This book is dedicated to the great pioneer
of baseball history and record keeping,
Henry Chadwick,
and to today's keepers of the flame,
the Society for American Baseball Research.

TOTAL

BASEBALL

EDITED BY

John Thorn and Pete Palmer

with David Reuther

A BASEBALL INK BOOK

WARNER BOOKS

A Warner Communications Company

Total Baseball Staff

Editors
John Thorn   *Pete Palmer*

Project Manager
David Reuther

Book Design and Production
Marc Cheshire

Fact Checkers
Bill Deane   *Richard Topp*   *Lloyd Johnson*

Copy Editors
Scott Kurtz   *Mark Hurst*

Proofreaders
G+H Soho, Ltd.
Jim Harris, President
Lisa Hoving   *James Waller*

Typographer
Gendell Graphics

Warner Books
Laurence J. Kirshbaum, President
Rick Horgan, Senior Editor
Milton Batalion, V.P, Manufacturing

A Warner Communications Company

Printed in the United States of America
First Printing: April 1989
1 3 5 7 9 10 8 6 4 2

Library of Congress Cataloging-in-Publication Data

Total baseball / edited by John Thorn & Pete Palmer.
p.   cm.
ISBN 0-446-51389-X
1. Baseball—United States—History.   I. Thorn, John. 1947-
II. Palmer, Pete.
GV863.A1T68   1989
796.357' 0973—dc19   88-87313

Contents

The Game Off the Field

PART TWO

The Annual Record

The Player Register

The Pitcher Register

The All-Time Leaders

The Rosters

Home-Road Statistics

Appendices

Acknowledgments

A book as large and complex as this could not have been published without the assistance of a legion of writers, researchers, and editorial/production staff. The principal contributors in these areas are credited on the preceding staff page and table of contents; others may be acknowledged within the text or in the separate introductions to the statistical sections of Part 2. Still others provided vital inspiration, investigative tips, and production help, yet go unmentioned in the body of the book; this section is for them, especially.

We are indebted to David Reuther, our friend and associate in many other books, and tireless project manager for this one. His contributions to the editorial, production, and business aspects of *Total Baseball*, from conception to publication, were truly indispensable.

Designer and production manager Marc Cheshire gave total commitment to this book for many months, working inhuman hours and fielding others' bobbles with equanimity, grace, and resourcefulness. We don't know anyone else who could have brought this book home the way he did.

Copy chief Scott Kurtz, who worked with us previously on *The Hidden Game of Baseball*, brought to the prose parts of this project his unique blend of copyediting skills and baseball knowledge. Working with him in this area were Mark Hurst and James Waller. Terry Brykczynski put his computer expertise to the task of file conversion from various word processing systems. Editorial assistants Susan Newkirk, Greg Vail, and Nina Bernard played an unsung but essential role in keeping track of those mountains of paper that ended up as this book.

Peter Bird, Jr., president of Gendell Graphics, supervised the mammoth job of setting the book. We thank him and his splendid staff for going the extra mile for us, especially in the final weeks of production.

Jim Harris, president of G&H/Soho Ltd., saw that the corrections and last-minute additions flowed smoothly from authors, fact checkers, and anxious editors to the final typeset pages. We thank the entire G&H/Soho crew, but make special mention of Lisa Hoving and James Waller.

Without the enthusiasm and commitment of Larry Kirshbaum, president of Warner Books, this book would have remained just another good idea in search of a publisher. Larry believed in *Total Baseball* from the moment he heard of it, and he put the prodigious energies and skills of Warner behind us. Rick Horgan, senior editor at Warner Books, offered critical guidance and support that made this a better book. Milton Batalion, vice president for manufacturing, could have thrown up his hands in dismay at the prospect of printing the biggest baseball book ever (and in less time than is conventionally given to a midsize novel); instead, he found a way to do it. And to all the other good folks at Warner who lent a hand, we extend our admiration and thanks.

Our friend Dick Perez provided a dozen of his typically wonderful sketches to embellish the title pages and part-titles. Dick is the preeminent artist of baseball, in whatever medium he chooses to work, and we appreciate his unique enhancement of *Total Baseball*.

The editors and writers of this book know a thing or two about baseball, yet we are still liable to an occasional lapse. Helping to keep these to a minimum were three experts for whose fact-checking services we are grateful: Bill Deane, Senior Associate of the National Baseball Library in Cooperstown; Lloyd Johnson, Executive Director of the Society for American Baseball Research; and Richard Topp, baseball historian and chairman of SABR's Biographical Research Committee. Also helpful in these areas were two unrelated Cohens, Eliot and Neil, both baseball experts.

For research help, particularly in the years before 1920, we extend heartfelt thanks to (alphabetically) SABR colleagues Bill Carle, Bob McConnell, David Neft, Bob Tiemann, and Frank Williams. Bill Carle helped us with biographical data, especially debut dates. Bob McConnell lent his personal expertise and his knowledge of the John Tattersall research collection to clearing up a variety of perplexing areas. David Neft supplied us with heretofore unknown RBI data for the National League of 1880–1885 and inspired us by his example, as the man who headed the Information Concepts, Inc., team that produced *The Baseball Encyclopedia* of 1969. Bob Tiemann provided game scores and sites for a host of pre-1900 games that were most helpful in deriving, for the first time, home-road stats for the nineteenth century. And Frank Williams continued his remarkable efforts in correcting pitcher won-lost records before 1920.

Other SABR members whose research is represented in *Total Baseball* include Bob Davids, the society's founder and the man who, in the words of Bill James, "has done more for baseball research than anyone else living"; and John Schwartz and Alex Haas, who combined with Davids to compile hit-by-pitch information from early newspaper box scores. The aid of Cliff Kachline, that extraordinary font of baseball knowledge, was invaluable even before this book began to take shape and continued to be so at many points in its development.

Tom Heitz, head of the National Baseball Library, was helpful as always with our occasional queries. Charlene Sanders of the Commissioner's Office offered some key help in solving a couple of last-minute mysteries.

Attorney Bob Stein displayed professionalism, perspicacity, and unfailing good humor as this book continued to change shape, seemingly from week to week.

And last, we thank some giants of baseball research whose work informs these pages but who are no longer with us to receive the tribute: in no particular order, Ernie Lanigan, John Tattersall, S. C. Thompson, Alex Haas, Preston D. Orem, Len Gettelson, and Lee Allen.

PART ONE

PART ONE

Introduction

Total Baseball is the most complete, most authoritative, and most informative—not to mention the biggest—baseball book ever published. It came into being because its creators saw that there was nothing else like it and because its publishers had faith that fans would want such a book: a virtual baseball library in one volume. (A dozen conventional books could be bound between these covers.) In fact, it could be said that Total Baseball is the first true baseball encyclopedia because it offers not only the game's numbers but also the stories behind them. An increasingly sophisticated baseball audience has shown its appetite for more accurate statistical data and more of it—both the traditional figures and the new, more analytical ones that are known by the term sabermetrics. We were convinced that these fans—and thousands of others who aren't quite so passionate about the stats—would also want to know more about the vast range of baseball knowledge that cannot be gleaned from the player records alone.

That is why this book is divided into two parts. The first consists of prose features on subjects of interest to all baseball fans, from the general reader who wishes to know more about the game's trivia and lore to the advanced fan who wants to know about its business and law. The origins of the farm system; black baseball before Jackie Robinson; complete balloting for the Hall of Fame, MVP, Cy Young, and Rookie of the Year awards; women in baseball; scandals and controversies; the ultimate baseball library . . . but why tease you with the pleasures that await you while (we hope) holding you captive with this Introduction? Simply be assured that Total Baseball will be totally absorbing, whether you begin with David Voigt's "History of Major League Baseball" and read straight through to the end of Part 1, or scan the Table of Contents for what appeals at the moment. The writers gathered together here are the experts in their fields, as befits an encyclopedic reference work, and even the most erudite reader will learn countless new things about this great game.

The same holds true for Part 2, which contains the playing and pitching registers, a variety of rosters, a year-by-year statistical summary of major league play since 1871, home-road statistics and more. The stats newly developed for this book—like the Clutch Hitting Index or Relief Ranking—will please the devotee of sabermetrics, who may know about Runs Created, Total Average, and the whole Linear Weights System but who has never before been offered these stats applied to all of baseball's 13,160 players. The traditional computations will appeal to baseball scholars, who know what a tangle of briars the historical record has become over the last 20 years, as individual player records have been altered without making corresponding changes to other players on the same team. (For more on this, see the much longer Introduction to Part 2.) And the cornucopia of stats old and new—for everyone from all-time leaders to cup-of-coffee nonentities—will provide days, months, and years of archaeological delight for baseball fans of all stripes.

Our plan for Total Baseball was to join the game's most knowledgeable writers, most of them members of the Society for American Baseball Research (SABR), with the game's great historical database, the one built up over two decades by Pete Palmer, and then to go for the most accurate, most entertaining, biggest, and best reference book ever devoted to baseball. Benefiting from the painstaking research of hundreds of friends and colleagues in SABR, we have corrected many errors and omissions in Macmillan's Baseball Encyclopedia, relying not upon the numbers enshrined by tradition or official edict but upon the evidence. How many hours have been spent scanning the handwritten official records of the early years of the century or reviewing box scores and scoresheets and game summaries! It would have been easier not to bother, to accept, for example, a game mistakenly entered twice in the record for 1910 so that Ty Cobb could keep his 1910 batting championship and career total of 4,191 hits. But there can be no statute of limitations on historical error; the researcher and historian must go where the evidence leads them, and if the result upsets some commonly held notions, so be it. (A scattered few statistics in Part One will differ from those in Part Two, for the production requirements of this book did not permit the far-flung writers of Part One to make use of the Palmer database, which corrects many errors of long standing.)

This book is as good as we know how to make it, but we do want to hear from you about our blunders (we know there will be some) or about your research (which may be as important to the second edition of Total Baseball as that of, say, Frank Williams or Bob McConnell was for this). We believe that history is process, not product, and our aim has been for Total Baseball to reflect the state of the art in baseball research and to convey its editors' love for the game. We hope you'll let us know if we succeeded.

The History

PEREZ

The History of Major League Baseball

David Q. Voigt

An Evolving Game: The Formative Years of Major League Baseball

Deeply embedded in the folklore of American sports is the story of baseball's supposed invention by a young West Point cadet, Abner Doubleday, in the summer of 1839 at the village of Cooperstown, New York. The yarn originated in 1907, in the final report of a committee commissioned by major league executives to inquire into the origins of "America's National Game."

The claim that the game was invented by the late Doubleday, who also won enduring fame as a Union general in the Civil War, was based on the dubious testimony of Abner Graves, a retired mining engineer. Indeed, Graves claimed to have actually witnessed the long-ago event. The Graves account appealed to committeeman Albert G. Spalding, a former star player and club owner, and concurrently a famous sporting goods tycoon and a fervently patriotic American. He persuaded his colleagues to accept the Doubleday invention account without further ado. With the release of the final version of the committee's report, the legend of baseball's immaculate conception began to worm its way into American mythology.

Ever since then, sports historians have repeatedly and futilely assailed the Doubleday account, arguing that Abner Doubleday never visited Cooperstown in 1839, that his diaries contain no reference to the game, and that the form of baseball he supposedly invented far too closely resembled the game as it was played in the early 1900s.

Indeed, sports historians have marshaled impressive evidence showing that American baseball, far from being an independent invention, evolved out of various ball-and-stick games that had been played in many areas of the world since the beginnings of recorded history. Among many suggested precursors of baseball, a Russian ball-and-stick game called *lapta* has been recently advanced by Soviet propagandists. But in early America, precursors of baseball included informal games of English origin such as paddleball, trap ball, one-old-cat, rounders, and town ball. The latter was a popular game in colonial New England and was played by adults and children with a bat and ball on an open field. Moreover, printed references to "base ball" in America date back to the eighteenth century. Among these accounts is one of Albigence Waldo, a surgeon with Washington's troops at Valley Forge who poetically told of soldiers batting balls and running bases in their free time. And in the early 1820s, the grandfather of the late novelist Samuel Hopkins Adams vividly recalled playing "base ball" on Mr. Mumford's pasture lot. Similarly in 1834 Robin Carver's *Book of Sports* related that an American version of rounders called 'base' or 'goal ball' was rivaling cricket in popularity among Americans. Indeed, cricket played a role in the evolution of organized baseball. From this British game came umpires and innings, and early baseball writers like Henry Chadwick used cricket terminology such as "batsman," "playing for the side," and "excellent field" in describing early baseball games. Likewise, the pioneer baseball innovator Harry Wright, a cricket professional turned baseball manager, drew heavily on his cricket background in promoting baseball as a professional team sport in the United States.

As an evolutionary blend of informal bat-and-ball games and the formal game of cricket, baseball needed no immaculate conception to become a popular American field sport. By the 1840s various forms of baseball vied for acceptance, including the popular Massachusetts and New York versions of the game. The Massachusetts game utilized an irregular four-sided field of play, with the four bases located at fixed, asymmetrical distances from each other and the "striker's," or batter's position away from the home base. "Scouts," or fielders, put men out by fielding a batted ball on the fly or on the first bounce, or by hitting a runner with a thrown ball. But this lively version of the game was overshadowed in the late 1840s by the "New York game," a popular version of which was devised by the members of the New York Knickerbocker Club. Organized in 1845 by a band of aspiring gentlemen and baseball enthusiasts, the Knickerbocker version was devised by one of their members, Alexander J. Cartwright. Cartwright prescribed a diamond-shaped infield with bases at ninety feet apart, a standard which has stood the test of time. The pitching distance was set at forty-five feet from the home base, and a pitcher was required to "pitch" a ball in a stiff-armed, underhanded fashion. The three-strikes-are-out rule was adopted, and a batter could also be put out by a fielder catching a batted ball in the air, or on the first bounce, or by throwing a fielded ball to the first baseman before the runner arrived. Other innovations included the nine-man team and three outs ending a team's batting in their half of an inning. Thus Cartwright's version of baseball became the basis of the game as presently played. Over the years, other innovations were added, including the nine-inning standard for games, changes in the pitching distance, and so one.

Once it was published and propagated by the Knickerbockers, the "New York game" was speedily adopted by other baseball clubs that sprang up in the New York City area and in other towns and cities of antebellum America. In the 1850s the rise of baseball clubs and team competition helped to meet the recreational needs of Americans who were caught up in an increasingly urban and industrial society. By the 1860s one of every six Americans lived in towns or cities, and

by then newspapers were covering games and noting the booming popularity of baseball. Mostly a northern and mid-western phenomenon, baseball fever ran highest in the New York City area, where in the 1850s games were being played "on every available green plot within a ten-mile circuit of the city." Spearheading the baseball boom were formally organized clubs with officers, clubhouses and playing grounds. Among the many clubs, the Knickerbockers sought to rule the game by posing as arbiters of play, rules, and decorum. Since no leagues or playing schedules existed, formal games in the 1850s were arranged by correspondence between club secretaries. The lordly Knickerbockers resisted such overtures, preferring to play among themselves, yet insisting on their preeminence over all other clubs. But the dynamic American game was not to be bound by gentlemanly monopolists or by arbitrary codes of amateurism. By the end of the 1850s, victories and the prospect of gate receipts were becoming more important factors. As more clubs embraced these goals, greater emphasis was placed on obtaining good players at whatever affronts to amateur standards.

In 1858 the Knickerbockers were dethroned as would-be overlords of baseball by the newly organized National Association of Base Ball Players. That year, representatives of twenty-five clubs formed the Association for the ostensible purpose of codifying rules and establishing guidelines for organized clubs and team competition. But the Association speedily established itself as the new arbiter of the game. Among its early rulings were the establishment of a pitcher's box and the standardization of the nine-inning game. The Association also approved the practice of charging paid admissions at games and that year saw 1,500 spectators pay 50¢ each to watch a game played between Brooklyn and New York "all-star" teams. Although the Association established no league or formal playing schedules, its authority was accepted and it lasted until 1871, when it was replaced by a lame organization called the National Association of Amateur Base Ball Players—to differentiate it from the newly founded National Association of Professional Base Ball Players. By 1860 some sixty clubs had joined the Association; mostly they came from the East and Midwest, but a sprinkling of college teams was included. By then, the mounting hostilities between the North and South account for the absence of southern clubs.

American baseball's popularity was at high tide when the Civil War broke out, but the South was excluded from major league baseball competition for many years. Indeed, one of the smaller legacies of the war between the states was major league baseball's east-west alignment of its franchises. And yet the war, which claimed 600,000 American lives, also popularized the game in all sections of the country, as soldiers in both armies played the game in camps and in prison compounds. This infusion of interest in the game set the stage for an even greater baseball boom which swept the North in the immediate postwar era.

Meanwhile, as the war raged toward its conclusion, baseball's popularity diminished for a time on the northern home front. Still, strong teams like the Brooklyn Excelsiors, the Brooklyn Eckfords, and the Brooklyn Atlantics delighted fans by their spirited competition. At the time, pitcher Jim Creighton of the Excelsiors became a popular hero by leading his team on a victorious eastern tour in 1860. In 1862 and 1863 the Eckfords laid claim to being America's best team, and the Brooklyn Atlantics, led by Dickey Pearce, boasted

consecutive unbeaten seasons in 1864 and 1865.

The game's popularity among returning soldiers helped to inspire a major baseball boom in post–Civil War America. By 1865 the game was widely touted as America's "national game," and its growing popularity was evidenced by the proliferation of organized clubs. In 1865, ninety-one clubs had joined the Association; the following year membership swelled to nearly two hundred; and 1867 saw more than three hundred clubs enrolled, including more than a hundred from midwestern towns and cities. At their own expense, the powerful Washington Nationals embarked on an unprecedented midwestern tour in 1867; they were beaten in one game by the previously unheralded Rockford (Illinois) Forest City nine. Although the Nationals' tour suggested that some type of organized competition was needed, it failed to produce such reforms as an organized league or a fixed playing schedule. However, editor Frank Queen of the *New York Clipper*, a popular sporting journal, hit upon the idea of giving gold awards annually to the best team and the nine best players. But such judgments were arbitrary and inadequate. Meanwhile, the style of play continued to improve in the late 1860s. Pitchers became more than passive servers as one of them, Arthur "Candy" Cummings, popularized a wrist-twisting, curved-ball delivery. Moreover, fielders became more mobile, baserunners took to sliding to avoid fielders' tags, and a rule change outlawed the one-bounce-and-out catch.

But baseball's dynamic postwar growth also confronted the shaky National Association with vexing problems. Rampant commercialism was one of them. As more clubs charged admission to games, many took to dividing receipts among the players. This trend swelled the ranks of "professional" players, whose presence posed a serious threat to the Association's amateur code. In 1863 Association leaders debated the problem, but vacillated by grudgingly allowing professionals to retain their memberships. The following year the Association defined a professional player as one who "plays base ball for money, place, or emolument." The definition embraced many players, some of whom drew straight salaries, or shared gate receipts, or occupied jobs that were awarded as a subterfuge to conceal their ball-playing activities. What's more, some of the professionals were jumping their contracts for better offers from other clubs. Dubbed "revolvers," they posed a major threat to the shaky authority of the National Association.

The Cincinnati Reds of 1869

By the late 1860s baseball was becoming more of a business, and playing competitive baseball was becoming a recognized career. As baseball writer Henry Chadwick observed in 1868, a new rank ordering among ball players was evidenced by the makeup of the Brooklyn Atlantics club. At the top was the club's elite professional team, followed by the club's amateur nine, with the lowly "muffins," or third-rate players, at the bottom. As baseball clubs came to be dominated by professional interests, some clubs financed their operations by selling stock shares and becoming joint stock companies, while others, which depended on shared gate receipts, operated as "cooperative nines."

Until 1869 the professional movement in baseball was mainly a covert trend, but in that year the Cincinnati Red Stocking club boldly announced its intention of fielding an all-salaried team which would compete against the top teams in the land. This forthright move was the brainchild of club

president Aaron B. Champion, a Cincinnati businessman and local booster. The Reds were not the first professional team, nor the first all-salaried team, nor the first team to go undefeated over a season. But as the first openly announced all-salaried team, the Reds, led by player-manager Harry Wright, who became known as the "Father of Professional Baseball," toured the country in 1869, winning some 60 games without a loss. The following year, the well-drilled Reds won another 24 before losing in June to the host Brooklyn Atlantics by an 8–7 score in eleven innings. Although the Reds' effort was financially unremunerative to its stockholders, who voted to return to amateur play after the 1870 season, the experiment inspired an enduring myth that professional baseball in America arose out of this episode. In truth the professional movement was already strongly entrenched. But the Reds' example inspired imitators and brought the smouldering amateur-professional controversy to a head. Thus when the National Association, at its annual meeting in 1870, sought to curb the professional movement, the professional delegates withdrew and formed their own organization in March 1871. This successful coup stunned the amateur National Association, which never recovered and died in 1874. It also marked the beginning of major league baseball in America. From 1871 to the present day, most changes in American baseball rules and style of play would be inspired by the professional major leagues.

The First Major League: The National Association of Professional Base Ball Players

America's first professional baseball league, the National Association of Professional Base Ball Players, was also the first major league. In its ranks were the strongest teams and the best players. The players controlled the league and enjoyed full freedom of contract and movement. Financial support came to those clubs whose stockholders or investors derived more prestige than monetary rewards from their sponsorship. And in this artist-patron relationship, player salaries had a higher priority than investor profits.

The National Association was created by a single evening's work on March 17, 1871. Structurally the league resembled the old amateur National Association, whose constitution was modified to serve professional interests and whose playing rules were adopted. Admission to the professional league required the payment of a ten-dollar entry fee, in stark contrast to the multimillion-dollar price tag now placed on a major league franchise. Like its predecessor, the professional National Association lacked a fixed schedule of games; each team was expected to play each rival five times in a season, with playing dates to be arranged by secretarial correspondence. The championship pennant was awarded to the team with the most victories, and a championship committee was empowered to rule on any disputed claims.

Although the National Association dominated organized baseball in 1871–1875, its structural defects portended its coming demise. The player-run organization wielded little control over players or teams. The easy admission policy made for a chronic dropout problem as disenchanted teams found it easy to turn their backs on ten dollars. Because of the absence of a fixed playing schedule, few contending teams played their required quota of games. Disputes over officiating stemmed from a reliance on volunteer umpires. Teams also quarreled over ticket pricing and the division of gate receipts. Indeed, most teams lost money, and such losses fueled the tension between players and investors. Critics accused the player-controlled league of failing to discipline players, especially the contract jumpers, drunkards, and alleged game fixers. Unresolved problems like these sowed the seeds of the league's eventual collapse, but while it lasted, the National Association also provided spectators with a sprightly brand of baseball.

Campaigns of the National Association, 1871–1875

The Association's 1871 campaign featured an exciting three-way battle between the Chicago White Stockings, Philadelphia Athletics, and Harry Wright's Boston Red Stockings. The Chicago team, which was housed in a new 7,000-seat wooden park and which boasted a $4,500 salaried star among its players, set a fast pace until the city's tragic fire destroyed the park. Forced to play their remaining games on the road, the White Stockings finished third and dropped out of the league until 1874. At the season's end, the Athletics and Red Stockings each had won 22 games, but the championship committee awarded the pennant to the Athletics, who had fewer losses. Harry Wright's plea that his Boston Reds had come closer to meeting their scheduled obligations was disallowed. Thus in spite of continuing controversy and a devastating fire, the National Association enjoyed an auspicious debut. Most clubs profited, and only one dropped out of the race. At the Association's annual meeting, the professionals tightened their hold on the league by electing one of their own, Bob Ferguson, to serve as president.

Eleven clubs entered the lists for the 1872 campaign, but hopes for a wide-open race were crushed by Harry Wright's powerful Boston team, which rolled to the championship on a 39–8 record. Stocked with stars like pitcher Al Spalding, infielder Ross Barnes (whose bunting prowess permitted him to take maximum advantage of the then-prevailing fair-foul hitting rule), and shortstop George Wright, the Red Stockings won the first of four consecutive pennants. They were the first of many powerful major league dynasties to come—a phenomenon which, over the course of major league baseball history, consistently made a mockery of the idea of competitive balance.

With nine teams competing in 1873, the Reds won a second pennant by staging a late-season drive to overtake the front-running Philadelphia "Phillies," or "Whites." Two Boston newcomers, catcher Jim White and outfielder Jim O'Rourke, contributed to the Reds' 43–16 winning gait. Although overall league revenues were disappointing, only one club dropped from contention during the course of the season.

In 1874, Wright's Reds posted a 52–18 record, to lap the New York Mutuals by 7½ games. That year Wright's team was the only one to play its full schedule of games, an impressive feat considering that Wright's team, in company with the Philadelphia Athletics, embarked upon a six-week baseball tour of Britain in hopes of persuading English sportsmen to adopt America's "national game." Like this first baseball mission, the Association's 1874 season was a financial bust. Although only one club dropped out of the race, accusations of gambling and fixed games clouded the league's reputation.

The 1875 season was the last campaign of the National Association. Thirteen teams entered the fray, but Boston's juggernaut, headed by Spalding, Barnes, O'Rourke, White, and George Wright, buried all rivals. With four Boston men

topping the league's hitters, the Reds posted a 71–8 record to finish 15 games up on their nearest pursuers. Of the thirteen contenders, seven failed to finish the 1875 season.

Now in full disarray, the sullied National Association reeled under problems of competitive imbalance, financial losses, and excessive player freedom. The time was ripe for a reformist coup, and a new breed of club directors, headed by William A. Hulbert of the Chicago White Stockings, moved to raise a rival major league that would better serve the interests of the club owners.

But the pioneering National Association was by no means a failure. For all its weaknesses, the Association had popularized professional baseball. Supporters like Henry Chadwick, the innovative sportswriter who now wore the title of "Father of Base Ball," publicized the league by his coverage of games and by his statistics-laden guidebooks. Chadwick's game coverage provided detailed accounts of games with box scores, including a lasting version which he devised in 1876. Such coverage enhanced the game's popularity and inspired widespread coverage by leading newspapers. Chadwick also served on the Association's rules committee, which approved a pitching change that allowed the underhanded pitchers to utilize wrist-snapping curveballs. But Chadwick's quixotic proposal to make baseball into a ten-man game failed to catch on.

The Association's most solid innovator was Harry Wright, who set high standards for professional promotion. Wright's Boston payroll was baseball's highest until the early 1880s. As Boston's manager, Wright presided over a $35,000 annual budget and dealt creatively with such problems as proper groundskeeping, equipment design and procurement, advertising, and the recruiting and training of players. Wright's mastery paid off in his team's astonishing success. He was honored in these years as the "Father of Professional Base Ball," and his envious colleagues also referred to the National Association as "Harry Wright's League."

The First Stable Major League: The National League, 1876–1879

President William A. Hulbert of the Chicago White Stockings was the driving force behind the coup that dethroned the National Association. Determined to field a strong team in Chicago, Hulbert in 1875 signed Boston pitcher Al Spalding to play with Chicago the following season, along with three other Boston stars: Ross Barnes, Jim White, and Cal McVey. Hulbert also signed Adrian Anson of the Athletics, who later became Chicago's longtime player-manager and the first major league hitter to notch over 3,000 hits.

Fearing possible reprisals from the player-run National Association, Hulbert moved to create a new league run by business-minded club investors. Backed by representatives from the St. Louis, Louisville, and Cincinnati clubs, Hulbert met with representatives of several eastern clubs—New York, Philadelphia, Boston, and Hartford—in February 1876. Out of this meeting came the National League of Professional Base Ball Clubs. The first permanent major league embraced Hulbert's thirteen-point plan of organization. In keeping with its title, the league emphasized the interests of member clubs over those of the players. Admitted as members were well-financed, joint-stock company clubs, each of which paid annual dues of $100 which were used to finance the league administrative body's handling of disputes, recordkeeping,

and officiating fees. The latter expense went for a staff of umpires, each to be paid $5 a game.

The eight charter clubs of the new National League were aligned on an east-west basis, and each team was granted a monopoly over its territory. For the 1876 season, each team agreed to play each rival ten times, with expulsion from the league the penalty for failing to do so. Adopting a high moral stance, NL leaders ordered member clubs to ban gambling, liquor sales, and Sunday games, and to draw up tightly written contracts aimed at preventing players from "revolving." For the players this was tough medicine, but with the strongest teams enrolled in the new league, there was little to do but submit. Indeed, the National Association never survived the NL coup and collapsed in 1876.

As the "Father of the National League," Hulbert presided over its fortunes from 1877 until his death in 1882. However, this most powerful of NL presidents to date owed much to his chief lieutenant, Al Spalding, who retired from the field to become the NL's most powerful advocate and defender. As a reward for his loyal support, Spalding's fledgling sporting goods company received the contract to supply the league's balls and to publish its annual guidebook. Beginning in 1877, Chadwick became the perennial editor of the league's official *Spalding Guide*.

Although its debut was auspicious, the NL's first four campaigns were marred by flagging profits, a major scandal, and opposition from a strong rival in the International Association. In 1876 Spalding pitched and managed the Chicago White Stockings to a 52–14 record, topping their closest pursuer by six games. Because of this runaway, attendance tailed off, prompting two teams, the Philadelphia Athletics and New York Mutuals, to forgo playing their final games in the west. For this breach of rules, Hulbert expelled the pair, thereby depriving the NL of franchises in the populous Philadelphia and New York areas until 1883. However, Hulbert made no effort to replace the two; hence only six teams took the field in 1877, the year the NL adopted a formal schedule of games. Spalding's decision to quit pitching that year dashed Chicago's hopes, but Louisville's hopes ran high until late in the season, when Wright's Boston Reds overtook them and won by seven games. But revelations that gamblers had bribed four Louisville players to lose key games marred Boston's victory. Faced with a major crisis, Hulbert responded by banishing the four players (Jim Devlin, George Hall, William Craver, and Al Nichols) for life. In the wake of the scandal, Louisville dropped from the league, followed by Hartford and St. Louis. To replace them, Indianapolis, Milwaukee, and Providence clubs joined the league. Meanwhile the NL also faced strong competition from the rival International Association. A loose league of mostly cooperative (gate-receipt-sharing) teams, the International Association threat prompted NL leaders to form a "League Alliance" of independent teams. By paying fees of ten dollars a year, League Alliance teams won the right to play exhibitions with NL teams, and the NL also pledged to honor their territorial rights and player contracts.

The hard-pressed NL suffered another profitless season in 1878, with Boston winning a second pennant by four games over Cincinnati. Still challenged by the International Association, the NL retaliated by raiding the circuit's teams and playing rosters. Over the winter of 1878–1879, Syracuse and Buffalo were persuaded to quit the Association for memberships in the NL, while Milwaukee and Indianapolis were

dropped from the NL. Troy and Cleveland were also admitted to bring the number of NL teams to eight. Such tactics undermined the International Association, which fielded an enfeebled minor league called the National Association in 1879.

In returning to an eight-team format in 1879, NL teams imposed rigid austerity measures. Among them, salaries were slashed and players compelled to buy their own uniforms and share the costs of meals. Moreover, player mobility was limited by the adherence to a reserve clause in player contracts. Limited to five players per team in 1879, by 1883 the reserve system was applied to most player contracts. Thereafter the reserve clause became a major bone of contention between owners and players. Meanwhile Providence won the 1879 pennant race; managed by George Wright and paced by John M. Ward's pitching, the Providence Grays won by 5 games over Wright's Boston Reds.

Major League Baseball's Golden Age, 1880–1889

As the decade of the 1880s dawned, major league baseball was only a pale reflection of the enormously popular spectacle that it would soon become. In 1880 the NL reigned supreme, but the league's financial performance was dismal. Thus far no NL club had matched the profits of Wright's 1875 Boston Reds, player salaries barely exceeded those of the 1869 Cincinnati Reds, annual membership changes underscored the league's instability, and the NL was unrepresented in the populous New York and Philadelphia areas.

At this point, however, a powerful stimulus came from the nation's booming economic and urban growth, and professional baseball expanded vigorously. The first to prosper was the NL, but its rising fortunes inspired rivals like the American Association (AA), which was recognized as a major league under the 1883 National Agreement. The following year another rival, the Union Association, vied for major league status, but the NL and AA joined forces to crush the pretender and maintain the dual major league system. The dual major league system lasted from 1883 to 1891, when it was replaced by a single major league. But in its heyday the dual major league system, with its annual World Series competition between the two leagues, proved to be popular and profitable. By 1889 leading clubs from both circuits counted annual profits of over $100,000. While most of the profits went to club owners, player salaries increased, averaging $2,000 a season, with a few stars getting as much as $5,000. Such gains by players were modest enough, but club owners still sought to limit player salaries. In opposing salary ceilings, players banded together under the Brotherhood of Professional Base Ball Players, which also opposed the unwritten reserve clause, unreasonable fines, and the sale of players from one club to another. In this decade the NL's Chicago team received $10,000 apiece from the sale of stars Mike "King" Kelly and John Clarkson to the Boston club.

The prosperity of the major league game was further evidenced by the expanded seasonal playing schedule. From 84 games a season in 1880 the NL increased its schedule to 132 games by 1889, while the AA upped its seasonal schedule to 140 games in 1889. To accommodate growing numbers of fans, including the 2 million who attended major league games in 1889, clubs erected new wooden parks with double-decked stands. To serve them, concessionaire Harry M. Stevens introduced the now classic baseball lunch of hot dogs, soda pop, and peanuts. And to sate the public's hunger for baseball news, daily newspapers expanded their coverage of games, and two weekly journals devoted to baseball—*Sporting Life* and *The Sporting News*—sprang to vigorous life in this decade. Moreover, at the peak of baseball's popularity, Spalding dispatched, in 1888–1889, two major league squads on a world tour in hopes of spreading the American game to other lands.

If Spalding's mission fell short of its goal abroad, at home the professional game was spreading to all corners of the land. In 1889 some 15 minor leagues were operating. Under the National Agreement of 1883, and its subsequent revisions, minor leagues were recognized as a part of organized baseball. Territorial rights and player rosters of such teams were protected by the major leagues. But black players and teams were increasingly excluded from organized baseball. In the past, gentlemen's agreements barred black teams from the amateur National Association and the professional National Association. At this time a few blacks played briefly in the major AA and in some minor leagues, but the presence of the segregated Negro league in Pennsylvania, in 1889, plus the existence of all-black independent professional teams, signaled the trend toward segregation of black players from organized baseball. Not until 1946 would the color barrier be lifted.

In this dynamic golden age, professional baseball's maturation as a field sport was speeded by a rash of rule changes. In 1881 the pitching distance was extended to fifty feet; in 1884 overhand pitching was legalized; in 1887 a uniform strike zone was established; in 1888 the three-strikes rule and in 1889 the four-balls rule were permanently adopted. These and other changes in playing rules resulted from pragmatic experiments by major league rules committees, whose constant tinkerings kept the game in a state of flux. Some short-lived changes, like the 1887 rule scoring bases on balls as hits and employing a modified four-strike rule, aimed at correcting the pitching-batting imbalance. But these quixotic rules inflated batting averages and produced eleven .400 hitters before they were discarded at the close of the 1887 season.

NL Campaigns of the 1880s

As the sole major league in 1880, the NL saw its fortunes rise with those of the Chicago dynasty. Winners of three consecutive pennants over the years 1880–1882, the Chicago team was led by player-manager Cap Anson, a popular hero and the leading hitter of the nineteenth century. Fielding a nucleus of stars, including colorful Mike "King" Kelly, pitchers Larry Corcoran and Fred Goldsmith, and catcher Frank "Silver" Flint, Chicago topped Providence by 15 games in 1880, by nine games in 1881, and by three games in 1882. In an unofficial postseason encounter with the rival American Association's Cincinnati champs, the two teams split a pair of games before AA officials canceled this 1882 harbinger of the World Series.

The rise of the AA threatened the dominant NL, which was left leaderless by Hulbert's death in 1882. At Spalding's suggestion, A. G. Mills was elected president. That fall the NL strengthened its position by dropping Troy and Worcester and planting teams in New York and Philadelphia. The NL playing schedule was increased to 98 games.

In the hotly contested 1883 race, Boston ended Chicago's reign by edging Anson's team by four games. That fall Mills ended the AA war by negotiating the National Agreement of 1883, which conceded major league status to the rival AA. Under the agreement, the AA adopted the reserve clause, the two leagues ceased raiding each other's players, and post-season World Series play between the two leagues was accepted. The agreement provided for major league control over lower levels of professional baseball by recognizing the territorial rights of minor league signatories. With frequent changes, this National Agreement remained in force until the American League war of 1900.

In 1884 the two major leagues faced competition from another major league aspirant. To combat this Union Association incursion, the NL and AA extended reserve coverage to all players and upped their playing schedules to 112 games. The surfeit of major league games contributed to lower attendance for all three embattled leagues, but the Union Association suffered more and was driven out. Least damaged was the NL, whose sprightly 1884 campaign saw pitcher Charles "Old Hoss" Radbourn employ the new rule legalizing overhand pitching with telling effect. Radbourn won 60 games to lead Providence to 10½-game victory over runner-up Boston. And in the first officially sanctioned World Series, Radbourn defeated the AA champion Mets in three straight games.

The following year Anson's White Stockings regained the heights as they won the first of two consecutive pennants. With ace pitcher John Clarkson winning 53 games, Chicago held off the New York Giants by two games to land the 1885 NL pennant. The Giants' surge owed to a piece of skullduggery by its owner. Having acquired a financial interest in the AA New York Mets, the Giants plucked ace pitcher Tim Keefe from them, and Keefe won 32 games for the Giants in 1885. Such trickery by the NL now had AA leaders wary of their rival, but in the World Series of 1885 AA prestige rose when the St. Louis Browns tied the powerful Chicagoans, and it soared further in 1886, when the Browns defeated Chicago in the $15,000 winner-take-all World Series of that year. The loss blighted Chicago's gritty 2½-game victory over Detroit in the 1886 NL campaign. Following the loss, Spalding sold King Kelly to Boston for $10,000. The sale electrified baseball fans, but it also signaled the end of the Chicago dynasty.

In the memorable 1887 campaign, Detroit won the pennant by 3½ games over the Philadelphia Phillies. Wildly inflated batting averages resulted from rule changes that modified the third-strike rule and scored bases on balls as hits. Detroit feasted under the new rules as Sam Thompson and the "big four" of Dan Brouthers, Jack Rowe, Hardie Richardson, and Jim White keyed a league-leading .343 (.299 when adjusted for that year's counting of walks as hits) team batting average. In World Series play, Detroit thrashed the Browns, winning ten of the fifteen games. That fall the rules committee scuttled the average-inflating rules and the NL increased its playing schedule to 132 games.

As Detroit faded, the New York Giants captured the next two NL pennants. Managed by Jim Mutrie and captained by John Ward, the well-balanced Giants defeated Chicago by 9 games and humbled the Browns in the 1888 World Series. The following year the Giants repeated, edging Boston by a single game and then trouncing the Brooklyn Bridegrooms in the World Series.

The profitable 1889 season marked the passing of the first golden age in major baseball history. Over the next two seasons the NL fought two costly interleague wars that overshadowed the pennant races. In 1890, as the NL battled the serious challenge of the Players League, the Brooklyn Bridegrooms, who were enticed to jump the AA for the NL, won by 6½ games over Anson's Chicago Colts. And in 1891, as the NL battled the AA, manager Frank Selee's Boston Beaneaters defeated Chicago by 3½ games. By then the interleague wars had ended with the NL the victor in both frays. Thus as the 1892 season dawned, the NL once again reigned supreme over major league baseball.

Rival Major Leagues of the 1880s: The American Association, Union Association, and Players League

The NL's most formidable nineteenth-century rival, the American Association of Base Ball Clubs, was organized by promoters who opposed the NL's monopoly. In wooing prospective clubs, the AA promoters saw an opportunity: New York, Philadelphia, Cincinnati, and St. Louis were good baseball cities that were not represented in the league. They also established a basic 25¢ admission price and allowed member clubs the option of selling booze and playing Sunday games. To entice good players, the AA promoters rejected the NL's reserve clause; and to ensure orderly play, a salaried corps of umpires was hired—an innovation soon imitated by the NL.

In its maiden season of 1882, the AA's six teams (Cincinnati, Louisville, St. Louis, Pittsburgh, Philadelphia, and Baltimore) prospered. All six finished the season, with Cincinnati winning the pennant by 11½ games over Philadelphia. Emergent stars of the AA included pitcher Will White and second baseman Bid McPhee of Cincinnati, first baseman Charles Comiskey of St. Louis, and outfielder Pete Browning and pitcher Tony Mullane of Louisville among the contenders.

In 1883 the AA expanded to eight clubs by adding Columbus and the New York Mets. By opposing the NL's reserve clause, the AA lured a number of disgruntled NL players into its ranks. Thus strengthened, the AA staged another profitable campaign, which saw the Philadelphia Athletics edge the St. Louis Browns by a single game. The AA's sprightly season prompted the NL to accommodate its rival. That fall NL president Mills and AA president Denny McKnight negotiated the National Agreement of 1883, which recognized the AA as a major league and instituted World Series play between the two leagues. For its part, the AA adopted the reserve clause.

The agreement between the NL and AA was barely concluded when a new league made a bid for major league recognition. The rival Union Association of Base Ball Clubs was organized in Pittsburgh in the fall of 1883. To entice players from the established majors, the UA leaders proclaimed their opposition to the reserve clause. A few major league players jumped to the new league, but most remained with the clubs out of fear of blacklisting, or in some cases because they were bought off by salary increases. With mostly unknown players in their ranks, the eight-team UA commenced playing a 128-game schedule in 1884. From the start the league suffered from unbalanced funding and talent distribution. The UA's principal backer, Henry V. Lucas, poured most of his money into his St. Louis Maroons, a team which won its first twenty-one games and made a shambles of the pennant race. Plagued by financial losses, only five charter teams survived the campaign. Nevertheless, the UA drained attendance from the established majors—especially

the AA, which unwisely expanded to counter the threat. In the fall of 1884, the UA folded when Lucas accepted an offer to enroll his St. Louis Maroons in the NL.

The collapse of the UA left the dual major league system intact, but relations between the NL and AA were strained. AA leaders accused their NL allies of duplicity for persuading the AA to expand to twelve teams to counter the UA's incursion. As a result the AA suffered heavier financial losses in its 1884 campaign, which the New York Mets won by 6½ games over Columbus. The Mets' victory was soured by their loss to Providence in the first officially sanctioned World Series. But even more damaging to the AA was the revelation the the Mets had come under the ownership of the NL New York Giants. Moreover, AA suspicions of NL duplicity were heightened by the UA peace settlement which brought the St. Louis Maroons into the NL, where they competed directly with the AA's St. Louis Browns.

As it turned out, the Maroons were no match for the Browns, whose profitable formula of cheap baseball, liquor sales, sideshows, Sunday games, and winning baseball was making a folk hero of the Browns' colorful president, Chris Von der Ahe. Beginning in 1885, player-manager Charles Comiskey led his team to four consecutive AA pennants. In 1885 the Browns won by 16 games over Cincinnati; in 1886, by 12 over Pittsburgh; in 1887, by 14 over Cincinnati; and in 1888, by 6½ over a beefed-up Brooklyn team. Star players like infielder Arlie Latham, outfielder Tip O'Neill, and pitchers Dave Foutz and Bob Caruthers paced the Browns to the first three pennants. Then, when Von der Ahe sold Foutz and Caruthers to Brooklyn in 1888, Comiskey came up with pitcher Silver King, whose 45 victories helped land a fourth consecutive pennant. In World Series play the Browns tied Chicago in 1885 and defeated Anson's team in 1886. But the team was drubbed by Detroit in 1887 and by the Giants in 1888.

Bitter rivalry between the Browns and Brooklyn Bridegrooms dominated the 1889 race, which ended with the Bridegrooms on top of the Browns by 2 games. But the Bridegrooms lost to the Giants in World Series play. Over the winter the St. Louis and Brooklyn factions battled over the choice of a new AA president, and in the stormy aftermath Brooklyn and Cincinnati joined the National League. The loss of these clubs, together with the loss of key players to the newly organized Players' League, crippled the AA. Forced to field weak teams in 1890, the AA ran a poor third to the NL and the Players' League. The AA's dismal race was won by Louisville, which only the year before had finished dead last in the AA with a 27–111 record.

The Players League War of 1890

The Players League of 1890 arose out of the long smoldering hostilities between major league players and owners, dating back to the NL seizure of power in 1876. Under NL control, players lost money and freedom of movement, and were subjected to harsh disciplinary codes backed by threats of expulsion and blacklisting. To the list of player grievances was added the reserve clause in player contracts, which players viewed as a device for lowering salaries and a denial of one's right to sell his services to the highest bidder. For their part, owners credited the clause for stabilizing teams and increasing profits. Although legal challenges sustained the players' position, such victories were too limited to overturn the re-

serve clause. Nor were players helped when rival leagues attacked the clause because the AA soon embraced the clause and the UA was driven out of business. Frustrated on these fronts, in 1885 the players resorted to collective action by forming the Brotherhood of Professional Base Ball Players. Initially organized as a benevolent association, the Brotherhood, under the leadership of star player and lawyer John Ward, became a collective-bargaining agency by 1887. In confronting the major league owners, the Brotherhood sought redress on such matters as the reserve clause, the sale of players, and the threatened salary ceiling.

In 1888 protracted negotiations between the Brotherhood and the owners broke down when the NL owners refused to budge on the salary ceiling issue, which had been accepted by the AA as part of the National Agreement. When the owners rejected Ward's ultimatum on the key issues, the Brotherhood moved to field a rival major league in 1890. With most of the best players in the fold, the Players' League attracted financial backers who accepted Ward's plan of sharing profits and power with the players. In 1890 the eight-team PL opened play with well-stocked teams planted in every NL city except Cincinnati.

Faced with a head-to-head battle for survival, the NL relied upon its war committee headed by Spalding. Spalding met the PL head-on by scheduling games on the same dates as PL teams, bribing PL players to jump ranks, initiating costly lawsuits over the reserve clause, lowering ticket prices, cajoling press support by threats to withdraw advertising, and raiding the AA and minor league rosters for players. Loyal managers like Anson, Wright, Bill McGunnigle, and Jim Mutrie persuaded good players to stay with the NL. Roster raids on AA teams lured stars like Billy Hamilton and Tommy Tucker; and promising rookies like pitchers Kid Nichols and Cy Young, infielder Bobby Lowe and outfielder Jess Burkett beefed up the NL teams.

Although beaten in the courts and at the turnstiles by the PL, which finished its season with Mike Kelly's Boston team beating out Ward's Brooklyn team by 6½ games, the PL's financial losses were too much for its backers to bear. In the fall of 1890, the disenchanted PL backers broke ranks and sued for peace. Magnanimous in victory, Spalding imposed no reprisals on PL players, but he gave no ground on the key issues. With the NL girding for war with the AA in the upcoming 1891 season, the salary ceiling implementation was delayed until the latest struggle was over.

The collapse of the PL afforded little relief for the stricken AA. In 1891 all-out war erupted between the NL and AA over the return of players and the relocation of franchises. When the AA's weak Cincinnati club folded, its popular manager Mike Kelly joined the Boston AA team, but after a few days he joined the Boston Nationals. With Kelly gone, the Boston AA team won the pennant by 8½ games over the Browns, but Boston fans flocked to watch Kelly captain the Boston Nationals to the NL pennant.

The 1891 season was the last for the AA. That fall four AA clubs, St. Louis, Louisville, Baltimore and Washington, quit the dying circuit to join the expanded twelve-club National League.

The "Big League": The National League, 1892–1899

The defeat of the AA in 1891 saddled the NL with a

$130,000 debt, which was incurred by buying out four of the defeated circuit's clubs. The remaining four AA teams—Baltimore, Louisville, St. Louis, and Washington—were added to the NL to form the twelve-club National League and American Association of Professional Base Ball Clubs. From 1892 to 1899 this monopolistic "big league" represented major league baseball. Enthralled by their newly created baseball "trust," the league's owners styled themselves as magnates presiding over a million-dollar entertainment industry. The magnates fully expected their monopoly league to produce unprecedented cash and glory. But such dreams were dashed by external factors, including a chronic national recession, the 1898 war with Spain, and the league's competitive imbalance. Eight seasons of play under the twelve-club format underscored its imbalance. With Boston, Baltimore, and Brooklyn winning all the races, fans in other cities lost interest. As profits dwindled, owners imposed a $2,400 ceiling on player salaries and battled one another over the division of gate receipts. Lacking strong leadership, each individual owner ran his club like a feudal fiefdom. Indeed, the blustering antics of the owners often upstaged players in newspaper accounts of this time. Some magnates hatched grandiose schemes aimed at making the monopoly league work more efficiently. Thus Andrew Freedman of the Giants advocated the annual pooling and redistribution of players and profits, provided that the "strongest and most lucrative franchises" got the best players. And another, Cincinnati owner John T. Brush, proposed harsh disciplinary measures aimed at curbing rowdy players, while also experimenting with minor league farm systems as a cheap source of talent.

Indeed, owner infighting over these and other issues damaged the big league's image, but the biggest threat to the league's credibility was the "syndicate" issue. The term "syndicatism" used at this time referred to interlocking club ownership schemes. Following bitter debate in 1898, two such interlocking directorates were approved by the owners. One of these schemes permitted owner Frank Robison of the Cleveland and St. Louis teams to transfer his best players to St. Louis; the other allowed owners Ferdinand Abell and Harry Vonderhorst of the Brooklyn and Baltimore teams to stock the Brooklyn team with the pick of those two squads. These operations made a farce of the 1899 pennant race and prompted the NL to return to an eight-club format in 1900; the cutback was accomplished by dropping Cleveland, Baltimore, Washington, and St. Louis from the NL.

The return to the eight-club format ended eight wayward seasons of major league baseball played under one unwieldy league format. Nevertheless, major league baseball continued to mature in the 1890s. Surprisingly enough, there were no franchise changes in these years. In 1898 the 154-game playing schedule was introduced, a format which dominated until 1961. And in 1893 a major change in playing rules fixed the pitching distance at 60'6" from home plate and also replaced the pitching box with a rubber slab atop a mound. This permanent change was introduced that year to correct the pitching-batting imbalance, a desirable goal which to this day remains elusive. The immediate effect of the lengthened pitching distance was not to give a mild boost to batting averages, but to send them soaring.

Thus in 1894 the Phillies posted a .349 team batting average, with the four-man outfield of Ed Delahanty, Sam Thompson, Billy Hamilton, and Tuck Turner combining for a .400-plus batting average. Sluggers also prospered, as

Thompson hit 129 homers in this era, and Washington outfielder Buck Freeman hit 25 homers in 1899; both these records endured for twenty years. (Later recounts gave the career record to Roger Connor and the single season mark to Ned Williams who had 27 tainted homers in 1884.) It took pitchers several seasons to adapt to the increased distance, but they did so by developing curves, changeups, and ball-doctoring trick deliveries to go with their fastballs. Meanwhile two offensive styles vied for acceptance in this era. For a brief time the "manly slugging" style feasted on pitchers, but the "scientific style" mastered by the Baltimore and Boston teams, which stressed bunting, stealing, sacrificing, and the hit-and-run, became the dominant offensive style of the next twenty years.

At this time other rule changes allowed player substitutions, established the infield fly rule, treated foul bunts as strikes, defined sacrifice flies and bunts, and introduced the pentagon-shaped home plate. On the playing fields, players wore stylized uniforms and most sported gloves, with catchers employing the big "Decker" mitt and wearing masks and chest protectors. When in action, teams played heady ball, using signals to trigger offensive and defensive movements. Defensively, infielders aligned themselves to turn double plays and outfielders coordinated their play by using backups, cutoffs and relays. Offensively, bunting, sacrificing, sliding, stealing, and hit-and-run plays were familiar tactics. But when teams like the Baltimore Orioles and Cleveland Spiders augmented their play with roughhouse tactics like spiking and jostling runners, baiting umpires, and bench jockeying, this "rowdy" brand of ball stirred the ire of reformers like Indianapolis owner John Brush. But hard-nosed baseball survived its critics, as did Sunday baseball. Despite fervent opposition from Sabbatarians, Sunday games were permitted by local option, although eastern cities held out against such games for twenty years. By then, major league clubs had outgrown the wooden parks of this era. A spate of ballpark fires late in this era inspired tougher safety codes that soon prompted the replacement of the vulnerable old wooden parks with concrete-and-steel edifices.

Big League Campaigns: The NL, 1892–1899

During the big league's eight-year existence, pennant monopolizing was the rule as only Boston, Baltimore, and Brooklyn teams won pennants. Managed by Frank Selee, the powerful Boston Beaneaters won back-to-back pennants in 1892–1893 and in 1897–1898. Paced by pitcher Kid Nichols (who won 297 games in this decade), Boston won the 1892 race played under a split-season format. Boston easily won the first half, but lost the second half by 3 games to manager Pat Tebeau's Cleveland Spiders, whose ace pitcher was the great Cy Young. In the postseason playoff, after the two teams played a scoreless tie, Boston swept the rest of the games to land the 1892 pennant.

In 1893 the unprofitable split-season format was dropped and the pitching distance was increased to 60'6". In a campaign marked by heavy hitting, Boston won by 5 games over Pittsburgh. Pittsburgh's Frank Killen won 34 games to lead hurlers, and outfielder Billy Hamilton batted .380. The following year saw Boston fall to the Baltimore Orioles, who rebounded from an eighth-place finish in 1893 to win the first of three consecutive pennants. Although plagued by poor pitching, the offense-minded Orioles batted .343, with every

regular topping the .300 mark at the plate. Future Hall of Famers on this star-studded team included Dan Brouthers, Hugh Jennings, John McGraw, Joe Kelley, Willie Keeler, and Wilbert Robinson. The Orioles won the 1894 pennant by 3 games over the Giants, but lost the first postseason Temple Cup Series, played between the first- and second-place finishers. In this inaugural Temple Cup Series, manager John Ward's Giants swept the Orioles in four straight games.

The following year manager Ned Hanlon's Orioles repeated as NL champions by edging the Cleveland Spiders by 3 games. A .324 team batting average and a brilliant 54–14 home won-loss record keyed the 1895 Orioles. But once again the Orioles failed in Temple Cup play, this time falling to the Spiders by four games to one. In 1896 the Orioles won a third consecutive NL pennant by 9½ games over the Spiders and swept their rivals in postseason Temple Cup play.

Bolstered by newcomers Billy Hamilton, Chick Stahl, and Jimmy Collins, Boston regained the heights in 1897–1898. Nichols won 30 games as the 1897 Beaneaters edged the Orioles by 2 games. But the Orioles won the postseason Temple Cup four games to one, the last year of this unremunerative and "shabby spectacle" which, one observer said, no more resembled the old World Series than a "crabapple does . . . a pippin."

Boston repeated in 1898, in a baseball campaign overshadowed by the Spanish-American War, beating the Orioles by 6 games. But by then the unprofitable "big league" was in its last throes. In a race marred by ludicrous syndicate ventures, in 1899 the Brooklyn Superbas won by 8 games over Boston. A syndicate team, the Superbas were managed by Hanlon, who stocked the Brooklyn team with the best players from the Brooklyn and Baltimore rosters. A similar venture that season had Robison's St. Louis-Cleveland syndicate loading the St. Louis team with the pick of these two clubs. But Robison's venture failed miserably as St. Louis finished fifth while the Cleveland team's 20–134 record was the worst by any major league team playing a 154-game schedule.

In the aftermath of the 1899 campaign, the owners scuttled the twelve-club big league and cut back to eight teams. Baltimore, Cleveland, Washington, and Louisville were dropped at a cost of $100,000, a buyout shared by the eight surviving teams. Born in debt, the monopoly big league died in debt, but the dawning twentieth century soon saw major league baseball prospering under a revived dual league format.

Major League Baseball's Silver Age, 1903–1920

The American League War, 1900–1902

The American League's struggle for major league recognition began in 1900, a propitious time for such an incursion. The NL owners had recently shed four teams, which left many unemployed players and some promising territories. Moreover, NL owners were distracted by an abortive attempt by other outsiders to revive the American Association, and by the NL's prosperous season of 1900. With a hefty boost from the nation's booming economy, most NL teams made money that year. In a close race the Brooklyn Superbas repeated as NL champs by beating a strong Pittsburgh team by 4½ games.

Such distractions favored the cause of the American League schemers. Prior to 1900, the newly proclaimed American League had operated as the Western League, a strong minor league based in the Midwest. Since 1894 the Western League's president, the able, dictatorial, and hard-drinking Byron "Ban" Johnson, had dreamed of making his circuit into a major league. To this end he had battled with NL owners over the drafting of his league's players, a practice which underscored his league's inferior status. Johnson's opportunity to press toward his goal came in 1899, when the NL cut back to eight teams. With the backing of lieutenants like Charles Comiskey and Connie Mack, Johnson renamed his circuit the American League, his clubs snapped up surplus NL players, and Comiskey moved his team to Chicago, where his White Stockings boldly confronted the NL's Cubs. With solid financial backing and a new ballpark, Comiskey's team of major league castoffs and promising youngsters captured the first AL pennant in a profitable campaign.

Emboldened by the AL's successful 1900 campaign, Johnson took note of the expiring National Agreement and unilaterally proclaimed the AL to be a major league. This 1901 declaration formally opened the American League war, and Johnson's promoters commenced hostilities by invading the NL's Philadelphia and Boston territories and occupying the former NL sites of Baltimore, Washington, Cleveland, and Detroit. To stock their teams, Johnson's financiers offered higher salaries to NL players, and in 1901 over a hundred NL players snapped at the bait. The jumpers included a bevy of stars, among them Cy Young, Clark Griffith, Jimmy Collins, and Nap Lajoie. Then, in a hotly contested and profitable pennant race, Comiskey's Chicago team edged Boston by 4 games to capture the 1901 AL pennant.

The timing of the AL's assault was excellent. In 1901–1902 the leaderless NL owners were locked in a bitter struggle over the choice of a league president. Two factions, one headed by owner Andrew Freedman of the Giants and the other by Spalding, battled to a standstill. In 1902 a temporary Control Commission headed the NL, which finally elected Henry Clay Pulliam as its president. In a complicated settlement the controversial Freedman sold his New York Giants interests for $125,000, on the condition that one of his cronies be permitted to plant an AL franchise in New York in 1903. By then, the AL had concluded another profitable season. With more NL players joining AL ranks, Connie Mack's Philadelphia Athletics landed the 1902 AL pennant by beating the Browns by 5 games.

In the fall of 1902, with most war-weary NL owners favoring a return to the dual major league structure, the NL sued for peace with the AL. Early in 1903 Johnson and Comiskey met with Pulliam and Cincinnati owner August "Garry" Herrmann and negotiated the National Agreement of 1903. Under its terms, the NL and AL would operate as separate but equal major leagues, bound by common playing rules, harmonized playing schedules, and mutually recognized territories and player contracts. The player contract accord restored the reserve clause and ended the AL's roster raids. The agreement also allowed an AL franchise to be located in New York, which Johnson secured by moving the financially shaky Baltimore Orioles to Manhattan, where in time the team prospered as the New York Yankees. Among other points, the Agreement reclassified the minor leagues and set new rules for the drafting of minor league players. Indeed, in this era minor league baseball grew lustily, reaching an all-time peak in 1913, when 46 leagues started the season. But if the Na-

tional Agreement stimulated the growth of organized base-ball, it did little to empower major league players. Major league players were denied representation on the controlling National Commission, and over the years 1902–1913 two attempts by players to organize unions were beaten down. And if the National Agreement included no salary ceiling plank, the Agreement unequivocally embraced the reserve clause and asserted the right of the National Commission to control baseball "by its own decrees . . . enforcing them without the aid of law, and [making it] answerable to no power outside its own."

The power to enforce these baseball laws came via a master stroke when the negotiators created a three-member National Commission charged with enforcing the National Agreement and keeping peace between the rival major leagues. As earlier demonstrated by the uneasy coexistence that marked the dual major league system of the 1880s, some such high-level exec-utive and judicial body was needed to settle disputes between two independent and highly competitive major leagues. It was a challenge that the National Commission successfully met for seventeen years.

Heading the National Commission were league presidents Johnson and Pulliam and Cincinnati magnate Garry Herr-mann, who served as the Commission's permanent chairman. On the face of it, this gave the NL two votes, but Johnson and Herrmann were close friends. Together they served during the lifetime of the National Commission, while four relatively weak presidents represented the NL, whose owners feared to empower any president. By contrast Johnson reigned as the most powerful president in major league history. As the AL's entrenched "czar," Johnson used his powers to safeguard his league against any NL treachery. In defending his league, Johnson personally held all AL franchise leases, ruled on ownership changes, fixed playing schedules, set basic admis-sion prices, and imposed his standards on owners and players. Inevitably such powers incurred enmities among AL owners, but until the Black Sox Scandal of 1919, Johnson's domina-tion of the AL held firm.

Over the years 1903–1920, with Herrmann's support, Johnson dominated the National Commission. In those years the Commission functioned as baseball's Supreme Court, set-tling disputes between clubs (mostly involving rights to player services), supporting the interests of club owners, disciplining players, defending umpires, fending off Federal League inter-lopers, defusing a players' union threat, and overseeing rela-tions with the minor leagues. But the most important achievement of the National Commission was its profitable administration of the revived World Series. Initially revived in 1903, the World Series got off to a shaky start when the Giants refused to play the AL champion in 1904. But in 1905 the two leagues adopted a new World Series format that placed the conduct of the classic under the control of the National Commission. With 10 percent of World Series reve-nues set aside for financing National Commission activities, the Commission faced a stern test. By capable administration the Commission met the challenge and the annual World Series became a profitable and permanent part of each major league season. By 1910 profits from World Series games had increased tenfold over those of 1905. But the Commission was responsible for any World Series chicanery; thus the rigged World Series of 1919 precipitated the downfall of the Na-tional Commission.

Peace and Prosperity: 1903–1920

By reviving the dual major league system with World Series play, the framers of the National Agreement harked back to the successful format of the golden 1880s. To that profitable format was added a National Commission charged with keep-ing the peace between the two major leagues. The combina-tion launched the major leagues on a stable course which produced no franchise changes for the next fifty years. In the 1903–1919 era the pattern was set and the two major leagues enjoyed a silver age of popularity and prosperity. In these years the popularity of the national pastime was buoyed by rising attendance, increased media coverage including motion pictures, and the ever-popular song, "Take Me Out to the Ball Game," introduced in 1908. The game's increasing popularity swelled annual profits, but as always these were unevenly distributed. In these years attendance at major league games increased steadily; from 4.7 million in 1903, attendance rose to 10 million in 1911, before falling under the impact of the Federal League incursion and the nation's involvement in the First World War. To house the growing numbers of fans, durable ballparks constructed of concrete and steel were built during the construction boom of 1909–1911. Capable of housing 30,000 or more fans, these parks served until the post–World War Two construction boom. At this time in-creasing profits boosted player salaries. By 1910 annual sala-ries ranged from $900 to $12,000, and by 1915 salaries of superstars like Ty Cobb, Tris Speaker, and Walter Johnson approached $20,000.

In this era stability also characterized the style of play. Only a few rule changes were made. Among them, a rule limited the height of pitching mounds to fifteen inches above the baseline level, the infield fly rule was invoked, a foul bunt on a third strike was ruled a strikeout, and earned run aver-ages by pitchers were included in annual records. On the playing fields teams employed the deadball style of play that resembled the "scientific game" of the 1890s. With new balls seldom being introduced into games, pitchers took command, using a variety of deliveries including spitballs and defacing balls with other foreign substances. In this era, earned run averages of 3.00 or below were seasonal norms, and seasonal batting averages, now affected by bigger parks and improved gloves, hovered around the .250 mark. Offensively, teams relied heavily on bunts, hit-and-run tactics, and base stealing to produce a few runs which power pitchers protected. Not surprisingly, pitching masters like Cy Young, Walter Johnson, Christy Mathewson, Grover Cleveland Alexander, Eddie Plank, and spitball artist Ed Walsh sparkled among the lead-ing stars of this era. But pitted against these dominant hurlers were some of the greatest hitters of all time. The masters of the deadball offense included Detroit's Ty Cobb, who won thirteen AL batting titles while scoring runs and stealing bases at unprecedented rates, and Pittsburgh's Honus Wag-ner, who won eight NL batting titles and stole 722 bases. Other hitting stars included Eddie Collins, Tris Speaker, Nap Lajoie, Sam Crawford, and the ill-fated Joe Jackson. The decline of the "deadball style" was foreshadowed by the 1910 introduction of the cork-centered ball. When widely used later in the era, it ended the conservative style of offensive play. The transformation was signaled in 1919, when Babe Ruth of the Red Sox hit 29 homers to set a new seasonal homer mark.

By 1919 the stability of the silver age had been undermined

by a series of disturbing events. In 1913 interlopers launched the Federal League and vied for major league recognition. That fall President James Gilmore lined up enough wealthy backers to plant Federal League teams in Chicago, Baltimore, Buffalo, Pittsburgh, Indianapolis, Brooklyn, St. Louis, and Kansas City. Over the next two seasons, the "Feds" took to raiding major league rosters with offers of higher salaries. The surfeit of games in 1914 and 1915 lowered major league revenues, but the Federal League invaders suffered more. There were two Federal League campaigns; Indianapolis won the 1914 pennant and Chicago took honors in 1915. The 1915 season was the last gasp of the Feds. Staggered by financial losses, the Feds surrendered when the established majors paid $5 million in compensation and awarded major league franchises to two Federal owners. But an antitrust suit pressed by dissident Baltimore owners against the majors eventually reached the U.S. Supreme Court. In 1922, Justice Oliver Wendell Holmes, speaking for a unanimous court, dismissed the suit and judged major league baseball to be mainly a sport and not a commonly accepted form of interstate commerce. But the 1922 decision was not a definitive ruling, and the major leagues would have to defend the reserve clause against future attacks in the courts and in the Congress of the United States. Nevertheless the FL challenge was the last full-scale incursion by a rival major league against the established majors.

Soon after the Federal League war, major league baseball faced another crisis brought on by America's entry into World War One. In supporting the nation's total war effort, dozens of major league players entered the armed services, and clubs staged patriotic displays, donating money and equipment to troops. For all that, in 1918 the provost marshal ruled major league baseball to be nonessential to the war effort, but his ruling permitted the majors to play a shortened 1918 campaign. That year attendance sank to 3 million, prompting tremulous owners to vote to shorten the 1919 playing schedule. However, to their surprise the war ended, and the attenuated 1919 campaign attracted 6.5 million fans. Caught short by this unexpected boom, officials sought to recoup money by upping the World Series schedule to a best-of-nine-games format.

As it turned out the expanded 1919 World Series precipitated the final crisis that ended the commissioner system. Embittered over their low salaries, eight Chicago White Sox players accepted bribes from gamblers to throw the World Series to the NL champion Cincinnati Reds. When revelations of this "Black Sox Scandal" came to light, it destroyed the National Commission and ended the old National Agreement. Chairman Herrmann resigned early in 1920, and that fall Federal Judge Kenesaw M. Landis was named the game's sole commissioner, an action confirmed by the new National Agreement of 1921. As the autocratic Landis defused the Black Sox Scandal by barring the eight accused Chicago players from organized baseball for life, the major league game lurched into a new golden age of cash and glory.

Deadball Dynasties: The American League, 1903–1920

Over the years 1903–1920, Ban Johnson's "great American League" surpassed its NL rival in attendance and also took an enduring lead over its rival in World Series victories. However, such dominance was not a result of the league's competitive balance; indeed, this dream was never realized in any era

of major league history until the early 1980s. In this early phase of AL history, four teams—Boston, Philadelphia, Chicago, and Detroit—dominated all AL pennant races.

The first of the AL minidynasties, the Boston Pilgrims relied in 1903 on the pitching of Cy Young, Bill Dineen, and Tom Hughes to trample the Philadelphia Athletics by 14½ games and then go on to win the first modern World Series over Pittsburgh. The following year Boston repeated, winning a close race by 1½ games over the New York Highlanders. That year manager John McGraw of the Giants refused to meet the Pilgrims in World Series play, but the controversy was resolved over the winter of 1904 with the establishment of a permanent World Series format.

In 1905 manager Connie Mack's Philadelphia Athletics got 87 victories from the pitching corps of Rube Waddell, Eddie Plank, Andy Coakley and Chief Bender, to edge the White Sox by 2 games. But with league-leading pitcher Waddell sidelined by an injury, the A's fell to the Giants in the World Series. As the A's faded in 1906, the most impotent of all pennant winners, the weak-hitting Chicago White Sox, won a close race by 3 games over the Highlanders. In winning, the White Sox batted .230 and scored a mere 570 runs. Yet in World Series play against the Cubs, whose 116 victories were the most ever by a team playing a 154-game schedule, the White Sox prevailed, winning four of the six games.

The next three AL pennants were captured by the Detroit Tigers, the league's most formidable dynasty to date. Managed by Hugh Jennings and powered by outfielders Sam Crawford and Ty Cobb, the latter the Georgia sensation who won the first of a record nine consecutive AL batting titles, the 1907 Tigers defeated Mack's Athletics by 1½ games. The following year the Tigers eked out a half-game win over player-manager Nap Lajoie's Cleveland team, and in 1909 the Tigers held off the Athletics by 3½ games. But in World Series action the Tigers resembled kittens. In 1907 and again in 1908 they fell to the Cubs, and in 1909 they lost to the Pirates.

Those three consecutive World Series losses infuriated AL president Johnson, but four straight AL victories over the years 1910–1913 restored the aplomb of the portly czar. In 1910 Mack's revamped Athletics, newly located in Shibe Park, used the pitching of Plank, Bender, Jack Coombs, and Cy Morgan, and the offensive and defensive skills of his "$100,000 infield" of Stuffy McGinnis, Eddie Collins, Jack Barry, and Frank "Home Run" Baker, to lap the Yankees by 14½ games and topple the Cubs in the World Series. The following year the A's repeated; this time they crushed the Tigers by 13½ games and then beat the Giants in World Series play.

Mack's A's faded to third in 1912, but the renamed Boston Red Sox, now playing in their new Fenway Park, breezed to a 14-game win over the Senators. "Smokey Joe" Wood's 34–5 pitching and Tris Speaker's .383 batting led the Red Sox, who followed their league win with a victory over the Giants in the World Series. With this latest Series, the AL took a lead in this fall competition, which they hold to this day.

The Federal League war was beginning when Mack led his resurgent A's to a 6½-game win over the Senators and another victory over the Giants in the 1913 World Series. In 1914 the Mackmen captured their fourth AL pennant in five years as they outran the Red Sox by 8½ games, but then they lost the World Series to the sweeping "miracle" Boston Braves who had come from last place on July 4 to take the NL flag. That

fall, racked by heavy financial losses incurred by the Federal League war, Mack sought to recoup by selling some of his stars. As a result, Mack's emasculated A's spent the next seven seasons in the AL cellar.

As the A's collapsed, the Red Sox and White Sox, both strengthened by player purchases from Mack, monopolized the next five AL races. By purchasing Jack Barry from Mack and snapping up minor league pitcher Babe Ruth, whom Mack had passed over, Boston was the first to cash in. The Red Sox won the 1915 pennant by 2½ games over the Tigers and went on to trounce the Phillies in World Series action. In this the last year of the Federal League war, Boston was one of only seven major league clubs to show a profit. But with the Feds out of the way in 1916, prosperity returned to the major leagues. Despite dealing Speaker to Cleveland, where his .386 batting ended Cobb's skein of nine straight AL batting titles, the Red Sox repeated. Ruth's 23 pitching victories led Boston to a 2-game victory over the White Sox and 5-game victory over the Dodgers in the World Series.

America's entry into the First World War in 1917 sent major league attendance plummeting as manager Clarence "Pants" Rowland drove his White Sox to a 9-game win over Boston. Shine-ball pitcher Eddie Cicotte's 28 victories led all AL hurlers, and Eddie Collins, Joe Jackson, and Happy Felsch supplied the power as the White Sox capped their victory with a win over the Giants in the World Series. But major league profits were low in 1917, and they touched rock bottom the following year, when the war effort forced the majors to cut their playing schedules to 128 games. The Red Sox rebounded to win the 1918 campaign by 2½ games over Cleveland. And by drubbing the Cubs in the World Series, the Red Sox notched their fifth World Series title in as many tries. However, at this point the Red Sox fell victim to their impecunious owner, Harry Frazee, whose player sales soon divested the team of its ablest stars, including Ruth. As the Red Sox faded, so did their record of World Series triumphs. To this day Red Sox fans are still waiting for a sixth World Series victory.

Boston's collapse opened the way for the powerful White Sox to win the shortened 1919 race by 3½ games over the surging Cleveland Indians. In the wake of the White Sox victory came the sordid World Series of 1919, which saw eight Chicago players conspire with gamblers to throw the extended Series to the Cincinnati Reds. In 1920 the much-publicized revelations of that piece of skullduggery forced owner Charles Comiskey to suspend his eight Black Sox players in the last week of the red-hot 1920 pennant campaign.

Stripped of their stars, the White Sox finished second, a game ahead of the Yankees and two games behind the victorious Cleveland Indians. The gritty Indians lost their star shortstop Ray Chapman when he was fatally beaned by pitcher Carl Mays of the Yankees. To the present day, this remains the only fatality in major league history that was the direct result of a playing field accident. In the memorable World Series of 1920, Cleveland and Brooklyn were tied at two games apiece when Indian second-sacker Bill Wambsganss busted a promising Dodger rally by pulling off the first and only unassisted triple play in World Series history. And in that same game Indian outfielder Elmer Smith hit the first World Series grand-slam homerun. Such heroics, plus three pitching victories by Stan Coveleski, boosted the Indians to a five-games-to-two triumph in the 1920 fall classic. Cleveland's victory also ended the Boston, Philadelphia, Chicago pennant monopoly of the AL's deadball era, while Ruth's 59 homers as a Yankee in 1920 heralded the incoming "big-bang" style of play that would characterize the coming decade of the 1920s.

Deadball Dynasties: The National League, 1901–1920

A similar pattern of competitive imbalance also marked the NL campaigns of the silver age. In this era three NL mini-dynasties—those of Pittsburgh, Chicago, and New York — monopolized the first 14 NL campaigns. Moreover, even as outsiders rose up to win three consecutive pennants over the years 1914–1916, the Giants and Cubs came back to win pennants in 1917–1918 before yielding to the Reds and Dodgers in this era's final two campaigns. Of the three monopolists, the Giants were the most dominating team. Under manager John McGraw, "the Napoleonic genius" who jumped the AL in 1902 to skipper the moribund Giants, the New Yorkers won six pennants, finished second eight times, and suffered only one losing season.

In 1901 the first of this dynastic trio, the Pittsburgh Pirates, won the first of three consecutive NL pennants. Pittsburgh's rise began in 1900, the year the NL cut back to eight teams. When his Louisville team was dropped in the NL's cutback, owner Barney Dreyfuss purchased the Pittsburgh club, which he strengthened by adding Louisville stars Fred Clarke and Honus Wagner to his Pirate team. Powered by player-manager Clarke and Wagner, and unscathed by the disastrous roster raids by AL teams that were weakening his opponents, Pittsburgh won the 1901 NL race by 7½ games over the Phillies; they then won the 1902 race by an awesome 27½ games over runner-up Brooklyn, and captured the 1903 flag by 6½ games over the Giants. In each of these campaigns, both Wagner and Clarke topped the .300 mark in batting. Moreover, Wagner's .355 hitting won the 1903 batting title while outfielder Ginger Beaumont's .357 batting won the 1902 batting title. The Pirate pitching staff was fronted by Deacon Phillippe, who won 66 games in these years, and by Jack Chesbro, who won 49 games in two seasons before jumping to the AL in 1903. In postseasonal play, the 1903 Pirates lost the first modern World Series to the Boston Red Sox.

Pittsburgh sank to fourth place in 1904 as the Giants surfaced to win consecutive pennants in 1904–1905. In 1904 the Giants won 106 games to beat the runner-up Chicago Cubs by 13 games. Power pitching by "Ironman" Joe McGinnity (35–8), Christy Mathewson (33–12), and "Dummy" Taylor (21–15) paced the light-hitting Giants to victory. But in the aftermath of the win, manager McGraw refused to meet the AL champion Boston Pilgrims in World Series play. That issue was resolved in 1905, the year McGraw drove his team to a 9-game win over the Pirates and then to an easy conquest of the Philadelphia Athletics in the World Series.

The following year, the Chicago Cubs emerged as the third NL dynasty of the deadball era. Pennant-starved since 1886, the Chicagoans recouped with a vengeance, winning an astonishing 530 games over the years 1906–1910. Such mastery was good enough to land four pennants in those five years. Skippered by player-manager Frank Chance, who, along with fellow infielders Johnny Evers and Joe Tinker, is now immortalized in baseball folklore, the 1906 Cubs won their record 116 games. Powered by Chance and third baseman Harry Steinfeldt, and armed by Mordecai "Three-Finger" Brown's 26–6 pitching, this superb team buried the Giants by 20

games, but lost the World Series to their hometown AL rivals, the "hitless wonder" White Sox.

The Cubs made it three victories in a row by winning in 1907–1908. The 1907 Cubs crushed Pittsburgh by 17 games, and in the unforgettable season of 1908, the Cubs edged the Giants by a single game. With two weeks remaining in the 1908 season, the Giants, Cubs, and Pirates were locked in a close race. Then, in a fateful encounter with the Cubs at the Polo Grounds, Fred Merkle of the Giants blundered by failing to touch second base as his Giants were scoring what looked like the winning run. In the stormy aftermath of this play, Umpire Hank O'Day ruled Merkle out for failing to touch the base and declared the game a tie because the swirling masses of Giant fans on the field made resumption of play impossible. Later NL president Harry Pulliam supported O'Day's decision and ruled that if necessary the game would be replayed at the close of the season. As it turned out, this was necessary because the Cubs and the Giants finished the season in a dead heat. To settle the outcome, the controversial game was replayed on October 8 at the Polo Grounds. The Cubs won the sudden-death game 4–2, as Brown outpitched Mathewson. In baseball folklore the Giant defeat permanently stigmatized "Bonehead" Fred Merkle as the blamesake of the Giants' defeat. As for the Cubs, they took full advantage of their quirky victory by defeating the Tigers for a second straight time in World Series action.

In 1909 the Cubs won 104 games, with Brown pitching 27 victories. But the Pirates won 110 that year to beat Chance's men by 6½ games. Wagner led the league in hitting, and pitchers Vic Willis and Howie Camnitz combined for 48 wins. In World Series action, the Pirates hung a third straight loss on the AL champion Tigers. But the Cubs rebounded in 1910, winning 104 games for a second straight year. This time it was enough to lap the Giants by 13, but the Cubs then fell to the Athletics in the World Series.

Over the years 1911–1913 the Giants dominated NL play. In winning three consecutive pennants, they piled up 303 victories; pitchers Mathewson and Rube Marquard accounted for 147 of these, while Giant hitters led the NL in batting each year. But in World Series appearances McGraw's men repeatedly swooned, losing to the Athletics in 1911 and 1913 and to the Red Sox in 1912.

Over the years 1914–1916, a whiff of competitive balance settled over the NL as three outsiders wrested pennants from the three dynasty teams. In 1914 the "miracle" Boston Braves stormed from 10 games back in mid-July to win 60 of their last 76 games; the surge was enough to crush the Giants by 10½ games. The following year, the Philadelphia Phillies landed their first NL pennant on the strength of 31 wins by pitcher Grover Cleveland Alexander and 24 homers by Gavvy Cravath. The Phillies beat out the Boston Braves by 7 games. And in 1916, manager Wilbert Robinson's Dodgers got 25 victories from pitcher Ed Pfeffer as they edged the Phillies by 2½ games. But this trio of outsiders produced only one World Series victory, which came when the Braves swept Mack's Athletics to win the 1914 classic. As for the other interlopers, both the Phillies and Dodgers fell to the Boston Red Sox.

Like the AL's, the NL's wartime campaigns of 1917–1918 were plagued by poor attendance which caused some tremulous owners to sell players in hopes of recouping losses. But the pennant monopolists held firm. The Giants won the 1917 race by 10 games over the Phillies, but then fell for a fourth

straight time in World Series play as the White Sox prevailed. And in 1918, after winning the attenuated NL race by 10½ games over the Giants, the Cubs bowed to the Red Sox in the World Series.

The deadball era was drawing to a close in 1919, which was the year that manager Pat "Whiskey Face" Moran drove his Cincinnati Reds to their first NL pennant. The Reds won by 9 games over the runner-up Giants as future Hall of Fame outfielder Edd Roush batted .321 to lead the league. The Reds also won the World Series, but the stench of the Black Sox Scandal sullied their victory. As breaking news stories of that scandal overshadowed stories of the 1920 pennant race, in progress when the news broke, the Brooklyn Dodgers went on to defeat the Giants by 7 games. But the Dodgers lost to an inspired Cleveland Indians team in the World Series. In the atmosphere of gloom caused by the Black Sox Scandal revelations, it was also apparent that the deadball era of stylized baseball play was ending. But a new era was unfolding in the 1920s that would launch the major leagues into new uplands of cash and glory.

Baseball's Second Golden Age, 1921–1931

Over the winter of 1920–1921, crestfallen club owners slavishly chose Federal Judge Kenesaw Mountain Landis to be baseball's high commissioner and empowered him to restore the game's scandal-sullied image. At the time few observers could have predicted that major league baseball was moving into another golden age of cash and glory that would be highlighted by the dazzling exploits of Babe Ruth, who already was enthralling fans by his mastery of the new "big-bang" offensive style. But the sparkling turnabout in baseball's fortunes was also buoyed by the optimistic spirit of America's "roaring twenties." This was a decade of booming prosperity, an expanding urban population, declining work hours, and hefty increases in recreational spending by the American people. By 1929, indeed, Americans were annually spending $4.9 billion for recreational pursuits. To be sure, much of this spending was diverted into movies, radios, and automobiles, but major sports like baseball, football, basketball, boxing, golf, and tennis were attracting millions of hero-worshipping fans. Such adulation made demigods of athletes like Red Grange, Jack Dempsey, Bobby Jones, and Bill Tilden, but all of these sporting heroes were overshadowed by Babe Ruth, who now became the most photographed American of the decade.

During baseball's "guilty season" of 1920, it was the fun-loving Ruth, not the stern moralist Commissioner Landis, who diverted the attention of fans from the Black Sox Scandal. In 1920 the Babe accomplished this feat by smacking 54 homers to break his own seasonal mark, which he had set only the year before. Ruth's latest achievement fully justified the astonishing $125,000 which the Yankees shelled out before the 1920 season to obtain the former Red Sox pitching ace, whose batting achievements caused him to be assigned to regular duty as an outfielder.

With the Yankees, the charismatic Ruth bestrode the baseball scene like a young colossus. The very embodiment of the big-bang offensive style, Ruth notched ten AL homer titles over the years 1920–1931. In the last six of those seasons, he smacked 302 homers, including a record 60 blows in 1927. At the close of the 1931 season Ruth's homer output exceeded

600, and when he retired in 1935, he had raised his total to 714, along with a lifetime batting average of .342.

Inspired by Ruth's example, the big-bang style dominated major league baseball offensives of this and all subsequent eras. While no other team matched the consistent power of the Yankees, in this era NL teams outslugged their AL counterparts. And if no player surpasses Ruth's consistent power, sluggers like Cy Williams, Hack Wilson, Chuck Klein, Harry Heilmann, and Rogers Hornsby ably mastered the big-bang style. In 1930 Wilson hit 56 homers to set an NL seasonal mark, but for sheer all-around batting consistency Hornsby and Heilmann had no peers. Over the years 1921–1927 Tiger outfielder Heilmann topped .390 four times, hit 104 homers, and won four AL batting titles.

Incredibly Hornsby bettered this performance. Over the years 1920–1925, Hornsby won six NL batting titles, topped the .400 mark in batting three times, and won two Triple Crowns. Hornsby's lifetime batting average of .358 is the best of any right-handed batter in major league history.

Such heroics by players of this era were the highlights of all-out seasonal offensives that dwarfed those of the deadball era. In this decade seasonal batting averages in both major leagues topped .280, with NL batters averaging a whopping .303 in 1930. At the same time, league-wide homer production, averaging 540 a season in the NL and 490 in the AL, helped raise per-game scoring to an average of five runs per team, while relegating base stealing to the status of a secondary tactic. Abetting the big-bang offensives of this era were innovations in technology and in pitching rules. Technology provided livelier balls, which were more frequently changed during games; indeed, fans were now permitted to keep balls hit into the stands. Meanwhile, rule changes of 1920–1921 barred the use of spitters and other doctored balls by all pitchers except for a few specified veterans. Such changes made for much battered pitchers with ERAs of 4.00 now regarded as an acceptable level of pitching performance. To cope with the situation, managers now relied more heavily on relief pitchers. Nevertheless, virtuoso starting pitchers like Johnson, Alexander, Grimes, Grove, Pennock, Hoyt, and Vance ranked among the top stars of this decade.

That fans welcomed the new offensive style was evidenced by the record-setting attendance marks of this era. Despite the lurid exposés of the Black Sox Scandal, a record 9.1 million fans attended major league games in 1920. Then, after falling below that mark for three seasons, attendance soared to an average of 9.6 million a season over the years 1924–1929 and peaked at 10.1 million in 1930. Helping to swell attendance in this era were Sunday games, which were legalized in all cities outside of Pennsylvania. Such support boosted revenues by 40 percent over the previous era and raised annual player salaries to an average of $7,000 by 1930. However, such average figures are misleading. In the NL, the Giants, Dodgers, Pirates, and Cardinals got most of the profits, and the AL Yankees alone accounted for 25 percent of that circuit's annual attendance. Player salaries also varied widely, ranging from less than $2,000 for fringe players to Ruth's princely $80,000 for the season of 1930; moreover, in this era the Yankee and Cub payrolls topped those of other teams.

That the Cardinals ranked with the most profitable NL clubs at this time owed to the genius of General Manager Branch Rickey. One of baseball's greatest innovators, Rickey had an impact on the game that extended far beyond this decade. At this time Rickey made a contender out of the impecunious Cardinals by reviving the farm system and using minor league farm clubs to develop and train young players. By purchasing minor league clubs and establishing working agreements with others, and by deploying scouts to sign young players at low costs, Rickey built and stocked a network of minor league farm clubs which supplied the Cardinals with a steady flow of star players. Despite opposition from Landis, Rickey's farm network flourished and was widely imitated. By cornering the market on young talent and selling surplus players to other major league teams, the Cardinals profited despite poor attendance. For his part, Rickey profited by reaping a percentage from each player sale.

As a baseball innovator, Rickey had a much more enduring impact on the game than Commissioner Landis. By banishing the Black Sox, disciplining players, and presiding in watch-dog fashion over annual World Series games, Landis contributed to restoring the game's honest image. But Landis's autocratic posturing grated on major league owners, some of whom resented his opposition to farm systems and his conservative approach to the sale of World Series radio broadcasting rights. Landis also stubbornly opposed the racial integration of organized baseball. Thus in this era outcast black players turned to their own leader, Andrew "Rube" Foster, who founded the Negro National League in 1920. In 1923 the Eastern Colored League took to the field as a second black major league, but gave way in 1928 to the Negro American League, which lasted until 1950. Such leagues fielded great black stars like future Hall of Famers Satchel Paige, Pop Lloyd, "Cool Papa" Bell, the slugging Josh Gibson, and Ray Dandridge. In this decade postseason exhibition games played between white and black major leaguers drew attention to the black stars, whose abilities matched and often surpassed those of white major leaguers.

But the limited exposure afforded to black stars contrasted starkly with the broad media coverage now lavished on the white majors. For this golden era of major league baseball history was gilded by newspaper coverage which touted the games and the player-heroes in romanticized style. Moreover, motion pictures and radio coverage opened new dimensions for promoting the game that suspicious owners of the age were slow to exploit. Conservative owners also took a dim view of the night baseball games which pioneer promoters were staging in the minors and in the black leagues. However, when the golden age ended amidst the worst economic depression of this century, such innovations would enable hard-pressed owners to better cope with the austerities of the 1930s.

Golden Age Campaigns: The AL, 1921–1931

In this era dreams of a competitively balanced AL went for naught as three teams—the Yankees, Senators, and Athletics—dominated the eleven pennant races. Foremost among these powers, the lordly Yankees used Ruth's explosive power to win six pennants and three world titles, while outdrawing all other AL teams by a wide margin. Once established, the Yankee dynasty lasted for forty years, during which time no more than three seasons passed by without the Yankees hoisting another AL pennant. In laying the foundations for this awesome domination, Yankee owners Jake Ruppert and Cap Huston repeatedly took advantage of their financially

strapped Boston colleague, Harry Frazee, to denude the latter's Boston Red Sox of its ablest stars. In 1919 the Yankees pried pitcher Carl Mays from Frazee, and at the end of that year, the Yankee owners paid Frazee $125,000 up-front money and also a $300,000 loan to snag their biggest catch of all in Babe Ruth. What's more, over the next few years Frazee paid off the loan by sending more players to New York. By then, picking the right Boston players was the job of General Manager Ed Barrow, who left his former post as Boston field manager to come to the Yankees. After joining the Yankees at the close of the 1920 season, Barrow's dealings with Frazee over the next three seasons made Yankees of such Boston stars as pitchers Waite Hoyt, Sam Jones, Joe Bush, Herb Pennock, and George Pipgras, catcher Wally Schang, and infielders Everett Scott and Joe Dugan.

Over the years 1921–1923, these acquisitions helped to carry the Yankees to three consecutive pennants while burying the once-proud Red Sox. In 1921, with Ruth smashing 59 homers and driving in 171 runs, and Mays pitching 27 victories, the Yankees defeated the Indians by 4½ games. The following year ex–Red Sox players Jones, Bush, and Scott were on hand to help the Yankees edge the Browns by a single game. However, consecutive World Series losses to the rival New York Giants, whose Polo Grounds the Yankees shared as tenants, blighted these victories. But in 1923 the Yankees, now owned outright by Ruppert, moved into their brand-new Yankee Stadium, where Ruth's opening-day homer signaled a coming turnabout. With Ruth batting .393 that season, leading the league in homers, and sharing the lead in RBIs, the Yankees swept to an easy 16-game romp over the runner-up Tigers. And then, after dropping two of the first three games of the 1923 World Series, the Yankees swept the Giants to land their first world title.

This initial display of Yankee dominance ended in 1924, when the team lost to the Washington Senators by two games. It was Washington's first AL pennant. Led by their "boy manager," second baseman Bucky Harris, the Senators went on to down the Giants in a seven-game World Series struggle. Pitching in relief, the veteran Walter Johnson notched the victory in the final game. The following year the Senators repeated, using a powerful .303 batting assault to top the Athletics by 8½ games. But in World Series action the 1925 Senators blew a three-games-to-one lead and lost to the Pirates in seven games.

As the AL's 1926 season began, any likelihood of a Yankee resurgence seemed a remote possibility. Only the year before, the Yankees languished in seventh place, as illness and insubordination tolled on Ruth's performance. But a contrite Ruth came back as strong as ever, and young infielders Lou Gehrig, Tony Lazzeri, and Mark Koenig revitalized the team. In a close race the Yankees edged the Indians by 3 games, but lost to the Cardinals in a memorable seven-game World Series battle. Rebounding from that defeat, the 1927 Yankees mounted one of the most devastating assaults in major league history. In crushing the runner-up Athletics by 19 games, the Yankees batted .307 and led the AL in all major offensive categories. Ruth's 60 homers set a seasonal mark that lasted for 34 years, and Gehrig weighed in with 47 homers and 175 RBIs. In World Series action the Yankees easily dispatched the Pirates in four games. The following year the Yankees repeated, although they were pressed hard by the Athletics, who finished 2½ games behind. Still the 1928 Yankees finished their season in fine fettle by scoring an avenging four-

game sweep of the Cardinals in the World Series.

The Yankees' latest stranglehold on the AL ended in 1929, when manager Connie Mack's power-packed Athletics captured the first of three consecutive pennants. The resurrection of the once-powerful Athletic dynasty was a triumph of patient rebuilding by Mack. After the veteran owner-manager broke up his formidable 1914 team, the Athletics spent the next seven years in the AL cellar. After quitting the depths in 1922, the team improved steadily. In 1928 the Athletics came close to dethroning the Yankees, and in 1929 the Mackmen mounted an offensive which rivaled that of the 1927 Yankees as they crushed the New Yorkers by 18 games. The team's .296 batting average was led by outfielder Al Simmons, who batted .365 with 34 homers and a league-leading 157 RBIs, and by first baseman Jimmy Foxx's .354-33-117 performance. The pitching staff, led by Lefty Grove (20–6), George Earnshaw (24–8), and Rube Walberg (18–11), was the league's best. In World Series play the Athletics crushed the Cubs in five games; one of the team's victories included a devastating 10-run outburst that turned an 8–0 deficit into a 10–8 victory.

Over the next two seasons, the Athletics continued their dominance. In 1930 they defeated the Senators by 8 games, and in 1931 they crushed the runner-up Yankees by 13½ games. In postseason action, the Athletics beat the Cardinals in five games to win the 1930 World Series, but in 1931 the team lost a seven-game struggle to the Cardinals. Indeed, the 1931 AL pennant was to be the last for manager Mack and for the Philadelphia Athletics. Financial losses caused by the nation's deepening Depression forced the aging manager to sell star players to weather the storm. In the past such drastic measures had worked, and Mack had been able to rebuild his team. But advancing age and changing baseball fortunes now conspired against Mack.

Golden Age Campaigns: The NL, 1921–1931

Although upstaged by Ruth and the Yankees and bested in six of eleven World Series clashes, NL teams of this era more than held their own against AL rivals. Indeed, NL sluggers outslugged their AL counterparts in nine of these seasons, NL pitchers posted better ERAs than AL hurlers, and in the inflationary 1930 season NL batters outhit and outslugged their rivals by wide margins. That year NL batters averaged .303 to the AL's .288, and NL sluggers powered 892 homers to 673 for the junior circuit.

And yet in this era the NL was no better balanced competitively than the AL. Of the eleven NL campaigns of this era, the Giants and Cardinals each won four, the Pirates won two, and the Cubs won the other. In 1924 manager McGraw's Giants became the first major league team of this century to win four consecutive pennants. This was a feat matched only by Harry Wright's Boston Red Stockings of the 1870s and by Charley Comiskey's St. Louis Browns of the 1880s. For their part, the Giants of this era turned the trick with a potent batting attack; in their four-year sway, Giant hitters averaged better than .300 and smashed 335 homers.

In stocking his first pennant winner, McGraw pulled off astute trades with the moribund Braves and Phillies to obtain pitcher Art Nehf, shortstop Dave Bancroft, and outfielders Irish Meusel and Casey Stengel. These acquisitions joined with future Hall of Famers Frank Frisch and Ross Youngs to lead the Giants to the 1921 pennant. That year the Giants edged the Pirates by 4 games, and in 1922 they repeated,

beating the runner-up Reds by 7 games. In both years the Giants met and defeated the Yankees in World Series play. In 1923 the Giants won a third straight flag by edging the Reds by 4½ games, but they lost the World Series to the Yankees. In 1924, with the addition of first baseman and future Hall of Famer Bill Terry, the Giants eked a narrow 1½-game victory over the Dodgers. In World Series play the Giants lost to the Senators in seven games. The 1924 pennant was McGraw's last as the Giants' manager and the last by a Giant team in this era.

As sicknesses took their toll on McGraw, coach Hugh Jennings, and outfielder Ross Youngs, the Pirates ended the Giants' four-year reign with an 8½-game victory over the New Yorkers. Future Hall of Famers—third baseman Harold "Pie" Traynor, and outfielders Max Carey and Hazen "Ki Ki" Cuyler—led the Pirates, who went on to score a dramatic come-from-behind victory over the Senators in the 1925 World Series.

As the squabbling Pirates faded to third place in 1926, the hitherto unsung Cardinals won their first NL pennant. It was the first of four championships in this era by this emergent new dynasty. The rise of the Cardinals was the handiwork of general manager Branch Rickey. From Rickey's expanding farm system came stalwarts like infielders Jim Bottomley and Tom Thevenow and outfielders Chick Hafey and Taylor Douthit. In 1921 player-manager Rogers Hornsby led the team to a 2-game victory over the Cincinnati Reds. And in a classic seven-game struggle, the Cardinals went on to defeat the Yankees in the World Series.

That fall Rickey enraged Cardinal fans by dealing the contentious Hornsby to the Giants for second baseman Frank Frisch. Frisch batted .337 to lead the 1927 Cardinals, while Hornsby batted .361 with the Giants. Nevertheless, both teams came up short, as the Pirates edged the runner-up Cardinals by 1½ games. Pittsburgh's .305 team batting average was sparked by future Hall of Fame outfielders Paul and Lloyd Waner; Paul's .380 clouting led the league, and brother Lloyd batted .355. But the Pirates were crushed by the Yankees in the 1927 World Series.

Under manager Bill McKechnie, the resilient Cardinals rebounded to win the 1928 campaign by 2 games over the Giants. But like the 1927 Pirates, the Cardinals too were swept by the Yankees in the World Series. As the Cardinals slipped to fourth place in 1929, the Cubs won their only pennant of this era. Managed by Joe McCarthy, the Cub revival was powered by a .303 team batting attack. Newly acquired Rogers Hornsby, who was pried loose from the Braves in a mammoth deal, led the Cubs with a .380 batting average. Behind Hornsby the team's power-packed outfield weighed in with Riggs Stephenson hitting .362, Hack Wilson batting .345 and driving in 159 runs, and "Ki Ki" Cuyler batting .360. The assault boosted the Cubs to a 10½-game victory over the Pirates, but the Chicagoans were no match for the rampaging Athletics in the World Series.

As the golden era ended, manager Gabby Street drove the Cardinals to consecutive pennants in 1930–1931. In 1930 the Cardinals struggled to a 2-game victory over the Cubs, who dumped manager McCarthy in the wake of the loss. In this vintage year of NL hitting, the Cardinals batted .314, but were outhit by the Giants, who smote .319 as a team! Every Cardinal starter in 1930 topped the .300 mark, and in World Series play the Cardinals outhit the Athletics. Nevertheless, the Athletics won the World Series in six games. The following year, as NL batting mirrored the falling national economy by dropping to .277, the Cardinals coasted to a 13-game victory over the Giants. A .286 team batting average and stout pitching by "Wild Bill" Hallahan, Burleigh Grimes, Paul Derringer, and Jess Haines paced the Cardinals, who defeated the Athletics in the World Series, four games to three. But falling attendance caused by the deepening Depression marred the 1931 NL season. Indeed, the decline signaled the end of the latest golden age and the beginning of a long era of austerity in major league baseball.

Austerity Baseball, 1932–1945

In company with most industrialized nations, America during these years suffered the calamitous effects of a lingering economic Depression followed hard after by years of total war. In America the great Depression blighted the 1930s by creating millions of jobless workers, holding wages far below their 1929 level, slowing population growth, and, of course, drastically reducing recreational spending. Although abetted by federal remedial programs, the national economy languished until 1940, when federal defense-spending programs spurred an economic revival. But the following year the nation faced a second ordeal, when it embarked upon four years of total war against the Axis powers.

Major league baseball felt the effects of the gathering Depression in 1931, when the AL suffered losses while the NL barely broke even. Once engulfed by the economic storm, both major leagues were hard hit as attendance fell to 8.1 million in 1932 and hit rock bottom with an overall total of 6.3 million in 1933. Thereafter attendance improved, but not until 1940 did annual attendance totals reach 10 million. A similar sickening decline affected the minor leagues. But the minors recovered strongly after 1933 and zoomed to a record total attendance of 18 million in 1940.

Since major league baseball's fate was at its gates, declining attendance translated into financial losses. In the AL, six previous years of domination by the Yankees and Athletics had the junior circuit trailing the NL in overall revenues. After losing a total of $156,000 in 1931, the AL suffered three desperate years during which overall losses topped $2 million. Slow improvement began with the 1935 season, but as always revenues were unevenly distributed. Strong clubs like the Yankees and Tigers fared far better than the financially battered Athletics, Browns, and Senators. Nor were conditions much better in the NL, which also lost heavily during the years 1932–1934. In that three-year span every NL team suffered at least two seasons of red ink. A turnabout began with the 1935 season, but over the next six seasons annual profits only twice totaled $500,000. Moreover, like those of the AL, NL revenues were unevenly distributed. The Cubs, Giants, Cardinals, and Reds fared far better than did the woebegone Braves and Phillies.

Under such financial pressures, salaries of major league players were slashed. Annual salary spending in the majors fell from $4 million in 1929 to $3 million in 1933, and as late as 1940 total payrolls still lagged behind the 1929 figure. Such cuts dropped the average player's salary to $6,000 in 1933, and the 1939 average salary of $7,300 still lagged behind the $7,500 figure of 1929. While such pay was good for those desperate times, job insecurity was rife among big league players of this era. Most players of this era needed no

reminders that budget-slashing owners could easily find cheap replacements in the minor leagues. But for the time being, the great stars of the black majors, which also suffered from Depression austerities, posed no competitive threat. However, winds of change were stirring against segregated institutions in America, including major league baseball's unwritten color bar.

Of course, owners also faced a survival-of-the-fittest struggle in this depressed decade. Better-located clubs like the Yankees, Tigers, Cubs, and Giants adapted far better than did the owners of the financially strapped Athletics, Senators, Browns, Braves, and Phillies. Caught up in a vicious cycle, these poorer owners were forced to sell players to better-heeled clubs, a policy which had the effect of worsening attendance. However, one club, the Cardinals, managed to sell players to much better advantage. Although plagued by poor attendance, including three seasons which produced an aggregate home attendance total of fewer than 900,000, and one of those a world championship season which attracted only 325,000 fans at home, the Cardinals still managed to hold their own financially. Player sales from Rickey's well-stocked minor league farm system enabled the Cardinals to recoup financially and at the same time field strong teams.

At this time eager purchasers of players included Tom Yawkey, the wealthy new owner of the Red Sox. In this decade Yawkey spent $1 million on players. As a result Red Sox attendance rose while that of his moribund NL rival the Boston Braves worsened. Other bullish owners included the owners of the Cubs, Reds, Tigers, and Dodgers. But the well-financed Yankees emulated Rickey's example and built an efficient farm system of their own. Directed by the ruthlessly efficient George Weiss, the Yankee farms strengthened the Yankees' stranglehold on the AL.

Still, Depression-imposed austerities challenged all clubs of this era to find new ways to beef up revenues. Perhaps the most drastic of these was the plan of the owner of the St. Louis Browns to move the club to the West Coast, a strategy which was aborted by the outbreak of World War Two. But for the most part promoters tried to find ways of wringing more money from ballpark fans. Among these, expanding concession sales, utilizing promotional schemes, and staging night baseball games were tactics borrowed from minor league promoters and the black majors. But night baseball proved to be the wave of the future for the major leagues. When introduced to the majors in 1935 by Cincinnati general manager Larry MacPhail, the popularity of night baseball had most major league clubs following suit by 1940. Yet another source of profits came from the sale of local radio rights to broadcast accounts of games, a scheme which some owners had tried, but most had stubbornly resisted back in the twenties. By 1939 radio income totaled 7.3 percent of club revenues, up from a negligible 0.3 percent in 1930. Similarly, sales of World Series radio rights, a windfall shared by all major league clubs, now fetched higher prices. And at the close of the decade, the new medium of television showed promise, but the onslaught of World War Two delayed its profitable exploitation.

In the near future such innovations would profoundly alter the major league scene, but for now survival dictated sticking to more conservative measures. Thus in this era no privately financed ballparks were constructed (as, indeed, had been the case in the 1920s with the exception of Yankee Stadium), but Cleveland's publicly financed Municipal Stadium foreshad-owed a future building boom that would replace most of the aging major league parks with modern facilities financed by public monies. When that day dawned, black players at last would be playing alongside whites in organized baseball. But in this era Commissioner Landis and his supporters continued their stubborn resistance in the face of mounting public support for organized baseball's integration. The breakthrough came, a year after Landis's death in 1945, as the first black player in this century signed a major league contract. Ironically, the integration of the white majors dealt a death blow to the flourishing black major leagues.

However, such impending changes were only dimly perceived by owners of this era. On the whole the 1930s were conservative years, with no significant rule changes invoked. In these years teams continued to master the big-bang style of play, with annual homer barrages, and pitching ERAs surpassing those of the 1920s. And if Ruth's departure in 1935 deprived the game of its most colorful hero of all time, new slugging stars like Hank Greenberg, Ted Williams, and Joe DiMaggio proved to be worthy successors. Their accomplishments and those of this era's teams were lavishly covered by sportswriters and by a new breed of radio sportscasters, whose ranks included some ex-players. Such coverage broadened baseball's appeal. So did the 1939 opening of the Baseball Hall of Fame at Cooperstown, New York, and the annual ritual of electing baseball immortals to the select circle. Indeed, the first annual election conducted in January of 1936 selected Ty Cobb, Babe Ruth, Honus Wagner, Christy Mathewson, and Walter Johnson as the five charter members. Over the years the number of enshrined players swelled to over 200, including stars from the segregated black majors. And so did the numbers of fans who annually made the pilgrimage to the Hall of Fame; from a few thousand a year in this era, the number of visitors now exceeds 250,000 annually.

The Crisis of World War Two

The major leagues were recovering from Depression-imposed austerities when the nation's entry into World War Two posed a second major crisis. From 1942 until the Allied victory in 1945, the nation's total war effort sapped baseball's manpower and threatened to curtail the 1945 playing season. Among the 12 million Americans summoned to military service during the war years were some 500 major league players and 3,500 minor leaguers. This talent drain shrank the minor leagues to nine circuits at one point, while only President Roosevelt's "green light" enabled the major leagues to continue playing throughout the war years.

That the major leagues continued playing the game in the face of wartime austerities owed to the resilience of its promoters and the continuing support of the fans. Although annual attendance fell from 10 million in 1941 to 8.8 million in 1942 and to a low point of 7.7 million in 1943, the numbers rebounded to 9 million in 1944 and then soared to a record 11.1 million in 1945. Indeed, baseball's continuing popularity won the support of political figures like J. Edgar Hoover and Senator A. B. Chandler, who were convinced that the game was serving the war effort by boosting morale, both on the homefront and among the troops abroad.

Nevertheless, it was no easy task keeping the game of baseball afloat amidst a total war effort. In these years owners were hard-pressed to find ways of coping with a variety of shortages. Among them, a crunching transportation and hotel

accommodation shortage forced promoters to cancel spring training programs in the southlands. And in 1945 the same problems forced the cancellation of that year's All-Star Game. Meanwhile a rubber shortage forced the major leagues to go with a dead "balata" ball (with a hard plastic at the core) in 1943, and all during the war a shortage of wood affected the quality of bats. Early in the war the threat of submarine attacks on coastal shipping also curtailed night games in East Coast centers, but by 1944 the restriction was lifted. Indeed, night games came to be welcomed by government officials, who regarded them as good recreation for defense workers.

But the worst shortage of all was in manpower. Indeed, never before nor since did the major leagues face a talent shortage of such proportions as occurred then. As draft boards denuded team rosters of able players, club officials scoured the land for draft rejects and other ineligibles; at this time, overage and underaged players were welcomed along with aliens. In questing after talented alien players, scouts turned up a mother lode in Latin America. Cuba turned out to be especially rich in prospects and at this time some fifty Cuban players were recruited. Indeed, at one point a young minor league promoter and war hero, Bill Veeck, proposed to buy the sickly NL Phillies franchise and stock it with black players from the Negro Leagues. Landis nixed the proposal.

For their part, owners needed stout hearts and a love of the game to keep going in the face of financial losses. In 1943 the majors lost $240,000, with the Cardinals and Tigers faring better than most other clubs. Hardest hit were the owners of the NL Phillies, who declared bankruptcy. The franchise was sold to the NL for $50,000, and after one abortive sale attempt NL officials sold the club to one of the DuPont Company heirs. Thus in the affluent hands of Bob Carpenter, this chronically weak NL franchise was soon revitalized.

At this time each owner was obliged to do his bit for the war effort. In response, clubs staged war bond sales, admitted servicemen free of charge to games, and allowed radio broadcasts of games to be transmitted free of charge to military bases. Although costly, such gestures paid off by increasing baseball's popularity. By 1944 the worst of the financial reverses caused by the war ended, and when the 1945 season returned overall profits of $1.2 million, it was apparent that major league baseball was once again on the upswing.

Such was not the case for the players who took a financial beating in each of these years. A government edict of 1943, which was part of a general effort to halt inflation by stabilizing wages, froze player salaries. The salary freezes came at a time when player salaries, which averaged $6,400 in 1942, were already at a low point. When the freeze on salaries continued through 1946, it stirred strong unionist sentiments among grousing players that erupted in the first postwar season.

Other changes unleashed by the war forced far-reaching changes on major league baseball. Fair employment policies adopted by the federal government and by some states now threatened major league baseball's long-established practice of racial segregation. Sensing the new trend toward racial integration, Branch Rickey in 1945 signed black major leaguer Jackie Robinson to a Dodger contract. Rickey also sent his scouts in search of other promising talent in the black majors. This was a timely move because Judge Landis's death in 1944 had removed a major stumbling block to the integration of the major leagues.

When the war ended in 1945 with a complete victory over the Axis powers, the prospects for major league baseball looked bright. But that year also brought news of the sale of the Yankees to a triumvirate of owners who paid $2.8 million for the club. And as it turned out, the postwar era would usher in yet another phase of Yankee domination.

Austerity Campaigns: The AL, 1932–1945

In the Depression era of 1932–1941, the AL extended its domination over the NL by winning seven of ten World Series encounters and six of the first nine All-Star Games. The annual All-Star Game was instituted in 1933 and quickly became a popular spectacle that marked the midpoint of each seasonal campaign. Meanwhile in the seasonal campaigns of this decade, AL batters topped their NL counterparts in batting average, homers, RBIs, and stolen bases, while NL hurlers posted lower ERAs than did AL pitchers. But there was an illusory quality to this apparent pattern of mastery. This was because the AL's dominance owed most to the powerful Yankees, who captured six of the AL's seven world titles in these years.

After a three-year hiatus, the Yankees recaptured the AL heights in 1932, crushing the Athletics by 13 games. Gehrig and Ruth combined for 75 homers and Yankee hitters batted .286. Under Manager Joe McCarthy, who was destined to become one of baseball's most victorious managers, pitching superiority also became a Yankee hallmark. In 1932, with Lefty Gomez leading the Yankees staff with 24 wins, the Yankee mound corps led the AL in ERA with 3.98. Thus fortified, the versatile Yankees went on to sweep the Cubs in a legendary World Series matchup, highlighted by Ruth's much-debated "called shot" homerun in the third game. And over the winter George Weiss was hired to build a Yankee farm system, a task which Weiss handled effectively. Within a few years the Yankee farm system laid the foundation for an awesome phase of Yankee domination.

Meanwhile, the other AL teams enjoyed a brief respite, as the Yankees fell behind the front-running Senators and Tigers over the next three seasons. As age tolled on Yankee stars like Ruth, the Senators, now skippered by another young player-manager, shortstop Joe Cronin, defeated the Yankees by 7 games to win the 1933 pennant race. League-leading hitting and sturdy pitching by Al Crowder and Earl Whitehill, who combined for 46 victories, carried the Senators, who went on to lose the World Series in five games to the Giants. Worse yet, in this rock-bottom Depression year, the Senators attracted only 437,000 home fans. Confronted with financial losses, owner Clark Griffith sold outfield star Goose Goslin to the Tigers. Goslin's loss dashed the Senators' hopes for 1934, and when the team slipped to the second division that year, Griffith sold Cronin—his son-in-law—to the Red Sox for $250,000.

As the Senators suffered, the Detroit Tigers prospered. In addition to landing Goslin in 1934, the Tigers also purchased catcher Mickey Cochrane from the Athletics. Installed as the Tigers' player-manager, Cochrane headed a Tiger resurgence that saw the team rise from a fifth-place finish in 1933 to consecutive AL titles in 1934–1935. In 1934 Cochrane and Goslin teamed with Hank Greenberg and Charley Gehringer to spearhead a .300 team batting attack. What's more, pitchers Schoolboy Rowe and Tommy Bridges combined for 46 wins as the Tigers defeated the Yankees by 7 games. The

sprightly effort attracted 919,000 home fans, who watched Detroit land its first AL pennant since 1909. Unhappily for the fans, they also saw the Tigers extend their World Series losing streak to four as the Cardinals prevailed in a seven-game struggle. But in 1935 the Tigers repeated as AL champions, edging the runner-up Yankees by 3 games. Greenberg led the team's .290 batting offensive by batting in 170 runs, and the purchase of Crowder from the Senators beefed up the team's pitching staff. Although a late-season injury kept Greenberg out of action in the 1935 World Series, the Tigers downed the Cubs in five games. It was Detroit's first World Series victory since 1887. But as it turned out, this victory was also the last World Series triumph by any AL team but the Yankees until 1948.

The second phase of Yankee domination over the AL began in 1936. The year before, Ruth's departure had removed the club's greatest drawing card, but this year young Joe DiMaggio appeared. Purchasing him from the San Francisco Seals of the Pacific Coast League for $25,000 and five other ball-players, the Yankees were taking a chance that DiMaggio would be able to play effectively in spite of his injured knee. Indeed, he was, although the outfielder did prove to be injury-prone. But in 1936 the highly touted DiMaggio was an immediate sensation. In his freshman year he hit .323 with 29 homers and 125 RBIs. That year Gehrig's 49 homers led the league and the Yankees batted .300 as a team with 182 homers. The Yankee assault lapped the runner-up Tigers by 19½ games and in World Series action the Yankees downed the Giants in six games. It was the first of four consecutive World Series titles by the Bronx Bombers. During this record-setting streak, Weiss's farm system provided a steady flow of talented replacements. Included were pitchers Spud Chandler, Steve Sundra, Marius Russo, and Atley Donald; outfielders Tommy Henrich and Charley Keller; and second baseman Joe Gordon. In 1937 the Yankees repeated by topping the Tigers by 13 games; in 1938 they beat out the beefed-up Red Sox by 9½ games; and in 1939 the Red Sox trailed the all-conquering Yankees by 17 games. In each of these seasons the Yankees blasted at least 166 homers. And in World Series play their mastery of their NL rivals increased steadily; in 1937 the Giants fell in five games, and in 1938 and 1939 the Yankees swept the Cubs and the Reds. Landing four consecutive world titles was an unprecedented achievement, but such domination also kindled an enduring wave of anti-Yankee hostility among fans and rival teams.

Mercifully for the rest of the AL contenders, a year's respite from Yankee domination came in 1940. The year before, Lou Gehrig's tragic illness ended the career of the great first baseman, whose "iron man" record of having played in 2,130 consecutive games still stands. In 1940 Gehrig's absence was keenly felt, and it enabled the Tigers and Indians to battle the Yankees on even terms. Cleveland's fireballing pitching ace, Bob Feller, won 27 games to lead his team's assault, but tensions between the Indian players and manager Oscar Vitt adversely affected the team's morale. Such tensions enabled the hard-hitting Tigers to close the gap. Batting a league-leading .286, the Tigers were paced by future Hall of Famer Hank Greenberg; the big outfielder batted .340 with a league-leading 41 homers and 150 RBIs. First baseman Rudy York weighed in with a .316 batting average, and his 33 homers and 134 RBIs complemented Greenberg's production. Second baseman Charley Gehringer, another destined Hall of Famer, batted .313 and drove in 81 runs, and outfielder Bar-

ney McCosky batted .340. To top it off, portly pitcher Bobo Newsom enjoyed a vintage season with a 21–5 record. In the last week of the season the Tigers deadlocked the Indians, and on the last day of the campaign the Tigers defeated the Indians to win the hotly contested race. In the decisive game, won by the Tigers 2–0, rookie Tiger pitcher Floyd Giebell outpitched the great Feller. Ironically it was Giebell's last major league victory. But in World Series action the Tigers lost to the Cincinnati Reds in seven games.

Hard after that defeat, the gathering storm of World War Two dealt the Tigers a crushing blow. After playing 19 games of the 1941 season, slugger Greenberg was drafted into the Army. As the Tigers slumped, the Yankees rebounded and romped to a runaway 17-game victory over the second-place Red Sox. But this last peacetime AL campaign was fraught with memorable events. For one, by hitting safely in 56 consecutive games, Yankee outfielder Joe DiMaggio sparked the Yankee surge and established an enduring major league record. For another, by batting .406 over the season, Boston outfielder Ted Williams became the last major league player to this day to top the .400 mark. And in the unforgettable World Series of 1941, by missing a third strike with two out in the ninth inning, thereby opening the floodgates for a game-winning Yankee rally in the fourth game, Dodger catcher Mickey Owen won enduring notoriety as the blamesake for the latest Yankee victory. The 1941 Series victory was the eighth straight by Yankee teams.

In the wake of the 1941 major league season, the Japanese attack on Pearl Harbor plunged the nation into full-scale war with the Axis powers. Soon thereafter, the military drafts sapped the playing strength of all teams, but the efficient Yankee farm system enabled the Yankees to retain enough able players to land two more pennants in 1942 and 1943. In 1942 the Yankees led the league in homers, fielding, and pitching to defeat the bridesmaid Red Sox by nine games. Yankee pitcher Ernie Bonham led all AL hurlers with a 21–5 mark, while Red Sox outfielder Ted Williams followed his brilliant 1941 season by notching a rare Triple Crown effort; Williams batted .356 with 36 homers and 137 RBIs. However, Yankee hopes of extending their World Series winning streak came a cropper as the Cardinals downed the New Yorkers in five games.

But the resilient Yankees bounced back in 1943. League-leading slugging and pitching, the latter fronted by Spud Chandler's 20–4, 1.64 ERA performance, carried the Yankees to a 13½-game win over the Washington Senators. To top off the victory, in World Series action the Yankees scored an avenging victory over the Cardinals, who were beaten in five games.

In 1944 the military draft finally denuded the Yankees, who fell to third. As the Yankees sagged, the Browns and the Tigers battled for the top position, and the struggle ended with the St. Louis Browns winning their first and only AL pennant. In edging the Tigers by a single game, the Browns' .252 team batting mark ranked near the bottom of the league. But stout pitching by Jack Kramer, Nelson Potter, and reliever George Caster, and shortstop Vern Stephens's league-leading 109 RBIs made the difference. Matched against their hometown rivals in World Series play, the Browns fell to the Cardinals in six games.

In the last wartime campaign, the 1945 Tigers eked a 1½-game victory over the Senators. Although the Tigers were outhit by five other teams, pitcher Hal Newhouser's 25–9,

1.81 ERA pitching and slugger Greenberg's timely return from military service sparked the Tigers. After missing four seasons of play, Greenberg returned to play in 78 games, during which he batted .311 and drove in 60 runs. In World Series play Greenberg's .304 batting and his two homers led the Tigers to victory over the Cubs in seven games, in what has been described as "the worst World Series ever played."

Austerity Campaigns: The NL, 1932–1945

Although offensively outclassed by the AL, the NL boasted the best pitching in these years. Indeed, pitching decided eight of the first ten NL campaigns of this era while also contributing to the senior circuit's better competitive balance. Over the years 1932–1941 the NL campaigns featured nine close races with five different pennant winners. Thus the longest reign of any would-be dynasty was two years, a feat achieved by the New York Giants and the Cincinnati Reds.

In 1932 the Chicago Cubs rose to the top of the NL and continued a quirky pattern, dating back to 1929, of winning a pennant every three years. In August the embattled Cubs replaced manager Rogers Hornsby with first baseman Charlie Grimm, a timely move that rallied the Cubs. Player-manager Grimm, in company with infielder Billy Herman and outfielders Riggs Stephenson and Johnny Moore, led the .278 team batting attack, while pitcher Lon Warneke (22–6) fronted the team's league-leading pitching staff. The Cubs went on to defeat the Pirates by four games, but were swept by the Yankees in the World Series.

As the Cubs swooned in 1933, another player-manager, first baseman Bill Terry, led the Giants to their first NL pennant since 1924. They did it by scoring a five-game victory over the Pirates. Terry batted .322, and outfielder Mel Ott's 23 homers keyed the Giants' league-leading homer assault. The pitching staff, fronted by lefty Carl Hubbell's 23 victories, was the league's best. And in World Series action the Giants beat the Senators in five games.

The following year the Giants again boasted league-leading pitching, but the hard-hitting Cardinals overtook the New Yorkers in the final week to win by 2 games. Dubbed the "Gas House Gang," these Cardinals symbolized the Depression austerities that affected the nation in this worst year of the economic hard times. The Cardinals drew only 325,000 home fans, but player-manager Frank Frisch, in company with Rip Collins, Ernie Orsatti, Joe Medwick, and Spud Davis, topped the .300 mark in batting to pace the team's league-leading .288 batting effort. But the brightest star was pitcher Dizzy Dean, who won 30 games to become the last major league hurler to crack the 30-game barrier for over thirty years; moreover, Dean's brother Paul won 19. In World Series play, the Cardinals rebounded from a 3–2 deficit in games to beat the Tigers.

The folksy Arkansas country boy Dizzy Dean won 28 games in 1935, but the Cubs trumped the Cardinal ace with their league-leading pitching staff. At the close of the campaign, the Cubs led the Cardinals by four games. Heading the Cub hurlers were Lon Warneke and lefty Bill Lee, each a 20-game winner. Five Cub regulars topped the .300 mark, including infielders Stan Hack and Billy Herman, outfielders Frank Demaree and Augie Galan, and catcher Gabby Hartnett, to pace the team's .288 batting offensive. And outfielder Chuck Klein, a timely acquisition from the moribund Phillies, powered 21 homers. But the Cubs were no match for the Tigers in World Series play; the Tigers defeated the Chicagoans in six games.

Over the next two seasons, Cub hitters topped all NL teams in batting, but each time the team finished second behind the Giants. Dominant pitching, paced by Carl Hubbell's 26 wins and Ott's league-leading 33 homers, led the 1936 Giants to a five-game win over the Cubs and Cardinals. In the second half of the campaign, many eyes were on lefty Hubbell, as the Giant hurler finished the season with 16 consecutive victories to threaten the record seasonal streak of 19 owned by Rube Marquard of the old Giants. Hubbell won the opener of the 1936 World Series, but the Yankees beat the lefty in the fourth game and went on to down the Giants in six games.

But postseasonal play was discounted, and Hubbell went on to add another eight victories in 1937. When the ace finally lost one on Memorial Day, his record (over two seasons) of 24 consecutive victories stood as the best by a major league pitcher. But more important to the Giants' cause in 1937, Hubbell went on to win 22 games and rookie Cliff Melton won 20 as the Giants hung on to beat the runner-up Cubs by 3 games. It was the second straight conquest for the Giants, but in World Series action they again fell to the Yankees, this time losing in five games.

For a last time in 1938, the Cubs used their magical three-year formula to land the NL pennant. In an epic campaign that saw Cincinnati Reds' pitcher Johnny Vander Meer pitch two consecutive no-hit games, and the front-running Pirates blow a big lead, the Cubs mounted a remarkable September surge to overhaul and topple the Pirates by 2 games. In a decisive game played in late September's gathering darkness at Wrigley Field, player-manager Gabby Hartnett hit his legendary "homer in the gloaming" as part of a three-game Cub sweep of the Pirates. Although the Cubs batted only .269 that year, the team's pitching staff was the best in the league. Nevertheless, the well-armed Cubs were swept by the Yankees in the 1938 World Series.

As the punchless Cubs sank to fourth place in 1939, manager Bill McKechnie drove the Cincinnati Reds to their first NL pennant since 1919. Since that victory, the Reds had been remembered primarily for pioneering night baseball and for Johnny Vander Meer's double no-hit feat. But recently the club had come under the ownership of radio tycoon Powel Crosley, whose player purchases were strengthening the team. Included were a prize pair of pitchers: Paul Derringer, who was purchased from the Cardinals, and Bucky Walters, who came via the Phillies. In 1939 this duo combined for 52 victories and headed the league's best pitching staff. Supported by sturdy hitting from outfielder Ival Goodman, first baseman Frank McCormick, and catcher Ernie Lombardi, the Reds held off the Cardinals to win by 4½ games. However, the Reds suffered the same fate as did the 1938 Cubs when the Yankees swept them in World Series play. Regrouping after this defeat, the Reds repeated in 1940 as they downed the rebuilt Dodgers by 12 games. For the winning Reds, mediocre hitting was overcome by league-leading pitching and fielding. And in the 1940 World Series it was the Reds who outlasted the Tigers in a seven-game struggle.

In the NL's last peacetime campaign before the outbreak of the Second World War, the Reds fell behind the rising Dodgers and the perennially contending Cardinals. In a close race the Dodgers held on to win by 2½ games over the Cardinals. In rebuilding the Dodgers, general manager Larry

MacPhail persuaded the club's banker trustees to bankroll the purchases of players from the Phillies and Cardinals. From the Cardinals came pitcher Curt Davis, and outfielders Medwick and young Pete Reiser. Snagging Reiser from the Cardinals' farm system was a real coup as he led the league in batting with a .343 mark. From the Phillies, MacPhail obtained pitcher Kirby Higbe and first baseman Dolph Camilli; and in 1941 Camilli's 34 homers and 120 RBIs led the league. With additional acquisitions, the 1941 Dodgers fielded few home-grown players. Indeed, player-manager Leo Durocher was a former Cardinal hand. But the Dodger assemblage of mercenaries led the NL in pitching and homers and tied with the Cardinals in hitting. During the frenzied campaign, the Dodgers attracted a million home fans, most of whom mourned their "Bums'" heart-breaking loss to the Yankees in the 1941 World Series.

As wartime exigencies riddled NL teams of playing talent, the Cardinals retained enough players to land three consecutive pennants over the years 1942–1944. Although Rickey left the Cardinals in 1942 to join the Dodgers as that team's general manager, his efficient farm system fueled the Cardinals. In dominating the NL, the Cardinals won 316 games in these years, each time leading the league in hitting and pitching. Managed by Billy Southworth, the 1942 Cardinals needed 106 wins to edge the Dodgers by 2 games. The following year 105 victories enabled the Cardinals to romp to an 18-game win over the runner-up Reds. And in 1944 another 105 victories easily carried the Redbirds to a 14½-game win over the second-place Pirates. In World Series play the Cardinals split with the Yankees, winning in five games in 1942 and losing by the same count in 1943. And in 1944 the Cardinals thrashed the Browns in six games. In these years young outfielder Stan Musial emerged as a superstar with the Cardinals, winning the first of what would be seven NL batting titles with a .357 mark in 1943.

It was the loss of Musial to military service in 1945 which helped the Cubs end the Cardinals' pennant monopoly. League-leading batting, fronted by first baseman Phil Cavaretta's major-league-leading .355 batting, and league-leading pitching carried the Cubs to a 3-game victory over the Cardinals. But the victory was soured by defeat at the hands of the Tigers in the 1945 World Series. Worse still, Cub fans to this day are still looking for another NL pennant.

Baseball's Postwar Era, 1946–1961

Victory in World War Two unleashed a host of pent-up changes which altered American society. Among the most welcomed was a steadily expanding economy which increased jobs, wages, and consumer spending. Bolstered by such growth industries as housing, television, and automobile production, the tide of economic prosperity transformed the nation into an affluent society of dynamic abundance. Moreover, most Americans shared in the fruits of this abundance. With plenty of discretionary income, Americans spent ever-increasing amounts for leisure and recreational purposes. From a total of $11 billion spent in 1946 on such pursuits, such spending topped $18 billion by 1960. By then, the most popular leisure activity was television viewing, with nearly 80 percent of American households of 1960 boasting at least one TV set. And the number of American households increased sharply along with the nation's booming population. A post-

war marriage boom fueled a fifteen-year-long baby boom to add to the nation's population growth. And in this era, millions of Americans forsook older cities for new suburban homes, a trend that sped the growth of new urban regions.

But postwar America was also faced with disturbing and controversial changes. At home, long-festering opposition to racial discrimination and segregation now saw black Americans using political action movements to batter away at sources of inequality. Similarly, increased union activity by organized workers was aimed at securing bigger shares of the fruits of abundance. And on the international front, the nation found itself thrust into a role as defender of the free world against Communist expansion. At this time a mounting arms race with the Soviet Union had America and the Russians stockpiling nuclear weapons and extending their rivalry into space exploration. This international ideological struggle translated at home into increased federal spending for defense and space programs, a continuation of the military draft, and a pervasive fear of Communism which spilled over into political campaigns.

At this time most of these forces and others impacted upon major league baseball. For openers, the rising national prosperity boosted attendance and revenues, but shifting population centers now tempted some club owners to abandon old sites for greener pastures elsewhere. By 1958 five such franchise shifts had occurred. In 1953 the NL Braves became the first breakaway franchise when they abandoned their traditional Boston haunts for Milwaukee; in 1954 the penurious AL Browns departed St. Louis for Baltimore, and the following year the equally penurious AL Athletics moved from Philadelphia to Kansas City. Such moves were controversial, for they destroyed a long-standing, fifty-year-old status quo in major league baseball. But the biggest public uproar echoed from Brooklyn and New York City, when fans of the NL Dodgers and Giants saw these teams move to the West Coast, respectively to Los Angeles and San Francisco. Following upon those moves, a rival major league, the Continental League, threatened to plant teams in some abandoned cities, but mostly in new population centers that now hungered for major league baseball. The urgent need to defuse the Continental League threat and the lesser need to assuage bereft New York fans prompted major league owners to expand the major leagues at the end of this era.

Meanwhile, these breakaway franchise movements, while increasing major league attendance and revenues, were weakening the minor leagues by pre-empting some of the strongest minor league territories. At the same time attendance at minor league games was being undermined by the increasing radio and television broadcasts of major league games. For the minor leagues, such blows were crushers. From an all-time peak in 1949, when the minors fielded 59 leagues with over 7,800 players and attracted 40 million fans, the number of minor leagues steadily dwindled. By the early 1960s, the number of minor leagues had shrunk to nineteen, with fewer than 2,500 playes and total annual attendance of less than 20 million fans. By then, major league owners were learning that there was a piper to pay; for the decline of the minors confronted the major leagues with a chronic, persistent problem of talent scarcity. To cope with the knotty talent shortage problem, major league clubs engaged in costly bidding wars for the services of promising young players. And in addition to bidding for "bonus babies," major league clubs recruited black players both at home and in Latin America. Since such

moves failed to solve the problem of talent scarcity, by the end of this era the majors were challenged to find ways of subsidizing the surviving minor leagues, to prevent these vital nurseries of playing talent from drying up.

But baseball's talent scarcity problem was also aggravated by the television revolution. As television producers soon learned that other sports attracted viewers, they took to subsidizing rival team sports such as professional football and basketball. As these and other sports gained in popularity, young athletes turned to them in increasing numbers. Indeed, at many schools and colleges baseball now ranked as a minor sport. But television bestowed blessings as well as problems upon baseball. In 1950 baseball telecasting provided $2.3 million in new revenues and by 1960 such annual income topped $12 million. As television income enhanced the value of major league franchises, its potential now became a major consideration in the relocation of franchises. For now, as at the present time, owners clung to the policy of negotiating their own local television contracts. But owners of this era worried over television's impact on live attendance at games. In 1946 a record 18.1 million fans attended major league games and in 1948 rising annual attendance peaked at 21.3 million. Thereafter annual attendance sagged, falling below the 20 million mark during the 1950s. For this turnabout, some owners blamed television for making a free show of the games. But aging parks, located in congested and declining center cities whose populations were shifting to suburban areas, also accounted for the decline. In other ways television altered the game. The steadily increasing number of night games now transformed major league baseball into a primarily nocturnal spectacle—except at Wrigley Field in Chicago. Night baseball was a trend encouraged by the televising of games as producers found night games to be more profitable. And by making celebrities of players, television triggered a rise in player salaries which would reach astonishing proportions in later years. Moreover, by scooping newspapers on the coverage of the outcome of games, television forced baseball writers to adopt a new, more probing style of baseball coverage. But such mixed blessings failed to deter owners of this era from reaping revenues from local and national television contracts. However, it is unlikely that any owner of this era could have envisioned a coming time when television revenue would exceed that of ticket sales at games.

Nor could many owners at the dawn of this era envision the revolutionary impact of the racial integration of baseball. Nevertheless, in 1947 major league baseball became a major front in the ongoing battle for racial equality. That year Branch Rickey's "great experiment" introduced Jackie Robinson as the first known black player in this century to play in the major leagues. Playing first base for the Brooklyn Dodgers that year, Robinson endured a trying ordeal of acceptance, but he passed the test magnificently. A .297 batting average sparked a championship season for the Dodgers and won Robinson the Rookie of the Year honors. More important, his success paved the way for other black stars to follow in his footsteps. By 1958 some hundred black Americans and some eighty black Hispanics played in the major leagues, mostly with NL teams, where their feats helped to exalt the NL over the AL. In Robinson's footsteps there followed such future Hall of Famers as Willie Mays, Roy Campanella, Ernie Banks, and Roberto Clemente. However, the opening of doors into the white major leagues doomed the black major leagues to extinction. By 1950 the era of the great black

majors was over. As for the white majors, the recruitment of black players only temporarily alleviated the growing talent shortage.

Meanwhile, the postwar surge in labor union activity in the nation at large was exerting its influence on the major leagues. In 1946 a mounting number of grievances against owners prompted major league players to organize under the newly formed American Baseball Guild. Headed by Boston attorney Robert Murphy, this fourth unionizing attempt by major league players now had players forming chapters on each team, electing player representatives, and demanding higher salaries, fringe benefits, and a pension plan. A strike threat that year was defused when owners conceded a minimum salary of $5,000, some fringe benefits, and a pension plan to be funded by national radio and television income. The latter concession was portentous; not only were owners committed to the pension principle, but an important precedent was set by giving players a share in national media revenue. Such concessions undercut the Guild, which soon died out. But when the owners attempted to abolish the pension system in 1953, player representatives from the sixteen clubs hired New York attorney J. Norman Lewis to represent their cause. Out of this crisis came the Major League Players Association; under Lewis's leadership, the Association fought a successful battle to retain the pension system. But the Association languished after this struggle and late in this era came under the leadership of Robert Cannon, who ran the Association as a company union until 1966. Then, under Marvin Miller's efficient leadership, the Association became a formidable collective-bargaining agency for the players.

Meanwhile, the Mexican League crisis of 1946 added to the growing tensions between players and owners. That year Mexican League promoters enticed a handful of major league players to jump to Mexican League teams with offers of high salaries. When Commissioner A. B. Chandler blacklisted the jumpers, one of them, Danny Gardella, sued in the federal courts. When a Circuit Court of Appeals found for Gardella, the threat to baseball's reserve clause was serious enough to persuade the owners to settle the case out of court. Subsequently, congressional investigations into baseball's monopolistic practices also threatened the reserve clause, but no legislation followed the work of Congressman Emmanuel Celler's probings.

Nevertheless, by creating the Major League Players Association and by linking pension payments to national television revenues, the militant players of this era laid the groundwork for massive salary breakthroughs to be reaped by a future generation of players. But for now the players had to content themselves with salaries which at least topped those of their forebears. During the 1950s, 75 percent of player salaries ranged from $10,000 to $25,000 a season. However, three superstars—Joe DiMaggio, Ted Williams, and Stan Musial—received annual salaries of $100,000 a season.

But if organized players showed signs of gaining wealth and power, the powers of baseball commissioners were waning. Indeed, when Landis died in 1944, it soon became apparent that the owners would not abide another powerful commissioner. Thus Landis's successor, Commissioner Chandler, was denied a second term in 1951. For his part, Chandler blamed his assertive stance on such issues as his support of the pension plan, his opposition to Sunday night ball, and his defense of the rights of minor league players, for his ouster. Be that as it may, the flamboyant Chandler was replaced by

Ford Frick, who served for fourteen years as the compliant tool of the owners. At this time the changing ranks of club owners included a new breed of wealthy businessmen who deferred to powerful owners like Walter O'Malley of the Dodgers and Dan Topping of the Yankees. By wielding influence on the owners' powerful executive committee, their powers far exceeded those of the commissioner.

Among the playing rule changes of this era, the 1950 recodification narrowed the strike zone and a 1954 rule permanently restored the sacrifice fly rule. Of important future significance was a 1959 rule which reacted to the designs of new, publicly financed ballparks in Milwaukee, Kansas City, Baltimore, San Francisco, and Los Angeles, and which anticipated the coming new park-building boom. This rule ordained that parks constructed after 1959 must conform to minimum distances of 325 feet from home plate to the right and left field fences.

On the playing fields, improved fielding was attributed to bigger, more flexible gloves. And the homer production of this era owed much to players wielding lighter, more tapered bats, to the required use of batting helmets, and to the frequent replacement of balls. A team now used as many as 12,000 balls in a season. Offensively such changes resulted in unprecedented homer barrages, with NL hitters averaging more than 1,100 homers a season during the 1950s. What's more, NL hitters regularly also bested AL batters in batting averages and stolen bases. Credit for this turnabout went to the greater number of black stars in the NL. Robinson became the first black star to win a Most Valuable Player Award, and after Robinson received that award in 1949, seven black stars, including sluggers Roy Campanella, Ernie Banks, and Willie Mays, won NL MVP awards in the 1950s. But the most celebrated stars of this era were DiMaggio, Williams, and Musial. DiMaggio retired after the 1951 season with a .325 lifetime batting average, while Williams and Musial starred throughout this era. When he retired in 1960, Williams, despite years lost for service in World War Two and the Korean conflict, owned a .344 lifetime batting average, six AL batting titles, 521 homers, and a pair of Triple Crowns. And when Musial retired in 1963, his credentials showed a .331 lifetime batting average, seven NL batting titles, and an NL record of 3,630 lifetime hits, evenly divided at home and on the road.

For the battered pitchers these postwar years were nightmarish. ERAs hovered around 4.00 in the NL and just below that seasonal mark in the AL. To cope with their batting tormentors, pitchers now relied more upon sliders and some clandestinely employed illegal deliveries like the spitball. Managers responded by deploying relief pitchers. At this time "short relievers," capable of dousing late-inning rallies, now became valued specialists whose exploits were measured by saves and honored late in the era with annual "Fireman of the Year" awards. Among the best of this era's "firemen" were Joe Page of the Yankees, Jim Konstanty of the Phillies, Roy Face of the Pirates, and the much-traveled Hoyt Wilhelm. Indeed, the knuckleball-throwing Wilhelm lasted twenty-one seasons. When he retired in 1972, he had appeared in 1,070 games, with 227 saves and a lifetime ERA of 2.52. But able starters were by no means extinct at this time. Among the very best, lefty Warren Spahn of the Braves went on to win 20 or more games in a dozen seasons, and retired with 363 lifetime victories. To honor the outstanding pitchers of each season, in 1956 the annual Cy Young Award was

instituted. The first recipient was Don Newcombe, the black pitching ace of the Brooklyn Dodgers. From 1956 through the 1966 season, only one award was given annually in the major leagues, but thereafter the best pitcher of the year in each league received a Cy Young Award.

Postwar Campaigns: The AL, 1946–1960

In this era the AL lagged behind the NL both in offensive performance and in annual attendance. For this reversal of fortunes, some observers faulted AL owners for taking a back seat to their NL counterparts in the signing of black stars and in the occupation of such choice sites as Los Angeles and San Francisco. But the AL's biggest problem was the overwhelming superiority of its own New York Yankees. By winning eleven of fifteen postwar-era campaigns, the Yankees made a mockery of the concept of competitive balance. Moreover, by their perennial dominance, the New Yorkers attracted the lion's share of AL attendance, to the detriment of their overmatched competitors. Indeed, such was the magnitude of the Yankee oppression that after 1948 no AL team but the Yankees won a World Series until 1966. For their part, the Yankees won nine world titles, thus singlehandedly maintaining the AL's domination in the annual test of strength between the two majors. Nevertheless, by the end of this era, the growing strength of the NL was evidenced by their team's victories in three of the last five World Series encounters and by victories in nine of this era's seventeen All Star Games.

But when each of the first three AL postwar campaigns produced a new champion, prospects for competitive balance looked bright. In 1946 the Boston Red Sox won their first AL pennant since 1918 to help foster this illusion. League-leading hitting by Red Sox batters, fronted by Ted Williams's .342-38-123 stickwork, and 45 wins posted by pitchers Dave "Boo" Ferriss and Tex Hughson, boosted the Red Sox to 104 wins and a 12-game romp over the defending Detroit Tigers. But after the Red Sox lost a hard-fought seven-game World Series battle at the hands of the Cardinals, another two decades would pass by before this club won another AL pennant.

As the Red Sox faded to third in 1947, the Yankees rebounded from a third-place finish to notch their first postwar pennant. DiMaggio batted .315 with 20 homers and 97 RBIs to lead the team's .271 batting assault. Besides leading the league in homers and batting, the Yankees also fielded the league's best pitching staff; Allie Reynolds, newly acquired from Cleveland, won 19, and rookies Specs Shea and Vic Raschi combined for 21 wins. Reliever Joe Page won 14 and tied for league leadership in saves with 17. It was enough to carry manager Bucky Harris's charges to a 12-game win over the second-place Tigers. Then, for a second time, the Yankees downed the Dodgers in World Series play.

The following year the Yankees, Red Sox, and Indians hooked up in a furious pennant struggle that ended in a tie between the Indians and Red Sox. To settle this first seasonal deadlock in AL history, the two teams played a sudden-death playoff game in Boston. By downing the Red Sox 8–3 in that game, Cleveland won the 1948 AL pennant and went on to beat the Boston Braves in the World Series. League-leading team batting (.282), homer production (155), pitching, and fielding powered the Indians, whose home attendance of more than 2 million fans was unsurpassed in this era. Player-manager Lou Boudreau led the Indians with a .355 average; outfielder Dale Mitchell batted .336, and outfielder Larry

Doby, who joined the team that season as the first black player in the AL, hit .301. Pitchers Bob Lemon, Bob Feller, and Gene Bearden accounted for 59 victories, but the pitching staff got an important boost when owner Bill Veeck acquired the legendary and aging Satchel Paige from the black majors. Paige contributed 6 victories and a save to the team's winning cause.

At this point the resurging Yankees dashed all hopes of continuing the league's pattern of competitive balance. Regrouping under manager Casey Stengel, the Yankees snatched ten of the next twelve AL pennants, including a record five in a row beginning with the 1949 conquest. In the torrid 1949 race, the injury-ridden Yankees edged the Red Sox by a game. Needing a pair of victories to overtake and conquer the Red Sox, the Yankees hosted the Bostonians in the closing days of the campaign and won both games. Key performances included relief pitcher Joe Page's 27 saves and 13 victories, and a .346-14-67 offensive effort by the ailing DiMaggio. Though he was sidelined much of the season by injuries, the Yankee Clipper's heroics helped to offset Williams's tremendous performance for the Red Sox. Williams's .343 batting average was barely edged out by George Kell, and his 43 homers and 159 RBIs led all rivals.

Over the next three seasons, the Yankees prevailed in three close races, edging the Tigers by 3 games in 1950, the Indians by 5 games in 1951, and the Indians by 2 games in 1952. Nor did they stop there. In winning for a fifth straight season in 1953, the Yankees enjoyed their only comfortable edge in their record skein as they downed the perennial bridesmaid Indians by 8½ games. In winning a record five consecutive AL pennants, the great Yankee pitching triumvirate of Allie Reynolds, Vic Raschi, and lefty Ed Lopat combined for a sparkling 255–117 won-loss record. That victory total included two no-hitters pitched by Reynolds in the 1951 campaign. In 1950, future Hall of Famer Ed "Whitey" Ford joined the Yankee staff; Ford's 9–1 pitching performance was a decisive factor in the team's winning stretch drive of that season. Offensively, manager Stengel relied on star performers like DiMaggio and catcher Yogi Berra and successfully platooned such able hitters as outfielders Hank Bauer and Gene Woodling. When age tolled on the great DiMaggio, who retired after the 1951 season, or when the Korean War military draft snagged young stars like Ford and Billy Martin, general manager George Weiss summoned rising stars like Mickey Mantle and Gil McDougald from the Yankee farm system. Shrewd trades by Weiss also landed key performers like Johnny Mize, pitcher Ed Lopat, and relief pitcher Bob Kuzava. In World Series action, the relentless Yankees captured five classics in a row. Three times, in 1949, 1952, and 1953, they toppled the Dodgers. In 1950 they swept the "Whiz Kid" Phillies, and in 1951 they defeated the "Miracle Giants" in six games. In two of these encounters, Kuzava's relief pitching was a deciding factor. And at the pinnacle of their success in 1953, the Yankees could boast of having won their last seven World Series encounters.

The following year, the Yankees won 103 games, their best record under Stengel's leadership, but manager Al Lopez's Cleveland Indians won the 1954 pennant with an AL record-breaking 111 victories. Second baseman Bobby Avila's .341 hitting won the league's batting title, and Larry Doby's league-leading 32 homers and 126 RBIs headed the team's league-leading 156 homer barrage. With a 2.78 ERA the team's pitching staff was unmatched; the starting trio of Early Wynn, Bob Lemon, and Mike Garcia accounted for 65 victories. But like the 1906 Chicago Cubs, who lost the World Series of that year after winning a major league record 116 games, the Indians fell to the New York Giants, who swept to victory in the 1954 World Series.

The 1954 victory was also Cleveland's last AL pennant to this day. What followed was another assertion of Yankee tyranny. Regrouping in 1955, the Yankees went on to win a string of four consecutive AL pennants. By this time most of the heroes of the 1949–1953 Yankees were gone. To replace the great pitching trio of Reynolds, Raschi, and Lopat, Weiss traded for pitchers Bob Turley and Don Larsen and summoned catcher Elston Howard, the first black player to wear a Yankee uniform, from the farm system. In a close race the 1955 Yankees edged the Indians by 3 games, with Berra winning his third MVP award for his latest offensive performance. Berra batted a workmanlike .272, and his 27 homers drove in 108 runs. Outfielder Mantle batted .306, and his league-leading 37 homers were accompanied by 99 RBIs. And Ford's 18 wins led AL hurlers. But in World Series action the Dodgers finally turned on their Yankee tormentors as they won the fall classic in seven games.

In 1956 Mantle's Triple Crown performance (.353-52-130) and Ford's 19 pitching victories paced the Yankees to an 8-game victory over the Indians. In the aftermath of that victory, the Yankees faced the Brooklyn Dodgers for a seventh and last subway World Series. The next time these two rivals met, the breakaway Dodgers would represent the West Coast city of Los Angeles. What followed was an epochal struggle which the Yankees won in seven games. But Larsen's brilliant pitching in the fifth game stamped this World Series with the mark of immortality. With the Series tied at two games, Larsen pitched a perfect game; it was the first no-hitter in World Series history and the first perfect game pitched in the majors in over thirty years. But the stubborn Dodgers carried the Series another two games before succumbing.

Over the next two seasons the Yankees won two more AL pennants. In 1957 the Bronx Bombers wielded league-leading batting and pitching to down the runner-up White Sox by 8 games. Mantle's .365-34-94 performance won the switch-hitting superstar another MVP Award. Rookie shortstop Tony Kubek's .297 hitting won him Rookie of the Year honors, and rookie Tom Sturdivant's 16 victories led the pitching staff. Nevertheless, the 1957 Yankees lost the World Series in seven games to the transplanted Milwaukee Braves. But the 1958 Yankees avenged that loss. Winning easily by 10 games over manager Al Lopez's White Sox, the Yankees led the AL in team batting, homers, and pitching. Turley's 21 victories led AL pitchers and Mantle's 42 homers led the league's sluggers. Then, in a rematch with the Braves, the gritty Yankees overcame a three-games-to-one deficit to win the 1958 World Series in seven games.

The following year slumping performances by Mantle and Turley contributed to the Yankee's third-place finish. The collapse enabled perennial runner-up manager Al Lopez to drive his Chicago White Sox to a 5-game victory over the Indians. The White Sox batted a weak .250, but they led the league in stolen bases, fielding, and pitching. Veteran pitcher Early Wynn, a future Hall of Famer, notched 22 victories in his last great seasonal performance, and relievers Turk Lown and George Staley fronted the league's best bullpen crew. But the White Sox lost the 1959 World Series to the Los Angeles Dodgers.

That fall the decision by AL owners to expand the league to ten teams in 1961 sounded the knell for the league's hallowed eight-club format and 154-game seasons. As the postwar era ended with the 1960 campaign, the Yankees rebounded to win by 8 games over the Baltimore Orioles. Although soon to pass from the Yankee scene, general manager Weiss pulled off another canny deal by obtaining outfielder Roger Maris from the Kansas City Athletics. With Maris leading the league in RBIs, and Mantle in homers, the well-armed Yankees faced the Pirates in the 1960 World Series. Yet despite a World Series record .338 team batting average, which produced three crushing victories over the Pirates, the Yankees lost the classic in seven games. Hard after this defeat, Weiss and manager Stengel were forced into retirement, although the pair soon surfaced in their familiar capacities with the NL's expansion New York Mets. Meanwhile, with the passing of the 1960 season, the AL prepared to enter the dawning era of expansion.

Postwar Campaigns: The NL, 1946–1961

In this era much of the credit for boosting NL stock above that of the AL belonged to Branch Rickey and Walter O'Malley of the Dodgers. Dodger general manager Rickey built the superb farm system which fueled the Dodger dynasty, and it was Rickey too who successfully pulled off the coup of baseball's racial integration. When Jackie Robinson made his successful debut in 1947, Rickey enjoyed a temporary corner on the market of black players whom his scouts recruited from the fading black majors and from Latin American countries. Moreover, when Dodger owner O'Malley engineered Rickey's ouster in 1950, the aging genius joined the Pirates and laid the groundwork for that forlorn team's rise to power. And as a final touch, it was Rickey's presence among the would-be promoters of the rival Continental League movement in 1959 that goaded major league owners into expanding their circuit in order to deflect the threat.

But the 1957 West Coast move of the Brooklyn Dodgers and New York Giants was O'Malley's doing. Indeed, these moves stirred the Continental League movement. And it was O'Malley, the most powerful and influential owner of this era, who persuaded his colleagues to embark upon the expansionist course. Thus while Rickey and O'Malley plied different courses of action, these embattled rivals together forced major league baseball to adapt to a changing American society.

But the rise of the Brooklyn Dodger dynasty in the NL of this era was mostly Rickey's handiwork. And an effective piece of domination it was. Of the sixteen NL campaigns of this era, the Dodgers won seven and narrowly missed winning three others. And yet the Dodgers, who won only two world titles, were upstaged by an even greater Yankee dynasty. Nevertheless, the Dodgers lorded over other NL teams. In these years the Braves won three pennants and a World Series; the Giants won two pennants and a World Series; and the four one-time winners—the Cardinals, Phillies, Pirates, and Reds—accounted for two World Series victories. At least it made the NL a better-balanced circuit than the Yankee-dominated AL of this era.

As the NL's postwar era unfolded, the outcomes of the first three campaigns produced an illusion of competitive balance similar to that in the AL. Here too the first three races produced three different winners. The 1946 race pitted the Dodgers against a Cardinal team which Rickey had assembled in his previous tenure at St. Louis. In a donnybrook race, the two teams finished the season in a dead heat. To settle the issue of this first true deadlock in NL history, a best-of-three playoff series was set, which the Cardinals won by sweeping the first two games. Overall, the Cardinals used league-leading pitching, batting, and fielding to assert their superiority. Pitcher Howie Pollet's league-leading 21 victories and 2.01 ERA led the pitching staff. And a pair of outfielders powered the Cardinal offensive: Musial's .365 hitting won the league batting crown, and Enos Slaughter's 130 RBIs topped all others. In the World Series the Cardinals toppled the favored Red Sox in seven games.

As it turned out, St. Louis fans would have to wait another seventeen seasons before a Cardinal team again scaled the heights. Meanwhile in 1947 attention of fans everywhere riveted upon the Dodgers and Jackie Robinson's debut as the first black player of the century to play in the majors. When Commissioner Chandler suspended manager Leo Durocher, Burt Shotton took over the reins of the club and stationed Robinson at first base. Advised by Rickey to turn his cheek against racist slurs, which came mostly from the Cardinals and Phillies, Robinson responded stoically and successfully. His .297 batting that year won him NL Rookie of the Year honors, and his example opened the way for more black players to follow. With outfielders Pete Reiser and Dixie Walker topping the .300 mark at bat, and with pitcher Ralph Branca winning a league-leading 21 games and bullpen master Hugh Casey saving a league-leading 18 games, the Dodgers beat the Cardinals by 5 games. That year the Dodgers also had the satisfaction of seeing their hated rivals, the Giants, finish in fourth place despite a record 221-homer barrage. But in World Series play, another local rival, the Yankees, downed the Dodgers in a grueling seven-game struggle.

In 1948 the Dodgers slipped to third as ex-Cardinal manager Billy Southworth drove the Boston Braves to a 6½-game victory over his former Redbird team. It was Boston's first NL pennant since 1914 and its last as a Beantown franchise. Boston's pitching trio of Johnny Sain (whose 24 victories led all NL hurlers), Warren Spahn, and Vern Bickford fronted the NL's most effective staff. And the team's league-leading .275 batting attack was fronted by outfielder Tommy Holmes (.325), and by infielders Al Dark (.322) and Bob Elliott (100 RBIs). But when the Braves met the Indians in World Series play, the Indians dispatched the Braves in five games. Landing the 1948 NL pennant was the last gasp of this faltering franchise, which five years later would move to more profitable pastures in Milwaukee.

As the Braves faded in 1949, the Dodgers asserted their dynastic power. Over the next five seasons the Dodgers won three NL races and lost two others by heartbreakingly narrow margins. In 1949 Robinson's league-leading .342 hitting helped the Dodgers eke a 1-game victory over the Cardinals. Joining the MVP Award-winning Robinson were black stars Roy Campanella, who batted .287, and pitcher Don Newcombe, whose 17 wins paced the staff. Outfielder Carl Furillo batted .322 and outfielder Duke Snider and first baseman Gil Hodges, who combined for 46 homers and 207 RBIs, paced the team's league-leading homer assault. But then, for a third time, the Dodgers bowed to the Yankees in the World Series.

In 1950 the Dodger "Boys of Summer" lost by 2 games to the Phillies' "Whiz Kids." Phillies' ace Robin Roberts averted a possible deadlock by outpitching Newcombe on the final day of the season. With youngsters Roberts and Curt Sim-

mons combining for 37 wins, and relief ace Jim Konstanty winning 16 and saving 22 for a Cy Young Award performance, the Phillies boasted the league's best pitching. At the plate the team was powered by Del Ennis, who drove in a league-leading 126 runs, and by young Richie Ashburn, who batted .303. But late in the season the team lost pitcher Simmons to the Korean War military draft. His absence tolled on the Phillies, who were swept by the Yankees in the World Series.

Over the winter of 1950, Dodger owner O'Malley forced Rickey out of his general manager post, but Rickey's departure spared him the agonies of the Dodgers' 1951 season. As the fateful campaign unfolded, the Dodgers soared to a 13½-game lead in early August. But in the September stretch, the "miracle" New York Giants rose to deadlock the Dodgers at the season's end. In the unforgettable playoff series between these traditional rivals, the Giants rallied to win the decisive game on outfielder Bobby Thomson's dramatic ninth-inning homer. In baseball folklore, Thomson's winning blast is immortalized as "the shot heard round the world." Indeed, it was a miraculous season as the Dodgers, paced by the hitting of Robinson and Campanella, led Giant hitters by 15 points. But black stars Monte Irvin (who batted .312-24-121) and rookie Willie Mays (who hit 20 homers) powered the Giants, who also got a .303 performance from team leader Al Dark and a .293 performance with 32 homers from the heroic Thomson. Moreover, Giant pitchers Sal Maglie and Larry Jansen each won 23 games, to pace the league-leading Giant pitching staff. However, the Giants' celebrated "Miracle of Coogan's Bluff" was tarnished by defeat at the hands of the Yankees in the 1951 World Series.

But at this point the snakebit Dodgers picked themselves up and went on to capture the next two NL pennants. In 1952 they outlasted the Giants by 4½ games, and the following year they coasted to a 13-game win over the transplanted Milwaukee Braves. In the hard-fought 1952 race the Giants suffered the loss of Mays to the military draft. It was a crushing blow for the Giants, but Dodger crushers led the league in homers. Snider, Hodges, and Campanella combined for 75, and this trio drove in nearly 300 runs. The pitching was shaky. Able starters Preacher Roe, Carl Erskine, and Billy Loes won 38 games, but reliever Joe Black made the difference. With a 15–4 record and 15 saves, Black enjoyed the best season of his brief career. The following year, Erskine picked up after the slumping Black and posted a 20–6 record to lead the staff. Behind him the mature Boys of Summer beat a hefty tattoo, leading the league in batting (.285) and homers (208). Rebounding from his previous year's slump, Furillo batted .344 to lead the league, and Campanella's .312-41-142 record won him another MVP Award. It added up to a two-year domination of the NL, but in World Series play the Dodger champs twice fell to their Yankee nemesis; in 1952 they lost the Series in seven games, and the following year they fell in six games.

Shortly after the 1953 Series loss, O'Malley picked the little-known Walter Alston to skipper the club. Although Alston would manage the team for twenty-three seasons, a longer skein than any of his managerial colleagues, his 1954 debut was inauspicious. That year the Dodgers lost to the Giants by 5 games. Offensively the Dodgers outbatted and outscored their rivals, but the Giants matched the Dodgers in homer production and fielded the league's best pitching staff. Returning from military service, Willie Mays led the league

in hitting with a .345 mark, and his 41 homers and 110 RBIs firmly established his credentials as one of the leading stars of the decade. That year also saw the ex–bonus baby Johnny Antonelli come into his own as a pitcher. His 21 victories and 2.30 ERA paced the Giant pitching staff, which was the league's best. But the Giants were cast as underdogs in the World Series against the powerful Cleveland Indians. However, a sensational fielding play by outfielder Mays doused a promising Indian rally in the first game, and key pinch hits by "Dusty" Rhodes in each of the first three games triggered winning rallies. The result was a four-game sweep of the Indians.

But the Giant victory was also the team's last as longtime residents of New York. Over the next two seasons, the battlewise Dodgers rebounded to win another pair of back-to-back pennants. Each year it was the Braves who finished second; in 1955 the Dodgers lapped the Milwaukee Braves by 13½ games, and the following year they held off their rivals by a single game. In 1955 outfielders Snider (.309-42-136) and Furillo (.314), and catcher Campanella (.318-32-107) paced the offensive. For his heroics, Campanella won his third MVP Award of the decade. Newcombe's 20 wins headed the dominant pitching staff. In the aftermath of the easy victory, the Dodgers also managed to defeat their Yankee tormentors for the first time as they won the 1955 World Series in seven games.

For the team's fanatical followers, this was to be the first and only world title they would see flying over Ebbets Field. In 1956 the Dodgers repeated, but only by the narrowest margin. League-leading performances by pitcher Newcombe (27 wins) and Clem Labine (19 saves) and a league-leading 43 homers by Duke Snider were needed to atone for the team's .258 batting. And in the aftermath of the grueling 1956 campaign, New York–area fans witnessed the last subway World Series matchup between the Yankees and Dodgers. Although the Dodgers won the first two games, they lost the Series in seven games. What's more, this Dodger team became the victims of the first no-hit game in World Series history when Yankee hurler Don Larsen hurled his perfect game in the fifth game.

As owner O'Malley laid plans for his team's postseasonal move to Los Angeles in 1957, his Dodger team fell to third. The following season, the team's first in Los Angeles, they fell further, to seventh place. In these years there was no stopping the well-balanced Milwaukee Braves. As the first breakaway franchise to win a major league pennant in this century, the 1957 Braves attracted over 2 million home fans, who saw the team down the Cardinals by 8 games. Outfielder Hank Aaron's 44 homers and 132 RBIs led the league's hitters, and veteran pitcher Spahn's 21 wins led the league's pitchers. Third baseman Ed Mathews supplied additional power with 32 homers and 94 RBIs, and starting pitchers Lew Burdette and Bob Buhl combined for 35 victories. Then in World Series play the underdog Braves treated their fans to Milwaukee's only world title to this date by downing the Yankees in seven games. The following year the Braves repeated, scoring an 8-game victory over the rising Pirates. Spahn's 22 victories again led NL hurlers and Burdette added 20 victories. At the bat Aaron showed the way with .326-30-95 hitting, with Mathews adding 31 homers and first baseman Frank Torre batting .309. But in a World Series rematch with the Yankees, the Braves blew a commanding three-games-to-one lead, and the avenging Yankees won in seven games. To the Yankees

went the honor of becoming the first team in over thirty years to rebound from such a deficit in World Series play.

As the decade of the fifties drew to a close, the transplanted Los Angeles Dodgers recovered from their seventh-place finish of 1958 to end the Braves' two-year reign. In a brilliant September stretch drive, the Dodgers won thirteen of fourteen games to deadlock the Braves at the end of the campaign. And for a change the Dodgers won the playoff series by sweeping the Braves in two games to claim the NL pennant. The Braves outhit, outhomered, and outpitched the Dodgers, but the Dodgers led the league in fielding, and outfielders Duke Snider (.308-23-88) and Wally Moon (.302-19-74) supplied power enough, and the bullpen saved 26 games. In World Series action against the White Sox, the Dodgers won in six games. The Dodgers' victories included a sweep of its three home games, which were played at the Los Angeles Coliseum, where a record 270,000 fans jammed the converted football stadium to witness the triumphs.

But the Dodgers fell to fourth in 1960 as the Pirates, a team constructed by Rickey, beat the Braves by 7 games. Manager Danny Murtaugh's "Bucs" batted a league-leading .276; shortstop Dick Groat's .325 batting led the NL hitters, and future Hall of Fame outfielder Roberto Clemente batted .314. Vern Law's 20 pitching victories led the starters, but reliever Roy Face was the bellwether of the staff. Face appeared in a league-leading 68 games, won 10 and saved 24, and posted an ERA of 2.90. In World Series play the Pirates were thrice battered by the Yankees, but they won the 1960 classic in seven games. Second baseman Bill Mazeroski's tenth-inning homer in the finale at Forbes Field secured Pittsburgh's first world title in thirty-five years.

The AL had already expanded to ten teams in 1961, when the NL played its last season under the traditional eight-club format with its hallowed 154-game schedule. In a close race the 1961 Cincinnati Reds edged the Dodgers by 4 games. Stout pitching, paced by starters Joey Jay, whose 21 wins led NL pitchers, and Jim O'Toole (19 wins), and 40 saves by the relief corps headed by Jim Brosnan and Bill Henry, carried the team. At bat the Reds batted .270, with outfielders Frank Robinson (.323-37-124) and Vada Pinson (.343-16-87) powering the attack. But when the Reds met the Yankees in World Series play, they succumbed in five games.

The Expansion Era Begins, 1961–1968

In this turbulent decade of American history, major league baseball's tradition-breaking expansion ranked as one of the lesser social disturbances. A time of massive social unrest, the strident sixties saw most established institutions targeted by would-be reformers. Sparking the fires of unrest were the assassinations of the Kennedy brothers and Martin Luther King, the great black civil rights leader. In the wake of these tragedies came storms of protest demonstrations supportive of increased freedom for individuals and for oppressed minorities. But as the decade wore on, the major focus of the protests centered on the nation's involvement in the Vietnam War. This country's latest struggle against the spread of international Communism began in the mid-1960s and lasted until 1973. An unpopular war, the Vietnam involvement consumed over 50,000 American soldiers' lives, polarized the nation into factions embattled over the morality of the war, and ended in a political and military defeat. Moreover, the violent protests

against the war spilled over into other social institutions. Thus demonstrations and protest movements by black Americans aimed at securing civil rights and economic betterment erupted at times into urban riots. And among other discontented minorites, many women organized into protest movements and demanded economic and political equality. At this time the widespread consciousness-raising appealed to many Americans, who supported such slogans as "Freedom Now" and affected new lifestyles in social relations, speech, clothing, and hairstyles. And by the end of the decade such supporters included numbers of major league ballplayers, who sought relief from long-established paternal controls imposed upon them by baseball law and custom.

Meanwhile, other forces of change were reshaping the nation and its national game. In this decade the nation's population soared past 200 million, with nearly half that number concentrated in some thirteen sprawling urban regions. Thus even as major league owners embarked upon an initial expansion course in 1960–1961, these new demographics portended further expansion of the two leagues along with the possible relocation of teams now situated in deteriorating urban areas.

Nevertheless, amidst all the disturbing changes the nation's economy continued to prosper. Although they were sapped by continuing inflation, the average wages of all workers rose to an annual figure of $8,000 by the end of the decade. As a result, annual spending for recreation rose to $18 billion, with television viewing continuing to reign as the most popular leisure outlet.

The continuing popularity of televised sports programs, now shown in color with ever-improving visual effects, was a boon to professional sports. While baseball profited from this popular medium, so did half a dozen rival sports. Among these, professional football expanded rapidly under the impetus of hefty national TV contracts which clubowners shared equally. By occupying most of the major urban regions, pro football now threatened baseball's pre-eminent position among the nation's favorite team sports. Indeed, in 1967 professional football's Super Bowl outscored the World Series in television ratings.

In stark contrast to pro football's bold expansionist course was major league baseball's limited expansion movement of these years. Baseball's initial expansion took place over the years 1961–1962 and was primarily an attempt to undercut the threat of the rival Continental League. Under this expansion, each major league added two teams and upped its seasonal playing schedule to 162. A significant departure, the addition of eight more games to playing schedules would drastically affect statistical comparisons of seasonal performances. Moreover, each new franchise owner paid $2 million, which was divided among the eight established clubs of each major league, and also participated in an expansion draft, which was used to enable the owners to stock their teams with players. But since established teams were permitted to withhold their best twenty-five players from the pool of eligibles, the new owners were forced to purchase unprotected cullings.

Under these procedures, the AL took the first expansion plunge in 1961. That year the AL added the Los Angeles Angels and a new edition of the Washington Senators. At the request of owner Cal Griffith, the original Senators relocated to Bloomington, Minnesota, where they became the Minnesota Twins. The furor evoked by that breakaway move forced AL owners to admit the new Washington Senators. It was an unwise move, as the franchise languished under weak owner-

ship and poor attendance. In 1972 the Senators moved to Arlington, Texas, where they fared better as the Texas Rangers. Nor did the AL Angels fare well in Los Angeles, where they were upstaged by O'Malley's Dodgers. However, this well-financed team found prosperity when it was moved to nearby Anaheim in 1965.

For its part the NL did better under its 1962 expansion. That year the NL occupied Houston, where the Colt .45s occupied temporary quarters while awaiting the construction of their new all-weather indoor Astrodome Stadium. When the Astrodome opened in 1965, this expansion team took on a new identity as the Houston Astros. Meanwhile, as part of a deal which allowed the AL to occupy the Los Angeles territory, the NL reoccupied the New York area by admitting the New York Mets. Although the Mets lost 120 games in their first season of play, the team was generously supported by suffering fans, who rejoiced in the return of NL baseball to the Gotham area. After playing its first two seasons in the old Polo Grounds, the Mets moved into newly built Shea Stadium, located in Queens.

Thus did the major leagues move into their first phase of expansion. But each passing season underscored the inadequacy of the ten-club format. Like the twelve-club NL of the 1890s, the ten-club array of the 1960s produced too many losers each season. Annual attendance was disappointing. By 1968, overall major league attendance topped that of 1960 by only 3 million admissions. And added to the problems of this phase of expansion were two controversial franchise shifts. In 1966 the NL's Milwaukee Braves abandoned that city for Atlanta, and in 1968 the AL's Athletics departed Kansas City for Oakland, California, where they poached upon the territory of the NL Giants. Each of these breakaway moves aroused protests from fans of the abandoned sites, and each prompted lawsuits which affected future expansion moves.

Meanwhile major league teams continued to face a growing shortage of playing talent. At most schools and colleges, where baseball now ranked as a minor sport, scouts complained that major sports like football and basketball were getting the best athletes. With the minor leagues shrinking alarmingly, major league owners in 1962 adopted a remedial Player Development Plan. Under this scheme, the minor leagues were reclassified, and each major league team agreed to subsidize at least five minor league teams. And to equitably distribute the limited supply of young prospects, the majors in 1965 adopted the radical plan of an annual free agent (rookie) draft. Under its provisions, each major league club in turn picked from a nationwide pool of high school and college prospects. Thus except for prospecting in foreign countries, the annual rookie draft ended the long and colorful era of free-enterprise scouting in America.

Along with the prevailing national mood of liberation for oppressed groups, the chronic player shortage helped to kindle reformist sentiments among this generation of major league players. More pampered and better trained, doctored, and defended than past generations of players, players of this decade demanded improved salaries, pensions, and working conditions. In these years player disdain for traditional authority was rife, and this was candidly spelled out in revelatory books, including bestsellers authored by pitchers Jim Brosnan and Jim Bouton. And in a precedent-shattering move in 1966, Dodger pitchers Sandy Koufax and Don Drysdale, acting on the advice of a lawyer, staged a successful joint holdout for hefty salary increases. That same year, player

representatives strengthened the moribund Major League Players Association (MLPA) by successfully engineering the election of Marvin Miller, an experienced labor negotiator, to serve as the Association's executive director. Landing Miller proved to be a master stroke for the players' cause. By rallying the players and by invoking federal labor relations laws, Miller forced the clubowners to recognize and to bargain collectively with the MLPA. During his seventeen years as executive director, Miller negotiated five Basic Agreements, or labor contracts, which wrung from owners unprecedented concessions and benefits. The Basic Agreements of 1966 and 1969 increased pension benefits and raised minimum salaries along with other gains. Thus by 1970 average player salaries, which totaled $17,000 in 1965, rose to $25,000. At the same time some twenty players were being paid annual salaries of at least $100,000 a year. But Miller's greatest coup of this decade was to win the solid support of major league players behind the MLPA. And by the end of this decade, major league umpires also won recognition and bargaining rights under their newly formed Major League Umpires Association.

Among the deserving recipients of increasing salaries were the growing numbers of black players in major league uniforms. By the end of the sixties, well over a hundred black Americans and scores of Latin Americans were playing in the majors. What's more, their offensive production made a reality of the prevailing Afro-American protest slogan that "black is beautiful." In these years black hitters dominated major league offenses. In the NL, black stars won seven homer titles, as many MVP awards, and six batting titles. And in the AL, blacks won three batting titles and three MVP awards. Among the reigning black superstars, Willie Mays of the Giants was voted Player of the Decade by *The Sporting News;* indeed, Mays posted a remote threat to overtake Ruth's lifetime homer mark, and at the end of his career he had powered 660 homers. But by the end of the decade more observers were touting Braves' outfielder Hank Aaron's chances of bettering Ruth. Meanwhile at this time, Frank Robinson became the first player to win an MVP Award in each major league, and outfielder Roberto Clemente of the Pirates won three NL batting titles.

Sparkling alongside such stars were white prodigies like Roger Maris, who blasted 61 homers in 162 games in 1961, to set a new seasonal mark for homer production; or Carl Yastrzemski, who won an AL Triple Crown; or Pete Rose, who broke in as a rookie in 1963 with the Cincinnati Reds and would later break Cobb's lifetime total of 4,191 hits.

Indeed, such offensive performances occurred despite the hitting famine caused by the dominant pitchers of this era. Abetting the hitting famine was the rule that expanded the strike zone for the 1963 season. But improved coaching techniques, improved gloves and defensive strategies, and, above all, the astute deployment of specialized relief pitchers tolled on hitters of the era. As a result, pitching ERAs averaged 3.30 in this era, and in 1968, the notorious "year of the pitcher," hurlers combined to produce an overall ERA of 2.98, which was the lowest earned run mark in nearly forty years. Not surprisingly, the impact of such virtuosity on hitting was traumatic. In 1967 major league hitters averaged .242, and in 1968 batting bottomed to a nadir of .237. It was that puny mark which prompted remedial action by the rules committee, whose members voted to narrow strike zones and lower pitching mounds for the 1969 season. Such medicine

broke the hitting famine, but while it lasted star pitchers made the most of their skills. In 1968 Cardinal ace Bob Gibson posted a 1.12 ERA and fanned a record 35 batters in three appearances in the World Series that fall. That same year, Denny McLain of the Tigers became the first hurler in over thirty years to break the 30-game victory barrier with a 31–6 performance; and Don Drysdale of the Dodgers posted a record 58 consecutive shutout innings. Moreover, in this decade fifteen pitchers would go on to join the ranks of the twenty all-time strikeout leaders.

However, many observers blamed the dominant pitching for lowering seasonal attendance marks in these years. From a record of 15 million in 1966, NL attendance slipped to 11.7 million in 1968, "the year of the pitcher." Nevertheless, annual NL attendance consistently bettered that of the AL; overall NL attendance of this era topped that of the AL by 16 million admissions. But a major factor accounting for NL attendance strength was the greater number of new ballparks in the senior circuit. In this decade, seven of the ten newly constructed parks were occupied by NL teams. Of these, nine were publicly financed, but the privately financed Dodger Stadium now attracted the lion's share of NL attendance.

But rising television revenues dispelled some of the anxieties over falling attendance. By 1967, revenues from local and national television contracts rose to $25 million, with no sign of abating. On the other hand, by urging more night games, by raising the value of major league franchises, by making celebrities of players, and by the presence of television entrepreneurs in the ranks of club owners, television was reshaping the game. To some alarmists television's influence was menacing. In 1964 the sale of the Yankees to the powerful CBS Network fed fears of excessive television influence. However, such fears were allayed by the declining fortunes of the Yankees under CBS management and by the 1973 resale of the team to private interests.

Campaigns of the Sixties: The AL, 1961–1968

By first expanding to ten teams in 1961, the AL led the NL both in attendance and in hitting. But when the NL followed suit in 1962, the AL was annually worsted in both categories. And when the hitting famine ravaged the major leagues late in this era, except for their leadership in homer hitting, AL batters suffered more.

To add to AL woes, the Yankees continued to monopolize pennants and overall attendance. Four more victories over the years 1961–1964 extended the Yankee's latest consecutive string of pennants to five, during which time the New Yorkers attracted 40 percent of the league's attendance. However, the latest Yankee surge was marred by losses in their last two World Series appearances. And in the wake of their loss to the Cardinals in the 1964 World Series, the Yankees collapsed suddenly and ignominiously. Thereafter, another twelve seasons would pass before a Yankee team again rose to the top of the league. But if rival clubs welcomed the tyrant's fall, they also discovered the draining impact of a weakened Yankee club on AL attendance.

In the AL's first expansion campaign, the 1961 Yankees powered their way to an 8-game win over the Tigers. With Roger Maris bashing a new seasonal record of 61 homers and Mantle poling 54, the Yankees unleashed a record seasonal team barrage of 240 homers. Maris also led the league in RBIs with 142, and Mantle knocked in 128. Ace pitcher Whitey Ford's 25 victories led the league's hurlers and reliever Luis Arroyo's 29 saves was tops in the league. While some observers blamed the Yankee power explosion on the expansion draft, which supposedly weakened pitching staffs around the league, the Yankees had no trouble downing the NL champion Reds in six games in the 1961 World Series.

In 1962 the Yankees won again, beating the Twins by 5 games. League-leading .267 batting and pitcher Ralph Terry's league-leading 23 victories spearheaded the attack. The switch-hitting Mantle's .321 batting topped the team, but this time around the Maris-Mantle slugging combination tailed off to a more modest 63 homers and 189 RBIs. Then, in a seven-game struggle that was drawn out by unprecedented rain delays, the Yankees defeated the Giants in the 1962 World Series. In the dramatic final game, Terry pitched a 1–0 shutout, but second baseman Bobby Richardson gloved a screaming liner by Giant slugger Willie McCovey to save the Yankee victory.

In retrospect the Yankee glory years ended with the 1962 victory. With Mantle sidelined much of the 1963 season, the Yankees batted only .252, but still romped to an easy 10½-game victory over the hard-hitting Twins. Superb pitching by Ford (whose 24 wins led the league) and by Bouton (who won 21 games) sparked the drive. But in World Series play the Yankees were swept by the Dodgers. Still, the Yankees mounted one last winning effort in 1964. Rallying from six games back in the late going, the team overtook the White Sox and Orioles to win by 1 game over the White Sox. Mantle's last great batting effort (.303-35-111) powered the team, and Ford, Bouton, and Al Downing combined for 48 pitching victories. But it took a nine-game winning streak in September, highlighted by the pitching of rookie Mel Stottlemyre, to turn the trick. However, the Yankees again fell in World Series play, this time losing to the Cardinals in seven games.

In the wake of that loss, like the wonderful one-hoss shay, the aging Yankees collapsed "all at once and nothing first." In 1965 the team sank to sixth place and in 1966 they finished last. The suddenness of the team's collapse was reflected in AL attendance figures; in 1965 AL attendance lagged 5 million behind that of the NL. Into the breach left by the faltering Yankees rushed other contenders, but no team held the heights for more than a single season. First to reach the top were the Minnesota Twins, who won the 1965 race by 7 games over the White Sox. Outfielder Tony Oliva topped all hitters with .321 batting and paced the team's league-leading .254 hitting. Aging slugger and future Hall of Famer Harmon Killebrew hit 25 homers. Pitcher Jim "Mudcat" Grant's 21 wins led all pitchers; Jim Kaat won 18, and reliever Al Worthington won 10 and saved 21. But for a third consecutive time the NL prevailed in World Series action, as the Twins lost to the Dodgers in seven games.

The AL ended its string of World Series losses in 1966, and with this victory the league's teams weaned themselves of Yankee dependence. Indeed, over the preceding eighteen seasons no AL team but the Yankees had won a world title. In exorcising that bugaboo, the Baltimore Orioles began by dispatching the Twins by 9 games. Outfielder Frank Robinson keyed the team's .258 batting assault with league-leading .316-49-122 hitting. The performance won Robinson a second Triple Crown and placed him in the records as the first player ever to win a Triple Crown in both major leagues. Infielders Brooks Robinson and John "Boog" Powell combined to drive in 209 runs, and the Oriole bullpen corps saved 51 games to

make life easier for the young starting pitchers. But in the 1966 World Series three of these pitching prodigies—Jim Palmer, Wally Bunker, and Steve Barber—hurled consecutive shutouts as the Orioles swept the favored Dodgers.

The rising Orioles were destined to become the AL's winningest team of the next 20 years, but in 1967 they slumped to sixth place, which opened the door of opportunity to yet another contender. In a close race the Boston Red Sox won their first pennant since 1946 by edging the Tigers by a game. In winning the Red Sox overcame the loss of promising young outfielder Tony Conigliaro, who suffered a career-threatening beaning; at the time of his accident, Conigliaro had 20 homers and 67 RBIs. But future Hall of Fame outfielder Carl Yastrzemski won a Triple Crown on .326-44-121 batting to front the team's league leadership in batting (.255) and homers (158). Pitcher Jim Lonborg's 22 wins led the league and reliever John Wyatt saved 20 games. But like their forebears of 1946, the 1967 Red Sox lost to the Cardinals in a seven-game World Series encounter.

In the last year of the ten-club format, the AL race produced the weakest seasonal hitting of this century. As the Red Sox faded, the Detroit Tigers won by 12 games over the reviving Orioles. Although batting a mere .235 as a team, the Tigers led the league in homers, paced by outfielder Willie Horton, who slugged 36. And considering that the best team in the league that year, the Oakland Athletics, batted .240, the Tigers' offensive was proportionately respectable. Moreover, the Tigers boasted pitcher Denny McLain, who won 31 games and lost 6 with a 1.96 ERA. Matched against the Cardinals in the 1968 World Series, the Tigers lost three of the first four games. But pitcher Mickey Lolich won two of the next three, to spark the Tigers to a dramatic comeback victory. It was Detroit's first world title since the war year of 1945.

As the year of 1968 ended, the owners voted to join with the NL in expanding the circuit to twelve teams beginning in 1969. Mercifully for beleaguered batters, the owners also accepted a rules committee proposal to penalize pitchers. Thenceforth in both major leagues the strike zone would be narrowed and pitching mounds would be lowered.

Campaigns of the Sixties: The NL, 1962–1968

Although the NL expanded a year after the AL took the first step, the senior circuit was quick to reassert its offensive superiority. In its brief seven-season span as a ten-team circuit, the NL won four of the seven World Series encounters and seven of eight All-Star Games. Moreover, in six of the seven seasons NL batters topped AL batters in hitting and in stolen bases. And although the AL was better-balanced competitively in this era, as the Dodgers and Cardinals were monopolizing six of the seven NL races, attendance at NL games far surpassed AL attendance.

In 1962 the NL opened its first season as an expanded circuit, with most teams drained of their reserve strength by the expansion draft. In the ensuing campaign, the Dodgers and Giants staged a torrid race. But a late September losing streak by the Dodgers enabled the Giants to draw even at the close of the playing season. To settle the issue, the fourth postseason playoff in NL history was scheduled, with the Dodgers astonishingly involved in all of them. And when Dodger relief pitchers blew a 4–2 lead in the ninth inning of the decisive third game, the Dodgers lost a playoff for the third time. For their part, the Dodgers were led that season by pitcher Don Drysdale, whose 25 wins led all pitchers, and by outfielder Tommy Davis, whose .346 batting and 153 RBIs led all NL hitters. But the hard-hitting Giants led the league in batting (.278) and in homers (204). Superstar Willie Mays led the Giant attack with .304 batting, 141 RBIs, and a league-leading 49 homers. Fellow outfielders Felipe Alou and Harvey Kuenn topped the .300 mark, and first baseman Orlando Cepeda weighed in with .306 batting, 35 homers, and 114 RBIs. Pitcher Jack Sanford won 24 games, and Juan Marichal and Billy O'Dell combined for 37, while reliever Stu Miller saved 19. However, the Giants lost a seven-game World Series duel to the Yankees.

Thereafter the Dodgers and Cardinals divided the remaining six NL championships of this era. In 1963 the Dodgers won by 6 games over the Cardinals. The team batted a modest .251, but Tommy Davis batted .326 to notch his second straight NL batting title, and shortstop Maury Wills batted .302 and led the league in stolen bases with 40. What really counted was the pitching, as the staff's 2.85 ERA was the league's best. That year lefty Sandy Koufax began a four-year skein of mastery that would propel him into the Hall of Fame. The ace's 25 wins and 1.88 ERA topped all hurlers, and reliever Ron Perranoski's 21 saves was the league's second best mark. In the 1963 World Series, the team's dominant pitching limited Yankee batters to a .171 batting average as the Dodgers swept to victory.

Dodger pitching again topped the league in 1964, with Koufax winning 19 and leading all hurlers with a 1.74 ERA, but poor hitting consigned Alston's men to sixth place. In a hotly contested five-team race, the Phillies led the pack by 6½ games with 12 games remaining on the schedule. But ten consecutive losses dropped the Phillies into a second-place tie with the Reds. The Phillies' swoon opened the gate for the Cardinals, who won 28 of their last 30 games. This brilliant stretch drive enabled the Redbirds to eke a one-game victory over the Phillies and Reds. The Cardinals' league-leading .272 batting made the difference. Infielders Bill White and Ken Boyer combined for 45 homers and 221 RBIs, and outfielder Curt Flood batted .311. But the timely acquisition of outfielder Lou Brock from the Cubs was decisive. Brock batted .348 in 103 games for the Cardinals and his 43 stolen bases ranked just behind Wills's total. And starting pitchers Bob Gibson, Ray Sadecki, and Curt Simmons combined to win 57 games. Yet so unexpected was the Cardinal victory that team manager Johnny Keane had signed a midseason pact to manage the Yankees the following year. The situation raised eyebrows when the Cardinals squared off against the Yankees in the 1964 World Series, but lame-duck Keane led the Cardinals to a seven-game victory over the Yankees.

In the wake of Keane's departure, the 1965 Cardinals dropped to seventh place. Into the power vacuum rushed the Dodgers, who gained the high ground and held it for two seasons against determined opposition from the Giants. Each Dodger victory was a near thing; in 1965 the Dodgers edged the Giants by 2 games, and the following year by 1½. In winning the 1965 pennant, the Dodgers batted a skimpy .245, with nary a .300 hitter in the regular lineup. But once again the Dodger pitching was superb; lefty Koufax won 26 on a 2.04 ERA, to top all NL hurlers, and Don Drysdale added 23 wins. And it was Koufax's shutout pitching in the seventh game of the World Series which led the team to victory over the Twins.

Over the winter Koufax and Drysdale staged an unprecedented joint holdout for salaries that were commensurate with their worth to the team. The two aces won salaries in the $100,000 range although these were grudgingly granted by owner O'Malley. But with Dodger home attendance topping the 2 million mark for the past eight seasons, such salaries were affordable. And in the case of Koufax, it was money well spent. In the close race of 1966 the lefty won 27 games with a 1.73 ERA, both league-leading figures. Drysdale slipped to 13–16, but reliever Phil "the Vulture" Regan saved 21 games. Such heroics were needed as the team batted only .256 with only Tommy Davis, in limited duty, topping the .300 mark. And in the 1966 World Series, the team's poor batting tolled as they were swept by the Orioles.

At the close of the 1966 campaign, the chronic arthritis in Koufax's pitching arm forced the ace to retire at the peak of his career. Thus disarmed, the weak-hitting Dodgers fell from contention. Not so the Cardinals, who perched atop the NL for the next two seasons as they twice drubbed the perennial bridesmaid Giants. In 1967 the Cardinals won by 10½ games, and in 1968 they won by 9. With Gibson sidelined for much of the 1967 season, the Cardinal bullpen responded by leading the league in saves. At bat the Cardinals hit .263, with Flood batting .335 and first baseman Orlando Cepeda batting .325 and driving in a league-leading 111 runs. Outfielder Lou Brock weighed in with .299 batting, and his 52 stolen bases led the league. In the 1967 World Series, Brock's .414 batting and seven stolen bases, and Gibson's three pitching wins and 26 strikeouts, highlighted the Cardinals' victory in the seven-game struggle with the Red Sox.

The following year a healthy Gibson won 22 games with a league-leading ERA of 1.12. In support of the black ace, pitchers Nelson Briles, Steve Carlton, and Ray Washburn combined to pitch 46 victories. Offensively, Brock's 62 steals led the league and Flood batted .301. As a team the Cardinals batted only .249, but in this "year of the pitcher," when overall NL batting stood at .243, it was enough. In the 1968 World Series, Gibson fanned a record 35 batters, but Flood's misjudging of Jim Northrup's fly ball in the seventh game allowed the Tigers to break through and complete their memorable come-from-behind victory.

As the curtain descended on the 1968 season, the major league owners now embarked on a second phase of expansion that would usher in a rich era of cash and glory for the major league game.

The Expanding Majors, 1969–1980

As the stormy sixties drew to a close, the nation united in applauding the successful moon landing by American astronauts in the summer of 1969. And if the strident countercultural protests lingered into the new decade, they lost their steam when the Vietnam War ended in 1973. The nation still had to weather a major political storm in 1974, when the Watergate scandal forced the resignation of President Richard Nixon, but the passing of that crisis marked the ending of the era of social turbulence. By then, a conservative reaction was ascendant and was marked by such themes as religious and patriotic revival and continuing fears of Communist expansionism.

In retrospect, mounting economic problems turned public attention from social protests to the harsh realities of earning a living. In 1973–1974 the nation suffered its worst economic recession since the thirties. A frightening accompaniment to the recession was mounting "stagflation"—a combination of inflation and rising unemployment. Indeed, by the end of the seventies an estimated 24 million Americans were living at or near the poverty level. To cope with the problem, millions of wives and mothers entered the labor force. As a result, the nation's birthrate declined sharply over the years 1973–1979. Nevertheless, abetted by the falling death rate, the population continued to grow; from a level of 204 million in 1970, the population reached 226 million by 1980.

The trend toward dual-income families in this era translated into rising incomes (albeit, inflated dollars) for most Americans. Nor did rising prices for consumer goods dampen the people's ardor for leisure and recreational pursuits. By the end of the decade, annual spending for recreation reached $40 billion. And because watching televised sports maintained its status as one of the most favored leisure outlets, the popularity of major team sports like baseball increased. For major league club owners of this era, this translated into heftier profits from television sources and surging attendance at the turnstiles.

Happily for major league baseball interests, such increasing prosperity followed hard after its latest expansion movement. In 1968 major league owners voted to add two teams to each league, thus increasing the 1969 major league membership to twenty-four teams. Under the new format, which imitated professional football's earlier and successful experiment, each league was realigned into six-team Eastern and Western Divisions. The 162-game seasonal schedule was retained, with each team playing its intradivisional opponents eighteen times and outsiders twelve times. At the close of a season, the new format called for the two divisional winners in each league to meet in a best-of-five-game playoff series to determine the league championship. Afterward, the champions of each league would meet in the usual World Series competition to determine the ultimate winner.

Supporters of this revolutionary new format touted its successful precedent in pro football and its competitive advantage over the recent ten-team system. Proponents also counted on the lure of each season's divisional races to sustain public interest; after all, such races would return four winners each season instead of two. Furthermore, a divisional winning team got to fly a pennant even if it subsequently lost out in the league championship playoffs. Finally, with six teams competing in each division, the worst any team might do was finish a season in sixth place. It was nice sleight-of-hand logic, and it worked.

Events speedily demonstrated the wisdom of such logic. For their part, baseball fans welcomed the new format once they got used to the new teams with their strange-sounding totems, including the presence of a Canadian team, the Montreal Expos, in the major league ranks. In the NL, the Expos joined the Eastern Division along with the Cardinals, Cubs, Mets, Phillies, and Pirates; in the NL's Western Division, the San Diego Padres were grouped with the Astros, Braves, Dodgers, Giants, and Reds. For its part, the AL installed its two new teams in its Western Division. There the newcoming Kansas City Royals and Seattle Pilots vied with the Angels, Athletics, Twins, and White Sox. However, this made for a perennially stronger Eastern Division, where the established Indians, Orioles, Red Sox, Senators, Tigers, and Yankees were now arrayed.

For the privilege of obtaining one of the new franchises, each newly admitted NL owner paid $10 million and each new AL owner paid $5.6 million; these initiation fees were divided as a windfall among the established clubs of each league. To stock the new teams with players, another expansion draft was held in each league. The latest draft allowed the new owners to purchase unprotected cullings from the rosters of established teams. And like the first expansion draft, this latest one placed the newcomers at a competitive disadvantage. In the NL the Expos and Padres long languished in their divisional cellars, and neither entry won a divisional pennant in this era. But such was not the case with the AL's newcoming Kansas City Royals club. In their first campaign the Royals finished fourth, and over the years 1975–1980 the Royals won four divisional races and a league championship. But on the other hand, the AL's new Seattle Pilots turned out to be a financial disaster. After finishing last in the AL West in 1969, the bankrupt club was sold to Milwaukee interests. There the Brewers prospered, but the relocation had the AL pulling NL chestnuts out of a legal fire. For having earlier allowed the Braves to abandon Milwaukee, the NL faced a menacing lawsuit (State of Wisconsin v. Milwaukee Braves), which was quashed by the AL's decision to relocate the Pilots. But in abandoning Seattle, the AL soon incurred a lawsuit by Seattle interests, a threat that the AL deflected by admitting a new Seattle team, the Mariners, in 1977. That year the AL's unilateral expansion move added two new teams, which raised the league's membership to fourteen clubs while that of the NL remained the same. In addition to the newly admitted Mariners, who joined the Western Division, the AL then added the Toronto Blue Jays to its Eastern Division. This precipitous move resulted in an unbalanced major league format which exists to this day; moreover, since 1977 AL teams have annually played a skewed 162-game schedule.

However, this mini-expansion ploy and another bold move of this era enabled the AL to gain parity with its NL rival. Indeed, drastic measures were needed to restore the AL's attendance deficit, which, over the years 1970–1976, lagged some 24 million admissions behind that of the NL. In an early effort to regain parity, AL owners in 1972 allowed the moribund Washington Senators to move to Arlington, Texas, where they played as the Texas Rangers in the league's Western Division. And to balance that move, the Milwaukee Brewers were relocated in the Eastern Division.

But the most controversial of all AL parity measures was the league's 1973 unilateral adoption of the designated hitter rule. An experiment that was successfully pioneered in the minors, the rule allowed a designated hitter to bat in place of a pitcher in a team's lineup. It must be admitted that the designated hitter rule helped to remedy the AL's chronic problem of weak hitting. Only the year before, overall AL batting had averaged an anemic .239. In 1973, with AL teams playing designated hitters, the seasonal batting average rose to .259. Thenceforth AL batting averages always surpassed seasonal NL figures. But the NL stubbornly resisted the innovation, and over the years 1973–1985 the use of designated hitters in World Series competition was limited to alternate years.

Meanwhile, the AL quest for parity was aided by a spate of new ballparks. Early in this era the NL opened five new parks. Belatedly, the AL followed suit, with four new parks and a major refurbishing of Yankee Stadium completed over the years 1972–1977. A new feature of some of the new parks, which affected fielding and batting, was the use of artificial playing surfaces. At the present time, ten major league parks are equipped with artificial playing surfaces. In the NL, where the Houston Astros pioneered in artificial surfacing in 1965, the Phillies, Pirates, Cardinals, Expos, and Reds now use artificial surfacing. In the AL, the Mariners, Royals, Twins, and Blue Jays now play home games on synthetic turfs.

Along with new parks, other innovations such as promotional giveaways and expanded concession sales and in-park entertainments contributed to soaring attendance at major league games in this era. After holding at 30 million admissions annually over the years 1973–1975, annual attendance at major league games soared to 43 million by 1980. But if rising attendance stimulated rising revenues, so did television. By 1980 income from national and local TV contracts accounted for 30 percent of baseball's $500 million in revenues of that year. Indeed, throughout the decade baseball's income from national network TV (which all clubs shared) increased steadily. From $17.5 million in 1971, such contracts returned $27.5 million in 1980. In 1980 this translated into a $1.8 million annual windfall for each team. And considering that such contracts covered only World Series games, league championship playoff games, the annual All-Star Game, and selected weekly and weekend games, such figures were impressive.

Indeed, major league owners might have wrung much more money from network TV sources had they not hewed to the policy of allowing clubs to contract individually with local TV stations. In 1975 local TV revenue totaled $31 million, and by 1980 this figure had nearly doubled. However, local TV income was unevenly distributed, which tended to favor some clubs over others. Thus clubs situated in more lucrative local television markets got the lion's share of this source of revenue. Still, at the close of this era local TV markets represented the fastest-growing segment of the television industry.

Nor was television income an unalloyed blessing. In this era some critics charged baseball owners with selling out to television interests when they permitted nocturnal broadcasts of World Series games. But the popularity of such games was evinced when an estimated 75 million TV fans witnessed the dramatic seventh game of the 1975 World Series. But if this demonstration of the game's popularity silenced some critics, others inveighed against the medium's impact on other areas of the game. Among such criticisms was the charge that TV was transforming ballplayers into highly paid and pampered celebrity entertainers.

Certainly player salaries in this decade soared to heights undreamed of by past generations of players. Even allowing for the bugaboo of inflation, the spiraling salary trend was dazzling. At the outset of this era, both a $100,000 salaried player and a $1 million total player payroll were exceptional. In 1971 player salaries averaged $34,000. But thereafter the average rose to $52,000 in 1976, to $90,000 in 1978, to $100,000 in 1979, and to an astonishing $185,000 in 1980. By 1980, indeed, payrolls of $10 million were common and were defended by director Marvin Miller of the Players Association, who argued that salaries amounted to less than 20 percent of annual revenues.

Truth to tell, much of the credit for enriching players of this era belonged to Miller. By threatening to lead his united players in a strike in 1969, Miller was able to negotiate a

second Basic Agreement, which raised the minimum salary, increased the pension fund, and won for players the right to use agents in bargaining for salaries with owners. Then when this contract expired and negotiations for a new Basic Agreement bogged down in 1972, the Players Association staged a thirteen-day strike which shortened that season's playing schedule by forcing the cancellation of games. In the aftermath of that strike, Miller negotiated a third Basic Agreement, which won for players the right to arbitrate their salary disputes. In retrospect it was this important concession that really fueled the spiraling salary trend.

In 1975 the players scored another major coup, when the Messersmith-McNally case was decided in their favor. That year Dodger pitcher Andy Messersmith refused to sign his 1975 contract and, after playing the season under his former contract, claimed his right to free agency under the existing reserve-clause procedure. Messersmith's appeal (along with that of pitcher Dave McNally, who chose to retire after the 1975 season) went to a three-member arbitration panel which upheld the players' claim by a 2–1 vote. Professional arbiter Peter Seitz joined with Miller in supporting Messersmith's appeal against the negative vote cast by owners' representative John Gaherin. Certainly the implications of this "Seitz decision" were far-reaching. The decision effectively circumvented the long-established reserve clause which had recently been tested by player Curt Flood (Flood v. Kuhn) before the U.S. Supreme Court. At the time, in 1972, the court rejected Flood's appeal by a 5–3 vote, but the court's ruling suggested that the players might overturn the reserve clause by means of collective bargaining or by legislation. The Messersmith decision was the outcome of collective bargaining. And when the owners failed to overturn the Seitz decision on a legal appeal, they staged a lockout of spring training camps in 1976, claiming that the latest Basic Agreement had expired with no new labor contract in place. However, a compromise reached by the embattled players and owners allowed the 1976 playing season to open on time. And over the following summer, negotiations produced a fourth Basic Agreement, which conceded free agency to six-year veterans. The latest Agreement instituted an annual re-entry draft procedure which enabled qualifying players to auction their services anew. As compensation for losing a veteran player in one of the re-entry drafts, an owner received an extra choice in the annual rookie draft. Thus over the years 1976–1980, some owners bid high prices for the services of veteran free agents. And in turn the gains scored by players in these annual drafts helped to boost the salaries granted by players who opted for salary arbitration procedures.

The combination of re-entry draft bids and salary arbitration awards resulted in spiraling salaries and produced a new breed of player plutocrats. In the first re-entry draft of 1976, outfielder Reggie Jackson received a five-year contract worth $2.93 million from Yankee owner George Steinbrenner. In 1979 the Houston Astros plucked pitcher Nolan Ryan from the re-entry draft by giving the hurler a $1 million annual contract. That same year outfielder Dave Parker wrung a five-year pact worth $900,000 annually from his Pittsburgh owners to dissuade him from entering the re-entry draft. Thus it was hardly surprising that when the fourth Basic Agreement expired in 1980 the owners determined to halt the salary spiral. Among their demands, owners wanted a veteran player in compensation for a player lost via the re-entry draft. And when negotiations broke down, the threat of another player strike darkened the 1980 season. But in the nick of time a compromise between the embattled groups postponed the debacle for a season.

Meanwhile, the plutocratic players basked in a suntime of cash and glory. As television celebrities, players of this era stood as a breed apart from those of past generations. More glamorized by television exposure, far more wealthy, and more pampered, some players now indulged in illegal drugs to the point of self-abuse. At this time baseball's growing problem of drug abuse mirrored a national epidemic of drug abuse which was one of the unhappier legacies from the embattled sixties.

Yet another survival from that feverish era was the hirsute appearance of many players of this decade. In addition to wearing gaudier uniforms, many players now sported long hair, mustaches, and beards in the fashion of nineteenth-century players. Formerly a symbol of social protest in the sixties, such hirsute appearances now became a widespread affectation of American males. Although some clubs opposed the trend, owner Charles Finley of the Oakland Athletics encouraged it by paying his players $300 apiece to grow facial hair. Once established, the trend spread widely among players and continues to this day. But appearances aside, this breed of players was more pampered, better doctored and trained, and more ably defended than any of their forebears. Indeed, lesser-paid managers were now hard pressed to discipline their charges. Moreover, players of the seventies were less easily replaced. In this era the total number of minor leaguers competing for big league jobs averaged about 3,000 in any season.

Continuing the trend of the last two decades, blacks and Hispanics predominated among the splendid performers of these years. In 1974 the number of black major league players peaked at 26 percent, but the figure leveled off at 20 percent by 1979. By then, Hispanic players comprised 10 percent of the major league players. As before, blacks and Hispanics continued to lead the majors in stolen bases, with superstar Lou Brock of the Cardinals setting a new seasonal mark of 118 thefts while en route to shattering Ty Cobb's lifetime total of 892 bases stolen. In 1974, Hank Aaron broke Ruth's lifetime homer mark and went on to set a new lifetime mark of 755 clouts. But in toppling the Babe's record, Aaron went to bat 3,965 more times than the great Yankee slugger. And when Willie Mays retired in 1973, his lifetime total of 660 homers ranked third on the all-time slugging list; behind Mays in the fourth position was Frank Robinson, who retired with 586. And in this decade, Aaron, Robinson, Mays, Brock, and Roberto Clemente joined the 3,000 hit club, while Rod Carew captured seven AL batting titles, including four in a row over the years 1972–1975. Moreover, in these years twelve black and Hispanic stars won MVP Awards, and pitchers Bob Gibson and Juan Marichal hurled their ways into baseball's Hall of Fame. Finally, it was fitting that the leading player celebrity of this era was Reggie Jackson, a slugging outfielder of mixed black and Hispanic parentage. Widely acclaimed for his homer clouting, Jackson's seven homers in two World Series appearances with the Yankees won him the sobriquet of "Mr. October" and a short-lived "Reggie" candy bar was named for him.

Although they were justly rewarded and celebrated for their feats on the playing fields, black players still faced lingering forms of discrimination. At this time studies showed that black players had to be better-than-average players to

make it into the majors. Thus there were few marginal black players on team rosters; moreover, teams were fearful of playing too many black players in a game lest it affect attendance. And retired black players seldom found jobs in baseball as field managers or in top administrative posts. However, Frank Robinson became the first black manager to be hired (and fired), and a few token black umpires also debuted in this era.

At the end of this era, *The Sporting News* chose the versatile white star Pete Rose as the recipient of its Player of the Decade Award. It was well deserved. In this era, Rose won a pair of NL batting titles and led the league in total hits four times. In 1978 the Cincinnati infielder, who was dubbed "Charlie Hustle," tied the NL's consecutive-game hitting record by batting safely in 44 consecutive games. That same year Rose joined the 3,000-hit club and continued his relentless drive to topple Ty Cobb's lifetime record of 4,191 hits.

White stars also predominated among pitchers of this era. In these years, Gaylord Perry, Tom Seaver, Phil Niekro, Don Sutton, and Steve Carlton hurled themselves to ultimate memberships in the exclusive 300-victory club. Carlton, Seaver, Perry, Sutton, and Nolan Ryan also were compiling strikeout totals that would later eclipse Walter Johnson's all-time mark. But with pitching ERAs now hovering above the 3.50 mark each season, managers continued to rely on specialized relief pitchers to bail out starters. Most prized were rally-busting short relievers like Mike Marshall of the Dodgers. In 1974 Marshall appeared in a record 106 games; by winning 15 and saving 21, Marshall won both the NL's Cy Young and Fireman of the Year awards for his efforts. Other acclaimed short relievers included Rollie Fingers of the Athletics, who won three Fireman of the Year awards, while saving 244 games. Fireballing Goose Gossage thrice led the AL in saves, and in 1978 he fanned 122 batters in his role as Yankee fireman. Sparky Lyle, who pitched for four different clubs in this era, saved 230 games. And late in this era, Bruce Sutter saved 133 games in five seasons with the Cubs.

With pitchers now penalized by a narrower strike zone and lowered mounds, such heroics were needed to cope with the batting resurgence. Offensively teams plied the big-bang tactic with gusto. At this time AL teams regained their power advantage and outhomered their NL rivals in eleven of the twelve seasons. Of course, the AL's 1977 mini-expansion made this a foregone conclusion. In the first year of that expansion, AL sluggers hammered a record 2,013 homers. By then, hitters in both leagues were swinging at cowhide-covered balls instead of the traditional horsehide-covered spheres. But this necessary innovation failed to produce the overall batting surge forecast by alarmed pundits. Except for the AL's unilateral adoption of the designated hitter rule, there were no significant rule changes in these years; most rule changes addressed statistical compilations. And at this time the major league policy of subsidizing the minor leagues was working. With each team spending at least $1.5 million a year to finance up to five minor league teams, by 1977 the minor leagues were stabilized at 17 leagues and 121 teams.

Internally the major leagues were mightily affected by the shift in the balance of power toward players and umpires. The powerful Players Association upset the power balance, as did the Major League Umpires Association. Indeed, umpires had long endured poor pay and job insecurity. But umpires of the 1970s had come a long way since the single-umpire system of the nineteenth century. Not until 1911 did both major leagues adopt a dual-umpire system for every game and the 1930s

first saw both major leagues employ three-man crews to work regular season games. By the 1969–1980 era, four-man crews worked each seasonal game and crews for postseasonal games numbered six. More important, the Major League Umpires Association (MLUA) now became a powerful bargaining agency. After winning collective-bargaining rights in 1970, the MLUA waged a successful strike in 1979, a walkout that lasted until mid-May. When the strike ended, the umpires could celebrate a major victory. Among the concessions they wrung from owners was a maximum salary of $50,000 for twenty-year veteran umps, hefty increases in expense allowances, safeguards against arbitrary dismissals, guaranteed pay for forty-five days in the event of a player strike, and—wonder of wonders—a two-week paid vacation. How the late Bill Klem, who earlier in this century worked each game behind the plate for thirteen seasons, would have welcomed that concession! What's more, umpire Ron Luciano became a minor celebrity and, in company with others, became the author of books.

Against such power blocs, the owners now deployed their power committees and hired negotiators. As for Commissioner Bowie Kuhn, he continued to occupy what by now was largely a ceremonial post, one mainly responsive to the wishes of the owners. In 1979 Walter O'Malley's death removed a powerful figure from the owners' camp. In passing, O'Malley left his enormously profitable franchise as his chief legacy; by 1977 the Dodgers were valued at $50 million, twice the value of most franchises. Thus as the decade of the 1980s dawned, baseball owners were challenged to find a new leader of O'Malley's stripe and new tactics to restore the balance of power in their favor.

Campaigns of the Seventies: the AL, 1969–1980

Upstaged by the NL in the first two expansion moves, the AL was forced to take drastic measures to gain parity with the NL in attendance and offensive performances. To this end such measures as new park construction and franchise shifts contributed, but most decisive were two bold unilateral moves whereby the AL adopted the designated hitter rule in 1973 and undertook its mini-expansion in 1977. By these strokes the AL ensured its perennial domination, both at bat and at the turnstiles.

But if AL leaders expected the new divisional format of the 1969 expansion move to produce competitive balance, they were disillusioned. Indeed, throughout this era pennant monopoly was the rule in both AL divisions. Over the twelve campaigns of 1969–1980, the Orioles and Yankees dominated the Eastern Division, while the Athletics and Royals ruled the West. By winning six Eastern Division races and finishing second four times, the Orioles now reigned as the winningest team in the majors. For their part, the reviving Yankees won four Eastern races, which left but two for outsiders to divide. In the AL West, it was much the same story. There the Oakland Athletics won five races, the Kansas City Royals won four, and the Minnesota Twins won two—leaving only one for an outsider to claim.

In the first expansion season of 1969, the Baltimore Orioles asserted their balanced power, which made them the most victorious major league team of this era. Under sophomore manager Earl Weaver, the Orioles stormed the Eastern Division, their 109 victories lapping the runner-up Tigers by 19 games. It was the first of three consecutive Eastern titles for

the Birds, with top-ranked pitching the key to each success. In 1969 the Oriole staff was the league's best, with Mike Cuellar (23–11) and Dave McNally (20–7) setting the pace. At bat the Orioles were powered by first baseman Boog Powell (.304-37-121) and outfielder Frank Robinson (.308-32-100). In the West, meanwhile, the Twins were winning the first of two consecutive titles. Victors by 9 games over the Athletics that year, the Twins led the league in batting and relief pitching. Offensive standouts included Rod Carew, whose .332 hitting topped the league, and Harmon Killebrew, whose league-leading 49 homers and 140 RBIs won the veteran slugger the MVP Award. But when the divisional titlists squared off in the first American League Championship Series, the Orioles brushed the Twins aside in three games. The sweep gave the Orioles a fourteen-game winning streak to take to the World Series. But after winning the opening game against the New York Mets, the Orioles surprisingly lost the next four.

In 1970 the crestfallen Orioles came back nearly as strong and downed the Yankees by 15 games to repeat as Eastern champs. Once again manager Earl Weaver's pitching corps was the league's best. Starters Mike Cuellar and Dave McNally each won 24 and Jim Palmer won 20. At the plate the Orioles batted .257, with outfielder Merv Rettenmund's .322 leading the team batting, and Powell (35-114) and Frank Robinson (25-78) supplying the power. In the West, the Twins also repeated, again topping the Athletics by 9 games and again leading the league in hitting and relief pitching. This time the team batted .262, but Killebrew (41-113) again powered the club. An injury to Carew limited his play, but even so the infielder batted .366. Taking up the slack this year were outfielders Tony Oliva (.325-23-107) and Cesar Tovar, who hit .300. However, when the Twins met the Orioles in LCS play, they were again swept. And this time the Orioles went on to score an avenging victory in World Series play. In crushing the Reds in five games, the Orioles blasted fifty hits; the star Oriole performer was future Hall of Famer Brooks Robinson, who batted .429 and dazzled the Reds with his brilliant fielding at third base.

It was a glorious victory for the Orioles, but astonishingly this well-armed team would not win another world title in this era. In 1971 the Orioles captured a third straight Eastern title by thrashing the Tigers by 12 games. It was a vintage season for Baltimore, which could boast league-leading hitting and pitching, including a quartet of 20-game winning pitchers in Cuellar, McNally, Palmer, and Pat Dobson. Offensively, outfielder Rettenmund (.318) fronted the team's .261 batting attack, and Powell, Frank Robinson, and Brooks Robinson powered the assault with a combined 70 homers and 283 RBIs. In the West, the fading Twins now yielded to the surging Oakland Athletics, who notched the first of five consecutive Western titles in 1971. In matching the Orioles' victory total of 101 games, the Athletics crushed the expansion Kansas City Royals by 16 games. For the A's, rookie pitcher Vida Blue won 24 games with a league-leading 1.82 ERA, and Jim "Catfish" Hunter won 21. Hunter's nickname was hung on the hurler by the team's flamboyant owner, Charley Finley, who also tried unsuccessfully to get Blue to change his first name to "True." Offensively, the A's lacked a .300 hitter, but third baseman Sal Bando (24-94) and outfielder Reggie Jackson (32-80) provided power aplenty. But when the Athletics met the Orioles in LCS play, they were swept by the Orioles. It was the third consecutive LCS sweep by the Orioles. However, the Orioles lost a seven-game World Series struggle to

the Pittsburgh Pirates, led by MVP Roberto Clemente.

In the wake of that loss, the Orioles fell from the top, and the balance of power now shifted to the West, where the volatile Athletics won the first of three consecutive AL championships. In the strike-shortened season of 1972, the A's won the Western title by 5½ games over the Chicago White Sox. Third sacker Joe Rudi batted .305, and first baseman Mike Epstein and outfielder Reggie Jackson combined for 51 homers as the A's rolled up 93 wins to head the AL. Moreover, the pitching staff was the league's best; Hunter and Ken Holtzman combined for 40 victories, and reliever Rollie Fingers won 11 and saved 21 games. In the East the strike-shortened schedule enabled the Tigers to eke a half-game victory over the runner-up Red Sox by dint of playing and winning one more game than the Bostonians. Manager Billy Martin's Tigers batted a mere .237, with no .300 hitter among the regulars, but lefty Mickey Lolich's 22 wins fronted the league's second-best pitching corps. In LCS play the weak-hitting Tigers held out for five games before succumbing to the A's, who went on to defeat the Reds in a seven-game World Series struggle. With slugger Jackson sidelined by an injury, unheralded catcher Gene Tenace took up the offensive slack. Tenace batted .348 and won three World Series games with timely hits.

Over the next two seasons, the Athletics continued their winning ways, twice downing the Orioles in LCS play and twice defeating NL contenders in World Series action. In 1973 the garishly clad A's defeated the Royals by 6 games in the West. Jackson's league-leading 32 homers and 117 RBIs powered the team, which also got superb pitching from Hunter (21–5), Holtzman (21–13), Blue (20–9), and reliever Fingers, who saved 22 games with a 1.92 ERA. That year the Orioles returned to the top in the East by downing the Red Sox by 8 games. In this first season under the designated hitter rule, the Orioles were paced by DH Tommy Davis, who batted .306 and drove in 89 runs. Palmer headed the pitching staff, which was the league's best, with a 22–9 mark; Cuellar won 18; and McNally and young Doyle Alexander combined for 29 wins. In the aftermath the Orioles battled the A's in a tense LCS matchup which went the full five games before Hunter's shutout pitching decided the issue. Then, in World Series action against the New York Mets, the Athletics rallied from a 3–2 deficit to land a second world title. Home runs by Reggie Jackson and Bert Campeneris settled the issue in Game Seven.

In 1974 the Athletics won a third consecutive World Series banner, a feat thus far unmatched under the major leagues' divisional format. In winning the Western race by 5 games over the Texas Rangers, the light-hitting (.247) A's were backed by the best pitching corps in the majors. Hunter's league-leading 25 wins and 2.49 ERA led the staff, who also got 19 wins from Holtzman, 17 wins from Blue, and 18 saves from the redoubtable Fingers. Although lacking a .300 hitter, the team was powered by Bando (22-103), Jackson (29-93), and outfielder Joe Rudi (.293-22-99). In the East, the Orioles won a fifth divisional flag by 2 games over the Yankees. League-leading fielding and sturdy pitching from Cuellar (22–10), McNally (16–10), and Ross Grimsley (18–13) carried the Orioles. In LCS competition the A's lost the opening game, but swept the next three to claim the league pennant. Pitted against the Dodgers in the World Series, the bickering Athletics, who squabbled among themselves and with their owner, nevertheless downed the Dodgers in five games. It was

the A's third straight World Series victory, and astonishingly the team's bullpen saved or won all twelve of the games won by the Athletics in their remarkable three-season skein.

But the 1974 league championship was the last by an Athletic team until 1988. Years of bickering between the players and owner Charley Finley wore on the team, and the loss of pitcher Hunter to the Yankees was a crushing blow. Hunter's loss was Finley's fault; after Finley reneged on the terms of Hunter's contract, Hunter sought arbitration, and the ruling allowed the pitcher to become a free agent. Nevertheless, in 1975 the A's won the Western title for a fifth straight year as they outlasted the Royals by 7 games. Despite the loss of Hunter, the team's pitching was the league's second best. Blue won 22 games, Holtzman 18, and Fingers won 10 and saved 24. Offensively, outfielder Claudell Washington led the team with .308 batting, and Jackson drove in 104 runs and hit a league-leading 36 homers. However, the league's power balance now shifted eastward, where the next five AL champions would be crowned. First of the Eastern powers to emerge were the 1975 Red Sox, who defeated the Orioles by 4½ games. The team's pitching was mediocre, but hefty .275 batting bolstered the assault. Rookie outfielder Fred Lynn's .331-21-105 hitting won him both Rookie of the Year and MVP honors, but outfielder Jim Rice (.309-22-102) came close to matching Lynn's production, while DH Cecil Cooper and catcher Carlton Fisk each topped the .300 mark. In the LCS faceoff, the Red Sox ended Oakland's domination with a three-game sweep. But in World Series action, the Red Sox lost an epochal seven-game struggle to the Cincinnati Reds.

Boston slipped to third in 1976, as another power rose in the AL East. After a twelve-year hiatus, the Yankees regained the heights and held the high ground for the next three seasons. For the Yankee renaissance much of the credit belonged to the team's wealthy and erratic owner, George Steinbrenner. After purchasing the team from the CBS Network in 1973, Steinbrenner brashly promised Yankee fans a pennant within three years, and in 1976 his words rang true. Moreover, the timing was propitious. In 1976 the team returned to its newly refurbished Yankee Stadium after spending two seasons at Shea Stadium in Queens. Under brash manager Billy Martin, whom Steinbrenner would fire and rehire five times, the Yankees romped over the runner-up Orioles by 10½ games. League-leading pitching, including 53 wins from starters Hunter, Dock Ellis, and Ed Figueroa, and a league-leading 23 saves from reliever Sparky Lyle eased the way. The team's .269 batting effort was led by outfielder Mickey Rivers, who batted .312, catcher Thurman Munson's .302 and 105 RBIs, and third baseman Graig Nettles's league-leading 32 homers. Meanwhile, the surging Kansas City Royals were breaking Oakland's stranglehold in the West. In downing owner Finley's decimated A's by 2½ games, the Royals matched the .269 batting mark of the Yankees. Third baseman George Brett's .333 topped the league's hitters, but DH Hal McRae was only a point behind at .332, and his 73 RBIs bettered Brett's total. The 1976 victory was the first of three straight Western titles by the Royals, who became the first of the AL's 1969 expansion teams to win a divisional pennant. In LCS play the Royals and Yanks battled for five games before first baseman Chris Chambliss won the pennant for the Yankees with a ninth-inning homer in the final game at Yankee Stadium. However, the Yankees were no match for Cincinnati's powerful "Big Red Machine," which swept to a four-game victory in the World Series.

Over the winter Steinbrenner strengthened his team by acquiring slugger Reggie Jackson in the re-entry draft. Jackson responded by batting .286 with 32 homers and 110 RBIs as the Yankees edged the Orioles by 2½ games in the 1977 Eastern race. Overall the team batted .281, with Rivers's .326 batting leading the team, Munson weighing in with .308-18-100 stickwork, and Nettles driving in 107 runs on 37 homers. Young Ron Guidry (16–7) led the starting pitchers, with Figueroa winning 16, newly acquired Don Gullett winning 14, and reliever Lyle saving 26. In the West, meanwhile, the Royals repeated as they downed the Texas Rangers by 8 games. The Royals batted .277, with outfielder Al Cowens (.312-23-112) leading the team, Brett batting .312, and McRae adding 21 homers and 92 RBIs. The Royal pitching staff was the league's best; Dennis Leonard won 20 games to lead the league, Paul Splittorff won 16, and the bullpen posted a league-leading 42 saves. In another LCS donnybrook, the Yankees edged the Royals in five games to land a second consecutive AL pennant. And in World Series action the Yankees trounced the Dodgers in six games. For the Yankees, the highlight came in the final game at the Stadium, when Jackson slugged three homers. In the afterglow of the victory, a candy bar was named for Jackson, who also wore the sobriquet of "Mr. October" for the remainder of his colorful career.

In an unforgettable encore performance, the Yankees repeated in 1978 after staging one of the most storied comebacks in baseball history. During much of the turbulent campaign, the Yankees trailed the slugging Red Sox. Midway in the campaign Steinbrenner sacked the volatile Martin for insubordination and replaced him with Bob Lemon. Under Lemon, the Yankees recuperated from a spate of injuries and crushed the Red Sox in two series to gain a tie by the season's end. In the sudden-death playoff game for the Eastern title, pitchers Ron Guidry and Goose Gossage held off the Red Sox, while homers by Jackson and shortstop Bucky Dent capped a 5–4 victory at Fenway Park. That year the Yankee pitchers posted a league-leading 3.10 ERA; Guidry's 25 wins (he lost only 3) and 1.74 ERA were the league's best, and Gossage won 10 and saved 27 games. Outfielder Lou Piniella's .314 batting led the team, which was powered by Jackson (27-97), Nettles (27-93), and Chambliss (who drove in 90 runs). Meanwhile, the upstaged Royals were winning a third consecutive Western title, this time by 5 games over the California Angels. With no .300 hitter in the regular lineup, the Royals batted .268; outfielder Amos Otis led the hitters with .298-22-96 batting. Starting pitchers Leonard and Splittorff combined for 40 victories, and reliever Al Hrabosky saved 20 as the Royals compiled the league's second-best pitching record. But the Yankees toppled the Royals in four games in LCS play. When World Series play began, the Yankees lost the first two games to the Dodgers, but then swept the next four games to cap a legendary campaign with a second straight world title.

Although Steinbrenner continued to spend heavily on free agents, the 1979 Yankees fell to fourth place in the Eastern Division. By winning 102 games, manager Earl Weaver led the Orioles to an 8-game win over the second-place Milwaukee Brewers. League-leading pitching, paced by Mike Flanagan's 23–9 effort, led the Orioles, whose offense was powered by first baseman Eddie Murray (.295-25-99) and outfielder Ken Singleton (.295-35-111). While the Orioles winged to the top in the AL East, the California Angels ended the Royals'

Western reign by scoring a 3-game victory. The Angels' victory ended years of frustration for owner Gene Autry, who had spent $15 million on playing talent since 1961. In 1978 two of Autry's recent acquisitions paid off as Rod Carew batted .318 and Don Baylor won the MVP Award for his .296-36-139 production. But the Angels' pitching corps compiled a vulnerable 4.34 ERA, and in LCS play the Orioles dispatched the Angels in four games. But the Orioles now faced their old Pirate tormentors in the World Series. In an eerie repeat of their 1971 matchup, after leading by three games to one in this 1979 encounter, the Orioles lost to the Pirates in seven games.

As the era ended, the Yankees rebounded to edge the Orioles by 3 games in the East. In the close race, Steinbrenner's latest re-entry draft acquisitions, infielder Bob Watson and pitcher Rudy May, made the difference. May won 15 games, and his 2.47 ERA led the league; Tommy John won 22, Guidry won 17, and the fireballing Gossage saved 33 games in relief. Watson's .307 batting led the hitters, but Jackson batted .300 and his 111 RBIs came with a league-leading 41 homers. This year, however, the Yankees were outmatched by the Royals. Rebounding to win the Western Division by 14 games over the Athletics, the Royals batted a league-leading .286. Brett's .390 batting, which included 24 homers and 118 RBIs, was the best batting mark in the majors since 1941. Outfielder Willie Wilson batted .326 and catcher-outfielder John Wathan batted .305. Pitcher Leonard won 20, and a Yankee castoff, lefty Larry Gura, won 18, with relief ace Dan Quisenberry saving 33 games to tie Gossage for the league lead. In LCS play the Royals, who had feasted on the Yankees during the season, swept the New Yorkers. In the wake of that loss, owner Steinbrenner sacked manager Dick Howser, despite the 103 victories the Yankees had compiled under Howser's leadership. By then, the Royals had lost to the Phillies in six games in the 1980 World Series. Thus the era ended with the NL boasting two straight World Series triumphs which the senior circuit would extend to four in the early 1980s.

Campaigns of the Seventies: the NL, 1969–1980

In this era the NL also failed to achieve the competitive balance envisioned by its 1969 expansion. Over the twelve NL campaigns of these years, both divisions were ruled by powerful dynasties. In the East, the Pirates won six races, the Phillies four, and the Mets two. In the West, the Reds won six races, the Dodgers three, with the Braves, Giants, and Astros as single-season winners.

Yet it was one of the league's lesser powers, the New York Mets, who made a rousing success of the first NL campaign under the new divisional format. Like the moonwalking American astronauts of that summer, the Mets also realized an "impossible dream," and their unlikely triumph became the sports story of that memorable year in the nation's history. In a baseball version of Horatio Alger's rags-to-riches yarns, the forlorn Mets shook off the effects of their horrendous 394–737 won-loss record, which the team had painfully compiled over seven zany seasons of NL play, and won the 1969 Eastern Division race by 8 games over a cocky Chicago Cub team. What's more, the Mets turned the trick by winning 38 of their last 49 games, mostly due to good pitching. Young Tom Seaver's league-leading 25 victories and Jerry Koosman's 17 headed a pitching staff whose 2.99 ERA ranked

second in the league. However, a puny .242 team batting average, fronted by outfielder Cleon Jones's .340-12-75, afforded little hope against the Western champion Atlanta Braves, winners by 3 games over the Giants. For the Braves, who led the NL in fielding, Hank Aaron's .300-44-97 batting, and Rico Carty's .342-16-58 effort in limited action, excelled. Pitcher Phil Niekro won 23 and Ron Reed won 18 as the staff turned in a 3.53 ERA. But in the NL's first League Championship Series, the impotent Mets turned tartars; scoring 27 runs in three games, they swept the favored Braves. However, the Mets appeared to be ludicrously mismatched against the versatile Orioles in the following World Series. But after losing the opening game, the Mets swept the Orioles in the next four games to realize their "impossible dream." In the afterglow, an outpouring of "Metomania" swept the country, and a dozen hastily written books celebrating the team's victory were churned out.

But the following year the powerful Pittsburgh Pirates ruthlessly banished any hopes of a continuing competitive balance in the NL East. Over the next six seasons, the Pirates captured five Eastern pennants, including three in a row over the years 1970–1972. In 1970 the Pirates baptized their newly occupied Three Rivers Stadium by downing the Cubs by 5 games and raising their first divisional flag. The Pirates batted .270, with Roberto Clemente hitting .352 and catcher Manny Sanguillen batting .325. With a 3.70 ERA, their pitching was shaky, but reliever Dave Giusti saved 26 games. Coincident with the Pirates' rise, another power moved to the top in the West as the Cincinnati Reds, now ensconced in their new Riverfront Stadium, scored a crushing 14½-game win over the runner-up Dodgers. At the plate the Reds matched the Pirates' batting, while leading the league in homers with 191. Catcher Johnny Bench's 45 homers and 148 RBIs led all sluggers and won him MVP honors. Infielders Pete Rose (.316) and Tony Perez (.317-40-129), and outfielder Bob Tolan (.316) added to the hit parade which was needed to bolster the pitching staff. The team's starting pitchers completed only 32 games, which inspired the bullpen to compile a league-leading 60 saves. And yet the staff's 3.71 ERA was only a point above that of the Pirates. In the LCS that year, the Reds swept the Pirates, but then the Reds fell to the avenging Orioles in the 1970 World Series.

The following year manager Danny Murtaugh led his Pirates to a 7-game win over the Cardinals in the NL East. At the plate the Pirates upped their batting to .274 as Clemente (.341) and Sanguillen (.319) maintained their pace, while outfielder Willie Stargell's league-leading 48 homers powered the team's league-leading 154-homer assault. In the West, poor pitching consigned the Reds to fourth place, leaving the field to the Giants and Dodgers. After leading most of the way, the Giants faltered in the stretch, but hung on to win by a game over the Dodgers. League-leading fielding buoyed the Giants, who batted only .247. Outfielder Bobby Bonds's .288-33-102 was the best effort by a regular. Future Hall of Fame pitcher Juan Marichal and Gaylord Perry combined for 34 victories as the staff's 3.33 ERA came close to matching the Pirates' mark of 3.31. In LCS play the Pirates lost the opening game, but swept to victory. And when matched against the Orioles in the World Series, the Pirates lost the first two games, but then rebounded to win in seven. The Pirate victory triggered a spate of destructive riots in Pittsburgh, but any fears by city fathers of future riots to come were banished by the shortcomings of the Pirate teams.

Although the 1972 Pirates romped to an 11-game victory over the Cubs in the East, another six seasons would pass before the Bucs won another NL pennant. Future Hall of Famer Roberto Clemente batted .312 and notched his 3,000th career hit as the Pirates matched their .274 batting mark of 1971. Outfielder Al Oliver batted .312 and infielder Richie Hebner batted .300, while Stargell powered the attack with 33 homers and 112 RBIs. Led by starting pitcher Steve Blass (19–8) and reliever Giusti (22 saves), the pitching staff posted a 2.81 ERA. In the West, meanwhile, the Reds rebounded to win by 10½ games over the Houston Astros. The acquisition of infielder Joe Morgan strengthened the Reds, who also got another MVP performance from Bench. The catcher's 40 homers and 125 RBIs led the league, and infielder Rose batted .307. But the pitching staff completed only 25 games. The best effort by a starter was Gary Nolan's 15–5 mark, but the bullpen, led by Clay Carroll's league-leading 37 saves, saved 60 games. In LCS action the Reds rallied from a 2–1 deficit to win the league pennant in five games. In the decisive game, played in Cincinnati, the Reds won 4–3. In the ninth inning of that game, Pirate reliever Bob Moose wild-pitched the winning run home. But when the Reds faced a 3–1 deficit in the World Series, their rally fell short as the Athletics hung on to win the world title in seven games.

Over the winter, Clemente's tragic death while on a mercy mission to Nicaragua was a crushing blow to the Pirate cause. Even so, the 1973 Pirates hung close, finishing third in a weak Eastern Division. On the strength of a lackluster 82–79 record, the Mets edged the Cardinals by 1½ games. Offensively the Mets batted a meager .246 with only 85 homers, but Seaver's 19–10 pitching and league-leading 2.08 ERA and reliever Tug McGraw's 25 saves compensated. In the West the Reds outlasted the Dodgers by 3½ games to win the divisional pennant. Led by Rose's league-leading .338 hitting, the Reds batted .254 and hit 137 homers. Perez batted .314-27-101, Morgan batted .290-26-82, and Bench drove in 104 runs. The Reds also led the league in stolen bases and fielding, and the pitching staff ranked fourth, just behind the Mets. Not surprisingly, the Reds were touted as LCS favorites, but the Mets edged them in five games to emerge as the NL's standard bearer in the World Series. Astonishingly the Mets took a 3–2 lead in the first five Series games against the Athletics. Had they hung on to win with their puny seasonal record, it would have gone into the record books as a quirky record. But the A's quashed this prospect by snagging the final two games to win the 1973 World Series.

As the impotent Mets faded in 1974, the Pirates rose again to win the next two Eastern races before yielding to the rising Phillies. Unsurpassed .274 team batting boosted the Pirates to a thin 1½-game win over the Cardinals in the East. Outfielders Richie Zisk (.313-17-100), Al Oliver (.321 and 85 RBIs), and Stargell (.301-25-96) powered the team, whose pitching staff posted a 3.49 ERA. But the league's balance of power was shifting westward, where the Dodgers and Reds would monopolize the next five NL pennants. In the 1974 Western Division race, the Dodgers defeated the Reds by 4 games. Backed by the most durable infield in baseball history, in Steve Garvey, Dave Lopes, Bill Russell, and Ron Cey, the 1974 Dodgers batted .272. First baseman Garvey, who would set an NL record in consecutive games played, led the assault that year with a .312-21-111 performance which won him MVP honors. Outfielder Jim Wynn added 32 homers and 108

RBIs. Pitchers Andy Messersmith and Don Sutton combined for 39 wins to head the league's top-ranked pitching staff, but reliever Mike Marshall won the pitching honors with his 15 victories and 21 saves. What's more, fireman Marshall appeared in a record 106 games. In the LCS playoff the Dodgers dispatched the Pirates in four games, but the Dodgers lost the World Series to the Athletics in five games.

It was the third consecutive Series victory for the Athletics, but the powerful Cincinnati Reds reversed the trend in 1975–1976. Dubbed "the Big Red Machine," the perennially pitching-poor Reds got only 22 complete games from their starters in 1975, but the team's crushing offense buried the runner-up Dodgers by 20 games. Heading the team's .271 batting offensive was second baseman Joe Morgan, who won MVP honors for his .327 batting and 94 RBIs. Third baseman Rose and outfielders Ken Griffey and George Foster topped .300 at bat, and first baseman Tony Perez and catcher Bench drove in a combined 219 runs. In the East the Pirates beat the Phils by 6½ games to win a second straight divisional title. The Pirates batted .263 and led the league in homers. Outfielder Dave Parker (.308-25-101) and first baseman Stargell (.295-22-90) powered the team, and catcher Manny Sanguillen batted .328. And the pitching staff's 3.02 ERA bettered the Reds. But the Reds swept the Pirates in LCS play and went on to beat the Red Sox in a tense seven-game World Series classic. In the final game at Boston the Reds overcame a 3–0 Boston lead. Morgan's single in the ninth inning provided the margin of victory as the Reds won 4–3. The victory was the Reds' first World Series triumph since 1940.

Nor did they stop there. The following year, as the NL celebrated its hundredth anniversary, the all-conquering Reds downed the Dodgers by 10 games in the West on the strength of league leadership in batting, homers, RBIs, stolen bases, and fielding. Morgan's .320-27-111 batting won the infielder a second straight MVP Award, Rose batted .323, and the outfield of Griffey (.336), Cesar Geronimo (.307), and George Foster (.306) all topped the .300 mark. Foster's 121 RBIs led the league, and the bullpen fronted by Rollie Eastwick led the league in saves. In the East it was the Phillies' misfortune to have to face this wrecking crew in LCS play. That year the Phillies finally won an Eastern title, the first of three consecutive victories, all coming at the expense of the Pirates. In 1976 the Phillies trounced the Pirates by 9 games. Slugging third baseman Mike Schmidt led the league in homers with 38 and drove in 107 runs, and the outfield of Jay Johnstone, Garry Maddox, and Greg Luzinski all topped the .300 mark, with Luzinski batting in 95 runs. Steve Carlton (20–7) headed a pitching staff that bettered the mediocre Reds' staff, but otherwise needed the 36 saves posted by the relief corps of Ron Reed, Tug McGraw, and Gene Garber. The LCS matchup between the Reds and the Phillies was a foregone conclusion which the Reds decided with a sweep. The Reds then went on to sweep the Yankees in the World Series to become the first NL team since 1922 to win back-to-back world titles.

But the Big Red Machine blew a gasket in 1977. The loss of ace pitcher Don Gullett to the re-entry draft (and the Yankees) and a dubious trade which sent first baseman Perez to the Expos created weaknesses that not even the mid-season acquisition of pitcher Tom Seaver from the Mets could assuage. Nor could Foster's herculean batting, which produced a league-leading 52 homers and 149 RBIs together with a .320 batting average. As the pitching-poor Reds faltered, the

Dodgers brushed them aside to win the Western title by 10 games. League leadership in homers (191) and pitching buoyed the Dodgers. A successful arm operation gave a new life to lefty Tommy John, whose 20 victories led the pitching staff. Offensively, outfielder Reggie Smith's .302-32-87 led the attack, with outfielder Dusty Baker and infielders Garvey and Ron Cey each topping the 30 mark in homers. Meanwhile, the Phillies repeated in the East, their 101 victories leading the league and topping the runner-up Pirates by 5 games. The Phillies led the league in batting at .279. Outfielder Luzinski's .309-30-130 was his best effort, and Schmidt again powered 38 homers while driving in 101 runs. Carlton led the pitchers with 23 victories, and Larry Christenson's 19–6 mark was his best in the majors; moreover, the bullpen's 43 saves topped the league. Still, the Dodgers defeated the Phillies in four games in the LCS. However, the Dodgers got their comeuppance from the Yankees, who won the 1977 World Series in six games.

Although the victory margin for both teams was skimpier, the 1978 divisional races repeated the scenario of the previous year. In the West the Dodgers repeated by edging the Reds by 2½ games. Once again the pitching staff was the league's best (3.12 ERA). Starters Burt Hooton, Tommy John, Don Sutton, and Doug Rau won 66 games, and reliever Terry Foster saved 22. Garvey headed the team's .264 batting attack with .316-21-113 stickwork; and Cey, Reggie Smith, and Rick Monday combined for 71 homers to head the team's league-leading homer barrage. In the East the Phillies won for a third straight year, but by a skimpy 1½-game margin over the Pirates. Luzinski's 35 homers and 101 RBIs paced a weak .258 batting assault; and Carlton (with 16 wins) and Dick Ruthven (with 13 wins), and relievers Ron Reed and McGraw led the Phils' pitching staff, which was the best in the Eastern Division, but a far cry from the Dodgers' mark of 1978. In LCS play the Dodgers again trounced the Phillies in four games, but again the Dodgers fell to their old Yankee nemesis in six games.

As the decade waned, the Pirates returned to power in the East by edging the runner-up Expos by 2 games. It was the sixth Eastern title of this era for the Pirates, who batted a lusty .272 but whose mediocre pitching staff depended heavily on its superb bullpen headed by Kent Tekulve, who appeared in 94 games and saved 31. Third baseman Bill Madlock's .328 batting led the team along with Parker (.310-25-94) and Stargell, whose 32 homers helped drive in 82 runs. At the same time in the West, the Reds also won their sixth divisional title of the era, beating the Astros by 1½ games. With Rose gone by way of the re-entry draft, his replacement Ray Knight batted .318 and, along with outfielders Griffey (.316) and Foster (.302-30-98), paced the team's .264 batting. Seaver's 16 victories led the team's mediocre pitching staff. The two rival dynasties met for a last time to date in LCS play with the Pirates sweeping the Reds. In World Series action the Pirates fell behind the Orioles three games to one, but swept the last three games for a stunning victory.

In 1980 the Phillies ended a thirty-year drought by winning an NL pennant. Goaded by manager Dallas Green, the Phillies won 21 of their last 28 games to eke a 1-game victory over the Expos in the East. An MVP performance by slugger Schmidt, who hit 48 homers and drove in 121 runs, powered the Phils, who also got .309 batting from outfielder Bake McBride, and .282 batting and inspired leadership from the transplanted Pete Rose. Lefty Carlton's 24 wins led the

league and won him the Cy Young Award, and Dick Ruthven won 17, while bullpen stalwart Tug McGraw saved 20 games. In the West the Dodgers and Astros finished in a dead heat as the front-running Astros lost their last three games to the visiting Dodgers. But in a sudden-death playoff for the Eastern Division title, Joe Niekro pitched the Astros to a 7–1 victory over the Dodgers at Dodger Stadium. The Astros got .309 hitting from outfielder Cesar Cedeno, and the team batted .261, but the punchless offense produced only 75 homers. But the Astros' pitching staff was the league's best. Joe Niekro won 20 games, Nolan Ryan won 11, and Vern Ruhle won 12. Ruhle's pitching compensated for the loss of power pitcher J. R. Richard, who had compiled a 10–4, 1.89 record when he sustained a career-ending stroke. In LCS play the Phils and Astros battled through five games, with the rebounding Phillies scoring two extra-inning victories in Houston to land the pennant. Thus emboldened, the Phillies went on to beat the Royals in a six-game World Series tussle. It was the Phillies' first world championship in the club's ninety-seven-year history as an NL team.

But in the season after Philadelphia's momentous victory, which saw the local police deploying mounted troopers and guard dogs to restrain the delirious Philadelphia fans, the major leagues were staggered by a crippling player strike.

Baseball's Embattled Eighties, 1981–1988

The conservative mood that gripped the nation in the late 1970s also held sway during these years and helped to catapult Ronald Reagan to landslide victories in the presidential elections of 1980 and 1984. Indeed, ex–movie actor Reagan was no stranger to baseball fans, many of whom saw him play the role of ex–pitching great Grover Cleveland Alexander on the silver screen. And now, as an avowed conservative, President Reagan sought to divert the nation's economy toward a free-enterprise course by such tactics as cutting federal taxes and reducing federal domestic spending programs. At the same time Reagan advocated a powerful national defense posture aimed at combating the spread of international communism.

But Reagan's first term was darkened by an economic recession which contributed to high unemployment. Especially hard hit by unemployment were minorities and blue-collar workers in declining industries. Among the declining industries were such former bellwether industries as steel and mining, whose sagging production was attributed to foreign competition. However, the American economy in the main continued to shift from its former heavy-industrial base to its present emphasis on high technology and information and services production.

Nevertheless, before Reagan's first term ended, such factors as federal tax cuts and falling inflation and interest rates spurred an economic recovery which continued into 1987. The boomlet reduced unemployment, but for most workers wage increases were small, and some 20 million Americans still remained at or near the poverty level in 1987. Indeed, some critics faulted Reagan's economic policies for favoring the well-to-do, whose ranks by 1987 included a million millionaires and a score of billionaires among a population of 240 million.

But prospects for continuing affluence dimmed as the year 1987 closed amidst fears of an impending recession. In Octo-

ber the nation's burgeoning national debt (estimated at $2.6 trillion) and a chronic foreign-trade imbalance triggered financial panics in domestic and foreign stock markets. Aggravated by the festering Iran-Contra scandal and the naval confrontation with Iran in the Persian Gulf, the economic crisis boded ill for the Reagan Administration and for the nation's future.

Moreover, other menacing problems clouded the nation's future. Among them was the epidemic of drug abuse which defied efforts at punitive control. According to a 1985 estimate, the multibillion-dollar illegal drug industry was being supported by 20 million American consumers. Included were scores of professional athletes who confronted their officials with the knotty problem of disciplining abusers without violating their civil rights.

And yet for all the sobering national problems, most Americans of these years enjoyed moderately prosperous lifestyles. For this accomplishment, the two-paycheck family trend was largely responsible. By 1987 working women, whose ranks included most wives, accounted for more than half of the American labor force. Buoyed by the additional income, most Americans continued to spend lavishly on leisure and recreational activities. According to one report, Americans in 1987 were spending well over $50 billion a year on gambling, sports betting, and physical activities alone. And among the host of available leisure activities, television viewing, especially televised sports programs, maintained a leading position.

Certainly America's continuing infatuation with major sports was a blessing for baseball as revenues from live attendance and television continued to grow at a record-setting pace. At the same time, however, spiraling player salaries pitted players against owners in a series of pitched battles on the labor front.

Indeed, embattled relations between players and owners was a leitmotif of this era. In 1981 the failure of owners and players to agree on a new labor contract triggered a crippling baseball strike—the worst in the history of major league baseball since the 1890 debacle. A major bone of contention was the owners' demand that a club receive a veteran player as compensation for losing a player in one of the annual re-entry drafts. When the deadline for an agreement expired with no compromise, the players struck on June 11, 1981. Once the strike began, it lasted some fifty days and wiped out a third of the season's playing schedule. The strike cost the united players at least $30 million in lost salaries, and the owners lost an estimated $116 million in revenues. However, the owners were partly compensated by $50 million in strike insurance. On the last day of July, a compromise ended the great player strike. The owners won their point on the player compensation issue, but they had to settle for an indirect approach. Thus when a team lost a player in a re-entry draft, the team got to choose a veteran player from a pool of surplus players provided by all major league teams. For their part, the players also successfully fended off the owners' demand for a ceiling on salaries. Agreement on these and lesser issues produced a fifth Basic Agreement, which ran through the season of 1984. The eleventh-hour agreement saved what was left of the 1981 season, but the salvage format devised by Commissioner Bowie Kuhn drew much criticism. Kuhn's plan called for a split-season campaign, a format which had been tried and discarded as unsatisfactory in 1892. Under Kuhn's scheme, the first-half winners were those teams which led their divisions at the time of the June 11 player walkout. The second-half winners would be the teams that led the divisions at the close of the campaign after the resumption of play in August. By ruling first-half winners ineligible to repeat as champions, Kuhn's plan of scheduling a round of playoffs to decide the divisional championships in each league was assured. Thus a separate best-of-five playoff series was scheduled to settle first the matter of the 1981 divisional championships. Thereafter, the winners engaged in the usual best-of-five game series to determine the champions of each league. Although the format worked as planned, it was faulted for producing lackadaisical play on the part of three of the four first-half winners and for reducing attendance in the second half of what writer Red Smith called "the dishonest season."

Nor did the great strike of 1981 end the tensions between the embattled players and owners. When the fifth Basic Agreement expired at the end of 1984 with no agreement in place, a new strike threat loomed in 1985. With salaries continuing their upward spiral, averaging $363,000 in 1984 with 36 players paid at least a million dollars that year, the owners determined to arrest the trend. Correctly zeroing in on salary arbitration as the cause of runaway salaries, the owners demanded that a player wait more than the current two-year period before becoming eligible for salary arbitration. In addition, the owners renewed their demand for a ceiling on salaries. Naturally the players resisted, and when no agreement was reached, the players struck on August 6, 1985. But this time the walkout lasted only two days; obviously neither side wanted a repeat of the 1981 ordeal. Following the resumption of negotiations, a sixth Basic Agreement was promulgated. The new contract compromised on the major issues. For their part, the owners failed to get a salary ceiling, but the players agreed to wait three years instead of two to become eligible for salary arbitration. The players won increased pension benefits, which now would pay a retired veteran with ten years of major league service an annual pension of $91,000! And the owners also won their demand to increase the popular League Championship Series playoffs to a best-of-seven-games format beginning with the 1985 season.

Still, the new four-year Basic Agreement failed to end the hostilities between players and owners. As salaries continued to soar, the owners unilaterally cut team player rosters to twenty-four men and proceeded to boycott the re-entry drafts of 1985–1986. Despite the presence of veteran stars on the auction blocks in those years, there were no bidders. In retaliation, the Players Association charged collusion and filed separate grievances for each of the two boycotted drafts. In September 1987 arbiter Thomas Roberts ruled in favor of the players in the first of those suits, that of 1985. At that time, however, Roberts delayed announcing the amount of punitive damages to be laid on the owners. Despite the setback, rumors of further collusion by owners seeking to cap player salaries were rife. In October 1987 one rumor had the owners' Player Relations Committee urging all owners to pay no player more than $2 million a season. Thus as the year ended another battle in the enduring war between players and owners loomed inasmuch as some 150 players were eligible to enter the upcoming 1987 re-entry draft.

Still, whatever the outcome of this impending struggle, the players of this era were obvious winners on the salary front. In 1982, the year after the great strike, salaries averaged $250,000. Two years later the average salary climbed to $330,000, almost the same as that of the highest-paid man-

ager, Tom Lasorda of the Dodgers. Then in 1986 the average salary peaked at $412,000 before falling slightly to $410,000 in 1987. The decrease was due in part to teams releasing veteran players and calling up minor leaguers, some of whom could be paid the minimum salary of $62,500. But the decrease was a minor one as annual payrolls for major league clubs in 1987 topped $295 million. Of course, payrolls varied from team to team; in 1987 the Yankee payroll of $18.5 million topped all others, while the $5.6 million payroll of the Seattle Mariners was the lowest of the twenty-six teams.

Average figures also failed to tell the full story of player gains of this era. Boosting average salary figures were the growing number of million-dollar-a-year players. In 1984 there were twenty; in 1985, thirty-six; in 1986, fifty-eight; and in 1987, fifty-seven. Among these plutocrats were a number of $2-million-a-year men, including slugger Mike Schmidt of the Phillies. In signing a two-year contract late in 1987, Schmidt successfully bucked the rumored attempt by owners to hold salaries at $2 million. In Schmidt's words, "I wanted the salary to read $2.25 million probably more for negotiating reasons for my fellow players. . . . I want my fellow players to know that's what top dollar is now." Small wonder then that salaries of baseball players now exceeded those of any rival team sports in America.

In defense of these astronomical player salaries, one could cite major league baseball's continuing prosperity. In this era, annual attendance at major league games repeatedly set new records. After the jarring strike of 1981 limited attendance to 22 million, attendance rebounded to a record 45 million the following year. And despite the national recession, that record fell in 1983. And, after falling by a mere 800,000 in 1984, attendance continued upward. In 1986 annual attendance totaled 47,500,000 and in 1987 it topped 52 million. As in every year since its mini-expansion in 1977, the AL led in attendance, and in 1987 the AL outdrew the NL by 2.5 million. But as always, attendance was unevenly distributed among the clubs. Until 1987 only the Dodgers had topped the 3 miilion mark in annual attendance, which they did on several occasions, but that year the NL Mets and Cardinals also cracked that barrier. Meanwhile, no AL team had broken the 3 million attendance barrier, but in 1987 the Toronto Blue Jays neared the mark, and in 1988 the Twins surpassed it. Moreover, the attendance picture was brightening for teams located in older cities like Chicago, Boston, New York, San Francisco, Cleveland, St. Louis, and Milwaukee, where demographic reports showed a reversal of population losses.

However, revenues from soaring attendance alone could not have supported the astonishing salaries of this era. What made the difference was television revenue, which some critics blamed for stimulating the trend by casting ballplayers in the company of highly paid TV celebrities. Be that as it may, in 1983 major league officials negotiated a $1.1 billion, six-year network television contract. When the contract took effect in 1984, revenues from network and local TV sources exceeded those of ticket sales. Although revenues from local TV contracts tended to favor teams that were located in the more lucrative local TV markets, the network TV contract in its final year of 1989 promised a hefty $230 million for all clubs to divide. Nevertheless, it was too soon to write finis to the old adage that "at the gate is baseball's fate." In 1985 a reported decline in network TV advertising sales raised the specter that the overexposure of televised sports programs would reverse the trend. Should ratings of televised sports

programs decline further, the amount of revenue from network TV would be further reduced.

At this time critics blamed drug abuse by players for lessening the popularity of major sports. But surprisingly baseball's popularity was little affected by revelations of drug abuse by players of this era. In 1980 director Ken Moffett of the Players Association admitted that as many as 40 percent of major league players might be drug abusers. In 1983 the problem reached serious proportions when three Kansas City Royals players were sentenced to jail terms as convicted users. That same year a Dodger pitcher was suspended, and in 1985 a San Diego Padres player was traded for similar offenses. And in 1985 baseball's public image was further tarnished by revelations coming from two Pittsburgh court trials of drug sellers. The testimony named seventeen players as drug users. Although these revelations had no discernible impact on the game's popularity, Commissioner Peter Ueberroth chose to treat the matter as a major scandal. But the commissioner's attempt to force all players to submit to periodic drug tests ran afoul of the Players Association, which insisted that the issue be addressed through collective-bargaining procedures. Still, Ueberroth suspended the accused players and, as a condition for reinstatement, forced each player to donate up to 10 percent of his salary to charities and to engage in antidrug campaigns. After ruling on this matter, Ueberroth announced at the opening of the 1986 season that the drug problem in baseball was solved. But this face-saving claim ignored the reality of the national epidemic of drug abuse and was mocked by the failure of President Reagan's vaunted 1986 antidrug crusade. Indeed, it is most unlikely that the game has been purged of drug abuse, and the problem of devising a punitive policy must surely be part of renewed contract negotiations when the current Basic Agreement expires in 1989.

That major league baseball's popularity was so little troubled by drug scandals, strikes, soaring salaries, or even the economic recession owed much to the dazzling style of play. Indeed, fans of this era witnessed the apotheosis of the big-bang offensives. In the AL, where sluggers consistently outhomered NL swingers by wide margins, homer records fell like sheaves. Over this seven-year span AL sluggers averaged 2,000 homers a year, with record-breaking seasons succeeding each other over the years 1985–1987. In 1985 AL sluggers bashed 2,178; in 1986, 2,240; and in 1987, a gargantuan 2,634 homers were struck. What's more, NL sluggers in 1987 weighed in with 1,824 homers to break their league's 1970 record.

Major league baseball's 1987 cannonade saw twenty-eight players hit 30 or more homers, including twenty American leaguers. Rookie Mark McGwire of the Oakland Athletics led the AL with 49—an all-time seasonal mark by a yearling, the feat won McGwire a unanimous vote for Rookie of the Year honors. Meanwhile, Andre Dawson of the Cubs matched McGwire's output and won the NL MVP Award despite his team's last-place finish in the NL East. Among the most consistent sluggers of this era, Mike Schmidt of the Phillies led NL sluggers four times, while Dale Murphy of the Braves twice topped the league. By the end of the 1988 season, Schmidt's total of 542 homers ranked him with the all-time leading clouters. And at the end of the 1987 season, Reggie Jackson retired from the AL wars with a lifetime total of 563 homers. Jackson's passing from the game left a lonesome gap in AL power circles which young Goliaths like

McGwire, Pete Incaviglia, Jose Canseco, George Bell, and Jesse Barfield seemed destined to fill.

But if this era's homer production was unprecedented, seasonal batting achievements were ordinary. Thanks to its designated hitter rule, AL batters annually surpassed NL hitters, with seasonal AL averages topping .260 while those of the NL hovered around the .255 mark. In the NL, black stars continued their batting leadership. Black stars won all seven of the NL batting titles of this era, with veteran Bill Madlock of the Pirates and young Tony Gwynn of the Padres each capturing a pair. It was otherwise in the AL, where a single dominating hitter, third baseman Wade Boggs of the Red Sox, captured four batting titles. An ideal leadoff hitter, the lefty-swinging Boggs batted .349 as a rookie in 1982. Over the next five seasons Boggs averaged a Cobbian .368. Moreover, in 1987 Boggs belted 24 homers to triple his best seasonal homer output thus far. In 1988, he became the first AL player to post six consecutive 200-hit seasons.

Among the memorable batting feats of this era, Pete Rose gained immortality on September 4, 1985, when the Cincinnati player-manager's single off pitcher Eric Show of the Padres broke Cobb's lifetime record of 4,191 hits. To be sure, Rose needed 2,300 more at bats than Cobb did to turn the trick, but the forty-four-year-old sparkplug put his feat into proper perspective when he said, "I might not be the best player, but I got the most hits." Indeed, and when Rose retired from active play at the end of the 1986 season, he had extended the total hit record to 4,256. While nothing touched Rose's accomplishment, the explosive 1987 season saw Don Mattingly of the Yankees match Dale Long's feat of homering in eight consecutive games, while Paul Molitor of the Brewers hit safely in 39 consecutive games, and rookie catcher Benito Santiago of the Padres hit safely in 34. Santiago's feat won for him NL Rookie of the Year honors.

In the offensive category of stolen bases, NL speedsters perennially topped their AL counterparts. At this time the newly crowned prince of thieves was outfielder Vince Coleman of the Cardinals. In 1985 Coleman set a rookie record with 110 steals, and at the end of the 1987 season he became the first player ever to swipe 100 or more bases in three consecutive seasons. However, Coleman had yet to top the latest seasonal record of 130 thefts, set by outfielder Rickey Henderson of the Oakland Athletics in 1982.

Not surprisingly the offensive pyrotechnics of these years had pundits wondering whatever had happened to pitching. Indeed, seasonal ERAs skyrocketed in both leagues, with the AL average well above 4.00 and that of the NL above 3.70. Of course this meant that the always volatile pitching-batting equilibrium was again out of whack. For the latest imbalance, observers proffered such explanations as livelier balls, narrowed strike zones, pitchers' fears of retaliation if they threw inside to batters, pitchers relying too much on breaking pitches, and managers relying more on their bullpen and demanding too little of their starters. Indeed, the numbers of complete games pitched by starting pitchers declined as managers relied more on specialized relief pitchers. Among the bullpen specialists, the most celebrated continued to be the firemen who were counted to come on late in a game to save a victory. Among the best were Dan Quisenberry, Goose Gossage, Bruce Sutter, Todd Worrell, Dave Righetti, Gene Garber (who notched his 200th career save in 1987), and Lee Smith, who set a record by recording 30 or more saves in three consecutive seasons.

Still, it seemed evident that more than yeomanlike relief work was needed to restore pitching to a proper balance. For now, managers complained of poorly trained pitchers, while pitchers blamed prevailing rules for favoring batters. Nor was it surprising that some pitchers were smuggling in illegal scuffed-ball and spitball deliveries.

However, good pitchers were by no means extinct. In this era Nolan Ryan hurled a record-setting fifth no-hitter in 1981. And at the end of the 1988 season, the forty-one-year-old fireballer, who had lost little of his earlier velocity, extended his all-time leading strikeout total to 4,775 whiffs. Indeed, in 1987 Ryan's 270 strikeouts led the NL, and his 2.76 ERA hardly justified his 8–16 won-loss record. Among the promising younger pitchers, Dwight Gooden of the Mets blazed his way to a 24–4, 1.53 ERA, with 268 strikeouts in 1985. And the following year Roger Clemens of the Red Sox also went 24–4 to become the first starting pitcher in fifteen years to win the AL MVP Award. Naturally Clemens also won the Cy Young Award that year, and when the ace went 20–9 in 1987, despite early-season ineffectiveness caused by his salary holdout, Clemens won a second Cy Young Award. By winning two straight, Clemens joined the select company of Sandy Koufax, Denny McLain, and Jim Palmer as the only pitchers to win back-to-back Cy Young Awards. And in 1988 Orel Hershiser's performance from August through October was unprecedented.

Campaigns of the Eighties: The AL, 1981–1988

The long-sought dream of an era of competitive balance now became a reality in the AL, as each of the seven campaigns produced a new league champion. What's more, eleven different teams won divisional titles, with only the Tigers, Royals, and Angels managing to win two. Of the dual winners, only the Royals were able to repeat as divisional champs, which they did in 1984–1985.

The AL's free-for-all pattern began with the singular campaign of 1981. When the long player strike gutted the middle of that season, a split-season format was adopted in hopes of renewing fan support for the arrested campaign. Under this format, the first half of the season ended when the players walked out on June 11, and the second half ran from the resumption of play in mid-August to the end of the regular playing schedule. Because the June 11 strike date had the Yankees leading the Orioles by 2 games in the East, and the Athletics leading the Rangers by 1½ games in the West, these teams were declared the first-half winners of their divisions. But when the split-season plan barred first-half winners from repeating as divisional champs, the Yankees dawdled to a sixth-place finish in the East's second-half race. Thus the Milwaukee Brewers won the second-half Eastern race by 1½ games over the Red Sox. In the West, the Athletics lost the second half to the Royals by 1 game.

At this point, the split-season script called for a best-of-five-games playoff series to determine the divisional championships. In the East the series went the full five games before the Yankees defeated the Brewers, but in the West the scrappy Athletics swept the Royals. Then in the ensuing League Championship Series the Yankees swept the Athletics. Although the Yankees won the 1981 AL pennant, their overall record was bettered by two other teams. The Yankee victory owed to its pitching staff, whose 2.90 ERA led the league; starters Ron Guidry and Dave Righetti combined for

19 wins, and reliever Goose Gossage saved 20 games. As for the Athletics, whose overall record was the AL's best, they led the league in homers. The Athletics were led by outfielder Rickey Henderson, who batted .319 and led the league in stolen bases, and pitcher Steve McCatty, whose 14 wins and 2.32 ERA led the league. As for the Yankees, their comeuppance came in the World Series. Matched against the resilient Dodgers, the Yankees took the first two games, but then were ignominiously swept. And by losing three games in relief, Yankee pitcher George Frazier added his name to the annals of World Series goats.

In the dog-eat-dog competition of the next six AL seasons, the Yankees failed to win another divisional title. In 1982 the Brewers squeaked to a 1-game win over the Orioles in the East. In winning, the Brewers batted .279 and the team's 216 homers topped the majors, with shortstop Robin Yount winning MVP honors for his .331-29-114 batting exploits. Outfielder Gorman Thomas led the league with 39 homers and drove in 112 runs. And infielders Cecil Cooper (.331-32-121) and Paul Molitor (.302-19-71) complemented Yount's stickwork. But the pitching was shaky, except for starters Pete Vuckovich and Mike Caldwell, who combined for 35 victories. Veteran reliever Rollie Fingers saved 29 games, so the late-season injury that sidelined this mustachioed ace was a crusher. In the West, the California Angels won a close race by 3 games over the Royals. A good hitting team, the Angels finished right behind the Brewers in hitting and homers, and their pitching bettered the Brewers. Starter Geoff Zahn's 18 wins led the staff. Offensively, a quartet of expensive recent acquisitions paced the attack, including infielders Rod Carew (.319) and Doug DeCinces (.301-30-97), and outfielders Fred Lynn (.299) and Reggie Jackson (39 homers and 102 RBIs). Jackson's 39 homers tied Thomas for the league leadership, and the veteran drove in 101 runs. When these two well-matched teams met in LCS play, for a time it seemed likely that Angel manager Gene Mauch might win his first pennant. The Angels took the first two games at home, but were swept by the Brewers in Milwaukee. Thus the Brewers became the first major league team to win an LCS after losing the first two games. But in World Series play it was the Cardinals who rebounded from a 3–2 deficit to defeat the Brewers. This latest loss was the fourth in a row by an AL entry.

But over the next three seasons, three different AL teams ended the NL streak by winning world titles. In 1983 the Orioles drove to a 6-game victory over the runner-up Tigers in the Eastern Division. Pitchers Scott McGregor (18–7), Mike Boddicker (16–8), Storm Davis (13–7), and reliever Tippy Martinez (with 21 saves) headed the league's second-best pitching staff. At bat the Orioles hit .269, and the team's 168 homers led the majors. Shortstop Cal Ripken, Jr.'s .318-27-102 batting won him MVP honors, while first baseman Eddie Murray weighed in with .306-33-111 clouting. Meanwhile, in the West the long-dormant Chicago White Sox stormed to a 20-game victory over the Royals. In landing their first divisional title, the White Sox drew 2 million fans, who saw young Ron Kittle win Rookie of the Year honors with his 35 homers and 100 RBIs. Although lacking a .300 hitter, the White Sox got plentiful power from outfielder Harold Baines (20-99), catcher Carlton Fisk (26-86), and DH Greg Luzinski (32-95). What's more, the White Sox boasted a pair of 20-game winners in Cy Young Award winner LaMarr Hoyt (24–10) and Rich Dotson (22–7). Behind Hoyt, the White Sox won the first LCS game, but the Orioles swept the next three games to

win the pennant. The Orioles then dropped the opening game of the 1983 World Series at home, but then swept the Phillies to end the AL's humiliating losing streak.

The following year another new champion surfaced in the AL East, which was now being touted as the strongest division in the majors. Riding the momentum of a 35–5 breakaway gait, the Detroit Tigers went on to win 104 games, enough to lap the Toronto Blue Jays by 15 games. It was indeed a vintage year for manager Sparky Anderson's all-conquering Tigers. Offensively the Tigers led the league in hitting (.271) and homers (187). Shortstop Alan Trammell batted .314, and outfielder Kirk Gibson and catcher Lance Parrish combined to produce 60 homers and 189 RBIs. To top it off, the Tigers also fielded the league's best pitching staff. Starters Jack Morris, Dan Petry, and Milt Wilcox turned in 54 victories and reliever Willie Hernandez, a recent acquisition from the Phillies, saved 32 games. In 32 of his 33 game-saving situations, Hernandez met the test—an achievement that won him both the Cy Young and MVP awards. Meanwhile, in the weaker Western Division the Royals eked a 3-game win over the Angels and Twins, but the Royals won only six more games than they lost. The Royals batted .268, with outfielder Willie Wilson and DH Hal McRae topping the .300 mark. But the pitching was mediocre and the staff depended heavily on reliever Dan Quisenberry, who saved 44 games. When the Tigers and Royals faced off in LCS play, the Tigers won the 1984 AL pennant by dispatching the Royals in three games. And in World Series action, the Tigers easily defeated the San Diego Padres in five games. By skippering the Tigers to victory, Sparky Anderson became the first manager to win World Series titles in both the American and National leagues.

But the Tigers' view from the top was a brief one. In 1985 they fell 15 games off the pace, leaving the Eastern field to the Blue Jays and Yankees. And at the close of the season, the Blue Jays topped the Yankees by 2 games, to win their first divisional title since joining the AL in the mini-expansion of 1977. The rise of the Blue Jays owed much to general manager Pat Gillick, who, by dint of shrewd trades and canny selections in annual surplus-player drafts, swiftly assembled a pennant contender. In 1985 the Blue Jays' pitching staff led the league, and outfielder Jesse Barfield (.289-27-84) powered an offense that produced a .269 team batting average and 158 homers. Pitcher Dave Stieb's 2.48 ERA led the league's pitchers, although his 14–13 record was disappointing. Starters Doyle Alexander and Jimmy Key combined for 31 victories, and Dennis Lamp posted an 11–0 record in relief. In the lightly regarded Western Division, meanwhile, the Royals became the only AL team of this brief era to repeat as divisional champs. In winning by a single game over the Angels, the Royals batted only .252, but powered 154 homers. Third baseman George Brett's .335-30-112 led the hitters, and first baseman Steve Balboni drove in 88 runs and hit 36 homers. The pitching was good. Young Bret Saberhagen's 20–6, 2.87 ERA won him the Cy Young Award, Charlie Leibrandt's 17 wins came on the league's second-best ERA, and reliever Dan Quisenberry saved 37 games. When the Blue Jays and Royals squared off in the newly extended seven-game LCS, the Blue Jays took a 3–1 lead, but the gritty Royals came on to win in seven games, beating the Blue Jays in their home roost the last two games. In the World Series, the resilient Royals staged yet another memorable comeback against the favored Cardinals. After losing the first two games at home, the

Royals fell behind 3–1, but rallied to win the next three games. This latest World Series victory extended the AL's winning streak to three.

In another topsy-turvy campaign, the 1986 Red Sox dethroned the Blue Jays in the East. The Red Sox took the lead in June and hung on to win the division pennant by 5½ games over the Yankees. A .271 team batting assault was fronted by batting champ Wade Boggs (.357-8-71) and outfielder Jim Rice (.324-20-110). Boston's overall pitching was mediocre, but starter Roger Clemens led all pitchers with a 24–4, 2.48 effort that won the big righthander both the MVP and Cy Young awards. While the Red Sox were winning in the East, the Royals faded in the West as arm miseries tolled on young Saberhagen. Thus the Angels won the division by 5 games over the Texas Rangers. Rookie first baseman Wally Joyner, who replaced the great Carew, batted .299-22-100 to head the Angels' weak .255 batting. But Angel pitching ranked second in the AL, with Mike Witt winning 18 on a sparkling 2.84 ERA, Kirk McCaskill and veteran Don Sutton combining for 32 wins, and reliever Donnie Moore saving 21 games. When the Angels took a 3–1 lead over the Red Sox in LCS play, it now appeared as if manager Gene Mauch might win his first pennant in twenty-five years at the helm of major league teams. Indeed, in the fifth game Mauch's Angels were one pitch away from a league title, but the Red Sox rallied to win the game on heroics by Dave Henderson. The Red Sox then took the next two games at home to land the 1986 AL pennant. In the World Series the Red Sox jumped to a 3–2 lead over the Mets and appeared on the verge of winning their first world title since 1918, but the Mets crushed the dream by winning the last two games at Shea Stadium.

As a climax to the eighty-six-year history of the AL, the 1987 season provided a storied campaign. In a frenetic season which saw AL sluggers set yet another homer mark and attendance climb to new heights, both divisional races were fiercely contested. In the East waged an epic struggle that ended in a 2-game victory by the Tigers. With seven games to play, the Blue Jays led by 3½ games, but incredibly they lost all seven, including three vital games to the Tigers in Detroit. Hefty .272 batting and a major-league-leading 225 homer barrage powered the Tigers, whose shaky pitching staff was bolstered by the September acquisition of veteran Doyle Alexander from the Braves. By posting a 5–0 record with the Tigers, Alexander was named Pitcher of the Month by *The Sporting News*. Among the offensive standouts, shortstop Alan Trammell batted .343-28-105, young catcher Matt Nokes, who replaced the departed Parrish, batted .289-32-87, and forty-year-old first baseman Darrell Evans hit 34 homers and drove in 99 runs. With Anderson's Tigers posting the best record in the majors, scant hope was afforded the Western-winning Minnesota Twins, who defeated the Royals by 2 games to win their first divisional title. Indeed, the Twins surrendered more runs (806) than they scored (786). But the Twins batted .261 and poled 196 homers; outfielder Kirby Puckett (.332-28-99) led the hitters, with outfielder Tom Brunansky and infielders Kent Hrbek and Gary Gaetti combining for 97 homers and 284 RBIs. On the other hand, Twins' pitchers allowed a horrendous 4.63 ERA. But the staff's most respectable member, Frank Viola, stood out as the winningest left-handed pitcher in the majors over the past four seasons. In 1986 Viola posted a 17–10, 2.90 ERA, and veteran Bert Blyleven recorded a 15–12 mark.

Matched against the Tigers in LCS play, the Twins were scorned as hometown dependents whose outstanding home record owed to the vagaries of their much-maligned domed stadium. But the Twins thrashed the Tigers in five games to win their first AL pennant in twenty-two years. Moreover, they went on to beat the crippled Cardinals in a seven-game World Series struggle by scoring all of their victories in their cozy "homer dome" before capacity crowds of screaming, hankie-waving fans. Thus the 1987 World Series stood out as the first where all victories were won on home fields. And the Twins were indeed fortunate to have hosted four of the games in their favorite bailiwick.

In 1988 a timely rule change which redefined the strike zone helped to quell the raging homer epidemic. In an anticlimactic season that saw batting and power hitting tail off, the well-balanced Oakland Athletics dominated the AL West from the start. The A's 104 victories topped the majors and lapped the runner-up Minnesota Twins by 13 games. League-leading pitching, paced by Dave Stewart's 21 wins and reliever Dennis Eckersley's 45 saves, carried the A's who were powered by young outfielder Jose Canseco's .307-42-124 batting. Canseco also stole 40 bases to become the first player to notch at least 40 homers and as many stolen bases. Meanwhile the AL East saw the only hotly contested divisional race in the majors, as the Boston Red Sox edged the Detroit Tigers by a single game; only 3½ games separated the Red Sox from the sixth place Yankees. Barely playing .500 ball at the All-Star break, the Red Sox changed managers—from John McNamara to Joe Morgan—and staged an extended winning streak that carried them to the top. Despite a late-season slump, they hung on to win. Leading the Boston attack, perennial batting champ Wade Boggs batted .366 to lead the majors and outfielder Mike Greenwell weighed in with a .325-22-119 performance. Ace pitchers Roger Clemens and Bruce Hurst each won 18 games and newly acquired reliever Lee Smith saved 29; still, the Red Sox needed the timely pitching of Mike Boddicker, who joined the staff from the Orioles late in the season and won seven games for Boston. However, the Red Sox were mismatched against the A's, who stormed to a sweeping victory in LCS play on the strength of Canseco's 3 homers and Eckersley's four saves in relief of the starters. In the World Series the A's were held in check by the Los Angeles Dodgers' pitchers, notably Orel Hershiser—whose three hits in Game Two exceeded the Series total of Canseco and Mark McGwire combined.

Campaigns of the Eighties: The NL, 1981–1988

Although less competitively balanced than the anarchical AL, the NL campaigns of this era were hotly contested. From 1981–87, only the Cardinals, winners of three NL pennants in these years, showed dynastic tendencies; the remaining four went singly to the Dodgers, Phillies, Padres, and Mets. In divisional races the Cardinals in the East and the Dodgers in the West each won three pennants, but no contender won in consecutive years. Indeed, in this brief era ten different NL teams won divisional championships.

When the long players' strike of 1981 gutted team playing schedules by an average of 55 games, the split-season format was unveiled upon resumption of play in August in hopes of salvaging the campaign. By dint of their 1½-game lead over the Cardinals on the June 11 strike day, the Phillies were declared first-half winners in the East; and by virtue of a mere half-game lead over the Reds on that fatal date, the Dodgers

became the first-half winners in the West. These were close calls to be sure, but no closer than the results of the second-half races. In the NL East, the Montreal Expos finished a half-game up on the luckless Cardinals, while the Houston Astros edged the snakebit Reds by 1½ games in the West. As frustrated runners-up in two close calls, the Cardinals and Reds with the best overall record in the NL received no recognition. However, the defiant Reds later raised their own homemade pennant as a symbol of protest. In the playoffs for the divisional titles, the Expos beat the Phillies in five games to win in the East, and the Dodgers rallied from a 2–1 deficit in games to beat the Astros in the West. The division-winning Expos and Dodgers then met in the usual League Championship Series, which the Dodgers won. Once again rallying from a 2–1 deficit, manager Lasorda's men edged the Expos. In winning the NL's forlorn 1981 championship, the Dodgers batted .262, led the league in homers with 82, and fielded the league's second-ranked pitching staff. Rookie pitcher Fernando Valenzuela won his first eight games and finished with a 13–7 mark to pace the staff, while outfielders Pedro Guerrero (.300-12-48) and Dusty Baker (.320-9-49) led the batting attack. In World Series play, the Dodgers once again dug themselves a hole by losing the first two games. But once again they rebounded, this time sweeping their old Yankee tormentors to win the 1981 world title.

With the game's image blighted by the "dishonest season" of 1981, the NL sorely needed a dramatic flourish to regain its credibility. Mercifully this was supplied by the extremely close divisional races of 1982. In the NL East a four-team struggle ended with the Cardinals topping the Phillies by 3 games. At bat the Cardinals hit .264, but with scant power (67 homers). Outfielder Lonnie Smith was the only regular to top the .300 mark, but first baseman Keith Hernandez batted .299 and drove in 94 runs, and outfielder George Hendrick powered the team with his .282-19-104 hitting. By way of compensation, the Cardinals led the league in fielding and stolen bases, and owned the league's second-best mound corps. Starters Joaquin Andujar and Bob Forsch each won 15 games, and ace reliever Bruce Sutter won 9 and saved a league-leading 36 games. In the West, meanwhile, the Braves won their first 13 games and hung on for dear life thereafter to edge the Dodgers by a game. Offensively, the Braves batted only .256, but led the league in homers with 146. Outfielder Dale Murphy's 36 homers generated a league-leading 109 RBIs, and third baseman Bob Horner hit 32 homers and drove in 97 runs. Veteran knuckleball hurler Phil Niekro's 17–4 effort headed the pitching staff, which needed every one of reliever Gene Garber's 30 saves. In LCS play the Braves' mediocre pitching tolled as the Cardinals swept to victory. In ensuing World Series play, the Cardinals fell behind the heavy-hitting Brewers 3–2, but rallied to win the final two games at home. This latest World Series victory was the fourth straight for NL contenders.

When the Cardinals succumbed to poor pitching in 1983, the Phillies snatched the Eastern title by 6 games over the Pirates. The Phillies did it with a brilliant stretch drive, winning twenty-one of their last twenty-five games. Offensively, the aging Phillies batted only .249, but third baseman Mike Schmidt's 40 homers led the league, and his 109 RBIs led the team. A sound pitching staff, fronted by John Denny's Cy Young Award-winning 19–6 effort and reliever Al Holland's 25 saves was a decisive factor in the victory. Meanwhile, in the West the Dodgers also mounted a September stretch drive to topple the Braves by 3 games. Like the Phillies, the Dodgers' .250 hitting was lackluster, but the team led the league in homers (146); outfielder Guerrero's 32 homers and 103 RBIs headed the assault. A major factor was the team's pitching staff, whose 3.10 ERA was the league's best. Valenzuela and Bob Welch combined for 30 victories, and reliever Steve Howe saved 18. In LCS play, veteran hurler Steve Carlton's two victories paced the Phillies to victory in four games. However, the Philadelphia "Wheeze Kids" fell to the Orioles in five games in the 1983 World Series.

As the Phillies sank to fourth place in 1984, the long-suffering Chicago Cubs notched their first pennant of any sort since 1945. In downing the Mets by 6½ games in the East, the Cubs staged a second-half rally, fronted by ex-Phillie infielder Ryne Sandberg's MVP-winning .314 batting. Dodger castoff Ron Cey contributed 25 homers and 97 RBIs, and young first baseman Leon "Bull" Durham weighed in with 23 homers and 96 RBIs. And the pitching staff was bolstered by yet another recent acquisition, Rick Sutcliffe, whose 16–1 record won him the Cy Young Award. Starter Steve Trout chipped in with 13 victories, and reliever Lee Smith won 9 games and saved 33. While the Cubs were winning in the East, another newcomer, the San Diego Padres, easily won the Western title by 12 games over the runner-up Braves. The Padres batted .259, with young outfielder Tony Gwynn leading the league with his .351 batting. The team's modest total of 109 homers was augmented by third baseman Graig Nettles and outfielder Kevin McReynolds, each of whom poled 20. More distinguished was the pitching staff, whose 3.48 ERA ranked third in the league. Able starters Eric Show, Ed Whitson, and Mark Thurmond combined for 43 victories, and veteran reliever Goose Gossage won 10 and saved 25 games. In LCS play the Cubs pounded out a pair of early victories at Wrigley Field, but the surprising Padres swept the next three games at home to become the first NL team ever to win an LCS after losing the first two games. Sad to say, however, the Padres' world title hopes went aglimmering as the Tigers trounced them in five games in the 1984 World Series.

The following year the Cardinals became the only major league team of this era to win a second league championship. In fending off the rising New York Mets by 3 games in the East, the Cardinals relied on league-leading batting and base stealing. Outfielder Willie McGee's league-leading .353 batting won him the MVP Award, and outfielder Vince Coleman won Rookie of the Year honors by stealing 110 bases—a new record for a rookie. Among other stalwarts, second baseman Tom Herr batted .302; first baseman Jack Clark, recently acquired from the Giants, hit 22 homers and drove in 87 runs; and shortstop Ozzie Smith, who won the league's Gold Glove Award for a sixth straight year, batted .276. What's more, Cardinal pitching ranked second in the league, with ex-Pirate John Tudor leading the hurlers with a 21–8, 1.93 ERA performance. Starters Andujar (21 wins) and Danny Cox (18 wins) lent sturdy support, as did relievers Jeff Lahti and Ken Dayley. The pair's 30 saves compensated for the loss of free agent Sutter. As the Cardinals were winning in the East, the Dodgers went on to win the Western title by 5½ games over the Reds. Offensively, the Dodgers' .261 hitting was led by outfielder Guerrero's .320-33-87 hitting. Better still, the Dodger pitching corps led the majors with a 2.96 ERA. The starting quartet of Orel Hershiser, Bob Welch, Jerry Reuss, and Fernando Valenzuela produced 64 wins, and the bullpen saved 31 games. In LCS play, the well-armed Dodgers took

the first two games of the newly established seven-game for-mat, but the Cardinals swept the next four to win the NL pennant. Pitted against the underdog Royals in the 1985 World Series, the Cardinals won three of the first four games, including the first two in the Royals' home lair. But the Royals won the fifth game at St. Louis and the final two games back home. The sixth game was marred by a disputed call at first base that gave the Royals a life of which they took full advantage. The Royals then won the final game in an 11–0 laugher, and their victory extended the recent AL World Series winning streak to three years.

The following year the New York Mets ended the AL's victory flurry with a dramatic win. In dominating the NL East, the 1986 Mets won 108 games to lap the runner-up Phillies by 21½ games. Offensively, the versatile Mets led the league in hitting (.263), poled 148 homers, and stole 118 bases. First baseman Keith Hernandez (.310-13-83) headed the charge, with outfielder Darryl Strawberry and catcher Gary Carter powering a combined 51 homers and 198 RBIs. As icing on their victory cake, the Mets fielded the best pitching staff in the majors. Starters Bob Ojeda (18–5), Dwight Gooden (17–6), Sid Fernandez (16–6) and Ron Dar-ling (15–6) were formidable, as was the bullpen duo of Roger McDowell (14 wins, 22 saves) and Jesse Orosco (8 wins, 21 saves). While the Mets were compiling the best record in the majors, the Houston Astros were winning the Western Divi-sion by 10 games over the Reds. Offensively, the Astros bat-ted .255 with 125 homers. Outfielder Kevin Bass batted .311-20-79 to head the hitters, while first baseman Glenn Davis powered 31 homers and drove in 101 runs. Backing the hitters was the league's second-best pitching staff, fronted by Mike Scott's 18–10 hurling, which was accompanied by a league-leading 2.22 ERA. While the outcome of the LCS appeared to be a foregone conclusion, the Astros hung tough before losing in six games to the Mets. The Red Sox also fell to the Mets in World Series play, but not before throwing a scare into manager Davey Johnson's crew. Indeed, the Red Sox took a 3–2 lead in games before the Mets rallied to win the final two games at Shea Stadium.

The following year most observers picked the swaggering Mets to repeat, but the resilient Cardinals took the 1987 Eastern title by 3 games. Although outhit by the league-leading Met batters, the Cardinals mustered .263 hitting, which they backed by stout relief pitching to pull off their victory. Offensively, the Cardinals' 94 homers were the fewest by any major league team this season, but first baseman Jack Clark bashed 35 and drove in 106 runs. Third baseman Terry Pendleton drove in 96 runs, while shortstop Ozzie Smith drove home 75 runs with nary a homer to his credit. But the Cardinals atoned with a sprightly running game led by out-fielder Vince Coleman, who topped 100 seasonal steals for the third straight season. Likewise the shaky pitching staff that completed only ten games was backed by a redoubtable relief crew whose ace, Todd Worrell, saved 33 games. Meanwhile in the NL West, the Giants won over the bridesmaid Reds by 6 games. The Giant victory was a dramatic turnabout for a team that in 1985 had finished last in their division with 100 losses. A fine balance of hitting and pitching made the differ-ence in 1987. At the plate the Giants batted .260 with 205 homers and were led by first baseman Will Clark's .308-35-91 pyrotechnics. Moreover, the pitching staff boasted the league's best ERA, even if the Giant starters completed only 28 games. What mattered was that relievers Scott Garrelts

and Jeff Robinson combined for 22 wins and 31 saves. When the Giants met the Cardinals in LCS play, injuries to Jack Clark and Pendleton cast the Cardinals as underdogs. But the Cardinals won their third NL title of the era by overcoming a 3–2 deficit in games with a pair of home-field victories. In World Series play, it was the crippled Cardinals who were favored over the unheralded Twins, but the American Leagu-ers won four games, all of them in their cozy domed stadium, to edge the Cardinals in seven games.

The pitching rule modification that stemmed the homer tide in 1988 wreaked havoc with NL batters in 1988 as only five regulars attained the .300 mark. Although no New York Met batter joined this circle, Darryl Strawberry boomed a league-leading 39 homers and drove in 101 runs and outfield mate Kevin McReynolds produced a .288-27-99; they pow-ered the Mets to 100 victories and an easy 15-game victory over the Pirates in the NL East. With a 2.91 ERA, the Mets also boasted the best pitching staff in the majors. David Cone led the starters at 20-3 and Dwight Gooden and Ron Darling combined for 35 wins. Relievers Randy Myers and Roger McDowell saved 42 games. In the West, meanwhile, the Los Angeles Dodgers took the lead in July and hung on to win by 7 games over the Cincinnati Reds who along the way got a rare perfect-game pitching performance from Tom Browning. But the Dodgers held claim to the best individual pitching per-formance of the year when their ace, Orel Hershiser, finished the regular season with a new record of 59 scoreless innings. In addition to a 23-8 record Hershiser led all NL pitchers in innings pitched, complete games, and shutouts. Offensively the modest Dodger attack was powered by newly acquired free agent Kirk Gibson (.290-25-76) and veteran outfielder Mike Marshall (.277-20-82). With pitcher Fernando Valenzuela sidelined by a shoulder injury and Gibson hobbled by a leg injury, the lightly regarded Dodgers were afforded little chance against the Mets in LCS play. But the Dodgers prevailed in seven games with Hershiser starting three games and relieving in another. And then they upset the Oakland Athletics in the World Series, despite crippling injuries to Gibson, pitcher John Tudor, and catcher Mike Scioscia.

Scanning the Future:
Baseball's Problems and Prospects

Carping purists notwithstanding, domed stadiums like Min-nesota's Metrodome, which contributed to the Twins' stun-ning 1987 World Series victory, are likely to become a familiar part of baseball's future landscape. In 1989 the To-ronto Blue Jays will occupy their new Toronto Skydome; and St. Petersburg, Florida, whose officials are eyeing a future major league franchise, will open their Florida-Suncoast Dome in the near future. Moreover, domed structures are under consideration in St. Louis, Chicago, Atlanta, and Tampa; the latter site, like St. Petersburg, is another beckon-ing site for future major league expansion.

As baseball's architecture has changed dramatically over the 116 years of major league baseball history, so have other aspects of the national game. Indeed, if major league base-ball's history offers any enduring lesson, it is that change is essential for sustaining the game's continuing growth and popularity. Thus as the game moves into the last decade of the twentieth century, its leaders cannot afford to assume compla-cently that its present popularity and prosperity are guaran-

teed to continue. The game's history teaches that in the past baseball has had to endure dismal busts along with dazzling booms. Indeed, the recent shock waves that buffeted the nation's economy must pose a grim reminder of the forces that nearly sixty years ago plunged the nation's economy and its national game into a decade of Depression.

To foster the game's continuing growth, baseball leaders should carefully monitor baseball's alliance with television. With half of major league baseball's annual revenues now coming from television, there is cause for alarm in some recent reports from the television industry warning that televised sports programming may be reaching a saturation point.

But at the present time baseball's overall popularity shows few signs of declining. Indeed, baseball's elevation to the status of a medal sport in the 1992 Olympic Games should boost interest in the game at the all-important school and college grassroots. Moreover, another round of major league expansion appears to be in the offing. Urban sites like Denver, Tampa, Phoenix, and New Jersey are likely targets for another expansion round that could end the current structural imbalance of the major leagues. But unless the two leagues agree on a joint expansion format, the likelihood of another unilateral expansion move such as occurred in 1977 looms large.

Like the issue of future expansion, the matter of resolving the designated hitter controversy also cries out for enlightened statesmanship by leaders of the two major leagues. Toward this end, in 1986 Commissioner Ueberroth moved to clarify the use of designated hitters in World Series play. Instead of the old practice of allowing the DH rule to be employed every other year, designated hitters now perform each year at World Series games played in AL parks. A reasonable compromise, it could be followed by wider accord on this divisive problem. Yet, as baseball history also shows, the two major leagues have always jealously guarded their independence. For this reason, overall statesmanlike leadership has always been hampered.

Still, such enlightened leadership is needed to resolve these and other knotty problems besetting the game. For one, the pitching-batting equation needs to be addressed anew. As the homer barrages of 1987 tolled on pitchers, rules makers were challenged to strike a balance in favor of the pitching side of the game. In 1988, the pendulum seemed to swing forcefully—at least in the NL—back toward the pitchers.

On the labor front, owners and players need to avoid any future replays of the crippling strike of 1981. When the present Basic Agreement expires at the end of 1989, the next contract must include safeguards against *sub rosa* conspiracies on the part of owners which now threaten the integrity of the free agent draft procedures. Moreover, the new contract must grapple with the damaging problem of drug abuse which has blighted the game's image. Admittedly, resolving such issues as these would require the wisdom of a Solomon.

On baseball's still festering racial front, Commissioner Ueberroth's recent move to foster the integration of minority group members, including ex-players, into the game's managerial and administrative posts has struck a hopeful note. Toward this end the newly created Baseball Network was beginning its work at the close of the 1987 season. The task was a formidable one, since in 1987 blacks and other minorities had attained only 17 of a total of 879 such positions in major league baseball.

In pondering the game's present and future problems and prospects, baseball leaders—now topped by Commissioner A. Bartlett Giamatti—would do well to survey the game's illustrious past. Since 1871, 13,000 players have played in the major leagues, and well over a billion fans have passed through turnstiles at major league ballparks. Indeed, the game's greatest assets always have been its players and devoted fans. Thus the key to baseball's continuing success is to maintain the quality of its players. To do that would ensure the steady support of its fans amidst all of the competing influences in American society.

## CHAPTER 2

Team Histories

Frederick Ivor-Campbell

There are today 26 major-league baseball teams—12 in the National League and 14 in the American—and their number is likely to grow in the next few years. From the organization of the first professional league—the National Association—in 1871, 108 clubs (plus those of the Negro major leagues) have played major-league ball at one time or another. Some played for as little as a few games in a single season, but others have played for more than a century, and one—the present Atlanta Braves—has played every season from 1871 to the present. The only existing franchise older than Atlanta's (which originated as the Boston Red Stockings, then became the Boston and Milwaukee Braves before moving to Atlanta) is the Chicago Cubs, which organized in 1870, a year before league play began. The White Stockings (as they were first known) missed two seasons (1872–1873) in the aftermath of the great Chicago fire, but have since then continuously represented the same city longer than any other club in baseball history.

Here are brief histories of the 26 current big-league clubs, arranged alphabetically by city or state. These are followed by summary histories of the 82 other clubs—now defunct—that at one time also represented their cities in the major leagues.

Atlanta Braves

The Atlanta Braves, who first played in 1871 as Boston's Red Stockings, are the only club to field a team every season of professional league baseball. When the game's first openly professional club, the Cincinnati Red Stockings, decided to revert to amateur status, manager/outfielder Harry Wright and three of his teammates took their talents (and club nickname) to Boston, where, with infielders Ross Barnes and Harry Schafer and pitcher Al Spalding, they formed the nucleus of a team that would dominate the five-year history of the first professional league, the National Association. After a close third-place finish in their first year, the Red Stockings won four pennants in convincing fashion, including a 71–8 record in 1875 with an .899 winning percentage that has never since been approached in major league ball.

When the National League replaced the NA in 1876, four of Boston's best players (including Spalding and Barnes) deserted the club for Chicago. But after a fourth-place finish in 1876, the Red Stockings lured pitcher Tommy Bond from Hartford and finished at the top in 1877 and '78. Bond dominated NL pitching, winning 80 games (40 each year), 22 more than his nearest rival. Although he won another 43 in 1879, Boston slipped to second.

In 1880 the Red Stockings suffered their first losing season as they fell to sixth. After another sixth-place finish the next year, Wright left to manage Providence, but Boston rebounded to third in 1882 and surprised everyone in 1883 by outplaying favored Chicago and Providence to capture their seventh pennant.

Providence knocked them out of the race late in 1884, and Boston remained out of contention the next four seasons. In 1889, though, with several players signed from the defunct Detroit Wolverines (including batting champ Dan Brouthers), and 49 wins from pitcher John Clarkson, the Beaneaters (as they were now more commonly known) waged a two-team race for the championship with the New York Giants. Boston won as many games as the Giants, but lost two more and finished a game back.

Frank Selee, who had managed two straight minor league pennant winners, was hired from Omaha along with his star pitcher, Charles "Kid" Nichols. Their arrival in 1890 ushered in Boston's second golden era. Before they left the club twelve years later, the Beaneaters had won five more NL pennants. Nichols won 27 games in his rookie season, but Boston—decimated by defections to the outlaw Players League—finished only fifth. With the return of some of the defectors in 1891, Clarkson won 33 games, Nichols recorded the first of seven consecutive 30-win seasons, and the Beaneaters returned to the top.

When the NL expanded in 1892 from eight teams to twelve, the schedule too was expanded, and the season divided into two halves. Boston won the first half, and the Cleveland Spiders the second. In a World Series to determine the league champion, the Beaneaters (who at 102–48 had the best over-all season record) defeated the Spiders.

The split season was abandoned and the schedule reduced in 1893—and Boston captured its third straight pennant. Center fielder Hugh Duffy hit .363. The next year, when hitters exploded for a league BA of .309, Duffy led the way with a .438 that is still the major-league record. His Beaneaters didn't win the pennant, but they became the first club in a decade (and the last until 1920) to hit over 100 home runs. Five Beaneaters drove in 100 runs or more, and the team set a big league record for runs scored (1,222) that still stands.

Boston dropped out of contention for a couple of years, but bounced back in 1897 to edge Baltimore for the pennant by two games. In the Temple Cup series, though (played between the first- and second-place teams for the world title), the Orioles overwhelmed Boston four games to one. The next year the schedule was expanded again, and again (as in 1892) Boston won 102 games to lead the league, winning their twelfth pennant. But as the league had abandoned the four-

year-old Temple Cup play, there was no World Series.

After coming in second in 1899, Boston dropped out of pennant contention for fourteen years, finishing as far back as 66½ games (in 1906) and losing as many as 108 (in 1909). Five times the club finished last, including the four years from 1909 to 1912. The Braves (as they were now known) rose to fifth in 1913 under new manager George Stallings, but seemed through the first half of 1914 to be securing for themselves another bed in the cellar.

In mid-July they stood a last-place eighth in a tight field. Six days and six wins later they were third. By mid-August they had climbed to second; on August 26 they replaced the New York Giants in first. For two weeks they alternated between first and second, then took off to win the pennant by 10½ games.

Boston's heroes were pitchers Dick Rudolph and Bill James, both in only their second full big league seasons. Rudolph won 27 games in 1914 and James won 26; then they added two more each in the Braves' World Series sweep of the heavily favored Philadelphia Athletics. But Rudolph crafted only one more 20-win season, and James won only 5 games in two final major-league campaigns.

Classy fielding kept the Braves competitive the next two years. In 1915 they spurted once again out of the cellar—but only to second place this time. They began their climb earlier the next year, but a seven-game losing streak in early September dropped them out of a tie for first. They rallied, but finished third. It was the Braves' last close race for thirty-two years.

In the twenty-nine years from 1917 through 1945 the Braves finished only three seasons as high as fourth, and only once as close as nine games from the top. With four years in the cellar and eleven in seventh place, the team finished near the bottom of the league more than half the time. In 1935 slugger Wally Berger led the league in home runs and RBIs, but the Braves lost a club-record 115 games in their worst season ever.

In 1946, with dynamic new ownership headed by contractor Lou Perini, a new manager—Billy Southworth, who had led the Cardinals to three pennants and two world championships—and the return of war veterans like pitchers Warren Spahn and John Sain, the Braves neared the end of their long depression with their first winning season in eight years. At the end of the season Boston acquired third baseman Bob Elliott from Pittsburgh. He enjoyed a career year in 1947, powering the Braves to third place. Spahn and Sain won 21 games each.

Spahn dropped to 15 wins in 1948, but Sain won 24. Four veterans—plus rookie shortstop Alvin Dark—hit over .300. With the league's best pitching and hitting, the Braves moved out in front in June, and shook off their last challengers with a September spurt that left them at the end champions by 6½ games.

But from there on, the Braves' path in Boston was downhill. Cleveland beat them in the World Series, and the club dropped to fourth for the next three years. Southworth resigned part way into the 1951 season. In 1952 the team fell to seventh; home attendance was less than one-fifth what it had been four years earlier. The next spring Perini moved the franchise to Milwaukee in the league's first realignment since 1900.

The move was a spectacular success. Not only did the Braves rebound to second place, but attendance jumped 649 percent over their previous year in Boston to set an NL record of more than 1.8 million. The league's best pitching staff was led by the trio that would anchor Milwaukee's years of greatness: veteran Warren Spahn, sophomore Lew Burdette, and rookie Bob Buhl. Sophomore third baseman Eddie Mathews led the league in home runs; with outfielder Henry Aaron, who came up the next year, Mathews would give the Braves a consistent source of power through their Milwaukee years.

A July-August surge in 1954 pulled the Braves within a few games of the top before they slipped back, but they set another attendance record and became the first NL club to draw more than two million at home in a season. In 1955 the Braves finished a distant second to the Dodgers, but 1956 produced a great three-way race that found the Braves slightly ahead through much of the season until five straight losses in early September brought them even with the surging Dodgers. It was a dogfight the rest of the way, not settled until the final day, when a Dodger victory over Pittsburgh left Milwaukee a game back in second.

The acquisition of veteran second baseman Red Schoendienst from St. Louis in June 1957 steadied the infield and gave the team a frequent baserunner for Mathews and Aaron to drive in. In August the Braves drew away from the pack, and recovered from a September slump to win the pennant by a convincing 8 games over St. Louis. The Yankees took them to seven games in the World Series, but Burdette's shutout in the finale brought the Braves their first world championship in forty-three years.

Milwaukee repeated as league champions just as convincingly in 1958, but in the autumn classic, after taking the first two games from the Yankees, they lost the Series in seven. The race was much tighter in 1959 until the Giants moved away from the Dodgers and Braves in August. But in September the Giants faltered as the others surged past them, and the season ended with the Braves and Dodgers tied. In a best-of-three playoff, the Dodgers took the pennant in two games—but both by only one run and the second only after twelve innings.

A portent for the Braves' future could be seen in the crowd of under 20,000 that attended the first playoff game in Milwaukee. After setting a third NL record in 1957, Milwaukee attendance had gradually declined, dropping below two million in 1958, the club's second pennant year, and even farther in this year of the tight pennant race. As the Braves declined on the field to a more distant second in 1960, then successively to fourth, fifth, and sixth, so too did the decline continue in the stands to well under a million. Perini sold his majority interest in the club. A tighter race in 1964 stirred a little more fan interest, but when attendance dropped in 1965 to a new Milwaukee low of just over half a million, the club pulled up stakes again and moved to Atlanta.

The Braves' won-lost records in 1965 and '66 were nearly identical. But in Atlanta attendance improved by almost a million. Of the Braves who had brought glory to Milwaukee, most were gone from the club or in decline. But Aaron was still at the height of his powers, and younger players were beginning to make their mark. Reliever Phil Niekro, for example, was converted to a starter in 1967 and responded with the league's best ERA.

After finishing no higher than fifth in their first three seasons in Atlanta, the Braves celebrated 1969, the first year of divisional play, with a late-season drive that carried them out of a tight five-team race to the championship of the West.

Veteran Orlando Cepeda, newly acquired from St. Louis, joined Aaron in supplying power, and Niekro won 23 games as the Braves won ten in a row to clinch the title in their next-to-last game. In the league's first Championship Series, though, the "Miracle" Mets of New York swept Atlanta in three games.

Aaron remained a presence in Atlanta for five more years, and Niekro, after a relatively dismal season in 1970, established himself over the years as one of the game's most durable and effective pitchers. But the team went nowhere. When they enjoyed an occasional good season (as in 1974, when they won 88 games), at least two other clubs did much better. Aaron returned to Milwaukee (to the AL Brewers) in 1975, and attendance sank to an Atlanta low. Yachtsman Ted Turner bought the club in 1976 and attendance rose, but the team sank to the bottom of the division for four years.

In 1982, though, with power from outfielder Dale Murphy and third baseman Bob Horner, and exceptional pitching from Niekro (17–4) and reliever Gene Garber (30 saves, a club record), Atlanta grabbed the division lead with a season-opening 13-game winning streak, and recovered from a mid-summer collapse to edge Los Angeles by one game for their second divisional crown. Once again, though, they were swept in the LCS, this time by St. Louis.

For the next two seasons Murphy's league-leading slugging carried the Braves to second place—a close 3 games behind Los Angeles in 1983 (in a race which pushed Atlanta attendance over two million for the first time), and a tie with Houston 12 games behind San Diego the next year. In the ensuing years, Murphy remained hot, but the Braves did not; they have finished no higher than fifth, nor closer than 20½ games from the top. In 1988 Murphy's star slipped from its accustomed height and the Braves suffered their worst season in fifty-three years.

Baltimore Orioles

The history of major league baseball in Baltimore dates back to 1872, to the Lord Baltimores of the National Association, and includes the great National League Orioles of the 1890s. The city was also represented in the American League's first big league seasons, 1901–1902. But when those Orioles moved to New York in 1903 and became the Highlanders (later the Yankees), Baltimore was left without a big league club for more than half a century, until the transfer of the Browns from St. Louis in 1954.

The current Orioles didn't get their start in St. Louis, though. Their first home was Milwaukee, where they finished in the AL cellar in 1901. Moving to St. Louis the next year, they lured several key players from the city's NL Cardinals—including 1901 batting champ Jesse Burkett, star shortstop Bobby Wallace, and the Cards' three best pitchers. They also took on the Cardinals' discarded nickname: the Browns.

The Browns finished a strong second to the Philadelphia Athletics in their first St. Louis season, but fell to sixth the next year and, except for a fourth-place finish in 1908 (thanks to the pitching of newly acquired veteran Rube Waddell), remained mired in the second division until 1920. Late in the 1913 season a young Branch Rickey was hired to manage the Browns. In his two full seasons he was unable to lift the club out of the second division, but he did sign college star George Sisler (whom he had coached at the University of Michigan),

who became, as the Browns' first baseman, one of the game's all-time greats.

In 1916, his first full season, Sisler led the Browns in hitting as they caught fire in August to record their first winning season in eight years. Pitcher Urban Shocker was obtained from the Yankees two years later and by 1920 had developed into a 20-game winner. Also in 1920, Sisler connected for what is still a major league record 257 hits and batted .407 to help move the Browns up to fourth, their first finish that high since 1908 (though their won-lost record of 76–77 remained on the losing side). The next year Shocker's 27 victories brought them a winning season and third place. And in 1922 the team recorded its finest record ever in St. Louis: 93 wins and a .604 winning percentage.

The 1922 Browns, led by Sisler's sizzling .420 BA, hit .313 as a team to lead the league. Left fielder Ken Williams ran away with the RBI title and beat out Babe Ruth and Tilly Walker for the home run crown. (Ruth, to be honest, did miss nearly a third of the season that year.) Sisler and Williams even finished one-two in AL stolen bases. And though Shocker slipped a bit to 24 wins, he led a pitching staff that recorded the league's lowest ERA. The team led the league in the standings throughout July and into August before the Yankees nudged ahead of them. The Browns hung close, but didn't regain the lead, remaining second, a heartbreaking single game back, at season's end.

Falling back to fifth the next year, as Sisler missed the whole season with a sinus infection, the Browns remained out of contention for the next twenty-one years, dropping to their lowest point in 1939, 64½ games out of first, with 111 losses. They recovered for three winning seasons in the war years 1942–1945, finishing a distant third in 1942, and capturing their only St. Louis pennant in 1944, edging the Detroit Tigers on the final day after trailing them through most of September. The World Series—an all-St. Louis affair—proved anticlimactic for the Browns as they lost to the Cardinals in six games.

The Browns finished third in 1945 before sinking back into the second division. Even the club's purchase by the dynamic Bill Veeck in July 1951 couldn't rouse them out of the depths. (A month after buying the Browns, Veeck made his best-remembered move; bringing in midget Eddie Gaedel for one plate appearance—he walked.)

Unable to earn either victories or money in St. Louis, Veeck in September 1953 sold the club to a Baltimore group, who moved the Browns and renamed them the Orioles. The new owners hired the brilliant Paul Richards to rebuild the team as manager, both in the front office and on the field. It took him (and Lee MacPhail, who became general manager and president in 1958) several years to move the Orioles above .500, but in 1960, young third baseman Brooks Robinson found he could hit as well as field, and rookie Jim Gentile drove in 98 runs; the team made its first run for the pennant since 1944. In first place in early September, they finished second when the Yanks won fifteen straight to pass them by.

The next year the O's did even better, winning six more games than they had in 1960 as Gentile hit 46 home runs and drove in 141. But it was an even better year for New York and Detroit, and Baltimore finished a distant third.

When Hank Bauer was brought in to manage the Orioles in 1964, the team entered its golden decades—twenty years which saw them win seven division titles, six pennants, and three world championships, with only two finishes below

third. With Robinson driving in runs and left fielder Boog Powell slugging at a league-leading pace, the O's finished 1964 with wins in seven of their final eight games. But the White Sox won their last nine and the Yankees put together an eleven-game streak near the end to take the flag and leave Baltimore third, two games back.

After another third-place finish in 1965, the Orioles acquired slugging Frank Robinson from Cincinnati and moved second-year pitcher Jim Palmer into the starting rotation. Palmer won 15 to lead a balanced staff, and Frank Robinson captured the Triple Crown. With both Robinsons and Powell driving in 100 runs or more, the O's romped to their first Baltimore pennant. They continued the romp in the World Series, holding Los Angeles to a total of just two runs as they swept to their first world title.

A drop in offensive production and the loss of Palmer to injuries for most of the season plunged Baltimore into a tie for sixth in 1967. Palmer was out the next year, too, but pitchers Dave McNally and Jim Hardin burst to the forefront with fine seasons to lift the club back to second.

Baltimore coach Earl Weaver, a pennant-winning manger in the O's farm system, replaced Hank Bauer at the Orioles' helm in mid-1968 to begin what became one of the longest and most successful managerial tenures of recent times. In fourteen full seasons Weaver led his club to six Eastern Division titles and six second-place finishes, with one season each in third and fourth. His teams featured fine hitters and fielders, but it is the pitching that stands out above the rest. In seven of the fourteen years the Oriole staff compiled the league's lowest ERA, including five consecutive seasons (1969-1973). Oriole pitchers put together in those fourteen years twenty-one 20-win seasons (eight of them by Jim Palmer), and garnered six Cy Young Awards.

In the first three years of divisional play (1969-71) Baltimore ran away with the East championship and swept to the pennant each time in the League Championship Series. The 1969 team (despite an embarrassingly easy loss to the New York Mets in the World Series) is often ranked among the greatest of all time. With overwhelming pitching and fielding, the Orioles took the division crown by 19 games, winning a club-record 109. In fielding, seven percentage points separated the AL's second-best team from the worst; the Orioles fielded three points better than the second-best team. And Oriole pitchers gave up nearly a run less per game than the league average.

Baltimore's performance in 1970 was nearly as impressive. Mike Cuellar and Dave McNally won 24 games each, and Jim Palmer contributed 20 more wins to the O's total of 108. This year they won the World Series as well as the pennant, rolling over Cincinnati in five games.

In the 1971 World Series, though, Pittsburgh came back from losses in the first two games to defeat the Orioles by a run in game seven. The O's captured divisional titles in 1973 and '74, but it was 1979 before they again triumphed in the LCS. Once again, however, they faced the Pirates in the World Series, and once again took the Series lead, only to fall again in the seventh game.

The 1979 pennant was Weaver's last, as late-season Oriole surges in 1980 and '82 fell just short. But in 1983 the O's—paced by the pitching of veteran Scott McGregor and rookie Mike Boddicker, and the hitting and fielding of Cal Ripken, Jr., and Eddie Murray at short and first—made new manager Joe Altobelli look good. After a comfortable divisional win,

they trounced Chicago's White Sox in the LCS and the Philadelphia Phillies in the World Series.

In decline since 1983 despite the return of Earl Weaver in 1985-1986, the Orioles finished last in the East in 1986. Though they rose to sixth in 1987, their .414 winning percentage was their lowest in thirty-two years. Then in 1988 they hit rock bottom, not only finishing last but also beginning the season with an AL record-setting twenty-one consecutive defeats.

Boston Red Sox

Since the end of World War Two, the Red Sox have won the American League pennant four times, only to lose the World Series each time in the seventh game. It was not always thus. In their first two decades they were the league's most successful club, winners of six pennants and five world championships. (No World Series was played the year of their second pennant.)

Organized in 1901 as one of four new eastern clubs in Ban Johnson's newly major league AL, Boston's Americans (or Pilgrims, Puritans, Plymouth Rocks, or Somersets, as they were variously called) quickly established themselves as one of the game's strongest teams. Star third baseman Jimmy Collins was lured from Boston's NL club to manage the new Americans, and he assembled a team that included such former NL standouts as slugger Buck Freeman and pitcher Cy Young. Finishing a strong second in the AL's inaugural major league season, the Pilgrims quickly supplanted their mediocre NL counterparts in the hearts and wallets of Boston fans.

After a third-place finish in 1902, the Pilgrims ran away from the rest of the league in 1903 to take their first pennant by 14½ games over Philadelphia. Young led the league in victories for the third straight season, Freeman took titles in home runs, total bases, and RBIs, and second-year outfielder Patsy Dougherty finished first in hits and runs scored. In the first modern World Series, Boston overcame Pittsburgh's favored Pirates, thereby confirming in the public mind the AL's claim to major league status.

Boston repeated as pennant winners in 1904, but by a much narrower margin, after a struggle with New York's Highlanders that wasn't settled until the next-to-last day of the season. The NL Giants refused to play Boston in a World Series that year.

Over the next few years, as the Pilgrims dropped into the league cellar, new owner John I. Taylor (whose father, *Boston Globe* publisher Charles Taylor, was said to have bought the club for his son to give him something useful to do) rid the team of many of the players who had brought it glory. Eventually Taylor was himself maneuvered out of the club presidency, but it turned out he had not been a wanton destroyer. In driving out the old guard he had been making room for new young players: pitcher Joe Wood, for example, and a sprightly outfield of Tris Speaker, Harry Hooper, and Duffy Lewis. The club—now known as the Red Sox—rose out of its depths in the final years of Taylor's presidency, even challenging the league leaders through much of 1909 before dropping away in late August. In 1911, in one of the last acts of his presidency, Taylor had, with his father, purchased land in Boston's Fenway section and build a new ballpark.

Sparked by the spectacular pitching of Joe Wood and

Speaker's play at the bat and in center field, the Red Sox of 1912 took the league lead in early June and were never headed, finishing with a club-record 105 victories. In the World Series they edged John McGraw's Giants and Christy Mathewson in one of the most exciting Series ever, four games to three, with one tie. Three years later, with a staff that boasted the AL's four top pitchers in winning percentage (including rookie Babe Ruth), the Sox captured their fourth pennant, staving off a late-season surge by Detroit to finish 2½ games in front. After a first-game loss to the Phillies in the World Series, Boston recovered to sweep the next four by one run apiece.

Joe Wood's ailing arm finally gave out, and Tris Speaker was traded to Cleveland at the start of the 1916 season following a salary dispute. But with Ruth winning 23 games to lead the team, the Sox slid past the White Sox and Tigers in mid-September to take their fifth flag, and waltzed over Brooklyn in the Series.

Incipient disaster struck the Red Sox that December when New York theatrical entrepreneurs Hugh Ward and Harry Frazee bought the club. They put little cash into the deal, counting on future profits to pay the bulk of the purchase price. Ward sailed for Australia, leaving Frazee to run the club. For a while the future looked bright. After a second-place finish in 1917, Frazee hired minor league executive Ed Barrow as manager, and when many of the team's regulars left for military service in World War One, Frazee bought and traded for worthy replacements. In a season shortened a month because of the war, the Sox edged Cleveland for their sixth pennant and defeated the Chicago Cubs for their fifth world championship.

Frazee's theater losses put him in a financial bind and gradually forced him to sell off the best of his players—mostly to the Yankees, who had plenty of money, and an office just a short hop from Frazee's New York theater. Though the Sox fell to sixth place in 1919, Babe Ruth kept attention fixed on the team as he went to the outfield and startled the baseball world with a record 29 home runs. But that winter Frazee sold Ruth to the Yankees for $100,000 and a $300,000 mortgage on Fenway Park.

The Red Sox were embarked on a fifteen-year sojourn in the second division that even a 1923 change in ownership was powerless to end. In the eleven years from 1922 through 1932 the Sox emerged from last place only twice. In 1932 they reached their nadir, losing 111 games and finishing 64 games out of first.

But in 1933, young, wealthy Tom Yawkey bought the club and promptly began what would be a lifetime effort to restore Boston to its former glory. His first efforts to buy success ready-made with such established stars as Lefty Grove, Jimmie Foxx, and Joe Cronin pulled the club out of the cellar but failed to lift it into pennant contention. But as general manager Eddie Collins began turning up young players to join the veterans, the Sox's fortunes rose. The emergence between 1938 and 1942 of players like Bobby Doerr, Ted Williams, and pitcher Tex Hughson brought Boston a level of success not seen since 1918. In four of the five years they finished second to the Yankees, achieving in 1942 their highest winning percentage since 1915.

The loss of most of these newcomers to military service in World War Two delayed further progress. But with the arrival of rookie pitching sensation Dave Ferriss in 1945, and the acquisition of slugging first baseman Rudy York that winter,

the club was prepared for its returning war veterans to join in bringing Boston its greatest season since 1912. With 104 victories, the 1946 Sox won their long-delayed seventh pennant by 12 games over second-place Detroit. Only in the World Series was there disappointment as the heavily favored Sox bowed in Game Seven by one run.

The Yankees ran away from the pack in 1947, but the three years that followed saw the Red Sox three times in the throes of pennant fever. In 1948, after falling back a bit in late September, the Sox won four at the very end to tie Cleveland for first—but lost the one-game playoff. The next year they were 12 games behind the Yankees on July 4, but pulled up gradually to take a one-game lead into the final two-game series in New York. One Sox win would give them the flag, but the Yankees took both games. In 1950 Boston played the league's best ball through July and August, to pull within a game of the Yankees on September 18, but then lost four in a row and all hope of the pennant.

In 1951 the Sox collapsed at season's end to finish third, 11 games back. They came no closer for the next fifteen years, finishing with eight consecutive losing seasons from 1959 through 1966, when they suffered their second successive ninth-place finish in a league now expanded to ten teams.

In 1967 the Sox awakened from their long slumber. A ten-game win streak in mid-July shot them out of mediocrity into the midst of a four-team race for the pennant that was not settled until Boston beat Minnesota and Detroit split a doubleheader on the final day, leaving the Sox on top. Carl Yastrzemski, who had replaced Ted Williams in left field seven years earlier, replaced him now in the fans' awe as he clinched the Triple Crown with a game-winning home run and six other hits in the final two must-win games. But Boston lost the World Series to St. Louis in seven games.

It was eight years before the Red Sox won another pennant, but they came close in 1972, losing the AL East crown by half a game to Detroit in the season's final series. They led the division two years later from mid-July through early September, then fell apart and finished third. But the next year, 1975, they maintained to the end the lead they first took in May, and swept Oakland in the League Championship Series for their ninth pennant. Television viewers will long remember Carlton Fisk's home run that won Game Six of the World Series from Cincinnati. But Red Sox fans also remember that the Sox lost Game Seven the next day, 4–3. Owner Tom Yawkey died the following July without the world championship he had sought for more than forty years.

Boston contended seriously in 1977 in a tight three-way race, pulling ahead for a time in June and again in August, but ultimately falling 2½ games short. The next year, though, the Sox pulled off another amazing finish. After blowing a 7½-game late-August lead to fall 3⅓ games behind New York in mid-September, they won their final eight scheduled games to tie the Yankees. But in the playoff, Yankee Bucky Dent's three-run pop-fly homer over Fenway's cozy left field wall proved Boston's ruin. The Sox rallied in the eighth to draw within a run, but with two out and a man on third in the ninth, Yastrzemski popped up and the season was history.

Yaz retired in 1983, full of years and honor, but outfielders Jim Rice and Dwight Evans remained from the 1975 champions. Joined by a new generation that included, in Wade Boggs, baseball's most consistent hitter since Ted Williams, and, in Roger Clemens, Boston's most exciting pitcher since Joe Wood, the Sox in 1986 won their tenth pennant, with an

amazing comeback over California from a 3–1 deficit in the LCS. In Game Six of the World Series they were within one pitch of capturing their first world title in 68 years. But they lost the game, and in Game Seven—once again—the Series.

In 1988 the Sox stumbled to the AL East crown, losing six of their final seven games. In the LCS they went down meekly in four straight games to Oakland.

California Angels

Of the ten teams added to the major leagues in the 1960s and '70s, the Angels were quickest to put together a winning season, finishing third in the American League in only their second year of play.

Former cowboy actor and singer Gene Autry brought the club into being as the Los Angeles Angels in December 1960. Playing their first season, 1961, in Los Angeles's Wrigley Field, a former minor league park with power alleys only five feet deeper than the foul poles, five Angels hit 20 or more home runs. Though the team finished seventh in the standings, they were second in homers only to the mighty Yankees.

What the Angels lost in home runs in 1962 (when they moved out of Wrigley Field into the L.A. Dodgers' new stadium), they more than made up in pitching. Paced by rookie Dean Chance, the Angels nearly doubled their wins on the road, and as late as mid-August stood in second place, within striking distance of New York. Though they tailed off in September, they finished a respectable third, 10 games back.

The team collapsed to ninth the next year, but in 1964 Chance's pitching and splendid relief by rookie Bob Lee overcame the Angels' continuing inertia at the bat to lift them back into the first division. Among Chance's league-leading 11 shutouts were six 1–0 victories.

Los Angeles became the California Angels in 1965 in anticipation of their move south to a new stadium in Anaheim the following year, but neither the name change nor the new location stirred them out of the second division. In 1967, though, with below-average run production but the league's third-best pitching, the Angels in midseason shot up from ninth to third before leveling off to fifth. After dismal seasons in 1968–1969, career years in 1970 by pitcher Clyde Wright (22 wins, including a no-hitter) and newly acquired left fielder Alex Johnson (202 hits and a league-high .329 BA) helped the Angels snap back with an 86–76 record that matched their previous best (1962).

The seven losing seasons which followed 1970 were somewhat redeemed by the arrival in 1972 of pitcher Nolan Ryan, who burst into superstardom as an Angel, setting a modern record of 383 strikeouts in 1973 and hurling four no-hitters in three years (1973–1975). Ryan's effectiveness dipped in 1978, but the club as a whole came to life, contending closely for the Western Division title all season until Kansas City shot ahead in September.

In 1979 Don Baylor became the first (and, so far, only) DH to be named league MVP, as a renewed offense powered California to its first division title. Baltimore stopped the Angels in the League Championship Series, though. The team's run production dropped off dramatically the next year and the club followed up its best season with its worst.

After another losing season in 1981 (during which Jim Fregosi was replaced as manager by twenty-year veteran Gene Mauch), California lured free-agent slugger Reggie Jackson from the Yankees. With Jackson leading a resurgent offense and Geoff Zahn headlining the league's second-best pitching staff, the Angels rebounded to a new team high of 93 wins in 1982, and their second division title. They defeated Milwaukee in the first two games of the LCS, but lost the next three. A disappointed manager Mauch retired.

Again, in 1983, the Angels followed a championship with a poor season—not quite as bad as 1980, but still their third worst ever. In 1984 they rebounded to .500, good enough for second in a weak division. As a foretaste of continuing improvement, pitcher Mike Witt concluded his rise to staff ace with a perfect game on the season's last day.

Gene Mauch came out of retirement to manage the Angels again in 1985. With pitching that featured splendid relief from newly acquired Donnie Moore (31 saves; 1.92 ERA), the team led the division much of the season, but lost three games of four to Kansas City in the final week to fall a game behind the Royals into second.

With Witt's 18 wins and 2.84 ERA pacing the staff and rookie first baseman Wally Joyner leading a revitalized offset, California won the 1986 division crown with ease. In the LCS against Boston, the Angels took three of the first four games, and in Game Five were within one pitch of capturing their first pennant. But the Boston Red Sox rallied to win.

In 1987 California for the third time followed up their division championship with a losing season, this time dropping the season finale to tie for last place in the AL West.

Chicago Cubs

The Chicago Cubs have represented the same city in the major leagues longer than any other club. Organized in 1870 to provide a professional challenge to Cincinnati's Red Stockings, the White Stockings (as they were originally known) were one of the founding members of the game's first professional league—the National Association—the next year.

Despite the great Chicago fire, which destroyed their ballpark, uniforms, and club business records late in the 1871 season, the White Stockings completed their schedule, finishing a close second to the Athletics of Philadelphia. But they dropped out of the NA for the next two years because of the fire's devastation. In 1875, in the midst of a second losing season following their return, the club arranged for four of champion Boston's best players to jump to Chicago for the 1876 season. That winter, White Stocking president William A. Hulbert and pitcher/manager Al Spalding (one of the jumpers) led in forming a new league to replace the NA.

Sparked by its Boston players and infielder Adrian "Cap" Anson (lured from the Athletics), the White Stockings in 1876 outscored their opponents by more than five runs per game and handily won the first championship of the new National League. The next year, though, when Spalding (whose pitching had brought Chicago 47 of its 52 victories in 1876) switched over to first base, the club fell off to fifth.

Spalding retired from the field in 1878 to attend to his young sporting goods firm (though he returned as club president from 1882 through 1891). In 1879 Anson was named to manage the team. Leading the league in batting, he restored the White Stockings to their winning ways, and in 1880 led them back to the top.

For twelve years the White Stockings ranked among baseball's best, garnering five pennants (1880–1882, 1885–1886)

and four second-place finishes. Anson's stern morality and strict discipline did not make him popular with his often rowdy teammates, but his consistency as a player set an example, and his innovative management made the most of his players' drive and aggressiveness. Anson's forcefulness, however, contributed to baseball's most grievous setback: his adamant refusal in the mid-1880s to take the field against black players prevented the racial integration of the major leagues that had up to then seemed imminent.

After a close finish behind Boston in 1891, the White Stockings' first era as a National League power ended. In each of the next eleven seasons they fell at least 15 games short of the top. The team's youthful ineptitude was reflected in the nicknames that succeeded "White Stockings": the "Colts," the "Orphans" (in 1898, after Anson—by then known as "Pop"—was fired after nineteen years at the helm), and finally, the "Cubs."

When Frank Selee (who had led Boston to greatness in the 1890s) was hired to manage the Cubs in 1902, he inherited a team that had ended the 1901 season 37 games out, its worst finish up to then. By 1903 he had turned catcher/outfielder Frank Chance into a first baseman, moved Joe Tinker from third to short, and brought up Johnny Evers from Troy to play second. The new double-play combination flourished not only in the field but at the bat. The Cubs finished third in 1903 with their best record in a dozen years.

That winter Selee traded for pitcher Mordecai "Three Finger" Brown, and in 1905 signed rookie hurler Ed Reulbach. After leading the Cubs to second place in 1904, Selee, ill with tuberculosis, took a leave of absence in the middle of the 1905 season. Chance took his place and brought the team to third.

Selee never returned, but he had gone a long way toward building a championship team. Trades for outfielder Jimmy Sheckard and third baseman Harry Steinfeldt, the signing of rookie pitcher Jack Pfiester, and the acquisition during the 1906 season of pitchers Orval Overall and Jack Taylor completed one of the greatest teams of all time. The Cubs passed the Giants to take the lead early in May and kept on rising. New York and Pittsburgh made a race of it through July, but the Cubs won 55 of their final 65 games to finish with a record 116 victories, 20 games ahead of second-place New York. The hitting of Steinfeldt and Chance led the Cubs to the top of the league in batting and slugging, and the club topped all others in fielding. But it was the Cub pitching that stood out most. Brown's 1.04 ERA was the league's best, with those of Pfiester and Reulbach second and third. The team ERA of 1.76 was the first below 2.00 since the pitching distance was increased to 60'6" in 1893. Over all, Chicago scored 80 more runs than its nearest rival, and yielded 89 fewer.

But in the World Series, the crosstown "hitless wonder" White Sox matched the Cubs' hitting and pitched twice as effectively to take the crown in six games. It was the third time the Cubs had failed to win the world title: in two of the earliest Series, they had tied the St. Louis Browns by 3–3–1 in 1885, and lost to them the next year, 2–4.

The Cubs' hitting and run production fell off in 1907, but their pitching did not (ERA: 1.73). With 107 wins, they captured their second straight pennant, by 17 games. This time their dominance carried over into the World Series as they swept Detroit after an opening-game tie.

The pennant race of 1908, in sharp contrast to those of the previous two years, was one of the tightest in baseball history. On September 22 the Cubs won two from the Giants to pull into a virtual tie for first (with Pittsburgh third, 1½ games back). The next day the Giants appeared to have beaten the Cubs with an RBI single in the last of the ninth. But young Fred Merkle, on first when the hit was made, seeing the runner on third cross the plate, failed to continue on to second himself and was forced out by alert Cub second baseman Johnny Evers for the third out, which negated the Giant run. Because of increasing darkness and the mood of excited fans on the field, the game was called and ruled a tie. After another week and a half in which all three teams took turns in front, Chicago defeated Pittsburgh to pull ahead by half a game, leaving the Pirates and Giants tied for second. But New York had one more game—and defeated the Boston Braves to pull into a tie with the Cubs. The "Merkle boner" game thus had to be replayed, and this time the Cubs won to take their third straight pennant. In the World Series they again beat Detroit in five games. Their second straight world title was also, to date, their last.

In 1909 the Cubs won 104 games as their pitching staff for the third time in four years recorded an ERA under 2.00, but the club trailed Pittsburgh throughout the season and finished second. In 1910, however, their 104 wins carried them to another pennant, by a comfortable 13 games. It was their last championship of the Chance era. After a World Series loss to the Philadelphia Athletics, and seasons in second and third place, Chance resigned, protesting the unwillingness of owner Charles Murphy to spend money for top players.

The Cubs got a new owner in 1916, and with him a new ballpark. Charles Weeghman, who had owned the Chicago Whales in the short-lived Federal League, purchased the Cubs when the FL went under, and moved them into the park he had built for the Whales. Although there has been recent talk of moving the Cubs out of what is now Wrigley Field, the introduction of night baseball in 1988 assures continuing play in this crown jewel of ballparks.

The team that next carried Chicago to the pennant, in the war-shortened season of 1918, featured only one name familiar to Cubs fans from earlier championship seasons—Fred Merkle. The man whose rookie boner as a Giant had made possible their pennant in 1908 was now their leading run producer. As in earlier pennant-winning seasons, fine pitching predominated, with veteran James "Hippo" Vaughn the league's best pitcher on the league's top staff.

Several years of decline followed the Cubs' World Series loss to the Boston Red Sox. The club hit bottom in 1925 with its first cellar finish in fifty-three years of league play, but a new era of greatness was at hand. In 1921 wealthy chewing-gum manufacturer William Wrigley had purchased control of the Cubs, with a determination to spend what was needed to produce a winner.

The seeds Wrigley planted eventually bore fruit. In 1926 he hired Joe McCarthy—a successful minor league manager—to lead the club, and drafted outfielder Lewis "Hack" Wilson from Toledo. Wilson immediately became one of the league's leading offensive threats, and the Cubs rebounded to the first division. In 1927 they even led the league through August before dropping back to fourth. A postseason trade brought them outfielder Hazen "Kiki" Cuyler, and a close third-place finish in 1928. Then the Cubs traded with the Braves for second baseman Rogers Hornsby, and in 1929 returned to the top. Led by Wilson's 159 RBIs and Hornsby's 149, five Cubs drove in more than 90 runs each. After battling Pittsburgh for the lead through mid-July, the Cubs hurtled ahead to take the

pennant by 10½ games, despite a late-season slump. The slump continued through the World Series, though, as the Athletics humbled the Cubs in five games.

Just four games from the end of the hot pennant race in 1930 (the year Wilson set the major league RBI record with 190), McCarthy—still smarting from criticism arising from the World Series loss—quit as manager. With Hornsby at the helm, the Cubs preserved a second-place finish. They dropped to third the next year, but returned to the top in 1932. Hornsby, near the end of his playing days, was dropped as manager in August, with the Cubs in second, and replaced by first baseman Charlie Grimm. Pitcher Lon Warneke, in his first full season as a starter, led the league in wins and ERA. The club enjoyed a hot streak in August to move out in front of slumping Pittsburgh and hung on to take the flag by four games. The Yankees provided the World Series humiliation this time, a four-game sweep that provided McCarthy (now the Yankee manager) with sweet revenge for the Chicago fans' criticism three years earlier.

It had become a pattern: three years, another pennant. In 1935 a balanced offense (led by catcher "Gabby" Hartnett and second baseman Billy Herman) and the league's best pitching brought the Cubs up from fourth in late June to first in September. They clinched the pennant with three games to go, with their twentieth win of a 21-game streak. In the World Series, Detroit stopped the Cubs in six games.

After two seasons in second, it was time for another pennant. Bill Lee, the Cubs' top pitcher in 1935, was now the league's finest, as was the Cubs' staff. With the club languishing 6½ games back in midseason, Grimm quit as manager and was replaced by catcher Hartnett. In September the Cubs came to life, rising to second early in the month. They overtook Pittsburgh on September 28 with their ninth consecutive win—on Hartnett's homer against the Pirates in the growing darkness with two away in the bottom of the ninth—and clinched the pennant four games later, on the next-to-last day of the season. It was their fourth pennant at three-year intervals—and their sixth straight World Series loss, another Yankee sweep.

In 1940, after fourteen straight winning seasons, the Cubs began a five-year stretch below .500. Jimmie Wilson replaced Hartnett as manager in 1941; then Grimm returned near the start of the 1944 season. The club finished a distant fourth that year, but in 1945, after a middling start, they won twenty-six of thirty midseason games to take a lead they never relinquished. Balanced pitching (sparked by Hank Borowy, who went 11–2 after coming over from the Yankees in July) and the hitting of veteran first baseman Phil Cavarretta (.355) and rookie center fielder Andy Pafko (110 RBIs) held off the pressing St. Louis Cardinals to preserve a sixteenth Cub pennant. But although they battled Detroit through a full seven games in the World Series, they ended up losing again—their ninth defeat in twelve tries.

For the next twenty-three years the Cubs remained out of pennant contention. But in 1969, the first year of divisional play, under the lively management of Leo Durocher, they took an early lead in the NL East. With a potent offense led by veteran sluggers Ron Santo, Ernie Banks, and Billy Williams, the team continued rising through early August. But the New York Mets rose even faster and farther; they didn't pause when Chicago leveled off in late August, and while the Cubs were losing eight straight in September the Mets were winning ten in a row. The Cubs wound up 8 games back.

The next year Chicago started well, slumped in late June, then fought back into the thick of the race in September before fading to another second-place finish. Three years later, in 1973, the Cubs entered July with a substantial lead. Although they fell to fifth by season's end, in the tightly packed division they were only 5 games back. It was to be their closest finish for eleven years.

In 1981 the Wrigley family, no longer able to bankroll a winner, sold the club to the Chicago Tribune Company. Three years later, with a new manager, Jim Frey, and an almost wholly different roster, the new management capped its rebuilding program with the acquisition from Cleveland, in mid-June 1984, of pitcher Rick Sutcliffe. As Sutcliffe fashioned a 16–1 record for his new club, the Cubs moved in front to stay on August 1, and kept on rising to capture their first division title by 6½ games.

Their fall was as rapid as their rise. After winning the first two games of the League Championship Series against San Diego, the pennant was swept out from under them as the Padres took the final three. In four losing seasons since 1984, the Cubs have finished no closer than 18½ games to the division winner.

Chicago White Sox

When minor league owner Charlie Comiskey transferred his club from St. Paul to Chicago as part of the move to upgrade the American League to major league status, he called it the White Stockings, after the Chicago team that dominated the National League in its early years. The new Chicago team revived memories of the old White Stockings, winning the AL championship in 1900, and repeating the triumph in 1901, the league's first major league season. Manager Clark Griffith (who had jumped to the White Stockings from Chicago's NL Cubs) was the team's star pitcher in 1901, winning 24 of 31 decisions as his team took the lead in May and held off the threatening Boston Somersets the rest of the way.

Griffith's effectiveness fell off in 1902, as did the team, (now called the White Sox) which took a sizable lead in July, only to slide back to fourth in August. Griffith left the next year and the White Sox sank to seventh. It would take eighteen years and baseball's greatest scandal for the Sox to finish that low again.

In 1904, after center fielder Fielder Jones replaced left fielder Nixey Callahan as manager, they rose into first place for a moment in August before settling back to third. The next year they made up a seven-game deficit in September to catch the Philadelphia Athletics, but the loss of two games to the A's stalled their drive and left them in second.

Nothing stalled the White Sox drive in 1906. Although they ranked at the very bottom of the league in hitting and entered June five games below .500, their pitching and hustle pulled them through. "Big Ed" Walsh, who had finally mastered the spitball after two years of trying, won 17 games, including a league-high 10 shutouts. Doc White contributed 18 wins with a league-best 1.52 ERA, and Frank Owen and Nick Altrock won 22 and 20, respectively. The Sox shot to the top in August with a 19-game win streak (including 8 shutouts). Early in September, New York's Highlanders passed them, but after the two teams had traded the lead back and forth for a couple of weeks the Sox spurted to take the pennant by 3 games. If the race was close, so were the individ-

ual games: the Sox achieved nearly one-third of their victories by the margin of a single run. The "hitless wonders" carried their momentum through the World Series, shocking the mighty crosstown Cubs (who had won a record 116 games that year) four games to two.

In 1907, after leading the league much of the first half, the Sox slipped to third. The next year Walsh pitched in the final seven games on his way to a career-high 40 wins. In a tight finish he pulled the Sox to within a half game of first-place Detroit before they dropped back to third with a loss to the Tigers on the final day.

It was 1915 before the Sox (piloted by rookie manager Clarence H. "Pants" Rowland) next finished that high, and 1916 before they again challenged seriously for the pennant. Comiskey, though accused of pinching pennies in his payment of players, was willing to spend what was needed to acquire them. After the 1914 season he purchased star second baseman Eddie Collins from the A's, and promising young Oscar "Happy" Felsch from minor league Milwaukee. The following August he acquired the great Joe Jackson from Cleveland. Together with the league's best pitching staff, they carried the Sox into the thick of a three-way race and a close second-place finish in 1916, and in 1917 to the pennant with the best winning percentage the club has ever compiled. Ten-year veteran pitcher Eddie Cicotte enjoyed his first 20-win season with a league-high 28 victories, and a league- and career-best 1.53 ERA. After dueling the Boston Red Sox most of the season, Chicago streaked out of reach in late August to finish with 100 wins and a 9-game lead. In the World Series against the New York Giants they captured their second (and, to date, their last) world title, in six games.

With several key players out much of 1918 for military or civilian war service, the White Sox finished out of the running, a dismal sixth. But in 1919, with the team back at full strength, the race once again went to Chicago. If their pitching didn't have quite the depth of the 1917 squad, its best hurlers were in peak form. Cicotte, after an off-year in 1918, attained a career high with 29 wins, as did Lefty Williams with 23 victories. Collins and Jackson enjoyed their best seasons in several years, and infielder Buck Weaver had never been better. Old-time pitcher/second baseman Kid Gleason was a rookie as a big league manager, but his Sox began strong and, after slipping briefly into second in midseason, pulled ahead in July to stay.

When the Sox lost the World Series to underdog Cincinnati, there were rumors of a fix, but nothing came to light for nearly a year. The White Sox looked better than ever in 1920. Though they fell back in May after a hot April, by mid-August they had risen to the thick of a tight three-team race. Felsch, Collins, and Weaver had never played better, Jackson was enjoying one of his very best seasons, and four pitchers were on their way to more than 20 wins. Chicago might not have caught Cleveland's rampaging Indians, but it didn't help that talk of a White Sox scandal revived late in the season, or that the grand jury convened only eight games from the end, or that eight Sox players were indicted and suspended with just three games to play. The teamed finished two games back, in second place.

The indicted players—among whom were Cicotte, Felsch, Jackson, Weaver, and Williams—were acquitted in court when three crucial confessions disappeared, but they were banned for life from organized baseball by commissioner K. M. Landis. The White Sox did not soon recover from the

loss. In 1921 they began fifteen years of wandering in the second division, including three seasons in the cellar and one seventh-place finish (in 1932) that, while not the league's most distant, remains the farthest out Chicago has ever finished, 56½ games behind champion New York.

Two of the club's greatest and most durable players arrived during these years: pitcher Ted Lyons (who won 260 games for the Sox over twenty-one years) in 1923, and in 1930 shortstop Luke Appling (who averaged .310 in his twenty years with the club). Owner Comiskey died in 1931, in the midst of his Sox's most dismal era, but Lyons and Appling were around long enough to enjoy a few fourth- and third-place seasons. But neither saw the Sox contend seriously for the pennant. After his playing career was over, Lyons managed the team for a few years—until 1948, when the Sox lost 101 games and finished last.

That year Frank Lane was lured from the presidency of the American Association to take charge as Chicago's general manager. He began reshaping the team, and after two more losing seasons the White Sox's fortunes began to rise. When Lane hired Paul Richards to manage the club in 1951, the Sox began what became a seventeen-year string of winning seasons.

In 1951, Richards's first season, the Sox spent a month in first place before drifting down to fourth, and the next year began a five-year stopover in third place. In 1954 they won 94 games but were out of the race by August—that was the year Cleveland won 111 and the second-place Yankees 103. Richards moved on to Baltimore, but Marty Marion, who replaced him, kept the Sox in third place. Their 91 wins in 1955 earned them a much tighter race than '54, one that found them in first place at the start of September, until four straight losses dropped them to third.

Frank Lane left at the end of the 1955 season, and young Chuck Comiskey (one of the grandchildren of Charlie Comiskey who now owned the club) took over the front office. A year later Comiskey replaced Marion with Al Lopez, who had piloted the great Cleveland club of 1954 and whose teams, in his six seasons of managing, had never finished below second. Lopez continued his success in Chicago: the Sox moved up to second (though well behind the Yankees) in 1957 and '58. In March 1959, Bill Veeck (who had in previous years owned the Cleveland Indians and the St. Louis Browns) bought a controlling interest in the White Sox from the Comiskey family and stepped into instant success.

With the Yankees suffering an off-year in 1959, Chicago and Cleveland battled for the lead throughout the summer, until the White Sox pulled away in late August. The same 94–60 record that had given them only a distant third in 1954 now carried them to their first pennant in forty years. The close and successful pennant race, and the club's dynamic new ownership, pushed Sox home attendance up more than 78 percent to a new club record.

As they had in 1906, pitching and hustle won the Sox their 1959 pennant. The league's best staff was led by veteran Early Wynn (enjoying his last big season with a league high of 22 wins) and young Bob Shaw (with a career high of 18), and featured the league's top relievers in Gerry Staley and Turk Lown. Shortstop Luis Aparicio, in the midst of a nine-year reign as stolen-base leader, set a personal high in runs scored as the club went 35–15 in one-run games. But in the World Series, Los Angeles stopped Chicago in six games.

The next year the Sox remained competitive until Septem-

ber, but finished third. After dropping to fourth and fifth the next two years (in a league now expanded to ten teams), they returned to second in 1963. The next year the Sox finished a season-long three-way race with nine straight wins, enough to pull them past Baltimore, but a game short of catching the Yankees, whose eleven-game streak a week earlier had put them out in front. After a third straight second-place finish in 1965, manager Lopez resigned for health reasons.

Under Eddie Stanky—and with the AL's stingiest pitching staff in forty-nine years—the Sox competed into the final week of a hot 1967 race, when five straight losses at the end dropped them to fourth. Only twice in the next thirteen years would they rise above .500; in 1970 they lost a club-record 106 games to finish at the bottom of the AL West. Two years later they took the division lead briefly in late August before dropping back to second, and in 1977 they held the lead through much of the summer before tailing off to third.

Bill Veeck had sold the club and repurchased it in 1976. But in January 1981, after three losing seasons and troubled by poor health and skyrocketing player salaries, he sold the Sox once again, to a group headed by Jerry Reinsdorf and Eddie Einhorn. With Reinsdorf heading the club's baseball operations and lawyer Tony LaRussa piloting the team on the field, the Sox became by 1983 one of the best teams in baseball. With their best record since 1920, the 1983 Sox carried the AL West by 20 games. Rookie slugger Ron Kittle led the attack, backed up by fourth-year outfielder Harold Baines and resurgent old-timers Greg Luzinski and Carlton Fisk. Pitchers LaMarr Hoyt and Rich Dotson attained personal bests to lead the majors in wins (with 24 and 22), and White Sox home attendance for the first time topped two million. In the League Championship Series, though, after a close win over Baltimore in the opener, Chicago lost the next three games and the pennant. The Sox's pitching and offense (except for Baines) collapsed the next season, and the team has not contended seriously since.

Cincinnati Reds

The Red Stockings was the nickname of two pioneering Cincinnati ballclubs—the first avowedly professional team, which was undefeated in 1869, and the charter member club in the National League of 1876–1880. After a year on the sidelines, the reformed Reds joined the new American Association and captured the 1882 pennant by 11½ games, with a .688 winning percentage that is still the club record. Seven Reds enjoyed career highs in batting, pitcher Will White led the association with 40 wins, and rookie second baseman John "Bid" McPhee proved himself already one of the game's classiest fielders. The Reds even won one of a pair of post-season exhibition games with Chicago's White Stockings, champions of the older and stronger National League.

McPhee remained eighteen years with the Reds and established himself as the finest second baseman of the nineteenth century. But the club would go thirty-seven years before it won another pennant. Twice in their seven remaining years in the AA the Reds finished second, and they enjoyed six winning seasons. Transferring from the AA to the NL in 1890, they finished fourth; at 10½ games out of first, it was their closest finish in the thirty-four years between 1884 and their next pennant-winning season, 1919.

The Reds wound up in the cellar for the first time in 1901.

The next year club owner John T. Brush sold out to a group of Cincinnati's political bosses, who in mid-August named August "Garry" Herrmann (formerly head of the water works commission) to run it. Herrmann promptly acquired two outfielders from Baltimore—Cy Seymour and Joe Kelley, who was appointed team manager—who helped pull the Reds up to .500 and to fourth place by season's end. Three winning seasons followed, but then came eleven years in which the Reds finished above .500 only once (and then by only one game). Herrmann, meanwhile had found his calling in baseball administration. He not only remained president of the Reds for twenty-five years, but he also chaired the three-man National Commission that oversaw organized baseball, from its establishment in 1903 until 1920 (when his resignation brought about the commission's demise).

A midseason trade in 1916 brought the Reds Christy Mathewson (at the end of his pitching career) to manage the team, plus outfielder Edd Roush. The next year, with Roush leading the league in batting, the Reds edged above .500 and into fourth place. In 1918 an August spurt boosted the Reds into third place, in a season shortened by a month at the end because of the World War. Roush enjoyed another banner year, but Mathewson left for the Army just before the season ended.

First baseman Hal Chase—suspected of throwing games—was traded away after the season and replaced by veteran Jake Daubert. Southpaw Slim Sallee was purchased from the Giants and righthander Ray Fisher from the Yankees. Pat Moran (who had led the Phillies to a pennant in 1915) was hired to replace Mathewson at the Cincinnati helm. Thus fortified, the Reds in 1919 won their second pennant. Three pitchers—Sallee (21–7), Hod Eller (20–9), and Dutch Ruether (19–7, 1.82 ERA)—reached career peaks, Fisher (14–5) enjoyed one of his best years, Roush won another batting title and finished second in NL RBIs, and three Reds finished in the league's top four in runs scored. The Reds broke quickly at the start, but faltered in May and didn't pass the Giants into first place for good until late July. But from then on, they increased their lead to the end, finishing 9 games in front. Rumors of a White Sox fix to throw the World Series clouded the Reds' Series triumph—and spoiled it entirely when, a year later, the scandal became public and the truth of the rumors was confirmed.

In 1920 Cincinnati led the league entering September, but Brooklyn spurted and the Reds slumped to a third-place finish, 10½ games out. They dropped to sixth in 1921, but recovered for five years in the first division, including three second-place finishes. But only in 1926 did the Reds contend closely for the flag. After leading the league much of the first half of the season, they found themselves in the second half tangled in a three-way battle with St. Louis and Pittsburgh. But after surging into a narrow lead with seven straight wins in mid-September, they lost their next five games and wound up 2 games back of the Cardinals in second place.

The Reds finished the eleven years after 1926 in the second division, hitting bottom with four straight cellar finishes in 1931–1934. President Herrmann retired after the 1927 season, and within two years a controlling interest in the Reds was sold to a wealthy Cincinnatian, Sidney Weil. But Weil lost his fortune in the stock market crash of 1929 and the Depression that followed. While he continued to run the Reds for four years, his stock in the club was held by the Central Trust Company. In his efforts to turn the club around, Weil

acquired catcher Ernie Lombardi from Brooklyn in March 1932, and pitcher Paul Derringer from the St. Louis Cardinals the following May. Neither made an immediate impact (Derringer lost 25 games in his first Red season and 21 the next), but both remained with the club long enough to star in its return to glory. Owner Weil, however, relinquished his control to the bank in 1933, at the depth of the Depression and of the team's fortunes.

The bank hired Larry MacPhail (who had rescued minor league Columbus by introducing night baseball there) to run the Reds. MacPhail in turn hired Frank Lane to develop a minor league farm system, and persuaded Cincinnati industrialist Powel Crosley, Jr., to invest in the club. On May 24, 1935, Crosley and MacPhail brought night ball to the major leagues (the Reds, with Derringer pitching, beat the Phillies 2–1), and with it a sharp upswing in attendance at Crosley Field. By June 1936, Crosley's increased investment in the Reds had made him the majority owner. The temperamental MacPhail quit suddenly in mid-September 1936, but the Reds replaced him with another successful minor league executive, Warren Giles, who ran the club until his selection in 1952 as president of the NL.

After rising to sixth place in 1935 and fifth the next year, the Reds dropped back into the cellar in 1937. But the following year, under new manager Bill McKechnie, they rose into the first division once again—even holding second place briefly in September before slipping to fourth. Derringer enjoyed the first of three peak seasons, young Johnny Vander Meer contributed 15 wins (including two consecutive no-hitters) and Bucky Walters, after his acquisition from the Phillies in June, compiled his first winning season since converting from third baseman to pitcher in 1935. Catcher Lombardi led the NL in batting, and first baseman Frank McCormick, in his first full season, led the team in RBIs and the league in hits. The stage was set for the club's first back-to-back pennants.

Several Reds reached the apex of their careers in 1939, among them Walters (27–11) and Derringer (25–7), who between them topped most of the league's pitching stats, and Frank McCormick, who led the league in RBIs and hits and finished second in batting. The club pulled out of the pack to the front before the end of May and held the lead to the end, although St. Louis closed the gap with a late-season surge before slipping 4½ games back.

Cincinnati's sweep by the Yankees in the World Series was something of a shock, but the club had recovered its poise by the next spring. Starting strong and—except for a small dip in August—pushing steadily upward throughout the season, the Reds shook off the persistent Dodgers in midseason and finished 12 games in front with their first 100-win season. Mc-Cormick and Lombardi powered the offense, and Walters for the second year in a row took NL crowns in wins and ERA. This time the team's triumph carried through the World Series as Walters and Derringer won two games apiece to edge the Detroit Tigers in seven games.

The Reds' pitching remained strong in 1941, but their hitting and run production fell off and the team struggled to finish third. They remained in the upper division through 1944, but then dropped into an eleven-year trough of losing seasons in which, while they never sank into the cellar, they never rose above fifth.

Ted Kluszewski was in his ninth season as the Reds' slugging first baseman when Cincinnati next offered a serious run for the pennant in 1956 under manager Birdie Tebbetts. Kluszewski led the club in hitting and RBIs, but his 35 home runs were good enough only for third behind rookie Frank Robinson's 38 and Wally Post's 36 on a team that hammered 221 during the season to tie the major league record set nine years earlier by the Giants. The Reds' offense (they led the league in runs scored) kept them in the thick of a three-team race throughout the season, and they finished only 2 games out. For the first time ever they drew more than a million fans at home.

The Reds dropped out of a tight race in August 1957, and suffered losing seasons the next three years. After the 1960 season, Gabe Paul, who had succeeded Warren Giles as club president and general manager, left to help organize the new Houston club, and the following spring owner Crosley died. Bill DeWitt, who replaced Paul as president (and ultimately purchased control of the club), acquired pitcher Joey Jay from the Milwaukee Braves and third baseman Gene Freese from the White Sox. Jay in 1961 won twelve games more than his previous season high—tying for the league lead with 21, and Freese homered 26 times and drove in 87 runs—both career highs. Most of the team improved on their 1960 stats, and despite a poor start that saw them enter May in last place, the Reds had risen to the top by mid-June. The streaking Dodgers caught them briefly in August, but then fell away as the Reds pushed their pennant-winning margin to 4 games. In the World Series, though, it was the Yankees in five games.

The Reds next threatened in 1964 when, in a wild three-way finish, they won nine straight in late September to take first place for a day before slipping into a tie for second, one game behind St. Louis. In 1965 a young Pete Rose recorded the first of his ten 200-hit seasons as the Reds battled among the leaders through much of the summer before dropping off to fourth.

That December, after a decade of standout offense in Cincinnati, Frank Robinson was traded to Baltimore. The next year, while Robinson won the Triple Crown in assisting his new team to the world championship, the Reds suffered their first losing season in six years and sank to seventh place. That winter, owner DeWitt completed the sale of the team to a group led by Cincinnati newspaper publisher Francis Dale, and including brothers James and William Williams who later acquired a controlling interest in the club.

In 1969, the first year of divisional play, the Reds rose, after a slow start, into the thick of a five-way race in the NL West before stumbling as Atlanta and San Francisco surged in the final three weeks. But the season provided a foretaste of the decade to come as the team captured league crowns in slugging and home runs.

At midseason in 1970 the Reds moved out of Crosley Field—their home for fifty-eight years—into the new Riverfront Stadium. Catcher Johnny Bench and third baseman Tony Perez, with the finest seasons of their long careers, paced an overwhelming Red offense as the team hammered out a new club-high 102 wins to reward rookie manager Sparky Anderson with victory in the NL West by 14½ games. In the League Championship Series the Reds continued their triumph with a three-game sweep of East winner Pittsburgh. But mighty Baltimore humbled the Reds in the World Series, 4–1.

Cincinnati's hitting and run production fell off sharply the next year, and the club dropped to fourth with their only losing season of the decade. But in 1972—spurred on after a

slow start by Johnny Bench's recovery of power, Gary Nolan's finest season on the mound, and the all-around mastery of newly acquired second baseman Joe Morgan—the Reds rebounded after a slow start to take a lead in June and pull away from everyone in July for an easy division win. Victory in the LCS came harder, as powerful Pittsburgh carried the series to the full five games before handing the Reds the pennant with a wild pitch in the last of the ninth inning of the final game. Cincinnati's defeat in the World Series was also close: the Reds won three, and Oakland's four wins were each achieved by a margin of just one run.

The Reds repeated as division titlists in 1973 with a second-half surge from fourth place that carried them past front-runner Los Angeles in September. But the much weaker New York Mets ended Cincinnati's pennant hopes in the LCS, 3–2.

In 1974 the Reds trailed the Dodgers all season and finished 4 games back in second place. But over the next two years they flattened all opposition and became known as the "Big Red Machine." In 1975, after hovering around .500 through mid-May, the Reds began an ascent that carried them to what are still club records: 108 victories and a winning margin of 20 games. The team featured balanced pitching (six starters won ten or more games), a balanced offense in which every regular drove in more than 45 runs (averaging nearly 77 apiece), the best fielding in the majors, and a big NL lead in stolen bases. After a three-game sweep of Pittsburgh in the LCS, the Reds subdued the stubborn Boston Red Sox in seven games for their first world title in thirty-five years, and their third overall.

They won their fourth the next year. Joe Morgan, at the peak of his career, led the NL in slugging, finished second to teammate George Foster in RBIs, and stole 60 bases. Balanced pitching and offense again put the Reds in front to stay in June, carrying the team to 102 wins and a 10-game lead over Los Angeles at the finish. The LCS produced another sweep—of Philadelphia this time. The World Series was also a sweep as the Reds dispatched the Yankees, outscoring them nearly three to one.

Two years of second-place finishes followed, and the Reds replaced Sparky Anderson at the helm with John McNamara, who led the club back to the top of the NL West in 1979. Pete Rose, after sixteen years in Cincinnati, had signed with the Phillies as a free agent, but Ray Knight (who replaced Rose at third base) minimized the loss with a team-high .318 batting average. Houston led the division much of the summer, but a sustained Reds' surge in August brought them even, then pulled them ahead in early September, where they hung on to take the title by just 1½ games. But that was the end of the Reds' decade of splendor, for Pittsburgh swept past them to the pennant in the LCS.

Joe Morgan left the club after the season, returning as a free agent to Houston, whence he had come eight years earlier. In 1980 the Reds dipped in midseason, recovering to make a race of it in August, only to fade a bit and finish third. The next year, in a season shortened and split in two by a players' strike, the Reds compiled the best overall record in the majors. But they came away empty-handed by finishing half a game behind Los Angeles in the first half-season and 1½ games back of Houston in the second half, losing a chance at postseason play when the powers that be decided to pit the half-season winners against each other for the right to play in the LCS.

As a penurious front office continued to trade away its stars or lose them to free agency, the dispirited Reds dropped to the bottom of the NL West in 1982 with a club-worst 101 losses. Manager McNamara yielded in midseason to coach Russ Nixon, who was himself replaced by Vern Rapp after another last-place finish in 1983. Robert Howsam, Sr., whose shrewd trading as general manager had been instrumental in building the mighty Reds of the 1970s, was called out of semiretirement to restore the club to respectability. Howsam signed free-agent slugger Dave Parker from Pittsburgh, and late in the 1984 season brought Pete Rose back as player-manager. Early in 1985 the NL approved the sale of the Reds to Marge Schott, a Cincinnati automobile dealer. With Parker enjoying his most productive seasons in several years, and newcomers Eric Davis and John Franco developing respectively into one of the league's leading run producers and one of its best relief pitchers, owner Schott's public enthusiasm for her team was rewarded with four straight second-place finishes (and a return in 1987 to a home attendance over two million for the first time in seven years). In 1987 the team even spent two months at the top of the NL West, until an August slump dropped them into a hole from which a late-season rally could not extricate them.

Cleveland Indians

Cleveland is the only club in the American League East without at least one divisional title. Since the advent of divisional play in 1969, the Indians have enjoyed only four winning seasons, finishing last in the East seven times. Their record was not always this dismal. Though no other major league club with their longevity has won as few pennants, the Indians before 1969 ranked consistently among the league's better teams. They finished in the top half of the league nearly 70 percent of the time through their first sixty-eight years, and only once (in 1914) wound up in the cellar.

The Indians (who were at first called the Blues because of the color of their uniforms) succeeded Cleveland's National League Spiders, who in 1899, their final season, lost a major league record 134 games. When the NL dropped the Spiders at the end of the season, Ban Johnson, president of the emerging American League, grasped the opportunity to move into this major market. In 1901, when Johnson proclaimed the AL a major league, Cleveland lured several players from NL clubs and played much better than the Spiders had, but still finished next-to-last in their first big league season. The next year the Bronchos (as they decided to call themselves) languished in last place through June. But during the season they acquired several players through trade and purchase—most notably star second baseman Napoleon "Nap" Lajoie and pitcher Bill Bernhard—who turned the Bronchos around in midseason and lifted them above .500 (and into fifth place) by season's end.

With Lajoie sparkling in the field and dominating the league at the plate, the fans soon settled on another nickname for the club—the Naps—that lasted as long as Lajoie remained in Cleveland. Late in the 1904 season, Lajoie was named manager. After enjoying moderate success in two of the next three seasons, the Naps in 1908 experienced their best year yet, and one of the team's most exciting finishes ever.

With a ten-game winning streak near the end of the season, they moved from fourth to first, only to be surpassed by

Detroit's ten-game streak. Both teams won their season finale, but the Tigers, because they had not made up an earlier rainout, took the pennant by half a game. Cleveland protested that if Detroit had played the missed game and lost, Cleveland would have gained a tie, forcing a playoff that might have brought them the championship. The dispute led to a rules change requiring ties or washouts to be replayed if their outcome could determine the pennant winner.

Poor seasons alternated with good the next few years. Lajoie quit as manager but remained as player. Pitching ace Addie Joss pitched a second no-hitter (he had hurled a perfect game at the height of the 1908 race), but before the start of the 1911 season, Joss was dead of tubercular meningitis. Outfielder Joe Jackson—acquired from the Athletics—hit .408 in his first full big league season. The club reached bottom in 1914 with a last-place finish that found them 18½ games out of *seventh* place, 48½ out of first. After the season Lajoie was waivered to Philadelphia (the fans then voted to rename the club the Indians), and the next August Jackson was sold to the Chicago White Sox as attendance dropped to its lowest level since 1901.

By the time the 1916 season began, though, new ownership had acquired the great Tris Speaker from Boston and brought up from the minors a pair of promising pitchers, Jim Bagby (Sr.) and Stan Coveleski. The club rose only one place that year, to sixth. But they stayed in the pennant fight through July and wound up winning 20 games more than they had the previous year. Attendance more than tripled over 1915.

Sparked by the three newcomers, the Indians rose to third in 1917, and to close second-place finishes the next two years. In 1920 everything came together. Speaker, who had taken over as manager the previous July, hit .388 and enjoyed one of his best years, as did Coveleski with 24 wins. Bagby, in the finest season of his career, led the league with 31 victories, and veteran pitcher Ray Caldwell (picked up from the Boston Red Sox the previous summer) added another 20. Six regulars hit over .300; the club as a whole hit .303.

Involved from mid-June in a close race with the Yankees, joined in August by the White Sox, Cleveland saw its home attendance climb above 900,000 for the first time, to set a club record that would last twenty-six years. The Yankees dropped back a bit in mid-September, but the White Sox hung close until the final week, when eight of their players were indicted and suspended as suspects in the Black Sox scandal of 1919. The Sox lost two of their final three games and all hope of tying Cleveland to force a playoff. The Indians defeated Brooklyn in a World Series that is best remembered for second baseman Bill Wambsganss's unassisted triple play in Game Five.

Cleveland led much of the way in 1921 before a late slump and a New York surge gave the Yankees their first pennant. Through the next quarter century the Indians came close to a pennant only twice. In 1926, with two veteran Georges—pitcher Uhle and first baseman Burns—enjoying their finest seasons, the Indians came to life in midseason and drew within three games of the Yankees by season's end. Fourteen years later, in 1940, behind the 27 wins of twenty-one-year-old Bob Feller and the inspired play (in the field and at the bat) of second-year shortstop Lou Boudreau, Cleveland made an even closer run for the flag. Throughout the summer the Indians were in or near first place, but six losses in nine games with a resurgent Detroit in late August and September left them a game back at the finish.

Two years later Boudreau, at age twenty-four, was named to manage the Tribe. His team stirred little interest through the war years. But in 1946, with Feller back from military service and pitching his best ever, Cleveland fans boosted home attendance above a million for the first time, even though the team's won-lost record was its worst in eighteen years. The next year, their first full season under new president Bill Veeck, the Indians climbed to fourth. More significantly, Veeck hired the league's first black player, Larry Doby, who became a mainstay of the Indians for the next eight years.

In 1948 the Indians began a nine-year era of excellence with a victory in one of the closest pennant races ever. Through June they ran a three-way race with the Yankees and the surprisingly lively Philadelphia Athletics; in July the Red Sox rose out of nowhere to make it a four-way struggle. In September the A's fell behind, but the three remaining clubs stayed close, and on September 24 found themselves in a three-way tie. Cleveland moved ahead with a four-game win streak, but Boston, after a pair of losses, won their final four (including two to eliminate New York). Cleveland's final-day loss to Detroit left them tied with Boston. In a one-game playoff in Boston the next day (the first playoff in AL history), manager-shortstop Boudreau capped his MVP season with two home runs to help give rookie Gene Bearden his twentieth win and the Tribe their second pennant. The exciting race drew more than 2.6 million Cleveland fans to Municipal Stadium, a new major league record and still Cleveland's season high. By contrast, the World Series against the Boston Braves was anticlimactic—a Cleveland triumph in six games.

By 1951 both owner Veeck and manager Boudreau had moved on, but under new manager Al Lopez the Indians fashioned a six-year stretch in which they finished second to the Yankees five times, and in 1954 they won their third pennant with 111 victories—the most in AL history. The Lopez years, 1951–1956, were punctuated by the power of players like Doby, Luke Easter, Al Rosen, and Vic Wertz. But it was pitching that gave the team its consistency. Bob Lemon and Early Wynn won between 17 and 23 games in every one of the six years, as did Mike Garcia through 1954. As Garcia and Feller (who won 22 in 1951) faded, Art Houtteman was acquired from Detroit for a couple of good years, and Herb Score came along for his two explosive seasons.

The 1954 season—Cleveland's year to break the Yankee grip on the AL—was in fact New York's best season in the eighteen years from 1943 through 1960, a period in which they won twelve pennants. The Yankees kept the race close until the end of July, and finished with 103 wins. But the Indians won an AL-record 111 games to beat New York by 8. Wynn and Lemon tied for the league lead with 23 wins apiece, and Garcia copped the ERA crown. Doby led the league in homers and RBIs, and second baseman Bobby Avila took the batting title. Heavily favored to defeat the Giants in the World Series, the Tribe and their fans were shocked when the NL champs swept them in four games.

After Lopez left to manage the White Sox in 1957, the Indians slipped below .500 for the first time in a decade. Rocky Colavito's power and Cal McLish's pitching brought them back in 1959, when they finished second to Lopez's Sox. Their next highest post-Lopez finish came nine years later, in 1968, when Luis Tiant and Sam McDowell pitched them into third.

Since 1968 the Indians have completed every season in the

bottom half of the AL East. Despite rosy predictions for 1987–1988, the results remained dismal as the Tribe finished last and then next-to-last.

Detroit Tigers

One of the more successful clubs in the American League, the Tigers have enjoyed winning seasons nearly 70 percent of the time. In eighteen of their sixty winning seasons, they have remained in contention into the final days, eleven times emerging triumphant as league or division champions. They have finished last in the league or AL East only three times, and have never had more than four losing seasons in a row.

Detroit was one of the clubs from Ban Johnson's Western League that (renamed the American League) raised itself to major league status in 1901 with a talent raid on the long-established National League. In their first six big league seasons, the Tigers displayed little bite, finishing four times in the second division and never threatening for the league lead.

In 1907 all that changed. Sparked by a young right fielder, Ty Cobb (who in his first full big league season led the league in batting, slugging, hits, RBIs, and stolen bases) and led by a dynamic new manager, Hugh "Eeyah" Jennings (who knew enough not to try to tell Cobb how to play the game), the Tigers clawed their way to the pennant in a four-way race. The outcome might have been different if two late-season games with second-place Philadelphia had not been rained out and tied. Today's rules would require that the games be made up.

The 1908 race was even closer, with four teams contending into late September. The race wasn't settled until the final day, when Detroit beat Chicago to edge Cleveland by half a game. Once again the pennant hinged on a rainout that had not been made up. And once again Cobb dominated the league's hitters (though he slipped to fourth in stolen bases).

The Tigers had a slightly easier time of it the next year. It was a three-way race into September, but Detroit then pulled away to finish 3½ games ahead of Philadelphia. Cobb, in his best season yet, took the Triple Crown and returned to the top in stolen bases. But the Tigers were unable to win a World Series. In 1907, after an opening-game tie, the Chicago Cubs swept the next four. The Cubs lost Game Three the next year, but won the other four. And in 1909 Pittsburgh and Detroit alternated victories, with the Pirates emerging world champions in seven games.

Jennings managed Detroit for eleven more seasons; then Cobb took the reins for six years before leaving for Philadelphia. But the Tigers won no more pennants in the Cobb era. Cobb himself continued to dominate the league offensively through 1919. In 1911 he achieved career highs in most offensive categories, including a batting average of .420, but the Tigers managed no better than a distant second to the Athletics. In 1915 they started strong and remained in the race throughout the season. Cobb stole what was for forty-seven years a modern-record 96 bases, and the team's 100 wins proved to be the highest total in their first thirty-three years. But after running neck and neck with the Red Sox through most of August, the Tigers slumped a bit in early September—just enough for the Sox to take the flag by 2½ games. A close third-place finish the next year marked the Tigers' last serious challenge for eighteen years.

In 1934, after six straight years in the second division, and only three years after their most distant finish ever (47 games out), the Tigers turned themselves around to win the pennant with a 101–53 record and a .656 winning percentage, the highest in Tiger history. Two newly acquired veterans—manager/catcher Mickey Cochrane and outfielder Goose Goslin—enjoyed fine seasons at the bat, as did first baseman Hank Greenberg (.339, 139 RBIs) in his first full season, and long-time Tiger second baseman Charlie Gehringer (.356, 127 RBIs). The two other infielders, third baseman Marv Owen and shortstop Billy Rogell enjoyed their finest seasons at the plate for a club whose batting average led the league at .300. It took the Tigers a month to get going, but by mid-July they had shot ahead of the Yankees, pulling farther away through August and September to win by 7 games. But once again, victory in the World Series eluded them as the St. Louis Cardinals blew them away 11–0 in Game Seven.

The Tigers' hitting fell off ten points in 1935, but their slugging jumped eleven points. Paced by Greenberg's 170 RBIs, Detroit—after another slow start—shot up so sharply in July and August that even a September slump gave the Yankees no opportunity to catch them. And finally, in their fifth try, the Tigers won a world championship, overcoming Chicago in six games despite the loss of Greenberg, who broke his wrist in Game Two. Part-owner Frank Navin, who had run the club for three decades, had finally seen his Tigers reach the very top. A month later, after falling from a horse, he suffered a heart attack and died.

Del Baker had replaced Cochrane as manager when Detroit next made a run for the pennant in 1940. In a tight race the Tigers caught up with Cleveland in early September and traded the lead with them for two weeks before pulling ahead to stay with two wins in a three-game series. In the pennant clincher, Detroit's Floyd Giebell outdueled Cleveland great Bob Feller 2–0 for his third—and last—big league victory. In the World Series the Tigers lost once again, as Cincinnati came from behind in Game Seven for a 2–1 win.

Two losing seasons followed, and Steve O'Neill replaced Baker at the helm. In 1944, the wartime Tigers, behind the splendid pitching of workhorses Dizzy Trout and Hal Newhouser (one-two in ERA and innings pitched, and winners of 27 and 29 games), joined the race in late August and found themselves tied with the St. Louis Browns for first going into the last game of the season. But the Browns beat the Yankees and Detroit lost to Washington as Trout failed in his try for a twenty-eighth win.

Hank Greenberg's release from military service in mid-1945 sparked another Tiger run for the pennant. They held the lead from mid-June through August, but in September a surging Washington caught up with them. The race once again went down to the final day, and the final inning, when Greenberg's grand slam overcame a St. Louis lead to give Detroit the flag over the idle Senators. Newhouser, with 25 wins and a 1.81 ERA, was named AL MVP for the second straight year. In the World Series his ERA shot up to 6.10, but he still managed to win two games (including the finale) as the Tigers took the Cubs in seven for their second world title.

In the twenty-three years that passed before their next pennant, the Tigers came close only twice. In 1950 they led the race through the middle of the season, but were caught by the Yankees late in August. After retaking the lead in early September, the two clubs ran neck-and-neck for a while before Detroit fell away to second.

Two years later the Tigers reached their nadir: their first cellar finish, their most losses ever (104), and their lowest winning percentage (.325). After a decade in which they finished no higher than fourth, they rebounded in 1961 as first baseman Norm Cash and left fielder Rocky Colavito both enjoyed the most explosive seasons of their careers. Compiling their best season record since 1934, Detroit led the league through parts of June and July. But this was the year of Maris and Mantle and 109 Yankee victories; when the season ended, the Tigers' 101 wins had earned them only second place.

They came much closer six years later in the great four-way race of 1967 that saw three clubs still contending on the final day, when the Tigers split a doubleheader to tie with Minnesota for second. If 1967 was a scramble, 1968 was all Detroit's. In what is now known as the year of the pitcher, Tiger Denny McLain won 31 games (the last major leaguer to win 30) to lead the team to a 103-win finish, 12 games ahead of Baltimore. Down 1–3 to the Cardinals in the World Series, the pitching of McLain in Game Six and Mickey Lolich in Games Five and Seven brought the Tigers back and gave them their third world championship.

A strike at the start of 1972 contributed to the Tigers' first divisional title, which culminated a four-way race in the AL East. Detroit defeated Boston two games out of three at season's end, to edge the Sox by half a game. But if the strike had not wiped out an unequal number of games, the end of the season could have seen the two clubs tied.

The Tigers lost the pennant to Oakland with a 1–2 loss in the finale of a close League Championship Series, and dropped out of contention for a decade. In 1974 they finished at the bottom of the division, and the next year lost 102 games to post the worst record in the majors.

Finally, after seven seasons in the second division, Detroit put together a strong second half in strike-divided 1981, fading only at the end to tie for second. Three years later the Tigers were back on top with one of their best years. Opening the season with 9 wins, they ended April at 18–2, stretched their mark to 35–5 by late May, and were never headed, finishing a team-record 15 games in front, with 104 wins, their most ever. Their balanced pitching staff led the league in ERA, even though none of their starters finished among the top ten. Tiger newcomer Willie Hernandez (who with Aurelio Lopez compiled a 19–4 record from the bullpen, with 46 saves) earned both Cy Young and MVP awards. After sweeping Kansas City in the LCS, the Tigers took the world championship—their fourth—from San Diego in five games.

In 1987 the Tigers caught Toronto's Blue Jays in the season's final series, tying them for the lead in the first game, moving to the front with a twelve-inning win in the second game, and clinching the division crown in the finale, 1–0. In the LCS, though, Minnesota stopped the favored Tigers, four games to one. In 1988 the Tigers led the AL East much of the way, but wound up second, one game behind Boston.

Houston Astros

The Colt .45s (as the Astros were originally known) had hoped to begin their history in the Harris County Domed Stadium, but when the start of the vast project was delayed, a temporary outdoor park was built for them next door in time for their 1962 inaugural. Heat, humidity, and giant mosquitoes held Colt home attendance below a million in each of their three outdoor seasons, but when, in 1965, they brought big league baseball indoors for the first time, the fans arrived—more than two million the first year. The original grass under the dome was real, but when the skylight panels were coated over so fielders wouldn't lose sight of high flies, the grass died. In 1966 the club (now known as the Astros) and the stadium (now called the Astrodome) brought to baseball yet another innovation—AstroTurf.

The Houston franchise, conceived as an entry in the abortive Continental League, first took the field instead (along with New York's Mets) in the National League, as part of the league's first expansion since shrinking from twelve teams to eight in 1900. Shrewd player selection by general manager Paul Richards kept the new team from being as bad as the Mets. Although they suffered just as long playing below .500 (seven years), they finished only once below New York in the standings.

When the NL added two more teams in 1969 and split into two divisions, the Astros for the first time made a serious title run. Though they wound up fifth in the West (ahead of only the expansion San Diego Padres), they rose to within two games of the top in August, and again in September, before a six-game losing streak dropped them out of contention. With an 81–81 record, they finished out of the ranks of losers for the first time.

After dropping below .500 again in 1970 and '71, the Astros made their second run for the division title in 1972. At the end of June they were neck and neck with Cincinnati for the lead, but the Reds pulled away over the rest of the season while Houston leveled off for an eventual second-place finish 10½ games back. With a record of 84–69, the Astros had fashioned their first winning season.

In 1975 they endured their worst year ever, losing 97 games to finish at the bottom of the West, 43½ games behind the Reds. But the next year pitcher J. R. Richard, with the first of several fine seasons, brought the club up to third with his 20 wins. By 1979 Richard was the NL's most overwhelming pitcher, leading the league with 313 strikeouts and a 2.71 ERA. His 18 wins and teammate Joe Niekro's 21 sparked a team that spent much of the summer in first place before falling to 1½ games behind Cincinnati at the end.

Houston and Los Angeles battled back and forth for the division lead throughout 1980. Richard began strong and seemed headed for his finest year. With a 10–4 record, he was starting pitcher in the All-Star Game. But shortly after mid-season he suffered a stroke that ended his big league career. Led by Joe Niekro and Vern Ruhle (who replaced Richard in the rotation and finished 12–4), the best pitching staff in baseball kept the Astros in the race to season's end, although three straight losses to the Dodgers had left the clubs tied for first. In a one-game playoff, Houston rebounded with a 7–1 win (Niekro's twentieth) to capture the division title. In the League Championship Series, the Astros took the Phillies to the tenth inning of the final game before bowing two games to three.

When a player strike cut the middle out of the 1981 season, intradivisional playoffs were scheduled between the winners of the two halves. Houston, the second-half champion, defeated first-half victor Los Angeles in the first two games, but lost the next three, and with them the division title.

After four years in the middle of the division, the Astros stormed back in 1986 with their best season ever, winning fifteen of their last nineteen games to conquer the West by ten

games. Pitcher Mike Scott, who had developed a deceptive split-finger fastball, won 18 to pace a strong Astro staff, leading the league in strikeouts and ERA. On September 25 he clinched the division crown with a no-hitter. In the LCS the Astros lost to the Mets, two games to four—but they held the New Yorkers at bay for fifteen innings of the final game before falling by a run in the sixteenth.

Kansas City Royals

Two years after the Athletics abandoned Kansas City for the West Coast, patent-medicine millionaire Ewing Kauffman bankrolled an expansion club for the city. Where the A's had been unable in thirteen years to fashion even one winning season, the Royals did it in 1971, their third year (when, ironically, they finished second in the AL West to the newly invincible Oakland A's). One of the most successful of all expansion clubs, the Royals in their first twenty years have finished either first or second in their division fourteen times.

In their fifth season, 1973, the year they moved into new Royals Stadium (the only major league park to be built exclusively for baseball in the past quarter century), the Royals also made their first serious run for the division title. A midsummer spurt carried them into first place in August before they leveled off to another second-place finish behind Oakland.

After a third second-place race with Oakland in 1975 (during which manager Jack McKeon was replaced by Whitey Herzog), the Royals won the division crown in 1976, taking the lead two months into the season and holding it to the end. Third baseman George Brett won his first AL batting championship and carried his hot bat into the League Championship Series, but the Yankees snatched the pennant on Chris Chambliss's home run in the bottom of the ninth inning of the final game.

For two more years the Royals dominated the AL West but failed to stop the Yankees in the LCS. In 1977, with a pitching staff that led the league in ERA and a balanced offense that included four players with more than 20 home runs and 80 RBIs, the Royals compiled a record of 102–60—their finest to date. Though they didn't move into the division lead until mid-August, they were nearly unstoppable the rest of the way. In the LCS they once again battled New York all the way, only to lose the Series and pennant for the second time in the final inning of game five.

The divisional race was a bit tighter in 1978, as California hung close to K.C. through much of August and into September, before the Royals finally pulled away. In the LCS, the Royals tied the Series with a big win in Game Two, but the Yankees came back to take the next two by one run each for their third straight flag.

The Royals slipped to second place in 1979, but the next year (led now by rookie manager Jim Frey) they overwhelmed the rest of a weak division. Despite a month-long decline in September, K.C. finished the season 14 games ahead of Oakland for their fourth divisional title. This was the year Brett chased .400 (ending at .390, the highest major league average since Ted Williams hit .406 in 1941), reliever Dan Quisenberry enjoyed his first big season (12 wins, 33 saves), and starter Dennis Leonard came back from an off-year to record his third 20-win season in four years. It was also the year the Royals finally beat the Yankees to capture their first pennant—with a three-game sweep in the LCS. In the World Series, though, it was Philadelphia in six games.

The player strike of 1981 divided the season into two halves. In the first half the Royals finished fifth, but part way through the second half Dick Howser (who had managed the Yankees to the East title the previous year) replaced Frey as Royals manager and brought the club in first, a game ahead of Oakland. But in the special playoffs, the A's (who had won the first-half race) beat K.C. for the division title with a three-game sweep.

Two more second-place finishes in 1982 (a close race with California) and 1983 (20 games behind the Chicago White Sox) were followed in 1984 by a fifth division championship in a three-way race with California and Minnesota. But Detroit swept away the Royals' pennant hopes in the LCS, in the minimum three games.

For Kansas City, 1985 was a season of catching up. Few picked the Royals to win the West, but with starters Charlie Leibrandt (17–9) and Bret Saberhagen (20–6) finishing two-three in the league ERA race, reliever Quisenberry leading the league in saves for the fourth straight year, and veteran George Brett healthy and enjoying one of his best seasons ever, the Royals chased California throughout the summer and caught them in the final week to take their sixth division crown by a single game. In the LCS against Toronto, K.C. fell behind 1–3, which would have eliminated them in earlier years. But, saved by the expansion of the Series from five games to seven, they came back with three straight wins for their second pennant. Repeating the suspense in the World Series, the Royals again fell behind 1–3, to St. Louis, before rallying once again to win three straight for their first world championship.

During the 1986 season, manager Howser left the club after he was found to have a brain tumor. The Royals dropped below .500 and finished third, their lowest rank in a dozen years. Howser was unable to return to the helm in 1987 as he had hoped and died during the summer. The Royals rallied at season's end to pull themselves above .500 and finish (for the eighth time) runner-up in the West, 2 games behind Minnesota. Although they improved on their 1987 won-lost record in 1988, they finished in third place.

Los Angeles Dodgers

When the Dodgers left Brooklyn for Los Angeles, an era ended. From baseball's earliest days Brooklyn had been prominent; the city's Atlantics were the nation's best in the mid-1860s, and since 1884 Brooklyn had been home to major league ball. But before the start of the 1958 season, its link to the big time was severed by an owner who saw greener fields to the west. He was right: the Dodgers in Los Angeles are one of the game's most profitable franchises, regularly attracting more than three million fans per year to Dodger Stadium.

The club's origins were modest. After winning the championship of the minor Inter-State League in 1883, Brooklyn moved up to the major league American Association in 1884 and endured three losing seasons in its first four years. But in 1888, after signing three regulars from New York's newly defunct Mets and buying pitching/hitting stars Bob Caruthers and Dave Foutz from the AA champion St. Louis Browns, Brooklyn finished second to St. Louis, and the next year dethroned the Browns for their first big league pennant. In

a projected ten-game World Series against the National League champion New York Giants, the Bridegrooms (as the Brooklyns had been nicknamed) won three of the first four games, but lost the next five.

Before the start of the 1890 season, Brooklyn transferred from the AA to the more prestigious NL. Many NL clubs performed below par that year, weakened by the loss of players to the outlaw Players League. But Brooklyn held on to most of its players and swept to its second straight pennant. In postseason play, poor weather and lack of fan support caused the World Series against AA winner Louisville to be called off after each team had won three games and tied one. The next year, with other NL teams renewed by players from the failed PL, Brooklyn finished sixth.

When the AA folded after the 1891 season, Brooklyn picked up slugger Dan Brouthers and pitcher George Haddock from pennant-winning Boston, and rebounded in 1892 to finish second and third in the two halves of a divided season. But for the next five years they finished no higher than fifth, and in 1898 sank to tenth in what was now a twelve-team league.

Help was on the way, however—help that today would be prohibited. Longtime Brooklyn president Charles Byrne had died, and the owners of the Baltimore Orioles—Harry Von der Horst and Ned Hanlon—seeing an opportunity to move into the more lucrative Brooklyn market, purchased a half interest in the Bridegrooms. Hanlon retained his Baltimore presidency, but took over as manager in Brooklyn, bringing along with him the core of his Oriole club—shortstop Hughie Jennings and outfielders Joe Kelley and Willie Keeler—plus its two best pitchers, Jim Hughes and Doc McJames.

The infusion of new talent worked wonders, as Brooklyn in 1899 (with a new nickname, the Superbas) took the NL lead in late May, during a twenty-two game winning streak, and held it the rest of the way. That winter, when Baltimore was dropped as the NL cut back from twelve teams to eight, Hanlon moved more Orioles to Brooklyn (including pitcher Joe "Iron Man" McGinnity), and once again led the Superbas to the pennant. That year they also won their first world championship in a series played with second-place Pittsburgh for the elegant Chronicle-Telegraph Cup.

Slow starts in 1901 and '02 kept the Superbas out of pennant contention, although they finished third and second. During this period Charley Ebbets, who had risen from ticket seller to president, took over majority ownership with the purchase of Von der Horst's stock, thereby quashing Hanlon's proposed move back to Baltimore. But Ebbets's clashes with Hanlon hastened the club's decline. In 1903 the team began a twelve-year sojourn in the second division, including a last-place finish in 1905 with their worst record ever (48–104, 56½ games out). Perhaps the most memorable events of these years were the change in nickname to Dodgers, and their move to brand-new Ebbets Field in 1913.

Hanlon was fired as manager after the disastrous 1905 season, but it was not until Wilbert Robinson took over in 1914 that the team began to pull out of its doldrums. Pitcher Jack Pfeffer, in his first full big-league season, won 23 games for the fifth-place Dodgers that year, and two years later led them to the pennant with 25 wins on a sparkling 1.92 ERA.

But the Dodgers lost the World Series to the Boston Red Sox, and in 1917 fell all the way to seventh. After three years in the second division, they bounced back in 1920, turning a three-way race into a rout with sixteen wins in their final eighteen games. After another World Series loss, to Cleveland, the Dodgers returned to the second division for another three years. In 1924 they began slowly, but leaped from twelve games back to an early-September lead, only to slip 1½ games behind the Giants at the finish.

Charley Ebbets died the following April, and Robinson was named to replace him. In his five years as president the club suffered on the field, finishing sixth each year. Fired as president but retained as manager, "Uncle Robbie" saw his Robins (as the Dodgers were now known) lead the league in 1930 most of the time from mid-May to a mid-August decline, then retake the lead for a day in mid-September before tailing off once more to finish fourth. That was Uncle Robbie's last hurrah. When the Robins provided no serious challenge in their fourth-place run the next year, he resigned after eighteen years at the wheel.

A succession of managers followed, but it was not until the Dodgers brought in the free-spending Larry MacPhail as general manager in 1938 that the club began to pull itself back into contention. The highlight of MacPhail's first year with the Dodgers was not the team's finish (seventh) but the introduction of night baseball to Ebbets Field (on June 15, when Cincinnati's Johnny Vander Meer defeated Brooklyn with his second consecutive no-hitter). MacPhail was also looking for new talent, and over the next couple of years he acquired a combination of youngsters and veterans that turned the Dodgers into one of the best teams in the league.

But MacPhail's most brilliant move may have been his conversion of shortstop Leo Durocher into manager Leo Durocher. The loud, driven Durocher alienated many (including MacPhail himself), but provided inspired leadership and a will to win that overcame complaints against him. After a third-place finish in 1939 and second place in 1940, the Dodgers battled the St. Louis Cardinals through all of 1941 before pulling ahead to clinch the pennant with just two games remaining. Veteran first baseman Dolf Camilli led the league in home runs and RBIs, sophomore outfielder Pete Reiser led the league in batting, slugging, and runs scored, and pitchers Kirby Higbe and Whitlow Wyatt tied for the league lead with 22 wins apiece, as the Dodgers for the first time since 1899 won 100 games. Only their loss to the Yankees in the World Series marred their finest season in forty-two years.

In 1942 they played even better, winning 104 games. But a late-season five-game slump dropped them behind the surging Cardinals, and they finished 2 games short of the flag.

MacPhail and many of his players left for the war, and though the club finished third in 1943 and 1945, it was not until 1946 that the Dodgers again presented a serious challenge. Once again the Cards and Dodgers made a two-team race of it, but this time the race ended in a tie, forcing the first league playoff ever. St. Louis won the pennant with wins in the first two games.

When MacPhail left for the Army, Branch Rickey was hired to run the club. MacPhail had left the club financially sound and a big drawing card; Rickey set about to make it a consistent winner. Famed as the developer of the Cardinal farm system, he was determined at Brooklyn to tap the one source of talent that the major leagues had willfully neglected: black players. He signed Jackie Robinson to Montreal (Brooklyn's leading farm team), and after a year there promoted him to the Dodgers for the 1947 season. Thus began the club's golden Brooklyn decade: ten years in which they won six pennants and—in 1955—a World Series. Two

other races went right to the wire; only once did they finish as low as third.

With manager Durocher suspended from baseball for a year for consorting with gamblers, the Dodgers in 1947 were led by grandfatherly Burt Shotton, brought out of his Florida retirement. Robinson's hustle put him at the top of the league in stolen bases and second in runs scored. The team pulled up from fourth in June to first in July, and held the lead to the end. In the World Series they lost to the Yankees in an exciting seven games.

Durocher returned to the helm in 1948, but was replaced by Shotton in midsummer, with the Dodgers in fifth place. Shotton saw the team rise to third that season, then battle back and forth with the Cardinals throughout 1949 before edging them by a game on the final day. Robinson, in his finest season, led the league in hitting and stolen bases, and finished among the leaders in most other offensive categories. Rookie pitcher Don Newcombe led the team in victories with 17, and Preacher Roe led the league in winning percentage. Again the World Series was a loss to the Yankees, this time in only five games.

In 1950 the Dodgers nearly caught the staggering Phillies, losing out only in the tenth inning of the final game. President Rickey left the club for Pittsburgh and was replaced by Walter O'Malley, who replaced manager Shotton with Charlie Dressen. The slugging of catcher Roy Campanella and first baseman Gil Hodges, and 20-win seasons by Roe (22–3) and Newcombe (20–9) kept the Dodgers in front through most of 1951, but New York's surging Giants closed from thirteen games back in August to tie for the lead at the finish. The teams split the first two playoff games. In Game Three the Dodgers were leading by two runs in the last of the ninth when Bobby Thomson's three-run homer gave New York the flag.

The next year, though, the Giants fell short and Brooklyn took the pennant with relative ease. But not the World Series. Although Brooklyn held a 3–2 lead after five games, the Yankees came back to take the final two.

The Dodgers repeated as NL champions in 1953 with their best season ever. Dodger bats overwhelmed the league, hitting 19 points and slugging 63 points above the league average, as the team outscored its nearest rival by more than a run per game. With a club-record 105 wins, the Dodgers cruised to the pennant by 13 games. But again the Yankees took the World Series, in six games.

Dressen wanted a three-year contract and was let go when he turned down another for only one year. Minor league manager Walter Alston wasn't so demanding, and signed for 1954 the first of a historic string of twenty-three one-year Dodger contracts that would see him into the Hall of Fame. After a second-place finish in Alston's rookie season, the Dodgers in 1955 took the lead from the start and—never challenged—walked away with their eleventh pennant. Outfielder Duke Snider, with one of his most productive seasons, led the league's most powerful squad; Newcombe (20–5) paced the league's best pitching staff.

Once more in the World Series, Brooklyn faced the Yankees, and once more the Series went seven games. But this time there was joy in Brooklyn—Johnny Podres shut out New York in the finale! In an exciting three-way fight in 1956, the Dodgers repeated as pennant-winners, taking their final three games to edge Milwaukee's Braves. Newcombe, in his greatest year, clinched the flag on the final day with his

twenty-seventh win. In the World Series, though, it was *déjà vu* time—a sixth Yankee triumph, in seven games. The golden decade was over.

The Dodgers (despite the league's best pitching) vacated the 1957 race in August, finishing third. Before the start of the next season, they had vacated Brooklyn as well, for Los Angeles. Playing in Memorial Coliseum (a converted football stadium) the L.A. Dodgers sank to seventh place in 1958. But the next year the reawakened bats of aging Duke Snider and Gil Hodges, the fiery pitching of young Don Drysdale, and the late-season pitching heroics of Roger Craig (recalled from Spokane) kept the team in the thick of a tight race that found them tied with the Braves at season's end. The Dodgers won the first playoff game in Milwaukee, and captured big league baseball's first West Coast pennant at home the next day, in the twelfth inning. Then they defeated the Chicago White Sox to give the West its first World Series winner.

After finishes of fourth and second, the Dodgers produced record-breaking excitement in 1962 as they moved into brand-new Dodger Stadium in the hills above Los Angeles. Between the new ballpark and the excitement generated on the field, more than 2.75 million fans passed through the turnstiles—a new attendance record that would last until the Dodgers themselves broke it fifteen years later. As pitcher Don Drysdale and left fielder Tommy Davis ignited the league with career-high seasons, and shortstop Maury Wills became the first major leaguer of the century to steal 100 bases, the team locked into a season-long struggle for first place with archrival San Francisco. But after holding a narrow lead much of the season, the Dodgers dropped their last four games to finish in yet another tie—their fourth.

The playoff must have reminded fans of 1951. As they had then, the Giants and Dodgers split the first two games, and the Dodgers once again brought a 4–2 lead into the ninth inning of Game Three. This time, though, it was not a home run that undid them, but a bases-loaded walk.

Sandy Koufax—who had won 14 games in 1962 (and the first of five straight ERA crowns) despite losing half the year with circulation problems in his fingers—rose to dominate the world of pitching the next four years. For three of those years his Dodgers dominated the NL. In 1963 Koufax's 25–5 season carried Los Angeles into the World Series against the Yankees, where two more wins helped put the New Yorkers away in the minimum four games. The next year Koufax slipped to 19 wins, but the Dodgers fell all the way to a tie for sixth.

They rebounded to the top in 1965. Koufax won 26 and Drysdale 23 in a tight four-team race that saw them fall behind the Giants in early September, only to retake the lead for good later in the month with 13 straight wins. The World Series against Minnesota went to the seventh game before Koufax nailed down another world title with his second shutout in three days.

The race in 1966 was just as close as in '65, with three teams switching leads throughout the season. But the Dodgers, third at the end of August, put together streaks of five and seven wins in September to move to the top, where Koufax clinched the pennant on the final day with his twenty-seventh victory. And then it was all over. After a losing effort in Game Two of the World Series (a Baltimore sweep), Koufax, at age thirty, retired because of arthritis in his pitching elbow. The Dodgers sank to eighth the next year and rose only to seventh in 1968.

In 1969, the first season of divisional play, Los Angeles found itself in the thick of a five-team race in the West until eight straight losses in late September dropped them to fourth. No one challenged Cincinnati in 1970, but the next year the Dodgers closed to within a game of the front-running Giants in September before their drive stalled.

A late-season Dodger slump let Cincinnati get to the top in 1973, but the Dodgers held their lead to the end in 1974. Newly acquired veteran outfielder Jimmy Wynn and first baseman Steve Garvey, in his first full season, led the club offensively; pitcher Mike Marshall set a modern major league record with 106 appearances in relief of a staff that was the league's best (which earned him the Cy Young Award). The Dodgers beat Pittsburgh handily in the League Championship Series for their fifth Los Angeles pennant, but lost the World Series to Oakland in five games.

Cincinnati proved untouchable in 1975 and '76, but in 1977 the Dodgers—under new manager Tom Lasorda, who moved up from the coaching staff when Alston retired— jumped to an early lead and held it all the way. Garvey's 33 home runs led a balanced offense in which four players hit 30 or more homers and drove in over 85 runs. Again the Dodgers won the LCS (in four games, against Philadelphia), and again they lost the World Series (to the Yankees, in six games).

Although the divisional race was closer— and the Dodgers broke baseball's three million attendance barrier for the first time—1978 was in most respects a replay of 1977. Garvey again led the club offensively, the Dodgers again beat out Cincinnati in the West and Philadelphia in a four-game LCS, and the Yankees again defeated the Dodgers in a six-game World Series.

A season-long back-and-forth battle with Houston in 1980 ended in a tie for first—the fifth tie for the Dodgers, three more than any other club. In the playoff (reduced from three games to one to bring the NL into line with AL practice), Houston won easily.

When the players went out on strike part way through 1981, the Dodgers, paced by the spectacular pitching of rookie Fernando Valenzuela, found themselves half a game in front of Cincinnati. In a special playoff with poststrike leader Houston, the Dodgers defeated the Astros in five games for the division title, and also went the distance in beating Montreal for the pennant—their twenty-first. Facing the Yankees for the eleventh time in World Series play, they lost the first two games, but swept the next four games to capture their sixth world title.

In 1982, after a poor start, the Dodgers fought back to take the lead in August and again in September before dropping back to second, a game out. More successful drives in 1983 and '85 led to their fifth and sixth division titles, but culminated in defeat in the LCS—to Philadelphia in 1983 and St. Louis two years later. In 1986 and '87 they posted identical 73–89 won-lost records—the team's worst in two decades.

But then in 1988, with an infusion of talent from the American League—most notably slugger Kirk Gibson and relief ace Jay Howell—and a spectacular season on the mound from starter Orel Hershiser (who concluded his 23–8 year with a major-league record 59 consecutive scoreless innings), the Dodgers bounced back to the top of the NL West. It took them the full seven games to down the favored Mets in the LCS for their twenty-second pennant, but in the World Series they humbled Oakland's powerful Athletics in just five games for their seventh world crown.

Milwaukee Brewers

When the new Seattle Pilots played their home opener in the refurbished minor league Sick's Stadium, 7,000 seats and the left field fence were still unfinished. The Pilots may not have needed the seats. Fewer than 700,000 fans came to see them play—the third worst attendance in the league—as they drifted into the cellar of the American League West with 98 losses. That winter the Pilots—renamed the Brewers—moved to Milwaukee, where a genuine big league stadium (vacated by the Braves five years earlier) awaited them.

Attendance improved nearly 38 percent in Milwaukee, although the Brewers of 1970 won only one game more than the Pilots had in Seattle. It would be eight more years before they experienced their first winning season. Meanwhile, in 1972, they switched divisions from West to East, trading places with the Washington Senators, who moved West to become the Texas Rangers.

At last—and with power—the Brewers broke their losing pattern in 1978. One key front-office move leading to the turnaround, the signing of free agent Larry Hisle (who the previous year with Minnesota had led the league in RBIs), was also a giant step in the escalation of major league player compensation. With a signing bonus and deferred payments on top of salary, Hisle's six-year contract averaged out to eleven times what he was paid in Minnesota, an annual average figure that would have paid almost 40 percent of the Brewers' player payroll the previous year.

Hisle proved his worth in 1978, leading an offense that sprang to life under rookie manager George Bamberger to top the league in hitting, slugging, homers, and runs scored. On the mound Mike Caldwell won 22 games in the best season of his career. Although the Brewers never threatened the Red Sox or Yankees for the lead, they did rise from below .500 in early June to finish a solid third, 24 games above .500.

A shoulder injury the next April marked the beginning of the end of Hisle's career and perhaps cost Milwaukee the division title. Even without Hisle the team compiled what is still their best winning percentage (.590), as outfielder Gorman Thomas (45 home runs, 123 RBIs) and several other Brewer hitters attained new career peaks of productivity. While they never seriously threatened front-running Baltimore, they rose past Boston in late August to finish second.

Most of the Milwaukee bats remained hot in 1980, but injuries, ragged pitching, and Bamberger's heart attack (which caused him to miss the first part of the season and retire in early September) contributed to a distant third-place finish. In strike-divided 1981, league-leading performances by two newly acquired pitchers—starter Pete Vuckovich (14–4) and reliever Rollie Fingers (28 saves)—helped give the Brewers the best overall record in the AL East, and the second-half championship. But in the special intradivisional playoffs with first-half winner New York, the Yankees captured the division crown three games to two.

The Brewers started slowly in 1982; at the end of May they were two games below .500, near the bottom of the division. A day later Buck Rogers, the Milwaukee coach who had replaced Bamberger as manager two years earlier, was himself replaced by coach Harvey Kuenn. By mid-July the team had risen to first place, and they led the West by more than six games as September neared. But Baltimore had cut the lead to three games by the time Milwaukee arrived for the season's final four games. One win would give the Brewers their first

division championship, but they lost the first three games by five, six, and eight runs. Don Sutton, who had been acquired from Houston a month earlier, faced Oriole Jim Palmer in the season finale: the Brewers made Sutton's job easy, scoring ten runs to Baltimore's two.

Milwaukee's offense—"Harvey's Wallbangers"—had been awesome, scoring more than a run per game above the league average. Just about every offensive category featured one or two Brewers among the league's top three: in hits they took all three top spots. Shortstop Robin Yount, who finished first in slugging, hits, total bases, and doubles, was named major league player of the year.

In postseason play California took a 2–1 lead in the League Championship Series, but Milwaukee came back to take the final two games and the pennant. In the World Series against St. Louis, the Brewers twice took the lead in games, but a Cardinal come-from-behind win in Game Seven ended Brewer hopes.

Milwaukee dropped to fifth in 1983, then to a last-place seventh the next year, 36½ games back—their most distant finish ever. It was not until 1987 that they returned to the winning track, finishing third with 91 victories. Had they remained in the AL West where they started, their record would have given them the division championship by 6 games.

As veterans Robin Yount and Paul Molitor continued to spark the team's offense, and starter Ted Higuera and reliever Dan Plesac headlined the AL East's best pitching staff, the Brewers in 1988 rose above .500 to stay at the end of August, and finished in a tie for third, just two games behind champion Boston.

Minnesota Twins

The Twins' beginnings as the Washington Senators were inauspicious. When American League president Ban Johnson established the Senators as part of his move in 1901 to raise the league to major league status, he staffed it with the manager and many of the players from his disbanded Kansas City franchise. Within a decade, four of the eight teams in the new major league had won two or more pennants, and three others had enjoyed at least one season in second place. But the Senators, after sixth-place finishes in their first two seasons, spent the next nine years in seventh or eighth. In 1904, their fourth season, they lost 113 games—still the team worst.

Even the arrival of promising young fireballer Walter Johnson didn't seem to help. By 1909 he was the league's second-best strikeout artist, but he lost 25 games and the Senators finished farther back than ever—56 games from the top. Johnson turned his record around the next two years, winning 25 games in 1910 and in 1911, but the team rose only to seventh.

When Clark Griffith—a forty-two-year-old former pitching great and one of the founders of the American League—was hired to manage the Senators after the 1911 season, the club's fortunes took an immediate turn for the better. Griffith revamped the lineup—most strikingly in the acquisition of first baseman Chick Gandil from minor league Montreal. The Senators won seventeen straight games after Gandil was put into the lineup, and found themselves in the midst of a pennant race. Boston's Red Sox eventually ran away from the field, but the Senators held off Philadelphia for second place.

Johnson won 32 games, and his 1.39 ERA led the league.

The next season was Johnson's finest. His league-leading 36 wins, 11 shutouts, and 1.09 ERA were also career bests and enabled Washington to overtake Cleveland late in the season for another second-place finish. But while Johnson continued to top 20 wins per season for several years before beginning to fade, his team was unable to stay competitive, only once in the next decade making a serious run at the pennant (in war-shortened 1918, when they finished 4 games back, in third).

Griffith wanted the Senators to spend more to attract good players; when his demands were rejected, he bought into a controlling interest in the club and named himself president. A year later, in 1921, he retired as field manager. Under a succession of veteran player-managers the team showed some improvement over the next three years, but Griffith's surprise appointment of twenty-seven-year-old second baseman Bucky Harris to manage the team in 1924 worked wonders. Left fielder Goose Goslin drove in more runs than Babe Ruth, and Walter Johnson put together his best season in years to head the league's best pitching staff. A hot streak in June shot the team from fifth to first, and a strong stretch drive in August and September brought them to the finish 2 games ahead of the Yankees. In the World Series a ground ball's lucky bounce over the head of the Giants' third baseman brought the Senators victory in the last of the twelfth inning of the seventh game.

Though the Senators, aided by the acquisition of veteran pitcher Stan Coveleski from Cleveland, fought off the A's to repeat as pennant winners in 1925, they were less successful in postseason play. Once again the Series went the full seven games, but this time Pittsburgh won the world title.

The Senators enjoyed winning seasons in five of the next seven years, as Johnson retired from the mound and replaced Harris as manager. But it was not until 1933, when Johnson was replaced by twenty-six-year-old shortstop Joe Cronin, that the team again pursued the pennant beyond midseason. Two veteran pitchers at the top of their form—Alvin "General" Crowder and Earl Whitehill—and a balanced offense led by Cronin and first baseman Joe Kuhel kept the Senators close to New York through July, and then, as the Yankees leveled off in August, shot the team up out of reach. Although they tailed off a bit at the end, the Senators won the pennant handily, compiling a .651 winning percentage that is still the club record. The New York Giants, though, took Washington's measure in the World Series and overcame them in five games.

The following October, after a drop from third place in June to a distant seventh at season's end had plunged home attendance nearly 25 percent below the previous year, Griffith—always close to the edge financially—traded Joe Cronin, his manager, star shortstop, and (since September) son-in-law, to the Boston Red Sox for a lesser shortstop and $225,000.

Only twice in their remaining quarter century in Washington did the Senators rise higher than fourth or finish closer than 17 games from the top. In 1943 they placed second, 13½ games behind the runaway Yankees. And two years later, after a poor start, they caught up with frontrunner Detroit in September, only to stall and finish 1½ games out. In their final six Washington seasons, they wound up in the cellar four times.

Calvin Griffith, Clark's adopted son, assumed the club presidency when his father died in 1955. Within three years

he was making plans to move the club to Minneapolis. There were threats from Congress and a plea from President Eisenhower not to move the Senators—and at first the league itself opposed the move. But Washington was not a good baseball town even when the Senators were playing well, and in October 1960 a solution was reached. The league would let Griffith move his club to Minnesota, and Washington would be granted a new expansion team.

Players like outfielders Bob Allison and Harmon Killebrew, and pitcher Camilo Pascual, who had enjoyed productive seasons before the move, were even more productive in Minnesota. Other standouts became regulars or joined the club after the move—Zoilo Versalles at shortstop, Rich Rollins at third, Jim Kaat on the mound, and (arriving in 1964) outfielder Tony Oliva and pitcher Jim "Mudcat" Grant. Infielder Rod Carew began his twelve-year stint with the Twins in 1967.

Former outfielder Sam Mele made his major league managerial debut during 1961, and in 1962 saw his Twins come close to catching the Yankees in mid-September, finishing second. The next year they didn't catch fire until August and wound up third. In 1964 they dropped below .500 into a tie for sixth. But after the end of June 1965 no one challenged them as they breezed to their first Minnesota pennant. Oliva led the league in batting for the second straight year, and Versalles (in what was far and away his finest season) led the league in total bases and runs scored. Mudcat Grant led the league with 21 victories (his only 20-win season) and 6 shutouts, and Kaat's 18 wins were the league's third best. In the World Series it took a three-hitter by Los Angeles's Sandy Koufax to stop the Twins in the seventh game.

After a poor start in 1966 that saw them enter July deep in fifth place, the Twins played better than anyone else the rest of the season to sneak ahead of Detroit into second. Killebrew, who had been injured much of the previous year, returned with his old power in '66, and Kaat enjoyed a career-high season with 25 wins.

The Twins began 1967 with another poor start. With the team in disarray and in sixth place, the easygoing Mele was replaced in June by hard-driving Cal Ermer, a longtime minor league manager. By mid-July the team had risen to second, and a month later (after dropping back to fourth) moved to the top in one of the greatest pennant races ever. Four clubs battled for the title, with three still in the running on the final day. But Boston defeated Minnesota to win the pennant, and Detroit split a doubleheader to tie the Twins for second. The next year Minnesota finished seventh.

Fiery rookie manager Billy Martin replaced Ermer in 1969 and, in this first season of divisional play, piloted the Twins to the championship of the West by a convincing 9 games. Killebrew exploded for the best season of his career (49 home runs, 140 runs driven in), and Carew won the first of his seven batting titles. The first League Championship Series, though, was a disaster for the Twins as Baltimore swept to the pennant in three games. Veteran manager Bill Rigney replaced the difficult Martin at the helm, and piloted Minnesota to an almost identical division crown in 1970, 9 games ahead of Oakland. Pitcher Jim Perry, with 24 victories, enjoyed his second straight 20-win season, and the best of his career. The LCS, though, was another repeat performance—a Baltimore sweep.

For the next thirteen years the Twins remained out of contention, although only in 1981 and '82 did they drop to the bottom of the division. Twice (in 1974 and '76) they recovered from poor starts to make a decent showing, and once (1979) they pushed into first in July before nosediving out of the race. But it was not until the flowering of a new generation of young players in 1984 that a Minnesota title threat could be taken seriously.

The Twins' decline on the field was matched by a decline in attendance, which even their move indoors in 1982 did not significantly redress. The Griffith family, unwilling to risk the high cost of luring proven talent, decided to give up the club after more than sixty years of family ownership. Early in 1984 a buyer was found in Carl Pohlad, a wealthy Minneapolis banker. By the time Pohlad's purchase was completed at the end of July, the Twins' young team had blossomed into the West's front-runner, paced by pitcher Frank Viola's sudden development into a winner, and by the arrival in May of rookie centerfield sparkplug Kirby Puckett. Although the Twins leveled off in August and lost their final six games, to fall to .500 and a tie for second, they had brought the crowds back to the ballpark. The team in 1984 for the first time ever drew more than 1.5 million fans to their home games, and remained well above a million the next two years despite a pair of losing seasons.

In 1987 the Minnesota fans were rewarded for their faithfulness. Although the Twins lost their last five games to finish only eight above .500 (and two ahead of surging Kansas City), their winning record at home was the best in the league, and their title in the West was never in doubt. More surprising was their decisive triumph over favored Detroit in the LCS, four games to one. In the first World Series to feature indoor play, the Twins won the four games played in their Metrodome to capture Minnesota's first world baseball championship in seven games.

Although the Twins in 1988 improved on their 1987 won-lost record—and Frank Viola, Kirby Puckett, and relief ace Jeff Reardon enjoyed career peaks—they finished well back of Oakland in the race for the division crown. But their home attendance, which had jumped 66 percent in 1987 to top 2 million for the first time, bounded another 45 percent in 1988 to make the Twins the first AL club ever to attract more than 3 million fans in a season.

Montreal Expos

In the spring of 1969, in an unfinished "temporary" ballpark that would be the Expos' home for eight years, major league baseball came to Canada. One of two clubs added to the National League in this first year of divisional play—Montreal in the East and San Diego in the West—the Expos finished 48 games out of first. But although they matched San Diego's 52–110 record and last-place divisional finish, they outdrew the Padres by better than two to one, with a home attendance of more than 1.2 million fans.

After a second last-place (but much improved at 73–89) season in 1970, the Expos moved a notch out of the cellar to fifth in 1971 and '72, and into pennant contention in 1973. Outfielder Ken Singleton became the first Expo to drive in 100 or more runs, rookie pitcher Steve Rogers compiled a sparkling 1.54 ERA (and a 10–5 won-lost record), and reliever Mike Marshall set a new major-league record with 92 pitching appearances (winning 14 games and saving a league-high 31). In the tightest race of the century, all six clubs

remained in contention into September, when Philadelphia dropped away. In mid-September Montreal won six straight to catch front-running Pittsburgh, only to lose nine of the next ten and drop back to fifth. Three wins in the final four games lifted them to fourth place, just 3½ games behind the champion New York Mets.

Center fielder Willie Davis (acquired from Los Angeles in a trade for Mike Marshall) led the Expos' offense in another fourth-place season in 1974, but the club sank back to a tie for last in 1975 and sole possession of the cellar a year later, with a 55–107 record nearly as bad as their first season (and a home attendance little more than half that of 1969).

But with the acquisition of heavy-hitting Tony Perez from Cincinnati, a new manager—the controversial Dick Williams—and strong seasons from catcher Gary Carter, sophomore outfielder Ellis Valentine, and rookie Andre Dawson, the club snapped back in 1977 to win 20 more games than the previous year and rise to fifth. And with their move into the new Olympic Stadium (built for the 1976 Olympics), Expo attendance rebounded from a club low to a new high.

After climbing another notch to fourth in 1978 (as the newly acquired Ross Grimsley became their first—and, to date, only—20-game winner), the Expos put on a run for the title that drove attendance in 1979 to over two million. Third baseman Larry Parrish, with a career-high season, led the club in batting and home runs in a balanced attack that saw five players drive in more than 70 runs. The pitching too was balanced, with six pitchers winning 10 games or more on a staff that compiled the league's lowest ERA. With a fast start in April, the Expos led the East through much of June and into July, when a surging Pittsburgh caught up with them. Both clubs climbed away from the pack to the end of the season. Montreal fell back a bit in August but caught up with the Pirates in September and carried the race to the final day before dropping off to second. The Expos' 95 victories remain the club record to date.

The 1980 race was just as exciting. A three-way struggle with Philadelphia and Pittsburgh through most of the summer narrowed to two teams in September as the Pirates fell away. In a crucial late-September series, the Expos beat the Phillies two games of three to take a half-game lead, but in the final series a week later Philadelphia won two games to clinch the crown.

In a 1981 season divided by a players' strike, Montreal finished the first part of the season in third place, but held off St. Louis to win the second part by half a game. The Expos then won the division championship in a special playoff with first-half winner Philadelphia—their first title—but lost the League Championship Series to Los Angeles.

As the Expos declined gradually over the next five years, most of the regulars left through trade, free agency, or retirement. But in 1987, two 1981 rookies who had remained in Montreal—outfielder Tim Raines and third baseman Tim Wallach—stood out in an Expo comeback that left them in third place, just four games back, with 91 wins and the second-best record in their history.

New York Mets

Branch Rickey's projected Continental League never materialized, but its New York and Houston franchises were admitted to the National League, expanding the league to ten clubs in 1962. Few major league teams have been as inept as the New York Mets were in their first season. Despite the presence on the club of such New York favorites as manager Casey Stengel, pitcher Roger Craig, and first baseman Gil Hodges, and of players like outfielders Richie Ashburn and Frank Thomas who were still near peak form, the Mets finished at the bottom of the league in batting, fielding, and pitching. They won only one game in four and suffered a twentieth-century record 120 losses. But New York fans—deprived of National League baseball since the defection of the Dodgers and Giants to the West Coast four years earlier—found their ineptitude lovable. By their third season, having moved out of the old Polo Grounds into brand-new Shea Stadium, the last-place Mets were regularly outdrawing the pennant-bound Yankees.

Former New York Giants catcher Wes Westrum replaced the aging Stengel as manager part way through the 1965 season, and the next year saw the club rise out of the cellar for the first time. But they fell back to tenth in 1967 (despite rookie Tom Seaver's 16 wins—a club record), and Westrum was replaced at the helm by Gil Hodges (who had retired from playing after a few games in 1963). With Jerry Koosman joining Seaver in the starting rotation and setting a new club record with 19 victories, Hodges led the Mets in 1968 back up to ninth place with their first season of more than 70 victories.

In 1969 the majors inaugurated divisional play, but the Mets got off to their usual indifferent start. At the end of May, however, they began to win consistently. By early June they were second in the NL East, though well back of the explosive Chicago Cubs. By September, though, the Cubs were faltering. The "Miracle Mets" caught and passed them with a ten-game winning streak and continued on to take the division title by eight games. Among the many Met heroes, Tom Seaver stands out. He won his last ten starts, sparking the team's final push to triumph and finishing with a league-high 25 wins that still stands as the club record. After a three-game sweep of West champion Atlanta in the league's first Championship Series, the Mets faced the mighty Baltimore Orioles—regarded by many as one of baseball's all-time greatest teams—for the world championship. The Met miracle continued as, after an opening game loss, the New Yorkers humbled the Orioles with four straight wins.

The Mets of 1970 remained competitive into mid-September as they sought to repeat their '69 triumph. But they fell back at the end while Pittsburgh spurted, and finished third. Two more third-place finishes followed in 1971 and '72. Just before the start of the 1972 season, Met coach Yogi Berra moved up to manage the club after Hodges suffered a fatal heart attack two days before his forty-eighth birthday.

In 1973 the NL East experienced the tightest major league race of the century. Chicago moved out in front of the pack early in the season, but folded in July and August. So did the Mets, who fell from third to a last-place sixth. But although they were last late in August, they were less than seven games out of first. A series of bursts in September, culminating in a seven-game winning streak, shot the Mets through the division into first place by September 21. Although they finished the season only three games above .500, they topped the division by 1½ games. In the LCS they held off the favored Cincinnati Reds to take the pennant in the maximum five games, but lost the World Series when Oakland overcame a 2–3 deficit to win the final two contests.

The Mets then entered a decade-long decline. Though they won as often in 1975 and '76 as they had in 1973, they didn't come close to winning the East, and dropped into a seven-year trough in 1977 which included five seasons in last place. Seaver was traded to Cincinnati in 1977, and Koosman (after two disastrous seasons) was sent to Minnesota in the fall of 1978 (where he won 20 the next year). The heirs of original owner Joan Whitney Payson (who had died in 1975) sold the club to Nelson Doubleday (of the publishing company) and Fred Wilpon in January 1980. In February the new owners hired Frank Cashen as general manager, hoping he could rebuild the Mets as he had the Baltimore Orioles in the late 1960s.

It took a few years to achieve the right blend, but when outfielder Darryl Strawberry was brought up from the minors early in 1983 and first baseman Keith Hernandez was acquired from St. Louis in June, the mix had nearly all the needed ingredients. In 1984, under new manager Davey Johnson, and with rookie pitchers Dwight Gooden and Ron Darling combining for 29 wins, the Mets rebounded to second place with their second-best season record up till then.

The rise continued in 1985. With catcher Gary Carter (newly acquired from Montreal) leading the club in homers and RBIs, and Gooden cementing his superstardom at age twenty with a phenomenal 24–4, 1.53 ERA season, the Mets won 98 games—eight more than the year before—and came within a game of tying St. Louis late in September before slipping 3 games back at the finish.

When the Mets acquired pitcher Bob Ojeda from the Boston Red Sox after the season, many predicted an easy division title for them in 1986. For once, the pundits were right. With Carter, Strawberry, and Hernandez powering the offense, and Ojeda, Darling, and Gooden all placing among the league's top five pitchers in ERA, the Mets won two of every three games (108 in all) to capture the division title by 21½ games.

The postseason battles were tougher. The Mets won the pennant from Houston with a 16-inning victory in Game Six of the LCS, but came within a strike of elimination by the Red Sox in Game Six of the World Series before rallying to take that game and the next for their second world crown.

Strawberry enjoyed his finest season yet in 1987, and pitchers Terry Leach and Rick Aguilera put together a combined won-lost record of 22–4. But Ojeda was lost to injury early in the season, and the Mets, though they hung close and posted 92 wins, lost out—as in 1985—to St. Louis by 3 games.

David Cone (20–3, 2.22 ERA) emerged in 1988 as the ace of the league's best pitching staff, which, with the power of Darryl Strawberry and Kevin McReynolds behind it, carried the Mets back to the top of the NL East, 15 games ahead of runner-up Pittsburgh. But after taking a 3-2 lead in the LCS, they lost the pennant to underdog Los Angeles in seven games.

New York Yankees

In its first twenty seasons, the club that became the New York Yankees won no league championship, and finished second only twice. But for the next forty-four years the Yankees dominated the American League, winning nearly two of every three pennants and twenty World Series. After another pennant drought of eleven years, the club in six years won five division titles, four pennants, and their twenty-first and twenty-second World Series. Their current pennant drought, which has lasted seven years so far, is the third longest in their history.

The Yankees began as the Baltimore Orioles in 1901. But AL president Ban Johnson really wanted a club in New York and, after outmaneuvering the politically influential Giants (who didn't want a competing big league team in their city), Johnson moved the Orioles to the northern end of Manhattan in 1903.

In 1904 the Highlanders (as they were known during their first years in New York because of the high land on which their park was built) chased the Boston Pilgrims through midsummer, catching them in August and trading first place back and forth into October. But after Jack Chesbro defeated Boston 3–2 on October 7 to give New York a half-game lead (it was his forty-first win, a twentieth-century major league record), the Pilgrims came back to win the next two. In the fourth game of the series, with Chesbro again pitching and the score tied 2–2 in the top of the ninth, a wild pitch over the New York catcher's head let in what proved to be Boston's pennant-clinching run.

The Highlanders again led the league in late September two years later, before tailing off to finish 3 games behind Chicago. But that was the last time they contended seriously for the title for fourteen years. Meanwhile they finished last twice, in 1908 losing a club-worst 103 games, and in 1912 suffering their most distant finish ever—55 games behind pennant-winning Boston.

In 1914 Colonel Jake Ruppert and Tillinghast Huston bought the Yankees, and the next year they purchased pitcher Bob Shawkey from the Philadelphia A's. Shawkey's 24 victories in 1916 led the Yankees to their first winning season in six years, and in 1919, on returning from military service, his 20 wins (plus the 9 of Carl Mays, who came to the club in a controversial midseason deal with the Red Sox) brought the Yankees to third—at 7½ games out, their closest finish in thirteen years.

That winter, on the recommendation of manager Miller Huggins, the Yankees paid a then-record $125,000 (plus a $300,000 loan) to the Red Sox for Babe Ruth. Ruth, with 54 home runs in 1920, obliterated the record of 29 he had set the year before, and Mays and Shawkey together won 46 games in a three-way pennant race that ended with New York a close third.

At season's end Ruppert hired Ed Barrow as Yankee general manager. While managing the Red Sox, Barrow had converted Ruth from a pitcher to outfielder. His December trade with Boston that gave the Yankees pitcher Waite Hoyt and catcher Wally Schang was just the improvement needed to bring the Yankees their first pennant in 1921. Ruth's 59 homers and his career-high 171 RBIs didn't hurt, either.

The prickly Carl Mays, staff ace in 1921 with a 27–9 record, slipped to 13–14 the next year. But the Yankees continued to decimate the Red Sox roster with trades that brought them pitchers "Bullet Joe" Bush and "Sad Sam" Jones, and infielders Everett Scott and Joe Dugan. Bush's 26 wins in 1922 made up for Mays's decline, and the Yankees captured their second straight championship.

Both races had been tight two-way struggles—with Cleveland in 1921 and the St. Louis Browns in 1922—and both pennants had been followed by a World Series loss to the Giants. But in 1923 the Yankees at last put everything together. After sharing the Giants' Polo Grounds since 1913,

they were at home in brand-new Yankee Stadium just across the Harlem River in the Bronx. With the addition of yet another pitcher from the Red Sox—Herb Pennock—and a .393 year from Ruth, they took the lead from the start and built it over the summer to a 16-game margin by the end. For the third time the Yankees faced the Giants in the World Series; this time they beat them, in six games, for their first world championship.

The Yankees lost a close race to Washington in 1924 and collapsed into seventh place in 1925—a year in which Ruth was lost much of the season to surgery and suspension. There were bright spots, though: center fielder Earle Combs, in his first full season, hit .342 to lead Yankee regulars, left fielder Bob Meusel filled Ruth's shoes as AL home run and RBI leader, and first baseman Lou Gehrig arrived to stay. With Ruth's return to full strength in 1926 and the establishment of a new middle infield of Tony Lazzeri and Mark Koenig, the Yankees took their fourth pennant in a race that was not as close as their 3-game winning margin would suggest. They lost a close World Series to the Cardinals.

Many observers rank the 1927 Yankees as baseball's greatest team ever. Certainly it was the Yankees' greatest team. They won more games (110) than any Yankee team before or since. Ruth hit his 60 home runs, and Gehrig drove in 175. Waite Hoyt led the league in ERA and rookie Wilcy Moore proved the league's premier reliever. As a team the Yankees led the league in hitting (.307) and slugging (.489, still a major league record); their pitchers compiled a 3.20 ERA that was 3/4 of a run per game lower than the ERA of the next best team. In the World Series they swept the Pittsburgh Pirates.

The resurgent Athletics made the 1928 race much closer, but New York won three in a row from the A's in mid-September to pull ahead, and held on for their sixth pennant. Another Series sweep (this time against the Cardinals) gave them their third world title.

For three years the A's left the Yankees in the shade. An ill Huggins yielded the club's reins in September 1929 and died before the season had ended. By the time the Yankees returned to the top in 1932, their manager was Joe McCarthy. He had led Chicago's Cubs to the NL pennant in 1929; in fifteen seasons at New York he would lead his club to eight more pennants and seven world championships. Only once would his Yankees finish as low as fourth.

A Yankee pennant and World Series triumph over the Cubs in 1932 was followed by three second-place finishes to Washington (in 1933) and Detroit (in 1934 and 1935). Ruth had retired by the time the Bronx Bombers returned to the top in 1936, but Gehrig was still in top form, catcher Bill Dickey and outfielder George Selkirk developed into formidable sluggers, and Joe DiMaggio arrived to take over center field. New York finished a club-record 19½ games in front and buried the Giants in the World Series.

Three more pennants and three more world titles followed in 1937–1939. Lefty Gomez emerged as the league's premier pitcher in 1937, and DiMaggio picked up the home run and slugging crowns. Again the Giants were vanquished in the World Series. Rookie second baseman Joe Gordon and sophomore outfielder Tommy Henrich joined Dickey, DiMaggio, and a declining Gehrig in leading the slugging Yankees to the 1938 crown and a Series sweep of the Cubs. A balanced attack in 1939 saw seven of the eight starters (including Babe Dahlgren, who replaced the dying Gehrig at first) drive in 80

runs or more as the Yankees won 106 to run away with their eleventh pennant—and eighth World Series, another sweep, with Cincinnati the victim. For the fourth year in a row the offense topped the league in slugging, and overshadowed the steady—if unspectacular—Yankee pitchers, who for the *sixth* consecutive season compiled the league's stingiest ERA.

After catching the leaders with a 19–4 spurt in late summer, the 1940 Yankees fell away to finish a close third. But then came another three convincing pennant wins and a pair of Series triumphs as the nation moved into World War Two. Outfielders DiMaggio and Charlie Keller dominated the Yankee offense in 1941, and rookie shortstop Phil Rizzuto hit .307. Though no Yankee pitcher won more than 15 games, seven won 9 or more (and reliever Johnny Murphy won 8 while saving a league-high 15). With 101 victories the team was lost from view to the rest of a league in which six of the eight clubs failed to break .500. In the World Series Brooklyn was the loser in five games.

Keller, DiMaggio, and Gordon provided the power, and Tiny Bonham (with 21 wins), Spud Chandler, and rookie Hank Borowy headed the league-leading pitching staff that propelled the Yankees to 103 wins and another easy pennant in 1942. But after winning their previous eight World Series, the Yankees were finally stopped, in five games, by the Cardinals.

By 1943 many Yankees were in military service. But pitchers Chandler, Bonham, Borowy, and Murphy were not, and they led the charge to the team's seventh pennant in eight years. In the Series the Yankees reversed the results of the previous year, turning back St. Louis in five.

When Jake Ruppert died in 1939, general manager Barrow succeeded him as president, a position he held until January 1945, when Dan Topping and Del Webb bought the club and installed Larry MacPhail as president, giving him a third of the club and a ten-year contract to run it. The volatile, innovative MacPhail had previously brought new life to Cincinnati and Brooklyn, and did bring night ball to Yankee Stadium. But manager McCarthy, who couldn't get along with MacPhail, quit early in the 1946 season, and the team finished a distant third.

DiMaggio and the others were back from the war by 1946, but it was not until 1947—under new manager Bucky Harris, and with sparkling pitching from Allie Reynolds (acquired from Cleveland), rookie Frank "Spec" Shea, and reliever Joe Page—that the Yankees returned to the top of the heap with an easy pennant win and a narrow World Series triumph over Brooklyn. On the day the Yankees won the Series, though, president MacPhail embarrassed the club and undid himself by brawling in public. Topping and Webb bought out his contract and share of the ownership. Topping took over the presidency, but promoted farm director George Weiss to run the club as general manager.

After the Yankees dropped a pair of season-ending games to the Red Sox to finish third in a tight 1948 race, Weiss replaced manager Harris with Casey Stengel, who in nine years of managing the Braves and Dodgers had only twice seen his club finish as high as fifth. But with Weiss providing a steady stream of talented players via the farm system and canny trades, the Yankees under Stengel proved all but invincible into the '60s.

Stengel's Yankees began by putting together a record string of five world championships. No major league club had

ever won five pennants in a row, let alone five World Series, and the Yankees didn't accomplish the feat easily. In 1949, for example, they saw the Red Sox come from 12 games back in midseason to pass them with a three-game series sweep in late September, only to rescue the flag with two close must-win victories over the Sox in the season's final games. In the World Series, Brooklyn was again the victim, in five games.

After losing much of 1949 to injury, DiMaggio returned with power in 1950, shortstop Rizzuto and catcher Yogi Berra enjoyed the finest seasons of their careers, and pitcher Whitey Ford broke into the majors, winning all nine of his decisions as a starter (he lost one game in relief). But the Yankees struggled even harder for the pennant than the year before, battling three other contenders before finally pulling in front to stay with five straight wins near to the end of the season. Though three of the games in the World Series were decided by just one run, New York took the Phillie "Whiz Kids" without a loss.

No Yankee drove in as many as 90 runs in 1951, and Whitey Ford was drafted for two years of military service. But the remaining pitchers doubled their shutout production and lowered the team ERA by more than half a run per game, enough to propel the club ahead of Cleveland in mid-September. In the World Series the Yankees shook the faith of the "miracle" Giants, four games to two. Cleveland challenged once again in 1952, and again fell just short, as did Brooklyn in carrying the World Series to seven games.

Finally, in 1953, Stengel's Yankees won with relative ease. Ford, back from the Army, won 18 to lead the club to a finish 8½ games up. Once again it was Brooklyn in the World Series, and once again the Yankees beat them.

In 1954 New York won 103 games—the most in Stengel's twelve-year tenure. But Cleveland won an AL-record 111 to take the flag by 8 games. In 1955, though, it was back to second place for Cleveland as New York, with Mickey Mantle now established as one of the game's most productive hitters, settled in for another four pennants. As August passed into September, three teams were within a game of each other at the top. But the Chicago White Sox faltered and fell away, leaving the Yankees and Indians to fight it out. With two weeks left, New York won eight straight to pass Cleveland for good. Facing the Dodgers in the World Series for the sixth time, the Yankees finally lost, as Johnny Podres shut them out in Game Seven to give Brooklyn its first world title since 1900.

From 1956 through 1958 the Yankees seldom found themselves out of first place. Only in 1957, when they leveled off in May before surging to the front in June, were they involved in anything resembling a close race. In postseason play, they went the full seven games all three years, winning twice—from the Dodgers for the sixth time in 1956, and from the Milwaukee Braves in 1958, after losing to them the year before.

In 1959 the Yankees started poorly and never did rise much above .500, finishing a distant third with their worst won-lost record in thirty-four years. After the season, Al Weiss sent an aging Hank Bauer to Kansas City in a trade that brought Roger Maris to New York. In 1960 Maris, with AL titles in slugging and RBIs, won the MVP award. He and Mantle dominated the power stats and led the charge back to the top as the Yankees won their final fifteen games to bury the faltering Orioles.

New York's 1960 pennant was the first in another five-flag

streak, but it was the last for Stengel. After Pittsburgh toppled the Yankees in the World Series on Bill Mazeroski's famous home run, president Topping retired both the seventy-year-old Stengel and general manager Weiss, sixty-five, who had been with the club for twenty-eight years.

With the season lengthened by eight games in 1961, Maris broke Ruth's home-run record and rookie manager Ralph Houk led the club to 109 wins, just one off the club record. Once again Maris and Mantle finished among the best in offensive power, and once again New York took the pennant by 8 games. Ford enjoyed a splendid 25–4 season and celebrated with two more wins in the World Series as the Yankees humbled Cincinnati in five games.

Pitcher Ralph Terry moved out of Ford's shadow in 1962 with 23 wins. Though the Yankees finished just five games ahead of Minnesota, there was little doubt about the outcome from midseason on. In a close World Series with San Francisco, Terry won two, including the clincher with a four-hit shutout.

Though New York won pennants the next two years, the 1962 world title was to be their last until the Steinbrenner era fifteen years later. Despite the loss to injuries of Mantle and Maris for much of 1963, New York dominated the AL, winning by 10½ games with 104 wins. But in postseason play the Yankees were themselves dominated by the Dodgers (now in Los Angeles), who held them to just four runs in a Series sweep.

Yogi Berra replaced Houk as manager for 1964. In a season-long three-way race with the White Sox and Orioles that found the clubs virtually tied in mid-September, only an eleven-game win streak gave the Yankees the space they needed for their final one-game margin of victory. Pitcher Jim Bouton won a pair in the World Series, but the Cardinals took the crown in seven. Berra was fired.

During the 1964 season Topping had sold the Yankees to CBS. The next year the club, which had gone forty years without a losing season, dropped to sixth place, and in 1966 fell to a last-place tenth, their first cellar finish in more than half a century. Even Houk's return as manager in 1967—though it led to some winning seasons—failed to restore the once-proud club to pennant contention, except once, in 1972, when it was mid-September before they fell out of a tight race to finish fourth.

In January 1973 a syndicate headed by Cleveland shipping magnate George Steinbrenner purchased the Yankees from CBS. Although he had vowed not to take a prominent role in running the club, Steinbrenner soon emerged as one of baseball's most active and intrusive owners. Through a series of shrewd trades, offers of big contracts to free agents, and what became a round robin of managerial changes, Steinbrenner's Yankees became competitive again in 1974 (finishing a close second to Baltimore after streaking from last in July to first in September) and returned to the top with three successive pennants and a pair of world championships.

Billy Martin (a former Yankee second baseman) in 1976, his first full season as manager, led the renewed club to a runaway division title. First baseman Chris Chambliss's homer in the last of the ninth of the final game of the League Championship Series gave the Yankees the pennant by the narrowest of margins over the Kansas City Royals. Cincinnati swept New York in the World Series, but the Yankees came back the next year to edge Baltimore and Boston in a three-way race that saw the teams shift back and forth in the

standings throughout the season. Slugger Reggie Jackson, signed as a free agent the previous autumn, turned the club's power trio of Chambliss, Graig Nettles, and Thurman Munson into a quartet as the Yankees recorded their first hundred-victory season in fourteen years. After another ninth-inning win over Kansas City in the LCS finale, New York won the World Series in six games over Los Angeles, and Jackson became "Mr. October" with five home runs—three of them in successive at-bats in the final game.

The 1978 season provided as exciting a race as baseball is likely to see. In mid-July it looked like a Red Sox romp, but the fourth-place Yankees put on a great surge, catching the faltering Sox with a four-game series sweep in early September. Boston dropped 3½ games back, but won their final eight games to catch New York on the final day. In the one-game tiebreaker, Yankee shortstop Bucky Dent lofted a wind-blown three-run homer over Boston's close left field wall in the seventh, and Jackson homered an inning later for New York's final run in the 5–4 win. Again the Royals were the victims in the LCS, as were the Dodgers in the World Series.

After dropping to fourth in 1979, the Yankees held off Baltimore in 1980 to win their fourth division title—but this time Kansas City swept to the pennant in three games. In 1981 the Yankees found themselves in first place when the players struck in June and were thus admitted to an intradivisional playoff with the season's second-half winner, Milwaukee. Narrowly defeating the Brewers for the division title, New York swept Oakland for the pennant in the LCS. But after taking the first two games from Los Angeles in the World Series, they were stopped cold as the Dodgers won the next four.

Since 1981, despite the infusion of stars from other clubs (like outfielder Rickey Henderson) and from the farm (like Don Mattingly), and despite constant roster manipulation, Steinbrenner has been unable to bring his Yankees back to the top. Billy Martin (who had first been fired in the midst of the 1978 pennant drive and was subsequently rehired and refired three times) was hired a fifth time to pilot the club. He lasted only into June 1988, when general manager Lou Piniella returned for a second stint as field manager. The Yankees remained in the thick of a tight divisional race until the loss of two late season series to ultimate champion Boston; three straight losses at season's end plunged them into fifth place, though only 3½ games out. Piniella was promptly replaced at the helm by Dallas Green, who had piloted the Phillies to the world title in 1980. It was the Yankees' sixteenth change of managers in Steinbrenner's sixteen years of ownership.

Oakland Athletics

The history of the Athletics is a tale of three cities—a story of the best of teams and of the worst of teams. With a thirteen-year sojourn in Kansas City between residence in Philadelphia and Oakland, the A's are the only club to include a stop in Middle America in their trek from the East Coast to West. They have won thirteen American League pennants (plus three Western Division championships that didn't lead to a pennant), second in the AL only to the incomparable Yankees. But they have also finished last in the league or division twenty-six times, and in sixteen seasons have lost 100 games or more—both AL worsts, by far. A club of extremes,

they have been either at the top or at the bottom in nearly one season out of two.

When Ban Johnson in 1901 established four eastern clubs for his American League, he chose Connie Mack to manage the new Philadelphia Athletics and gave him a quarter ownership of the club. Mack, who had been managing the league's Milwaukee franchise, settled in at Philadelphia and set a record for managerial longevity—fifty years—that is unlikely ever to be surpassed.

In his first fourteen years the A's dominated the league, with six pennants and two close second-place finishes. After finishing fourth in 1901, the club won its first pennant the next year, pulling away from the field with spurts in August and September. Rube Waddell led the team with 24 wins, and six regulars hit over .300. The next two years saw the A's fade in August, but in 1905, after forging ahead in early August and hanging on to the lead with two crucial wins over Chicago's surging White Sox in late September, the A's opened October with a five-game winning streak to clinch their second flag. Waddell, with 26 wins, once again led the club (followed closely by Eddie Plank's 25) and compiled a league-leading 1.48 ERA. In the Athletics' first World Series appearance, though, New York's Christy Mathewson provided most of the pitching heroics, shutting out the A's three times in the Giants' 4–1 Series triumph.

Another August decline in 1906 was followed in 1907 by a comeback struggle from fifth place in late May to a 2½-game lead in mid-September. But the loss of a crucial game to Detroit several days later, and the failure to make up a rainout and a tie, left the A's 1½ games behind the Tigers at the finish.

In 1908 the A's suffered their first losing season, but they rebounded in 1909 to chase the Tigers throughout the summer before tailing off to second. In 1910, with a pitching staff that compiled a stunning 1.79 ERA (paced by Jack Coombs, whose 31 wins included 13 shutouts) and with league-leading fielding and hitting, the A's pulled ahead for good in June, increasing their lead through the rest of the season to finish 14½ games in front. In the World Series they continued to dominate, outscoring the Chicago Cubs 35–15 as they took their first world title, in five games. The A's repeated just as convincingly in 1911. With their "$100,000 infield" of Stuffy McInnis, Eddie Collins, Jack Barry, and Frank "Home Run" Baker averaging .323 at the bat, and Jack Coombs winning 28 games to again lead the club (and the league), the A's overtook Detroit in August to win by 13½ games. In the World Series, Baker hit two important home runs against the Giants, and the A's defeated Mathewson twice, avenging their 1905 humiliation with a victory in six games.

A third-place finish in 1912 broke the pennant streak, but the Athletics came back for two more in 1913 and '14, in both seasons pulling away in early June for easy wins. In the 1913 World Series the A's again felled the Giants, this time in just five games, but the next year they were in turn humiliated by the upstart Boston Braves, who stunned Philadelphia with the first sweep since the renewal of World Series play in 1903.

That winter, Mack began to dismantle his championship club, selling second baseman Collins to the White Sox and releasing pitchers Coombs, Eddie Plank, and Chief Bender. (Third baseman Baker, homesick for the country life, sat out the 1915 season before moving on to the Yankees). Though Mack received $50,000 for Collins, his unconditional release of the three pitchers suggests that he had another reason than

financial need for purging his club. (Suspicion of corrupt play in the 1914 World Series has been hinted.)

Whatever Mack's reasons, the changes did not help the club. The A's sank immediately to last place, where they remained for seven years. In 1915 they lost 109 games and finished 58½ games out. The next year they lost 117 games to set a league record for ineptitude that has never been equalled.

It was a decade before Mack was able to restore the club to respectability. In 1924 he brought up Al Simmons, and the next year Jimmie Foxx and pitcher Lefty Grove. Thus renewed, the A's in 1925 battled Washington to the end of August before backing off to second. In 1927 they won 91 games, though their second-place finish was 19 games back of the overwhelming Yankees. In 1928 the A's battled from well back of New York in midseason to overtake them for a day or two in September, only to lose three of four games in a critical Yankee series and slip back to second.

From 1929 through 1931, though, the A's interrupted New York's domination of the AL with three spectacular seasons. In 1929 sophomore pitcher George Earnshaw blossomed into the league's big winner with 24 victories and Grove led the league's stingiest staff with a league-low 2.81 ERA. Six players drove in 79 runs or more (led by Simmons' league-high 157) in powering the A's to 104 wins and an impressive finish 18 games ahead of the second-place Yankees.

After swamping the Cubs in the World Series, the A's repeated as pennant winners in 1930. Simmons led the league in batting (.381), and Grove led its pitchers in just about everything; wins (28), ERA, strikeouts—even saves (9). Again the World Series was no contest as the A's downed the Cardinals in six.

Earnshaw won more than 20 games for his third successive season in 1931, Simmons repeated as batting leader (.390), and Grove enjoyed what would be the finest season of his career (31–4, 2.06 ERA) in carrying the A's to 107 wins—their best record ever. But in Game Seven of the World Series their dominance of the baseball world ended in a Cardinal victory.

Following a second-place finish in 1932, Mack began selling off his stars again. This time the reason was primarily economic. Home attendance—never robust—fell off sharply after 1931, as the Great Depression and the A's decline made their impact felt. By 1935 the Athletics were back in the cellar, where they finished in ten of Mack's final sixteen years as manager.

In 1946 Mack, who since 1940 had been the A's majority stockholder, divided his shares among his three sons, provoking a family squabble over control of the club. In 1950 the two eldest, Roy and Earle, bought out Connie Jr. and pressured their eighty-seven-year-old father to retire. But with Connie Sr. gone, attendance (which had risen to new highs in the baseball boom that followed World War Two) dropped off again. When in 1954 the A's finished 60 games behind champion Cleveland and attendance dropped to an eighteen-year low, the Macks sold the club to Chicagoan Arnold Johnson, who moved it to Kansas City.

Attendance jumped more than a million the first season in Kansas City (putting the A's over one million for the first time ever), and the team rose a couple of places to sixth. But 1955 was the high point of their thirteen-year stay in the Midwest; the K.C. A's never again rose above seventh, and they finished last six times.

Owner Johnson died in March 1960, and that December his heirs sold the club to the enterprising but abrasive Charles O. Finley. Finley brought in a succession of new managers over the next few years, and in 1965 outfitted his players in new bright green-and-yellow uniforms. But with the league's expansion to ten teams in 1961, the A's had two places lower to sink—and did. After finishing tenth in 1967 for the third time in four years, Finley moved the club to Oakland, California.

Attendance was slow to improve in Oakland—unlike the team. In 1968, their first year on the coast, they put together their first winning season in sixteen years. The next year, with the start of divisional play, the A's took second in the AL West. Reggie Jackson, in only his second full big league season, enjoyed his finest year, with 47 home runs, 118 RBIs, and AL highs in slugging (.608) and runs scored (123).

After another second-place finish in 1970, the A's were ready for a return to glory. In the next five years they won five division titles, winning both the AL pennant and the World Series in the three middle years, 1972–1974. In 1971, with a new manager, Dick Williams, and three pitchers (Vida Blue, Catfish Hunter, and reliever Rollie Fingers) who reached their prime all at once, the A's enjoyed their best season in forty years and won the West by 16 games. Baltimore swept them away in the League Championship Series, but they came back to take the West again the next year. Detroit took them to the limit in the LCS, as did Cincinnati in the World Series, but in both series the A's prevailed in the deciding game by the margin of a single run.

The next year, 1973, Jackson led the league in slugging, homers, and RBIs, Ken Holtzman joined Blue and Hunter in the 20-win column, and home attendance crept over a million (by a few hundred souls) for the first time in Oakland as the A's ran their string of Western Division titles to three. Once again they were pushed to the limit in the postseason—by Baltimore in the LCS and the New York Mets in the World Series—and once again they emerged as world champions.

Manager Williams quit in a dispute with Finley and was replaced by Al Dark, but the outcome in 1974 (except for a drop in attendance to under a million) was the same. Hunter bore more of the pitching load and wound up tied for the AL lead with 25 wins. His 2.49 ERA also led the league, as the staff ended Baltimore's five-year hold on the ERA title. The A's toppled the Orioles in the LCS and (in the first World Series held entirely on the West Coast) won their third consecutive world title in five closely fought games with Los Angeles.

Free-agent Catfish Hunter deserted to the Yankees, and Baltimore regained the ERA crown in 1975, but pitchers Paul Lindblad and newcomer Dick Bosman combined for a 20–5 record to supplement the efforts of Blue, Holtzman, and Fingers and carry Oakland to an unprecedented fifth straight division title. But there the magic stopped, as Boston swept to the pennant in the LCS.

In the off-season Finley, with moves reminiscent of Connie Mack, tried to sell off his star players: Blue, Jackson, Fingers, Holtzman, and outfielder/first baseman Joe Rudi, one of the team's steadiest hitters. The proposed sales made some sense: the players planned to leave the club at the end of their 1976 option year, and Finley by disposing of them before they played out their option could at least be compensated for his loss. The Jackson and Holtzman deals were approved, but baseball commissioner Bowie Kuhn blocked the sale of the

others, citing the "best interests of baseball."

The weakened A's came back from a poor start to close within 2½ games of the Kansas City Royals in 1976, but they dropped to last place the next year. After another last-place finish in 1979, Finley hired fiery Billy Martin to manage the club. Martin brought the A's in second in 1980, and first in the first half of strike-divided 1981. They won the Western Division championship by sweeping Kansas City in the special intradivisional playoffs, but were in turn swept by the Yankees in the LCS.

Finley's sale of the club in 1981 to the folks who bring us Levi's jeans signaled a turn toward normalcy and popularity. Despite a losing season in 1982, the club set a home attendance record as over 1.7 million fans came to watch Ricky Henderson's successful assault on the stolen-base record. In 1987 the A's finished right at .500—for the first time in their history a perfectly average team.

But in 1988 the A's once more became the league's best. With reliever Dennis Eckersley (who blossomed to become the league's top closer), starter Dave Stewart (with his second straight 20-win season), and a cadre of fine middle relievers pacing the league's best pitching staff, and with sluggers Jose Canseco, Dave Henderson, and Mark McGwire driving in 317 of the club's 800 runs, the A's won a major-league high 104 games to finish 13 games ahead of Minnesota in the AL West, and they topped 2 million in home attendance for the first time. They swept Boston in the LCS for their thirteenth pennant but faltered in the World Series, losing to underdog Los Angeles in five games.

Philadelphia Phillies

It took the Phillies thirty-two years to win their first pennant, and ninety-seven to win their first world championship. They have finished last in their league or division twenty-seven times—more than one season in four. In the nine years from 1975 through 1983, though, they were one of the most formidable teams in baseball.

Alfred J. Reach, a sporting goods entrepreneur and former player, and Colonel John Rogers, a Philadelphia lawyer and politician, organized the Phillies in 1883 to bring Philadelphia back into the National League after a six-year absence. In their first season, the Phillies won only 17 of 98 decisions to finish an eighth-place last, as far out of seventh as the seventh-place team was from first. Bad as the Phillies have sometimes been since, their 1883 winning percentage of .173 remains their very worst.

Reach hired the respected Harry Wright to manage the Phillies in 1884, and while Wright failed to lead them to a pennant in his ten years at the helm, he did make them respectable. His fourth-place 1886 team, in fact, compiled a winning percentage of .623 that remained the club's best for ninety years. In 1887 the Phillies, with three pitchers winning more than 20 games, finished second, just 3½ games behind Detroit—their closest finish until their first pennant twenty-eight years later.

The Phillies remained in the upper division twelve of the next fourteen years. For five years—1891–1895—they fielded an outfield of Ed Delahanty, Billy Hamilton, and Sam Thompson—Hall of Famers who rank among the top hitters of all time. In the three heavy-hitting seasons that followed the lengthening of the pitching distance to its present 60'6" in

1893, Delahanty, Hamilton, and Thompson—with help from players like catcher Jack Clements (.394 in 1895) and utility outfielder Tuck Turner (.416 in 1894)—sparked the Phillies to three team batting titles with BAs of over .300. In 1894 three Phillie outfielders hit over .400 (Hamilton just missed, at .399), and the team hit .349—still the major league record.

In 1899, with Delahanty's .408 leading the way, the Phillies once again topped .300 to lead the league. Though the team finished third, they won 94 games, a club high they would not surpass for seventy-seven years. President Reach sold his interest in the club after a dispute with co-owner Rogers, and Rogers lost star second baseman Larry Lajoie in a salary dispute to the Athletics (Philadelphia's new entry in the rival American League). But the Phillies chased front-runner Pittsburgh through much of 1901. Though they slumped in August, they recovered to finish second.

It was the end of an era. Delahanty deserted to the AL the next season, and the Phillies dropped to seventh. Rogers sold the club to a syndicate. By 1904 the team was in last place, losing 100 games for the first time.

They rose into the first division the next season, but didn't mount a serious pennant run until 1911, when the pitching of rookie Grover Cleveland Alexander kept them in the thick of the race into midseason. Two years later they enjoyed first place through most of June before fading to a distant second.

In 1915 Alexander brought his ERA down more than a run per game to a league- and career-best of 1.22, hurling 12 shutouts among his 31 wins. Right fielder Gavvy Cravath and first baseman Fred Luderus finished one-two among NL sluggers, and Cravath won home run and RBI crowns. For half a season all eight clubs were in the thick of a tight race, with the Cubs and Phillies at the top of the heap. But in July the Cubs folded, and in August and September the Phillies took off to outdistance the late-surging Boston Braves by 7 games for their first pennant.

The World Series was a Phillies' heartbreak. Four of the five games were decided by a single run—but the runs belonged to the Boston Red Sox, who swept four after the Phillies had taken the opener.

Alexander shut out a record-tying 16 opponents the following year, winning a career-high 33, and teammate Eppa Rixey had his first big year with 22 wins. Through most of the season, the club trailed the leading Dodgers, but caught them in September, only to fall away again in the final week.

After Alexander's 30 wins had brought the Phillies another second-place finish in 1917, the club dealt him to Chicago and embarked on thirty-one years of wandering in the desert. After fourteen losing seasons (eight of them in last place), they climbed to fourth, two games above .500, in 1932, but dropped back the next year into the second division (including nine last-place finishes) for sixteen more years.

Several outstanding players spent time in Philadelphia during these years: Dave Bancroft (a rookie in their pennant season), Cy Williams, Freddy Leach, Chuck Klein, Lefty O'Doul, and Dick Bartell. Of these, only Williams and Klein retired as Phillies. The financially strapped management traded away the others at the height of their careers in deals that included cash as well as players. Even Klein—perhaps the greatest of them all—was sold twice before returning a third time to Philly to end his career.

The Phillies in 1930 produced a season that ranks among the most extraordinary of all time. With Klein and O'Doul leading the way at .386 and .383, every regular hit at least

.280, to give the Phillies a team BA of .315. But Phillie pitchers yielded a record 1199 runs while compiling the worst big league ERA ever—6.71. The club lost 102 games and finished last.

The Phillies' move in 1938 out of tiny, antiquated Baker Bowl into the Athletics' Shibe Park did nothing for attendance—or for performance, as the team strung together a club-record five consecutive last-place finishes from 1938 to 1942, in which they averaged 107 losses per season and finished between 43 and 62½ games out of first.

In February 1943 the league took control of the debt-ridden club and sold it to a group headed by New York sportsman William D. Cox. Cox didn't last long; before the year was out he was barred from baseball for betting on the Phillies. His controlling interest was sold to Robert M. Carpenter, who installed his son, Robert Jr., as president. The younger Carpenter hired former pitcher Herb Pennock as general manager with instructions to build a farm system, and a new era began in the club's history.

Outfielder Del Ennis had come up to hit .313 in 1946, but Pennock died (in January 1948) before he could see the full fruits of his labor. First baseman Dick Sisler would be purchased in March; rookie outfielder Richie Ashburn would lead Phillie batters in 1948 with a .333 BA. Willie Jones wouldn't nail down third base for another year, and rookie pitchers Robin Roberts and Curt Simmons wouldn't overawe the opposition for a couple of seasons yet. But the team that would be dubbed the "Whiz Kids" was gathering. Triple-A manager Eddie Sawyer was brought up in late July.

In 1949, the loss of first baseman Eddie Waitkus (shot in the chest by a crazed young woman) and midseason complacency threatened to strand the Phillies in the second division. But Sawyer fired up his players in a special team meeting, and the Phillies rallied to finish third with the club's best record in thirty-two years.

With new red-pinstripe uniforms and a recovered Eddie Waitkus, the 1950 Phillies pulled away from a tightly bunched first division in July and August, but late in September fell to within two games of onrushing Brooklyn. The Dodgers took the first game of a season-ending two-game series to narrow the gap to one. But in the finale the Phillies' Sisler homered to break a tenth-inning tie. When Brooklyn failed to score in the bottom of the tenth, the Whiz Kids had their pennant.

Curt Simmons, who was called up for military service in September after winning 17 games, missed the World Series. As in 1915, the result for Philadelphia was frustration and heartbreak, as the Phillies were swept by the Yankees—in the first three games by a single run.

Roberts's pitching kept the Phillies in the first division for four of the next five years, but the team made no serious run at another pennant. And when Roberts began to lose his effectiveness the team sank farther, to fifth for two years, then to four years in the cellar, culminating in 1961 with the longest big league losing streak of the century: 23 games.

The club stuck with new manager Gene Mauch, and the 1962 Phillies edged above .500 for the first time in nine years (though finishing seventh in a league newly expanded to ten teams). In 1963 they moved up to fourth with a strong second half. In 1964, with the acquisition of pitcher Jim Bunning from Detroit and infielder Richie (later Dick) Allen's productive rookie season, Mauch's Phillies moved way out in front in August. But they blew their lead with ten straight losses in

late September while Cincinnati was winning nine and St. Louis eight in a row. Only victories in their final two games salvaged a second-place tie.

The Phillies produced winning seasons the next three years but never challenged the leaders. With Mauch replaced as manager during the 1968 campaign, the team embarked on seven straight losing seasons, including three years at the bottom of the NL East.

Pitcher Steve Carlton, acquired from St. Louis in an off-season trade, accounted for nearly half the Phillies' 59 wins in 1972. His 27 victories for the league's worst team gave the club a ray of hope for the future and earned Carlton the Cy Young Award. Carlton lost a league-high 20 games the next year, but as he regained his form over the next three seasons, so too the Phillies gradually rose to the top of the division.

In 1974 sophomore third baseman Mike Schmidt burst to the forefront of the league's power hitters. The Phillies dropped out of contention in August, but wound up third, their best finish since the league split into divisions in 1969. The next year outfielder Greg Luzinski joined Schmidt among the league's top sluggers, and the club rose to second, with their first winning season since 1967.

The Phillies had entered their golden age—nine straight winning seasons (a club record), including five division titles, two pennants, and their first world championship. In 1976 they enjoyed their finest regular season ever. With Schmidt and Luzinski providing the power, Carlton returning to the ranks of 20-game winners and Jim Lonborg climaxing a long comeback with 18 wins, the Phillies took the division lead in May and pulled away, recovering from a late-season dive to finish well ahead of Pittsburgh. Their 101 wins, .6235 winning percentage, and nine-game margin of victory remain club records.

The Phillies were swept by Cincinnati in the League Championship Series, but came back the next season to duplicate their record 101 wins for another comfortable first-place finish. Carlton won 23 (and his second Cy Young Award), and Luzinski enjoyed the best season of his career, driving in 130 runs. After defeating Los Angeles in the LCS opener, though, the Phillies lost the pennant with three straight losses.

In 1978, even though Schmidt and Carlton had off-years, the Phillies led much of the season and captured the division title a third straight time. But it was a tight race, and they barely survived a late-season Pittsburgh surge to finish 1½ games in front. For the third time, their triumph in the East was followed by defeat in the LCS—for the second time at the hands of Los Angeles in four games.

Danny Ozark, in his seventh year as Phillies manager, was replaced by Dallas Green late in a disappointing 1979 season that saw the club stumble after a strong start before rallying in September to finish fourth. But Schmidt was back in top form, and Pete Rose had arrived via free agency to add his bat and hustle.

In a three-way race in 1980 that remained close through August, the Phillies hung tight without being able to move into the lead. But as Pittsburgh folded in late August and early September, the Phillies edged in front briefly, then battled back and forth with Montreal. Tied with the Expos as the clubs met in Montreal for the season's final three games, Philadelphia took the first 2–1, then—in eleven innings—the second, to clinch their fourth division title in five years. Schmidt, with perhaps his finest season, drove in 121 runs and was named NL MVP; Carlton, with 24 wins, won his third Cy

Young Award; and veteran reliever Tug McGraw enjoyed his best season in years.

In an LCS in which four of the five games went into extra innings, the Phillies prevailed over Houston, capturing their first pennant since the Whiz Kids era thirty years earlier. And in the World Series, fortune finally smiled on the team as they overcame Kansas City in six games.

The Phillies won the first half of the strike-divided 1981 season. In the special intradivisional playoff against Montreal, Philadelphia fought back to tie the series after losing the first two games—only to lose the finale.

The Carpenter family—citing the prohibitive cost of running a major league club—sold the team. Manager Dallas Green also left and was replaced by Pat Corrales, who kept the club in the thick of the 1982 race until the final month, when the Phillies slipped 3½ games back, to second. Carlton's 23 wins earned him a record fourth Cy Young trophy.

Mike Schmidt again dominated the Phillies' offense in 1983, but Carlton yielded to John Denny as the team's pitching ace. Newly acquired reliever Al Holland emerged as one of the league's best. After general manager Paul Owens took over for Corrales as manager in midseason, the Phillies came alive and took the division title by 6 games. Carlton dominated the LCS with an 0.66 ERA and two wins as the Phillies won their fourth pennant. But their golden age ended in the World Series, when Baltimore triumphed in five games.

The Phillies dropped to .500 and fourth place in 1984, and suffered a losing fifth-place season in 1985. They rebounded to second in 1986 (but 21½ games behind New York), then dropped back below .500 in 1987. Mike Schmidt continued to power the offense—the only member of the 1980 world champions still a Phillie. Despite an impressive lineup of everyday players in 1988, the Phils collapsed, finishing in the division cellar for the first time in fifteen years.

Pittsburgh Pirates

Pittsburgh became a big league city in 1882, when its Allegheny baseball club joined with five other teams to form the American Association. Allegheny president H. D. McKnight was named president of the new league, but Allegheny made little stir until the club hired Horace Phillips to manage it and replaced its team in 1885 with players from the defunct Columbus Club, which had finished second in the AA the year before. The new Alleghenys finished a distant third in 1885, but after purchasing Pud Galvin from Buffalo they improved in 1886 to a respectable second behind the invincible St. Louis Browns.

Flushed with success, Allegheny in 1887 became the first club to desert the AA for the older and more highly regarded National League. There they found the competition stiffer and sank back into the second division. In 1890, when most of the team jumped to the rival Pittsburgh Players' League club, Allegheny (known that year as the Innocents) suffered the worst season in Pittsburgh major league history, finishing last, 66½ games out of first place (and 23 out of seventh), with a won-lost record of 23–113.

When the PL folded after just one season, Allegheny merged with its PL counterpart to form the Pittsburgh Athletic Company, thereby retrieving many of its old regulars. The club also hired a second baseman—Lou Bierbaur—whose signing (or theft, as his old club saw it) gave the

Innocents a new and more enduring nickname: the Pirates. The renewed club still finished last in 1891, but thirty-six games closer to the top than the year before, and only fractionally out of seventh place.

In 1893 a rules change moved the pitcher 10½ feet farther back from home plate. Of all the NL clubs, the Pirates benefited most from the change: their batting average jumped 63 points—28 more than that of the league as a whole—while their pitchers suffered less than most. The club finished second, with a .628 winning percentage that was their best of the century. Lefty Frank Killen, a twenty-two-year-old pitcher acquired from Washington, led the club's resurgence with a league-leading 34 wins.

Although catcher Connie Mack was called upon to manage the club toward the end of the 1894 season and led them to winning seasons the next two years, the Pirates did not make another serious run for the pennant until 1900. With a team transformed yet again by players from a defunct club—this time the Louisville Colonels—the Pirates battled Brooklyn's Superbas almost to the end of the season before dropping 4½ games back, a solid second. Although they lost the postseason Chronicle-Telegraph Cup games (that year's World Series) to the Superbas, the Pirates were embarked on an era of greatness.

In the merger that brought the Louisville players to Pittsburgh, the Colonels' owner Barney Dreyfuss acquired half ownership of the Pirates. A year later he bought the other half. His perennial hope for the club was a first-division finish; in twenty-six of his thirty-two years of Pirate ownership his hope was rewarded.

Four of the former Louisville players—outfielder-turned-shortstop Honus Wagner, outfielder/manager Fred Clarke, third baseman/outfielder Tommy Leach, and pitcher Deacon Phillippe—and one carryover from the old Pirates, pitcher Sam Leever, remained with Pittsburgh long enough to help lead them to four pennants and, in 1909, their first world championship. In the sixteen years Clarke managed the Pirates (a club record), they also finished second five times, and slipped out of the first division only in Clarke's final two seasons at the helm.

In contrast to the club's devastation by the Players' League raid of 1890, the Pirates were unaffected in 1901 by raiders from the American League (which that year turned itself into a major league largely by drawing off talent from National League clubs). Only third baseman Jimmy Williams defected to the Americans, and he was ably replaced by Tommy Leach, as the Pirates, with the league's best pitching (Jesse Tannehill and Deacon Phillippe finished one-two in ERA, and Jack Chesbro at 21–10 led in winning percentage), captured their first pennant by a comfortable 7½ games over the Philadelphia Phillies.

The Pirates repeated as pennant winners in 1902 and 1903. The 1902 team was one of the most overwhelming of all time. One Pirate or another led the league in nearly every offensive category: Ginger Beaumont in hits and batting; Tommy Leach in home runs (with 6); and Honus Wagner in slugging, RBIs, runs scored, doubles, and stolen bases. Pitcher Jack Chesbro's 28 wins led the league, and the top five NL pitchers in winning percentage were all Pirates. The club held the lead the whole season, finishing 27½ games ahead of second-place Brooklyn, still a major league record.

Pitchers Chesbro and Tannehill deserted to the AL's New York Highlanders the next season, but their loss merely made

Pittsburgh's pennant-winning margin (6½ games) smaller than it might have been. Wagner beat out teammate Fred Clarke for the NL batting crown and finished second to Clarke in slugging. Beaumont took the titles in hits, runs, and total bases. Pitcher Sam Leever, with his finest season, led the club with 25 wins and the league in ERA and winning percentage. Owner Dreyfuss arranged with the AL champion Boston Pilgrims for a best-of-nine World Series—the first between NL and AL champions—but the Pirates lost it in eight games as their tired pitchers at last succumbed to overwork.

Although the Pirates twice finished second over the next four years, they didn't come close to capturing another pennant until 1908, when, in one of the tightest NL races ever, they were edged out by the Chicago Cubs and finished one game back, tied with New York's Giants for second. The following year, though, they moved in June into the new concrete-and-steel Forbes Field and celebrated by returning to the top of the league with a club record 110 wins—holding off the dogged Cubs throughout the season to take the flag by 6½ games. And this time they won the World Series, too, although they needed the full seven games to subdue Detroit's Tigers. Honus Wagner remained the league's dominant offensive force, but aging pitchers Leever and Phillippe were overshadowed by a new crop of standouts: Vic Willis, Howie Camnitz, Nick Maddox, and Lefty Leifield—and the astonishing rookie Babe Adams, who after going 12–3 (with a 1.11 ERA) during the season, won three more games in the World Series.

The Series triumph ended an era. Wagner was past his prime and wound down his long career over the next several seasons as the Pirates dropped out of contention for a dozen years, including four (1914–1917) in the hated second division. Only Babe Adams remained of the world championship team when Pittsburgh next made a contest of the pennant race in 1921, taking an early lead and holding it most of the summer until an August-September decline dropped them to second place, 4 games back.

Former Pirate infielder Bill McKechnie replaced George Gibson as manager during the following season with the club in fifth place, and saw the Pirates spurt to second before fading to third at the finish. Two more third-place seasons—with the Pirates finishing just 3 games out of first in 1924—paved the way for another pennant in 1925.

The 1925 Pirates fielded several stars: shortstop Glenn Wright, who led the club with 121 RBIs; sophomore right fielder Kiki Cuyler, who led the team in hitting (.357) and the league in runs scored; third baseman Pie Traynor, who shone on the field and at the bat; and Max Carey, who beat out Cuyler for the league stolen base title and enjoyed his finest season (.343) at the plate. The team as a whole hit .307 to lead the league and ran away with the pennant, spurting to catch the front-running Giants in midseason and pushing ahead to an 8½-game lead by season's end. The World Series was tougher, but the Pirates prevailed over the Washington Senators, defeating veteran Walter Johnson in a seventh-game slugfest 9–7. Babe Adams, hero of the 1909 Series and now, at forty-three, near the end of a long career, pitched one shutout inning in Game Four.

Rookie outfielder Paul Waner arrived the next season and hit .336, but the team, which had led the race going into August, fell into decline late in the month and finished third, 4½ games out. Max Carey sparked an unsuccessful player

uprising against the management and was sold to Brooklyn just before the Pirate collapse in August, and manager McKechnie was replaced after the season by former Washington manager Donie Bush.

In 1927, his first season at the helm, Bush sailed the Pirate ship to its sixth pennant, even though Kiki Cuyler was benched for half the season for refusing to bat second in the order. But Paul Waner's younger brother Lloyd arrived to join Paul in the outfield, and the pair tore up the league, finishing one-two in hits (237 and 223) as Paul also took crowns in batting (.380; Lloyd was third at .355), RBIs and total bases, while Lloyd led in runs scored. In and out of first place throughout the season, the Pirates moved into the lead a final time at the start of September and held on to edge the St. Louis Cardinals by 1½ games. In the World Series, though (played with Cuyler on the bench), the Pirates were swept by a Yankee team widely acclaimed as the greatest of all time.

Barney Dreyfuss died in February 1932. Ownership of the Pirates passed to his widow, who named their son-in-law Bill Benswanger president. The team finished a competitive second in 1932 and 1933, but then fell back until 1938, when—with Pie Traynor now manager—they moved out in front in midseason and held their lead comfortably until late September, when ten straight Chicago victories (including three against Pittsburgh) dropped the Pirates to second place, where they finished, 2 games back.

The Pirates showcased some great players in their lean years, like shortstop Arky Vaughan in the 1930s and early '40s, and slugger Ralph Kiner, who won or shared the league home run title all seven of his seasons with Pittsburgh in the 1940s and '50s. But after 1938 the club finished no closer than eight games from the top for twenty-one years. They finished as high as second only twice (in 1944 and 1958), and in the eight years 1950–1957 wound up each season either last or next-to-last, reaching their nadir in 1952 with 112 losses and a last-place finish 54½ games out of first.

The Pirates had been purchased in 1946 by a four-man syndicate that included singer Bing Crosby and real estate tycoon John W. Galbreath. Galbreath later bought a majority interest in the club and, as president, hired Branch Rickey to rebuild the Pirates into contenders. Barney Dreyfuss had resisted the development of minor league farm systems (a Rickey innovation at St. Louis and Brooklyn), preferring to scour unaffiliated minor league teams himself for young talent. Rickey's ministrations helped build a foundation for the Pirate resurgence of 1958–1960.

No one threatened the 1958 Milwaukee Braves' preeminence in the NL after July, but Pittsburgh came closer than anyone, finishing second, eight games back. Six of the eight regulars who would lead the Pirates to their next championship in 1960 were already in the lineup, including Dick Groat, Bill Mazeroski, and Roberto Clemente; and the leading pitchers of 1958—Bob Friend, Vern Law, and reliever Roy Face—topped the 1960 staff, too.

In 1959 the Pirates fell back to fourth place, barely above .500, but the next year they began strong and, shaking off their last challenger in late July, built up a 7-game margin of victory by season's end. League batting champion Groat paced a balanced offense that led the league in hitting, and pitcher Law, with 20 wins, enjoyed the finest season of his career. Facing the Yankees in the World Series, the Pirates were overwhelmed in the three games they lost, but they won the world title with four close wins, capped by Mazeroski's

famous home run in the bottom of the ninth inning of the final game.

Pittsburgh again led the league in batting in 1961, with Clemente (whose .351 batting average led the league) and first baseman Dick Stuart (35 home runs, 117 RBIs) enjoying especially fine seasons. But the Pirate pitching fell apart (Vern Law lost most of the season to arm trouble), and the club dropped to sixth place.

When the Pirates next made a serious run for the pennant, in 1966, Harry Walker managed the team and center fielder Matty Alou (newly acquired from San Francisco) won the batting crown. (His brother Felipe of Atlanta was runner-up—the only one-two brother finish ever.) In a season-long three-way race, the Pirates took a lead in August but lost it early in September and finished third, 3 games out. They dropped to sixth again the next season and remained out of the pennant race for three years.

In 1970 the majors experienced their second season of divisional play, John Galbreath's son Daniel was named Pirates' president, and Danny Murtaugh returned a third time to pilot the Pirates. (His second stint was for half a season in 1967.) The team began slowly and entered June with a record under .500. But they were already on their way up, and by mid-July, when they moved out of aging Forbes Field into the brand-new Three Rivers Stadium, they were at the top of the NL East. They slipped into a three-way tangle in mid-September, but shot ahead later in the month to take the division title by 5 games. Most of the team was new since 1960—the power was now supplied by first baseman Bob Robertson and outfielder Willie Stargell. But Roberto Clemente was still in top form, and Bill Mazeroski was still at second base, though nearing the end of his career.

In the 1970 League Championship Series, the Pirates were swept by Cincinnati. But they came back the next season to overwhelm the East in a race that was no race after June, then defeated San Francisco for their eighth pennant, three games to one. Their slugging—paced by Stargell's league-leading 48 home runs—led the league, and reliever Dave Giusti saved a league-leading 30 games in support of a balanced pitching staff. Clemente hit .414 in the World Series (with half his hits going for extra bases) as the Pirates overcame a 0–2 deficit to edge Baltimore in seven games for their fourth world title.

In 1972, after a slow start, Pittsburgh (now managed by their former center fielder Bill Virdon) rocketed to their third straight division championship—by 11 games over Chicago. The club lost, narrowly, to Cincinnati in the LCS, then suffered an even greater loss when Clemente was killed that winter in a plane crash. They played poorly the next season, yet even with a losing record finished third, only 2½ games behind the champion New York Mets in a five-way divisional race. Danny Murtaugh returned as manager a fourth (and final) time late in the season and piloted the club to two more NL East titles the next two years.

The 1974 championship drive featured a comeback from last place in early July to first by late August, followed by a nip-and-tuck race in September with St. Louis that was settled by a tenth-inning Pirate victory over Chicago in the season's final game. Stargell's bat was joined by those of Al Oliver and Richie Zisk as the Pirates outhit the rest of the league. In the LCS, though, the Los Angeles Dodgers overcame Pittsburgh handily, three games to one.

The Pirates won the 1975 race more easily, holding the lead from early June as right fielder Dave Parker, in his first full big league season, led the club in home runs and RBIs, and the league in slugging. But once again, for the fourth time in five tries, Pittsburgh lost the pennant in the LCS—swept this time by the awesome Cincinnati Reds, winners of 108 regular season games.

A distant second-place finish in 1976 was followed that December by manager Murtaugh's untimely death. His successor, Chuck Tanner, kept the Pirates competitive in his first two seasons, steering them to within 5 games of the champion Phillies in 1977, then—with an amazing August-September spurt from way below .500—to within 1½ games of the Phillies in 1978.

In 1979 the Pirates again started slowly but began to move up in May and pushed to the front, ahead of Montreal, in late July. By mid-September, though, the Expos had caught up, and it was not until the final day that an Expo loss and Pirate win gave Pittsburgh its sixth NL East title. Parker and the aging Stargell (now called "Pops") were still the club's big bats, but submariner Kent Tekulve had emerged as the bullpen ace, and one of six Pirate pitchers to win 10 games or more.

In the LCS the Pirates repaid Cincinnati for their 1975 humiliation, sweeping to the pennant in three games. In the World Series they seemed to have met their match in Baltimore, falling behind three games to one. But Pops rallied his "family" to victory in the final three must-win contests, and Pittsburgh for a fifth time reigned at the top of the baseball world.

For seven years the Pirates drifted downhill. The club's family spirit disintegrated, fans deserted the team, and it seemed for a time that the Pirates would leave Pittsburgh. But in 1985 a group of local corporations and individuals purchased the club from the Galbreaths, determined (with the assistance of a loan from the city of Pittsburgh) to keep the Pirates in town. Syd Thrift, a trader of consummate skill, was named general manager, and Chicago White Sox coach Jim Leyland was hired to his first job as a big league pilot. Under the new regime the club improved gradually, until in 1988 it once again proved itself a serious contender for the NL championship of the East. Thrift had built a team second only to New York's mighty Mets, one that drew more than 1.8 million fans at home—a club record. But Thrift's unwillingness to share with his superiors the top-level decision making bulked larger, in the eyes of the Pirate directors, than his achievement and he was fired at the season's end.

St. Louis Cardinals

The club that is now the Cardinals first fielded a team in 1881, and the next season became a charter member of the American Association, a new major league formed in part to offer fans the beer and Sunday baseball forbidden by the older National League. Chris Von der Ahe, one of the club's founders and its first president, at first saw in baseball simply a source of customers for his St. Louis saloon and beer garden, but he developed a love for the game itself as his Brown Stockings—or Browns—developed into one of the era's greatest teams.

After a losing season in 1882, Von der Ahe hired Ted Sullivan, a noted judge of baseball talent, to manage the Browns. Sullivan brought in third baseman Arlie Latham and pitcher Tony Mullane to strengthen a team that already

boasted a fine pitcher in Jumbo McGinnis (25–18 in 1882) and one of the game's premier first baseman in Charlie Comiskey. Although Sullivan quit before the end of his first season because of the continued interference of the volatile Von der Ahe, the Browns finished second in the AA, just a game behind champion Philadelphia.

When Mullane bolted the Browns in 1884, the club slipped to fourth. But help was on the way. In July Von der Ahe purchased the Bay City, Michigan, club to acquire its heavy-hitting pitcher Dave Foutz, and in September added another hitting pitcher, "Parisian Bob" Caruthers, to the roster. In 1885—with Comiskey now the manager, left fielder Tip O'Neill blossoming into one of baseball's best hitters, and Caruthers and Foutz winning 40 and 33 games—the Browns rose to the top, 16 games ahead of second-place Cincinnati. They finished on top four years in a row, tying Chicago's White Stockings (3–3–1) in the 1885 World Series and defeating them four games to two the next year for the AA's only Series triumph over their NL rivals.

Pitcher Silver King joined the club in 1887, and outfielder Tommy McCarthy arrived the following year. They helped keep the Browns at the top of the AA through 1888 (although the team lost the World Series both years). But Von der Ahe's sale of Foutz and Caruthers to Brooklyn following the 1887 season boosted Brooklyn to second place in 1888. The next year Brooklyn edged the Browns for the pennant, and the club's first era of greatness was over.

When the AA folded after the 1891 season, the Browns were taken into the NL, but fared poorly there, finishing ninth and eleventh of the twelve clubs in the divided season of 1892. They rose no higher than ninth in the remaining years of Von der Ahe's ownership, dropping into the cellar (63½ games out) in 1897 and returning to the bottom with a club-worst 111 losses the next season.

New owners Frank and Stanley Robison (who also controlled the Cleveland club) transferred the best Cleveland players and their manager to St. Louis in 1899. Dubbed the Perfectos, the revitalized St. Louis club fell short of perfection, but did rise to a first-division fifth place that year and (now known as the Cardinals) rose to fourth in 1901 before sinking back into the second division for a dozen years.

After Stanley Robison died in 1911 (his brother Frank had died in 1905), the club passed into the possession of Frank's daughter Helene Britton, who ran it behind the scenes until, in 1916, she sold it to a syndicate headed by her attorney James C. Jones. Jones hired Branch Rickey away from the AL Browns to run the club.

Rickey took over a team with two chief assets: manager Miller Huggins and a promising young infielder, Rogers Hornsby. Huggins had managed the Cards to third place in 1914, before Hornsby arrived, and after a pair of losing seasons brought them up to third again in 1917. Huggins was lost to the New York Yankees the next year, and Rickey left the club temporarily for military service in the Great War. When Rickey returned in 1919, he took over as manager himself, and in 1921 and 1922 saw the team finish third, closer to the leaders than the club had finished since joining the NL in 1891. Led by Hornsby's .397 and .401 batting, the team hit over .300 both seasons.

Sam Breadon, one of the Jones group of owners, increased his investment in the Cardinals until by 1920 he was majority stockholder and club president, with Rickey as vice president and general manager. Breadon moved the Cards out of the inadequate wooden Cardinal Park during the 1920 season into the more modern Sportsman's Park, owned by the Browns (and built on the site of Von der Ahe's original grounds).

Early in the 1925 season, with the Cards in last place, Breadon replaced Rickey as field manager with second baseman Hornsby. The switch worked. In 1925 the Cards rebounded to fourth, and in 1926 they captured their first pennant since the glory days of the old Browns four decades earlier—edging Cincinnati in the final week of the season after an August spurt had shot them into pennant contention. The season was made perfect by victory in the World Series over Miller Huggins's Yankees.

But Breadon and his irascible player-manager had a falling out, and Hornsby found himself traded that winter to the New York Giants for second baseman Frank Frisch and pitcher Jimmy Ring. The trade enraged Cardinal fans, but the team finished a close second in 1927, and returned to the top (under new manager Bill McKechnie) in a tight race the following season.

McKechnie, fired after the Yankees swept the Cards in the 1928 World Series and rehired in the midst of a Cardinal slump the next season, left to manage the Boston Braves in 1930. Former catcher Gabby Street, who replaced him, led the Cards back to the top again for successive pennants in 1930 and 1931, and in 1931 to a World Series victory over the Philadelphia Athletics. The 1930 race saw the club shoot from below .500 in mid-June to 30 games above .500 by season's end, overtaking three other teams to clinch the flag just three games from the finish. The 1931 team ran away with the pennant, leading all the way and finishing 13 games in front. Outfielder Chick Hafey and first baseman Jim Bottomley finished first and third in NL batting, and pitcher Bill Hallahan led the league in strikeouts (for the second year in a row) and tied for the lead in wins, with 19. Four of the league's top five base stealers—led by Frank Frisch and including outfielder Pepper Martin in his first full season—were Cardinals.

When the Cards dropped to sixth place in 1932 and showed little improvement the following year, Breadon replaced manager Street with Frisch. As when he had named Hornsby to manage, Breadon's move paid immediate dividends. Though the club finished fifth that season, their record improved after Frisch took over, and the next year, in a season-long uphill struggle, the Cards won thirteen of their final fifteen games to pass the front-running New York Giants in the final week.

Writers labeled the 1934 Cardinals the "Gashouse Gang" for their rowdy and daring play. In addition to team veterans Frisch and Martin (who had been shifted from the outfield to third base), the gang included shortstop Leo Durocher, left fielder Joe "Ducky" Medwick, and the team's leading hitter and slugger, first baseman Rip Collins, who in a career-best season led the league in slugging average and tied for first in home runs.

Cardinal pitching was headed by the league-leading Jerome "Dizzy" Dean (30–7) and his rookie brother Paul (19–11). Of the team's final nine wins, Diz and Paul accounted for seven. Each won another pair in the Cards' World Series triumph over Detroit.

The next two seasons the Cardinals moved into the lead late in the season only to wind up second. After the team slipped into the second division in 1938, Breadon replaced Frisch as manager with Ray Blades, who led a late-season run

for the flag in 1939 but finished second. When the Cards failed to contend in 1940, Breadon brought up Rochester manager Billy Southworth for a second time. Southworth had failed as McKechnie's replacement in 1929, but this time he stuck, becoming one of the club's greatest helmsmen.

Through all these years Branch Rickey was revolutionizing baseball as he built the game's first and most extensive "farm system" of minor league clubs. The Cardinals' farm teams would—until the other major league clubs caught on and caught up—provide St. Louis with a competitive advantage in the recruitment and development of young players.

In the closing days of the 1941 season, perhaps the Cardinal system's greatest product arrived at the big club: Stan Musial. Southworth brought the club in a close second that year after a season-long back-and-forth struggle with Brooklyn. The next year—Musial's first full season—the Cardinals enjoyed their winningest season ever: 106 victories. They needed them all, too, for Brooklyn won 104 games, leading the race until mid-September, when the Cardinals passed them and held on to a narrow lead by winning twelve of their final thirteen games. St. Louis pitchers Mort Cooper and Johnny Beazley finished one-two in National League wins and ERA, while Enos Slaughter and Musial paced the Cardinal offense. The club maintained its momentum in the World Series, taking the Yankees in five games.

St. Louis retained its preeminence for two more years as baseball gradually lost players to military service in World War Two. Slaughter and Beazley were gone by 1943. But Cooper remained to compile two more 20-plus winning seasons, and Musial was not called until after the 1944 season. With 105 wins in both 1943 and 1944, the Cards ran away with two more pennants, losing to the Yankees in the 1943 World Series, but taking their sixth world title the next year from their St. Louis landlords, the AL champion Browns.

Owner Breadon had fired Branch Rickey in 1942 (objecting to the personal profit Rickey made from selling the club's unneeded farm players), and Southworth left to manage the Boston Braves after the 1945 season (in which the Cards failed to catch the leading Chicago Cubs, finishing second). Rickey went to head the Brooklyn Dodgers, building for them a farm system and tapping the large reservoir of black players. In 1946, the last year of all-white major league ball, the Cards (managed now by Eddie Dyer) and the Dodgers waged a two-team pennant race, ending the season in the first major league tie for first place. St. Louis won the first two games in a best-of-three playoff and went on to surprise the favored Boston Red Sox in the World Series. With the war over, the team was back at full strength. Slaughter led the league in RBIs, and Musial led it in most other offensive categories; pitcher Howie Pollett led the league in ERA (as he had in 1943 before leaving for the war) and in wins, with 21.

But St. Louis was slow to integrate its club and lost ground to teams like Brooklyn, whose black players brought an immediate upswing in the club's success. The Cards began poorly in 1947, but recovered to finish second to Brooklyn, though never offering a serious challenge for the flag. After the season Breadon sold the club to Fred Saigh and Robert Hannegan (the U.S. Postmaster General). Musial enjoyed his finest season in 1948, but the club finished second again in a lackluster race. The next year, though, the Cards and Dodgers tangled in a season-long struggle for first place that was not resolved until the season's last day—with Brooklyn on top.

The Cardinals threatened to move to Milwaukee, but beer magnate August Busch, Jr., purchased the club early in 1953 and the same year bought Sportsman's Park from the Browns (who were moving to Baltimore). With Busch's infusion of money and enthusiasm, the club slowly revived. They made runs for the pennant in 1957, 1960, and 1963, but each time tailed off sharply in the final week of the season.

The Cards were playing below .500, in seventh place, in mid-June 1964 when the arrival (via a trade with the Cubs) of speedy young Lou Brock sparked a revival of both the team and player. Brock, who had been hitting .251 in Chicago, with 10 stolen bases, hit .348 the rest of the season and stole 33 more bases as the Cards hurtled into the midst of a four-way race for the pennant that was settled only when they took the flag with an 11–5 win on the final day. After surprising the Yankees in the World Series, the Cardinals were themselves surprised when manager Johnny Keane left to take the Yankee helm. The club slipped into the second division for a couple of years under the management of their great former second baseman Red Schoendienst.

But owner Busch built them a striking new stadium in 1966, and the next season the team rebounded to the top again, running away from the field in the last half of the season behind the heavy hitting of Orlando Cepeda, the bat and speed of Lou Brock, and a pitching staff of remarkable breadth and balance. Bob Gibson's three World Series wins over Boston edged the Cards to a ninth world title and set the stage for Gibson's astonishing season the following year.

With his 22 wins leading the Cards to another pennant in 1968, Gibson hurled 13 shutouts and compiled an ERA of just 1.12—both feats the best in more than half a century, both ranking among the top five big league performances ever. After winning a pair of World Series games, though, Gibson lost Game Seven as Detroit took the crown.

Red Schoendienst continued as Cardinal manager through 1976—a club record twelve years—but led the team to no more championships. When divisional play was inaugurated in 1969, geography was ignored as the Cards were installed in the East to add strength to what seemed the weaker division. But it was fourteen years before they won their first divisional championship. Four times they finished second, losing twice by only 1½ games, in the back-to-back tight races of 1973 and 1974.

Dorrell "Whitey" Herzog was in his first full season as Cardinal manager before the club again finished that near the top. In the strike-shortened divided season of 1981, the Cards compiled the best overall record in the NL East, but because they had finished the two halves of the season second to Philadelphia and Montreal they were ineligible for postseason play.

With the defensive wizard shortstop Ozzie Smith (acquired from San Diego) and rookie speedster Willie McGee bolstering an already strong team, the Cardinals of 1982, after prevailing against the Phillies in the race for the East, swept West champion Atlanta for the pennant and captured their tenth World Series crown in a seven-game struggle with Milwaukee.

After two seasons out of the running, the Cards in 1985 gained the power of veteran Jack Clark (acquired from San Francisco) and the speed of rookie Vince Coleman. With career-best seasons from Willie McGee and newly acquired pitcher John Tudor, the team edged the New York Mets for the division title and defeated Los Angeles for the pennant—but lost the World Series in seven games to Kansas City.

Jack Clark missed two-thirds of the 1986 season to injury, and the Cards finished below .500, but they rebounded to edge the Mets again for the championship of the East in 1987 as Clark and Vince Coleman enjoyed their finest seasons at the bat. But the reinjured Clark made only a token appearance as the Cards edged San Francisco for the league championship, and he missed the World Series entirely as St. Louis bowed to Minnesota in seven games. That winter Clark signed as a free agent with the Yankees and in 1988 the Cardinals dropped to fifth place, 25 games out.

San Diego Padres

In their first fifteen years the Padres put together only one winning season. In their sixteenth, they won the National League pennant. Founded in the 1969 expansion that saw the two major leagues divide into East and West divisions, the Padres finished last in the six-team NL West their first six seasons, ending each year from 28½ to 42 games behind the division champion.

Their first season was their worst. With 110 losses, the Padres finished not only 41 games out of first but 29 games out of *fifth*. First baseman Nate Colbert, with 24 home runs, provided San Diego's brightest ray of hope. He proved to be one of the Padres' standout performers through their last-place years, and in 1971 became the first Padre to drive in more than 100 runs.

Big league baseball was not an instant hit in San Diego. Home attendance barely topped half a million in the Padres' first year, and though it rose a little over the next few seasons, the increase was not enough to make the club viable. Owner C. Arnholt Smith decided early in 1974 to sell the franchise to a buyer who planned to move the team to Washington, D.C. New uniforms had been manufactured and the club's files were packed for the move, when the builder of the Mc-Donald's fast-food empire, longtime baseball fan Ray Kroc, stepped in with an offer to buy the Padres for cash and keep them in San Diego. His bid was accepted.

Though Kroc's 1974 Padres finished last with the same 60–102 record they had posted the year before, his sense of showmanship drew spectators. Home attendance shot up 76 percent, rising above a million for the first time. The Padres then began to draw fans on their own merits as they finally pulled themselves out of the cellar. Pitcher Randy Jones, who in 1974 had led the league with 22 losses, turned his record around and for two years shone as one of the game's finest pitchers. He halved his 1974 ERA to a league-leading 2.24, winning 20 games as the Padres rose to fourth place in 1975 and posted a winning percentage over .400 for the first time. The next year Jones won a league-high 22 games and earned the Cy Young Award—the first major award to come to a San Diego player.

Although 1976 proved to be Jones's last winning season, the Padres were by then attracting other top-quality players. Outfielder Dave Winfield came up as a rookie in 1973, and the following year became the team RBI leader, a position he held in six of his seven full seasons with the Padres. Reliever Rollie Fingers signed as a free agent. In each of his four seasons in San Diego (1977–1980) he led the team in saves, twice also leading the league. In 1978 the Padres acquired veteran pitcher Gaylord Perry from Texas and installed rookie Ozzie Smith at shortstop. Perry's sparkling 21–6 sea-

son gave San Diego its second Cy Young winner, and together with Smith's play in the field, Winfield's bat (.308, 97 RBIs) and Fingers's 37 saves, brought the Padres their first winning season.

All these stars had gone—and owner Kroc had recently died—by the time the Padres recorded a second winning season six years later, and won the division title and NL pennant with a new blend of experience and youth. Sparked by recently acquired veterans Steve Garvey at first, Graig Nettles at third, and Goose Gossage in the bullpen, and by a bevy of younger stars like batting champ Tony Gwynn and hard-hitting outfielder Kevin McReynolds, the Padres moved into first place to stay in early June. From August 3 to the end of the season, they played only .500 ball but still won the championship of the weak Western Division by 12 games. Underdogs in the League Championship Series, the Padres lost the first two games in Chicago, but took the pennant with three come-from-behind wins at home.

Their decline began with their World Series loss to Detroit. The end of 1985 saw them tied for third, and in 1986 they slipped below .500 and into fourth place. In 1987 Gwynn won his second batting title, and rookie catcher Benito Santiago capped the season with a 34-game hitting streak to cop Rookie of the Year honors. But with most of the 1984 standouts faded or traded, the Padres' decline was complete: the club for the ninth time in its nineteen years finished last.

In late May 1988, with the team at 16–30, Padre general manager Jack McKeon took over as field manager from Larry Bowa and piloted the Padres to their third best season ever. With nine wins in their final ten games, the Padres boosted their season record above .500 (to 83–78), and leaped from sixth to third in the division standings.

San Francisco Giants

The expulsion of Troy and Worcester from the National League after the 1882 season cleared the way for the league to reestablish clubs in the major markets of Philadelphia and New York. Manufacturer John B. Day was awarded the New York franchise. Purchasing the defunct Troy club, he divided their players between the new NL Gothams and his other club, the Metropolitans of the American Association, and set them up on adjoining grounds north of Central Park, on a field once used for polo.

The Mets fared better than the Gothams, finishing fourth in 1883 to the Gothams' sixth, and winning the AA pennant the next year while the Gothams rose only to fifth in the NL. Since the NL, with greater prestige and higher ticket prices, offered potentially greater profit, Day switched some of his Mets to the Gothams in 1885, including ace hurler Tim Keefe and manager Jim Mutrie. The results were immediate: the Mets sank to seventh place while the Gothams (dubbed "my Giants" by an enthusiastic Mutrie) rose to the thick of a pennant race with Chicago. At the finish Chicago was on top by two games, but the Giants had won more than three games out of four for a .759 winning percentage that is not only the club's best ever, but one of the highest in major-league history. Pitchers Keefe and Mickey Welch together won 76 of the team's 85 victories, and first-baseman Roger Connor led the league in batting.

The Giants won their first pennant in 1888 by nine games over Chicago, and their second the next year in a one-game

squeaker over Boston. Keefe and Welch, still going strong, combined for 61 wins in '88 and 55 in '89. Continuing their winning ways in the World Series, the Giants triumphed easily over St. Louis in 1888, and overcame a 1-3 deficit to vanquish Brooklyn the next year.

In 1890, ravaged by the loss of players to the rival Players League, the Giants finished sixth, but they recovered several players when the PL folded at the end of the season. (They also moved into the PL ballpark, named it after their original Polo Grounds, and played there 67 years). They rose to third in 1891, but Day could no longer afford to maintain the team and sold out to financier Edward Talcott. Talcott brought back former Giant star J. M. Ward to manage the club, and in 1894 saw the team rise to a close second-place finish behind Baltimore. Pitchers Amos Rusie and Jouett Meekin tied for the league lead with 36 wins apiece. In postseason Temple Cup play, the Giants swept Baltimore in four games for their third world championship.

That winter Talcott sold control of the club to Tammany Hall politician Andrew Freedman. Giant fortunes sank under Freedman's abrasive and heavy-handed rule. As he ran through a succession of managers, the Giants fell to ninth (of twelve clubs) in 1895 and—apart from a third-place finish in 1897—rose no higher than seventh while he controlled the franchise. In 1902, his final year of ownership, the Giants suffered their lowest winning percentage—.353—and most distant finish ever—53½ games behind champion Pittsburgh.

In the midst of the 1902 season, though, a skirmish in the war between the NL and the upstart American League led to a Giant turnaround. John T. Brush, owner of the NL Cincinnati Reds, bought the AL Baltimore Orioles, then released Oriole manager John McGraw and several key players to sign with NL clubs. Five joined the Giants, including McGraw, catcher Roger Bresnahan, and pitcher Joe "Iron Man" McGinnity. That winter, Brush sold the Reds and Orioles and bought the Giants.

In 1903, with Bresnahan hitting .350 and McGinnity winning a league-high 31 games (closely followed by third-year Giant Christy Mathewson's 30 wins), manager McGraw saw his Giants win thirty-six more games than they had in 1902 and finish a solid second in the standings. In McGraw's twenty-nine full seasons at the helm, the team would win ten pennants and finish second eleven times.

Just two years after their worst season ever, McGraw in 1904 led the Giants to one of their best. Their 106 wins and 13-game winning margin remain Giant highs to this day. The club led the NL in pitching, hitting, fielding, and base stealing. McGinnity led league pitchers in several categories with a career-best 35–8, 1.61 ERA season. Mathewson, right behind with 33 wins, led the league in strikeouts.

The only Giant disappointment of 1904 was McGraw's refusal to face Boston in a World Series. His rejection of the AL champions as worthy opponents was the last shot fired in the war between the two leagues. By the time the Giants had repeated as NL pennant winners a year later, the World Series was an official and permanent feature of the baseball landscape. Mathewson led NL pitchers in 1905 with 31 wins and an ERA of 1.27, and outfielder "Turkey Mike" Donlin, acquired from Cincinnati the previous July, erupted with the best season of his career, batting a team-high .356 and scoring a league-high 124 runs. The Giants won only one game less than the year before and held a comfortable lead throughout the season. Matty's three shutouts against the Philadelphia

Athletics in the World Series secured the club's fourth world crown.

It was 1911 before the Giants won their next pennant. Despite 96 wins in 1906 they finished a distant second to Chicago's mighty Cubs, who won a record 116 games. In 1908 the Giants came within a disputed play of the pennant. On September 23, playing Chicago (with whom they were tied at the top of a three-way race), Giant baserunner Fred Merkle failed to run to second on a single by Al Bridwell that would have driven in the winning run from third. Merkle was forced at second after the ball (or a second ball—the argument still rages) was recovered amid the horde of fans who overran the field. The force out at second negated the run, and the game was ruled a tie. At season's end, when the two clubs found themselves again tied at the top, the "Merkle boner" game was replayed. The Cubs won the game and flag, leaving the Giants in a second-place tie with Pittsburgh.

In 1911 the Giants pulled away from the Cubs in September for the first of three straight pennants. (Early in the season most of the Polo Grounds was rebuilt in concrete after fire destroyed the wooden stands.) The following year the Giants took the lead in May and held it comfortably the rest of the way. In 1913 they didn't move into first until late June, but then quickly put the flag out of reach and finished 12½ games ahead of the faltering Phillies. Mathewson led the team in victories over the three years, with 74, followed closely by Rube Marquard (who with 73 wins enjoyed the three best seasons of his career). Matty led the NL in ERA in 1911 and 1913; Giant rookie Jeff Tesreau took the honors in 1912 (winning 17 games that season and 22 the next). Giant pitching led the league all three seasons, as did their hitting, which featured a balanced offense paced by infielders Larry Doyle and Art Fletcher and catcher John "Chief" Meyers.

In the World Series, though, the Giants three times fell short of the title. Philadelphia's Athletics defeated them handily in 1911 and 1913, but the Giants carried the 1912 Series against the Boston Red Sox to the tenth inning of the final game before a pair of Giant fielding lapses enabled Boston to rally for the win.

Boston's "miracle" Braves, in their 1914 surge from last place to the pennant, passed the front-running Giants for good in early September. The next year, five of the eight NL clubs found themselves bunched within 3½ games of one another at the lower end of the standings as the season ended—with the Giants at the very bottom. And in a 1916 Giant season characterized by dips and surges, even a 26-game winning streak in September couldn't raise the team higher than fourth. But in 1917 a balanced pitching staff—paced by Ferdie Schupp's one big season (21–7, 1.95 ERA)—hurled the Giants to the front early in June and kept them there to the finish. Once more, though, the World Series proved a disappointment, with a loss to the Chicago White Sox in six games.

Three years of second-place finishes followed, in the midst of which the Giants changed owners. Brush had died in 1912 and was succeeded as president by his son-in-law Harry Hempstead. But in January 1919 Brush's heirs sold the club to financier and racehorse fancier Charles A. Stoneham, with manager McGraw a minority stockholder.

In 1921 McGraw brought home the first of four straight winners for Stoneham. Seven regulars hit over .300 (led by third baseman Frank Frisch's .341); first baseman George Kelly's 23 home runs topped the NL. The club hung close to

Pittsburgh through August, then broke into a lead which the fading Pirates could not challenge. In postseason play the Giants lost the first two games to the Yankees, but charged back to win their fifth world title. The next year outfielder Emil "Irish" Meusel celebrated his first full season in New York with a team-high 132 RBIs, as the Giants fended off a midseason challenge from St. Louis to pull away to a comfortable margin at the end. The World Series was especially sweet: a four-game sweep of the Yankees.

Cincinnati and Pittsburgh hung just behind the Giants through much of 1923, but never quite caught up. The Giants' league-leading offense was led by individual NL highs in RBIs (Meusel), runs scored (outfielder Ross Youngs), and hits and total bases (Frisch). But the Yankees finally caught the Giants in the World Series, 4–2.

George Kelly took the NL RBI title in 1924. The club's hitting remained the league's best, and by early August the Giants had taken a ten-game lead. But they then leveled off while Brooklyn and Pittsburgh surged. Brooklyn, in fact, took over the lead for a day in early September, but the Giants emerged triumphant at the end by 1½ games. The World Series, though, was as heartbreaking as the pennant race had been heartstopping: the Giants lost to Washington in the last of the twelfth inning of the seventh game when a Senator grounder bounced over the head of rookie third baseman Fred Lindstrom to drive in the Series-ending run.

Close finishes—2 games out—in 1927 and 1928 were the nearest McGraw's Giants came to another pennant. Player relations with the demanding manager had seldom been harmonious, and they had reached a low point when, ill and tired, he quit early in the 1932 season with the team in last place, naming first baseman Bill Terry to replace him. Under Terry the Giants rose only to sixth that season, but McGraw had built a squad fit for a new era of greatness. He had persuaded Terry to leave a career with Standard Oil for one with the Giants; he had saved Mel Ott's unique but effective batting stance from revision by well-meaning minor league managers by keeping Ott out of the minors; and he had rescued pitcher Carl Hubbell from mediocrity by encouraging the screwball pitch other managers had tried to suppress.

Hubbell and Ott formed the heart of the club that would win a trio of pennants under Terry's management. In 1933 the Giants moved to the front in June and, despite a late-September slump, finished well ahead of runner-up Pittsburgh. Ott, with what was for him an off-year, powered the Giant offense with 23 homers and 103 RBIs, while Hubbell led the league in wins, shutouts, and ERA. Hubbell also hurled two wins against Washington in the World Series, and Ott won it all for New York with a tenth-inning home run in Game Five. McGraw, still the club's vice president, threw a party for "his" Giants after the Series. The following February he died, at age sixty.

As they had the previous season, the Giants of 1934 emerged from the crowd to take and hold first place into late September. They rose higher than they had in 1933 and didn't slump as far at the end. But their five end-of-season losses were enough to drop them 2 games behind the surging Cardinals at the finish. Again in 1935 they led the league much of the season. But they had begun to level off in mid-July and finished the season well back in third. Charles Stoneham died in January 1936, and his son Horace—who at age thirty-three had already run the club for a year—assumed the club presidency.

In 1936, and again in 1937, the Giants came from behind to take the flag. Hubbell sparked their second-half resurgence in 1936, winning his final 16 decisions of the season as the Giants rose from fourth to first. In the World Series, though, Hubbell, after one win, was stopped by the Yankees in his try for a second. The Yankees took the Series in six games.

Again the next year the Giants hid behind the leaders most of the season until a surge in late August coincided with a Chicago decline and shot the Giants to the front. The Cubs recovered, but New York continued its winning ways and finished ahead by 3 games. But again the Yankees dominated the World Series, winning 4–1.

Hubbell's years of greatness were now over, and while the Giants led the NL through the first half of 1938, they finished third, 5 games out. It would be twelve years before they again finished that close to the top. Mel Ott replaced Terry as manager in 1942, but the Giants sank to the cellar in 1943 with their second-worst season ever, and finished last again three years later. One bright spot: in 1947 they rose to fourth with a barrage of 221 home runs (led by Johnny Mize's 51) that remained the major league record (though tied by Cincinnati in 1956) until the 1961 Yankees topped it with 240.

Halfway through the 1948 season the baseball world was startled to learn that Leo Durocher, the fiery manager of the Brooklyn Dodgers, had switched his allegiance to their arch foes, the Giants. Durocher discarded the three top Giant home run hitters of 1947 (but presciently retained the fourth, Bobby Thomson), and added agile infielders Alvin Dark and Eddie Stanky to the roster. By 1950, with the blossoming of Sal Maglie into a first-rank pitcher and the timely midseason purchase of hurler Jim Hearn, the Giants were once more a challenger, spurting in the second half from below .500 to within 5 games of the top.

After losing their first eleven games the next year, the Giants began a long climb. A sixteen-game August winning streak and a seven-game streak at season's end tied them with Brooklyn and forced a three-game playoff. After a win and a loss, the Giants entered the last of the ninth inning of Game Three trailing 1–4. Two singles and a double cut the deficit by a run and brought on Dodger Ralph Branca to face Bobby Thomson, whose two-run homer had provided the Giants' margin of victory in Game One. Thomson homered again, and the Giants won the pennant. Their defeat by the Yankees in the World Series dimmed the miracle a bit, but couldn't detract from the career bests of pitchers Maglie and Larry Jansen, who tied for the NL lead with 23 wins apiece, and of former Negro League great Monte Irvin, who hit .312 and led the league in RBIs.

The next year Irvin was lost until August with a broken ankle, Jansen (with a back problem) fell off to 11–11, and Willie Mays—a promising rookie in 1951—left early in the season for a hitch in the Army. Still, the Giants hung close to Brooklyn for much of the summer and finished second. In 1953, though, they fell apart in midseason and wound up in fifth, 35 games out.

Mays returned in 1954 to enjoy one of his strongest seasons at the bat, and pitchers Johnny Antonelli (newly acquired from Milwaukee), sophomore Ruben Gomez, and reliever Marv Grissom all burst forth with the best seasons of their careers. The Giants pulled away from Brooklyn in July and held on with a late-season rush to finish 5 games up. Underdogs to powerful Cleveland in the World Series, they stunned the Indians (and the rest of the baseball world) with a four-

game sweep. It was their eighth world title—and, so far, their last.

Manager Durocher retired after a distant third-place finish in 1955, and Bill Rigney, who replaced him (the first of seven straight rookie managers to be hired by the Giants over the next twenty years), presided over a pair of sixth-place seasons in the club's final years in New York. Persuaded by the Dodgers' Walter O'Malley that California was the land of baseball opportunity, Giant owner Stoneham announced in August 1957 his decision to move the club to San Francisco before the next season.

The move succeeded. Home attendance doubled, even though the team had to play in a former minor league park that seated fewer than 23,000 fans. When new Candlestick Park opened in 1960 attendance climbed to nearly 1.8 million, a new club high. Better still, rookie sensations like Orlando Cepeda in 1958 and Willie McCovey in 1959, plus the continuing mastery of Willie Mays, made the Giants competitive once again. In their first fourteen San Francisco seasons, they compiled winning records—a longer string than they had ever known in New York.

Candlestick Park, though, proved a cold and windy place to watch baseball, and after its inaugural season fans began to drift away. Attendance picked up some in 1962, however, as the Giants battled for first all summer with the Los Angeles Dodgers. Mays, Cepeda, and Felipe Alou headlined the league's best offense, and a pair of veteran pitchers—Jack Sanford and Billy O'Dell—garnered the most wins of their careers (24 and 19) as part of a balanced staff that also got 16 wins from veteran Billy Pierce and 18 from the emerging great Juan Marichal. Still, the Giants trailed the Dodgers most of the season until a Dodger loss and Giant win on the final day threw the teams into a tie and another playoff. As in 1951, the Giants won the first game and lost the second, and overcame a ninth-inning deficit in the finale to win the pennant. Also as in 1951, they lost the World Series to the Yankees, although this time they held on until the final out of Game Seven before losing their grip on the crown.

The 1963 Giants offered little challenge to the leaders after June, but the next three years found them locked to the end in tight struggles for the flag. Although they finished fourth in 1964, they were still in contention with just two games to play, in one of the closest four-way races ever. The next year they took the lead from the Dodgers early in September, only to lose it in the final week. And in 1966, in a season-long three-way race with the Dodgers and Pirates, the Giants weren't eliminated until the final day.

The turbulence of these races was reflected in the team itself. Cepeda (until traded to St. Louis in 1966) continually railed against his managers and his low pay. Alvin Dark, after four winning seasons as manager, was fired in 1964 when some of his racist comments ended up in print. And Marichal was fined and suspended for nine days in 1965 for hitting Dodger catcher John Roseboro over the head with his bat.

After a pair of distant second-place finishes, the Giants in 1969 (with the fine work of Marichal and McCovey augmented by the speed and power of young outfielder Bobby Bonds) found themselves in the thick of a five-way race for the championship of the newly created NL West. The race wasn't settled until the final week, when Atlanta's ten-game winning streak knocked the Giants out of first. Two years later, with Bonds the chief source of offensive power and fine pitching from starters Marichal and Gaylord Perry and reliever Jerry Johnson, the Giants moved out in front at the start of the season and held their lead all the way. A September slump coinciding with a Dodger surge narrowed the lead to one game in midmonth, but the Giants held on for the division crown. In their first experiences with a League Championship Series, though, they succumbed to Pittsburgh with three losses after an opening-game win.

The LCS loss signaled the end of an era. McCovey was past his prime and Marichal had enjoyed his last big year. Mays, after twenty Giant seasons, was sold to the Mets in 1972 so he could close out his career in New York, where it began. That year the Giants suffered their first losing season in San Francisco, and attendance for the first time dropped below what it had been in their final New York season.

Attendance had reached such a low point by the mid-1970s that Stoneham negotiated the club's sale to a Canadian brewery which planned to move it to Toronto. But San Francisco's mayor George Moscone delayed the sale until a buyer could be found who would keep the Giants in the city. San Francisco realtor Robert Lurie stepped forth with half the purchase price, and Arizona cattleman Arthur "Bud" Herseth provided the rest. (Toronto settled for an expansion club, the Blue Jays.)

After six years out of the running, the Giants in 1978 played at the top of the NL East through much of the summer before dropping to third (and home attendance jumped more than a million above the previous year). But they fell below .500 the next two years—making seven losing seasons in the nine that followed their division title of 1971.

In 1982 the Giants—paced by the slugging of Jack Clark and Greg Minton's sparkling relief pitching—made one of the most impressive comebacks since divisional play was instituted in 1969, driving from ten games below .500 in late June to just 2 games from champion Atlanta at season's end. But they dropped to fifth the following year, and to a last-place sixth in 1984 and 1985.

When Roger Craig was called on to manage the final weeks of the 1985 season, there was no stopping the Giants' slide to a club-record 100 losses. But the next year, inspiring a "can do" spirit among the players, Craig turned the club around. Veteran hurler Mike Krukow won a career-high 20 games, eight players contributed more than 40 RBIs each, and the team captured 26 of their 83 wins in their final at-bat. In first place at midseason, the Giants slipped (in part because of injuries) to third by season's end, but the fans were back— over 700,000 more than a year earlier.

The club set a new home attendance record of more than 1.9 million in 1987 as it returned to the top of the NL West for the first time in sixteen years. Sophomore first baseman Will Clark led a balanced offense, and several shrewd in-season acquisitions by the front office spurred a second-half drive from five games back to a 6-game lead at the finish. But after taking a 3–2 advantage over St. Louis in the LCS, the Giants failed to score in the final two games and the Cardinals captured the flag. In 1988, injuries to several key players contributed to the team's decline to fourth place, 11½ games out.

Seattle Mariners

The Mariners are one of only two major-league teams never to have won a pennant or divisional title (the Texas Rangers are

the other), the only team without a single winning season or first-division finish—and (at home in Seattle's Kingdome) the only team to have played all its home games indoors. The Mariners have become stronger in recent years. Only once in their first seven years did their winning percentage rise above .450, but in three of the past five seasons it has done so. In 1987, winning eight of their last ten games (including the final four) the Mariners closed the season at 78–84 (.481), only 7 games behind champion Minnesota, in fourth place—their best record yet.

Organized in 1977, the Mariners returned major league baseball to the Pacific Northwest eight years after the Seattle Pilots had moved to Milwaukee after only one season. With a 64–98 inaugural season, the Mariners avoided last place in the American League West only because the Oakland A's had plummeted faster and farther. The hitting of first baseman Dan Meyer, outfielder Leroy Stanton, and rookie center fielder Ruppert Jones—who combined for 73 home runs—and the relief pitching of rookie Enrique (Romo) Romero, who contributed 16 saves and 8 wins, provided most of the high points of that first season.

There was less to cheer about the next year as the production of the first-season heroes fell off and the Mariners took possession of the cellar from mid-May on, losing a club-record 104 games. They finished 12 games out of sixth place, 35 out of first. Much of the offense that was generated came from outfielder Leon Roberts. Acquired from Houston over the winter, Roberts put together his best season and became the Mariners' first .300 hitter.

The club moved up a notch in 1979, to sixth place. Meyer and Jones regained much of their 1977 power, first baseman Bruce Bochte hit .316 and drove in 100 runs, and DH Willie Horton, near the end of a long career, enjoyed one of his finest seasons, driving in 106 runs and leading the club with 29 homers.

As the Mariners, with the league's weakest hitting, dropped back into the cellar the next year, attendance fell to a new low, and some of the original owners decided to sell out. In January 1981 California real-estate magnate George Argyros purchased control of the club, and later bought out the remaining partners to take sole ownership.

In strike-divided 1981 the Mariners finished sixth and fifth in the two halves of the season. Second baseman Julio Cruz continued among the league's top base stealers, and right fielder Tom Paciorek's second-place .326 BA put a Seattle hitter high among the league's best for the first time. Paciorek was traded away that winter, but his replacement, veteran Al Cowens, came through with one of his best seasons in 1982. And Mariner pitching improved dramatically—from the bottom of the league in ERA in 1981 to fourth best in '82. Newcomers Bill Caudill and rookie Ed Vande Berg, working in relief, combined for 21 wins and 31 saves. Starter Floyd Bannister led the league in strikeouts while winning 12 games (tying Caudill for the team lead), and veteran Gaylord Perry added 10 victories, including his 300th career win in May. The team finished above .450 for the first time, fourth in the AL West, a new high.

Caudill's 26 saves in 1983 couldn't prevent a slide back into last place. But the club's farm system was beginning to produce quality talent, and 1984 saw the arrival of two standouts: first baseman Alvin Davis, whose 27 homers and 116 RBIs earned him AL Rookie of the Year honors, and pitcher Mark Langston, a 17-game winner in 1984 and AL strikeout leader

in three of his first four seasons. Rookie third baseman Jim Presley hit 10 home runs in 70 games and blossomed into one of the club's leading power hitters the next year.

After sixth-place finishes in 1984 and '85, the Mariners fell off to last again in 1986. Langston's 19 wins led the team's 1987 rebound to fourth, with Lee Guetterman's 11–4 pitching and the power of Davis and Presley providing valuable assists. Infielder Harold Reynolds stole his sixtieth base in the final game to preserve his lead in that department and to give the Mariners their first league leader in an offensive category. The end of 1988, though, found the team once more settled in the cellar of the AL West.

Texas Rangers

As part of the first American League expansion, a new Washington club was added to the league in November 1960, to replace the old Senators, who were moving to Minnesota to become the Twins. The old Senators had languished in the second division their final 14 years in Washington, and the new Senators scarcely improved on that record. In each of their first four seasons they lost 100 games or more, tying for last place in 1961 and holding down the bottom all by themselves for two years before rising to ninth in 1964.

Although as an expansion team the new Senators had to make do at first with expendable players from the established clubs, they were not devoid of talent. In their first season, pitcher Dick Donovan led the league with a 2.40 earned run average, though injuries and the lack of offensive support held his won-lost record to 10–10. Perhaps their most promising player, he was traded with two teammates to Cleveland for outfielder Jimmy Piersall. Piersall proved a major disappointment in Washington, batting only .244 while Donovan was winning 20 games for his new club.

Not all the Senators' trades proved disastrous. In late 1964 they sent another promising pitcher—Claude Osteen—to the Dodgers in a deal that brought them five players, including third baseman Ken McMullen and outfielder Frank Howard. Osteen blossomed into a consistent winner in Los Angeles, but McMullen brought strength to the Washington infield and Howard became one of the league's offensive stars.

The Senators' blend of youth and experience jelled in 1969 under rookie manager Ted Williams, as several key players—including McMullen and Howard—enjoyed career-best seasons. The club finished above .500 for the first time, driving with a late-season spurt to within a game of third-place Boston in the league's Eastern Division.

But 1969 was a one-year phenomenon. After losing seasons in 1970 and '71 (and the loss of much of their fan support), owner Bob Short pulled up stakes and moved the club to Arlington, Texas (midway between Fort Worth and Dallas), where, as the Texas Rangers, they have been ever since. Their first summer in Texas resembled their first in Washington: they lost 100 games (despite a strike-shortened season) and finished last. Williams was replaced by a new rookie manager—Whitey Herzog—but the club did no better in 1973.

Before the season's end Herzog gave way to Billy Martin. Martin came too late to save the Rangers from another lost season, but the next year he spurred the team to the kind of turnaround Williams had managed five years earlier. Behind the 25–12 pitching of Ferguson Jenkins (acquired in the off-season from the Cubs) and the hitting of league MVP Jeff

Burroughs and rookie first baseman Mike Hargrove, the Rangers spurted in the second half of 1974 from a sub-.500 record to second place in the American League West, only 5 games behind Oakland.

Since 1974 the Rangers' fortunes have been up and down. After two losing seasons they rebounded in 1977 to their finest season yet (94–68, .580) and second place, behind strong pitching and the blooming of Jim Sundberg as a hitter to go along with his league-leading catching. Fergie Jenkins's return to the club (after two years in Boston), the sparkling 11–5 season of rookie Steve Comer, and a September surge kept the club competitive in 1978. Jim Kern's brilliant relief work the next season helped the club recover from a nosedive in July and August to edge Minnesota for a strong third-place finish.

After a losing season in 1980, the Rangers bounced back in 1981 to record their second-best winning percentage ever (.543)—and finishes of second and third in the two halves of the strike-divided season. Then they slipped below .500 again for four more years. Pitcher Charlie Hough's knuckleball, and strong seasons at the bat from Pete O'Brien, Larry Parrish, and rookies Scott Fletcher and Pete Incaviglia helped new manager Bobby Valentine turn the Rangers around once again in 1986, lifting them to the club's fifth second-place finish after last-place seasons in 1984 and '85.

Once more, though, the turnaround was brief: in 1987 losses in their final games of the season dropped the Rangers into a tie at the bottom of the division, and in 1988 they finished only two games out of the cellar, in sixth place.

Toronto Blue Jays

For a while, in February 1977, it looked as if the National League's San Francisco Giants would move to Toronto, where there were buyers eager for the club. But when the Giants were sold in March to new owners determined to keep them in San Francisco, the American League jumped in to establish Toronto as an American League city, setting up an expansion club, the Blue Jays.

It took seven years for the Jays to lift themselves out of last place in the seven-team American League East. For five years they had the cellar all to themselves, never finishing closer than 11 games behind the *sixth*-place club.

In their first season, the Jays' 107 losses left them 45½ games out of first, as the team performed at the bottom of the division in hitting, fielding, and pitching. In 1978 their fielding improved dramatically, but the Jays still lost over 100 games, and there was little doubt after April who would finish last.

The next year was the team's worst ever. While every other Eastern Division club was compiling a winning record, Toronto plunged relentlessly downward and, despite a brief rally in September, finished 28½ games out of sixth place (50½ out of first), with 109 losses.

The club's turnaround began in 1980. It was late June before the Jays began their drop away from the rest of the division, and for the first time they finished with fewer than 100 losses. Pitchers Jim Clancy and Dave Stieb lowered their ERAs below 4.00 for the first time, and newly acquired second baseman Damaso Garcia combined with shortstop Alfredo Griffin to form the league's best double-play combination. There were still two more seasons in the cellar, but in strike-divided 1981 the Jays played a creditable second half for the first time, and in 1982 they spurted in September to tie the Indians for sixth at season's end. Garcia in 1982 became a .300 hitter and a leading base stealer, Clancy put together his first winning season and Stieb his second, and Stieb's five shutouts led the league.

In 1983, with seven of the Blue Jays' eight principal pitchers enjoying winning seasons, and the Jays' hitters leading the league in team batting and slugging, Toronto recorded its first winning season—in fourth place, only 9 games out of first. Their balanced pitching and offense carried them to a repeat 89–73 record in 1984—this time for second place (though they finished a distant 15 games behind Detroit).

In 1985 the Blue Jays topped their division with 99 victories, edging the Yankees by 2 games. Their pitching was better than ever. Doyle Alexander won 17 games, Jimmy Key and Dave Stieb contributed 14 each, and reliever Dennis Lamp compiled an impressive 11–0 record. Stieb led the league in ERA, with Key fourth. Tony Fernandez, in his first full big league season, sparkled as expected at short, but also proved unexpectedly solid at the bat. Eight Jays drove in more than 50 runs, with outfielders George Bell (95), Jesse Barfield (84), and Lloyd Moseby (71) pacing the club's balanced attack.

In the LCS the Jays won three of their first four games against Kansas City, but lost the next three—and the pennant. Equally discouraging was their drop to fourth place in 1986. Barfield, Bell, and Fernandez all improved at the plate, but the league-leading pitchers of 1985 dropped back to the middle of the pack in '86 (though rookie Mark Eichorn sparkled in long relief).

Toronto sprang back stronger than ever in 1987. Jim Clancy (15–11, 3.54 ERA) enjoyed his best season yet, as did Jimmy Key (17–8), whose 2.76 ERA led the league. Once again, as in 1985, the team ERA was the league's lowest. And the offense remained strong. (George Bell, league RBI leader with 134, was named the American League MVP at season's end.) The Jays led their division going into the season's final series against second-place Detroit, though four straight losses had reduced the lead to just one game. Needing to win two of the three games to take the AL East title, or one to tie the Tigers and force a playoff, the Jays' slumping bats remained quiet, and Toronto lost the first two games. In the season finale, Jimmy Key hurled a three-hitter, striking out eight. But one of the hits was a home run—the only run of the game, as it turned out. Toronto's seven-game losing streak had cost them what would have been their second title in three years.

In 1988, a rocky season made worse by George Bell's feud with manager Jimy Williams (who wanted the unwilling outfielder to serve as designated hitter), the Jays surged at the end—with six straight wins—into a tie for third place, only two games out of first. The season was highlighted by the emergence of Fred McGriff as one of the game's most powerful batsmen, and by ace Dave Stieb's two successive one-hitters in late September—both of which were no-hitters through 8⅔ innings.

Defunct Clubs

In addition to the many Negro League teams, some 108 ballclubs have played in the major leagues since the first

professional association was formed in 1871. The twenty-six that still do are described above; here are the other eighty-two, listed according to the league and year in which they first played major league ball. Official club names precede the name of the city; nicknames follow.

National Association, 1871–1875

Two of the twenty-three clubs that played at one time or another in baseball's first professional league still play in the majors: the Atlanta Braves (then the Boston Red Stockings) and the Chicago Cubs (then the White Stockings). The other twenty-one:

Athletic of Philadelphia: NA 1871–1875, NL 1876. Organized in 1860 as an amateur club, the Athletics became one of the dominant teams of the decade. As professionals they won the first NA pennant in 1871. After one year in the NL, they were expelled for failing to make the final western trip of the season.

Forest City of Cleveland, NA 1871–1872. In the midst of a second losing season, the club disbanded in August 1872.

Forest City of Rockford, Ill., NA 1871. As an amateur club, Forest City (with its sixteen-year-old pitcher Al Spalding) was the only team to defeat the famous Washington Nationals on their pioneering midwestern tour of 1867. As professionals, Forest City finished seventh of the nine NA teams in 1871.

Kekionga of Fort Wayne, NA 1871. The Kekiongas won the first NA game ever played, but dropped out of the association before the end of the season.

Mutual of New York, NA 1871–1875, NL 1876. Organized as an amateur club in 1857, the Mutuals were said to be backed financially by New York's notorious William M. "Boss" Tweed. Frequently accused of corrupt practices, the club was one of the leading eastern teams of the late 1860s. They were declared national champions of 1868, and proclaimed themselves national champions of 1870. On the demise of the NA the Mutuals entered the NL, but were expelled after one season (along with the Athletics) for failing to play their final games in the West.

Olympic of Washington, D.C., NA 1871–1872. Unsuccessful in 1872 after playing well the year before, the Olympics disbanded about midseason.

Union of Troy, N.Y., NA 1871–1872. The Haymakers, as they were popularly known, dropped out of the NA halfway through the 1872 season.

Atlantic of Brooklyn, NA 1872–1875. One of the greatest of the amateur clubs, the Atlantics (organized in 1855) went undefeated in 1864 and 1865, and won three successive national championships, 1864–1866. But in four NA seasons their combined won-lost record was only 49–139, including a dismal 2–42 in 1875.

Eckford of Brooklyn, NA 1872. Another great early amateur club—like the Atlantics, organized in 1855—they won the national championship in 1862, and again (with an undefeated season of ten games) the next year. The Eckfords actually joined the NA in August 1871, replacing Kekionga, but their 1871 games were later erased from the record because they had failed to enter the association at the start of the season.

Lord Baltimore of Baltimore, NA 1872–1874. After twice finishing third, the Lord Baltimores (or "Canaries," for their yellow silk jerseys) disbanded two games before the end of the

1874 season, while in last place.

Mansfield of Middletown, Ct., NA 1872. Disbanded in late August.

National of Washington, D.C., NA 1872–1873, 1875. Organized as amateurs in 1859, the Nationals were the first eastern club to tour as far west as Chicago and St. Louis. After skipping the 1874 race, the Nationals re-entered the NA in 1875, but dropped out in July.

Maryland of Baltimore, NA 1873. Dropped out after only six games.

Philadelphia, NA 1873–1875. Known successively as the "White Stockings," "Pearls," and "Phillies," the team finished a strong second to Boston in their first season, but slipped to fourth and fifth the next two years.

Resolute of Elizabeth, N.J., NA 1873. Disbanded in August with a 2–21 record.

Hartford Dark Blues, NA 1874–1875, NL 1876–1877. After a weak first year, Hartford finished third in its next three seasons, as standings are reckoned today. But by the 1876 guidelines (which used the number of games won rather than winning percentage), Hartford that year placed second. In 1877 the club played its home games in Brooklyn, N.Y.

Centennial of Philadelphia, NA 1875. Dropped out in late May.

New Haven Elm Citys, NA 1875. Failed to play out their schedule.

St. Louis Brown Stockings, NA 1875, NL 1876–1877. George Bradley pitched all but 5 of the Browns' 39 wins in 1875, when they finished fourth, and all 45 victories in 1876, when they finished a strong third (in number of victories; they were second in winning percentage). With Bradley lost to Chicago the next year, St. Louis dropped below .500—and out of the league.

St. Louis Red Stockings, NA 1875. A successful amateur club that decided to take a fling at pro ball, the Red Stockings played only a few games in the NA.

Western of Keokuk, Iowa, NA 1875. Disbanded in mid-June.

National League, 1876–

When the NL was founded to replace the ill-organized NA, it included six of the stronger NA clubs plus independent clubs in Cincinnati and Louisville. The league's composition was in continual flux to the end of the century as clubs were dropped and added, shrinking the league to as few as six teams and expanding it to as many as twelve. Two clubs that first played major league ball in the NL still do: the Philadelphia Phillies and the San Francisco (originally New York) Giants, both organized in 1883. (The Boston and Chicago franchises—that continue to this day as the Atlanta Braves and Chicago Cubs—had their starts in the National Association.) Those that have not survived:

Cincinnati Red Stockings, NL 1876–1880. From last place in 1876 (and 1877, when their games were not counted because of the club's reorganization and failure to pay its dues), the Reds—with seven new regulars—rose to second in 1878, only to fall back to fifth in 1879, and last again in 1880. That fall, when they refused to accept a new rule abolishing liquor sales and Sunday baseball on club grounds, they were dropped from league membership.

Louisville Grays, NL 1876–1877. The strong Louisville team would have won the pennant in 1877 but for the crook-

edness of four players who threw several games late in the season. The expulsion of the four showed the NL's determination to wipe out corruption, but it also led to the club's departure from the league. Moreover, it prompted the stillbirth of a St. Louis team that had planned to sign some of the four for 1878.

Indianapolis Browns, NL 1878. Finished fifth of six teams.

Milwaukee Grays (or Cream Citys), NL 1878. Finished a last-place sixth.

Providence Grays, NL 1878–1885. One of the great teams in the NL's early years, Providence won pennants in 1879 and 1884, finishing no lower than third in seven of their eight seasons. In 1884, pitcher Charlie "Old Hoss" Radbourn won a record 59 games, then pitched the Grays to victory in baseball's first World Series with a three-game sweep of the American Association champion New York Mets. But their glory year was followed in short order by what turned out to be their final year.

Buffalo Bisons, NL 1879–1885. Buffalo moved up to the majors after winning the International Association pennant in 1878. Jim "Pud" Galvin pitched nearly 70 percent of Buffalo's victories as he led them to four first-division finishes in seven big league seasons. First baseman Dan Brouthers, in his five years with Buffalo, twice won the batting title and led NL sluggers five times.

Cleveland Blues, NL 1879–1884. Cleveland's fortunes rested in large measure with pitcher Jim McCormick (who also managed the club their first two seasons). In 1880, their best season, McCormick won a career-high 45 games to bring the Blues in third. In 1883 Cleveland was in first place when McCormick's injured arm put him out for the season after he had won twenty-three games. The Blues dropped to fourth. The club folded after a seventh-place finish in 1884, a season that saw McCormick and two other Blues jump to the UA.

Star of Syracuse, NL 1879. After finishing a close second to Buffalo in the International League in 1878, the Stars moved up with the Bisons to the NL, but disbanded after a single unsuccessful season.

Troy, N.Y., Trojans, NL 1879–1882. After four losing seasons the franchise was expelled to make room for a club in New York City.

Worcester, Mass., Ruby Legs, NL 1880–1882. After a pair of losing minor league seasons, Worcester was admitted to the NL to replace the defunct Stars of Syracuse. After finishing a respectable fifth in 1880, Worcester dropped into the cellar for two seasons before being ousted in 1883 for a new Philadelphia club.

Detroit Wolverines, NL 1881–1888. Buffalo's sale of its "big four" (Dan Brouthers, Hardy Richardson, Jack Rowe, and Deacon White) to Detroit late in 1885 transformed a perennial also-ran into a contender. The club finished second in 1886 and won the pennant in 1887. In a World Series played in ten different cities, the Wolverines trounced St. Louis ten games to five. In 1888, after finishing fifth, they expired.

Kansas City Cowboys, NL 1886. They finished seventh, 58½ games out.

Washington Senators, NL 1886–1889. In their four seasons, the Senators finished out of the cellar only once: next to last in 1887.

Indianapolis Hoosiers, NL 1887–1889. After dropping below Washington into the cellar in 1887, the Hoosiers and Senators traded places for their final two years.

American Association, 1882–1891

Three of the six clubs that formed the AA in 1882 still represent their cities in the majors today: Allegheny (Pittsburgh), Cincinnati, and St. Louis. Brooklyn, which entered the AA two years later, today represents Los Angeles. The others:

Athletic of Philadelphia, AA 1882–1890. After finishing a distant second in the AA's first season, the Athletics in 1883 took the pennant from St. Louis by a single game. First baseman Harry Stovey, who led AA batters in most offensive categories that year, was even more impressive in 1884, hitting .404 and slugging .648 to lead the league. But the A's dropped to seventh and never again challenged for the crown. Expelled from the AA after the 1890 season for financial reasons, they were replaced by the Philadelphia club from the defunct Players League.

Baltimore Orioles, AA 1882–1889, 1890–1891, NL 1892–1899. After eight seasons out of pennant contention (including four in last place), the Orioles dropped out of the AA to play minor league ball in 1890. But toward the end of the season, when Brooklyn's new franchise went under, the Orioles returned to complete Brooklyn's season (finishing a combined last). After rising to third in 1891, the AA's final year, the Orioles were invited into the expanding NL, where they dropped to a twelfth-place last (54½ games out) in 1892.

Ned Hanlon, hired to manage Baltimore early in the 1892 season, set about building a championship club. By 1894, with a lineup that included six future Hall of Famers, Hanlon led his club to a narrow pennant victory over New York, though the Giants swept the Orioles in the first Temple Cup World Series, 4–0.

For five years Hanlon's brand of scrappy, hustling play made the Orioles the terror of the NL. Led by shortstop Hughie Jennings and outfielders Willie Keeler and Joe Kelley, the club repeated as NL champions in 1895 and 1896, and finished second to Boston the next two years. They lost the Temple Cup to Cleveland (1–4) in 1895, but swept the Spiders the next year 4–0, and took the cup again in 1897, defeating Boston 4–1 in what turned out to be the Series swan song.

Baltimore owners Hanlon and Harry Von der Horst purchased a half-interest in the Brooklyn club in 1899 (retaining a half-interest in Baltimore), and switched Jennings, Kelley, and Keeler to Brooklyn. Hanlon also went over as manager, leaving third baseman John McGraw in charge of the Orioles. McGraw hit .391 and rookie pitcher Joe McGinnity won 28 games to bring the team in fourth. But Hanlon's Superbas won the pennant, and when the NL cut back to eight teams after the season, Baltimore got the ax.

Eclipse of Louisville/Louisville Colonels (or Cyclones), AA 1882–1891, NL 1892–1899. The club, which changed its official name from Eclipse to Louisville after the 1883 season, was one of only two teams to play all ten seasons of the major league AA. (St. Louis—the present Cardinals—was the other.) Louisville finished above .500 in five of its first six years, but only once in that time closed within ten games of the top—in 1884, when Guy Hecker's 52 wins brought the team in third. Slugger Pete Browning paced the Colonel offense in their early years, winning batting titles in 1882 (his rookie season) and 1885, and hammering a second-best .402 in 1887. (A bat made for him by woodworker John Hillerich inspired the creation of the Louisville Slugger.)

By 1889, though, the club had sunk to last place, finishing 66½ games out of first, with 111 losses. The next year, although Hecker and Browning defected to the outlaw PL, the club was less affected by deserters than other AA teams. The Colonels (paced by the league's best hitter, William "Chicken" Wolf, and its best pitcher, Scott Stratton) made one of the greatest turnarounds in big league history, winning the pennant by 10 games over second-place Columbus. In the World Series against Brooklyn, poor weather and small crowds ended play after the teams had tied once and won three apiece.

Even though the Colonels finished next to last in 1891, they were one of four clubs taken into the NL after the AA folded. They never finished higher than ninth in the NL, and for three straight years (1894–1896) they occupied the cellar. When the league cut back from twelve teams to eight after the 1899 season, Louisville merged with the Pittsburgh Pirates.

Columbus Colts (or Senators), AA 1883–1884. From sixth place in 1883, Columbus climbed to second in 1884 behind the 34–13 pitching of rookie Ed Morris. But when the AA dropped back from twelve clubs to eight in 1885, Columbus was out.

Metropolitan of New York, AA 1883–1887. After success in minor league and independent play since 1880, the Mets entered the AA in 1883 as the association expanded from six clubs to eight. Sparked by the 41–17 pitching of Tim Keefe (who was picked up from disbanded Troy), the Mets finished fourth. The next season, with first baseman Dave Orr hitting .354 in his first full major league season and pitcher Jack Lynch matching Keefe with 37 wins apiece, the Mets won the AA pennant handily. But they lost baseball's first World Series to the Providence Grays. When manager Jim Mutrie, third baseman Dude Esterbrook, and pitcher Keefe were transferred in 1885 to the New York Giants (the two clubs had the same owner), the Mets sank to seventh place, where they finished in their final three seasons.

Indianapolis Blues, AA 1884. Finished eleventh of twelve clubs, 46 games behind.

Toledo Blue Stockings, AA 1884. Catcher Fleet Walker (who played in 42 games) and his brother Welday (5 games) were the major leagues' first black players—and the only blacks until Jackie Robinson broke the color bar for good in 1947.

Washington, D.C., AA 1884. The popularity of the city's UA Nationals proved too much for this inept AA club, which went under in early August.

Virginia of Richmond, AA 1884. When Washington disbanded in August, the Wilmington club of the Eastern League was invited to join the AA as its replacement. Wilmington declined (and later jumped to the UA), but Virginia—also a member of the EL—accepted the invitation and took over Washington's remaining games. Washington-Virginia finished a combined 24–81, in last place.

Cleveland Spiders, AA 1887–1888, NL 1888–1899. After two losing seasons in the AA, the Spiders moved to the NL, where they continued below .500 for three more years. But in 1892 Cy Young's league-leading pitching brought them the second-half championship of the league's experimental split season. Cleveland lost the World Series to first-half winner Boston, losing five after tying the first game.

Second-place finishes in 1895 and 1896 qualified the Spiders for the Temple Cup series against champion Baltimore.

In 1895 they beat the Orioles for the world title four games to one, but were swept the next year 0–4.

In 1899, when owner Frank Robison transferred all the team's best players to St. Louis (which he also owned), Cleveland suffered the worst season in major league history, winning only 20 games while losing a record 134. They finished 35 games behind eleventh-place Washington and 84 games out of first. After the season the Spiders died, as the NL cut back from twelve teams to eight.

Kansas City Blues, AA 1888–1889. Finished last in 1888, next to last in 1889.

Columbus Colts (or Solons), AA 1889–1891. In 1890, with the AA weakened by the replacement of half its franchises with new clubs and by defections to the outlaw PL, Columbus (which retained several of its regulars) rose from its 1889 sixth-place finish to second behind Louisville. When the PL folded and the defectors returned in 1891, Columbus dropped back to sixth.

Brooklyn Gladiators, AA 1890. Formed as a replacement for the Brooklyn club that forsook the AA for the NL in 1890, the Gladiators floundered and were replaced by Baltimore late in the season.

Rochester Hop Bitters, AA 1890. Played .500 ball, finishing fifth.

Syracuse Stars, AA 1890. Finished sixth.

Toledo Maumees, AA 1890. Finished fourth.

Cincinnati Porkers, AA 1891. Also known as "Kelly's Killers" for their manager Mike "King" Kelly, the club went bankrupt in August and was replaced by Milwaukee.

Milwaukee Brewers, AA 1891. This Western League club moved up to the AA in August. Taking five players and the 43–57 record from the defunct Cincinnati club, Milwaukee went 21–15 the rest of the way to lift the Cincinnati-Milwaukee combination from seventh to fifth by season's end.

Washington Senators, AA 1891, NL 1892–1899. Despite a cellar finish in the AA's final year, the Senators were taken into the expanding NL. Of its nine losing seasons, the best was a tie for sixth in the twelve-team NL of 1897.

Union Association, 1884

Formed in opposition to the reserve rule that governed players in the NL and AA, the UA struggled through one season. The first eight clubs listed here began the season. The other five are listed according to the month they entered the UA as replacement teams. All thirteen—like the UA itself—are long extinct:

Altoona, Pa., Unions, UA 1884. The first of several UA clubs to drop out of competition during the season, Altoona disbanded on May 31, but reorganized as an independent club two days later with many of the same players.

Baltimore Monumentals, UA 1884. Bill Sweeney's league-leading 40 wins accounted for 70 percent of third-place Baltimore's victories.

Boston Unions, UA 1884. Outfielder Tom McCarthy, the UA's only Hall of Famer, hit .215 in this, his rookie big league season. Boston finished fourth.

Chicago Browns/Pittsburgh Stogies, UA 1884. Financial woes caused the Chicago Browns to relocate in Pittsburgh in late August, but the club quit altogether less than a month later.

Cincinnati Outlaw Reds, UA 1884. With three 20-game winners—including Jim McCormick, who won 21 after de-

fecting from the NL in midseason—Cincinnati compiled a strong 69–36 record, but still finished 21 games behind champion St. Louis.

Keystone of Philadelphia, UA 1884. In early August Keystone dropped out of the league and reorganized as an independent semipro club.

National of Washington, D.C., UA 1884. Finished sixth, 46½ games back.

St. Louis Maroons, UA 1884, NL 1885–1886. Batting 47 points above the league average, the Maroons scored 184 runs more than the next-best club to run away with the pennant. They were the only UA club to survive 1884 as a major league team, but in the NL they were unable to fashion a winning season or finish higher than sixth.

Kansas City Unions, UA 1884. Formed to replace Altoona, Kansas City went 16–63 in its partial season.

Wilmington, Del., Quicksteps, UA 1884. After the Quicksteps had gone 51–12 to sew up the Eastern League championship, they jumped to the UA in August to replace Philadelphia's Keystones. But as several players failed to make the jump with them, the move was a disaster on the field (2–16) and financially. They failed in mid-September.

Milwaukee Grays, UA 1884. One of only two teams left in the deteriorating Northwestern League, Milwaukee moved up to the UA in September to complete the schedule of dropout Wilmington.

St. Paul White Caps, UA 1884. With the disbanding of the Northwestern League in September, St. Paul joined the UA to take over Pittsburgh's remaining games.

Players League, 1890

Formed in rebellion against the Brush classification plan, the PL drew many of the finest players from the NL and AA, and proved the most popular league with the fans. But when only one club turned a profit, the clubs' financial backers deserted and the league died. Two clubs were admitted to the AA, and many of the rest merged with their National League counterparts:

Boston Red Stockings, PL 1890, AA 1891. Boston won the PL pennant with such stars as Dan Brouthers, Old Hoss Radbourne, Hardy Richardson, and manager King Kelly. The only PL club to make money, Boston joined the AA the next year and won another pennant. But when the popular Kelly defected to Boston's NL Beaneaters (who also won a pennant for the city in 1891), the fans defected too, and the Red Stockings died along with the AA at the end of the season.

Brooklyn Wonders, PL 1890. At the end of a season in which they edged New York for second place, the Wonders merged with Brooklyn's NL pennant-winners.

Buffalo Bisons, PL 1890. After a last-place finish 20 games back of their nearest competitor, the Bisons simply went out of business.

Chicago Pirates, PL 1890. Mark Baldwin and Charles "Silver" King tied for the league lead with 32 wins each, pitching Chicago into fourth place. Both went to Pittsburgh the next year, although the franchise was absorbed by Chicago's NL Colts.

Cleveland Infants, PL 1890. Like Cleveland's NL Spiders of 1890, the Infants finished next to last. But one of their three managers, infielder Oliver Wendell "Patsy" Tebeau, would go on to lead the Spiders to their finest seasons.

Philadelphia Quakers, PL 1890, *Athletic* AA 1891. Although they finished sixth in their PL season, the Quakers compiled a winning record. When the Athletics of the AA were expelled following the 1890 season, the Quakers were admitted in their place and awarded the name "Athletic." The team finished fourth in 1891, but was not among the four clubs taken into the NL when the AA folded, because Philadelphia already had an NL team (the Phillies).

New York Giants, PL 1890. Paced by the hitting of first baseman Roger Connor and outfielder Jim O'Rourke, New York's PL Giants finished third. In November the club merged with the city's NL Giants.

Pittsburgh Burghers, PL 1890. After a sixth-place finish, the Pittsburgh PL club and the NL Allegheny Club combined to form the new Pittsburgh Athletic club, which still represents Pittsburgh in the NL.

American League, 1901–

When Western League president Ban Johnson renamed the circuit in 1900 and proclaimed it a major league the next year, he little knew how stable it would be. For over half a century (1903–1953) the same eight clubs represented the same eight cities. Even today, although the league has expanded and several clubs have moved to new cities, not one franchise has perished.

Federal League, 1914–1915

After an inaugural season as a six-team minor league in 1913, the FL expanded to eight teams and declared war on the NL and AL for their players. After two big league seasons, and despite two of the game's most exciting pennant races ever, the league died for lack of patronage, and with it went its eight franchises:

Baltimore Terrapins, FL 1914–1915. Jack Quinn and George Suggs, with 26 and 25 wins, pitched Baltimore to third place in 1914. But when Quinn and Suggs lost their stuff the next year, the club sank out of sight, 24 games behind seventh-place Brooklyn.

Brooklyn Tip-Tops (or Brookfeds), FL 1914–1915. Not even the acquisition of batting and base-stealing champ Benny Kauff could stop Brooklyn from slipping from fifth in 1914 to seventh the next year.

Buffalo Buffeds, 1914–1915. Finished fourth in 1914, sixth the next year.

Chicago Chifeds (or Whales), FL 1914–1915. After leading the league through July and much of August in 1914, only to lose out after a late-season struggle with Indianapolis, the Whales came back in 1915 to triumph in an even tighter race that saw the three top teams separated at the finish by only half a game. Owner Charles Weeghman was permitted to buy the NL Cubs in 1916, and many Whales joined the Cubs in play at what was then Weeghman Park and now is known as Wrigley Field.

Indianapolis Federals (or Hoosiers), FL 1914; *Newark Peps*, FL 1915. Five regulars hit over .300 (paced by Benny Kauff's league-leading .370) in 1914, and the team as a whole hit twenty-two points above the league average. From fourth place in August the Hoosiers fought back to capture the flag from Chicago by 1½ games, with seven consecutive wins at the end. The only major league pennant-winner to move to a new city the next year, the Hoosiers became the Peps in 1915.

Though they remained competitive into September, an eight-game losing streak dropped them out of the race and they finished fifth.

Kansas City Packers, FL 1914–1915. After a sixth-place finish in 1914, the Packers competed in a five-way race through much of 1915. But from first place on August 21 they dropped to fifth a week later and finished fourth.

Pittsburgh Rebels, FL 1914–1915. After avoiding last place in 1914 only by St. Louis's late-season nosedive, Pittsburgh turned itself around the next year, luring first baseman Ed Konetchy from their NL rival Pirates, and pitcher Frank Allen from the NL Brooklyn Robins. Both enjoyed the best season of their careers to lead the Rebels into first place in

late August, where they remained until they were dropped to third by losing three out of four at the end to the champion Whales.

St. Louis Terriers, FL 1914–1915. After finishing last in 1914, St. Louis added veteran pitcher Eddie Plank to its roster. From a club with two 20-game losers, the Terriers became in 1915 a team with three 20-game winners (including Plank), pulling up from fifth late in August to catch the leaders with a nine-game winning streak. At the finish, though, they ranked second—by less than one percentage point, the narrowest big league pennant margin ever. For 1916, Terriers' owner Phil Ball took over the AL St. Louis Browns.

CHAPTER 3

Postseason Play

Frederick Ivor-Campbell

As we all know, major-league baseball doesn't end with the end of the season. There follows the *post-season*—the League Championship Series and the World Series—when even the most casual fan is stirred to follow the games which determine, eventually, the world's best team.

Once there was much more baseball played in the postseason. In the 1880s, for example, nearly every major-league club played a couple of weeks of postseason games, generally exhibitions against clubs they didn't face during the regular season—like teams from the other major league, or a minor league.

Before there was a World Series there were city and regional series. In 1882 Cleveland defeated Cincinnati for the championship of Ohio, and the next year teams in Philadelphia and New York played for the championships of those cities. These were informal series, arranged by the clubs themselves without official league sanction, and varied in the number of games scheduled according to the desires of the clubs involved.

The same held true for the early World Series, which had their beginnings in 1884. Two years earlier, the champions of the National League and the brand-new American Association played a pair of postseason contests (in which each team recorded a shutout against the other). Some would like to call these games the first World Series, but no one in 1882 saw them as more than exhibition games. In fact, because the NL didn't yet recognize the legitimacy of the AA and forbade its clubs to play those of the new league, the NL champion Chicago White Stockings had to release their players from their season contracts so they could face AA champion Cincinnati as technically independent players.

That winter the two major leagues made their peace, and although a proposed series between the 1883 NL and AA titlists was called off, the 1884 champion Providence Grays (NL) and the Metropolitan Club of New York (AA) played three games "for the championship of the United States." The winning Grays were acclaimed in the press as "champions of the world," and the World Series was born.

The brief 1884 Series set the stage for more elaborate World Series to follow. From 1885 through 1890 the NL and AA pennant winners met in Series that ranged in length from six games to 15.

The demise of the AA after the 1891 season caused a one-year gap in World Series play. When the National League expanded from eight clubs to twelve the next year (by absorbing four teams from the defunct AA), it divided the regular season into two halves, with the first-half winner playing the winner of the second half for the world title. Boston defeated Cleveland in the first official World Series, but the unpopular divided season was not repeated (that is, until the strike year of 1981).

Two years later a new World Series scheme was devised when one William C. Temple offered a prize cup to the winner of a postseason series between the first- and second-place finishers in the NL. For four years these best-of-seven Temple Cup games served as the officially recognized world championship. But by the end of four lopsided Series (only one of which was won by the pennant-winning club), fan interest—never robust—had declined so much that the trophy was returned to its donor and the series abandoned.

In 1900, partisans of second-place Pittsburgh felt that their Pirates were the equal of pennant-winning Brooklyn, and a Pittsburgh newspaper, the *Chronicle-Telegraph*, offered a silver trophy cup to the winner of a best-of-five series between the clubs, to be played entirely in Pittsburgh. Described in the press as the "world's championship series," the games confirmed the superiority of Brooklyn's Superbas, who needed only four games to subdue the hometown Pirates.

The upgrading of the American League from minor- to major-league status in 1901 made a return to interleague World Series play theoretically possible, but it was not until after the NL and AL had made peace in 1903 that the first modern Series was contested. The owners of NL champion Pittsburgh and AL champion Boston arranged a best-of-nine postseason Series in 1903, which proved both popular and financially successful—a firm foundation for future Series. When the NL pennant-winning Giants refused to meet repeating AL titlist Boston in 1904, press and fan disappointment led baseball's National Commission to establish the World Series officially and permanently in 1905.

The end of the 1903 season saw not only the first modern World Series, but also a revival of city and regional series (which had lapsed when the AA folded) in Chicago, Philadelphia, St. Louis, and Ohio. In 1905 the National Commission offered to oversee these series, too, and give them the stability of official sanction. Until the manpower needs of the World War halted the 1918 season a month early (discouraging postseason play apart from the World Series), most of the city and regional series—and occasional series between other clubs, like Cleveland and Pittsburgh, and the Boston Red Sox and New York Giants—were played under National Commission auspices. (Details of the City Series will be found in the appendix to this volume.)

After the war's end, only Chicago's Cubs and White Sox resumed a city series; they played 16 series between 1921 and 1942, when World War II intervened. For 26 years thereafter the World Series alone remained of the once multifaceted major-league postseason—until the AL and NL split into two divisions each in 1969 and ushered in a new layer of playoffs:

the League Championship Series. (In 1981, to recoup some of the money and fan interest lost during a midseason players' strike that split the season in half, a one-time third layer of postseason playoffs was added, pitting the first-half and second-half winners in each division against each other for the division titles—an aberration that made even more of a mockery of the divisional races than the strike itself had done.) From 1969 through 1984 the LCS were played as best-of-five series, but in 1985 they were expanded to match the best-of-seven World Series.

Key to the Statistics

The statistics in this section of *Total Baseball* are standard—there is little point in applying newer analytical measures to performances that run to seven games or fewer. We do offer, however, stats that were not standard at the time, such as earned run averages for years before 1912 and runs batted in before 1920 (which were determined from box scores and play-by-plays) and saves before 1969. Beyond our powers of reconstruction were the following: runs batted in for the World Series of 1884, 1885, and 1900; stolen bases for 1884 and 1885; and batter strikeouts for 1885, 1894–1897, and 1900.

Ignoring the odd 1887 custom of counting walks as base hits, we present the cumulative box score for that year's World Series in accordance with modern practice. Other curiosities of early postseason play include the use of neutral sites for some games in 1885 and 1888 and for the majority of

games in 1887, and the use of players who did not appear in so much as an inning for that team during the regular season (Tom Forster, New York Mets, 1884; Bug Holliday, Chicago, 1885; Sy Sutcliffe, Detroit, 1887; Jumbo Davis, Brooklyn 1889).

The length of the World Series varied from three games in 1884 all the way up to fifteen in 1887 and ten the following year. The best-of-seven format came in with the Temple Cup Series of 1894 and has been the norm for World Series ever since (excepting 1900, 1903, and 1919–1921). In recent years this format has become the norm for League Championship Series as well.

If a player appeared at more than one position during the Series, the number of games he played at each is noted (for example, a man who divided seven games at shortstop and third base would carry the notation *ss-4, 3b-3*). Other abbreviations are as follows:

POS	Position	SB	Stolen Bases
AVG	Batting average	W	Wins
G	Games	L	Losses
AB	At bats	ERA	Earned run average
R	Runs	GS	Games started
H	Hits	CG	Complete games
2B	Doubles	SHO	Shutouts
3B	Triples	SV	Saves
HR	Home runs	IP	Innings pitched
RB	Runs batted in	ER	Earned runs
BB	Bases on Balls	SO	Strikeouts

After a flurry of boasts and challenges, Met manager Jim Mutrie and the Grays' Frank Bancroft arranged a three-game series in New York to determine which team was the nation's best. These were not the first games between NL and AA pennant winners. In 1882, the AA's first season, champion Cincinnati met NL titlist Chicago twice as part of its postseason schedule, in games viewed simply as exhibition contests. (Each team won one). The next year a postseason series was proposed between champions Boston (NL) and the Athletics of Philadelphia (AA), but the Athletics fared so poorly in exhibitions against lesser NL teams that they refused to face Boston.

The 1884 Series was touted as "for the championship of the United States," but the influential weekly *Sporting Life* established precedent for future Series hype by naming victorious Providence "Champions of the World." The weather turned cold and windy as the Series got under way. A hardy opening game crowd of 2,500 saw the Grays' great Charlie "Old Hoss" Radbourn blank the Mets on two singles. Met pitcher Tim Keefe, wild at the start, paved the way for two first-inning Providence runs by hitting the first two men to face him and assisted them around the bases with a pair of wild pitches. Paul Hines singled in the third for the Grays' first hit and scored as a passed ball and two more wild pitches brought him home. Keefe yielded only four other hits, but they came back to back in the seventh to produce the Grays' final three runs.

The 1,000 spectators at Game Two witnessed the Series' closest contest. Keefe and Radbourn overwhelmed their opposition for four innings, but in the top of the fifth the Grays bunched three of their five hits for three two-out runs as Jerry Denny homered over the center field fence. The Mets responded with a run in the last of the fifth, but scored no more before darkness ended the game after seven innings.

The Grays had clinched the championship with their second win, and when they saw only a few hundred diehards in the stands for Game Three, they wanted to go home. The Mets must have regretted their insistence on playing the game. Although darkness halted it after only six innings, rookie Met pitcher Buck Becannon (replacing Keefe, who umpired) and awful Mets fielding gave Providence eleven or twelve runs (scorers lost count), while Radbourn held the New Yorkers to a pair of unearned tallies.

Providence Grays (NL), 3; New York Mets (AA), 0

PRO (N)

PLAYER/POS	AVG	G	AB	R	H	2B	3B	HR	RB	BB	SO	SB
Cliff Carroll, of	.100	3	10	2	1	0	0	0		1	1	
Jerry Denny, 3b	.444	3	9	3	4	0	1	1		0	3	
Jack Farrell, 2b	.444	3	9	3	4	2	0	0		0	0	
Barney Gilligan, c	.444	3	9	3	4	2	0	0		0	1	
Paul Hines, of	.250	3	8	5	2	0	0	0		3	0	
Arthur Irwin, ss	.222	3	9	2	2	0	1	0		0	2	
Charlie Radbourn, p	.100	3	10	1	1	0	0	0		3	3	
Paul Radford, of	.000	3	7	1	0	0	0	0		0	1	
Joe Start, 1b	.100	3	10	0	1	0	0	0		0	2	
TOTAL	.235		81	20	19	4	2	1		5	13	

PITCHER	W	L	ERA	G	GS	CG	SV	SHO	IP	H	ER	BB	SO
Charlie Radbourn	3	0	0.00	3	3	3	0	1	22.0	11	0	0	16
TOTAL	3	0	0.00	3	3	3	0	1	22.0	11	0	0	16

NY (A)

PLAYER/POS	AVG	G	AB	R	H	2B	3B	HR	RB	BB	SO	SB
Buck Becannon, p	.500	1	2	0	1	0	0	0		0	0	
Steve Brady, of	.000	3	10	1	0	0	0	0		0	1	
Dude Esterbrook, 3b	.300	3	10	0	3	1	0	0		0	3	
Tom Forster, 2b	.000	1	3	0	0	0	0	0		0	1	
Bill Holbert, c	.000	1	2	0	0	0	0	0		0	1	
Tim Keefe, p	.200	2	5	0	1	0	0	0		0	4	
Ed Kennedy, of	.000	3	7	0	0	0	0	0		0	2	
Candy Nelson, ss	.100	3	10	0	1	0	0	0		0	1	
Dave Orr, 1b	.111	3	9	0	1	0	0	0		0	0	
Charlie Reipschlager, c	.000	2	5	1	0	0	0	0		0	1	
Chief Roseman, of	.333	3	9	1	3	0	0	0		0	1	
Dasher Troy, 2b	.200	2	5	0	1	0	0	0		0	1	
TOTAL	.143		77	3	11	1	0	0		0	16	

PITCHER	W	L	ERA	G	GS	CG	SV	SHO	IP	H	ER	BB	SO
Buck Becannon	0	1	3.00	1	1	1	0	0	6.0	9	2	2	1
Tim Keefe	0	2	3.60	2	2	2	0	0	15.0	10	6	3	12
TOTAL	0	3	3.43	3	3	3	0	0	21.0	19	8	5	13

GAME 1 AT NY OCT 23

NY	000 000 000	0	2	0
PRO	201 000 30X	6	5	2

Pitchers: KEEFE vs RADBOURN
Attendance: 2,500

GAME 2 AT NY OCT 24

PRO	000 030 0	3	5	4
NY	000 010 0	1	3	1

Pitchers: RADBOURN vs KEEFE
Home Runs: Denny-PRO
Attendance: 1,000
(Game called at end of seventh, darkness)

GAME 3 AT NY OCT 25

PRO	120 044	11	9	3
NY	000 011	2	6	9

Pitchers: RADBOURN vs BECANNON
Attendance: 300
(Game called at end of sixth, darkness)

Before the start of the final game, the two clubs agreed to throw out Game Two, which had been forfeited to Chicago, leaving the Series tied at two wins apiece, plus the one tie. But after the Browns won the seventh game for their third victory, Chicago manager Cap Anson decided his club should retain its forfeit win after all, and a select committee agreed, leaving the Series in a tie instead of a White Stocking defeat.

Game One, in Chicago, was called for darkness after eight innings, with the score tied 5–5. The Browns scored first with a run in the second and added four more in the top of the fourth. But Chicago came back with a run in the last of the fourth, and in the bottom of the eighth scored four more on a walk, two singles, and Fred Pfeffer's game-tying three-run homer.

The Series moved to St. Louis for the next three games. Chicago was leading 5–4 in the sixth inning of Game Two when Browns manager Charlie Comiskey pulled his team off the field, objecting to the umpiring of David Sullivan. Umpire Sullivan later forfeited the game to the White Stockings; he worked no more in the Series. The Browns won Game Three, scoring five unearned runs with two out in the top of the first, and holding on for a 7–4 win. Chicago lost again the next day in a much closer game. The Browns scored first with a run in the third inning, but Abner Dalrymple's two-run homer in the fifth gave the White Stockings a 2–1 lead. In the bottom of the eighth, however, St. Louis scored twice and held on for the 3–2 win.

The Series took to the road for its final three games. In Pittsburgh for Game Five, Chicago overwhelmed the Browns 9–2, scoring four runs in the first inning, and their final three just before darkness ended the game after seven innings.

Game Six and Seven were played in Cincinnati. The White Stockings won the sixth game by the same 9–2 score as Game Five. The Browns' two runs were unearned, as Chicago's Jim McCormick stopped St. Louis on just two hits, both singles. The Brown's victory in the finale was a runaway 13–4, called in the eighth for darkness. St. Louis' six-run fourth inning typified the game's sloppy play, the runs scoring on five hits, four errors, and two passed balls.

Chicago White Stockings (NL), 3; St. Louis Browns (AA), 3; tie, 1

CHI (N)

PLAYER/POS	AVG	G	AB	R	H	2B	3B	HR	RB	BB	SO	SB
Cap Anson, 1b	.423	7	26	8	11	1	1	0		2		
Tom Burns, ss-4,3b-3	.080	7	25	3	2	0	1	0		0		
John Clarkson, p-2,of-2	.154	4	13	1	2	1	0	0		0		
Abner Dalrymple, of	.269	7	26	4	7	2	0	1		2		
Silver Flint, c	.143	4	14	0	2	0	0	0		0		
George Gore, of	.000	1	3	1	0	0	0	0		1		
Bug Holliday, of	.000	1	4	0	0	0	0	0		0		
King Kelly, of-4,c-3	.346	7	26	9	9	3	1	0		2		
Jim McCormick, p	.176	5	17	1	3	0	0	0		0		
Fred Pfeffer, 2b	.407	7	27	5	11	2	0	1		0		
Billy Sunday, of	.273	6	22	5	6	2	0	0		2		
N. Williamson, 3b-4,ss-3	.087	7	23	1	2	0	0	0		4		
TOTAL	.243		226	38	55	11	3	2		13		

PITCHER	W	L	ERA	G	GS	CG	SV	SHO	IP	H	ER	BB	SO
John Clarkson	0	1	1.13	2	2	2	0	0	16.0	15	2	1	15
Jim McCormick	3	2	2.00	5	5	5	0	0	36.0	27	8	6	19
TOTAL	3	3	1.73	7	7	7	0	0	52.0	42	10	7	34

STL (A)

PLAYER/POS	AVG	G	AB	R	H	2B	3B	HR	RB	BB	SO	SB
Sam Barkley, 2b	.087	7	23	3	2	0	0	0		2		
Doc Bushong, c	.154	4	13	1	2	0	0	0		0		
Bob Caruthers, p-3,of-2	.200	5	15	1	3	0	1	0		1		
Charlie Comiskey, 1b	.292	7	24	6	7	0	0	0		0		
Dave Foutz, p	.167	4	12	1	2	0	0	0		0		
Bill Gleason, ss	.231	7	26	5	6	2	0	0		1		
Arlie Latham, 3b	.318	7	22	5	7	3	0	0		2		
Hugh Nicol, of	.000	1	2	0	0	0	0	0		0		
Tip O'Neill, of	.208	7	24	4	5	0	0	0		0		
Yank Robinson, of-4,c-3	.174	7	23	5	4	0	1	0		1		
Curt Welch, of	.148	7	27	5	4	1	1	0		0		
TOTAL	.199		211	36	42	6	3	0		7		

PITCHER	W	L	ERA	G	GS	CG	SV	SHO	IP	H	ER	BB	SO
Bob Caruthers	1	1	2.42	3	3	3	0	0	26.0	25	7	4	16
Dave Foutz	2	2	0.61	4	4	4	0	0	29.1	30	2	9	14
TOTAL	3	3	1.46	7	7	7	0	0	55.1	55	9	13	30

GAME 1 AT CHI OCT 14

STL	010	400	00	5	7 2
CHI	000	100	04	5	5 10

Pitchers: CARUTHERS vs CLARKSON
Home Runs: Pfeffer-CHI
Attendance: 2,000
(Game called at end of eighth, darkness)

GAME 2 AT STL OCT 15

CHI	110	003		5	6 5
STL	300	10X		4	2 4

Pitchers: McCORMICK vs FOUTZ
Attendance: 2,000
(Game forfeited to Chicago in bottom of sixth)

GAME 3 AT STL OCT 16

CHI	111	000	001	4	8 7
STL	500	002	00X	7	8 4

Pitchers: CLARKSON vs CARUTHERS
Attendance: 3,000

GAME 4 AT STL OCT 17

CHI	000	020	000	2	8 3
STL	001	000	02X	3	6 7

Pitchers: McCORMICK vs FOUTZ
Home Runs: Dalrymple-CHI
Attendance: 3,000

GAME 5 AT PIT OCT 22

CHI	400	110	3	9	7 1
STL	010	000	1	2	4 7

Pitchers: CLARKSON vs FOUTZ
Attendance: 500
(Game called at end of seventh, darkness)

GAME 6 AT CIN OCT 23

CHI	200	111	040	9	11 7
STL	002	000	000	2	2 7

Pitchers: McCORMICK vs CARUTHERS
Attendance: 1,500

GAME 7 AT CIN OCT 24

CHI	200	020	00	4	9 9
STL	004	621	0X	13	13 5

Pitchers: McCORMICK vs FOUTZ
Attendance: 1,200
(Game called in eighth, darkness)

It was a winner-take-all Series, with the club that won four games pocketing the entire proceeds. Attendance, very good for those days, averaged over 7,000 per game and brought the victorious Browns about $14,000.

The first three games were played in Chicago. The White Stockings won the opener on a sparkling five-hit shutout by their ace John Clarkson. But St. Louis's Bob Caruthers improved on Clarkson's performance the next day, blanking Chicago on just two singles as his Browns turned thirteen hits and thirteen Chicago errors into twelve runs (in a game shortened by darkness to eight innings). The White Stockings improved their fielding in the next game (which was also called after eight innings), and this time their bats came alive. With eleven hits (including home runs by Mike "King" Kelly and George Gore) combining with seven St. Louis errors, they regained the Series advantage with an easy 11–4 win.

When the venue shifted to St. Louis, though, the Browns battled back. In a back-and-forth battle in Game Four, Chicago tied the game at 5–5 with a pair of runs in the sixth, but St. Louis scored three final runs a half inning later, winning when darkness ended play in the middle of the seventh.

Game Five repeated Game Two's innovation: two umpires (instead of the usual one), plus a "referee" who stood between the pitcher and second base. The umpiring satisfied everyone, but Chicago, handicapped by their scheduled pitcher's sore arm, lost when they sent shortstop Ned Williamson and right fielder Jimmy Ryan into the box. In the 6½ innings before dark, St. Louis got to Williamson and Ryan for eleven hits and ten runs as their Nat Hudson held Chicago batters to three hits and three unearned runs.

The finale proved to be the Series' best-played and closest game. Chicago's Clarkson shut out the Browns through seven innings as his mates built a three-run lead—one of them scored on Fred's Pfeffer's homer in the fourth. Rain (and a rowdy crowd which poured onto the field) halted play for a while in the fifth. But the game resumed and the rain subsided. In the last of the eighth, Charlie Comiskey scored the Browns' first run on a single, errant throw and run-scoring fly out, and Arlie Latham tripled home two more runners later in the inning to tie the game. The score remained 3–3 into the last of the tenth, when the Browns' Curt Welch singled (for

only the fourth St. Louis hit), went to second on an infield hit, and took third on a sacrifice. Welch then attempted to steal home but catcher Kelly had smelled out the play and called for a pitch out. Clarkson's delivery was poor and bobbled by Kelly, allowing Welch to steal home with a "$15,000 slide" for the Browns' triumph.

St. Louis Browns (AA), 4; Chicago White Stockings (NL), 2

STL (A)

PLAYER/POS	AVG	G	AB	R	H	2B	3B	HR	RB	BB	SO	SB
Doc Bushong, c	.188	6	16	4	3	1	0	0	2	4	5	0
Bob Caruthers, p-3,of-3	.250	6	24	6	6	1	2	0	5	1	4	1
Charlie Comiskey, 1b	.292	6	24	2	7	1	0	0	2	0	4	0
Dave Foutz, p-2,of-2	.200	4	15	2	3	1	1	0	3	0	3	0
Bill Gleason, ss	.208	6	24	3	5	0	0	0	5	1	3	0
Nat Hudson, p-1,of-1	.167	2	6	1	1	0	1	0	0	1	3	0
Arlie Latham, 3b-6,c-1	.174	6	23	4	4	0	1	0	3	3	4	2
Tip O'Neill, of	.400	6	20	4	8	0	2	2	5	4	5	2
Yank Robinson, 2b	.316	6	19	5	6	1	1	0	3	2	3	2
Curt Welch, of	.350	6	20	7	7	2	0	0	1	3	4	2
TOTAL	.262		191	38	50	7	8	2	29	19	38	9

PITCHER	W	L	ERA	G	GS	CG	SV	SHO	IP	H	ER	BB	SO
Bob Caruthers	2	1	2.42	3	3	3	0	1	26.0	18	7	6	12
Dave Foutz	1	1	3.60	2	2	2	0	0	15.0	16	6	6	7
Nat Hudson	1	0	2.57	1	1	1	0	0	7.0	3	2	3	3
TOTAL	4	2	2.81	6	6	6	0	1	48.0	37	15	15	22

CHI (N)

PLAYER/POS	AVG	G	AB	R	H	2B	3B	HR	RB	BB	SO	SB
Cap Anson, 1b-6,c-2	.238	6	21	3	5	1	0	0	1	4	0	1
Tom Burns, 3b-6,of-1	.286	6	21	2	6	2	1	0	1	0	2	0
John Clarkson, p-4,of-1	.067	4	15	0	1	0	0	0	1	0	2	1
Abner Dalrymple, of	.190	6	21	2	4	1	1	0	2	0	5	1
Silver Flint, c	.000	1	3	0	0	0	0	0	0	1	0	1
George Gore, of	.174	6	23	4	4	0	0	1	2	3	3	0
King Kelly, c-5,ss-2,1b-1,3b-1	.208	6	24	4	5	0	0	1	1	2	2	1
Jim McCormick, p	.000	1	3	0	0	0	0	0	0	0	0	0
Fred Pfeffer, 2b	.286	6	21	7	6	0	0	1	4	2	1	2
Jimmy Ryan, of-6,p-1,ss-1	.250	6	20	4	5	1	0	0	2	0	1	1
Ned Williamson, ss-6,p-2,c-1,of-1	.056	6	18	2	1	0	1	0	3	4	5	1
TOTAL	.195		190	28	37	5	3	3	18	15	22	8

PITCHER	W	L	ERA	G	GS	CG	SV	SHO	IP	H	ER	BB	SO
John Clarkson	2	2	2.01	4	4	3	0	1	31.1	25	7	12	28
Jim McCormick	0	1	6.75	1	1	1	0	0	8.0	13	6	2	4
Jimmy Ryan	0	0	9.00	1	0	0	0	0	5.0	8	5	4	4
Ned Williamson	0	1	4.50	2	1	0	0	0	2.0	4	1	1	2
TOTAL	2	4	3.69	8	6	4	0	1	46.1	50	19	19	38

GAME 1 AT CHI OCT 18

STL	000 000 000	0	5	3
CHI	200 001 03X	6	10	4

Pitchers: FOUTZ vs CLARKSON
Attendance: 6,000

GAME 2 AT CHI OCT 19

STL	200 230 50	12	13	2
CHI	000 000 00	0	2	10

Pitchers: CARUTHERS vs McCORMICK
Home Runs: O'Neill-STL (2)
Attendance: 8,000
(Game called at end of eighth, darkness)

GAME 3 AT CHI OCT 20

CHI	200 112 32	11	11	2
STL	010 002 01	4	9	7

Pitchers: CLARKSON, Williamson (8) vs CARUTHERS
Home Runs: Kelly-CHI, Gore-CHI
Attendance: 6,000
(Game called at end of eighth, darkness)

GAME 4 AT STL OCT 21

CHI	300 002 0	5	6	4
STL	011 033 X	8	7	4

Pitchers: CLARKSON vs FOUTZ
Attendance: 8,000
(Game called in seventh, darkness)

GAME 5 AT STL OCT 22

CHI	011 100 00	3	3	3
STL	214 003 0X	10	11	3

Pitchers: WILLIAMSON, Ryan (2) vs HUDSON
Attendance: 10,000
(Game called in eighth, darkness)

GAME 6 AT STL OCT 23

CHI	010 101 000 0	3	6	2
STL	000 000 030 1	4	5	3

Pitchers: CLARKSON vs CARUTHERS
Home Runs: Pfeffer-CHI
Attendance: 8,000

Even though their star slugger Dan Brouthers was sidelined for all but one game by a sprained ankle, the Wolverines—in baseball's longest World Series, played in ten different cities—followed up their only pennant with an easy triumph over repeating AA champion St. Louis. The Browns won the opener at home, though, 6–1. They played errorless ball (rare in that era) as pitcher Bob Caruthers held Detroit scoreless until the ninth inning, and drove in the Browns' second run himself with a first-inning single.

The Wolverines came back to win the next three games. They took an early lead in Game Two and held on for a 5–3 win in St. Louis to even the Series. Then, in the Series' tightest game (played in Detroit) the Wolverines defeated Caruthers 2–1 in the last of the thirteenth when their pitcher Charlie Getzien led off with a single, advanced to second and third on ground outs, and scored on an infield error. In Game Four (in Pittsburgh) Detroit's Charles "Lady" Baldwin stopped the Browns on two hits for an easy 8–0 win.

Caruthers hurled a seven-hitter in Brooklyn for St. Louis's second win, but Detroit took the next four. Getzien contributed a two-hit shutout in New York, and Baldwin overcame Caruthers 3–1 in Philadelphia the next day. Getzien yielded eight hits the day after that in Boston, but Caruthers gave up thirteen, including two home runs to Sam Thompson, and Detroit took the game 9–2. Back in Philadelphia for Game Nine, St. Louis broke a 1–1 tie with a run in the top of the sixth. But the Wolverines scored two in the seventh and a final run in the eighth. The win gave Detroit a 7–2 Series advantage.

Game Ten, scheduled for the next day in Washington, was postponed because of rain until the following morning. Detroit's Hardy Richardson opened the game with a home run, but the Wolverines lost an opportunity to clinch the Series as the Browns overwhelmed Getzien with sixteen hits for an 11–4 victory featuring a triple play. But that afternoon, in Baltimore, Detroit took the deciding game as decisively as they had lost in the morning, knocking the Browns' Dave Foutz for fourteen hits (including four by Richardson and three—including a home run—by Larry Twitchell) as Baldwin held St. Louis to two hits in a 13–3 win.

The Browns and Wolverines split the final four meaningless games, played in Brooklyn,

Detroit Wolverines (NL), 10; St. Louis Browns (AA), 5

DET (N)

PLAYER/POS	AVG	G	AB	R	H	2B	3B	HR	RB	BB	SO	SB
Lady Baldwin, p	.235	5	17	1	4	1	0	0	1	2	2	1
Charlie Bennett, c-10,1b-3	.262	11	42	6	11	2	1	0	9	3	5	5
Dan Brouthers, 1b	.667	1	3	0	2	0	0	0	0	0	0	0
Pete Conway, p	.000	4	12	0	0	0	0	0	0	0	2	0
Fred Dunlap, 2b	.150	11	40	5	6	0	1	0	1	0	4	4
Charlie Ganzel, 1b-10,c-7	.224	14	58	5	13	1	0	0	2	1	2	3
Charlie Getzien, p	.300	6	20	5	6	2	0	0	2	3	6	1
Ned Hanlon, of	.220	15	50	5	11	1	1	0	4	5	1	7
Hardy Richardson, of-10,2b-5,3b-1	.197	15	66	12	13	5	2	1	4	1	9	7
Jack Rowe, ss	.333	15	63	12	21	1	1	0	7	2	1	5
Cy Sutcliffe, 1b-3,c-1	.091	4	11	1	1	0	0	0	0	1	1	1
Sam Thompson, of	.362	15	58	8	21	2	0	2	7	3	3	5
Larry Twitchell, of	.250	6	20	5	5	1	0	1	3	0	1	1
Deacon White, 3b-14,1b-1	.207	15	58	8	12	1	1	0	3	2	0	2
TOTAL	.243		518	73	126	17	7	4	43	23	37	42

PITCHER	W	L	ERA	G	GS	CG	SV	SHO	IP	H	ER	BB	SO
Lady Baldwin	4	1	1.50	5	5	5	0	1	42.0	28	7	10	4
Pete Conway	2	2	3.00	4	4	4	0	0	33.0	31	11	6	10
Charlie Getzien	4	2	2.48	6	6	6	0	1	58.0	61	16	15	17
TOTAL	10	5	2.30	15	15	15	0	2	133.0	120	34	31	31

STL (A)

PLAYER/POS	AVG	G	AB	R	H	2B	3B	HR	RB	BB	SO	SB
Jack Boyle, c	.208	6	24	1	5	0	0	0	1	0	4	0
Doc Bushong, c	.241	9	29	3	7	0	0	0	1	4	1	0
Bob Caruthers, p-8,of-3	.239	10	46	2	11	0	0	0	3	1	1	3
Charlie Comiskey, 1b-14,of-1	.306	15	62	8	19	2	0	0	2	1	1	4
Dave Foutz, of-11,p-3,1b-1	.169	15	59	4	10	2	1	0	1	2	3	0
Bill Gleason, ss	.163	13	49	3	8	0	0	0	1	3	2	1
Silver King, p	.071	4	14	0	1	0	0	0	0	0	3	0
Arlie Latham, 3b	.293	15	58	12	17	1	0	0	1	9	2	15
Harry Lyons, ss	.286	2	7	3	2	0	0	0	0	1	0	0
Tip O'Neill, of	.200	15	65	7	13	2	1	1	5	0	2	0
Yank Robinson, 2b	.326	15	46	5	15	5	1	0	4	10	6	4
Curt Welch, of	.207	15	58	6	12	3	1	1	6	0	2	1
TOTAL	.232		517	54	120	15	4	2	25	31	27	28

PITCHER	W	L	ERA	G	GS	CG	SV	SHO	IP	H	ER	BB	SO
Bob Caruthers	4	4	2.13	8	8	8	0	0	71.2	64	17	12	19
Dave Foutz	0	3	3.46	3	3	3	0	0	26.0	36	10	9	6
Silver King	1	3	2.03	4	4	4	0	0	31.0	26	7	2	21
TOTAL	5	10	2.38	15	15	15	0	0	128.2	126	34	23	46

Detroit, Chicago, and St. Louis. For the first time in a World Series, two umpires officiated at all the games.

GAME 1 AT STL OCT 10

STL	200 040 000	6	12	0
DET	000 000 001	1	4	5

Pitchers: CARUTHERS vs GETZIEN
Attendance: 4,208

GAME 2 AT STL OCT 11

DET	022 000 100	5	10	2
STL	000 000 120	3	8	7

Pitchers: CONWAY vs FOUTZ
Attendance: 6,408

GAME 3 AT DET OCT 12

STL	010 000 000 000 0	1	13	7
DET	000 000 010 000 1	2	6	1

Pitchers: CARUTHERS vs GETZIEN
Attendance: 4,509

GAME 4 AT PIT OCT 13

DET	410 012 000	8	11	1
STL	000 000 000	0	2	6

Pitchers: BALDWIN vs KING
Attendance: 2,447

GAME 5 AT BRO OCT 14

STL	200 002 100	5	5	4
DET	000 020 000	2	7	5

Pitchers: CARUTHERS vs CONWAY
Attendance: 6,796

GAME 6 AT NY OCT 15

DET	330 000 003	9	12	1
STL	000 000 000	0	2	8

Pitchers: GETZIEN vs FOUTZ
Attendance: 5,797

GAME 7 AT PHI OCT 17

STL	000 000 001	1	8	1
DET	030 000 00X	3	6	1

Pitchers: CARUTHERS vs BALDWIN
Home Runs: O'Neill-STL
Attendance: 6,478

GAME 8 AT BOS OCT 18

DET	031 003 200	9	13	2
STL	100 001 000	2	8	5

Pitchers: GETZIEN vs CARUTHERS
Home Runs: Thompson-DET (2)
Attendance: 2,891

GAME 9 AT PHI OCT 19

STL	000 101 000	2	9	2
DET	000 100 21X	4	6	3

Pitchers: KING vs CONWAY
Attendance: 2,389

GAME 10 AT WAS OCT 21 (AM)

DET	200 010 001	4	8	3
STL	200 031 41X	11	16	5

Pitchers: GETZIEN vs CARUTHERS
Home Runs: Latham-STL, Welch-STL, Richardson-DET
Attendance: 1,261

GAME 11 AT BAL OCT 21 (PM)

STL	110 010 000	3	2	7
DET	100 344 10X	13	14	7

Pitchers: FOUTZ vs BALDWIN
Home Runs: Twitchell-DET
Attendance: 2,707
(Detroit wins best of 15 series 8 to 3)

GAME 12 AT BRO OCT 22

DET	000 100 0	1	5	3
STL	410 000 X	5	10	2

Pitchers: CONWAY vs KING
Attendance: 1,138
(Game called in seventh, darkness)

GAME 13 AT DET OCT 24

DET	020 100 120	6	12	3
STL	100 010 001	3	4	5

Pitchers: BALDWIN vs CARUTHERS
Attendance: 3,389

GAME 14 AT CHI OCT 25

STL	000 002 100	3	10	5
DET	300 010 00X	4	4	4

Pitchers: KING vs GETZIEN
Attendance: 378

GAME 15 AT STL OCT 26

STL	340 110	9	11	5
DET	011 000	2	8	7

Pitchers: CARUTHERS vs BALDWIN
Attendance: 659
(Game called after sixth, cold)

St. Louis, AA champions for the fourth straight year, battled the Giants closely through several games, but blowout losses in Games Six and Eight undid them. The first three games were played in New York. In a splendidly pitched opener, Brown ace Charles "Silver" King held New York to two hits and a walk while Giant ace Tim Keefe limited the Browns to three hits and a walk, striking out nine on his way to a narrow 2–1 win. St. Louis evened the Series in Game Two behind the shutout pitching of Elton "Icebox" Chamberlain. Tommy McCarthy scored the Browns' first run in the second inning when, after singling, he moved around to third on two passed balls by Giant catcher Buck Ewing and came home on Ewing's failed attempt to throw out a runner stealing second. Two more runs in the ninth gave St. Louis more than enough insurance for the win.

The Giants scored twice in the first inning of Game Three, and increased their lead to 4–0 before allowing St. Louis a pair of harmless runs in the final innings. They also scored first and led all the way in Game Four (played in Brooklyn) as another St. Louis rally fell short. The Browns took a 4–1 lead into the bottom of the eighth in Game Five (in New York), but a five-run Giant rally reversed the lead—and the outcome—as the game was called for darkness with St. Louis at bat in the ninth.

Giant Mickey Welch hurled a three-hitter (in Philadelphia) the next day, but St. Louis, capitalizing on walks and a questionable "safe" call at home, carried a 4–1 lead into the sixth inning. New York exploded in the late innings for 11 runs, however, and when darkness ended the game after eight the Giants were just one win away from the title.

The final four games were played in St. Louis. The Browns spoiled New York's hope of quick victory in Game Seven, coming from behind to tie the score with three runs in the fourth, and—after New York had scored twice in the sixth—recovering again with a four-run eighth for a 7–5 lead before darkness again halted play after eight innings. But the Browns' win only delayed the inevitable. The Giants hammered Icebox Chamberlain for twelve hits in Game Eight (including home runs by Buck Ewing and Mike Tiernan) to clinch their first world championship with an 11–3 win.

New York Giants (NL), 6;
St. Louis Browns (AA), 4

NY (N)

PLAYER/POS	AVG	G	AB	R	H	2B	3B	HR	RB	BB	SO	SB
Willard Brown, c	.375	2	8	1	3	1	0	0	0	0	0	0
Roger Connor, 1b	.304	7	23	7	7	1	2	0	3	4	0	4
Ed Crane, p	.143	2	7	1	1	0	0	0	0	2	0	1
Buck Ewing, c-6,1b-1	.346	7	26	5	9	0	2	1	6	1	3	5
Bill George, p-1,1b-1	.333	2	9	2	3	1	0	1	4	0	2	0
George Gore, of-2,3b-1	.455	3	11	5	5	1	0	0	0	2	2	2
Gil Hatfield, p-1,2b-1,ss-1	.250	2	8	2	2	0	0	0	1	1	2	1
Tim Keefe, p	.091	4	11	2	1	0	0	0	0	0	2	1
Pat Murphy, c	.100	3	10	1	1	0	0	0	1	0	0	0
Jim O'Rourke, of-7,1b-2,ss-1	.222	10	36	4	8	0	0	0	1	4	2	3
Danny Richardson, 2b	.167	9	36	6	6	2	0	0	6	3	5	3
Mike Slattery, of-10,2b-1	.205	10	39	6	8	2	0	0	5	0	5	6
Mike Tiernan, of	.342	10	38	8	13	0	0	1	6	8	2	5
Ledell Titcomb, p-1,of-1	.500	1	4	1	2	1	0	0	1	0	0	0
Monte Ward, ss	.379	8	29	4	11	1	0	0	6	1	0	6
Mickey Welch, p	.286	2	7	2	2	0	0	0	1	0	0	0
Art Whitney, 3b-9,of-1	.324	10	37	7	12	0	1	0	12	1	4	2
TOTAL	.277		339	64	94	10	5	3	55	27	30	38

PITCHER	W	L	ERA	G	GS	CG	SV	SHO	IP	H	ER	BB	SO
Ed Crane	1	1	2.12	2	2	2	0	0	17.0	15	4	6	12
Bill George	0	1	7.20	1	1	1	0	0	10.0	15	8	3	4
Gil Hatfield	0	0	12.60	1	0	0	0	0	5.0	12	7	3	2
Tim Keefe	4	0	0.51	4	4	4	0	0	35.0	18	2	9	30
Ledell Titcomb	0	1	6.75	1	1	0	0	0	4.0	5	3	2	2
Mickey Welch	1	1	2.65	2	2	2	0	0	17.0	10	5	9	2
TOTAL	6	4	2.97	11	10	9	0	0	88.0	75	29	32	52

STL (A)

PLAYER/POS	AVG	G	AB	R	H	2B	3B	HR	RB	BB	SO	SB
Jack Boyle, c-4,of-1	.438	4	16	4	7	0	1	0	4	2	2	3
Icebox Chamberlain, p	.000	5	13	3	0	0	0	0	0	4	3	1
Charlie Comiskey, 1b-10,of-1	.268	10	41	6	11	1	1	0	3	1	1	4
Jim Devlin, p	.000	1	3	0	0	0	0	0	0	0	0	0
Ed Herr, of	.091	3	11	2	1	0	0	0	0	0	5	1
Silver King, p	.067	5	15	1	1	0	0	0	0	1	6	0
Arlie Latham, 3b	.250	10	40	10	10	0	0	0	3	5	6	11
Harry Lyons, of	.118	5	17	0	2	0	0	0	1	1	5	0
Tommy McCarthy, of	.244	10	41	10	10	1	0	1	9	0	0	6
Jocko Milligan, c-8,1b-1	.400	8	25	5	10	2	1	0	4	3	3	0
Tip O'Neill, of	.243	10	37	8	9	1	0	2	11	6	3	0
Yank Robinson, 2b	.250	10	36	7	9	2	1	0	7	6	12	2
Bill White, ss	.143	10	35	4	5	1	0	0	4	3	6	1
TOTAL	.227		330	60	75	8	4	3	46	32	52	29

PITCHER	W	L	ERA	G	GS	CG	SV	SHO	IP	H	ER	BB	SO
Icebox Chamberlain	2	3	5.32	5	5	5	0	1	44.0	52	26	16	13
Jim Devlin	1	0	2.57	1	0	0	0	0	7.0	5	2	2	5
Silver King	1	3	2.31	5	5	4	0	0	35.0	37	9	9	12
TOTAL	4	6	3.87	11	10	9	0	1	86.0	94	37	27	30

The final two games meant nothing to the outcome, and both clubs used reserve pitchers in Game Nine. But St. Louis rewarded the small crowd with a two-run rally in the ninth to tie the game at 11-all and scored three more runs in the tenth to win it. The finale the next day again featured heavy hitting on both sides, including a trio of home runs (one of them Tip O'Neill's second in two days) and an 18–7 St. Louis romp.

GAME 1 AT NY OCT 16

STL	001	000	000	1	3	5
NY	011	000	00X	2	2	4

Pitchers: KING vs KEEFE
Attendance: 4,876

GAME 2 AT NY OCT 17

STL	010	000	002	3	7	4
NY	000	000	000	0	6	1

Pitchers: CHAMBERLAIN vs WELCH
Attendance: 5,575

GAME 3 AT NY OCT 18

STL	000	000	011	2	5	5
NY	200	100	10X	4	5	2

Pitchers: KING vs KEEFE
Attendance: 5,780

GAME 4 AT NY OCT 19

NY	104	010	000	6	8	2
STL	001	000	020	3	7	4

Pitchers: CRANE vs CHAMBERLAIN
Attendance: 3,062

GAME 5 AT BRO OCT 20

NY	003	001	00	4	5	5
STL	100	000	05	6	9	2

Pitchers: KING vs KEEFE
Attendance: 9,124
(Game called at end of eighth, darkness)

GAME 6 AT PHI OCT 22

NY	000	103	35	12	13	5
STL	301	000	01	5	3	7

Pitchers: WELCH vs CHAMBERLAIN
Attendance: 3,281
(Game called at end of eighth, darkness)

GAME 7 AT STL OCT 24

NY	030	002	00	5	11	3
STL	000	300	04	7	8	3

Pitchers: CRANE vs KING
Attendance: 4,624
(Game called at end of eighth, darkness)

GAME 8 AT STL OCT 25

NY	103	100	006	11	12	2
STL	000	100	110	3	5	6

Pitchers: KEEFE vs CHAMBERLAIN
Home Runs: Ewing-NY, Tiernan-NY
Attendance: 4,865
(New York wins best of 10 series, 6 to 2)

GAME 9 AT STL OCT 26

STL	140	020	202	3	14	15	4
NY	035	000	120	0	11	14	5

Pitchers: King, DEVLIN (4) vs GEORGE
Home Runs: O'Neill-STL
Attendance: 711

GAME 10 AT STL OCT 27

STL	010	505	421	18	17	3
NY	310	000	021	7	13	8

Pitchers: CHAMBERLAIN vs TITCOMB, Hatfield (5)
Home Runs: George-NY, O'Neill-STL, McCarthy-STL
Attendance: 412

Six wins was the magic number this year, and it was agreed that—unlike most previous Series—play would not continue beyond the deciding game. At first it seemed Brooklyn might prevail, with an assist from the dark of night. The Giants wanted the opening game called for darkness after the seventh inning, when they led 10–8. But the umpires held off until Brooklyn, in the deepening gloom, had scored four runs in the last of the eighth to go ahead 12–10.

The next day, in Brooklyn before more than 16,000 spectators (by far the largest World Series crowd to that time), Giant Ed "Cannonball" Crane held the Grooms to four hits as New York evened the Series. But Brooklyn won the next two for a 3–1 Series advantage. In Game Three, ahead 8–7 in the sixth inning, the Grooms began stalling, waiting for darkness to fall. The score was still 8–7 when the game was finally halted in the top of the ninth with one out and three Giants on base.

Darkness for a third time gave Brooklyn the victory in Game Four. New York overcame a 7–2 Bridegroom lead to tie the score with five runs in the top of the sixth, but in the bottom of the inning Brooklyn's Tom "Oyster" Burns homered in the dark for three runs. The umpires then halted the game.

The five remaining contests went the distance, and the Giants won them all. Cannonball Crane in Game Five gave up eight hits, but homered in his own behalf, driving in two runs in his Giants' 11–3 rout. Game Six was a pitching duel between New York's Hank O'Day and Brooklyn's William "Adonis" Terry. The Grooms scored a run in the second inning, but New York tied the game with two outs in the last of the ninth (when Monte Ward singled, stole second and third, and scored on Roger Connor's single), and won it with two away in the eleventh as Ward drove in a speedy Mike Slattery from second with an infield hit.

Back-to-back homers by Giants Dan Richardson and Jim O'Rourke highlighted an eight-run second inning in Game Seven. The Giants' eventual 11–7 win gave them their first Series advantage. In Game Eight, two of Brooklyn's five hits were home runs. But the Giants outscored the Grooms 12–2 over the first four innings and beat them 16–7.

With their backs to the wall, the Bridegrooms scored first in

Game Nine and held a 2–1 lead after five innings. But New York tied the score in the sixth and went ahead 3–2 on a passed ball in the seventh. Meanwhile Giant pitcher

Hank O'Day (although he walked five batters) blanked the Grooms on just two hits after the first inning to bring New York its second straight world championship.

New York Giants (NL), 6;
Brooklyn Bridegrooms (AA), 3

NY (N)

PLAYER/POS	AVG	G	AB	R	H	2B	3B	HR	RB	BB	SO	SB
Willard Brown, c	.600	1	5	3	3	0	0	1	2	0	0	0
Roger Connor, 1b	.343	9	35	9	12	2	2	0	12	3	2	8
Ed Crane, p	.278	5	18	3	5	1	1	1	5	1	2	0
Buck Ewing, c	.250	8	36	5	9	4	0	0	7	2	5	1
George Gore, of	.333	5	21	5	7	1	1	0	1	3	0	2
Tim Keefe, p	.500	2	4	1	2	1	0	0	0	1	1	0
Hank O'Day, p	.167	3	6	0	1	0	0	0	0	2	2	0
Jim O'Rourke, of	.389	9	36	7	14	2	2	2	7	2	2	3
Danny Richardson, 2b	.314	9	35	8	11	1	1	3	8	3	5	3
Mike Slattery, of	.188	4	16	6	3	0	0	0	1	3	1	1
Mike Tiernan, of	.289	9	38	12	11	1	1	1	5	5	3	3
Monte Ward, ss	.417	9	36	10	15	0	1	0	7	5	2	10
Mickey Welch, p	.333	1	3	0	1	1	0	0	0	0	1	0
Art Whitney, 3b	.229	9	35	4	8	2	1	0	3	1	0	0
TOTAL	.315		324	73	102	16	10	8	58	31	26	31

PITCHER	W	L	ERA	G	GS	CG	SV	SHO	IP	H	ER	BB	SO
Ed Crane	4	1	3.72	5	5	4	0	0	38.2	29	16	32	19
Tim Keefe	0	1	8.18	2	1	1	1	0	11.0	17	10	2	4
Hank O'Day	2	0	1.17	3	2	2	0	0	23.0	10	3	14	12
Mickey Welch	0	1	9.00	1	1	0	0	0	5.0	11	5	3	1
TOTAL	6	3	3.94	11	9	7	1	0	77.2	67	34	51	36

BRO (A)

PLAYER/POS	AVG	G	AB	R	H	2B	3B	HR	RB	BB	SO	SB
Oyster Burns, of	.229	9	35	8	8	3	0	2	11	5	6	0
Doc Bushong, c	.000	3	8	0	0	0	0	0	0	1	0	0
Bob Caruthers, p	.250	4	8	1	2	0	0	0	1	3	3	0
Bob Clark, c	.417	4	12	3	5	2	0	0	3	2	2	0
Hub Collins, 2b	.371	9	35	13	13	3	0	1	2	7	5	6
Pop Corkhill, of	.208	9	24	4	5	1	0	1	5	6	2	1
Jumbo Davis, ss	.000	1	4	0	0	0	0	0	0	0	0	0
Dave Foutz, 1b-9,p-1	.286	9	35	7	10	2	0	1	9	4	2	3
Mickey Hughes, p	.333	3	3	1	1	1	0	0	0	1	2	0
Tom Lovett, p	.000	1	1	0	0	0	0	0	0	0	0	0
Darby O'Brien, of	.161	9	31	8	5	0	1	0	4	12	6	6
George Pinckney, 3b	.258	9	31	2	8	2	0	0	3	4	2	2
Germany Smith, ss	.172	8	29	2	5	2	1	0	2	3	2	2
Adonis Terry, p-5,1b-1	.167	5	18	1	3	0	0	0	1	1	1	1
Joe Visner, c-3,of-2	.125	5	16	2	2	1	0	0	0	2	3	0
TOTAL	.231		290	52	67	17	2	5	41	51	36	21

PITCHER	W	L	ERA	G	GS	CG	SV	SHO	IP	H	ER	BB	SO
Bob Caruthers	0	2	3.75	4	2	2	1	0	24.0	28	10	6	6
Dave Foutz	0	0	7.20	1	0	0	0	0	5.0	5	4	2	2
Mickey Hughes	1	0	7.71	1	1	0	0	0	7.0	14	6	3	3
Tom Lovett	0	1	24.00	1	1	0	0	0	3.0	8	8	2	1
Adonis Terry	2	3	5.97	5	5	4	0	0	37.2	47	25	18	14
TOTAL	3	6	6.22	12	9	6	1	0	76.2	102	53	31	26

GAME 1 AT NY OCT 18

NY	020 210 50	10 12 2
BRO	510 000 24	12 16 3

Pitchers: KEEFE vs TERRY
Home Runs: Collins-BRO,
  Richardson-NY
Attendance: 8,848
(Game called at end of eighth,
  darkness)

GAME 2 AT BRO OCT 19

NY	111 120 000	6 10 4
BRO	110 000 000	2 4 8

Pitchers: CRANE vs CARUTHERS
Attendance: 16,172

GAME 3 AT NY OCT 22

NY	200 032 00	7 15 2
BRO	023 120 00	8 12 3

Pitchers: WELCH, O'Day (6) vs
  HUGHES, Caruthers (8)
Home Runs: Corkhill-BRO,
  O'Rourke-NY
Attendance: 5,181
(Game called at end of eighth,
  darkness)

GAME 4 AT BRO OCT 23

NY	001 105	7 9 8
BRO	202 033	10 7 1

Pitchers: CRANE vs TERRY
Home Runs: Burns-BRO
Attendance: 3,045
(Game called at end of sixth,
  darkness)

GAME 5 AT BRO OCT 24

NY	004 040 021	11 12 2
BRO	000 111 000	3 8 2

Pitchers: CRANE vs CARUTHERS
Home Runs: Brown-NY,
  Richardson-NY, Crane-NY
Attendance: 2,901

GAME 6 AT NY OCT 25

BRO	010 000 000 00	1 6 4
NY	000 000 001 01	2 7 1

Pitchers: TERRY vs O'DAY
Attendance: 2,556

GAME 7 AT NY OCT 26

BRO	004 030 000	7 5 3
NY	180 001 10X	11 14 4

Pitchers: LOVETT, Caruthers (4) vs
  CRANE, Keefe (5)
Home Runs: Richardson-NY,
  O'Rourke-NY
Attendance: 3,312

GAME 8 AT BRO OCT 28

NY	541 203 001	16 15 4
BRO	200 000 023	7 5 4

Pitchers: CRANE vs TERRY, Foutz (5)
Home Runs: Foutz-BRO, Tiernan-NY,
  Burns-BRO
Attendance: 2,584

GAME 9 AT NY OCT 29

BRO	200 000 000	2 4 2
NY	100 001 10X	3 8 5

Pitchers: TERRY vs O'DAY
Attendance: 3,067

The Bridegrooms, AA pennant winners in 1889, switched to the NL and returned to World Series play as champions of their new league. Louisville, meanwhile, rose from a last-place finish in 1889 to replace Brooklyn at the top of the AA. The Series, though, seemed meaningless to many who believed that pennant-winning Boston of the outlaw Players League (which had drawn off many of the best NL and AA players) could beat both Louisville and Brooklyn if given the opportunity.

The first four games of the Series were played in Louisville before an ever decreasing number of spectators. The largest crowd—5,600—saw the Cyclones humiliated in the opener 9–0 as Brooklyn's Adonis Terry stopped them on two singles. The Grooms won the second game, too, breaking a 2–2 tie with a pair of runs in the fourth and holding on for a 5–3 win.

Louisville played catch-up throughout Game Three and entered the last of the eighth still behind 7–4. But a walk, three hits, a sacrifice fly, and a passed ball brought the score to 7-all—where it remained when darkness ended the game. Only 1,050 spectators attended the final contest in Louisville, but they saw the first Louisville win. The Cyclones scored three runs in the first inning, but Brooklyn countered with three an inning later, and both teams scored single runs in the third. Louisville's Red Ehret blanked the Grooms the rest of the way, but Brooklyn's Tom Lovett yielded the Cyclones a winning run in the seventh when Tim Shinnick tripled and was sacrificed home.

Rain postponed the first game in Brooklyn for two days, but when it was played—on a cold, muddy day before a small crowd of 1,000—the Grooms took the lead on Oyster Burns's two-run homer in the first inning and held it all the way for their third win. As the weather grew colder, the crowds declined for the final two games. Louisville captured its second win by a 9–8 margin when a three-run Brooklyn rally in the eighth inning of Game Six stalled one run short of a tie. Only abut 300 diehards saw the Cyclones even the Series in the finale, 6–2 behind Red Ehret's four-hitter. A tie-breaking eighth game seemed called for, but there was not enough interest in playing any further in the bitter cold.

Brooklyn Bridegrooms (NL), 3; Louisville Cyclones (AA), 3; tie, 1

BRO (N)

PLAYER/POS	AVG	G	AB	R	H	2B	3B	HR	RB	BB	SO	SB
Oyster Burns, of-4,3b-3	.222	7	27	6	6	2	0	1	5	3	4	0
Doc Bushong, c	.000	2	6	0	0	0	0	0	0	0	1	0
Bob Caruthers, of	.000	2	6	0	0	0	0	0	0	2	0	0
Bob Clark, c	.667	1	3	2	2	0	1	0	1	0	0	0
Hub Collins, 2b	.310	7	29	7	9	0	1	0	1	3	0	2
Tom Daly, c-6,1b-1	.182	6	22	1	4	2	0	0	3	0	4	2
Patsy Donovan, of	.471	5	17	5	8	1	0	0	3	2	1	3
Dave Foutz, 1b-7,of-1	.300	7	30	6	9	2	1	0	4	0	1	1
Tom Lovett, p-4,of-1	.067	5	15	0	1	0	0	0	0	0	4	0
Darby O'Brien, of	.125	6	24	3	3	0	1	0	3	1	5	3
George Pinckney, 3b	.357	4	14	4	5	0	2	0	3	2	1	1
Germany Smith, ss	.276	7	29	3	8	0	2	0	7	0	3	1
Adonis Terry, p-3,of-3	.050	4	20	5	1	1	0	0	0	6	3	1
TOTAL	.231		242	42	56	8	8	1	30	19	27	14

PITCHER	W	L	ERA	G	GS	CG	SV	SHO	IP	H	ER	BB	SO
Tom Lovett	2	2	2.83	4	4	4	0	0	35.0	29	11	6	14
Adonis Terry	1	1	3.60	3	3	3	0	1	25.0	25	10	10	8
TOTAL	3	3	3.15	7	7	7	0	1	60.0	54	21	16	22

LOU (A)

PLAYER/POS	AVG	G	AB	R	H	2B	3B	HR	RB	BB	SO	SB
Ned Bligh, c	.000	2	3	0	0	0	0	0	0	0	1	0
Ed Daily, of-4,p-2	.136	6	22	1	3	1	1	0	3	1	2	2
Red Ehret, p	.429	3	7	1	3	0	1	0	0	0	0	0
Charlie Hamburg, of	.269	7	26	3	7	1	0	0	2	0	3	0
George Meakim, p	.500	1	2	0	1	0	0	0	0	0	0	0
Harry Raymond, ss-5,ss-3	.148	7	27	5	4	1	1	0	1	2	5	1
John Ryan, c	.053	6	19	0	1	0	0	0	2	0	1	1
Tim Shinnick, 2b	.292	7	24	3	7	1	1	0	3	2	2	2
Scott Stratton, p-3,of-1	.222	4	9	4	2	1	0	0	0	2	1	3
Harry Taylor, 1b	.300	7	30	6	9	1	0	0	2	2	3	3
Phil Tomney, ss	.200	3	5	1	1	0	0	0	0	3	1	0
Farmer Weaver, of	.259	7	27	4	7	1	0	0	4	1	2	5
Pete Weckbecker, c	.000	1	4	0	0	0	0	0	0	0	1	0
Chicken Wolf, 3b-5,of-3	.360	7	25	4	9	3	1	0	8	3	0	2
TOTAL	.235		230	32	54	10	5	0	25	16	22	19

PITCHER	W	L	ERA	G	GS	CG	SV	SHO	IP	H	ER	BB	SO
Ed Daily	0	2	2.65	2	2	2	0	0	17.0	12	5	8	5
Red Ehret	2	0	1.35	3	2	1	0	0	20.0	12	3	6	13
George Meakim	0	0	0.00	1	0	0	0	0	4.0	6	0	1	1
Scott Stratton	1	1	2.37	3	3	1	0	0	19.0	26	5	4	8
TOTAL	3	3	1.95	9	7	5	1	0	60.0	56	13	19	27

GAME 1 AT LOU OCT 17

BRO	300	030	30	9	11	1
LOU	000	000	00	0	2	6

Pitchers: TERRY vs STRATTON
Attendance: 5,600

GAME 2 AT LOU OCT 18

BRO	020	201	000	5	5	3
LOU	101	000	001	3	6	5

Pitchers: LOVETT vs DAILY
Attendance: 2,860

GAME 3 AT LOU OCT 20

BRO	020	130	10	7	10	2
LOU	001	012	03	7	11	3

Pitchers: Terry vs Stratton, Meakim (4)
Attendance: 2,500

GAME 4 AT LOU OCT 21

BRO	031	000	000	4	7	2
LOU	301	000	10X	5	9	2

Pitchers: LOVETT vs EHRET
Attendance: 1,050

GAME 5 AT BRO OCT 25

LOU	010	010	000	2	5	6
BRO	210	200	20X	7	7	0

Pitchers: DAILY vs LOVETT
Home Runs: Burns-BRO
Attendance: 1,000

GAME 6 AT BRO OCT 27

LOU	012	101	220	9	13	3
BRO	100	004	030	8	12	3

Pitchers: STRATTON, Ehret (7) vs TERRY
Attendance: 600

GAME 7 AT BRO OCT 28

LOU	103	000	020	6	8	3
BRO	200	000	000	2	4	1

Pitchers: EHRET vs LOVETT
Attendance: 300

Interleague squabbling prevented a World Series in 1891, and the AA folded before the next season. Four AA clubs were taken into the NL, expanding the NL to twelve teams. To create a postseason championship series, the regular season was divided in half, with first-half winner Boston meeting second-half victor Cleveland for both the league and world titles.

The first game, in Cleveland, was a pitching and fielding classic. Boston's Jack Stivetts and Cleveland's Cy Young blanked the opposition for eleven innings before darkness halted the game. Young yielded just six hits and Stivetts four—all singles. Just as remarkable in an era when errors were commonplace, Cleveland committed only one and Boston none; several outstanding plays were made in the field.

Boston center fielder Hugh Duffy was the offensive and defensive star of Game Two. He drove in three of the Beaneaters' four runs (with a fly out, a triple, and a double), and scored the fourth himself after tripling a second time. And in the bottom of the ninth he snared a leadoff liner with a great running catch. As it was, Cleveland scored once in the inning to pull within a run of a tie; Duffy's catch prevented a certain tie and a possible Cleveland win. Game Three was just as close. Pitchers Stivetts and Young each gave up two early runs, but then blanked their foes until the seventh inning, when Boston's Tommy McCarthy singled in Stivetts (who had doubled) with what proved the winning run.

The Series moved to Boston for the next three games. In Game Four, Boston ace Kid Nichols shut out the Spiders, scattering seven hits and fanning eight. Cleveland's Nig Cuppy yielded only six hits, but one was a home run ball to Hugh Duffy for two runs in the third inning, and another was a two-run single to Joe Quinn in the sixth. Cleveland pitcher John Clarkson helped his own cause the next day with a three-run homer in the Spider's six-run second inning. But Boston pitcher Jack Stivetts—with the score now 7–5 Cleveland in the sixth—tripled in a run and scored the tying run. In the seventh, Stivetts scored Boston's twelfth (and final) run after singling, while holding Cleveland scoreless through the final four innings.

Two days later the Beaneaters brought the Series to an end with their fifth straight win. The Spiders scored first, with a three-run third, but pitcher Kid Nichols

Boston Beaneaters, 5; Cleveland Spiders, 0; tie, 1

BOS (N)

PLAYER/POS	AVG	G	AB	R	H	2B	3B	HR	RB	BB	SO	SB
Charlie Bennett, c	.286	2	7	2	2	0	0	1	1	0	2	1
Hugh Duffy, of	.462	6	26	3	12	3	2	1	9	1	0	3
Charlie Ganzel, c	.500	2	8	1	4	0	0	0	2	1	0	0
King Kelly, c	.000	2	8	0	0	0	0	0	0	0	2	1
Herman Long, ss	.222	6	27	4	6	0	0	0	1	0	0	2
Bobby Lowe, of	.130	6	23	2	3	0	0	0	0	1	2	1
Tommy McCarthy, of	.381	6	21	2	8	2	0	0	2	6	1	3
Billy Nash, 3b	.167	6	24	3	4	0	0	0	4	2	3	2
Kid Nichols, p	.286	2	7	1	2	0	0	0	2	0	1	1
Joe Quinn, 2b	.286	6	21	2	6	1	1	0	4	1	2	0
Harry Staley, p	.000	1	4	0	0	0	0	0	0	0	3	0
Jack Stivetts, p	.250	3	12	3	3	1	1	0	1	0	2	0
Tommy Tucker, 1b	.261	6	23	2	6	0	0	1	2	0	1	0
TOTAL	.265		211	25	56	7	4	3	28	12	19	14

PITCHER	W	L	ERA	G	GS	CG	SV	SHO	IP	H	ER	BB	SO
Kid Nichols	2	0	1.00	2	2	2	0	1	18.0	17	2	4	13
Harry Staley	1	0	3.00	1	1	1	0	0	9.0	10	3	1	0
Jack Stivetts	2	0	0.93	3	3	3	0	1	29.0	21	3	7	17
TOTAL	5	0	1.29	6	6	6	0	2	56.0	48	8	12	30

CLE (N)

PLAYER/POS	AVG	G	AB	R	H	2B	3B	HR	RB	BB	SO	SB
Jesse Burkett, of	.320	6	25	3	8	1	0	0	1	0	2	4
Cupid Childs, 2b	.409	6	22	3	9	0	2	0	0	5	1	0
John Clarkson, p	.250	2	8	1	2	0	0	1	3	0	1	0
Nig Cuppy, p	.000	1	3	0	0	0	0	0	0	0	2	0
George Davis, 3b-2	.167	3	6	0	1	0	0	0	0	0	1	0
Jimmy McAleer, of	.182	6	22	0	4	0	0	0	1	2	2	1
Ed McKean, ss	.440	6	25	2	11	0	0	0	6	1	3	0
Jack O'Connor, of	.136	6	22	1	3	0	0	0	0	2	3	0
Patsy Tebeau, 3b	.000	5	18	1	0	0	0	0	0	0	2	1
Jake Virtue, 1b	.125	6	24	1	3	0	0	0	0	2	5	1
Cy Young, p	.091	3	11	0	1	0	0	0	0	0	5	0
Chief Zimmer, c	.261	6	23	2	6	1	1	0	2	0	3	0
TOTAL	.230		209	15	48	2	3	1	13	12	30	7

PITCHER	W	L	ERA	G	GS	CG	SV	SHO	IP	H	ER	BB	SO
John Clarkson	0	2	5.29	2	2	2	0	0	17.0	24	10	5	9
Nig Cuppy	0	1	1.13	1	1	1	0	0	8.0	6	1	4	1
Cy Young	0	2	3.00	3	3	3	0	1	27.0	26	9	3	9
TOTAL	0	5	3.46	6	6	6	0	1	52.0	56	20	12	19

held them scoreless after that and singled home Boston's tying and go-ahead runs himself as the Beaneaters tagged Cy Young for eight runs over the final six innings.

GAME 1 AT CLE OCT 17

CLE 000 000 000 00 0 4 1
BOS 000 000 000 00 0 6 0
Pitchers: YOUNG vs STIVETTS
Attendance: 6,000

GAME 2 AT CLE OCT 18

BOS 101 010 010 4 10 2
CLE 001 100 001 3 10 2
Pitchers: STALEY vs CLARKSON
Attendance: 6,700

GAME 3 AT CLE OCT 19

CLE 200 000 000 2 8 0
BOS 110 000 10X 3 9 2
Pitchers: YOUNG vs STIVETTS
Attendance: 5,000

GAME 4 AT BOS OCT 21

CLE 000 000 000 0 7 3
BOS 002 002 00X 4 6 0
Pitchers: CUPPY vs NICHOLS
Home Runs: Duffy-BOS
Attendance: 6,547

GAME 5 AT BOS OCT 22

CLE 060 010 000 7 9 4
BOS 000 324 30X 12 14 3
Pitchers: CLARKSON vs STIVETTS
Home Runs: Clarkson-CLE, Tucker-BOS
Attendance: 3,466

GAME 6 AT BOS OCT 24

CLE 003 000 000 3 10 5
BOS 002 211 11X 8 11 5
Pitchers: YOUNG vs NICHOLS
Home Runs: Bennett-BOS
Attendance: 2,300

As the divided season of 1892 was not repeated, no "world series" was held in 1893. But in 1894 Pittsburgh sportsman William C. Temple offered an elegant trophy to the winner of a series between the NL's first- and second-place finishers. For four years the Temple Cup games determined the world championship. In this first matchup, second-place New York swept the feisty pennant-winning Orioles.

Game One, in Baltimore, was a shutout through four innings as New York's Amos Rusie and Baltimore's Duke Esper held their opponents at bay. But Giant George Van Haltren tripled in the fifth inning and scored the game's first run on a fly to left. The Giants also scored single runs in the sixth, seventh, and eighth innings, while Rusie continued his shutout pitching through the eighth. In the ninth Oriole John McGraw singled, and he came around on a sacrifice, stolen base, and single to spoil the shutout. But the Oriole effort was too little to deprive Rusie of his win.

Some two hundred policemen patrolled the second game the next day to protect the umpires and New York's players and fans from the abusive Orioles and the crowd in the stands whom the Oriole players egged on. Baltimore scored first with two runs in the second and, after losing and regaining the lead, completed the eighth inning tied 5–5. But in the top of the ninth, the Giants put together their second four-run inning of the game. Once again the Orioles came up with a run in the last of the ninth, but once again came up short.

More than 22,000 spectators showed up for Game Three as the Series shifted to New York—a huge crowd for that era, even for a Saturday. As in Game One, the Giants' Amos Rusie hurled a 4–1 victory. New York broke a 1–1 tie with a run in the fifth on a throwing error and a ground out, and scored the game's final runs an inning later. Threatening weather held down attendance at Game Four to about 12,000. Baltimore jumped to a quick lead with two runs in the top of the first, but New York pitcher Jouett Meekin held the Orioles to just one run after that as the Giants piled up runs for a 16–3 advantage by the time darkness forced an end to play after eight innings. Meekin, in winning his second game of the Series, connected for three hits himself—half as many as he permitted the whole Oriole team.

New York Giants, 4; Baltimore Orioles, 0

NY (N)

PLAYER/POS	AVG	G	AB	R	H	2B	3B	HR	RB	BB	SO	SB
Eddie Burke, of	.389	4	18	3	7	1	0	0	2	1		1
George Davis, 3b	.313	4	16	5	5	2	2	0	5	2		2
Jack Doyle, 1b	.588	4	17	4	10	1	1	0	6	1		6
Duke Farrell, c	.400	4	15	5	6	0	0	0	2	1		1
Shorty Fuller, ss	.286	4	14	4	4	0	0	0	2	2		1
Jouett Meekin, p	.556	2	9	2	5	0	0	0	3	0		0
Yale Murphy, of	.000	1	1	0	0	0	0	0	0	0		0
Amos Rusie, p	.429	2	7	1	3	1	0	0	1	0		0
Mike Tiernan, of	.294	4	17	5	5	0	1	0	3	2		0
George Van Haltren, of	.500	4	14	3	7	1	1	0	0	2		2
Monte Ward, 2b	.294	4	17	1	5	0	0	0	6	0		0
TOTAL	.393		145	33	57	6	5	0	30	11		13

PITCHER	W	L	ERA	G	GS	CG	SV	SHO	IP	H	ER	BB	SO
Jouett Meekin	2	0	1.59	2	2	2	0	0	17.0	13	3	8	6
Amos Rusie	2	0	0.50	2	2	2	0	0	18.0	14	1	3	9
TOTAL	4	0	1.03	4	4	4	0	0	35.0	27	4	11	15

BAL (N)

PLAYER/POS	AVG	G	AB	R	H	2B	3B	HR	RB	BB	SO	SB
Frank Bonner, ss-1,of-1	.000	2	5	0	0	0	0	0	0	0		0
Steve Brodie, of	.000	4	15	2	0	0	0	0	0	2		1
Dan Brouthers, 1b	.188	4	16	2	3	0	0	0	0	1		3
Duke Esper, p	.000	1	2	0	0	0	0	0	0	1		0
Kid Gleason, p	.200	2	5	0	1	0	1	0	1	0		0
Bill Hawke, p	.000	1	2	0	0	0	0	0	0	0		0
George Hemming, p	.000	1	3	0	0	0	0	0	0	1		0
Hughie Jennings, ss	.143	4	14	0	2	0	0	0	1	0		0
Willie Keeler, of	.250	3	12	1	3	0	0	0	1	1		0
Joe Kelley, of	.333	4	15	2	5	1	1	0	0	3		1
John McGraw, 3b	.250	4	16	2	4	0	0	0	2	0		1
Heinie Reitz, 2b	.333	4	15	1	5	0	0	0	4	1		1
Wilbert Robinson, c	.267	4	15	1	4	0	0	0	1	1		1
TOTAL	.200		135	11	27	1	2	0	10	11		8

PITCHER	W	L	ERA	G	GS	CG	SV	SHO	IP	H	ER	BB	SO
Duke Esper	0	1	4.00	1	1	1	0	0	9.0	13	4	1	3
Kid Gleason	0	1	9.69	2	1	1	0	0	13.0	25	14	6	3
Bill Hawke	0	1	9.00	1	1	0	0	0	4.0	9	4	1	0
George Hemming	0	1	1.13	1	1	1	0	0	8.0	10	1	3	2
TOTAL	0	4	6.09	5	4	3	0	0	34.0	57	23	11	8

GAME 1 AT BAL OCT 4

NY	000 011 110	4	13	2
BAL	000 000 001	1	7	1

Pitchers: RUSIE vs ESPER
Attendance: 9,000

GAME 2 AT BAL OCT 5

NY	004 000 014	9	14	3
BAL	022 000 101	6	7	2

Pitchers: MEEKIN vs GLEASON
Attendance: 11,000

GAME 3 AT NY OCT 6

BAL	000 100 000	1	7	4
NY	100 012 00X	4	10	4

Pitchers: HEMMING vs RUSIE
Attendance: 22,000

GAME 4 AT NY OCT 8

BAL	201 000 00	3	6	3
NY	101 351 50	16	20	4

Pitchers: HAWKE, Gleason (5) vs MEEKIN
Attendance: 12,000
(Game called at end of eighth, darkness)

Baltimore, repeating as NL pennant winner, returned to Temple Cup play against new runner-up Cleveland. The first 4½ innings of the opener—played in Cleveland—featured a scoreless duel between Baltimore veteran John "Sadie" McMahon and the Spiders' great Cy Young. After Cleveland scored the game's first run in the last of the fifth, the teams traded runs and the lead, completing the eighth inning tied 3–3. In the top of the ninth, doubles by Wilbert Robinson and John McGraw restored the edge to Baltimore. But in the bottom of the inning, four straight Spider hits pushed across the tying run and filled the bases. One runner was forced at home for the first out, but a grounder that just missed being a double-play ball drove in the winning Cleveland run.

The next three games were not so closely contested. A large and enthusiastic Cleveland crowd watched its Spiders jump on Baltimore for three runs in the bottom of Game Two and coast to a 7–2 win behind the strong pitching of Nig Cuppy, who held the Orioles to five singles. Cleveland repeated itself in Game Three, again exploding for three runs in the bottom of the first on the way to a seven-run total. Cy Young was just as effective in the box as Cuppy had been, scattering four hits over seven shutout innings before Baltimore put together three singles in the eighth for their only run.

When the teams shifted to Baltimore for Game Four, the Orioles sprang to life. While their pitcher Duke Esper strangled the Spiders on just five singles—only two Cleveland runners advanced as far as second base—Oriole batters tagged Nig Cuppy for five runs and their first Temple Cup win in two years of trying.

It proved to be their only win of the Series. The next day, in the first close struggle since the opener, Cy Young and Baltimore's rookie ace Bill Hoffer dueled scorelessly through six innings. But in the top of the seventh, Young doubled to start what became a three-run rally, and an inning later the Spiders scored twice more. Baltimore scored a single run in the last of the seventh, and, with two out in the ninth, loaded the bases on two walks and a hit batsman. A Cleveland error brought in the Orioles' second run as the bases remained full for Steve Brodie. But despite the pleas of Baltimore partisans to hit a homer or triple, Brodie "failed miserably" and Cleveland copped the cup.

Cleveland Spiders, 4;
Baltimore Orioles, 1

CLE (N)

PLAYER/POS	AVG	G	AB	R	H	2B	3B	HR	RB	BB	SO	SB
Harry Blake, of	.250	5	20	1	5	3	0	0	2	0		0
Jesse Burkett, of	.450	5	20	3	9	2	0	0	2	0		1
Cupid Childs, 2b	.190	5	21	4	4	1	0	0	2	1		1
Nig Cuppy, p	.167	2	6	1	1	1	0	0	1	0		0
Jimmy McAleer, of	.286	5	21	2	6	0	0	0	2	0		1
Chippy McGarr, 3b	.368	5	19	3	7	2	0	0	1	1		2
Ed McKean, ss	.300	5	20	2	6	1	1	0	4	3		1
Patsy Tebeau, 1b	.286	5	21	3	6	1	0	0	3	1		0
Cy Young, p	.250	3	12	3	3	1	0	0	1	0		0
Chief Zimmer, c	.333	4	18	2	6	3	0	0	3	3		0
TOTAL	.298		178	24	53	14	1	0	21	9		6

PITCHER	W	L	ERA	G	GS	CG	SV	SHO	IP	H	ER	BB	SO
Nig Cuppy	1	1	3.18	2	2	2	0	0	17.0	14	6	4	6
Cy Young	3	0	2.33	3	3	3	0	0	27.0	28	7	4	2
TOTAL	4	1	2.66	5	5	5	0	0	44.0	42	13	8	8

BAL (N)

PLAYER/POS	AVG	G	AB	R	H	2B	3B	HR	RB	BB	SO	SB
Steve Brodie, of	.200	5	20	1	4	0	0	0	2	0		0
Scoops Carey, 1b	.263	5	19	0	5	1	0	0	1	0		0
Boileryard Clarke, c	.286	2	7	1	2	0	0	0	0	0		2
Duke Esper, p	.000	1	3	0	0	0	0	0	0	1		0
Kid Gleason, 2b	.105	5	19	0	2	0	0	0	0	0		0
Bill Hoffer, p	.000	2	7	0	0	0	0	0	0	0		0
Hughie Jennings, ss	.368	5	19	3	7	2	0	0	2	1		1
Willie Keeler, of	.235	5	17	3	4	0	0	0	1	3		0
Joe Kelley, of	.368	5	19	1	7	0	0	0	5	1		1
John McGraw, 3b	.400	5	20	4	8	2	0	0	1	2		2
Sadie McMahon, p	.000	2	7	0	0	0	0	0	0	0		0
Wilbert Robinson, c	.250	3	12	1	3	1	0	0	0	0		0
TOTAL	.249		169	14	42	6	0	0	12	8		6

PITCHER	W	L	ERA	G	GS	CG	SV	SHO	IP	H	ER	BB	SO
Duke Esper	1	0	0.00	1	1	1	0	1	9.0	5	0	0	3
Bill Hoffer	0	2	4.24	2	2	2	0	0	17.0	21	8	6	4
Sadie McMahon	0	2	5.94	2	2	2	0	0	16.2	27	11	3	2
TOTAL	1	4	4.01	5	5	5	0	1	42.2	53	19	9	9

GAME 1 AT CLE OCT 2

BAL	000 001 021	4	12	0
CLE	000 011 012	5	14	3

Pitchers: McMAHON vs YOUNG
Attendance: 8,000

GAME 2 AT CLE OCT 3

BAL	010 001 000	2	5	4
CLE	300 012 10X	7	10	5

Pitchers: HOFFER vs CUPPY
Attendance: 10,000

GAME 3 AT CLE OCT 5

BAL	000 000 010	1	7	1
CLE	300 000 31X	7	13	1

Pitchers: McMAHON vs YOUNG
Attendance: 12,000

GAME 4 AT BAL OCT 7

CLE	000 000 000	0	5	1
BAL	012 000 20X	5	9	1

Pitchers: CUPPY vs ESPER
Attendance: 9,100

GAME 5 AT BAL OCT 8

CLE	000 000 320	5	11	3
BAL	000 000 101	2	9	5

Pitchers: YOUNG vs HOFFER
Attendance: 5,000

Baltimore captured its third consecutive pennant and for the second year in a row faced runner-up Cleveland in the Temple Cup games. But this time the Orioles emerged triumphant—with a sweep in which their margin of victory was never less than four runs.

Aces Bill Hoffer of Baltimore and the Spiders' Cy Young faced each other in the opener, in Baltimore. Hoffer walked four men, but gave up only five hits while the Orioles bombarded Young for thirteen. When the game ended, Hoffer and Baltimore had a 7–1 win.

Bobby Wallace (who had not yet discovered his role at shortstop that would propel him into the Hall of Fame) pitched for Cleveland in Game Two. He lost the game in the first inning when two Spider errors, a hit batsman, three hits, and a steal of home put four Baltimore runs on the board. The Orioles added two runs in the third and another in the fifth, while their promising twenty-year-old pitcher Joe Corbett held the Spiders to two runs on seven hits.

The Orioles' Hoffer gave up ten hits to Cleveland in Game Three—two more than the Birds made off Spider Nig Cuppy. But all the hits off Hoffer were singles, and he walked only one. Half of Cleveland's hits went toward producing just two runs. Their second run tied the score in the fifth inning, but in the sixth Baltimore regained the lead as John McGraw singled, stole second, took third on an error, and came home on an outfield fly. In the eighth the Orioles bunched four of their eight hits for three insurance runs.

The Series moved to Cleveland for the fourth game. Young Joe Corbett was again sent into the box for Baltimore, this time to face Nig Cuppy. For six innings the game was a scoreless duel. Baltimore hit safely in every inning but the second, but failed to score until the seventh, when Joe Kelley's double and Jack Doyle's single scored the only run they would need. But the Orioles added a second run in that inning and three more in the eighth. Two of the four Cleveland hits against Corbett put men on base in the eighth inning, and Corbett walked two in the ninth to raise Cleveland's hopes. But no Spider scored, and with the 5–0 win the Orioles were world champions at last.

Baltimore Orioles, 4; Cleveland Spiders, 0

BAL (N)

PLAYER/POS	AVG	G	AB	R	H	2B	3B	HR	RB	BB	SO	SB
Steve Brodie, of	.067	4	15	1	1	0	0	0	3	0		1
Joe Corbett, p	.500	2	6	1	3	1	0	0	0	1		0
Jack Doyle, 1b	.294	4	17	3	5	1	0	0	4	0		2
Bill Hoffer, p	.286	2	7	1	2	0	2	0	0	0		0
Hughie Jennings, ss	.333	4	15	5	5	2	0	0	3	1		1
Willie Keeler, of	.471	4	17	4	8	1	2	0	4	0		1
Joe Kelley, of	.471	4	17	3	8	1	0	0	4	0		2
John McGraw, 3b	.267	4	15	4	4	0	0	0	1	0		4
Joe Quinn, 3b	.000	1	3	1	0	0	0	0	0	0		0
Heinie Reitz, 2b	.133	4	15	1	2	0	0	0	2	1		0
Wilbert Robinson, c	.267	4	15	1	4	1	0	0	2	0		0
TOTAL	.296		142	25	42	7	4	0	23	3		11

PITCHER	W	L	ERA	G	GS	CG	SV	SHO	IP	H	ER	BB	SO
Joe Corbett	2	0	0.50	2	2	2	0	1	18.0	11	1	7	10
Bill Hoffer	2	0	1.50	2	2	2	0	0	18.0	15	3	5	10
TOTAL	4	0	1.00	4	4	4	0	1	36.0	26	4	12	20

CLE (N)

PLAYER/POS	AVG	G	AB	R	H	2B	3B	HR	RB	BB	SO	SB
Harry Blake, of	.071	4	14	1	1	0	0	0	0	1		1
Jesse Burkett, of	.333	4	15	1	5	0	0	0	0	2		0
Cupid Childs, 2b	.231	4	13	2	3	0	0	0	0	4		1
Nig Cuppy, p	.143	2	7	0	1	0	0	0	0	0		0
Jimmy McAleer, of	.133	4	15	0	2	0	0	0	1	1		1
Chippy McGarr, 3b	.063	4	16	0	1	0	0	0	0	0		2
Ed McKean, ss	.313	4	16	0	5	1	1	0	1	1		1
Jack O'Connor, 1b	.286	4	14	1	4	0	0	0	1	1		0
Patsy Tebeau, 1b	.000	1	1	0	0	0	0	0	0	0		0
Bobby Wallace, p-1	.200	3	5	0	1	0	0	0	0	0		0
Cy Young, p	.000	1	3	0	0	0	0	0	0	0		0
Chief Zimmer, c	.214	4	14	0	3	1	0	0	1	2		0
TOTAL	.195		133	5	26	2	1	0	4	12		6

PITCHER	W	L	ERA	G	GS	CG	SV	SHO	IP	H	ER	BB	SO
Nig Cuppy	0	2	4.76	2	2	2	0	0	17.0	19	9	0	4
Bobby Wallace	0	1	4.50	1	1	1	0	0	8.0	10	4	2	4
Cy Young	0	1	6.00	1	1	1	0	0	9.0	13	6	1	0
TOTAL	0	4	5.03	4	4	4	0	0	34.0	42	19	3	8

GAME 1 AT BAL OCT 2

BAL	002 001 310	7	13	1
CLE	000 001 000	1	5	4

Pitchers: HOFFER vs YOUNG
Attendance: 4,000

GAME 2 AT BAL OCT 3

BAL	402 010 00	7	10	3
CLE	001 001 00	2	7	3

Pitchers: CORBETT vs WALLACE
Attendance: 3,100
(Game called at end of eighth, darkness)

GAME 3 AT BAL OCT 5

BAL	011 001 030	6	8	2
CLE	001 010 000	2	10	2

Pitchers: HOFFER vs CUPPY
Attendance: 2,000

GAME 4 AT CLE OCT 8

CLE	000 000 000	0	4	2
BAL	000 000 23X	5	11	1

Pitchers: CUPPY vs CORBETT
Attendance: 1,500

Boston had edged Baltimore in a close race for the NL pennant, but the Orioles turned the tables on the Beaneaters in Temple Cup play. The Series was a high-scoring affair, the winner of each game averaging eleven runs, the loser eight.

The opener, in Boston, set the tone for the games. Baltimore sent four runners across the plate in the top of the first inning, and Boston followed in its half with three. The Beaneaters recorded only twelve hits in the game to the Orioles' twenty, but they also received seven walks from Baltimore hurler Jerry Nops, and five of those runners scored. The lead switched back and forth in the middle innings, but Boston scored two final runs in the eighth and hung on for a 13–12 win.

Baltimore's Joe Corbett gave up sixteen hits (one a home run) and four walks in Game Two as Boston scored eleven times. But Boston's two pitchers, Fred Klobedanz and Jack Stivetts, were even more generous, handing out seventeen hits (including three homers—one of them to opposing pitcher Corbett, who also hit a double and two singles) and five walks as the Orioles evened the Series with their thirteen-run attack.

Game Three was the Series' lowest in run production, with Baltimore scoring four in the second inning and another four in the third for an 8–3 win. But rain ended the game before Boston could complete its time at bat in the last of the eighth, which erased from the record four more Oriole runs scored earlier in the inning. Rather than waste the two free days before the Series resumed in Baltimore, the two clubs played a pair of exhibition games in Worcester and Springfield, Massachusetts. Baltimore won them both, 11–10 and 8–6.

The Orioles continued their roll in Series Game Four, with another close but high-scoring victory, 12–11. It looked at first like a blowout as Baltimore scored six runs in the first inning and five more in the second. But Ted Lewis relieved Boston starter Jack Stivetts and held Baltimore to just one further run as the Beaneaters fought back to within one run of a tie before faltering in the ninth.

Boston batters hit Oriole Bill Hoffer safely fifteen times in Game Five, but only three Beaneaters scored. Baltimore, with two fewer hits, garnered six more runs than Boston and, with their fourth win, the right to hold the cup for another year. But at-

tendance at the final game was so small the embarrassed Baltimore management refused to release the figures, and the league gave the cup back to Mr. Temple rather than sponsor another unprofitable Series. There was no postseason championship contest in 1898 or 1899.

Baltimore Orioles, 4;
Boston Beaneaters, 1

BAL (N)

PLAYER/POS	AVG	G	AB	R	H	2B	3B	HR	RB	BB	SO	SB
Frank Bowerman, c-1,1b-1	.500	2	8	2	4	0	1	0	4	0		0
Boileryard Clarke, c	.563	4	16	5	9	1	1	1	4	1		0
Joe Corbett, p	.667	2	6	2	4	1	0	1	2	0		0
Jack Doyle, 1b	.526	5	19	7	10	2	0	0	9	0		2
Bill Hoffer, p	.250	2	8	2	2	1	0	0	0	0		0
Hughie Jennings, ss	.318	5	22	5	7	2	0	0	3	4		0
Willie Keeler, of	.391	5	23	5	9	2	0	0	2	4		0
Joe Kelley, of	.313	4	16	7	5	3	0	0	5	5		0
John McGraw, 3b	.300	5	20	6	6	1	1	0	6	7		0
Jerry Nops, p	.286	2	7	0	2	0	0	0	1	1		0
Tom O'Brien, of	.400	1	5	2	2	1	0	0	0	0		0
Heinie Reitz, 2b	.250	5	20	4	5	1	0	1	4	2		0
Jake Stenzel, of	.381	5	21	7	8	1	1	0	3	2		2
TOTAL	.382		191	54	73	16	4	3	43	26		4

PITCHER	W	L	ERA	G	GS	CG	SV	SHO	IP	H	ER	BB	SO
Joe Corbett	1	0	9.00	2	1	1	0	0	12.0	21	12	8	5
Bill Hoffer	2	0	3.38	2	2	2	0	0	16.0	25	6	4	2
Jerry Nops	1	1	12.86	2	2	1	0	0	14.0	23	20	9	3
TOTAL	4	1	8.14	6	5	4	0	0	42.0	69	38	21	10

BOS (N)

PLAYER/POS	AVG	G	AB	R	H	2B	3B	HR	RB	BB	SO	SB
Marty Bergen, c	.500	1	4	0	2	0	0	0	1	0		1
Jimmy Collins, 3b	.182	5	22	2	4	0	0	0	4	1		0
Hugh Duffy, of	.524	5	21	6	11	1	0	0	7	1		0
Billy Hamilton, of	.500	4	16	6	8	1	0	0	2	5		2
Charlie Hickman, p-1,of-1	.250	1	4	0	1	1	0	0	1	0		0
Fred Klobedanz, p	1.000	2	5	3	5	0	0	0	0	0		0
Fred Lake, c	.000	1	4	0	0	0	0	0	0	0		0
Ted Lewis, p	.500	3	6	1	3	1	0	0	1	1		0
Herman Long, ss	.286	5	21	4	6	1	1	1	5	2		1
Bobby Lowe, 2b	.391	5	23	6	9	2	0	0	6	1		1
Kid Nichols, p	.000	1	3	0	0	0	0	0	0	1		0
Chick Stahl, of	.400	5	20	6	8	1	0	0	6	3		2
Jack Stivetts, p-2,of-1	.000	3	7	1	0	0	0	0	0	1		1
Jim Sullivan, p	.000	1	1	0	0	0	0	0	0	0		0
Fred Tenney, 1b	.300	5	20	4	6	0	0	0	2	4		2
George Yeager, c	.500	3	12	2	6	1	1	0	2	2		0
TOTAL	.365		189	41	69	9	2	1	38	21		10

PITCHER	W	L	ERA	G	GS	CG	SV	SHO	IP	H	ER	BB	SO
Charlie Hickman	0	1	3.60	1	1	0	0	0	5.0	7	2	2	0
Fred Klobedanz	0	1	9.35	2	1	0	0	0	8.2	12	9	8	0
Ted Lewis	1	1	6.17	3	1	0	0	0	11.2	18	8	9	4
Kid Nichols	0	0	12.00	1	1	0	0	0	6.0	14	8	0	3
Jack Stivetts	0	1	17.55	2	1	0	0	0	6.2	16	13	7	0
Jim Sullivan	0	0	3.00	1	0	0	0	0	3.0	6	1	0	0
TOTAL	1	4	9.00	10	5	0	0	0	41.0	73	41	26	7

GAME 1 AT BOS OCT 4

BAL	401 023 200	12 20	4
BOS	300 125 02X	13 12	4

Pitchers: NOPS vs Nichols, LEWIS (7)
Attendance: 9,600

GAME 2 AT BOS OCT 5

BAL	130 160 110	13 17	2
BOS	002 620 100	11 16	3

Pitchers: CORBETT vs KLOBEDANZ, Stivetts (5)
Home Runs: Reitz-BAL, Clarke-BAL, Corbett-BAL, Long-BOS
Attendance: 6,500

GAME 3 AT BOS OCT 6

BAL	044 000 0	8 9	2
BOS	003 000 0	3 10	2

Pitchers: HOFFER vs LEWIS, Klobedanz (4)
Attendance: 5,000
(Game called in eighth, rain)

GAME 4 AT BAL OCT 9

BOS	000 024 320	11 16	3
BAL	650 001 00X	12 14	3

Pitchers: STIVETTS, Lewis (3) vs NOPS, Corbett (7)
Attendance: 2,500

GAME 5 AT BAL OCT 11

BOS	020 000 001	3 15	3
BAL	023 000 22X	9 13	2

Pitchers: HICKMAN, Sullivan (7) vs HOFFER
Attendance: 700

Pennant-winning Brooklyn led the NL in hitting, but runner-up Pittsburgh claimed the best pitching. Honus Wagner was the only Pirate regular to hit over .300, but he enjoyed what turned out to be his finest season offensively, leading the league with a .381 batting average. Pittsburghers believed their club superior to Brooklyn and a best-of-five "world championship" series was arranged, with all the games to be played in Pittsburgh for a silver cup donated by the *Pittsburgh Chronicle-Telegraph.* Brooklyn, however, proved that its pennant was no fluke.

Two of the game's best pitchers faced off in the opener: Pittsburgh's Rube Waddell, who had led the league in ERA, and Joe "Iron Man" McGinnity, whose 29 regular-season wins totaled nine more than those of the league's runners-up. McGinnity prevailed, shutting out the Pirates until two unearned runs came across in the top of the ninth. Pirate errors also gave Brooklyn a pair of unearned runs, but Waddell lost the game on hits—thirteen in all, including six in the Superbas' three-run third inning.

In Game Two, Brooklyn's Frank Kitson held Pittsburgh to four hits, and although his Superbas scored only one earned run, six Pirate errors gave them their second win, 4–2.

The Pirates staved off a Series sweep with sharp pitching and heavy hitting in Game Three. Deacon Phillippe shut out Brooklyn on six hits as the Pirates jumped on Harry Howell for thirteen. All the Pirate hits were singles, but combined with Brooklyn errors they were good for ten runs, seven of them unearned.

Three Brooklyn singles and a fumble by Pirate pitcher Sam Leever in the fourth inning of Game Four gave the Superbas three runs and a 4–0 lead the Pirates could not overcome. Brooklyn hurler McGinnity scattered nine Pirate hits and, supported by flawless fielding, held Pittsburgh to a single run to bring Brooklyn its first World Series triumph in three tries—and its last until 1955. The Brooklyn players voted to award their trophy to McGinnity for his fine pitching. The cup may be seen today—along with the Temple Cup and the current World Series trophy—at baseball's Hall of Fame in Cooperstown.

Brooklyn Superbas, 3; Pittsburgh Pirates, 1

BRO (N)

PLAYER/POS	AVG	G	AB	R	H	2B	3B	HR	RB	BB	SO	SB
Lave Cross, 3b	.278	4	18	2	5	0	1	0		0		1
Bill Dahlen, ss	.176	4	17	3	3	0	0	0		0		1
Tom Daly, 2b	.154	4	13	2	2	1	0	0		3		0
Duke Farrell, c	.375	2	8	0	3	0	0	0		0		1
Harry Howell, p	.000	1	3	0	0	0	0	0		0		0
Hughie Jennings, 1b	.167	4	18	1	3	1	0	0		1		0
Fielder Jones, of	.278	4	18	3	5	0	0	0		1		1
Willie Keeler, of	.353	4	17	0	6	0	0	0		1		0
Joe Kelley, of	.176	4	17	2	3	0	0	0		2		0
Frank Kitson, p	.000	1	3	0	0	0	0	0		1		0
Joe McGinnity, p	.143	2	7	1	1	0	0	0		0		0
Deacon McGuire, c	.375	2	8	1	3	1	0	0		0		0
TOTAL	.231		147	15	34	3	1	0		9		4

PITCHER	W	L	ERA	G	GS	CG	SV	SHO	IP	H	ER	BB	SO
Harry Howell	0	1	3.38	1	1	1	0	0	8.0	13	3	2	3
Frank Kitson	1	0	1.00	1	1	1	0	0	9.0	4	1	1	2
Joe McGinnity	2	0	0.00	2	2	2	0	0	18.0	14	0	3	5
TOTAL	3	1	1.03	4	4	4	0	0	35.0	31	4	6	10

PIT (N)

PLAYER/POS	AVG	G	AB	R	H	2B	3B	HR	RB	BB	SO	SB
Ginger Beaumont, of	.267	4	15	2	4	0	0	0		1		1
Fred Ely, ss	.286	4	14	1	4	0	0	0		1		2
Tommy Leach, of	.176	4	17	4	3	0	0	0		1		0
Sam Leever, p	.250	2	4	0	1	0	0	0		0		1
Tom O'Brien, 1b	.125	4	16	1	2	1	0	0		0		0
Jack O'Connor, c	.250	2	4	0	1	0	0	0		1		0
Deacon Phillippe, p	.000	1	4	1	0	0	0	0		0		0
Claude Ritchey, 2b	.333	4	15	3	5	1	0	0		1		0
Pop Schriver, ph	.000	1	1	0	0	0	0	0		0		0
Rube Waddell, p	.200	2	5	0	1	0	0	0		0		0
Honus Wagner, of	.400	4	15	2	6	1	0	0		0		2
Jimmy Williams, 3b	.214	4	14	0	3	0	0	0		1		0
Chief Zimmer, c	.111	3	9	1	1	0	0	0		0		1
TOTAL	.233		133	15	31	3	0	0		6		7

PITCHER	W	L	ERA	G	GS	CG	SV	SHO	IP	H	ER	BB	SO
Sam Leever	0	2	1.29	2	2	1	0	0	14.0	13	2	4	4
Deacon Phillippe	1	0	0.00	1	1	1	0	1	9.0	6	0	2	5
Rube Waddell	0	1	2.08	2	1	1	0	0	13.0	15	3	3	7
TOTAL	1	3	1.25	5	4	3	0	1	36.0	34	5	9	16

GAME 1 AT PIT OCT 15

BRO	003	101	000	5	13 1
PIT	000	000	002	2	5 4

Pitchers: McGINNITY vs WADDELL
Attendance: 4,000

GAME 2 AT PIT OCT 16

BRO	010	003	000	4	7 0
PIT	000	100	100	2	4 6

Pitchers: KITSON vs LEEVER
Attendance: 1,800

GAME 3 AT PIT OCT 17

BRO	000	000	000	0	6 3
PIT	310	020	13X	10	13 1

Pitchers: HOWELL vs PHILLIPPE
Attendance: 2,500

GAME 4 AT PIT OCT 18

BRO	100	311	000	6	8 0
PIT	000	001	000	1	9 3

Pitchers: McGINNITY vs LEEVER,
  Waddell (6)
Attendance: 2,335

When the Boston Pilgrims of the young American League accepted a challenge from owner Barney Dreyfuss of the National League Pirates, the modern World Series was born. (In 1901–02, the National and American Leagues were warring, and did not stage a postseason series.) Pittsburgh was favored to win but entered the Series weakened by injuries to pitching ace Sam Leever and shortstop Honus Wagner, and by the loss of pitcher Ed Doheny to mental illness.

Deacon Phillippe, the Pirates' one healthy starter, faced Cy Young in the opener, winning handily as Pirate batters, with two out in the top of the first, jumped on Young (and a porous defense) for four runs. Right fielder Jimmy Sebring starred offensively for the Pirates, with four RBIs and the Series's first home run. Boston came back in Game Two as Bill Dinneen shut out the Pirates on three hits. His teammates scored three runs off the sore-armed Leever and reliever Bucky Veil, two coming on homers by Patsy Dougherty. (They were the last World Series home runs for five years.)

Phillippe, with only a day's rest, started Game Three and again pitched Pittsburgh into the Series lead, holding Boston to four hits. After a Sunday travel day to Pittsburgh and a day of rain, Phillippe defeated Boston a third time, though he yielded three ninth-inning runs before emerging with a 5–4 win.

The tide began to turn against the Pirates the next day, as Boston knocked five ground-rule triples into the overflow crowd, scoring ten runs in the sixth and seventh innings to give Young an 11–2 victory. Dinneen bested Leever for a second time in Game Six, holding the Pirates scoreless in eight of their nine innings for a 6–3 win. And in Game Seven, Phillippe finally lost, Young winning his second game as Boston numbered 5 more triples among its 11 hits.

After another travel Sunday and another rainout, Phillippe for the fifth time faced the Pilgrims. He pitched well, giving up three runs (only two of them earned). But Bill Dinneen pitched better, holding the Pirates to four hits as he shut them out for the second time to give Boston the Series.

Boston Pilgrims (AL), 5; Pittsburgh Pirates (NL), 3

BOS (A)

PLAYER/POS	AVG	G	AB	R	H	2B	3B	HR	RB	BB	SO	SB
Jimmy Collins, 3b	.250	8	36	5	9	1	2	0	1	1	1	3
Lou Criger, c	.231	8	26	1	6	0	0	0	4	2	3	0
Bill Dinneen, p	.250	4	12	1	3	0	0	0	0	0	2	0
Patsy Dougherty, of	.235	8	34	3	8	0	2	2	5	2	6	0
Duke Farrell, ph	.000	2	2	0	0	0	0	0	1	0	0	0
Hobe Ferris, 2b	.290	8	31	3	9	0	1	0	5	0	6	0
Buck Freeman, of	.281	8	32	6	9	0	3	0	4	2	2	0
Tom Hughes, p	.000	1	0	0	0	0	0	0	0	0	0	0
Candy La Chance, 1b	.222	8	27	5	6	2	1	0	4	3	2	0
Jack O'Brien, ph	.000	2	2	0	0	0	0	0	0	0	1	0
Freddy Parent, ss	.281	8	32	8	9	0	3	0	4	1	1	0
Chick Stahl, of	.303	8	33	6	10	1	3	0	3	1	2	2
Cy Young, p	.133	4	15	1	2	0	1	0	3	0	3	0
TOTAL	.252		282	39	71	4	16	2	34	14	29	5

PITCHER	W	L	ERA	G	GS	CG	SV	SHO	IP	H	ER	BB	SO
Bill Dinneen	3	1	2.06	4	4	4	0	2	35.0	29	8	8	28
Tom Hughes	0	1	9.00	1	1	0	0	0	2.0	4	2	2	0
Cy Young	2	1	1.85	4	3	3	0	0	34.0	31	7	4	17
TOTAL	5	3	2.15	9	8	7	0	2	71.0	64	17	14	45

PIT (N)

PLAYER/POS	AVG	G	AB	R	H	2B	3B	HR	RB	BB	SO	SB
Ginger Beaumont, of	.265	8	34	6	9	0	1	0	1	2	4	2
Kitty Bransfield, 1b	.207	8	29	3	6	0	2	0	1	1	6	1
Fred Clarke, of	.265	8	34	3	9	2	1	0	2	1	5	1
Brickyard Kennedy, p	.500	1	2	0	1	1	0	0	0	0	0	0
Tommy Leach, 3b	.273	8	33	3	9	0	4	0	7	1	4	1
Sam Leever, p	.000	2	4	0	0	0	0	0	0	0	0	0
Ed Phelps, c-7	.231	8	26	1	6	2	0	0	1	1	6	0
Deacon Phillippe, p	.222	5	18	1	4	0	0	0	1	0	3	0
Claude Ritchey, 2b	.111	8	27	2	3	1	0	0	2	4	7	1
Jimmy Sebring, of	.367	8	30	3	11	0	1	1	3	1	4	0
Harry Smith, c	.000	1	3	0	0	0	0	0	0	0	0	0
Gus Thompson, p	.000	1	1	0	0	0	0	0	0	0	0	0
Bucky Veil, p	.000	1	2	0	0	0	0	0	0	0	2	0
Honus Wagner, ss	.222	8	27	2	6	1	0	0	3	3	4	3
TOTAL	.237		270	24	64	7	9	1	21	14	45	9

PITCHER	W	L	ERA	G	GS	CG	SV	SHO	IP	H	ER	BB	SO
Brickyard Kennedy	0	1	5.14	1	1	0	0	0	7.0	11	4	3	3
Sam Leever	0	2	5.40	2	2	1	0	0	10.0	13	6	3	2
Deacon Phillippe	3	2	2.86	5	5	5	0	0	44.0	38	14	3	22
Gus Thompson	0	0	4.50	1	0	0	0	0	2.0	3	1	0	1
Bucky Veil	0	0	1.29	1	0	0	0	0	7.0	6	1	5	1
TOTAL	3	5	3.34	10	8	6	0	0	70.0	71	26	14	29

GAME 1 AT BOS OCT 1

PIT	401	100	100	7	12 2
BOS	000	000	201	3	6 4

Pitchers: PHILLIPPE vs YOUNG
Home Runs: Sebring-PIT
Attendance: 16,242

GAME 2 AT BOS OCT 2

PIT	000	000	000	0	3 2
BOS	200	001	00X	3	9 0

Pitchers: LEEVER, Vail (2) vs DINNEEN
Home Runs: Dougherty-BOS(2)
Attendance: 9,415

GAME 3 AT BOS OCT 3

PIT	012	000	010	4	7 0
BOS	000	100	010	2	4 2

Pitchers: PHILLIPPE vs HUGHES, Young (3)
Attendance: 18,801

GAME 4 AT PIT OCT 6

BOS	000	010	003	4	9 1
PIT	100	010	30X	5	12 1

Pitchers: DINNEEN vs PHILLIPPE
Attendance: 7,600

GAME 5 AT PIT OCT 7

BOS	000	006	410	11	14 2
PIT	000	000	020	2	6 4

Pitchers: YOUNG vs KENNEDY, Thompson (8)
Attendance: 12,322

GAME 6 AT PIT OCT 8

BOS	003	020	100	6	10 1
PIT	000	000	300	3	10 3

Pitchers: DINNEEN vs LEEVER
Attendance: 11,556

GAME 7 AT PIT OCT 10

BOS	200	202	010	7	11 4
PIT	000	101	001	3	10 3

Pitchers: YOUNG vs PHILLIPPE
Attendance: 17,038

GAME 8 AT BOS OCT 13

PIT	000	000	000	0	4 3
BOS	000	201	00X	3	8 0

Pitchers: PHILLIPPE vs DINNEEN
Attendance: 7,455

After a year's gap caused by the Giants' refusal to play the American League champion Boston Pilgrims, the World Series—now established on an official and permanent basis—resumed with a pitching classic. Even though the A's ERA league leader Rube Waddell had ostensibly injured his shoulder and could not pitch in the Series—rumor had it that gamblers had reached him—the Philadelphia staff recorded a Series ERA of only 1.47. But the Giants' staff—led by Christy Mathewson's three shutouts—registered a matchless ERA of 0.00, permitting only three unearned runs to score in their only Series loss. Every victory in the Series was a shutout.

Mathewson, a 31-game winner in the regular season, continued his winning ways in the Series opener. Though three of the four hits he yielded were doubles, he permitted no more than one hit in any inning, and stopped the only scoring threat, fielding a squeeze bunt to throw out the runner at the plate in the sixth inning.

The A's came back to tie the Series the next day. This time it was Chief Bender's turn to hurl a four-hit shutout. Joe McGinnity also pitched well for the Giants, but New York errors in the third and eighth innings let in three unearned runs—the only runs, as it turned out, to be scored against the Giants in the Series.

Mathewson, pitching with only two days' rest in Game Three, once again permitted only four hits (all singles this time), and Philadelphia's flawed fielding let in seven unearned runs to help give Matty an easy 9–0 win. In Game Four, McGinnity, the hard-luck loser of Game Two, tried again. This time the Giants supported him almost flawlessly, while he gave up only five singles on his way to victory in the Series' tightest game. An A's error led to a single Giant run, and a loss for Eddie Plank, who had pitched even better than McGinnity, giving up only four hits while fanning six.

Chief Bender, the A's winner in Game Two, pitched a five-hitter in Game Six, but he also yielded three walks, all of which contributed to the two Giant runs. Mathewson, though he gave up six hits, walked none, retiring the final ten batters to conclude his record third shutout—and the Series.

New York Giants (NL), 4;
Philadelphia Athletics (AL), 1

NY (N)

PLAYER/POS	AVG	G	AB	R	H	2B	3B	HR	RBI	BB	SO	SB
Red Ames, p	.000	1	0	0	0	0	0	0	0	0	0	0
Roger Bresnahan, c	.313	5	16	3	5	2	0	0	1	4	0	1
George Browne, of	.182	5	22	4	4	0	0	0	1	0	2	2
Bill Dahlen, ss	.000	5	15	1	0	0	0	0	1	3	2	3
Art Devlin, 3b	.250	5	16	0	4	1	0	0	1	1	3	3
Mike Donlin, of	.263	5	19	4	5	1	0	0	1	2	1	2
Billy Gilbert, 2b	.235	5	17	1	4	0	0	0	2	0	2	1
Christy Mathewson, p	.250	3	8	1	2	0	0	0	0	1	1	0
Dan McGann, 1b	.235	5	17	1	4	2	0	0	4	2	7	0
Joe McGinnity, p	.000	2	5	0	0	0	0	0	0	0	2	0
Sam Mertes, of	.176	5	17	2	3	1	0	0	2	2	5	0
Sammy Strang, ph	.000	1	1	0	0	0	0	0	0	0	1	0
TOTAL	.203		153	15	31	7	0	0	13	15	26	12

PITCHER	W	L	ERA	G	GS	CG	SV	SHO	IP	H	ER	BB	SO
Red Ames	0	0	0.00	1	0	0	0	0	1.0	1	0	1	1
Christy Mathewson	3	0	0.00	3	3	3	0	3	27.0	14	0	1	18
Joe McGinnity	1	1	0.00	2	2	1	0	1	17.0	10	0	3	6
TOTAL	4	1	0.00	6	5	4	0	4	45.0	25	0	5	25

PHI (A)

PLAYER/POS	AVG	G	AB	R	H	2B	3B	HR	RBI	BB	SO	SB
Chief Bender, p	.000	2	5	0	0	0	0	0	0	0	1	0
Andy Coakley, p	.000	1	2	0	0	0	0	0	0	0	1	0
Lave Cross, 3b	.105	5	19	0	2	0	0	0	0	1	1	0
Monte Cross, ss	.176	5	17	0	3	0	0	0	0	0	7	0
Harry Davis, 1b	.200	5	20	0	4	1	0	0	0	0	1	0
Topsy Hartsel, of	.294	5	17	1	5	1	0	0	0	2	1	2
Danny Hoffman, ph	.000	1	1	0	0	0	0	0	0	0	1	0
Bris Lord, of	.100	5	20	0	2	0	0	0	2	0	5	0
Danny Murphy, 2b	.188	5	16	0	3	1	0	0	0	0	1	0
Eddie Plank, p	.167	2	6	0	1	0	0	0	0	0	2	0
Mike Powers, c	.143	3	7	0	1	1	0	0	0	0	0	0
Ossee Schreckengost, c	.222	3	9	2	2	1	0	0	0	0	0	0
Socks Seybold, of	.125	5	16	0	2	0	0	0	0	2	3	0
TOTAL	.161		155	3	25	5	0	0	2	5	25	2

PITCHER	W	L	ERA	G	GS	CG	SV	SHO	IP	H	ER	BB	SO
Chief Bender	1	1	1.06	2	2	2	0	1	17.0	9	2	6	13
Andy Coakley	0	1	2.00	1	1	1	0	0	9.0	8	2	5	2
Eddie Plank	0	2	1.59	2	2	2	0	0	17.0	14	3	4	11
TOTAL	1	4	1.47	5	5	5	0	1	43.0	31	7	15	26

GAME 1 AT PHI OCT 9

NY	000 020 001	3	10	1
PHI	000 000 000	0	4	0

Pitchers: MATHEWSON vs PLANK
Attendance: 17,955

GAME 2 AT NY OCT 10

PHI	001 000 020	3	6	2
NY	000 000 000	0	4	2

Pitchers: BENDER vs McGINNITY, Ames (9)
Attendance: 24,992

GAME 3 AT PHI OCT 12

NY	200 050 002	9	9	1
PHI	000 000 000	0	4	5

Pitchers: MATHEWSON vs COAKLEY
Attendance: 10,991

GAME 4 AT NY OCT 13

PHI	000 000 000	0	5	2
NY	000 100 00X	1	4	1

Pitchers: PLANK vs McGINNITY
Attendance: 13,598

GAME 5 AT NY OCT 14

PHI	000 000 000	0	6	0
NY	000 010 01X	2	5	1

Pitchers: BENDER vs MATHEWSON
Attendance: 24,187

The Cubs and White Sox have played more postseason City Series than any other clubs, but this was their only all-Chicago World Series. The Cubs were the clear favorites: league leaders in batting, fielding, and pitching (with a team ERA of only 1.76). They were one of baseball's greatest teams ever, with a still-record 116 wins, finishing 20 games ahead of the second-place Giants. The White Sox, by contrast, although their pitching and fielding were good enough to rank second in the American League, were the junior circuit's weakest hitters, batting as a team only .230, 32 points below the Cubs. But in the Series the "hitless wonders" prevailed. Though they hit only .198 and yielded eight unearned runs to the Cubs' two, the Sox bunched their hits for 20 earned runs—double the Cubs' total. Meanwhile, Sox pitchers held the Cubs to a .196 BA, and produced a team ERA less than half that of Cub pitchers.

Game One was a pitcher's duel as the Cubs' Mordecai (Three Finger) Brown and the Sox' Nick Altrock traded four-hitters and one earned run apiece. But Brown lost the game when his error in the seventh led to the Sox' second run. The Cubs snapped back to take Game Two on Ed Reulbach's one-hit 7–1 win. Although Reulbach issued six walks, he didn't really need the five unearned runs handed his club by Sox errors.

In Game Three the Sox regained the Series lead as Ed Walsh two-hit the Cubs, fanning 12 for the Series' first shutout. The Cubs' Jack Pfiester also pitched shutout ball in eight of his nine innings, but George Rohe's bases-loaded triple in the sixth gave the Sox more than enough to defeat him. Brown brought the Cubs back the next day, evening the Series with a two-hit shutout of his own, winning when Altrock yielded his only run on pairs of singles and sacrifice bunts in the seventh.

The rest of the Series belonged to the hitless wonders, who rocked three Cub pitchers for 12 hits and eight runs to take Game Five, and buried Brown and Orval Overall under 14 hits and another eight runs in Game Six to capture their first world championship.

Chicago White Sox (AL), 4;
Chicago Cubs (NL), 2

CHI (A)

PLAYER/POS	AVG	G	AB	R	H	2B	3B	HR	RB	BB	SO	SB
Nick Altrock, p	.250	2	4	0	1	0	0	0	0	0	1	1	0
George Davis, ss	.308	3	13	4	4	3	0	0	6	0	1	1
Jiggs Donahue, 1b	.333	6	18	0	6	2	1	0	4	3	3	0
Patsy Dougherty, of	.100	6	20	1	2	0	0	0	1	3	4	2
Eddie Hahn, of	.273	6	22	4	6	0	0	0	0	1	1	0
Frank Isbell, 2b	.308	6	26	4	8	4	0	0	4	0	6	1
Fielder Jones, of	.095	6	21	4	2	0	0	0	0	3	3	0
Ed Mc Farland, ph	.000	1	1	0	0	0	0	0	0	0	0	0
Bill O'Neill, of	.000	1	1	1	0	0	0	0	0	0	0	0
Frank Owen, p	.000	1	2	0	0	0	0	0	0	0	1	0
George Rohe, 3b	.333	6	21	2	7	1	2	0	4	3	1	2
Billy Sullivan, c	.000	6	21	0	0	0	0	0	0	0	9	0
Lee Tannehill, ss	.111	3	9	1	1	0	0	0	0	0	2	0
Babe Towne, ph	.000	1	1	0	0	0	0	0	0	0	0	0
Ed Walsh, p	.000	2	4	1	0	0	0	0	0	0	3	0
Doc White, p	.000	3	3	0	0	0	0	0	0	0	1	0
TOTAL	.198		187	22	37	10	3	0	19	18	35	6

PITCHER	W	L	ERA	G	GS	CG	SV	SHO	IP	H	ER	BB	SO
Nick Altrock	1	1	1.00	2	2	2	0	0	18.0	11	2	2	5
Frank Owen	0	0	3.00	1	0	0	0	0	6.0	6	2	3	2
Ed Walsh	2	0	1.20	2	2	1	0	1	15.0	7	2	6	17
Doc White	1	1	1.80	3	2	1	1	0	15.0	12	3	7	4
TOTAL	4	2	1.50	8	6	4	1	1	54.0	36	9	18	28

CHI (N)

PLAYER/POS	AVG	G	AB	R	H	2B	3B	HR	RB	BB	SO	SB
Mordecai Brown, p	.333	3	6	0	2	0	0	0	0	0	4	0
Frank Chance, 1b	.238	6	21	3	5	1	0	0	0	2	1	2
Johnny Evers, 2b	.150	6	20	2	3	1	0	0	1	1	3	2
Doc Gessler, ph	.000	2	1	0	0	0	0	0	0	1	0	0
Solly Hofman, of	.304	6	23	3	7	1	0	0	2	3	5	1
Johnny Kling, c	.176	6	17	2	3	1	0	0	0	4	3	0
Pat Moran, ph	.000	2	2	0	0	0	0	0	0	0	0	0
Orval Overall, p	.250	2	4	1	1	1	0	0	0	1	1	0
Jack Pfiester, p	.000	2	2	0	0	0	0	0	0	0	1	0
Ed Reulbach, p	.000	2	3	0	0	0	0	0	0	1	0	1	0
Frank Schulte, of	.269	6	26	1	7	3	0	0	3	1	3	0
Jimmy Sheckard, of	.000	6	21	0	0	0	0	0	0	1	2	4	1
Harry Steinfeldt, 3b	.250	6	20	2	5	1	0	0	2	1	0	0
Joe Tinker, ss	.167	6	18	4	3	0	0	0	1	2	2	3
TOTAL	.196		184	18	36	9	0	0	11	18	28	9

PITCHER	W	L	ERA	G	GS	CG	SV	SHO	IP	H	ER	BB	SO
Mordecai Brown	1	2	3.20	3	3	2	0	1	19.2	14	7	4	12
Orval Overall	0	0	2.25	2	0	0	0	0	12.0	10	3	3	8
Jack Pfiester	0	2	6.10	2	1	1	0	0	10.1	7	7	3	11
Ed Reulbach	1	0	2.45	2	2	1	0	0	11.0	6	3	8	4
TOTAL	2	4	3.40	9	6	4	0	1	53.0	37	20	18	35

GAME 1 AT CHI-N OCT 9

CHI-A　000 011 000　　2 4 1
CHI-N　000 001 000　　1 4 2
Pitchers: ALTROCK vs BROWN
Attendance: 12,693

GAME 2 AT CHI-A OCT 10

CHI-N　031 001 020　　7 10 2
CHI-A　000 010 000　　1 1 2
Pitchers: REULBACH vs WHITE, Owen (4)
Attendance: 12,595

GAME 3 AT CHI-N OCT 11

CHI-A　000 003 000　　3 4 1
CHI-N　000 000 000　　0 2 2
Pitchers: WALSH vs PFIESTER
Attendance: 13,667

GAME 4 AT CHI-A OCT 12

CHI-N　000 000 100　　1 7 1
CHI-A　000 000 000　　0 2 1
Pitchers: BROWN vs ALTROCK
Attendance: 18,385

GAME 5 AT CHI-N OCT 13

CHI-A　102 401 000　　8 12 6
CHI-N　300 102 000　　6 6 0
Pitchers: WALSH, White (7) vs Reulbach, PFIESTER (3), Overall (4)
Attendance: 23,257

GAME 6 AT CHI-A OCT 14

CHI-N　100 010 001　　3 7 0
CHI-A　340 000 01X　　8 14 3
Pitchers: BROWN, Overall (2) vs WHITE
Attendance: 19,249

The two-run lead that Detroit took into the bottom of the ninth inning of Game One proved to be its biggest of the Series. And it was short-lived, as Chicago—after Frank Chance's leadoff single—took advantage of a hit batsman, a fumble at third base, and a dropped third strike to even the score. Three scoreless extra innings later, darkness ended the game in a 3–3 tie.

The Tigers pitched well enough in the Series. Wild Bill Donovan and George Mullin, who provided more than 80 percent of Detroit's pitching, allowed only four earned runs each for a combined 1.89 ERA. But Cub pitchers gave up only four earned runs *as a team*, suffocating the Tigers with a team ERA of 0.75. And while Tiger fielders made one less error than the Cubs, their misplays proved more costly, permitting eight unearned runs to the Cubs' two.

Detroit's three-run eighth in the opener provided half of their Series scoring. Nine Tiger hits in Game Two produced only one run, while the Cubs bunched six of their nine hits into two innings for three runs and the Series' first win. In Games Three and Four, while the Tigers were twice again limited to a single run, the Cubs increased their run production to five and six, clustering 40 percent of their hits into two three-run innings, one in each game. Mordecai (Three Finger) Brown wrapped up the Series for Chicago with a shutout, as his Cubs blended a hit in each of the first two innings with three stolen bases and a Tiger error for the game's only two runs.

Detroit's twenty-year-old Ty Cobb, the American League batting, RBI, and stolen base leader in his first full big league season, hit an anemic .200 in the World Series, stealing no bases and driving in no Tiger runs. If there was an offensive hero, it was Cub centerfielder Jimmy Slagle. At age thirty-four, nearing the end of a ten-year major league career, he led both clubs with four RBIs (nearly quadruple his season's per-game output) and six stolen bases.

Chicago Cubs (NL), 4;
Detroit Tigers (AL), 0; tie, 1

CHI (N)

PLAYER/POS	AVG	G	AB	R	H	2B	3B	HR	RB	BB	SO	SB
Mordecai Brown, p	.000	1	3	0	0	0	0	0	0	1	0	0
Frank Chance, 1b	.214	4	14	3	3	1	0	0	0	3	2	3
Johnny Evers, 2b-5,ss-1	.350	5	20	2	7	2	0	0	1	0	1	3
Del Howard, 1b-1	.200	2	5	0	1	0	0	0	0	0	2	1
Johnny Kling, c	.211	5	19	2	4	0	0	0	1	1	4	0
Pat Moran, ph	.000	1	0	0	0	0	0	0	0	0	0	0
Orval Overall, p	.200	2	5	0	1	0	0	0	2	0	1	0
Jack Pfiester, p	.000	1	2	0	0	0	0	0	0	0	1	0
Ed Reulbach, p	.200	2	5	0	1	0	0	0	1	0	0	0
Frank Schulte, of	.250	5	20	3	5	0	0	0	2	1	2	0
Jimmy Sheckard, of	.238	5	21	0	5	2	0	0	2	0	4	1
Jimmy Slagle, of	.273	5	22	3	6	0	0	0	4	2	3	6
Harry Steinfeldt, 3b	.471	5	17	2	8	1	1	0	2	1	2	1
Joe Tinker, ss	.154	5	13	4	2	0	0	0	1	3	3	1
Heinie Zimmerman, 2b	.000	1	1	0	0	0	0	0	0	0	1	0
TOTAL	.257		167	19	43	6	1	0	16	12	26	16

PITCHER	W	L	ERA	G	GS	CG	SV	SHO	IP	H	ER	BB	SO
Mordecai Brown	1	0	0.00	1	1	1	0	1	9.0	7	0	1	4
Orval Overall	1	0	1.00	2	2	1	0	0	18.0	14	2	4	11
Jack Pfiester	1	0	1.00	1	1	1	0	0	9.0	9	1	1	3
Ed Reulbach	1	0	0.75	2	1	1	0	0	12.0	6	1	3	4
TOTAL	4	0	0.75	6	5	4	0	1	48.0	36	4	9	22

DET (A)

PLAYER/POS	AVG	G	AB	R	H	2B	3B	HR	RB	BB	SO	SB
Jimmy Archer, c	.000	1	3	0	0	0	0	0	0	0	1	0
Ty Cobb, of	.200	5	20	1	4	0	1	0	0	0	3	0
Bill Coughlin, 3b	.250	5	20	0	5	0	0	0	0	1	4	1
Sam Crawford, of	.238	5	21	1	5	1	0	0	3	0	3	0
Bill Donovan, p	.000	2	8	0	0	0	0	0	0	0	3	0
Davy Jones, of	.353	5	17	1	6	0	0	0	0	4	0	3
Ed Killian, p	.500	1	2	1	1	0	0	0	0	0	0	0
George Mullin, p	.000	2	6	0	0	0	0	0	0	0	1	0
Charley O'Leary, ss	.059	5	17	0	1	0	0	0	0	1	3	0
Fred Payne, c-1	.250	2	4	0	1	0	0	0	1	0	0	1
Claude Rossman, 1b	.400	5	20	1	8	0	1	0	2	1	0	1
Germany Schaefer, 2b	.143	5	21	1	3	0	0	0	0	0	3	0
Boss Schmidt, c-3	.167	4	12	0	2	0	0	0	0	2	1	0
Ed Siever, p	.000	1	1	0	0	0	0	0	0	0	0	0
TOTAL	.209		172	6	36	1	2	0	6	9	22	6

PITCHER	W	L	ERA	G	GS	CG	SV	SHO	IP	H	ER	BB	SO
Bill Donovan	0	1	1.71	2	2	2	0	0	21.0	17	4	5	16
Ed Killian	0	0	2.25	1	0	0	0	0	4.0	3	1	1	1
George Mullin	0	2	2.12	2	2	2	0	0	17.0	16	4	6	8
Ed Siever	0	1	4.50	1	1	0	0	0	4.0	7	2	0	1
TOTAL	0	4	2.15	6	5	4	0	0	46.0	43	11	12	26

GAME 1 AT CHI OCT 8

DET	000	000	030	000	3	9	3
CHI	000	100	002	000	3	10	5

Pitchers: Donovan vs Overall, Reulbach (10)
Attendance: 24,377

GAME 2 AT CHI OCT 9

DET	010	000	000	1	9	1
CHI	010	200	00X	3	9	1

Pitchers: MULLIN vs PFIESTER
Attendance: 21,901

GAME 3 AT CHI OCT 10

DET	000	001	000	1	6	1
CHI	010	310	00X	5	10	1

Pitchers: SIEVER, Killian (5) vs REULBACH
Attendance: 13,114

GAME 4 AT DET OCT 11

CHI	000	020	301	6	7	2
DET	000	100	000	1	5	2

Pitchers: OVERALL vs DONOVAN
Attendance: 11,306

GAME 5 AT DET OCT 12

CHI	110	000	000	2	7	1
DET	000	000	000	0	7	2

Pitchers: BROWN vs MULLIN
Attendance: 7,370

The Tigers won their final game of the season to take their second straight pennant, and the Cubs won their third pennant in a row by defeating the Giants in a replay of an earlier tie. Ty Cobb and Detroit improved on their 1907 Series performance, as Cobb led his club in batting, hits, and RBIs, and the Tigers won a game. But the Cubs as a team hit 90 percentage points higher than Detroit, and outscored them 24–15, to take the Series with relative ease.

In Game One, the Tigers took advantage of the Cubs' ragged fielding to score two runs in the eighth for a 6–5 lead. But in the top of the ninth, the Cubs erupted for five runs on six consecutive singles and a double steal, to win the game. The next day Chicago's Orval Overall held Detroit to four hits and one ninth-inning run. The Tigers' Wild Bill Donovan pitched even better for seven innings, holding Pittsburgh to a single in the sixth. But in the eighth, Joe Tinker's two-run homer—the first in a World Series since 1903—began an assault that ended only after six Cubs had crossed the plate.

Detroit finally manufactured a Series win, pummeling Jack Pfiester in Game Three for ten hits (six of them in the sixth inning) and an 8–3 victory. But that was their last burst. As the Series moved to Detroit for Games Four and Five, the Tiger offense collapsed. Three Finger Brown, the winner as a reliever in Game One, won Game Four as a starter, shutting out the Tigers on four hits. The Cubs needed only three of their ten hits, combining them with a couple of walks and stolen bases, and a muffed fly ball, to score twice in the third inning and once in the ninth.

Only 6,210 spectators—the smallest World Series crowd of the century—saw Overall strike out four Tigers in the first inning of Game Five (one reached first on a wild pitch) in what became a three-hit shutout. Meanwhile, his Cubs unloaded for ten hits, defeating Donovan a second time, scoring runs in the first and fifth innings. Overall—after yielding a leadoff walk to Cobb in the fifth—retired Cobb on a force play and set down the final 11 men to face him.

Chicago Cubs (NL), 4;
Detroit Tigers (AL), 1

CHI (N)

PLAYER/POS	AVG	G	AB	R	H	2B	3B	HR	RB	BB	SO	SB
Mordecai Brown, p	.000	2	4	0	0	0	0	0	0	0	2	0
Frank Chance, 1b	.421	5	19	4	8	0	0	0	2	3	1	5
Johnny Evers, 2b	.350	5	20	5	7	1	0	0	2	1	2	2
Solly Hofman, of	.316	5	19	2	6	0	1	0	4	1	4	2
Del Howard, ph	.000	1	1	0	0	0	0	0	0	0	0	0
Johnny Kling, c	.250	5	16	2	4	1	0	0	2	2	2	0
Orval Overall, p	.333	3	6	0	2	0	0	0	0	0	1	0
Jack Pfiester, p	.000	1	2	0	0	0	0	0	0	0	2	0
Ed Reulbach, p	.000	2	3	0	0	0	0	0	0	0	1	0
Frank Schulte, of	.389	5	18	4	7	0	1	0	2	2	1	2
Jimmy Sheckard, of	.238	5	21	2	5	2	0	0	1	2	3	1
Harry Steinfeldt, 3b	.250	5	16	3	4	0	0	0	3	2	5	1
Joe Tinker, ss	.263	5	19	2	5	0	0	1	4	0	2	2
TOTAL	.293		164	24	48	4	2	1	20	13	26	15

PITCHER	W	L	ERA	G	GS	CG	SV	SHO	IP	H	ER	BB	SO
Mordecai Brown	2	0	0.00	2	1	1	0	1	11.0	6	0	1	5
Orval Overall	2	0	0.98	3	2	2	0	1	18.1	7	2	7	15
Jack Pfiester	0	1	7.87	1	1	0	0	0	8.0	10	7	3	1
Ed Reulbach	0	0	4.70	2	1	0	0	0	7.2	9	4	1	5
TOTAL	4	1	2.60	8	5	3	0	2	45.0	32	13	12	26

DET (A)

PLAYER/POS	AVG	G	AB	R	H	2B	3B	HR	RB	BB	SO	SB
Ty Cobb, of	.368	5	19	3	7	1	0	0	4	1	2	2
Bill Coughlin, 3b	.125	3	8	0	1	0	0	0	1	0	1	0
Sam Crawford, of	.238	5	21	2	5	1	0	0	1	1	2	0
Bill Donovan, p	.000	2	4	0	0	0	0	0	0	1	1	1
Red Downs, 2b	.167	2	6	1	1	1	0	0	1	1	2	0
Davy Jones, ph	.000	3	2	1	0	0	0	0	0	1	1	0
Ed Killian, p	.000	1	0	0	0	0	0	0	0	0	0	0
Matty Mc Intyre, of	.222	5	18	2	4	1	0	0	0	3	2	1
George Mullin, p	.333	1	3	1	1	0	0	0	1	1	0	0
Charley O'Leary, ss	.158	5	19	2	3	0	0	0	0	0	3	0
Claude Rossman, 1b	.211	5	19	3	4	0	0	0	3	1	4	1
Germany Schaefer, 2b-3,3b-2	.125	5	16	0	2	0	0	0	0	1	4	1
Boss Schmidt, c	.071	4	14	0	1	0	0	0	1	0	2	0
Ed Summers, p	.200	2	5	0	1	0	0	0	1	0	2	0
Ira Thomas, c-1	.500	2	4	0	2	1	0	0	1	1	0	0
George Winter, p-1	.000	2	0	0	0	0	0	0	0	0	0	0
TOTAL	.203		158	15	32	5	0	0	14	12	26	6

PITCHER	W	L	ERA	G	GS	CG	SV	SHO	IP	H	ER	BB	SO
Bill Donovan	0	2	4.24	2	2	2	0	0	17.0	17	8	4	10
Ed Killian	0	0	11.57	1	1	0	0	0	2.1	5	3	3	1
George Mullin	1	0	0.00	1	1	1	0	0	9.0	7	0	1	8
Ed Summers	0	2	4.30	2	1	0	0	0	14.2	18	7	4	7
George Winter	0	0	0.00	1	0	0	0	0	1.0	1	0	1	0
TOTAL	1	4	3.68	7	5	3	0	0	44.0	48	18	13	26

GAME 1 AT DET OCT 10

CHI	004 000 105	10	14	2
DET	100 000 320	6	10	4

Pitchers: Reulbach, Overall (7), BROWN (8) vs Killian, SUMMERS (3)
Attendance: 10,812

GAME 2 AT CHI OCT 11

DET	000 000 001	1	4	1
CHI	000 000 06X	6	7	1

Pitchers: DONOVAN vs OVERALL
Home Runs: Tinker-CHI
Attendance: 17,760

GAME 3 AT CHI OCT 12

DET	100 005 020	8	11	4
CHI	000 300 000	3	7	2

Pitchers: MULLIN vs PFIESTER, Reulbach (9)
Attendance: 14,543

GAME 4 AT DET OCT 13

CHI	002 000 001	3	10	0
DET	000 000 000	0	4	1

Pitchers: BROWN vs SUMMERS, Winter (9)
Attendance: 12,907

GAME 5 AT DET OCT 14

CHI	100 010 000	2	10	0
DET	000 000 000	0	3	0

Pitchers: OVERALL vs DONOVAN
Attendance: 6,210

Babe Adams, a twenty-seven-year-old rookie pitcher, was only the fifth biggest winner on the Pittsburgh staff. But his fine 12–3 record was supported by a team-best 1.11 ERA, and manager Fred Clarke started him in the Series opener against Detroit's ace George Mullin (who had led the American League with a career-high 29 wins). Mullin pitched well, giving up only one earned run—manager/outfielder Clarke's homer in the fourth inning. But four Tiger errors led to three Pirate runs in the fifth and sixth. Meanwhile, Adams, after yielding a run in the first, pitched shutout ball the rest of the way for the win.

Detroit came back in Game Two with seven runs (including Ty Cobb's theft of home) as Wild Bill Donovan held the Pirates to two runs on five hits. In Game Three the Pirates took an early lead, which Detroit, despite rallies in the seventh and ninth innings, was unable to overcome. Errors determined most of the scoring, as only one of Detroit's six runs and two of Pittsburgh's eight were earned.

Mullin shut out the Pirates on five hits in Game Four, striking out ten men as Detroit scored five runs (all earned, despite Pittsburgh's six errors) to drive out starter Lefty Leifield after four innings. The seesaw Series continued in Game Five, with Babe Adams winning his second game behind his Pirates' ten-hit, eight-run attack. Adams gave up leadoff homers to Davy Jones in the first and Sam Crawford in the eighth. But Pittsburgh's Clarke more than countered these with his three-run shot in the seventh. (All three homers were hit into temporary seats in center field.)

Back in Detroit for Game Six, the Tigers evened the Series for the third time, Mullin winning his second game in a close contest that saw Pittsburgh pull within a run of tying the game in the ninth before a runner thrown out at home and a game-ending double play cut their rally dead.

In the finale it was Babe Adams once again, scattering six Tiger hits for an easy 8–0 win, his third of the Series. Detroit had done better than ever, but still lost their third World Series in three consecutive attempts. A quarter century would pass before they would have a chance to try again.

Pittsburgh Pirates (NL), 4; Detroit Tigers (AL), 3

PIT (N)

PLAYER/POS	AVG	G	AB	R	H	2B	3B	HR	RB	BB	SO	SB
Ed Abbaticchio, ph	.000	1	1	0	0	0	0	0	0	0	0	0
Bill Abstein, 1b	.231	7	26	3	6	2	0	0	2	3	10	1
Babe Adams, p	.000	3	9	0	0	0	0	0	0	1	1	0
Bobby Byrne, 3b	.250	7	24	5	6	1	0	0	0	1	4	1
Howie Camnitz, p	.000	2	1	0	0	0	0	0	0	0	0	0
Fred Clarke, of	.211	7	19	7	4	0	0	2	7	5	3	3
George Gibson, c	.240	7	25	2	6	2	0	0	2	1	1	2
Ham Hyatt, of-1	.000	2	4	1	0	0	0	0	1	1	0	0
Tommy Leach, of-7,3b-1	.360	7	25	8	9	4	0	0	2	2	1	1
Lefty Leifield, p	.000	1	1	0	0	0	0	0	0	0	1	0
Nick Maddox, p	.000	1	4	0	0	0	0	0	0	0	1	0
Dots Miller, 2b	.250	7	28	2	7	1	0	0	4	2	5	3
Paddy O'Connor, ph	.000	1	1	0	0	0	0	0	0	0	1	0
Deacon Phillippe, p	.000	2	1	0	0	0	0	0	0	0	1	0
Honus Wagner, ss	.333	7	24	4	8	2	1	0	6	4	2	6
Vic Willis, p	.000	2	4	0	0	0	0	0	0	0	1	0
Chief Wilson, of	.154	7	26	2	4	1	0	0	1	0	2	1
TOTAL	.224		223	34	50	13	1	2	25	20	34	18

PITCHER	W	L	ERA	G	GS	CG	SV	SHO	IP	H	ER	BB	SO
Babe Adams	3	0	1.33	3	3	3	0	1	27.0	18	4	6	11
Howie Camnitz	0	1	9.82	2	1	0	0	0	3.2	8	4	2	2
Lefty Leifield	0	1	11.25	1	1	0	0	0	4.0	7	5	1	0
Nick Maddox	1	0	1.00	1	1	1	0	0	9.0	10	1	2	4
Deacon Phillippe	0	0	0.00	2	0	0	0	0	6.0	2	0	1	2
Vic Willis	0	1	3.97	2	1	0	0	0	11.1	10	5	8	3
TOTAL	4	3	2.80	11	7	4	0	1	61.0	55	19	20	22

DET (A)

PLAYER/POS	AVG	G	AB	R	H	2B	3B	HR	RB	BB	SO	SB
Donie Bush, ss	.261	7	23	5	6	1	0	0	3	5	3	1
Ty Cobb, of	.231	7	26	3	6	3	0	0	5	2	2	2
Sam Crawford, of-7,1b-1	.250	7	28	4	7	3	0	1	4	1	1	1
Jim Delahanty, 2b	.346	7	26	2	9	4	0	0	4	2	5	0
Bill Donovan, p	.000	2	4	0	0	0	0	0	0	1	0	0
Davy Jones, of	.233	7	30	6	7	0	0	1	1	2	1	1
Tom Jones, 1b	.250	7	24	3	6	1	0	0	2	2	0	1
Matty Mc Intyre, of-1	.000	4	3	0	0	0	0	0	0	0	1	0
George Moriarty, 3b	.273	7	22	4	6	1	0	0	1	3	1	0
George Mullin, p-4	.188	6	16	1	3	1	0	0	0	1	3	0
Charley O'Leary, 3b	.000	1	3	0	0	0	0	0	0	0	0	0
Boss Schmidt, c	.222	6	18	0	4	2	0	0	4	2	0	0
Oscar Stanage, c	.200	2	5	0	1	0	0	0	0	2	2	0
Ed Summers, p	.000	2	3	0	0	0	0	0	0	0	2	0
Ed Willett, p	.000	2	2	0	0	0	0	0	0	0	0	0
Ralph Works, p	.000	1	0	0	0	0	0	0	0	0	0	0
TOTAL	.236		233	28	55	16	0	2	26	20	22	6

PITCHER	W	L	ERA	G	GS	CG	SV	SHO	IP	H	ER	BB	SO
Bill Donovan	1	1	3.00	2	2	1	0	0	12.0	7	4	8	7
George Mullin	2	1	2.25	4	3	3	0	1	32.0	23	8	8	20
Ed Summers	0	2	8.59	2	2	0	0	0	7.1	13	7	4	4
Ed Willett	0	0	0.00	2	0	0	0	0	7.2	3	0	0	1
Ralph Works	0	0	9.00	1	0	0	0	0	2.0	4	2	0	2
TOTAL	3	4	3.10	11	7	4	0	1	61.0	50	21	20	34

GAME 1 AT PIT OCT 8

DET	100	000	000	1	6	4
PIT	000	121	00X	4	5	0

Pitchers: MULLIN vs ADAMS
Home Runs: Clarke-PIT
Attendance: 29,264

GAME 2 AT PIT OCT 9

DET	023	020	000	7	9	3
PIT	200	000	000	2	5	1

Pitchers: DONOVAN vs CAMNITZ, Willis (3)
Attendance: 30,915

GAME 3 AT DET OCT 11

PIT	510	000	002	8	10	3
DET	000	000	420	6	10	5

Pitchers: MADDOX vs SUMMERS, Willett (1), Works (8)
Attendance: 18,277

GAME 4 AT DET OCT 12

PIT	000	000	000	0	5	6
DET	020	300	00X	5	8	0

Pitchers: LEIFIELD, Phillippe (5) vs MULLIN
Attendance: 17,036

GAME 5 AT PIT OCT 13

DET	100	002	010	4	6	1
PIT	111	000	41X	8	10	2

Pitchers: SUMMERS, Willett (8) vs ADAMS
Home Runs: D.Jones-DET, Crawford-DET, Clarke-PIT
Attendance: 21,706

GAME 6 AT DET OCT 14

PIT	300	000	001	4	7	3
DET	100	211	00X	5	10	3

Pitchers: WILLIS, Camnitz (6), Phillippe (7) vs MULLIN
Attendance: 10,535

GAME 7 AT DET OCT 16

PIT	020	203	010	8	7	0
DET	000	000	000	0	6	3

Pitchers: ADAMS vs DONOVAN, Mullin (4)
Attendance: 17,562

Pitcher Jack Coombs burst into stardom in 1910, emerging as the ace of a Philadelphia pitching staff which dominated the American League with an ERA of only 1.79. Coombs himself led league pitchers with 31 wins and 13 shutouts, and finished second to Chicago's Ed Walsh with an ERA of 1.30—all career bests. He continued his domination into the World Series, pitching three complete-game victories in the Athletics' surpisingly easy triumph over the Cubs.

The Series' finest pitching performance, though, was turned in by the A's Chief Bender in the opener. Only two batters reached base over the first eight innings—on a single and walk—and both of them were cut down trying to steal second. In the ninth, two Cub singles and two Athletic errors produced an unearned run, but as the A's had scored four runs (Bender himself providing the margin of victory with the game's second RBI in the second inning), the Cubs' run did no damage.

Coombs started Game Two and gave up a Cub run in the top of the first inning. But Athletic bats were hot in the Series (their team .316 batting average stood as a Series record for fifty years), and their 14 hits in this game (including four doubles and six runs in the seventh) sank Three Finger Brown and gave Coombs an easy win. Connie Mack also started Coombs in Game Three, two days later, and again the result was a lopsided win. Coombs himself drove in three of his team's 12 runs, and right fielder Danny Murphy added three more with the Series' only home run.

Bender pitched Game Four and suffered the A's only loss, as the Cubs tied the game at 3–3 with a run in the bottom of the ninth, and won it for reliever Three Finger Brown with a two-out RBI single an inning later.

Coombs faced Brown a second time in Game Five. Both clubs made nine hits, but the A's put four of them together with a walk, a wild pitch, and two stolen bases for five runs in the eighth to sink Brown as they had in Game Two, breaking a tight game wide open for Coombs's third win and the Athletics' first world championship.

Philadelphia Athletics (AL), 4; Chicago Cubs (NL), 1

PHI (A)

PLAYER/POS	AVG	G	AB	R	H	2B	3B	HR	RB	BB	SO	SB
Frank Baker, 3b	.409	5	22	6	9	3	0	0	4	2	1	0
Jack Barry, ss	.235	5	17	3	4	2	0	0	3	1	3	0
Chief Bender, p	.333	2	6	1	2	0	0	0	1	1	1	0
Eddie Collins, 2b	.429	5	21	5	9	4	0	0	3	2	0	4
Jack Coombs, p	.385	3	13	0	5	1	0	0	3	0	3	0
Harry Davis, 1b	.353	5	17	5	6	3	0	0	2	3	4	0
Topsy Hartsel, of	.200	1	5	2	1	0	0	0	0	0	1	2
Jack Lapp, c	.250	1	4	0	1	0	0	0	1	0	2	0
Bris Lord, of	.182	5	22	3	4	2	0	0	1	1	3	0
Danny Murphy, of	.350	5	20	6	7	3	0	1	9	1	0	1
Amos Strunk, of	.278	4	18	2	5	1	1	0	2	2	5	0
Ira Thomas, c	.250	4	12	2	3	0	0	0	1	4	1	0
TOTAL	.316		177	35	56	19	1	1	30	17	24	7

PITCHER	W	L	ERA	G	GS	CG	SV	SHO	IP	H	ER	BB	SO
Chief Bender	1	1	1.93	2	2	2	0	0	18.2	12	4	4	14
Jack Coombs	3	0	3.33	3	3	3	0	0	27.0	23	10	14	17
TOTAL	4	1	2.76	5	5	5	0	0	45.2	35	14	18	31

CHI (N)

PLAYER/POS	AVG	G	AB	R	H	2B	3B	HR	RB	BB	SO	SB
Jimmy Archer, c-2,1b-1	.182	3	11	1	2	1	0	0	0	0	3	0
Ginger Beaumont, ph	.000	3	2	1	0	0	0	0	0	1	1	0
Mordecai Brown, p	.000	3	7	0	0	0	0	0	0	0	1	0
Frank Chance, 1b	.353	5	17	1	6	1	1	0	4	0	3	0
King Cole, p	.000	1	2	0	0	0	0	0	0	0	2	0
Solly Hofman, of	.267	5	15	2	4	0	0	0	2	4	3	0
Johnny Kane, pr	.000	1	0	0	0	0	0	0	0	0	0	0
Johnny Kling, c-3	.077	5	13	0	1	0	0	0	1	1	2	0
Harry Mc Intire, p	.000	2	1	0	0	0	0	0	0	0	1	0
Tom Needham, ph	.000	1	1	0	0	0	0	0	0	0	0	0
Orval Overall, p	.000	1	1	0	0	0	0	0	0	0	0	0
Jack Pfiester, p	.000	1	2	0	0	0	0	0	0	0	1	0
Ed Reulbach, p	.000	1	0	0	0	0	0	0	0	0	0	0
Lew Richie, p	.000	1	0	0	0	0	0	0	0	0	0	0
Frank Schulte, of	.353	5	17	3	6	3	0	0	2	2	3	0
Jimmy Sheckard, of	.286	5	14	5	4	2	0	0	1	7	2	1
Harry Steinfeldt, 3b	.100	5	20	0	2	1	0	0	1	0	4	0
Joe Tinker, ss	.333	5	18	2	6	2	0	0	0	2	2	1
Heinie Zimmerman, 2b	.235	5	17	0	4	1	0	0	2	1	3	1
TOTAL	.222		158	15	35	11	1	0	13	18	31	3

PITCHER	W	L	ERA	G	GS	CG	SV	SHO	IP	H	ER	BB	SO
Mordecai Brown	1	2	5.50	3	2	1	0	0	18.0	23	11	7	14
King Cole	0	0	3.38	1	1	0	0	0	8.0	10	3	3	5
Harry Mc Intire	0	1	6.75	2	0	0	0	0	5.1	4	4	3	3
Orval Overall	0	1	9.00	1	1	0	0	0	3.0	6	3	1	1
Jack Pfiester	0	0	0.00	1	1	0	0	0	6.2	9	0	1	1
Ed Reulbach	0	0	9.00	1	1	0	0	0	2.0	3	2	2	0
Lew Richie	0	0	0.00	1	0	0	0	0	1.0	1	0	0	0
TOTAL	1	4	4.70	10	5	1	0	0	44.0	56	23	17	24

GAME 1 AT PHI OCT 17

CHI	000	000	001	1	3 1
PHI	021	000	01X	4	7 2

Pitchers: OVERALL, McIntire (4) vs BENDER
Attendance: 26,891

GAME 2 AT PHI OCT 18

CHI	100	000	101	3	8 3
PHI	002	010	60X	9	14 4

Pitchers: BROWN, Richie (8) vs COOMBS
Attendance: 24,597

GAME 3 AT CHI OCT 20

PHI	125	000	400	12	15 1
CHI	120	000	020	5	6 5

Pitchers: COOMBS vs Reulbach, McINTIRE (3), Pfiester (3)
Home Runs: Murphy-PHI
Attendance: 26,210

GAME 4 AT CHI OCT 22

PHI	001	200	000 0	3	11 3
CHI	100	100	001 1	4	9 1

Pitchers: BENDER vs Cole, BROWN (9)
Attendance: 19,150

GAME 5 AT CHI OCT 23

PHI	100	010	050	7	9 1
CHI	010	000	010	2	9 2

Pitchers: COOMBS vs BROWN
Attendance: 27,374

Connie Mack's pitching aces out-dueled Christy Mathewson, and Frank Baker hit two crucial home runs to become "Home Run" Baker forever more, as the A's avenged their 1905 Series loss to the Giants. Game One, though, belonged to Matty and New York. Philadelphia scored first, but the Giants tied the game with an unearned run in the fourth inning, and won it with two doubles in the seventh, setting at naught Chief Bender's otherwise splendid 11-strikeout performance.

The A's came back to take three in a row. In Game Two Eddie Plank held the Giants to one run and Baker hit the first of his homers, breaking a tie in the sixth with a two-run blast off Rube Marquard. The next day, the A's and Jack Coombs handed Mathewson his first World Series loss. Both pitchers went the distance in an 11-inning duel that saw Matty hold the A's scoreless through eight, only to give up a game-tying home run to Baker in the ninth, and two unearned runs in the eleventh. Coombs, meanwhile, pitched two-hit, one-run ball through ten innings. In the last of the eleventh, a third Giant hit and an A's error let in a second Giant run, but the rally died when Beals Becker was cut down for the final out trying to steal second.

After a week of rain, Mathewson and Bender squared off in Game Four. The Giants jumped on Bender for two runs in the first, and held the lead until the fourth. But in the last of the fourth, three successive A's doubles and a run-scoring fly put the A's in front to stay as Bender held New York scoreless over the final 8 innings.

In Game Five, a three-run homer by the A's Rube Oldring off Rube Marquard in the third provided the only scoring through 6½ innings. But the Giants crept back with one run in the seventh, and two more in the last of the ninth tied the score. Plank replaced Coombs for the A's in the tenth and took the loss as Larry Doyle led off with a double, took third on a missed force play, and scored on Fred Merkle's fly to deep right.

After five closely contested games, Game Six was a laugher. It, too, was close at first—tied 1–1 after 3½ innings. But the A's scored four runs in the fourth on singles and errors, once in the sixth, and seven times in the seventh on a barrage of hits, an error, and a two-run wild pitch. Chief Bender, who gave up only four hits and two unearned runs, was the beneficiary of this largesse, taking his second win of the Series and giving the A's their second consecutive world title.

Philadelphia Athletics (AL), 4;
New York Giants (NL), 2

PHI (A)

PLAYER/POS	AVG	G	AB	R	H	2B	3B	HR	RB	BB	SO	SB
Frank Baker, 3b	.375	6	24	7	9	2	0	2	5	1	5	0
Jack Barry, ss	.368	6	19	2	7	4	0	0	2	0	2	2
Chief Bender, p	.091	3	11	0	1	0	0	0	0	0	1	0
Eddie Collins, 2b	.286	6	21	4	6	1	0	0	1	2	2	2
Jack Coombs, p	.250	2	8	1	2	0	0	0	0	0	0	0
Harry Davis, 1b	.208	6	24	3	5	1	0	0	5	0	3	0
Jack Lapp, c	.250	2	8	1	2	0	0	0	0	0	1	0
Bris Lord, of	.185	6	27	2	5	2	0	0	1	0	5	0
Stuffy Mc Innis, 1b	.000	1	0	0	0	0	0	0	0	0	0	0
Danny Murphy, of	.304	6	23	4	7	3	0	0	3	0	3	0
Rube Oldring, of	.200	6	25	2	5	2	0	1	3	0	5	0
Eddie Plank, p	.000	2	3	0	0	0	0	0	0	0	2	0
Amos Strunk, pr	.000	1	0	0	0	0	0	0	0	0	0	0
Ira Thomas, c	.083	4	12	1	1	0	0	0	1	1	2	0
TOTAL	.244		205	27	50	15	0	3	21	4	31	4

PITCHER	W	L	ERA	G	GS	CG	SV	SHO	IP	H	ER	BB	SO
Chief Bender	2	1	1.04	3	3	3	0	0	26.0	16	3	8	20
Jack Coombs	1	0	1.35	2	2	1	0	0	20.0	11	3	6	16
Eddie Plank	1	1	1.86	2	1	1	0	0	9.2	6	2	0	8
TOTAL	4	2	1.29	7	6	5	0	0	55.2	33	8	14	44

NY (N)

PLAYER/POS	AVG	G	AB	R	H	2B	3B	HR	RB	BB	SO	SB
Red Ames, p	.500	2	2	0	1	0	0	0	0	0	1	0
Beals Becker, ph	.000	3	3	0	0	0	0	0	0	0	0	0
Doc Crandall, p-2	.500	3	2	1	1	1	0	0	1	2	0	0
Josh Devore, of	.167	6	24	1	4	1	0	0	3	1	8	0
Larry Doyle, 2b	.304	6	23	3	7	3	1	0	1	2	1	2
Art Fletcher, ss	.130	6	23	1	3	1	0	0	1	0	4	0
Buck Herzog, 3b	.190	6	21	3	4	2	0	0	2	3	2	2
Rube Marquard, p	.000	3	2	0	0	0	0	0	0	0	2	0
Christy Mathewson, p	.286	3	7	0	2	0	0	0	0	1	3	0
Fred Merkle, 1b	.150	6	20	1	3	1	0	0	1	2	6	0
Chief Meyers, c	.300	6	20	2	6	2	0	0	2	0	3	0
Red Murray, of	.000	6	21	0	0	0	0	0	0	2	5	0
Fred Snodgrass, of	.105	6	19	1	2	0	0	0	1	2	7	0
Art Wilson, c	.000	1	1	0	0	0	0	0	0	0	0	0
Hooks Wiltse, p	.000	2	1	0	0	0	0	0	0	0	1	0
TOTAL	.175		189	13	33	11	1	0	10	14	44	4

PITCHER	W	L	ERA	G	GS	CG	SV	SHO	IP	H	ER	BB	SO
Red Ames	0	1	2.25	2	1	0	0	0	8.0	6	2	1	6
Doc Crandall	1	0	0.00	2	0	0	0	0	4.0	2	0	0	2
Rube Marquard	0	1	1.54	3	2	0	0	0	11.2	9	2	1	8
Christy Mathewson	1	2	2.00	3	3	2	0	0	27.0	25	6	2	13
Hooks Wiltse	0	0	18.90	2	0	0	0	0	3.1	8	7	0	2
TOTAL	2	4	2.83	12	6	2	0	0	54.0	50	17	4	31

GAME 1 AT NY OCT 14

PHI	010	000	000	1	6 2
NY	000	100	10X	2	5 0

Pitchers: BENDER vs MATHEWSON
Attendance: 38,281

GAME 2 AT PHI OCT 16

NY	010	000	000	1	5 3
PHI	100	002	00X	3	4 0

Pitchers: MARQUARD, Crandall (8) vs PLANK
Home Runs: Baker-PHI
Attendance: 26,286

GAME 3 AT NY OCT 17

PHI	000	000	001	02	3 9 2
NY	001	000	000	01	2 3 5

Pitchers: COOMBS vs MATHEWSON
Home Runs: Baker-PHI
Attendance: 37,216

GAME 4 AT PHI OCT 24

NY	200	000	000	2	7 3
PHI	000	310	00X	4	11 1

Pitchers: MATHEWSON, Wiltse (8) vs BENDER
Attendance: 24,355

GAME 5 AT NY OCT 25

PHI	003	000	000	0	3 7 1
NY	000	000	102	1	4 9 2

Pitchers: Coombs, PLANK (10) vs Marquard, Ames (4), CRANDALL (8)
Home Runs: Oldring-PHI
Attendance: 33,228

GAME 6 AT PHI OCT 26

NY	100	000	001	2	4 3
PHI	001	401	70X	13	13 5

Pitchers: AMES, Wiltse (5), Marquard (7) vs BENDER
Attendance: 20,485

The Giants outhit the Red Sox by 50 percentage points, and their pitchers let in one less earned run per game. But this was the Series in which Fred Snodgrass's famous muff of a routine fly to center in the tenth inning of the final game helped turn a slim Giant lead into a Red Sox world championship. In all fairness, it must be admitted that Snodgrass followed his muff with a brilliant catch off the next batter, and indecision by the catcher and first baseman permitted a pop foul to drop, keeping the Sox alive to score the tying and winning runs. For that matter, this final game might not have been needed at all if Snodgrass and Beals Becker hadn't both been cut down trying to steal second in the eleventh inning of Game Two, which ended in a tie because of darkness. If either had gone on to score, the Giants would have won the Series in seven games.

Boston's Smokey Joe Wood followed up his spectacular 34–5 regular season with Series wins in Games One and Four, before being rocked for six runs in the first inning of Game Seven for a loss. Relieving in the eighth inning of the finale, he stopped the Giants for two innings, but gave up what would have been the losing run in the tenth had not the Giants' fielding in the last of the inning turned the game around, giving Wood the win and the Sox the Series.

Although Wood won three games, the best pitching of the Series was turned in by the Giants' Rube Marquard and Boston's Hugh Bedient. Marquard (who in the regular season had tied a major league record with 19 consecutive wins) won two of his club's three victories (Games Three and Six), allowing three runs—only one of them earned. Bedient, in two starts and two relief appearances, matched Marquard's 0.50 earned run average, winning a duel with Christy Mathewson in Game Five, and hurling seven effective innings against Matty in the finale.

Mathewson was the Series' hard-luck pitcher: his one tie and two losses were all decided by unearned runs.

Boston Red Sox (AL), 4; New York Giants (NL), 3; tie, 1

BOS (A)

PLAYER/POS	AVG	G	AB	R	H	2B	3B	HR	RB	BB	SO	SB
Neal Ball, ph	.000	1	1	0	0	0	0	0	0	0	1	0
Hugh Bedient, p	.000	4	6	0	0	0	0	0	0	0	0	0
Hick Cady, c	.136	7	22	1	3	0	0	0	1	0	3	0
Bill Carrigan, c	.000	2	7	0	0	0	0	0	0	0	0	0
Ray Collins, p	.000	2	5	0	0	0	0	0	0	0	2	0
Clyde Engle, ph	.333	3	3	1	1	1	0	0	2	0	0	0
Larry Gardner, 3b	.179	8	28	4	5	2	1	1	4	2	5	0
Charley Hall, p	.750	2	4	0	3	1	0	0	0	1	0	0
Olaf Henricksen, ph	1.000	2	1	0	1	1	0	0	1	0	0	0
Harry Hooper, of	.290	8	31	3	9	2	1	0	2	4	4	2
Duffy Lewis, of	.156	8	32	4	5	3	0	0	2	2	2	0
Buck O'Brien, p	.000	2	2	0	0	0	0	0	0	0	2	0
Tris Speaker, of	.300	8	30	4	9	1	2	0	2	4	2	1
Jake Stahl, 1b	.281	8	32	3	9	2	0	0	2	0	6	2
Heinie Wagner, ss	.167	8	30	1	5	1	0	0	0	3	6	1
Joe Wood, p	.286	4	7	1	2	0	0	0	0	1	1	0
Steve Yerkes, 2b	.250	8	32	3	8	0	2	0	4	2	3	0
TOTAL	.220		273	25	60	14	6	1	21	19	36	6

PITCHER	W	L	ERA	G	GS	CG	SV	SHO	IP	H	ER	BB	SO
Hugh Bedient	1	0	0.50	4	2	1	0	0	18.0	10	2	7	7
Ray Collins	0	0	1.88	2	1	0	0	0	14.1	14	3	0	6
Charley Hall	0	0	3.38	2	0	0	0	0	10.2	11	4	9	1
Buck O'Brien	0	2	5.00	2	2	0	0	0	9.0	12	5	3	4
Joe Wood	3	1	3.68	4	3	2	0	0	22.0	27	9	3	21
TOTAL	4	3	2.80	14	8	3	0	0	74.0	74	23	22	39

NY (N)

PLAYER/POS	AVG	G	AB	R	H	2B	3B	HR	RB	BB	SO	SB
Red Ames, p	.000	1	0	0	0	0	0	0	0	0	0	0
Beals Becker, of-1	.000	2	4	1	0	0	0	0	0	2	0	0
Doc Crandall, p	.000	1	1	0	0	0	0	0	0	0	1	0
Josh Devore, of	.250	7	24	4	6	0	0	0	0	7	5	4
Larry Doyle, 2b	.242	8	33	5	8	1	0	1	2	3	2	2
Art Fletcher, ss	.179	8	28	1	5	1	0	0	3	1	4	1
Buck Herzog, 3b	.400	8	30	6	12	4	1	0	4	1	3	2
Rube Marquard, p	.000	2	4	0	0	0	0	0	0	1	0	0
Christy Mathewson, p	.167	3	12	0	2	0	0	0	0	0	4	0
Moose Mc Cormick, ph	.250	5	4	0	1	0	0	0	1	0	0	0
Fred Merkle, 1b	.273	8	33	5	9	2	1	0	3	0	7	1
Chief Meyers, c	.357	8	28	2	10	0	1	0	3	2	3	1
Red Murray, of	.323	8	31	5	10	4	1	0	5	2	2	0
Tillie Shafer, ss	.000	3	0	0	0	0	0	0	0	0	0	0
Fred Snodgrass, of	.212	8	33	2	7	2	0	0	2	2	5	1
Jeff Tesreau, p	.375	3	8	0	3	0	0	0	2	1	3	0
Art Wilson, c	1.000	2	1	0	1	0	0	0	0	0	0	0
TOTAL	.270		274	31	74	14	4	1	25	22	39	12

PITCHER	W	L	ERA	G	GS	CG	SV	SHO	IP	H	ER	BB	SO
Red Ames	0	0	4.50	1	0	0	0	0	2.0	3	1	1	0
Doc Crandall	0	0	0.00	1	0	0	0	0	2.0	1	0	0	2
Rube Marquard	2	0	0.50	2	2	2	0	0	18.0	14	1	2	9
Christy Mathewson	0	2	1.26	3	3	3	0	0	28.2	23	4	5	10
Jeff Tesreau	1	2	3.13	3	3	1	0	0	23.0	19	8	11	15
TOTAL	3	4	1.71	10	8	6	0	0	73.2	60	14	19	36

GAME 1 AT NY OCT 8

BOS	000 001 300	4	6	1
NY	002 000 001	3	8	1

Pitchers: WOOD vs TESREAU, Crandall (8)
Attendance: 35,730

GAME 2 AT BOS OCT 9

NY	010 100 030 10	6	11	5
BOS	300 010 010 10	6	10	1

Pitchers: Mathewson vs Collins, Hall (8), Bedient (11)
Attendance: 30,148

GAME 3 AT BOS OCT 10

NY	010 010 000	2	7	1
BOS	000 000 001	1	7	0

Pitchers: MARQUARD vs O'BRIEN, Bedient (9)
Attendance: 34,624

GAME 4 AT NY OCT 11

BOS	010 100 001	3	8	1
NY	000 000 100	1	9	1

Pitchers: WOOD vs TESREAU, Ames (8)
Attendance: 36,502

GAME 5 AT BOS OCT 12

NY	000 000 100	1	3	1
BOS	002 000 00X	2	5	1

Pitchers: MATHEWSON vs BEDIENT
Attendance: 34,683

GAME 6 AT NY OCT 14

BOS	020 000 000	2	7	2
NY	500 000 00X	5	11	4

Pitchers: O'BRIEN, Collins (2) vs MARQUARD
Attendance: 30,622

GAME 7 AT BOS OCT 15

NY	610 002 101	11	16	4
BOS	010 000 210	4	9	3

Pitchers: TESREAU vs WOOD, Hall (2)
Home Runs: Doyle-NY, Gardner-BOS
Attendance: 32,694

GAME 8 AT BOS OCT 16

NY	001 000 000 1	2	9	2
BOS	000 000 100 2	3	8	5

Pitchers: MATHEWSON vs Bedient, WOOD (8)
Attendance: 17,034

Third baseman Frank Baker and catcher Wally Schang drove in more than 60 percent of the Athletics' runs, as Philadelphia dispatched the Giants in five games. Chief Bender led A's pitchers with two wins, and rookie Bullet Joe Bush hurled a nifty five-hitter in Game Three, but the Series highlights were two duels between the A's Eddie Plank and the Giant's Christy Mathewson. The A's heavy hitting made Bender's wins possible and Bush's win easy, but pitching dominated the Plank-Matty games.

Bender yielded 11 hits in the opener, as did the Giants' pitchers. But five of the game's six extra-base hits belonged to the A's—including Baker's two-run homer and triples by Schang and Eddie Collins—and Bender emerged victorious. In Game Two, Plank and Mathewson pitched shutout ball through nine innings, but in the top of the tenth Matty himself singled in the game's first run and scored the second. Taking a 3–0 lead into the bottom of the inning, he set the A's down in order for New York's only Series win.

In Game Three, Schang's solo homer and Collins's three hits (including his second Series triple) and three RBIs led a 12-hit A's attack which, with Bush's fine pitching, put Philadelphia back into the Series lead. Bender won again in Game Four, shutting out the Giants through six innings as his A's scored six runs. But in the seventh, New York's Fred Merkle homered for three runs, and a single, double, and triple in the eighth brought in two more Giant runs. With his lead cut to a single run, Bender bore down in the ninth and retired the side in order.

Plank avenged his earlier loss with a brilliant two-hitter in Game Five, facing the minimum three batters in eight of the nine innings. (His own error in the fifth—a dropped pop-up—led to the Giants' only run.) Mathewson pitched well, too, yielding only six singles. But four of them came in the first and third innings, combining with two sacrifice flies and an error for three runs. Only one Athletic batter reached base in the final six innings, but with Plank pitching as he was, the game and the title were in Philadelphia's pocket.

Philadelphia Athletics (AL), 4;
New York Giants (NL), 1

PHI (A)

PLAYER/POS	AVG	G	AB	R	H	2B	3B	HR	RB	BB	SO	SB
Frank Baker, 3b	.450	5	20	2	9	0	0	1	7	0	2	1
Jack Barry, ss	.300	5	20	3	6	3	0	0	2	0	0	0
Chief Bender, p	.000	2	8	0	0	0	0	0	1	0	1	0
Joe Bush, p	.250	1	4	0	1	0	0	0	0	0	1	0
Eddie Collins, 2b	.421	5	19	5	8	0	2	0	3	1	2	3
Jack Lapp, c	.250	1	4	0	1	0	0	0	0	0	1	0
Stuffy Mc Innis, 1b	.118	5	17	1	2	1	0	0	2	0	2	0
Eddie Murphy, of	.227	5	22	2	5	0	0	0	0	2	0	0
Rube Oldring, of	.273	5	22	5	6	0	1	0	0	0	1	1
Eddie Plank, p	.143	2	7	0	1	0	0	0	0	0	0	0
Wally Schang, c	.357	4	14	2	5	0	1	1	6	2	4	0
Amos Strunk, of	.118	5	17	3	2	0	0	0	0	2	2	0
TOTAL	.264		174	23	46	4	4	2	21	7	16	5

PITCHER	W	L	ERA	G	GS	CG	SV	SHO	IP	H	ER	BB	SO
Chief Bender	2	0	4.00	2	2	2	0	0	18.0	19	8	1	9
Joe Bush	1	0	1.00	1	1	1	0	0	9.0	5	1	4	3
Eddie Plank	1	1	0.95	2	2	2	0	0	19.0	9	2	3	7
TOTAL	4	1	2.15	5	5	5	0	0	46.0	33	11	8	19

NY (N)

PLAYER/POS	AVG	G	AB	R	H	2B	3B	HR	RB	BB	SO	SB
George Burns, of	.158	5	19	2	3	2	0	0	1	1	5	1
Claude Cooper, pr	.000	2	0	0	0	0	0	0	0	0	0	1
Doc Crandall, p-2	.000	4	4	0	0	0	0	0	0	0	0	0
Al Demaree, p	.000	1	1	0	0	0	0	0	0	0	0	0
Larry Doyle, 2b	.150	5	20	1	3	0	0	0	2	0	1	0
Art Fletcher, ss	.278	5	18	1	5	0	0	0	4	1	1	1
Eddie Grant, ph	.000	2	1	0	0	0	0	0	0	0	0	0
Buck Herzog, 3b	.053	5	19	1	1	0	0	0	0	0	1	0
Rube Marquard, p	.000	2	1	0	0	0	0	0	0	0	0	0
Christy Mathewson, p	.600	2	5	1	3	0	0	0	1	1	0	0
Moose Mc Cormick, ph	.500	2	2	1	1	0	0	0	0	0	0	0
Larry Mc Lean, c-4	.500	5	12	0	6	0	0	0	2	0	0	0
Fred Merkle, 1b	.231	4	13	3	3	0	0	1	3	1	2	0
Chief Meyers, c	.000	1	4	0	0	0	0	0	0	0	0	0
Red Murray, of	.250	5	16	2	4	0	0	0	1	2	2	2
Tillie Shafer, of-5,3b-1	.158	5	19	2	3	1	1	0	1	2	3	0
Fred Snodgrass, 1b-1,of-1	.333	2	3	0	1	0	0	0	0	0	0	0
Jeff Tesreau, p	.000	2	2	0	0	0	0	0	0	0	1	0
Art Wilson, c	.000	3	3	0	0	0	0	0	0	0	2	0
Hooks Wiltse, 1b	.000	2	2	0	0	0	0	0	0	0	1	0
TOTAL	.201		164	15	33	3	1	1	15	8	19	5

PITCHER	W	L	ERA	G	GS	CG	SV	SHO	IP	H	ER	BB	SO
Doc Crandall	0	0	3.86	2	0	0	0	0	4.2	4	2	0	2
Al Demaree	0	1	4.50	1	1	0	0	0	4.0	7	2	1	0
Rube Marquard	0	1	7.00	2	1	0	0	0	9.0	10	7	3	3
Christy Mathewson	1	1	0.95	2	2	2	0	1	19.0	14	2	2	7
Jeff Tesreau	0	1	6.48	2	1	0	0	0	8.1	11	6	1	4
TOTAL	1	4	3.80	9	5	2	0	1	45.0	46	19	7	16

GAME 1 AT NY OCT 7

PHI	000	320	010	6	11	1
NY	001	030	000	4	11	0

Pitchers: BENDER vs MARQUARD, Crandall (6), Tesreau (8)
Home Runs: Baker-PHI
Attendance: 36,291

GAME 2 AT PHI OCT 8

NY	000	000	000 3	3	7	2
PHI	000	000	000 0	0	8	2

Pitchers: MATHEWSON vs PLANK
Attendance: 20,563

GAME 3 AT NY OCT 9

PHI	320	000	210	8	12	1
NY	000	010	100	2	5	1

Pitchers: BUSH vs TESREAU, Crandall (7)
Home Runs: Schang-PHI
Attendance: 36,896

GAME 4 AT PHI OCT 10

NY	000	000	320	5	8	2
PHI	010	320	00X	6	9	0

Pitchers: MARQUARD vs BENDER
Home Runs: Merkle-NY
Attendance: 20,568

GAME 5 AT NY OCT 11

PHI	102	000	000	3	6	1
NY	000	010	000	1	2	2

Pitchers: PLANK vs MATHEWSON
Attendance: 36,682

The Athletics, easy winners of their fourth pennant in five years, were clear favorites over Boston. But the "Miracle Braves"—who moved from last place to first between July 18 and August 25 and kept going to take the pennant by 10½ games—had the momentum and swept the Series.

Boston pitcher Dick Rudolph (who won 27 games during the season) limited the A's to five hits and an unearned run, to take the opener behind the Braves' heavy hitting, 7–1. But the rest of the games were not won so easily.

Philadelphia's Eddie Plank held the Braves scoreless through eight innings of Game Two, and gave up only one run in the ninth. But the Braves' Bill James (26–7 during the season) allowed only two hits and no runs at all.

Game Three was a seesaw affair not settled until the twelfth inning. Through ten innings, starters Lefty Tyler of Boston and Joe Bush of the A's traded runs. Philadelphia scored one in the top of the first, but Braves' catcher Hank Gowdy doubled in the tying run in the second. The teams traded runs again in the fourth, but no one else crossed the plate until the tenth, when Frank Baker's bases-loaded single drove in two. For the third time, the Braves came back to tie it up. Gowdy opened the last of the tenth with the Series' only home run, and after a walk and single, a sacrifice fly knotted the score. Bill James came on to pitch no-hit ball through the eleventh and twelfth. Bush remained in for the A's, retiring the side in the eleventh. But an inning later Gowdy opened with his third crucial hit of the game, a double. Les Mann replaced him as runner, and after a walk, bunt, and wild throw to third, Mann scampered home with the winning run.

Two of Connie Mack's most promising young pitchers, Bob Shawkey and Herb Pennock (who would later find stardom as New York Yankees), shared the A's pitching in Game Four, and gave up only six hits between them. But a walk and an error led to a Boston run in the fourth, and although Shawkey himself doubled in the tying run a half inning later, two more Braves scored in the last of the fifth on Johnny Evers's single. Pennock came on to pitch three innings of shutout relief, but Rudolph held the A's hitless over the final four innings to preserve his second win and the Braves' crown.

Boston Braves (NL), 4; Philadelphia Athletics (AL), 0

BOS (N)

PLAYER/POS	AVG	G	AB	R	H	2B	3B	HR	RB	BB	SO	SB
Ted Cather, of	.000	1	5	0	0	0	0	0	0	0	1	0
Joe Connolly, of	.111	3	9	1	1	0	0	0	1	1	1	0
Charlie Deal, 3b	.125	4	16	1	2	2	0	0	0	0	0	2
Josh Devore, ph	.000	1	1	0	0	0	0	0	0	0	1	0
Johnny Evers, 2b	.438	4	16	2	7	0	0	0	2	2	2	1
Larry Gilbert, ph	.000	1	0	0	0	0	0	0	0	1	0	0
Hank Gowdy, c	.545	4	11	3	6	3	1	1	3	5	1	1
Bill James, p	.000	2	4	0	0	0	0	0	0	0	4	0
Les Mann, of-2	.286	3	7	1	2	0	0	0	1	0	1	0
Rabbit Maranville, ss	.308	4	13	1	4	0	0	0	3	1	1	2
Herbie Moran, of	.077	3	13	2	1	1	0	0	0	1	1	1
Dick Rudolph, p	.333	2	6	1	2	0	0	0	0	1	1	0
Butch Schmidt, 1b	.294	4	17	2	5	0	0	0	2	0	2	1
Lefty Tyler, p	.000	1	3	0	0	0	0	0	0	0	1	0
Possum Whitted, of	.214	4	14	2	3	0	1	0	2	3	1	1
TOTAL	.244		135	16	33	6	2	1	14	15	18	9

PITCHER	W	L	ERA	G	GS	CG	SV	SHO	IP	H	ER	BB	SO
Bill James	2	0	0.00	2	1	1	0	1	11.0	2	0	6	9
Dick Rudolph	2	0	0.50	2	2	2	0	0	18.0	12	1	4	15
Lefty Tyler	0	0	3.60	1	1	0	0	0	10.0	8	4	3	4
TOTAL	4	0	1.15	5	4	3	0	1	39.0	22	5	13	28

PHI (A)

PLAYER/POS	AVG	G	AB	R	H	2B	3B	HR	RB	BB	SO	SB
Frank Baker, 3b	.250	4	16	0	4	2	0	0	2	1	3	0
Jack Barry, ss	.071	4	14	1	1	0	0	0	0	1	3	1
Chief Bender, p	.000	1	2	0	0	0	0	0	0	0	0	0
Joe Bush, p	.000	1	5	0	0	0	0	0	0	0	2	0
Eddie Collins, 2b	.214	4	14	0	3	0	0	0	1	2	1	1
Jack Lapp, c	.000	1	1	0	0	0	0	0	0	0	0	0
Stuffy Mc Innis, 1b	.143	4	14	2	2	1	0	0	0	3	3	0
Eddie Murphy, of	.188	4	16	2	3	2	0	0	0	2	2	0
Rube Oldring, of	.067	4	15	0	1	0	0	0	0	0	5	0
Herb Pennock, p	.000	1	1	0	0	0	0	0	0	0	0	0
Eddie Plank, p	.000	2	2	0	0	0	0	0	0	0	1	0
Wally Schang, c	.167	4	12	1	2	1	0	0	0	1	4	0
Bob Shawkey, p	.500	1	2	0	1	1	0	0	1	0	1	0
Amos Strunk, of	.286	2	7	0	2	0	0	0	0	0	2	0
Jimmy Walsh, of-2	.333	3	6	0	2	1	0	0	1	3	1	0
Weldon Wyckoff, p	1.000	1	1	0	1	1	0	0	0	0	0	0
TOTAL	.172		128	6	22	9	0	0	5	13	28	2

PITCHER	W	L	ERA	G	GS	CG	SV	SHO	IP	H	ER	BB	SO
Chief Bender	0	1	10.13	1	1	0	0	0	5.1	8	6	2	3
Joe Bush	0	1	3.27	1	1	1	0	0	11.0	9	4	4	4
Herb Pennock	0	0	0.00	1	0	0	0	0	3.0	2	0	2	3
Eddie Plank	0	1	1.00	1	1	1	0	0	9.0	7	1	4	6
Bob Shawkey	0	1	3.60	1	1	0	0	0	5.0	4	2	2	0
Weldon Wyckoff	0	0	2.45	1	0	0	0	0	3.2	3	1	1	2
TOTAL	0	4	3.41	6	4	2	0	0	37.0	33	14	15	18

GAME 1 AT PHI OCT 9

BOS	020 013 010	7 11 2
PHI	010 000 000	1 5 0

Pitchers: RUDOLPH vs BENDER, Wyckoff (6)
Attendance: 20,562

GAME 2 AT PHI OCT 10

BOS	000 000 001	1 7 1
PHI	000 000 000	0 2 1

Pitchers: JAMES vs PLANK
Attendance: 20,562

GAME 3 AT BOS OCT 12

PHI	100 100 000 200	4 8 2
BOS	010 100 000 201	5 9 1

Pitchers: BUSH vs Tyler, JAMES (11)
Home Runs: Gowdy-BOS
Attendance: 35,520

GAME 4 AT BOS OCT 13

PHI	000 010 000	1 7 0
BOS	000 120 00X	3 6 0

Pitchers: SHAWKEY, Pennock (6) vs RUDOLPH
Attendance: 34,365

Boston's five runs in Game Five were the most scored by either team in a Series characterized by outstanding pitching. It was also one of the most closely contested Series: the deciding run was not scored until the ninth inning in three of the games, and only in Game One was the margin of victory as much as two runs.

Grover Cleveland Alexander pitched the opener for the Phillies, and while the Red Sox tagged him for eight hits, they were all singles, and not until the eighth inning did one manage to drive a runner home. Boston's Ernie Shore pitched just as well, giving up only five singles and four walks. But two Phillie hits produced a run in the fourth, and an alternating pair of walks and infield hits in the eighth broke the tie with two runs for the Phillies' only win.

The next three games were 2–1 Boston victories. Rube Foster held the Phillies to three hits in Game Two, and led his team at the bat, going 3 for 4, including a double in the fifth. But it was his single in the ninth with a man on second that produced what proved to be the winning run as he retired the side in the bottom of the ninth to preserve his win. Dutch Leonard duplicated Foster's three-hit pitching two days later as the Series moved to Boston's spacious new Braves Field for Game Three. Before a new Series record crowd of 42,300, Leonard defeated the great Alexander, as the Sox' Duffy Lewis—with his third hit of the game—singled over second base to score Harry Hooper from third with two out in the bottom of the ninth.

Ernie Shore returned to the mound for Boston in Game Four, and although he gave up more hits (seven) than he had in Game One, his Sox had scored their two runs before the Phillies put across their one in the eighth.

Rube Foster was not as effective in Game Five as he had been in Game Two, twice giving the Phillies a two-run lead as Phillie first baseman Fred Luderus drove in three runs with a double and a home run. But from the fifth inning on, Foster held Philadelphia scoreless on two hits, while Duffy Lewis evened the score with a two-run homer in the eighth, and Harry Hooper (who had tied the score earlier with a home run in the third) won the game and the Series with a second homer in the top of the ninth.

Boston Red Sox (AL), 4;
Philadelphia Phillies (NL), 1

BOS (A)

PLAYER/POS	AVG	G	AB	R	H	2B	3B	HR	RB	BB	SO	SB
Jack Barry, 2b	.176	5	17	1	3	0	0	0	1	1	2	0
Hick Cady, c	.333	4	6	0	2	0	0	0	0	1	2	0
Bill Carrigan, c	.000	1	2	0	0	0	0	0	0	1	1	0
Rube Foster, p	.500	2	8	0	4	1	0	0	1	0	2	0
Del Gainer, 1b	.333	1	3	1	1	0	0	0	0	0	0	0
Larry Gardner, 3b	.235	5	17	2	4	0	1	0	0	1	0	0
Olaf Henricksen, ph	.000	2	2	0	0	0	0	0	0	0	0	0
Dick Hoblitzel, 1b	.313	5	16	1	5	0	0	0	1	0	1	1
Harry Hooper, of	.350	5	20	4	7	0	0	2	3	2	4	0
Hal Janvrin, ss	.000	1	1	0	0	0	0	0	0	0	0	0
Dutch Leonard, p	.000	1	3	0	0	0	0	0	0	0	2	0
Duffy Lewis, of	.444	5	18	1	8	1	0	1	5	1	4	0
Babe Ruth, ph	.000	1	1	0	0	0	0	0	0	0	0	0
Everett Scott, ss	.056	5	18	0	1	0	0	0	0	0	3	0
Ernie Shore, p	.200	2	5	0	1	0	0	0	0	0	3	0
Tris Speaker, of	.294	5	17	2	5	0	1	0	0	4	1	0
Pinch Thomas, c	.200	2	5	0	1	0	0	0	0	0	0	0
TOTAL	.264		159	12	42	2	2	3	11	11	25	1

PITCHER	W	L	ERA	G	GS	CG	SV	SHO	IP	H	ER	BB	SO
Rube Foster	2	0	2.00	2	2	2	0	0	18.0	12	4	2	13
Dutch Leonard	1	0	1.00	1	1	1	0	0	9.0	3	1	0	6
Ernie Shore	1	1	2.12	2	2	2	0	0	17.0	12	4	8	6
TOTAL	4	1	1.84	5	5	5	0	0	44.0	27	9	10	25

PHI (N)

PLAYER/POS	AVG	G	AB	R	H	2B	3B	HR	RB	BB	SO	SB
Pete Alexander, p	.200	2	5	0	1	0	0	0	0	0	1	0
Dave Bancroft, ss	.294	5	17	2	5	0	0	0	1	2	2	0
Beals Becker, of	.000	2	0	0	0	0	0	0	0	0	0	0
Ed Burns, c	.188	5	16	1	3	0	0	0	0	1	2	0
Bobby Byrne, ph	.000	1	1	0	0	0	0	0	0	0	0	0
George Chalmers, p	.333	1	3	0	1	0	0	0	0	0	1	0
Gavvy Cravath, of	.125	5	16	2	2	1	1	0	1	2	6	0
Oscar Dugey, pr	.000	2	0	0	0	0	0	0	0	0	0	1
Bill Killefer, ph	.000	1	1	0	0	0	0	0	0	0	0	0
Fred Luderus, 1b	.438	5	16	1	7	2	0	1	6	1	4	0
Erskine Mayer, p	.000	2	4	0	0	0	0	0	0	0	2	0
Bert Niehoff, 2b	.063	5	16	1	1	0	0	0	0	1	5	0
Dode Paskert, of	.158	5	19	2	3	0	0	0	0	1	2	0
Eppa Rixey, p	.500	1	2	0	1	0	0	0	0	0	0	0
Milt Stock, 3b	.118	5	17	1	2	1	0	0	0	1	0	0
Possum Whitted, of-5,1b-1	.067	5	15	0	1	0	0	0	1	1	0	1
TOTAL	.182		148	10	27	4	1	1	9	10	25	2

PITCHER	W	L	ERA	G	GS	CG	SV	SHO	IP	H	ER	BB	SO
Pete Alexander	1	1	1.53	2	2	2	0	0	17.2	14	3	4	10
George Chalmers	0	1	2.25	1	1	1	0	0	8.0	8	2	3	6
Erskine Mayer	0	1	2.38	2	2	1	0	0	11.1	16	3	2	7
Eppa Rixey	0	1	4.05	1	0	0	0	0	6.2	4	3	2	2
TOTAL	1	4	2.27	6	5	4	0	0	43.2	42	11	11	25

GAME 1 AT PHI OCT 8

BOS	000	000	010	1	8 1
PHI	000	100	02X	3	5 1

Pitchers: SHORE vs ALEXANDER
Attendance: 19,343

GAME 2 AT PHI OCT 9

BOS	100	000	001	2	10 0
PHI	000	010	000	1	3 1

Pitchers: FOSTER vs MAYER
Attendance: 20,306

GAME 3 AT BOS OCT 11

PHI	001	000	000	1	3 0
BOS	000	100	001	2	6 1

Pitchers: ALEXANDER vs LEONARD
Attendance: 42,300

GAME 4 AT BOS OCT 12

PHI	000	000	010	1	7 0
BOS	001	001	00X	2	8 1

Pitchers: CHALMERS vs SHORE
Attendance: 41,096

GAME 5 AT PHI OCT 13

BOS	011	000	021	5	10 1
PHI	200	200	000	4	9 1

Pitchers: FOSTER vs Mayer, RIXEY (3)
Home Runs: Hooper-BOS (2),
Lewis-BOS, Luderus-PHI
Attendance: 20,306

In close pennant races, the Red Sox repeated as league champions and Brooklyn won its first pennant since 1900. The first three games of the Series were tightly contested, and the outcomes were determined by only one run apiece. For 6½ innings in the opener, Brooklyn's Rube Marquard dueled Boston's Ernie Shore about equally. But in the last of the seventh the Sox capitalized on a double, some sloppy Brooklyn fielding, and a couple of sacrifice hits for three runs, adding another off reliever Jeff Pfeffer in the eighth for a 6–1 lead. The Robins fought back in the ninth, driving out Shore and drawing within one run of a tie before reliever Carl Mays retired the final man with the bases loaded.

Game Two was even tighter. Boston starter Babe Ruth gave up a first-inning inside-the-park homer to Hy Myers, but in the third he drove in Everett Scott (who had tripled) to tie the game at 1–1. Then for the next ten innings he and Robin pitcher Sherry Smith shut off all scoring. Ruth continued to blank Brooklyn in the fourteenth, and in the last of the inning a walk, sacrifice, and single over the head of the third baseman gave Boston and Ruth the victory.

Brooklyn veteran Jack Coombs took a 4–0 lead into the sixth inning of Game Three before weakening. But after giving up a third Boston run on Larry Gardner's one-out homer in the seventh, he was relieved by Jeff Pfeffer, who set the Sox down in order the rest of the way. In saving what proved to be Coombs's last World Series appearance (as well as the Robins' only Series win), Pfeffer preserved Coombs's perfect Series won-lost record at 5–0.

Games Four and Five proved anticlimactic. In Game Four, Gardner's second homer of the Series—inside the park for three runs in the second inning—overcame the Robins' two runs in the first. The Sox added a run here and there to increase their lead, while Sox starter Dutch Leonard shut Brooklyn out through the final eight innings for a comfortable 6–2 win. And in what became the Series finale, Ernie Shore held the Robins to three singles and one unearned run as his Sox took advantage of a bad-hop triple in the second and two third-inning errors by Robin shortstop Ivy Olson to take the lead—and their fourth world championship.

Boston Red Sox (AL), 4; Brooklyn Robins (NL), 1

BOS (A)

PLAYER/POS	AVG	G	AB	R	H	2B	3B	HR	RBI	BB	SO	SB
Hick Cady, c	.250	2	4	1	1	0	0	0	0	0	3	0
Bill Carrigan, c	.667	1	3	0	2	0	0	0	0	1	0	0
Rube Foster, p	.000	1	1	0	0	0	0	0	0	0	1	0
Del Gainer, ph	1.000	1	1	0	1	0	0	0	1	0	0	0
Larry Gardner, 3b	.176	5	17	2	3	0	0	2	6	0	2	0
Olaf Henricksen, ph	.000	1	0	1	0	0	0	0	0	1	0	0
Dick Hoblitzel, 1b	.235	5	17	3	4	1	0	0	2	6	0	0
Harry Hooper, of	.333	5	21	6	7	1	1	0	1	3	1	0
Hal Janvrin, 2b	.217	5	23	2	5	3	0	0	1	0	6	0
Dutch Leonard, p	.000	1	3	0	0	0	0	0	0	1	3	0
Duffy Lewis, of	.353	5	17	3	6	2	1	0	1	2	1	0
Carl Mays, p	.000	2	1	0	0	0	0	0	0	0	1	0
Mike Mc Nally, pr	.000	1	0	1	0	0	0	0	0	0	0	0
Babe Ruth, p	.000	1	5	0	0	0	0	0	1	0	2	0
Everett Scott, ss	.125	5	16	1	2	0	1	0	1	1	1	0
Ernie Shore, p	.000	2	7	0	0	0	0	0	0	0	2	0
Chick Shorten, of	.571	2	7	0	4	0	0	0	2	0	1	0
Pinch Thomas, c	.143	3	7	0	1	0	1	0	0	0	1	0
Tilly Walker, of	.273	3	11	1	3	0	1	0	1	1	2	0
Jimmy Walsh, of	.000	1	3	0	0	0	0	0	0	0	0	0
TOTAL	.238		164	21	39	7	6	2	18	18	25	1

PITCHER	W	L	ERA	G	GS	CG	SV	SHO	IP	H	ER	BB	SO
Rube Foster	0	0	0.00	1	0	0	0	0	3.0	3	0	0	1
Dutch Leonard	1	0	1.00	1	1	1	0	0	9.0	5	1	4	3
Carl Mays	0	1	5.06	2	1	0	1	0	5.1	8	3	3	2
Babe Ruth	1	0	0.64	1	1	1	0	0	14.0	6	1	3	4
Ernie Shore	2	0	1.53	2	2	1	0	0	17.2	12	3	4	9
TOTAL	4	1	1.47	7	5	3	1	0	49.0	34	8	14	19

BRO (N)

PLAYER/POS	AVG	G	AB	R	H	2B	3B	HR	RBI	BB	SO	SB
Larry Cheney, p	.000	1	0	0	0	0	0	0	0	0	0	0
Jack Coombs, p	.333	1	3	0	1	0	0	0	1	0	0	0
George Cutshaw, 2b	.105	5	19	2	2	1	0	0	2	1	1	0
Jake Daubert, 1b	.176	4	17	1	3	0	1	0	0	2	3	0
Wheezer Dell, p	.000	1	0	0	0	0	0	0	0	0	0	0
Gus Getz, ph	.000	1	1	0	0	0	0	0	0	0	0	0
Jimmy Johnston, of-2	.300	3	10	1	3	0	1	0	0	1	0	0
Rube Marquard, p	.000	2	3	0	0	0	0	0	0	0	1	0
Fred Merkle, 1b-1	.250	3	4	0	1	0	0	0	1	2	0	0
Chief Meyers, c	.200	3	10	0	2	0	1	0	0	1	0	0
Otto Miller, c	.125	2	8	0	1	0	0	0	0	0	1	0
Harry Mowery, 3b	.176	5	17	2	3	0	0	0	1	3	2	0
Hy Myers, of	.182	5	22	2	4	0	0	1	3	0	3	0
Ivy Olson, ss	.250	5	16	1	4	0	1	0	2	2	2	0
Ollie O'Mara, ph	.000	1	1	0	0	0	0	0	0	0	1	0
Jeff Pfeffer, p-3	.250	4	4	0	1	0	0	0	0	0	0	0
Nap Rucker, p	.000	1	0	0	0	0	0	0	0	0	0	0
Sherry Smith, p	.200	1	5	0	1	1	0	0	0	0	0	0
Casey Stengel, of-3	.364	4	11	2	4	0	0	0	0	0	1	0
Zack Wheat, of	.211	5	19	2	4	0	1	0	1	2	2	1
TOTAL	.200		170	13	34	2	5	1	11	14	19	1

PITCHER	W	L	ERA	G	GS	CG	SV	SHO	IP	H	ER	BB	SO
Larry Cheney	0	0	3.00	1	0	0	0	0	3.0	4	1	1	5
Jack Coombs	1	0	4.26	1	1	0	0	0	6.1	7	3	1	1
Wheezer Dell	0	0	0.00	1	0	0	0	0	1.0	1	0	0	0
Rube Marquard	0	2	6.55	2	2	0	0	0	11.0	12	8	6	9
Jeff Pfeffer	0	1	1.69	3	1	0	1	0	10.2	7	2	4	5
Nap Rucker	0	0	0.00	1	0	0	0	0	2.0	1	0	0	3
Sherry Smith	0	1	1.35	1	1	1	0	0	13.1	7	2	6	2
TOTAL	1	4	3.04	10	5	1	1	0	47.1	39	16	18	25

GAME 1 AT BOS OCT 7

BRO	000	100	004	5	10	4
BOS	001	010	31X	6	8	1

Pitchers: MARQUARD, Pfeffer (8) vs SHORE, Mays (9)
Attendance: 36,117

GAME 2 AT BOS OCT 9

BRO	100	000	000	000 00	1	6	2
BOS	001	000	000	000 01	2	7	1

Pitchers: SMITH vs RUTH
Home Runs: H.Myers-BRO
Attendance: 41,373

GAME 3 AT BRO OCT 10

BOS	000	002	100	3	7	1
BRO	001	120	00X	4	10	0

Pitchers: MAYS, Foster (6) vs COOMBS, Pfeffer (7)
Home Runs: Gardner-BOS
Attendance: 21,087

GAME 4 AT BRO OCT 11

BOS	030	110	100	6	10	1
BRO	200	000	000	2	5	4

Pitchers: LEONARD vs MARQUARD, Cheney (5), Rucker (8)
Home Runs: Gardner-BOS
Attendance: 21,662

GAME 5 AT BOS OCT 12

BRO	010	000	000	1	3	3
BOS	012	010	00X	4	7	2

Pitchers: PFEFFER, Dell (8) vs SHORE
Attendance: 42,620

Easy winners in their pennant races, the White Sox and Giants traded pairs of victories in the Series before the Sox came up with a second pair to take the title in six games. In the opener, Happy Felsch's solo homer in the fourth inning gave Sox starter Eddie Cicotte the margin he needed to defeat Giant Slim Sallee 2–1, and in Game Two Red Faber went all the way, as his Sox broke a 2–2 tie in the fourth inning with five runs on six singles for Chicago's second win.

The clubs traveled to New York for Games Three and Four, and Giant pitchers rewarded their fans with a pair of shutouts to even the Series. In Game Three, a triple, double, and single against the Sox' Cicotte in the fourth inning produced the only scoring, as Giant Rube Benton blanked the Sox on five hits, walking none. Giant ace Ferdie Schupp (a 21-game winner during the season) did the honors in Game Four, scattering seven hits, as Benny Kauff, with his first Series hit in the fourth inning, homered inside the park to deep center against Red Faber for the deciding run. Two later runs against Faber and two more in the eighth (on Kauff's second homer) against reliever Dave Danforth made Schupp's win easy.

But Faber, the loser in Game Four, came in to pitch two innings of perfect relief two days later in Chicago for his second win, as the Sox rebounded from a 2–5 deficit with three runs in the bottom of the seventh to tie the game and three more an inning later to win it.

After a day of rest and a return to New York, Faber was given his third start. He pitched well enough, but his third win and the Series clincher was really the gift of some infamous Giant fielding. In the fourth inning, the first two Sox batters—Eddie Collins and Joe Jackson—reached on a high throw to first and a dropped fly. Happy Felsch, the third man up, reached on a fielder's choice as Giant third baseman Heinie Zimmerman chased Collins across the plate in a botched rundown. Jackson and Felsch scored the second and third unearned runs as Chick Gandil singled off the hapless Rube Benton. The Giants recovered to score two runs an inning later, but Faber shut them out the rest of the way to give his Sox the Series.

Chicago White Sox (AL), 4; New York Giants (NL), 2

CHI (A)

PLAYER/POS	AVG	G	AB	R	H	2B	3B	HR	RB	BB	SO	SB
Eddie Cicotte, p	.143	3	7	0	1	0	0	0	0	0	2	0
Eddie Collins, 2b	.409	6	22	4	9	1	0	0	2	2	3	3
Shano Collins, of	.286	6	21	2	6	1	0	0	0	0	2	0
Dave Danforth, p	.000	1	0	0	0	0	0	0	0	0	0	0
Red Faber, p	.143	4	7	0	1	0	0	0	0	0	3	0
Happy Felsch, of	.273	6	22	4	6	1	0	1	3	1	5	0
Chick Gandil, 1b	.261	6	23	1	6	1	0	0	5	0	2	1
Joe Jackson, of	.304	6	23	4	7	0	0	0	2	1	0	1
Nemo Leibold, of	.400	2	5	1	2	0	0	0	2	1	1	0
Byrd Lynn, ph	.000	1	1	0	0	0	0	0	0	0	1	0
Fred Mc Mullin, 3b	.125	6	24	3	3	1	0	0	2	1	6	0
Swede Risberg, ph	.500	2	2	0	1	0	0	0	1	0	0	0
Reb Russell, p	.000	1	0	0	0	0	0	0	0	0	0	0
Ray Schalk, c	.263	6	19	1	5	0	0	0	0	2	1	1
Buck Weaver, ss	.333	6	21	3	7	1	0	0	1	0	2	0
Lefty Williams, p	.000	1	0	0	0	0	0	0	0	0	0	0
TOTAL	.274		197	21	54	6	0	1	18	11	28	6

PITCHER	W	L	ERA	G	GS	CG	SV	SHO	IP	H	ER	BB	SO
Eddie Cicotte	1	1	1.96	3	2	2	0	0	23.0	23	5	2	13
Dave Danforth	0	0	18.00	1	0	0	0	0	1.0	3	2	0	2
Red Faber	3	1	2.33	4	3	2	0	0	27.0	21	7	3	9
Reb Russell	0	0	INF	1	1	0	0	0	0.0	2	1	1	0
Lefty Williams	0	0	9.00	1	0	0	0	0	1.0	2	1	0	3
TOTAL	4	2	2.77	10	6	4	0	0	52.0	51	16	6	27

NY (N)

PLAYER/POS	AVG	G	AB	R	H	2B	3B	HR	RB	BB	SO	SB
Fred Anderson, p	.000	1	0	0	0	0	0	0	0	0	0	0
Rube Benton, p	.000	2	4	0	0	0	0	0	0	0	3	0
George Burns, of	.227	6	22	3	5	0	0	0	2	2	6	1
Art Fletcher, ss	.200	6	25	2	5	1	0	0	0	0	2	0
Buck Herzog, 2b	.250	6	24	1	6	0	1	0	2	1	4	0
Walter Holke, 1b	.286	6	21	2	6	2	0	0	1	0	6	0
Benny Kauff, of	.160	6	25	2	4	1	0	2	5	0	2	1
Lew Mc Carty, c-2	.400	3	5	1	2	0	1	0	1	0	0	0
Pol Perritt, p	1.000	3	2	0	2	0	0	0	0	0	0	0
Bill Rariden, c	.385	5	13	2	5	0	0	0	2	2	1	0
Dave Robertson, of	.500	6	22	3	11	1	1	0	1	0	0	2
Slim Sallee, p	.167	2	6	0	1	0	0	0	0	0	2	0
Ferdie Schupp, p	.250	2	4	0	1	0	0	0	0	1	0	1	0
Jeff Tesreau, p	.000	1	0	0	0	0	0	0	0	0	0	0
Jim Thorpe, of	.000	1	0	0	0	0	0	0	0	0	0	0
Joe Wilhoit, ph	.000	2	1	0	0	0	0	0	0	1	0	0
Heinie Zimmerman, 3b	.120	6	25	1	3	0	1	0	0	0	0	0
TOTAL	.256		199	17	51	5	4	2	16	6	27	4

PITCHER	W	L	ERA	G	GS	CG	SV	SHO	IP	H	ER	BB	SO
Fred Anderson	0	1	18.00	1	0	0	0	0	2.0	5	4	0	3
Rube Benton	1	1	0.00	2	2	1	0	1	14.0	9	0	1	8
Pol Perritt	0	0	2.16	3	0	0	0	0	8.1	9	2	3	3
Slim Sallee	0	2	5.28	2	2	1	0	0	15.1	20	9	4	4
Ferdie Schupp	1	0	1.74	2	2	1	0	1	10.1	11	2	2	9
Jeff Tesreau	0	0	0.00	1	0	0	0	0	1.0	0	0	1	1
TOTAL	2	4	3.00	11	6	3	0	2	51.0	54	17	11	28

GAME 1 AT CHI OCT 6

NY	000 010 000	1	7	1
CHI	001 100 00X	2	7	1

Pitchers: SALLEE vs CICOTTE
Home Runs: Felsch-CHI
Attendance: 32,000

GAME 2 AT CHI OCT 7

NY	020 000 000	2	8	1
CHI	020 500 00X	7	14	1

Pitchers: Schupp, ANDERSON (2), Perritt (4), Tesreau (8) vs FABER
Attendance: 32,000

GAME 3 AT NY OCT 10

CHI	000 000 000	0	5	3
NY	000 200 00X	2	8	2

Pitchers: CICOTTE vs BENTON
Attendance: 33,616

GAME 4 AT NY OCT 11

CHI	000 000 000	0	7	0
NY	000 110 12X	5	10	1

Pitchers: FABER, Danforth (8) vs SCHUPP
Home Runs: Kauff-NY (2)
Attendance: 27,746

GAME 5 AT CHI OCT 13

NY	200 200 100	5	12	3
CHI	001 001 33X	8	14	6

Pitchers: SALLEE, Perritt (8) VS Russell, Cicotte (1), Williams (7), FABER (8)
Attendance: 27,323

GAME 6 AT NY OCT 15

CHI	000 300 001	4	7	1
NY	000 020 000	2	6	3

Pitchers: FABER vs BENTON, Perritt (6)
Attendance: 33,969

Although both clubs had lost key players to military service, so had other major league teams, and after a season shortened by a month because of the war, the Red Sox and Cubs found themselves opponents in an early-September World Series.

In the opener, Babe Ruth pushed his string of consecutive scoreless World Series innings to 22, holding the Cubs to six singles as he went the distance. The Cubs' Hippo Vaughn pitched just as well, but two of the five singles he yielded followed a leadoff walk in the fourth and produced the game's only run. Chicago evened the Series in Game Two, bunching four of their seven hits after a walk in the second inning to take a 3-0 lead. Successive triples in Boston's ninth spoiled Lefty Tyler's shutout but not his victory.

Hippo Vaughn lost another close one in Game Three when he gave up two runs in the fourth inning on a hit batsman and a succession of singles. The Cubs got him one run back in the fifth, but the Sox' Carl Mays held Chicago to that one run as he hurled Boston back into the Series lead. Ruth pushed the Sox farther ahead the next day in another squeaker. As he continued his mastery over Cub hitters, he drove Boston into the lead with a two-run triple in the fourth inning (his only Series hit). But in the eighth a run-scoring ground out ended his record setting string of scoreless innings at 29⅔, and a single drove in another run to tie the game. The Sox, though, scored a third run on a Chicago error in the last of the eighth, and reliever Bullet Joe Bush shut down a threat in the ninth to save Ruth's win.

Vaughn, in his third start, finally found what was needed for victory—a shutout, on five hits, as the Cubs added hits to walks from Boston's Sad Sam Jones in the third and eighth to push across their three runs. But in Game Six the Sox scored two unearned runs on a dropped line drive to right in the third inning. It was their only scoring off Lefty Tyler, but Boston's Carl Mays was on his way to a one-run three-hitter that brought the Red Sox their fifth world championship in five tries. To date, although they have tried four more times, they have not won a sixth.

Boston Red Sox (AL), 4; Chicago Cubs (NL), 2

BOS (A)

PLAYER/POS	AVG	G	AB	R	H	2B	3B	HR	RB	BB	SO	SB
Sam Agnew, c	.000	4	9	0	0	0	0	0	0	0	0	0
Joe Bush, p	.000	2	2	0	0	0	0	0	0	1	0	0
Jean Dubuc, ph	.000	1	1	0	0	0	0	0	0	0	1	0
Harry Hooper, of	.200	6	20	0	4	0	0	0	0	2	2	0
Sam Jones, p	.000	1	1	0	0	0	0	0	0	1	0	0
Carl Mays, p	.200	2	5	1	1	0	0	0	0	1	0	0
Stuffy Mc Innis, 1b	.250	6	20	2	5	0	0	0	1	1	1	0
Hack Miller, ph	.000	1	1	0	0	0	0	0	0	0	0	0
Babe Ruth, p-2,of-2	.200	3	5	0	1	0	1	0	2	0	2	0
Wally Schang, c	.444	5	9	1	4	0	0	0	1	2	3	1
Everett Scott, ss	.095	6	21	0	2	0	0	0	1	1	1	0
Dave Shean, 2b	.211	6	19	2	4	1	0	0	0	4	3	1
Amos Strunk, of	.174	6	23	1	4	1	1	0	0	0	5	0
Fred Thomas, 3b	.125	6	16	0	2	0	0	0	0	1	2	0
George Whiteman, of	.250	6	20	2	5	0	1	0	1	2	1	1
TOTAL	.186		172	9	32	2	3	0	6	16	21	3

PITCHER	W	L	ERA	G	GS	CG	SV	SHO	IP	H	ER	BB	SO
Joe Bush	0	1	3.00	2	1	1	1	0	9.0	7	3	3	0
Sam Jones	0	1	3.00	1	1	1	0	0	9.0	7	3	5	5
Carl Mays	2	0	1.00	2	2	2	0	0	18.0	10	2	3	5
Babe Ruth	2	0	1.06	2	2	1	0	1	17.0	13	2	7	4
TOTAL	4	2	1.70	7	6	5	1	1	53.0	37	10	18	14

CHI (N)

PLAYER/POS	AVG	G	AB	R	H	2B	3B	HR	RB	BB	SO	SB
Turner Barber, ph	.000	3	2	0	0	0	0	0	0	0	0	0
Charlie Deal, 3b	.176	6	17	0	3	0	0	0	0	0	1	0
Phil Douglas, p	.000	1	0	0	0	0	0	0	0	0	0	0
Max Flack, of	.263	6	19	2	5	0	0	0	0	4	1	1
Claude Hendrix, p-1	1.000	2	1	0	1	0	0	0	0	0	0	0
Charlie Hollocher, ss	.190	6	21	2	4	0	1	0	1	1	1	1
Bill Killefer, c	.118	6	17	2	2	1	0	0	2	2	0	0
Les Mann, of	.227	6	22	0	5	2	0	0	2	0	0	0
Bill Mc Cabe, ph	.000	3	1	1	0	0	0	0	0	0	0	0
Fred Merkle, 1b	.278	6	18	1	5	0	0	0	1	4	3	0
Bob O'Farrell, c-1	.000	3	3	0	0	0	0	0	0	0	0	0
Dode Paskert, of	.190	6	21	0	4	1	0	0	2	2	2	0
Charlie Pick, 2b	.389	6	18	2	7	1	0	0	0	1	1	1
Lefty Tyler, p	.200	3	5	0	1	0	0	0	2	2	0	0
Hippo Vaughn, p	.000	3	10	0	0	0	0	0	0	0	5	0
Chuck Wortman, 2b	.000	1	1	0	0	0	0	0	0	0	0	0
Rollie Zeider, 3b	.000	2	0	0	0	0	0	0	0	2	0	0
TOTAL	.210		176	10	37	5	1	0	10	18	14	3

PITCHER	W	L	ERA	G	GS	CG	SV	SHO	IP	H	ER	BB	SO
Phil Douglas	0	1	0.00	1	0	0	0	0	1.0	1	0	0	0
Claude Hendrix	0	0	0.00	1	0	0	0	0	1.0	0	0	0	0
Lefty Tyler	1	1	1.17	3	3	1	0	0	23.0	14	3	11	4
Hippo Vaughn	1	2	1.00	3	3	3	0	1	27.0	17	3	5	17
TOTAL	2	4	1.04	8	6	4	0	1	52.0	32	6	16	21

GAME 1 AT CHI SEPT 5

BOS	000	100	000	1	5	0
CHI	000	000	000	0	6	0

Pitchers: RUTH vs VAUGHN
Attendance: 19,274

GAME 2 AT CHI SEPT 6

BOS	000	000	001	1	6	1
CHI	030	000	000	3	7	1

Pitchers: BUSH vs TYLER
Attendance: 20,040

GAME 3 AT CHI SEPT 7

BOS	000	200	000	2	7	0
CHI	000	010	000	1	7	1

Pitchers: MAYS vs VAUGHN
Attendance: 27,054

GAME 4 AT BOS SEPT 9

CHI	000	000	020	2	7	1
BOS	000	200	01X	3	4	0

Pitchers: Tyler, DOUGLAS (8) vs RUTH, Bush (9)
Attendance: 22,183

GAME 5 AT BOS SEPT 10

CHI	001	000	002	3	7	0
BOS	000	000	000	0	5	0

Pitchers: VAUGHN vs JONES
Attendance: 24,694

GAME 6 AT BOS SEPT 11

CHI	000	100	000	1	3	2
BOS	002	000	00X	2	5	0

Pitchers: TYLER, Hendrix (8) vs MAYS
Attendance: 15,238

In the bottom of the first inning of Game One, White Sox pitcher Eddie Cicotte hit the first batter to face him, a prearranged signal to gamblers that "the fix was on"—that the Sox would throw the Series. The eight Chicago conspirators—pitching aces Cicotte and Lefty Williams, outfielders Joe Jackson and Happy Felsch, and infielders Chick Gandil, Buck Weaver, Fred McMullin and Swede Risberg—received no more than a fraction of the $100,000 promised them but "honored" their end of the deal. Cicotte (winner of 29 regular-season games, with a 1.82 ERA) gave up seven hits and six runs in the opening innings of Game One en route to a 1–9 loss, and Williams, though he held the Reds to four hits in Game Two, uncharacteristically walked six and fanned only one, a performance bad enough for a 2–4 loss.

Dickie Kerr, Chicago's third-best pitcher and not in on the fix, won Game Three with a three-hit shutout. But although Cicotte pitched well in Game Four, Chicago lost a third time as the Reds' Jimmy Ring hurled a three-hit shutout of his own (all three hits coming, ironically, off the bats of conspirators Jackson, Felsch, and Gandil).

Cincinnati's Hod Eller beat Chicago in Game Five with the Series' third successive three-hit shutout. Loser Lefty Williams once again yielded only four hits, but three came in a four-run sixth inning which also saw a walk and a throwing error by Felsch. (The win, the Reds' fourth, did not decide the Series, which had been expanded to the best five of nine in the exuberance which followed the end of the Great War.)

Chicago exerted itself to win the next two games. In Game Six, Kerr's second win depended on crucial hits by Jackson and Gandil in the tenth inning; and in Game Seven Cicotte held the Reds to one run as Jackson and Felsch drove in all the Sox' four.

But in Game Eight, Williams gave up two singles and two doubles before being pulled with only one away in the first. Jackson homered in the third. And he doubled and Gandil tripled to drive in three Chicago runs in the eighth. But by then the Reds had scored ten runs on their way to an easy win and their tainted world title.

Cincinnati Reds (NL), 5; Chicago White Sox (AL), 3

CIN (N)

PLAYER/POS	AVG	G	AB	R	H	2B	3B	HR	RB	BB	SO	SB
Jake Daubert, 1b	.241	8	29	4	7	0	1	0	1	1	2	1
Pat Duncan, of	.269	8	26	3	7	2	0	0	8	2	2	0
Hod Eller, p	.286	2	7	2	2	1	0	0	0	0	2	0
Ray Fisher, p	.500	2	2	0	1	0	0	0	0	0	0	0
Heinie Groh, 3b	.172	8	29	6	5	2	0	0	2	6	4	0
Larry Kopf, ss	.222	8	27	3	6	0	2	0	3	3	2	0
Dolf Luque, p	.000	2	1	0	0	0	0	0	0	0	1	0
Sherry Magee, ph	.500	2	2	0	1	0	0	0	0	0	0	0
Greasy Neale, of	.357	8	28	3	10	1	1	0	4	2	5	1
Bill Rariden, c	.211	5	19	0	4	0	0	0	2	0	0	1
Morrie Rath, 2b	.226	8	31	5	7	1	0	0	2	4	1	2
Jimmy Ring, p	.000	2	5	0	0	0	0	0	0	0	2	0
Edd Roush, of	.214	8	28	6	6	2	1	0	7	3	0	2
Dutch Ruether, p-2	.667	3	6	2	4	1	2	0	4	1	0	0
Slim Sallee, p	.000	2	4	0	0	0	0	0	0	0	0	0
Jimmy Smith, pr	.000	1	0	0	0	0	0	0	0	0	0	0
Ivey Wingo, c	.571	3	7	1	4	0	0	0	1	3	1	0
TOTAL	.255		251	35	64	10	7	0	34	25	22	7

PITCHER	W	L	ERA	G	GS	CG	SV	SHO	IP	H	ER	BB	SO
Hod Eller	2	0	2.00	2	2	2	0	1	18.0	13	4	2	15
Ray Fisher	0	1	2.35	2	1	0	0	0	7.2	7	2	2	2
Dolf Luque	0	0	0.00	2	0	0	0	0	5.0	1	0	0	6
Jimmy Ring	1	1	0.64	2	1	1	0	1	14.0	7	1	6	4
Dutch Ruether	1	0	2.57	2	2	1	0	0	14.0	12	4	4	1
Slim Sallee	1	1	1.35	2	2	1	0	0	13.1	19	2	1	2
TOTAL	5	3	1.63	12	8	5	0	2	72.0	59	13	15	30

CHI (A)

PLAYER/POS	AVG	G	AB	R	H	2B	3B	HR	RB	BB	SO	SB
Eddie Cicotte, p	.000	3	8	0	0	0	0	0	0	0	3	0
Eddie Collins, 2b	.226	8	31	2	7	1	0	0	1	1	2	1
Shano Collins, of	.250	4	16	2	4	1	0	0	0	0	0	0
Happy Felsch, of	.192	8	26	2	5	1	0	0	3	1	4	0
Chick Gandil, 1b	.233	8	30	1	7	0	1	0	5	1	3	1
Joe Jackson, of	.375	8	32	5	12	3	0	1	6	1	2	0
Bill James, p	.000	1	2	0	0	0	0	0	0	0	1	0
Dickie Kerr, p	.167	2	6	0	1	0	0	0	0	0	0	0
Nemo Leibold, of	.056	5	18	0	1	0	0	0	0	2	3	1
Grover Lowdermilk, p	.000	1	0	0	0	0	0	0	0	0	0	0
Byrd Lynn, c	.000	1	1	0	0	0	0	0	0	0	0	0
Erskine Mayer, p	.000	1	0	0	0	0	0	0	0	0	0	0
Fred Mc Mullin, ph	.500	2	2	0	1	0	0	0	0	0	0	0
Eddie Murphy, ph	.000	3	2	0	0	0	0	0	0	0	1	0
Swede Risberg, ss	.080	8	25	3	2	0	1	0	0	5	3	1
Ray Schalk, c	.304	8	23	1	7	0	0	0	2	4	2	1
Buck Weaver, 3b	.324	8	34	4	11	4	1	0	0	0	2	0
Roy Wilkinson, p	.000	2	2	0	0	0	0	0	0	0	1	0
Lefty Williams, p	.200	3	5	0	1	0	0	0	0	0	3	0
TOTAL	.224		263	20	59	10	3	1	17	15	30	5

PITCHER	W	L	ERA	G	GS	CG	SV	SHO	IP	H	ER	BB	SO
Eddie Cicotte	1	2	2.91	3	3	2	0	0	21.2	19	7	5	7
Bill James	0	0	5.79	1	0	0	0	0	4.2	8	3	3	2
Dickie Kerr	2	0	1.42	2	2	2	0	1	19.0	14	3	3	6
Grover Lowdermilk	0	0	9.00	1	0	0	0	0	1.0	2	1	1	0
Erskine Mayer	0	0	0.00	1	0	0	0	0	1.0	0	0	1	0
Roy Wilkinson	0	0	1.23	2	0	0	0	0	7.1	9	1	4	3
Lefty Williams	0	3	6.61	3	3	1	0	0	16.1	12	12	8	4
TOTAL	3	5	3.42	13	8	5	0	1	71.0	64	27	25	22

The Indians outscored the Robins in the Series, 21 runs to 8. Yet after losing the opener in Brooklyn, the Robins fought back to take the next two, and held the Series lead as the teams traveled to Cleveland for the next four games.

Both clubs garnered five hits in Game One, but an error, walk, single, and double gave the Indians two runs in the second and a lead they never yielded, as Stan Coveleski outlasted Rube Marquard for the win. In Game Two, both clubs increased their hit totals to seven, but the Robins bunched six of theirs into three innings for three runs, while Burleigh Grimes, only once yielding two hits in an inning, shut the Indians out. The two runs Brooklyn scored in the first inning of Game Three were all Sherry Smith needed to give the Robins their second win behind his three-hit pitching. But Brooklyn scored only twice more in the Series as the Indians swept to the championship with four wins in Cleveland.

With the Indians scoring four runs in Game Four before Brooklyn put its one run on the board, Coveleski breezed to his second five-hit Series run. Jim Bagby had it even easier the next day. The Robins tagged him for 13 hits, but not until the ninth inning were they able to put them together for a run. Meanwhile Bagby and his teammates were registering a couple of Series firsts as they moved to an eight-run lead. Right fielder Elmer Smith opened the scoring in the first inning with the first World Series grand slam, and Bagby himself homered for three more in the fourth—the first pitcher to hit a Series home run.

But the 1920 Series is best remembered for second baseman Bill Wambsganss's unassisted triple play in the fifth inning. With runners on first and second going on pitcher Clarence Mitchell's liner, Wambsganss snared the ball for the first out, stepped on second to force one runner, and tagged the runner coming in from first to retire the side.

In Game Six Duster Mails, a late-season addition to the team, shut out Brooklyn on three hits in a 1–0 squeaker over Sherry Smith. Coveleski won the clincher the next day, also via the shutout, with his third five-hitter of the Series and his third Series win.

Cleveland Indians (AL), 5;
Brooklyn Robins (NL), 2

CLE (A)

PLAYER/POS	AVG	G	AB	R	H	2B	3B	HR	RB	BB	SO	SB
Jim Bagby, p	.333	2	6	1	2	0	0	1	3	0	0	0
George Burns, 1b-4	.300	5	10	1	3	1	0	0	2	3	3	0
Ray Caldwell, p	.000	1	0	0	0	0	0	0	0	0	0	0
Stan Coveleski, p	.100	3	10	2	1	0	0	0	0	0	4	0
Joe Evans, of	.308	4	13	0	4	0	0	0	0	1	0	0
Larry Gardner, 3b	.208	7	24	1	5	1	0	0	2	1	1	0
Jack Graney, of-2	.000	3	3	0	0	0	0	0	0	0	2	0
Charlie Jamieson, of-5	.333	6	15	2	5	1	0	0	1	1	0	1
Doc Johnston, 1b	.273	5	11	1	3	0	0	0	0	2	1	1
Harry Lunte, 2b	.000	1	0	0	0	0	0	0	0	0	0	0
Duster Mails, p	.000	2	5	0	0	0	0	0	0	0	1	0
Les Nunamaker, c-1	.500	2	2	0	1	0	0	0	0	0	0	0
Steve O'Neill, c	.333	7	21	1	7	3	0	0	2	4	3	0
Joe Sewell, ss	.174	7	23	4	4	0	0	0	0	2	1	0
Elmer Smith, of	.308	5	13	1	4	0	1	1	5	1	1	0
Tris Speaker, of	.320	7	25	6	8	2	1	0	1	3	1	0
Pinch Thomas, c	.000	1	0	0	0	0	0	0	0	0	0	0
George Uhle, p	.000	2	0	0	0	0	0	0	0	0	0	0
Bill Wambsganss, 2b	.154	7	26	3	4	0	0	0	1	2	1	0
Joe Wood, of	.200	4	10	2	2	1	0	0	0	1	2	0
TOTAL	.244		217	21	53	9	2	2	17	21	21	2

PITCHER	W	L	ERA	G	GS	CG	SV	SHO	IP	H	ER	BB	SO
Jim Bagby	1	1	1.80	2	2	1	0	0	15.0	20	3	1	3
Ray Caldwell	0	1	27.00	1	1	0	0	0	0.1	2	1	1	0
Stan Coveleski	3	0	0.67	3	3	3	0	0	27.0	15	2	2	8
Duster Mails	1	0	0.00	2	1	1	0	1	15.2	6	0	6	6
George Uhle	0	0	0.00	2	0	0	0	0	3.0	1	0	0	3
TOTAL	5	2	0.89	10	7	5	0	2	61.0	44	6	10	20

BRO (N)

PLAYER/POS	AVG	G	AB	R	H	2B	3B	HR	RB	BB	SO	SB
Leon Cadore, p	.000	2	0	0	0	0	0	0	0	0	0	0
Tommy Griffith, of	.190	7	21	1	4	2	0	0	3	0	2	0
Burleigh Grimes, p	.333	3	6	1	2	0	0	0	0	0	0	0
Jimmy Johnston, 3b	.214	4	14	2	3	0	0	0	0	0	2	1
Pete Kilduff, 2b	.095	7	21	0	2	0	0	0	0	1	4	0
Ed Konetchy, 1b	.174	7	23	0	4	0	1	0	2	3	2	0
Ernie Krueger, c-3	.167	4	6	0	1	0	0	0	0	0	0	0
Bill Lamar, ph	.000	3	3	0	0	0	0	0	0	0	0	0
Al Mamaux, p	.000	3	1	0	0	0	0	0	0	0	1	0
Rube Marquard, p	.000	2	1	0	0	0	0	0	0	0	0	0
Bill Mc Cabe, pr	.000	1	0	0	0	0	0	0	0	0	0	0
Otto Miller, c	.143	6	14	0	2	0	0	0	0	0	1	2	0
Clarence Mitchell, p-1	.333	2	3	0	1	0	0	0	0	0	0	0
Hy Myers, of	.231	7	26	0	6	0	0	0	1	0	1	0
Bernie Neis, of-2	.000	4	5	0	0	0	0	0	0	1	0	0
Ivy Olson, ss	.320	7	25	2	8	1	0	0	0	3	1	0
Jeff Pfeffer, p	.000	1	1	0	0	0	0	0	0	0	0	0
Ray Schmandt, ph	.000	1	1	0	0	0	0	0	0	0	0	0
Jack Sheehan, 3b	.182	3	11	0	2	0	0	0	0	0	1	0
Sherry Smith, p	.000	2	6	0	0	0	0	0	0	0	2	0
Zack Wheat, of	.333	7	27	2	9	2	0	0	2	1	2	0
TOTAL	.205		215	8	44	5	1	0	8	10	20	1

PITCHER	W	L	ERA	G	GS	CG	SV	SHO	IP	H	ER	BB	SO
Leon Cadore	0	1	9.00	2	1	0	0	0	2.0	4	2	1	1
Burleigh Grimes	1	2	4.19	3	3	1	0	1	19.1	23	9	9	4
Al Mamaux	0	0	4.50	3	0	0	0	0	4.0	2	2	0	5
Rube Marquard	0	1	1.00	2	1	0	0	0	9.0	7	1	3	6
Clarence Mitchell	0	0	0.00	1	0	0	0	0	4.2	3	0	3	1
Jeff Pfeffer	0	0	3.00	1	0	0	0	0	3.0	4	1	2	1
Sherry Smith	1	1	0.53	2	2	2	0	1	17.0	10	1	3	3
TOTAL	2	5	2.44	14	7	3	0	1	59.0	53	16	21	21

GAME 1 AT BRO OCT 5

CLE	020	100	000	3	5	0
BRO	000	000	100	1	5	1

Pitchers: COVELESKI vs MARQUARD, Mamaux (7), Cadore (9)
Attendance: 23,753

GAME 2 AT BRO OCT 6

CLE	000	000	000	0	7	1
BRO	101	010	00X	3	7	0

Pitchers: BAGBY, Uhle (7) vs GRIMES
Attendance: 22,559

GAME 3 AT BRO OCT 7

CLE	000	100	000	1	3	1
BRO	200	000	00X	2	6	1

Pitchers: CALDWELL, Mails (1), Uhle (8) vs SMITH
Attendance: 25,088

GAME 4 AT CLE OCT 9

BRO	000	100	000	1	5	1
CLE	202	000	10X	5	12	2

Pitchers: CADORE, Mamaux (2), Marquard (3), Pfeffer (6) vs COVELESKI
Attendance: 25,734

GAME 5 AT CLE OCT 10

BRO	000	000	001	1	13	1
CLE	400	310	00X	8	12	2

Pitchers: GRIMES, Mitchell (4) vs BAGBY
Home Runs: E.Smith-CLE, Bagby-CLE
Attendance: 26,884

GAME 6 AT CLE OCT 11

BRO	000	000	000	0	3	0
CLE	000	001	00X	1	7	3

Pitchers: SMITH vs MAILS
Attendance: 27,194

GAME 7 AT CLE OCT 12

BRO	000	000	000	0	5	2
CLE	000	110	10X	3	7	3

Pitchers: GRIMES, Mamaux (8) vs COVELESKI
Attendance: 27,525

Since both the Giants and Yankees called the Polo Grounds home, all eight games were played there, with the two clubs alternating from game to game as the hometeam. Pitching dominated the first two games—especially Yankee pitching. In Game One, Giant third baseman Frank Frisch went 4 for 4 against Carl Mays. But Mays gave up only one other hit and walked no one, to fashion a shutout. The next day Art Nehf of the Giants allowed the Yankees only three singles. But the Yankees capitalized on two of them, together with one of Nehf's seven walks, a couple of Giant errors, and Bob Meusel's steal of home to score three times, as pitcher Waite Hoyt shut out the Giants on two singles to put the Yanks two up in the Series.

In Game Three the hitters finally came alive. With the score tied 4–4 in the last of the seventh, the Giants unloaded for eight hits which, with two walks and a sacrifice fly, produced eight runs and the first Giant win. They evened the Series the next day, scoring three runs in the eighth to take a 3–1 lead, adding another in the ninth. Babe Ruth's first World Series home run, a solo shot in the bottom of the ninth, thrilled the fans but had no effect on the game's outcome.

The Yankees regained the Series lead in Game Five. Waite Hoyt was not as sharp as he had been in the opener, yielding ten hits. But the only run scored against him came as the result of a first-inning error, a deficit his Yankee teammates overcame for a 3–1 win. In Game Six the Yankees took a quick 3–0 lead in the first. The Giants tied it in the top of the second on home runs by Irish Meusel and Frank Snyder, but Chick Fewster hit a two-run shot a half inning later to restore the Yankee lead. In the fourth inning, though, the Giants parlayed four singles and an error into four runs and a lead that held up for a Series-tying win.

The Yankees scored only one run the rest of the way as the Giants took the final two games on unearned runs. In Game Seven, Mays and the Giants' Phil Douglas dueled into the seventh tied 1–1. But in the last of the seventh, Giant Frank Snyder's double drove in Johnny Rawlings, who had reached on an error, for the game's deciding run. In Game Eight, Hoyt held the Giants to four hits and completed his third game without giving up an earned run. But a Giant runner had scored in the first inning when a grounder shot through the legs of shortstop Roger Peckinpaugh. It turned out to be the game's only run, as Art Nehf and his Giants'

New York Giants (NL), 5; New York Yankees (AL), 3

NY (N)

PLAYER/POS	AVG	G	AB	R	H	2B	3B	HR	RB	BB	SO	SB
Dave Bancroft, ss	.152	8	33	3	5	1	0	0	3	1	5	0
Jesse Barnes, p	.444	3	9	3	4	0	0	0	0	0	0	0
George Burns, of	.333	8	33	2	11	4	1	0	2	3	5	1
Phil Douglas, p	.000	3	7	0	0	0	0	0	0	0	2	0
Frankie Frisch, 3b	.300	8	30	5	9	0	1	0	1	4	3	3
George Kelly, 1b	.233	8	30	3	7	1	0	0	4	3	10	0
Irish Meusel, of	.345	8	29	4	10	2	1	1	7	2	3	1
Art Nehf, p	.000	3	9	0	0	0	0	0	0	1	3	0
Johnny Rawlings, 2b	.333	8	30	2	10	3	0	0	4	0	3	0
Earl Smith, c-2	.000	3	7	0	0	0	0	0	0	1	0	0
Frank Snyder, c-6	.364	7	22	4	8	1	0	1	3	0	2	0
Fred Toney, p	.000	2	0	0	0	0	0	0	0	0	0	0
Ross Youngs, of	.280	8	25	3	7	1	1	0	4	7	2	2
TOTAL	.269		264	29	71	13	4	2	28	22	38	7

PITCHER	W	L	ERA	G	GS	CG	SV	SHO	IP	H	ER	BB	SO
Jesse Barnes	2	0	1.65	3	0	0	0	0	16.1	10	3	6	18
Phil Douglas	2	1	2.08	3	3	2	0	0	26.0	20	6	5	17
Art Nehf	1	2	1.38	3	3	3	0	1	26.0	13	4	13	8
Fred Toney	0	0	23.63	2	2	0	0	0	2.2	7	7	3	1
TOTAL	5	3	2.54	11	8	5	0	1	71.0	50	20	27	44

NY (A)

PLAYER/POS	AVG	G	AB	R	H	2B	3B	HR	RB	BB	SO	SB
Frank Baker, 3b-2	.250	4	8	0	2	0	0	0	0	1	0	0
Rip Collins, p	.000	1	0	0	0	0	0	0	0	0	0	0
Al De Vormer, c-1	.000	2	1	0	0	0	0	0	0	0	0	0
Chick Fewster, of	.200	4	10	3	2	0	0	1	2	3	3	0
Harry Harper, p	.000	1	0	0	0	0	0	0	0	0	0	0
Waite Hoyt, p	.222	3	9	0	2	0	0	0	0	1	0	1
Carl Mays, p	.111	3	9	0	1	0	0	0	0	0	1	0
Mike Mc Nally, 3b	.200	7	20	3	4	1	0	0	1	1	3	2
Bob Meusel, of	.200	8	30	3	6	2	0	0	3	2	5	1
Elmer Miller, of	.161	8	31	3	5	1	0	0	2	5	5	0
Roger Peckinpaugh, ss	.179	8	28	2	5	1	0	0	0	4	3	0
Bill Piercy, p	.000	1	0	0	0	0	0	0	00	0	0	0
Wally Pipp, 1b	.154	8	26	1	4	1	0	0	2	2	3	1
Jack Quinn, p	.000	1	2	0	0	0	0	0	0	0	1	0
Tom Rogers, p	.000	1	0	0	0	0	0	0	0	0	0	0
Babe Ruth, of	.313	6	16	3	5	0	0	1	4	5	8	2
Wally Schang, c	.286	8	21	1	6	1	1	0	1	5	4	0
Bob Shawkey, p	.500	2	4	2	2	0	0	0	0	0	1	0
Aaron Ward, 2b	.231	8	26	1	6	0	0	0	4	2	6	0
TOTAL	.207		241	22	50	7	1	2	20	27	44	6

PITCHER	W	L	ERA	G	GS	CG	SV	SHO	IP	H	ER	BB	SO
Rip Collins	0	0	54.00	1	0	0	0	0	0.2	4	4	1	0
Harry Harper	0	0	20.25	1	1	0	0	0	1.1	3	3	2	1
Waite Hoyt	2	1	0.00	3	3	3	0	1	27.0	18	0	11	18
Carl Mays	1	2	1.73	3	3	3	0	1	26.0	20	5	0	9
Bill Piercy	0	0	0.00	1	0	0	0	0	1.0	2	0	0	2
Jack Quinn	0	1	9.82	1	0	0	0	0	3.2	8	4	2	2
Tom Rogers	0	0	6.75	1	0	0	0	0	1.1	3	1	0	1
Bob Shawkey	0	1	7.00	2	1	0	0	0	9.0	13	7	6	5
TOTAL	3	5	3.09	13	8	6	0	2	70.0	71	24	22	38

flawless fielding blanked the Yankees to give manager John McGraw his first world championship since 1905.

GAME 1 AT NY -N OCT 5

NY-A	100 011 000	3	7	0
NY-N	000 000 000	0	5	0

Pitchers: MAYS vs DOUGLAS, Barnes (9)
Attendance: 30,202

GAME 2 AT NY -A OCT 6

NY-N	000 000 000	0	2	3
NY-A	000 100 02X	3	3	0

Pitchers: NEHF vs HOYT
Attendance: 34,939

GAME 3 AT NY -N OCT 7

NY-A	004 000 010	5	8	0
NY-N	004 000 81X	13	20	0

Pitchers: Shawkey, QUINN (3), Collins (7), Rogers (8) vs Toney, BARNES (3)
Attendance: 36,509

GAME 4 AT NY -A OCT 9

NY-N	000 000 031	4	9	1
NY-A	000 010 001	2	7	1

Pitchers: DOUGLAS vs MAYS
Home Runs: Ruth-NY(A)
Attendance: 36,372

GAME 5 AT NY -N OCT 10

NY-A	001 200 000	3	6	1
NY-N	100 000 000	1	10	1

Pitchers: HOYT vs NEHF
Attendance: 35,758

GAME 6 AT NY -A OCT 11

NY-N	030 401 000	8	13	0
NY-A	320 000 000	5	7	2

Pitchers: Toney, BARNES (1) vs Harper, SHAWKEY (2), Piercy (9)
Home Runs: E.Meusel-NY(N), Snyder-NY(N), Fewster-NY(A)
Attendance: 34,283

GAME 7 AT NY -N OCT 12

NY-A	010 000 000	1	8	1
NY-N	000 100 10X	2	6	0

Pitchers: MAYS vs DOUGLAS
Attendance: 36,503

GAME 8 AT NY -A OCT 13

NY-N	100 000 000	1	6	0
NY-A	000 000 000	0	4	1

Pitchers: NEHF vs HOYT
Attendance: 25,410

The Giants didn't quite sweep the Series—a tie in Game Two interrupted their string of victories—but they shut down the Yankee offense, holding Yankee scoring to three runs or less per game, and Babe Ruth to two hits and a .118 BA. This Series restored the best-of-seven-games format after three years of best-of-nine.

The Giants had to come from behind to take Game One. Yankee Bullet Joe Bush and Giant Art Nehf hurled shutout ball through five innings before the Yankees scored single runs in the sixth and seventh innings (Ruth driving in the Series' first run for the second year in a row with his single in the sixth). But in the eighth, Bush gave up four straight singles and two runs before Waite Hoyt relieved him with the score tied and men on first and third. Hoyt set down all three men he faced, but the first out—Ross Youngs's fly to center—drove in what proved to be the Giants' winning run.

The Giants led off Game Two with three first-inning runs on Irish Meusel's home run, but scored no more as Bob Shawkey stopped them for nine innings while his Yankees picked up runs in the first, fourth (on Aaron Ward's homer), and eighth to tie it all up. At the end of the tenth, with forty-five minutes left before sundown, the umpires called the game for darkness and provoked a storm of seat cushions and bottles from the stands.

The Giants resumed their winning ways in Game Three behind Jack Scott's shutout. Scott—picked up by the Giants in mid-season—gave up only four Yankee hits, walking one, in the Series' top pitching performance. In Game Four the Yankees scored twice in the first inning, but in the fifth the Giants pounced on Carl Mays for four hits and two runs before the first out was recorded. Before the inning ended, a ground out and another hit had brought two more Giants across the plate, enough to survive Aaron Ward's second Series home run for a 4–3 win.

Game Five, the clincher, showed Nehf the winner by two runs at game's end, but the game went back and forth before the outcome was decided. Nehf gave up only five hits—all singles—but all of them contributed toward scoring Yankee runs in the first, fifth, and seventh innings. The Giants took the lead in the second with a pair of runs, but again fell behind until four hits and a walk in the eighth undid Yankee pitcher Joe Bush's fine effort, giving the Giants three additional runs and John McGraw his third world title.

New York Giants (NL), 4;
New York Yankees (AL), 0; tie, 1

NY (N)

PLAYER/POS	AVG	G	AB	R	H	2B	3B	HR	RB	BB	SO	SB
Dave Bancroft, ss	.211	5	19	4	4	0	0	0	2	2	1	0
Jesse Barnes, p	.000	1	4	0	0	0	0	0	0	0	1	0
Bill Cunningham, of	.200	4	10	0	2	0	0	0	2	2	1	0
Frankie Frisch, 2b	.471	5	17	3	8	1	0	0	2	1	0	1
Heinie Groh, 3b	.474	5	19	4	9	0	1	0	0	2	1	0
George Kelly, 1b	.278	5	18	0	5	0	0	0	2	0	3	0
Lee King, of	1.000	2	1	0	1	0	0	0	1	0	0	0
Hugh Mc Quillan, p	.250	1	4	1	1	1	0	0	0	0	0	0
Irish Meusel, of	.250	5	20	3	5	0	0	1	7	0	1	0
Art Nehf, p	.000	2	3	0	0	0	0	0	0	2	0	0
Rosy Ryan, p	.000	1	0	0	0	0	0	0	0	0	0	0
Jack Scott, p	.250	1	4	0	1	0	0	0	0	0	1	0
Earl Smith, c-1	.143	4	7	0	1	0	0	0	0	0	2	0
Frank Snyder, c	.333	4	15	1	5	0	0	0	0	0	1	0
Casey Stengel, of	.400	2	5	0	2	0	0	0	0	0	1	0
Ross Youngs, of	.375	5	16	2	6	0	0	0	2	3	1	0
TOTAL	.309		162	18	50	2	1	1	18	12	15	1

PITCHER	W	L	ERA	G	GS	CG	SV	SHO	IP	H	ER	BB	SO
Jesse Barnes	0	0	1.80	1	1	1	0	0	10.0	8	2	2	6
Hugh Mc Quillan	1	0	3.00	1	1	1	0	0	9.0	8	3	2	4
Art Nehf	1	0	2.25	2	2	1	0	0	16.0	11	4	3	6
Rosy Ryan	1	0	0.00	1	0	0	0	0	2.0	1	0	0	2
Jack Scott	1	0	0.00	1	1	1	0	1	9.0	4	0	1	2
TOTAL	4	0	1.76	6	5	4	0	1	46.0	32	9	8	20

NY (A)

PLAYER/POS	AVG	G	AB	R	H	2B	3B	HR	RB	BB	SO	SB
Frank Baker, ph	.000	1	1	0	0	0	0	0	0	0	0	0
Joe Bush, p	.167	2	6	0	1	0	0	0	1	0	0	0
Joe Dugan, 3b	.250	5	20	4	5	1	0	0	0	0	1	0
Waite Hoyt, p	.500	2	2	0	1	0	0	0	0	0	0	0
Sam Jones, p	.000	1	2	0	0	0	0	0	0	0	0	0
Carl Mays, p	.000	1	2	0	0	0	0	0	0	0	0	0
Norm Mc Millan, of	.000	1	2	0	0	0	0	0	0	0	0	0
Mike Mc Nally, 2b	.000	1	0	0	0	0	0	0	0	0	0	0
Bob Meusel, of	.300	5	20	2	6	1	0	0	2	1	3	1
Wally Pipp, 1b	.286	5	21	0	6	1	0	0	3	0	2	1
Babe Ruth, of	.118	5	17	1	2	1	0	0	1	2	3	0
Wally Schang, c	.188	5	16	0	3	1	0	0	0	0	3	0
Everett Scott, ss	.143	5	14	0	2	0	0	0	1	1	0	0
Bob Shawkey, p	.000	1	4	0	0	0	0	0	0	0	1	0
Elmer Smith, ph	.000	2	2	0	0	0	0	0	0	0	2	0
Aaron Ward, 2b	.154	5	13	3	2	0	0	2	3	3	3	0
Whitey Witt, of	.222	5	18	1	4	1	1	0	0	1	2	0
TOTAL	.203		158	11	32	6	1	2	11	8	20	2

PITCHER	W	L	ERA	G	GS	CG	SV	SHO	IP	H	ER	BB	SO
Joe Bush	0	2	4.80	2	2	1	0	0	15.0	21	8	5	6
Waite Hoyt	0	1	1.13	2	1	0	0	0	8.0	11	1	2	4
Sam Jones	0	0	0.00	2	0	0	0	0	2.0	1	0	1	0
Carl Mays	0	1	4.50	1	1	0	0	0	8.0	9	4	2	1
Bob Shawkey	0	0	2.70	1	1	1	0	0	10.0	8	3	2	4
TOTAL	0	4	3.35	8	5	2	0	0	43.0	50	16	12	15

GAME 1 AT NY -N OCT 4

NY-A	000 001 100		2	7	0
NY-N	000 000 03X		3	11	3

Pitchers: BUSH, Hoyt (8) vs Nehf, RYAN (8)
Attendance: 36,514

GAME 2 AT NY -A OCT 5

NY-N	300 000 000 0		3	8	1
NY-A	100 100 010 0		3	8	0

Pitchers: Barnes vs Shawkey
Home Runs: E.Meusel-NY(N), Ward-NY(A)
Attendance: 37,020

GAME 3 AT NY -N OCT 6

NY-A	000 000 000		0	4	1
NY-N	002 000 10X		3	12	1

Pitchers: HOYT, Jones (8) vs J.SCOTT
Attendance: 37,620

GAME 4 AT NY -A OCT 7

NY-N	000 040 000		4	9	1
NY-A	200 000 100		3	8	0

Pitchers: McQUILLAN vs MAYS, Jones (9)
Home Runs: Ward-NY(A)
Attendance: 36,242

GAME 5 AT NY -N OCT 8

NY-A	100 010 100		3	5	0
NY-N	020 000 03X		5	10	0

Pitchers: BUSH vs NEHF
Attendance: 38,551

After two Series played entirely in the Polo Grounds, the Giants and Yankees in 1923 had Yankee Stadium across the river to play alternate games in. Celebrating the opener in the new "house that Ruth built," the Yankees took an early three-run lead. In the third inning, though, the Giants drove out starter Waite Hoyt, emerging with four runs. Yankee reliever Joe Bush prevented further Giant scoring for several innings as the Yankees picked up a tying run in the seventh. But with the game still knotted in the top of the ninth, Giant Casey Stengel legged out an inside-the-park homer to win it.

Babe Ruth gave Herb Pennock his first World Series win with a pair of homers in Game Two. The first, a solo blast over the roof in right, broke a 1–1 tie in the fourth, and the second, an inning later, concluded Yankee scoring in their 4–2 win that evened the Series. Stengel sent the Giants ahead in the seventh inning of Game Three, lifting a home run over the fence this time for the game's only score. The run gave Art Nehf the win in his duel with Sad Sam Jones, and again gave the Giants the Series lead.

Giant Ross Youngs's fourth hit of Game Four, an inside-the-park homer into the Polo Grounds' deep outfield, gave the Giants a fourth run to lead off the bottom of the ninth, but as a rally it fell short; the Yankees, who had already scored eight, took the game to even the Series. In Game Five Joe Bush gave up only three Giant hits—a single, double, and triple to Irish Meusel. Irish scored the only Giant run, but his Yankee brother Bob drove in three runs with his three hits—sharing RBI honors with Joe Dugan, whose four hits included the Series' third inside-the-park home run, a three-run shot in the second inning. Final score: 8–1.

In Game Six, Herb Pennock yielded four Giant runs in his seven innings on the mound and seemed on the edge of defeat. But in the top of the eighth, Art Nehf (who had pitched one-hit ball since Ruth homered for a Yankee run in the first) lost his stuff. With one out, two singles followed by two walks (on eight pitches) forced in a run. Rosy Ryan replaced Nehf and walked in another run. Ruth struck out, but Bob Meusel's single and a wild throw from center cleared the bases to put the Yankees ahead 6–4, where they remained to game's end for the first of their twenty-two world championships.

New York Yankees (AL), 4; New York Giants (NL), 2

NY (A)

PLAYER/POS	AVG	G	AB	R	H	2B	3B	HR	RB	BB	SO	SB
Joe Bush, p-3	.429	4	7	2	3	1	0	0	1	1	1	0
Joe Dugan, 3b	.280	6	25	5	7	2	1	1	5	3	0	0
Hinky Haines, of	.000	2	1	1	0	0	0	0	0	0	0	0
Harvey Hendrick, ph	.000	1	1	0	0	0	0	0	0	0	0	0
Fred Hoffmann, ph	.000	2	1	0	0	0	0	0	0	0	1	0
Waite Hoyt, p	.000	1	1	0	0	0	0	0	0	0	1	0
Ernie Johnson, ss-1	.000	2	0	1	0	0	0	0	0	0	0	0
Sam Jones, p	.000	2	2	0	0	0	0	0	0	0	1	0
Bob Meusel, of	.269	6	26	1	7	1	2	0	8	0	3	0
Herb Pennock, p	.000	3	6	0	0	0	0	0	0	0	2	0
Wally Pipp, 1b	.250	6	20	2	5	0	0	0	2	4	1	0
Babe Ruth, of-6,1b-1	.368	6	19	8	7	1	1	3	3	8	6	0
Wally Schang, c	.318	6	22	3	7	1	0	0	0	1	2	0
Everett Scott, ss	.318	6	22	2	7	0	0	0	3	0	1	0
Bob Shawkey, p	.333	1	3	0	1	0	0	0	0	1	0	0
Aaron Ward, 2b	.417	6	24	4	10	0	0	1	2	1	3	1
Whitey Witt, of	.240	6	25	1	6	2	0	0	4	1	1	0
TOTAL	.293		205	30	60	8	4	5	29	20	22	1

PITCHER	W	L	ERA	G	GS	CG	SV	SHO	IP	H	ER	BB	SO
Joe Bush	1	1	1.08	3	1	1	0	0	16.2	7	2	4	5
Waite Hoyt	0	0	15.43	1	1	0	0	0	2.1	4	4	1	0
Sam Jones	0	1	0.90	2	1	0	1	0	10.0	5	1	2	3
Herb Pennock	2	0	3.63	3	2	1	1	0	17.1	19	7	1	8
Bob Shawkey	1	0	3.52	1	1	0	0	0	7.2	12	3	4	2
TOTAL	4	2	2.83	10	6	2	2	0	54.0	47	17	12	18

NY (N)

PLAYER/POS	AVG	G	AB	R	H	2B	3B	HR	RB	BB	SO	SB
Dave Bancroft, ss	.083	6	24	1	2	0	0	0	1	1	2	1
Virgil Barnes, p	.000	2	1	0	0	0	0	0	0	0	1	0
Jack Bentley, p	.600	5	5	0	3	1	0	0	0	0	0	0
Bill Cunningham, of-3	.143	4	7	0	1	0	0	0	0	1	0	1
Frankie Frisch, 2b	.400	6	25	2	10	0	1	0	1	0	0	0
Dinty Gearin, pr	.000	1	0	0	0	0	0	0	0	0	0	0
Hank Gowdy, c-2	.000	3	4	0	0	0	0	0	0	1	0	0
Heinie Groh, 3b	.182	6	22	3	4	0	1	0	2	3	1	0
Travis Jackson, ph	.000	1	1	0	0	0	0	0	0	0	0	0
Claude Jonnard, p	.000	2	0	0	0	0	0	0	0	0	0	0
George Kelly, 1b	.182	6	22	1	4	0	0	0	1	1	2	0
Freddie Maguire, pr	.000	2	0	1	0	0	0	0	0	0	0	0
Hugh Mc Quillan, p	.000	2	3	0	0	0	0	0	0	0	1	0
Irish Meusel, of	.280	6	25	3	7	1	1	1	2	0	2	0
Art Nehf, p	.167	2	6	0	1	0	0	0	0	0	4	0
Jimmy O'Connell, ph	.000	2	1	0	0	0	0	0	0	0	1	0
Rosy Ryan, p	.000	3	2	0	0	0	0	0	0	0	1	0
Jack Scott, p	.000	2	1	0	0	0	0	0	0	0	0	0
Frank Snyder, c	.118	5	17	1	2	0	0	1	2	0	2	0
Casey Stengel, of	.417	6	12	3	5	0	0	2	4	4	0	0
Mule Watson, p	.000	1	0	0	0	0	0	0	0	0	0	0
Ross Youngs, of	.348	6	23	2	8	0	1	3	2	0	0	0
TOTAL	.234		201	17	47	2	3	5	17	12	18	1

PITCHER	W	L	ERA	G	GS	CG	SV	SHO	IP	H	ER	BB	SO
Virgil Barnes	0	0	0.00	2	0	0	0	0	4.2	4	0	0	4
Jack Bentley	0	1	9.45	2	1	0	0	0	6.2	10	7	4	1
Claude Jonnard	0	0	0.00	2	0	0	0	0	2.0	1	0	1	1
Hugh Mc Quillan	0	1	5.00	2	1	0	0	0	9.0	11	5	4	3
Art Nehf	1	1	2.76	2	2	1	0	1	16.1	10	5	6	7
Rosy Ryan	1	0	0.96	3	0	0	0	0	9.1	11	1	3	3
Jack Scott	0	1	12.00	2	1	0	0	0	3.0	9	4	1	2
Mule Watson	0	0	13.50	1	1	0	0	0	2.0	4	3	1	1
TOTAL	2	4	4.25	16	6	1	0	1	53.0	60	25	20	22

GAME 1 AT NY -A OCT 10

NY-N	004 000 001	5	8 0
NY-A	120 000 100	4	12 1

Pitchers: Watson, RYAN (3) vs Hoyt, BUSH (3)
Home Runs: Stengel-NY(N)
Attendance: 55,307

GAME 2 AT NY -N OCT 11

NY-A	010 210 000	4	10 0
NY-N	010 001 000	2	9 2

Pitchers: PENNOCK vs McQUILLAN, Bentley (4)
Home Runs: Ward-NY(A), E.Meusel-NY(N), Ruth-NY(A) (2)
Attendance: 40,402

GAME 3 AT NY -A OCT 12

NY-N	000 000 100	1	4 0
NY-A	000 000 000	0	6 1

Pitchers: NEHF vs JONES, Bush (8)
Home Runs: Stengel-NY(N)
Attendance: 62,430

GAME 4 AT NY -N OCT 13

NY-A	061 100 000	8	13 1
NY-N	000 000 031	4	13 1

Pitchers: SHAWKEY, Pennock (8) vs J.SCOTT, Ryan (2), McQuillan (3), Jonnard (8), Barnes (9)
Home Runs: Youngs-NY(N)
Attendance: 46,302

GAME 5 AT NY -A OCT 14

NY-N	010 000 000	1	3 2
NY-A	340 100 00X	8	14 0

Pitchers: BENTLEY, J.Scott (2), Barnes (4), Jonnard (8) vs BUSH
Home Runs: Dugan-NY(A)
Attendance: 62,817

GAME 6 AT NY -N OCT 15

NY-A	100 000 050	6	5 0
NY-N	100 111 000	4	10 1

Pitchers: PENNOCK, Jones (8) vs NEHF, Ryan (8)
Home Runs: Ruth-NY(A), Snyder-NY(N)
Attendance: 34,172

Four of the seven games in this exciting Series were decided by one run—two of them after twelve innings. Pitcher Walter Johnson, in his first World Series after eighteen big-league seasons and 376 victories, opened for Washington against the Giants' Art Nehf. Although fourteen Giants reached base on hits or walks in the first nine innings, only two scored—George Kelly and Bill Terry, both of whom homered. In the bottom of the ninth, the Senators scored their second run to send the game into extra innings. Johnson shut out the Giants for two more frames, but in the top of the twelfth, two walks and three singles put New York ahead by two. Washington came back with a run and had a man on third. But Kelly at second base stopped Goose Goslin's grounder with his bare hand, and Nehf had the Giants' first win.

Goslin and manager/second baseman Bucky Harris homered in Game Two to give the Senators a 3–0 lead through six innings. The Giants scored once in the seventh and drove out starter Tom Zachary with two more in the ninth to tie the game, but in the last of the ninth Senator Roger Peckinpaugh doubled in the tie breaker to even the Series.

The Giants took an early lead in Game Three and held it to retake the Series lead, but Washington (led by Goslin's three-run homer in the third) unleashed a 13-hit, seven-run attack the next day to even the Series once more. In Game Five, though, New York pulled ahead again, defeating Johnson a second time as winning pitcher Jack Bentley put the Giants into the lead for good with a two-run homer in the fifth. In Game Six, Washington's two runs in the fifth inning overcame a first-inning Giant run and gave Tom Zachary all he needed for the Senators' third win, which set the stage for one of the most memorable games in Series history.

Washington scored first in Game Seven on manager Harris's homer in the fourth inning, but the Giants scored three runs in the sixth (two of them on Senator errors) to go ahead 3–1. In the last of the eighth, though, Harris's grounder to third bounced over the head of rookie Freddie Lindstrom for two more Senator runs and a 3–3 tie. Walter Johnson came in to face the Giants in the ninth, and shut them out through the twelfth, fanning five. Then in the bottom of the twelfth, with one out, Muddy Ruel (given a second chance after Giant catcher Hank Gowdy caught his foot in his mask and missed Ruel's pop foul) doubled to left. Pitcher Johnson then reached first when

Washington Senators (AL), 4; New York Giants (NL), 3

WAS (A)

PLAYER/POS	AVG	G	AB	R	H	2B	3B	HR	RB	BB	SO	SB
Ossie Bluege, ss-5,3b-4	.192	7	26	2	5	0	0	0	2	3	4	1
Goose Goslin, of	.344	7	32	4	11	1	0	3	7	0	7	0
Bucky Harris, 2b	.333	7	33	5	11	0	0	2	7	1	4	0
Walter Johnson, p	.111	3	9	0	1	0	0	0	0	0	0	0
Joe Judge, 1b	.385	7	26	4	10	1	0	0	0	5	2	0
Nemo Leibold, of-1	.167	3	6	1	1	1	0	0	0	1	0	0
Firpo Marberry, p	.000	4	2	0	0	0	0	0	0	0	0	0
Joe Martina, p	.000	1	0	0	0	0	0	0	0	0	0	0
Earl Mc Neely, of	.222	7	27	4	6	3	0	0	1	4	4	1
Ralph Miller, 3b	.182	4	11	0	2	0	0	0	2	1	0	0
George Mogridge, p	.000	2	5	0	0	0	0	0	0	0	5	0
Curly Ogden, p	.000	1	0	0	0	0	0	0	0	0	0	0
Roger Peckinpaugh, ss	.417	4	12	1	5	2	0	0	2	1	0	1
Sam Rice, of	.207	7	29	2	6	0	0	0	1	3	2	2
Muddy Ruel, c	.095	7	21	2	2	1	0	0	0	6	1	0
Allan Russell, p	.000	1	0	0	0	0	0	0	0	0	0	0
Mule Shirley, ph	.500	3	2	1	1	0	0	0	1	0	0	0
By Speece, p	.000	1	0	0	0	0	0	0	0	0	0	0
Bennie Tate, ph	.000	3	0	0	0	0	0	0	1	3	0	0
Tommy Taylor, 3b	.000	3	2	0	0	0	0	0	0	0	2	0
Tom Zachary, p	.000	2	5	0	0	0	0	0	0	1	3	0
TOTAL	.246		248	26	61	9	0	5	24	29	34	5

PITCHER	W	L	ERA	G	GS	CG	SV	SHO	IP	H	ER	BB	SO
Walter Johnson	1	2	2.25	3	2	2	0	0	24.0	30	6	11	20
Firpo Marberry	0	1	1.13	4	1	0	2	0	8.0	9	1	4	10
Joe Martina	0	0	0.00	1	0	0	0	0	1.0	0	0	0	1
George Mogridge	1	0	2.25	2	2	0	0	0	12.0	7	3	6	5
Curly Ogden	0	0	0.00	1	1	0	0	0	0.1	0	0	1	1
Allan Russell	0	0	3.00	1	0	0	0	0	3.0	4	1	0	0
By Speece	0	0	9.00	1	0	0	0	0	1.0	3	1	0	0
Tom Zachary	2	0	2.04	2	2	1	0	0	17.2	13	4	3	3
TOTAL	4	3	2.15	15	7	3	2	0	67.0	66	16	25	40

NY (N)

PLAYER/POS	AVG	G	AB	R	H	2B	3B	HR	RB	BB	SO	SB
Harry Baldwin, p	.000	1	0	0	0	0	0	0	0	0	0	0
Virgil Barnes, p	.000	2	4	0	0	0	0	0	0	1	2	0
Jack Bentley, p-3	.286	5	7	1	2	0	0	1	2	1	1	0
Wayland Dean, p	.000	1	0	0	0	0	0	0	0	0	0	0
Frankie Frisch, 2b-7,3b-1	.333	7	30	1	10	4	1	0	0	4	1	1
Hank Gowdy, c	.259	7	27	4	7	0	0	1	2	2	2	0
Heinie Groh, ph	1.000	1	1	0	1	0	0	0	0	0	0	0
Travis Jackson, ss	.074	7	27	3	2	0	0	0	1	1	4	1
Claude Jonnard, p	.000	1	0	0	0	0	0	0	0	0	0	0
George Kelly, 1b-4,of-4,2b-1	.290	7	31	7	9	1	0	1	4	1	8	0
Fred Lindstrom, 3b	.333	7	30	1	10	2	0	0	4	3	6	0
Hugh Mc Quillan, p	1.000	3	1	0	1	0	0	0	1	1	0	0
Irish Meusel, of	.154	4	13	0	2	0	0	0	1	2	0	0
Art Nehf, p	.429	3	7	1	3	0	0	0	0	0	1	0
Rosy Ryan, p	.500	2	2	1	1	0	0	1	2	0	0	0
Frank Snyder, ph	.000	1	1	0	0	0	0	0	0	0	0	0
Billy Southworth, of-2	.000	5	1	0	0	0	0	0	0	0	0	0
Bill Terry, 1b-4	.429	5	14	3	6	0	1	1	1	3	1	0
Mule Watson, p	.000	1	0	0	0	0	0	0	0	0	0	0
Hack Wilson, of	.233	7	30	1	7	1	0	0	3	1	9	0
Ross Youngs, of	.185	7	27	3	5	1	0	0	2	5	6	1
TOTAL	.261		253	27	66	9	2	4	22	25	40	3

PITCHER	W	L	ERA	G	GS	CG	SV	SHO	IP	H	ER	BB	SO
Harry Baldwin	0	0	0.00	1	0	0	0	0	2.0	1	0	0	1
Virgil Barnes	0	1	5.68	2	2	0	0	0	12.2	15	8	1	9
Jack Bentley	1	2	3.71	3	2	1	0	0	17.0	18	7	8	10
Wayland Dean	0	0	4.50	1	0	0	0	0	2.0	3	1	0	2
Claude Jonnard	0	0	INF	1	0	0	0	0	0.0	0	0	1	0
Hugh Mc Quillan	0	0	2.57	3	1	0	1	0	7.0	2	2	6	2
Art Nehf	1	1	1.83	3	2	1	0	0	19.2	15	4	9	7
Rosy Ryan	1	0	3.18	2	0	0	0	0	5.2	7	2	4	3
Mule Watson	0	0	0.00	1	0	0	1	0	0.2	0	0	0	0
TOTAL	3	4	3.24	17	7	2	2	0	66.2	61	24	29	34

shortstop Travis Jackson bobbled what ought to have been a third-out grounder. With men on second and first, Earl McNeely bounced to Lindstrom at third. But again the ball bounded over Lindstrom's head, and Ruel raced home with Johnson's first Series win and Washington's first world championship.

GAME 1 AT WAS OCT 4

NY	010 100 000 002	4	14	1
WAS	000 001 001 001	3	10	1

Pitchers: NEHF vs JOHNSON
Home Runs: Kelly-NY, Terry-NY
Attendance: 35,760

GAME 2 AT WAS OCT 5

NY	000 000 102	3	6	0
WAS	200 010 001	4	6	1

Pitchers: BENTLEY vs ZACHARY, Marberry (9)
Home Runs: Goslin-WAS, Harris-WAS
Attendance: 35,922

GAME 3 AT NY OCT 6

WAS	000 200 011	4	9	2
NY	021 101 01X	6	12	0

Pitchers: MARBERRY, Russell (4), Martina (7), Speece (8) vs McQuillan, RYAN (9), Jonnard (9), Watson (9)
Home Runs: Ryan-NY
Attendance: 47,608

GAME 4 AT NY OCT 7

WAS	003 020 020	7	13	3
NY	100 001 011	4	6	1

Pitchers: MOGRIDGE, Marberry (8) vs BARNES, Baldwin (6), Dean (8)
Home Runs: Goslin-WAS
Attendance: 49,243

GAME 5 AT NY OCT 8

WAS	000 100 010	2	9	1
NY	001 020 03X	6	13	0

Pitchers: JOHNSON vs BENTLEY, McQuillan (8)
Home Runs: Bentley-NY, Goslin-WAS
Attendance: 49,211

GAME 6 AT WAS OCT 9

NY	100 000 000	1	7	1
WAS	000 020 00X	2	4	0

Pitchers: NEHF, Ryan (8) vs ZACHARY
Attendance: 34,254

GAME 7 AT WAS OCT 10

NY	000 003 000 000	3	8	3
WAS	000 100 020 001	4	10	4

Pitchers: Barnes, McQuillan (8), Nehf (10), BENTLEY (11) vs Ogden, Mogridge (1), Marberry (6), JOHNSON (9)
Home Runs: Harris-WAS
Attendance: 31,667

Repeating as pennant winners, the Senators found themselves again locked in a tight Series, this time with the Pirates, who hadn't won a pennant since 1909. Again Walter Johnson pitched the Series opener, winning this time with a strong five-hit, ten-strikeout performance, giving up only one run on Pie Traynor's homer in the fifth. Home runs by Pirates Kiki Cuyler and Glenn Wright and Senator Joe Judge accounted for four of the five runs scored in Game Two, in which Pirate Vic Aldridge dueled Senator Stan Coveleski to a narrow 3–2 win, evening the Series.

Washington took Games Three and Four, though, for a 3–1 Series advantage, Goose Goslin's solo homer in the sixth inning providing the margin of victory in Game Three, and homers by Goslin (for three runs) and Joe Harris the next day providing all the scoring as Johnson shut the Pirates out.

Harris hit his third Series homer in Game Five, but Pirate bats overwhelmed Coveleski as he lost to Aldridge for a second time. And although Goslin's third homer gave the Senators an early lead in Game Six, Pittsburgh's Ray Kremer shut Washington out from the third inning on as his teammates pulled even with two runs in the bottom of the third, and Eddie Moore's homer in the fifth gave him the run he needed for a win that sent the Series into a seventh game.

Both clubs went with their best in the finale as Johnson, winner of Games One and Four, faced Aldridge, victor in Games Two and Five. But Aldridge was wild, issuing three walks and two wild pitches in addition to two hits before being yanked with only one out in the top of the first. Johnson was hardly more effective: although he lasted the whole game, he gave up 15 hits and five earned runs. But if there was a Series goat, it would have to be Senator shortstop Roger Peckinpaugh, the American League MVP. Though he drove in a run in the first and homered for another in the eighth, his dropped pop fly in the seventh and wild throw in the eighth (his seventh and eighth errors of the Series) opened the way to four unearned runs and Pittsburgh's 9–7 triumph.

Pittsburgh Pirates (NL), 4;
Washington Senators (AL), 3

PIT (N)

PLAYER/POS	AVG	G	AB	R	H	2B	3B	HR	RB	BB	SO	SB
Babe Adams, p	.000	1	0	0	0	0	0	0	0	0	0	0
Vic Aldridge, p	.000	3	7	0	0	0	0	0	0	0	0	0
Clyde Barnhart, of	.250	7	28	1	7	1	0	0	5	3	5	1
Carson Bigbee, of-1	.333	4	3	1	1	1	0	0	1	0	0	1
Max Carey, of	.458	7	24	6	11	4	0	0	2	2	3	3
Kiki Cuyler, of	.269	7	26	3	7	3	0	1	6	1	4	0
Johnny Gooch, c	.000	3	3	0	0	0	0	0	0	0	0	0
George Grantham, 1b-4	.133	5	15	0	2	0	0	0	0	0	3	1
Ray Kremer, p	.143	3	7	0	1	0	0	0	1	0	5	0
Stuffy Mc Innis, 1b-3	.286	4	14	0	4	0	0	0	1	0	2	0
Lee Meadows, p	.000	1	1	0	0	0	0	0	0	1	1	0
Eddie Moore, 2b	.231	7	26	7	6	1	0	1	2	5	2	0
Johnny Morrison, p	.500	3	2	1	1	0	0	0	0	0	0	0
Red Oldham, p	.000	1	0	0	0	0	0	0	0	0	0	0
Earl Smith, c	.350	6	20	0	7	1	0	0	0	1	2	0
Pie Traynor, 3b	.346	7	26	2	9	0	2	1	4	3	1	1
Glenn Wright, ss	.185	7	27	3	5	1	0	1	3	1	4	0
Emil Yde, p-1	.000	2	1	0	0	0	0	0	0	0	0	0
TOTAL	.265		230	25	61	12	2	4	25	17	32	7

PITCHER	W	L	ERA	G	GS	CG	SV	SHO	IP	H	ER	BB	SO
Babe Adams	0	0	0.00	1	0	0	0	0	1.0	2	0	0	0
Vic Aldridge	2	0	4.42	3	3	2	0	0	18.1	18	9	9	9
Ray Kremer	2	-1	3.00	3	2	2	0	0	21.0	17	7	4	9
Lee Meadows	0	1	3.38	1	0	0	0	0	8.0	6	3	0	4
Johnny Morrison	0	0	2.89	3	1	0	0	0	9.1	11	3	1	7
Red Oldham	0	0	0.00	1	0	0	1	0	1.0	0	0	0	2
Emil Yde	0	1	11.57	1	1	0	0	0	2.1	5	3	3	1
TOTAL	4	1	3.69	13	7	4	1	0	61.0	59	25	17	32

WAS (A)

PLAYER/POS	AVG	G	AB	R	H	2B	3B	HR	RB	BB	SO	SB
Spencer Adams, 2b-1	.000	2	1	0	0	0	0	0	0	0	0	0
Win Ballou, p	.000	2	0	0	0	0	0	0	0	0	0	0
Ossie Bluege, 3b	.278	5	18	2	5	1	0	0	2	1	4	0
Stan Coveleski, p	.000	2	3	0	0	0	0	0	0	0	2	0
Alex Ferguson, p	.000	2	4	0	0	0	0	0	0	0	3	0
Goose Goslin, of	.308	7	26	6	8	1	0	3	6	3	3	0
Joe Harris, of	.440	7	25	5	11	2	0	3	6	3	4	0
Bucky Harris, 2b	.087	7	23	2	2	0	0	0	1	1	3	0
Walter Johnson, p	.091	3	11	0	1	0	0	0	0	0	3	0
Joe Judge, 1b	.174	7	23	2	4	1	0	1	3	3	2	0
Nemo Leibold, ph	.500	3	2	1	1	1	0	0	0	1	0	0
Firpo Marberry, p	.000	2	0	0	0	0	0	0	0	0	0	0
Earl Mc Neely, of-2	.000	4	0	2	0	0	0	0	0	0	0	1
Buddy Myer, 3b	.250	3	8	0	2	0	0	0	0	1	2	0
Roger Peckinpaugh, ss	.250	7	24	1	6	1	0	1	3	1	2	1
Sam Rice, of	.364	7	33	5	12	0	0	0	3	0	1	0
Muddy Ruel, c	.316	7	19	0	6	1	0	0	1	3	2	0
Dutch Ruether, ph	.000	1	1	0	0	0	0	0	0	0	1	0
Hank Severeid, c	.333	1	3	0	1	0	0	0	0	0	0	0
Bobby Veach, ph	.000	2	1	0	0	0	0	0	0	1	0	0
Tom Zachary, p	.000	1	0	0	0	0	0	0	0	0	0	0
TOTAL	.262		225	26	59	8	0	8	25	17	32	2

PITCHER	W	L	ERA	G	GS	CG	SV	SHO	IP	H	ER	BB	SO
Win Ballou	0	0	0.00	2	0	0	0	0	1.2	0	0	1	1
Stan Coveleski	0	2	3.77	2	2	1	0	0	14.1	16	6	5	3
Alex Ferguson	1	1	3.21	2	2	1	0	0	14.0	13	5	6	11
Walter Johnson	2	1	2.08	3	3	3	0	1	26.0	26	6	4	15
Firpo Marberry	0	0	0.00	2	0	0	1	0	2.1	3	0	0	2
Tom Zachary	0	0	10.80	1	0	0	0	0	1.2	3	2	1	0
TOTAL	3	4	2.85	12	7	5	1	1	60.0	61	19	17	32

The Yankees, returning to the World Series after a two-year absence, faced the Cardinals, who had won their first pennant since joining the National League in 1892. Both clubs led their league in slugging and runs scored; this power erupted occasionally in the Series, but over all, pitching dominated as each staff bettered its regular-season earned run average by nearly a run per game.

Herb Pennock of the Yankees pitched a splendid three-hitter in the opener. After yielding two hits and a run in the first inning, he shut out the Cards the rest of the way, holding them hitless until the ninth. Cardinal starter Bill Sherdel also pitched effectively, but three walks in the first and a hit-sacrifice-hit sandwich in the sixth brought in enough runs to beat him.

In Game Two, the veteran Grover Cleveland Alexander evened the Series, striking out ten and holding the Yankees to four singles (three of them in the two-run second) as Billy Southworth and Tommy Thevenow homered for four of St. Louis's six runs. Two days later Jesse Haines put the Cards into the lead, winning the game both ways with a five-hit shutout and a two-run homer.

New York's big bats finally awoke in Game Four. Five Yankees doubled, and Babe Ruth hit three home runs (a World Series record) in a 14-hit, 10-run assault on half the Cardinal pitching staff. Yankee pitcher Waite Hoyt also gave up 14 hits, but 12 were singles and only five runs scored. In contrast, Game Five was a pitchers' duel. Pennock and Sherdel again faced each other and held the opposition to two runs apiece through nine innings. But in the tenth, rookie Tony Lazzeri's sacrifice fly gave New York a 3–2 lead, which Pennock held in the last of the tenth for his second win.

With St. Louis down three games to two, the Series moved to hostile New York for the final games. This didn't seem to trouble the Cardinals, who erupted in Game Six for their own ten-run game, four of them driven in by Les Bell's first-inning single and seventh-inning home run. Alexander pitched a complete game for his second Series win, and came back the next day to relieve Haines in the seventh with a 3–2 lead and the bases full. He struck out Lazzeri to end the inning and kept the Yankees off the bases until he issued Babe Ruth his eleventh Series walk with two away in the ninth. But Ruth, trying to steal second, was caught, and the Cards were world champions.

St. Louis Cardinals (NL), 4;
New York Yankees (AL), 3

STL (N)

PLAYER/POS	AVG	G	AB	R	H	2B	3B	HR	RB	BB	SO	SB
Pete Alexander, p	.000	3	7	1	0	0	0	0	0	0	2	0
Hi Bell, p	.000	1	0	0	0	0	0	0	0	0	0	0
Les Bell, 3b	.259	7	27	4	7	1	0	1	6	2	5	0
Jim Bottomley, 1b	.345	7	29	4	10	3	0	0	5	1	2	0
Taylor Douthit, of	.267	4	15	3	4	2	0	0	1	3	2	0
Jake Flowers, ph	.000	3	3	0	0	0	0	0	0	0	1	0
Chick Hafey, of	.185	7	27	2	5	2	0	0	0	0	7	0
Jesse Haines, p	.600	3	5	1	3	0	0	1	2	0	1	0
Bill Hallahan, p	.000	1	0	0	0	0	0	0	0	0	0	0
Wattie Holm, of-4	.125	5	16	1	2	0	0	0	1	1	2	0
Rogers Hornsby, 2b	.250	7	28	2	7	1	0	0	4	2	2	1
Vic Keen, p	.000	1	0	0	0	0	0	0	0	0	0	0
Bob O'Farrell, c	.304	7	23	2	7	1	0	0	2	2	2	0
Art Reinhart, p	.000	2	0	0	0	0	0	0	0	0	0	0
Flint Rhem, p	.000	1	1	0	0	0	0	0	0	0	1	0
Bill Sherdel, p	.000	2	5	0	0	0	0	0	0	0	2	0
Billy Southworth, of	.345	7	29	6	10	1	1	1	4	0	1	0
Tommy Thevenow, ss	.417	7	24	5	10	1	0	1	4	0	1	0
Specs Toporcer, ph	.000	1	0	0	0	0	0	0	0	1	0	0
TOTAL	.272		239	31	65	12	1	4	30	11	30	2

PITCHER	W	L	ERA	G	GS	CG	SV	SHO	IP	H	ER	BB	SO
Pete Alexander	2	0	1.33	3	2	2	1	0	20.1	12	3	4	17
Hi Bell	0	0	9.00	1	0	0	0	0	2.0	4	2	1	1
Jesse Haines	2	0	1.08	3	2	1	0	1	16.2	13	2	9	5
Bill Hallahan	0	0	4.50	1	0	0	0	0	2.0	2	1	3	1
Vic Keen	0	0	0.00	1	0	0	0	0	1.0	0	0	0	0
Art Reinhart	0	1	INF	1	0	0	0	0	0.0	1	4	4	0
Flint Rhem	0	0	6.75	1	1	0	0	0	4.0	7	3	2	4
Bill Sherdel	0	2	2.12	2	2	1	0	0	17.0	15	4	8	3
TOTAL	4	3	2.71	13	7	4	1	1	63.0	54	19	31	31

NY (A)

PLAYER/POS	AVG	G	AB	R	H	2B	3B	HR	RB	BB	SO	SB
Spencer Adams, ph	.000	2	0	0	0	0	0	0	0	0	0	0
Pat Collins, c	.000	3	2	0	0	0	0	0	0	0	1	0
Earle Combs, of	.357	7	28	3	10	2	0	0	2	5	2	0
Joe Dugan, 3b	.333	7	24	2	8	1	0	0	2	1	1	0
Mike Gazella, 3b	.000	1	0	0	0	0	0	0	0	0	0	0
Lou Gehrig, 1b	.348	7	23	1	8	2	0	0	4	5	4	0
Waite Hoyt, p	.000	2	6	0	0	0	0	0	0	0	1	0
Sam Jones, p	.000	1	0	0	0	0	0	0	0	0	0	0
Mark Koenig, ss	.125	7	32	2	4	1	0	0	2	0	6	0
Tony Lazzeri, 2b	.192	7	26	2	5	1	0	0	3	1	6	0
Bob Meusel, of	.238	7	21	3	5	1	1	0	0	6	1	0
Ben Paschal, ph	.250	5	4	0	1	0	0	0	1	1	2	0
Herb Pennock, p	.143	3	7	1	1	1	0	0	0	0	2	0
Dutch Ruether, p-1	.000	3	4	0	0	0	0	0	0	0	0	0
Babe Ruth, of	.300	7	20	6	6	0	0	4	5	11	2	1
Hank Severeid, c	.273	7	22	1	6	1	0	0	1	1	2	0
Bob Shawkey, p	.000	3	2	0	0	0	0	0	0	0	1	0
Urban Shocker, p	.000	2	0	0	0	0	0	0	0	0	0	0
Myles Thomas, p	.000	2	0	0	0	0	0	0	0	0	0	0
TOTAL	.242		223	21	54	10	1	4	20	31	31	1

PITCHER	W	L	ERA	G	GS	CG	SV	SHO	IP	H	ER	BB	SO
Waite Hoyt	1	1	1.20	2	2	1	0	0	15.0	19	2	1	10
Sam Jones	0	0	9.00	1	0	0	0	0	1.0	2	1	2	1
Herb Pennock	2	0	1.23	3	2	2	0	0	22.0	13	3	4	8
Dutch Ruether	0	1	4.15	1	1	0	0	0	4.1	7	2	2	1
Bob Shawkey	0	1	5.40	3	1	0	0	0	10.0	8	6	2	7
Urban Shocker	0	1	5.87	2	1	0	0	0	7.2	13	5	0	3
Myles Thomas	0	0	3.00	2	0	0	0	0	3.0	3	1	0	0
TOTAL	3	4	2.86	14	7	3	0	0	63.0	65	20	11	30

GAME 1 AT NY OCT 2

STL	100	000	000	1	3	1
NY	100	001	00X	2	6	0

Pitchers: SHERDEL, Haines (8) vs PENNOCK
Attendance: 61,658

GAME 2 AT NY OCT 3

STL	002	000	301	6	12	1
NY	020	000	000	2	4	0

Pitchers: ALEXANDER vs SHOCKER, Shawkey (8), Jones (9)
Home Runs: Southworth-STL, Thevenow-STL
Attendance: 63,600

GAME 3 AT STL OCT 5

NY	000	000	000	0	5	1
STL	000	310	00X	4	8	0

Pitchers: RUETHER, Shawkey (5), Thomas (8) vs HAINES
Home Runs: Haines-STL
Attendance: 37,708

GAME 4 AT STL OCT 6

NY	101	142	100	10	14	1
STL	100	300	001	5	14	0

Pitchers: HOYT vs Rhem, REINHART (5), H.Bell (5), Hallahan (7), Keen (9)
Home Runs: Ruth-NY (3)
Attendance: 38,825

GAME 5 AT STL OCT 7

NY	000	001	001	1	3	9	1
STL	000	100	100	0	2	7	1

Pitchers: PENNOCK vs SHERDEL
Attendance: 39,552

GAME 6 AT NY OCT 9

STL	300	010	501	10	13	2
NY	000	100	100	2	8	1

Pitchers: ALEXANDER vs SHAWKEY, Shocker (8), Thomas (8)
Home Runs: L.Bell-STL
Attendance: 48,615

GAME 7 AT NY OCT 10

STL	000	300	000	3	8	0
NY	001	001	000	2	8	3

Pitchers: HAINES, Alexander (7) vs HOYT, Pennock (7)
Home Runs: Ruth-NY
Attendance: 38,093

The Pirates, who struggled to a narrow pennant win in a four-team race, were no slouches at the bat. Their team BA of .305 led the National League, and in the Waner brothers—Paul and Lloyd—and Pie Traynor they had three of the league's five top hitters. But in the World Series they came up against a Yankee team that is still widely regarded as the game's greatest ever. With 110 season victories and a 19-game margin over second-place Philadelphia, the Yankees led the American League in nearly every offensive category. Three Yankees—Earle Combs, Lou Gehrig, and Babe Ruth—hit over .350, and divided among them league crowns in runs, hits, doubles, triples, home runs (Ruth's 60), RBIs, and slugging average. The Yankees not only hit: their pitching staff boasted the league's lowest earned run average.

In the Series, though, it was Pittsburgh's erratic play that brought about the first American League sweep. The Pirates scored four times off Yankee starter Waite Hoyt in Game One, and might have won the game. But Paul Waner misplayed a Gehrig fly for a run-scoring triple in the first, and in the third, two Pirate errors led to three more Yankee runs. A final run in the fifth was all New York needed to win, 5–4.

The Yankees won the next two games more convincingly, with strong pitching and timely hitting. George Pipgras held Pittsburgh to two runs in Game Two as his Yankees bunched seven of their 11 hits into the third and eighth innings (also taking advantage of two walks and a hit batsman in the eighth) for their six runs. And in Game Three—as Herb Pennock pitched perfectly into the eighth inning before yielding two hits and a run—Yankee batters again bunched most of their hits into two innings, scoring two runs on Gehrig's first-inning triple and six more in the seventh, climaxed by Ruth's three-run homer.

Pittsburgh took advantage of two Yankee errors in the seventh inning of Game Four to score two runs and tie the game at three-all. But in the last of the ninth, after the Pirates' Johnny Miljus had struck out Gehrig and Bob Meusel with the bases loaded, his second wild pitch of the inning undid him—Combs scored from third with the Series' winning run.

New York Yankees (AL), 4;
Pittsburgh Pirates (NL), 0

NY (A)

PLAYER/POS	AVG	G	AB	R	H	2B	3B	HR	RB	BB	SO	SB
Benny Bengough, c	.000	2	4	1	0	0	0	0	0	1	0	0
Pat Collins, c	.600	2	5	0	3	1	0	0	0	3	0	0
Earle Combs, of	.313	4	16	6	5	0	0	0	2	1	2	0
Joe Dugan, 3b	.200	4	15	2	3	0	0	0	0	0	0	0
Cedric Durst, ph	.000	1	1	0	0	0	0	0	0	0	0	0
Lou Gehrig, 1b	.308	4	13	2	4	2	2	0	4	3	3	0
Johnny Grabowski, c	.000	1	2	0	0	0	0	0	0	0	0	0
Waite Hoyt, p	.000	1	3	0	0	0	0	0	0	0	0	0
Mark Koenig, ss	.500	4	18	5	9	2	0	0	2	0	2	0
Tony Lazzeri, 2b	.267	4	15	1	4	1	0	0	2	1	4	0
Bob Meusel, of	.118	4	17	1	2	0	0	0	1	1	7	1
Wilcy Moore, p	.200	2	5	0	1	0	0	0	0	0	3	0
Herb Pennock, p	.000	1	4	1	0	0	0	0	1	0	1	0
George Pipgras, p	.333	1	3	0	1	0	0	0	0	0	1	0
Babe Ruth, of	.400	4	15	4	6	0	0	2	7	2	2	1
TOTAL	.279		136	23	38	6	2	2	19	13	25	2

PITCHER	W	L	ERA	G	GS	CG	SV	SHO	IP	H	ER	BB	SO
Waite Hoyt	1	0	4.91	1	1	0	0	0	7.1	8	4	1	2
Wilcy Moore	1	0	0.84	2	1	1	1	0	10.2	11	1	2	2
Herb Pennock	1	0	1.00	1	1	1	0	0	9.0	3	1	0	1
George Pipgras	1	0	2.00	1	1	1	0	0	9.0	7	2	1	2
TOTAL	4	0	2.00	5	4	3	1	0	36.0	29	8	4	7

PIT (N)

PLAYER/POS	AVG	G	AB	R	H	2B	3B	HR	RB	BB	SO	SB
Vic Aldridge, p	.000	1	2	0	0	0	0	0	0	0	0	0
Clyde Barnhart, of	.313	4	16	0	5	1	0	0	4	0	0	0
Fred Brickell, ph	.000	2	2	1	0	0	0	0	0	0	0	0
Mike Cvengros, p	.000	2	0	0	0	0	0	0	0	0	0	0
Joe Dawson, p	.000	1	0	0	0	0	0	0	0	0	0	0
Johnny Gooch, c	.000	3	5	0	0	0	0	0	0	1	1	0
George Grantham, 2b	.364	3	11	0	4	1	0	0	0	1	1	0
Heinie Groh, ph	.000	1	1	0	0	0	0	0	0	0	0	0
Joe Harris, 1b	.200	4	15	0	3	0	0	0	1	0	0	0
Carmen Hill, p	.000	1	2	0	0	0	0	0	0	1	0	0
Ray Kremer, p	.500	1	2	1	1	1	0	0	0	0	1	0
Lee Meadows, p	.000	1	2	0	0	0	0	0	0	0	0	0
Johnny Miljus, p	.000	2	2	0	0	0	0	0	0	0	2	0
Hal Rhyne, 2b	.000	1	4	0	0	0	0	0	0	0	0	0
Earl Smith, c-2	.000	3	8	0	0	0	0	0	0	0	0	0
Roy Spencer, c	.000	1	1	0	0	0	0	0	0	0	0	0
Pie Traynor, 3b	.200	4	15	1	3	1	0	0	0	0	1	0
Lloyd Waner, of	.400	4	15	5	6	1	1	0	0	1	0	0
Paul Waner, of	.333	4	15	0	5	1	0	0	3	0	1	0
Glenn Wright, ss	.154	4	13	1	2	0	0	0	2	0	0	0
Emil Yde, pr	.000	1	0	1	0	0	0	0	0	0	0	0
TOTAL	.223		130	10	29	6	1	0	10	4	7	0

PITCHER	W	L	ERA	G	GS	CG	SV	SHO	IP	H	ER	BB	SO
Vic Aldridge	0	1	7.36	1	1	0	0	0	7.1	10	6	4	4
Mike Cvengros	0	0	3.86	2	0	0	0	0	2.1	3	1	0	2
Joe Dawson	0	0	0.00	1	0	0	0	0	1.0	0	0	0	0
Carmen Hill	0	0	4.50	1	1	0	0	0	6.0	9	3	1	6
Ray Kremer	0	1	3.60	1	1	0	0	0	5.0	5	2	3	1
Lee Meadows	0	1	9.95	1	1	0	0	0	6.1	7	7	1	6
Johnny Miljus	0	1	1.35	2	0	0	0	0	6.2	4	1	4	6
TOTAL	0	4	5.19	9	4	0	0	0	34.2	38	20	13	25

After squandering a 13½-game lead and falling briefly behind the Athletics in early September, the Yankees recovered to meet the Cardinals—winners of another tight National League race—in the Series. With Herb Pennock lost to arm trouble, the Yankees made do with just three pitchers in extending their Series win streak to eight games.

The four games offered little suspense, but for Yankee fans there were thrills aplenty. The Bronx Bombers' nine home runs (including four by Lou Gehrig and three by Babe Ruth) nearly equalled St. Louis's total scoring (ten runs), and Gehrig himself drove in as many runs (nine) as the entire Cardinal offense. Ruth and Gehrig started things off with successive doubles and a run in the first inning of the opener, and when Bob Meusel followed Ruth's second double with a home run in the fourth, the Yanks had more than they would need to support Waite Hoyt's three-hitter. The Cardinals' Jim Bottomley homered off Hoyt in the seventh, but successive singles by Mark Koenig, Ruth, and Gehrig produced a fourth Yankee run and concluded the scoring.

Gehrig homered in the first inning of Game Two to get New York off to a 3–0 lead against forty-one-year-old Grover Cleveland Alexander. The Cards snapped back to tie the game, but the Yankees retook the lead with a run in the last of the second and put together four hits, two walks, and a hit batsman for four more in the third. A final Yankee run in the seventh capped a 9–3 four-hit win for pitcher George Pipgras.

Jim Bottomley gave St. Louis its first lead of the Series with a two-run triple in the first inning of Game Three. But Yankee Tom Zachary gave up only one more run, taking the third Yankee win as Gehrig drove in three runs with homers in the second and fourth, and his teammates scored three more in the sixth (thanks in large part to two Cardinal errors and Meusel's steal of home) and a final (unearned) run an inning later.

New York completed its second straight Series sweep with another 7–3 win two days later. Waite Hoyt gained his second victory, mostly on the strength of five solo Yankee homers, including three by Babe Ruth.

New York Yankees (AL), 4;
St. Louis Cardinals (NL), 0

NY (A)

PLAYER/POS	AVG	G	AB	R	H	2B	3B	HR	RB	BB	SO	SB
Benny Bengough, c	.231	4	13	1	3	0	0	0	0	1	1	0
Pat Collins, c	1.000	1	1	0	1	1	0	0	0	0	0	0
Earle Combs, ph	.000	1	0	0	0	0	0	0	1	0	0	0
Joe Dugan, 3b	.167	3	6	0	1	0	0	0	1	0	0	0
Leo Durocher, 2b	.000	4	2	0	0	0	0	0	0	0	1	0
Cedric Durst, of	.375	4	8	3	3	0	0	1	2	0	1	0
Lou Gehrig, 1b	.545	4	11	5	6	1	0	4	9	6	0	0
Waite Hoyt, p	.143	2	7	0	1	0	0	0	0	0	0	0
Mark Koenig, ss	.158	4	19	1	3	0	0	0	0	0	1	0
Tony Lazzeri, 2b	.250	4	12	2	3	1	0	0	0	1	0	2
Bob Meusel, of	.200	4	15	5	3	1	0	1	3	2	5	2
Ben Paschal, of	.200	3	10	0	2	0	0	0	1	1	0	0
George Pipgras, p	.000	1	2	0	0	0	0	0	1	0	0	0
Gene Robertson, 3b	.125	3	8	1	1	0	0	0	2	1	0	0
Babe Ruth, of	.625	4	16	9	10	3	0	3	4	1	2	0
Tom Zachary, p	.000	1	4	0	0	0	0	0	0	0	1	0
TOTAL	.276		134	27	37	7	0	9	25	13	12	4

PITCHER	W	L	ERA	G	GS	CG	SV	SHO	IP	H	ER	BB	SO
Waite Hoyt	2	0	1.50	2	2	2	0	0	18.0	14	3	6	14
George Pipgras	1	0	2.00	1	1	1	0	0	9.0	4	2	4	8
Tom Zachary	1	0	3.00	1	1	1	0	0	9.0	9	3	1	7
TOTAL	4	0	2.00	4	4	4	0	0	36.0	27	8	11	29

STL (N)

PLAYER/POS	AVG	G	AB	R	H	2B	3B	HR	RB	BB	SO	SB
Pete Alexander, p	.000	2	1	0	0	0	0	0	1	0	0	0
Ray Blades, ph	.000	1	1	0	0	0	0	0	0	0	1	0
Jim Bottomley, 1b	.214	4	14	1	3	0	1	1	3	2	6	0
Taylor Douthit, of	.091	3	11	1	1	0	0	0	1	1	1	0
Frankie Frisch, 2b	.231	4	13	1	3	0	0	0	1	2	2	2
Chick Hafey, of	.200	4	15	0	3	0	0	0	0	1	4	0
Jesse Haines, p	.000	1	2	0	0	0	0	0	0	0	0	0
George Harper, of	.111	3	9	1	1	0	0	0	0	2	2	0
Andy High, 3b	.294	4	17	1	5	2	0	0	1	1	3	0
Wattie Holm, of-1	.167	3	6	0	1	0	0	0	1	0	1	0
Syl Johnson, p	.000	2	0	0	0	0	0	0	0	0	0	0
Rabbit Maranville, ss	.308	4	13	2	4	1	0	0	0	1	1	1
Pepper Martin, pr	.000	1	0	1	0	0	0	0	0	0	0	0
Clarence Mitchell, p	.000	1	2	0	0	0	0	0	0	0	0	0
Ernie Orsatti, of-1	.286	4	7	1	2	1	0	0	0	1	3	0
Flint Rhem, p	.000	1	0	0	0	0	0	0	0	0	0	0
Bill Sherdel, p	.000	2	5	0	0	0	0	0	0	0	2	0
Earl Smith, c	.750	1	4	0	3	0	0	0	0	0	0	0
Tommy Thevenow, ss	.000	1	0	0	0	0	0	0	0	0	0	0
Jimmie Wilson, c	.091	3	11	1	1	1	0	0	1	0	3	0
TOTAL	.206		131	10	27	5	1	1	9	11	29	3

PITCHER	W	L	ERA	G	GS	CG	SV	SHO	IP	H	ER	BB	SO
Pete Alexander	0	1	19.80	2	1	0	0	0	5.0	10	11	4	2
Jesse Haines	0	1	4.50	1	1	0	0	0	6.0	6	3	3	3
Syl Johnson	0	0	4.50	2	0	0	0	0	2.0	4	1	1	1
Clarence Mitchell	0	0	1.59	1	0	0	0	0	5.2	2	1	2	2
Flint Rhem	0	0	0.00	1	0	0	0	0	2.0	0	0	0	1
Bill Sherdel	0	2	4.72	2	2	0	0	0	13.1	15	7	3	3
TOTAL	0	4	6.09	9	4	0	0	0	34.0	37	23	13	12

GAME 1 AT NY OCT 4

STL	000	000	100	1	3 1
NY	100	200	01X	4	7 0

Pitchers: SHERDEL, Johnson (8) vs HOYT
Home Runs: Meusel-NY, Bottomley-STL
Attendance: 61,425

GAME 2 AT NY OCT 5

STL	030	000	000	3	4 1
NY	314	000	10X	9	8 2

Pitchers: ALEXANDER, Mitchell (3) vs PIPGRAS
Home Runs: Gehrig-NY
Attendance: 60,714

GAME 3 AT STL OCT 7

NY	010	203	100	7	7 2
STL	200	010	000	3	9 3

Pitchers: ZACHARY vs HAINES, Johnson (7), Rhem (8)
Home Runs: Gehrig-NY (2)
Attendance: 39,602

GAME 4 AT STL OCT 9

NY	000	100	420	7	15 2
STL	001	100	001	3	11 0

Pitchers: HOYT vs SHERDEL, Alexander (7)
Home Runs: Ruth-NY (3), Durst-NY, Gehrig-NY
Attendance: 37,331

The surprising success of a surprise starter and the ultimate in big innings highlighted the return of the Athletics to World Series play after a gap of fifteen years. In the opener, A's manager Connie Mack passed over the aces of his pitching staff in favor of Howard Ehmke, an aging journeyman who that season had started only eight times and pitched under 55 innings. But Ehmke, who (per Mack's instructions) had studied the Cubs' hitters in a series of late-season games, held the Cubs scoreless through the first eight innings of Game One (yielding an unearned run in the last of the ninth) while fanning 13 batters for a new Series record. Chicago's Charlie Root also pitched effectively until Jimmie Foxx's solo homer in the seventh gave the A's the game's first score. A pair of errors by Cub shortstop Woody English in the ninth set up two unearned runs against reliever Guy Bush and gave Ehmke and the A's all the lead they needed.

Home runs by Foxx and Al Simmons drove in five of the A's nine runs in Game Two as Philadelphia took a 2–0 Series lead. But Guy Bush held Mack's sluggers to nine singles and one run in Game Three as his Cubs scored three runs in the sixth to take their first win.

The Cubs seemed well on their way to tying the Series in Game Four as they entered the last of the seventh with an 8–0 lead. But Simmons led off with a homer to erase Charlie Root's shutout, and five of the next six batters singled. Art Nehf relieved Root, but the first batter to face him—Mule Haas—lofted a fly to center which Hack Wilson lost in the sun for a three-run inside-the-park homer, and the score was 8–7. After walking Mickey Cochrane, Nehf was replaced by Sheriff Blake, who gave up two singles and saw the tying run come home before Pat Malone took the mound with two men still on base and only one away. Malone struck out two in a row to end the inning—but not until he first hit a batter and gave up a double by Jimmy Dykes for the two runs that gave the A's a 10–8 win and a 3–1 Series advantage.

Game Five, although inevitably anticlimactic, was not decided until the final at-bat. Chicago scored twice off Ehmke in the fourth as Malone shut out the A's with only two hits through eight. But in the last of the ninth a single and Haas's home run tied the score, and—with two men out—Simmons doubled, Foxx was walked intentionally, Bing Miller doubled, and the Series was history.

Philadelphia Athletics (AL), 4; Chicago Cubs (NL), 1

PHI (A)

PLAYER/POS	AVG	G	AB	R	H	2B	3B	HR	RB	BB	SO	SB
Max Bishop, 2b	.190	5	21	2	4	0	0	0	1	2	3	0
Joe Boley, ss	.235	5	17	1	4	0	0	0	1	0	3	0
George Burns, ph	.000	1	2	0	0	0	0	0	0	0	1	0
Mickey Cochrane, c	.400	5	15	5	6	1	0	0	0	7	0	0
Jimmy Dykes, 3b	.421	5	19	2	8	1	0	0	4	1	1	0
George Earnshaw, p	.000	2	5	1	0	0	0	0	0	0	4	0
Howard Ehmke, p	.200	2	5	0	1	0	0	0	0	0	0	0
Jimmie Foxx, 1b	.350	5	20	5	7	1	0	2	5	1	1	0
Walter French, ph	.000	1	1	0	0	0	0	0	0	0	1	0
Lefty Grove, p	.000	2	2	0	0	0	0	0	0	0	1	0
Mule Haas, of	.238	5	21	3	5	0	0	2	6	1	3	0
Bing Miller, of	.368	5	19	1	7	1	0	0	4	0	2	0
Jack Quinn, p	.000	1	2	0	0	0	0	0	0	0	2	0
Eddie Rommel, p	.000	1	0	0	0	0	0	0	0	0	0	0
Al Simmons, of	.300	5	20	6	6	1	0	2	5	1	4	0
Homer Summa, ph	.000	1	1	0	0	0	0	0	0	0	1	0
Rube Walberg, p	.000	2	1	0	0	0	0	0	0	0	0	0
TOTAL	.281		171	26	48	5	0	6	26	13	27	0

PITCHER	W	L	ERA	G	GS	CG	SV	SHO	IP	H	ER	BB	SO
George Earnshaw	1	1	2.63	2	2	1	0	0	13.2	14	4	6	17
Howard Ehmke	1	0	1.42	2	2	1	0	0	12.2	14	2	3	13
Lefty Grove	0	0	0.00	2	0	0	2	0	6.1	3	0	1	10
Jack Quinn	0	0	9.00	1	1	0	0	0	5.0	7	5	2	2
Eddie Rommel	1	0	9.00	1	0	0	0	0	1.0	2	1	1	0
Rube Walberg	1	0	0.00	2	0	0	0	0	6.1	3	0	0	8
TOTAL	4	1	2.40	10	5	2	2	0	45.0	43	12	13	50

CHI (N)

PLAYER/POS	AVG	G	AB	R	H	2B	3B	HR	RB	BB	SO	SB
Footsie Blair, ph	.000	1	1	0	0	0	0	0	0	0	0	0
Sheriff Blake, p	1.000	2	1	0	1	0	0	0	0	0	0	0
Guy Bush, p	.000	2	3	1	0	0	0	0	0	1	3	0
Hal Carlson, p	.000	2	0	0	0	0	0	0	0	0	0	0
Kiki Cuyler, of	.300	5	20	4	6	1	0	0	4	1	7	0
Woody English, ss	.190	5	21	1	4	2	0	0	0	1	6	0
Mike Gonzalez, c-1	.000	2	1	0	0	0	0	0	0	0	1	0
Charlie Grimm, 1b	.389	5	18	2	7	0	0	1	4	1	2	0
Gabby Hartnett, ph	.000	3	3	0	0	0	0	0	0	0	3	0
Cliff Heathcote, ph	.000	2	1	0	0	0	0	0	0	0	0	0
Rogers Hornsby, 2b	.238	5	21	4	5	1	1	0	1	1	8	0
Pat Malone, p	.250	3	4	0	1	1	0	0	0	0	2	0
Norm Mc Millan, 3b	.100	5	20	0	2	0	0	0	0	2	6	1
Art Nehf, p	.000	2	0	0	0	0	0	0	0	0	0	0
Charlie Root, p	.000	2	5	0	0	0	0	0	0	0	3	0
Riggs Stephenson, of	.316	5	19	3	6	1	0	0	3	2	2	0
Zack Taylor, c	.176	5	17	0	3	0	0	0	0	3	3	0
Chick Tolson, ph	.000	1	1	0	0	0	0	0	0	0	1	0
Hack Wilson, of	.471	5	17	2	8	0	1	0	4	3	0	0
TOTAL	.249		173	17	43	6	2	1	15	13	50	1

PITCHER	W	L	ERA	G	GS	CG	SV	SHO	IP	H	ER	BB	SO
Sheriff Blake	0	1	13.50	2	0	0	0	0	1.1	4	2	0	1
Guy Bush	1	0	0.82	2	1	1	0	0	11.0	12	1	2	4
Hal Carlson	0	0	6.75	2	0	0	0	0	4.0	7	3	1	3
Pat Malone	0	2	4.15	3	2	1	0	0	13.0	12	6	7	11
Art Nehf	0	0	18.00	2	0	0	0	0	1.0	2	2	1	0
Charlie Root	0	1	4.72	2	2	0	0	0	13.1	12	7	2	8
TOTAL	1	4	4.33	13	5	2	0	0	43.2	48	21	13	27

GAME 1 AT CHI OCT 8

PHI	000 000 102	3	6	1
CHI	000 000 001	1	8	2

Pitchers: EHMKE vs ROOT, Bush (8)
Home Runs: Foxx-PHI
Attendance: 50,740

GAME 2 AT CHI OCT 9

PHI	003 300 120	9	12	0
CHI	000 030 000	3	11	1

Pitchers: EARNSHAW, Grove (5) vs MALONE, Blake (4), Carlson (6), Nehf (9)
Home Runs: Simmons-PHI, Foxx-PHI
Attendance: 49,987

GAME 3 AT PHI OCT 11

CHI	000 003 000	3	6	1
PHI	000 010 000	1	9	1

Pitchers: BUSH vs EARNSHAW
Attendance: 29,921

GAME 4 AT PHI OCT 12

CHI	000 205 100	8	10	2
PHI	000 000 10X	10	15	2

Pitchers: Root, Nehf (7), Malone (7), Carlson (8) vs Quinn, Walberg (6), ROMMEL (7), Grove (8)
Home Runs: Grimm-CHI, Haas-PHI, Simmons-PHI
Attendance: 29,921

GAME 5 AT PHI OCT 14

CHI	002 000 000	2	8	1
PHI	000 000 003	3	6	0

Pitchers: MALONE vs Ehmke, WALBERG (4)
Home Runs: Haas-PHI
Attendance: 29,921

Pitching 85 percent of the Series with a combined ERA of 1.02, Philadelphia aces George Earnshaw and Lefty Grove chilled the hot Cardinals, who had hit .314 and averaged 6½ runs per game during the season. The A's hit only .197 themselves in the Series, but more than half their hits went for extra bases as they outscored St. Louis 21–12 and took their second consecutive world championship in six games.

Grove faced Cardinal spitballer Burleigh Grimes in the opener, giving up nine hits, including four singles in the Cards' two-run third. The Athletics, for their part, touched Grimes for only five hits, all in separate innings. But every hit—a double, two triples, and home runs by Al Simmons and Mike Cochrane—resulted in a run, and Grove and the A's emerged 5–2 victors. In the first inning of Game Two, Cochrane again homered, sending Earnshaw on his way to Philadelphia's second win, 6–1.

When the Series moved to St. Louis, though, the Cards came alive. Wild Bill Hallahan (their leading winner during the season, with 15) spaced seven hits for a shutout. Taylor Douthit's fourth-inning home run off Rube Walberg was the first Cardinal hit, but the Cards knocked out nine more for four more runs before they were finished. A pair of unearned runs evened the Series the next day when A's third baseman Jimmy Dykes's wild throw to first in the fourth inning let in a tie-breaking second Cardinal run and led to a third against the ultimate loser Lefty Grove. Meanwhile, Cardinal veteran Jesse Haines, after yielding three Philadelphia hits and a run in the first inning, shut out the A's on one hit the rest of the way.

Earnshaw and Grove combined to restore the Series lead to the Athletics in Game Five with a three-hit shutout. Grove, who took over when Earnshaw left for a pinch hitter in the eighth, garnered his second Series win as Jimmie Foxx homered off Grimes in the top of the ninth for the game's only runs. After a travel day to Philadelphia, Earnshaw pitched again for the A's in Game Six, and pushed the Cardinals' scoreless streak to 21 innings before allowing them a token run in the ninth. But by then seven A's had crossed the plate and the Series was theirs.

Philadelphia Athletics (AL), 4; St. Louis Cardinals (NL), 2

PHI (A)

PLAYER/POS	AVG	G	AB	R	H	2B	3B	HR	RB	BB	SO	SB
Max Bishop, 2b	.222	6	18	5	4	0	0	0	0	7	3	0
Joe Boley, ss	.095	6	21	1	2	0	0	0	1	0	1	0
Mickey Cochrane, c	.222	6	18	5	4	1	0	2	4	5	2	0
Jimmy Dykes, 3b	.222	6	18	2	4	3	0	1	5	5	3	0
George Earnshaw, p	.000	3	9	0	0	0	0	0	0	0	5	0
Jimmie Foxx, 1b	.333	6	21	3	7	2	1	1	3	2	4	0
Lefty Grove, p	.000	3	6	0	0	0	0	0	0	0	3	0
Mule Haas, of	.111	6	18	1	2	0	1	0	1	1	3	0
Eric Mc Nair, ph	.000	1	1	0	0	0	0	0	0	0	0	0
Bing Miller, of	.143	6	21	0	3	2	0	0	3	0	4	0
Jim Moore, of-1	.333	3	3	0	1	0	0	0	0	1	1	0
Jack Quinn, p	.000	1	0	0	0	0	0	0	0	0	0	0
Bill Shores, p	.000	1	0	0	0	0	0	0	0	1	0	0
Al Simmons, of	.364	6	22	4	8	2	0	2	4	2	2	0
Rube Walberg, p	.000	1	2	0	0	0	0	0	0	0	1	0
TOTAL	.197		178	21	35	10	2	6	21	24	32	0

PITCHER	W	L	ERA	G	GS	CG	SV	SHO	IP	H	ER	BB	SO
George Earnshaw	2	0	0.72	3	3	2	0	0	25.0	13	2	7	19
Lefty Grove	2	1	1.42	3	2	2	0	0	19.0	15	3	3	10
Jack Quinn	0	0	4.50	1	0	0	0	0	2.0	3	1	0	1
Bill Shores	0	0	13.50	1	0	0	0	0	1.1	3	2	0	0
Rube Walberg	0	1	3.86	1	1	0	0	0	4.2	4	2	1	3
TOTAL	4	2	1.73	9	6	4	0	0	52.0	38	10	11	33

STL (N)

PLAYER/POS	AVG	G	AB	R	H	2B	3B	HR	RB	BB	SO	SB
Sparky Adams, 3b	.143	6	21	0	3	0	0	0	0	1	0	4	0
Hi Bell, p	.000	1	0	0	0	0	0	0	0	0	0	0
Ray Blades, of-3	.111	5	9	2	1	0	0	0	0	2	2	0
Jim Bottomley, 1b	.045	6	22	1	1	1	0	0	0	2	9	0
Taylor Douthit, of	.083	6	24	1	2	0	0	1	2	0	2	0
George Fisher, ph	.500	2	2	0	1	1	0	0	0	0	1	0
Frankie Frisch, 2b	.208	6	24	0	5	2	0	0	0	0	0	1
Charlie Gelbert, ss	.353	6	17	2	6	0	1	0	2	3	3	0
Burleigh Grimes, p	.400	2	5	0	2	0	0	0	0	0	1	0
Chick Hafey, of	.273	6	22	2	6	5	0	0	2	1	3	0
Jesse Haines, p	.500	1	2	0	1	0	0	0	1	0	0	0
Bill Hallahan, p	.000	2	2	0	0	0	0	0	0	1	1	0
Andy High, 3b	.500	1	2	1	1	0	0	0	0	0	0	0
Syl Johnson, p	.000	2	0	0	0	0	0	0	0	0	0	0
Jim Lindsey, p	1.000	2	1	0	1	0	0	0	0	0	0	0
Gus Mancuso, c	.286	2	7	1	2	0	0	0	0	1	2	0
Ernie Orsatti, ph	.000	1	1	0	0	0	0	0	0	0	0	0
George Puccinelli, ph	.000	1	1	0	0	0	0	0	0	0	0	0
Flint Rhem, p	.000	1	1	0	0	0	0	0	0	0	1	0
George Watkins, of	.167	4	12	2	2	0	0	1	1	1	3	0
Jimmie Wilson, c	.267	4	15	0	4	1	0	0	2	0	1	0
TOTAL	.200		190	12	38	10	1	2	11	11	33	1

PITCHER	W	L	ERA	G	GS	CG	SV	SHO	IP	H	ER	BB	SO
Hi Bell	0	0	0.00	1	0	0	0	0	1.0	0	0	0	0
Burleigh Grimes	0	2	3.71	2	2	2	0	0	17.0	10	7	6	13
Jesse Haines	1	0	1.00	1	1	1	0	0	9.0	4	1	4	2
Bill Hallahan	1	1	1.64	2	2	1	0	1	11.0	9	2	8	8
Syl Johnson	0	0	7.20	2	0	0	0	0	5.0	4	4	3	4
Jim Lindsey	0	0	1.93	2	0	0	0	0	4.2	1	1	1	2
Flint Rhem	0	1	10.80	1	1	0	0	0	3.1	7	4	2	3
TOTAL	2	4	3.35	11	6	4	0	1	51.0	35	19	24	32

GAME 1 AT PHI OCT 1

STL	002	000	000	2	9	0
PHI	010	101	11X	5	5	0

Pitchers: GRIMES vs GROVE
Home Runs: Cochrane-PHI, Simmons-PHI
Attendance: 32,295

GAME 2 AT PHI OCT 2

STL	010	000	000	1	6	2
PHI	202	200	00X	6	7	2

Pitchers: RHEM, Lindsey (4), Johnson (7) vs EARNSHAW
Home Runs: Cochrane-PHI, Watkins-STL
Attendance: 32,295

GAME 3 AT STL OCT 4

PHI	000	000	000	0	7	0
STL	000	110	21X	5	10	0

Pitchers: WALBERG, Shores (5), Quinn (7) vs HALLAHAN
Home Runs: Douthit-STL
Attendance: 36,944

GAME 4 AT STL OCT 5

PHI	100	000	000	1	4	1
STL	001	200	00X	3	5	1

Pitchers: GROVE vs HAINES
Attendance: 39,946

GAME 5 AT STL OCT 6

PHI	000	000	002	2	5	0
STL	000	000	000	0	3	1

Pitchers: Earnshaw, GROVE (8) vs GRIMES
Home Runs: Foxx-PHI
Attendance: 38,844

GAME 6 AT PHI OCT 8

STL	000	000	001	1	5	1
PHI	201	211	00X	7	7	0

Pitchers: HALLAHAN, Johnson (3), Lindsey (6), Bell (8) vs EARNSHAW
Home Runs: Dykes-PHI, Simmons-PHI
Attendance: 32,295

For the second year in a row, the A's met the Cardinals in the Series, and once again pitchers Lefty Grove and George Earnshaw provided more than 80 percent of the Athletics' pitching, performing splendidly and winning three games between them. But this time Cardinal pitchers Wild Bill Hallahan and Burleigh Grimes outshone them, winning two games apiece to bring St. Louis the world championship.

Grove gave up four hits and two runs in the first inning of the opener, but shut out the Cards the rest of the way as the A's scored six off Paul Derringer to take the Series lead. Earnshaw also held St. Louis to two runs the next day—both manufactured by Pepper Martin's daring baserunning. But they were more than enough for Hallahan, who shut out the A's on three singles.

The Cardinals took their first Series lead in Game Three, scoring five times off Grove and reliever Roy Mahaffey while Grimes held the A's hitless through seven innings and scoreless through eight before giving up a harmless two-run homer to Al Simmons in the bottom of the ninth. But the A's came back to even the Series the next day on Earnshaw's two-hit shutout.

Pepper Martin, the Cardinal hero of Game Two, homered for two runs in Game Five, and drove in two more of St. Louis's five runs with a sacrifice fly and a single. Meanwhile pitcher Hallahan held Philadelphia to a lone run, returning the Series lead to the Cardinals with his second win.

Game Six pitted Grove and Derringer against each other again as in the opener, and again Grove emerged the victor, holding the Cardinals to one run and five hits. The Athletics scored four unearned runs in the fifth off the unfortunate Derringer who, after an error put a runner on base to open the inning, gave up two singles and walked four, including two with the bases full, before leaving the game. Four more Philadelphia runs in the seventh (two of them scoring on a dropped fly ball) gave the A's the Series' only lopsided win.

In the finale, Grimes once again held the A's scoreless through eight before giving up two runs in the ninth. And once again the runs proved harmless against an early Cardinal lead, as Hallahan came on to retire Max Bishop for the final out.

St. Louis Cardinals (NL), 4; Philadelphia Athletics (AL), 3

STL (N)

PLAYER/POS	AVG	G	AB	R	H	2B	3B	HR	RB	BB	SO	SB
Sparky Adams, 3b	.250	2	4	0	1	0	0	0	0	0	1	0
Ray Blades, ph	.000	2	2	0	0	0	0	0	0	0	2	0
Jim Bottomley, 1b	.160	7	25	2	4	1	0	0	2	2	5	0
Ripper Collins, ph	.000	2	2	0	0	0	0	0	0	0	1	0
Paul Derringer, p	.000	3	2	0	0	0	0	0	0	0	1	0
Jake Flowers, 3b-4	.091	5	11	1	1	1	0	0	0	1	0	0
Frankie Frisch, 2b	.259	7	27	2	7	2	0	0	1	1	2	1
Charlie Gelbert, ss	.261	7	23	0	6	1	0	0	3	0	4	0
Burleigh Grimes, p	.286	2	7	0	2	0	0	0	2	0	2	0
Chick Hafey, of	.167	6	24	1	4	0	0	0	0	0	5	1
Bill Hallahan, p	.000	3	6	0	0	0	0	0	0	0	3	0
Andy High, 3b	.267	4	15	3	4	0	0	0	0	0	2	0
Syl Johnson, p	.000	3	2	0	0	0	0	0	0	0	2	0
Jim Lindsey, p	.000	2	0	0	0	0	0	0	0	0	0	0
Gus Mancuso, c-1	.000	2	1	0	0	0	0	0	0	0	0	0
Pepper Martin, of	.500	7	24	5	12	4	0	1	5	2	3	5
Ernie Orsatti, of	.000	1	3	0	0	0	0	0	0	0	3	0
Flint Rhem, p	.000	1	0	0	0	0	0	0	0	0	0	0
Wally Roettger, of	.286	3	14	1	4	1	0	0	0	0	3	0
George Watkins, of	.286	5	14	4	4	1	0	1	2	2	1	1
Jimmie Wilson, c	.217	7	23	0	5	0	0	0	2	1	1	0
TOTAL	.236		229	19	54	11	0	2	17	9	41	8

PITCHER	W	L	ERA	G	GS	CG	SV	SHO	IP	H	ER	BB	SO
Paul Derringer	0	2	4.26	3	2	0	0	0	12.2	14	6	7	14
Burleigh Grimes	2	0	2.04	2	2	1	0	0	17.2	9	4	9	11
Bill Hallahan	2	0	0.49	3	2	2	1	1	18.1	12	1	8	12
Syl Johnson	0	1	3.00	3	1	0	0	0	9.0	10	3	1	6
Jim Lindsey	0	0	5.40	2	0	0	0	0	3.1	4	2	3	2
Flint Rhem	0	0	0.00	1	0	0	0	0	1.0	1	0	0	1
TOTAL	4	3	2.32	14	7	3	1	1	62.0	50	16	28	46

PHI (A)

PLAYER/POS	AVG	G	AB	R	H	2B	3B	HR	RB	BB	SO	SB
Max Bishop, 2b	.148	7	27	4	4	0	0	0	0	3	5	0
Joe Boley, ss	.000	1	1	0	0	0	0	0	0	0	1	0
Mickey Cochrane, c	.160	7	25	2	4	0	0	0	1	5	2	0
Doc Cramer, ph	.500	2	2	0	1	0	0	0	2	0	0	0
Jimmy Dykes, 3b	.227	7	22	2	5	0	0	0	2	5	1	0
George Earnshaw, p	.000	3	8	0	0	0	0	0	0	0	2	0
Jimmie Foxx, 1b	.348	7	23	3	8	0	0	1	3	6	5	0
Lefty Grove, p	.000	3	10	0	0	0	0	0	0	0	7	0
Mule Haas, of	.130	7	23	1	3	1	0	0	2	3	5	0
Johnnie Heving, ph	.000	1	1	0	0	0	0	0	0	0	0	0
Waite Hoyt, p	.000	1	2	0	0	0	0	0	0	0	0	0
Roy Mahaffey, p	.000	1	0	0	0	0	0	0	0	0	0	0
Eric Mc Nair, 2b-1	.000	2	2	1	0	0	0	0	0	0	1	0
Bing Miller, of	.269	7	26	3	7	1	0	0	1	0	4	0
Jim Moore, of-1	.333	2	3	0	1	0	0	0	0	0	1	0
Eddie Rommel, p	.000	1	0	0	0	0	0	0	0	0	0	0
Al Simmons, of	.333	7	27	4	9	2	0	2	8	3	3	0
Phil Todt, ph	.000	1	0	0	0	0	0	0	0	1	0	0
Rube Walberg, p	.000	2	0	0	0	0	0	0	0	0	0	0
Dib Williams, ss	.320	7	25	2	8	1	0	0	1	2	9	0
TOTAL	.220		227	22	50	5	0	3	20	28	46	0

PITCHER	W	L	ERA	G	GS	CG	SV	SHO	IP	H	ER	BB	SO
George Earnshaw	1	2	1.88	3	3	2	0	1	24.0	12	5	4	20
Lefty Grove	2	1	2.42	3	3	2	0	0	26.0	28	7	2	16
Waite Hoyt	0	1	4.50	1	1	0	0	0	6.0	7	3	0	1
Roy Mahaffey	0	0	9.00	1	0	0	0	0	1.0	1	1	1	0
Eddie Rommel	0	0	9.00	1	0	0	0	0	1.0	3	1	0	0
Rube Walberg	0	0	3.00	2	0	0	0	0	3.0	3	1	2	4
TOTAL	3	4	2.66	11	7	4	0	1	61.0	54	18	9	41

GAME 1 AT STL OCT 1

PHI	004 000 200	6	11	0
STL	200 000 000	2	12	0

Pitchers: GROVE vs DERRINGER, Johnson (8)
Home Runs: Simmons-PHI
Attendance: 38,529

GAME 2 AT STL OCT 2

PHI	000 000 000	0	3	0
STL	010 000 10X	2	6	1

Pitchers: EARNSHAW vs HALLAHAN
Attendance: 35,947

GAME 3 AT PHI OCT 5

STL	020 200 001	5	12	0
PHI	000 000 002	2	2	0

Pitchers: GRIMES vs GROVE, Mahaffey (9)
Home Runs: Simmons-PHI
Attendance: 32,295

GAME 4 AT PHI OCT 6

STL	000 000 000	0	2	1
PHI	100 002 00X	3	10	0

Pitchers: JOHNSON, Lindsey (6) vs EARNSHAW
Home Runs: Foxx-PHI
Attendance: 32,295

GAME 5 AT PHI OCT 7

STL	100 002 011	5	12	0
PHI	000 000 100	1	9	0

Pitchers: HALLAHAN vs HOYT, Walberg (7), Rommel (9)
Home Runs: Martin-STL, Watkins-STL
Attendance: 32,295

GAME 6 AT STL OCT 9

PHI	000 040 400	8	8	1
STL	000 001 000	1	5	2

Pitchers: GROVE vs DERRINGER, Johnson (5), Lindsey (7), Rhem (9)
Attendance: 39,401

GAME 7 AT STL OCT 10

PHI	000 000 002	2	7	1
STL	202 000 00X	4	5	0

Pitchers: EARNSHAW, Walberg (8) vs GRIMES, Hallahan (9)
Attendance: 20,805

Lou Gehrig, who hit .529 and scored nearly a quarter of New York's runs, led both clubs in batting, slugging, hits, runs, and RBIs as the Yankees crushed the Cubs in four games. But the Series is best remembered for Babe Ruth's "called" shot in Game Three, when he pointed his bat at pitcher Charlie Root in the fifth inning and broke the game's 4–4 tie a moment later with a massive home run into the center field bleachers. Debate has raged ever since about whether Ruth intended his gesture as a home run prediction. Whether intended or not, it erased from public memory Gehrig's home run that followed Ruth's (and the homers both men had hit earlier in the game), and made memorable an otherwise undistinguished Series.

Chicago scored in the first inning of each game, taking early leads in three of the four, but held no lead beyond the sixth inning. In Game One, the Cubs connected for ten hits to the Yankees' eight, but managed to score only half as many runs as the New Yorkers, who put what had been a close game out of reach with five runs in the sixth (on four walks, two singles, and a ground out) and three more in the seventh (a walk, two singles, a hit batsman, a sacrifice fly, and a wild pitch).

Chicago's Lon Warneke walked four batters in Game Two, and three of them went on to score as the Yankees countered single Cub runs in the first and third with pairs of their own on two walks and two singles in each frame. (A fifth Yankee run—on two singles without bases on balls—concluded the scoring for the game.)

Game Three featured not only the two homers each by Ruth and Gehrig, but home runs by the Cubs' Kiki Cuyler and Gabby Hartnett. Hartnett's solo shot in the last of the ninth brought Chicago to within two runs of New York for the Series' closest finish.

Four first-inning singles, Frank Demaree's three-run homer, and a Yankee error gave the Cubs a 4–1 advantage early in Game Four—their biggest lead of the Series. But by game's end, 19 Yankee hits (including two home runs by Tony Lazzeri and one by Earle Combs) had created 13 Yankee runs, and the world title was theirs.

New York Yankees (AL), 4; Chicago Cubs (NL), 0

NY (A)

PLAYER/POS	AVG	G	AB	R	H	2B	3B	HR	RB	BB	SO	SB
Johnny Allen, p	.000	1	0	0	0	0	0	0	0	0	0	0
Sammy Byrd, of	.000	1	0	0	0	0	0	0	0	0	0	0
Ben Chapman, of	.294	4	17	1	5	2	0	0	6	2	4	0
Earle Combs, of	.375	4	16	8	6	1	0	1	4	4	3	0
Frankie Crosetti, ss	.133	4	15	2	2	1	0	0	0	2	3	0
Bill Dickey, c	.438	4	16	2	7	0	0	0	4	2	1	0
Lou Gehrig, 1b	.529	4	17	9	9	1	0	3	8	2	1	0
Lefty Gomez, p	.000	1	3	0	0	0	0	0	0	0	2	0
Myril Hoag, pr	.000	1	0	1	0	0	0	0	0	0	0	0
Tony Lazzeri, 2b	.294	4	17	4	5	0	0	2	5	2	1	0
Wilcy Moore, p	.333	1	3	0	1	0	0	0	0	0	2	0
Herb Pennock, p	.000	2	1	0	0	0	0	0	0	0	0	0
George Pipgras, p	.000	1	5	0	0	0	0	0	0	0	5	0
Red Ruffing, p-1	.000	2	4	0	0	0	0	0	0	1	1	0
Babe Ruth, of	.333	4	15	6	5	0	0	2	6	4	3	0
Joe Sewell, 3b	.333	4	15	4	5	1	0	0	3	4	0	0
TOTAL	.313		144	37	45	6	0	8	36	23	26	0

PITCHER	W	L	ERA	G	GS	CG	SV	SHO	IP	H	ER	BB	SO
Johnny Allen	0	0	40.50	1	1	0	0	0	0.2	5	3	0	0
Lefty Gomez	1	0	1.00	1	1	1	0	0	9.0	9	1	1	8
Wilcy Moore	1	0	0.00	1	0	0	0	0	5.1	2	0	0	1
Herb Pennock	0	0	2.25	2	0	0	2	0	4.0	2	1	4	4
George Pipgras	1	0	4.50	1	1	0	0	0	8.0	9	4	3	1
Red Ruffing	1	0	4.00	1	1	1	0	0	9.0	10	4	6	10
TOTAL	4	0	3.25	7	4	2	2	0	36.0	37	13	11	24

CHI (N)

PLAYER/POS	AVG	G	AB	R	H	2B	3B	HR	RB	BB	SO	SB
Guy Bush, p	.000	2	1	0	0	0	0	0	0	1	0	0
Kiki Cuyler, of	.278	4	18	2	5	1	1	1	2	0	3	1
Frank Demaree, of	.286	2	7	1	2	0	0	1	4	1	0	0
Woody English, 3b	.176	4	17	2	3	0	0	0	1	2	2	0
Burleigh Grimes, p	.000	2	1	0	0	0	0	0	0	0	1	0
Charlie Grimm, 1b	.333	4	15	2	5	2	0	0	1	2	2	0
Marv Gudat, ph	.000	2	2	0	0	0	0	0	0	0	1	0
Stan Hack, ph	.000	1	0	0	0	0	0	0	0	0	0	0
Gabby Hartnett, c	.313	4	16	2	5	2	0	1	1	1	3	0
Rollie Hemsley, c-1	.000	3	3	0	0	0	0	0	0	0	3	0
Billy Herman, 2b	.222	4	18	5	4	1	0	0	1	1	3	0
Billy Jurges, ss	.364	3	11	1	4	1	0	0	1	0	1	2
Mark Koenig, ss-1	.250	2	4	1	1	0	1	0	1	1	0	0
Pat Malone, p	.000	1	0	0	0	0	0	0	0	0	0	0
Jakie May, p	.000	2	2	0	0	0	0	0	0	0	0	0
Johnny Moore, of	.000	2	7	1	0	0	0	0	0	2	1	0
Charlie Root, p	.000	1	2	0	0	0	0	0	0	0	1	0
Bob Smith, p	.000	1	0	0	0	0	0	0	0	0	0	0
Riggs Stephenson, of	.444	4	18	2	8	1	0	0	4	0	0	0
Bud Tinning, p	.000	2	0	0	0	0	0	0	0	0	0	0
Lon Warneke, p	.000	2	4	0	0	0	0	0	0	0	3	0
TOTAL	.253		146	19	37	8	2	3	16	11	24	3

PITCHER	W	L	ERA	G	GS	CG	SV	SHO	IP	H	ER	BB	SO
Guy Bush	0	1	14.29	2	2	0	0	0	5.2	5	9	6	2
Burleigh Grimes	0	0	23.63	2	0	0	0	0	2.2	7	7	2	0
Pat Malone	0	0	0.00	1	0	0	0	0	2.2	1	0	4	4
Jakie May	0	1	11.57	2	0	0	0	0	4.2	9	6	3	4
Charlie Root	0	1	10.38	1	1	0	0	0	4.1	6	5	3	4
Bob Smith	0	0	9.00	1	0	0	0	0	1.0	2	1	0	1
Bud Tinning	0	0	0.00	2	0	0	0	0	2.1	0	0	0	3
Lon Warneke	0	1	5.91	2	1	1	0	0	10.2	15	7	5	8
TOTAL	0	4	9.26	13	4	1	0	0	34.0	45	35	23	26

GAME 1 AT NY SEPT 28

CHI	200	000	220	6	10	1
NY	000	305	31X	12	8	2

Pitchers: BUSH, Grimes (6), Smith (8) vs RUFFING
Home Runs: Gehrig-NY
Attendance: 41,459

GAME 2 AT NY SEPT 29

CHI	101	000	000	2	9	0
NY	202	010	00X	5	10	1

Pitchers: WARNEKE vs GOMEZ
Attendance: 50,709

GAME 3 AT CHI OCT 1

NY	301	020	001	7	8	1
CHI	102	100	001	5	9	4

Pitchers: PIPGRAS, Pennock (9) vs ROOT, Malone (5), May (7), Tinning (9)
Home Runs: Ruth-NY (2), Gehrig-NY (2), Cuyler-CHI, Hartnett-CHI
Attendance: 49,986

GAME 4 AT CHI OCT 2

NY	102	002	404	13	19	4
CHI	400	001	001	6	9	1

Pitchers: Allen, MOORE (1), Pennock (7) vs Bush, Warneke (1), MAY (4), Tinning (7), Grimes (9)
Home Runs: Demaree-CHI, Lazzeri-NY (2), Combs-NY
Attendance: 49,844

Although John McGraw had retired from managing the Giants in 1932, he continued to regard them as "his" team. Led now by first baseman Bill Terry, the Giants faced a club also led by an active player, shortstop Joe Cronin in his rookie managerial season.

Giant ace Carl Hubbell dominated the first game, striking out ten while limiting the Senators to five singles and a pair of unearned runs. Mel Ott set the tone for New York with a two-out two-run homer in the first inning, and singled home a third Giant run in the third to build a lead Washington would not overcome. The next day the Senators scored first, on Goose Goslin's solo homer in the third. But that was the only run scored off Giant pitcher Hal Schumacher, and when the Giants drove out Senator starter Alvin Crowder with six runs in the sixth they had their second win well in hand.

The Senators revived when the Series moved to Washington for Game Three. Each of second baseman Buddy Myer's three hits scored or drove in a run, providing a growing cushion for pitcher Earl Whitehill, who recorded the Series' only shutout.

Games Four and Five went to New York, but not without a struggle. In the fourth game, manager Terry's home run broke the ice in the fourth inning, but Giant pitcher Hubbell muffed a bunt in the seventh which led to the tying run. Hubbell and Senator starter Monty Weaver dueled without further scoring until shortstop Blondy Ryan's single in the top of the eleventh put New York up by one. Hubbell let men reach second and third with one out in the last of the eleventh, but an intentional walk set up the hoped-for double play to end the game.

New York had built a three-run lead in Game Five when Senator Fred Schulte evened the score in the last of the sixth with a three-run homer. Relievers Jack Russell and Dolf Luque then dueled scorelessly into the tenth, when Giant Mel Ott (whose homer had begun the Series' scoring in the first inning of Game One) homered once again for what proved the Series' final run. Luque shut down the Senators in their half of the tenth, and "McGraw's Giants" were for the fourth time the world's finest. But before the advent of another spring, McGraw was dead.

New York Giants (NL), 4;
Washington Senators (AL), 1

NY (N)

PLAYER/POS	AVG	G	AB	R	H	2B	3B	HR	RB	BB	SO	SB
Hi Bell, p	.000	1	0	0	0	0	0	0	0	0	0	0
Hughie Critz, 2b	.136	5	22	2	3	0	0	0	0	1	0	0
Kiddo Davis, of	.368	5	19	1	7	1	0	0	0	0	3	0
Freddie Fitzsimmons, p	.500	1	2	0	1	0	0	0	0	0	0	0
Carl Hubbell, p	.286	2	7	0	2	0	0	0	0	0	0	0
Travis Jackson, 3b	.222	5	18	3	4	1	0	0	2	1	3	0
Dolf Luque, p	1.000	1	1	0	1	0	0	0	0	0	0	0
Gus Mancuso, c	.118	5	17	2	2	1	0	0	2	3	0	0
Jo-Jo Moore, of	.227	5	22	1	5	1	0	0	1	1	3	0
Lefty O'Doul, ph	1.000	1	1	1	1	0	0	0	2	0	0	0
Mel Ott, of	.389	5	18	3	7	0	0	2	4	4	4	0
Homer Peel, of-1	.500	2	2	0	1	0	0	0	0	0	0	0
Blondy Ryan, ss	.278	5	18	0	5	0	0	0	1	1	5	0
Hal Schumacher, p	.286	2	7	0	2	0	0	0	3	0	3	0
Bill Terry, 1b	.273	5	22	3	6	1	0	1	1	0	0	0
TOTAL	.267		176	16	47	5	0	3	16	11	21	0

PITCHER	W	L	ERA	G	GS	CG	SV	SHO	IP	H	ER	BB	SO
Hi Bell	0	0	0.00	1	0	0	0	0	1.0	0	0	0	0
Freddie Fitzsimmons	0	1	5.14	1	1	0	0	0	7.0	9	4	0	2
Carl Hubbell	2	0	0.00	2	2	2	0	0	20.0	13	0	6	15
Dolf Luque	1	0	0.00	1	0	0	0	0	4.1	2	0	2	5
Hal Schumacher	1	0	2.45	2	2	1	0	0	14.2	13	4	5	3
TOTAL	4	1	1.53	7	5	3	0	0	47.0	37	8	13	25

WAS (A)

PLAYER/POS	AVG	G	AB	R	H	2B	3B	HR	RB	BB	SO	SB
Ossie Bluege, 3b	.125	5	16	1	2	1	0	0	0	1	6	0
Cliff Bolton, ph	.000	2	2	0	0	0	0	0	0	0	0	0
Joe Cronin, ss	.318	5	22	1	7	0	0	0	2	0	2	0
General Crowder, p	.250	2	4	0	1	0	0	0	0	0	0	0
Goose Goslin, of	.250	5	20	2	5	1	0	1	1	1	3	0
Dave Harris, of-1	.000	3	2	0	0	0	0	0	0	2	0	0
John Kerr, pr	.000	1	0	0	0	0	0	0	0	0	0	0
Joe Kuhel, 1b	.150	5	20	1	3	0	0	0	1	1	4	0
Heinie Manush, of	.111	5	18	2	2	0	0	0	0	2	1	0
Alex Mc Coll, p	.000	1	0	0	0	0	0	0	0	0	0	0
Buddy Myer, 2b	.300	5	20	2	6	1	0	0	2	2	3	0
Sam Rice, ph	1.000	1	1	0	1	0	0	0	0	0	0	0
Jack Russell, p	.000	3	2	0	0	0	0	0	0	1	2	0
Fred Schulte, of	.333	5	21	1	7	1	0	1	4	1	1	0
Luke Sewell, c	.176	5	17	1	3	0	0	0	1	2	0	1
Lefty Stewart, p	.000	1	1	0	0	0	0	0	0	0	1	0
Tommy Thomas, p	.000	2	0	0	0	0	0	0	0	0	0	0
Monte Weaver, p	.000	1	4	0	0	0	0	0	0	0	2	0
Earl Whitehill, p	.000	1	3	0	0	0	0	0	0	0	0	0
TOTAL	.214		173	11	37	4	0	2	11	13	25	1

PITCHER	W	L	ERA	G	GS	CG	SV	SHO	IP	H	ER	BB	SO
General Crowder	0	1	7.36	2	2	0	0	0	11.0	16	9	5	7
Alex Mc Coll	0	0	0.00	1	0	0	0	0	2.0	0	0	0	0
Jack Russell	0	1	0.87	3	0	0	0	0	10.1	8	1	0	7
Lefty Stewart	0	1	9.00	1	1	0	0	0	2.0	6	2	0	0
Tommy Thomas	0	0	0.00	2	0	0	0	0	1.1	1	0	0	2
Monte Weaver	0	1	1.74	1	1	0	0	0	10.1	11	2	4	3
Earl Whitehill	1	0	0.00	1	1	1	0	1	9.0	5	0	2	2
TOTAL	1	4	2.74	11	5	1	0	1	46.0	47	14	11	21

GAME 1 AT NY OCT 3

WAS	000 100 001	2	5 3
NY	202 000 00X	4	10 2

Pitchers: STEWART, Russell (3), Thomas (8) vs HUBBELL
Home Runs: Ott-NY
Attendance: 46,672

GAME 2 AT NY OCT 4

WAS	001 000 000	1	5 0
NY	000 006 00X	6	10 0

Pitchers: CROWDER, Thomas (6), McColl (7) vs SCHUMACHER
Home Runs: Goslin-WAS
Attendance: 35,461

GAME 3 AT WAS OCT 5

NY	000 000 000	0	5 0
WAS	210 000 10X	4	9 1

Pitchers: FITZSIMMONS, Bell (8) vs WHITEHILL
Attendance: 25,727

GAME 4 AT WAS OCT 6

NY	000 100 000 01	2	11 1
WAS	000 000 100 00	1	8 0

Pitchers: HUBBELL vs WEAVER, Russell (11)
Home Runs: Terry-NY
Attendance: 26,762

GAME 5 AT WAS OCT 7

NY	020 001 000 1	4	11 1
WAS	000 003 000 0	3	10 0

Pitchers: Schumacher, LUQUE (6) vs Crowder, RUSSELL (6)
Home Runs: Schulte-WAS, Ott-NY
Attendance: 28,454

Pitching brothers Dizzy and Paul Dean won seven games in ten days to give the Cardinals the pennant on the final day of the season. In the Series they continued their winning ways, chalking up all four Cardinal victories. Dizzy pitched the opener in Detroit. Given a 3–0 lead, thanks to five Tiger errors in the first three innings, he breezed to an 8–3 win.

Detroit's Schoolboy Rowe brought the Tigers back with a pitching masterpiece in Game Two. After giving up single runs in the second and third innings, he allowed only one runner to reach base over the next nine as his Tigers tied the score in the ninth, and won it on two walks and a single in the twelfth.

Paul Dean nearly pitched a shutout in Game Three, yielding a harmless run with two out in the ninth after the Cards had built him a 4–0 lead. Brother Diz figured in a curious and painful play in Game Four. Pinch-running in the fourth inning, he was beaned by a would-be double-play throw as he ran to second. The tying run scored from third on the play, but Detroit's pitcher Eldon Auker shut out the Cards through the final five innings, and his teammates scored six more runs to bury St. Louis 10–4, evening the Series at two apiece. Diz was rushed to the hospital, but as no damage was found he started Game Five the next day. He pitched well enough, but Detroit's Tommy Bridges pitched better, giving the Cardinals only one run to the Tigers' three.

Paul Dean evened the Series again with a win against Rowe in a closely contested sixth game. A grounder through Dean's legs allowed the Tigers to tie the game in the sixth inning, but Paul redeemed his error in the seventh when he singled in the tie-breaking—and as it turned out, winning—run. Dizzy came back after only a day's rest to hurl a six-hit shutout in the finale. He also scored the game's first run and drove in the sixth with a double and single in his team's seven-run third. Three innings later, frustrated Tiger fans, angered by Cardinal Joe Medwick's rough slide into their third baseman, pelted Medwick with food and bottles, halting the game for twenty minutes until Commissioner Landis ordered Medwick from the game. The delay only forestalled Detroit's defeat, as the Cards took the title game 11–0.

St. Louis Cardinals (NL), 4; Detroit Tigers (AL), 3

STL (N)

PLAYER/POS	AVG	G	AB	R	H	2B	3B	HR	RB	BB	SO	SB
Tex Carleton, p	.000	2	1	0	0	0	0	0	0	0	0	0
Ripper Collins, 1b	.367	7	30	4	11	1	0	0	3	1	2	0
Pat Crawford, ph	.000	2	2	0	0	0	0	0	0	0	0	0
Spud Davis, ph	1.000	2	2	0	2	0	0	0	1	0	0	0
Dizzy Dean, p-3	.250	4	12	3	3	2	0	0	1	0	3	0
Paul Dean, p	.167	2	6	0	1	0	0	0	2	0	1	0
Bill De Lancey, c	.172	7	29	3	5	3	0	1	4	2	8	0
Leo Durocher, ss	.259	7	27	4	7	1	1	0	0	0	0	0
Frankie Frisch, 2b	.194	7	31	2	6	1	0	0	4	0	1	0
Chick Fullis, of	.400	3	5	0	2	0	0	0	0	0	0	0
Jesse Haines, p	.000	1	0	0	0	0	0	0	0	0	0	0
Bill Hallahan, p	.000	1	3	0	0	0	0	0	0	0	1	0
Pepper Martin, 3b	.355	7	31	8	11	3	1	0	4	3	3	2
Joe Medwick, of	.379	7	29	4	11	0	1	1	5	1	7	0
Jim Mooney, p	.000	1	0	0	0	0	0	0	0	0	0	0
Ernie Orsatti, of	.318	7	22	3	7	0	1	0	2	3	1	0
Jack Rothrock, of	.233	7	30	3	7	3	0	0	6	1	2	0
Dazzy Vance, p	.000	1	0	0	0	0	0	0	0	0	0	0
Bill Walker, p	.000	2	2	0	0	0	0	0	0	0	2	0
Burgess Whitehead, ss	.000	1	0	0	0	0	0	0	0	0	0	0
TOTAL	.279		262	34	73	14	5	2	32	11	31	2

PITCHER	W	L	ERA	G	GS	CG	SV	SHO	IP	H	ER	BB	SO
Tex Carleton	0	0	7.36	2	1	0	0	0	3.2	5	3	2	2
Dizzy Dean	2	1	1.73	3	3	2	0	1	26.0	20	5	5	17
Paul Dean	2	0	1.00	2	2	2	0	0	18.0	15	2	7	11
Jesse Haines	0	0	0.00	1	0	0	0	0	0.2	1	0	0	2
Bill Hallahan	0	0	2.16	1	1	0	0	0	8.1	6	2	4	6
Jim Mooney	0	0	0.00	1	0	0	0	0	1.0	1	0	0	0
Dazzy Vance	0	0	0.00	1	0	0	0	0	1.1	2	0	1	3
Bill Walker	0	2	7.11	2	0	0	0	0	6.1	6	5	6	2
TOTAL	4	3	2.34	13	7	4	0	1	65.1	56	17	25	43

DET (A)

PLAYER/POS	AVG	G	AB	R	H	2B	3B	HR	RB	BB	SO	SB
Eldon Auker, p	.000	2	4	0	0	0	0	0	0	0	2	0
Tommy Bridges, p	.143	3	7	0	1	0	0	0	0	1	4	0
Mickey Cochrane, c	.214	7	28	2	6	1	0	0	1	4	3	0
General Crowder, p	.000	2	1	0	0	0	0	0	0	0	0	0
Frank Doljack, of-1	.000	2	2	0	0	0	0	0	0	0	0	0
Pete Fox, of	.286	7	28	1	8	6	0	0	2	1	4	0
Charlie Gehringer, 2b	.379	7	29	5	11	1	0	1	2	3	0	1
Goose Goslin, of	.241	7	29	2	7	1	0	0	2	3	1	0
Hank Greenberg, 1b	.321	7	28	4	9	2	1	1	7	4	9	1
Ray Hayworth, c	.000	1	0	0	0	0	0	0	0	0	0	0
Chief Hogsett, p	.000	3	0	0	0	0	0	0	0	0	1	0
Firpo Marberry, p	.000	2	0	0	0	0	0	0	0	0	0	0
Marv Owen, 3b	.069	7	29	0	2	0	0	0	1	0	5	1
Billy Rogell, ss	.276	7	29	3	8	1	0	0	4	1	4	1
Schoolboy Rowe, p	.000	3	7	0	0	0	0	0	0	0	5	0
Gee Walker, ph	.333	3	3	0	1	0	0	0	1	0	1	0
Jo-Jo White, of	.130	7	23	6	3	0	0	0	0	8	4	1
TOTAL	.224		250	23	56	12	1	2	20	25	43	5

PITCHER	W	L	ERA	G	GS	CG	SV	SHO	IP	H	ER	BB	SO
Eldon Auker	1	1	5.56	2	2	1	0	0	11.1	16	7	5	2
Tommy Bridges	1	1	3.63	3	2	1	0	0	17.1	21	7	1	12
General Crowder	0	1	1.50	2	1	0	0	0	6.0	6	1	1	2
Chief Hogsett	0	0	1.23	3	0	0	0	0	7.1	6	1	3	3
Firpo Marberry	0	0	21.60	2	0	0	0	0	1.2	5	4	1	0
Schoolboy Rowe	1	1	2.95	3	2	2	0	0	21.1	19	7	0	12
TOTAL	3	4	3.74	15	7	4	0	0	65.0	73	27	11	31

GAME 1 AT DET OCT 3

STL	021	014	000	8	13	4
DET	001	001	010	3	8	5

Pitchers: J.DEAN vs CROWDER, Marberry (6), Hogsett (6)
Home Runs: Medwick-STL, Greenberg-DET
Attendance: 42,505

GAME 2 AT DET OCT 4

STL	011	000	000	000	2	7	3
DET	000	100	001	001	3	7	0

Pitchers: Hallahan, W.WALKER (9) vs ROWE
Attendance: 43,451

GAME 3 AT STL OCT 5

DET	000	000	001	1	8	2
STL	110	020	00X	4	9	1

Pitchers: BRIDGES, Hogsett (5) vs P.DEAN
Attendance: 34,073

GAME 4 AT STL OCT 6

DET	003	100	150	10	13	1
STL	011	200	000	4	10	5

Pitchers: AUKER vs Carleton, Vance (3), W.WALKER (5), Haines (8), Mooney (9)
Attendance: 37,492

GAME 5 AT STL OCT 7

DET	010	002	000	3	7	0
STL	000	000	100	1	7	1

Pitchers: BRIDGES vs J.DEAN, Carleton (9)
Home Runs: Gehringer-DET, DeLancey-STL
Attendance: 38,536

GAME 6 AT DET OCT 8

STL	100	020	100	4	10	2
DET	001	002	000	3	7	1

Pitchers: P.DEAN vs ROWE
Attendance: 44,551

GAME 7 AT DET OCT 9

STL	007	002	200	11	17	1
DET	000	000	000	0	6	3

Pitchers: J.DEAN vs AUKER, Rowe (3), Hogsett (3), Bridges (4), Marberry (8), Crowder (9)
Attendance: 40,902

With a 21-game September winning streak, the Cubs vaulted over the Giants and Cardinals to face Detroit in the Series, and for a moment it seemed as if their momentum might carry them past the Tigers as well. Chicago scored two runs off Schoolboy Rowe in the top of the first in the opener, and right fielder Frank Demaree homered to open the ninth as Lon Warneke blanked the Tigers on four hits. But Detroit retaliated quickly in Game Two, driving out starter Charlie Root in the first inning with four runs (including Hank Greenberg's two-run homer) before Root had had a chance to record even one out. Tiger pitcher Rocky Bridges gained an easy 8–3 win, but Greenberg broke a wrist and was finished for the Series.

In Game Three the Cubs scored three times before Detroit countered with their first run in the sixth. But a walk and four Tiger hits in the eighth put the Bengals ahead 4–3, and Billy Rogell's baserunning as he turned a foiled steal into a rundown permitted a fifth Tiger to cross the plate. Two Cub runs in the last of the ninth tied the score, but Detroit pulled out the victory in the eleventh as a pair of singles sandwiched Fred Lindstrom's error at third to give them an unearned run.

Detroit's Alvin "General" Crowder followed up the Tigers' advantage the next day with a neat five-hit 2–1 win. Once again the Cubs bobbled away the game, this time with two sixth-inning errors that enabled Detroit to score the winning run without a hit. Chuck Klein's two-run homer saved Chicago from elimination in Game Five as Lon Warneke and Bill Lee shut out the Tigers through eight before letting in a harmless run in the ninth.

Chicago's Larry French and Tiger Rocky Bridges yielded 12 hits apiece in Game Six. Cub second baseman Billy Herman singled in a run in the third to tie the score, and homered for two more runs in the fifth to put the Cubs ahead. But the Tigers tied it up an inning later, and took their first world title ever when Goose Goslin singled in Mickey Cochrane with two out in the bottom of the ninth.

Detroit Tigers (AL), 4;
Chicago Cubs (NL), 2

DET (A)

PLAYER/POS	AVG	G	AB	R	H	2B	3B	HR	RB	BB	SO	SB
Eldon Auker, p	.000	1	2	0	0	0	0	0	0	0	1	0
Tommy Bridges, p	.125	2	8	1	1	0	0	0	1	0	3	0
Flea Clifton, 3b	.000	4	16	1	0	0	0	0	0	2	4	0
Mickey Cochrane, c	.292	6	24	3	7	1	0	0	1	4	1	0
General Crowder, p	.333	1	3	1	1	0	0	0	0	1	0	0
Pete Fox, of	.385	6	26	1	10	3	1	0	4	0	1	0
Charlie Gehringer, 2b	.375	6	24	4	9	3	0	0	4	2	1	1
Goose Goslin, of	.273	6	22	2	6	1	0	0	3	5	0	0
Hank Greenberg, 1b	.167	2	6	1	1	0	0	1	2	1	0	0
Chief Hogsett, p	.000	1	0	0	0	0	0	0	0	0	0	0
Marv Owen, 1b-4,3b-2	.050	6	20	2	1	0	0	0	1	2	3	0
Billy Rogell, ss	.292	6	24	1	7	2	0	0	1	2	5	0
Schoolboy Rowe, p	.250	3	8	0	2	1	0	0	0	0	1	0
Gee Walker, of-1	.250	3	4	1	1	0	0	0	0	1	0	0
Jo-Jo White, of	.263	5	19	3	5	0	0	0	1	5	7	0
TOTAL	.248		206	21	51	11	1	1	18	25	27	1

PITCHER	W	L	ERA	G	GS	CG	SV	SHO	IP	H	ER	BB	SO
Eldon Auker	0	0	3.00	1	1	0	0	0	6.0	6	2	2	1
Tommy Bridges	2	0	2.50	2	2	2	0	0	18.0	18	5	4	9
General Crowder	1	0	1.00	1	1	1	0	0	9.0	5	1	3	5
Chief Hogsett	0	0	0.00	1	0	0	0	0	1.0	0	0	1	0
Schoolboy Rowe	1	2	2.57	3	2	2	0	0	21.0	19	6	1	14
TOTAL	4	2	2.29	8	6	5	0	0	55.0	48	14	11	29

CHI (N)

PLAYER/POS	AVG	G	AB	R	H	2B	3B	HR	RB	BB	SO	SB
Tex Carleton, p	.000	1	1	0	0	0	0	0	0	1	1	0
Phil Cavaretta, 1b	.125	6	24	1	3	0	0	0	0	0	5	0
Frank Demaree, of	.250	6	24	2	6	1	0	2	2	1	4	0
Larry French, p	.250	2	4	1	1	0	0	0	0	0	2	0
Augie Galan, of	.160	6	25	2	4	1	0	0	2	2	2	0
Stan Hack, 3b-6,ss-1	.227	6	22	2	5	1	1	0	0	2	2	1
Gabby Hartnett, c	.292	6	24	1	7	0	0	1	2	0	3	0
Roy Henshaw, p	.000	1	1	0	0	0	0	0	0	0	0	0
Billy Herman, 2b	.333	6	24	3	8	2	1	1	6	0	2	0
Billy Jurges, ss	.250	6	16	3	4	0	0	0	1	4	4	0
Chuck Klein, of-3	.333	5	12	2	4	0	0	1	2	0	2	0
Fabian Kowalik, p	.500	1	2	1	1	0	0	0	0	0	0	0
Bill Lee, p	.000	2	1	0	0	0	0	0	1	0	0	0
Fred Lindstrom, of-4,3b-1	.200	4	15	0	3	1	0	0	0	1	1	0
Ken O'Dea, ph	1.000	1	1	0	1	0	0	0	1	0	0	0
Charlie Root, p	.000	2	0	0	0	0	0	0	0	0	0	0
Walter Stephenson, ph	.000	1	1	0	0	0	0	0	0	0	1	0
Lon Warneke, p	.200	3	5	0	1	0	0	0	0	0	0	0
TOTAL	.238		202	18	48	6	2	5	17	11	29	1

PITCHER	W	L	ERA	G	GS	CG	SV	SHO	IP	H	ER	BB	SO
Tex Carleton	0	1	1.29	1	1	0	0	0	7.0	6	1	7	4
Larry French	0	2	3.38	2	1	1	0	0	10.2	15	4	2	8
Roy Henshaw	0	0	7.36	1	0	0	0	0	3.2	2	3	5	2
Fabian Kowalik	0	0	2.08	1	0	0	0	0	4.1	3	1	1	1
Bill Lee	0	0	3.48	2	1	0	1	0	10.1	11	4	5	5
Charlie Root	0	1	18.00	2	1	0	0	0	2.0	5	4	1	2
Lon Warneke	2	0	0.54	3	2	1	0	1	16.2	9	1	4	5
TOTAL	2	4	2.96	12	6	2	1	1	54.2	51	18	25	27

GAME 1 AT DET OCT 2

CHI	200 000 001	3	7	0
DET	000 000 000	0	4	3

Pitchers: WARNEKE vs ROWE
Home Runs: Demaree-CHI
Attendance: 47,391

GAME 2 AT DET OCT 3

CHI	000 010 200	3	6	1
DET	400 300 10X	8	9	2

Pitchers: ROOT, Henshaw (1), Kowalik (4) vs BRIDGES
Home Runs: Greenberg-DET
Attendance: 46,742

GAME 3 AT CHI OCT 4

DET	000 001 040 01	6	12	2
CHI	020 010 002 00	5	10	3

Pitchers: Auker, Hogsett (7), ROWE (8) vs Warneke, Lee (8), FRENCH (10)
Home Runs: Demaree-CHI
Attendance: 45,532

GAME 4 AT CHI OCT 5

DET	001 001 000	2	7	0
CHI	010 000 000	1	5	2

Pitchers: CROWDER vs CARLETON, Root (8)
Home Runs: Hartnett-CHI
Attendance: 49,350

GAME 5 AT CHI OCT 6

DET	000 000 001	1	7	1
CHI	002 000 10X	3	8	0

Pitchers: ROWE vs WARNEKE, Lee (7)
Home Runs: Klein-CHI
Attendance: 49,237

GAME 6 AT DET OCT 7

CHI	001 020 000	3	12	0
DET	100 101 001	4	12	1

Pitchers: FRENCH vs BRIDGES
Home Runs: Herman-CHI
Attendance: 48,420

The Giants managed to win two games, but this first Series between the cross-river rivals in thirteen years was really no contest. Babe Ruth was gone, but Lou Gehrig was still there, and Joe DiMaggio had arrived. The Yankees outhit the Giants by 56 percentage points and outscored them by 20 runs.

Giant ace Carl Hubbell, who had won his final 16 decisions of the regular season, continued his streak in the Series opener. The Yankees scored first on George Selkirk's third-inning homer, but Giant shortstop Dick Bartell homered to even things in the fifth. Hubbell held the Yankees to that one run, but the Giants roughed up Red Ruffing for five more runs, to give the Polo Grounders a brief Series advantage.

Game Two was a Yankee blowout, as the Yankees hammered five Giant pitchers for 18 runs—four of them on Tony Lazzeri's grand slam in the third—to give Lefty Gomez an easy win. By contrast, Game Three was a pitchers' duel. Although the Giants touched Bump Hadley and Pat Malone for 11 hits, only Jimmy Ripple's fifth-inning homer produced a run. Giant Freddie Fitzsimmons was much more stingy with hits, yielding only four. But one was Gehrig's home run in the second inning, and another was Frank Crosetti's game-winning RBI single in the eighth.

Gehrig homered again in the third inning of Game Four to give the Yankees an insurmountable lead—and Hubbell his first loss in months. Down three games to one, the Giants struggled back in Game Five. They took a first-inning 3–0 lead, but the Yankees clawed their way back, and by the end of six the score was 4–4. There it stayed until the tenth, when a double, sacrifice, and fly to center put the Giants ahead by a run. Hal Schumacher, who had pitched the whole game, held the Yankees scoreless one more time for the win.

Fitzsimmons, who had pitched so well in his third-game loss, didn't last four innings in Game Six. Though the Giants scored first, Yankee Jake Powell (who led all Series hitters at .455) tied the game with a two-run homer in the top of the second. Two more runs in the fourth drove out Fitzsimmons, but the game stayed close until the top of the ninth, when five Yankees singles and three walks produced seven runs and a Series-ending 13–5 rout.

New York Yankees (AL), 4;
New York Giants (NL), 2

NY (A)

PLAYER/POS	AVG	G	AB	R	H	2B	3B	HR	RB	BB	SO	SB
Frankie Crosetti, ss	.269	6	26	5	7	2	0	0	3	3	5	0
Bill Dickey, c	.120	6	25	5	3	0	0	1	5	3	4	0
Joe DiMaggio, of	.346	6	26	3	9	3	0	0	3	1	3	0
Lou Gehrig, 1b	.292	6	24	5	7	1	0	2	7	3	2	0
Lefty Gomez, p	.250	2	8	1	2	0	0	0	3	0	3	0
Bump Hadley, p	.000	1	2	0	0	0	0	0	0	0	1	0
Roy Johnson, ph	.000	2	1	0	0	0	0	0	0	0	1	0
Tony Lazzeri, 2b	.250	6	20	4	5	0	0	1	7	4	4	0
Pat Malone, p	1.000	2	1	0	1	0	0	0	0	0	0	0
Johnny Murphy, p	.500	1	2	1	1	0	0	0	0	1	0	0
Monte Pearson, p	.500	1	4	0	2	1	0	0	0	0	0	0
Jake Powell, of	.455	6	22	8	10	1	0	1	5	4	4	1
Red Rolfe, 3b	.400	6	25	5	10	0	0	0	4	3	1	0
Red Ruffing, p-2	.000	3	5	0	0	0	0	0	0	1	2	0
Bob Seeds, pr	.000	1	0	0	0	0	0	0	0	0	0	0
George Selkirk, of	.333	6	24	6	8	0	1	2	3	4	4	0
TOTAL	.302		215	43	65	8	1	7	41	26	35	1

PITCHER	W	L	ERA	G	GS	CG	SV	SHO	IP	H	ER	BB	SO
Lefty Gomez	2	0	4.70	2	2	1	0	0	15.1	14	8	11	9
Bump Hadley	1	0	1.13	1	1	0	0	0	8.0	10	1	1	2
Pat Malone	0	1	1.80	2	0	0	1	0	5.0	2	1	1	2
Johnny Murphy	0	0	3.38	1	0	0	1	0	2.2	1	1	1	1
Monte Pearson	1	0	2.00	1	1	1	0	0	9.0	7	2	2	7
Red Ruffing	0	1	4.50	2	2	0	0	0	14.0	16	7	5	12
TOTAL	4	2	3.33	9	6	2	2	0	54.0	50	20	21	33

NY (N)

PLAYER/POS	AVG	G	AB	R	H	2B	3B	HR	RB	BB	SO	SB
Dick Bartell, ss	.381	6	21	5	8	3	0	1	3	4	4	0
Slick Castleman, p	.500	1	2	0	1	0	0	0	0	0	0	0
Dick Coffman, p	.000	2	0	0	0	0	0	0	0	0	0	0
Harry Danning, c-1	.000	2	2	0	0	0	0	0	0	0	1	0
Kiddo Davis, ph	.500	4	2	1	1	0	0	0	0	0	0	0
Freddie Fitzsimmons, p	.500	2	4	0	2	0	0	0	0	0	1	0
Frank Gabler, p	.000	2	0	0	0	0	0	0	0	1	0	0
Harry Gumbert, p	.000	2	0	0	0	0	0	0	0	0	0	0
Carl Hubbell, p	.333	2	6	0	2	0	0	0	1	0	0	0
Travis Jackson, 3b	.190	6	21	1	4	0	0	0	1	1	3	0
Mark Koenig, 2b-1	.333	3	3	0	1	0	0	0	0	0	1	0
Hank Leiber, of	.000	2	6	0	0	0	0	0	0	2	2	0
Sam Leslie, ph	.667	3	3	0	2	0	0	0	0	0	0	0
Gus Mancuso, c	.263	6	19	3	5	2	0	0	1	3	3	0
Eddie Mayo, 3b	.000	1	1	0	0	0	0	0	0	0	0	0
Jo-Jo Moore, of	.214	6	28	4	6	2	0	1	1	1	4	0
Mel Ott, of	.304	6	23	4	7	2	0	1	3	3	1	0
Jimmy Ripple, of	.333	5	12	2	4	0	0	1	3	3	3	0
Hal Schumacher, p	.000	2	4	0	0	0	0	0	0	1	3	0
Al Smith, p	.000	1	0	0	0	0	0	0	0	0	0	0
Bill Terry, 1b	.240	6	25	1	6	0	0	0	5	1	4	0
Burgess Whitehead, 2b	.048	6	21	1	1	0	0	0	2	1	3	0
TOTAL	.246		203	23	50	9	0	4	20	21	33	0

PITCHER	W	L	ERA	G	GS	CG	SV	SHO	IP	H	ER	BB	SO
Slick Castleman	0	0	2.08	1	0	0	0	0	4.1	3	1	2	5
Dick Coffman	0	0	32.40	2	0	0	0	0	1.2	5	6	1	1
Freddie Fitzsimmons	0	2	5.40	2	2	1	0	0	11.2	13	7	2	6
Frank Gabler	0	0	7.20	2	0	0	0	0	5.0	7	4	4	0
Harry Gumbert	0	0	36.00	2	0	0	0	0	2.0	7	8	4	2
Carl Hubbell	1	1	2.25	2	2	1	0	0	16.0	15	4	2	10
Hal Schumacher	1	1	5.25	2	2	1	0	0	12.0	13	7	10	11
Al Smith	0	0	81.00	1	0	0	0	0	0.1	2	3	1	0
TOTAL	2	4	6.79	14	6	3	0	0	53.0	65	40	26	35

GAME 1 AT NY -N SEPT 30

NY-A	001	000	000	1	7	2
NY-N	000	011	04X	6	9	1

Pitchers: RUFFING vs HUBBELL
Home Runs: Bartell-NY(N), Selkirk-NY(A)
Attendance: 39,419

GAME 2 AT NY -N OCT 2

NY-A	207	001	206	18	17	0
NY-N	010	300	000	4	6	1

Pitchers: GOMEZ vs SCHUMACHER, Smith (3), Coffman (3), Gabler (5), Gumbert (9)
Home Runs: Dickey-NY(A), Lazzeri-NY(A)
Attendance: 43,543

GAME 3 AT NY -A OCT 3

NY-N	000	010	000	1	11	0
NY-A	010	000	01X	2	4	0

Pitchers: FITZSIMMONS vs HADLEY, Malone (9)
Home Runs: Gerhig-NY(A), Ripple-NY(N)
Attendance: 64,842

GAME 4 AT NY -A OCT 4

NY-N	000	100	010	2	7	1
NY-A	013	000	01X	5	10	1

Pitchers: HUBBELL, Gabler (8) vs PEARSON
Home Runs: Gehrig-NY(A)
Attendance: 66,669

GAME 5 AT NY -A OCT 5

NY-N	300	001	000	1	5	8	3
NY-A	011	002	000	0	4	10	1

Pitchers: SCHUMACHER vs Ruffing, MALONE (7)
Home Runs: Selkirk-NY(A)
Attendance: 50,024

GAME 6 AT NY -N OCT 6

NY-A	021	200	017	13	17	2
NY-N	200	010	110	5	9	1

Pitchers: GOMEZ, Murphy (7) vs FITZSIMMONS, Castleman (4), Coffman (9), Gumbert (9)
Home Runs: Moore-NY(N), Ott-NY(N), Powell-NY(A)
Attendance: 38,427

For the second year in a row, the Yankees overwhelmed the Giants, this time in just five games. Giant ace Carl Hubbell, who took the opener in 1936, was unable to repeat this year. For five innings he held the Yankees to one hit. But in the sixth everything fell apart. Before Hubbell was taken out, two walks, five singles, and a Giant error had let in five runs. And the two runners Hubbell left on base scored later on a second Giant error and two walks by reliever Dick Coffman. The Yankees' Lefty Gomez also yielded six hits, but wider spacing and better field support held the Giants to one run in the fifth. Tony Lazzeri's homer in the eighth made the final score 8–1.

The Yankees spread their runs a bit more evenly in Game Two. For the second time the Giants gained a 1–0 lead. Rookie phenom Cliff Melton held the Yankees scoreless through four, but four straight hits for two runs at the start of the fifth drove him out. Reliever Ad Gumbert stopped the Yankees in the rest of the inning but gave up four more hits—and four more runs—in the sixth before Coffman stepped in to stop the assault. But Coffman gave up two final Yankee runs in the seventh, to complete a second straight 8–1 Yankee win, as Red Ruffing held the Giants scoreless through the final eight innings.

The Yankees had scored five times off Hal Schumacher in Game Three before the Giants got their one run in the seventh. But Yankee starter Monte Pearson made the game tighter as he yielded a single and two walks to load the bases in the ninth before Johnny Murphy came on to record the final out.

Giant bats finally came alive in the second inning of Game Four. Seven singles, plus a walk and a missed play at the plate gave the club a 6–1 lead, which starter Hubbell protected for the only Giant win of the Series.

Solo homers by Myril Hoag in the second and Joe DiMaggio in the third gave the Yankees a 2–0 lead early in Game Five, but Giant Mel Ott tied it up with a two-run shot off Lefty Gomez in the last of the third. But Gomez shut the Giants down the rest of the way, and in the fifth with what proved the game winner (scoring himself on Lou Gehrig's double for the final run of the Series).

New York Yankees (AL), 4;
New York Giants (NL), 1

NY (A)

PLAYER/POS	AVG	G	AB	R	H	2B	3B	HR	RB	BB	SO	SB
Ivy Andrews, p	.000	1	2	0	0	0	0	0	0	0	1	0
Frankie Crosetti, ss	.048	5	21	2	1	0	0	0	0	3	2	0
Bill Dickey, c	.211	5	19	3	4	0	1	0	3	2	2	0
Joe DiMaggio, of	.273	5	22	2	6	0	0	1	4	0	3	0
Lou Gehrig, 1b	.294	5	17	4	5	1	1	1	3	5	4	0
Lefty Gomez, p	.167	2	6	2	1	0	0	0	1	2	1	0
Bump Hadley, p	.000	1	0	0	0	0	0	0	0	0	0	0
Myril Hoag, of	.300	5	20	4	6	1	0	1	2	0	1	0
Tony Lazzeri, 2b	.400	5	15	3	6	0	1	1	2	3	3	0
Johnny Murphy, p	.000	1	0	0	0	0	0	0	0	0	0	0
Monte Pearson, p	.000	1	3	0	0	0	0	0	0	1	1	0
Jake Powell, ph	.000	1	1	0	0	0	0	0	0	0	1	0
Red Rolfe, 3b	.300	5	20	3	6	2	1	0	1	3	2	0
Red Ruffing, p	.500	1	4	0	2	1	0	0	3	0	0	0
George Selkirk, of	.263	5	19	5	5	1	0	0	6	2	0	0
Kemp Wicker, p	.000	1	0	0	0	0	0	0	0	0	0	0
TOTAL	.249		169	28	42	6	4	4	25	21	21	0

PITCHER	W	L	ERA	G	GS	CG	SV	SHO	IP	H	ER	BB	SO
Ivy Andrews	0	0	3.18	1	0	0	0	0	5.2	6	2	4	1
Lefty Gomez	2	0	1.50	2	2	2	0	0	18.0	16	3	2	8
Bump Hadley	0	1	33.75	1	1	0	0	0	1.1	6	5	0	0
Johnny Murphy	0	0	0.00	1	0	0	1	0	0.1	0	0	0	0
Monte Pearson	1	0	1.04	1	1	0	0	0	8.2	5	1	2	4
Red Ruffing	1	0	1.00	1	1	1	0	0	9.0	7	1	3	8
Kemp Wicker	0	0	0.00	1	0	0	0	0	1.0	0	0	0	0
TOTAL	4	1	2.45	8	5	3	1	0	44.0	40	12	11	21

NY (N)

PLAYER/POS	AVG	G	AB	R	H	2B	3B	HR	RB	BB	SO	SB
Dick Bartell, ss	.238	5	21	3	5	1	0	0	1	0	3	0
Wally Berger, ph	.000	3	3	0	0	0	0	0	0	0	1	0
Don Brennan, p	.000	2	0	0	0	0	0	0	0	0	0	0
Lou Chiozza, of	.286	2	7	0	2	0	0	0	0	1	1	0
Dick Coffman, p	.000	2	1	0	0	0	0	0	0	0	1	0
Harry Danning, c	.250	3	12	0	3	1	0	0	2	0	2	0
Harry Gumbert, p	.000	2	0	0	0	0	0	0	0	0	0	0
Carl Hubbell, p	.000	2	6	1	0	0	0	0	0	1	0	0
Hank Leiber, of	.364	3	11	2	4	0	0	0	2	1	1	0
Sam Leslie, ph	.000	2	1	0	0	0	0	0	0	1	0	0
Gus Mancuso, c-2	.000	3	8	0	0	0	0	0	1	0	1	0
Johnny Mc Carthy, 1b	.211	5	19	1	4	1	0	0	1	1	2	0
Cliff Melton, p	.000	3	2	0	0	0	0	0	0	1	1	0
Jo-Jo Moore, of	.391	5	23	1	9	1	0	0	1	0	1	0
Mel Ott, 3b	.200	5	20	1	4	0	0	1	3	1	4	0
Jimmy Ripple, of	.294	5	17	2	5	0	0	0	0	3	1	0
Blondy Ryan, ph	.000	1	1	0	0	0	0	0	0	0	1	0
Hal Schumacher, p	.000	1	1	0	0	0	0	0	0	0	1	0
Al Smith, p	.000	2	0	0	0	0	0	0	0	0	0	0
Burgess Whitehead, 2b	.250	5	16	1	4	2	0	0	0	2	0	1
TOTAL	.237		169	12	40	6	0	1	12	11	21	1

PITCHER	W	L	ERA	G	GS	CG	SV	SHO	IP	H	ER	BB	SO
Don Brennan	0	0	0.00	2	0	0	0	0	3.0	1	0	1	1
Dick Coffman	0	0	4.15	2	0	0	0	0	4.1	2	2	5	1
Harry Gumbert	0	0	27.00	2	0	0	0	0	1.1	4	4	1	1
Carl Hubbell	1	1	3.77	2	2	1	0	0	14.1	12	6	4	7
Cliff Melton	0	2	4.91	3	2	0	0	0	11.0	12	6	6	7
Hal Schumacher	0	1	6.00	1	1	0	0	0	6.0	9	4	4	3
Al Smith	0	0	3.00	2	0	0	0	0	3.0	2	1	0	1
TOTAL	1	4	4.81	14	5	1	0	0	43.0	42	23	21	21

GAME 1 AT NY -A OCT 6

NY-N	000 010 000	1	6	2
NY-A	000 007 01X	8	7	0

Pitchers: HUBBELL, Gumbert (6), Coffman (6), Smith (8) vs GOMEZ
Home Runs: Lazzeri-NY(A)
Attendance: 60,573

GAME 2 AT NY -A OCT 7

NY-N	100 000 000	1	7	0
NY-A	000 024 20X	8	12	1

Pitchers: MELTON, Gumbert (5), Coffman (6) vs RUFFING
Attendance: 57,675

GAME 3 AT NY -N OCT 8

NY-A	012 110 000	5	9	0
NY-N	000 000 100	1	5	4

Pitchers: PEARSON, Murphy (9) vs SCHUMACHER, Melton (7), Brennan (9)
Attendance: 37,385

GAME 4 AT NY -N OCT 9

NY-A	101 000 001	3	6	0
NY-N	060 000 10X	7	12	3

Pitchers: HADLEY, Andrews (2), Wicker (8) vs HUBBELL
Home Runs: Gehrig-NY(A)
Attendance: 44,293

GAME 5 AT NY -N OCT 10

NY-A	011 020 000	4	8	0
NY-N	002 000 000	2	10	0

Pitchers: GOMEZ vs MELTON, Smith (6), Brennan (8)
Home Runs: DiMaggio-NY(A), Hoag-NY(A), Ott-NY(N)
Attendance: 38,216

As they had six years earlier, the Cubs faced the Yankees in the World Series, and as they had six years earlier, New York swept the Series in four games. Although Cub batters made nearly as many hits as the Yankees, they did much less damage, driving in 13 fewer runs. In Game One, Yankee ace Red Ruffing scattered nine Cub hits, holding Chicago to a single run. The Cubs' Bill Lee was nearly as effective in scattering hits, but a base on balls in the second (the game's only walk) followed by a pair of singles sandwiched around an error accounted for two runs—all the Yankees would need for the win (though they scored once more in the sixth).

In Game Two the Cubs outhit the Yankees 11 to 7, but scored only half as many runs as the New Yorkers. Chicago's Dizzy Dean, pitching on craft and guile with his fastball gone, managed to keep the game close until the final innings. With a 3–2 lead going into the eighth, though, he gave up a two-run homer to Frank Crosetti, and the same to Joe DiMaggio in the ninth before being relieved. Yankee fireman Johnny Murphy, meanwhile, held Chicago scoreless over the final two innings to preserve Lefty Gomez's win.

Utility outfielder Joe Marty drove in both Chicago runs in Game Three with a grounder to third in the fifth and a homer in the eighth. (His .500 BA was tops for both teams, and he drove in five of the Cubs' nine Series runs.) But again the Cubs fell short, as Yankee rookie second baseman Joe Gordon homered to tie the score in the bottom of the fifth with the first of what would be five Yankee runs by the time Bill Dickey's homer in the eighth ended the scoring for the day.

Cub second baseman Billy Herman's wild throw with two out in the second inning of Game Four led to three unearned runs, and a Yankee lead they would not relinquish. Though their lead was cut to one run (4–3) when Chicago scored twice in the top of the eighth, the Yankees took advantage of two wild pitches and two walks to turn their four hits into four runs that crushed Cub hopes and gave the New Yorkers a record third consecutive world championship.

New York Yankees (AL), 4; Chicago Cubs (NL), 0

NY (A)

PLAYER/POS	AVG	G	AB	R	H	2B	3B	HR	RB	BB	SO	SB
Frankie Crosetti, ss	.250	4	16	1	4	2	1	1	6	2	4	0
Bill Dickey, c	.400	4	15	2	6	0	0	1	2	1	0	1
Joe DiMaggio, of	.267	4	15	4	4	0	0	1	2	1	1	0
Lou Gehrig, 1b	.286	4	14	4	4	0	0	0	0	2	3	0
Lefty Gomez, p	.000	1	2	0	0	0	0	0	0	0	0	0
Joe Gordon, 2b	.400	4	15	3	6	2	0	1	6	1	3	1
Tommy Henrich, of	.250	4	16	3	4	1	0	1	1	0	1	0
Myril Hoag, of-1	.400	2	5	3	2	1	0	0	1	0	0	0
Johnny Murphy, p	.000	1	0	0	0	0	0	0	0	0	0	0
Monte Pearson, p	.333	1	3	1	1	0	0	0	0	1	0	0
Jake Powell, of	.000	1	0	0	0	0	0	0	0	0	0	0
Red Rolfe, 3b	.167	4	18	0	3	0	0	0	1	0	3	1
Red Ruffing, p	.167	2	6	1	1	0	0	0	1	1	0	0
George Selkirk, of	.200	3	10	0	2	0	0	0	1	2	1	0
TOTAL	.274		135	22	37	6	1	5	21	11	16	3

PITCHER	W	L	ERA	G	GS	CG	SV	SHO	IP	H	ER	BB	SO
Lefty Gomez	1	0	3.86	1	1	0	0	0	7.0	9	3	1	5
Johnny Murphy	0	0	0.00	1	0	0	1	0	2.0	2	0	1	1
Monte Pearson	1	0	1.00	1	1	1	0	0	9.0	5	1	2	9
Red Ruffing	2	0	1.50	2	2	2	0	0	18.0	17	3	2	11
TOTAL	4	0	1.75	5	4	3	1	0	36.0	33	7	6	26

CHI (N)

PLAYER/POS	AVG	G	AB	R	H	2B	3B	HR	RB	BB	SO	SB
Clay Bryant, p	.000	1	2	0	0	0	0	0	0	0	1	0
Tex Carleton, p	.000	1	0	0	0	0	0	0	0	0	0	0
Phil Cavaretta, of-3	.462	4	13	1	6	1	0	0	0	0	1	0
Ripper Collins, 1b	.133	4	15	1	2	0	0	0	0	0	3	0
Dizzy Dean, p	.667	2	3	0	2	0	0	0	0	0	0	0
Frank Demaree, of	.100	3	10	1	1	0	0	0	0	1	2	0
Larry French, p	.000	3	2	0	0	0	0	0	0	0	0	0
Augie Galan, ph	.000	2	2	0	0	0	0	0	0	0	1	0
Stan Hack, 3b	.471	4	17	3	8	1	0	0	1	1	2	0
Gabby Hartnett, c	.091	3	11	0	1	0	1	0	0	0	2	0
Billy Herman, 2b	.188	4	16	1	3	0	0	0	0	1	4	0
Billy Jurges, ss	.231	4	13	0	3	1	0	0	0	1	3	0
Tony Lazzeri, ph	.000	2	2	0	0	0	0	0	0	0	1	0
Bill Lee, p	.000	2	3	0	0	0	0	0	0	0	1	0
Joe Marty, of	.500	3	12	1	6	1	0	1	5	0	2	0
Ken O'Dea, c-1	.200	3	5	1	1	0	1	0	1	2	1	0
Vance Page, p	.000	1	0	0	0	0	0	0	0	0	0	0
Carl Reynolds, of-3	.000	4	12	0	0	0	0	0	0	1	3	0
Charlie Root, p	.000	1	0	0	0	0	0	0	0	0	0	0
Jack Russell, p	.000	2	0	0	0	0	0	0	0	0	0	0
TOTAL	.243		136	9	33	4	1	2	8	6	26	0

PITCHER	W	L	ERA	G	GS	CG	SV	SHO	IP	H	ER	BB	SO
Clay Bryant	0	1	6.75	1	1	0	0	0	5.1	6	4	5	3
Tex Carleton	0	0	INF	1	0	0	0	0	0.0	1	2	2	0
Dizzy Dean	0	1	6.48	2	1	0	0	0	8.1	8	6	1	2
Larry French	0	0	2.70	3	0	0	0	0	3.1	1	1	1	2
Bill Lee	0	2	2.45	2	2	0	0	0	11.0	15	3	1	8
Vance Page	0	0	13.50	1	0	0	0	0	1.1	2	2	0	0
Charlie Root	0	0	3.00	1	0	0	0	0	3.0	3	1	0	1
Jack Russell	0	0	0.00	2	0	0	0	0	1.2	1	0	1	0
TOTAL	0	4	5.03	13	4	0	0	0	34.0	37	19	11	16

GAME 1 AT CHI OCT 5

NY	020 000 100	3	12	1
CHI	001 000 000	1	9	1

Pitchers: RUFFING vs LEE, Russell (9)
Attendance: 43,642

GAME 2 AT CHI OCT 6

NY	020 000 022	6	7	2
CHI	102 000 000	3	11	0

Pitchers: GOMEZ, Murphy (8) vs J.DEAN, French (9)
Home Runs: Crosetti-NY, DiMaggio-NY
Attendance: 42,108

GAME 3 AT NY OCT 8

CHI	000 010 010	2	5	1
NY	000 022 01X	5	7	2

Pitchers: BRYANT, Russell (6), French (7) vs PEARSON
Home Runs: Dickey-NY, Gordon-NY, Marty-CHI
Attendance: 55,236

GAME 4 AT NY OCT 9

CHI	000 100 020	3	8	1
NY	030 001 04X	8	11	1

Pitchers: LEE, Root (4), Page (7), French (8), Carleton (8), J.Dean (8) vs RUFFING
Home Runs: Henrich-NY, O'Dea-CHI
Attendance: 59,847

The Yankees won their fourth consecutive World Series with their second sweep in a row. This time the victim was Cincinnati, in the Series for the first time since their tainted triumph over the Black Sox two decades earlier. New York had lost the power of Lou Gehrig (whose illness forced his retirement early in the season), but in the Series rookie outfielder Charlie Keller took up the slack. He led both clubs in batting, slugging, home runs, RBIs, hits, and runs, and hit one of the Series' two triples. His eight runs scored equalled those of the whole Cincinnati team.

The Yankees' Red Ruffing and Cincinnati's Paul Derringer hurled matching four-hitters through eight innings of Game One. With the score tied 1–1, Ruffing set the Reds down in order in the ninth. But in the bottom of the ninth Keller tripled off Derringer with one away, and scored the deciding run on catcher Bill Dickey's single.

Babe Dahlgren, Gehrig's replacement at first base, doubled in the third and later scored the Yankees' first run in Game Two, and homered in the next inning for New York's fourth and final run of the game. Red starter Bucky Walters stopped the Yankees after that, but they had more than enough runs for the win, as Monte Pearson held the Reds hitless through seven and wound up with a two-hit shutout.

Keller provided the margin of victory with a pair of two-run homers in the first and fifth innings of Game Three. Joe DiMaggio's two-run homer in the third and Bill Dickey's solo shot that followed Keller's homer in the fifth accounted for the rest of New York's runs in their 7–3 win.

No one scored through six innings of Game Four. Keller and Dickey then homered in the top of the seventh, but Red Rolfe's error at third in the last of the inning opened the way for the Reds to go ahead with three unearned runs. They earned a fourth run an inning later, but the Yankees tied it up with two in the ninth (one unearned) and took the lead in the tenth with three more runs (two unearned) on a walk, a single, and three more Red errors. Reliever Johnny Murphy held off a Red threat in the last of the tenth and the Series was over.

New York Yankees (AL), 4; Cincinnati Reds (NL), 0

NY (A)

PLAYER/POS	AVG	G	AB	R	H	2B	3B	HR	RB	BB	SO	SB
Frankie Crosetti, ss	.063	4	16	2	1	0	0	0	0	1	2	2	0
Babe Dahlgren, 1b	.214	4	14	2	3	2	0	1	2	0	4	0
Bill Dickey, c	.267	4	15	2	4	0	0	2	5	1	2	0
Joe DiMaggio, of	.313	4	16	3	5	0	0	1	3	1	1	0
Lefty Gomez, p	.000	1	1	0	0	0	0	0	0	0	1	0
Joe Gordon, 2b	.143	4	14	1	2	0	0	0	1	0	2	0
Bump Hadley, p	.000	1	3	0	0	0	0	0	0	0	0	0
Oral Hildebrand, p	.000	1	1	0	0	0	0	0	0	0	1	0
Charlie Keller, of	.438	4	16	8	7	1	1	3	6	1	2	0
Johnny Murphy, p	.000	1	2	0	0	0	0	0	0	0	1	0
Monte Pearson, p	.000	1	2	0	0	0	0	0	0	0	1	0
Red Rolfe, 3b	.125	4	16	2	2	0	0	0	0	0	0	0
Red Ruffing, p	.333	1	3	0	1	0	0	0	0	0	1	0
George Selkirk, of	.167	4	12	0	2	1	0	0	0	3	2	0
Steve Sundra, p	.000	1	0	0	0	0	0	0	0	0	1	0
TOTAL	.206		131	20	27	4	1	7	18	9	20	0

PITCHER	W	L	ERA	G	GS	CG	SV	SHO	IP	H	ER	BB	SO
Lefty Gomez	0	0	9.00	1	1	0	0	0	1.0	3	1	0	1
Bump Hadley	1	0	2.25	1	0	0	0	0	8.0	7	2	3	2
Oral Hildebrand	0	0	0.00	1	1	0	0	0	4.0	2	0	0	3
Johnny Murphy	1	0	2.70	1	0	0	0	0	3.1	5	1	0	2
Monte Pearson	1	0	0.00	1	1	1	0	1	9.0	2	0	1	8
Red Ruffing	1	0	1.00	1	1	1	0	0	9.0	4	1	1	4
Steve Sundra	0	0	0.00	1	0	0	0	0	2.2	4	0	1	2
TOTAL	4	0	1.22	7	4	2	0	1	37.0	27	5	6	22

CIN (N)

PLAYER/POS	AVG	G	AB	R	H	2B	3B	HR	RB	BB	SO	SB
Wally Berger, of	.000	4	15	0	0	0	0	0	1	0	4	0
Nino Bongiovanni, ph	.000	1	1	0	0	0	0	0	0	0	0	0
Frenchy Bordagaray, pr	.000	2	0	0	0	0	0	0	0	0	0	0
Harry Craft, of	.091	4	11	0	1	0	0	0	0	0	6	0
Paul Derringer, p	.200	2	5	0	1	0	0	0	0	0	0	0
Lonny Frey, 2b	.000	4	17	0	0	0	0	0	0	1	4	0
Lee Gamble, ph	.000	1	1	0	0	0	0	0	0	0	1	0
Ival Goodman, of	.333	4	15	3	5	1	0	0	1	1	2	1
Lee Grissom, p	.000	1	0	0	0	0	0	0	0	0	0	0
Willard Hershberger, c-2	.500	3	2	0	1	0	0	0	1	0	0	0
Ernie Lombardi, c	.214	4	14	0	3	0	0	0	2	0	1	0
Frank Mc Cormick, 1b	.400	4	15	1	6	1	0	0	1	0	1	0
Whitey Moore, p	.000	1	1	0	0	0	0	0	0	0	0	0
Billy Myers, ss	.333	4	12	2	4	0	1	0	0	2	3	0
Al Simmons, of	.250	1	4	1	1	1	0	0	0	0	0	0
Junior Thompson, p	1.000	1	1	0	1	0	0	0	0	0	0	0
Bucky Walters, p	.000	2	3	0	0	0	0	0	0	0	0	0
Billy Werber, 3b	.250	4	16	1	4	0	0	0	2	2	0	0
TOTAL	.203		133	8	27	3	1	0	8	6	22	1

PITCHER	W	L	ERA	G	GS	CG	SV	SHO	IP	H	ER	BB	SO
Paul Derringer	0	1	2.35	2	2	1	0	0	15.1	9	4	3	9
Lee Grissom	0	0	0.00	1	0	0	0	0	1.1	0	0	1	0
Whitey Moore	0	0	0.00	1	0	0	0	0	3.0	0	0	0	2
Junior Thompson	0	1	13.50	1	1	0	0	0	4.2	5	7	4	3
Bucky Walters	0	2	4.91	2	1	1	0	0	11.0	13	6	1	6
TOTAL	0	4	4.33	7	4	2	0	0	35.1	27	17	9	20

GAME 1 AT NY OCT 4

CIN	000	100	000	1	4	0
NY	000	010	001	2	6	0

Pitchers: DERRINGER vs RUFFING
Attendance: 58,541

GAME 2 AT NY OCT 5

CIN	000	000	000	0	2	0
NY	003	100	00X	4	9	0

Pitchers: WALTERS vs PEARSON
Home Runs: Dalhgren-NY
Attendance: 59,791

GAME 3 AT CIN OCT 7

NY	202	030	000	7	5	1
CIN	120	000	000	3	10	0

Pitchers: Gomez, HADLEY (2) vs THOMPSON, Grissom (5), Moore (7)
Home Runs: Keller-NY (2), DiMaggio-NY, Dickey-NY
Attendance: 32,723

GAME 4 AT CIN OCT 8

NY	000	000	202	3	7	7	1
CIN	000	000	310	0	4	11	4

Pitchers: Hildebrand, Sundra (5), MURPHY (7) vs Derringer, WALTERS (8)
Home Runs: Keller-NY, Dickey-NY
Attendance: 32,794

The Tigers outpitched and out-slugged the Reds, and scored six more runs than the Reds did. What they failed to do was win the Series.

Tiger ace Bobo Newsom, who had enjoyed what would be his finest season in a long career, carried his mastery into the Series opener. Detroit gave him an early lead, driving out Red starter Paul Derringer with five runs in the second inning, and added a pair of runs in the fifth on Bruce Campbell's home run. Newsom, meanwhile, held the Reds to single runs in the fourth and eighth.

Cincinnati's Bucky Walters walked the first two Tigers he faced in Game Two, and both scored. But two Red runs in the second tied the game, Jimmy Ripple's two-run homer an inning later gave them the lead, and pitcher Walters scored an insurance run in the fourth after doubling. Another Tiger walk in the sixth led to their third run, but Walters retired the remaining Tigers in order.

The Series moved to Detroit and the lead to the Tigers in Game Three. Detroit's Rocky Bridges yielded ten hits and four runs, but his teammates responded with 13 hits and seven runs, including a pair of two-run homers by Rudy York and Pinky Higgins in the seventh. Cincinnati again evened the Series the next day, though, with five runs to support Derringer's five-hit, two-run pitching. Although Newsom's father had suffered a fatal heart attack the day after seeing his son win the opener, the son pitched Game Five, and improved on his previous performance with a three-hit shutout. Hank Greenberg's homer in the third inning accounted for the first three of the Tigers' eight runs in their lopsided win.

The Reds returned home needing to win the final two games. Like Newsom, Bucky Walters bettered his earlier win with a shutout in Game Six, and drove in two of the Reds' four runs, one with a solo homer in the eighth. In the Series finale, Newsom and Derringer found themselves evenly matched. The Tigers scored a run in the third, while Newsom held Cincinnati scoreless through six. But in the seventh, leadoff doubles by Frank McCormick and Jimmy Ripple, plus a successful bunt and a fly to deep center, gave the Reds two runs—all they needed as Derringer stopped the Tigers through the final six innings for the victory.

Cincinnati Reds (NL), 4; Detroit Tigers (AL), 3

CIN (N)

PLAYER/POS	AVG	G	AB	R	H	2B	3B	HR	RB	BB	SO	SB
Morrie Arnovich, of	.000	1	1	0	0	0	0	0	0	0	0	0
Bill Baker, c	.250	3	4	1	1	0	0	0	0	0	1	0
Joe Beggs, p	.000	1	0	0	0	0	0	0	0	0	0	0
Harry Craft, ph	.000	1	1	0	0	0	0	0	0	0	0	0
Paul Derringer, p	.000	3	7	0	0	0	0	0	0	0	1	0
Lonny Frey, ph	.000	3	2	0	0	0	0	0	0	0	0	0
Ival Goodman, of	.276	7	29	5	8	2	0	0	5	0	3	0
Johnny Hutchings, p	.000	1	0	0	0	0	0	0	0	0	0	0
Eddie Joost, 2b	.200	7	25	0	5	0	0	0	2	1	2	0
Ernie Lombardi, c-1	.333	2	3	0	1	1	0	0	0	1	0	0
Frank Mc Cormick, 1b	.214	7	28	2	6	1	0	0	1	1	1	0
Mike Mc Cormick, of	.310	7	29	1	9	3	0	0	2	1	6	0
Whitey Moore, p	.000	3	2	0	0	0	0	0	0	0	1	0
Billy Myers, ss	.130	7	23	0	3	0	0	0	2	2	5	0
Elmer Riddle, p	.000	1	0	0	0	0	0	0	0	0	0	0
Lew Riggs, ph	.000	3	3	1	0	0	0	0	0	0	2	0
Jimmy Ripple, of	.333	7	21	3	7	2	0	1	6	4	2	0
Junior Thompson, p	.000	1	1	0	0	0	0	0	0	0	1	0
Jim Turner, p	.000	1	2	0	0	0	0	0	0	0	0	0
Johnny Vander Meer, p	.000	1	0	0	0	0	0	0	0	0	0	0
Bucky Walters, p	.286	2	7	2	2	1	0	1	2	0	1	0
Billy Werber, 3b	.370	7	27	5	10	4	0	0	2	4	2	0
Jimmie Wilson, c	.353	6	17	2	6	0	0	0	1	1	2	1
TOTAL	.250		232	22	58	14	0	2	21	15	30	1

PITCHER	W	L	ERA	G	GS	CG	SV	SHO	IP	H	ER	BB	SO
Joe Beggs	0	0	9.00	1	0	0	0	0	1.0	3	1	0	1
Paul Derringer	2	1	2.79	3	3	2	0	0	19.1	17	6	10	6
Johnny Hutchings	0	0	9.00	1	0	0	0	0	1.0	2	1	1	0
Whitey Moore	0	0	3.24	3	0	0	0	0	8.1	8	3	6	7
Elmer Riddle	0	0	0.00	1	0	0	0	0	1.0	0	0	0	2
Junior Thompson	0	1	16.20	1	1	0	0	0	3.1	8	6	4	2
Jim Turner	0	1	7.50	1	1	0	0	0	6.0	8	5	0	4
Johnny Vander Meer	0	0	0.00	1	0	0	0	0	3.0	2	0	3	2
Bucky Walters	2	0	1.50	2	2	2	0	1	18.0	8	3	6	6
TOTAL	4	3	3.69	14	7	4	0	1	61.0	56	25	30	30

DET (A)

PLAYER/POS	AVG	G	AB	R	H	2B	3B	HR	RB	BB	SO	SB
Earl Averill, ph	.000	3	3	0	0	0	0	0	0	0	0	0
Dick Bartell, ss	.269	7	26	2	7	2	0	0	3	3	3	0
Tommy Bridges, p	.000	1	3	0	0	0	0	0	0	0	1	0
Bruce Campbell, of	.360	7	25	4	9	1	0	1	5	4	4	0
Frank Croucher, ss	.000	1	0	0	0	0	0	0	0	0	0	0
Pete Fox, ph	.000	1	1	0	0	0	0	0	0	0	0	0
Charlie Gehringer, 2b	.214	7	28	3	6	0	0	0	1	2	0	0
Johnny Gorsica, p	.000	2	4	0	0	0	0	0	0	0	2	0
Hank Greenberg, of	.357	7	28	5	10	2	1	1	6	2	5	0
Pinky Higgins, 3b	.333	7	24	2	8	3	1	1	6	3	3	0
Fred Hutchinson, p	.000	1	0	0	0	0	0	0	0	0	0	0
Barney Mc Cosky, of	.304	7	23	5	7	1	0	0	1	7	0	0
Archie Mc Kain, p	.000	1	0	0	0	0	0	0	0	0	0	0
Bobo Newsom, p	.100	3	10	1	1	0	0	0	0	0	1	0
Schoolboy Rowe, p	.000	2	1	0	0	0	0	0	0	0	1	0
Clay Smith, p	.000	1	1	0	0	0	0	0	0	0	1	0
Billy Sullivan, c-4	.154	5	13	3	2	1	0	0	0	5	2	0
Birdie Tebbetts, c-3	.000	4	11	0	0	0	0	0	0	0	0	0
Dizzy Trout, p	.000	1	1	0	0	0	0	0	0	0	1	0
Rudy York, 1b	.231	7	26	3	6	0	1	1	2	4	7	0
TOTAL	.246		228	28	56	9	3	4	24	30	30	0

PITCHER	W	L	ERA	G	GS	CG	SV	SHO	IP	H	ER	BB	SO
Tommy Bridges	1	0	3.00	1	1	1	0	0	9.0	10	3	1	5
Johnny Gorsica	0	0	0.79	2	0	0	0	0	11.1	6	1	4	4
Fred Hutchinson	0	0	9.00	1	0	0	0	0	1.0	1	1	1	1
Archie Mc Kain	0	0	3.00	1	0	0	0	0	3.0	4	1	0	0
Bobo Newsom	2	1	1.38	3	3	3	0	1	26.0	18	4	4	17
Schoolboy Rowe	0	2	17.18	2	2	0	0	0	3.2	12	7	1	1
Clay Smith	0	0	2.25	1	0	0	0	0	4.0	1	1	3	1
Dizzy Trout	0	1	9.00	1	1	0	0	0	2.0	6	2	1	1
TOTAL	3	4	3.00	12	7	4	0	1	60.0	58	20	15	30

GAME 1 AT CIN OCT 2

DET	050 020 000	7 10 1
CIN	000 100 010	2 8 3

Pitchers: NEWSOM vs DERRINGER, Moore (2), Riddle (9)
Home Runs: Campbell-DET
Attendance: 31,793

GAME 2 AT CIN OCT 3

DET	200 001 000	3 3 1
CIN	022 100 00X	5 9 0

Pitchers: ROWE, Gorsica (4) vs WALTERS
Home Runs: Ripple-CIN
Attendance: 30,640

GAME 3 AT DET OCT 4

CIN	100 000 012	4 10 1
DET	000 100 42X	7 13 1

Pitchers: TURNER, Moore (7), Beggs (8) vs BRIDGES
Home Runs: York-DET, Higgins-DET
Attendance: 52,877

GAME 4 AT DET OCT 5

CIN	201 100 010	5 11 1
DET	001 001 000	2 5 1

Pitchers: DERRINGER vs TROUT, Smith (3), McKain (7)
Attendance: 54,093

GAME 5 AT DET OCT 6

CIN	000 000 000	0 3 0
DET	003 400 01X	8 13 0

Pitchers: THOMPSON, Moore (4), Vander Meer (5), Hutchings (8) vs NEWSOM
Home Runs: Greenberg-DET
Attendance: 55,189

GAME 6 AT CIN OCT 7

DET	000 000 000	0 5 0
CIN	200 000 01X	4 10 2

Pitchers: ROWE, Gorsica (1), Hutchinson (8) vs WALTERS
Home Runs: Walters-CIN
Attendance: 30,481

GAME 7 AT CIN OCT 8

DET	001 000 000	1 7 0
CIN	000 000 20X	2 7 1

Pitchers: NEWSOM vs DERRINGER
Attendance: 26,854

Dodger catcher Mickey Owen's dropped third strike in Game Four was the Series' memorable boner, but it was not the chief cause of Brooklyn's downfall. Yankee pitching was. Three Yankee starters hurled complete-game wins, with each giving the Dodgers only one earned run. And relief ace Johnny Murphy hurled two-hit shutout ball in six innings over two games, winning one.

Yankee Joe Gordon opened the Series scoring with a solo homer in the second inning of Game One, and the Yankees added runs in the fourth and sixth. Owen tripled in the Dodgers' first run in the fifth, and pinch hitter Lew Riggs singled in an unearned run in the seventh. But Yankee starter Red Ruffing held on to his slim lead through the final two innings for the win.

Dodger ace Whitlow Wyatt gave the Yankees single runs in the second and third innings of Game Two, but held them scoreless the rest of the way. Meanwhile, the Dodgers tied the game in the fifth, and scored an unearned run in the sixth to finish the scoring and give Brooklyn its only win of the Series.

Freddie Fitzsimmons, with the Dodgers' best pitching of the Series, dueled Yankee Marius Russo through seven scoreless innings in Game Three. But Fitzsimmons's final out of the seventh—a line drive by Russo that bounced off Fitzsimmons's leg into the glove of shortstop Pee Wee Reese—broke his kneecap. Hugh Casey, who replaced Fitzsimmons in the eighth, retired the first batter, but then gave up four straight singles for two runs before being removed. The Yankees scored no more, and Brooklyn came up with a run in the last of the eighth. But Russo stopped the Dodgers in order in the ninth to preserve his lead for the Yankees' second win.

In Game Four, for the first time in the Series, the margin of victory was more than one run, thanks to catcher Owen's famous boner. Brooklyn held the lead 4–3 with two out in the top of the ninth. Dodger reliever Casey, who had shut out the Yankees since coming on in the fifth inning, then struck out Tommy Henrich for what should have been the game-ending out. But Owen let the ball get by him, and before the third out was recorded Casey had given up a single, two doubles, and two walks—and four runs, for Brooklyn's third loss.

The Yankees scored twice off Wyatt in the second inning of Game Five, and once more in the fifth (on Henrich's home run), as Tiny Bonham held Brooklyn to four hits and a single run to clinch the ninth Yankee world title.

New York Yankees (AL), 4;
Brooklyn Dodgers (NL), 1

NY (A)

PLAYER/POS	AVG	G	AB	R	H	2B	3B	HR	RB	BB	SO	SB
Tiny Bonham, p	.000	1	4	0	0	0	0	0	0	0	4	0
Frenchy Bordagaray, pr	.000	1	0	0	0	0	0	0	0	0	0	0
Marv Breuer, p	.000	1	1	0	0	0	0	0	0	0	0	0
Spud Chandler, p	.500	1	2	0	1	0	0	0	1	0	0	0
Bill Dickey, c	.167	5	18	3	3	1	0	0	1	3	1	0
Joe DiMaggio, of	.263	5	19	1	5	0	0	0	1	2	2	0
Atley Donald, p	.000	1	2	0	0	0	0	0	0	0	1	0
Joe Gordon, 2b	.500	5	14	2	7	1	1	1	5	7	0	0
Tommy Henrich, of	.167	5	18	4	3	1	0	1	1	3	3	0
Charlie Keller, of	.389	5	18	5	7	2	0	0	5	3	1	0
Johnny Murphy, p	.000	2	2	0	0	0	0	0	0	0	0	0
Phil Rizzuto, ss	.111	5	18	0	2	0	0	0	0	3	1	1
Red Rolfe, 3b	.300	5	20	2	6	0	0	0	0	2	1	0
Buddy Rosar, c	.000	1	0	0	0	0	0	0	0	0	0	0
Red Ruffing, p	.000	1	3	0	0	0	0	0	0	0	0	0
Marius Russo, p	.000	1	4	0	0	0	0	0	0	0	1	0
George Selkirk, ph	.500	2	2	0	1	0	0	0	0	0	0	0
Johnny Sturm, 1b	.286	5	21	0	6	0	0	0	2	0	2	1
TOTAL	.247		166	17	41	5	1	2	16	23	18	2

PITCHER	W	L	ERA	G	GS	CG	SV	SHO	IP	H	ER	BB	SO
Tiny Bonham	1	0	1.00	1	1	1	0	0	9.0	4	1	2	2
Marv Breuer	0	0	0.00	1	0	0	0	0	3.0	3	0	1	2
Spud Chandler	0	1	3.60	1	1	0	0	0	5.0	4	2	2	2
Atley Donald	0	0	9.00	1	1	0	0	0	4.0	6	4	3	2
Johnny Murphy	1	0	0.00	2	0	0	0	0	6.0	2	0	1	3
Red Ruffing	1	0	1.00	1	1	1	0	0	9.0	6	1	3	5
Marius Russo	1	0	1.00	1	1	1	0	0	9.0	4	1	2	5
TOTAL	4	1	1.80	8	5	3	0	0	45.0	29	9	14	21

BRO (N)

PLAYER/POS	AVG	G	AB	R	H	2B	3B	HR	RB	BB	SO	SB
Johnny Allen, p	.000	3	0	0	0	0	0	0	0	0	0	0
Dolph Camilli, 1b	.167	5	18	1	3	1	0	0	1	1	6	0
Hugh Casey, p	.500	3	2	0	1	0	0	0	0	0	1	0
Pete Coscarart, 2b	.000	3	7	1	0	0	0	0	0	1	2	0
Curt Davis, p	.000	1	2	0	0	0	0	0	0	0	0	0
Freddie Fitzsimmons, p	.000	1	2	0	0	0	0	0	0	0	0	0
Herman Franks, c	.000	1	1	0	0	0	0	0	0	0	0	0
Larry French, p	.000	2	0	0	0	0	0	0	0	0	0	0
Augie Galan, ph	.000	2	2	0	0	0	0	0	0	0	1	0
Billy Herman, 2b	.125	4	8	0	1	0	0	0	0	2	0	0
Kirby Higbe, p	1.000	1	1	0	1	0	0	0	0	0	0	0
Cookie Lavagetto, 3b	.100	3	10	1	1	0	0	0	0	2	0	0
Joe Medwick, of	.235	5	17	1	4	1	0	0	0	1	2	0
Mickey Owen, c	.167	5	12	1	2	0	1	0	2	3	0	0
Pee Wee Reese, ss	.200	5	20	1	4	0	0	0	2	0	0	0
Pete Reiser, of	.200	5	20	4	4	1	1	1	3	1	6	0
Lew Riggs, 3b-2	.250	3	8	0	2	0	0	0	1	1	1	0
Dixie Walker, of	.222	5	18	3	4	2	0	0	0	2	1	0
Jimmy Wasdell, of-1	.200	3	5	0	1	0	0	0	2	0	0	0
Whit Wyatt, p	.167	2	6	1	1	1	0	0	0	0	1	0
TOTAL	.182		159	11	29	7	2	1	11	14	21	0

PITCHER	W	L	ERA	G	GS	CG	SV	SHO	IP	H	ER	BB	SO
Johnny Allen	0	0	0.00	3	0	0	0	0	3.2	1	0	3	0
Hugh Casey	0	2	3.38	3	0	0	0	0	5.1	9	2	2	1
Curt Davis	0	1	5.06	1	1	0	0	0	5.1	6	3	3	1
Freddie Fitzsimmons	0	0	0.00	1	1	0	0	0	7.0	4	0	3	1
Larry French	0	0	0.00	2	0	0	0	0	1.0	0	0	0	0
Kirby Higbe	0	0	7.36	1	1	0	0	0	3.2	6	3	2	1
Whit Wyatt	1	1	2.50	2	2	2	0	0	18.0	15	5	10	14
TOTAL	1	4	2.66	13	5	2	0	0	44.0	41	13	23	18

GAME 1 AT NY OCT 1

BRO	000 010 100	2	6	0
NY	010 101 00X	3	6	1

Pitchers: DAVIS, Casey (6), Allen (7) vs RUFFING
Home Runs: Gordon-NY
Attendance: 68,540

GAME 2 AT NY OCT 2

BRO	000 021 000	3	6	2
NY	011 000 000	2	9	1

Pitchers: WYATT vs CHANDLER, Murphy (6)
Attendance: 66,248

GAME 3 AT BRO OCT 4

NY	000 000 020	2	8	0
BRO	000 000 010	1	4	0

Pitchers: RUSSO vs Fitzsimmons, CASEY (8), French (8), Allen (9)
Attendance: 33,100

GAME 4 AT BRO OCT 5

NY	100 200 004	7	12	0
BRO	000 220 000	4	9	1

Pitchers: Donald, Breuer (5), MURPHY (8) VS Higbe, French (4), Allen (5), CASEY (5)
Home Runs: Reiser-BRO
Attendance: 33,813

GAME 5 AT BRO OCT 6

NY	020 010 000	3	6	0
BRO	001 000 000	1	4	1

Pitchers: BONHAM vs WYATT
Home Runs: Henrich-NY
Attendance: 34,072

Cardinal rookies Stan Musial and Whitey Kurowski drove in game-winning runs for rookie-pitcher Johnny Beazley in Games Two and Five as the major leagues' youngest team upset the Yankees. New York won only the opener, building a seven-run lead for starter Red Ruffing, who shut out St. Louis on one hit through 8⅓ innings before giving up four hits and four harmless runs in the last of the ninth.

The Cardinals scored first in Game Two on catcher Walker Cooper's two-run double in the first inning. Kurowski tripled in a third Cardinal run in the seventh, but pitcher Beazley, after holding the Yankees scoreless through seven innings, gave up three runs in the eighth on two singles and Charlie Keller's two-run homer. St. Louis regained the lead a half inning later when Musial singled home Enos Slaughter (who had doubled), and stifled a threat in the ninth as Slaughter's great throw from right field nailed a Yankee runner at third.

Second-year Cardinal pitcher Ernie White turned in the Series' top mound performance with a six-single, no-walk shutout in Game Three (aided by outfielders Musial and Slaughter, who hauled in a pair of potential home run blasts in the seventh inning). The Cards managed only five singles themselves, but they combined one with a walk, sacrifice, and ground out for a run in the third, and sandwiched a Yankee error with two hits in the ninth for an unearned insurance run.

Game Four saw the Series' heaviest hitting. New York scored once in the first, but the Cards exploded in the fourth for six runs on six hits and two walks. The Yankees tied it up two innings later, with Keller's three-run homer the feature of the five-run inning. St. Louis took the lead for good with two runs in the seventh, and added a ninth run in the ninth.

Beazley and Ruffing tangled in Game Five. Phil Rizzuto's solo homer put New York ahead in the first inning. Slaughter's fourth-inning home run tied the score, but the Yankees regained the lead with a run later in the inning. The Cards retied the game in the sixth, and took the final lead when Kurowski homered for two runs in the top of the ninth. The Yankees threatened in the last of the ninth, putting their first two men on with a single and error. But catcher Cooper picked a runner off second, second baseman Jimmy Brown redeemed his earlier error with a sparkling catch, then fielded a routine grounder for the final out and the Cardinal triumph.

St. Louis Cardinals (NL), 4;
New York Yankees (AL), 1

STL (N)

PLAYER/POS	AVG	G	AB	R	H	2B	3B	HR	RB	BB	SO	SB
Johnny Beazley, p	.143	2	7	0	1	0	0	0	0	0	5	0
Jimmy Brown, 2b	.300	5	20	2	6	0	0	0	1	3	0	0
Mort Cooper, p	.200	2	5	1	1	0	0	0	2	0	1	0
Walker Cooper, c	.286	5	21	3	6	1	0	0	4	0	1	0
Creepy Crespi, pr	.000	1	0	1	0	0	0	0	0	0	0	0
Harry Gumbert, p	.000	2	0	0	0	0	0	0	0	0	0	0
Johnny Hopp, 1b	.176	5	17	3	3	0	0	0	0	1	1	0
Whitey Kurowski, 3b	.267	5	15	3	4	0	1	1	5	2	3	0
Max Lanier, p	1.000	2	1	0	1	0	0	0	1	0	0	0
Marty Marion, ss	.111	5	18	2	2	0	1	0	3	1	2	0
Terry Moore, of	.294	5	17	2	5	1	0	0	2	2	3	0
Stan Musial, of	.222	5	18	2	4	1	0	0	2	4	0	0
Ken O'Dea, ph	1.000	1	1	0	1	0	0	0	1	0	0	0
Howie Pollet, p	.000	1	0	0	0	0	0	0	0	0	0	0
Ray Sanders, ph	.000	2	1	1	0	0	0	0	0	1	0	0
Enos Slaughter, of	.263	5	19	3	5	1	0	1	2	3	2	0
Harry Walker, ph	.000	1	1	0	0	0	0	0	0	0	1	0
Ernie White, p	.000	1	2	0	0	0	0	0	0	0	0	0
TOTAL	.239		163	23	39	4	2	2	23	17	19	0

PITCHER	W	L	ERA	G	GS	CG	SV	SHO	IP	H	ER	BB	SO
Johnny Beazley	2	0	2.50	2	2	2	0	0	18.0	17	5	3	6
Mort Cooper	0	1	5.54	2	2	0	0	0	13.0	17	8	4	9
Harry Gumbert	0	0	0.00	2	0	0	0	0	0.2	1	0	0	0
Max Lanier	1	0	0.00	2	0	0	0	0	4.0	3	0	1	1
Howie Pollet	0	0	0.00	1	0	0	0	0	0.1	0	0	0	0
Ernie White	1	0	0.00	1	1	1	0	1	9.0	6	0	0	6
TOTAL	4	1	2.60	10	5	3	0	1	45.0	44	13	8	22

NY (A)

PLAYER/POS	AVG	G	AB	R	H	2B	3B	HR	RB	BB	SO	SB
Tiny Bonham, p	.000	2	2	0	0	0	0	0	0	1	0	0
Hank Borowy, p	.000	1	1	0	0	0	0	0	0	0	1	0
Marv Breuer, p	.000	1	0	0	0	0	0	0	0	0	0	0
Spud Chandler, p	.000	2	2	0	0	0	0	0	0	0	1	0
Frankie Crosetti, 3b	.000	1	3	0	0	0	0	0	0	0	1	0
Roy Cullenbine, of	.263	5	19	3	5	1	0	0	2	1	2	1
Bill Dickey, c	.263	5	19	1	5	0	0	0	0	1	0	0
Joe DiMaggio, of	.333	5	21	3	7	0	0	0	3	0	1	0
Atley Donald, p	.000	1	2	0	0	0	0	0	0	0	0	0
Joe Gordon, 2b	.095	5	21	1	2	1	0	0	0	0	7	0
Buddy Hassett, 1b	.333	3	9	1	3	1	0	0	2	0	1	0
Charlie Keller, of	.200	5	20	2	4	0	0	2	5	1	3	0
Jerry Priddy, 1b-3,3b-1	.100	3	10	0	1	1	0	0	1	1	0	0
Phil Rizzuto, ss	.381	5	21	2	8	0	0	1	1	2	1	2
Red Rolfe, 3b	.353	4	17	5	6	2	0	0	0	1	2	0
Buddy Rosar, ph	1.000	1	1	0	1	0	0	0	0	0	0	0
Red Ruffing, p-2	.222	4	9	0	2	0	0	0	0	0	2	0
George Selkirk, ph	.000	1	1	0	0	0	0	0	0	0	0	0
Tuck Stainback, pr	.000	2	0	0	0	0	0	0	0	0	0	0
Jim Turner, p	.000	1	0	0	0	0	0	0	0	0	0	0
TOTAL	.247		178	18	44	6	0	3	14	8	22	3

PITCHER	W	L	ERA	G	GS	CG	SV	SHO	IP	H	ER	BB	SO
Tiny Bonham	0	1	4.09	2	2	1	1	0	11.0	9	5	3	3
Hank Borowy	0	0	18.00	1	1	0	0	0	3.0	6	6	3	1
Marv Breuer	0	0	INF	1	0	0	0	0	0.0	2	0	0	0
Spud Chandler	0	1	1.08	2	1	0	1	0	8.1	5	1	1	3
Atley Donald	0	1	6.00	1	0	0	0	0	3.0	3	2	2	1
Red Ruffing	1	1	4.08	2	2	1	0	0	17.2	14	8	7	11
Jim Turner	0	0	0.00	1	0	0	0	0	1.0	0	0	1	0
TOTAL	1	4	4.50	10	5	2	1	0	44.0	39	22	17	19

GAME 1 AT STL SEPT 30

NY	000 110 032	7	11 0
STL	000 000 004	4	7 4

Pitchers: RUFFING, Chandler (9) vs M.COOPER, Gumbert (8), Lanier (9)
Attendance: 34,769

GAME 2 AT STL OCT 1

NY	000 000 030	3	10 2
STL	200 000 110	4	6 0

Pitchers: BONHAM vs BEAZLEY
Home Runs: Keller-NY
Attendance: 34,255

GAME 3 AT NY OCT 2

STL	001 000 001	2	5 1
NY	000 000 000	0	6 1

Pitchers: WHITE vs CHANDLER, Breuer (9), Turner (9)
Attendance: 69,123

GAME 4 AT NY OCT 4

STL	000 600 201	9	12 1
NY	100 005 000	6	10 1

Pitchers: M.Cooper, Gumbert (6), Pollet (6), LANIER (7) vs Borowy, DONALD (4), Bonham (7)
Home Runs: Keller-NY
Attendance: 69,902

GAME 5 AT NY OCT 5

STL	000 101 002	4	9 4
NY	100 100 000	2	7 1

Pitchers: BEAZLEY vs RUFFING
Home Runs: Rizzuto-NY, Slaughter-STL, Kurowski-STL
Attendance: 69,052

Although both clubs had lost players to military service since the previous World Series, history seemed to be repeating itself. The Cardinals lost to the Yankees in the opener and won the second game, as they had the previous year. But this year it was the Yankees who took the next three games and the Series, as fine Cardinal pitching gave way to even finer Yankee mound work.

Yankee pitcher Spurgeon (Spud) Chandler, coming off his finest season (20–4, 1.64 ERA), continued to overwhelm the opposition in the Series. He held the Cards to two runs (only one earned) in Game One, and the Yankees took advantage of a wild pitch to score two runs of their own in the sixth inning, breaking a 2–2 tie for a 4–2 win. Cardinal shortstop Marty Marion homered in the third inning for the first Cardinal run the next day, and first baseman Ray Sanders homered for two more runs in a three-run fourth. Cardinal ace Mort Cooper held New York to one run on four hits through eight innings, but he weakened in the last of the ninth, giving up a double and triple to the first two batters. But only two runs scored as he retired the next three men for St. Louis's only victory.

The Cardinals carried a 2–1 lead into the last of the eighth inning of Game Three, when a pair of errors, two walks, and five Yankee hits (including Billy Johnson's three-run triple) undid them. Yankee fireman Johnny Murphy retired the Cards in order in the ninth to save Hank Borowy's win. Max Lanier and Harry Brecheen held New York to just two runs (and six hits) in Game Four, but Yankee pitcher Marius Russo gave up only one run—and that was scored only because of two Yankee errors in the seventh inning.

In the fifth and (as it turned out) final game, St. Louis couldn't score even an unearned run, although they knocked Spud Chandler for ten hits. But they were all singles and were spaced harmlessly over eight of the nine innings. Three St. Louis pitchers held the Yankees to just seven hits, six of them singles. But in the sixth inning Bill Dickey followed one of the Yankee singles with the game's only extra-base hit—a home run—to produce the game's only scoring, and bring the Yankees yet another world championship, their tenth.

New York Yankees (AL), 4;
St. Louis Cardinals (NL), 1

NY (A)

PLAYER/POS	AVG	G	AB	R	H	2B	3B	HR	RB	BB	SO	SB
Tiny Bonham, p	.000	1	2	0	0	0	0	0	0	0	0	0
Hank Borowy, p	.500	1	2	1	1	1	0	0	0	0	1	0
Spud Chandler, p	.167	2	6	0	1	0	0	0	0	0	2	0
Frankie Crosetti, ss	.278	5	18	4	5	0	0	0	1	2	3	1
Bill Dickey, c	.278	5	18	1	5	0	0	1	4	2	2	0
Nick Etten, 1b	.105	5	19	0	2	0	0	0	2	1	2	0
Joe Gordon, 2b	.235	5	17	2	4	1	0	1	2	3	3	0
Billy Johnson, 3b	.300	5	20	3	6	1	1	0	3	0	3	0
Charlie Keller, of	.222	5	18	3	4	0	1	0	2	2	5	1
Johnny Lindell, of	.111	4	9	1	1	0	0	0	0	1	4	0
Bud Metheny, of	.125	2	8	0	1	0	0	0	0	0	2	0
Johnny Murphy, p	.000	2	0	0	0	0	0	0	0	0	0	0
Marius Russo, p	.667	1	3	1	2	2	0	0	0	1	1	0
Tuck Stainback, of	.176	5	17	0	3	0	0	0	0	0	2	0
Snuffy Stirnweiss, ph	.000	1	1	1	0	0	0	0	0	0	0	0
Roy Weatherly, ph	.000	1	1	0	0	0	0	0	0	0	0	0
TOTAL	.220		159	17	35	5	2	2	14	12	30	2

PITCHER	W	L	ERA	G	GS	CG	SV	SHO	IP	H	ER	BB	SO
Tiny Bonham	0	1	4.50	1	1	0	0	0	8.0	6	4	3	9
Hank Borowy	1	0	2.25	1	1	0	0	0	8.0	6	2	3	4
Spud Chandler	2	0	0.50	2	2	2	0	1	18.0	17	1	3	10
Johnny Murphy	0	0	0.00	2	0	0	1	0	2.0	1	0	1	0
Marius Russo	1	0	0.00	1	1	1	0	0	9.0	7	0	1	2
TOTAL	4	1	1.40	7	5	3	1	1	45.0	37	7	11	26

STL (N)

PLAYER/POS	AVG	G	AB	R	H	2B	3B	HR	RB	BB	SO	SB
Al Brazle, p	.000	1	3	0	0	0	0	0	0	0	1	0
Harry Brecheen, p	.000	3	0	0	0	0	0	0	0	0	0	0
Mort Cooper, p	.000	2	5	0	0	0	0	0	0	0	3	0
Walker Cooper, c	.294	5	17	1	5	0	0	0	0	0	1	0
Frank Demaree, ph	.000	1	1	0	0	0	0	0	0	0	0	0
Murry Dickson, p	.000	1	0	0	0	0	0	0	0	0	0	0
Debs Garms, of-1	.000	2	5	0	0	0	0	0	0	0	2	0
Johnny Hopp, of	.000	1	4	0	0	0	0	0	0	0	1	0
Lou Klein, 2b	.136	5	22	0	3	0	0	0	0	1	2	0
Howie Krist, p	.000	1	0	0	0	0	0	0	0	0	0	0
Whitey Kurowski, 3b	.222	5	18	2	4	1	0	0	1	0	3	0
Max Lanier, p	.250	3	4	0	1	0	0	0	1	0	0	0
Danny Litwhiler, of-4	.267	5	15	0	4	1	0	0	2	2	4	0
Marty Marion, ss	.357	5	14	1	5	2	0	1	2	3	1	1
Stan Musial, of	.278	5	18	2	5	0	0	0	0	2	2	0
Sam Narron, ph	.000	1	1	0	0	0	0	0	0	0	0	0
Ken O'Dea, c-1	.667	2	3	0	2	0	0	0	0	0	0	0
Ray Sanders, 1b	.294	5	17	3	5	0	0	1	2	3	4	0
Harry Walker, of	.167	5	18	0	3	1	0	0	0	0	2	0
Ernie White, pr	.000	1	0	0	0	0	0	0	0	0	0	0
TOTAL	.224		165	9	37	5	0	2	8	11	26	1

PITCHER	W	L	ERA	G	GS	CG	SV	SHO	IP	H	ER	BB	SO
Al Brazle	0	1	3.68	1	1	0	0	0	7.1	5	3	2	4
Harry Brecheen	0	1	2.45	3	0	0	0	0	3.2	5	1	3	3
Mort Cooper	1	1	2.81	2	2	1	0	0	16.0	11	5	3	10
Murry Dickson	0	0	0.00	1	0	0	0	0	0.2	0	0	1	0
Howie Krist	0	0	INF	1	0	0	0	0	0.0	1	0	0	0
Max Lanier	0	1	1.76	3	2	0	0	0	15.1	13	3	3	13
TOTAL	1	4	2.51	11	5	1	0	0	43.0	35	12	12	30

GAME 1 AT NY OCT 5

STL	010	010	000	2	7 2
NY	000	202	00X	4	8 2

Pitchers: LANIER vs CHANDLER
Home Runs: Gordon-NY
Attendance: 68,676

GAME 2 AT NY OCT 6

STL	001	300	000	4	7 2
NY	000	100	002	3	6 0

Pitchers: M.COOPER vs BONHAM, Murphy (9)
Home Runs: Marion-STL, Sanders-STL
Attendance: 68,578

GAME 3 AT NY OCT 7

STL	000	200	000	2	6 4
NY	000	001	05X	6	8 0

Pitchers: BRAZLE, Krist (8), Brecheen (8) VS BOROWY, Murphy (9)
Attendance: 69,990

GAME 4 AT STL OCT 10

NY	000	100	010	2	6 2
STL	000	000	100	1	7 1

Pitchers: RUSSO vs Lanier, BRECHEEN (8)
Attendance: 36,196

GAME 5 AT STL OCT 11

NY	000	002	000	2	7 1
STL	000	000	000	0	10 1

Pitchers: CHANDLER vs M.COOPER, Lanier (8), Dickson (9)
Home Runs: Dickey-NY
Attendance: 33,872

The Cardinals—a much stronger team in the regular season—entered the World Series against their landlord Browns (who owned Sportsman's Park, where both teams played) as clear favorites. They won the Series in six games, but if the Browns' fielding had been as good as their pitching the outcome might have been different.

The Browns won the opener on Denny Galehouse's strong pitching. Galehouse gave up seven hits and four walks, but held the Cards scoreless for 8⅔ innings before yielding a run in the ninth. Cardinal ace Mort Cooper also pitched well in six of his seven innings. He allowed the Browns only two hits, but they came back to back in the fourth inning—a single followed by George McQuinn's home run—to give the Browns all the scoring they needed.

Brown pitcher Nelson Potter's two errors (a fumble and a wild throw) on a bunt in the third inning of Game Two led to an unearned run, and third baseman Mark Christman's fumble an inning later set up a second unearned run. The Browns tied the score with a pair of runs on three two-out hits in the seventh—enough to have won an error-free game—but lost when the Cardinals singled a run across in the last of the eleventh.

Two Brown errors led to a pair of unearned runs in Game Three, but Jack Kramer held the Cards scoreless apart from that, striking out ten. Meanwhile, Brown hitters tied together five singles with two out in the third inning for three runs, adding a fourth run on a wild pitch before the inning ended. In the seventh the Browns tacked on two more runs for a comfortable win and a 2–1 Series advantage.

The Cardinals came back to earn victory in Games Four and Five, knocking three Brown pitchers for 12 hits in Game Four (including Stan Musial's two-run homer in the first) and a 5–1 win for pitcher Harry Brecheen, then rapping Denny Galehouse for two solo homers in Game Five (by Danny Litwhiler and Ray Sanders) for the game's only scoring as Mort Cooper fanned 12 Browns while shutting them out.

Two of the Cardinals' three runs in the fourth inning of Game Six were made possible by Brown shortstop Vern Stephens's throwing error. They provided the margin of victory, as Cardinal pitchers Max Lanier and Ted Wilks held the Browns to three hits and a single run, and brought the Cards their second world title in three years.

St. Louis Cardinals (NL), 4;
St. Louis Browns (AL), 2

STL (N)

PLAYER/POS	AVG	G	AB	R	H	2B	3B	HR	RB	BB	SO	SB
Augie Bergamo, of-2	.000	3	6	0	0	0	0	0	0	1	2	3	0
Harry Brecheen, p	.000	1	4	0	0	0	0	0	0	0	1	0
Bud Byerly, p	.000	1	0	0	0	0	0	0	0	0	0	0
Mort Cooper, p	.000	2	4	0	0	0	0	0	0	0	2	0
Walker Cooper, c	.318	6	22	1	7	2	1	0	2	3	2	0
Blix Donnelly, p	.000	2	1	0	0	0	0	0	0	0	1	0
George Fallon, 2b	.000	2	2	0	0	0	0	0	0	0	1	0
Debs Garms, ph	.000	2	2	0	0	0	0	0	0	0	0	0
Johnny Hopp, of	.185	6	27	2	5	0	0	0	0	0	8	0
Al Jurisich, p	.000	1	0	0	0	0	0	0	0	0	0	0
Whitey Kurowski, 3b	.217	6	23	2	5	1	0	0	1	1	4	0
Max Lanier, p	.500	2	4	0	2	0	0	0	1	0	0	0
Danny Litwhiler, of	.200	5	20	2	4	1	0	1	1	2	7	0
Marty Marion, ss	.227	6	22	1	5	3	0	0	2	2	3	0
Stan Musial, of	.304	6	23	2	7	2	0	1	2	2	0	0
Ken O'Dea, ph	.333	3	3	0	1	0	0	0	2	0	0	0
Ray Sanders, 1b	.286	6	21	5	6	0	0	1	1	5	8	0
Freddy Schmidt, p	.000	1	1	0	0	0	0	0	0	0	1	0
Emil Verban, 2b	.412	6	17	1	7	0	0	0	2	2	0	0
Ted Wilks, p	.000	2	2	0	0	0	0	0	0	0	2	0
TOTAL	.240		204	16	49	9	1	3	15	19	43	0

PITCHER	W	L	ERA	G	GS	CG	SV	SHO	IP	H	ER	BB	SO
Harry Brecheen	1	0	1.00	1	1	1	0	0	9.0	9	1	4	4
Bud Byerly	0	0	0.00	1	0	0	0	0	1.1	0	0	0	1
Mort Cooper	1	1	1.13	2	2	1	0	1	16.0	9	2	5	16
Blix Donnelly	1	0	0.00	2	0	0	0	0	6.0	2	0	1	9
Al Jurisich	0	0	27.00	1	0	0	0	0	0.2	2	2	1	0
Max Lanier	1	0	2.19	2	2	0	0	0	12.1	8	3	8	11
Freddy Schmidt	0	0	0.00	1	0	0	0	0	3.1	1	0	1	1
Ted Wilks	0	1	5.68	2	1	0	1	0	6.1	5	4	3	7
TOTAL	4	2	1.96	12	6	2	1	1	55.0	36	12	23	49

STL (A)

PLAYER/POS	AVG	G	AB	R	H	2B	3B	HR	RB	BB	SO	SB
Floyd Baker, 2b	.000	2	2	0	0	0	0	0	0	0	2	0
Milt Byrnes, ph	.000	3	2	0	0	0	0	0	0	1	2	0
Mike Chartak, ph	.000	2	2	0	0	0	0	0	0	0	2	0
Mark Christman, 3b	.091	6	22	0	2	0	0	0	1	0	6	0
Ellis Clary, ph	.000	1	1	0	0	0	0	0	0	0	0	0
Denny Galehouse, p	.200	2	5	0	1	0	0	0	0	1	1	0
Don Gutteridge, 2b	.143	6	21	1	3	1	0	0	0	3	5	0
Red Hayworth, c	.118	6	17	1	2	1	0	0	1	3	1	0
Al Hollingsworth, p	.000	1	1	0	0	0	0	0	0	0	0	0
Sig Jakucki, p	.000	1	0	0	0	0	0	0	0	0	0	0
Jack Kramer, p	.000	2	4	0	0	0	0	0	0	0	2	0
Mike Kreevich, of	.231	6	26	0	6	3	0	0	0	0	5	0
Chet Laabs, of-4	.200	5	15	1	3	1	1	0	0	2	6	0
Frank Mancuso, c-1	.667	2	3	0	2	0	0	0	1	0	0	0
George McQuinn, 1b	.438	6	16	2	7	2	0	1	5	7	2	0
Gene Moore, of	.182	6	22	4	4	0	0	0	0	3	6	0
Bob Muncrief, p	.000	2	1	0	0	0	0	0	0	0	1	0
Nelson Potter, p	.000	2	4	0	0	0	0	0	0	0	1	0
Tex Shirley, p	.000	2	0	0	0	0	0	0	0	0	0	0
Vern Stephens, ss	.227	6	22	2	5	1	0	0	0	3	3	0
Tom Turner, ph	.000	1	1	0	0	0	0	0	0	0	0	0
Al Zarilla, of-3	.100	4	10	1	1	0	0	0	1	0	4	0
TOTAL	.183		197	12	36	9	1	1	9	23	49	0

PITCHER	W	L	ERA	G	GS	CG	SV	SHO	IP	H	ER	BB	SO
Denny Galehouse	1	1	1.50	2	2	2	0	0	18.0	13	3	5	15
Al Hollingsworth	0	0	2.25	1	0	0	0	0	4.0	5	1	2	1
Sig Jakucki	0	1	9.00	1	1	0	0	0	3.0	5	3	0	4
Jack Kramer	1	0	0.00	2	1	1	0	0	11.0	9	0	4	12
Bob Muncrief	0	1	1.35	2	0	0	0	0	6.2	5	1	4	4
Nelson Potter	0	1	0.93	2	2	0	0	0	9.2	10	1	3	6
Tex Shirley	0	0	0.00	2	0	0	0	0	2.0	2	0	1	1
TOTAL	2	4	1.49	12	6	3	0	0	54.1	49	9	19	43

GAME 1 AT STL-N OCT 4

STL-A	000	200	000	2 2 0
STL-N	000	000	001	1 7 0

Pitchers: GALEHOUSE vs M.COOPER, Donnelly (8)
Home Runs: McQuinn-STL(A)
Attendance: 33,242

GAME 2 AT STL-N OCT 5

STL-A	000	002	000 0	2 7 4
STL-N	001	100	000 1	3 7 0

Pitchers: Potter, MUNCRIEF (7) vs Lanier, DONNELLY (8)
Attendance: 35,076

GAME 3 AT STL-A OCT 6

STL-N	100	000	100	2 7 0
STL-A	004	000	20X	6 8 2

Pitchers: WILKS, Schmidt (3), Jurisich (7), Byerly (7) vs KRAMER
Attendance: 34,737

GAME 4 AT STL-A OCT 7

STL-N	202	001	000	5 12 0
STL-A	000	000	010	1 9 1

Pitchers: BRECHEEN vs JAKUCKI, Hollingsworth (4), Shirley (8)
Home Runs: Musial-STL(N)
Attendance: 35,455

GAME 5 AT STL-A OCT 8

STL-N	000	001	010	2 6 1
STL-A	000	000	000	0 7 1

Pitchers: M.COOPER vs GALEHOUSE
Home Runs: Sanders-STL(N), Litwhiler-STL(N)
Attendance: 36,568

GAME 6 AT STL-N OCT 9

STL-A	010	000	000	1 3 2
STL-N	000	300	00X	3 10 0

Pitchers: POTTER, Muncrief (4), Kramer (7) vs LANIER, Wilks (6)
Attendance: 31,630

As World War Two ended during the summer, military major leaguers began returning to their clubs. Hank Greenberg's return in July provided the spark needed for Detroit's narrow pennant victory, and his three-run homer in Game Two of the World Series proved to be the decisive blow in the Tigers' successful struggle for the world title.

Chicago started strong as Cub ace Hank Borowy shut out the Tigers on six singles while his teammates drove out Tiger ace Hal Newhouser with seven runs in the first three innings, to win 9–0. Chicago continued its assault the next day with a run in the top of the fourth, but in the fifth inning Tiger Doc Cramer—with two out and two on—singled in the tying run, and Greenberg followed with his tie-breaking homer for three additional runs. Detroit pitcher Virgil Trucks (who had returned from the Navy in time to pitch in the regular-season finale) held the Cubs scoreless after the fourth inning for the Tiger win.

Chicago's Claude Passeau moved the Cubs back into the Series lead with a one-hit shutout in Game Three, but Tiger Dizzy Trout's five-hitter in Game Four again evened the Series. The Tigers bunched four of their seven hits in the fourth inning for all four of their runs.

Detroit took the Series lead for the first time with an 8–4 win in Game Five. Borowy and Newhouser faced each other as they had in the opener, but this time Borowy was hit hard. Driven out when four Tigers opened the sixth inning with safe hits, he took the loss as Newhouser went the distance for the win.

In Game Six, Chicago concluded the seventh inning of a heavy-hitting game leading 7–3. Detroit tied the score with four runs in the top of the eighth (capped by Greenberg's home run), but in the last of the twelfth the Cubs' Stan Hack doubled home the winning run to keep Chicago's hopes alive.

Two days later in the finale, Cub manager Charlie Grimm started Borowy, who had relieved for four shutout innings to win Game Six. But this third appearance in four days proved too much. Removed after the first three batters to face him singled, he took the loss, as the Tigers went on to score nine runs to the Cubs' three.

Detroit Tigers (AL), 4; Chicago Cubs (NL), 3

DET (A)

PLAYER/POS	AVG	G	AB	R	H	2B	3B	HR	RB	BB	SO	SB
Al Benton, p	.000	3	0	0	0	0	0	0	0	0	0	0
Red Borom, ph	.000	2	1	0	0	0	0	0	0	0	0	0
Tommy Bridges, p	.000	1	0	0	0	0	0	0	0	0	0	0
George Caster, p	.000	1	0	0	0	0	0	0	0	0	0	0
Doc Cramer, of	.379	7	29	7	11	0	0	0	4	1	0	1
Roy Cullenbine, of	.227	7	22	5	5	2	0	0	4	8	2	1
Zeb Eaton, ph	.000	1	1	0	0	0	0	0	0	0	1	0
Hank Greenberg, of	.304	7	23	7	7	3	0	2	7	6	5	0
Joe Hoover, ss	.333	1	3	1	1	0	0	0	0	1	0	0
Chuck Hostetler, ph	.000	3	3	0	0	0	0	0	0	0	0	0
Bob Maier, ph	1.000	1	1	0	1	0	0	0	0	0	0	0
Eddie Mayo, 2b	.250	7	28	4	7	1	0	0	2	2	2	0
John Mc Hale, ph	.000	3	3	0	0	0	0	0	0	0	1	0
Ed Mierkowicz, of	.000	1	0	0	0	0	0	0	0	0	0	0
Les Mueller, p	.000	1	0	0	0	0	0	0	0	0	0	0
Hal Newhouser, p	.000	3	8	0	0	0	0	0	1	1	1	0
Jimmy Outlaw, 3b	.179	7	28	1	5	0	0	0	3	2	1	1
Stubby Overmire, p	.000	1	1	0	0	0	0	0	0	0	0	0
Paul Richards, c	.211	7	19	0	4	2	0	0	6	4	3	0
Bob Swift, c	.250	3	4	1	1	0	0	0	0	0	2	0
Jim Tobin, p	.000	1	1	0	0	0	0	0	0	0	0	0
Dizzy Trout, p	.167	2	6	0	1	0	0	0	0	0	0	0
Virgil Trucks, p	.000	2	4	0	0	0	0	0	0	1	1	0
Hub Walker, ph	.500	2	2	1	1	1	0	0	0	0	0	0
Skeeter Webb, ss	.185	7	27	4	5	0	0	0	1	3	1	0
Rudy York, 1b	.179	7	28	1	5	1	0	1	3	3	4	0
TOTAL	.223		242	32	54	10	0	2	32	33	22	3

PITCHER	W	L	ERA	G	GS	CG	SV	SHO	IP	H	ER	BB	SO
Al Benton	0	0	1.93	3	0	0	0	0	4.2	6	1	0	5
Tommy Bridges	0	0	16.20	1	0	0	0	0	1.2	3	3	3	1
George Caster	0	0	0.00	1	0	0	0	0	0.2	0	0	0	1
Les Mueller	0	0	0.00	1	0	0	0	0	2.0	0	0	1	1
Hal Newhouser	2	1	6.10	3	3	2	0	0	20.2	25	14	4	22
Stubby Overmire	0	1	3.00	1	1	0	0	0	6.0	4	2	2	2
Jim Tobin	0	0	6.00	1	0	0	0	0	3.0	4	2	1	0
Dizzy Trout	1	1	0.66	2	1	1	0	0	13.2	9	1	3	9
Virgil Trucks	1	0	3.38	2	2	1	0	0	13.1	14	5	5	7
TOTAL	4	3	3.84	15	7	4	0	0	65.2	65	28	19	48

CHI (N)

PLAYER/POS	AVG	G	AB	R	H	2B	3B	HR	RB	BB	SO	SB
Heinz Becker, ph	.500	3	2	0	1	0	0	0	0	1	1	0
Cy Block, pr	.000	1	0	0	0	0	0	0	0	0	0	0
Hank Borowy, p	.167	4	6	1	1	1	0	0	0	0	3	0
Phil Cavaretta, 1b	.423	7	26	7	11	2	0	1	5	4	3	0
Bob Chipman, p	.000	1	0	0	0	0	0	0	0	0	0	0
Paul Derringer, p	.000	3	0	0	0	0	0	0	0	0	0	0
Paul Erickson, p	.000	4	0	0	0	0	0	0	0	0	0	0
Paul Gillespie, c-1	.000	3	6	0	0	0	0	0	0	0	0	0
Stan Hack, 3b	.367	7	30	1	11	3	0	0	4	4	2	0
Roy Hughes, ss	.294	6	17	1	5	1	0	0	3	4	5	0
Don Johnson, 2b	.172	7	29	4	5	2	1	0	0	0	8	1
Mickey Livingston, c	.364	6	22	3	8	3	0	0	4	1	1	0
Peanuts Lowrey, of	.310	7	29	4	9	1	0	0	0	1	2	0
Clyde Mc Cullough, ph	.000	1	1	0	0	0	0	0	0	0	1	0
Lennie Merullo, ss	.000	3	2	0	0	0	0	0	0	0	0	0
Bill Nicholson, of	.214	7	28	1	6	1	1	0	8	2	5	0
Andy Pafko, of	.214	7	28	5	6	2	1	0	2	2	5	1
Claude Passeau, p	.000	3	7	1	0	0	0	0	1	0	4	0
Ray Prim, p	.000	2	0	0	0	0	0	0	0	0	0	0
Ed Sauer, ph	.000	2	2	0	0	0	0	0	0	0	2	0
Bill Schuster, ss-1	.000	2	1	1	0	0	0	0	0	0	0	0
Frank Secory, ph	.200	5	5	0	1	0	0	0	0	0	2	0
Hy Vandenberg, p	.000	3	1	0	0	0	0	0	0	0	1	0
Dewey Williams, c-1	.000	2	2	0	0	0	0	0	0	0	1	0
Hank Wyse, p	.000	3	3	0	0	0	0	0	0	0	2	0
TOTAL	.259		247	29	64	16	3	1	27	19	48	2

PITCHER	W	L	ERA	G	GS	CG	SV	SHO	IP	H	ER	BB	SO
Hank Borowy	2	2	4.00	4	3	1	0	1	18.0	21	8	6	8
Bob Chipman	0	0	0.00	1	0	0	0	0	0.1	0	0	1	0
Paul Derringer	0	0	6.75	3	0	0	0	0	5.1	5	4	7	1
Paul Erickson	0	0	3.86	4	0	0	0	0	7.0	8	3	3	5
Claude Passeau	1	0	2.70	3	2	1	0	1	16.2	7	5	8	3
Ray Prim	0	1	9.00	2	1	0	0	0	4.0	4	4	1	1
Hy Vandenberg	0	0	0.00	3	0	0	0	0	6.0	1	0	3	3
Hank Wyse	0	1	7.04	3	1	0	0	0	7.2	8	6	4	1
TOTAL	3	4	4.15	23	7	2	0	2	65.0	54	30	33	22

GAME 1 AT DET OCT 3

CHI	403	000	200	9 13 0
DET	000	000	000	0 6 0

Pitchers: BOROWY vs NEWHOUSER, Benton (3), Tobin (5), Mueller (8)
Home Runs: Cavaretta-CHI
Attendance: 54,637

GAME 2 AT DET OCT 4

CHI	000	100	000	1 7 0
DET	000	040	00X	4 7 0

Pitchers: WYSE, Erickson (7) vs TRUCKS
Home Runs: Greenberg-DET
Attendance: 53,636

GAME 3 AT DET OCT 5

CHI	000	200	100	3 8 0
DET	000	000	000	0 1 2

Pitchers: PASSEAU vs OVERMIRE, Benton (7)
Attendance: 55,500

GAME 4 AT CHI OCT 6

DET	000	400	000	4 7 1
CHI	000	001	000	1 5 1

Pitchers: TROUT vs PRIM, Derringer (4), Vandenberg (6), Erickson (8)
Attendance: 42,923

GAME 5 AT CHI OCT 7

DET	001	004	102	8 11 0
CHI	001	000	201	4 7 2

Pitchers: NEWHOUSER vs BOROWY, Vandenberg (6), Chipman (6), Derringer (7), Erickson (9)
Attendance: 43,463

GAME 6 AT CHI OCT 8

DET	010	000	240	000	7 13 0
CHI	000	041	200	001	8 15 3

Pitchers: Trucks, Caster (5), Bridges (6), Benton (7), TROUT (8) vs Passeau, Wyse (7), Prim (8), BOROWY (9)
Home Runs: Greenberg-DET
Attendance: 41,708

GAME 7 AT CHI OCT 10

DET	510	000	120	9 9 1
CHI	100	100	010	3 10 0

Pitchers: NEWHOUSER vs BOROWY, Derringer (1), Vandenberg (2), Erickson (6), Passeau (8), Wyse (9)
Attendance: 41,590

With World War Two over, the majors were at full strength for the first time in five years. Boston's big bats were back, and the Sox ran away with the American League pennant. St. Louis had Stan Musial back, but they struggled to their pennant, finishing the regular schedule tied with Brooklyn, and defeating them in the first major league tie-breaker playoff, two games to one.

Favored Boston edged St. Louis in the opener, but it took a home run by Rudy York in the top of the tenth to spoil Cardinal ace Howie Pollet's strong showing. Harry Brecheen brought the Cards back the next day with the first of his three Series wins—a four-hit shutout.

Boston regained the lead in Game Three. Sox ace Dave Ferriss spaced six hits and a walk, one per inning, in shutting out the Cardinals, and Rudy York hit his second game-winning homer, this time a three-run shot in the first inning. The next day, though, St. Louis exploded for a record-tying 20 hits—four apiece by Enos Slaughter, Joe Garagiola and Whitey Kurowski—to give Cardinal pitcher George Munger (who had completed only two of his seven regular-season starts) an easy complete-game 12–3 victory.

For the third time the Red Sox took the Series lead, winning Game Five 6–3 behind Joe Dobson's four-hit pitching (the Cards' three runs were unearned), but St. Louis tied the Series for the third time with a win in Game Six. Brecheen, in his second start, again pitched splendidly, holding Boston to a single run in the seventh inning, long after the Cards had driven out Sox starter Mickey Harris with three runs in the third.

The final game, like the Series itself, was a seesaw battle. Boston scored the first run in the top of the first, but St. Louis tied the score an inning later. The Cards took a two-run lead on three hits in the fifth, but the Sox came back in the eighth to tie it up as Dom DiMaggio doubled off reliever Brecheen to drive in a pair of pinch hitters who had singled and doubled off starter Murry Dickson. The Series' final run came a half inning later. Slaughter opened with a single, but moved no farther as the next two batters were retired. Then Harry Walker hit a liner over short. Slaughter, off with the crack of the bat, never paused and beat the relay to the plate with what proved the winning run, as Brecheen held the Sox in the ninth for his third win of the Series and the Cardinals' seventh world title.

St. Louis Cardinals (NL), 4; Boston Red Sox (AL), 3

STL (N)

PLAYER/POS	AVG	G	AB	R	H	2B	3B	HR	RB	BB	SO	SB
Johnny Beazley, p	.000	1	0	0	0	0	0	0	0	0	0	0
Al Brazle, p	.000	1	2	0	0	0	0	0	0	0	0	0
Harry Brecheen, p	.125	3	8	2	1	0	0	0	1	0	1	0
Murry Dickson, p	.400	2	5	1	2	2	0	0	1	0	1	0
Erv Dusak, of	.250	4	4	0	1	1	0	0	0	2	2	0
Joe Garagiola, c	.316	5	19	2	6	2	0	0	4	0	3	0
Nippy Jones, ph	.000	1	1	0	0	0	0	0	0	0	1	0
Whitey Kurowski, 3b	.296	7	27	5	8	3	0	0	2	0	3	0
Marty Marion, ss	.250	7	24	1	6	2	0	0	4	1	1	0
Terry Moore, of	.148	7	27	1	4	0	0	0	2	2	6	0
Red Munger, p	.250	1	4	0	1	0	0	0	0	0	2	0
Stan Musial, 1b	.222	7	27	3	6	4	1	0	4	4	2	1
Howie Pollet, p	.000	2	4	0	0	0	0	0	0	0	1	0
Del Rice, c	.500	3	6	2	3	1	0	0	0	0	2	0
Red Schoendienst, 2b	.233	7	30	3	7	1	0	0	1	0	2	1
Dick Sisler, ph	.000	2	2	0	0	0	0	0	0	0	0	0
Enos Slaughter, of	.320	7	25	5	8	1	1	1	2	4	3	1
Harry Walker, of	.412	7	17	3	7	2	0	0	6	4	2	0
Ted Wilks, p	.000	1	0	0	0	0	0	0	0	0	0	0
TOTAL	.259		232	28	60	19	2	1	27	19	30	3

PITCHER	W	L	ERA	G	GS	CG	SV	SHO	IP	H	ER	BB	SO
Johnny Beazley	0	0	0.00	1	0	0	0	0	1.0	1	0	0	1
Al Brazle	0	1	5.40	1	0	0	0	0	6.2	7	4	6	4
Harry Brecheen	3	0	0.45	3	2	2	0	1	20.0	14	1	5	11
Murry Dickson	0	1	3.86	2	2	0	0	0	14.0	11	6	4	7
Red Munger	1	0	1.00	1	1	1	0	0	9.0	9	1	3	2
Howie Pollet	0	1	3.48	2	2	1	0	0	10.1	12	4	4	3
Ted Wilks	0	0	0.00	1	0	0	0	0	1.0	2	0	0	0
TOTAL	4	3	2.32	11	7	4	0	1	62.0	56	16	22	28

BOS (A)

PLAYER/POS	AVG	G	AB	R	H	2B	3B	HR	RB	BB	SO	SB
Jim Bagby, p	.000	1	1	0	0	0	0	0	0	0	0	0
Mace Brown, p	.000	1	0	0	0	0	0	0	0	0	0	0
Paul Campbell, pr	.000	1	0	0	0	0	0	0	0	0	0	0
Leon Culberson, of-3	.222	5	9	1	2	0	0	1	1	1	2	1
Dom DiMaggio, of	.259	7	27	2	7	3	0	0	3	2	2	0
Joe Dobson, p	.000	3	3	0	0	0	0	0	0	0	2	0
Bobby Doerr, 2b	.409	6	22	1	9	1	0	1	3	2	2	0
Clem Dreisewerd, p	.000	1	0	0	0	0	0	0	0	0	0	0
Dave Ferriss, p	.000	2	6	0	0	0	0	0	0	0	1	0
Don Gutteridge, 2b-2	.400	3	5	1	2	0	0	0	1	0	0	0
Mickey Harris, p	.333	2	3	0	1	0	0	0	0	0	1	0
Pinky Higgins, 3b	.208	7	24	1	5	1	0	0	2	2	0	0
Tex Hughson, p	.333	3	3	0	1	0	0	0	0	0	1	0
Earl Johnson, p	.000	3	1	0	0	0	0	0	0	0	0	0
Bob Klinger, p	.000	1	0	0	0	0	0	0	0	0	0	0
Tom Mc Bride, of-2	.167	5	12	0	2	0	0	0	1	0	1	0
Catfish Metkovich, ph	.500	2	2	1	1	0	0	0	0	0	0	0
Wally Moses, of	.417	4	12	1	5	0	0	0	1	1	2	0
Roy Partee, c	.100	5	10	1	1	0	0	0	1	1	2	0
Johnny Pesky, ss	.233	7	30	2	7	0	0	0	0	1	3	1
Rip Russell, 3b-1	1.000	2	2	1	2	0	0	0	0	0	0	0
Mike Ryba, p	.000	1	0	0	0	0	0	0	0	0	0	0
Hal Wagner, c	.000	5	13	0	0	0	0	0	0	0	1	0
Ted Williams, of	.200	7	25	2	5	0	0	0	1	5	5	0
Rudy York, 1b	.261	7	23	6	6	1	1	2	5	6	4	0
Bill Zuber, p	.000	1	0	0	0	0	0	0	0	0	0	0
TOTAL	.240		233	20	56	7	1	4	18	22	28	2

PITCHER	W	L	ERA	G	GS	CG	SV	SHO	IP	H	ER	BB	SO
Jim Bagby	0	0	3.00	1	0	0	0	0	3.0	6	1	1	1
Mace Brown	0	0	27.00	1	0	0	0	0	1.0	4	3	1	0
Joe Dobson	1	0	0.00	3	1	1	0	0	12.2	4	0	3	10
Clem Dreisewerd	0	0	0.00	1	0	0	0	0	0.1	0	0	0	0
Dave Ferriss	1	0	2.03	2	2	1	0	1	13.1	13	3	2	4
Mickey Harris	0	2	3.72	2	2	0	0	0	9.2	11	4	4	5
Tex Hughson	0	1	3.14	3	2	0	0	0	14.1	14	5	3	8
Earl Johnson	1	0	2.70	3	0	0	0	0	3.1	1	1	2	1
Bob Klinger	0	1	13.50	1	0	0	0	0	0.2	2	1	1	0
Mike Ryba	0	0	13.50	1	0	0	0	0	0.2	2	1	1	0
Bill Zuber	0	0	4.50	1	0	0	0	0	2.0	3	1	1	1
TOTAL	3	4	2.95	19	7	2	0	1	61.0	60	20	19	30

GAME 1 AT STL OCT 6

BOS	010 000 001 1	3	9	2
STL	000 001 010 0	2	7	0

Pitchers: Hughson, JOHNSON (9) vs POLLET
Home Runs: York-BOS
Attendance: 36,218

GAME 2 AT STL OCT 7

BOS	000 000 000	0	4	1
STL	001 020 00X	3	6	0

Pitchers: HARRIS, Dobson (8) vs BRECHEEN
Attendance: 35,815

GAME 3 AT BOS OCT 9

STL	000 000 000	0	6	1
BOS	300 000 01X	4	8	0

Pitchers: DICKSON, Wilks (8) vs FERRISS
Home Runs: York-BOS
Attendance: 34,500

GAME 4 AT BOS OCT 10

STL	033 010 104	12	20	1
BOS	000 000 020	3	9	4

Pitchers: MUNGER vs HUGHSON, Bagby (3), Zuber (6), Brown (8), Ryba (9), Dreisewerd (9)
Home Runs: Slaughter-STL, Doerr-BOS
Attendance: 35,645

GAME 5 AT BOS OCT 11

STL	010 000 002	3	4	1
BOS	110 001 30X	6	11	3

Pitchers: Pollet, BRAZLE (1), Beazley (8) vs DOBSON
Home Runs: Culberson-BOS
Attendance: 35,982

GAME 6 AT STL OCT 13

BOS	000 000 100	1	7	0
STL	003 000 01X	4	8	0

Pitchers: HARRIS, Hughson (3), Johnson (8) vs BRECHEEN
Attendance: 35,768

GAME 7 AT STL OCT 15

BOS	100 000 020	3	8	0
STL	010 020 01X	4	9	1

Pitchers: Ferriss, Dobson (5), KLINGER (8), Johnson (8) vs Dickson, BRECHEEN (8)
Attendance: 36,143

Two of the most memorable plays in World Series history brought Brooklyn victory in Games Four and Six, but when the Series had ended the Yankees were world champions for the eleventh time. Dodger ace Ralph Branca set New York down in order through the first four innings of Game One. But the first five batters to face him in the fifth inning reached base. Branca was lifted, but before the inning was over five Yankees had crossed the plate— more than enough for their first win.

The Yankees went two-up the next day, rocking four Brooklyn pitchers for 15 hits and an easy 10–3 win. Brooklyn finally made its presence felt in Game Three, another heavy-hitting affair, scoring six times in the second inning to establish a lead the Yankees could not overcome. Both teams recorded 13 hits, but Dodger fireman Hugh Casey extinguished the last Yankee flame in the seventh inning, and preserved a narrow 9–8 Dodger lead the rest of the way.

Shortstop Pee Wee Reese's error and a bases-loaded walk gave the Yankees an unearned run in the first inning of Game Four, and they earned a second run in the fourth. Meanwhile, Yankee pitcher Bill Bevens, although he averaged a walk an inning, had allowed no Dodger hits and only one run as the game entered the last of the ninth. Bevens retired two in the ninth, but walked his ninth and tenth batters (one intentionally), then lost both his no-hitter and the game as Dodger pinch hitter Cookie Lavagetto doubled home the two baserunners to even the Series at two-all.

Yankee Spec Shea (the winning pitcher in Game One) held Brooklyn to four hits and one run in Game Five. Joe DiMaggio homered in the fifth inning for New York's second run, enough to put the Yankees back in the Series lead. The Dodgers rebounded in Game Six to build an early 4–0 lead. But the Yankees tied the score in the last of the third and took a lead in the fourth. Brooklyn regained the lead in the sixth with four runs, but when DiMaggio hit a long fly to left with two on in the Yankee half of the inning, it looked as if the score would be tied. But substitute left fielder Al Gionfriddo (in what turned out to be his last big league game) raced to the bullpen fence 415 feet out to rob DiMag of the home run. New York scored a run in the ninth, but thanks to Gionfriddo's catch it was not enough to win the game.

Brooklyn scored first in the finale with a pair of second-inning runs, but Yankee relievers Bill

New York Yankees (AL), 4; Brooklyn Dodgers (NL), 3

NY (A)

PLAYER/POS	AVG	G	AB	R	H	2B	3B	HR	RB	BB	SO	SB
Yogi Berra, c-4,of-2	.158	6	19	2	3	0	0	1	2	1	2	0
Bill Bevens, p	.000	2	4	0	0	0	0	0	0	0	2	0
Bobby Brown, ph	1.000	4	3	2	3	2	0	0	3	1	0	0
Spud Chandler, p	.000	1	0	0	0	0	0	0	0	0	0	0
Allie Clark, of-1	.500	3	2	1	1	0	0	0	1	1	0	0
Joe DiMaggio, of	.231	7	26	4	6	0	0	2	5	6	2	0
Karl Drews, p	.000	2	0	0	0	0	0	0	0	0	2	0
Lonny Frey, ph	.000	1	1	0	0	0	0	0	0	1	0	0
Tommy Henrich, of	.323	7	31	2	10	2	0	1	5	2	3	0
Ralph Houk, ph	1.000	1	1	0	1	0	0	0	0	0	0	0
Billy Johnson, 3b	.269	7	26	8	7	0	3	0	2	3	4	0
Johnny Lindell, of	.500	6	18	3	9	3	1	0	7	5	2	0
Sherm Lollar, c	.750	2	4	3	3	2	0	0	1	0	0	0
George Mc Quinn, 1b	.130	7	23	3	3	0	0	0	1	5	8	0
Bobo Newsom, p	.000	2	0	0	0	0	0	0	0	0	0	0
Joe Page, p	.000	4	4	0	0	0	0	0	0	0	1	0
Jack Phillips, 1b-1	.000	2	2	0	0	0	0	0	0	0	0	0
Vic Raschi, p	.000	2	0	0	0	0	0	0	0	0	0	0
Allie Reynolds, p	.500	2	4	2	2	0	0	0	1	0	0	0
Phil Rizzuto, ss	.308	7	26	3	8	1	0	0	2	4	0	2
Aaron Robinson, c	.200	3	10	2	2	0	0	0	1	2	1	0
Spec Shea, p	.400	3	5	0	2	1	0	0	1	0	2	0
Snuffy Stirnweiss, 2b	.259	7	27	3	7	0	1	0	3	8	8	0
Butch Wensloff, p	.000	1	0	0	0	0	0	0	0	0	0	0
TOTAL	.282		238	38	67	11	5	4	36	38	37	2

PITCHER	W	L	ERA	G	GS	CG	SV	SHO	IP	H	ER	BB	SO
Bill Bevens	0	1	2.38	2	1	1	0	0	11.1	3	3	11	7
Spud Chandler	0	0	9.00	1	0	0	0	0	2.0	2	2	3	1
Karl Drews	0	0	3.00	2	0	0	0	0	3.0	2	1	1	0
Bobo Newsom	0	1	19.29	2	1	0	0	0	2.1	6	5	2	0
Joe Page	1	1	4.15	4	0	0	1	0	13.0	12	6	2	7
Vic Raschi	0	0	6.75	2	0	0	0	0	1.1	2	1	0	1
Allie Reynolds	1	0	4.76	2	2	1	0	0	11.1	15	6	3	6
Spec Shea	2	0	2.35	3	3	1	0	0	15.1	10	4	8	10
Butch Wensloff	0	0	0.00	1	0	0	0	0	2.0	0	0	0	0
TOTAL	4	3	4.09	19	7	3	1	0	61.2	52	28	30	32

BRO (N)

PLAYER/POS	AVG	G	AB	R	H	2B	3B	HR	RB	BB	SO	SB
Dan Bankhead, pr	.000	1	0	1	0	0	0	0	0	0	0	0
Rex Barney, p	.000	3	1	0	0	0	0	0	0	0	0	0
Hank Behrman, p	.000	5	0	0	0	0	0	0	0	0	0	0
Bobby Bragan, ph	1.000	1	1	0	1	1	0	0	1	0	0	0
Ralph Branca, p	.000	3	4	0	0	0	0	0	0	0	1	0
Hugh Casey, p	.000	6	1	0	0	0	0	0	0	0	1	0
Bruce Edwards, c	.222	7	27	3	6	1	0	0	2	2	7	0
Carl Furillo, of	.353	6	17	2	6	2	0	0	3	3	0	0
Al Gionfriddo, of-1	.000	4	3	2	0	0	0	0	0	1	0	1
Hal Gregg, p	.000	3	3	0	0	0	0	0	0	1	1	0
Joe Hatten, p	.333	4	3	1	1	0	0	0	0	0	0	0
Gene Hermanski, of	.158	7	19	4	3	0	1	0	1	3	3	0
Gil Hodges, ph	.000	1	1	0	0	0	0	0	0	0	1	0
Spider Jorgensen, 3b	.200	7	20	1	4	2	0	0	3	2	4	0
Cookie Lavagetto, 3b-3	.143	5	7	0	1	1	0	0	3	0	2	0
Vic Lombardi, p-2	.000	3	3	0	0	0	0	0	0	0	0	0
Eddie Miksis, 2b-1,of-1	.250	5	4	1	1	0	0	0	0	0	1	0
Pee Wee Reese, ss	.304	7	23	5	7	1	0	0	4	6	3	3
Pete Reiser, of-3	.250	5	8	1	2	0	0	0	3	1	0	0
Jackie Robinson, 1b	.259	7	27	3	7	2	0	0	3	2	4	2
Eddie Stanky, 2b	.240	7	25	4	6	1	0	0	2	3	2	0
Harry Taylor, p	.000	1	0	0	0	0	0	0	0	0	0	0
Arky Vaughan, ph	.500	3	2	0	1	1	0	0	0	1	0	0
Dixie Walker, of	.222	7	27	1	6	1	0	1	4	3	1	1
TOTAL	.230		226	29	52	13	1	1	26	30	32	7

PITCHER	W	L	ERA	G	GS	CG	SV	SHO	IP	H	ER	BB	SO
Rex Barney	0	1	2.70	3	1	0	0	0	6.2	4	2	10	3
Hank Behrman	0	0	7.11	5	0	0	0	0	6.1	9	5	5	3
Ralph Branca	1	1	8.64	3	1	0	0	0	8.1	12	8	5	8
Hugh Casey	2	0	0.87	6	0	0	1	0	10.1	5	1	1	3
Hal Gregg	0	1	3.55	3	1	0	0	0	12.2	9	5	8	10
Joe Hatten	0	0	7.00	4	1	0	0	0	9.0	12	7	7	5
Vic Lombardi	0	1	12.15	2	2	0	0	0	6.2	14	9	1	5
Harry Taylor	0	0	INF	1	1	0	0	0	0.0	2	0	1	0
TOTAL	3	4	5.55	27	7	0	1	0	60.0	67	37	38	37

Bevens and Joe Page shut them out through the final seven innings as their teammates gradually built a Series-clinching 5–2 victory.

GAME 1 AT NY SEPT 30

BRO	100 001 100	3	6	0
NY	000 050 00X	5	4	0

Pitchers: BRANCA, Behrman (5), Casey (7) vs SHEA, Page (6)
Attendance: 73,365

GAME 2 AT NY OCT 1

BRO	001 100 001	3	9	2
NY	101 121 40X	10	15	1

Pitchers: LOMBARDI, Gregg (5), Behrman (7), Barney (7) vs REYNOLDS
Home Runs: Walker-BRO, Henrich-NY
Attendance: 69,865

GAME 3 AT BRO OCT 2

NY	002 221 100	8	13	0
BRO	061 200 00X	9	13	1

Pitchers: NEWSOM, Raschi (2), Drews (3), Chandler (4), Page (6) vs Hatten, Branca (5), CASEY (7)
Home Runs: DiMaggio-NY, Berra-NY
Attendance: 33,098

GAME 4 AT BRO OCT 3

NY	100 100 000	2	8	1
BRO	000 010 002	3	1	3

Pitchers: BEVENS vs Taylor, Gregg (1), Behrman (8), CASEY (9)
Attendance: 33,443

GAME 5 AT BRO OCT 4

NY	000 110 000	2	5	0
BRO	000 001 000	1	4	1

Pitchers: SHEA vs BARNEY, Hatten (7), Behrman (7), Casey (8)
Home Runs: DiMaggio-NY
Attendance: 34,379

GAME 6 AT NY OCT 5

BRO	202 004 000	8	12	1
NY	004 100 001	6	15	2

Pitchers: Lombardi, BRANCA (3), Hatten (6), Casey (9) vs Reynolds, Drews (3), PAGE (5), Newsom (6), Raschi (7), Wensloff (8)
Attendance: 74,065

GAME 7 AT NY OCT 6

BRO	020 000 000	2	7	0
NY	010 201 10X	5	7	0

Pitchers: GREGG, Behrman (4), Hatten (6), Barney (6), Casey (7) vs Shea, Bevens (2), PAGE (5)
Attendance: 71,548

Boston outpitched and outhit Cleveland, and the clubs tied in runs scored. But the Braves scored most of their runs in one game, and the Indians, spreading theirs more evenly, took the Series. Boston ace Johnny Sain dueled Bob Feller in the opener. Feller gave up only two singles, but one of them followed a walk and a sacrifice (and a controversial pickoff play at second, in which the Boston runner was ruled safe although photos later showed him clearly out) and drove in the game's only run. Both teams registered eight hits in Game Two, but Cleveland's led to four runs, while Indian hurler Bob Lemon held Boston to just one—and that was unearned.

Cleveland's rookie sensation Gene Bearden shut out the Braves on five hits in Game Three as the Series moved to Cleveland's huge Municipal Stadium. Bearden himself, after doubling in the third, scored on a Boston error what proved to be the winning run. A record 81,897 fans saw Sain face Steve Gromek in Game Four. Only five Indians hit Sain safely, but a first-inning single and double put Cleveland on the board, and Larry Doby's home run two innings later made the score 2–0. Boston's Marv Rickert homered in the seventh to narrow Cleveland's lead, but that ended the scoring.

Another attendance record was set at Game Five as 86,288 fans gathered to watch Bob Feller sew up the title for Cleveland. They went home disappointed. In a game that featured five of the Series' eight home runs, Boston jumped ahead on Bob Elliott's three-run blast in the first. Dale Mitchell opened Cleveland's half of the inning with a home run, but Elliott neutralized it in the third with his second homer. The Indians drove out Boston starter Nelson Potter with four runs in the fourth inning (three coming on Jim Hegan's homer). But Warren Spahn (who had lost Game Two) hurled one-hit shutout relief over the final five frames as his Braves tied the game on Bill Salkeld's homer in the sixth, and blew out Feller and two relievers with six runs in the seventh. The fourth Indian pitcher, Satchel Paige (in his only World Series appearance), retired two batters to end the inning, but the damage had been done.

A day later though, back in Boston, Cleveland edged the Braves 4–3 for the title. Gene Bearden's relief pitching allowed two inherited baserunners to score in the eighth, but halted Boston's rally one run short of a tie.

Cleveland Indians (AL), 4; Boston Braves (NL), 2

CLE (A)

PLAYER/POS	AVG	G	AB	R	H	2B	3B	HR	RB	BB	SO	SB
Gene Bearden, p	.500	2	4	1	2	1	0	0	0	0	1	0
Ray Boone, ph	.000	1	1	0	0	0	0	0	0	0	1	0
Lou Boudreau, ss	.273	6	22	1	6	4	0	0	3	1	1	0
Russ Christopher, p	.000	1	0	0	0	0	0	0	0	0	0	0
Allie Clark, of	.000	1	3	0	0	0	0	0	0	0	1	0
Larry Doby, of	.318	6	22	1	7	1	0	1	2	2	4	0
Bob Feller, p	.000	2	4	0	0	0	0	0	0	0	2	0
Joe Gordon, 2b	.182	6	22	3	4	0	0	1	2	1	2	1
Steve Gromek, p	.000	1	3	0	0	0	0	0	0	0	1	0
Jim Hegan, c	.211	6	19	2	4	0	0	1	5	1	4	1
Wally Judnich, of	.077	4	13	1	1	0	0	0	1	1	4	0
Ken Keltner, 3b	.095	6	21	3	2	0	0	0	2	2	3	0
Bob Kennedy, of	.500	3	2	0	1	0	0	0	1	0	1	0
Ed Klieman, p	.000	1	0	0	0	0	0	0	0	0	0	0
Bob Lemon, p	.000	2	7	0	0	0	0	0	0	0	0	0
Dale Mitchell, of	.174	6	23	4	4	1	0	1	1	2	0	0
Bob Muncrief, p	.000	1	0	0	0	0	0	0	0	0	0	0
Satchel Paige, p	.000	1	0	0	0	0	0	0	0	0	0	0
Hal Peck, of	.000	1	0	0	0	0	0	0	0	0	0	0
Eddie Robinson, 1b	.300	6	20	0	6	0	0	0	1	1	0	0
Al Rosen, ph	.000	1	1	0	0	0	0	0	0	0	0	0
Joe Tipton, ph	.000	1	1	0	0	0	0	0	0	0	1	0
Thurman Tucker, of	.333	1	3	1	1	0	0	0	0	1	0	0
TOTAL	.199		191	17	38	7	0	4	16	12	26	2

PITCHER	W	L	ERA	G	GS	CG	SV	SHO	IP	H	ER	BB	SO
Gene Bearden	1	0	0.00	2	1	1	1	1	10.2	6	0	1	4
Russ Christopher	0	0	INF	1	0	0	0	0	0.0	2	1	0	0
Bob Feller	0	2	5.02	2	2	1	0	0	14.1	10	8	5	7
Steve Gromek	1	0	1.00	1	1	1	0	0	9.0	7	1	1	2
Ed Klieman	0	0	INF	1	0	0	0	0	0.0	1	3	2	0
Bob Lemon	2	0	1.65	2	2	1	0	0	16.1	16	3	7	6
Bob Muncrief	0	0	0.00	1	0	0	0	0	2.0	1	0	0	0
Satchel Paige	0	0	0.00	1	0	0	0	0	0.2	0	0	0	0
TOTAL	4	2	2.72	11	6	4	1	1	53.0	43	16	16	19

BOS (N)

PLAYER/POS	AVG	G	AB	R	H	2B	3B	HR	RB	BB	SO	SB
Red Barrett, p	.000	2	0	0	0	0	0	0	0	0	0	0
Vern Bickford, p	.000	1	0	0	0	0	0	0	0	0	0	0
Clint Conatser, of	.000	2	4	0	0	0	0	0	1	0	0	0
Alvin Dark, ss	.167	6	24	2	4	1	0	0	0	0	2	0
Bob Elliott, 3b	.333	6	21	4	7	0	0	2	5	2	2	0
Tommy Holmes, of	.192	6	26	3	5	0	0	0	1	0	0	0
Phil Masi, c	.125	5	8	1	1	1	0	0	1	0	0	0
Frank Mc Cormick, 1b-1	.200	3	5	0	1	0	0	0	0	2	0	0
Mike Mc Cormick, of	.261	6	23	1	6	0	0	0	2	0	4	0
Nelson Potter, p	.500	2	2	0	1	0	0	0	0	0	0	0
Marv Rickert, of	.211	5	19	2	4	0	0	1	2	0	4	0
Connie Ryan, ph	.000	2	1	0	0	0	0	0	0	0	1	0
Johnny Sain, p	.200	2	5	0	1	0	0	0	0	0	0	0
Bill Salkeld, c	.222	5	9	2	2	0	0	1	1	5	1	0
Ray Sanders, ph	.000	1	1	0	0	0	0	0	0	0	0	0
Sibby Sisti, 2b	.000	2	1	0	0	0	0	0	0	0	0	0
Warren Spahn, p	.000	3	4	0	0	0	0	0	1	0	0	0
Eddie Stanky, 2b	.286	6	14	0	4	1	0	0	1	7	1	0
Earl Torgeson, 1b	.389	5	18	2	7	3	0	0	1	2	1	1
Bill Voiselle, p	.000	2	2	0	0	0	0	0	0	0	0	0
TOTAL	.230		187	17	43	6	0	4	16	16	19	1

PITCHER	W	L	ERA	G	GS	CG	SV	SHO	IP	H	ER	BB	SO
Red Barrett	0	0	0.00	2	0	0	0	0	3.2	1	0	0	1
Vern Bickford	0	1	2.70	1	1	0	0	0	3.1	4	1	5	1
Nelson Potter	0	0	8.44	2	1	0	0	0	5.1	6	5	2	1
Johnny Sain	1	1	1.06	2	2	2	0	1	17.0	9	2	0	9
Warren Spahn	1	1	3.00	3	1	0	0	0	12.0	10	4	3	12
Bill Voiselle	0	1	2.53	2	1	0	0	0	10.2	8	3	2	2
TOTAL	2	4	2.60	12	6	2	0	1	52.0	38	15	12	26

GAME 1 AT BOS OCT 6

CLE	000 000 000	0 4 0
BOS	000 000 01X	1 2 2

Pitchers: FELLER vs SAIN
Attendance: 40,135

GAME 2 AT BOS OCT 7

CLE	000 210 001	4 8 1
BOS	100 000 000	1 8 3

Pitchers: LEMON vs SPAHN, Barrett (5), Potter (8)
Attendance: 39,633

GAME 3 AT CLE OCT 8

BOS	000 000 000	0 5 1
CLE	001 100 00X	2 5 0

Pitchers: BICKFORD, Voiselle (4), Barrett (8) vs BEARDEN
Attendance: 70,306

GAME 4 AT CLE OCT 9

BOS	000 000 100	1 7 0
CLE	101 000 00X	2 5 0

Pitchers: SAIN vs GROMEK
Home Runs: Doby-CLE, Rickert-BOS
Attendance: 81,897

GAME 5 AT CLE OCT 10

BOS	301 001 600	11 12 0
CLE	100 400 000	5 6 2

Pitchers: Potter, SPAHN (4) vs FELLER, Klieman (7), Christopher (7), Paige (7), Muncrief (8)
Home Runs: Elliott-BOS (2), Mitchell-CLE, Hegan-CLE, Salkeld-BOS
Attendance: 86,288

GAME 6 AT BOS OCT 11

CLE	001 002 010	4 10 0
BOS	000 100 020	3 9 0

Pitchers: LEMON, Bearden (8) vs VOISELLE, Spahn (8)
Home Runs: Gordon-CLE
Attendance: 40,103

Casey Stengel, in the first of his twelve years as Yankee manager, edged his team past the Boston Red Sox for his first of ten American League pennants, then past the Dodgers for his first of seven world championships. New York and Brooklyn traded 1–0 wins to begin the Series. In Game One Yankee Allie Reynolds dueled Dodger rookie Don Newcombe scorelessly through 8½ innings—until Tommy Henrich led off the last of the ninth with a Yankee home run. Dodger Jackie Robinson scored after doubling off Vic Raschi in the second inning of Game Two for that game's only score, while Dodger ace Preacher Roe permitted the Yankees just six scattered hits—never more than one per inning.

The teams entered the ninth inning of Game Three tied 1–1. But in the top of the ninth, Dodger starter Ralph Branca, after loading the bases on two walks and a single, gave up another single to pinch hitter Johnny Mize for two runs. Jerry Coleman's single off reliever Jack Banta drove in another run before the third out was made. In the last of the ninth, Yankee fireman Joe Page (who had held Brooklyn scoreless since coming on with the bases loaded in the fourth) finally weakened. But after yielding solo homers to Luis Olmo and Roy Campanella, he struck out pinch hitter Bruce Edwards for New York's second win.

The Yankees' victory in Game Four came a little easier. They scored first, driving out starter Don Newcombe with three runs in the fourth, and rapping reliever Joe Hatten for three more runs an inning later. Brooklyn retaliated in the sixth, sending Yankee starter Ed Lopat to the showers with seven singles for four runs. But Allie Reynolds came on for 3⅓ innings of no-hit relief to preserve the Yankees lead—and his Series 0.00 earned run average.

After four closely contested games, the Yankees erupted in Game Five for ten runs in the first six innings as Brooklyn was held to just two. In the last of the seventh, the Dodgers came back, driving out starter Vic Raschi with a four-run rally, capped by Gil Hodges's three-run homer. But Joe Page came on to get the final out of the seventh, and held the Dodgers scoreless over the final two innings to bring the Yankees' world titles to an even dozen.

New York Yankees (AL), 4; Brooklyn Dodgers (NL), 1

NY (A)

PLAYER/POS	AVG	G	AB	R	H	2B	3B	HR	RB	BB	SO	SB
Hank Bauer, of	.167	3	6	0	1	0	0	0	0	0	0	0
Yogi Berra, c	.063	4	16	2	1	0	0	0	1	1	3	0
Bobby Brown, 3b-3	.500	4	12	4	6	1	2	0	5	2	2	0
Tommy Byrne, p	1.000	1	1	0	1	0	0	0	0	0	0	0
Gerry Coleman, 2b	.250	5	20	0	5	3	0	0	4	0	4	0
Joe DiMaggio, of	.111	5	18	2	2	0	0	1	2	3	5	0
Tommy Henrich, 1b	.263	5	19	4	5	0	0	1	1	3	0	0
Billy Johnson, 3b	.143	2	7	1	1	0	0	0	0	0	2	1
Johnny Lindell, of	.143	2	7	0	1	0	0	0	0	0	2	0
Ed Lopat, p	.333	1	3	0	1	1	0	0	1	0	0	0
Cliff Mapes, of	.100	4	10	3	1	1	0	0	0	2	4	0
Johnny Mize, ph	1.000	2	2	0	2	0	0	0	2	0	0	0
Gus Niarhos, c	.000	1	0	0	0	0	0	0	0	0	0	0
Joe Page, p	.000	3	4	0	0	0	0	0	0	0	2	0
Vic Raschi, p	.200	2	5	0	1	0	0	0	1	1	1	0
Allie Reynolds, p	.500	2	4	0	2	1	0	0	0	0	1	0
Phil Rizzuto, ss	.167	5	18	2	3	0	0	0	1	3	1	1
Charlie Silvera, c	.000	1	2	0	0	0	0	0	0	0	0	0
Snuffy Stirnweiss, ph	.000	1	0	0	0	0	0	0	0	0	0	0
Gene Woodling, of	.400	3	10	4	4	3	0	0	0	3	0	0
TOTAL	.226		164	21	37	10	2	2	20	18	27	2

PITCHER	W	L	ERA	G	GS	CG	SV	SHO	IP	H	ER	BB	SO
Tommy Byrne	0	0	2.70	1	1	0	0	0	3.1	2	1	2	1
Ed Lopat	1	0	6.35	1	1	0	0	0	5.2	9	4	1	4
Joe Page	1	0	2.00	3	0	0	1	0	9.0	6	2	3	8
Vic Raschi	1	1	4.30	2	2	0	0	0	14.2	15	7	5	11
Allie Reynolds	1	0	0.00	2	1	1	1	1	12.1	2	0	4	14
TOTAL	4	1	2.80	9	5	1	2	1	45.0	34	14	15	38

BRO (N)

PLAYER/POS	AVG	G	AB	R	H	2B	3B	HR	RB	BB	SO	SB
Jack Banta, p	.000	3	1	0	0	0	0	0	0	0	0	0
Rex Barney, p	.000	1	0	0	0	0	0	0	0	0	0	0
Ralph Branca, p	.000	1	3	0	0	0	0	0	0	0	3	0
Tommy Brown, ph	.000	2	2	0	0	0	0	0	0	0	1	0
Roy Campanella, c	.267	5	15	2	4	1	0	1	2	3	1	0
Billy Cox, 3b-1	.333	2	3	0	1	0	0	0	0	0	1	0
Bruce Edwards, ph	.500	2	2	0	1	0	0	0	0	0	1	0
Carl Erskine, p	.000	2	0	0	0	0	0	0	0	0	0	0
Carl Furillo, of-2	.125	3	8	0	1	0	0	0	0	1	0	0
Joe Hatten, p	.000	2	0	0	0	0	0	0	0	0	0	0
Gene Hermanski, of	.308	4	13	1	4	0	1	0	2	3	3	0
Gil Hodges, 1b	.235	5	17	2	4	0	0	1	4	1	4	0
Spider Jorgensen, 3b-3	.182	4	11	2	2	2	0	0	0	2	2	0
Mike Mc Cormick, of	.000	1	0	0	0	0	0	0	0	0	0	0
Eddie Miksis, 3b-2	.286	3	7	0	2	1	0	0	0	0	1	0
Paul Minner, p	.000	1	0	0	0	0	0	0	0	0	0	0
Don Newcombe, p	.000	2	2	0	0	0	0	0	0	0	3	0
Luis Olmo, of	.273	4	11	2	3	0	0	1	2	0	2	0
Erv Palica, p	.000	1	0	0	0	0	0	0	0	0	0	0
Marv Rackley, of	.000	2	5	0	0	0	0	0	0	0	2	0
Pee Wee Reese, ss	.316	5	19	2	6	1	0	1	2	1	0	1
Jackie Robinson, 2b	.188	5	16	2	3	1	0	0	2	4	2	0
Preacher Roe, p	.000	1	3	0	0	0	0	0	0	0	3	0
Duke Snider, of	.143	5	21	2	3	1	0	0	0	0	8	0
Dick Whitman, ph	.000	1	1	0	0	0	0	0	0	0	1	0
TOTAL	.210		162	14	34	7	1	4	14	15	38	1

PITCHER	W	L	ERA	G	GS	CG	SV	SHO	IP	H	ER	BB	SO
Jack Banta	0	0	3.18	3	0	0	0	0	5.2	5	2	1	4
Rex Barney	0	1	16.88	1	1	0	0	0	2.2	3	5	6	2
Ralph Branca	0	1	4.15	1	1	0	0	0	8.2	4	4	4	6
Carl Erskine	0	0	16.20	2	0	0	0	0	1.2	3	3	1	0
Joe Hatten	0	0	16.20	2	0	0	0	0	1.2	4	3	2	0
Paul Minner	0	0	0.00	1	0	0	0	0	1.0	1	0	0	0
Don Newcombe	0	2	3.09	2	2	1	0	0	11.2	10	4	3	11
Erv Palica	0	0	0.00	1	0	0	0	0	2.0	1	0	1	1
Preacher Roe	1	0	0.00	1	1	1	0	1	9.0	6	0	0	3
TOTAL	1	4	4.30	14	5	2	0	1	44.0	37	21	18	27

GAME 1 AT NY OCT 5

BRO	000	000	000	0	2	0
NY	000	000	001	1	5	1

Pitchers: NEWCOMBE vs REYNOLDS
Home Runs: Henrich-NY
Attendance: 66,224

GAME 2 AT NY OCT 6

BRO	010	000	000	1	7	2
NY	000	000	000	0	6	1

Pitchers: ROE vs RASCHI
Attendance: 70,053

GAME 3 AT BRO OCT 7

NY	001	000	003	4	5	0
BRO	000	100	002	3	5	0

Pitchers: Byrne, PAGE (4) vs BRANCA, Banta (9)
Home Runs: Reese-BRO, Olmo-BRO, Campanella-BRO
Attendance: 32,788

GAME 4 AT BRO OCT 8

NY	000	330	000	6	10	0
BRO	000	004	000	4	9	1

Pitchers: LOPAT, Reynolds (6) VS NEWCOMBE, Hatten (4), Erskine (6), Banta (7)
Attendance: 33,934

GAME 5 AT BRO OCT 9

NY	203	113	000	10	11	1
BRO	001	001	400	6	11	2

Pitchers: RASCHI, Page (7) vs BARNEY, Banta (3), Erskine (6), Hatten (6), Palica (7), Minner (9)
Home Runs: DiMaggio-NY, Hodges-BRO
Attendance: 33,711

Philadelphia's Whiz Kids, who had capped an exciting pennant race with the Phillies' first flag in thirty-five years, carried the excitement into the World Series but couldn't quite catch up with the Yankees. New York scored only one run in the opener; Philadelphia didn't score any. The Phillies did score a run in the second game, but the Yankees scored two. In Game Three the Phillies scored two runs, the Yankees three.

Jim Konstanty, the National League's ace reliever (and MVP), started his first major league game in four years to lead off the Series, and held the Yankees to just four hits in eight innings of work. But Bobby Brown's double in the fourth was followed by two long flies which moved Brown around to the plate—all the scoring New York needed as Vic Raschi held the Phillies to two singles and a walk.

Robin Roberts and Allie Reynolds dueled in Game Two. New York scored first with a run on a walk and two singles in the second inning, but two Phillie singles and a fly to left tied the game in the last of the fifth. There matters stood until the top of the tenth, when Joe DiMaggio led off with a home run to the upper deck in left. Reynolds held the Phillies in the bottom of the tenth for the second Yankee win.

The Phillies took a lead for the only time in the Series when they broke a 1–1 tie with a run in the seventh inning of Game Three. But New York scored on a Phillie error to tie the game again in the eighth, and in the last of the ninth—with two outs—Yankees Gene Woodling, Phil Rizzuto, and Jerry Coleman singled to produce the winning run.

Rookie sensation Whitey Ford started Game Four and held Philadelphia scoreless into the ninth inning as his Yankees scored twice in the first and three more times in the sixth. He was taken out with two away in the ninth after two singles, a hit batsman, and a Yankee error had permitted two Phillies to score. But reliever Allie Reynolds struck out the final batter to secure for the Yankees a Series sweep.

New York Yankees (AL), 4;
Philadelphia Phillies (NL), 0

NY (A)

PLAYER/POS	AVG	G	AB	R	H	2B	3B	HR	RB	BB	SO	SB
Hank Bauer, of	.133	4	15	0	2	0	0	0	1	0	0	0
Yogi Berra, c	.200	4	15	2	3	0	0	1	2	2	1	0
Bobby Brown, 3b	.333	4	12	2	4	1	1	0	1	0	0	0
Gerry Coleman, 2b	.286	4	14	2	4	1	0	0	3	2	0	0
Joe Collins, 1b	.000	1	0	0	0	0	0	0	0	0	0	0
Joe Di Maggio, of	.308	4	13	2	4	1	0	1	2	3	1	0
Tom Ferrick, p	.000	1	0	0	0	0	0	0	0	0	0	0
Whitey Ford, p	.000	1	3	0	0	0	0	0	0	0	2	0
Johnny Hopp, 1b	.000	3	2	0	0	0	0	0	0	0	0	0
Jackie Jensen, pr	.000	1	0	0	0	0	0	0	0	0	0	0
Billy Johnson, 3b	.000	4	6	0	0	0	0	0	0	0	3	0
Ed Lopat, p	.500	1	2	0	1	0	0	0	0	0	1	0
Cliff Mapes, of	.000	1	4	0	0	0	0	0	0	0	1	0
Johnny Mize, 1b	.133	4	15	0	2	0	0	0	0	0	1	0
Vic Raschi, p	.333	1	3	0	1	0	0	0	0	0	0	0
Allie Reynolds, p	.333	2	3	0	1	0	0	0	0	1	2	0
Phil Rizzuto, ss	.143	4	14	1	2	0	0	0	0	3	0	1
Gene Woodling, of	.429	4	14	2	6	0	0	0	1	2	0	0
TOTAL	.222		135	11	30	3	1	2	10	13	12	1

PITCHER	W	L	ERA	G	GS	CG	SV	SHO	IP	H	ER	BB	SO
Tom Ferrick	1	0	0.00	1	0	0	0	0	1.0	1	0	1	0
Whitey Ford	1	0	0.00	1	1	0	0	0	8.2	7	0	1	7
Ed Lopat	0	0	2.25	1	1	0	0	0	8.0	9	2	0	5
Vic Raschi	1	0	0.00	1	1	1	0	1	9.0	2	0	1	5
Allie Reynolds	1	0	0.87	2	1	1	1	0	10.1	7	1	4	7
TOTAL	4	0	0.73	6	4	2	1	1	37.0	26	3	7	24

PHI (N)

PLAYER/POS	AVG	G	AB	R	H	2B	3B	HR	RB	BB	SO	SB
Richie Ashburn, of	.176	4	17	0	3	1	0	0	1	0	4	0
Jimmy Bloodworth, 2b	.000	1	0	0	0	0	0	0	0	0	0	0
Putsy Caballero, ph	.000	3	1	0	0	0	0	0	0	0	1	0
Del Ennis, of	.143	4	14	1	2	1	0	0	0	0	1	0
Mike Goliat, 2b	.214	4	14	1	3	0	0	0	1	1	2	0
Granny Hamner, ss	.429	4	14	1	6	2	1	0	0	1	2	1
Ken Heintzelman, p	.000	1	2	0	0	0	0	0	0	0	0	0
Ken Johnson, pr	.000	1	0	0	0	0	0	0	0	0	0	0
Willie Jones, 3b	.286	4	14	1	4	1	0	0	0	0	3	0
Jim Konstanty, p	.250	3	4	0	1	0	0	0	0	0	1	0
Stan Lopata, c-1	.000	2	1	0	0	0	0	0	0	0	1	0
Jackie Mayo, of-1	.000	3	0	0	0	0	0	0	0	1	0	0
Russ Meyer, p	.000	2	0	0	0	0	0	0	0	0	0	0
Bob Miller, p	.000	1	0	0	0	0	0	0	0	0	0	0
Robin Roberts, p	.000	2	2	0	0	0	0	0	0	0	1	0
Andy Seminick, c	.182	4	11	0	2	0	0	0	0	1	3	0
Ken Silvestri, c	.000	1	0	0	0	0	0	0	0	0	0	0
Dick Sisler, of	.059	4	17	0	1	0	0	0	1	0	5	0
Eddie Waitkus, 1b	.267	4	15	0	4	1	0	0	0	2	0	0
Dick Whitman, ph	.000	3	2	0	0	0	0	0	0	1	0	0
TOTAL	.203		128	5	26	6	1	0	3	7	24	1

PITCHER	W	L	ERA	G	GS	CG	SV	SHO	IP	H	ER	BB	SO
Ken Heintzelman	0	0	1.17	1	1	0	0	0	7.2	4	1	6	3
Jim Konstanty	0	1	2.40	3	1	0	0	0	15.0	9	4	4	3
Russ Meyer	0	1	5.40	2	0	0	0	0	1.2	4	1	0	1
Bob Miller	0	1	27.00	1	1	0	0	0	0.1	2	1	0	0
Robin Roberts	0	1	1.64	2	1	1	0	0	11.0	11	2	3	5
TOTAL	0	4	2.27	9	4	1	0	0	35.2	30	9	13	12

GAME 1 AT PHI OCT 4

NY	000 100 000	1	5	0
PHI	000 000 000	0	2	1

Pitchers: RASCHI vs KONSTANTY, Meyer (9)
Attendance: 30,746

GAME 2 AT PHI OCT 5

NY	010 000 000 1	2	10	0
PHI	000 010 000 0	1	7	0

Pitchers: REYNOLDS vs ROBERTS
Home Runs: DiMaggio-NY
Attendance: 32,660

GAME 3 AT NY OCT 6

PHI	000 001 100	2	10	2
NY	001 000 011	3	7	0

Pitchers: Heintzelman, Konstanty (8), MEYER (9) vs Lopat, FERRICK (9)
Attendance: 64,505

GAME 4 AT NY OCT 7

PHI	000 000 002	2	7	1
NY	200 003 00X	5	8	2

Pitchers: MILLER, Konstanty (1), Roberts (8) vs FORD, Reynolds (9)
Home Runs: Berra-NY
Attendance: 68,098

The Giants—who caught Brooklyn with a tremendous late-season drive, then defeated them for the pennant on Bobby Thomson's ninth-inning home run in Game Three of the tie-breaker playoff series—carried their momentum through Game Three of the World Series before bowing to the Yankees. Dave Koslo (the only Giant starter not to see action in the playoff) pitched the Series opener and held the Yankees to one run. Monte Irvin's steal of home for the Giants' second run in the top of the first was enough for the win, but Al Dark made Koslo's lead more secure with a three-run homer in the sixth.

The Yankees evened the Series in Game Two, scoring two early runs (one of them Joe Collins's home run) off Larry Jansen, and holding on for the win behind Ed Lopat's five-hit pitching. But the Giants regained the lead in Game Three with five unearned runs (three of them on Whitey Lockman's homer) in a fifth inning prolonged by two Yankee errors, as pitchers Jim Hearn and Sheldon Jones combined to hold the Bronx Bombers to five hits and a pair of runs (though Hearn issued eight walks).

But that was the end of the Giants' drive. Although they scored first in games Four and Five with first-inning runs, they couldn't hold the lead either time. In Game Four Allie Reynolds held the Giants to two runs as his Yankees scored six—including a two-run homer by Joe DiMaggio in the fifth inning that proved to be the last home run of his career. DiMag drove in three more Yankee runs in Game Five, as did Phil Rizzuto, and rookie infielder Gil McDougald contributed a grand slam as the Bombers earned their nickname in obliterating Giant pitching with 13 runs. Ed Lopat, meanwhile, hurled his second five-hitter of the Series for his second win.

Yankee Hank Bauer tripled with the bases full in the sixth inning of Game Six to break a tie and give the Yankees a 4–1 lead. The Giants loaded the bases with three straight singles to open the top of the ninth, and scored two runners on successive flies to left, to come within one run of a tie. But pinch hitter Sal Yvars (in his only Series at-bat) lined out to right and the Yankees had their fourteenth world title.

New York Yankees (AL), 4; New York Giants (NL), 2

NY (A)

PLAYER/POS	AVG	G	AB	R	H	2B	3B	HR	RB	BB	SO	SB
Hank Bauer, of	.167	6	18	0	3	0	1	0	3	1	1	0
Yogi Berra, c	.261	6	23	4	6	1	0	0	0	2	1	0
Bobby Brown, 3b-4	.357	5	14	1	5	1	0	0	0	2	1	0
Gerry Coleman, 2b	.250	5	8	2	2	0	0	0	0	1	2	0
Joe Collins, 1b-6,of-1	.222	6	18	2	4	0	0	1	3	2	1	0
Joe Di Maggio, of	.261	6	23	3	6	2	0	1	5	2	4	0
Bobby Hogue, p	.000	2	0	0	0	0	0	0	0	0	0	0
Johnny Hopp, ph	.000	1	0	0	0	0	0	0	0	1	0	0
Bob Kuzava, p	.000	1	0	0	0	0	0	0	0	0	0	0
Ed Lopat, p	.125	2	8	0	1	0	0	0	0	1	0	0
Mickey Mantle, of	.200	2	5	1	1	0	0	0	0	2	1	0
Billy Martin, pr	.000	1	0	1	0	0	0	0	0	0	0	0
Gil Mc Dougald, 3b-5,2b-4	.261	6	23	2	6	1	0	1	7	2	2	0
Johnny Mize, 1b-2	.286	4	7	2	2	1	0	0	1	2	0	0
Tom Morgan, p	.000	1	0	0	0	0	0	0	0	0	0	0
Joe Ostrowski, p	.000	1	0	0	0	0	0	0	0	0	0	0
Vic Raschi, p	.000	2	2	0	0	0	0	0	0	0	2	1	0
Allie Reynolds, p	.333	2	6	0	2	0	0	0	0	1	0	1	0
Phil Rizzuto, ss	.320	6	25	5	8	0	0	1	3	2	3	0
Johnny Sain, p	.000	1	1	0	0	0	0	0	0	0	0	0
Gene Woodling, of-5	.167	6	18	6	3	1	1	1	1	1	5	3	0
TOTAL	.246		199	29	49	7	2	5	25	26	23	0

PITCHER	W	L	ERA	G	GS	CG	SV	SHO	IP	H	ER	BB	SO
Bobby Hogue	0	0	0.00	2	0	0	0	0	2.2	1	0	0	0
Bob Kuzava	0	0	0.00	1	0	0	0	0	1.0	0	0	0	0
Ed Lopat	2	0	0.50	2	2	2	0	0	18.0	10	1	3	4
Tom Morgan	0	0	0.00	1	0	0	0	0	2.0	2	0	1	3
Joe Ostrowski	0	0	0.00	1	0	0	0	0	2.0	1	0	0	1
Vic Raschi	1	1	0.87	2	2	0	0	0	10.1	12	1	8	4
Allie Reynolds	1	1	4.20	2	2	1	0	0	15.0	16	7	11	8
Johnny Sain	0	0	9.00	1	0	0	0	0	2.0	4	2	2	2
TOTAL	4	2	1.87	12	6	3	1	0	53.0	46	11	25	22

NY (N)

PLAYER/POS	AVG	G	AB	R	H	2B	3B	HR	RB	BB	SO	SB
Al Corwin, p	.000	1	0	0	0	0	0	0	0	0	0	0
Alvin Dark, ss	.417	6	24	5	10	3	0	1	4	2	3	0
Clint Hartung, of	.000	2	4	0	0	0	0	0	0	0	0	0
Jim Hearn, p	.000	2	3	0	0	0	0	0	0	0	1	0
Monte Irvin, of	.458	6	24	3	11	0	1	0	2	2	1	2
Larry Jansen, p	.000	3	2	0	0	0	0	0	0	0	0	0
Sheldon Jones, p	.000	2	0	0	0	0	0	0	0	0	0	0
Monte Kennedy, p	.000	2	0	0	0	0	0	0	0	0	0	0
Alex Konikowski, p	.000	1	0	0	0	0	0	0	0	0	0	0
Dave Koslo, p	.000	2	5	0	0	0	0	0	0	0	2	0
Whitey Lockman, 1b	.240	6	25	1	6	2	0	1	4	1	2	0
Jack Lohrke, ph	.000	2	2	0	0	0	0	0	0	0	1	0
Sal Maglie, p	.000	1	1	0	0	0	0	0	0	0	0	0
Willie Mays, of	.182	6	22	1	4	0	0	0	1	2	2	0
Ray Noble, c	.000	2	2	0	0	0	0	0	0	0	1	0
Bill Rigney, ph	.250	4	4	0	1	0	0	0	0	1	1	0
Hank Schenz, pr	.000	1	0	0	0	0	0	0	0	0	0	0
George Spencer, p	.000	2	0	0	0	0	0	0	0	0	0	0
Eddie Stanky, 2b	.136	6	22	3	3	0	0	0	1	3	2	0
Hank Thompson, of	.143	5	14	2	2	0	0	0	0	5	0	0
Bobby Thomson, 3b	.238	6	21	1	5	1	0	0	2	5	0	0
Wes Westrum, c	.235	6	17	1	4	1	0	0	0	5	3	0
Davey Williams, ph	.000	2	1	0	0	0	0	0	0	0	0	0
Sal Yvars, ph	.000	1	1	0	0	0	0	0	0	0	0	0
TOTAL	.237		194	18	46	7	1	2	15	25	22	2

PITCHER	W	L	ERA	G	GS	CG	SV	SHO	IP	H	ER	BB	SO
Al Corwin	0	0	0.00	1	0	0	0	0	1.2	1	0	0	1
Jim Hearn	1	0	1.04	2	1	0	0	0	8.2	5	1	8	1
Larry Jansen	0	2	6.30	3	2	0	0	0	10.0	8	7	4	6
Sheldon Jones	0	0	2.08	2	0	0	1	0	4.1	5	1	1	2
Monte Kennedy	0	0	6.00	2	0	0	0	0	3.0	3	2	1	4
Alex Konikowski	0	0	0.00	1	0	0	0	0	1.0	1	0	0	0
Dave Koslo	1	1	3.00	2	2	1	0	0	15.0	12	5	7	6
Sal Maglie	0	1	7.20	1	1	0	0	0	5.0	8	4	2	3
George Spencer	0	0	18.90	2	0	0	0	0	3.1	6	7	3	0
TOTAL	2	4	4.67	16	6	1	1	0	52.0	49	27	26	23

GAME 1 AT NY-A OCT 4

NY-N	200	003	000	5	10 1
NY-A	010	000	000	1	7 1

Pitchers: KOSLO vs REYNOLDS, Hogue (7), Morgan (8)
Home Runs: Dark-NY(N)
Attendance: 65,673

GAME 2 AT NY-A OCT 5

NY-N	000	000	100	1	5 1
NY-A	110	000	01X	3	6 0

Pitchers: JANSEN, Spencer (7) vs LOPAT
Home Runs: Collins-NY(A)
Attendance: 66,018

GAME 3 AT NY-N OCT 6

NY-A	000	000	011	2	5 2
NY-N	010	050	00X	6	7 2

Pitchers: RASCHI, Hogue (5), Ostrowski (7) vs HEARN, Jones (8)
Home Runs: Lockman-NY(N), Woodling-NY(A)
Attendance: 52,035

GAME 4 AT NY-N OCT 8

NY-A	010	120	200	6	12 0
NY-N	100	000	001	2	8 2

Pitchers: REYNOLDS vs MAGLIE, Jones (6), Kennedy (9)
Home Runs: DiMaggio-NY(A)
Attendance: 49,010

GAME 5 AT NY-N OCT 9

NY-A	005	202	400	13	12 1
NY-N	100	000	000	1	5 3

Pitchers: LOPAT vs JANSEN, Kennedy (4), Spencer (6), Corwin (7), Konikowski (9)
Home Runs: McDougald-NY(A), Rizzuto-NY(A)
Attendance: 47,530

GAME 6 AT NY-A OCT 10

NY-N	000	010	002	3	11 1
NY-A	100	003	00X	4	7 0

Pitchers: KOSLO, Hearn (7), Jansen (8) VS RASCHI, Sain (7), Kuzava (9)
Attendance: 61,711

In four of the seven games, home runs provided the margin of victory. Homers accounted for five of the six runs scored in the opener, with Duke Snider's two-run blast in the sixth putting Brooklyn ahead to stay. Star Dodger reliever Joe Black, in only his third start of the year, held New York to six hits and two runs in defeating Yankee ace Allie Reynolds.

Four home runs enlivened the next three games but did not govern the outcomes. Billy Martin's three-run shot was the centerpiece of the Yankee assault in Game Two, but New York would have won without it behind Vic Raschi's one-run three-hitter. Brooklyn needed no homers to regain the Series advantage in Game Three. In the top of the ninth, with the Dodgers leading by a run, Pee Wee Reese and Jackie Robinson singled (driving out starter Ed Lopat) and pulled a double steal. Both then scored on a passed ball. Yankee pinch hitter Johnny Mize homered in the last of the ninth, but Preacher Roe escaped without further scoring for a complete-game 5–3 win.

Black opposed Reynolds again in Game Four and bettered his earlier performance, holding New York to three hits and one run (a Mize homer) in seven innings. But Reynolds improved even more, fanning ten as he shut the Dodgers out.

Snider hit his second homer of the Series and Mize his third in the fifth inning of Game Five. Mize's shot put New York ahead, but Brooklyn tied the game in the seventh and took a 6–5 lead when Snider doubled home a run in the eleventh. Dodger right fielder Carl Furillo's leaping catch in the last of the eleventh robbed Mize of another home run, and starter Carl Erskine held on for the win, giving Brooklyn a 3–2 Series lead.

Snider's home run in the last of the sixth ended Vic Raschi's shutout in Game Six, but Yogi Berra, the first Yankee up in the seventh, tied the game and spoiled Billy Loes's shutout with his home run, and pitcher Raschi singled home the go-ahead run two outs later. Yankee sophomore Mickey Mantle's blast in the eighth (the first of his record 18 World Series home runs) made the score 3–1. Snider's fourth homer of the Series gave the Dodgers a second run in the eighth, but Allie Reynolds relieved Raschi and prevented further scoring, sending the Series to a seventh game.

Joe Black traded three shutout innings with Yankee Ed Lopat in the finale before both clubs scored single runs in the fourth and fifth innings. Mantle homered off Black in the sixth for a third Yankee run that proved the Series

New York Yankees (AL), 4; Brooklyn Dodgers (NL), 3

NY (A)

PLAYER/POS	AVG	G	AB	R	H	2B	3B	HR	RB	BB	SO	SB
Hank Bauer, of	.056	7	18	2	1	0	0	0	1	4	3	0
Yogi Berra, c	.214	7	28	2	6	1	0	2	3	2	4	0
Ewell Blackwell, p	.000	1	1	0	0	0	0	0	0	0	0	0
Joe Collins, 1b	.000	6	12	1	0	0	0	0	0	1	3	0
Tom Gorman, p	.000	1	0	0	0	0	0	0	0	0	0	0
Ralph Houk, ph	.000	1	1	0	0	0	0	0	0	0	0	0
Bob Kuzava, p	.000	1	1	0	0	0	0	0	0	0	0	0
Ed Lopat, p	.333	2	3	0	1	0	0	0	1	1	1	0
Mickey Mantle, of	.345	7	29	5	10	1	1	2	3	3	4	0
Billy Martin, 2b	.217	7	23	2	5	0	0	1	4	2	2	0
Gil Mc Dougald, 3b	.200	7	25	5	5	0	0	1	3	5	2	1
Johnny Mize, 1b-4	.400	5	15	3	6	1	0	3	6	3	1	0
Irv Noren, of-3	.300	4	10	0	3	0	0	0	1	1	3	0
Vic Raschi, p	.167	3	6	0	1	0	0	0	1	1	2	0
Allie Reynolds, p	.000	4	7	0	0	0	0	0	0	0	2	0
Phil Rizzuto, ss	.148	7	27	2	4	1	0	0	0	5	2	0
Johnny Sain, p-1	.000	2	3	0	0	0	0	0	0	0	0	0
Ray Scarborough, p	.000	1	0	0	0	0	0	0	0	0	0	0
Gene Woodling, of-6	.348	7	23	4	8	1	1	1	1	3	3	0
TOTAL	.216		232	26	50	5	2	10	24	31	32	1

PITCHER	W	L	ERA	G	GS	CG	SV	SHO	IP	H	ER	BB	SO
Ewell Blackwell	0	0	7.20	1	1	0	0	0	5.0	4	4	3	4
Tom Gorman	0	0	0.00	1	0	0	0	0	0.2	1	0	0	0
Bob Kuzava	0	0	0.00	1	0	0	1	0	2.2	0	0	0	2
Ed Lopat	0	1	4.76	2	2	0	0	0	11.1	14	6	4	3
Vic Raschi	2	0	1.59	3	2	1	0	0	17.0	12	3	8	18
Allie Reynolds	2	1	1.77	4	2	1	1	1	20.1	12	4	6	18
Johnny Sain	0	1	3.00	1	0	0	0	0	6.0	6	2	3	3
Ray Scarborough	0	0	9.00	1	0	0	0	0	1.0	1	1	0	1
TOTAL	4	3	2.81	14	7	2	2	1	64.0	50	20	24	49

BRO (N)

PLAYER/POS	AVG	G	AB	R	H	2B	3B	HR	RB	BB	SO	SB
Sandy Amoros, ph	.000	1	0	0	0	0	0	0	0	0	0	0
Joe Black, p	.000	3	6	0	0	0	0	0	0	1	6	0
Roy Campanella, c	.214	7	28	0	6	0	0	0	1	1	6	0
Billy Cox, 3b	.296	7	27	4	8	2	0	0	0	3	4	0
Carl Erskine, p	.000	3	6	1	0	0	0	0	0	0	1	0
Carl Furillo, of	.174	7	23	1	4	2	0	0	0	3	3	0
Gil Hodges, 1b	.000	7	21	1	0	0	0	0	1	5	6	0
Tommy Holmes, of	.000	3	1	0	0	0	0	0	0	0	0	0
Ken Lehman, p	.000	1	0	0	0	0	0	0	0	0	0	0
Billy Loes, p	.333	2	3	0	1	0	0	0	0	0	1	1
Bobby Morgan, 3b	.000	2	1	0	0	0	0	0	0	0	0	0
Rocky Nelson, ph	.000	4	3	0	0	0	0	0	0	1	2	0
Andy Pafko, of-5	.190	7	21	0	4	0	0	0	2	0	4	0
Pee Wee Reese, ss	.345	7	29	4	10	0	0	1	4	2	1	1
Jackie Robinson, 2b	.174	7	23	4	4	0	0	1	2	7	5	2
Preacher Roe, p	.000	3	2	0	0	0	0	0	0	0	0	0
Johnny Rutherford, p	.000	1	0	0	0	0	0	0	0	0	0	0
George Shuba, of-3	.300	4	10	0	3	1	0	0	0	0	4	0
Duke Snider, of	.345	7	29	5	10	2	0	4	8	1	5	1
TOTAL	.215		233	20	50	7	0	6	18	24	49	5

PITCHER	W	L	ERA	G	GS	CG	SV	SHO	IP	H	ER	BB	SO
Joe Black	1	2	2.53	3	3	1	0	0	21.1	15	6	8	9
Carl Erskine	1	1	4.50	3	2	1	0	0	18.0	12	9	10	10
Ken Lehman	0	0	0.00	1	0	0	0	0	2.0	2	0	1	0
Billy Loes	0	1	4.35	2	1	0	0	0	10.1	11	5	5	5
Preacher Roe	1	0	3.18	3	1	1	0	0	11.1	9	4	6	7
Johnny Rutherford	0	0	9.00	1	0	0	0	0	1.0	1	1	1	1
TOTAL	3	4	3.52	13	7	3	0	0	64.0	50	25	31	32

winner, as three Yankee relievers held Brooklyn scoreless through the final four frames.

GAME 1 AT BRO OCT 1

NY	010	000	010	2	6	2
BRO	010	002	01X	4	6	0

Pitchers: REYNOLDS, Scarborough (8) vs BLACK
Home Runs: Robinson-BRO, Snider-BRO, Reese-BRO, McDougald-NY
Attendance: 34,861

GAME 2 AT BRO OCT 2

NY	000	115	000	7	10	0
BRO	000	100	000	1	3	1

Pitchers: RASCHI vs ERSKINE, Loes (6), Lehman (8)
Home Runs: Martin-NY
Attendance: 33,792

GAME 3 AT NY OCT 3

BRO	001	010	012	5	11	0
NY	010	000	011	3	6	2

Pitchers: ROE vs LOPAT, Gorman (9)
Home Runs: Berra-NY, Mize-NY
Attendance: 66,698

GAME 4 AT NY OCT 4

BRO	000	000	000	0	4	1
NY	000	100	01X	2	4	1

Pitchers: BLACK, Rutherford (8) VS REYNOLDS
Home Runs: Mize-NY
Attendance: 71,787

GAME 5 AT NY OCT 5

BRO	010	030	100	01	6	10	0
NY	000	050	000	00	5	5	1

Pitchers: ERSKINE vs Blackwell, SAIN (6)
Home Runs: Snider-BRO, Mize-NY
Attendance: 70,536

GAME 6 AT BRO OCT 6

NY	000	000	210	3	9	0
BRO	000	001	010	2	8	1

Pitchers: RASCHI, Reynolds (8) vs LOES, Roe (9)
Home Runs: Snider-BRO (2), Berra-NY, Mantle-NY
Attendance: 30,037

GAME 7 AT BRO OCT 7

NY	000	111	100	4	10	4
BRO	000	110	000	2	8	1

Pitchers: Lopat, REYNOLDS (4), Raschi (7), Kuzava (7) vs BLACK, Roe (6), Erskine (8)
Home Runs: Woodling-NY, Mantle-NY
Attendance: 33,195

Although the Yankees easily won the American League pennant, the Dodgers seemed even more overwhelming, with a team batting average of .285 and a club-record 105 season wins. But when the Series was over, the Yankees had added a record fifth straight world championship to their record fifth straight pennant.

Dodger ace Carl Erskine lasted only one inning of the Series opener, giving up three walks and two triples for four Yankee runs. By the middle of the seventh inning, the Dodgers had tied the score at 5–5. But Yankee Joe Collins homered to break the tie in the last of the seventh, and reliever Johnny Sain ensured his own win with a two-run double an inning later. The Dodgers outhit New York in Game Two, and held a 2–1 lead entering the bottom of the seventh. But Billy Martin (who hit .500 and slugged .958 in the Series) tied the game with a leadoff homer in the seventh, and Mickey Mantle won it with a two-run blast in the eighth.

Down 0–2, Brooklyn evened the Series at home with victories in Games Three and Four. Erskine redeemed his poor start in Game One with a record-setting 14-strikeout performance in Game Three. But it was a narrow win, settled only when Roy Campanella homered in the last of the eighth to break a 2–2 tie. In Game Four, Duke Snider made Billy Loes's three-run pitching a winning performance, driving in four of the Dodgers' seven runs with two doubles and a homer.

But Brooklyn never even took the lead in the final two games. Four Yankee home runs (including a Mantle grand slam) rocked Dodger pitching in Game Five as the Bombers built a lead which Dodger home runs in the eighth and ninth were unable to overcome. In Game Six the Yankees built a 3–0 lead over Erskine in the first two innings. Brooklyn fought back with a run in the sixth, and tied the game on Carl Furillo's two-run homer in the top of the ninth. But with men on first and second in the last of the ninth, Yankee Billy Martin singled in the game-ending, Series-winning run. It was Martin's twelfth hit, a new record for a six-game Series.

New York Yankees (AL), 4;
Brooklyn Dodgers (NL), 2

NY (A)

PLAYER/POS	AVG	G	AB	R	H	2B	3B	HR	RB	BB	SO	SB
Hank Bauer, of	.261	6	23	6	6	0	1	0	1	2	4	0
Yogi Berra, c	.429	6	21	3	9	1	0	1	4	3	3	0
Don Bollweg, 1b-1	.000	3	2	0	0	0	0	0	0	0	2	0
Joe Collins, 1b	.167	6	24	4	4	1	0	1	2	3	8	0
Whitey Ford, p	.333	2	3	0	1	0	0	0	0	0	0	0
Tom Gorman, p	.000	1	1	0	0	0	0	0	0	0	1	0
Bob Kuzava, p	.000	1	1	0	0	0	0	0	0	0	1	0
Ed Lopat, p	.000	1	3	0	0	0	0	0	0	0	2	0
Mickey Mantle, of	.208	6	24	3	5	0	0	2	7	3	8	0
Billy Martin, 2b	.500	6	24	5	12	1	2	2	8	1	2	1
Jim Mc Donald, p	.500	1	2	0	1	1	0	0	1	1	1	0
Gil Mc Dougald, 3b	.167	6	24	2	4	0	1	2	4	1	3	0
Johnny Mize, ph	.000	3	3	0	0	0	0	0	0	0	1	0
Irv Noren, ph	.000	2	1	0	0	0	0	0	0	1	0	0
Vic Raschi, p	.000	1	2	0	0	0	0	0	0	0	1	0
Allie Reynolds, p	.500	3	2	0	1	0	0	0	0	1	1	0
Phil Rizzuto, ss	.316	6	19	4	6	1	0	0	0	3	2	1
Johnny Sain, p	.500	2	2	1	1	1	0	0	2	0	1	0
Art Schallock, p	.000	1	0	0	0	0	0	0	0	0	0	0
Gene Woodling, of	.300	6	20	5	6	0	0	1	3	6	2	0
TOTAL	.279		201	33	56	6	4	9	32	25	43	2

PITCHER	W	L	ERA	G	GS	CG	SV	SHO	IP	H	ER	BB	SO
Whitey Ford	0	1	4.50	2	2	0	0	0	8.0	9	4	2	7
Tom Gorman	0	0	3.00	1	0	0	0	0	3.0	4	1	0	1
Bob Kuzava	0	0	13.50	1	0	0	0	0	0.2	2	1	0	1
Ed Lopat	1	0	2.00	1	1	1	0	0	9.0	9	2	4	3
Jim Mc Donald	1	0	5.87	1	1	0	0	0	7.2	12	5	0	3
Vic Raschi	0	1	3.38	1	1	1	0	0	8.0	9	3	3	4
Allie Reynolds	1	0	6.75	3	1	0	1	0	8.0	9	6	4	9
Johnny Sain	1	0	4.76	2	0	0	0	0	5.2	8	3	1	1
Art Schallock	0	0	4.50	1	0	0	0	0	2.0	2	1	1	1
TOTAL	4	2	4.50	13	6	2	1	0	52.0	64	26	15	30

BRO (N)

PLAYER/POS	AVG	G	AB	R	H	2B	3B	HR	RB	BB	SO	SB
Wayne Belardi, ph	.000	2	2	0	0	0	0	0	0	0	1	0
Joe Black, p	.000	1	0	0	0	0	0	0	0	0	0	0
Roy Campanella, c	.273	6	22	6	6	0	0	1	2	2	3	0
Billy Cox, 3b	.304	6	23	3	7	3	0	1	6	1	4	0
Carl Erskine, p	.250	3	4	0	1	0	0	0	0	0	1	0
Carl Furillo, of	.333	6	24	4	8	2	0	1	4	1	3	0
Jim Gilliam, 2b	.296	6	27	4	8	3	0	2	4	0	2	0
Gil Hodges, 1b	.364	6	22	3	8	0	0	1	1	3	3	1
Jim Hughes, p	.000	1	1	0	0	0	0	0	0	0	1	0
Clem Labine, p	.000	3	2	0	0	0	0	0	0	0	0	0
Billy Loes, p	.667	1	3	0	2	0	0	0	0	0	0	0
Russ Meyer, p	.000	1	1	0	0	0	0	0	0	0	1	0
Bob Milliken, p	.000	1	0	0	0	0	0	0	0	0	0	0
Bobby Morgan, ph	.000	1	1	0	0	0	0	0	0	0	0	0
Johnny Podres, p	1.000	1	1	0	1	0	0	0	0	0	0	0
Pee Wee Reese, ss	.208	6	24	0	5	0	1	0	0	4	1	0
Jackie Robinson, of	.320	6	25	3	8	2	0	0	2	1	0	1
Preacher Roe, p	.000	1	3	0	0	0	0	0	0	0	2	0
George Shuba, ph	1.000	2	1	1	1	0	0	1	2	0	0	0
Duke Snider, of	.320	6	25	3	8	3	0	1	5	2	6	0
Don Thompson, of	.000	2	0	0	0	0	0	0	0	0	0	0
Ben Wade, p	.000	2	0	0	0	0	0	0	0	0	0	0
Dick Williams, ph	.500	3	2	0	1	0	0	0	0	0	1	0
TOTAL	.300		213	27	64	13	1	8	26	15	30	2

PITCHER	W	L	ERA	G	GS	CG	SV	SHO	IP	H	ER	BB	SO
Joe Black	0	0	9.00	1	0	0	0	0	1.0	1	1	0	2
Carl Erskine	1	0	5.79	3	3	1	0	0	14.0	14	9	9	16
Jim Hughes	0	0	2.25	1	0	0	0	0	4.0	3	1	1	3
Clem Labine	0	2	3.60	3	0	0	1	0	5.0	10	2	1	3
Billy Loes	1	0	3.38	1	1	0	0	0	8.0	8	3	2	8
Russ Meyer	0	0	6.23	1	0	0	0	0	4.1	8	3	4	5
Bob Milliken	0	0	0.00	1	0	0	0	0	2.0	2	0	1	0
Johnny Podres	0	1	3.38	1	1	0	0	0	2.2	1	1	2	0
Preacher Roe	0	1	4.50	1	1	1	0	0	8.0	5	4	4	4
Ben Wade	0	0	15.43	2	0	0	0	0	2.1	4	4	1	2
TOTAL	2	4	4.91	15	6	2	1	0	51.1	56	28	25	43

GAME 1 AT NY SEPT 30

BRO	000	013	100	5	12	2
NY	400	010	13X	9	12	0

Pitchers: Erskine, Hughes (2), LABINE (6), Wade (8) vs Reynolds, SAIN (6)
Home Runs: Gilliam-BRO, Hodges-BRO, Shuba-BRO, Berra-NY, Collins-NY
Attendance: 69,374

GAME 2 AT NY OCT 1

BRO	000	200	000	2	9	1
NY	100	000	12X	4	5	0

Pitchers: ROE vs LOPAT
Home Runs: Martin-NY, Mantle-NY
Attendance: 66,786

GAME 3 AT BRO OCT 2

NY	000	010	010	2	6	0
BRO	000	011	01X	3	9	0

Pitchers: RASCHI vs ERSKINE
Home Runs: Campanella-BRO
Attendance: 35,270

GAME 4 AT BRO OCT 3

NY	000	020	001	3	9	0
BRO	300	102	10X	7	12	0

Pitchers: FORD, Gorman (2), Sain (5), Schallock (7) vs LOES, Labine (9)
Home Runs: McDougald-NY, Snider-BRO
Attendance: 36,775

GAME 5 AT BRO OCT 4

NY	105	000	311	11	11	1
BRO	010	010	041	7	14	1

Pitchers: McDONALD, Kuzava (8), Reynolds (9) vs PODRES, Meyer (3), Wade (8), Black (9)
Home Runs: Woodling-NY, Mantle-NY, Martin-NY, McDougald-NY, Cox-BRO, Gilliam-BRO
Attendance: 36,775

GAME 6 AT NY OCT 5

BRO	000	001	002	3	8	3
NY	210	000	001	4	13	0

Pitchers: Erskine, Milliken (5), LABINE (7) vs Ford, REYNOLDS (8)
Home Runs: Furillo-BRO
Attendance: 62,370

The Indians, who had won a league-record 111 games to break the American League domination of the New York Yankees, entered the World Series as strong favorites to humble the Giants. It was not to be.

Cleveland would have won the opener had it not been played in New York's Polo Grounds, with their short foul lines and deep center field. Most of the game was a pitchers' duel. Vic Wertz (the only Indian to hit safely in all four games) tripled off Sal Maglie to give Cleveland a two-run lead in the top of the first, but three Giant singles and a walk in the third off Bob Lemon tied the score. Lemon then settled down to hold New York scoreless through the ninth. Cleveland threatened in the eighth when the first two batters reached base, bringing Wertz to the plate. As he had already hit Maglie safely three times, Don Liddle was brought in to pitch to him. Wertz responded with a fly to deep center that would have been a home run in Cleveland, but in New York turned into the most famous catch in World Series history as Willie Mays raced out and tracked down the ball about 425 feet from the plate. Marv Grissom replaced Liddle on the mound and issued a walk to load the bases, but he retired the next two batters and (despite Wertz's double in the top of the tenth) held Cleveland scoreless the rest of the way. In the last of the tenth, Lemon retired the first batter, but Mays walked and stole second, and Hank Thompson was walked intentionally to set up the double play. Pinch hitter Dusty Rhodes then entered the hall of heroes with a short fly to right that—though it would have been an out in Cleveland—fell into the Polo Grounds stands for three runs and a Giant victory.

The rest of the Series was anti-climax. In the second game Rhodes, with half the Giants' four hits, drove in two runs on a single and another homer, providing the margin of victory for Giant ace Johnny Antonelli, who allowed only one of Cleveland's 14 baserunners to score. Game Three was no contest. New York had scored all six of its runs before the Indians managed to come up with single runs in both the seventh and eighth. Pinch hitter Hank Majeski's three-run homer put Cleveland on the board in the fifth inning of Game Four. But as New York had already scored seven times, even a fourth Cleveland run in the seventh proved too little to prevent a Giant sweep.

New York Giants (NL), 4;
Cleveland Indians (AL), 0

NY (N)

PLAYER/POS	AVG	G	AB	R	H	2B	3B	HR	RBI	BB	SO	SB
Johnny Antonelli, p	.000	2	3	0	0	0	0	0	0	1	0	0
Alvin Dark, ss	.412	4	17	2	7	0	0	0	0	1	1	0
Ruben Gomez, p	.000	1	4	0	0	0	0	0	0	0	2	0
Marv Grissom, p	.000	1	1	0	0	0	0	0	0	0	1	0
Monte Irvin, of	.222	4	9	1	2	1	0	0	2	0	3	0
Don Liddle, p	.000	2	3	0	0	0	0	0	0	0	2	0
Whitey Lockman, 1b	.111	4	18	2	2	0	0	0	0	1	2	0
Sal Maglie, p	.000	1	3	0	0	0	0	0	0	0	2	0
Willie Mays, of	.286	4	14	4	4	1	0	0	3	4	1	1
Don Mueller, of	.389	4	18	4	7	0	0	0	1	0	1	0
Dusty Rhodes, of-2	.667	3	6	2	4	0	0	2	7	1	2	0
Hank Thompson, 3b	.364	4	11	6	4	1	0	0	2	7	1	0
Wes Westrum, c	.273	4	11	0	3	0	0	0	3	1	3	0
Hoyt Wilhelm, p	.000	2	1	0	0	0	0	0	0	0	1	0
Davey Williams, 2b	.000	4	11	0	0	0	0	0	0	1	2	0
TOTAL	.254		130	21	33	3	0	2	20	17	24	1

PITCHER	W	L	ERA	G	GS	CG	SV	SHO	IP	H	ER	BB	SO
Johnny Antonelli	1	0	0.84	2	1	1	1	0	10.2	8	1	7	12
Ruben Gomez	1	0	2.45	1	1	0	0	0	7.1	4	2	3	2
Marv Grissom	1	0	0.00	1	0	0	0	0	2.2	1	0	3	2
Don Liddle	1	0	1.29	2	1	0	0	0	7.0	5	1	1	2
Sal Maglie	0	0	2.57	1	1	0	0	0	7.0	7	2	2	2
Hoyt Wilhelm	0	0	0.00	2	0	0	1	0	2.1	1	0	0	3
TOTAL	4	0	1.46	9	4	1	2	0	37.0	26	6	16	23

CLE (A)

PLAYER/POS	AVG	G	AB	R	H	2B	3B	HR	RBI	BB	SO	SB
Bobby Avila, 2b	.133	4	15	1	2	0	0	0	0	2	1	0
Sam Dente, ss	.000	3	3	1	0	0	0	0	0	1	0	0
Larry Doby, of	.125	4	16	0	2	0	0	0	0	2	4	0
Mike Garcia, p	.000	2	0	0	0	0	0	0	0	0	0	0
Bill Glynn, 1b-1	.500	2	2	1	1	1	0	0	0	0	1	0
Mickey Grasso, c	.000	1	0	0	0	0	0	0	0	0	0	0
Jim Hegan, c	.154	4	13	1	2	1	0	0	0	1	1	0
Art Houtteman, p	.000	1	0	0	0	0	0	0	0	0	0	0
Bob Lemon, p-2	.000	3	6	0	0	0	0	0	0	1	1	0
Hank Majeski, 3b-1	.167	4	6	1	1	0	0	1	3	0	1	0
Dale Mitchell, ph	.000	3	2	0	0	0	0	0	0	1	0	0
Don Mossi, p	.000	3	0	0	0	0	0	0	0	0	0	0
Hal Naragon, c	.000	1	0	0	0	0	0	0	0	0	0	0
Ray Narleski, p	.000	2	0	0	0	0	0	0	0	0	0	0
Hal Newhouser, p	.000	1	0	0	0	0	0	0	0	0	0	0
Dave Philley, of-2	.125	4	8	0	1	0	0	0	0	1	3	0
Dave Pope, of-2	.000	3	3	0	0	0	0	0	0	1	1	0
Rudy Regalado, 3b-1	.333	4	3	0	1	0	0	0	1	0	0	0
Al Rosen, 3b	.250	3	12	0	3	0	0	0	0	1	0	0
Al Smith, of	.214	4	14	2	3	0	0	1	2	2	2	0
George Strickland, ss	.000	3	9	0	0	0	0	0	0	0	2	0
Vic Wertz, 1b	.500	4	16	2	8	2	1	1	3	2	2	0
Wally Westlake, of	.143	2	7	0	1	0	0	0	0	1	3	0
Early Wynn, p	.500	1	2	0	1	1	0	0	0	0	1	0
TOTAL	.190		137	9	26	5	1	3	9	16	23	0

PITCHER	W	L	ERA	G	GS	CG	SV	SHO	IP	H	ER	BB	SO
Mike Garcia	0	1	5.40	2	1	0	0	0	5.0	6	3	4	4
Art Houtteman	0	0	4.50	1	0	0	0	0	2.0	2	1	1	1
Bob Lemon	0	2	6.75	2	2	1	0	0	13.1	16	10	8	11
Don Mossi	0	0	0.00	3	0	0	0	0	4.0	3	0	0	1
Ray Narleski	0	0	2.25	2	0	0	0	0	4.0	1	1	1	2
Hal Newhouser	0	0	INF	1	0	0	0	0	0.0	1	1	1	0
Early Wynn	0	1	3.86	1	1	0	0	0	7.0	4	3	2	5
TOTAL	0	4	4.84	12	4	1	0	0	35.1	33	19	17	24

GAME 1 AT NY SEPT 29

CLE	200 000 000 0	2	8	0
NY	002 000 000 3	5	9	3

Pitchers: LEMON vs Maglie, Liddle (8), GRISSOM (8)
Home Runs: Rhodes-NY
Attendance: 52,751

GAME 2 AT NY SEPT 30

CLE	100 000 000	1	8	0
NY	000 020 10X	3	4	0

Pitchers: WYNN, Mossi (8) vs ANTONELLI
Home Runs: Smith-CLE, Rhodes-NY
Attendance: 49,099

GAME 3 AT CLE OCT 1

NY	103 011 000	6	10	1
CLE	000 000 110	2	4	2

Pitchers: GOMEZ, Wilhelm (7) vs GARCIA, Narleski (6), Mossi (9)
Home Runs: Wertz-CLE
Attendance: 71,555

GAME 4 AT CLE OCT 2

NY	021 040 000	7	10	3
CLE	000 030 100	4	6	2

Pitchers: LIDDLE, Wilhelm (7), Antonelli (8) vs LEMON, Newhouser (5), Narleski (5), Mossi (6), Garcia (8)
Home Runs: Majeski-CLE
Attendance: 78,102

The Dodgers and Yankees, after a year's absence, faced each other again in the World Series—their sixth Series confrontation in fifteen years. And after Brooklyn had lost the first two games it began to look as though 1955 might also mark the Yankees' sixth Series triumph over the Dodgers. But this was Brooklyn's year.

The opener was a hitters' game, but closely contested. Both teams scored twice in the second inning and once in the third, but Yankee first baseman Joe Collins's leadoff homer in the last of the fourth gave New York its first lead of the game, and his two-run blast in the sixth made the score 6–3. Brooklyn clawed back in the eighth for two runs—including Jackie Robinson's steal of home—to pull within one run of a tie, but they came no closer. In Game Two, Yankee pitcher Tommy Byrne held the Dodgers to five hits and two runs, and won his own game at the bat with a two-run single that capped the Yankees' four-run fourth.

The Series turned around as the Dodgers captured the next three games in Brooklyn. Roy Campanella's two-run homer in the first inning of Game Three gave Brooklyn a quick lead. New York tied the game with a pair of runs in the second (one of them a homer by Mickey Mantle, who appeared in only three Series games because of a leg injury). But two more Dodger runs in the last of the second drove out Yankee starter Bob Turley and put them ahead to stay as Dodger hurler Johnny Podres held the Yankees to three runs. Home runs by Campanella, Gil Hodges, and Duke Snider accounted for six of Brooklyn's eight runs in Game Four as the Dodgers evened the Series at two-all. Sandy Amoros's second-inning homer initiated the scoring in Game Five, and Snider's blasts in the third and fifth (which made him the first player to hit four home runs in two different Series) gave Brooklyn a 4–1 lead, which even late-inning Yankee homers by Bob Cerv and Yogi Berra could not overcome.

New York bounced back in Game Six, scoring all five of their runs in the first inning (including three on Bill Skowron's homer) to give Whitey Ford a comfortable lead, which he held with a one-run four-hitter. But in the finale, Gil Hodges drove in two Brooklyn runs with a single in the fourth and a sacrifice fly in the sixth. They were all Brooklyn got, but they proved more than enough to carry the Dodgers to their first world title in fifty-five years, as left fielder Sandy Amoros stifled New York's only real scoring

Brooklyn Dodgers (NL), 4; New York Yankees (AL), 3

BRO (N)

PLAYER/POS	AVG	G	AB	R	H	2B	3B	HR	RB	BB	SO	SB
Sandy Amoros, of	.333	5	12	3	4	0	0	1	3	4	4	0
Don Bessent, p	.000	3	1	0	0	0	0	0	0	0	1	0
Roy Campanella, c	.259	7	27	4	7	3	0	2	4	3	3	0
Roger Craig, p	.000	1	0	0	0	0	0	0	0	1	0	0
Carl Erskine, p	.000	1	1	0	0	0	0	0	0	0	0	0
Carl Furillo, of	.296	7	27	4	8	1	0	1	3	3	5	0
Jim Gilliam, 2b-5,of-4	.292	7	24	2	7	1	0	0	3	8	1	1
Don Hoak, 3b-1	.333	3	3	0	1	0	0	0	0	2	0	0
Gil Hodges, 1b	.292	7	24	2	7	0	0	1	5	3	2	0
Frank Kellert, ph	.333	3	3	0	1	0	0	0	0	0	1	0
Clem Labine, p	.000	4	4	0	0	0	0	0	0	0	3	0
Billy Loes, p	.000	1	1	0	0	0	0	0	0	0	0	0
Russ Meyer, p	.000	1	2	0	0	0	0	0	0	0	1	0
Don Newcombe, p	.000	3	3	0	0	0	0	0	0	0	0	0
Johnny Podres, p	.143	2	7	1	1	0	0	0	0	0	1	0
Pee Wee Reese, ss	.296	7	27	5	8	1	0	0	2	3	5	0
Jackie Robinson, 3b	.182	6	22	5	4	1	1	0	1	1	2	1
Ed Roebuck, p	.000	1	0	0	0	0	0	0	0	0	0	0
George Shuba, ph	.000	1	1	0	0	0	0	0	0	0	0	0
Duke Snider, of	.320	7	25	5	8	1	0	4	7	2	6	0
Karl Spooner, p	.000	2	0	0	0	0	0	0	0	0	0	0
Don Zimmer, 2b	.222	4	9	0	2	0	0	0	0	2	2	5
TOTAL	.260		223	31	58	8	1	9	30	33	38	2

PITCHER	W	L	ERA	G	GS	CG	SV	SHO	IP	H	ER	BB	SO
Don Bessent	0	0	0.00	3	0	0	0	0	3.1	3	0	1	1
Roger Craig	1	0	3.00	1	1	0	0	0	6.0	4	2	5	4
Carl Erskine	0	0	9.00	1	1	0	0	0	3.0	3	3	2	3
Clem Labine	1	0	2.89	4	0	0	1	0	9.1	6	3	2	2
Billy Loes	0	1	9.82	1	1	0	0	0	3.2	7	4	1	5
Russ Meyer	0	0	0.00	1	0	0	0	0	5.2	4	0	2	4
Don Newcombe	0	1	9.53	1	1	0	0	0	5.2	8	6	2	4
Johnny Podres	2	0	1.00	2	2	2	0	1	18.0	15	2	4	10
Ed Roebuck	0	0	0.00	1	0	0	0	0	2.0	1	0	0	0
Karl Spooner	0	1	13.50	2	1	0	0	0	3.1	4	5	3	6
TOTAL	4	3	3.75	17	7	2	1	1	60.0	55	25	22	39

NY (A)

PLAYER/POS	AVG	G	AB	R	H	2B	3B	HR	RB	BB	SO	SB
Hank Bauer, of-5	.429	6	14	1	6	0	0	0	0	1	0	1
Yogi Berra, c	.417	7	24	5	10	1	0	1	2	3	1	0
Tommy Byrne, p-2	.167	3	6	0	1	0	0	0	2	0	2	0
Andy Carey, ph	.500	2	2	0	1	0	1	0	1	0	0	0
Tom Carroll, pr	.000	2	0	0	0	0	0	0	0	0	0	0
Bob Cerv, of-4	.125	5	16	1	2	0	0	1	1	0	4	0
Gerry Coleman, ss	.000	3	3	0	0	0	0	0	0	0	1	0
Rip Coleman, p	.000	1	0	0	0	0	0	0	0	0	0	0
Joe Collins, 1b-5,of-1	.167	5	12	6	2	0	0	2	3	6	4	1
Whitey Ford, p	.000	2	6	1	0	0	0	0	0	1	1	0
Bob Grim, p	.000	3	2	0	0	0	0	0	0	0	0	0
Elston Howard, of	.192	7	26	3	5	0	0	1	3	1	8	0
Johnny Kucks, p	.000	2	0	0	0	0	0	0	0	0	0	0
Don Larsen, p	.000	1	2	0	0	0	0	0	0	0	0	0
Mickey Mantle, of-2	.200	3	10	1	2	0	0	1	1	0	2	0
Billy Martin, 2b	.320	7	25	2	8	1	1	0	4	1	5	0
Gil Mc Dougald, 3b	.259	7	27	2	7	0	0	1	1	2	6	0
Tom Morgan, p	.000	2	0	0	0	0	0	0	0	0	0	0
Irv Noren, of	.063	5	16	0	1	0	0	0	1	1	1	0
Phil Rizzuto, ss	.267	7	15	2	4	0	0	0	1	5	1	2
Eddie Robinson, 1b-1	.667	4	3	0	2	0	0	0	1	2	1	0
Bill Skowron, 1b-3	.333	5	12	2	4	2	0	1	3	0	1	0
Tom Sturdivant, p	.000	2	0	0	0	0	0	0	0	0	0	0
Bob Turley, p	.000	3	1	0	0	0	0	0	0	0	0	0
TOTAL	.248		222	26	55	4	2	8	25	22	39	3

PITCHER	W	L	ERA	G	GS	CG	SV	SHO	IP	H	ER	BB	SO
Tommy Byrne	1	1	1.88	2	2	1	0	0	14.1	8	3	8	8
Rip Coleman	0	0	9.00	1	0	0	0	0	1.0	5	1	0	1
Whitey Ford	2	0	2.12	2	2	1	0	0	17.0	13	4	8	10
Bob Grim	0	1	4.15	3	1	0	1	0	8.2	8	4	5	8
Johnny Kucks	0	0	6.00	2	0	0	0	0	3.0	4	2	1	1
Don Larsen	0	1	11.25	1	1	0	0	0	4.0	5	5	2	2
Tom Morgan	0	0	4.91	2	0	0	0	0	3.2	3	2	3	1
Tom Sturdivant	0	0	6.00	2	0	0	0	0	3.0	5	2	2	0
Bob Turley	0	1	8.44	3	1	0	0	0	5.1	7	5	4	7
TOTAL	3	4	4.20	18	7	2	1	0	60.0	58	28	33	38

threat with a spectacular running catch in the sixth that started a double play and preserved Johnny Podres's second Series win.

GAME 1 AT NY SEPT 28

BRO	021	000	020	5	10 0
NY	021	102	00X	6	9 1

Pitchers: NEWCOMBE, Bessent (6), Labine (8) vs FORD, Grim (9)
Home Runs: Furillo-BRO, Snider-BRO, Howard-NY, Collins-NY (2)
Attendance: 63,869

GAME 2 AT NY SEPT 29

BRO	000	110	000	2	5 2
NY	000	400	00X	4	8 0

Pitchers: LOES, Bessent (4), Spooner (5), Labine (8) vs BYRNE
Attendance: 64,707

GAME 3 AT BRO SEPT 30

NY	020	000	100	3	7 0
BRO	220	200	20X	8	11 1

Pitchers: TURLEY, Morgan (2), Kucks (5), Sturdivant (7) vs PODRES
Home Runs: Campanella-BRO, Mantle-NY
Attendance: 34,209

GAME 4 AT BRO OCT 1

NY	110	102	000	5	9 0
BRO	001	330	10X	8	14 0

Pitchers: LARSEN, Kucks (5), R.Coleman (6), Morgan (7), Sturdivant (8) VS Erskine, Bessent (4), LABINE (5)
Home Runs: McDougald-NY, Campanella-BRO, Hodges-BRO, Snider-BRO
Attendance: 36,242

GAME 5 AT BRO OCT 2

NY	000	100	110	3	6 0
BRO	021	010	01X	5	9 2

Pitchers: GRIM, Turley (7) vs CRAIG, Labine (7)
Home Runs: Cerv-NY, Berra-NY, Amoros-BRO, Snider-BRO (2)
Attendance: 36,796

GAME 6 AT NY OCT 3

BRO	000	100	000	1	4 1
NY	500	000	00X	5	8 0

Pitchers: SPOONER, Meyer (1), Roebuck (7) vs FORD
Home Runs: Skowron-NY
Attendance: 64,022

GAME 7 AT NY OCT 4

BRO	000	101	000	2	5 0
NY	000	000	000	0	8 1

Pitchers: PODRES vs BYRNE, Grim (6), Turley (8)
Attendance: 62,465

The 1956 Series was a mirror image of 1955. With both teams repeaters as league champions, the Yankees this year followed Brooklyn's winning pattern of the previous Series: losing the first two games, winning the next three, then splitting the final pair.

Sal Maglie outlasted Yankee ace Whitey Ford in the opener. Maglie gave up nine hits and three runs (on homers by Mickey Mantle and Billy Martin), but struck out ten and took the win as Jackie Robinson and Gil Hodges contributed homers for four of Brooklyn's six runs. Dodger ace Don Newcombe was blown out by six Yankee runs (capped by Yogi Berra's grand slam) in the first two innings of Game Two. But Brooklyn came back with six unearned runs in their half of the second (three of them on Duke Snider's homer) and proceeded to run through seven Yankee pitchers for a 13–8 win and a two-game Series edge.

Whitey Ford tried again in Game Three, and this time held on for a complete-game 5–3 win, supported by Billy Martin's game-tying solo homer in the second and forty-year-old Enos Slaughter's go-ahead three-run shot in the sixth. Tom Sturdivant duplicated Ford's effectiveness and success the next day with a six-hit 6–2 win to even the Series.

Sal Maglie pitched Game Five for Brooklyn and improved on his winning performance of Game One, yielding only two runs and holding New York hitless until Mantle's two-out homer in the fourth inning. But no one was a match for Yankee pitcher Don Larsen that day. There was a close out on a deflected Dodger liner in the second inning, and center fielder Mantle made a fine running catch to prevent a hit in the fifth. But Larsen retired the rest routinely, and when Dale Mitchell fanned in the ninth Larsen had his perfect game—a feat still unique in World Series history.

Brooklyn reliever Clem Labine was started in Game Six against Yankee fastballer Bob Turley. No runner scored for either side until the last of the tenth inning when, with two out, Jackie Robinson lined a Turley pitch over the head of the left fielder, scoring Jim Gilliam from second and forcing New York into a seventh game.

The finale proved an anticlimactic disaster for Brooklyn. Once again Dodger starter Newcombe was driven out—this time by Yogi Berra's two two-run homers and Elston Howard's solo shot. By the time it was over, Bill Skowron had increased the Yankee run total to nine with a grand slam, and Yankee starter Johnny Kucks had shut Brooklyn out on three

New York Yankees (AL), 4;
Brooklyn Dodgers (NL), 3

NY (A)

PLAYER/POS	AVG	G	AB	R	H	2B	3B	HR	RB	BB	SO	SB
Hank Bauer, of	.281	7	32	3	9	0	0	1	3	0	5	1
Yogi Berra, c	.360	7	25	5	9	2	0	3	10	4	1	0
Tommy Byrne, p-1	.000	2	1	0	0	0	0	0	0	0	0	0
Andy Carey, 3b	.158	7	19	2	3	0	0	0	0	1	6	0
Bob Cerv, ph	1.000	1	1	0	1	0	0	0	0	0	0	0
Gerry Coleman, 2b	.000	2	2	0	0	0	0	0	0	0	0	0
Joe Collins, 1b-5	.238	6	21	2	5	2	0	0	2	2	3	0
Whitey Ford, p	.000	2	4	0	0	0	0	0	0	0	3	0
Elston Howard, of	.400	1	5	1	2	1	0	1	1	0	0	0
Johnny Kucks, p	.000	3	3	0	0	0	0	0	0	0	1	0
Don Larsen, p	.333	2	3	1	1	0	0	0	0	1	0	0
Mickey Mantle, of	.250	7	24	6	6	1	0	3	4	6	5	1
Billy Martin, 2b-7,3b-1	.296	7	27	5	8	0	0	2	3	1	6	0
Maury Mc Dermott, p	1.000	1	1	0	1	0	0	0	0	0	0	0
Gil Mc Dougald, ss	.143	7	21	0	3	0	0	0	1	3	6	0
Tom Morgan, p	1.000	2	1	1	1	0	0	0	0	0	0	0
Norm Siebern, ph	.000	1	1	0	0	0	0	0	0	0	0	0
Bill Skowron, 1b-2	.100	3	10	1	1	0	0	1	4	0	3	0
Enos Slaughter, of	.350	6	20	6	7	0	0	1	4	4	0	0
Tom Sturdivant, p	.333	2	3	0	1	0	0	0	0	0	1	0
Bob Turley, p	.000	3	4	0	0	0	0	0	0	0	1	0
George Wilson, ph	.000	1	1	0	0	0	0	0	0	0	1	0
TOTAL	.253		229	33	58	6	0	12	33	21	43	2

PITCHER	W	L	ERA	G	GS	CG	SV	SHO	IP	H	ER	BB	SO
Tommy Byrne	0	0	0.00	1	0	0	0	0	0.1	1	0	0	1
Whitey Ford	1	1	5.25	2	2	1	0	0	12.0	14	7	2	8
Johnny Kucks	1	0	0.82	3	1	1	0	1	11.0	6	1	3	2
Don Larsen	1	0	0.00	2	2	1	0	1	10.2	1	0	4	7
Maury Mc Dermott	0	0	3.00	1	0	0	0	0	3.0	2	1	3	3
Tom Morgan	0	1	9.00	2	0	0	0	0	4.0	6	4	4	3
Tom Sturdivant	1	0	2.79	2	1	1	0	0	9.2	8	3	8	9
Bob Turley	0	1	0.82	3	1	1	0	0	11.0	4	1	8	14
TOTAL	4	3	2.48	16	7	5	0	2	61.2	42	17	32	47

BRO (N)

PLAYER/POS	AVG	G	AB	R	H	2B	3B	HR	RB	BB	SO	SB
Sandy Amoros, of	.053	6	19	1	1	0	0	0	1	2	4	0
Don Bessent, p	.500	2	2	0	1	0	0	0	1	1	1	0
Roy Campanella, c	.182	7	22	2	4	1	0	0	3	3	7	0
Gino Cimoli, of	.000	1	0	0	0	0	0	0	0	0	0	0
Roger Craig, p	.500	2	2	0	1	0	0	0	0	0	0	0
Don Drysdale, p	.000	1	0	0	0	0	0	0	0	0	0	0
Carl Erskine, p	.000	2	1	0	0	0	0	0	0	0	1	0
Carl Furillo, of	.240	7	25	2	6	2	0	0	1	2	3	0
Jim Gilliam, 2b-6,of-1	.083	7	24	2	2	0	0	0	2	7	3	1
Gil Hodges, 1b	.304	7	23	5	7	2	0	1	8	4	4	0
Ransom Jackson, ph	.000	3	3	0	0	0	0	0	0	0	2	0
Clem Labine, p	.250	2	4	0	1	1	0	0	0	0	2	0
Sal Maglie, p	.000	2	5	0	0	0	0	0	0	0	2	0
Dale Mitchell, ph	.000	4	4	0	0	0	0	0	0	0	1	0
Charlie Neal, 2b	.000	1	4	0	0	0	0	0	0	0	1	0
Don Newcombe, p	.000	2	1	0	0	0	0	0	0	0	0	0
Pee Wee Reese, ss	.222	7	27	3	6	0	1	0	2	6	6	0
Jackie Robinson, 3b	.250	7	24	5	6	1	0	1	2	5	2	0
Ed Roebuck, p	.000	3	0	0	0	0	0	0	0	0	0	0
Duke Snider, of	.304	7	23	5	7	1	0	1	4	6	8	0
Rube Walker, ph	.000	2	2	0	0	0	0	0	0	0	0	0
TOTAL	.195		215	25	42	8	1	3	24	32	47	1

PITCHER	W	L	ERA	G	GS	CG	SV	SHO	IP	H	ER	BB	SO
Don Bessent	1	0	1.80	2	0	0	0	0	10.0	8	2	3	5
Roger Craig	0	1	12.00	2	1	0	0	0	6.0	10	8	3	4
Don Drysdale	0	0	9.00	1	0	0	0	0	2.0	2	2	1	1
Carl Erskine	0	1	5.40	2	1	0	0	0	5.0	4	3	2	2
Clem Labine	1	0	0.00	2	1	1	0	1	12.0	8	0	3	7
Sal Maglie	1	1	2.65	2	2	2	0	0	17.0	14	5	6	15
Don Newcombe	0	1	21.21	2	2	0	0	0	4.2	11	11	3	4
Ed Roebuck	0	0	2.08	3	0	0	0	0	4.1	1	1	0	5
TOTAL	3	4	4.72	16	7	3	0	1	61.0	58	32	21	43

singles. For New York it was world title number seventeen.

Overall, the Yankees pitched better, hit oftener, and scored more runs than the Braves. But the Braves had Lew Burdette, and with him they won the Series.

The opener pitted the Braves' established great Warren Spahn against New York's emerging great Whitey Ford. Ford prevailed, with a five-hit 3–1 win as Spahn was chased in the sixth. Burdette, winner of 17 regular-season games, started Game Two against veteran Bobby Shantz, the American League ERA leader. After a scoreless first inning, both pitchers gave up a run in the second and another in the third. Two go-ahead runs in the top of the fourth ended the Braves' scoring, but they were enough, as Burdette blanked New York through the final six innings to even the Series. Before he was finished, Burdette would stretch his consecutive scoreless innings to 24.

The Yankees exploded in Game Three, in Milwaukee, running through six Brave pitchers for a 12–3 rout. Braves fans even ended up cheering Yankee second baseman Tony Kubek—a Milwaukee native—who opened the scoring with a solo homer in the first, scored again after singling in the fourth (on Mickey Mantle's home run), and concluded the Yankee scoring in the seventh with his second homer, with two aboard.

Warren Spahn carried a 4–1 Braves lead into the ninth inning of Game Four, but after retiring the first two batters in the ninth, he gave up singles to Yogi Berra and Gil McDougald, and a game-tying home run to Elston Howard. In the top of the tenth, Hank Bauer tripled in a go-ahead Yankee run, but Milwaukee's Johnny Logan doubled to tie it up in the last of the tenth, and Eddie Mathews homered to give Spahn a shaky victory.

Burdette faced Ford in Game Five. In the sixth inning the Braves put half their hits—three singles—back to back for a run. It was all they needed as Burdette spaced seven singles for the shutout. Back in New York the next day, all the scoring came on home runs. Each club hit a pair, but Berra's in the third was the only one with a man aboard. Brave blasts in the fifth (Frank Torre) and seventh (Hank Aaron) tied the score, but Bauer answered Aaron's homer in the last of the seventh with what proved the winning shot. Bob Turley, who yielded just two hits while fanning eight (the Series high) claimed the Yankee victory.

In the finale, Burdette, with only two days' rest, scattered four hits over the first eight innings as the Braves gave him a 5–0 lead. In

Milwaukee Braves (NL), 4; New York Yankees (AL), 3

MIL (N)

PLAYER/POS	AVG	G	AB	R	H	2B	3B	HR	RB	BB	SO	SB
Hank Aaron, of	.393	7	28	5	11	0	1	3	7	1	6	0
Joe Adcock, 1b	.200	5	15	1	3	0	0	0	2	0	2	0
Bob Buhl, p	.000	2	1	0	0	0	0	0	0	0	1	0
Lew Burdette, p	.000	3	8	0	0	0	0	0	0	1	2	0
Gene Conley, p	.000	1	0	0	0	0	0	0	0	0	0	0
Wes Covington, of	.208	7	24	1	5	1	0	0	1	2	6	1
Del Crandall, c	.211	6	19	1	4	0	0	1	1	1	1	0
John De Merit, pr	.000	3	0	0	0	0	0	0	0	0	0	0
Bob Hazle, of	.154	4	13	2	2	0	0	0	0	1	2	0
Ernie Johnson, p	.000	3	1	0	0	0	0	0	0	0	1	0
Nippy Jones, ph	.000	3	2	0	0	0	0	0	0	0	0	0
Johnny Logan, ss	.185	7	27	5	5	1	0	1	2	3	6	0
Felix Mantilla, 2b-3	.000	4	10	1	0	0	0	0	0	1	0	0
Eddie Mathews, 3b	.227	7	22	4	5	3	0	1	4	8	5	0
Don Mc Mahon, p	.000	3	0	0	0	0	0	0	0	0	0	0
Andy Pafko, of-5	.214	6	14	1	3	0	0	0	0	0	1	0
Juan Pizarro, p	.000	1	1	0	0	0	0	0	0	0	0	0
Del Rice, c	.167	2	6	0	1	0	0	0	0	1	2	0
Carl Sawatski, ph	.000	2	2	0	0	0	0	0	0	0	2	0
Red Schoendienst, 2b	.278	5	18	0	5	1	0	0	2	0	1	0
Warren Spahn, p	.000	2	4	0	0	0	0	0	0	1	2	0
Frank Torre, 1b	.300	7	10	2	3	0	0	2	3	2	0	0
Bob Trowbridge, p	.000	1	0	0	0	0	0	0	0	0	0	0
TOTAL	.209		225	23	47	6	1	8	22	22	40	1

PITCHER	W	L	ERA	G	GS	CG	SV	SHO	IP	H	ER	BB	SO
Bob Buhl	0	1	10.80	2	2	0	0	0	3.1	6	4	6	4
Lew Burdette	3	0	0.67	3	3	3	0	2	27.0	21	2	4	13
Gene Conley	0	0	10.80	1	0	0	0	0	1.2	2	2	1	0
Ernie Johnson	0	1	1.29	3	0	0	0	0	7.0	2	1	1	8
Don Mc Mahon	0	0		3	0	0	0	0	5.0	3	0	3	5
Juan Pizarro	0	0	10.80	1	0	0	0	0	1.2	3	2	2	1
Warren Spahn	1	1	4.70	2	2	1	0	0	15.1	18	8	2	2
Bob Trowbridge	0	0	45.00	1	0	0	0	0	1.0	2	5	3	1
TOTAL	4	3	3.48	16	7	4	0	2	62.0	57	24	22	34

NY (A)

PLAYER/POS	AVG	G	AB	R	H	2B	3B	HR	RB	BB	SO	SB
Hank Bauer, of	.258	7	31	3	8	2	1	2	6	1	6	0
Yogi Berra, c	.320	7	25	5	8	1	0	1	2	4	0	0
Tommy Byrne, p	.500	2	2	0	1	0	0	0	0	0	1	0
Andy Carey, 3b	.286	2	7	0	2	1	0	0	1	1	0	0
Gerry Coleman, 2b	.364	7	22	2	8	2	0	0	2	3	1	0
Joe Collins, 1b-5	.000	6	5	0	0	0	0	0	0	0	3	0
Art Ditmar, p	.000	2	1	0	0	0	0	0	0	0	1	0
Whitey Ford, p	.000	2	5	0	0	0	0	0	0	0	1	0
Bob Grim, p	.000	2	0	0	0	0	0	0	0	0	0	0
Elston Howard, 1b-3	.273	6	11	2	3	0	0	1	3	1	3	0
Tony Kubek, of-5,3b-2	.286	7	28	4	8	0	0	2	4	0	4	0
Johnny Kucks, p	.000	1	0	0	0	0	0	0	0	0	0	0
Don Larsen, p	.000	2	2	1	0	0	0	0	0	2	1	0
Jerry Lumpe, 3b-3	.286	6	14	0	4	0	0	0	2	1	1	0
Mickey Mantle, of-5	.263	6	19	3	5	0	0	1	2	3	1	0
Gil Mc Dougald, ss	.250	7	24	3	6	0	0	0	2	3	3	1
Bobby Richardson, 2b-1	.000	2	0	0	0	0	0	0	0	0	0	0
Bobby Shantz, p	.000	3	1	0	0	0	0	0	0	0	0	0
Harry Simpson, 1b-4	.083	5	12	0	1	0	0	0	1	0	4	0
Bill Skowron, 1b	.000	2	4	0	0	0	0	0	0	0	0	0
Enos Slaughter, of	.250	5	12	2	3	1	0	0	0	3	2	0
Tom Sturdivant, p	.000	2	1	0	0	0	0	0	0	0	0	0
Bob Turley, p	.000	3	4	0	0	0	0	0	0	0	2	0
TOTAL	.248		230	25	57	7	1	7	25	22	34	1

PITCHER	W	L	ERA	G	GS	CG	SV	SHO	IP	H	ER	BB	SO
Tommy Byrne	0	0	5.40	2	0	0	0	0	3.1	1	2	2	1
Art Ditmar	0	0	0.00	2	0	0	0	0	6.0	2	0	0	2
Whitey Ford	1	1	1.13	2	2	1	0	0	16.0	11	2	5	7
Bob Grim	0	1	7.71	2	0	0	0	0	2.1	3	2	0	2
Johnny Kucks	0	0	0.00	1	0	0	0	0	0.2	1	0	1	1
Don Larsen	1	1	3.72	2	1	0	0	0	9.2	8	4	5	6
Bobby Shantz	0	1	4.05	3	1	0	0	0	6.2	8	3	2	7
Tom Sturdivant	0	0	6.00	2	1	0	0	0	6.0	6	4	1	2
Bob Turley	1	0	2.31	3	2	1	0	0	11.2	7	3	6	12
TOTAL	3	4	2.89	19	7	2	0	0	62.1	47	20	22	40

the bottom of the ninth, though, three Yankee singles loaded the bases with two out. But third baseman Eddie Mathews snared Bil Skowron's sharp grounder and stepped on the bag for a force out that preserved Burdette's second shutout and gave Milwaukee its first world championship.

GAME 1 AT NY OCT 2

MIL	000 000 100	1	5	0
NY	000 012 00X	3	9	1

Pitchers: SPAHN, Johnson (6), McMahon (7) vs FORD
Attendance: 69,476

GAME 2 AT NY OCT 3

MIL	011 200 000	4	8	0
NY	011 000 000	2	7	2

Pitchers: BURDETTE vs SHANTZ, Ditmar (4), Grim (8)
Home Runs: Logan-MIL, Bauer-NY
Attendance: 65,202

GAME 3 AT MIL OCT 5

NY	302 200 500	12	9	0
MIL	010 020 000	3	8	1

Pitchers: Turley, LARSEN (2) vs BUHL, Pizarro (1), Conley (3), Johnson (5), Trowbridge (7)
Home Runs: Kubek-NY (2), Mantle-NY, Aaron-MIL
Attendance: 45,804

GAME 4 AT MIL OCT 6

NY	100 000 003 1	5	11	0
MIL	000 400 000 3	7	7	0

Pitchers: Sturdivant, Shantz (5), Kucks (8), Byrne (8), GRIM (10) vs SPAHN
Home Runs: Aaron-MIL, Torre-MIL, Howard-NY, Mathews-MIL
Attendance: 45,804

GAME 5 AT MIL OCT 7

NY	000 000 000	0	7	0
MIL	000 001 00X	1	6	1

Pitchers: FORD, Turley (8) vs BURDETTE
Attendance: 45,811

GAME 6 AT NY OCT 9

MIL	000 010 100	2	4	0
NY	002 000 10X	3	7	0

Pitchers: Buhl, JOHNSON (3), McMahon (8) vs TURLEY
Home Runs: Berra-NY, Torre-MIL, Aaron-MIL, Bauer-NY
Attendance: 61,408

GAME 7 AT NY OCT 10

MIL	004 000 010	5	9	1
NY	000 000 000	0	7	3

Pitchers: BURDETTE vs LARSEN, Shantz (3), Ditmar (4), Sturdivant (6), Byrne (8)
Home Runs: Crandall-MIL
Attendance: 61,207

After four games, Milwaukee held a 3–1 Series advantage, but New York rebounded to take the final three games and avenge their loss to the Braves the year before. As in the previous series, Warren Spahn faced Whitey Ford in the opener. The durable Spahn emerged the victor when Bill Bruton singled home the Braves' winning run off reliever Ryne Duren in the last of the tenth. In Game Two, home runs by Bruton and pitcher Lew Burdette (for three runs) helped put the Braves ahead 7–1 in the first inning. Milwaukee scored off five Yankee hurlers in their eventual 13–5 win.

Don Larsen and Ryne Duren combined for a shutout in Game Three to give New York its first victory. Hank Bauer drove in all four Yankee runs with a two-run single in the fifth and his third home run in three games in the seventh. Warren Spahn held Bauer hitless in Game Four, blanking New York on two hits to defeat Whitey Ford and bring Milwaukee within a win of the championship.

Yankee Bob Turley came up with a shutout of his own the next day, though, fanning ten men along the way. Gil McDougald's solo homer in the third inning was all the offense Turley needed, but as insurance the Yankees bunched six of their ten hits into the sixth inning for six more runs.

Spahn and Ford, with only two days' rest, confronted each other a third time in Game Six. Ford lasted less than two innings, but Spahn (despite Hank Bauer's fourth Series home run in the first inning) endured into extra innings, when McDougald put New York ahead with a leadoff homer in the tenth. Two outs and two hits later, Spahn was removed, and Bill Skowron's single off reliever Don McMahon drove home another Yankee run. Milwaukee scored once in the last of the tenth and threatened further damage with men on first and third. But Bob Turley came on to retire the final batter and send the Series to a seventh game.

In the sixth inning of the finale, the Braves' Del Crandall homered against Turley (who had relieved Don Larsen in the third) to tie the game 2–2. But four Yankee runs off starter Lew Burdette in the top of the eighth (including Skowron's three-run homer) made the score 6–2, where it remained, as Turley held on to bring Casey Stengel his seventh (and last) Series triumph—and the Yankees their eighteenth.

New York Yankees (AL), 4; Milwaukee Braves (NL), 3

NY (A)

PLAYER/POS	AVG	G	AB	R	H	2B	3B	HR	RB	BB	SO	SB
Hank Bauer, of	.323	7	31	6	10	0	0	4	8	0	5	0
Yogi Berra, c	.222	7	27	3	6	3	0	0	2	1	0	0
Andy Carey, 3b	.083	5	12	1	1	0	0	0	0	0	3	0
Murry Dickson, p	.000	2	0	0	0	0	0	0	0	0	0	0
Art Ditmar, p	.000	1	1	0	0	0	0	0	0	0	0	0
Ryne Duren, p	.000	3	3	0	0	0	0	0	0	0	2	0
Whitey Ford, p	.000	3	4	1	0	0	0	0	0	2	2	0
Elston Howard, of	.222	6	18	4	4	0	0	0	2	1	4	1
Tony Kubek, ss	.048	7	21	0	1	0	0	0	1	1	7	0
Johnny Kucks, p	1.000	2	1	0	1	0	0	0	0	0	0	0
Don Larsen, p	.000	2	2	0	0	0	0	0	0	1	0	0
Jerry Lumpe, 3b-3,ss-2	.167	6	12	0	2	0	0	0	0	1	2	0
Duke Maas, p	.000	1	0	0	0	0	0	0	0	0	0	0
Mickey Mantle, of	.250	7	24	4	6	0	1	2	3	7	4	0
Gil Mc Dougald, 2b	.321	7	28	5	9	2	0	2	4	2	4	0
Zach Monroe, p	.000	1	0	0	0	0	0	0	0	0	0	0
Bobby Richardson, 3b	.000	4	5	0	0	0	0	0	0	0	0	0
Norm Siebern, of	.125	3	8	1	1	0	0	0	0	0	3	2
Bill Skowron, 1b	.259	7	27	3	7	0	0	2	7	1	4	0
Enos Slaughter, ph	.000	4	3	1	0	0	0	0	0	1	1	0
Marv Throneberry, ph	.000	1	1	0	0	0	0	0	0	0	1	0
Bob Turley, p	.200	4	5	0	1	0	0	0	2	0	1	0
TOTAL	.210		233	29	49	5	1	10	29	21	42	1

PITCHER	W	L	ERA	G	GS	CG	SV	SHO	IP	H	ER	BB	SO
Murry Dickson	0	0	4.50	2	0	0	0	0	4.0	4	2	0	1
Art Ditmar	0	0	0.00	1	0	0	0	0	3.2	2	0	0	2
Ryne Duren	1	1	1.93	3	0	0	1	0	9.1	7	2	6	14
Whitey Ford	0	1	4.11	3	3	0	0	0	15.1	19	7	5	16
Johnny Kucks	0	0	2.08	2	0	0	0	0	4.1	4	1	1	0
Don Larsen	1	0	0.96	2	2	0	0	0	9.1	9	1	6	9
Duke Maas	0	0	81.00	1	0	0	0	0	0.1	2	3	1	0
Zach Monroe	0	0	27.00	1	0	0	0	0	1.0	3	3	1	1
Bob Turley	2	1	2.76	4	2	1	1	1	16.1	10	5	7	13
TOTAL	4	3	3.39	19	7	1	2	1	63.2	60	24	27	56

MIL (N)

PLAYER/POS	AVG	G	AB	R	H	2B	3B	HR	RB	BB	SO	SB
Hank Aaron, of	.333	7	27	3	9	2	0	0	2	4	6	0
Joe Adcock, 1b	.308	4	13	1	4	0	0	0	0	1	3	0
Billy Bruton, of	.412	7	17	2	7	0	0	1	2	5	5	0
Lew Burdette, p	.111	3	9	1	1	0	0	1	0	3	0	0
Wes Covington, of	.269	7	26	2	7	0	0	0	4	2	4	0
Del Crandall, c	.240	7	25	4	6	0	0	1	3	3	10	0
Harry Hanebrink, ph	.000	2	2	0	0	0	0	0	0	0	0	0
Johnny Logan, ss	.120	7	25	3	3	2	0	0	2	2	4	0
Felix Mantilla, ss-1	.000	4	0	1	0	0	0	0	0	0	0	0
Eddie Mathews, 3b	.160	7	25	3	4	2	0	0	3	6	11	1
Don Mc Mahon, p	.000	3	0	0	0	0	0	0	0	0	0	0
Andy Pafko, of	.333	4	9	0	3	1	0	0	1	0	0	0
Juan Pizarro, p	.000	1	0	0	0	0	0	0	0	0	0	0
Bob Rush, p	.000	1	2	0	0	0	0	0	0	0	2	0
Red Schoendienst, 2b	.300	7	30	5	9	3	1	0	0	2	1	0
Warren Spahn, p	.333	3	12	0	4	0	0	0	3	0	6	0
Frank Torre, 1b	.176	7	17	0	3	0	0	0	1	2	0	0
Carl Willey, p	.000	1	0	0	0	0	0	0	0	0	0	0
Casey Wise, ph	.000	2	1	0	0	0	0	0	0	0	1	0
TOTAL	.250		240	25	60	10	1	3	24	27	56	1

PITCHER	W	L	ERA	G	GS	CG	SV	SHO	IP	H	ER	BB	SO
Lew Burdette	1	2	5.64	3	3	1	0	0	22.1	22	14	4	12
Don Mc Mahon	0	0	5.40	3	0	0	0	0	3.1	3	2	3	5
Juan Pizarro	0	0	5.40	1	0	0	0	0	1.2	2	1	1	3
Bob Rush	0	1	3.00	1	1	0	0	0	6.0	3	2	5	2
Warren Spahn	2	1	2.20	3	3	2	0	1	28.2	19	7	8	18
Carl Willey	0	0	0.00	1	0	0	0	0	1.0	0	0	0	2
TOTAL	3	4	3.71	12	7	3	0	1	63.0	49	26	21	42

GAME 1 AT MIL OCT 1

NY	000	120	000	0	3	8	1
MIL	000	200	010	1	4	10	0

Pitchers: Ford, DUREN (8) vs SPAHN
Home Runs: Skowron-NY, Bauer-NY
Attendance: 46,367

GAME 2 AT MIL OCT 2

NY	100	100	003	5	7	0
MIL	710	000	23X	13	15	1

Pitchers: TURLEY, Maas (1), Kucks (1), Dickson (5), Monroe (8) vs BURDETTE
Home Runs: Bruton-MIL, Burdette-MIL, Mantle-NY (2), Bauer-NY
Attendance: 46,367

GAME 3 AT NY OCT 4

MIL	000	000	000	0	6	0
NY	000	020	02X	4	4	0

Pitchers: RUSH, McMahon (7) vs LARSEN, Duren (8)
Home Runs: Bauer-NY
Attendance: 71,599

GAME 4 AT NY OCT 5

MIL	000	001	110	3	9	0
NY	000	000	000	0	2	1

Pitchers: SPAHN vs FORD, Kucks (8), Dickson (9)
Attendance: 71,563

GAME 5 AT NY OCT 6

MIL	000	000	000	0	5	0
NY	001	006	00X	7	10	0

Pitchers: BURDETTE, Pizarro (6), Willey (8) vs TURLEY
Home Runs: McDougald-NY
Attendance: 65,279

GAME 6 AT MIL OCT 8

NY	100	001	000	2	4	10	1
MIL	110	000	000	1	3	10	4

Pitchers: Ford, Ditmar (2), DUREN (6), Turley (10) vs SPAHN, McMahon (10)
Home Runs: Bauer-NY, McDougald-NY
Attendance: 46,367

GAME 7 AT MIL OCT 9

NY	020	000	040	6	8	0
MIL	100	001	000	2	5	2

Pitchers: Larsen, TURLEY (3) vs BURDETTE, McMahon (8)
Home Runs: Crandall-MIL, Skowron-NY
Attendance: 46,367

It took a nosedive from first to third by San Francisco and a Dodger playoff victory over Milwaukee (who had finished the season tied with the Dodgers), to bring Los Angeles the city's first major league pennant. But once they had made it to the Series, the Dodgers dispatched the White Sox in six games.

The opener, though, belonged to Chicago. In their first World Series in forty years, the White Sox overwhelmed Los Angeles with 11 runs in the first four innings as pitchers Early Wynn and Gerry Staley combined to blank the Dodgers. Chicago's big gun was veteran slugger Ted Kluszewski (acquired from Pittsburgh in late August), whose single and two homers drove in five runs. Chicago scored twice in the first inning the next day, but Dodger starter Johnny Podres settled down to blank the Sox over the next five innings as home runs by Charlie Neal in the fifth and pinch hitter Chuck Essegian and Neal (again) in the seventh put the Dodgers ahead by two. Rookie reliever Larry Sherry gave up a third Chicago run in the eighth on Al Smith's double, but a second runner was nailed at the plate, and Sherry set down the side in the ninth to save Podres's win.

When the Series moved to Los Angeles' cavernous Coliseum for the West Coast's first World Series games ever, fans turned out in record numbers, setting a new Series mark in each of the next three games. Dodger starter Don Drysdale yielded 11 hits and four walks in Game Three, but the only run scored against him came on a double-play after Larry Sherry had relieved him with two men on in the eighth. As Los Angeles had already scored twice, and added a third run in their half of the eighth, Drysdale emerged with the win and Sherry with his second save. In Game Four, the Sox's Sherm Lollar's three-run homer had tied the score by the time Sherry relieved Dodger starter Roger Craig in the eighth, so Gil Hodges's solo homer in the last of the eighth gave Sherry the win this time—and Los Angeles a 3–1 Series advantage.

Chicago's Bob Shaw dueled Dodger Sandy Koufax through seven innings of Game Five before 92,706 spectators (still a Series high). The Sox scored only once off Koufax, but one run was enough for their second win as a pair of Sox relievers continued Shaw's shutout through the final two innings.

Back in Chicago for Game Six, the Dodgers unloaded on Early Wynn and Dick Donovan for eight runs in the third and fourth innings. Ted Kluszewski's

three-run homer in the last of the fourth led to Larry Sherry's fourth relief appearance—and his second Series win, as he held the Sox scoreless the rest of the game to bring the world championship to the West Coast for the first time.

Los Angeles Dodgers (NL), 4; Chicago White Sox (AL), 2

LA (N)

PLAYER/POS	AVG	G	AB	R	H	2B	3B	HR	RB	BB	SO	SB
Chuck Churn, p	.000	1	0	0	0	0	0	0	0	0	0	0
Roger Craig, p	.000	2	3	0	0	0	0	0	0	0	2	0
Don Demeter, of	.250	6	12	2	3	0	0	0	0	1	3	0
Don Drysdale, p	.000	1	2	0	0	0	0	0	0	0	0	0
Chuck Essegian, ph	.667	4	3	2	2	0	0	2	2	1	1	0
Ron Fairly, of-4	.000	6	3	0	0	0	0	0	0	0	1	0
Carl Furillo, of-1	.250	4	4	0	1	0	0	0	2	0	1	0
Jim Gilliam, 3b	.240	6	25	2	6	0	0	0	0	2	2	2
Gil Hodges, 1b	.391	6	23	2	9	0	1	1	2	1	2	0
Johnny Klippstein, p	.000	1	0	0	0	0	0	0	0	0	0	0
Sandy Koufax, p	.000	2	2	0	0	0	0	0	0	0	1	0
Clem Labine, p	.000	1	0	0	0	0	0	0	0	0	0	0
Norm Larker, of	.188	6	16	2	3	0	0	0	0	2	3	0
Wally Moon, of	.261	6	23	3	6	0	0	1	2	2	2	1
Charlie Neal, 2b	.370	6	27	4	10	2	0	2	6	0	1	1
Joe Pignatano, c	.000	1	0	0	0	0	0	0	0	0	0	0
Johnny Podres, p-2	.500	3	4	1	2	1	0	0	1	0	0	0
Rip Repulski, of	.000	1	0	0	0	0	0	0	0	1	0	0
Johnny Roseboro, c	.095	6	21	0	2	0	0	0	1	0	2	0
Larry Sherry, p-4	.500	5	4	0	2	0	0	0	0	0	1	0
Duke Snider, of-3	.200	4	10	1	2	0	0	1	2	2	0	0
Stan Williams, p	.000	1	0	0	0	0	0	0	0	0	0	0
Maury Wills, ss	.250	6	20	2	5	0	0	0	1	0	3	1
Don Zimmer, ss	.000	1	1	0	0	0	0	0	0	0	0	0
TOTAL	.261		203	21	53	3	1	7	19	12	27	5

PITCHER	W	L	ERA	G	GS	CG	SV	SHO	IP	H	ER	BB	SO
Chuck Churn	0	0	27.00	1	0	0	0	0	0.2	5	2	0	0
Roger Craig	0	1	8.68	2	2	0	0	0	9.1	15	9	5	8
Don Drysdale	1	0	1.29	1	1	0	0	0	7.0	11	1	4	5
Johnny Klippstein	0	0	0.00	1	0	0	0	0	2.0	1	0	0	2
Sandy Koufax	0	1	1.00	2	1	0	0	0	9.0	5	1	1	7
Clem Labine	0	0	0.00	1	0	0	0	0	1.0	0	0	0	1
Johnny Podres	1	0	4.82	2	2	0	0	0	9.1	7	5	6	4
Larry Sherry	2	0	0.71	4	0	0	2	0	12.2	8	1	2	5
Stan Williams	0	0	0.00	1	0	0	0	0	2.0	0	0	2	1
TOTAL	4	2	3.23	15	6	0	2	0	53.0	52	19	20	33

CHI (A)

PLAYER/POS	AVG	G	AB	R	H	2B	3B	HR	RB	BB	SO	SB
Luis Aparicio, ss	.308	6	26	1	8	1	0	0	0	2	3	1
Norm Cash, ph	.000	4	4	0	0	0	0	0	0	0	2	0
Dick Donovan, p	.333	3	3	0	1	0	0	0	0	0	1	0
Sammy Esposito, 3b	.000	2	2	0	0	0	0	0	0	0	1	0
Nellie Fox, 2b	.375	6	24	4	9	3	0	0	0	4	1	0
Billy Goodman, 3b	.231	5	13	1	3	0	0	0	1	0	5	0
Ted Kluszewski, 1b	.391	6	23	5	9	1	0	3	10	2	0	0
Jim Landis, of	.292	6	24	6	7	0	0	0	1	1	7	1
Sherm Lollar, c	.227	6	22	3	5	0	0	1	5	1	3	0
Turk Lown, p	.000	3	0	0	0	0	0	0	0	0	0	0
Jim Mc Anany, of	.000	3	5	0	0	0	0	0	0	1	0	0
Ray Moore, p	.000	1	0	0	0	0	0	0	0	0	0	0
Bubba Phillips, 3b-3,of-1	.300	3	10	0	3	1	0	0	0	0	0	0
Billy Pierce, p	.000	3	0	0	0	0	0	0	0	0	0	0
Jim Rivera, of	.000	5	11	1	0	0	0	0	0	3	1	0
Johnny Romano, ph	.000	1	1	0	0	0	0	0	0	0	0	0
Bob Shaw, p	.250	2	4	0	1	0	0	0	0	0	2	0
Al Smith, of	.250	6	20	1	5	3	0	0	1	4	4	0
Gerry Staley, p	.000	4	1	0	0	0	0	0	0	1	1	0
Earl Torgeson, 1b-1	.000	3	1	1	0	0	0	0	0	1	0	0
Early Wynn, p	.200	3	5	0	1	1	0	0	1	0	2	0
TOTAL	.261		199	23	52	10	0	4	19	20	33	2

PITCHER	W	L	ERA	G	GS	CG	SV	SHO	IP	H	ER	BB	SO
Dick Donovan	0	1	5.40	3	1	0	1	0	8.1	4	5	3	5
Turk Lown	0	0	0.00	3	0	0	0	0	3.1	2	0	1	3
Ray Moore	0	0	9.00	1	0	0	0	0	1.0	1	1	0	1
Billy Pierce	0	0	0.00	3	0	0	0	0	4.0	2	0	2	3
Bob Shaw	1	1	2.57	2	2	0	0	0	14.0	17	4	2	2
Gerry Staley	0	1	2.16	4	0	0	1	0	8.1	8	2	0	3
Early Wynn	1	1	5.54	3	3	0	0	0	13.0	19	8	4	10
TOTAL	2	4	3.46	19	6	0	2	0	52.0	53	20	12	27

GAME 1 AT CHI OCT 1

LA	000	000	000	0	8	3
CHI	207	200	00X	11	11	0

Pitchers: CRAIG, Churn (3), Labine (4), Koufax (5), Klippstein (7) vs WYNN, Staley (8)
Home Runs: Kluszewski-CHI (2)
Attendance: 48,013

GAME 2 AT CHI OCT 2

LA	000	010	300	4	9	1
CHI	200	000	010	3	8	0

Pitchers: PODRES, Sherry (7) vs SHAW, Lown (7)
Home Runs: Neal-LA (2), Essegian-LA
Attendance: 47,368

GAME 3 AT LA OCT 4

CHI	000	000	010	1	12	0
LA	000	000	21X	3	5	0

Pitchers: DONOVAN, Staley (7) vs DRYSDALE, Sherry (8)
Attendance: 92,394

GAME 4 AT LA OCT 5

CHI	000	000	400	4	10	3
LA	004	000	01X	5	9	0

Pitchers: Wynn, Lown (3), Pierce (4), STALEY (7) vs Craig, SHERRY (8)
Home Runs: Lollar-CHI, Hodges-LA
Attendance: 92,650

GAME 5 AT LA OCT 6

CHI	000	100	000	1	5	0
LA	000	000	000	0	9	0

Pitchers: SHAW, Pierce (7), Donovan (8) VS KOUFAX, Williams (8)
Attendance: 92,706

GAME 6 AT CHI OCT 8

LA	002	600	001	9	13	0
CHI	000	300	000	3	6	1

Pitchers: Podres, SHERRY (4) vs WYNN, Donovan (4), Staley (5), Pierce (8), Moore (9)
Home Runs: Snider-LA, Moon-LA, Kluszewski-CHI, Essegian-LA
Attendance: 47,653

Through six games and 8½ innings of the seventh, the Yankees had outscored the Pirates by 29 runs. But as Pirate second baseman Bill Mazeroski stepped to the plate to open the last of the ninth, the Series was even at three games apiece, and Game Seven was tied 9–9. The stage was set for Mazeroski to fulfill that ultimate baseball fantasy, and he did, on pitcher Ralph Terry's second pitch.

Yankee Roger Maris opened the Series scoring with a solo homer in the first inning of Game One, and Elston Howard added two more Yankee runs with a homer in the ninth. But between the home runs New York scored only one run to the Pirates' six (including a two-run homer by Mazeroski in the fourth).

The Yankees avenged their first-game loss with a blowout in Game Two—their first of three. Pittsburgh hit safely 13 times, but scored only three runs. New York, though, turned 19 hits (and a Pirate error) into 16 runs—five of them driven in by Mickey Mantle's two home runs. Continuing their assault in New York the next day, the Bronx Bombers scored six runs in the first inning and four in the fourth as Whitey Ford blanked the Pirates on four hits. Mantle homered again, and second baseman Bobby Richardson drove in a Series single-game record six runs with a grand slam and a single.

Pirate ace Vernon Law—the winner of Game One—started Game Four and, with relief help once again from Roy Face, held the Yankees to two runs to even the Series. Law's bat proved crucial, too, as he doubled in Pittsburgh's first run and scored the third in a three-run fifth that provided all the Pirate scoring. In Game Five, the Pirates' Mazeroski doubled in what proved the two decisive runs in a three-run second as Harvey Haddix and Roy Face (who recorded his third save of the Series) duplicated the previous day's achievement of limiting New York to two runs.

But once again the Yankees came back. Bobby Richardson drove in three of New York's 12 runs with two triples to establish a new Series record of 12 RBIs as the Yankees, behind Whitey Ford's second shutout, sent the Series into a seventh game.

Home runs dominated the finale. Rocky Nelson's two-run shot in the first opened the scoring, and Yankee homers by Bill Skowron in the fifth and Yogi Berra in the sixth contributed four of the five runs that put New York ahead 5–4. Pirate Hal Smith's three-run homer in the bottom of the eighth restored the lead to Pittsburgh, 9–7, and after the Yankees had

Pittsburgh Pirates (NL), 4;
New York Yankees (AL), 3

PIT (N)

PLAYER/POS	AVG	G	AB	R	H	2B	3B	HR	RB	BB	SO	SB
Gene Baker, ph	.000	3	3	0	0	0	0	0	0	0	1	0
Smoky Burgess, c	.333	5	18	2	6	1	0	0	0	2	1	0
Tom Cheney, p	.000	3	0	0	0	0	0	0	0	0	0	0
Joe Christopher, ph	.000	3	0	2	0	0	0	0	0	0	0	0
Gino Cimoli, of-6	.250	7	20	4	5	0	0	0	1	2	4	0
Roberto Clemente, of	.310	7	29	1	9	0	0	0	3	0	4	0
Roy Face, p	.000	4	3	0	0	0	0	0	0	0	2	0
Bob Friend, p	.000	3	1	0	0	0	0	0	0	0	0	0
Joe Gibbon, p	.000	2	0	0	0	0	0	0	0	0	0	0
Fred Green, p	.000	3	1	0	0	0	0	0	0	0	0	0
Dick Groat, ss	.214	7	28	3	6	2	0	0	2	0	1	0
Harvey Haddix, p	.333	2	3	0	1	0	0	0	0	0	1	0
Don Hoak, 3b	.217	7	23	3	5	2	0	0	3	4	1	0
Clem Labine, p	.000	3	0	0	0	0	0	0	0	0	0	0
Vern Law, p	.333	3	6	1	2	1	0	0	1	0	1	0
Bill Mazeroski, 2b	.320	7	25	4	8	2	0	2	5	0	3	0
Vinegar Bend Mizell, p	.000	2	0	0	0	0	0	0	0	0	0	0
Rocky Nelson, 1b-3	.333	4	9	2	3	0	0	1	2	1	1	0
Bob Oldis, c	.000	2	0	0	0	0	0	0	0	0	0	0
Dick Schofield, ss-2	.333	3	3	0	1	0	0	0	0	0	1	0
Bob Skinner, of	.200	2	5	2	1	0	0	0	1	1	0	1
Hal Smith, c	.375	3	8	1	3	0	0	1	3	0	0	0
Dick Stuart, 1b	.150	5	20	0	3	0	0	0	0	0	3	0
Bill Virdon, of	.241	7	29	2	7	3	0	0	5	1	3	1
George Witt, p	.000	3	0	0	0	0	0	0	0	0	0	0
TOTAL	.256		234	27	60	11	0	4	26	12	26	2

PITCHER	W	L	ERA	G	GS	CG	SV	SHO	IP	H	ER	BB	SO
Tom Cheney	0	0	4.50	3	0	0	0	0	4.0	4	2	1	6
Roy Face	0	0	5.23	4	0	0	3	0	10.1	9	6	2	4
Bob Friend	0	2	13.50	3	2	0	0	0	6.0	13	9	3	7
Joe Gibbon	0	0	9.00	2	0	0	0	0	3.0	4	3	1	2
Fred Green	0	0	22.50	3	0	0	0	0	4.0	11	10	1	3
Harvey Haddix	2	0	2.45	2	1	0	0	0	7.1	6	2	2	6
Clem Labine	0	0	13.50	3	0	0	0	0	4.0	13	6	1	2
Vern Law	2	0	3.44	3	3	0	0	0	18.1	22	7	3	8
Vinegar Bend Mizell	0	1	15.43	2	1	0	0	0	2.1	4	4	2	1
George Witt	0	0	0.00	3	0	0	0	0	2.2	5	0	2	1
TOTAL	4	3	7.11	28	7	0	3	0	62.0	91	49	18	40

NY (A)

PLAYER/POS	AVG	G	AB	R	H	2B	3B	HR	RB	BB	SO	SB
Luis Arroyo, p	.000	1	1	0	0	0	0	0	0	0	0	0
Yogi Berra, of-4,c-3	.318	7	22	6	7	0	0	1	8	2	0	0
Johnny Blanchard, c-2	.455	5	11	2	5	2	0	0	2	0	0	0
Clete Boyer, 3b-4,ss-1	.250	4	12	1	3	2	1	0	1	0	1	0
Bob Cerv, of-3	.357	4	14	1	5	0	0	0	0	0	3	0
Jim Coates, p	.000	3	1	0	0	0	0	0	0	0	1	0
Joe De Maestri, ss-3	.500	4	2	1	1	0	0	0	0	0	1	0
Art Ditmar, p	.000	2	0	0	0	0	0	0	0	0	0	0
Ryne Duren, p	.000	2	0	0	0	0	0	0	0	0	0	0
Whitey Ford, p	.250	2	8	1	2	0	0	0	0	2	2	0
Eli Grba, pr	.000	2	0	0	0	0	0	0	0	0	0	0
Elston Howard, c-4	.462	5	13	4	6	1	1	1	4	1	4	0
Tony Kubek, ss-7,of-2	.333	7	30	6	10	1	0	0	3	2	2	0
Dale Long, pr	.333	3	3	0	1	0	0	0	0	0	0	0
Hector Lopez, of-1	.429	3	7	0	3	0	0	0	0	0	0	0
Duke Maas, p	.000	1	0	0	0	0	0	0	0	0	0	0
Mickey Mantle, of	.400	7	25	8	10	1	0	3	11	8	9	0
Roger Maris, of	.267	7	30	6	8	1	0	2	2	2	4	0
Gil Mc Dougald, 3b	.278	6	18	4	5	1	0	0	2	3	3	0
Bobby Richardson, 2b	.367	7	30	8	11	2	2	1	12	1	1	0
Bobby Shantz, p	.333	3	3	0	1	0	0	0	0	0	0	0
Bill Skowron, 1b	.375	7	32	7	12	0	0	2	6	0	6	0
Bill Stafford, p	.000	2	1	0	0	0	0	0	0	0	1	0
Ralph Terry, p	.000	2	2	0	0	0	0	0	0	0	1	0
Bob Turley, p	.250	2	4	0	1	0	0	0	0	1	0	0
TOTAL	.338		269	55	91	13	4	10	54	18	40	0

PITCHER	W	L	ERA	G	GS	CG	SV	SHO	IP	H	ER	BB	SO
Luis Arroyo	0	0	13.50	1	0	0	0	0	0.2	2	1	0	1
Jim Coates	0	0	5.68	3	0	0	0	0	6.1	6	4	1	3
Art Ditmar	0	2	21.60	2	2	0	0	0	1.2	6	4	1	0
Ryne Duren	0	0	2.25	2	0	0	0	0	4.0	2	1	1	5
Whitey Ford	2	0	0.00	2	2	2	0	2	18.0	11	0	2	8
Duke Maas	0	0	4.50	1	0	0	0	0	2.0	2	1	0	1
Bobby Shantz	0	0	4.26	3	0	0	1	0	6.1	4	3	1	1
Bill Stafford	0	0	1.50	2	0	0	0	0	6.0	5	1	1	2
Ralph Terry	0	2	5.40	2	1	0	0	0	6.2	7	4	1	5
Bob Turley	1	0	4.82	2	2	0	0	0	9.1	15	5	4	0
TOTAL	3	4	3.54	20	7	2	1	2	61.0	60	24	12	26

tied the game in the top of the ninth (on three singles and a ground out), Mazeroski's immortal shot over the wall in left gave Pittsburgh its first world championship in thirty-five years.

GAME 1 AT PIT OCT 5

NY	100	100	002	4	13	2
PIT	300	201	00X	6	8	0

Pitchers: DITMAR, Coates (1), Maas (5), Duren (7) vs LAW, Face (8)
Home Runs: Maris-NY, Mazeroski-PIT, Howard-NY
Attendance: 36,676

GAME 2 AT PIT OCT 6

NY	002	127	301	16	19	1
PIT	000	100	002	3	13	1

Pitchers: TURLEY, Shantz (9) vs FRIEND, Green (5), Labine (6), WITT (6), Gibbon (7), Cheney (9)
Home Runs: Mantle-NY (2)
Attendance: 37,308

GAME 3 AT NY OCT 8

PIT	000	000	000	0	4	0
NY	600	400	00X	10	16	1

Pitchers: MIZELL, Labine (1), Green (1), Witt (4), Cheney (6), Gibbon (8) vs FORD
Home Runs: Richardson-NY, Mantle-NY
Attendance: 70,001

GAME 4 AT NY OCT 9

PIT	000	030	000	3	7	0
NY	000	100	100	2	8	0

Pitchers: LAW, Face (7) vs TERRY, Shantz (7), Coates (8)
Home Runs: Skowron-NY
Attendance: 67,812

GAME 5 AT NY OCT 10

PIT	031	000	001	5	10	2
NY	011	000	000	2	5	2

Pitchers: HADDIX, Face (7) vs DITMAR, Arroyo (2), Stafford (3), Duren (8)
Home Runs: Maris-NY
Attendance: 62,753

GAME 6 AT PIT OCT 12

NY	015	002	220	12	17	1
PIT	000	000	000	0	7	1

Pitchers: FORD vs FRIEND, Cheney (3), Mizell (4), Green (6), Labine (6), Witt (9)
Attendance: 38,580

GAME 7 AT PIT OCT 13

NY	000	014	022	9	13	1
PIT	220	000	051	10	11	0

Pitchers: Turley, Stafford (2), Shantz (3), Coates (8), TERRY (8) vs Law, Face (6), Friend (9), HADDIX (9)
Home Runs: Nelson-PIT, Skowron-NY, Berra-NY, Smith-PIT, Mazeroski-PIT
Attendance: 36,683

Slugger Mickey Mantle sat out most of the Series with a thigh infection, but rookie manager Ralph Houk enjoyed an otherwise splendid finish to a splendid season as his Yankees mauled the Reds, 27 runs to 13. Yankee ace Whitey Ford, coming off one of his finest seasons (25–4), carried his mound mastery into the Series opener, holding Cincinnati to two singles and a walk as he hurled his third straight World Series shutout. New York recorded only six hits, but two of them were home runs by Elston Howard and Bill Skowron.

Gordy Coleman's two-run homer the next day in the top of the fourth inning broke Cincinnati's scoring drought and gave the Reds a 2–0 lead. Yogi Berra tied the score half an inning later with a two-run blast for New York, but that was all they would get. Red starter Joey Jay blanked the Yankees the rest of the way as his teammates put across four more runs to even the Series. Bob Purkey pitched for the Reds in Game Three and blanked New York on one hit through the first six innings, taking a 1–0 lead into the top of the seventh. A pair of Yankee singles sandwiched around a passed ball evened the score, but the Reds regained the lead with a run in the last of the seventh. But Yankee pinch hitter Johnny Blanchard homered to retie the game in the eighth and—while Yankee relief ace Luis Arroyo stopped the Reds through the final two innings—Roger Maris hit his sixty-second home run of the year to win the game and regain the Series lead for New York.

Cincinnati never again threatened. In Game Four, Whitey Ford held the Reds to four harmless singles until he was removed in the sixth because of an ankle injury. (In the third inning he passed Babe Ruth's World Series record of 29⅔ consecutive scoreless innings.) Reliever Jim Coates continued Ford's shutout as the Yankees scored seven runs for the decisive win. The fifth and final game also was no contest. Cincinnati did score five runs—three on Frank Robinson's third-inning home run and two on Wally Post's shot in the fifth. But the Yankees ran through eight Red pitchers, scoring 13 times. Seven of their 15 hits went for extra bases, including Johnny Blanchard's second home run of the Series, and a triple and homer by utility outfielder Hector Lopez.

New York Yankees (AL), 4;
Cincinnati Reds (NL), 1

NY (A)

PLAYER/POS	AVG	G	AB	R	H	2B	3B	HR	RB	BB	SO	SB
Luis Arroyo, p	.000	2	0	0	0	0	0	0	0	0	0	0
Yogi Berra, of	.273	4	11	2	3	0	0	1	3	5	1	0
Johnny Blanchard, of-2	.400	4	10	4	4	1	0	2	3	2	0	0
Clete Boyer, 3b	.267	5	15	0	4	2	0	0	3	4	0	0
Jim Coates, p	.000	1	1	0	0	0	0	0	0	0	1	0
Buddy Daley, p	.000	2	1	0	0	0	0	0	0	1	0	0
Whitey Ford, p	.000	2	5	1	0	0	0	0	0	1	0	0
Billy Gardner, ph	.000	1	1	0	0	0	0	0	0	0	0	0
Elston Howard, c	.250	5	20	5	5	3	0	1	1	2	3	0
Tony Kubek, ss	.227	5	22	3	5	0	0	0	1	1	4	0
Hector Lopez, of-3	.333	4	9	3	3	0	1	1	7	2	3	0
Mickey Mantle, of	.167	2	6	0	1	0	0	0	0	0	2	0
Roger Maris, of	.105	5	19	4	2	1	0	1	2	4	6	0
Jack Reed, of	.000	3	0	0	0	0	0	0	0	0	0	0
Bobby Richardson, 2b	.391	5	23	2	9	1	0	0	0	0	0	1
Bill Skowron, 1b	.353	5	17	3	6	0	0	1	5	3	4	0
Bill Stafford, p	.000	1	2	0	0	0	0	0	0	0	0	0
Ralph Terry, p	.000	2	3	0	0	0	0	0	0	0	1	0
TOTAL	.255		165	27	42	8	1	7	26	24	25	1

PITCHER	W	L	ERA	G	GS	CG	SV	SHO	IP	H	ER	BB	SO
Luis Arroyo	1	0	2.25	2	0	0	0	0	4.0	4	1	2	3
Jim Coates	0	0	0.00	1	0	0	1	0	4.0	1	0	1	2
Buddy Daley	1	0	0.00	2	0	0	0	0	7.0	5	0	0	3
Whitey Ford	2	0	0.00	2	2	1	0	1	14.0	6	0	1	7
Bill Stafford	0	0	2.70	1	1	0	0	0	6.2	7	2	2	5
Ralph Terry	0	1	4.82	2	2	0	0	0	9.1	12	5	2	7
TOTAL	4	1	1.60	10	5	1	1	1	45.0	35	8	8	27

CIN (N)

PLAYER/POS	AVG	G	AB	R	H	2B	3B	HR	RB	BB	SO	SB
Gus Bell, ph	.000	3	3	0	0	0	0	0	0	0	0	0
Don Blasingame, 2b	.143	3	7	1	1	0	0	0	0	0	3	0
Jim Brosnan, p	.000	3	0	0	0	0	0	0	0	0	0	0
Leo Cardenas, ph	.333	3	3	0	1	1	0	0	0	0	1	0
Elio Chacon, 2b-3	.250	4	12	2	3	0	0	0	0	1	2	0
Gordie Coleman, 1b	.250	5	20	2	5	0	0	1	2	0	1	0
Johnny Edwards, c	.364	3	11	1	4	2	0	0	2	0	0	0
Gene Freese, 3b	.063	5	16	0	1	1	0	0	0	3	4	0
Dick Gernert, ph	.000	4	4	0	0	0	0	0	0	0	1	0
Bill Henry, p	.000	2	0	0	0	0	0	0	0	0	0	0
Ken Hunt, p	.000	1	0	0	0	0	0	0	0	0	0	0
Joey Jay, p	.000	2	4	0	0	0	0	0	0	0	2	0
Darrell Johnson, c	.500	2	4	0	2	0	0	0	0	0	0	0
Ken Johnson, p	.000	1	0	0	0	0	0	0	0	0	0	0
Sherman Jones, p	.000	1	0	0	0	0	0	0	0	0	0	0
Eddie Kasko, ss	.318	5	22	1	7	0	0	0	1	0	2	0
Jerry Lynch, ph	.000	4	3	0	0	0	0	0	0	1	1	0
Jim Maloney, p	.000	1	0	0	0	0	0	0	0	0	0	0
Jim O'Toole, p	.000	2	3	0	0	0	0	0	0	0	1	0
Vada Pinson, of	.091	5	22	0	2	1	0	0	0	0	1	0
Wally Post, of	.333	5	18	3	6	1	0	1	2	0	1	0
Bob Purkey, p	.000	2	3	0	0	0	0	0	0	0	3	0
Frank Robinson, of	.200	5	15	3	3	2	0	1	4	3	4	0
Jerry Zimmerman, c	.000	2	0	0	0	0	0	0	0	0	0	0
TOTAL	.206		170	13	35	8	0	3	11	8	27	0

PITCHER	W	L	ERA	G	GS	CG	SV	SHO	IP	H	ER	BB	SO
Jim Brosnan	0	0	7.50	3	0	0	0	0	6.0	9	5	4	5
Bill Henry	0	0	19.29	2	0	0	0	0	2.1	4	5	2	3
Ken Hunt	0	0	0.00	1	0	0	0	0	1.0	0	0	1	1
Joey Jay	1	1	5.59	2	2	1	0	0	9.2	8	6	6	6
Ken Johnson	0	0	0.00	1	0	0	0	0	0.2	0	0	0	0
Sherman Jones	0	0	0.00	1	0	0	0	0	0.2	0	0	0	0
Jim Maloney	0	0	27.00	1	0	0	0	0	0.2	4	2	1	1
Jim O'Toole	0	2	3.00	2	2	0	0	0	12.0	11	4	7	4
Bob Purkey	0	1	1.64	2	1	1	0	0	11.0	6	2	3	5
TOTAL	1	4	4.91	15	5	2	0	0	44.0	42	24	24	25

GAME 1 AT NY OCT 4

CIN	000	000	000	0	2	0
NY	000	101	00X	2	6	0

Pitchers: O'TOOLE, Brosnan (8) vs FORD
Home Runs: Howard-NY, Skowron-NY
Attendance: 62,397

GAME 2 AT NY OCT 5

CIN	000	211	020	6	9	0
NY	000	200	000	2	4	3

Pitchers: JAY vs TERRY, Arroyo (8)
Home Runs: Coleman-CIN, Berra-NY
Attendance: 63,083

GAME 3 AT CIN OCT 7

NY	000	000	111	3	6	1
CIN	001	000	100	2	8	0

Pitchers: Stafford, Daley (7), ARROYO (8) vs PURKEY
Home Runs: Blanchard-NY, Maris-NY
Attendance: 32,589

GAME 4 AT CIN OCT 8

NY	000	112	300	7	11	0
CIN	000	000	000	0	5	1

Pitchers: FORD, Coates (6) vs O'TOOLE, Brosnan (6), Henry (9)
Attendance: 32,589

GAME 5 AT CIN OCT 9

NY	510	502	000	13	15	1
CIN	003	020	000	5	11	3

Pitchers: Terry, DALEY (3) vs JAY, Maloney (1), K.Johnson (2), Henry (3), Jones (4), Purkey (5), Brosnan (7), Hunt (9)
Home Runs: Blanchard-NY, Robinson-CIN, Lopez-NY, Post-CIN
Attendance: 32,589

After edging Los Angeles for the pennant in a three-game playoff to break a regular-season tie, San Francisco battled to the final out of Game Seven before falling to New York in the World Series. The teams alternated wins throughout the Series. In the opener Roger Maris doubled two runs home for a quick Yankee lead. Whitey Ford gave up a run in the second (ending his record streak for consecutive scoreless World Series innings pitched at 33⅔) and a tying run an inning later. But he blanked the Giants after that, and won the game on Clete Boyer's homer in the seventh.

Giant Jack Sanford blanked the Yankees on three hits in Game Two, but in Game Three Yankee Bill Stafford restored the Series edge to New York with a four-hit 3–2 win (a shutout until Giant Ed Bailey's ninth-inning home run). Both clubs hit safely nine times in Game Four. But one of the Giants' hits was Chuck Hiller's tie-breaking grand slam in the seventh—more than enough for a Giant win and another Series tie. In Game Five Sanford brought a three-hit 2–2 tie into the last of the eighth. But after he had notched his tenth strikeout, two singles and Tom Tresh's home run drove him out and gave Yankee pitcher Ralph Terry all the margin he needed to avenge his second-game loss to Sanford, and put the Yankees ahead in the Series for the third time.

When play resumed in San Francisco after several days of rain, Billy Pierce held New York to just three hits. One was Roger Maris's solo homer in the fifth, but Pierce's Giants unloaded on Whitey Ford for five runs, driving Ford out and keeping Giant hopes alive.

The finale pitted Terry against Sanford for the third time. Both pitched effectively, but Terry carried a 1–0 lead into the last of the ninth. Pinch hitter Matty Alou led off with a bunt single, but Terry fanned the next two batters. Then Willie Mays doubled to right, but Roger Maris's slick fielding stopped Alou at third. As Terry faced Willie McCovey (who had homered off him in Game Two), he pondered the home run he had given up to Bill Mazeroski two years earlier to lose the 1960 World Series to Pittsburgh. McCovey lined Terry's third pitch toward right—but right at second baseman Bobby Richardson, who grabbed it for the Yankees' twentieth world title. It would be fifteen years before they saw another.

New York Yankees (AL), 4; San Francisco Giants (NL) 3

NY (A)

PLAYER/POS	AVG	G	AB	R	H	2B	3B	HR	RB	BB	SO	SB
Yogi Berra, c-1	.000	2	2	0	0	0	0	0	0	0	2	0
Johnny Blanchard, ph	.000	1	1	0	0	0	0	0	0	0	1	0
Clete Boyer, 3b	.318	7	22	2	7	1	0	1	4	1	3	0
Marshall Bridges, p	.000	2	0	0	0	0	0	0	0	0	0	0
Jim Coates, p	.000	2	0	0	0	0	0	0	0	0	0	0
Buddy Daley, p	.000	1	0	0	0	0	0	0	0	0	0	0
Whitey Ford, p	.000	3	7	0	0	0	0	0	0	0	1	0
Elston Howard, c	.143	6	21	1	3	1	0	0	1	1	4	0
Tony Kubek, ss	.276	7	29	2	8	1	0	0	1	1	3	0
Dale Long, 1b	.200	2	5	0	1	0	0	0	1	0	1	0
Hector Lopez, ph	.000	2	2	0	0	0	0	0	0	0	0	0
Mickey Mantle, of	.120	7	25	2	3	1	0	0	0	4	5	2
Roger Maris, of	.174	7	23	4	4	1	0	1	5	5	2	0
Bobby Richardson, 2b	.148	7	27	3	4	0	0	0	0	3	1	0
Bill Skowron, 1b	.222	6	18	1	4	0	1	0	1	1	5	0
Bill Stafford, p	.000	1	3	0	0	0	0	0	0	0	1	0
Ralph Terry, p	.125	3	8	0	1	0	0	0	0	0	6	0
Tom Tresh, of	.321	7	28	5	9	1	0	1	4	1	4	2
TOTAL	.199		221	20	44	6	1	3	17	21	39	4

PITCHER	W	L	ERA	G	GS	CG	SV	SHO	IP	H	ER	BB	SO
Marshall Bridges	0	0	4.91	2	0	0	0	0	3.2	4	2	2	3
Jim Coates	0	1	6.75	2	0	0	0	0	2.2	1	2	1	3
Buddy Daley	0	0	0.00	1	0	0	0	0	1.0	1	0	1	0
Whitey Ford	1	1	4.12	3	3	1	0	0	19.2	24	9	4	12
Bill Stafford	1	0	2.00	1	1	1	0	0	9.0	4	2	2	5
Ralph Terry	2	1	1.80	3	3	2	0	1	25.0	17	5	2	16
TOTAL	4	3	2.95	12	7	4	0	1	61.0	51	20	12	39

SF (N)

PLAYER/POS	AVG	G	AB	R	H	2B	3B	HR	RB	BB	SO	SB
Felipe Alou, of	.269	7	26	2	7	1	1	0	1	1	4	0
Matty Alou, of-4	.333	6	12	2	4	1	0	0	1	0	1	0
Ed Bailey, c-3	.071	6	14	1	1	0	0	1	2	0	3	0
Bobby Bolin, p	.000	2	0	0	0	0	0	0	0	0	0	0
Ernie Bowman, ss-1	.000	2	1	1	0	0	0	0	0	0	0	0
Orlando Cepeda, 1b	.158	5	19	1	3	1	0	0	2	0	4	0
Jim Davenport, 3b	.136	7	22	1	3	1	0	0	1	4	7	0
Tom Haller, c	.286	4	14	1	4	1	0	1	3	0	2	0
Chuck Hiller, 2b	.269	7	26	4	7	3	0	1	5	3	4	0
Harvey Kuenn, of	.083	4	12	1	1	0	0	0	0	1	1	0
Don Larsen, p	.000	3	0	0	0	0	0	0	0	0	0	0
Juan Marichal, p	.000	1	2	0	0	0	0	0	0	0	1	0
Willie Mays, of	.250	7	28	3	7	2	0	0	1	1	5	1
Willie Mc Covey, 1b-2,of-2	.200	4	15	2	3	0	1	1	1	1	3	0
Stu Miller, p	.000	2	0	0	0	0	0	0	0	0	0	0
Bob Nieman, ph	.000	1	0	0	0	0	0	0	0	1	0	0
Billy O'Dell, p	.333	3	3	0	1	0	0	0	0	0	0	0
John Orsino, c	.000	1	1	0	0	0	0	0	0	0	0	0
Jose Pagan, ss	.368	7	19	2	7	0	0	1	2	0	1	0
Billy Pierce, p	.000	2	5	0	0	0	0	0	0	0	1	0
Jack Sanford, p	.429	3	7	0	3	0	0	0	0	0	2	0
TOTAL	.226		226	21	51	10	2	5	19	12	39	1

PITCHER	W	L	ERA	G	GS	CG	SV	SHO	IP	H	ER	BB	SO
Bobby Bolin	0	0	6.75	2	0	0	0	0	2.2	4	2	2	2
Don Larsen	1	0	3.86	3	0	0	0	0	2.1	1	1	2	0
Juan Marichal	0	0	0.00	1	1	0	0	0	4.0	2	0	2	4
Stu Miller	0	0	0.00	2	0	0	0	0	1.1	1	0	2	0
Billy O'Dell	0	1	4.38	3	1	0	1	0	12.1	12	6	3	9
Billy Pierce	1	1	2.40	2	2	1	0	0	15.0	8	4	2	5
Jack Sanford	1	2	1.93	3	3	1	0	1	23.1	16	5	8	19
TOTAL	3	4	2.66	16	7	2	1	1	61.0	44	18	21	39

GAME 1 AT SF OCT 4

NY	200 000 121	6 11 0
SF	011 000 000	2 10 0

Pitchers: FORD vs O'DELL, Larsen (7), Miller (9)
Home Runs: Boyer-NY
Attendance: 43,852

GAME 2 AT SF OCT 5

NY	000 000 000	0 3 1
SF	100 000 10X	2 6 0

Pitchers: TERRY, Daley (8) vs SANFORD
Home Runs: McCovey-SF
Attendance: 43,910

GAME 3 AT NY OCT 7

SF	000 000 002	2 4 3
NY	000 000 30X	3 5 1

Pitchers: PIERCE, Larsen (7), Bolin (8) vs STAFFORD
Home Runs: Bailey-SF
Attendance: 71,434

GAME 4 AT NY OCT 8

SF	020 000 401	7 9 1
NY	000 002 001	3 9 1

Pitchers: Marichal, Bolin (5), LARSEN (6), O'Dell (7) vs Ford, COATES (7), Bridges (7)
Home Runs: Haller-SF, Hiller-SF
Attendance: 66,607

GAME 5 AT NY OCT 10

SF	001 010 001	3 8 2
NY	000 101 03X	5 6 0

Pitchers: SANFORD, Miller (8) vs TERRY
Home Runs: Pagan-SF, Tresh-NY
Attendance: 63,165

GAME 6 AT SF OCT 15

NY	000 010 010	2 3 2
SF	000 320 00X	5 10 1

Pitchers: FORD, Coates (5), Bridges (8) vs PIERCE
Home Runs: Maris-NY
Attendance: 43,948

GAME 7 AT SF OCT 16

NY	000 100 000	1 7 0
SF	000 000 000	0 4 1

Pitchers: TERRY vs SANFORD, O'Dell (8)
Attendance: 43,948

The Yankees won the American League pennant by 10½ games, but in the Series they were overwhelmed by Dodger pitching. The opener pitted two all-time greats against each other: Yankee Whitey Ford (24–7 that season) and Sandy Koufax (25–5). For an inning it was close. Ford fanned two of the first three batters to face him, and Koufax struck out the side. But in the top of the second the Dodgers' Frank Howard doubled with one out, and before Ford could record the second out, two singles and John Roseboro's home run had put four Dodger runs across. Koufax ran his consecutive Ks to five and had tied the Series single-game record of 14 by the time Tom Tresh tagged him for a two-run homer in the eighth. That was New York's only scoring, and Koufax ended the game with a new-record fifteenth strikeout an inning later.

Veteran Johnny Podres pitched shutout ball through 8⅓ innings of Game Two as his Dodgers built him a four-run lead (one of the runs a homer by ex-Yankee Bill Skowron). New York scored a run in the last of the ninth, but it was not enough to keep the Dodgers from returning to Los Angeles with a 2–0 Series advantage.

A first-inning walk, a wild pitch, and a single moved Dodger Jim Gilliam around the bases for the only scoring in Game Three as Yankee Jim Bouton hooked up in a duel with Don Drysdale. Bouton left after seven innings for Yankee relief ace Hal Reniff, who held Los Angeles hitless through the final frames. When Drysdale completed his shutout, only three singles had been hit against him, and he had struck out nine.

Ford and Koufax tangled again in the fourth game. Ford pitched much more impressively than he had in the opener, walking just one and yielding only two hits in seven innings. One of the Dodger hits was Frank Howard's solo homer in the fifth inning, but Mickey Mantle evened the score with a home run off Koufax in the seventh. But in the last of the seventh, Yankee first baseman Joe Pepitone lost sight of a throw from the third baseman for an error that sent batter Jim Gilliam all the way to third, and Willie Davis followed with a fly to center that scored Gilliam with the go-ahead run. No one else scored against Ford (or Reniff, who relieved him in the eighth), but no other Yankee scored against Koufax either, and the Dodgers, with just two hits, captured the game and the Series.

Los Angeles Dodgers (NL), 4; New York Yankees (AL), 0

LA (N)

PLAYER/POS	AVG	G	AB	R	H	2B	3B	HR	RB	BB	SO	SB
Tommy Davis, of	.400	4	15	0	6	0	2	0	2	0	2	1
Willie Davis, of	.167	4	12	2	2	2	0	0	3	0	6	0
Don Drysdale, p	.000	1	1	0	0	0	0	0	0	2	0	0
Ron Fairly, of	.000	4	1	0	0	0	0	0	0	3	0	0
Jim Gilliam, 3b	.154	4	13	3	2	0	0	0	0	3	1	0
Frank Howard, of	.300	3	10	2	3	1	0	1	1	0	2	0
Sandy Koufax, p	.000	2	6	0	0	0	0	0	0	0	2	0
Ron Perranoski, p	.000	1	0	0	0	0	0	0	0	0	0	0
Johnny Podres, p	.250	1	4	0	1	0	0	0	0	0	0	0
Johnny Roseboro, c	.143	4	14	1	2	0	0	1	3	0	4	0
Bill Skowron, 1b	.385	4	13	2	5	0	0	1	3	1	3	0
Dick Tracewski, 2b	.154	4	13	1	2	0	0	0	0	1	2	0
Maury Wills, ss	.133	4	15	1	2	0	0	0	0	1	3	1
TOTAL	.214		117	12	25	3	2	3	12	11	25	2

PITCHER	W	L	ERA	G	GS	CG	SV	SHO	IP	H	ER	BB	SO
Don Drysdale	1	0	0.00	1	1	1	0	1	9.0	3	0	1	9
Sandy Koufax	2	0	1.50	2	2	2	0	0	18.0	12	3	3	23
Ron Perranoski	0	0	0.00	1	0	0	1	0	0.2	1	0	0	1
Johnny Podres	1	0	1.08	1	1	0	0	0	8.1	6	1	1	4
TOTAL	4	0	1.00	5	4	3	1	1	36.0	22	4	5	37

NY (A)

PLAYER/POS	AVG	G	AB	R	H	2B	3B	HR	RB	BB	SO	SB
Yogi Berra, ph	.000	1	1	0	0	0	0	0	0	0	0	0
Johnny Blanchard, of-1	.000	1	3	0	0	0	0	0	0	0	0	0
Jim Bouton, p	.000	1	2	0	0	0	0	0	0	0	2	0
Clete Boyer, 3b	.077	4	13	0	1	0	0	0	0	1	6	0
Harry Bright, ph	.000	2	2	0	0	0	0	0	0	0	2	0
Al Downing, p	.000	1	1	0	0	0	0	0	0	0	1	0
Whitey Ford, p	.000	2	3	0	0	0	0	0	0	0	0	0
Steve Hamilton, p	.000	1	0	0	0	0	0	0	0	0	0	0
Elston Howard, c	.333	4	15	0	5	0	0	0	1	0	3	0
Tony Kubek, ss	.188	4	16	1	3	0	0	0	0	0	3	0
Phil Linz, ph	.333	3	3	0	1	0	0	0	0	0	1	0
Hector Lopez, of-2	.250	3	8	1	2	2	0	0	0	0	1	0
Mickey Mantle, of	.133	4	15	1	2	0	0	1	1	1	5	0
Roger Maris, of	.000	2	5	0	0	0	0	0	0	0	1	0
Joe Pepitone, 1b	.154	4	13	0	2	0	0	0	0	1	3	0
Hal Reniff, p	.000	3	0	0	0	0	0	0	0	0	0	0
Bobby Richardson, 2b	.214	4	14	0	3	1	0	0	0	1	3	0
Ralph Terry, p	.000	1	0	0	0	0	0	0	0	0	0	0
Tom Tresh, of	.200	4	15	1	3	0	0	1	2	1	6	0
Stan Williams, p	.000	1	0	0	0	0	0	0	0	0	0	0
TOTAL	.171		129	4	22	3	0	2	4	5	37	0

PITCHER	W	L	ERA	G	GS	CG	SV	SHO	IP	H	ER	BB	SO
Jim Bouton	0	1	1.29	1	1	0	0	0	7.0	4	1	5	4
Al Downing	0	1	5.40	1	1	0	0	0	5.0	7	3	1	6
Whitey Ford	0	2	4.50	2	2	0	0	0	12.0	10	6	3	8
Steve Hamilton	0	0	0.00	1	0	0	0	0	1.0	0	0	0	1
Hal Reniff	0	0	0.00	3	0	0	0	0	3.0	0	0	1	1
Ralph Terry	0	0	3.00	1	0	0	0	0	3.0	3	1	1	0
Stan Williams	0	0	0.00	1	0	0	0	0	3.0	1	0	0	5
TOTAL	0	4	2.91	10	4	0	0	0	34.0	25	11	11	25

GAME 1 AT NY OCT 2

LA	041	000	000	5	9	0
NY	000	000	020	2	6	0

Pitchers: KOUFAX vs FORD, Williams (6), Hamilton (9)
Home Runs: Roseboro-LA, Tresh-NY
Attendance: 69,000

GAME 2 AT NY OCT 3

LA	200	100	010	4	10	1
NY	000	000	001	1	7	0

Pitchers: PODRES, Perranoski (9) vs DOWNING, Terry (6), Reniff (9)
Home Runs: Skowron-LA
Attendance: 66,455

GAME 3 AT LA OCT 5

NY	000	000	000	0	3	0
LA	100	000	00X	1	4	1

Pitchers: BOUTON, Reniff (8) vs DRYSDALE
Attendance: 55,912

GAME 4 AT LA OCT 6

NY	000	000	100	1	6	1
LA	000	010	10X	2	2	1

Pitchers: FORD, Reniff (8) vs KOUFAX
Home Runs: F.Howard-LA, Mantle-NY
Attendance: 55,912

With late-season spurts the Cardinals edged the Reds and Phillies for their first pennant in eighteen years and the Yankees overtook the White Sox and Orioles for their fifteenth in eighteen years and their twenty-ninth over all. But when the Series was over, the long era of Yankee dominance had come to an end.

St. Louis won the opener, a 24-hit slugfest in which Curt Flood's RBI triple in the sixth proved the decisive blow. But New York came back to take the next two games. Rookie Mel Stottlemyre won Game Two, holding the Cards to three runs as his Yankees scored eight. (Loser Bob Gibson struck out nine Yankees, though, on his way to a new Series record of 31.) Game Three, by contrast, featured a pitchers' duel between Jim Bouton and Cardinal veteran Curt Simmons. Cardinal reliever Barney Schultz, who replaced Simmons for the last of the ninth with the score 1–1, lost the game on his first pitch when Mickey Mantle homered to deep right (his sixteenth World Series home run, which moved him ahead of Babe Ruth into the all-time Series lead).

Cardinal Ray Sadecki (the winner in Game One) left with one out in the first inning of Game Four after four Yankee batters hit safely, but relievers Roger Craig and Ron Taylor stopped New York on just two singles the rest of the way. The Cards were also held to six hits, but one was Ken Boyer's grand slam in the sixth, which erased a 3–0 Yankee lead and gave St. Louis runs enough to even the Series at two games apiece.

Gibson and Stottlemyre faced off a second time in Game Five. Gibson carried a 2–0 lead into the last of the ninth, when with two out Tom Tresh tagged him for a game-tying home run. In the top of the tenth, though, the Cards regained the lead on Tim Mc-Carver's three-run homer and held on for the win as Gibson notched his thirteenth K of the game.

Bouton and Simmons tangled again in Game Five. Another 1–1 duel was shattered this time in the top of the sixth when Roger Maris and Mantle tagged Simmons for back-to-back home runs. New York put the game away in the eighth with five runs off Cardinal relievers—four of them on Joe Pepitone's grand slam.

With the series tied 3–3, Gibson and Stottlemyre were called upon to settle the title. Gibson pitched the whole game, striking out nine. Mantle touched him for a three-run homer in the sixth inning, and Clete Boyer and Phil Linz hit solo shots in the ninth.

St. Louis Cardinals (NL), 4; New York Yankees (AL), 3

STL (N)

PLAYER/POS	AVG	G	AB	R	H	2B	3B	HR	RB	BB	SO	SB
Ken Boyer, 3b	.222	7	27	5	6	1	0	2	6	1	5	0
Lou Brock, of	.300	7	30	2	9	2	0	1	5	0	3	0
Gerry Buchek, 2b	1.000	4	1	1	1	0	0	0	0	0	0	0
Roger Craig, p	.000	2	1	0	0	0	0	0	0	0	0	0
Curt Flood, of	.200	7	30	5	6	0	1	0	3	3	1	0
Bob Gibson, p	.222	3	9	1	2	0	0	0	0	0	3	0
Dick Groat, ss	.192	7	26	3	5	1	1	0	1	4	3	0
Bob Humphreys, p	.000	1	0	0	0	0	0	0	0	0	0	0
Charlie James, ph	.000	3	3	0	0	0	0	0	0	0	1	0
Julian Javier, 2b	.000	1	1	0	0	0	0	0	0	0	0	0
Dal Maxvill, 2b	.200	7	20	0	4	1	0	0	1	1	4	0
Tim Mc Carver, c	.478	7	23	4	11	1	1	1	5	5	1	1
Gordie Richardson, p	.000	2	0	0	0	0	0	0	0	0	0	0
Ray Sadecki, p	.500	2	2	0	1	0	0	0	1	0	1	0
Barney Schultz, p	.000	4	1	0	0	0	0	0	0	0	0	0
Mike Shannon, of	.214	7	28	6	6	0	0	1	2	0	9	1
Curt Simmons, p	.500	2	4	0	2	0	0	0	0	1	0	0
Bob Skinner, ph	.667	4	3	0	2	1	0	0	1	1	0	0
Ron Taylor, p	.000	2	1	0	0	0	0	0	0	0	1	0
Carl Warwick, ph	.750	5	4	2	3	0	0	0	1	1	0	0
Bill White, 1b	.111	7	27	2	3	1	0	0	2	2	6	0
TOTAL	.254		240	32	61	8	3	5	29	18	39	3

PITCHER	W	L	ERA	G	GS	CG	SV	SHO	IP	H	ER	BB	SO
Roger Craig	1	0	0.00	2	0	0	0	0	5.0	2	0	3	9
Bob Gibson	2	1	3.00	3	3	2	0	0	27.0	23	9	8	31
Bob Humphreys	0	0	0.00	1	0	0	0	0	1.0	0	0	0	1
Gordie Richardson	0	0	40.50	2	0	0	0	0	0.2	3	3	2	0
Ray Sadecki	1	0	8.53	2	2	0	0	0	6.1	12	6	5	2
Barney Schultz	0	1	18.00	4	0	0	1	0	4.0	9	8	3	1
Curt Simmons	0	1	2.51	2	2	0	0	0	14.1	11	4	3	8
Ron Taylor	0	0	0.00	2	0	0	1	0	4.2	0	0	1	2
TOTAL	4	3	4.29	18	7	2	2	0	63.0	60	30	25	54

NY (A)

PLAYER/POS	AVG	G	AB	R	H	2B	3B	HR	RB	BB	SO	SB
Johnny Blanchard, ph	.250	4	4	0	1	1	0	0	0	0	1	0
Jim Bouton, p	.143	2	7	0	1	0	0	0	1	0	2	0
Clete Boyer, 3b	.208	7	24	2	5	1	0	1	3	1	5	1
Al Downing, p	.000	3	2	0	0	0	0	0	0	0	2	0
Whitey Ford, p	1.000	1	1	0	1	0	0	0	0	1	2	0
Pedro Gonzalez, 3b	.000	1	1	0	0	0	0	0	0	0	0	0
Steve Hamilton, p	.000	2	0	0	0	0	0	0	0	0	0	0
Mike Hegan, ph	.000	3	1	1	0	0	0	0	0	0	1	0
Elston Howard, c	.292	7	24	5	7	1	0	0	2	4	6	0
Phil Linz, ss	.226	7	31	5	7	1	0	2	2	2	5	0
Hector Lopez, of-1	.000	3	2	0	0	0	0	0	0	0	0	0
Mickey Mantle, of	.333	7	24	8	8	2	0	3	8	6	8	0
Roger Maris, of	.200	7	30	4	6	0	0	1	1	1	4	0
Pete Mikkelsen, p	.000	4	0	0	0	0	0	0	0	0	0	0
Joe Pepitone, 1b	.154	7	26	1	4	1	0	1	5	2	3	0
Hal Reniff, p	.000	1	0	0	0	0	0	0	0	0	0	0
Bobby Richardson, 2b	.406	7	32	3	13	2	0	0	3	0	2	1
Rollie Sheldon, p	.000	2	0	0	0	0	0	0	0	0	0	0
Mel Stottlemyre, p	.125	3	8	0	1	0	0	0	0	0	6	0
Ralph Terry, p	.000	1	0	0	0	0	0	0	0	0	0	0
Tom Tresh, of	.273	7	22	4	6	2	0	2	7	6	7	0
TOTAL	.251		239	33	60	11	0	10	33	25	54	2

PITCHER	W	L	ERA	G	GS	CG	SV	SHO	IP	H	ER	BB	SO
Jim Bouton	2	0	1.56	2	2	1	0	0	17.1	15	3	5	7
Al Downing	0	1	8.22	3	1	0	0	0	7.2	9	7	2	5
Whitey Ford	0	1	8.44	1	1	0	0	0	5.1	8	5	1	4
Steve Hamilton	0	0	4.50	2	0	0	1	0	2.0	3	1	0	2
Pete Mikkelsen	0	1	5.79	4	0	0	0	0	4.2	4	3	2	4
Hal Reniff	0	0	0.00	1	0	0	0	0	0.1	2	0	0	0
Rollie Sheldon	0	0	0.00	2	0	0	0	0	2.2	0	0	2	2
Mel Stottlemyre	1	1	3.15	3	3	1	0	0	20.0	18	7	6	12
Ralph Terry	0	0	0.00	1	0	0	0	0	2.0	2	0	3	3
TOTAL	3	4	3.77	19	7	2	1	0	62.0	61	26	18	39

But as St. Louis had scored six times off Stottlemyre and his replacement Al Downing before the Yankees scored their first runs, the game ended with the Cards victors and world champions. Yogi Berra, New York's rookie manager, was fired the next day. The following season the Yankees finished sixth.

GAME 1 AT STL OCT 7

NY	030 010 010	5 12 2
STL	110 004 03X	9 12 0

Pitchers: FORD, Downing (6), Sheldon (8), Mikkelsen (9) vs SADECKI, Schultz (7)
Home Runs: Tresh-NY, Shannon-STL
Attendance: 30,805

GAME 2 AT STL OCT 8

NY	000 101 204	8 12 0
STL	001 000 011	3 7 0

Pitchers: STOTTLEMYRE vs GIBSON, Schultz (9), Craig (9)
Home Runs: Linz-NY
Attendance: 30,805

GAME 3 AT NY OCT 10

STL	000 010 000	1 6 0
NY	010 000 001	2 5 2

Pitchers: Simmons, SCHULTZ (9) vs BOUTON
Home Runs: Mantle-NY
Attendance: 67,101

GAME 4 AT NY OCT 11

STL	000 004 000	4 6 1
NY	300 000 000	3 6 1

Pitchers: Sadecki, CRAIG (1), Taylor (6) vs DOWNING, Mikkelsen (7), Terry (8)
Home Runs: K.Boyer-STL
Attendance: 66,312

GAME 5 AT NY OCT 12

STL	000 020 000 3	5 10 1
NY	000 000 002 0	2 6 2

Pitchers: GIBSON vs Stottlemyre, Reniff (8), MIKKELSEN (8)
Home Runs: Tresh-NY, McCarver-STL
Attendance: 65,633

GAME 6 AT STL OCT 14

NY	000 012 050	8 10 0
STL	100 000 011	3 10 1

Pitchers: BOUTON, Hamilton (9) VS SIMMONS, Taylor (7), Schultz (8), Richardson (8), Humphreys (9)
Home Runs: Maris-NY, Mantle-NY, Pepitone-NY
Attendance: 30,805

GAME 7 AT STL OCT 15

NY	000 003 002	5 9 2
STL	000 330 10X	7 10 1

Pitchers: STOTTLEMYRE, Downing (5), Sheldon (5), Hamilton (7), Mikkelsen (8) vs GIBSON
Home Runs: Brock-STL, Mantle-NY, K.Boyer-STL, C.Boyer-NY, Linz-NY
Attendance: 30,346

The Twins (bringing the World Series to Minnesota for the first time ever) featured heavy hitting, while Dodger hopes rested on great pitching and speed on the bases. For a while it looked as if batting power would triumph as the Twins took the first two games at home. They drove out Dodger starter Don Drysdale with seven runs in the first three innings of the opener—including home runs by Don Mincher and Zoilo Versalles—on the way to a convincing 8–2 win, and followed up with a 5–1 triumph the next day over Dodger ace Sandy Koufax (who had declined to pitch Game One on Yom Kippur, the holiest day of the Jewish year) and star reliever Ron Perranoski, who was tagged for three of the Twins' runs.

But when the Series moved to Los Angeles, Dodger pitching began to assert itself. Claude Osteen held Minnesota to five hits and no runs, while Los Angeles bunched seven of their ten hits in the middle three innings for four runs. Drysdale evened the Series in Game Four, avenging his first-game pounding with a second Dodger five-hitter. Twins Harmon Killebrew and Tony Oliva tagged him for a pair of solo homers, but that was Minnesota's only scoring—more than balanced by seven Dodger runs, including homers by Wes Parker and Lou Johnson. In Game Five the next day, Koufax avenged his earlier loss, carrying Los Angeles to its first Series lead with a shutout in which he allowed only four singles and a walk, while fanning ten Twins. Speedster Willie Davis stole three bases and Maury Wills stole another as the Dodgers parlayed fourteen hits into a 7–0 victory.

Back in Minnesota for Game Six, the Twins rallied, using the long ball to even the Series again with a 5–1 win. Bob Allison opened the scoring with a two-run shot off Dodger starter Claude Osteen in the fourth, and Minnesota pitcher Mudcat Grant insured his own win with a three-run blast two innings later.

In the finale, though, the visiting team won for the only time in the Series. Koufax again struck out ten men, stopping the Twins on three hits for his second shutout. Lou Johnson's second Series homer (a fourth-inning solo shot to left off Twin starter Jim Kaat that was barely fair) was all the Dodgers needed for their fifth world championship, but Ron Fairly followed Johnson with a double and Wes Parker singled home an insurance run that drove Kaat out and concluded the Series scoring.

Los Angeles Dodgers (NL), 4; Minnesota Twins (AL) 3

LA (N)

PLAYER/POS	AVG	G	AB	R	H	2B	3B	HR	RB	BB	SO	SB
Jim Brewer, p	.000	1	0	0	0	0	0	0	0	0	0	0
Willie Crawford, ph	.500	2	2	0	1	0	0	0	0	0	1	0
Willie Davis, of	.231	7	26	3	6	0	0	0	0	0	2	3
Don Drysdale, p-2	.000	3	5	0	0	0	0	0	0	0	4	0
Ron Fairly, of	.379	7	29	7	11	3	0	2	6	0	1	0
Jim Gilliam, 3b	.214	7	28	2	6	1	0	0	2	1	0	0
Lou Johnson, of	.296	7	27	3	8	2	0	2	4	1	3	0
John Kennedy, 3b	.000	4	1	0	0	0	0	0	0	0	0	0
Sandy Koufax, p	.111	3	9	0	1	0	0	0	0	1	5	0
Jim Lefebvre, 2b	.400	3	10	2	4	0	0	0	0	0	0	0
Don Le John, ph	.000	1	1	0	0	0	0	0	0	0	1	0
Bob Miller, p	.000	2	0	0	0	0	0	0	0	0	0	0
Wally Moon, ph	.000	2	2	0	0	0	0	0	0	0	0	0
Claude Osteen, p	.333	2	3	0	1	0	0	0	0	0	0	0
Wes Parker, 1b	.304	7	23	3	7	0	1	1	2	3	3	2
Ron Perranoski, p	.000	2	0	0	0	0	0	0	0	0	0	0
Howie Reed, p	.000	2	0	0	0	0	0	0	0	0	0	0
Johnny Roseboro, c	.286	7	21	1	6	1	0	0	3	5	3	1
Dick Tracewski, 2b	.118	6	17	0	2	0	0	0	0	1	5	0
Maury Wills, ss	.367	7	30	3	11	3	0	0	3	1	3	3
TOTAL	.274		234	24	64	10	1	5	21	13	31	9

PITCHER	W	L	ERA	G	GS	CG	SV	SHO	IP	H	ER	BB	SO
Jim Brewer	0	0	4.50	1	0	0	0	0	2.0	3	1	0	1
Don Drysdale	1	1	3.86	2	2	1	0	0	11.2	12	5	3	15
Sandy Koufax	2	1	0.38	3	3	2	0	2	24.0	13	1	5	29
Bob Miller	0	0	0.00	2	0	0	0	0	1.1	0	0	0	0
Claude Osteen	1	1	0.64	2	2	1	0	1	14.0	9	1	5	4
Ron Perranoski	0	0	7.36	2	0	0	0	0	3.2	3	3	4	1
Howie Reed	0	0	8.10	2	0	0	0	0	3.1	2	3	2	4
TOTAL	4	3	2.10	14	7	4	0	3	60.0	42	14	19	54

MIN (A)

PLAYER/POS	AVG	G	AB	R	H	2B	3B	HR	RB	BB	SO	SB
Bob Allison, of	.125	5	16	3	2	1	0	1	2	2	9	1
Earl Battey, c	.120	7	25	1	3	0	1	0	2	0	5	0
Dave Boswell, p	.000	1	0	0	0	0	0	0	0	0	0	0
Mudcat Grant, p	.250	3	8	3	2	1	0	1	3	0	1	0
Jimmie Hall, of	.143	2	7	0	1	0	0	0	0	1	5	0
Jim Kaat, p	.167	3	6	0	1	0	0	0	0	2	5	0
Harmon Killebrew, 3b	.286	7	21	2	6	0	0	1	2	6	4	0
Johnny Klippstein, p	.000	2	0	0	0	0	0	0	0	0	0	0
Jim Merritt, p	.000	2	0	0	0	0	0	0	0	0	0	0
Don Mincher, 1b	.130	7	23	3	3	0	0	1	1	2	7	0
Joe Nossek, of-5	.200	6	20	0	4	0	0	0	0	0	1	0
Tony Oliva, of	.192	7	26	2	5	1	0	1	2	1	6	0
Camilo Pascual, p	.000	1	1	0	0	0	0	0	0	0	0	0
Jim Perry, p	.000	2	0	0	0	0	0	0	0	0	0	0
Bill Pleis, p	.000	1	0	0	0	0	0	0	0	0	0	0
Frank Quilici, 2b	.200	7	20	2	4	2	0	0	1	4	3	0
Rich Rollins, ph	.000	3	2	0	0	0	0	0	0	0	1	0
Sandy Valdespino, of-2	.273	5	11	1	3	1	0	0	0	0	1	0
Zoilo Versalles, ss	.286	7	28	3	8	1	1	1	4	2	7	1
Al Worthington, p	.000	2	0	0	0	0	0	0	0	0	0	0
Jerry Zimmerman, c	.000	2	1	0	0	0	0	0	0	0	0	0
TOTAL	.195		215	20	42	7	2	6	19	19	54	2

PITCHER	W	L	ERA	G	GS	CG	SV	SHO	IP	H	ER	BB	SO
Dave Boswell	1	0	3.38	1	0	0	0	0	2.2	3	1	2	3
Mudcat Grant	2	1	2.74	3	3	2	0	0	23.0	22	7	2	12
Jim Kaat	1	2	3.77	3	3	1	0	0	14.1	18	6	2	6
Johnny Klippstein	0	0	0.00	2	0	0	0	0	2.2	2	0	2	3
Jim Merritt	0	0	2.70	2	0	0	0	0	3.1	2	1	0	1
Camilo Pascual	0	1	5.40	1	1	0	0	0	5.0	8	3	1	0
Jim Perry	0	0	4.50	2	0	0	0	0	4.0	5	2	2	4
Bill Pleis	0	0	9.00	1	0	0	0	0	1.0	2	1	0	0
Al Worthington	0	0	0.00	2	0	0	0	0	4.0	2	0	2	2
TOTAL	4	4	3.15	17	7	3	0	0	60.0	64	21	13	31

GAME 1 AT MIN OCT 6

LA	010	000	001	2	10	1
MIN	016	001	00X	8	10	0

Pitchers: DRYSDALE, Reed (3), Brewer (5), Perranoski (7) vs GRANT
Home Runs: Fairly-LA, Mincher-MIN, Versalles-MIN
Attendance: 47,797

GAME 2 AT MIN OCT 7

LA	000	000	100	1	7	3
MIN	000	002	12X	5	9	0

Pitchers: KOUFAX, Perranoski (7), Miller (8) vs KAAT
Attendance: 48,700

GAME 3 AT LA OCT 9

MIN	000	000	000	0	5	0
LA	000	211	00X	4	10	1

Pitchers: PASCUAL, Merritt (6), Klippstein (8) vs OSTEEN
Attendance: 55,934

GAME 4 AT LA OCT 10

MIN	000	101	000	2	5	2
LA	110	103	01X	7	10	0

Pitchers: GRANT, Worthington (6), Pleis (8) vs DRYSDALE
Home Runs: Killebrew-MIN, Parker-LA, Oliva-MIN, Johnson-LA
Attendance: 55,920

GAME 5 AT LA OCT 11

MIN	000	000	000	0	4	1
LA	202	100	20X	7	14	0

Pitchers: KAAT, Boswell (3), Perry (6) vs KOUFAX
Attendance: 55,801

GAME 6 AT MIN OCT 13

LA	000	000	100	1	6	1
MIN	000	203	00X	5	6	1

Pitchers: OSTEEN, Reed (6), Miller (8) vs GRANT
Home Runs: Allison-MIN, Grant-MIN, Fairly-LA
Attendance: 49,578

GAME 7 AT MIN OCT 14

LA	000	200	000	2	7	0
MIN	000	000	000	0	3	1

Pitchers: KOUFAX vs KAAT, Worthington (4), Klippstein (6), Merritt (7), Perry (9)
Home Runs: Johnson-LA
Attendance: 50,596

The Orioles, with their first pennant since moving from St. Louis in 1954, won the franchise's first World Series ever, crushing Series repeater Los Angeles in four games. Back-to-back home runs by Frank and Brooks Robinson in the top of the first inning of the opener gave Baltimore a quick three-run lead, and the O's added a fourth run an inning later before the Dodgers attempted to come back with single runs in the second and third innings. But by then Oriole reliever Moe Drabowsky had come on to pitch, and he stopped the Dodgers on one hit the rest of the way, striking out eleven (including six in a row in the fourth and fifth innings). The Dodgers would not score again in the Series.

Sophomore Jim Palmer (a week shy of his twenty-first birthday) hurled a four-hit shutout at Los Angeles in Game Two, defeating the great—but critically sore-armed—Sandy Koufax, who, though only thirty years old himself, was pitching the final game of his career. Three errors by center fielder Willie Davis in the fifth (including a pair of flies lost in the sun) led to three unearned runs—the first scoring against Koufax. Frank Robinson's leadoff triple in the sixth and Boog Powell's single gave the Orioles an earned run before a double play ended the inning. Koufax was replaced after the inning by a succession of Dodger relievers as Baltimore went on to win 6–0.

Wally Bunker did the honors for the Orioles in Game Three, emerging the victor of a pitching duel with Dodger Claude Osteen on the strength of a fifth-inning home run by Paul Blair, a tremendous 430-foot shot to left. Osteen yielded only two other Orioles hits—both singles—in his seven innings, and Dodger reliever Phil Regan retired the side in the eighth. But one run was all Bunker needed for his shutout win.

Dave McNally, who had given up the Dodgers' only Series runs in Game One, mended his ways with a four-hit shutout in Game Four. He needed the shutout for the Oriole sweep, for Dodger Don Drysdale was also in top form. Drysdale, too, gave up only four hits. But one of them was Frank Robinson's second home run of the Series, a fourth-inning solo shot to left for the game's only scoring.

Baltimore Orioles (AL), 4;
Los Angeles Dodgers (NL) 0

BAL (A)

PLAYER/POS	AVG	G	AB	R	H	2B	3B	HR	RB	BB	SO	SB
Luis Aparicio, ss	.250	4	16	0	4	1	0	0	0	2	0	0
Paul Blair, of	.167	4	6	2	1	0	0	1	1	1	0	0
Curt Blefary, of	.077	4	13	0	1	0	0	0	0	2	3	0
Wally Bunker, p	.000	1	2	0	0	0	0	0	0	0	1	0
Moe Drabowsky, p	.000	1	2	0	0	0	0	0	0	0	1	0
Andy Etchebarren, c	.083	4	12	2	1	0	0	0	0	2	4	0
Davy Johnson, 2b	.286	4	14	1	4	1	0	0	1	0	1	0
Dave Mc Nally, p	.000	2	3	0	0	0	0	0	0	0	1	0
Jim Palmer, p	.000	1	4	0	0	0	0	0	0	0	2	0
Boog Powell, 1b	.357	4	14	1	5	1	0	0	1	0	1	0
Brooks Robinson, 3b	.214	4	14	2	3	0	0	1	1	1	0	0
Frank Robinson, of	.286	4	14	4	4	0	1	2	3	2	3	0
Russ Snyder, of	.167	3	6	1	1	0	0	0	1	2	0	0
TOTAL	.200		120	13	24	3	1	4	10	11	17	0

PITCHER	W	L	ERA	G	GS	CG	SV	SHO	IP	H	ER	BB	SO
Wally Bunker	1	0	0.00	1	1	1	0	1	9.0	6	0	1	6
Moe Drabowsky	1	0	0.00	1	0	0	0	0	6.2	1	0	2	11
Dave Mc Nally	1	0	1.59	2	2	1	0	1	11.1	6	2	7	5
Jim Palmer	1	0	0.00	1	1	1	0	1	9.0	4	0	3	6
TOTAL	4	0	0.50	5	4	3	0	3	36.0	17	2	13	28

LA (N)

PLAYER/POS	AVG	G	AB	R	H	2B	3B	HR	RB	BB	SO	SB
Jim Barbieri, ph	.000	1	1	0	0	0	0	0	0	0	1	0
Jim Brewer, p	.000	1	0	0	0	0	0	0	0	0	0	0
Wes Covington, ph	.000	1	1	0	0	0	0	0	0	0	1	0
Tommy Davis, of-3	.250	4	8	0	2	0	0	0	0	1	1	0
Willie Davis, of	.063	4	16	0	1	0	0	0	0	0	4	0
Don Drysdale, p	.000	2	2	0	0	0	0	0	0	0	1	0
Ron Fairly, of-2,1b-1	.143	3	7	0	1	0	0	0	0	2	4	0
Al Ferrara, ph	1.000	1	1	0	1	0	0	0	0	0	0	0
Jim Gilliam, 3b	.000	2	6	0	0	0	0	0	1	2	0	0
Lou Johnson, of	.267	4	15	1	4	1	0	0	0	1	1	0
John Kennedy, 3b	.200	2	5	0	1	0	0	0	0	0	0	0
Sandy Koufax, p	.000	1	2	0	0	0	0	0	0	0	0	0
Jim Lefebvre, 2b	.167	4	12	1	2	0	0	1	1	3	4	0
Bob Miller, p	.000	1	0	0	0	0	0	0	0	0	0	0
Joe Moeller, p	.000	1	0	0	0	0	0	0	0	0	0	0
Nate Oliver, pr	.000	1	0	0	0	0	0	0	0	0	0	0
Claude Osteen, p	.000	1	2	0	0	0	0	0	0	0	1	0
Wes Parker, 1b	.231	4	13	0	3	2	0	0	0	1	3	0
Ron Perranoski, p	.000	2	0	0	0	0	0	0	0	0	0	0
Phil Regan, p	.000	2	0	0	0	0	0	0	0	0	0	0
Johnny Roseboro, c	.071	4	14	0	1	0	0	0	0	0	3	0
Dick Stuart, ph	.000	2	2	0	0	0	0	0	0	0	1	0
Maury Wills, ss	.077	4	13	0	1	0	0	0	0	3	3	1
TOTAL	.142		120	2	17	3	0	1	2	13	28	1

PITCHER	W	L	ERA	G	GS	CG	SV	SHO	IP	H	ER	BB	SO
Jim Brewer	0	0	0.00	1	0	0	0	0	1.0	0	0	0	1
Don Drysdale	0	2	4.50	2	2	1	0	0	10.0	8	5	3	6
Sandy Koufax	0	1	1.50	1	1	0	0	0	6.0	6	1	2	2
Bob Miller	0	0	0.00	1	0	0	0	0	3.0	2	0	2	1
Joe Moeller	0	0	4.50	1	0	0	0	0	2.0	1	1	1	0
Claude Osteen	0	1	1.29	1	1	0	0	0	7.0	3	1	1	3
Ron Perranoski	0	0	5.40	2	0	0	0	0	3.1	4	2	1	2
Phil Regan	0	0	0.00	2	0	0	0	0	1.2	0	0	1	2
TOTAL	0	4	2.65	11	4	1	0	0	34.0	24	10	11	17

GAME 1 AT LA OCT 5

BAL	310	100	000	5	9	0
LA	011	000	000	2	3	0

Pitchers: McNally, DRABOWSKY (3) vs DRYSDALE, Moeller (3), Miller (5), Perranoski (8)
Home Runs: F.Robinson-BAL, B.Robinson-BAL, Lefebvre-LA
Attendance: 55,941

GAME 2 AT LA OCT 6

BAL	000	031	020	6	8	0
LA	000	000	000	0	4	6

Pitchers: PALMER vs KOUFAX, Perranoski (7), Regan (8), Brewer (9)
Attendance: 55,947

GAME 3 AT BAL OCT 8

LA	000	000	000	0	6	0
BAL	000	010	000	1	3	0

Pitchers: OSTEEN, Regan (8) vs BUNKER
Home Runs: Blair-BAL
Attendance: 54,445

GAME 4 AT BAL OCT 9

LA	000	000	000	0	4	0
BAL	000	100	000	1	4	0

Pitchers: DRYSDALE vs McNALLY
Home Runs: F.Robinson-BAL
Attendance: 54,458

The Cardinals cruised into the Series leading by 10½ games, whereas the Red Sox eked out their pennant over Minnesota and Detroit only by a dramatic win at season's end. The Sox continued to claw their way through six games of the Series before finally falling to superior pitching and hitting in the seventh game. Cardinal hurler Bob Gibson (who had missed a third of the season with a broken leg) edged Boston in the opener 2–1 with a six-hitter that included ten strikeouts. The only run against him came on a solo homer by opposing pitcher Jose Santiago in the third that tied the game. But Santiago was undone when Cardinal Lou Brock singled off him to open the seventh, then stole second, and moved around to score on a pair of ground outs.

Boston ace Jim Lonborg evened the Series the next day with a brilliant one-hit shutout. Sox Triple Crown winner Carl Yastrzemski accounted for four of Boston's five runs with homers in the fourth and seventh innings. Cardinal Nelson Briles outlasted a succession of Boston pitchers for a go-ahead 5–2 win in Game Three, and Gibson, with a five-hit shutout in Game Four, put St. Louis up three games to one.

But Boston's Lonborg kept Red Sox hopes alive with another pitching gem—a three-hitter in which the only extra-base hit was Roger Maris's harmless home run in the last of the ninth, after the Sox had already scored three runs (two of them unearned). Boston's bats came alive as the Series moved to Boston for Game Six, and the Sox evened the Series with an 8–4 win. The Cards used eight pitchers in a futile effort to hold off the Boston assault. Boston's score would have been greater had not all four Boston homers (including three in the fourth inning by Yastrzemski, Reggie Smith, and Rico Petrocelli—his second of the game) been solo shots.

With the Series tied at three-all, the Series' two-game winners, Gibson and Lonborg, faced off in the finale. It turned out to be no contest. Lonborg gave up ten hits and seven runs (including a homer by pitcher Gibson in the fifth and a three-run blast by Julian Javier an inning later) in six innings. Four Boston relievers held the Cards scoreless the rest of the game, but it was too late. Gibson's three-hitter included ten strikeouts and yielded only two Boston runs.

St. Louis Cardinals (NL), 4; Boston Red Sox (AL) 3

STL (N)

PLAYER/POS	AVG	G	AB	R	H	2B	3B	HR	RB	BB	SO	SB
Eddie Bressoud, ss	.000	2	0	0	0	0	0	0	0	0	0	0
Nelson Briles, p	.000	2	3	0	0	0	0	0	0	0	0	0
Lou Brock, of	.414	7	29	8	12	2	1	1	3	2	3	7
Steve Carlton, p	.000	1	1	0	0	0	0	0	0	0	0	0
Orlando Cepeda, 1b	.103	7	29	1	3	2	0	0	1	0	4	0
Curt Flood, of	.179	7	28	2	5	1	0	0	3	3	3	0
Phil Gagliano, ph	.000	1	1	0	0	0	0	0	0	0	0	0
Bob Gibson, p	.091	3	11	1	1	0	0	1	1	1	2	0
Joe Hoerner, p	.000	2	0	0	0	0	0	0	0	0	0	0
Dick Hughes, p	.000	2	3	0	0	0	0	0	0	0	3	0
Larry Jaster, p	.000	1	0	0	0	0	0	0	0	0	0	0
Julian Javier, 2b	.360	7	25	2	9	3	0	1	4	0	6	0
Jack Lamabe, p	.000	3	0	0	0	0	0	0	0	0	0	0
Roger Maris, of	.385	7	26	3	10	1	0	1	7	3	1	0
Dal Maxvill, ss	.158	7	19	1	3	0	1	0	1	4	1	0
Tim Mc Carver, c	.125	7	24	3	3	1	0	0	2	2	2	0
Dave Ricketts, ph	.000	3	3	0	0	0	0	0	0	0	0	0
Mike Shannon, 3b	.208	7	24	3	5	1	0	1	2	1	4	0
Ed Spiezio, ph	.000	1	1	0	0	0	0	0	0	0	0	0
Bobby Tolan, ph	.000	3	2	1	0	0	0	0	0	1	1	0
Ray Washburn, p	.000	2	0	0	0	0	0	0	0	0	0	0
Ron Willis, p	.000	3	0	0	0	0	0	0	0	0	0	0
Hal Woodeshick, p	.000	1	0	0	0	0	0	0	0	0	0	0
TOTAL	.223		229	25	51	11	2	5	24	17	30	7

PITCHER	W	L	ERA	G	GS	CG	SV	SHO	IP	H	ER	BB	SO
Nelson Briles	1	0	1.64	2	1	1	0	0	11.0	7	2	1	4
Steve Carlton	0	1	0.00	1	1	0	0	0	6.0	3	0	2	5
Bob Gibson	3	0	1.00	3	3	3	0	1	27.0	14	3	5	26
Joe Hoerner	0	0	40.50	2	0	0	0	0	0.2	4	3	1	0
Dick Hughes	0	1	5.00	2	2	0	0	0	9.0	9	5	3	7
Larry Jaster	0	0	0.00	1	0	0	0	0	0.1	2	0	0	0
Jack Lamabe	0	1	6.75	3	0	0	0	0	2.2	5	2	0	4
Ray Washburn	0	0	0.00	2	0	0	0	0	2.1	1	0	1	2
Ron Willis	0	0	27.00	3	0	0	0	0	1.0	2	3	4	1
Hal Woodeshick	0	0	0.00	1	0	0	0	0	1.0	1	0	0	0
TOTAL	4	3	2.66	20	7	4	0	1	61.0	48	18	17	49

BOS (A)

PLAYER/POS	AVG	G	AB	R	H	2B	3B	HR	RB	BB	SO	SB
Jerry Adair, 2b-4	.125	5	16	0	2	0	0	0	0	1	0	3	1
Mike Andrews, 2b-3	.308	5	13	2	4	0	0	0	1	0	1	0
Gary Bell, p	.000	3	0	0	0	0	0	0	0	0	0	0
Ken Brett, p	.000	2	0	0	0	0	0	0	0	0	0	0
Joe Foy, 3b-3	.133	6	15	2	2	1	0	0	1	1	5	0
Russ Gibson, c	.000	2	2	0	0	0	0	0	0	0	0	0
Ken Harrelson, of	.077	4	13	0	1	0	0	0	1	1	3	0
Elston Howard, c	.111	7	18	0	2	0	0	0	1	1	2	0
Dalton Jones, 3b-4	.389	6	18	2	7	0	0	0	1	1	3	0
Jim Lonborg, p	.000	3	9	0	0	0	0	0	0	0	7	0
Dave Morehead, p	.000	2	0	0	0	0	0	0	0	0	0	0
Dan Osinski, p	.000	2	0	0	0	0	0	0	0	0	0	0
Rico Petrocelli, ss	.200	7	20	3	4	1	0	2	3	3	8	0
Mike Ryan, c	.000	1	2	0	0	0	0	0	0	0	1	0
Jose Santiago, p	.500	3	2	1	1	0	0	1	1	0	1	0
George Scott, 1b	.231	7	26	3	6	1	1	0	0	3	6	0
Norm Siebern, of-1	.333	3	3	0	1	0	0	0	1	0	0	0
Reggie Smith, of	.250	7	24	3	6	1	0	2	3	2	2	0
Lee Stange, p	.000	1	0	0	0	0	0	0	0	0	0	0
Jerry Stephenson, p	.000	1	0	0	0	0	0	0	0	0	0	0
Jose Tartabull, of-6	.154	7	13	1	2	0	0	0	0	1	2	0
George Thomas, of-1	.000	2	2	0	0	0	0	0	0	0	1	0
Gary Waslewski, p	.000	2	1	0	0	0	0	0	0	0	1	0
John Wyatt, p	.000	2	0	0	0	0	0	0	0	0	0	0
Carl Yastrzemski, of	.400	7	25	4	10	2	0	3	5	4	1	0
TOTAL	.216		222	21	48	6	1	8	19	17	49	1

PITCHER	W	L	ERA	G	GS	CG	SV	SHO	IP	H	ER	BB	SO
Gary Bell	0	1	5.06	3	1	0	1	0	5.1	8	3	1	1
Ken Brett	0	0	0.00	2	0	0	0	0	1.1	0	0	1	1
Jim Lonborg	2	1	2.63	3	3	2	0	1	24.0	14	7	2	11
Dave Morehead	0	0	0.00	2	0	0	0	0	3.1	0	0	4	3
Dan Osinski	0	0	6.75	2	0	0	0	0	1.1	2	1	0	0
Jose Santiago	0	2	5.59	3	2	0	0	0	9.2	16	6	3	6
Lee Stange	0	0	0.00	1	0	0	0	0	2.0	3	0	0	0
Jerry Stephenson	0	0	9.00	1	0	0	0	0	2.0	3	2	1	0
Gary Waslewski	0	0	2.16	2	1	0	0	0	8.1	4	2	2	7
John Wyatt	1	0	4.91	2	0	0	0	0	3.2	1	2	3	1
TOTAL	3	4	3.39	21	7	2	1	1	61.0	51	23	17	30

GAME 1 AT BOS OCT 4

STL	001	000	100	2	10	0
BOS	001	000	000	1	6	0

Pitchers: GIBSON vs SANTIAGO, Wyatt (8)
Home Runs: Santiago-BOS
Attendance: 34,796

GAME 2 AT BOS OCT 5

STL	000	000	000	0	1	1
BOS	000	101	30X	5	9	0

Pitchers: HUGHES, Willis (6), Hoerner (7), Lamabe (7) vs LONBORG
Home Runs: Yastrzemski-BOS (2)
Attendance: 35,188

GAME 3 AT STL OCT 7

BOS	000	001	100	2	7	1
STL	120	001	01X	5	10	0

Pitchers: BELL, Waslewski (3), Stange (6), Osinski (8) vs BRILES
Home Runs: Shannon-STL, Smith-BOS
Attendance: 54,575

GAME 4 AT STL OCT 8

BOS	000	000	000	0	5	0
STL	402	000	00X	6	9	0

Pitchers: SANTIAGO, Bell (1), Stephenson (3), Morehead (5), Brett (8) vs GIBSON
Attendance: 54,575

GAME 5 AT STL OCT 9

BOS	001	000	002	3	6	1
STL	000	000	001	1	3	2

Pitchers: LONBORG vs CARLTON, Washburn (7), Willis (9), Lamabe (9)
Home Runs: Maris-STL
Attendance: 54,575

GAME 6 AT BOS OCT 11

STL	002	000	200	4	8	0
BOS	010	300	40X	8	12	1

Pitchers: Hughes, Willis (4), Briles (5), LAMABE (7), Hoerner (7), Jaster (7), Washburn (7), Woodeshick (8) vs Waslewski, WYATT (6), Bell (8)
Home Runs: Petrocelli-BOS (2), Yastrzemski-BOS, Smith-BOS, Brock-STL
Attendance: 35,188

GAME 7 AT BOS OCT 12

STL	002	023	000	7	10	1
BOS	000	010	010	2	3	1

Pitchers: GIBSON vs LONBORG, Santiago (7), Morehead (9), Osinski (9), Brett (9)
Home Runs: Gibson-STL, Javier-STL
Attendance: 35,188

In this "year of the pitcher," Tiger Denny McLain's 31 wins were the most for a major leaguer in thirty-seven years. Cardinal Bob Gibson's 1.12 ERA was the majors' best since Dutch Leonard's 1.01 in 1914, and his 13 season shutouts tied for third best of all time. In the Series, though, it was Detroit's second-best pitcher—Mickey Lolich—who emerged as the hero.

McLain came off second-best against Gibson in the opener. He yielded only three hits in his five innings, but two Cardinal singles in the fourth combined with a pair of walks and a Tiger error for three runs. Gibson, meanwhile, was in the process of striking out a Series-record 17 batters on the way to a five-hit shutout. But Lolich brought Detroit back in Game Two. He struck out nine, and his third-inning home run (the only one of his major league career) for the second Tiger run provided all the scoring needed for a Detroit victory, although the Tigers kept putting runs across for an eventual 8–1 win.

Home runs accounted for most of the scoring in Game Three. Veteran Al Kaline's two-run shot in the third opened the scoring, but Cardinal Tim McCarver's three-run blast in the fifth put St. Louis ahead. Tiger Dick McAuliffe's solo shot later in the inning brought Detroit within one run of a tie, but the Cardinals put the game away on Orlando Cepeda's three-run homer in the seventh.

McLain faced Gibson again in Game Four, and again came off second-best. Cardinal Lou Brock led off the game with a home run, and before the end of the third inning McLain was gone. Gibson gave up a solo homer to Tiger Jim Northrup in the fourth, but that was the only Detroit run he allowed. Gibson homered himself and struck out ten in an easy 10–1 win.

Down three games to one, the Tigers were saved from elimination by Lolich's arm. Although three Cardinal hits in the top of the first (including Orlando Cepeda's second homer of the Series) gave St. Louis a quick three runs, Lolich held the Cards scoreless the rest of the game as his Tigers fought back with two runs in the fourth and three more in the seventh (with a rally started by Lolich's single). McLain finally came through in Game Six, evening the Series with an easy 13–1 victory, in which Jim Northrup's grand slam provided the big blow of a ten-run third inning.

Lolich and Gibson—both 2–0 in the Series—faced off in the finale. Gibson broke his own World Series strikeout record in the third inning (finishing with 8 for the game and 35 for the Series), and both pitchers hurled shutout ball through six innings. But four two-out Tiger hits in the top of the seventh—including a misplayed fly ball in center field—put three runs on the board, and another run in the ninth made the score 4–0. In the last of the ninth, Mike Shannon's solo homer spoiled Lolich's shutout, but not his third Series win—or the Tigers' comeback world title.

Detroit Tigers (AL), 4; St. Louis Cardinals (NL) 3

DET (A)

PLAYER/POS	AVG	G	AB	R	H	2B	3B	HR	RB	BB	SO	SB
Gates Brown, ph	.000	1	1	0	0	0	0	0	0	0	0	0
Norm Cash, 1b	.385	7	26	5	10	0	0	1	5	3	5	0
Wayne Comer, ph	1.000	1	1	0	1	0	0	0	0	0	0	0
Pat Dobson, p	.000	3	0	0	0	0	0	0	0	0	0	0
Bill Freehan, c	.083	7	24	0	2	1	0	0	2	4	8	0
John Hiller, p	.000	2	0	0	0	0	0	0	0	0	0	0
Willie Horton, of	.304	7	23	6	7	1	1	1	3	5	6	0
Al Kaline, of	.379	7	29	6	11	2	0	2	8	0	7	0
Fred Lasher, p	.000	1	0	0	0	0	0	0	0	0	0	0
Mickey Lolich, p	.250	3	12	2	3	0	0	1	2	1	5	0
Tom Matchick, ph	.000	3	3	0	0	0	0	0	0	0	1	0
Eddie Mathews, 3b-1	.333	2	3	0	1	0	0	0	1	1	1	0
Dick Mc Auliffe, 2b	.222	7	27	5	6	0	0	1	3	4	6	0
Denny Mc Lain, p	.000	3	6	0	0	0	0	0	0	0	4	0
Don Mc Mahon, p	.000	2	0	0	0	0	0	0	0	0	0	0
Jim Northrup, of	.250	7	28	4	7	0	1	2	8	1	5	0
Ray Oyler, ss	.000	4	0	0	0	0	0	0	0	0	0	0
Daryl Patterson, p	.000	2	0	0	0	0	0	0	0	0	0	0
Jim Price, ph	.000	2	2	0	0	0	0	0	0	0	1	0
Joe Sparma, p	.000	1	0	0	0	0	0	0	0	0	0	0
Mickey Stanley, ss-7,of-4	.214	7	28	4	6	0	1	0	0	2	4	0
Dick Tracewski, 3b-1	.000	2	0	1	0	0	0	0	0	0	0	0
Don Wert, 3b	.118	6	17	1	2	0	0	0	2	6	5	0
Earl Wilson, p	.000	1	1	0	0	0	0	0	0	0	1	0
TOTAL	.242		231	34	56	4	3	8	33	27	59	0

PITCHER	W	L	ERA	G	GS	CG	SV	SHO	IP	H	ER	BB	SO
Pat Dobson	0	0	3.86	3	0	0	0	0	4.2	5	2	1	0
John Hiller	0	0	13.50	2	0	0	0	0	2.0	6	3	3	1
Fred Lasher	0	0	0.00	1	0	0	0	0	2.0	1	0	0	1
Mickey Lolich	3	0	1.67	3	3	3	0	0	27.0	20	5	6	21
Denny Mc Lain	1	2	3.24	3	3	1	0	0	16.2	18	6	4	13
Don Mc Mahon	0	0	13.50	2	0	0	0	0	2.0	4	3	0	1
Daryl Patterson	0	0	0.00	2	0	0	0	0	3.0	1	0	1	0
Joe Sparma	0	0	54.00	1	0	0	0	0	0.1	2	2	0	0
Earl Wilson	0	1	6.23	1	1	0	0	0	4.1	4	3	6	3
TOTAL	4	3	3.48	18	7	4	0	0	62.0	61	24	21	40

STL (N)

PLAYER/POS	AVG	G	AB	R	H	2B	3B	HR	RB	BB	SO	SB
Nelson Briles, p	.000	2	4	0	0	0	0	0	0	0	4	0
Lou Brock, of	.464	7	28	6	13	3	1	2	5	3	4	7
Steve Carlton, p	.000	2	0	0	0	0	0	0	0	0	0	0
Orlando Cepeda, 1b	.250	7	28	2	7	0	0	2	6	2	3	0
Ron Davis, of	.000	2	7	0	0	0	0	0	0	0	2	0
Johnny Edwards, ph	.000	1	1	0	0	0	0	0	0	0	1	0
Curt Flood, of	.286	7	28	4	8	1	0	0	2	2	2	3
Phil Gagliano, ph	.000	3	3	0	0	0	0	0	0	0	0	0
Bob Gibson, p	.125	3	8	2	1	0	0	1	2	1	2	0
Wayne Granger, p	.000	1	0	0	0	0	0	0	0	0	0	0
Joe Hoerner, p	.500	3	2	0	1	0	0	0	0	0	1	0
Dick Hughes, p	.000	1	0	0	0	0	0	0	0	0	0	0
Larry Jaster, p	.000	1	0	0	0	0	0	0	0	0	0	0
Julian Javier, 2b	.333	7	27	1	9	1	0	0	3	3	4	1
Roger Maris, of-5	.158	6	19	5	3	1	0	0	1	3	3	0
Dal Maxvill, ss	.000	7	22	1	0	0	0	0	0	0	3	5	0
Tim Mc Carver, c	.333	7	27	3	9	0	2	1	4	3	2	0
Mel Nelson, p	.000	1	0	0	0	0	0	0	0	0	0	0
Dave Ricketts, ph	1.000	1	1	0	1	0	0	0	0	0	0	0
Dick Schofield, ss-1	.000	2	0	0	0	0	0	0	0	0	1	0
Mike Shannon, 3b	.276	7	29	3	8	1	0	1	4	1	5	0
Ed Spiezio, ph	1.000	1	1	0	1	0	0	0	0	0	0	0
Bobby Tolan, ph	.000	1	1	0	0	0	0	0	0	0	1	0
Ray Washburn, p	.000	2	3	0	0	0	0	0	0	0	1	0
Ron Willis, p	.000	3	0	0	0	0	0	0	0	0	0	0
TOTAL	.255		239	27	61	7	3	7	27	21	40	11

PITCHER	W	L	ERA	G	GS	CG	SV	SHO	IP	H	ER	BB	SO
Nelson Briles	0	1	5.56	2	2	0	0	0	11.1	13	7	4	7
Steve Carlton	0	0	6.75	2	0	0	0	0	4.0	7	3	1	3
Bob Gibson	2	1	1.67	3	3	3	0	1	27.0	18	5	4	35
Wayne Granger	0	0	0.00	1	0	0	0	0	2.0	0	0	1	1
Joe Hoerner	0	1	3.86	3	0	0	1	0	4.2	5	2	5	3
Dick Hughes	0	0	0.00	1	0	0	0	0	0.1	2	0	0	0
Larry Jaster	0	0	INF	1	0	0	0	0	0.0	2	3	1	0
Mel Nelson	0	0	0.00	1	0	0	0	0	1.0	0	0	0	1
Ray Washburn	1	1	9.82	2	2	0	0	0	7.1	7	8	7	6
Ron Willis	0	0	8.31	3	0	0	0	0	4.1	2	4	4	3
TOTAL	3	4	4.65	19	7	3	1	1	62.0	56	32	27	59

GAME 1 AT STL OCT 2

DET	000 000 000	0	5	3
STL	000 300 10X	4	6	0

Pitchers: McLAIN, Dobson (6), McMahon (8) vs GIBSON
Home Runs: Brock-STL
Attendance: 54,692

GAME 2 AT STL OCT 3

DET	011 003 102	8	13	1
STL	000 001 000	1	6	1

Pitchers: LOLICH vs BRILES, Carlton (6), Willis (7), Hoerner (9)
Home Runs: Horton-DET, Lolich-DET, Cash-DET
Attendance: 54,692

GAME 3 AT DET OCT 5

STL	000 040 300	7	13	0
DET	002 010 000	3	4	0

Pitchers: WASHBURN, Hoerner (6) vs WILSON, Dobson (5), McMahon (6), Patterson (7), Hiller (8)
Home Runs: Kaline-DET, McCarver-STL, McAuliffe-DET, Cepeda-STL
Attendance: 53,634

GAME 4 AT DET OCT 6

STL	202 200 040	10	13	0
DET	000 100 000	1	5	4

Pitchers: GIBSON vs McLAIN, Sparma (3), Patterson (4), Lasher (6), Hiller (8), Dobson (8)
Home Runs: Brock-STL, Gibson-STL, Northrup-DET
Attendance: 53,634

GAME 5 AT DET OCT 7

STL	300 000 000	3	9	0
DET	000 200 30X	5	9	1

Pitchers: Briles, HOERNER (7), Willis (7) vs LOLICH
Home Runs: Cepeda-STL
Attendance: 53,634

GAME 6 AT STL OCT 9

DET	0 210 010 000	13	12	1
STL	00 0 000 001	1	9	1

Pitchers: McLAIN vs WASHBURN, Jaster (3), Willis (3), Hughes (3), Carlton (4), Granger (7), Nelson (9)
Home Runs: Northrup-DET, Kaline-DET
Attendance: 54,692

GAME 7 AT STL OCT 10

DET	000 000 301	4	8	1
STL	000 000 001	1	5	0

Pitchers: LOLICH vs GIBSON
Home Runs: Shannon-STL
Attendance: 54,692

Atlanta's Hank Aaron homered in each game and drove in a series-high seven runs. But the "Miracle Mets" as a team outhomered the Braves six to five, outhit them by seventy-two percentage points, and scored nearly twice as many runs.

Twice in the first game the Braves came from behind to lead by a run, but in the top of the eighth, five New York hits and poor Atlanta fielding buried starter Phil Niekro under five runs. In Game Two, home runs by Tommie Agee and Ken Boswell helped New York take an early 8–0 lead that even Aaron's three-run homer in the fifth couldn't damage.

In the third game the lead changed hands three times on home runs. Aaron began the barrage with a two-run shot in the first inning. Agee's homer in the third followed by Boswell's for two runs in the fourth put the Mets ahead—until Orlando Cepeda's two-run homer in the fifth gave Atlanta another lead. But in the bottom of the fifth, Met rookie Wayne Garrett's two-run blast reversed the lead one last time and, after four final shutout innings by twenty-two-year-old reliever Nolan Ryan, the Mets had swept to their first pennant.

New York Mets (East), 3; Atlanta Braves (West) 0

NY (E)

PLAYER/POS	AVG	G	AB	R	H	2B	3B	HR	RB	BB	SO	SB
Tommie Agee, of	.357	3	14	4	5	1	0	2	4	2	5	2
Ken Boswell, 2b	.333	3	12	4	4	0	0	2	5	1	2	0
Wayne Garrett, 3b	.385	3	13	3	5	2	0	1	3	2	2	1
Rod Gaspar, of	.000	3	0	0	0	0	0	0	0	0	0	0
Gary Gentry, p	.000	1	0	0	0	0	0	0	0	0	0	0
Jerry Grote, c	.167	3	12	3	2	1	0	0	1	1	4	0
Bud Harrelson, ss	.182	3	11	2	2	1	1	0	3	1	2	0
Cleon Jones, of	.429	3	14	4	6	2	0	1	4	1	2	2
Jerry Koosman, p	.000	1	2	1	0	0	0	0	0	1	2	0
Ed Kranepool, 1b	.250	3	12	2	3	1	0	0	1	1	2	0
J. C. Martin, ph	.500	2	2	0	1	0	0	0	2	0	0	0
Tug Mc Graw, p	.000	1	0	0	0	0	0	0	0	0	0	0
Nolan Ryan, p	.500	1	4	1	2	0	0	0	0	0	1	0
Tom Seaver, p	.000	1	3	0	0	0	0	0	0	0	0	0
Art Shamsky, of	.538	3	13	3	7	0	0	0	1	0	3	0
Ron Taylor, p	.000	2	0	0	0	0	0	0	0	0	0	0
Al Weis, 2b	.000	3	1	0	0	0	0	0	0	0	0	0
TOTAL	.327		113	27	37	8	1	6	24	10	25	5

PITCHER	W	L	ERA	G	GS	CG	SV	SHO	IP	H	ER	BB	SO
Gary Gentry	0	0	9.00	1	1	0	0	0	2.0	5	2	1	1
Jerry Koosman	0	0	11.57	1	1	0	0	0	4.2	7	6	4	5
Tug Mc Graw	0	0	0.00	1	0	0	1	0	3.0	1	0	1	1
Nolan Ryan	1	0	2.57	1	0	0	0	0	7.0	3	2	2	7
Tom Seaver	1	0	6.43	1	1	0	0	0	7.0	8	5	3	2
Ron Taylor	1	0	0.00	2	0	0	1	0	3.1	3	0	0	4
TOTAL	3	0	5.00	7	3	0	2	0	27.0	27	15	11	20

ATL (W)

PLAYER/POS	AVG	G	AB	R	H	2B	3B	HR	RB	BB	SO	SB
Hank Aaron, of	.357	3	14	3	5	2	0	3	7	0	1	0
Tommie Aaron, ph	.000	1	1	0	0	0	0	0	0	0	0	0
Felipe Alou, ph	.000	1	1	0	0	0	0	0	0	0	0	0
Bob Aspromonte, ph	.000	3	3	0	0	0	0	0	0	0	0	0
Clete Boyer, 3b	.111	3	9	0	1	0	0	0	3	2	3	0
Jim Britton, p	.000	1	0	0	0	0	0	0	0	0	0	0
Rico Carty, of	.300	3	10	4	3	2	0	0	0	3	1	0
Orlando Cepeda, 1b	.455	3	11	2	5	2	0	1	3	1	2	1
Bob Didier, c	.000	3	11	0	0	0	0	0	0	0	2	0
Paul Doyle, p	.000	1	0	0	0	0	0	0	0	0	0	0
Gil Garrido, ss	.200	3	10	0	2	0	0	0	0	1	1	0
Tony Gonzalez, of	.357	3	14	4	5	1	0	1	2	1	4	0
Sonny Jackson, ss	.000	1	0	0	0	0	0	0	0	0	0	0
Pat Jarvis, p	.000	1	2	0	0	0	0	0	0	0	2	0
Mike Lum, of-1	1.000	2	2	0	2	1	0	0	0	0	0	0
Felix Millan, 2b	.333	3	12	2	4	1	0	0	0	3	0	0
Gary Neibauer, p	.000	1	0	0	0	0	0	0	0	0	0	0
Phil Niekro, p	.000	1	3	0	0	0	0	0	0	0	1	0
Milt Pappas, p	.000	1	1	0	0	0	0	0	0	0	1	0
Ron Reed, p	.000	1	0	0	0	0	0	0	0	0	0	0
George Stone, p	.000	1	1	0	0	0	0	0	0	0	1	0
Bob Tillman, c	.000	1	0	0	0	0	0	0	0	0	0	0
Cecil Upshaw, p	.000	3	1	0	0	0	0	0	0	0	1	0
TOTAL	.255		106	15	27	9	0	5	15	11	20	1

PITCHER	W	L	ERA	G	GS	CG	SV	SHO	IP	H	ER	BB	SO
Jim Britton	0	0	0.00	1	0	0	0	0	0.1	0	0	1	0
Paul Doyle	0	0	0.00	1	0	0	0	0	1.0	2	0	1	3
Pat Jarvis	0	1	12.46	1	1	0	0	0	4.1	10	6	0	6
Gary Neibauer	0	0	0.00	1	0	0	0	0	1.0	0	0	0	1
Phil Niekro	0	1	4.50	1	1	0	0	0	8.0	9	4	4	4
Milt Pappas	0	0	11.57	1	0	0	0	0	2.1	4	3	0	4
Ron Reed	0	1	21.60	1	1	0	0	0	1.2	5	4	3	3
George Stone	0	0	9.00	1	0	0	0	0	1.0	2	1	0	0
Cecil Upshaw	0	0	2.84	3	0	0	0	0	6.1	5	2	1	4
TOTAL	0	3	6.92	11	3	0	0	0	26.0	37	20	10	25

GAME 1 AT ATL OCT 4

NY	020 200 050	9 10 1
ATL	012 010 100	5 10 2

Pitchers: SEAVER, Taylor (8) vs NIEKRO, Upshaw (9)
Home Runs: Gonzalez-ATL, H.Aaron-ATL
Attendance: 50,122

GAME 2 AT ATL OCT 5

NY	132 210 200	11 13 1
ATL	000 150 000	6 9 3

Pitchers: Koosman, TAYLOR (5), McGraw (7) VS REED, Doyle (2), Pappas (3), Britton (6), Upshaw (6), Neibauer (9)
Home Runs: Agee-NY, Boswell-NY, H.Aaron-ATL, Jones-NY
Attendance: 50,270

GAME 3 AT NY OCT 6

ATL	200 020 000	4 8 1
NY	001 231 00X	7 14 0

Pitchers: JARVIS, Stone (5), Upshaw (6) VS Gentry, Ryan (3)
Home Runs: H.Aaron-ATL, Agee-NY, Boswell-NY, Cepeda-ATL, Garrett-NY
Attendance: 53,195

Minnesota led the league in batting, Baltimore in pitching. In the LCS, pitching prevailed as the Twins were held to a series batting average 113 points below their season mark.

Still, Minnesota nearly won the first game with three runs on only four hits. But the Orioles tied the score on Boog Powell's homer in the bottom of the ninth and won the game three innings later on Paul Blair's suicide squeeze bunt with two away. In Game Two, Minnesota's Dave Boswell scattered seven Baltimore hits over 10⅔ scoreless innings before giving way to Ron Perranoski in the eleventh. But Oriole pitcher Dave McNally was more than a match for Boswell. He gave up only three Twin hits—none in the final 7⅔ innings of the 11 he pitched—and took the win when Baltimore pinch hitter Curt Motton lined a single off Perranoski to score Powell from second with the game's only run.

In the third game, the Twins fell apart as the Orioles battered seven Minnesota pitchers for eighteen hits. Baltimore's Jim Palmer gave up more than a hit an inning himself, but coasted to the pennant 11–2.

Baltimore Orioles (East), 3; Minnesota Twins (West) 0

BAL (E)

PLAYER/POS	AVG	G	AB	R	H	2B	3B	HR	RB	BB	SO	SB
Mark Belanger, ss	.267	3	15	4	4	0	1	1	1	1	0	0
Paul Blair, of	.400	3	15	1	6	2	0	1	6	2	2	0
Don Buford, of	.286	3	14	3	4	1	0	0	1	3	0	0
Mike Cuellar, p	.000	1	2	0	0	0	0	0	0	0	1	0
Andy Etchebarren, c	.000	2	4	0	0	0	0	0	0	0	0	0
Dick Hall, p	.000	1	0	0	0	0	0	0	0	0	0	0
Elrod Hendricks, c	.250	3	8	2	2	2	0	0	3	1	2	0
Davy Johnson, 2b	.231	3	13	2	3	0	0	0	0	2	1	0
Marcelino Lopez, p	.000	1	0	0	0	0	0	0	0	0	0	0
Dave May, ph	.000	1	1	0	0	0	0	0	0	0	0	0
Dave Nc Nally, p	.000	1	4	0	0	0	0	0	0	0	2	0
Curt Motton, ph	.500	2	2	0	1	0	0	0	1	0	0	0
Jim Palmer, p	.000	1	5	0	0	0	0	0	0	0	3	0
Boog Powell, 1b	.385	3	13	2	5	0	0	1	1	2	0	0
Merv Rettenmund, ph	.000	1	0	0	0	0	0	0	0	0	0	0
Pete Richert, p	.000	1	0	0	0	0	0	0	0	0	0	0
Brooks Robinson, 3b	.500	3	14	1	7	1	0	0	0	0	0	0
Frank Robinson, of	.333	3	12	1	4	2	0	1	2	3	3	0
Chico Salmon, ph	.000	1	1	0	0	0	0	0	0	0	0	0
Eddie Watt, p	.000	1	0	0	0	0	0	0	0	0	0	0
TOTAL	.293		123	16	36	8	1	4	15	13	14	0

PITCHER	W	L	ERA	G	GS	CG	SV	SHO	IP	H	ER	BB	SO
Mike Cuellar	0	0	2.25	1	1	0	0	0	8.0	3	2	1	7
Dick Hall	1	0	0.00	1	0	0	0	0	0.2	0	0	0	1
Marcelino Lopez	0	0	0.00	1	0	0	0	0	0.1	1	0	2	0
Dave Nc Nally	1	0	0.00	1	1	1	0	1	11.0	3	0	5	11
Jim Palmer	1	0	2.00	1	1	1	0	0	9.0	10	2	4	4
Pete Richert	0	0	0.00	1	0	0	0	0	1.0	0	0	2	2
Eddie Watt	0	0	0.00	1	0	0	0	0	2.0	0	0	0	2
TOTAL	3	0	1.13	7	3	2	0	1	32.0	17	4	12	27

MIN (W)

PLAYER/POS	AVG	G	AB	R	H	2B	3B	HR	RB	BB	SO	SB
Bob Allison, of	.000	2	8	0	0	0	0	0	0	1	0	0
Dave Boswell, p	.000	1	4	0	0	0	0	0	0	0	4	0
Leo Cardenas, ss	.154	3	13	0	2	0	1	0	0	0	7	0
Rod Carew, 2b	.071	3	14	0	1	0	0	0	0	1	4	0
Dean Chance, p	.000	1	0	0	0	0	0	0	0	0	0	0
Joe Grzenda, p	.000	1	0	0	0	0	0	0	0	0	0	0
Tom Hall, p	.000	1	0	0	0	0	0	0	0	0	0	0
Harmon Killebrew, 3b	.125	3	8	2	1	1	0	0	0	6	2	0
Chuck Manuel, ph	.000	1	0	0	0	0	0	0	0	1	0	0
Bob Miller, p	.000	1	0	0	0	0	0	0	0	0	0	0
George Mitterwald, c	.143	2	7	0	1	0	0	0	0	0	1	3	0
Graig Nettles, ph	1.000	1	1	0	1	0	0	0	0	0	0	0
Tony Oliva, of	.385	3	13	3	5	2	0	1	2	1	3	1
Ron Perranoski, p	.000	3	1	0	0	0	0	0	0	0	1	0
Jim Perry, p	.000	1	3	0	0	0	0	0	0	0	0	0
Rich Reese, 1b	.167	3	12	0	2	0	0	0	2	1	1	0
Rich Renick, ph	.000	1	1	0	0	0	0	0	0	0	0	0
John Roseboro, c	.200	2	5	0	1	0	0	0	0	0	0	0
Cesar Tovar, of	.077	3	13	0	1	0	0	0	0	1	2	1
Ted Uhlaender, of	.167	2	6	0	1	0	0	0	0	0	0	0
Dick Woodson, p	1.000	1	1	0	1	0	0	0	0	0	0	0
Al Worthington, p	.000	1	0	0	0	0	0	0	0	0	0	0
TOTAL	.155		110	5	17	3	1	1	5	12	27	2

PITCHER	W	L	ERA	G	GS	CG	SV	SHO	IP	H	ER	BB	SO
Dave Boswell	0	1	0.84	1	1	0	0	0	10.2	7	1	7	4
Dean Chance	0	0	13.50	1	0	0	0	0	2.0	4	3	0	2
Joe Grzenda	0	0	0.00	1	0	0	0	0	0.2	0	0	0	0
Tom Hall	0	0	0.00	1	0	0	0	0	0.2	0	0	0	0
Bob Miller	0	1	5.40	1	1	0	0	0	1.2	5	1	0	0
Ron Perranoski	0	1	5.79	3	0	0	0	0	4.2	8	3	0	2
Jim Perry	0	0	3.38	1	1	0	0	0	8.0	6	3	3	3
Dick Woodson	0	0	10.80	1	0	0	0	0	1.2	3	2	3	2
Al Worthington	0	0	6.75	1	0	0	0	0	1.1	3	1	0	1
TOTAL	0	3	4.02	11	3	0	0	0	31.1	36	14	13	14

GAME 1 AT BAL OCT 4

MIN	000 010 200 000	3	4	2
BAL	000 110 001 001	4	10	1

Pitchers: Perry, PERRANOSKI (9) VS Cuellar, Richert (9), Watt (10), Lopez (12), HALL (12)
Home Runs: F.Robinson-BAL, Belanger-BAL, Oliva-MIN, Powell-BAL
Attendance: 39,324

GAME 2 AT BAL OCT 5

MIN	000 000 000 00	0	3	1
BAL	000 000 000 01	1	8	0

Pitchers: BOSWELL, Perranoski (11) VS McNALLY
Attendance: 41,704

GAME 3 AT MIN OCT 6

BAL	030 201 023	11	18	0
MIN	100 010 000	2	10	2

Pitchers: PALMER vs MILLER, Woodson (2), Hall (4), Worthington (5), Grzenda (6), Chance (7), Perranoski (9)
Home Runs: Blair-BAL
Attendance: 32,735

The heavy-hitting, slick-fielding Orioles, who also boasted the majors' top pitching staff, entered the Series clear favorites against the upstart Mets. But the "Miracle Mets," after losing the opener, polished off Baltimore with four straight wins.

The clubs' big winners, Met Tom Seaver (25–7) and Mike Cuellar (23–11) faced each other in the opener. Baltimore's leadoff batter, Don Buford, greeted Seaver with a home run, and a three-run Oriole rally with two out in the fourth made the score 4–0 before the Mets scored their first Series run in the seventh. Cuellar held New York to that one run for the victory.

No one scored for three innings of Game Two off Oriole Dave McNally or even hit Met Jerry Koosman safely. But Met Donn Clendenon led off the fourth with a home run as Koosman continued to no-hit Baltimore for three more innings. In the seventh, though, Baltimore's Paul Blair spoiled Koosman's no-hitter with a leadoff single, and after stealing second, scored the tying run on Brooks Robinson's single. But those were the only hits the O's would get, and in the top of the ninth three successive two-out Met singles produced what proved to be the winning run.

Met pitchers Gary Gentry and Nolan Ryan (with the assist of two spectacular catches by center fielder Tommie Agee that saved a total of five runs) combined for a shutout in Game Three. Agee's leadoff homer against Jim Palmer in the first was all the scoring the Mets would need, but they added four more runs before the game ended. Game Four was the Series' tightest. Seaver went the distance for the win, holding a 1–0 lead until a sacrifice fly scored the tying Baltimore run in the top of the ninth. In the bottom of the tenth, the Mets finally won it as a bunt thrown to first hit the runner and bounded away, allowing pinch runner Rod Gaspar to score all the way from second.

Dave McNally and Jerry Koosman tangled a second time in Game Five, and again Koosman and the Mets emerged victorious. McNally's two-run homer in the third gave him a lead which Frank Robinson expanded with a solo shot. But in an eerie sixth inning reprise of Game Four of the 1957 World Series featuring Nippy Jones, the Mets' Cleon Jones was struck by a pitch on the foot and awarded first base after inspection by the home plate umpire revealed tell-tale shoe polish on the ball. Each Jones produced a key run, Cleon coming home on Donn Clendenon's home run which followed immediately. Al Weis

New York Mets (NL), 4;
Baltimore Orioles (AL) 1

NY (N)

PLAYER/POS	AVG	G	AB	R	H	2B	3B	HR	RB	BB	SO	SB
Tommie Agee, of	.167	5	18	1	3	0	0	1	1	2	5	1
Ken Boswell, 2b	.333	1	3	1	1	0	0	0	0	0	0	0
Don Cardwell, p	.000	1	0	0	0	0	0	0	0	0	0	0
Ed Charles, 3b	.133	4	15	1	2	1	0	0	0	0	2	0
Donn Clendenon, 1b	.357	4	14	4	5	1	0	3	4	2	6	0
Duffy Dyer, ph	.000	1	1	0	0	0	0	0	0	0	0	0
Wayne Garrett, 3b	.000	2	1	0	0	0	0	0	0	2	1	0
Rod Gaspar, of-1	.000	2	2	1	0	0	0	0	0	0	0	0
Gary Gentry, p	.333	1	3	0	1	1	0	0	2	0	2	0
Jerry Grote, c	.211	5	19	1	4	2	0	0	1	1	3	0
Bud Harrelson, ss	.176	5	17	1	3	0	0	0	0	3	4	0
Cleon Jones, of	.158	5	19	2	3	1	0	0	2	0	1	0
Jerry Koosman, p	.143	2	7	0	1	1	0	0	0	0	4	0
Ed Kranepool, 1b	.250	1	4	1	1	0	0	1	1	0	0	0
J.C. Martin, ph	.000	1	0	0	0	0	0	0	0	0	0	0
Nolan Ryan, p	.000	1	0	0	0	0	0	0	0	0	0	0
Tom Seaver, p	.000	2	4	0	0	0	0	0	0	0	2	0
Art Shamsky, of-1	.000	3	6	0	0	0	0	0	0	0	0	0
Ron Swoboda, of	.400	4	15	1	6	1	0	0	1	1	3	0
Ron Taylor, p	.000	2	0	0	0	0	0	0	0	0	0	0
Al Weis, 2b	.455	5	11	1	5	0	0	1	3	4	2	0
TOTAL	.220		159	15	35	8	0	6	13	15	35	1

PITCHER	W	L	ERA	G	GS	CG	SV	SHO	IP	H	ER	BB	SO
Don Cardwell	0	0	0.00	1	0	0	0	0	1.0	0	0	0	0
Gary Gentry	1	0	0.00	1	1	0	0	0	6.2	3	0	5	4
Jerry Koosman	2	0	2.04	2	2	1	0	0	17.2	7	4	4	9
Nolan Ryan	0	0	0.00	1	0	0	1	0	2.1	1	0	2	3
Tom Seaver	1	1	3.00	2	2	1	0	0	15.0	12	5	3	9
Ron Taylor	0	0	0.00	2	0	0	1	0	2.1	0	0	1	3
TOTAL	4	1	1.80	9	5	2	2	0	45.0	23	9	15	28

BAL (A)

PLAYER/POS	AVG	G	AB	R	H	2B	3B	HR	RB	BB	SO	SB
Mark Belanger, ss	.200	5	15	2	3	0	0	0	0	1	2	1	0
Paul Blair, of	.100	5	20	1	2	0	0	0	0	2	5	1
Don Buford, of	.100	5	20	1	2	1	0	1	2	2	4	0
Mike Cuellar, p	.400	2	5	0	2	0	0	0	1	0	3	0
Clay Dalrymple, ph	1.000	2	2	0	2	0	0	0	0	0	0	0
Andy Etchebarren, c	.000	2	6	0	0	0	0	0	0	0	1	0
Dick Hall, p	.000	1	0	0	0	0	0	0	0	0	0	0
Elrod Hendricks, c	.100	3	10	1	1	0	0	0	0	1	0	0
Davy Johnson, 2b	.063	5	16	1	1	0	0	0	0	2	1	0
Dave Leonhard, p	.000	1	0	0	0	0	0	0	0	0	0	0
Dave May, ph	.000	2	1	0	0	0	0	0	0	1	1	0
Dave Mc Nally, p	.200	2	5	1	1	0	1	1	2	0	2	0
Curt Motton, ph	.000	1	1	0	0	0	0	0	0	0	0	0
Jim Palmer, p	.000	1	2	0	0	0	0	0	0	1	0	0
Boog Powell, 1b	.263	5	19	0	5	0	0	0	0	1	4	0
Merv Rettenmund, pr	.000	1	0	0	0	0	0	0	0	0	0	0
Pete Richert, p	.000	1	0	0	0	0	0	0	0	0	0	0
Brooks Robinson, 3b	.053	5	19	0	1	0	0	0	2	0	3	0
Frank Robinson, of	.188	5	16	2	3	0	0	1	1	4	3	0
Chico Salmon, pr	.000	2	0	0	0	0	0	0	0	0	0	0
Eddie Watt, p	.000	2	0	0	0	0	0	0	0	0	0	0
TOTAL	.146		157	9	23	1	0	3	9	15	28	1

PITCHER	W	L	ERA	G	GS	CG	SV	SHO	IP	H	ER	BB	SO
Mike Cuellar	1	0	1.13	2	2	1	0	0	16.0	13	2	4	13
Dick Hall	0	1	INF	1	0	0	0	0	0.0	1	0	1	0
Dave Leonhard	0	0	4.50	1	0	0	0	0	2.0	1	1	1	1
Dave Mc Nally	0	1	2.81	2	2	1	0	0	16.0	11	5	5	13
Jim Palmer	0	1	6.00	1	1	0	0	0	6.0	5	4	4	5
Pete Richert	0	0	INF	1	0	0	0	0	0.0	0	0	0	0
Eddie Watt	0	1	3.00	2	0	0	0	0	3.0	4	1	0	3
TOTAL	1	4	2.72	10	5	2	0	0	43.0	35	13	15	35

homered in the seventh for a 3–3 tie. With McNally now gone, two doubles off Eddie Watt in the eighth brought in the go-ahead Met run, and a pair of errors let in a run for insurance. Koosman held Baltimore scoreless in the ninth and the Met miracle was complete.

GAME 1 AT BAL OCT 11

NY   000 000 100   1 6 1
BAL 100 300 00X   4 6 0

Pitchers: SEAVER, Cardwell (6), Taylor (7) vs CUELLAR
Home Runs: Buford-BAL
Attendance: 50,429

GAME 2 AT BAL OCT 12

NY   000 100 001   2 6 0
BAL   000 000 100   1 2 0

Pitchers: KOOSMAN, Taylor (9) vs McNALLY
Home Runs: Clendenon-NY
Attendance: 50,850

GAME 3 AT NY OCT 14

BAL   000 000 000   0 4 1
NY   120 001 01X   5 6 0

Pitchers: PALMER, Leonhard (7) VS GENTRY, Ryan (7)
Home Runs: Agee-NY, Kranepool-NY
Attendance: 56,335

GAME 4 AT NY OCT 15

BAL   000 000 001 0   1 6 1
NY   010 000 000 1   2 10 1

Pitchers: Cuellar, Watt (8), HALL (10), Richert (10) vs SEAVER
Home Runs: Clendenon-NY
Attendance: 57,367

GAME 5 AT NY OCT 16

BAL   003 000 000   3 5 2
NY   000 002 12X   5 7 0

Pitchers: McNally, WATT (8) vs KOOSMAN
Home Runs: McNally-BAL, F.Robinson-BAL, Clendenon-NY, Weis-NY
Attendance: 57,397

Pitching was the game and three the magic number, as Cincinnati swept Pittsburgh, scoring three runs in each game while holding the Pirates to just three runs for the whole series.

Pirate pitcher Dock Ellis matched the Reds' Gary Nolan for nine scoreless innings in Game One before a pinch-hit triple, a single, and a double undid him for three runs in the top of the tenth. In Game Two Pittsburgh scored its first series run, but Red center fielder Bobby Tolan scored three for Baltimore—including a home run—to give Cincinnati its second win.

The Pirates took a lead for the only time in the series with a run in the top of the first inning of Game Three. But Tony Perez and Johnny Bench homered in the bottom of the inning to put the Reds up 2–1. The Pirates tied the score in the fifth, but three Red relievers combined to shut them out over the final four innings, while Tolan sank the Pirate ship with his second game-winner in two days: a single in the eighth that drove in Cincinnati's third—and final—run.

Cincinnati Reds (West), 3;
Pittsburgh Pirates (East) 0

CIN (W)

PLAYER/POS	AVG	G	AB	R	H	2B	3B	HR	RB	BB	SO	SB
Johnny Bench, c	.222	3	9	2	2	0	0	1	1	3	1	0
Angel Bravo, ph	.000	1	1	0	0	0	0	0	0	0	0	0
Bernie Carbo, of	.000	2	6	0	0	0	0	0	0	0	3	0
Clay Carroll, p	.000	2	0	0	0	0	0	0	0	0	0	0
Ty Cline, of-1	1.000	2	1	2	1	0	1	0	0	1	0	0
Tony Cloninger, p	.000	1	1	0	0	0	0	0	0	1	0	0
Dave Concepcion, ss	.000	3	3	0	0	0	0	0	0	0	0	0
Wayne Granger, p	.000	1	0	0	0	0	0	0	0	0	0	0
Don Gullett, p	.000	2	1	0	0	0	0	0	0	0	0	0
Tommy Helms, 2b	.273	3	11	0	3	0	0	0	0	0	1	0
Lee May, 1b	.167	3	12	0	2	1	0	0	2	0	2	0
Hal Mc Rae, of-1	.000	2	4	0	0	0	0	0	0	0	1	0
Jim Merritt, p	.000	1	2	0	0	0	0	0	0	0	2	0
Gary Nolan, p	.333	1	3	0	1	0	0	0	0	0	0	0
Tony Perez, 3b-3,1b-1	.333	3	12	4	4	2	0	1	2	1	1	0
Pete Rose, of	.231	3	13	1	3	0	0	0	1	0	0	0
Jimmy Stewart, of	.000	1	2	0	0	0	0	0	0	0	0	0
Bobby Tolan, of	.417	3	12	3	5	0	0	1	2	1	1	1
Milt Wilcox, p	.000	1	0	0	0	0	0	0	0	0	0	0
Woody Woodward, ss-3,3b-3	.100	3	10	0	1	0	0	0	0	0	1	0
TOTAL	.220		100	9	22	3	1	3	8	8	12	1

PITCHER	W	L	ERA	G	GS	CG	SV	SHO	IP	H	ER	BB	SO
Clay Carroll	0	0	0.00	2	0	0	1	0	1.1	2	0	0	2
Tony Cloninger	0	0	5.40	1	1	0	0	0	5.0	7	3	4	1
Wayne Granger	0	0	0.00	1	0	0	0	0	0.2	1	0	0	0
Don Gullett	0	0	0.00	2	0	0	2	0	3.2	1	0	2	3
Jim Merritt	1	0	1.69	1	1	0	0	0	5.1	3	1	0	2
Gary Nolan	1	0	0.00	1	1	0	0	0	9.0	8	0	4	6
Milt Wilcox	1	0	0.00	1	0	0	0	0	3.0	1	0	2	5
TOTAL	3	0	1.29	9	3	0	3	0	28.0	23	4	12	19

PIT (E)

PLAYER/POS	AVG	G	AB	R	H	2B	3B	HR	RB	BB	SO	SB
PLAYER, POS	AVG	G	AB	R	H	2B	3B	HR	RB	BB	SO	SB
Gene Alley, ss	.000	2	7	0	0	0	0	0	0	1	2	0
Matty Alou, of	.250	3	12	1	3	1	0	0	0	2	1	0
Dave Cash, 2b	.125	2	8	1	1	1	0	0	0	1	1	0
Roberto Clemente, of	.214	3	14	1	3	0	0	0	1	0	4	0
Dock Ellis, p	.000	1	2	0	0	0	0	0	0	0	1	0
Joe Gibbon, p	.000	2	0	0	0	0	0	0	0	0	0	0
Dave Giusti, p	.000	2	0	0	0	0	0	0	0	0	0	0
Richie Hebner, 3b	.667	2	6	0	4	2	0	0	0	2	1	0
Johnny Jeter, of-1	.000	3	2	0	0	0	0	0	0	0	2	0
Bill Mazeroski, 2b	.000	1	2	0	0	0	0	0	0	2	0	0
Bob Moose, p	.000	1	4	0	0	0	0	0	0	0	1	0
Al Oliver, 1b	.250	2	8	0	2	0	0	0	0	1	1	0
Jose Pagan, 3b	.333	1	3	0	1	0	0	0	0	1	1	0
Freddie Patek, ss	.000	1	3	0	0	0	0	0	0	1	2	0
Bob Robertson, 1b-1	.200	2	5	0	1	1	0	0	0	0	0	0
Manny Sanguillen, c	.167	3	12	0	2	0	0	0	0	0	1	0
Willie Stargell, of	.500	3	12	0	6	1	0	0	1	1	1	0
Luke Walker, p	.000	1	2	0	0	0	0	0	0	0	1	0
TOTAL	.225		102	3	23	6	0	0	3	12	19	0

PITCHER	W	L	ERA	G	GS	CG	SV	SHO	IP	H	ER	BB	SO
Dock Ellis	0	1	2.79	1	1	0	0	0	9.2	9	3	4	1
Joe Gibbon	0	0	0.00	2	0	0	0	0	0.1	0	0	1	0
Dave Giusti	0	0	3.86	2	0	0	0	0	2.1	3	1	1	1
Bob Moose	0	1	3.52	1	1	0	0	0	7.2	4	3	2	4
Luke Walker	0	1	1.29	1	1	0	0	0	7.0	5	1	1	5
TOTAL	0	3	2.67	7	3	0	0	0	27.0	22	8	8	12

For the second year in a row, Baltimore swept Minnesota in the LCS. In the first two games the Orioles' attack featured the big inning. The score was tied 2–2 in the first game as the Orioles came to bat in the top of the fourth. But by the time the Twins came to bat in the inning, they were seven runs behind—thanks in part to a grand slam by Baltimore pitcher Mike Cuellar. Harmon Killebrew's two-run homer in the fifth helped bring the Twins within three, but they came no closer.

Except for home runs to Killebrew and Tony Oliva in the fourth inning, Oriole pitcher Dave Mc-Nally stopped the Twins in Game Two, and Baltimore held a close 4–3 lead after eight. If they had been playing at home, they wouldn't have needed to bat at all in the ninth. But they did come to bat in the top of the ninth, and they once again buried Minnesota under a seven-run inning.

In the third game, for the second year in a row, Oriole pitcher Jim Palmer breezed through the series clincher. Baltimore scored five runs for him in the first three innings, and another in the eighth—four more than he needed to carry his club to another pennant.

Baltimore Orioles (East), 3; Minnesota Twins (West) 0

BAL (E)

PLAYER/POS	AVG	G	AB	R	H	2B	3B	HR	RB	BB	SO	SB
Mark Belanger, ss	.333	3	12	5	4	0	0	0	0	1	1	0
Paul Blair, of	.077	3	13	0	1	0	0	0	0	1	4	0
Don Buford, of	.429	2	7	2	3	1	0	1	3	2	0	0
Mike Cuellar, p	.500	1	2	1	1	0	0	1	4	0	1	0
Andy Etchebarren, c	.111	2	9	1	1	0	0	0	0	0	3	0
Dick Hall, p	.500	1	2	0	1	0	0	0	0	0	1	0
Elrod Hendricks, c	.400	1	5	2	2	0	0	0	0	0	1	0
Davy Johnson, 2b	.364	3	11	4	4	0	0	2	4	1	1	0
Dave Nc Nally, p	.400	1	5	1	2	1	0	0	1	0	1	0
Jim Palmer, p	.250	1	4	1	1	1	0	0	1	0	0	0
Boog Powell, 1b	.429	3	14	2	6	2	0	1	6	0	3	0
Merv Rettenmund, of	.333	1	3	1	1	0	0	0	1	2	1	1
Brooks Robinson, 3b	.583	3	12	4	7	2	0	1	0	1	0	0
Frank Robinson, of	.200	3	10	3	2	0	0	1	2	5	2	0
TOTAL	.330		109	27	36	7	0	6	24	12	19	1

PITCHER	W	L	ERA	G	GS	CG	SV	SHO	IP	H	ER	BB	SO
Mike Cuellar	0	0	12.46	1	1	0	0	0	4.1	10	6	1	2
Dick Hall	1	0	0.00	1	0	0	0	0	4.2	1	0	0	3
Dave Nc Nally	1	0	3.00	1	1	1	0	0	9.0	6	3	5	5
Jim Palmer	1	0	1.00	1	1	1	0	0	9.0	7	1	3	12
TOTAL	3	0	3.33	4	3	2	0	0	27.0	24	10	9	22

MIN (W)

PLAYER/POS	AVG	G	AB	R	H	2B	3B	HR	RB	BB	SO	SB
Bob Allison, ph	.000	3	2	0	0	0	0	0	0	0	1	1	0
Brant Alyea, of-2	.000	3	7	1	0	0	0	0	0	2	3	0
Bert Blyleven, p	.000	1	0	0	0	0	0	0	0	0	0	0
Leo Cardenas, ss	.182	3	11	1	2	0	0	0	1	1	1	0
Rod Carew, ph	.000	2	2	0	0	0	0	0	0	0	1	0
Tom Hall, p	.000	2	1	0	0	0	0	0	0	0	1	0
Jim Holt, of	.000	3	5	0	0	0	0	0	0	0	2	0
Jim Kaat, p	.000	1	1	0	0	0	0	0	0	0	0	0
Harmon Killebrew, 3b-2,1b-1	.273	3	11	2	3	0	0	2	4	2	4	0
Chuck Manuel, ph	.000	1	1	0	0	0	0	0	0	0	1	0
George Mitterwald, c	.500	2	8	2	4	1	0	0	2	0	2	0
Tony Oliva, of	.500	3	12	2	6	2	0	1	1	0	1	0
Ron Perranoski, p	.000	2	0	0	0	0	0	0	0	0	0	0
Jim Perry, p	.000	2	1	0	0	0	0	0	0	1	0	0
Frank Quilici, 2b-2	.000	3	2	0	0	0	0	0	0	0	1	0
Paul Ratliff, c	.250	1	4	0	1	0	0	0	0	0	1	0
Rich Reese, 1b	.143	2	7	0	1	0	0	0	0	1	1	0
Rich Renick, 3b-1	.200	2	5	0	1	0	0	0	0	0	1	0
Danny Thompson, 2b	.125	3	8	0	1	1	0	0	0	1	0	0
Luis Tiant, p	.000	1	0	0	0	0	0	0	0	0	0	0
Cesar Tovar, of-3,2b-1	.385	3	13	2	5	0	1	0	1	0	0	0
Stan Williams, p	.000	2	0	0	0	0	0	0	0	1	0	0
Dick Woodson, p	.000	1	0	0	0	0	0	0	0	0	0	0
Bill Zepp, p	.000	2	0	0	0	0	0	0	0	0	0	0
TOTAL	.238		101	10	24	4	1	3	10	9	22	0

PITCHER	W	L	ERA	G	GS	CG	SV	SHO	IP	H	ER	BB	SO
Bert Blyleven	0	0	0.00	1	0	0	0	0	2.0	2	0	0	2
Tom Hall	0	1	6.75	2	1	0	0	0	5.1	6	4	4	6
Jim Kaat	0	1	9.00	1	1	0	0	0	2.0	6	2	2	1
Ron Perranoski	0	0	19.29	2	0	0	0	0	2.1	5	5	1	3
Jim Perry	0	1	13.50	2	1	0	0	0	5.1	10	8	1	3
Luis Tiant	0	0	13.50	1	0	0	0	0	0.2	1	1	0	0
Stan Williams	0	0	0.00	2	0	0	0	0	6.0	2	0	1	2
Dick Woodson	0	0	9.00	1	0	0	0	0	1.0	2	1	1	0
Bill Zepp	0	0	6.75	2	0	0	0	0	1.1	2	1	2	2
TOTAL	0	3	7.62	14	3	0	0	0	26.0	36	22	12	19

GAME 1 AT MIN OCT 3

BAL	020	701	000	10	13 0
MIN	110	130	000	6	11 2

Pitchers: Cuellar, HALL (5) vs PERRY, Zepp (4), Woodson (5), Williams (6), Perranoski (9)
Home Runs: Cuellar-BAL, Buford-BAL, Powell-BAL, Killebrew-MIN
Attendance: 26,847

GAME 2 AT MIN OCT 4

BAL	102	100	007	11	13 0
MIN	000	300	000	3	6 2

Pitchers: McNALLY vs HALL, Zepp (4), Williams (5), Perranoski (8), Tiant (9)
Home Runs: F.Robinson-BAL, Killebrew-MIN, Oliva-MIN, Johnson-BAL
Attendance: 27,490

GAME 3 AT BAL OCT 5

MIN	000	010	000	1	7 2
BAL	113	000	10X	6	10 0

Pitchers: KAAT, Blyleven (3), Hall (5), Perry (7) vs PALMER
Home Runs: Johnson-BAL
Attendance: 27,608

With a near-sweep of Cincinnati, the Orioles helped Baltimore fans forget their 1969 Series humiliation by the New York Mets. Baltimore's first two wins, though, were closely contested. In the opener in Cincinnati (the first World Series game played on artificial grass), a Red run in the first inning and Lee May's third-inning two-run homer off Oriole starter Jim Palmer gave Cincinnati a 3–0 lead. But Orioles Boog Powell and Elrod Hendricks tagged Red starter Gary Nolan for home runs in the fourth and fifth that evened the score, and Brooks Robinson—whose otherworldly defense at third gave Reds righthanded hitters nightmares throughout the Series—homered in the seventh for a one-run Baltimore lead that held up as Palmer settled down to pitch one-hit ball from the fourth inning until he was relieved for the final out of the ninth.

Game Two was just as close. The Reds scored four runs in the first three innings, but Baltimore came back with six in the fourth and fifth. Johnny Bench's leadoff homer in the last of the sixth brought the Reds within one, but that was the end of the scoring for either side. In Game Three Oriole Dave McNally gave up nine hits and three runs. But he himself hit a grand slam in the sixth inning to cement what became a 9–3 victory.

On the verge of a Series sweep, the Orioles scored three runs in the last of the third inning of Game Four to take a 4–2 lead. But the Reds' Pete Rose homered in the fifth, and although Baltimore got the run back in the sixth, Lee May's three-run blast in the eighth overcame the Oriole lead and gave the Reds a narrow 6–5 win as Red reliever Clay Carroll permitted only one Oriole to hit safely over the final 3⅔ innings.

Mike Cuellar, driven out of Game Two in the third inning, hurled the complete game for Baltimore in Game Five, even though Cincinnati hammered him for four hits (three of them doubles) and three runs in the top of the first inning. But as Oriole home runs by Frank Robinson and Merv Rettenmund highlighted a Baltimore onslaught that produced fifteen hits and nine runs, Cuellar settled down, holding Cincinnati to a walk and a pair of harmless singles over the final eight innings to bring Baltimore its second world title in five years.

Baltimore Orioles (AL), 4; Cincinnati Reds (NL) 1

BAL (A)

PLAYER/POS	AVG	G	AB	R	H	2B	3B	HR	RBI	BB	SO	SB
Mark Belanger, ss	.105	5	19	0	2	0	0	0	0	1	1	2	0
Paul Blair, of	.474	5	19	5	9	1	0	0	3	2	4	0
Don Buford, of	.267	4	15	3	4	0	0	1	1	3	2	0
Terry Crowley, ph	.000	1	1	0	0	0	0	0	0	0	0	0
Mike Cuellar, p	.000	2	4	0	0	0	0	0	0	0	2	0
Moe Drabowsky, p	.000	2	1	0	0	0	0	0	0	0	1	0
Andy Etchebarren, c	.143	2	7	1	1	0	0	0	0	2	3	0
Dick Hall, p	.000	1	1	0	0	0	0	0	0	0	1	0
Elrod Hendricks, c	.364	3	11	1	4	1	0	1	4	1	2	0
Davy Johnson, 2b	.313	5	16	2	5	2	0	0	2	5	2	0
Marcelino Lopez, p	.000	1	0	0	0	0	0	0	0	0	0	0
Dave Mc Nally, p	.250	1	4	1	1	0	0	1	4	0	2	0
Jim Palmer, p	.143	2	7	1	1	0	0	0	0	0	3	0
Tom Phoebus, p	.000	1	0	0	0	0	0	0	0	0	0	0
Boog Powell, 1b	.294	5	17	6	5	1	0	2	5	5	2	0
Merv Rettenmund, of-1	.400	2	5	2	2	0	0	1	2	1	0	0
Pete Richert, p	.000	1	0	0	0	0	0	0	0	0	0	0
Brooks Robinson, 3b	.429	5	21	5	9	2	0	2	6	0	2	0
Frank Robinson, of	.273	5	22	5	6	0	0	2	4	0	5	0
Chico Salmon, ph	1.000	1	1	1	1	0	0	0	0	0	0	0
Eddie Watt, p	.000	1	0	0	0	0	0	0	0	0	0	0
TOTAL	.292		171	33	50	7	0	10	32	20	33	0

PITCHER	W	L	ERA	G	GS	CG	SV	SHO	IP	H	ER	BB	SO
Mike Cuellar	1	0	3.18	2	2	1	0	0	11.1	10	4	2	5
Moe Drabowsky	0	0	2.70	2	0	0	0	0	3.1	2	1	1	1
Dick Hall	0	0	0.00	1	0	0	1	0	2.1	0	0	0	0
Marcelino Lopez	0	0	0.00	1	0	0	0	0	0.1	0	0	0	0
Dave Mc Nally	1	0	3.00	1	1	1	0	0	9.0	9	3	2	5
Jim Palmer	1	0	4.60	2	2	0	0	0	15.2	11	8	9	9
Tom Phoebus	1	0	0.00	1	0	0	0	0	1.2	1	0	0	0
Pete Richert	0	0	0.00	1	0	0	1	0	0.1	0	0	0	0
Eddie Watt	0	1	9.00	1	0	0	0	0	1.0	2	1	1	3
TOTAL	4	1	3.40	12	5	2	2	0	45.0	35	17	15	23

CIN (N)

PLAYER/POS	AVG	G	AB	R	H	2B	3B	HR	RBI	BB	SO	SB
Johnny Bench, c	.211	5	19	3	4	0	0	1	3	1	2	0
Angel Bravo, ph	.000	4	2	0	0	0	0	0	0	1	1	0
Bernie Carbo, of-2	.000	4	8	0	0	0	0	0	0	2	3	0
Clay Carroll, p	.000	4	1	0	0	0	0	0	0	0	1	0
Darrel Chaney, ss	.000	3	1	0	0	0	0	0	0	0	1	0
Ty Cline, ph	.333	3	3	0	1	0	0	0	0	0	0	0
Tony Cloninger, p	.000	2	2	0	0	0	0	0	0	0	1	0
Dave Concepcion, ss	.333	3	9	0	3	0	1	0	3	0	0	0
Pat Corrales, ph	.000	1	1	0	0	0	0	0	0	0	0	0
Wayne Granger, p	.000	2	0	0	0	0	0	0	0	0	0	0
Don Gullett, p	.000	3	1	0	0	0	0	0	0	0	1	0
Tommy Helms, 2b	.222	5	18	1	4	0	0	0	0	0	1	0
Lee May, 1b	.389	5	18	6	7	2	0	2	8	2	2	0
Jim Mc Glothlin, p	.000	1	2	0	0	0	0	0	0	0	1	0
Hal Mc Rae, of	.455	3	11	1	5	2	0	0	3	0	1	0
Jim Merritt, p	.000	1	1	0	0	0	0	0	0	0	1	0
Gary Nolan, p	.000	2	3	0	0	0	0	0	0	0	0	0
Tony Perez, 3b	.056	5	18	2	1	0	0	0	0	3	4	0
Pete Rose, of	.250	5	20	2	5	1	0	1	2	2	0	0
Jimmy Stewart, ph	.000	2	2	0	0	0	0	0	0	0	1	0
Bobby Tolan, of	.211	5	19	5	4	1	0	1	1	3	2	1
Ray Washburn, p	.000	1	0	0	0	0	0	0	0	0	0	0
Milt Wilcox, p	.000	2	0	0	0	0	0	0	0	0	0	0
Woody Woodward, ss-3	.200	4	5	0	1	0	0	0	0	0	0	0
TOTAL	.213		164	20	35	6	1	5	20	15	23	1

PITCHER	W	L	ERA	G	GS	CG	SV	SHO	IP	H	ER	BB	SO
Clay Carroll	1	0	0.00	4	0	0	0	0	9.0	5	0	2	11
Tony Cloninger	0	1	7.36	2	1	0	0	0	7.1	10	6	5	4
Wayne Granger	0	0	33.75	2	0	0	0	0	1.1	7	5	1	1
Don Gullett	0	0	1.35	3	0	0	0	0	6.2	5	1	4	4
Jim Mc Glothlin	0	0	8.31	1	1	0	0	0	4.1	6	4	2	2
Jim Merritt	0	1	21.60	1	1	0	0	0	1.2	3	4	1	0
Gary Nolan	0	1	7.71	2	2	0	0	0	9.1	9	8	3	9
Ray Washburn	0	0	13.50	1	0	0	0	0	1.1	2	2	0	0
Milt Wilcox	0	1	9.00	2	0	0	0	0	2.0	3	2	0	2
TOTAL	1	4	6.70	18	5	0	0	0	43.0	50	32	20	33

GAME 1 AT CIN OCT 10

BAL	000 210 100	4	7	2
CIN	102 000 000	3	5	0

Pitchers: PALMER, Richert (9) vs NOLAN, Carroll (7)
Home Runs: May-CIN, Powell-BAL, Hendricks-BAL, B.Robinson-BAL
Attendance: 51,531

GAME 2 AT CIN OCT 11

BAL	000 150 000	6	10	2
CIN	301 000 000	5	7	0

Pitchers: Cuellar, PHOEBUS (3), Drabowsky (5), Lopez (7), Hall (7) VS McGlothlin, WILCOX (5), Carroll (5), Gullett (8)
Home Runs: Tolan-CIN, Powell-BAL, Bench-CIN
Attendance: 51,531

GAME 3 AT BAL OCT 13

CIN	010 000 200	3	9	0
BAL	201 014 10X	9	10	1

Pitchers: CLONINGER, Granger (6), Gullett (7) vs McNALLY
Home Runs: F.Robinson-BAL, Buford-BAL, McNally-BAL
Attendance: 51,773

GAME 4 AT BAL OCT 14

CIN	011 010 030	6	8	3
BAL	013 001 000	5	8	0

Pitchers: Nolan, Gullett (3), CARROLL (6) VS Palmer, WATT (8), Drabowsky (9)
Home Runs: B.Robinson-BAL, Rose-CIN, May-CIN
Attendance: 53,007

GAME 5 AT BAL OCT 15

CIN	300 000 000	3	6	0
BAL	222 010 02X	9	15	0

Pitchers: MERRITT, Granger (2), Wilcox (3), Cloninger (5), Washburn (7), Carroll (8) vs CUELLAR
Home Runs: F.Robinson-BAL, Rettenmund-BAL
Attendance: 45,341

For the first time, an LCS went more than the minimum three games, as Pittsburgh rebounded from a loss in the opener to take the next three from San Francisco.

The Pirates scored first, with two runs in the third inning of Game One, but the Giants came back with a run in the bottom of the inning and put the game away in the fifth as Tito Fuentes and Willie McCovey both hit two-out two-run homers. Pirate first baseman Bob Robertson avenged his club's opening-game defeat the next day, battering four of the Giants' six pitchers for three home runs and a double—and five RBIs—in the Pirates' 9–5 win. Robertson continued his assault in Game Three, homering off Juan Marichal in the second. The Giants came back with a run in the sixth, but third baseman Richie Hebner put the game away with a second Pirate home run off Marichal in the eighth.

Both clubs scored five times in the first two innings of Game Four. But Pirate relievers Bruce Kison and Dave Giusti then pinned the Giants down for the final seven innings, while Roberto Clemente and Al Oliver combined for four RBIs in the sixth to capture the flag.

Pittsburgh Pirates (East), 3;
San Francisco Giants (West), 1

PIT (E)

PLAYER/POS	AVG	G	AB	R	H	2B	3B	HR	RB	BB	SO	SB
Gene Alley, ss	.500	1	2	1	1	0	0	0	0	0	0	0
Steve Blass, p	.000	2	1	0	0	0	0	0	0	0	1	0
Dave Cash, 2b	.421	4	19	5	8	2	0	0	1	0	1	1
Roberto Clemente, of	.333	4	18	2	6	0	0	0	4	1	6	0
Gene Clines, of	.333	3	1	1	1	0	0	1	1	0	1	0
Vic Davalillo, ph	.000	2	2	0	0	0	0	0	0	0	1	0
Dock Ellis, p	.000	1	3	0	0	0	0	0	0	0	2	0
Dave Giusti, p	.000	4	1	0	0	0	0	0	0	0	0	0
Richie Hebner, 3b	.294	4	17	3	5	1	0	2	4	0	4	0
Jackie Hernandez, ss	.231	4	13	2	3	0	0	0	1	0	4	0
Bob Johnson, p	.000	1	2	0	0	0	0	0	0	0	1	0
Bruce Kison, p	.000	1	2	0	0	0	0	0	0	0	0	0
Milt May, ph	.000	1	1	0	0	0	0	0	0	0	0	0
Bill Mazeroski, ph	1.000	1	1	1	1	0	0	0	0	0	0	0
Bob Miller, p	.000	1	0	0	0	0	0	0	0	0	0	0
Bob Moose, p	.000	1	0	0	0	0	0	0	0	0	0	0
Al Oliver, of	.250	4	12	2	3	0	0	1	5	1	3	0
Jose Pagan, 3b	.000	1	1	0	0	0	0	0	0	0	0	0
Bob Robertson, 1b	.438	4	16	5	7	1	0	4	6	0	2	0
Manny Sanguillen, c	.267	4	15	1	4	0	0	0	1	1	1	1
Willie Stargell, of	.000	4	14	1	0	0	0	0	0	2	6	0
TOTAL	.271		144	24	39	4	0	8	23	5	33	2

PITCHER	W	L	ERA	G	GS	CG	SV	SHO	IP	H	ER	BB	SO
Steve Blass	0	1	11.57	2	2	0	0	0	7.0	14	9	2	11
Dock Ellis	1	0	3.60	1	1	0	0	0	5.0	6	2	4	1
Dave Giusti	0	0	0.00	4	0	0	3	0	5.1	1	0	2	3
Bob Johnson	1	0	0.00	1	1	0	0	0	8.0	5	0	3	7
Bruce Kison	1	0	0.00	1	0	0	0	0	4.2	2	0	2	3
Bob Miller	0	0	6.00	1	0	0	0	0	3.0	3	2	3	3
Bob Moose	0	0	0.00	1	0	0	0	0	2.0	0	0	0	0
TOTAL	3	1	3.34	11	4	0	3		35.0	31	13	16	28

SF (W)

PLAYER/POS	AVG	G	AB	R	H	2B	3B	HR	RB	BB	SO	SB
Jim Barr, p	.000	1	1	0	0	0	0	0	0	0	0	0
Bobby Bonds, of	.250	3	8	0	2	0	0	0	0	2	4	0
Ron Bryant, p	.000	1	0	0	0	0	0	0	0	0	0	0
Don Carrithers, p	.000	1	0	0	0	0	0	0	0	0	0	0
John Cumberland, p	.000	1	0	0	0	0	0	0	0	0	0	0
Dick Dietz, c	.067	4	15	0	1	0	0	0	0	2	5	0
Frank Duffy, ph	.000	1	1	0	0	0	0	0	0	0	1	0
Tito Fuentes, 2b	.313	4	16	4	5	1	0	1	2	1	3	0
Alan Gallagher, 3b	.100	4	10	0	1	0	0	0	0	0	2	0
Steve Hamilton, p	.000	1	0	0	0	0	0	0	0	0	0	0
Jim Ray Hart, 3b-1	.000	3	5	0	0	0	0	0	0	0	2	0
Ken Henderson, of	.313	4	16	3	5	1	0	0	2	2	1	1
Jerry Johnson, p	.000	1	0	0	0	0	0	0	0	0	0	0
Dave Kingman, of-2	.111	4	9	0	1	0	0	0	0	1	3	0
Hal Lanier, 3b	.000	1	1	0	0	0	0	0	0	0	0	0
Juan Marichal, p	.000	1	3	0	0	0	0	0	0	0	1	0
Willie Mays, of	.267	4	15	2	4	2	0	1	3	3	3	1
Willie Mc Covey, 1b	.429	4	14	2	6	0	0	2	6	4	2	0
Don Mc Mahon, p	.000	2	0	0	0	0	0	0	0	0	0	0
Gaylord Perry, p	.250	2	4	0	1	0	0	0	0	0	0	0
Jimmy Rosario, pr	.000	1	0	0	0	0	0	0	0	0	0	0
Chris Speier, ss	.357	4	14	4	5	1	0	1	1	1	1	0
TOTAL	.235		132	15	31	5	0	5	14	16	28	2

PITCHER	W	L	ERA	G	GS	CG	SV	SHO	IP	H	ER	BB	SO
Jim Barr	0	0	9.00	1	0	0	0	0	1.0	3	1	0	2
Ron Bryant	0	0	4.50	1	0	0	0	0	2.0	1	1	1	2
Don Carrithers	0	0	INF	1	0	0	0	0	0.0	3	3	0	0
John Cumberland	0	1	9.00	1	1	0	0	0	3.0	7	3	0	4
Steve Hamilton	0	0	9.00	1	0	0	0	0	1.0	1	1	0	3
Jerry Johnson	0	0	13.50	1	0	0	0	0	1.1	1	2	1	2
Juan Marichal	0	1	2.25	1	1	1	0	0	8.0	4	2	0	6
Don Mc Mahon	0	0	0.00	2	0	0	0	0	3.0	0	0	0	3
Gaylord Perry	1	1	6.14	2	2	1	0	0	14.2	19	10	3	11
TOTAL	1	3	6.09	11	4	2	0	0	34.0	39	23	5	33

GAME 1 AT SF OCT 2

PIT	002 000 200	4	9	0
SF	001 040 00X	5	7	2

Pitchers: BLASS, Moose (6), Giusti (8) VS PERRY
Home Runs: Fuentes-SF, McCovey-SF
Attendance: 40,977

GAME 2 AT SF OCT 3

PIT	010 210 401	9	15	0
SF	110 000 002	4	9	0

Pitchers: ELLIS, Miller (6), Giusti (9) VS CUMBERLAND, Barr (4), McMahon (5), Carrithers (7), Bryant (7), Hamilton (9)
Home Runs: Robertson-PIT (3), Clines-PIT, Mays-SF
Attendance: 42,562

GAME 3 AT PIT OCT 5

SF	000 001 000	1	5	2
PIT	010 000 01X	2	4	1

Pitchers: MARICHAL vs JOHNSON, Giusti (9)
Home Runs: Robertson-PIT, Hebner-PIT
Attendance: 38,322

GAME 4 AT PIT OCT 6

SF	140 000 000	5	10	0
PIT	230 004 00X	9	11	2

Pitchers: PERRY, Johnson (6), McMahon (8) VS Blass, KISON (3), Giusti (7)
Home Runs: Speier-SF, McCovey-SF, Hebner-PIT, Oliver-PIT
Attendance: 35,487

Baltimore, dividing its fifteen runs evenly among the three games, swept the ALCS for the third year in a row.

Oakland's Vida Blue took a 3–1 lead into the seventh inning of Game One, but with two away and men on first and third, an Oriole single and two doubles pushed across four runs to beat him 5–3, as Oriole starter Dave McNally and reliever Eddie Watt held the A's scoreless from the fifth inning on. In the second game Oakland managed only one run off Mike Cuellar, while the Orioles hammered Catfish Hunter for five runs on four homers—two of them by Boog Powell, including one in the eighth with a man aboard.

Reggie Jackson retaliated for the A's in Game Three with two home runs off Jim Palmer, and Sal Bando added a third. But Palmer permitted no other A's to score, and—supported by a Baltimore run in the first and two each in the fifth and seventh—preserved an Oriole lead throughout the game, for the third year in a row clinching the pennant for Baltimore with a complete-game victory.

Baltimore Orioles (East), 3;
Oakland A's (West) 0

BAL (E)

PLAYER/POS	AVG	G	AB	R	H	2B	3B	HR	RB	BB	SO	SB
Mark Belanger, ss	.250	3	8	1	2	0	0	0	1	3	2	0
Paul Blair, of	.333	3	9	1	3	1	0	0	2	0	3	0
Don Buford, of	.429	2	7	1	3	0	1	0	0	2	1	0
Mike Cuellar, p	.333	1	3	0	1	0	0	0	0	0	2	0
Andy Etchebarren, c	.000	2	5	0	0	0	0	0	0	0	0	0
Elrod Hendricks, c	.500	2	4	1	2	0	0	1	2	1	1	0
Davy Johnson, 2b	.300	3	10	2	3	2	0	0	0	3	1	0
Dave Nc Nally, p	.000	1	2	0	0	0	0	0	0	0	0	0
Curt Motton, ph	1.000	1	1	0	1	1	0	0	1	0	0	0
Jim Palmer, p-1	.200	2	5	1	1	0	0	0	0	0	1	0
Boog Powell, 1b	.300	3	10	4	3	0	0	2	3	3	3	0
Merv Rettenmund, of	.250	3	8	0	2	1	0	0	1	0	3	0
Brooks Robinson, 3b	.364	3	11	2	4	1	0	1	3	0	1	0
Frank Robinson, of	.083	3	12	2	1	1	0	0	1	1	4	0
Eddie Watt, p	.000	1	0	0	0	0	0	0	0	0	0	0
TOTAL	.274		95	15	26	7	1	4	14	13	22	0

PITCHER	W	L	ERA	G	GS	CG	SV	SHO	IP	H	ER	BB	SO
Mike Cuellar	1	0	1.00	1	1	1	0	0	9.0	6	1	1	2
Dave Nc Nally	1	0	3.86	1	1	0	0	0	7.0	7	3	1	5
Jim Palmer	1	0	3.00	1	1	1	0	0	9.0	7	3	3	8
Eddie Watt	0	0	0.00	1	0	0	1	0	2.0	2	0	0	1
TOTAL	3	0	2.33	4	3	2	1	0	27.0	22	7	5	16

OAK (W)

PLAYER/POS	AVG	G	AB	R	H	2B	3B	HR	RB	BB	SO	SB
Sal Bando, 3b	.364	3	11	3	4	2	0	1	1	1	0	0
Curt Blefary, ph	.000	1	1	0	0	0	0	0	0	0	1	0
Vida Blue, p	.000	1	3	0	0	0	0	0	0	0	3	0
Bert Campaneris, ss	.167	3	12	0	2	1	0	0	0	0	1	0
Tommy Davis, 1b-2	.375	3	8	1	3	1	0	0	0	0	0	0
Dave Duncan, c	.500	2	6	0	3	1	0	0	2	0	0	0
Mike Epstein, 1b-1	.200	2	5	0	1	0	0	0	0	0	3	0
Rollie Fingers, p	.000	2	0	0	0	0	0	0	0	0	0	0
Mudcat Grant, p	.000	1	0	0	0	0	0	0	0	0	0	0
Dick Green, 2b	.286	3	7	0	2	0	0	0	0	1	1	0
Mike Hegan, ph	.000	1	1	0	0	0	0	0	0	0	0	0
Catfish Hunter, p	.000	1	3	0	0	0	0	0	0	0	1	0
Reggie Jackson, of	.333	3	12	2	4	1	0	2	2	0	1	0
Darold Knowles, p	.000	1	0	0	0	0	0	0	0	0	0	0
Bob Locker, p	.000	1	0	0	0	0	0	0	0	0	0	0
Angel Mangual, of	.167	3	12	1	2	1	1	0	2	0	1	0
Rick Monday, of	.000	1	3	0	0	0	0	0	0	1	2	0
Joe Rudi, of	.143	2	7	0	1	1	0	0	0	1	0	0
Diego Segui, p	.000	1	2	0	0	0	0	0	0	0	0	0
Gene Tenace, c	.000	1	3	0	0	0	0	0	0	1	1	0
TOTAL	.229		96	7	22	8	1	3	7	5	16	0

PITCHER	W	L	ERA	G	GS	CG	SV	SHO	IP	H	ER	BB	SO
Vida Blue	0	1	6.43	1	1	0	0	0	7.0	7	5	2	8
Rollie Fingers	0	0	7.71	2	0	0	0	0	2.1	2	2	1	2
Mudcat Grant	0	0	0.00	1	0	0	0	0	2.0	3	0	0	2
Catfish Hunter	0	1	5.63	1	1	1	0	0	8.0	7	5	2	6
Darold Knowles	0	0	0.00	1	0	0	0	0	0.1	1	0	0	0
Bob Locker	0	0	0.00	1	0	0	0	0	0.2	0	0	2	0
Diego Segui	0	1	5.79	1	1	0	0	0	4.2	6	3	6	4
TOTAL	0	3	5.40	8	3	1	0	0	25.0	26	15	13	22

GAME 1 AT BAL OCT 3

OAK	020	100	000	3	9	0
BAL	000	100	40X	5	7	1

Pitchers: BLUE, Fingers (8) vs McNALLY, Watt (8)
Attendance: 42,621

GAME 2 AT BAL OCT 4

OAK	000	100	000	1	6	0
BAL	011	000	12X	5	7	0

Pitchers: HUNTER vs CUELLAR
Home Runs: B.Robinson-BAL, Powell-BAL (2), Hendricks-BAL
Attendance: 35,003

GAME 3 AT OAK OCT 5

BAL	100	020	200	5	12	0
OAK	001	001	010	3	7	0

Pitchers: PALMER vs SEGUI, Fingers (5), Knowles (7), Locker (7), Grant (8)
Home Runs: Jackson-OAK (2), Bando-OAK
Attendance: 33,176

In its third successive Series, Baltimore faced its third different opponent and beat the Pirates in the first two games. A walk, a wild pitch, two Baltimore errors, and a single in the second inning of the opener gave Pittsburgh an early 3–0 lead. But Oriole pitcher Dave McNally shut out the Pirates on two hits the rest of the game as Frank Robinson, Merv Rettenmund and Don Buford homered to give Baltimore a 5–3 victory. Jim Palmer took the win in Game Two as Baltimore hammered Pirate pitching for fourteen hits and eleven runs before Palmer issued Richie Hebner a three-run homer—Pittsburgh's only scoring—in the eighth.

The Pirates overtook the Orioles when the Series moved to Pittsburgh. Steve Blass pitched a three-hitter in Game Three, and while Frank Robinson's solo homer in the seventh ended Blass's shutout, a three-run shot by Pirate Bob Robertson in the last of the inning cemented a 5–1 Pittsburgh win. The next evening (in the first World Series night game ever), Baltimore scored three times in the top of the first inning, but two Pirate runs later in the inning and another run in the third tied the game. It remained tied until Pirate pinch hitter Milt May singled home the game winner with two away in the seventh.

With the Series now even at two wins apiece, Pittsburgh's Nelson Briles stopped the Orioles in Game Five on a pair of singles. Bob Robertson's leadoff homer in the second proved all the Pirates needed for the win, but Briles himself drove in an insurance run later in the inning and Pittsburgh went on to win 4–0.

The Pirates tried to win it all in Game Six, scoring single runs against the O's Jim Palmer in the second inning and the third (Roberto Clemente's home run). But Pirate starter Bob Moose was replaced after giving up a solo homer to Don Buford in the sixth, and a tying Baltimore run came home an inning later. A ninth-inning pinch hitter for Palmer produced nothing, but Baltimore won in the last of the tenth, when Frank Robinson scored on Brooks Robinson's sacrifice fly to shallow center.

Steve Blass, who had defeated Oriole Mike Cuellar in Game Three, faced him again in the finale and again emerged the victor of a pitching duel. Clemente's two-out homer in the fourth inning provided the game's only run until the eighth, when both teams scored single runs. Blass retired Baltimore in order in the ninth and the Pirates were world champions.

Pittsburgh Pirates (NL), 4; Baltimore Orioles (AL) 3

PIT (N)

PLAYER/POS	AVG	G	AB	R	H	2B	3B	HR	RB	BB	SO	SB
Gene Alley, ss	.000	2	2	0	0	0	0	0	0	1	0	0
Steve Blass, p	.000	2	7	0	0	0	0	0	0	0	1	0
Nelson Briles, p	.500	1	2	0	1	0	0	0	1	0	1	0
Dave Cash, 2b	.133	7	30	2	4	1	0	0	1	3	1	1
Roberto Clemente, of	.414	7	29	3	12	2	1	2	4	2	2	0
Gene Clines, of	.091	3	11	2	1	0	1	0	0	1	1	1
Vic Davalillo, of-2	.333	3	3	1	1	0	0	0	0	0	0	0
Dock Ellis, p	.000	1	1	0	0	0	0	0	0	0	1	0
Dave Giusti, p	.000	3	0	0	0	0	0	0	0	0	0	0
Richie Hebner, 3b	.167	3	12	2	2	0	0	1	3	3	3	0
Jackie Hernandez, ss	.222	7	18	2	4	0	0	0	1	2	5	1
Bob Johnson, p	.000	2	3	0	0	0	0	0	0	0	2	0
Bruce Kison, p	.000	2	2	0	0	0	0	0	0	1	2	0
Milt May, ph	.500	2	2	0	1	0	0	0	1	0	0	0
Bill Mazeroski, ph	.000	1	1	0	0	0	0	0	0	0	0	0
Bob Miller, p	.000	3	0	0	0	0	0	0	0	0	0	0
Bob Moose, p	.000	3	0	0	0	0	0	0	0	0	1	0
Al Oliver, of-4	.211	5	19	1	4	2	0	0	2	2	5	0
Jose Pagan, 3b	.267	4	15	0	4	2	0	0	2	0	1	0
Bob Robertson, 1b	.240	7	25	4	6	0	0	2	5	4	8	0
Charlie Sands, ph	.000	1	1	0	0	0	0	0	0	0	1	0
Manny Sanguillen, c	.379	7	29	3	11	1	0	0	0	0	3	2
Willie Stargell, of	.208	7	24	3	5	1	0	0	1	7	9	0
Bob Veale, p	.000	1	0	0	0	0	0	0	0	0	0	0
Luke Walker, p	.000	1	0	0	0	0	0	0	0	0	0	0
TOTAL	.235		238	23	56	9	2	5	21	26	47	5

PITCHER	W	L	ERA	G	GS	CG	SV	SHO	IP	H	ER	BB	SO
Steve Blass	2	0	1.00	2	2	2	0	0	18.0	7	2	4	13
Nelson Briles	1	0	0.00	1	1	1	0	1	9.0	2	0	2	2
Dock Ellis	0	1	15.43	1	1	0	0	0	2.1	4	4	1	1
Dave Giusti	0	0	0.00	3	0	0	1	0	5.1	3	0	2	4
Bob Johnson	0	1	9.00	2	1	0	0	0	5.0	5	5	3	3
Bruce Kison	1	0	0.00	2	0	0	0	0	6.1	1	0	2	3
Bob Miller	0	1	3.86	3	0	0	0	0	4.2	7	2	1	2
Bob Moose	0	0	6.52	3	1	0	0	0	9.2	12	7	2	7
Bob Veale	0	0	13.50	1	0	0	0	0	0.2	1	1	2	0
Luke Walker	0	0	40.50	1	1	0	0	0	0.2	3	3	1	0
TOTAL	4	3	3.50	19	7	3	1	1	61.2	45	24	20	35

BAL (A)

PLAYER/POS	AVG	G	AB	R	H	2B	3B	HR	RB	BB	SO	SB
Mark Belanger, ss	.238	7	21	4	5	0	1	0	0	5	2	1
Paul Blair, of-3	.333	4	9	2	3	1	0	0	0	0	1	0
Don Buford, of	.261	6	23	3	6	1	0	2	4	3	3	0
Mike Cuellar, p	.000	2	3	0	0	0	0	0	0	1	2	0
Pat Dobson, p	.000	3	2	0	0	0	0	0	0	0	2	0
Tom Dukes, p	.000	2	0	0	0	0	0	0	0	0	0	0
Andy Etchebarren, c	.000	1	2	0	0	0	0	0	0	0	0	0
Dick Hall, p	.000	1	0	0	0	0	0	0	0	0	0	0
Elrod Hendricks, c	.263	6	19	3	5	1	0	0	1	3	3	0
Grant Jackson, p	.000	1	0	0	0	0	0	0	0	0	0	0
Davy Johnson, 2b	.148	7	27	1	4	0	0	0	3	0	1	0
Dave Leonhard, p	.000	1	0	0	0	0	0	0	0	0	0	0
Dave Mc Nally, p	.000	4	4	0	0	0	0	0	0	0	3	0
Jim Palmer, p	.000	2	4	0	0	0	0	0	0	2	2	0
Boog Powell, 1b	.111	7	27	1	3	0	0	0	1	1	3	0
Merv Rettenmund, of-6	.185	7	27	3	5	0	0	1	4	0	4	0
Pete Richert, p	.000	1	0	0	0	0	0	0	0	0	0	0
Brooks Robinson, 3b	.318	7	22	2	7	0	0	0	5	3	1	0
Frank Robinson, of	.280	7	25	5	7	0	0	2	2	2	8	0
Tom Shopay, ph	.000	5	4	0	0	0	0	0	0	0	0	0
Eddie Watt, p	.000	2	0	0	0	0	0	0	0	0	0	0
TOTAL	.205		219	24	45	3	1	5	22	20	35	1

PITCHER	W	L	ERA	G	GS	CG	SV	SHO	IP	H	ER	BB	SO
Mike Cuellar	0	2	3.86	2	2	0	0	0	14.0	11	6	6	10
Pat Dobson	0	0	4.05	3	1	0	0	0	6.2	13	3	4	6
Tom Dukes	0	0	0.00	2	0	0	0	0	4.0	2	0	0	1
Dick Hall	0	0	0.00	1	0	0	1	0	1.0	1	0	0	0
Grant Jackson	0	0	0.00	1	0	0	0	0	0.2	0	0	1	0
Dave Leonhard	0	0	0.00	1	0	0	0	0	1.0	0	0	1	0
Dave Mc Nally	2	1	1.98	4	2	1	0	0	13.2	10	3	5	12
Jim Palmer	1	0	2.65	2	2	0	0	0	17.0	15	5	9	15
Pete Richert	0	0	0.00	1	0	0	0	0	0.2	0	0	0	1
Eddie Watt	0	1	3.86	2	0	0	0	0	2.1	4	1	0	2
TOTAL	3	4	2.66	19	7	1	1	0	61.0	56	18	26	47

GAME 1 AT BAL OCT 9

PIT	030	000	000	3	3	0
BAL	013	010	00X	5	10	3

Pitchers: ELLIS, Moose (3), Miller (7) VS McNALLY
Home Runs: F.Robinson-BAL, Rettenmund-BAL, Buford-BAL
Attendance: 53,229

GAME 2 AT BAL OCT 11

PIT	000	000	030	3	8	1
BAL	010	361	00X	11	14	1

Pitchers: R.JOHNSON, Kison (4), Moose (4), Veale (5), Miller (6), Giusti (8) vs PALMER, Hall (9)
Home Runs: Hebner-PIT
Attendance: 53,239

GAME 3 AT PIT OCT 12

BAL	000	000	100	1	3	3
PIT	100	001	30X	5	7	0

Pitchers: CUELLAR, Dukes (7), Watt (8) vs BLASS
Home Runs: F.Robinson-BAL, Robertson-PIT
Attendance: 50,403

GAME 4 AT PIT OCT 13

BAL	300	000	000	3	4	1
PIT	201	000	10X	4	14	0

Pitchers: Dobson, Jackson (6), WATT (7), Richert (8) vs Walker, KISON (1), Giusti (8)
Attendance: 51,378

GAME 5 AT PIT OCT 14

BAL	000	000	000	0	2	1
PIT	021	010	00X	4	9	0

Pitchers: McNALLY, Leonhard (5), Dukes (6) vs BRILES
Home Runs: Robertson-PIT
Attendance: 51,377

GAME 6 AT BAL OCT 16

PIT	011	000	000	0	2	9	1
BAL	000	001	100	1	3	8	0

Pitchers: Moose, R.Johnson (7), Giusti (7), MILLER (10) vs Palmer, Dobson (10), McNALLY (10)
Home Runs: Clemente-PIT, Buford-BAL
Attendance: 44,174

GAME 7 AT BAL OCT 17

PIT	000	100	010	2	6	1
BAL	000	000	100	1	4	0

Pitchers: BLASS vs CUELLAR, Dobson (9), McNally (9)
Home Runs: Clemente-PIT
Attendance: 47,291

Pittsburgh traded wins with Cincinnati through the first four games—winning the first and third—and took a lead into the ninth inning of the fifth game before a home run and a wild pitch undid them.

Cincinnati got eight hits in each of the first two games. In the first game, though, only Joe Morgan's first-inning homer produced a run, and the Reds lost 1–5. But the next day, five first-inning hits gave the Reds four runs and a lead the Pirates could not overcome.

Pirate catcher Manny Sanguillen brought Pittsburgh back in Game Three with a home run in the fifth and the game-winning RBI in the eighth. But Reds pitcher Ross Grimsley evened the series for Cincinnati the next day with a two-hitter, in the series' only complete-game performance.

Game Five was Pittsburgh's for 8½ innings. The Pirates scored first, and held the lead into the bottom of the ninth. But Johnny Bench opened the Reds' half of the ninth with a game-tying home run, and Tony Perez and Denis Menke followed him with singles. Bob Moose came in and retired the next two men, though George Foster (running for Perez) took third on a fly to right. Moose then threw away the pennant with a run-scoring, series-ending wild pitch.

Cincinnati Reds (West), 3; Pittsburgh Pirates (East) 2

CIN (W)

PLAYER/POS	AVG	G	AB	R	H	2B	3B	HR	RB	BB	SO	SB
Johnny Bench, c	.333	5	18	3	6	1	1	1	2	1	3	2
Jack Billingham, p	.000	1	2	0	0	0	0	0	0	0	1	0
Pedro Borbon, p	.000	3	0	0	0	0	0	0	0	0	0	0
Clay Carroll, p	.000	2	0	0	0	0	0	0	0	0	0	0
Darrel Chaney, ss	.188	5	16	3	3	0	0	0	1	1	1	1
Dave Concepcion, ss-1	.000	3	2	0	0	0	0	0	0	0	0	0
George Foster, pr	.000	1	0	1	0	0	0	0	0	0	0	0
Cesar Geronimo, of	.100	5	20	2	2	0	0	1	1	0	2	0
Ross Grimsley, p	.500	1	4	0	2	1	0	0	1	0	1	0
Don Gullett, p	.500	2	2	0	1	0	0	0	0	0	0	0
Joe Hague, ph	.000	3	1	0	0	0	0	0	0	2	1	0
Tom Hall, p	.000	2	1	0	0	0	0	0	0	0	0	0
Jim Mc Glothlin, p	.000	1	0	0	0	0	0	0	0	0	0	0
Hal Mc Rae, ph	.000	1	0	0	0	0	0	0	0	0	0	0
Denis Menke, 3b	.250	5	16	1	4	1	0	0	4	3	0	0
Joe Morgan, 2b	.263	5	19	5	5	0	0	2	3	1	2	1
Gary Nolan, p	.000	1	2	0	0	0	0	0	0	0	1	0
Tony Perez, 1b	.200	5	20	0	4	1	0	0	2	0	7	0
Pete Rose, of	.450	5	20	1	9	4	0	0	2	1	2	0
Bobby Tolan, of	.238	5	21	3	5	1	1	0	4	0	4	0
Ted Uhlaender, ph	.500	2	2	0	1	0	0	0	0	0	0	0
TOTAL	.253		166	19	42	9	2	4	16	10	28	4

PITCHER	W	L	ERA	G	GS	CG	SV	SHO	IP	H	ER	BB	SO
Jack Billingham	0	0	3.86	1	1	0	0	0	4.2	5	2	2	4
Pedro Borbon	0	0	2.08	3	0	0	0	0	4.1	2	1	0	1
Clay Carroll	1	1	3.38	2	0	0	0	0	2.2	2	1	3	0
Ross Grimsley	1	0	1.00	1	1	1	0	0	9.0	2	1	0	5
Don Gullett	0	1	8.00	2	2	0	0	0	9.0	12	8	0	5
Tom Hall	1	0	1.23	2	0	0	0	0	7.1	3	1	3	8
Jim Mc Glothlin	0	0	0.00	1	0	0	0	0	1.0	0	0	0	0
Gary Nolan	0	0	1.50	1	1	0	0	0	6.0	4	1	1	4
TOTAL	3	2	3.07	13	5	1	0	0	44.0	30	15	9	27

PIT (E)

PLAYER/POS	AVG	G	AB	R	H	2B	3B	HR	RB	BB	SO	SB
Gene Alley, ss	.000	5	16	1	0	0	0	0	0	0	3	0
Steve Blass, p	.000	2	6	0	0	0	0	0	0	0	3	0
Nelson Briles, p	.000	1	2	0	0	0	0	0	0	0	1	0
Dave Cash, 2b	.211	5	19	0	4	0	0	0	3	0	0	0
Roberto Clemente, of	.235	5	17	1	4	1	0	1	2	3	5	0
Gene Clines, ph	.000	3	2	1	0	0	0	0	0	0	0	0
Vic Davalillo, ph	.000	1	0	0	0	0	0	0	0	1	0	0
Dock Ellis, p-1	.000	2	1	0	0	0	0	0	0	0	0	0
Dave Giusti, p	.000	3	1	0	0	0	0	0	0	0	0	0
Richie Hebner, 3b	.188	5	16	2	3	1	0	0	1	1	3	0
Ramon Hernandez, p	.000	3	0	0	0	0	0	0	0	0	0	0
Bob Johnson, p	.000	2	1	0	0	0	0	0	0	0	1	0
Bruce Kison, p	.000	2	0	0	0	0	0	0	0	0	0	0
Milt May, c	.500	1	2	0	1	0	0	0	1	0	0	0
Bill Mazeroski, ph	.500	2	2	0	1	0	0	0	0	0	1	0
Bob Miller, p	.000	1	0	0	0	0	0	0	0	0	0	0
Bob Moose, p	.000	2	0	0	0	0	0	0	0	0	0	0
Al Oliver, of	.250	5	20	3	5	2	1	1	3	0	4	0
Bob Robertson, 1b	.000	4	0	0	0	0	0	0	0	0	1	0
Manny Sanguillen, c	.313	5	16	4	5	1	0	1	2	0	0	0
Willie Stargell, 1b-5,of-1	.063	5	16	1	1	1	0	0	1	2	5	0
Rennie Stennett, of-5,2b-1	.286	5	21	2	6	0	0	0	1	1	0	0
Luke Walker, p	.000	1	0	0	0	0	0	0	0	0	0	0
TOTAL	.190		158	15	30	6	1	3	14	9	27	0

PITCHER	W	L	ERA	G	GS	CG	SV	SHO	IP	H	ER	BB	SO
Steve Blass	1	0	1.72	2	2	0	0	0	15.2	12	3	6	5
Nelson Briles	0	0	3.00	1	1	0	0	0	6.0	6	2	1	3
Dock Ellis	0	1	0.00	1	1	0	0	0	5.0	5	0	1	3
Dave Giusti	0	1	6.75	3	0	0	1	0	2.2	5	2	0	3
Ramon Hernandez	0	0	2.70	3	0	0	1	0	3.1	1	1	0	3
Bob Johnson	0	0	3.00	2	0	0	0	0	6.0	4	2	2	7
Bruce Kison	1	0	0.00	2	0	0	0	0	2.1	1	0	0	3
Bob Miller	0	0	0.00	1	0	0	0	0	1.0	0	0	0	1
Bob Moose	0	1	54.00	2	1	0	0	0	0.2	5	4	0	0
Luke Walker	0	0	18.00	1	0	0	0	0	1.0	3	2	0	0
TOTAL	2	3	3.30	18	5	0	2	0	43.2	42	16	10	28

GAME 1 AT PIT OCT 7

CIN	100	000	000	1	8	0
PIT	300	020	00X	5	6	0

Pitchers: GULLETT, Borbon (7) vs BLASS, R.Hernandez (9)
Home Runs: Morgan-CIN, Oliver-PIT
Attendance: 50,476

GAME 2 AT PIT OCT 8

CIN	400	000	010	5	8	1
PIT	000	111	000	3	7	1

Pitchers: Billingham, HALL (5) vs MOOSE, Johnson (1), Kison (6), R.Hernandez (7), Giusti (9)
Home Runs: Morgan-CIN
Attendance: 50,584

GAME 3 AT CIN OCT 9

PIT	000	010	110	3	7	0
CIN	002	000	000	2	8	1

Pitchers: Briles, KISON (7), Giusti (8) VS Nolan, Borbon (7), CARROLL (7), McGlothlin (9)
Home Runs: Sanguillen-PIT
Attendance: 52,420

GAME 4 AT CIN OCT 10

PIT	000	000	100	1	2	3
CIN	100	202	20X	7	11	1

Pitchers: ELLIS, Johnson (6), Walker (7), Miller (8) vs GRIMSLEY
Home Runs: Clemente-PIT
Attendance: 39,447

GAME 5 AT CIN OCT 11

PIT	020	100	000	3	8	0
CIN	001	010	002	4	7	1

Pitchers: Blass, R.Hernandez (8), GIUSTI (9), Moose (9) vs Gullett, Borbon (4), Hall (6), CARROLL (9)
Home Runs: Geronimo-CIN, Bench-CIN
Attendance: 41,887

Oakland turned back the Tigers in the first two games, but Detroit evened the series before succumbing in the fifth game.

In Game One, Tiger Al Kaline homered off Rollie Fingers in the eleventh to give starter Mickey Lolich a 2–1 lead. But in the last of the inning, pinch hitter Gonzalo Marquez singled off Tiger reliever Chuck Seelbach with two on to drive in the tying run, and Gene Tenace scored to win it on the same play as right fielder Kaline threw the ball away. Blue Moon Odom increased the A's series lead with a three-hit shutout in Game Two, but Detroit's Joe Coleman retaliated with 14 strikeouts and a shutout of his own to save the Tigers from elimination in Game Three.

In Game Four the A's pulled out of a 1–1 tie with two runs in the top of the tenth. But Detroit in its half of the inning went through three Oakland relievers for three runs and the win. In the finale, after Odom, the A's starter, had given Detroit a run and a brief lead in the first, he and Vida Blue divided eight shutout innings between them as the A's scored twice to capture their first pennant since Connie Mack won his last in Philadelphia forty-one years earlier.

Oakland A's (West), 3; Detroit Tigers (East) 2

OAK (W)

PLAYER/POS	AVG	G	AB	R	H	2B	3B	HR	RB	BB	SO	SB
Matty Alou, of	.381	5	21	2	8	4	0	0	2	0	2	1
Sal Bando, 3b	.200	5	20	4	4	0	0	0	0	0	3	0
Vida Blue, p	.000	4	1	0	0	0	0	0	0	0	0	0
Bert Campaneris, ss	.429	2	7	3	3	0	0	0	0	1	0	2
Tim Cullen, ss	.000	2	1	0	0	0	0	0	0	0	0	0
Dave Duncan, c	.000	2	2	0	0	0	0	0	0	1	1	0
Mike Epstein, 1b	.188	5	16	1	3	0	0	1	1	4	5	1
Rollie Fingers, p	.000	3	1	0	0	0	0	0	0	0	0	0
Dick Green, 2b	.125	5	8	0	1	1	0	0	0	0	0	0
Dave Hamilton, p	.000	1	0	0	0	0	0	0	0	0	0	0
Mike Hegan, 1b-1	.000	3	1	1	0	0	0	0	0	0	0	0
George Hendrick, of-1	.143	5	7	2	1	0	0	0	0	0	1	0
Ken Holtzman, p	.000	1	1	0	0	0	0	0	0	0	1	0
Joe Horlen, p	.000	1	0	0	0	0	0	0	0	0	0	0
Catfish Hunter, p	.167	2	6	0	1	0	0	0	0	0	2	0
Reggie Jackson, of	.278	5	18	1	5	1	0	0	2	1	6	2
Ted Kubiak, 2b-3,ss-1	.500	4	4	0	2	0	0	0	1	0	0	0
Bob Locker, p	.000	2	0	0	0	0	0	0	0	0	0	0
Angel Mangual, ph	.000	3	3	0	0	0	0	0	0	0	1	0
Gonzalo Marquez, ph	.667	3	3	1	2	0	0	0	1	0	0	0
Dal Maxvill, ss-4,2b-1	.125	5	8	0	1	0	0	0	0	1	2	1
Don Mincher, ph	.000	1	1	0	0	0	0	0	0	0	1	0
Blue Moon Odom, p-2	.250	3	4	0	1	1	0	0	0	0	1	0
Joe Rudi, of	.250	5	20	1	5	1	0	0	2	1	4	0
Gene Tenace, c-5,2b-2	.059	5	17	1	1	0	0	0	0	1	3	5
TOTAL	.224		170	13	38	8	0	1	10	12	35	7

PITCHER	W	L	ERA	G	GS	CG	SV	SHO	IP	H	ER	BB	SO
Vida Blue	0	0	0.00	4	0	0	1	0	5.1	4	0	1	5
Rollie Fingers	1	0	1.69	3	0	0	0	0	5.1	4	1	1	3
Dave Hamilton	0	0	INF	1	0	0	0	0	0.0	1	0	1	0
Ken Holtzman	0	1	4.50	1	1	0	0	0	4.0	4	2	2	2
Joe Horlen	0	1	INF	1	0	0	0	0	0.0	0	1	1	0
Catfish Hunter	0	0	1.17	2	2	0	0	0	15.1	10	2	5	9
Bob Locker	0	0	13.50	2	0	0	0	0	2.0	4	3	0	1
Blue Moon Odom	2	0	0.00	2	2	1	0	1	14.0	5	0	2	5
TOTAL	3	2	1.76	16	5	1	1	1	46.0	32	9	13	25

DET (E)

PLAYER/POS	AVG	G	AB	R	H	2B	3B	HR	RB	BB	SO	SB
Ed Brinkman, ss	.250	1	4	0	1	1	0	0	0	0	0	0
Ike Brown, 1b	.500	1	2	0	1	0	0	0	2	0	1	0
Gates Brown, ph	.000	3	2	1	0	0	0	0	0	1	0	0
Norm Cash, 1b	.267	5	15	1	4	0	0	1	2	2	3	0
Joe Coleman, p	.500	1	2	0	1	0	0	0	0	1	0	0
Bill Freehan, c	.250	3	12	2	3	1	0	1	3	0	1	0
Woody Fryman, p	.000	2	3	0	0	0	0	0	0	0	0	0
Tom Haller, ph	.000	1	1	0	0	0	0	0	0	0	0	0
John Hiller, p	.000	3	0	0	0	0	0	0	0	0	0	0
Willie Horton, of-3	.100	5	10	0	1	0	0	0	0	1	3	0
Al Kaline, of	.263	5	19	3	5	0	0	1	1	2	2	0
John Knox, pr	.000	1	0	0	0	0	0	0	0	0	0	0
Lerrin La Grow, p	.000	1	0	0	0	0	0	0	0	0	0	0
Mickey Lolich, p	.000	2	7	0	0	0	0	0	0	0	2	0
Dick Mc Auliffe, ss-4,2b-1	.200	5	20	3	4	0	0	1	1	1	4	0
Jim Northrup, of	.357	5	14	0	5	0	0	0	1	2	3	0
Aurelio Rodriguez, 3b	.000	5	16	0	0	0	0	0	0	2	2	0
Fred Scherman, p	.000	1	0	0	0	0	0	0	0	0	0	0
Chuck Seelbach, p	.000	2	0	0	0	0	0	0	0	0	0	0
Duke Sims, c-2,of-2	.214	4	14	0	3	2	1	0	0	1	2	0
Mickey Stanley, of-3	.333	4	6	0	2	0	0	0	0	0	0	0
Tony Taylor, 2b	.133	4	15	0	2	2	0	0	0	0	2	0
Chris Zachary, p	.000	1	0	0	0	0	0	0	0	0	0	0
TOTAL	.198		162	10	32	6	1	4	10	13	25	0

PITCHER	W	L	ERA	G	GS	CG	SV	SHO	IP	H	ER	BB	SO
Joe Coleman	1	0	0.00	1	1	1	0	1	9.0	7	0	3	14
Woody Fryman	0	2	3.65	2	2	0	0	0	12.1	11	5	2	8
John Hiller	1	0	0.00	3	0	0	0	0	3.1	1	0	1	1
Lerrin La Grow	0	0	0.00	1	0	0	0	0	1.0	0	0	0	1
Mickey Lolich	0	1	1.42	2	2	0	0	0	19.0	14	3	5	10
Fred Scherman	0	0	0.00	1	0	0	0	0	0.2	1	0	0	1
Chuck Seelbach	0	0	18.00	2	0	0	0	0	1.0	4	2	0	0
Chris Zachary	0	0	INF	1	0	0	0	0	0.0	0	1	1	0
TOTAL	2	3	2.14	13	5	1	0	1	46.1	38	11	12	35

GAME 1 AT OAK OCT 7

DET	010 000 000 01	2	6	2
OAK	001 000 000 02	3	10	1

Pitchers: LOLICH, Seelbach (11) VS Hunter, Blue (9), FINGERS (9)
Home Runs: Cash-DET, Kaline-DET
Attendance: 29,536

GAME 2 AT OAK OCT 8

DET	000 000 000	0	3	1
OAK	100 040 00X	5	8	0

Pitchers: FRYMAN, Zachary (5), Scherman (5), LaGrow (6), Hiller (7) VS ODOM
Attendance: 31,088

GAME 3 AT DET OCT 10

OAK	000 000 000	0	7	0
DET	000 200 01X	3	8	1

Pitchers: HOLTZMAN, Fingers (5), Blue (6), Locker (7) vs COLEMAN
Home Runs: Freehan-DET
Attendance: 41,156

GAME 4 AT DET OCT 11

OAK	000 000 100 2	3	9	2
DET	001 000 003	4	10	1

Pitchers: Hunter, Fingers (8), Blue (9), Locker (10), HORLEN (10), Hamilton (10) VS Lolich, Seelbach (10), HILLER (10)
Home Runs: McAuliffe-DET, Epstein-OAK
Attendance: 37,615

GAME 5 AT DET OCT 12

OAK	010 100 000	2	4	0
DET	100 000 000	1	5	2

Pitchers: ODOM, Blue (6) vs FRYMAN, Hiller (9)
Attendance: 50,276

Oakland slugger Reggie Jackson missed the Series with a pulled hamstring, but Gene Tenace (the A's backup catcher during the season) took up the slack, hitting four of the club's five homers and driving in nine of their sixteen runs.

Six of the seven games were decided by a single run. Oakland won the first two in Cincinnati, 3–2 and 2–1. Tenace made the difference in the opener, driving in all the A's runs with a two-run homer in the second inning and a solo shot in the fifth. In the second game, A's starting pitcher Catfish Hunter singled in a run in the second inning which proved the margin of his victory. His 8⅔-inning performance was the longest mound outing in a Series which saw the two clubs together use nearly seven pitchers per game.

Cincinnati took the first game in Oakland, 1–0. The A's' Blue Moon Odom dueled the Reds' Jack Billingham scorelessly on one hit through six innings before giving up the game's only run on a single-sacrifice-single in the seventh. Billingham, too, yielded only three hits in eight-plus innings before yielding to ace reliever Clay Carroll, who retired the side in the ninth.

Oakland won Game Four, 3–2. Tenace opened the scoring with a solo homer in the fifth. The Reds' Bobby Tolan doubled in a pair in the eighth to put Cincinnati ahead, but in the last of the ninth four successive A's singles scored two runs, with Tenace scoring the game winner on pinch hitter Angel Mangual's hit. Tenace homered again in Game Five for three runs, but it wasn't enough as the Reds tied the score in the eighth and won on Pete Rose's RBI single in the ninth.

The Reds produced the Series' only blowout with five runs in the seventh inning of Game Six to make the score 8–1, where it remained. The finale saw Tenace drive in a run in the top of the first for a narrow Oakland lead which held until the Reds tied the game in the fifth. In the sixth the A's scored twice—Tenace doubling in the go-ahead run. Cincinnati scored once more in the eighth as a runner inherited by A's reliever Rollie Fingers came home on a sacrifice fly. But Fingers permitted no other runs to score, and the A's took the crown with their fourth one-run victory.

Oakland Athletics (AL), 4; Cincinnati Reds (NL) 3

OAK (A)

PLAYER/POS	AVG	G	AB	R	H	2B	3B	HR	RBI	BB	SO	SB
Matty Alou, of	.042	7	24	0	1	0	0	0	0	0	3	1
Sal Bando, 3b	.269	7	26	2	7	1	0	0	1	2	5	0
Vida Blue, p	.000	4	1	0	0	0	0	0	0	2	1	0
Bert Campaneris, ss	.179	7	28	1	5	0	0	0	0	1	4	0
Dave Duncan, c-1	.200	3	5	0	1	0	0	0	0	1	3	0
Mike Epstein, 1b	.000	6	16	1	0	0	0	0	0	5	3	0
Rollie Fingers, p	.000	6	1	0	0	0	0	0	0	0	0	0
Dick Green, 2b	.333	7	18	0	6	2	0	0	1	0	4	0
Dave Hamilton, p	.000	2	0	0	0	0	0	0	0	0	0	0
Mike Hegan, 1b-5	.200	6	5	0	1	0	0	0	0	0	2	0
George Hendrick, of	.133	5	15	3	2	0	0	0	0	1	2	0
Ken Holtzman, p	.000	3	5	0	0	0	0	0	0	0	0	0
Joe Horlen, p	.000	1	0	0	0	0	0	0	0	0	0	0
Catfish Hunter, p	.200	3	5	0	1	0	0	0	1	2	1	0
Ted Kubiak, 2b	.333	4	3	0	1	0	0	0	0	0	0	0
Allan Lewis, pr	.000	6	0	2	0	0	0	0	0	0	0	0
Bob Locker, p	.000	1	0	0	0	0	0	0	0	0	0	0
Angel Mangual, of-2	.300	4	10	1	3	0	0	0	1	0	0	0
Gonzalo Marquez, ph	.600	5	5	0	3	0	0	0	1	0	0	0
Don Mincher, ph	1.000	3	1	0	1	0	0	0	1	0	0	0
Blue Moon Odom, p-2	.000	4	4	0	0	0	0	0	0	0	3	0
Joe Rudi, of	.240	7	25	1	6	0	0	1	1	2	5	0
Gene Tenace, c-6,1b-1	.348	7	23	5	8	1	0	4	9	4	0	0
TOTAL	.209		220	16	46	4	0	5	16	21	37	1

PITCHER	W	L	ERA	G	GS	CG	SV	SHO	IP	H	ER	BB	SO
Vida Blue	0	1	4.15	4	1	0	1	0	8.2	8	4	5	5
Rollie Fingers	1	1	1.74	6	0	0	2	0	10.1	4	2	4	11
Dave Hamilton	0	0	6.75	2	0	0	0	0	1.1	2	1	2	1
Ken Holtzman	1	0	2.13	3	2	0	0	0	12.2	11	3	3	4
Joe Horlen	0	0	27.00	1	0	0	0	0	1.1	3	4	1	1
Catfish Hunter	2	0	2.81	3	2	0	0	0	16.0	12	5	6	11
Bob Locker	0	0	0.00	1	0	0	0	0	0.1	1	0	0	0
Blue Moon Odom	0	1	1.59	2	2	0	0	0	11.1	5	2	6	13
TOTAL	4	3	3.05	22	7	0	3	0	62.0	46	21	27	46

CIN (N)

PLAYER/POS	AVG	G	AB	R	H	2B	3B	HR	RBI	BB	SO	SB
Johnny Bench, c	.261	7	23	4	6	1	0	1	1	5	5	2
Jack Billingham, p	.000	3	5	0	0	0	0	0	0	0	4	0
Pedro Borbon, p	.000	6	0	0	0	0	0	0	0	0	0	0
Clay Carroll, p	.000	5	0	0	0	0	0	0	0	0	0	0
Darrel Chaney, ss-3	.000	4	7	0	0	0	0	0	0	2	2	0
Dave Concepcion, ss-5	.308	6	13	2	4	0	1	0	2	2	2	1
George Foster, of-1	.000	2	0	0	0	0	0	0	0	0	0	0
Cesar Geronimo, of	.158	7	19	1	3	0	0	0	3	1	4	1
Ross Grimsley, p	.000	4	2	0	0	0	0	0	0	0	2	0
Don Gullett, p	.000	1	2	0	0	0	0	0	0	0	0	0
Joe Hague, of-1	.000	3	3	0	0	0	0	0	0	0	0	0
Tom Hall, p	.000	4	2	0	0	0	0	0	0	0	1	0
Julian Javier, ph	.000	4	2	0	0	0	0	0	0	0	0	0
Jim Mc Glothlin, p	.000	1	1	0	0	0	0	0	0	0	0	0
Denis Menke, 3b	.083	7	24	1	2	0	0	1	2	2	6	0
Joe Morgan, 2b	.125	7	24	4	3	2	0	0	1	6	3	2
Gary Nolan, p	.000	2	3	0	0	0	0	0	0	0	3	0
Tony Perez, 1b	.435	7	23	3	10	2	0	0	2	4	4	0
Pete Rose, of	.214	7	28	3	6	0	0	1	2	4	4	1
Bobby Tolan, of	.269	7	26	2	7	1	0	0	6	1	4	5
Ted Uhlaender, ph	.250	4	4	0	1	1	0	0	0	0	1	0
TOTAL	.209		220	21	46	8	1	3	21	27	46	12

PITCHER	W	L	ERA	G	GS	CG	SV	SHO	IP	H	ER	BB	SO
Jack Billingham	1	0	0.00	3	2	0	1	0	13.2	6	0	4	11
Pedro Borbon	0	-1	3.86	6	0	0	0	0	7.0	7	3	2	4
Clay Carroll	0	1	1.59	5	0	0	1	0	5.2	6	1	4	3
Ross Grimsley	2	1	2.57	4	1	0	0	0	7.0	7	2	3	2
Don Gullett	0	0	1.29	1	1	0	0	0	7.0	5	1	2	4
Tom Hall	0	0	0.00	4	0	0	1	0	8.1	6	0	2	7
Jim Mc Glothlin	0	0	12.00	1	1	0	0	0	3.0	2	4	2	3
Gary Nolan	0	1	3.38	2	2	0	0	0	10.2	7	4	2	3
TOTAL	3	2	2.17	26	7	0	3	0	62.1	46	15	21	37

GAME 1 AT CIN OCT 14

OAK	020	010	000	3	4	0
CIN	010	100	000	2	7	0

Pitchers: HOLTZMAN, Fingers (6), Blue (7) VS NOLAN, Borbon (7), Carroll (8)
Home Runs: Tenace-OAK (2)
Attendance: 52,918

GAME 2 AT CIN OCT 15

OAK	011	000	000	2	9	2
CIN	000	000	001	1	6	0

Pitchers: HUNTER, Fingers (9) VS GRIMSLEY, Borbon (6), Hall (8)
Home Runs: Rudi-OAK
Attendance: 53,224

GAME 3 AT OAK OCT 18

CIN	000	000	100	1	4	2
OAK	000	000	000	0	3	2

Pitchers: BILLINGHAM, Carroll (9) VS ODOM, Blue (8), Fingers (8)
Attendance: 49,410

GAME 4 AT OAK OCT 19

CIN	000	000	020	2	7	1
OAK	000	010	002	3	10	1

Pitchers: Gullett, Borbon (8), CARROLL (9) vs Holtzman, Blue (8), FINGERS (9)
Home Runs: Tenace-OAK
Attendance: 49,410

GAME 5 AT OAK OCT 20

CIN	100	110	011	5	8	0
OAK	030	100	000	4	7	2

Pitchers: McGlothlin, Borbon (4), Hall (5), Carroll (7), GRIMSLEY (8), Billingham (9) vs Hunter, FINGERS (5), Hamilton (9)
Home Runs: Rose-CIN, Tenace-OAK, Menke-CIN
Attendance: 49,410

GAME 6 AT CIN OCT 21

OAK	000	010	000	1	7	1
CIN	000	111	50X	8	10	0

Pitchers: BLUE, Locker (6), Hamilton (7), Horlen (7) vs Nolan, GRIMSLEY (7), Borbon (6), Hall (7)
Home Runs: Bench-CIN
Attendance: 52,737

GAME 7 AT CIN OCT 22

OAK	100	002	000	3	6	1
CIN	000	010	010	2	4	2

Pitchers: Odom, HUNTER (5), Holtzman (8), Fingers (8) vs Billingham, BORBON (6), Carroll (6), Grimsley (7), Hall (8)
Attendance: 56,040

The Mets received strong pitching throughout the series, and their offense came through just often enough to defeat Cincinnati in five games.

Though three Reds pitchers held New York to three hits in Game One, the single Met run in the second seemed for a time enough for a win. But Tom Seaver gave up a home run to Pete Rose in the eighth and lost the game in the ninth when Johnny Bench homered. Not wanting another last-inning loss in Game Two, the Mets unloaded for four runs in the top of the ninth to add to their one in the fourth. But this time one would have been enough as Jon Matlack blanked the Reds on two hits.

The Mets made it easy for Jerry Koosman in Game Three in New York, scoring nine times in the first four innings. Things were more difficult for shortstop Bud Harrelson, who exchanged blows with Pete Rose following Rose's hard slide in the fifth inning. A bench-clearing melee ensued, and fans in the left field stands showered Rose with debris until a delegation of Tom Seaver, Willie Mays and Rusty Staub visited the area to calm nerves and eliminate the threat of a forfeit. In Game Four, though, Met bats were stifled once again as four Reds pitchers combined for a 12-inning three-hitter. The Reds won the game and tied the series on Rose's sweetly vengeful twelfth-inning homer.

In the finale the Mets took a quick two-run lead. Cincinnati tied the game in the top of the fifth, but New York retaliated with four more in the bottom of the inning. Seaver—and Tug Mc-Graw in the ninth—held the Reds scoreless the rest of the way.

New York Mets (East), 3;
Cincinnati Reds (West) 2

NY (E)

PLAYER/POS	AVG	G	AB	R	H	2B	3B	HR	RB	BB	SO	SB
Ken Boswell, ph	.000	1	1	0	0	0	0	0	0	0	0	0
Wayne Garrett, 3b	.087	5	23	1	2	1	0	0	1	0	5	0
Jerry Grote, c	.211	5	19	2	4	0	0	0	2	1	3	0
Don Hahn, of	.235	5	17	2	4	0	0	0	1	2	4	0
Bud Harrelson, ss	.167	5	18	1	3	0	0	0	2	1	1	0
Cleon Jones, of	.300	5	20	3	6	2	0	0	3	2	4	0
Jerry Koosman, p	.500	1	4	1	2	0	0	0	1	0	0	0
Ed Kranepool, of	.500	1	2	0	1	0	0	0	2	0	0	0
Jon Matlack, p	.000	1	2	0	0	0	0	0	0	1	2	0
Willie Mays, of	.333	1	3	1	1	0	0	0	1	0	0	0
Tug Mc Graw, p	.000	2	1	0	0	0	0	0	0	0	1	0
Felix Millan, 2b	.316	5	19	5	6	0	0	0	2	2	1	0
John Milner, 1b	.176	5	17	2	3	0	0	0	1	5	3	0
Harry Parker, p	.000	1	0	0	0	0	0	0	0	0	0	0
Tom Seaver, p	.333	2	6	1	2	2	0	0	1	1	1	0
Rusty Staub, of	.200	4	15	4	3	0	0	3	5	3	2	0
George Stone, p	.000	1	1	0	0	0	0	0	0	1	1	0
TOTAL	.220		168	23	37	5	0	3	22	19	28	0

PITCHER	W	L	ERA	G	GS	CG	SV	SHO	IP	H	ER	BB	SO
Jerry Koosman	1	0	2.00	1	1	1	0	0	9.0	8	2	0	9
Jon Matlack	1	0	0.00	1	1	1	0	1	9.0	2	0	3	9
Tug Mc Graw	0	0	0.00	2	0	0	1	0	5.0	4	0	3	3
Harry Parker	0	1	9.00	1	0	0	0	0	1.0	1	1	0	0
Tom Seaver	1	1	1.62	2	2	1	0	0	16.2	13	3	5	17
George Stone	0	0	1.35	1	1	0	0	0	6.2	3	1	2	4
TOTAL	3	2	1.33	8	5	3	1	1	47.1	31	7	13	42

CIN (W)

PLAYER/POS	AVG	G	AB	R	H	2B	3B	HR	RB	BB	SO	SB
Ed Armbrister, of-1	.167	3	6	0	1	0	0	0	0	0	5	0
Johnny Bench, c	.263	5	19	1	5	2	0	1	1	2	2	0
Jack Billingham, p	.000	2	3	0	0	0	0	0	0	0	1	0
Pedro Borbon, p	.000	4	0	0	0	0	0	0	0	0	0	0
Clay Carroll, p	.000	3	0	0	0	0	0	0	0	0	0	0
Darrel Chaney, ph	.000	5	9	0	0	0	0	0	0	3	4	0
Ed Crosby, ss	.500	2	2	0	1	0	0	0	0	0	1	0
Dan Driessen, 3b	.167	4	12	0	2	1	0	0	1	0	2	0
Phil Gagliano, ph	.000	3	3	0	0	0	0	0	0	0	2	0
Cesar Geronimo, of	.067	4	15	0	1	0	0	0	0	0	7	0
Ken Griffey, of-2	.143	3	7	0	1	1	0	0	0	0	1	0
Ross Grimsley, p	.000	2	0	0	0	0	0	0	0	0	0	0
Don Gullett, p	.000	3	1	0	0	0	0	0	0	0	0	0
Tom Hall, p	.000	3	0	0	0	0	0	0	0	0	0	0
Hal King, ph	.500	3	2	0	1	0	0	0	0	1	1	0
Andy Kosco, of	.300	3	10	0	3	0	0	0	0	2	3	0
Denis Menke, ss-2,3b-2	.222	3	9	1	2	0	0	1	1	1	2	0
Joe Morgan, 2b	.100	5	20	1	2	1	0	0	1	2	2	0
Roger Nelson, p	.000	1	0	0	0	0	0	0	0	0	0	0
Fred Norman, p	.000	1	1	0	0	0	0	0	0	0	1	0
Tony Perez, 1b	.091	5	22	1	2	0	0	1	2	0	4	0
Pete Rose, of	.381	5	21	3	8	1	0	2	2	2	2	0
Larry Stahl, ph	.500	4	4	1	2	0	0	0	0	0	1	0
Dave Tomlin, p	.000	1	0	0	0	0	0	0	0	0	0	0
TOTAL	.186		167	8	31	6	0	5	8	13	42	0

PITCHER	W	L	ERA	G	GS	CG	SV	SHO	IP	H	ER	BB	SO
Jack Billingham	0	1	4.50	2	2	0	0	0	12.0	9	6	4	9
Pedro Borbon	1	0	0.00	4	0	0	1	0	4.2	3	0	0	3
Clay Carroll	1	0	1.29	3	0	0	0	0	7.0	5	1	1	2
Ross Grimsley	0	1	12.27	2	1	0	0	0	3.2	7	5	2	3
Don Gullett	0	1	2.00	3	1	0	0	0	9.0	4	2	3	6
Tom Hall	0	0	67.50	3	0	0	0	0	0.2	3	5	4	1
Roger Nelson	0	0	0.00	1	0	0	0	0	2.1	0	0	1	0
Fred Norman	0	0	1.80	1	1	0	0	0	5.0	1	1	3	3
Dave Tomlin	0	0	16.20	1	0	0	0	0	1.2	5	3	1	1
TOTAL	2	3	4.50	20	5	0	1	0	46.0	37	23	19	28

GAME 1 AT CIN OCT 6

NY	010	000	000	1	3	0
CIN	000	000	011	2	6	0

Pitchers: SEAVER vs Billingham, Hall (9), BORBON (9)
Home Runs: Rose-CIN, Bench-CIN
Attendance: 53,431

GAME 2 AT CIN OCT 7

NY	000	100	004	5	7	0
CIN	000	000	000	0	2	0

Pitchers: MATLACK vs GULLETT, Carroll (6), Borbon (9)
Home Runs: Staub-NY
Attendance: 54,041

GAME 3 AT NY OCT 8

CIN	002	000	000	2	8	1
NY	151	200	00X	9	11	1

Pitchers: GRIMSLEY, Hall (2), Tomlin (3), Nelson (4), Borbon (7) vs KOOSMAN
Home Runs: Staub-NY (2), Menke-CIN
Attendance: 53,967

GAME 4 AT NY OCT 9

CIN	000	000	100	001	2	8	0
NY	001	000	000	000	1	3	2

Pitchers: Norman, Gullett (6), CARROLL (10), Borbon (12) vs Stone, McGraw (7), PARKER (12)
Home Runs: Perez-CIN, Rose-CIN
Attendance: 50,786

GAME 5 AT NY OCT 10

CIN	001	010	000	2	7	1
NY	200	041	00X	7	13	1

Pitchers: BILLINGHAM, Gullett (5), Carroll (5), Grimsley (7) vs SEAVER, McGraw (9)
Attendance: 50,323

The Orioles finally met their match in an LCS as Oakland took its second consecutive pennant. Baltimore started strong, chasing A's starter Vida Blue with four runs in the first inning as Jim Palmer—pitching the series opener for a change—blanked the A's on five hits. But Oakland snapped back in Game Two, with five of their six runs coming on homers by Sal Bando (two, for three runs), Joe Rudi, and Bert Campaneris.

Oriole Mike Cuellar and the A's Ken Holtzman cut down opposing batters for 10½ innings in Game Three before Oakland's Campaneris broke the 1–1 tie in the bottom of the eleventh with a leadoff home run. The next day Jim Palmer was driven out in the second inning by three Oakland runs, and the A's added to their lead with another run in the sixth. But Andy Etchebarren led a four-run Oriole comeback in the seventh with a three-run homer, and Bobby Grich's solo shot in the next inning gave the Orioles the margin they needed to win the game and tie the series.

The A's took it all in the finale, though, needing only one of their three runs as Catfish Hunter stopped Oakland cold on five scattered hits.

Oakland A's (West), 3; Baltimore Orioles (East) 2

OAK (W)

PLAYER/POS	AVG	G	AB	R	H	2B	3B	HR	RB	BB	SO	SB
Jesus Alou, dh-1	.333	4	6	0	2	0	0	0	1	0	1	0
Mike Andrews, 1b-1,dh-1	.000	2	1	0	0	0	0	0	0	0	0	0
Sal Bando, 3b	.167	5	18	2	3	0	0	2	3	3	6	0
Vida Blue, p	.000	2	0	0	0	0	0	0	0	0	0	0
Pat Bourque, dh	.000	2	1	0	0	0	0	0	0	1	1	0
Bert Campaneris, ss	.333	5	21	3	7	1	0	2	3	2	2	3
Billy Conigliaro, of	.000	1	4	0	0	0	0	0	0	0	2	0
Vic Davalillo, 1b-2,of-2	.625	4	8	2	5	1	1	0	1	1	0	0
Rollie Fingers, p	.000	3	0	0	0	0	0	0	0	0	0	0
Ray Fosse, c	.091	5	11	2	1	1	0	0	3	2	2	0
Dick Green, 2b	.077	5	13	0	1	1	0	0	1	1	4	0
Ken Holtzman, p	.000	1	0	0	0	0	0	0	0	0	0	0
Catfish Hunter, p	.000	2	0	0	0	0	0	0	0	0	0	0
Reggie Jackson, of	.143	5	21	0	3	0	0	0	0	0	6	0
Deron Johnson, dh	.100	4	10	0	1	0	0	0	0	2	6	0
Ted Kubiak, 2b	.000	3	2	0	0	0	0	0	0	0	1	0
Allan Lewis, pr	.000	2	0	1	0	0	0	0	0	0	0	0
Angel Mangual, of	.111	3	9	1	1	0	0	0	0	0	3	0
Blue Moon Odom, p-2	.000	1	0	0	0	0	0	0	0	0	0	0
Horacio Pina, p	.000	1	0	0	0	0	0	0	0	0	0	0
Joe Rudi, of	.222	5	18	1	4	0	0	1	3	3	1	0
Gene Tenace, 1b-5,c-3	.235	5	17	3	4	1	0	0	0	2	4	0
TOTAL	.200		160	15	32	5	1	5	15	17	39	3

PITCHER	W	L	ERA	G	GS	CG	SV	SHO	IP	H	ER	BB	SO
Vida Blue	0	1	10.29	2	2	0	0	0	7.0	8	8	5	3
Rollie Fingers	0	1	1.93	3	0	0	1	0	4.2	4	1	2	4
Ken Holtzman	1	0	0.82	1	1	1	0	0	11.0	3	1	1	7
Catfish Hunter	2	0	1.65	2	2	1	0	0	16.1	12	3	5	6
Blue Moon Odom	0	0	1.80	2	0	0	0	0	5.0	6	1	2	4
Horacio Pina	0	0	0.00	1	0	0	0	0	2.0	3	0	1	1
TOTAL	3	2	2.74	11	5	2	1	0	46.0	36	14	16	25

BAL (E)

PLAYER/POS	AVG	G	AB	R	H	2B	3B	HR	RB	BB	SO	SB
Doyle Alexander, p	.000	1	0	0	0	0	0	0	0	0	0	0
Frank Baker, ss	.000	2	0	0	0	0	0	0	0	0	0	0
Don Baylor, of-3	.273	4	11	3	3	0	0	0	1	3	5	0
Mark Belanger, ss	.125	5	16	0	2	0	0	0	1	1	1	0
Paul Blair, of	.167	5	18	2	3	0	0	0	1	5	0	0
Larry Brown, 3b	.000	1	0	0	0	0	0	0	0	0	0	0
Al Bumbry, of	.000	2	7	1	0	0	0	0	0	2	2	1
Rich Coggins, of	.444	2	9	1	4	1	0	0	0	0	0	0
Terry Crowley, of-1	.000	2	2	0	0	0	0	0	0	0	0	0
Mike Cuellar, p	.000	1	0	0	0	0	0	0	0	0	0	0
Tommy Davis, dh	.286	5	21	1	6	1	0	0	2	1	0	0
Andy Etchebarren, c	.357	4	14	1	5	1	0	1	4	0	1	0
Bobby Grich, 2b	.100	5	20	1	2	0	0	1	1	2	5	0
Grant Jackson, p	.000	2	0	0	0	0	0	0	0	0	0	0
Dave Nc Nally, p	.000	1	0	0	0	0	0	0	0	0	0	0
Jim Palmer, p	.000	3	0	0	0	0	0	0	0	0	0	0
Boog Powell, 1b	.000	1	4	1	0	0	0	0	0	0	1	0
Merv Rettenmund, of	.091	3	11	1	1	0	0	0	0	3	2	0
Bob Reynolds, p	.000	2	0	0	0	0	0	0	0	0	0	0
Brooks Robinson, 3b	.250	5	20	1	5	2	0	0	2	1	1	0
Eddie Watt, p	.000	1	0	0	0	0	0	0	0	0	0	0
Earl Williams, 1b-4,c-1	.278	5	18	2	5	2	0	1	4	2	2	0
TOTAL	.211		171	15	36	7	0	3	15	16	25	1

PITCHER	W	L	ERA	G	GS	CG	SV	SHO	IP	H	ER	BB	SO
Doyle Alexander	0	1	4.91	1	1	0	0	0	3.2	5	2	0	1
Mike Cuellar	0	1	1.80	1	1	1	0	0	10.0	4	2	3	11
Grant Jackson	1	0	0.00	2	0	0	0	0	3.0	0	0	1	0
Dave Nc Nally	0	1	5.87	1	1	0	0	0	7.2	7	5	2	7
Jim Palmer	1	0	1.84	3	2	1	0	1	14.2	11	3	8	15
Bob Reynolds	0	0	3.18	2	0	0	0	0	5.2	5	2	3	5
Eddie Watt	0	0	0.00	1	0	0	0	0	0.1	0	0	0	0
TOTAL	2	3	2.80	11	5	2	0	1	45.0	32	14	17	39

GAME 1 AT BAL OCT 6

OAK	000	000	000	0	5 1
BAL	400	000	11X	6	12 0

Pitchers: BLUE, Pina (1), Odom (3), Fingers (8) vs PALMER
Attendance: 41,279

GAME 2 AT BAL OCT 7

OAK	100	002	021	6	9 0
BAL	100	001	010	3	8 0

Pitchers: HUNTER, Fingers (8) VS McNALLY, Reynolds (8), G.Jackson (9)
Home Runs: Campaneris-OAK, Rudi-OAK, Bando-OAK (2)
Attendance: 48,425

GAME 3 AT OAK OCT 9

BAL	010 000 000 00			1	3 0
OAK	000 000 010 01			2	4 3

Pitchers: CUELLAR vs HOLTZMAN
Home Runs: Williams-BAL, Campaneris-OAK
Attendance: 34,367

GAME 4 AT OAK OCT 10

BAL	000	000	410	5	8 0
OAK	030	001	000	4	7 0

Pitchers: Palmer, Reynolds (2), Watt (7), G.JACKSON (7) vs Blue, FINGERS (7)
Home Runs: Etchebarren-BAL, Grich-BAL
Attendance: 27,497

GAME 5 AT OAK OCT 11

BAL	000	000	000	0	5 2
OAK	001	200	00X	3	7 0

Pitchers: ALEXANDER, Palmer (4) vs HUNTER
Attendance: 24,265

For the second year in a row, the A's were outpitched and outscored by their Series opposition, and this time they were outhit as well. But again, when the dust of Game Seven had risen, they still wore the crown. A's starter Ken Holtzman, who because of the American League's new designated hitter rule had not batted all season, doubled for the A's first hit in the third inning of Game One and scored the first Oakland run on a Met error. The A's scored again in the inning, enough for the win as Holtzman and two relievers held New York to a single run.

The Mets evened things in a Game Two that lasted a record 4 hours 13 minutes, scoring four runs with two out in the top of the twelfth inning for a lead the A's were not able to overcome. (Three of the runs scored on a pair of errors by second-baseman Mike Andrews, prompting a flap that rocked the baseball world as A's owner Charlie Finley tried—unsuccessfully—to "fire" Andrews by declaring him injured.) Final score of the slugfest: 10–7.

In a somewhat more normal third game, the Mets grabbed an early lead on Wayne Garrett's leadoff homer in the bottom of the first and scored a second run on two singles and wild pitch for a 2–0 lead that held up until Oakland tied the game in the eighth. In the eleventh, the A's Ted Kubiak worked his way around the bases on a walk, passed ball, and single for a lead that reliever Rollie Fingers held in the bottom of the inning.

New York evened the Series on Rusty Staub's three-run homer in the first inning of Game Four (scoring three more times later for a 6–1 win). The Mets moved in front on a sparkling 2–0 three-hitter by Jerry Koosman and Tug McGraw in Game Five, but lost their edge as the Series returned to Oakland for Game Six, losing when Reggie Jackson's doubles in the first and third drove in two runs to give the A's a lead New York was unable to overtake.

Oakland made the finale look easy. Bert Campaneris and Jackson both hit two-run homers in the third inning, and Campaneris scored a fifth run two innings later before New York finally got on the board in the sixth. In the ninth inning the Mets scored a second run with two outs, but reliever Darold Knowles came on for a record seventh pitching appearance and retired the final batter for his second Series save.

Oakland Athletics (AL), 4; New York Mets (NL) 3

OAK (A)

PLAYER/POS	AVG	G	AB	R	H	2B	3B	HR	RB	BB	SO	SB
Jesus Alou, of-6	.158	7	19	0	3	1	0	0	3	0	0	0
Mike Andrews, 2b-1	.000	2	3	0	0	0	0	0	0	1	1	0
Sal Bando, 3b	.231	7	26	5	6	1	1	0	1	4	7	0
Vida Blue, p	.000	2	4	0	0	0	0	0	0	0	4	0
Pat Bourque, 1b	.500	2	2	0	1	0	0	0	0	0	0	0
Bert Campaneris, ss	.290	7	31	6	9	0	1	1	3	1	7	3
Billy Conigliaro, ph	.000	3	3	0	0	0	0	0	0	0	1	0
Vic Davalillo, of-4,1b-1	.091	6	11	0	1	0	0	0	0	2	1	0
Rollie Fingers, p	.333	6	3	0	1	0	0	0	0	0	1	0
Ray Fosse, c	.158	7	19	0	3	1	0	0	0	1	4	0
Dick Green, 2b	.063	7	16	0	1	0	0	0	0	1	6	0
Ken Holtzman, p	.667	3	3	2	2	2	0	0	0	0	0	0
Catfish Hunter, p	.000	2	5	0	0	0	0	0	0	0	3	0
Reggie Jackson, of	.310	7	29	3	9	3	1	1	6	2	7	0
Deron Johnson, 1b-2	.300	6	10	0	3	1	0	0	0	1	4	0
Darold Knowles, p	.000	7	0	0	0	0	0	0	0	0	0	0
Ted Kubiak, 2b	.000	4	3	1	0	0	0	0	0	1	1	0
Allan Lewis, pr	.000	3	0	1	0	0	0	0	0	0	0	0
Paul Lindblad, p	.000	3	1	0	0	0	0	0	0	0	0	0
Angel Mangual, of-1	.000	5	6	0	0	0	0	0	0	0	3	0
Blue Moon Odom, p-2	.000	3	1	0	0	0	0	0	0	0	1	0
Horacio Pina, p	.000	2	0	0	0	0	0	0	0	0	0	0
Joe Rudi, of	.333	7	27	3	9	2	0	0	4	3	4	0
Gene Tenace, 1b-7,c-3	.158	7	19	0	3	1	0	0	3	11	7	0
TOTAL	.212		241	21	51	12	3	2	20	28	62	3

PITCHER	W	L	ERA	G	GS	CG	SV	SHO	IP	H	ER	BB	SO
Vida Blue	0	1	4.91	2	2	0	0	0	11.0	10	6	3	8
Rollie Fingers	0	1	0.66	6	0	0	2	0	13.2	13	1	4	8
Ken Holtzman	2	1	4.22	3	3	0	0	0	10.2	13	5	5	6
Catfish Hunter	1	0	2.03	2	2	0	0	0	13.1	11	3	4	6
Darold Knowles	0	0	0.00	7	0	0	2	0	6.1	4	0	5	5
Paul Lindblad	1	0	0.00	3	0	0	0	0	3.1	4	0	1	1
Blue Moon Odom	0	0	3.86	2	0	0	0	0	4.2	5	2	2	2
Horacio Pina	0	0	0.00	2	0	0	0	0	3.0	6	0	2	0
TOTAL	4	3	2.32	27	7	0	4	0	66.0	66	17	26	36

NY (N)

PLAYER/POS	AVG	G	AB	R	H	2B	3B	HR	RB	BB	SO	SB
Jim Beauchamp, ph	.000	4	4	0	0	0	0	0	0	0	1	0
Ken Boswell, ph	1.000	3	3	1	3	0	0	0	0	0	0	0
Wayne Garrett, 3b	.167	7	30	4	5	0	0	2	2	5	11	0
Jerry Grote, c	.267	7	30	2	8	0	0	0	0	0	1	0
Don Hahn, of	.241	7	29	2	7	1	1	0	2	1	6	0
Bud Harrelson, ss	.250	7	24	2	6	1	0	0	1	5	3	0
Ron Hodges, ph	.000	1	0	0	0	0	0	0	0	1	0	0
Cleon Jones, of	.286	7	28	5	8	2	0	1	1	4	2	0
Jerry Koosman, p	.000	2	4	0	0	0	0	0	0	0	3	0
Ed Kranepool, ph	.000	4	3	0	0	0	0	0	0	0	0	0
Ted Martinez, pr	.000	2	0	0	0	0	0	0	0	0	0	0
Jon Matlack, p	.250	3	4	0	1	0	0	0	0	2	1	0
Willie Mays, of-2	.286	3	7	1	2	0	0	0	1	0	1	0
Tug Mc Graw, p	.333	5	3	1	1	0	0	0	0	0	1	0
Felix Millan, 2b	.188	7	32	3	6	1	1	0	1	1	1	0
John Milner, 1b	.296	7	27	2	8	0	0	0	2	5	1	0
Harry Parker, p	.000	3	0	0	0	0	0	0	0	0	0	0
Ray Sadecki, p	.000	4	0	0	0	0	0	0	0	0	0	0
Tom Seaver, p	.000	2	5	0	0	0	0	0	0	0	2	0
Rusty Staub, of	.423	7	26	1	11	2	0	1	6	2	2	0
George Stone, p	.000	2	0	0	0	0	0	0	0	0	0	0
George Theodore, of-1	.000	2	2	0	0	0	0	0	0	0	0	0
TOTAL	.253		261	24	66	7	2	4	16	26	36	0

PITCHER	W	L	ERA	G	GS	CG	SV	SHO	IP	H	ER	BB	SO
Jerry Koosman	1	0	3.12	2	2	0	0	0	8.2	9	3	7	8
Jon Matlack	1	2	2.16	3	3	0	0	0	16.2	10	4	5	11
Tug Mc Graw	1	0	2.63	5	0	0	1	0	13.2	8	4	9	14
Harry Parker	0	1	0.00	3	0	0	0	0	3.1	2	0	2	2
Ray Sadecki	0	0	1.93	4	0	0	0	0	4.2	5	1	1	6
Tom Seaver	0	1	2.40	2	2	0	0	0	15.0	13	4	3	18
George Stone	0	0	0.00	2	0	0	1	0	3.0	4	0	1	3
TOTAL	3	4	2.22	21	7	0	3	0	65.0	51	16	28	62

Dodger pitcher Don Sutton—who had brought his won-lost record from 10–9 to 19–9 with a nine-game winning streak in the regular season—continued his winning ways in the LCS, surrendering only seven hits and one run in seventeen innings and taking both the opener and clincher of the four-game series. Los Angeles's Andy Messersmith followed up Sutton's opening-game shutout with six shutout innings of his own in Game Two before Pittsburgh scored its first two runs of the series in the seventh. They tied the score, but the Dodgers countered with three more in the top of the eighth to assure their second win.

The Pirates captured their only victory in Game Three, as Richie Hebner and Willie Stargell homered for five of the Bucs' seven runs, while Bruce Kison and Ramon Hernandez shut out the Dodgers on four hits.

Pittsburgh finally got to Sutton for a run when Stargell homered in the seventh inning of Game Four. But it was too little, and too late to stem a twelve-run Dodger attack led by Steve Garvey's four hits (two of them home runs) and four RBIs.

Los Angeles Dodgers (West), 3; Pittsburgh Pirates (East) 1

LA (W)

PLAYER/POS	AVG	G	AB	R	H	2B	3B	HR	RB	BB	SO	SB
Rick Auerbach, ph	1.000	1	1	0	1	1	0	0	0	0	0	0
Bill Buckner, of	.167	4	18	0	3	1	0	0	0	0	2	0
Ron Cey, 3b	.313	4	16	2	5	3	0	1	1	3	2	0
Willie Crawford, of	.250	2	4	1	1	0	0	0	1	1	1	0
Al Downing, p	.000	1	1	0	0	0	0	0	0	0	0	0
Joe Ferguson, of-3,c-2	.231	4	13	3	3	0	0	0	2	5	1	0
Steve Garvey, 1b	.389	4	18	4	7	1	0	2	5	1	1	0
Charley Hough, p	.000	1	0	0	0	0	0	0	0	0	0	0
Von Joshua, ph	.000	1	0	0	0	0	0	0	0	1	0	0
Lee Lacy, pr	.000	1	0	0	0	0	0	0	0	0	0	0
Davey Lopes, 2b	.267	4	15	4	4	0	1	0	3	5	1	3
Mike Marshall, p	.000	2	0	0	0	0	0	0	0	0	0	0
Ken Mc Mullen, ph	.000	1	1	0	0	0	0	0	0	0	1	0
Andy Messersmith, p	.000	1	3	0	0	0	0	0	0	0	1	0
Manny Mota, of-1	.333	3	3	0	1	0	0	0	1	0	0	0
Tom Paciorek, of	1.000	1	1	0	1	0	0	0	0	0	0	0
Doug Rau, p	.000	1	0	0	0	0	0	0	0	0	0	0
Bill Russell, ss	.389	4	18	1	7	0	0	0	3	1	0	0
Eddie Solomon, p	.000	1	0	0	0	0	0	0	0	0	0	0
Don Sutton, p	.286	2	7	0	2	0	0	0	0	1	1	2	0
Jimmy Wynn, of	.200	4	10	4	2	2	0	0	2	9	1	1
Steve Yeager, c	.000	3	9	1	0	0	0	0	0	3	3	1
TOTAL	.268		138	20	37	8	1	3	19	30	16	5

PITCHER	W	L	ERA	G	GS	CG	SV	SHO	IP	H	ER	BB	SO
Al Downing	0	0	0.00	1	0	0	0	0	4.0	1	0	1	0
Charley Hough	0	0	7.71	1	0	0	0	0	2.1	4	2	0	2
Mike Marshall	0	0	0.00	2	0	0	0	0	3.0	0	0	0	1
Andy Messersmith	1	0	2.57	1	1	0	0	0	7.0	8	2	3	0
Doug Rau	0	1	40.50	1	1	0	0	0	0.2	3	3	1	0
Eddie Solomon	0	0	0.00	1	0	0	0	0	2.0	2	0	1	1
Don Sutton	2	0	0.53	2	2	1	0	1	17.0	7	1	2	13
TOTAL	3	1	2.00	9	4	1	0	1	36.0	25	8	8	17

PIT (E)

PLAYER/POS	AVG	G	AB	R	H	2B	3B	HR	RB	BB	SO	SB
Ken Brett, p	.000	1	1	0	0	0	0	0	0	0	1	0
Gene Clines, of	.000	2	1	1	0	0	0	0	0	0	0	0
Larry Demery, p	.000	2	0	0	0	0	0	0	0	0	0	0
Dave Giusti, p	.000	3	0	0	0	0	0	0	0	0	0	0
Richie Hebner, 3b	.231	4	13	1	3	0	0	1	4	1	4	0
Ramon Hernandez, p	.000	2	1	0	0	0	0	0	0	0	1	0
Art Howe, ph	.000	1	1	0	0	0	0	0	0	0	0	0
Ed Kirkpatrick, 1b	.000	3	9	0	0	0	0	0	0	2	0	0
Bruce Kison, p	.000	1	3	0	0	0	0	0	0	0	2	0
Mario Mendoza, ss	.200	3	5	0	1	0	0	0	1	1	0	0
Al Oliver, of	.143	4	14	1	2	0	0	0	1	2	2	0
Dave Parker, of-2	.125	3	8	0	1	0	0	0	0	0	1	0
Juan Pizarro, p	.000	1	0	0	0	0	0	0	0	0	0	0
Paul Popovich, ss	.600	3	5	1	3	0	0	0	0	0	0	0
Jerry Reuss, p	.000	2	2	0	0	0	0	0	0	0	0	0
Bob Robertson, 1b	.000	1	5	1	0	0	0	0	0	0	0	0
Jim Rooker, p	.500	1	2	0	1	0	0	0	0	0	0	0
Manny Sanguillen, c	.250	4	16	0	4	1	0	0	0	0	0	0
Willie Stargell, of	.400	4	15	3	6	0	0	2	4	1	2	0
Rennie Stennett, 2b	.063	4	16	1	1	0	0	0	0	1	1	0
Frank Taveras, ss	.000	2	2	0	0	0	0	0	0	0	0	1
Richie Zisk, of-2	.300	3	10	1	3	0	0	0	0	0	3	0
TOTAL	.194		129	10	25	1	0	3	10	8	17	1

PITCHER	W	L	ERA	G	GS	CG	SV	SHO	IP	H	ER	BB	SO
Ken Brett	0	0	7.71	1	0	0	0	0	2.1	3	2	2	1
Larry Demery	0	0	27.00	2	0	0	0	0	1.0	3	3	2	0
Dave Giusti	0	1	21.60	3	0	0	0	0	3.1	13	8	5	1
Ramon Hernandez	0	0	0.00	2	0	0	0	0	4.1	3	0	1	2
Bruce Kison	1	0	0.00	1	1	0	0	0	6.2	2	0	6	5
Juan Pizarro	0	0	0.00	1	0	0	0	0	0.2	0	0	1	0
Jerry Reuss	0	2	3.72	2	2	0	0	0	9.2	7	4	8	3
Jim Rooker	0	0	2.57	1	1	0	0	0	7.0	6	2	5	4
TOTAL	1	3	4.89	13	4	0	0	0	35.0	37	19	30	16

GAME 1 AT PIT OCT 5

LA	010 000 002	3	9	2
PIT	000 000 000	0	4	0

Pitchers: SUTTON vs REUSS, Giusti (8)
Attendance: 40,638

GAME 2 AT PIT OCT 6

LA	100 100 030	5	12	0
PIT	000 000 200	2	8	3

Pitchers: MESSERSMITH, Marshall (8) VS Rooker, GIUSTI (8), Demery (8), Hernandez (8)
Home Runs: Cey-LA
Attendance: 49,247

GAME 3 AT LA OCT 8

PIT	502 000 000	7	10	0
LA	000 000 000	0	4	5

Pitchers: KISON, Hernandez (7) vs RAU, Hough (1), Downing (4), Solomon (8)
Home Runs: Stargell-PIT, Hebner-PIT
Attendance: 55,953

GAME 4 AT LA OCT 9

PIT	000 000 100	1	3	1
LA	102 022 23X	12	12	0

Pitchers: REUSS, Brett (3), Demery (6), Giusti (7), Pizarro (8) vs SUTTON, Marshall (9)
Home Runs: Garvey-LA (2), Stargell-PIT
Attendance: 54,424

After spotting Baltimore a win in the opener, Oakland took the next three games and their third consecutive pennant. Although the A's got nine hits in Game One—their series high—the Orioles hit harder, burying Oakland under home runs by Paul Blair, Brooks Robinson, and Bobby Grich. In Game Two, though, Ken Holtzman shut out Baltimore on five hits and Ray Fosse homered. Bando homered again in the third game for the only Oakland run as Jim Palmer limited the A's to four hits. But one run was enough to defeat Baltimore, for Vida Blue shut them out on a masterly two-hitter.

Oriole starter Mike Cuellar walked nine men in 4⅔ innings of Game Four, including four in the fifth to force in Oakland's first run. Two innings later Reggie Jackson's double (the only Oakland hit of the game) off reliever Ross Grimsley drove in Oakland's second run, while starter Catfish Hunter was blanking the O's through seven-plus innings. After failing to score for thirty consecutive innings, the Orioles got to reliever Rollie Fingers for a run with two out in the bottom of the ninth. But Fingers then struck out Don Baylor, and the A's had their pennant.

Oakland A's (West), 3;
Baltimore Orioles (East) 1

OAK (W)

PLAYER/POS	AVG	G	AB	R	H	2B	3B	HR	RB	BB	SO	SB
Jesus Alou, ph	1.000	1	1	0	1	0	0	0	0	0	0	0
Sal Bando, 3b	.231	4	13	4	3	0	0	2	2	4	0	0
Vida Blue, p	.000	1	0	0	0	0	0	0	0	0	0	0
Bert Campaneris, ss	.176	4	17	0	3	0	0	0	3	0	3	1
Rollie Fingers, p	.000	2	0	0	0	0	0	0	0	0	0	0
Ray Fosse, c	.333	4	12	1	4	1	0	1	3	1	2	0
Dick Green, 2b	.222	4	9	0	2	0	0	0	0	2	1	0
Jim Holt, 1b-1	.000	2	0	0	0	0	0	0	0	1	0	0
Ken Holtzman, p	.000	1	0	0	0	0	0	0	0	0	0	0
Catfish Hunter, p	.000	2	0	0	0	0	0	0	0	0	0	0
Reggie Jackson, dh-3,of-1	.167	4	12	0	2	1	0	0	1	5	2	0
Angel Mangual, dh	.250	1	4	0	1	0	0	0	0	0	0	0
Dal Maxvill, 2b	.000	1	1	0	0	0	0	0	0	0	1	0
Billy North, of	.063	4	16	3	1	1	0	0	0	2	1	1
Blue Moon Odom, p-1	.000	3	0	0	0	0	0	0	0	0	0	0
Joe Rudi, of	.154	4	13	0	2	0	1	0	1	3	2	0
Gene Tenace, 1b	.000	4	11	1	0	0	0	0	0	1	4	1
Manny Trillo, pr	.000	1	0	1	0	0	0	0	0	0	0	0
Claudell Washington, of-3	.273	4	11	1	3	1	0	0	0	0	0	0
Herb Washington, pr	.000	2	0	0	0	0	0	0	0	0	0	0
TOTAL	.183		120	11	22	4	1	3	11	22	16	3

PITCHER	W	L	ERA	G	GS	CG	SV	SHO	IP	H	ER	BB	SO
Vida Blue	1	0	0.00	1	1	1	0	1	9.0	2	0	0	7
Rollie Fingers	0	0	3.00	2	0	0	1	0	3.0	3	1	1	3
Ken Holtzman	1	0	0.00	1	1	1	0	1	9.0	5	0	2	3
Catfish Hunter	1	1	4.63	2	2	0	0	0	11.2	11	6	2	6
Blue Moon Odom	0	0	0.00	1	0	0	0	0	3.1	1	0	0	1
TOTAL	3	1	1.75	7	4	2	1	2	36.0	22	7	5	20

BAL (E)

PLAYER/POS	AVG	G	AB	R	H	2B	3B	HR	RB	BB	SO	SB
Frank Baker, ss	.000	2	0	0	0	0	0	0	0	0	0	0
Don Baylor, of	.267	4	15	0	4	0	0	0	0	0	2	0
Mark Belanger, ss	.000	4	9	0	0	0	0	0	0	1	3	0
Paul Blair, of	.286	4	14	3	4	0	0	1	2	2	2	0
Al Bumbry, ph	.000	2	1	0	0	0	0	0	0	0	1	0
Enos Cabell, of-1	.250	3	4	0	1	0	0	0	0	0	0	0
Rich Coggins, of	.000	3	11	0	0	0	0	0	0	0	3	0
Mike Cuellar, p	.000	2	0	0	0	0	0	0	0	0	0	0
Tommy Davis, dh	.267	4	15	0	4	0	0	0	1	0	1	0
Andy Etchebarren, c	.333	2	6	0	2	0	0	0	0	0	0	0
Wayne Garland, p	.000	1	0	0	0	0	0	0	0	0	0	0
Bobby Grich, 2b	.250	4	16	2	4	1	0	1	2	0	1	0
Ross Grimsley, p	.000	2	0	0	0	0	0	0	0	0	0	0
Elrod Hendricks, c	.167	3	6	1	1	0	0	0	0	1	3	0
Grant Jackson, p	.000	1	0	0	0	0	0	0	0	0	0	0
Dave Nc Nally, p	.000	1	0	0	0	0	0	0	0	0	0	0
Curt Motton, ph	.000	1	1	0	0	0	0	0	0	0	0	0
Jim Palmer, p-1	.000	2	0	0	0	0	0	0	0	0	0	0
Boog Powell, 1b	.125	2	8	0	1	0	0	0	0	1	0	0
Bob Reynolds, p	.000	1	0	0	0	0	0	0	0	0	0	0
Brooks Robinson, 3b	.083	4	12	1	1	0	0	1	1	1	0	0
Earl Williams, 1b	.000	2	6	0	0	0	0	0	0	0	2	0
TOTAL	.177		124	7	22	1	0	3	7	5	20	0

PITCHER	W	L	ERA	G	GS	CG	SV	SHO	IP	H	ER	BB	SO
Mike Cuellar	1	1	2.84	2	2	0	0	0	12.2	9	4	13	6
Wayne Garland	0	0	0.00	1	0	0	0	0	0.2	1	0	1	0
Ross Grimsley	0	0	1.69	2	0	0	0	0	5.1	1	1	2	2
Grant Jackson	0	0	0.00	1	0	0	0	0	0.1	0	0	0	1
Dave Nc Nally	0	1	1.59	1	1	0	0	0	5.2	6	1	2	2
Jim Palmer	0	1	1.00	1	1	1	0	0	9.0	4	1	1	4
Bob Reynolds	0	0	0.00	1	0	0	0	0	1.1	0	0	3	1
TOTAL	1	3	1.80	9	4	1	0	0	35.0	22	7	22	16

GAME 1 AT OAK OCT 5

BAL	100	140	000	6	10	0
OAK	001	010	001	3	9	0

Pitchers: CUELLAR, Grimsley (9) vs HUNTER, Odom (5), Fingers (9)
Home Runs: Blair-BAL, Robinson-BAL, Grich-BAL
Attendance: 41,609

GAME 2 AT OAK OCT 6

BAL	000	000	000	0	5	2
OAK	000	101	03X	5	8	0

Pitchers: McNALLY, Garland (6), Reynolds (7), G.Jackson (8) vs HOLTZMAN
Home Runs: Bando-OAK, Fosse-OAK
Attendance: 42,810

GAME 3 AT BAL OCT 8

OAK	000	100	000	1	4	2
BAL	000	000	000	0	2	1

Pitchers: BLUE vs PALMER
Home Runs: Bando-OAK
Attendance: 32,060

GAME 4 AT BAL OCT 9

OAK	000	010	100	2	1	0
BAL	000	000	001	1	5	1

Pitchers: HUNTER, Fingers (8) vs CUELLAR, Grimsley (5)
Attendance: 28,136

Although the A's were in a turmoil of dislike for owner Charlie Finley—and for each other—they played well enough together to take their third consecutive world championship in just five games. Still, victory didn't come easily, as three of Oakland's wins came by identical 3–2 scores (as did the Dodgers' one victory), and their biggest winning margin was three runs in Game Four. It was the first World Series held entirely on the West Coast.

The A's and Dodgers split the first two games in Los Angeles. Oakland won the opener on the strength of Reggie Jackson's home run in the second inning, pitcher Ken Holtzman's double in the fifth (he moved around on a wild pitch and squeeze bunt), and a Dodger throwing error in the eighth. The Dodgers evened the Series on Joe Ferguson's two-run homer in the sixth inning of the second game, which gave Los Angeles a 3–0 lead that an Oakland rally in the ninth failed to catch.

Los Angeles outhit Oakland in Game Three, but two of the A's runs were unearned, coming after Dodger catcher Ferguson bobbled what should have been a third-out play in the third inning.

Pitcher Ken Holtzman, who had now gone two regular seasons without a time at bat, produced in Game Four his second hit of the Series, this one a homer in the third inning for the game's first run. The Dodgers' Bill Russell tripled off him for two runs a half inning later, but in the last of the sixth inning Oakland regained the lead on three walks interspersed with a pair of singles and an RBI grounder to short. Four runs scored—more in this one inning than either team scored in any of the other four games.

Oakland took an early 2–0 lead in Game Five, with single runs in the first and second innings (the latter a Ray Fosse home run). The Dodgers put together a pinch-hit double, a walk, a pair of sacrifices (bunt and fly), and a single to tie the score in the sixth. But Joe Rudi hit the first pitch of Oakland's half of the seventh into the stands in left for the run that decided the game and the Series.

Oakland Athletics (AL), 4; Los Angeles Dodgers (NL) 1

OAK (A)

PLAYER/POS	AVG	G	AB	R	H	2B	3B	HR	RB	BB	SO	SB
Jesus Alou, ph	.000	1	1	0	0	0	0	0	0	0	1	0
Sal Bando, 3b	.063	5	16	3	1	0	0	0	2	2	5	0
Vida Blue, p	.000	2	4	0	0	0	0	0	0	0	4	0
Bert Campaneris, ss	.353	5	17	1	6	2	0	0	2	0	2	1
Rollie Fingers, p	.000	4	2	0	0	0	0	0	0	0	1	0
Ray Fosse, c	.143	5	14	1	2	0	0	1	1	1	5	0
Dick Green, 2b	.000	5	13	1	0	0	0	0	0	1	4	0
Larry Haney, c	.000	2	0	0	0	0	0	0	0	0	0	0
Jim Holt, 1b-1	.667	4	3	0	2	0	0	0	2	0	0	0
Ken Holtzman, p	.500	2	4	2	2	1	0	1	1	1	1	0
Catfish Hunter, p	.000	2	2	0	0	0	0	0	0	0	2	0
Reggie Jackson, of	.286	5	14	3	4	1	0	1	1	5	3	1
Angel Mangual, ph	.000	1	1	0	0	0	0	0	0	0	1	0
Dal Maxvill, 2b	.000	2	0	0	0	0	0	0	0	0	0	0
Billy North, of	.059	5	17	3	1	0	0	0	0	2	5	1
Blue Moon Odom, p	.000	2	0	0	0	0	0	0	0	0	0	0
Joe Rudi, of-5,1b-2	.333	5	18	1	6	0	0	1	4	0	3	0
Gene Tenace, 1b	.222	5	9	0	2	0	0	0	0	3	4	0
Claudell Washington, of	.571	5	7	1	4	0	0	0	0	1	1	0
Herb Washington, pr	.000	3	0	0	0	0	0	0	0	0	0	0
TOTAL	.211		142	16	30	4	0	4	14	16	42	3

PITCHER	W	L	ERA	G	GS	CG	SV	SHO	IP	H	ER	BB	SO
Vida Blue	0	1	3.29	2	2	0	0	0	13.2	10	5	7	9
Rollie Fingers	1	0	1.93	4	0	0	2	0	9.1	8	2	2	6
Ken Holtzman	1	0	1.50	2	2	0	0	0	12.0	13	2	4	10
Catfish Hunter	1	0	1.17	2	1	0	1	0	7.2	5	1	2	5
Blue Moon Odom	1	0	0.00	2	0	0	0	0	1.1	0	0	1	2
TOTAL	4	1	2.05	12	5	0	3	0	44.0	36	10	16	32

LA (N)

PLAYER/POS	AVG	G	AB	R	H	2B	3B	HR	RB	BB	SO	SB
Rick Auerbach, pr	.000	1	0	0	0	0	0	0	0	0	0	0
Jim Brewer, p	.000	1	0	0	0	0	0	0	0	0	0	0
Bill Buckner, of	.250	5	20	1	5	1	0	1	1	0	1	0
Ron Cey, 3b	.176	5	17	1	3	0	0	0	3	3	0	0
Willie Crawford, of-2	.333	3	6	1	2	0	0	1	1	0	0	0
Al Downing, p	.000	1	1	0	0	0	0	0	0	0	0	0
Joe Ferguson, of-4,c-2	.125	5	16	2	2	0	0	1	2	4	6	1
Steve Garvey, 1b	.381	5	21	2	8	0	0	0	1	0	3	0
Charley Hough, p	.000	1	0	0	0	0	0	0	0	0	0	0
Von Joshua, ph	.000	4	4	0	0	0	0	0	0	0	0	0
Lee Lacy, ph	.000	1	1	0	0	0	0	0	0	0	1	0
Davey Lopes, 2b	.111	5	18	2	2	0	0	0	0	3	4	2
Mike Marshall, p	.000	5	0	0	0	0	0	0	0	1	0	0
Andy Messersmith, p	.500	2	4	0	2	0	0	0	0	0	2	0
Tom Paciorek, ph	.500	3	2	1	1	1	0	0	0	0	0	0
Bill Russell, ss	.222	5	18	0	4	0	1	0	2	0	2	0
Don Sutton, p	.000	2	3	0	0	0	0	0	0	0	2	0
Jimmy Wynn, of	.188	5	16	1	3	1	0	1	2	4	4	0
Steve Yeager, c	.364	4	11	0	4	1	0	0	1	1	4	0
TOTAL	.228		158	11	36	4	1	4	10	16	32	3

PITCHER	W	L	ERA	G	GS	CG	SV	SHO	IP	H	ER	BB	SO
Jim Brewer	0	0	0.00	1	0	0	0	0	0.1	0	0	0	1
Al Downing	0	1	2.45	1	1	0	0	0	3.2	4	1	4	3
Charley Hough	0	0	0.00	1	0	0	0	0	2.0	0	0	1	4
Mike Marshall	0	1	1.00	5	0	0	1	0	9.0	6	1	1	10
Andy Messersmith	0	2	4.50	2	2	0	0	0	14.0	11	7	7	12
Don Sutton	1	0	2.77	2	2	0	0	0	13.0	9	4	3	12
TOTAL	1	4	2.79	12	5	0	1	0	42.0	30	13	16	42

GAME 1 AT LA OCT 12

OAK	010	010	010	3	6	2
LA	000	010	001	2	11	1

Pitchers: Holtzman, FINGERS (5), Hunter (9) vs MESSERSMITH, Marshall (9)
Home Runs: Jackson-OAK, Wynn-LA
Attendance: 55,974

GAME 2 AT LA OCT 13

OAK	000	000	002	2	6	0
LA	010	002	00X	3	6	1

Pitchers: BLUE, Odom (8) vs SUTTON, Marshall (9)
Home Runs: Ferguson-LA
Attendance: 55,989

GAME 3 AT OAK OCT 15

LA	000	000	011	2	7	2
OAK	002	100	00X	3	5	2

Pitchers: DOWNING, Brewer (4), Hough (5), Marshall (7) vs HUNTER, Fingers (8)
Home Runs: Buckner-LA, Crawford-LA
Attendance: 49,347

GAME 4 AT OAK OCT 16

LA	000	200	000	2	7	1
OAK	001	004	00X	4	7	0

Pitchers: MESSERSMITH, Marshall (7) VS HOLTZMAN, Fingers (8)
Home Runs: Holtzman-OAK
Attendance: 49,347

GAME 5 AT OAK OCT 17

LA	000	002	000	2	5	1
OAK	110	000	10X	3	6	1

Pitchers: Sutton, MARSHALL (6) vs Blue, ODOM (7), Fingers (8)
Home Runs: Fosse-OAK, Rudi-OAK
Attendance: 49,347

The Reds, who had steamrolled the National League during the season, continued their roll in the LCS. Red pitcher Don Gullett gave up three Pirate runs in the first game, but he drove in three himself with a home run and a single. Pitching the series' only complete game, he won easily behind his club's twelve-hit, eight-run attack. The Reds won just as handily in Game Two, with Fred Norman and reliever Rawley Eastwick holding the Pirates to one run as Tony Perez drove in half the Reds' six runs—two of them with a first-inning homer.

In Game Three the Pirates struggled gamely against elimination. Cincinnati scored first in the second, but in the sixth Al Oliver put Pittsburgh ahead with a two-run homer. In the eighth, though, Pete Rose restored the Reds' lead (and nullified rookie John Candelaria's fourteen-strikeout effort over 7⅔ innings) with his two-run shot. The Pirates were granted a brief reprieve when Red reliever Eastwick walked in the tying run in the bottom of the ninth. But in the tenth the Reds scored twice on three hits, and when Eastwick's replacement Pedro Borbon shut the Pirates down in the bottom of the tenth, Cincinnati had its series sweep.

Cincinnati Reds (West), 3; Pittsburgh Pirates (East) 0

CIN (W)

PLAYER/POS	AVG	G	AB	R	H	2B	3B	HR	RB	BB	SO	SB
Ed Armbrister, ph	.000	2	0	0	0	0	0	0	0	1	0	0
Johnny Bench, c	.077	3	13	1	1	0	0	0	0	1	6	1
Pedro Borbon, p	.000	1	0	0	0	0	0	0	0	0	0	0
Clay Carroll, p	.000	1	0	0	0	0	0	0	0	0	0	0
Dave Concepcion, ss	.455	3	11	2	5	0	0	1	1	1	2	2
Terry Crowley, ph	.000	1	0	0	0	0	0	0	0	0	0	0
Rawly Eastwick, p	.000	2	0	0	0	0	0	0	0	0	0	0
George Foster, of	.364	3	11	3	4	0	0	0	0	1	2	1
Cesar Geronimo, of	.000	3	10	0	0	0	0	0	0	1	7	0
Ken Griffey, of	.333	3	12	4	4	1	0	0	4	0	3	3
Don Gullett, p	.500	1	4	1	2	0	0	1	3	0	0	0
Will Mc Enaney, p	.000	1	0	0	0	0	0	0	0	0	0	0
Joe Morgan, 2b	.273	3	11	2	3	3	0	0	1	3	2	4
Gary Nolan, p	.000	1	2	0	0	0	0	0	0	0	2	0
Fred Norman, p	.000	1	1	0	0	0	0	0	0	1	0	0
Tony Perez, 1b	.417	3	12	3	5	0	0	1	4	1	2	0
Merv Rettenmund, ph	.000	2	1	0	0	0	0	0	0	1	0	0
Pete Rose, 3b	.357	3	14	3	5	0	0	1	2	0	2	0
TOTAL	.284		102	19	29	4	0	4	18	9	28	11

PITCHER	W	L	ERA	G	GS	CG	SV	SHO	IP	H	ER	BB	SO
Pedro Borbon	0	0	0.00	1	0	0	1	0	1.0	0	0	0	1
Clay Carroll	0	0	0.00	1	0	0	0	0	1.0	0	0	0	1
Rawly Eastwick	1	0	0.00	2	0	0	1	0	3.2	2	0	2	1
Don Gullett	1	0	3.00	1	1	1	0	0	9.0	8	3	2	5
Will Mc Enaney	0	0	6.75	1	0	0	0	0	1.1	1	1	0	1
Gary Nolan	0	0	3.00	1	1	0	0	0	6.0	5	2	0	5
Fred Norman	1	0	1.50	1	1	0	0	0	6.0	4	1	5	4
TOTAL	3	0	2.25	8	3	1	2	0	28.0	20	7	10	18

PIT (E)

PLAYER/POS	AVG	G	AB	R	H	2B	3B	HR	RB	BB	SO	SB
Ken Brett, p	.000	2	0	0	0	0	0	0	0	0	0	0
John Candelaria, p	.000	1	3	0	0	0	0	0	0	0	3	0
Larry Demery, p	.000	1	0	0	0	0	0	0	0	0	0	0
Duffy Dyer, ph	.000	1	0	0	0	0	0	0	1	1	0	0
Dock Ellis, p	.000	1	0	0	0	0	0	0	0	0	0	0
Dave Giusti, p	.000	1	0	0	0	0	0	0	0	0	0	0
Richie Hebner, 3b	.333	3	12	2	4	1	0	0	2	1	1	0
Ramon Hernandez, p	.000	1	0	0	0	0	0	0	0	0	0	0
Ed Kirkpatrick, ph	.000	2	2	0	0	0	0	0	0	0	0	0
Bruce Kison, p	.000	1	0	0	0	0	0	0	0	0	0	0
Al Oliver, of	.182	3	11	1	2	0	0	1	2	2	0	0
Dave Parker, of	.000	3	10	2	0	0	0	0	0	1	3	0
Willie Randolph, 2b-1	.000	2	2	1	0	0	0	0	0	0	1	0
Jerry Reuss, p	.000	1	1	0	0	0	0	0	0	0	0	0
Craig Reynolds, ss-1	.000	2	1	0	0	0	0	0	0	0	0	0
Bob Robertson, 1b-1	.500	3	2	0	1	0	0	0	1	1	0	0
Bill Robinson, ph	.000	2	2	0	0	0	0	0	0	0	1	0
Jim Rooker, p	.000	1	1	0	0	0	0	0	0	0	1	0
Manny Sanguillen, c	.167	3	12	0	2	0	0	0	0	0	0	0
Willie Stargell, 1b	.182	3	11	1	2	1	0	0	0	1	3	0
Rennie Stennett, 2b-3,ss-1	.214	3	14	0	3	0	0	0	0	0	1	0
Frank Taveras, ss	.143	3	7	0	1	0	0	0	1	1	2	0
Kent Tekulve, p	.000	2	0	0	0	0	0	0	0	0	0	0
Richie Zisk, of	.500	3	10	0	5	1	0	0	0	2	2	0
TOTAL	.198		101	7	20	3	0	1	7	10	18	0

PITCHER	W	L	ERA	G	GS	CG	SV	SHO	IP	H	ER	BB	SO
Ken Brett	0	0	0.00	2	0	0	0	0	2.1	1	0	0	1
John Candelaria	0	0	3.52	1	1	0	0	0	7.2	3	3	2	14
Larry Demery	0	0	18.00	1	0	0	0	0	2.0	4	4	1	1
Dock Ellis	0	0	0.00	1	0	0	0	0	2.0	2	0	0	2
Dave Giusti	0	0	0.00	1	0	0	0	0	1.1	0	0	0	1
Ramon Hernandez	0	1	27.00	1	0	0	0	0	0.2	3	2	0	0
Bruce Kison	0	0	4.50	1	0	0	0	0	2.0	2	1	1	1
Jerry Reuss	0	1	13.50	1	1	0	0	0	2.2	4	4	4	1
Jim Rooker	0	1	9.00	1	1	0	0	0	4.0	7	4	0	5
Kent Tekulve	0	0	6.75	2	0	0	0	0	1.1	3	1	1	2
TOTAL	0	3	6.58	12	3	0	0	0	26.0	29	19	9	28

The Oakland A's ran their domination of the American League West to five years, but an aroused Boston team stifled their try for a fourth straight pennant.

In the first game Luis Tiant held Oakland to three hits as his teammates—aided by four Oakland errors—scored seven times before giving the A's an unearned run in the eighth. Oakland scored first in Game Two on Reggie Jackson's two-run homer in the first inning and added a run in the fourth. But Carl Yastrzemski's two-run shot in the last of the fourth, followed by a Carlton Fisk double and a Fred Lynn single, drove out A's starter Vida Blue, and the tying run scored on a double play. Single Boston runs in the sixth, seventh, and eighth put the game away.

The A's started Ken Holtzman for the second time in Game Three, after only two days of rest. He held the Sox scoreless for three innings, but was driven from the game in the fifth. Boston scored four times before Oakland put a run on the board, and retained the lead to the game's conclusion.

Boston Red Sox (East), 3; Oakland A's (West) 0

BOS (E)

PLAYER/POS	AVG	G	AB	R	H	2B	3B	HR	RB	BB	SO	SB
Juan Beniquez, dh	.250	3	12	2	3	0	0	0	1	0	1	2
Rick Burleson, ss	.444	3	9	2	4	2	0	0	1	1	0	0
Reggie Cleveland, p	.000	1	0	0	0	0	0	0	0	0	0	0
Cecil Cooper, 1b	.400	3	10	0	4	2	0	0	1	0	2	0
Denny Doyle, 2b	.273	3	11	3	3	0	0	0	1	0	1	0
Dick Drago, p	.000	2	0	0	0	0	0	0	0	0	0	0
Dwight Evans, of	.100	3	10	1	1	1	0	0	1	1	2	0
Carlton Fisk, c	.417	3	12	4	5	1	0	0	2	0	2	1
Fred Lynn, of	.364	3	11	1	4	1	0	0	3	0	0	0
Roger Moret, p	.000	1	0	0	0	0	0	0	0	0	0	0
Rico Petrocelli, 3b	.167	3	12	1	2	0	0	1	2	0	3	0
Luis Tiant, p	.000	1	0	0	0	0	0	0	0	0	0	0
Rick Wise, p	.000	1	0	0	0	0	0	0	0	0	0	0
Carl Yastrzemski, of	.455	3	11	4	5	1	0	1	2	1	1	0
TOTAL	.316		98	18	31	8	0	2	14	3	12	3

PITCHER	W	L	ERA	G	GS	CG	SV	SHO	IP	H	ER	BB	SO
Reggie Cleveland	0	0	5.40	1	1	0	0	0	5.0	7	3	1	2
Dick Drago	0	0	0.00	2	0	0	2	0	4.2	2	0	1	2
Roger Moret	1	0	0.00	1	0	0	0	0	1.0	1	0	1	0
Luis Tiant	1	0	0.00	1	1	1	0	0	9.0	3	0	3	8
Rick Wise	1	0	2.45	1	1	0	0	0	7.1	6	2	3	2
TOTAL	3	0	1.67	6	3	1	2	0	27.0	19	5	9	14

OAK (W)

PLAYER/POS	AVG	G	AB	R	H	2B	3B	HR	RB	BB	SO	SB
Glenn Abbott, p	.000	1	0	0	0	0	0	0	0	0	0	0
Sal Bando, 3b	.500	3	12	1	6	2	0	0	2	0	3	0
Vida Blue, p	.000	1	0	0	0	0	0	0	0	0	0	0
Dick Bosman, p	.000	1	0	0	0	0	0	0	0	0	0	0
Bert Campaneris, ss	.000	3	11	1	0	0	0	0	0	1	1	0
Rollie Fingers, p	.000	1	0	0	0	0	0	0	0	0	0	0
Ray Fosse, c	.000	1	2	0	0	0	0	0	0	0	1	0
Phil Garner, 2b	.000	3	5	0	0	0	0	0	0	0	1	0
Tommy Harper, ph	.000	1	0	0	0	0	0	0	0	1	0	0
Jim Holt, 1b-1	.333	3	3	0	1	1	0	0	0	0	0	0
Ken Holtzman, p	.000	2	0	0	0	0	0	0	0	0	0	0
Don Hopkins, dh	.000	1	0	0	0	0	0	0	0	0	0	0
Reggie Jackson, of	.417	3	12	1	5	0	0	1	3	0	2	0
Paul Lindblad, p	.000	2	0	0	0	0	0	0	0	0	0	0
Ted Martinez, 2b	.000	1	0	0	0	0	0	0	0	0	0	0
Billy North, of	.000	3	10	0	0	0	0	0	0	1	2	0
Joe Rudi, 1b-2,of-1	.250	3	12	1	3	2	0	0	0	0	1	0
Gene Tenace, c-3,1b-1	.000	3	9	0	0	0	0	0	0	3	2	0
Jim Todd, p	.000	3	0	0	0	0	0	0	0	0	0	0
Cesar Tovar, 2b-1	.500	2	2	2	1	0	0	0	0	0	1	0
Claudell Washington, of-2,dh-1	.250	3	12	1	3	1	0	0	1	0	2	0
Billy Williams, dh-2	.000	3	8	0	0	0	0	0	0	1	1	0
TOTAL	.194		98	7	19	6	0	1	7	9	14	0

PITCHER	W	L	ERA	G	GS	CG	SV	SHO	IP	H	ER	BB	SO
Glenn Abbott	0	0	0.00	1	0	0	0	0	1.0	0	0	0	0
Vida Blue	0	0	9.00	1	1	0	0	0	3.0	6	3	0	2
Dick Bosman	0	0	0.00	1	0	0	0	0	0.1	0	0	0	0
Rollie Fingers	0	1	6.75	1	0	0	0	0	4.0	5	3	1	3
Ken Holtzman	0	2	4.09	2	2	0	0	0	11.0	12	5	1	7
Paul Lindblad	0	0	0.00	2	0	0	0	0	4.2	5	0	1	0
Jim Todd	0	0	9.00	3	0	0	0	0	1.0	3	1	0	0
TOTAL	0	3	4.32	11	3	0	0	0	25.0	31	12	3	12

GAME 1 AT BOS OCT 4

OAK 000 000 010   1 3 4
BOS 200 000 50X   7 8 3

Pitchers: HOLTZMAN, Todd (7), Lindblad (7), Bosman (7), Abbott (8) vs TIANT
Attendance: 35,578

GAME 2 AT BOS OCT 5

OAK 200 100 000   3 10 0
BOS 000 301 11X   6 12 0

Pitchers: Blue, Todd (4), FINGERS (5) VS Cleveland, MORET (6), Drago (7)
Home Runs: Jackson-OAK, Yastrzemski-BOS, Petrocelli-BOS
Attendance: 35,578

GAME 3 AT OAK OCT 7

BOS 000 130 010   5 11 1
OAK 000 001 020   3 6 2

Pitchers: WISE, Drago (8) vs HOLTZMAN, Todd (5), Lindblad (5)
Attendance: 49,358

The Red Sox entered the Series as underdogs to the mighty Reds, who had won 108 regular-season games. In the opening game, though, the Reds were surprised by veteran Sox starter Luis Tiant, who shut them out on five hits with the Series' first complete-game pitching effort in four years. Tiant also opened the Boston seventh with a single, starting a rally that ended only when he fouled out to end the inning after six runs had scored.

Boston took a 2–1 lead into the ninth inning of Game Two before Johnny Bench doubled to drive out starter Bill Lee, and Dave Concepcion and Ken Griffey drove in runs off reliever Dick Drago to turn the tide for Cincinnati. The Reds moved ahead in the Series with a tenth-inning victory in Game Three, a slugfest in which each club hit three home runs and used five pitchers. Boston tied the score on Dwight Evans's two-run homer in the ninth, but in the last of the tenth, the Reds' Joe Morgan drove one over the center fielder's head with the bases full to end the game.

Tiant pitched Game Four for Boston. Four of the nine hits against him went for extra bases, and each drove in a run. But the Sox bunched six of their eleven hits in the fourth inning for five runs—their only scoring, but enough for the win. Tiant himself scored the fifth run after singling. The Reds moved nearer the title in Game Five, though, as Tony Perez homered twice for four runs in a 6–2 win for a 3–2 Series advantage.

A day of travel to Boston and three days of rain between Games Five and Six brought Tiant back to the mound for a third time. Rookie standout Fred Lynn gave Tiant a three-run lead with a first-inning homer, but Ken Griffey's triple and Johnny Bench's long single drove in the tying Red runs in the fifth. Two more Red runs in the seventh and Cesar Geronimo's leadoff homer in the eighth drove out Tiant, but Boston pinch hitter Bernie Carbo homered to center in the last of the eighth for three runs that tied the score again. After a trio of Boston relievers had held Cincinnati in check through the top of the twelfth inning, the Sox leadoff hitter in the last of the twelfth, Carlton Fisk, ended the game dramatically with a home run to left on the first pitch that came within inches of being foul.

After the pyrotechnics of Game Six (ranked by some as the greatest World Series game ever), the seventh game, close as it was, came as an anticlimax. Boston scored three runs in the third inning, but the Reds began their comeback with Tony Perez's two-run homer in the sixth, tied the game an inning later, and took a 4–3 lead on Joe Morgan's bloop RBI single in the ninth. Red reliever Will McEnaney came on to set the Sox down in order in the last of the ninth, and the Reds went home with their first world title in thirty-five years.

Cincinnati Reds (NL), 4; Boston Red Sox (AL) 3

CIN (N)

PLAYER/POS	AVG	G	AB	R	H	2B	3B	HR	RB	BB	SO	SB
Ed Armbrister, ph	.000	4	1	1	0	0	0	0	0	2	0	0
Johnny Bench, c	.207	7	29	5	6	2	0	1	4	2	4	0
Jack Billingham, p	.000	3	2	0	0	0	0	0	0	0	0	0
Pedro Borbon, p	.000	3	1	0	0	0	0	0	0	0	0	0
Clay Carroll, p	.000	5	0	0	0	0	0	0	0	0	0	0
Darrel Chaney, ph	.000	2	2	0	0	0	0	0	0	0	1	0
Dave Concepcion, ss	.179	7	28	3	5	1	0	1	4	0	1	3
Terry Crowley, ph	.500	2	2	0	1	0	0	0	0	0	1	0
Pat Darcy, p	.000	2	1	0	0	0	0	0	0	0	0	0
Dan Driessen, ph	.000	2	2	0	0	0	0	0	0	0	0	0
Rawly Eastwick, p	.000	5	1	0	0	0	0	0	0	0	0	0
George Foster, of	.276	7	29	1	8	1	0	0	2	1	1	0
Cesar Geronimo, of	.280	7	25	3	7	0	1	2	3	3	5	0
Ken Griffey, of	.269	7	26	4	7	3	1	0	4	4	2	2
Don Gullett, p	.286	3	7	1	2	0	0	0	0	0	2	0
Will Mc Enaney, p	1.000	5	1	0	1	0	0	0	0	0	0	0
Joe Morgan, 2b	.259	7	27	4	7	1	0	0	3	5	1	2
Gary Nolan, p	.000	2	1	0	0	0	0	0	0	0	0	0
Fred Norman, p	.000	2	2	0	0	0	0	0	0	0	0	0
Tony Perez, 1b	.179	7	28	4	5	0	0	3	7	3	9	1
Merv Rettenmund, ph	.000	3	3	0	0	0	0	0	0	0	1	0
Pete Rose, 3b	.370	7	27	3	10	1	1	0	2	5	1	0
TOTAL	.242		244	29	59	9	3	7	29	25	30	9

PITCHER	W	L	ERA	G	GS	CG	SV	SHO	IP	H	ER	BB	SO
Jack Billingham	0	0	1.00	3	1	0	0	0	9.0	8	1	5	7
Pedro Borbon	0	0	6.00	3	0	0	0	0	3.0	3	2	2	1
Clay Carroll	1	0	3.18	5	0	0	0	0	5.2	4	2	2	3
Pat Darcy	0	1	4.50	2	0	0	0	0	4.0	3	2	2	1
Rawly Eastwick	2	0	2.25	5	0	0	1	0	8.0	6	2	3	4
Don Gullett	1	1	4.34	3	3	0	0	0	18.2	19	9	10	15
Will Mc Enaney	0	0	2.70	5	0	0	1	0	6.2	3	2	2	5
Gary Nolan	0	0	6.00	2	2	0	0	0	6.0	6	4	1	2
Fred Norman	0	1	9.00	2	1	0	0	0	4.0	8	4	3	2
TOTAL	4	3	3.88	30	7	0	2	0	65.0	60	28	30	40

BOS (A)

PLAYER/POS	AVG	G	AB	R	H	2B	3B	HR	RB	BB	SO	SB
Juan Beniquez, of-2	.125	3	8	0	1	0	0	0	0	1	1	0
Rick Burleson, ss	.292	7	24	1	7	1	0	0	2	4	2	0
Jim Burton, p	.000	2	0	0	0	0	0	0	0	0	0	0
Bernie Carbo, of-2	.429	4	7	3	3	1	0	2	4	1	1	0
Reggie Cleveland, p	.000	3	2	0	0	0	0	0	0	0	2	0
Cecil Cooper, 1b	.053	5	19	0	1	1	0	0	1	0	3	0
Denny Doyle, 2b	.267	7	30	3	8	1	1	0	0	2	1	0
Dick Drago, p	.000	2	0	0	0	0	0	0	0	0	0	0
Dwight Evans, of	.292	7	24	3	7	1	1	1	5	3	4	0
Carlton Fisk, c	.240	7	25	5	6	0	0	2	4	2	4	0
Doug Griffin, ph	.000	1	1	0	0	0	0	0	0	0	0	0
Bill Lee, p	.167	2	6	0	1	0	0	0	0	0	3	0
Fred Lynn, of	.280	7	25	3	7	1	0	1	5	3	5	0
Rick Miller, of-2	.000	3	2	0	0	0	0	0	0	0	0	0
Bob Montgomery, ph	.000	1	1	0	0	0	0	0	0	0	0	0
Roger Moret, p	.000	3	0	0	0	0	0	0	0	0	0	0
Rico Petrocelli, 3b	.308	7	26	3	8	1	0	0	4	3	6	0
Dick Pole, p	.000	1	0	0	0	0	0	0	0	0	0	0
Diego Segui, p	.000	1	0	0	0	0	0	0	0	0	0	0
Luis Tiant, p	.250	3	8	2	2	0	0	0	0	0	2	0
Jim Willoughby, p	.000	3	0	0	0	0	0	0	0	0	0	0
Rick Wise, p	.000	2	2	0	0	0	0	0	0	0	1	0
Carl Yastrzemski, 1b-4,of-4	.310	7	29	7	9	0	0	0	4	4	1	0
TOTAL	.251		239	30	60	7	2	6	30	30	40	0

PITCHER	W	L	ERA	G	GS	CG	SV	SHO	IP	H	ER	BB	SO
Jim Burton	0	1	9.00	2	0	0	0	0	1.0	1	1	3	0
Reggie Cleveland	0	1	6.75	3	1	0	0	0	6.2	7	5	3	5
Dick Drago	0	1	2.25	2	0	0	0	0	4.0	3	1	1	1
Bill Lee	0	0	3.14	2	2	0	0	0	14.1	12	5	3	7
Roger Moret	0	0	0.00	3	0	0	0	0	1.2	2	0	3	1
Dick Pole	0	0	INF	1	0	0	0	0	0.0	0	1	2	0
Diego Segui	0	0	0.00	1	0	0	0	0	1.0	0	0	0	0
Luis Tiant	2	0	3.60	3	3	2	0	1	25.0	25	10	8	12
Jim Willoughby	0	1	0.00	3	0	0	0	0	6.1	3	0	2	2
Rick Wise	1	0	8.44	2	1	0	0	0	5.1	6	5	2	2
TOTAL	3	4	3.86	22	7	2	0	1	65.1	59	28	25	30

GAME 1 AT BOS OCT 11

CIN	000	000	000	0	5 0
BOS	000	000	60X	6	12 0

Pitchers: GULLETT, Carroll (7), McEnaney (7) vs TIANT
Attendance: 35,205

GAME 2 AT BOS OCT 12

CIN	000	100	002	3	7 1
BOS	100	001	000	2	7 0

Pitchers: Billingham, Borbon (6), McEnaney (7), EASTWICK (8) vs Lee, Drago (9)
Attendance: 35,205

GAME 3 AT CIN OCT 14

BOS	010	001	102 0	5	10 2
CIN	000	230	000 1	6	7 0

Pitchers: Wise, Burton (5), Cleveland (5), WILLOUGHBY (7), Moret (10) VS Nolan, Darcy (5), Carroll (7), McEnaney (7), EASTWICK (9)
Home Runs: Fisk-BOS, Bench-CIN, Concepcion-CIN, Geronimo-CIN, Carbo-BOS, Evans-BOS
Attendance: 55,392

GAME 4 AT CIN OCT 15

BOS	000	500	000	5	11 1
CIN	200	200	000	4	9 1

Pitchers: TIANT vs NORMAN, Borbon (4), Carroll (5), Eastwick (7)
Attendance: 55,667

GAME 5 AT CIN OCT 16

BOS	100	000	001	2	5 0
CIN	000	113	01X	6	8 0

Pitchers: CLEVELAND, Willoughby (6), Pole (8), Segui (8) vs GULLETT, Eastwick (9)
Home Runs: Perez-CIN (2)
Attendance: 56,393

GAME 6 AT BOS OCT 21

CIN	000	030	210 000	6	14 0
BOS	300	000	030 001	7	10 1

Pitchers: Nolan, Norman (3), Billingham (3), Carroll (5), Borbon (6), Eastwick (8), McEnaney (9), DARCY (10) VS Tiant, Moret (8), Drago (9), WISE (12)
Home Runs: Lynn-BOS, Geronimo-CIN, Carbo-BOS, Fisk-BOS
Attendance: 35,205

GAME 7 AT BOS OCT 22

CIN	000	002	101	4	9 0
BOS	003	000	000	3	5 2

Pitchers: Gullett, Billingham (5), CARROLL (7), McEnaney (9) vs Lee, Moret (7), Willoughby (7), BURTON (9), Cleveland (9)
Home Runs: Perez-CIN
Attendance: 35,205

Philadelphia outhit Cincinnati in two of the three games, but couldn't turn enough hits into runs, as the Reds for the second year in a row swept the LCS. The Phillies scored first in Game One with a run in the first inning. But pitcher Don Gullett held them scoreless for the next seven innings as his Reds caught up in the third, moved ahead in the sixth, and took a five-run lead into the last of the ninth. The Phillies scored twice in their half of the inning, but the rally fell short.

In the second game the Phillies outhit the Reds ten to six, scoring the game's first two runs while their starter Jim Lonborg threw a no-hitter for five innings. But in the sixth a walk and two singles drove Lonborg out and set the Reds off on a two-inning six-run spree for their second win.

Again in Game Three the Phillies outhit the Reds, this time going into the last of the ninth ahead by two runs. But George Foster and Johnny Bench hit back-to-back homers off Ron Reed to tie the score, and two relievers (and a single and two walks) later, the Reds brought home another pennant as Ken Griffey's high-bouncing chop glanced off first baseman Bobby Tolan's outstretched glove.

Cincinnati Reds (West), 3; Philadelphia Phillies (East) 0

CIN (W)

PLAYER/POS	AVG	G	AB	R	H	2B	3B	HR	RB	BB	SO	SB
Ed Armbrister, ph	.000	1	0	0	0	0	0	0	0	0	0	0
Johnny Bench, c	.333	3	12	3	4	1	0	1	1	1	2	1
Pedro Borbon, p	.000	2	2	1	0	0	0	0	0	0	2	0
Dave Concepcion, ss	.200	3	10	4	2	1	0	0	0	2	1	0
Dan Driessen, ph	.000	1	1	0	0	0	0	0	0	0	0	0
Rawly Eastwick, p	.000	2	0	0	0	0	0	0	0	0	0	0
Doug Flynn, 2b	.000	1	0	0	0	0	0	0	0	0	0	0
George Foster, of	.167	3	12	2	2	0	0	2	4	0	4	0
Cesar Geronimo, of	.182	3	11	0	2	0	1	0	2	1	3	0
Ken Griffey, of	.385	3	13	2	5	0	1	0	2	2	1	2
Don Gullett, p	.500	1	4	1	2	1	0	0	3	0	0	0
Mike Lum, ph	.000	1	1	0	0	0	0	0	0	0	0	0
Joe Morgan, 2b	.000	3	7	2	0	0	0	0	0	6	1	2
Gary Nolan, p	.000	1	0	0	0	0	0	0	0	1	0	0
Tony Perez, 1b	.200	3	10	1	2	0	0	0	3	1	2	0
Pete Rose, 3b	.429	3	14	3	6	2	1	0	2	1	0	0
Manny Sarmiento, p	.000	1	1	0	0	0	0	0	0	0	0	0
Pat Zachry, p	.000	1	0	0	0	0	0	0	0	0	0	0
TOTAL	.253		99	19	25	5	3	3	17	15	16	5

PITCHER	W	L	ERA	G	GS	CG	SV	SHO	IP	H	ER	BB	SO
Pedro Borbon	0	0	0.00	2	0	0	1	0	4.1	4	0	1	0
Rawly Eastwick	1	0	12.00	2	0	0	0	0	3.0	7	4	2	1
Don Gullett	1	0	1.13	1	1	0	0	0	8.0	2	1	3	4
Gary Nolan	0	0	1.59	1	1	0	0	0	5.2	6	1	2	1
Manny Sarmiento	0	0	18.00	1	0	0	0	0	1.0	2	2	1	0
Pat Zachry	1	0	3.60	1	1	0	0	0	5.0	6	2	3	3
TOTAL	3	0	3.33	8	3	0	1	0	27.0	27	10	12	9

PHI (E)

PLAYER/POS	AVG	G	AB	R	H	2B	3B	HR	RB	BB	SO	SB
Richie Allen, 1b	.222	3	9	1	2	0	0	0	0	3	2	0
Bob Boone, c	.286	3	7	0	2	0	0	0	1	1	0	0
Larry Bowa, ss	.125	3	8	1	1	1	0	0	1	3	0	0
Ollie Brown, of	.000	1	2	0	0	0	0	0	0	1	1	0
Steve Carlton, p	.000	1	2	0	0	0	0	0	0	0	0	0
Dave Cash, 2b	.308	3	13	1	4	1	0	0	1	0	0	0
Gene Garber, p	.000	2	0	0	0	0	0	0	0	0	0	0
Terry Harmon, pr	.000	1	0	1	0	0	0	0	0	0	0	0
Tom Hutton, ph	.000	1	1	0	0	0	0	0	0	0	0	0
Jay Johnstone, of-2	.778	3	9	1	7	1	1	0	2	1	0	0
Jim Kaat, p	.500	1	2	0	1	0	0	0	0	0	0	0
Jim Lonborg, p	.000	1	1	0	0	0	0	0	0	0	0	0
Greg Luzinski, of	.273	3	11	2	3	2	0	1	2	1	4	0
Garry Maddox, of	.231	3	13	2	3	1	0	0	2	2	0	0
Jerry Martin, of	.000	1	1	1	0	0	0	0	0	0	0	0
Tim Mc Carver, c-1	.000	2	4	0	0	0	0	0	0	0	1	0
Tug Mc Graw, p	.000	2	0	0	0	0	0	0	0	0	0	0
Johnny Oates, c	.000	1	1	0	0	0	0	0	0	0	0	0
Ron Reed, p	.000	2	0	0	0	0	0	0	0	0	0	0
Mike Schmidt, 3b	.308	3	13	1	4	2	0	0	2	0	1	0
Bobby Tolan, 1b-1,of-1	.000	3	2	0	0	0	0	0	0	0	0	0
Tom Underwood, p	.000	1	0	0	0	0	0	0	0	0	0	0
TOTAL	.270		100	11	27	8	1	1	11	12	9	0

PITCHER	W	L	ERA	G	GS	CG	SV	SHO	IP	H	ER	BB	SO
Steve Carlton	0	1	3.86	1	1	0	0	0	7.0	8	3	5	6
Gene Garber	0	1	40.50	2	0	0	0	0	0.2	2	3	1	0
Jim Kaat	0	0	3.00	1	1	0	0	0	6.0	2	2	2	1
Jim Lonborg	0	1	1.69	1	1	0	0	0	5.1	2	1	2	2
Tug Mc Graw	0	0	11.57	2	0	0	0	0	2.1	4	3	1	5
Ron Reed	0	0	7.71	2	0	0	0	0	4.2	6	4	2	2
Tom Underwood	0	0	0.00	1	0	0	0	0	0.1	1	0	2	0
TOTAL	0	3	5.47	10	3	0	0	0	26.1	25	16	15	16

GAME 1 AT PHI OCT 9

CIN	001	002	030	6	10	0
PHI	100	000	002	3	6	1

Pitchers: GULLETT, Eastwick (9) VS CARLTON, McGraw (8)
Home Runs: Foster-CIN
Attendance: 62,640

GAME 2 AT PHI OCT 10

CIN	000	004	200	6	6	0
PHI	010	010	000	2	10	1

Pitchers: ZACHRY, Borbon (6) vs LONBORG, Garber (6), McGraw (7), Reed (7)
Home Runs: Luzinski-PHI
Attendance: 62,651

GAME 3 AT CIN OCT 12

PHI	000	100	221	6	11	0
CIN	000	000	403	7	9	2

Pitchers: Kaat, Reed (7), GARBER (9), Underwood (9) vs Nolan, Sarmiento (6), Borbon (7), EASTWICK (8)
Home Runs: Foster-CIN, Bench-CIN
Attendance: 55,047

Returning to postseason play after a dozen years' absence, the Yankees found themselves evenly matched with the first-time-champion Royals. They didn't really need their two ninth-inning runs in the first game: the two they scored in the first inning proved cushion enough for Catfish Hunter's one-run five-hitter. But Kansas City came back the next day, scoring first, losing the lead in the third, then regaining it for good in the sixth.

The Royals again took a first-inning lead in Game Three, but this time the Yankees, once they went ahead in the sixth, didn't let go. Kansas City held on to its early lead in Game Four, building on it throughout the game for a second win, despite Yankee Graig Nettles' two home runs.

But Game Five—like the series itself—was a seesaw affair. For the fourth time the Royals scored first, with a pair in the first on John Mayberry's home run. But the Yankees tied the game when they came to bat, and K.C. retook the lead in the second. New York went ahead again in the third and increased its lead to 6–3 in the sixth. But in the top of the eighth, George Brett's three-run homer tied the score once again, setting the stage for Chris Chambliss to win for the Yankees their thirtieth American League pennant with his first-pitch home run in the bottom of the ninth.

New York Yankees (East), 3; Kansas City Royals (West) 2

NY (E)

PLAYER/POS	AVG	G	AB	R	H	2B	3B	HR	RB	BB	SO	SB
Sandy Alomar, dh-1	.000	2	1	0	0	0	0	0	0	0	0	0
Chris Chambliss, 1b	.524	5	21	5	11	1	1	2	8	0	1	2
Dock Ellis, p	.000	1	0	0	0	0	0	0	0	0	0	0
Ed Figueroa, p	.000	2	0	0	0	0	0	0	0	0	0	0
Oscar Gamble, of	.250	3	8	1	2	1	0	0	1	1	1	0
Ron Guidry, pr	.000	1	0	0	0	0	0	0	0	0	0	0
Elrod Hendricks, ph	1.000	1	1	0	1	0	0	0	0	0	0	0
Catfish Hunter, p	.000	2	0	0	0	0	0	0	0	0	0	0
Grant Jackson, p	.000	2	0	0	0	0	0	0	0	0	0	0
Sparky Lyle, p	.000	1	0	0	0	0	0	0	0	0	0	0
Elliott Maddox, of	.222	3	9	0	2	1	0	0	1	0	1	0
Jim Mason, ss	.000	2	0	0	0	0	0	0	0	0	0	0
Carlos May, dh	.200	3	10	1	2	1	0	0	0	1	4	0
Thurman Munson, c	.435	5	23	3	10	2	0	0	3	0	1	0
Graig Nettles, 3b	.235	5	17	2	4	1	0	2	4	3	3	0
Lou Piniella, dh-3	.273	4	11	1	3	1	0	0	0	0	1	0
Willie Randolph, 2b	.118	5	17	0	2	0	0	0	1	3	1	1
Mickey Rivers, of	.348	5	23	5	8	0	1	0	0	1	1	0
Fred Stanley, ss	.333	5	15	1	5	2	0	0	2	2	0	0
Dick Tidrow, p	.000	3	0	0	0	0	0	0	0	0	0	0
Otto Velez, ph	.000	1	1	0	0	0	0	0	0	0	0	0
Roy White, of	.294	5	17	4	5	3	0	0	3	5	1	1
TOTAL	.316		174	23	55	13	2	4	21	16	15	4

PITCHER	W	L	ERA	G	GS	CG	SV	SHO	IP	H	ER	BB	SO
Dock Ellis	1	0	3.38	1	1	0	0	0	8.0	6	3	2	5
Ed Figueroa	0	1	5.84	2	2	0	0	0	12.1	14	8	2	5
Catfish Hunter	1	1	4.50	2	2	1	0	0	12.0	10	6	1	5
Grant Jackson	0	0	8.10	2	0	0	0	0	3.1	4	3	1	3
Sparky Lyle	0	0	0.00	1	0	0	1	0	1.0	0	0	1	0
Dick Tidrow	1	0	3.68	3	0	0	0	0	7.1	6	3	4	0
TOTAL	3	2	4.70	11	5	1	1	0	44.0	40	23	11	18

KC (W)

PLAYER/POS	AVG	G	AB	R	H	2B	3B	HR	RB	BB	SO	SB
Doug Bird, p	.000	1	0	0	0	0	0	0	0	0	0	0
George Brett, 3b	.444	5	18	4	8	1	1	1	5	2	1	0
Al Cowens, of	.190	5	21	3	4	0	1	0	0	1	1	2
Larry Gura, p	.000	2	0	0	0	0	0	0	0	0	0	0
Tom Hall, p	.000	1	0	0	0	0	0	0	0	0	0	0
Andy Hassler, p	.000	2	0	0	0	0	0	0	0	0	0	0
Dennis Leonard, p	.000	2	0	0	0	0	0	0	0	0	0	0
Mark Littell, p	.000	3	0	0	0	0	0	0	0	0	0	0
Buck Martinez, c	.333	5	15	0	5	0	0	0	4	1	3	0
John Mayberry, 1b	.222	5	18	4	4	0	0	1	3	1	0	0
Hal Mc Rae, dh-3,of-2	.118	5	17	2	2	1	1	0	1	1	4	0
Steve Mingori, p	.000	3	0	0	0	0	0	0	0	0	0	0
Dave Nelson, dh-1	.000	2	2	0	0	0	0	0	0	0	1	0
Amos Otis, of	.000	1	1	0	0	0	0	0	0	0	0	0
Freddie Patek, ss	.389	5	18	2	7	2	0	0	4	0	1	0
Marty Pattin, p	.000	2	0	0	0	0	0	0	0	0	0	0
Tom Poquette, of	.188	5	16	1	3	2	0	0	4	2	3	0
Jamie Quirk, dh-2	.143	4	7	1	1	0	1	0	2	0	2	0
Cookie Rojas, 2b	.333	4	9	2	3	0	0	0	1	0	0	1
Paul Splittorff, p	.000	2	0	0	0	0	0	0	0	0	0	0
Bob Stinson, c-1	.000	2	1	0	0	0	0	0	0	0	0	0
John Wathan, c	.000	1	0	0	0	0	0	0	0	0	0	0
Frank White, 2b	.125	4	8	2	1	0	0	0	0	0	1	0
Jim Wohlford, of	.182	5	11	3	2	0	0	0	0	3	1	2
TOTAL	.247		162	24	40	6	4	2	24	11	18	5

PITCHER	W	L	ERA	G	GS	CG	SV	SHO	IP	H	ER	BB	SO
Doug Bird	1	0	1.93	1	0	0	0	0	4.2	4	1	0	1
Larry Gura	0	1	4.22	2	2	0	0	0	10.2	18	5	1	4
Tom Hall	0	0	0.00	1	0	0	0	0	0.1	1	0	0	0
Andy Hassler	0	1	6.14	2	1	0	0	0	7.1	8	5	6	4
Dennis Leonard	0	0	19.29	2	2	0	0	0	2.1	9	5	2	0
Mark Littell	0	1	1.93	3	0	0	0	0	4.2	4	1	1	3
Steve Mingori	0	0	2.70	3	0	0	1	0	3.1	4	1	0	1
Marty Pattin	0	0	27.00	2	0	0	0	0	0.1	0	1	1	0
Paul Splittorff	1	0	1.93	2	0	0	0	0	9.1	7	2	5	2
TOTAL	2	3	4.40	18	5	0	1	0	43.0	55	21	16	15

GAME 1 AT KC OCT 9

NY	200	000	002	4	12	0
KC	000	000	010	1	5	2

Pitchers: HUNTER vs GURA, Littell (9)
Attendance: 41,077

GAME 2 AT KC OCT 10

NY	012	000	000	3	12	5
KC	200	002	03X	7	9	0

Pitchers: FIGUEROA, Tidrow (6) vs Leonard, SPLITTORFF (3), Mingori (9)
Attendance: 41,091

GAME 3 AT NY OCT 12

KC	300	000	000	3	6	0
NY	000	203	00X	5	9	0

Pitchers: HASSLER, Pattin (6), Hall (6), Mingori (6), Littell (6) vs ELLIS, Lyle (9)
Home Runs: Chambliss-NY
Attendance: 56,808

GAME 4 AT NY OCT 13

KC	030	201	010	7	9	1
NY	020	000	101	4	11	0

Pitchers: Gura, BIRD (3), Mingori (7) vs HUNTER, Tidrow (4), Jackson (7)
Home Runs: Nettles-NY (2)
Attendance: 56,355

GAME 5 AT NY OCT 14

KC	210	000	030	6	11	1
NY	202	002	001	7	11	1

Pitchers: Leonard, Splittorff (1), Pattin (4), Hassler (5), LITTELL (7) vs Figueroa, Jackson (8), TIDROW (9)
Home Runs: Mayberry-KC, Brett-KC, Chambliss-NY
Attendance: 56,821

The Reds led the National League in virtually every offensive category and in fielding as well. In the Series (which, incidentally, was the first to employ the designated hitter), the Big Red Machine continued its roll over the Yankees to become the first National League club in fifty-four years to repeat as world champions, as well as the first team to sweep both a League Championship and World Series. Red catcher Johnny Bench led the attack with eight hits, half of them for extra bases, for a batting average of .533 and a 1.133 average in slugging.

Joe Morgan's home run for Cincinnati in the first inning of Game One was the first hit of the Series, but New York pushed across a tying run half an inning later on a sacrifice fly. Red pitchers Don Gullett and Pedro Borbon held the Yankees scoreless after that as the Reds regained the lead with a run in the third and extended it in the sixth and seventh for a 5–1 win.

Game Two turned out to be the Reds' only narrow victory. They scored first, with three runs in the second inning. In the fourth the Yankees scored their first run, and they tied the score with two more runs in the seventh. But with two men out in the last of the ninth, a throwing error by Yankee shortstop Fred Stanley allowed the Reds' batter Ken Griffey to reach second, from where he scored the winning run on Tony Perez's line single to left.

In Game Three, four hits and a pair of stolen bases put Cincinnati ahead 3–0 in the second inning, and Dan Driessen homered in the fourth to make it 4–0 before the Yankees scored their first run. Another quartet of hits in the eighth gave the Reds two more runs and a 6–2 win.

New York took the lead for the only time in the Series when Chris Chambliss doubled in Thurman Munson in the first inning of Game Four. (Munson had singled with the third of what became six straight hits.) But the Reds' George Foster drove in a tying run in the fourth, and Johnny Bench followed him with a two-run homer. New York scored again an inning later to come close, but Bench's second home run, a three-run blast in the ninth, put the game out of reach, and a pair of ground-rule doubles touched by New York fans nailed the final run in the Yankee coffin.

Cincinnati Reds (NL), 4; New York Yankees (AL) 0

CIN (N)

PLAYER/POS	AVG	G	AB	R	H	2B	3B	HR	RB	BB	SO	SB
Johnny Bench, c	.533	4	15	4	8	1	1	2	6	0	1	0
Jack Billingham, p	.000	1	0	0	0	0	0	0	0	0	0	0
Pedro Borbon, p	.000	1	0	0	0	0	0	0	0	0	0	0
Dave Concepcion, ss	.357	4	14	1	5	1	1	0	3	1	3	1
Dan Driessen, dh	.357	4	14	4	5	2	0	1	1	2	0	1
George Foster, of	.429	4	14	3	6	1	0	0	4	2	3	0
Cesar Geronimo, of	.308	4	13	3	4	2	0	0	1	2	2	2
Ken Griffey, of	.059	4	17	2	1	0	0	0	1	0	1	1
Don Gullett, p	.000	1	0	0	0	0	0	0	0	0	0	0
Will Mc Enaney, p	.000	2	0	0	0	0	0	0	0	0	0	0
Joe Morgan, 2b	.333	4	15	3	5	1	1	1	2	2	2	2
Gary Nolan, p	.000	1	0	0	0	0	0	0	0	0	0	0
Fred Norman, p	.000	1	0	0	0	0	0	0	0	0	0	0
Tony Perez, 1b	.313	4	16	1	5	1	0	0	2	1	2	0
Pete Rose, 3b	.188	4	16	1	3	1	0	0	1	2	2	0
Pat Zachry, p	.000	1	0	0	0	0	0	0	0	0	0	0
TOTAL	.313		134	22	42	10	3	4	21	12	16	7

PITCHER	W	L	ERA	G	GS	CG	SV	SHO	IP	H	ER	BB	SO
Jack Billingham	1	0	0.00	1	0	0	0	0	2.2	0	0	0	1
Pedro Borbon	0	0	0.00	1	0	0	0	0	1.2	0	0	0	0
Don Gullett	1	0	1.23	1	1	0	0	0	7.1	5	1	3	4
Will Mc Enaney	0	0	0.00	2	0	0	2	0	4.2	2	0	1	2
Gary Nolan	1	0	2.70	1	1	0	0	0	6.2	8	2	1	1
Fred Norman	0	0	4.26	1	1	0	0	0	6.1	9	3	2	2
Pat Zachry	1	0	2.70	1	1	0	0	0	6.2	6	2	5	6
TOTAL	4	0	2.00	8	4	0	2	0	36.0	30	8	12	16

NY (A)

PLAYER/POS	AVG	G	AB	R	H	2B	3B	HR	RB	BB	SO	SB
Doyle Alexander, p	.000	1	0	0	0	0	0	0	0	0	0	0
Chris Chambliss, 1b	.313	4	16	1	5	1	0	0	1	0	2	0
Dock Ellis, p	.000	1	0	0	0	0	0	0	0	0	0	0
Ed Figueroa, p	.000	1	0	0	0	0	0	0	0	0	0	0
Oscar Gamble, of-2	.125	3	8	0	1	0	0	0	1	0	0	0
Elrod Hendricks, ph	.000	2	2	0	0	0	0	0	0	0	0	0
Catfish Hunter, p	.000	1	0	0	0	0	0	0	0	0	0	0
Grant Jackson, p	.000	1	0	0	0	0	0	0	0	0	0	0
Sparky Lyle, p	.000	2	0	0	0	0	0	0	0	0	0	0
Elliott Maddox, of-1,dh-1	.200	2	5	0	1	0	1	0	0	1	2	0
Jim Mason, ss	1.000	3	1	1	1	0	0	1	1	0	0	0
Carlos May, dh	.000	4	9	0	0	0	0	0	0	0	1	0
Thurman Munson, c	.529	4	17	2	9	0	0	0	2	0	1	0
Graig Nettles, 3b	.250	4	12	0	3	0	0	0	2	3	1	0
Lou Piniella, of-2,dh-2	.333	4	9	1	3	1	0	0	0	0	0	0
Willie Randolph, 2b	.071	4	14	1	1	0	0	0	0	1	3	0
Mickey Rivers, of	.167	4	18	1	3	0	0	0	0	1	2	1
Fred Stanley, ss	.167	4	6	1	1	1	0	0	1	3	1	0
Dick Tidrow, p	.000	2	0	0	0	0	0	0	0	0	0	0
Otto Velez, ph	.000	3	3	0	0	0	0	0	0	0	3	0
Roy White, of	.133	4	15	0	2	0	0	0	0	3	0	0
TOTAL	.222		135	8	30	3	1	1	8	12	16	1

PITCHER	W	L	ERA	G	GS	CG	SV	SHO	IP	H	ER	BB	SO
Doyle Alexander	0	1	7.50	1	1	0	0	0	6.0	9	5	2	1
Dock Ellis	0	1	10.80	1	1	0	0	0	3.1	7	4	0	1
Ed Figueroa	0	1	5.63	1	1	0	0	0	8.0	6	5	5	2
Catfish Hunter	0	1	3.12	1	1	1	0	0	8.2	10	3	4	5
Grant Jackson	0	0	4.91	1	0	0	0	0	3.2	4	2	0	3
Sparky Lyle	0	0	0.00	2	0	0	0	0	2.2	1	0	0	3
Dick Tidrow	0	0	7.71	2	0	0	0	0	2.1	5	2	1	1
TOTAL	0	4	5.45	9	4	1	0	0	34.2	42	21	12	16

GAME 1 AT CIN OCT 16

NY	010	000	000	1	5	1
CIN	101	001	20X	5	10	1

Pitchers: ALEXANDER, Lyle (7) vs GULLETT, Borbon (8)
Home Runs: Morgan-CIN
Attendance: 54,826

GAME 2 AT CIN OCT 17

NY	000	100	200	3	9	1
CIN	030	000	001	4	10	0

Pitchers: HUNTER vs Norman, BILLINGHAM (7)
Attendance: 54,816

GAME 3 AT NY OCT 19

CIN	030	100	020	6	13	2
NY	000	100	100	2	8	0

Pitchers: ZACHRY, McEnaney (7) vs ELLIS, Jackson (4), Tidrow (8)
Home Runs: Driessen-CIN, Mason-NY
Attendance: 56,667

GAME 4 AT NY OCT 21

CIN	000	300	004	7	9	2
NY	100	010	000	2	8	0

Pitchers: NOLAN, McEnaney (7) vs FIGUEROA, Tidrow (9), Lyle (9)
Home Runs: Bench-CIN (2)
Attendance: 56,700

The Phillies took the first game, but the Dodgers proved better over all at turning hits into runs and swept the next three. Philadelphia jumped ahead in the first inning of Game One, and had built a 5–1 lead by the seventh, when Ron Cey tied the score with a Dodger grand slam. But the Phillies came back with two runs on three singles in the top of the ninth and held on for the win. As in Game One, both clubs again got nine hits apiece in Game Two, but this time Dodger pitcher Don Sutton scattered the Phillies' hits for a single run over nine innings, while Phillie starter Jim Lonborg—in the four innings he pitched—yielded five runs, including a grand slam to Dusty Baker.

In Game Three Los Angeles outhit the Phillies, but the Dodgers were nearly undone when starter Burt Hooton walked in three Philadelphia runs in the second inning. The Phillies took a two-run lead into the ninth, but after two men were out the Dodgers rebounded, thanks largely to a couple of old pros. Pinch hitter Vic Davalillo, age 38, beat out a drag bunt on a disputed call, and 39-year-old Manny Mota doubled to deep left. Two more Dodger singles scored three runs that proved enough for the win.

The Dodgers didn't even need all of their five hits to take the final game behind Tommy John's one-run seven-hitter, for one of those hits was another Dusty Baker home run with a man aboard.

Los Angeles Dodgers (West), 3; Philadelphia Phillies (East) 1

LA (W)

PLAYER/POS	AVG	G	AB	R	H	2B	3B	HR	RB	BB	SO	SB
Dusty Baker, of	.357	4	14	4	5	1	0	2	8	2	3	0
Glenn Burke, of	.000	4	7	0	0	0	0	0	0	0	3	0
Ron Cey, 3b	.308	4	13	4	4	1	0	1	4	2	4	1
Vic Davalillo, ph	1.000	1	1	1	1	0	0	0	0	0	0	0
Mike Garman, p	.000	2	0	0	0	0	0	0	0	0	0	0
Steve Garvey, 1b	.308	4	13	2	4	0	0	0	0	2	1	1
Ed Goodson, ph	.000	1	1	0	0	0	0	0	0	0	0	0
Jerry Grote, c-1	.000	2	0	0	0	0	0	0	0	1	0	0
Burt Hooton, p	1.000	1	1	0	1	1	0	0	0	0	0	0
Charley Hough, p	.000	1	0	0	0	0	0	0	0	0	0	0
Tommy John, p	.200	2	5	0	1	0	0	0	0	0	2	0
Lee Lacy, ph	1.000	1	1	1	1	0	0	0	0	0	0	0
Davey Lopes, 2b	.235	4	17	2	4	0	0	0	3	2	0	0
Rick Monday, of	.286	3	7	1	2	1	0	0	0	0	2	1
Manny Mota, ph	1.000	1	1	1	1	1	0	0	0	0	0	0
Doug Rau, p	.000	1	0	0	0	0	0	0	0	0	0	0
Lance Rautzhan, p	.000	1	0	0	0	0	0	0	0	0	0	0
Rick Rhoden, p	.000	1	1	0	0	0	0	0	0	0	0	0
Bill Russell, ss	.278	4	18	3	5	1	0	0	2	0	0	0
Reggie Smith, of	.188	4	16	2	3	0	1	0	1	2	5	1
Elias Sosa, p	.000	2	1	0	0	0	0	0	0	0	0	0
Don Sutton, p	.000	1	3	0	0	0	0	0	0	0	0	0
Steve Yeager, c	.231	4	13	1	3	0	0	0	2	1	3	0
TOTAL	.263		133	22	35	6	1	3	20	14	22	3

PITCHER	W	L	ERA	G	GS	CG	SV	SHO	IP	H	ER	BB	SO
Mike Garman	0	0	0.00	2	0	0	1	0	1.1	0	0	0	1
Burt Hooton	0	0	16.20	1	1	0	0	0	1.2	2	3	4	1
Charley Hough	0	0	4.50	1	0	0	0	0	2.0	2	1	0	3
Tommy John	1	0	0.66	2	2	1	0	0	13.2	11	1	5	11
Doug Rau	0	0	0.00	1	0	0	0	0	1.0	0	0	0	1
Lance Rautzhan	1	0	0.00	1	0	0	0	0	0.1	0	0	0	0
Rick Rhoden	0	0	0.00	1	0	0	0	0	4.1	2	0	2	0
Elias Sosa	0	1	10.13	2	0	0	0	0	2.2	5	3	0	0
Don Sutton	1	0	1.00	1	1	1	0	0	9.0	9	1	0	4
TOTAL	3	1	2.25	12	4	2	1	0	36.0	31	9	11	21

PHI (E)

PLAYER/POS	AVG	G	AB	R	H	2B	3B	HR	RB	BB	SO	SB
Bob Boone, c	.400	4	10	1	4	0	0	0	0	0	0	0
Larry Bowa, ss	.118	4	17	2	2	0	0	0	1	1	0	0
Ollie Brown, ph	.000	2	2	0	0	0	0	0	0	0	1	0
Warren Brusstar, p	.000	2	0	0	0	0	0	0	0	0	0	0
Steve Carlton, p	.500	2	4	0	2	0	0	0	1	0	2	0
Larry Christenson, p	.000	1	0	0	0	0	0	0	0	1	1	0
Gene Garber, p	.000	3	0	0	0	0	0	0	0	0	0	0
Richie Hebner, 1b-3	.357	4	14	2	5	2	0	0	0	0	1	0
Tom Hutton, 1b-1	.000	3	3	0	0	0	0	0	0	0	0	0
Davy Johnson, 1b	.250	1	4	0	1	0	0	0	2	0	1	0
Jay Johnstone, of	.200	2	5	0	1	0	0	0	0	0	1	0
Jim Lonborg, p	.000	1	1	0	0	0	0	0	0	0	1	0
Greg Luzinski, of	.286	4	14	2	4	1	0	1	2	3	3	1
Garry Maddox, of	.429	2	7	1	3	0	0	0	2	0	1	0
Jerry Martin, of-1	.000	3	4	0	0	0	0	0	0	0	2	0
Bake Mc Bride, of	.222	4	18	2	4	0	0	1	2	1	2	0
Tim Mc Carver, c-2	.167	3	6	1	1	0	0	0	0	1	3	0
Tug Mc Graw, p	.000	2	0	0	0	0	0	0	0	0	0	0
Ron Reed, p	.000	3	0	0	0	0	0	0	0	0	0	0
Mike Schmidt, 3b	.063	4	16	2	1	0	0	0	1	2	3	0
Ted Sizemore, 2b	.231	4	13	1	3	0	0	0	0	2	0	0
TOTAL	.225		138	14	31	3	0	2	12	11	21	1

PITCHER	W	L	ERA	G	GS	CG	SV	SHO	IP	H	ER	BB	SO
Warren Brusstar	0	0	3.38	2	0	0	0	0	2.2	2	1	1	2
Steve Carlton	0	1	6.94	2	2	0	0	0	11.2	13	9	8	6
Larry Christenson	0	0	8.10	1	1	0	0	0	3.1	7	3	0	2
Gene Garber	1	1	3.38	3	0	0	0	0	5.1	4	2	0	3
Jim Lonborg	0	1	11.25	1	1	0	0	0	4.0	5	5	1	1
Tug Mc Graw	0	0	0.00	2	0	0	1	0	3.0	1	0	2	3
Ron Reed	0	0	1.80	3	0	0	0	0	5.0	3	1	2	5
TOTAL	1	3	5.40	14	4	0	1	0	35.0	35	21	14	22

GAME 1 AT LA OCT 4

PHI	200	021	002	7	9	0
LA	000	010	400	5	9	2

Pitchers: Carlton, GARBER (7), McGraw (9) vs John, Garman (5), Hough (6), SOSA (8)
Home Runs: Luzinski-PHI, Cey-LA
Attendance: 55,968

GAME 2 AT LA OCT 5

PHI	001	000	000	1	9	1
LA	001	401	10X	7	9	1

Pitchers: LONBORG, Reed (5), Brusstar (7) vs SUTTON
Home Runs: McBride-PHI, Baker-LA
Attendance: 55,973

GAME 3 AT PHI OCT 7

LA	020	100	003	6	12	2
PHI	030	000	020	5	6	2

Pitchers: Hooton, Rhoden (2), Rau (7), Sosa (8), RAUTZHAN (8), Garman (9) vs Christensen, Brusstar (4), Reed (5), GARBER (7)
Attendance: 63,719

GAME 4 AT PHI OCT 8

LA	020	020	000	4	5	0
PHI	000	100	000	1	7	0

Pitchers: JOHN vs CARLTON, Reed (6), McGraw (7), Garber (9)
Home Runs: Baker-LA
Attendance: 64,924

As in 1976, the Royals met the Yankees in the LCS, and as in 1976 the series went five games, with the Royals outscoring New York by a single run. But this time Kansas City won the first game, and as the teams traded victories through the first four games and K.C. took a lead into the ninth inning of Game Five, it began to look as though this year the Royals might take the pennant.

Royal hitters began things with a bang, scoring six of their seven runs in Game One in the first three innings for an insurmountable lead. New York came back to take the second game 6–2 behind Ron Guidry's three-hitter, but the Royals reversed the score the next day as Dennis Leonard limited the Yankees to four hits. Yankee reliever Sparky Lyle shut K.C. down over the final five innings of Game Four after the Royals had drawn within a run of New York in the fourth inning, and the series was tied.

In the finale, Kansas City drew first blood with two runs in the bottom of the first and led by one run after eight. But with the pennant in sight, the Royals gave up three Yankee runs in the top of the ninth, scoring nothing themselves as reliever Lyle held them off to give the Yankees their thirty-first flag.

New York Yankees (East), 3; Kansas City Royals (West) 2

NY (E)

PLAYER/POS	AVG	G	AB	R	H	2B	3B	HR	RB	BB	SO	SB
Paul Blair, of	.400	3	5	1	2	0	0	0	0	0	0	0
Chris Chambliss, 1b	.059	5	17	0	1	0	0	0	0	3	4	0
Bucky Dent, ss	.214	5	14	1	3	1	0	0	2	1	0	0
Ed Figueroa, p	.000	1	0	0	0	0	0	0	0	0	0	0
Ron Guidry, p	.000	2	0	0	0	0	0	0	0	0	0	0
Don Gullett, p	.000	1	0	0	0	0	0	0	0	0	0	0
Reggie Jackson, of-4,dh-1	.125	5	16	1	2	0	0	0	1	2	2	1
Cliff Johnson, dh-4	.400	5	15	2	6	2	0	1	2	1	2	0
Thurman Munson, c	.286	5	21	3	6	1	0	1	5	0	2	0
Graig Nettles, 3b	.150	5	20	1	3	0	0	0	1	0	3	0
Lou Piniella, of-4,dh-1	.333	5	21	1	7	3	0	0	2	0	1	0
Willie Randolph, 2b	.278	5	18	4	5	1	0	0	2	1	0	0
Mickey Rivers, of	.391	5	23	5	9	2	0	0	2	0	2	1
Fred Stanley, ss	.000	2	0	0	0	0	0	0	0	0	0	0
Dick Tidrow, p	.000	2	0	0	0	0	0	0	0	0	0	0
Mike Torrez, p	.000	2	0	0	0	0	0	0	0	0	0	0
Roy White, of-1,dh-1	.400	4	5	2	2	2	0	0	0	1	0	0
TOTAL	.263		175	21	46	12	0	2	17	9	16	2

PITCHER	W	L	ERA	G	GS	CG	SV	SHO	IP	H	ER	BB	SO
Ed Figueroa	0	0	10.80	1	1	0	0	0	3.1	5	4	2	3
Ron Guidry	1	0	3.97	2	2	1	0	0	11.1	9	5	3	8
Don Gullett	0	1	18.00	1	1	0	0	0	2.0	4	4	2	0
Sparky Lyle	2	0	0.96	4	0	0	0	0	9.1	7	1	0	3
Dick Tidrow	0	0	3.86	2	0	0	0	0	7.0	6	3	3	3
Mike Torrez	0	1	4.09	2	1	0	0	0	11.0	11	5	5	5
TOTAL	3	2	4.50	12	5	1	0	0	44.0	42	22	15	22

KC (W)

PLAYER/POS	AVG	G	AB	R	H	2B	3B	HR	RB	BB	SO	SB
Doug Bird, p	.000	3	0	0	0	0	0	0	0	0	0	0
George Brett, 3b	.300	5	20	2	6	0	2	0	2	1	0	0
Al Cowens, of	.263	5	19	2	5	0	0	1	5	1	3	0
Larry Gura, p	.000	2	0	0	0	0	0	0	0	0	0	0
Andy Hassler, p	.000	1	0	0	0	0	0	0	0	0	0	0
Pete La Cock, 1b	.000	1	1	0	0	0	0	0	0	1	1	0
Joe Lahoud, dh	.000	1	1	2	0	0	0	0	0	2	0	0
Dennis Leonard, p	.000	2	0	0	0	0	0	0	0	0	0	0
Mark Littell, p	.000	2	0	0	0	0	0	0	0	0	0	0
John Mayberry, 1b	.167	4	12	1	2	1	0	1	3	1	2	0
Hal Mc Rae, dh-3,of-2	.444	5	18	6	8	3	0	1	2	3	1	0
Steve Mingori, p	.000	3	0	0	0	0	0	0	0	0	0	0
Amos Otis, of	.125	5	16	1	2	1	0	0	2	2	3	2
Freddie Patek, ss	.389	5	18	4	7	3	1	0	5	1	2	0
Marty Pattin, p	.000	1	0	0	0	0	0	0	0	0	0	0
Tom Poquette, of	.167	2	6	0	1	0	0	0	0	0	0	0
Darrell Porter, c	.333	5	15	3	5	0	0	0	0	3	0	0
Cookie Rojas, dh	.250	1	4	0	1	0	0	0	0	0	1	1
Paul Splittorff, p	.000	2	0	0	0	0	0	0	0	0	0	0
John Wathan, 1b-2,c-1,dh-1	.000	4	6	0	0	0	0	0	0	0	3	0
Frank White, 2b	.278	5	18	1	5	1	0	0	2	0	4	1
Joe Zdeb, of	.000	4	9	0	0	0	0	0	0	0	2	1
TOTAL	.258		163	22	42	9	3	3	21	15	22	5

PITCHER	W	L	ERA	G	GS	CG	SV	SHO	IP	H	ER	BB	SO
Doug Bird	0	0	0.00	3	0	0	0	0	2.0	4	0	0	1
Larry Gura	0	1	18.00	2	1	0	0	0	2.0	7	4	1	2
Andy Hassler	0	1	4.76	1	1	0	0	0	5.2	5	3	0	3
Dennis Leonard	1	1	3.00	2	1	1	0	0	9.0	5	3	2	4
Mark Littell	0	0	3.00	2	0	0	0	0	3.0	5	1	3	1
Steve Mingori	0	0	0.00	3	0	0	0	0	1.1	0	0	0	1
Marty Pattin	0	0	1.50	1	0	0	0	0	6.0	6	1	0	0
Paul Splittorff	1	0	2.40	2	2	0	0	0	15.0	14	4	3	4
TOTAL	2	3	3.27	16	5	1	0	0	44.0	46	16	9	16

GAME 1 AT NY OCT 5

KC	222	000	010	7	9	0
NY	002	000	000	2	9	0

Pitchers: SPLITTORFF, Bird (9) vs GULLETT. Tidrow (3), Lyle (9)
Home Runs: McRae-KC, Mayberry-KC, Munson-NY, Cowens-KC
Attendance: 54,930

GAME 2 AT NY OCT 6

KC	001	001	000	2	3	1
NY	000	023	01X	6	10	1

Pitchers: HASSLER, Littell (6), Mingori (8) vs GUIDRY
Home Runs: Johnson-NY
Attendance: 56,230

GAME 3 AT KC OCT 7

NY	000	010	001	2	4	1
KC	011	012	10X	6	12	1

Pitchers: TORREZ. Lyle (6) vs LEONARD
Attendance: 41,285

GAME 4 AT KC OCT 8

NY	121	100	001	6	13	0
KC	002	200	000	4	8	2

Pitchers: Figueroa, Tidrow (4), LYLE (4) vs GURA, Pattin (3), Mingori (9), Bird (9)
Attendance: 41,135

GAME 5 AT KC OCT 9

NY	001	000	013	5	10	0
KC	201	000	000	3	10	1

Pitchers: Guidry, Torrez (3), LYLE (8) vs Splittorff, Bird (8), Mingori (8), LEONARD (9), Gura (9), Littell (9)
Attendance: 41,133

This was the Series in which Yankee Reggie Jackson established his reputation as "Mr. October" with a record five home runs, including three in successive at-bats in the final game, and the Yankees showed that after a decade or so of decline they were once again the world's best. Los Angeles scored first in the opening game with a pair of first-inning runs. But New York gained back half the ground in the bottom of the first and tied the game on Willie Randolph's leadoff homer in the sixth. The clubs traded runs in the eighth and ninth to take the game into extra innings. The impasse was not breached until the last of the twelfth, when Randolph doubled and Paul Blair singled him home.

Game Two, by contrast, was a runaway Dodger victory. Home runs in the first three innings by Ron Cey, Steve Yeager, and Reggie Smith made the score 5–0 before New York scored its lone run in the fourth. Burt Hooton hurled the Dodger win, a five-hitter. And for good measure, Dodger Steve Garvey homered in the ninth inning. The Yankees returned to form two days later in Los Angeles, though, scoring three runs in the top of the first on pairs of doubles and singles (and a Dodger error). Dodger Dusty Baker's three-run homer tied the game in the third, but single Yankee runs in the next two innings provided pitcher Mike Torrez with runs enough for the win.

Two of the four hits yielded by emerging Yankee ace Ron Guidry in Game Four were pitcher Rick Rhoden's double followed by Davey Lopes's home run in the third inning. But the Yankees had already scored three times in the second, and Reggie Jackson homered in the sixth as Guidry held Los Angeles scoreless after the third for a 4–2 win. A Yankee assault against Dodger pitcher Don Sutton in Game Five included back-to-back home runs by Thurman Munson and Jackson in the eighth inning. But Los Angeles rocked Yankee pitching even harder, with homers by Steve Yeager and Reggie Smith producing five of the Dodgers' ten runs as the club evaded elimination with its second win.

The Dodgers scored first in the sixth game when Steve Garvey's first-inning triple drove in two runners. Yankee Chris Chambliss matched that an inning later with a two-run homer. Smith restored the lead to Los Angeles with a solo shot in the third inning, but Jackson put the Yankees back in front with the first of his three home runs, a two-run blast in the fourth. By the time he had homered again for two in the fifth and for the third time in the eighth, the

New York Yankees (AL), 4; Los Angeles Dodgers (NL) 2

NY (A)

PLAYER/POS	AVG	G	AB	R	H	2B	3B	HR	RB	BB	SO	SB
Paul Blair, of-3	.250	4	4	0	1	0	0	0	1	0	0	0
Chris Chambliss, 1b	.292	6	24	4	7	2	0	1	4	0	2	0
Ken Clay, p	.000	2	0	0	0	0	0	0	0	0	0	0
Bucky Dent, ss	.263	6	19	0	5	0	0	0	2	2	1	0
Ron Guidry, p	.000	1	2	0	0	0	0	0	0	0	1	0
Don Gullett, p	.000	2	2	0	0	0	0	0	0	0	2	0
Catfish Hunter, p	.000	2	0	0	0	0	0	0	0	0	0	0
Reggie Jackson, of	.450	6	20	10	9	1	0	5	8	3	4	0
Cliff Johnson, c-1	.000	2	1	0	0	0	0	0	0	0	0	0
Sparky Lyle, p	.000	2	2	0	0	0	0	0	0	0	2	0
Thurman Munson, c	.320	6	25	4	8	2	0	1	3	2	8	0
Graig Nettles, 3b	.190	6	21	1	4	1	0	0	2	2	3	0
Lou Piniella, of	.273	6	22	1	6	0	0	0	3	0	3	0
Willie Randolph, 2b	.160	6	25	5	4	2	0	1	1	2	2	0
Mickey Rivers, of	.222	6	27	1	6	2	0	0	1	0	2	1
Fred Stanley, ss	.000	1	0	0	0	0	0	0	0	0	0	0
Dick Tidrow, p	.000	2	1	0	0	0	0	0	0	0	1	0
Mike Torrez, p	.000	2	6	0	0	0	0	0	0	0	4	0
Roy White, ph	.000	2	2	0	0	0	0	0	0	0	0	0
George Zeber, ph	.000	2	2	0	0	0	0	0	0	0	2	0
TOTAL	.244		205	26	50	10	0	8	25	11	37	1

PITCHER	W	L	ERA	G	GS	CG	SV	SHO	IP	H	ER	BB	SO
Ken Clay	0	0	2.45	2	0	0	0	0	3.2	2	1	1	0
Ron Guidry	1	0	2.00	1	1	1	0	0	9.0	4	2	3	7
Don Gullett	0	1	6.39	2	2	0	0	0	12.2	13	9	7	10
Catfish Hunter	0	1	10.38	2	1	0	0	0	4.1	6	5	0	1
Sparky Lyle	1	0	1.93	2	0	0	0	0	4.2	2	1	0	2
Dick Tidrow	0	0	4.91	2	0	0	0	0	3.2	5	2	0	1
Mike Torrez	2	0	2.50	2	2	2	0	0	18.0	16	5	5	15
TOTAL	4	2	4.02	13	6	3	0	0	56.0	48	25	16	36

LA (N)

PLAYER/POS	AVG	G	AB	R	H	2B	3B	HR	RB	BB	SO	SB
Dusty Baker, of	.292	6	24	4	7	0	0	1	5	0	2	0
Glenn Burke, of	.200	3	5	0	1	0	0	0	0	0	1	0
Ron Cey, 3b	.190	6	21	2	4	1	0	1	3	3	5	0
Vic Davalillo, ph	.333	3	3	0	1	0	0	0	0	1	0	0
Mike Garman, p	.000	2	0	0	0	0	0	0	0	0	0	0
Steve Garvey, 1b	.375	6	24	5	9	1	1	1	3	1	4	0
Ed Goodson, ph	.000	1	1	0	0	0	0	0	0	0	1	0
Jerry Grote, c	.000	1	1	0	0	0	0	0	0	0	0	0
Burt Hooton, p	.000	2	5	0	0	0	0	0	0	0	2	0
Charley Hough, p	.000	2	0	0	0	0	0	0	0	0	0	0
Tommy John, p	.000	1	2	0	0	0	0	0	0	0	0	0
Lee Lacy, of-2	.429	4	7	1	3	0	0	0	0	2	1	0
Rafael Landestoy, pr	.000	1	0	0	0	0	0	0	0	0	0	0
Davey Lopes, 2b	.167	6	24	3	4	0	1	1	2	4	3	2
Rick Monday, of	.167	4	12	0	2	0	0	0	0	0	3	0
Manny Mota, ph	.000	3	3	0	0	0	0	0	0	1	0	0
Johnny Oates, c	.000	1	1	0	0	0	0	0	0	0	0	0
Doug Rau, p	.000	2	0	0	0	0	0	0	0	0	0	0
Lance Rautzhan, p	.000	1	0	0	0	0	0	0	0	0	0	0
Rick Rhoden, p	.500	2	2	1	1	1	0	0	0	0	0	0
Bill Russell, ss	.154	6	26	3	4	0	1	0	2	1	3	0
Reggie Smith, of	.273	6	22	7	6	1	0	3	5	4	3	0
Elias Sosa, p	.000	2	0	0	0	0	0	0	0	0	0	0
Don Sutton, p	.000	2	6	0	0	0	0	0	0	0	1	0
Steve Yeager, c	.316	6	19	2	6	1	0	2	5	1	1	0
TOTAL	.231		208	28	48	5	3	9	28	16	36	2

PITCHER	W	L	ERA	G	GS	CG	SV	SHO	IP	H	ER	BB	SO
Mike Garman	0	0	0.00	2	0	0	0	0	4.0	2	0	1	3
Burt Hooton	1	1	3.75	2	2	1	0	0	12.0	8	5	2	9
Charley Hough	0	0	1.80	2	0	0	0	0	5.0	3	1	0	5
Tommy John	0	1	6.00	1	1	0	0	0	6.0	9	4	3	7
Doug Rau	0	1	11.57	2	1	0	0	0	2.1	4	3	0	1
Lance Rautzhan	0	0	0.00	1	0	0	0	0	0.1	0	0	2	0
Rick Rhoden	0	1	2.57	2	2	0	0	0	7.0	4	2	1	5
Elias Sosa	0	0	11.57	2	0	0	0	0	2.1	3	3	1	1
Don Sutton	1	0	3.94	2	2	1	0	0	16.0	17	7	7	3
TOTAL	2	4	4.09	16	6	2	0	0	55.0	50	25	17	34

Yankees' twenty-first world title was well in hand.

GAME 1 AT NY OCT 11

LA	200 000 001 000	3	6	0
NY	100 001 010 001	4	11	0

Pitchers: Sutton, Rautzhan (8), Sosa (8), Garman (9), RHODEN (12) vs Gullett, LYLE (9)
Home Runs: Randolph-NY
Attendance: 56,668

GAME 2 AT NY OCT 12

LA	212 000 001	6	9	0
NY	010 000 000	1	5	0

Pitchers: HOOTON vs HUNTER, Tidrow (3), Clay (6), Lyle (9)
Home Runs: Cey-LA, Yeager-LA, Smith-LA, Garvey-LA
Attendance: 56,691

GAME 3 AT LA OCT 14

NY	300 110 000	5	10	0
LA	003 000 000	3	7	1

Pitchers: TORREZ vs JOHN, Hough (7)
Home Runs: Baker-LA
Attendance: 55,992

GAME 4 AT LA OCT 15

NY	030 001 000	4	7	0
LA	002 000 000	2	4	0

Pitchers: GUIDRY vs RAU, Rhoden (2), Garman (9)
Home Runs: Lopes-LA, Jackson-NY
Attendance: 55,995

GAME 5 AT LA OCT 16

NY	000 000 220	4	9	2
LA	100 432 00X	10	13	0

Pitchers: GULLETT, Clay (5), Tidrow (6), Hunter (7) vs SUTTON
Home Runs: Yeager-LA, Smith-LA, Munson-NY, Jackson-NY
Attendance: 55,955

GAME 6 AT NY OCT 18

LA	201 000 001	4	9	0
NY	020 320 01X	8	8	1

Pitchers: HOOTON, Sosa (4), Rau (5), Hough (7) vs TORREZ
Home Runs: Chambliss-NY, Smith-LA, Jackson-NY (3)
Attendance: 56,407

Steve Garvey hit half the Dodgers' eight home runs and Tommy John hurled the first LCS shutout in four years as Los Angeles, for the second year in a row, defeated the Phillies for the pennant in four games. Philadelphia's five runs in Game One would have been enough to win any of the other games, but not this one as the Dodgers outhomered the Phillies four to one (including two by Garvey) and scored nine times. Dodger Davey Lopes hit the game's only home run the next day (with a man aboard), but it was more than enough support for John's four-hit shutout.

The series' most decisive win went to the Phillies in Game Three. Steve Carlton allowed four Dodger runs to score, but he made up for it by driving in his own four runs on a homer and sacrifice fly. His teammates added five more, rendering futile Garvey's third series home run.

But Garvey's fourth homer, in Game Four, helped carry the Dodgers into the tenth inning, when Bill Russell—capitalizing on Gary Maddox's muff of Ron Cey's fly to center—singled home Cey with the Dodgers' unearned pennant winner.

Los Angeles Dodgers (West), 3; Philadelphia Phillies (East), 1

LA (W)

PLAYER/POS	AVG	G	AB	R	H	2B	3B	HR	RB	BB	SO	SB
Dusty Baker, of	.467	4	15	1	7	2	0	0	1	3	0	0
Ron Cey, 3b	.313	4	16	4	5	1	0	1	3	2	4	0
Joe Ferguson, ph	.000	2	2	0	0	0	0	0	0	0	1	0
Terry Forster, p	.000	1	0	0	0	0	0	0	0	0	0	0
Steve Garvey, 1b	.389	4	18	6	7	1	1	4	7	0	1	0
Jerry Grote, c	.000	1	0	0	0	0	0	0	0	0	0	0
Burt Hooton, p	.000	1	2	0	0	0	0	0	0	0	1	0
Charley Hough, p	.000	1	0	0	0	0	0	0	0	0	0	0
Tommy John, p	.000	1	3	0	0	0	0	0	0	0	0	0
Lee Lacy, ph	.000	2	2	0	0	0	0	0	0	0	0	0
Davey Lopes, 2b	.389	4	18	3	7	1	1	2	5	0	1	1
Rick Monday, of	.200	3	10	2	2	0	1	0	0	1	5	0
Manny Mota, ph	1.000	2	1	0	1	1	0	0	0	0	0	0
Billy North, of	.000	4	8	0	0	0	0	0	0	0	1	0
Doug Rau, p	.000	1	0	0	0	0	0	0	0	0	0	0
Lance Rautzhan, p	.000	1	0	0	0	0	0	0	0	0	0	0
Rick Rhoden, p	.000	1	1	0	0	0	0	0	0	0	0	0
Bill Russell, ss	.412	4	17	1	7	1	0	0	2	1	1	0
Reggie Smith, of	.188	4	16	2	3	1	0	1	0	2	0	0
Don Sutton, p	.000	1	2	0	0	0	0	0	0	0	2	0
Bob Welch, p	.000	1	2	0	0	0	0	0	0	0	1	0
Steve Yeager, c	.231	4	13	2	3	0	0	1	2	2	2	1
TOTAL	.286		147	21	42	8	3	8	21	9	22	2

PITCHER	W	L	ERA	G	GS	CG	SV	SHO	IP	H	ER	BB	SO
Terry Forster	1	0	0.00	1	0	0	0	0	1.0	1	0	0	2
Burt Hooton	0	0	7.71	1	1	0	0	0	4.2	10	4	0	5
Charley Hough	0	0	4.50	1	0	0	0	0	2.0	1	1	0	1
Tommy John	1	0	0.00	1	1	1	0	1	9.0	4	0	2	4
Doug Rau	0	0	3.60	1	1	0	0	0	5.0	5	2	2	1
Lance Rautzhan	0	0	6.75	1	0	0	0	0	1.1	3	1	2	0
Rick Rhoden	0	0	2.25	1	0	0	0	0	4.0	2	1	1	3
Don Sutton	0	1	6.35	1	1	0	0	0	5.2	7	4	2	0
Bob Welch	1	0	2.08	1	0	0	0	0	4.1	2	1	0	5
TOTAL	3	1	3.41	9	4	1	0	1	37.0	35	14	9	21

PHI (E)

PLAYER/POS	AVG	G	AB	R	H	2B	3B	HR	RB	BB	SO	SB
Bob Boone, c	.182	3	11	0	2	0	0	0	0	0	1	0
Larry Bowa, ss	.333	4	18	2	6	0	0	0	0	1	2	0
Warren Brusstar, p	.000	3	0	0	0	0	0	0	0	0	0	0
Jose Cardenal, 1b	.167	2	6	0	1	0	0	0	0	1	1	0
Steve Carlton, p	.500	1	4	2	2	0	0	1	4	0	0	0
Larry Christenson, p	.000	1	1	0	0	0	0	0	0	0	1	0
Rawly Eastwick, p	.000	1	0	0	0	0	0	0	0	0	0	0
Barry Foote, ph	.000	1	1	0	0	0	0	0	0	0	1	0
Orlando Gonzalez, ph	.000	1	1	0	0	0	0	0	0	0	1	0
Richie Hebner, 1b-2	.111	3	9	0	1	0	0	0	1	0	0	0
Randy Lerch, p	.000	1	2	0	0	0	0	0	0	0	1	0
Greg Luzinski, of	.375	4	16	3	6	0	1	2	3	1	2	0
Garry Maddox, of	.263	4	19	1	5	0	0	0	2	0	3	0
Jerry Martin, of-3	.222	4	9	1	2	1	0	1	2	1	3	0
Bake Mc Bride, of-2	.222	3	9	2	2	0	0	1	1	0	2	0
Tim Mc Carver, c-1	.000	2	4	2	0	0	0	0	0	1	2	0
Tug Mc Graw, p	.000	3	0	0	0	0	0	0	0	0	0	0
Jim Morrison, ph	.000	1	1	0	0	0	0	0	0	0	1	0
Ron Reed, p	.000	2	0	0	0	0	0	0	0	0	0	0
Dick Ruthven, p	.000	1	1	0	0	0	0	0	0	0	1	0
Mike Schmidt, 3b	.200	4	15	1	3	2	0	0	1	2	2	0
Ted Sizemore, 2b	.385	4	13	3	5	0	1	0	1	1	1	0
TOTAL	.250		140	17	35	3	2	5	16	9	21	0

PITCHER	W	L	ERA	G	GS	CG	SV	SHO	IP	H	ER	BB	SO
Warren Brusstar	0	0	0.00	3	0	0	0	0	2.2	2	0	1	0
Steve Carlton	1	0	4.00	1	1	1	0	0	9.0	8	4	2	8
Larry Christenson	0	1	12.46	1	1	0	0	0	4.1	7	6	1	3
Rawly Eastwick	0	0	9.00	1	0	0	0	0	1.0	3	1	0	1
Randy Lerch	0	0	5.06	1	1	0	0	0	5.1	7	3	0	0
Tug Mc Graw	0	1	1.59	3	0	0	0	0	5.2	3	1	5	5
Ron Reed	0	0	2.25	2	0	0	0	0	4.0	6	1	0	2
Dick Ruthven	0	1	5.79	1	1	0	0	0	4.2	6	3	0	3
TOTAL	1	3	4.66	13	4	1	0	0	36.2	42	19	9	22

It took Bucky Dent's pop-fly home run against Boston in an Eastern Division tiebreaker to carry the Yankees into the LCS. But once there they took the pennant, downing the Royals for the third year in a row. Reggie Jackson's three-run homer in the eighth inning of Game One capped a sixteen-hit, seven-run Yankee attack, as pitchers Jim Beattie and Ken Clay combined to limit Kansas City to two hits and a single run. The Royals, though, made it look just as easy the next day as their own sixteen hits and ten runs evened the series.

Twice in Game Three George Brett gave the Royals a lead with a home run, and he tied the game with a third homer in the fifth. But Jackson's two-run homer in the fourth brought the Yankees back, and Thurman Munson's two-run shot in the eighth gave New York a close win. Game Four was just as close, but more of a pitcher's duel. Dennis Leonard, who went the distance, gave up only four hits, but two of them were home runs to Graig Nettles and Roy White. Yankee starter Ron Guidry allowed a run in the first, but shut out the Royals for the next seven innings. Goose Gossage preserved Guidry's good work—and the pennant—in the ninth.

New York Yankees (East), 3;
Kansas City Royals (West), 1

NY (E)

PLAYER/POS	AVG	G	AB	R	H	2B	3B	HR	RB	BB	SO	SB
Jim Beattie, p	.000	1	0	0	0	0	0	0	0	0	0	0
Paul Blair, of-3,2b-1	.000	4	6	1	0	0	0	0	0	0	1	0
Chris Chambliss, 1b	.400	4	15	1	6	0	0	0	2	0	4	0
Ken Clay, p	.000	1	0	0	0	0	0	0	0	0	0	0
Bucky Dent, ss	.200	4	15	0	3	0	0	0	4	0	0	0
Brian Doyle, 2b	.286	3	7	0	2	0	0	0	1	1	1	0
Ed Figueroa, p	.000	1	0	0	0	0	0	0	0	0	0	0
Rich Gossage, p	.000	2	0	0	0	0	0	0	0	0	0	0
Ron Guidry, p	.000	1	0	0	0	0	0	0	0	0	0	0
Catfish Hunter, p	.000	1	0	0	0	0	0	0	0	0	0	0
Reggie Jackson, dh-3,of-1	.462	4	13	5	6	1	0	2	6	3	4	0
Cliff Johnson, ph	.000	1	1	0	0	0	0	0	0	0	0	0
Sparky Lyle, p	.000	1	0	0	0	0	0	0	0	0	0	0
Thurman Munson, c	.278	4	18	2	5	1	0	1	2	0	0	0
Graig Nettles, 3b	.333	4	15	3	5	0	1	1	2	0	1	0
Lou Piniella, of	.235	4	17	2	4	0	0	0	0	0	3	0
Mickey Rivers, of	.455	4	11	0	5	0	0	0	0	2	0	0
Fred Stanley, 2b	.200	2	5	0	1	0	0	0	0	0	2	0
Gary Thomasson, of	.000	3	1	0	0	0	0	0	0	0	0	0
Dick Tidrow, p	.000	1	0	0	0	0	0	0	0	0	0	0
Roy White, of-3,dh-1	.313	4	16	5	5	1	0	1	1	1	2	0
TOTAL	.300		140	19	42	3	1	5	18	7	18	0

PITCHER	W	L	ERA	G	GS	CG	SV	SHO	IP	H	ER	BB	SO
Jim Beattie	1	0	1.69	1	1	0	0	0	5.1	2	1	5	3
Ken Clay	0	0	0.00	1	0	0	1	0	3.2	0	0	3	2
Ed Figueroa	0	1	27.00	1	1	0	0	0	1.0	5	3	0	0
Rich Gossage	1	0	4.50	2	0	0	1	0	4.0	3	2	0	3
Ron Guidry	1	0	1.13	1	1	0	0	0	8.0	7	1	1	7
Catfish Hunter	0	0	4.50	1	1	0	0	0	6.0	7	3	3	5
Sparky Lyle	0	0	13.50	1	0	0	0	0	1.1	3	2	0	0
Dick Tidrow	0	0	4.76	1	0	0	0	0	5.2	8	3	2	1
TOTAL	3	1	3.86	9	4	0	2	0	35.0	35	15	14	21

KC (W)

PLAYER/POS	AVG	G	AB	R	H	2B	3B	HR	RB	BB	SO	SB
Doug Bird, p	.000	2	0	0	0	0	0	0	0	0	0	0
Steve Braun, of-1	.000	2	5	0	0	0	0	0	0	0	1	0
George Brett, 3b	.389	4	18	7	7	1	1	3	3	0	1	0
Al Cowens, of	.133	4	15	2	2	0	0	0	1	0	2	0
Larry Gura, p	.000	1	0	0	0	0	0	0	0	0	0	0
Al Hrabosky, p	.000	3	0	0	0	0	0	0	0	0	0	0
Clint Hurdle, of-2	.375	4	8	1	3	0	1	0	1	2	3	0
Pete La Cock, 1b-3	.364	4	11	1	4	2	1	0	1	3	1	1
Dennis Leonard, p	.000	2	0	0	0	0	0	0	0	0	0	0
Hal Mc Rae, dh	.214	4	14	0	3	0	0	0	2	2	2	1
Steve Mingori, p	.000	1	0	0	0	0	0	0	0	0	0	0
Amos Otis, of	.429	4	14	2	6	2	0	0	1	3	5	4
Freddie Patek, ss	.077	4	13	2	1	0	0	1	2	1	4	0
Marty Pattin, p	.000	1	0	0	0	0	0	0	0	0	0	0
Tom Poquette, ph	.000	1	1	0	0	0	0	0	0	0	0	0
Darrell Porter, c	.357	4	14	1	5	1	0	0	3	2	0	0
Paul Splittorff, p	.000	1	0	0	0	0	0	0	0	0	0	0
John Wathan, 1b	.000	1	3	0	0	0	0	0	0	0	0	0
Frank White, 2b	.231	4	13	1	3	0	0	0	2	0	0	0
Willie Wilson, of	.250	3	4	0	1	0	0	0	0	0	2	0
TOTAL	.263		133	17	35	6	3	4	16	14	21	6

PITCHER	W	L	ERA	G	GS	CG	SV	SHO	IP	H	ER	BB	SO
Doug Bird	0	1	9.00	2	0	0	0	0	1.0	2	1	0	1
Larry Gura	1	0	2.84	1	1	0	0	0	6.1	8	2	2	2
Al Hrabosky	0	0	3.00	3	0	0	0	0	3.0	3	1	0	2
Dennis Leonard	0	2	3.75	2	2	1	0	0	12.0	13	5	2	11
Steve Mingori	0	0	7.36	1	0	0	0	0	3.2	5	3	3	0
Marty Pattin	0	0	27.00	1	0	0	0	0	0.2	2	2	0	0
Paul Splittorff	0	0	4.91	1	1	0	0	0	7.1	9	4	0	2
TOTAL	1	3	4.76	11	4	1	0	0	34.0	42	18	7	18

GAME 1 AT KC OCT 3

NY	011 020 030	7 16 0
KC	000 001 000	1 2 2

Pitchers: BEATTIE, Clay (6) vs LEONARD, Mingori (5), Hrabosky (8), Bird (9)
Home Runs: Jackson-NY
Attendance: 41,143

GAME 2 AT KC OCT 4

NY	000 000 220	4 12 1
KC	140 000 32X	10 16 1

Pitchers: FIGUEROA, Tidrow (2), Lyle (7) vs GURA, Pattin (7), Hrabosky (8)
Home Runs: Patek-KC
Attendance: 41,158

GAME 3 AT NY OCT 6

KC	101 010 020	5 10 1
NY	010 201 02X	6 10 0

Pitchers: Splittorff, BIRD (8), Hrabosky (8) vs Hunter, GOSSAGE (7)
Home Runs: Brett-KC (3), Jackson-NY, Munson-NY
Attendance: 55,535

GAME 4 AT NY OCT 7

KC	100 000 000	1 7 0
NY	010 001 00X	2 4 0

Pitchers: LEONARD vs GUIDRY, Gossage (9)
Home Runs: Nettles-NY, R.White-NY
Attendance: 56,356

The outcome was the same as in 1977: the Yankees over the Dodgers in six games. But this year New York overcame a two-game deficit by sweeping the next four, a feat never before achieved in a World Series.

Los Angeles overwhelmed New York in the opener. Home runs in the second and fourth innings by Dusty Baker and Davey Lopes (two, for five RBIs), and another run in the fifth, gave the Dodgers a 7–0 lead before Reggie Jackson's leadoff homer in the seventh gave New York its first score. The Yankees scored four more times, but so did the Dodgers for an 11–5 win. Game Two was closer. The Yankees scored first and held a lead through the top of the sixth, but Ron Cey's three-run homer in the bottom of the inning gave Los Angeles the runs they needed to win 4–3.

Yankee Ron Guidry, coming off a spectacular 25–3 regular season, pitched Game Three as the Series moved to New York. He gave up eight hits and issued seven walks. But only one baserunner scored, thanks in large part to several memorable stops and throws by third baseman Graig Nettles. Meanwhile, Roy White's home run in the first inning began Yankee scoring in what would become a 5–1 win.

It took ten innings for New York to win Game Four. Starters Tommy John and Ed Figueroa hurled shutout ball until Dodger Reggie Smith tagged Figueroa for a three-run homer in the top of the fifth. The Yankees clawed back in the sixth. Reggie Jackson singled in one run, then—in a play that stirred great controversy—got in the way (the Dodgers claimed intentionally) of a throw from second on an attempted double play, deflecting the ball to the outfield and permitting a second run to score. In the eighth, Thurman Munson doubled home the tying Yankee run, and in the last of the tenth Lou Piniella's two-out drive to center scored baserunner Roy White with the game winner.

Game Five was a Yankee blowout. No one hit home runs, but the Yankees hit sixteen singles (a Series record) and two doubles for twelve runs (five of them driven in by Munson's three hits) to give Yankee pitcher Jim Beattie (nine hits, two runs) an easy win. Back in Los Angeles for the sixth game, the Yankees won the crown on the hitting of two men at the bottom of the batting order: Denny Doyle and Bucky Dent. With three hits each, they combined for five RBIs in the 7–2 win. For good measure, Reggie Jackson concluded the Series scoring with a mighty two-run homer in the seventh.

New York Yankees (AL), 4;
Los Angeles Dodgers (NL), 2

NY (A)

PLAYER/POS	AVG	G	AB	R	H	2B	3B	HR	RB	BB	SO	SB
Jim Beattie, p	.000	1	0	0	0	0	0	0	0	0	0	0
Paul Blair, of	.375	6	8	2	3	1	0	0	0	1	4	0
Chris Chambliss, 1b	.182	3	11	1	2	0	0	0	0	1	1	0
Ken Clay, p	.000	1	0	0	0	0	0	0	0	0	0	0
Bucky Dent, ss	.417	6	24	3	10	1	0	0	7	1	2	0
Brian Doyle, 2b	.438	6	16	4	7	1	0	0	2	0	0	0
Ed Figueroa, p	.000	2	0	0	0	0	0	0	0	0	0	0
Rich Gossage, p	.000	3	0	0	0	0	0	0	0	0	0	0
Ron Guidry, p	.000	1	0	0	0	0	0	0	0	0	0	0
Mike Heath, c	.000	1	0	0	0	0	0	0	0	0	0	0
Catfish Hunter, p	.000	2	0	0	0	0	0	0	0	0	0	0
Reggie Jackson, dh	.391	6	23	2	9	1	0	2	8	3	7	0
Cliff Johnson, ph	.000	2	2	0	0	0	0	0	0	0	1	0
Jay Johnstone, of	.000	2	0	0	0	0	0	0	0	0	0	0
Paul Lindblad, p	.000	1	0	0	0	0	0	0	0	0	0	0
Thurman Munson, c	.320	6	25	5	8	3	0	0	7	3	7	1
Graig Nettles, 3b	.160	6	25	2	4	0	0	0	1	0	6	0
Lou Piniella, of	.280	6	25	3	7	0	0	0	4	0	0	1
Mickey Rivers, of-4	.333	5	18	2	6	0	0	0	1	0	2	1
Jim Spencer, 1b-3	.167	4	12	3	2	0	0	0	0	2	4	0
Fred Stanley, 2b	.200	3	5	0	1	1	0	0	0	1	0	0
Gary Thomasson, of	.250	3	4	0	1	0	0	0	0	0	1	0
Dick Tidrow, p	.000	2	0	0	0	0	0	0	0	0	0	0
Roy White, of	.333	6	24	9	8	0	0	1	4	4	5	2
TOTAL	.306		222	36	68	8	0	3	34	16	40	5

PITCHER	W	L	ERA	G	GS	CG	SV	SHO	IP	H	ER	BB	SO
Jim Beattie	1	0	2.00	1	1	1	0	0	9.0	9	2	4	8
Ken Clay	0	0	11.57	1	0	0	0	0	2.1	4	3	2	2
Ed Figueroa	0	1	8.10	2	2	0	0	0	6.2	9	6	5	2
Rich Gossage	1	0	0.00	3	0	0	0	0	6.0	1	0	1	4
Ron Guidry	1	0	1.00	1	1	1	0	0	9.0	8	1	7	4
Catfish Hunter	1	1	4.15	2	2	0	0	0	13.0	13	6	1	5
Paul Lindblad	0	0	11.57	1	0	0	0	0	2.1	4	3	0	1
Dick Tidrow	0	0	1.93	2	0	0	0	0	4.2	4	1	0	5
TOTAL	4	2	3.74	13	6	2	0	0	53.0	52	22	20	31

LA (N)

PLAYER/POS	AVG	G	AB	R	H	2B	3B	HR	RB	BB	SO	SB
Dusty Baker, of	.238	6	21	2	5	0	0	1	1	1	3	0
Ron Cey, 3b	.286	6	21	2	6	0	0	1	4	3	3	0
Vic Davalillo, dh-1	.333	2	3	0	1	0	0	0	0	0	0	0
Joe Ferguson, c	.500	2	4	1	2	2	0	0	0	0	1	0
Terry Forster, p	.000	3	0	0	0	0	0	0	0	0	0	0
Steve Garvey, 1b	.208	6	24	1	5	1	0	0	0	1	7	1
Jerry Grote, c	.000	2	0	0	0	0	0	0	0	0	0	0
Burt Hooton, p	.000	2	0	0	0	0	0	0	0	0	0	0
Charley Hough, p	.000	2	0	0	0	0	0	0	0	0	0	0
Tommy John, p	.000	2	0	0	0	0	0	0	0	0	0	0
Lee Lacy, dh	.143	4	14	0	2	0	0	0	1	1	3	0
Davey Lopes, 2b	.308	6	26	7	8	0	0	3	7	2	1	2
Rick Monday, of-4,dh-1	.154	5	13	2	2	1	0	0	0	4	3	0
Manny Mota, ph	.000	1	0	0	0	0	0	0	0	0	0	0
Billy North, of	.125	4	8	2	1	1	0	0	0	2	1	1
Johnny Oates, c	1.000	1	1	0	1	0	0	0	0	1	0	0
Doug Rau, p	.000	1	0	0	0	0	0	0	0	0	0	0
Lance Rautzhan, p	.000	2	0	0	0	0	0	0	0	0	0	0
Bill Russell, ss	.423	6	26	1	11	2	0	0	2	2	2	1
Reggie Smith, of	.200	6	25	3	5	0	0	1	5	2	6	0
Don Sutton, p	.000	2	0	0	0	0	0	0	0	0	0	0
Bob Welch, p	.000	3	0	0	0	0	0	0	0	0	0	0
Steve Yeager, c	.231	5	13	2	3	1	0	0	0	1	2	0
TOTAL	.261		199	23	52	8	0	6	22	20	31	5

PITCHER	W	L	ERA	G	GS	CG	SV	SHO	IP	H	ER	BB	SO
Terry Forster	0	0	0.00	3	0	0	0	0	4.0	5	0	1	6
Burt Hooton	1	1	6.48	2	2	0	0	0	8.1	13	6	3	6
Charley Hough	0	0	8.44	2	0	0	0	0	5.1	10	5	2	5
Tommy John	1	0	3.07	2	2	0	0	0	14.2	14	5	4	6
Doug Rau	0	0	0.00	1	0	0	0	0	2.0	1	0	3	0
Lance Rautzhan	0	0	13.50	2	0	0	0	0	2.0	4	3	0	0
Don Sutton	0	2	7.50	2	2	0	0	0	12.0	17	10	4	8
Bob Welch	0	1	6.23	3	0	0	1	0	4.1	4	3	2	6
TOTAL	2	4	5.47	17	6	0	1	0	52.2	68	32	16	40

The Pirates—with a better season's record than Cincinnati and stronger hitting and pitching—proved their superiority in the LCS as well, dominating the statistics and sweeping the series. Yet the games were closer than the stats alone would suggest. Pittsburgh won the first game by three runs—but they didn't come until Willie Stargell's homer in the eleventh inning broke a 2–2 tie.

In Game Two, Cincinnati scored first. The Pirates tied the game with a run in the fourth and took a narrow lead with another in the fifth. But the Reds came back on a game-tying pair of doubles in the ninth, and it wasn't until the tenth that Pittsburgh eked out its victory with a run on two singles and Don Robinson's shutout relief.

Only in the third game did the Pirates take a commanding lead, with six runs in the first four innings (two of them on home runs by Stargell and Bill Madlock). The Reds outhit Pittsburgh eight to seven, but only Johnny Bench's homer brought them a run, as Bert Blyleven overcame them in the series' only complete-game pitching performance.

Pittsburgh Pirates (East), 3; Cincinnati Reds (West), 0

PIT (E)

PLAYER/POS	AVG	G	AB	R	H	2B	3B	HR	RB	BB	SO	SB
Matt Alexander, pr	.000	1	0	1	0	0	0	0	0	0	0	0
Jim Bibby, p	.000	1	0	0	0	0	0	0	0	1	0	0
Bert Blyleven, p	.333	1	3	1	1	0	0	0	0	0	1	0
John Candelaria, p	.000	1	3	0	0	0	0	0	0	0	2	0
Mike Easler, ph	.000	1	1	0	0	0	0	0	0	0	0	0
Tim Foli, ss	.333	3	12	1	4	1	0	0	3	0	0	0
Phil Garner, 2b-3,ss-1	.417	3	12	4	5	0	1	1	1	1	0	0
Grant Jackson, p	.000	2	1	0	0	0	0	0	0	0	0	0
Bill Madlock, 3b	.250	3	12	1	3	0	0	1	2	2	0	2
John Milner, of	.000	3	9	0	0	0	0	0	0	2	0	0
Omar Moreno, of	.250	3	12	3	3	0	1	0	0	2	2	1
Ed Ott, c	.231	3	13	0	3	0	0	0	0	0	2	0
Dave Parker, of	.333	3	12	2	4	0	0	0	2	2	3	1
Dave Roberts, p	.000	1	0	0	0	0	0	0	0	0	0	0
Don Robinson, p	.000	2	0	0	0	0	0	0	0	0	0	0
Bill Robinson, of	.000	3	3	0	0	0	0	0	0	0	0	0
Enrique Romo, p	.000	2	0	0	0	0	0	0	0	0	0	0
Willie Stargell, 1b	.455	3	11	2	5	2	0	2	6	3	2	0
Rennie Stennett, 2b	.000	1	0	0	0	0	0	0	0	0	0	0
Kent Tekulve, p	.000	2	1	0	0	0	0	0	0	0	1	0
TOTAL	.267		105	15	28	3	2	4	14	13	13	4

PITCHER	W	L	ERA	G	GS	CG	SV	SHO	IP	H	ER	BB	SO
Jim Bibby	0	0	1.29	1	1	0	0	0	7.0	4	1	4	5
Bert Blyleven	1	0	1.00	1	1	1	0	0	9.0	8	1	0	9
John Candelaria	0	0	2.57	1	1	0	0	0	7.0	5	2	1	4
Grant Jackson	1	0	0.00	2	0	0	0	0	2.0	1	0	1	2
Dave Roberts	0	0	INF	1	0	0	0	0	0.0	0	0	1	0
Don Robinson	1	0	0.00	2	0	0	1	0	2.0	0	0	1	3
Enrique Romo	0	0	0.00	2	0	0	0	0	0.1	3	0	1	1
Kent Tekulve	0	0	3.00	2	0	0	0	0	3.0	2	1	2	2
TOTAL	3	0	1.48	12	3	1	1	0	30.1	23	5	11	26

CIN (W)

PLAYER/POS	AVG	G	AB	R	H	2B	3B	HR	RB	BB	SO	SB
Rick Auerbach, ph	.000	2	2	0	0	0	0	0	0	0	1	0
Doug Bair, p	.000	1	0	0	0	0	0	0	0	0	0	0
Johnny Bench, c	.250	3	12	1	3	0	1	1	1	2	2	0
Dave Collins, of	.357	3	14	0	5	1	0	0	1	0	2	2
Dave Concepcion, ss	.429	3	14	1	6	1	0	0	0	0	3	0
Hector Cruz, of-1	.200	2	5	1	1	0	0	0	0	0	1	0
Dan Driessen, 1b	.083	3	12	1	1	0	0	0	0	0	1	0
George Foster, of	.200	3	10	1	2	0	0	1	2	4	3	0
Cesar Geronimo, of	.143	2	7	0	1	0	0	0	0	0	5	0
Tom Hume, p	.000	3	1	0	0	0	0	0	0	0	1	0
Ray Knight, 3b	.286	3	14	0	4	1	0	0	0	0	2	1
Mike La Coss, p	.000	1	0	0	0	0	0	0	0	0	0	0
Charlie Leibrandt, p	.000	1	0	0	0	0	0	0	0	0	0	0
Joe Morgan, 2b	.000	3	11	0	0	0	0	0	0	3	1	1
Fred Norman, p	.000	1	1	0	0	0	0	0	0	0	0	0
Frank Pastore, p	.000	1	0	0	0	0	0	0	0	1	1	0
Tom Seaver, p	.000	1	2	0	0	0	0	0	0	0	1	0
Mario Soto, p	.000	1	0	0	0	0	0	0	0	0	0	0
Harry Spilman, ph	.000	2	2	0	0	0	0	0	0	0	0	0
Dave Tomlin, p	.000	3	0	0	0	0	0	0	0	0	0	0
TOTAL	.215		107	5	23	4	1	2	5	11	26	4

PITCHER	W	L	ERA	G	GS	CG	SV	SHO	IP	H	ER	BB	SO
Doug Bair	0	1	9.00	1	0	0	0	0	1.0	2	1	1	0
Tom Hume	0	1	6.75	3	0	0	0	0	4.0	6	3	0	2
Mike La Coss	0	1	10.80	1	1	0	0	0	1.2	1	2	4	0
Charlie Leibrandt	0	0	0.00	1	0	0	0	0	0.1	0	0	0	0
Fred Norman	0	0	18.00	1	0	0	0	0	2.0	4	4	1	1
Frank Pastore	0	0	2.57	1	1	0	0	0	7.0	7	2	3	1
Tom Seaver	0	0	2.25	1	1	0	0	0	8.0	5	2	2	5
Mario Soto	0	0	0.00	1	0	0	0	0	2.0	0	0	0	1
Dave Tomlin	0	0	0.00	3	0	0	0	0	3.0	3	0	2	3
TOTAL	0	3	4.34	13	3	0	0	0	29.0	28	14	13	13

GAME 1 AT CIN OCT 2

```
PIT  002 000 000 03   5 10 0
CIN  000 200 000 00   2  7 0
```

Pitchers: Candelaria, Romo (8), Tekulve (8), JACKSON (10), D.Robinson (11) vs Seaver, HUME (9), Tomlin (11)
Home Runs: Garner-PIT, Foster-CIN, Stargell-PIT
Attendance: 55,006

GAME 2 AT CIN OCT 3

```
PIT  000 110 000 1   3 11 0
CIN  010 000 001 0   2  8 0
```

Pitchers: Bibby, Jackson (8), Romo (8), Tekulve (8), Roberts (9), D.ROBINSON (9) vs Pastore, Tomlin (8), Hume (8), BAIR (10)
Attendance: 55,000

GAME 3 AT PIT OCT 5

```
CIN  000 001 000   1 8 1
PIT  112 200 01X   7 7 0
```

Pitchers: LaCOSS, Norman (2), Leibrandt (4), Soto (5), Tomlin (7), Hume (8) vs BLYLEVEN
Home Runs: Stargell-PIT, Madlock-PIT, Bench-CIN
Attendance: 42,240

Baltimore, returning to post-season play after a four-year absence, struggled with first-timer California through three games before blowing them away in the fourth. Game One went into the last of the tenth, tied 3–3, when Oriole pinch hitter John Lowenstein, up with two men on, ended it with a two-out, two-strike shot that just cleared the left field wall.

Game Two looked like a blowout for Baltimore. Eddie Murray drove in four runs, and the rest of the team added five more to give the O's a 9–1 lead by the end of three. But California chipped away at the lead in the latter half of the game and drew within one in the ninth, before Brian Downing hit into a forceout with the bases full to end their scoring.

The Angels' late rally in Game Three was more successful. Down by a run in the bottom of the ninth, they scored twice, on a walk, a dropped outfield fly, and Larry Harlow's game-winning double. The final game, though, was all Baltimore's, as Scott McGregor—pitching the series' only complete game—blanked the Angels on six hits. The Orioles scored two in the third and another in the fourth, before Pat Kelly put Angel pennant hopes out of reach with a three-run homer in the O's five-run seventh.

Baltimore Orioles (East), 3; California Angels (West), 1

BAL (E)

PLAYER/POS	AVG	G	AB	R	H	2B	3B	HR	RB	BB	SO	SB
Mark Belanger, ss	.200	3	5	0	1	0	0	0	1	1	2	0
Al Bumbry, of	.250	4	16	5	4	0	1	0	0	4	3	2
Terry Crowley, ph	.500	2	2	0	1	0	0	0	1	0	0	0
Rich Dauer, 2b	.182	4	11	0	2	0	0	0	0	0	1	0
Doug De Cinces, 3b	.308	4	13	4	4	1	0	0	3	1	1	0
Rick Dempsey, c	.400	3	10	3	4	2	0	0	2	1	0	1
Mike Flanagan, p	.000	1	0	0	0	0	0	0	0	0	0	0
Kiko Garcia, ss	.273	4	11	1	3	0	0	0	2	2	4	0
Pat Kelly, dh-2,of-1	.364	3	11	3	4	0	0	1	4	1	3	2
John Lowenstein, of-3	.167	4	6	2	1	0	0	1	3	2	2	0
Dennis Martinez, p	.000	1	0	0	0	0	0	0	0	0	0	0
Lee May, dh	.143	2	7	0	1	0	0	0	1	1	3	0
Scott Mc Gregor, p	.000	1	0	0	0	0	0	0	0	0	0	0
Eddie Murray, 1b	.417	4	12	3	5	0	0	1	5	5	2	0
Jim Palmer, p	.000	1	0	0	0	0	0	0	0	0	0	0
Gary Roenicke, of	.200	2	5	1	1	0	0	0	1	0	0	0
Ken Singleton, of	.375	4	16	4	6	2	0	0	2	1	2	0
Dave Skaggs, c	.000	1	4	0	0	0	0	0	0	0	0	0
Billy Smith, 2b	.000	1	4	0	0	0	0	0	0	0	1	0
Don Stanhouse, p	.000	3	0	0	0	0	0	0	0	0	0	0
TOTAL	.278		133	26	37	5	1	3	25	18	24	5

PITCHER	W	L	ERA	G	GS	CG	SV	SHO	IP	H	ER	BB	SO
Mike Flanagan	1	0	5.14	1	1	0	0	0	7.0	6	4	1	2
Dennis Martinez	0	0	3.24	1	1	0	0	0	8.1	8	3	0	4
Scott Mc Gregor	1	0	0.00	1	1	1	0	1	9.0	6	0	1	4
Jim Palmer	0	0	3.00	1	1	0	0	0	9.0	7	3	2	3
Don Stanhouse	1	1	6.00	3	0	0	0	0	3.0	5	2	3	0
TOTAL	3	1	2.97	7	4	1	0	1	36.1	32	12	7	13

CAL (W)

PLAYER/POS	AVG	G	AB	R	H	2B	3B	HR	RB	BB	SO	SB
Don Aase, p	.000	2	0	0	0	0	0	0	0	0	0	0
Jim Anderson, ss	.091	4	11	0	1	0	0	0	0	0	1	0
Mike Barlow, p	.000	1	0	0	0	0	0	0	0	0	0	0
Don Baylor, dh-3,of-1	.188	4	16	2	3	0	0	1	2	1	2	0
Bert Campaneris, ss	.000	1	0	0	0	0	0	0	0	0	0	0
Rod Carew, 1b	.412	4	17	4	7	3	0	0	1	0	0	1
Bobby Clark, of	.000	1	3	0	0	0	0	0	0	0	2	0
Mark Clear, p	.000	1	0	0	0	0	0	0	0	0	0	0
Willie Davis, ph	.500	2	2	1	1	1	0	0	0	0	0	0
Brian Downing, c	.200	4	15	1	3	0	0	0	1	1	1	0
Dan Ford, of	.294	4	17	2	5	1	0	2	4	0	0	0
Dave Frost, p	.000	2	0	0	0	0	0	0	0	0	0	0
Bobby Grich, 2b	.154	4	13	0	2	1	0	0	2	1	1	0
Larry Harlow, of-2	.125	3	8	0	1	1	0	0	1	1	2	0
Chris Knapp, p	.000	1	0	0	0	0	0	0	0	0	0	0
Carney Lansford, 3b	.294	4	17	2	5	0	0	0	3	1	2	1
Dave La Roche, p	.000	1	0	0	0	0	0	0	0	0	0	0
Rick Miller, of	.250	4	16	2	4	0	0	0	0	0	1	0
John Montague, p	.000	2	0	0	0	0	0	0	0	0	0	0
Merv Rettenmund, dh	.000	2	2	0	0	0	0	0	0	2	1	0
Nolan Ryan, p	.000	1	0	0	0	0	0	0	0	0	0	0
Frank Tanana, p	.000	1	0	0	0	0	0	0	0	0	0	0
Dickie Thon, ss	.000	1	0	1	0	0	0	0	0	0	0	0
TOTAL	.234		137	15	32	7	0	3	14	7	13	2

PITCHER	W	L	ERA	G	GS	CG	SV	SHO	IP	H	ER	BB	SO
Don Aase	1	0	1.80	2	0	0	0	0	5.0	4	1	2	6
Mike Barlow	0	0	0.00	1	0	0	0	0	1.0	0	0	0	0
Mark Clear	0	0	4.76	1	0	0	0	0	5.2	4	3	2	3
Dave Frost	0	1	18.69	2	1	0	0	0	4.1	8	9	5	1
Chris Knapp	0	1	7.71	1	1	0	0	0	2.1	5	2	1	0
Dave La Roche	0	0	6.75	1	0	0	0	0	1.1	2	1	1	1
John Montague	0	1	9.00	2	0	0	0	0	4.0	4	4	2	2
Nolan Ryan	0	0	1.29	1	1	0	0	0	7.0	4	1	3	8
Frank Tanana	0	0	3.60	1	1	0	0	0	5.0	6	2	2	3
TOTAL	1	3	5.80	12	4	0	0	0	35.2	37	23	18	24

GAME 1 AT BAL OCT 3

CAL	101	001	000	0	3	7	1
BAL	002	100	000	3	6	6	0

Pitchers: Ryan, MONTAGUE (8) vs Palmer, STANHOUSE (10)
Home Runs: Ford-CAL, Lowenstein-BAL
Attendance: 52,787

GAME 2 AT BAL OCT 4

CAL	100	001	132	8	10	1
BAL	441	000	00X	9	11	1

Pitchers: FROST, Clear (2), Aase (8) vs FLANAGAN, Stanhouse (8)
Home Runs: Ford-CAL, Murray-BAL
Attendance: 52,108

GAME 3 AT CAL OCT 5

BAL	000	101	100	3	8	3
CAL	100	100	002	4	9	0

Pitchers: D.Martinez, STANHOUSE (9) vs Tanana, AASE (6)
Home Runs: Baylor-CAL
Attendance: 43,199

GAME 4 AT CAL OCT 6

BAL	002	100	500	8	12	1
CAL	000	000	000	0	6	0

Pitchers: McGREGOR vs KNAPP, LaRoche (3), Frost (4), Montague (7), Barlow (9)
Home Runs: Kelly-BAL
Attendance: 43,199

Veteran Willie Stargell was "Pops," and in the Series he showed his Pirate "family" the way. Seven of his twelve hits went for extra bases, and he drove in a Series-high seven runs. What Stargell began, submarine reliever Kent Tekulve finished, appearing in five of the seven games and recording a record-tying three saves.

Stargell drove in a pair of runs in the opener—one of them with an eighth-inning homer—but Pittsburgh's four runs fell short of the five Baltimore had scored in the first inning. The only extra-base hits in Game Two came from the bat of Eddie Murray, who homered and doubled to drive in both Baltimore runs. But three singles and a sacrifice fly had already given Pittsburgh two runs in the second inning, and two more Pirate singles and a walk in the top of the ninth made the score 3–2. Tekulve came on in the last of the ninth to preserve the lead, fanning two as he retired the side in order.

Baltimore bounced back, though, to take the next two games in convincing fashion. The score favored the Orioles 8–4 when Tekulve came on to set the birds down in order over the final two innings. But Baltimore starter Scott McGregor had by then settled into his groove, retiring the final eleven Pirates with relative ease to preserve his lead and the Oriole win. It took four Orioles pitchers to hold the Pirates in Game Four. Stargell led the Bucs' seventeen-hit attack with a homer, double, and single, and the Pirates led 6–3 entering the eighth inning. But Baltimore loaded the bases in the top of the eighth, prompting Pirate manager Chuck Tanner to bring Tekulve in again. This one time the strategy failed, as Tekulve saw six runs score before he retired his first batter.

Down three games to one, the Pirates rebounded in Game Five, scoring seven times in the final three innings for a 7–1 victory. Baltimore starter Jim Palmer matched John Candelaria's shutout pitching through six innings of Game Six before the Pirates tagged him for pairs of runs in the seventh and eighth. Tekulve, meanwhile, continued Candelaria's shutout through the final three innings, retiring the last seven men in order, four by strikeout. Baltimore scored first in the finale on Rich Dauer's leadoff home run in the third inning, but Stargell put the Pirates ahead with a two-run homer in the sixth. Tekulve came in with two Orioles on base in the eighth to stifle the threat, and (after the Pirates had scored a pair of insurance runs in the top of the ninth) set Baltimore

down in order to complete the Pirate comeback.

Pittsburgh Pirates (NL), 4; Baltimore Orioles (AL), 3

PIT (N)

PLAYER/POS	AVG	G	AB	R	H	2B	3B	HR	RB	BB	SO	SB
Matt Alexander, of	.000	1	0	0	0	0	0	0	0	0	0	0
Jim Bibby, p	.000	2	4	0	0	0	0	0	0	0	1	0
Bert Blyleven, p	.000	2	3	0	0	0	0	0	0	0	0	0
John Candelaria, p	.333	2	3	0	1	0	0	0	0	0	2	0
Mike Easler, ph	.000	2	1	0	0	0	0	0	0	1	0	0
Tim Foli, ss	.333	7	30	6	10	1	1	0	3	2	0	0
Phil Garner, 2b	.500	7	24	4	12	4	0	0	5	3	1	0
Grant Jackson, p	.000	4	1	0	0	0	0	0	0	0	0	0
Bruce Kison, p	.000	1	0	0	0	0	0	0	0	0	0	0
Lee Lacy, ph	.250	4	4	0	1	0	0	0	0	0	1	0
Bill Madlock, 3b	.375	7	24	2	9	1	0	0	3	5	1	0
John Milner, of	.333	3	9	2	3	1	0	0	1	2	0	0
Omar Moreno, of	.333	7	33	4	11	2	0	0	3	1	7	0
Steve Nicosia, c	.063	4	16	1	1	0	0	0	0	0	2	0
Ed Ott, c	.333	3	12	2	4	1	0	0	3	0	2	0
Dave Parker, of	.345	7	29	2	10	3	0	0	4	2	7	0
Don Robinson, p	.000	4	0	0	0	0	0	0	0	0	0	0
Bill Robinson, of-6	.263	7	19	2	5	1	0	0	2	0	4	0
Enrique Romo, p	.000	2	1	0	0	0	0	0	0	0	0	0
Jim Rooker, p	.000	2	2	0	0	0	0	0	0	0	1	0
Manny Sanguillen, ph	.333	3	3	0	1	0	0	0	0	1	0	0
Willie Stargell, 1b	.400	7	30	7	12	4	0	3	7	0	6	0
Rennie Stennett, ph	1.000	1	1	0	1	0	0	0	0	0	0	0
Kent Tekulve, p	.000	5	2	0	0	0	0	0	0	0	0	0
TOTAL	.323		251	32	81	18	1	3	32	16	35	0

PITCHER	W	L	ERA	G	GS	CG	SV	SHO	IP	H	ER	BB	SO
Jim Bibby	0	0	2.61	2	2	0	0	0	10.1	10	3	2	10
Bert Blyleven	1	0	1.80	2	1	0	0	0	10.0	8	2	3	4
John Candelaria	1	1	5.00	2	2	0	0	0	9.0	14	5	2	4
Grant Jackson	1	0	0.00	4	0	0	0	0	4.2	1	0	2	2
Bruce Kison	0	1	108.00	1	1	0	0	0	0.1	3	4	2	0
Don Robinson	1	0	5.40	4	0	0	0	0	5.0	4	3	6	3
Enrique Romo	0	0	3.86	2	0	0	0	0	4.2	5	2	3	4
Jim Rooker	0	0	1.04	2	1	0	0	0	8.2	5	1	3	4
Kent Tekulve	0	1	2.89	5	0	0	3	0	9.1	4	3	3	10
TOTAL	4	3	3.34	24	7	0	3	0	62.0	54	23	26	41

BAL (A)

PLAYER/POS	AVG	G	AB	R	H	2B	3B	HR	RB	BB	SO	SB
Benny Ayala, of-3	.333	4	6	1	2	0	0	1	2	1	0	0
Mark Belanger, ss-4	.000	5	6	1	0	0	0	0	0	1	1	0
Al Bumbry, of	.143	7	21	3	3	0	0	0	1	2	1	0
Terry Crowley, ph	.250	5	4	0	1	1	0	0	2	1	0	0
Rich Dauer, 2b-5	.294	6	17	2	5	1	0	1	1	0	1	0
Doug De Cinces, 3b	.200	7	25	2	5	0	0	1	3	5	5	1
Rick Dempsey, c-6	.286	7	21	3	6	2	0	0	1	3	0	0
Mike Flanagan, p	.000	3	5	0	0	0	0	0	0	1	2	0
Kiko Garcia, ss	.400	6	20	4	8	2	1	0	6	1	3	0
Pat Kelly, ph	.250	5	4	0	1	0	0	0	0	1	1	0
John Lowenstein, of-3	.231	6	13	2	3	1	0	0	3	1	3	0
Tippy Martinez, p	.000	3	0	0	0	0	0	0	0	0	0	0
Dennis Martinez, p	.000	2	0	0	0	0	0	0	0	0	0	0
Lee May, ph	.000	2	1	0	0	0	0	0	0	1	1	0
Scott Mc Gregor, p	.000	2	4	1	0	0	0	0	0	2	1	0
Eddie Murray, 1b	.154	7	26	3	4	1	0	1	2	4	4	1
Jim Palmer, p	.000	2	4	0	0	0	0	0	0	0	3	0
Gary Roenicke, of-5	.125	6	16	1	2	1	0	0	0	0	6	0
Ken Singleton, of	.357	7	28	1	10	1	0	0	2	2	5	0
Dave Skaggs, c	.333	1	3	1	1	0	0	0	0	0	0	0
Billy Smith, 2b-2	.286	4	7	1	2	0	0	0	0	2	0	0
Don Stanhouse, p	.000	3	0	0	0	0	0	0	0	0	0	0
Sammy Stewart, p	.000	1	1	0	0	0	0	0	0	0	1	0
Tim Stoddard, p	1.000	4	1	0	1	0	0	0	1	0	0	0
Steve Stone, p	.000	1	0	0	0	0	0	0	0	0	0	0
TOTAL	.232		233	26	54	10	1	4	23	26	41	2

PITCHER	W	L	ERA	G	GS	CG	SV	SHO	IP	H	ER	BB	SO
Mike Flanagan	1	1	3.00	3	2	1	0	0	15.0	18	5	2	13
Tippy Martinez	0	0	6.75	3	0	0	0	0	1.1	3	1	0	1
Dennis Martinez	0	0	18.00	2	1	0	0	0	2.0	6	4	0	0
Scott Mc Gregor	1	1	3.18	2	2	1	0	0	17.0	16	6	2	8
Jim Palmer	0	1	3.60	2	2	0	0	0	15.0	18	6	5	8
Don Stanhouse	0	1	13.50	3	0	0	0	0	2.0	6	3	3	0
Sammy Stewart	0	0	0.00	1	0	0	0	0	2.2	4	0	1	0
Tim Stoddard	1	0	5.40	4	0	0	0	0	5.0	6	3	1	3
Steve Stone	0	0	9.00	1	0	0	0	0	2.0	4	2	2	2
TOTAL	3	4	4.35	21	7	2	0	0	62.0	81	30	16	35

In the tightest LCS yet, the Phillies took the opener 3–1 on the series' only home run—Greg Luzinski's two-run blast in the sixth inning. It was the only game not to go into extra innings.

The Astros evened the series in Game Two—demolishing a 3–3 tie with four runs in the tenth—and took the series lead in a Game Three pitchers' duel that saw Astro Joe Niekro hurl ten scoreless innings. Reliever Dave Smith continued the shutout and took the win as Joe Morgan's triple and Denny Walling's sacrifice fly off ace Phillie reliever Tug McGraw scored the game's only run in the bottom of the eleventh.

The Phillies rebounded, though, with their own set of extra-inning victories. In Game Four, a single and two doubles pushed across two go-ahead runs in the top of the tenth, and McGraw preserved the edge for his second series save. And in the finale—which saw the lead change hands three times—after Del Unser scored on Gary Maddox's tenth-inning double, Dick Ruthven held off Houston to bring the Phillies their first pennant in thirty years.

Philadelphia Phillies (East), 3; Houston Astros (West), 2

PHI (E)

PLAYER/POS	AVG	G	AB	R	H	2B	3B	HR	RB	BB	SO	SB
Ramon Aviles, pr	.000	1	0	1	0	0	0	0	0	0	0	0
Bob Boone, c	.222	5	18	1	4	0	0	0	2	1	2	0
Larry Bowa, ss	.316	5	19	2	6	0	0	0	0	3	3	1
Warren Brusstar, p	.000	2	1	0	0	0	0	0	0	0	1	0
Marty Bystrom, p	.000	1	2	0	0	0	0	0	0	0	1	0
Steve Carlton, p	.000	2	4	0	0	0	0	0	0	0	1	0
Larry Christenson, p	.000	1	2	0	0	0	0	0	0	0	1	0
Greg Gross, of-1	.750	4	4	2	3	0	0	0	1	0	0	0
Greg Luzinski, of	.294	5	17	3	5	2	0	1	4	0	6	0
Garry Maddox, of	.300	5	20	2	6	2	0	0	3	2	2	2
Bake Mc Bride, of	.238	5	21	0	5	0	0	0	0	1	5	2
Tug Mc Graw, p	.000	5	1	0	0	0	0	0	0	0	0	0
Keith Moreland, c-1	.000	2	1	0	0	0	0	0	1	0	0	0
Dickie Noles, p	.000	2	0	0	0	0	0	0	0	0	0	0
Ron Reed, p	.000	3	0	0	0	0	0	0	0	0	0	0
Pete Rose, 1b	.400	5	20	3	8	0	0	0	2	5	3	0
Dick Ruthven, p	.000	2	2	0	0	0	0	0	0	0	2	0
Kevin Saucier, p	.000	2	0	0	0	0	0	0	0	0	0	0
Mike Schmidt, 3b	.208	5	24	1	5	1	0	0	1	1	6	1
Lonnie Smith, of-2	.600	3	5	2	3	0	0	0	0	0	0	1
Manny Trillo, 2b	.381	5	21	1	8	2	1	0	4	0	2	0
Del Unser, of-2	.400	5	5	2	2	1	0	0	1	0	2	0
George Vukovich, of-1	.000	4	3	0	0	0	0	0	0	0	0	0
TOTAL	.289		190	20	55	8	1	1	19	13	37	7

PITCHER	W	L	ERA	G	GS	CG	SV	SHO	IP	H	ER	BB	SO
Warren Brusstar	1	0	3.38	2	0	0	0	0	2.2	1	1	1	0
Marty Bystrom	0	0	1.69	1	1	0	0	0	5.1	7	1	2	1
Steve Carlton	1	0	2.19	2	2	0	0	0	12.1	11	3	8	6
Larry Christenson	0	0	4.05	1	1	0	0	0	6.2	5	3	5	2
Tug Mc Graw	0	1	4.50	5	0	0	2	0	8.0	8	4	4	5
Dickie Noles	0	0	0.00	2	0	0	0	0	2.2	1	0	3	0
Ron Reed	0	1	18.00	3	0	0	0	0	2.0	3	4	1	1
Dick Ruthven	1	0	2.00	2	1	0	0	0	9.0	3	2	5	4
Kevin Saucier	0	0	0.00	2	0	0	0	0	0.2	1	0	2	0
TOTAL	3	2	3.28	20		5	0	2	49.1	40	18	31	19

HOU (W)

PLAYER/POS	AVG	G	AB	R	H	2B	3B	HR	RB	BB	SO	SB
Joaquin Andujar, p	.000	1	0	0	0	0	0	0	0	0	0	0
Alan Ashby, c	.125	2	8	0	1	0	0	0	1	0	0	0
Dave Bergman, 1b	.333	4	3	0	1	0	1	0	2	0	0	0
Bruce Bochy, c	.000	1	1	0	0	0	0	0	0	0	0	0
Enos Cabell, 3b	.238	5	21	1	5	1	0	0	0	1	3	0
Cesar Cedeno, of	.182	3	11	1	2	0	0	0	1	1	0	0
Jose Cruz, of	.400	5	15	3	6	1	1	0	4	8	1	0
Ken Forsch, p	1.000	2	2	0	2	0	0	0	0	0	0	0
Danny Heep, ph	.000	1	1	0	0	0	0	0	0	0	0	0
Art Howe, 1b-4	.200	5	15	0	3	1	1	0	2	2	2	0
Frank La Corte, p	.000	2	1	0	0	0	0	0	0	0	0	0
Rafael Landestoy, 2b-3,ss-1	.222	5	9	3	2	0	0	0	2	1	0	1
Jeffrey Leonard, of-1	.000	3	3	0	0	0	0	0	0	0	2	0
Joe Morgan, 2b	.154	4	13	1	2	1	1	0	0	6	1	0
Joe Niekro, p	.000	1	3	0	0	0	0	0	0	0	1	0
Terry Puhl, of-4	.526	5	19	4	10	2	0	0	3	3	2	2
Luis Pujols, c	.100	4	10	1	1	0	1	0	0	3	0	0
Craig Reynolds, ss	.154	4	13	2	2	1	0	0	0	3	1	0
Vern Ruhle, p	.000	1	3	0	0	0	0	0	0	0	1	0
Nolan Ryan, p	.000	2	4	1	0	0	0	0	0	1	2	0
Joe Sambito, p	.000	3	0	0	0	0	0	0	0	0	0	0
Dave Smith, p	.000	3	0	0	0	0	0	0	0	0	0	0
Denny Walling, of-2,1b-1	.111	3	9	2	1	0	0	0	2	1	0	0
Gary Woods, of-3	.250	4	8	0	2	0	0	0	1	1	3	1
TOTAL	.233		172	19	40	7	5	0	18	31	19	4

PITCHER	W	L	ERA	G	GS	CG	SV	SHO	IP	H	ER	BB	SO
Joaquin Andujar	0	0	0.00	1	0	0	1	0	1.0	0	0	0	0
Ken Forsch	0	1	4.15	2	1	1	0	0	8.2	10	4	1	6
Frank La Corte	1	1	3.00	2	0	0	0	0	3.0	7	1	2	2
Joe Niekro	0	0	0.00	1	1	0	0	0	10.0	6	0	1	2
Vern Ruhle	0	0	3.86	1	1	0	0	0	7.0	8	3	1	3
Nolan Ryan	0	0	5.40	2	2	0	0	0	13.1	16	8	3	14
Joe Sambito	0	1	4.91	3	0	0	0	0	3.2	4	2	2	6
Dave Smith	1	0	3.86	3	0	0	0	0	2.1	4	1	2	4
TOTAL	2	3	3.49	15		5	1	1	49.0	55	19	13	37

GAME 1 AT PHI OCT 7

HOU	001	000	000	1	7	0
PHI	000	002	10X	3	8	1

Pitchers: FORSCH vs CARLTON, McGraw (8)
Home Runs: Luzinski-PHI
Attendance: 65,277

GAME 2 AT PHI OCT 8

HOU	001	000	110	4	7	8	1
PHI	000	200	010	1	4	14	2

Pitchers: Ryan, Sambito (7), D.Smith (7), LaCORTE (9), Andujar (10) vs Ruthven, McGraw (8), REED (9), Saucier (10)
Attendance: 65,476

GAME 3 AT HOU OCT 10

PHI	000	000	000	00	0	7	1
HOU	000	000	000	01	1	6	1

Pitchers: Christensen, Noles (7), McGRAW (8) vs Niekro, D.SMITH (11)
Attendance: 44,443

GAME 4 AT HOU OCT 11

PHI	000	000	030	2	5	13	0
HOU	000	110	001	0	3	5	1

Pitchers: Carlton, Noles (6), Saucier (7), Reed (7), BRUSSTAR (8), McGraw (10) vs Ruhle, D.Smith (8), SAMBITO (8)
Attendance: 44,952

GAME 5 AT HOU OCT 12

PHI	020	000	050	1	8	13	2
HOU	100	001	320	0	7	14	0

Pitchers: Bystrom, Brusstar (6), Christensen (7), Reed (7), McGraw (8), RUTHVEN (9) vs Ryan, Sambito (8), Forsch (8), LaCORTE (9)
Attendance: 44,802

Kansas City and New York met for the fourth time in the LCS, and this time the Royals swept to their first pennant. In the first game the Yankees scored first, with second-inning home runs by Rick Cerone and Lou Piniella, but the Royals' Frank White doubled in a pair later in the inning to tie it, and Willie Aikens's hit in the third gave K.C. the lead. They held it to the end as Larry Gura shut out New York the rest of the way.

The Royals scored three runs in the third inning of Game Two, on Willie Wilson's two-run triple and an RBI double by U. L. Washington. Yankee starter Rudy May stopped K.C. after that, but the Royals already had enough for the win as Dennis Leonard in eight innings held New York to two runs, and Dan Quisenberry kept the lid on in the ninth.

Game Three was decided by home runs. White scored first for the Royals with a solo shot in the fifth. New York took the lead briefly with a two-run sixth, but lost it—and the pennant—in the top of the seventh when Goose Gossage, relieving starter Tommy John with two out and a man on, gave up an infield single to Washington and a home run to George Brett.

Kansas City Royals (West), 3;
New York Yankees (East), 0

KC (W)

PLAYER/POS	AVG	G	AB	R	H	2B	3B	HR	RB	BB	SO	SB
Willie Aikens, 1b	.364	3	11	0	4	0	0	0	2	0	1	0
George Brett, 3b	.273	3	11	3	3	1	0	2	4	1	0	0
Larry Gura, p	.000	1	0	0	0	0	0	0	0	0	0	0
Clint Hurdle, of	.000	3	2	0	0	0	0	0	0	0	1	0
Pete La Cock, 1b	.000	1	0	0	0	0	0	0	0	0	0	0
Dennis Leonard, p	.000	1	0	0	0	0	0	0	0	0	0	0
Hal Mc Rae, dh	.200	3	10	0	2	0	0	0	0	1	3	0
Amos Otis, of	.333	3	12	2	4	1	0	0	0	0	3	2
Darrell Porter, c	.100	3	10	2	1	0	0	0	0	1	0	0
Dan Quisenberry, p	.000	2	0	0	0	0	0	0	0	0	0	0
Paul Splittorff, p	.000	1	0	0	0	0	0	0	0	0	0	0
U. L. Washington, ss	.364	3	11	1	4	1	0	0	1	2	3	0
John Wathan, of	.000	3	6	1	0	0	0	0	0	3	1	0
Frank White, 2b	.545	3	11	3	6	1	0	1	3	0	1	1
Willie Wilson, of	.308	3	13	2	4	2	1	0	4	1	2	0
TOTAL	.289		97	14	28	6	1	3	14	9	15	3

PITCHER	W	L	ERA	G	GS	CG	SV	SHO	IP	H	ER	BB	SO
Larry Gura	1	0	2.00	1	1	1	0	0	9.0	10	2	1	4
Dennis Leonard	1	0	2.25	1	1	0	0	0	8.0	7	2	1	8
Dan Quisenberry	1	0	0.00	2	0	0	1	0	4.2	4	0	2	1
Paul Splittorff	0	0	1.69	1	1	0	0	0	5.1	5	1	2	3
TOTAL	3	0	1.67	5	3	1	1	0	27.0	26	5	6	16

NY (E)

PLAYER/POS	AVG	G	AB	R	H	2B	3B	HR	RB	BB	SO	SB
Bobby Brown, of	.000	3	10	1	0	0	0	0	0	1	2	0
Rick Cerone, c	.333	3	12	1	4	0	0	1	2	0	1	0
Ron Davis, p	.000	1	0	0	0	0	0	0	0	0	0	0
Bucky Dent, ss	.182	3	11	0	2	0	0	0	0	0	1	0
Oscar Gamble, of-1,dh-1	.200	2	5	1	1	0	0	0	0	1	1	0
Rich Gossage, p	.000	1	0	0	0	0	0	0	0	0	0	0
Ron Guidry, p	.000	1	0	0	0	0	0	0	0	0	0	0
Reggie Jackson, of	.273	3	11	1	3	1	0	0	0	1	4	0
Tommy John, p	.000	1	0	0	0	0	0	0	0	0	0	0
Joe Lefebvre, of	.000	1	0	0	0	0	0	0	0	0	0	0
Rudy May, p	.000	1	0	0	0	0	0	0	0	0	2	0
Bobby Murcer, dh	.000	1	4	0	0	0	0	0	0	0	2	0
Graig Nettles, 3b	.167	2	6	1	1	0	0	1	1	0	1	0
Lou Piniella, of	.200	2	5	1	1	0	0	1	1	2	1	0
Willie Randolph, 2b	.385	3	13	0	5	2	0	0	1	1	3	0
Aurelio Rodriguez, 3b	.333	2	6	0	2	1	0	0	0	0	0	0
Eric Soderholm, dh	.167	2	6	0	1	0	0	0	0	0	0	0
Jim Spencer, ph	.000	1	1	0	0	0	0	0	0	0	0	0
Tom Underwood, p	.000	2	0	0	0	0	0	0	0	0	0	0
Bob Watson, 1b	.500	3	12	0	6	3	1	0	0	0	0	0
TOTAL	.255		102	6	26	7	1	3	5	6	16	0

PITCHER	W	L	ERA	G	GS	CG	SV	SHO	IP	H	ER	BB	SO
Ron Davis	0	0	2.25	1	0	0	0	0	4.0	3	1	1	3
Rich Gossage	0	1	54.00	1	0	0	0	0	0.1	3	2	0	0
Ron Guidry	0	1	12.00	1	1	0	0	0	3.0	5	4	4	2
Tommy John	0	0	2.70	1	1	0	0	0	6.2	8	2	1	3
Rudy May	0	1	3.38	1	1	1	0	0	8.0	6	3	3	4
Tom Underwood	0	0	0.00	2	0	0	0	0	3.0	3	0	0	3
TOTAL	0	3	4.32	7	3	1	0	0	25.0	28	12	9	15

GAME 1 AT KC OCT 8

NY	020	000	000	2 10 1
KC	022	000	12X	7 10 0

Pitchers: GUIDRY, Davis (4), Underwood (8) vs GURA
Home Runs: Cerone-NY, Piniella-NY, G.Brett-KC
Attendance: 42,598

GAME 2 AT KC OCT 9

NY	000	020	000	2 8 0
KC	003	000	00X	3 6 0

Pitchers: MAY vs LEONARD, Quisenberry (9)
Home Runs: Nettles-NY
Attendance: 42,633

GAME 3 AT NY OCT 10

KC	000	010	300	4 12 1
NY	000	002	000	2 8 0

Pitchers: Splittorff, QUISENBERRY (6) vs John, GOSSAGE (7), Underwood (8)
Home Runs: White-KC, G.Brett-KC
Attendance: 56,588

Both clubs had won divisional titles three years in a row—1976–1978—only to lose the League Championship Series. But both overcame the jinx in 1980 to face off in the World Series—the Phillies for the first time in thirty years, the Royals for the first time ever. Kansas City began with a rush in the opener, scoring two runs on Amos Otis's homer in the second inning and two more on Willie Aikens's blast an inning later. But the Phillies came back to take the lead in their half of the third with a five-run rally capped by Bake McBride's three-run homer. Single Phillie runs in each of the next two innings kept them out of reach of Aikens's second two-run shot in the eighth for a narrow 7–6 win. The Phillies extended their Series advantage with a 6–4 win in the second game, rebounding from a two-run deficit with four runs in the eighth inning.

The two clubs traded single runs throughout Game Three. Royal George Brett's first-inning homer began the scoring. The Phillies got the run back in the second inning, the Royals took the lead back in the fourth, Phillie Mike Schmidt homered to tie it again in the fifth, Amos Otis countered with a homer in the seventh, and Pete Rose singled in another tying Phillie run in the eighth. Phillie reliever Tug McGraw (who had a save in the opening game) came on to pitch the last of the tenth inning, but couldn't hold the tie, though two men were out before Willie Aikens singled in the Royals' winning run. The Royals evened the Series with their second victory the next day, scoring four times in the first inning and once in the second (with Willie Aikens for the second time in the Series hitting two home runs in a game), then holding on for a 5–3 win.

But the Phillies recovered to win the next two, and their first world crown. Mike Schmidt's fourth-inning two-run homer began the Phillies' scoring in Game Five. The Royals replied with one run in the fifth, and Amos Otis's home run an inning later tied the game. A second K.C. run in the inning put the Royals ahead until the top of the ninth, when pinch hitter Del Unser doubled home Schmidt to tie the game, and Manny Trillo drove home Unser with the go-ahead run. Tug McGraw, who had held K.C. scoreless through two innings of relief, loaded the bases in the last of the ninth with three walks, but at last fanned Jose Cardenal for the final out. In Game Six, with the Phillies ahead 4–0 in the eighth inning, McGraw relieved starter Steve Carlton with two men on, and

loaded the bases with a walk. One Royal scored on a sacrifice fly before McGraw got his third out. In the ninth, another McGraw walk and two singles again loaded the bases with only one away, but Frank White popped out foul, the ball bouncing off Bob Boone's catcher's mitt into Pete Rose's hand, and Willie Wilson struck out for the twelfth time to end the Series.

Philadelphia Phillies (NL), 4;
Kansas City Royals (AL), 2

PHI (N)

PLAYER/POS	AVG	G	AB	R	H	2B	3B	HR	RB	BB	SO	SB
Bob Boone, c	.412	6	17	3	7	2	0	0	4	4	0	0
Larry Bowa, ss	.375	6	24	3	9	1	0	0	2	0	0	3
Warren Brusstar, p	.000	1	0	0	0	0	0	0	0	0	0	0
Marty Bystrom, p	.000	1	0	0	0	0	0	0	0	0	0	0
Steve Carlton, p	.000	2	0	0	0	0	0	0	0	0	0	0
Larry Christenson, p	.000	1	0	0	0	0	0	0	0	0	0	0
Greg Gross, of-3	.000	4	2	0	0	0	0	0	0	0	0	0
Greg Luzinski, dh-2,of-1	.000	3	9	0	0	0	0	0	0	1	5	0
Garry Maddox, of	.227	6	22	1	5	2	0	0	1	1	3	0
Bake Mc Bride, of	.304	6	23	3	7	1	0	1	5	2	1	0
Tug Mc Graw, p	.000	4	0	0	0	0	0	0	0	0	0	0
Keith Moreland, dh	.333	3	12	1	4	0	0	0	1	0	1	0
Dickie Noles, p	.000	1	0	0	0	0	0	0	0	0	0	0
Ron Reed, p	.000	2	0	0	0	0	0	0	0	0	0	0
Pete Rose, 1b	.261	6	23	2	6	1	0	0	1	2	2	0
Dick Ruthven, p	.000	1	0	0	0	0	0	0	0	0	0	0
Kevin Saucier, p	.000	1	0	0	0	0	0	0	0	0	0	0
Mike Schmidt, 3b	.381	6	21	6	8	1	0	2	7	4	3	0
Lonnie Smith, of-5,dh-1	.263	6	19	2	5	1	0	0	1	1	1	0
Manny Trillo, 2b	.217	6	23	4	5	2	0	0	2	0	0	0
Del Unser, of	.500	3	6	2	3	2	0	0	2	0	1	0
Bob Walk, p	.000	1	0	0	0	0	0	0	0	0	0	0
TOTAL	.294		201	27	59	13	0	3	26	15	17	3

PITCHER	W	L	ERA	G	GS	CG	SV	SHO	IP	H	ER	BB	SO
Warren Brusstar	0	0	0.00	1	0	0	0	0	2.1	0	0	1	0
Marty Bystrom	0	0	5.40	1	1	0	0	0	5.0	10	3	1	4
Steve Carlton	2	0	2.40	2	2	0	0	0	15.0	14	4	9	17
Larry Christenson	0	1	108.00	1	1	0	0	0	0.1	5	4	1	0
Tug Mc Graw	1	1	1.17	4	0	0	2	0	7.2	7	1	8	10
Dickie Noles	0	0	1.93	1	0	0	0	0	4.2	5	1	2	6
Ron Reed	0	0	0.00	2	0	0	1	0	2.0	2	0	0	2
Dick Ruthven	0	0	3.00	1	1	0	0	0	9.0	9	3	0	7
Kevin Saucier	0	0	0.00	1	0	0	0	0	0.2	0	0	2	0
Bob Walk	1	0	7.71	1	1	0	0	0	7.0	8	6	3	3
TOTAL	4	2	3.69	15	6	0	3	0	53.2	60	22	27	49

KC (A)

PLAYER/POS	AVG	G	AB	R	H	2B	3B	HR	RB	BB	SO	SB
Willie Aikens, 1b	.400	6	20	5	8	0	1	4	8	6	8	0
George Brett, 3b	.375	6	24	3	9	2	1	1	3	2	4	1
Jose Cardenal, of	.200	4	10	0	2	0	0	0	0	0	3	0
Dave Chalk, 3b	.000	1	0	1	0	0	0	0	0	1	0	1
Onix Concepcion, pr	.000	3	0	0	0	0	0	0	0	0	0	0
Rich Gale, p	.000	2	0	0	0	0	0	0	0	0	0	0
Larry Gura, p	.000	2	0	0	0	0	0	0	0	0	0	0
Clint Hurdle, of	.417	4	12	1	5	1	0	0	2	1	1	1
Pete La Cock, 1b	.000	1	0	0	0	0	0	0	0	0	0	0
Dennis Leonard, p	.000	2	0	0	0	0	0	0	0	0	0	0
Renie Martin, p	.000	3	0	0	0	0	0	0	0	0	0	0
Hal Mc Rae, dh	.375	6	24	3	9	3	0	0	1	2	2	0
Amos Otis, of	.478	6	23	4	11	2	0	3	7	3	3	0
Marty Pattin, p	.000	1	0	0	0	0	0	0	0	0	0	0
Darrell Porter, c-4	.143	5	14	1	2	0	0	0	0	3	4	0
Dan Quisenberry, p	.000	6	0	0	0	0	0	0	0	0	0	0
Paul Splittorff, p	.000	1	0	0	0	0	0	0	0	0	0	0
U L Washington, ss	.273	6	22	1	6	0	0	0	2	0	6	0
John Wathan, c-2,of-1	.286	3	7	1	2	0	0	0	1	2	1	0
Frank White, 2b	.080	6	25	0	2	0	0	0	0	1	5	1
Willie Wilson, of	.154	6	26	3	4	1	0	0	0	4	12	2
TOTAL	.290		207	23	60	9	2	8	22	26	49	6

PITCHER	W	L	ERA	G	GS	CG	SV	SHO	IP	H	ER	BB	SO
Rich Gale	0	1	4.26	2	2	0	0	0	6.1	11	3	4	4
Larry Gura	0	0	2.19	2	2	0	0	0	12.1	8	3	3	4
Dennis Leonard	1	1	6.75	2	2	0	0	0	10.2	15	8	2	5
Renie Martin	0	0	2.79	3	0	0	0	0	9.2	11	3	3	2
Marty Pattin	0	0	0.00	1	0	0	0	0	1.0	0	0	0	2
Dan Quisenberry	1	2	5.23	6	0	0	1	0	10.1	10	6	3	0
Paul Splittorff	0	0	5.40	1	0	0	0	0	1.2	4	1	0	0
TOTAL	2	4	4.15	17	6	0	1	0	52.0	59	24	15	17

GAME 1 AT PHI OCT 14

KC	022 000 020	6 9 1
PHI	005 110 00X	7 11 0

Pitchers: LEONARD, Martin (4), Quisenberry (8) vs WALK, McGraw (8)
Home Runs: Otis-KC, Aikens-KC (2), McBride-PHI
Attendance: 65,791

GAME 2 AT PHI OCT 15

KC	000 001 300	4 11 0
PHI	000 020 04X	6 8 1

Pitchers: Gura, QUISENBERRY (7) vs CARLTON, Reed (9)
Attendance: 65,775

GAME 3 AT KC OCT 17

PHI	010 010 010 0	3 14 1
KC	100 100 100 1	4 11 0

Pitchers: Ruthven, McGRAW (10) vs Gale, Martin (5), QUISENBERRY (8)
Home Runs: Schmidt-PHI, G.Brett-KC, Otis-KC
Attendance: 42,380

GAME 4 AT KC OCT 18

PHI	010 000 110	3 10 1
KC	410 000 00X	5 10 2

Pitchers: CHRISTENSEN, Noles (1), Saucier (6), Brusstar (6) vs LEONARD, Quisenberry (8)
Home Runs: Aikens-KC (2)
Attendance: 42,363

GAME 5 AT KC OCT 19

PHI	000 200 002	4 7 0
KC	000 012 000	3 12 2

Pitchers: Bystrom, Reed (6), McGRAW (7) vs Gura, QUISENBERRY (7)
Home Runs: Schmidt-PHI, Otis-KC
Attendance: 42,369

GAME 6 AT PHI OCT 21

KC	000 000 010	1 7 2
PHI	002 011 00X	4 9 0

Pitchers: GALE, Martin (3), Splittorff (5), Pattin (7), Quisenberry (8) vs CARLTON, McGraw (8)
Attendance: 65,838

The Expos, who triumphed over the NL East in the second half of the season, won the first two play-off games at home by identical 3–1 scores over the first-half champion Phillies. The Phillies rapped Expo ace Steve Rogers for ten hits in Game One, but Keith Moreland's solo home run in the second was the only hit to produce a run. The homer tied the score briefly, but the Expos regained the lead in the last of the second inning on Chris Speier's double and increased it to 3–1, two innings later. The Expos scored their three runs early in Game Two on Speier's second-inning single and Gary Carter's two-run homer an inning later. Expo starter Bill Gullickson blanked the Phillies on three hits through 7⅔ innings, but three two-out hits in the eighth scored a Phillie run and brought on reliever Jeff Reardon, who ended the threat for his second save in as many days.

When the Series moved to Philadelphia, the Phillies recovered to even things with a pair of wins. After an easy 13-hit 6–2 victory in Game Three, they took a 4–0 lead into the fourth inning of Game Four. Montreal fought back to tie the game, fell behind again, then re-tied the score at 5–5 in the top of the seventh. The final innings featured a duel between relievers Tug McGraw and Jeff Reardon. McGraw stopped the Expos on one hit through three innings, and took the win when Reardon, after retiring eight Phillies in a row, gave up a leadoff homer to pinch hitter George Vukovich in the bottom of the tenth.

Steve Rogers won the division title for Montreal in the finale, hurling a six-hit shutout against the Phillies and driving in the first two of the Expos' three runs with a bases-loaded single through the box in the fifth inning.

Montreal Expos, 3;
Philadelphia Phillies, 2

MON (E)

PLAYER/POS	AVG	G	AB	R	H	2B	3B	HR	RB	BB	SO	SB
Stan Bahnsen, p	.000	1	0	0	0	0	0	0	0	0	0	0
Ray Burris, p	.000	1	2	0	0	0	0	0	0	0	2	0
Gary Carter, c	.421	5	19	3	8	3	0	2	6	1	1	0
Warren Cromartie, 1b	.227	5	22	1	5	2	0	0	1	0	9	0
Andre Dawson, of	.300	5	20	1	6	0	1	0	0	1	6	2
Terry Francona, of	.333	5	12	0	4	0	0	0	0	2	2	2
Woody Fryman, p	.000	1	0	0	0	0	0	0	0	0	0	0
Bill Gullickson, p	.000	1	3	0	0	0	0	0	0	0	1	0
Wallace Johnson, ph	.500	2	2	0	1	0	0	0	0	1	0	0
Bill Lee, p	.000	1	0	0	0	0	0	0	0	0	0	0
Jerry Manuel, 2b	.071	5	14	0	1	0	0	0	0	2	5	0
Brad Mills, ph	.000	1	0	0	0	0	0	0	0	1	0	0
John Milner, ph	.500	2	2	0	1	0	0	0	0	1	0	0
Larry Parrish, 3b	.150	5	20	3	3	1	0	0	1	1	3	0
Mike Phillips, 2b	.000	1	1	0	0	0	0	0	0	0	0	0
Jeff Reardon, p	.000	3	1	0	0	0	0	0	0	0	1	0
Steve Rogers, p	.400	2	5	0	2	0	0	0	2	0	1	0
Scott Sanderson, p	.000	1	1	0	0	0	0	0	0	0	1	0
Elias Sosa, p	.000	2	0	0	0	0	0	0	0	0	0	0
Chris Speier, ss	.400	5	15	4	6	2	0	0	3	4	2	0
Tim Wallach, of-3	.250	4	4	1	1	1	0	0	0	0	4	0
Jerry White, of	.167	5	18	3	3	1	0	0	1	2	2	3
TOTAL	.255		161	16	41	10	1	2	16	18	36	7

PITCHER	W	L	ERA	G	GS	CG	SV	SHO	IP	H	ER	BB	SO
Stan Bahnsen	0	0	0.00	1	0	0	0	0	1.1	1	0	1	1
Ray Burris	0	1	5.06	1	1	0	0	0	5.1	7	3	4	4
Woody Fryman	0	0	6.75	1	0	0	0	0	1.1	3	1	1	0
Bill Gullickson	1	0	1.17	1	1	0	0	0	7.2	6	1	1	3
Bill Lee	0	0	0.00	1	0	0	0	0	0.2	2	0	0	1
Jeff Reardon	0	1	2.08	3	0	0	2	0	4.1	1	1	1	2
Steve Rogers	2	0	0.51	2	2	1	0	1	17.2	16	1	3	5
Scott Sanderson	0	0	6.75	1	1	0	0	0	2.2	4	2	2	2
Elias Sosa	0	0	3.00	2	0	0	0	0	3.0	4	1	0	1
TOTAL	3	2	2.05	13	5	1	2	1	44.0	44	10	13	19

PHI (E)

PLAYER/POS	AVG	G	AB	R	H	2B	3B	HR	RB	BB	SO	SB
Luis Aguayo, pr	.000	2	0	1	0	0	0	0	0	0	0	0
Ramon Aviles, ph	.000	1	0	0	0	0	0	0	0	1	0	0
Bob Boone, c	.000	3	5	0	0	0	0	0	0	0	0	0
Larry Bowa, ss	.176	5	17	0	3	1	0	0	1	1	0	0
Warren Brusstar, p	.000	2	0	0	0	0	0	0	0	0	0	0
Steve Carlton, p	.250	2	4	0	1	0	0	0	0	0	0	0
Larry Christensen, p	.000	1	2	0	0	0	0	0	0	0	1	0
Dick Davis, of	.000	1	2	0	0	0	0	0	0	0	1	0
Greg Gross, of-2	.000	4	4	0	0	0	0	0	0	0	0	0
Sparky Lyle, p	.000	3	0	0	0	0	0	0	0	0	0	0
Garry Maddox, of	.333	2	3	0	1	1	0	0	0	0	0	0
Gary Matthews, of	.400	5	20	3	8	0	1	1	1	0	2	0
Bake Mc Bride, of	.200	4	15	1	3	1	0	0	0	0	5	0
Tug Mc Graw, p	.000	2	0	0	0	0	0	0	0	0	0	0
Keith Moreland, c	.462	4	13	2	6	0	0	1	3	1	1	0
Dickie Noles, p	.000	1	0	0	0	0	0	0	0	1	0	0
Ron Reed, p	.000	4	0	0	0	0	0	0	0	0	0	0
Pete Rose, 1b	.300	5	20	1	6	1	0	0	2	2	0	0
Dick Ruthven, p	.000	1	1	0	0	0	0	0	0	0	0	0
Mike Schmidt, 3b	.250	5	16	3	4	1	0	1	2	4	2	0
Lonnie Smith, of	.263	5	19	1	5	1	0	0	0	0	4	0
Manny Trillo, 2b	.188	5	16	1	3	0	0	0	1	4	0	0
George Vukovich, of-3	.444	5	9	1	4	0	0	1	2	0	3	0
TOTAL	.265		166	14	44	6	1	4	12	13	19	0

PITCHER	W	L	ERA	G	GS	CG	SV	SHO	IP	H	ER	BB	SO
Warren Brusstar	0	0	4.91	2	0	0	0	0	3.2	5	2	1	3
Steve Carlton	0	2	3.86	2	2	0	0	0	14.0	14	6	8	13
Larry Christensen	1	0	1.50	1	1	0	0	0	6.0	4	1	1	8
Sparky Lyle	0	0	0.00	3	0	0	0	0	2.1	4	0	2	1
Tug Mc Graw	1	0	0.00	2	0	0	0	0	4.0	2	0	0	2
Dickie Noles	0	0	4.50	1	1	0	0	0	4.0	4	2	2	5
Ron Reed	0	0	3.00	4	0	0	0	0	6.0	5	2	3	4
Dick Ruthven	0	1	4.50	1	1	0	0	0	4.0	3	2	1	0
TOTAL	2	3	3.07	16	5	0	0	0	44.0	41	15	18	36

GAME 1 AT MON OCT 7

PHI	010 000 000	1	10	1
MON	110 100 00X	3	8	0

Pitchers: CARLTON, R.Reed (7) vs ROGERS, Reardon (9)
Home Runs: Moreland-PHI
Attendance: 34,327

GAME 2 AT MON OCT 8

PHI	000 000 010	1	6	2
MON	012 000 00X	3	7	0

Pitchers: RUTHVEN, Brusstar (5), Lyle (7), McGraw (8) vs GULLICKSON, Reardon (8)
Home Runs: Carter-MON
Attendance: 45,896

GAME 3 AT PHI OCT 9

MON	010 000 010	2	8	4
PHI	020 002 20X	6	13	4

Pitchers: BURRIS, Lee (6), Sosa (7) vs CHRISTENSON, Lyle (7), R.Reed (8)
Attendance: 36,835

GAME 4 AT PHI OCT 10

MON	000 112 100 0	5	10	1
PHI	202 001 000 1	6	9	0

Pitchers: Sanderson, Bahnsen (3), Sosa (5), Fryman (6), REARDON (7) vs Noles, Brusstar (5), LyLE (6), R.Reed (7), McGRAW (8)
Home Runs: Carter-MON, Schmidt-PHI, Matthews-PHI, G.Vukovich-PHI
Attendance: 38,818

GAME 5 AT PHI OCT 11

MON	000 021 000	3	8	1
PHI	000 000 000	0	6	0

Pitchers: ROGERS vs CARLTON, R.Reed (9)
Attendance: 47,384

Cincinnati, with the league's best overall season record, failed to win either half season in the NL West, and watched from the sidelines as first-half winner Los Angeles, down 0–2, recovered to win the final three games—and the division title—from second-half victor Houston. In the opener, Astro Alan Ashby's two-run homer in the last of the ninth broke a 1–1 tie and gave Nolan Ryan a two-hit victory. The next day, Astro Denny Walling's two-out bases-loaded single in the last of the eleventh scored Phil Garner with the game's only run.

When the clubs shifted to Los Angeles for the remainder of the series, the Dodgers came alive. In Game Three, a first-inning double by Dusty Baker and home run by Steve Garvey drove in three Dodger runs. Pitcher Burt Hooton and two relievers held Houston to three hits in what became a 6–1 Dodger victory. The next day, Dodger Fernando Valenzuela and Astro Vern Ruhle hurled matching four-hitters. But Pedro Guerrero's home run in the fifth inning and a pair of Dodger singles sandwiched around a sacrifice and intentional walk in the seventh gave Los Angeles two runs, while Valenzuela held Houston to a single run in the ninth. In the finale, Jerry Reuss blanked the Astros on five hits while his Dodgers blended three of their seven hits with a walk and Astro error for three runs in the sixth. Two more hits produced a final run an inning later.

Los Angeles Dodgers, 3; Houston Astros, 2

LA (W)

PLAYER/POS	AVG	G	AB	R	H	2B	3B	HR	RB	BB	SO	SB
Dusty Baker, of	.167	5	18	2	3	1	0	0	1	2	0	0
Terry Forster, p	.000	1	0	0	0	0	0	0	0	0	0	0
Steve Garvey, 1b	.368	5	19	4	7	0	1	2	4	0	2	0
Pedro Guerrero, 3b	.176	5	17	1	3	1	0	1	1	2	4	1
Burt Hooton, p	.000	1	3	0	0	0	0	0	0	0	0	0
Steve Howe, p	.000	2	0	0	0	0	0	0	0	0	0	0
Jay Johnstone, ph	.000	1	1	0	0	0	0	0	0	0	0	0
Ken Landreaux, of	.200	5	20	1	4	1	0	0	1	0	1	0
Davey Lopes, 2b	.200	5	20	1	4	1	0	0	0	3	7	1
Mike Marshall, ph	.000	1	1	0	0	0	0	0	0	0	1	0
Rick Monday, of	.214	5	14	1	3	0	0	0	1	2	4	0
Tom Niedenfuer, p	.000	1	0	0	0	0	0	0	0	0	0	0
Jerry Reuss, p	.000	2	8	0	0	0	0	0	0	0	8	0
Bill Russell, ss	.250	5	16	1	4	1	0	0	2	3	1	0
Steve Sax, 2b	.000	1	0	0	0	0	0	0	0	0	0	0
Mike Scioscia, c	.154	4	13	0	2	0	0	0	1	1	2	0
Reggie Smith, ph	.000	2	1	0	0	0	0	0	1	0	1	0
Dave Stewart, p	.000	2	0	0	0	0	0	0	0	0	0	0
Derrel Thomas, of	.000	4	2	1	0	0	0	0	0	0	1	0
Fernando Valenzuela, p	.000	2	4	0	0	0	0	0	0	0	1	0
Bob Welch, p	.000	1	0	0	0	0	0	0	0	0	0	0
Steve Yeager, c	.400	2	5	1	2	1	0	0	0	0	1	0
TOTAL	.198		162	13	32	6	1	3	12	13	34	2

PITCHER	W	L	ERA	G	GS	CG	SV	SHO	IP	H	ER	BB	SO
Terry Forster	0	0	0.00	1	0	0	0	0	0.1	0	0	0	0
Burt Hooton	1	0	1.29	1	1	0	0	0	7.0	3	1	3	2
Steve Howe	0	0	0.00	2	0	0	0	0	2.0	1	0	0	2
Tom Niedenfuer	0	0	0.00	1	0	0	0	0	0.1	1	0	1	1
Jerry Reuss	1	0	0.00	2	2	1	0	1	18.0	10	0	5	7
Dave Stewart	0	2	40.50	2	0	0	0	0	0.2	4	3	0	1
Fernando Valenzuela	1	0	1.06	2	2	1	0	0	17.0	10	2	3	10
Bob Welch	0	0	0.00	1	0	0	0	0	1.0	0	0	1	1
TOTAL	3	2	1.17	12	5	2	0	1	46.1	29	6	13	24

HOU (W)

PLAYER/POS	AVG	G	AB	R	H	2B	3B	HR	RB	BB	SO	SB
Alan Ashby, c	.111	3	9	1	1	0	0	1	2	2	0	0
Cesar Cedeno, 1b	.231	4	13	0	3	1	0	0	0	2	2	2
Jose Cruz, of	.300	5	20	0	6	1	0	0	0	1	3	1
Kiko Garcia, ss-1	.000	2	4	0	0	0	0	0	0	0	1	0
Phil Garner, 2b	.111	5	18	1	2	0	0	0	0	3	3	0
Art Howe, 3b	.235	5	17	1	4	0	0	1	1	2	1	0
Bob Knepper, p	.000	1	1	0	0	0	0	0	0	0	0	0
Frank La Corte, p	.000	2	0	0	0	0	0	0	0	0	0	0
Joe Niekro, p	.000	1	2	0	0	0	0	0	0	0	0	0
Joe Pittman, ph	.000	2	2	0	0	0	0	0	0	0	0	0
Terry Puhl, of	.190	5	21	2	4	1	0	0	0	0	1	1
Luis Pujols, c	.000	2	6	0	0	0	0	0	0	0	1	0
Craig Reynolds, ss-1	.333	2	3	1	1	0	0	0	0	0	1	0
Dave Roberts, ph	.000	1	1	0	0	0	0	0	0	0	1	0
Vern Ruhle, p	.000	1	1	0	0	0	0	0	0	0	1	0
Nolan Ryan, p	.250	2	4	0	1	0	0	0	0	1	1	0
Joe Sambito, p	.000	2	0	0	0	0	0	0	0	0	0	0
Tony Scott, of	.150	5	20	0	3	0	0	0	2	1	6	0
Billy Smith, p	.000	1	0	0	0	0	0	0	0	0	0	0
Dave Smith, p	.000	2	0	0	0	0	0	0	0	0	0	0
Harry Spilman, ph	.000	1	1	0	0	0	0	0	0	0	0	0
Dickie Thon, ss	.182	4	11	0	2	0	0	0	0	1	0	0
Denny Walling, 1b-2	.333	3	6	0	2	0	0	0	1	0	1	0
Gary Woods, ph	.000	2	2	0	0	0	0	0	0	0	1	0
TOTAL	.179		162	6	29	3	0	2	6	13	24	4

PITCHER	W	L	ERA	G	GS	CG	SV	SHO	IP	H	ER	BB	SO
Bob Knepper	0	1	5.40	1	1	0	0	0	5.0	6	3	2	4
Frank La Corte	0	0	0.00	2	0	0	0	0	3.2	2	0	1	5
Joe Niekro	0	0	0.00	1	1	0	0	0	8.0	7	0	3	4
Vern Ruhle	0	1	2.25	1	1	0	0	0	8.0	4	2	2	1
Nolan Ryan	1	1	1.80	2	2	1	0	0	15.0	6	3	3	14
Joe Sambito	1	0	16.20	2	0	0	0	0	1.2	5	3	2	2
Billy Smith	0	0	0.00	1	0	0	0	0	0.1	0	0	0	0
Dave Smith	0	0	3.86	2	0	0	0	0	2.1	2	1	0	4
TOTAL	2	3	2.45	12	5	2	0	0	44.0	32	12	13	34

GAME 1 AT HOU OCT 6

LA	000	000	100	1	2	0
HOU	000	001	002	3	8	0

Pitchers: Valenzuela, STEWART (9) vs RYAN
Home Runs: Garvey-LA, Ashby-HOU
Attendance: 44,836

GAME 2 AT HOU OCT 7

LA	000 000	000 00	0	9	1
HOU	000 000	000 01	1	9	0

Pitchers: Reuss, S.Howe (1), STEWART (11), Forster (11), Niedenfuer (11) vs Niekro, D.Smith (9), SAMBITO (11)
Attendance: 42,398

GAME 3 AT LA OCT 9

HOU	001	000	000	1	3	2
LA	300	000	03X	6	10	0

Pitchers: KNEPPER, LaCorte (6), Sambito (8), B.Smith (8) vs HOOTON, S.Howe (8), Welch (9)
Home Runs: Garvey-LA, A.Howe-HOU
Attendance: 46,820

GAME 4 AT LA OCT 10

HOU	000	000	001	1	4	0
LA	000	010	10X	2	4	0

Pitchers: RUHLE vs VALENZUELA
Home Runs: Guerrero-LA
Attendance: 55,983

GAME 5 AT LA OCT 11

HOU	000	000	000	0	5	3
LA	000	003	10X	4	7	2

Pitchers: RYAN, D.Smith (7), LaCorte (7) vs REUSS
Attendance: 55,979

Fine pitching characterized the series, with the losing team held to one run in four of the five games. In the exception Expo Ray Burris hurled a shutout.

Montreal put men on base in each inning of the opener. But the pitching of Burt Hooton and Bob Welch—plus some fine Dodger fielding—kept the Expos from scoring until the ninth, when their one run was too little to overcome the Dodger lead. Burris's shutout evened the series in Game Two as the Expos scored three times against rookie sensation Fernando Valenzuela. The Expos took the series lead in Game Three, overcoming a 0–1 deficit with a two-out four-run burst in the sixth (capped by Jerry White's three-run homer).

In the end, though, the Dodgers prevailed. Through seven innings of Game Four, Hooton and the Expos' Bill Gullickson dueled at 1–1. But in the top of the eighth, Steve Garvey homered with a man aboard, and four more Dodger runs in the ninth put the game away. The finale—Burris vs. Valenzuela again—featured another 1–1 duel, this one reaching into the top of the ninth when, with two out, Dodger Rick Monday homered off reliever Steve Rogers. In the bottom of the ninth, Valenzuela walked two batters after retiring two, but Welch came on to save the game and the pennant.

Los Angeles Dodgers (West), 3; Montreal Expos (East), 2

LA (W)

PLAYER/POS	AVG	G	AB	R	H	2B	3B	HR	RB	BB	SO	SB
Dusty Baker, of	.316	5	19	3	6	1	0	0	3	1	0	0
Bobby Castillo, p	.000	1	0	0	0	0	0	0	0	0	0	0
Ron Cey, 3b	.278	5	18	1	5	1	0	0	3	3	2	0
Terry Forster, p	.000	1	0	0	0	0	0	0	0	0	0	0
Steve Garvey, 1b	.286	5	21	2	6	0	0	1	2	0	4	0
Pedro Guerrero, of	.105	5	19	1	2	0	0	1	2	1	4	0
Burt Hooton, p	.000	2	5	0	0	0	0	0	0	0	2	0
Steve Howe, p	.000	2	0	0	0	0	0	0	0	0	0	0
Jay Johnstone, ph	.000	2	2	0	0	0	0	0	0	0	0	0
Ken Landreaux, of-3	.100	5	10	0	1	1	0	0	0	3	2	0
Davey Lopes, 2b	.278	5	18	0	5	0	0	0	0	1	3	5
Rick Monday, of-2	.333	3	9	2	3	0	0	1	1	0	4	0
Tom Niedenfuer, p	.000	1	0	0	0	0	0	0	0	0	0	0
Alejandro Pena, p	.000	2	0	0	0	0	0	0	0	0	0	0
Jerry Reuss, p	.000	1	2	0	0	0	0	0	0	0	0	0
Bill Russell, ss	.313	5	16	2	5	0	1	0	1	1	1	0
Steve Sax, 2b	.000	1	0	0	0	0	0	0	0	0	0	0
Mike Scioscia, c	.133	5	15	1	2	0	0	1	1	2	1	0
Reggie Smith, ph	1.000	1	1	0	1	0	0	0	1	0	0	0
Derrel Thomas, 3b-1,of-1	1.000	2	1	2	1	0	0	0	0	0	0	0
Fernando Valenzuela, p	.000	2	5	0	0	0	0	0	1	0	0	0
Bob Welch, p	.000	3	0	0	0	0	0	0	0	0	0	0
Steve Yeager, c	.500	1	2	1	1	0	0	0	0	0	0	0
TOTAL	.233		163	15	38	3	1	4	15	12	23	5

PITCHER	W	L	ERA	G	GS	CG	SV	SHO	IP	H	ER	BB	SO
Bobby Castillo	0	0	0.00	1	0	0	0	0	1.0	0	0	0	1
Terry Forster	0	0	0.00	1	0	0	0	0	0.1	0	0	0	1
Burt Hooton	2	0	0.00	2	2	0	0	0	14.2	11	0	6	7
Steve Howe	0	0	0.00	2	0	0	0	0	2.0	1	0	0	2
Tom Niedenfuer	0	0	0.00	1	0	0	0	0	0.1	2	0	0	0
Alejandro Pena	0	0	0.00	2	0	0	0	0	2.1	1	0	0	0
Jerry Reuss	0	1	5.14	1	1	0	0	0	7.0	7	4	1	2
Fernando Valenzuela	1	1	2.45	2	2	0	0	0	14.2	10	4	5	10
Bob Welch	0	0	5.40	3	0	0	1	0	1.2	2	1	0	2
TOTAL	3	2	1.84	15	5	0	1	0	44.0	34	9	12	25

MON (E)

PLAYER/POS	AVG	G	AB	R	H	2B	3B	HR	RB	BB	SO	SB
Ray Burris, p	.000	2	6	0	0	0	0	0	0	0	4	0
Gary Carter, c	.438	5	16	3	7	1	0	0	4	4	2	0
Warren Cromartie, 1b	.167	5	18	0	3	1	0	0	2	0	2	0
Andre Dawson, of	.150	5	20	2	3	0	0	0	0	0	4	0
Terry Francona, of-1	.000	2	1	0	0	0	0	0	0	0	1	0
Woody Fryman, p	.000	1	0	0	0	0	0	0	0	0	0	0
Bill Gullickson, p	.000	2	3	0	0	0	0	0	0	1	2	0
Bill Lee, p	.000	1	0	0	0	0	0	0	0	0	0	0
Jerry Manuel, pr	.000	1	0	0	0	0	0	0	0	0	0	0
John Milner, ph	.000	1	1	0	0	0	0	0	0	0	1	0
Larry Parrish, 3b	.263	5	19	2	5	2	0	0	2	1	1	0
Tim Raines, of	.238	5	21	1	5	2	0	0	1	0	3	0
Jeff Reardon, p	.000	1	0	0	0	0	0	0	0	0	0	0
Steve Rogers, p	.000	2	2	0	0	0	0	0	0	0	1	0
Rodney Scott, 2b	.167	5	18	0	3	0	0	0	0	1	3	1
Elias Sosa, p	.000	1	0	0	0	0	0	0	0	0	0	0
Chris Speier, ss	.188	5	16	0	3	0	0	0	0	2	0	0
Tim Wallach, ph	.000	1	1	0	0	0	0	0	0	0	0	0
Jerry White, of	.313	5	16	2	5	1	0	1	3	3	1	1
TOTAL	.215		158	10	34	7	0	1	8	12	25	2

PITCHER	W	L	ERA	G	GS	CG	SV	SHO	IP	H	ER	BB	SO
Ray Burris	1	0	0.53	2	2	1	0	1	17.0	10	1	3	4
Woody Fryman	0	0	36.00	1	0	0	0	0	1.0	3	4	1	1
Bill Gullickson	0	2	2.51	2	2	0	0	0	14.1	12	4	6	12
Bill Lee	0	0	0.00	1	0	0	0	0	0.1	1	0	0	0
Jeff Reardon	0	0	27.00	1	0	0	0	0	1.0	3	3	0	0
Steve Rogers	1	1	1.80	2	1	1	0	0	10.0	8	2	1	6
Elias Sosa	0	0	0.00	1	0	0	0	0	0.1	1	0	1	0
TOTAL	2	3	2.86	10	5	2	0	1	44.0	38	14	12	23

GAME 1 AT LA OCT 13

MON	000	000	001	1	9	0
LA	020	000	03X	5	8	0

Pitchers: GULLICKSON, Reardon (8) vs HOOTON, Welch (8), Howe (9)
Home Runs: Guerrero-LA, Scioscia-LA
Attendance: 51,273

GAME 2 AT LA OCT 14

MON	020	001	000	3	10	1
LA	000	000	000	0	5	1

Pitchers: BURRIS vs VALENZUELA, Niedenfuer (7), Forster (7), Pena (7), Castillo (9)
Attendance: 53,463

GAME 3 AT MON OCT 16

LA	000	100	000	1	7	0
MON	000	004	00X	4	7	1

Pitchers: REUSS, Pena (8) vs ROGERS
Home Runs: White-MON
Attendance: 54,372

GAME 4 AT MON OCT 17

LA	001	000	024	7	12	1
MON	000	100	000	1	5	1

Pitchers: HOOTON, Welch (8), Howe (9) vs GULLICKSON, Fryman (8), Sosa (9), Lee (9)
Home Runs: Garvey-LA
Attendance: 54,499

GAME 5 AT MON OCT 19

LA	000	010	001	2	6	0
MON	100	000	000	1	3	1

Pitchers: VALENZUELA, Welch (9) vs Burris, ROGERS (9)
Home Runs: Monday-LA
Attendance: 36,491

The home field didn't seem to offer any advantage. First-half winner New York captured both games played in Milwaukee, but when the Series moved to Yankee Stadium for the final three games, the second-half champion Brewers evened the series.

Milwaukee took a 2–0 lead early in the opener, but New York erupted for four runs in the fourth on Oscar Gamble's two-run homer and Rick Cerone's double, and held on to win 5–3. In Game Two, rookie starter Dave Righetti fanned ten Brewers in his six innings and Goose Gossage's brilliant relief earned him his second save in two days as the Yankees took a 3–0 win on homers by Lou Piniella and Reggie Jackson.

Milwaukee, struggling against elimination, took the lead in the seventh inning of Game Three on Ted Simmons' two-run homer. New York tied the score at 3–3 in their half of the inning, but Paul Molitor broke the tie in the eighth with a solo homer. Simmons doubled home an insurance run later in the inning for a 5–3 Brewer win. The Brewers tagged Yankee pitching for only four hits in Game Four, but three of them came in the fourth inning and combined with a sacrifice fly to produce the Brewers' two runs. New York scored once in the sixth, but baserunning errors an inning later ended their only other scoring threat.

In the finale Milwaukee scored two early runs, but the Yankees (as they had done in the opener) took the lead with a four-run fourth—this time on home runs by Reggie Jackson and Oscar Gamble, and Rick Cerone's single. Cerone later hit an insurance homer, as the home team finally won a game—and captured the division crown.

New York Yankees, 3; Milwaukee Brewers, 2

NY (E)

PLAYER/POS	AVG	G	AB	R	H	2B	3B	HR	RB	BB	SO	SB
Bobby Brown, pr	.000	1	0	0	0	0	0	0	0	0	0	0
Rick Cerone, c	.333	5	18	1	6	2	0	1	5	0	2	0
Ron Davis, p	.000	3	0	0	0	0	0	0	0	0	0	0
Barry Foote, ph	.000	1	0	0	0	0	0	0	0	0	0	0
Oscar Gamble, dh	.556	4	9	2	5	1	0	2	3	1	2	0
Rich Gossage, p	.000	3	0	0	0	0	0	0	0	0	0	0
Ron Guidry, p	.000	2	0	0	0	0	0	0	0	0	0	0
Reggie Jackson, of	.300	5	20	4	6	0	0	2	4	1	5	0
Tommy John, p	.000	1	0	0	0	0	0	0	0	0	0	0
Rudy May, p	.000	1	0	0	0	0	0	0	0	0	0	0
Larry Milbourne, ss	.316	5	19	4	6	1	0	0	0	0	1	0
Jerry Mumphrey, of	.095	5	21	2	2	0	0	0	0	0	1	1
Bobby Murcer, ph	.000	2	1	0	0	0	0	0	0	1	0	0
Graig Nettles, 3b	.059	5	17	1	1	0	0	0	1	3	1	0
Lou Piniella, dh	.200	4	10	1	2	1	0	1	3	0	0	0
Willie Randolph, 2b	.200	5	20	0	4	0	0	0	1	1	4	0
Rick Reuschel, p	.000	1	0	0	0	0	0	0	0	0	0	0
Dave Revering, 1b	.000	2	0	0	0	0	0	0	0	0	0	0
Dave Righetti, p	.000	2	0	0	0	0	0	0	0	0	0	0
Bob Watson, 1b	.438	5	16	2	7	0	0	0	1	1	1	0
Dave Winfield, of	.350	5	20	2	7	3	0	0	0	1	5	0
TOTAL	.269		171	19	46	8	0	6	18	9	22	1

PITCHER	W	L	ERA	G	GS	CG	SV	SHO	IP	H	ER	BB	SO
Ron Davis	1	0	0.00	3	0	0	0	0	6.0	1	0	2	6
Rich Gossage	0	0	0.00	3	0	0	3	0	6.2	3	0	2	8
Ron Guidry	0	0	5.40	2	2	0	0	0	8.1	11	5	3	8
Tommy John	0	1	6.43	1	1	0	0	0	7.0	8	5	2	0
Rudy May	0	0	0.00	1	0	0	0	0	2.0	1	0	0	1
Rick Reuschel	0	1	3.00	1	1	0	0	0	6.0	4	2	1	3
Dave Righetti	2	0	1.00	2	1	0	0	0	9.0	8	1	3	13
TOTAL	3	2	2.60	13	5	0	3	0	45.0	36	13	13	39

MIL (E)

PLAYER/POS	AVG	G	AB	R	H	2B	3B	HR	RB	BB	SO	SB
Sal Bando, 3b	.294	5	17	1	5	3	0	0	1	2	3	0
Dwight Bernard, p	.000	2	0	0	0	0	0	0	0	0	0	0
Thad Bosley, dh	.000	1	0	0	0	0	0	0	0	0	0	0
Mike Caldwell, p	.000	2	0	0	0	0	0	0	0	0	0	0
Cecil Cooper, 1b	.222	5	18	1	4	0	0	0	3	1	3	0
Jamie Easterly, p	.000	2	0	0	0	0	0	0	0	0	0	0
Marshall Edwards, of	.000	2	1	0	0	0	0	0	0	0	1	0
Rollie Fingers, p	.000	3	0	0	0	0	0	0	0	0	0	0
Jim Gantner, 2b	.143	4	14	1	2	1	0	0	0	0	2	0
Moose Haas, p	.000	2	0	0	0	0	0	0	0	0	0	0
Roy Howell, dh-3	.400	4	5	0	2	0	0	0	0	2	2	0
Randy Lerch, p	.000	1	0	0	0	0	0	0	0	0	0	0
Bob Mc Clure, p	.000	3	0	0	0	0	0	0	0	0	0	0
Paul Molitor, of	.250	5	20	2	5	0	0	1	1	2	5	0
Don Money, 2b-1,dh-1	.000	2	3	0	0	0	0	0	0	0	0	0
Charlie Moore, of-2,dh-2	.222	4	9	0	2	0	0	0	1	1	2	0
Ben Oglivie, of	.167	5	18	0	3	1	0	0	1	0	7	0
Ed Romero, 2b	.500	1	2	1	1	0	0	0	0	0	1	0
Ted Simmons, c	.211	5	19	1	4	1	0	1	4	2	2	0
Jim Slaton, p	.000	4	0	0	0	0	0	0	0	0	0	0
Gorman Thomas, of-3,dh-2	.118	5	17	2	2	0	0	1	1	1	9	0
Pete Vuckovich, p	.000	2	0	0	0	0	0	0	0	0	0	0
Robin Yount, ss	.316	5	19	4	6	0	1	0	1	2	2	1
TOTAL	.222		162	13	36	6	1	3	13	13	39	1

PITCHER	W	L	ERA	G	GS	CG	SV	SHO	IP	H	ER	BB	SO
Dwight Bernard	0	0	0.00	2	0	0	0	0	2.1	0	0	0	0
Mike Caldwell	0	1	4.32	2	1	0	0	0	8.1	9	4	0	4
Jamie Easterly	0	0	6.75	2	0	0	0	0	1.1	2	1	0	1
Rollie Fingers	1	0	3.86	3	0	0	1	0	4.2	7	2	1	5
Moose Haas	0	2	9.45	2	2	0	0	0	6.2	13	7	1	1
Randy Lerch	0	0	1.50	1	1	0	0	0	6.0	3	1	4	3
Bob Mc Clure	0	0	0.00	3	0	0	0	0	3.1	4	0	0	2
Jim Slaton	0	0	3.00	4	0	0	0	0	6.0	6	2	0	2
Pete Vuckovich	1	0	0.00	2	1	0	0	0	5.1	2	0	3	4
TOTAL	2	3	3.48	21	5	0	1	0	44.0	46	17	9	22

GAME 1 AT MIL OCT 7

NY	000	400	001	5	13 1
MIL	011	010	000	3	8 3

Pitchers: Guidry, DAVIS (5), Gossage (8) vs HAAS, Bernard (4), McClure (5), Slaton (6), Fingers (8)
Home Runs: Gamble-NY
Attendance: 35,064

GAME 2 AT MIL OCT 8

NY	000	100	002	3	7 0
MIL	000	000	000	0	7 0

Pitchers: RIGHETTI, Davis (7), Gossage (7) vs CALDWELL, Slaton (7)
Home Runs: Piniella-NY, Jackson-NY
Attendance: 26,395

GAME 3 AT NY OCT 9

MIL	000	000	320	5	9 0
NY	000	100	200	3	8 2

Pitchers: Lerch, FINGERS (7) vs JOHN, May (8)
Home Runs: Simmons-MIL, Molitor-MIL
Attendance: 56,411

GAME 4 AT NY OCT 10

MIL	000	200	000	2	4 2
NY	000	001	000	1	5 0

Pitchers: VUCKOVICH, Easterly (6), Slaton (7), McClure (8), Fingers (9) vs REUSCHEL, Davis (7)
Attendance: 52,077

GAME 5 AT NY OCT 11

MIL	011	000	100	3	8 0
NY	000	400	12X	7	13 0

Pitchers: HAAS, Caldwell (4), Bernard (4), McClure (6), Slaton (7), Easterly (8), Vuckovich (8) vs Guidry, RIGHETTI (5), Gossage (8)
Home Runs: Thomas-MIL, Jackson-NY, Gamble-NY, Cerone-NY
Attendance: 47,505

First-half winner Oakland, with the league's best win-loss record over the full season, swept the division title from second-half champ Kansas City (who, with a full-season record of 50–53, had become the only club in major-league history to qualify for postseason play with a losing record). Twice in the opener the Royals loaded the bases against Mike Norris with fewer than two outs, but both times failed to score. Meanwhile, after a Royal error had prolonged the A's fourth inning, Wayne Gross homered for three unearned Oakland runs. Dwayne Murphy's eighth-inning solo shot gave the A's a fourth run. The game ended with Norris possessor of a four-hit shutout.

Game Two was closer. Oakland's Tony Armas doubled in a run in the top of the first, and doubled home another in the eighth (his fourth hit of the game) to break a 1–1 tie and provide the margin needed for pitcher Steve McCatty's six-hit win. The A's Rick Langford yielded ten hits in Game Three (including Kansas City's only extra-base hit of the series, a double), but only one Royal scored, meanwhile the A's were sending four runs across the plate—three of them by Rickey Henderson, who reached base four times on pairs of hits and walks.

Oakland Athletics, 3;
Kansas City Royals, 0

KC (W)

PLAYER/POS	AVG	G	AB	R	H	2B	3B	HR	RB	BB	SO	SB
Willie Aikens, 1b	.333	3	9	0	3	0	0	0	0	3	2	0
George Brett, 3b	.167	3	12	0	2	0	0	0	0	0	0	0
Cesar Geronimo, pr	.000	1	0	0	0	0	0	0	0	0	0	0
Larry Gura, p	.000	1	0	0	0	0	0	0	0	0	0	0
Clint Hurdle, of	.273	3	11	0	3	0	0	0	0	1	1	0
Mike Jones, p	.000	1	0	0	0	0	0	0	0	0	0	0
Dennis Leonard, p	.000	1	0	0	0	0	0	0	0	0	0	0
Renie Martin, p	.000	2	0	0	0	0	0	0	0	0	0	0
Lee May, 1b	.000	1	0	0	0	0	0	0	0	0	0	0
Hal Mc Rae, dh	.091	3	11	0	1	1	0	0	0	1	1	0
Amos Otis, of	.000	3	12	0	0	0	0	0	1	0	4	0
Dan Quisenberry, p	.000	1	0	0	0	0	0	0	0	0	0	0
U. L. Washington, ss	.222	3	9	0	2	0	0	0	0	0	1	0
John Wathan, c	.300	3	10	1	3	0	0	0	0	1	1	0
Frank White, 2b	.182	3	11	1	2	0	0	0	0	1	1	0
Willie Wilson, of	.308	3	13	0	4	0	0	0	0	1	0	0
TOTAL	.204		98	2	20	1	0	0	2	7	11	0

PITCHER	W	L	ERA	G	GS	CG	SV	SHO	IP	H	ER	BB	SO
Larry Gura	0	1	7.36	1	1	0	0	0	3.2	7	3	3	3
Mike Jones	0	1	2.25	1	1	0	0	0	8.0	9	2	0	2
Dennis Leonard	0	1	1.13	1	1	0	0	0	8.0	7	1	1	3
Renie Martin	0	0	0.00	2	0	0	0	0	5.1	1	0	2	2
Dan Quisenberry	0	0	0.00	1	0	0	0	0	1.0	1	0	0	0
TOTAL	0	3	2.08	6	3	0	0	0	26.0	25	6	6	10

OAK (W)

PLAYER/POS	AVG	G	AB	R	H	2B	3B	HR	RB	BB	SO	SB
Tony Armas, of	.545	3	11	1	6	2	0	0	3	1	1	0
Dave Beard, p	.000	1	0	0	0	0	0	0	0	0	0	0
Rick Bosetti, of	.000	1	0	0	0	0	0	0	0	0	0	0
Keith Drumright, dh	.250	1	4	0	1	0	0	0	0	0	0	0
Wayne Gross, 3b-1	.400	2	5	1	2	0	0	1	3	0	0	0
Mike Heath, c	.000	2	8	0	0	0	0	0	0	0	1	0
Rickey Henderson, of	.182	3	11	3	2	0	0	0	0	2	0	2
Cliff Johnson, dh	.286	2	7	0	2	1	0	0	0	0	1	0
Mickey Klutts, 3b	.143	2	7	0	1	0	0	0	0	0	1	0
Rick Langford, p	.000	1	0	0	0	0	0	0	0	0	0	0
Steve Mc Catty, p	.000	1	0	0	0	0	0	0	0	0	0	0
Dave Mc Kay, 2b	.273	3	11	0	3	0	0	1	1	1	1	0
Kelvin Moore, 1b	.000	2	8	0	0	0	0	0	0	0	2	0
Dwayne Murphy, of	.545	3	11	4	6	1	0	1	2	1	1	0
Jeff Newman, c	.000	1	3	0	0	0	0	0	0	0	1	0
Mike Norris, p	.000	1	0	0	0	0	0	0	0	0	0	0
Rob Picciolo, ss	.333	1	3	0	1	0	0	0	0	0	0	0
Jim Spencer, 1b	.250	1	4	0	1	1	0	0	0	0	0	0
Fred Stanley, ss	.000	3	6	0	0	0	0	0	0	1	1	0
Tom Underwood, p	.000	1	0	0	0	0	0	0	0	0	0	0
TOTAL	.253		99	10	25	5	0	3	9	6	10	2

PITCHER	W	L	ERA	G	GS	CG	SV	SHO	IP	H	ER	BB	SO
Dave Beard	0	0	0.00	1	0	0	1	0	1.1	0	0	0	2
Rick Langford	1	0	1.23	1	1	0	0	0	7.1	10	1	0	3
Steve Mc Catty	1	0	1.00	1	1	1	0	0	9.0	6	1	4	3
Mike Norris	1	0	0.00	1	1	1	0	1	9.0	4	0	3	2
Tom Underwood	0	0	0.00	1	0	0	0	0	0.1	0	0	0	1
TOTAL	3	0	0.67	5	3	2	1	1	27.0	20	2	7	11

GAME 1 AT KC OCT 6

OAK	000 300 010	4	8	2
KC	000 000 000	0	4	1

Pitchers: NORRIS vs LEONARD, Martin (9)
Home Runs: Gross-OAK, Murphy-OAK
Attendance: 40,592

GAME 2 AT KC OCT 7

OAK	100 000 010	2	10	1
KC	000 000 010	1	6	0

Pitchers: McCATTY vs JONES, Quisenberry (9)
Attendance: 40,274

GAME 3 AT OAK OCT 9

KC	000 100 000	1	10	3
OAK	101 200 00X	4	7	0

Pitchers: GURA, Martin (4) vs LANGFORD, Underwood (8), Beard (8)
Home Runs: McKay-OAK
Attendance: 40,002

The A's scored only four runs to their opponents' twenty as the Yankees swept the series. And only two of the six Yankee pitchers permitted an Oakland runner to score, while not one of Oakland's eight pitchers held New York scoreless. Even so, two of the three games were closely contested.

Oakland's Mike Norris gave up a bases-loaded double to Graig Nettles in the first inning of Game One before settling down to pitch shutout ball. But the three runs Nettles drove in were more than enough, as Tommy John and two relievers held the A's to a single run.

Game Two was the series' only blowout, and even it remained close for three innings. But, led by a pair of three-run homers from Nettles and Lou Piniella, the Yankees parlayed nineteen hits into thirteen runs as Yankee reliever George Frazier held the A's scoreless over the final five frames.

Game Three remained tight until the ninth. Through eight innings the only run came on Yankee Willie Randolph's homer off Oakland starter Matt Keough. But in the top of the ninth, Graig Nettles tagged reliever Tom Underwood for his second bases-clearing double of the series. The three runs weren't really needed, as Dave Righetti, Ron Davis, and Goose Gossage combined to shut out the A's for the full nine.

New York Yankees (East), 3;
Oakland A's (West), 0

NY (E)

PLAYER/POS	AVG	G	AB	R	H	2B	3B	HR	RBI	BB	SO	SB
Bobby Brown, of-2	1.000	3	1	2	1	0	0	0	0	0	0	0
Rick Cerone, c	.100	3	10	1	1	0	0	0	0	0	0	0
Ron Davis, p	.000	2	0	0	0	0	0	0	0	0	0	0
Barry Foote, c-1	1.000	2	1	0	1	0	0	0	0	0	0	0
George Frazier, p	.000	1	0	0	0	0	0	0	0	0	0	0
Oscar Gamble, dh-2,of-1	.167	3	6	2	1	0	0	0	0	1	5	3	0
Rich Gossage, p	.000	2	0	0	0	0	0	0	0	0	0	0
Reggie Jackson, of	.000	2	4	1	0	0	0	0	0	1	1	0	1
Tommy John, p	.000	1	0	0	0	0	0	0	0	0	0	0
Rudy May, p	.000	1	0	0	0	0	0	0	0	0	0	0
Larry Milbourne, ss	.462	3	13	4	6	0	0	0	1	0	0	0
Jerry Mumphrey, of	.500	3	12	2	6	1	0	0	0	3	2	0
Bobby Murcer, dh	.333	1	3	0	1	0	0	0	0	1	1	0
Graig Nettles, 3b	.500	3	12	2	6	2	0	1	9	1	0	0
Lou Piniella, dh-2,of-1	.600	3	5	2	3	0	0	1	3	0	0	0
Willie Randolph, 2b	.333	3	12	2	4	0	0	1	2	0	1	0
Dave Revering, 1b	.500	2	2	0	1	0	0	0	0	0	0	0
Dave Righetti, p	.000	1	0	0	0	0	0	0	0	0	0	0
Andre Robertson, ss	.000	1	1	0	0	0	0	0	0	0	0	0
Aurelio Rodriguez, 3b	.000	1	0	0	0	0	0	0	0	0	0	0
Bob Watson, 1b	.250	3	12	0	3	0	0	0	1	1	0	1
Dave Winfield, of	.154	3	13	2	2	1	0	0	2	1	2	1
TOTAL	.336		107	20	36	4	0	3	20	13	10	2

PITCHER	W	L	ERA	G	GS	CG	SV	SHO	IP	H	ER	BB	SO
Ron Davis	0	0	0.00	2	0	0	0	0	3.1	0	0	2	4
George Frazier	1	0	0.00	1	0	0	0	0	5.2	5	0	1	5
Rich Gossage	0	0	0.00	2	0	0	1	0	2.2	1	0	0	2
Tommy John	1	0	1.50	1	1	0	0	0	6.0	6	1	1	3
Rudy May	0	0	8.10	1	0	0	0	0	3.1	6	3	0	5
Dave Righetti	1	0	0.00	1	1	0	0	0	6.0	4	0	2	4
TOTAL	3	0	1.33	8	2	0	1	0	27.0	22	4	6	23

OAK (W)

PLAYER/POS	AVG	G	AB	R	H	2B	3B	HR	RBI	BB	SO	SB
Tony Armas, of	.167	3	12	0	2	0	0	0	0	0	5	0
Dave Beard, p	.000	1	0	0	0	0	0	0	0	0	0	0
Rick Bosetti, of-1,dh-1	.250	2	4	1	1	1	0	0	0	0	1	0
Mike Davis, ph	1.000	1	1	0	1	0	0	0	0	0	0	0
Keith Drumright, dh-1	.000	3	4	0	0	0	0	0	0	1	0	0
Wayne Gross, 3b	.000	3	5	0	0	0	0	0	0	0	0	0
Mike Heath, c-2,of-1	.333	3	6	1	2	0	0	0	0	0	1	0
Rickey Henderson, of	.364	3	11	0	4	2	1	0	1	1	2	2
Cliff Johnson, dh	.000	2	6	0	0	0	0	0	0	2	2	0
Jeff Jones, p	.000	1	0	0	0	0	0	0	0	0	0	0
Matt Keough, p	.000	1	0	0	0	0	0	0	0	0	0	0
Brian Kingman, p	.000	1	0	0	0	0	0	0	0	0	0	0
Mickey Klutts, 3b	.429	3	7	1	3	0	0	0	0	0	1	0
Steve Mc Catty, p	.000	1	0	0	0	0	0	0	0	0	0	0
Dave Mc Kay, 2b	.273	3	11	0	3	0	0	0	1	0	2	0
Kelvin Moore, 1b	.222	3	9	2	2	0	0	0	0	0	1	0
Dwayne Murphy, of	.250	3	8	0	2	1	0	0	1	2	3	0
Jeff Newman, c	.000	2	5	0	0	0	0	0	0	0	2	0
Mike Norris, p	.000	1	0	0	0	0	0	0	0	0	0	0
Bob Owchinko, p	.000	1	0	0	0	0	0	0	0	0	0	0
Rob Picciolo, ss	.200	2	5	1	1	0	0	0	0	0	2	0
Jim Spencer, 1b	.000	2	2	0	0	0	0	0	0	0	0	0
Fred Stanley, ss	.333	2	3	0	1	0	0	0	0	1	0	1	0
Tom Underwood, p	.000	2	0	0	0	0	0	0	0	0	0	0
TOTAL	.222		99	4	22	4	1	0	4	6	23	2

PITCHER	W	L	ERA	G	GS	CG	SV	SHO	IP	H	ER	BB	SO
Dave Beard	0	0	40.50	1	0	0	0	0	0.2	5	3	0	0
Jeff Jones	0	0	4.50	1	0	0	0	0	2.0	2	1	1	0
Matt Keough	0	1	1.08	1	1	0	0	0	8.1	7	1	6	2
Brian Kingman	0	0	81.00	1	0	0	0	0	0.1	3	3	0	0
Steve Mc Catty	0	1	13.50	1	1	0	0	0	3.1	6	5	2	2
Mike Norris	0	1	3.68	1	1	0	0	0	7.1	6	3	2	4
Bob Owchinko	0	0	5.40	1	0	0	0	0	1.2	3	1	0	0
Tom Underwood	0	0	13.50	2	0	0	0	0	1.1	4	2	2	2
TOTAL	0	3	6.84	9	3	0	0	0	25.0	36	19	13	10

GAME 1 AT NY OCT 13

OAK	000	010	000	1	6	1
NY	300	000	00X	3	7	1

Pitchers: NORRIS, Underwood (8) vs JOHN, Davis (7), Gossage (8)
Attendance: 55,740

GAME 2 AT NY OCT 14

OAK	001	200	000	3	11	1
NY	100	701	40X	13	19	0

Pitchers: McCATTY, Beard (4), Jones (5), Kingman (7), Owchinko (7) vs May, FRAZIER (4)
Home Runs: Piniella-NY, Nettles-NY
Attendance: 48,497

GAME 3 AT OAK OCT 15

NY	000	001	003	4	10	0
OAK	000	000	000	0	5	2

Pitchers: RIGHETTI, Davis (7), Gossage (9) vs KEOUGH, Underwood (9)
Home Runs: Randolph-NY
Attendance: 47,302

What the Yankees had done to the Dodgers three years earlier, the Dodgers now did to the Yankees in this, their eleventh meeting in the Series: they took the crown with four straight wins after losing the first two games. In the opener Bob Watson's first-inning three-run homer gave New York an insurmountable lead. Yankee starter Ron Guidry pitched seven strong innings, yielding just one run on a Steve Yeager homer, but two eighth-inning Dodger runs charged to reliever Ron Davis made things exciting until Yankee third baseman Graig Nettles dampened the rally with a splendid diving catch of Steve Garvey's line drive. In Game Two, Tommy John (now a Yankee) shut out his old teammates on three hits for seven innings. Reliever Goose Gossage completed the shutout, earning his second save in two days in the 3–0 Yankee victory.

But as the Series moved to Los Angeles, the Dodgers took the upper hand. Rookie ace Fernando Valenzuela experienced rocky going in the early innings of Game Three, yielding six hits (including home runs to Bob Watson and Rick Cerone) and four runs in the second and third innings. But Ron Cey's first-inning home run had given Los Angeles three early runs, and Dodger hitters added two more in the fifth as Valenzuela settled down to blank New York on three hits over the final six innings. The next day the Dodgers evened the Series with another close win. New York scored four times before the Dodgers got their first runs, but L.A. tied the game at 6–6 in the sixth and took an 8–6 lead an inning later. Reggie Jackson homered in the eighth to bring New York within one run of a tie, but they came no closer.

In Game Five, for the third day in a row, the Dodgers overcame a Yankee lead to claim a one-run victory. Dodger pitcher Jerry Reuss gave the Yankees a run on two hits in the second inning, but shut them out on just three additional hits the rest of the way. Yankee starter Ron Guidry, meanwhile, stopped the Dodgers on two hits through the first six innings, but then gave up back-to-back homers to Pedro Guerrero and Steve Yeager in the seventh—runs enough for a 2–1 Dodger win. The final game was close for four innings, but in the fifth and sixth the Dodgers broke it open with seven runs and coasted in on Steve Howe's 3⅔ innings of shutout relief to a 9–2 win and, including 1900, their sixth world championship.

Los Angeles Dodgers (NL), 4; New York Yankees (AL), 2

LA (N)

PLAYER/POS	AVG	G	AB	R	H	2B	3B	HR	RB	BB	SO	SB
Dusty Baker, of	.167	6	24	3	4	0	0	0	1	1	6	0
Bobby Castillo, p	.000	1	0	0	0	0	0	0	0	0	0	0
Ron Cey, 3b	.350	6	20	3	7	0	0	1	6	3	3	0
Terry Forster, p	.000	2	0	0	0	0	0	0	0	0	0	0
Steve Garvey, 1b	.417	6	24	3	10	1	0	0	0	2	5	0
Dave Goltz, p	.000	2	0	0	0	0	0	0	0	0	0	0
Pedro Guerrero, of	.333	6	21	2	7	1	1	2	7	2	6	0
Burt Hooton, p	.000	2	4	1	0	0	0	0	0	1	3	0
Steve Howe, p	.000	3	2	0	0	0	0	0	0	0	2	0
Jay Johnstone, ph	.667	3	3	1	2	0	0	1	3	0	0	0
Ken Landreaux, of-3	.167	5	6	1	1	1	0	0	0	0	2	1
Davey Lopes, 2b	.227	6	22	6	5	1	0	0	2	4	3	4
Rick Monday, of-4	.231	5	13	1	3	1	0	0	0	3	6	0
Tom Niedenfuer, p	.000	2	0	0	0	0	0	0	0	0	0	0
Jerry Reuss, p	.000	2	3	0	0	0	0	0	0	1	2	0
Bill Russell, ss	.240	6	25	1	6	0	0	0	2	0	1	1
Steve Sax, 2b-1	.000	2	1	0	0	0	0	0	0	0	0	0
Mike Scioscia, c	.250	3	4	1	1	0	0	0	0	1	0	0
Reggie Smith, ph	.500	2	2	0	1	0	0	0	0	0	1	0
Dave Stewart, p	.000	2	0	0	0	0	0	0	0	0	0	0
Derrel Thomas, of-3,3b-2,ss-1	.000	5	7	2	0	0	0	0	0	1	1	2	0
Fernando Valenzuela, p	.000	1	3	0	0	0	0	0	0	1	0	0
Bob Welch, p	.000	1	0	0	0	0	0	0	0	0	0	0
Steve Yeager, c	.286	6	14	2	4	1	0	2	4	0	2	0
TOTAL	.258		198	27	51	6	1	6	26	20	44	6

PITCHER	W	L	ERA	G	GS	CG	SV	SHO	IP	H	ER	BB	SO
Bobby Castillo	0	0	9.00	1	0	0	0	0	1.0	0	1	5	0
Terry Forster	0	0	0.00	2	0	0	0	0	2.0	1	0	3	0
Dave Goltz	0	0	5.40	2	0	0	0	0	3.1	4	2	1	2
Burt Hooton	1	1	1.59	2	2	0	0	0	11.1	8	2	9	3
Steve Howe	1	0	3.86	3	0	0	1	0	7.0	7	3	1	4
Tom Niedenfuer	0	0	0.00	2	0	0	0	0	5.0	3	0	1	0
Jerry Reuss	1	1	3.86	2	2	1	0	0	11.2	10	5	3	8
Dave Stewart	0	0	0.00	2	0	0	0	0	1.2	1	0	2	1
Fernando Valenzuela	1	0	4.00	1	1	1	0	0	9.0	9	4	7	6
Bob Welch	0	0	INF	1	1	0	0	0	0.0	3	2	1	0
TOTAL	4	2	3.29	18	6	2	1	0	52.0	46	19	33	24

NY (A)

PLAYER/POS	AVG	G	AB	R	H	2B	3B	HR	RB	BB	SO	SB
Bobby Brown, of-2	.000	4	1	1	0	0	0	0	0	0	1	0
Rick Cerone, c	.190	6	21	2	4	1	0	1	3	4	2	0
Ron Davis, p	.000	4	0	0	0	0	0	0	0	0	0	0
Barry Foote, ph	.000	1	1	0	0	0	0	0	0	0	1	0
George Frazier, p	.000	3	2	0	0	0	0	0	0	0	1	0
Oscar Gamble, of-2	.333	3	6	1	2	0	0	0	1	1	0	0
Rich Gossage, p	.000	3	1	0	0	0	0	0	0	0	1	0
Ron Guidry, p	.000	2	5	0	0	0	0	0	0	0	3	0
Reggie Jackson, of	.333	3	12	3	4	1	0	1	1	2	3	0
Tommy John, p	.000	3	2	0	0	0	0	0	0	0	0	0
Dave La Roche, p	.000	1	0	0	0	0	0	0	0	0	0	0
Rudy May, p	.000	3	1	0	0	0	0	0	0	0	0	0
Larry Milbourne, ss	.250	6	20	2	5	2	0	0	3	4	0	0
Jerry Mumphrey, of	.200	5	15	2	3	0	0	0	0	3	2	1
Bobby Murcer, ph	.000	4	3	0	0	0	0	0	0	0	0	0
Graig Nettles, 3b	.400	3	10	1	4	1	0	0	0	1	1	0
Lou Piniella, of-3	.438	6	16	2	7	1	0	0	3	0	1	0
Willie Randolph, 2b	.222	6	18	5	4	1	1	2	3	9	0	1
Rick Reuschel, p	.000	2	2	0	0	0	0	0	0	0	1	0
Dave Righetti, p	.000	1	1	0	0	0	0	0	0	0	1	0
Andre Robertson, pr	.000	1	0	0	0	0	0	0	0	0	0	0
Aurelio Rodriguez, 3b-3	.417	4	12	1	5	0	0	0	0	1	2	0
Bob Watson, 1b	.318	6	22	2	7	1	0	2	7	3	0	0
Dave Winfield, of	.045	6	22	0	1	0	0	0	1	5	4	1
TOTAL	.238		193	22	46	8	1	6	22	33	24	4

PITCHER	W	L	ERA	G	GS	CG	SV	SHO	IP	H	ER	BB	SO
Ron Davis	0	0	23.14	4	0	0	0	0	2.1	4	6	5	4
George Frazier	0	3	17.18	3	0	0	0	0	3.2	9	7	3	2
Rich Gossage	0	0	0.00	3	0	0	2	0	5.0	2	0	2	5
Ron Guidry	1	1	1.93	2	2	0	0	0	14.0	8	3	4	15
Tommy John	1	0	0.69	3	2	0	0	0	13.0	11	1	0	8
Dave La Roche	0	0	0.00	1	0	0	0	0	1.0	0	0	0	2
Rudy May	0	0	2.84	3	0	0	0	0	6.1	5	2	1	5
Rick Reuschel	0	0	4.91	2	1	0	0	0	3.2	7	2	3	2
Dave Righetti	0	0	13.50	1	1	0	0	0	2.0	5	3	2	1
TOTAL	2	4	4.24	18	6	0	2	0	51.0	51	24	20	44

GAME 1 AT NY OCT 20

LA	000	010	020	3	5	0
NY	301	100	00X	5	6	0

Pitchers: REUSS, Castillo (3), Goltz (4), Niedenfuer (5), Stewart (8) vs GUIDRY, Davis (8), Gossage (8)
Home Runs: Watson-NY, Yeager-LA
Attendance: 56,470

GAME 2 AT NY OCT 21

LA	000	000	000	0	4	2
NY	000	010	02X	3	6	1

Pitchers: HOOTON, Forster (7), Howe (8), Stewart (8) vs JOHN, Gossage (8)
Attendance: 56,505

GAME 3 AT LA OCT 23

NY	022	000	000	4	9	0
LA	300	020	00X	5	11	1

Pitchers: Righetti, FRAZIER (3), May (5), Davis (8) vs VALENZUELA
Home Runs: Cey-LA, Watson-NY, Cerone-NY
Attendance: 56,236

GAME 4 AT LA OCT 24

NY	211	002	010	7	13	1
LA	002	013	20X	8	14	2

Pitchers: Reuschel, May (4), Davis (5), FRAZIER (5), John (7) vs Welch, Goltz (1), Forster (4), Niedenfuer (5), HOWE (7)
Home Runs: Johnstone-LA, Randolph-NY, Jackson-NY
Attendance: 56,242

GAME 5 AT LA OCT 25

NY	010	000	000	1	5	0
LA	000	000	20X	2	4	3

Pitchers: GUIDRY, Gossage (8) vs REUSS
Home Runs: Guerrero-LA, Yeager-LA
Attendance: 56,115

GAME 6 AT NY OCT 28

LA	000	134	010	9	13	1
NY	001	001	000	2	7	2

Pitchers: HOOTON, Howe (6) vs John, FRAZIER (5), Davis (6), Reuschel (6), May (7), LaRoche (9)
Home Runs: Guerrero-LA, Randolph-NY
Attendance: 56,513

The official records show Atlanta ahead and threatening only once in a three-game series swept by the Cardinals. But in the original Game One, Phil Niekro held a slim 1–0 Atlanta lead in the fifth inning when rain wiped out the game just before it could become official.

In the first official game, the Braves scored nothing at all as Bob Forsch held them to three hits. Atlanta's Pascual Perez gave up only one run through the first five innings, but the Cardinals exploded for five runs in the sixth to put the game away. Following another rainout, Niekro tried again in Game Two. He gave up a run in the first, but Atlanta came back with three before he yielded a second run in the sixth. Gene Garber, who relieved Niekro, gave up the tying run in the eighth and lost the game in the bottom of the ninth on Ken Oberkfell's RBI liner over the center fielder's head.

Joaquin Andujar shut out the Braves through six innings of Game Three before giving up two runs in the seventh. But by then St. Louis had scored five times. Bruce Sutter retired the last seven Braves in relief of Andujar, and the Cardinals had their pennant.

St. Louis Cardinals (East), 3; Atlanta Braves (West), 0

STL (E)

PLAYER/POS	AVG	G	AB	R	H	2B	3B	HR	RB	BB	SO	SB
Joaquin Andujar, p	.000	1	1	0	0	0	0	0	0	0	1	0
Doug Bair, p	.000	1	0	0	0	0	0	0	0	0	0	0
Steve Braun, ph	.000	1	1	0	0	0	0	0	0	0	0	0
Bob Forsch, p	.667	1	3	1	2	0	0	0	1	0	0	0
David Green, of	1.000	2	1	1	1	0	0	0	0	0	0	0
George Hendrick, of	.308	3	13	2	4	0	0	0	2	1	2	0
Keith Hernandez, 1b	.333	3	12	3	4	0	0	0	1	2	3	0
Tommy Herr, 2b	.231	3	13	1	3	1	0	0	0	1	2	0
Willie Mc Gee, of	.308	3	13	4	4	0	2	1	5	0	5	0
Ken Oberkfell, 3b	.200	3	15	1	3	0	0	0	2	0	0	0
Darrell Porter, c	.556	3	9	3	5	3	0	0	1	5	2	0
Lonnie Smith, of	.273	3	11	3	3	0	0	0	1	0	1	0
Ozzie Smith, ss	.556	3	9	0	5	0	0	0	3	3	0	1
John Stuper, p	.000	1	1	0	0	0	0	0	0	0	0	0
Bruce Sutter, p	.000	2	1	0	0	0	0	0	0	0	0	0
TOTAL	.330		103	17	34	4	2	1	16	12	16	1

PITCHER	W	L	ERA	G	GS	CG	SV	SHO	IP	H	ER	BB	SO
Joaquin Andujar	1	0	2.70	1	1	0	0	0	6.2	6	2	2	4
Doug Bair	0	0	0.00	1	0	0	0	0	1.0	2	0	3	0
Bob Forsch	1	0	0.00	1	1	0	1	0	9.0	3	0	0	6
John Stuper	0	0	3.00	1	1	0	0	0	6.0	4	2	1	4
Bruce Sutter	1	0	0.00	2	0	0	1	0	4.1	0	0	0	1
TOTAL	3	0	1.33	6	3	1	1	1	27.0	15	4	6	15

ATL (W)

PLAYER/POS	AVG	G	AB	R	H	2B	3B	HR	RB	BB	SO	SB
Steve Bedrosian, p	.000	2	0	0	0	0	0	0	0	0	0	0
Bruce Benedict, c	.250	3	8	1	2	1	0	0	0	2	1	0
Brett Butler, of-1	.000	2	1	0	0	0	0	0	0	0	0	0
Rick Camp, p	.000	1	0	0	0	0	0	0	0	0	0	0
Chris Chambliss, 1b	.000	3	10	0	0	0	0	0	0	1	0	0
Gene Garber, p	.000	2	1	0	0	0	0	0	0	0	0	0
Terry Harper, of	.000	1	1	0	0	0	0	0	0	0	0	0
Bob Horner, 3b	.091	3	11	0	1	0	0	0	0	0	2	0
Glenn Hubbard, 2b	.222	3	9	1	2	0	0	0	1	0	3	0
Rick Mahler, p	.000	1	0	0	0	0	0	0	0	0	0	0
Donnie Moore, p	.000	2	0	0	0	0	0	0	0	0	0	0
Dale Murphy, of	.273	3	11	1	3	0	0	0	0	0	2	1
Phil Niekro, p	.000	1	0	0	0	0	0	0	1	0	0	0
Pascual Perez, p	.000	2	3	0	0	0	0	0	0	0	1	0
Biff Pocoroba, ph	.000	1	1	0	0	0	0	0	0	0	0	0
Rafael Ramirez, ss	.182	3	11	1	2	0	0	0	1	1	1	0
Jerry Royster, of-3,3b-1	.182	3	11	0	2	0	0	0	0	0	2	0
Bob Walk, p	.000	1	0	0	0	0	0	0	0	0	0	0
Claudell Washington, of	.333	3	9	0	3	0	0	0	0	2	2	0
Larry Whisenton, ph	.000	2	2	0	0	0	0	0	0	0	1	0
TOTAL	.169		89	5	15	1	0	0	3	6	15	1

PITCHER	W	L	ERA	G	GS	CG	SV	SHO	IP	H	ER	BB	SO
Steve Bedrosian	0	0	18.00	2	0	0	0	0	1.0	3	2	1	2
Rick Camp	0	1	36.00	1	1	0	0	0	1.0	4	4	1	0
Gene Garber	0	1	8.10	2	0	0	0	0	3.1	4	3	1	3
Rick Mahler	0	0	0.00	1	0	0	0	0	1.2	3	0	2	0
Donnie Moore	0	0	0.00	2	0	0	0	0	2.2	2	0	0	1
Phil Niekro	0	0	3.00	1	1	0	0	0	6.0	6	2	4	5
Pascual Perez	0	1	5.19	2	1	0	0	0	8.2	10	5	2	4
Bob Walk	0	0	9.00	1	0	0	0	0	1.0	2	1	1	1
TOTAL	0	3	6.04	12	3	0	0	0	25.1	34	17	12	16

GAME 1 AT STL OCT 7

ATL	000	000	000	0	3	0
STL	001	005	01X	7	13	1

Pitchers: PEREZ, Bedrosian (6), Moore (6), Walk (8) vs FORSCH
Attendance: 53,008

GAME 2 AT STL OCT 9

ATL	002	010	000	3	6	0
STL	100	001	011	4	9	1

Pitchers: Niekro, GARBER (7) vs Stuper, Bair (7), SUTTER (8)
Attendance: 53,408

GAME 3 AT ATL OCT 10

STL	040	010	001	6	12	0
ATL	000	000	200	2	6	1

Pitchers: ANDUJAR, Sutter (7) vs CAMP, Perez (2), Moore (5), Mahler (7), Bedrosian (8), Garber (9)
Home Runs: McGee-STL
Attendance: 52,173

For the first time in LCS play, a club won the first two games but lost the series. The Angels overcame a 1–3 deficit to take Game One, with four runs in the third and three more later, while starter Tommy John settled down to stop the Brewers through the final six innings. In Game Two Bruce Kison prevailed, as the Angels built a 4–0 lead over Milwaukee and Pete Vuckovich before Kison gave up what proved to be a harmless two-run homer to Paul Molitor in the fifth.

With three chances to clinch the pennant, California three times fell short. In the third game, their three eighth-inning runs couldn't catch the Brewers, who already had five. In Game Four, Don Baylor's eighth-inning grand slam completed Angel scoring at five runs, but Milwaukee had already scored seven, and they added two more. In the finale, Kison held a 3–2 lead when he was relieved after five innings. But Cecil Cooper singled off Luis Sanchez in the seventh (with two out and the bases loaded) for two runs and a Brewer lead. Bob McClure and Pete Ladd held off the Angels through the final two innings, and the Brewers were on their way to their first World Series.

Milwaukee Brewers (East), 3; California Angels (West), 2

MIL (E)

PLAYER/POS	AVG	G	AB	R	H	2B	3B	HR	RB	BB	SO	SB
Dwight Bernard, p	.000	1	0	0	0	0	0	0	0	0	0	0
Mark Brouhard, of	.750	1	4	4	3	1	0	1	3	0	0	0
Mike Caldwell, p	.000	1	0	0	0	0	0	0	0	0	0	0
Cecil Cooper, 1b	.150	5	20	1	3	2	0	0	4	0	6	0
Marshall Edwards, dh-2,of-1	.000	3	1	2	0	0	0	0	0	0	0	1
Jim Gantner, 2b	.188	5	16	1	3	0	0	0	2	1	1	0
Moose Haas, p	.000	1	0	0	0	0	0	0	0	0	0	0
Roy Howell, dh	.000	1	3	0	0	0	0	0	0	0	1	0
Pete Ladd, p	.000	3	0	0	0	0	0	0	0	0	0	0
Bob Mc Clure, p	.000	1	0	0	0	0	0	0	0	0	0	0
Paul Molitor, 3b	.316	5	19	4	6	1	0	2	5	2	3	1
Don Money, dh	.182	4	11	2	2	0	0	0	1	3	1	0
Charlie Moore, of	.462	5	13	3	6	0	0	0	0	1	2	0
Ben Oglivie, of	.133	4	15	1	2	0	0	1	1	0	3	0
Ted Simmons, c	.167	5	18	3	3	0	0	0	1	1	4	0
Jim Slaton, p	.000	2	0	0	0	0	0	0	0	0	0	0
Don Sutton, p	.000	1	0	0	0	0	0	0	0	0	0	0
Gorman Thomas, of	.067	5	15	1	1	0	0	1	3	2	7	0
Pete Vuckovich, p	.000	2	0	0	0	0	0	0	0	0	0	0
Robin Yount, ss	.250	5	16	1	4	0	0	0	0	5	0	0
TOTAL	.219		151	23	33	4	0	5	20	15	28	2

PITCHER	W	L	ERA	G	GS	CG	SV	SHO	IP	H	ER	BB	SO
Dwight Bernard	0	0	0.00	1	0	0	0	0	1.0	0	0	0	0
Mike Caldwell	0	1	15.00	1	1	0	0	0	3.0	7	5	1	2
Moose Haas	1	0	4.91	1	1	0	0	0	7.1	5	4	5	7
Pete Ladd	0	0	0.00	3	0	0	2	0	3.1	0	0	0	5
Bob Mc Clure	1	0	0.00	1	0	0	0	0	1.2	2	0	0	0
Jim Slaton	0	0	1.93	2	0	0	1	0	4.2	3	1	1	3
Don Sutton	1	0	3.52	1	1	0	0	0	7.2	8	3	2	9
Pete Vuckovich	0	1	4.40	2	2	1	0	0	14.1	15	7	7	8
TOTAL	3	2	4.19	12	5	1	3	0	43.0	40	20	16	34

CAL (W)

PLAYER/POS	AVG	G	AB	R	H	2B	3B	HR	RB	BB	SO	SB
Don Baylor, dh	.294	5	17	2	5	1	1	1	10	2	0	0
Juan Beniquez, of	.000	2	0	0	0	0	0	0	0	0	0	0
Bob Boone, c	.250	5	16	3	4	0	0	1	4	0	2	0
Rod Carew, 1b	.176	5	17	2	3	1	0	0	0	4	4	1
Bobby Clark, of	.000	2	0	0	0	0	0	0	0	0	0	0
Doug De Cinces, 3b	.316	5	19	5	6	2	0	0	0	1	5	0
Brian Downing, of	.158	5	19	4	3	1	0	0	0	3	2	0
Tim Foli, ss	.125	5	16	2	2	0	0	0	1	0	3	0
Dave Goltz, p	.000	1	0	0	0	0	0	0	0	0	0	0
Bobby Grich, 2b	.200	5	15	1	3	1	0	0	1	2	7	0
Andy Hassler, p	.000	2	0	0	0	0	0	0	0	0	0	0
Reggie Jackson, of	.111	5	18	2	2	0	0	1	2	2	7	0
Ron Jackson, ph	1.000	1	1	0	1	0	0	0	0	0	0	0
Tommy John, p	.000	2	0	0	0	0	0	0	0	0	0	0
Bruce Kison, p	.000	2	0	0	0	0	0	0	0	0	0	0
Fred Lynn, of	.611	5	18	4	11	2	0	1	5	2	3	0
Luis Sanchez, p	.000	2	0	0	0	0	0	0	0	0	0	0
Rob Wilfong, ph	.000	2	1	0	0	0	0	0	0	0	1	0
Mike Witt, p	.000	1	0	0	0	0	0	0	0	0	0	0
Geoff Zahn, p	.000	1	0	0	0	0	0	0	0	0	0	0
TOTAL	.255		157	23	40	8	1	4	23	16	34	1

PITCHER	W	L	ERA	G	GS	CG	SV	SHO	IP	H	ER	BB	SO
Dave Goltz	0	0	7.36	1	0	0	0	0	3.2	4	3	2	2
Andy Hassler	0	0	0.00	2	0	0	0	0	2.2	0	0	0	2
Tommy John	1	1	5.11	2	2	1	0	0	12.1	11	7	6	6
Bruce Kison	1	0	1.93	2	2	1	0	0	14.0	8	3	3	12
Luis Sanchez	0	1	6.75	2	0	0	0	0	2.2	4	2	1	1
Mike Witt	0	0	6.00	1	0	0	0	0	3.0	2	2	2	3
Geoff Zahn	0	1	7.36	1	1	0	0	0	3.2	4	3	1	2
TOTAL	2	3	4.29	11	5	2	0	0	42.0	33	20	15	28

GAME 1 AT CAL OCT 5

MIL	021	000	000	3	7 2
CAL	104	210	00X	8	10 0

Pitchers: CALDWELL, Slaton (4), Ladd (7), Bernard (8) vs JOHN
Home Runs: Thomas-MIL, Lynn-CAL
Attendance: 64,406

GAME 2 AT CAL OCT 6

MIL	000	020	000	2	5 0
CAL	021	100	00X	4	6 0

Pitchers: VUCKOVICH vs KISON
Home Runs: Re.Jackson-CAL, Molitor-MIL
Attendance: 64,179

GAME 3 AT MIL OCT 8

CAL	000	000	030	3	8 0
MIL	000	300	20X	5	6 0

Pitchers: ZAHN, Witt (4), Hassler (7) vs SUTTON, Ladd (8)
Home Runs: Molitor-MIL, Boone-CAL
Attendance: 50,135

GAME 4 AT MIL OCT 9

CAL	000	001	040	5	5 3
MIL	030	301	02X	9	9 2

Pitchers: JOHN, Goltz (4), Sanchez (8) vs HAAS, Slaton (8)
Home Runs: Baylor-CAL, Brouhard-MIL
Attendance: 51,003

GAME 5 AT MIL OCT 10

CAL	101	100	000	3	11 1
MIL	100	100	20X	4	6 4

Pitchers: Kison, SANCHEZ (6), Hassler (7) vs Vuckovich, McCLURE (7), Ladd (9)
Home Runs: Oglivie-MIL
Attendance: 54,968

The Series was anticipated as a matchup of Cardinal speed and Brewer power. In the event, though, St. Louis outslugged the Brewers and wound up with their tenth world championship.

The Brewers, in their first World Series, looked unstoppable in the opening game. Hammering four Cardinal pitchers for seventeen hits (including a record five for Paul Molitor), they scored ten runs while pitcher Mike Caldwell was shutting out the Cards on three hits. In the second game Milwaukee continued the onslaught, building an early 3–0 lead. But St. Louis finally got on the scoreboard with two runs in the last of the third, and tied the game at 4–4 in the sixth on Darrell Porter's two-RBI double. And the Cards won the game on a bases-loaded walk in the eighth as relievers Doug Bair and Bruce Sutter held the Brewers scoreless over the final four innings.

St. Louis pushed into the Series lead in Game Three, thanks mostly to the 6⅓ shutout innings of starter Joaquin Andujar and the fielding and batting of center fielder Willie McGee. McGee drove in four of the six Cardinal runs with a pair of homers and prevented an extra-base hit and a two-run Brewer homer with leaping catches in the first and final innings. The Cards pressed their advantage in Game Four with four early runs. But in the last of the seventh (with the score now 5–1), an error by Cardinal pitcher Dave La Point opened the way for Milwaukee to win the game with six two-out runs on a barrage of hits (and the added assistance of a pair of walks and a wild pitch).

Brewer pitcher Mike Caldwell wasn't as effective in Game Five as he had been in the opener, yielding fourteen hits and four runs in 8⅓ innings of work. But he was never behind in the game as his teammates, with eleven hits of their own (four of them by Robin Yount, including a home run) and several fielding gems put Milwaukee ahead again in the Series with a 6–4 win.

The Cards had their backs to the wall as the Series moved to St. Louis for the final games. But in Game Six the Cards responded to their opening-game humiliation with a laugher of their own, 13–1, on John Stuper's four-hitter. And in the finale they rocked Brewer ace Pete Vuckovich and three relievers for fifteen hits and a 6–3 victory that gave starter Joaquin Andujar his second Series win and reliever Bruce Sutter his second save.

St. Louis Cardinals (NL), 4;
Milwaukee Brewers (AL), 3

STL (N)

PLAYER/POS	AVG	G	AB	R	H	2B	3B	HR	RB	BB	SO	SB
Joaquin Andujar, p	.000	2	0	0	0	0	0	0	0	0	0	0
Doug Bair, p	.000	3	0	0	0	0	0	0	0	0	0	0
Steve Braun, dh	.500	2	2	0	1	0	0	0	2	1	0	0
Glenn Brummer, c	.000	1	0	0	0	0	0	0	0	0	0	0
Bob Forsch, p	.000	2	0	0	0	0	0	0	0	0	0	0
David Green, of-4,dh-3	.200	7	10	3	2	1	1	0	0	1	3	0
George Hendrick, of	.321	7	28	5	9	0	0	0	5	2	2	0
Keith Hernandez, 1b	.259	7	27	4	7	2	0	1	8	4	2	0
Tommy Herr, 2b	.160	7	25	2	4	2	0	0	5	3	3	0
Dane Iorg, dh	.529	5	17	4	9	4	1	0	1	0	0	0
Jim Kaat, p	.000	4	0	0	0	0	0	0	0	0	0	0
Jeff Lahti, p	.000	2	0	0	0	0	0	0	0	0	0	0
Dave La Point, p	.000	2	0	0	0	0	0	0	0	0	0	0
Willie Mc Gee, of	.240	6	25	6	6	0	0	2	5	1	3	0
Ken Oberkfell, 3b	.292	7	24	4	7	1	0	0	1	2	1	2
Darrell Porter, c	.286	7	28	1	8	2	0	1	5	1	4	0
Mike Ramsey, 3b-2	.000	3	1	1	0	0	0	0	0	0	1	0
Lonnie Smith, of-6,dh-1	.321	7	28	6	9	4	1	0	1	1	5	2
Ozzie Smith, ss	.208	7	24	3	5	0	0	0	1	3	0	1
John Stuper, p	.000	2	0	0	0	0	0	0	0	0	0	0
Bruce Sutter, p	.000	4	0	0	0	0	0	0	0	0	0	0
Gene Tenace, dh-1	.000	5	6	0	0	0	0	0	0	1	2	0
TOTAL	.273		245	39	67	16	3	4	34	20	26	7

PITCHER	W	L	ERA	G	GS	CG	SV	SHO	IP	H	ER	BB	SO
Joaquin Andujar	2	0	1.35	2	2	0	0	0	13.1	10	2	1	4
Doug Bair	0	1	9.00	3	0	0	0	0	2.0	2	2	2	3
Bob Forsch	0	2	4.97	2	2	0	0	0	12.2	18	7	3	4
Jim Kaat	0	0	3.86	4	0	0	0	0	2.1	4	1	2	2
Jeff Lahti	0	0	10.80	2	0	0	0	0	1.2	4	2	1	1
Dave La Point	0	0	3.24	2	1	0	0	0	8.1	10	3	2	3
John Stuper	1	0	3.46	2	2	1	0	0	13.0	10	5	5	5
Bruce Sutter	1	0	4.70	4	0	0	2	0	7.2	6	4	3	6
TOTAL	4	3	3.84	21	7	1	2	0	61.0	64	26	19	28

MIL (A)

PLAYER/POS	AVG	G	AB	R	H	2B	3B	HR	RB	BB	SO	SB
Dwight Bernard, p	.000	1	0	0	0	0	0	0	0	0	0	0
Mike Caldwell, p	.000	3	0	0	0	0	0	0	0	0	0	0
Cecil Cooper, 1b	.286	7	28	3	8	1	0	1	6	1	1	0
Marshall Edwards, of	.000	1	0	0	0	0	0	0	0	0	0	0
Jim Gantner, 2b	.333	7	24	5	8	4	1	0	4	1	1	0
Moose Haas, p	.000	2	0	0	0	0	0	0	0	0	0	0
Roy Howell, dh	.000	4	11	1	0	0	0	0	0	0	3	0
Pete Ladd, p	.000	1	0	0	0	0	0	0	0	0	0	0
Bob Mc Clure, p	.000	5	0	0	0	0	0	0	0	0	0	0
Doc Medich, p	.000	1	0	0	0	0	0	0	0	0	0	0
Paul Molitor, 3b	.355	7	31	5	11	0	0	0	3	2	4	1
Don Money, dh-4	.231	5	13	4	3	1	0	0	1	2	3	0
Charlie Moore, of	.346	7	26	3	9	3	0	0	2	1	0	0
Ben Oglivie, of	.222	7	27	4	6	0	1	1	1	2	4	0
Ted Simmons, c	.174	7	23	2	4	0	0	2	3	5	3	0
Jim Slaton, p	.000	2	0	0	0	0	0	0	0	0	0	0
Don Sutton, p	.000	2	0	0	0	0	0	0	0	0	0	0
Gorman Thomas, of	.115	7	26	0	3	0	0	0	3	2	7	0
Ned Yost, c	.000	1	0	0	0	0	0	0	0	1	0	0
Robin Yount, ss	.414	7	29	6	12	3	0	1	6	2	2	0
TOTAL	.269		238	33	64	12	2	5	29	19	28	1

PITCHER	W	L	ERA	G	GS	CG	SV	SHO	IP	H	ER	BB	SO
Dwight Bernard	0	0	0.00	1	0	0	0	0	1.0	0	0	0	1
Mike Caldwell	2	0	2.04	3	2	1	0	1	17.2	19	4	3	6
Moose Haas	0	0	7.36	2	1	0	0	0	7.1	8	6	3	4
Pete Ladd	0	0	0.00	1	0	0	0	0	0.2	1	0	2	0
Bob Mc Clure	0	2	4.15	5	0	0	2	0	4.1	5	2	3	5
Doc Medich	0	0	18.00	1	0	0	0	0	2.0	5	4	1	0
Jim Slaton	1	0	0.00	2	0	0	0	0	2.2	1	0	2	1
Don Sutton	0	1	7.84	2	2	0	0	0	10.1	12	9	1	5
Pete Vuckovich	0	1	4.50	2	2	0	0	0	14.0	16	7	5	4
TOTAL	3	4	4.80	19	7	1	2	1	60.0	67	32	20	26

GAME 1 AT STL OCT 12

MIL	200	112	004	10	17	0
STL	000	000	000	0	3	1

Pitchers: CALDWELL vs FORSCH, Kaat (6), LaPoint (8), Lahti (9)
Home Runs: Simmoms-MIL
Attendance: 53,723

GAME 2 AT STL OCT 13

MIL	012	010	000	4	10	1
STL	002	002	01X	5	8	0

Pitchers: Sutton, McCLURE (7), Ladd (8) vs Stuper, Kaat (5), Bair (5), SUTTER (7)
Home Runs: Simmons-MIL
Attendance: 53,723

GAME 3 AT MIL OCT 15

STL	000	030	201	6	6	1
MIL	000	000	020	2	5	3

Pitchers: ANDUJAR, Kaat (7), Bair (7), Sutter (7) vs VUCKOVICH, McClure (9)
Home Runs: McGee-STL (2), Cooper-MIL
Attendance: 56,556

GAME 4 AT MIL OCT 16

STL	130	001	000	5	8	1
MIL	000	000	60X	7	10	2

Pitchers: LaPoint, BAIR (7), Kaat (7), Lahti (7) vs Haas, SLATON (6), McClure (8)
Attendance: 56,560

GAME 5 AT MIL OCT 17

STL	001	000	102	4	15	2
MIL	101	010	12X	6	11	1

Pitchers: FORSCH, Sutter (8) vs CALDWELL, McClure (9)
Home Runs: Yount-MIL
Attendance: 56,562

GAME 6 AT STL OCT 19

MIL	000	000	001	1	4	4
STL	020	326	00X	13	12	1

Pitchers: SUTTON, Slaton (6), Medich (6), Bernard (8) vs STUPER
Home Runs: Porter-STL, Hernandez-STL
Attendance: 53,723

GAME 7 AT STL OCT 20

MIL	000	012	000	3	7	0
STL	000	103	02X	6	15	1

Pitchers: Vuckovich, McCLURE (6), Haas (6), Caldwell (8) vs ANDUJAR, Sutter (8)
Home Runs: Oglivie-MIL
Attendance: 53,723

The Dodgers earned only four runs off Philadelphia pitching, and even though they doubled their run total to eight on unearned runs, the Phillies scored twice that number to take the pennant in four games.

Mike Schmidt homered off Jerry Reuss in the first inning of the opener for the game's only run. Phillie starter Steve Carlton loaded the bases in the eighth, but Al Holland came on to get the third out and preserve the shutout. The Phillies also scored only one run in the second game, on Gary Matthews's homer off Fernando Valenzuela in the second. But this time the run only tied the score, and in the fifth Pedro Guerrero tripled in two unearned runs to give Valenzuela the Dodgers' only win.

The Phillies' Charlie Hudson hurled the series' only complete game—a four-hitter—to win Game Three. Gary Matthews's four hits in Game Three and Four included his second and third series homers, and drove in half the Phillies' fourteen runs as they took the two games by identical 7–2 scores.

Philadelphia Phillies (East), 3; Los Angeles Dodgers (West), 1

PHI (E)

PLAYER/POS	AVG	G	AB	R	H	2B	3B	HR	RB	BB	SO	SB
Steve Carlton, p	.200	2	5	0	1	0	0	0	0	0	3	0
Ivan De Jesus, ss	.250	4	12	0	3	0	0	0	1	3	3	0
John Denny, p	.000	1	1	0	0	0	0	0	0	0	0	0
Bob Dernier, of	.000	1	0	0	0	0	0	0	0	0	0	0
Bo Diaz, c	.154	4	13	0	2	1	0	0	0	2	1	0
Greg Gross, of-3	.000	4	5	1	0	0	0	0	0	2	2	0
Von Hayes, of-1	.000	2	2	0	0	0	0	0	0	0	0	0
Al Holland, p	.000	2	0	0	0	0	0	0	0	0	0	0
Charles Hudson, p	.000	1	4	0	0	0	0	0	0	0	3	0
Joe Lefebvre, of-1	.000	2	2	0	0	0	0	0	1	0	1	0
Sixto Lezcano, of	.308	4	13	2	4	0	0	1	2	1	1	0
Garry Maddox, of	.273	3	11	0	3	1	0	0	1	0	1	0
Gary Matthews, of	.429	4	14	4	6	0	0	3	8	2	1	1
Joe Morgan, 2b	.067	4	15	1	1	0	0	0	0	2	1	0
Tony Perez, ph	1.000	1	1	0	1	0	0	0	0	0	0	0
Ron Reed, p	.000	2	0	0	0	0	0	0	0	0	0	0
Pete Rose, 1b	.375	4	16	3	6	0	0	0	0	1	1	1
Juan Samuel, pr	.000	1	0	0	0	0	0	0	0	0	0	0
Mike Schmidt, 3b	.467	4	15	5	7	2	0	1	2	2	3	0
Ossie Virgil, ph	.000	1	1	0	0	0	0	0	0	0	1	0
TOTAL	.262		130	16	34	4	0	5	15	15	22	2

PITCHER	W	L	ERA	G	GS	CG	SV	SHO	IP	H	ER	BB	SO
Steve Carlton	2	0	0.66	2	2	0	0	0	13.2	13	1	5	13
John Denny	0	1	0.00	1	1	0	0	0	6.0	5	0	3	3
Al Holland	0	0	0.00	2	0	0	1	0	3.0	1	0	0	3
Charles Hudson	1	0	2.00	1	1	1	0	0	9.0	4	2	2	9
Ron Reed	0	0	2.70	2	0	0	0	0	3.1	4	1	1	3
TOTAL	3	1	1.03	8	4	1	1	0	35.0	27	4	11	31

LA (W)

PLAYER/POS	AVG	G	AB	R	H	2B	3B	HR	RB	BB	SO	SB
Dusty Baker, of	.357	4	14	4	5	1	0	1	1	2	0	0
Joe Beckwith, p	.000	2	0	0	0	0	0	0	0	0	0	0
Greg Brock, 1b	.000	3	9	1	0	0	0	0	0	0	3	0
Jack Fimple, c	.143	3	7	0	1	0	0	0	1	0	3	0
Pedro Guerrero, 3b	.250	4	12	1	3	1	1	0	2	3	3	0
Rick Honeycutt, p	.000	2	0	0	0	0	0	0	0	0	0	0
Rafael Landestoy, ph	.000	2	2	0	0	0	0	0	0	0	1	0
Ken Landreaux, of	.143	4	14	0	2	0	0	0	1	1	3	0
Candy Maldonado, ph	.000	2	2	0	0	0	0	0	0	0	1	0
Mike Marshall, 1b-3,of-2	.133	4	15	1	2	1	0	1	2	1	6	0
Rick Monday, ph	.000	1	0	0	0	0	0	0	0	0	0	0
Jose Morales, ph	.000	2	2	0	0	0	0	0	0	0	1	0
Tom Niedenfuer, p	.000	2	0	0	0	0	0	0	0	0	0	0
Alejandro Pena, p	1.000	1	1	0	1	0	0	0	0	0	0	0
Jerry Reuss, p	.000	2	3	0	0	0	0	0	0	0	3	0
Bill Russell, ss	.286	4	14	1	4	0	0	0	0	2	4	1
Steve Sax, 2b	.250	4	16	0	4	0	0	0	0	1	0	1
Derrel Thomas, of	.444	4	9	0	4	1	0	0	0	0	3	1
Fernando Valenzuela, p	.000	1	3	0	0	0	0	0	0	1	0	0
Bob Welch, p	.000	1	0	0	0	0	0	0	0	0	0	0
Steve Yeager, c	.167	2	6	0	1	1	0	0	0	0	0	0
Pat Zachry, p	.000	2	0	0	0	0	0	0	0	0	0	0
TOTAL	.209		129	8	27	5	1	2	7	11	31	3

PITCHER	W	L	ERA	G	GS	CG	SV	SHO	IP	H	ER	BB	SO
Joe Beckwith	0	0	0.00	2	0	0	0	0	2.1	1	0	2	3
Rick Honeycutt	0	0	21.60	2	0	0	0	0	1.2	4	4	0	2
Tom Niedenfuer	0	0	0.00	2	0	0	1	0	2.0	0	0	1	3
Alejandro Pena	0	0	6.75	1	0	0	0	0	2.2	4	2	1	3
Jerry Reuss	0	2	4.50	2	2	0	0	0	12.0	14	6	3	4
Fernando Valenzuela	1	0	1.13	1	1	0	0	0	8.0	7	1	4	5
Bob Welch	0	1	6.75	1	1	0	0	0	1.1	0	1	2	0
Pat Zachry	0	0	2.25	2	0	0	0	0	4.0	4	1	2	2
TOTAL	1	3	3.97	13	4	0	1	0	34.0	34	15	15	22

The White Sox and Orioles entered the LCS evenly matched, with similar season's records and stats. But in the LCS, Baltimore all but shut down Chicago's run production. Both teams had 28 hits, but the Sox, held to four for extra bases, found themselves outslugged by 116 percentage points and outscored by 16 runs.

Chicago won the first game, scoring two of their three series runs as LaMarr Hoyt shut Baltimore out for eight innings before letting in a run in the ninth. But the White Sox had concluded their effective scoring. In Game Two, Oriole rookie Mike Boddicker shut them out on five hits, striking out fourteen. In Game Three the Sox scored their final run. The Orioles got only two more hits than Chicago, but blended them with nine walks, a hit batsman, and a Sox error to score eleven runs. In the fourth game, Oriole pitchers Storm Davis and Tippy Martinez saw that ten Chicago hits scored no runs. Britt Burns held Baltimore scoreless, too, through nine innings. But Tito Landrum's solo homer in the top of the tenth drove Burns out, and two more Oriole runs provided more than enough scoring to win Baltimore the flag.

Baltimore Orioles (East), 3;
Chicago White Sox (West), 1

BAL (E)

PLAYER/POS	AVG	G	AB	R	H	2B	3B	HR	RB	BB	SO	SB
Benny Ayala, dh	.000	1	0	0	0	0	0	0	0	1	0	0
Mike Boddicker, p	.000	1	0	0	0	0	0	0	0	0	0	0
Al Bumbry, of	.125	3	8	0	1	1	0	0	1	0	2	0
Todd Cruz, 3b	.133	4	15	0	2	0	0	0	1	0	5	0
Rich Dauer, 2b	.000	4	14	0	0	0	0	0	1	1	0	0
Storm Davis, p	.000	1	0	0	0	0	0	0	0	0	0	0
Rick Dempsey, c	.167	4	12	1	2	0	0	0	0	1	1	0
Jim Dwyer, of-1	.250	2	4	1	1	1	0	0	0	1	0	0
Mike Flanagan, p	.000	1	0	0	0	0	0	0	0	0	0	0
Dan Ford, of-1	.200	2	5	0	1	1	0	0	0	0	1	0
Tito Landrum, of-3	.200	4	10	2	2	0	0	1	1	0	2	0
John Lowenstein, of	.167	2	6	0	1	1	0	0	2	1	2	0
Tippy Martinez, p	.000	2	0	0	0	0	0	0	0	0	0	0
Scott Mc Gregor, p	.000	1	0	0	0	0	0	0	0	0	0	0
Eddie Murray, 1b	.267	4	15	5	4	0	0	1	3	3	3	1
Joe Nolan, ph	.000	1	0	0	0	0	0	0	1	0	0	0
Jim Palmer, pr	.000	1	0	0	0	0	0	0	0	0	0	0
Cal Ripken, ss	.400	4	15	5	6	2	0	0	1	2	3	0
Gary Roenicke, of	.750	3	4	4	3	1	0	1	4	5	0	0
John Shelby, of-2	.222	3	9	1	2	0	0	0	0	1	3	1
Ken Singleton, dh	.250	4	12	0	3	2	0	0	1	2	2	0
Sammy Stewart, p	.000	2	0	0	0	0	0	0	0	0	0	0
TOTAL	.217		129	19	28	9	0	3	17	16	24	2

PITCHER	W	L	ERA	G	GS	CG	SV	SHO	IP	H	ER	BB	SO
Mike Boddicker	1	0	0.00	1	1	1	0	1	9.0	5	0	3	14
Storm Davis	0	0	0.00	1	1	0	0	0	6.0	5	0	2	2
Mike Flanagan	1	0	1.80	1	1	0	0	0	5.0	5	1	0	1
Tippy Martinez	1	0	0.00	2	0	0	0	0	6.0	5	0	3	5
Scott Mc Gregor	0	1	1.35	1	1	0	0	0	6.2	6	1	3	2
Sammy Stewart	0	0	0.00	2	0	0	1	0	4.1	2	0	1	2
TOTAL	3	1	0.49	8	4	1	1	1	37.0	28	2	12	26

CHI (W)

PLAYER/POS	AVG	G	AB	R	H	2B	3B	HR	RB	BB	SO	SB
Juan Agosto, p	.000	1	0	0	0	0	0	0	0	0	0	0
Harold Baines, of	.125	4	16	0	2	0	0	0	0	1	3	0
Floyd Bannister, p	.000	1	0	0	0	0	0	0	0	0	0	0
Salome Barojas, p	.000	2	0	0	0	0	0	0	0	0	0	0
Britt Burns, p	.000	1	0	0	0	0	0	0	0	0	0	0
Julio Cruz, 2b	.333	4	12	0	4	0	0	0	0	3	4	2
Richard Dotson, p	.000	1	0	0	0	0	0	0	0	0	0	0
Jerry Dybzinski, ss	.250	2	4	0	1	0	0	0	0	0	0	0
Carlton Fisk, c	.176	4	17	0	3	1	0	0	0	1	3	0
Scott Fletcher, ss	.000	3	7	0	0	0	0	0	0	1	0	0
Jerry Hairston, of	.000	2	3	0	0	0	0	0	0	1	1	0
La Marr Hoyt, p	.000	1	0	0	0	0	0	0	0	0	0	0
Ron Kittle, of	.286	3	7	1	2	1	0	0	0	1	2	0
Jerry Koosman, p	.000	1	0	0	0	0	0	0	0	0	0	0
Dennis Lamp, p	.000	3	0	0	0	0	0	0	0	0	0	0
Rudy Law, of	.389	4	18	1	7	1	0	0	0	0	1	2
Vance Law, 3b	.182	4	11	0	2	0	0	0	1	1	3	0
Greg Luzinski, dh	.133	4	15	0	2	1	0	0	0	1	5	0
Tom Paciorek, 1b-3,of-2	.250	4	16	1	4	0	0	0	1	1	2	0
Aurelio Rodriguez, 3b	.000	2	0	0	0	0	0	0	0	0	0	0
Mike Squires, 1b-3	.000	4	4	0	0	0	0	0	0	0	0	0
Dick Tidrow, p	.000	1	0	0	0	0	0	0	0	0	0	0
Greg Walker, 1b-1	.333	2	3	0	1	0	0	0	0	1	2	0
TOTAL	.211		133	3	28	4	0	0	2	12	26	4

PITCHER	W	L	ERA	G	GS	CG	SV	SHO	IP	H	ER	BB	SO
Juan Agosto	0	0	0.00	1	0	0	0	0	0.1	0	0	0	0
Floyd Bannister	0	1	4.50	1	1	0	0	0	6.0	5	3	1	5
Salome Barojas	0	0	18.00	2	0	0	0	0	1.0	4	2	0	0
Britt Burns	0	1	0.96	1	1	0	0	0	9.1	6	1	5	8
Richard Dotson	0	1	10.80	1	1	0	0	0	5.0	6	6	3	3
La Marr Hoyt	1	0	1.00	1	1	1	0	0	9.0	5	1	0	4
Jerry Koosman	0	0	54.00	1	0	0	0	0	0.1	1	2	2	0
Dennis Lamp	0	0	0.00	3	0	0	0	0	2.0	0	0	2	1
Dick Tidrow	0	0	3.00	1	0	0	0	0	3.0	1	1	3	3
TOTAL	1	3	4.00	12	4	1	0	0	36.0	28	16	16	24

GAME 1 AT BAL OCT 5

CHI	001	001	000	2	7	0
BAL	000	000	001	1	5	1

Pitchers: HOYT vs McGREGOR, Stewart (7), T.Martinez (8)
Attendance: 51,289

GAME 2 AT BAL OCT 6

CHI	000	000	000	0	5	2
BAL	010	102	00X	4	6	0

Pitchers: BANNISTER, Barojas (7), Lamp (8) vs BODDICKER
Home Runs: Roenicke-BAL
Attendance: 52,347

GAME 3 AT CHI OCT 7

BAL	310	020	014	11	8	1
CHI	010	000	000	1	6	1

Pitchers: FLANAGAN, Stewart (6) vs DOTSON, Tidrow (6), Koosman (9), Lamp (9)
Home Runs: Murray-BAL
Attendance: 46,635

GAME 4 AT CHI OCT 8

BAL	000	000	000	3	3	9	0
CHI	000	000	000	0	0	10	0

Pitchers: Davis, T.MARTINEZ (7) vs BURNS, Barojas (10), Agosto (10), Lamp (10)
Home Runs: Landrum-BAL
Attendance: 45,477

Near neighbors Baltimore and Philadelphia met in a World Series for the first time. Both clubs were led by new managers: Baltimore by Joe Altobelli, who inherited a team built under longtime Oriole manager Earl Weaver; and the Phillies by general manager Paul Owens, who replaced Pat Corrales with himself in midseason. Both started their top game winners in the opener, and the result was a pitchers' duel, with all three runs scored on solo homers. Phillie John Denny gave up the first home run to Jim Dwyer in the first inning, but after that (with late-inning help from Al Holland) he blanked the Orioles, while Baltimore's Scott McGregor, after 5⅔ scoreless innings gave up home runs to Joe Morgan and (the game-loser two innings later) to Garry Maddox.

The Orioles swept the next four games. In Game Two, Mike Boddicker yielded just three singles (and no walks) to Phillie batters. Though one of the singles led to a run in the fourth inning, giving the Phillies a 1–0 lead, Oriole John Lowenstein tied the score with a home run in the fifth. Three more Oriole hits in the inning and a sacrifice fly made the score 3–1, and three two-out singles in the seventh inning brought in a fourth Baltimore run.

Philadelphia again scored first in Game Three, on leadoff home runs in the second and third innings by Gary Matthews and Joe Morgan. But the Orioles finally got to veteran starter Steve Carlton in the sixth for one run and drove him out after a second run scored an inning later. Carlton suffered the loss when the baserunner he left scored the tie-breaking run from second on an error by shortstop Ivan DeJesus.

The Phillies also lost Game Four by a single run. Baltimore scored first with two runs in the top of the fourth, but Philadelphia recovered with one run in the fourth and two an inning later. They would not lead again in the Series. Baltimore scored twice in the sixth to go ahead again, and once more in the seventh. The Phillies scored once more with two down in the last of the ninth to draw within one run of a tie, but Joe Morgan lined out to second to end the game.

Home runs by Rick Dempsey and Eddie Murray (who hit two) accounted for four of Baltimore's five runs in the final game—more than enough to support Scott McGregor's five-hit shutout pitching.

Baltimore Orioles (AL), 4; Philadelphia Phillies (NL), 1

BAL (A)

PLAYER/POS	AVG	G	AB	R	H	2B	3B	HR	RB	BB	SO	SB
Benny Ayala, ph	1.000	1	1	1	1	0	0	0	1	0	0	0
Mike Boddicker, p	.000	1	3	0	0	0	0	0	0	1	0	1	0
Al Bumbry, of	.091	4	11	0	1	1	0	0	1	0	1	0
Todd Cruz, 3b	.125	6	16	1	2	0	0	0	0	1	3	0
Rich Dauer, 2b	.211	5	19	2	4	1	0	0	3	0	3	0
Storm Davis, p	.000	1	2	0	0	0	0	0	0	0	2	0
Rick Dempsey, c	.385	5	13	3	5	4	0	1	2	2	2	0
Jim Dwyer, of	.375	2	8	3	3	1	0	1	1	1	0	0
Mike Flanagan, p	.000	1	0	0	0	0	0	0	0	0	1	0
Dan Ford, of-4	.167	5	12	1	2	0	0	1	1	1	5	0
Tito Landrum, of	.000	3	0	0	0	0	0	0	0	0	0	1
John Lowenstein, of	.385	4	13	2	5	1	0	1	1	0	3	0
Tippy Martinez, p	.000	3	0	0	0	0	0	0	0	0	0	0
Scott Mc Gregor, p	.000	2	5	0	0	0	0	0	0	0	0	0
Eddie Murray, 1b	.250	5	20	2	5	0	0	2	3	1	4	0
Joe Nolan, c	.000	2	2	0	0	0	0	0	0	1	0	0
Jim Palmer, p	.000	1	0	0	0	0	0	0	0	0	0	0
Cal Ripken, ss	.167	5	18	2	3	0	0	0	1	3	4	0
Gary Roenicke, of-2	.000	3	7	0	0	0	0	0	0	0	2	0
Len Sakata, 2b	.000	1	1	0	0	0	0	0	0	0	0	0
John Shelby, of	.444	5	9	1	4	0	0	0	1	0	4	0
Ken Singleton, ph	.000	2	1	0	0	0	0	0	0	1	1	0
Sammy Stewart, p	.000	3	2	0	0	0	0	0	0	0	0	0
TOTAL	.213		164	18	35	8	0	6	17	10	37	1

PITCHER	W	L	ERA	G	GS	CG	SV	SHO	IP	H	ER	BB	SO
Mike Boddicker	1	0	0.00	1	1	1	0	0	9.0	3	0	0	6
Storm Davis	1	0	5.40	1	1	0	0	0	5.0	6	3	1	3
Mike Flanagan	0	0	4.50	1	1	0	0	0	4.0	6	2	1	1
Tippy Martinez	0	0	3.00	3	0	0	0	2	3.0	3	1	0	0
Scott Mc Gregor	1	1	1.06	2	2	1	0	1	17.0	9	2	2	12
Jim Palmer	1	0	0.00	1	0	0	0	0	2.0	2	0	1	1
Sammy Stewart	0	0	0.00	3	0	0	0	0	5.0	2	0	2	6
TOTAL	4	1	1.60	12	5	2	2	1	45.0	31	8	7	29

PHI (N)

PLAYER/POS	AVG	G	AB	R	H	2B	3B	HR	RB	BB	SO	SB
Larry Andersen, p	.000	2	0	0	0	0	0	0	0	0	0	0
Marty Bystrom, p	.000	1	0	0	0	0	0	0	0	0	0	0
Steve Carlton, p	.000	1	3	0	0	0	0	0	0	0	1	0
Ivan De Jesus, ss	.125	5	16	0	2	0	0	0	0	1	2	0
John Denny, p	.200	2	5	1	1	0	0	0	1	0	1	0
Bob Dernier, pr	.000	1	0	1	0	0	0	0	0	0	0	0
Bo Diaz, c	.333	5	15	1	5	1	0	0	0	1	2	0
Greg Gross, of	.000	2	6	0	0	0	0	0	0	0	0	0
Von Hayes, of-1	.000	4	3	0	0	0	0	0	0	0	1	0
Willie Hernandez, p	.000	3	0	0	0	0	0	0	0	0	0	0
Al Holland, p	.000	2	0	0	0	0	0	0	0	0	0	0
Charles Hudson, p	.000	2	2	0	0	0	0	0	0	0	1	0
Joe Lefebvre, of-2	.200	3	5	0	1	1	0	0	0	2	1	0
Sixto Lezcano, of-3	.125	4	8	0	1	0	0	0	0	0	2	0
Garry Maddox, of-3	.250	4	12	1	3	1	0	1	1	0	2	0
Gary Matthews, of	.250	5	16	1	4	0	0	1	1	2	2	0
Joe Morgan, 2b	.263	5	19	3	5	0	1	2	2	2	3	1
Tony Perez, 1b-2	.200	4	10	0	2	0	0	0	0	0	2	0
Ron Reed, p	.000	3	0	0	0	0	0	0	0	0	0	0
Pete Rose, 1b-3,of-1	.313	5	16	1	5	1	0	0	1	1	3	0
Juan Samuel, ph	.000	3	1	0	0	0	0	0	0	0	0	0
Mike Schmidt, 3b	.050	5	20	0	1	0	0	0	0	0	6	0
Ossie Virgil, c-1	.500	3	2	0	1	0	0	0	1	0	0	0
TOTAL	.195		159	9	31	4	1	4	9	7	29	1

PITCHER	W	L	ERA	G	GS	CG	SV	SHO	IP	H	ER	BB	SO
Larry Andersen	0	0	2.25	2	0	0	0	0	4.0	4	1	0	1
Marty Bystrom	0	0	0.00	1	0	0	0	0	1.0	0	0	0	1
Steve Carlton	0	1	2.70	1	1	0	0	0	6.2	5	2	3	7
John Denny	1	1	3.46	2	2	0	0	0	13.0	12	5	3	9
Willie Hernandez	0	0	0.00	3	0	0	0	0	4.0	0	0	1	4
Al Holland	0	0	0.00	2	0	0	1	0	3.2	1	0	0	5
Charles Hudson	0	2	8.64	2	2	0	0	0	8.1	9	8	1	6
Ron Reed	0	0	2.70	3	0	0	0	0	3.1	4	1	2	4
TOTAL	1	4	3.48	16	5	0	1	0	44.0	35	17	10	37

GAME 1 AT BAL OCT 11

PHI	000	001	010	2	5	0
BAL	100	000	000	1	5	1

Pitchers: DENNY, Holland (8) vs McGREGOR, Stewart (9), T.Martinez (9)
Home Runs: Morgan-PHI, Maddox-PHI, Dwyer-BAL
Attendance: 52,204

GAME 2 AT BAL OCT 12

PHI	000	100	000	1	3	0
BAL	000	030	10X	4	9	1

Pitchers: HUDSON, Hernandez (5), Andersen (6), Reed (8) vs BODDICKER
Home Runs: Lowenstein-BAL
Attendance: 52,132

GAME 3 AT PHI OCT 14

BAL	000	001	200	3	6	1
PHI	011	000	000	2	8	2

Pitchers: Flanagan, PALMER (5), Stewart (7), T.Martinez (9) vs CARLTON, Holland (7)
Home Runs: Matthews-PHI, Morgan-PHI, Ford-BAL
Attendance: 65,792

GAME 4 AT PHI OCT 15

BAL	000	202	100	5	10	1
PHI	000	120	001	4	10	0

Pitchers: DAVIS, Stewart (6), T.Martinez (8) vs DENNY, Hernandez (6), Reed (6), Andersen (8)
Attendance: 66,947

GAME 5 AT PHI OCT 16

BAL	011	210	000	5	5	0
PHI	000	000	000	0	5	1

Pitchers: McGREGOR vs HUDSON, Bystrom (5), Hernandez (6), Reed (9)
Home Runs: Murray-BAL (2), Dempsey-BAL
Attendance: 67,064

After two games in Chicago, the Cubs appeared headed for their first pennant in thirty-nine years. Rick Sutcliffe and Warren Brusstar shut out the Padres 13–0 in an opener enlivened by five Cub home runs. In a quieter second game, the Cubs built a 4–1 lead over the first four innings and held on for the win.

When the series moved to San Diego, though, the Padres came to life. In the fifth and sixth innings of Game Three, they obliterated a 1–0 Cub lead with seven runs, as Ed Whitson and Goose Gossage held the Cubs scoreless after the second inning for what turned into an easy Padres win.

Game Four was not so easy. San Diego scored first in the third inning, lost their lead in the fourth, tied in the fifth, went ahead in the seventh, and fell back into a 5–5 tie in the eighth. But in the bottom of the ninth, Padre Steve Garvey's two-run homer sent the series into a fifth game.

Leon Durham put the Cubs ahead with a two-run homer in the first inning of the finale, and Jody Davis added to the lead with a solo shot in the second. Rick Sutcliffe, meanwhile, was setting down Padres as he added five shutout innings to his seven from Game One. But he gave up two runs in the sixth, and after first baseman Durham saw a grounder go through his legs to let in the tying run in the seventh, the Cubs watched the pennant slip away as Tony Gwynn's double and Garvey's single drove in the game's three final runs.

San Diego Padres (West), 3; Chicago Cubs (East), 2

SD (W)

PLAYER/POS	AVG	G	AB	R	H	2B	3B	HR	RB	BB	SO	SB
Kurt Bevacqua, ph	.000	2	2	0	0	0	0	0	0	0	0	0
Greg Booker, p	.000	1	0	0	0	0	0	0	0	0	0	0
Bobby Brown, of	.000	3	4	1	0	0	0	0	0	1	2	1
Dave Dravecky, p	.000	3	0	0	0	0	0	0	0	0	0	0
Tim Flannery, ph	.500	3	2	2	1	0	0	0	0	0	0	0
Steve Garvey, 1b	.400	5	20	1	8	1	0	1	7	1	2	0
Rich Gossage, p	.000	3	0	0	0	0	0	0	0	0	0	0
Tony Gwynn, of	.368	5	19	6	7	3	0	0	3	1	2	0
Greg Harris, p	.000	1	0	0	0	0	0	0	0	0	0	0
Andy Hawkins, p	.000	3	0	0	0	0	0	0	0	0	0	0
Terry Kennedy, c	.222	5	18	2	4	0	0	0	1	1	3	0
Craig Lefferts, p	.000	3	0	0	0	0	0	0	0	0	0	0
Tim Lollar, p	.000	1	1	0	0	0	0	0	0	0	1	0
Carmelo Martinez, of	.176	5	17	1	3	0	0	0	0	2	4	0
Kevin Mc Reynolds, of	.300	4	10	2	3	0	0	1	4	3	1	0
Graig Nettles, 3b	.143	4	14	1	2	0	0	0	2	1	1	0
Mario Ramirez, ph	.000	2	2	0	0	0	0	0	0	0	0	0
Luis Salazar, of-2,3b-1	.200	3	5	0	1	0	1	0	0	0	1	0
Eric Show, p	.000	2	1	0	0	0	0	0	0	0	1	0
Champ Summers, ph	.000	2	2	0	0	0	0	0	0	0	1	0
Garry Templeton, ss	.333	5	15	2	5	1	0	0	2	2	0	1
Mark Thurmond, p	1.000	1	1	0	1	0	0	0	0	0	0	0
Ed Whitson, p	.000	1	3	0	0	0	0	0	0	0	1	0
Alan Wiggins, 2b	.316	5	19	4	6	0	0	0	1	2	2	0
TOTAL	.265		155	22	41	5	1	2	20	14	22	2

PITCHER	W	L	ERA	G	GS	CG	SV	SHO	IP	H	ER	BB	SO
Greg Booker	0	0	0.00	1	0	0	0	0	2.0	2	0	1	2
Dave Dravecky	0	0	0.00	3	0	0	0	0	6.0	2	0	0	5
Rich Gossage	0	0	4.50	3	0	0	1	0	4.0	5	2	1	5
Greg Harris	0	0	31.50	1	0	0	0	0	2.0	9	7	3	2
Andy Hawkins	0	0	0.00	3	0	0	0	0	3.2	0	0	2	1
Craig Lefferts	2	0	0.00	3	0	0	0	0	4.0	1	0	1	1
Tim Lollar	0	0	6.23	1	1	0	0	0	4.1	3	3	4	3
Eric Show	0	1	13.50	2	2	0	0	0	5.1	8	8	4	2
Mark Thurmond	0	1	9.82	1	1	0	0	0	3.2	7	4	2	1
Ed Whitson	1	0	1.13	1	1	0	0	0	8.0	5	1	2	6
TOTAL	3	2	5.23	19	5	0	1	0	43.0	42	25	20	28

CHI (E)

PLAYER/POS	AVG	G	AB	R	H	2B	3B	HR	RB	BB	SO	SB
Thad Bosley, ph	.000	2	2	0	0	0	0	0	0	0	2	0
Larry Bowa, ss	.200	5	15	1	3	1	0	0	1	1	0	0
Warren Brusstar, p	.000	3	1	0	0	0	0	0	0	0	0	0
Ron Cey, 3b	.158	5	19	3	3	1	0	1	3	3	3	0
Henry Cotto, of	1.000	3	1	1	1	0	0	0	0	0	0	0
Jody Davis, c	.389	5	18	3	7	2	0	2	6	0	3	0
Bob Dernier, of	.235	5	17	5	4	2	0	1	1	5	4	2
Leon Durham, 1b	.150	5	20	3	3	0	0	2	4	1	4	0
Dennis Eckersley, p	.000	2	1	0	0	0	0	0	0	0	1	0
George Frazier, p	.000	1	0	0	0	0	0	0	0	0	0	0
Richie Hebner, ph	.000	2	1	0	0	0	0	0	0	0	0	0
Steve Lake, c	1.000	1	1	0	1	1	0	0	0	0	0	0
Davey Lopes, of-1	.000	2	1	0	0	0	0	0	0	0	0	0
Gary Matthews, of	.200	5	15	4	3	0	0	2	5	6	4	1
Keith Moreland, of	.333	5	18	3	6	2	0	0	2	1	1	0
Ryne Sandberg, 2b	.368	5	19	3	7	2	0	0	2	3	2	3
Scott Sanderson, p	.000	1	2	0	0	0	0	0	0	0	1	0
Lee Smith, p	.000	2	0	0	0	0	0	0	0	0	0	0
Tim Stoddard, p	.000	2	0	0	0	0	0	0	0	0	0	0
Rick Sutcliffe, p	.500	2	6	1	3	0	0	1	1	0	2	0
Steve Trout, p	.500	2	2	0	1	0	0	0	0	0	0	0
Tom Veryzer, ss-2,3b-1	.000	3	1	0	0	0	0	0	0	0	0	0
Gary Woods, of	.000	1	1	0	0	0	0	0	0	0	1	0
TOTAL	.259		162	26	42	11	0	9	25	20	28	6

PITCHER	W	L	ERA	G	GS	CG	SV	SHO	IP	H	ER	BB	SO
Warren Brusstar	0	0	0.00	3	0	0	0	0	4.1	6	0	0	1
Dennis Eckersley	0	1	8.44	1	1	0	0	0	5.1	9	5	0	0
George Frazier	0	0	10.80	1	0	0	0	0	1.2	2	2	0	1
Scott Sanderson	0	0	5.79	1	1	0	0	0	4.2	6	3	1	2
Lee Smith	0	1	9.00	2	0	0	1	0	2.0	3	2	0	3
Tim Stoddard	0	0	4.50	2	0	0	0	0	2.0	1	1	2	2
Rick Sutcliffe	1	1	3.38	2	2	0	0	0	13.1	9	5	8	10
Steve Trout	1	0	2.00	2	1	0	0	0	9.0	5	2	3	3
TOTAL	2	3	4.25	14	5	0	1	0	42.1	41	20	14	22

GAME 1 AT CHI OCT 2

```
SD    000 000 000    0  6  1
CHI   203 062 00X   13 16  0
```
Pitchers: SHOW, Harris (7), Booker (7) vs SUTCLIFFE, Brusstar (8)
Home Runs: Dernier-CHI, Matthews-CHI (2), Sutcliffe-CHI, Cey-CHI
Attendance: 36,282

GAME 2 AT CHI OCT 3

```
SD    000 101 000    2  5  0
CHI   102 100 00X    4  8  1
```
Pitchers: THURMOND, Hawkins (4), Dravecky (6), Lefferts (8) vs TROUT, Smith (9)
Attendance: 36,282

GAME 3 AT SD OCT 4

```
CHI   010 000 000    1  5  0
SD    000 034 00X    7 11  0
```
Pitchers: ECKERSLEY, Frazier (6), Stoddard (8) vs WHITSON, Gossage (9)
Home Runs: McReynolds-SD
Attendance: 58,346

GAME 4 AT SD OCT 6

```
CHI   000 300 020    5  8  1
SD    002 010 202    7 11  0
```
Pitchers: Sanderson, Brusstar (5), Stoddard (7), SMITH (8) vs Lollar, Hawkins (2), Dravecky (6), Gossage (8), LEFFERTS (9)
Home Runs: Davis-CHI, Durham-CHI, Garvey-SD
Attendance: 58,354

GAME 5 AT SD OCT 7

```
CHI   210 000 000    3  5  1
SD    000 002 40X    6  8  0
```
Pitchers: SUTCLIFFE, Trout (7), Brusstar (8) vs Show, Hawkins (2), Dravecky (4), LEFFERTS (6), Gossage (8)
Home Runs: Durham-CHI, Davis-CHI
Attendance: 58,359

The heavily favored Tigers swept the series, but not without difficulty, despite a fourteen-hit, three-homer, 8–1 romp in the opener.

Games Two and Three were much tighter. In the second game, after Detroit had built a 3–0 lead over the first three innings, Royal rookie starter Bret Saberhagen settled down and blanked the Tigers for the next five innings as K.C. inched its way to a tie with runs in the fourth, seventh, and eighth. Through the ninth and tenth innings, Tiger reliever Aurelio Lopez and Royal Dan Quisenberry dueled scorelessly, but in the top of the eleventh Johnny Grubb doubled home two Tiger runs. Lopez struggled but held the Royals scoreless in the last of the eleventh for the win.

In Game Three, the Royals' Charlie Leibrandt and Tigers' Milt Wilcox and Willie Hernandez hurled matching three-hitters. But the Tigers secured the game—and the pennant—when Chet Lemon scored on a broken double play in the second inning for the game's only run.

Detroit Tigers (East), 3; Kansas City Royals (West), 0

DET (E)

PLAYER/POS	AVG	G	AB	R	H	2B	3B	HR	RB	BB	SO	SB
Doug Baker, ss	.000	1	0	0	0	0	0	0	0	0	0	0
Dave Bergman, 1b-1	1.000	2	1	1	1	0	0	0	0	0	0	1
Tom Brookens, 2b-1,3b-1	.000	2	2	0	0	0	0	0	0	0	1	0
Marty Castillo, 3b	.250	3	8	0	2	0	0	0	2	0	3	1
Darrell Evans, 1b-3,3b-1	.300	3	10	1	3	1	0	0	1	1	0	1
Barbaro Garbey, dh-2	.333	3	9	1	3	0	0	0	0	0	1	0
Kirk Gibson, of	.417	3	12	2	5	1	0	1	2	2	1	1
Johnny Grubb, dh	.250	1	4	0	1	1	0	0	2	0	0	0
Willie Hernandez, p	.000	3	0	0	0	0	0	0	0	0	0	0
Larry Herndon, of	.200	2	5	1	1	0	0	0	1	1	2	0
Ruppert Jones, of	.000	2	5	1	0	0	0	0	0	1	1	0
Rusty Kuntz, of	.000	1	1	0	0	0	0	0	0	0	0	0
Chet Lemon, of	.000	3	13	1	0	0	0	0	0	0	1	0
Aurelio Lopez, p	.000	1	0	0	0	0	0	0	0	0	0	0
Jack Morris, p	.000	1	0	0	0	0	0	0	0	0	0	0
Lance Parrish, c	.250	3	12	1	3	1	0	1	3	0	3	0
Dan Petry, p	.000	1	0	0	0	0	0	0	0	0	0	0
Alan Trammell, ss	.364	3	11	2	4	0	1	1	3	3	1	0
Lou Whitaker, 2b	.143	3	14	3	2	0	0	0	0	0	3	0
Milt Wilcox, p	.000	1	0	0	0	0	0	0	0	0	0	0
TOTAL	.234		107	14	25	4	1	4	14	8	17	4

PITCHER	W	L	ERA	G	GS	CG	SV	SHO	IP	H	ER	BB	SO
Willie Hernandez	0	0	2.25	3	0	0	1	0	4.0	3	1	1	3
Aurelio Lopez	1	0	0.00	1	0	0	0	0	3.0	4	0	1	2
Jack Morris	1	0	1.29	1	1	0	0	0	7.0	5	1	1	4
Dan Petry	0	0	2.57	1	1	0	0	0	7.0	4	2	1	4
Milt Wilcox	1	0	0.00	1	1	0	0	0	8.0	2	0	2	8
TOTAL	3	0	1.24	7	3	0	1	0	29.0	18	4	6	21

KC (W)

PLAYER/POS	AVG	G	AB	R	H	2B	3B	HR	RB	BB	SO	SB
Steve Balboni, 1b	.100	3	10	0	1	0	0	0	0	1	4	0
Buddy Biancalana, ss	.000	2	1	0	0	0	0	0	0	0	1	0
Bud Black, p	.000	1	0	0	0	0	0	0	0	0	0	0
George Brett, 3b	.231	3	13	0	3	0	0	0	0	0	2	0
Onix Concepcion, ss	.000	3	7	0	0	0	0	0	0	0	0	0
Mark Huismann, p	.000	1	0	0	0	0	0	0	0	0	0	0
Dane Iorg, ph	.500	2	2	0	1	0	0	0	1	0	0	0
Lynn Jones, of-2	.200	3	5	1	1	0	0	0	0	0	0	0
Mike Jones, p	.000	1	0	0	0	0	0	0	0	0	0	0
Charlie Leibrandt, p	.000	1	0	0	0	0	0	0	0	0	0	0
Hal Mc Rae, ph	1.000	2	2	0	2	1	0	0	1	0	0	0
Darryl Motley, of	.167	3	12	0	2	0	0	0	1	1	3	0
Jorge Orta, dh	.100	3	10	1	1	0	1	0	1	0	2	0
Greg Pryor, 3b	.000	1	0	0	0	0	0	0	0	0	0	0
Dan Quisenberry, p	.000	1	0	0	0	0	0	0	0	0	0	0
Bret Saberhagen, p	.000	1	0	0	0	0	0	0	0	0	0	0
Pat Sheridan, of	.000	3	6	1	0	0	0	0	0	3	3	0
Don Slaught, c	.364	3	11	0	4	0	0	0	0	0	0	0
U. L. Washington, ph	.000	2	1	0	0	0	0	0	0	0	1	0
John Wathan, dh	.000	1	1	0	0	0	0	0	0	0	0	0
Frank White, 2b	.083	3	12	1	1	0	0	0	0	0	3	0
Willie Wilson, of	.154	3	13	0	2	0	0	0	0	1	2	0
TOTAL	.170		106	4	18	1	1	0	4	6	21	0

PITCHER	W	L	ERA	G	GS	CG	SV	SHO	IP	H	ER	BB	SO
Bud Black	0	1	5.40	1	1	0	0	0	5.0	7	3	1	3
Mark Huismann	0	0	10.13	1	0	0	0	0	2.2	6	3	1	2
Mike Jones	0	0	6.75	1	0	0	0	0	1.1	1	1	0	0
Charlie Leibrandt	0	1	1.13	1	1	1	0	0	8.0	3	1	4	6
Dan Quisenberry	0	1	3.00	1	0	0	0	0	3.0	2	1	1	1
Bret Saberhagen	0	0	2.25	1	1	0	0	0	8.0	6	2	1	5
TOTAL	0	3	3.54	6	3	1	0	0	28.0	25	11	8	17

GAME 1 AT KC OCT 2

DET	200	110	121	8	14	0
KC	000	000	100	1	5	1

Pitchers: MORRIS, Hernandez (8) vs BLACK, Huismann (6), M.Jones (8)
Home Runs: Herndon-DET, Trammell-DET, Parrish-DET
Attendance: 41,973

GAME 2 AT KC OCT 3

DET	201	000	000	02	5	8	1
KC	000	100	110	00	3	10	3

Pitchers: Petry, Hernandez (8), LOPEZ (9) vs Saberhagen, QUISENBERRY (9)
Home Runs: Gibson-DET
Attendance: 42,019

GAME 3 AT DET OCT 5

KC	000	000	000	0	3	3
DET	010	000	00X	1	3	0

Pitchers: LEIBRANDT vs WILCOX, Hernandez (9)
Attendance: 52,168

Few objective observers expected the Padres (playing in their first World Series) to best the mighty Tigers—and they didn't. Detroit's first two batters in Game One hit safely to produce the Series' first scoring before an out had been recorded. San Diego countered with three two-out hits in their half of the first to go ahead 2–1. But Detroit starter Jack Morris settled down to shut out the Padres over the final eight innings, and his Tigers scored the tying and winning runs in the fifth on Larry Herndon's two-run homer. The Tigers scored again in Game Two before the first out was recorded and drove out Padre starter Ed Whitson with three first-inning runs on five singles. But this time Detroit was shut out (by relievers Andy Hawkins and Craig Lefferts) over the final eight, while San Diego scored single runs in the first and fourth and the winning runs in the fifth on a three-run homer by the normally light-hitting Kurt Bevacqua.

The Tigers won Game Three on walks—a Series-record eleven—as the Series moved to Detroit. After scoring their first two runs in the second on a single and Marty Castillo's home run, they continued on to put across two more in the inning on a pair of hits alternated with three walks (the last with the bases full). Three more walks an inning later, followed by a hit batsman, gave Detroit its final run in what became a 5–2 win.

Alan Trammell's two-run homer in the first inning of Game Four put the Tigers ahead to stay. Tiger pitcher Jack Morris gave up a solo home run to Terry Kennedy in the second, but Trammell swatted a second two-run shot an inning later for a 4–1 lead. Morris let a second Padre runner score on a wild pitch in the ninth, but then retired Kennedy for the third out and his second Series win. Kirk Gibson's two home runs framed Tiger scoring in the final game. His two-run shot in the first inning opened the game's scoring. San Diego tied it up with runs in the third and fourth, but Detroit took a 5–3 lead with runs in the fifth and seventh (the latter on Lance Parrish's homer). The unlikely Kurt Bevacqua brought the Padres within a run of tying the game with his second Series homer in the eighth (doubling his regular-season total), but Gibson ended the scoring—and Padre hopes—with a three-run blast half an inning later.

Detroit Tigers (AL), 4; San Diego Padres (NL), 1

DET (A)

PLAYER/POS	AVG	G	AB	R	H	2B	3B	HR	RB	BB	SO	SB
Doug Bair, p	.000	1	0	0	0	0	0	0	0	0	0	0
Dave Bergman, 1b	.000	5	5	0	0	0	0	0	0	0	1	0
Tom Brookens, 3b	.000	3	3	0	0	0	0	0	0	0	1	0
Marty Castillo, 3b	.333	3	9	2	3	0	0	1	2	2	1	0
Darrell Evans, 1b-4,3b-2	.067	5	15	1	1	0	0	0	1	4	4	0
Barbaro Garbey, dh-3	.000	4	12	0	0	0	0	0	0	0	2	0
Kirk Gibson, of	.333	5	18	4	6	0	0	2	7	4	4	3
Johnny Grubb, dh-2	.333	4	3	0	1	0	0	0	0	0	0	0
Willie Hernandez, p	.000	3	0	0	0	0	0	0	0	0	0	0
Larry Herndon, of	.333	5	15	1	5	0	0	1	3	3	2	0
Howard Johnson, ph	.000	1	1	0	0	0	0	0	0	0	0	0
Ruppert Jones, of	.000	2	3	0	0	0	0	0	0	0	1	0
Rusty Kuntz, ph	.000	2	1	0	0	0	0	0	0	1	0	1
Chet Lemon, of	.294	5	17	1	5	0	0	0	1	2	2	2
Aurelio Lopez, p	.000	2	0	0	0	0	0	0	0	0	0	0
Jack Morris, p	.000	2	0	0	0	0	0	0	0	0	0	0
Lance Parrish, c	.278	5	18	3	5	1	0	1	2	3	2	1
Dan Petry, p	.000	2	0	0	0	0	0	0	0	0	0	0
Bill Scherrer, p	.000	3	0	0	0	0	0	0	0	0	0	0
Alan Trammell, ss	.450	5	20	5	9	1	0	2	6	2	2	1
Lou Whitaker, 2b	.278	5	18	6	5	2	0	0	0	4	4	0
Milt Wilcox, p	.000	1	0	0	0	0	0	0	0	0	0	0
TOTAL	.253		158	23	40	4	0	7	23	24	27	7

PITCHER	W	L	ERA	G	GS	CG	SV	SHO	IP	H	ER	BB	SO
Doug Bair	0	0	0.00	1	0	0	0	0	0.2	0	0	0	1
Willie Hernandez	0	0	1.69	3	0	0	2	0	5.1	4	1	0	0
Aurelio Lopez	1	0	0.00	2	0	0	0	0	3.0	1	0	1	4
Jack Morris	2	0	2.00	2	2	2	0	0	18.0	13	4	3	13
Dan Petry	0	1	9.00	2	2	0	0	0	8.0	14	8	5	4
Bill Scherrer	0	0	3.00	3	0	0	0	0	3.0	5	1	0	0
Milt Wilcox	1	0	1.50	1	1	0	0	0	6.0	7	1	2	4
TOTAL	4	1	3.07	14	5	2	2	0	44.0	44	15	11	26

SD (N)

PLAYER/POS	AVG	G	AB	R	H	2B	3B	HR	RB	BB	SO	SB
Kurt Bevacqua, dh	.412	5	17	4	7	2	0	2	4	1	2	0
Bruce Bochy, ph	1.000	1	1	0	1	0	0	0	0	0	0	0
Greg Booker, p	.000	1	0	0	0	0	0	0	0	0	0	0
Bobby Brown, of	.067	5	15	1	1	0	0	0	2	0	4	0
Dave Dravecky, p	.000	2	0	0	0	0	0	0	0	0	0	0
Tim Flannery, 2b	1.000	1	1	0	1	0	0	0	0	0	0	0
Steve Garvey, 1b	.200	5	20	2	4	2	0	0	2	0	2	0
Rich Gossage, p	.000	2	0	0	0	0	0	0	0	0	0	0
Tony Gwynn, of	.263	5	19	1	5	0	0	0	0	3	2	1
Greg Harris, p	.000	1	0	0	0	0	0	0	0	0	0	0
Andy Hawkins, p	.000	3	0	0	0	0	0	0	0	0	0	0
Terry Kennedy, c	.211	5	19	2	4	1	0	1	3	1	1	0
Craig Lefferts, p	.000	3	0	0	0	0	0	0	0	0	0	0
Tim Lollar, p	.000	1	0	0	0	0	0	0	0	0	0	0
Carmelo Martinez, of	.176	5	17	0	3	0	0	0	0	1	9	0
Graig Nettles, 3b	.250	5	12	2	3	0	0	0	2	5	0	0
Ron Roenicke, of-1	.000	2	0	0	0	0	0	0	0	0	0	0
Luis Salazar, of-2,3b-1	.333	4	3	0	1	0	0	0	0	0	0	0
Eric Show, p	.000	1	0	0	0	0	0	0	0	0	0	0
Champ Summers, ph	.000	1	1	0	0	0	0	0	0	0	1	0
Garry Templeton, ss	.316	5	19	1	6	1	0	0	0	0	3	0
Mark Thurmond, p	.000	2	0	0	0	0	0	0	0	0	0	0
Ed Whitson, p	.000	1	0	0	0	0	0	0	0	0	0	0
Alan Wiggins, 2b	.364	5	22	2	8	1	0	0	1	0	2	1
TOTAL	.265		166	15	44	7	0	3	14	11	26	2

PITCHER	W	L	ERA	G	GS	CG	SV	SHO	IP	H	ER	BB	SO
Greg Booker	0	0	9.00	1	0	0	0	0	1.0	0	1	4	0
Dave Dravecky	0	0	0.00	2	0	0	0	0	4.2	3	0	1	5
Rich Gossage	0	0	13.50	2	0	0	0	0	2.2	3	4	1	2
Greg Harris	0	0	0.00	1	0	0	0	0	5.1	3	0	3	5
Andy Hawkins	1	1	0.75	3	0	0	0	0	12.0	4	1	6	4
Craig Lefferts	0	0	0.00	3	0	0	1	0	6.0	2	0	1	7
Tim Lollar	0	1	21.60	1	1	0	0	0	1.2	4	4	4	0
Eric Show	0	1	10.13	2	1	0	0	0	2.2	4	3	1	2
Mark Thurmond	0	1	10.13	2	2	0	0	0	5.1	12	6	3	2
Ed Whitson	0	0	40.50	1	1	0	0	0	0.2	5	3	0	0
TOTAL	1	4	4.71	17	5	0	1	0	42.0	40	22	24	27

GAME 1 AT SD OCT 9

DET	100 020 000	3	8	0
SD	200 000 000	2	8	1

Pitchers: MORRIS vs THURMOND, Hawkins (6), Dravecky (8)
Home Runs: Herndon-DET
Attendance: 57,908

GAME 2 AT SD OCT 10

DET	300 000 000	3	7	3
SD	100 130 00X	5	11	0

Pitchers: PETRY, Lopez (5), Scherrer (6), Bair (7), Hernandez (8) vs Whitson, HAWKINS (1), Lefferts)7)
Home Runs: Bevacqua-SD
Attendance: 57,911

GAME 3 AT DET OCT 12

SD	001 000 100	2	5	0
DET	041 000 00X	5	7	0

Pitchers: LOLLAR, Booker (2), Harris (3) vs WILCOX, Scherrer (7), Hernandez (7)
Home Runs: Castillo-DET
Attendance: 51,970

GAME 4 AT DET OCT 13

SD	010 000 001	2	10	2
DET	202 000 00X	4	7	0

Pitchers: SHOW, Dravecky (3), Lefferts (7), Gossage (8) vs MORRIS
Home Runs: Trammell-DET (2), Kennedy-SD
Attendance: 52,130

GAME 5 AT DET OCT 14

SD	001 200 010	4	10	1
DET	300 010 13X	8	11	1

Pitchers: Thurmond, HAWKINS (1), Lefferts (5), Gossage (7) vs Petry, Scherrer (4), LOPEZ (5), Hernandez (8)
Home Runs: Gibson-DET (2), Parrish-DET, Bevacqua-SD
Attendance: 51,901

The Dodgers' league-leading pitchers held St. Louis to three runs over the first two games, even though the Cardinals recorded eight hits per game. But the Cards' league-leading hitters put their blows to better advantage in the next four games of the expanded LCS, scoring twenty-six times for four wins and the pennant.

Fernando Valenzuela captured Game One for the Dodgers, thanks in part to some ragged fielding by the usually sharp Cardinal infield. And as Orel Hershiser was holding St. Louis to two runs in Game Two, an errant Cardinal pickoff throw and heavy Dodger hitting gave him an increasingly comfortable lead.

When the series shifted to St. Louis for Game Three, the Cardinals revived, scoring twice in each of the first two innings for a quick lead, which they held for their first win. In Game Four they unloaded for nine runs in the second inning, and in Game Five—with the game and series tied in the bottom of the ninth—Ozzie Smith hit his first lefthanded home run ever to give St. Louis the series lead.

Back in Los Angeles, the Dodgers scored first in Game Six, and held a 4–1 lead after six innings. But three Cardinals scored on four hits in the seventh, and though Dodger Mike Marshall's eighth-inning home run restored the lead to Los Angeles, Cardinal Jack Clark settled things with a three-run homer in the ninth.

St. Louis Cardinals (East), 4; Los Angeles Dodgers (West), 2

STL (E)

PLAYER/POS	AVG	G	AB	R	H	2B	3B	HR	RB	BB	SO	SB
Joaquin Andujar, p	.250	2	4	1	1	1	0	0	0	0	1	0
Steve Braun, ph	.000	2	2	0	0	0	0	0	0	0	0	0
Bill Campbell, p	.000	3	0	0	0	0	0	0	0	0	0	0
Cesar Cedeno, of-4	.167	5	12	2	2	1	0	0	0	2	3	0
Jack Clark, 1b	.381	6	21	4	8	0	0	1	4	5	5	0
Vince Coleman, of	.286	3	14	2	4	0	0	0	1	0	2	1
Danny Cox, p	.000	1	2	0	0	0	0	0	0	1	1	0
Ken Dayley, p	.500	5	2	0	1	0	0	0	0	0	0	0
Bob Forsch, p	.000	1	0	0	0	0	0	0	0	0	0	0
Brian Harper, ph	.000	1	1	0	0	0	0	0	0	0	0	0
Tommy Herr, 2b	.333	6	21	2	7	4	0	1	6	5	2	1
Rick Horton, p	.000	3	0	0	0	0	0	0	0	0	0	0
Mike Jorgensen, ph	.000	2	2	0	0	0	0	0	0	0	1	0
Jeff Lahti, p	.000	2	0	0	0	0	0	0	0	0	0	0
Tito Landrum, of-4	.429	5	14	2	6	0	0	0	4	1	1	1
Willie Mc Gee, of	.269	6	26	6	7	1	0	0	3	3	6	2
Tom Nieto, c	.000	1	3	1	0	0	0	0	0	1	2	0
Terry Pendleton, 3b	.208	6	24	2	5	1	0	0	4	1	3	0
Darrell Porter, c	.267	5	15	1	4	1	0	0	0	5	4	0
Ozzie Smith, ss	.435	6	23	4	10	1	1	1	3	3	1	1
John Tudor, p	.000	2	4	1	0	0	0	0	0	1	1	0
Andy Van Slyke, of	.091	5	11	1	1	0	0	0	1	2	1	0
Todd Worrell, p	.000	4	0	0	0	0	0	0	0	0	0	0
TOTAL	.279		201	29	56	10	1	3	26	30	34	6

PITCHER	W	L	ERA	G	GS	CG	SV	SHO	IP	H	ER	BB	SO
Joaquin Andujar	0	1	6.97	2	2	0	0	0	10.1	14	8	4	9
Bill Campbell	0	0	0.00	3	0	0	0	0	2.1	3	0	0	2
Danny Cox	1	0	3.00	1	1	0	0	0	6.0	4	2	5	4
Ken Dayley	0	0	0.00	5	0	0	2	0	6.0	2	0	1	3
Bob Forsch	0	0	5.40	1	0	0	0	0	3.1	3	2	2	0
Rick Horton	0	0	9.00	3	0	0	0	0	3.0	4	3	2	1
Jeff Lahti	1	0	0.00	2	0	0	0	0	2.0	2	0	0	1
John Tudor	1	1	2.84	2	2	0	0	0	12.2	10	4	3	8
Todd Worrell	1	0	1.42	4	0	0	0	0	6.1	4	1	2	3
TOTAL	4	2	3.46	23	6	0	2	0	52.0	46	20	19	31

LA (W)

PLAYER/POS	AVG	G	AB	R	H	2B	3B	HR	RB	BB	SO	SB
Dave Anderson, ss-3,3b-1	.000	4	5	1	0	0	0	0	0	3	1	0
Bob Bailor, 3b	.000	2	1	0	0	0	0	0	0	0	0	0
Greg Brock, 1b-4	.083	5	12	2	1	0	0	1	2	2	2	0
Enos Cabell, 1b-3	.077	5	13	1	1	0	0	0	0	0	3	0
Bobby Castillo, p	.000	1	2	0	0	0	0	0	0	0	1	0
Carlos Diaz, p	.000	2	0	0	0	0	0	0	0	0	0	0
Mariano Duncan, ss	.222	5	18	2	4	2	1	0	1	1	3	1
Pedro Guerrero, of	.250	6	20	2	5	1	0	0	4	5	2	2
Orel Hershiser, p	.286	2	7	1	2	0	0	0	1	0	2	0
Rick Honeycutt, p	.000	2	0	0	0	0	0	0	0	0	0	0
Ken Howell, p	.000	1	0	0	0	0	0	0	0	0	0	0
Jay Johnstone, ph	.000	1	1	0	0	0	0	0	0	0	0	0
Ken Landreaux, of	.389	5	18	4	7	3	0	0	2	1	1	0
Bill Madlock, 3b	.333	6	24	5	8	1	0	3	7	0	2	1
Candy Maldonado, of-3	.143	4	7	0	1	0	0	0	1	0	3	0
Mike Marshall, of	.217	6	23	1	5	2	0	1	3	1	3	0
Len Matuszek, 1b-1,of-1	1.000	3	1	1	1	0	0	0	0	0	0	0
Tom Niedenfuer, p	.000	3	1	0	0	0	0	0	0	0	1	0
Jerry Reuss, p	.000	1	0	0	0	0	0	0	0	0	0	0
Steve Sax, 2b	.300	6	20	1	6	3	0	0	1	1	5	0
Mike Scioscia, c	.250	6	16	2	4	0	0	0	1	4	0	0
Fernando Valenzuela, p	.200	2	5	0	1	0	0	0	0	0	0	0
Bob Welch, p	.000	1	1	0	0	0	0	0	0	0	1	0
Terry Whitfield, ph	.000	1	0	0	0	0	0	0	0	0	0	0
Steve Yeager, c	.000	1	2	0	0	0	0	0	0	1	1	0
TOTAL	.234		197	23	46	12	1	5	23	19	31	4

PITCHER	W	L	ERA	G	GS	CG	SV	SHO	IP	H	ER	BB	SO
Bobby Castillo	0	0	3.38	1	0	0	0	0	5.1	4	2	2	4
Carlos Diaz	0	0	3.00	2	0	0	0	0	3.0	5	1	1	2
Orel Hershiser	1	0	3.52	2	2	1	0	0	15.1	17	6	6	5
Rick Honeycutt	0	0	13.50	2	0	0	0	0	1.1	4	2	2	1
Ken Howell	0	0	0.00	1	0	0	0	0	2.0	0	0	0	2
Tom Niedenfuer	0	2	6.35	3	0	0	1	0	5.2	5	4	2	5
Jerry Reuss	0	1	10.80	1	1	0	0	0	1.2	5	2	1	0
F. Valenzuela	1	0	1.88	2	2	0	0	0	14.1	11	3	10	13
Bob Welch	0	1	6.75	1	1	0	0	0	2.2	5	2	6	2
TOTAL	2	4	3.86	15	6	1	1	0	51.1	56	22	30	34

Were it not for the expansion of the LCS to a best-of-seven series, the Blue Jays would have won the pennant. But after winning three of the first four games, the Jays lost their steam and K.C. swept to their second pennant.

The pitching of Toronto ace Dave Stieb proved a key to the club's fortunes. Three times he started for the Jays. In the opener he threw eight shutout innings as the Jays won easily. In Game Four he continued to dominate batters, though three walks in the sixth helped the Royals score a go-ahead run before Toronto pulled it out (for reliever Tom Henke) with a three-run ninth. Had the series ended there, Stieb would have been a hero. But it didn't, and he was called upon again for Game Seven—perhaps with inadequate rest. This time he faltered. After giving up single runs in the second and fourth innings, he loaded the bases in the sixth with two walks and a hit batsman. Jim Sundberg unloaded them with a wind-blown triple, later scoring himself, and the Royals were on the road to victory.

George Brett keyed Kansas City's triumph. His four hits in Game Three (including two home runs) gave the club its first victory, and his RBI ground out in Game Five and go-ahead homer in Game Six proved game-winners in contests the Royals had to win.

Kansas City Royals (West), 4; Toronto Blue Jays (East), 3

KC (W)

PLAYER/POS	AVG	G	AB	R	H	2B	3B	HR	RB	BB	SO	SB
Steve Balboni, 1b	.120	7	25	1	3	0	0	0	0	1	2	8	0
Buddy Biancalana, ss	.222	7	18	2	4	1	0	0	1	1	6	0
Bud Black, p	.000	3	0	0	0	0	0	0	0	0	0	0
George Brett, 3b	.348	7	23	6	8	2	0	3	5	7	5	0
Onix Concepcion, ss	.000	4	1	0	0	0	0	0	0	0	0	0
Steve Farr, p	.000	2	0	0	0	0	0	0	0	0	0	0
Mark Gubicza, p	.000	2	0	0	0	0	0	0	0	0	0	0
Dane Iorg, ph	.500	4	2	0	1	1	0	0	0	2	0	0
Danny Jackson, p	.000	2	0	0	0	0	0	0	0	0	0	0
Lynn Jones, of	.000	5	0	0	0	0	0	0	0	0	0	0
Charlie Leibrandt, p	.000	3	0	0	0	0	0	0	0	0	0	0
Hal Mc Rae, dh	.261	6	23	1	6	2	0	0	3	1	6	0
Darryl Motley, of	.333	2	3	1	1	0	0	0	0	1	2	0
Jorge Orta, dh-1	.000	2	5	0	0	0	0	0	0	0	1	0
Jamie Quirk, ph	.000	1	1	0	0	0	0	0	0	0	0	0
Dan Quisenberry, p	.000	4	0	0	0	0	0	0	0	0	0	0
Bret Saberhagen, p	.000	2	0	0	0	0	0	0	0	0	0	0
Pat Sheridan, of	.150	7	20	4	3	0	0	2	3	2	3	0
Lonnie Smith, of	.250	7	28	2	7	2	0	0	1	3	6	1
Jim Sundberg, c	.167	7	24	3	4	1	1	1	6	1	7	0
Frank White, 2b	.200	7	25	1	5	0	0	0	3	1	2	0
Willie Wilson, of	.310	7	29	5	9	0	0	1	2	1	5	1
TOTAL	.225		227	26	51	9	1	7	26	22	51	2

PITCHER	W	L	ERA	G	GS	CG	SV	SHO	IP	H	ER	BB	SO
Bud Black	0	0	1.69	3	1	0	0	0	10.2	11	2	4	8
Steve Farr	1	0	1.42	2	0	0	0	0	6.1	4	1	1	3
Mark Gubicza	1	0	3.24	2	1	0	0	0	8.1	4	3	4	4
Danny Jackson	1	0	0.00	2	1	1	0	1	10.0	10	0	1	7
Charlie Leibrandt	1	2	5.28	3	2	0	0	0	15.1	17	9	4	6
Dan Quisenberry	0	1	3.86	4	0	0	1	0	4.2	7	2	0	3
Bret Saberhagen	0	0	6.14	2	2	0	0	0	7.1	12	5	2	6
TOTAL	4	3	3.16	18	7	1	1	1	62.2	65	22	16	37

TOR (E)

PLAYER/POS	AVG	G	AB	R	H	2B	3B	HR	RB	BB	SO	SB
Jim Acker, p	.000	2	0	0	0	0	0	0	0	0	0	0
Doyle Alexander, p	.000	2	0	0	0	0	0	0	0	0	0	0
Jesse Barfield, of	.280	7	25	3	7	1	0	1	4	3	7	1
George Bell, of	.321	7	28	4	9	3	0	0	1	0	4	0
Jeff Burroughs, ph	.000	1	1	0	0	0	0	0	0	0	0	0
Jim Clancy, p	.000	1	0	0	0	0	0	0	0	0	0	0
Tony Fernandez, ss	.333	7	24	2	8	2	0	0	2	1	2	0
Cecil Fielder, ph	.333	3	3	0	1	1	0	0	0	0	1	0
Damaso Garcia, 2b	.233	7	30	4	7	4	0	0	1	3	3	0
Jeff Hearron, c	.000	2	0	0	0	0	0	0	0	0	0	0
Tom Henke, p	.000	3	0	0	0	0	0	0	0	0	0	0
Garth Iorg, 3b	.133	6	15	1	2	0	0	0	0	1	3	0
Cliff Johnson, dh	.368	7	19	1	7	2	0	0	2	1	4	0
Jimmy Key, p	.000	2	0	0	0	0	0	0	0	0	0	0
Dennis Lamp, p	.000	3	0	0	0	0	0	0	0	0	0	0
Gary Lavelle, p	.000	1	0	0	0	0	0	0	0	0	0	0
Manny Lee, 2b	.000	1	0	0	0	0	0	0	0	0	0	0
Lloyd Moseby, of	.226	7	31	5	7	1	0	0	4	2	3	1
Rance Mulliniks, 3b	.364	5	11	1	4	1	0	1	3	2	2	0
Al Oliver, dh	.375	5	8	0	3	1	0	0	3	0	0	0
Dave Stieb, p	.000	3	0	0	0	0	0	0	0	0	0	0
Lou Thornton, pr	.000	2	0	1	0	0	0	0	0	0	0	0
Willie Upshaw, 1b	.231	7	26	2	6	2	0	0	1	1	4	0
Ernie Whitt, c	.190	7	21	1	4	1	0	0	2	2	4	0
TOTAL	.269		242	25	65	19	0	2	23	16	37	2

PITCHER	W	L	ERA	G	GS	CG	SV	SHO	IP	H	ER	BB	SO
Jim Acker	0	0	0.00	2	0	0	0	0	6.0	2	0	0	5
Doyle Alexander	0	1	8.71	2	2	0	0	0	10.1	14	10	3	9
Jim Clancy	0	1	9.00	1	0	0	0	0	1.0	2	1	1	0
Tom Henke	2	0	4.26	3	0	0	0	0	6.1	5	3	4	4
Jimmy Key	0	1	5.19	2	2	0	0	0	8.2	15	5	2	5
Dennis Lamp	0	0	0.00	3	0	0	0	0	9.1	2	0	1	10
Gary Lavelle	0	0	INF	1	0	0	0	0	0.0	0	1	1	0
Dave Stieb	1	1	3.10	3	3	0	0	0	20.1	11	7	10	18
TOTAL	3	4	3.77	17	7	0	0	0	62.0	51	26	22	51

GAME 1 AT TOR OCT 8

KC	000 000 001	1	5	1
TOR	023 100 00X	6	11	0

Pitchers: LEIBRANDT, Farr (3), Gubicza (5), Jackson (8) vs STIEB, Henke (9)
Attendance: 39,115

GAME 2 AT TOR OCT 9

KC	002 100 001 1	5	10	3
TOR	000 102 010 2	6	10	0

Pitchers: Black, QUISENBERRY (8) vs Key, Lamp (4), Lavelle (8), HENKE (8)
Home Runs: Wilson-KC, Sheridan-KC
Attendance: 34,029

GAME 3 AT KC OCT 11

TOR	000 050 000	5	13	1
KC	100 112 01X	6	10	1

Pitchers: Alexander, Lamp (6), CLANCY (8) vs Saberhagen, Black (5), FARR (5)
Home Runs: Brett-KC (2), Barfield-TOR, Mulliniks-TOR, Sundberg-KC
Attendance: 40,224

GAME 4 AT KC OCT 12

TOR	000 000 003	3	7	0
KC	000 001 000	1	2	0

Pitchers: Stieb, HENKE (7) vs LEIBRANDT, Quisenberry (9)
Attendance: 41,112

GAME 5 AT KC OCT 13

TOR	000 000 000	0	8	0
KC	110 000 00X	2	8	0

Pitchers: KEY, Acker (6) vs JACKSON
Attendance: 40,046

GAME 6 AT TOR OCT 15

KC	101 012 000	5	8	1
TOR	101 001 000	3	8	2

Pitchers: GUBICZA, Black (6), Quisenberry (9) vs ALEXANDER, Lamp (6)
Home Runs: Brett-KC
Attendance: 37,557

GAME 7 AT TOR OCT 16

KC	010 104 000	6	8	0
TOR	000 010 001	2	8	1

Pitchers: Saberhagen, LEIBRANDT (4), Quisenberry (9) vs STIEB, Acker (6)
Home Runs: Sheridan-KC
Attendance: 32,084

The underdog Royals surprised St. Louis with superior hitting and pitching, and even outstole the speedy Cards six bases to two. Still, had an umpire not muffed a call at first base in Game Six, St. Louis might have emerged from the fray wearing the world crown.

The Cardinals broke a 1–1 tie in the fourth inning of the opener with back-to-back doubles off Royal starter Danny Jackson, and held on behind the strong pitching of John Tudor and reliever Todd Worrell for a 3–1 win. In Game Two, except for the fourth inning, when he yielded a single and two doubles (for two runs) before retiring his first batter, Cardinal starter Danny Cox held the Royals in check. Royal starter Charlie Leibrandt hurled even more effectively, holding St. Louis to two hits—until the ninth inning, when four Cardinal hits (three of them doubles) produced four runs and a second Card victory.

Kansas City finally demonstrated its punch in Game Three. Frank White hit a two-run homer in the fifth, and the Royals scored four more times to win behind the six-hit hurling of sophomore sensation Bret Saberhagen. The next day, though, Royal bats died again against John Tudor, who shut them out on five hits. Three Royal pitchers yielded only six hits to Cardinal batters, but two were home runs to Tito Landrum and Willie McGee, and one was a triple to Terry Pendleton, who scored on a sacrifice squeeze.

Down three games to one, the Royals hammered eleven hits in Game Five for six runs to win behind Danny Jackson's five-hitter. Seven Royal hits in the first eight innings of Game Six, though, scored no runs against Cardinal starter Danny Cox and reliever Ken Dayley. But in the last of the ninth, with the Cards ahead 1–0 and Todd Worrell now pitching, Royal pinch hitter Jorge Orta was ruled safe at first on what the cameras showed clearly as an out. This miscall, followed by a pop foul that first baseman Jack Clark should have caught but didn't, opened the door to Cardinal disintegration. A single and passed ball put Royals at second and third, and after an intentional walk to set up the double play, pinch hitter Dane Iorg singled home the tying and winning Royal runs.

The Cardinals threw seven pitchers at Kansas City in the finale in a vain attempt to halt the Royals' fourteen-hit, eleven-run attack, while Bret Saberhagen stopped the Cards cold on five hits to bring the Royals their first world title.

Kansas City Royals (AL), 4;
St. Louis Cardinals (NL), 3

KC (A)

PLAYER/POS	AVG	G	AB	R	H	2B	3B	HR	RB	BB	SO	SB
Steve Balboni, 1b	.320	7	25	2	8	0	0	0	3	5	4	0
Joe Beckwith, p	.000	1	0	0	0	0	0	0	0	0	0	0
Buddy Biancalana, ss	.278	7	18	2	5	0	0	0	2	5	4	0
Bud Black, p	.000	2	1	0	0	0	0	0	0	0	1	0
George Brett, 3b	.370	7	27	5	10	1	0	0	1	4	7	1
Onix Concepcion, ss-2	.000	3	0	1	0	0	0	0	0	0	0	0
Dane Iorg, ph	.500	2	2	0	1	0	0	0	2	0	0	0
Danny Jackson, p	.000	2	6	0	0	0	0	0	0	0	5	0
Lynn Jones, of-4	.667	6	3	0	2	1	1	0	0	0	0	0
Charlie Leibrandt, p	.000	2	4	0	0	0	0	0	0	0	2	0
Hal Mc Rae, ph	.000	3	1	0	0	0	0	0	0	1	0	0
Darryl Motley, of-4	.364	5	11	1	4	0	0	1	3	0	1	0
Jorge Orta, ph	.333	3	3	0	1	0	0	0	0	0	0	0
Greg Pryor, 3b	.000	1	0	0	0	0	0	0	0	0	0	0
Dan Quisenberry, p	.000	4	0	0	0	0	0	0	0	0	0	0
Bret Saberhagen, p	.000	2	7	1	0	0	0	0	0	0	4	0
Pat Sheridan, of-4	.222	5	18	0	4	2	0	0	1	0	7	0
Lonnie Smith, of	.333	7	27	4	9	3	0	0	4	3	8	2
Jim Sundberg, c	.250	7	24	6	6	2	0	1	6	4	0	0
John Wathan, ph	.000	2	1	0	0	0	0	0	0	0	1	0
Frank White, 2b	.250	7	28	4	7	3	0	1	6	3	4	0
Willie Wilson, of	.367	7	30	2	11	0	1	0	3	1	4	3
TOTAL	.288		236	28	68	12	2	2	26	28	56	6

PITCHER	W	L	ERA	G	GS	CG	SV	SHO	IP	H	ER	BB	SO
Joe Beckwith	0	0	0.00	1	0	0	0	0	2.0	1	0	0	3
Bud Black	0	1	5.06	2	1	0	0	0	5.1	4	3	5	4
Danny Jackson	1	1	1.69	2	2	1	0	0	16.0	9	3	5	12
Charlie Leibrandt	0	1	2.76	2	2	0	0	0	16.1	10	5	4	10
Dan Quisenberry	1	0	2.08	4	0	0	0	0	4.1	5	1	3	3
Bret Saberhagen	2	0	0.50	2	2	2	0	1	18.0	11	1	1	10
TOTAL	4	3	1.89	13	7	3	0	1	62.0	40	13	18	42

STL (N)

PLAYER/POS	AVG	G	AB	R	H	2B	3B	HR	RB	BB	SO	SB
Joaquin Andujar, p	.000	2	1	0	0	0	0	0	0	0	1	0
Steve Braun, ph	.000	1	1	0	0	0	0	0	0	0	0	0
Bill Campbell, p	.000	3	0	0	0	0	0	0	0	0	0	0
Cesar Cedeno, of	.133	5	15	1	2	1	0	0	1	2	2	0
Jack Clark, 1b	.240	7	25	1	6	2	0	0	4	3	9	0
Danny Cox, p	.000	2	4	0	0	0	0	0	0	0	2	0
Ken Dayley, p	.000	4	0	0	0	0	0	0	0	0	0	0
Ivan De Jesus, ph	.000	1	1	0	0	0	0	0	0	0	0	0
Bob Forsch, p	.000	2	0	0	0	0	0	0	0	0	0	0
Brian Harper, ph	.250	4	4	0	1	0	0	0	1	0	1	0
Tommy Herr, 2b	.154	7	26	2	4	2	0	0	0	2	2	0
Rick Horton, p	.000	3	1	0	0	0	0	0	0	0	1	0
Mike Jorgensen, of-1	.000	2	3	0	0	0	0	0	0	0	0	0
Jeff Lahti, p	.000	3	0	0	0	0	0	0	0	0	0	0
Tito Landrum, of	.360	7	25	3	9	2	0	1	1	0	2	0
Tom Lawless, pr	.000	1	0	0	0	0	0	0	0	0	0	0
Willie Mc Gee, of	.259	7	27	2	7	2	0	1	2	1	3	1
Tom Nieto, c	.000	2	5	0	0	0	0	0	1	1	2	0
Terry Pendleton, 3b	.261	7	23	3	6	1	1	0	3	3	2	0
Darrell Porter, c	.133	5	15	0	2	0	0	0	0	2	5	0
Ozzie Smith, ss	.087	7	23	1	2	0	0	0	0	4	0	1
John Tudor, p	.000	3	5	0	0	0	0	0	0	0	4	0
Andy Van Slyke, of	.091	6	11	0	1	0	0	0	0	0	5	0
Todd Worrell, p	.000	3	1	0	0	0	0	0	0	0	1	0
TOTAL	.185		216	13	40	10	1	2	13	18	42	2

PITCHER	W	L	ERA	G	GS	CG	SV	SHO	IP	H	ER	BB	SO
Joaquin Andujar	0	1	9.00	2	1	0	0	0	4.0	10	4	4	3
Bill Campbell	0	0	2.25	3	0	0	0	0	4.0	4	1	2	5
Danny Cox	0	0	1.29	2	2	0	0	0	14.0	14	2	4	13
Ken Dayley	1	0	0.00	4	0	0	0	0	6.0	1	0	3	5
Bob Forsch	0	1	12.00	2	1	0	0	0	3.0	6	4	1	3
Rick Horton	0	0	6.75	3	0	0	0	0	4.0	4	3	5	5
Jeff Lahti	0	0	12.27	3	0	0	0	1	3.2	10	5	0	2
John Tudor	2	1	3.00	3	3	1	0	1	18.0	15	6	7	14
Todd Worrell	0	1	3.86	3	0	0	0	1	4.2	4	2	2	6
TOTAL	3	4	3.96	25	7	1	2	1	61.1	68	27	28	56

GAME 1 AT KC OCT 19

STL	001	100	001	3	7	1
KC	010	000	000	1	8	0

Pitchers: TUDOR, Worrell (7) vs JACKSON, Quisenberry (8), Black (9)
Attendance: 41,650

GAME 2 AT KC OCT 20

STL	000	000	004	4	6	0
KC	000	200	000	2	9	0

Pitchers: Cox, DAYLEY (8), Lahti (9) vs LEIBRANDT, Quisenberry (9)
Attendance: 41,656

GAME 3 AT STL OCT 22

KC	000	220	200	6	11	0
STL	000	001	000	1	6	0

Pitchers: SABERHAGEN vs ANDUJAR, Campbell (5), Horton (6), Dayley (8)
Home Runs: White-KC
Attendance: 53,634

GAME 4 AT STL OCT 23

KC	000	000	000	0	5	1
STL	011	010	00X	3	6	0

Pitchers: BLACK, Beckwith (6), Quisenberry (8) vs TUDOR
Home Runs: Landrum-STL, McGee-STL
Attendance: 53,634

GAME 5 AT STL OCT 24

KC	130	000	011	6	11	2
STL	100	000	000	1	5	1

Pitchers: JACKSON vs FORSCH, Horton (2), Campbell (4), Worrell (6), Lahti (8)
Attendance: 53,634

GAME 6 AT KC OCT 26

STL	000	000	010	1	5	0
KC	000	000	002	2	10	0

Pitchers: Cox, Dayley (8), WORRELL (9) vs Leibrandt, QUISENBERRY (8)
Attendance: 41,628

GAME 7 AT KC OCT 27

STL	000	000	000	0	5	0
KC	023	060	00X	11	14	0

Pitchers: TUDOR, Campbell (3), Lahti (5), Horton (5), Andujar (5), Forsch (5), Dayley (7) vs SABERHAGEN
Home Runs: Motley-KC
Attendance: 41,658

Houston pitcher Mike Scott overwhelmed the Mets in Games One and Four, and would have faced them a third time in Game Seven if the Astros had won Game Six. They tried, scoring three runs in the first as Bob Knepper shut out the Mets on two hits through eight innings. But in the top of the ninth New York tied the game and held on into extra innings. No one scored again until the Mets put a run across in the fourteenth. Astro Billy Hatcher tied it up again later in the fourteenth with a home run just inside the left field foul pole. Two innings later the Mets (aided by a pair of wild pitches) scored three runs. Again the Astros came back, scoring twice, but fell just short as Jesse Orosco struck out Kevin Bass with two men on base to win his third game of the series and give New York the pennant.

In the series opener Houston scored just one run off Dwight Gooden, but it was enough, as Mike Scott, fanning fourteen, shut out the Mets on five hits. New York came back with five runs in Game Two to win behind Bob Ojeda, who gave up ten hits but only one run. In Game Three the Astros held the lead into the last of the sixth, when New York tied the score with four runs. Houston retook the lead in the seventh with a run, but Met Len Dykstra won it for New York with a two-run homer in the bottom of the ninth.

The Astros' win in Game Four evened the series. Houston had scored three runs by the time Scott (on his way to a three-hitter) gave the Mets their only run in the eighth. Houston's Nolan Ryan gave up only two hits in the first nine innings of Game Five (one of them Darryl Strawberry's game-tying solo homer in the fifth), striking out twelve. But New York's Gooden also yielded only one run in ten innings of work. Astro Charlie Kerfeld shut out the Mets in the tenth and eleventh, and the Mets' Orosco stopped Houston in the eleventh and twelfth. But in the last of the twelfth, Met catcher Gary Carter singled home a run off Kerfeld to end the game (and his series-long batting slump)—setting the stage for the sixteen-inning marathon the next day.

New York Mets (East), 4; Houston Astros (West), 2

NY (E)

PLAYER/POS	AVG	G	AB	R	H	2B	3B	HR	RB	BB	SO	SB
Rick Aguilera, p	.000	2	0	0	0	0	0	0	0	0	0	0
Wally Backman, 2b	.238	6	21	5	5	0	0	0	2	2	4	1
Gary Carter, c	.148	6	27	1	4	1	0	0	2	2	5	0
Ron Darling, p	.000	1	1	0	0	0	0	0	0	0	0	0
Lenny Dykstra, of	.304	6	23	3	7	1	1	1	3	2	4	1
Kevin Elster, ss	.000	4	3	0	0	0	0	0	0	0	1	0
Sid Fernandez, p	.000	1	1	0	0	0	0	0	0	0	0	0
Dwight Gooden, p	.000	2	5	0	0	0	0	0	0	0	2	0
Danny Heep, of-1	.250	5	4	0	1	0	0	0	1	0	2	0
Keith Hernandez, 1b	.269	6	26	3	7	1	1	0	3	3	6	0
Howard Johnson, ph	.000	2	2	0	0	0	0	0	0	0	0	0
Ray Knight, 3b	.167	6	24	1	4	0	0	0	2	1	5	0
Lee Mazzilli, ph	.200	5	5	0	1	0	0	0	0	0	3	0
Roger Mc Dowell, p	.000	2	1	0	0	0	0	0	0	0	0	0
Kevin Mitchell, of	.250	2	8	1	2	0	0	0	0	0	1	0
Bob Ojeda, p	.000	2	5	1	0	0	0	0	0	0	2	0
Jesse Orosco, p	.000	4	0	0	0	0	0	0	0	0	0	0
Rafael Santana, ss	.176	6	17	0	3	0	0	0	0	0	3	0
Doug Sisk, p	.000	1	0	0	0	0	0	0	0	0	0	0
Darryl Strawberry, of	.227	6	22	4	5	1	0	2	5	3	12	1
Tim Teufel, 2b	.167	2	6	0	1	0	0	0	0	0	0	0
Mookie Wilson, of	.115	6	26	2	3	0	0	1	1	1	7	1
TOTAL	.189		227	21	43	4	2	3	19	14	57	4

PITCHER	W	L	ERA	G	GS	CG	SV	SHO	IP	H	ER	BB	SO
Rick Aguilera	0	0	0.00	2	0	0	0	0	5.0	2	0	2	2
Ron Darling	0	0	7.20	1	1	0	0	0	5.0	6	4	2	5
Sid Fernandez	0	1	4.50	1	1	0	0	0	6.0	3	3	1	5
Dwight Gooden	0	1	1.06	2	2	0	0	0	17.0	16	2	5	9
Roger Mc Dowell	0	0	0.00	2	0	0	0	0	7.0	1	0	0	3
Bob Ojeda	1	0	2.57	2	2	1	0	0	14.0	15	4	4	6
Jesse Orosco	3	0	3.38	4	0	0	0	0	8.0	5	3	2	10
Doug Sisk	0	0	0.00	1	0	0	0	0	1.0	1	0	1	0
TOTAL	4	2	2.29	15	6	1	0	0	63.0	49	16	17	40

HOU (W)

PLAYER/POS	AVG	G	AB	R	H	2B	3B	HR	RB	BB	SO	SB
Larry Andersen, p	.000	2	0	0	0	0	0	0	0	0	0	0
Alan Ashby, c	.130	6	23	2	3	1	0	1	2	2	1	0
Kevin Bass, of	.292	6	24	0	7	2	0	0	4	4	2	0
Jeff Calhoun, p	.000	1	0	0	0	0	0	0	0	0	0	0
Jose Cruz, of	.192	6	26	0	5	0	0	0	2	1	8	0
Glenn Davis, 1b	.269	6	26	3	7	1	0	1	3	1	3	0
Bill Doran, 2b	.222	6	27	3	6	0	0	1	3	2	2	0
Phil Garner, 3b	.222	3	9	1	2	1	0	0	2	1	2	0
Billy Hatcher, of	.280	6	25	4	7	0	0	1	2	3	2	3
Charlie Kerfeld, p	.000	3	0	0	0	0	0	0	0	0	0	0
Bob Knepper, p	.000	2	5	0	0	0	0	0	0	1	2	0
Davey Lopes, ph	.000	3	2	1	0	0	0	0	0	1	0	0
Aurelio Lopez, p	.000	2	0	0	0	0	0	0	0	0	0	0
Jim Pankovits, ph	.000	2	2	0	0	0	0	0	0	0	1	0
Terry Puhl, ph	.667	3	3	0	2	0	0	0	0	0	0	1
Craig Reynolds, ss	.333	4	12	1	4	0	0	0	0	1	3	0
Nolan Ryan, p	.000	2	4	0	0	0	0	0	0	0	2	0
Mike Scott, p	.000	2	6	0	0	0	0	0	0	0	5	0
Dave Smith, p	.000	2	0	0	0	0	0	0	0	0	0	0
Dickie Thon, ss	.250	6	12	1	3	0	0	1	1	0	1	0
Denny Walling, 3b	.158	5	19	1	3	1	0	0	2	0	4	0
TOTAL	.218		225	17	49	6	0	5	17	17	40	8

PITCHER	W	L	ERA	G	GS	CG	SV	SHO	IP	H	ER	BB	SO
Larry Andersen	0	0	0.00	2	0	0	0	0	5.0	1	0	2	3
Jeff Calhoun	0	0	9.00	1	0	0	0	0	1.0	1	1	1	0
Charlie Kerfeld	0	1	2.25	3	0	0	0	0	4.0	2	1	1	4
Bob Knepper	0	0	3.52	2	2	0	0	0	15.1	13	6	1	9
Aurelio Lopez	0	1	8.10	2	0	0	0	0	3.1	7	3	4	3
Nolan Ryan	0	1	3.86	2	2	0	0	0	14.0	9	6	1	17
Mike Scott	2	0	0.50	2	2	2	0	1	18.0	8	1	1	19
Dave Smith	0	1	9.00	2	0	0	0	0	2.0	2	2	3	2
TOTAL	2	4	2.87	16	6	2	0	1	62.2	43	20	14	57

GAME 1 AT HOU OCT 8

NY	000	000	000	0	5	0
HOU	010	000	00X	1	7	1

Pitchers: GOODEN, Orosco (8) vs SCOTT
Home Runs: Davis-HOU
Attendance: 44,131

GAME 2 AT HOU OCT 9

NY	000	230	000	5	10	0
HOU	000	000	100	1	10	2

Pitchers: OJEDA vs RYAN, Andersen (6), Lopez (8), Kerfeld (9)
Attendance: 44,391

GAME 3 AT NY OCT 11

HOU	220	000	100	5	8	1
NY	000	004	002	6	10	1

Pitchers: Knepper, Kerfeld (8), SMITH (9) vs Darling, Aguilera (6), OROSCO (8)
Home Runs: Doran-HOU, Strawberry-NY, Dykstra-NY
Attendance: 55,052

GAME 4 AT NY OCT 12

HOU	020	010	000	3	4	1
NY	000	000	010	1	3	0

Pitchers: SCOTT vs FERNANDEZ, McDowell (7), Sisk (9)
Home Runs: Ashby-HOU, Thon-HOU
Attendance: 55,038

GAME 5 AT NY OCT 14

HOU	000	010	000	000	1	9	1
NY	000	000	001	2	4	0

Pitchers: Ryan, KERFELD (10) vs Gooden, OROSCO (11)
Home Runs: Strawberry-NY
Attendance: 54,986

GAME 6 AT HOU OCT 15

NY	000	000	003	000	010	3	7	11	0
HOU	300	000	000	000	010	2	6	11	1

Pitchers: Ojeda, Aguilera (6), McDowell (9), OROSCO (14) vs Knepper, Smith (9), Andersen (11), LOPEZ (14), Calhoun (16)
Home Runs: Hatcher-HOU
Attendance: 45,718

For the second time in the two years of the expanded LCS, a club that would have been eliminated in a five-game series came back to take the pennant in seven games. The first two games were one-sided. California scored five early runs off Roger Clemens and breezed to an easy 8–1 win in the opener. Boston retaliated in Game Two with nine runs, breaking the game open with six unanswered runs in the seventh and eighth innings.

Game Three was close until the Angels scored for three runs with two out in the seventh to break a 1–1 tie. In Game Four, the Angels were handed a tie in the last of the ninth when Boston reliever Calvin Schiraldi hit a batter with the bases loaded and won in the eleventh on Bobby Grich's RBI single.

The Red Sox, down three games to one, were on the brink of elimination in Game Five, with two out in the ninth, when Dave Henderson, after fouling off one third-strike pitch, hit the next for a two-run homer that gave Boston a one-run lead. The Angels tied the game in the last of the ninth, but Henderson's sacrifice fly in the eleventh put the Sox ahead for good.

Boston needed two more wins and got them with surprising ease, 10–4 and 8–1, as Oil Can Boyd and Clemens redeemed their earlier losses.

Boston Red Sox (East), 4;
California Angels (West), 3

BOS (E)

PLAYER/POS	AVG	G	AB	R	H	2B	3B	HR	RB	BB	SO	SB
Tony Armas, of	.125	5	16	1	2	1	0	0	0	0	2	0
Marty Barrett, 2b	.367	7	30	4	11	2	0	0	5	2	2	0
Don Baylor, dh	.346	7	26	6	9	3	0	1	2	4	5	0
Wade Boggs, 3b	.233	7	30	3	7	1	1	0	2	4	1	0
Oil Can Boyd, p	.000	2	0	0	0	0	0	0	0	0	0	0
Bill Buckner, 1b	.214	7	28	3	6	1	0	0	3	0	2	0
Roger Clemens, p	.000	3	0	0	0	0	0	0	0	0	0	0
Steve Crawford, p	.000	1	0	0	0	0	0	0	0	0	0	0
Dwight Evans, of	.214	7	28	2	6	1	0	1	4	3	3	0
Rich Gedman, c	.357	7	28	4	10	1	0	1	6	0	4	0
Mike Greenwell, ph	.500	2	2	0	1	0	0	0	0	0	0	0
Dave Henderson, of	.111	5	9	3	1	0	0	1	4	2	2	0
Bruce Hurst, p	.000	2	0	0	0	0	0	0	0	0	0	0
Spike Owen, ss	.429	7	21	5	9	0	1	0	3	2	2	1
Jim Rice, of	.161	7	31	8	5	1	0	2	6	1	8	0
Ed Romero, ss	.000	1	2	0	0	0	0	0	0	0	0	0
Joe Sambito, p	.000	3	0	0	0	0	0	0	0	0	0	0
Calvin Schiraldi, p	.000	4	0	0	0	0	0	0	0	0	0	0
Bob Stanley, p	.000	3	0	0	0	0	0	0	0	0	0	0
Dave Stapleton, 1b	.667	4	3	2	2	0	0	0	0	1	0	0
TOTAL	.272		254	41	69	11	2	6	35	19	31	1

PITCHER	W	L	ERA	G	GS	CG	SV	SHO	IP	H	ER	BB	SO
Oil Can Boyd	1	1	4.61	2	2	0	0	0	13.2	17	7	3	8
Roger Clemens	1	1	4.37	3	3	0	0	0	22.2	22	11	7	17
Steve Crawford	1	0	0.00	1	0	0	0	0	1.2	1	0	2	1
Bruce Hurst	1	0	2.40	2	2	1	0	0	15.0	18	4	1	8
Joe Sambito	0	0	13.50	3	0	0	0	0	0.2	1	1	1	0
Calvin Schiraldi	0	1	1.50	4	0	0	1	0	6.0	5	1	3	9
Bob Stanley	0	0	3.18	3	0	0	0	0	5.2	7	2	3	1
TOTAL	4	3	3.58	18	7	1	1	0	65.1	71	26	20	44

CAL (W)

PLAYER/POS	AVG	G	AB	R	H	2B	3B	HR	RB	BB	SO	SB
Bob Boone, c	.455	7	22	4	10	0	0	1	2	1	3	0
Rick Burleson, 2b-2,dh-1	.273	4	11	0	3	0	0	0	0	0	0	0
John Candelaria, p	.000	2	0	0	0	0	0	0	0	0	0	0
Doug Corbett, p	.000	3	0	0	0	0	0	0	0	0	0	0
Doug De Cinces, 3b	.281	7	32	2	9	3	0	1	3	0	2	0
Brian Downing, of	.222	7	27	2	6	0	0	1	7	4	5	0
Chuck Finley, p	.000	3	0	0	0	0	0	0	0	0	0	0
Bobby Grich, 2b-3,1b-3	.208	6	24	1	5	0	0	1	3	0	8	0
George Hendrick, of-2,1b-1	.083	3	12	0	1	0	0	0	0	0	2	0
Jack Howell, ph	.000	2	1	0	0	0	0	0	0	1	1	0
Reggie Jackson, dh	.192	6	26	2	5	2	0	0	2	2	7	0
Ruppert Jones, of-5	.176	6	17	4	3	1	0	0	2	5	2	0
Wally Joyner, 1b	.455	3	11	3	5	2	0	1	2	2	0	0
Gary Lucas, p	.000	4	0	0	0	0	0	0	0	0	0	0
Kirk Mc Caskill, p	.000	2	0	0	0	0	0	0	0	0	0	0
Donnie Moore, p	.000	3	0	0	0	0	0	0	0	0	0	0
Jerry Narron, c-3	.500	4	2	1	1	0	0	0	0	1	1	0
Gary Pettis, of	.346	7	26	4	9	1	0	1	4	3	5	0
Vern Ruhle, p	.000	1	0	0	0	0	0	0	0	0	0	0
Dick Schofield, ss	.300	7	30	4	9	1	0	1	2	1	5	1
Don Sutton, p	.000	2	0	0	0	0	0	0	0	0	0	0
Devon White, of-3	.500	4	2	1	1	0	0	0	0	0	1	0
Rob Wilfong, 2b	.308	4	13	1	4	1	0	0	2	0	2	0
Mike Witt, p	.000	2	0	0	0	0	0	0	0	0	0	0
TOTAL	.277		256	30	71	11	0	7	29	20	44	1

PITCHER	W	L	ERA	G	GS	CG	SV	SHO	IP	H	ER	BB	SO
John Candelaria	1	1	0.84	2	2	0	0	0	10.2	11	1	6	7
Doug Corbett	1	0	5.40	3	0	0	0	0	6.2	9	4	2	2
Chuck Finley	0	0	0.00	3	0	0	0	0	2.0	1	0	0	1
Gary Lucas	0	0	11.57	4	0	0	0	0	2.1	3	3	1	2
Kirk Mc Caskill	0	2	7.71	2	2	0	0	0	9.1	16	8	5	7
Donnie Moore	0	1	7.20	3	0	0	1	0	5.0	8	4	2	0
Vern Ruhle	0	0	13.50	1	0	0	0	0	0.2	2	1	0	0
Don Sutton	0	0	1.86	2	1	0	0	0	9.2	6	2	1	4
Mike Witt	1	0	2.55	2	2	1	0	0	17.2	13	5	2	8
TOTAL	3	4	3.94	22	7	1	1	0	64.0	69	28	19	31

GAME 1 AT BOS OCT 7

CAL	041	000	030	8	11	0
BOS	000	001	000	1	5	1

Pitchers: WITT vs CLEMENS, Sambito (8), Stanley (8)
Attendance: 32,993

GAME 2 AT BOS OCT 8

CAL	000	110	000	2	11	3
BOS	110	010	33X	9	13	2

Pitchers: McCASKILL, Lucas (8), Corbett (8) vs HURST
Home Runs: Joyner-CAL, Rice-BOS
Attendance: 32,786

GAME 3 AT CAL OCT 10

BOS	010	000	020	3	9	1
CAL	000	001	31X	5	8	0

Pitchers: BOYD, Sambito (7), Schiraldi (8) vs CANDELARIA, Moore (8)
Home Runs: Schofield-CAL, Pettis-CAL
Attendance: 64,206

GAME 4 AT CAL OCT 11

BOS	000	001	020	00	3	6	1
CAL	000	000	003	01	4	11	2

Pitchers: Clemens, SCHIRALDI (9) vs Sutton, Lucas (7), Ruhle (7), Finley (8), CORBETT (8)
Home Runs: DeCinces-CAL
Attendance: 64,223

GAME 5 AT CAL OCT 12

BOS	020	000	004	01	7	12	0
CAL	001	002	201	00	6	13	0

Pitchers: Hurst, Stanley (7), Sambito (9), CRAWFORD (9), Schiraldi (11) vs Witt, Lucas (9), MOORE (9), Finley (11)
Home Runs: Gedman-BOS, Boone-CAL, Grich-CAL, Baylor-BOS, Henderson-BOS
Attendance: 64,223

GAME 6 AT BOS OCT 14

CAL	200	000	110	4	11	1
BOS	205	010	20X	10	16	1

Pitchers: McCASKILL, Lucas (3), Corbett (4), Finley (7) vs BOYD, Stanley (8)
Home Runs: Downing-CAL
Attendance: 32,998

GAME 7 AT BOS OCT 15

CAL	000	000	010	1	6	2
BOS	030	400	10X	8	8	1

Pitchers: CANDELARIA, Sutton (4), Moore (8) vs CLEMENS, Schiraldi (8)
Home Runs: Rice-BOS, Evans-BOS
Attendance: 33,001

In their three most recent Series appearances—1946, 1967, and 1975—the Red Sox had battled to a seventh game, only to lose. This time they came within one strike of winning the crown in the sixth game—but wound up losing again in Game Seven.

Boston surprised the favored Mets by taking the first two games in New York. Bruce Hurst (with relief from Calvin Schiradli in the ninth) pitched a four-hitter. New York's Ron Darling hurled just as well but lost when a seventh-inning walk, a wild pitch, and an error by second baseman Tim Teufel moved Jim Rice around the bases with the game's only run. Game Two, close for three innings, turned into a 9–3 Boston blowout as the Sox racked four of the five Met pitchers for eighteen hits, including home runs by Dave Henderson and Dwight Evans.

When the Series moved to Boston, though, the Mets revived to rap Sox starter Oil Can Boyd and two relievers for thirteen hits and seven runs (starting with Len Dykstra's leadoff home run in the first inning) as former Sox pitcher Bob Ojeda subdued his old teammates, giving up just one run on five hits in his seven innings of work. The next day Ron Darling redeemed his first-game loss with seven shutout innings as his teammates built him a 6–0 lead (five of the runs scoring on homers by Dykstra and a pair by Gary Carter). The game ended at 6–2, with the Series even at two wins apiece.

Boston recovered in its final home appearance, taking a 4–0 lead and holding it until Teufel spoiled Bruce Hurst's try for a second shutout by homering in the eighth inning. Hurst yielded a second run with two out in the ninth, but struck out Len Dykstra on three pitches to seal his second win.

The ninth inning of Game Six ended with the score tied 3–3. Boston's Dave Henderson led off the tenth with a home run and two more Sox hits made the score 5–3. Boston reliever Calvin Schiraldi retired the first two Mets in the last of the tenth on long flies, but then three Mets singled, driving in one run and driving out Schiraldi. Bob Stanley, his replacement, had two strikes on Mookie Wilson when a wild pitch let in the tying run, and then Wilson's grounder went through first baseman Bill Buckner's legs as the winning Met bounded across the plate.

The Red Sox nearly recovered in Game Seven. Second-inning home runs by Dwight Evans and Rich Gedman, a walk, sacrifice, and single gave Boston a 3–0 lead which they held into the sixth inning. But then starter Bruce

New York Mets (NL), 4; Boston Red Sox (AL), 3

NY (N)

PLAYER/POS	AVG	G	AB	R	H	2B	3B	HR	RBI	BB	SO	SB
Rick Aguilera, p	.000	1	0	0	0	0	0	0	0	0	0	0
Wally Backman, 2b	.333	6	18	4	6	0	0	0	1	3	2	1
Gary Carter, c	.276	7	29	4	8	2	0	2	9	0	4	0
Ron Darling, p	.000	3	3	0	0	0	0	0	0	0	1	0
Lenny Dykstra, of	.296	7	27	4	8	0	0	2	3	2	7	0
Kevin Elster, ss	.000	1	0	0	0	0	0	0	0	0	0	0
Sid Fernandez, p	.000	3	0	0	0	0	0	0	0	0	0	0
Dwight Gooden, p	.500	2	2	1	1	0	0	0	0	0	0	0
Danny Heep, dh-2,of-1	.091	5	11	0	1	0	0	0	2	1	1	0
Keith Hernandez, 1b	.231	7	26	1	6	0	0	0	4	5	1	0
Howard Johnson, 3b-1,ss-1	.000	2	5	0	0	0	0	0	0	0	2	0
Ray Knight, 3b	.391	6	23	4	9	1	0	1	5	2	2	0
Lee Mazzilli, of-1	.400	4	5	2	2	0	0	0	0	0	0	0
Roger Mc Dowell, p	.000	5	0	0	0	0	0	0	0	0	0	0
Kevin Mitchell, of-2,dh-1	.250	5	8	1	2	0	0	0	0	0	3	0
Bob Ojeda, p	.000	2	2	0	0	0	0	0	0	0	1	0
Jesse Orosco, p	1.000	4	1	0	1	0	0	0	1	0	0	0
Rafael Santana, ss	.250	7	20	3	5	0	0	0	2	2	5	0
Doug Sisk, p	.000	1	0	0	0	0	0	0	0	0	0	0
Darryl Strawberry, of	.208	7	24	4	5	1	0	1	1	4	6	3
Tim Teufel, 2b	.444	3	9	1	4	1	0	1	1	1	2	0
Mookie Wilson, of	.269	7	26	3	7	1	0	0	0	1	6	3
TOTAL	.271		240	32	65	6	0	7	29	21	43	7

PITCHER	W	L	ERA	G	GS	CG	SV	SHO	IP	H	ER	BB	SO
Rick Aguilera	1	0	12.00	1	0	0	0	0	3.0	8	4	1	4
Ron Darling	1	1	1.53	3	3	0	0	0	17.2	13	3	10	12
Sid Fernandez	0	0	1.35	3	0	0	0	0	6.2	6	1	1	10
Dwight Gooden	0	2	8.00	2	2	0	0	0	9.0	17	8	4	9
Roger Mc Dowell	1	0	4.91	5	0	0	0	0	7.1	10	4	6	2
Bob Ojeda	1	0	2.08	2	2	0	0	0	13.0	13	3	5	9
Jesse Orosco	0	0	0.00	4	0	0	2	0	5.2	2	0	0	6
Doug Sisk	0	0	0.00	1	0	0	0	0	0.2	0	0	1	1
TOTAL	4	3	3.29	21	7	0	2	0	63.0	69	23	28	53

BOS (A)

PLAYER/POS	AVG	G	AB	R	H	2B	3B	HR	RBI	BB	SO	SB
Tony Armas, ph	.000	1	1	0	0	0	0	0	0	0	1	0
Marty Barrett, 2b	.433	7	30	1	13	2	0	0	4	5	2	0
Don Baylor, dh-3	.182	4	11	1	2	1	0	0	1	1	3	0
Wade Boggs, 3b	.290	7	31	3	9	3	0	0	3	4	2	0
Oil Can Boyd, p	.000	1	0	0	0	0	0	0	0	0	0	0
Bill Buckner, 1b	.188	7	32	2	6	0	0	0	1	0	3	0
Roger Clemens, p	.000	2	4	1	0	0	0	0	0	0	1	0
Steve Crawford, p	.000	3	1	0	0	0	0	0	0	0	0	0
Dwight Evans, of	.308	7	26	4	8	2	0	2	9	4	3	0
Rich Gedman, c	.200	7	30	1	6	1	0	1	1	0	10	0
Mike Greenwell, ph	.000	4	3	0	0	0	0	0	0	1	2	0
Dave Henderson, of	.667	7	15	6	10	1	1	2	5	2	6	0
Bruce Hurst, p	.000	3	3	0	0	0	0	0	0	0	3	0
Al Nipper, p	.000	2	0	0	0	0	0	0	0	0	0	0
Spike Owen, ss	.300	7	20	2	6	0	0	0	2	5	6	0
Jim Rice, of	.333	7	27	6	9	1	1	0	0	6	9	0
Ed Romero, ss	.000	3	1	0	0	0	0	0	0	0	0	0
Joe Sambito, p	.000	2	0	0	0	0	0	0	0	0	0	0
Calvin Schiraldi, p	.000	3	1	0	0	0	0	0	0	0	0	0
Bob Stanley, p	.000	5	1	0	0	0	0	0	0	0	1	0
Dave Stapleton, 1b	.000	3	1	0	0	0	0	0	0	0	0	0
TOTAL	.290		238	27	69	11	2	5	26	28	53	0

PITCHER	W	L	ERA	G	GS	CG	SV	SHO	IP	H	ER	BB	SO
Oil Can Boyd	0	1	7.71	1	1	0	0	0	7.0	9	6	1	3
Roger Clemens	0	0	3.18	2	2	0	0	0	11.1	9	4	6	11
Steve Crawford	1	0	6.23	3	0	0	0	0	4.1	5	3	0	4
Bruce Hurst	2	0	1.96	3	3	1	0	0	23.0	18	5	6	17
Al Nipper	0	1	7.11	2	1	0	0	0	6.1	10	5	2	2
Joe Sambito	0	0	27.00	2	0	0	0	0	0.1	2	1	2	0
Calvin Schiraldi	0	2	13.50	3	0	0	1	0	4.0	7	6	3	2
Bob Stanley	0	0	0.00	5	0	0	1	0	6.1	5	0	1	4
TOTAL	3	4	4.31	21	7	1	2	0	62.2	65	30	21	43

Hurst lost his touch: four hits and a walk later the score was tied. A succession of five Sox relievers tried to hold the line, but the Mets scored five runs to Boston's two in the final innings for an 8–5 triumph.

GAME 1 AT NY OCT 18

BOS	000	000	100	1	5	0
NY	000	000	000	0	4	1

Pitchers: HURST, Schiradli (9) vs DARLING, McDowell (8)
Attendance: 55,076

GAME 2 AT NY OCT 19

BOS	003	120	201	9	18	0
NY	002	010	000	3	8	1

Pitchers: Clemens, CARWFORD (5), Stanley (7) vs GOODEN, Aguilera (6), Orosco (7), Fernandez (9), Sisk (9)
Home Runs: Henderson-BOS, Evans-BOS
Attendance: 55,063

GAME 3 AT BOS OCT 21

NY	400	000	210	7	13	0
BOS	001	000	000	1	5	0

Pitchers: OJEDA, McDowell (8) vs BOYD, Sambito (8), Stanley (8)
Home Runs: Dykstra-NY
Attendance: 33,595

GAME 4 AT BOS OCT 22

NY	000	300	210	6	12	0
BOS	000	000	020	2	7	1

Pitchers: DARLING, McDowell (7), Orosco (7) vs NIPPER, Crawford (7), Stanley (9)
Home Runs: Dykstra-NY, Carter-NY (2)
Attendance: 33,920

GAME 5 AT BOS OCT 23

NY	000	000	011	2	10	1
BOS	011	020	00X	4	12	0

Pitchers: GOODEN, Fernandez (5) vs HURST
Home Runs: Teufel-NY
Attendance: 34,010

GAME 6 AT NY OCT 25

BOS	110	000	100 2	5	13	3
NY	000	020	010 3	6	8	2

Pitchers: Clemens, SCHIRALDI (8), Stanley (10) vs Ojeda, McDowell (7), Orosco (8), AGUILERA (9)
Home Runs: Henderson-BOS
Attendance: 55,078

GAME 7 AT NY OCT 27

BOS	030	000	020	5	9	0
NY	000	003	32X	8	10	0

Pitchers: Hurst, SCHIRALDI (7), Sambito (7), Stanley (7), Nipper (8), Crawford (8) vs Darling, Fernandez (4), McDOWELL (8), Orosco (9)
Home Runs: Evans-BOS, Gedman-BOS, Knight-NY, Strawberry-NY
Attendance: 55,032

The Giants scored four times in the fourth inning of Game Five, winning the game and taking a 3–2 series advantage. But Cardinal pitchers shut them out the rest of the series (an NLCS record 22 innings) to capture the flag.

St. Louis won the opener 5–3, with pitcher Greg Mathews's two-run single in the sixth providing his margin of victory. The Giants came back in Game Two, supporting Dave Dravecky's two-hit shutout with home runs by Will Clark and Jeffrey Leonard. But the Cards retook the series lead in Game Three, overcoming a 0–4 deficit with two runs on Jim Lindeman's homer in the sixth and four more in the seventh (capped by Lindeman's sacrifice fly) for an eventual 6–5 win.

The Giants snapped back with a pair of wins, scoring four runs on three homers in Game Four (including Leonard's fourth in successive games—an LCS record), and six runs in Game Five. But Dravecky and the Giants lost a heartbreaker in Game Six when right fielder Candy Maldonado lost Tony Pena's fly in the lights for a triple. Pena scored on a sacrifice fly for the game's only run, as John Tudor and two late-inning relievers blanked the Giants. Danny Cox pitched an easier shutout in the finale as his Cardinals hammered seven Giant pitchers for twelve hits and six runs.

St. Louis Cardinals (East), 4; San Francisco Giants (West) 3

STL (E)

PLAYER/POS	AVG	G	AB	R	H	2B	3B	HR	RB	BB	SO	SB
Jack Clark, ph	.000	1	1	0	0	0	0	0	0	0	1	0
Vince Coleman, of	.269	7	26	3	7	1	0	0	4	4	6	1
Danny Cox, p	.333	2	6	0	2	0	0	0	1	0	2	0
Ken Dayley, p	.000	3	0	0	0	0	0	0	0	0	0	0
Dan Driessen, 1b-4	.250	5	12	1	3	2	0	0	1	1	1	0
Curt Ford, of	.333	4	9	2	3	0	0	0	0	1	1	0
Bob Forsch, p	.000	3	0	0	0	0	0	0	0	0	0	0
Tommy Herr, 2b	.222	7	27	6	6	0	0	0	3	0	1	1
Rick Horton, p	.000	1	0	0	0	0	0	0	0	0	0	0
Lance Johnson, pr	.000	1	0	1	0	0	0	0	0	0	0	1
Tom Lawless, 3b-2,of-1	.333	3	6	0	2	0	0	0	0	1	1	0
Jim Lindeman, 1b	.308	5	13	1	4	0	0	1	3	0	3	0
Joe Magrane, p	.000	1	1	0	0	0	0	0	0	0	0	0
Greg Mathews, p	1.000	2	2	0	2	0	0	0	2	0	0	0
Willie Mc Gee, of	.308	7	26	2	8	1	1	0	2	0	5	0
John Morris, of	.000	2	3	0	0	0	0	0	0	0	0	0
Jose Oquendo, of-5,3b-1	.167	5	12	3	2	0	0	1	4	3	2	0
Tom Pagnozzi, ph	.000	1	1	0	0	0	0	0	0	0	0	0
Tony Pena, c	.381	7	21	5	8	0	1	0	0	3	4	1
Terry Pendleton, 3b	.211	6	19	3	4	0	1	0	1	0	6	0
Ozzie Smith, ss	.200	7	25	2	5	0	1	0	1	3	4	0
John Tudor, p	.000	2	4	0	0	0	0	0	0	0	4	0
Todd Worrell, p-3,of-1	.000	3	1	0	0	0	0	0	0	0	1	0
TOTAL	.260		215	23	56	4	4	2	22	16	42	4

PITCHER	W	L	ERA	G	GS	CG	SV	SHO	IP	H	ER	BB	SO
Danny Cox	1	1	2.12	2	2	2	0	1	17.0	17	4	3	11
Ken Dayley	0	0	0.00	3	0	0	2	0	4.0	1	0	2	4
Bob Forsch	1	1	12.00	3	0	0	0	0	3.0	4	4	1	3
Rick Horton	0	0	0.00	1	0	0	0	0	3.0	2	0	0	2
Joe Magrane	0	0	9.00	1	1	0	0	0	4.0	4	4	2	3
Greg Mathews	1	0	3.48	2	2	0	0	0	10.1	6	4	3	10
John Tudor	1	1	1.76	2	2	0	0	0	15.1	16	3	5	12
Todd Worrell	0	0	2.08	3	0	0	1	0	4.1	4	1	1	6
TOTAL	4	3	2.95	17	7	2	3	1	61.0	54	20	17	51

SF (W)

PLAYER/POS	AVG	G	AB	R	H	2B	3B	HR	RB	BB	SO	SB
Mike Aldrete, of-3	.100	5	10	0	1	0	0	0	0	1	2	0
Bob Brenly, c	.235	6	17	3	4	1	0	1	2	3	7	0
Will Clark, 1b	.360	7	25	3	9	2	0	1	3	3	6	1
Chili Davis, of	.150	6	20	2	3	1	0	0	0	1	4	0
Kelly Downs, p	.000	1	0	0	0	0	0	0	0	0	0	0
Dave Dravecky, p	.167	2	6	0	1	0	0	0	0	0	1	0
Scott Garrelts, p	.000	2	0	0	0	0	0	0	0	0	0	0
Atlee Hammaker, p	.000	2	3	0	0	0	0	0	0	0	2	0
Mike Krukow, p	.000	1	2	0	0	0	0	0	0	1	0	0
Mike La Coss, p	.000	2	0	0	0	0	0	0	0	0	0	0
Craig Lefferts, p	.000	3	0	0	0	0	0	0	0	0	0	0
Jeffrey Leonard, of	.417	7	24	5	10	0	0	4	5	3	4	0
Candy Maldonado, of	.211	5	19	2	4	1	0	0	2	0	3	0
Bob Melvin, c-2	.429	3	7	0	3	0	0	0	0	1	1	0
Eddie Milner, of-4	.143	6	7	0	1	0	0	0	0	0	3	0
Kevin Mitchell, 3b	.267	7	30	2	8	1	0	1	2	0	3	1
Joe Price, p	.000	2	1	0	0	0	0	0	0	0	1	0
Rick Reuschel, p	.000	2	2	0	0	0	0	0	0	0	1	0
Don Robinson, p	.000	3	0	0	0	0	0	0	0	0	0	0
Chris Speier, 2b-1	.000	3	5	0	0	0	0	0	0	0	2	0
Harry Spilman, ph	.500	3	2	1	1	0	0	1	1	0	0	0
Rob Thompson, 2b-6	.100	7	20	4	2	0	1	1	2	5	7	2
Jose Uribe, ss	.269	7	26	1	7	1	0	0	2	0	4	1
TOTAL	.239		226	23	54	7	1	9	20	17	51	5

PITCHER	W	L	ERA	G	GS	CG	SV	SHO	IP	H	ER	BB	SO
Kelly Downs	0	0	0.00	1	0	0	0	0	1.1	1	0	0	0
Dave Dravecky	1	1	0.60	2	2	1	0	1	15.0	7	1	4	14
Scott Garrelts	0	0	6.75	2	0	0	0	0	2.2	2	2	4	4
Atlee Hammaker	0	1	7.87	2	2	0	0	0	8.0	12	7	0	7
Mike Krukow	1	0	2.00	1	1	1	0	0	9.0	9	2	1	3
Mike La Coss	0	0	0.00	2	0	0	0	0	3.1	1	0	3	2
Craig Lefferts	0	0	0.00	3	0	0	0	0	2.0	3	0	1	0
Joe Price	1	0	0.00	2	0	0	0	0	5.2	3	0	1	7
Rick Reuschel	0	1	6.30	2	2	0	0	0	10.0	15	7	2	2
Don Robinson	0	1	9.00	3	0	0	0	0	3.0	3	3	0	3
TOTAL	3	4	3.30	20	7	2	0	1	60.0	56	22	16	42

GAME 1 AT STL OCT 6

SF	100	100	010	3	7 1
STL	001	103	00X	5	10 1

Pitchers: REUSCHEL, Lefferts (7), Garrelts (8) vs MATHEWS, Worrell (8), Dayley (8)
Home Runs: Leonard-SF
Attendance: 55,331

GAME 2 AT STL OCT 7

SF	020	100	020	5	10 0
STL	000	000	000	0	2 1

Pitchers: DRAVECKY vs TUDOR, Forsch (9)
Home Runs: Clark-SF, Leonard-SF
Attendance: 55,331

GAME 3 AT SF OCT 9

STL	000	002	400	6	11 1
SF	031	000	001	5	7 1

Pitchers: Magrane, FORSCH (5), Worrell (7) vs Hammaker, D.ROBINSON (7), Lefferts (7), LaCoss (8)
Home Runs: Lindeman-STL, Leonard-SF, Spilman-SF
Attendance: 57,913

GAME 4 AT SF OCT 10

STL	020	000	000	2	9 0
SF	000	120	01X	4	9 2

Pitchers: COX vs KRUKOW
Home Runs: Thompson-SF, Leonard-SF, Brenly-SF
Attendance: 57,997

GAME 5 AT SF OCT 11

STL	101	100	000	3	7 0
SF	101	400	00X	6	7 1

Pitchers: Mathews, FORSCH (4), Horton (4), Dayley (7) vs Reuschel, PRICE (5)
Home Runs: Mitchell-SF
Attendance: 59,363

GAME 6 AT STL OCT 13

SF	000	000	000	0	6 0
STL	010	000	00X	1	5 0

Pitchers: DRAVECKY, D.Robinson (7) vs TUDOR, Worrell (8), Dayley (9)
Attendance: 55,331

GAME 7 AT STL OCT 14

SF	000	000	000	0	8 1
STL	040	002	00X	6	12 0

Pitchers: HAMMAKER, Price (3), Downs (3), Garrelts (5), Lefferts (6), LaCoss (6), D.Robinson (8) vs COX
Home Runs: Oquendo-STL
Attendance: 55,331

The Tigers, with the best over-all won-lost record in the majors, were favored to defeat the ninth-ranked Twins, although Minnesota held the home field advantage and the major leagues' best record at home. Tiger pitcher Doyle Alexander—he had been 9–0 since joining Detroit in mid-August—took a 5–4 lead into the last of the eighth in Game One. But a single and double drove him out, and before the inning was over three more Twins had scored to sew up their first win. Detroit scored twice in the second inning the next day, but the Twins responded later in the inning with three runs, two on Tim Laudner's double off Tiger ace Jack Morris, and increased their lead in the fourth and fifth to seal Morris's first loss in Minnesota after eleven wins.

The Tigers won a game after the series moved to Detroit, when Pat Sheridan's two-run homer in the eighth inning of Game Three restored a lead they had squandered in the middle innings. But that was it for Detroit, as the Twins surprised everyone by subduing the Tigers in their den. In Game Four they took the lead for good on Greg Gagne's fourth-inning home run. And in Game Five, after initiating the scoring with four runs in the second, Minnesota pushed on to a 9–5 win and their first pennant in twenty-two years.

Minnesota Twins (West) 4; Detroit Tigers (East), 1

MIN (W)

PLAYER/POS	AVG	G	AB	R	H	2B	3B	HR	RB	BB	SO	SB
Keith Atherton, p	.000	1	0	0	0	0	0	0	0	0	0	0
Don Baylor, dh	.400	2	5	0	2	0	0	0	1	0	0	0
Juan Berenguer, p	.000	4	0	0	0	0	0	0	0	0	0	0
Bert Blyleven, p	.000	2	0	0	0	0	0	0	0	0	0	0
Tom Brunansky, of	.412	5	17	5	7	4	0	2	9	4	3	0
Randy Bush, dh	.250	4	12	4	3	0	1	0	2	3	2	3
Sal Butera, c	.667	1	3	0	2	0	0	0	0	0	0	0
Mark Davidson, pr	.000	1	0	0	0	0	0	0	0	0	0	0
Gary Gaetti, 3b	.300	5	20	5	6	1	0	2	5	1	3	0
Greg Gagne, ss	.278	5	18	5	5	3	0	2	3	3	4	0
Dan Gladden, of	.350	5	20	5	7	2	0	0	5	2	1	0
Kent Hrbek, 1b	.150	5	20	4	3	0	0	1	1	3	0	0
Gene Larkin, ph	1.000	1	1	0	1	1	0	0	1	0	0	0
Tim Laudner, c	.071	5	14	1	1	1	0	0	2	2	5	0
Steve Lombardozzi, 2b	.267	5	15	2	4	0	0	0	1	2	2	0
Al Newman, 2b	.000	1	2	0	0	0	0	0	0	0	0	0
Kirby Puckett, of	.208	5	24	3	5	1	0	1	3	0	5	1
Jeff Reardon, p	.000	4	0	0	0	0	0	0	0	0	0	0
Dan Schatzeder, p	.000	2	0	0	0	0	0	0	0	0	0	0
Les Straker, p	.000	1	0	0	0	0	0	0	0	0	0	0
Frank Viola, p	.000	2	0	0	0	0	0	0	0	0	0	0
TOTAL	.269		171	34	46	13	1	8	33	20	25	4

PITCHER	W	L	ERA	G	GS	CG	SV	SHO	IP	H	ER	BB	SO
Keith Atherton	0	0	0.00	1	0	0	0	0	0.1	1	0	0	0
Juan Berenguer	0	0	1.50	4	0	0	1	0	6.0	1	1	3	6
Bert Blyleven	2	0	4.05	2	2	0	0	0	13.1	12	6	3	9
Jeff Reardon	1	1	5.06	4	0	0	2	0	5.1	7	3	3	5
Dan Schatzeder	0	0	0.00	2	0	0	0	0	4.1	2	0	0	5
Les Straker	0	0	16.88	1	1	0	0	0	2.2	3	5	4	1
Frank Viola	1	0	5.25	2	2	0	0	0	12.0	14	7	5	9
TOTAL	4	1	4.50	16	5	0	3	0	44.0	40	22	18	35

DET (E)

PLAYER/POS	AVG	G	AB	R	H	2B	3B	HR	RB	BB	SO	SB
Doyle Alexander, p	.000	2	0	0	0	0	0	0	0	0	0	0
Dave Bergman, 1b-1,dh-1	.250	4	4	0	1	0	0	0	2	0	1	0
Tom Brookens, 3b	.000	5	13	0	0	0	0	0	0	0	3	0
Darrell Evans, 1b-5,3b-1	.294	5	17	0	5	0	0	0	0	4	2	0
Kirk Gibson, of	.286	5	21	4	6	1	0	1	4	3	8	3
Johnny Grubb, dh-1	.571	4	7	0	4	0	0	0	0	0	1	0
Mike Heath, c	.286	3	7	1	2	0	0	1	2	0	0	0
Mike Henneman, p	.000	3	0	0	0	0	0	0	0	0	0	0
Willie Hernandez, p	.000	1	0	0	0	0	0	0	0	0	0	0
Larry Herndon, of-2,dh-1	.333	3	9	1	3	1	0	0	2	1	1	0
Eric King, p	.000	2	0	0	0	0	0	0	0	0	0	0
Chet Lemon, of	.278	5	18	4	5	0	0	2	4	1	4	0
Bill Madlock, dh	.000	1	5	0	0	0	0	0	0	0	3	0
Jack Morris, p-1,dh-1	.000	2	0	1	0	0	0	0	0	0	0	0
Jim Morrison, 3b-1,dh-1	.400	2	5	1	2	0	0	0	0	0	1	0
Matt Nokes, c-3,dh-2	.143	5	14	2	2	0	0	1	2	1	4	0
Dan Petry, p	.000	1	0	0	0	0	0	0	0	0	0	0
Jeff Robinson, p	.000	1	0	0	0	0	0	0	0	0	0	0
Pat Sheridan, of-4	.300	5	10	2	3	1	0	1	2	0	2	1
Frank Tanana, p	.000	1	0	0	0	0	0	0	0	0	0	0
Walt Terrell, p	.000	1	0	0	0	0	0	0	0	0	0	0
Mark Thurmond, p	.000	1	0	0	0	0	0	0	0	0	0	0
Alan Trammell, ss	.200	5	20	3	4	1	0	0	2	1	2	0
Lou Whitaker, 2b	.176	5	17	4	3	0	0	1	1	7	3	0
TOTAL	.240		167	23	40	4	0	7	21	18	35	5

PITCHER	W	L	ERA	G	GS	CG	SV	SHO	IP	H	ER	BB	SO
Doyle Alexander	0	2	10.00	2	2	0	0	0	9.0	14	10	1	5
Mike Henneman	1	0	10.80	3	0	0	0	0	5.0	6	6	6	3
Willie Hernandez	0	0	0.00	1	0	0	0	0	0.1	2	0	0	0
Eric King	0	0	1.69	2	0	0	0	0	5.1	3	1	2	4
Jack Morris	0	1	6.75	1	1	1	0	0	8.0	6	6	3	7
Dan Petry	0	0	0.00	1	0	0	0	0	3.1	1	0	1	4
Jeff Robinson	0	0	0.00	1	0	0	0	0	0.1	1	0	0	0
Frank Tanana	0	1	5.06	1	1	0	0	0	5.1	6	3	4	1
Walt Terrell	0	0	9.00	1	1	0	0	0	6.0	7	6	4	4
Mark Thurmond	0	0	0.00	1	0	0	0	0	0.1	0	0	0	0
TOTAL	1	4	6.70	14	5	1	0	0	43.0	46	32	20	25

GAME 1 AT MIN OCT 7

```
DET  001 001 120   5 10 0
MIN  010 030 04X   8 10 0
```
Pitchers: ALEXANDER, Henneman (8), Hernandez (8), King (8) vs Viola, REARDON (8)
Home Runs: Heath-DET, Gibson-DET, Gaetti-MIN (2)
Attendance: 53,269

GAME 2 AT MIN OCT 8

```
DET  020 000 010   3 7 1
MIN  030 210 00X   6 6 0
```
Pitchers: MORRIS vs BLYLEVEN, Berenguer (8)
Home Runs: Lemon-DET, Whitaker-DET, Hrbek-MIN
Attendance: 55,245

GAME 3 AT DET OCT 10

```
MIN  000 202 200   6 8 1
DET  005 000 02X   7 7 0
```
Pitchers: Straker, Schatzeder (3), Berenguer (8), REARDON (8) vs Terrell, HENNEMAN (7)
Home Runs: Gagne-MIN, Brunansky-MIN, Sheridan-DET
Attendance: 49,730

GAME 4 AT DET OCT 11

```
MIN  001 111 010   5 7 1
DET  100 011 000   3 7 1
```
Pitchers: VIOLA, Atherton (6), Berenguer (6), Reardon (9) vs TANANA, Petry (6), Thurmond (9)
Home Runs: Puckett-MIN, Gagne-MIN
Attendance: 51,939

GAME 5 AT DET OCT 12

```
MIN  040 000 113   9 15 1
DET  000 300 011   5 9 1
```
Pitchers: BLYLEVEN, Schatzeder (7), Berenguer (8), Reardon (8) vs ALEXANDER, King (2), Henneman (7), Robinson (9)
Home Runs: Brunansky-MIN, Nokes-DET, Lemon-DET
Attendance: 47,448

Although the Twins compiled a dismal record on the road during the season (29–52), their play at home (56–25) topped the majors. In postseason play they won all six games played in their Metrodome, including the four that won them the world championship. They overwhelmed St. Louis in the Series opener, the first World Series game ever played indoors. The Cardinals scored first, in the second inning, but Twin ace Frank Viola (with relief from Keith Atherton in the ninth) stopped them after that as his teammates unloaded for seven runs in the fourth inning (capped by Dan Gladden's grand slam) on their way to a 10–1 win. The Cardinals scored four runs in Game Two, but again the Twins enjoyed a big fourth inning— bunching six of their ten hits together for six runs—and scored two other runs on homers by Gary Gaetti and Tim Laudner.

When the Series moved to St. Louis, the Cardinals grabbed the home advantage to post their three wins. In Game Three, Cardinal pitchers John Tudor and Todd Worrell combined for a five-hitter as the Cards came from behind with a three-run seventh to win 3–1. The next day St. Louis broke a 1–1 tie with their own fourth-inning explosion, for six runs. The big blow was a three-run homer by utility infielder Tom Lawless—only the second home run of his big league career. Final score: 7–2. After five scoreless innings in Game Five, St. Louis moved out to a 4–0 lead in the sixth and seventh innings. Gaetti's eighth-inning triple put two Minnesota runs across, but the Cards held on for a 4–2 win.

Back in Minneapolis, St. Louis built up a 5–2 lead in Game Six before the Twins retaliated with four runs in the fifth inning (with Don Baylor's three-run homer providing the tying runs) and four more an inning later with Kent Hrbek's grand slam. A final Twins run in the eighth ended the scoring at 11–5.

The Cardinals scored first in Game Seven, with a pair of runs in the second inning, but the Twins edged their way to a tie with single runs in the second and fifth, and an inning later took the lead on three walks and an infield single. As Twin starter Frank Viola held St. Louis scoreless on two hits after the second inning, Minnesota made the score 4–2 with a final run in the eighth, and ace reliever Jeff Reardon retired the Cards in order in the ninth to bring Minnesota its first world championship.

Minnesota Twins (AL) 4;
St. Louis Cardinals (NL), 3

MIN (A)

PLAYER/POS	AVG	G	AB	R	H	2B	3B	HR	RB	BB	SO	SB
Keith Atherton, p	.000	2	0	0	0	0	0	0	0	0	0	0
Don Baylor, dh-3	.385	5	13	3	5	0	0	1	3	1	1	0
Juan Berenguer, p	.000	3	0	0	0	0	0	0	0	0	0	0
Bert Blyleven, p	.000	2	1	0	0	0	0	0	0	0	1	0
Tom Brunansky, of	.200	7	25	5	5	0	0	0	2	4	4	1
Randy Bush, dh-2	.167	4	6	1	1	1	0	0	2	0	1	0
Sal Butera, c	.000	1	0	0	0	0	0	0	0	0	0	0
Mark Davidson, of-1	.000	2	1	0	0	0	0	0	0	0	0	0
George Frazier, p	.000	1	0	0	0	0	0	0	0	0	0	0
Gary Gaetti, 3b	.259	7	27	4	7	2	1	1	4	2	5	2
Greg Gagne, ss	.200	7	30	5	6	1	0	1	3	1	6	0
Dan Gladden, of	.290	7	31	3	9	2	1	1	7	3	4	2
Kent Hrbek, 1b	.208	7	24	4	5	0	0	1	6	5	3	0
Gene Larkin, 1b-1,dh-1	.000	5	3	1	0	0	0	0	0	1	0	0
Tim Laudner, c	.318	7	22	4	7	1	0	1	4	5	3	0
Steve Lombardozzi, 2b	.412	6	17	3	7	1	0	1	4	2	3	0
Al Newman, 2b-3	.200	4	5	0	1	0	0	0	0	1	1	0
Joe Niekro, p	.000	1	0	0	0	0	0	0	0	0	0	0
Kirby Puckett, of	.357	7	28	5	10	1	1	0	3	2	1	1
Jeff Reardon, p	.000	4	0	0	0	0	0	0	0	0	0	0
Dan Schatzeder, p	.000	3	0	0	0	0	0	0	0	0	0	0
Roy Smalley, ph	.500	4	2	0	1	1	0	0	0	2	0	0
Les Straker, p	.000	2	2	0	0	0	0	0	0	0	2	0
Frank Viola, p	.000	3	1	0	0	0	0	0	0	0	1	0
TOTAL	.269		238	38	64	10	3	7	38	29	36	6

PITCHER	W	L	ERA	G	GS	CG	SV	SHO	IP	H	ER	BB	SO
Keith Atherton	0	0	6.75	2	0	0	0	0	1.1	0	1	1	0
Juan Berenguer	0	1	10.38	3	0	0	0	0	4.1	5	5	0	1
Bert Blyleven	1	1	2.77	2	2	0	0	0	13.0	13	4	2	12
George Frazier	0	0	0.00	1	0	0	0	0	2.0	1	0	0	2
Joe Niekro	0	0	0.00	1	0	0	0	0	2.0	1	0	1	1
Jeff Reardon	0	0	0.00	4	0	0	1	0	4.2	5	0	0	3
Dan Schatzeder	1	0	6.23	3	0	0	0	0	4.1	4	3	3	3
Les Straker	0	0	4.00	2	2	0	0	0	9.0	9	4	3	6
Frank Viola	2	1	3.72	3	3	0	0	0	19.1	17	8	3	16
TOTAL	4	3	3.75	21	7	0	1	0	60.0	60	25	13	44

STL (N)

PLAYER/POS	AVG	G	AB	R	H	2B	3B	HR	RB	BB	SO	SB
Vince Coleman, of	.143	7	28	5	4	0	0	0	2	2	10	6
Danny Cox, p	.000	3	2	0	0	0	0	0	0	0	1	0
Ken Dayley, p	.000	4	1	0	0	0	0	0	0	0	1	0
Dan Driessen, 1b	.231	4	13	3	3	2	0	0	1	1	1	0
Curt Ford, of-4	.308	5	13	1	4	0	0	0	2	1	1	0
Bob Forsch, p	.000	3	2	0	0	0	0	0	0	0	0	0
Tommy Herr, 2b	.250	7	28	2	7	0	0	1	1	2	2	0
Rick Horton, p	.000	2	0	0	0	0	0	0	0	0	0	0
Lance Johnson, pr	.000	1	0	0	0	0	0	0	0	0	0	1
Steve Lake, c	.333	3	3	0	1	0	0	0	1	0	0	0
Tom Lawless, 3b	.100	3	10	1	1	0	0	1	3	0	4	0
Jim Lindeman, 1b-6,of-1	.333	6	15	3	5	1	0	0	2	0	3	0
Joe Magrane, p	.000	2	0	0	0	0	0	0	0	0	0	0
Greg Mathews, p	.000	1	1	0	0	0	0	0	0	0	0	0
Willie Mc Gee, of	.370	7	27	2	10	2	0	0	4	0	9	0
John Morris, of	.000	1	2	0	0	0	0	0	0	0	1	0
Jose Oquendo, 3b-4,of-3	.250	7	24	2	6	0	0	0	2	1	4	0
Tom Pagnozzi, dh-1	.250	2	4	0	1	0	0	0	0	0	0	0
Tony Pena, c-6,dh-1	.409	7	22	2	9	1	0	0	4	3	2	1
Terry Pendleton, dh-2	.429	3	7	2	3	0	0	0	1	1	1	2
Ozzie Smith, ss	.214	7	28	3	6	0	0	0	2	2	3	2
John Tudor, p	.000	2	2	0	0	0	0	0	0	0	2	0
Lee Tunnell, p	.000	2	0	0	0	0	0	0	0	0	0	0
Todd Worrell, p	.000	4	0	0	0	0	0	0	0	0	0	0
TOTAL	.259		232	26	60	8	0	2	25	13	44	12

PITCHER	W	L	ERA	G	GS	CG	SV	SHO	IP	H	ER	BB	SO
Danny Cox	1	2	7.71	3	2	0	0	0	11.2	13	10	8	9
Ken Dayley	0	0	1.93	4	0	0	1	0	4.2	2	1	0	3
Bob Forsch	1	0	9.95	3	0	0	0	0	6.1	8	7	5	3
Rick Horton	0	0	6.00	2	0	0	0	0	3.0	5	2	0	1
Joe Magrane	0	1	8.59	2	2	0	0	0	7.1	9	7	5	5
Greg Mathews	0	0	2.45	1	1	0	0	0	3.2	2	1	2	3
John Tudor	1	1	5.73	2	2	0	0	0	11.0	15	7	3	8
Lee Tunnell	0	0	2.08	2	0	0	0	0	4.1	4	1	2	1
Todd Worrell	0	0	1.29	4	0	0	2	0	7.0	6	1	4	3
TOTAL	3	4	5.64	23	7	0	3	0	59.0	64	37	29	36

GAME 1 AT MIN OCT 17

STL	010	000	000		1	5	1
MIN	000	720	10X		10	11	0

Pitchers: MAGRANE, Forsch (4), Horton (7) vs VIOLA, Atherton (9)
Home Runs: Gladden-MIN, Lombardozzi-MIN
Attendance: 55,171

GAME 2 AT MIN OCT 18

STL	000	010	120		4	9	0
MIN	010	601	00X		8	10	0

Pitchers: COX, Tunnell (4), Dayley (7), Worrell (8) vs BLYLEVEN, Berenguer (8), Reardon (9)
Home Runs: Gaetti-MIN, Laudner-MIN
Attendance: 55,257

GAME 3 AT STL OCT 20

MIN	000	001	000		1	5	1
STL	000	000	30X		3	9	1

Pitchers: Straker, BERENGUER (7), Schatzeder (7) vs TUDOR, Worrell (8)
Attendance: 55,347

GAME 4 AT STL OCT 21

MIN	001	010	000		2	7	1
STL	001	600	00X		7	10	1

Pitchers: VIOLA, Schatzeder (4), Niekro (5), Frazier (7) vs Mathews, FORSCH (4), Dayley (7)
Home Runs: Gagne-MIN, Lawless-STL
Attendance: 55,347

GAME 5 AT STL OCT 22

MIN	000	000	020		2	6	1
STL	000	003	10X		4	10	1

Pitchers: BLYLEVEN, Atherton (7), Reardon (7) vs COX, Dayley (8), Worrell (8)
Attendance: 55,347

GAME 6 AT MIN OCT 24

STL	110	210	000		5	11	2
MIN	200	044	01X		11	15	0

Pitchers: TUDOR, Horton (5), Forsch (6), Dayley (6), Tunnell (7) vs Straker, SCHATZEDER (4), Berenguer (6), Reardon (9)
Home Runs: Herr-STL, Baylor-MIN, Hrbek-MIN
Attendance: 55,293

GAME 7 AT MIN OCT 25

STL	020	000	000		2	6	1
MIN	010	011	01X		4	10	0

Pitchers: Magrane, COX (5), Worrell (6) vs VIOLA, Reardon (9)
Attendance: 55,376

The Mets had defeated the Dodgers in 10 of 11 regular season games, but in the LCS the pitching of Dodger ace Orel Hershiser and rookie Tim Belcher, and the timely hitting of Mike Scioscia and Kirk Gibson, propelled L.A. to the pennant. The Dodgers scored a first-inning run in the opener and carried a 2–0 lead into the ninth. But three Met runs in the top of the ninth (the final two scoring with two outs on a fly to short center that bounced off the glove of a diving John Shelby) gave New York the victory.

Dodger pitcher Tim Belcher singled with two away in the second inning of Game Two to start a four-run rally—the margin of victory in Belcher's 6–3 win. In Game Three (played in a steady downpour after a rainout the night before), the Mets overcame a 3–4 deficit, rapping four Dodger pitchers for five runs in the last of the eighth to take the series lead.

Kirk Gibson's twelfth-inning solo homer the next night put the Dodgers ahead 5–4, after Mike Scioscia's ninth-inning home run had pulled them into a tie. In the last of the twelfth, Orel Hershiser (who had pitched seven innings to no decision in the previous game) took the mound with two out and the bases full, and saved the game as center fielder Shelby, on the run, snared Kevin McReynolds' looping fly.

Gibson homered again in Game Four—for three runs that provided the winning margin in a 7–4 Dodger victory. One game from the pennant, as the series moved back to Los Angeles, the Dodgers for the first time failed to score first and saw the series evened a third time as David Cone held them to five hits and one run while the Mets scored five. But in the finale, the Dodgers unloaded on Ron Darling for six runs in the first two innings and Hershiser blanked the Mets on five hits.

Los Angeles Dodgers (West), 4; New York Mets (East), 3

LA (W)

PLAYER/POS	AVG	G	AB	R	H	2B	3B	HR	RB	BB	SO	SB
Tim Belcher, p	.125	2	8	1	1	0	0	0	0	0	3	0
Mike Davis, ph	.000	4	2	0	0	0	0	0	0	1	0	0
Rick Dempsey, c-3	.400	4	5	1	2	2	0	0	2	1	0	0
Kirk Gibson, of	.154	7	26	4	4	0	0	2	6	3	6	2
Jose Gonzalez, of-3	.000	4	0	2	0	0	0	0	0	0	0	0
Alfredo Griffin, ss	.160	7	25	1	4	1	0	0	3	0	5	0
Jeff Hamilton, 3b	.217	7	23	2	5	0	0	0	1	3	4	0
Mickey Hatcher, 1b-6,of-1	.238	6	21	4	5	2	0	0	3	3	0	0
Danny Heep, ph	.000	3	1	0	0	0	0	0	0	1	1	0
Orel Hershiser, p	.000	4	9	1	0	0	0	0	1	1	2	0
Brian Holton, p	1.000	3	1	1	1	0	0	0	0	0	0	0
Rick Horton, p	.000	4	0	0	0	0	0	0	0	0	0	0
Jay Howell, p	.000	2	0	0	0	0	0	0	0	0	0	0
Tim Leary, p	.000	2	1	0	0	0	0	0	0	0	0	0
Mike Marshall, of	.233	7	30	3	7	1	1	0	5	2	9	0
Jesse Orosco, p	.000	4	0	0	0	0	0	0	0	0	0	0
Alejandro Pena, p	.000	3	0	0	0	0	0	0	0	0	0	0
Steve Sax, 2b	.267	7	30	7	8	0	0	0	3	3	3	5
Mike Scioscia, c	.364	7	22	3	8	1	0	1	2	1	2	0
Mike Sharperson, ss-1,3b-1	.000	2	1	0	0	0	0	0	0	1	1	0
John Shelby, of	.167	7	24	3	4	0	0	0	3	5	12	2
Franklin Stubbs, 1b-3	.250	4	8	0	2	0	0	0	0	0	4	0
John Tudor, p	.000	1	2	0	0	0	0	0	0	0	2	0
Tracy Woodson, 1b	.250	3	4	0	1	0	0	0	0	0	1	0
TOTAL	.214		243	31	52	7	1	3	30	25	54	9

PITCHER	W	L	ERA	G	GS	CG	SV	SHO	IP	H	ER	BB	SO
Tim Belcher	2	0	4.11	2	2	0	0	0	15.1	12	7	4	16
Orel Hershiser	1	0	1.09	4	3	1	1	1	24.2	18	3	7	15
Brian Holton	0	0	2.25	3	0	0	1	0	4.0	2	1	1	2
Rick Horton	0	0	0.00	4	0	0	0	0	4.1	4	0	2	3
Jay Howell	0	1	27.00	2	0	0	0	0	0.2	1	2	2	1
Tim Leary	0	1	6.23	2	1	0	0	0	4.1	8	3	3	3
Jesse Orosco	0	0	7.71	4	0	0	0	0	2.1	4	2	3	0
Alejandro Pena	1	1	4.15	3	0	0	1	0	4.1	1	2	5	1
John Tudor	0	0	7.20	1	1	0	0	0	5.0	8	4	1	1
TOTAL	4	3	3.32	25	7	1	3	1	65.0	58	24	28	42

NY (E)

PLAYER/POS	AVG	G	AB	R	H	2B	3B	HR	RB	BB	SO	SB
Rick Aguilera, p	.000	3	1	0	0	0	0	0	0	0	1	0
Wally Backman, 2b	.273	7	22	2	6	1	0	0	2	2	5	1
Gary Carter, c	.222	7	27	0	6	1	1	0	4	1	3	0
David Cone, p	.000	3	4	0	0	0	0	0	0	0	0	0
Ron Darling, p-2	.000	2	3	0	0	0	0	0	0	0	2	0
Lennie Dykstra, of	.429	7	14	6	6	3	0	1	3	4	0	0
Kevin Elster, ss	.250	5	8	1	2	1	0	0	1	3	0	0
Sid Fernandez, p	.000	1	1	0	0	0	0	0	0	0	0	0
Dwight Gooden, p	.200	3	5	0	1	0	0	0	0	0	2	0
Keith Hernandez, 1b	.269	7	26	2	7	0	0	1	5	6	7	1
Gregg Jefferies, 3b	.333	7	27	2	9	2	0	0	1	4	0	0
Howard Johnson, ss-5,3b-1	.056	6	18	3	1	0	0	0	0	1	6	1
Terry Leach, p	.000	3	0	0	0	0	0	0	0	0	0	0
Dave Magadan, ph	.000	3	3	0	0	0	0	0	0	0	2	0
Lee Mazzilli, ph	.500	3	2	0	1	0	0	0	0	0	1	0
Roger Mc Dowell, p	.000	4	0	0	0	0	0	0	0	0	0	0
Kevin Mc Reynolds, of	.250	7	28	4	7	2	0	2	4	3	5	2
Randy Myers, p	.000	3	0	0	0	0	0	0	0	0	0	0
Mackey Sasser, c-1	.200	4	5	0	1	0	0	0	0	0	1	0
Darryl Strawberry, of	.300	7	30	5	9	2	0	1	6	2	5	0
Tim Teufel, 2b	.000	1	3	0	0	0	0	0	0	0	1	0
Mookie Wilson, of-3	.154	4	13	2	2	0	0	0	1	1	2	0
TOTAL	.242		240	27	58	12	1	5	27	28	42	6

PITCHER	W	L	ERA	G	GS	CG	SV	SHO	IP	H	ER	BB	SO
Rick Aguilera	0	0	1.29	3	0	0	0	0	7.0	3	1	2	4
David Cone	1	1	4.50	3	2	1	0	0	12.0	10	6	5	9
Ron Darling	0	1	7.71	2	2	0	0	0	7.0	11	6	4	7
Sid Fernandez	0	1	13.50	1	1	0	0	0	4.0	7	6	1	5
Dwight Gooden	0	0	2.95	3	2	0	0	0	18.1	10	6	8	20
Terry Leach	0	0	0.00	3	0	0	0	0	5.0	4	0	1	4
Roger Mc Dowell	0	1	4.50	4	0	0	0	0	6.0	6	3	2	5
Randy Myers	2	0	0.00	3	0	0	0	0	4.2	1	0	2	0
TOTAL	3	4	3.94	22	7	1	0	0	64.0	52	28	25	54

GAME 1 AT LA OCT 4

NY	000	000	003	3	8	1
LA	100	000	100	2	4	0

Pitchers: Gooden, MYERS (8) vs Hershiser, J.HOWELL (9)
Attendance: 55,582

GAME 2 AT LA OCT 5

NY	000	200	001	3	6	0
LA	140	010	00X	6	7	0

Pitchers: CONE, Aguilera (3), Leach (6), McDowell (8) vs BELCHER, Orosco (9), Pena (9)
Home Runs: Hernandez-NY
Attendance: 55,780

GAME 3 AT NY OCT 8

LA	021	000	010	4	7	2
NY	001	002	05X	8	9	2

Pitchers: Hershiser, J.Howell (8), PENA (8), Horton (8) vs Darling, McDowell (7), MYERS (8), Cone (9)
Attendance: 44,672

GAME 4 AT NY OCT 9

LA	200 000 002 001	5	7	1
NY	000 301 000 000	4	10	2

Pitchers: Tudor, Holton (6), Horton (7), PENA (9), Leary (12), Orosco (12), Hershiser (12) vs Gooden, Myers (9), McDOWELL (11)
Home Runs: Strawberry-NY, McReynolds-NY, Scioscia-LA, Gibson-LA
Attendance: 54,014

GAME 5 AT NY OCT 10

LA	000	330	001	7	12	0
NY	000	030	010	4	9	1

Pitchers: BELCHER, Horton (8), Holton (8) vs FERNANDEZ, Leach (5), McDowell (8)
Home Runs: Gibson-LA, Dykstra-NY
Attendance: 52,069

GAME 6 AT LA OCT 11

NY	101	021	000	5	11	0
LA	000	010	000	1	5	2

Pitchers: CONE vs LEARY, Holton (5), Horton (6), Orosco (8)
Home Runs: McReynolds-NY
Attendance: 55,885

GAME 7 AT LA OCT 12

NY	000	000	000	0	5	2
LA	150	000	00X	6	10	0

Pitchers: DARLING, Gooden (2), Leach (5), Aguilera (7) vs HERSHISER
Attendance: 55,693

Jose Canseco's three home runs and Dennis Eckersley's sparkling relief pitching highlighted Oakland's sweep to the pennant. In his six shutout innings, Eckersley gave up just one hit and a pair of walks while fanning five, to record an LCS record four saves.

Canseco's fourth-inning solo shot off the Sox's Bruce Hurst put the A's out in front in Game One. Boston tied it up in the seventh, but two former Boston players—Carney Lansford, who doubled, and Dave Henderson, who singled him home—put Oakland back in front, and Eckersley (also an ex-Bostonian) held the Sox through the final two innings.

Oakland's Storm Davis and Boston's Roger Clemens dueled scorelessly through five innings of Game Two. The Sox took advantage of an Oakland error to score twice in the sixth, but four Oakland hits in the seventh (including a two-run homer by Canseco), a balk, and a wild pitch put the A's up 3–2. Rich Gedman's home run for Boston in the last of the seventh tied the score, but in the ninth Oakland's rookie shortstop Walt Weiss singled home what proved the game winner off Sox ace reliever Lee Smith.

Boston unloaded for five runs in the first two innings of Game Three. But Weiss's double and home runs by Mark McGwire and Carney Lansford in the last of the second brought the A's within one run of a tie, and Ron Hassey's two-run homer an inning later gave the A's a lead that they held to the end. Dave Henderson's two-run blast in the eighth capped the A's 10–6 victory.

Canseco's first-inning homer in Game Four put the A's ahead to stay, as starter Dave Stewart and relievers Rick Honeycutt and Eckersley combined for a four-hit, 4–1 pennant clincher.

Oakland Athletics (West), 4; Boston Red Sox (East), 0

OAK (W)

PLAYER/POS	AVG	G	AB	R	H	2B	3B	HR	RB	BB	SO	SB
Don Baylor, dh	.000	2	6	0	0	0	0	0	0	1	2	0
Greg Cadaret, p	.000	1	0	0	0	0	0	0	0	0	0	0
Jose Canseco, of	.313	4	16	4	5	1	0	3	4	1	2	1
Storm Davis, p	.000	1	0	0	0	0	0	0	0	0	0	0
Dennis Eckersley, p	.000	4	0	0	0	0	0	0	0	0	0	0
Mike Gallego, 2b	.083	4	12	1	1	0	0	0	0	0	3	0
Ron Hassey, c	.500	4	8	2	4	1	0	1	3	1	1	0
Dave Henderson, of	.375	4	16	2	6	1	0	1	4	1	7	0
Rick Honeycutt, p	.000	3	0	0	0	0	0	0	0	0	0	0
Stan Javier, of	.500	2	4	0	2	0	0	0	1	1	0	0
Carney Lansford, 3b	.294	4	17	4	5	1	0	1	2	0	2	0
Mark Mc Gwire, 1b	.333	4	15	4	5	0	0	1	3	1	5	0
Gene Nelson, p	.000	2	0	0	0	0	0	0	0	0	0	0
Dave Parker, dh-2,of-1	.250	4	12	1	3	1	0	0	0	0	4	0
Tony Phillips, of-2,2b-1	.286	2	7	0	2	1	0	0	0	1	4	0
Eric Plunk, p	.000	1	0	0	0	0	0	0	0	0	0	0
Luis Polonia, of-1	.400	3	5	0	2	0	0	0	0	1	1	0
Terry Steinbach, c	.250	2	4	0	1	0	0	0	0	2	0	0
Dave Stewart, p	.000	2	0	0	0	0	0	0	0	0	0	0
Walt Weiss, ss	.333	4	15	2	5	2	0	0	2	0	4	0
Bob Welch, p	.000	1	0	0	0	0	0	0	0	0	0	0
Curt Young, p	.000	1	0	0	0	0	0	0	0	0	0	0
TOTAL	.299		137	20	41	8	0	7	20	10	35	1

PITCHER	W	L	ERA	G	GS	CG	SV	SHO	IP	H	ER	BB	SO
Greg Cadaret	0	0	27.00	1	0	0	0	0	0.1	1	1	0	0
Storm Davis	0	0	0.00	1	1	0	0	0	6.1	2	0	5	4
Dennis Eckersley	0	0	0.00	4	0	0	4	0	6.0	1	0	2	5
Rick Honeycutt	1	0	0.00	3	0	0	0	0	2.0	0	0	2	0
Gene Nelson	2	0	0.00	2	0	0	0	0	4.2	5	0	1	0
Eric Plunk	0	0	0.00	1	0	0	0	0	0.1	1	0	0	1
Dave Stewart	1	0	1.35	2	2	0	0	0	13.1	9	2	6	11
Bob Welch	0	0	27.00	1	1	0	0	0	1.2	6	5	2	0
Curt Young	0	0	0.00	1	0	0	0	0	1.1	1	0	0	2
TOTAL	4	0	2.00	16	4	0	4	0	36.0	26	8	18	23

BOS (E)

PLAYER/POS	AVG	G	AB	R	H	2B	3B	HR	RB	BB	SO	SB
Marty Barrett, 2b	.067	4	15	2	1	0	0	0	0	1	0	0
Todd Benzinger, 1b-3	.091	4	11	0	1	0	0	0	0	1	3	0
Mike Boddicker, p	.000	1	0	0	0	0	0	0	0	0	0	0
Wade Boggs, 3b	.385	4	13	2	5	0	0	0	3	3	4	0
Ellis Burks, of	.235	4	17	2	4	1	0	0	1	0	3	0
Roger Clemens, p	.000	1	0	0	0	0	0	0	0	0	0	0
Dwight Evans, of	.167	4	12	1	2	1	0	0	1	3	5	0
Wes Gardner, p	.000	1	0	0	0	0	0	0	0	0	0	0
Rich Gedman, c	.357	4	14	1	5	0	0	1	1	2	1	0
Mike Greenwell, of	.214	4	14	2	3	1	0	1	3	3	0	0
Bruce Hurst, p	.000	2	0	0	0	0	0	0	0	0	0	0
Spike Owen, dh	.000	1	0	0	0	0	0	0	0	1	0	0
Larry Parrish, 1b-2	.000	4	6	0	0	0	0	0	0	0	2	0
Jody Reed, ss	.273	4	11	0	3	1	0	0	0	2	1	0
Jim Rice, dh	.154	4	13	0	2	0	0	0	1	2	4	0
Ed Romero, pr	.000	1	0	0	0	0	0	0	0	0	0	0
Kevin Romine, pr	.000	2	0	1	0	0	0	0	0	0	0	0
Lee Smith, p	.000	2	0	0	0	0	0	0	0	0	0	0
Mike Smithson, p	.000	1	0	0	0	0	0	0	0	0	0	0
Bob Stanley, p	.000	2	0	0	0	0	0	0	0	0	0	0
TOTAL	.206		126	11	26	4	0	2	10	18	23	0

PITCHER	W	L	ERA	G	GS	CG	SV	SHO	IP	H	ER	BB	SO
Mike Boddicker	0	1	20.25	1	1	0	0	0	2.2	8	6	1	2
Roger Clemens	0	0	3.86	1	1	0	0	0	7.0	6	3	0	8
Wes Gardner	0	0	5.79	1	0	0	0	0	4.2	6	3	2	8
Bruce Hurst	0	2	2.77	2	2	1	0	0	13.0	10	4	5	12
Lee Smith	0	1	8.10	2	0	0	0	0	3.1	6	3	1	4
Mike Smithson	0	0	0.00	1	0	0	0	0	2.1	3	0	0	1
Bob Stanley	0	0	9.00	2	0	0	0	0	1.0	2	1	1	0
TOTAL	0	4	5.29	10	4	1	0	0	34.0	41	20	10	35

GAME 1 AT BOS OCT 5

OAK	000	100	010	2	6	0
BOS	000	000	100	1	6	0

Pitchers: Stewart, HONEYCUTT (7), Eckersley (8) vs HURST
Home Runs: Canseco-OAK
Attendance: 34,104

GAME 2 AT BOS OCT 6

OAK	000	000	301	4	10	1
BOS	000	002	100	3	4	1

Pitchers: Davis, Cadaret (7), NELSON (7), Eckersley (9) vs Clemens, Stanley (8), SMITH (8)
Home Runs: Canseco-OAK, Gedman-BOS
Attendance: 34,605

GAME 3 AT OAK OCT 8

BOS	320	000	100	6	12	0
OAK	042	010	12X	10	15	1

Pitchers: BODDICKER, Gardner (3), Stanley (8) vs Welch, NELSON (2), Young (6), Plunk (7), Honeycutt (7), Eckersley (8)
Home Runs: Greenwell-BOS, McGwire-OAK, Lansford-OAK, Hassey-OAK, Henderson-OAK
Attendance: 49,261

GAME 4 AT OAK OCT 9

BOS	000	001	000	1	4	0
OAK	101	000	02X	4	10	1

Pitchers: HURST, Smithson (5), Smith (7) vs STEWART, Honeycutt (8), Eckersley (9)
Home Runs: Canseco-OAK
Attendance: 49,406

Mickey Hatcher's home run in the first inning of Game One set the tone for the Dodgers' surprising triumph over Oakland's mighty A's. Hatcher, who homered only once during the season, initiated the Series scoring with a two-run blast to left center. Half an inning later the A's Jose Canseco—baseball's leading slugger, with 42 season homers—erased the Dodger lead with his first career grand slam. But while Hatcher went on to hit safely six more times in the Series—including another home run—Canseco's first hit was also his last, as he went 0 for 19 the rest of the way. The Dodgers scored once in the sixth inning to draw within one run of a tie, but remained behind until the last of the ninth when, with two out and one on, Kirk Gibson pinch hit for pitcher Alejandro Peña. Gibson, the Dodgers' top source of power during the season, was so hobbled by leg injuries that he had, till that moment, sat out the game in the training room. But with two strikes on him he belted a home run off baseball's premier reliever, Dennis Eckersley, to win the game. It was Gibson's only Series appearance.

Dodger ace Orel Hershiser blanked the A's on three hits in Game Two and led the offense with three hits of his own. His single in the third inning began a five-run Dodger rally (capped by Mike Marshall's three-run homer), and his fourth-inning double drove in the Dodgers' sixth and final run.

When the Series moved to Oakland, the A's recovered for a dramatic win in Game Three, as Mark McGwire (who had homered 32 times during the season) broke a 1–1 tie with his only Series hit, a solo homer in the last of the ninth. In Game Four, Dodger reliever Jay Howell, who had yielded the losing home run the day before, got McGwire to pop up with the bases full to end the seventh inning, and blanked the A's the rest of the way to preserve a narrow 4–3 Dodger victory.

Hershiser returned to pitch Game Five. He allowed two runs in his four-hitter, but Mickey Hatcher had given the Dodgers the lead with a two-run homer in the first inning, and Mike Davis (who had homered just twice during the season) drove a 3–0 pitch into the stands for two more runs in the fourth. Veteran catcher Rick Dempsey (substituting for injured first-stringer Mike Scioscia) doubled home a fifth Los Angeles run in the sixth, and the Dodgers were on their way to a seventh world title.

Los Angeles Dodgers (NL), 4; Oakland Athletics (AL), 1

LA (N)

PLAYER/POS	AVG	G	AB	R	H	2B	3B	HR	RB	BB	SO	SB
Dave Anderson, dh	.000	1	1	0	0	0	0	0	0	0	1	0
Tim Belcher, p	.000	2	0	0	0	0	0	0	0	0	0	0
Mike Davis, dh-2,of-1	.143	4	7	3	1	0	0	2	2	4	0	2
Rick Dempsey, c	.200	2	5	0	1	1	0	0	1	1	2	0
Kirk Gibson, ph	1.000	1	1	1	1	0	0	1	2	0	0	0
Jose Gonzalez, of-3	.000	4	2	0	0	0	0	0	0	0	2	0
Alfredo Griffin, ss	.188	5	16	2	3	0	0	0	0	2	4	0
Jeff Hamilton, 3b	.105	5	19	1	2	0	0	0	0	1	4	0
Mickey Hatcher, of	.368	5	19	5	7	1	0	2	5	1	3	0
Danny Heep, of-1,dh-1	.250	3	8	0	2	1	0	0	0	0	2	0
Orel Hershiser, p	1.000	2	3	1	3	2	0	0	1	0	0	0
Brian Holton, p	.000	1	0	0	0	0	0	0	0	0	0	0
Jay Howell, p	.000	2	0	0	0	0	0	0	0	0	0	0
Tim Leary, p	.000	2	0	0	0	0	0	0	0	0	0	0
Mike Marshall, of	.231	5	13	2	3	0	0	1	3	0	5	0
Alejandro Pena, p	.000	2	0	0	0	0	0	0	0	0	0	0
Steve Sax, 2b	.300	5	20	3	6	0	0	0	1	0	1	1
Mike Scioscia, c	.214	4	14	0	3	0	0	0	1	0	2	0
John Shelby, of	.222	5	18	0	4	1	0	0	1	2	7	1
Franklin Stubbs, 1b	.294	5	17	3	5	2	0	0	2	1	3	0
John Tudor, p	.000	1	0	0	0	0	0	0	0	0	0	0
Tracy Woodson, 1b-3	.000	4	4	0	0	0	0	0	0	1	0	0
TOTAL	.246		167	21	41	8	1	6	19	13	36	4

PITCHER	W	L	ERA	G	GS	CG	SV	SHO	IP	H	ER	BB	SO
Tim Belcher	1	0	6.23	2	2	0	0	0	8.2	10	6	6	10
Orel Hershiser	2	0	1.00	2	2	2	0	1	18.0	7	2	6	17
Brian Holton	0	0	0.00	1	0	0	0	0	2.0	0	0	1	0
Jay Howell	0	1	3.38	2	0	0	1	0	2.2	3	1	1	2
Tim Leary	0	0	1.35	2	0	0	0	0	6.2	6	1	2	4
Alejandro Pena	1	0	0.00	2	0	0	0	0	5.0	2	0	1	7
John Tudor	0	0	0.00	1	1	0	0	0	1.1	0	0	0	1
TOTAL	4	1	2.03	12	5	2	1	1	44.1	28	10	17	41

OAK (A)

PLAYER/POS	AVG	G	AB	R	H	2B	3B	HR	RB	BB	SO	SB
Don Baylor, ph	.000	1	1	0	0	0	0	0	0	0	1	0
Todd Burns, p	.000	1	0	0	0	0	0	0	0	0	0	0
Greg Cadaret, p	.000	3	0	0	0	0	0	0	0	0	0	0
Jose Canseco, of	.053	5	19	1	1	0	0	1	5	2	5	1
Storm Davis, p	.000	2	1	0	0	0	0	0	0	0	1	0
Dennis Eckersley, p	.000	2	0	0	0	0	0	0	0	0	0	0
Mike Gallego, 2b	.000	1	0	0	0	0	0	0	0	0	0	0
Ron Hassey, c-4	.250	5	8	0	2	0	0	0	1	3	3	0
Dave Henderson, of	.300	5	20	1	6	2	0	0	1	2	7	0
Rick Honeycutt, p	.000	3	0	0	0	0	0	0	0	0	0	0
Glenn Hubbard, 2b	.250	4	12	2	3	0	0	0	0	1	2	1
Stan Javier, of-2	.500	3	4	0	2	0	0	0	2	0	1	0
Carney Lansford, 3b	.167	5	18	2	3	0	0	0	1	2	2	0
Mark Mc Gwire, 1b	.059	5	17	1	1	0	0	1	1	3	4	0
Gene Nelson, p	.000	3	0	0	0	0	0	0	0	0	0	0
Dave Parker, of-2,dh-2	.200	4	15	0	3	0	0	0	0	2	4	0
Tony Phillips, 2b-1,of-1	.250	2	4	1	1	0	0	0	0	1	2	0
Eric Plunk, p	.000	2	0	0	0	0	0	0	0	0	0	0
Luis Polonia, of-2	.111	3	9	1	1	0	0	0	0	0	2	0
Terry Steinbach, c-2,dh-1	.364	3	11	0	4	1	0	0	0	0	2	0
Dave Stewart, p	.000	2	3	1	0	0	0	0	0	0	3	0
Walt Weiss, ss	.063	5	16	1	1	0	0	0	0	0	2	1
Bob Welch, p	.000	1	0	0	0	0	0	0	0	0	0	0
Curt Young, p	.000	1	0	0	0	0	0	0	0	0	0	0
TOTAL	.177		158	11	28	3	0	2	11	17	41	3

PITCHER	W	L	ERA	G	GS	CG	SV	SHO	IP	H	ER	BB	SO
Todd Burns	0	0	0.00	1	0	0	0	0	0.1	0	0	0	0
Greg Cadaret	0	0	0.00	3	0	0	0	0	2.0	2	0	3	3
Storm Davis	0	2	11.25	2	2	0	0	0	8.0	14	10	1	7
Dennis Eckersley	0	1	10.80	2	0	0	0	0	1.2	2	2	1	2
Rick Honeycutt	1	0	0.00	3	0	0	0	0	3.1	0	0	0	5
Gene Nelson	0	0	1.42	3	0	0	0	0	6.1	4	1	3	3
Eric Plunk	0	0	0.00	2	0	0	0	0	1.2	0	0	0	3
Dave Stewart	0	1	3.14	2	2	0	0	0	14.1	12	5	5	5
Bob Welch	0	0	1.80	1	1	0	0	0	5.0	6	1	3	8
Curt Young	0	0	0.00	1	0	0	0	0	1.0	1	0	0	0
TOTAL	1	4	3.92	20	5	0	0	0	43.2	41	19	13	36

GAME 1 AT LA OCT 15

OAK	040 000 000	4	7 0
LA	200 001 002	5	7 0

Pitchers: Stewart, ECKERSLEY (9) vs Belcher, Leary (3), Holton (6), PENA (8) Home Runs: Hatcher-LA, Canseco-OAK, Gibson-LA
Attendance: 55,983

GAME 2 AT LA OCT 16

OAK	000 000 000	0	3 0
LA	005 100 00X	6	10 1

Pitchers: DAVIS, Nelson (4), Young (6), Plunk (7), Honeycutt (8) vs HERSHISER
Home Runs: Marshall-LA
Attendance: 56,051

GAME 3 AT OAK OCT 18

LA	000 010 000	1	8 1
OAK	001 000 001	2	5 0

Pitchers: Tudor, Leary (2), Pena (6), J.HOWELL (9) vs Welch, Cadaret (6), Nelson (6), HONEYCUTT (8)
Home Runs: McGwire-OAK
Attendance: 49,316

GAME 4 AT OAK OCT 19

LA	201 000 100	4	8 1
OAK	100 001 100	3	9 2

Pitchers: BELCHER, J.Howell (7) vs STEWART, Cadaret (7), Eckersley (9)
Attendance: 49,317

GAME 5 AT OAK OCT 20

LA	200 201 000	5	8 0
OAK	001 000 010	2	4 0

Pitchers: HERSHISER vs DAVIS, Cadaret (5), Nelson (5), Honeycutt (8), Plunk (9), Burns (9)
Home Runs: Hatcher-LA, Davis-LA
Attendance: 49,317

CHAPTER 4

The All-Star Game

Frederick Ivor-Campbell

Although the tradition of All-Star Games in baseball dates back to an 1858 series between teams of stars from Brooklyn and New York (they were called "picked nines" in those days), the current All-Star series began when Arch Ward, sports editor of the *Chicago Tribune*, persuaded hesitant league owners to go along with his proposal for a game between stars from the American and National leagues, to be played in Chicago during that city's Century of Progress Exposition in 1933.

All-Star managers (who, except for the first game, have been the pilots of the previous year's pennant winners) shared with fans the selection of players for the first two games. From 1935 through 1946 the manager selected his whole squad. Since 1947, he has chosen his pitchers and all other players except the eight members of the starting lineup. The fans chose the starters in 1947–1957; after an incident of ballot-box stuffing by Cincinnati partisans in 1957, the major league players, coaches, and managers made the choice in 1958–1969; in 1970 the selection of starting lineups was returned to the fans.

The American League dominated the early years of the series, winning the first three games, and extending their winning margin to eight games (12–4) by 1949. The National League cut the lead in half with four straight wins, and by 1964 had drawn even in the series (17–17–1). Since then, the National Leaguers have won 20 All-Star Games while losing only four, and now hold a commanding 37–21 lead in the series. Even if the American Leaguers were to begin winning every year, it would take them until 2004 to catch up.

GAME 1
Comiskey Park, Chicago
July 6, 1933
AL, 4–2

```
NL   000 002 000     2  8  0
AL   012 001 00X     4  9  1
```
Pitchers: HALLAHAN, Warneke (3),
  Hubbell (7) vs GOMEZ, Crowder (4),
  Grove (7)
Home Runs: Ruth-A, Frisch-N
Attendance: 49,200

Baseball's two grand old managers—Connie Mack and John McGraw—were chosen to lead the American and National League squads in the first All-Star Game, and American starting pitcher Lefty Gomez of the Yankees took home honors both as the first All-Star winning pitcher and as the first player to drive in an All-Star run (singling in Jimmie Dykes in the second inning). But it was another "grand old man"—Babe Ruth—who made the game's headlines. At thirty-eight, in his next-to-last season as a Yankee, he lined a two-run homer in the third to make the score 3–0, and as right fielder in the eighth he robbed Chick Hafey of a hit with a remarkable running catch of Hafey's line drive.

Frank Frisch homered for the Nationals, following up Pepper Martin's RBI with a solo shot in the National League's two-run sixth. But the American stars countered with an insurance run in the bottom of the sixth, as Earl Averill singled in Joe Cronin to end the scoring. Carl Hubbell for the Nationals and Lefty Grove for the Americans blanked the opposition through the final innings.

GAME 2
Polo Grounds, New York
July 10, 1934
AL, 9–7

```
AL   000 261 000     9 14  1
NL   103 030 000     7  8  1
```
Pitchers: Gomez, Ruffing (4),
  HARDER (5) vs Hubbell,
  Warneke (4), MUNGO (5),
  J.Dean (6), Frankhouse (9)
Home Runs: Frisch-N, Medwick-N
Attendance: 48,363

This was the game in which Carl Hubbell struck out Babe Ruth, Lou Gehrig, Jimmie Foxx, Al Simmons, and Joe Cronin in order in the first two innings. Hubbell also walked two and gave up two hits in his three innings of work, but allowed no run to score as his Nationals took a 4–0 lead on homers by Frank Frisch in the first and Joe Medwick (for three runs) in the third off American starter (and first-game winner) Lefty Gomez.

But with Hubbell gone, the Americans pounced on Lon Warneke and Van Lingle Mungo for four runs each in the fourth and fifth innings. The Nationals battled back for three off Red Ruffing in their half of the fifth, to come within a run of tying the game. But Mel Harder relieved Ruffing with none out and put out the fire, one-hitting the National stars over the final five innings. The Americans picked up an insurance run in the sixth off Dizzy Dean before Dean and Fred Frankhouse shut them down, too, through the final three frames.

GAME 3
Municipal Stadium, Cleveland
July 8, 1935
AL, 4–1

```
NL   000 100 000     1  4  1
AL   210 010 00X     4  8  0
```
Pitchers: WALKER, Schumacher (3),
  Derringer (7), J.Dean (8) vs
  GOMEZ, Harder (7)
Home Runs: Foxx-A
Attendance: 69,812

Lefty Gomez started his third All-Star Game, and pitched a record six innings to pick up his second All-Star win. For three innings he shut out the Nationals as the Americans built a lead behind him on Jimmie Foxx's two-run homer in the first, and Rollie Hemsley's triple and Joe Cronin's run-scoring fly in the second.

The National Leaguers tried to catch up in the fourth, when they put together two of their three hits off Gomez—a double by Arky Vaughan and a single by Bill Terry—and scored a run. But an inning later Foxx nullified the National run, singling Joe Vosmik home for his third RBI.

Gomez blanked the National stars through two more innings before yielding to Mel Harder, who came in to close his second All-Star Game. Harder had created an All-Star record the previous year with his five consecutive scoreless innings pitched, and extended the record to eight, with three more shutout innings to end the game.

GAME 4
Braves Field, Boston
July 7, 1936
NL, 4–3

```
AL   000 000 300     3  7  1
NL   020 020 00X     4  9  0
```
Pitchers: GROVE, Rowe (4),
  Harder (7) vs J.DEAN, Hubbell (4),
  C.Davis (7), Warneke (7)
Home Runs: Galan-N, Gehrig-A
Attendance: 25,534

The National League, which had not yet won an All-Star Game, scored first in the second when Gabby Hartnett tripled in a run off Lefty Grove—rookie Joe DiMaggio missing his try for a shoe-top catch of Hartnett's drive to right field. Pinky Whitney then singled in Hartnett. Augie Galan homered off Schoolboy Rowe (and the right field foul pole) in the fifth, and DiMaggio's bobble of Billy Herman's single a batter later put Herman in position to score an unearned fourth run, on Joe Medwick's single, that proved to be the margin of victory.

The Americans, shut out through six by Dizzy Dean and Carl Hubbell, nearly tied the game in the seventh off Curt Davis as Lou Gehrig homered and Luke Appling singled in two more. But Lon Warneke took over and, after loading the bases with a walk, escaped disaster as shortstop Leo Durocher snared DiMaggio's vicious line drive to his right for the third out. Warneke shut the Americans out over the final two innings to preserve the one-run lead and the National League's first All-Star win.

GAME 5
Griffith Stadium, Washington
July 7, 1937
AL, 8–3

NL	000	111	000	3	13	0
AL	002	312	00X	8	13	2

Pitchers: J.DEAN, Hubbell (4), Blanton (4), Grissom (5), Mungo (6), Walters (8) vs GOMEZ, Bridges (4), Harder (7)
Home Runs: Gehrig-A
Attendance: 31,391

President Franklin Roosevelt attended the game. Lou Gehrig homered and doubled to drive in half the American League's eight runs in an easy American win. Lefty Gomez started his fourth All-Star Game in five years, winning his third. And American reliever Mel Harder pitched the final innings for the fourth All-Star Game in a row, pushing his record for consecutive All-Star shutout innings to 13. But the game is remembered not for any of these things, but for Earl Averill's line drive in the third inning which fractured Dizzy Dean's toe and led to the premature end of his spectacular career. (Dean recovered from the broken toe, but tried to resume his pitching too soon. In favoring the toe, he changed his delivery and irreparably injured his pitching arm.)

The Americans began their scoring when Gehrig, who preceded Averill in the batting order, homered off Dean in the third, with one aboard. They added to their score in each of the next three innings, so that although the Nationals countered with single runs in the three middle innings, they only fell farther behind.

GAME 6
Crosley Field, Cincinnati
July 6, 1938
NL, 4–1

AL	000	000	001	1	7	4
NL	100	100	20X	4	8	0

Pitchers: GOMEZ, Allen (4), Grove (7) vs VANDER MEER, Lee (4), Brown (7)
Attendance: 27,607

For the fifth (and final) time, Lefty Gomez started for the American League, and although he gave up only two hits and no earned runs in his three innings, he was saddled with the loss when an error by shortstop Joe Cronin paved the way for a National League run in the first.

The Nationals scored their only earned run in the fourth when Mel Ott tripled and Ernie Lombardi singled him home. But in the seventh they recorded two more unearned runs when Leo Durocher bunted to move Frank McCormick to second. Both McCormick and Durocher scored as third baseman Jimmie Foxx threw wildly to first and right fielder Joe DiMaggio (who chased the ball down) missed home plate with his throw.

In the ninth DiMaggio singled and Cronin doubled him home in partial atonement for their errors. But as Johnny Vander Meer and Big Bill Lee had each blanked the American stars on one hit in their three-inning stints, and some fine outfield catches had kept them from scoring more than this one run off Mace Brown, the Americans' errors cost them the game.

GAME 7
Yankee Stadium, New York
July 11, 1939
AL, 3–1

NL	001	000	000	1	7	1
AL	000	210	00X	3	6	1

Pitchers: Derringer, LEE (4), Fette (7) vs Ruffing, BRIDGES (4), Feller (6)
Home Runs: J.DiMaggio-A
Attendance: 62,892

Six Yankees started for the American League, and one of them—Joe DiMaggio—hit the game's only home run. But it was a young Cleveland pitcher—twenty-year-old Bob Feller, playing in his first All-Star Game—who turned in the most memorable performance.

The Nationals scored first, with a run in the third on three hits off the American League starter, Red Ruffing. But the Americans came back with two runs in the fourth on a walk, two singles, and a bobbled grounder by shortstop Arky Vaughan. DiMaggio hit his insurance homer an inning later.

In the top of the sixth, after two singles and an error had loaded the bases with National stars, with only one out, Feller replaced Tommy Bridges to face Vaughan (who had earlier singled and scored his team's only run). One pitch got Feller out of the inning as Vaughan grounded into a 4–6–3 double play. Feller shut out the National stars over the final three innings, striking out Johnny Mize and Stan Hack in the ninth to end the game and give the Americans their fifth All-Star victory.

GAME 8
Sportsman's Park, St. Louis
July 9, 1940
NL, 4–0

AL	000	000	000	0	3	1
NL	300	000	01X	4	7	0

Pitchers: RUFFING, Newsom (4), Feller (7) vs DERRINGER, Walters (3), Wyatt (5), French (7), Hubbell (9)
Home Runs: West-N
Attendance: 32,373

The National Leaguers made short work of the Americans, scoring three times in the first inning and holding the opposing stars to three hits for the All-Star Game's first shutout. Before American League starter Red Ruffing retired a single National batter in the bottom of the first inning, three of the game's four runs had been scored, on singles by Arky Vaughan and Billy Herman and Max West's home run to right center.

Ruffing then settled down, and he and Buck Newsom held the Nationals to just three additional hits through the seventh. Bob Feller gave up the Nationals' fourth run in the eighth, on a walk, a sacrifice, and Harry Danning's single.

Five National League pitchers combined for the shutout, permitting only five batters to reach base while striking out seven. Starter Paul Derringer, who struck out three men in his two innings, was awarded the win.

GAME 9
Briggs Stadium, Detroit
July 8, 1941
AL, 7–5

```
NL  000 001 220    5 10 2
AL  000 101 014    7 11 3
```
Pitchers: Wyatt, Derringer (3),
 Walters (5), PASSEAU (7) vs Feller,
 Lee (4), Hudson (7), SMITH (8)
Home Runs: Vaughn-N (2),
 Williams-A
Attendance: 54,674

The National Leaguers entered the last of the ninth with a 5–3 lead and hopes of nailing down their first back-to-back All-Star victories. The American stars had scored their first run in the fourth. The Nationals tied the score in the top of the sixth, but the Americans countered with a run later in the inning. The Nationals' Arky Vaughan then made a bid to be the game's hero, homering in the seventh off Sid Hudson with a man aboard to restore the National lead, and homering again an inning later off Edgar Smith for two more runs.

A double and single by the DiMaggio brothers Joe and Dom brought the Americans a run closer in the eighth, but they still needed two to tie as they faced Claude Passeau in the bottom of the ninth. Two one-out singles and a walk loaded the bases, and a force play at second (that just missed being a game-ending double play) scored Ken Keltner from third. With two men now out and the Americans still down a run, Ted Williams homered on a letter-high fastball against the upper parapet in right for three more runs and another American League victory.

GAME 10
Polo Grounds, New York
July 6, 1942
AL, 3–1

```
AL  300 000 000    3 7 0
NL  000 000 010    1 6 1
```
Pitchers: CHANDLER, Benton (5) vs
 M.COOPER, Vander Meer (4),
 Passeau (7), Walters (9)
Home Runs: Boudreau-A, York-A,
 Owen-N
Attendance: 33,694

Home runs accounted for all the scoring as the American League, in something of a reverse of the 1940 game, scored three times in the top of the first to defeat the Nationals. Lou Boudreau, leading off, hit the game winner off Mort Cooper's second pitch, into the upper deck in left field. A double and two outs later, Rudy York put one over the fence near the short right field foul line for two more runs.

The Americans hit safely only four more times, and scored no more runs, but they already had more than enough, as Spud Chandler and Al Benton combined to shut out the National League stars for seven innings, until Mickey Owen, pinch-hitting for pitcher Claude Passeau in the eighth, hit his only home run of the summer.

This was the second All-Star Game played in the Polo Grounds. It had been Brooklyn's turn to host the game at Ebbets Field, but because the proceeds were destined for the war effort, the site was shifted to the larger stadium. The game might as well have been held in Brooklyn, though, as a pregame rain held attendance to well below the Polo Grounds' capacity.

GAME 11
Shibe Park, Philadelphia
July 13, 1943
AL, 5–3

```
NL  100 000 101    3 10 3
AL  031 010 00X    5 8 1
```
Pitchers: M.COOPER, Vander
 Meer (3), SeweLL (6), Javery (7) vs
 LEONARD, Newhouser (4),
 Hughson (7)
Home Runs: Doerr-A, V.DiMaggio-N
Attendance: 31,938

For the first time, the All-Star Game was played at night. And for the only time in All-Star history, no Yankee played—although six had been named to the American League squad. But Yankee Joe McCarthy (serving for the sixth time as American manager) was piqued by criticism that he favored his own players, and retaliated by keeping them all on the bench.

The only DiMaggio in this wartime game was Pittsburgh's Vince, and he provided most of the National League power—batting 3 for 3, with eight total bases and two of his team's three runs. But after the Nationals had jumped to a one-run lead in the first, Bobby Doerr of the Americans homered off Mort Cooper with two aboard in the second to put the American stars ahead. They added to their lead with a run in the third and another in the fifth. DiMaggio scored in the seventh after tripling off Tex Hughson and added a homer against Hughson in the ninth, but his heroics were not enough to overcome the American League's march to its third win in a row, and its eighth in eleven tries.

GAME 12
Forbes Field, Pittsburgh
July 11, 1944
NL, 7–1

```
AL  010 000 000    1 6 3
NL  000 040 21X    7 12 1
```
Pitchers: Borowy, HUGHSON (4),
 Muncrief (5), Newhouser (7),
 Newsom (8) vs Walters,
 RAFFENSBERGER (4), Sewell (6),
 Tobin (9)
Attendance: 29,589

For the second time the game was played at night, and for the seventh time Joe McCarthy managed the American League team. But unlike Game 11—he let his Yankees play. He started Yankee pitcher Hank Borowy, who not only shut out the Nationals in his three innings but drove in a run in the second to give his team the lead.

But that was all the American stars got. For the first four innings it was enough, but in the fifth a double, four singles, a walk, an error, and a stolen base brought in four National League runs. In the seventh, Whitey Kurowski doubled in two more National runs, and in the eighth a missed third strike, two walks, and a fly ball produced a seventh and final tally.

No home runs were hit in the game, only the second time that had happened in All-Star play. But Phil Cavarretta of the Nationals tripled—and reached base four additional times on a single and three walks for a new All-Star on-base record.

GAME 13
Fenway Park, Boston
July 9, 1946
AL, 12-0

```
NL   000 000 000    0  3  0
AL   200 130 24X   12 14  1
```
Pitchers: PASSEAU, Higbe (4),
Blackwell (5), Sewell (8) vs FELLER,
Newhouser (4), Kramer (7)
Home Runs: Keller-A, Williams-A (2)
Attendance: 34,906

No All-Star Game was played in 1945 because of restrictions on wartime travel, but when the classic resumed in 1946 the American stars avenged their 1944 loss with the most decisive All-Star victory to date: 12–0. American pitchers Bob Feller, Hal Newhouser, and Jack Kramer combined to hold the National stars to three singles and a walk, as their teammates pounded National pitching for 14 hits, including two doubles and three home runs.

But the game belonged to Ted Williams. Back after three years at war, and playing before his hometown fans, he equaled Phil Cavarretta's 1944 on-base record in spectacular fashion, with one walk, two singles, and two home runs: one a drive into the center field bleachers and the other the first homer ever hit off Rip Sewell's looping "eephus" pitch. He scored the game's first run in the first inning as Charlie Keller followed his walk with a homer, and went on to break an All-Star record by scoring three more times, while driving in a record five runs.

GAME 14
Wrigley Field, Chicago
July 8, 1947
AL, 2-1

```
AL   000 001 100   2  8  0
NL   000 100 000   1  5  1
```
Pitchers: Newhouser, SHEA (4),
Masterson (7), Page (8) vs
Blackwell, Brecheen (4), SAIN (7),
Spahn (8)
Home Runs: Mize-N
Attendance: 41,123

Johnny Mize homered for the National League off rookie Spec Shea in the fourth inning for the game's first run, after three one-hit innings by the two lanky starters, Ewell Blackwell of the Nationals and Hal Newhouser of the Americans. Mize's run remained the only score until the sixth inning, when the American Leaguers tied the game on two singles and a double-play grounder.

Sharp baserunning by Bobby Doerr—plus a little luck—led to the Americans' second run an inning later. Doerr singled, then stole second. He took third when pitcher Johnny Sain's pickoff throw bounced off Doerr's back into the outfield. Pinch hitter Stan Spence then singled Doerr home with what proved to be the game's final—and winning—run. The Nationals put men on first and third in the eighth, but shortstop Lou Boudreau's spectacular stop of a hot grounder and sharp throw to first retired the side and ended the threat.

GAME 15
Sportsman's Park, St. Louis
July 13, 1948
AL, 5-2

```
NL   200 000 000   2  8  0
AL   011 300 00X   5  6  0
```
Pitchers: Branca, SCHMITZ (4),
Sain (4), Blackwell (6) vs
Masterson, RASCHI (4),
Coleman (7)
Home Runs: Musial-N, Evers-A
Attendance: 34,009

Vic Raschi pitched three shutout innings for the American stars and drove in two go-ahead runs with a fourth-inning single as the American League—for the third time since the All-Star Game originated in 1933—won its third classic in a row. The Nationals scored first on Stan Musial's two-run homer in the top of the first. But that was all they got, as starter Walt Masterson settled down and shut out the Nationals through the second and third innings. Raschi then came on for his shutout stint, and Joe Coleman stopped the Nationals without even a hit over the final three innings.

Meanwhile, the Americans scored a run in the second on Hoot Evers's homer, and tied the game with another run in the third on two walks, a double steal, and an outfield fly. Then in the fourth, when two walks and a single had loaded the bases, pitcher Raschi singled in the third and fourth American runs. Joe DiMaggio's pinch-hit fly scored a fifth run. Johnny Sain and Ewell Blackwell shut out the Americans the rest of the way, but the damage had been done.

GAME 16
Ebbets Field, Brooklyn
July 12, 1949
AL, 11-7

```
AL   400 202 300   11 13  1
NL   212 002 000    7 12  5
```
Pitchers: Parnell, TRUCKS (2),
Brissie (4), Raschi (7) vs Spahn,
NEWCOMBE (2), Munger (5),
Bickford (6), Pollet (7), Blackwell (8),
Roe (9)
Home Runs: Musial-N, Kiner-N
Attendance: 32,577

Each team scored seven earned runs in this game which saw a total of 25 hits, including seven doubles and two home runs. But two first-inning National League errors let in four unearned American runs to provide the margin for the American League's fourth consecutive All-Star win. Stan Musial and Ralph Kiner each drove in two National runs with homers, but Eddie Joost singled in two runs for the Americans and Joe DiMaggio singled and doubled in three more to lead the American attack. For the second year in a row, Vic Raschi shut out the National stars for three innings, this time holding the American lead over the final third of the game.

The game was notable as the first to include black players: three Dodgers (Jackie Robinson, Roy Campanella, and Don Newcombe) for the National League, and Larry Doby for the American. With the Americans now ahead 12–4, it also marked the farthest extent of American League domination of the midsummer classic.

GAME 17
Comiskey Park, Chicago
July 11, 1950
NL, 4-3

```
NL   020 000 001 000 01   4 10 0
AL   001 020 000 000 00   3  8 1
```
Pitchers: Roberts, Newcombe (4), Konstanty (6), Jansen (7), BLACKWELL (12) vs Raschi, Lemon (4), Houtteman (7), Reynolds (10), GRAY (13), Feller (14)
Home Runs: Kiner-N, Schoendienst-N
Attendance: 46,127

For the first time, the All-Star Game went into extra innings, and for the first time the National League won a game as the visiting team. Three pitchers each hurled three innings of shutout ball: Bob Lemon and Allie Reynolds for the American League and Ewell Blackwell (who finished the game and got the win) for the Nationals. But top pitching honors were earned by National Leaguer Larry Jansen, who struck out six and gave up only one hit over *five* shutout innings (7-11).

The National stars scored first with two runs in the second. The Americans came back with one in the third, and tied and took the lead in the fifth on George Kell's run-scoring fly and an RBI single by Ted Williams (who, it was later learned, had broken his left elbow making an off-the-wall catch in the first inning). But in the top of the ninth, Ralph Kiner of the Nationals hit a game-tying homer, and 4½ scoreless innings later Red Schoendienst—on the first pitch of the fourteenth inning—homered off American Ted Gray with what proved to be the game winner.

GAME 18
Briggs Stadium, Detroit
July 10, 1951
NL, 8-3

```
NL   100 302 110   8 12 1
AL   010 110 000   3 10 2
```
Pitchers: Roberts, MAGLIE (3), Newcombe (6), Blackwell (9) vs Garver, LOPAT (4), Hutchinson (5), Parnell (8), Lemon (9)
Home Runs: Musial-N, Elliott-N, Wertz-A, Kell-A, Hodges-N, Kiner-N
Attendance: 52,075

In a game moved from Philadelphia to help Detroit celebrate its 250th birthday, hometowners Vic Wertz and George Kell of the Tigers hit solo homers in the fourth and fifth innings to bring the American stars within a run of the Nationals. But they came no closer, as the National Leaguers pulled away for a convincing 8-3 victory.

The Nationals, aided by six innings of shutout pitching (including three by Don Newcombe), produced four home runs of their own to drive in six of their eight runs. With the score tied 1-1 going into the fourth inning, Stan Musial greeted Ed Lopat's first pitch with a shot to the right field upper deck, and Bob Elliott added two more runs later in the inning with a homer to left. Gil Hodges increased the National League lead to 6-3 with a two-run homer in the sixth, and Ralph Kiner concluded the Nationals' scoring with a solo upper-deck shot to left center in the eighth. For the first time in All-Star play, the National League had won two games in a row.

GAME 19
Shibe Park, Philadelphia
July 8, 1952
NL, 3-2

```
AL   000 20   2 5 0
NL   100 20   3 3 0
```
Pitchers: Raschi, LEMON (3), Shantz (5) vs Simmons, RUSH (4)
Home Runs: J. Robinson-N, Sauer-N
Attendance: 32,785

No sun shone for this rain-shortened game, but two hometown pitchers did. Curt Simmons of the Phillies held the American stars to one hit as he shut them out over the first three innings. And the Athletics' Bobby Shantz—in the midst of an MVP season—struck out the side in the fifth for the Americans.

But home runs and rain determined the final outcome. Jackie Robinson opened the scoring with a homer off Vic Raschi in the bottom of the first to give the Nationals a 1-0 lead. In the fourth the Americans came back to take the lead briefly with two runs on a double, a walk, and two singles off eventual winner Bob Rush. But in the bottom of the inning, Hank Sauer's home run off Bob Lemon with one aboard returned the lead to the National League. And there it stayed through a scoreless fifth, when the rain, which had fallen throughout the game, at last brought the soggy festivities to the All-Star series' first premature conclusion.

GAME 20
Crosley Field, Cincinnati
July 14, 1953
NL, 5-1

```
AL   000 000 001   1  5 0
NL   000 020 12X   5 10 0
```
Pitchers: Pierce, REYNOLDS (4), Garcia (6) Paige (8) vs Roberts, SPAHN (4), Simmons (6), Dickson (8)
Attendance: 30,846

For the first 4½ innings, pitchers for both sides held the opposition scoreless, with one hit each. Then the National Leaguers got to Allie Reynolds for two runs in the bottom of the fifth on a hit batsman, a walk, and two singles.

This proved margin enough for the National League's fourth consecutive victory, as four National pitchers held the Americans to just two hits through eight innings before three singles in the ninth gave the American Leaguers their only run. For good measure, though, the National stars added a run in the seventh, and two more in the eighth (with three singles and a walk off Satchel Paige in his only All-Star appearance).

Enos Slaughter of the Nationals provided much of the game's excitement. With two singles, a walk, and a stolen base, he drove in one run and scored two others, and defensively made a spectacular diving catch in right field. Pee Wee Reese's double in the seventh (scoring Slaughter) was the game's only extra-base hit.

GAME 21
Municipal Stadium, Cleveland
July 13, 1954
AL, 11–9

```
NL   000 520 020    9 14 0
AL   004 121 03X   11 17 1
```
Pitchers: Roberts, Antonelli (4), Spahn (6), Grissom (6), CONLEY (8), Erskine (8) vs Ford, Consuegra (4), Lemon (4), Porterfield (5), Keegan (8), STONE (8), Trucks (9)
Home Runs: Rosen-A (2), Boone-A, Kluszewski-N, Bell-N, Doby-A
Attendance: 68,751

American starter Whitey Ford gave up only one hit in three shutout innings, and National starter Robin Roberts shut out the American stars through two. But in the bottom of the third Al Rosen tagged Roberts for a three-run homer, and Ray Boone followed with a solo shot. By the end of the game new All-Star records had been set for hits (31), runs (20), and pitchers used (13), and the record of 6 home runs had been equaled.

The Nationals topped the American four-run third with five straight hits off Sandy Consuegra in the fourth, for five runs. The Americans tied the game with a run in their half of the fourth, but Ted Kluszewski homered in the fifth for two more National League runs. In the bottom of the fifth, Rosen homered again, for two, to bring the Americans even again.

A run in the sixth put the Americans ahead, but Gus Bell's two-run blast in the eighth returned the Nationals to the top by one. They were threatening to lengthen that lead when Dean Stone entered the contest in relief of Bob Keegan with two out and Red Schoendienst on third. Before Stone's first delivery, Schoendienst broke for home and was tagged out, setting the stage for Stone to become the winning pitcher without making a pitch. American Larry Doby tied it up again later in the eighth with a home run, and Nellie Fox drove in the game's final two runs a few batters later with a bases-loaded single.

In the ninth, the Nationals' Stan Musial blasted two over the fence—both foul—with a man aboard. But Virgil Trucks retired him and Gil Hodges, who followed, to preserve the American League's first victory in five games.

GAME 22
County Stadium, Milwaukee
July 12, 1955
NL, 6–5

```
AL   400 001 000 000   5 10 2
NL   000 000 230 001   6 13 1
```
Pitchers: Pierce, Wynn (4), Ford (7), SULLIVAN (8) vs Roberts, Haddix (4), Newcombe (7), Jones (8), Nuxhall (8), CONLEY (12)
Home Runs: Mantle-A, Musial-N
Attendance: 45,314

Down 0–5 in the seventh inning, the National Leaguers came back to tie the game and send it into extra innings. The Americans attacked early, scoring four runs off Robin Roberts (three of them on Mickey Mantle's home run to center) before the game's first out had been recorded. They added a fifth run in the sixth inning. Meanwhile, pitchers Billy Pierce and Early Wynn were shutting the Nationals down on four hits.

In the seventh, though, two singles, a walk, and an American error gave the Nationals two runs, and in the eighth, four two-out singles and another error tied the game. Joe Nuxhall for the Nationals and the Americans' Frank Sullivan prevented further scoring through the eleventh. In the top of the twelfth, Gene Conley replaced Nuxhall and struck out the side: Al Kaline, Mickey Vernon, and Al Rosen. Sullivan returned for the Americans to face Stan Musial in the bottom of the twelfth. Musial hit the first pitch—a fastball—over the screen in right and the game was over.

GAME 23
Griffith Stadium, Washington
July 10, 1956
NL, 7–3

```
NL   001 211 200   7 11 0
AL   000 003 000   3 11 0
```
Pitchers: FRIEND, Spahn (4), Antonelli (6) vs PIERCE, Ford (4), Wilson (5), Brewer (6), Score (8), Wynn (9)
Home Runs: Mays-N, Williams-A, Mantle-A, Musial-N
Attendance: 28,843

Four of the game's greatest sluggers—Willie Mays, Stan Musial, Ted Williams, and Mickey Mantle—hit home runs, three of them off two of the game's greatest pitchers—Whitey Ford and Warren Spahn. But the star of the game was National League third baseman Ken Boyer, who went 3 for 5, scoring one run and driving in another, while making three spectacular diving and leaping plays in the field.

The National stars scored five times—including twice in the fourth on Mays's homer off Ford—before the Americans put a run on the board. But in the bottom of the sixth, Williams homered for two runs off Spahn, and Mantle followed him with another homer to bring the Americans within two. But that was the end of their scoring, as Johnny Antonelli relieved Spahn to stop the American stars the rest of the way. The Nationals scored twice more in the seventh—one of the runs coming on Musial's homer—ensuring them a comfortable 7–3 victory.

GAME 24
Busch Stadium, St. Louis
July 9, 1957
AL, 6–5

```
AL   020 001 003   6 10 0
NL   000 000 203   5  9 1
```
Pitchers: BUNNING, Loes (4), Wynn (7), Pierce (7), Mossi (9), Grim (9) vs SIMMONS, Burdette (2), Sanford (6), Jackson (7), Labine (9)
Attendance: 30,693

Cincinnati fans stuffed the ballot boxes and elected Reds to start everywhere but first base. Commissioner Ford Frick removed two elected starters, but left five Reds in the lineup. They could not bring the National League the victory, though.

The Americans scored twice in the second on singles and walks to take a lead they held to the finish. Although reliever Lew Burdette—after walking in the second run—stopped the American stars through the fifth, Jim Bunning and Billy Loes were combining to keep the Nationals from scoring through the first six innings. The Americans, meanwhile, added a third run in the top of the sixth on a double, a wild pitch, and a single.

The Nationals scored their first two in the seventh, on two singles and a double, to draw within a run of a tie. But in the top of the ninth the Americans combined two singles, an error, a sacrifice bunt, and Minnie Minoso's pinch double for three more runs. They needed them all, for the Nationals responded in their half of the ninth with three runs of their own on a blend of walks, hits (including Willie Mays's triple), and a wild pitch. With two out and a runner at second, Gil Hodges lined one deep to left center. But Minoso, now in left field, snared the drive on the run to end the game.

GAME 25
Memorial Stadium, Baltimore
July 8, 1958
AL, 4–3

NL	210	000	000	3	4	2
AL	110	011	00X	4	9	2

Pitchers: Spahn, FRIEND (4), Jackson (6), Farrell (7) vs Turley, Narleski (2), WYNN (6), O'Dell (7)
Attendance: 48,829

Although American League pitchers held the National Leaguers to only four hits (all singles), the Nationals took a quick lead, and held it for half the game before they were overtaken. Willie Mays and Stan Musial singled in the top of the first, both scoring as American starter Bob Turley proceeded to give up a sacrifice fly, hit a batter, walk a man, and unload a wild pitch.

The Americans came back with one run in their half of the first, but the Nationals drove Turley out with their third run as Mays (who had reached on a fielder's choice) worked his way around the bases on a steal, an error, and Bob Skinner's single. Once again the Americans answered with a run, but they didn't tie the game until Mickey Vernon scored on a bases-loaded ground out in the fifth. An inning later they took the lead when pinch hitter Gil McDougald singled home Frank Malzone.

Billy O'Dell set down the Nationals in order over the final three innings to preserve the lead and give the American Leaguers their second consecutive victory. They have not won two in a row since.

GAME 26
Forbes Field, Pittsburgh
July 7, 1959
NL, 5–4

AL	000	100	030	4	8	0
NL	100	000	22X	5	9	1

Pitchers: Wynn, Duren (4), Bunning (7), FORD (8), Daley (8) vs Drysdale, Burdette (4), Face (7), ANTONELLI (8), Elston (9)
Home Runs: Mathews-N, Kaline-A
Attendance: 35,277

For the third year in a row, the game was decided by one run, with the National League celebrating the city of Pittsburgh's bicentennial by breaking the American League's win streak at two.

Eddie Mathews homered for the Nationals in the bottom of the first for the only run in the first three innings, as Don Drysdale stopped the Americans without a hit or walk, fanning four. Al Kaline tied the game in the top of the fourth with an American home run for the only score of the middle three innings, as Ryne Duren one-hit the Nationals, like Drysdale striking out four.

In the last of the seventh, though, a double and two singles off Jim Bunning put the Nationals ahead by two runs. The NL lead lasted only briefly, however, as the Americans moved back into the lead with three runs in the eighth off Roy Face, with two singles, a walk, and a double after Face had retired the first two men. But in their half of the eighth the Nationals hit on Whitey Ford, tying the game with a single-sacrifice-single, and scoring the game winner on Willie Mays's triple to center.

GAME 27
Memorial Coliseum, Los Angeles
August 3, 1959
AL, 5–3

AL	012	000	110	5	6	0
NL	100	010	100	3	6	3

Pitchers: WALKER, Wynn (4), Wilhelm, (6), O'Dell (7), McLish (8) vs DRYSDALE, Conley (4), Jones (6), Face (8)
Home Runs: Malzone-A, Berra-A, F. Robinson-N, Gilliam-N, Colavito-A
Attendance: 55,105

To raise extra money for the players' pension fund and other causes, a second All-Star Game was scheduled for 1959, the first ever to be played in August, and the first on the West Coast. The American stars avenged their earlier defeat with a 5–3 win, out-homering the Nationals three to two.

The National Leaguers scored first on a first-inning double and sacrifice fly, but Frank Malzone tied the score with the game's first home run. Yogi Berra homered an inning later with one on for a 3–1 American lead, but Frank Robinson brought the Nationals back to within one with his homer in the fifth. The Americans replaced that run in the top of the seventh on a walk, two errors, and a single, but Junior Gilliam countered with a home run in the last of the inning. Rocky Colavito scored the game's final run for the Americans in the eighth with the game's final homer.

Don Drysdale, the pitching standout of the July game, struck out five this time, but also walked three and gave up three runs on homers to take the loss.

GAME 28
Municipal Stadium, Kansas City
July 11, 1960
NL, 5–3

NL	311	000	000	5	12	4
AL	000	001	020	3	6	1

Pitchers: FRIEND, McCormick (4), Face (6), Buhl (8), Law (9) vs MONBOUQUETTE, Estrada (3), Coates (4), Bell (6), Lary (8), Daley (9)
Home Runs: Banks-N, Crandall-N, Kaline-A
Attendance: 30,619

The day was hot—the temperature broke 100—and so were the National League bats. Willie Mays went 3 for 4, including a leadoff triple and a double; Ernie Banks homered and doubled; Del Crandall homered and singled; and Joe Adcock doubled and singled for three-fourths of the Nationals' 12 hits as the National League scored five unanswered runs in the first three innings to take an unbeatable lead. Starter Bob Friend, meanwhile, blanked the Americans on one hit through three innings and Mike McCormick held them scoreless for two more before yielding the first American run in the sixth on Nellie Fox's bases-loaded single. Roy Face then came on to douse the fire, getting Luis Aparicio to ground into a double play.

Four American League pitchers stopped the National stars after the third inning, and Al Kaline homered for two more American runs in the eighth. In the ninth the Americans put men on first and second with one away. But their comeback fell short, as Vern Law came on to retire Brooks Robinson and Harvey Kuenn and preserve the National victory.

GAME 29
Yankee Stadium, New York
July 13, 1960
NL, 6-0

NL	021 000 102	6 10 0
AL	000 000 000	0 8 0

Pitchers: LAW, Podres (3), S.Williams (5), Jackson (7), Henry (8), McDaniel (9) vs FORD, Wynn (4), Staley (6), Lary (8), Bell (9)
Home Runs: Mathews-N, Mays-N, Musial-N, Boyer-N
Attendance: 38,362

Only two days after the first All-Star Game, the squads met a second time before fewer than 39,000 fans in capacious Yankee Stadium. It was no contest. Vern Law, who had completed and saved the first game, started and won this one. His two shutout innings set the pace for the five National pitchers who followed him to fashion the first National League shutout in twenty years. The American stars got only two fewer hits than the Nationals (8 to 10), but only one was for extra bases, whereas four of the National League hits were home runs.

Eddie Mathews began the scoring with a two-run homer in the second, and Willie Mays (on his way to a second straight 3-for-4 game) homered for the third National run an inning later. No one scored through the three middle innings, but in the seventh Stan Musial broke his own record with his sixth All-Star homer—a mighty shot three tiers up in right—and in the ninth Ken Boyer completed the rout with a two-run shot to left.

GAME 30
Candlestick Park, San Francisco
July 11, 1961
NL, 5-4

AL	000 001 002 1	4 4 2
NL	010 100 010 2	5 11 5

Pitchers: Ford, Lary (4), Donovan (4), Bunning (6), Fornieles (8), WILHELM (8) vs Spahn, Purkey (4), McCormick (6), Face (9), Koufax (9), MILLER (9)
Home Runs: Killebrew-A, Altman-N
Attendance: 44,115

National League pitchers began the game where they had left off the year before. For five innings Warren Spahn and Bob Purkey shut out the American stars without a hit or base on balls. In the sixth, Harmon Killebrew homered off Mike McCormick to end the American drought, but it was the only hit McCormick yielded through the eighth.

Meanwhile, the Nationals had taken a 3–1 lead with runs in the second and fourth innings and George Altman's homer in the eighth. But in the top of the ninth, Candlestick's notorious winds helped put the Americans back in the game. Their second and third hits of the game brought in one run, and their fourth (and last) hit put another man on base. The tying run came in when the wind first of all blew pitcher Stu Miller off the mound for a balk to advance the runners, and then twisted a grounder out of third baseman Ken Boyer's grasp for a run-scoring error. In the tenth, the wind may have contributed to the Americans' go-ahead run as Boyer's throw to first sailed into the outfield, allowing Nellie Fox (who had walked) to score from first.

But in the last of the tenth the wind finally came to the aid of the Nationals, rendering useless the famous knuckleball of American reliever Hoyt Wilhelm, who gave up the tying run on hits by Hank Aaron and Willie Mays and lost the game when Roberto Clemente singled in Mays from second.

GAME 31
Fenway Park, Boston
July 31, 1961
Tie, 1-1

NL	000 001 000	1 5 1
AL	100 000 000	1 4 0

Pitchers: Purkey, Mahaffey (3), Koufax (5), Miller (7) vs Bunning, Schwall (4), Pascual (7)
Home Runs: Colavito-A
Attendance: 31,851

In the second All-Star Game of 1961, the weather again played a crucial role, as heavy rain at the end of the ninth inning forced the first (and, so far, only) All-Star tie.

Rocky Colavito's home run for the Americans in the first inning turned out to be his squad's only run, as four National League pitchers combined to shut out the American stars on only three singles the rest of the way. The American League pitching was just as effective, with starter Jim Bunning and finisher Camilo Pascual each pitching three no-hit innings. Don Schwall, who pitched the middle three innings, gave up all five National League hits and the Nationals' one run. But even that might have been prevented.

In the sixth, with two on and two out, American shortstop Luis Aparicio waited for a slow grounder, failing to get the ball in time to throw the batter out and end the inning. The Nationals scored on the next play, Bill White's hot ground single up the middle, which Aparicio stopped brilliantly to prevent more than one run from scoring, but which did drive in the game's tying—and final—run.

GAME 32
D.C. Stadium, Washington
July 10, 1962
NL, 3-1

NL	000 002 010	3 8 0
AL	000 001 000	1 4 0

Pitchers: Drysdale, MARICHAL (4), Purkey (6), Shaw (8) vs Bunning, PASCUAL (4), Donovan (7), Pappas (9)
Attendance: 45,480

The stadium was new, President Kennedy threw out the first ball, and starters Don Drysdale of the Nationals and Jim Bunning of the Americans both pitched three innings of one-hit shutout ball. But Maury Wills stole the show. Entering the game in the sixth inning to run for forty-one-year-old Stan Musial, who had singled, Wills stole second, then scored on Dick Groat's single up the middle for the game's first run. Another single, a long fly out, and a ground out scored Groat with the second (and, as it turned out, winning) run.

Two singles and a fly out by Roger Maris brought in an American run in the bottom of the sixth off Bob Purkey. But that was all they got, as Purkey and Bob Shaw one-hit the American stars through the final three innings.

In the eighth inning Wills manufactured an insurance run for the Nationals. On first with a leadoff single, he somehow reached third on Jim Davenport's single to short left, racing from second to third as left fielder Rocky Colavito threw in to second. He scored after tagging on a foul out to right.

GAME 33
Wrigley Field, Chicago
July 30, 1962
AL, 9–4

AL	001	201	302	9	10	0
NL	010	000	111	4	10	4

Pitchers: Stenhouse, HERBERT (3), Aguirre (6), Pappas (9) vs Podres, MAHAFFEY (3), Gibson (5), Farrell (7), Marichal (8)
Home Runs: Runnels-A, Wagner-A, Colavito-A, Roseboro-N
Attendance: 38,359

With this second game of 1962, the leagues ended their four-year experiment of playing two All-Star games a year. The Americans out-homered the Nationals to spoil the National League's attempt to even the series at 16 wins apiece. But no matter—the American stars would win only once again in the next twenty years.

The National stars scored first on a double and single in the second, but Pete Runnels evened the score in the third with a solo homer, and Leon Wagner put the Americans ahead with a two-run shot an inning later. After Tom Tresh doubled home a fourth American run in the sixth, Rocky Colavito put the game out of reach with a three-run blast in the seventh.

The Nationals tried to come back with runs in the seventh and eighth, but the Americans neutralized them with two more of their own in the ninth (on two errors, two Juan Marichal wild pitches, a double, and a long fly out). With the score now 9–3, John Roseboro's solo homer in the last of the ninth put the Nationals in the home-run column, but that was all.

GAME 34
Municipal Stadium, Cleveland
July 9, 1963
NL, 5–3

NL	012	010	010	5	6	0
AL	012	000	000	3	11	1

Pitchers: O'Toole, JACKSON (3), Culp (5), Woodeshick (6), Drysdale (8) vs McBride, BUNNING (4), Bouton (6), Pizarro (7), Radatz (8)
Attendance: 44,160

Willie Mays sparked the National League to victory with his baserunning and timely hitting. Although he had only one hit—a single—he scored two runs and drove in two others in the Nationals' 5–3 win.

The National stars scored first when Mays walked in the second inning, stole second, and came in on a single by Dick Groat. The Americans tied the game in the last of the second, but in the top of the third Mays singled in one run, stole second again, and scored his second run on Ed Bailey's single.

Once again the Americans came back in the bottom of the third to tie the game on Albie Pearson's double, followed by two singles sandwiched around an infield out. But these were their last runs, as four National pitchers shut them out on four singles the rest of the way. Meanwhile, Mays drove in what proved to be the winning run with a ground out in the fifth. In the eighth the Nationals scored a final run when Ron Santo singled home Bill White, who had singled and stolen second.

GAME 35
Shea Stadium, New York
July 7, 1964
NL, 7–4

AL	100	002	100	4	9	1
NL	000	210	004	7	8	0

Pitchers: Chance, Wyatt (4), Pascual (5), RADATZ (7) vs Drysdale, Bunning (4), Short (6), Farrell (7), MARICHAL (9)
Home Runs: B.Williams-N, Boyer-N, Callison-N
Attendance: 50,850

A new stadium in the midst of a World's Fair was the venue for this game in which the National League at last drew even with the American at 17 wins apiece.

The American stars jumped into the lead with an unearned run in the first, but the Nationals (after Dean Chance had shut them out through three innings) overtook the Americans in the fourth, on home runs by Billy Williams and Ken Boyer, and Dick Groat doubled in a third run in the fifth. In the top of the sixth the Americans tied the score when Brooks Robinson tripled in a pair, and took the lead again an inning later on a sacrifice fly that barely scored Elston Howard ahead of Willie Mays's throw from center.

The Americans held their slim lead into the bottom of the ninth. But Mays walked (after fouling off five third strikes), stole second, and scored the tying run on a single to short right and an errant throw home. One intentional walk and two outs later, Johnny Callison hit Dick Radatz's 1–2 fastball over the fence in right to win the game.

GAME 36
Metropolitan Stadium, Bloomington, Minnesota
July 13, 1965
NL, 6–5

NL	320	000	100	6	11	0
AL	000	140	000	5	8	0

Pitchers: Marichal, Maloney (4), Drysdale (5), KOUFAX (6), Farrell (7), Gibson (8) vs Pappas, Grant (2), Richert (4), McDOWELL (6), Fisher (8)
Home Runs: Mays-N, Torre-N, Stargell-N, McAuliffe-A, Killebrew-A
Attendance: 46,706

For a while it looked as though the Nationals would run away with the game. Willie Mays led off with a home run in the first, and Joe Torre added two runs with a homer later in the inning. In the second Willie Stargell homered for two more runs to make the score 5–0. National starter Juan Marichal stopped the Americans on one hit through three innings.

But the American stars battled back. A single, a walk, and another single off Marichal's replacement, Jim Maloney, brought in one run in the fourth. Maloney retired the first two men in the fifth, but then he gave up a walk followed by a home run to Dick McAuliffe, and a scratch single followed by a Harmon Killebrew homer—and the score was tied at 5–5.

Only one more run was scored. In the seventh, Willie Mays, who had walked and gone to third on Hank Aaron's single, scored on Ron Santo's infield hit to short. The Nationals held off American threats in the eighth and ninth to take the All-Star series lead for the first time.

GAME 37
Busch Memorial Stadium, St. Louis
July 12, 1966
NL, 2-1

```
AL   010 000 000 0   1 6 0
NL   000 100 000 1   2 6 0
```

Pitchers: McLain, Kaat (4), Stottlemyre (6), Siebert (8), RICHERT (10) vs Koufax, Bunning (4), Marichal (6), G.PERRY (9)
Attendance: 49,936

The celebration of another new stadium and the city's bicentennial—and a temperature of 106°F—greeted participants in the 1966 classic. Pitching dominated: seven pitchers hurled two innings or more each of shutout ball. American starter Denny McLain threw three perfect innings, but the National League's Sandy Koufax gave the Americans a run in the second when he let loose a wild pitch after Brooks Robinson had tripled.

The Nationals tied the score in the fourth with three singles off Jim Kaat, but that ended the scoring for both sides through the regulation nine innings. In the top of the tenth, Gaylord Perry stopped the American stars. But in the last half of the inning, National Leaguer Tim McCarver singled off Pete Richert, was sacrificed to second, and came across with the winning run on Maury Wills's single to right.

GAME 38
Anaheim Stadium, Anaheim, California
July 11, 1967
NL, 2-1

```
NL   010 000 000 000 001   2 9 0
AL   000 001 000 000 000   1 8 0
```

Pitchers: Marichal, Jenkins (4), Gibson (7), Short (9), Cuellar (11), DRYSDALE (13), Seaver (15) vs Chance, McGlothlin (4), Peters (6), Downing (9), HUNTER (11)
Home Runs: Allen-N, B.Robinson-A, Perez-N
Attendance: 46,309

This was a game of strikeouts, home runs, and extra innings. Every one of the twelve pitchers used in the game struck out at least one batter. American Leaguers Gary Peters (who pitched three perfect middle innings) and Catfish Hunter struck out four apiece, while Ferguson Jenkins of the Nationals tied the All-Star record with six. The game total of 30 strikeouts shattered the previous record of 20 set in 1955.

Apart from the splendid pitching, three home runs provided the only excitement—and the only scoring—in this longest All-Star Game. Richie Allen of the Nationals scored first, homering to center off Dean Chance in the second inning. The Americans' Brooks Robinson tied the score in the sixth with a shot off Jenkins. And 8½ innings later, in the top of the fifteenth, National Leaguer Tony Perez homered off Hunter for the game's third and final run. Tom Seaver set down the Americans in the bottom of the fifteenth, and the game—after a record 3 hours and 41 minutes—was history.

GAME 39
Astrodome, Houston
July 9, 1968
NL, 1-0

```
AL   000 000 000   0 3 1
NL   100 000 00X   1 5 0
```

Pitchers: TIANT, Odom (3), McLain (5), McDowell (7), Stottlemyre (8), John (8) vs DRYSDALE, Marichal (4), Carlton (6), Seaver (7), Reed (9), Koosman (9)
Attendance: 48,321

This game could be described by what was missing: fresh air and real grass (it was the first All-Star Game held indoors), hitting (the eight hits were a new low for a nine-inning All-Star Game), and earned runs (the game's only run came with the help of an error). In fact, if it weren't for thirty-seven-year-old Willie Mays, the game might not have had any runs at all. Starting only because of an injury to Pete Rose, National Leaguer Mays led off the bottom of the first with a single, and took second when first baseman Harmon Killebrew mishandled pitcher Luis Tiant's pickoff throw for an error. Mays took third as the rattled Tiant threw a wild pitch to walk Curt Flood, and scored when Willie McCovey grounded into a double play.

The pitching on both sides was superb, but the National Leaguers shone especially bright. Tom Seaver gave up two of the Americans' three hits (all of which were doubles), but struck out five in his two innings. Juan Marichal hurled two perfect innings, fanning three. And none of the six National pitchers walked a man. One American, Killebrew, couldn't walk. Stretching for a throw at first, the slugger tore a hamstring and missed the next two months, the most serious All-Star Game casualty since Ted Williams's broken elbow 18 years earlier.

GAME 40
R.F.K. Memorial Stadium, Washington, D.C.
July 23, 1969
NL, 9-3

```
NL   125 100 000   9 11 0
AL   011 100 000   3  6 2
```

Pitchers: CARLTON, Gibson (4), Singer (5), Koosman (7), Dierker (8), P.Niekro (9) vs STOTTLEMYRE, Odom (3), Knowles (3), McLain (4), McNally (5), McDowell (7), Culp (9)
Home Runs: Bench-N, Howard-A, McCovey-N (2), Freehan-A
Attendance: 45,259

After four one-run victories in a row, the National Leaguers finally broke loose, massing 10 of their 11 hits in the first four innings for nine runs and a crushing win. Scoring an unearned run in the first on a dropped outfield fly, and two in the second on Johnny Bench's home run, the Nationals erupted in the third for five runs off Blue Moon Odom before two outs had been recorded. Willie McCovey's two-run homer began the third-inning scoring, and an error, single, and two doubles added three more runs before Odom was mercifully relieved. McCovey homered again in the fourth for the Nationals' final tally.

The American bats were not wholly silent, but the solo homers by Frank Howard and Bill Freehan in the second and third, and a third run in the fourth, couldn't counter the Nationals' attack.

The final five innings of the game were as quiet as the opening four had been noisy. No runs scored, and the two teams together managed only three hits.

GAME 41
Riverfront Stadium, Cincinnati
July 14, 1970
NL, 5-4

```
AL  000 001 120 000   4 12 0
NL  000 000 103 001   5 10 0
```

Pitchers: Palmer, McDowell (4), J.Perry (7), Hunter (9), Peterson (9), Stottlemyre (9), WRIGHT (11) vs Seaver, Merritt (4), G.Perry (6), Gibson (8), OSTEEN (10)
Home Runs: Dietz-N
Attendance: 51,838

In a new stadium, opened only two weeks earlier, no one scored for the first five innings, as Jim Palmer and Sam McDowell of the Americans and Tom Seaver and Jim Merritt of the Nationals held the opposition to two hits per team. The Americans finally scored a run in the sixth, and another in the seventh. The Nationals got one back in the last of the seventh, but the Americans increased their lead to 4–1 in the eighth when Brooks Robinson tripled home two baserunners.

Fans had already begun to leave the park when the Nationals' Dick Dietz homered off Catfish Hunter to lead off the last of the ninth. Two pitchers, three singles, and a sacrifice fly later, the game was tied and headed for extra innings. Claude Osteen held the Americans scoreless from the tenth through the twelfth, and the Nationals also failed to score in the tenth and eleventh. But in the last of the twelfth, with two out, Pete Rose, Billy Grabarkewitz, and Jim Hickman singled. Hometowner Rose, racing home from second on Hickman's hit, crashed into catcher Ray Fosse with a force that injured both players and still provokes controversy—but which also gave the National League its eighth straight victory.

GAME 42
Tiger Stadium, Detroit
July 13, 1971
AL, 6-4

```
NL  021 000 010   4 5 0
AL  004 002 00X   6 7 0
```

Pitchers: ELLIS, Marichal (4), Jenkins (6), Wilson (7) vs BLUE, Palmer (4), Cuellar (6), Lolich (8)
Home Runs: Bench-N, Aaron-N, Jackson-A, F.Robinson-A, Killebrew-A, Clemente-N
Attendance: 53,559

With an assist from a favorable wind, six all-time greats homered to account for all the scoring as the American League broke its eight-game All-Star drought with a 6–4 victory. Johnny Bench put the Nationals in front with a two-run homer in the second inning off Vida Blue, and Hank Aaron—with his first All-Star home run—added a third run off Blue an inning later. But the Americans, shut out by Dock Ellis through the first two innings, rocked him in the bottom of the third as Reggie Jackson and Frank Robinson wrested the lead from the Nationals with a pair of two-run homers. (Robinson's made him the first player to hit an All-Star home run for both leagues.)

Ferguson Jenkins yielded the game's fifth homer, Harmon Killebrew's two-run shot for the Americans in the sixth. Roberto Clemente brought the Nationals a run closer with his solo homer off Mickey Lolich in the eighth, but that ended the team's scoring, and (for a year, anyway) the National League's All-Star stranglehold.

GAME 43
Atlanta Stadium, Atlanta
July 25, 1972
NL, 4-3

```
AL  001 000 020 0   3 6 0
NL  000 002 001 1   4 8 0
```

Pitchers: Palmer, Lolich (4), G.Perry (6), Wood (8), McNALLY (10) vs Gibson, Blass (3), Sutton (4), Carlton (6), Stoneman (7), McGRAW (9)
Home Runs: Aaron-N, Rojas-A
Attendance: 53,107

The American Leaguers tried to extend their All-Star win streak to two games, and for a time it looked as though they might do it. In the third, they scored the only run of the first half of the game as Jim Palmer and Mickey Lolich held the Nationals to two hits through the first five innings. In the sixth Hank Aaron thrilled the hometown crowd with a two-run homer deep to left to shift the lead to the National League. But Cookie Rojas restored the American lead with his own two-run shot in the eighth.

The Americans held their lead into the bottom of the ninth, but after two singles and a force out, the score was tied. Tug McGraw set down the American stars in order in the tenth, but American reliever Dave McNally was not so fortunate. He walked leadoff batter Nate Colbert, who was sacrificed to second. Joe Morgan then sent the American Leaguers back into the ranks of losers with a sharp RBI single to right center. His single also gave the Nationals their seventh win in seven extra-inning games.

GAME 44
Royals Stadium, Kansas City
July 24, 1973
NL, 7-1

```
NL  002 122 000   7 10 0
AL  010 000 000   1  5 0
```

Pitchers: WISE, Osteen (3), Sutton (5), Twitchell (6), Giusti (7), Seaver (8), Brewer (9) vs Hunter, Holtzman (2), BLYLEVEN (3), Singer (4), Ryan (6), Lyle (8), Fingers (9)
Home Runs: Bench-N, Bonds-N, W.Davis-N
Attendance: 40,849

Once again a new stadium was chosen to host the All-Star Game, and once again the National League emerged victorious. The Americans scored first, with a run in the second when Reggie Jackson scored from second on a single after doubling off the center field wall. But that was the beginning and end of their offense, as six National pitchers shut them out on three hits the rest of the way.

Meanwhile the National League hitters came to life, producing seven runs in four innings. Two walks and two singles in the third brought in two runs, and Johnny Bench's homer in the fourth made the score 3–1. In the fifth, Bobby Bonds—in the midst of his finest season—homered for two more National runs. And in the sixth, Willie Davis's home run completed the game's scoring, bringing in the Nationals' sixth and seventh runs.

The final third of the game was anticlimactic, as only two hits were made after the sixth inning. But Bonds brought the crowd to life briefly in the seventh, stretching one of those hits into a double with some audacious baserunning (ensuring his selection as the game's MVP).

GAME 45
Three Rivers Stadium, Pittsburgh
July 23, 1974
NL, 7–2

AL	002 000 000	2	4	1
NL	010 210 12X	7	10	1

Pitchers: G.Perry, TIANT (4), Hunter (6), Fingers (8) vs Messersmith, BRETT (4), Matlack (6), McGlothen (7), Marshall (8)
Home Runs: R.Smith-N
Attendance: 50,706

Steve Garvey, who was elected to the National League starting lineup on write-in votes (his name was omitted from the fans' All-Star ballot), sparked the Nationals to yet another convincing win over the hapless American stars. After singling in the second inning, he scored the game's first run on Ron Cey's double.

The Americans took the lead with two runs in the top of the third, capitalizing on two walks and an error sandwiched between Thurman Munson's leadoff double and Dick Allen's single. They might have scored more had not Garvey snared Bobby Murcer's hot grounder for an assist on the third out.

Garvey doubled in the tying run in the fourth, and Cey's RBI ground out restored the Nationals' lead. Lou Brock added a run in the fifth with a single and some inspired baserunning, and Reggie Smith homered for another in the seventh. Don Kessinger's triple and a wild pitch by Rollie Fingers in the eighth contributed to two final National League runs.

GAME 46
County Stadium, Milwaukee
July 15, 1975
NL, 6–3

NL	021 000 003	6	13	1
AL	000 003 000	3	10	1

Pitchers: Reuss, Sutton (4), Seaver (6), MATLACK (7), R.Jones (9) vs Blue, Busby (3), Kaat (5), HUNTER (7), Gossage (9)
Home Runs: Garvey-N, Wynn-N, Yastrzemski-A
Attendance: 51,480

When National stars Steve Garvey and Jim Wynn led off the second with back-to-back homers and their teammates added another run in the third, it looked as if the National League might be on its way to another easy win. But the American pitchers shut down the National League offense for the next five innings, and Carl Yastrzemski made a contest of it with a three-run homer in the sixth off Tom Seaver to tie the score.

In the top of the ninth, though, the Americans all but gave the game away. Left fielder Claudell Washington dropped a fly on the run (it was scored a hit) and misplayed a line drive that went for a double. Goose Gossage came in to relieve Catfish Hunter on the mound and hit the next batter to load the bases. Bill Madlock then drove in two of the baserunners with a single through the drawn-in infield, and Pete Rose knocked in the third run of the inning with a sacrifice fly.

Randy Jones set the Americans down in order in the bottom of the ninth, and—voilà!—the National League had won again.

GAME 47
Veterans Stadium, Philadelphia
July 13, 1976
NL, 7–1

AL	000 100 000	1	5	0
NL	202 000 03X	7	10	0

Pitchers: FIDRYCH, Hunter (3), Tiant (5), Tanana (7) vs R.JONES, Seaver (4), Montefusco (6), Rhoden (8), K.Forsch (9)
Home Runs: Foster-N, Lynn-A, Cedeno-N
Attendance: 63,974

Tom Seaver gave up a home run to Fred Lynn in the fourth inning, but that was the Americans' only score as the Nationals held the American stars to five hits while celebrating the nation's bicentennial with ten hits and seven runs.

Rookie standout Mark Fidrych was chosen to start for the Americans and was promptly rapped for two runs. Pete Rose led off with a single and was tripled home by Steve Garvey, who scored himself on a ground out. The Nationals doubled their score in the third inning as George Foster tagged Catfish Hunter for two runs with a mighty home run to left center, and capped their assault with three more in the eighth off Frank Tanana, including a two-run homer by Cesar Cedeno.

The fans had elected five members of Cincinnati's "big red machine" to the National League starting lineup, and Sparky Anderson, the Reds' and National squad's manager, added two more. They provided the bulk of the Nationals' offense, with seven hits, four RBIs, and four runs scored.

GAME 48
Yankee Stadium, New York
July 19, 1977
NL, 7–5

NL	401 000 020	7	9	1
AL	000 002 102	5	8	0

Pitchers: SUTTON, Lavelle (4), Seaver (6), R.Reuschel (8), Gossage (9) vs PALMER, Kern (3), Eckersley (4), LaRoche (6), Campbell (7), Lyle (8)
Home Runs: Morgan-N, Luzinski-N, Garvey-N, Scott-A
Attendance: 56,683

The Nationals' Joe Morgan homered off Jim Palmer to open the game, and before Palmer escaped the first inning three more National Leaguers had crossed the plate on a single, double, and Greg Luzinski's homer. Palmer got through the second inning without further damage, but before he was relieved in the third Steve Garvey had homered to give the Nationals a 5–0 lead.

The Americans fought back against Tom Seaver in the sixth and seventh. Seaver retired two in the sixth, but then gave up two singles, and two runs as Richie Zisk doubled the runners home. Two more singles in the seventh produced a third American run.

But the Nationals—assisted by pitcher Sparky Lyle's wild pitch and hit batsman—put a sixth and seventh run on the board in the eighth with a double and single. The Americans added two final runs of their own in the bottom of the ninth on George Scott's homer off Goose Gossage, but fell short of victory once again.

GAME 49
San Diego Stadium,
July 11, 1978
NL, 7-3

AL	201	000	000	3	8	1
NL	003	000	04X	7	10	0

Pitchers: Palmer, Keough (3), Sorensen (4), Kern (7), Guidry (7), GOSSAGE (8) vs Blue, Rogers (4), Fingers (6), SUTTER (8), P.Niekro (9)
Attendance: 51,549

Rod Carew led off both the first and third innings with triples—an All-Star record— scoring both times as the Americans took a 3-0 lead into the bottom of the third. But then Jim Palmer, who had shut the Nationals out on one hit through the first two innings, lost his touch. After yielding a leadoff single, he retired two batters, but then issued three walks to force in a run, and when Steve Garvey singled past the shortstop two more runs scored to tie the game.

No one scored through the next 4½ innings, with Larry Sorensen turning in the game's top pitching performance as he shut the Nationals out on one hit through the three middle innings. But in the last of the eighth, Gosse Gossage (the National League closer the previous year) took the mound this year for the Americans. Garvey greeted him with a leadoff triple and scored what proved to be the winning run on a wild pitch. A walk and three singles added three insurance runs before the inning ended. Bruce Sutter and Phil Niekro blanked the Americans in the ninth, and the Nationals has extended their current win streak to seven.

GAME 50
Kingdome, Seattle
July 17, 1979
NL, 7-6

NL	211	001	011	7	10	0
AL	302	001	000	6	10	0

Pitchers: Carlton, Andujar (2), Rogers (4), G.Perry (6), Sambito (6), LaCoss (6), SUTTER (8) vs Ryan, Stanley (3), Clear (5), KERN (7), Guidry (9)
Home Runs: Lynn-A, Mazzilli-N
Attendance: 58,905

Mike Schmidt tripled and George Foster doubled to drive in the game's first runs as the Nationals began their scoring in the top of the first. The Americans fought back to take the lead later in the inning as Don Baylor doubled home one run and Fred Lynn homered for two more. The Nationals tied the score with a run in the second and went ahead again in the third when Schmidt scored after doubling. But the Americans recaptured the lead in the bottom of the third, scoring twice on a single, wild pitch, ground out, hit batsman, single, and error.

Three innings later the Nationals again tied the game, but the Americans went ahead for the third time with a run in their half of the sixth. Outstanding throws by right fielder Dave Parker, who notched two assists, helped to keep the Americans from pulling away. In the eighth the Nationals' Lee Mazzilli homered for yet another tie, and an inning later Ron Guidry walked Mazzilli with the bases loaded to force in the Nationals' go-ahead seventh run. When Bruce Sutter kept the Americans from scoring in the bottom of the ninth, the National Leaguers had for the second time defeated the Americans eight years in a row.

GAME 51
Dodger Stadium,
Los Angeles
July 8, 1980
NL, 4-2

AL	000	020	000	2	7	1
NL	000	012	10X	4	7	0

Pitchers: Stone, JOHN (4), Farmer (6), Stieb (7), Gossage (8) vs Richard, Welch (3), REUSS (6), Bibby (7), Sutter (8)
Home Runs: Lynn-A, Griffey-N
Attendance: 56,088

For 4⅔ innings J.R. Richard and Bob Welch held the American stars scoreless. But then Rod Carew singled and Fred Lynn drove in the game's first runs with his third All-Star homer.

The Americans' Steve Stone and Tommy John pitched even better, setting the Nationals down in order through four innings. John continued the perfect streak through the first two outs of the fifth, but then Ken Griffey homered, and the Americans' spell on the National Leaguers was broken.

While three National pitchers limited the Americans to a single and a walk over the final four innings, three singles and an error sent the Nationals into the lead in the sixth. A passed ball surrounded by two wild pitches moved Dave Concepcion around the bases in the seventh (he had reached on a fielder's choice) for the Nationals' fourth run. They didn't really need it, though, as Bruce Sutter—the winning pitcher in the two previous All-Star games—saved this one with two final innings of no-hit ball for the Nationals' ninth successive win.

GAME 52
Municipal Stadium,
Cleveland
August 9, 1981
NL, 5-4

NL	000	011	120	5	9	1
AL	010	003	000	4	11	1

Pitchers: Valenzuela, Seaver (2), Knepper (3), Hooton (5), Ruthven (6), BLUE (7), Ryan (8), Sutter (9) vs Morris, Barker (3), K.Forsch (5), Norris (6), Davis (7), FINGERS (8), Stieb (8)
Home Runs: Singleton-A, Carter-N (2), Parker-N, Schmidt-N
Attendance: 72,086

The game, delayed until August by the midseason players' strike, drew an All-Star record crowd of more than 72,000 fans, and the managers set a new record by using 56 players. But the game itself followed a familiar pattern.

The Americans scored first in the second inning on Ken Singleton's home run off Tom Seaver, and held their slim lead into the fifth on Len Barker's two innings of perfect pitching. But Ken Forsch replaced Barker in the fifth and Gary Carter homered off his first pitch to tie the score. Dave Parker's homer off Mike Norris an inning later put the Nationals ahead for the first time, but the Americans came right back in the bottom of the inning, putting together four singles and a sacrifice fly for three runs and a two-run advantage.

Gary Carter's second home run of the game—this time off Ron Davis's first pitch—brought the Nationals within one in the seventh, and Mike Schmidt's two-run blast off Rollie Fingers in the eighth restored their lead. Three National pitchers shut out the Americans without a hit over the final three innings as closer Bruce Sutter picked up his second consecutive All-Star save and the National Leaguers their tenth consecutive victory.

GAME 53
Olympic Stadium, Montreal
July 13, 1982
NL, 4–1

```
AL  100 000 000   1  8  2
NL  021 001 00X   4  8  1
```

Pitchers: ECKERSLEY, Clancy (4), Bannister (5), Quisenberry (6), Fingers (8) vs ROGERS, Carlton (4), Soto (6), Valenzuela (8), Minton (8), Howe (9), Hume (9)
Home Runs: Concepcion-N
Attendance: 59,057

In the first All-Star Game held outside the United States, the American League for the third year in a row put the first run on the board, but for the eleventh year in a row the final score showed the National League the winner. Two singles, a wild pitch, and a sacrifice fly gave the Americans a run in the top of the first. But starter Steve Rogers of the host Expos held the Americans scoreless for the remainder of his three innings while the Nationals struck back for two runs in the second on Dave Concepcion's home run, and added another in the third when Ruppert Jones—who had tripled to open the inning—scored on a sacrifice fly.

Six National League pitchers (and shortstop Ozzie Smith's spectacular stop and throw to first with two on in the eighth) joined Rogers in holding the American stars scoreless after the first inning. Two hometowners put together the Nationals' final run in the sixth. Al Oliver, leading off, doubled down the line in left and took third as the ball got by left fielder Rickey Henderson. Two outs later Gary Carter lined a pitch to center, scoring Oliver as Willie Wilson's dive for the ball came up short.

GAME 54
Comiskey Park, Chicago
July 6, 1983
AL, 13–3

```
NL  100 110 000    3  8  3
AL  117 000 22X   13 15  2
```

Pitchers: SOTO, Hammaker (3), Dawley (3), Dravecky (5), Perez (7), Orosco (7), L.Smith (8) vs STIEB, Honeycutt (4), Stanley (6), Young (8), Quisenberry (9)
Home Runs: Rice-A, Lynn-A
Attendance: 43,801

The game returned to the park where it had originated fifty years earlier, and the American League, after eleven years of All-Star losses, unleashed its pent-up fury to produce the greatest margin of victory in thirty-seven years. The game began, though, as an embarrassment of errors. American starter Dave Stieb struck out the side in the first, but along the way two errors (one of them Stieb's) let in a run. An unearned run in the bottom of the first tied the score and another in the second put the American League ahead for good (making a loser out of the unfortunate National starter Mario Soto).

The hitting began in earnest in the last of the third as the Americans scored seven times for a new one-inning record. Among their six hits (also a record for an All-Star inning) were a homer by Jim Rice, a triple by George Brett, and a bases-loaded blast by Fred Lynn—his fourth All-Star home run and the first grand slam in All-Star history. With the score now 9–1, the National League's single runs in the fourth and fifth were exercises in futility, and the Americans' two each in the seventh and eighth served chiefly to boost the winning total to 13—another All-Star high.

GAME 55
Candlestick Park,
San Francisco
July 10, 1984
NL, 3–1

```
AL  010 000 000   1  7  2
NL  110 000 01X   3  8  0
```

Pitchers: STIEB, Morris (3), Dotson (5), Caudill (7), Hernandez (8) vs LEA, Valenzuela (3), Gooden (5), Soto (7), Gossage (9)
Home Runs: Brett-A, Carter-N, Murphy-N
Attendance: 57,756

Only four times in the previous fifty-four All-Star Games had a pitcher struck out the side in order. In this game, three more pitchers did it. And, on this fiftieth anniversary of Carl Hubbell's five consecutive strikeouts, two of those pitchers combined to break Hubbell's record with six back-to-back whiffs, who threw out the first ball, also saw an All-Star nine-inning record set with 21 total Ks (11 by National League pitchers, 10 by American).

In the fourth inning, National star Fernando Valenzuela mowed down three of the game's premier sluggers: Dave Winfield, Reggie Jackson, and George Brett. If the three men Dwight Gooden retired on strikes an inning later (Lance Parrish, Chet Lemon, and rookie Alvin Davis) were slightly less formidable, still, it was an impressive performance for a nineteen-year-old rookie (the youngest player in All-Star history). The three that American Leaguer Bill Caudill struck out in the seventh were no slouches either: Tim Raines, Ryne Sandberg (in the midst of an MVP season), and Keith Hernandez.

Three of the four runs scored in the game were homers. The National League's run in the first was unearned, but the Americans' George Brett homered to center to tie the game in the second, and the Nationals' go-ahead run later in the inning came on Gary Carter's blast to left. In the eighth, National Leaguer Dale Murphy also put one over the left field fence to end the scoring.

GAME 56
H. Humphrey Metrodome,
Minneapolis
July 16, 1985
NL, 6–1

```
NL  011 020 002   6  9  1
AL  100 000 000   1  5  0
```

Pitchers: HOYT, Ryan (4), Valenzuela (7), Reardon (8), Gossage (9) vs MORRIS, Key (3), Blyleven (4), Stieb (6), Moore (7), Petry (9), Hernandez (9)
Attendance: 54,960

The American Leaguers scored first, as Rickey Henderson led off the bottom of the first with a single and circled the bases on a steal, error, and sacrifice fly. But the five National pitchers blanked the Americans the rest of the way on only four more singles.

Meanwhile, the National stars methodically dismantled the Americans for their thirty-sixth All-Star victory. In the top of the second, after Darryl Strawberry singled and stole second, Terry Kennedy, whose error had led to the American League run, redeemed himself by singling Strawberry home. An inning later, with two out, Tom Herr doubled and scored the go-ahead (and winning) run on Steve Garvey's single.

In the fifth the Nationals scored two more runs on a hit batsman, Tim Wallach's ground-rule double, and Ozzie Virgil's single, and finished their scoring in the ninth with another pair on three walks and Willie McGee's double—another ground-rule bounce out of play off the lively Metrodome surface. Goose Gossage struck out the final two American batters in the bottom of the ninth, and the Nationals had increased their winning margin in the series to a new high of seventeen games.

GAME 57
Astrodome, Houston
July 15, 1986
AL, 3-2

AL	020	000	100	3	5	0
NL	000	000	020	2	5	1

Pitchers: CLEMENS, Higuera (4), Hough (7), Righetti (8), Aase (9) vs GOODEN, Valenzuela (4), Scott (7), Fernandez (8), Krukow (9)
Home Runs: Whitaker-A, White-A
Attendance: 45,774

National League pitchers struck out 12 Americans, led by Fernando Valenzuela's five in a row, which matched the mark set by Carl Hubbell in 1934. (Two years earlier Valenzuela had helped set a multipitcher All-Star record of six consecutive strikeouts.) In the eighth inning Sid Fernandez, after walking two, struck out the next three.

Though the American Leaguers struck out fewer men, their pitching was more effective over all. Starter Roger Clemens hurled three perfect innings (3 balls and 21 strikes), and Teddy Higuera one-hit the Nationals over the next three. Charlie Hough struck out three in the eighth after yielding the Nationals' only extra-base hit (a double) to Chris Brown. But catcher Rich Gedman couldn't handle Hough's knuckleball, and Brown advanced to third on the first strikeout (ruled a wild pitch) and scored on the second, a passed ball which also enabled batter Hubie Brooks to reach first safely. Brooks moved up on a balk and scored the Nationals' second run on Steve Sax's single.

But home runs had already undone the Nationals. With two gone in the second, Dave Winfield doubled off starter Dwight Gooden, and Lou Whitaker clubbed an 0-2 pitch over the fence in right. And in the seventh, Frank White (hitting for Whitaker) knocked Mike Scott's 0-2 pitch over the fence in left center for what proved the margin of American League victory.

GAME 58
Oakland-Alameda County
Stadium, Oakland
July 14, 1987
NL, 2-0

NL	000	000	000	000	2	2	8	2
AL	000	000	000	000	0	0	6	1

Pitchers: Scott, Sutcliffe (3), Hershiser (5), R.Reuschel (7), Franco (8), Bedrosian (9), L.SMITH (10), S. Fernandez (13) vs Saberhagen, Morris (4), Langston (6), Plesac (8), Righetti (9), Henke (9), J.HOWELL (12)
Attendance: 49,671

None of the previous fifty-seven All-Star Games had gone more than five innings without at least one run crossing the plate. But this game went more than twice that before National Leaguer Tim Raines tripled in two runs in the top of the thirteenth for the game's only scoring. It was the National League's eighth win in eight extra-inning All-Star games.

Both teams missed scoring opportunities in the ninth inning. Raines singled for the Nationals with only one out, and became the game's first runner to reach third when a throw from first on his attempted steal went into center field. But a fly to short right and a foul out left him stranded. In the bottom of the ninth, the Americans came close to winning the game as Dave Winfield headed for home from second on a missed 4-6-1 double play. But National pitcher Steve Bedrosian, covering first, snared the off-center throw from short and fired it home to catch Winfield for the third out.

The Americans again reached third in the eleventh as Larry Parrish singled and moved around on a sacrifice and ground out. But pitcher Lee Smith (whose three shutout innings earned him the win) struck out Tony Fernandez to end the threat.

GAME 59
Riverfront Stadium,
Cincinnati
July 12, 1988
AL, 2-1

AL	001	100	000	2	6	2
NL	000	100	000	1	5	0

Pitchers: VIOLA, Clemens (3), Gubicza (4), Stieb (6), Russell (7), Jones (8), Plesac (8), Eckersley (9) vs GOODEN, Knepper (4), Cone (5), Gross (6), Davis (7), Walk (7), Hershiser (8), Worrell (9)
Attendance: 55,837

Oakland's Terry Steinbach was not among the ten top American League catchers in batting; because of time lost to injuries, he was not even his club's leading catcher in games played. But the fans voted him to start in the All-Star Game, and he won it for the American Leaguers with a home run in his first trip to the plate and a sacrifice fly his next time up. Steinbach's homer—a drive off Dwight Gooden that led off the third inning—caromed off the glove of a leaping Darryl Strawberry over the wall in right for the game's first score. His sacrifice fly—high and deep to left in the fourth inning—scored Dave Winfield (aboard with his record seventh All-Star double) to put the Americans ahead 2-0.

Steinbach also contributed negatively to the National League run later in the fourth. His throwing error on Vince Coleman's steal of second enabled Coleman to advance to third, whence he scored on a wild pitch by Mark Gubicza.

American starter Frank Viola, the midseason league leader in wins, was awarded the victory for his two perfect innings pitched. Dennis Eckersley, the majors' top reliever, preserved the win for the Americans with a perfect ninth inning.

## CHAPTER 5

The Changing Game

Bill Felber

In the season of 1906, at the arguable heights of their careers, the Hall of Fame–bound trio of Joe Tinker, Johnny Evers, and Frank Chance completed approximately 50 double plays. Seven decades later, their deservedly anonymous successors in a second-division Chicago Cubs infield—Mick Kelleher, Manny Trillo, and Pete LaCock, recorded about twice that number. May we infer that the finest middle infield of a bygone era would be rejected as unfit for duty on a perfectly nondescript modern pro team?

For the five-year period between 1921 and 1925, Rogers Hornsby batted better than .400. In the past forty-five years, not a single major league hitter has reached that level of excellence for as much as one season, let alone half a decade. May we conclude that were he in his prime today, Hornsby would shame Wade Boggs into anonymity?

The answers to those questions are, if not two resounding "noes," at least two very cautious "not necessarilys."

Baseball is not played in a time capsule, and neither its record book nor its archives can be read as if it were. The game played on the artificial turf of Royals Stadium that you watch today on television holds the same lure as the contest your grandfather carriaged to Chicago's old West Side Park to see. Teams contest for the same end, using fundamentally the same objects in a format scribed basically by the same rules. But technological, sociological, strategic, and cultural forces have over decades refined those elements so that today's performances cannot be accurately measured relative to yesterday's, nor judgment as to the superiority of either made with precision, save in the mind's eye, which is the only pertinent arbiter of such standards anyway.

Baseball today is different from the game of the turn of the century in as many ways as American culture is different from the horse-and-buggy era. Imagine paying a quarter for admission to the ballpark, another quarter for access to the grandstand, and a third quarter for a seat. Imagine games played before audiences of a few hundred or maybe a thousand. Imagine visiting teams arriving in town on trains, bunking two to a bed, then caravaning to the ball yard in a grand parade through the town's streets. But never at night. And never, ever on Sunday. Now imagine baseball as the only sport of widespread popularity. No football to speak of, no basketball, no hockey; no golf, no tennis, no track of consequence, horseracing only for the elite, and boxing only for the disreputable. There was such a time only about a century ago.

In many ways, the game of baseball has changed precisely because America itself has changed. Whether all that change has been for the good may be argued. You might contend, for instance, that a part of laudable Americana died out when the practice of uniformed players publicly trolleying to the game—a means of stirring fan attention—was halted in the first decade of the twentieth century. But most, if not all, aspects of baseball's growth alongside society were inevitable. The 50¢ admission charge established by the National League in 1876 held forth for many years, but so did the rather unsavory practice of treating players as peons, to the point of doubling up on sleeping arrangements. Philadelphia Athletics pitcher Rube Waddell once actually had it written into his contract that teammate (and bunkmate) Ossee Schrekengost would be barred from eating animal crackers in bed . . . because the crumbs irritated the pitcher! Players today sleep in the most modern of hotels, and they do not always even share rooms, much less beds. And as the cost of living and the cost of operating a franchise have both increased strikingly in the interim, so have the size of the grandstand and the cost of a general admission ticket, the latter about fifteenfold.

In any era and at any price, a great championship battle has always held the populace in relative thrall. Millions of fans watched on their living room televisions in October 1986 as the Mets rallied to defeat first the Astros and then the Red Sox to win the World Series. Those fans studied every decisive play from a half dozen angles on instant replay; they second-guessed managerial moves and controversial umpires' decisions. But was that excitement any greater, measure for measure, than the grip in which the cities of Boston and Baltimore were held during the final days of the race for the 1897 National League pennant?

There was neither television nor radio then, but that did not stay the enthusiasm of hundreds of thousands of rooters nationwide as the pulsating battle for supremacy wound to a close. The principals were the two most dominant sporting teams of their generation: the Boston Beaneaters and Baltimore Orioles had divided the previous six pennants. Now, with less than a week remaining in the 1897 season, they were locked in a virtual tie for first, each having won better than seven of every ten games played and fated by the schedule to meet for three conclusive games in Baltimore. So all-encompassing was interest in the games' outcomes that Associated Press telegraphers dispatched play-by-play accounts to every major subscribing newspaper east of the Rockies. More than three dozen correspondents—an unheard-of number for the era—covered the games in person. Twenty more telegraphers tapped out accounts to cities where fans had gathered in theaters or outside newspaper offices to follow the events on chalkboards. In Boston, fan interest was so great that the game reports received triple the front-page space accorded to the activities of President William McKinley, who was in Boston at that very time! Throngs numbering in the thousands massed daily along Washington Street, Boston's Newspaper

Row, to watch mechanical re-creations. There was a published report of 4,000 fans jamming Boston's Music Hall to watch a similar simulation. The games at Baltimore's Union Grounds drew as many as 25,000 spectators—more than twice the previous record attendance for that facility!

The excitement of a great pennant race is a constant. Only the modes of sensing that excitement change. Consider only a few of the more obvious changes:

The player pool has changed, albeit at times tardily, to reflect the nation's accepted ethnic population base. And when that pool has expanded to encompass Southerners, Irish, Jews, Latins, or blacks, it has done so in fundamental reaction to changes in national acceptance: the gradual dying out of post–Civil War prejudice; the assimilation of the immigrant population; the eventual willingness of white society to acknowledge blacks as equals.

Technology has worked on the sport in ways as basic as improved methods of construction of the ball and glove; as grandiose and obvious as the abandonment of the unfenced pasture in favor of the comparative luxury of the wooden park, thence to the brick-and-concrete stadium, and finally to the multipurpose facility of recent decades.

Sociological alterations, as exemplified by population shifts from the cities to the suburbs and the replacement of the trolley in favor of the automobile, have leveled inner-city ballparks like Pittsburgh's Forbes Field and replaced them with fringe-area facilities readily accessible only by car.

Attitudinal adjustments of the nation have been mirrored in the game on the field. We were a prim-and-proper country in 1908, and our baseball was a prim-and-proper game, heavy on the bunt and complete game, and very short on the home run. We were a comparatively profligate bunch in the late 1920s, winning and losing with abandon on Wall Street, and we liked baseball heroes like Babe Ruth and Hack Wilson, who hit 'em far during the day and swigged 'em often at night. The difference of only two decades is strikingly underscored in a baseball statistic that might also speak volumes about off-field attitudes: for the five years between 1906 and 1910, the Chicago White Sox hit a total of only 27 home runs. Ruth hit more than that by himself in every season save one between 1919 and 1933.

Baseball's labor-management machinations have at least generally mirrored national patterns. The present major leagues can trace their ancestry back to the 1870s, an age when even the legality of organized labor was questioned. The motivation behind the organizers of the National League was to take control of the competition away from a players' cooperative. The 1890s, the era of some of the most violent union-management conflicts (the Haymarket riot, the Pullman strike, et al.), also witnessed the last direct player challenge to the authority of ownership, the Brotherhood War, which produced the Players League. Unionization very gradually gained favor, although both nationally and in baseball that process took decades. And true player free agency, as with worker rights, often arrived only through the aegis of the courts, if indeed it even exists today.

Finally, as the educational level of America itself has changed, the strategies of baseball have evolved. The dominant function of today's "relief ace" could hardly have been envisioned by the game's greatest minds as little as two or three decades ago. The stolen base, home run, sacrifice—all have come and gone, and in some cases come again, as strategic coups.

It is as judgmental to speculate whether changes that make the game of 1989 different from the game of 1907 are for the better as it is to posit whether Joe Tinker was a better shortstop than Mick Kelleher or Dave Rosello.

No one would contend that baseball has been, or is today, any more than a general mirror of its times. But neither can it seriously be suggested that the National Pastime has failed to change with the changing years. For purposes of this discussion, it is vital to recognize both of these realities. And paradoxically, only by appreciating the game's evolution can you begin to sense the marvelous continuum represented therein.

So by what context does one measure Hornsby's feats of the 1920s relative to Boggs's of today? By the context of the technological, strategic, societal, and cultural changes that have wrought both of them. Could Joe Tinker play shortstop for the Cubs of today? For that matter, could Ozzie Smith have adapted to the scrub fields, primitive travel demands, incompetent training aides and all-but-useless equipment of eighty years ago? These questions cannot be answered with finality. But without considering the many changing aspects of the game, attempts to even provide an answer become frivolous.

What follows is an effort—by examining some of the major causes of change—to provide context to discussion of the evolving nature of baseball, a sport that through more than a century has possessed only one enduring and vital characteristic: it has, from the outset, been America's leading national pastime.

The Leagues

On St. Patrick's Day in 1871, representatives of ten teams met in New York City to organize what became known as the National Association. The delegates set a $10 entry fee for each club, elected a gentleman from Troy, N.Y., named James Kerns, as president, and drew up a set of rules calling for each team to play every other team in a best-of-five-game series. The champion would receive a pennant.

The National Association survived only a brief five years. But it is remembered today as the first league organized for the conduct of professional baseball in America. And its legacy proved lasting. Since that St. Patrick's Day meeting in 1871, not a day has passed without at least one major league in operation in the United States.

The National Association collapsed in 1876, both because of problems that were inherent in its structure and because of what was perceived at the time as the unwholesome atmosphere surrounding some of its games. The latter was readily recognizable at many game sites. Open betting on the day's results often took place at the park, and players in uniforms were among those making wagers. The result was suspected bribery and open intimidation of umpires and players. Heavy wagerers directed profanity at players whose errors jeopardized their stakes. The open selling of liquor further exacerbated ill feelings in what remained a temperate national climate. But the Association faced other problems as well. Players refused to honor contracts, often jumping from team to team, without penalty. Or they simply deserted. No wonder it was a comparatively simple matter for one of the owners of the Chicago team, William Hulbert, to foment what would prove to be a revolution during the winter of 1875-1876.

Hulbert, in company with Albert Spalding, who was recog-

nized as the top pitcher of the day, formulated a list of rules designed to obviate the major problems plaguing the National Association. Among steps taken was the drawing up of a formal player contract designed to stifle once and for all the practice of "jumping." In January 1876, Hulbert met secretly with representatives of the Cincinnati, Louisville, and St. Louis clubs to outline his plan. They agreed. Hulbert then confronted the more powerful Eastern bloc of teams with his intention of establishing a reform league. He also outlined the principles. Bookmaking and liquor selling would be banned from parks. Sunday baseball was frowned upon, and the penalty for players taking bribes or betting on games was established as expulsion, with no hope of reinstatement. The membership fee was raised tenfold, to $100, in an attempt to guarantee stability. A 50¢ admission price was established. The National League had been born.

The rise of the National League and the several challenges to its supremacy are amply documented in this volume, so this essay will defer to Messrs. Voight, Dellinger, Mann, Hailey, Tygiel, et al. Let's proceed to the changes in baseball on the field as distinct from those in league structures, legal issues, franchise locations, and race relations.

Night Ball

By the early 1930s, talk was being heard of the revolutionary prospect of playing major league games under artificial lighting. That the concept was feasible there could be no doubt: a baseball game had been played at night as long ago as 1880, only two years after the introduction of electric light, and the Des Moines, Iowa club of the Western League installed lights to play league games in 1930. (Research is under way now to substantiate a claim that a game in St. Louis in the mid-1890s was begun in darkness and completed under arc lights—making it the first major league night game.) The idea, which caught on in a Depression era of dwindling attendance, was to stave off financial collapse. It was Cincinnati executive Larry MacPhail who finally advanced the notion of staging big league games around the normal working fan's hours. Mc-Phail had good reason to lobby for the change; his Cincinnati franchise had drawn an anemic 206,000 fans in all of 1934, not enough to offset expenses. MacPhail and Reds' club owner Powel Crosley petitioned the National League for the right to play seven 1935 games at night, and the league reluctantly agreed, taking note of the extenuating circumstance of the depressed attendance in Cincinnati. The first of those games, played on May 24, pitted Cincinnati against Philadelphia, and skeptics were moved to silence when it attracted an audience of better than 20,000 to what proved to be a 2–1 Reds' victory. By 1941, night ball was a fact in the majority of major league parks, and by shortly after the war's end only Wrigley Field in Chicago among all major league stadiums lacked lighting. Today, most major league games—and virtually all minor league games—are played during evening hours. Attendance figures partially reflect the reason: prior to the advent of night baseball, it was considered exceptional if a ballclub drew a half million fans for a season, and the entire National League schedule of 1933 attracted only about 3.1 million fans. Today, several clubs can anticipate drawing virtually that many in a single home season, and a minimum attendance of about 1.5 million is required merely to break even.

The Bat, Ball, and Glove

The bat, ball, and glove are baseball's utensils. Virtually every child old enough to root, root, root for the home-team owns at least one of each. Their omnipresence serves as immutable evidence of the game's cultural popularity.

Yet today's equipment is as changed from its predecessors of generations ago as is baseball itself. Even the seemingly simple functions of each have been redefined, in part a cause and in part an effect of the changing game.

Only a few of those changes are reflected in the rulebook; to most the book has proved adaptable. Examination of the adjustments made to baseball's basic tools illuminates the courses of change that the game of baseball itself has taken.

For obvious reasons, rule makers have always felt the need to at least broadly define how the ball should be made. Curiously that definition has changed very little over the course of more than a century. Notice how similar the two definitions are that follow—the first from an 1861 convention of the National Association of Base Ball Players, and the second taken from the Official Baseball Rules of 1987:

1861. *The ball must weigh not less than five and one half, nor more than five and three fourths ounces avoirdupois. It must measure not less than nine and one half, nor more than nine and three fourths inches in circumference. It must be composed of India rubber and yarn, covered with leather.*

Present. *The ball shall be a sphere formed by yarn wound around a small core of cork, rubber, or similar material, covered with two strips of white horsehide or cowhide, tightly stitched together. It shall weigh not less than five nor more than five and one quarter ounces avoirdupois and measure not less than nine nor more than nine and one quarter inches in circumference.*

How greatly has the ball changed in a century and a quarter? It is about five percent smaller, about nine percent lighter. Rather than an India rubber center, it may have—and in professional ball does have—a cork center. The stitching must be tight . . . but precisely how tight is not defined. And that's it. In every other respect, the ball put in play in the first professional games of 1861 would pass muster by modern rules.

That is not to say that the baseball of Civil War days and the Rawlings Official model of today are virtually identical. Today's ball is far more resilient and travels greater distances. This is due to several factors.

Most obviously the modern baseball undergoes far less wear and tear. For many years it was customary for a game ball, even a mushy, discolored or lopsided one, to be kept in play until it was irretrievably lost. And the key word was "irretrievably." In the nineteenth century, if a ball was hit into the stands, it was obtained by ushers for continued play. If hit out of sight, it was searched for . . . for as long as five minutes. Then and only then might the host team be required to furnish a second ball. The idea of going through a few dozen balls per game— common today—would have seemed frivolously wasteful to Great-Grandpa.

That policy moderated with the passing years, but it was not until 1920 that league officials stipulated the use only of clean and new baseballs, both in an effort to enhance offense and out of concern for player safety (since worn and discolored balls frequently were hard to control or even see). Those directives lent a new measure of consistency to the game, so that the ball a batter swung at in the bottom of the ninth was

not different from the one used in the first-pitch ceremonies.

The only rules change of significance affecting the ball came in 1910, and it authorized the use of a cushioned cork center as an alternative to the rubber-centered ball that had been in vogue until that time. The cork-centered ball was found to be more lively, an especially desirable trait considering the depressed (and, to the baseball-going public, depressing) batting averages. The cork-centered ball was introduced in time for the 1910 World Series between the Philadelphia Athletics and Chicago Cubs, and the two clubs batted .272, which was about twenty points higher than the regular season league average. For the 1911 regular season, both leagues used the cork-centered ball: National League averages rose by only four points; but in the American League the climb was a heady thirty points, and the league leader, Detroit's Ty Cobb, hit a stunning .420. A total of twenty-one American League regulars bettered .300 that season; only eight had done so the year before. In the National League, Chicago's Frank Schulte hit 21 home runs. Schulte had tied for the home run title in 1910 with 10.

All other changes in the makeup of the ball itself—tighter winding of the yarn, introduction of different and supposedly better kinds of yarn, raised or depressed stitches, the change from horsehide to cowhide in 1974—have been products of technology, not of the rule makers. About 1920, as batting averages soared and Babe Ruth began to crash home runs in unheard-of profusion, there was controversy over the substitution of Australian wool for the generic type in making baseball yarn. Surely, fans speculated, this new wool must be the reason behind the livelier ball. In fact, the explanation probably had more to do with improved methods of winding the wool than with the wool itself.

The same rulebook that has licensed virtually no change in the parameters of the baseball itself has brooked only minor adjustment with the bat, and then, generally, only by way of greater specificity. Again, compare the rules governing play in 1861 with the slightly more elaborate section from the modern rulebook:

1861. *The bat must be round and must not exceed two and one half inches in diameter in the thickest part. It must be made of wood, and may be of any length to suit the striker.*

Present. *The bat shall be a smooth, rounded stick not more than two and three quarter inches in diameter at the thickest part and not more than forty-two inches in length. The bat shall be one piece of solid wood, or formed from a block of wood consisting of two or more pieces of wood bonded together with an adhesive in such way that the grain direction in all pieces is essentially parallel to the length of the bat. Any such laminated bat shall contain only wood or adhesive.*

The modern rule also contains an allowance for a small "cupping" of up to one inch at the bat's end, and for use of a grip-improving substance on the bat handle. But again, the stipulated differences of more than a century of development are comparatively minimal. There is a length limit where once there was none, but, at least in practice, the limit is functionally irrelevant. In today's major leagues, it is virtually unheard-of for a bat to exceed thirty-six inches in length, much less forty-two. The modern bat has gained one quarter of an inch in girth over its ancestor, and it need no longer necessarily be of a single piece of wood, if laminated in such a way that the effect of a single piece of wood is achieved.

More so than with the ball, changes in the bat have tended to develop stylistically, and under the influence of the batters themselves. Bats, of course, always have been highly personalized objects. With such a broad allowance by the rules (no weight limit, no functional length limit), hitters have tended to individualize their preference within widely recognized norms. In the place-hitting era of the nineteenth century, for instance, heavy "wagon tongue" models with thick barrels capable of plopping the ball squarely were coveted (the flat-sided bats permitted in some years in the 1880s never caught on). Cap Anson, legendary star of the Chicago White Stockings, used just such a bat, reputedly weighing in at a manly three pounds and then some. In the 1920s, Babe Ruth menaced opposing pitchers with a forty-eight-ounce model bat, sometimes even wielding a fifty-two-ounce club. But Ruth saw to it that the bat handle was tapered to accommodate his smaller than normal hands. Heinie Groh, third baseman of the Cincinnati Reds and New York Giants, was no slugger of Ruthian proportion. Yet Groh's innovative "bottle" bat—with its narrow handle expanding precipitously at the hitting area to a broad surface— not only served as a personal trademark, but helped him to a .292 lifetime average and a starting role on four pennant winners.

The modern bat bears no resemblance to any of those models. It is sleeker, usually no more than thirty-five inches in length and no heavier than thirty-three ounces. The reason is simple: batting instructors, who once looked upon mass as the key factor behind a mighty poke, now focus on bat speed instead. The faster a batter can savage a bat through the strike zone, the greater the force applied to the ball. And the greater force applied, the farther the ball travels. Presto, light bats.

As for gloves . . . well, in the game's early days they did not exist. Players were expected to catch the ball bare-handed. For a time they received something of an aid in that effort by a rule recording an out if a ball was caught on the first bounce. That made things a little easier. The use of gloves was never formally barred, as, for instance, was the use of black players in the old National Association rulebook; it simply was looked upon as sort of sissified. There is no clear record of who first conceived the notion of fielding with a glove. Al Spalding wrote that the first to don a glove was an 1875 player for the National Association's St. Louis team named Charlie Waitt. In a game that year Waitt donned a street-dress leather glove on his fielding hand. Waitt, reportedly, was ridiculed league-wide. But as more prominent players adopted Waitt's concept, the notion gradually came to be accepted. It was not until the retirement in 1894 of Jeremiah Denny, however, that the era of the bare-handed fielder passed.

Two points ought quickly to be made about the use of early-day gloves. First, their function was utterly different than it is today. The first gloves, lacking webbing and lacing, merely provided protection for the hands, which fielded the ball. Today's larger, better-padded, webbed, laced and pocketed gloves might more appropriately be described as "fielding devices," because it is they, not the fielder's hands, that do much of the actual fielding work.

Secondly and as verification of the first point, players of the nineteenth century often wore gloves on both hands. For the throwing hand, they would simply snip the glove at the fingers for dexterity. Those photographs that remain of players of the era—and especially the ones portraying fielding sequences— confirm that unusual tendency.

It was not until 1895 that stipulations concerning use of

gloves were included in the rules: those limited the size of gloves to ten ounces and fourteen inches circumference for all players except catchers and first basemen, who were permitted to use any size glove. (Today's rulebook, conversely, takes a page and a half to specify dimensions, materials, lacings, and webbings for gloves. Today there are thirteen different size limitations on the standard fielder's glove alone, ranging from palm width to the length of each separate finger.) The transition from the glove as protection to the glove as a tightly defined fielding aid came gradually but inexorably.

The first advance was development of a "pocket," that spot in the palm of the hand where the ball was most easily and most naturally caught. As with the origination of the glove itself, there is no firm and fast date for the pocket's appearance: it simply sort of happened. And it did not happen immediately. To the contrary, for several years after the introduction of the glove fielders adopted a sort of "reverse pocket," they would excise the leather from the palm area and leave that area bare, presumably for more "touch." In all probability, the "pocket" was not invented by glove makers, but by players themselves, taking advantage of the natural stretching the glove's leather underwent with use. Today we call this "breaking a glove in." Today, however, "pockets" are preformed by the manufacturer.

Credit commonly is given to a pitcher, spitballer Bill Doak of the St. Louis Cardinals, for advancing glove technology from the primordial state. In 1920, Doak approached a glove manufacturer with a plan for a new personalized glove. Many players liked personalized glove models, but Doak's was different. It envisioned a preformed pocket, not one that would be fashioned through constant wear. And it included a square of reinforced webbing between the thumb and finger sections as an additional aid to fielding. Previously the fingers simply had been tied together if they were not allowed to act independently. So advanced was Doak's model, by the way, that it remained popular for almost thirty years. And every subsequent advance in glove design, whether it was the hinged heel, short- or long-fingered design, or advanced webbing, can be traced to a concept originated by Doak.

In the 1930s, rule makers mandated the use only of leather in the making of gloves—the first change in rules on the subject since the initial size and weight limitations were set in 1895. And in 1939, acting in response to Hank Greenberg's introduction of an oversized mitt with a netted webbing, they outlawed the use of netting, limited webbing to four inches from thumb to palm (the present rule is four and one half inches), and restricted the size of first basemen's gloves as well. Weight restrictions were dropped in 1950, and size limitations were further defined.

To that date, no limitation had ever been placed on the size of the catcher's mitt; after all, the larger the catcher's mitt, the harder it was for a catcher to dig the ball out and make a throw to base. But in 1960 Baltimore manager Paul Richards discovered that there was something at least potentially worse than having catchers who could not evict the ball from an oversized mitt. And that was having catchers who could not catch the ball at all.

Richards's problem was that his most effective pitcher was Hoyt Wilhelm, and Wilhelm's most effective pitch was a knuckleball that proved as difficult to catch as it was to hit. Baltimore catchers soared to the top of the league passed-ball rankings. Richards's solution was to devise a catcher's mitt of nearly fifty inches in circumference, a huge thing perhaps

twice the standard size. If Baltimore catchers could not throw out base stealers with the new mitt, they could at least have a fighting chance at halting Wilhelm's pitch. Shortly after the appearance of Richards' oversized mitt, the rule was amended to set a thirty-eight-inch circumference and fifteen-and-one-half-inch diameter limit on catchers' gloves as well.

Even after catchers' gloves were restricted in size, however, questions remained about enforcement of the 1950 size limits. So in 1972 the rules committee drafted the present thirteen-point measuring system. Fortunately there is no record of a game ever being halted while a manager challenged the legality of a fielder's glove on all thirteen points.

Spring Training

The precise origin of spring training, that marvelously contrived ritual that today amounts to a one-month paid vacation in the sun for athletes, media, and club officials, is unknown. With few exceptions, early ballplayers trained at home on their own. It is known that in 1870 the Chicago White Stockings organized a trip to New Orleans, but that may have been mere barnstorming rather than preparing players for the coming season. The generally accepted beginning of spring training for purposes of conditioning is 1886, when the White Stockings and Philadelphia traveled, respectively, to Little Rock and Charleston. The precise regimen of spring training has varied greatly from decade to decade. Today, for instance, little actual "training" is done at spring training, since players, many of whom earn several hundred thousands of dollars, are expected to report in shape, and the emphasis is on narrowing a roster of forty players to the requisite twenty-four for opening day. Spring training today amounts in large measure to an extended advertisement for the season to come, with a bit of tryout camp thrown in for effect.

But that was not always the case. Early day players commonly received salaries of a few hundred or a few thousand dollars, supplementing that with off-season jobs—like bartending—of questionable value to their athletic careers. These players literally required a period of a month or so to work back into shape. In the early 1900s, the New York Giants trained in the little Texas town of Marlin, and their training was, by the strictest definition, training. Each day began and ended with what amounted to a two-mile forced march along the railroad tracks from the hotel to the park. The routine consisted of batting and fielding practice, along with drills on the fundamentals of play. If there was a scrimmage, it usually was an intrasquad effort, or perhaps a game against a local team or minor league club. In 1906 the sixteen major league teams trained in ten different states, as far north as Illinois; the notion of grouping in Florida and Arizona to make practice games between major league aggregations more convenient would not gain full currency for the better part of another decade. In 1911, the Yankees set up their spring camp in Bermuda. At most early camps, conditioning was overseen by the players themselves, since as a rule teams employed only the manager and a single coach—if that.

The Pitcher

How prized is the pitcher?

Consider that of the nine positions, candidates for eight are

winnowed principally by their skill with the bat. Shortstops and catchers may progress a few levels through the professional ranks on the strength of superior range or arms; outfielders may emerge by dint of speed, or catchers thanks to a God-given arm. But fundamentally not even an Ozzie Smith or a Benito Santiago moves far past rookie league ball until they establish at least a minimal offensive ability.

The only exception is the pitcher.

And pitchers always have been the exception, even before the designated hitter rule legislated most of them out of that *terra incognita* known as the batter's box. In any analysis of Ty Cobb's value as a player, the first thing that comes up is his lifetime .367 batting average. But no one would think of discussing Sandy Koufax's value to the Dodgers in terms of his .097 batting average.

In fact, the pitcher is the one and only player whose defensive contribution is so vital that the ability to hit is considered irrelevant. Red Ruffing, the fine righthander for the New York Yankees of the 1930s and 1940s, compiled one of the best batting records of any pitcher in the past three quarters of a century, including a .268 career average. But when he was voted into the Hall of Fame in 1967, it was on the strength of a 273-225 record, 3.80 earned run average, and on his status as the leading moundsman for seven pennant winners.

Pitching has been the staple of the successful big league franchise virtually since there has been big league baseball. Connie Mack is variously quoted as having called it anywhere from 70 to 90 percent of the game. The precise figure is not important. What is important is that Mr. Mack's axiom remains generally accepted today.

And yet despite the constancy of the importance of quality pitching, both pitching styles and the rules governing pitching have undergone more major changes than any other aspect of on-field play—so much so that the best pitchers of 1987 have virtually nothing in common with the best pitchers of a century ago . . . and little resemblance to their predecessors of as little as two to three decades back.

Much of the evolution took place during the game's formative years and came via efforts by the rule makers to settle on the proper balance of batting to pitching. In the early years of professional ball—the 1860s and 1870s—pitching bore more similarity to the style employed today in fast-pitch softball than in baseball. The ball was delivered underhand and without a wrist snap—although pitchers fudged so much on the latter point that by 1872 the wrist movement was legalized—from a box set at a distance of 45 feet from the plate. Legalization of the wrist snap spawned the development of various "trick" pitches, notably the curveball, which is commonly credited to William "Candy" Cummings, a much-traveled moundsman of that era who compiled a 124-72 record in the only six seasons he played in top-level professional baseball. Whether Cummings or any of several other pitchers of his era actually first perfected the technique of making a ball curve, Candy generally got the credit—enough to have been elected to the Hall of Fame for that accomplishment in 1939.

Nineteenth-century pitchers worked under virtually everchanging conditions. For instance, the pitcher's "box" was moved back to 50 feet from home plate after the season of 1880; then in 1893 it was eliminated altogether in favor of the "rubber" placed at 60 feet, 6 inches. The underhand delivery requirement gradually was modified to allow what in effect was a sidearm pitch in 1883 and a full overhand delivery the

following year. Rules governing the ball-and-strike count—at one time nine balls were required to give the batter a walk—changed frequently until they were stabilized at four and three, respectively, in 1889. At various times pitchers were required to deliver a high or low pitch, as requested by the batter; windups were banned, then permitted again; the size of the "box" was altered almost routinely before being consigned to extinction.

It would be difficult to generalize as to whether all of those changes helped or hurt pitchers. Certainly batting averages tended to improve as the distance between the mound and plate increased. Yet the underhand pitching style—much easier on the arm—enabled most teams to play an entire schedule with only one or two pitchers. And the best of them attained results that would be unthinkable today.

By way of illustration, compare the statistics Providence's Hoss Radbourn compiled in 1884 with the record of the last pitcher to win thirty or more games, Detroit's Denny McLain in 1968, and of the pitcher with the best statistics in 1988, Los Angeles' Orel Hershiser.

	Radbourn	McLain	Hershiser
Games	75	41	35
Innings Pitched	678.2	336	267
Victories	60	31	23
Complete Games	73	28	15
Earned Run Average	1.38	1.96	2.26
Strikeouts	441	280	178
Shutouts	11	6	8

Radbourn's statistics seem even more impressive when it is noted that his Providence team played only a 112-game schedule. Yet of course the comparisons are fair only as an illustration of how greatly the pitching environment—the rules, conditions, and strategies—changed between 1884 and 1968 or the present.

At least as dynamic a force as the rulebook in the evolution of the modern pitcher has been the development of pitching strategy, notably new pitches. For while the broad regulations under which pitchers work today are not vastly different from 1893, the arsenal of pitches that have come into vogue—and occasionally passed from it—has ranged widely and sometimes wildly.

Cummings's introduction (if, indeed, it was Cummings) of the curveball marked the first major deviation toward finesse from what up to that time had fundamentally been a power pitcher's game. Phonnie Martin threw a drop, or slowball, and Al Spalding and Tim Keefe were masters of the change of pace. These innovations took hold, but bolder experimentation was limited to a handful of hurlers. While pitchers of the latter part of the nineteenth-century occasionally dabbled in "outshoots" or "rises," the best continued to build their reputations with speed. "Cyclone" Young in Cleveland and Amos Rusie, New York's "Hoosier Thunderbolt," were the best and in all likelihood the fastest of them. Young won 27 games for Cleveland in 1891, his first full season, and then over a twenty-two-year career accumulated 511 victories, a total whose magnificence is best illustrated by the fact that the all-time runner-up, Washington's Walter Johnson, trails by roughly 100. Young's 2,799 strikeouts—a record when he retired—further testify to his velocity. As for Rusie, he won 36 games in 1894 and led the league in strikeouts five times

between 1890 and 1895. He also led five times in walks, initiating the popular linkage between hard throwers and control trouble.

By the mid-1890s, earned run averages rose as a reaction to the shift of the mound back to 60 feet, 6 inches. The legendary Baltimore Orioles of Wee Willie Keeler had batted .343 as a team in 1894, and did not even lead the league—Philadelphia did, at .349! In response, pitchers began to experiment more readily with changes of speed, and with the ball itself. In Chicago, Clark Griffith scraped the ball against his spikes and discovered that the scuffs added to the break of his curve. Griffith became a twenty-game winner for six consecutive seasons. Philadelphia's Al Orth, a fastballer through and through, mastered the art of changing speeds and won 203 games in fifteen years.

Equally as significant as changes in the approaches to pitching was the increase in the numbers of pitchers needed. In 1876, Chicago's Al Spalding had been able to pitch in all but five of his team's sixty-six games. But by the early 1880s the top teams were using two pitchers, and within another decade—as the increased pitching distance, longer playing schedules, and more tiresome overhand motion became accepted—staffs of fewer than four to five were uncommon. The Detroit team of the 1884 National League utilized perhaps the first pitching "staff" per se, with four hurlers—Frank Meinke, Stump Weidman, Charley Getzien, and Dupee Shaw each working between 147 and 289 innings. Detroit's strategy did not count for much—the club finished last—but within a decade Baltimore rode what amounted to a four- to six-pitcher rotation to the league championship. That staff's ace, Sadie McMahon, pitched only about one quarter of the total number of innings worked by the sextet. In 1876, the eight National League teams basically employed a total of thirteen pitchers; by 1886 that number was twenty-four; by 1896, for twelve teams, it was fifty-one.

By the turn of the century, the repopularization of two theretofore lightly used pitches helped re-establish the pitcher as the game's dominant player. Christy Mathewson, a fresh-faced college graduate from Bucknell, brought with him to the New York Giants a pitch he called the "fadeaway," actually a reworked version of something known in the 1880s as an "outshoot." Today it is called the screwball. The pitch, which acts like a reverse curve, when thrown by a right-handed pitcher breaks toward a righthanded batter. Mathewson might very well have become a great pitcher even without the fadeaway, but with it he won 373 games, four times winning 30 or more, and five times helping the Giants to pennants. So difficult was the pitch to throw and control that no other major league pitcher of the era could master it.

The other dominant pitch of the first part of the twentieth-century was the spitball, advocated principally by two men, Jack Chesbro and Ed Walsh.

Chesbro came to the major leagues with Pittsburgh in 1899, and by 1901, when he incorporated the spitball into his routine— it would not be illegal to doctor a baseball with a foreign substance for two more decades—he became a twenty-game winner. He won 28 games with the pennant-winning Pirates in 1902, so greatly increasing his value that he became one of a cadre of early-day "free agents" who were recruited to the fledgeling American League during a three-year interleague "war." With the New York team of the young league in 1904, Chesbro's spitball took him to a twentieth-century record 41 victories, although it also set up one of

the most ironic finishes to any pennant race. Because of its wild break, the spitball was considered one of the least predictable of pitches. Chesbro had walked only 88 batters that season, fewer than two every nine innings. His control of the devious delivery was impeccable.

On the final weekend of that season, Boston and New York— virtually tied for first—engaged in a five-game series, with the winner of three games to be the champion. Chesbro's forty-first victory came in the series opener, but Boston claimed the ensuing two. In the climactic fourth game—the opening contest of a last-day doubleheader—Chesbro, seeking his forty-second win, held a 2-2 tie entering the ninth. An infield hit, a sacrifice, and a groundout moved Boston's pennant-winning run to third base with two out. The great pitcher had been masterful to that point, walking just one and striking out five. But in that most pivotal of situations, a Chesbro spitball bounced in the dirt and skipped toward the backstop, a wild pitch that cost New York a pennant.

Walsh, like Chesbro, perfected control of the elusive spitter, and parlayed that to remarkable feats. A moundsman of modest ability prior to employing the pitch in 1906, he won 17 games that first season, 24 the next, and an astonishing 40 the year after that. Yet irony played a central role in Walsh's career as well, for perhaps his best performance in that 40-win season of 1908 came in defeat. At the climax of a peripatetic three-team race involving Cleveland, Detroit, and Chicago, Walsh's White Sox came to Cleveland needing a victory to remain in contention. Walsh pitched a four-hitter and struck out 15 batters . . . but Cleveland's Addie Joss achieved a rare perfect game and won 1–0. The only run scored—no, not on a wild pitch—on a passed ball.

Other so-called "freak" pitches came into vogue during that era as well. Pitchers altered balls not only with spit or spikes, but with emery paper, paraffin, mud, slippery elm, and who knows what else. But the ranks of pitchers who relied on tampering for their success still constituted a minority. Most, like Washington's Walter Johnson, continued to rely on the basic fastball.

Of course, most pitchers did not have a fastball of the caliber of Walter Johnson's to rely on.

And on that basis, pitchers and batters lived in happy coexistence for about a decade, pausing only to occasionally admire the ascendancy of a new star like Philadelphia's Grover Cleveland Alexander. Master both of the fastball and curve, Alexander emerged in 1911 as a rookie 28-game winner, and by 1915 he was leading the Phillies to the National League pennant on the strength of a 31-victory season. With Philadelphia and later with the Chicago Cubs, he led the league in victories six times between 1911 and 1920, becoming generally acknowledged as the pre-eminent pitcher of the latter half of what is commonly called baseball's "dead ball" era.

Alexander, along with Walter Johnson, continued to pitch in form beyond 1920, but that was not true of major league pitchers as a whole. A series of factors, some mechanical, some societal, reshaped the game again following World War One, and in most instances it was the pitchers who suffered in the reshaping.

The catalyst for much of that reshaping, ironically, was a former pitcher. And a very good one. As a twenty-year-old rookie in 1915, Babe Ruth won 18 games to help the Boston Red Sox to the world's championship. By the following season, Ruth, a 23-game winner who added a twenty-fourth in the

World Series, was coming to be recognized as the Sox's ace. He led the American League in earned run average (1.75), starts (41), and shutouts (9), and the following season paced it in complete games (35) as well.

But by 1918 Ruth the pitcher was recognized as less of a hero than Ruth the slugger. He pitched in 20 games that season— and won 13 of them—but started nearly three times as often in the outfield, a response both to his hitting and to the fans' clamoring to see him hit. Although by no means an everyday player, the Babe tied for the league lead in home runs that season (his total was a modest 11). But more significantly he drew crowds, both to Fenway Park and on the road. So in 1919 Boston manager Ed Barrow converted him almost exclusively to the outfield. Ruth's response was to break the all-time record for home runs—with 29—and to lead the league in runs scored, runs batted in, and slugging average as well. Traded to New York in 1920, Ruth almost immediately became the most celebrated player in the game's history. He hit a then-unthinkable 54 home runs, broke existing records for runs scored, runs batted in, bases on balls, and slugging average. To the public, Ruth was "the Sultan of Swat," "the Bazoo of Bang," "the Infant Swatigy," "the Colossus of Clout." Batting averages and home run production rose league-wide as other players strove to imitate him. American League batters, who hit .248 with 136 home runs in 1917, had raised those figures to .292 and 477 by 1921. In the National League, the increases for the same period were from .249 and 202 to .289 and 460. Part of that 150 to 200 percent increase in the home run count could, perhaps, be attributed to the banning—enforced gradually as of 1920—of the spitball and other so-called "doctored" pitches, part to improved craftsmanship on the part of the baseball makers, and part to the desire of league officials to replace soiled, scuffed balls with cleaner, whiter ones. But in large measure, the change was simply a strategical one: batters swung harder and tried to drive the ball farther than ever before. Once a poke-and-run contest, baseball had become—thanks in good measure to Ruth—a slugger's game. And the fans loved it: American League attendance soared from 1.7 million in 1918 to more than 5 million in 1920.

Unfortunately for pitchers, they proved less than capable of adapting to the new and more thrilling style. The rule change barring use of the spitball, emery ball, shine ball, and other similar pitches removed at least a potential weapon from all arsenals, save those of seventeen men who had used the spitter in the major leagues prior to its being banned. (They were permitted to continue throwing the pitch, which did not actually die out until the last of those seventeen, Burleigh Grimes, retired in 1934.) New pitches were not effectively developed to take the void. A few toyed with a knuckleball, and in the late 1920s a nondescript pitcher for the St. Louis Browns named George Blaeholder devised what eventually came to be known as the slider. But for the most part, pitchers relied on the fastball, curve, and a very occasional changeup. With pitchers as with batters, raw power replaced guile and cunning as the chief weapon.

The result was predictable: for the better part of two decades, batting averages, home run totals, and earned run averages soared. Look at the table of league earned run averages for the American and National Leagues between 1920 and 1930:

YEAR	NL ERA	AL ERA
1920	3.13	3.79
1921	3.78	4.28
1922	4.10	4.03
1923	3.99	3.99
1924	3.87	4.23
1925	4.27	4.39
1926	3.84	4.02
1927	3.91	4.12
1928	3.98	4.04
1929	4.71	4.24
1930	4.97	4.65

In the National League, earned run averages increased by a full 59 percent in that one decade alone. Home run totals more than tripled. Strikeouts, the pitcher's logical counterweapon against the big flailer, also increased, but by a far less imposing 6 percent. The differences are less dramatic in the American League, but still large. And although pitchers reasserted their competitiveness, if not their mastery, during the 1930s, the average ERA by 1940 had fallen only to the 4.00 level. By 1940, however, bat-happy baseball society had been conditioned to view a 4.00 ERA as good.

The era between 1920 and 1960 produced some exceptional pitchers, but few changes in pitching style. In the mid-1930s, a rookie righthander in Detroit named Eldon Auker bothered batters with an underhand delivery that would have been reminiscent of the style in the 1870s. Auker's "submarine" pitch was necessitated by an arm injury that made it difficult for him to throw in the normal overhand fashion. He won 130 games in a 10-year career, pitched on two pennant winners and one world champion, and his style would be resurrected in the modern era by relief pitchers like Ted Abernathy, Kent Tekulve, Dan Quisenberry, and Gene Garber. In the National League, the New York Giants' Carl Hubbell also reached back into time for a cudgel. Hubbell resurrected Mathewson's fadeaway, renamed it the screwball, and mystified National League opponents sufficiently to record five straight 20-victory seasons between 1933 and 1937, leading the Giants to three pennants.

A more conventional, and more overpowering, form belonged to Lefty Grove, who pitched seventeen years for the Philadelphia Athletics and Boston Red Sox. Grove's trademarks were a fastball that many have called the swiftest ever and a surly disposition. Four times a league leader in victories and nine times the ERA king, Grove was the only pitcher to win 300 games in the hot-hitting era of the 1920s and 1930s, an achievement often cited by those who point to him as the best ever. His career ERA of 3.06 is more than one full point lower than the league average for the years (1925-1941) in which he worked.

Pitching rules, which had remained virtually untouched since 1920, underwent several adjustments between 1950 and 1969, and all of them appeared to bear on the relative effectiveness of pitchers. The strike zone was tightened in 1950— the new boundaries being the armpit and bottom of the knee (they had been the top of the shoulder and bottom of the knee). When home runs climbed to record levels by 1961, the old strike zone was restored, and earned run averages decreased sharply, to a post-1920 low of 2.98 in the American League in 1968. Rule makers responded to that by lowering

the mound several inches and reducing the strike zone again. Averages and home runs climbed again, as they did in the American League in 1973 when the designated hitter rule was introduced.

But it would be overly simple and wrong to point merely to the rule book as the fulcrum for all variations in pitching performance in the past three and a half decades. Probably the most significant factor was the development of relief pitching. Beyond that, pitchers perfected pitches they had only toyed with before. The knuckleball was not new—it had been thrown since the early part of the century, and in the 1940s the Washington Senators employed a foursome of knuckling starters. But no one used it as effectively as Hoyt Wilhelm and then Phil and Joe Niekro. Wilhelm pitched in an unprecedented 1,070 games over twenty-one years and established what at the time was the all-time record for saves, with 227. Phil Niekro won over 300 games and, in tandem with his brother Joe, in 1987 broke the record for most victories by members of one family.

A sort of variation on the knuckleball, also developed years ago and resurrected recently, was the forkball or "split-fingered fastball." Credit for its development generally is given to 1940s New York Yankee pitcher Ernie Bonham, but the first famous exponent was Elroy Face, a relief pitcher for the Pittsburgh Pirates of the 1950s and '60s. In 1959 Face compiled an 18-1 record by the simple expedient of jamming the ball between his fingers before releasing it: this gave it an unnatural dip as it crossed home plate. In the late 1970s, another reliever, Bruce Sutter of the Chicago Cubs, reinvented the same pitch, which he termed a "split-fingered fastball." Sutter saved 37 games for the 1979 Cubs, an accomplishment of no small measure when it is recognized that his team only won 80 times that season. In Sutter's wake, entire pitching staffs began learning the split-fingered pitch. Roger Craig became a one-man traveling demonstration of the pitch's success. As Detroit pitching coach, he taught it to the Tigers in 1984 and they responded by winning the world championship. Then Craig taught it to journeyman Houston righthander Mike Scott, and he blossomed into an 18-game winner capable of recording over 300 strikeouts while leading his team to a divisional flag in 1986. Craig himself became manager at San Francisco, where his staff of split-fingerers helped the Giants win the NL West title in 1987.

The most widely used new pitch, however, was the one invented by Blaeholder fifty years before—the slider. Acting much like a fastball but with a sharp break, the slider supplanted the more leisurely curveball in the repertoire of dozens of major leaguers. Perhaps the pitch's most famous exponent was Steve Carlton, who used it to become the second-winningest lefthander of all time, behind only Warren Spahn. So disarming was Carlton's slider that he staged a dramatic contest in the mid-1980s with fastballer Nolan Ryan to see which man would become the first pitcher in history to record 4,000 strikeouts.

But if the evolution of pitching suggests anything, it is that no one style, no single delivery, and no simple rules change is perpetually dominant. In the 1960s, no two pitchers could have been more stylistically different than Juan Marichal, the high-kicker of the San Francisco Giants, and Sandy Koufax, the stylish lefthander of the Los Angeles Dodgers. Marichal dabbled in every move, every trick ever devised. He threw the fastball, the curveball, the slider, the changeup, the screwball, and he delivered each of them overhanded, three-quartered, or sidearmed, almost at his whim. Koufax relied on a fastball, a curve, and exemplary control. Yet in 1963, for instance, each man won 25 games, and the name of each appeared among the league leaders in winning percentage, earned run average, strikeouts, complete games, and innings pitched. Between 1963 and 1966, Marichal averaged better than 23 victories, Koufax 24.

Perhaps the most frequently debated question is whether today's pitcher throws harder than his predecessor. It is, of course, almost impossible to answer. To the degree that improved training and conditioning programs encourage greater speed, it is logical to believe that the fastest hurlers of today—Nolan Ryan or Dwight Gooden at their best—must be swifter than Grove or Walter Johnson or Cy Young. Ryan's fastball—in his prime—was clocked on radar guns at about 100 miles per hour. Old-timers, of course, did not have the advantage, or disadvantage, of pitching to radar guns, so assessments of their speed must necessarily be more crude. Bob Feller's fastball, for instance, once was clocked against a speeding motorcycle. The finding? About 100 miles per hour. The testimony of old-timers varies. Many picked Walter Johnson, but Johnson himself picked Smoky Joe Wood. Billy Herman selected Van Lingle Mungo. Contemporaries like Wes Ferrell said Lefty Grove was faster than Feller, but numerous sportswriters sided with Feller as the fastest ever. Connie Mack, who played and managed across six decades, opted for Amos Rusie, the old-time "Hoosier Thunderbolt." But Mack's opinion could have been influenced by nostalgia: he batted against Rusie. Nolan Ryan generally is considered the fastest of the 1980s' pitchers, but for a time it was not even presumed that he was the fastest Houston Astro. Until his crippling stroke, J. Rodney Richard was conceded that title by at least some who saw both.

The Playing Field

Charles "Hoss" Radbourn was a pitcher of considerable note in the National League of the 1880s . . . and a hitter of no special renown. In 1882 he won 31 games for Providence and hit only one home run. But this story isn't about any of his 31 victories. It isn't really even about his home run. It's about playing conditions.

On August 17 of that year Radbourn was playing right field—as he occasionally did when not hurling—for Providence, which was at home against Detroit. Now the Providence field was not unlike most baseball fields of the day: it was, in the literal sense, a field. There was little groundskeeping and often no outfield barriers; even if there were, well-heeled fans who wished to simply pulled their carriages up onto the depths of the playing surface and watched from there.

On this particular date, the game developed into what cliché-prone sportswriters of a later era might refer to as a "tight pitchers battle" between John Ward of Providence and Stump Weidman of Detroit. Through seventeen innings each man held the opponent scoreless. When Radbourn advanced to the plate with one man out in the eighteenth, the sky was growing dark.

In his then-brief big league career, the Hoss had never hit a home run. He was not alone in that distinction, for four-base hits were a rare sight. (That season's league leader, George Wood of Detroit, hit only 7; the league record was 9.) But

Radbourn lashed at Weidman's pitch and sent it scurrying past Wood in left field. As some witnesses reported it, the ball rolled close to the leg of an especially spirited black horse hitched to a wagon.

Wood, of course, raced to the spot and reached for the ball. He was prevented by, of all things, the horse's hind hoof, which swished through the air and barely missed conking him. Wood reached again; again the horse kicked. Radbourn, meanwhile, raced past second.

The visitors were desperate. Wood grabbed for a handful of grass, hopeful of appeasing the critter. That did not work. Finally Ned Hanlon obtained a stick, reached in, and swatted the ball clear of danger. It was too late; as Hanlon prepared to throw, Radbourn was being carried from the field in triumph.

The mere concept of what ought to constitute a major league ballpark has evolved through at least five distinct transformations, each markedly different from its predecessor, and each spurred by changes both in the game's strategy and in the nation's sociology. The conditions attending to Charley Radbourn's home run in Providence in 1882 may seem bizarre to us. But no more bizarre, perhaps, than artificial turf will seem three generations hence.

The first parks, used in the first few decades of professional ball, were simple open spaces with ruts worn by the players marking the baselines. At games that attracted large crowds, the playing area often was defined by the fans themselves, who formed a cordon around the circumference. In 1871, the Forest City team representing Rockford, Illinois, in the National Association played on a field called by ballpark expert Phil Lowry "the strangest in major league history." Trees virtually lined the baselines, so players chasing pop-ups took their chances with physical peril if they watched the ball rather than their step. Third base was on a hill, home plate in a depression, and the outfield was framed by a gutter draining an adjacent horse racing track.

There were few of the niceties we presently associate with a ballpark for several reasons, not the least of which was that, since the game itself was new, club owners often lacked the capital necessary to develop the grounds beyond a rudimentary level. A grandstand might hold up to about 1,500 customers if it was expansive, but usually it held fewer. It was desirable, but by no means certain, that the ground be level and free of gravel. Horse droppings might literally pockmark areas of play. Except in Rockford, trees were not much of a hazard, but even at the best of diamonds infields were poorly sculpted and ill cared for. There were rarely such things as a scoreboard or dugout, and where outfield fences existed—they first came into being at Brooklyn's Union Grounds—they might be as close as 180 feet from home or as distant as 500 feet at all points. Some of the fields—Brooklyn's, for instance—doubled in the winter as skating rinks, at which time they were deliberately flooded. Imagine that happening at Yankee Stadium today!

Gradually over a span of years, ballfields assumed a more standardized and slightly more familiar appearance. By the mid-1880s, most playing fields had attained at least a semienclosed status. But distances to the fences commonly were dictated as much by topography as by any other consideration. Chicago's Lake Front Park was, when built in 1883, considered the archetypical modern facility, seating almost 10,000. Yet its cramped site near the lake permitted only a 180-foot carry to left field and only 300 feet to dead center. Such a field would be considered inadequate for fifteen-year-

olds today. But at Boston's spacious Huntington Avenue Grounds of a few years later, the barrier to left was a comfortable 440 feet from home plate; it was 635 feet to the fence in center. For part of the 1896 season, St. Louis's Robison Field did not even have a fence entirely circling the grounds. At one point in right field that year, it was possible to hit a ball (in play) through a gap in the barrier, and if so, the ball could roll unimpeded for more than 600 feet . . . to a lake!

If there was a single, overriding concern about ballparks in the game's first few decades, it was the danger of fire. Because wood was the common building material, facilities were susceptible to that danger, and it intruded on the occasion of a game more than once, sometimes with dire results. Baltimore's Union Park was damaged by fire in 1894; the same season a blaze destroyed Boston's South End Grounds in the third inning of a game between the Orioles and Beaneaters. A game was halted by fire at Chicago's West Side Park; several years earlier a contest actually had continued at the nearby Twenty-third Street Grounds while fire consumed the grandstand. Brooklyn's Washington Park fell to flames in 1889, and New York's Polo Grounds was virtually destroyed in 1911.

With all of its inherent and obvious disadvantages, the wooden ballpark may seem to have been anachronistic as early as 1910 or so; furthermore, this role in the development of the game may seem to have been quite fleeting. Was it really anachronistic? Yes. Was its role fleeting? No. The era of wood, from the opening of Brooklyn's Union Grounds in 1862 until the closing of the last wooden grandstand, at Philadelphia's Baker Bowl in 1938, encompasses three quarters of a century, or better than half of the lifespan of the professional game to date.

The demise of the wooden park was occasioned by a number of factors, the fire hazard not being the least of them. Some wooden parks were deemed to be particularly dangerous. In 1903, a wooden rail gave way at Baker Bowl in Philadelphia, and hundreds of fans fell from balcony seats, twelve to their deaths. In 1907 and again in 1908, the building inspector for the city of Cincinnati submitted a detailed bill of particulars on the hazards at the Palace of the Fans. Cracked girders, decayed supports, unsafe flooring, and a defective bleacher platform were only some of the problems. Construction problems were documented in St. Louis and other cities as well. But the gradually widening acceptance of baseball as a cultural event also played a part in the transition to more permanent structures. The average attendance climbed from 100,000 per franchise in 1890 to 362,000 in 1905. Larger, stronger, and more durable stadiums were needed. Because of the game's growing popularity, club owners were able to provide such facilities. Motivation also came from the fact that as new parks were constructed, the clubs could increase the numbers of more costly box seats, thus increasing potential revenues.

Concrete and steel became the materials of choice. In Philadelphia in 1909, club owner Benjamin Shibe conceived and executed plans for a baseball park at the site of a former brickyard at the corner of Twenty-first and Lehigh. The facility would be easily accessible from the city's center by trolley line and would supplant the old, wooden Columbia Park, which had the added disadvantage of being located near several breweries, thus subjecting patrons to the constant odor of hops and yeast.

But Shibe Park not only smelled better, it became the grandest facility of its type ever conceived. A French Renais-

sance-style dome at the home plate entrance gave the stadium a distinctive, almost churchlike appearance. The concrete grandstand and bleachers followed the first and third base foul lines, with seating provided for 20,000. A huge scoreboard was installed in left field. The facility's price tag was placed at a breathtaking half million dollars.

The opening of Shibe Park set a standard that was soon and widely matched. In Pittsburgh, Barney Dreyfuss already had begun construction of a replacement for the old Exposition Park, the riverfront facility that had been in use since 1890. The park that Dreyfuss named Forbes Field opened on June 30 at the site near Schenley Park and included elevators, lighting in the grandstand, telephones, and even maids in the ladies' rooms. He also conceived of providing access to the upper levels of the triple-decked grandstand by means of ramps rather than stairs, a practice that has continued to this day. The larger capacity of Forbes paid almost immediate dividends when the Pirates celebrated their inaugural season by winning the world championship.

If there is one hallmark of the concrete and steel stadiums raised in a dozen different cities between the years 1909 and 1923, it is their individuality. When Charles Comiskey developed plans for his new concrete and steel structure at Thirty-fifth and Shields in Chicago in 1910, he asked his own star, pitcher Ed Walsh, to take a hand in the work. It may not be surprising that Comiskey Park, both at its opening and for decades afterward, was considered one of the most tasking layouts for hitters, with 363-foot foul lines, 382-foot power alleys, and a center field distance that ranged to 455 feet. Particularly in the deadball era, the center field fence may as well not have existed at all. In Brooklyn's 22,000 seat Ebbets Field, which opened in 1913, the original carry to the barrier in left was 419 feet. Yet a street limited the distance to the fence in right field to a mere 301. (Construction of bleachers in the 1930s brought the left field wall within a more manageable distance as well.)

Of course, the most unusual design of all the old parks was New York's bathtub-shaped Polo Grounds, which replaced the wooden facility of the same name after it was damaged by fire in 1911. The "new" Polo Grounds featured foul poles only about 260 feet distant from the plate, with a center field that arced to distances of nearly 500 feet.

With a few exceptions, the classic-era parks served their host teams well for generations. But gradually in the 1940s and 1950s, and increasingly so in the 1960s, interior wear and exterior conditions rendered many of those parks unsatisfactory, at least in the eyes of their tenants. Those conditions were varied, but they can be summarized as follows:

Access The classic-era parks had been dependent on trolley, subway, or bus lines to deliver fans to their gates. But by the 1950s, America was a motorized nation, and club owners came to feel the need for proximity to modern freeways, as well as expansive parking lots. Brooklyn club owner Walter O'Malley moved his team out of Ebbets Field and to Los Angeles when the borough failed to deliver on such a facility. The Giants, beset at the Polo Grounds by many of the same problems, fled the same year to San Francisco.

Size When most of the classic-era parks were constructed, crowds of 30,000 were considered exceptional. By the mid-1960s, however, operational costs forced some clubs to average that much per home date just to show a profit. Neither Forbes Field in Pittsburgh, Shibe Park in Philadelphia nor Crosley Field in Cincinnati was capable of seating much more

than 35,000; when new and larger multipurpose stadiums were built in those cities, the clubs hastened to move into them.

Cost Without exception, classic-era parks had been constructed using private capital. By the 1960s, the cost of developing the kind of 50,000-seat stadium required by a major league team was virtually prohibitive. But municipalities, which had come over the years to view teams as community assets, proved willing in many cases to support the construction. This happened as early as the 1930s in Cleveland, and again in 1954, when the city of Baltimore captured the former Browns from St. Louis. Since Dodger Stadium opened in Los Angeles in 1962, there have been eighteen new stadiums opened for major league use, and the construction or renovation of every single one has been undertaken with public money. Oftentimes, that public involvement has taken place as one part of a larger urban-development effort, with the new park situated on once-blighted or undeveloped land near the core city and forming the centerpiece of a massive redevelopment project. This has been the case in cities like St. Louis, Seattle, Minneapolis-St. Paul, and Pittsburgh, and it continues to be discussed in other locales, notably San Francisco.

But concurrent with that last trend, a new and significant factor has been introduced. Whereas in the past ballparks were forced by the exigency of private construction to conform to their surroundings, thus imbuing each park inevitably with an individual flavor, public involvement reversed the equation. Since the opening of Shea Stadium in New York and the Astrodome in Houston, surroundings were altered to conform to the concept of an "ideal" park, rather than the opposite. Freed from the constrictions of neighborhood geography—and in an effort to maximize utility—designers gave their parks a symmetry bordering on sameness. The result: Many have said it is almost impossible to distinguish Riverfront Stadium in Cincinnati from Three Rivers Stadium in Pittsburgh or Veterans Stadium in Philadelphia.

In truth, neither stadium designers nor club owners fell headlong into the new age of modern "superpark" design, with whatever advantages or shortcomings the era may contain. In fact, the postclassic era dawned with a two-decade transitional period during which the factors noted above were gradually assimilated into the classic motif.

Cleveland's Municipal Stadium provided the introduction to this transitional period. Constructed in 1932 by the city of Cleveland, it was vast (potentially holding more than 80,000), virtually symmetrical, yet situated close to the central city on the lakefront. Evidence that the concept of coexistence between a private ballclub and public stadium had not yet taken firm hold is the fact that for about fifteen years after Municipal Stadium was built, the Indians occupied it only in fits and starts, generally playing their weekend games there, but maintaining the staid old League Park as their weekday habitat. Not until 1947 did the Indians become full-time tenants of the big ballpark.

For the first time in 1953, and again in 1954 and 1955, public facilities were developed with the specific aim of attracting major league teams. It worked in all three cases: to lure the Braves from Boston to Milwaukee, the Browns from St. Louis to Baltimore, and the Athletics from Philadelphia to Kansas City. The moves were unprecedented for the previous half-century, yet sensible in that all three teams left cities which had proved incapable of supporting two clubs. The stadiums in Milwaukee and Baltimore were constructed basi-

cally from scratch; in Kansas City, Municipal Stadium had served for many years as a minor league facility, but extensive renovation was undertaken. In none of the three cases did the stadiums abandon the city for the open country, but neither were they reliant on mass transit either.

The era of the modern public superstadium ironically probably dates from the opening of the last private stadium, Dodger Stadium in Los Angeles in 1962. Yet the species' zenith was achieved in 1965, when the Harris County Domed Stadium, the Astrodome, opened in Houston. A multimillion-dollar project in an era when that was a breathtaking sum, the Astrodome broke away from so many traditional rules and patterns of stadium design that it literally changed the way the game was played.

The first and most obvious change, of course, was the roof that covered the facility. Baseball had come indoors. No more would rain, wind, or other weather be a factor in a game's outcome. Beyond that, since grass would not grow under the dome's roof, an artificial turf had to be installed. This "AstroTurf," as it came to be called, was faster and more durable than grass, and also was harder on the players' legs, so it required adaptations in teams' strategy. Swifter, more agile fielders replaced slow-footed but hard-hitting predecessors. Speed, whether for base stealing or cutting off base hits, supplanted brawn in the game played inside on artificial turf.

Within a span of little more than a decade, artificial turf became the most-copied aspect of any single new ballpark built in America since the owners of the Union Grounds in Brooklyn fenced in their lot. Not only did it not wear out, not only was it easier to maintain during rain, but it stood up better under the strain of multipurpose use for such nonbaseball occasions as football games and musical concerts. Municipalities installed the stuff virtually everywhere a stadium was built for use by more than one team: in Philadelphia, Cincinnati, and Pittsburgh in the span of one year alone. The city of St. Louis originally built a new Busch Stadium in 1966 with a grass surface, but replaced it with turf after a few years. So faddish had artificial turf become that in 1970, when Kansas City officials developed plans for separate and individually designed football and baseball stadiums, they still installed artificial turf on the baseball field. In fact, of the fourteen municipally funded ballparks opened since the Astrodome in 1965 and still in use, only five—Atlanta-Fulton County, Anaheim, Oakland-Alameda County, Jack Murphy in San Diego, and Arlington Stadium in Texas—use a natural-grass surface today. The trend is most pronounced in the National League, where six of the twelve teams play on artificial turf. The trend toward indoor stadiums, by the way, is only slightly less dramatic. There are presently four such, three having opened in the past decade (in Seattle, Montreal, and Minneapolis-St. Paul). Finally, the trend toward multiuse stadiums, which at one stage not long ago appeared inexorable, may be abating. Of the sixteen facilities opened since Dodger Stadium in 1962 and still in use, all but two (Arlington Stadium and Royals Stadium) have seen some multisports use. But two others (Shea and Oakland-Alameda) have reverted to baseball-only status, although in each case the reversion was due to factors beyond the control of the ballclub.

The future of each of these trends is important because the size, shape, and atmosphere of the ballpark is one of the most consequential non-talent factors affecting play. The parameters of those factors may change: from trees or no trees in foul territory to real or artificial grass. But it is now and always has been up to the individual clubs to adjust successfully to windless King County Stadium or windy Candlestick Park. What can be said, and what could always be said, is that in baseball, more so than in any other sport, the term "home field advantage" is meant to be taken literally.

Strategy Before 1920

There is no single "correct" way to win a pennant. If a club can hit the cover off the ball, it might have a chance. If it can field with the best, that might be enough. And if its pitchers are dominant, that, too, might do it.

Then again, maybe not.

If the history of major league baseball demonstrates anything, it is that the search for a single winning formula is as elusive as the search for a rainbow's end.

Since the National League of Professional Baseball Clubs first organized for play in 1876, there have been 219 recognized "major league" seasons played, most by the two currently operating leagues, but also including a handful of "third majors." The table below lists the number of times the team leaders in five major performance categories—which may be read as indicative of a particular basic strategic bent—also won the league or divisional pennant. The five categories (and the strategies they may represent) are batting average (batting), slugging average (slugging), stolen bases (speed), fielding average (fielding), and earned run average (pitching). (The figures for stolen bases are measured against only 196 seasons, rather than 213, since no reasonably accurate records of stolen bases were kept until the mid-1880s.)

Category	Winning League Leaders	Percentage
Batting Average	83	38.1
Slugging Average	92	42.0
Stolen Bases	44	22.0
Fielding Average	67	30.5
Earned Run Average	100	45.6

It stands to reason that if, through the seasons, ballclubs had found one strategy to be more important than any other, that finding should be indicated in a superior correlation between league leadership and pennants won. In fact, as the table above indicates, any such superiority is quite minimal, if it exists at all. The 46 percent correlation between leadership in earned run average and championships is only about 4 percent higher than the correlation between winning and slugging. Given the size of the sample, that difference cannot even be considered statistically reliable, much less relevant.

The table certainly cannot be read as conclusive. No one would affirm, for instance, that raw stolen-base totals are the sole measurement of emphasis on speed; that fielding average is the only gauge of defensive ability; or that ERA is the one yardstick by which to assess pitching strength. Yet if achievement in those five categories can at least be read as a barometer of strategic superiority, then what the table does suggest is that the least productive strategy contributes to victory approximately one quarter of the time, the most productive less than half the time.

Why do strategies change? Why don't the modern Mets approach the challenge of winning in the same fashion as the

White Stockings of bygone days? Many of the reasons are obvious. Plainly, changing conditions and rules dictate some of the strategic adjustments. The White Stockings and their counterparts of the 1880s would, for instance, have considered it folly to pay more than one or two pitchers and an equal number of substitutes. Rules regulated the appearances of nonregulars, and in a time of 80-game schedules and underhanded deliveries, more bodies simply were not required. Night baseball and modernday transcontinental travel demands, too, place greater strains on players.

Changes in park sizes, styles, and equipment contribute to strategic alterations as well. When, in the first quarter of the twentieth century, improved manufacturing techniques made for a better grade of ball, managers found it more productive to eschew the erstwhile popular sacrifice in favor of waiting for a home run. The increasing popularity of artificial turf created an intensified interest in defensive range and speed. And sociological adjustments played a part as well. The 1920 outlawing of the spitball and other "trick" pitches that involved defacing of the ball—occasioned, at least in good measure, by sociological factors—plainly contributed to generally higher batting averages throughout the 1920s and 1930s. The *de facto* banning of the beanball and its first cousin, the knockdown pitch, in recent years resulted in some degree from public complaints about the pitch's potential danger.

But another, less obvious contributor to the constant ebb and flow of baseball strategy is simple managerial practice. If a particular team employs a new, or more often resurrected, strategy to success, the prospect is great that competitors will incorporate that strategy into their own plans. Often, these strategic adjustments are of a more transitory duration, but in terms of their impact on individual pennant races they can be just as important.

It is overly simplistic to equate particular strategies with specific time periods—to suggest, for instance, that because earned run averages tended to be lower during the first decade of the 1900s, the emphasis at that time was on pitching. Or to argue that teams stressed offense in the 1920s and 1930s because batting averages swelled, or to suggest that speed has become the dominant force of the present generation. In fact, between 1900 and 1919—the commonly recognized dead-ball era—the league batting champion won 20 pennants, the slugging champion 19, and the earned run average champion only 16. Conversely, between 1920 and 1949—the period of unbridled hitting—32 pennants were won by clubs that led their league in ERA, only 24 by slugging leaders, and only 22 by batting average leaders. And only 10 of the 36 league stolen base leaders since 1969 have won divisional pennants, a correlation that is slightly greater than the average for all time, but hardly compelling in making the argument for a contemporary strategic shift to speed.

Those numbers do not render the era labels meaningless, but they do suggest that the successful managers—of every generation—may be following their own strategies, rather than the obvious ones.

The art of strategy probably is as old as the game itself. The first player in the first game approached the batting area for the first time and, scanning the defense, wondered whether it would be wiser to take a strike, go to right, or rip one over the left fielder's head. When Candy Cummings discovered—if Candy Cummings indeed discovered—that he could make a baseball curve, he was engaging in the development of strategy. So was the anonymous manager who—faced with the dilemma of none out in the ninth and the winning run at third—brainstormed bringing both his infield and outfield in to a shallow depth, the better to cut off the run at home. When, in the 1880s, Chicago's legendarily innovative King Kelly—perhaps apocryphally—dashed from his seat on the bench, yelled "Kelly now substituting," and snagged a foul fly to save the game, he was enhancing strategy: at least, he was until that particular practice was outlawed, and substitutions were permitted only during time-outs.

Perhaps the first recognized employer of what we might today consider strategy on a prolonged basis was Ross Barnes, the second baseman of the champion Chicago White Stockings of the National League's inaugural season in 1876. The league at the time had a rule that stipulated as fair any ball which landed in fair territory, irrespective of whether it subsequently rolled foul before passing a base. By that standard, many of the "bunts" of today—and a number of chops as well—would be fair balls. Barnes developed the skill of striking such "fair-foul" hits, and he did it so well that he led the league in batting that first season, with a .429 average. Alas for Barnes, as would be the case of some subsequent strategists of later ages—notably spitballers—rule makers reacted to his achievement by outlawing the strategy that made it possible. And when in 1877 the requirement was established that a ground ball must pass first or third base in fair territory to be legitimately fair, Barnes' average plummeted by over 150 points, to .272.

As would be expected, the development of strategy during the game's first decades occurred in very broad and general terms. There was, for instance, little thought given to the strategic advantages of relief pitchers, platooning, pinch hitting, pinch running, or defensive replacement, for the simple reason that until 1891 substitutions—save for injury—were not even permitted. Naturally, the growing awareness of the value of maintaining a reserve of players first focused on the pitcher's mound.

As early as 1876, the first season of club-based professional leagues, managers employed diverse approaches to pitching strategy. Four of the eight teams, including the Chicago champions, stayed fundamentally with a single hurler. In the case of Chicago manager Al Spalding, that pitcher was Spalding himself, who pitched in 61 of the team's 66 games. But three other clubs divided the mound work roughly equally between two men of reasonably balanced skills. In the case of third-place Hartford, for instance, Tommy Bond pitched 408 innings with a 1.68 ERA, while old-timer Candy Cummings curve-balled his way through 216 innings with a 1.67 ERA. And fourth-place Boston went so far as to divide the work among three pitchers, each pitching between 170 and 220 innings. Boston manager Harry Wright might have seemed very much the trend setter had he stuck with that notion. But the very next year Wright jettisoned all three of his 1876 arms and signed Bond away from Hartford to pitch 58 of the club's 61 games. It was the "Wright" move; Boston won the 1877 flag. Cincinnati employed a three-man staff that year . . . and finished last.

If we define a pitching "staff" as consisting of at least four pitchers, each sharing a roughly equivalent part of the responsibility, then credit for devising the first one probably belongs to Jack Chapman, who directed the fortunes of several early-day National League teams. Chapman found himself in De-

troit in 1884, surrounded by little offense and even less in the way of reliable pitching. The team's earned run average in 1883 had been 3.56, second worst in the league and considerably higher than the overall 3.13 league average. This was still very much an era when a single hurler could carry a team's fortunes: In Providence, Charles Radbourn would win 60 games and pitch 679 innings, the equivalent of 75 complete games. Other mound stars included Pud Galvin (46-22) in Buffalo, Larry Corcoran (35-23) in Chicago, and Mickey Welch (39-21) in New York. Chapman had no one who could hope to match such standouts head-on day after day, so he did not try. Instead, he rotated five men, none pitching more than 30 percent of the team's innings. The result: well, it wasn't much. Detroit still finished last. Chapman took his approach to Buffalo in 1885, where the notion of a four-man pitching rotation lasted longer than Chapman himself; it remained throughout the season, but he was dismissed after a 12-19 start.

From the mid-1880s, experimentation with multipitcher staffs became more common, but no team won a pennant utilizing such an approach until Chapman's successor in Detroit, Bill Watkins, resurrected the notion in 1887. That club, too, featured five pitchers, none of whom did very much more than a third of the work. Like Chapman, Watkins plainly was trying to mask a weakness. His everyday lineup featured some of the game's greats: outfielder Sam Thompson won the batting (.372) and RBI (166) titles, and the team led the league in runs scored, doubles, triples, batting average, slugging, and fielding average. But as usual, all of the great pitchers toiled for other teams: Tim Keefe and Welch in New York, John Clarkson in Chicago, Galvin in Pittsburgh. Watkins had only two proven arms—Lady Baldwin (42-13 in 1886) and Charles Getzien (30-11)—and two lightly used reserves, Pete Conway, acquired from Kansas City, and a twenty-three-year-old named Larry Twitchell. When Kansas City's team folded after the 1886 season, Watkins signed the team's top pitcher, Stump Weidman. He also promoted Twitchell to a semiregular status, and those moves, combined with the availability of Conway for a full year, left Watkins so deep in pitching that he could actually afford to let Weidman go to the New York team of the American Association at midseason. Following is the record of that Detroit staff for 1887:

Pitcher	Games	Innings	Wins-Losses	ERA
Getzien	43	367	29–13	3.73
Baldwin	24	211	13–10	3.84
Weidman	21	183	13–7	5.36
Conway	17	146	8–9	2.90
Twitchell	15	112	11–1	4.33

Suddenly the names of Detroit pitchers began showing up in the strangest of places, like among the league leaders in key pitching categories. Getzien led in percentage and was third in wins, Conway ranked second in ERA and allowed fewer hits per nine innings pitched than anyone. The next season a very funny thing happened: several teams ditched their reliance on a single pitcher in favor of a staff. There remained a few holdouts: Boston's John Clarkson pitched 483 innings in 1888, 620 in 1889, and 460 as late as 1891. But within a decade of the Detroit staff's accomplishment, Boston's Kid

Nichols could lead the league in innings pitched with a comparatively modest 368. The era of a team asking one man to pitch as many as 400 innings was not quite dead yet—it would resurface here and there through the first decade of the twentieth century—but it was dying.

The change to a multiple-pitcher staff may have been hastened by Detroit's inability to snare one of the strong arms—a Clarkson or a Galvin—but changing conditions and rules would have made it inevitable even so. Occasionally, a strategy works so well that it must be legislated against. Ross Barnes's was one such. But the all-time champions, both in devising new strategies and in getting them banned, almost certainly were the Baltimore Orioles teams that flourished under manager Ned Hanlon in the 1890s.

In many respects, those Orioles were an ingenious lot of unprecedented proportion. The record should show that they won three consecutive pennants (1894–1896); that they compiled offensive statistics which are phenomenal by contemporary standards and were impressive even in the context of their times; and that they dominated in other aspects of the game as well. In 1894, the Orioles' team batting average was .343, the second highest ever recorded. (The highest, notably, came that very same season.) The Orioles batted .324 as a team in 1895 and .328 in 1896, leading the league. It should be noted that the overall league averages those years were .309, .296, and .290, but even so, the Orioles could hit! They could run as well. In those same three seasons, Baltimore players averaged 358 stolen bases per year. Again, some contextual reference is necessary. Different methods of figuring stolen bases in force at the time invalidate any comparisons between those numbers and present standards, which would make team totals in excess of 300 exceptional. But even judging by the context of their era, the Orioles were demons; the average of the other NL teams of that era was 242 stolen bases, a 48 percent differential per season!

Hanlon's Orioles achieved that mastery by a singular combination of remarkable skill and superior innovative capacity. Among the strategies team members are credited with devising or popularizing:

The hit-and-run play. Stories as to the origin of this strategem, whereby according to a preconceived plan a runner breaks for the next base while the batter attempts to drive the ball through a hole vacated by the fielder covering the steal effort, are both numerous and hoary, and no definitive judgment can be rendered. Cap Anson, longtime manager of the Chicago White Stockings, is among those purported to have claimed this strategy as his own. But the best available evidence tends to support the claim of the Orioles' chief contemporary rivals, the Boston Beaneaters, and their manager, Frank Selee. John McGraw, the famous manager who played for the Orioles, insisted on the validity of Baltimore's claim. But even if Hanlon's Orioles cannot be established as the originators, they certainly brought the play to its first and lasting popularity. As worked most frequently by Baltimore on frustrated opponents, John McGraw, leading off, would reach base, and then Willie Keeler, a superlative hitter (lifetime .345 batting average) whose principal asset was bat control, would direct the ball to the appropriate defensive weakspot, often resulting in runners at first and third with none out.

The Baltimore chop. There is no question as to the origin of this play, which has waned in strategic significance with the advent of the home run as a game factor. But Orioles' hitters

mastered it and used that mastery to advantage. The chop was deceptively simple: a hitter would employ an exaggerated downward swing to drive the pitch almost directly into the ground in front of the plate. On the hard Baltimore dirt, the result would be a simple infield bouncer, but one recoiling so high off the ground that there was no defense; infielders could merely wait in vain frustration for the ball to descend while the batter scampered to first base unchallenged.

The bunt single. The sacrifice, of course, had been around for many years prior to the emergence of the Orioles. But Baltimore players like McGraw, Hughie Jennings, and Joe Kelley were among the first to widely use the bunt as an offensive weapon, a means for reaching base. Dickey Pearce of the old Brooklyn Atlantics pioneered in this regard, and Ross Barnes followed. But McGraw especially was brash in his use of the bunt: it was occasionally remarked in awe that he might even attempt to lay one down on Boston third baseman James Collins, then considered the standard for measurement of excellence at the position.

The Orioles weren't the only innovators of the 1890s. In Boston, the Beaneaters honed their skill at the double steal, wherein the runner at first broke for second, and when the catcher attempted to retire him the runner on third tried to score. This rather daring technique required not only nerves and teamwork but superior speed, and the Beaneaters had plenty of the latter commodity with the likes of Billy Hamilton, whose more than 900 career stolen bases represented the all-time record until Lou Brock's day. The Brooklyn club of the same era is generally credited with originating the tricky cutoff play, whereby an infielder intercepts an outfielder's throw to the plate in an effort to retire the batter if he, thinking the ball will be thrown through, attempts to advance an extra base.

But the Orioles devised other, less gentlemanly strategies as well. Their first baseman, "Dirty Jack" Doyle, got his nickname by tripping, jostling, or holding opposing runners by the belt; Jennings at shortstop or McGraw at third were equally as likely to obstruct a runner. Oriole outfielders were known for hiding extra balls in the tall grass to be put in play in emergencies. It was said that catcher Wilbert Robinson always kept his pockets full of pebbles, which he dropped in the shoes of batters as he squatted behind them. On offense, the Orioles were by no means above cutting bases when an umpire's back was turned. They could do all of those things because most games of the era were officiated by a single arbiter, who could not hope to watch everything taking place on the broad expanse. Ultimately, public disgust at the Orioles' open flaunting of rules caused league officials to authorize umpiring teams. Over time, the practice grew to using four umpires. The trend started with the Orioles.

Possibly the most convincing evidence of the prominent role played by Hanlon's Orioles in the development of baseball strategy is the fact that the two superior minds of the subsequent generation of baseball officials were former Orioles: McGraw and Hughie Jennings. It was they who, while piloting teams of the first few years of the twentieth century to pennants, popularized strategic innovations that would eventually assume permanent, prominent roles in the planning of every major league franchise.

Jennings took over leadership of the new American League's Detroit Tigers in 1907 following his retirement as an active player, and he became an immediate success. The Tigers, a 71-78 team the previous year under Bill Armour,

leaped immediately to 92-58 and the championship. They followed that up with pennants in 1908 and 1909 as well, the first American League club to win three years running. In part, Jennings's success was a product of his being in the right place at the right time; his managerial star ascended in almost precise concert with the development of Ty Cobb, who came up as an eighteen-year-old rookie in 1905 and won batting titles in twelve of the thirteen years from 1907-1919. But give Jennings some credit as well for analyzing his team's strengths and weaknesses, and for inventing methods of overcoming the latter.

The prime example of that trait involved his handling of the Tigers' catchers. Even in the years of their first two championships, catching was a comparative liability for them. The regular, Boss Schmidt, hit just .244 and .265, and he seemed especially bedazzled by lefthanded pitchers. Jennings had dealt summarily enough with other weak links by releasing them. But he did not want to dispatch Schmidt because of his still sharp defensive skills and above-average throwing arm. Instead, Jennings replaced Schmidt in the lineup against left-handers, with righthanded Ira Thomas and then with Oscar Stanage after Thomas was traded. What Jennings was using was a platoon system, and it gradually caught on. Yankee manager George Stallings applied the notion with outfielders Willie Keeler and Birdie Cree in 1909, then took the idea with him to Boston when he assumed control of the Braves in 1914. There his judicious mixing of a half dozen outfielders helped bring him a pennant.

Research compiled by Bill James for his *Historical Abstract* suggests that the notion of platooning actually started with Bill Armour, Jennings's predecessor at Detroit in 1906, rotating Schmidt and Freddie Payne (though the idea may have begun as far back as the 1880s with Frank Bancroft). But Armour's platoon system attracted little notice, and he himself was soon fired. It plainly is Jennings who deserves credit for popularizing the idea by demonstrating over a period of several seasons that it could work with a pennant contender.

In the National League, McGraw pioneered strategy of a very different, but equally lasting type. There came to the Giants in 1908 a twenty-year-old rookie pitcher named Otis Crandall—the players called him "Doc"—who showed exceptional potential. Crandall won 12 games, but he lacked overpowering speed, stamina, was hit hard in the later innings of games, and did his best work in relief of other pitchers. To minimize the weakness and take best advantage of the strengths, McGraw in 1909 designated Crandall as the club's "relief" pitcher, chosen to enter in midgame and rescue a faltering teammate. In an era when starting pitchers were rarely removed—about two thirds of all starts that year were complete games—the concept of a pitcher actually specializing in midgame appearances seemed demeaning. Yet that is precisely what "Doc" Crandall did: starting only 7 games, entering 23 in relief of other Giants, and winning 5 of those games, with 4 of what would come to be classified as saves and just 1 defeat. Over the next three seasons, two thirds of Crandall's 120 appearances were in relief. He won 20 times, saved 11 more, and lost just 6. He was not considered the equal of Christy Mathewson, Rube Marquard, or Jeff Tesreau, but he would have ranked in value with any other of the Giants starters.

As intriguing as it was, Crandall's success did not spur an immediate flood of imitators. Managers, who found quality

starting pitching difficult enough to locate, could not bring themselves to isolate one or more of their better arms for emergency duty. One of the few mimics was Patsy Donovan of the Boston Red Sox, who in 1910 converted righthander Charley Hall from an occasional, ineffective starter into a reliever of fairly consistent quality. Between 1910 and 1913, Hall made 136 pitching appearances for Boston, just 51 of them as a starter, and in relief he won 20 of 24 decisions, saving 11 others. Fittingly the 1912 World Series pitted Hall's Red Sox against Crandall's Giants. Hall was the more widely used, pitching 10 2/3 innings in two games with a 3.38 ERA. Crandall saw action in just one game, and he did not allow a run, as the Giants eventually lost four games to three.

While McGraw and Jennings innovated, game strategy during the dead-ball era between 1901 and 1920 appeared to stress strong pitching, baserunning, playing for a single run, and an emphasis on one or two players who, had 1980s hyperbole been in fashion then, would have been called "superstars." The most obvious of the latter was Cobb, who batted .350 in 1907, .385 in 1910, .420 in 1911, and .410 in 1912. In 1910, for example, Cobb's batting average was nearly 100 points higher than any of his teammates, and his slugging average was 125 points superior. He was not the only early 1900s example of the near "one-man team." In Cleveland in 1911, outfielder Joe Jackson batted .408, slugged .590, collected 233 hits, with 45 doubles, 19 triples, and 126 runs scored. The second highest totals on the team in each category were: .304, .396, 142, 25, 9, and 89. In 1909, Pittsburgh's Honus Wagner led his team to the pennant with a .339 average. The second highest average among the Pirate regulars belonged to player-manager Fred Clarke, at .287.

With the home run not yet developed as a viable option, and with league earned run averages ranging between 2.30 and 2.70, managers often resorted to the sacrifice or the stolen base, mindful of the importance of every run. It is not possible today to reconstruct totals of sacrifices, but stolen base records are available, and their counts rose higher and swifter than at any other period of the game until the 1970s, as the evolution of the individual and team stolen base records indicates. In 1900, two years after the modern system for counting steals was developed (prior to that, any baserunner's extra-base advance—whether via a pitched or hit ball had been counted), Brooklyn led the majors with 274 steals, while St. Louis's Patsy Donovan and New York's George Van Maltren set the individual standard with 45. Frank Isbell of the new American League's Chicago team broke the modern individual record in 1901 with 52, and Isbell's Sox stole 280. In 1903 Frank Chance of the National League Chicago Cubs and Jimmy Sheckard of the Dodgers upped the individual mark to 67, and in 1904 the New York Giants raised the team record to 283. The Giants broke their own record in 1905, stealing 291, and Cobb shattered the modern individual record in 1909 with 76 steals.

Neither record lasted one season: in 1910, Eddie Collins of the Philadelphia Athletics stole 81, and the Cincinnati Reds 310. And even those standards were erased within one year, Cobb stealing 83 and the New York Giants 347 in 1911. Clyde Milan of Washington broke Cobb's record with 88 in 1912; then Cobb broke Milan's mark in 1915, stealing 96.

There you have it: the individual record broken seven times, the team record five times, all in a span of fifteen seasons. Cobb's record did not fall for forty-seven years, until Maury Wills stole 104 bases for Los Angeles in 1962. And the Giants team record of 347 steals is unsurpassed to this very day.

Wouldn't it be natural for a record in a newly established category to be broken several times in quick succession, then finally to reach a comparatively unattainable plateau? Yes. But consider that even the original team mark of 274 set by the 1900 Dodgers would have stood into the 1970s. The first twenty years of the century were not a case of a record gradually being raised beyond reach; they were a case of teams simply stressing the running game. The very worst team at accumulating stolen bases in the century's first decade, the 1906 Boston Braves (who stole 93), would have won either the American or National League stolen base championships 38 times between 1925 and 1960.

Strategy: 1920-Present

The reasons behind the switch—which occurred about 1920—from a strategy based on the sacrifice and stolen base to one focusing on the extra-base hit are numerous and complex. Changes in rules, park design, equipment, and fan interest all played a part. The impact of those factors on the changed game is underscored in the dramatically altered statistics of the game in the 1920s and later, as compared with its predecessor. The raw numbers of runs being scored provides the clearest contrast.

Prior to the season of 1920, the major league record in this century for runs scored in a season by an individual was 147, Ty Cobb scoring that many in 1911. The record since the establishment of the 16-team, 154-game schedule, set in 1911, was 11,164. But in 1920, New York's Babe Ruth easily broke Cobb's individual record by scoring 158. He broke it again in 1921 with 177, establishing the standard that still exists. In all, Cobb's former record was topped 13 times in the American League alone between 1920 and 1940. Meanwhile, the total runs scored record rose to 11,935 in 1921, then broke through the 12,000 barrier the following year, to 12,059. It was broken again in 1925 (12,592), again in 1929 (12,747), and again in 1930 (13,695). And that record stood for more than three decades, until it was surpassed in 1962, by which time each major league had added two teams and eight more games to the playing schedule.

Power records similarly surged. Tris Speaker's dead-ball era record for doubles—53 set in 1912—fell to Speaker himself in 1923 (59), and was surpassed in eight more seasons during the 1920s and 1930s; in 1936 alone five players matched or bettered that pre-1920 record. The pre-1920 record for home runs—Ruth's 29 in 1919—bears no comparison, of course, with subsequent achievements. It had been raised three times by Ruth himself by 1927, and was bettered in every single American League season until the war year of 1944, when New York's Nick Etten led the league with only 22. Slugging averages, which ranged between .310 and .340 during the dead-ball era, jumped by an average of more than 20 points in both leagues in 1920 alone, and by 30 more points the following year. The increase in the American League alone was nearly 14 percent between 1919 and 1921. The league slugging average soared to .421 by 1930 in the American League, to .448 in the National.

With the increase in power came a concurrent acceptance of the base on balls as occasionally being strategically prudent. Managers, operating on the theory that discretion might

be the better part of valor, instructed or allowed pitchers to "work around" certain hitters like Ruth who were capable of doing far more damage with a home run than a walk. For the pre-1920s, when pitchers looked on a base on balls as pariah, the Chicago Cubs' Jimmy Sheckard held the record by drawing 147 of them in 1911. That lasted only as long as it took Ruth to be walked 148 times in 1920. The Babe raised that standard to 170 in 1923. The league record of 4,282 walks issued in the National League in 1911 lasted until 1925, when American League pitchers walked 4,315 batters. The record was hiked biennially to 4,402, 4,611, 4,855 and 4,924 in the same league between 1932 and 1938.

Finally, in the 1920s and 1930s, the notion of the relief pitcher as defined by McGraw years earlier first gained true prominence. In 1919, the St. Louis Cardinals' Oscar Tuero had become the first primarily relief pitcher to lead the league in appearances; he pitched in 45 games, 28 out of the bullpen. The achievement drew little notice, primarily because his team finished seventh. But in 1923, the pennant-winning Giants' Claude Jonnard and Rosy Ryan tied for the league lead in appearances, each with 45. Ryan started 15 games that season, Jonnard but 1. The following season, Firpo Marberry of the AL champion Washington Senators led the league with 50 appearances, only 15 of them starts. Marberry repeated as the most-called-upon in 1925 with 55 appearances, all in relief, in another pennant-winning year. Marberry's role was by no means yet established; he would lead the league four more times in appearances, three times as a reliever, once as a starter. But the idea of a specialist in quality relief pitching for first-rank teams had at last begun to gain acceptance. When the 1927 New York Yankees blitzed the American League to win 110 games, their most frequently called upon pitcher was rookie Wilcy Moore, who won 19 games despite starting only 12. Moore pitched 38 times out of the bullpen. In 1901, National League pitchers had completed 976 games, representing nearly 90 percent of the schedule. By 1919, that figure had fallen to about 60 percent. In 1922, for the first time in history, National League pitchers completed fewer than half of all their starts. By 1930, the percentage had fallen to 43 percent in 1930, and it held at roughly that level through the 1930s and 1940s.

As the perceived importance of the complete game waned, a sort of temporary strategical miasma ensued; managers, less unwilling to turn to the bullpen, had not perfected effective strategies for its use. That began to change in the early 1940s, when Brooklyn's Leo Durocher developed the notion of a bullpen "ace," a late-inning stopper capable both of helping his team regain leads and of buttressing a successful but tiring starter's work by holding his advantage through the final innings. For the first time, a manager appeared not to expect his starter to finish, or at least not to mind if he didn't. Dodger starters completed only 66 games in 1941—one of the lowest totals ever by a pennant winner—and only 67 more the following season. But Durocher used the hard-throwing Hugh Casey to win 14 games in relief and save 20 those two years. The notion was copied. Boston's Joe Cronin won the 1946 American League pennant thanks in good measure to the relief pitching of Bob Klinger, who appeared 27 times in relief and saved a league-high 9 games. The New York Yankees' Joe Page won a total 21 games and saved 33 in virtually exclusive bullpen action in 1947-1948.

The notion of relievers as failed starters was gradually eroding. As late as 1946, more than half the major league mound staffs were led in appearances by a starter, and it was still possible for a starter, Cleveland's Bob Feller, to lead the league in that category. But the trend was plain. In 1947, relievers led in appearances on ten of the sixteen staffs. By 1952, the figure was thirteen of sixteen. In Philadelphia in 1950, a relief pitcher, Jim Konstanty, won the Most Valuable Player Award by pitching in a record 74 games, saving 22 of them and leading his team to the National League pennant. In Brooklyn, Joe Black won 15 games and saved 15 more for the pennant-winning 1952 Dodgers. In Cleveland in 1954, Al Lopez presented a relief duo: lefthander Don Mossi and righty Ray Narleski appeared in 82 games between them, saving 20. The major league save record (although it was not an official statistic until 1969), which had stood at 22 since being set by Marberry in 1926, was swollen to 27 by Page in 1949. Boston's Ellis Kinder matched that in 1953, and New York's Luis Arroyo topped it in 1961 with 29. Prior to 1949, only Marberry in all of baseball history had saved 20 games in a year. Between 1949 and 1961, 10 pitchers did it.

Player platooning, basically a dormant activity after the early 1920s, was revived as a practice in the late 1940s, principally by Stengel. A platoon player himself under McGraw with the 1920s Giants, Stengel in 1949 and 1950 alternated third basemen Bobby Brown, a lefthander, and righty Bill Johnson. In 1951, Gil McDougald supplanted Johnson as the righthanded half of the platoon. The Yankees won the world championship all three years. By 1955 Stengel had expanded his platoon system, alternating righthanded Bill Skowron with lefty Joe Collins at first base, and subbing righthanded Elston Howard for Irv Noren occasionally in the outfield. Howard and utility man Tony Kubek both were platooned at several positions in 1957 and 1958. Again successful managers took their cues from Stengel. Fred Haney's use of the first base platoon of Joe Adcock and Frank Torre helped the Braves to the 1958 pennant. The only manager to beat out Stengel for the AL pennant between 1949 and 1960, Al Lopez, used a platoon system to do so in Chicago in 1959, alternating righty Bubba Phillips and lefty Billy Goodman at third base, and righty Jim McAnany and lefty Jim Rivera in right field. In Pittsburgh in 1960, manager Danny Murtaugh often alternated at three positions: Hal Smith or Smoky Burgess at catcher, Dick Stuart or Rocky Nelson at first, and Gino Cimoli or Bill Virdon in center. But for Fred Hutchinson's use of platoons at three positions in 1961 (Jerry Zimmerman and John Edwards at catcher, Elio Chacon and Don Blasingame at second, Wally Post and Jerry Lynch in left), Cincinnati very possibly might not have held off the Dodgers to win by four games. By the mid 1960s, most teams were platooning at least one position.

The other significant change in strategy to evolve during the 1950s (and early 1960s) was a growing acceptance of the strikeout as an acceptable price to pay for home run power. In retrospect, that acceptance can clearly be seen as a delayed reaction, for home run totals had begun to mount sharply in 1953. For the past two decades, major league batters had averaged between 1,300 and 1,700 home runs; in 1953, they hit 2,076, a record 1,197 of them coming in the National League alone. That represented a 22 percent increase over the previous season. From 1953 through 1960, the record was raised only about 10 percent, and in fact the raw numbers of home runs flattened and occasionally declined between the 1950s peak season, 1956, and 1960. But strikeouts rose sharply. In 1953, major league batters struck out 10,220

times; by 1960, that total had risen steadily to more than 12,800, a climb of more than 25 percent. The strikeout explosion continued unabated through the 1960s, whether home runs rose (as they did in 1961 and 1962) or fell. In fact, between 1961 and 1966, home run production remained virtually level in the major leagues, despite the addition of two expansion teams. But strikeouts rose by more than 25 percent over the same period. The increase (part of which was attributable to strategical concessions and part to rules changes), showed itself in the individual strikeout totals as well. The pre-1956 record for most strikeouts in a season was Vince DiMaggio's 134, set in 1938. Washington's Jim Lemon broke it that season with 138. In 1961, Detroit's Jake Wood broke it again, fanning 141 times. Harmon Killebrew of Minnesota raised the mark to 142 the following season; then the Chicago White Sox' Dave Nicholson increased it to 175 in 1963. By 1969, when San Francisco's Bobby Bonds whiffed 187 times, the record was thought unassailable. Not so—Bonds himself beat it in 1970 with 189 strikeouts. Since 1966, there have been only six seasons when the league leader struck out as few times as DiMaggio did when he set the record.

The game of the 1970s and 1980s features at least three more easily identifiable refinements; two of them strategic, the third brought about by one of the game's rare major rules changes. Those three are the further specification of the role of the relief pitcher, the regeneration of stress on the running game, and the implementation of the designated hitter.

The use of the bullpen as a strategic factor has progressed constantly from Luis Arroyo's days in New York until the present. Again, clear evidence is found in the record book. Arroyo's previously unmatched total of 29 saves might have inspired great admiration, yet the following season in Pittsburgh Elroy Face saved 28 games, and in 1964 and 1965 Arroyo's record was matched, then surpassed: first by Dick Radatz in Boston, then by Chicago's Ted Abernathy, who accumulated 31. Kansas City's Jack Aker broke the record the following season with 32, but that lasted only until 1970, when Cincinnati's Wayne Granger saved 35 games. The Reds' Clay Carroll raised the record to 37 in 1972, and Detroit's John Hiller saved 38 in 1973; then in 1983 Kansas City's Dan Quisenberry took the record past 40, saving 45 games. Bruce Sutter of St. Louis matched that total in 1984, and Dave Righetti saved 46 in 1986, to establish, at least for the moment, a new record.

Arroyo's remarkable 29 saves in 1961 would have led the major leagues in only one season of the past ten.

As noteworthy as the increase in record performance, however, is the willingness of major league managers and others to focus solely on the save as a measure of bullpen effectiveness. This demonstrates how completely the primary role of the bullpen has changed—from rescuing incompetent starters from the jaws of defeat to ensuring wins as a part of a carefully worked-out strategy. In 1974, Mike Marshall of the Los Angeles Dodgers became the first relief pitcher to win the Cy Young Award; his credentials included 15 victories, but also a league-leading 21 saves (and an incredible 106 games). Three years later, New York's Sparky Lyle would win the AL award with 13 wins and 26 saves. By 1979, a reliever's victory total had become extraneous: Bruce Sutter was recognized as the National League's top pitcher that season despite winning just 6 games. He saved 37. Rollie Fingers did the same thing for Milwaukee in 1981, winning just 6 but saving 28 . . . and he was named the league MVP to boot! Willie Hernandez

won the 1984 Cy Young Award and the MVP for Detroit on the basis of only 9 victories, but 32 saves.

It is difficult to assert with precision why the stolen base, which had been approached with apathy by power-happy major league teams for decades, was reinvigorated as an acceptable procedure. The simplest of explanations may hold: that players entered the major league ranks who could run, but not hit with power. The changing playing conditions, notably the wider use of artificial surfaces, may well have played a part, as may have the infusion of black and Caribbean Basin players. Managerial choice certainly had something to do with it; men like Al Lopez, Chuck Tanner, and Whitey Herzog found it easier to succeed with the versatility and greater athleticism afforded by the baserunning threat than by the occasionally lumbering, one-dimensional slugger.

But if the reasons behind the stolen base's surge are speculative and complex, affixing the date of its arrival as a mainstream strategem is less so. It came from Venezuela to Chicago in the person of Luis Aparicio in 1956.

Prior to Aparicio, there had not been a genuine base-stealing threat—a fellow capable of swiping 50 or more bases in a season—in more than a decade. And the efforts of the comparative handful of fellows who could perform such feats of speed in those days—George Case in Washington and Stuffy Stirnweiss in New York—got lost in the glare of the home run era. Consequently, major league stolen base totals had sagged to inconsequence. From 1920, when more than 1,700 bases had been stolen, these were the figures for five-year intervals through 1955:

Year	NL	AL	Total
1925	672	711	1,383
1930	481	598	1,079
1935	403	477	880
1940	475	478	953
1945	525	453	978
1950	372	278	650
1955	377	317	694

Aparicio sounded the call to the new emphasis on speed. As a rookie in 1956, he led the American League in steals. His total of 21 was certainly nothing special, even for the sluggish 1950s, but the notion of a baserunner as a weapon had not yet caught on, even in Chicago. The following season, 1957, Aparicio won the stolen base title again, this time with 28 thefts. In 1959, he stole 56 (Willie Mays, the National League champion, stole 27). Aparicio would go on to win the stolen base crown in nine successive seasons, topping 40 steals in four of the next five years.

But by 1959, Aparicio no longer was the whole story. Stolen base totals had turned upward virtually league-wide. National Leaguers stole 439 bases that season, their highest total in nearly a decade. In 1960, Los Angeles shortstop Maury Wills joined Aparicio at the 50-steal plateau and National Leaguers stole more than 500. Then in 1962 Wills eclipsed Aparicio and all base stealers in the game's history by running successfully 104 times, breaking Cobb's record of 96 that had stood since 1915. The Dodgers as a team stole 198, the most by any major league club since 1918.

Baserunners seemed to establish a cause-and-effect relationship with pennants, notably in the National League. Wills was a key factor in the Dodgers' championships in 1963,

1965, and 1966. St. Louis obtained Lou Brock from the Cubs in midseason of 1964 and promptly took off from mediocrity to the world's championship as he stole 43 bases (including 33 for the Cards). With Brock at the heart of the Cardinals' offense, they won again in 1967 and 1968. In 1965, major league runners stole nearly 1,450 bases, a level that hearkened back to the dead-ball era for comparison. And that figure was no fluke: In 1969, more than 1,000 bases were stolen in the American League alone, more than had been swiped in all major league games as recently as 1960. By 1975, the major league tally had surpassed 2,500; by 1987, it was over 3,500.

As was the case in the pre-1920s, every team had its "rabbit," and there were so many that speed alone was no longer a guarantor of team success. In 1974, Brock broke Wills's single-season record by stealing 118 bases. But his Cardinals finished second in the NL East. In 1976, Chuck Tanner's Oakland A's stole 341 bases, missing by only six the all-time record that McGraw's Giants had established in 1911. Bill North stole 75 that season, Bert Campaneris 54, and Don Baylor 52. Eight different Oakland players stole 20 or more. Yet the A's finished second behind Kansas City, which stole "only" 218.

Today the stolen base records—along with those for saves—are being rewritten routinely. The fact is best illustrated by noting that of the top nineteen base stealers in the game's history as of the end of the 1987 season, thirteen played all or most of their careers since 1960. And that does not include young chargers like St. Louis's Vince Coleman, who in only three seasons already has stolen 326 bases.

The era of the designated hitter certainly has its strategic implications, but all of the game's deep thinkers of the ages couldn't have devised a way to use it had not rule makers seen fit in 1973 to legalize it—on a league-option basis. The premise of the DH is as simple as the realization that most pitchers are miserable batters. It allows one player to bat repeatedly for the pitcher without requiring the pitcher's removal from the game. The two major leagues split over the DH when it was written into the rulebook, and they have remained divided ever since—the American League adopting it, the National League remaining with the traditional nine-player format. In time, the rule also has been adopted by virtually every other college and professional league. It has as well been accepted as a part of the World Series, used from 1976 through 1985 in alternating years, and since 1986 has been used in games played in the home ballpark of the American League champion.

Most American League teams have used the DH position as a refuge for older, perhaps slower ballplayers who are no longer capable of measuring up to the daily demands of the field, but are still considered effective offensively. In that sense, the very first DH, the New York Yankees' Ron Blomberg, was an accurate precursor: Blomberg batted .293 over eight major league seasons, but never carried a big league reputation at either first base or left field. Blomberg's legacy was exemplified by the fourteen men who served as their teams' principal DHs during 1988: Jim Rice, Tony Armas, Harold Baines, Darrell Evans, Pat Tabler, Joe Meyer, Gene Larkin, Dave Parker, Steve Balboni, Gino Petralli, Rance Mulliniks, Larry Sheets, Larry Parrish, Dave Kingman, Jorge Orta, Ron Kittle, and Ken Phelps. Several—Rice, Armas, Baines, Parker—had at one time been considered adequate to exceptional all-around players. But only a handful—Meyer, Larkin, Petralli—could not be said to be in the twilight of their careers. Without the DH, most of the others might already have confronted retirement.

The designated hitter rule was adopted by the American League as an effort to increase offensive production, and in that way spur fan interest. As noted earlier, the late 1960s had been a pitcher-dominated era of the game. The AL earned run average, which in recent times had ranged between 3.67 and 4.16, had fallen through the mid-1960s to a low of 2.98 by 1968; by 1972 it had moderated only to 3.07. (National League earned run averages had fallen in the same fashion through the 1960s, but by 1972 had regained much of their normal levels.) AL attendance fell as well: from a league-wide 12.1 million in 1969 to just over 12 million in 1970, to 11.9 million in 1971 and 11.4 million in 1972. In simple terms, club owners worried that pitchers like Oakland's Catfish Hunter and Vida Blue, Baltimore's Jim Palmer, and Detroit's Mickey Lolich might through their very brilliance be stifling fan interest. The change seemed to accomplish its task of injecting more offense into the AL game; in 1973, the league earned run average climbed three quarters of a point, to 3.82, one of the most dramatic one-season shifts in the game's history. Other statistics reflected the rules change as well: the league batting average rose from .239 to .259; teams scored 29 percent more runs, and hit 32 percent more home runs.

The principal points of debate concerning the DH have been twofold: whether it inappropriately undermines one of baseball's appealing tenets, that all participants be complete athletes; and whether it diminishes the strategic interplay.

Its detractors argue that, logically, the DH must negatively impact on strategy by removing one of the questions a manager must repeatedly consider during the course of a game: whether to remove a reasonably effective but trailing pitcher and replace him with a pinch hitter. The fewer decisions the manager must make, the reasoning goes, the more muted become baseball's strategic nuances. And as strategy dulls, so does the game.

Among those arguing against that reasoning has been Bill James, who in his *Baseball Historical Abstract* argued that the DH actually enhances strategy. James's contention was that with a normally inept-hitting pitcher at bat, managers actually were forced into a series of obvious moves that could not be viewed as options at all. A reasonably competent DH, by contrast, gave managers some choice in the decision of whether to bunt, steal, swing away, or hit and run.

CHAPTER 6

A Baseball Calendar

John Thorn

What follows is a random walk through baseball history, organized on a day-by-day basis. There is no point in your contending that one feat should have been included and another not, for the events were chosen without system; another compiler no doubt would present a quite different calendar.

This humble offering makes no claim to being comprehensive. The full banquet of *A Baseball Book of Days* awaits another day; this is merely a tray of appetizers, with events majestic and picayune competing for your notice. Bill Buckner rubs elbows with Fred Merkle, Tom Browning with Joe Borden, Babe Ruth (while kneeling) with Eddie Gaedel. Enjoy.

JANUARY 1

1857 Tim Keefe born.
1935 Hank Greenberg born, 1911; the two-time MVP drove in 183 runs, then hit 58 homers the following year.

JANUARY 2

1836 Dickey Pearce born; with the pre-Civil War Brooklyn Atlantics, he invented modern shortstop play and the bunt hit.
1933 Kid Gleason dies.
1951 Bill Madlock born.

JANUARY 3

1912 Frenchy Bordagaray born; fined $500 for spitting at an umpire, he protested, "Maybe I did wrong, but the penalty was a little more than I expectorated."
1920 Babe Ruth is sold to the Yankees.

JANUARY 4

1890 Ossie Vitt born; "Hits are my bread and butter."
1931 Roger Connor dies; his 138 career homers stood as the record until Ruth topped it in 1921.

JANUARY 5

1864 Ban Johnson born.
1898 Riggs Stephenson born.
1920 The sale from the Red Sox to the Yankees of Babe Ruth, after a season in which he hit a record 29 homers, is announced to the press.
1934 Yanks release two Hall of Famers on the same day—Joe Sewell and Herb Pennock.
1943 Big league clubs decide to train in the North due to World War Two.

JANUARY 6

1920 Early Wynn born; he pitched 23 seasons, more than any American Leaguer, and won the Cy Young Award at age 39, going 22–10 for the 1959 White Sox.
1920 New York Yankees announce purchase of Babe Ruth from Boston Red Sox.
1976 Ted Turner buys Braves for $11 million.

JANUARY 7

1913 Johnny Mize born; the big first sacker led the NL in homers four times and on a record six occasions hit three homers in a game.
1924 NY buys Earle Combs from Louisville, where in 1923 he hit for an average of .380 with 241 hits.

JANUARY 8

1927 After 22 years with the Detroit Tigers, Ty Cobb signs with the Philadelphia A's.
1947 Hank Greenberg is sold by Tigers to Pittsburgh, where he hits 25 homers and tutors Ralph Kiner.

JANUARY 9

1903 Frank Farrell and Bill Devery buy AL franchise for New York, picking up abandoned Baltimore; this team would be called the Highlanders, and later the Yankees.
1918 Brooklyn trades Casey Stengel to Pittsburgh in deal that brings them Burleigh Grimes; two decades later, Dodgers will dump Stengel as manager and hire Grimes.
1936 Ralph Terry born.

JANUARY 10

1835 Harry Wright born.
1930 Art "The Great" Shires, first baseman for the White Sox, TKO's Boston Braves' catcher Al Spohrer in a boxing match at Boston Garden.
1938 Willie McCovey born.

JANUARY 11

1876 Elmer Flick was born; he batted .378 for the 1900 Phillies but lost the batting title to Wagner; five years later his .306 was good enough to lead the AL.
1890 Max Carey born.

JANUARY 12

1927 Zack Wheat, released on 1/1 by Dodgers, signs with Athletics—rest home for Eddie Collins, Ty Cobb, and in 1928, Tris Speaker.
1932 Cincinnati's Edd Roush, the premier center fielder of his day, retires from baseball.
1950 Randy Jones born.
1961 Cub owner William Wrigley announces team will be managed by eight coaches.

JANUARY 13

1901 Fred Schulte born.
1944 Larry Jaster born; as a Cardinal rookie in 1965, he tied for the NL in shutouts with five—all of them against the champion Dodgers.

JANUARY 14

1919 Charles Hempstead sells the New York Giants to Charles Stoneham, John McGraw, and Francis X. McQuade, 1919; the Stonehams controlled the Giants for the next 56 years.
1952 Terry Forster born.

JANUARY 15

1959 Joe Cronin is named AL president, the first player to reach such heights in the game's management.
1981 Johnny Mize elected to Hall of Fame.

JANUARY 16

1873 Jimmy Collins born.
1911 Dizzy Dean born.
1974 Whitey Ford and Mickey Mantle, teammates through the Yankees' glory years of the 1950s and 1960s, are elected to the Hall of Fame.

JANUARY 17

1931 Don Zimmer born.
1933, 1952: Two major league catchers, unrelated but with the same last name, were born on the same day, 19 years apart — Darrell Porter (1952) and J.W. Porter (1933).

JANUARY 18

1938 Curt Flood born; his 1970 suit against organized baseball, though defeated in the U.S. Supreme Court, ushered in the free-agency revolution.

JANUARY 19

1945 Stan Musial enlists in the U.S. Navy; coming back to the Cards in 1946, he didn't skip a beat, hitting .365 to lead the league.

JANUARY 20

1871 The Boston Red Stockings are formed at the Parker House in the Hub; they were led by the Wright brothers, Harry and George, both former Cincinnati Red Stockings.

JANUARY 21

1947 Carl Hubbell, Lefty Grove, Frank Frisch, and Mickey Cochrane are elected to the Hall of Fame.

JANUARY 22

1949 Mike Caldwell born.
1959 Ken Williams dies; the St. Louis Browns' outfielder, who hit 39 homers in 1922, was one of only two men to snatch the title from Babe Ruth in the period 1918-1931.

JANUARY 23

1962 Jackie Robinson is the first black elected to the Hall of Fame.
1979 Willie Mays is elected to the Hall of Fame; Hack Wilson and Warren Giles are named by the Veterans Committee.

JANUARY 24

1938 Jim Mutrie dies; proud manager of the New York Gothams, he called them his "Giants," and so they became; he led them and the rival-league Mets to pennants.
1941 Tommy Bond dies.
1960 Russ Ford dies.
1969 Tom Zachary dies; gave up Babe Ruth's sixtieth homer in 1927.

JANUARY 25

1928 Baseball immortal Tris Speaker given unconditional release by Washington.
1978 Gaylord Perry is traded from the Texas Rangers to San Diego for Dave Tomlin and $125,000; with the Padres he goes 21-6 and wins his second Cy Young Award.

JANUARY 26

1904 George Blaeholder born; ostensible inventor of slider in 1920s.
1950 Sluggers Jimmie Foxx (534 homers) and Mel Ott (511) are named to the Hall of Fame.

JANUARY 27

1882 Charlie "Bumpus" Jones born; on October 15, 1892, he made his major league debut by pitching a no-hitter, his only big league win as a starter.
1937 Flood waters of Ohio River inundate Crosley Field.

JANUARY 28

1847 George Wright born.
1891 Bill Doak born; he wrote the request on behalf of 17 other spitball pitchers that they be allowed to throw the pitch, banned in 1920, for the rest of their careers.

JANUARY 29

1961 Outfield greats and stolen-base kings Max Carey and Billy Hamilton elected to Hall of Fame; between them they had 1,650 thefts, and in 1922 Carey stole 51 bases in 53 tries.

JANUARY 30

1923 The Red Sox trade Herb Pennock, future Hall of Famer, to the Yanks for three nondescript players and cash; over the next six years, he wins 115 games.
1943 Davey Johnson born.
1954 Braves trade Johnny Antonelli, Don Liddle, Ebba St. Claire to NY for Bobby Thomson and Sam Calderone.

JANUARY 31

1919 Jackie Robinson born.
1931 Ernie Banks born.
1947 Nolan Ryan born.
1977 Joe Sewell is named to the Hall of Fame; the toughest strikeout in baseball history, he fanned only 114 times in a 14-year career.

FEBRUARY 1

1875 Billy Sullivan born; catcher for the "hitless wonder" White Sox, 1906 World Champions.
1898 Pop Anson is fired as White Stockings' manager.
1928 Hugh Jennings dies.
1944 Paul Blair born; acknowledged as top defensive center fielder of his day.

FEBRUARY 2

1876 NL founded at Grand Central Hotel in New York on Broadway and West 3rd Street.
1908 Wes Ferrell born; hit a record 38 homers besides winning 193 games.
1936 Ty Cobb leads the balloting in the first election for the Hall of Fame; he is joined by Babe Ruth, Honus Wagner, Christy Mathewson and Walter Johnson.
1979 Twins trade six-time batting champ Rod Carew to Angels.

FEBRUARY 3

1890 Larry MacPhail born; his Cincinnati Reds were the first major league team to play under the lights.

FEBRUARY 4

1878 Germany Schaefer born; the only man to steal first base, he prompted a rule change that forbade running the bases in backward order.
1909 John Clarkson dies; he won 53 games to lead Chicago to the 1885 NL flag, and won 208 in five-year span.
1969 Bowie Kuhn named baseball commissioner.

FEBRUARY 5

1891 Roger Peckinpaugh born.
1897 Hoss Radbourn dies.
1921 Yankees buy 20-acre plot of land in Bronx which will become site of new Yankee Stadium.
1934 Henry Aaron born; the home run king hit 755 in his 23 seasons.

FEBRUARY 6

1895 Babe Ruth born; the incomparable Bambino won 89 games as a Red Sox pitcher before joining the Yankees, for whom he would win five more from 1920 to 1933.

FEBRUARY 7

1942 The Reds trade Ernie Lombardi to the Braves; in his only year in Boston, he took the NL batting championship with a mark of .330.
1949 Joe DiMaggio signs $100,000 contract, first in baseball.
1959 Nap Lajoie dies.

FEBRUARY 8

1924 Joe Black born.
1956 At age 93 and after 50 years as field manager of the A's, Connie Mack dies.

FEBRUARY 9

1887 Heinie Zimmerman born.
1927 In trade of Hall of Famers, Giants send George Kelly to Cincy for Edd Roush.
1971 Satchel Paige becomes the first player to enter the Hall of Fame by virtue of his accomplishments in the Negro Baseball Leagues.

FEBRUARY 10

1884 Billy Evans born; he is one of only five umpires enshrined in Cooperstown.
1894 Herb Pennock born.
1917 Allie Reynolds born.

FEBRUARY 11

1862 Curt Welch born; his steal of home in the bottom of the tenth won the 1886 World Series for St. Louis.
1946 John Paciorek born; made debut as 18-year-old with Astros by reaching base in all five at-bats, scoring four runs and driving in five—and never played in big leagues again.
1950 KiKi Cuyler dies; his bases-loaded double in the eighth inning of Game Seven won the 1925 World Series.

FEBRUARY 12

1870 Jesse Burkett born.
1903 Chick Hafey born; an outfielder for the Cards and Reds, he had a career bat mark of .317.

FEBRUARY 13

1883 "Prince Hal" Chase born; the fancy-fielding first baseman led NL batters with an average of .339 in 1916.

FEBRUARY 14

1887 Michael "King" Kelly is sold by Chicago to Boston for an unprecedented $10,000.
1915 Red Barrett born, once pitched a complete game while throwing only 58 pitches.

FEBRUARY 15

1900 George Earnshaw born.
1916 After sitting out all of 1915, "Home Run" Baker is sold by the decimated Philadelphia A's to New York for $35,000.
1948 Ron Cey born.
1963 Bump Hadley dies.
1980 Gaylord Perry traded from Padres to Texas with Tucker Ashford and Joe Carroll for Willie Montanez.

FEBRUARY 16

1866 Billy Hamilton born.
1961 Dazzy Vance dies; he didn't notch his first big league victory until age 31, then won 197 and led the league in strikeouts seven straight seasons.
1967 Red Ruffing elected to Hall of Fame.

FEBRUARY 17

1964 Luke Appling is elected to the Hall of Fame; "Old Aches and Pains" hit a homer in an Old Timers' Game at age 75.

FEBRUARY 18

1897 Zip Zabel born; pitched 18 1/3 innings of relief in one game, allowing no earned runs.
1927 Luis Arroyo born.
1938 Manny Mota born; he holds the record for most career pinch hits, 150.

FEBRUARY 19

1969 Doc White dies; the songwriting dentist was the left-handed ace of the "hitless wonder" White Sox.

FEBRUARY 20

1859 Tony Mullane born; ambidextrous twirler won more post-1876 games than any pitcher eligible for the Hall of Fame yet still outside it.
1890 Sam Rice born; he ended his 20-year career only 13

hits shy of 3,000—but that was in 1934, when folks didn't make such a fuss over records.

FEBRUARY 21

1903 Tom Yawkey born.
1958 Alan Trammell born.
1969 Ted Williams is named manager of the Senators; in his debut year, they went from 31 games under .500 to 10 over.
1972 Tom Seaver becomes highest paid pitcher in baseball history when he signed $172,500 a year contract with Mets.

FEBRUARY 22

1874 Bill Klem born; he said he never called one wrong ("in my heart") in 35 years in the majors.
1923 Christy Mathewson is named president of Braves.

FEBRUARY 23

1929 Elston Howard born.
1941 Ron Hunt born; he set a modern record in 1971 by taking first base 50 times after being drilled by a pitch.

FEBRUARY 24

1874 Honus Wagner born; he was generally regarded by those who saw him as the game's greatest all-around player.

FEBRUARY 25

1919 Monte Irvin born.
1934 John McGraw dies.
1972 The Phillies obtain Steve Carlton from the Cardinals for Rick Wise, 1972; all Carlton did that year was win 27 and the Cy Young Award.

FEBRUARY 26

1887 Grover "Old Pete" Alexander born; he won 373 games, of which 90 were shutouts—and an incredible 16 of these came in 1916 alone.
1935 Babe Ruth signs three-year contract with Braves.

FEBRUARY 27

1964 Mickey Mantle signs his first $100,000 contract with the Yankees.

FEBRUARY 28

1963 Eppa Rixey dies; pitched 21 years for poor clubs yet won 266 games.
1972 Dizzy Trout dies.

MARCH 1

1969 Mickey Mantle announces his retirement; the three-time MVP hit 536 homers plus a record 18 in the World Series.

MARCH 2

1909 Mel Ott born; only five-nine and 165 pounds, he used an unorthodox swing to launch 511 homers, then an NL record.

MARCH 3

1860 John Montgomery Ward born; only Ruth surpassed his dual success as pitcher and regular player.

MARCH 4

1891 Dazzy Vance born.

1897 Lefty O'Doul born.
1921 Boston's long-time right fielder Harry Hooper switches the color of his sox from red to white as he is traded for Shano Collins and Nemo Leibold.

MARCH 5

1860 Sam Thompson born; his ratio of RBIs to games-played is the highest of all time.

MARCH 6

1900 Lefty Grove born; the game's greatest southpaw, he was 31-4 in 1931 and 300-141 lifetime.
1938 Phils trade Dolf Camilli to Dodgers for Eddie Morgan and $45,000.
1961 New York Metropolitan Baseball Club, Inc., receives certificate of membership in NL.

MARCH 7

1924 Pat Moran dies of Bright's disease in spring training.
1950 J.R. Richard born; the six-eight pitcher had been amassing Hall of Fame calibre stats when he suffered a stroke during the 1980 season.
1979 Semi-pro and sandlot umpires used when major league umpires strike.

MARCH 8

1930 Babe Ruth ends his holdout, signing for $80,000; asked why he should earn more than President Hoover, he replied, "Why not? I had a better year."
1942 Dick Allen born.
1966 Stengel elected to Hall of Fame.

MARCH 9

1912 Arky Vaughan born; the Pirate shortstop hit .385 in 1935, an NL level since unequaled.

MARCH 10

1959 Bill Veeck buys control of White Sox for $2.7 million.
1963 Pete Rose, a non-roster player appearing in his first exhibition game, goes 2 for 2, both doubles.

MARCH 11

1953 Fred Toney dies.
1972 Zack Wheat dies.
1976 Larry Gardner dies.

MARCH 12

1930 Vern "Deacon" Law born; he took Cy Young Award honors in 1960.

MARCH 13

1872 Willie Keeler born.
1886 Frank Baker born.
1954 Bobby Thomson, newly acquired by Braves, suffers triple fracture of right ankle in game against Yanks; door opened for 2B Aaron.
1975 Frank Robinson makes debut as majors' first black manager.

MARCH 14

1932 Dodgers trade Ernie Lombardi, Babe Herman, Wally Gilbert to Reds for Tony Cuccinello, Joe Stripp, Clyde Sukeforth.

1954   Aaron starts first exhibition game; got three hits, including homer, vs. Red Sox.
1980   Chuck Klein is elected to the Hall of Fame; the slugging Phils' outfielder recorded 44 assists in 1930.

MARCH 15

1946   Bobby Bonds born; he was the most frequent member of the "30-30" club (homers and steals) and came within one homer of going "40-40," a mark first reached by Oakland's Jose Canseco in 1988.

MARCH 16

1906   Lloyd Waner born; "Little Poison" starred in the Pittsburgh outfield alongside brother Paul ("Big Poison") from 1927 through 1940.

MARCH 17

1919   "Pistol Pete" Reiser born.
1969   St. Louis Cardinals trade Orlando Cepeda to Atlanta for Joe Torre.

MARCH 18

1953   In the first franchise shift in half a century, the Boston Braves announce they are moving to Milwaukee.

MARCH 19

1871   "Iron Man" Joe McGinnity born; five times he pitched both games of doubleheaders and he was still pitching in the minors at age 54.

MARCH 20

1821   William H. Cammeyer born; he created baseball's first enclosed park, the Union Grounds in Brooklyn.
1933   George Altman born; after middling career in U.S., went on to stardom in Japan.
1984   Stan Coveleski dies.

MARCH 21

1976   Toronto granted AL franchise for 1977.
1977   Mark "The Bird" Fidrych, coming off a Rookie of the Year performance, hurts his left knee and never fully recovers.

MARCH 22

1972   Yankees obtain reliever Sparky Lyle from Boston Red Sox for Danny Cater and Mario Guerrero.

MARCH 23

1863   Joe Gunson born; invented catcher's mitt.
1886   Cy Slapnicka born; the peerless "ivory hunter" of his day, he scouted and signed the 16-year-old Bob Feller.

MARCH 24

1893   George Sisler born; twice he hit over .400, and in 1920 he stroked 257 hits, a record.

MARCH 25

1887   Clyde Milan born; the fleet Washington outfielder set an AL record with 88 steals in 1912.
1909   Emil "Dutch" Leonard born.

MARCH 26

1973   George Sisler dies.

MARCH 27

1879   Miller Huggins born.
1902   Name "Cubs" is coined by *Chicago Daily News*.
1906   Toad Ramsey dies; erratic lefty fanned 499 in 1886.
1927   Joe Start dies; "Old Reliable" first baseman played first base at the top grade of competition from 1860 through 1886 spanning the amateur and professional eras.
1938   Luke Appling breaks his leg in an exhibition game with the Cubs; he went on to miss half the season.

MARCH 28

1907   Red Sox manager Chick Stahl commits suicide.
1909   Pitcher Lon Warneke born; the "Arkansas Hummingbird" of the Cubs and Cards was 193-121 lifetime.

MARCH 29

1867   Denton True "Cy" Young born; with 511 career wins, is it any wonder they named an award after him?

MARCH 30

1904   James "Ripper" Collins born; switch-hitting first sacker hit 35 homers in 1934 and led Cardinal batters in World Series.

MARCH 31

1868   Happy Jack Stivetts born; won 20 games five times and hit 35 career homers.

APRIL 1

1914   At the age of 37, Rube Waddell dies; the eccentric lefthander fanned 349 batters in 1904, a record that stood for over 60 years.
1939   Phil Niekro born.
1963   Mets purchase outfielder Duke Snider from Los Angeles Dodgers.
1972   Seattle franchise transfers to Milwaukee.
1982   Walt Terrell and Ron Darling traded from Texas to Mets for Lee Mazilli.

APRIL 2

1870   Hugh Jennings born.
1907   Luke Appling born.
1927   Billy Pierce born; a top AL pitcher in the 1950s who was traded to the Giants in 1962, he took to his new home by going 12-0 at Candlestick Park.

APRIL 3

1974   The Dodgers receive 17-year-old Pedro Guerrero from Cleveland for pitcher Bruce Ellingsen.
1930   Wally Moon born.
1856   Guy Hecker born; as pitcher he won 52 games in 1884 and two years later won AA batting title with mark of .342.

APRIL 4

1974   In the earliest opening in major league history, the Cincinnati Reds defeat the Atlanta Braves 7-6 in 11 innings. In his first time at bat, Henry Aaron hit a three-run homer off Jack Billingham. It was his 714th, tying Babe Ruth's career record.

APRIL 5

1951   Rennie Stennett born; in a nine-inning game on Sep-

tember 16, 1975, he got seven hits in seven trips to the plate.

APRIL 6

1903, 1908 Of only 10 catchers in the Hall of Fame, two were born on this day—Mickey Cochrane in 1903 and Ernie Lombardi in 1908.
1973 Ron Blomberg of the Yankees becomes the first major league designated hitter.
1982 Blizzard in New York cancels Opening Day and next three games.
1871 Boston (NA) wins first game, 41-10

APRIL 7

1873 John McGraw born.
1918 Bobby Doerr born.
1979 Ken Forsch of Houston pitches a no-hit, no-run game against Atlanta to duplicate the no-hitter hurled by his brother Bob of the Cardinals on April 16, 1978.
1984 Jack Morris throws the first no-hitter by a Tiger in 26 years, winning 4-0 over Chicago.

APRIL 8

1969 Montreal Expos defeat Mets, 10-9, in major league baseball's first international game.
1974 At Atlanta, Henry Aaron breaks Babe Ruth's career record by slugging his 715th home run off southpaw Al Downing in the fourth inning.

APRIL 9

1888 Jim "Hippo" Vaughn born.
1913 Ebbets Field opens with the Dodgers losing to the Phillies, 1-0.
1965 The Houston Astrodome opens with an exhibition game between the Astros and Yankees.
1981 Handed the Opening Day assignment when Jerry Reuss was injured, rookie Fernando Valenzuela shuts out the Astros; he went on to win the Rookie and Cy Young Awards.

APRIL 10

1897 Ross Youngs born.
1906 Mike Donlin marries Mabel Hite; they form a vaudeville team, providing a model for future Giant Rube Marquard and his wife, Blossom Seeley.
1913 The Washington Senators defeat the Yankees, 2-1, in their home opener. Walter Johnson allows a run in the first inning, but will not give up another run for 56 consecutive innings.
1950 Ken Griffey born.
1971 Veterans' Stadium in Philadelphia opens.
1976 At Milwaukee, Yanks lead 9-6 into bottom of ninth. Lyle gives up a grand slam to Don Money, but first base ump McKean says he had called timeout before pitch—Milwaukee loses, 9-7.

APRIL 11

1912 Rube Marquard begins 19-game win streak with 18-3 win vs. Brooklyn.
1955 Chuck Tanner hits a homer on first pitch he sees in major leagues.
1962 The New York Mets play their first game and lose, 11-4, to the Cardinals at St. Louis.
1969 Seattle Pilots play their first game— shutting out White Sox, 7-0.

APRIL 12

1880 Addie Joss born.
1909 First game played in what is now known as Connie Mack Stadium.
1916 Tris Speaker traded from Boston to Cleveland for Sam Jones, Fred Thomas, and $50,000.
1980 In the second inning of Milwaukee's 18-1 victory over the Red Sox, Cecil Cooper and Don Money each belt a grand-slam homer.

APRIL 13

1875 Norman "Kid" Elberfeld born.
1914 Baltimore beats Buffalo, 3–2, in first Federal League game.
1916 Babe Adams, Pittsburgh veteran, pitches a one-hitter against the Cardinals.
1953 For the first time in half a century, a new city is represented in the American and National Leagues. The Braves move from Boston to Milwaukee and opened in Cincinnati where Max Surkont set down the Reds 2-0.
1964 Bret Saberhagen born.
1972 First full major league player strike in history ends after 10 days.
1984 Pete Rose gets hit number 4,000— exactly 21 years after his first hit.

APRIL 14

1910 Two one-hit games pitched in American League, Walter Perry Johnson accomplishing the feat for Washington and Frank Smith for Chicago. Frank Baker of the Athletics and Ray Demmitt of the Browns, respectively, kept Johnson and Smith out of the glory circle. One year earlier George Mullin pitched a one-hit game for Tigers against White Sox.
1917 Eddie Cicotte pitches no-hit, no-run game for White Sox against St. Louis, passing three men and having one error behind him.
1917 Ray Bates, Athletics, batting twice in the seventh inning against Charley Jamieson and Yancey Ayers of Washington, drives three men in with a triple and two more with a double—five runs batted in one inning. The Mackmen then make 10 runs, winning 16-4.
1920 Babe Ruth plays his first game with the Yankees. He gets two singles off Scott Perry of the Athletics and muffs a line fly in the eighth that gave the Mackmen two runs and the decision, 3-1.
1941 Pete Rose born.
1969 In the first major league game played outside the United States, the Montreal Expos defeat St. Louis, 8-7, at Jarry Park.

APRIL 15

1909 Fans discover that the "K" in Leon Ames' name stands for Kalamity. The Giant pitcher retires the Superbas for nine innings without a hit, but New York cannot make a run for him and the game lasts four more innings. Brooklyn, with Kaiser Wilhelm pitching, wins 3-0. The New York outfielders did not have a putout. Six years later Rube Marquard blanked Brooklyn in hits and runs, winning over lefthander Nap Rucker, 2-0.
1947 Jackie Robinson plays his first major league game at first base for the Dodgers. He goes 0 for 3 at bat, but scores the deciding run in a 5-3 victory over the Boston Braves at

Brooklyn. He becomes the first black to appear in the majors since 1884.

1958   Big league ball comes to California as the Giants defeat the Dodgers in their home opener at Seals Stadium in San Francisco.

1968   Astros and Mets play 23-1/2 innings of scoreless ball before bobble by Al Weis leads to Houston run in 24th frame.

APRIL 16

1887   No one had ever hit a homer in in his first major league at-bat; this day, two American Association rookies— Mike Griffin of Baltimore and George "White Wings" Tebeau of Cincinnati—accomplish the feat.

1895   Phillies, managed by Arthur Irwin, stop off at Hagerstown, Md. to play an exhibition game and make 46 hits for a total of 92 bases, including 14 home runs.

1898   Grandstand at Sportsman's Park, St. Louis, destroyed by fire while Cardinals were playing Cubs. About 40 persons are seriously hurt in stampede to get out of the grounds.

1903   Paul Waner born.

1906   John Lush, Phillies, pitches a freak game against New York, passing and fanning 10 men. He won 4-2.

1918   The Pittsburgh Pirates, in their first game of the year, are held to one hit—a double by Casey Stengel in the fourth inning. Pete Schneider pitched for the Reds.

1935   Babe Ruth makes his National League debut with a single and home run for the Boston Braves.

1940   Bob Feller of Indians pitches history's only Opening Day no-hitter.

APRIL 17

1820   Alexander Joy Cartwright, Jr., was born on this day; in 1845 he was a principal organizer of the Knickerbocker Base Ball Club of New York.

1892   The first Sunday game in the National League is played between Cincinnati and St. Louis.

1898   Bobby Mathews dies.

1908   White Sox almost live up to their names of Hitless Wonders. Rube Waddell of the Browns gives them just one blow, this being the product of Jake Atz.

1915   Fritz Maisel, Yankees, steals his way from first to the plate in the ninth inning of game with Athletics.

1953   Mickey Mantle of Yankees blasts longest measured home run, clearing left field wall in Washington for flight of 565 feet.

1964   Pittsburgh's Willie Stargell hits the first home run at Shea Stadium.

APRIL 18

1880   Sam Crawford born.

1890   Brooklyn and Syracuse, of the American Association, play a nine inning game in which 43 runs were scored, a record for their league. Brooklyn won, 22-21, getting the deciding run in the ninth.

1901   Jimmy Sheckard of the Superbas, is hissed by Philadelphia fans every time he bats because he had jumped from American to National League. In spite of the hostile crowd, Sheckard whacks the Phillie pitchers for three triples. Sheckard's leap earned him the appellation of "Grasshopper Jim".

1905   George Winter, Red Sox, holds Washington to one hit, made by infielder Mullin, but is beaten, 1-0.

1923   Yankee Stadium opens, with Babe Ruth dedicating it by clouting three-run homer for 4-1 victory over Boston.

1946   Jim "Catfish" Hunter born; he won 20 or more games in five straight years, taking Cy Young honors in 1974.

APRIL 19

1890   Opening games of first and only season of Players League played. Buffalo, with Connie Mack catching, defeat Cleveland, 23-2, the Bisons getting 16 passes from pitcher Henry Gruber.

1890   Re-entering the National League, Cincinnati Reds are beaten in their first championship game by Chicago, 5-4, Cyclone Jim Duryea pitching against Bill Hutchison.

1897   Giants play exhibition game with Elizabeth, N.J., team and win, 40-1. George Van Haltren cracks out seven hits.

1900   Detroit Americans held hitless by Morris F. "Doc" Amole of Buffalo.

1909   Bucky Walters born.

1981   The International League game between Rochester and Pawtucket which started at 8:00 the previous evening is suspended at 4:07 on Easter morning after 32 innings, with the score tied at 2-2. When the game was resumed on June 23, Pawtucket scored one run in the 33rd to win. It was easily the longest game in organized baseball history.

APRIL 20

1892   Dave Bancroft born.

1903   Yankees, playing first game in American League, are beaten by Washington 3-1, as Jack Chesbro lost to Al "The Curveless Wonder" Orth.

1910   Addie "The Human Slat" Joss of the Indians retires the White Sox without a hit, winning over Doc White, 1-0. He passed two men and one error, a fumble by Bradley, was made behind him. Joss had 10 assists.

1912   Fenway Field, Boston, opens, Red Sox winning in 11 innings from Yankees, 7-6. Benny Kauff then played his first game in the major leagues.

1912   White Sox and Browns play 15 innings to a scoreless draw, Jim Scott pitching against George Baumgardner.

1920   Manager Gavvy Cravath of the Phils inserts himself as a pinch hitter and beat New York with a three-run homer, his last in the majors.

1961   Don Mattingly born.

APRIL 21

1887   Joe McCarthy born.

1898   Bill Duggleby, Phillies, batting for the first time in a major league game, hits ball over right field fence with bases full against Cy Seymour of Giants, a feat without precedent or antecedent.

1910   Emery ball introduced to American League by Russ Ford of Yankees. With it he wins over Athletics, 1-0 and fans nine men, striking out "Home Run" Harry Davis all four times he appears.

APRIL 22

1876   Boston beats Philadelphia, 6-5, in first NL game, with Jim (Orator) O'Rourke making first hit.

1898   Pair of no-hit games in National League, Jay Hughes of Baltimore accomplishing feat against Boston and Theo Breitenstein of Cincinnati against Pittsburgh. This is Hughes' second game in the majors. In the first he had blanked Washington.

1905   Free game for 30,000 Highlanders (Yankee) fans re-

sults from club's failure to issue rainchecks previous day, when storm broke early.

1915 Napoleon Lajoie, second basing for the Athletics, against Boston, has five errors, managing to make one putout and three assists cleanly.

1915 Pinstripes appear on Yankee uniform for the first time.

1918 Mickey Vernon born.

1970 Tom Seaver of the Mets fans the last 10 Padres he faces for a 2-1 victory. He gave up only two hits while whiffing a total of 19 San Diego players.

APRIL 23

1900 Jim Bottomley born.

1916 Jack Graney, Indians, makes two home runs in game with Browns off Earl Hamilton and Jim Park.

1919 For the fifth time Walter Johnson starts the season by pitching a shutout. He wins over Scott Perry of Athletics in 13 innings, 1-0.

1921 Warren Spahn born.

1952 Hoyt Wilhelm of the Giants wins his first major league game, and in the process hits a home run in his first at bat, followed by a triple. Although he pitched in 1,069 games after this day, he never hit another homer or triple.

1983 Milt Wilcox's perfect game at Chicago is ruined on a two-out ninth inning single.

APRIL 24

1894 Baltimore Orioles, taking their last turn at bat against Boston, are behind, 3-1. Before they conclude their part of the ninth, McGraw, Jennings & Co. make 14 runs off Jack Stivetts and Kid Nichols, the last named making a fizzle of his rescue attempt.

1894 Howard Ehmke born; a questionable infield single in September 1923 was all that kept him from pitching successive no-hitters.

1909 Walter Johnson, who the year before had pitched three shutouts in four days against the Highlanders, loses to them by a score of 17–0.

1915 Pitcher Babe Ruth is withdrawn from the game with Philadelphia by manager Bill Carrigan so that Hick Cady— lifetime, one home run—could pinch hit for him.

1964 Sandy Koufax strikes out 18 Chicago Cubs.

APRIL 25

1876 Chicago shuts out Louisville, 4-0 in Chicago's first National League game and the NL's first whitewash. Pitcher-manager A. G. Spalding blasts three hits.

1884 John "Pop" Lloyd born; the finest shortstop to come out of the Negro Leagues, he was referred to as the "black Wagner."

1901 George Stallings' Detroit Tigers make AL debut by scoring 10 runs in last inning to beat Milwaukee, 14-13.

APRIL 26

1900 Hack Wilson born.

1904 Tyrus Raymond Cobb, Tiger manager, plays his first game in organized baseball with Augusta, Ga., club of South Atlantic League against Columbia, S.C., at Augusta. Batting seventh he made a double and a home run in four at bats.

1905 Jack McCarthy, Cub center fielder, figures in three double plays in game with Pirates, nailing three men who tried to score. No other major league outfielder ever has started three double plays in the same game.

APRIL 27

1896 Rogers Hornsby born; between 1921 and 1925, he averaged better than .400 while topping that mark three times.

1912 Keen students of the calendar, the Pirates make 27 hits off three Cincinnati pitchers and win, 23-4.

1916 Enos Slaughtor born.

1944 Jim Tobin of the Braves pitches a no-hitter over the Dodgers at Boston, winning 2-0. He also hits a homer.

1947 Babe Ruth Day is held at Yankee Stadium.

APRIL 28

1898 National League game scheduled for Philadelphia has to be called off on account of snow.

1901 White Sox unable to make anything except singles off Bock Baker of Cleveland— but they gathered 23 of them.

1901 Tigers, the original cardiac kids, for fourth time in succession since their debut, get runs necessary to defeat Hugh Duffy's Milwaukee team in the last inning.

1927 Charlie Maxwell born; Tiger outfielder specialized in hitting homers on Sunday.

1934 Goose Goslin of Tigers grounds into four double plays in one game.

APRIL 29

1876 First extra inning game played in National League, Hartford wins from Boston, 3-2 in 10 rounds.

1906 New York sees its first Sunday major league game as the Yanks and A's play a benefit for victims of the San Francisco earthquake.

1911 Yankee pitchers—Jim Vaughn and Jack Quinn— pitch seven balls to Stuffy McInnis, Athletics. Off these he made five singles, hitting the first pitch three times and the second twice.

1933 Luke Sewell of Washington Senators tags out two Yankees at home on the same play.

1934 Luis Aparicio born.

1981 Steve Carlton gets strikeout number 3,000.

APRIL 30

1887 James F. "Tip" O'Neill of the Browns, batting three times in the fifth and sixth innings against Morrison of Cleveland, makes two home runs and a triple. In other parts of the contest he obtained a single and a double. O'Neill ran up a batting average of .492 in the American Association that year, when players were allowed four strikes, and a base on balls was counted as a base hit. It was then that the term "safe hit" crept into the pastime—to distinguish real hits from those obtained on passes.

1922 Charlie Robertson of White Sox pitches last perfect game in majors until Don Larsen's masterpiece in the 1956 World Series.

1961 Willie Mays wallops four home runs against the Braves in Milwaukee.

MAY 1

1920 Brooklyn Superbas (today's Dodgers) and Boston Braves, playing in Boston, go 26 innings before quitting with score tied, 1-1. Leon Cadore and Joe Oeschger go full distance for contesting teams. Also on this day, Babe Ruth made his first home run as a Yankee, hitting it off Herb Pennock of Boston.

1926 Satchel Paige debuts for Chattanooga in the Negro Southern League.
1959 Thirty-nine-year-old Early Wynn of the White Sox is the whole show against the Red Sox as he pitches a one-hitter, strikes out 14, and hit a double and home run for a 1-0 victory.

MAY 2

1887 Eddie Collins born.
1909 Honus Wagner steals his way from first to the plate in the first inning in game with Cubs.
1917 The unique double no-hit game, in which Fred Toney keeps the Cubs hitless for nine innings and Jim Vaughn does the same thing to the Reds. In the tenth, Vaughn, weakening, is reached for hits by Larry Kopf and Jim Thorpe and Cincinnati wins, 1-0.
1920 No rest for the weary Superbas. They play and lose a 13-inning, 4-3 game with Phillies, after having figured in a 26-inning tie on previous afternoon with Braves.
1939 Lou Gehrig benches himself after playing 2,130 consecutive games.
1947 Davey Lopes born.
1954 Stan Musial sets major league mark with five homers in doubleheader against Giants (later tied by Nate Colbert).

MAY 3

1891 Eppa Rixey born.
1905 Red Ruffing born.
1920 Superbas become undisputed long distance champions of world by figuring in their third extra-inning game in three successive days. This time they lose to Boston in 19 innings, bringing their three-day total to 58. In each game Brooklyn used only one pitcher and so did the opposition, Leon Cadore and Joe Oeschger being paired in the first, Burleigh Grimes and George Smith in the second and Sherrod Smith and Dana Fillingim in the third.
1950 Baffled by new rule, Vic Raschi of Yanks commits record number of four balks in one game, two less than the league record at that time for a full season.

MAY 4

1871 In first game of first professional league, the National Association, Fort Wayne's Bobby Mathews tosses a 2-0 shutout at the Forest City nine of Cleveland.
1889 Jerry Denny, Indianapolis, makes six hits in six times at bat off Jim Galvin and Harry Staley of Pittsburgh. Hoosiers win game, 17-12.
1969 Astros turn seven double plays against San Francisco.

MAY 5

1904 Cy Young, in the midst of a 24 inning hitless streak, hurls a perfect game against the A's.
1917 Ernie Koob, Browns, pitches hitless game against White Sox and wins, 1-0 over Eddie Cicotte, who three weeks previously had prevented St. Louis from getting a hit.

MAY 6

1915 Babe Ruth starts on his home run career in the American League, hitting for the circuit in a game with the Yankees against Jack Warhop.
1917 Bob Groom of the St. Louis Browns imitates moundmate Ernie Koob and pitches a no-hit game against the Chicago White Sox— the second day in succession against this team and a major league record.

1931 Willie Mays born.
1953 Bobo Holloman of Browns pitches no-hitter in his first major league start, but proves flash in pan and is sold to Toronto 11 weeks later.
1982 Gaylord Perry gets win number 300.

MAY 7

1906 Bill Donovan, Detroit pitcher, steals his way around the bases in one inning on catcher Fritz Buelow of Cleveland.
1925 Pittsburgh shortstop Glenn Wright makes unassisted triple play.
1930 Dick Williams born.
1959 Roy Campanella Night at the Los Angeles Coliseum; record U.S. crowd of 93,103 witnesses exhibition game between Dodgers and Yankees.

MAY 8

1858 Dan Brouthers born.
1878 Outfielder Paul Hines of Providence pulls a triple play against Boston; for over a century, historians disputed whether it was unassisted or not.
1906 Athletics, crippled, have to play a pitcher in left against Red Sox. That pitcher—Chief Bender—hits two home runs.
1968 Jim "Catfish" Hunter of Oakland pitches a perfect game against the Twins. There was not even a tough fielding play behind Hunter, who fanned 11. He also got three hits and four RBIs.

MAY 9

1901 Earl Moore of Cleveland holds White Sox hitless for nine innings, but in tenth the Chicagoans get two hits and win the game, 4 to 2.
1961 Jim Gentile of the Orioles hits consecutive grand slam homers in the first and second innings.
1961 Tony Gwynn born.

MAY 10

1868 Ed Barrow born; he headed the Yankees for 24 years.
1910 Heinie Zimmerman of the Cubs, in a game with the Giants, has as many errors at short as hits—four.

MAY 11

1894 Hugh Jennings, Baltimore, is hit three times by pitched balls in a game with Philadelphia by Wilfred "Kid" Carsey. Amos Rusie hit him in the temple in 1897 and nearly killed him.
1897 Charles A. "Duke" Farrell, catching for Washington, throws out eight of 10 Orioles who tried to steal second—a major league record.
1903 Charlie Gehringer born.
1904 Cy Young leads Red Sox to 1-0 victory over Detroit in 15 innings, his pitching rival being Ed Killian.
1984 Tigers run away to best start in major league history at 26-4.

MAY 12

1871 Highest shutout score in game between professional teams—Mutuals of New York defeat Resolutes of Elizabeth, N.J., 39-0.
1910 Chief Bender almost pitches a perfect game for the Athletics against Cleveland. He slips up by passing Terry Turner in the sixth. Ira Thomas nailed Turner when he tried

to steal, so only 27 men faced the Chippewa Chieftain.
1925 Yogi Berra born.
1955 Sam "Toothpick" Jones of the Cubs pitches a no-hit, no-run game. In the ninth against Pittsburgh, he walks the bases full and then fans the next three batters.
1957 Lou Whitaker born.
1970 Ernie Banks gets home run number 500.

MAY 13

1911 Grover Cleveland Alexander, relieving George Chalmers in the ninth inning of game against Cincinnati, pitches eight hitless rounds. Phillies win in 16th, 5-4.
1967 Mickey Mantle hits home run number 500.

MAY 14

1881 Ed Walsh born.
1899 Earle Combs born.
1913 Walter Johnson, after keeping his opponents away from the plate for 56 innings, is scored on by the Browns, who had beaten him the year before, after he had won 16 straight.
1936 Dick Howser born.
1942 Tony Perez born.

MAY 15

1952 Having pitched four no-hitters in minors, Virgil Trucks of Tigers hurls his first in majors (against Senators) this day and adds another before season is out (August 25 against Yankees).
1953 George Brett born.

MAY 16

1894 While Oriole third baseman John McGraw and Beantown first baseman Tommy Tucker engage in fist fight on baselines, fire breaks out in bleachers and burns down Boston ballpark along with 170 other buildings.
1905 Cubs sustain their third straight shutout at hands of Giants, Red Ames winning over them, 4-0. Dummy Taylor beat them on May 13, 1-0 and Joe McGinnity conquered them the next day, 4-0.
1955 Jack Morris born.
1965 Nineteen-year-old Jim Palmer wins his first major league victory and hits his first homer as the Orioles beat the Yanks 7-5.

MAY 17

1888 After having struck out 11 Pirates on May 15, Tim Keefe, Giants, goes back at them with one day's rest and whiffs 11 more.

MAY 18

1897 William "Scrappy" Joyce of Giants makes four triples in game with Pittsburgh— only time this has been done in major league history.
1912 Rallying behind the suspended Ty Cobb, Detroit players refuse to play; a makeshift team, assembled to avoid forfeit of the franchise, loses to the A's, 24-2.
1937 Brooks Robinson born.
1946 Reggie Jackson born.

MAY 19

1910 Cy Young wins number 500.
1968 After hitting 10 home runs in six games, Frank Howard of the Senators is stopped by Detroit's Earl Wilson.

MAY 20

1921 Hal Newhouser born; he led the AL in wins in 1944-46 with 29, 25, and 26.
1931 Ken Boyer born.
1946 Bobby Murcer born.
1983 Wildfire Schulte dies.

MAY 21

1902 Earl Averill born.
1952 Nineteen successive Dodger batters reach base in the first inning against Cincinnati.

MAY 22

1901 Frank "Noodles" Hahn, Cincinnati lefthander, fans 16 Boston batters in nine innings, whiffing everybody in the lineup.
1902 Al Simmons born; for 11 years in a row he batted over .300 and drove in more than 100 runs, and for five years in a row topped 200 hits.

MAY 23

1883 Snorkey Base Ball Club of Philadelphia defeats Hoppers, 34-11. Snorkeys are one-armed, Hoppers one-legged. All but one man are Reading RR employees who lost a limb in work-related accidents.
1888 Zack Wheat born.
1890 Large day for New York teams. The Giants stole 17 bases on catcher Bill Wilson of Pittsburgh and the Players League team, with Hank O'Day pitching, won from Chicago, 23-9.
1895 Louisville has to forfeit a game to Brooklyn because the supply of balls is exhausted.

MAY 24

1918 Third 19 inning game played in American League, Cleveland winning from New York, 3-2 on Joe Wood's second home run of contest. Stanley Coveleski pitched for winners, Allen Russell and George Mogridge for losers.
1935 In first major league night game, Reds beat Phils by 2-1 at Crosley Field, Cincinnati.
1936 Tony Lazzeri, batting eighth for the Yanks, drives in 11 runs with one triple and three home runs—two of them grand slams—in a 25-2 rout of the A's.

MAY 25

1935 Babe Ruth hits last major league homer, off Guy Bush in Pittsburgh, clearing right field roof after having hit two homers earlier in same game.

MAY 26

1913 Walter Johnson retires Athletics in sixth inning on three pitched balls.
1959 Harvey Haddix of Pittsburgh pitches 12 perfect innings before losing to Milwaukee 1-0 in the 13th on an error, a sacrifice, and Joe Adcock's double.

MAY 27

1885 Giants run up their highest shutout score and one of the largest on record as they defeat Buffalo, 24-0. Hall of Famer Jim Galvin pitched for the losers, Hall of Famer Mickey Welch for the winners.
1888 William H. "Adonis" Terry of Brooklyn Association

team pitches hitless and runless game against Louisville, winning over Toad Ramsey, 4-0.

1937 Carl Hubbell wins his 24th straight game over two seasons, a record, as he comes out of the bullpen to vanquish the Reds, 3-2.

MAY 28

1896 Warren Giles born.

1914 Harry Hooper, Duffy Lewis and Tris Speaker of the Red Sox make triple steal on Rip Hageerman and Fred Carisch of the Indians. Triple steal led to triple squeal and Umpire Oliver Chill banished Birmingham, Carisch, and Ivy Olson from game.

1956 Dale Long of the Pirates connects for his eighth home run in eight consecutive games, a record later tied by Don Mattingly.

MAY 29

1909 Frank Baker smacks the first of his many home runs over the right field wall at Shibe Park.

1916 Giants set all-time record by winning 17th consecutive road game; also won 26 straight at home that year, but finished fourth!

1920 John Lavan, Cardinals, "pulls a John Anderson" in the game with Chicago, stealing third with Jacques Fournier there. Because of this mental lapse the Cubs win, 8-5.

1971 Joe Morgan, Denis Menke, Cesar Geronimo, Jack Billingham, and Ed Armbrister come to Reds from Astros for Lee May, Tommy Helms, and Jimmy Stewart, 1971.

MAY 30

1887 Bill George, lefthanded pitcher of Giants, passes 17 of the Chicagos in a nine inning game.

1894 Robert Lowe, Boston, after being held hitless in morning game by Cincinnati pitchers, takes revenge on "Icebox" Chamberlain in the afternoon by making four home runs (two in one inning) and a single.

1895 Attendance at game in Philadelphia so large, crowd covered most of right field. Dusty Miller, covering that position for the Reds, thus was able to throw out four Phillies at first who drove the ball through the infield.

1922 Max Flack of Cubs and Cliff Heathcote of Cards trade uniforms between A.M. and P.M. games, with both outfielders seeing action in both games of doubleheader.

MAY 31

1899 Charles S. "Chick" Stahl, Boston, makes six hits in six times at bat against Cleveland.

1975 Spoiler Cesar Tovar registers the only hit off Catfish Hunter—the fifth time he has had his team's only hit in a game.

JUNE 1

1895 Roger Connor, St. Louis, batting six times in a game with New York, makes six hits.

1910 Miller Huggins of Cardinals does not have time at bat charged against him in six trips to plate in game with Philadelphia, walking four times and sacrificing twice.

1925 Lou Gehrig pinch hits for Pee Wee Wanninger and starts his 2,130-game playing streak.

1975 Nolan Ryan of the Angels pitches his fourth no-hitter, a 1-0 win over the Orioles. It was his 100th major league victory.

JUNE 2

1864 Wilbert Robinson born.

1890 Ed Delahanty, this day the shortstop of the Cleveland Brotherhood team, makes six hits in six times at bat.

1941 Lou Gehrig dies.

JUNE 3

1851 New York Knickerbockers wear first uniforms—straw hats, blue full-length trousers and white shirts.

1932 Lou Gehrig becomes the first modern player in the century to hit four homers in a game, but the headlines go to John McGraw's resignation as Giant manager.

JUNE 4

1968 Don Drysdale of the Dodgers blanks the Pirates, 5-0, for his sixth straight shutout en route to a record 58 scoreless innings; twenty years later, his mark would be topped by Orel Hershiser.

JUNE 5

1874 Jack Chesbro born; the spitballing righthander set a modern record for wins in a season with 41 in 1904.

1911 In the Boston-Chicago game, reliever Smokey Joe Wood strikes out three pinch hitters in the ninth to secure the win, 5-4.

JUNE 6

1907 Bill Dickey born; the great Yankee receiver caught 100 or more games for 13 years in a row.

JUNE 7

1884 Charlie Sweeney, pitching for Providence, sets a game-strikeout record of 19 that will stand until Roger Clemens tops it in 1986.

1892 Jack Doyle of Cleveland, first pinch hitter in NL, singles.

1906 Cubs beat up Giants, scoring 11 runs in the first inning off Christy Mathewson, Joe McGinnity, and George Ferguson and winning, 19-0.

JUNE 8

1926 Babe Ruth launches what may be the longest home run ever—over 600 feet—and homers again in 11th for 11-9 win at Navin Field.

1950 At Fenway Park, the Red Sox slaughter the Browns 29-4. Bobby Doerr has three homers, Ted Williams and Walt Dropo two each, and Al Zarilla has four doubles.

1961 Eddie Mathews, Henry Aaron, Joe Adcock, and Frank Thomas of Milwaukee hit successive homers in the seventh inning against Cincinnati.

JUNE 9

1903 Pirates, after having blanked their opponents in 57 successive innings, are scored on in the fourth by the Phillies. Kaiser Wilhelm was the pitcher yielding the run.

1914 Honus Wagner becomes first player in modern baseball to get 3,000 hits.

JUNE 10

1890 Pitcher Jack Stivetts, St. Louis Browns, makes two home runs and a pair of singles in an American Association game with Toledo.

1892 Wilbert Robinson of Orioles hits 7 for 7 in a nine inning game, a feat not to be matched for more than eighty years. He also batted in 11 runs, a record topped only by Jim Bottomley's 12 in 1924.
1944 Fifteen-year-old southpaw Joe Nuxhall becomes the youngest to play in the majors in this century.
1959 Rocky Colavito of Cleveland hit four homers against the Orioles.
1981 Pete Rose ties Musial's NL record with his 3,630th hit.

JUNE 11

1879 Roger Bresnahan born; the Hall of Fame catcher came to the majors as a pitcher and threw a shutout in his debut.
1904 Bob Wicker leads Cubs to 1-0 victory over Giants in 12 innings, thus branding Joe McGinnity with his first defeat of the year, following 12 victories in a row.

JUNE 12

1880 J. Lee Richmond, Worcester, retires Cleveland without a hit or run and prevents anyone from reaching first, recording the first perfect game in the major leagues.
1939 National Baseball Museum and Hall of Fame is dedicated at Cooperstown, N.Y., on baseball's proclaimed centennial.

JUNE 13

1851 Jim Mutrie born.
1873 Bill Bergen born; he was so good a receiver that he lasted 11 years despite batting only .170.
1922 Mel Parnell born.

JUNE 14

1870, 1876 Longest winning streak in history snapped as Cincinnati's Red Stockings drop 8-7 decision in 11 innings to Brooklyn's Atlantics. Six years later, George Hall of the Philadelphia Athletics—who on this day in 1870 had been stationed in center field for those same Atlantics—would become the first big leaguer to hit for the cycle.
1912 Clyde "Deerfoot" Milan, Washington, steals five bases in game with Cleveland.
1969 Reggie Jackson of Oakland has his biggest batting day as he knocks in 10 runs with two homers, a double, and two singles against the Red Sox in Boston. Oakland won 21-7.

JUNE 15

1902 Corsicana defeats Texarkana 51-3 in a Texas League game. Nig Clarke of Corsicana hits eight home runs.
1938 Johnny Vander Meer of Reds pitches his second consecutive no-hit, no-run game spoiling Dodgers' arc light opener at Ebbets Field.
1938 Billy Williams born.
1958 Wade Boggs born.

JUNE 16

1881 For the fifth time on record a National League player makes six hits in six times at bat. This player is left fielder Louis Pessano "Buttercup" Dickerson of Worcester, the first Italian-American to play in the majors.
1938 Slugger Jimmie Foxx does not get much chance to hit as the Browns walk him six times in succession. The Red Sox win anyway, 12-8.

JUNE 17

1880 John Montgomery Ward pitches a perfect game for Providence against Buffalo.
1890 Perhaps the first baseball strikes on record is engineered by Jack Clements, one of the few southpaw catchers ever in baseball. Clements, who had caught four games on the preceding Saturday and Monday, refused to play more than one game on this day and thus unilaterally canceled a doubleheader.
1960 Ted Williams hits home run number 500.

JUNE 18

1894 Boston's first inning welcome to Tony Mullane of Baltimore consists of 16 runs, as 21 men come to bat. Mullane takes his lumps until the seventh inning, when he is finally relieved in a 24-7 thrashing.
1907 Andy Coakley, Cincinnati pitcher, cripples two Giants with successive pitches, beaning Roger Bresnahan (who was given last rites as he lay unconscious) and then breaking Dan McGann's right wrist.
1939 Lou Brock born; he broke Ty Cobb's season record for stolen bases with 118 in 1974, and passed him for the lifetime title three years later.
1953 Red Sox rookie Gene Stephens becomes only player in modern history to blast three hits in same inning as Boston raps Tigers for 17 runs in seventh inning.
1975 Another Red Sox rookie, Fred Lynn, drives in 10 runs against Detroit with three homers, a double, and a single; he won both Rookie of the Year and MVP awards.

JUNE 19

1846 The first match game of baseball under Alexander Cartwright's rules is played at the Knickerbockers' grounds in Hoboken, New Jersey.
1903 Lou Gehrig born.
1909 Walter Johnson, in a game against Yankees, turns loose four wild pitches, passes seven men and hit a man, yet wins nevertheless, 7-4.

JUNE 20

1912 Josh Devore, Giants, in ninth inning of game with Braves, steals four bases. New York wins, 21-12, but Boston gets 10 runs in the last inning off Ernie Shore, then making his big-time debut.
1915 St. Louis Browns show up in Detroit without any uniforms. The Tigers lend them their spare uniforms, then whip them, 1-0.
1980 Freddie Patek, one of baseball's smallest players, hits three home runs and a double to lead California in a 20-2 trouncing of the Red Sox in Fenway Park.

JUNE 21

1887 Toad Ramsey fans 17 Cleveland batters in an American Association game at Louisville.
1938 In two successive doubleheaders (four games), Pinky Higgins of the Red Sox bangs out 12 consecutive hits (with two walks interspersed).
1949 Cleveland catcher Jim Hegan pulls unassisted double play.
1964 Jim Bunning pitches a perfect game for the Phillies over the Mets.
1970 Detroit's Cesar Gutierrez goes 7 for 7 in a 12-inning

game with Cleveland; the last to go 7-for-7 was Wilbert Robinson of the Baltimore Orioles in 1892.

JUNE 22

1889 Louisville of the American Association drops its 26th straight game, setting up a major league record that has never been equaled.
1900 Phillies and Superbas play weird game, Quakers forfeiting it in the 11th when they trailed 20-13.
1903 Carl Hubbell born.
1947 Ewell Blackwell almost duplicates the Vander Meer double no-hit record by following his June 18 gem over Boston with 8-1/3 hitless innings against the Dodgers before the bubble bursts.

JUNE 23

1895 George Weiss born.
1915 Bruno Phillip Haas, pitching his first major league game for the Athletics, passes 16 Yankees, makes three wild pitches, and is beaten, 15-7.
1917 Babe Ruth, peeved because Umpire Brick Owens called a ball that gave Ray Morgan, first Washington batter, his base, tries to slug Brick and is put out of the game. Ernie Shore then becomes Boston's pitcher and retires in order the 26 men who face him, plus getting credit for the 27th out when catcher Sam Agnew threw out Morgan trying to steal.
1971 Rick Wise of the Phils hits a home run in the fourth consecutive game that he pitched in June.

JUNE 24

1955 Harmon Killebrew, 18, hits his first major league roundtripper off Billy Hoeft at Griffith Stadium.

JUNE 25

1881 George Gore of Chicago steals seven bases against Providence.

JUNE 26

1901 Red Sox show up unexpectedly in Philadelphia to play a game when they were scheduled to play in Baltimore.
1970 Frank Robinson hits two grand slam homers for the Orioles as they clobber Washington 12-2.

JUNE 27

1876 Diminutive Davy Force (nicknamed "Tom Thumb"), shortstop of the Philadelphia Athletics, becomes the first National Leaguer to garner six hits in a game.
1948 Don Baylor born.
1958 Billy Pierce of the White Sox retires 26 Washington batters in a row before pinch hitter Ed Fitzgerald doubles for the only hit. Pierce wins, 1-0.
1971 Rick Wise of the Phils pitches a no-hitter against the Reds and hits two homers in 4-0 win.
1984 Dwight Evans hits for the cycle.

JUNE 28

1907 Branch Rickey, behind the bat for the Yankees, lets the Senators steal 13 bases.
1917 Lee Magee of the Yankees has four assists from center field in a game with the Athletics.

JUNE 29

1897 Chicago White Stockings set a scoring record for all

time by winning over Louisville, 36-7. Anson's team scores in every inning and knocks out 32 hits.
1936 Harmon Killebrew born.
1956 Pedro Guerrero born.
1968 Jim Northrup of Detroit hits a grand slam, third in five days; he had hit two on June 24.

JUNE 30

1894 Reporting with $500 bonus money pinned to his back pocket, Louisville NL rookie Fred Clarke breaks in with 5 for 5 against Cannonball Gus Weyhing of Phils.
1909 Pittsburgh's Forbes Field opens, with Cubs winning over Pirates, 3-2, as Ed Reulbach nipped Vic Willis.

JULY 1

1857 Roger Connor born.
1861 John Clarkson born.
1902 Rube Waddell, pitching his first game in Philadelphia for Connie Mack, manages a peculiar feat. In three innings—the third, sixth, and ninth—he retires the same three batsmen on strikes, these being Billy Gilbert, Harry Howell, and Jack Cronin. The Rube whiffed 13 Orioles and faced only 27 batters.
1905 Frank Owen, White Sox, pulls Iron Man stunt on Browns, beating them twice, 32-2 and 2-0.
1920 Walter Johnson pitches no-hit game against Boston, Bucky Harris' fumble on Harry Hooper in seventh being only thing that stood between Johnson and a perfect game.
1951 Bob Feller pitches the third no-hitter of his career to tie the record (since broken by Nolan Ryan) of Cy Young and Larry Corcoran, 1951.

JULY 2

1903 Ed Delahanty falls off railway bridge; his body is recovered a week later after being washed over Niagara Falls.
1933 Carl Hubbell of the Giants hurls an 18 inning shutout, allowing Cardinals six hits and no walks.

JULY 3

1941 The Yankees' Joe DiMaggio hits in his 45th straight game, breaking the record set by Willie Keeler in 1897.
1947 Cleveland purchases Larry Doby—first black player in the American League.
1966 Tony Cloninger of Atlanta hits two grand slams, single, drives in nine.

JULY 4

1859 Mickey Welch born.
1905 Athletics win from Reds Sox, 4-2, in 20 innings, Rube Waddell besting Cy Young.
1908 George "Hooks" Wiltse pitches 10 inning no-hit game for Giants against Phillies, winning over George McQuillan, 1-0. Hooks blew his perfect game when, on an 0-2 count, he hit the Phillie pitcher, 27th man to face him, on the arm.
1906 Tightest game to that time (since topped by Sandy Koufax and Bob Hendley in 1965) played by Pirates and Cubs, each team making only one hit. Lefty Leifeld of Bucs loses to Mordecai Brown, 1-0.
1912 Ty Cobb steals second, third, and home in the fifth inning of the opener of a twin bill with St. Louis Browns; Tiger teammate George Mullin throws a no-hitter in nightcap to celebrate his birthday.
1930 George Steinbrenner born.

1939 Jim Tabor of the Red Sox hits two grand slams.

JULY 5

1897 For the seventh time in eight games, Boston plates the winning run in the ninth inning. Philadelphia is their victim this time, as the Beaneaters score five in the final frame to win, 8-5.

1947 Larry Doby breaks color line in American League, pinch hitting for Cleveland Indians against White Sox, 1947.

JULY 6

1891 Steve O'Neill born.

1933 The first All Star Game is played at Comiskey Park, with the AL defeating the NL, 4-2, on Babe Ruth's two-run homer.

1954 Willie Randolph born.

1956 Jim Busby hits second grand slam in two days; these are only two of his 13-year career.

1982 Indian Bob Johnson dies.

JULY 7

1904 Jack Chesbro, Yankees, after winning 14 games in a row, is beaten by Norwood Gibson of Red Sox, 4-1.

1906 Satchel Paige born; 42 years later to the day, he would sign a major league contract with Cleveland.

1911 Joe Wood, pitching for Red Sox, holds Browns to one hit and fans 15 men, losing no-hitter when Burt Shotton cracks a hit in the ninth.

JULY 8

1902 How's this for a debut? Danny Murphy, due to play his first game with Athletics, does not reach park in Boston until after game has started and so only received opportunity to bat six times. He made six hits, including a home run off Cy Young with the bases full.

1912 Rube Marquard, after winning 19 games in a row for the Giants, is stopped by Jimmy Lavender of the Cubs, 7-3.

1941 In most dramatic finish to an All-Star Game, Ted Williams connects off Claude Passeau for a three-run homer with two outs in the ninth to give AL 7-5 win.

JULY 9

1859 Fred Tenney born; first baseman pioneered the 3-6-3 double play.

1951 Harry Heilmann dies.

1955 Willie Wilson born.

1969 The Cubs' Jimmy Qualls singled off the Mets' Tom Seaver with one out in the ninth, breaking up a perfect game.

1986 Red Lucas dies.

JULY 10

1868 Bobby Lowe born; Boston second baseman was first to hit four homers in a game (1894).

1932 Philadelphia's Athletics defeat the Indians, 18-17, in 18 frames; winning pitcher Ed Rommel allows 29 hits and 14 runs in relief, Cleveland's Johnny Burnett gets nine hits.

1935 Paul Hines dies.

1954 Andre Dawson born.

JULY 11

1914 George Herman Ruth plays his first game in the American League. He pitches seven innings for the Red Sox and gets the win over Cleveland.

JULY 12

1911 Ty Cobb scores hitless run in first inning of game with Athletics. After getting pass from Harry Krause, he steals second, third and the plate,

1951 Allie Reynolds, the Super Chief of the Bronx Bombers, no-hits Cleveland, 1-0, the first of two such classics he will throw this year.

JULY 13

1890 Stan Coveleski born.

1900 Frank (Noodles) Hahn, Cincinnati southpaw, no-hits Phillies, 4-0.

1934 Babe Ruth hits home run number 700.

1963 Early Wynn, after struggling through six unsuccessful starts, attains his 300th and final win.

JULY 14

1897 After having made nine hits in nine times at bat the day before in a doubleheader with Louisville, Ed Delahanty of the Phils cracks four more hits in five trips to the plate.

1898 Happy Chandler born.

1969 Joe Niekro of the Padres defeats Atlanta, 1-0; the losing pitcher is his brother Phil, 1969.

JULY 15

1876 St. Louis' George Bradley pitches first NL no-hitter, whipping the Hartford Blues, 2-0.

1901 Christy Mathewson pitches no-hit game against St. Louis.

1969 Rod Carew ties Pete Reiser's single-season record with his seventh steal of home.

JULY 16

1866 Lipman Pike of the Athletics, first Jew in professional baseball, hits six homers (five consecutive) against the Alerts, also of Philadelphia.

1902 After pitching 41 consecutive runless innings, Jack Chesbro of the Pirates is scored on by Boston in the seventh inning—a new record for the National League.

1909 Tigers and Senators, in Detroit, play 18 innings to a runless draw. Ed "Kickapoo" Summers goes entire route for Detroit.

1920 Rube Benton of the Giants tires out Earl Hamilton of the Pirates in a 17 inning pitching battle won by New York by the odd score of 7-0.

1948 Dodger manager Leo Durocher switches to become Giant manager.

JULY 17

1908 Every National League game a shutout. Boston beat Pittsburgh, 4-0; Philadelphia beat St. Louis, 3-0; Cincinnati beat Brooklyn, 2-0; and Chicago beat New York, 1-0.

1917 Lou Boudreau born.

1941 Joe DiMaggio's 56-game hitting streak stopped by Al Smith and Jim Bagby in Cleveland night game, with third baseman Ken Keltner making two great plays against the Yankee Clipper.

1961 Ty Cobb dies.

JULY 18

1882 Ambidextrous hurler Tony Mullane of Louisville pitches with both hands in a major league game at Baltimore.

Normally a righthander, Mullane switches to the left hand in the fourth inning. He does quite well for several innings but eventually loses to Baltimore, 9-8.

JULY 19

1902 John McGraw assumes management of Giants and is beaten by Philadelphia, 4-3.

1909 Neal Ball, Indian shortstop, makes first unassisted triple play in game against Boston. With Charley Wagner running from second and Jake Stahl from first, he takes liner hit by Amby McConnell, touches second, and then tags Stahl.

1910 Cy Young registers his 500th victory in the major leagues when he leads Cleveland to 5-2 win over Washington in 11 innings. No pitcher before Young had won 500 games and no pitcher after him is likely to.

1920 For the fifth time during the year, Babe Ruth hits two home runs in game. Dickie Kerr of the White Sox yields both, one in the fourth and one in the ninth. The first homer is Ruth's 28th and creates a new home run record for the major leagues.

1955 Reliever Babe Birrer of Detroit pitches four innings and connects for two three-run homers.

1960 Juan Marichal breaks in with the Giants by pitching a one-hit shutout, defeating Robin Roberts and the Phillies.

JULY 20

1858 First admission charge to a baseball game (50¢) charged for Brooklyn vs. New York All-Star Game at Fashion Race Course in Long Island.

1901 Heinie Manush born.

JULY 21

1881 Johnny Evers born; the grouchy second sacker was named MVP for his role on the Miracle Braves of 1914.

1886 For the first time on record, a major league team makes 10 runs in an extra inning. The Kansas City Cowboys win over Detroit, 12-2 in 11 rounds, with Charlie Getzien absorbing the late pounding. He was fined $100 for the outcome of the game.

1975 Felix Millan of Mets hits four singles, but each time is wiped out as Joe Torre grounds into a double play.

JULY 22

1893 Jesse "Pop" Haines born; he defeated the Yanks twice in the 1926 World Series, including Game Seven.

JULY 23

1896 Cy Young almost pitches no-hit game against Phillies. With two out in ninth, Ed Delahanty gets his team's first and only blow, a single.

1918 Pee Wee Reese born.

1922 Ray Grimes drives in a run in 17th straight game (27 total).

1936 Don Drysdale born.

1944 Bill Nicholson of Chicago Cubs is ordered intentionally passed with bases filled by New York Giants manager Mel Ott in eighth inning, after he had rocked them with four consecutive homers in two days; though Cubs rally to tie game at 10-all, Giants win, 12-10.

JULY 24

1911 A group of American League All-Stars play the Indians in a benefit game for the late Addie Joss.

1911 Owen Wilson of the Pirates, who next year would hit a record 36 triples, hits three in one game against Brooklyn.

1983 George Brett hits his "pine tar" home run vs. Yankees.

JULY 25

1883 Charles Radbourn, Providence Grays, sends the Clevelands down to a hitless and runless defeat, winning over One-Armed Daily, 8-0. One error was made behind him, he struck out six men and passed no one.

1913 Relieving Tom Hughes in the fourth inning, Walter Johnson keeps the Browns to one run and seven hits in 11⅓ rounds and fans 16 of them.

1918 Walter Johnson wins over St. Louis, 1-0, in 15 innings, Allan Sothoron pitching against him.

1930 The A's come up with a triple steal in the first inning and again in the fourth against Cleveland. This is the only time two triple steals were achieved in one game.

JULY 26

1876 Cal McVey goes 6 for 7, as he did day before; this gives him 15 hits over three games.

1923 Hoyt Wilhelm born.

1928 Bob Meusel hits for cycle for third time in career, a record tied only by Babe Herman, who did it all three times in 1931.

1933 Fired as Card manager the previous day, Rogers Hornsby signs to manage Browns, so he doesn't even have to move out of his apartment in St. Louis.

JULY 27

1880 Joe Tinker born.

1885 John Clarkson pitches no-hit game for Chicago against Providence.

1918 Harry Heitman debuts with the Dodgers by yielding hits to the first four men to face him; he leaves the park, enlists in the Navy, and never pitches in the majors again.

1946 Rudy York hits two grand slams.

JULY 28

1875 Joe Borden of the Boston Red Stockings throws baseball's first no-hitter, defeating the Chicago White Stockings, 4-0 at Boston.

1949 Vida Blue born.

1954 Jim Bagby, Sr. dies; he won 31 games for the champion Indians of 1920.

1986 Joe Oeschger dies.

JULY 29

1886 Toad Ramsey, Louisville lefty, one-hits Baltimore while fanning 16 of his 499 victims that year.

JULY 30

1889 Casey Stengel born.

1959 Willie McCovey, just up from Phoenix, collects four hits in four trips in his debut with the San Francisco Giants. His hits included two triples in a 7-2 triumph over the Phillies, and they came off no patsy— future Hall of Famer Robin Roberts.

JULY 31

1891 Amos Rusie, Giants, no-hits Brooklyn.

1910 The Cubs have to stop play in their game with the Cardinals at the end of the seventh to catch a train, possibly

costing King Cole a no-hit contest. He didn't give any blows in the seven innings that were played and no men were left on bases, four who walked being erased either on double plays or trying to steal.

1922 Hank Bauer born.
1954 Joe Adcock of Milwaukee unloads on the Dodgers for a record 18 total bases—four homers and a two-bagger.
1975 Max Flack dies.

AUGUST 1

1903 Only one New York Highlander—Kid Elberfeld—is able to get hits off Rube Waddell of Athletics. He raps four hits while the rest of his teammates are fanning 13 times. New York wins, 3-2.
1954 Joe Adcock's slugging rampage of previous day is followed by his beaning by Clem Labine at Ebbets Field.
1972 Nate Colbert of San Diego drives in 13 runs in a doubleheader victory on five homers and two singles.
1978 Pete Rose's hitting streak is halted at 44 games, tying Willie Keeler's NL mark.

AUGUST 2

1979 Yankee catcher Thurman Munson dies in the crash of a plane he was piloting at the Canton, Ohio, airport. He was only 32.

AUGUST 3

1894 Harry Heilmann born.
1930 Smokey Joe Williams of the Homestead Grays beat Chet Brewer of the Kansas City Monarchs, 1-0 in 12 innings. Williams gave up only one hit and fanned 27.
1948 Satchel Paige makes first major league start.
1960 Detroit trades manager Jimmy Dykes to Cleveland for manager Joe Gordon.

AUGUST 4

1867 Jake Beckley born.
1884 Jim Galvin pitches no-hit game for Buffalo against Detroit.
1910 Jack Coombs, Athletics, and Ed Walsh, White Sox, have 16 inning battle in which no runs are scored. Philadelphia's star allowed three hits and fanned 18 men; Chicagoan permitted six blows and whiffed 10.
1962 Roger Clemens born.
1982 Outfielder Joel Youngblood knocks in the winning run in the New York Mets' 7-4 victory over the Cubs in Chicago. In the course of the day-game he is traded to the Montreal Expos, who are playing that night in Philadelphia. Youngblood caught a plane for Philly and appeared in right field for the Expos in the fourth inning. He later contributes a single. He becomes the only person to play (and also collect hits) for two teams in two different cities in the same day.

AUGUST 5

1890 Cy Young pitches his first game in National League, turning in 8-1 victory for Cleveland over Chicago.
1931 Tommy Bridges of the Tigers retires the first 26 Senators before pinch hitter Dave Harris gets a bloop single. Bridges wins, 13-0.

AUGUST 6

1884 After having made two home runs the previous day off Jim McCormick of Cleveland, Adrian Anson of Chicago hits three circuit drives in succession off Sam Moffett—a total of five homers in two successive days.

AUGUST 7

1887 Bill McKechnie born; he was the only NL skipper to win pennants with three different clubs.
1906 Umpire James E. Johnstone barred from Polo Grounds by New York management; game forfeited to Cubs.

AUGUST 8

1903 For the second time in eight days, Joe McGinnity pitches two games for Giants. He defeats Brooklyn twice, scores being 6-1 and 4-3, and allows 13 hits.
1936 Frank Howard born.

AUGUST 9

1887 Charley Buffinton pitches one-hit game against Chicago. Two days before, he had limited Indianapolis to one safety.
1889 Pittsburgh defeats Washington, 15-3, Billy Sunday, famous evangelist, making four of the winners' runs and stealing four bases on the Senators' catcher—Connie Mack.
1906 Jack Taylor of Cardinals extends his incredible pitching streak of complete games to 187 (plus 15 relief appearances in which he needed no help). Incredibly, his streak began on June 13, 1901—more than five years distant.
1975 Davey Lopes of the Dodgers steals his 32nd consecutive base without being caught in a win over the Mets. This broke Max Carey's 1922 record. Lopes tacked on six more steals before being nipped on August 24.

AUGUST 10

1933 Rocky Colavito born.
1944 Red Barrett of the Boston Braves throws only 58 pitches in a complete-game shutout of the Reds.

AUGUST 11

1907 In the second game of a twin bill, shortened by agreement, Ed Karger of the Cardinals pitches a seven inning perfect game against Boston.

AUGUST 12

1880 Christy Mathewson born.
1892 Ray Schalk born.
1966 Art Shamsky of the Reds comes off the bench to pinch hit in the eighth and hits a home run. He stays in the game and connects again in the 10th and 11th innings, but Cincinnati still loses to Pittsburgh.

AUGUST 13

1906 Jack Taylor is knocked out of the box by Brooklyn in the third frame, ringing a close to his streak of of 1,727 consecutive innings without requiring relief.
1917 Sid Gordon born.
1930 Wilmer "Vinegar Bend" Mizell born.
1940 Pitcher Tony Cloninger born.

AUGUST 14

1888 Tim Keefe is beaten by Cubs, 4-2, after winning 19 straight.
1930 Earl Weaver born.
1958 Vic Power, Cleveland first baseman, steals home twice; he stole only one other base all year.

He connected against the Angels, who beat the Yankees, 4-3.

AUGUST 15

1859   Charles Comiskey born.
1886   Guy Hecker, Louisville, scores seven runs in game with Baltimore that Colonels win, 22-5. He bats seven times and registers three home runs, two doubles and one single. Guy pitched this game, allowing four hits.
1916   Babe Ruth wins a 13 inning pitching battle with Walter Johnson, 1-0, Jack Barry's third hit of the day sending in the only run.
1926   Babe Herman doubles into a double play, and though three Dodgers wind up at third on the play, Herman gets credit for driving in game's winning run against Braves.

AUGUST 23

1922   George Kell born.
1982   With a reputation for doctoring the ball which dated back many years, 43-year-old Seattle pitcher Gaylord Perry is ejected in the seventh inning for throwing a spitball against the Red Sox.

AUGUST 16

1948   Babe Ruth dies of cancer at age of 53.

AUGUST 24

1852   Jim "Orator" O'Rourke born; he caught a complete big-league game (the Giants' 1904 pennant clincher) at the age of 52.
1887   Harry Hooper born.
1923   Carl Mays of Yanks beats A's for 23rd consecutive time, a streak that began on August 30, 1918, when he was with the Red Sox.

AUGUST 17

1882   Behind pitcher John Ward and right fielder Hoss Radbourn, who hit the game-winning homer, Providence beats Detroit, 1-0, in 18 innings.
1920   Ray Chapman, Cleveland shortstop, becomes lone casualty in major league history, dying from accidental beaning by Carl Mays the previous day.

AUGUST 25

1889   Brooklyn and Cincinnati go to Hamilton, Ohio, to play a Sunday game, where they manage to play 3-1/3 innings before the cops hauled them in. Each Sabbath violator was fined $8.85.
1894   Chicago catcher Pop Schriver catches ball thrown by Clark Griffith from top of Washington Monument, 555 feet high.
1906   White Sox, after winning 19 in a row, are stopped by Washington.
1946   Rollie Fingers born.

AUGUST 18

1893   Burleigh Grimes born.
1934   Roberto Clemente born.
1960   Ron Darling born.
1965   Henry Aaron of the Braves hits a Curt Simmons pitch on top of the pavilion roof at Sportsman's Park, St. Louis, for an apparent home run. However, umpire Chris Pelekoudas calls him out for being out of the batter's box when he connected.

AUGUST 26

1916   Joe Bush, Athletics, pitches hitless and runless ball against Cleveland, Jack Graney, first batter, who walked, being only man to reach base.
1935   Zeke Bonura, of all people, steals home in the 15th frame to give White Sox win over Yanks, 9-8.

AUGUST 19

1880   Larry Corcoran pitches no-hit game for Chicago against Boston.
1911   After having won 22 straight games from Cincinnati, Christy Mathewson is beaten by them, 7-4. His conqueror is Art Fromme.
1951   Eddie Gaedel, 43-inch midget, draws walk as pinch hitter for Browns.

AUGUST 27

1897   Roger Bresnahan, later a Hall of Fame catcher, makes his debut as an 18-year-old pitcher for Washington. He shut out St. Louis 3-0 on six hits.
1911   Ed Walsh pitches no-hit game for White Sox against Red Sox; Clyde Engle, who walked, is the one man to reach first.
1943   Lou Pinella born.
1982   Rickey Henderson not only breaks Lou Brock's season stolen base record of 118, but swipes three more bases in the A's 5-4 loss at Milwaukee. This gives Henderson 122 thefts in 127 games.

AUGUST 20

1886   Double one-hit game in American Association, Kilroy pitching for Baltimore and Miller for Athletics.
1908   Al Lopez born; in 17 years at the helm of the Indians and White Sox, he finished first or second 12 times.
1944   Graig Nettles born.
1945   Tommy Brown, 17-year-old shortstop of the Dodgers, becomes the youngest major league player to hit a home run, smacking one off Preacher Roe of the Pirates.

AUGUST 28

1909   Queerest one-hit game on record in majors: William Denton "Dolly" Gray, Washington, pitches it against White Sox and is beaten, 6-4. He gives eight bases on balls in the second, of which seven come in succession, and forces in five runs. Pat Dougherty's scratch hit over Bob Unglaub's head, opening third inning, was Chicago's lone blow.
1926   Emil Levsen of the Indians pitches two complete game wins over the Red Sox, 6-1 and 5-1. He did not fan a batter in either game.

AUGUST 21

1926   Ted Lyons of the White Sox pitches a 6-0 no-hitter over the Red Sox in one hour and seven minutes.

AUGUST 22

1911   Josh Devore of Giants raps five hits— each on the first pitch.
1961   Roger Maris, en route to a new home run record, becomes the first player to hit his 50th home run in August.

AUGUST 29

1896   Curt Welch dies; 10 years earlier, he stole home in the

bottom of the tenth to win the World Series for the St. Louis Browns.

1973   Nolan Ryan of the Angels gives up one tainted hit in a 5-0 win over the Yankees. Two Angel infielders play Alphonse and Gaston with Thurman Munson's pop fly, and it drops between them.

AUGUST 30

1899   Kiki Cuyler born.
1905   Ty Cobb plays his first game with Detroit, hitting a double off Jack Chesbro of the Yankees.
1918   Ted Williams born.

AUGUST 31

1875   Eddie Plank born.
1894   Sliding Billy Hamilton, Phillies, steals seven bases in eight inning game with Washington, tying George Gore's National League record.
1903   For the third time inside of a month, Joe McGinnity pitches and wins two games for New York. Philadelphia is beaten by scores of 4-1 and 9-2.
1935   Frank Robinson born.
1937   Rudy York of the Tigers hits his 17th and 18th home runs of the month to set a new record; Detroit beats the Washington Senators, 12-3.
1950   Gil Hodges of the Dodgers hits four homers and a single and bats in nine runs in a 19-3 rout of the Braves at Brooklyn.

SEPTEMBER 1

1890   Pirates beaten three times in one day by Brooklyn—in morning, 10-9, though they score nine runs in the ninth, and in afternoon, 3-2 and 8-4. All three games go nine innings.
1900   Hub Pruett born; the mediocre rookie southpaw gained fame with the Browns in 1922 by fanning Ruth in 10 of the Babe's first 11 at-bats against him.
1912   Smokey Joe Wood of the Red Sox beats Walter Johnson of the Senators, 1-0, in a specially arranged pitching duel at Boston. This was the 14th straight win for Wood; Johnson had won 16 straight earlier in the season. When the season ended, Wood had 34 wins, Johnson 32.
1931   Lou Gehrig hits third grand slam in four days.

SEPTEMBER 2

1850   Al Spalding born.
1933   Marv Throneberry born.
1970   Billy Williams of the Cubs plays his 1,117th consecutive game, a National League record.

SEPTEMBER 3

1897   Willie Keeler and Jack Doyle, Baltimore, each make six hits in six times at bat off Red Donahue and Percy Coleman of St. Louis, this being the only major league game on record in which two players accomplished feat. Baltimore naturally won, 22-1.

SEPTEMBER 4

1916   In sentimental hurling duel that marks final appearance for both, Christy Mathewson of Reds outlasts Three-Finger Brown of Cubs, 10-8.

SEPTEMBER 5

1874   Nap Lajoie born.

1908   Nap Rucker, Brooklyn lefthander, pitches no-hit game against Boston, striking out 14 men.
1918   Because of war-curtailed season, World Series starts a month early and Babe Ruth of Red Sox outpitches Jim Vaughn of Cubs, 1-0, in opener.

SEPTEMBER 6

1883   Largest inning in major league history, as the Chicago White Stockings score 18 runs in the seventh off Stump Weidman and Dick Burns of Detroit. Game winds up with Ansonites on top, 26-6. Tommy Burns of Chicago bats three times in the seventh and makes three hits.
1888   Red Faber born; he pitched in 20 seasons, and was the AL's last legal spitballer when he retired in 1933.
1897   Willie Keeler gets 15th hit over three consecutive games.
1912   Jeff Tesreau of the Giants, slightly assisted by some New York correspondents who use their persuasive powers on an official scorer, pitches no hit game against Phillies, winning over Eppa Rixey, 3 to 0. A ball hit to Merkle was first put down as a hit and later changed into an error.

SEPTEMBER 7

1911   Rookie Grover Alexander of the Phils takes a 1-0 thriller from 44-year-old Cy Young, who was closing out his career with the Boston Braves.

SEPTEMBER 8

1896   Baltimore, after having won three games from Louisville the previous day, takes two more falls out of the Colonels, the scores being 10-9 and 3-1. Five victories and five defeats in two days are major league records.
1907   Buck Leonard born.
1965   Bert Campaneris of the A's plays all 9 positions. Only Cesar Tovar of the Twins has matched this feat.

SEPTEMBER 9

1877   Frank Chance born.
1894   Joe Kelley of Orioles, makes nine hits in nine times at bat in doubleheader with Cleveland, off Sullivan and Young. Five of these drives were for extra bases, four being doubles and one being a triple.
1898   Frankie Frisch born.
1899   Waite Hoyt born.
1965   Sandy Koufax of the Dodgers pitches a perfect game against the Cubs, fanning 14 and winning 1-0. His opponent, Bob Hendley, allows the Dodgers only one hit, a double by Lou Johnson.

SEPTEMBER 10

1896   George Kelly born; "Highpockets" of the Giants hit seven homers over six consecutive games in 1924.

SEPTEMBER 11

1882   Tony Mullane, Louisville, pitches no-hit game against Cincinnati.
1912   The Athletics' Eddie Collins steals six bases in a game with Detroit, an AL record; eleven days later, he would do it again.

SEPTEMBER 12

1947   Ralph Kiner smacks two homers to conclude four game stretch in which he hit eight.

1962 Tom Cheney of the Senators sets a record by fanning 21 Orioles in a 16-inning game which he wins, 2-1.
1969 Jerry Koosman and Don Cardwell of Mets each throw 1-0 shutouts over Pirates; each gets game-winning RBI.
1976 Minnie Minoso becomes oldest player to get a hit in a regulation game. He was almost 54 at the time.

SEPTEMBER 13

1883 Hugh Daily, Cleveland's one-armed pitcher, no-hits the Phillies.

SEPTEMBER 14

1903 John McGraw tries young pitcher named Leon Ames against Cardinals and in his debut he gives them neither hit nor run—the game, however, lasts only five innings.
1915 Giants, despite making 14 hits off Larry Cheney of Cubs, can't score a run and are beaten, 7-0.
1951 In his first big league game, Bob Nieman of the Browns homers in his first two at-bats.

SEPTEMBER 15

1902 First double play by historic combination of Tinker-to-Evers-to-Chance.
1938 Gaylord Perry born.
1963 The three Alou brothers—Felipe, Matty, and Jesus—play briefly in the Giant outfield at the same time in a regular game. This necessitated benching Willie Mays.
1969 Steve Carlton of the Cardinals fans 19 Mets but loses, 4-3, as Ron Swoboda drives in all four runs with two homers.

SEPTEMBER 16

1924 Sunny Jim Bottomley blasts five Dodger pitchers to go 6 for 6, plus all-time record of 12 runs batted in, shading old mark of 11 set by Wilbert Robinson, who had to watch this performance painfully as Dodger manager.
1975 The Pirates annihilated the Cubs in Wrigley Field 22-0. It was the most one-sided shutout since 1900. Rennie Stennett got 7 hits in 7 at-bats.
1988 Tom Browning of the Reds becomes the 14th pitcher to throw a perfect game, defeating L.A. at Cincinnati, 1-0.

SEPTEMBER 17

1879 Andrew "Rube" Foster born; the top pitcher in black baseball for a decade, in 1920 he formed the Negro National League.
1912 Casey Stengel, purchased conditionally from Montgomery, breaks in with Brooklyn by blasting Pittsburgh pitching for four hits and a walk in five tries, also stealing a base in 7-3 victory, whereupon Dodgers complete terms of purchase before Stengel is showered and dressed.
1984 Reggie Jackson, now with the California Angels, becomes the 13th player to hit 500 big league homers. His wallop against Kansas City's Bud Black came 17 years to the day after his first big league hit.
1984 Dwight Gooden fans 16 Phils in a 2-1 victory, equaling the number of Pirates fanned in his last outing—tying the record for strikeouts in consecutive starts.

SEPTEMBER 18

1897 Denton T. Young, Cleveland, retires Cincinnati without a hit or run.
1911 Larry Doyle of Giants steals home twice in same game.

1968 After Gaylord Perry had pitched a no-hitter over the Cardinals the day before, Ray Washburn retaliates with a no-hitter over the Giants in the same San Francisco park.

SEPTEMBER 19

1926 Edwin "Duke" Snider born; the Dodger center fielder hit 40 or more home runs in five straight years.
1943 Joe Morgan born.

SEPTEMBER 20

1882 On closing day of the season Larry Corcoran, Chicago White Stockings, pitches no-hit, no-run game against Worcester, winning over Frank Mountain, 5-0.
1900 Honus Wagner steals five bases in game with St. Louis, Cardinals' catcher being Wilbert Robinson.
1958 Baltimore's Hoyt Wilhelm, still winless (0-6) as a starter after his relief career foundered, revives his fortunes by no-hitting New York.

SEPTEMBER 21

1865 Bill Joyce born.
1934 Dizzy Dean and brother Paul shut out Dodgers in twin bill. Diz throws three-hitter in opener, then Paul outdoes him by hurling no-hitter in nightcap,
1942 Sam McDowell born.

SEPTEMBER 22

1904 Jim O'Rourke, although 52 years old, catches a full game for the Giants and goes 1 for 4 at bat.
1920 Bob Lemon born; after coming to the Indians as a third baseman in 1941, he found his true vocation on the mound, winning 20 games seven times.

SEPTEMBER 23

1886 Pud Galvin of Pittsburgh walks three Brooklyn batters to load the bases, but then picks George Smith off first base, Bill McClellan off third, and Jim McTamany off second.
1908 Fred Merkle did not touch second in ninth inning of game with Cubs and game ended in a tie, 1-1, instead of a New York victory, 2-1. This oversight cost the Giants the pennant, for the season ended in a tie and the Cubs won the one-game playoff.

SEPTEMBER 24

1939 Eighteen years after his major league debut, Johnny Cooney of Braves hits first major league homer, a wrong-field slice in Polo Grounds; next day, he adds another.
1957 Ted Williams is retired by Hal Griggs, snapping a streak of 16 straight times on base, a record.

SEPTEMBER 25

1929 Yank manager Miller Huggins dies.
1946 Bill Veeck, owner of Cleveland, offers free admission to game with Chisox; 12,800 show up to see Chi win, 4-1.
1965 Satchel Paige becomes at 59 the oldest to play in the majors as he takes the mound for Kansas City and pitches three scoreless innings over the Red Sox. He gave out only one hit—that to Carl Yastrzemski.

SEPTEMBER 26

1908 Ed Reulbach, Cubs, performs the greatest iron man stunt on record in majors by twice blanking Brooklyn. Scores were 5-0 and 3-0. Superbas got five singles in first game, three

in second, and never got nearer the plate than second base.

1912 Cubs have Reds shut out 9-0 up to the ninth. Cincinnati then makes 10 runs off Jimmy Lavender, Fred Toney and Larry Cheney, but in their part the Cubs rebounded for two runs against Ralph Works and Rube Benton and won, 11-10.

1954 Karl Spooner hurls second shutout in second major league start, equaling record of Al Spalding, John M. Ward, Jim Hughes, and Al Worthington.

1981 Houston's Nolan Ryan pitches his fifth career no-hit, no-run game, a 5-0 victory over the Los Angeles Dodgers at the Astrodome.

SEPTEMBER 27

1881 Troy defeats Cleveland at Troy, 10-8, in rainstorm; the last game of the season, it draws a whopping crowd of 12.

1919 Babe Ruth ceases hitting home runs for the season, four bagger number 29 being manufactured at Washington in the third inning off Jordan and giving him a record of one or more circuit clouts at every American League Park.

1928 Lefty Grove of A's fans White Sox in seventh inning with nine pitched balls, second time he turned trick this season (also August 23 vs. Cleveland).

1930 The Cubs' Hack Wilson hits his final two homers of the season, giving him 56 for a NL record.

1935 The Cubs win their 21st consecutive game without a loss or tie (the 1916 New York Giants won 26 with one tie) and clinch the pennant.

SEPTEMBER 28

1920 George Sisler equals and breaks American League record of hits for season (made by Ty Cobb in 1911) in game with Indians, getting 248th safety, a homer, in sixth and 249th safety, a triple, in eighth.

1938 Gabby Hartnett's homer in gathering darkness breaks 5-5 tie with Pirates and puts Cubs into first place to stay.

1941, 1960 A big date for Ted Williams: he closes the 1941 season by going 6 for 8 to hit .406, and 19 years later he closes his career by hitting a homer in his last time at bat.

SEPTEMBER 29

1913 Walter Johnson wins his 36th game of the season as the Senators beat the A's, 1-0.

1963 In what is both his debut and his finale, John Paciorek of Houston goes 3 for 3 with two walks, three RBI's, and four runs scored.

1988 Orel Hershiser of the Dodgers throws ten shutout innings against the Padres before departing the tie game, thus running his streak of scoreless frames to 59 and surpassing by one the record set in 1968 by Don Drysdale.

SEPTEMBER 30

1916 Giants, after winning 26 straight games and creating new major league record, beaten by Braves, 8-3. George Tyler stops the McGrawites and makes Brooklyn champion of National League.

1926 Robin Roberts born; the 28 games he won for the Phils in 1952 are the NL's high-water mark of the last half-century.

1927 Babe Ruth hits 60th homer, surpassing his own record by one. The victim is Tom Zachary of the Senators.

1931 Babe Herman sets record by hitting for cycle third time in this season; only Bob Meusel has ever hit for cycle thrice in career.

1951 Jackie Robinson hits a home run in the 14th inning to give the Dodgers a 9-8 win over the Phils and a tie in the National League race with the Giants.

1972 Roberto Clemente hits a double in the fourth inning against the Mets for his 3,000th hit in the majors. It proves to be his last hit as he died in an airplane crash in December.

1984 Mike Witt throws a perfect game.

1988 For the second consecutive time, Dave Stieb of Toronto is only one strike away from a no-hitter, then allows a dink hit and settles for a one-hitter.

OCTOBER 1

1933 Nick Altrock pinch hits for Washington at age of 57.

1961 Roger Maris sets a new season record for home runs when he hit his 61st off Tracy Stallard of the Red Sox to give the Yankees a 1-0 victory.

OCTOBER 2

1908 Addie Joss of Cleveland pitches a perfect game, winning 1-0 over the White Sox. Ed Walsh gives up only four hits and fans 15 in a dazzling encounter.

1949 Browns use a different pitcher in each of nine innings against White Sox.

1968 Bob Gibson breaks Sandy Koufax's Series record by whiffing 17 Tigers while winning the first game.

1978 In a one-game season playoff, Bucky Dent of the Yankees hits a 3-run homer in the seventh inning to help defeat the Red Sox 5-4 and give winning hurler Ron Guidry a remarkable 25-3 season won-lost record.

OCTOBER 3

1872 Fred Clarke born.

1895 Harry Wright dies in Atlantic City.

1897 Cap Anson closes out a memorable 27-year career which started in the National Association 1871. He hits two home runs against St. Louis. At age 46, he is the oldest player to homer in the majors.

1947 Cookie Lavagetto's pinch double with two out and two aboard in the ninth inning of World Series game at Ebbets Field ruins Bill Bevens' no-hitter and beats Yanks, 3 to 2.

1951 Bobby Thomson's dramatic homer off Ralph Branca in ninth with two aboard gives Giants 5-4 victory over Dodgers in third and final playoff game for pennant.

OCTOBER 4

1948 Cleveland shortstop, manager, and MVP Lou Boudreau goes 4 for 4 off Red Sox pitching to win the AL's first one-game playoff for a pennant.

1955 The Brooklyn Dodgers win their first World Series with Johnny Podres blanking the Yankees 2-0 in the final game, aided by Sandy Amoros' great catch.

OCTOBER 5

1941 Brooklyn catcher Mickey Owen drops a third strike of what would have been the last out of a Dodger victory over the Yankees. Given a second chance, the Yankees score four runs to win the game, and eventually the Series.

OCTOBER 6

1824 Henry Chadwick born in England; the prolific writer may have done more than anyone to make baseball America's national pastime.

1908 On final game of AL season, with pennant at stake for

winner and third place awaiting loser, Bill Donovan's two-hitter gives Detroit the decision over Chicago.
1966   Jim Palmer, 20, becomes the youngest hurler to hurl a World Series shutout as the Orioles beat the Dodgers, 6-0. Sandy Koufax is the loser, and it marks his last appearance in a game.

OCTOBER 7

1862   Pitcher Jim Creighton, at age 21 baseball's first star, injures himself against the Unions of Morrisania and, "after suffering for a few days, expired."
1905   Chuck Klein born.
1913   Living up to his nickname, John Franklin "Home Run" Baker connects with homer that enables A's to beat Giants in World Series opener, 6-4.

OCTOBER 8

1926   Grover Alexander leaves bullpen in seventh inning of seventh World Series game to strike out Tony Lazzeri with bases loaded and two out, then holds Yanks scoreless the next two innings to win.
1956   In what is still the only no-hitter in Series history, Don Larsen of the Yankees pitches a perfect game against Brooklyn.

OCTOBER 9

1889   Rube Marquard born.
1898   Joe Sewell born.
1924   Jake Daubert dies after routine operation, age 39.
1934   Dizzy Dean blanks the Tigers, 11-0, in the Seventh Game, and the Cardinals take the Series, 4-3.
1972   Oakland's Gene Tenace homers in his first two World Series at-bats.

OCTOBER 10

1904   After winning 41 games all season, spitballer Jack Chesbro unleashes ninth inning wild pitch on last day to cost New York the AL pennant.
1906   Cubs' Ed Reulbach pitches first World Series one-hitter vs. White Sox.
1980   With the Kansas City Royals down 2-1 in the seventh inning of the third AL championship playoff game, George Brett hits a three-run homer off relief ace Goose Gossage of the Yankees to give the Royals a 4-2 win and a three-game sweep of the Series.

OCTOBER 11

1854   Pitcher Will White born; the brother of Deacon White, he won more than 40 games three times and was the first player to wear glasses.

OCTOBER 12

1906   Joe Cronin born.
1929   A's rally for 10 runs in eighth inning to win over Cubs, 10-8, on Mule Haas' lost-in-the-sun three-run homer that eluded Hack Wilson.
1982   Paul Molitor of Milwaukee collects five hits, a Series record, in the 10-0 opener over the Cardinals in St. Louis. Mike Caldwell tosses the shutout for the Brewers.

OCTOBER 13

1876   Rube Waddell born.
1931   Eddie Mathews born.

1960   Bill Mazeroski opens the bottom of the ninth with a home run off Ralph Terry of the Yankees to give the Pirates a 10-9 victory and the championship.

OCTOBER 14

1896   Oscar Charleston born; the top black player of the 1920s.
1905   Christy Mathewson blanks the Athletics 2-0 to give the Giants the championship four games to one. All games ended in shutouts, with Matty getting three, Joe McGinnity one, and Chief Bender one.
1976   Yankees win pennant on Chris Chambliss' ninth inning homer off Kansas City's Mark Littell in Game Five of AL Playoffs.

OCTOBER 15

1892   Jack Stivetts throws five perfect innings at Washington, 6-0, before game is called because of darkness (second of twin bill).
1894   Bumpus Jones, who had shown up unannounced in Cincy clubhouse day before, starts and pitches no-hitter, only major league victory.
1945   Jim Palmer born; a three-time Cy Young Award winner, he won 20 or more in eight of nine years in the 1970s.
1986   The Mets defeat Houston in the NL LCS, winning Game Six by a score of 7-6 in 16 innings. In a game that lasted four hours, forty-two minutes, the Mets scored three in the ninth to tie the game at 3-3; and the Astros scored one in the 14th to stay alive at 4-4 and two in the bottom of the 16th to give the Mets a mighty scare.

OCTOBER 16

1883   Will Harridge born.
1900   Goose Goslin born.
1912   Fred Snodgrass drops an easy fly ball in the 10th inning that permits the Red Sox to score two runs and win the Series from the Giants.
1969   Behind Jerry Koosman and homers by Al Weis and Donn Clendenon, the Mets beat the Orioles to take the Series in five games.

OCTOBER 17

1848   Candy Cummings born; the diminutive hurler (five-nine, 120 pounds) was the first to make a baseball curve.
1960   At Blackstone Hotel in Chicago, NL awards franchises to NY and Houston for 1962.

OCTOBER 18

1950   Connie Mack retires after 50 years as Philadelphia A's manager.
1977   Reggie Jackson hits three home runs on three pitches as the Yanks clinch the World Series with a sixth-game victory over Los Angeles.

OCTOBER 19

1876   Mordecai Peter Centennial Brown, known as Three-Finger, born; he overcame his handicap to develop the nastiest curve of the dead-ball era.
1946   Allie Reynolds traded to NY by Cleveland for Joe Gordon and Eddie Bockman: as an Indian, his won-lost record was 51-47; as a Yank, it was 131-60.
1949   A's trade Nellie Fox to Chicago for catcher Joe Tipton.

OCTOBER 20

1931 Mickey Mantle born.
1938 Juan Marichal born; the Dominican dandy had a dazzling array of pitches and deliveries that produced six 20-game seasons.

OCTOBER 21

1910 Giants defeat Yanks, four games to two, in first NY City Series; Matty wins all four Giant victories.
1928 Whitey Ford born; the Yankees' "Chairman of the Board" won 236 games plus an all-time high of 10 more in World Series competition.
1975 The Reds use eight pitchers in the sixth game of the Series, but Carlton Fisk breaks up the thrilling contest with a homer in the 12th inning to give the Red Sox a 7-6 win.
1981 Cards get Willie McGee from Yanks for Bob Sykes.

OCTOBER 22

1907 Jimmie Foxx born.
1975 Following a thrilling 12-inning loss in Boston the night before, the Reds get a ninth inning single from Joe Morgan and win Game Seven and the Series.

OCTOBER 23

1884 The New York Metropolitans host the Providence Grays in the first World Series game, losing 6-0 to Hoss Radbourn.
1979 Billy Martin fights marshmallow salesman in bar in Bloomington, Minnesota; he is fired five days later.

OCTOBER 24

1929 Jim Brosnan born; taking up where Henry Wiggen left off, the pitcher-author wrote *The Long Season* in 1960.

OCTOBER 25

1884 Old Hoss Radbourn of Providence wins his third straight Series victory over the New York Mets of the American Association, 12-2. This concluded the three-game Series.
1889 Smokey Joe Wood born; his 1912 performance with the Red Sox was the equal of any as he went 34-5 while adding three more wins in the Series—including the final game.
1937 Boston Bees sign Casey Stengel as manager.
1965 Leo Durocher named to manage Cubs, ending college of coaches scheme.
1986 Only one strike away from losing the World Series to the Boston Red Sox, the Mets stage a miraculous rally in the tenth inning of Game Six. Down 5-3 in the bottom of the tenth with two out, no one on, and two strikes on Gary Carter, the Mets go on to score the winning run on Bill Buckner's misplay of a Mookie Wilson grounder. New York will win Game Seven two days later.

OCTOBER 26

1899 Judy Johnson born; he starred at third base for the Hilldale Club, the Homestead Grays, and the Pittsburgh Crawfords.
1917 Miller Huggins signs two-year contract to manage Yanks.
1934 Bosox get Joe Cronin from Washington for $250,000 and Lyn Lary; in deal Senators' owner Clark Griffith dealt his own son-in-law.

1960 The American League approves the transfer of the Senators to Minnesota and announces new franchises will be awarded to Washington and Los Angeles, This is the first expansion of the major leagues in this century.

OCTOBER 27

1859 Buck Ewing born; his contemporaries called him not only the greatest catcher of his time but also the top all-around player.
1890 Chicken Wolf has three hits and three RBIs to lead Louisville over the American Association champion Brooklyn team 9-8. The weather at the Brooklyn grounds was so cold and blustery, only 300 people came out to see the contest. After one more game, the Series, all tied up at three games apiece, was called off because of cold weather.
1922 Ralph Kiner born.

OCTOBER 28

1935 Bob Veale born, 45 years and a day after the above-mentioned exploits of Chicken Wolf. Veale will one day pitch for a Pirate staff that includes Ray Lamb and Bob Moose.
1981 After losing the first two Series games to the Yankees, the Los Angeles Dodgers come back to sweep the final four and take the Series. The Yankees fall apart in the final game, 9-2. It was at the time the latest played Series game in this century.

OCTOBER 29

1929 Stock Market Crash; Harry Heilmann, .344 hitter in 1929, released on waivers to Cincy.
1939 Pete Richert born; debuted with Dodgers by fanning first six men he faced (April 12, 1962).
1953 The sale of the St. Louis AL franchise is completed, and the venerable Browns become the Baltimore Orioles.
1969 Tom Seaver gets first of three Cy Young Awards.

OCTOBER 30

1898 Bill Terry born.
1973 Tom Seaver wins second Cy Young Award, becoming first non-20 game winner to take the honor.

OCTOBER 31

1867 Ed Delahanty born.
1900 Cal Hubbard was born; the massive umpire (six-three, 250) is the only man enshrined in both Cooperstown and Canton, home of the Pro Football Hall of Fame.

NOVEMBER 1

1859 Bid McPhee born; greatest second baseman of the years before 1900.
1951 Catcher Roy Campanella of Brooklyn is voted the NL's MVP for the first of what will prove to be three times.
1960 Fernando Valenzuela born.

NOVEMBER 2

1927 Ban Johnson, founder of AL, resigns as league president.
1974 Henry Aaron traded to Brewers for Dave May; in Japan, he defeats Sadaharu Oh in homer contest 10-9, at Korakuen Stadium in Tokyo.

NOVEMBER 3

1918 Bob Feller born; he pitched three no-hitters, 12 one-hitters, and would have topped 300 wins but for World War Two.

NOVEMBER 4

1874 Bobby Wallace born.
1911 Joe Medwick born.
1950 Grover Cleveland Alexander dies.
1959 Ernie Banks wins his second straight MVP Award; he led NL shortstops in fielding while poling out 45 homers and driving in 143 runs.
1976 First free-agent draft is held, Montreal selects Reggie Jackson with first choice.

NOVEMBER 5

1869 Cincinnati Reds play last game of year, beating Mutuals of New York, 17-8; Reds' record for year is 57-0-1.
1968 Denny McLain takes MVP and Cy Young honors for his 31-6 record; no one had won more since Grover Alexander in 1916.

NOVEMBER 6

1887 Walter Johnson born; relying purely on speed and control, The Big Train won more games than anyone but Cy Young, and threw more shutouts than anybody.

NOVEMBER 7

1928 Manager—and less replaceably, .387 hitter—Rogers Hornsby was traded from Boston to the Cubs for $200,000 and five players.
1938 Jim Kaat born.

NOVEMBER 8

1894 King Kelly dies at Boston.
1896 Bucky Harris born.
1951 Yankee catcher Yogi Berra wins the first of his eventually three MVP Awards.

NOVEMBER 9

1931 Whitey Herzog born.
1935 Bob Gibson born.
1960 Casey Stengel, fired as the Yankees' manager after his 10th pennant in 12 years, says, "I'll never make the mistake of being 70 years old again."

NOVEMBER 10

1934 Norm Cash born; his on-base average of .488 in 1961 has not been topped since.
1955 Jack Clark born.
1965 Willie Mays, Giants, named NL's MVP.

NOVEMBER 11

1891 Rabbit Maranville born; inventor of the basket catch, the five-five shortstop played from 1912-1935.
1917 Grover Alexander traded to Cubs with Bill Killefer for Mike Prendergast, Pickles Dillhoefer, and $60,000.

NOVEMBER 12

1920 Judge Kenesaw Mountain Landis is named to the newly created position of Commissioner of Baseball.
1975 Tom Seaver gets third Cy Young Award.

NOVEMBER 13

1939 Wes Parker born.
1973 Reggie Jackson of Oakland is voted MVP as he leads the AL in homers, RBIs, and slugging.

NOVEMBER 14

1900 Ban Johnson, president of the Western League, announces his intention to upgrade his circuit to major rank.
1929 Joe McGinnity dies.
1954 Willie Hernandez born.
1956 Mantle is unanimous MVP.

NOVEMBER 15

1920 Waite Hoyt and Wally Schang are traded to the New York Yankees by Boston's Harry Frazee, the man who gave the Yanks Babe Ruth.
1942 Joe Gunson dies.
1969 Billy Southworth dies.
1985 Riggs Stephenson dies; for his 14-year career, he batted .336.

NOVEMBER 16

1951 Herb Washington born.
1980 George Brett of the Royals, coming off a .390 season, is named his league's MVP.

NOVEMBER 17

1923 Mike Garcia born.
1959 Willie McCovey, Giants, named NL Rookie of the Year.
1965 Among 156 nominees, retired Air Force general William D. "Spike" Eckert is selected as the game's new commissioner, replacing Ford Frick.

NOVEMBER 18

1888 Led by Al Spalding, the Chicago White Sox and "All Americans" sail from San Francisco for Honolulu, first stop on their world tour.
1888 "Colby Jack" Coombs born.

NOVEMBER 19

1921 Roy Campanella born; a superb receiver and power hitter, he was MVP in 1951, 1953, and 1955.
1979 Nolan Ryan is the first free agent to sign a million a year contract (Houston Astros).

NOVEMBER 20

1866 Kenesaw Mountain Landis born.
1869 Clark Griffith born.
1962 Chisox release Early Wynn, who has 299 wins; signs with Cleveland in June 1963, wins one game.
1980 Mike Schmidt of the Phillies wins the first of his three MVP Awards.

NOVEMBER 21

1905 Fred Lindstrom born.
1920 Stan Musial born; along with only Schmidt and Campanella, he was a three-time MVP in the NL.
1934 Yanks buy Joe DiMaggio from SF Seals for $25,000 and four players—he had hit in 61 straight in 1933.
1956 Brooklyn's Don Newcombe becomes first to win NL's MVP and Cy Young Award.

1962 Dick Stuart goes from Pittsburgh to Red Sox with Jack Lamabe, for Don Schwall and Jim Pagliaroni; hits 42 homers with 118 RBIs in first year in AL.

NOVEMBER 22

1892 Urban Shocker born.
1907 Dick Bartell born.
1950 Lyman Bostock born.
1957 Mantle wins MVP, 233 points to 232 by Williams, who hit .388 at age 39; this is second time Williams lost MVP honors by one vote—see entry for November 27.
1977 Goose Gossage leaves the Pirates as a free agent to sign a six-year contract for $2.75 million with the Yankees.

NOVEMBER 23

1940 Luis Tiant born.
1965 The Mets acquire 44-year-old pitcher Warren Spahn from the Braves, for whom he had won 20 or more 13 times.

NOVEMBER 24

1944 Active as baseball's commissioner until the last, Judge Landis dies.
1953 Walter Alston named Dodger manager.

NOVEMBER 25

1906 Arthur Soden, owner of the Boston team in the NL since 1877, sells out to the Dovey brothers; the team's nickname became the Doves.
1914 Joe DiMaggio born.

NOVEMBER 26

1866 Hugh Duffy born.
1908 Lefty Gomez born.
1975 Fred Lynn of the Red Sox is voted the AL's MVP, the first rookie so named.

NOVEMBER 27

1947 Joe DiMaggio is elected MVP over triple-crown winner Williams, 202 votes to 201. One writer fails to give Williams even a 10th-place vote, worth two points.
1954 Orioles and Yankees swap 18 players.
1967 Senators get Bill Denehy and $100,000 from Mets for manager Gil Hodges.

NOVEMBER 28

1972 Frank Robinson is traded from the Dodgers to the Angels, for whom he becomes that new phenomenon, the designated hitter.
1975 Steve Stone signs as free agent with Baltimore.

NOVEMBER 29

1922 Minnie Minoso born; he played in five decades by virtue of two pinch hit appearances at age 57.
1971 Gaylord Perry and Frank Duffy are traded from San Francisco to Cleveland for Sam McDowell.
1976 Yankees sign free agent outfielder Reggie Jackson for $3.5 million dollars.

NOVEMBER 30

1898 Fred "Firpo" Marberry born.
1920, 1948 Former pitching great Rube Foster organizes the Negro National League, and on this date 28 years later it disbands.

DECEMBER 1

1911 Walter Alston born; in 1955 he led the Brooklyn Dodgers to their only championship and won three more with the Dodgers of Los Angeles.

DECEMBER 2

1847 Deacon White born; he played every position over a long career while batting .303.

DECEMBER 3

1925 Harry Simpson born; traded in midseason five times in five years, he was given one of the game's great nicknames, "Suitcase."

DECEMBER 4

1868 Jesse Burkett born; with Hornsby and Cobb, he forms a trio of those who have hit .400 three times.

DECEMBER 5

1973 Montreal trades reliever Mike Marshall to the Dodgers—for whom in the next season he would pitch in 106 games and win the Cy Young Award—for Willie Davis.

DECEMBER 6

1899 Jocko Conlan born; the one-time White Sox outfielder was an NL umpire from 1941 through 1964.

DECEMBER 7

1947 Johnny Bench born; he was the top catcher of the 1970s, twice the NL homer champ and MVP.

DECEMBER 8

1939 Mindful of Lou Gehrig's illness, the writers waive the five-year rule and vote him into the Hall of Fame by acclamation.

DECEMBER 9

1965 Branch Rickey dies; he was one of the game's great innovators and one of the nation's great men.

DECEMBER 10

1981 In a six-player deal, St. Louis and San Diego trade shortstops, with Ozzie Smith going to the Cards and Garry Templeton to the Padres.

DECEMBER 11

1959 The Yanks acquire Roger Maris in a seven-player deal that also moves Don Larsen to Kansas City.

DECEMBER 12

1903 In a deal with the Cards, the Cubs get Three-Finger Brown and Jack O'Neill for Jack Taylor and Larry McLean.

DECEMBER 13

1927 Detroit trades outfielder Heinie Manush to the Browns, for whom he would hit .378.

DECEMBER 14

1932 The Browns trade Goose Goslin to Senators, whom he will lead to the 1933 pennant.

DECEMBER 15

1900 In the most lopsided deal ever, the Reds trade Christy Mathewson, with 373 wins ahead of him, for Amos Rusie, whose 243 career wins were all behind him.

DECEMBER 16

1982 The Mets reacquire Tom Seaver from the Reds for three players.

DECEMBER 17

1849 O.P. Caylor born; the sportswriter was so celebrated for his baseball knowledge that in 1885-1887 he was hired to manage first the Reds and then the Mets.

DECEMBER 18

1886 Ty Cobb born; beginning in 1907, he won 12 AL batting titles in the next 13 years.

DECEMBER 19

1934 Al Kaline born; in 1955, he became the youngest ever to win a batting crown.

DECEMBER 20

1926 In a shocking trade of baseball's best second sackers, the Cards send Rogers Hornsby to New York and receive Frankie Frisch.

DECEMBER 21

1911 Josh Gibson born; from his debut with the Homestead Grays in 1930 to his death in 1947, he was the home run king of black baseball.

DECEMBER 22

1915 For two years a rival to the American and National Leagues, the Federal League disbands.

DECEMBER 23

1942 Southpaw Jerry Koosman born; as a rookie with the Mets in 1968, he tied an NL record with seven shutouts.

DECEMBER 24

1913 Louis Sockalexis dies; the Penobscot Indian who hit .338 as a Cleveland rookie gave that team its nickname.

DECEMBER 25

1855 James "Pud" Galvin born; the "Little Steam Engine" hurled more innings and more complete games than anyone but Cy Young.

DECEMBER 26

1837 Morgan Bulkeley born; the president of the Hartford team known as the Dark Blues, he served as the NL's president in its inaugural year of 1876.
1927 Stu Miller born; the changeup artist was said to throw pitches at three speeds— slow, slower, and slowest.

DECEMBER 27

1912 Jim Tobin born; the Boston Braves' pitcher hit three homers in a game in 1942 and two years later threw a no-hitter.
1914 Postseason All-Star tour—AL led by Connie Mack, NL by Frank Bancroft—disbands at San Diego after 44 games across U.S. and Hawaii.

DECEMBER 28

1856 Harry Stovey born; an early slugger, he led his league in homers five times and in triples four times.
1900 Ted Lyons born; pitched entire 21-year career for tail-end Chicago White Sox, completing nearly 75 percent of his starts.

DECEMBER 29

1888 Asa Brainard dies; pitched for unbeaten Cincinnati Red Stocking nine of 1869 and married the girl who sewed the team's red stockings.
1947 George Blaeholder dies.

DECEMBER 30

1944 The White Sox buy Browns' infielder Floyd Baker, who would set a record of sorts by hitting only one home run in 13 years' play.
1955 Sandy Koufax born; the Dodger lefty dominated the game in 1961-1966, when he went 129-47 with four no-hitters, five ERA crowns, and three Cy Young Awards.

DECEMBER 31

1857 King Kelly born; his daring baserunning prompted the cry of "Slide, Kelly, Slide!"
1973 Pittsburgh Pirate star Roberto Clemente is killed in the crash of a plane flying in relief supplies to Nicaraguan earthquake victims.

The Players

CHAPTER 7

Lives of the Players

John B. Holway and Bob Carroll

On the following pages you'll find biographical sketches of 400 men, all in one way or another connected to baseball. Two questions naturally arise. First, why 400? And second, why *these* 400? To deal with the easier question first, we were limited by space. If we were going to say anything worthwhile, we had to forget about doing 13,000-plus baseballers and concentrate our attention somewhere in the 350–500 range. We also knew that we would include a number of men for reasons other than how well they played. For example, Earl Weaver never made the majors as a second baseman and Judge Landis played a punk shortstop, but we knew they belonged on our list. When we counted up the "nonplayers," we had about fifty-five. A couple were waffley: was Clark Griffith a pitcher, a manager, or an executive?

Why not 396 or 413? Look, we had to draw a line somewhere. If we drew it at 407, we'd have no earthly reason for excluding player 408.

Once we settled on 400 total, we were ready for the hard part. Who?

We had to have the 200 members of the Hall of Fame. Most of them would have been included under any reasonable criteria anyway. The few arguable enshrinees belong in our 400 just because they *are* enshrinees, sort of a self-fulfilling immortality.

A few individuals not yet in the Hall of Fame made the cut as managers or contributors. We were ruthless here and probably a little hard on managers. Well, they're used to rejection.

Four other factors weighed heavily in our choices of players.

We wanted a strong sampling of players from all nine positions—nine and a half counting DH's. Pitching may be 75 percent of baseball, as Connie Mack used to say, but we weren't about to present 300 pitchers and 100 position players. Neither did we want 112 slugging left fielders and 8 catchers. We decided that we'd include roughly 30 players at each position. Those who will say they can name a dozen shortstops more valuable than our last couple of second basemen may be right; they'll also be irrelevant. We ended up being hoisted a little by our own petard; we kept grieving over terrific pitchers we'd left out, but we already had included over 100 hurlers.

Obviously we had to consider quality. Everyone has an opinion, but most of us could agree on the greatest-of-the-great—maybe even on the great. It was the "darned good's" that gave us trouble. Example: no one would leave out Ted Williams and few would skip Billy Williams. But what about Cy, Dick, Earl, or Ken?

Pete Palmer, Bill James, and a few others have done a lot of valuable work using statistical analysis in ranking players from different eras of baseball history. We used their various rankings as a starting point, but we couldn't follow them slavishly. They do not always agree in their rankings. Furthermore, many nineteenth-century players and the great black players of the pre-Jackie Robinson days are not subject to the same statistical analysis. And finally there are players we felt we must include for reasons other than pure competency.

Which brings us to our third consideration—fame. Quite often, as we made our final cuts, we were faced with two or three or more players who seemed virtually interchangeable. When we could find no statistical reason to include one and not the others, we made a judgment as to which player was the best known to a modern reader. If our estimate was correct, we included the one you would most like to read about.

Two large groups of players were helped by our including fame in our calculations: nineteenth-century players and players from the Negro Leagues. Both groups are at a disadvantage in that their statistical records are incomplete and those that exist do not always relate well to modern major league baseball's numbers. Was a 30-game winner in 1880 the equivalent of a 15-game winner today? What does a .350 batting average in the Negro National League of 1935 really mean? We must depend on contemporary accounts to rank these players. Of course, those accounts are highly subjective. We know we'll be hearing, "How can you leave out so-and-so and include whoozis?"

Our fourth and final consideration applied to only a few players. These were borderline candidates. They could have been in or out. If one player had a more interesting story than another of apparently equal worthiness, we told the more entertaining tale.

We have to say something about why a few men were not included. Fame was a consideration but not when all other factors said no. Smead Jolley was famous but overrated as a hitter, and in the field he was unsafe at any speed. Jose Canseco is famous, but he needs a few more years of excellent play to be included. All of the Black Sox were notorious; we included Eddie Cicotte and Joe Jackson, with some misgivings, because their records prior to their shame were too good to ignore.

We passed on players who had supreme moments of accomplishment but failed to measure up over the long hall. Johnny Vander Meer and Bobby Thomson came awfully close anyway. Bobo Holloman and Pat Seerey didn't.

We did not use any absolute statistical cutoffs. Dave Kingman hit 442 home runs, Riggs Stephenson hit .336, and Tony Mullane won 285 games. We thought some other players were better.

In preparing the biographical sketches, we wanted to show first of all why we included each man in our 400. Much of this

involves repeating numbers. For the most part, we tried to rely on traditional categories that nearly everyone understands: batting average, ERA, RBIs, strikeouts, etc. There are often more meaningful statistics, pioneered by Palmer, James, and others, but this does not seem like the proper forum to explain them. We refer you to the Introduction to the statistical portion of this book.

We tried to avoid speculation of the if-he-hadn't-been-struck-by-lightning-he-would-have-hit-a-hundred-homers kind. We don't pretend to know what might have happened if there'd been no war, if the fences had been moved in, if Herb Score had ducked, if Cap Anson had played for the 1927 Yankees. We have our hands full with what did happen; let others worry about might have been.

The notorious "park factor" is part of this. By now, everyone must know that it's easier to hit in Wrigley Field than in the Astrodome—and on and on. We mentioned park factors in a few sketches when it seemed unavoidable, but to harp on it for every player affected would have put us all to sleep.

A few purists may find a note of levity in some of the sketches. Does that mean we do not view the annual pennant struggles as being on a par with, say, the struggle for world peace? Golly, we hope so. We can certainly be accused of enjoying our subjects. When baseball isn't fun anymore, we're *all* going to be in trouble.

Hank Aaron

Outfielder, Mil (N) 1954–65,
Atl (NL) 1966–74, Mil (A) 1975–76

If charisma were a baseball stat, Aaron would have been benched. No question he was great, but was he *box office*? Yearly, while lesser lights adorned magazine covers, the unassuming Alabaman quietly went his Hall of Fame way, winning baseball games with his quick feet, strong arm, and powerful bat. No Rodney Dangerfield, he always got respect; he *deserved* adulation.

His numbers were terrific: four times he led the league in home runs, four times in RBIs, thrice he scored the most runs, twice he had the most hits, and twice he topped all National Leaguers in batting average. In 1957, when his Braves were world champs, he was MVP, but most fans recognized him as a great player quicker than they'd have recognized him on the street. He made a more exciting stat line than an interview. It didn't help that he played in Milwaukee and Atlanta, places New York-based media *still* have to look up before they can point to them on a map. Worst of all, he was pleasant, modest, hard-working, and uncontroversial.

Then, as he neared the end of his career, this unpretentious superstar was thrust into the full glare of media hype as he fought the battle of his life—taking on Babe Ruth's ghost. "Hammerin' Hank" finished the 1973 season with 713 career home runs, only one less than Ruth's lifetime 714. After enduring a whole winter of "experts" speculating when he would, whether he could, and even *if* he should break the record, Aaron tied it in his first at-bat of 1974. A few days later, on April 8, at 9:07 EST, before 53,775 Atlanta fans, he elevated Al Downing's pitch into the record books as number 715. Before retiring in 1976, Aaron brought his record total up to 755.

More than a decade later, the "greatest home run hitter"

ruckus remains unsettled. Aaronites like to point out that Hank faced some un-Ruthian obstacles in playing most of his career in a "pitcher's park," facing more "good" pitchers and batting under lights. Ah, yes, say the pro-Ruthians, but the Babe had charisma!

Although he was never spectacular, on the basis of consistency Aaron was awesome. Among all players, he ranks third in games and hits, second in at-bats, runs, and total runs (runs plus RBIs), and first in home runs and RBIs—and grounding into double plays. His average season over twenty-three years was .305, 33 home runs, 100 RBIs. He hit 40 home runs or better eight times, the last when he was thirty-nine years old. Just running out his homers covered over fifty-one miles. He was named to the Hall of Fame in 1982.

When Reggie Jackson hit his 400th homer, he was asked if he could catch Aaron's 755. Reggie shook his head. Aaron, he said, was still an entire career away.

Charles "Babe" Adams

Pitcher, StL (N) 1906, Pit (N) 1907–26

The 1909 World Series had Detroit's Ty Cobb and Pittsburgh's Honus Wagner, but the star of the classic was Adams, a twenty-seven-year-old Pirate rookie. The quiet righthander from Indiana—a creditable 12–3 in 1909 but hardly the Buc ace — might not have pitched at all had star hurler Howie Camnitz not come down with an attack of quinsy. Pittsburgh manager Fred Clarke had been tipped that Adams threw with the "same style but faster" than AL pitcher Dolly Gray, who'd stumped Detroit batters during the season. Playing the hunch, Clarke sent the boy to do a man's job in the Series opener. Adams responded with a six-hitter, then six-hit the Tigers again in the fifth and seventh games to make the Pirates world champs.

Babe's best pitches were a good fastball (which earned him his nickname as a kid) but especially a curveball that could freeze batters in their tracks. His real talent, however, was his control. It took him to 194 Pirate wins over eighteen seasons, including 22–12 in 1911 and 21–10 in 1913. In 1914, he pitched a twenty-one-inning game without allowing a single walk. He averaged just 1.29 walks per nine innings over his career, with a pinpoint 0.62 record in 1920 (18 walks in 263 innings), tying with Christy Mathewson (1913) for best of all time.

Grover Cleveland "Pete" Alexander

Pitcher, Phi (N) 1911–17, 1930,
Chi (N) 1918–26, StL (N) 1926–29

When Grover Cleveland Alexander retired in 1930, he saw his name at the top of the "Games Won" column in the National League record book. A recount eventually added one more win to Christy Mathewson's lifetime total to leave them tied at 373 (Matty has now lost a win after all, returning him to 372), which was kind of fitting because one or the other was certainly the best NL righthander of the first half of the twentieth century. Alexander went into the Hall of Fame in 1938, two years after Mathewson. Military service in World War One cost Alex one-plus years after three straight 30-win

seasons, and a shell that burst in his ear may have triggered the epilepsy and led to the alcoholism that plagued him for the rest of his days; a gas attack in a training drill eventually cost Mathewson his life. Matty's out pitch was his fadeaway; Alex had a good fastball and better curve, all delivered with an easy, just-tossin' motion. Both had the kind of control that could carve a roast. Alex won two of the three games in which they faced each other.

Not even Matty ever had a moment like Alex's in the 1926 World Series. The grizzled veteran, nearing forty, won his second Series game for the Cardinals in Game Six and then allegedly went out to save St. Louis from alcohol by drinking it all himself. The next day, more hung over than the Gardens of Babylon, he was summoned to the mound in the seventh inning of the final game. The Cards led 3–2, but the Yankees had slugger Tony Lazzeri up with two outs and the bases loaded. Alex worked the count to 1-and-2, including a heart-stopping foul down the left field line, then whooshed strike three past Lazzeri's bat. After two more shutout innings, the Cards were champs and Alexander was a legend. The incident served as the climax of the movie *The Winning Team*, with Ronald Reagan portraying Alexander.

The Lazzeri strikeout crowned a career that glittered with three 30-win seasons and five 20-win seasons. His 90 career shutouts are second only to Walter Johnson's 110. His lifetime ERA of 2.56 included seasons of 1.22, 1.55, 1.72, and 1.86.

Alexander's 277 strikeouts in 1911 was the rookie record until Dwight Gooden broke it. But his 28 wins still stand as the freshman mark. Four of his wins were consecutive shut-outs. In 1915 he led the Phillies to a pennant, winning 31 and clinching the flag with a one-hitter. He won one more in the Series against Boston—the last Series win for the Phils until 1980.

All this was doubly impressive because he pitched his home games from 1911 to 1917 in little Baker Bowl, with a right field wall just off the second baseman's hip, and from 1918 to 1925 at hitter-friendly Wrigley Field. In 1916 Alexander tied a forty-year-old mark with 16 shutouts—and nine of these were registered at Baker Bowl.

As his career closed, Alex's alcoholism was so bad he couldn't shake hands without taking three stabs at it, and his wife hid her perfume so he wouldn't drink that. He ended up re-enacting the Lazzeri strikeout with a flea circus on Broadway. In 1950, he died alone in a rented room.

Dick Allen

Third Baseman/First Baseman,
Phi (N) 1963–69, 1975–76, StL (N) 1970, LA (N) 1971,
Chi (A) 1972–74, Oak (A) 1977

Dick ("Don't call me Richie!") Allen had baseball talent and opera-star temperament. When his mood was right, he was a one-man offense who could carry a team for a week or a month. When his mood was wrong, he could pout or even disappear for an equal length of time. He found spring training a waste of time and avoided as much of it as possible. He drove enemy pitchers and friendly managers crazy with equal nonchalance.

He came to the Phillies a professed third baseman in 1963, led the league in errors a couple of times, and from 1969 until he retired in 1977 was more or less a first baseman. Allen

lived by his bat: seven seasons over .300, ten seasons with 20 or more homers, and six seasons of 90-plus RBIs.

In 1970 the Phillies traded him to the Cardinals, who kept him a year and then passed him on to the Dodgers. In both cases, the teams improved their records, but decided Allen would never win the Employee of the Month award. In 1972 he was sent to the White Sox and patient manager Chuck Tanner (a.k.a. Job). Allen responded with an MVP year, hitting .308 and leading the AL in homers (37) and RBIs (113). After that, he got bored or sulky or whatever. By 1974, even Tanner was miffed over such Allen foibles as taking the last month of the season off to go tend his prize horses. Always his own man but often his worst enemy (despite heated competition among former teammates), Allen was ever an enigma.

Walter Alston

Manager, Bkn (N) 1954–57,
LA (N) 1958–76. First base, StL (N) 1936

For twenty-three years—all on one-year contracts — Alston managed the Dodgers, overseeing their migration from Brooklyn to Los Angeles and presiding as they became base-ball's most financially successful franchise. The Dodgers topped two million in attendance seven times with Walter in the dugout, their prosperity based on consistent wins. Alston brought them to four world championships, seven pennants, and eight second-place finishes. Only John McGraw, who managed thirty-one years, won more National League games or pennants.

Alston's entire major league playing career consisted of one at bat. Lon Warneke struck him out. But twenty years of playing and managing in the minors taught him to handle a team with patience and straightforward honesty. He was managing Nashua in the Dodgers' system in 1946, when the presence of black players was a hot potato. He volunteered to be the first white manager for a couple of talented black prospects and sent Roy Campanella and Don Newcombe on to stardom.

His Dodger teams had many stars but were renowned for their pitchers. Sandy Koufax and Don Drysdale are Hall of Famers, and countless others starred while hurling in the Dodger blue. Some of the credit goes to Alston and his patient handling. Named Major League Manager of the Year by *The Sporting News* in 1955, 1959, and 1963, Alston was elected to the Baseball Hall of Fame in 1983.

George "Sparky" Anderson

Manager, Cin (N) 1970–78,
Det (A) 1979–88. Second base, Phi (N) 1959

To paraphrase Will Rogers, Anderson never met a man he didn't talk to death. If he could have hit as well as he talks, he'd have been an All-Star player. Instead he batted a mute .218 in his only major league season as a player. Despite his own lack of prowess, the loquacious leader has become one of baseball's great managers. Employing a slow fuse with prob-lem players, a quick hook for pitchers, and an outlook more upbeat than a Basie riff, Anderson is the only man to win a World Series in both leagues, to win 100 games in both

leagues, and to be Manager of the Year in both leagues. In 1970, his first year at the helm, he guided Cincinnati's Big Red Machine to a pennant, then followed with more in 1972, 1973, 1975, and 1976; the latter two years also produced World Championships. It was the first time since John McGraw's New York Giants in 1921–1922 that a National League team had won back-to-back championships. In 1984 he led the Tigers to a world title. All told, he's guided his teams to seven first-place finishes and five seconds. His postseason record, 34–21 and .619, is the best of any manager.

Adrian "Cap" Anson

First Baseman/Third Baseman, Rock (NA) 1871,
Phil (NA) 1872-75, Chi (N) 1876–97. Manager,
Chi (N) 1879–1897, NY (N) 1898

Anson was the biggest star of the nineteenth century, one of the men who popularized baseball. During his twenty-seven-season career (1871–1897), he became the first man to make over 3,000 hits, even though nineteenth-century teams played fewer games per season than today's clubs. Twenty-five times he went over .300; three times he topped .390. He had good power for the dead-ball days. In 1884 he slugged five homers in two games, a feat that would not be matched until 1925.

He wasn't much of a fielder, though. His 58 errors in 1884 is still a record for first basemen. Even fielding with bare hands, that's a ton.

Cap managed Chicago's NL team (then called the "White Stockings") to five pennants between 1880 and 1886. He was a pioneer in the use of the hit-and-run, signals, platoons, a pitching rotation, and spring training. A big man—six-two, 220 pounds—he was a stiff-backed martinet who marched his men onto the field in military formation and used his fists to enforce his rules, the least popular being his no-drinking edict. Once he threw Chicago team owner A. G. Spalding off the field for challenging one of his decisions.

When he was finally let go by Chicago, his fans raised $50,000 for him. He turned it down.

Luis Aparicio

Shortstop, Chi (A) 1956–62, 1968–70,
Bal (A) 1963–67, Bos (A)1971–73

"Little Looie" played 2,581 games, more than any other shortstop, led the American League in stolen bases nine times (in a row), topped AL shortstops in fielding average eight times, and in 1984 became the first Venezuelan voted into the Hall of Fame. But he wasn't the be-all and end-all of short fielders. His lifetime batting average of .262 embraces *nada* power, and his .308 on-base average is embarrassing for a guy who was almost always used to lead off. Small wonder he never scored 100 runs and rarely led even his own team. What he did on offense was steal bases—506 of them. On the other hand, he was thrown out over 100 times.

He was smooth defensively—he won nine Gold Gloves. After being among the league leaders in total chances early in his career, his putouts and assists declined as his fielding average went up, indicating sure hands but the loss of the kind of range that wins extra ballgames. But no shortstop was

ever more durable, and the amiable Aparicio helped win flags for the White Sox in 1959 and for the Orioles in 1966. He was arguably the best player in the AL in 1960 when Roger Maris was named the MVP. That year Luis hit only .277 but stole 51 bases, led all shortstops in assists and fielding average, and knocked in 62 runs as a leadoff man.

Luke Appling

Shortstop, Chi (A) 1930–50. Manager, KC (A) 1967

Shortstops who can hit are as rare as Chicago pennants. Luke Appling could hit, and he spent twenty years wearing a White Sox uniform while other teams popped champagne corks at seasons' end. Although he never got into a World Series, he played in seven All-Star Games and averaged .444 there. He led the AL in batting in 1936, hitting .388, still the highest average by a shortstop in this century. He copped another crown in 1943, with .328. His are the only batting crowns won by a Sox hitter in spacious Comiskey Park. His career average of .310 came on 2,749 hits, and while he was never a power hitter (45 homers), he both scored and batted in over 1,000 runs. In 1964, he was elected to the Hall of Fame.

His specialty was fouling off pitches until he got one he wanted. According to legend, he once fouled twelve straight into the stands when the hard-strapped White Sox management refused him a dozen souvenir balls for friends. According to another version, it was fourteen straight after being turned down for two passes.

Originally a poor fielder, he led AL shortstops in errors six times. But he improved greatly over his career and finished with a record seven years leading in assists.

Nicknamed "Old Aches and Pains" because he led the league in hypochondria every year, he somehow survived aching ankles, pink eye, perpetual flu, a permanently sore back, headaches, inflamed throats, chills, vertigo, a real broken finger, and a fractured leg to play twenty years and usually top the Sox in games played. Among AL shortstops, only Aparicio put in more time at the position. At age seventy-five, he was healthy enough to slug a home run in the first Cracker Jack Old-Timers' Game in Washington, in 1984.

Richie Ashburn

Outfielder, Phi (N) 1948–59,
Chi (N) 1960–61, NY (N) 1962

Ashburn was one of the three best defensive center fielders ever. From 1948 through 1958 he led National League outfielders in chances per game every year but 1955 (when he finished second by 0.1). Sure, the other Phillie outfielders never won any dash medals, and ace Robin Roberts threw fly balls like they'd been ordered C.O.D., but Ashburn's gift for covering center made it all work. Willie Mays got the Gold Gloves; Ashburn got the outs —about 50 more each season. According to Pete Palmer's analytical stats, only Tris Speaker and Max Carey rank ahead of Richie as fly chasers, and then by a margin so small you'd get a recount in most states.

Ashburn's arm never got him a blue ribbon, but it got the Phillies a pennant in 1950, when he gunned down the Dodgers' Cal Abrams at the plate to preserve a tie in the season's

final game. The Phillies won the game and the flag in the tenth.

Richie broke in with the Phillies in 1948, topping the NL in steals and hitting in 23 straight games, the rookie record until Santiago passed it in 1987. He led the league in batting in 1955 and 1958. He hit over .300 in nine of his fifteen seasons. He was a leadoff man who homered only slightly more often than swallows visit Capistrano, but he led the NL in hits three times and bases on balls four times. His career on-base average was near .400.

He closed out with .306 for the expansion Mets, providing some respectability to an otherwise comical outfit. He has since gone on to become one of the top broadcasters in the game for the Phillies.

Earl Averill

Outfielder, Cle (A) 1929–39,
Det (A) 1939–40, Bos (N) 1941

After three excellent seasons with San Francisco of the PCL, Averill was purchased by the Indians in 1929 for $50,000. In his first major league at bat, he homered. He stood only five-nine and weighed just 172, but he generated home run power. For a half dozen years in the 1930s, he was one of the most feared batters in baseball. A back injury and a malformed spine affected his swing in 1937, left him as just an ordinary hitter, and prematurely shortened his career.

When Averill joined the Hall of Fame in 1975, he complained that he had had to wait thirty-four years. "Stats alone are enough," he said. His numbers were impressive, all right: .318 career batting average, 238 home runs, 1,164 RBIs, and 1,224 runs scored. During his ten best seasons, he averaged 23 home runs, 12 triples. 108 RBIs and 115 runs scored. He also led all outfielders in putouts twice. But hitting stats were inflated by an animated baseball during the time Averill was at his peak. Probably a better gauge of his ability is that he was the only outfielder selected to the first six All-Star Games.

The most famous incident in his career came in the 1937 All-Star Game, when a line drive off his bat broke pitcher Dizzy Dean's toe. Dean tried to come back from the injury too soon, altered his pitching motion, and ruined his arm. Ironically it was during that same 1937 season that Averill's back problem began to cut into his career.

Frank "Home Run" Baker

Third Baseman, Phi (A) 1908–14,
NY (A) 1916–19, 1921–22

Although he led the American League in homers four straight years (1911–1914) with his fifty-two-ounce bat, Baker's season high was an un-Ruthian 12 in 1913. He spent most of his career in the dead-ball era, when the baseball was as lively as an octogenarian's libido. His "Home Run" nickname stemmed from two timely shots off Christy Mathewson and Rube Marquard to win a pair of games in the 1911 World Series.

Later third basemen punched more round-trippers with a bouncier baseball, but few could match Baker's all-around

play. Named to the Hall of Fame in 1955, his career Relative Batting Average (batting average adjusted to the league average) of .307 is surpassed only by Wade Boggs and George Brett among hot corner practitioners. He was anchor man of the Philadelphia's "$100,000 infield" (with first baseman Stuffy McInnis, second baseman Eddie Collins, and shortstop Jack Barry), a quartet so adept that the A's won four flags in five years. In World Series play, Baker hit .409 in 1910, .375 in 1911, and .450 in 1913. When he slipped to .250 in 1914, the A's lost the Series four straight.

Baker sat out the 1915 season in a salary dispute. (He also missed the 1920 season due to the death of his wife.) Connie Mack began selling off his stars, and Baker was sold to the Yankees in 1916 for a then-tidy $37,500. He was New York's biggest drawing card until Babe Ruth arrived in 1920 and redefined the job description for "home run hitter."

Dave "Beauty" Bancroft

Shortstop, Phi (N) 1915–19, NY (N) 1920–23,
Bos (N) 1924–27, Bkn (N) 1928–29,
NY (N) 1930. Manager, Bos (N) 1924–27

Bancroft is less famous than some, but he's one of the three top fielding shortstops ever, along with Ozzie Smith and Art Fletcher. No shortstop has ever handled more chances than Bancroft did in 1922—984 (Smith's busiest season was 933 in 1980). Of course strikouts were fewer in Beauty's day than in Ozzie's, meaning more opportunities for fielders, and the ball is more lively today. But gloves were much smaller in 1922, which explains why three times Bancroft committed 60 errors or more.

Beauty, who was named to the Hall of Fame in 1971, was a winner. Manager Pat Moran gave him credit for sparking the Phils from sixth place to the pennant as a rookie in 1915. Traded to New York in 1920, Bancroft was made captain right away, and the next year the Giants won their first of four straight flags. He teamed with Frankie Frisch on the double play, and with George Kelly at first base and Heinie Groh at third, to form one of the game's top infields. Bancroft got his nickname from his habit of yelling "Beauty!" whenever his pitcher made a good pitch.

A switch-hitting leadoff man who crowded the plate, Bancroft coaxed plenty of walks but was a light hitter until the lively ball appeared in 1920. That year he hit .299 and followed it up with three consecutive .300 seasons, skipped a year, and then hit .300 twice more.

Bancroft was a sparkplug on the field, a fiery team leader with great instincts for the game who also managed during his four seasons in Boston. When he first joined the Giants, they asked if he wanted to go over their signs. "I don't have to," Beauty said, "I know them already."

Ernie Banks

Shortstop/First Baseman, Chi (N) 1953–71

Likable, popular Ernie hit more home runs than any other shortstop, 47 in 1958. He's also the first National Leaguer to win back-to-back MVPs (Yogi Berra did it in the AL).

A slim man for a slugger, Ernie had fast wrists and swung a

light, thirty-one-ounce bat, producing a powerful buggy-whip action. His 44 home runs in 1955 included a record 5 grand slams. He led the NL with his 47 homers in 1958 and again with 41 in 1960, to complete four straight years of 40-plus homers. But his homer totals are slightly inflated because he played in "the friendly confines of Wrigley Field" (his words)—Ernie hit 290 at home, 222 away.

Banks's batting average was modest, and he was a disaster on base. He was thrown out more than he stole, 53–50. Although he was a solid fielder and set an NL season record for shortstops in fielding average with .985 (only 12 errors) in 1959, Banks did not win many games with his glove. And he could never lead the Cubs to a pennant—they finished fifth in both his MVP years. Banks was at first base, where he had moved in 1962, when the Cubs collapsed in 1969 and lost the pennant to the Mets. But at age thirty-eight, Ernie still contributed 23 home runs and 106 runs batted in and led NL first basemen in fielding percentage.

His sunny disposition and his chirpy "Let's play two!" made him "Mr. Cub," a favorite of Wrigley's bleacher bums. In 1977 he was elected to the Hall of Fame.

Edward Barrow

Executive, Bos (AL) 1917–20, NY (A) 1921–45.
Manager, Det (A) 1903–04, Boston (A) 1918–20

The beetle-browed Barrow discovered Honus Wagner, switched Babe Ruth to the outfield, developed the Yankees' farm system, and masterminded them to fourteen flags and ten world championships.

This former bare-knuckle fighter and hotelman also pioneered night ball (at Paterson, New Jersey, in 1896), sanctioned the only woman to pitch in organized baseball (Lizzie Arlington, Eastern League, in 1897), was the first man to paint distances on outfield fences (Yankees, 1923), and to put large numbers on players' uniforms (Yanks, 1929).

After starting as a concession manager in 1894, he managed, operated, and part-owned several minor league teams, including Wheeling, West Virginia, where author Zane Grey played outfield. Barrow also was a fight promoter, and he sometimes hired heavyweight champs John L. Sullivan, James Corbett, and Jim Jeffries as umpires.

In 1917 Barrow became manager of the Red Sox. He led them to the world championship in 1918, when he began the transition of Ruth from pitcher to everyday player. Sox owner Harry Frazee sold Ruth to New York in 1920, and Barrow followed in 1921 as general manager.

Upon his arrival he told Yankee owner Colonel Jacob Ruppert, "If you ran your brewery the way you run this club, you'd go broke." Babe's 54 homers in 1920 had not been enough to move New York out of third place, but the next year, Barrow's first, the Yanks finally won their first flag. As he and assistant George Weiss built up a farm system, the Yankees would win six pennants in Barrow's first eight years, another in 1932, and another four between 1936 and 1939.

Barrow became president of the Yankees after the death of Ruppert in 1939 and held that position until the team was sold in 1945. He is memorialized with plaques in Cooperstown and one in center field of Yankee Stadium, the park he did so much to build.

Dick Bartell

Shortstop, Pit (N) 1927–30, Phi (N) 1931–34,
NY (N) 1935–38, Chi (N) 1939, Det (A) 1940–41,
NY (N) 1941–43, 1946

In his autobiography, *Rowdy Richard*, Bartell modestly argued that he ought to be in the Hall of Fame. He found few backers outside his immediate family, but the old battler has a better case for the Hall than if he were running for Mr. Congeniality. In Palmer's Linear Weights System, Bartell's 27 Games Won put him ahead of five shortstops now in the Hall—Ernie Banks, Travis Jackson, Joe Tinker, Pee Wee Reese, and Luis Aparicio.

A pepperpot who usually batted first or second in the order, he hit over .300 six times in his career. In 1933, he tied a record with four doubles in one game. Dick was at the top of his game in 1936 and 1937. In the former year he hit .298 for the Giants and led all shortstops in assists, double plays, and total chances per game. His teammate, Carl Hubbell, was the MVP with 26 victories, but Bartell played every day and may have had more total value. In the World Series Dick hammered Yankee pitchers at a .381 clip in a losing cause. The Giants won the NL pennant again in 1937, as Dick hit .306 and again led in total chances per game.

In 1940 Bartell was traded to Detroit in the AL. He hit only .233, but the Tigers won nine games more than they had the year before without him and rose all the way from fifth to first. Dick was the World Series goat, though, when, with the Tigers leading the seventh game 1–0, he took a throw from the outfield with his back to the plate and let the Reds' Frank McCormick score the tying run. Detroit eventually lost 2–1.

Bartell was sent back to the Giants the next year, after a slow start in which he saw little action. He batted .303 for New York over the rest of the season. The Tigers fell back to fifth.

For all his participation on pennant winners, the image that remains (and the one Bartell himself perpetuates in his autobiography) is one of a hot-headed scrapper who enjoyed fighting and baseball in that order.

Don Baylor

Designated Hitter/Outfielder, Bal (N) 1970–75,
Oak (A) 1976, Cal (A) 1977–82, NY (A) 1983–85,
Bos (A) 1986–87, Min (A) 1987, Oak (A) 1988-

Look up DH in the baseball dictionary and you'll see a picture of Baylor. He has been one of the most effective at that ersatz position of all the American Leaguers who've tried it. He was even the AL MVP in 1979 when he decorated his .296 batting average with 36 homers and league highs in RBIs (139) and runs scored (120). Actually he was in the outfield in 97 and DH'd in only 65 that year, but who's counting? Baylor's defensive limitations make him somewhat of a designated hitter even when he has a glove on.

All told, Baylor has officially DH'd in nearly 1,300 of his more than 2,200 games. Except for six seasons in California, he's been pretty much of a have-bat/will-travel around the AL. It's moved him into rarefied sluggers' air: more than 300 homers and nearly 1,300 RBIs. Although he's hired for his bat, he also has an admirable reputation as a team leader and

steadying influence in the clubhouse. While such things are not subject to statistical evaluation, most of the teams he's hit for have been winners.

Jake "Eagle Eye" Beckley

First Baseman, Pit (N) 1888–89, 1891–96, Pit (P) 1890, NY (N) 1896–97, Cin (N) 1897–1903, StL (N) 1904–07

One of the last of the handlebar-mustache players and a big star at the turn of the century, Beckley played more games than any first baseman in history, 2,377—Gehrig was more than 200 behind. Jake rapped out 2,931 hits, paving the way to his Hall of Fame election in 1971. He batted over .300 thirteen times, and hit three home runs in one game in 1897, a feat that would not be repeated for twenty-five years (by Ken Williams in 1922).

It was hard to hit homers then. Not only were the baseballs deader than Saturday night in Des Moines, but the fences were deeper because they built ballparks to the shapes of city blocks. The center field fence could be some 550 feet away with an area in front roped off for carriages. Players could sooner mail the ball to the fence than hit it there. Triples were a better indicator of power. Jake hit 246, more than anyone in his day, and fourth best all time, behind Ty Cobb, Sam Crawford, and Honus Wagner. Twice he hit three in one game.

When the players revolted against management in 1890 and formed the short-lived Players League, Beckley was one of the many stars who jumped with them. "I'm only in this game for the money," he said candidly.

But he played with verve too. Sometimes he turned the bat around and bunted with the handle. His favorite stunt was a cute hidden ball trick. Jake liked to hide the ball under first base, and then pull it out and shock the runner who'd just seen him barehanded. Somehow the naive runners never caught on.

John Beckwith

Shortstop/Catcher, Negro Leagues, 1919–38: Chicago Giants, Chicago American Giants, Baltimore Black Sox, Homestead Grays, Harrisburg Giants, Lincoln Giants, Bacharach Giants, New York Black Yankees, Newark Dodgers, Brooklyn Royal Giants

Beckwith was only nineteen when he knocked the first ball ever hit over the left field fence at Redland Field, Cincinnati, in 1920. A righthanded pull hitter, he went on to rank as one of the great long-ball sluggers in the black leagues, clouting a reported 72 and 54 home runs in two of his seasons in Chicago. After he moved East in the late 1920s, he topped all hitters there, including Josh Gibson, in home runs in 1930 and 1931.

John could also hit for average, belting black and white big leaguers equally well—.323 in the black majors and .311 in twenty-nine games against top white big leaguers. His two best seasons were 1924, when he led all hitters with a .452 average, and 1930, when he posted an amazing .546.

A big man at 230 pounds, Beckwith could play any position on the field and would even pitch occasionally. He was a moody, antisocial man whose personality may have kept him

on the move from team to team. But it also helped enhance his reputation as one of the most fearsome sluggers of his day.

David "Buddy" Bell

Third Baseman, Cle (A) 1972–78, Tex (A) 1979–85, Cin (N) 1986–87, Hou (N) 1988-

Buddy has never made it to a World Series or even to the playoffs, so he has never gotten much national publicity. But he is among the top four defensive third basemen, according to Palmer's linear weights. His hard-nosed, give-all-for-the-team style of play has made him a crowd favorite at each of his stops and won him six consecutive Gold Gloves. Bell was a sixteenth-round Cleveland draft pick as an outfielder and wasn't moved to third until his second year with the Indians.

A consistent .280-.290 hitter throughout his career, Bell's best season was 1979, his first in Texas. He played in every game, led the league in at-bats, and hit .299, with 200 hits, 42 doubles, 18 home runs, and 101 RBIs. He gave the Rangers two more .290 seasons and two .300 years before being packed off to Cincinnati, where he had his first 20-home run season. Bell left holding the Ranger records for doubles, RBIs, extra-base hits, and total bases.

Over his career, Buddy has amassed nearly 2,500 hits, and his 180-plus homers, when added to his father Gus's 206, give the Bells a shot at first place in the father-son home run derby.

James "Cool Papa" Bell

Outfielder, Negro Leagues, 1922–46; St. Louis Stars, Pittsburgh Crawfords, Detroit Wolves, Kansas City Monarchs, Chicago American Giants, Memphis Red Sox, Homestead Grays

That Bell could switch off the light and jump into bed before the room got dark, as Satchel Paige always claimed, may be a slight exaggeration. (Bell says he did it but admits that the light switch had a short in it.) But he *was* fast enough to score from second on a fly, which he did against Dizzy Dean in Yankee Stadium in 1935, and to score from first on a sacrifice, which he did against Bob Lemon in 1948, when Bell was forty-five years old. According to legend at least, Cool Papa was the fastest man in spikes.

Like Ruth, George Sisler, and Stan Musial, Bell started as a pitcher at age nineteen with the St. Louis Stars. He threw a knuckleball and won his first three games, calmly sleeping before a big game against Rube Foster's American Giants to win his nickname, "Cool Papa."

Bell, who stood over six feet, could also hit the long ball righthanded. His manager, Big Bill Gatewood, who taught Satchel Paige the hesitation pitch, converted the rookie Bell into a switch-hitting outfielder and told him to hit the ball on the ground. Infielders like Judy Johnson admit that if the ball took two hops, you might as well put it in your pocket.

Eventually Bell joined two of the most famous teams in blackball annals, the Crawfords (with Paige, Josh Gibson, Johnson, and Oscar Charleston), and the Grays (with Gibson and Buck Leonard).

Bell's lifetime batting average, though records are still incomplete, is tenth on the Negro League list. Surprisingly he is

ninth among home run hitters. In games against white big leaguers Bell hit .392.

Although he never had a chance at the white majors himself, Cool Papa helped some others. He was hitting .411 in 1946, but he sat out the final doubleheader so the batting title would go to young Monte Irvin and help boost him into integrated ball. Bell also counseled Jackie Robinson to give up playing shortstop and concentrate on second, the position he settled on with the Dodgers. He said his greatest thrill was the day Jackie made good in the majors.

In 1974 Cool Papa was named to the Baseball Hall of Fame.

Johnny Bench

Catcher, Cin (N) 1967–83

Bench was all but elected to Cooperstown in 1970 at the age of twenty-two when he slugged 45 home runs with 148 RBIs and was named MVP. It was a bit of an overreaction. He proved to be an outstanding player and a certain Hall of Famer during the rest of his career, but he never quite matched that 1970 season. His second best season came two years later in 1972, when he hit 40 home runs and won his second MVP.

With eleven seasons of 20-plus home runs, Bench demolished the home run record for catchers with 325 (to Yogi Berra's 313). But his batting average was unimpressive, and even his high RBI totals were dependent on the wealth of opportunities offered anyone batting mid-lineup for Cincinnati's Big Red Machine.

Johnny had a splendid Series in 1976, hitting .529 in his direct competition with Yankee Thurman Munson, the AL's top catcher. Bench's two homers and five RBIs was the *coup de grace* in Game Four of the Reds' sweep.

No one, including Bench, could live up to Bench's reputation as a catcher. In his first year, 1968, he led in both assists and passed balls. As esteem for his throwing arm grew, runners tested it less, and his caught-stealing numbers declined. Whether he was the best came second to whether everyone *thought* he was the best.

He called the pitches as Cincinnati's Big Red Machine rolled to six division titles, four NL pennants, and two World Series. But he handled only one 20-game winner, and the Reds' pitching usually had the same relationship to the team as his heel had to Achilles.

Albert "Chief" Bender

Pitcher, Phi (A) 1903–14, Bal (F) 1915,
Phi (N) 1916–17, Chi (A) 1925

This half-Chippewa Indian from the White Earth reservation in Minnesota was the money pitcher on Connie Mack's champion A's of the 1905–14 era, the man Connie said he'd pick if he had one game he had to win. Connie never spoke with a forked tongue, yet oddly Bender pitched only one must-win game in his life, the final game of the 1905 World Series, and lost it 2–0. Altogether the Chief won six out of ten Series games for Philadelphia. In 1910 Eddie Plank was hurt, and Bender and Jack Coombs pitched the entire Series, winning

4–1. In 1913, when Coombs was hurt, Mack asked Bender to pitch out of turn and promised to pay the Chief's mortgage of $2,500 if he would do it. Said Connie: "I knew then the Giants were done for." Bender won both his starts.

A product of the Carlisle Indian School, Bender never pitched in the minors and won the first big league game he pitched, a four-hitter, when he was nineteen. He was a big man (six-two), who pitched with a high kick and an overhand delivery. His out pitch, in those days before doctoring was illegal, was the "talcum ball," which he rubbed with talcum powder to make it smooth. He claimed it gave the ball a sharp drop.

Although he won 210 games in his sixteen seasons, the Chief won 20 games only twice (in 1910 and 1913). But he had some terrific ERA years. Three times he went under 2.00. Even in the dead-ball era, that wasn't chopped liver. No one sold off his Hall of Fame stock when he was elected in 1953. If he was no superstar, he was a very good pitcher with a great team—one that included Eddie Collins and Home Run Baker—behind him.

Lawrence "Yogi" Berra

Catcher, NY (A) 1946–63, NY (N) 1965.
Manager NY (A) 1964, 1984–85, NY (N) 1972–75

Yogi just might have been the best catcher the game has ever seen. Certainly he's the most *seen* catcher, having appeared on TV in a record 14 World Series, ten of them as a member of the world champs. He holds the records for most Series games (75) and most hits (71). Yogi is also the only catcher ever to call a perfect World Series game.

After shuttling between catching and the outfield, Berra was handed the first-string catcher's job by new manager Casey Stengel in 1949, and the Yankees won the first of five straight pennants. The two facts are not a coincidence. Yogi was "the man who holds us together," Stengel said in 1955, when Yogi won his third MVP.

One of the game's great bad-ball hitters, Berra hit only .285, but Oriole manager Paul Richards called him the most dangerous hitter in baseball after the seventh inning. He totaled 358 homers, and his 313 as a catcher are more than any backstop except Bench. Yogi could field, too, once going 148 straight games and 950 chances without an error, both records for catchers. His handling of pitchers always earned good reviews, and the Yankee staff numbers indicate the kudos were deserved.

Berra's best year was 1950, when he hit .322 with 124 RBIs but lost the MVP to teammate Phil Rizzuto. Berra did win the award in 1951, 1954, and 1955. In 1972, he was elected to the Hall of Fame.

Though an intelligent student of baseball (and an intelligent person), Berra was considered a buffoon by people who think reading the headlines on the sports page makes them experts. Yogi's favorite reading was comic books, he finished out of the money in the Mark Harmon Look-alike Contest, and his natural shyness sometimes makes him seem slow on the uptake. His malaprops have made him the most quoted person in baseball history, although it's getting harder every year to know what he said and what they *said* he said. Either way, he's moving up fast on Bill Shakespeare in Bartlett's. Some Yogi-isms: "He was a big clog in their machine." "It

gets late early there [left field]." "Nobody goes there anymore, it's too crowded." "Take it with a grin of salt." Or the immortal "It's never over till it's over." When Yogi was given a benefit on his retirement, he graciously thanked "all those who made this day necessary."

Thus it came as a surprise when Berra was named to manage the Yankees in 1964. Despite injuries to Mantle, Whitey Ford, and others, they came from six games back to win. But Yogi lost the Series to Johnny Keane's Cards, then was summarily replaced by Keane. He went crosstown to coach the Mets and managed them to a pennant in 1973. His winning percentage as a manager is an impressive .522.

Max Bishop

Second Baseman, Phi (A) 1924–33, Bos (A) 1934–35

Bishop was called "Camera Eye" for the way he looked over pitches. He led the AL second basemen in fielding in 1926 and 1928, but his range was only ordinary. He seldom stole a base and had little power at bat. Although he hit .316 in 1928, he was more comfortable at .270 and often a good deal lower.

What made Bishop valuable was his ability to draw walks. The Philadelphia A's of 1929–1931 had plenty of people who could hit a ton; Bishop gave them someone to drive home. Only 165 pounds, he never played in more than 130 games in a season, but in seven of the eight years when he played in at least 114 games, he walked over 100 times. From 1928 through 1931, he scored over 100 runs each season.

An extreme example of his unique talent came in 1929. He played in 129 games and made only 110 hits for a poor .232 batting average. But he walked a league-leading 128 times, nearly one a game, and scored 102 runs. His on-base percentage was .395!

Bert Blyleven

*Pitcher, Min (A) 1970–76, Tex (A) 1976–77,
Pit (N) 1978–80, Cle (A) 1981–85, Min (A) 1985-*

One of six foreign-born pitchers to win over 200 games, handsome Bert Blyleven was born in Holland. Had he stayed there, he might have wasted his long fingers plugging dikes instead of throwing the most wicked curves since the Burma Road. Bert's roundhouse was voted best in the league by AL managers, but the hitters knew it before the ballots were passed out. He didn't get to number seven on the all-time strikeout list by throwing tulips.

Blyleven is a control pitcher. When his hook isn't hooking, he spends a lot of time watching the ball sail into the seats. He surrendered an amazing 50 home runs in 1986, although pitching in the Metrodome surely had something to do with that.

He has been one of the top AL pitchers of his generation. Unfortunately he had some of his best years for teams ranging from bad to mediocre, making his more than 250 wins all the more impressive. In 1973 Bert was 20–17 for third-place Minnesota, his only 20-win season. Eleven years later, he almost made it at 19–7 for the tail-end Indians.

In one of his rare sojourns with a strong team, he was 12–5 for the 1979 Pirates and won a playoff game and a World Series tilt. His complaints the next year that he was being underused and overrelieved by manager Chuck Tanner did not endear him to Pirate fans but won him a ticket back to the American League. His subsequent record would tend to support his argument. He helped the Twins to the AL pennant in 1987 with a pair of LCS wins and added another in the World Series victory over the Cardinals.

Wade Boggs

Third Baseman, Bos (N) 1982-

If Boggs were to be run over in an elephant stampede tomorrow, he would still be remembered as one of the best hitters of the 1980s—perhaps *the* best. Certainly his batting averages put him in the lead. As a rookie in 1982, he batted a terrific .349. It turned out to be an "off" year. Every year since then, he's topped .350 except for 1984, when he slumped to .325. Three times he's been over .360. All this has added up to five AL batting crowns in his first seven seasons. He is probably the only player in baseball who could lead his league in hitting and see his career average go *down*.

Criticized for shoddy defense when he first arrived in Boston, he's worked hard to improve that. He also showed surprising power in 1987, when he hit 24 home runs. Nevertheless his job in the Red Sox scheme is to get on base and be driven in. He's done that so well that he's currently riding a streak of six straight seasons of scoring 100 or more runs.

According to published reports, Boggs eats chicken before every game as a sort of charm. Perhaps it wards off krypton.

Bobby Bonds

*Outfield, SF (N) 1968–74, NY (A) 1975,
Cal (A) 1976–77, Chi (A) 1978, Tex (A) 1978,
Cle (A) 1979, StL (N) 1980, Chi (N) 1981*

Bonds combined power and speed like no player before him. In 1969 he became only the fourth player to hit 30 home runs and steal 30 bases in a season, and then he went on to repeat that feat four more times, to take permanent possession. He was also the first man to 30–30 in both leagues.

Bobby stole 461 bases and hit 332 homers, 35 of them as leadoff man, 11 of those in one season, both records at the time. He is one of two men to hit a grand slam in his first big league game, and the first to do it since 1898.

Twice he led the league in runs scored and once in total bases, but where he was a real pacesetter was in strikeouts. That was Bonds' weakness. He set the major league record when he whiffed 187 times in 1979 and then broke it with 189 in 1970. He averaged one K in every four at-bats and ranks number six on the all-time strikeout list.

After seven seasons with the Giants, Bonds became a nomad, spending the next seven years with seven teams, all of them looking for his instant offense. In 1979, at age thirty-three, he hit 25 home runs and stole 34 bases for Cleveland, missing a sixth 30–30 season.

His son Barry has hit 53 home runs in his first three seasons in Pittsburgh, putting the Bondses on the brink of becoming the all-time father-son home run champs.

Bob Boone

Catcher, Phi (A) 1972–81, Cal (A) 1982-

Boone has caught more games than any other man in big league history, passing Hall of Famer Al Lopez (1,918 games) in 1987.

As a defensive catcher, Boone has been one of the best. He led league catchers in assists in 1973 and 1984. His 89 assists in 1973 were the most for a rookie since Johnny Bench had 108 in 1968. With California since 1982, he has thrown out better than 45 percent of runners attempting to steal, including 58 percent in his first year with the Angels. He won his first Gold Glove in 1978 with a .991 fielding average, breaking Bench's ten-year streak. Since then he's earned three more.

Boone's record as a handler of pitchers has been a mixed bag. The ERAs of both of his clubs went up after he joined them, and when he left the Phils, the club ERA went down. Nevertheless on his arrival in California, the Angels immediately rose from fifth to first. In all, he's guided his staffs to six division flags. And although Tim McCarver was Steve Carlton's personal catcher in Philadelphia in the late 1970s, Steve's wins went up from 18 to 24 when Boone took over in 1980.

Not much of a hitter during the regular season, Boone has had a splendid postseason record at bat—.311, including .400 for the Phils in the 1977 LCS and .455 for the Angels in the 1986 championship series. He appeared in one World Series, with Philadelphia in 1980, and batted .412.

Bob and father Ray, a longtime infielder for Cleveland and Detroit, are the second father and son after the Bells to each have 100 career home runs.

"Sunny Jim" Bottomley

First Baseman, StL (N) 1922–32, Cin (N) 1933–35, StL (A) 1936–37. Manager StL (A) 1937

Swaggering, popular, his hat cocked rakishly on the side of his head, Sunny Jim is in the record books for batting in 12 runs in one game. He did it in 1924 on two homers, a double, and three singles. That game, more than his career record, got him elected to the Hall of Fame in 1974.

In his sixteen major league seasons, Bottomley batted .300 eight times and batted in 100 or more runs six years in a row. Certainly not a wimp record but less impressive than it would be if it had occurred at any time in history other than the hit-happy 1920s and 1930s. In those days .300 hitters were as common as hip flasks at a hop. Bottomley was not particularly adept defensively, leading NL first basemen in errors four times.

Jim helped the Cardinals win four flags, in 1926, 1928, 1930, and 1931. He was named MVP in 1928 after leading the league in RBIs and triples and tying for homers with Hack Wilson.

In 1931 Jim figured in the closest batting race in history. Though injured, he hit .3482, losing to Bill Terry with .3486, and to his own roommate, Chick Hafey, who had .3489. If batting averages had been adjusted according to difficulty of the home ballpark, the Giants' Terry, playing in the cavernous Polo Grounds, would have won fair and square.

Lou Boudreau

Shortstop, Cle (A) 1938–50, Bos (A) 1951–52. Manager, Cle (A) 1942–50, Bos (A) 1952–54, KC (A) 1955–57, Chi (N) 1960

Boudreau got a lot of ink by pulling the "Boudreau Shift" against Ted Williams in 1946, bunching six of his Cleveland players on the right side of second base and daring Williams to take a shot. Actually Boudreau's manager Roger Peckinpaugh had first used the shift against Ted in 1941. But the maneuver earned Lou a reputation as a creative strategist, a fame unsupported by his record, which, except for one unforgettable year, was a losing one.

Lou Boudreau's greatest asset as a manager was that he could write the name *Lou Boudreau* in at shortstop every day. His hitting and his fielding combined to make him one of the half dozen best shortstops in this century.

A fine fielder, he led AL shortstops in fielding average a record-tying eight times, in double plays five times, and in putouts four. His 134 double plays in 1943 was a record, as was his .982 fielding average in 1947. His arm was only so-so, and others had more flat-out range, but Boudreau's knowledge of hitters allowed him to compensate by positioning himself where the action was.

In 1942, at the age of twenty-four, Lou applied for the Cleveland manager's job and got it, becoming the youngest man to manage a full season. The Indians finished fourth, the same spot they had held under Peckinpaugh. The Tribe moved up to third in 1943, then slipped to fifth in 1944, although Boudreau won the batting title with .327.

By 1947, when the Indians finished a ho-hum fourth, new owner Bill Veeck tried to trade Boudreau to the St. Louis Browns, a fate considered only slightly more humane than the guillotine. Angry Cleveland fans cast a newspaper vote 90 percent in favor of keeping Lou and trading Veeck. The owner decided to stick with Lou for one more year.

What a year! "Lou was determined to prove I was a jerk," Bill wrote. "And he did." In that magical 1948 Boudreau had the kind of season Frank Merriwell used to dream about. He hit .355, with 18 homers and 106 RBIs. He was always—or seemed always —to be at the center of a rally. One day he sat out with a slight injury, then came off the bench to pinch-hit for a win. More, he inspired his team; several players had career years. A furious four-way pennant race ended with the Indians and Red Sox tied. In the playoff at Boston, Boudreau daringly named a rookie lefty, Gene Bearden, to start. He himself smacked two home runs to destroy the Sox 8–3. The Indians then bested the Braves in the Series. Lou was AL MVP with more than 100 votes to spare.

Everything after that was an anticlimax. Lou managed four teams, finishing between third and eighth, before becoming a broadcaster for the Cubs and the father-in-law of Denny McLain.

In 1970 he was elected to the Hall of Fame.

Ken Boyer

Third Baseman, StL (N) 1955–65, NY (N) 1966–67, Chi (A) 1967–68, LA (N) 1968–69. Manager, StL 1978–80.

The best of six brothers who all played professional ball, Ken

was a third baseman in the Brooks Robinson mold, diving into the hole to snare hard grounders or running them down backhand behind the bag. Pie Traynor called him the best he ever saw.

Five times Ken led NL third basemen in double plays. Six times he won Gold Gloves. He even played center field one season, 1957, and led all NL outfielders in fielding average. His kid brother Clete, a Yankees' third baseman, was perhaps even better afield, but lacked Ken's bat. Ken hit over .300 five times and drove in 90 runs or better seven years in a row.

He sparked the Cards to the flag in 1964, hitting .295 with, 24 home runs and a league-leading 119 RBIs, and won the MVP. It was to be his last big season before a bad back slowed him down.

In the Series that year Ken beat Clete's Yanks in Game Four with a grand slam to even the Series. Then he helped win the seventh with a homer and three runs scored. It was the only time brothers hit homers in the same Series game.

Harry Brecheen

Pitcher, StL (N) 1940–52, StL (A) 1953

Brecheen was the Cardinal pitcher in 1946 when Enos Slaughter raced home from first to beat the Red Sox in the seventh game of the World Series. It gave Harry his third win of the Series, making him the first man to notch three since Stan Coveleski twenty-six years earlier and the only lefthander until Mickey Lolich twenty-two years later. The moment was a teensy tainted: pitching in relief, Brecheen had just allowed two inherited runners to score, blowing the lead he'd been sent in to hold. He nailed the win by shutting out the Sox in the ninth.

Two years later, 1948, Brecheen posted a 20–7 mark and the NL's lowest ERA. He won 14 games or better six years in a row for the Cardinals and pitched in three World Series, winning four and losing one. After eleven seasons with the proud Cardinals, he moved over to the humble Browns and discovered where their humility came from. He went 5–13 despite a decent 3.07 ERA. The next year the Browns moved to Baltimore and Harry became the pitching coach.

Nicknamed "the Cat" for the way he would pounce off the mound to field his position, Harry's World Series ERA of 0.83 is the second-best ever.

Roger Bresnahan

Catcher, Was (N) 1897, Chi (N) 1900, Bal (A) 1901–02,
NY (N) 1902–08, StL (N) 1909–12, Chi (N) 1913–15.
Manager, StL (N) 1090–12, Chi (N) 1915

Bresnahan is best known as the man who introduced shin guards for catchers in 1907, though some insist they had been worn earlier by black infielders. Some white catchers also reportedly wore protection under their socks. But Roger was the first white big leaguer to wear them openly, which brought jeering from fans and other players. He is said to have borrowed the idea from cricket. He also pioneered a crude leather batting helmet as early as 1908, after nearly being killed by a beaning.

Bresnahan caught Christy Mathewson and Joe McGinnity for the Giants. He, McGinnity, and manager John McGraw had arrived from Baltimore, picked up a last-place club, made a 32-game winner out of McGinnity and a 29-game winner out of Matty, and raised the team to second in 1903 and first in 1904 and 1905. In 1905 Roger achieved a feat that may never be duplicated—he caught four World Series shutouts, three of them by Matty. He also batted .313.

At bat, Bresnahan favored the thick-handled bats popular then. His best season was 1903, when he batted .350 with 42 extra-base hits and 34 stolen bases. He was unusually fast for a catcher, enough to bat first or second in the lineup. He had started out as a pitcher and then played center field, not becoming a regular catcher until 1905. He was a natural leader and, like his boss, McGraw, a fiery umpire baiter with frequent suspensions.

In 1945 Bresnahan became the first catcher elected to Cooperstown, two years ahead of Mickey Cochrane, who was a much better hitter and arguably better defensively and as a handler of pitchers.

Roger said he was born in Tralee, Ireland, so he was nicknamed "The Duke of Tralee." Actually, he was born (and died) in Toledo, Ohio.

George Brett

Third Baseman/First Baseman KC (A) 1973-

A curly-haired heart throb, Brett was the jewel in batting coach Charlie Lau's crown. He'd never gotten to .300 in the minor leagues, yet hitting off his front foot with the distinctive one-hand followthrough Lau taught, the lefthanded hitter went on to win two American League batting titles.

His .390 in 1980 came within a point of John McGraw's 1899 mark for highest batting average by a third baseman and was the closest assault on .400 since Ted Williams's .406 in 1941. Also in 1980, Brett knocked in 118 runs in 117 games to become the first player since Joe DiMaggio in 1948 to drive in over one run per game played.

Three times (in 1975, 1976, and 1979) George has led the AL in both hits and triples during the same season, a feat matched only by Ty Cobb. In 1979 he became one of only five players to slug 20 doubles, triples, and home runs in the same season.

Brett has thrived in postseason play, leading Kansas City to the playoffs six times, 1976–1985, and hitting .349 in playoff and Series competition. His nine homers—three in one 1976 game—are a record in the playoffs. One of his homers, a three-run shot off the Yanks' Goose Gossage, won the 1980 playoff, ending three years of consecutive playoff losses to New York.

Ironically George may be remembered longest for one at-bat at Yankee Stadium in 1985 and the homer he did-didn't-did hit. In the ninth inning, Brett put the ball in the stands to give Kansas City the lead. But Yankee manager Billy Martin convinced the umpire to take a homer away from him because there was too much pine tar on the bat handle. The usually calm Brett blew up like the Hindenburg. His frenzied, screaming protest is still among the most popular and amusing TV replays. A couple of days later, AL President Lee McPhail overruled his umpires and restored the homer on the grounds that they should have called the bat for excess pine tar *before* Brett batted.

Tommy Bridges

Pitcher, Det (A) 1930–46

In his first major league appearance, Bridges entered the game in relief against the Yankees, got Babe Ruth to ground out, and struck out Lou Gehrig. He went on from there to carve out an outstanding career with the Tigers. The slightly built righthander's trademark was a hard-breaking, heart-breaking curve that skittered sharply down and away. It helped make him one of the top AL pitchers of the 1930s, a milieu that included Lefty Grove, Ted Lyons, Red Ruffing, and Lefty Gomez—Hall of Famers all.

Tommy won 20 games three years in a row, 1934–1936, and helped pitch the Tigers to pennants in the first two. He also led the league in strikeouts in 1935 and 1936. But Bridges was also prone to control problems; he walked over 100 batters six times and averaged 3.79 walks per nine innings pitched. Nevertheless his career ERA of 3.57 wasn't bad at all in an era when the league averaged well above four. Bridges missed perfect-game immortality in 1932, when he gave up a single to pinch hitter Dave Harris (.327) with two out in the ninth.

He pitched in four World Series, winning four games and losing one. The win they all remember came in the 1935 Series, when, leading 4–3 in the ninth inning of Game Six, he gave up a leadoff triple to Stan Hack of the Cubs. Tom slammed the door with a strikeout, a grounder, and a fly to make the Tigers champs.

Lou Brock

Outfielder, Chi (N) 1961–64, StL (N) 1964–79

According to traditionalists, the trade that sent Brock from the Cubs to the Cardinals in 1964 for pitcher Ernie Broglio was the greatest steal since Brinks. "Steal," of course, is a significant word when discussing Brock—he once held the season record for stolen bases with his 118 in 1974. Actually the Cards also got a couple of guys named Jack Spring and Paul Toth, and the Cubs received Bobby Shantz and Doug Clemens, but Shantz was near the end of the line and the others never had one to begin with. So when Broglio won only seven games for Chicago in three years before disappearing into a trivia question and Brock played in the Cardinal outfield for sixteen years, made over 3,000 hits, and led the Cards to three pennants, the deal looked pretty darn good for the Redbirds.

But wait! According to some revisionist statisticians, Brock wasn't the bargain he was cracked up to be. They point out that Lou didn't walk enough for a leadoff man, so that his 3,023 career hits and .293 batting average become only a .341 on-base percentage. They also murmur seductively that he struck out way too often—1,730 times. And even though Brock finished up as the all-time base-stealing champ with 938 and led the NL eight times, revisionists ho-hum. They weigh the rally-killing effect of a caught-stealing against the marginal value of a successful theft, and downgrade the whole maneuver as something that just keeps 'em happy in the cheap seats. Finally revisionists point out that Brock was barely adequate in left field and had an arm you could stuff in a Christmas stocking.

Against all that evidence, the traditionalists can only mumble that Lou led the league in runs scored twice and wound up with 1,610. That he hit 149 homers and batted in 900, both above par for leadoff batters. That he hit .300 in one World Series, .400-plus in two, and twice stole seven bases in a Series, for an all-time record of fourteen. He also scored sixteen runs in twenty-one Series games and knocked in thirteen. And, the traditionalists quibble, for all those seasons he played in St. Louis, opponents *thought* he was doing things that beat them and had the losses to show for it.

In 1985, the first chance they got, the baseball writers elected Brock to the Hall of Fame. Shows whose side they're on.

Dennis "Dan" Brouthers

First Baseman, Troy (N) 1879–80,
Buf (N) 1881–85, Det (N) 1886–88, Bos (N) 1889,
Bos (P) 1890, Bos (AA) 1891, Bkn (N) 1892–93,
Bal (N) 1894–95, Lou (N) 1895, Phi (N) 1896

Brouthers (pronounced "Broothers") was the Mickey Mantle of the 1880s. He hit only 106 home runs—no one hit many in those days—but many of Dan's were tape-measure blows. In 1886 one knocked the fans out of a tower *behind* the park in Boston. He led the National League in home runs twice (1881 and 1886), not counting a career-high 14 in 1884.

A big man for his era (six-two, 220 pounds), Brouthers possessed a great batting eye and rarely struck out. He is said to have originated the phrase "Keep your eye on the ball." And that he did. His lifetime batting average of .343 is ninth-best all-time. He was the first man to win back-to-back batting titles, in 1882 and 1883; he won five overall. He drove in 100 or more runs five times and led in slugging average six straight seasons (1881–1886); his .520 lifetime slugging average was by far the best in the nineteenth century.

With Buffalo in the early 1880s, Brouthers played lead assassin in baseball's first Murderers' Row: "the Big Four" that also included Hardy Richardson, Jack Rowe, and Deacon White. All four were sold to Detroit after the 1885 season for a then princely $7,500. They won the pennant in 1887 and beat American Association champ St. Louis in a challenge Series, ten games to five. "We slugged 'em to death," Dan said.

Dan moved up to Boston in 1889, where he played in three leagues in three years. His Players League and AA teams won pennants. Finally, at Baltimore in 1894 he teamed with John McGraw to help the Orioles win their first flag.

Brouthers ended as a night watchman at the Polo Grounds. He died in 1932 and was inducted into the Hall of Fame in 1945.

Mordecai "Three Finger" Brown

Pitcher, StL (N) 1903,
Chi (N) 1904–12, 1916, Cin (N) 1913, StL (F) 1914,
Bkn (F) 1914, Chi (F) 1915.
Manager StL (F) 1914

When Brown was seven, he stuck his right hand in his uncle's corn shredder, cutting off the top two joints of his index finger

and paralyzing his little finger. The accident probably put him in the Hall of Fame. The damaged fingers gave Mordecai a natural knuckler, and he used it to star for the Cubs in their great years, 1905–1910. The shredder became a tourist attraction.

His biggest win was one of the most famous games ever played, the 1908 makeup of the Cubs-Giants game suspended when Fred Merkle failed to touch second base. Merkle's "boner" nullified a Giant win and left the teams tied at season's end. The makeup game was in New York in a park loaded with partisan fans, who thought they had been cheated out of victory. Brown and other Cubs received fistfuls of "black hand letters"—death threats—before they took the field. When Chicago starter Jack Pfeister got in trouble in the first inning, manager Frank Chance quickly called in Brown, who walked to the mound amid savage catcalls while a policeman stood guard. Brown was 29–9 in 1908 with a 1.47 ERA, while his mound opponent, Christy Mathewson, was 37–11, 1.43, but Brown had the edge that day, winning 4–2.

It was one of nine straight victories Mordecai scored over Matty going back to 1905. Their lifetime record versus each other: 13–11, Brown.

From 1904 through 1910, Brown had ERAs of 1.86, 2.17, 1.04, 1.39, 1.47, 1.31, and 1.86. That 1.04 is the record and the only time he led the NL. Low ERAs were the norm during those dead-ball days, but such consistency was scary. Speaking of consistency, he won 20 or more for six straight seasons from 1906 through 1911. Brown totaled a tidy 239 career wins, with a .649 winning percentage. In addition, he recorded 48 saves. By the modern definition of saves, he led the league four years in a row, topped by 13 in 1910. Of course, he had a first-rate team — the Tinker-to-Evers-to-Chance Cubs—playing behind him. Or maybe they had a great pitcher out front. He three-fingered Chicago to pennants in 1906, 1907, 1908, and 1910, and then took the Chicago Feds to the flag in 1915 with 17–8, 2.09.

Louis "Pete" Browning

Outfielder, Lou (AA) 1882–89, Cle (P) 1890, Pit (N) 1891, Cin (N) 1891–92, Lou (N) 1892–93, StL (N) 1894, Bkn (N) 1894

The original Louisville Slugger, Browning hit a career .343 back in the 1880s mostly for Louisville of the AA. Pete, who lived and died in the city by the Ohio River, was the first man to have his bats made to order for him, by John Hillerich, who went on to found the famous bat-making firm.

Although he led the American Association in batting twice and the Players League once, Pete's best year was 1887, when he finished second. He hit .471 under that year's rule which counted walks as hits. With the walks factored out, he dropped to "only" .402. His worst year was .253 in 1889. He blamed it on too much "German tea," swore off the stuff, and hit .391 the next season.

A pure hitter, Browning was pollution in the field with a lifetime .882 fielding average.

Morgan G. Bulkeley

Executive

Ever since Bulkeley was elected to the Hall of Fame in 1937, Cooperstown apologists have been hard-pressed to explain the error. They point out that old Bulks was a successful businessman and banker, head of Aetna Life Insurance for years, governor of Connecticut (1889–1893), U.S. senator (1905–1911), and a distinguished citizen of many public and personal virtues all his long life—all of which should get him into the Hall of Fame about as much as wearing a tutu should get you into the Marines.

As to what he did for baseball: well, he was president of the Hartford Dark Blues baseball club in 1874–1875. Remember them? Then, because they needed a figurehead, he let them make him President of the brand-new National League in 1876. He doesn't seem to have done anything during his year in office, but that's pretty much what the real power in the league—founder William Hulbert—wanted. When he didn't show up at the 1877 meeting, the club presidents elected Hulbert president since he'd been doing Bulkeley's job anyway. About thirty years later, Bulkeley's name was on the report of the committee that decided Abner Doubleday invented baseball, but Bulkeley doesn't appear to have been any more active in that than he'd been as NL prexy. At least *that's* in his favor. We are also told that he remained "close" to the game all his life. Define "close."

In point of fact, Bulkeley was a fine person who got into the Hall of Fame because the selectors of 1937 didn't know beans about baseball's history and figured the first NL president *must* have been a pioneer. They were wrong.

Jim Bunning

Pitcher, Det (A) 1955–63, Phi (N) 1964–67, 1970–71, Pit (N) 1968–69, LA (N) 1969

Bunning not only won 100 games in each league, he pitched a no-hitter in each. His NL effort was a perfect game, one of only thirteen in the history of the game, thrown against the last-place Mets on Father's Day in 1964. Jim won 20 only once, 20–8 with the fourth-place Tigers in 1957, but he won 19 in 1962 for the Tigers and three straight times for the Phillies (1964–66).

At six-three, Bunning was an intimidating power pitcher. He led the AL twice in strikeouts and the NL once. When he retired, he had 2,855 strikeouts, then second only to Walter Johnson.

With a degree in economics and nine children to support, Jim went into Republican politics in his home state of Kentucky when he left baseball. He lost a bid to become governor, but later won a seat in the U.S. Congress.

Selva "Lew" Burdette

Pitcher, NY (A) 1950, Bos (N) 1951–52, Mil (N) 1953–63, StL (N) 1963–64, Chi (N) 1964–65, Phi (N) 1965, Cal (N) 1966–67

Burdette was born in Nitro, West Virginia, and media types

liked to refer to him as "Nitro Lew" during his career because it gave their accounts an excitingly explosive ambience. Burdette's temper could go off occasionally. And his curve—especially his wet curve—could drop like a bomb. But his career was anything but rocketlike.

He was twenty-seven before he became a journeyman starter with the Braves in 1953, playing a righthanded second banana to Warren Spahn's lefthanded lead. He was thirty when he became a very good pitcher in 1956, winning 19 and leading the NL in ERA. He was nearing thirty-two the next year when, after 17 regular-season wins, he became a great pitcher in the World Series. In that fall of 1957, he defeated the Yankees three times, throwing three complete-game seven-hitters. Two of them —including the seventh game— were shutouts. His Series ERA was 0.67.

Having hit his peak, he stayed for a while, winning 60 games in the next three seasons, including a 1–0 no-hit win in 1960. Then came a slow decline into spot starter and reliever, until he closed up shop with 203 career victories in 1967. The media types missed the proper metaphor. Nitro is in coal country, and West Virginia coal burns slow but gives off excellent heat.

Jesse Burkett

Outfield, NY (N) 1890,
Cle (N) 1891–98, StL (N) 1899–1901,
StL (A) 1902–04, Bos (A) 1905

Burkett was known as the "Crab." He was argumentative, surly, and unpopular with both opponents and teammates. He once punched a rival manager in the nose and another time left a game under police guard for fomenting a riot. When he wasn't fighting, he was complaining. He griped *almost* as often as he cracked out base hits.

Burkett hit .400 three times, a feat accomplished by only two other men, Ty Cobb and Rogers Hornsby. He hit .423 in 1895, .410 in 1896, and .402 in 1899. The first two marks led the NL, but his 1899 average left him second to Big Ed Delahanty's .408. How he must have grumbled about that! Two years later, the Crab got his third NL batting title with a solid .382. Those were hitters' years. The pitcher's mound had been moved back to its present position of sixty feet, six inches from home plate in 1894, and the batters were able to tee off on those longer throws. It would take several years for the pitchers to catch up.

But Jesse would have hit, anyway. With the kind of speed that enabled him to steal 392 bases in his career and beat out many infield hits, Jesse boasted he could *bunt* .300. He bunted so well, in fact, that he could foul off third strikes indefinitely. His prowess inspired the creation of the present rule calling a bunted foul with two strikes an out.

Jesse started out as a pitcher for the Giants, but promptly proved a much better hitter and was moved to the outfield by the Cleveland Spiders. But he never seemed to get the hang of the outfield and, also hampered by the small gloves of the day, was perennially among the league leaders in errors. His .341 lifetime batting average made up for his bobbles and made his personality almost tolerable.

Owen "Donie" Bush

Shortstop, Det (A) 1908–21, Was (A) 1921–23.
Manager, Was (A) 1923, Pit (N) 1927–29, Chi (A) 1930–31,
Cin (N) 1933

At five-six and 140 pounds, Bush didn't hit much—.250 lifetime—but he drew a lot of walks for the Tigers and scored a lot of runs ahead of Ty Cobb, Sam Crawford, and Bobby Veach. Bush led the league in walks five of six times from 1909 through 1914, stole 30 or more bases eight times and scored 90 or more runs another eight times, including a league-best 113 in 1917. Meanwhile, Detroit was winning pennants in 1908–1909, finishing second in 1911 and 1915, and third in 1910 and 1919.

A good fielder, Bush's greatest strength was as a field general for almost thirteen years on those strong Tiger teams. He would later manage in the big leagues for seven years, winning a World Series with Pittsburgh in 1927.

As a minor league manager at Minneapolis, Bush took a big kid named Williams in tow and patiently polished him into a big leaguer. Williams's teammate Bobby Doerr says Donie was the perfect manager for Ted, holding the reins neither too tight nor too loose. Once after Ted had doubled, Bush hollered to him to be careful of a pickoff. "Don't worry, Skip," Williams called back, "I got here by myself and I can get home by myself."

Roy Campanella

Catcher, Negro Leagues, 1937–45,
Baltimore Elite Giants, Bkn (N) 1948–57

For a decade with the Brooklyn Dodgers (1948–1957), Campanella was one of the two best catchers in baseball. His only serious rival was the Yankees' Yogi Berra. The Dodgers and Yankees dominated their leagues during that period, and each catcher received three MVP awards. An auto accident in 1958 left Campy substantially paralyzed and ended his career. In 1969 he was elected to the Hall of Fame.

The squat, powerful Campanella began playing in the Negro Leagues with the Baltimore Elite Giants while still a teenager. He played in All-Star Games in 1941, 1944, and 1945. He was the second black player (after Jackie Robinson) signed by the Dodgers, and he joined Nashua in the Brooklyn farm system in 1946.

In 1948, a month into the season, he was called up to the Dodgers and quickly established himself as the NL's top catcher. Campanella was excellent defensively, an acknowledged master in handling pitchers, and durable. His rookie year was the only one of his ten in the majors in which he didn't catch in over 100 games.

Campy's Dodgers won NL pennants in 1949, 1952, 1953, 1955 and 1956. The 1955 crew defeated the Yankees in the World Series to become the first Brooklyn world champs in this century. Although he was always steady as Gibraltar behind the plate, Campanella's hitting fluctuated wildly. But in his best seasons he was a terror. In 1951 he hit .325 with 33 home runs and 108 RBIs to win his first MVP Award. Two years later, in 1953, he won his second MVP with .312, 41 homers, and a league-leading 142 RBIs. At the time, both the home run and RBI marks were records for catchers. He

slipped to his poorest season in 1954, batting only .207. But in the championship year of 1955 he bounced back with .318, 32, and 107 to gain his third MVP. His career totals were .276, 242, 856, with the home run total being the most ever hit by a catcher up to that time.

Campanella's autobiography, *It's Good to Be Alive*, told the story of his courageous struggle to overcome the effects of his auto accident. It was later made into a movie for television.

Rod Carew

Second Baseman/First Baseman, Min (A) 1967–78,
Cal (A) 1979–85

Only Ty Cobb won more batting championships than Carew, the moody Panamanian who sprayed 3,053 hits where they ain't. He won seven AL titles for Minnesota, including four in a row from 1972 through 1975. In 1969, when Rod won his first batting crown with .332, he stole home 7 times, tying a mark set by Brooklyn's Pete Reiser. In 1972 Rod hit a league-leading .318 without a single homer, the only batting champ ever to do that. Fifteen of his hits were bunts. Carew's high mark was .388 in 1977, like Ted Williams' mark of 1957 the second highest batting average in the majors since 1941. That year he also led in runs scored (128) and triples (16). He was named MVP.

Carew spent his last seven years with the Angels in a poor park for hitters. Although he won no more batting championships in California, he was over .300 in his first five seasons there. He retired with a .328 career average.

The main raps against Carew related to his defense. He played second base through 1975, but critics carped that his arm was too weak for the job. Shifted to first base for his remaining ten seasons, he caught flack as a single-hitter in a power position.

Max Carey

Outfielder, Pit (N) 1910–26, Bkn (N) 1926–29.
Manager, Bkn (N) 1932–33

Pittsburgh's Max Carey was probably the best center fielder National League batters ever cursed. The only thing that covered more grass at Forbes Field was smoke from the steel mills. In Palmer's Linear Weights, only Tris Speaker ranks with Max as an outfield bandit.

Born Maximillian Carnerius, the former divinity student led the league in putouts nine times and retired with an NL record of 6,363, a mark later broken by Willie Mays in a longer career. Carey's 339 assists are still the twentieth-century NL record.

A good-but-not-great hitter, Carey averaged .285 and led the league twice in triples, more on speed than power. He was a great baserunner—fifth on the all-time stolen base list with 738. He led the league in thefts ten times, and once, in 1922, he stole 51 bases in 53 attempts.

In 1925, his final full year with Pittsburgh, at age thirty-five, he stole second, third, and home in the same inning on two different days in August. Playing in the World Series that year with a broken rib, he batted .458, stole three bases, and

in the seventh game clipped Walter Johnson for four hits and scored three times to help win the world championship 9–7.

In 1961 Carey was elected to the Hall of Fame.

Steve Carlton

Pitcher, StL (N) 1965–71, Phi (N) 1972–86, SF (N) 1986,
Chi (A) 1986, Cle (A) 1987, Min (A) 1987–88

For most of his career Carlton answered a short "——" to questions from the press and refused to grant interviews. He let his pitching do his talking, but as a consequence his training methods remained a mystery. One report had him preparing for a game with meditation while floating weightless in total darkness. However he prepared, it worked.

With Spahn and Koufax, Carlton was one of the three best NL lefthanders of all time. He won 329 games, second only to Spahn among lefties. He had 4,131 strikeouts—19 in one game – more than anyone except Nolan Ryan. (He's also second to Ryan in walks with 1,828.) He won four Cy Youngs, one of them unanimous.

He's the only man to win a Cy Young with a last-place team. That was in 1972, after he'd been swapped from the Cardinals. Steve was an amazing 27–10 with the Phils, who won only 32 without him that year. He was Triple Crown winner—wins, ERA, and strikeouts (27, 1.97, 310). It earned him a record salary from the Phillies the following year— $167,000, a figure that is laughable today. Carlton took special delight during 1972 in whipping his old team, the Cards, who had refused to give him a raise after his 20–9 season helped them take second place in 1971. He beat the Birds four times, allowing a total of only two runs. One of the wins was his 100th. He also got his 300th victory, over St. Louis Cardinals.

Steve had four more 20-win seasons as the Phillies moved from being "phutile" in the early 1970s to contenders, finally becoming world champions in 1980. He won two games in the 1980 World Series, including the Game Six clincher.

Using a fastball, curve, and legendary slider, the six-four lefty was a workhorse, leading the NL in innings pitched five times. When he suffered a strained shoulder in 1985, he went on the disabled list for the first time in his career.

Gary Carter

Catcher, Mon (N) 1974–84, NY (N) 1985-

Although cynics admit Carter ranks as the top catcher of the 1980s, they criticize his personality. After all, the guy is friendly, open, cooperative, thoughtful, enthusiastic, and has never been involved in a scandal. *What's he hiding*?

Granting for the moment that he just might be what he seems as a person, the next question might be: is he what he seems to be as a catcher? Long regarded as the best-throwing backstop in the NL, he has slipped a bit in the past few years. He makes up for his aging arm in part with good footwork and a quick release. He is widely admired as a handler of pitchers, but since coming to the Mets in 1985 he's had more to work with than most NL catchers. He is given much of the credit for the development of young Dwight Gooden into a star. In summary, for all his virtues behind the plate, Carter would

not be a virtual shoo-in for the Hall of Fame were it not for his bat.

His career batting average is in the middling range, but his power stats are excellent: more than 300 career home runs, with a high of 32 in 1985; four seasons with over 100 RBIs, including a league-leading 106 in 1984.

In the strike-shortened 1981 season, Gary hit only .251 for the Expos but slugged .421 in the divisional series to help get them into the playoff and .438 there, as they lost to the Dodgers. In the 1986 World Series he hit two key home runs in the third-game win and ignited the tenth-inning rally in Game Six that culminated in Bill Buckner's fatal error.

Alexander Joy Cartwright

Founder

The first man to formulate baseball's rules, Cartwright may have "invented" baseball in 1845 when he organized the New York Knickerbockers, who played their first match game in Hoboken, New Jersey, on the nineteenth day of June in the following year (and lost 23–1).

The Knicks were a company of volunteer firemen, and Cartwright a bank teller, when the historic marriage was made. It was a game for gentlemen, and Cartwright once fined a Knick sixpence for swearing. The rules for the "New York Game" included three strikes per out, and three outs per inning. But balls hit over the fence were fouls, a ball caught on one bounce was an out, and the first team to score 21 runs ("aces") was declared the winner. A committee later provided formally for nine-men teams, nine innings to the game, and ninety feet between bases.

Then he went west to California where he found the '49ers in the big Gold Rush, spreading his new game, like Johnny Appleseed, at every village he stopped, and carrying with him the ball of that historic first game. He eventually reached Honolulu, where he found business success and became a respected civic leader. He died in 1892, but the publicity surrounding the Abner Doubleday legend with the foundation of the Hall of Fame at Cooperstown led to an investigation of Cartwright's role in the origin of the game. He was enshrined in the Hall in 1938.

Bob Caruthers

Pitcher, StL (AA) 1884–87, Bkn (AA) 1888–89,
1890–91, StL (N) 1892

Twice a 40-game winner, 138-pound Bob Caruthers retired with a 218–97 record for an amazing .692 percentage, the highest of any pitcher with a significant number of decisions. In a nine-year career Caruthers pitched for five championship teams and one runner-up. His only losing team was sixth place Brooklyn in 1891, but he was still 18–14.

As a twenty-one-year old rookie with the old St Louis Browns, Bob led the American Association in wins, percentage, and ERA (40–13, .755, 2.07). The next year he was 30–14. In the postseason series against Cap Anson's NL White Stockings, he won a one-hit shutout over Jim McCormick. When he tried to come back the next day, he was blasted for twelve hits. But he won the sixth and final game,

4–3, over Hall of Famer John Clarkson in ten innings. Parisian Bob—so named for his off-season trip to France— was 29–9 in 1887, as the Browns won their third straight flag.

After a 29–15 season with second-place Brooklyn, he had his best year in 1889, 40–11, as the Brooks won the AA pennant.

As the rules governing pitching tightened and the number of balls needed for a base on balls fell, Caruthers's walks increased. His wins dropped to 23, then 18. After starting 1892 at 2–8 for St. Louis, he called it a career.

Norm Cash

First Baseman, Chi (A) 1958–59, Det (A) 1960–74

Cash hit .300 only once, and it was a big one—.361 in 1961, his second year as the Tigers' first baseman. He also slugged 41 HRs and knocked in 132.

The next year Norm fell 118 points to .263, a record fall for a batting champ. He never approached 100 RBIs again or hit higher than .283, but he remained a dangerous batter. He had more RBIs per official at-bats than his roommate, Al Kaline, in part because he drew 1,043 walks. He finished with 1,046 runs scored, 1,103 RBIs, and 377 homers. Four times he cleared the roof at Tiger Stadium.

The popular and personable first sacker was somewhat immobile in the field, but he had sure hands and twice led AL first basemen in fielding. He hit .385 in the 1968 World Series to help the Tigers win in seven.

A good football player at Sul Ross State, Cash had been a thirteenth-round draft choice of the NFL Chicago Bears, but he chose to play baseball.

Cesar Cedeno

Outfielder, Hou (N) 1970–81, Cin (N) 1982–85,
StL (N) 1985, LA (N) 1986

Leo Durocher once called Cedeno another Willie Mays. Then, in his third and fourth seasons, the young Dominican made the mistake of compiling back-to-back .320 years. From there on, he staggered through the remainder of his career under that back-breaking tonnage of *potential*. Cedeno might have come closer to imitating Mays if he'd played anywhere but Houston, where his long drives were outs. It didn't help that he got into only two postseason series with Houston and didn't do well in either.

For one brief period he was the player everyone predicted he'd be. In 1985 the Cardinals picked him up in late season. In 28 games, he hit .434 to help St. Louis to the division title. Again he slumped in postseason play, hitting only .167 in the LCS and .133 in the Series.

His career totals of 2,087 hits for a .285 average, 976 RBIs, and 199 home runs would look a lot better if so much hadn't been expected of him. His best mark—550 stolen bases—put him in ninth place all-time when he retired.

Orlando Cepeda

First Baseman, SF (N) 1958–66, StL (N) 1966–68,

Atl (N) 1969–72, Oak (A) 1972, Bos (A) 1973, KC (A) 1974

Cepeda's first big league home run was also the first major league homer ever hit on the West Coast. It came in 1958 against Los Angeles. Orlando hit 24 more to win the Rookie of the Year and helped pull the Giants from sixth to third. He was only twenty years old. His father, Perucho, a shortstop, had been hailed as the greatest player in Puerto Rico. Orlando's first seven seasons gave rise to predictions that he would become the greatest Latin player. In those seven seasons, he topped .300 six times, had at least 96 RBIs each year, and totaled 222 home runs. His 46 homers and 142 RBIs led the NL in 1961. Despite his success in San Francisco, his stay was stormy as he fought managers and fans who tagged him as lazy.

A bad knee had begun to limit his play, and surgery in 1965 cost him most of the season. The Cards took a chance on him, and he was named Comeback of the Year in 1966 with 20 homers and 73 RBIs. The next year, as the Cardinals won the pennant, he was a unanimous choice for MVP. He hit a career high .325, with 25 home runs and a league-high 111 RBIs. Cepeda hit a disappointing .103 in the World Series.

Further knee problems pulled down the rest of his career, although he showed occasional flashes of his old power. His career totals of .297, 379 homers, and 1,365 RBI put him in rarefied atmosphere. However, a postcareer, ten-month prison sentence for marijuana possession has thus far weighed more heavily with Cooperstown selectors.

Henry Chadwick

Pioneer

Having played cricket and rounders in his native England, Chadwick came to America with his family in 1837 at age thirteen. He first played baseball in 1847 and pronounced it a descendant of the earlier English games. When nearly a decade later he first saw games between skilled players, he recognized baseball's potential to become America's national game. His writings and influence helped make that potential a fact.

In the late 1850s, he began covering baseball games as a reporter for several newspapers, most notably the *New York Clipper* and the *Brooklyn Eagle*. In connection with this, he developed the box score and devised a system of scoring that is little changed today.

Chadwick continued to write and comment on baseball for more than fifty years. He originated the first guide, *Beadle's Dime Baseball Player*, in 1860, edited *DeWitt's Guide* through the 1870s and *Spalding's Base Ball Guide* from 1881 to 1908. His *The Game of Base Ball* (1868) was the first hardcover book published on the subject.

Widely influential for his writings, he also had a direct influence in shaping the game by serving on various rules committees, beginning in 1858. He opposed gambling, drunkenness, and rowdiness among players, sometimes to no avail. Chadwick considered himself one of "the intelligent majority" who preferred scientific hitting over slugging and fielding prowess.

Among the honors he received during his lifetime were an honorary membership in the National League in 1894 (though the $600-a-year pension the league granted two years later had more practical value) and a medal awarded at the St. Louis World's Fair.

The "Father of Baseball," as he was called, died from pneumonia in 1908 after attending Opening Day in Brooklyn. Flags around the league flew at half-staff in his honor. In 1938 he was named to the Hall of Fame.

Frank "Husk" Chance

First Baseman, Chi (N) 1898–1912, NY (A) 1913–14. Manager, Chi (N) 1905–12, NY (A) 1913–14, Bos (A) 1923

Because of the popularity of F. P. Adams' poem bemoaning that his favorites, the Giants, were often victims of double plays by the Cubs' Tinker-to-Evers-to-Chance, there is a tendency to view the trio's election to Cooperstown in 1946 as some sort of P.R. fluke. In point of fact, a strong case can be made for Tinker's and Evers's enshrinements as players. Chance, however, had too short a career as a regular to rank with the game's foremost first basemen. Nevertheless he's the most deserving Hall of Famer of the three. He was called "The Peerless Leader" for good reason.

Chance never played in the minors. He broke in as a catcher before winning the first base job in 1903. By 1904 he was captain of the team, and in 1905 at age twenty-seven he succeeded Frank Selee as manager.

As the Cubs manager he led the Chicago to glory in 1906–1910, when they won four flags in five years. They also won two World Series under Chance, which is two more than they've won since. In his first full year at the helm, the Cubbies won 116 games, a record that still stands, despite the fact that modern teams play more games. They *averaged* 106 wins in the five-year span. Of course, he had good players, but so did John McGraw in New York and Fred Clarke in Pittsburgh.

Even counting two seventh-place years with the New York Highlanders (1913–14) and one last-place finish with the Red Sox (1923), Frank's winning percentage of .593 is sixth best ever.

And he wasn't a bad first baseman, big for his day and very powerful. He played only six full years. The victim of frequent beanings, Frank played his last full season in 1908. He hit .272 and slammed three hits against Mathewson in the unforgettable playoff that gave the Cubs the flag. In the World Series victory over Detroit, he hit .421. He averaged .310 in Series play overall, and his ten Series stolen bases are topped only by Eddie Collins and Lou Brock. His career batting average was a strong .297 during the most inert days of the dead-ball era. He usually batted himself cleanup, just another indication that he knew what to do with a good player when he had one.

A. B. "Happy" Chandler

Commissioner

The popular, outgoing Kentucky U.S. senator (and former governor) was a surprise choice to become commissioner of baseball in 1945, filling the office held by Judge Kenesaw Mountain Landis until his death in 1944. Chandler was the choice of the Yankees' Leland "Larry" MacPhail. Other can-

didates had included Ford Frick, Jim Farley, J. Edgar Hoover, and Tom Dewey.

As commissioner, Chandler proved well liked by fans, press, and even most players. Undoubtedly many of his decisions worked to the benefit of baseball. His downfall was that he *made* decisions when most baseball owners would have preferred a figurehead.

Early in his tenure, he was confronted with the decision of the Dodgers' Branch Rickey to sign Jackie Robinson and other black players. Chandler was already on record as favoring black entrance to the heretofore all-white major leagues. Over the objections of the other fifteen owners, the commissioner stood behind Rickey, making baseball open to all.

Early in 1946, Chandler faced another crisis when eighteen major league players jumped to the Mexican League for promises of higher salaries. Chandler banned the players from major league baseball for five years. Many believe that this decision more than any other eventually led to his downfall as commissioner because it left baseball's reserve clause open to the courts. The player ban was lifted in 1950, and most of the players returned to their former clubs—some, such as pitcher Sal Maglie, to outstanding success. However, a suit filed by outfielder Danny Gardella shook baseball to its foundations.

One of Chandler's more controversial decisions was a suspension handed out to popular manager Leo Durocher for the 1947 season. The action was apparently precipitated by Durocher's being seen in the company of known gamblers. Chandler was criticized at the time for not taking action against some owners, including MacPhail, who also numbered gamblers among their acquaintances. His defense was that Durocher's suspension was the culmination of a long string of controversial incidents.

In 1951 he received only nine of sixteen owner votes for his re-election. A two-thirds endorsement was necessary. Chandler resigned and returned to Kentucky, where he was again elected governor. In 1982 he was named to the Baseball Hall of Fame.

Ray Chapman

Shortstop, Cle (A) 1912–20

Chapman was the only major leaguer ever killed in a game. On August 16, 1920, as his Indians fought toward their first pennant, he froze on a Carl Mays pitch. The ball fractured his skull and he died the next day. He was only twenty-nine years old.

At the time Chapman was the AL's leading shortstop. He had hit .300 in three of his last four seasons and was among the leaders each year in stolen bases. A clever hit-and-run man, he led in walks in 1918. In the field he had the best range in the league.

In the furor after his death, most "trick" pitches were banned, among them the spitball. Ironically Mays's pitch had been a fastball. More important, the leagues mandated more frequent disposal of discolored or bruised baseballs; this produced conditions that were safer for batters. This step may also have done more to usher in the prodigious batting boom of the 1920s than even the injection of rabbit hormones into the ball.

Oscar Charleston

Outfielder, Negro Leagues, 1915–50, Indianapolis ABCs, Lincoln Stars, Chicago American Giants, St. Louis Giants, Harrisburg Giants, Hilldale, Homestead Grays, Pittsburgh Crawfords, Toledo Crawfords, Indianapolis Crawfords, Philadelphia Stars, Brooklyn Brown Dodgers

Charleston is often cited as the greatest player of the Negro Leagues. Contemporaries lauded him as "the black Tris Speaker" for his center field play, "the black Ty Cobb" for his base running, and "the black Babe Ruth" for his hitting. While such analogies are useful in showing the range of Charleston's abilities, they have a counterfeit aura that is unfair to a unique performer. His combination of speed and strength places him among the foremost players, black or white, of all time. New York Giants' manager John McGraw said Charleston was the best player, period. Then he sighed: "If only I could calcimine him."

As a center fielder, Charleston was able to play unusually shallow because his great speed and judgment allowed him to get back for deep fly balls. He ranged far to his left and right, enabling the other outfielders to play closer to the foul lines. His arm has been reported as "weak", but all sources agree on its accuracy.

Charleston ran bases with speed (he was clocked at 23 seconds for the 220-yard dash) and savagery. He was quick-tempered and possessed legendary strength. Many who saw him remark on his "mean streak," indicating he preferred running over an opponent or spiking him than sliding around him to avoid a tag. On the other hand, some of the same observers indicate that Charleston picked his victims judiciously, always choosing those he knew he could physically bully.

He hit with great power and consistency. While statistics are incomplete, it is known that he batted .366 in the Negro National League in 1920 and followed that with .434 in 1921. He is unofficially credited with a lifetime league average of .353, and he batted .318 with 11 home runs in fifty-three barnstorming games against white major leaguers. He led the NNL in home runs several times, and many of his homers were of the tape-measure variety.

He started in 1915, became a player-manager in the late 1920s, and was active as a manager until his death in 1954. When Branch Rickey decided to break white baseball's color line, he had Charleston scout the Negro Leagues. Among his recommendations were Jackie Robinson and Roy Campanella.

Charleston was elected to the Hall of Fame in 1976.

Jack Chesbro

Pitcher, Pit (N) 1899–1902, NY (A) 1903–09, Bos (A) 1909

Until Ralph Branca threw the "Shot Heard 'Round the World" to Bobby Thomson in 1951, Chesbro was notorious for tossing the most infamous pitch in history. It was probably a spitter, and it definitely sailed over the head of New York Highlander catcher Red Kleinow and, according to baseball lore, it absolutely cost New York the 1904 pennant.

It was the final day of the season at old Hilltop Park (now the site of the New York Medical Center). The Highlanders

were a game and a half behind Boston but could have won the pennant by sweeping a doubleheader against the Red Sox (then called the Puritans). Chesbro pitched the first game for New York. The score was 1–1 with two out in the Boston ninth. Boston's Lou Criger was on third and the count was 2–0. Then Chesbro threw *the pitch*. Jack, and later Mrs. Chesbro, always maintained that Kleinow should have caught the ball, but neither was a disinterested observer and there was no instant replay. New York won the second game of the doubleheader (though by then Boston couldn't have cared less).

The New York press elected Chesbro goat and never let him forget it for the rest of his life. No one ever seemed to notice that the team could have won by rallying in its half of the ninth (or by scoring two more runs in any of the earlier innings). It was like pulling teeth to get anyone in New York to admit that the Highlanders wouldn't have had a sniff at the pennant had it not been for Chesbro. He'd earlier earned the nickname "Happy Jack" for his pleasant disposition while working in the state mental hospital in Middletown, New York. To smile after that pitch no doubt required steel facial muscles.

Ironically, up to that awful pitch the stocky righthander was enjoying one of the best seasons of any pitcher in the twentieth century: it would end up 41–12, with a 1.82 ERA. He started 51 games, completed 48, pitched 455 innings, and whiffed 240—still the Yankee record.

Chesbro won 21 and 28 with Pittsburgh in 1901–02, then jumped to New York. He won 21 in his first year there, but missed pitching in the 1903 World Series with the Pirates. He won 19 in 1905 and 24 in 1906, but people kept asking, "Yeah, but what about that pitch in 1904?"

Chesbro was named to the Hall of Fame in 1946 for what he did on all his *other* pitches.

Clarence "Cupid" Childs

Second Baseman, Phi (N) 1888, Syr (AA) 1890,
Cle (N) 1891–98, StL (N) 1899, Chi (N) 1900–01

Childs was one of the leading infielders of the 1890s. At his peak with the Cleveland Spiders he was a steady .300 hitter and considered one of the best fielding second basemen in the NL. With players such as Childs, pitcher Cy Young, short-stop Ed McKean, outfielder Jesse Burkett, and first baseman/manager Patsy Tebeau, the Spiders challenged the Baltimore Orioles as the leading team of the mid-1890s.

Childs scored at least 90 runs each season from 1890 through 1898, including an NL-leading 136 in 1892. He topped .300 six times, with a career high of .355 in 1896. That season he led all NL second basemen in putouts, assists, and doubleplays. He also led in errors, one of four times he topped the league in that category. Despite his high miscue totals, his contemporaries regarded him as an outstanding fielder who collected errors on balls that many fielders would not have reached.

In 1899 Childs was one of the Cleveland players switched to St. Louis in a move to build a powerhouse Cardinal team by the Robison brothers, who owned both franchises. The Cleveland franchise was destroyed by the loss of its best players, while the Cardinals finished a disappointing fifth.

Eddie "Knuckles" Cicotte

Pitcher, Det (A) 1905, Bos (A) 1908–12,
Chi (A) 1912–20

Cicotte was a key conspirator in the infamous "Black Sox" scandal over the 1919 World Series. He tearfully confessed: "I did it for the wife and kiddies." Although neither he nor any of the other seven Soiled Sox were ever convicted of their misdeeds in a court of law—the evidence mysteriously disappeared before the trial—they were banned from baseball for life.

Until the revelations of the scandal, Cicotte was one of the AL's most successful pitchers, using trick pitches such as the knuckleball, shine ball, emery ball, and spitball. From 1908 through 1916, he won between 10 and 18 games each season. In 1917, when the Sox won the AL pennant, he was 28–12, leading the league in wins, innings pitched and ERA. After an off-year, he bounced back with his best season in 1919: he led in both wins and percentage with a 29–7 mark. In spite of Cicotte's success, White Sox owner Charles Comiskey paid him considerably less than several lesser pitchers in the league received. Apparently this left him open to entreaties by gamblers that he help throw the 1919 World Series to underdog Cincinnati.

He lost two Series games to the Reds, both under circumstances that appeared more suspicious when the fix conspiracy became public. That did not occur until near the end of the 1920 season, one in which Cicotte had a 21–10 record.

After he was barred from baseball, Cicotte lived quietly in Detroit, using a pseudonym to protect the wife and children for whom he claimed to have entered the conspiracy.

Fred Clarke

Outfielder, Lou (N) 1894–99, Pit (N) 1900–1915.
Manager, Lou (N) 1897–99, Pit (N) 1900–15

Clarke was a sure-handed, speedy outfielder and an excellent hitter with surprising power for a 160-pounder. He hit .406 in 1897, topped .300 eleven times, and finished with a career .315 average. He totaled 2,708 hits, scored 1,626 runs, batted in 1,015, and stole 506 bases.

But he was an even better manager. He won four pennants at Pittsburgh and finished second five times. He came to Pittsburgh from Louisville in 1900 when the NL pared down from twelve to eight teams. Honus Wagner, Tommy Leach, Deacon Phillippe, and Claude Ritchey were among the other former Louisville players who joined the Pirates. In his first year as Pirate skipper, 1900, Fred and the other Louisville imports lifted them from seventh to the thick of the pennant fight—they eventually finished second.

He brought the Buccos in first the next three years, 1901–1903. In 1903 he took them to the first World Series, losing to Boston only after eight hard-fought games.

In 1909 the Pirates won 110, a total exceeded only by the 1906 Cubs and 1954 Indians. In the World Series, Fred's three-run homer in the seventh inning of Game Five broke open a 3–3 tie, as Pittsburgh went on to defeat Ty Cobb's Tigers. Clarke drove in seven runs in the Series.

He was elected to the Hall of Fame in 1951.

John Clarkson

Pitcher, Wor (N) 1882, Chi (N) 1884–87,
Bos (N) 1890–92, Cle (N) 1892–94

One of the greatest pitchers of the nineteenth century, Clarkson combined a curve and cunning to win 326 games, but his manager in Chicago insisted that he "pitched on praise" and needed continuous ego boosting to be effective. If scolded, the handsome, high-strung righthander would loose all confidence and sulk. The temperamental pitcher ended his years in an insane asylum.

Clarkson joined Chicago in 1884 and the next year led the NL in victories while compiling a 53–16 record. He won 35 in 1886 and 38 in 1887, again leading in victories in the latter year.

Before the 1888 season he and outfielder/catcher King Kelly were sold to Boston for $10,000 each, an incredible sum at that time. Clarkson justified the price by continuing his outstanding pitching, winning 33 in 1889, 49 in 1890 (when he also led the NL in winning percentage and ERA), 25 in 1891, and 33 in 1892.

In 1963 he was named to the Hall of Fame.

Roberto Clemente

Outfielder, Pit (N) 1955–72

The first Hispanic to be elected to the Hall of Fame and the second ballplayer to be honored on a U.S. stamp, Clemente won four batting titles.

A proud, even vain, man, Clemente was sensitive to prejudice against Latin players and quick to speak out against real or imagined slights. He believed he deserved more MVP Awards than the one that won in 1966. Whether that was true or not, Roberto was handicapped by playing his entire career in Pittsburgh instead of New York or Los Angeles. Critics also pointed out that he missed many games and labeled him a hypochondriac. Clemente's physical ills were real, the worst being a chronic bad back stemming from a 1956 auto accident. He played in over 100 games in each of his eighteen major league seasons, but the criticism remained.

Clemente finished with a .317 career batting average, an even 3,000 base hits, 1,416 runs scored, and 1,305 RBIs. Standing deep in the righthand batter's box, he put all of his body into an all-or-nothing swing, but though he cracked 240 homers, he was not really a home run hitter. His forte was the line drive, often lashing pitches to the opposite field for extra-base hits.

His arm became legendary. He set the NL record by leading in assists five times. His season high was 27 in 1961. He won 12 straight Gold Gloves.

Roberto led the Pirates to two world championships, hitting .362 in the World Series. His great showcase was in 1971, when he hit .414 and played with an inspiring recklessness in leading the Pirates to a seven-game victory over the Baltimore Orioles. Only then did some of his severest critics admit his greatness.

He died in a plane crash on New Year's Eve, 1972, on a mercy flight carrying supplies to earthquake victims in Nicaragua. The usual five-year waiting period was waived, and he was named to the Hall of Fame in 1973.

Harlond Clift

Third Baseman, StL (A) 1934–43, Was (A) 1943–45

Clift was an outstanding player whose competent light was hidden beneath bushels of ineptitude provided by his St. Louis Browns teammates. It was difficult for fans in the 1930s to think of anyone with the laughing-stock Browns as a serious talent. Of course, the Browns' attendance was so low in the 1930s—in only two seasons did they draw over 200,000—that there were few in the stands to admire Clift or chuckle at his teammates.

An exceptional fielder, he was the first third baseman to start 50 double plays in a season. And while that record was in part due to a penchant that Brownies' pitchers had for putting runners on base, the rest of Clift's fielding stats support the idea that he had range and reliability beyond most AL third sackers.

He was certainly the most productive hitter among the league's third basemen. He hit .300 a couple of times, but his career batting average was an unexceptional .272. But he walked a lot, going over the 100 mark seven times in eight seasons. And he hit with more power than any third baseman ever had. In 1937 he set a record for third basemen with 29 homers. The next year he upped that to 34. In both years he drove in more than 100 runs.

Ty Cobb

Outfielder, Det (A) 1905–26, Phi (A) 1927–28.
Manager, Det (A) 1921–26

In 1936 Cobb was the first man elected to Cooperstown, mostly by voters who grew up in his era. Babe Ruth was second. The majority of today's critics would reverse the order and maybe drop Cobb a few more pegs besides. The reason, of course, is that the modern game, with its emphasis on home runs, has evolved in a Ruthian rather than a Cobbian direction.

Cobb's strengths were his ability to reach first, steal a base or two, and then score. After all these years, he's still first in batting average (.366), second in hits (4,190), second in steals (892), and first in runs scored (2,245). He collected eleven AL batting titles, hit over .400 three times, led in steals six times and in runs scored five. In other words, he was the best at the things he tried to be best *at*.

He was no home run hitter, managing only 118 in twenty-four seasons. But for most of those seasons, going for homers against the dead ball was a losing proposition. He *did* lead in slugging average eight times, proving he wasn't just a powder-puff hitter with extra puffs. The ball was invigorated during the last third of Cobb's career, but that was a little late to ask the old dog to learn a new trick. Still, in 1925 he hit three homers in one game, just showing off.

Admittedly, for all his heavy hitting his Tigers won only three pennants and no World Series. In nineteen of his twenty-two seasons in Detroit, the Tabbies missed the brass ring. The fault, dear Brutus, was not in their star; it was on their pitcher's mound. Cobb was the best player of his time—or at least the first two-thirds of his time.

Considering all that, it's a bit disconcerting to find a few modernists working overtime to chisel Cobb down to a so-so

level. Essentially, the argument is that modern players are bigger, faster, better trained, and face more difficult challenges. None of the old-timers could make it big today, they say. Cobb might hit .260.

Well, games and times change, all right. Fifty years from now, our grandchildren will be looking at a different game and some of them will be wondering what *we* ever saw in Mike Schmidt or Hank Aaron. The problem with that kind of thinking is that it keeps the player from the past anchored in his time while giving any benefits of a later age to the moderns. One critic snickered at Cobb's batting stance; he held his hands apart and then choked up or swung from the end, according to the pitch. Tyrus, the critic insisted, would be tied up by Dwight Gooden or Nolan Ryan. The critic apparently credits Cobb with the IQ of an ashtray. It would take him about half of one at-bat to figure out what he had to do to adjust. Moreover, our "modern" Cobb would have the same advantages in diet, training, and baseball experiences the other moderns have. *He*'d be bigger, faster, and better trained. He might not hit .366—though we shouldn't bet against it—but he'd be right up there showing other moderns his heels.

Relative comparisons from one era to another work better when they have some statistical reality—like Bill Terry's .401 in 1930, when just about everybody else hit .300, being adjusted down (but we still leave him at the top for that year!). Given Cobb's situation, he excelled all others in batting average.

Now, if the critics want to stomp on Cobb, they can put their clodhoppers on his personality. "The Georgia Peach" was no peach. He was mean, vindictive, selfish, vain, a bully, a racist, paranoid, cruel, and hot-tempered. He spiked infielders just for the hell of it, fought—that is, physically attacked—anyone who crossed him, would do literally anything to be first in literally anything.

But it was just because of those nasty attributes that Cobb would have found a way to win in any age. The Cobb *persona* made him a great player, gave him a shipload of records, and put him into the Hall of Fame first. And when he died, three baseball people showed up at the funeral, probably only because they were expecting free eats afterward.

"We may never see his like again," Connie Mack once said of him. Indeed we won't.

Gordon "Mickey" Cochrane

Catcher, Phi (A) 1925–33, Det (A) 1934–37.
Manager, Det (A) 1934–38

They used to argue who was the greatest catcher ever, Cochrane or Bill Dickey. Modern statistical techniques have moved Gabby Hartnett into the discussion. Josh Gibson has his backers. And later ages shout the praises of Yogi Berra and Johnny Bench. But the final cut usually comes down to "Cochrane or —."

When Mickey gets the edge, it's usually on "leadership," which is measured as easily as the distance to Oz. Nevertheless, Cochrane played on five AL pennant winners in a seven-year stretch, and that's at least tertiary evidence that he was officer material. As a matter of fact, he managed two of those teams (Detroit in 1934–1935) while taking his regular turn behind the plate.

If Mickey had a fault, it was that his fire burned too bright. He was such an intense, take-charge competitor that he used himself up some seasons. Connie Mack called him the biggest factor in the Athletics' three straight pennants (1929–1931), but there must have been times when nobody wanted to be in the same room with Cochrane.

He was considered an exceptional defender once he underwent intensive instruction from old pro Cy Perkins. So it shocked everyone when Pepper Martin, the "Wild Horse of the Osage," stole five bases on him in the 1931 World Series—"ran wild" is the way it's usually put. Most people blamed the Philadelphia pitchers.

Cochrane got high marks in his day for handling pitchers, and there's not much doubt that he did it well. Of course, having guys like Lefty Grove, George Earnshaw, and Tommy Bridges to work with gave him a leg up.

We can measure what he did at the plate better than what he did behind it. From the time Mack purchased his contract for $50,000 in 1925, through his sale to the Tigers for $100,000 in 1934, until a Bump Hadley pitch ended his career and nearly killed him in 1937, Black Mike averaged .320, the best career mark for any catcher. He had good speed for a catcher (64 stolen bases) and usually batted second. He scored 1,041 runs—four times over 100. He was a line drive hitter, but in 1932, when he drove in 112 runs, he also knocked 23 homers. He won Most Valuable Player Awards in 1928 and 1934, although neither year was his best with a bat.

He was named to the Hall of Fame in 1947.

Rocco "Rocky" Colavito

Outfielder, Cle (A) 1955–59, 1965–67, Det (A) 1960–63,
KC (A) 1964, Chi (A) 1967, LA (N) 1968, NY (A) 1968

Colavito hit with power—374 career homers, three seasons over 40—and threw like a cannon. He hit four home runs in a row in a 1959 game against Baltimore. And though he was as slow as a tax refund, he was sure-handed. He played in 234 straight games in 1964–1966 before anybody said "E, Colavito." He only led the league in assists once, but that was because runners knew enough not to challenge him. There ought to be a stat for runners who *don't* tag up and score on a fly; Rocky was responsible for a lot of those.

In 1959, when he led the AL in homers with 42, he was the most adored player in Cleveland, maybe the most popular *person*. So naturally, the Indians' braintrust traded him to Detroit for singles hitter Harvey Kuenn. And right then and there a lot of Cleveland baseball fans started looking for another kind of summer entertainment. Some of them haven't forgiven the Indians yet.

Eddie "Cocky" Collins

Second Baseman,
Phi (A) 1906–14, 1927–30, Chi (A) 1915–26.
Manager, Chi (A) 1925–26

Photos of Collins in his prime show a wimpy-looking guy, thin but hippy, with come-fly-with-me ears, a generous nose, and a chin that barely clears his neck. He wasn't a hunk, but he was a real beauty at second base. For twenty-five years,

1906–1930, Collins suited up for major league games, and for nineteen of those he was the regular at a position that lends itself to injuries. He was the pivot man in the A's $100,000 infield that helped win four pennants from 1910 through 1914. Then he did the same job for the world champion White Sox of 1917 and the 1919 club, a hose of a different color.

Batting lefthanded, he cracked out 3,311 hits for a .333 career batting average. He was a perfect leadoff or number two hitter, drawing five walks for every strikeout, but for much of his career he batted third, where his lack of home run power limited his RBIs. He ended with 1,299, which puts him behind a lot of sluggers. Once on base, though, he got around, scoring 1,818 runs, including seven seasons of 100-plus. He led the American League three years in a row (1912–14).

He stole more bases than anyone but Lou Brock and Ty Cobb. And he is the only man since 1900 to steal six bases in one game. He did it on September 11, 1912. Eleven days later he did it again. He set the mark for most World Series steals, with 14, later tied by Brock. However, his stolen base percentage was only a break-even 65 percent.

No second baseman has accepted more chances than Collins, nor led the league in fielding as many times—nine.

Connie Mack, who managed both Collins and Nap Lajoie, called Eddie the best second baseman he ever saw. Even so, Collins went into the Hall of Fame in 1939, two years after Lajoie.

Jimmy Collins

Third Baseman, Lou (N) 1895,
Bos (N) 1895–1900, Bos (A) 1901–07, Phi (A) 1907–08.
Manager, Bos (A) 1901–06

Back at the turn of the century, Collins revolutionized third base play. Before his time, most third sackers anchored themselves on the basepath. Collins was one of the first men to play in or back depending upon the situation. It allowed him to range over more ground than any other third baseman of his time.

As a brash rookie in 1895, he dared the greatest bunters of a bunting era—Keeler, McGraw, Jennings, Burkett, Hamilton —to test him. When they did, he charged in to bare-hand the ball and whip it to first, S.O.P. for third basemen now but a real marvel in his day.

In 1897 Jimmy played the hot corner on the Boston Beaneaters' great infield of Fred Tenney, Bobby Lowe, and Herman Long, which led Boston to the pennant. He hit .328 with a National League–leading 15 homers. His best year afield was 1900; he handled 601 putouts and assists, which is still the record.

In 1901 Jim jumped to the new Boston Americans, as player/manager, hit .332, and brought the club in second. In 1903 he led them to the pennant and that fall became the first manager to win a World Series. Collins' club had no chance to defend its honors against the NL in 1904; no Series was played that year, but his Bostons won a second consecutive AL pennant.

He was elected to the Hall of Fame in 1945.

Earle Combs

Outfielder, NY (A) 1924–35

Combs (it rhymes with "tombs") was the whippet-fast leadoff man for the Ruth-Gehrig Yankees. Possessing a warm and generous personality, he seemed unruffled that the Yankee sluggers got the spotlight; his job was to get on and get home. From 1925 through 1932 he scored at least 100 runs each season. In 1927, when the Babe hit 60 homers, Combs batted .356, scored 137 runs, and led the AL in hits (231) and triples (23). When Gehrig drove in 184 runs in 1931, Combs scored 120. The next year he touched home 143 times. He had a career batting average of .325, led the AL three times in three-base hits, and scored 1,186 runs.

He was at his best in three World Series (1926, 1927, and 1932), hitting a cumulative .350 and scoring 17 runs in fifteen games. A broken finger limited him to a single pinch-hitting appearance in the 1928 Series; he drove in a run in the final-game win with a sacrifice fly.

His arm didn't intimidate anyone. Speed was his trademark in center field. He used it well, leading AL outfielders in putouts a couple times. He suffered a fractured skull when he crashed into an outfield fence in 1934 and retired after one more year.

He was named to the Hall of Fame in 1970.

Charles Comiskey

First Baseman, StL (AA) 1882–89, 1891, Chi (P) 1890,
Cin (N) 1892–94. Manager, StL (AA) 1883–89,
Chi (P) 1890, StL (AA) 1891, Cin (N) 1892–94

Comiskey helped Ban Johnson create the American League and was one of its strongest voices until his death in 1931. He founded the White Sox and owned the AL team for its first thirty-one years. He gave Chicago two world champions, four pennants, and the ballpark that bears his name. He was called the "Old Roman" because of his handsome, Barrymore profile, and wavy, silver hair.

He was also, to put it charitably, a cheapskate. An example of Comiskey's miserliness: pitcher Dickie Kerr, one of the honest Sox in the 1919 World Series, won twice against the Reds and half his own team, then won 21 in 1920 and 19 in 1921. Comiskey paid him $4,500 and refused to give him a raise. Kerr quit. He could make $5,000 playing semipro!

The fact that Comiskey paid some of his greatest players coolie wages has been used by some revisionist historians to justify the action of the eight Black Sox players in selling the 1919 World Series down the river. Whether Commie "deserved" what he got, America's baseball fans didn't.

Before owning the White Sox, Comiskey played first base for the old St. Louis Browns of the American Association. He wasn't much as a hitter—lifetime .264—but he's credited with revolutionizing the position by letting the pitcher cover on grounders wide of the bag. As captain and manager, beginning at age twenty-five, he pioneered moving his fielders around for different hitters. He led the Browns to four straight AA flags, 1885–1888.

Some have found it curious that Comiskey could treat his White Sox players like indentured servants yet was one of the players who supported the Players League in 1890.

Davey Concepcion

Shortstop, Cin (N) 1970-

Among major league shortstops from Venezuela, Concepcion ranks second in reputation only to Luis Aparicio. Luis may have had a little more range at his best, but Davey popularized the technique of bouncing long throws from the hole to first to get runners who would have beaten high-arc tosses. With career batting averages in the .260s, neither set any hitting records. Davey had more power—he surprised with 16 homers in 1979— but Luis stole a couple hundred more bases.

Although Concepcion topped .300 only twice (and never in a championship year), he got hot in the October playoffs and Series. He averaged over .400 in the 1975 and 1979 playoffs and over .300 in the 1970, 1972, and 1976 Series. In the 1975 classic, Concepcion came up in the ninth inning of Game Two, with the Reds losing 2–1, two out, and Johnny Bench on second. He slapped a single to tie the score, stole second, and scored on Ken Griffey's double to win the game.

John "Jocko" Conlan

Umpire

A long-time minor league outfielder with two brief shots at the White Sox, Conlan got into umpiring by accident in 1935 in Chicago. One of the regular umpires was overcome by the heat. Jocko, who was on the bench, was rushed in to pinch-ump and did well.

In Conlan's first year as a real umpire, 1941, he ejected twenty-six men. His favorite target was Leo Durocher. He gradually mellowed, learned to use psychology and snappy retorts instead of his thumb to keep order. His trademarks were a polka-dot bow tie and a quick grin.

He spent twenty-seven seasons as an NL umpire, worked six World Series, six All-Star Games, and four pennant-deciding playoffs. In 1974, he was elected to the Hall of Fame.

Tom Connolly

Umpire

Connolly was born in England and came to the U.S. with his family at age fifteen in 1885. Enamored of baseball, he studied the rule book assiduously and became an NL umpire in 1898. He quit in 1900 because the weak league president wouldn't support his rulings. Hired by the AL, he umpired the first league game, Chicago versus Cleveland, on April 24, 1901. He was also chosen to umpire the first World Series in 1903.

In those days umpires worked alone, one to a game (two in the Series), and took the taunts of both players and fans. Connally once rowed out of Boston at midnight under threat from irate fans. Pitcher Joe McGinnity reportedly spit in his face, was fined and suspended, and jumped to the NL. But even the irascible Ty Cobb learned to back off when Tom's neck turned red. Eventually, Connally was able to go ten years straight without ejecting a dissenter.

After thirty-three years behind the mask, Tom became chief of AL umpires for twenty-three more, calling it quits in 1954 at the age of eighty-three. He lived to be ninety-one. In 1953, he was named to the Hall of Fame along with Bill Klem, the first two umpires so honored.

Roger Connor

First Baseman, Tro (N) 1880–82, NY (N) 1883–89, 1891, 1893–94, NY (P) 1890, Phi (N) 1892, StL (N) 1894–97. Manager, StL (N) 1896

Whose career home run record did Babe Ruth break? Connor's, of course. Roger hit 136 (some sources say 132) of the old dead balls for four bases. The mark stood until 1921, when Babe broke it on his way to 59.

Oddly, Connor only once led his league in homers (13 in the 1890 Players League), but he got as high as 17 in 1887. Triples were his specialty—he was tops in that department twice, in double figures eleven times, and cracked a personal high of 25 in 1894. He hit 233 altogether, and only four men have topped that— Crawford, Cobb, Wagner, and Beckley.

At six-two and 210 pounds, Connor was a big man for his day. He was one of the men New York manager Jim Mutrie meant when he called his team "giants," a name that stuck in the imagination longer than the team stuck in New York. In 1888 and 1889, Connor helped the Giants to two pennants. He was named to the Hall of Fame in 1976.

Walker Cooper

Catcher, StL (N) 1940–45, 1956–57, NY (N) 1946–49, Cin (N) 1949–50, Bos (N) 1950–52, Mil (N) 1953, Pit (N) 1954, Chi (N) 1954–55

Lon Warneke, who pitched to him and against him and umpired behind him, called Cooper a better catcher than Bill Dickey or Gabby Hartnett. That tells us never to buy real estate from Mr. Warneke. Still, the six-three Coop gave the Cardinals, Giants, Braves, and nearly every other team in the NL solid catching for years and years. He hit .300 several times and ended with a .285 career average. In three World Series, he averaged .300. When he got too old to do the job behind the plate, he remained an effective pinch-hitter.

The Giants wanted him so badly in 1946 they paid the Cardinals $175,000 for him while he was still in the Navy. In 1947 he hit 35 home runs for New York, but that was uncharacteristic. His next highest season total was 20.

He wasn't Dickey or Hartnett, but he was a darn sight better than most.

Stan Coveleski

Pitcher, Phi (A) 1912, Cle (A) 1916–24, Was (A) 1925–27, NY (A) 1928

Baseball got Coveleski out of the Pennsylvania coal mines (five cents an hour, seventy-two hours a week). "I only saw the sun on Sundays," he cracked. "I would have been great in night baseball." And the spitter got him into the majors with Cleveland in 1916 at the age of twenty-seven. In his first year,

the introverted righthander was 15–13 with a sixth-place club. Over the next few years, the Indians moved up in the standings. Coveleski followed a 19-win sophomore season with four straight 20-plus-win years (22, 24, 24, and 23). In 1920, when the Indians won the pennant, Jim Bagby led the staff with 31 wins to Coveleski's 24. But in the World Series against Brooklyn, Coveleski ran up the best performance since Mathewson's three shutouts in the 1905 classic, winning 3–1, 5–1, and 3–0 for an 0.67 ERA.

Only of average build, Covie was a workhorse, three times hurling 300 innings. One reason was the spitter, which is easy on arms. The other was Stan's philosophy: let them hit the first pitch. They seldom hit it far. Stan allowed only 1 home run per 46 innings, even in tiny League Park with its 290-foot right field fence. He had superb control of the spitter. Supposedly, he once went seven straight innings without throwing a called ball.

After Covie won 23 in 1921, Cleveland slipped in the standings and his victory totals declined. He led the AL in ERA in 1923 but won only 13. Traded to Washington in 1925, he responded with another league-leading ERA and a 20–5 record, as the Senators won the pennant. He'd lost his World Series magic, however, and lost twice to the world champion Pirates.

Stan's older brother Harry was known as the "Giant Killer" when, as a rookie with the Phils in 1908, he beat the Giants three times down the stretch. More than Fred Merkle's "boner," Harry's efforts knocked New York out of pennant contention.

Clifford "Gavvy" Cravath

Outfielder, Bos (A) 1908, Chi (A) 1909, Was (A) 1909, Phi (N) 1912–20. Manager, Phi (N) 1919–20

Born a generation too soon, Cravath was the home run king in the dead-ball years immediately preceding the Babe Ruth Revolution. In a seven-year span—1913–1919—the Phillies' outfielder led the NL in homers five times and tied once. A short right field target in Philadelphia's Baker Bowl helped quite a bit, but Gavvy, a righthanded batter deserves credit for knowing what to do with it.

He flunked two earlier trials in the AL and didn't get to the Phillies until 1912, when he was thirty-one. A genial practical joker, he kept his teammates loose with his jokes and pitchers up tight with his bat. In 1915 he helped Philadelphia to a pennant with a league-high 115 RBIs and a then twentieth-century record of 24 homers.

Sam Crawford

Outfielder, Cin (N) 1899–1902, Det (A) 1903–17

Wahoo Sam (he was born in Wahoo, Nebraska) played right field beside Ty Cobb on the Tigers, hit behind him—and once even pinch-hit for him—but was overshadowed by him, much as Gehrig was overshadowed by Ruth.

Cobb disliked Crawford. Supposedly Tyrus Rex was convinced the modest right fielder was jealous of his accomplishments. More likely he resented Crawford for already being a star when Cobb arrived in Detroit. Another possibility was that Cobb envied Crawford for being both a great player and a likable person.

Nevertheless Cobb campaigned for years to get Crawford into the Hall of Fame. It was an uncharacteristic act on Cobb's part, but perhaps moved his eventual destination out one ring. Crawford shouldn't have needed any campaign. He was elected to the Hall of Fame in 1957 and deservedly so.

Sam was the greatest triples hitter in history, with 312 to Ty's 297. Only two other men, Honus Wagner and Tris Speaker, are even over 200, and no modern player has hit half as many. Crawford lashed 26 of them in 1914 for an AL record (tied by Joe Jackson), and led the league six times. It's a given, today, to assume that Crawford would have hit tons of home runs with a livelier ball. He *did* lead the NL in homers with 16 in 1901 and the AL with 7 in 1908 and 8 in 1914, but mostly he hit screaming line drives that might have bounced off (or punctured) modern fences.

Sam had six 100-plus-RBI seasons and led the AL three times. Many of Cobb's record 2,245 runs scored were batted in by Sam.

He left the majors after 1917, just 36 hits shy of 3,000. The figure was no big deal then, or he might have hung around and picked them up. Two years later he could still hit .360 in the Pacific Coast League.

Joe Cronin

Shortstop/Manager, Pit (N) 1926–27, Was (A) 1928–34, Bos (A) 1935–45

Cronin spent fifty years in baseball, rising from All-Star shortstop to pennant-winning manager, to general manager, and finally to AL president. He was even nominated for commissioner. Horatio Alger should have written his bio.

Born in San Francisco just after the 1906 earthquake, Joe joined the Washington Senators in 1928 and was a full-fledged star by 1930, when he hit .346 and drove in 126. He was the AL's MVP. In all, he had eight seasons with over 100 RBIs, ten full seasons over .300, and 170 homers. Only seven shortstops have ever scored 100 runs and batted in 100 in the same season. Honus Wagner did it three times, Cronin four. He sure didn't hit like a shortstop. He didn't field like one either, at least not like the best. He wasn't embarrassing, but he would never have made the mythical AL All-Star team seven times with his glove.

In 1933, a near-beardless youth of twenty-six, he was named manager of the Senators. Darned if he didn't win the pennant that year, and no Senator manager ever won another. The next year he married the boss's niece in September. And in October the boss sold him to the Red Sox for $225,000.

He continued as player/manager for the Bosox, although he mainly pinch-hit after 1941. In 1943 he pinch-hit five homers, an AL record. In 1946, after he'd become strictly a bench manager, his Red Sox won the pennant. Two years later he moved upstairs to become the Boston general manager, and in 1959 he was elected AL prexy, serving until 1973. He was the AL's chairman of the board until his death in 1984.

A hearty, affable man, modest to a fault, Cronin was a great player, an adequate manager (albeit with a tendency to chew up his pitching staff), and a popular executive. He was named to the Hall of Fame in 1956.

Arthur "Candy" Cummings

Pitcher, NY (NA) 1872, Bal (NA) 1873, Phi (NA) 1874, Hartford (NA) 1875, Hartford (NL) 1876, Cin (NL) 1877

Cummings was elected to the Hall of Fame in 1939 as the inventor of the curveball, and historians have been perplexed ever since. Well, he said he came up with the curve in 1866 after seeing a spinning clamshell curve as it was skipped across the water. Clamshell spinning and curveball tossing are unrelated throwing techniques, but let that pass. Cummings apparently used his clam-curve against Harvard the next year, and the scholars were baffled. So was President Andrew Johnson, another early observer. (Johnson was baffled by just about everything while he was in the White House.)

Cummings was a pitcher for the Excelsiors of Brooklyn when the revolutionary discovery was made. Back then pitchers had to throw underhand with both feet on the ground, but they were only forty-five feet away from the batter. Cummings discovered that he could make the ball curve with the wind in his face but not with it at his back.

Anyway, the curve brought Cummings success, and in 1870 Henry Chadwick, the most knowledgeable authority of the day, said that he was the best pitcher in the land. Chadwick sometimes agreed with Cummings's clam-curve-creation claims, but at other times talked about seeing curves in the 1850s.

Between 1872 and 1875, Cummings won 124 games in the National Association, the league that preceded the NL. He also picked up his nickname—"candy" meant "best" in nineteenth-century slang. But he was just a little wisp of a thing, barely 120 pounds, and the overwork caught up with him. By 1878 he was done.

Many others disputed Cummings's claim to being the first curveball pitcher. Among them were Alphonse Martin, Bobby Mathews, Fred Goldsmith, and Joseph Mann. Most likely it was invented independently by many different pitchers over a couple of decades.

Hazen "Kiki" Cuyler

Outfielder, Pit (N) 1921–27, Chi (N) 1928–35, Cin (N) 1935–37, Bkn (N) 1938

Cuyler broke in with Pittsburgh in 1924, hitting .354, and he was hailed as "another Cobb." The next year he made the prophets look good as he hit .357, with 17 homers, 26 triples, and 45 doubles. He drove in 102 runs and scored 144. He even stole 41 bases. In one span, he had ten consecutive hits. The Pirates won the pennant. That October, Cuyler homered to win the second Series game against Washington. He came up in the seventh game with the bases loaded against Walter Johnson, crossed himself, and doubled in two for the victory.

After a .321 season in 1926, when he led the NL in runs scored and stolen bases, he ran into *l'affaire de Bush* in 1927. Manager Donie Bush wanted Cuyler to bat second (which was a little strange because Cuyler was the best home run threat on the club). Kiki was superstitious about the slot, insisting he couldn't and wouldn't hit second. Bush benched Cuyler, accused him of not hustling, and put a lesser player in Cuyler's position. The Pirates still won the pennant but lost the Series four straight. Around Pittsburgh there are fans to this day who'll swear the Bucs, with Cuyler, would have wiped up those 1927 Yankees. After the season, Cuyler was shipped to the Cubs for no one very useful. The Pirates took thirty-three years to win another pennant.

Meanwhile, Cuyler hit .360 for the Cub pennant winners of 1929. In 1930 he slumped to .355. But he had 228 hits, 155 runs scored, and 134 RBIs. In all, he hit .300 ten times. He was still around in 1932 to hit a solid .291 when the Cubs won again.

He never became "another Cobb" but, except for that silliness about batting second, it's hard to fault him. He ended with a .321 batting average, scored 1,305 runs, batted in 1,065. He hit line drives, so his homer total was a modest 127, but he had 394 doubles and 157 triples. He led the league in stolen bases four times, used his speed well in the outfield, and had a good arm. He was quiet, never drank or smoked, and only Donie Bush ever accused him of malingering. He was named to the Hall of Fame in 1968.

Some people want to pronounce his nickname "Kee-Kee," as if he was a belly dancer. Actually he got it when other outfielders called for him to take fly balls: "Cuy! Cuy!"

Ray Dandridge

Third Baseman, Negro Leagues, 1933–48, Detroit Stars, Newark Dodgers, Newark Eagles, New York Cubans

Dandridge, old-timers from the Negro Leagues say, could field like Brooks Robinson and hit like Pie Traynor and George Kell. Even allowing for hyperbole, Dandridge was a terrific third baseman—perhaps the best never to play in the white major leagues.

Ray was so bowlegged that "You could drive a freight train through there," Monte Irvin says, "but not a baseball." He was a marvelous fielder, cat-quick, with a powerful arm.

Not a power hitter, Dandridge concentrated on hitting the ball where it was pitched. He hit .347 against white big league pitching in barnstorming exhibitions. His best mark in the Negro National League was .370 in 1944.

Much of Ray's career was spent in the Mexican League and in the Cuban winter league. He spurned an offer from Cleveland in 1948 because it didn't carry a bonus. The next year he signed with the New York Giants, who sent him to the Minneapolis Millers of the American Association. He said he was twenty-nine; in actuality, he was past thirty-six.

He was AA Rookie of the Year in '49 and the league's MVP the next year when he hit .311 for the champion Millers. The Giants brought other players with lesser records to the majors but— perhaps because of his age—kept Dandridge in the minors, a great disappointment to him. He retired after the 1955 season.

In 1987 he was named to the Baseball Hall of Fame.

Andre Dawson

Outfielder, Mon (N) 1976–86, Chi (N) 1987-

Rookie of the Year in 1977, Dawson played ten full seasons in Montreal. He earned a reputation as an excellent fielder and dangerous hitter. In the early 1980s major league players voted him the best all-around player in the NL. He also

earned bad knees and several operations on Expo Stadium's artificial surface. When he became a free agent in 1987, he sought out the Chicago Cubs, signed a blank contract, and told them to fill in the figure. Despite his uncertain knees, he could have signed with other teams for considerably more money. But Wrigley Field had real grass, reachable walls, and Dawson had hit .346 in Chicago over the preceding ten years. The Cubs acquired a bargain. Dawson hit only .287, but smashed 49 homers and drove in 137 runs, both NL highs in '87. He was voted the MVP Award and signed a new (much more lucrative) contract for 1988.

Leon Day

Pitcher, Negro Leagues, 1934–50,
Bacharach Giants, Brooklyn Eagles, Newark Eagles,
Baltimore Elite Giants

The five-seven 140-pound Day was an all-around performer who pitched and played second base and center field. Although many statistics are missing, it is known that he hit over .300 in nearly every season. But his fame rests on his pitching. Day holds the Negro League record with 18 strikeouts in one game in 1940—one of his victims was Roy Campanella (who fanned three times). Day won three of four games he pitched against the legendary Satchel Paige, including victories in the East-West (All-Star) Game and the 1942 Negro World Series.

Day's career was interrupted by World War Two service in Europe. In 1945 he defeated Ewell Blackwell for the European Service Championship before 50,000 G.I.'s in Nuremburg. In his first game back home in 1946, he tossed a no-hit game with 17 strikeouts.

Jay Hanna "Dizzy" Dean

Pitcher, StL (N) 1930–37, Chi (N) 1938–41, StL (A) 1947

After winning 20 games for the 1933 Cardinals, Dizzy was joined on the St. Louis staff by his younger brother. "Me and Paul will probably win 40 games," Dizzy predicted for 1934. He was wrong. They won 49, with Diz winning 30 to lead the Cards to the pennant. "It ain't braggin' if yuh can do it," explained Diz. In the World Series, each brother won two games. Always the headline maker, Dizzy broke up a double play while pinch-running in Game Four by blocking the relay with his forehead. It was feared he might be lost for the remainder of the Series until the next day's headline reported: X-RAY OF DEAN'S HEAD REVEALS NOTHING. At least, that's the way they tell the story, and if it isn't true, it should be.

Dizzy clowned, bragged, and pitched his way to immortality. Even his marvelous work on the mound was sometimes overshadowed by colorful "Dean stories." Supposedly, one day he was interviewed by three different reporters, one after the other. He told each a new "story of Dizzy's life" with different birthdates, birthplaces, and even gave himself three different Christian names. "All those felluhs wanted a exclusive," he explained.

In 1935 Dean won 28 and followed with 24 in 1936. He was in the midst of another fine year in 1937 when a line drive off

Earl Averill's bat in the All-Star Game broke his toe. He tried to come back too soon, altered his motion to favor the toe, and ruined his arm. He was twenty-six and had won 134 games.

Traded to the Cubs in 1938, he used a "nuffin' ball" to sore-arm his way to a 7–1 record for the pennant winners. In a courageous World Series appearance, he held the mighty Yankees at bay for seven innings before the roof fell in. It was his last hurrah.

After retiring, Diz became a colorful national play-by-play announcer who enriched the English language with exciting new grammar, such as "He slud into third." Brief though his career was, it was so brilliant at its height and Dean himself brought so much more to baseball than his pitching talent, that he was elected to the Hall of Fame in 1953.

Ed Delahanty

Outfielder, Phi (N) 1888–89, 1891–01,
Cle (P) 1890, Was (A) 1902–03

The Phillies had the trio of Delahanty, Billy Hamilton, and Sam Thompson in the same outfield from 1891 to 1895. They all were magnificent hitters and all three are in the Hall of Fame. Did the Phillies destroy the rest of the league? They did not; they finished fourth four times and third in '95. Makes you wonder about the rest of the team, doesn't it?

"Big Ed" Delahanty weighed only about 170 pounds, but he went up a couple tons when he had a bat in his hands. He was long regarded as the only man to lead both major leagues in batting, topping the NL with .408 in 1899 and the AL with .376 in 1902, but the latter mark has now been shown to place second to Nap Lajoie's .378. His lifetime .346 is the fourth-best of all time. From 1894 to 1896, he hit .407, .404, and .397. That .407 was only fourth-best in the league, and it was a period of high batting averages, still . . .

Oldest of four ball-playing brothers, Ed hit with power and speed; his 19 homers in 1893 was one of the highest totals of the nineteenth century. In 1896 he became the second man to hit four home runs in one game.

A notorious bad-ball hitter, Ed "often" stepped across the plate to smash a fat pitch, according to legend.

And try this one. He once reputedly knocked a baseball in half. They sure don't build 'em the way they used to!

Tall tales aside, Delahanty was a magnificent hitter who went into the Hall of Fame in 1945.

Unfortunately, he was also a drunk. Beset by drinking, debts, and divorce, he was suspended by his team in the summer of 1903. He caught a train from Chicago for New York, got boisterously loaded, and was kicked off the team train at Niagara Falls. Still drunk, he staggered onto a bridge, fell into the river, and was swept over the falls. He was thirty-five years old.

Bill Dickey

Catcher, NY (A) 1928–43, 1946.
Manager, NY (A) 1946

Dickey's reputation appears to have slipped of late, but it's a trick of perception. He was a great catcher, but there have been several great catchers since, and new statistical tech-

niques indicate some of Dickey's contemporaries (and some of those who followed) may have been better than anyone realized at the time. So the question that used to be so popular—who's the greatest catcher, Dickey or Cochrane?—has a few more multiple choices.

Then, too, there's the out-of-sight, out-of-mind philosophy. Dickey caught his last game in 1946. The people who watched him half a century ago figured they were looking at something special in catchers. They could cite several facts to prove their eyes weren't playing tricks.

Dickey caught 100 games or more for thirteen straight years, a record. His .362 batting average in 1936 was a record for a catcher. He had a career average of .313, with 202 home runs and 1,209 RBIs. He was on eleven AL All-Star teams, and the first game wasn't played until his fifth year as a regular. He played in eight World Series, hit 5 homers, and his 24 World Series RBIs are the eighth-highest total ever. Dickey knew how to make 'em count. He had several clutch World Series hits. His ninth-inning single won the Opening Game in 1939. And his two-run homer won the Game Five in 1943.

Defensive prowess is hard to prove—next to impossible with a catcher —but Dickey got raves when he played and was called in later to show Yogi Berra the way to do it.

Dickey wasn't the rah-rah type. He led quietly, but the point is, *he led*. One day in 1932 he took exception to the way a runner slid in at home, so he flattened the guy and broke his jaw. It was out of character for Dickey and got him fined and suspended, but it probably made the next fellow sliding home against the Yankees think twice about how he did it.

If there's an argument against him, it's that Dickey played on so many winning teams that he was bound to look good. How's that for a Catch-22? It's kind of like the Yogi-ism that "Nobody goes there 'cause it's too crowded." Would the Yankees have been good with another catcher? Sure. Would they have been *as* good? Hah!

Dickey was named to the Hall of Fame in 1954.

Martin Dihigo

Pitcher/Outfielder, Negro Leagues, 1923–45,
Cuban Stars (East), New York Cubans, Homestead Grays,
Hilldale, Darby Daisies

Dihigo was one of the most versatile athletes in the history of baseball. In a career that lasted from 1923 to 1950, he starred as a pitcher, as a hitter, as an outfielder, and occasionally as an infielder.

As a pitcher, counting several seasons in Mexico, Venezuela, and the Dominican Republic, Dihigo was 256–136. His stock in trade was a blazing fastball.

As a batter, he hit over .400 three times in Cuba and the States. He led the Eastern Colored League in homers in 1926 and the American Negro League in batting with .386 in 1929. Reportedly, his longest home run came in Pittsburgh in 1936, a 500-foot shot that landed on a hospital roof.

In the outfield, he had exceptional range, and his throwing arm was claimed to be among the best ever. Supposedly, a contest was once held in Cuba wherein a *jai alai* player, using his basketlike *cesto*, slung a ball from home plate against the center field wall on one bounce. Dihigo threw the ball over the wall.

As a manager, he led the New York Cubans to the Negro National League playoff in 1935 and starred both on the mound and at the plate.

Dihigo was a big man (six-three, 220 pounds), but he was amazingly agile. Friendly, extremely popular, and with a great sense of humor, in 1977 he became the first Cuban ever to be elected to the Baseball Hall of Fame.

Dom DiMaggio

Outfielder, Bos (A) 1940–42, 1946–53

Red Sox fans used to sing: "He's better than his brother Joe – Dominick DiMaaaggiiiooooh!" Well, he wasn't. Dom was five-nine and 168 pounds, about 90 percent Joe's size and he was about 90 percent the player Joe was. But 90 percent of Joe DiMaggio is better than 100 percent of most of the guys who've ever drawn major league salaries. Dom wore glasses and because not very many players wore them he was called "The Little Professor," which is a better moniker than "Joe's Kid Brother."

Okay, comparisons are inevitable. Dom didn't have Joe's home run power; he was in double figures for homers only twice (in Fenway!) in his career. Nor did he hit as often; Joe's .325 is 27 points better than Dom's .298. But Dom was a leadoff man, and he did that very well. He led the AL in runs scored in 1950 and '51. He was more likely to walk than Joe, pulling his .380 OBA to within 14 points of his big brother's. Surprisingly, Dom was more likely to strike out than Joe. He had 571 strikeouts (to Joe's 369) in a lot fewer at-bats. Proving that Joe was a better hitter is kind of like proving that beans give gas—everybody but Boston already knows it.

They were both good center fielders. We can give Dom an edge there. He led AL center fielders in chances per game three times when one of the other AL center fielders was Joe. Some would argue that Dom got less help from his left and right fielders and *had* to accept more chances. The point is, he did it.

In the final game of the 1946 World Series, Dom twisted an ankle while tying the game with a double in the top of the eighth. Enos Slaughter made his famous dash all the way home from first in the bottom of the inning to win the game, but said later he wouldn't have tried it if Dom had still been in center.

Joe DiMaggio

Outfielder, NY (A) 1936–42, 1946–51

Jolting Joe, the "Yankee Clipper," sells coffee makers, married Marilyn Monroe, hit in 56 straight games, and was voted baseball's greatest living player. (Extensive research has failed to uncover anyone who ever wanted to be known as baseball's greatest dead player.)

Revisionists blame the New York media for the DiMaggio mystique. Like everyone outside the Big Apple thought he was just another ballplayer! Actually, in some cities around the AL where Yankee-hating was a religious test, DiMag received a special dispensation. Fans who would have kicked Tommy Henrich's dog still cheered for DiMaggio.

The revisionists miss the point. Declaring anyone the

"greatest" anything may be pretty silly, but when it's done it comes from the heart, not from the stats. DiMaggio warmed more baseball fans' chests than hot-dog heartburn. He was adored, idealized, lionized. The symbol.

As a symbol, he was handsome, quiet, a little aloof. They would have called him a Greek god but he was an Italian. Even that worked because he was a symbol for loyal Italian-Americans at a time when Mussolini's fascists stood for a lot of nasty things.

And—oh boy!—did he ever look good on the field! Graceful out there in center, he wasn't slow but it always seemed as if the film had been slowed down a bit so you could catch the nuances. At the plate, he stood with his feet planted wide apart and his bat ready but straight-up, motionless. And when you saw him swing, you never forgot it—no matter where the ball went.

Joe's stats were terrific, maybe not the best ever, but close enough to support the emotions of his fans. He lost three years to the service, but still ended with 2,214 hits, 361 home runs, 1,390 runs scored, 1,537 RBIs, and a .325 career batting average. He led the league in homers twice, RBIs twice, batting average twice. When he batted in 155 runs in 1948, he had more RBIs than games. Only one hitter has done that since. He played 13 years and was named to 13 AL All-Star teams. He was the AL MVP three times, including the 1941 season, in which he hit in a record 565 consecutive games.

Joltin' Joe went into the Hall of Fame in 1955, just as soon as he was eligible. What else?

Larry Doby

Outfielder, Cle (A) 1947–55, 1958, Chi (A) 1956–57, 1959,
Det (A) 1959. Manager, Chi (A) 1978

Doby was the first black to play in the AL, joining Cleveland in 1947 as a second baseman. He was switched to center field the next season, after extensive tutelage by Tris Speaker, and helped the Indians win their first pennant since Speaker played center in 1920. Doby hit .301 for the season; his home run off Johnny Sain won Game Four of the World Series that year.

Although Doby became an outstanding center fielder, he was more feared for his bat. He is one of the few men to drive one over the distant center field wall at Griffith Stadium in Washington (Ruth, Williams, and Mantle are the others). Larry was the first black player to lead either major league in home runs with his 32 in 1952. He led again with the same total in 1954 and also topped the AL in RBIs with 126, as the Indians won the pennant with an AL record win total of 111. He ended his career with 242 homers, 969 RBIs, and a .283 batting average.

In addition to power, speed, and consistency, Larry had a temper that sometimes brought criticism but in the long run probably earned respect for blacks. With the black Newark Eagles, Larry teamed with Monte Irvin in 1946 to win the black world championship over Satchel Paige's Kansas City Monarchs.

Doby had a brief stint as interim manager of the Chicago White Sox in 1978.

Bobby Doerr

Second Baseman, Bos (A) 1937–44, 1946–51

The Red Sox of the late 1940s won more games than any team in baseball, but kept coming up just short of a pennant—except in 1946 when they blew the World Series. No one in his right mind ever blamed Doerr for the shortfalls that gave Bosox fans short falls. From the day he took over Boston's second base in 1937 until a chronic bad back forced him to hang up his glove at thirty-three in 1951, he was a rock—so reliable in the field they should have checked his glove for a 23-jewel movement. In 1948, smack in the middle of a pennant race, Bobby went almost three months—414 chances—without an error. Doerr didn't make spectacular plays. He didn't have to. He anticipated and was already in position. He's still in the all-time top ten second basemen in putouts and assists, surrounded by guys who played longer.

Bobby was no slouch with a bat either. He adjusted to Fenway's Green Monster early, so that his numbers in Boston are way better than on the road, but that's a way of life for righthanded Red Soxers. Averaging it out, he hit a solid .288, with 223 home runs and 1,247 RBIs. In 1944—admittedly a war year—he got his average up to .325 and led the AL in slugging average. Doerr was named MVP that season. During his career, he played in nine All-Star Games.

Doerr had a knack for the clutch, though it sometimes was wasted. He hit .409 in the 1946 Series. In the do-or-die ninth inning of the seventh game, with the Sox down, 4–3, he singled the tying run into scoring position. The next three men made outs. In 1949, in the final game against the Yankees, with the pennant on the line, he slugged a three-run triple against Vic Raschi. The Sox lost anyway.

In 1986 the Veterans Committee put him in the Hall of Fame at Cooperstown.

Don Drysdale

Pitcher, Bkn (N) 1956–57, LA (N) 1958–69

When Drysdale pitched for the Dodgers, the *batters* had to be dodgers. The big righthander could have written *Winning Through Intimidation*. At six-five, he delivered his 90-plus m.p.h. fastball with a big sidearm motion—"all spikes, elbows, and fingernails"—that made righthanded batters think they were under a rocket attack from third base. They say that, halfway through some of his games the groundskeeper had to come out and sprinkle sand in the batter's box. Batter's fears were justified. Big Don hit 154 batters, about 1 every 22 innings. It's the all-time record. Off the field, Drysdale was always a considerate gentleman; but when he walked onto the field he was Freddy on Elm Street. He broke one batter's hand and was suspended for throwing beanballs. He threatened to sue and was reinstated. Adding to the terror, Don had a temper and everyone knew it. After giving up one home run, he threw the ball into the stands. He claimed that it "slipped."

Through the 1960s, Drysdale and Sandy Koufax were the Dodgers' one-two mound punch. One year they negotiated their contracts as an entry. Together, they put Los Angeles in three World Series during the decade.

Don compiled a 209–166 record over his fourteen-year

career. His ERA was 2.95 and he totaled 2,486 strikeouts, three times leading the NL. He won the Cy Young Award in 1962 with a 25–9 mark. In 1968 he threw six straight shutouts on his way to a record of 58 consecutive scoreless innings which stood until Orel Hershiser surpassed it in 1988.

He was named to the Baseball Hall of Fame in 1984.

Hugy Duffy

Outfielder, Chi (N) 1888–89, Chi (P) 1890, Bos (AA) 1891, Bos (N) 1892–1900, Mil (A) 1901, Phi (N) 1904–06. Manager, Mil (A) 1901, Phi (N) 1904–06, Chi (A) 1910–11, Bos (A) 1921–22

Pint-sized Duffy had the biggest batting average ever, .440 (originally thought to be .438) in 1894, the hottest-hitting year ever, when the entire *league* batted .309. Hugh hit 41 percent better than average, which isn't the record, but is pretty darned good. He also tied for the home run lead with 18 and led in RBIs with 145. It helped put him in the Hall of Fame in 1945.

Rejected by the White Sox in 1889 as too small ("We've got a batboy," Cap Anson said), Duffy was signed by the Bostons in 1892. There he joined another New England Irishman now in Cooperstown, Tommy McCarthy, to form the best defensive duo of the era. Boston fans called them the "Heavenly Twins." Frustrated batters called them less printable things.

Duffy ended his seventeen-year with a .328 batting average, 1,554 runs scored, 1,299 RBIs, and 599 stolen bases.

Fred "Sure Shot" Dunlap

Second Baseman, Cle (N) 1880–83, StL (U) 1884, StL (N) 1885–86, Det (N) 1886–87, Pit (N) 1888–90, NY (P) 1890, Was (AA) 1891. Manager, Pit (N) 1889

Dunlap was the biggest star of the one-year Union Association, which is sort of like being the most coveted Cracker Jacks prize. Labeled the "King of Second Basemen" in the 1880s, he was a noble hitter and fielder, but what set him above infield commoners was a powerful arm, which earned him the nickname "Sure Shot." Reportedly, he didn't so much throw the ball as sling it. He was an established NL star who'd twice hit .300 for Cleveland when Union Association dollars lured him to that ill-fated league and made him the highest-paid player in baseball.

Dunlap hit .412 in 1884 and led the Union Association in almost everything—batting average, slugging average, hits, runs, home runs, and every second base fielding category but errors —as his St Louis team won the only ever UA flag.

When the UA folded the next year, Fred folded as a slugger. Back in the NL, his batting average plunged 100 points. He never hit .300 again, but he continued his reign at second for several more seasons.

Leo "The Lip" Durocher

Manager, Bkn (N) 1939–46, 1948, NY (N) 1949–55,

Chi (N) 1966–72, Hou (N) 1972–3 Shortstop, NY (A) 1925, 1928–29, Cin (N) 1930–33, StL (N) 1933–37, Bkn (N) 1938–41, 1943, 1945

Loud-mouthed, pugnacious Leo was the Billy Martin of the 1940s. He baited umpires, picked fights, won more games than Stengel, and made his lifelong credo—"Nice guys finish last"—a part of the American language.

He broke in with the 1928 Yankees as a scrappy good-field-no-hit infielder, who delighted in getting Babe Ruth's goat. His gung-ho attitude and gone-south bat earned him the moniker "The All-American Out." By 1934 he was with the Cards, regarded as the best-fielding shortstop in the NL. He reportedly gave them their Gas House Gang nickname and helped spark them to the 1934 pennant.

In 1939 Brooklyn boss Larry MacPhail, a firebrand himself, tapped Durocher to lead the Dodgers. Lippy punched a golf caddy, fought with MacPhail, gambled, was fired, rehired, and raised the Bums from sixth to third, to second, and finally to first in 1941.

In 1946 Leo feuded with MacPhail, then owner of the Yanks, consorted with gangster Bugsy Siegel, married movie star Lorraine Day upon her divorce, and finally was suspended for 1947 by Baseball Commissioner Happy Chandler.

Leo returned to the Dodger helm in 1948 but was let go in midseason. He shocked his fans by moving over to the hated Giants. He had his greatest success in New York. In 1951 he nurtured young Willie Mays through a horrendous career-opening slump and won one of the most thrilling pennant races in history, as Bobby Thomson sank the Dodgers with his "shot heard 'round the world."

Three years later Leo won his third flag, his first World Series— and his third Manager of the Year Award. After the 1955 season, he worked for several years in television.

In 1966 Leo returned to the dugout as manager of the Cubs, where he served until late in the 1972 season. Although he brought the Cubbies into contention, he was unable to get them over the hump. Then he managed Houston at the end of 1972 and all of '73.

Many have written that Durocher was no more than an ordinary manager with a poor or noncontending team, but that he could ride a winner down a hot pennant race better than any other skipper. Leo's 2,010 victories rank him sixth all-time among managers. His 1,710 losses are seventh.

Jimmy Dykes

Manager, Chi (A) 1934–46, Phi (A) 1951–53, Bal (A) 1954, Cin (N) 1958, Det (A) 1959–60, Cle (A) 1960–61. Third Baseman, Phi (A) 1918–32, Chi (A) 1933–39

Dykes managed for twenty-one years in the major leagues and never won a pennant. His teams finished in the first division only eight times and never higher than third. Yet he was regarded as an outstanding manager who got more out of his often-talentless teams than could reasonably be expected. Patient, humorous, knowledgeable, he lost 1,538 games—ninth all-time—but won a creditable 1,407. A quotable, non-stop talker, he said that winning without good players was like trying to steal first base. His best-known statement was to label Yankees' skipper Joe McCarthy a "push-button manager," meaning that McCarthy had only to push the right

button to trot out another .300 hitter or quality pitcher. Dykes, of course, had few buttons.

Dykes was an infielder with the Philadelphia A's throughout the 1920s and played on the championship teams of 1929–31. A good and versatile fielder, he performed mostly at third base, but played extensively at second and occasionally at short and first. Initially a poor hitter, he developed into a reliable batsman and finished his career with a .280 batting average, 2,256 hits, and 1,071 RBIs.

Billy Evans

Umpire

Evans began as a sportswriter and umpired his first minor league game only because the assigned man didn't show up. In 1906 his ability got him promoted all the way from a Class C minor league to the AL. He was only twenty-two.

Billy umpired back when it took guts to wear a blue suit. He once had his skull fractured by a bottle during a riot in a ballpark. Another time he tangled with Ty Cobb under the stands and was nearly choked to death. But Evans learned to substitute diplomacy for belligerence and became one of the great umpires of the game. A friendly, fastidious man, he helped gain respect for all umps.

In Game Two of the 1909 World Series, Evans and Bill Klem had to ask the bleacherites whether a ball had landed fair or foul because temporary seats jutted out onto the field and hid the deep foul line. The next day four umpires worked the game, a practice that was eventually adopted for all major league games.

After 1927 Evans left umpiring to become the general manager for the Cleveland Indians. He also wrote a sports column, and later served as vice-president of the Detroit Tigers.

In 1973 Evans was elected to the Baseball Hall of Fame.

Darrell Evans

Third Baseman/First Baseman, Atl (N) 1969–76, SF (N) 1976–83, Det (A) 1983-

Evans combined a home run bat and an ability to draw walks into a twenty-year major league career. His career batting average hovered around .250.

Evans says his career turned around when he saw a UFO while sitting on his porch in California in 1976. He'd just been traded from Atlanta, where he'd been hitting .173, to San Francisco. He took the sighting as a good omen and began hitting with renewed energy.

In 1985, in friendly Tiger Stadium, Darrell led the AL with 40 homers at the age of thirty-eight, the oldest HR champ ever and the only man to hit 40 in both leagues. Two years later he slugged 34, the oldest man to reach that height.

Dwight Evans

Outfielder, Bos (A) 1972-

In his first years with the Red Sox, Evans was regarded as a good defensive outfielder but a poor hitter. Slowly he won respect for his bat. His strength was not his batting average, although he finally cracked .300 in his eighteenth AL season. Evans learned to draw walks, leading the league three times, and at the same time turned into one of the AL's better home run hitters. His 22 in the strike-shortened 1981 season tied for first in the league, but he has also had three seasons with more than 30 homers. Whether making circus World Series catches or driving long shots over or against the Fenway Wall, Evans became a darling of Boston fans.

His leaping one-handed catch of Joe Morgan's home run bid in the eleventh inning of the Sixth Game in the 1975 World Series was one of the most heart-stopping ever seen. He then threw to the infield to double off Ken Griffey for the third out, setting the stage for Carlton Fisk's game-winning homer in the twelfth.

Johnny Evers

Second Baseman, Chi (N) 1902–13, Bos (N) 1914–17, 1929, Phi (N) 1917, Chi (A) 1922. Manager, Chi (N) 1913, 1921; Chi (A) 1924

Rumor to the contrary, Evers did not earn his way into Cooperstown in 1946 by being the middle word in the refrain of F. P. Adams's poem about "Tinker to Evers to Chance." However, like a bowl of chicken soup, it didn't hurt. Except for an un-Evers-like .341 in 1912, his batting averages look sad beside those of AL contemporaries Nap Lajoie and Eddie Collins. Still, at the time Johnny played, what with the dead ball, there weren't many players at any position who hit with Lajoie or Collins. Evers's batting averages were consistently above the league average. Little Johnny was undeniably the top NL second baseman of the twentieth century's first two decades.

The Cubbie double-play combination that set F. P. Adams's pen in motion never led the league in twin killings—and small wonder. The Chicago pitchers kept baserunners to a minimum. What made "T to E to C" exceptional was their timing; on those rare occasions when a DP was crucial, they were the best in the business.

They were the main men in Chicago's four pennants between 1906 and 1910. Of the three, the 140-pound Evers was probably the most valuable player both in the field and at the plate. The hardest to get along with, too. His nickname was "The Crab." Even Tinker didn't like him; except for obligatory *You take its* and *I got its*, they didn't speak for years. Grouchy as he was, little Johnny was also skilled, pugnacious, and ingenious.

Evers was the culprit who called for the ball and tagged second base, putting out poor Fred Merkle and throwing the 1908 race into a tie. It worked in part because he'd warned the umpire that he would do it if the occasion arose. When Merkle made a beeline for the clubhouse instead of touching second and Johnny put the ball on the bag, the umpire had no choice but to call Fred out.

Sold to Boston in 1914, Evers joined shortstop Rabbit Maranville and sparked the miracle come-from-behind flag. He was voted MVP. Johnny was usually hot in the Series; he hit .350 in both 1908 and '09. He hit .438 in this one, and his single drove in the winning run in the fourth and final game.

William "Buck" Ewing

Catcher, Tro (N) 1880–82, NY (N) 1883–89, 1891–92,
NY (P) 1890, Cle (N) 1893–94, Cin (N) 1895–97. Manager,
NY (P) 1890, Cin (N) 1895–99, NY (N) 1900

Ewing was the subject of an early lithograph dramatizing the day he stole second and third, then announced, "And now I'm going to steal home"—and did. In 1919, twenty-five years after he stepped down as a regular, no less authority than the *Reach Guide* linked him with Ty Cobb and Honus Wagner as the three top stars of all time. Very likely, Buck was the greatest all-around player of the nineteenth century.

He wasn't the greatest with the bat, but he was a strong hitter, averaging .303 over eighteen seasons. He led the NL with 10 home runs in 1883 and hit 20 triples the next year. And, as the lithograph showed, he was a daring and dangerous baserunner.

In the field, Ewing was just about as good as it got. He could and did play every position, but he was most famous as a catcher, the most demanding defensive slot. He was quick and had an exceptional arm. In fact, his arm was so strong that he regularly threw out runners without rising from his catcher's crouch, a feat unheard of before his time.

A field leader *par excellence*, Ewing captained New York's NL champions of 1888–1889. After he retired as a player, he managed for several years, compiling a 489–395 mark. He was named to the Baseball Hall of Fame in 1939.

Connie Mack, a catcher himself, called Ewing the greatest ever. Buck's teammate, Mickey Welch, called him the greatest *player*, period. Buck was the first catcher to throw from the crouch and one of the first to use the big mitt.

His biggest rival was "King" Kelly of Chi, though Kelly played the outfield, too. Both were consistent—.311 for Ewing, .313 for Kelly. Ewing had power (a league-leading 10 homers in 1883) but Kelly had more (with 12 in '84).

Buck was fast enough to lead off, often stealing over 50 bases a year; but, then again, so did Kelly.

In 1893 Ewing played all nine positions. But Kelly played all but pitcher.

Kelly and Ewing—what little there was to choose between them was in their handling of pitchers, and in this Ewing had no peer.

Urban "Red" Faber

Pitcher, Chi (A) 1914–33

The last of the AL's "legal" spitball pitchers, Faber spent his entire career with the White Sox. In 1921 he scored one of the finest pitching feats ever. Playing for the seventh-place White Sox, he was 25–15, with a league-leading ERA of 2.48. To prove it was no fluke, he went 21–17 the next year and again led in ERA, as the White Sox climbed to fifth.

Faber had won 20 earlier with strong teams behind him, but 1921 was the beginning of the post-Black Sox era, when Chicago plunged into the second division for almost two decades. In fifteen of Red's twenty seasons, Chicago finished in the second division. Yet, he had only six losing years and finished with 254 victories.

Disdaining strikeouts, Faber wanted batters to hit his pitch— his spitter—right into the dirt. He once pitched a nine-inning game with 67 pitches, or less than 3 pitches per out.

In the 1917 World Series, Red won 3 games and lost 1. He sat out the 1919 Black Sox Series with an injury, watching eight of his teammates lose on purpose.

In 1964 he was elected to the Baseball Hall of Fame.

Elroy Face

Pitcher, Pit (N) 1953, 1955–68, Det (A) 1968,
Mon (N) 1969

In 1959 Face and his newfangled forkball set an amazing record, 18–1, in relief for the second-place Pirates. Because the practice today is to bring in the "closer" almost exclusively to protect a lead, relief pitchers now accumulate more saves than ever before, but wins are rare. Face often relieved with the score tied or the Pirates a run or two behind. Of course, he "vultured" a few, also—blowing the lead, then getting the victory when the Pirates came from behind to win.

When Pittsburgh reached the World Series the next year, Face saved the first 3 games, as the Pirates beat the Yankees in 7 games on Bill Mazeroski's homer. With the different utilization of relief pitchers in his day, Face saved 193 games in his sixteen-year career. He won 96 games in relief and 8 more as a starter. His "out" pitch was the forkball, which he threw as an off-speed pitch. Now it is better known as the split-fingered fastball.

Ferris Fain

First Baseman, Phi (A) 1947–52, Chi (A) 1953–54,
Det (A) 1955, Cle (A) 1955

Fain was a singles hitter in a HR position. He won two batting crowns, hitting .344 in 1951 and .327 in 1952, but had only one other .300 year. His OBP, however, was consistently high, as he drew at least 94 walks in seven of his nine seasons. In fact, his lifetime OBP of .425 is the eighth best of all players.

Although he led AL first basemen in errors five times, he was considered an exceptional fielder, with unusual range. He led in assists four times.

Fain became a star in the Pacific Coast League and complained that he had to take a pay cut when he came to the majors.

Bob Feller

Pitcher, Cle (N) 1936–41, 1945–56

Feller came out of Iowa as a phenom—a schoolboy with a legendary fastball. Unlike so many prodigies, Feller made good on his promise. He just may have been the best pitcher ever. Many veterans say Bob was the fastest they ever saw, but Feller had a dangerous curve as well. He set the standard as the strikeout pitcher of his time.

As a seventeen-year-old kid, just off the farm, in 1936, Bobby whiffed 8 Cardinals in three innings in his first big league exhibition. In Bob's AL debut he fanned 15. At the age of nineteen in '38 Feller set a record with 18 strikeouts.

That year Bob led the league in both strikeouts (240) and walks (208).

In 1939, at the age of twenty, Bob had his first big year—24–9, for the third-place Indians. Again he led in Ks and BBs. At twenty-one Bob hurled the only Opening Day no-hitter, went on to a 27–11 mark, fanned a league-high 261, and won *The Sporting News*' vote as Player of the Year. His no-hitter was the first of three. He also had a record 12 one-hitters, seven of them spoiled by the scratchiest of hits. Crowds flocked to see him duel Williams or DiMaggio. "It's just me against them," he exulted, "man to man."

Bob was 25–13 in 1941, as the Indians almost won the flag. Then, with his mountaintop years just ahead, he volunteered for combat duty as a naval gunner in the Pacific. He would go on to win eight battle stars. The war took almost four full years out of the very peak of Bob's career, ages twenty-three through twenty-six. His own estimate, probably conservative, is that it cost him 1,000 strikeouts and 100 wins, enough to give him over 3,500 whiffs and 360 victories.

Instead he ended with 2,581 Ks (once third on the all-time list, now farther down) and 266 wins. Bob also had a then-record 1,764 walks. In his first full season back, in 1946, Feller added a slider and struck out 348, one short of an AL record set by Rube Waddell in 1904. Feller had three more 20-win seasons in the postwar years.

Feller often pitched relief between starts and saved 21 games in addition to his 266 wins.

Bob never won a World Series game. In 1948 he lost an opening-game two-hitter, 1–0, when the Braves' Phil Masi was called safe on a pickoff play. Films clearly showed Masi was out, but Masi scored the only run of the game.

Feller was elected to the Baseball Hall of Fame in 1962.

Rick Ferrell

Catcher, StL (A) 1929–33, 1941–43, Bos (A) 1933–37,
Was (A) 1937–41, 1944–45, 1947

Ferrell was the catcher for the AL in the first All-Star Game and caught all nine innings. Durability was one of his virtues. He held the AL record for most games caught with 1,805 until Carlton Fisk surpassed it in 1988. A fine defensive catcher with a strong arm, he was considered one of the best handlers of pitchers around. Ferrell was a fair hitter, who topped .300 four times, but had little home run power. His brother Wes, a pitcher, hit 10 more career homers, but Rick seldom struck out and drew more than his share of walks.

From 1934 into 1938, Rick caught his kid brother Wes, one of the more successful brother batteries in history. They were so in tune, it was said, that Rick could catch a whole game without signs. When they were on opposite sides, Rick did well against Wes, once homering off him.

Rick had a rare knack for handling knuckleball pitchers. In 1945 he caught for Washington, a team with four knuckle-ballers as starters.

He was elected to the Baseball Hall of Fame in 1984.

Wes Ferrell

Pitcher, Cle (A) 1927–33,
Bos (A) 1934–37, Was (A) 1937–38,

NY (A) 1939, Bkn (N) 1940, Bos (N) 1941

Ferrell won 20 or more games for the Indians in each of his first four full years, starting in 1929. Possessed of a blazing fastball and a blazing temper, the handsome righthander was a little wild on the mound. In two of those seasons, his walks outnumbered his strikeouts.

A sore arm in 1933 cost him his fastball and he was traded to Boston the next year, where he joined his catcher brother Rick. Wes became a junkball pitcher and twice won 20 for the Bosox. He had his best season in 1935 when he was 25–14 with the fourth-place Red Sox and led the AL in wins, complete games, and innings pitched. He finished his career with a 193–128 record and .601 percentage. His 4.04 career ERA looks better in the context of his time than it does when compared with earlier and later eras.

Ferrell may have been the best-hitting-pitcher of all. He had a career batting average of .280 and his 38 home runs are the most by any pitcher. Wes's best home run year was 1931 with 9. That year he also tossed a no-hitter, a rare feat in the high-hitting 1930s.

An amateur astrologer, Wes guided his career by the stars and said they accurately predicted his ups and downs.

Rollie Fingers

Pitcher, Oak (A) 1968–76, SD (N) 1977–80,
Mil (A) 1981–82, 1984–85

In his seventeen-year career, Fingers saved 341 games. That's more preserving than Grandma used to do at canning time and it's also the all-time record for relief pitchers. His 107 relief wins are third on the list.

Rollie was the main man out of the Oakland bullpen in the early 1970s when the A's won five division titles, three pennants, and three World Championships. In the 1974 World Series, his 1 win and 2 saves earned him the MVP nod. His 6 saves in three Series is a record.

Fingers pitched for San Diego from 1977 to 1980 and had his two top save seasons there, with 35 in 1977 and 37 the next year. Both marks led the NL. He was named Relief Man of the Year by Rolaids and Fireman of the Year by *The Sporting News* in both seasons.

Returning to the AL with Milwaukee in 1981, he led the AL in saves with 28 in a strike-shortened season. He was named both MVP and Cy Young winner. An arm injury in 1982 kept him out of the World Series and caused him to miss the 1983 season.

Famous for his handlebar mustache, the spare, six-foot-four righthander relied on good control of his fastball. Later in his career, Fingers added a slider.

Charles O. Finley

Owner, KC (A) 1961–67, Oak (A) 1968–80

Only George Steinbrenner, among ballclub owners, has been more controversial than Finley, an insurance tycoon who bought the old Kansas City A's and moved them to Oakland. He feuded with his players, with fans, and with Commissioner Bowie Kuhn. He also built a dynasty around Reggie

Jackson, Catfish Hunter, Sal Bando, Rollie Fingers, Vida Blue, and others. His A's won five straight division titles, 1971–1975, and three consecutive World Championships.

Free agency eventually did Finley's A's in. Unwilling to pay the ever-increasing salaries, Finley tried to sell off a few of his stars before they became free agents, but the deals were blocked by the commissioner. Finley went to court but lost. And then he lost the players. Ironically, it was some of his controversial labor relations with players that inadvertently helped hasten free agency.

Finley hired and fired managers at a pace that seemed breakneck in those pre-Steinbrenner days. He also drew fans with sometimes outrageous promotions. He put a jackass in his bullpen and named it "Charley O." He burst with ideas—many of which were originally laughed at but many of which have also come to pass. He favored night World Series games, colorful uniforms, and designated hitters. He also advocated interleague play and *orange* baseballs.

Stubborn and volatile, Finley changed baseball in his twenty years with the A's. For the worse, his critics said. For the better, time seems to be saying.

Carlton Fisk

Catcher, Bos (A) 1969–80, Chi (A) 1981-

The image of Fisk using body English to coax his game-winning homer to stay fair in the twelfth inning of Game Six in the 1975 World Series is locked in the minds of millions of baseball fans who saw it on television. But Fisk was more than a one-hit hero.

He won the Rookie of the Year Award with the Red Sox in 1972, hitting .293 with 22 home runs. Although he's topped .300 twice, his batting average has normally been well below that of his first year. However, he's maintained his long-ball power. In 1985, at age thirty-seven, he hit 37 homers. In 1987 he surpassed 300 career home runs. And in 1988 he established a new mark for games caught in the AL.

Durable, strong-armed, and an outstanding handler of pitchers, Fisk ranks among the best catchers in the history of the game. In 1981 he left Boston via free agency and signed with the White Sox.

Freddie Fitzsimmons

Pitcher, NY (N) 1925–37, Bkn (N) 1937–43.
Manager, Phi (N) 1943–45

Fitzsimmons combined with southpaw Carl Hubbell to give the Giants an excellent righty-lefty one-two punch in the late 1920s and early 1930s. Although Hubbell was the Giants' "Meal Ticket," the team also fed on a steady diet of wins by "Fat Freddie." Fitzsimmons combined a wide assortment of pitches, excellent control, and an odd windup involving a turn toward second base (a la Luis Tiant) to go 20–9 in 1928 and 19–7 in 1930. Twice he won 18.

Traded to Brooklyn in 1937, he was used as a spot starter with great success. His 16–2 mark in 1940 led the NL in winning percentage. In 1941, at the age of forty, Fitzsimmons started Game Three of the World Series to become the oldest starter in Series history. For seven innings he shut out the mighty Yankees, but a drive off the bat of his mound opponent, Marius Russo, hit him flush on the knee and put him out of the game. The Yankees scored twice in the next inning to win, 2–1.

Fitzsimmons finished his career at 217–146.

Elmer Flick

Outfielder, Phi (N) 1898–1902; Cle (A) 1902–10

Although he's chiefly famous for winning the 1905 AL batting crown with an average of just .306, Flick was actually one of the top hitters at the turn of the century. In 1905 the league batting average was only .241; Willie Keeler, another pretty good hitter, was the only other regular in the league to get above .300. Elmer's best mark, .378 in 1900, almost won the NL title; he lost to Honus Wagner's .381 on the final day.

For three years straight, 1905 to 1907, Flick led the AL in triples. His career batting average was .315.

Flick was so good, in fact, that when he hit .302 for Cleveland in 1907, Detroit offered to swap their young star outfielder for Elmer even up. Cleveland preferred to stick with Flick and so passed up the offer of Ty Cobb. Unfortunately, injuries all but ended Elmer's career the next year; he played in only 99 more games.

He was named to the Baseball Hall of Fame in 1963.

Curt Flood

Outfielder, Cin (N) 1956–57, StL (N) 1958–69,
Was (A) 1971

Flood was one of the most important and influential players in the history of baseball, though his significance was unrelated to his undeniable talent. During the 1960s Flood helped the Cardinals to three pennants as their center fielder. A good hitter (career average .293), Curt excelled in the outfield. He was voted Gold Gloves from 1963 through 1969.

However, when the Cardinals attempted to trade him to the Phillies after the '69 season, he refused. "I do not feel I am a piece of property to be bought and sold irrespective of my wishes," he wrote to Commissioner Bowie Kuhn. He turned down a $100,000 contract with the Phillies to challenge baseball's reserve clause in federal court. The case went all the way to the U.S. Supreme Court, where his plea was rejected, 5–3. Nevertheless, the narrowness of the ruling forced baseball's owners to agree to an arbitration system, which eventually ended the reserve clase.

Flood, a serious, introspective man, briefly attempted a comeback in 1971 and then retired. Though he received none of the benefits of baseball's current free agency, he—more than any other player—is responsible for it.

Ed "Whitey" Ford

Pitcher, NY (A) 1950, 1953–67

The "Chairman of the Board," Ford ranks as one of the greatest lefthanded pitchers of all time. His 236–106 career record yields a winning percentage of .690, third all-time and

the best of any 200-game winner in this century. He led the AL in victories three times, ERA and shutouts twice. He won the 1951 Cy Young Award at a time when only one was given to cover both leagues.

But Whitey's fame rests primarily on his ability as a "money pitcher," and pitching for eleven Yankee pennant winners gave him ample opportunity to earn his reputation. His World Series performances alone were enough. He started the most games (22), pitched the most innings (146), gave up the most hits (134), struck out the most batters (94), walked the most (34), and won the most (10). He also ranks first in losses (8), but his 2.71 ERA speaks better for the quality of his efforts.

A fun-loving native New Yorker, Whitey first pitched for the Yankees in 1950, when he went 9–1 and added his first Series win after a midseason call-up. He then entered the service for two years, but upon his return, picked up where he'd left off. Yankees Manager Casey Stengel used him judiciously throughout the 1950s; in only 1955 did Ford start more than 30 games, limiting the number of wins (and losses) he could earn in a given season. After Stengel was replaced in 1961, the number of Whitey's starts per year increased sharply. He won 25 games in 1961 and 24 in 1963.

Ford pitched with his head more than his arm. He was the master of a variety of pitches, including a few frowned upon in the rulebook. He was moderately wild in his early years, but developed into one of the best control artists in the league.

In 1974 Ford was elected to the Baseball Hall of Fame.

Bill Foster

Pitcher, Negro Leagues, 1923–37, Memphis Red Sox, Chicago American Giants, Homestead Grays, Kansas City Monarchs, Cole's American Giants

Big Bill, Rube Foster's younger half-brother, was considered one of the two best lefthanded pitchers in the black leagues. He ranks first in wins and his 18 victories in 1927 are the third-highest season total.

Foster's two most famous wins came for the Chicago American Giants over "Bullet Joe" Rogan, ace of the rival Kansas City Monarchs, in the 1926 championship playoff. Bill's team was down 3 games to 2, when he beat Rogan 2–0 and 5–0 in a double-header to clinch the pennant.

Foster's best seasons were 1927 (18–3) and '32 (14–6).

Andrew "Rube" Foster

League President/Owner/Manager/Pitcher, Negro Leagues, 1902–26, Chicago Union Giants, Cuban-X Giants, Philadelphia Giants, Leland Giants, Chicago American Giants

"The Father of Black Baseball," Foster first attracted attention with his pitching. In 1902, he won four of the Philadelphia Cuban-X Giants' five wins against the Philadelphia Giants in a playoff billed as for the "Colored Championship of the World." The next year he switched to the Giants and led them to the title.

In 1910, in partnership with the son-in-law of Charles Comiskey, he formed the Chicago American Giants to play at the White Sox's old South Side Park. Although there was no league, Foster's Giants were generally recognized as the leading black team throughout the decade. As their manager, Foster built his teams on speed and pitching, insisted on disciplined play and initiated several strategies that became standard.

Black baseball was generally in a chaotic state when Foster and the owners of six Midwestern teams formed the Negro National League. Foster was named president and his Giants won the first three pennants. The NNL raised standards for players, drew fans with pennant races, and, according to many, saved black baseball. As president, Foster worked fifteen-hour days but drew no regular salary. He did receive a percentage of league-game attendance, but contributed part of that to the league. He preached that if blacks maintained a high level of play, when the whites were ready to open the doors, the blacks would be ready to walk through.

In 1926 Foster suffered a nervous breakdown from overwork. He died four years later, but black baseball had been put on a solid footing.

In 1981 Foster was named to the Baseball Hall of Fame.

George Foster

Outfielder, SF (N) 1969–71, Cin (N) 1971–81, NY (N) 1982–86, Chi (A) 1986

Foster earned the nickname "The Destroyer" as well as the NL's 1977 MVP Award for his heavy hitting with Cincinnati's Big Red Machine in the 1970s. A quiet, introspective man with deep religious convictions, he conversely presented one of baseball's most menacing presences when standing at the plate with his black bat and glowering expression. From 1976–78 he led the NL in RBIs, with 121, 149, and 120. He also was home run leader in 1977–1978, with 52 and 40.

Traded to the Mets in 1982, he found himself playing half his games in a poor hitter's park and without the flock of teammates clogging the bases, waiting to be driven home, that he had known in Cincinnati. Although he twice drove in 90 runs, he could never regain the slugging level he'd attained with the Reds, and his fielding—never good—became a major liability.

He completed his career with 348 home runs and 1,239 RBIs.

Nellie Fox

Second Baseman, Phi (A) 1947–49, Chi (A) 1950–63, Hou (N) 1964–65

Little Nellie (five-ten, 160 pounds) was a plucky second baseman, known for his choke-up batting grip and huge wad of tobacco. He was the heart of the Go-Go White Sox of the 1950s, teaming first with Chico Carrasquel and then with Luis Aparicio as the AL's premier keystone combo. He led the league's second basemen five times in turning double plays.

Considered a poor hitter when he first arrived in the majors, Fox learned to punch out short drives and led the AL seven straight years (1954–1960) in singles and four years in total hits. He batted .300 or better six times and finished with a .288 career batting average. He struck out about as often as

Chicago has an honest election, and ranks as the third-hardest batter to whiff in history.

But more than for his stats, Nellie was known for his all-out hustling play and infectious spirit. When the White Sox won their first pennant in forty years in 1959, Fox was named Most Valuable Player, though several other players had better statistics.

Jimmie Foxx

*First Baseman, Phi (A) 1925–35, Bos (A) 1936–42,
Chi (N) 1942, 1944–45*

Foxx, the Maryland strongman discovered appropriately by Home Run Baker, ranks with the greatest sluggers of all time. When he retired, his 534 homers ranked second to Babe Ruth and only Ruth and Roger Maris hit more in one season than Jimmie's 58 in 1932.

"Double X" loved to show off his bulging biceps by cutting the sleeves off his shirts. "Even his hair has muscles," winced Lefty Gomez, who threw a pitch that Jimmie walloped into the farthest corner of the third deck in Yankee Stadium. "It took forty-five minutes to walk up there," Lefty said.

Originally a catcher, Foxx found that way blocked with the A's by Mickey Cochrane. He switched to first base and became one of the key players in Philadelphia's 1929–1931 dynasty. In those three seasons he hit 100 home runs and drove in 343.

In 1932 the good-natured, moon-faced Foxx launched an assault on Babe Ruth's five-year-old mark of 60 homers. Although he fell short with 58, fans noted he had 2 home runs washed out by rainouts. His homers, 169 RBIs, and .361 batting average won him the MVP award. He won again in 1933 with a Triple Crown year: 48 home runs, 163 RBIs, and a .356 batting average.

Traded to the Red Sox after tying for the home run crown with 36 in 1935, he took advantage of Fenway Park's short left field fence to produce several fine years. In 1938 his league-leading 175 RBIs and .349 batting average earned him his third Most Valuable Player award. Curiously, his 50 homers did not lead the league, but his more modest 35 the next year did.

"The Beast," as he was affectionately known, finished his career with 1,921 RBIs (sixth all-time) and a .325 batting average. His lifetime .609 slugging average ranks fourth behind only Ruth, Williams, and Gehrig.

In 1951 Foxx was elected to the Baseball Hall of Fame.

Bill Freehan

Catcher, Det (A) 1961, 1963–76

Signed for a $100,000 bonus by the Tigers, Freehan turned out to be an excellent investment. He solved their catching problems for thirteen seasons (1963–1975). Freehan was a terrific catcher who won five Gold Gloves and holds the AL record for career fielding percentage (.993) for catchers. He hit an even .300 in 1964, but most of his batting marks were considerably lower, and he ended with a .262 career average. That was offset by his 200 career home runs. He got high marks as a team leader and helped the Tigers to a World

Championship in 1968 and an American League East pennant in 1972.

Larry French

Pitcher, Pit (N) 1929–34, Chi (N) 1935–41, Bkn (N) 1942

Four men have broken into the majors with one-hitters. French is the only man who went out with one. He tossed it for the Dodgers in September of 1942 at the age of thirty-four. Then he marched into the Navy for the next twenty-seven years, emerging as a four-stripe captain. His career mark of 197–171 left him only 3 victories shy of becoming the first pitcher to win 200 without a 20-win season.

A lefthanded knuckleballer, French spent the first half of his career with the lowly Pirates, then joined the Cubs in 1935 in time to help them to the pennant with a 17–10 mark.

Chicago won again in 1938, but Larry had his worst season to become the only man ever to lose 19 games with a pennant winner.

Ford Frick

Commissioner/League President

Starting as a sportswriter (and Ruth's "ghost"), Frick spent forty-three years in baseball. As NL president (1934–1951), he was pivotal in the Jackie Robinson Revolution. When the Cardinals threatened to strike rather than play against Robinson in 1947, Frick told them bluntly: "I don't care if half the league strikes. Those who do will . . . be suspended, and I do not care if it wrecks the NL for five years. This is the United States of America, and one citizen has as much right to play as another."

He was also one of the forces behind the establishment of a Hall of Fame; in 1970 he was elected to the Hall himself.

As Baseball Commissioner (1951–1968), Frick presided over expansion to Milwaukee, Los Angeles, San Francisco, Minneapolis-St. Paul, Houston, Baltimore, Oakland, and Atlanta. He negotiated a $13-million TV package with NBC, and oversaw the end of the reserve clause and the birth of the free agent draft.

His most controversial ruling was probably his decision that an asterisk be placed beside Roger Maris's 61-homer record, an edict that was never enforced.

Frankie Frisch

*Second Baseman, NY (N) 1919–26, StL (N) 1927–37.
Manager, StL (N) 1933–38, Pit (N) 1940–46,
Chi (N) 1949–51*

"The Fordham Flash" stepped straight from the Rams' campus into the major leagues with the Giants in 1919. He was a key man on New York's four straight pennant winners from 1921 through 1924. A slashing switch-hitter, he "never hit a home run when a single would win the game" but cracked plenty of singles, doubles, and triples. He led the NL with 223 hits in 1923, had thirteen seasons of batting over .300, scored over 100 seven times, and batted in over 100 three times. His

career marks included 1,532 runs scored, 1,244 RBIs, and a .316 batting average.

For several years he was considered the likely heir to John McGraw as manager of the Giants, but the feisty Frisch rebelled at McGraw's dictatorial methods. In 1927 he was traded to St. Louis in exchange for Rogers Hornsby, a swap that shocked and angered Cardinal fans.

Though never the hitter that Hornsby was, Frisch was a better fielder and his equal as a team leader. He played on Cardinal pennant winners in 1928, 1930–1931, and after becoming player-manager, in 1934. All told, he played on eight pennant winners and six runners-up. He was named NL MVP in 1931, but he is probably better known as the scrappy leader of the Cardinal "Gashouse Gang" that won the 1934 world championship.

In sixteen years as a manager, and despite being saddled with weak teams in Chicago during his final seasons, he compiled a .513 winning percentage.

He was elected to the Hall of Fame in 1947.

Jim "Pud" Galvin

Pitcher, StL (NA) 1875, Buf (N) 1879–85,
Pit (AA) 1885–86, Pit (N) 1887–89, 1891–92, Pit (P) 1890,
StL (N) 1892. Manager, Buf (N) 1885

Supposedly Galvin picked up the nickname "Pud" for making "pudding" out of batters. On the other hand, the five-eight pitcher checked in at 190 pounds at his lightest and once ballooned to 320. When he ran, what did he jiggle like a bowl of?

He was the greatest fat pitcher, and the hardest-working. In the early 1880s, when pound-for-pound Galvin was as good as any pitcher around, slabmen threw underhand from a shorter distance. Usually two pitchers worked every other game, and regulars always had high numbers. But Galvin was ridiculous.

One year he pitched 656 innings, the next year 636. He had one 593-inning season and six more over 400. He was effective, too. Although his teams ran from fair to rotten, he had two seasons with 46 wins, one with 37, and seven years with from 20 to 29. He pitched 2 no-hitters and 57 shutouts. He walked almost no one—1.13 per nine innings. And he had the greatest pick-off move of his day—once nailing three baserunners in the same inning!

In fourteen seasons, he won 361 games to rank sixth all-time. His 310 losses are the second-most ever. He's also second all-time in innings pitched (5,941) and complete games (639).

A placid, gentle man, Galvin opened a saloon in Pittsburgh after he retired from baseball. Reportedly the place was always packed, but he went broke anyway. Then the nine bartenders he'd hired each opened a bar.

In 1965 he was named to the Hall of Fame.

Lou Gehrig

First Baseman, NY (A) 1923–39

Gehrig played in the shadow of Ruth and, later, DiMaggio. He played in an era of great first basemen—Foxx, Mize,

Greenberg, and Terry. He also played a record 2,130 straight games, and became in his quiet way perhaps the best first baseman ever. They called him "The Iron Horse"; he hauled the Yankees to seven pennants.

"I'm not a headline guy," Lou said. When he hit .545 in the 1928 World Series, Ruth hit .625. When Gehrig hit a home run in the 1932 Series, Ruth had just hit his "called shot" homer ahead of him. When Lou slugged 4 home runs in one game, John McGraw retired the same day to steal the headlines.

When Gehrig was voted MVP in 1927, he was paid $6,000. Ruth got $80,000. That was the year Babe hit 60 homers to 47 for Lou.

But Lou set some marks even Babe couldn't touch—184 RBIs in 1931. That year Lou produced 301 runs (runs scored plus RBIs, minus home runs), the all-time record. His 23 grand slams are also a record. In the 1932 World Series, Lou was truly Ruthian. In four games he hit 3 home runs, batted .529, and knocked in a four-game record eight runs.

Before Lou's death at the age of thirty-seven, he had hit 493 homers, then the third-highest ever, behind Ruth and Foxx. Some old-timers say Gehrig hit the ball as hard as they did, but he hit it on a line with overspin; they lifted it into the air for greater distance.

Gehrig had 1,991 RBIs, third behind Ruth and Aaron. Of course, Babe was on base to score a lot of those runs. On the other hand, Gehrig often came up with the bases empty after Babe had cleared them. Yankee Stadium didn't help him—he actually hit better on the road. He led the AL in RBIs five times.

Gehrig won the Triple Crown in 1934 (.363, 49 homers, 165 RBIs) but finished only fifth in the MVP voting. He won the award in 1936 with 49 home runs, 167 runs scored, and 152 RBIs.

In 1939 Gehrig finally took himself out of the lineup. With death approaching, he told sixty-one thousand fans in Yankee Stadium, "I consider myself the luckiest man on the face of the earth."

The normal waiting period was waived and he was elected to the Baseball Hall of Fame in 1939.

Charlie Gehringer

Second Baseman, Det (A) 1924–42

A lefthanded hitter, Gehringer slapped hits to all fields. He made 2,839 base hits over nineteen years, including 184 home runs, 146 triples, and—tenth all-time—574 doubles. He topped .300 in thirteen of his sixteen full seasons, led the AL with a .371 mark in 1937 to earn MVP honors, drove in 100-plus runs seven times and 1,427 for his career.

In the field his hallmarks were grace and efficiency. He made even the hardest plays look easy. Seven times he led AL second basemen in assists, nine times in fielding average.

He was tough in World Series play. His home run in the fifth game in 1934 beat Dizzy Dean of the Cardinals. A year later he singled in the ninth against the Cubs and scored the winning run that gave Detroit the championship.

But he hardly ever showed emotion or said anything about *anything*. Reporters liked to quote him—". . ." They called him the "Mechanical Man." He was as colorful as a glass of water.

He was elected to the Baseball Hall of Fame in 1949.

Bob "Hoot" Gibson

Pitcher, StL (N) 1959–75

In 1968 Gibson registered the lowest ERA in NL history, 1.12; hurled 13 shutouts, second-best in NL annals; went 22–9; and then fanned a record 35 in the World Series, including 17 in one game to shut out the Tigers and 31-game winner Denny McLain. It was a pitcher's year, but *wow*!

A fire-breathing, flame-throwing competitor, Bob was the best righthanded pitcher of the power-pitching 1960s. He won two Cy Youngs and one MVP.

In three World Series Bob was 7–2, had a 1.89 ERA, and struck out 92 men in 81 innings. In his first Series, against the Yanks in 1964, he lost the second game, then came back to win games Five and Seven. Three years later, 1967, Gibson broke his leg in midseason but threw away his crutches to win 3 against Boston that fall, a six-hitter, a five-hitter, and a three-hitter, in that order.

The broken leg in 1967 came after two 20-win seasons and before three more 20-win years. He also won 19 twice. In 1971 he threw a no-hitter against Pittsburgh, the world champions that year. When Gibson retired, he was the winningest pitcher in St Louis history (251–174) and second all-time in strikeouts (3,117).

Immensely intimidating on the mound, Bob put every ounce of power into his pitches—primarily a fastball and slider. He had a reputation as a headhunter, but insists he "hardly ever threw at a batter." But, he admits, "When I did, I hit 'em."

He was elected to the Baseball Hall of Fame in 1981.

Josh Gibson

Catcher, Negro Leagues, 1930–46, Homestead Grays, Pittsburgh Crawfords

"There is a catcher," said Walter Johnson, the Hall of Fame pitcher, "that any big league club would like to buy for $200,000. His name is Gibson. He can do everything. He hits the ball a mile, catches so easily he might as well be in a rocking chair, throws like a bullet. Bill Dickey isn't as good a catcher. Too bad this Gibson is a colored fellow."

Because black players were barred from the white major leagues during Gibson's time, there is no way to know for certain that he was the best catcher of all time. He may have been only one of the half dozen best. No lower ranking seems possible for the man they called "the Black Babe Ruth."

Actually accounts of his catching skills vary. Some say he was a little weak on pop fouls, but everyone agrees he had a good arm.

There's no dispute about his hitting. It was magnificent. The barrel-chested, 215-pound slugger hit home runs of tremendous length. One was measured with a tape at 575 feet, but it may not have been his longest. He also hit them often. One estimate, including barnstorming, Mexican League, Caribbean, and semipro games, puts his total at about 950. In Negro League and semi-pro games he was credited with 75

homers in 1931 and 69 in 1934. His batting average for seventeen years with the Homestead Grays and Pittsburgh Crawfords was over .350. He topped .400 at least twice. Combining with Buck Leonard in a "Ruth-Gehrig" tandem, Gibson led the Grays to nine straight pennants (1937–1945).

A warm, fun-loving man, Gibson was popular everywhere he played and, next to Satchel Paige, the Negro Leagues' greatest drawing card. For a time, he and Paige were battery mates.

Gibson was thirty-three years old when Jackie Robinson signed to play for the Dodgers. Reportedly he was bitter at having been passed over. Many believe he would have been signed by a white major league team in 1947, but he died of a brain hemorrhage in January of that year.

In 1972 he became the second Negro League player elected to the Hall of Fame.

Warren Giles

National League President, 1951–69

Wounded as a lieutenant in World War One, Giles was elected president of the Moline (Illinois) team in the Three-I League in 1919, to start a baseball career that spanned fifty years. He helped Branch Rickey build the Cardinals' farm system into baseball's best. In 1937 he took over as general manager of the last-place Cincinnati Reds. Two years later he had them in the World Series. In 1940 they were world champions.

As NL president, Giles oversaw league expansion to the West Coast, the attendance boom that followed the Vietnam War, and the battles with the players' union.

He was elected to the Hall of Fame in 1979.

Vernon "Lefty" Gomez

Pitcher, NY (A) 1930–42, Was (A) 1943

"Goofy" Gomez, inventor of the revolving goldfish bowl for tired goldfish, is one of the wittiest men ever to pitch a baseball. He entertained his teammates with his antics and one-liners. And sometimes—when he wasn't pitching—drew a smile from the opposition. His credo was "I'd rather be lucky than good." Actually he was both.

He was lucky to pitch for powerful Yankees' teams of the 1930s. They gave him baseball's most consistent support with their bats and gloves and enabled him to pitch in five World Series. And he was lucky to pitch half the time in Yankee Stadium, where "Death Valley" in the left field power alley swallowed up long drives from righthanded hitters.

But he was good too—one of the best lefthanders of the century. He won 20 games four times, including a sensational 26–5 year in 1934. He led the AL in strikeouts three times, with a top mark of 194 in 1938. He won 189 and lost 102. And in five World Series, he won six without a single loss.

He took his pitching seriously, but he had the ability to laugh at himself. He said the secret of his success was "clean living and a fast outfield—I'm the guy who made Joe DiMaggio famous."

Gomez was elected to the Hall of Fame in 1972.

Joe Gordon

Second Baseman, NY (A) 1938–43, 1946,
Cle (A) 1947–50. Manager, Cle (A) 1958–60, Det (A) 1960,
KC (A) 1961, 1969

Anyone with Gordon's surname is likely to be nicknamed "Flash," but Joe lived up to the label with his acrobatic defensive skills. He ranged over the Yankee infield, making plays that other second basemen dream about. One game he made eleven assists. He was at the head of AL second sackers in assists four times. Of course, the flip side was that in getting to balls others couldn't, he sometimes fumbled them. He led or tied in errors four times too. It was worth the price. In the first six years he cavorted at second base for the Yankees, they went to five World Series.

He seldom hit for average, but he had home run power. The one year he topped .300—.322 in 1942—he was named AL MVP. After he returned from military service, he struggled though a .210 season, and the Yankees, figuring he was washed up, dealt him to Cleveland. There he combined with Lou Boudreau to form what many still consider the most deadly double-play combination ever.

In 1948 he had his greatest season, batting .280, with 32 homers and 124 RBIs, as the Indians won the world championship. He completed his career with 253 home runs and 975 RBIs.

Leon "Goose" Goslin

Outfield, Was (A) 1921–30, 1933, 1938,
StL (A) 1930–32, Det (A) 1934–37

Except for the years Ted Williams managed the team, Goslin was the best hitter ever to wear a Washington uniform. He was with the Senators for all of the 1920s and looked in on them twice in the 1930s, slumming. The Senators were a pretty terrible team through most of their stay in the AL. Everybody knows the line: "Washington: first in war, first in peace, and last in the American League." But actually they weren't so awful when Goslin was with them; they won three pennants, the only ones they'd ever win.

Goslin showed up at the end of the 1921 season, and by the next year he was a fixture in left field. "Fixture" is a little harsh. He was neither the worst nor the slowest outfielder in the AL, just sort of lumbering.

But when he had the lumber in his hands, he was a star. He hit .300 or over in his first seven full years as a Senator. In 1924 he led the AL in RBIs with 129, hit .344 and knocked 12 homers, which was a fair number for anyone playing half his games in cavernous Griffith Stadium. The Senators won their first pennant and only World Series, as Goslin at one point set a record with 6 consecutive hits. The next year the Senators won their second pennant, as Goslin led the AL in triples, while hitting .334 with 18 homers and 113 RBIs. He hit .354 and .334 in the next two seasons, then topped the AL in 1928 with a .379 mark in the closest batting race in AL history; Goose singled in his last at-bat of the season to edge Heinie Manush by .001.

He hurt his arm horsing around in 1929, and for a time it looked like curtains. The Senators dealt him to the Browns ("St. Louis: gateway to the West and to the bottom of the

American League") and his arm came back. After a couple of good years in St. Louis (the Brownies even finished fifth in 1931), he was sent back to Washington with thanks in 1933. And darned if the Senators didn't win their third and last-ever pennant that year!

Next, it was off to Detroit for Goose and pennants in 1934 and 1935, something they hadn't seen in Detroit since 1909.

Goslin finished up with a career batting average of .316 and 248 home runs, but his best thing was batting in runs—1,609.

He was elected to the Hall of Fame in 1968.

Rich "Goose" Gossage

Pitcher, Chi (A) 1972–76, Pit (N) 1977,
NY (A) 1978–83, SD (N) 1984–87, Chi (N) 1988-

In his heyday, 1975–86, the big, mustachioed Goose glowered at the hitters, then blew his fastball by them. He didn't have a whole lot more than heat and intimidation, but for an inning or two he was devastating. He led the AL in saves with the fifth-place White Sox in 1975. The next year, desperate for starters, the Sox put him into the rotation. He struggled to 9–17 and was traded to Pittsburgh. Returned to his natural habitat, the bullpen, he saved 26, won 11, and set an NL record for relievers with 151 strikeouts.

In 1978 Goose signed with the Yankees as a free agent. He led the AL with 27 saves and won 10 as New York caught Boston on the last day of the season and then won the pennant in a playoff. Gossage spent six seasons in New York, earning a reputation as one of the top relievers in the game. In 1984 he moved again as a free agent, this time to San Diego, where he helped the Padres to their first pennant.

Hank Gowdy

Catcher, NY (N) 1910–11, 1923–25,
Bos (N) 1911–17, 1919–23, 1929–30

A quality catcher and fair hitter. Gowdy was the first major league player to enter military service in World War One. He was the regular receiver for the "Miracle Braves" of 1914. In the four-game World Series sweep over the A's, he hit .545, with three doubles, a triple, and a home run.

Ten years later, catching for the Giants in the 1924 Series, he was a goat in the final game. Hank tripped over his face mask on an easy pop foul by Muddy Ruel, who then doubled and scored the winning run.

Hank Greenberg

First Baseman, Det (A) 1930, 1933–41,
1945–46, Pit (N) 1947

One of the most fearsome home run hitters of all time, Greenberg played only nine full seasons, yet amassed 331 homers and 1,276 RBIs. Although he was an impressive six-four and 210 pounds, his success stemmed more from hard work than natural gifts. Thought too tall and awkward to play baseball, he applied himself with diligence and made himself into an adequate defensive first baseman. In 1940, when the Tigers

wanted to get Rudy York's bat into the lineup, Hank went to left field, and did the job well enough that the Tigers won the pennant.

In 1934 he led the Tigers to the World Series with 26 homers, 139 RBIs, and a league-leading 63 doubles. In 1935 he was even better, winning his first MVP Award with 36 home runs and 170 RBIs, both leading the AL. The Tigers were world champions.

The following year a broken wrist limited him to 12 games, but in 1937 he came back with 40 home runs and 183 RBIs, the third-highest RBI total ever. Perhaps his 1938 season is his most famous. That year he chased Babe Ruth's record down to the wire, finishing with 58 home runs. No right-handed hitter has ever exceeded that total. He had a knack for hitting more than one in a game, accomplishing that eleven times during the year. Two years later, as the Tigers' new left fielder, he won his second MVP on 41 homers and 150 RBIs, and the Tigers again won the pennant.

Then in 1941, only 19 games into the season, Greenberg was inducted into the Army. He was thirty-one. He did not return to the Tigers until midway through 1945. Fittingly his ninth-inning grand slam on the final day of the season won Detroit another pennant. After once more leading the AL in homers (with 44) and RBIs (with 127) in 1946, he was sold to Pittsburgh before the 1947 season for $75,000. The Pirates shortened the distant left field fence at Forbes Field in his honor by erecting a bullpen, quickly labeled "Greenberg Gardens." Hank hit 25 homers in 1947, then retired, but the Pirates' young slugger, Ralph Kiner, who'd been Greenberg's roommate on the Pirates, credited Greenberg's instruction and example with much of his subsequent success as a home run hitter.

Greenberg was elected to the Hall of Fame in 1956.

Gus Greenlee

Owner, Negro League

The flamboyant Greenlee, cigar-chomping Pittsburgh racketeer and numbers lord, never would have passed Judge Landis's scrutiny as a white owner. But he may have saved black baseball in the dreary days of the Depression.

Gus owned the Pittsburgh Crawfords, acclaimed by many as the best black team of all time, with Satchel Paige, Josh Gibson, Oscar Charleston, Cool Papa Bell, Judy Johnson, and other greats of black baseball. He waged a spirited war against Homestead Grays' owner Cum Posey for supremacy in Pittsburgh. Cum got his own racketeer to bankroll him, and the two fought both in the park and out.

Greenlee signed Paige from Birmingham and promoted him into the greatest drawing card in black ball. He also publicized Pepper Bassett, who caught Satch sitting in a rocking chair.

In 1933 Gus helped revive the Negro National League after the Depression had put it out for a year. He served as league president from 1933 to 1937. He also provided the inspiration for the East-West or All-Star Game, played in Comiskey Park a month after the first white All-Star Game there. It proved a financial life-saver, with upwards of 50,000 fans some years. The only profit many black clubs made all year was their share of receipts from that one game.

Gus also owned a stable of boxers, including world light-heavyweight champ John Henry Lewis. Like the ball team, the hobby lost money but was a cover for his numbers activities.

In 1937 Dominican dictator Rafael Trujillo bought Gus's stars out from under him, the Pittsburgh police finally raided his numbers store, and Gus at last was on the ropes.

Bobby Grich

Second Baseman, Bal (A) 1970–76, Cal (A) 1977–86

One of the most underrated players in the game, Grich was an outstanding all-around player who was generally thought of as only a glove man. His fielding, of course, *was* exceptional. In 1985 he made only two errors all season, to set a new standard for second basemen with a .997 fielding average. In 1973 he had a .995 mark. His career percentage of .984 is also the record. He won four Gold Gloves.

What was often overlooked was his hitting. He hit .304 in 1981 and got into the .290s a couple of times, but he was more comfortable at .250-.260. Nevertheless his ability to draw walks—twice over 100—kept him on base and allowed him to score 1,033 runs. He had good home run power with 224 career round-trippers. In the strike-shortened 1981 season he tied for the AL homer title with 22. Two years earlier he blasted 30 and drove in 101 runs.

Part of Grich's image problem was his postseason play. With Baltimore and California he appeared in five LCS's, always on the losing side. And in 24 LCS games he hit only .182.

Clark Griffith

Pitcher, StL (AA) 1891, Bos (AA) 1891, Chi (N) 1893-1900, Chi (A) 1901–02, NY (A) 1903–07, Cin (N) 1909–10, Was (A) 1912-14. Manager, Chi (A) 1901–02, NY (A) 1903–08, Cin (N) 1909–11, Was (A) 1912–20

"The Old Fox," Griffith was elected to the Hall of Fame in 1946 as one of the game's pioneers. He could just as easily have gone in for his pitching. And he wasn't a bad manager either. Clark was born in a Missouri log cabin. His father was shot and killed when Clark was two. The boy held Jesse James's horse, was a trapper, cowpuncher, faro dealer, and singer in frontier saloons before taking up baseball.

Only five-eight, he learned to use guile from Old Hoss Radbourn, another great little man. He got the hitters out with brains, a primitive slider (Cy Young called it a "dinky-dinky pitch")— and a little scuffing of the ball. He won 20 or more games for Chicago six straight years, from 1894 through 1899. Jumping to the AL in 1901, Griff pitched (24–7) and managed the White Sox to the first flag in the new league's history. He took over as the Yankees (then known as the Highlanders) first manager when the club moved to New York in 1903. It was his last season as a full-time pitcher. His career mark was a sparkling 240–141.

Although the Highlanders nearly won the 1904 American League pennant, and finished second again in 1906, Griff was let go in mid-1908. He always felt he'd been mistreated by the New York owners, fans, and press. It led to his life-long

loathing of the Yankees.

After managing Cincinnati for three years, AL president Ban Johnson prevailed upon him to help rescue the failing Washington franchise in 1912. Griffith became manager and mortgaged his ranch to buy 10 percent of the stock. With Walter Johnson pitching and Griffith managing, the Senators finished second two years in a row, then began a slow drift toward the second division as financial problems continued to beset the team.

In 1920 Griffith purchased controlling interest in the Senators, resigned as field manager, and took over as president. Although the team won a world championship in 1924 and pennants in 1925 and 1933, it was always financially strapped. Unable to compete with the richer AL clubs, Griffith was often forced to sell his better players to keep operating. In 1934 he even had to sell his manager-shortstop and son-in-law, Joe Cronin, for $225,000. Griffith was a leader in popularizing night games, the use of on-field entertainers such as Al Schacht, and in the signing of Latin players—all dictated by the constant financial woes of the Senators. Perhaps his greatest achievement was keeping baseball in the nation's capital during his lifetime. He should receive accolades for his off-field friendships with James A. Farley, Postmaster-General, and President Franklin D. Roosevelt; these friendships were responsible for the famous "Green Light" to wartime baseball.

Burleigh Grimes

Pitcher, Pit (N) 1916–17, 1928–29, 1934, Bkn (N) 1918–26,
NY (N) 1927, Bos (N) 1930, StL (N) 1930–31, 1933–34,
Chi (N) 1932–33, NY (A) 1934.
Manager, Bkn (N) 1937–38

Grimes threw the last legal spitball in 1934. But "Old Stubblebeard"—a nickname derived from his habit of not shaving on days he pitched —won games as much on willpower as "wetpower." Pitching for the Cardinals in the 1931 World Series, he threw a two-hitter in Game Three to beat Lefty Grove. Came the final game, he had an inflamed appendix. The trainer put ice packs on his stomach between innings while Grimes shut out Philadelphia for eight innings. He weakened in the ninth, but still got two outs before a reliever nailed down the win.

"Boiley," as they called him in Brooklyn, was a workhorse who led the NL in innings pitched three times and topped 300 innings in five different seasons. A gruff, hard-bitten type he was only too willing to knock down any batter with the temerity to dig in at the plate.

His greatest seasons were with Brooklyn, where he four times won 20 games between 1918 and 1926. In 1920 he helped the Dodgers to a pennant with a 23–11 mark.

In the World Series that year, he shut out Cleveland on seven hits in Game Two, but Game Five is the one everyone remembers. Cleveland loaded the bases in the first inning; the scouting report said to throw the Indians' outfielder Elmer Smith spitballs. Grimes did and Smith took issue with the scouting report by hitting the first grand-slam home run in Series history. In the fourth inning Grimes gave up the first Series home run by a pitcher, to Cleveland's Jim Bagby. The weirdness wasn't over. Grimes was replaced by Clarence Mitchell, who then batted in the fifth inning and lined the ball

to Tribe second baseman Bill Wambsganss, who turned it into an unassisted triple play!

After leaving Brooklyn, Grimes was 19–8 for the Giants in 1927 and 25-14 for Pittsburgh in 1928. He got to St. Louis in 1930 and helped them win two straight pennants.

One of the small group identified as spitballers and allowed to keep throwing the pitch after it was outlawed in 1920, Grimes both lasted longer than the rest and won more games. He finished up in 1934 with a 270–212 mark. His career ERA of 3.53 was acquired in an age of heavy hitting, when any season mark under 4.00 was hot pitching.

He was elected to the Hall of Fame in 1964.

Henry "Heinie" Groh

Third Baseman, NY (N) 1912–13, 1922–26,
Cin (N) 1913–21, Pit (N) 1927.
Manager, Cin (N) 1918

Only five-eight, Heinie was famous for his bat, shaped like a big milk bottle. Its handle ballooned into a thick barrel, which he held high over his right shoulder. He looked sort of like a cartoon. But don't laugh. In the 1922 World Series, he used it to hit .474. The next year Heinie reportedly drove around with license plate #474.

The Giants picked up Groh in 1922 from Cincinnati, where he'd been an outstanding third baseman for years, and he helped them win pennants for three straight years. A good fielder and dangerous hitter (.293 lifetime), he believed his odd bat gave him better control on bunts.

Robert "Lefty" Grove

Pitcher, Phi (A) 1925–33, Bos (A) 1934–41

Grove boggles the mind, to say nothing of how he boggled AL batters. The consensus pick as best lefthander in history, Lefty might also have been the best pitcher, period. Some hitters insist he was faster than Johnson or Feller. His ball didn't have a hop at all—but still they couldn't hit it.

He was terrific from the day in 1920 when he first began pitching for Jack Dunn's Baltimore Orioles of the International League. But Dunn wasn't about to sell him to a major league team until he got his price—and the price went up every year. By the close of the 1924 season, Grove had won 108 games for Dunn and had yet to pitch in the majors. Connie Mack finally came up with $100,600, a new record. Grove was twenty-five when he pitched his first game for the A's.

Although it took him a couple of years to begin rolling up big victory totals, Lefty led the AL in strikeouts as a rookie. In walks, too—earning a reputation for wildness that was unmerited after that first season. He was, however, wild after a loss. He set new records for clubhouse tantrums, but it was noted he always punched lockers with his right hand. His theory on kicking water buckets was "Always be sure the bucket is empty."

After leading the league in ERA and strikeouts in 1926, he really got rolling. In the next seven seasons, he won 20 or more seven times, led in wins four times, led in winning percentage four times, in ERA four, in strikeouts five, and in shutouts

twice. Death and taxes are less consistent. His 31–4 record in 1931 is his gaudiest season and earned him the MVP.

The A's won pennants from 1929 through 1931, but by 1934 the Depression was killing attendance and Connie Mack needed money. He sold Grove to the Red Sox for $125,000 (a $24,400 capital gain). Lefty's fabled fastball was a memory, and it took him an 8–8 season to change over to a "curves and control" pitcher. Then he won 20 for the eighth time and followed with a couple of 17-win seasons. He also took four more ERA titles. On July 25, 1941, he became the sixth modern pitcher to win 300 games. At 300–141 his .680 career percentage ranks fourth all-time but doesn't include his 55 saves. His lifetime ERA of 3.06, when normalized to the league average and adjusted for home park, was the best ever—even topping Walter Johnson's.

In 1947 he was named to the Hall of Fame.

Ron Guidry

Pitcher, NY (A) 1975-

In 1978 Guidry had one of the most effective years of any pitcher any time any place. The slightly built Louisiana left-hander was 25–3, to lead the AL in both wins and percentage. Also tops were his 1.74 ERA and 9 shutouts. In 273 innings, he allowed a skimpy 187 hits. He struck out 248 but walked only 72. Led by Guidry, the Yankees moved from 10 1/2 games back on July 24 to tie the fading Red Sox on the last day of the season, then won the playoff on Bucky Dent's homer. Naturally it had to be Ron, on short rest, who started and won the playoff victory. He added two more wins in the postseason.

He won the Cy Young Award hands down and finished second in the MVP voting.

"Louisiana Lightning" was never quite the same world-beater again, though he had several fine seasons, including 21–9 in 1983 and 22–6 in 1985.

Stan Hack

Third Baseman, Chi (N) 1932–47. Manager,
Chi (N) 1954–56, StL (N) 1958

"Smiling Stan" played on four Cubs pennant winners and hit .348 in the Series (.471 in 1938), though the Cubs lost all four. *The Sporting News* chose him as its all-star third baseman three years in a row, 1940–1942.

A lifetime .301 hitter, he cracked out 2,193 hits in sixteen years. He also drew 1,092 walks and scored 1,239 runs. He seldom hit with much power, but he was consistent.

Hack's most famous hit came in the sixth game of the 1935 Series against the Tigers. Down three games to two, and tied in this game 3–3, Stan led off the ninth inning and smote one of Tommy Bridges' curves over the Tiger center fielder's head for a triple. A sacrifice fly ball would give the Cubs the lead. But Billy Jurges struck out, Larry French bounced out, and when Augie Galan finally got the fly, it was too late. A half inning later the Tigers won the game and the Series.

Charles "Chick" Hafey

Outfielder, StL (N) 1924–31, Cin (N) 1932–35, 1937

Hafey had everything you could ask for in a ballplayer except good health. He hit for a good average with fair power. He was fast. He could field. And he had the best throwing arm of any NL outfielder during his time.

The quiet, modest slugger was at the same time known for playing practical jokes on his teammates. He first became a regular with the Cardinals in 1926, as the team fought toward its first pennant. He was beaned several times during the season, affecting his sight. He was advised to wear glasses, a rarity among players of his day. His sight fluctuated so that he actually used three different pairs, depending on the state of his eyes.

From 1927 through 1931 he hit above .300 each season for the Cards, who won pennants in 1928, 1930, and 1931. He drove in over 100 runs in three of those seasons, and had a career-high 29 home runs in 1929—this despite a chronic sinus infection that required several operations.

In 1931 Hafey won the closest batting race in NL history, nosing out Bill Terry by .0003. Terry hit .3495 to Hafey's .3498. Chick had been a holdout several times before; when he asked for a raise to $17,000 after winning the batting championship, St. Louis traded him to Cincinnati. He had several good seasons with the Reds before retiring in 1935. A comeback attempt in 1937 was unsuccessful.

Hafey was elected to the Hall of Fame in 1971.

Jesse "Pop" Haines

Pitcher, Cin (N) 1918, StL (N) 1920–37

Haines was a temperamental workhorse who relied on a good fastball and tricky knuckleball to win 210 games, all with the St. Louis Cardinals. Until Bob Gibson surpassed his mark, he was the Cards' all-time winner. He didn't join the team until he was twenty-six years old but stayed until he was forty-five—hence his nickname "Pop."

He won 20 or more three times and pitched a no-hitter in 1924. During his time with the Redbirds, they won five pennants and three world championships. Haines was 3–1 in World Series play.

Haines was 13–4 in 1926, as the Cards won their first pennant. In the Series he shut out the Yanks, the last time that would happen for sixteen years.

Oddly Haines was most famous for being relieved in a ball game. In the seventh game of the 1926 Series, he was leading 3–2 when he developed a blister from throwing the knuckler and loaded the bases in the seventh inning with two out and Tony Lazzeri up. Manager Rogers Hornsby waved in Grover Alexander from the bullpen. Alexander's strikeout of Lazzeri is one of the most famous events in baseball history.

Haines was elected to the Hall of Fame in 1970.

Billy Hamilton

Outfielder, KC (AA) 1888–89,

Phi (N) 1890–95, Bos (N) 1896–1901

"Sliding Billy" epitomized the jackrabbit era of the 1890s. Only five-six, he stole 937 bases—117 in 1889, 102 in 1890, and 115 in 1891—and led his league in steals in seven of his fourteen seasons. The 117 steals was a record until Lou Brock broke it eighty-five years later. Of course they were not all what we call stolen bases today. Going from first to third on a single was counted as a "steal."

Hamilton was the most efficient leadoff man ever. He had more runs scored than games played—a record—1,692 runs in 1,593 games. He also holds the all-time record for runs scored in a single season with 196 in 1894. He led the league four times. He was able to accomplish these things for several reasons in addition to his undeniable speed. In the first place, he was an exceptional hitter, leading the NL twice—.340 in 1891 and .380 in 1893. His career average was .344, eighth best of all time. Second, he walked a lot. He topped the NL in bases on balls five times. Third, he was followed in the batting order through most of his career by other outstanding hitters.

In 1894, his record year for scoring runs, he played center field for the Phillies and hit .399. Left fielder Ed Delahanty hit .400, and right fielder Sam Thompson hit .404. And substitute outfielder Tuck Turner hit .416 in 80 games! Even so, the Phillies finished fourth.

In 1896 the Phillies traded him to Boston for veteran third baseman Billy Nash. He joined Hall of Famer Hugh Duffy in the Beaneaters' outfield and helped his new team win pennants in 1897–1898.

Hamilton was elected to the Hall of Fame in 1961.

Ned Hanlon

Outfielder, Cle (N) 1880, Det (N) 1881–1888,
Pit (N) 1889, 1891, Pit (P) 1890, Bal (N) 1892.
Manager, Pit (N) 1889, 1891, Pit (P) 1890,
Bal (N) 1892–98, Bkn (N) 1899–1905,
Cin (N) 1906–07

Ned Hanlon was the original dirty tricks manager with the old Baltimore Orioles and Brooklyn Superbas of the Gay Nineties. With Willie Keeler, John McGraw, Joe Kelley, Hughie Jennings, and the rest, Hanlon's teams bunted and hit-and-ran their way to five flags.

They also reportedly:

• raised the foul lines so bunts would stay fair
• grabbed runners' belts as they rounded third base
• hid extra balls in the outfield grass to throw in on long hits
• flashed mirrors in the faces of the other teams' batters and fielders
• rolled on the ground and pinched their arms to fake being hit by pitches
• buried cement in front of home plate, then beat balls down on it so they'd bounce high enough to beat out—the famous "Baltimore Chop."

After a dozen years as a good field/no hit outfielder, Hanlon took over the Orioles in 1892, when they finished twelfth. He picked on young McGraw mercilessly until John offered to "punch his big head"—exactly the reaction Ned wanted.

The next year he had the O's up to eighth, and by 1894 to first. They won three straight flags, then finished second twice. Moving to Brooklyn, he won flags his first two years,

1899–1900, then began a descent to last. But Ned still ended with a .530 winning percentage.

After baseball he went into real estate and made a fortune.

Mel Harder

Pitcher, Cle (A) 1928–47

Harder won over 223 games in twenty years of pitching for Cleveland, including 20-win seasons in 1934–1935. Only Bob Feller won more for the Tribe. He had the honor of pitching the opening game in Municipal Stadium against Lefty Grove before 82,000 fans. He lost 1–0. In the 1934 All-Star Game, he hurled five scoreless innings.

After retiring from the mound, Mel coached the Indian pitchers in 1949 through 1963, the glory years of their magnificent pitching staffs. He was credited with helping Feller, Bob Lemon, Early Wynn, Mike Garcia, Herb Score, and others. It was said that "he had a camera in his head" because of his uncanny ability to spot pitching flaws.

Mike Hargrove

First Baseman, Tex (A) 1974–78, SD (N) 1979,
Cle (A) 1979–85

Hargrove was called "the Human Rain Delay" because of his long, involved ritual before taking his stance in the batter's box. He'd walk up near the plate and take exactly three deliberate practice swings. Then he would step into the box and meticulously dig in his left foot. Next he'd adjust his helmet. Arrange his uniform. Tug his belt. At last, he was ready. But after the first pitch, he'd go through it all again. He drove pitchers crazy. But it worked. He hit .290 for his twelve seasons, led his league in walks twice, and had four seasons of over 100 walks. His lifetime OBP of .401, when normalized to the league average and adjusted for home park, is among the top twenty of this century.

Will Harridge

American League President, 1931–59

Harridge worked for the Wabash Railroad handling travel arrangements for AL teams and umpires. He had never seen a major league game until he became private secretary to AL President Ban Johnson in 1911. Twenty years later the efficient but colorless, conservative Harridge was promoted to chief and served twenty-eight years, 1931–1959.

He preferred to stay in the background, but he never hesitated to enforce league rules and decorum. In 1931, shortly after taking office and in the middle of a heated pennant race, he suspended Yankee catcher Bill Dickey for a month for slugging another player. Harridge was a strong advocate of the All-Star Game. He opposed night baseball until he saw that such games made baseball more available to families. He hated gimmicks and showboating, and was not amused when Bill Veeck used a midget as a pinch hitter.

He fined Boston's Ted Williams for spitting at fans. But when Ted won the 1941 All-Star Game with a ninth-inning

homer, Harridge lost his reserve. He almost kissed Ted, he said, and would have "if there weren't so many people around."

Harridge was named to the Hall of Fame in 1972.

Stanley "Bucky" Harris

Second Baseman, Was (A) 1919–28, Det (A) 1929, 1931.
Manager, Was (A) 1924–28, Det (A) 1929–33, Bos (A) 1934,
Was (A) 1935–42, Phi (N) 1943, NY (A) 1947–48,
Was (A) 1950–54, Det (A) 1955–56

Harris broke in as a regular second baseman with the Senators in 1920, hitting .300 for the only time in his career. In 1924 "the Boy Manager" became the Senators' skipper at age twenty-seven. He took the team to its first pennant and a World Series victory over the Giants. With Washington down three games to two, Harris knocked in both runs to win Game Six 2–1 and tie the Series. The next day Bucky drove in three runs to pull his team to a 3–3 tie after nine innings. They won in the twelfth on the famous hit that bounced over third baseman Fred Lindstrom's head. Harris hit .333 for the Series, with seven RBIs, and two homers—he hit only nine other home runs in his career.

Though the Senators repeated as pennant winners in 1925, they lost the Series to the Pirates. In 1929 Harris moved to Detroit as player-manager and began a career as the "Available Man." All told, he managed for twenty-nine years. He had two more sessions in Washington (1935–1942 and 1950–1954), two in Detroit (1929–1933 and 1955–1956), one year in Boston (1934), two-thirds of a season with the Phillies (1943), and two years with the Yankees (1947–1948). Most of the time he was saddled with teams that had little chance to win; twenty of them finished in the second division. But Harris was respected as a manager who got the most out of his limited material.

He won his last pennant and world championship with the Yankees in 1947 but lost a three-way race to Boston and Cleveland in 1948. The Yanks promptly fired Harris and hired Casey Stengel.

Bucky ranks third all-time in managerial wins with 2,159 and second in losses with 2,219. He was elected to the Hall of Fame in 1975.

Charles "Gabby" Hartnett

Catcher, Chi (N) 1922–40, NY (N) 1941.
Manager, Chi (N) 1938–40

While AL fans argued the merits of Cochrane and Dickey, NL fans had no problem identifying their circuit's best catcher. Hartnett was the cream of the NL, and to some the best of all. Although he was often described as a "beefy man with a tomato face who talked a lot," his nickname was actually hung on him ironically when as a Cubs rookie in 1922 he said virtually nothing. He developed his communication skills, of course, but for twenty seasons his batting and catching skills spoke louder.

An excellent defensive catcher with a powerful arm and a take-charge handler of pitchers, he caught 1,790 games. In twelve seasons, he played in over 100 games. He led National League catchers in fielding six times.

His lifetime batting average was .297, and at one time he held the record for home runs by a catcher, with 236. He drove in 1,179 runs, with a personal high of 122 in 1930. While he was with them, the Cubs won four pennants. He appeared in five All-Star Games and was NL MVP in 1935.

He was behind the plate in the 1932 World Series when Babe Ruth hit his "called shot" off Charley Root. Gabby always insisted the Babe didn't point.

In 1934 he caught Carl Hubbell's great All-Star Game feat of striking out Ruth, Gehrig, Foxx, Simmons, and Cronin. "Just throw them what you throw me," he told Hub, "I can't hit it, and neither will they."

But Hartnett's greatest moment—perhaps the greatest in Chicago baseball history—was his "homer in the gloaming" against Pittsburgh as darkness fell on Wrigley Field, September 28, 1938. Gabby had become Cubs manager in midseason and led the club from 6½ games behind to 1½ behind the Pirates. The teams met in Chicago for a series that would decide the pennant. In the leadoff game, the score was tied after eight innings, and the umps warned that the ninth would be the last. There were two out in the bottom of the ninth, 34,465 crazed fans in the stands, and Mace Brown had an 0–2 count against Gabby. Hartnett hit the next ball into the bleachers and the Cubs went on to the flag.

Gabby was named to the Hall of Fame in 1955.

Guy Hecker

Pitcher/First Baseman/Manager, Lou (AA) 1882–89,
Pit (N) 1890. Manager, Pit (N) 1890

In 1884 Hecker led the old American Association with a 52–20 mark and 1.80 ERA. Two years later he led the league in batting with .342. Guy was surely the best hitting pitcher until Ferrell. He averaged .284 for his career and even stole 48 bases in 1887. On August 15, 1886, he allowed Baltimore four hits in a complete-game victory while registering six hits himself, including three homers and two doubles. He also scored a record of seven runs.

Hecker's pitching was his forte, however. In four years 1883–1886, he *averaged* 34–23 for a team that finished third, fourth, fifth, and fifth. In his big year, 1884, he also led in complete games, innings pitched, and strikeouts.

Jim Hegan

Catcher, Cle (A) 1941–42, 1946–57, Det (A) 1958,
Phi (N) 1958–59, SF (N) 1959, Chi (N) 1960

The top defensive catcher in the AL in the post-World War Two period, Hegan holds a record that may never be broken—he handled eighteen 20-game winners with the Indians, 1946–1957. The glory years of Cleveland pitching coincided with the tenure of Jim (and pitching coach Mel Harder). Three of Hegan's stars—Bob Feller, Bob Lemon, and Early Wynn—are in the Hall of Fame. Two of them—Feller and Wynn—call him the best receiver ever.

In 1946, in his first season as a regular, Hegan handled Feller's 348-strikeout season. That year the Indians were 45–43 with him, 21–43 without. In 1954 his pitchers won 111

games, the most ever in the AL. In between he caught three no-hitters, by Feller, Lemon, and Don Black.

A poor hitter with a career .228 batting average, Hegan had his best offensive season in the Indians' world championship season of 1948. He batted .248, hit 14 homers, and drove in 61 runs.

Harry "Slug" Heilmann

Outfielder, Det (A) 1914, 1916–29, Cin (N) 1930, 1932

Heilmann was a good hitter who became a great hitter when the lively ball was introduced in 1920. Line drives that fielders had previously reached began whizzing by their gloves before they could react. Harry was a line drive machine. His homer totals were only average; his biggest year was 21 in 1923. But he hit plenty of gappers for doubles and triples. For much of his career he batted behind Ty Cobb, helping him to his all-time record in runs scored. Harry had 1,551 RBIs and topped 100 in eight seasons.

"Slug" didn't help his team in the outfield. He was slow and awkward. For two years the Tigers tried to put him at first base. He led AL first basemen in errors both years, so they sent him back to the outfield, where he had fewer opportunities to be slow and awkward.

But with a bat in his hand, Heilmann rivaled the NL's Rogers Hornsby as the greatest righthanded hitter of the time. He led the AL in hitting four times, oddly—in alternating odd years. In 1921, he led with .393; in 1923 it was .403; in 1925, .393; and in 1927, .398. In his "off-years" between titles, he bided his time with .356, .346, and .367. His career average was .342.

Heilmann was a low-key, articulate man, who told droll stories of his playing days. After retiring, he put those talents to work as a popular play-by-play radio broadcaster for the Tigers.

He was named to the Hall of Fame in 1952.

Ricky Henderson

Outfielder, Oak (A) 1979–84, NY (A) 1985-

The greatest thief since Willie Sutton, Henderson demolished the single-season stolen base record in 1982, when he swiped 130 for Oakland. Three times he has gone over 100, and he's led the AL in steals eight times. After only ten years in the majors, he ranks third all-time in stolen bases behind Lou Brock and Ty Cobb (Billy Hamilton's 937 total in the 1890s is not counted because it was accomplished under different rules.)

An ideal leadoff man, Rickey usually bats in the .290-.310 range, draws plenty of walks (he's twice led the American League), and scores and scores and scores; he's averaged over 100 runs scored per season for his career.

Henderson also hits with occasional power. Only Bobby Bonds tops him in leadoff home runs, and Rickey will probably surpass that mark as well.

Tommy Henrich

Outfielder, NY (A) 1937–42, 1946–50

"Old Reliable" Henrich played right field on eight Yankee champions in eleven years. Yankee fans like to say that the Keller-DiMaggio-Henrich outfield was the best ever, but Yankee fans are like that. Tommy was a first-rate player, but his .282 batting average and 183 homers do not quite put him in "best" circles. On the other hand, DiMaggio called him the smartest player in the majors, and nobody gave tests to prove otherwise.

One thing, Tommy was always in the middle of the action.

In the 1941 Series, he was at bat when Mickey Owen dropped that third strike. Henrich alertly raced to first, igniting the game-winning rally in Game Six.

He got the game-winning hits in three of the four Yankee victories in the 1947 Series, including the deciding seventh game.

He played hurt most of 1949 but was such a clutch hitter in the 115 games he limped into that he finished sixth in the MVP voting. He finished the season with a flourish, whipping the home run that beat Boston on the final day to clinch the flag, the first of Casey Stengel's record-breaking five straight pennants. Then, in the opening game of the World Series, Tommy slugged a homer off Newcombe in the bottom of the ninth to beat the Dodgers, 1–0.

Billy Herman

Second Baseman, Chi (N) 1931–41, Bkn (N) 1941–43, 1946, Bos (N) 1946, Pit (N) 1947. Manager, Pit (N) 1947, Bos (A) 1964–66

Herman was a great hit-and-run man and smart second baseman, who played on four NL champs with the Cubs and Dodgers, winning every third year—1932, 1935, 1938, and 1941.

Billy succeeded Rogers Hornsby at second base for the Cubs in 1932, hit .314, improved the defense, and helped the team move up from third to the flag. He set an NL record by handling over 900 chances at second for five straight years. For his first seven seasons in Chicago, Billy teamed with shortstop Billy Jurges in a double-play combination that had even old-time Cubs fans asking "Who-to-who-to-Chance?" Herman's best year was 1935, when he hit .341, cracked 227 hits to lead the NL, and scored 113 runs. His career batting average was .304.

Early in the 1941 season, Billy was sent off to Brooklyn. "I just bought a pennant," Dodger owner Larry MacPhail crowed. He was right. Billy and his new partner young Pee Wee Reese meshed beautifully and the Dodgers won their first flag in twenty-one years.

Herman was elected to the Hall of Fame in 1975.

Floyd "Babe" Herman

Outfielder, Bkn (N) 1926–31, 1945,

Cin (N) 1932, 1935–36, Chi (N) 1933–34, Pit (N) 1935,
Det (A) 1937

Poor Babe is remembered as the man who hit .393 and couldn't win the batting crown, and as the daffy Dodger who got hit on the head with a fly ball and somehow tripled into a triple play.

True on the first count. Libel on the other two.

Babe hit .393 in 1930, when players were benched for hitting .290 and optioned to Topeka for hitting .280. Bill Terry won the batting championship with .401, the last time a National Leaguer topped the .400 mark.

In 1935 he hit the first night-game home run in big league history. Even after he left Brooklyn, someone was always willing to hire him for his hitting and look the other way while he tried to play the outfield. For his thirteen major league seasons, he averaged .324 with his bat and slightly higher with his glove.

Herman was not the naive simpleton that the writers and historians created. He was a thoughtful, intelligent man, and he did not triple into a triple play. He doubled into a double play. It happened like this: With the bases loaded at Ebbets Field, Herman slammed a drive off the wall, and the ball bounced all the way back to second base. One run scored, and someone yelled to throw home. Dazzy Vance, halfway home, turned and scrambled back to third base, where Chick Fewster had already arrived from first base. Herman, running full out but head down, heard the yell and thought Fewster must be scoring, so he raced for third. He slid in safely—even stylishly—to find the other two already there. They called Fewster and Herman out and gave him credit for a double. Ever after, when the Dodgers put three men on base, some wag was sure to ask, "Which base?"

As for getting hit on the head with a fly, Herman stoutly denied it. "How about the shoulder, Babe?" someone asked. "No," he said, "the shoulder don't count."

Keith Hernandez

First Baseman, StL (N) 1974–83, NY (N) 1983-

If Hernandez ever melts down his Gold Gloves, he can fill every cavity in New York. As of 1988, he's won eight and figures to be good for a few more before he's done. He is easily the premier fielding first baseman of today. The only argument is whether he is the best of all time. The fact that he already holds the record for career assists by a first baseman (but is not in the top ten of games played) supports the "Aye" vote.

A consistent .300 hitter with line-drive power, Keith led the NL with a .344 batting average in 1979 and was voted co-MVP with Willie Stargell. In 1982 he hit .299 and drove in 94 runs, as the Cardinals won the world championship. His surprise trade to the Mets the next season is still a sore point with Cardinals' fans. Mets fans think of it as akin to Christmas morning.

Hernandez played on his second world champion team with New York in 1986 and a divisional championship in 1988. The handsome lefthanded hitter is considered a leader in the clubhouse and on the field.

Dorrel "Whitey" Herzog

Manager, Tex (A) 1973, KC (A) 1975–79, StL (N) 1980-.
Outfielder, Was (A) 1956–58, KC (A) 1958–60,
Bal (A) 1961–62, Det (A) 1963

Herzog's playing career was eight years of undistinguished outfielding. His managing career ranks as one of the best and brightest.

He took over at Kansas City in mid-1975 and brought them home second. Three consecutive division titles followed, but the Royals lost the LCS all three times. When Kansas City finished second in 1979, he was fired.

He crossed the state to St. Louis, where he's had his greatest success. His Cardinals won the world championship in 1982 and pennants in 1985 and 1987. In none of those years was St. Louis favored in preseason appraisals.

Whitey's best Series may have been 1987. Playing without his top hitter, Jack Clark, and with substitutes in several positions, he still took the Series to seven games against Minnesota.

"Whitey-ball" in the 1980s has been tailored to Busch Stadium, with its artificial surface and deep power alleys. Typically his lineup is mostly made up of speedy, good-fielding, line-drive hitters, with at least one strong power hitter to bat cleanup. His pitching staff normally hosts more than the usual number of lefthanders.

Gil Hodges

First Baseman, Bkn (N) 1943, 1947–57, LA (N) 1958–61,
NY (N) 1962–63. Manager, Was (A) 1963–67,
NY (N) 1968–71

Gil was one of the top guns in the Dodgers' Murderers' Row, 1948–1959. He slugged 370 homers during an eighteen-year career, drove in 1,274, and was considered a top fielder among National League first basemen. He played on seven Dodger pennant winners, six in Brooklyn and the last in 1959 for Los Angeles.

Hodges was an even-tempered gentleman of immense strength, both in physique and character. His inner strength helped him persevere during the extended batting slumps that he was prone to as a player. Most fans know Hodges's frustrating 1952 Series when he went 0-for-21. Dodger fans were sending him batting tips and lighting candles in church for him. Fewer recall that he hit .364 the next year in the Series or that he drove in both runs of the final game in 1955, as the Dodgers won their first world championship.

As manager of the dreadful Washington Senators (1963–1967), he needed every ounce of his patience. When he brought the team up to sixth in 1967, people said his next project would be parting the Red Sea.

Actually he undertook something more difficult—he became manager of the Mets. Throughout the 1960s the Mets had always been good for a laugh but rarely good for a win. They didn't disappoint the stand-up comics in 1968, Hodges's first year at the helm, finishing ninth. Then, in 1969, with Hodges platooning a lineup of mostly retreads and with a young pitching staff boasting Tom Seaver, Jerry Koosman, and Tug McGraw, the team became the Amazing Mets. They

won the NL East, brushed aside Atlanta in the LCS, and humbled Baltimore in a five-game World Series—"The Miracle of Flushing Meadows."

Harry Hooper

Outfielder, Bos (A) 1909–20, Chi (A) 1921–25

Hooper was an excellent rightfielder with a legendary throwing arm. He played with Tris Speaker and Duffy Lewis in what old-timers called the best outfield ever. There have been several "best-ever" outfields since, but the trio brought the Red Sox two world titles—in 1912 and 1915. Speaker was the star, of course, but after Spoke moved on to Cleveland, Lewis and Hooper helped the Sox win another World Series in 1916. And *then*, when Duffy wasn't around in 1918, Hooper was still there for a fourth championship. If you get the idea that Harry was a winner, you're probably running on all cylinders.

In the final game of the 1912 World Series, he went back as far as he could, then leaped, speared Larry Doyle's drive barehanded, and fell backward into the stands. His robbery kept the Sox alive to win in the tenth.

In 1915, after hitting only two home runs all season, he hit two in the final game of the World Series with the last one providing the margin of victory. In the 1916 Series, he hit .333 and scored six runs in five days.

Harry was a leadoff hitter with a modest .281 lifetime batting average, but he drew a lot of walks, which allowed him to score 1,429 runs in his career.

Hooper was elected to the Hall of Fame in 1971.

Rogers Hornsby

Second Baseman, StL (N) 1915–26, 1933,
NY (N) 1927, Bos (N) 1928, Chi (N) 1929–32,
StL (A) 1933–37. Manager, StL (N) 1925–26,
Bos (N) 1927, Chi (N) 1930–32, StL (A) 1933–37, 1952,
Cin (N) 1952–53

Hornsby always said he could have made it to the majors on his fielding even if he'd only been an ordinary hitter. Well, maybe. The question is, how long would he have stayed there? Using his chances-handled-per-game as a gauge, he started out with pretty good range but slowed down fast. By 1920, when he first showed himself to be a great hitter, he was average at best in the field. And throughout the 1920s just about every good team in the NL had a second baseman covering more ground than the Rajah.

Of course, none of them hit as well. Hornsby never had to make a living with his glove; he was a magnificent hitter. Many call him the greatest righthanded hitter of all time. Proving that takes all sorts of adjustments as you try to relate one era to another, so there might have been a righthander to rank ahead of Hornsby, but he has to be in the top handful. Take a deep breath and listen:

His career batting average of .358 is second only to Ty Cobb, who batted southpaw. Hornsby is the only righthanded batter to hit .400 three times, and his .424 in 1924 is a record for this century. He won six straight batting titles from 1920 to 1925 and added a seventh in 1928. He made 250 hits in 1922, led the league four times, and cracked over 200 seven

times. He led the NL in home runs twice, led in triples once and tied once, led in doubles four times. He led or tied in runs five times and in RBIs four times. He won two Triple Crowns and two MVPs. Whew!

In the feet-of-clay department, the Rajah had a royal disdain for the opinions and feelings of everybody he ever met. He was brusque, blunt, hypercritical, dictatorial, moody, and argumentative. He alienated almost everyone sooner or later. St. Louis traded him right after he'd player-managed them to a world championship in 1926. The Giants traded him in 1927 after he hit .361. He predicted he'd lead the league again in 1928. He did, and the Braves traded immediately him to the Cubs for 1929.

Except for that 1926 pennant in his second year as skipper, he had no success as a major league manager. He never had any other Hornsbys playing for him, and he was satisfied with nothing less.

His only vice—outside of a personality that could sand wood—was betting on horses. He was bad at it. What he was, was a hitter. He never drank, smoked, read, or went to movies because he wanted to protect his batting eye.

Hornsby was elected to the Hall of Fame in 1942.

Frank Howard

Outfielder, LA (N) 1958–64, Was (A) 1965–71,
Tex (A) 1972, Det (A) 1972–73.
Manager, SD (N) 1981, NY (N) 1983

When six-seven, 255-pound Howard came up to bat, the pitcher must have figured someone had moved the mound closer to the plate. "Hondo" was intimidating and he could deliver. He hit some of the mightiest blasts ever seen and left painted seats in the upper decks all over both leagues as mementoes of his homers. Even Ted Williams, his manager at Washington, shook his head in admiration.

Of course Howard struck out a lot too, flailing at low outside curves. But when he connected, the balls flew. Playing for the Dodgers, he walloped a long home run in the 1963 World Series to beat Whitey Ford, 2–1, and complete a four-game sweep of the Yankees. With Washington, he hit 136 home runs from 1968 through 1970. In 1968, the Year of the Pitcher, Howard had a streak of ten homers in twenty at-bats. Number ten, against Lolich, hit the roof of Tiger Stadium.

He was a bit clumsy in the outfield but was no Babe Herman. And he played hard, was always hustling. He finished with 382 career homers and everyone's respect.

Waite Hoyt

Pitcher, NY (N) 1918, 1932, Bos (A) 1919–20,
NY (A) 1921–30, Det (A) 1930–31, Phi (A) 1931,
Bkn (N) 1932, 1937–38, Pit (N) 1933–37

"The secret of success," Hoyt once said, "is to pitch for the New York Yankees." This Broadway playboy, vaudeville singer, part-time undertaker, and baseball broadcaster won 237 games, mostly for the great Yankees of Ruth and Gehrig.

Signed by John McGraw when he was only fifteen, Hoyt pitched only one inning for the Giants before he was sent to the Boston Red Sox in 1919. His record was mediocre over

two seasons, except for one brilliant eleven-inning perfecto stint sandwiched between hits in a thirteen-inning game against the Yankees. Impressed, New York acquired him in 1921 and made him a regular starter. Hoyt won 19 as the Yankees won their first pennant. He was sensational in the World Series that fall, pitching three complete games without allowing an earned run. Nevertheless, an error cost him the final game of the Series, 1–0.

He was the ace of the Yankees' staff throughout the 1920s, with his top seasons coming in 1927, when he was 22–7 and led the AL in ERA, and in 1928, when he went 23–7. After leaving the Yankees in 1930, he pitched for many teams with only occasional success as a starter. He was, however, an effective relief pitcher for four seasons with the Pirates in the mid-1930s.

Hoyt, who was elected to the Hall of Fame in 1969, was a popular play-by-play man for Cincinnati for twenty-four years.

Cal Hubbard

Umpire, 1936–50

Hubbard is the only man in the baseball, college football, and pro football Halls of Fame. A 250-pound behemoth when most football linemen were 200–210 pounds, Big Cal played end and tackle at both Centenary and Geneva Colleges in the mid-1920s, then went on to an all-pro career with the New York Giants and Green Bay Packers of the NFL. A devastating defensive player and road-clearing blocker, he starred on four championship teams.

Cal had taken up umpiring in the summers while still a football player and moved smoothly into his new career. He became an AL umpire in 1936 and served for fifteen years. He was known for his intimate knowledge of the rules and for the efficient and authoritative way he ran a game. A hunting accident prematurely ended his active career, but he continued as supervisor of umpires for the AL for another fifteen years.

Carl Hubbell

Pitcher, NY (N) 1928–43

In one of baseball's small ironies, the intelligent, level-headed Hubbell will forever be known as a "screwball" pitcher. The adjective refers, of course, to what he threw, not what he was. The pitch, thrown with a clockwise snap of his left wrist, left Carl with a left arm so twisted that the palm of his hand faces out! It also made him the NL's premier lefthander of the 1930s.

Reportedly, when he was a Tiger farmhand, Detroit manager Ty Cobb discouraged him from throwing "that thing." Fortunately, Carl continued to toss what is, in effect, a reverse curve, and when the Giants bought his contract, he got the chance to use it against major league batters. They hated it!

He had five straight winning seasons under his belt, twice posting 18 wins, when he suddenly blossomed into "Super Pitcher" in 1933. Carl considered his greatest game to be a 1933 18-inning shutout without giving up a base on balls. In July, he went 46 straight innings without allowing a run. He pitched ten shutouts in all that year, had a 23–12 mark for the champion Giants, with the unbelievably low (for those years) ERA of 1.66. He won the MVP.

In the Series that fall, Hub beat Washington in the opener, giving up two unearned runs. In Game Four he went eleven innings, giving up another unearned run. In the eleventh he loaded the bases on a single, a walk, and a bunt that didn't roll foul. Then he calmly ended the game on a double play to win 2–1. His ERA for the Series was 0.00.

In 1934 he went 21–12, with a league-leading 2.30 ERA. In the All-Star Game that year he struck out Babe Ruth, Lou Gehrig, Jimmie Foxx, Al Simmons, and Joe Cronin in succession.

After a 23–12 year in 1935, "King Carl," the Giants' "Meal Ticket," took them to another pennant in 1936 with his second MVP year, a 26–6 gem that saw him again lead the NL in ERA. That year Hubbell began a 24-game regular-season winning streak that extended into 1937. His 22–8 mark in 1937 gave him five straight 20-win seasons and gave New York one more flag.

Carl became a spot starter for his final six seasons, with his only losing mark being 11–12 in 1940. He finished with a 253–154 career record, and was elected to the Hall of Fame in 1947. Not bad for a screwball!

Miller Huggins

Second Baseman, Cin (N) 1904–09, StL (N) 1910–16. Manager, StL (N) 1913–17, NY (A) 1918–29

Huggins wasn't a bad little second baseman for thirteen years in the NL, but his main claim to fame is as manager of the Yankees' "Murderers' Row" of the 1920s.

He began as the Cardinals' manager in 1913. The Redbirds had never won a pennant up till then, and Hug didn't change the *status quo*. He did, however, twice get them as high as third. That earned him a chance with the Yankees in 1918. New York was another team that had never won a pennant but had some prospects for improvement. Hug got them up to fourth and then third in 1919.

The Yankees bought Babe Ruth in 1920, and when they finished third went out and bought more talent. By 1921 they were ready. Almost as interesting as the yearly pennant races was the relationship between the five-four, 140-pound Huggins and his overgrown Peck's Bad Boy, Ruth. Hug fought with him, fined him, suspended him, was hung over the rear platform of trains by him, and above all won pennants with him—six of them in eight years, 1921–1928, including three world championships. In 1925 Babe was making $52,000 and hitting .246, when he stayed out three nights in a row. Hug called Babe and all the players into the dugout and slapped a $5,000 fine on him, ten times the previous record. Ruth complained to owner Jacob Ruppert, who backed Hug. The fine stuck. The Babe apologized.

Many consider Hug's 1927 Yankees the greatest team of all time. Both his 1927 and 1928 teams swept the World Series in four straight games.

The little guy died suddenly of blood poisoning in 1929. Even Ruth cried at the news. Their monuments now stand side by side in Yankee Stadium's center field. In 1964 Huggins joined Ruth in the Hall of Fame.

William Hulbert

National League Founder, President 1877–82

Hulbert's Hall of Fame plaque is incorrectly identified as "Morgan Bulkeley." The real Bulkeley was a figurehead president in the NL's first year; Hulbert founded the National League. What they did in Cooperstown was sort of like citing that dog that used to listen to "his master's voice" as the inventor of the phonograph.

From 1871 to 1875, the loose, rowdy, gambler-ridden National Association made a stab at being a league. Hulbert, the Chicago team owner, thought it might be nice to have a league with enforced rules, regular schedules, civilized behavior, and scores that weren't known on the mornings of the games. In 1876 he called together some like-minded owners, convinced them there was hope for the future, and formed the National League. The only mistake he made was to get Bulkeley from Hartford to pretend to be president as a sop to the eastern teams. Hulbert had a problem with the east; he'd just lured four of Boston's best players to Chicago.

Well, the next year—after Chicago had won the first NL pennant—Bulkeley didn't show up at the league meeting, so there was nothing to do but elect Hulbert as president. He did things like kick New York and Philadelphia out of the league for failing to fulfill their schedules, ban four players for life for fixing games, come down hard on drunks and rowdies, and generally run things with a firm hand until his death in 1882.

In the 1800s, he was referred to as the "Savior of the Game," which is a bit much but beats "What's-his-name-from-Hartford" hands down.

Jim "Catfish" Hunter

Pitcher, KC (A) 1965–67, Oak (A) 1968–74,
NY (A) 1975–79

Hunter was the ace of the A's great teams in the first half of the 1970s and helped the Yankees win three straight pennants in the second half of the decade. And he started as a batting practice pitcher!

In 1964 A's owner Charles O. Finley signed Hunter to a $50,000 bonus contract. And because Finley thought "Jim Hunter" lacked oomph and because his bonus baby liked to hunt and fish, the owner hung the nickname "Catfish" on him. Considering the possibilities in the animal kingdom, it could have been worse.

In his first season, the eighteen-year-old righthander pitched only batting practice for the A's. At one point, Finley had a publicity photo taken with Hunter sitting on the lap of Satchel Paige, who was sitting in a rocker. Maybe you had to be there.

In 1965 the nineteen-year-old Hunter became a regular starter for the A's and went 8–8. The next year he was named to the AL All-Star team; his record was 9–11 with the seventh-place A's. He pitched a perfect game in 1968 but didn't have his first winning season until 1970, when he was 18–14. By then Finley had moved the A's to Oakland, and his young players were becoming stars.

Starting in 1971, Hunter was 21–11, 21–7, and 21–5, and he won the Cy Young Award in 1974 with a 25–12 mark and a league-leading 2.49 ERA. The A's won pennants and world

championships from 1972 to 1974. But all was not happy in A's-ville. Hunter sued Finley for breach of contract and ended up winning a bigger award than the Cy Young: he was declared a free agent and signed a five-year contract with the Yankees for an estimated $3.75 million.

His best year in New York was his first, 25–14, his fifth straight 20-win season. He slumped after that, but was still a useful starter in the three pennant-winning seasons (1976–1978). After the 1979 season, he retired. His career totals were 224–166. In 1987 he was elected to the Hall of Fame.

Monford "Monte" Irvin

Outfielder, Negro Leagues, 1938–48, Newark Eagles,
NY (N) 1949–55, Chi (N) 1956

Irvin got to the New York Giants after a fine career in the Negro Leagues, where he was credited with two batting titles with the Newark Eagles, .396 in 1941 and .398 in 1946. In the latter year, Irvin played shortstop for Newark, and he and second baseman Larry Doby helped bring the Eagles the black world championship of 1946 over Satchel Paige's Kansas City Monarchs.

Irvin signed with the New York Giants in 1949 and played briefly with the team that year. He was thirty years old, and all agree that his skills had diminished from the level he had shown in the Negro Leagues. The "diminished" Irvin hit .299 in 1950. In 1951 he upped that to .312, led the NL in RBIs with 121, and knocked out 24 homers. Down the stretch, as the Giants chased the Dodgers to a playoff and ultimate victory, he hit over .400. In the World Series, he hit .458 and even stole home in the opening game.

A broken leg in 1952 almost ended Irvin's career, but he bounced back with .323 in 1953. In eight years but only five full seasons, his NL batting average was .293, with 99 homers.

In 1968 Irvin joined the Commissioner's Office as a public relations expert. Irvin represented Commissioner Kuhn at Atlanta when Henry Aaron broke Babe Ruth's home run record.

Irvin was elected to the Hall of Fame in 1973.

Joe Jackson

Outfielder, Phi (A) 1908–09, Cle (A) 1910–15,
Chi (A) 1915–20

One of the great natural hitters, Shoeless Joe threw his career and his honor away for thirty pieces of silver. Joe averaged .356 for his career, the third best ever, using his favorite bat, "Black Betsy," and a swing so pretty it would make Will Clark weep. Babe Ruth said he copied Joe's swing. Ironically it was Ruth's popularity that helped fans forget the shame that Jackson and his coconspirators brought to baseball.

An illiterate millhand, Joe hit .408 as a Cleveland rookie in 1911. He finished second to Ty Cobb's .420. The next year Joe hit .395 and finished second again to Cobb (.410). Except for ten games in 1908–1909, Joe always hit .300. But a trade to the White Sox in 1915 threw him in with the proverbial bad company.

The White Sox were building a great team, but it was a team split. Joe resented the Sox' educated second baseman Eddie Collins and his cadre of followers. The other side, the ones who griped about the admittedly low salaries owner Charles Comiskey paid, the ones who figured baseball was a stick and they had the wrong end, the ones who hung with the sharpies who looked for an edge, *that* side accepted Joe. They were his friends. They didn't laugh at his naiveté, snicker at his lack of sophistication, or make fun of his southern drawl.

Despite the division on the team, it won the 1917 pennant and World Series. Because 1918 was a war year, Joe took a shipyard job and played only in 17 games. Others were missing. When everyone returned in 1919, the Sox paraded to another pennant and were installed as heavy favorites over Cincinnati in the World Series. But the chiselers on the team had a different idea. They conspired with gamblers to throw the Series for a promised $20,000. In Jackson, who was grossly underpaid at $8,000, the sharpies found a willing conspirator.

The story broke late in the 1920 season, while Jackson was hitting .382. Eight players were indicted in Chicago. Jackson admitted his guilt, but none of the players were convicted in court. There was no doubt of what they'd done, but the carefully assembled evidence suddenly and mysteriously disappeared. No matter, Judge Landis, the baseball commissioner, banned the "Black Sox" from the game for life. Jackson, as well as others in the group of "eight men out," played outlaw ball under an assumed name. Even fat and out of shape he never lost that great swing.

Larry Jackson

Pitcher, StL (N) 1955–62, Chi (N) 1963–66,
Phi (N) 1966–68

Jackson won 184 games for the Cardinals and Cubs in the 1950s and 1960s. Although in double figures twelve of his fourteen seasons, Larry had only one 20-game season. In 1964 he was 24–11 for the eighth-place Cubs, finishing second in the Cy Young voting.

He didn't get much help from his teams, so Larry helped himself in the field, leading all pitchers in chances accepted and fielding average several seasons.

Reggie Jackson

Outfielder. KC (A) 1967, Oak (A) 1968–75, 1987,
Bal (A) 1976, NY (A) 1977–81,
Cal (A) 1982–86

"Mr. October," Jackson was perhaps the most electrifying hitter of the 1970s. "I'd like to be able to light the fire a little bit," he said. And he did.

Reggie was at his best in the World Series, hitting .357, ninth best ever. His Series slugging average of .755 is tops all time. He's probably most famous for driving three home runs on three pitches in the final game of the 1977 Series to sink the Dodgers. Reggie was a winner. In twelve years, 1971–1982, his teams—the A's, Yanks, and Angels—won ten

division crowns and five world championships. Jackson won the MVP in 1973, when he led the league with 32 homers and 117 RBIs for Oakland's champs. Perhaps Reggie's longest homer was walloped in the 1971 All-Star Game. It hit a light tower above the roof of Tiger Stadium like a rifle shot.

Jackson is sixth on the all-time home run list with 563. He won four home run crowns and drove in 1,702 runs. He also struck out more than any other man in history, 2,597 times— once in every four at-bats. But he considered the strikeouts a bargain price for the homers.

Intelligent, outspoken, egomaniacal, Reggie fought with his team owners, Charles Finley and George Steinbrenner, and with his managers, especially Billy Martin, who benched him once for loafing.

Jackson wanted to be "the straw that stirs the drink," the highest-paid star, with his own eponymous candy bar. If there were an Ego Hall of Fame, Jackson would be the first one in. But the doors of Cooperstown will open for him too.

Travis Jackson

Shortstop, NY (N) 1922–36

Jackson was a member of the Giants' "Hall of Fame Infield" of 1925–27. While Jackson played short and Fred Lindstrom third, they were joined by George Kelly, Bill Terry, Frankie Frisch, and Rogers Hornsby.

However, Jackson and the others had many better years. Travis played on New York pennant winners in 1923, 1924, 1933, and 1936, his final season. He was a reliable shortstop with good range, and inevitably was given the nickname "Stonewall." (Like, you couldn't hit a ball through him. Get it?) He led NL shortstops in assists four times, total chances three times, and fielding average twice. Defensively his strongest feature was his powerful throwing arm.

If Jackson had an edge over a half dozen good-fielding shortstops of his day, it was that he hit better. He topped .300 six times and finished with a career mark of .291. That wasn't sensational for the hit-happy time he played in, but it was excellent for a shortstop. He even learned to jerk the ball down the Polo Grounds' short foul lines. One year he hit 21 homers. His 929 RBIs are also high for someone playing his position.

Ferguson Jenkins

Pitcher, Phi (N) 1965–66, Chi (N) 1966–73, 1982–83,
Tex (A) 1974–75, 1978–81, Bos (A) 1976–77

Pitching in the hitters' haven, Wrigley Field, Jenkins strung six consecutive 20-win seasons together. In 1971 he was the NL's Cy Young winner with a 24–13 mark and 2.77 ERA. He pitched 325 innings that season, one of the five years he topped 300.

Jenkins combined excellent control with a good fastball and curve. Traded to Texas in 1974, he responded with a 25–12 season, leading the AL in wins. In a nineteen-season career, he never pitched for a pennant winner, yet he compiled a 284–226 mark.

Hughie Jennings

*Shortstop, Lou (AA) 1891,
Lou (N) 1892–93, Bal (N) 1893–99,
Bkn (N) 1899–1900, 1903, Phi (N) 1901–02,
Det (A) 1907, 1909, 1912, 1918.
Manager, Det (A) 1907–20*

A law school graduate, Jennings played on the famous rip 'n' run Baltimore Orioles of the Gay Nineties. He was their shortstop and captain, and they won the pennant his first three years, 1894–1896, plus the Temple Cup playoffs the next year. Hugh helped with averages of .332, .385, .398, .353, and .328—the best years he ever had, thanks in part to the new, longer pitching distance, which was inflating everyone's batting stats. In 1895 Hughie scored 159 runs and knocked in 125 more, with only four home runs.

Jennings's specialty was getting hit with the pitch, which he did 49 times in 1896, the record until Ron Hunt broke it in 1971. The Orioles weren't above faking it a bit, by taking a close pitch, then rolling around in supposed pain, while raising a welt by pinching themselves. However, Jennings had his skull fractured by an Amos Rusie pitch in 1897. That one was almost certainly legitimate.

Hughie took over as Detroit manager in 1907 and won pennants in his first three seasons. Only Ralph Houk of the Yankees matched that. In eleven more years of trying, Jennings never won again, but he finished in the first division seven times. His greatest player was, of course, Ty Cobb, whom he disliked but coddled. His other players were treated sternly, often sarcastically.

Jennings's nickname was "Eeyah," because he used to shout it from the coaching box. He said it was Hawaiian for "Watch out!"

He was elected to the Hall of Fame in 1945.

Tommy John

*Pitcher, Cle (A) 1963–64,
Chi (A) 1965–71, LA (N) 1972–74,
(injured 1975) 1976–78, NY (A) 1979–82, 1986-,
Cal (A) 1982–85, Oak (A) 1985*

John is the bionic man, with two arms and two careers. In July of 1974 he had only a fair 124–106 lifetime mark, but was coming off his best season, a career high of 16 wins for the Dodgers. He was 13–3 for 1974, and seemed headed for a great year when he tore a ligament in his elbow.

Dr. Frank Jobe sewed a new one back in. It was history's first ligament transplant. Tommy said he asked Dr. Jobe to give him Koufax's arm but said he got Mrs. Koufax's by mistake. He could throw again, but he had no fastball—he didn't even have a medium ball. Still, he could throw curves and get them over the plate. And he knew how to pitch.

In 1976 he was 10–10 for the Dodgers and was named the Comeback Player of the Year. That was nice, but he was just beginning his second career. In 1977, he was 20–7. After joining the New York Yankees as a free agent in 1979, he won 21 and 22. And he pitched on and on: 1988 was his twenty-fifth season.

Bancroft "Ban" Johnson

American League President, 1901–27

A former sportswriter, Johnson built the AL from the old Western League, a minor loop which he and Charles Comiskey took over in 1893. In 1900 they changed its name and in 1901 proclaimed it a major league. They raided the NL for star players and managers and built the league into what they claimed it to be.

By 1903 Johnson had forced the NL to make peace, leading to the first modern World Series—won by Ban's AL Boston boys over Pittsburgh. In fact, the AL would win fourteen of the first twenty-four Series.

Johnson ran his league with tunnel vision. A humorless workaholic, his word was law among the original AL team owners. He banned liquor from his ballparks and fined for profanity and rowdyism. He backed his umpires, raising their status. Although nominally the president of the AL, he was called the "Czar of Baseball" because he dominated the three-man commission that governed the game until 1920.

But his power slipped as new owners who resented his dictatorial ways entered the AL. Even his old ally, Comiskey, turned against him. When the Black Sox scandal broke in 1920, Johnson demanded a full investigation, causing a final break with Comiskey, who owned the Sox. One result was that the commission was replaced by one czar, Judge Landis. Ban fought his loss of power for six years before resigning.

He was elected to the Hall of Fame in 1937.

"Indian Bob" Johnson

*Outfielder, Phi (A) 1933–42, Was (A) 1943, Bos (A)
1944–45*

The lesson of Johnson's career was "Play for a contender or they'll never remember." It was his misfortune to join the Philadelphia A's in 1933, just when Connie Mack was selling off his high-priced stars and the team was heading for the bottom of the AL like a lead submarine. So for ten years with the awful A's and three more with a couple of other *nolo contenderes*, Johnson played the outfield, hit a ton, and today is too obscure for a good trivia question.

Even when he'd do things like go 6-for-6 (in 1934) or bat in six runs in one inning (1937), the A's were so far out of contention that their contests were carried on sports pages after "In other games . . ." Of course, fans knew about him then—he was elected to seven All-Star Games—they just forgot quickly because none of his hits ever meant anything in a pennant race.

What hitting? Five seasons over .300 and a .296 career mark; three years with 30 or better homers among a total of 288; seven straight 100-RBI years (eight altogether) for teams that considered each baserunner a moral victory.

Now, just for a second, close your eyes and picture that record in Yankee pinstripes.

William "Judy" Johnson

Third Baseman, Negro League, 1921–38, Hilldale,

Homestead Grays, Darby Daisies, Pittsburgh Cranfords

Johnson was one of the three best third baseman during the 1920s and 1930s. A steady defensive player, he was dependable rather than flashy. At bat he was an intelligent, scientific hitter who consistently exceeded .300 and was acclaimed for his ability to come through in the clutch. Known for his quiet, down-to-business manner, Johnson was considered a steadying influence on younger players.

He played on the famous Philadelphia Hilldales (1921–1929), hitting .364 in the 1924 black World Series. His inside-the-park grand slam won Game Four. In 1929 he hit .383 with 22 stolen bases. The next year he joined the Homestead Grays as player-manager. Judy also played on the 1935 Pittsburgh Crawfords, perhaps the best black team of all time, with Satchel Paige, Cool Papa Bell, Oscar Charleston, and Josh Gibson.

In later years, Johnson scouted first for the Philadelphia A's and later found Dick Allen for the Phillies. He was named to the Hall of Fame in 1975.

Walter Johnson

Pitcher, Was (A) 1907–27.
Manager, Was (A) 1929–32, Cle (A) 1933–35

Johnson is high up on everyone's list of nominees as the greatest pitcher of all time. His statistics alone are staggering. Working for a Washington team that finished in the second division in ten of his twenty-one seasons, he nevertheless won 416 games (second only to Cy Young), pitched in 5,923 innings (third most of all time), threw an all-time record 110 shutouts, and compiled a 2.17 ERA, the seventh-best career mark. For years his 3,508 strikeouts was considered an unbreakable record, but a later, more free-swinging age has changed that; even though he has been surpassed by Nolan Ryan, Steve Carlton, and Don Sutton, he still may be the greatest strikeout artist ever.

He won more than 30 games in two seasons, more than 20 in ten other years. He led the AL in wins six times, in ERA five times, and in strikeouts twelve!

He did nearly all of this with a fabled fastball, thrown with an easy side-arm motion. It came in straight as string, but the hitters couldn't get around on it. Only late in his career did Johnson bother to develop a curve. He had good control, and for all his innings pitched only in one season did he walk more than 100 batters.

He won more more 1–0 games—and lost more—than any other man. In 1908, Johnson's first full year in the league, he won three shutouts in four days, giving up twelve hits in the three games, yet he had to settle for a 14–14 record for a last-place club. In 1913 he battled for fifteen innings to win 1–0; in 1918 he struggled twenty innings for a 1–0 win, giving up only one walk the whole game.

Of all his great seasons, 1913 was no doubt the acme. He was 36–7, to lead in wins and percentage. His ERA was 1.09. In a league-leading 346 innings he gave up only 230 hits, an average of less than six per nine innings. He struck out 243 to lead the league and walked—now get this—only 38! Oh, yes, he pitched eleven shutouts and had 55⅔ straight shutout innings, a mark which stood until 1968. He even set the

record for fielding that year, with no errors in 103 chances. Naturally he was MVP.

Even with a sore arm in 1921 (when he had an 8–10 record), he could still pitch a no-hitter. It was his only one; strangely, he never pitched one in spacious Griffith Stadium.

Johnson finally made it to the World Series in 1924 at the age of thirty-six. The old man was 23–7 and led the league in his usual categories: wins, ERA, strikeouts, and shutouts. The writers gave him another MVP.

As much as batters hated to bat against him, everybody liked "the Big Train." Open, honest, modest, soft-spoken, considerate, shy, he never drank or smoked but didn't condemn those who did. A big evening for him was going to a movie or just talking baseball. If he wasn't the greatest pitcher ever, you'd want him to be. In 1936 he was one of the first five players elected to the Hall of Fame.

Adrian "Addie" Joss

Pitcher, Cle (A) 1902–10

Joss's death at age thirty-one cut off one of baseball's most brilliant pitching careers. He was the hardest man in history to reach base against, just 8.7 runners per nine innings; only 1.4 of them were walks. At six-three, 185 pounds, the long-armed Joss pitched with an exaggerated pinwheel motion that earned him the nickname of "the Human Hairpin." Addie pivoted away from the hitter before the pitch, then came side-armed with a "jump" ball that—the batters swore—dipped, leveled off, and dipped again, something like Frank Merriwell's fictional curve that broke both ways on the way to the plate. It earned him a lifetime 1.88 ERA, second best ever to Ed Walsh's 1.82.

Joss broke in with Cleveland in 1902. He fanned four of the first six men he faced and ended with a one-hitter, a single by Jesse Burkett. A few days later Addie just missed another no-hitter; with one out in the ninth, an error and two singles spoiled it.

As a rookie, he was 17–13 with fifth-place Cleveland and 18–13 the next year, as the club rose to third. In two years Addie started 60 games and completed 59. For his career he finished 234 out of 260.

He won 20 or more each year from 1905 through 1908, with a high of 27 in 1907.

Joss's best year came in 1908, when Cleveland made a run for the pennant against Ed Walsh's White Sox and Ty Cobb's Tigers. Addie won seven of his club's first eleven games. The three teams were neck and neck (and neck) on October 2, when Joss faced Walsh. Big Ed was 40–14 at that point. Ed pitched a four-hitter; Addie topped him 1–0 with a perfect game. Though Cleveland lost to Detroit by ½ game, Joss was 24–11 with a 1.16 ERA.

Addie was a fine barbershop singer and often harmonized on the sidelines with Walsh.

Joss threw another no-hitter in 1910 but hurt his elbow and ended the season early with a 5–5 record. The next spring he fainted on the trip north; eleven days later he was dead of tubercular meningitis.

Although he played only nine years, his record was so outstanding that the usual ten-year requirement was waived when he was elected to the Hall of Fame in 1978.

Jim Kaat

Pitcher, Was (A) 1959–60, Min (A) 1961–73,
Chi (A) 1973–75, Phi (N) 1976–79, NY (A) 1979–80,
StL (N) 1980–83

"I've never craved center stage," Kaat said, but only Warren Spahn, Eddie Plank, and Steve Carlton won more among lefties than Jim's 283. Three times a 20-game winner, he used a good fastball, guile, and a brutal conditioning program to pitch for a record twenty-five seasons. His best year was 1966 with Minnesota, when he led the league with 25 wins and won the *Sporting News*'s Pitcher of the Year Award. His other 20-win seasons came with the White Sox in 1974–1975.

Not only did Kaat put in a lot of years, he put in some workhorse seasons, going over 300 innings twice and over 200 twelve other times, in spite of several serious injuries.

Kaat helped himself in ways other than with his arm. His .185 career batting average was fair for a pitcher and his 134 career sacrifices is the record for hurlers. He may have been the best-fielding pitcher ever, winning sixteen straight Golden Gloves.

Al Kaline

Outfielder, Det (A) 1953–74

Kaline accepted a $30,000 bonus to sign with Detroit in 1953. Two years later, without having spent a day in the minors, the twenty-year-old Kaline won the 1955 AL batting title with .340, the youngest champ ever. Al never hit that high again, but for twenty-two years he was an outstanding player for Detroit. Though never again spectacular with a bat, he was steady, accumulating 1,622 runs scored and 1,583 RBIs. Kaline finished with 3,007 hits, a .297 batting average, and 399 home runs. He played in eighteen All-Star Games.

Kaline was a sensational defensive outfielder, with a powerful, accurate arm. He won eleven Gold Gloves. In 1971 he went through 133 games without an error.

Although Al battled injuries his whole career—he broke his cheek bone, collar bone, rib, foot, finger, and arm at various times—he set an AL record with twenty years of 100 games or more.

He played in only one World Series. In 1968 he hit .379 with eight RBIs to lead the Tigers to a victory in seven games over the Cardinals.

He was elected to the Hall of Fame in 1980.

Willie Kamm

Third Baseman, Chi (A) 1923–31, Cle (A) 1931–35

The White Sox bought Kamm from San Francisco of the Pacific Coast League in 1923 for the then sensational price of $100,000 to try to plug the hole at third left by banned Black Soxer Buck Weaver. In a career trapped in the second division, Willie earned a reputation as one of the best-fielding third basemen ever. He led the AL at his position eight times in fielding average and was consistently among the leaders in all fielding categories except errors. Although he had no home run power, he was a good contact hitter, with a .281 career

batting average. His .308 in 1928 was his single-season best.

Tim Keefe

Pitcher, Troy (N) 1880–82, NY (AA) 1883–84,
NY (N) 1885–89, 1891, NY (P) 1890,
Phi (N) 1891–93

Keefe was one of the first great changeup artists. For six straight years, 1883–1888, the unassuming righthander combined a fair fastball and curve with his changeup to win 32 games or more. Twice he went over 40. He ended his career with 344 victories.

In 1888 he won 19 straight, including one twelve-inning effort. That's the year he and fellow Irishman Mickey Welch pitched the Giants to the NL flag. Tim was top in wins, percentage, ERA, strikeouts, and shutouts. In the championship series against the American Association's St. Louis Browns that October, he won all four of New York's victories.

Tim's finest day came in 1883. He won both ends of a July 4 doubleheader—a one-hitter in the morning and a two-hitter in the afternoon.

He was named to the Hall of Fame in 1964.

Willie Keeler

Outfielder, NY (N) 1892–93, 1910,
Bkn (N) 1893, 1899–1902, Bal (N) 1894–98,
NY (A) 1903–09

At 5'4½" and 140 pounds, "Wee Willie" looked like the batboy. He choked up a foot on his thirty-inch bat, the lightest in the league, stood stiff-legged, leaning over the plate, and chopped down on the ball, the famous "Baltimore Chop." The ball bounced into the air, and before it came down, Willie was safe at first. Or if the infielders charged in, he'd bounce it over their heads. His "I hit 'em where they ain't" has been quoted more often than the Gettysburg Address.

He hit .432 in 1897, second best ever, to lead the NL, and followed with a league-topping .379 in 1898. He had two other seasons over .390. His .345 career average ranks him fifth all-time. He had over 200 hits eight years in a row. The ultimate singles hitter, 2,536 of his 2,962 hits were for one base.

Keeler hit in 44 straight games in 1897. No one kept such records then, but in all the years since, only Rose has tied it and only DiMaggio has surpassed it.

A brilliant bunter, he is one of the men responsible for the modern foul-strike rule. He could bunt fouls by the hour until they changed the rule and began calling them outs after two strikes.

Known as an outstanding right fielder, he played his first major league games as a lefthanded-throwing third baseman. A practical joker in moments of leisure, Keeler was deadly serious on the field. He was elected to the Hall of Fame in 1939.

George Kell

Third Baseman, Phi (A) 1943–46, Det (A) 1946–52,

Bos (A) 1952–54, Chi (A) 1954–56, Bal (A) 1956–57

Kell gave the Tigers and several other AL clubs some steady fielding and .300 hitting after World War Two. He led the league in batting average in 1949, just inching out Ted Williams by .0002 with a .3429 mark. Kell was safely in front of Williams as he approached his last at-bat of the season. Teammates urged him to let a pinch hitter bat in his place since an out would lose him the title. He refused and took his place in the on-deck circle, but before he could bat a teammate ended the inning and the season by hitting into a double play. In nine seasons, Kell batted over .300. Never a power hitter, Kell is one of the few modern hitters to have over 100 RBIs with fewer than 10 home runs, a feat he achieved in 1950.

Kell had an excellent throwing arm and was sure-handed. He led AL third basemen in fielding average seven times, in assists four times, and in putouts and double plays twice.

In 1983 he was named to the Hall of Fame.

Charlie Keller

*Outfielder, NY (A) 1939–43, 1945–49, 1952,
Det (A) 1950–51*

Until a congenital back problem forced him to the sidelines, Keller seemed destined to take his place as one of the greatest of all the Yankees' hitters. "King Kong" played with Joe DiMaggio and Tommy Henrich in the Yankee outfield that helped win four flags in five years, 1939–1943. He used the New York short porch to propel as many as 33 home runs and averaged 98 RBIs a year. Though Keller hit .300 only three times, pitchers respected him and regularly gave him 100 walks. He was a hard man to double up.

Charlie was a great October hitter. In 1939 he hit .438 in the World Series; his two homers and four RBIs won the third game, 7–3, and it was he who barreled into the Reds' Ernie Lombardi to score the deciding run in the tenth inning of the final game. In the 1941 Series, Keller hit .389. In the fourth game, after Henrich reached first on Mickey Owen's passed ball, Charlie doubled in the two runs that won the game. Then he scored the run that won the fifth and final game. In 1942 his two-run homer in the second game tied the score in the eighth, though the Cardinals went on to win the game and the Series.

Following another pennant winner in 1943, he went into the Navy. He returned in 1945 and played until 1951, but the back problem limited him to only one more season of more than 83 games. He retired to raise horses on his Maryland farm, Yankeeland.

Joe Kelley

*Outfielder, Bos (N) 1891, 1908,
Pit (N) 1891–92, Bal (N) 1892–98, Bkn (N) 1899–01,
Bal (A) 1902, Cin (N) 1902–06.
Manager, Cin (N) 1902–05, Bos (N) 1908*

Kelley was the heavy-hitting left fielder for the famous Baltimore Orioles of the 1890s. Joe played on six pennant winners in seven years, 1894–1900. The final two were with the Brooklyn Superbas, whom he captained.

He hit over .300 for eleven consecutive seasons. In 1894, when he hit .393, he went 9-for-9 in a doubleheader, still the record. Three years later he hit .388. His lifetime average was .319.

Kelley was a speedy outfielder with a powerful arm. He used to come to the park at nine in the morning to practice his bunting and running. A handsome if vain man, he kept a mirror under his cap and liked to sneak looks at himself in the outfield.

He was elected to the Hall of Fame in 1971.

George "Highpockets" Kelly

*First Baseman, NY (N) 1915–17, 1919–26, Pit (N) 1917,
Cin (N) 1927–30, Chi (N) 1930, Bkn (N) 1932*

Kelly was the slick-fielding, clutch-hitting first baseman for a Giants team that won four straight NL pennants, 1921–1924. John McGraw, the New York manager, said that Kelly made "more important hits" for him than any player he ever had. He led the NL in RBIs with 94 in 1920, then knocked home over 100 in each of the pennant-winning seasons. In 1924 he led the league again with 136.

A good home run hitter, he led the NL in 1921 with 23 and set a record in 1924 with 7 homers in 6 games.

The lanky "Highpockets" had one of the most powerful arms in the league. His on-the-money throw across the infield completed a brilliant double play to end the 1921 World Series. He consistently ranked high in assists and holds the NL records for most putouts and most chances in a season.

He was named to the Hall of Fame in 1973.

Mike "King" Kelly

*Outfielder/Catcher/Manager,
Cin (N) 1878–79, Chi (N) 1880–86,
Bos (N) 1887–89, 1891–92, Bos (P) 1890,
Cin-Mil (AA) 1891,
Bos (AA) 1891, NY (N) 1893*

With his dark hair, black mustache, and flashing white smile, the King was a matinee idol and the subject of a popular song, "Slide, Kelly, Slide." ("If your batting doesn't fail ya, they will take ya to Australia / Slide, Kelly, on your belly, slide, slide, slide.")

Mike rode to the park in a silk hat, ascot, and patent leather shoes, in a carriage pulled by two white horses (and sometimes by his "cranks," or fans). He was one of the best-dressed men in America. He went on the stage reciting "Casey at the Bat" and made $3,000 for the use of his picture on advertisements. He was a big gambler and was often seen at the races.

Mike was one of the first hitters to perfect the hit-and-run, one of the first catchers to give finger signals, and one of the first outfielders to play close to back up infield plays. And despite the song, he was one of the first runners to use the hook slide. His most famous slide knocked the ball out of George Wright's hand to clinch the 1882 flag.

He also liked to catch the ump asleep (they had only one then) and cut from first base to third base without going near second. He'd take a similar shortcut from second base to home.

In all, Kelly sparked Anson's White Stockings to five flags in seven years, 1880–1886. He led the NL in hitting with .354 in 1884 and .388 in 1886.

In 1887 Boston bought him for a record price, and he became "the $10,000 Beauty." He reputedly kept $5,000 of his purchase price for the use of his likeness for promotional purposes. Mike hit .322 his first year with them and stole 84 bases.

Kelly also managed and batted the Bostons to the Players League flag in 1890.

Mike played all nine positions. Once, while sitting on the bench, a foul fly came back. "Kelly now catching," he shouted and made the catch. They changed the substitute rule after that.

Anson always said, "Mike's only enemy is himself." He died of pneumonia at the age of thirty-six, penniless after giving his only suit of clothes to a tramp while on a boat to Boston to recite "Casey" one more time. The city gave him a grand funeral send-off.

He was named to the Hall of Fame in 1945.

Ken Keltner

Third Baseman, Cle (A) 1937–44, 1946–49,
Bos (A) 1950

Keltner was the AL's top-fielding third baseman in the 1940s. He led AL third sackers in fielding average three times, assists four times, and double plays five times. With Keltner on third and Lou Boudreau at short, Cleveland fans saw some of the best fielding of the decade. Ken's habit of taking a quick look at the ball in his hand before he gunned it to first was imitated by Cleveland schoolboys. Keltner is best known for the two fine plays he made to stop Joe DiMaggio's hit streak at 56.

A fair hitter with some long-ball power, his best year was 1948, when he hit 31 homers, knocked in 119 runs, and hit .297, as the Indians won a tight race and the Series.

Bill Killefer

Catcher, StL (A) 1909–10,
Phi (N) 1911–17, Chi (N) 1918–21.
Manager, Chi (N) 1921–25, StL (A) 1930–33

Killefer was a typical catcher of the dead-ball era—a good handler of pitchers, strong-armed, reliable on defense, and a rotten hitter. He averaged .238 over thirteen seasons and crushed a grand career total of 4 home runs.

His primary claim to fame is that he was Grover Alexander's favorite catcher. They first hooked up in 1911, Alex's rookie year with the Phillies. Their partnership continued when they were traded in tandem to the Cubs after the 1917 season and lasted until Killefer took over as the Cubs' manager and retired as a player in 1921.

There seems little doubt that he was an intelligent player whose handling helped Alexander be one of baseball's greatest pitchers. There's no way of knowing how many games Alex might have won with a catcher who had less brains and more RBIs.

Harmon Killebrew

First Baseman/Third Baseman/Outfielder,
Was (A) 1954–60, Min (A) 1961–74,
KC (A) 1975

A few eyebrows went up among the Old School observers when Killebrew was elected to the Hall of Fame in 1984. The Killer didn't fit the traditional mold of so many enshrined in Cooperstown. He didn't hit for breathtaking batting averages; not once in his career did he bat above .288 for a full season, and his career average was a mere .256. Shortstops do better. He was no jackrabbit on the bases; he stole 19 in twenty-two seasons. Catchers do better. He didn't dazzle anyone with his glove; he played three positions without ever winning even a Pyrite Glove, much less real gold. He wasn't even a colorful character, just a modest, nice guy who came to work, did his job, and went home to his wife and children.

Killebrew was a one-dimensional player.

Of course, that one dimension—smashing home runs in gargantuan quantities—produced more runs for his team than all the singles of a half dozen "good" hitters. And unless there's been a sudden and secret change in the rules, the object of hitting is to score runs.

Killebrew lifted 573 lordly blasts over the fences. Only one AL player hit more—Babe Ruth. In home run frequency, Harmon is third behind only Ruth and Ralph Kiner. Such slugging helped win the Killer spots on *The Sporting News*'s All-Star teams at three different positions—3B, 1B, and OF. Eight times he went over 40 homers; six times he led or tied for the league lead. Harmon was MVP in 1969, when he led the league with 49 homers and 140 RBIs. He had 1,584 RBIs for his career.

And while that .256 batting average draws no raves, he drew 1,559 walks, which puts his on-base percentage up over .375.

Ralph Kiner

Outfielder, Pit (N) 1946–53, Chi (N) 1953–54, Cle (A) 1955

Kiner never said, "Home run hitters drive Cadillacs"; Fritz Ostermueller did. But he was talking about Ralph.

Kiner was like Killebrew a "one-dimensional ballplayer," who was worth more than most two- or three-dimensional players who ever lived. Such is the structure of baseball that blasting one three-run home run will help a team more than a leaping one-handed catch, or two or three steals of second. Moaned Warren Spahn: "Kiner can wipe out your lead with one swing."

No one except Babe Ruth ever dominated home run hitting the way Kiner did from 1946 to 1952, as he led or tied for the NL leadership in his first seven major league seasons. Aaron, Mays, Killebrew, Jackson, Foxx, and others hit more, but Ralph averaged 40 every 550 at-bats; only Babe did better. In 1947 he hit 51; in 1949 he raised that to 54, the second-highest total in NL history.

Like the Babe, Ralph got a lot of walks, going over 100 six times. He was usually found on *The Sporting News*'s All-Star team, and by 1951 Ralph was the highest-paid player in the league.

But the big difference between them was that the Yankees,

with a strong supporting cast, won pennants on Babe's homers; the Pirates were usually last in spite of Ralph's.

Kiner, who was elected to the Hall of Fame in 1975, became a TV commentator for the Mets in the year of their inception, 1962, and remains behind the mike as one of the hardiest of all baseball's voices.

Chuck Klein

Outfielder, Phi (N) 1928–33, 1937–44,
Chi (N) 1934–36, Pit (N) 1939

Philadelphia's Baker Bowl, the Phillies' home through the 1930s, had a short right field that was batter-friendly, to say the least. No player ever took better advantage of the situation than Klein, a powerful lefthanded hitter whose pokes against and over the Bowl's cozy wall helped him produce a startling five-year record.

In 1929, his first full season, he led the NL with 43 home runs, while hitting .356 and driving in 145 runs. He beat Mel Ott by one for the homer crown when Phillie pitchers walked Mel five straight times on the final day, including once with the bases full.

The next year he was awesome: .386, 40 homers, 170 RBIs—but did not lead the league in any of those categories in that hit-happy year. He continued his assault in 1931: .337, 31 home runs, and 121 RBIs, the last two figures leading the league.

He was named MVP in 1932, when he led again in homers with 38, while driving in 137 and hitting .348. In 1933 he climaxed his five years of excellence with a Triple Crown: .368, 28, 120.

Traded to the Cubs in 1934, he continued to be a productive hitter, but without his best friend, the wall, his great days were over. He finished his career with an even 300 homers and a .320 batting average.

The wall even helped Klein to a defensive record. In 1930 he threw out 44 runners from his up-close and personal right field spot.

Other players had the same wall to shoot for in the era; nobody used it better.

He was named to the Hall of Fame in 1980.

Bill Klem

Umpire, 1905–40

In a career that stretched from 1905 through 1940, Bill Klem was considered the greatest umpire of all time. He's credited by some with being the first umpire to use hand signals and the first to use the smaller chest protector.

Klem officiated in eighteen World Series, a record.

When Bill broke in, there was only one ump per game, and he literally dodged bottles from angry fans. When a player advanced on Klem to argue, he drew a line in the dirt with his shoe and called it "the Rio Grande." One step over, and the player was out.

Bill kind of resembled a catfish, but saying so to his face was another cause for automatic ejection. He once slugged it

out with outfielder Goose Goslin in a hotel elevator.

Baseball was "more than a game, it's a religion," Klem said. "I never missed one," he always said of his calls. But after he retired, he would add, "in here," tapping his heart.

Klem was elected to the Hall of Fame in 1953.

Johnny Kling

Catcher, Chi (N) 1900–08, 1910–11, Bos (N) 1911–12,
Cin (N) 1913. Manager, Bos (N) 1912

Kling was the peppery catcher for the great Tinker-to-Evers-to-Chance Cub teams of the century's first decade. A good defensive catcher, he pulled his weight as a hitter with a career average of .272. That was a little unusual in those days, when backstops were catchers first and hitters only if convenient. He was also rated as one of the best handlers of pitchers in the game. Certainly the record of the Cubs' moundmen during that period did nothing to tarnish that reputation.

The Cubs, with "Noisy" Kling behind the plate, won three straight pennants, 1906–1908. He sat out 1909, and they finished second. When he returned in 1910, they won another flag.

Casimir "Jim" Konstanty

Pitcher, Cin (N) 1944, Bos (N) 1946, Phi (N) 1948–54,
NY (A) 1954–56, StL (N) 1956

Big, bespectacled Jim was one of the early relief chiefs, and like so many, he had one truly great year. In 1950 he led the NL with 22 saves and 16 relief wins for the Whiz Kid Phils, who just nipped the Dodgers for the pennant on the last day of the 1950 season. He was named MVP.

He was the surprise starter in the World Series against New York, when Phillie ace Robin Roberts needed rest after pitching the season finale. He dueled Vic Raschi for eight innings, gave up just one run on a double and two flies, and lost 1–0.

Jerry Koosman

Pitcher, NY (N) 1967–78, Min (A) 1979–81,
Chi (A) 1981–83, Phi (N) 1984–85

Quietly Koosman emerged as a solid 222-game winner trapped mostly with inferior teams. As a rookie in 1968, Jerry was 19–12, with a 2.08 ERA, setting a rookie record with 7 shutouts. (His other record was striking out 62 times in 1968 as a batter.)

Koosman had a sore arm in 1969 but still posted a 17–9 record to join Seaver in sparking the Mets to their dramatic World Series win. Kooz's contribution: a two-hit shutout of the Orioles in Game Two, a 5–3 victory in Game Five, and an overall Series ERA of 2.04.

Jerry added another win in the 1973 Series. He won 21 games for the 1976 Mets and 20 for the 1979 Twins. In 1983 he went 11–7 to help the White Sox reach the playoffs.

Sanford "Sandy" Koufax

Pitcher, Bkn (N) 1955–57, LA (N) 1958–66

For five fabulous years, 1962–1966, Sandy Koufax did things with a baseball that no other lefty has done: five ERA titles, four no-hitters, three Cy Youngs, and one MVP.

And much of it was achieved pitching while in excruciating pain.

Wild as a youngster, Koufax labored for six years to compile a 36–40 record. Then he found his groove and became a star.

In 1965 Koo struck out 382, breaking Waddell's season record of 349. He also threw a perfect game.

In 1966 he won more games, 27, and pitched more shutouts, 11, than any NL lefty in one year in this century.

Then his arm went bad, and he walked away at the age of thirty "while I could still comb my hair."

Koufax won only 165 games, but no man who won twice that many ever reached the same heights. In 1972, at thirty-six, he was the youngest man ever elected to Cooperstown.

As a fastball hurler, Koufax ranked with Ryan, Johnson, Feller, Grove, and Gooden. Unlike Grove and Johnson, Sandy had a dandy curve too. He whiffed 18 men in one game twice, in 1959 and 1962.

His World Series ERA was 0.95, although his won-lost record was only 4–3. Four of the ten runs against him were unearned.

Bowie Kuhn

Commissioner, 1969–84

A Princeton lawyer, Bowie Kuhn replaced "the unknown soldier," General William Eckert, as commissioner for three controversial terms. Considered the owners' commissioner—as indeed every commissioner is—Kuhn resisted players' demands for more money, saying greedy players would bankrupt the teams. Player-negotiator Marvin Miller called it Kuhn's "annual poor-mouth speech."

Ironically many owners also opposed Kuhn, and he was bypassed in the negotiations with Miller. Charles Finley of Oakland led the "dump Bowie" movement, which almost succeeded until two owners changed their votes. Kuhn would later void Finley's sales of $3.5 million worth of stars, which helped to drive the combative Finley out of the game.

One of Kuhn's moves was to sanction playing the World Series at night. He appeared at the first night game on a cold October evening wearing no top coat to dramatize how "mild" the weather was. But he was wearing thermal skivvies underneath.

Napoleon "Larry" Lajoie

Second Baseman, Phi (N) 1896–1900, Phi (A) 1901–02,
1915–16, Cle (A) 1902–14.
Manager, Cle (A) 1905–09.

One of the best second basemen of all time and, by all accounts, the most graceful, Lajoie was also one of the most successful righthanded hitters. An established star with the NL Phillies, where he'd hit .380 in 1899, he jumped to Connie Mack's AL Philadelphia A's in 1901. The presence of Lajoie, Cy Young, and a few others helped legitimize the AL as a major league. Lajoie's .426 in the league's first year is still the highest batting average ever achieved in the AL.

The following year an injunction by the Phillies forced AL president Ban Johnson to shift Lajoie to Cleveland, where he spent the bulk of his career. In 1902, 1903, and 1904 he led the AL twice more in batting with averages of .378, .355, and .381.

Lajoie's status was such that the team was named after him during his tenure—the Cleveland Naps. He managed the club from 1905 to part of 1909 and got them as high as second in 1909. Late in the 1910 campaign, he gave up the reins because he felt the cares of managing were hurting his play.

Lajoie was a powerful line-drive hitter who pulled the ball. In 1910 the popular second baseman was locked in a tight batting race with Ty Cobb, despised by nearly everyone in the AL. The winner of the race was to receive a gift of a new Chalmers automobile. On the final day of the season the St. Louis Browns' manager ordered his young third baseman to play extremely deep on Lajoie during a doubleheader, ostensibly because of Larry's ability to smash the ball. Lajoie went 8 for 8, with seven of the hits being bunts, but lost the title to Cobb by .0007. He was given the auto anyway. In 1981 Paul MacFarlane of *The Sporting News* discovered that Ty got credit for an extra hit that year and Lajoie should have won the title. Commissioner Kuhn ruled that, damn the facts, the records remain as they had been.

Lajoie hit over .300 in sixteen of his twenty-one seasons and finished with 3,242 hits for a .338 average. He accumulated 1,599 RBIs and scored 1,503. He led AL second basemen in fielding six times.

In 1937 he was named to the Hall of Fame.

Kenesaw Mountain Landis

Commissioner, 1920–44

Baseball's first commissioner and only true czar, Landis demanded and got autocratic power to clean up the Black Sox scandal ruthlessly. By doing so, he restored public confidence in the integrity of baseball. He went on to rule the game with a power never wielded since. Historian David Q. Voigt calls him one of the five most influential men in baseball history.

A shock of white hair, a thin, unsmiling mouth, and a crushed fedora hat—this was the image of Landis, who restored integrity to the game and ruled it for more than two decades.

As a federal judge, Landis had won fame by fining John D. Rockefeller's Standard Oil trust $29 million and for jailing ninety-four Socialist Labor Party leaders during World War One. But he refused to rule in the Federal League's suit against the NL and AL, saying it "would be a blow against a national institution." It won him the job as commissioner.

Landis banned the Black Sox for life, though no court had convicted them. He banned several other players for less publicized fixing charges. He suspended Babe Ruth for barnstorming without permission.

On the other hand, he was zealous in defending player rights. He opposed the farm system, and though he could not stop it, he released two hundred Tiger and Cardinal farm

hands into free agency on the grounds that they were being "covered up" by the teams.

Team owners bridled under his iron rule and never again granted a commissioner such powers. He was elected to the Hall of Fame in 1944, a month after his death.

Tony Lazzeri

*Second Baseman, NY (A) 1926–37, Chi (N) 1938,
Bkn (N) 1939, NY (N) 1939*

Poor Lazzeri. As a twenty-two-year-old Yankee rookie, he was the victim of the most famous strikeout in history. He whiffed with the bases loaded against a hung-over Grover Alexander in the 1926 World Series. But with a tiny change of wind, Tony could have been the hero; before striking out he hit a long drive to left that faded foul by a few inches. "A few feet more," said Alex, "and he'd have been the hero and I'd have been the bum."

Like his nemesis Alexander, Lazzeri was a victim of epilepsy. And like Alex, he overcame it to have an outstanding career.

Ironically Lazzeri hit a World Series grand slam ten years later in 1936.

Overall he played second base for six Yankee pennant winners and helped the Cubs to a flag in 1938. He drove in over 100 runs in seven different seasons and finished with a .292 career batting average.

Tony also had one of the greatest minor league years ever— 202 runs, 222 RBIs, and 60 HRs for San Francisco of the Pacific Coast League in 1925 (of course, they played a 197-game season).

Bob Lemon

*Pitcher, Cle (A) 1941–42, 1946–58.
Manager, KC (A) 1970–72,
Chi (A) 1977–78, NY (A) 1978–82*

Lemon was the ace of perhaps the finest pitching staff in AL history—the Indians of 1948–1956, with Bob Feller, Early Wynn, Mike Garcia, Herb Score, and others. Lem won 207 games for Cleveland, yet didn't become a pitcher until he was nearly twenty-six years old.

As a third baseman, he played ten games with the Tribe before going into military service for World War Two. He demonstrated that he was not a good enough hitter to replace Ken Keltner at third for the Indians. Moreover, his arm was erratic. He seemed unable to throw a ball straight.

When he returned to the Tribe in 1946, the decision was made to turn his liability into a virtue by making him a pitcher. He showed promise in 1947 when he won 11. By 1948 he was a star. As the Indians won their first pennant in 28 years, he pitched a no-hitter, 10 shutouts, and won 20 games. He added two more wins in the World Series.

He had seven 20-win seasons from 1948 to 1956. Three times he led the AL in victories, including 1955, when he won "only" 18.

Lem helped himself with his glove and bat. Often used as a pinch hitter, his 37 home runs are second all-time among pitchers.

In 1978 Lem took over as manager of the Yankees when they were 10½ games behind the Red Sox and split with dissension. With patient handling—plus a raft of Red Sox injuries—Bob achieved one of the unforgettable modern miracles by bringing the Yankees back to a last-day tie with Boston and a playoff victory.

Lemon was elected to the Hall of Fame in 1976.

Walter "Buck" Leonard

*First Baseman, Negro League, 1933–50, Brooklyn Royal
Giants, Homestead Grays*

They called Leonard "the black Gehrig." Like Lou, Buck was a durable first baseman with plenty of lefthanded power. He teamed with Josh Gibson to give the Homestead Grays a mighty one-two home run punch as the Grays won nine straight Negro National League flags, 1937–1945. When Gibson left the club, 1940–1941, for Mexico, the Grays won on Buck's power alone.

In 1939 Leonard led all black batters with .492. He also slugged 7 homers in the short season, hitting them at a rate of 66/550 at-bats. Runner-up Gibson hit 6 (a rate of 59/550). Buck's entire career has not yet been compiled, but one estimate of his Negro League record puts his batting average at .336. He was also one of black baseball's most popular players.

He was elected to the Hall of Fame in 1972.

Freddie Lindstrom

*Third Baseman/Outfielder, NY (N) 1924–32,
Pit (N) 1933–34, Chi (N) 1935–36*

Lindstrom was a victim of pebbles. It was his bad luck that when he was an eighteen-year-old Giants rookie in the seventh game of the 1924 Series, not one but two balls hit pebbles and bounced over his head. The first, in the eighth inning, let in the tying run. The second, in the twelfth, lost the game for the Giants.

Ironically Lindstrom went on to be considered one of the NL's best-fielding third basemen until a foot injury in 1931 forced him to the outfield.

When he became a Giants regular in 1925 and began showing his hitting ability, New York fans called him "the Boy Wonder." A consistent .300 hitter, his top seasons were 1928, when he led the NL with 231 hits and batted .358, and 1930, when he hit .379 and swatted 22 home runs.

In 1935 he helped the Cubs to a pennant as an outfielder.

He was elected to the Hall of Fame in 1976.

John Henry "Pop" Lloyd

*Shortstop, Negro League, 1905–31, Macon Acmes, Cuban-
X Giants, Philadelphia Giants, Leland Giants, Lincoln
Giants, Chicago American Giants, Brooklyn Royal
Giants, Columbus Buckeyes, Bacharach Giants,
Hilldale, New York Black Yankees*

"You could put Wagner and Lloyd in a bag together," Connie

Mack once said, "and whichever you pulled out, you wouldn't go wrong." They called Lloyd "the black Wagner," and Honus said he considered it an honor.

Starting in 1905, Lloyd established himself as the finest shortstop in black baseball and one of the finest ever. He played for independent black teams and in Cuba, where he was adored. They called him *Cuchara*, which means "scoop" or "shovel." Much like Wagner, he would scoop up a grounder and fire it to first in a hail of dust and pebbles that he'd also shoveled up with the ball.

His finest hour came in 1909 against Ty Cobb and the Tigers in five exhibition games in Havana. Cobb did not steal a base, as Lloyd tagged him out three times. Lloyd hit .500 against the Tiger pitchers; Cobb hit .369 against the Cubans. The Georgia Peach was so angry and embarrassed he stomped off the field, vowing never to play blacks again.

At bat, Lloyd was a scientific hitter, spraying line drives where the ball was pitched. Although he was in his mid-thirties when the Negro National League was formed, Lloyd played for a dozen years and compiled a league average of .342. His best season was 1928 when he hit .564 and led the league in home runs at the age of 44.

More than a great shortstop and hitter, Lloyd was the model gentleman of black ball, as Mathewson was the paragon role model of the white game. "Gosh bob it!" was his strongest oath.

In 1977 he was elected to the Hall of Fame.

Sherm Lollar

Catcher, Cle (A) 1946, NY (A) 1947–48,
StL (A) 1949–51, Chi (A) 1952–63

Lollar put the Stop-Stop in the Go-Go White Sox of the 1950s. The underrated catcher anchored the Sox, a team built on speed, defense, and pitching. On the base paths, Sherm literally anchored the Sox' running attack as he brought out various allusions to snails, molasses, and Ernie Lombardi. Nevertheless, as one of the few Sox with punch in his bat, he earned his keep on offense. In their pennant year of 1959, he socked 22 homers.

He excelled in defense. He was a rock behind the plate and an excellent handler of pitchers, absolutely crucial in the Sox scheme. And when the opposition tried a little go-going of its own, it was usually gone. In 1954 Sherm played for five months straight without permitting a single stolen base.

Ernie Lombardi

Catcher, Bkn (N) 1931, Cin (N) 1932–41,
Bos (N) 1942, NY (N) 1943–47

Lombardi was the slowest runner in the Hall of Fame, including executives, pioneers, and exhibits. "Schnozz" was a big, muscular guy, with a banana nose, an easygoing manner, and feet of pure lead. His lack of foot speed was legendary. Infielders played shallow in the outfield and could still throw him out. It was said he had to hit .400 to bat .300. He was a cinch double play anytime they got the runner at second; if they couldn't trust the infielder's arm, he could carry it to first.

Nonetheless, Lombardi was one of baseball's greatest catchers. He is one of two catchers to ever lead his league in hitting, and the only one to do it twice. The first time was in 1938, when he hit .342 and was voted the MVP. Five years later, he repeated with .330. His career average was .306. He hit with tremendous power—he had to because he never got a "leg" hit— but on a line. His home run totals were modest: a high of 20 in 1939 and 190 for his career.

He was considered barely adequate as a defensive catcher in his day, whenever he let a pitch get even a few steps away from him, it was a passed ball for sure. He was on the receiving end of Johnny Vander Meer's two no-hitters and one of the keys to Cincinnati's two straight pennants in 1939–1940.

Lombardi was criticized unfairly for his famous "snooze" in the fourth and final game of the 1939 World Series. What actually happened is this:

With Yankee runners at the corners and the score tied in the tenth, Joe DiMaggio singled the go-ahead run home. The right fielder misplayed the ball and Charlie Keller, running from first, came charging homeward. He hit Lombardi where the chest protector doesn't cover, and while Ernie fell to the ground in agony, DiMaggio scored. The play didn't lose the Series, but it probably kept Ernie out of Cooperstown until 1986, nine years after his death.

Davey Lopes

Second Baseman, LA (N) 1972–81, Oak (A) 1982–84,
Chi (N) 1984–86, Hou (N) 1986–87

Lopes was the kind of player who earns a reputation as "pesty." Translated, that means he won a lot of games for his team without piling up big statistics. He was okay in the field, but no world beater. He never led NL second basemen in fielding, but he did top them a couple of times in errors. He had a .263 career batting average and hit 28 homers in 1979, but it was the only time he socked more than 17. He *did* steal bases, leading the league in 1975–1976 and totaling 557. What made that part of his game significant was that he was almost never caught. He had one string of 38 straight successes.

Davey was a member of the Dodger infield with Steve Garvey, Bill Russell, and Ron Cey, a group that played together from 1973 to 1980. By doing all the little things, Lopes played in four World Series.

Al Lopez

Catcher, Bkn (N) 1928, 1930–35, Bos (N) 1936–40,
Pit (N) 1940–46, Cle (A) 1947. Manager, Cle (A) 1951–56,
Chi (A) 1957–65, 1968–69

Until Bob Boone broke it in 1987, Lopez had the record for most games caught. A good take-charge backstop, he played for nineteen seasons, mostly with second division clubs, and hit a decent .261. He learned a lot of baseball and a lot more patience. Both helped him become one of baseball's greatest managers.

Taking over the helm at Cleveland in 1951, he chased the Yankees to three straight second-place finishes. The ex-catcher's Tribe teams were built on great pitching, with Bob

Feller, Bob Lemon, Early Wynn, and Mike Garcia, and home runs. Unfortunately for Cleveland, the Yankees always seemed to have enough pitching and more of everything else. But in 1954 the *Señor*'s Indians won 111 games, the AL record, to win the pennant.

Al moved to the White Sox in 1957 and won his second flag two years later. He did it with mirrors, since the Sox had almost no power. Owner Bill Veeck said a typical rally was two bloopers, an error, a passed ball, and two walks. A hit batsman would be "the final crusher." Thirty-five of their wins were by one run.

Lopez was a popular leader. If he had any fault, said Veeck, it was that "he was too decent." From 1949 to 1964 Lopez was the only manager other than a Yankee to win an AL pennant. He also brought his clubs in second ten times.

In 1977 he was elected to the Hall of Fame.

Dick Lundy

Shortstop, Negro League, 1916–48,
Bacharach Giants, Lincoln Giants, Hilldale, Baltimore
Black Sox, Philadelphia Stars, Newark Dodgers,
New York Cubans, Newark Eagles, Jacksonville Eagles

"King Richard" was one of the top shortstops of blackball history, possessing a strong arm, sure hands, and exceptional range. Although batting records are incomplete, the clever switch-hitter hit in the .330 range over his long career. He hit .400 four times between 1921 and 1930 in the United States and Cuba.

Big, graceful, and a natural leader, Lundy played on several championship teams. In 1925, when he and "Pop" Lloyd, the nonpareil of black shortstops, were both members of the Atlantic City Bacharach Giants, Lloyd moved over to second base because of the younger man's then-superior range. Lundy replaced Lloyd as manager of the Bacharachs and led them from fourth to two straight pennants, while hitting .329 and .306. In 1933–1934 he was a starting shortstop in the first two black All-Star Games.

Adolfo "Dolf" Luque

Pitcher, Bos (N) 1914–15, Cin (N) 1918–29,
Bkn (N) 1930–31, NY (N) 1932–35

One of Cuba's first major league pitching stars, Luque was the leading pitcher in the NL in 1923. He was 27–8 for the second-place Reds, with a league-leading 1.93 ERA. Two years later, he led the NL in ERA again with a 2.63 mark. In twenty years of pitching, twelve with the Reds, he won 193 games.

The pride of Havana even found a new career at age 43. He became the bullpen stopper of the New York Giants and led the NL in relief wins with 8.

Always hot-tempered, he reportedly stomped into the opposing team's dugout one day in response to some unkind words and popped Casey Stengel on the nose.

Albert "Sparky" Lyle

Pitcher, Bos (A) 1967–71,
NY (A) 1972–78, Tex (A) 1979–80,
Phi (N) 1980–82, Chi (A) 1982

Lyle won 99 games in relief and saved 238. Every one of his 899 pitching appearances was in relief. The durable left-hander was a big factor in getting the Yankees into the 1976 and 1977 World Series, with 23 saves the first year and 26 the next, when he also won 13 and earned the Cy Young Award.

Sparky used his slider to write a fine postseason record in 1977. With New York losing the LCS two games to one, Lyle pitched 5⅔ shutout innings to beat Kansas City and even the series. The next day he went 1⅓ more scoreless innings as the Yanks rallied to win. Two days later he pitched 3⅓ more innings of one-hit ball to beat the Dodgers in the World Series opener.

Then in 1978 his world was shattered when the Yanks paid millions to sign free agent Goose Gossage. Goose pushed Sparky right off the bullpen bench, and he spent the season in mop-up rolls. He told of it in his book, *The Bronx Zoo*.

A flake and clubhouse cutup, Sparky once leaped nude onto a birthday cake, only to learn later that it was intended for Yankee manager Ralph Houk.

Fred Lynn

Outfielder, Bos (A) 1974–80, Cal (A) 1981–84,
Bal (A) 1985–88, Det (A) 1988–

Lynn had one of baseball's most remarkable rookie years in 1975—he is the only man to win the MVP his first year in the majors. The Red Sox won the pennant as Lynn, their center fielder, hit .331, led the league in doubles and runs, cracked 21 homers, and batted in 105 runs.

Fred continued to hit with good power, getting up to 39 home runs in 1979, when he won the batting title with .333. In 1982 Lynn helped California win the division title, then walloped .611 in the LCS. He's won four Gold Gloves.

Yet Fred's career has been a disappointment in view of its brilliant beginning. His batting average has fallen through the 1980s, as have his RBIs. Many of his problems stem from frequent injuries—too frequent, say his critics.

Ted Lyons

Pitcher, Chi (A) 1923–42, 1946.
Manager, Chi (A) 1946–48

Lyons pitched twenty-one seasons for the White Sox. During those years, the Sox finished in the second division sixteen times. Fans in other cities celebrated pennants; in Chicago they celebrated Ted Lyons. Possibly the most popular player ever to take the mound in the Windy City, he earned fans' devotion with his upbeat personality, indomitable spirit, and by being one of the greatest pitchers of all time.

He came straight out of Baylor University, skipped the minors, and relieved in the first major league game he ever saw. By the next year he was a regular starter. Using a good fastball, curve, and knuckler, he won 20-plus three times with

the second-division White Sox: in 1925, 1927, and for the last time in 1930.

In 1931 a sore arm cost him his fastball and nearly his career. Although he was no longer the dominating pitcher he had been in the 1920s, he used control and guile to remain the Sox stopper through the 1930s. Near the end of the decade, he became a "Sunday" pitcher, always pitching on that day because the biggest crowds showed up then.

Lyons won 260 games for the Sox, many fewer than he might have won for stronger teams, but he never complained. In 1955 he was named to the Hall of Fame.

Connie Mack (Cornelius McGillicuddy)

Catcher, Was (N) 1886–89, Buf (P), 1890, Pit (N) 1891–96.
Manager, Pit (N) 1894–96, Phi (A) 1901–50.

For fifty years Mack managed the Philadelphia A's, building and destroying two dynasties. He had some of the greatest and some of the worst teams in history—his 1916 A's lost 117 games. Mack finished first nine times and last sixteen times. His lifetime 3,776–4,025 record is first among all managers in both wins and losses.

A lean, sweet-faced man in derby hat and stiff collar, even in the dugout, he was known to everyone as "Mr. Mack." To some he was a skinflint. But lack of money was his lifelong problem. With a modest fortune behind him, he might have dominated the AL, as the Yankees did in the 1920s and 1930s.

Born during the American Civil War, he quit school in the sixth grade to work in a cotton mill. He was a weak-hitting (.251) catcher for a while in the 1880s before sinking his life savings in Buffalo of the Players League. When the league folded after one year, Mack was wiped out.

After three years of managing lackluster Pittsburgh in the 1890s, and a four-year stint with Milwaukee of the Western League, he was given the Philadelphia franchise in the new AL in 1901, with backing from Ben Shibe. Some said the team would be a "White Elephant," a symbol of wasted capital, but Mack brought the A's in first in 1902. The White Elephant became the team's symbol. He developed stars such as Rube Waddell, Eddie Plank, Chief Bender, Eddie Collins, and Home Run Baker and won five flags in ten years, 1905–1914.

John McGraw's Giants beat him in the 1905 World Series, but Mack got revenge in 1911 and 1913.

But the Miracle Braves of 1914 shocked him in four straight; the Federal League was raiding his stars and bidding salaries up. Mack began selling his stars, plunged to the bottom in 1915, and stumbled in last for seven years in a row. Anyone else would have been canned, but Connie was, after all, a stockholder.

Patiently Mack founded another dynasty with Foxx, Simmons, and Cochrane, and even shelled out a record $100,600 for Lefty Grove. They brought him three more flags, 1929–1931, before the Depression broke, and he sold his stars to pay the rent.

He was elected to the Hall of Fame in 1937. He was still managing in 1950 at eighty-seven, still looking for that third dynasty. New York gave him a tickertape parade. He died in 1956 at the age of ninety-three, after his heirs had sold the club to a corporation in Kansas City.

Raleigh "Biz" Mackey

Catcher, Negro League, 1918–47, San Antonio Giants, Indi-
anapolis ABCs, Hilldale, Darby Daisies, Philadelphia
Stars, Washington Elite Giants, Baltimore Elite Giants,
Newark Eagles

Mackey is usually named as the finest defensive catcher of the Negro Leagues. Josh Gibson hit with much more power, but Mackey was his superior with a glove. "He was the master of defense," his protégé, Roy Campanella, would say. "For real catching skills, I don't think Cochrane was the master that Mackey was."

Pitchers loved to throw to Biz. He built up their confidence, called their game, "stole" borderline strikes for them. A jolly, bubbly man, he "jived" the hitters to take their mind off the game. Infielders loved to cover bases for him. "You didn't have to move your glove six inches," Judy Johnson said. The ball reached second light as a feather.

And he could hit, from either side—.364 in 1923, .363 in 1924, .317 lifetime.

In 1935 Biz met fifteen-year-old Campanella and shaped him into a Hall of Famer. "You saw Campy catch, you saw Mackey," oldsters say. In 1941 Biz could still outpoll Campy in the balloting for the black All-Star Game by 30,000 votes.

Biz retired as a forklift operator in Los Angeles. When the Dodgers gave Campy a "night" in 1959 before 93,000 fans at the Coliseum, Roy called on Biz to stand and take their applause. He died soon afterwards.

Larry MacPhail

Executive, Owner

Night ball, radio broadcasts, batting helmets, air travel, old-timers' day, fireworks, three championship dynasties, loud feuds with his managers—chances are anything that Veeck, Finley, or Steinbrenner thought up, MacPhail had already done.

Wounded and gassed in World War One, the fiery redhead had even tried to kidnap the German Kaiser in a daring adventure. (All he got was the Kaiser's ashtray.)

Back home Larry took over the Cardinals' Columbus farm team and pioneered in the advent of night games and air travel by baseball clubs. He also slugged a cop in a hotel lobby and was fired by St. Louis.

As general manager of Cincinnati in 1935, MacPhail brought the first lights to a major league park ("Every night will be a Sunday") and laid the groundwork for the Reds' champs of 1939–1940.

Moving to the moribund Dodgers in 1938, Larry brought Red Barber in to broadcast home games, hired manager Leo Durocher, and built a winner in 1941.

After another tour in the Army as a colonel, MacPhail bought a one-third interest in the Yankees. He installed lights in Yankee Stadium and brought the Yanks to a pennant and world championship in 1947. During the victory celebration, he engaged in a loud public brawl. The next day his partners terminated his contract as club administrator and bought him out.

He was elected to the Hall of Fame in 1978. His legacy lived on in his son Lee, president of the AL (1974–1983), and

grandson, Andy, general manager of the Minnesota Twins.

Bill Madlock

Third Baseman, Tex (A) 1973, Chi (N) 1974–76, SF (N) 1977–79, Pit (N) 1979–85, LA (N) 1985–87, Det (N) 1987

Madlock won four batting titles to put him in rarefied company. The first two came with the Cubs in 1975–1976. Then after a disappointing two and a half seasons in San Francisco, he was traded in mid-1979 to the Pirates and hit .328 down the stretch to help them win the pennant. In the World Series that year, he hit .375.

Although he won batting titles for the Pirates in 1981 and 1983, the team slipped lower in the standings. Many Pittsburgh fans placed some of the blame on Madlock—unfairly it would seem. He had never been a power hitter or an outstanding fielder, but these failings became increasingly criticized as the Pirates slumped. He played with injuries, but when he sat out games, he was accused of malingering. Much of the criticism actually stemmed from his habit of speaking his mind honestly about a deteriorating situation with the ball club. Pirate fans, not liking the message, wanted to shoot the messenger.

He later helped Los Angeles and Detroit win division titles.

Sherry Magee

Outfielder, Phi (N) 1904–14, Bos (N) 1915–17, Cin (N) 1917–19

Magee was an excellent hitter in the dead-ball era. He stole a lot of bases (441), hit a lot of doubles (425), and led the league twice in RBIs, twice in slugging average, and once in batting. He finished his career in 1919 with a .291 career average and 1,182 RBIs. His reputation would be higher today except for two quirks of fate. First, after eleven seasons with the Phillies, he was traded to the Braves in 1915, just before the Phils' first pennant and just after the "Miracle Braves" pennant, thus depriving him of a World Series showcase. Second, and worse, he is often confused with Lee Magee, a contemporary who was banned from baseball on fixing charges.

Sal Maglie

Pitcher, NY (N) 1945, 1950–55, Cle (A) 1955–56, Bkn (N) 1956–57, NY (A) 1957–58, StL (N) 1958

Maglie was one of the jumpers who signed with the Mexican League in 1946. It cost him a four-year suspension from the majors. When he returned in 1950 at age thirty-three, he was 18–4.

He had a 23–6 mark in 1951, the year of the Miracle of Coogan's Bluff. It was Sal who kept the Giants in the race the first half before their other hurlers caught fire.

In 1956 the thirty-nine-year-old Maglie stunned New York by moving to the Dodgers, where he went 13–5. Sal pitched one crucial September game against fifth-place Philadelphia, when a loss would have put Brooklyn out of the race. He responded with a no-hitter, and the Bums captured the flag.

They called him "the Barber" because he shaved the hitters close with inside pitches (and because he had a permanent five o'clock shadow himself). As a coach, he passed on his philosophy to Jim Bouton: "If you're 2–0 on a guy, go ahead and flatten his ass."

Jim Maloney

Pitcher, Cin (N) 1960–70, Cal (A) 1971

Before a sore arm ended his career at age thirty-one, Maloney pitched three no-hitters and five one-hitters. Some say he was faster than Koufax.

In 1963 he struck out eight straight Braves—Eddie Mathews was eighth—before Hank Aaron grounded out. Jim was 23–7 that year for the fifth-place Reds. (He also led in wild pitches, keeping the hitters honest.)

Two years later he was 20–9, as Cincy finished fourth. Two of his wins were no-hitters; the first went ten innings against the last-place Mets before two hits in the eleventh beat him 1–0.

Mickey Mantle

Outfielder, NY (A) 1951–68

The most powerful switch-hitter ever, Mantle was a magnificent talent who was beset throughout his entire career by injuries. A high school football injury left him with a chronic bone infection in his legs. He had a shoulder operation, a broken foot, a torn hamstring. He taped his legs every day he played; even so, he sometimes took to the field in pants soaked with blood. He compounded his injury problems by refusing to follow exercise programs and partying into the wee hours with his Yankee buddies. His attitude was "live now"; no male member of his family had lived past forty.

Joining the Yankees in 1951 as the designated successor to Joe DiMaggio, Mantle had a difficult rookie year, was farmed out, and considered quitting baseball. A visit from his terminally ill father, who had named him Mickey after Mickey Cochrane, convinced the young slugger to go on. He returned to the Yankees but injured a knee in the second game of the World Series that year.

In 1952 he began to show his awesome talent, hitting .311. He quickly became known for his tape measure home runs. Among others during his career, he walloped one to the facade on Yankee Stadium's roof, estimated at 600 feet, hit a 565-footer in Washington, and blasted one in Chicago, which, Yankee Manager Casey Stengel said left seats "flyin' around for five minutes."

In eighteen seasons he twice topped 50 homers, led the AL in home runs four times, and finished with a total of 536. He scored a Triple Crown in 1956, played in twenty All-Star Games, and earned three MVP Awards (in 1956, 1957, and 1962).

Mantle played in twelve World Series. He hit the most Series homers (18), scored the most runs (42), and batted in the most (40).

He was named to the Hall of Fame in 1974.

Heinie Manush

Outfielder, Det (A) 1923–27, StL (A) 1928–30,
Was (A) 1930–35, Bos (A) 1936, Bkn (N) 1937–38,
Pit (N) 1938–39

Manush was an outstanding hitter during the 1920s and 1930s with several AL teams. He compiled a lifetime batting average of .330. A line drive hitter, he knocked out more triples (160) than home runs (110). As a Detroit rookie in 1923, Heinie played beside Harry Heilmann and Ty Cobb, who gave him batting tips. Three years later he dueled Babe Ruth for the batting title. He went 6 for 9 in the final doubleheader to hit .378 and beat the Babe by six points.

In 1928 he cracked out 241 base hits to again hit .378 but lost the batting crown to Goose Goslin by one point. Two years later the two men would be traded for each other.

Walter "Rabbit" Maranville

Shortstop, Bos (N) 1912–20, 1929–35, Pit (N) 1921–24,
Chi (N) 1925, Bkn (N) 1926, StL (N) 1927–28.
Manager, Chi (N) 1925

The real miracle behind the 1914 "Miracle Braves" was a hoppity little five-five shortstop named Maranville (accent on the "an"). He hit only .246, but he put on a *nonpareil* show at shortstop.

Sporting a "vest pocket catch" and a better range than General Electric, Rabbit handled more chances than any shortstop ever had before and teamed with Evers to lead the league in double plays (far more than Evers had ever made with Tinker and Chance).

Maranville was sick for the first few weeks in 1914, as the Braves stumbled in the cellar. Then after July 14 he, and they, stormed to the pennant. In the World Series he even hit .308 as the Braves swept the mighty A's in four straight.

Braves' manager George Stallings hailed Maranville as another Cobb, but the only way he might have had Cobb's bat would have been to swipe it from the rack. His career average was .258. An incorrigible prankster, he was famous for his mischief. A free spirit, he was sometimes free with spirits; "there's a lot less alcohol consumed since 1926," he once said, "because that's when I stopped drinking."

He played for twenty-three seasons and was considered a top gloveman to the end. He was elected to the Hall of Fame in 1954.

Fred "Firpo" Marberry

Pitcher, Was (A) 1923–32, 1936, Det (A) 1933–35,
NY (N) 1936

One of the earliest relief artists, Marberry was the forerunner of the great relief pitchers of today. Nicknamed for the Argentine fighter Luis Firpo, Marberry had a similar, powerful physique. He both started and relieved, but his reputation was built on relieving as he led the AL in saves five times. He helped Washington to two flags (1924–1925) and Detroit to one (1934).

Marberry had 15 saves in 1924, plus 2 in the World Series,

15 more in 1925 as the Senators won again, and 22 in 1926. He was 15–5 with 3 saves for Detroit in 1934 to help them to their first flag in a quarter century, and he ended with a 147–89 won-lost mark and 101 saves.

Juan Marichal

Pitcher, SF (N) 1960–73, Bos (A) 1974, LA (N) 1975

Facing Marichal was like facing a dozen different pitchers. His high leg kick was his trademark, but once the leg came down, the ball could zip toward the batter from any angle— sidearm, three-quarters, over the top—as he delivered fastballs, curves, and sliders in a multiplicity of speeds, yet always with marvelous control. From 1963 through 1969, the brilliant righthander from the Dominican Republic was the major league's winningest pitcher.

After winning 18 for the Giants in 1962, Marichal won 20 or more in six of the next seven seasons. He was 25–8 in 1963, including a no-hitter, to lead the NL in wins and 25–6 in 1966 to lead in percentage. In 1968 he was back on top in wins: 26–9. And the next season he led in ERA. He completed 244 of his 457 starts; manager Al Dark said, "Put your club a run ahead in the late innings, and Marichal is the greatest pitcher I ever saw."

He did not have a losing season until 1972. He averaged nearly 6 strikeouts per nine innings while walking less than 2.

Usually easy-going, with a ready, impish grin, Marichal's reputation was tarnished by one out-of-character moment. In 1965, during a game with the Dodgers, he was brushed back by the pitch. Then the return throw from Dodger catcher John Roseboro whizzed close by his ear. Suddenly getting it from in front and behind, Marichal turned and clubbed Roseboro on the head with his bat. He was fined $1,750, an NL record at the time, and suspended for nine days.

In 1983 Marichal was named to the Hall of Fame.

Roger Maris

Outfielder, Cle (A) 1957–58, KC (A) 1958–59,
NY (A) 1960–66, StL (N) 1967–68

Maris may never be forgiven. He broke the Babe's sacrosanct record of 60 home runs in a season. How dare he! When Hank Aaron passed Ruth's career total, there was anger among the unreasoning, but the 714 never had the magic of 60. And Aaron roared past and added 30 more after he broke it. Maris topped 60 by only one in a season eight games longer than the Babe's. And Aaron was a great player. Maris wasn't.

"I don't want to be Babe Ruth," Maris protested. He needn't have said it. There were too many others anxious to prove that he wasn't. So Maris struck more home runs than any other major league batter had ever hit in a single season and spent the rest of his life hearing what a bum he was. Commissioner Ford Frick even ordered an asterisk placed beside Roger's 61, though he might have preferred a scarlet letter.

Maris was no bum. He was an intelligent, likable man, a bit reserved—a private sort of person—totally unprepared to turn the media blitz that drowned him to his advantage. He was a talented player. All right, not a great player, but a good

one. He was sure in the outfield, with a fine arm. He never hit for much of an average, and he ended his twelve-year career with only a .260 mark, but he had good home run power. In eleven *other* seasons he totaled 214 homers.

He was AL MVP the year *before* his 61-homer season, with 39 home runs and a league-leading 112 RBIs. In 1961, besides the homers, he led in runs (132) and RBIs (142), so his second MVP wasn't just for breaking Ruth's record. In 1962, he had 33 homers and 100 RBIs. He had some injuries after that, and the numbers fell off, but he was the regular right fielder when healthy for five straight Yankees pennant winners (1960–1964). He finished up in 1967–1968, as a regular for two Cardinals teams that won flags.

If he'd hit 59, he'd have been a hero.

Richard "Rube" Marquard

Pitcher, NY (N) 1908–15, Bkn (N) 1915–20,
Cin (N) 1921, Bos (N) 1922–25

The Giants bought Marquard from Indianapolis for a record $11,000 in 1908 and rushed him into the pennant race before he was ready. The result was an "$11,000 Lemon" until careful nurturing by coach Wilbert Robinson turned him into a "beauty" in 1911. Rube was 24–7 to help win the flag. It was the first of three 20-victory years for the lefthander and three straight flags for the Giants. In the 1911 Series he had a 1.54 ERA but lost his only decision.

In 1912, when he was 26–11, Marquard won his first 19 games to tie Tim Keefe's record. He actually won 20 if modern scoring rules are applied; one "win" was scored a save. In the World Series that year, he had an 0.50 ERA and won two of the Giants' three victories.

In 1913 he was 23–10, giving him 73 victories in three years.

Those were his three best years. He had a brief comeback with Brooklyn under Robinson in 1916. He was 13–6, and the Dodgers won the flag. He upped that to 19–12 the next year, but led the NL in losses in 1918. He helped the Dodgers to another pennant with a 10–7 mark in 1920.

Although nicknamed after another star lefthander, Rube Waddell, Marquard was no Rube. He was sophisticated, a flashy dresser, no drinker (unlike Waddell), and married a Broadway actress.

He was elected to the Hall of Fame in 1971.

Mike Marshall

Pitcher, Det (A) 1967, Sea (A) 1969,
Hou (N) 1970, Mon (N) 1970–73, LA (N) 1974–76,
Atl (N) 1976–77, Tex (A) 1977,
Min (A) 1978–80, NY (N) 1981

A doctor of physiology, Marshall jogged four miles a day and set a record pitching in 106 games in 1974. That year he was 15–12 with 21 saves for the Dodgers, all tops in the NL for relievers that year. That performance earned him the Cy Young Award, the first ever won by a reliever. Two other times (1973 and 1979) he went over 90 games.

Mike designed his own conditioning program, but his education intimidated coaches and managers. He fought with Mayo Smith, Sal Maglie, and Harry Walker, with little success, until he joined Montreal under Gene Mauch, who let him do what he wanted. Marshall's saves shot up to 23 in 1971 and 31 in 1973.

In Minnesota in 1979 he used his screwball to save 32 games, his all-time high.

He ended his fourteen-season career with 92 relief wins and 188 saves.

Billy Martin

Second Base, NY (A) 1950–57, KC (A) 1957, Det (A) 1958,
Cle (A) 1959, Cin (N) 1960, Mil (N) 1961, Min (A) 1961.
Manager, Min (A) 1969, Det (A) 1971–73, Tex (A) 1974–75,
NY (A) 1975–78, 1979, 1983, 1988, Oak (A) 1980–83

"Everybody looks up to Billy Martin," one player said. "That's because he probably just knocked them down."

As a Yankee second baseman in the 1950s, he earned a reputation for light-hitting, heads-up play, and ready fists. He'd once considered becoming a middleweight boxer, and he was only too anxious to demonstrate his prowess. A brawl in the Copacabana night club in 1957 led to a trade to Kansas City and four final nomadic seasons.

He became a major league manager with the Twins in 1969, and the Martin pattern emerged. His clubs invariably improved their record from the previous year—the Twins jumped to the division title. Then Martin would be involved in a well-publicized fight, usually involving alcohol, and would be fired. One season in Minnesota, three in Detroit, two in Texas, and three in Oakland.

His saddest moments came with the Yankees, where he was hired and fired five times. Hired first in 1975, he took them to the pennant in 1976 and a world championship in 1977, only to be fired after 94 games in 1978. He was rehired in 1979 for the final two-thirds of the season, then fired again. After his three years in Oakland, he was back with the Yankees for all of 1983, most of 1985, and part of 1988.

Martin, when sober and with his temper under control, is a bright, articulate man. He has many friends who are intensely loyal, and he has shown himself to be a talented manager. Unfortunately his destructive side has had one enduring victim—himself.

Eddie Mathews

Third Baseman, Bos (N) 1952, Mil (N) 1953–65,
Atl (N) 1966, Hou (N) 1967, Det (A) 1967–68.
Manager, Atl (N) 1972–74

Lefthanded hitting Mathews was the greatest home run hitter among third basemen until Mike Schmidt. Mathews's 512 homers made him only the seventh man to hit 500, and he had four seasons with over 40, including league-leading marks of 47 in 1953 and 46 in 1959. Although he hit over .300 three times, his career average was only .271; however, he supplemented his 2,315 hits with 1,444 walks, leading the NL four times in that department.

He played fifteen of his seventeen seasons in a Braves uniform, beginning with the team's last season in Boston and ending with its first year in Atlanta. In between were thirteen

seasons in Milwaukee. He combined with Hank Aaron to form perhaps the best one-two punch of all time. Their total of 863 home runs while together ranks ahead of Mays-McCovey (800) and Ruth-Gehrig (772). Mathews usually batted third ahead of Aaron to take advantage of his ability to draw walks. He scored 1,509 runs, often being plated by Aaron. Eddie drove in 1,453 runs himself.

Curiously, with all his outstanding seasons in Milwaukee, two of the most ordinary were the pennant winning years of 1957–1958.

The handsome slugger was elected to the Hall of Fame in 1978.

Don Mattingly

First Baseman, NY (A) 1982–

Mattingly won the AL batting title with a .343 mark in 1984, his first full major league season, and he has been one of the most consistent hitters in baseball since. Perhaps no hitter in baseball today has combined high average with home run power to the same extent. He's topped 200 hits three times, 30 homers three times, and 100 RBIs four times. His 145 RBIs in 1985 led the AL. He led in doubles in 1984–1986. The 1985 MVP, he has been voted the top player in baseball in more than one poll.

Mattingly made headlines in 1988 with his criticism of the atmosphere Yankees' owner George Steinbrenner produced on the ballclub.

Christy Mathewson

Pitcher, NY (N) 1900–16, Cin (N) 1916.
Manager, Cin (N) 1916–18

One of the first five men elected to Cooperstown in 1936, Matty was handsome, intelligent, clean-cut, clean-living, the most popular pitcher of his day and possibly the best. They called Matty "Big Six," after New York's most famous fire engine. In an era of roughnecks, Matty was a college man who sang in the Bucknell glee club, belonged to the literary society, was president of his class, and could beat twelve foes at checkers at the same time. He refused to pitch on Sunday. The childless John McGraw virtually made him his son. Matty was the model for the Frank Merriwell of Yale books and the "Baseball Joe" stories that molded young boys' characters when Great Grandpa was a kid. Christy's own book, *Pitching in a Pinch*, is still a delight to read.

Connie Mack once compared Mathewson with Walter Johnson, who was also one of the first five in the Hall of Fame. "With Johnson, it was brute force," Mack said. "With Mathewson, it was knowledge and judgment, perfect control, and form."

Mathewson was famous for his "fadeaway," a screwball. With it, Matty won 30 three years in a row (1903–1905), posting ERAs of 1.27, 1.43, and 1.14 those seasons. He won 37 in 1908 and had nine other seasons with 20 or more wins. He brought the Giants five pennants. Matty's 80 shutouts are surpassed only by Walter Johnson and Grover Alexander. In the 1905 World Series, Matty pitched three shutouts in six days, giving up just 14 hits—and only one walk!

Mathewson had great control. In 1908 he had 391 innings pitched, 259 strikeouts, and only 42 walks. In 1913 he averaged only 0.6 walks per nine innings; he went 68 straight innings without a walk. He once won a game with 67 pitches.

Yet he wasn't out for records and always held something in reserve in those pre-relief days.

Before the Perrys and Niekros, Christy and his brother Henry held the record for wins by brothers—372 by Christy, none by Henry, whose big league career produced only one decision. Christy joined the Army in World War One and was the victim of poison gas. He suffered pulminary tuberculosis brought on by the gas, and died in 1925 at the age of forty-one.

Carl Mays

Pitcher, Bos (A) 1915–19, NY (A) 1919–23,
Cin (N) 1924–28, NY (N) 1929

Mays, of course, is the man whose submarine pitch killed Cleveland shortstop Ray Chapman in 1920. That tragic incident has obscured the fact that he was one of the best pitchers of his day.

Mays had a reputation for throwing at batters—and once he threw at a fan—but he denied intent to hit Chapman, and the game situation—leadoff batter, start of the inning—argues strongly that it was an accident. Actually, Mays hit only seven batters that year, far from the league high. Still, at least two teams threatened not to play against him after that. But Carl calmly won his next start 8–0. He was 26–11 for the Yankees that year, and 27–9 the next season when the Yanks won their first pennant.

A morose loner, Mays was unpopular with teammates and extremely so with fans after the Chapman tragedy. Mays "has no friends and doesn't want any," one player said of him. Mays's response: That's what made him a great pitcher. In addition to his two great Yankee years, he earlier won 21 and 22 with the Red Sox, and in the mid-1920s won 20 and 19 for the Reds. He played on six pennant winners at Boston and New York.

Willie Mays

Outfielder, Negro League, 1948–50,
Birmingham Black Barons,
NY (N) 1951–52, 1954–57, SF (N) 1958–72,
NY (N) 1972–73

The most exciting player of the 1960s, Mays hit 660 home runs, raced around the bases or into deepest center field, his hat flying off behind him. "The only man who could have caught that ball," one announcer said, "just hit it."

His catch off Vic Wertz in the 1954 World Series is sometimes cited as the greatest ever—a long sprint, an over-the-shoulder catch near the wall 460 feet away, a spin, and a bullet throw back to the infield. The hat flew off, of course—Willie later admitted he wore hats a size too small to make them do that.

New Yorkers gloried in their three great center fielders, "Willie, Mickey, and the Duke." The most ebullient—and to many the best—Willie was the "Say Hey Kid" who played

stickball with the kids in Harlem and hardball in the Polo Grounds at night.

He won eleven straight Gold Gloves and set the record for career putouts by an outfielder and the NL record for total chances.

He also stole 337 bases, led the league four times, and was the first man in the 300/300 club—300 steals, 300 homers. He was one of the few stolen-base kings who wasn't spinning his wheels, with a 77 percent success ratio (anything below 66 percent is a net negative).

Willie came up to the Giants in 1951. He started by going 0 for 22. But manager Leo Durocher stuck with him, pepped him up, and both Willie and the Giants caught fire. The team came from 13½ games behind to catch the Dodgers and win the playoff on Bobby Thomson's home run. "The only reason I pitched to Thomson," Dodger manager Chuck Dressen said, "was because Willie was the next hitter."

After military service in 1953, Mays returned to lead the Giants to the 1954 pennant with an NL-high .345 and 41 homers. He was named MVP. "If he could cook," said Leo, "I'd marry him."

Willie led the league in homers four times, topping 50 twice.

Moving to San Francisco in 1958 hurt his home run totals (as Aaron's move to Atlanta helped his). Still, Willie slugged four in one game in 1961. In 1962 he hit 49 with 141 RBIs to lead the Giants to a playoff victory over Los Angeles.

In 1965 he slugged 52 homers, 17 of them in August, to pass 500 and win his second MVP. *The Sporting News* named him the Player of the 1960s.

In 1979 he was elected to the Hall of Fame.

Bill Mazeroski

Second Baseman, Pit (N) 1956–72

Possibly the greatest-fielding second baseman who ever lived, Maz's 1,706 double plays is the all-time record for second-sackers. Around Pittsburgh, they called him "no-hands"—the ball seemed to go from the shortstop's shovel pass and ricochet to first with him hardly touching it. He led the league in assists nine times, double plays eight, putouts five, and fielding average three.

Bill also hit the most dramatic World Series homer ever struck, a *sayonara* blow in the ninth to win the seventh game of the 1960 Series and make the Pirates world champions.

Generally he wasn't too bad at bat, and in a friendlier park he would have been even better. He had a respectable .260 career batting average, with fair home run power. His Series-ending homer in 1960 was his second round-tripper of the Series: his two-run blast provided the margin of victory in Game One.

Joe McCarthy

Manager, Chi (N) 1926–30, NY (A) 1931–46,
Bos (A) 1948–50

If McCarthy was a "push-button manager," as rival skipper Jimmy Dykes once said, no manager ever pushed them more effectively. In twenty-four years as a major league manager,

his teams won seven world championships, nine pennants, and never finished out of the first division. His .614 winning percentage for nearly 3,500 games is the record, as is his .698 for nine World Series.

A minor league second baseman who never played a game in the majors, McCarthy won American Association pennants at Louisville and was hired by the Cubs in 1926. He instituted discipline on the free-spirited club and in 1929 led them to the NL pennant. They lost the World Series to the A's. The following year McCarthy resigned in September with the Cubs in second place.

The Yankees hired him for the 1931 season expressly to bring the team back to the heights it had enjoyed in the 1920s. Despite some resentment by some of the older Yankee players, including Babe Ruth, who had expected to be named manager, McCarthy brought the team home second in his first season and won the pennant and his first world championship in 1932.

He kept them in second place for the next three years while retooling the team. By 1936, with the arrival of rookie Joe DiMaggio, he had a dynasty. His Yankees won four straight world championships, slipped to third in 1940, then rebounded for three more pennants and two World Series wins. He resigned in 1945 because of ill health and a personality clash with new Yankee owner Larry MacPhail.

McCarthy accepted the job as manager of the Red Sox in 1948. The team had an awesome lineup of hitters but lacked pitching. Nevertheless he finished second two years in a row, losing the pennant in a playoff in 1948 and on the last day of the season in 1949. He retired during the 1950 season for health reasons.

Nicknamed "Marse Joe," McCarthy was a strict disciplinarian as a manager, but a warm, friendly man in his off-field moments.

He was elected to the Hall of Fame in 1957.

Tommy McCarthy

Outfielder, Bos (U) 1884, Bos (N) 1885, 1892–95,
Phi (N) 1886–87, StL (AA) 1888–91, Bkn (N) 1896.
Manager, StL (AA) 1890

McCarthy broke in with the Union Association in 1884, but did not really establish himself until he joined the American Association's St. Louis Browns in 1888. He helped the Browns win the '88 pennant and gained a reputation as an outstanding defensive player. He stole 93 bases in 1888 and led the AA in stolen bases in 1890.

His greatest years were with Boston's pennant-winning teams of the early 1890s. He and Hugh Duffy became known as the "Heavenly Twins" for their defensive plays in the outfield. Although McCarthy hit .346 in 1893 and .349 the following year, he was not a great hitter; he averaged .292 for his career. His strengths were his speed, his powerful throwing arm, and his scientific approach. He was an excellent bunter, and he and Duffy were brilliant hit-and-run artists and deadly on the double steal. McCarthy also popularized the practice of trapping fly balls and throwing runners out at second, sometimes starting double plays.

He was named to the Hall of Fame in 1946.

Jim McCormick

Pitcher, Ind (N) 1878, Cle (N) 1879–84, Cin (U) 1884, Prov (N) 1885, Chi (N) 1885–87. Manager, Cle (N) 1879–80

Way back in 1880, husky, mustachioed McCormick was probably the MVP of the young NL. He won 45, tops in the league, hurled 657 innings, held hitters to a 1.85 ERA—and managed Cleveland to a third-place finish. He was twenty-four years old.

For much of his career, 1878–1887, Jim suffered with losing clubs—he lost 40 games for sixth-place Cleveland in 1879. Still, he won 40-plus twice and was ERA king twice.

Not until 1885–1886 did he land with a flag winner, Anson's White Sox. He rewarded them with seasons of 21–7 and 31–11.

His totals for his ten-year career were 264–214, 2.43 ERA.

Willie McCovey

First Baseman, SF (N) 1959–73, 1977–80, SD (N) 1974–76, Oak (A) 1976

McCovey slugged 18 grand slams, an NL record, and led the league in homers three times, but according to Willie "the hardest ball I ever hit" was an out. The Giants were losing 1–0 in the ninth inning of the seventh game of the 1962 World Series, but they had the tying run on third and the winning run at second. Willie lined a bullet at Yankees' second baseman Bobby Richardson for the final out. A foot either way and the Giants would have been champs.

In the second game of the Series, McCovey had blasted one against a Candlestick Park light tower off the same pitcher, Ralph Terry.

Although extremely shy in his first years, Willie became a friendly, gregarious team leader. He hit 521 homers and batted in 1,555 runs during his twenty-two seasons.

Willie broke in 1959 with a perfect 4 for 4 against Robin Roberts. He hit .354 that year to win the Rookie of the Year Award.

Ten years later he was MVP with 45 homers and 126 RBIs, both league-leading totals, and a .320 batting average.

He was named to the Hall of Fame in 1986.

Joe "Iron Man" McGinnity

Pitcher, Bal (N) 1899, Bkn (N) 1900, Bal (A) 1901–02, NY (N) 1902–08

McGinnity got his nickname from working in an iron foundry in his youth, but it just as easily could have come from winning seven games in six days in the minors in 1896, or from pitching five doubleheaders in the majors. Joe also pitched a two-year record for this century of 434 innings in 1903 and 408 the next year, and he was still hurling minor league ball at the age of fifty-four.

Three of those doubleheader victories came in one month—August 1, 8, and 31, 1903. Joe won a league-leading 31 games for the second-place Giants that year. He pitched 44 complete games.

McGinnity threw an underhand curveball, with a motion so low his hand almost touched the ground. The fastball broke down, and the curve appeared to break up. Joe called it "Old Sal," and it may have put less strain on his arm than an overhand curve would have. He pitched for twenty-six years, though only ten in the majors. After leaving the Giants, Joe could still win 29 and 30 in the International League. He won 247 in the majors, but his total wins, majors and minors, came to 471.

McGinnity won 28 games as a rookie with Baltimore in 1899, but his greatest seasons were with the Giants (1902–08), for whom he won 31 in 1903 and 35 in 1904.

McGinnity had a reputation for throwing at hitters. He scored one hit batsman for every 19 men he faced—a record.

He was named to the Hall of Fame in 1946.

John McGraw

Third Baseman, Bal (AA) 1891, Bal (N) 1892–99, StL (N) 1900, Bal (A) 1901–02, NY (N) 1902–06. Manager, Bal (N) 1899, Bal (A) 1901–02, NY (N) 1902–32

A brawling, brilliant bully, McGraw and his Giants won ten pennants in twenty-one years, 1904–24. He dominated the NL for three decades as the Giants' manager after nearly a decade as a scrappy third baseman for the old Orioles of the 1890s.

As a manager, his strategic cleverness and his determination to control every aspect of his team won him the title "Little Napoleon." In 1892 McGraw joined the Baltimore Orioles of Keeler, Jennings, Hanlon *et al.* Mac could trip and spike with the rest of them, and he and Keeler are among those who are credited with inventing the hit-and-run. The O's won the flag in 1894–1896, with McGraw hitting .325 or better each year, the first of nine straight years he would hit .300. The O's won the Temple Cup playoffs in 1896–1897.

In 1899 Mac served as player-manager and hit .391; most of the star players had been sent to Brooklyn and the O's team finished fourth. Of all nineteenth-century players, no one had a higher on-base percentage than McGraw's .456.

He led Baltimore in the new AL 1901–1902, finishing fifth and seventh. John also fought with umpires and when league president Ban Johnson backed the umps, Mac jumped to New York in the NL, taking fellow Irishmen Joe McGinnity and Roger Bresnahan with him.

The Giants finished last in 1902, but leaped all the way to second in 1903 and first in 1904. McGraw haughtily refused to play a World Series against Johnson's AL. Mac won again in 1905, and this time he played the Series and demolished the AL Athletics in five games.

He lost a pennant narrowly in 1908 after the Merkle "boner," but stoutly defended Merkle from criticism.

A master psychologist, McGraw played on superstition and in 1911 put a Kansas lunatic, Charlie Faust, in uniform as a good luck mascot; the team charged from third place to the flag, the first of three straight.

By 1911 McGraw was already recognized as a managerial genius, he drove his players hard, called pitches from the bench, and was one of the first managers to grasp the concept of relief pitching, using Claude Elliott, George Ferguson, and Doc Crandall in that role in the first decade of the century. He

won another pennant in 1917.

McGraw captured an unprecedented four straight pennants in 1921–1924, a record that would stand until Casey Stengel broke it in 1953. But though the Giants stayed in the first division through most of his remaining years, he had won his last flag. Players began to rebel against his vicious, profane tongue lashings. In 1932 the Giants dived to eighth and he resigned after thirty-three seasons as a manager. His 2,840 career victories rank second only to Connie Mack.

He was named to the Hall of Fame in 1937.

Bill McKechnie

Third Baseman, Pit (N) 1907, 1910–12, 1918, 1920,
Bos (N) 1913, NY (A) 1913, Ind (F) 1914, Nwk (F) 1915,
NY (N) 1916, Cin (N) 1916–17. Manager, Nwk (F) 1915,
Pit (N) 1922–26, StL (N) 1928–29, Bos (N) 1930–37,
Cin (N) 1938–46

A light-hitting infielder during his playing career, McKechnie became one of baseball's most respected managers, winning pennants with three different NL teams. Known as "the Deacon" because of his years singing in a church choir and his cadaverous "parson" looks, his virtues as a skipper were his deep knowledge of baseball, his likable personality, and his infinite patience.

His first manager's job was with Newark in the short-lived Federal League. In 1922 he took over in Pittsburgh and brought them from the second division to a pennant and World Championship in 1925. When the team slipped to third in 1926, he was fired.

He was hired by the Cardinals in 1928 and immediately won the pennant. However, the team lost the World Series in four games. Midway through 1929 he was fired again.

In 1930 he was hired as skipper of the Boston Braves and stayed for eight years. Although Boston was the only NL team he managed that did not win a pennant, he earned wide respect for his efforts in sometimes making "silk purses" out of the material at hand. When he led them to fifth place in 1937, he was named Manager of the Year.

McKechnie moved to Cincinnati in 1938, the scene of his greatest teams. He won pennants in 1939 and 1940 and the World Series in the latter year.

McKechnie was elected to the Hall of Fame in 1962.

John "Bid" McPhee

Second Baseman, Cin (AA) 1882–89, Cin (N) 1890–99.
Manager, Cin (N) 1901–02

McPhee was utterly boring. He played eighteen seasons before 1900, every one at the same position, second base; every one for the same team, Cincinnati (the team changed leagues in 1890 or McPhee would have stayed in the same one). He played hard but clean. In all of his eighteen seasons he was never fined. He was never even thrown out of a game! At a time when rough and rowdy baseballers were providing a wealth of wicked anecdotes, McPhee showed up every day in shape, stayed sober, did his job, and went home to a good night's sleep. The only thing remotely interesting about him was that he refused to wear a glove until 1897, more than a

decade after they'd become common.

Oh yes, he was an excellent leadoff man, walked a lot, and scored 1,684 runs on his .275 batting average. He led the AA in triples in 1887 and totaled 189 for his career. But except for an obvious ability to score runs and an assumption that such an ability might lead to a number of victories, he really wasn't anything special with a bat. See? Boring.

He was at his most monotonous at second base. Game after game, season after season, batters would knock balls his way, and he just kept plucking them from the ground or the air and putting the batters out. He did this with such tedious regularity that he led his league's second basemen in fielding ten times, finished second four seasons, and was never lower than fourth. He was the leader in double plays eleven years, in putouts eight, and in assists six. He set the record for fielding average with .978 in 1896, the year before he started wearing a glove. That might be slightly interesting except that someone broke his record after a mere twenty-three years. True, in more than one hundred years, no second baseman has exceeded his 1886 total of 529 putouts. And true, he also holds the career mark in putouts with 6,545, ranks fourth in assists with 6,905, and second in total chances with 14,241. But what are those things compared to stories of droll nights on the town or a few hundred home runs? What a yawn! No wonder he's not in the Hall of Fame.

Hal McRae

DH/Outfielder, Cin (N) 1968, 1970–72, KC (A) 1973–87

McRae became a star with the Kansas City Royals as a designated hitter. He was named the top DH in the AL five times. Perhaps only Don Baylor rivals him at that job. McRae, a disciple of the Charlie Lau school of hitting, managed to combine good home run power (191 career homers) with a good batting average (.290 lifetime). His 133 RBIs in 1982 were the most ever by a DH and won him the nickname of "Mr. Ribbie" among teammates.

He hit a career-high .332 in 1976 but was narrowly nosed out for the batting title by teammate George Brett. An inside-the-park home run gave Brett the title; McRae later asserted that the ball might have been caught and suggested that Brett had received favorable treatment through the season to keep the batting title in white hands. He was offered the manager's job at Kansas City in midseason of 1987 but declined because there was no assurance that he would be rehired for a full season.

Joe Medwick

Outfielder, StL (N) 1932–40, 1947–48,
Bkn (N) 1940–43, 1946, NY (N) 1943–45,
Bos (N) 1945

A rough-house, tough guy from the Cardinals' Gashouse Gang, Medwick was one of the top sluggers of the 1930s. A notorious bad-ball hitter, he led the NL in RBIs three straight years, 1936–38, and won the batting Triple Crown in 1937 (.374, 31, 154). He was named MVP that year.

He picked up the odd nickname "Ducky Wucky" in the minors because of his unusual waddle.

In the seventh game of the 1934 World Series, he slid hard into the Tigers' third baseman—too hard, thought Tiger fans, who pelted him with garbage until Commissioner Landis ordered him out of the game.

Sold to the Dodgers for $125,000 in 1940, he helped them win the 1941 pennant but suffered a near-fatal beaning by former teammate Bob Bowman. Though he recovered and played until 1948, he was never the same hitter he had been.

His career totals include a .324 batting average, 202 home runs, and 1,383 RBIs.

In 1968 he was elected to the Hall of Fame.

Jose Mendez

Pitcher, Negro League, 1908–26, Cuban Stars,
Stars of Cuba, All Nations, Los Angeles White Sox,
Chicago American Giants, Detroit Stars,
Kansas City Monarchs

Baseball's troubadour of the tropics, Mendez was an outstanding Cuban pitcher in the early twentieth century. His success against touring major league clubs made him a national hero. Among others, he won games against Eddie Plank in 1910 and Christy Mathewson in 1911. In 1908 he beat the Cincinnati Reds three times, without allowing a run in twenty-five innings. In the summers, Mendez played with the U.S. multiracial All Nations club, the forerunner of the Kansas City Monarchs. Late in his career, as manager of the Monarchs, he put himself in to pitch the final game of the 1924 Black World Series and won, 5–0. Musically talented, Mendez played the cornet for dances after games and later traveled the Caribbean, playing the guitar and teaching baseball.

Andy Messersmith

Pitcher, Cal (A) 1968–72, LA (N) 1973–75, 1979,
Atl (N) 1976–77, NY (A) 1978

Every player today should say a prayer of thanks to Messersmith. It was he, along with Dave McNally, who overturned the sacrosanct reserve clause, leading to the present six-year re-entry draft that has made millionaires of .240 hitters.

He was an excellent pitcher when healthy, winning 20 games for the Angels in 1971. He was traded to the Dodgers after the 1972 season and had a brilliant 20–6 mark in 1974. It was then that he and McNally challenged the reserve clause in their contracts that forced them to re-sign the next year with the same team. Five years earlier Curt Flood had filed suit in an attempt to overturn the clause but had lost in the Supreme Court by a narrow vote. This time the players won on a split decision. The ruling was that by playing the 1975 season without signing contracts, they had fulfilled their "option year." Although McNally chose to retire, Messersmith signed with Atlanta in 1976 for a huge salary increase. Unfortunately a sore arm limited his effectiveness with the Braves, but he had opened the door to free agentry for all players.

Marvin Miller

Labor Negotiator

Miller, "the players' commissioner," was the enemy of the owners and the real commissioner, but fewer than half a dozen men have turned the baseball world upside down as he did. In 1981 he led the first extended players' strike in history, ushering in a new era in baseball negotiations. A labor economist with the steelworkers' union, Miller was chosen by the players to head their union in 1966, in the most serious challenge to the owners' control since the Players League in 1890.

Miller negotiated five labor contracts with the owners. In the first the owners increased their contribution to the pension fund, increased the minimum major league salary, and agreed to reconsider the reserve clause. The second recognized the Major League Players Association as the official bargaining agent for players (except with regard to salaries), allowed players to be represented by agents when negotiating salaries, and permitted arbitration in disputes that could not be otherwise settled.

In 1972 Miller led a brief strike to force the negotiation of a third contract. This one extended arbitration and resulted in a further increase in salaries.

In 1975, when Andy Messersmith and Dave McNally were declared free agents by a federal court (by having played out the option years of their contracts), the reserve clause was dead. Miller's fourth contract compromised by limiting free agency to six-year veterans, who would become available through re-entry drafts.

Again salaries soared. Owners demanded compensation for players lost to free agency, and this led to the 1981 strike of fifty days. Again Miller reached a compromise; owners were to receive some compensation in the form of established players from a general pool, but the union had proved its strength. Miller retired in 1984.

Minnie Minoso

Thirdbase, Negro League, 1946–48, New York Cubans,
outfielder, Cle (A) 1949–51, 1958–59, Chi (A) 1951–57,
1960–61, 1964, 1976, 1980, StL (N) 1962, Was (A) 1963

Minoso didn't have a full season in the majors until he was twenty-eight, but when he burst on the scene with the Go-Go White Sox in 1951, he immediately became one of the most exciting players in the AL. He led in stolen bases, 1951–53, in triples three times, in doubles once, and once in hits. He compiled a career batting average of .298, lashed out 1,963 hits, and had 1,023 RBIs, most of it crammed into eleven exciting seasons.

Of the seventeen seasons he is credited with playing, one was a nine-game "cup of coffee" in 1949, two were fan-pleasing, end-of-season returns in 1976 and 1980, and three were as a reserve in the early 1960s, when he was over forty years old.

Johnny Mize

First Baseman, StL (N) 1936–41,

NY (N) 1942, 1946–49, NY (A) 1949–53

Mize won four home run crowns, three RBI titles, a batting championship, and finished among the top three in various offensive categories a total of fifty-four times. His 51 homers with the Giants in 1947 are an NL record for lefthanded hitters. The burly first baseman slugged 359 career home runs, hitting three in a game six different times. His .312 batting average and 1,337 RBIs mark him as one of baseball's great sluggers.

In both 1939 and 1940 he finished second in the voting for the NL MVP. In 1939 he led in homers (28) and batting average (.349); the next year he topped in homers (43) and RBIs (137).

After a long career with the Cardinals and Giants, "the Big Cat" joined the Yankees in mid-1949 as a part-time first baseman and full-time pinch hitter. In 1952 he became the second man in World Series history to pinch-hit a home run. For the entire Series he batted .400, with 3 homers and a slugging average of 1.067.

Mize was named to the Hall of Fame in 1981.

Joe Morgan

Second Baseman, Hou (N) 1963–71, 1980,
Cin (N) 1972–79, SF (N) 1981–82, Phi (N) 1983,
Oak (A) 1984

Little Joe stood only five-seven but he played more games at second base than any man but Eddie Collins and won back-to-back MVPs in 1975–1976.

Morgan began his career with Houston, where he twice scored over 100 runs and developed an ability to draw walks. Traded to Cincinnati in 1972, he came into his own as an offensive star with the Big Red Machine. In 1975 he won his first MVP with a .327 batting average, 17 homers, 107 runs scored, 94 RBIs, and 67 stolen bases. The next year he hit .320, with 27 homers, 113 runs scored, 111 RBIs, and 60 stolen bases.

For his career, he hit 268 home runs, scored 1,651 runs, and batted in 1,134. He stole 689 bases and is third all-time in walks with 1,865.

In the field, Morgan won five Gold Gloves, and in 1977–1978 put together a string of 91 straight games without an error. Still, the stubborn fact is that Joe was not a great fielder. Apparently the writers went on form and not substance in voting him those Gold Gloves. For instance, he led the league in assists only once, a sign that he didn't cover a great deal of ground.

But above all, Morgan was a winner. He led the Reds to five division titles and three World Series. After signing with Houston in 1980, he took them to a division title. And in 1983 he was one of several veterans (they were called "the Wheeze Kids") who brought the Phillies a pennant.

Jack Morris

Pitcher, Det (A) 1977–

Jack is the workhorse of two Tiger champions, 1984 and 1987. Always near the top in innings pitched, he won 20 games twice—20–13 in 1983 and 21–8 in 1986. He also led the AL in victories in the strike-shortened 1981 season, going 14–7. In the 1980s, as this is written, no AL pitcher had won more games.

Morris's ERAs were not spectacular, but he was a master at preventing unearned runs, especially in the postseason.

A convert to the split-fingered fastball, Morris had a no-hitter going into the ninth inning in Chicago in 1984. A fan tried to jinx him by yelling about the no-hitter. "I know, I'm working on it," Jack shot back, "and I'm going to get it too." And he did.

Thurman Munson

Catcher, NY (A) 1969–79

A fiery plane crash on August 2, 1979, cut short Munson's career after slightly less than ten full seasons and knocked the bottom out of the Yankees' team. The Yankees' captain was an outstanding catcher in the tradition of Bill Dickey, Yogi Berra, and Elston Howard.

He led New York to three straight pennants, 1976–1978, and was voted the AL MVP in 1976, when he batted .302, hit 17 homers, and drove in 105 runs.

A basketball star in college, Munson was fast enough to bat second in the lineup. He packed a home run punch in his bat, but was primarily a line drive hitter.

Munson hit .302 and was AL Rookie of the Year in 1970. He was named to the AL All-Star team in 1971 and then every year from 1973 to '78. A durable backstop, he played at least 125 games a year from his rookie season until his death; his total of 1,423 games exceeds those of several excellent catchers who played far longer. His career batting average was .292.

At the close of the memorable pennant race of 1978, in the playoff versus Kansas City, he trumped Brett's three homers with a two-run shot of his own in the eighth to win the third game.

In the World Series a year earlier, Munson had nearly matched Bench's .533 with a .529 of his own in a battle of super catchers.

He was a proud man with a venomous tongue, and he bridled in 1977, when Reggie Jackson joined the team at a higher salary. The angry energy that flared between the two men nevertheless spurred the dissension-ridden Yanks to two flags.

Dale Murphy

Outfielder, Atl (N) 1976–

Nice guys may not always finish last, but Murphy, one of baseball's nicest people, has had little luck in NL pennant races. In eleven seasons as a Braves' regular, the best his team has done is one appearance in the 1982 League Championship Series. No one has blamed Murph.

The righthanded slugger came to the Braves as a catcher but was switched to first base in 1978, his first season as a regular. Two years later he was moved again, this time to center field, where he became one of the best.

His strong suit is his powerful bat. He won back-to-back

MVP Awards in 1982–1983, leading the NL in RBIs and slugging average both years. In 1984–1985, he led in homers. He's paid the price for his more than 330 homers, striking out over 100 times in nine different seasons.

Eddie Murray

First Baseman, Bal (A) 1977–

One of the better power hitters of the 1980s, Murray averaged over 100 RBIs per season for his first eleven seasons, yet led the AL only once—in the strike-shortened 1981 season. He also tied for the lead in homers that season with 22. Probably the most powerful switch-hitter since Mickey Mantle, Murray was the model of consistency for Baltimore until injuries cut into his homer and RBI titles. Fans who had cheered him on with cries of "Ed-dee, Ed-dee!" turned against him and booed. Murray demanded a trade, and generally handled the situation poorly. Though he played in only two World Series (1979, 1983), he had the Orioles in the thick of six pennant races. His batting average in those Septembers was .318, says *Sports Illustrated*'s Peter Gammons.

Murray, who commands a multimillion dollar salary, donates a generous portion of it to provide summer camps for city kids in memory of his mother.

Stan "The Man" Musial

Outfielder/First Baseman, StL (N) 1941–44, 1946–63

At one time Musial held almost every NL batting record except homers, and he was close to that too—some fifty major league and NL marks. His 3,630 career hits were second only to Cobb. Now Rose, Aaron, Mays, and others have passed most of them.

Popular with fans and writers alike, Stan was three times MVP, four times coming in second. He used an odd, "peek-a-boo" batting stance—lefthanded, curled up, almost as if he was looking around a corner, his bat barrel held back and straight up. It worked for him. Stan led the NL seven times in batting.

Son of a Polish immigrant miner, Stan started as a minor league pitcher until he hurt his arm and switched to the outfield.

After playing twelve end-of-season games for the Cardinals in 1941, he led them to the world championship in 1942. He specialized in doubles and triples, and won two batting championships in his first four years (not counting Navy service in 1945). The Cards were NL champs all four of those seasons and world champs three of them.

In 1948 Stan suddenly blossomed as a home run threat. His batting average, doubles, and triples stayed high too. He was slugging average champion three times before the change and three times after it.

Musial won his last batting title in 1957 at the age of thirty-six (.351).

As a forty-one-year-old grandfather in 1962, he could still hit .330, third best in the league.

Stan once hit five homers in a doubleheader. His most famous home run won the 1955 All-Star Game in the twelfth inning. "I'll get you out of here in a hurry," he told Yogi Berra, the AL catcher, then whacked the first pitch over the wall.

His career totals: .331, 475 home runs, 725 doubles, 177 triples, 1,949 runs, and 1,951 RBIs.

He was elected to the Hall of Fame in 1969.

Graig Nettles

Third Baseman, Min (A) 1967–69, Cle (A) 1970–72, NY (A) 1973–83, SD (N) 1984–86, Atl (N) 1987, Mon (N) 1988–

One of the best glove men to play third base, Nettles finally began winning Gold Gloves when Brooks Robinson retired, although he'd been an acknowledged master for several years. His eye-popping stops in the 1978 World Series were a big factor in the Yankee victory. And Series watchers saw him pull his spectacular act again in 1981. Only Robinson played more games at third or accepted more fielding chances.

Although his lifetime batting average is below .250, Graig hit with power. His nearly 400 homers put him third among third basemen, after Mike Schmidt and Eddie Mathews. He led the AL in homers with 32 in 1976 and followed with a career-high 37 the next season.

Don Newcombe

Pitcher, Negro League, 1944–45, Newark Eagles; Bkn (N) 1949–51, 1954–57, LA (N) 1958, Cin (N) 1958–60, Cle (A) 1960

Big Don was Rookie of the Year with the Dodgers in 1949, with a 17–8 mark and an NL-leading five shutouts. He jumped to 19–11 in 1950 and 20–9 in '51. Then he lost two years to the Army. It took the 1954 season to get him back to where he'd been, but in the next two seasons, he was brilliant: 20–5 and 27–7 to win the first Cy Young Award.

Suddenly, in 1957, he struggled. The next year he slipped further and was traded to Cincinnati. After a brief comeback to 13–8 with the sixth-place Reds in 1959, he fell off the charts.

After his brilliant beginning, Newk finished his career with a disappointing 149–90 record.

The problem was alcohol. It ruined his career and nearly his life. But, heroically, he pulled himself back and now counsels other baseball alcoholics as a member of the Dodgers' front office.

Hal Newhouser

Pitcher, Det (A) 1939–53, Cle (A) 1954–55

Wrongly stigmatized as a wartime phenom, Newhouser was actually the AL's top lefthander for the 1940s. Ted Williams called him one of the three best hurlers he ever faced. Other stars played part or all of the war years without having their records denigrated. But Newhouser was so dominant in 1944–1945 that it's sometimes forgotten he had two 20-win years and won more than half of his 207 career victories after the war.

In 1944 he overcame the wildness that had plagued him in

his first seasons with the Tigers. He was voted AL MVP for his 29–9 record and 2.22 ERA. The next year he was 25–9 and led the AL in shutouts (8) and ERA (1.81). The Tigers won the AL pennant in 1945, and though he didn't pitch well in the World Series win over the Cubs, he was still credited with 2 victories. In both 1944 and 1945 he led the AL in strikeouts.

The stars were all back in 1946, but Newhouser sailed on. He had the most wins of any pitcher at 26–9 and again led the league in ERA with 1.94. He had his greatest strikeout year at 275, but finished second to Bob Feller's 348. "Prince Hal" was the AL's top winner again in 1948, with 21.

Charles "Kid" Nichols

Pitcher, Bos (N) 1890–1901, StL (N) 1904–05,
Phi (N) 1905–06. Manager, StL (N) 1904–05

Perhaps the best of the pre-1900 pitching greats, Nichols' seven straight seasons of 30 or more wins is topped by no one. He won 20 or more games for ten straight seasons and had eleven 20-win seasons altogether.

Pitching without a windup, "Kid" had control and speed but no curve. He took over as ace of the Bostons in 1890 at the age of twenty and pitched them to five pennants, 1891–93 and 1897–98.

His best year was 1892 (35–16). He won 3 complete game victories in three days in September, then in the Temple Cup playoff against second-place Cleveland, he dueled Cleveland ace Cy Young (36–11) for eleven scoreless innings before darkness forced a stoppage of play.

Nichols was 30–14 for a fourth-place team in 1896. The next year he beat the Orioles two out of three in September to clinch a flag. His 30-win streak was finally broken in 1898— he won 29.

Seventh all-time in wins, with a 360–203 record, the Kid also notched 533 complete games for fourth on the all-time list. In 502 games with Boston, he was relieved only 25 times.

Phil Niekro

Pitcher, Mil (N) 1964–65, Atl (N) 1966–83, 1987,
NY (A) 1984–85, Cle (A) 1986–87, Tor (A) 1987

For twenty-four years, to the age of forty-eight, Niekro tossed his knuckler, most of the time for weak Atlanta teams in a notorious hitters' park. When he approached win number 300, some experts were surprised; they'd never thought of him as a star. But he was. Hitters knew it long before the writers suspected. Bobby Murcer said hitting Niekro's knuckler was like "eating jelly with chopsticks."

For his 300th win, Phil decided not to throw a single knuckler—until the last batter, when he struck Jeff Burroughs out with three of them.

Not only did Phil win 318, he saved 30 others, a rarity for modern starters. Among his 274 losses were 47 shutouts— only Johnson and Young had more.

Niekro wandered seven years in the minors and didn't become a regular starter with the Braves until 1967 when he was twenty-eight. He led the NL with a 1.87 ERA that season and was 11–9 with seventh-place Atlanta.

Niekro's club—the Braves—held him down. Atlanta finished last six times with him, and he led the league in defeats four times, a record. He somehow managed to win 20 three times. In 1979 he led the NL in both wins and losses with a 21–20 mark.

Phil's home park also hurt. It was part of the reason he led the league four times in throwing gopher pitches.

Phil was 23–13 in 1969 to lead Atlanta to the division title.

He holds the record for most wins after the age of forty— 121. He's the second-oldest man (forty-three and a half) to hit a homer.

When he retired in 1987 he had 3,342 strikeouts and was third all-time in bases on balls, fourth in innings pitched, and first in wild pitches, 200. He once threw 6 wild ones in one game—four in one inning.

Pedro "Tony" Oliva

Outfielder, Min (A) 1962–76

There's no telling what the Oliva's batting marks might have been if he'd had a healthy knee. Instead, he had five operations, each one slowing him down a little more. As a Minnesota rookie in 1964, he lined out 217 hits, the AL rookie record. He also tied the rookie mark for total bases and, incidentally, led in batting, .323. Naturally, he was Rookie of the Year.

Tony led the league in batting the next year too, as the Twins won the flag and almost won the Series. He tied Johnny Pesky's mark of leading the league in hits each of his first two seasons.

And then he hurt his knee. Two subpar seasons followed, but by 1969 he was back over .300.

In 1971 Oliva was having his best year ever, .375, when he fell and hurt his knee again. His average dropped to .337, and though he hung on to win his third batting title, he was through as an outfielder and as a great hitter. He became exclusively a DH until he finally retired in 1976 with a career average of .304 and 220 home runs.

Incidentally, he was born Pedro Oliva and became Tony when he used his brother's passport to get out of Cuba. A third brother, Juan Carlos, stayed in Havana and became one of Cuba's top pitchers.

James "Orator Jim" O'Rourke

Outfielder, Middletown (NA) 1872,
Bos (NA) 1873–75, Bos (N) 1876–78, 1880, Prov (N) 1879,
Buf (N) 1881–84, NY (N) 1885–89, 1891–92, 1904,
NY (P) 1890, Was (N) 1893.
Manager, Buf (N) 1881–84, Was (N) 1893

O'Rourke reportedly had only average speed and a weak arm, but he was a star in the National Association for four seasons before the National League was formed, averaging .317. He helped the Boston Red Stockings to five pennants (three in the National Association), then switched to Providence and helped them win a flag in 1879. Ten years later he was the regular left fielder for the New York Giants champions of 1888–89. In between, he spent four seasons as player-manager of Buffalo's NL club.

From 1876 on, he hit over .300 in eleven major league seasons, averaging .310. After retiring he managed and umpired, and at the age of 52 caught a nine-inning game for the Giants, their pennant clincher in 1904. He even got his 2,304th major league hit and scored his 1,446th run.

And *then* he became president of a minor league.

His nickname stemmed from his Yale Law School background and his flowery, bombastic speech.

In 1945 he was named to the Baseball Hall of Fame.

Amos Otis

Outfielder, NY (N) 1967, 1969, KC (A) 1970–83,
Pit (N) 1984

Otis is another underrated player. He helped Kansas City win four division titles and one World Series between 1976 and 1980. He hit a strong .277, with 193 home runs and 1,008 RBIs. He hit .429 in the 1978 League Championship Series in a futile effort to upset the Yanks.

Two years later Amos hit .333, as the Royals won the LCS. He then hit .478 in the World Series against Philadelphia, including a home run in Game Five to bring Kansas City to within one run of victory.

Otis was one of the best baserunners of his day. When he led the AL in stolen bases in 1971 with 52, he was caught only eight times. The year before that he had done even better with 33 out of 34—the only time they caught him was on a steal of home.

He was a fine fielder too. In his first two years, 1970–71, he went 165 straight games without an error. He led the league's outfielders in putouts, double plays, and total chances both years.

Mel Ott

Outfielder, NY (N) 1926–47.
Manager, NY (N) 1942–48

With his quick, distinctive leg kick as he stepped into the ball, Ott used to golf high flies into the chummy upper deck of the Polo Grounds, 256 feet away. He hit almost two thirds of his homers at home. When he retired after twenty-two seasons, he had 511 homers, the third highest total at the time, and a .304 career average. He set new NL career records for runs (1,859), RBIs (1,860), and walks (1,708). The run and RBI marks were first broken by Stan Musial; the walks by Joe Morgan.

Ott's famous leg kick helped him compensate for his lack of size; he weighed only 165–170 pounds. It was a graceful kick, unlike that of Sadaharu Oh, who lifted his front knee and pulled his foot back with his bat cocked forward. Mel lifted his front foot high, his weight perfectly balanced on the fulcrum of his bat handle at his belt. Babe Ruth, Ducky Medwick, Rudy York, and other big men used modified versions of it.

Ott arrived in New York with a straw suitcase at the age of sixteen and adopted Manager John McGraw as a father. He stayed to become one of the Giants' all-time most popular players and six-time home run champ.

Six times Mel led the league in walks and ten times drew 100 or more. Four times he drew 5 walks in one game; the first time was on the final day of the 1929 season, when Phillies pitchers gave him five intentional walks, one with the bases loaded, so he couldn't tie Philadelphia's Chuck Klein for the homer title.

Mel hit .389 in the 1933 World Series and won the deciding game with a home run in the tenth inning. It was his eighth season on the Giants, though he was only twenty-five years old.

Ott became player-manager of the Giants in 1942. It was in reference to Ott that Leo Durocher made his famous pronouncement that "Nice guys finish last."

He was elected to the Baseball Hall of Fame in 1951.

Leroy "Satchel" Paige

Pitcher, Negro League, 1926–50, Chattanooga Black Lookouts, Birmingham Black Barons, Cleveland Cubs, Pittsburgh Crawfords, Kansas City Monarchs, New York Black Yankees, Satchel Paige's All-Stars, Philadelphia Stars, Cle (A) 1948–50, StL (A) 1951–53, KC (A) 1965

If Satch wasn't the greatest black pitcher of all time (and many say he was), he was by far the most famous. He began pitching semipro in 1924, and made his professional debut in 1926, age twenty-two; he was 9–6 the next year, and pitched the Birmingham Black Barons into the playoffs. His white major league debut was in 1948 with Cleveland, age forty-two; he was 6–1, set attendance records, and helped the Indians to the pennant. When they said he should be Rookie of the Year, he asked what year they meant.

Satch got his name from toting bags at the Mobile railroad station at the age of seven. He got his hesitation pitch from throwing rocks at other kids, fooling them into ducking too soon. After a stretch in reform school for stealing toys, Satchel learned his control from Black Baron vets who taught him to throw over a Coke bottle cap until he could "nip frosting off a cake." Satch called it his "be ball," " 'cause it be where I want it to be." He got his fastball from the Lord.

Joining the Pittsburgh Crawfords in 1931, Paige teamed with Josh Gibson in one of the greatest batteries of all time. In 1934 he led all Negro League pitchers with a 16–2 mark and threw a 17-strikeout no-hitter against the Homestead Grays. Barnstorming in the offseason, he dueled many a game against Dizzy Dean and later Bob Feller. Much of his pitching was on tour, traveling packed into a car, knees against chin, to prairie towns, where, "if I didn't pitch, they didn't want the team—in *town*, let alone the park." From there he sailed to Latin America, where his fabled bronze arm went dead.

The Kansas City Monarchs took a chance on him, and Paige miraculously pitched his arm back into shape. He usually pitched two or three innings a night to draw a crowd. One of his great moments came when he deliberately walked the bases "drunk" to face his old buddy Gibson, then whiffed Josh. In the 1942 Series against the Grays, he and Hilton Smith held Josh to a .125 average and swept all 4 games.

Satch loved fast cars and fast women. He was always dallying, then racing to the park, police sirens screaming either in escort or pursuit. Fined twenty-five dollars for speeding, he peeled off fifty dollars and told the judge, "Here. I'm comin' back tomorrow."

When Satch signed with Cleveland for the 1948 pennant

stretch, *The Sporting News* called it a publicity stunt. "Everybody told me he was through," said the Indians' boss, Bill Veeck. "That was understandable. They thought he was human." Satch pitched a shutout in his second start, drew two hundred thousand fans to his first three starts, plus thousands more who couldn't get in.

In 1951 Veeck took Satch to the Browns, where he had his own rocking chair in the bullpen and could still win 12 games and save 10. Finally, in 1965, aged fifty-nine, Paige pitched three innings for the Kansas City Athletics to draw a bonus, the oldest man ever to pitch in the majors. He allowed one hit.

Satch's wit has entered the language. His most famous saying is "Never look back. Something may be gaining on you."

Jim Palmer

Pitcher, Bal (A) 1965–67, 1969–84

Winner of three Cy Youngs, Palmer won 20 games eight times and helped the Orioles win six flags. The handsome righthander is the greatest jockey shorts salesman in baseball history, and his seminude posters advertising underwear are almost as famous in Europe and Asia as they are in the United States.

Jim won 268 games despite suffering a sore arm after shutting out the Dodgers as a twenty-year-old in the 1966 Series. The injury kept him out of the majors for virtually two years.

When he got back, Palmer won 20 or more four straight seasons, from 1970 to 1973. After an off-year, he put together another four-straight, 20-plus streak, 1975–78. He won three Cy Young awards, 1973, 1975, and 1976. He led the AL in ERA in 1973 and '75.

Throughout his career, Jim shared a stormy, symbiotic relationship with Manager Earl Weaver. They yelled at each other but respected each other and, in the end, helped each other achieve greatness.

As a high fastball pitcher, Palmer gave up a lot of home runs—but never a grand slam.

He was also excellent in preventing unearned runs, a neglected side of pitching. He modestly says that's because he gave up few ground balls to make errors on. But his World Series record shows that, even when his mates did kick a ball, Jim slammed the door.

Dave Parker

Outfielder, Pit (N) 1973–83, Cin (N) 1984–87, Oak (A) 1988–

Parker's career divides into three distinct stages.

First, 1975–1979: the superstar. Starting with his first full year, Parker was a .300 hitter, with back-to-back NL batting championships in 1977 and 1978, 30 home runs in 1978, MVP in the 1979 All-Star Game, a leader of the 1979 World Championship team, and a reputation as a hustling "complete" player, with speed and the best right field arm in baseball.

Second, 1980–1983: the disappointment. After signing a five-year $5-million contract to become the highest-paid player in baseball, his batting average and power fell off alarmingly, as did his availability. He was constantly injured and obviously overweight. He reacted to criticism by Pittsburgh fans by criticizing the fans. He became arguably the most unpopular player ever to wear a Pirate uniform. One day he was nearly skulled by a battery thrown from the stands. Only later was it learned that he had become deeply involved in drug abuse.

Third, 1984–?: the aging slugger: Parker signed with Cincinnati as a free agent. Given a new start, he apparently conquered his addiction and produced excellent power stats for the Reds, twice topping 30 homers and leading the NL in RBIs in 1985. No longer an all-around player, he was traded to Oakland for 1988 as a prospective DH. A thumb injury cut into his season, but he showed flashes of home run power.

Roger Peckinpaugh

Shortstop, Cle (A) 1910–13, NY (A) 1913–21, Was (A) 1922–26, Chi (A) 1927. Manager, NY (A) 1914, Cle (A) 1928–33, 1941

Peckinpaugh was a fine-fielding shortstop with bad luck. In the eight years he played for the Yankees he led AL shortstops in assists three times. In any later age, that sort of range would have had him canonized by the New York media, but Roger did his work in those years when the Giants were *the* team in New York and the Yankees were a distant "other." The Yanks won the pennant in 1921, his last season with them, but the Giants beat them in the World Series, as Peckinpaugh's error let in the winning run in the final game.

Traded to Washington, he helped the Senators win a pennant and World Series in 1924, but his contributions were overshadowed by those of the "Boy Manager," Bucky Harris, and Walter Johnson, who finally had the chance to pitch for a winner after years with poor teams.

Peckinpaugh was a liability at bat early in his career, but gradually improved to ordinary. He actually hit .305 in 1919. In 1925 he hit a sprightly .294 and fielded brilliantly all season to lead the Senators to another pennant. This time he was named AL MVP just before the World Series.

But the 1925 Series was a nightmare for Roger. By the eighth inning of the final game, he had made 7 errors. Suddenly, in the top of the eighth, he became a hero—he hit a home run to put the Senators in the lead. Alas! In the bottom of the eighth, the Pirates tied the game, and poor Roger made error number 8—a Series record for any position that still stands—to keep the inning going. The Pirates scored twice more to become champions. In Peckinpaugh's greatest season, he became the World Series' greatest goat.

Herb Pennock

Pitcher, Phi (A) 1912–15, Bos (A) 1915–17, 1918–22, 1934, NY (A) 1923–33

Pennock was a smooth lefthander whose effortless style took him to a 240–162 career. Anything but overpowering, he blended curves and excellent control with the excellent bat support he usually received. Although he threw 35 shutouts over his twenty-two seasons, he was the kind of pitcher who

pitched just well enough to win. In World Series competition, he was 5–0.

He came to the big leagues right out of high school, joining the Athletics and winning 11 games for the 1914 team at age twenty. When Connie Mack dismantled his team after the loss to the Braves in the 1914 World Series, Pennock was sold to the Red Sox, another strong team. By 1920 the Sox owner began selling his stars. In 1923 Pennock was passed on to the Yankees, with whom he had his best seasons. He was 21–9 in 1924 and 23–11 in 1926, and had two other seasons with 19 wins.

At 160 pounds, Pennock was seldom a staff workhorse. He led the AL with 277 innings pitched in 1925, but he usually threw 50–60 fewer innings. He nearly always gave up more hits than innings, although his low number of walks somewhat compensated for that. He once pitched an 11-hit shutout. His career ERA of 3.61 isn't spectacular. But, while the spectacular pitchers came and went, Pennock and his soft curves prevailed.

In 1948 he was elected to the Baseball Hall of Fame.

Atanacio "Tony" Perez

First Baseman/Third Baseman, Cin (N) 1964–76, 1984–86,
Mon (N) 1977–79, Bos (A) 1980–82, Phi (N) 1983

One of the biggest cogs in the Big Red Machine of the 1970s, Perez helped put the Reds in four World Series. He knocked in 90 or more runs eleven straight seasons, 1967–1977. His career totals read 1,652 RBIs and 1,272 runs scored. He hit 379 homers, with a high of 40 in 1970. He hit .300 a couple of times and finished with a respectable .279 for twenty-three seasons. Yet, amazingly, he never led his league in a single important offensive statistic.

But he was consistent. He was also a good enough glove man to play third base for five seasons for Cincinnati so slugger Lee May could play first.

He hit .435 in the 1972 World Series. In the 1975 Series, Tony went 0 for 15, then exploded with 2 homers and 4 RBIs to win the fifth game, 6–2. He added another homer and 2 RBIs in the final game to key a 4–3 win.

Gaylord Perry

Pitcher, SF (N) 1962–71, Cle (A) 1972–75,
Tex (A) 1976–77, 1980, SD (N) 1978–79, NY (A) 1980,
Atl (N) 1981, Sea (A) 1982–83,
KC (A) 1983

The only man to win a Cy Young Award in both leagues, Perry had as much fun outwitting the umpires with his spitter as he did fooling the hitters with it. He even wrote a hilarious book about it, revealing for instance that KY Jelly and Preparation H work as well as the old standbys: spit, sweat, and Vaseline. The trick was to lubricate the fingers enough to squirt the ball out without spin, like squirting a watermelon seed. The ball then behaves like a knuckleball but is easier to control. Perry was still winning games at the age of forty-three.

Perry won 20-plus twice for the Giants in the 1960s before he was traded to the AL after the 1971 season. NL umps were

glad to see Perry go. Umpire Chris Pelekoudas gave him a giant jar of Vaseline as a going-away present.

His first year in the AL, Perry was 24–16 with the fifth-place Indians. He was the first man to top 20 in both leagues in nearly fifty years.

By 1978 he was back in the NL, where his 21–6 mark for San Diego earned him his second Cy Young. It was his fifth 20-win season.

In twenty-two years Perry played on only one division champ. With support like that, a guy needs a little extra edge to win 314 games.

Charles "Deacon" Phillippe

Pitcher, Lou (N) 1899, Pit (N) 1900–11

Phillippe was the best control pitcher in the twentieth century, giving up a stingy 1.25 walks per nine innings.

The Deacon's best year was 24–7 in 1903, his fourth 20-victory year in five years in the league. In the first World Series that fall, Phillippe pitched 5 complete games in thirteen days (a total of 44 innings pitched) and gave up only 3 walks. He won his first 3 starts in a period of six days. But he lost Game Six on ground rule triples into the crowd. The next day he pitched his fifth complete game in eleven days and was shut out, 3–0, as Boston took the Series.

The Deacon had his fifth 20-win year in 1905 and was still around to pitch 6 innings in the 1909 Series without allowing an earned run.

Billy Pierce

Pitcher, Det (A) 1945, 1948,
Chi (A) 1949–61, SF (N) 1962–64

Pierce was the epitome of "stylish lefty," the kind who looks good even when he loses. But Billy didn't lose that often. The White Sox got him and $10,000 from the Tigers in 1949 for an aging catcher. It was the kind of deal that should have got the Sox four-to-seven at Joliet.

Billy stepped in immediately as the Sox ace; that wasn't any great honor in 1949, but after Chicago added such as Nellie Fox, Minnie Minoso, and Chico Carrasquel for a few broken bats or bubble gum cards or some other trade imbalance, the White Sox became a consistent first-division team. Billy led the AL in ERA in 1955, won 20 games in 1956 and '57, and totaled 186 wins for his thirteen years with the Sox. In 1959 he helped them win their first pennant in forty years.

In 1962 he joined the Giants and led them to a flag with a record of 16–6 that included a 12–0 record at Candlestick Park.

Eddie Plank

Pitcher, Phi (A) 1901–14, StL (F) 1915, StL (A) 1916–17

Plank came out of Gettysburg College to win 327 games. He held the record for most wins by a lefthander until Warren Spahn surpassed that mark in 1963, forty-six years after Eddie retired. He won 20 or more games eight times, seven

with the Philadelphia A's and one with St. Louis of the Federal League. He pitched for six AL championship teams with the A's. He was only 2–5 in World Series games, but 4 of his losses were shutouts. His Series ERA was 1.32. He threw a lot of shutouts himself—69—the most for a lefty and fifth-best of all time.

Plank drove batters crazy *before* he threw the ball. He'd fuss around the mound, fidgeting with his uniform, talking to the ball ("Only nine more to go," etc.), shaking off signs. By the time he threw the ball, the batter was ready to swing at anything.

Of course, Plank didn't throw just anything. He had a good fastball and curve, which he delivered sidearm with good control. He struck out 2,246 batters and walked fewer than half that many. Despite all his good years, he never led the league in wins, strikeouts, or ERA.

He was named to the Baseball Hall of Fame in 1946.

Cumberland "Cum" Posey

Outfielder, Owner, Negro League, Homestead Grays, Detroit Wolves

Posey's Homestead Grays wrote a record never approached by any other U.S. pro team in any sport—they won nine straight pennants from 1937 to 1945 with Josh Gibson, Buck Leonard, and Cool Papa Bell generating the power. Only the Tokyo Giants, with nine straight Japanese championships, can match them. Yet they may not have been the greatest Grays teams of all.

The 1926 club, starring Joe Williams, won 43 straight (mostly against white semipro teams). The 1930 Grays, with Williams, Gibson, and Charleston, won 11 out of 12 from the western champion Monarchs. And the 1931 club boasted a record of 136–17, again mostly against semipros. They even challenged the white major league Pirates to a winner-take-all series, but Pittsburgh refused.

Posey's father was a wealthy barge captain, his mother the first black to graduate from Ohio State. At various times Cum attended Penn State, Pitt, and Duquesne universities, but failed to graduate from any of them. He was considered the best colored basketball player in America in 1913 and also managed the Murdock Grays, a steel mill team. Eventually he founded the Loendi Big Five, which claimed the U.S. basketball championship of 1919. He gained control of the Homestead Grays in the early 1920s, played for the team until 1928, and managed it until 1935.

But when the Depression struck, Posey lost his stars to racketeer Gus Greenlee's well-bankrolled Pittsburgh Crawfords. Cum got his own racketeer, Sonnyman Jackson, and fought back, eventually driving Greenlee out of the league.

In 1937 Cum bought Gibson back for $2,500, and the team went 152–11 to embark on their pennant streak.

The Grays shuttled between Pittsburgh and Washington by bus, playing two or three games a day, league and semi-pro. Rain could wipe out all profit for the week, until World War II brought prosperity at last. In 1945 Posey's Grays sometimes drew thirty thousand fans to Griffith Stadium hours after the AL Senators had played before three thousand in the same park.

But when baseball was at last integrated after the war, the raids of major league clubs soon destroyed Cum's life investment. Luke Easter was snatched up by the Indians for only $10,000. Posey moaned, "It's like coming into a man's store and stealing the merchandise right off the shelves."

John "Boog" Powell

First Baseman, Bal (A) 1961–74, Cle (A) 1975–76, LA (N) 1977

Powell drove some long blasts out of parks—469 feet in Baltimore in 1962, over the roof of Tiger Stadium in 1969. He and Frank Robinson provided the power that brought the Orioles four pennants and two world titles between 1966 and 1971. Big Boog (six-four, 230 pounds) crushed 339 home runs, with a high of 39 in 1964.

Boog hit .357 in the 1966 World Series as Baltimore swept the Dodgers in four straight. In 1969 he hit .385 to help sweep Minnesota in the LCS and .429 to key the sweep again a year later. In the 1970 Series his home runs won the first two games to get the O's off to a five-game victory over the Big Red Machine.

Del Pratt

Second Baseman, StL (A) 1912–17, NY (A) 1918–20, Bos (A) 1921–22, Det (A) 1923–24

Pratt had a knack for picking losers. He went from the 1912 Browns to the 1918 Yanks, 1921 Red Sox, and 1923 Tigers, spending most of his thirteen-year career in the second division.

Del was a fair singles hitter with a high of .324 in 1921. Curiously, he hit .302 as a Browns' rookie, then missed that level for seven straight seasons. But in 1920, with the livelier ball, he suddenly remembered how to do it and hit over .300 in each of his last five seasons, bowing out with .302 in 1924. Another oddity about Pratt was that he played over 100 games in each of his seasons. He quit with 1,996 hits; if he'd been keeping track, he might have tried to hang around for one more year.

He was a good glove man, although he slowed down rapidly near the end. He led AL second basemen in putouts five times.

He was somewhat of a clubhouse lawyer and was traded away from the Yankees following the 1920 season after a dispute over the division of New York's World Series money for finishing in third place in the AL. The Yankees won the pennant in 1921 and Pratt's new team, Boston, finished fifth, reducing his bonus to nothing. Well, penny wise and pound foolish . . .

The way Pratt got to the Yankees was that he and a teammate sued the Browns' owner for calling them "lazy" and intimating they lost games purposely. The players settled out of court and then—surprise! surprise!—were traded.

John Picus "Jack" Quinn

Pitcher, NY (A) 1909–12, 1919–21, Bos (N) 1913, Bal (F) 1914–15, Chi (A) 1918, Bos (A) 1922–25,

Phi (A) 1925–30, Bkn (N) 1931–32,
Cin (N) 1933

An old spitballer, Quinn pitched almost 1,000 pro games in almost thirty years, 1907–1935. He hit his last home run in the majors at the age of forty-six and won his last game when he was forty-seven. Or maybe forty-seven and forty-eight—there's a disagreement as to when he was born. Anyway, he was old! Spitballers, like knuckleballers, tend to have long careers.

Trapped in a coal mine fire as a youth, Jack had a checkered baseball career. He bounced around the Yanks (Highlanders) when they were down, 1909–1912, the minors, the Federal League, the Yanks again when they were rebuilding, 1919–1921, the Red Sox when they were down, 1922–1924, then caught the A's on the upswing, 1925–1930. He hurled two Series games in 1930 at the age of forty-six (or thereabouts)—the oldest man to do so.

During all that time, he kept his spitball low and usually over the plate. His only 20-win season was with the Feds in 1914, which makes it a bit suspect, but he won 18 three times in the AL. Well, no one ever said he was great, just good for a long, long time.

Dan Quisenberry

Pitcher, KC (A) 1979–88, StL (N) 1988

The submarine baller Quisenberry was baseball's premier reliever of the 1980s, leading the AL in saves five years out of six, 1980–1985. He was Fireman of the Year four times and was one of the top reasons Kansas City got into four playoffs in that period.

Calling himself "just a garbage man," Quiz saved 45 in 1983, a record until Dave Righetti of the Yankees topped it in 1986.

Dan has a dry sense of humor. "I have seen the future," he was fond of saying. "It is much like the present, only longer." As for his underhand style, he shrugged. "I found a delivery in my flaw."

Dick Radatz

Pitcher, Bos (A) 1962–66, Cle (A) 1966–67,
Chi (N) 1967, Det (A) 1969, Mon (N) 1969

For nearly four years, 1962–1965, Fenway Park's leftfield wall was only the second-most-fearsome "Monster" in Red Sox land. Number one was the six-six, 250-pound fastballer who stomped in from the bullpen and turned batters to mush. Radatz won two Fireman of the Year Awards for the Red Sox, 1962 and 1964, when he led the AL in saves. He led in relief wins three straight years, 1962–1964. His 16 relief wins in 1964 set an AL record (since broken).

The Monster intimidated hitters, averaging more than a strikeout an inning, and after every win he'd shove his fist triumphantly into the air. And just when they didn't think he could get any better, he lost it. As soon as he lost a foot off his fastball, he was done. He didn't have anything else to throw.

His final figures: 52–43 and 122 saves—100 in four years.

Charles "Ol' Hoss" Radbourn

Pitcher, Buf (N) 1880, Pro (N) 1881–85,
Bos (N) 1886–89, Bos (P) 1890, Cin (N) 1891

Radbourn was hardly a "hoss." He stood only five-nine and weighed 168. But he earned his name by winning 60 games in one year, 1884—that's 678 innings, over 441 strikeouts, and a 1.38 ERA. He won the NL pennant for Providence. By season's end he was pitching every day until he could barely lift his arm to comb his hair. Then he won three more against the AA champs in the freezing cold in the championship series.

Hoss had a great curveball. He also had an "in-shoot," or screwball. He delivered both underhand, although overhand pitching had been legalized that year. The pitching distance was only fifty feet, but batters could ask for a high or low ball, in effect cutting the strike zone in half.

Charlie had already won 31 in 1882 and 49 in 1883 when the historic 1884 season with Providence began.

The temperamental Radbourn resented young Charlie Sweeney trying to push him out as ace. He was suspended for loafing, but when Sweeney got drunk and jumped the club, they begged Rad to come back. The only pitcher on the roster, he pitched nearly every game until Providence clinched the flag. He pitched 30 of 32 remaining games, won 26 of them—18 in a row, including 5 shutouts and 4 one-run games. His winning streak was broken when he lost, 2–0.

Rad had several more good years to bring his career record to 308–191. Then he bought a bar and retired. In 1894 he shot himself hunting, losing one eye and half his face. He ended his days in the back of a pool hall, refusing to come out. He died at the age of forty-two. Sweeney died five years later, reportedly in San Quentin on a murder rap.

Radbourn was elected to the Baseball Hall of Fame in 1939.

Tim Raines

Outfielder, Mon (N) 1979–

Raines may be the top player in the NL in the 1980s. A compact switch-hitter, his main weapon is blinding speed, but he also hits with occasional power. As a rookie in 1981, he stole 71 bases in only 88 games. He led the NL in steals in his first four seasons, with a high of 90 in 1983. Entering the 1988 season, he had the best base-stealing percentage in history for players with 300 or more steals: 511 out of 585 for 87 percent. He led the league in runs scored in 1983 and 1987. In 1986, he topped the NL with a .334 batting average. He opted for free agency in 1987, but no team made a legitimate offer, an absurd situation that was later ruled to have resulted from collusion on the part of owners. They couldn't have been more obvious if they'd held a meeting on "60 Minutes." Raines eventually re-signed with Montreal, but he missed spring training and the first month of the season. When he hit .330, he set a lot of people wondering about the need for spring training.

Willie Randolph

Second Baseman, Pit (N) 1975, NY (A) 1976–

Randolph was one of the sparkplugs who drove the Yankees to five titles in six years, 1976–1981. Solid defensively and excellent on double plays, he enjoyed his best year at bat in 1980 (.294). His worst was 1981 (.232, two HRs); however, his two-run homer in the League Championship Series won the third game to clinch the pennant. Although held back by injuries the last few years, he hit a career-high .305 in 1987. One of his strengths has been that he walks about twice as often as he strikes out.

Dick Redding

Pitcher, Negro League, 1911–38, Lincoln Giants, Lincoln Stars, Indianapolis ABCs, Chicago American Giants, Brooklyn Royal Giants, Bacharach Giants

Cannonball Dick could knock the bat out of a man's hand back in the pre-World War One era. He is credited with twelve no-hitters, though this is unverified and probably mostly against semipro foes.

From 1912 to 1914 Dick teamed with Joe Williams on the Lincoln Giants to form perhaps black baseball's strongest one-two pitching punch ever. Real old-timers insist the two were both faster than the younger and more famous Satchel Paige.

Thereafter Dick and Joe became fierce rivals. In 1920 Redding beat Joe with a no-hitter at Ebbets Field in probably the finest game he ever pitched.

An illiterate Georgian, he was credited with 17 straight wins as a rookie in 1911. In 1915 he reportedly won 20 straight. He pitched the Indianapolis ABC's to a championship in 1917, then spent 1918 seeing combat service in France.

No stats were kept until the Eastern League was formed in 1923, when Dick was over the hill and managing the Brook Royals, one of the weakest clubs. He was a losing pitcher then.

He often faced Ruth and Gehrig in exhibitions; his job was to groove soft pitches to them to please the customers.

Harold "Pee Wee" Reese

Shortstop, Bkn (N) 1940–42, 1946–57, LA (N) 1958

Reese was shortstop on seven pennant-winning Dodger teams, from 1941 to 1956. An average hitter, he nevertheless led the NL in runs scored in 1949 with 132 and totaled 1,338 for his career. A good baserunner, he played during a time when base stealing was not stressed. His 30 steals led the league in 1952, and his career total of 232 stolen bases is one of the better marks for the era. He was at his best in the field and in providing leadership as captain of the team. Reese once faked a splinter in his eye to give his reliever more time to warm up. The performance was so convincing that the hurler dropped the ball and came over to see if he could help. A Southerner, one of Pee Wee's greatest accomplishments was winning Jackie Robinson's acceptance on the team.

His nickname stemmed not from his lack of size (five-ten, 160), but from the fact he was a marbles champion as a lad.

Although he hit .300 only once and never amassed exceptional stats, he finished in the top ten in MVP voting in eight of his sixteen seasons.

Reese was elected to the Baseball Hall of Fame in 1984.

Ed Reulbach

*Pitcher, Chi (N) 1905–13, Bkn (N) 1913–14,
Nwk (F) 1915, Bos (N) 1916–17*

Reulbach is the only man ever to pitch a doubleheader shutout, which he did in the stretch of the 1908 pennant race, won by the Cubs in a playoff of the Merkle game. When the Cubs' other starters came out of the hectic Giant series (that included the Merkle game) in September, exhausted, Ed agreed to pitch the doubleheader against the seventh-place Dodgers, whom he had already beaten seven times. He shut them out for eighteen innings, and the Cubs went on to win in a playoff.

Ed had pitched marathons before—in 1905 he had won an eighteen-inning game, then went twenty innings to win another.

For three years, 1906–08, Reulbach had a remarkable record—60–15. He led the league in winning percentage all three seasons (only Lefty Grove has matched that)—as the Cubs swept three pennants. In the 1906 Series against the Hitless Wonder White Sox, Ed pitched a one-hitter in Game Two.

Reulbach died July 17, 1961, the same day as Ty Cobb.

Rick Reuschel

*Pitcher, Chi (N) 1972–81, 1983–84,
NY (A) 1981, Pit (N) 1985–87, SF (N) 1987–*

Reuschel was an outstanding starter for the Cubs' throughout the 1970s, winning 20 in 1977 and 18 in 1979 for so-so teams. Traded to the Yankees in 1981, he was expected to thrive with the Yankees' bats behind him. Instead, his career was nearly ended by a sore arm. He tried a comeback with the Cubs and finally signed a minor league contract with the Pirates in 1985.

He made a remarkable comeback with the last-place Bucs, 14–8. Traded to the Giants in 1987, he helped them win their division and continued with an outstanding season in 1988, winning 19 and contending for Cy Young honors.

"Big Daddy"—he's a well-upholstered six foot three—throws with a deceptively easy motion; he almost seems to be lobbing the ball. But he has surprising velocity, good movement, changes speeds well, and has fine control.

Jim Rice

Outfielder, Bos (A) 1974–

Rice was made for Fenway Park and took advantage of it. He and Fred Lynn enjoyed splendid rookie seasons in 1975 to lift the Red Sox from ninth to the flag. An injury kept Rice out of

the World Series, which Boston lost to the Reds in seven games.

Jim's best season was the thrilling 1978 pennant race with New York, won by the Yankees in a playoff. Rice led the league in homers (46), RBIs (139), triples (15), and hits (213), with a .315 batting average. He was voted MVP over New York's Ron Guidry in a hotly debated vote.

Rice led in home runs three times and RBIs twice. On the downside, he was also among the all-time leaders in hitting into double plays. But you know who the leader is? Hank Aaron. Not bad company to be in.

Edgar "Sam" Rice

Outfielder, Was (A) 1915–33, Cle (A) 1934

Rice stopped only 13 hits short of 3,000, hit .322, topped .300 fourteen times, stole 351 bases, had good range in the outfield and a strong arm, and played on all three Washington pennant winners. He rarely struck out; in 1929 Sam came to bat 616 times and whiffed only 9 of them. He had no power; he once hit 182 singles in one season; most batters don't get that many hits.

A victim of a tragic killer tornado that killed most of his family, Sam wandered aimlessly, joining a shipping concern. As a sailor in Mexico, he began to play baseball. Rice joined the Senators as a pitcher in 1915. When Detroit hurler Hooks Dauss tripled off him, Sam cut his toe plate off forever.

In 1924 Rice put together a thirty-one-game hit streak, led the AL with 216 hits, and batted .334 as the Senators won their first pennant.

In 1925 he hit .350 and cracked 227 hits to lead the Senators into the World Series, then slapped 12 hits in the Series, a record (later broken by Bobby Richardson of the Yankees). In Game Three he made the most famous play of his life; he chased down Pirate Earl Smith's drive but fell into the stands as he reached the ball. An out or a home run? Rice would never answer directly. "The ump called him out." He would smile mysteriously. He left a letter to be opened at his death. In it, he at last answered the question. He caught the ball.

Rice was elected to the Baseball Hall of Fame in 1963.

Branch Rickey

Executive. Manager, StL (A) 1913–15, StL (N) 1919–25

Rickey invented the farm system and integrated the game. One would have been enough to put him among the five most influential men in baseball history. Rickey's decision to sign Jackie Robinson to a Dodger contract took great courage. His motives were not completely pure. Robinson, Roy Campanella, and Don Newcombe, and other black stars helped win seven pennants for the Dodgers.

Rickey had powerful fundamentalist religious scruples against playing ball on Sunday. As a player and manager, he was not available on Sundays. He wasn't missed that much as a player. He was a catcher, but he hit only .239 in 119 major league games and once was victimized for 13 stolen bases in a game. He was however a brilliant teacher and innovator. After a period as both field manager and business manager of

the Browns, he joined the Cardinals as president of the club in 1916. After 1925 he concentrated on his front office job.

In 1919 Branch conceived the farm system. Unable to outbid the rich clubs for players, he decided to grow his own, and his minor league chain was one reason for the Cardinals' five flags in nine years, 1926–1934. Eventually he had eight hundred players under contract on fifty teams.

Rickey had taken over a team $175,000 in debt and made it a champ. He also instituted ladies' day, the Knothole Gang to get kids interested in the game, the batting cage, and the sliding pit.

After the season in 1942, he moved to the Dodgers and laid the groundwork for the champions of 1947 to 1955. He eventually sold his stock in the club for a cool million.

He moved on to Pittsburgh in 1951. There Rickey left a legacy that produced a flag in 1960 after he had gone. His trial balloon of a Continental League pushed baseball to expand in the 1960s.

He was elected to the Baseball Hall of Fame in 1967.

Eppa Rixey

Pitcher, Phi (N) 1912–17, 1919–20, Cin (N) 1921–33

The winningest National League lefthander until Warren Spahn—and still the losingest—Rixey was a control artist who seldom walked anyone and seldom whiffed anyone. If Spahn hadn't broken his record, he said, nobody would have known about him. That's an exaggeration, but he seldom pitched for teams that were likely to make him a household name at World Series time.

Straight off the University of Virginia campus, Rixey began on the 1912 Phillies in the shadow of Pete Alexander. He was 11–12 on the 1915 champs and lost his only World Series game.

He was 22–10 for the second-place Phils in 1916, lost 21 for them in 1917, then went into the Army for a year in France. He lost 22 in 1920 as the Phillies finished last.

Switching to the sixth-place Reds, Rixey won 20-plus three times, including a league-leading 25–13 in 1922, when they rose to second. The six-five stringbean with a big sweeping motion was voted the Reds' all-time lefthander in a 1969 fan vote. He pitched for twenty-one years, amassing a career record of 266–251. His home run ratio, one per forty-eight innings, was the best in the Ruthian era.

He was named to the Baseball Hall of Fame in 1963.

Cal Ripken, Jr.

Shortstop, Bal (A) 1981–

Ripken is the best power-hitting shortstop since Ernie Banks. Originally a third baseman, he was switched to short in 1982, his first full year with the Orioles. When he slugged 28 home runs and batted in 93 runs, he was named Rookie of the Year. His second season was even better. He led the AL in hits (211), doubles (47), and runs (121), while hitting .318, with 27 homers and 102 RBIs. The Orioles were World Champions and Ripkin was named MVP.

Although he's been chosen on the AL All-Star team each year since 1983, his batting average and RBIs have slipped,

mirroring the Orioles' slippage in the standings. Extremely durable, Ripken had a consecutive-game streak of over 1,000 games by the end of 1988.

Phil "Scooter" Rizzuto

Shortstop, NY (A) 1941–42, 1946–56

Rizzuto played on ten Yankee pennant winners and in nine World Series. A superior fielder, he led AL shortstops in fielding in 1949 and 1950. Those were his best offensive years, too, as he scored over 100 runs each season. His 1950 season won him the MVP, as he hit .324, fifty-one points above his career average.

A Yankee broadcaster, the five-foot-six Rizzuto has remained highly visible in New York, and his "Holy cow!" has become his trademark.

As a rookie in 1941, he was called to the mound by Lefty Gomez. "Kid, is your mother in the stands?" Lefty asked. "Yes, sir, Mr. Gomez," Phil replied. "Well, stay here and talk to me a little; she'll think you're giving advice to the great Lefty Gomez." That day Phil hit his first home run and circled the bases with his face wreathed in smiles.

Robin Roberts

Pitcher, Phi (N) 1948–61,
Bal (A) 1962–65, Hou (N) 1965–66,
Chi (N) 1966

Roberts had great control and a fastball. He came close to a rare 30 wins with 28 in 1952, and came within 14 of winning 300 games.

His moment supreme came in October 1950, when he hurled the Whiz Kids to their first flag in thirty-five years. After pitcher Curt Simmons was drafted, the Phils lost their comfortable lead and went into the final game—against the Dodgers—only one game ahead. Robin, taking up the slack, was making his third start in five days. He battled Don Newcombe into the tenth inning, 1–1, before Dick Sisler's home run finally won it for Robin.

In the Series a weary Roberts started Game Two, but this time he was the loser, 2–1, in the tenth on a home run by Joe DiMaggio. It was his only World Series. Though he won 20-plus for six years in a row and led the league in five of them, the Phils never got closer than third again.

He was voted MVP in 1952, when he was 28–7 with a fourth-place team. He was 6–0 against the champion Dodgers.

Roberts had excellent control—1.7 walks per game lifetime. In 1953–1954 he had the least walks and most strikeouts per game in the NL. But he gave up more than 500 home runs, including a then-record 46 in 1956, as hitters knew they could dig in on him.

Roberts was a workhorse, leading the league in complete games and innings pitched five times each. It finally cost him the snap in his fastball. Roberts was 10–22 in 1957, 1–10 in 1961. But he learned to pitch with finesse, went to the AL, and won another 52 games.

In 1976 he was named to the Baseball Hall of Fame.

Brooks Robinson

Third Baseman, Bal (A) 1955–77

Robbie led AL third basemen in fielding average a record ten times, he won sixteen straight Gold Gloves, and he set the existing career records in assists, putouts, double plays, and fielding average. And he made some postseason plays that brought millions of viewers to their feet, cheering.

His best year at bat was 1964, when he hit .317 and led in RBIs and all the fielding categories for his position. The BBWA named him MVP. In twenty-three seasons, he had 268 homers, 1,357 RBIs, and a .267 batting average.

The postseason brought out the best in Brooks at bat as well. He hit .429 in the 1970 Series, sparkled in the field, and was named Series MVP. The next year he hit .364 in the ALCS and .318 in the Series.

Personable and extremely popular with Oriole fans, he could have been elected King of Baltimore during his playing days. He was elected to the Baseball Hall of Fame in 1983.

Frank Robinson

Outfielder, Cin (N) 1956–65, Bal (A) 1966–71,
LA (N) 1972, Cal (A) 1973–74, Cle (A) 1974–76.
Manager, Cle (A) 1975–77, SF (N) 1981–84, Bal (A) 1988–

From 1956, when he blasted 38 home runs to tie the rookie record, until 1976, when he hit his last, Robbie was one of the best-hitting outfielders of all time. His career marks include 586 homers, 1,812 RBIs, 1,829 runs, 2,943 hits, and a .294 batting average. In 1970 he hit two grand slams in a single game.

Frank is also the Jackie Robinson of managing, the first black man to lead a white big league team. He managed the Indians to two fourth-place finishes and a fifth from 1975 to 1977, and later managed San Francisco and Baltimore.

An aggressive, intelligent leader, he's the first man to win MVPs in each league—1961 with the Reds and 1966 with the Orioles. He led them both to pennants, and in the latter year, his first in the AL, won the Triple Crown as well. The two Robinsons, Frank and Brooks, provided the punch for four Oriole champions: 1966, 1969, 1970, and 1971.

In 1982 he was named to the Baseball Hall of Fame.

Jackie Robinson

Infield, Negro League, 1945, Kansas City Monarchs,
Bkn (N) 1947–56

Aggressive, exciting, driven with an inner fire, Robinson battled his opponents, history, and himself. He made integration succeed, and in doing so helped the Dodgers win six flags. Historian David Q. Voigt calls him one of the five most pivotal men in baseball history—and he ranks right up there in American history as well.

He could drop a bunt, line a homer, or steal a base—whatever was needed to win. "If it wasn't for him," the Cards' Red Schoendienst once said, "the Dodgers would be in the second division."

Jack's story is familiar: football star at UCLA, an Army

court martial (and acquittal) for refusing to sit in the back of the bus, a year with the Kansas City Monarchs (hitting .345), the surprise announcement that he would be the first black to sign in the white majors, the promise to Branch Rickey to turn the other cheek to insults, the jockeying, the knockdown pitches, the threat of a strike, and the triumphant rookie year of 1947.

Robinson was not the best black prospect, Negro Leaguers agree. But he was college-educated and had played with whites, two intangibles that Rickey sought above sheer talent.

Jackie was twenty-eight before he reached the white majors, his athletic peak behind him. Yet he revolutionized the game with his running, dancing off base to rattle the pitcher, and 19 steals of home—5 in one year. It was a new brand of ball, and blacks who followed Robinson's footsteps perfected it.

Jack's best season was 1949. He led the league in batting and stolen bases, knocked in 124 runs, and won the MVP, as the Dodgers won the pennant by a single game.

In 1951 the Dodgers were fighting to stave off the Giants' amazing drive. On the final day, against the Phils, with the bases loaded, Jack made a spectacular catch of Eddie Waitkus's drive up the middle to preserve the tie. In the fourteenth he walloped a homer to win it and end the season all tied up. The Giants, however, won the three-game playoff for the pennant, somewhat obscuring one of Robinson's greatest seasons.

Robinson played for only ten years. He finished with a .311 career batting average, but more important, he led his team to six pennants.

After retiring, Robinson became active in politics and spoke out militantly on civil rights. He was one of the first to denounce the game for not hiring black managers. At last, the tensions took their toll, the fires burned out, and he died at the age of fifty-three, leaving the game unalterably changed.

He was named to the Baseball Hall of Fame in 1962.

Wilbert Robinson

Catcher, Phi (AA) 1886–90,
Bro-Bal (AA) 1890, Bal (AA) 1891, Bal (N) 1892–99,
StL (N) 1900, Bal (A) 1901–02.
Manager, Bal (A) 1902, Bkn (N) 1914–31

Uncle Wilbert was chubby and cherubic, a former catching star with the great Orioles, later the lovable manager of Brooklyn's Daffiness Boys and winner of two pennants.

He's one of only two men to get seven hits in a nine-inning game—he drove in 11 runs that same day in 1892. A lifetime .273 hitter, Robbie had three .330-plus years with the Orioles.

In 1911 he joined his old teammate and friend John McGraw as Giant coach. His patient handling helped make an $11,000 beauty out of the former "$11,000 lemon," Rube Marquard.

But the friendship with McGraw broke up in an argument over a missed sign in the 1913 World Series, and Robbie went to manage the crosstown Dodgers. He raised attendance, started a Bonehead Club for stupid plays, and became its first member when he handed the wrong lineup card to the umpire. He agreed to catch a baseball dropped from a plane; the ball turned out to be a grapefruit and splattered all over his chest, and thinking the wet was blood Robbie though he'd

been killed. He once benched a player because he couldn't spell his name for the lineup card.

Incredibly lax as a disciplinarian, Robbie nevertheless had a knack for developing pitchers.

Robbie won Brooklyn's first twentieth-century flag in 1916. He finished fifth in 1919, hired hunchbacked Eddie Bennett as batboy, and finished first in 1920. He left Bennett home and lost the last four games of the World Series in Cleveland. He fired Eddie and fell back to fifth in 1921. He almost won again in 1924 but lost to McGraw by one and a half games.

He was elected to the Baseball Hall of Fame in 1945.

Wilbur "Bullet Joe" Rogan

Pitcher, Negro League, 1917–46, Los Angeles White Sox,
Kansas City Monarchs

Little (five-six) Rogan pitched for the Kansas City Monarchs a decade before Satchel Paige, and most black vets who saw them both believe that Joe was the better. Monarch second baseman Newt Allen said, "Satchel had the stuff, but Rogan had the brains."

Joe's 109 wins are second best for the black leagues. Satch is fourth with 100, though several of Paige's seasons have not yet been compiled, and he won 63 more in the white majors and minors. On the other hand, Rogan did not begin pitching in the big time until he was thirty.

Satch was languid and loose, Bullet Joe stocky and dour. Paige threw his fastball in a cup, Rogan threw a farago of curves, sliders, and palm balls all over the plate. Satchel was a comedian at bat, Joe hit cleanup on one of the greatest murderers' rows in blackball annals.

Casey Stengel also called Rogan "one of the best, if not the best, pitchers that ever lived." He discovered Rogan in the Arizona desert with a black cavalry team on the Mexican border in 1918. Stengel, a Kansas City native, tipped off the Monarch owner, and Joe's pro career was launched at the age of thirty.

He pitched and batted the Monarchs to three straight flags, 1923–1925, hitting .426, .450, and .355. On the mound he was 12–9, 19–10, and 12–2 in the 100-game Negro League seasons. He was probably the MVP in 1924 or 1925—if not both.

His postseason record was .421 at bat, 8–4 on the mound.

In fifteen games against white big leaguers, Joe hit .389. In one 1929 game, Al Simmons went 0 for 5 against Joe, and struck out three times.

Eddie Rommel

Pitcher, Phi (A) 1920–32

In 1922 Rommel had one of the finest seasons of all time—27–13 for the seventh-place A's (they were a last-place team without him), a feat almost as amazing as Carlton's 27–10 with the last-place Phils of 1972.

The next year he led the league in losses, 18–19 with the sixth-place A's. In five roller coaster years, 1921–1925, Ed and his knuckler led the league in victories two times and in losses twice.

By the time the A's dynasty blossomed, Ed was past his

prime. Nevertheless, he was 28–11 during the pennant-winning seasons of 1929 to 1931.

He later became an outstanding AL umpire.

Pete "Charlie Hustle" Rose

Outfielder/First Baseman/Third Baseman/Second Baseman, Cin (N) 1963–78, 1984–86, Phi (N) 1979–83, Mon (N) 1984. Manager, Cin (N) 1984–

The most exciting player of his age, Charlie Hustle monopolized center stage with his unsuccessful pursuit of Joe DiMaggio's hit streak in 1978 and his successful pursuit of Ty Cobb's lifetime hit record in 1985.

Rose played more games than any other man (3,562), batted more times (14,053), made more hits (4,256), stands second in doubles (746), and fourth in runs (2,165). He had fourteen .300 years and ten 200-hit seasons (Cobb had only nine), won three batting titles, and made the NL All-Star team in seventeen seasons at five positions. He was Rookie of the Year in 1963, MVP in 1973, and played in his last World Series in 1983.

He was a hell-for-leather baserunner who wasn't very fast. He was a great hitter who lacked home run power. On any given day in his career there were probably a couple of hundred players in the majors with more talent. None made as much out of his talent as Rose. He didn't drink or smoke and kept himself in perfect shape. He worked and he hustled. In an exhibition game with the lordly Yankees in the early 1960s, he ran out a walk. "Charlie Hustle," they sneered. Rose turned the putdown into a compliment.

He played hard every day. He played wherever he was needed. And he loved every inning. Long after some of those Yankees who sneered had retired, in part because they disdained conditioning as much as Pete's gung-ho style, Rose was winning games with head-first dives and key hits.

Above all, Rose was a winner. Pete played on four pennant winners in Cincinnati during the 1970s, then he signed a lucrative contract with the Phillies in 1979 and helped them to two more pennants in the 1980s. *The Sporting News* voted him Player of the 1970s, then Man of the Year in 1985.

"There are a lot of players better than me," Rose said, "but I do the same thing day in and day out, year in and year out."

Al Rosen

Third Baseman, Cle (A) 1947–56

For a few years, Al Rosen was one of the most feared hitters in the American League. He played thirty-five games for the Indians from 1947 to 1949, but couldn't move Ken Keltner off third base until 1950. That year his 37 homers set an AL rookie record not broken until 1987. In 1953 he was AL MVP, narrowly missing the Triple Crown with a .336 batting average, while leading the league with 43 homers (still the record for AL third basemen) and 145 RBIs.

In 1954 he was on his way to an equally impressive season when he suffered a broken finger. The injury permanently affected his grip on the bat. He returned to the lineup and helped the Indians set the AL record with 111 victories in winning the pennant, but his batting stats fell off badly. He

retired two years later. In the five years from 1950 to 1954, he averaged .298, 31 home runs, and 114 RBIs.

Edd Roush

Outfielder, Chi (A) 1913, Ind (F) 1914, Nwk (F) 1915, NY (N) 1916, 1927–29, Cin (N) 1916–26, 1931

Roush was the Tris Speaker of the NL. He made circus catches and won batting titles—.341 in 1917, his first year as a Cincinnati regular, and .321 in 1919. He just missed the one in between, losing by two points to Brooklyn's Zach Wheat.

Edd's 1919 title helped the Reds win the flag, but he hit only .214 in the Series. Not that it mattered; that was the year the Black Sox decided to lose the Series.

Roush swung the heaviest bat in the league, a 48-ounce club, but he wasn't a home run hitter; only 68 of his 2,376 career hits went the distance. He was a singles hitter, but darned consistent. In both 1921 and 1922 he hit .352; then in 1923 he slumped to .351.

Roush was an independent cuss who held out year after year just so he could miss spring training. When he *really* got into a money dispute in 1930, he held out the entire season.

He was named to the Baseball Hall of Fame in 1962.

Charles "Red" Ruffing

Pitcher, Bos (A) 1924–30, NY (A) 1930–42, 1945–46, Chi (A) 1947

Mired with the bottom-of-the-barrel Red Sox of the late 1920s, Ruffing seemed to go with the flow, compiling a 39–96 record with appropriate sky-high ERAs. In 1928 he was 10–25; the next year 9–22.

Traded to the Yankees in 1930, he became the new improved version. Buoyed by better defense and far more hitting, Ruffing's pitching "became much better," as though a weight had been lifted. His victories shot up as his ERA dropped. Four straight years (1936–1939), he won 20, and he had eight other seasons of at least 14 wins. His total Yankee record was 231-124. In six World Series he was 7–2, with a 2.63 ERA.

The burly redhead was primarily a fastball pitcher, but though he was often lauded for his "pinpoint" control, he walked more than 100 in three different seasons and finished his career with a total of 1,541 free passes.

Ruffing had hoped for a career as an outfielder, but a childhood accident cost him four toes on his left foot. No longer able to run, he became a pitcher. However, he remained an excellent hitter for a pitcher, averaging .269 with 36 career home runs. He was often used as a pinch-hitter.

He was named to the Baseball Hall of Fame in 1967.

Amos Rusie

Pitcher, Ind (N) 1889, NY (N) 1890–95, 1897–98, Cin (N) 1901

Rusie helped revolutionize the game. The Hoosier Thunder-

bolt was the fastest pitcher of the 1890s. In 1893 they moved the pitching distance back five feet (and six inches) to its present distance because of him and a few others. At the old fifty-foot distance (measured from the front of the box, not the back), Rusie had struck out 345, 337, and 303 from 1890 to 1892. After they moved it back, his whiffs dropped to 208—and everyone's batting average jumped up.

Rusie was as wild as he was fast. He whiffed 1,957 batters and walked 1,716. His 289 walks (in 548 innings) in 1890 is the record. In four seasons he led the league in both walks and strikeouts. Amos was a workhorse, often going over 300 innings pitched and twice over 400.

In the eight years he pitched for the Giants, Rusie won 20 or more in each of those eight years. His top year was 1894, 36-13, plus 2 more wins in the Temple Cup playoff over Baltimore. His ERA that year of 2.78 was awesome compared to the NL average of 5.32.

In 1895 he was 22-21, as the Giants finished twelfth. He sat out 1896 in a dispute with his owner, who tried to subtract a fine he had levied from the pitcher's salary for the coming year. Rusie went to court, and the other owners paid the fine and Rusie's 1896 salary rather than see the reserve clause tested. As the league's top box-office draw he returned in 1897 and went 29-8, as he lifted the Giants from seventh to second.

His wins fell to 20 in 1898, and he blamed it on the wear on his arm. When the club tried to cut his pay again, from $3,000 to $2,000, Rusie sat out for two years. In 1901 he was traded to Cincinnati, but his arm was gone and he retired after three games. The Giants did better on their end of the trade, picking up a kid pitcher named Christy Mathewson.

Rusie, who compiled a 243–160 mark in only nine full seasons, was named to the Baseball Hall of Fame in 1977.

Babe Ruth

Outfielder, Bos (A) 1914–19, NY (A) 1920–34, Bos (N) 1935

There has never been another figure in American sports like the Babe. Gargantuan—nay, Rabelaisian—in his appetites, prodigious in his production, he is the most famous athlete this nation has ever produced. Maris and Aaron topped his records, but they can never top him in American mythology.

Ruth revolutionized the game. Authorities disagree whether his home runs gave birth to the lively ball or vice versa. They also disagree on whether Babe created attendance records with his homers or whether the postwar Roaring Twenties prosperity created them. But Babe gave the game a lift after the Black Sox scandal and personified his time as no other American has.

No one has dominated the game as the Babe did.

He began as a lefthanded pitcher with the Red Sox. He went 18–8 in his first full season, 23–12 as a sophomore, and 24–13 in 1917, his third year. He led the AL in ERA in 1916. Yet his hitting was so impressive that he became a part-time outfielder in 1918 and won his first home run crown, with 11 in ninety-five games. In 1919, still batting against the dead ball, he crushed 29 homers, breaking a record that had stood for thirty-five years.

In 1920 he was sold to the Yankees for an announced figure of $100,000 (in truth it was far more). He arrived in New York the same year the lively ball arrived in baseball. *They*

hit a new record 54 homers (in only 458 at bats!), batted .376, and led in RBIs with 137. The next year the Babe had arguably the greatest season any batter ever had: 59 home runs, 171 RBIs, 177 runs, a .378 batting average, and an otherworldly slugging percentage of .846. Only one batter was able to top his 59 homers during the next forty years—the Babe with 60 in 1927.

All told, he led in home runs twelve times, in RBIs six, in runs scored eight, in walks eleven, in slugging percentage thirteen times, and in batting average only once (in 1924 with .378).

His career totals: 714 homers, 2,211 RBIs, 2,174 runs, a record 2,056 walks, a record .690 slugging average, and a .342 batting average.

Equally important to the Ruthian Mystique was the Public Ruth, the hefty child-man the fans loved. The Private Ruth ate too much, drank too deeply, partied too long, womanized too indiscriminately, cursed like a wounded Marine, held petty grudges, and sometimes bullied lesser mortals. The Public Ruth signed autographs, was naughty but nice, hit home runs for hospitalized boys, grinned on cue, and even "called his shot" before a home run in the 1932 World Series. The "called shot" illustrates how pervasive was the Ruthian Mystique; any other batter would have been merely pointing and yelling at the Cubs' pitcher, as the Chicago players always insisted he did. But the public chose to believe The Ruth had pointed to the center field bleachers moments before hitting his fifteenth and final World Series home run out there. The fans believed he could do anything, so they let him.

In 1936, a year after he retired, he was named to the Baseball Hall of Fame.

Nolan Ryan

Pitcher, NY (N) 1966, 1968–71, Cal (A) 1972–79, Hou (N) 1980–

There's no way to know if Ryan threw faster than any of the great fastballers of the past, but no one has ever thrown so fast for *so long* as Ryan. In his twenty-second major league season, at the age of forty-one, he can still strike out over 200 batters with heat. As a sheer athlete, he is the greatest pitcher who ever lived. No one else has pitched five no-hitters. His 383 strikeouts in one year (1973) stands as the record—and that was accomplished in the first year of the DH, so he had no patsies in his opposing lineups. His total K's are over 4,700, more than 600 past his nearest rival. His 270-plus wins were accomplished with mostly average or less support. "My job is to give my team a chance to win," he said. "I have no control over how many runs they score."

Actually, Ryan's control was for many years the only flaw in his pitching. He led his league eight times in walks. In 1977 he walked 204 in 299 innings (he also struck out 341). His career total of walks will probably stand as the record as long as will his strikeout total—which may be until well past the time this page has turned to dust. But, as his fastball has slowed— relatively—his control has improved.

Surprisingly, he's never won a Cy Young Award. But consider his 1974 season: most innings pitched, 333; fewest hits per nine innings, 5.97; most strikeouts per nine innings, 9.92; and a 22-16 record with a *last-place team.*

Ryne Sandberg

Second Baseman, Phi (N) 1981; Chi (N) 1982–

Sandberg has been the top NL second baseman of the 1980s and may be rated one of the best ever by the time he's done. He played third base in 1982, his first season in Cubland, but since has settled in at second to make it his own. He could probably play any field position. He has an above-average range and arm, and if he lacks the flash of some more acrobatic second-sackers, he's a whole lot steadier. He hustles all the time—not always the easiest thing to do in Chicago where they lose a lot of 10–2 games. He's got some home run power and a steady bat.

In 1984, when the Cubs won their division (yes, Virginia, there is a first place!), Sandberg hit .314, with 19 homers and 19 triples! He led the league in three-baggers and in runs scored (114). He was a runaway MVP.

Ron Santo

Third Baseman, Chi (N) 1960–73, Chi (A) 1974

The Brooks Robinson of the NL, Santo gave the Cubs some fine third base play in the 1960s. If he wasn't quite the fielder Brooks was, he outhit, outhomered, and out-RBI'ed Robby. Santo, Billy Williams, and Ernie Banks provided a tremendous power trio for Chicago.

Ron is the fourth highest home run hitter among third basemen, with 342, behind Mike Schmidt, Eddie Mathews, and Graig Nettles. He had ten seasons of 90 or more RBIs. In his best year, 1969, he drove in 129, as the Cubs made their strongest bid for a flag.

The pitchers feared him; he led in walks four times.

In the field Ron was double-play champ five times, putout king six times straight, and assist leader seven straight. Among NL third basemen, only Schmidt rivals him in total chances.

Ray Schalk

Catcher, Chi (A) 1912–28, NY (A) 1929.
Manager, Chi (A) 1927–28

Schalk was small for a catcher (five-nine, 165 pounds), and his nickname "Cracker" reportedly referred to his view from behind, which was said to resemble a cracker box. At any rate he was a cracker jack catcher. He caught 100 or more games in twelve seasons, including eleven in a row. He led AL catchers in fielding eight times.

In 1920 Schalk caught four 20-game winners (Red Faber, Ed Cicotte, Lefty Williams, and Dickie Kerr), a feat matched only by Baltimore's Elrod Hendricks. Over the years Ray caught four no-hitters (Jim Scott, Joe Benz, Cicotte, and Charlie Robertson), a feat matched by no one. The last one was a perfect game. Until his death in 1970 Schalk sent telegrams of congratulation to every no-hit catcher.

Schalk caught spitters, shine balls, emery balls, and knucklers. It earned him a fistful of broken fingers. Fast enough to steal 30 bases in 1916, a record for catchers, Schalk was the first catcher to back up first and third bases. He could make putouts at all four bases and did.

Ray had a strong arm, and he holds the AL record for career assists by a catcher. He had a good record against Cobb especially.

Offensively he wasn't an asset. His career batting average was only .256, and he had no power. He lived by his glove, wits, durability, and honesty. With the White Sox of 1919, that last quality was important, as eight of Schalk's teammates conspired to lose the World Series that year.

Schalk was named to the Hall of Fame in 1955.

Wally Schang

Catcher, Phi (A) 1913–17, 1930, Bos (A) 1918–20,
NY (A) 1921–25, StL (A) 1926–29, Det (A) 1931

Wally Schang just had a knack for showing up at the right time.

In 1913, his rookie year, the Philadelphia A's won the pennant and World Series. They followed with another pennant in his sophomore season. Traded to Boston in 1918, he arrived just in time to enjoy the Red Sox' last world championship. Three years later, he was dealt to the Yankees, who had never finished first. But Wally's luck held, and they took the flag in his first three seasons in pinstripes. They even won the world championship in 1923. In 1926 he was traded again—to the St. Louis Browns. Not even Wally and a world of rabbits' feet could help the Brownies, but he did get himself traded back to Philadelphia in 1930. The A's were already world champs from 1929, but with Schang backing up Mickey Cochrane, they repeated.

All in all, Schang played on seven pennant winners in his nineteen years, but it wasn't all serendipity; he contributed.

Schang was an excellent defensive catcher with a deadly arm; in a 1920 game he threw out six runners. He also had a nice sting in his bat. He is the first switch-hitter to hit a lefty and a righty home run in a single game. He hit over .300 six times and had a career .286 average. On days he wasn't catching, he was sometimes put in the outfield or at third base to keep his bat in the lineup.

Mike Schmidt

Third Baseman, Phi (N) 1972-

Schmidt is not only the greatest hitter to play third base—everyone knows that—he is also arguably the greatest fielder. His homers are famous; less well known is his 404 assists in 1974, the most ever by an NL third baseman. Three years later his 396 assists were the *second* highest total in NL history. He won eight Gold Gloves in a row.

Mike also won eight home run crowns, four RBI titles, and three MVPs. His home run to at-bat ratio ranks in the top ten all-time, and he is one of only 14 major leaguers to hit over 500 home runs.

He pays a high price—nearly one strikeout every four at-bats, or about three for every home run. But it's worth it. He put the Phillies into the playoffs six times, and he is one of only 14 major leaguers to hit over 500 home runs.

He's been amazingly durable. Until his season-ending rotator tear in 1988, he had never been sidelined for an extended period.

Tom Seaver

Pitcher, NY (N) 1967–77, 1983, Cin (N) 1977–82,
Chi (A) 1984–86, Bos (A) 1986

Of all the great pitchers since World War Two, Seaver may have been the best. He won 311 games, struck out 3,640 batters, compiled a career ERA of 2.86, but most important he seemed able to win with both good and losing teams. As Rookie of the Year in 1967, he was 16–13 with the seventh-place Mets, and he just kept doing that sort of thing. In twenty years of pitching, his winning percentage exceeded his team's in sixteen seasons.

On the other hand, he could ride a winning team. He was 25–7 for the "Amazin' Mets" world champs in 1969, when he won his first Cy Young Award. The second came for his 19–10 mark and NL-leading ERA with the 1973 pennant winners. Two years later he was 22–9 with an ERA of 2.38 and won his third Cy Young.

Although he led the NL in strikeouts five times, had ten seasons with over 200 strikeouts, and still holds the NL record with 19 whiffs in a nine-inning game, he was never a "thrower." He exhibited excellent control and pitch selection from the start. He just happened to be a heady control pitcher who also threw a ninety-eight-mile-per-hour fastball throughout most of his career. His power came from tremendous lower body strength and a low pitching motion designed to take full advantage of his leg muscles. When he was throwing correctly, his right knee would drag on the ground with each pitch.

Tom resembled Christy Mathewson—clean-cut, handsome, intelligent, a student of pitching, and a devotee of the *New York Times* crossword puzzle. Ironically, when all votes are in, it may be a toss-up as to who was the best righthander a New York NL team ever had.

Joe Sewell

Shortstop, Cle (A) 1920–30, NY (A) 1931–33

Sewell was rushed into the Cleveland infield when shortstop Ray Chapman was killed during the 1920 pennant race. He hit .329 in the stretch to help rally the club back from the tragedy and win a three-way race.

Overshadowed by teammates such as Tris Speaker, and later by Ruth and Gehrig, little Joe quietly made a place among the top shortstops of all time. A good defensive player, he had a career batting average of .312 and both scored and batted in over 1,000 runs.

With his forty-ounce bat, Joe punched the ball where they ain't. Nine times he hit over .300, playing in a hitter's dream era. In 1923 he reached .353 and knocked in 109 runs. In 1925 he hit .336, cracked 204 hits, and batted in 98 runs with only one HR.

Sewell is famous for not striking out—only 114 times in 7,132 at-bats. In 1925 he whiffed an incredible four times in 608 at-bats.

He also ran up a streak of 1,103 consecutive games.

His brother Luke caught for many years. The two were teammates on the Indians.

Joe was named to the Hall of Fame in 1977.

James "Cy" Seymour

Outfielder, NY (N) 1896–1900, 1906–10,
Bal (A) 1901–02, Cin (N) 1902–06, Bos (N) 1913

Seymour won 20 games twice for the Giants of 1897–98. He was fast but wild as a starving wolf, leading the league three times in walks. Meanwhile, his hitting was improving every year, and when it topped .300 it was suggested that he do the rest of his throwing from the outfield.

He was with Cincinnati in 1905, when he had one heckuva year. He led the NL in—get this—hits, doubles, triples, RBI, batting average and slugging average. But he only finished second with his eight home runs because his teammate, one Fred Odwell, hit nine. Mr. Odwell is perhaps the most obscure and unusual home run champ of all time, having hit exactly one homer before 1905 and never hitting another after that one year when he deprived his fellow Red of a triple crown.

Urban Shocker

Pitcher, NY (A) 1916–17, 1925–28, StL (A) 1918–24

The spitballer Shocker won 20 four years in a row for the Browns in 1920–1923, as St. Louis finished fourth, third, second, and fifth. In 1921 he led the league in wins, going 27–12 with a third-place club. In 1922 he led in strikeouts and went 24–17, almost pitching the Brownies to the pennant over the Yankees. Shocker would be remembered much better today if he had spent his prime years with the Yankees. His first two seasons (1916–1917) were in New York, and he was traded back to them in 1925. That was the year Babe Ruth got his famous bellyache and the team fell to seventh; Shocker would have been better off staying with the Browns. He won 19 and 18 the next two years, as the Yankees won pennants, but heart disease took his life in 1928 at the age of thirty-seven.

Al Simmons

Outfielder, Phi (A) 1924–32, 1940–41, 1944,
Chi (A) 1933–35, Det (A) 1936, Was (A) 1937–38,
Bos (N) 1939, Cin (A) 1939, Bos (A) 1943

In 1930, when Bucketfoot Al was at his best, Connie Mack said he wished he had nine players named Simmons. Actually he didn't even have one; Al's real name was Alois Szymanski.

When he first joined the A's in 1924, everybody hooted. He had a classic "foot-in-the-bucket" batting stance with his left foot pointing at third base, just the way kids are taught *not* to do it from the time they pick up a bat. Critics said he'd better change or he'd be back in Milwaukee double quick. He hit .308 as a rookie, but really convinced them the next year when he went to .384 and pounded out 253 hits, the second highest total in AL history. After that, when he stood there like he was going to kill ants on the foul line, the critics just said, "Nice stance, Mr. Simmons."

Al hit .392 in 1927, but his top years were the three A's pennant seasons of 1929–31. In 1929 he led in RBIs, with 34 homers and a .365 batting average; *The Sporting News*

named him the AL MVP. In 1930 he led in batting with .381, and had 36 homers and 165 RBIs. Then in 1931 he upped his average to .390 and led the league again.

Mack started selling his stars as the Depression hurt him pretty hard. Simmons was sent to Chicago in 1933, and though he had a few more good years, the great ones were over. He finished with 2,927 hits, 307 home runs, 1,827 RBIs, and a .334 batting average.

In Game Four of the 1929 World Series, he ignited the famous ten-run seventh inning rally, when the A's came from an 8–0 deficit. Al led off with a blast over the roof against the Cubs' Charlie Root. Before the inning ended, Simmons singled to set up the ninth run and scored number ten himself.

He was named to the Hall of Fame in 1953.

Ted Simmons

Catcher, StL (N) 1968–80, Mil (A) 1981–85,
Atl (N) 1986–

Simmons was an outstanding hitter for a catcher. Unfortunately he wasn't an outstanding *catcher* for a catcher. His receiving, pitcher handling, and throwing were adequate at best. In 1973 he led NL catchers in assists, but much of that may reflect the liberties runners were taking. Ted always seemed like a first baseman waiting to happen.

At bat rather than behind it, he was one of the best, hitting over .300 seven times in his sixteen seasons as a regular. Five times he had 20 or more homers, and he had eight seasons of 90 or more RBIs.

George Sisler

First Baseman, StL (A) 1915–22, 1924–27, Was (A) 1928,
Bos (N) 1928–30. Manager, StL (A) 1924–26

The original "Gorgeous George," Sisler was the best first baseman who ever lived until 1923. He was one of the best *players* ever—until 1923.

Consider: from 1916 to 1919, when the dead ball was still the order of the day, he hit .338 for the Browns. There was another hitter in St. Louis at the time, a fellow named Hornsby. Sisler outhit him. Sisler only hit 38 home runs, but no one was hitting many then. He did steal 45 bases in 1918 to lead the AL. And he also was already regarded as the equal of Hal Chase with a glove, which would make him the best-fielding honest first baseman up till then.

So in 1920 they brought in the lively ball, and everyone's batting average went up—but nobody's more than Sisler's. From 1920 through 1922 he hit .407, .371, and .420. His hit totals were 257 (the all-time record), 216, and 246. He hit 19 homers in 1920, led in stolen bases in 1921 and 1922, batted in over 100 runs, and scored over 125 each season. And all the time he kept fielding up a storm. Ty Cobb, who handed out compliments as often as he handed out hundred-dollar bills, said Sisler was "the nearest thing to a perfect ballplayer."

And then came 1923. Sisler missed the whole year with a sinus infection that caused double vision. And when he came back in 1924, he was just a very good ballplayer. He played seven more years, but he never regained the magic.

He was elected to the Hall of Fame in 1939.

Enos "Country" Slaughter

Outfielder, StL (N) 1938–42, 1946–53,
NY (A) 1954–59, KC (A) 1955–56, Mil (N) 1959

In ten dramatic seconds in the 1946 World Series, Slaughter dashed all the way from first base to immortality. His mad race to score the winning run for the Cardinals in the final game was the greatest highlight of his career, but it was certainly not the only highlight.

He had ten seasons hitting .300 or better, finishing with a career mark right at an even .300. He led the NL in RBIs in 1946, and though he wasn't a big home run hitter (169 in nineteen seasons), he led the league in triples twice. He was a fine fielder with a good arm. He played on two world championship teams with the Cardinals in 1942 and 1946; then in the 1950s he helped the Yankees win three pennants.

And until Pete Rose came along, Slaughter was known as the epitome of hustle. When people said "a player like Slaughter," they didn't mean a .300 hitter or a strong-armed outfielder; they meant a smart, aggressive player who never walked anywhere on a ballfield when he could run and who'd cut your throat to win a game.

He was named to the Hall of Fame in 1985.

Oswald "Ozzie" Smith

Shortstop, SD (N) 1978–81, StL (N) 1982–

The acrobatic Wizard of Oz may be the best defensive shortstop of all time. "He's changed fielding for shortstops," admits Hall of Fame shortstop Lou Boudreau. Smith's famous back flip when he runs to his position at the start of a game is for show, but it illustrates the kind of defensive plays he can make. His range is exceptional, and while his arm is not, his ability to make accurate, off-balance throws makes up for any lack of strength. No shortstop has ever made more assists than Oz in 1980 (621). He helped take the Cards to three World Series, in 1982, 1985, and 1987.

Originally a good field/no hit player, Smith has turned himself into a valuable offensive performer. He's become adept at drawing walks, held his strikeout totals low, and moved his batting average up. He hit .303 in 1987. Although he has no home run power, his ability to steal bases somewhat makes up for that. When he hit a rare home run in the 1985 LCS, he explained, "I was trying to hit the top half of the ball and hit the bottom by mistake."

At a salary of $2 million a year, Ozzie is also changing the old dictum that singles hitters drive Fords.

Reggie Smith

Outfielder, Bos (A) 1966–73, StL (N) 1974–76,
LA (N) 1976–81, SF (N) 1982

Until injuries wore him down, Smith was one of the best all-around players in baseball. He was also generally unrecognized as such. He joined the Red Sox in 1967, played a mean center field, contributed 15 homers, and helped the team to the pennant. He got one vote for Rookie of the Year.

Over the next six seasons, he hit .300 three times for the

Sox and cracked as many as 30 home runs, yet never finished in the top twenty in MVP voting.

Traded to the NL, he got a little more recognition. With the Cardinals in 1974, he hit .309 and drove in 100 runs. In 1977 he led the Dodgers to a pennant with 32 homers and a .307 batting average. He was fourth in the MVP voting, the only time he ever made the top ten.

Though he may have been overlooked when he played, his career totals mark him as a star: 314 home runs, 2,020 hits, 1,092 RBIs, and a .287 batting average.

Edwin "Duke" Snider

Outfielder, Bkn (N) 1947–57, LA (N) 1958–62,
NY (N) 1963, SF (N) 1964

"Willie, Mickey, and the Duke" gave New Yorkers the game's three hardest hitting center fielders from 1951 to 1957. For the last four of those years the most consistent home run hitter of the three was Snider. He hit 40 or more homers five years in a row, an NL record tied only by Ralph Kiner. He was helped by often being the only lefthanded batter in the Dodgers' lineup, and Ebbets Field's cozy confines didn't hurt.

Snider was a smooth-fielding center fielder for six Dodger pennant winners. He was usually at his best in the World Series. His lifetime 11 Series home runs and 26 RBIs are the best marks for any National Leaguer. He hit four homers in both the 1952 Series and in the 1955 Series, when the Dodgers finally defeated the Yankees for the world championship.

The popular, articulate Duke is the all-time Dodger home run leader. His career totals are 407 homers, 1,333 RBIs, 1,259 runs scored, and a .295 batting average.

He was named to the Hall of Fame in 1980.

Warren Spahn

Pitcher, Bos (N) 1942, 1946–52, Mil (N) 1953–64,
NY (N) 1965, SF (N) 1965

The winningest lefthander of all time, Spahn won 20 or more games 13 times, tying Christy Mathewson's NL record. He needed only 11 more wins to top Grover Alexander's 373 lifetime victories. Yet he didn't win his first major league game until he was twenty-five years old.

He seemed to get better as he got older. His good control became great; his fastball slipped a little, but he added a screwball and slider to his curve and change-up; and, of course, he got smarter and smarter. His ability to place his pitches and vary the speeds kept batters always off-stride.

He led the NL in strikeouts four straight years (1949–1952), in ERA twice, and in victories eight times, including five straight (1957–61). His 63 shutouts are the most by an NL lefty.

Spahn had his first 20-win season in 1947; then, curiously, he fell to 15 wins in 1948 when the Boston Braves won the pennant. Nevertheless the Braves' shallow pitching staff was described as "Spahn, [Johnny] Sain, and pray for rain." He was still at the top of his game in 1957–1958, when the Milwaukee Braves won pennants. In 1957 he was voted the Cy Young Award.

In 1960, at the age of thirty-nine, he pitched his first no-

hitter. The next year, five days past his fortieth birthday, he pitched his second.

Spahn was elected to the Hall of Fame in 1973. He would have been elected earlier, but he found it so hard to hang up the spikes that he kept on pitching in the minors in 1966–67, delaying the onset of his eligibility for the Hall.

Al Spalding

Pitcher, Boston (NA) 1871–75, Chi (N) 1876–78.
Manager, Chi (N) 1876–77. Executive

Spalding might have won 300 if we knew how many he pitched as a teenager in top independent ball. His wins are unknown, but they included one as a seventeen-year-old in 1867 over George Wright's Washingtons, 29–23.

Al's official record starts when the National Association was founded in 1871. Playing for Boston, his totals were 20–10, 37–8, 41–15, and 52–18. In 1875 he posted an amazing 57–5, including 24 in a row, pitching in every game his team played. He also hit .300 each of the last four years, as the Bostons won four straight flags.

Lured to Chicago with the formation of the National League in 1876, Spalding helped write the new league's constitution. He was that first year's biggest winner at 47–13, as Chicago won the flag.

Then his arm finally gave out. He left behind a lifetime W-L percentage of .787. Of course it's the record.

Al opened a sporting goods business and issued the first Spalding Baseball Guide in 1877.

In 1882 he took over as president of the champion Chicagos with stars such as Cap Anson, George Gore, Larry Corcoran, and Fred Goldsmith.

He led a world tour of teams in 1888 and was instrumental in the NL's successful war with the Players League in 1890. He helped plan the Chicago World's Fair of 1893. In 1905 he organized a commission to determine where baseball was born: Chadwick had said England; Spalding chauvinistically said America, supporting the Abner Doubleday legend, a claim he repeated in 1911 in his history of baseball, *America's National Game*.

Spalding ran for the U.S. Senate in 1910 and lost. He died in 1915, but his name remained an essential part of the game, on every official NL ball used until the year 1976.

He was named to the Hall of Fame in 1939.

Tris Speaker

Outfielder, Bos (A) 1907–15, Cle (A) 1916–26,
Was (A) 1927, Phi (A) 1928. Manager, Cle (A) 1919–26

Speaker revolutionized center field play, taking advantage of the dead ball to play behind second base almost as a fifth infielder. He made unassisted double plays on short flies (the only man to do it in a World Series), was the pivot man on 4–8–3 plays, and even took pickoff throws from the pitcher. Yet he could still go back to get flies over his head. He is second in lifetime putouts and total chances in the outfield and first in assists—35 of them as a rookie in 1909. He may have been the first outfielder to test the wind by throwing grass in the air.

Tris won only one batting title, but he topped .375 six times and had a lifetime mark of .344. In 1916 he broke Ty Cobb's streak of five straight batting crowns. His 793 doubles are first on the all-time list, and his 223 triples are sixth. "Spoke's" 3,515 hits knocked in 1,559 runs and he scored 1,881 times. He almost never struck out. He stole 433 bases.

And he did it all after breaking his right arm as a kid in Texas and learning to throw and hit lefty instead.

Speaker broke in with the Red Sox in 1909 and soon formed, with Harry Hooper and Duffy Lewis, perhaps the best defensive outfield ever. He was MVP in 1912 as the Sox won pennants that year and in 1915. Traded to Cleveland in 1916, he became player-manager in 1919 and led the Indians to their first pennant in 1920. He hit .388.

He was named to the Hall of Fame in 1937.

Willie Stargell

Outfielder/First Baseman, Pit (N) 1962–82

The only man to hit a ball clear out of Dodger Stadium, a feat he accomplished twice, Stargell is also the only man to hit four into the upper deck of Three Rivers Stadium. He hit seven over the roof of old Forbes Field (only nine others have done it even once).

Forbes was tough on Willie. In one stretch, 1965–1966, he hit only 19 home runs at home, 41 on the road. His totals took a jump after the Pirates moved to Three Rivers, though even that is a pitchers' park. Willie led the league in homers in 1971 and 1973.

In 1979 Stargell won three MVPs—in the regular season (tying Keith Hernandez), the playoffs, and the World Series.

In the World Series versus the Orioles, Willie came up in the seventh game with Pittsburgh losing 1–0 in the sixth. He crashed his third home run of the Series, to give the Pirates the championship.

In twenty-one years, he thumped 475 homers, batted in 1,540 runs, and compiled a .282 batting average. He paid a high price for his homers, striking out once every four at-bats.

Not included in Willie's numbers are "intangibles." Much of his 1979 MVP Award was for leadership. As captain of the Pirates, he led with a combination of quiet example and symbols. He passed out "Stargell Star" decals for outstanding plays and invented (and exemplified) the "We are family" slogan which tied the team together.

He was elected to the Hall of Fame in 1988.

Daniel "Rusty" Staub

Outfielder/First Baseman, Hou (N) 1963–68,
Mon (N) 1969–71, 1979, NY (N) 1972–75, 1981–85,
Det (A) 1976–79, Tex (A) 1980

"*Le grand orange*" (the big redhead), as Montreal fans called him, Staub played well for some undistinguished teams (the Astros, Expos, Mets, and Tigers), usually flirting with .300 and 100 RBIs.

His best year, 1967, he hit .333 in the Hitters' Horror, the Astrodome. He led the league with 44 doubles.

Rusty finally found a winner with the Mets in 1973. He hit only .269 during the season but shone in the World Series,

hitting .423. His five RBIs won Game Four 6–1.

After he got too "grand" to play the outfield, he became an outstanding DH for the Tigers, twice batting in over 100 runs. Then he finished as a deadly pinch hitter for the Mets. In his final season, he became the eleventh man to register 100 career pinch hits.

George Steinbrenner

Owner

The Yankees' controversial owner has often been more newsworthy than his team. He took over the team in the early 1970s when the once lordly Yankees had wallowed in the depths of the AL for nearly a decade. His stated intention was to return the Yankees to their former glory. He has made the moves that brought four pennants to New York, 1976–1978 and 1981, and the club has been competitive in most years.

Steinbrenner has shown an admirable willingness to spend huge amounts of money in pursuit of excellence. He's signed such free agents as Catfish Hunter, Reggie Jackson, Goose Gossage, Dave Winfield, and Jack Clark. His employees are well paid for their efforts.

On the other hand, his constant switching of managers—seventeen changes since Steinbrenner bought the team—has become a national joke. Billy Martin has been hired and fired five times. His verbal battles with his own players, his public second-guessing, and his interference in the daily operation of the team have opened him to criticism from those who believe his influence is counterproductive.

He has brought back to the Yankees many fans who had switched allegiance to the Mets. At the same time, he's sent a large number of former Yankee fans scurrying to Shea Stadium. Volatile, yet often charming, the only thing absolutely predictable about Steinbrenner is that he will make more headlines.

Charles "Casey" Stengel

Outfielder, Bkn (N) 1912–17, Pit (N) 1918–19,
Phi (N) 1920–21, NY (N) 1921–23, Bos (N) 1924–25.
Manager, Bkn (N) 1934–36, Bos (N) 1938–43,
NY (N) 1949–60, NY (N) 1962–65

Stengel won ten pennants in twelve years, hid a bird under his hat, and doubled up a Senate hearing with the funniest monologue in the history of the *Congressional Record*, which, as Will Rogers said, "is goin' some."

Casey put in fourteen seasons as a useful NL outfielder, compiling a .284 batting average and a reputation as a prankster. The bird, for example, he had captured in the outfield, then let escape when he strode to the plate and doffed his cap to the fans.

Stengel embarked on a managerial career in the minors and low majors, frequently getting a pink slip. ("I say fired," he said, "because there is no doubt I had to leave.")

Leading the lowly Dodgers in 1934, he achieved brief fame when Giant manager Bill Terry sneered, "Is Brooklyn still in the league?" The insulted Bums knocked New York out of the pennant.

With the old Boston Braves, 1938–1943, Casey finished

seventh four times in a row. When he was hit by a Boston cab and broke his leg, the city voted the cabbie MVP.

Case went back to the minors, won a flag at Milwaukee and another at Oakland in the Pacific Coast League.

Then fate struck with a surprise call from the Yankees. In Stengel's first year, 1949, the club was hit with a record number of injuries. All summer he juggled his lineup and platooned players, a strategy that would become his trademark. On the last day of the season, the Yankees caught the Red Sox for the pennant. They beat the Dodgers in the World Series to begin an amazing string of five straight world championships, 1949–1953.

In 1954 he won 103 games—and finished second to Cleveland's 111. His Yanks won four pennants in a row (1955–1958) and two more world championships, missed a year, then won Casey's final pennant in 1960. His ten pennants and seven world titles in twelve years is considered by some the greatest managerial accomplishment of all time.

The Yankees fired him as too old, but he took on the new challenge of wet-nursing the perfectly awful Mets through their first four seasons. Though the team finished a well-deserved last each year, they did show improvement each season.

Casey's warmth, his pixie sense of humor, and his unique, rambling, ungrammatical, nonstop monologues made him perhaps baseball's most loved figure since Babe Ruth.

He was named to the Hall of Fame in 1966.

Norman "Turkey" Stearnes

Outfielder, Negro leagues, 1921–41: Montgomery Grey Sox, Detroit Stars, New York Lincoln Giants, Kansas City Monarchs, Cole's American Giants, Chicago American Giants, Philadelphia Stars, Detroit Black Sox

Stearnes is the all-time HR champ of the Negro leagues, beating the more famous Gibson 171–137. (Josh, it is true, had more HR/AB.) Turkey led or tied the league seven times from 1923–1932; Josh, six. He averaged 30 every 550 at bats. Stearnes led the league in BA once, with .430 in 1935. His lifetime mark was .341. Against white big leaguers, he hit .313. His fellow Detroiter, Hank Greenberg, heard the stories and asked Cool Papa Bell if they were true. Bell assured him that they were.

Turkey weighed only 168 and swung from an odd left-handed stance, choking up on the bat, with his right toe pointing up. Yet he smashed some long blows, including a 450-footer into the upper deck of Comiskey Park. He played an excellent center field and was fast enough to lead off, which he often did with a home run. In 1935 he and Mule Suttles played together on the western league champion Chicago American Giants, Stearnes batting lead-off and Suttles clean-up.

Stearnes played his best in the postseason, hitting .474 in nine games, including four HRs. In the 1929 playoff against St. Louis—and Mule Suttles, the black leagues' number-two man in homers—Turkey hit .481 with 11 RBIs and the first homer ever hit over the 450' wall at Hamtramck Stadium.

"If they don't put him in the Hall of Fame," says Bell, "they shouldn't put *anybody* in."

Harry Stovey

Outfielder/First Baseman, Wor (N) 1880–82, Phi (AA) 1883–89, Bos (P) 1890, Bos (N) 1891–92, Bal (N) 1892–93, Bkn (N) 1893

Stovey hit .326 for the old Philadelphia AA club in 1884 while leading the league in triples and runs. Of course it was an expansion year, with three leagues and thirty-three teams.

A husky righthanded hitter, renowned for his gentlemanly conduct, he topped his league in homers five times, with a high of 19 in 1889. He retired in 1893 with 121 career home runs, the record at the time. It was later broken by Roger Connor in 1895 and by many more since.

Despite stealing as many as 97 bases in a season and scoring more than one run per game over his career, Stovey finished with only a .288 batting average. His strengths were his strong arm, power, and speed. He reportedly once circled the bases in fourteen seconds.

Bruce Sutter

Pitcher, Chi (N) 1976–80, StL (N) 1981–84, Atl (N) 1985–86, injured in 1987, 1988

Sutter was one of the most effective relief pitchers in history. His split-finger fastball baffled NL hitters and sent other NL pitchers to learning how to throw it.

He came to the NL with the Cubs in 1976 and in his second season saved 31 games. His 6 wins and league-leading 37 saves earned him the Cy Young Award for 1979.

Traded to the Cardinals in 1981, he continued to star. His 36 saves in 1982 helped the team to the world championship in 1982. In 1984 he had a career-high 45 saves, to lead the NL for the fifth time.

He signed with Atlanta as a free agent for 1985, but after a disappointing season, he underwent elbow surgery. He pitched in only 16 games in 1986 and missed all of the 1987 season. He pitched with occasional success in 1988.

Don Sutton

Pitcher, LA (N) 1966–80, 1988, Hou (N) 1981–82, Mil (A) 1982–83, Oak (A) 1985, Cal (A) 1985–87

Sutton won 20 games only once, but he kept plugging away to become one of the big winners of all time. He was probably both hurt and helped by the five-day rotation, which cuts about five starts out of each season but might mean longer careers: Sutton pitched for twenty-three seasons.

Don was 21–10 for the 1976 Dodgers for his only 20-win year, but he had eleven other seasons with 15 wins or more. One of his best years was 1980. He was only 13–5, but he led the NL in ERA.

Sutton never pitched a no-hitter, but he has five one-hitters, tying the NL record.

He was accused of throwing "doctored" pitches, but his long career is evidence of either his legality or his legerdemain.

Jesse Tannehill

*Pitcher, Cin (N) 1894, 1911, Pit (N) 1897–1902,
NY (A) 1903, Bos (A) 1904–08, Was (A) 1908–09*

A great control pitcher, lefthander Tannehill won 20 games six times from 1898 to 1905 and had a 197–116 career record. He averaged only 1.6 walks per nine innings. He helped pitch the Pirates to the 1901 and 1902 NL pennants. He won the 1901 ERA title with a 2.18 mark.

The Pirates won the 1903 pennant without Tannehill; he and Happy Jack Chesbro jumped to the AL New York Highlanders (Yankees) that year. It cost him a chance to appear in the first World Series.

He was a disappointing 15–15 in New York and was traded to Boston, the winner of the 1903 Series. His 21–11 season helped Boston win the 1904 pennant, but again he lost his World Series chance when the NL's Giants refused to meet the AL champs.

With Cy Young, Bill Dineen, and Tannehill doing most of the pitching, Boston set a team record low of 1.5 walks per nine innings in 1904.

Jack Taylor

Pitcher, Chi (N) 1898–1903, 1906–07, StL (N) 1904–06

Taylor won 20 games four times and 151 during his career, but his claim to fame is an uncanny ability to finish what he started. On June 20, 1901, he pitched a complete game. Through his next 186 starts—more than five years' worth—he would pitch a complete game every time he started. One game went nineteen innings; another went eighteen. He finished them both. On another occasion, he pitched both ends of a doubleheader. Fifteen times he relieved other, less stouthearted hurlers, and each time finished the game. Taylor wasn't a particularly imposing physical specimen. At five-ten and 170 pounds, he was average or a little less for a pitcher of his day. Finally, on August 9, 1906, he was relieved in a game.

Although he pitched only ten years in the NL, two of them partial seasons, Taylor had six seasons of over 300 innings and completed 278 of his 286 starts.

Gene Tenace

*Catcher, Oak (A) 1969–76, SD (N) 1977–80,
StL (N) 1981–82, Pit (N) 1983*

Tenace was the steady catcher for the Oakland A's dynasty that won three World Series, 1972–74. A decent enough defensive catcher, he was actually very dangerous with the bat, despite a dreary .241 batting average. Over his career, he was nearly as likely to get a walk as to get a hit—984 walks to 1,060 hits. He led the AL twice in bases on balls and had a .380 on-base average.

When he did get a hit, the odds were five-to-one it would go out of the park. Nearly 20 percent of his hits were homers—201.

Tenace first showed he could be something out of the ordinary in the 1972 World Series. He'd just limped through a .225 season with 5 homers, followed by an .059 LCS. He

looked like a soft touch to the Reds. So in his first two Series at bats he homered, not only setting a record but also providing the A's with all the runs they needed in a 3–2 win. For the Series he hit .348 and had 4 homers and 9 RBIs.

Bill Terry

*First Baseman, NY (N) 1923–36.
Manager, NY (N) 1932–41*

Terry was the last NL batter to hit .400, but it doesn't impress some modern commentators, who point out that when Memphis Bill hit .401 in 1930, the whole blessed league hit .303. Still, anyone who knocks out 254 hits as Terry did in 1930 deserves respect. And it wasn't that he was a one-year wonder. He played fourteen seasons and topped .300 eleven times. Besides his .400 year, he had averages of .372, .354, .350, .349, and .341—the last mark also being his career average. This is not Mario Mendoza!

He wasn't Lou Gehrig either, of course. His 154 career homers don't look all that great against Gehrig or Foxx, two AL first basemen of the period. There are two answers to that. The first is obvious: Terry wasn't the home run hitter that either of those brawny gentlemen were. He was a line drive hitter who hit to all fields. And that's part of the second answer: he played his home games in the Polo Grounds, which had wonderfully short foul lines for dead pull hitters and horrifyingly deep power alleys for anyone who wasn't. Terry made the decision to go with the percentages, which was considered smart baseball in his day. One tipoff is that in five of the six years from 1927 through 1932, he averaged 20 homers a year. The sixth year was 1930 when he hit only 9. That looks suspiciously as though he cut his swing just a little when he saw a chance to hit .400.

Some oldtime sportswriters are kind of happy to see Terry low-rated. He was the kind of player who, if he thought you were a jerk, said so. Some call that "refreshing honesty"; others call it "arrogance." Whatever. Once the reputation was set, he couldn't say anything to please some writers. There was one day in 1934, after he'd become manager of the Giants: a writer asked him what he thought of the Dodgers, at a time when everyone knew the Dodgers were pretty awful. Terry, trying to be one of the guys, made a little joke. "Is Brooklyn still in the league?" he asked. Naturally it got blown all out of proportion, especially when the Dodgers beat the Giants a couple of times at the end of the season to knock them out of the pennant.

One thing about Terry: he was a much better fielder than the home run-hitting first sackers of his time. And he also became a better manager, winning three pennants and a world title in 1933 when he was a player-manager.

Roy Thomas

*Outfielder, Phi (N) 1899–1908, 1910–11,
Pit (N) 1908, Bos (N) 1909*

Thomas was a valuable powder-puff hitter for the Phillies in the twentieth century's first decade. He topped .300 five times and averaged .290 for his thirteen NL seasons, but in the power department he ranked just ahead of Eddie Gaedel.

Despite excellent speed, he never hit more than 15 doubles in any season. In 1900 he had 168 hits and 161 were singles. He actually hit 53 triples and 7 homers in his career, but the outfielders played him in so close that anything that skipped through was a sure three bases.

When it came to drawing walks, Thomas was a major talent, leading the NL seven times. His on-base average was .407. It was due to his skill. At five-eleven, he had about the same strike zone as anyone else, and he certainly didn't intimidate pitchers. Yet in seven of eight years, 1899–1906, he walked over 100 times. His ability to get on, steal bases, and score, added to his excellent flyhawking, made him a Phillie favorite.

Sam Thompson

Outfielder, Det (N) 1885–88,
Phi (N) 1889–98, Det (A) 1906

Big Sam played in two Hall of Fame outfields. In the early 1890s, he, Billy Hamilton, and Ed Delahanty made a heavy-lumber trio for the Phillies. In 1894 Hamilton hit .404, Delahanty .407, and Thompson .407. The second Hall of Fame outfield was in 1906, when the Detroit Tigers had suffered so many injuries that they asked Sam out of retirement. For the final eight games of the season, he lined up with Ty Cobb and Sam Crawford. He hit a mere .226, but he was forty-six years old at the time.

Thompson started with the old NL Detroit Wolverines in 1885. At first they didn't have a uniform to fit his six-two, 220-pound frame, and he squeezed into what was available. Running out a double, he split his pants right up the middle.

The modest, good-humored slugger became the most popular player in Detroit. In 1887, when they won the NL pennant, he led the NL with a .372 batting average and 166 RBIs.

Thompson compiled a .331 career batting average. One of the best home run hitters of the nineteenth-century, he led the NL with 20 in 1889 and 18 in 1895. His 128 career homers rank him second only to Roger Connor for the era. And his ratio of RBIs to games played is the best *all time*.

An outstanding fielder, he was renowned for his powerful arm. Reportedly he popularized throwing all the way from the outfield to the catcher on one bounce.

In 1974 he was named to the Hall of Fame.

Luis Tiant

Pitcher, Cle (A) 1964–69, Min (A) 1970,
Bos (A) 1971–78, NY (A) 1979–80, Pit (N) 1981,
Cal (A) 1982

The herky-jerky Cuban dervish Tiant won 20 games four times and finished with a 229–172 record in a career that looked to be over in the middle. After four merely good years with Cleveland, he was suddenly great in 1968 with a 21–9 mark and a league-leading 1.60 ERA. But the next year he led the AL in losses at 9–20. Traded to Minnesota, he appeared washed up with no arm left.

Boston took a chance on him, but he struggled to 1–7 in 1971. But the next year he was the Comeback of the Year

with 15–6 and his second ERA title (1.91). He won 20 games three times for the Red Sox but was at his best in 1975, when his season's record was 18–14. The Sox won the division; then Luis started them on a three-game sweep in the LCS with a three-hitter over Oakland. He opened the World Series against the powerful Reds with another shutout, threw a 163-pitch, complete game victory in Game Four, and went seven innings in Game Six before weakening.

After games Luis would entertain writers, puffing his long Cuban cigar and telling stories. Some say he took the cigar with him into the shower.

Tiant's father, Luis Sr., had been a skinny lefthanded junk pitcher in the Negro Leagues. Neither had seen the other pitch until the older man got a visa to leave Havana and was given an emotional welcome to Fenway Park.

Joe Tinker

Shortstop, Chi (N) 1902–12, 1916, Cin (N) 1913,
Chi (F) 1914–15. Manager, Cin (N) 1913,
Chi (F) (1914–15, Chi (N) 1916.

Sometimes the whole is more than the sum of its parts, and that sort of rep seems to forever follow Tinker, Evers, and Chance. Bound together in F. P. Adams's famous bit of doggerel and in their simultaneous election to the Hall of Fame in 1946, the impression persists that they were three ordinary guys who somehow made magic only as a trio. The impression is unfair. Each was an excellent player, and no doubt they could have proved their worth as individuals.

Manager Chance's Cubs depended on pitching, speed, and defense. They won four pennants and two world championships from 1906 to 1910 using that recipe. None of the Cubbies hit much in those dead-ball days; the 1907 world champs didn't have a .300 hitter, their RBI leader had 70, and the Cubs' best home run man had 2. Of course, most other NL teams were similar.

In that context, Tinker was a pretty decent hitter for his time. His .263 average ranks right up there with those of shortstops of later, better-hitting eras. He usually knocked in 60–70 runs a season, and he hit 6 homers in 1908. He was practically a slugger! For some reason, Lord knows why, he always hit Christy Mathewson well, and since the Giants were always trying to nudge the Cubs out of first place, that was a very valuable talent. Once on base, Joe also had the required speed, stealing 336 bases over his career.

But Joe was paid to field. And that he did very well, leading NL shortstops five times in average, in assists twice, and in putouts twice. He even led once in double plays. Only once, you ask? Isn't that the maneuver T-to-E-to-C were supposedly such whizzes at? Well, they were—everyone who saw them agrees—but the Cubs' pitchers just didn't give them as many chances to get two as some other combinations had. In the case of double plays, it looks like the sum wasn't equal to the parts.

Joe Torre

Catcher/First Baseman/Third Baseman, Mil (N) 1960–65,
Atl (N) 1966-68, StL (N) 1969–74, NY (N) 1975-77.

Manager, NY (N) 1977–81, Atl (N) 1982–84

Torre started out with the Braves as a catcher because he kept getting fat. The idea was that catchers don't have to run much, something fat guys hate to do. Everything went well for a while. Joe didn't have the best arm in the world, but it wasn't embarrassing. He did all the other catching chores okay, and he was a terrific hitter. They selected him for the NL All-Star team from 1963 through 1967. The only thing was that catchers need rest every couple of days. In Joe's case, he usually spent his day of rest at first base so they could keep his bat in the lineup.

In 1969 he was traded to the Cardinals, who put him at first base full-time. Along about then, Joe figured he'd better get serious about a diet. It wasn't quite as quick as with the frog who turned into a prince, but in 1971, slim, trim Torre emerged as a third baseman and had the season of his life. He led the NL in batting (.363), hits (230), and RBIs (137). He was named MVP.

Although he never got back to that level, Torre had a lot of good seasons in his eighteen years. He finished with a .297 career average, 252 homers, and 1,185 RBIs.

Cristobal Torriente

Outfielder, Negro League, 1914–32, Cuban Stars, Chicago American Giants, Kansas City Monarchs, Detroit Stars, Gilkerson's Union Giants, Atlanta Black Crackers, Cleveland Cubs

Many authorities pick the big Cuban on the all-time All-Negro League outfield. In 1919 Torriente, Oscar Charleston, and speedster Jimmy Lyons patrolled the outfield for the Chicago American Giants, making perhaps the best trio ever among black teams.

Torriente was called the Ruth of Cuba, and in 1920 the two faced each other in Havana, one on one. Torri got three homers, two off first baseman Highpockets Kelly and one off Ruth himself. The Babe went 0-for-4 against Cuban hurling. Two home runs were usually good enough to lead the league for an entire season in the cavernous parks down there, making Torri's feat the more remarkable.

Cris wore bracelets, which he shook before going to bat, and a red bandana around his neck, for his Cuban club, the *Rojos,* or Reds.

He was Cuban batting champion three times, stolen base champ four times, and triple and home run champ five times each. In 1919–1920 he led in every batting department.

Torriente's highest averages were .401 in Cuba, 1915–1916, and .402 in the States in 1920. He led the Negro League in 1923 with .389.

Torri pitched occasionally and even played a lefthanded second base. He was also a notorious playboy, and he died an alcoholic at an early age.

Alan Trammell

Shortstop, Det (A) 1977–

Trammell is a good glove in the process of becoming an outstanding bat. He and second baseman Lou Whitaker have held down the keystone positions for the Tigers for eleven seasons. A four-time Gold Glove winner, Trammell's home runs climbed from 2 in 1978, his first full season, to 14 in 1983, to 28 in 1987. His batting average, though its climb has not been so steady, began in the .260s and peaked with .343 in 1987, as the Tigers won the Eastern Division.

In 1984, when the Tigers won the World Series, Trammell was named Series MVP for his .450 average, including two homers and six RBIs in five games.

Harold "Pie" Traynor

Third Baseman, Pit (N) 1920–37.
Manager, Pit (N) 1934–39.

Traynor used to be figured as the best-ever third baseman, but his halo has tarnished a little of late, as sluggers like Eddie Mathews, Brooks Robinson, Graig Nettles, and Mike Schmidt have appeared. There even seems to be some effort to show that he wasn't even the best when he was playing, but that's a little harder to swallow.

Traynor, who usually batted fifth for the Pirates, was no home run hitter; he knocked a mere 58 in his 1,941 games. Of course, half those games were in Forbes Field, where any righthanded batter who swung for the distant left field fence would have been considered a little goofy. Traynor doubled and tripled at a pretty good clip.

He seems to have driven runs home pretty well too, with seven seasons of 100-plus RBIs, but some critics worry that he didn't walk a whole lot. They also point out that batting averages were at an all-time high in the twenty years between the World Wars, making his .320 less impressive. However, it *does* happen to be the best for any of the third basemen who played during that period.

Traynor was regarded as the top-fielding third baseman of his day. A Pittsburgh sportswriter once wrote: "He doubled down the left field foul line, but Traynor threw him out." He led NL third sackers in putouts seven times, assists three times, and, surprisingly, only once in fielding average. There's no way to really rank him against modern third basemen. His career and single-season marks have been far surpassed by post-World War Two players, perhaps because more business comes to the hot corner now that most players try to pull the ball. Fielding stats being what they are, they neither prove nor disprove that he was the best gloveman playing third during his time. Most of the fans, teammates, and opponents thought he was, but they could be wrong.

Maybe they gave him extra for personality; Traynor was a genial, articulate man, with more friends than bookkeepers have decimal points. *The Sporting News* named him to its All-Star Major League team seven times between 1925 and 1933. He finished in the top ten in NL MVP voting six times through the same period. Let's put it this way, the people who looked at third basemen when Pie was playing thought he was Pie à la mode. Some moderns disagree. Of course, there are also people around today who can prove that Elvis lives, nobody ever walked on the moon, and fast food is good for you.

Traynor was named to the Hall of Fame in 1948.

Paul "Dizzy" Trout

Pitcher, Det (A) 1939–52, Bos (A) 1952, Bal (A) 1957

It was a wartime year, but in 1944 Trout was 27–14 and led the AL in ERA, complete games, innings pitched, and shutouts. Dizzy's teammate Hal Newhouser got the headlines with 29–9, but Trout may have been even better. He finished second to Hal in the MVP voting, 232 to 236.

In 1945 Diz was only 18–15 (while Newhouser was 25–9), but in the stretch, he pitched six games in nine days and won four of them, as the Tigers won the pennant on the final day. In the Series he had an 0.64 ERA but had to split his two decisions. He won the fourth game 4–1 and lost the sixth game in relief in the twelfth inning.

After the war, Trout's record slipped more than Newhouser's, but for two years they were terrific.

Trout's son Steve is a current major league pitcher, and their total of more than 250 wins makes them the winningest father-son combo.

George Uhle

Pitcher, Cle (A) 1919–28, 1936, Det (A) 1929–33,
NY (N) 1933, NY (A) 1933–34

One of the best hitting pitchers ever, with a .288 career batting average, Uhle (pronounced "Yoo-lee") was also one of the first to throw a slider, two decades before it became widespread in the 1940s. He was 26–16 for third-place Cleveland in 1923 and 27–11 for the second-place Tribe in 1926, leading in wins, complete games, and innings pitched each year. He was also first in putting men on base the latter year, with 300 hits and 118 walks, or a dangerous 11.8 per nine innings. George pitched a 20-inning game in 1929. He finished his seventeen-year career with exactly 200 wins.

Arthur "Dazzy" Vance

Pitcher, Pit (N) 1915, NY (A) 1915, 1918,
Bkn (N) 1922–32, 1935, StL (N) 1933–34, Cin (N) 1934

One of the Dodgers' Daffiness Boys, Dazzy didn't win his first big league game until he was thirty-one in 1922. Vance had pitched five complete games in seven days in the minors, causing a chronic sore arm which almost ended his career. He bounced around the minors for ten years until manager Wilbert Robinson of the Dodgers tried starting him every fifth day, instead of every fourth, the common practice.

Vance responded magnificently. His high-kick windup and extremely long arms (he had an eighty-three-inch reach) gave him a roaring fastball. Pitching with a tattered sleeve to confuse the hitters, he led the NL in strikeouts seven straight years, a record, in ERA three years, and in wins two.

Dazzy was the best pitcher in the league in 1924, with 28–6, as the Bums almost beat the Giants for the pennant. He won the MVP, even though Rogers Hornsby hit a mere .424 that year.

In 1925 the Bums fell to seventh, but Vance led in wins again, with 22–8. One was a one-hitter, and another, five days later, a rare 1920s no-hitter (against the Phils). In 1928 the Dodgers were sixth, but Vance was 22–10.

Vance was as famous for clowning as for pitching. He liked to party, often staying out until the detectives in the lobby yawned and went to bed. Then he would slip in unnoticed.

He was the key man in the famous play when Babe Herman doubled into a double play. Vance was on second base, but instead of scoring on Herman's drive, he rounded third and then went back to find Herman and one other runner sliding in from the opposite direction.

Vance was named to the Hall of Fame in 1955.

Floyd "Arky" Vaughan

Shortstop, Pit (N) 1932–41, Bkn (N) 1942–43, 1947–48

Next to Honus Wagner, Vaughan may have been the best-hitting shortstop ever, hitting over .300 twelve times, including his first ten years in the NL. His .385 in 1935 is the twentieth-century record for shortstops. In fourteen seasons he averaged .318 and led the league in runs scored three times. Vaughan had a good eye and rarely whiffed; from 1934 to 1936 he was the top NL hitter in drawing walks.

Though he was not a power hitter, Arky hit 19 homers one season and led the league in triples three different years. He slugged two home runs in the 1941 All-Star Game, the first man to do so.

He fielded his position well and led NL shortstops in putouts and assists three times each.

Vaughan was respected around the league for his honesty and integrity. In 1943, believing Brooklyn manager Leo Durocher had unfairly suspended another player and then lied about him to reporters, he handed in his uniform, threatening to leave the team until Durocher backed down. He retired at the end of the season and didn't return to the Dodgers until 1947, when Durocher was suspended for the season.

Vaughan was named to the Hall of Fame in 1985.

James "Hippo" Vaughn

Pitcher, NY (A) 1908, 1910–12, Was (A) 1912,
Chi (N) 1913–21

Like Harvey Haddix, lefthander Vaughn is remembered for one outstanding game, somewhat obscuring the fact that he pitched a number of excellent games. Indeed he was one of the best pitchers around during the World War One period. He didn't really settle in until he was twenty-six years old in 1914. But in seven years with the Cubs, he won 20 or more games five times, 10 once, and 17 once.

In 1918 he was 22–10 to lead the NL in wins, tops in ERA at 1.74, and led in strikeouts and innings pitched. In the World Series that year, he pitched three complete games and gave up only three earned runs, yet he was only 1–2.

Now about *The* game. On May 2 in Chicago, he hurled nine no-hit innings against Cincinnati. What made this no-hitter really special was that Fred Toney, pitching for the Reds, also tossed a no-hitter. So they went into the top of the tenth and Hard Luck Hippo gave up a single to light-hitting Larry Kopf. An outfield error followed, putting the runner on third. The next batter, Jim Thorpe, topped a little roller down

the third base line. Vaughn was called Hippo because he ran like one, but he was on the ball quickly and shoveled it to the catcher. Too late. The runner slid in with the run. In the bottom of the tenth, Toney retired the Cubs hitless again.

Bill Veeck

Owner, Cle (A), StL (A), Chi (A)

Veeck sent a midget to bat, integrated the AL, invented the exploding scoreboard, put players' names on their uniforms, and gave baseball its first two-million-attendance team, the 1948 Indians. He even tried to field an integrated Phillies club in 1943 until Judge Landis shot down his quest for ownership.

With his open collar, his wooden leg (a souvenir of the Marines), and his extroverted twinkle, Bill was a fans' owner who lounged in the bleachers, chain-drinking beer and listening to gripes. He owned three different AL teams at various times.

He learned the game at the hotdog stand in Wrigley Field, where his father was general manager for the Cubs. Later, Bill himself became general manager of the minor league Milwaukee Brewers.

After the war Veeck brought Cleveland a pennant in 1948. His promotions brought in fans and he brought in the players, including Larry Doby, the AL's first black player and forty-two-year-old Satchel Paige. In the early 1950s, Veeck tried to save the Browns. Some of his gimmicks were outrageous, such as sending midget Eddie Gaedel to pinch-hit (he walked) and having the fans manage a game by holding up decision cards. As White Sox owner, he gave the team its first flag in forty years in 1959.

His iconoclastic ways alienated the other owners but enchanted the fans. He wrote about his adventures entertainingly in *Veeck as in Wreck*. He even wrote about his sabbatical as a race track owner in a book entitled *30 Tons a Day*.

George "Rube" Waddell

Pitcher, Lou (N) 1897, 1899, Pit (N) 1900–1901,
Chi (N) 1901, Phi (A) 1902–07, StL (N) 1908–10

Lefthander Waddell had a terrific fastball, a biting curve, and exceptional control of his pitches. His life was fast, veered wildly, and had no control whatsoever. He is usually called eccentric, or erratic, or flaky, or unstable, or capricious. He was nutty. Completely uneducated, he fits the old line "If he had a brain, he would be dangerous."

He missed games because he was fishing, or helping the local firemen, or playing marbles, or drunk, or because he just forgot. He missed a World Series because he hurt his arm wrestling. He once dived into a river to save a drowning man—who turned out to be a log.

Everybody liked Rube, even all the managers who fired him, because they never knew if he'd show up or what he'd do if he got there. He *was* likable—a big, overgrown six-year-old.

People told all kinds of stories about him. He was so fast he poured ice water on his arm to slow himself down; he hit birds on the wing by throwing stones; he told his fielders to sit down

while he struck out the side; and he did cartwheels off the mound after whipping Cy Young in a twenty-inning showdown. Actually, he did beat Young, 4–2, in twenty innings, and he may have done the outfield stunt a couple of times in exhibition games.

The only manager ever to have the patience to put up with him for an extended period was Connie Mack, who would have probably called the Mad Hatter "a little odd." Especially if he could pitch.

In truth, Waddell was a heckuva pitcher for Mack for four seasons, and a good pitcher for a couple more years after that. He led in strikeouts for six straight seasons, with 349 in 1904, a record that would stand until 1973. He won 96 games from 1902 through 1905 (but he lost 56 and the A's had strong teams). He got his ERA down to 1.48 in 1905 (but five other pitchers were under 2.00).

Finally, even Mack couldn't take it any longer, and he traded Waddell to the Browns in 1908. The fact that Waddell's pitching was slipping probably made it a little easier. Yet in his first game against the A's, Waddell struck out sixteen batters.

By 1910 Rube was back in the minors. A year or so after that, he was visiting in Kentucky when a flood hit. In an act that recalls how he used to help firemen, Waddell stood for hours armpit deep in freezing water, passing sandbags to repair a dike. He contracted tuberculosis and died in 1914.

He was elected to the Hall of Fame in 1946.

John "Honus" Wagner

Shortstop, Lou (N) 1897–99,
Pit (N) 1900–17. Manager, Pit (N) 1917

Some say Wagner was the best player of all time. He was voted into Cooperstown in 1936 right behind Cobb and ahead of Ruth. The argument goes that a great shortstop is inherently more valuable than a great outfielder. Certainly that's true in the field. What might be more to the point is to rank Wagner against Cobb and Ruth as a hitter. Even allowing for the differences in liveliness of the baseballs each batted against in his prime, Cobb and Ruth were probably more dangerous at bat.

Nevertheless Honus hit .300 seventeen years in a row and won eight batting titles in twelve years, 1900–1911. He had a career mark of .329, with 3,430 hits, 651 doubles, 252 triples (third best all-time), 101 homers, 1,740 runs, and 1,732 RBIs. He led the NL in stolen bases five times. He finished with 722, fifth best all-time. He reputedly stole second, third, and home three times in his career.

In Wagner's only showdown against Cobb, in the 1909 World Series, Ty called to him from first base, "Watch out, Krauthead, I'm coming down." The two-hundred-pound Honus knocked Ty's teeth loose with the tag. Wagner batted .333 to Cobb's .200, and stole six bases to Ty's two, as Pittsburgh beat Detroit in seven. (Wagner's stolen base mark stood until Lou Brock broke it in 1967.)

Wagner was so long-armed and bowlegged, they said he could tie his shoes without bending down. His batting stance, says writer Bob Broeg, resembled a man sitting on a bar stool. He used the hands-apart grip and swung at anything near the plate.

Whether Wagner was the best-*fielding* shortstop of all

time, which you hear sometimes, or just one of the best of his day is hard to tell from fielding stats. He didn't become a full-time shortstop until his seventh NL season. He seems to have been a little rough at first, but he had great range. After he'd been at it for a few years, he led NL shortstops a couple of times in fielding average.

They say that when he fielded a grounder, his big hands scooped up dirt, ball, and all, and that he'd let everything fly, showering the first baseman in pebbles. Honus, who could embroider a story like Aunt Tillie could a seat cushion, said a dog once ran onto the field and snatched the ball; he said he threw both dog and ball to first for the out.

If his stories were incredible, at least you could tell them to your mother, he said. One estimate puts him as the most beloved man in baseball during the time between King Kelly and Babe Ruth. If so, he deserved the adoration. He always had time for a friend; he helped rookies; he had a drink now and then, but he was never a drunk; he was brighter than most but suffered fools with patience; and he never, *never*, acted the star. He also refused to let a cigarette company put his picture in their packs because he didn't want to encourage kids to smoke. He made them stop distributing one print, making the few in circulation the most valuable baseball cards in the world.

Bobby Wallace

Shortstop, Cle (N) 1894–98, StL (N) 1899–1901, 1917–18, StL (A) 1902–16. Manager, StL (A) 1911–12, Cin (N) 1937

When Bobby Wallace was elected to the Hall of Fame in 1953, a lot of people asked who-in-hell he was. More than thirty-five years later, when fans file past his plaque at Cooperstown, most of them ask the same question.

To answer: Wallace was the first AL shortstop in the Hall, beating Joe Cronin by three years. He played in the majors for twenty-five years, although you could only count him as a regular for about fifteen. He hit .300 three times, but most years he was down around .250 and a couple of years he was lower yet.

He started as a pitcher with the old Cleveland Spiders of the NL, then moved to third base for a couple of seasons. In 1899 he became a St. Louis Cardinal and switched to shortstop. By 1902 he was so highly regarded that the St. Louis Browns of the new AL paid him a $6,500 advance and signed him to a five-year contract for $32,500, thus making him the highest-paid player in baseball. In sum, he was the Ozzie Smith of his day.

He was generally accepted as the best AL shortstop from 1902 until about 1910, which is a pretty good run. The ranking was based almost entirely on his glove. As usual, fielding statistics don't prove a whole lot. Wallace led in fielding percentage and assists three times each. Big deal! His most significant fielding figure is that he averaged 6.1 chances per game; only four shortstops have ever done better.

Naturally, playing for the Browns meant no World Series appearances and mostly losing teams. It's to Wallace's credit that somebody remembered him forty years later, and it's to the Hall of Fame's credit that they elected a shortstop (in 1953) just because he could field. They've only done that once or twice.

Ed Walsh

Pitcher, Chi (A) 1904–16, Bos (N) 1917

The greatest spitballer, Walsh compiled the lowest lifetime ERA in history, 1.82. He was also one of the great ironmen of all time, four times leading the league in innings pitched, with an AL record of 464 in 1908. That's the year he won 40 games and almost pitched his "Hitless Wonder" White Sox to the flag. From 1907 through 1910, Walsh's ERAs were 1.60, 1.42, 1.41, and 1.27. That last one came in 1910, when he lost 20 games for a sixth-place club that hit .211 with seven home runs—for the whole team! He's the only man to lead the league in both ERA and losses at the same time.

A muscular product of the coal mines, Big Ed was square-shouldered and handsome. And he knew it. "He could strut sitting down," someone said.

In 1906 he was 17–13 with a team that hit .230. Ten of his wins were shutouts. In the World Series against the rival Cubs, Ed whiffed a then-record 12 men to win the third game on a two-hitter.

Walsh's finest season was 1908, when Chicago, Cleveland, and Detroit raced down to the wire. His team hit only 3 homers all year, one of them by Ed himself. He started 49 games and relieved in 17 more. He threw 11 shutouts, and won 40 games while losing only 15. He also saved 6.

Ed pitched seven games in the last nine days, including a doubleheader win over Boston, in which he gave one run, one walk, and seven hits. He threw fifteen runners out himself! The next day he pitched another nine innings, his third complete game in two days. In a head-to-head showdown against Cleveland ace Addie Joss, Ed fanned 15 and gave up only four hits—but Joss trumped him with a perfect game.

The next day Walsh was called in to relieve with the bases loaded, two out in the ninth, and Nap Lajoie at bat. He fooled Larry with a fastball instead of a spitter and got him on a called strike three. He would call it the greatest thrill of his career.

Walsh continued to work hard—370 innings in 1910, 369 in 1911, 393 in 1912. He won 27 games in each of the last two years, including a no-hitter. His arm gave out in 1913 and several comeback tries failed. He finished with 195 wins, 57 of them shutouts.

He was named to the Hall of Fame in 1946.

William "Bucky" Walters

Pitcher, Bos (N) 1931–34, 1950, Phi (N) 1934–38, Cin (N) 1938–48. Manager, Cin (N) 1948–49

For two magnificent years, 1939–1940, Walters was the premier pitcher in baseball. With Paul Derringer, he led the Reds to their first flags since 1919 after two decades of frustration.

In 1939 Bucky, 27–11, led in wins, ERA, complete games, and strikeouts, easily winning the MVP. In 1940 he led in wins again (22–10), plus ERA and complete games. Walters added two wins in the World Series, holding the Tigers to a 1.50 ERA.

In 1944 Walters had a 23–8 mark for the third-place Reds. He lost a perfect game on a two-out single in the eighth. When the 1948 season began, Bucky needed only two more

wins to reach 200 and looked like a dead-bang cinch. But he'd also been named as the Reds' manager that year. He only got around to pitching in seven games and won none of them. Nevertheless, his 198–160 record isn't bad for a fellow who began as a third baseman and never pitched a game until he was in his fifth major league season.

Lloyd Waner

Outfielder, Pit (N) 1927–41, 1944–45, Bos (N) 1941,
Cin (N) 1941, Phi (N) 1942, Bkn (N) 1944

A good singles hitter, Lloyd rode to Cooperstown on the coattails of his big brother Paul. The two played next to each other for Pittsburgh from 1927 through 1940.

Lloyd was a steady .300 hitter in an era of steady .300 hitters. As a rookie in 1927, he made 223 hits, a rookie record; 198 of them were singles, still a record for anyone. He led the NL with 133 runs scored. He hit .355, plus .400 in the World Series, as the Yankees crushed the Pirates in four straight.

He made 221 hits in 1928 and 234 in 1929, when he led the league with 20 triples. An illness cost him most of the 1930 season, but he came back to lead the league with 214 hits in 1931.

Lloyd rarely struck out—only 173 times, an average of once in every 45 at-bats. In 1941 he played in 77 games without a single strikeout. The bad news was that he didn't walk very often either, not nearly often enough for a lifetime leadoff man.

His greatest attribute was his speed. It made him an excellent center fielder. Lloyd led the league in putouts four times.

Lloyd was known as "Little Poison" and Paul as "Big Poison," which is Dodger-fan talk for "little person" and "big person." Lloyd didn't drink, while Paul was a notorious toper. The two had started out as roomies but later split up.

Lloyd "rejoined" Paul in the Hall of Fame in 1967, two years after Paul's death. Certainly the fact that they formed a duo for so many years must have had some influence on the voters, but Lloyd's 2,459 hits, .316 batting average, and excellence in the outfield give him some good credentials on his own.

Paul Waner

Outfield, Pit (N) 1926–40, Bkn (N) 1941,
1943–44, Bos (N) 1941–42, NY (A) 1944–45

"Big Poison" wasn't a big man, at five-eight, 153 pounds, but he was a big talent. Paul hit over .300 twelve straight years. He collected 200 hits eight times, tying Willie Keeler's record.

Waner won three batting titles in 1927, 1934, and 1936. His .380 in 1927 won him the NL MVP Award.

Paul learned to hit swinging at corncobs in Oklahoma. He stood deep in the box, feet together, and aimed at the top of the ball, swinging down as in a golf shot, a theory he later taught as coach. A line drive hitter, he led in doubles and triples twice each.

He wasn't a home run threat, although he hit 15 in 1929. He recognized that approach as a losing game in spacious Forbes Field and became adept at lining the ball down either

foul line. The worst that could happen was a foul ball. If the ball hit fair, he had extra bases. In twenty years, Paul had 3,152 hits, including 603 doubles and 190 triples. His batting average was .333, and he scored 1,626 runs and drove in 1,309.

In his prime he was a fine defensive outfielder with the arm to play right field at Forbes.

Paul was notorious for his drinking. One year manager Pie Traynor convinced him to lay off the sauce. When Paul's batting average dropped to .240, Traynor took him out and bought him a drink. But despite humorous stories about his hungover hitting, the boozing probably kept him from a couple of batting titles and left him only an ordinary player in his last few years.

The story is that Paul beat out a grounder off an infielder's glove one day in 1942 for what could have been his 3,000th hit. However, he signaled the scorer to call it an error, preferring to wait for a clean blow for the big one. The infielder's comment has not survived.

Waner was named to the Hall of Fame in 1952.

John Montgomery Ward

Pitcher/Shortstop, Prov (N) 1878–82,
NY (N) 1883–89, 1893–94, Bkn (P) 1890, Bkn (N) 1891–92.
Manager, NY (N) 1884, 1893–94, Bkn (P) 1890,
Bkn (N) 1891–92

When Monte Ward was named to the Hall of Fame in 1964, the only question was whether he should go in as a pitcher, a shortstop, or as an executive. One of the most remarkable figures in baseball history, he excelled at nearly everything he did.

He broke in as an eighteen-year-old pitcher with Providence in 1878 and led the NL in ERA. The next year he pitched his team to a pennant with a 47–17 mark. In 1880 he pitched the second perfect game in NL history and finished with a 40–23 record. An arm injury ended his pitching career after he'd won 161 games. In 1883 he played center field despite his lame arm—throwing lefthanded!

Undaunted, he became the league's top shortstop, hitting .300 three times, and glueing the infield as captain of the 1888–1889 league champion New York Giants. He led the NL twice in stolen bases and finished with 2,123 career hits and 1,408 runs scored.

A handsome society lion, married to an actress, Ward studied law at night at Columbia, graduating with honors. In 1886 he led the formation of the Players' Brotherhood, the first attempt to improve players' rights. When the Brotherhood got no satisfaction, they formed their own league, the Players League, in 1890. One hundred players jumped their teams in support. Ward played for and managed the Brooklyn club in the league. When the owners sought an injunction against the players, Ward argued the case in court and won.

He won the battles but not the war. Even though the new league drew better than the NL or American Association, the financial backers of the Players League teams became nervous and many pulled out. Ward's league folded after one year, and the players meekly signed new reserve contracts with their old owners.

Ward returned to the Giants, and as player-manager took them to a Temple Cup victory in 1894.

Lon Warneke

Pitcher, Chi (N) 1930–36, 1942–45, StL (N) 1937–42

"The Arkansas Hummingbird," Warneke was one of the top righthanders of the 1930s, winning 20 games three times and helping the Cubs to two pennants. In 1932 he topped the NL in wins and percentage with a 22–6 mark. He also led in ERA and shutouts. The Cubs won the pennant but lost the World Series to the Yankees. In 1935, when the Cubs won the flag again, Lon went 20–13 and won twice in the World Series.

Although the modest Warneke was one of Chicago's most popular players, he was traded to the Cardinals in 1937. He helped them win the 1942 pennant—after he had been traded back to Chicago. He beat Brooklyn in a crucial September game to give the Cards a slim lead. "Now hold it," he told his old mates, and they did.

Warneke, who finished with a 193–121 career mark, later was a National League umpire from 1949 to 1955.

Earl Weaver

Manager, Bal (A) 1968–82, 1985–86

Weaver presided over the Orioles' dynasty of the 1970s, leading them to six division titles, four pennants, and one world championship. His winning percentage of .583 ranks in the top ten all-time. Although it was said his teams relied on "pitching and the three-run homer" to win, and the formula has been copied by several teams in the 1980s, Weaver was actually a highly innovative manager. He schooled his players in fundamentals, pioneered the use of computer charts, extended the use of platooning, and even wrote a training manual used by the entire Orioles' organization. Always open to new ideas, his motto became the title of his autobiography: *It's What You Learn After You Know It All That Counts.*

A minor league second baseman who never got beyond Double-A, his success once he turned to managing won him promotion to the Orioles in 1968. Although one of his hurlers cracked, "The only thing Earl knows about pitching is that he couldn't hit it," he and coach George Bamberger produced twenty-two 20-game winners and six Cy Young winners. Several pitchers, including Mike Cueller, Steve Stone, and Mike Torrez came from other organizations to achieve their best seasons with the Orioles.

Weaver was known for his rages against umpires. He was ejected from ninety-one games during his career. Once he was booted from both ends of a doubleheader. However, Weaver was so respected as a psychologist that some believe that many of his tantrums were staged to arouse his team.

George Weiss

Executive

"The last of the empire builders," Weiss, more than any other man, was responsible for the unprecedented success of the New York Yankees from the mid-1930s until the mid-1960s: twenty-two pennants and seventeen world championships.

He began with the Eastern League New Haven franchise in 1919 and advanced to become general manager of Balti-

more of the International League in 1929. In 1932 he was made farm director of the Yankees and kept an overpowering fountain of talent flowing to the majors for the next fifteen years. Many of the greatest players ever to wear Yankee pinstripes came up through Weiss's farms.

In 1948 he became general manager of the Yankees. One of his first moves was to hire Casey Stengel as manager, despite Stengel's reputation as a clown. With Weiss supplying the players and Stengel managing them, the Yankees won ten pennants between 1949 and 1960.

Both he and Stengel were let go as "too old" after the 1960 season. Weiss became president of the expansion Mets in 1961, hired Stengel as manager, and together they laid the groundwork for the future success of that team. In the meantime, the Yankees that Weiss had built continued to win pennants through 1964, and then collapsed into the poorest Yankees' decade since before World War One.

Weiss was named to the Hall of Fame in 1971.

Mickey Welch

Pitcher, Troy (N) 1880–82, NY (N) 1883–92

"Smiling Mickey" was able to grin 311 times as the winning pitcher in games played between 1880 and 1892. He was the third pitcher to win 300 games, preceded only by Pud Galvin and teammate Tim Keefe. Although Welch was not noted for his speed, he was effective with changes of speed on his curveball and screwball.

Welch led the NL in walks for three straight years, 1884–1886, but averaged over 500 innings pitched for each of those years. In 1885 he won 44 games (including a streak of seventeen victories in a row) for the Giants. He finally had a clause written into his contract that he would only pitch every two days.

He and Keefe combined as a one-two pitching punch for the Giants in the late 1880s, helping the team to pennants in 1888 and 1889.

Welch was elected to the Hall of Fame in 1973.

Willie "Devil" Wells

Shortstop, Negro League, 1925–49, St. Louis Stars, Detroit Wolves, Kansas City Monarchs, Chicago American Giants, Cole's American Giants, Newark Eagles, Memphis Red Sox, New York Black Yankees, Baltimore Elite Giants

Wells is among the top six Negro League home run hitters of all time. Though not considered a slugger, Wells owns the all-time Negro League home run record, with 27 in 1927, aided by a short left field fence in his St. Louis home park.

In 1930 Willie led the Negro National League with .404.

Wells's batting average in the black big leagues was .332. Against white big leaguers, he was even better: .369, with 6 homers in 31 games.

At shortstop, Wells had sure hands but did not have a strong arm. He compensated with an uncanny ability to play the hitters. He is usually considered the top shortstop in black baseball during the latter 1920s and 1930s. He was chosen to play in the East-West All-Star Game eight times.

A notorious target of beanball pitches, Wells created an

early batting helmet by taking a miner's hardhat and knocking off the gas jet.

He began managing in 1936 with the Newark Eagles and is ranked as one of the finest skippers in Negro League history. His Eagles won the NNL pennant in 1946. Among his players were Ernie Banks, Don Newcombe, Larry Doby, and Monte Irvin.

Zack Wheat

Outfielder, Bkn (N) 1909–26, Phi (A) 1927

Wheat was a graceful fielder with an amazingly accurate arm and a reliable line drive hitter. For years there was a sign on the Ebbets Field wall: "Zack Wheat caught 345 flies last year; Tanglefoot fly paper caught 10 million." The only thing that had to be repainted from season to season was the appropriate number of putouts by Wheat; he was the Brooklyn left fielder for eighteen years.

Although he led the NL in hitting only once—.335 in 1918—Wheat topped .300 fourteen times and finished with a .317 career average. He cracked 2,884 hits, scored 1,289 runs, and batted in 1,261. His line drives were usually smoked. Once the lively ball was introduced, drives that had been catchable zoomed past the fielders. Wheat's best batting marks came when he was in his late thirties. In 1924 at the age of thirty-eight, he hit .375, with 14 homers and 97 RBIs. The next year he drove in 103 runs, while hitting .359. Noted for his ability to hit curveballs, Wheat had no weaknesses at bat or in the field, but he did have thin, weak ankles that were often injured.

Although he played on Dodger pennant winners in 1916 and 1920, Wheat always maintained that his favorite game was the twenty-six-inning, 1–1 tie between Brooklyn and Boston in 1920.

He was elected to the Hall of Fame in 1959.

James "Deacon" White

Third Baseman/Catcher, Cle (NA) 1871–72,
Bos (NA) 1873–75, Chi (N) 1876, Bos (N) 1877,
Cin (N) 1878–80, Buf (N) 1881–85, Det (N) 1886–88,
Pit (N) 1889, Buf (P) 1890. Manager Cin (N) 1879

White was one of the most remarkable players of the nineteenth century. His career was long, productive, and filled with firsts. For example, on May 4, 1871, when the Cleveland Forest Citys played the Fort Wayne Kekiongas in the *first* game of the spanking new National Association, who strode up to the plate to become the *first* batter ever in a recognized professional league? White. And a few moments later, who doubled to make the *first* hit and the *first* extra-base hit? White. And a short while after that, who became the *first* to be put out on a double play? White.

After the 1872 campaign, he left Cleveland for the Boston Red Stockings, who then became the *first* team to win two consecutive pennants, then three consecutive, and then four. And speaking of four, White, Al Spalding, Ross Barnes, and Cal McVey, among Boston's best players, were called "the Big Four" (historically, the *first* "Big Four") when they deserted for Chicago in 1876. The resulting ruckus brought about the formation of the National League, and Chicago won the NL's *first* pennant, as White became its *first* RBI leader.

Back to Boston in 1877, White became Beantown's *first* batting champion (.387) as the Red Stockings won their *first* NL pennant. Deacon next formed the catching half of baseball's *first* brother battery with pitcher Will White, the *first* player to wear glasses on the field.

In the early 1880s at Buffalo, White became part of the *second* "Big Four," along with Dan Brouthers, Hardy Richardson, and Jack Rowe. In 1885 all four were sold to Detroit in the *first* big player deal. And in 1887 they led Detroit to its *first* (and last) NL pennant. White hit .303 at the age of forty.

White's nickname suited him; he never drank, smoked, or cursed, and he carried his Bible with him when the team was on the road.

Frank White

Second Baseman, KC (A) 1973–

An often unsung hero, White has been an outstanding second baseman for all of the Royals' better teams. At first used as a utility man, he settled in as the regular at second in 1976, the year the Royals won their first-division championship. Although he's only led AL second basemen twice in fielding average, his range factor has been excellent. He has won eight Gold Gloves, symbolic of the best fielder. His career fielding average is in the top ten all-time.

His career batting average is below .260, but he has shown home run power. In both 1985 and 1986 he hit 22 homers.

Sol White

Second Baseman, Executive, Negro League, 1887–1926,
Pittsburgh Keystones, Washington Capital Citys, Wheeling
(O.B.), New York Gorhams, York Monarchs (O.B.), Cuban
Giants, Genuine Cuban Giants, Fort Wayne (O.B.), Page
Fence Giants, Cuban X-Giants, Columbia Giants, Philadel-
phia Giants, Lincoln Giants, Quaker Giants, Cleveland
Browns, Newark Stars

If Rube Foster was the "father of black baseball," White was the grandfather. Born in 1868, he was nineteen when major league baseball's bars clanged shut on blacks in 1887, and he lived to see the end of sixty years of baseball *apartheid* in 1947. White played with white minor league teams in the 1880s (once playing against Ban Johnson); then after *apartheid*, he played for the Cuban Giants, the Page Fence Giants, and the Philadelphia Giants. Finally he joined the Cuban X-Giants, along with black pioneers Charley "Tokahoma" Grant, Rube Foster, Home Run Johnson, Frank Grant, Pop Lloyd, etc.

White managed the 1903 Philadelphia Giants, who beat Newark of the International League four straight but lost the first black World Series to Foster's X-Giants two games to three. He hired Foster and got revenge the following year two-to-one.

In his *History of Colored Baseball*, White wrote of the financial pressures on black teams in 1906 and of walking around towns for hours looking for hotels which would accept

them. The average white big leaguer made $2,000 a year, he wrote; the average black, $466.

White took Pop Lloyd, Dick Redding, Louis Santop, and Spotswood Poles to the New York Lincoln Giants in 1911. The Lincolns were perhaps the strongest black team in pre-World War One days.

After retiring, White coached at Wilberforce College and wrote a sports column. In his *History* he had urged blacks to keep up their skills so they would be ready when the doors were opened again. He was seventy-nine in 1947 when his prophecy came true in Brooklyn.

Hoyt Wilhelm

Pitcher, NY (N) 1952–56, StL (N) 1957,
Cle (A) 1957–58, Bal (A) 1958–62, Chi (A) 1963–68,
Cal (A) 1969, Atl (N) 1969–71, Chi (N) 1970,
LA (N) 1971–72

The first relief pitcher honored by Cooperstown, Hoyt used his knuckler to pitch until he was forty-eight. Hoyt's 1,070 games are a record for pitchers. Although he saved 227 games, he never in any season led in saves. He did lead in relief wins twice, and his 123 relief victories are the all-time record.

The way a staff's stopper is used has changed since Wilhelm's day. When he pitched, a top reliever was often brought in when a game was close, no matter which team was leading, a system that led to many wins but reduced the chance for saves. The most common modern practice is to bring in a club's closer primarily in save situations with the team ahead. Although saves have increased greatly, a relief win now often means that the reliever must first lose the lead he was sent in to protect.

Wilhelm's top save total was 27 in 1964 with the White Sox. He also had 12 relief wins that year. Yet the only category he led in was relief losses with 9.

An infantryman in World War Two, Hoyt was wounded and received the Purple Heart during the Battle of the Bulge. He was twenty-eight before he reached the majors and slugged a home run in his first major league at-bat. He never hit another. (His lifetime batting average was .088.)

Although many pitchers had used the knuckleball before Wilhelm, perhaps no pitcher had ever used it so much to the exclusion of other pitches. Certainly no pitcher popularized it so.

Hoyt baffled the batters—and catchers—with his knuckler. Five of his receivers set records for the most passed balls in an inning, and he gave up a whopping total of unearned runs.

As a rookie with the New York Giants in 1952, Wilhelm led the NL in appearances (71), ERA (2.43), and winning percentage with a 15–3 mark.

In late 1958 he was given an infrequent start by the Orioles and responded with a no-hitter over the Yankees. The next year he was used primarily as a starter; he was 15–11 and led the AL in ERA. But after a few starts in 1960, he was returned to the bullpen.

Wilhelm was elected to the Hall of Fame in 1985.

J. L. Wilkinson

Executive, owner, Negro League, 1909–48, All Nations,
Kansas City Monarchs

The white owner of the famous Kansas City Monarchs, Wilkinson was one of the pioneers of night baseball who gave Satchel Paige his second chance and Jackie Robinson his first. His lights saved Negro baseball in the Depression and helped to save the white minors as well.

Wilkinson's first club, the All Nations—a multiracial team of blacks, whites, and orientals, plus a woman—barnstormed the prairies before World War One. He was one of the founders of the Negro NL in 1920. His Monarchs were black world champs in 1924, league champs in 1925, and reached the playoffs in 1926.

When the Depression struck, Wilkie bought portable lights, playing his first night game in Enid, Oklahoma, two weeks before Des Moines opened with its lights and the same night that Independence, Kansas, played organized baseball's first night game. Wilkinson took his lights to St. Louis, Detroit, Pittsburgh, and elsewhere, helping spread the idea to countless cities.

In 1937, when Paige's career seemed dead because of a sore arm, Wilkie took a chance on him and the arm magically healed. Satch helped win pennants in 1937, 1939–1942, and 1946, and brought in much needed dollars. Satch got 15 percent off the top.

In 1945 Wilkinson also gave a job to a rookie shortstop named Robinson.

When the white big league raids decimated the black leagues, no club lost more than the Monarchs. Wilkinson sold out his interest in 1948.

Billy Williams

Outfield, Chi (N) 1959–74, Oak (A) 1975–76

Williams played in 1,117 straight games, the NL record.

The NL Rookie of the Year in 1961, Williams established himself in left field for the Cubs and remained for fourteen seasons. His final two years were spent as a DH with Oakland.

Nicknamed "Sweet Swinging" because of his batting swing, the popular Williams slugged 426 home runs and drove in 1,475 runs, while fashioning a .290 career batting average. He, Ernie Banks, and Ron Santo gave the Cubs a terrific power trio throughout the 1960s, but the Cubbies were never quite able to win a pennant.

Billy usually hit around 25–30 homers a year, reaching his peak, 42, in 1970. Two years later *The Sporting News* named him Player of the Year, when he led the NL in batting and slugging with .333 and .606.

He was named to the NL All-Star team six times. In 1987 he was elected to the Hall of Fame.

Smokey Joe Williams

Pitcher, Negro League, 1897–1932, San Antonio Bronchos,
Leland Giants, Chicago Giants, Lincoln Giants, Chicago
American Giants, Bacharach Giants, Brooklyn Royal

Giants, Homestead Grays

In a 1952 poll conducted by the *Pittsburgh Courier* a panel of black veterans and sportswriters picked Williams as the best black pitcher of all time. He defeated Satchel Paige by a single vote. He was considered faster than Paige.

A big half-black, half-Commanche, Joe resembled Walter Johnson in age, build, and style—both threw blazing fastballs and little else. In their one head-to-head confrontation, Joe won 1–0.

It was one of 19 wins (and 7 losses) Joe recorded against white big leaguers in exhibition games. He defeated seven Hall of Famers—Johnson, Grover Alexander, Chief Bender, Rube Marquard (twice), Waite Hoyt, and Satchel Paige. Two of his losses came after the age of forty; two more were 1–0 decisions.

Joe's best game was a ten-inning, 20-strikeout no-hitter against John McGraw's NL champion Giants in 1917. He lost it 1–0 on an error. Reportedly he gained his nickname after the game when Ross Youngs remarked, "That was a hell of a game, Smokey." Until then Williams had been called Cyclone Joe. In 1930 he fanned twenty-seven Kansas City Monarchs in a twelve-inning night game. The primitive lights and tobacco juice on the ball didn't hurt.

Williams and Paige faced each other twice in the early 1930s. They split the two games. "Smokey Joe could throw harder than all of them," Paige declared.

Joe's rival was Cannonball Redding. They started as teammates on the 1911–1914 New York Lincolns, forming one of the best one-two pitching punches in history.

Ken Williams

Outfield, Cin (N) 1915–16,
StL (A) 1918–27, Bos (A) 1928–29

Overshadowed by Babe Ruth and by his own teammate, George Sisler, Williams was a good hitter who in his best season almost batted the Browns to a pennant in 1922. They lost to the Yankees by a single game, and might have won had Sisler not injured his shoulder just before a crucial head-to-head series in the stretch. Ken knocked in 155 runs and won the home run crown with 39. (It should be noted that Ruth missed a quarter of the season that year.) Williams hit thirty-two of his homers in Sportsman's Park.

Ken played in a fine outfield alongside Jack Tobin and Baby Doll Jacobson. All of them were later picked as outfielders on various Browns all-time teams.

Although he never matched his 1922 numbers, the tall lefthanded hitter finished second in the AL in homers in 1921, 1923, and 1925.

Ted Williams

Outfielder, 1939–42, 1946–60.
Manager, Was (A) 1969–71, Tex (A) 1972

Either Williams or Babe Ruth was the greatest hitter of all time, and you could probably cover the difference with an ant's umbrella. Despite losing nearly five seasons in various wars, Williams put together a statistical record that would

stand against anyone's. Whether that makes Williams one-two as the greatest *player* of all time is another question altogether.

First the career figures: .344 career batting average, 521 home runs, 1,798 runs, 1,839 RBIs, 2,019 walks, and a .634 slugging average.

And what about individual seasons? He won six AL batting championships, including the famous .406 of 1941; four home run titles, including a personal high of 43 in 1949; six times leading in runs scored; four times in RBIs; eight times in walks; and nine times in slugging average.

And how about the clutch? Remember Williams's home run with two out in the ninth to win the 1941 All-Star Game? Or the 1946 All-Star homer off Rip Sewell's blooper pitch? Or that he could have sat down the final day in 1941 and finished with a rounded-off .400 (.3995) but insisted on playing and lifted his average to .406? Or that he homered in his last major league at-bat?

And remember he won two MVPs, in 1946 and 1949, and his fans never stopped complaining about the ones he didn't win. And remember *The Sporting News* named him Player of the Decade for the 1950s, which raised a few eyebrows among the fans of Musial, Mays, and Mantle, to name only the M's.

One thing seems certain: Williams will get better every year in our memories as we look at his statistical record. There was never a question that he was the best hitter when he was playing. He was criticized for other things and we tend to forget those. They said he was no better than adequate in the field with a so-so arm, with the footnote that he played Fenway's left field wall very well. They complained that the Red Sox won only a single pennant in all the Williams years, with the footnote that there were some serious pitching problems nearly every year in Boston. They grumbled that he was sometimes boorish, with the footnote that he was often charming.

Most of the gripes were about intangible things. If you were playing a computer baseball game and could pick your roster from players from any era, you'd probably start with Williams if Ruth was already taken.

Williams was elected to the Hall of Fame in 1966.

Vic Willis

Pitcher, Bos (N) 1898–1905,
Pit (N) 1906–09, StL (N) 1910

Willis holds the NL record for complete games in this century, with 45 in 1902, as well as for losses, with 29 in 1905 for the seventh-place Bostonians. But the curveballer won 20 or more eight times, including four of his first five years, 1898–1902. He finished with a hefty 247–206 record.

As a twenty-two-year-old rookie in 1898, Vic helped pitch Boston to the flag with a 24–13 record. In 1899 he was 27–10 with a no-hitter.

After an off-year in 1900, Willis came back in 1901 to go 20–17 for a fifth-place team. The next year he was 27–19, led in innings pitched and strikeouts, and set a modern record with 45 complete games.

Vic had two big losing years in 1904–1905, when he was 18–25 and 11–29 as Boston stumbled in next-to-last. But a trade to third-place Pittsburgh in 1906 brought him back to a

22–11 record, the first of four straight 20-win years. In the last one, 1909, Willis was 22–11 to lead the Pirates to the world championship.

Willis's 247 victories appear to be some sort of Hall of Fame dividing line. Every eligible pitcher with a career predominantly in the twentieth century who won more than Willis has been elected to the Hall.

Maury Wills

Shortstop, LA (N) 1959–66, 1969–72, Pit (N) 1967–68,
Mon (N) 1969. Manager, Sea (A) 1980–81

Wills brought the stolen base back into baseball. No NL player had stolen 50 bases since Max Carey in 1923 when Wills grabbed that many in 1960. Two years later he shattered Ty Cobb's 1915 record of 96 and became the first man to break 100 in this century. (Nineteenth-century rules counted extra bases taken on others' hits as steals.) Maury's 104 steals lit the way for the Brocks, Hendersons, and Colemans and changed the nature of the game.

Wills was the shortstop for Los Angeles, a team long on pitching and short on power. His steals were of more value to the Dodgers than they might have been to a team of greater batting proficiency. He led the NL in stolen bases six straight years, 1960–1965, and he finished his fourteen-year career with 586. In addition to the 104 in 1962, which won him the MVP Award, he stole 94 in 1965.

Wills spent eight years in the minors before finally being given a chance with the Dodgers midway through the 1959 season. Although he had no home run power, Wills was more than a one-dimensional player. He had a career batting average of .281, and he twice won Gold Gloves as a shortstop. With Wills at short, the Dodgers won four pennants.

His son Bump Wills played six years (1977–1982) in the majors and was also an excellent base stealer.

Lewis "Hack" Wilson

Outfield, NY (N) 1923–25, Chi (N) 1926–31,
Bkn (N) 1932–34, Phi (N) 1934

It was often said of Wilson that "he was a lowball hitter and a highball drinker." The line could still get a chuckle after his career went down the tube at age thirty-four but lost its mirth when he died at forty-eight. For five years he was the most fearsome slugger in the NL; then, almost overnight, he became a has-been.

He was one of the strangest-looking men ever to play in the majors. He stood only five-six but weighed around 210. He had an eighteen-inch neck and wore a size-six shoe. Because someone thought he resembled the famous strongman George Hackenschmidt, Wilson was tagged "Hack," but that probably didn't do him justice. What he really looked like was Barney Rubble with Wilma Flintstone's feet.

After he'd played a couple of years for the Giants and been found wanting, the Cubs picked him up for a song—a little ditty called $5,000—in 1926. Right away he started hitting homers and driving in runs. From 1926 through 1930 he led the NL in homers four times, drove in over 100 runs each year, and hit over .300. The really big seasons were 1929,

when he hit .345 and had 159 RBIs to help the Cubs to the pennant, and 1930, which made everything else look like a preamble. In 1930 he hit .356, he scored 146 runs, he hammered out 56 homers—still the NL record—and he drove in a grand total of (drum roll) 191 runs!

Hack was thirty years old and it was "top-of-the-world-ma"! And if you remember what happened next in the Cagney movie, just about the same thing happened to Hack in 1931. His boozing was at the base. Manager Rogers Hornsby got on his case about the cases he was consuming. Hack sulked and drank more. And when he hit .261, with 13 homers and 61 RBIs, they exiled him to Brooklyn. By 1934, he was done hitting lowballs.

He was elected to the Hall of Fame in 1979.

Dave Winfield

Outfield, SD (N) 1973–80, NY (A) 1981–

Probably the best all-around athlete in the majors in the last quarter century, the six-six, 220-pound Winfield was drafted to play both pro football and pro basketball but opted instead to step directly from the University of Minnesota into a regular job in the San Diego outfield in 1973. Although the San Diego park was a poor one for righthanded power hitters and the Padres team was annually awful, he established himself as one of the NL's best players, hitting .300 twice, leading in RBIs in 1979, and earning two Gold Gloves.

Frustrated at playing for a losing team, he signed an estimated $25-million contract as a free agent with the Yankees in 1981. He has seldom been out of the news since. Discounting 1981, the strike year, he has batted in at least 100 runs every year as a Yankee except 1987, when he drove home 97. His home run totals have been as high as 37 and as low as 19 (in 1984, when he batted .340). He has brightened innumerable highlight films with leaping outfield catches. He has been a team leader and has conducted himself as a model citizen, and his Winfield Foundation is known for its charitable work with underprivileged youth.

There's a downside. He has also been involved in numerous verbal skirmishes and even a lawsuit with Yankee owner George Steinbrenner. The Yankees have played in only one World Series (1981) since his arrival, and he hit only .045 there. And the seagulls of Toronto will never forgive him for his mighty outfield toss that nailed one of their numbers.

George Wright

Shortstop, Bos (NA), 1871–75,
Bos (N) 1876–78, 1880–81, Prov (N) 1879, 1882.
Manager, Prov (N) 1879

Baseball's Wright brothers weren't related to the airplane inventors, but they got professional baseball off the ground in 1869 with the first completely pro team. George starred at shortstop for older brother Harry's pioneer pro club, the Cincinnati Red Stockings, which went unbeaten that year while playing all comers from east coast to west. George hit .629, with 49 homers in the Reds' 57 counted games.

George had been named shortstop on pioneer baseball writer Henry Chadwick's first All-Star team in 1868. He was

the first shortstop to play out beyond the baselines, thereby increasing his range. He was valued even more for his fielding than his hitting. And small wonder! The Red Stockings won games by scores of 85–7, 40–0, and 103–8. Who needed another hitter?

The Wrights moved to Boston of the new National Association following the 1870 campaign and won four straight flags, 1872–1875. George's batting average ranged from .409 to .336.

When the NL was founded in 1876, George was the first man to come to bat. He hit a grounder to shortstop.

His batting began dropping off, however, and with the advent of sidearm and curveball pitching in 1877, it was down to .255, but Boston won the flag and repeated in 1878. In 1879 he moved to Providence as player-manager and beat Harry's Bostonians for the flag, giving him eight pennants in nine years.

George founded a sporting goods company in Boston. When he took on a partner in 1879, the company became Wright & Ditson. An all-around athlete, George had starred at cricket before turning full-time to baseball. After retiring from the diamond, he returned to cricket. He introduced golf to the Boston area and was instrumental in introducing hockey to the United States. He also supported tennis, and his two sons won national championships.

George was named to the Hall of Fame in 1937.

William "Harry" Wright

Outfielder/Pitcher, Bos (NA) 1871–75,
Bos (N) 1876–77. Manager, Bos (NA) 1871–75,
Bos (N) 1876–81, Pro (N) 1882–83,
Phi (N) 1884–93

Henry Chadwick, "the father of baseball," called Wright the "father of pro baseball."

Harry organized the game's first completely professional team, the Cincinnati Red Stockings, paving the way for the first pro league, the National Association. He designed the basic uniform that is still worn today, knee-length knickers instead of pantaloons. And he patented the first scorecard.

A professional cricket player, in 1858 Harry decided to try the new American game of baseball. He joined the New York Knickerbockers as an outfielder. He occasionally pitched in relief, throwing a change-up he called a "dew drop."

In 1867 Harry joined the Cincinnati Red Stockings as a pitcher. Since 1865 he had been a paid bowler for the Cincinnati Union Cricket Club. By 1868, with several pros on the team, the Red Stockings were Midwest champions. The next year his younger brother George, a star shortstop, joined the team, and the Red Stockings took the field as the first fully professional baseball team. The Red Stockings toured the country and won every game in 1869. The winning streak continued until June 14, 1870, when they were finally bested by the Atlantics of Brooklyn in a memorable extra-inning thriller. The publicity the Reds generated stirred public interest in professional baseball and eventually led to the establishment of the National Association, the first pro baseball league, in 1871.

With the formation of the National Association, Harry became manager of the Boston team, called the Red Stockings since the Cincinnati team had disbanded, with George as

shortstop. They won four pennants, in 1872–1875. The Red Stockings joined the newly formed National League in 1876, its first year. Harry won pennants in 1877 and 1878.

Harry continued as a manager in the NL until 1893. Although he won no more pennants, several of his teams come close. He was universally respected for his integrity and innovative ideas.

Among the changes he reportedly advocated that were later instituted: the fifty-foot and then the fifty-five-foot pitching distance, six balls for a walk instead of nine, pre-game practice, a livelier ball with a cork center, and overhand pitching.

One idea that was tried out but did not prevail: a flat bat.

Harry Wright was named to the Hall of Fame in 1953.

Early Wynn

Pitcher, Was (A) 1939, 1941–44, 1946–48,
Cle (A) 1949–57, 1963, Chi (A) 1958–62

Wynn pitched his first major league game at age nineteen, but he didn't get any (ahem) early wins. Throwing for the Senators in the 1940s, he was erratic—a burly batch of talent with no clear idea of what to do. He was 18–12 in 1943 and 8–17 the next year, 17–15 in 1947 and 8–19 in 1948, with a 5.82 ERA. The Senators finally said the heck with him and shipped him to Cleveland.

Indians' pitching coach Mel Harder taught him the fine art of pitching, sharpened his pitches, and by 1950, the new, improved model was 18–8 with the AL's best ERA. Cleveland had the best pitching in the world in the 1950s, with Bob Feller, Bob Lemon, Mike Garcia, and their equal—sometimes better—Wynn. As an Indian, he won 20 games four times, 18 once, 17 twice.

In a sense, Wynn was a throwback, a 1950s pitcher with the attitude of an old 1890s Oriole. The plate was *his*. Any batter with the audacity to dig in could expect the next pitch to be aimed at his sinuses. They said Wynn would have brushed back his grandmother. "Only if she dug in," said Early. He didn't so much win games as wrestle for them, earning victory by intimidation, force of will, anger, and downright cussedness.

He walked scads and struck out a ton, eventually leading the AL twice in both departments. In all, he walked 1,775, yet he wasn't really wild; he just refused to give a batter a good pitch.

In 1958, Al Lopez, his former Indians' manager, acquired him for the White Sox. His 22–10 record in 1959 helped the Sox win their first pennant in forty years and earned the thirty-nine-year-old Wynn the Cy Young Award. By 1960 Early needed 29 more victories for 300. He developed a gouty elbow. It took him four years and a lot of pain, but on July 13, 1963, he became baseball's fourteenth 300-game winner.

In 1972 he was elected to the Hall of Fame.

Jim Wynn

Outfielder, Hou (N) 1963–73, LA (N) 1974–75,
Atl (N) 1976, NY (A) 1977, Mil (A) 1977

Wynn, at five-ten and 160 pounds, was called "the Toy Can-

non" because he generated so much power for his size. For most of his career, he played half his games in the Astrodome, the second worst park to hit a ball out of (the first worst is Yellowstone). Nevertheless, he popped 37 homers in 1967 and 33 in 1969. Joe Morgan, a pretty fair hitter, finished second on the team both years with 10 and 15.

Playing for the Astros in the 1960s had other disadvantages. There usually weren't a lot of runners for Jimmy to knock in; he topped 100 RBIs once for Houston but was over 80 three other years. And there was seldom anyone to knock Wynn home when he got on; Wynn walked over 100 times in seven different seasons, four as an Astro. His 148 free passes in 1969 tied the NL record.

In 1974 Wynn was traded to the Dodgers. Chavez Ravine is no hitter's paradise, but finally he was with a winner. He hit 32 homers, scored 108 runs, and batted in 104, to help the Dodgers to a pennant. Wynn finished fifth in the MVP voting, and everyone wondered where he'd been all these years.

The answer was he'd been hiding at Loop 610, Kirby and Fannin Streets, Houston, Texas.

Carl Yastrzemski

Outfielder/First Baseman, Bos (A) 1961–83

For one month—September 1967—Ted Williams said, Yaz was the greatest player who ever lived. Almost single-handedly the Boston left fielder lifted the Red Sox from ninth in 1966 to the flag. In a final doubleheader victory over pursuing Minnesota, Carl got 7-for-8 to sink the Twins. He won the Triple Crown and played a sensational left field with his glove and arm. Naturally he was MVP. He hit .400 in the World Series against St. Louis, with three homers.

Yaz won three batting titles, including .301 in 1968, the lowest ever to win. But that was the Year of the Pitcher, when the *average* American Leaguer hit .230. In a normal year Carl would have hit .331; in the 1930 NL, .388.

Carl began as a line drive hitter. Then at age twenty-seven he began lifting weights and came out slugging in 1967, the "Impossible Dream" season, with 44 homers. He had two more 40-homer seasons and finished with 452. His career .285 batting average is more impressive in light of his 1,844 RBIs, 1,816 runs scored, and 1,845 walks.

He led the league in assists six times, more than any other outfielder in AL history, and he got 190 intentional walks, more than any other AL hitter since such records were kept starting in 1955.

Tom Yawkey

Owner, Bos (A) 1933–77

A wealthy lumberman and mine owner, Yawkey was the adopted son of onetime Detroit owner William Yawkey. He bought the moribund Red Sox in 1933 and set out to buy a pennant by acquiring star players such as Joe Cronin, Lefty Grove, Jimmie Foxx, and Wes Ferrell. It didn't work, mostly because the Yankees were in the league, but he did revive fan interest that had all but disappeared in the years that the Sox spent scraping the bottom of the AL. Yawkey finally won pennants in 1946, 1967, and 1975. He never saw them win a

World Series though—they lost in seven games every time.

Generous and popular with his players, Yawkey often worked out with them before games and was interested in their affairs. Critics said that he overpaid and pampered his stars, thus diminishing their desire to win. He was also accused of bucking racial integration; the Sox were the last team to have a black player, and that was not until 1959.

He served as AL vice president in 1956–1973.

Yawkey was elected to the Hall of Fame in 1980.

Rudy York

First Baseman, Det (A) 1934, 1937–45,
Bos (A) 1946–47, Chi (A) 1947, Phi (A) 1948.
Manager, Bos (A) 1959

As a rookie catcher in 1937, the scarfaced part-Cherokee smashed 18 home runs for Detroit in August alone, the record for one month. In all, he slugged 35 in only 375 at-bats.

In 1940, with the Tigers well-stocked with catchers and needing York's big bat in the lineup, slugger Hank Greenberg was moved to left field and York was installed at first base. The change did nothing for the Tiger defense ("Rudy York is part Indian and part first baseman" was a popular line), but it gave them a pennant-winning attack. Greenberg was named MVP; York hit 33 homers, drove in 134 runs, and batted .316.

He led the AL in homers and RBIs in 1943, and helped the Tigers win another flag in 1945. Traded to the Red Sox in 1946, he again found himself on a pennant winner. In thirteen seasons, York hit 277 home runs and had 1,152 RBIs.

Denton "Cy" Young

Pitcher, Cle (N) 1890–98, StL (N) 1899–1900,
Bos (A) 1901–08, Cle (A) 1909–11, Bos (N) 1911.
Manager, Bos (A) 1907

Young's career record looks like a misprint: 511–313. Surely there must be a couple of decimal points missing! If nothing else, it prepares you to gosh-and-golly through some of the other high points: Young was number one in innings pitched with 7,356 and in complete games with 751. He had 16 seasons of 20 or more wins (including 14 in a row), five seasons of winning 30 or more; 76 shutouts; a 2.63 career ERA; three no-hitters, with the one in 1904 a perfect game. Ridiculous!

They called him Cy either because he threw baseballs against a fence until it looked like a cyclone had hit it or because he showed up at the Cleveland Spiders' park in 1890 carrying a cardboard suitcase, wearing a cheap, too-small suit, and looking like what you'd get if you mail-ordered for a hick. But from his first pitch, he was the Spiders' best pitcher, and he continued being the staff ace for whatever team he played for during the next twenty years. His last two seasons he slipped, but there was nothing wrong with his arm; he just got too fat to field bunts.

Young's arm was a wonder. He never had a sore arm, even though he pitched over 400 innings five times and over 300 eleven other seasons. He'd go home to his Ohio farm in October, do chores all winter, and show up ready for another 400 innings the next spring.

Cy threw twelve pitches before each game and was ready to go. On the mound he wheeled away from the hitter to hide the ball, then uncorked one of four deliveries, including an overhand curve, a sidearm curve, and a "tobacco ball." Young was a great control pitcher, averaging 1.5 walks per game. He once went twenty innings in a game without giving a walk. Eleven times he led the league in fewest walks and most strikeouts.

If they'd had a Cy Young Award when he pitched, he probably would have won only a couple at most. There was usually somebody having a more phenomenal individual season—Kid Nichols, Amos Rusie, Joe McGinnity, Christy Mathewson, Three-Finger Brown, Addie Joss, or Ed Walsh. A few pitchers in history have been terrific for enough seasons that they might actually rank ahead of Young on the all-time scale. Maybe Lefty Grove, Walter Johnson, Bob Feller, Tom Seaver, Matty, or Alexander. Cy had some advantages over most of them. He was almost always on winning teams. He didn't have to fret a lively ball. In its first years, the AL he jumped to in 1901 was definitely weaker than the NL. If you could choose any pitcher who has ever played to pitch for you in a big game, you probably wouldn't pick Young. But if your opponent picked him, he might beat you. After all, Cy was the winning pitcher 511 times.

He was elected to the Hall of Fame in 1937.

Ross Youngs

Outfielder, NY (N) 1917–26

Virtually John McGraw's "son"—Mac called him "the greatest outfielder I ever saw"—Youngs played on the Giants' four straight pennant winners in 1921 through 1924. When he hit .375 in the 1922 Series to Ruth's .118, Mac said he wouldn't trade him for the Babe. It got a big laugh over at the Yankee office. Hyperbole aside, Youngs was a splendid right fielder—a fast runner, fearless, with excellent judgment and a fine arm. A smart baserunner, too. At bat, the stocky lefthanded hitter had double and triple power and hit .300 from the moment he first came to bat in the Polo Grounds.

In 1924 he hit .356. If he wasn't Ruth, he was definitely one of the best players in the NL. Then, in 1925, something was wrong. He struggled at bat all season and finished at .264. In the off-season, he was diagnosed as suffering from Bright's Disease. He played through 1926 on guts, teaching young Mel Ott everything he knew about playing right field. By will alone he hit .302. By 1927 he was bedridden, and in October he died at the age of thirty.

He was elected to the Hall of Fame in 1972.

Robin Yount

Shortstop/Outfielder, Mil (A) 1974–

Yount became the Brewers' regular shortstop in 1974 at age eighteen and held the job with his glove for a few years until his bat caught up. By the 1980s he was hitting for average and power.

The tousle-headed Yount was the best player in the AL in 1982. Robin smacked two home runs off Jim Palmer to clinch the flag for Milwaukee on the final day, to end with 29 homers, .331, and the best slugging average in the league. He won the MVP by a landslide. Yount stayed hot in the World Series, hitting .414 with a record-setting two four-hit games, as the Brewers lost to the Cardinals in seven games.

After 1,479 games at shortstop, a shoulder injury in 1984 finally sent Yount to center field, where he has continued to rank among the AL's best players.

## CHAPTER 8

Demographics
Richard Topp

What do ballplayers do when they leave the game? How tall or short was the average player a hundred years ago? Did Tony Mullane really pitch with both hands? Did John M. Ward hurt his right arm while pitching, then play the next season as a lefthanded-throwing centerfielder? Was Christy Mathewson born in 1880, as the reference books have stated throughout this century—or was this his "baseball age," with his true birth year being 1878?

These are the questions that stir the souls of baseball sleuths, notably those of that 7,000-strong band called the Society for American Baseball Research. As a past chairman of SABR's Biographical Research Committee, I have had many notable finds cross my desk over the years. Here is a small sampling of what I study.

Alternate Occupations

A venerable children's fortune-telling rhyme, recited while counting objects or skipping along, went:

> Tinker, Tailor,
> Soldier, Sailor,
> Rich man, Poor man,
> Beggerman, Thief.

In the Middle Ages, that may have been all the known professions a man could be.

Baseball has been true to the above verse, and more so. Prior to the skyrocketing salaries of today, which often set up a man with income for the rest of his life, the player's post-playing occupations came from all walks of life. Bob Addy was the tinker, or more like a tinsmith. He practiced his craft in the mining towns near Pocatello, Idaho. The only tailor and the only beggar who came from the majors was Lew Say. Lew played from 1873 to 1884. He was a tailor by trade but was known to walk the streets of Baltimore begging for handouts.

There have been many soldiers and sailors—from the Civil War to Vietnam. Abner Doubleday, the mythical founder of the National Pastime, is forever etched in history as the captain who gave the order to return fire in response to Confederate shelling of Fort Sumter. That action started the Civil War. Also in the War Between the States we find George Zettlein, a twenty-year-old sailor under the command of Admiral Farragut at the battle of Mobile Bay. Doug Allison was a drummer boy for the Pennsylvania volunteers. James Price, the 1884 New York Giants' manager, was a captain in the New York Regiment. The War with Spain was short. Arlie Pond was a medical officer in the Philippines and later served as assistant surgeon general to Walter Reed. Laurie Reis joined at forty, well after his playing days were over.

Both world wars produced a huge exodus of players; the clubs were severely depleted. The 1918 season was ordered halted by the provost marshall on Labor Day. President Franklin Roosevelt had a change of heart in 1942; he ordered baseball to continue, to serve as a release for defense workers. Again the rosters were depleted, the minors were all but dried up, and the majors were forced to use youngsters and 4-F's. The two long-time doormats of the American League prospered—the St. Louis Browns of 1944 won their first and only pennant, and the 1945 Washington Senators finished in second. The Korean and Vietnam conflicts also took players away from the major leagues, although mostly they served in reserve units for short terms of duty. And people will always wonder how many homers Ted Williams would have hit if he hadn't gone off to war two times . . .

Outside of the present players with their inflated salaries, who were the rich men? Herman Franks could have been the wealthiest because of his investments. Hank Greenberg married into the Gimbel Department Store fortune. And George Halas went into another sport to find fortune. Al Spalding started a little sporting goods store in Chicago that still bears his name. But the champ has to be Frank Olin, a journeyman infielder who played 49 games in the 1880s. When he passed on control of Olin Industries in 1944 to his sons, he was worth over 60 million dollars.

What about the poor men? Well, there have been many. Some are in great need to this day, having retired before the 1947 pension plan went into effect. Some greats were truly poor like Pud Galvin, the first 300-game winner, who died in squalor. Hack Wilson was living in a tool shed as a custodian of a local park in Baltimore. As with Galvin, a collection was taken up to pay for Wilson's funeral. Bill Cissell died of starvation in a Chicago slum: he had a part-time job at Comiskey Park with the ground crew, but was unable to find work in the off-season. And it's rumored that Jimmie Foxx was informed of his election to the Hall of Fame while he was a resident of Miami's Skid Row.

As for the thieves, where did they go wrong? Harry Decker passed bad checks; Bill Geer was a fence for stolen goods.

There's more to the above rhyme—in 1888 another poet named Bolton added "Doctor, Lawyer, and Indian Chief."

Medical men are spread out over the life of baseball. Bobby Brown is the American League president. Doc White was a dentist. Doc Medich even performed his duties on a fan who was suffering from chest pains. Wyman Andrus, a one-gamer with Providence in 1885, went to medical school with fellow Canadian Pete Wood. Both graduated on the same day in 1893. The 1906 World Series had three doctors—Doc Gessler, Doc White, and Frank Owen. Billy Nash was often referred to as a doctor; even his obituary called him that. The

truth was that he was an orderly and never entered medical school.

The most prominent lawyer among ballplayers has to be John Montgomery Ward. Ward engineered the first player revolt, and helped form the Players' League in 1890. Another is Bob Gibson, a four-game pitcher in 1890 who made it to the Federal bench where he served for twenty-six years.

There has never been an Indian chief, but one player came close: Allie Reynolds was nominated by the Creek Nation but lost the election.

In 1974 John Le Carré wrought another turn on the nursery rhyme—this one was a novel called *Tinker, Tailor, Soldier, Spy*. Our spy is Moe Berg, a man "who speaks twelve languages and can't hit in any of them!" Berg went to Japan with a group of All-Stars not simply because he spoke Japanese, but to do intelligence work in the threatening period before Pearl Harbor.

When players go on road trips, the unwritten rule is to enjoy the city's nightlife after the game. Moe enjoyed talking to professors at Columbia, Harvard, and Chicago Universities.

Why would a contending team like the Washington Senators of 1932 and 1933 be interested in a catcher who batted .077 with Cleveland the year before? Was it convenient for the government to have Moe close by? Moe did work for the newly formed OSS, a forerunner to the CIA. He was sent to Germany and various neutral countries before World War Two and during it. We may never know the precise extent of what Moe did in his spy career, as much of this information is still classified.

Let's take a look at the other noble professions . . .

The acting professions saw many players do vaudeville in the offseason. Marty McHale made a career out of it. Cap Anson did a vaudeville act with his daughter and introduced a small ditty called "Take Me Out to the Ball Game," which has since become baseball's national anthem. Rube Marquard appeared on stage with his wife Blossom Seeley. Mike Donlin, Rabbit Maranville, Babe Ruth, Rube Waddell, and a legion of other players also trod the boards.

One of the earliest baseball movies was a short produced by the Vitagraph Studios in 1909. The movie showed Honus Wagner teaching a little boy the art of batting. The little boy, one Moses Horwitz, stayed in acting as Moe Howard, one of the Three Stooges. Babe Ruth appeared in a few silent movies, but his hitting was better than his acting. Chuck Connors acted in movies and had a hit television show, "The Rifleman." Peanuts Lowrey, who grew up behind the M-G-M studios, did one scene as a child with Thelma Todd. Johnny Berardino is currently a doctor on a daytime soap opera.

Carmen Fanzone, a utility player in the 1970s with the Red Sox and Cubs, plays trumpet in Doc Severinsen's band on Johnny Carson's television show.

Some players had a calling and became "men of the cloth." The most famous is Billy Sunday, but Doc White also did a little evangelical work. Al Travers, one of a bunch of students who substituted for the 1912 striking Tigers, became a Catholic priest. Morrie Arnovich studied to be a rabbi. Al Worthington is currently a Baptist preacher.

Saloonkeeper seems to be the most-honored profession among players. Fred Pfeffer ran a saloon in the theater district of Chicago; it was a watering hole for actors and ballplayers.

Accountants are few and far between. Ross Barnes became

one after the foul-fair rule was changed and cut his batting average by over 100 points. Joe Quest was an accountant for the City Clerk of Chicago . . . who was Cap Anson.

The insurance industry has produced many a good living—Cy Block and Marv Rotblatt have been quite successful there.

Edd Roush was a gravedigger and later a cemetery manager in Oakland, Indiana. Richie Hebner was also a gravedigger for many years.

Patsy Dougherty was the only bank teller of note; he died at his window of a heart attack in 1940.

Frank Isbell and Three-Finger Brown owned gasoline stations.

Joe Borden, who in 1875 pitched the first no-hitter, was demoted to groundskeeper near the end of the 1876 season.

Charlie Waitt, the first man to wear a glove, died on the job; he was a window washer in San Francisco when he fell.

Firemen of note were John Clapp in Ithaca, New York, and Bill Gleason in St. Louis. Chicken Wolf was riding on a fire truck in Louisville when he fell off and suffered a severe head injury; subsequently he became hopelessly insane.

Officers of the law pop up now and then. Tony Mullane, the celebrated contract jumper, was a Chicago Police detective; so was George Rooks. Bill Craver, expelled from baseball for game-fixing in 1877, became a policeman in Troy, New York. Johnny Ryan was killed while making an arrest in 1902. Jimmy Ryan was a court bailiff. And believe it or not, a major leaguer was once a member of the Royal Canadian Mounted Police—Jean-Pierre Roy. The most unusual encounter was in 1894, when policeman George Strief arrested robber Pud Galvin in Pittsburgh.

There have been major leaguers who played other sports in the off-season. Professional football claims Ernie Nevers, Garland Buckeye, Jim Thorpe, Red Badgro, Shorty Des Jardien, George Halas, Paddy Driscoll, etc. Ace Parker is the only pro football Hall of Famer to hit a homer in his first major league at-bat.

Basketball has its share, too, in Gene Conley, Dave DeBusschere, Chuck Connors, Frank Baumholtz, Danny Ainge, and more.

Jack Graney led the long parade of ex-players into the broadcasting booth; now every team has at least one doing the color.

Many players wrote, or rather "ghosted," newspaper columns, but Tim Murnane became the first ex-player-turned-reporter, followed shortly by Sam Crane.

Last but not least is politicians, an occupation that in public opinion polls ranks below used-car salesman for credibility. Only two players were governors: John Tener of Pennsylvania and Fred Brown, a lifetime nine-gamer who became the chief executive of New Hampshire. Brown was also the only senator; he rode to victory in the Roosevelt landslide of 1932.

Four congressmen served: Tener, Pius Schwert (New York), Wilmer "Vineger Bend" Mizell (North Carolina), and Jim Bunning (Kentucky).

Mayors and local office holders are numerous; the mayor of the biggest city has to be the 1954 batting champion, Bobby Avila, who is the mayor of Veracruz, Mexico.

Let's not leave the used-car dealers out in the cold. Tony Piet was one of the largest dealers in Chicago. Smokey Burgess also did well selling the "American dream."

The list of ballplayers' occupations mirrors the way the rest of America earns a living. Because of the steady flow of

players into retirement and the limited number of baseball jobs, very few manage to stay in the game.

Height and Weight

Is the baseball player of today bigger and stronger than his counterpart of fifty years ago? What about of a hundred years ago?

Below is a look at the rookies of three selected periods in time.

	1880–1889	1930–1939	1980–1986
Rookies	922	1,037	1,167
Ave. Height (Inches)	69.90*	71.60	73.24
Ave. Weight (lbs.)	170.52*	178.76	186.79

*Based on 479 known heights and 471 known weights.

The present-day player is 4.8 percent taller than one hundred years ago and 2.3 percent taller than fifty years ago. The average weight, due to a better diet, shoots up 9.5 percent over one hundred years and 4.5 percent over the 1930s player.

Of course there are some differences. In the 1950s Eddie Gaedel brought down the averages with his 3'7" and 65 pounds. So did Bobby Shantz (at 5'6" and 139) and Albie Pearson (5'5" and 140). These players and others throw a monkey wrench into the theory that players today are bigger and better.

But Gaedel, Shantz, and Pearson appeared thirty years ago, and in that time we have seen Greg Luzunski closing out his career at 279 pounds. And Ron Reed, an ex-basketball player, pitching at 6'6" jacks up the average.

The 1970s and 1980s also saw the influx of talent from the Dominican Republic, players not in the same height and weight class as Luzinski or Reed, and little men like Harry Chappas (5'3" and 150) and Fred Patek (5'5" and 148). Those players would bring the average down.

Ex-basketball players seem to inflate the present-day averages. Gene Conley was 6'6", Dave DeBusschere was 6'6", and Frank Howard was 6'7". But the biggest of all was Johnny Gee, the Pittsburgh-New York pitcher of the 1940s who came in at 6' 9".

In 1984 Luzinski and Ron Kittle of the White Sox pulled a double steal. No one on the Yankees was expecting Greg to break toward the plate, so he made it. Later research was done, and it was found that Luzinski became the heaviest player to steal home, breaking a long-time unwritten record of Zeke Bonura, who did it while weighing 260!

In 1961 Albie Pearson roomed on the road with Big Ted Kluszewski, a giant of his time at 6'2" and 225. It was rumored that Big Klu made up Albie's bed in a dresser drawer.

The 1880s and 1890s were not limited to little men as the averages would lead us to believe. Cap Anson and Pud Galvin were nearing the magic 300-pound mark in their last seasons. Dave Orr, a power hitter of the 1880s, was averaging 250! King Kelly, the barrel-chested star, certainly weighed more than the 170 he is listed as weighing. And "Big Dan" Brouthers lived up to his name with an average weight of 207 on his 6'2" frame.

Yes, there were more little guys a hundred years ago than today—people like Davy "Tom Thumb" Force, who tipped the scales at 5'4" and 130. Larry Corcoran came in at 120 while winning 177 games in eight years. Wee Willie McGill was 5'6" and a 20-game winner at 17. Research has found the next closest man to Eddie Gaedel in weight—he was Harry Keenan, a 16-year-old pitcher with Cincinnati in 1891 who was 95 pounds dripping wet!

One wonders what it may have been like to see a confrontation between certain managers and players, especially between Miller "Mighty Mite" Huggins (5'6" and 140) and his star Babe Ruth.

When Bill Veeck was hiding Eddie Gaedel in the Browns' office before his great debut in 1951, Eddie was asking how tall Wee Willie Keeler was. I guess Wee Willie was a man Eddie "looked up" to; after all, the Hall of Famer was 5'4" and 140.

Gaedel wasn't the only midget in baseball; there was Don Davidson, the long-time traveling secretary of the Braves. On road trips a Braves player would get Don's room changed to a high floor, since Davidson had trouble reaching the buttons on the elevators.

The twentieth century had its small men, too. Most encyclopedias show Pete Burg, an infielder with the 1910 Boston Braves, as 5'10". It was discovered not long ago that while playing in the New England League a photo was taken of Pete standing next to a six-foot-tall teammate. The Brockton, Massachusetts newspaper captioned the picture, saying that Pete was the smallest in baseball at 5'1". It seems nobody believed any player could be that small, so someone had "corrected" this stat for the future as 5'10".

The Chicago White Sox of 1950s and '60s had a great double-play combination of Nellie Fox and Luis Aparicio. Not many people know that when the club was home, the Sox players would run out from the dugout and Fox and Aparicio would race to second base. The winner would get to stand on the base during the national anthem, so as to appear taller.

Switch-Hitters

In a late-season game in 1897, Roger Denzer, a right-handed Chicago pitcher, faced Brooklyn in a meaningless game. Both clubs were soon to finish thirty-plus games out of first; the Boston Beaneaters and the Baltimore Orioles had a nice two-team race.

The next day the Chicago *Inter-Ocean* took note of the Brooklyn win. There was nothing special in the loss by Denzer—he was 2–8 that season. But the reporter noted an oddity: at a time when left-handed batters were a distinct minority, the Brooklyn lineup had seven of them. This kind of line-up stacking or platooning had been done years before as managers were experimenting with the right-left situation. Brooklyn manager Billy Barnie may have wondered that day what it would be like to have a team of switch-hitters, so he wouldn't have to pinch-hit, could keep a good fielder in position, and could still have an advantage in batting for nine innings. A sign of things to come, but switch-hitters were a rare commodity in those distant days. In contrast, the 1965 Dodgers had the pieces fall into place and won a pennant with an all-switch-hitting infield: Wes Parker at first, Jim LeFebvre at second, Maury Wills at short, and Junior Gilliam at third.

The first switch-hitter was Bob Ferguson, who played in the National Association, National League, and American Association from 1871–1884. But the first really great switch-hitter was undoubtedly George Davis, a player from 1890 to 1909. In his twenty years he ranks fourth among switch-hitters in games, at-bats, average, and doubles. Davis ranks number one in triples with 166 and is number two behind Mantle in RBIs. The nineteenth century saw other solid switch-hitters in Tommy Tucker, Dan McGann, Tom Daly, and John Anderson.

Max Carey and Frankie Frisch were the big-gun switch-hitters in the first half of the twentieth century. Frisch and Carey also had speed going for them. Frisch stole 419 bases and from 1921 to 1930 averaged 187 hits a season. Carey ranks fifth on the all-time stolen base list; one year he stole 51 bases in 53 attempts. But in order to steal a base you must first get on. Carey's speed also produced 159 triples; this was possible because he played for most of his career in vast Forbes Field.

On June 25, 1937, Augie Galan of the Cubs made the record books for hitting homers while batting right- and left-handed in a game. He connected off Fred Fitzsimmons of the Dodgers in the fourth inning as a lefty, and in the eighth he hit one as a righty off Ralph Birkofer. But later research revealed that Wally Schang of the Philadelphia Athletics had been the first to hit homers as a lefty and righty—in a 1916 game.

Mickey Mantle on many occasions connected with two homers in a game from both sides. In the early 1950s, reliever Satchel Paige was a victim one day of a Mantle left-handed barrage, following the starting pitcher's victimization by Mantle's righty exploits. He told his manager the Yanks would be tough this year with those twin brothers they brought up.

For sheer power it was Mickey Mantle all the way. His 536 career home runs leads every other switch-hitter by a wide margin. So do his strikeouts. Pete Rose, on the other hand, was a throwback to the early days of the 1920s and 1930s, a contact hitter. Rose hit the magic 200-hit mark ten times in his twenty-four-year career. Sure he had over 1,100 strikeouts in his career, but that's an average of only 47 or 48 per season, whereas Mantle had an average of 95. Rose didn't have blazing speed; he never placed among stolen base leaders, but he was fast enough to wipeout all competitors in doubles with 746. Ted Simmons ranks second, 269 behind "Charlie Hustle."

The modern player is stronger and faster, and the advent of players like Reggie Smith, Ted Simmons, Willie Wilson, and Ken Singleton make the switch-hitter a permanent part of the baseball scene.

Who knows what the future may bring. Could the lefty-righty confrontations between managers be a thing of the past? Not so fast—there is something else that managers haven't experimented with for many, many years. Switch-pitchers.

Back in 1882 Tony Mullane pitched with both hands. There are also reports of Icebox Chamberlain and John Clarkson doing the same in the 1880s. Tony Mullane was a double threat; he was switch-hitter and a switch-thrower as well. In the 1940s Ed Head and Cal McLish were experimenting with this in spring training, but none dared do it in a regular-season game. Catcher Paul Richards pitched ambidextrously in the minors.

Was it Yogi Berra who once said, "I'd give my right arm to be ambidextrous"?

All-Time Switch-Hitting Leaders*

Games		At-Bat		Average	
Pete Rose	3562	Pete Rose	14053	Frank Frisch	.316
Max Carey	2476	Max Carey	9363	Pete Rose	.303
Mickey Mantle	2401	Frank Frisch	9112	Mickey Mantle	.298
George Davis	2377	George Davis	9060	George Davis	.297
Ted Simmons	2378	Ted Simmons	8573	Eddie Murray	.296
Frank Frisch	2310	R. Schoendienst	8479	Rip Collins	.296
Larry Bowa	2247	Larry Bowa	8418	Willie Wilson	.295
Red Schoendienst	2216	Mickey Mantle	8102	Tommy Tucker	.290
Ken Singleton	2082	Don Kessinger	7651	John Anderson	.290
Don Kessinger	2078	Maury Wills	7588	Red Schoendienst	.289

Doubles		Triples		Home Runs	
Pete Rose	746	George Davis	166	Mickey Mantle	536
Ted Simmons	477	Max Carey	159	Reggie Smith	314
Frank Frisch	466	Frank Frisch	138	Eddie Murray	305
George Davis	454	Pete Rose	135	Ken Singleton	246
Red Schoendienst	427	John Anderson	124	Ted Simmons	246
Max Carey	419	Duke Farrell	123	Pete Rose	160
Reggie Smith	363	Willie Wilson	112	Roy White	160
Mickey Mantle	344	Lu Blue	109	Tom Tresh	153
Augie Galan	336	Tom Daly	103	Rip Collins	135
John Anderson	326	Dan McGann	103	Roy Smalley	135

Runs		Runs Batted In		Hits	
Pete Rose	2165	Mickey Mantle	1509	Pete Rose	4256
Mickey Mantle	1677	George Davis	1435	Frank Frisch	2880
George Davis	1545	Ted Simmons	1378	George Davis	2688
Max Carey	1545	Pete Rose	1314	Max Carey	2665
Frank Frisch	1532	Frank Frisch	1244	Ted Simmons	2451
Donie Bush	1280	Eddie Murray	1106	Red Schoendienst	2449
Red Schoendienst	1223	Reggie Smith	1092	Mickey Mantle	2415
Jim Gilliam	1163	Ken Singleton	1065	Larry Bowa	2191
Lu Blue	1151	John Anderson	976	Maury Wills	2134
Reggie Smith	1123	Duke Farrell	912	Ken Singleton	2029

*Listing courtesy of Robert McConnell, Wilmington, Delaware. Includes the 1987 season.

Handicaps

The word "handicap" comes from an Old English term describing how beggars asked for money in the streets. They would take off their caps and hold them out for coins to be dropped in. The term was "cap in hand," later altered to "hand and cap."

The disabled must work harder to equal their able-bodied opponents or teammates. The ones that played baseball showed courage just to make the team.

The first known physically handicapped player was Hugh "One-Arm" Daily, a major-league pitcher for six years in the 1880s. The nickname hinted that Hugh had an entire arm missing, but actually he was only missing his left hand, which had been severed in an explosion. Hugh won 73 games in his career, and on September 13, 1883, he pitched a no-hitter against the Phillies.

In those days gloves were optional, but that wasn't the case with Pete Gray of the 1945 St. Louis Browns. Gray played the outfield wearing his glove on his left hand. He would then catch a fly ball, toss it into the air, stuff his glove under his right arm stump, catch the ball, and throw it. Sounds difficult? Pete did this in about one second.

Gray won the right for a tryout with the Browns when he tore up the Southern Association with his batting. He hit .333 and stole 68 bases in 1944 with Memphis. Gray won the Southern Association's MVP Award that year. Pete batted only .218 for the Browns, but his determination was admired by teammates. Disabled war vets were inspired by Pete's exploits, proving that a handicap was only a setback to a career, not an end to it. After all, Andy Russell won the Oscar for best supporting actor around this time too, in *The Best Years of Our Lives,* and he was missing both arms!

Among other amputees were four fairly good pitchers. Mordecai "Three-Finger" Brown lost one finger and part of another in a farm accident as a boy, but the remaining fingers forced him to hold the ball differently from the norm. Brown's pitching was unmatched. In a five-year span, 1906–1910, he put a hex on the National League, winning 127 games while losing 32. But his control was even better: in that same period Brown pitched 1,461 innings while allowing 230 earned runs

for an ERA of 1.42! Brown's pitching in 1906 helped the Cubs win a record 116 games. He won 26 of them and posted an ERA of 1.04, with 10 shutouts.

I wonder if missing the toes on one foot had anything to do with Red Ruffing winning 273 games in his career?

Monty Stratton, a White Sox pitcher in the 1930s, won 36 games in five years for an also-ran club, but a hunting accident cost him a leg. Although he never pitched again in the majors, he made a comeback in the Texas League. In 1946 Stratton was 18–8 in 27 games for the Sherman Twins—20 were complete games.

Losing a leg usually means losing a major league career, as happened to Monty Stratton or Jimmy Wood. Wood injured his leg during the 1873 season leading to an abscess. Doctors trying to treat the leg managed to break it, and were forced to amputate the leg to save his life. Wood's reward was being named manager of the White Stockings for 1874 and 1875.

Bert Shepard did one better on Stratton—he played in the majors with an artificial leg. The Washington Senators hired the minor league war vet to show that the disabled can play. He pitched only one game in the 1945 season, for only 5⅓ innings, but nevertheless he did it—and he allowed only three hits and one earned run!

Another famous handicapped player was William Ellsworth Hoy, known for the rest of his life as "Dummy." Neither his teammates nor Hoy himself saw the name as being offensive. In fact, the seven known deaf-mutes in baseball, that seemingly pejorative nickname seems to come up all the time, just as American Indian players are often called "Chief."

When Hoy broke in with Oshkosh in 1886 under manager Frank Selee, he was regarded as a freak. But his determination was admirable. Hoy was responsible for two customs used in baseball today. He would screech and hold his arm out when he caught a fly ball. This was to tell the other fielders that it was his catch. Notice outfielders using this hand signal today. Also he would ask the umpire to use a hand signal to let him know if the pitch was a ball or strike, a method that is universally practiced today.

Hoy was quite an outfielder, once throwing out three runners at the plate in one game, all from center field. On October 7, 1961, Hoy was honored by being allowed to throw out the first ball of Game Three of the 1961 World Series. Two months later he was dead at the ripe age of ninety-nine.

Ed "Dummy" Dundon was the first deaf-mute in the majors with the Columbus Buckeyes in 1883, but he didn't last long, playing in 52 games over two years.

Tom "Dummy" Lynch came along in 1884 for one game as a pitcher with the White Stockings; he only lasted seven innings. Lynch and Hoy were valedictorians at their respective schools for the deaf. Lynch went to the "Harvard" of deaf schools—Gallaudet in Washington, D.C.

The 1901 New York Giants took a big step in hiring the handicapped. They had three deaf-mutes on the roster that year. "Dummy" Taylor won 18 for the seventh-place team. "Dummy" Leitner came over the Athletics and pitched in two games. And pitcher "Dummy" Deegan hurled 17 innings in two games.

The last deaf-mute in the majors was Dick Sipek, the only one who was not called "Dummy." (Similarly, Ben Tincup was the first Indian not called "Chief.") Sipek, an outfielder who much admired "Dummy" Hoy, played 82 games for the 1945 Reds. Hoy would show up at Cincinnati games just to watch and talk with Sipek.

Tom Sunkel, a pitcher for the Cardinals, Giants, and Dodgers was blind in one eye. Research has uncovered that Harry Wright was the only blind manager. In 1890, while managing the Phillies, Wright was stricken with a common head cold in mid-May. This head cold spread and infected his nervous system, and Wright as a result began to go blind. On May 22 Wright was out as manager and was bedridden. Jack Clements took over the club for the next 19 games; then Al Reach, the Phillies president, took them on the road for an 11-game swing; and Bob Allen ran the club until August 11. Finally Harry Wright came back for the last 46 games of the season. Although he still could not see very well, his team finished in third place.

Age

On May 25, 1988, in a nursing home at Findlay, Ohio, John Francis Daley celebrated his 101st birthday. Daley played in only 17 games for the St. Louis Browns in 1912, but until his death later that year he was the oldest ex-player in history. Only one other player reached the magic century mark.

Interviews with Daley have resulted in some colorful tales. He related the story of how his family moved from Pittsburgh: all the home furnishings were loaded on a raft to journey down the river. He grew up listening to stories of baseball from a local citizen, Cal McVey, a man who played with the famous unbeaten Red Stockings of 1869 and in the majors from 1871 to 1879. Daley remembered representing the Browns in a meeting to form a players' union. There he was sitting between Eddie Collins and Ty Cobb. Cobb leaned over and whispered about a new company back home in Georgia, "Put your money on Coca-Cola—you'll make a killing!"

The other century player was Ralph Darwin Miller, a pitcher in only two seasons, 1898 and 1899. Ralph was the last surviving player from nineteenth-century baseball; he died on May 8, 1873, only fifty-four days after reaching 100. It was too late for any celebration, since his death was only noticed by the sports world a few years later.

The youngest player ever was Fred Chapman, a pitcher with the Philadelphia Athletics in 1887. Fred celebrated his fifteenth birthday after the season on November 25. Chapman was younger than Joe Nuxhall, who was at one time thought to have been the youngest.

In 1944 the Cincinnati Reds were hit hard by the military draft, so they were willing to try out anybody who showed some promise. It was Joe's father who was offered a tryout—Joe just went along for the ride, but somehow he ended up trying out for himself. The Reds were impressed with the son more than with his father, so Joe made his debut against the powerful Cardinals in 10–0 rout of Cincinnati. Joe pitched only two-thirds of an inning, giving up seven earned runs, two hits, and walking five in his sole major league appearance until 1952.

Looking back at baseball history, we find that the 1885 Cincinnati Reds were the oldest team in terms of how long their players went on to live. They had four players who lived into their nineties and one who reached his eighties. Dummy Hoy, Frank Foreman, Arlie Latham, and George Hogriever made it past 90, and Bid McPhee was 83 when he died. The team also had another six players to reach 70! The 1895 Reds

had an average lifetime age of 69.5 years.

A switch on the 1895 Reds was the 1884 Chicago White Stockings, a team that had four hitters with more than 20 homers, a team that boasted the "Stonewall Infield." The average age at death for this club was a mere 55 years. Sure, Dalrymple, Andrus, and Goldsmith were well past 90 when they died; and Anson, Sunday, and Pfeffer were past 70. But eight players on the twenty-man roster died before the age of 45.

The oldest player actually to play in a game is Satchel Paige, who pitched three innings in 1965 for Kansas City. Paige claimed to be born on July 7, 1906. But that date is suspect. I was told, during an interview with an old boyhood pal and teammate of Satch's, that July 7 is correct, but the year should be 1900. Satch was very protective of his age. Upon his induction to the Hall of Fame, he was asked what his birthdate was. Satch said he didn't know, adding that his mother had written it down in the family Bible but the goat had eaten it!

The youngest team to take the field for a game was the 1963 Houston Colt .45s. On September 27 of that year the starting lineup had Jay Dahl (17), Jerry Grote (20), Rusty Staub (19), Jim Wynn (21), Aaron Pointer (21), Brock Davis (18), Joe Morgan (20), Glenn Vaughan (19), and Sonny Jackson (19). Dahl became the youngest in the majors to die—an auto accident ended his life at 19.

Again the war years produced the widest margin of age for a single team. The 1944 Dodgers had Eddie Miksis at 17, and Gene Mauch, Ralph Branca, and Cal McLish at 18. At the other end of the spectrum, Paul Waner was 41 and Johnny Cooney 43.

Jim O'Rourke, the last survivor of the National Association, and the last survivor of the first National League game in 1876, played his final game in 1904. At 52 "Orator Jim" was the oldest player to play a full game. Strange as it seems, only four years later his son made his debut. Only one other father and son have had as few as four years between their respective retirement and debut—Jim and Mike Hegan.

In 1912 the Detroit Tigers went on strike to protest Ty Cobb's suspension. In order to avoid a forfeit against Philadelphia, the Tigers enlisted college boys and put 46-year-old coach Deacon McGuire in to catch; manager Hughie Jennings was forced to pinch-hit in the ninth at age 43. Jennings later returned in 1918 to play one game at first base, at the age of 49.

The oldest manager, of course, was Connie Mack; he called it quits in 1950 at the age of 87, after fifty-three years at the helm. Roger Peckinpaugh, on the other hand, became manager of the New York Yankees at twenty-three. Tom Sheehan was the oldest to be appointed as manager in 1960 at 66 years of age.

Achievements by youthful players are numerous. Robin Yount played the most games before age 20. Wee Willie McGill was a 17-year-old 20-game winner.

Other milestones were Tommy Brown of the 1944 Dodgers, who was the youngest to homer at 16. A 17-year-old Bob Feller struck out 17 players in one game. And Tony Conigliaro hit 24 homers at age 19.

But with age comes wisdom. Minnie Minoso and Nick Altrock have played in five decades. Altrock started in 1898, pitching for Louisville, and while spending 46 years as a Washington coach would pinch-hit now and then: his last time was in 1933. Minnie Minoso began his career in 1949 with Cleveland and "retired" in 1964. When Bill Veeck bought the White Sox for a second time, Minnie came back as a publicity stunt and was a designated hitter in three games in 1976. News stories said Minnie had made the elite club of four-decade players; it was also noted that Altrock was the only one who played in five. Minnie came back in 1980 to tie the record. And in 1986 he said he was ready for 1990!

Youngest Team at Death

1884 Chicago White Stockings

Tom Lee	21
Joe Brown	29
Sy Sutcliffe	29
Larry Corcoran	32
Silver Flint	35
Ned Williamson	36
King Kelly	36
Tom Burns	44
Walt Kinzie	52
George Crosby	53
Tom Lynch	60
Cap Anson	70
Billy Sunday	72
Fred Pfeffer	72
John Hibbard	73
George Gore	76
Abner Dalrymple	82
Fred Andrus	87
Fred Goldsmith	87
Mike Corcoran	?

Average age = 55 years

Oldest Team at Death

1895 Cincinnati Reds

Dummy Hoy	99
Frank Foreman	94
Arlie Latham	92
George Hogriever	91
Bid McPhee	83
Harry Spies	76
Dusty Miller	76
Mike Kahoe	75
Frank Dwyer	74
Bill Phillips	72
Morgan Murphy	71
Bill Merritt	67
Germany Smith	64
Tom Parrott	63
Bill Grey	61
Billy Rhines	52
Farmer Vaughn	49
Buck Ewing	47
Bug Holliday	43
Eddie Burke	41
Lem Bailey	?

Average age = 69.5 years

## CHAPTER 9

Foreign-Born Players

Bill Deane

In discussing the impact and contributions of foreign-born major leaguers, we must first define "foreign-born." For the purposes of this study, we will consider anyone born outside of what is now the United States, regardless of circumstances, with the exclusion of nineteenth-century players born in England or Ireland and twentieth-century Latin-American-born players. These groups are excluded only because their sizes would lopside the data.

Using these guidelines, there have been 285 major leaguers (1876–1988), plus four National Association (1871–1875) players, born on foreign soil. These can be divided into nine distinct regional groups: Canada; the Atlantic and Caribbean; the British Isles; Germany; Southern Europe; Northern Europe; Central Europe; Eastern Europe; and Asia and the Pacific. The following table shows the number of members from each group, broken down by era:

Foreign-Born Top-Level Baseball Players by Debut Year

REGION*	1871–1900	1901–1930	1931–1960	1961–1988	TOTAL
Canada	44	36	36	34	150
Atlantic/Caribbean	1	1	5	15	22
British Isles	6	22	2	4	34
Germany	11	11	2	7	31
Southern Europe	1	2	7	5	15
Northern Europe	5	7	0	2	14
Central Europe	3	3	1	0	7
Eastern Europe	1	5	5	0	11
Asia/Pacific	1	1	0	4	6
TOTALS	73	88	58	71	290

*See explanations in text.

Following is a summary of the contributions of each regional group:

Canada

Canadians represent more than half of the foreign-born players under discussion. Of the 150 Canadian-born big leaguers, 81 were born in Ontario; 18 in Quebec; 10 in New Brunswick; 8 in British Columbia; 7 each in Nova Scotia and Saskatchewan; 5 in Alberta; 3 in Manitoba; 2 on Prince Edward Island; 1 in Newfoundland; and 8 in undetermined places in Canada.

The first Canadian-born major leaguer was Bill Phillips, a first baseman who began his ten-year career in 1879 and batted .266 lifetime. Among the best of the Canadians are Tip O'Neill, Art Irwin, Russ Ford, George Selkirk, Jeff Heath, Pete Ward, Ferguson Jenkins, John Hiller, and Terry Puhl.

O'Neill, a pitcher-turned-outfielder, had a monster year in 1887, when he batted .435 and led the American Association in practically every offensive category. His career average was .326, including two batting crowns.

Heath was often charged with not living up to his "potential." He was hardly a washout, however, twice leading the AL in triples, twice topping .340, and finishing his career with 194 homers, 887 RBI and a .293 average. His .509 lifetime slugging average ranks among the top 40 in baseball history.

Jenkins is likely to become the first Canadian-born Hall of Famer. He posted a 284–226 career pitching record, with seven 20-win seasons, 3,192 strikeouts, and a Cy Young Award.

Hiller recovered from a heart attack to become one of the AL's premier relievers in the 1970s. His career mark was 87–76, with 125 saves and a 2.83 ERA.

Puhl of the Astros is an excellent all-around athlete with a 12-year .281 average. Other Canadians active in 1988 included Angels' pitcher Kirk McCaskill, Blue Jays' outfielder Rob Ducey, and Rangers' hurler Stephen Wilson.

Some other Canadians made contributions of a trivial nature. Selkirk is the man who replaced Babe Ruth in the Yankees' outfield. Art Irwin, who employed a buckskin contraption to protect a pair of broken fingers in 1883, has been called the trendsetter in the use of fielders' gloves. And Glen Gorbous, who had a short stint as a big league outfielder, is credited with the longest measured baseball throw, one of 445'10" in 1957.

Atlantic/Caribbean

In 1871, the initial season of the National Association (NA), the Troy Haymakers employed a third baseman by the name of Esteban Bellan, a native of Havana, Cuba. Bellan played in three NA seasons and was the only Latin-American to play at the top level of pro baseball before 1902. Beginning in 1911, Latins (mostly Cubans) began trickling into the majors at the rate of one or two per year. After the major league color line was broken in 1947, the Latin population mushroomed. There have now been close to 500 Latin-born major leaguers from Cuba (26 percent), Puerto Rico (25 percent), the Dominican Republic (23 percent), Venezuela, Mexico, Panama, Nicaragua, Colombia, and Honduras.

Although twentieth-century Latins are excluded from the tables in this chapter, they cannot be totally ignored in a discussion of foreign-born stars. The best include Hall of Famers Roberto Clemente (Puerto Rico), Luis Aparicio (Venezuela), and Juan Marichal (Dominican Republic), along with Puerto Rican Orlando Cepeda and Cubans Dolf Luque, Minnie Minoso, Luis Tiant, Tony Oliva, and Tony Perez. Current Latin stars include Cuban Jose Canseco (Athletics), Mexican Fernando Valenzuela (Dodgers) and Dominicans George Bell and Tony Fernandez (Blue Jays), Pedro Guerrero (Cardinals), Julio Franco (Indians), and Juan Samuel (Phillies).

Aside from Latins, there have been 21 big leaguers born in the Atlantic/Caribbean area, including 8 from the Virgin Islands (V.I.), 5 from the Bahamas, 4 from the (Panama)

Canal Zone (an English-speaking, soon-to-be-relinquished American-owned territory), 3 from Jamaica, and 1 (Edmund Porray) born aboard ship in the Atlantic Ocean.

The most prominent member of this group is Rod Carew, born in Gatun in the Canal Zone. Carew retired following the 1985 season with a .328 career average, 3,053 hits, seven batting titles, and an MVP Award.

Other notables include Al McBean (V.I.), a 1960s relief ace; Jose Morales (V.I.), a 12-year .287 hitter who retired as the number one single-season and number three career pinch-hit collector; and current Angels' star Chili Davis (Jamaica). Other members active in 1988 included the Angels' Devon White (Jamaica), the Rangers' Jerry Browne (V.I.), and the Cubs' Rolando Roomes (Jamaica).

British Isles

Dozens of Irish- and English-born players graced the diamonds in the first few decades of big league ball. By the early part of this century the immigration flow had abated, and Irish and English players became the exception; thus the year 1901 was selected as our cutoff point in categorizing these players as "foreign-born."

Before 1901, there were five players born in Scotland and one from Wales. The first among these was David Abercrombie (Scotland), a one-game shortstop in 1871. The best were two pitchers: Jim McCormick (Scotland), who posted a 264–214 record in ten seasons; and Ted Lewis (Wales), who was 94–64 over a six-year career.

In the present century, there have been 14 players from England, 9 from Ireland, 4 from Scotland, and 1 from Wales, to debut in the majors. The cream of this crop is Scotland's Bobby Thomson, author of the 1951 "shot heard 'round the world" and 263 other big league homers.

Active in 1988 was pitcher Danny Cox of the Cardinals (from England).

Germany

The first German-born top-level player was Joseph Miller in 1872. Nineteen other Germans, typically nicknamed "Fritz" or "Dutch," entered the scene before World War One, but only four made it in the half century thereafter.

Probably the best German import was hurler Charlie "Pretzels" Getzien, who had a lifetime 145–139 record, including 30–11 and 29–13 seasons in 1886–1887.

Two German-born players competed in the majors in 1988: Giants' reliever Craig Lefferts and Oakland A's second baseman Glenn Hubbard.

Southern Europe

This region has produced six big leaguers from France, five from Italy, three from Spain, and one—former Dodgers' player and executive Al Campanis—from Greece.

The first Southern European in the majors was Joseph Woerlin (France), a one-game shortstop in 1895. Two French-born players were in the majors in 1988: Phillies' infielder Steve Jeltz and Twins' pitcher Charlie Lea.

Lea has probably been the most successful of the Southern Europe group. He sports a 62–48 career record, including a no-hitter, as he rebounds from a rotator cuff injury to his pitching shoulder.

Northern Europe

Five players born in Sweden, four in the Netherlands, three in Norway, and one each from Denmark and Finland comprise this group. The first was National Association pitcher-outfielder Reinder (Rynie) Wolters (Netherlands).

Two members stand out. One is Norwegian outfielder-first baseman John Anderson, a turn-of-the-century switch-hitter who batted .290 lifetime. The other is the only current entry, Twins' pitcher Bert Blyleven, whose career totals through 1988 include 254 victories and 3,431 strikeouts.

Central Europe

Only seven players are included in this group, starting with Hungarian pitcher Josef Strauss (1884) and ending with Austrian hurler Kurt Krieger (1951). In between were four players born in the Austro-Hungarian empire and one from Switzerland.

The latter was pitcher Otto Hess, the most successful of this group. Hess won 70 games, including 20 for the 1906 Indians, and was also used as an outfielder, first baseman, and pinch hitter.

Eastern Europe

There have been five natives of Russia, four of Poland, and two of Czechoslovakia to play in the major leagues.

The first was Russian outfielder Jake Gettman in 1897. The most recent was Polish pitcher Moe Drabowsky, who hurled in the bigs between 1956 and 1972, and was a relief star in his later years. Another Eastern European standout was Czechoslovakia's Elmer Valo, who batted .282 in a twenty-year career (1940–1961).

Asia/Pacific

There have been two major leaguers born in Australia, and one each from China, Japan, Okinawa, and American Samoa.

The first and best of these was Australian second baseman Joe Quinn, who collected 1,797 hits in a 17-year career (1884–1901). Another Aussie, Craig Shipley, recently played with the Dodgers.

Other notables from this small group are Samoan slugger Tony Solaita, who hit 50 of his 372 professional homers in the majors; and Japanese pitcher Masanori Murakami.

CHAPTER 10

Baseball Families

Larry Amman

Just as the Wright brothers were first in flight, so were Wright brothers first in baseball. In the National Association's inaugural season of 1871, the Boston team featured Harry Wright as manager and reserve outfielder, and George at shortstop. Brother Sam joined them on the bench for the 1876 season, after an apprenticeship in New Haven the year before.

Since then there have been 319 brother combinations in the majors. The only season in which there was not at least one such pair was 1899. There were seven new ones in 1987 and two in 1988.

The first thing that strikes the eye as one reads the list is the large number who were teammates, however briefly—more than 25 percent.

Another observation one must make is how one-sided the big league performance was between so many of the combinations. For example, there are twenty-five members of the Hall of Fame who had brothers in the majors. Yet how many baseball fans have ever heard of the brothers of Bill Dickey, Christy Mathewson, or Honus Wagner? As another example, how many people remember the brothers of Steve Sax, Eddie Murray, Graig Nettles, and Robin Yount? All four of these current big names have brothers who played in the majors briefly.

Of course, being the brother of a major leaguer never guarantees success, nor even a shot at the big leagues. The five Delahantys, the three Boyers, and the two Ferrells all had other brothers who played minor league ball only.

Because the combinations in which more than one brother excelled are so rare, we can focus on the more outstanding ones.

In terms of balanced, outstanding achievement no group of three or more brothers can match the DiMaggios. The enduring folk hero status of Joe DiMaggio unfortunately has not done anything to keep alive the memory of his brothers, Vince and Dom. All three were gifted outfielders, good hitters, and fine all-around athletes. Vince, the oldest of these sons of a San Francisco fisherman, played for five different National League teams. In 1941 he had 21 homers and 100 RBIs for Pittsburgh. Four years later he hit four grand slams for the Phillies.

Dom DiMaggio was the youngest and smallest of the three brothers. Although lacking any of the power of the other two, he was the fastest on the bases and yielded nothing to his two brothers in the grace and skill he exhibited in the outfield. His lifetime batting average was just under .300.

In the 1941 All-Star Game, Dom went to right field as a late-inning substitute to play alongside Joe in center. This was a first in the mid-summer classic. In the eighth inning, Joe doubled and Dom singled him home. In the 1949 All-Star Game, Joe drove in Dom with what proved to be the margin of victory for the junior circuit.

Dominic, or the "Little Professor" as he was called, started four different All-Star games, including the 1946 contest. That year he was voted to start in center field ahead of his brother. On the season, Dom outhit Joe by 26 points (.316 to .290).

In the 1943 All-Star Game, Vince went 3 for 3, including a ninth-inning home run. While both brothers were away in the military, Vince was ". . . maintaining the family tradition of excellence in All-Star Games."

The first time two brothers played against each other in an All-Star Game was in 1969. Carlos May of the White Sox came to bat as a pinch-hitter with brother Lee of the Reds playing first base.

For the title of the best brother pitching combination, the competition is very close between the Niekros of Ohio and the Perrys of Williamston, North Carolina. In 1987 the ancient knuckleballing duo of Phil and Joe Niekro passed Jim and Gaylord Perry in wins. The two families remain very close in most statistical categories.

The Perry brothers had one full season as teammates—1974 with Cleveland, when the two combined for 39 victories, almost half of the team total. A year earlier, when Jim was with Detroit, the two made their only start against each other. Gaylord took the loss for Cleveland. Jim got a no-decision. In the 1970 All-Star Game, the National League pitcher in the sixth and seventh innings was Gaylord Perry of the Giants. On the mound for the American League in the seventh and eighth innings was Jim Perry of the Twins. This is the only time two brothers were rival pitchers in the mid-summer classic. Both have also won the Cy Young Award.

For Joe and Phil Niekro, pitching against each other was not that uncommon. It happened nine different times. The most noteworthy occasion came on September 26, 1978, in Atlanta. Before this, his last start of the season, Phil was 19–17 for the Braves; Joe was 12–14 for the Astros. Houston won 2–0, much to the dismay of victor Joe. He loathed the idea of pitching against his brother in these circumstances.

Harry and Stan Coveleski of the coal-mining country in Pennsylvania were brother hurlers who refused to start games against each other. Stan, the younger, was in his first full season in the majors in 1916 at Cleveland while Harry was winning 20 for the third consecutive year at Detroit. Harry developed arm trouble and did not pitch another full season, but Stan went on to five 20-win seasons and a niche in the Hall of Fame.

Virtually every baseball fan has heard of the game on September 15, 1963, in which Felipe, Matty, and Jesus Alou formed the San Francisco outfield for one inning. A better

story about this Dominican family, however, is the race for the 1966 National League batting title.

Going into the season, Felipe, with the Atlanta Braves, had established himself as a hitter of high average and respectable power. Younger brother Matty's career so far had been disappointing. With no power, his lifetime batting average was .260. In the off-season the Giants had traded him to Pittsburgh.

With the Bucs, Matty came under the special tutelage of manager Harry Walker. "Harry the Hat" taught his pupil to chop down on the ball and to hit to left field instead of trying to pull. This, plus over 20 bunt and 30 infield singles, propelled Matty to the top of the league batting race. Second or third to him almost all year was Atlanta leadoff man and first baseman Felipe Alou. Matty won the crown with a .342 average, while Felipe finished second at .327. The elder brother, however, led the circuit in runs, hits, and total bases.

It was only fitting that Harry Walker was the cause of the enormous jump in Matty's batting average. In 1947 Harry Walker the outfielder was traded from the Cardinals to the Phillies early in the season. There he won the batting title with an average 100 points higher than the year before. This was the second batting title in the family. In 1944 older brother Dixie had led the senior circuit with a .357 mark at Brooklyn.

Brother rivalries and brother teammates come into very sharp focus under the media glare of the World Series. The fall classics from 1921 to 1932 featured Bob Meusel of the Yankees versus older brother Emil or "Irish" of the Giants. These two California outfielders were very similar in physical appearance and in capabilities.

Before the 1921 Series one writer summed up the pair:

Bob hits harder than Emil though he is not as consistent in garnering his hits. Bob also excels Emil as a thrower, but Emil is the more finished fielder. Bob is a left field hitter, and Emil often hits to right, so the play of "Meusel flied to Meusel" may be repeated frequently during the Series.

Indeed, it was so in all three series. In Game Three of the 1923 fall classic, each brother robbed the other of an extra-base hit. Over all, Irish emerged superior to Bob in every category—even in extra-base hits. Bob, however, had the last laugh, driving in the go-ahead run in Game Six of 1923 to give the Yankees their first world title.

For their entire careers, the Meusels startle the observer with the closeness of all their statistics. Irish averaged .310 to Bob's .309, both for 11 seasons. Bob leads in all other categories, but not by much. If Irish's totals were increased by prorating them based on his 100 fewer games, the two would look like clones. Each man led his league in RBIs one time.

Two brothers whose lifetime batting averages are identical are Bob and Roy Johnson. Both of these Oklahoma Indians hit .296 as American League outfielders in the 1930s. Bob amassed 2,000 hits and almost 300 home runs, playing mostly for Connie Mack. Elder brother Roy was a speedy singles and doubles hitter. He exceeded his brother only in stolen bases in his considerably shorter career.

The 1927 World Series featured Lloyd Waner leading off and playing center field for Pittsburgh while older brother Paul hit third and patrolled right field. In just his second season, Paul had won the batting title. Rookie Lloyd finished second in hits and third in batting average. The two combined for 460 hits during the season and were 11 for 30 in the World Series as the Yankees swept the Pirates in four games.

The Waners played parts of 16 seasons together, much longer than any other pair. Paul hit 17 points higher in batting and almost 70 points higher in slugging. However, "Big Poison" was actually shorter than Lloyd. Paul's moniker came from all the doubles and triples he delivered.

In 1934 Dizzy and Paul Dean had the greatest year any pitching brothers have ever enjoyed. "Me 'n' Paul" together won 49 games during the regular season and all four of the games the Cardinals won from the Tigers in the World Series. In 1935 their combined victory total was only two less. These two 19-win seasons were Paul's only full years in the majors.

An even more memorable year in St. Louis Cardinal history was 1942. In the last week of August, the Red Birds were five games behind the defending champion Brooklyn Dodgers. Five weeks later the Cardinals clinched first place with a record September rush. Winning five games in the last month for a total of 22 on the season was Mort Cooper. Catching him was younger brother Walker, in his first season as a regular. Mort won his September games with great flair. He was called the "fashion plate" for wearing the number on his back which equaled the victory he was seeking that day. The Cardinals beat the Yankees in a five-game World Series to shock all of baseball. Walker Cooper contributed several timely hits to the Series upset.

Mort also won 20 for the 1943 and 1944 pennant winners and had a victory in each of the World Series. Both brothers were named to *The Sporting News* All-Star team in 1944. Walker hit an even .300 for three Fall Classics.

The Coopers may have been the best of the 15 brother battery combinations, but Wes and Rick Ferrell have to be a close second. Rick caught his younger brother for five straight seasons. Wes won 20 the first two years together.

The next great brother act in the World Series was in 1964, when Ken and Clete Boyer were the opposing third basemen. Elder brother Ken was the National League's Most Valuable Player with a league-leading 119 RBIs for St. Louis. Clete had hit an anemic .219 for the Yankees. Still, this was his chance to show the baseball world he was Ken's equal in the field.

Although neither hit for a high average in the seven games, both did well with the glove. Ken gave his team all its runs in Game Four with a grand-slam homer. St. Louis won that contest 4–3. In the seventh game, Ken scored the first run and later homered. Brother Clete helped make the finish exciting as he hit one of the two solo home runs off Bob Gibson in the ninth inning. Like the Coopers, the Boyers were born and raised in the "Show Me" state. Both parents were in the stands maintaining their strict neutrality and feeling great pride.

The integrity of play when brothers square off against each other has been taken for granted for many years. This wasn't always the case. In 1933 Joe Sewell, playing third base for the Yankees, and Luke Sewell, catching for Washington, found themselves on opposite sides of a hot pennant race. They had been teammates at Cleveland for a number of years.

Reporting on a crucial game in the 1933 American League race, Shirley Povich of the *Washington Post* wrote:

It was brother versus brother in the seventh when Joe Sewell made a whale of a stop and throw to cut down Luke. It's things like that help prove the honesty of baseball.

The shadow of the Black Sox Scandal still hung over the game.

Now for a trivia windup: There have been five brother shortstop–second base combinations in big league history: Granny and Garvin Hamner of the 1945 Phillies, Lou and Dino Chiozza of the 1935 Phillies, Milt and Frank Bolling of the 1958 Tigers, Eddie and Johnny O'Brien of the Pirates in the mid-1950s, and Cal and Bill Ripken of the 1987 Orioles. The O'Briens were one of seven sets of twins in the majors.

Josh Clarke with Louisville in the National League in 1898 and George "White Wings" Tebeau of Cleveland in 1894–1895 must have felt some sense of constraint in criticizing their managers. In both cases it was a brother: Fred Clarke and Patsy Tebeau. Both pilots were regular players those seasons as well. Ed Hengle, who never played in the majors, managed his brother Moxie in the Union Association for the entry that began the season in Chicago. By the end of the campaign, both Mengels were gone, and the club had moved to Pittsburgh.

Wes and Rick Ferrell have something in common with Jesse and Lee Tannehill. In each case the pitching brother—Wes and Jesse—had a higher career batting average and more home runs than the brother who played every day.

No, Henry and Tommie Aaron were not the first "soul-brother" brother combination in major-league baseball. The game's first black siblings were Fleet and Welday Walker, who both played for Toledo of the American Association in 1884. That circuit was then considered a major league.

Brothers' Combined Totals

Seasons		Games		Hits		Doubles		Triples	
Alou	47	Alou	5,129	Waner	5,611	DiMaggio	906	Waner	308
Niekro	46	Waner	4,541	Alou	5,094	Waner	884	Delahanty	280
Delahanty	41	DiMaggio	4,245	DiMaggio	4,853	Delahanty	769	Wagner	256
Perry	39	Boyer	3,872	Delahanty	4,211	Alou	765	Clarke	233
Waner	38	Aaron	3,735	Aaron	3,987	Sewell	709	Connor	225
Boyer	36	Delahanty	3,595	Sewell	3,619	Johnson	671	DiMaggio	212
Sewell	35	Sewell	3,532	Boyer	3,559	Aaron	666	Meusel	187
DiMaggio	34	May	3,236	Wagner	3,489	Wagner	658	Johnson	178
Ferrell	33	Cruz	3,077	Johnson	3,343	Meusel	618	Ewing	178
Forsch	31	Johnson	3,016	Meusel	3,214	Boyer	523	Wheat	177
Aaron	30								

Home Runs		Runs		RBI's		Batting Average (10 seasons)		Steals	
Aaron	768	DiMaggio	2,927	DiMaggio	2,739	Manush	.329	Wagner	726
DiMaggio	573	Waner	2,827	Aaron	2,391	Wagner	.326	Delahanty	685
Boyer	444	Delahanty	2,309	Delahanty	2,153	Waner	.325	Clarke	557
May	444	Aaron	2,276	Waner	1,907	Connor	.314	Milan	501
Nettles	406	Alou	2,213	Meusel	1,887	Delahanty	.311	Cruz	322
Allen	358	Johnson	1,956	Johnson	1,839	*Brett	.310	Alou	294
Murray	358	Sewell	1,794	Boyer	1,803	Meusel	.309	Meusel	253
Johnson	346	Wagner	1,762	May	1,780	Wheat	.309	Moriarty	250
Alou	269	Boyer	1,761	Wagner	1,750	Clarke	.308	Aaron	249
Torre	264	Clarke	1,744	Sewell	1,747	O'Rourke	.308	Connor	235

Brother Pitching Totals

Games		Innings		Wins		Losses		Strikeouts		Shutouts		Complete Games	
Niekro	1,566	Niekro	8,690	Niekro	538	Niekro	478	Perry	5,110	Perry	85	Clarkson	571
Perry	1,407	Perry	8,637	Perry	529	Perry	439	Niekro	5,089	Niekro	74	Radbourn	491
McDaniel	1,006	Clarkson	5,616	Clarkson	383	*Forsch	244	Mathewson	2,504	Coveleski	51	Weyhing	455
*Forsch	982	*Forsch	4,813	Radbourn	309	Weyhing	239	Clarkson	2,326	Clarkson	43	Mathewson	436
Clarkson	705	Mathewson	4,793	Coveleski	296	Clarkson	232	*Forsch	2,140	*Forsch	37	Perry	412
				*Forsch	278							Niekro	352
*Still active												Coveleski	308

Fathers and Sons

Shortly after breaking into the majors, Dale Berra was asked about similarities between himself and his famous father, Yogi. The younger Berra replied, "Our similarities are different."

Like the many malapropisms of Yogi Berra, this one by his son may appear foolish on the surface, but it contains quite a bit of underlying wisdom. In fact, it can serve as a metaphor for father-son combinations in major league baseball.

Of the 110 combinations, only 30 feature both generations at the same position. There are 16 father-son pitcher combinations, four cases where both father and son caught, one where both played first, two where both played shortstop, and seven where both father and son were outfielders. Very few fathers and sons at any position have career totals that are at all close.

Another important generalization is the great increase in father-son combinations since World War Two, especially in the last twenty years. The first son of a former big leaguer to break into the majors was Jack Doscher in 1903 as a pitcher for the Chicago Cubs—one of the three teams with whom his father, Herm, had toiled as a utility player twenty years earlier. By 1945 the number of father-son combinations was 36. In 1965 the total was 66. That means almost 40 percent of today's number has been added in the last two decades.

Is the son of a big league ballplayer more apt to develop into a major leaguer than the average boy? Some people think not. In the 1950s, Hall of Famer George Sisler was asked this very question. The two-time .400 hitter shook his head over how two of his offspring had made the majors. He pointed out that baseball players are absentee fathers. They don't have much opportunity to teach their boys the fundamentals of the game or to practice with them.

If not their fathers, perhaps other well-qualified profession-als have instructed the second generation. A worthwhile

study could be conducted to determine how many second-generation players who have broken in during the last two decades attended baseball camps as boys. If the number is significant, this could explain the big increase during this period.

Certainly, the Sisler family deserves special attention. Father George broke into the majors just before World War One as a pitcher for the St. Louis Browns. After being switched to first base, he spent fifteen years as one of the greatest performers ever at that position. Accordingly, it is only fitting that he should have one son, Dick, who was a good hitter and another son, Dave, who pitched in the majors briefly. Dick's home run on the last day of the 1950 season, which gave the Philadelphia Whiz Kids the pennant, has given him an identity independent of his father. Also, these two men both managed in the majors for a short time. Currently they are the only father-son combination in this category.

Baseball families fall into one of three categories: famous fathers only, famous sons only, and equals.

Let us consider the famous son category first. Another way of describing these men would be to call them "fathers of . . . " Two families stand out in this category. They are the Muellers and the Walkers.

Walter Mueller was a reserve outfielder for the Pirates for four seasons in the 1920s. His son, Don, hit .296 in twelve seasons as a National League outfielder. In 1954 Mueller and teammate Willie Mays battled all season for the batting title on the pennant-winning Giants. Mays finished first in hitting by three points, but Mueller led the league in hits with 212.

Dixie Walker was a pitcher for the Washington team from 1909 through 1912. His lifetime record was 24–30. Both his sons, Fred (or "Dixie") and Harry, won batting titles.

These two are the only clear cases of a son of All-Star quality who had a father whose career in the majors was forgettable. Other families with "fathers of . . . " are Coleman, Grimsley, and Smalley.

In contrast, the list of "sons of . . . " is a long one. There are seven baseball fathers in the Hall of Fame. Six—Averill, Berra, Collins, Lindstrom, Mack, and Walsh—had offspring who fit this category. Four more families—Bagby, Camilli, Trosky, and Wood—had fathers of All-Star quality and sons who are footnotes to their careers. Hegan, Wills, and Trout are families where the sons had respectable careers and characteristics similar to those of the fathers, but the older generation was clearly superior.

We must consider first whether some of the "sons of . . . " got to the majors, or second, stayed longer than they merited, because of the family name. I would cite Collins, Walsh, and Wood to prove the former proposition, and Dale Berra and Marc Sullivan as support for the latter.

The younger Berra and Sullivan not only had the temerity to go into their father's business, but, like Bill and Cal Ripken, Jr. of Baltimore, they had dad for their boss. The Ripkens (in 1988) and Dale Berra (in 1985) saw their fathers dismissed as managers early in the season. Cal Ripken, Sr. was not only the first father to manage two sons at once, but the first without major league playing experience to manage his sons.

Sullivan, whose father owned part of the Red Sox, traded his son to the Houston Astros organization before the 1988 season, where he could commiserate with the Berras on the difficulties of combining a baseball career with family obligations.

By far the most interesting category is that of the fathers and sons whose careers parallel or equal each other.

The two Billy Sullivans caught for both the White Sox and the Tigers. Both played other positions as well as caught in one World Series. Sullivan Senior caught the older Ed Walsh; Junior caught the younger Ed Walsh—both at Chicago. Junior hit for what appears a much higher average, but we must remember that Senior played in the Dead-Ball Era, and Junior in the high-hitting 1930s.

Jim and Mike Hegan were a father-son combination well known for defensive ability. Father Jim was a great handler of pitchers for Cleveland. Mike played first base and the outfield for several American League teams. Both appeared in two World Series. Mike broke into the majors just four seasons after his father's finale. This is as close as any father and son have come to playing in the majors at the same time.

The father-son pitching combinations have few parallels. Both Thornton Lee and son Don gave up homers to Ted Williams. The two Jim Bagbys are the only father and son who both pitched in a World Series.

Joe Schultz, Junior, received some unwanted publicity in Jim Bouton's book *Ball Four,* for being Bouton's manager. Schultz and his father, Joe Senior, each spent almost a decade in the majors as reserve players. Senior was 46 for 170 as a pinch-hitter. Junior went 43 for 160 in that same role.

For balance in contribution and overall quality, the Bells and the Boones are supreme. It is only fitting that Buddy Bell should have spent a portion of his fine career with the Cincinnati Reds, the team on which his father, Gus, spent his best years. Currently the two have identical career batting averages of .281. Buddy may pass his father in home runs—the last major category in which he trails. Bob Boone has long emerged from the shadow of his father, Ray. The younger Boone broke the record for the most games caught in a career in 1987. Still, he won't come close to the offensive accomplishments of his father, who had his finest years with the Detroit Tigers in the 1950s. Both men appeared in a World Series.

Bell and Boone are the only families in which both father and son have played in All-Star Games. Gus was 2 for 6, hitting a home run his first time up; Buddy is 1 for 7, hitting a triple in his first plate appearance. Ray Boone went 1 for 5 in All-Star games with a homer; Bob is 2 for 5 in three games.

In Game One of the 1984 World Series, a two-run double by San Diego catcher Terry Kennedy was noted by the television announcers as something significant. This was the first time in the history of the fall classic that both a father and son had a World Series RBI. Terry's father, Bob, knocked in a run for Cleveland as an outfielder in the 1948 Series. There have been seven families in which the father and son both played in a World Series. Five have been mentioned already; there is also Ernie and Don Johnson. The father was a substitute infielder for the Yankees in the 1923 Series. Don was the regular second baseman for the Cubs in the 1945 fall classic. Stan Javier in 1988 with Oakland makes seven; his father, Julian, played in four World Series.

An interesting father-son parallel to watch for in the future is that between Bobby and Barry Bonds. The son, an outfielder for Pittsburgh, has his father's penchant for home runs, stolen bases, and strikeouts.

The Bondses are not the first black father-son combination. That honor goes to the Hairstons. Father Sam caught two games for the White Sox in 1951. Son Jerry was a respected

pinch-hitter for that team for over a decade.

What does the future hold for baseball fathers and sons? Will Bob Boone be the first son of a big leaguer to be voted into the Hall of Fame? Will Ken Griffey and his son both be in the majors at the same time? Will the Treshes or the Boones provide the first father-son-grandson combination in the majors? We can be sure there will be many more combinations and more interesting parallels.

Father-Son Hitters

	Years	Games	Runs	Hits	Homers	RBIs	BA	Steals
AVERILL								
Earl, Sr.	13	1,669	1,224	2,020	238	1,165	.318	69
Earl, Jr.	9	449	137	249	44	159	.242	3
BELL								
Gus	15	1,741	865	1,823	206	942	.281	30
Buddy	17	2,371	1,146	2,499	201	1,103	.280	55
BERRA								
Yogi	19	2,120	1,175	2,150	358	1,430	.285	30
Dale	11	853	236	603	49	278	.236	32
BONDS								
Bobby	14	1,849	1,258	1,886	332	1,024	.268	461
Barry	3	404	268	388	65	165	.258	85
BOONE								
Ray	13	1,373	645	1,260	151	737	.275	21
Bob	17	2,093	635	1,699	104	764	.252	34
CAMILLI								
Dolf	12	1,490	936	1,482	239	950	.977	60
Doug	9	313	56	153	18	80	.199	0
HEGAN								
Jim	17	1,666	550	1,087	92	525	.228	15
Mike	12	965	281	504	53	229	.242	28
KENNEDY								
Bob	16	1,483	514	1,176	63	514	.254	45
Terry	11	1,190	418	1,104	103	555	.266	3
SCHOFIELD								
Ducky	19	1,321	394	699	21	211	.227	12
Dick	6	636	273	544	43	203	.230	77
SISLER								
George	15	2,055	1,283	2,812	99	1,175	.340	375
Dick	8	799	302	720	55	360	.276	6
SMALLEY								
Roy, Jr.	11	872	277	601	61	305	.227	4
Roy, III	13	1,653	745	1,454	163	694	.257	27
SULLIVAN								
Billy, Sr.	16	1,146	363	777	20	378	.212	98
Billy, Jr.	12	962	347	820	29	388	.289	30
TRESH								
Mike	12	1,027	326	788	2	297	.249	19
Tom	9	1,192	595	1,041	153	530	.245	45
WILLS								
Maury	14	1,942	1,067	2,134	20	458	.281	586
Bump	6	831	472	807	36	302	.266	196

Father-Son Pitchers

	Years	Games	W-L	SO	CG	ERA
Jim Bagby						
Sr.	9	316	127–89	450	132	3.10
Jr.	10	303	97–96	431	84	3.96
Joe Coleman						
Sr.	10	223	52–76	444	60	4.38
Jr.	15	484	142–135	1728	94	3.69
Lew Krausse						
Sr.	2	23	5–1	17	3	4.48
Jr.	12	321	68–91	721	21	4.00
Lee						
Thornton	16	374	117–124	937	155	3.56
Don	9	244	40–44	467	13	3.61
Pillette						
Herman	4	107	34–32	148	33	3.45
Duane	8	188	38–66	305	34	4.40
Mel Queen						
Sr.	8	146	27–40	328	15	5.09
Jr.	9	140	20–17	302	6	3.14
Sisler						
George	7	24	5–6	63	9	2.35
Dave	7	247	38–44	355	12	4.33
Trout						
Paul	15	521	170–161	1,256	158	3.23
Steve	11	282	84–89	639	29	4.13
Ed Walsh						
Sr.	14	430	195–126	2,346	250	1.82
Jr.	4	79	11–24	107	15	5.57

Baseball Families

KEY
tm teammates
F-S father-son

BROTHERS

AARON Henry & Tommie *tm*
ACOSTA Jose & Merito
ADAMS Bobby & Dick *F-S also*
ALLEN Dick, Hank & Ron *tm*
ALLISON Art & Doug *tm*
ALOMAR Roberto & Sandy Jr.
ALOU Felipe, Matty & Jesus *tm*
ANDREWS Rob & Mike
ASPROMONTE Bob & Ken

BAILEY Ed & Jim *tm*
BANDO Chris & Sal
BANNON Jimmy & Tom
BARNES Jesse & Virgil
BARRETT Marty & Tom
BAXES Jim & Mike
BELL Charlie & Frank
BENNETT Dave & Dennis *tm*
BERGEN Bill & Marty
BIGBEE Carson & Lyle *tm*
BLANKENSHIP Homer & Ted *tm*
BLUEGE Ossie & Otto
BOLLING Frank & Milt *tm*
BOONE Danny & Ike
BOYER Clete, Ken & Cloyd *tm*
BOYLE Buzz & Jim
BOYLE Eddie & Jack
BRADY Steve & Tom
BRASHEAR Kitty & Roy
BREEDEN Danny & Hal *tm*
BRETT George & Ken
BREWER Mike & Tony
BRINKMAN Chuck & Ed
BROWN Dick & Larry
BROWN Jackie & Paul
BROWN Oscar & Ollie

CAMNITZ Harry & Howie *tm*
CAMP Kid & Llewellan *tm*
CANTWELL Mike & Tom
CARLYLE Cleo & Roy
CASEY Dan & Dennis *tm*
CHIOZZA Dino & Lou *tm*
CHRISTOPHER Lloyd & Russ
CLAPP Aaron & John
CLARKE Fred & Josh *tm*
CLARKE Sumpter & Rufe
CLARKSON Dad, John & Walter *tm*
CLIBURN Stan & Stew
COFFMAN Dick & Slick
COHEN Andy & Syd
CONIGLIARO Billy & Tony
CONNELL Gene & Joe
CONNOR Joe & Roger
CONWAY Jim & Pete
CONWAY Bill & Dick *tm*
COONEY Jimmy & Johnny *tm F-S also*
COOPER Mort & Walker *tm*
CORCORAN Larry & Mike *tm*
COSCARART Joe & Pete
COVELESKI Harry & Stan
COVINGTON Sam & Tex
CROSS Amos, Frank & Lave *tm*
CRUZ Hector, Jose & Tommy *tm*
CUCCINELLO Al & Tony

DAILY Con & Ed
DALY Joe & Tom
DANNING Harry & Ike
DARINGER Cliff & Rolla
DAVALILLO Vic & Yo-Yo
DAVENPORT Claude & Dave
DEAN Dizzy & Paul *tm*
DEASLEY Jim & Pat
DELAHANTY Ed, Frank, Jim, Joe & Tom *tm*
DEMONTREVILLE Gene & Lee
DICKEY Bill & George
DILLON Packy & Joe *tm*
DIMAGGIO Vince, Joe & Dom
DONAHUE Jiggs & Pat

DONOVAN Jerry & Tom
DORGAN Jerry & Mike
DOWNS Kelly & Dave
DOYLE Brian & Doyle
DRAKE Sammy & Solly
DUGAN Bill & Ed *tm*

EDWARDS Dave, Marshall & Mike (twins)
ENS Jewel & Mutz
ERAUTT Eddie & Joe
EVERS Joe & Johnny
EWING Buck & John *tm*

FALK Bibb & Chet
FERRELL Rick & Wes *tm*
FERRY Cy & Jack
FINNEY Hal & Lou
FISHER Bob & Newt
FISHER Chauncey & Tom
FOGARTY Jim & Joe
FORD Gene & Russ
FOREMAN Brownie & Frank *tm*
FORSCH Bob & Ken
FOUTZ Dave & Frank
FOWLER Art & Jesse
FREESE Gene & George
FRIEL Bill & Pat
FULLER Harry & Shorty

GAGLIANO Phil & Ralph
GANZEL Charlie & John *F-S also*
GARBARK Bob & Mike
GARDELLA Al & Danny *tm*
GARRETT Adrian & Wayne
GASTON Alex & Milt *tm*
GEISS Bill & Emil
GILBERT Harry & John *tm*
GILBERT Charlie & Tookie *F-S also*
GLEASON Bill & Jack *tm*
GLEASON Harry & Kid
GRABOWSKI Al & Reggie
GRAVES Joe & Sid
GREGG Dave & Vean
GRIMES Ray & Roy (twins) *F-S also*
GRISSOM Lee & Marv
GROH Heine & Lew
GUMBERT Ad & Billy
GWYNN Chris & Tony

HACKETT Mert & Walter *tm*
HAFEY Bud & Tom
HAIRSTON Jerry & John *F-S also*
HAMNER Garvin & Granny *tm*
HANDLEY Gene & Lee
HARGRAVE Bubbles & Pinky
HATFIELD Gil & John
HAYWORTH Ray & Red
HEMPHILL Charlie & Frank
HENGLE Emery (Moxie) & Ed *tm*
HEVING Joe & Johnnie
HIGH Andy, Charlie & Hugh
HILL Hugh & Still Bill
HINCHMAN Bill & Harry *tm*
HITCHCOCK Billy & Jim
HOGAN George & Happy
HOVLIK Hick & Joe
HOWARD Del & Ivon
HUGHES Jim & Mickey
HUGHES Ed & Tom
HUNTER Bill & George

IORG Dane & Garth
IRWIN Arthur & John

JEFFCOAT George & Hal
JIMENEZ Elvio & Manny
JONES Darryl & Lynn
JONES Gary & Steve
JOHNSON Bob & Roy
JOHNSON Chet & Earl
JOHNSTON Doc & Jimmy
JONNARD Bubber & Claude (twins)
JORGENS Arndt & Orville

KAPPEL Heinie & Joe
KELL George & Skeeter

KELLER Charlie & Hal
KELLNER Alex & Walt *tm*
KELLY George & Ren
KENNEDY Jim & Junior
KEOUGH Marty & Joe *F-S also*
KILLEFER Bill & Red
KILROY Matt & Mike *tm*
KLAUS Billy & Bobby
KLING Bill & Johnny
KNODE Mike & Ray
KNOTHE Fritz & George
KOPF Larry & Wally
KRSNICH Mike & Rocky

LACHEMANN Marcel & Rene
LANNING Johnny & Tom
LANSFORD Carney & Joe
LARY Al & Frank
LELIVELT Bill & Jack
LILLARD Bill & Gene *tm*
LOBERT Frank & Hans
LOOK Bruce & Dean
LOWDERMILK Grover & Lou *tm*
LUSH Billy & Ernie

MACHA Ken & Mike
MADDUX Greg & Mike
MAHLER Mickey & Rick *tm*
MAISEL Fritz & George
MANCUSO Frank & Gus
MANGUAL Angel & Pepe
MANSELL John, Mike & Tom *tm*
MANUSH Frank & Heine
MARION Marty & Red
MASKREY Harry & Leech *tm*
MATHEWSON Christy & Henry *tm*
MATTOX Cloy & Jim
MAY Carlos & Lee
MAYER Erskine & Sam
MCDANIEL Lindy & Von *tm*
MCFARLAN Alex & Dan
MCFARLAND Lamont & Charles
MCGEEHAN Connie & Dan
MCLAUGHLIN Barney & Frank *tm*
MEUSEL Bob & Irish
MILAN Clyde & Horace *tm*
MILLER Jake & Russ
MILLER Bing & Ralph *tm*
MITCHELL John & Charlie
MOFFETT Joe & Sam
MORIARTY Bill & George
MORRISON Johnny & Phil *tm*
MORRISSEY John & Tom
MUELLER Clarence & Walter *F-S also*
MURRAY Eddie & Rich
MYERS Billy & Lynn

NETTLES Graig & Jim
NEWKIRK Floyd & Joel
NIEKRO Joe & Phil *tm*
NIXON Otis & Donnell
NYMAN Chris & Nyls

O'BRIEN Eddie & Johnny (twins) *tm*
OGDEN Curley & Jack
OLIVO Chi Chi & Diomedes
O'NEILL Jack, Jim, Mike & Steve *tm*
ONSLOW Eddie & Jack
O'ROURKE Jim & John *F-S also*
ORTIZ Baby & Roberto *tm*
O'TOOLE Denny & Jim
OWEN Dave & Spike

PACIOREK John, Tom & Jim
PARKER Jay & Doc
PARROTT Jiggs & Tom *tm*
PASCUAL Camilo & Carlos
PATTERSON Ham & Pat
PEITZ Heine & Joe *tm*
PEPLOSKI Henry & Pepper
PERRY Gaylord & Jim *tm*
PEREZ Pascual & Melido
PFEFFER Big Jeff & Jeff
PIERSON Dave & Dick
PIKE Jay & Lip
PIPGRAS Ed & George

POTTER Dykes & Squire

RADBOURN George & Old Hoss
RAJSICH Dave & Gary
REACH Al & Bob
RECCIUS John & Phil (twins) *tm*
REUSCHEL Paul & Rick *tm*
REYNOLDS Hal & Don
RICKETTS Dick & Dave
RIDDLE Elmer & Johnny *tm*
RIPKIN Cal & Billy *tm F-S also*
ROBINSON Bruce & Dave
ROBINSON Fred & Wilbert
ROENICKE Gary & Ron
ROETTGER Oscar & Wally
ROMO Vicente & Romero Enrique
ROOF Gene & Phil
ROSENBERG Harry & Lou
ROTH Braggo & Frank
ROWE Dave & Jack
ROY Charlie & Luther
RUSSELL Allan & Lefty

SADOWSKI Bob, Eddie & Ted
SAUER Ed & Hank
SAX Dave & Steve *tm*
SAY Jimmie & Lou *tm*
SCANLAN Doc & Frank
SCHANG Bobby & Wally
SCHAREIN Art & George
SCHMIDT Boss & Walt
SCHULTE Herman & Leonard
SEWELL Luke, Joe & Tommie *tm*
SHAFFER Orator & Taylor *tm*
SHANNON Joe & Red *tm*
SHANTZ Billy & Bobby *tm*
SHERLOCK Monk & Vince
SHERRY Larry & Norm *tm*
SISLER Dave & Dick *F-S also*
SMITH Charlie & Fred
SOWDERS Bill, John & Len
STAFFORD John & Jim
STANICEK Steve & Pete
STANLEY Buck & Joe
STOVALL George & Jessie
SURHOFF Bill & Rich
SUTHERLAND Darrell & Gary

TANNEHILL Jesse & Lee
TEBEAU Patsy & White Wings *tm*
THIELMAN Henry & Jake
THOMAS Bill & Roy *tm*
THOMPSON Homer & Tommy *tm*
THRONEBERRY Faye & Marv
TOBIN Jim & Johnny
TORRE Frank & Joe *tm*
TRAFFLEY Bill & John
TREACEY Fred & Pete *tm*
TREVINO Alex & Bobby
TWOMBLY Babe & George
TYLER Fred & Lefty *tm*
TYRONE Jim & Wayne

UNDERWOOD Pat & Tom

VAN CUYK Chris & Johnny

WADE Ben & Jake
WAGNER Butts & Honus
WALKER Dixie Sr. & Ernie *F-S also*
WALKER Dixie Jr. & Harry
WALKER Gee & Hub *tm*
WALKER Fleet & Welday *tm*
WANER Lloyd & Paul *tm*
WATT Al & Frank
WEILAND Bob & Ed
WESTLAKE Jim & Wally
WEYHING Gus & John
WHEAT Mack & Zack
WHITE Deacon & Will *tm*
WHITNEY Art & Frank
WILLIAMS Gus & Harry
WILTSE Hooks & Snake
WINGO Al & Ivy
WOOD Fred & Pete *tm*
WRIGHT George, Harry & Sam *tm*

YOCHIM Len & Ray
YOUNT Larry & Robin

FATHERS-SONS

ADAMS Bobby-Mike
ALOMAR Sandy-Roberto &
  Sandy Jr.
ARAGON Angel-Jack
AVERILL Earl-Earl

BAGBY Jim Sr. & Jr.
BARNHART Clyde-Vic
BEAMON Charlie-Charlie
BELL Gus-Buddy
BERRA Yogi-Dale
BERRY Charlie-Charlie
BERRY Joe-Joe
BONDS Bobby-Barry
BOONE Ray-Bob
BRICKELL Fred-Fritzie
BRUCKER Earle Sr. & Jr.
BRUMLEY Mike-Tony

CAMILLI Dolf-Doug
CAMPANIS Alex-Jim
CARREON Camilo-Mark
COLEMAN Joe-Joe
COLLINS Ed Sr. & Jr.
CONNOLLY Ed Sr. & Jr.
COONEY Jimmy-Jimmy & John
CORRIDEN Red-John
CROUCH Bill-Wilmar

DOSCHER Herm-Jack

ELLSWORTH Dick-Steve
ESCHEN Jim-Larry

FRANCONA Tito-Terry

GABRIELSON Len-Len

GANZEL Charlie-Babe
GILBERT Larry-Charlie & Tookie
GRAHAM Peaches-Jack
GREEN Fred-Gary
GRIMES Ray-Oscar
GRIMSLEY Ross-Ross

HAIRSTON Sam-Jerry & John
HEGAN Jim-Mike
HEINTZELMAN Ken-Tom
HOOD Wally Sr. & Jr.

JAVIER Julian-Stan
JOHNSON Adam-Adam
JOHNSON Ernie-Don

KEOUGH Marty-Matt
KENNEDY Bob-Terry
KRAUSE Lew Sr. & Jr.
KUNKEL Bill-Jeff

LANDRUM Joe-Tom
LANIER Max-Hal
LAW Vern-Vance
LEE Thornton-Don
LERCHEN Dutch-George
LIEBHARDT Glenn-Glenn
LINDSTROM Fred-Charlie
LIVELY Jack-Bud

MACK Connie-Earle
MAGGERT Harl-Harl
MALAY Charlie-Joe
MARTIN Barney-Jerry
MATTICK Wally-Bobby
MAY Pinky-Milt
MEINKE Frank-Bob

MILLS Willie-Art
MONTEAGUDO Rene-Aurelio
MOORE Eugene Sr. & Jr.
MORTON Guy Sr. & Jr.
MUELLER Walter-Don

NARLESKI Bill-Ray
NICHOLS Chet Sr. & Jr.
NORTHEY Ron-Scott

OKRIE Frank-Len
O'ROURKE Patsy-Joe
O'ROURKE Jim-Queenie
OSBORNE Tiny-Bobo

PARTENHEIMER Steve-Dan
PILLETTE Herman-Duane

QUEEN Mel-Mel

RIPKEN Cal-Cal & Billy
RIPLEY Walt-Allen

SAVIDGE Ralph-Don
SCHOFIELD Ducky-Dick
SCHULTZ Joe Sr. & Jr.
SHEELY Earl-Bub
SIEBERT Dick-Paul
SISLER George-Dick & Dave
SKINNER Bob-Joel
SMALLEY Roy Jr.-Roy III
ST. CLAIRE Ebba-Randy
STENHOUSE Dave-Mike
STEPHENSON Joe-Jerry
STILLWELL Ron-Kurt
STOTTLEMYRE Mel-Todd

SULLIVAN Billy Sr.-Jr.
SULLIVAN Haywood-Marc
SUSCE George-George

TANNER Chuck-Bruce
TARTABULL Jose-Danny
TORRES Ricardo-Gil
TRESH Mike-Tom
TROSKY Hal Sr. & Jr.
TROUT Paul-Steve

UNSER Al-Del

VIRGIL Ozzie Sr. & Jr.

WAKEFIELD Howard-Dick
WALKER Dixie-Dixie & Harry
WALSH Ed-Ed
WHITE JoJo-Mike
WILLS Maury-Bump
WINE Bobby-Robbie
WOOD Joe-Joe

YOUNG Del-Del

**GREAT GRANDFATHER-GREAT
GRANDSON**

Jim Bluejacket & Bill Wilkinson

GRANDFATHER-GRANDSON

George Rooks-Lou Possehl
Shano Collins-Bob Gallagher
Bill Brubaker-Dennis Rasmussen
Marty & Ed Hermann
Lloyd & Jim Spencer

## CHAPTER 11

No Minor League Experience

Cappy Gagnon

If a group of baseball experts were asked to pick the all-time greatest players, a handful of names would be on everyone's list: Ruth, Williams, Gehrig, Cobb, Musial, Mays, Aaron, etc. Great players, all of them, but none of them made it to the big leagues without first prepping in the minors. In fact, among the more than 13,000 men who've appeared in the big show, only a very small number were able to complete a ten-year career without first spending some time in the bushes.

Without the ten-year requirement, many more players would qualify, but this would not be a true indicator of talent, because the list would include players like the Detroit Tigers "fill-ins" of 1912, the midget Eddie Gaedel, and the mascot Charles "Victory" Faust, among others. In addition, many players particularly batterymen, were recruited off sandlots or campuses to replace injured players, or to get a cup-of-coffee tryout.

Two other types of players went straight to the big leagues, frequently with disastrous results. The first were the 1950s bonus babies. According to the rules at that time, a player signing for more than a $4,000 bonus was required to stay in the majors for at least two years after signing. Most of these players were not ready for big league competition, but because they could not be sent down, they were unable to receive the minor league seasoning which lower-rated prospects were getting.

Among American League players adversely affected by this rule during the 1955 season were Kenny Kuhn of the Indians, Tommy Carroll of the Yankees, and Jim Small and "Diamond Jim" Brady of the Tigers. Kuhn was a schoolboy star from Louisville; Small, a speedster from Portland; Carroll and Brady were signed off the campus of the University of Notre Dame. At the time of signing, most of these bonus babies were faced with the choice of college or the majors. For those like Carroll and Jim Brady, Ph.D., who had both, there was a fallback position if their major-league careers ended without the anticipated stardom. But many other players found a lot of disappointment in their mid-twenties when they found themselves without a baseball career or a college education.

The other type of player who was rushed to the majors was the high school or college "phenom." To paraphrase a comment at the time, most of these phenoms did not "phenominate." The most famous example of this type was David Clyde. In 1973 the Texas Rangers ended the season with the worst record in the major leagues (57–105), costing the manager (Whitey Herzog) his job. The ballclub was in deep financial trouble, and drastic measures were called for. A Texas high-schooler, just eighteen, Clyde was the obvious choice for a quick fix.

Barely out of high school, Clyde pitched his first big league game with all the attendant hype. The game was an artistic and financial success. The year's biggest crowd saw him win. Unfortunately, the bubble burst soon thereafter. He developed a sore arm and a taste for drinking and nightlife that his new manager (Billy Martin) was unable to control, for reasons which are well known now. Eddie Bane, of Arizona State, was the collegiate equivalent of Clyde, at least on the field.

Various factors play a role in determining how quickly a player will advance to the majors. In the long-ago, a small number of "bird dogs"—injured and retired players mostly—scoured the country for fresh talent. Playing and living conditions were harsh in the big leagues, and there was little coaching to polish a player's skills. The minors, or occasionally the colleges, were the crucible to teach fundamentals and "inside play." In those pre-expansion, pre-TV days, minor league teams would locate, sign, teach and develop their own players until they could get a good price from a higher league or the majors. This practice continued into the 1950s.

Bonus baby rules from 1947 until the establishment of the combined draft in the 1960s altered this system. Although many players arrived in the majors straight out of high school or college, their lack of experience doomed most of them to a trip to the minors after their enforced bench sitting was over. For Kuhn, Brady, Carroll, and Small, their careers never lived up to their schoolboy promise. Harmon Killebrew was one of the few bonus babies who was able later to make it big after a stretch in the minors.

Some players, however, have had the right combination of polished talent and maturity, or have managed to be selected by a team with a spot on the roster at the right position, or have had a manager who was willing to give a young player a trial or have simply been lucky. It was then up to the player to avoid slumps and injuries.

At least forty men have skipped the minors and completed ten or more seasons without being farmed out. Seven of them played for only one team. Six jumped directly from high school. Fifteen reached the Hall of Fame, with at least one more likely to make it (Dave Winfield). The group would make a pretty good All-Star squad, except that there are no full-time catchers (Fred Tenney made his mark as a first baseman).

There are some asterisks to attach to the players on this list. For example, although Walter Johnson did not play in organized baseball before he signed with the Senators, he did play nearly a full season with a Weiser (Idaho) semipro team in 1907. Similarly, Red Murray played a few years of semipro ball in Elmira (N.Y.) while in his first college (Lock Haven Normal School in Pennsylvania).

Bob Horner is a more complicated case. He successfully

fought the Atlanta Braves' management during the 1980 season when they tried to send him down to the minors, but when he could find no takers in the free-agent market after the 1986 season, he spent 1987 playing in Japan. Since this was in their "major" league and he returned to the American majors for the 1988 season, I have listed him. Horner was a slugging shortstop for the Arizona State Sun Devils when he was signed by the Braves.

Ernie Banks and Larry Doby are more troublesome variations of the Horner problem. Gentleman Ernie played for the Negro League Kansas City Monarchs for three years prior to joining the Cubs in 1953; Doby played five years with the Newark Eagles, as a second baseman, before joining the Indians in 1947. Doby's composite career may someday gain him Hall of Fame admission. Only the cruel color line of organized baseball prevented many deserving players from reaching the majors. Some Negro League researchers believe that major league status should be conferred on the Negro Leagues.

Most of the players on this list went to college before being picked for the majors. They should probably rate a special category, since colleges have served as the equivalent of a big league farm system for many years. Among the collegians on this list are three who later had their colleges attached to their names: the Fordham Flash (Frisch), Gettysburg Eddie (Plank), and Colby Jack (Coombs). The rough-and-tumble players of the early game often ridiculed collegians.

Some of the collegians on this list were, for a time, better known on campus as basketball players (Koufax, Groat, Yost, Chapman, and Winfield). After setting scoring records at Duke, Groat also played a year of NBA basketball with the Fort Wayne Pistons.

Charles Albert "Chief" Bender jumped to the majors directly from the Carlisle Indian School. He was the first of five players on this list to be brought to the big leagues by Connie Mack. The others were Barry, Coombs, Plank, and Dugan. Connie liked smart players with good personal habits and seemed to favor collegians.

Barry's development as a shortstop moved Stuffy McInnis to first base and gave the $100,000 infield defensive wizards at all four spots. Barry later became one of the college game's most successful coaches, at Holy Cross, which sent many other players to the Athletics, including Dugan.

Coombs wrote one of the bestselling and most popular texts on baseball play while coaching Duke University. He is also a little tainted to be on this list, having played in the outlaw Vermont League in 1905. Plank, like Bender, was a Hall of Famer.

Ethan Allen also wrote a fine text on baseball and created All-Star Baseball, a terrific table game. Like Koufax, Allen was a product of the University of Cincinnati. Dave Winfield is another author from this list. Although his book angered his employer, Winfield has enjoyed a reputation as a thoughtful man. His athletic ability and tremendous physique were very impressive. Winfield was drafted by all three major pro sports. Cy Williams was also an all-around athlete; at Notre Dame, Cy and Knute Rockne were backup ends on the 1910 football team. Cy also lettered in track as a hurdler. He made the most of his education, graduating as an architect and gaining as much prominence in his postplaying career as when he won four home run titles in the National League.

Most of the men on this list possessed a high degree of intelligence along with their ability to hit, run, and throw.

This may be a result of the high percentage of collegians, or it may have been the quality which kept them in the majors without minor league preparation.

Ted Lyons (Baylor) and Eppa Rixey (Virginia) won 526 games between them during twenty-one-year careers. Pete Donohue and Wild Bill Donovan won 320 games, led their leagues in eleven pitching categories, and had five 20-win seasons. Sisler was such an all-around player that he was both a pitcher and a first baseman in the majors. Brought to the majors by the St. Louis Browns, he played for his former college coach at Michigan, the immortal Branch Rickey. Pitcher George Uhle hit .302 in his brief rookie year, foreshadowing that he would become the greatest hitting pitcher in the history of the game.

An interesting aspect of the first-year accomplishments of these players is that except for three of the pitchers (Bender, Plank, and Powell) they broke in with modest production. Few were regulars. Most came up to teams with second-division records and a hole to fill, although Connie Mack brought up Coombs and Bender to pennant-winning teams and Barry to a second-place finisher. Milt Gaston also came up to a defending league champ when he joined the 1924 Yankees.

Bibb Falk also came up to a defending league champ, but since the 1920 White Sox were decimated by the Black Sox Scandal, there was a lot of room for new blood. Falk later became a prominent college coach at Texas, the school which has produced the second-most current major league players and which is among the top three all-time.

Carl Scheib, Eddie Yost, and Johnny Antonelli were sixteen, seventeen, and eighteen, respectively, when they first appeared in a big league game, during the forties. The first two were helped by the wartime depletion of talent. Johnny Antonelli was one of the biggest bonus babies of the forties, signing for a reported $65,000 during the Braves' 1948 pennant-winning season. Yost needed federal government intervention to stay on this list.

"The Walking Man" grew up in Brooklyn. He attended NYU in the fall of 1944, playing basketball. He skipped college baseball, playing semipro ball in New Jersey on weekends. While Senator scout Joe Cambria was on a rare scouting mission (rare because it was not in a Spanish-speaking country), he spotted Yost. It is alleged that Yost was signed on the spot. He went to the majors right away, playing in a few games at the end of the 1944 season.

Yost spent all of 1945 and much of 1946 in the Navy. When the 1947 season began, Clark Griffith decided that Eddie should serve a little time in Chattanooga. The Senators' manager, Ossie Bluege, the former great Nat third sacker, agreed with this assessment. Eddie also agreed, but there was a congressional act that protected jobs for ex-servicemen. This law said that Eddie had to be retained until July 15. Yost would likely have languished on the bench until he could be sent down, except that veteran Cecil Travis slumped badly and, on May 21, Eddie got a chance to play third as a temporary regular. He lasted fourteen years with the Senators.

Among this precocious group, three players stand above the others for the uniqueness of their accomplishment: Bob Feller, Al Kaline, and Mel Ott. They each went directly from high school to the majors, without the benefit of college or semipro experience, and completed Hall of Fame careers without ever changing teams. Except for the years taken from Feller during the war, all of these players have had more than

twenty years of big league service. In effect, they wore only one uniform after high school! They could be the subject of a story, "From High School to Cooperstown, with Only One Stop in Between."

The chart that follows summarizes the accomplishment of the players referred to in this chapter:

KEY: YRS = Seasons in the majors; POS = Primary Position(s) played during rookie season; TMS = Number of teams on during career; AGE = Years and month of age during April of Rookie year; OPPORTUNITY = Finish of team during season prior to rookie year; player's rookie year; RESULT = Won-lost record (pitchers) or batting average (others) during the rookie year.

NAME	YRS	POS	TEAMS	AGE	OPPORTUNITY	RESULT
Allen, Ethan	13	OF	6	22/3	3, 1926	.308
Antonelli, Johnny	12	P	3	18/0	3, 1948	0-0
Banks, Ernie	19	SS	1	22/3	5, 1953	.314
Barry, Jack	11	2B-SS	2	21/0	2, 1908	.222
Bender, Chief	16	P	4	20/1	1, 1902	17-15
Chapman, Sam	11	OF	2	22/0	7, 1938	.259
Coombs, Jack	15	P	3	23/5	1, 1906	10-10
Doby, Larry	13	OF	3	22/5	6, 1947	.156
Donohue, Pete	12	P	4	20/5	3, 1921	7-6
Donovan, Wild Bill	18	P	4	21/6	7, 1898	1-6
Dugan, Joe	14	SS	5	19/11	8, 1917	.194
Falk, Bibb	12	OF	2	21/3	1, 1920	.294
Feller, Bob	18	P	1	17/5	3, 1936	5-3
Frisch, Frank	20	2B-3B	2	20/7	2, 1919	.226
Gaston, Milton	11	P	5	28/3	1, 1924	5-3
Groat, Dick	14	SS	4	21/5	7, 1952	.284
Horner, Bob	11	3B	3	20/8	6, 1978	.266
Hunter, Catfish	15	P	2	20/0	10, 1965	8-8
Johnson, Walter	21	P	1	19/5	7, 1907	5-9
Kaline, Al	23	OF	1	18/4	8, 1953	.250
Koufax, Sandy	13	P	1	19/4	2, 1955	2-2
Lyons, Ted	21	P	1	22/4	5, 1923	2-1
MacFayden, Danny	17	P	6	20/10	8, 1926	0-1
Magee, Sherry	16	OF	3	18/8	7, 1904	.277
Murray, Red	11	OF	3	22/1	6, 1905	.257
O'Dell, Digger	13	P	5	21/2	8, 1954	1-1
Ott, Mel	22	OF	1	17/1	2, 1926	.383
Plank, Eddie	17	P	3	25/8	0*, 1901	17-11
Powell, Jack	11	P	3	22/9	2, 1897	15-9
Rixey, Eppa	21	P	2	21/11	4, 1912	10-10
Scheib, Carl	11	P	2	16/3	8, 1943	0-1
Sisler, George	16	1B-OF-P	3	22/1	6, 1915	.285,4-4
Tenney, Fred	17	C	2	22/5	1, 1894	.388
Uhle, George	17	P	4	20/7	2, 1919	10-5
Wallace, Bobby	25	SS	3	19/5	3, 1894	.154
Williams, Cy	19	OF	2	24/4	2, 1912	.242
Winfield, Dave	16	OF	2	21/6	6, 1973	.277
Yost, Eddie	18	3B	3	17/6	2, 1944	.143
Zachary, Tom	19	P	7	22/1	5, 1918	2-0

*Eddie Plank's rookie year was also the rookie year of his team (Philadelphia) and league (the AL).

## CHAPTER 12

Baseball Nicknames

James K. Skipper, Jr.

Nicknames for professional baseball players date from the 1860s. Yet from that time to the present, there has been little systematic research on how players receive their nicknames, what the nicknames mean, and how they might be classified. This essay will attempt such an analysis by starting with pitchers enshrined in the Baseball Hall of Fame. Using this limited population has several advantages. First, it allows for a manageable number for a report of this length. Second, the players discussed are important in the history of the game. Third, the players are well enough known that the analysis can concentrate on their nicknames without having to detail their careers and accomplishments.

Excluding John Montgomery Ward, Martin Dihigo, and George Herman Ruth, who played more games at other positions than pitcher, and Al Spalding and Clark Griffith, who were elected principally for their executive talents, 48 hurlers are in the Hall of Fame. If we define a nickname as a name which is not derived from a person's given names, but one which is added to, substituted for, or used alternatively with those given names, 40 of the pitchers in the Hall of Fame, or 83 percent, have nicknames. This percentage is over three times greater than the 25.6 percent of all major league players with "official" nicknames (i.e., those that have been recorded and documented) through 1979, as I reported in an earlier study. Thus ability may be an important variable associated with the tendency for a player to attract a nickname, but certainly not the only one. Eight of the all-time-great pitchers do not have official nicknames. They are: John Clarkson (1882–1894), Adrian Joss (1902–1910), Stanley Coveleski (1912–1928), Robert Lemon (1941–1958), Warren Spahn (1942–1965), Robin Roberts (1948–1966), James (Hoyt) Wilhelm (1952–1972), and Sanford Koufax (1955–1966).

There are many ways in which nicknames might be classified. The ultimate test of any system is its usefulness. I have chosen to begin this review with two generic categories based on whether the origin of the nickname indicates a direct relation to the game of baseball, or to something else. Then I have let the nicknames themselves and the circumstances surrounding their origin suggest subcategories. In instances of multiple nicknames and conflicting accounts of origins, it is the most commonly used nickname which is classified, and the account which I believe is most convincing. Even so, judgment calls are involved.

Nicknames Directly Related to Baseball

Surprisingly, just 10 of the pitchers have nicknames that are directly related to baseball. There are two apparent cate-gories. Eight of the pitchers received their nicknames *during their major league careers* and two *before they reached the majors*. William Cummings (1866–1877), who is credited by some with developing the curveball, was called "Candy." The term "candy" referred to his "doing such a sweet job pitching the baseball." James Galvin (1875–1892) received the nickname of "Pud" for making pudding out of opposing batters. He was also called "Gentle Jeems," due to his laidback personality, and "the Little Steam Engine," because of his vigorous pitching style.

Charles Radbourn (1880–1891) was tagged "Old Hoss" after the proverbial old farm horse who was always faithful and ready to work. Radbourn won 18 games in the space of a month during the last portion of the 1884 season. Joseph McGinnity (1899–1908) earned the nickname "Iron Man" by winning five games in six days for Brooklyn in 1900. "Iron Man" refers to his indestructibility. Another account, however, is that the nickname really stems from McGinnity's off-season job in an iron foundry.

Walter Johnson's (1907–1927) fastball led to two nicknames, "Barney" after Barney Oldfield, who was driving race cars at a mile a minute, and "the Big Train," since at the start of his career trains were the fastest vehicles yet developed. Burleigh Grimes (1916–1934) was the last of the spitball pitchers. He did not shave on the days he pitched because the slippery elm he chewed and used to moisten the ball irritated his skin. This led to his nickname of "Ol' Stubblebeard." "The Meal Ticket" was applied to Carl Hubbell (1928–1943) in 1933, due to his ability to win crucial games and prevent losing streaks for the New York Giants. He was also called "King Carl" in reference to the majesty of his pitching. Finally, Robert Feller's (1936–1956) blazing fastball gave rise to his "Rapid Robert" nickname while pitching for the Cleveland Indians in 1936, even before he had graduated from high school.

Denton Young (1890–1911) was addressed as "Cy," short for "Cyclone," before he had won a major league game. At a tryout with Canton of the Tri-State League in 1890, not only did Young's fastballs get by the batter, they splintered the boards of the backstop. A bystander remarked, " 'Pears as though a cyclone struck 'em." A nickname was born. "Cy" became a popular baseball nickname, and many future players would inherit Young's "Cy," even though they had little in common with him. Richard Marquard (1908–1925) also received his nickname, "Rube," before he became a major leaguer. Marquard was compared to George "Rube" Waddell (see below) by *Indianapolis Star* sportswriters after he had won his first game for that city's minor league team in the American Association of 1908. The nickname stuck with him for his entire career.

Nicknames Not Directly Related to Baseball

The nicknames of Hall of Fame pitchers which are not directly related to the game of baseball illustrate eight broad categories which may be used in the future to classify other players' nicknames.

Place nicknames are the first category. The fastball pitcher Amos Rusie (1889–1901) grew up in Indiana and was called "the Hoosier Thunderbolt." Herbert Pennock (1912–1934) was born in Kennett Square, Pennsylvania, and had the nickname "the Knight of Kennett Square." Similarly, Edward Plank (1901–1917) was born in Gettysburg, Pennsylvania, attended Gettysburg College, and was a guide at the Civil War battlefield during the off-season. He was known as "Gettysburg Eddie." Juan Marichal (1960–1975) hailed from the Dominican Republic and was referred to as the "Dominican Dandy."

Nicknames which designate either *age or ethnic identification* represent two more categories. Players who begin their careers at an early age are often called "Kid," as was the case of Charles Nichols (1890–1906). He received his nickname in 1887 at age seventeen, when he won 21 games for Kansas City in the Western League. Waite Hoyt (1918–1938) signed a major league contract at age fifteen and immediately acquired the nickname of "School Boy." Jessie Haines (1918–1937), on the other hand, did not acquire the nickname of "Pop" until the latter stage of his career. Charles Bender (1903–1925) was of Indian extraction and was called "Chief." An ethnic designation was given to almost every Indian ballplayer from the 1890s to the 1950s.

Distinguishing physical characteristics define another category. "Lefty" is *the* most common nickname in baseball history. Two pitchers in the Hall of Fame have that nickname, Robert Grove (1925–1941) and Vernon Gomez (1930–1943). Grove was also called "Mose," short for Moses, because of his silvery hair, and Gomez, "the Gay Castilian," referring to his fun-loving personality and Spanish heritage. In addition, Gomez also earned the tag "Goofy" early in his career after he told a sportswriter he had invented a revolving goldfish bowl so that the fish would be able to see everything without having to swim! Hair color is the source of the second most popular set of baseball nicknames. "Red" and "Whitey" are the most common. These nicknames are represented in the Hall of Fame by pitchers Urban "Red" Faber (1914–1933), Charles "Red" Ruffing (1924–1947), and Edward "Whitey" Ford (1950–1967). Variation in body size also results in many nicknames with some form of "Big" being most popular— Edward Walsh (1904–1917) was "Big Ed"; Christopher Mathewson (1900–1916) was "Big Six." However, with Mathewson, some believe the "Big Six" sobriquet referred either to a New York typographical union, or a large New York City fire engine, both of which had the same nickname. In more modern times, Donald Drysdale (1956–1969) at 6′5″ tall was called "Big D." A body deformity or missing part may also be a reason for a nickname, as in the case of Mordecai Brown (1903–1916). He lost half of his right index finger (pitching hand) as a youth in a mining accident and was accorded the nickname of "Three Finger."

Personality and behavioral traits are a parallel category to physical characteristics as a source of nicknames. Michael Welch (1880–1892) was given the nickname "Smiling Mickey" by cartoonist E. V. Munkitvick because he always had a smile on his face, and John Chesbro (1899–1909) was known as "Happy Jack" for the same reason. Chesbro was also called "Algy," which was a popular slang term for sissy, which in his case meant exactly the opposite. Timothy Keefe (1880–1893), a 344-game winner, was dubbed "Sir Timothy" in honor of his royal achievements and lordly bearing. George Waddell (1897–1910) fit the classic stereotype of the country yokel in appearance, mannerisms, speech, and other behaviors. He liked nothing better than chasing fire engines, marching in parades, and tending bar, which on several occasions took precedence over his pitching chores. Fans began calling him "Rube" from the start of his career. "Rube," like "Cy," had been applied to many players after Waddell. White Sox manager Lena Blackburne is credited as the first to tag Jerome Dean (1930–1947) as "Dizzy." Pitching for a U.S. Army team in 1928, Dean was mowing down one White Sox batter after another. Blackburne screamed at his batters, "Don't let that Dizzy rookie fool ya." The nickname was reinforced in 1930, when Dean joined the St. Louis Cardinals, because of his zany behavior and colloquial speech.

Sometimes an incident occurs in one's life which is so significant that it leads to a nickname. This category may be called *"critical incident."* Grover Cleveland Alexander (1911–1930) was referred to as "Old Pete," although he was addressed as "Pete" or "Alex." The nickname stems from a hunting trip in Texas during which Alexander fell from a buckboard and landed on his face in a large pool of alkali and mud resembling peat. Clarence Vance (1915–1935) was known as "Dazzy" by age eleven. He picked up the term as a youth in his native Nebraska from a cowboy who said of his beautiful pistol, "Ain't it a dazzy." Vance started using the word "dazzy" so much that it became his nickname. Later he called his change-of-pace pitch a "dazzy"! Leroy Paige (1948–1953, 1965) also was bestowed with his nickname of "Satchel" at an early age. As a seven-year-old porter in the Mobile, Alabama, railroad station, he managed to rig up ropes around his shoulders and waist, which made it possible for him to carry so many satchels at once that you could hardly see him.

In addition to ballplayers being nicknamed after each other, they are also nicknamed after other *real people or fictional characters.* For instance, Robert Gibson (1959–1975) was called "Hoot," after the cowboy movie star of the 1930s and 1940s, Edmund "Hoot" Gibson.

The last category is *amphigoric.* The nicknames either make no sense, or they do not refer to that to which the nickname refers to in any other case. Eppa Rixey (1912–1933) was dubbed "Eppa Jephtha" by Cincinnati writer Bill Phelon, who took pleasure in such bizarre nomenclature. Theodore Lyons (1923–1946) was christened "Tex" early in his career, even though he had no association with the state of Texas. A sportswriter started using "Tex" when he could not discover Lyons's first name in time to make his column deadline. Early Wynn (1939–1963) was nicknamed "Gus" in 1937 by minor league teammate Ellis Clary, who said he just looked like a Gus! For purposes of publicity, James Hunter (1965–1979) was given the nickname "Catfish" at his signing in 1964 by Oakland owner Charles Finley. Hunter had no association with the nickname, or the fish, before that time.

Observations

What can be concluded from this brief review of the nick-

names of pitchers in the Baseball Hall of Fame? First, the answer is yes to the question of whether baseball players' nicknames can be classified. Even this limited population allows for the development of empirical categories. Second, based on this sample, it appears that a substantial majority of players' nicknames are not directly related to the game of baseball. Third, subject to more extensive analysis, it would seem that physical and personality and behavioral characteristics may account for the largest number of nicknames. Fourth, it is quite possible (given conclusions two and three) that some players would have had the same nicknames whether they played baseball or not. We are aware of them, however, because they did play baseball, and records have been kept. Finally, the categories themselves are heuristic,

which is to say, they suggest other categories—for example, nicknames that stem from childhood as contrasted from those that do not; nicknames which can be used as terms of address, such as "Red" or "Satchel," as compared to those which are used primarily as terms of reference, such as "Gettysburg Eddie" and "Iron Man."

At this stage the categories are neither demonstrative nor definitive, neither all-inclusive nor mutually exclusive. They are not etched in stone. They will have to be extended, modified and revised, divided and subdivided, before their usefulness is maximized. They do, however, provide a foundation upon which to build our understanding of baseball players' nicknames.

## CHAPTER 13

Mascots and Superstitions

Don Nelson

When the New York Mets received their supply of lucky buckeyes just in time for the 1987 stretch run, some people probably figured that the division championship was in the bag. After all, hadn't rally caps served the Mets well in 1986? The buckeyes, believed to have mystical powers, were sent in from some solicitous Mets fans at the far-off Jack Daniel's Distillery in Lynchburg, Tennessee (population 361).

Rubbing lucky buckeyes did not work for the Mets and against the Cardinals in 1987, but modern ballplayers are at a distinct disadvantage compared to those of the past. Years ago, players and teams had the powerful help of hairpins and chewing gum, for instance, to accomplish the same things. Jake Powell, during his last season in the minors, found 202 lucky hairpins and rapped out 202 hits that year. (Jake played outfield for the Senators, Yanks, and Phils in the 1930s and '40s.) And Waite Hoyt claimed to have won 23 games for the Yankees in 1928 by merely sticking gum to the button of his cap. Nothing illegal about that.

This is not to say that ballplayers are no longer superstitious. Wade Boggs eats chicken before every game; Manager Sparky Anderson avoids stepping on the foul lines; players walk around in stinking socks, afraid to change them for fear of breaking a good streak of some kind.

The book *Superstition!* by Willard Heap says, "Baseball is considered America's national sport and baseball players undoubtedly lead all other athletes in their devotion to superstition. As a class they are probably more susceptible to jinxes than any other body of professional players in the world." That passage, written in 1972, may still be true, but ballplayers as a class today are apparently more confident of their skills and less fearful of Jonahs, jinxes, hexes, and hoodoos. At least that is what some research suggests.

I looked at baseball people's relationship to that most unlucky of numbers: 13. I examined the preseason rosters of all major league clubs in 1967 and at ten-year intervals (in 1977 and 1987) to see if there were any trends regarding how many players, coaches, and managers have been assigned uniform number 13. I took as my total sample all those players who had been assigned uniform numbers 11, 12, 13, 14, and 15. If routinely assigned, each number from 11 through 15 should represent about 20 percent of the "population" of these numbers. The middle number, 13, has never come close to its "normal" share. But on the other hand, the percentage of those who defied superstition and put on the dreaded number has more than doubled over the 20-year period. Uniform number 7 (lucky 7, that is) has declined in use by 18 percent over the same period.

Only a handful of performers ventured out with a big 13 on their backs in 1967, including three pitchers—Blue Moon Odom, Steve Barber and Turk Farrell. By 1977, Blue Moon still had his lucky (?) 13, but he was cut before the season began. By then, not only pitchers were throwing caution to the wind. Shortstop Dave Concepcion and catchers Joe Ferguson and Lance Parrish, to name a few, likewise laughed at folklore and donned the dreaded 13.

In 1987, Concepcion and Ferguson were still tempting fate with their 13s—Ferguson by now was a coach. Their ranks were joined by the likes of Lee Mazzilli, Mike Pagliarulo, Ruppert Jones, and Ozzie Guillen. Is this a trend? I would say so. By 1997, number 13 may approach a "normal" distribution of 20 percent of all numbers 11 through 15.

Ralph Branca was one of the first to venture out in full view of the multitudes wearing a 13 on his shirt. And we all know what Bobby Thomson did to *him* in the 1951 National League playoffs. Odom believed in countering superstitions with aggressive taunts. Besides displaying a 13 on his back, he also liked to step *on* the foul lines. Concepcion, on the other hand, has been a bit more cautious. He crosses himself before batting, perhaps to nullify the 13 hex.

What is a superstition anyway? A superstition is defined as a belief that some action or circumstance not logically or casually related to a course of events influences the outcome. We must be careful to differentiate between superstitions and rituals.

Thus when John McGraw hired someone to haul around a wagonload of good-luck barrels where his players could see them, that was pure superstition. But when Hank Aaron slowly and deliberately put on his batting helmet before stepping into the batter's box, that was ritual. The barrels were totally unrelated to the game and performance, whereas Aaron's repeated ceremony must have put him in just the right mood to hoist 'em out.

Talismans and trinkets and hairpins and barrels are all interesting as good-luck charms and bad-luck baubles. But these are all inanimate objects. Some of the more interesting tales of superstition involve living icons: the use of boys, dogs, blacks, and hunchbacks as good-luck mascots.

Team photos from the 19th century often include mascots, usually little boys, black and white. An 1888 team photo includes two greyhounds. Even the baseball writers had mascots, judging from a picture of a group of scribes with a young boy. Rubbing a black's hair brought luck; touching a hunchback's hump also was sure to yield base hits for batters and strikes for pitchers. Understand that times were different then in terms of racial attitudes and respect for the handicapped.

Mascots and superstitions in general had their greatest impact on the game early in this century. It was an "Age of Magic," as John Holway called it, writing in *The National Pastime*. Magic began to be a presence on baseball diamonds

just before 1910, continued forcefully throughout the teens, but largely seemed to vanish in a ghostly haze by the early 1930s.

We pick up the magic trail in 1908. That fiery Southerner Ty Cobb "discovered" a black urchin, "Li'l Rastus," whom he "kept around" for good luck, yet whom he also kept hidden from public view, according to Anthony Papalas, writing in the 1984 *Baseball Research Journal*. Li'l Rastus seemed to be bringing a run of luck, but when a losing streak and missing equipment showed up simultaneously, he was kicked out of the clubhouse. Li'l Rastus defected to the Cubs for the World Series and the Chicagoans beat the Tigers. He made somewhat of a comeback with the Bengals in 1909. George Mullin once "stole" him from under Cobb's bunk and put him under his own. Mullin worked a shutout the next day and got three hits, Papalas reports. But the Tigers lost the world title again, this time to the Pirates.

It was also in 1909 that Louis Van Zelst, a dwarf-hunch-back with a body misshapen from a childhood accident, be-came the A's mascot. The A's made a good stretch run that year, but lost the pennant to the Tigers.

In 1910 Connie Mack gave Van Zelst a full contract as batboy; the little fellow traveled with the team in uniform, inviting players to pat his hump. The A's won the pennant and the Series.

In 1911 the ultimate confrontation between opposing human good-luck charms was assured when Mack's A's, with little Louis and McGraw's Giants clashed for the world title. For, as Holway writes, the Giants "themselves carried one of the most famous good-luck charms in the annals of baseball, Charles Victor Faust."

Faust, though (perhaps) retarded or psychotic or both, was neither animal nor boy nor black nor physically disfigured. Thomas Busch, writing in the 1983 *Baseball Research Journal*, tells of how Faust came from Kansas to New York hoping to play for the Giants, but wound up as a mascot. Busch described him as 6' 2" and weak-eyed, "a gawky, awkward, grinning farmboy who, whether walking or running, moved with a loping trot that reminded one of a jackrabbit hopping across a prairie." Holway was more concise, calling Faust "a lunatic Kansas hayseed." Busch was not so sure of Faust's lunacy. He thought he may have been a "skillful self-pro-moter" or even an "eccentric genius" of the Veeck-Finley mold. In today's parlance, he may have been merely a flake.

Whatever, Faust actually appeared as a pitcher in two Giants games, something no dog, young boy, or deformed dwarf ever did.

Meanwhile, back at the 1911 World Series, Van Zelst outcharmed Faust (whose middle name had taken on a Y as in Victor*y*). The A's prevailed.

As an added fillip to that season and the Series, Holway relates that the Giants' Leon "Red" Ames "was considered a hoodoo pitcher, the unluckiest man in baseball, until an ac-tress gave him a lucky necktie soon after Faust joined the team; helped by both Faust and the tie, Ames won five of his last six (regular season) games.

"In game six [of the Series, however, Chief] Bender went up against Ames, who had foolishly thrown away his lucky tie. In the fourth inning, the Giants fell apart, allowing four runs, three on errors, including one fumble by Ames. The A's were champs again."

Van Zelst stayed with the A's, mascoting them to pennants in 1913 and 1914. The Athletics beat the Giants again in the 1913 fall classic. Faust, who had fallen out of favor with McGraw, was not on the bench to counteract Louis's spell.

The 1914 Series is interesting in that Van Zelst, Mack, and the A's were pitted against the Miracle Braves and George Stallings, "probably the most superstitious man ever to man-age in the major leagues," according to Holway. "[Stallings] had so many lucky charms that he kept them in a trunk which the equipment manager lugged from city to city," Holway says.

The Braves' miraculous dash from last place to first began after Stallings added another trinket to his trunk, "a lucky 10¢ piece blessed by a Cuban witch doctor known as the 'black pope.' " Van Zelst could not overcome Stallings' voo-doo, and the Braves swept the A's.

Luck ran out for both little hunchbacked Louis and the grinning, gap-toothed Charles Victor(y) Faust in 1915. Louis didn't go to spring training, sickened, and died at age twenty before the season began. Without Van Zelst, the A's finished last that year and the following six as well.

Faust died in a hospital for the insane far from New York in mid-1915 at age thirty-four. The Giants also landed in the cellar that year.

The next memorable mascot to come along—and arguably the luckiest and longest-lasting of the lot—showed up in a Chicago White Sox uniform in 1917. As a batboy, little Eddie Bennett won the Series for the Sox in 1917, but he was up against more sinister forces on his own team in 1919—they were the losing Black Sox. Bennett moved to Brooklyn in 1920; the Dodgers promptly won the pennant. The Yankees knew a good thing when they saw it. They decided that Babe Ruth wasn't enough. Bennett became the Yankees' full-time batboy and official mascot in 1921, and, of course, the Yankees grabbed the flag. The hunchbacked man-child stayed with the club until he was seriously injured in an automobile accident in midseason of 1933, according to *Mur-derers' Row* author G. H. Fleming.

During his years with the Bronx Bombers, with Ruth and Lou Gehrig and others rubbing his back for luck, the team won seven pennants and four world championships. Like Faust and Van Zelst, Bennett met an untimely and early end, dying from alcoholism in 1935 at the age of thirty-two.

Did the Age of Magic die with him?

Today lucky uniform number 7 is out; unlucky 13 is in. Mascots, barrels, and hairpins are out; cork, sandpaper, and Vaseline are in. Still, baseball players treat foul lines like hot wires. Striking out the first batter is still a bad omen. And speaking of a no-hitter while it is being pitched always brings a barrage of hits. As long as we have Rally Caps and Homer Hankies, the Age of Magic will live on.

CHAPTER 14

Phantom Ballplayers
Clifford S. Kachline

Garbage in, garbage out is an expression that gained currency with the advent of the computer age. The logic behind the catch phrase, however, prevailed long before the electronic marvels came into being. Baseball, in fact, has had its own version of the maxim almost since the game's earliest days, largely as a consequence of recordkeepers who sometimes unwittingly entered erroneous data into the record books.

Numerous examples of the *garbage in, garbage out* principle have been discovered in baseball's statistical archives through the years. But statistics aren't the only area where the phenomenon has shown up. Another involves what researchers of the sport refer to as "phantoms"—players credited with having performed in the major leagues but who in reality never did appear in a big league game.

Phantoms are hardly a recent phenomenon. They have existed almost as long as boxscores have been published. Some were the product of misunderstandings by—or misinformation given to—official scorers or the parties who compiled the boxscores. A few of these crept into the leagues' official records. Others were created by mistakes on the part of telegraph operators or by typographical errors and appeared only in newspaper boxscores.

Little if any attention was paid to the situation until the 1950s. The original edition of *The Official Encyclopedia of Baseball,* published by A. S. Barnes and Co. in 1951, provided fans for the first time with a supposedly complete alphabetical tabulation of every man who ever played in the majors, together with his basic yearly big league stats. The publication stimulated the interest of the sport's researchers. When editors Hy Turkin and S. C. Thompson deleted the names of some players—most of whom were previously shown as having a one-game career—from subsequent revised editions, the matter of phantoms started to become a source of fascination.

Who really were the "impostors" that were listed in earlier editions? What had prompted the editors to include them in the first place? And what evidence had been found to prove conclusively that they never played in the big leagues?

The introduction of *The Baseball Encyclopedia* by the Macmillan Publishing Company in 1969 focused additional attention on the subject. In compiling data for that publication, David Neft and his crew of Information Concepts, Inc. researchers continued the process of purging phantoms from the records. Since then, further investigation by Neft, Pete Palmer, Bill Haber, Al Kermisch, and others has led to the expunging of several more players.

In many instances confirming the status of a phantom was a complicated chore. The task sometimes was made more difficult because the player's name was included in the official league statistics. In other cases, especially those involving nineteenth-century performers, the fact that official league records no longer exist compounded the problem because it made it impossible to determine who was credited by the official scorer and/or league statistician with appearing in the game or games in question. (The American League's official game-by-game player sheets of 1901–1904 reportedly were destroyed by fire decades ago, while the official National League data also vanished for the pre-1902 period except for the 1899 season.)

An example of a phantom who appears in the league records is Albert W. Olsen. For thirty-five years he was carried in the *Encyclopedias* and shown as participating in one game—as a pinch hitter—for the Boston Red Sox in 1943. Olsen did train with the Red Sox that spring, but he was shipped to San Diego of the Pacific Coast League before opening day and spent the entire season in the minors. In addition, it was his exploits as a lefthanded pitcher, not as a hitter, that originally attracted the Red Sox.

Nevertheless, American League records list Olsen as playing for Boston in a game in Chicago on May 16, 1943. Newspaper boxscores credited him with drawing a walk while batting for pitcher Dick Newsome and subsequently stealing a base. However, recent research has confirmed that the supposed "Olsen" actually was a newcomer to the Red Sox roster—outfielder Leon Culberson, who had just been called up from Louisville (of the American Association) and was making his major league debut.

How could such a mistake have occurred? There probably were no phone lines from the pressbox to the dugouts in those days, and in the absence of being able to call down to check the player's name, it's conceivable that someone in the pressbox referred to a Red Sox spring training scorecard and may have found the pinch hitter was wearing the same number that originally had been assigned to Olsen. Fortunately, investigation has revealed the player was identified as "Culbeson" by at least one Boston paper.

To add to the irony, Culberson was installed as the Red Sox' leadoff man in the second game of the day's doubleheader and contributed a single and triple in five at-bats. He went on to play 81 games with Boston that season, counting his "Olsen" unveiling.

A manager's pique led to a phantom known as J. A. Costello getting into the early *Encyclopedias*. Curiously, the incident also took place in Chicago and likewise involved a player's big league debut. It occurred in the morning half of a holiday bill between Cleveland and the White Sox on July 4, 1912. Late in the contest, Indians' Manager Harry Davis, still burning over an umpire's decision, sent the newcomer into the game to replace center fielder Joe Birmingham and in-

structed him to announce himself to umpire Gene Hart as "Costello."

In reality, the player was Kenneth Nash, who had only recently joined Cleveland from Boston University law school. He subsequently appeared in ten additional games with Cleveland that season under his correct surname, mostly as a shortstop, and then played with the St. Louis Cardinals for part of 1914. Nash later became a prominent state representative, state senator, and judge in his home state of Massachusetts.

The 1903 official National League records contain a phantom who long baffled researchers. Among the Pittsburgh player sheets is one headed "George Gray" with entries for two games as an outfielder—on May 28 and May 31. Four years earlier the Pirates had a pitcher named George "Chummy" Gray, and it's possible the scorer or league statistician remembered him while filling in the player's first name. When the first *Official Encyclopedia* appeared in 1951, the player was identified as William (rather than George) Gray, a native of Pittsburgh.

It turns out that the two George (or William) Gray entries properly belonged to not one, but two different players. The Pirates' left fielder in the May 28 game really was Romer Carl "Reddy" Grey, younger brother of novelist Zane Grey. He had been obtained on loan from the Worcester club of the Eastern League to fill in that afternoon in the final game of a series in Boston.

On the other hand, while boxscores in Cincinnati newspapers listed the Pittsburgh left fielder for the May 31 game in Cincinnati as "Gray," the player actually was Ernest Diehl, a Cincinnati sandlotter who had been recruited by the injury-riddled Pirates. The game represented Diehl's first appearance in the major leagues and his only game that season, but he played 12 more games with Pittsburgh the following year. It should be noted that ever since the original Turkin/Thompson tome, the *Encyclopedias* have credited Diehl with playing one game with Pittsburgh in 1903, but until recent years they also carried William Gray with two games.

A majority of baseball's phantoms were the product of typographical errors—instances where a linotypist or a typesetter mistakenly included one or more incorrect letters in a name, or where a printer inserted a correction line in the wrong place. In compiling data for the *Encyclopedias,* the authors/researchers relied not only on the so-called official league records but also combed boxscores published in *The Sporting News, Sporting Life, The New York Clipper,* and various local newspapers. In the process they occasionally came upon what appeared to be a previously unlisted "new" player who, in the final analysis, proved to be someone else. Even today, misspellings of this type in newspapers can cause great befuddlement.

A classic illustration of a phantom who was created by a typographical error is the player carried in the early *Encyclopedias* as John P. Morgan. He was listed as appearing in one game as a third baseman with the Philadelphia Athletics in 1916. A study of A's boxscores for the season disclosed the source of the mix-up: It was *The Sporting News*'s boxscore of the August 3 game at Cleveland. *(Sporting Life* had dropped boxscores by this time.) The Philadelphia half of *TSN*'s box has "Morgan, 2b," while on the very same line in Cleveland's half is "Gandil, 1b."

Careful examination reveals the Morgan/Gandil type slug was a correction line that the printer inserted in the wrong

place. It was intended for the Washington-at-Cleveland boxscore of the previous day (August 2) in which the Senators' second baseman, Harry Morgan, appeared on the same line as Chick Gandil and contained the identical AB-H-PO-A-E figures given for each player in the misaligned August 2 line.

This explanation may well leave you, the reader, with several questions, to wit: (1.) Who did play third for the A's that day, and was he properly credited in the official records? (2.) Why did the *Encyclopedia* compilers show Morgan as a third baseman instead of a second baseman? (3.) How did they come up with "John P." for the impostor's name?

The answers are: (1.) Lee McElwee and, yes, he was credited with this game; (2.) because veteran Nap Lajoie played the entire game at his usual second base position for the A's, the researcher who made this "discovery" apparently assumed it should have read "Morgan, 3b" rather than "2b"; (3.) an infielder named John P. Morgan was active in the minor leagues that season, and the *Encyclopedia* editors probably figured the A's had given him a trial. Numerous other phantoms were similarly tagged with the first names of then-current minor leaguers.

Typos involving misspelled names led to a number of one-game phantoms. Two examples will serve to demonstrate the point. They are John H. Carlock (1912, Cleveland) and a player listed simply as Deniens (no first name given) with the 1914 Chicago Federals. *Sporting Life* had "Carlock, ph" for Cleveland in an August 24, 1912, game at Boston, but Cleveland newspapers and *The Sporting News* reported the pinch-hitter was Fred Carisch, a reserve catcher with the Indians. Official AL records also credit Carisch with that appearance. "Deniens, c" turned out to be Clem Clemens, a catcher in 13 games with the 1914 ChiFeds. One can readily visualize how handwritten names "Carisch" and "Clemens" could have been misinterpreted by a telegrapher or linotypist for "Carlock" and "Deniens."

The origins of some other phantoms are more mysterious. Take the case of Lou Proctor. The *Encyclopedias* credited him with one appearance with the 1912 St. Louis Browns. *The Sporting News* and *Sporting Life,* which may have obtained their boxscores from the same source, show "Proctor, ph" and "Procter, pi," respectively, in a May 13 game at Boston. However, a Boston newspaper referred to the pinch hitter as Albert "Pete" Compton, a catcher with the Browns that season (whose real first name was, of all things, Anna). While AL records contain no reference to Proctor, they unfortunately also fail to include the May 13 appearance among Compton's 100 games. Rumor has it that Proctor was a prankish Western Union telegrapher who inserted his own name as a pinch hitter.

The presence on one team of two players with the same or an almost similar surname can lead to problems. The Washington Senators figured in three such mixups. Ironically, in one instance research by Kermisch has established that a player long labeled a phantom was, in fact, the real McCoy. The player in question was Charles C. Conway. In 1911 the Senators had both Conway, a rookie outfielder up from Youngstown (Ohio-Pennsylvania), and William "Wid" Conroy, veteran infielder-outfielder, on their spring roster. When the season began, Conroy was idled by a stone bruise of the foot. Meantime, Conway appeared in two games during opening week, finishing up in right field on April 15 and starting at that position three days later, before the Senators returned him to Youngstown. Unfortunately, *Sporting Life* and *The*

Sporting News each showed "Conroy" as the replacement in the first contest, but both had "Conway, rf" in their April 18 boxscore. Although the early *Encyclopedias* listed Conway and credited him with playing two games, the Macmillan compilers dropped his name 20 years ago on the erroneous premise that it was the veteran Conroy who participated in the April 15-18 games. Actually, Conroy didn't make the first of his 106 appearances that year until April 27.

An equally confusing puzzle centered on a 1914 Washington pitcher known as Barron or Barton. The early *Encyclopedias* carried both John J. Barron (later changed to Frank John Barron) and Carroll R. "Buck" Barton and credited each with pitching in one game for the '14 Senators. Actually only one pitcher was involved (and just one appearance), but which pitcher was it? Player contract data of the period reveal that Washington signed Carroll R. Barton in 1913 and retained rights to him while he pitched for Newport News (Virginia League) that season and again in 1914. During the same two years John J. Barron was pitching in the New England League. To complicate matters further, Washington signed Frank J. Barron in 1914 and shipped him to Newport News, where he became a teammate of Barton. While Barron posted a dismal 1-3 record, Barton was a 16-game winner that year.

So who was the 1914 Washington pitcher? The American League player records contain an entry headed "Barron" with data for an August 18 game, and boxscores of the contest likewise have "Barron" pitching one inning—the ninth—for the Senators against the visiting St. Louis Browns. The player's correct identity was confirmed when, shortly before his death in 1964, Frank Barron disclosed in an interview that while still studying for his law degree at West Virginia University he was signed by Clark Griffith in 1914, was assigned to Newport News and later pitched one inning for Washington before resuming his law studies.

The third Washington mix-up relates to a 1944 player identified in the *Encyclopedias* as Armando Viera Valdes. Official AL records contain a sheet for Armand (without the final "o") Valdes and note that he made a pinch-hitting appearance for the Senators in a May 3 game at Boston, but Richard Topp's research has disclosed that the pinch hitter was Rogelio "Roy" Valdes, a fellow Cuban but no relative of Armando.

With many major leaguers lost to military service in 1944, scout Joe Cambria lined up several Cubans to fill voids on the Senators' roster. Early in the year he signed an outfielder who was listed in the 1944 *American League Red Book* as Armand (without the "o") Valdes. Several weeks thereafter—too late for inclusion in the *Red Book*—Cambria signed Rogelio Valdes, a catcher. Both spent the early weeks of the season with Washington (each was later optioned to Williamsport of the Eastern League), and presumably the official scorer and/or league statistician picked up the incorrect first name from the Senator roster in the *AL Red Book*.

As in the case of Charles Conway, another player once regarded as a phantom has turned out to be a legitimate athlete after all. The Turkin-Thompson tomes listed him as William Krouse, a second baseman in one game with Cincinnati in 1901. Compilers of the Macmillan encyclopedia decided he was an imposter and dropped him, crediting his appearance to Bill Fox, the Reds' regular keystoner. However, research has revealed that the "Krouse, 2b" for Cincinnati in the July 27, 1901 game at Chicago was a recently-released minor leaguer whose correct name was Charles "Famous" Krause. Krause, who was on his way home to Detroit at the

time, was given a chance with the Reds because Fox was sidelined with a split finger, but the newcomer performed so poorly that he was dumped after that one appearance.

The accompanying table lists the phantoms who have been eliminated from the all-time roster of major league players since the first Turkin/Thompson *Official Encyclopedia* of 1951. In the absence of an official clearinghouse for such data, no claim is made that the list is complete. Where it is available, brief information on the reason for the deletion of the player is given. Unfortunately, documentation by Turkin/Thompson and the ICI group that compiled the 1969 *Encyclopedia* disappeared years ago.

With today's sophisticated technology and record-keeping procedures, the margin for error in the identification of players—and in the official statistics—has been reduced considerably. Still, a slipup that occurred in the 1984 official American League averages (Alvaro Espinoza was omitted completely, even though he appeared in one game with Minnesota) emphasizes that mistakes still are possible.

A factor that poses the potential for error is the frequency of teams having two players with the same—or nearly identical—surname. In 1987, for instance, the Atlanta Braves' pitching staff at one time or another included two Smiths (Zane and Pete) as well as a Cary (Chuck) and Clary (Marty), while the St. Louis Cardinals had two relief specialists named Dayley (Ken) and Dawley (Bill) and also a Perry (Pat) and a Terry (Scott), two pitchers who coincidentally were traded for each other during the season. Meanwhile, Seattle's lineup often included both Phil Bradley and Scott Bradley, while Craig Reynolds and Ronn Reynolds occasionally appeared in the same lineup for Houston, and Baltimore, of course, had the brothers Ripken. Other examples—such as Sandberg (Ryne) and Sundberg (Jim) of the Cubs and infielders Jeltz (Steve) and Jelks (Greg) of the Phillies—could be cited, but the duo that could cause the greatest difficulty for researchers circa 2000 consists of pitchers Don Robinson and Jeff Robinson, both of whom pitched for San Francisco and Pittsburgh in 1987.

Couple this with the typographical errors that still show up in newspaper boxscores, and you can see that the days of *garbage in, garbage out* are likely to continue.

Tabulation of Phantoms

Baldwin,——. 1907 Boston NL, 1 game as C. One of James C. Ball's 10 games.

Barton, Carroll R. 1914 Washington AL, 1 game as P. Same as game credited to Frank J. Barron.

Bigler, Ivan E. 1917 St. Louis AL, 1 game as 1B. Typographical error; one of George H. Sisler's 135 games.

Boylan,——. 1887 Philadelphia NL, 1 game as 2B. One of Charles J. Bastian's 60 games.

Carlock, John H. 1912 Cleveland AL, 1 game as PH. Typographical error; one of Frederick B. Carisch's 26 games.

Christman, H. B. 1888 Kansas City AA, 1 game as C. Documentation behind deletion no longer available.

Collins, Frank. 1892 St. Louis NL, 1 game as OF. Documentation behind deletion no longer available.

Costello, J. A. 1912 Cleveland AL, 1 game as OF. One of 11 games played by Kenneth L. Nash, who used pseudonym in debut.

Davis, Thomas J. 1890 Cleveland NL, 1 game as OF. One of George Stacey Davis' 136 games.

Davis, ——. 1903 Chicago NL, 1 game as OF. Documentation behind deletion no longer available.

Deniens,——. 1914 Chicago FL, 1 game as C. Typographical error; one of Clement L. Clemens' 13 games.

Drennan, K. John. 1904 Detroit AL, 1 game as 1B. Typographical error; one of William "Wild Bill" Donovan's 46 games.

Dugan, E. 1884 Kansas City UA, 3 games as OF. Same player as William H. Dugan, who played 9 games with Richmond AA the same year.

Gray, William. 1903 Pittsburgh NL, 2 games as OF. One game belongs to Romer C. Grey; other game belongs to Ernest G. Diehl.

King, Frederick. 1901 Milwaukee AL, 1 game as C. Game belongs to John A. Butler, later with St. Louis and Brooklyn NL, who used pseudonym in debut.

Lane,——. 1901 Boston NL, 1 game as 3B. Typographical error; one of Bobby Lowe's 129 games.

Leonard,——. 1892 St. Louis NL, 1 game as OF. Documentation behind deletion no longer available.

Mares,——. 1894 Louisville NL, 1 games as OF. Documentation behind deletion no longer available.

McCauley, William. 1884 St. Louis AA, 1 game as C. Game belongs to James A. McCauley, who also played in 1885–1886.

Meddlebrook,——. 1884 Baltimore UA, 1 game as OF. Documentation behind deletion no longer available.

Merson,——. 1914 Brooklyn FL, 1 game as PH. Typographical error; one of George J. Anderson's 98 games.

Miller, Bert. 1897 Philadelphia NL, 3 games as 2B. Games belong to Frank A. Miller, formerly listed as Frederick Miller, who also played one game each with Washington NL and St. Louis NL in 1892.

Miller, Henry D. 1892 Chicago NL, 4 games as P. Games belong to Harry DeMiller, who was erroneously listed for 1 game as 3B with 1892 St. Louis NL.

Moore, Guy W. 1922 St. Louis NL, 1 game as OF. Documentation behind deletion no longer available.

Morgan, John P. 1916 Philadelphia AL, 1 game as 3B. Typographical error; one of Leland S. McElwee's 54 games.

Olsen, Albert W. 1943 Boston AL, 1 game as PH. Game belongs to Leon Culberson, who played 81 games that season.

Pratt, Thomas J. 1884 Baltimore AA, 1 game as OF. Documentation behind deletion no longer available.

Proctor, Lou. 1912 St. Louis AL, 1 game as PH. Game belongs to Anna S. "Pete" Compton, who played in 101 games that season.

Ritchie,——. 1910 St. Louis NL, 1 game as PH. Documentation behind deletion no longer available.

Schauer,——. 1890 Columbus AA, 1 game as 1B. Documentation behind deletion no longer available.

Seymour, Thomas. 1882 Pittsburgh AA, 1 game as P. Player's correct name was Jacob Semer.

Smith, Charles H. "Pacer." 1877 Chicago/Cincinnati NL, 34 games as 2B-OF-C. Record belongs to Harry W. Smith, who also played 1 game with 1889 Louisville AA.

Smith, E. J. 1890 Buffalo PL, 1 game as 1B. One of John Irwin's 77 games.

Strands, Lewis. 1915 Chicago FL, 1 game as 2B. One of John J. Farrell's 70 games.

Thayer, Edward L. 1876 New York NL, 1 game as 2B. Player's correct name was George T. Fair.

Turbot,——. 1902 St. Louis NL, 1 game as OF. Documentation behind deletion no longer available.

Valdes, Armando V. 1944 Washington AL, 1 game as PH. Game belongs to a different player, Rogelio "Roy" Valdes.

Young, David. 1895 St. Louis NL, 1 game as 3B. Documentation behind deletion no longer available.

## CHAPTER 15

Scandals and Controversies

Stephen S. Hall

Scandal is in the eye of the beholder. The biggest scandal of baseball's 1876 season was the failure of the New York Mutuals and Philadelphia Athletics to fulfill their obligatory season-ending western road trip, resulting in their expulsion from the National League. Yet when black players were virtually excluded from the first eight decades of organized ball, few saw it as a long-running institutional scandal. When the likable but wayward Babe Ruth cut a broad swath through most notions of civilized behavior, the Sultan of Swat's charmed, forgiving public responded with winks and nods. But when Walter O'Malley, in a business decision calculated to maximize profits (surely one of baseball's most enduring and honored traditions), moved his Dodgers to Los Angeles after the 1957 season, he traumatized an entire generation of Brooklyn fans. Which was more scandalous behavior?

From its earliest days, baseball has indulged gamblers, fixers, drunkards, brawlers, disreputable moguls, bad actors, felons, homicidal maniacs, crooked umpires, vindictive owners, pyromaniacal fans, and at least one ax murderer. Just as a Dickens novel reflects all the voices and vices of Victorian London, baseball hears from all precincts of the American experience, including the seedy.

Gambling, Bribery, and Game-Fixing

Baseball's greatest scandal is unquestionably the fixing of the 1919 World Series, but the Black Sox scandal merely climaxed more than five decades of dubious collusion between players and gamblers. Half a century before the World Series fix, in 1872, the *New York Times* harumphed editorially that the aim of baseball was "to employ professional players to perspire in public for the benefit of gamblers . . ." Many small scandals lit the way to the disgrace of 1919.

Baseball began as a gentlemanly avocation, but any disputatious athletic event quickly caught the attention of gamblers. As early as 1857, crowds at Elysian Fields in Hoboken, New Jersey, one of amateur baseball's most hallowed venues, came to bet on games. It was but a short step from gambling to influencing the outcome of games. Soon word drifted eastward that gamblers on the West Coast were not averse to firing their guns into the air at crucial moments to disrupt the concentration of fielders—and, of course, to protect their investments.

A slang term, "hippodroming," soon emerged to indicate a game played with the illusion of spontaneity when, in fact, the outcome had already been fixed. Gamblers reportedly harassed members of the Brooklyn Excelsiors in an 1860 game with the Brooklyn Atlantics—after which the Excelsiors refused to play the Atlantics again. Another team, the

Haymakers of Troy, New York, was suspected of hippodroming, largely because its owners included renowned New York gamblers like John Morrissey. Rumors of fixed games so dogged baseball in its early years that a Buffalo writer once suggested, "Any professional base ball club will 'throw' a game if there is money in it. A horse race is a pretty safe thing to speculate on, in comparison with an average ball match."

Gamblers freely circulated in baseball parks, occasioning such warnings as the BETTING POSITIVELY PROHIBITED sign that graced the wall of the Washington Nationals' ballpark in 1867. A forerunner of bookmaking, called pool selling, sprung up in conjunction with baseball, and by the 1870s as much as $70,000 might be riding on a single game. With all the betting, it was inevitable that gamblers would approach players with bribes—even during the "amateur" era. Players of that era—ill educated, often immigrants—were particularly susceptible; the under-the-table payments they received as amateurs did little to instill moral probity. Indeed, patronage jobs were often offered in lieu of outright salaries by such well-connected owners as Boss Tweed, part owner of the New York Mutuals. A lot of baseball players found well-paying jobs in such unlikely spots as the U.S. Treasury Department in Washington and the coroner's office in New York.

Indeed, a scant six years after the formation of the amateur National Association, organized baseball confronted its first gambling scandal. On September 28, 1865, the heavily favored New York Mutuals lost to the Brooklyn Eckfords, 28–11. It later developed that two Mutuals players, Ed Duffy and William Wansley, offered money to Mutuals shortstop Thomas Devyr to throw the game. For their role in the conspiracy, which was investigated by the Judicial Committee of the National Association, Duffy and Wansley were banned from match play; the Mutuals, in desperate need of a shortstop, helped to have charges against Devyr dismissed. By 1870, all three players had won reinstatement—a prophetic indication that organized baseball was not yet prepared to take a firm stand against gambling.

A little-known footnote to the amazing 60–0 season of the 1869 Cincinnati Red Stockings, baseball's first avowedly professional team, is that the lone blemish in their record came as the result of a tie with the hippodroming Haymakers of Troy, who walked off the field in the sixth inning of a 17–17 game on some reportedly dubious pretext to save their gambling bosses from a probable loss. Five years into the professional era, the legendary baseball writer Henry Chadwick felt compelled to charge in print that players were in cahoots with gamblers and had staged "rather questionable" games during the 1874 campaign. The charges remained just that—accusations—until the Louisville Grays scandal of 1877. It was, according to historian J. E. Findling, "the first documented

case of player crookedness after the founding of the National League."

The senior circuit was barely a year old when Chadwick's worst fears came true. The National League had been organized in February of 1876, at least in part as a response to growing public disenchantment with baseball's wayward ways—the influence of gamblers, the appearance of fixed games, the drunken, salacious antics of players. In August of 1877 the league-leading Louisville Grays embarked on a long eastern road trip. After a disastrous stretch of seven losses and a tie, in part facilitated by suspiciously inept play, the team returned home. Sportswriters openly hinted that Louisville had dumped its games and deliberately blown the pennant.

Since a Louisville newspaper magnate served as club president, the *Courier-Journal* ran speculative articles intended to smoke out the suspected fixers. The ploy worked when one of the players confessed. On October 30, 1877, the Louisville directors expelled four players—Jim "Terror" Devlin, George "Gentleman George" Hall, Bill "Butcher" Craver, and Al "Slippery Elm" Nichols—for life. Nichols, a utility player, had befriended a "pool seller" named James McCloud, who paid Devlin and Hall $100 to throw a game. An examination of Western Union telegrams conclusively established links between the gambler and the players. Craver refused to cooperate in the investigation, thus earning his expulsion, but Devlin, Hall, and Nichols were accused of selling games and "tampering with players." In their defense, they claimed that the Louisville management had failed to pay their salaries as promised—not an unlikely charge, given the parlous finances of the nineteenth-century clubs. All four were banned for life, and the Louisville Grays were disbanded before the start of the 1878 season. The *Louisville Courier-Journal* attributed the dissolution to "the rascality of last year's players and the general conviction that dishonest players on other clubs were more the rule than the exception . . ."

Umpires were not immune to the emoluments of gamblers either. As a player for the Chicago White Stockings, Richard Higham's desultory attitude and outright ineptitude had aroused suspicion. As umpire, Higham handled many games involving the Detroit Wolverines at the outset of the 1882 season, and a number of observers—including Wolverine owner William Thompson—believed that many of the close calls went against Detroit. Thompson, who also happened to be mayor of Detroit, assigned a private detective to investigate Higham. The detective ultimately uncovered the scam: Higham placed bets by telegram with a well-known gambler on the very games he was scheduled to umpire, then made calls favoring the team he'd bet on. Baseball officials confronted Higham with the evidence and banished him from the game. It represented no midlife crisis for Higham, however—he promptly became a bookie based in Chicago. This expulsion marks the only documented case of dishonesty by an umpire in the history of major league baseball.

The influence—or at least suspicion—of gambling did not subside after the Louisville Grays and Higham scandals. Contemporary commentators speak of "a little odor" hovering over the pennant races of 1891 and 1892, but no details ever emerged. Then, at the turn of the century, baseball took a two-decade running start toward the scandal that would forever blacken its name.

The lassitude with which baseball viewed the gambling establishment by 1900 affected every part of the game. Players openly associated with gamblers; and, indeed, in some cases that was a politic thing to do, for those gamblers happened to be team owners. The original bankrollers of the New York Highlanders, Frank Farrell and William "Big Bill" Devery, typified the unhealthy cross-pollination of sports and gaming. Devery went unbowed by his reputation as New York's most corrupt police commissioner, and Farrell's notorious gambling habits placed him many chits above the middling pool seller. One of their favorite pals was the player known as "Prince Hal": Hal Chase, probably the most corrupt ballplayer ever.

Chase began his career with the Highlanders in 1905 and was an extraordinarily gifted fielder at first base. He was also a well-known gambler who thought nothing of betting on his own team, and sometimes even against it. Many of his managers—including George Stallings of the Highlanders, Frank Chance of the Yankees (as the Highlanders came to be called), and Christy Mathewson in Cincinnati—suggested at one time or another that he threw games. It is typical of the *laissez-faire* days before the Black Sox scandal that when Stallings publicly complained about Chase, American League President Ban Johnson did not investigate the alleged game fixing, but rather dressed down Chase's manager for smearing the reputation of a big gate attraction. By 1918, when he was suspended by the Reds for gambling and attempting to bribe an opposing pitcher, Chase's appearance on the field was sometimes greeted with cynical cries of "What are the odds?"

At least once, and probably on many occasions, Chase offered bribes to teammates and opposing players to give substandard performances. He concluded his malodorous career with the 1919 New York Giants; true to form, he was indefinitely suspended in August, along with third baseman Heinie Zimmerman. It later emerged that Chase and Zimmerman offered an $800 bribe to Giant pitcher Rube Benton to throw a game; bribes were also offered to Benny Kauff, Lee Magee, Fred Toney, and Jean Dubuc. Despite no public explanation, Giants manager John McGraw later suggested that Chase and Zimmerman's questionable play against Cincinnati helped the Reds win the pennant—lending, if true, a rarely noted but fitting symmetry to that year's corrupt World Series. Prince Hal's crowning achievement in this record of deceit was to bring gamblers and fixers together to throw the 1919 World Series.

Hal Chase's machinations were merely the most obvious symptoms of pervasive corruption in the period 1900–1920, according to baseball historian David Quentin Voight. There was a reported attempt to bribe players in the first two World Series, in 1903 and 1905; in the former year, Boston catcher Lou Criger was offered a bribe to "lay down," while in the latter year, Philadelphia pitcher Rube Waddell did not play due to an injury, when he had allegedly received a $17,000 offer not to play. It was widely believed that gamblers tried to fix the 1908 season. In 1916, the New York Giants were rumored to have helped the Dodgers beat out the Phillies in the pennant race, and the 1918 World Series may have been tampered with as well. There was even the bizarre attempt, on the last day of the 1910 season, to bribe an official scorer, so that Cleveland's popular Nap Lajoie could beat out the detested Ty Cobb for the batting crown. The unsuccessful attempt—to change an error into a hit for Lajoie—resulted in dismissal for St. Louis Browns coach Harry Howell; St. Louis manager Jack O'Connor, too, got fired for ordering his third

baseman to play so deep that Lajoie got seven bunt singles in the season-ending doubleheader. Yet these transgressions were more of degree than nature. Since at least the 1890s, it was commonplace for teams to reward opposition players with clothes, cigars, even money for a good performance against rivals; it no doubt took but a short step to rewarding bad performances as well.

All the corruption came home to roost in 1919. Even before the very first pitch had been thrown in what became Cincinnati's "improbable" World Series victory over the Chicago White Sox, rumors swirled that the fix was on. It took a year for the rumors to come true. The initial reaction was to dismiss the allegations, including reports that gamblers had offered Cincinnati pitcher Hod Eller a $5,000 bribe which he turned down.

But the 1920 season was a cauldron of renewed rumors of bribery and game fixing. No less than seven clubs—the Giants, Cubs, Yankees, Braves, Red Sox, Indians, and White Sox—were suspected of throwing games that season. Cub players Lee Magee and Claude Hendrix were blacklisted, Hendrix toward the end of the 1920 season for trying to fix a game with the Phillies. Finally, in September 1920, a Chicago grand jury convened to investigate charges about the 1919 World Series. Meanwhile, an article appeared on September 27, 1920, in the *Philadelphia North American* in which local gambler Bill Maharg went beyond innuendo and blew open the scandal. Maharg described how White Sox pitcher Eddie Cicotte volunteered to fix the Series; how Maharg and his partner, former major leaguer Billy Burns, promised to pay $100,000 to eight White Sox players; how the gamblers double-crossed the players by paying them only $10,000 at first; how the players double-crossed the gamblers by winning a game they were supposed to lose; and how Burns and Maharg got double-crossed by a rival fixer, New York gambler (and former boxing champion) Abe Attell, who *also* was bribing the players. The following day, Cicotte agreed to testify to the grand jury and named the names ever after branded the "Black Sox": pitchers Cicotte and Claude Williams, batting star Joe Jackson, infielders Buck Weaver (who had "guilty knowledge" of the fix but refused to take part in it), Swede Risberg, and Chick Gandil, outfielder Oscar "Happy" Felsch, and even a utility man, Fred McMullin. Not only did they throw the 1919 World Series to the Reds, but, in a disreputable postscript to their season of infamy, they dumped the 1920 pennant race to the Indians, too.

In grand jury testimony, Gandil emerged as the ringleader, pocketing $35,000. Cicotte received $10,000; Jackson got $5,000 (he was earning about $6,000 a year from the tight-fisted White Sox owner Charles Comiskey). Arnold Rothstein, the notorious gangster, reputedly masterminded the fix, although his role was never legally proven and he was never charged with a crime. The scandal left no one untainted. Joe Jackson wrote a letter to Comiskey shortly after the calamitous Series, stating that the Series outcome was questionable and volunteering to meet with the owner to provide details, but Comiskey—said to be concerned about the effect of such revelations on attendance and profits, not to mention his equity in the franchise—never followed up on Jackson's offer.

Following the mysterious disappearance of their confessions and other legal skullduggery, the "eight" Black Sox won acquittal during their June 1921 conspiracy trial; none of the big-fish gamblers and fixers went to trial. But the newly appointed baseball commissioner, Kenesaw Mountain Landis,

in an extraordinarily usurptive move aimed at restoring public confidence in the game, suspended all eight players for life. The sentence was particularly brutal for Weaver, who had not participated in the scam, and Jackson. "Shoeless Joe," in throwing the series, batted .375, and it was his apparently accurate throw to the plate in the tense fourth game, inexplicably cut off by pitcher Cicotte, which convinced cognoscenti in the stands beyond a doubt that the White Sox were deliberately tossing the games. In the roundelay of accusations that later emerged, Rube Benton charged that Hal Chase made $40,000 betting on the Reds; others charged that Benton knew of the fix and had made $3,200; and St. Louis infielder Joe Gedeon won $600 following a tip from Swede Risberg.

Bill James, in his *Historical Baseball Abstract,* estimates that a total of thirty-eight major league ballplayers were implicated in scandals during the period 1917–1927, and that nineteen were formally banned or effectively blacklisted (James's list includes several players, however, who were suspended not for corruption, but for such offenses as contract jumping). In addition to the Chase and Black Sox scandals, James cites the allegations of Jimmy O'Connell, who claimed to have offered $500 to Philadelphia player Heinie Sand to fix a game in 1924; O'Connell and Giants coach Cozy Dolan were banned for life, but Frankie Frisch denied he'd known about the fix.

Under Landis's stern tutelage, baseball took a far less tolerant view of gamblers, though tales of the corrupt teens continued to trickle out. In 1926, player-managers Ty Cobb of the Tigers and Tris Speaker of the Indians both resigned under a cloud; the public later learned that ex-pitcher Dutch Leonard alleged that they had conspired to fix the last game of the 1919 season so that Detroit could win third-place money and that Smoky Joe Wood allegedly placed bets for Cobb and Speaker. And in 1927, "Black Sox" Swede Risberg publicly charged that some fifty players had known of a four-game series in 1917 that the Tigers threw to the White Sox.

Compared to the tormented twenties, the Depression and war years seemed peaceably upright. But never entirely so. In 1943, for example, Phillies owner William D. Cox received a swift and permanent suspension from Landis for betting on Philadelphia games. It would be perhaps naive to think that Landis's crowd-pleasing gestures totally eliminated gambling from the game, but they certainly sent a message to players and administrators alike that, if caught, the price would be steep. The antigambling fervor carried over into the commissionership of A. B. "Happy" Chandler, who in the spring of 1947 suspended Brooklyn manager Leo Durocher for one year for "conduct detrimental to baseball." Personality clashes and baseball politics apparently influenced Chandler's decision, but he had previously warned Durocher against associating with gamblers and other "unsavory" characters, including actor George Raft. Durocher, not heeding the warning, had actually been living in Raft's home the previous fall.

Commissioner Bowie Kuhn prided himself on an aggressive Landis-style stance against even the *appearance* of association with gamblers, and so in 1969 presented an ultimatum to four prominent baseball people, including Oakland owner Charles O. Finley and Atlanta Brave directors Bill Bartholomay, John Louis, and Del Coleman. All four had interests in the Parvin-Dohrmann Co., which owned and operated the Fremont, Stardust, and Aladdin casinos in Las Vegas. Faced with choosing baseball or gaming, Finley sold

his stock, and all but Coleman resigned their directorships. Somewhat more controversial (and problematic) was Kuhn's insistence that players or coaches employed by baseball teams could not accept public relations work at casinos. Thus Mets batting instructor Willie Mays (in 1979) and Yankee spring training instructor Mickey Mantle (in 1983) were forced to give up their baseball jobs in order to serve as greeters at Atlantic City casinos. Shortly after Kuhn left office, incoming Commissioner Peter Ueberroth revoked the orders.

Baseball's last great gambling scandal unwittingly reaffirmed the old Graig Nettles adage about going from Cy Young to Sayonara. Detroit pitcher Denny McLain made the trip in four years, winning the prestigious award outright in 1968 with a 31–6 record and sharing it again in 1969, only to bounce out of the majors by 1972. Around the beginning of 1970, word circulated that a Detroit grand jury had begun investigating McLain. Against a backdrop of personal financial difficulties, McLain's rumored involvement with gamblers prompted a meeting with Bowie Kuhn, at which the pitcher admitted investing $5,700 in a bookmaking operation at a bar he frequented in Flint, Michigan. The confession preceded by several days a *Sports Illustrated* article on February 17, 1970, which described McLain's involvement in the bookmaking operation. The article went on to suggest that when McLain failed to pay out $46,600 on a winning bet in 1967, organized crime enforcer Tony Giacalone allegedly stomped on the pitcher's foot, dislocating several toes and causing him to miss at least two September starts during Detroit's heated pennant race with Boston. The article further alleged that Detroit mobster Billy Giacalone, brother of Tony, bet heavily on Boston to win the pennant, and also against Detroit in their final game of the season, which McLain started and the Tigers lost; in all, McLain lost his last three decisions of the 1967 season. The bookie connection and the allegations earned an indefinite suspension from Kuhn, although the commissioner later stated there was no proof of McLain's having bet on baseball games.

Unindicted but never clear of the clouds over his head, McLain returned to the Tigers in July. He received two more suspensions that season amid increasingly bizarre behavior: threatening a parking lot attendant, dumping a bucket of ice water on two sportswriters, and violating federal law by carrying a gun on a commercial airliner. McLain was traded to the Senators, and tried comebacks with Oakland and Atlanta before bouncing entirely out of baseball in 1972. In 1985, he was found guilty in a Florida trial and sentenced to twenty-three years in jail on charges of racketeering, loan sharking, extortion, and possession of cocaine with intent to distribute. After serving nearly thirty months, McLain won his appeal and regained freedom. (Late in 1988, however, he pled guilty to several of the charges and once again faced a jail term.) In allegedly dabbling both in gambling and drugs, McLain bridged the gap between baseball's more traditional vices and the modern fascination with controlled substances.

Alcohol and Controlled Substances

John Barleycorn's name has never been entered into a major league scorecard, but alcohol has undoubtedly affected the outcome of games and certainly determined the length of careers. Two anecdotes a century apart suggest just how endemic drink—and drunks—have been to the game. When the

Philadelphia Athletics won the pennant in 1871 (and in those days, it was a *real* pennant), the flag flew not from a stadium flagpole, nor did someone hoist it up in the clubhouse. No, it was promptly hung in a Philadelphia saloon. In 1974, after both Whitey Ford and Mickey Mantle won election to the Hall of Fame, restauranteur Toots Shor remarked, "It shows what you can accomplish if you stay up all night drinking whiskey all the time." In the 1970s and 1980s, drug use became pervasive, leading to baseball's worst scandal since the days of the Black Sox.

Nineteenth-century ballplayers were inordinately fond of what they called "German tea," and "lushers" were common on every team. In 1880, in a dispute as political as it was moral, the Cincinnati ball club was expelled from the National League for selling liquor at the stadium (as well as for playing on Sunday). Shortly before his death in 1882, National League president William A. Hulbert issued lifetime suspensions to the "ten chronic lushers" in the league. "Drinking, late hours, and wenching were more common in the early decades of professionalism than they are now," historian Harold Seymour wrote in 1963, "or at least more regularly publicized in the newspapers."

Drinking by ballplayers had become so bad that it had attracted the notice and interest of temperance groups, as well as self-ordained protectors of the game's image. Thus in the 1880s, *The Sporting News* attacked such popular gate attractions as Mike "King" Kelly, Jim McCormick, Pete Browning, and Curt Welch for their notorious drinking. The most flagrant violator was probably Welch. An outfielder for St. Louis, Welch could be seen out in the field sneaking sips of beer, which he hid behind the billboards of Sportsman's Park. This may in part explain why he was known for his circus catches.

In 1886, Chicago White Stockings owner A. G. Spalding went on the warpath against his boozing players. He dangled $350 bonuses in front of two of his stars, Kelly and McCormick, if they would curtail their heavy drinking. They did not. Prior to their departure for spring training that year, the White Stockings even gathered en masse in Spalding's sporting goods store in Chicago to take public vows of temperence, with Chicago manager Adrian "Cap" Anson administering the oaths. Spalding then packed them off to the thermal waters of Hot Springs, Arkansas; the express purpose, according to one writer, was "to boil out the alcoholic microbes." Lushing being a league-wide problem, many teams added Hot Springs to their February itineraries.

Many outstanding players have achieved notoriety with their drinking escapades. Chicago manager Anson got into a drunken fistfight in a saloon and was arrested on one occasion; Rube Waddell, the turn-of-the-century lefthander, often disappeared after long benders. The most tragic victim of drinking may well have been Ed Delahanty. Suspended by the Washington Senators for disciplinary problems in Detroit in July of 1903, Big Ed headed back east by train, got drunk and abusive on board, and had to be put off in Canada, just north of the Niagara River. He started to walk across the railroad bridge that led to the U.S., got into a tussle with the night watchman, and tumbled into the Niagara River; eight days later, his body washed up below Niagara Falls, some eleven miles downstream from the bridge.

In the era of prohibition, Babe Ruth was a walking advertisement for the ease with which alcohol could be obtained. That fine Yankee tradition was upheld by Mantle and Ford,

aided and abetted by their drinking partner Billy Martin. But alcoholism unquestionably shortened the career of Cub outfielder Hack Wilson, and drinking problems came to be associated with such players as Paul Waner, Jimmie Foxx, Don Newcombe, Ryne Duren, and Dennis Martinez, to mention but a few. For many decades, during which sportswriting shared more with hagiography than journalism, incidents of alcohol abuse never reached the public. It could be argued that only upon the publication of *Ball Four* by Jim Bouton in 1970 did the hangover earn its rightful spot in the locker room.

While baseball clubs naturally condemned alcohol and drug use, teams continued to sell beer in the stands, of course. This hypocritical policy reached a sodden apotheosis on June 4, 1974, in Cleveland's Municipal Stadium, when the Indians sponsored a 10¢ beer night. Increasingly rowdy as the game progressed, drunken Cleveland fans spilled out onto the field and pelted the visiting Texas Rangers with firecrackers. By the bottom of the ninth inning of a 5–5 game, dozens of fans streamed onto the field, threatened Texas players, and ignited a riot requiring police action to quell. Cleveland lost the game on a forfeit.

Alcohol abuse continued to be a problem into the 1980s. In 1980, Dodger pitcher Bob Welch publicly acknowledged a drinking problem that occasioned a five-week stay in The Meadows, which would become a popular substance-abuse treatment center. That same year, Kansas City catcher Darrell Porter checked in for drug and alcohol counseling.

Baseball players reflected general social trends with their increasing experimentation with drugs during the 1960s and 1970s, although a lot of disposable income and free time contributed to crash courses in recreational pharmacology. Access to drugs was easy. Many players routinely used "greenies," amphetamine-barbiturate combos, that allegedly gave them a lift before games. In some cases, the pills were distributed by club physicians, and the problem had become sufficiently widespread that in 1971 Commissioner Bowie Kuhn instituted baseball's first Drug Education and Prevention Program. Its effectiveness was questionable: in 1980, the team physician for the Phillies' Reading farm team was arrested for illegally writing prescriptions for amphetamines. The charges were later dismissed, but the doctor, Patrick A. Mazza, testified that he prescribed the pep pills at the request of seven Philadelphia players.

Baseball formally entered the era of mind-altering drugs on August 25, 1980, when Texas pitcher Ferguson Jenkins was arrested at the Toronto airport for possession of two ounces of marijuana, two grams of hashish, and four grams of cocaine; he was later found guilty of cocaine possession. Unofficially, baseball had tipped its hand during the previous decade. Pitcher Bill Lee, then of Montreal, had openly admitted use of marijuana. More startlingly, Pittsburg pitcher Dock Ellis, reportedly suffering a hangover on a day he didn't expect to pitch, flung a no-hitter (with eight walks) against the San Diego Padres on June 12, 1970. Ellis later denied that he was working on a hangover; he was working, rather, on a tab of LSD.

By the 1980s, the list of baseball's drug abusers began to read like a crime wave in a "good neighborhood." July 1982—San Diego infielder Alan Wiggins was arrested for cocaine possession. November 1982—Dodger relief pitcher Steve Howe began the first of three treatment regimens for drug abuse, which culminated with his suspension for the entire 1984 season. October 1983—four Kansas City Royal players (Willie Aikens, Vida Blue, Jerry Martin, and Willie Wilson) pled guilty to charges of attempting to possess cocaine and later served time in prison. January 1984—Atlanta pitcher Pasquel Perez was arrested in the Dominican Republic with half of a gram of cocaine; found guilty, he paid about $400 in fines. May 1984—Anthony J. Peters, a former ice cream salesman in Milwaukee, received twenty-two years in jail for selling cocaine; at least ten players on the Milwaukee Brewers, Chicago White Sox, and Cleveland Indians were customers, and players Dick Davis, Paul Molitor, and Claudell Washington all reportedly admitted cocaine use during interviews with federal agents. 1985—San Francisco outfielder Chili Davis publicly admitted using cocaine in 1983, but stopped when the Federal Bureau of Investigation reportedly questioned him about it.

These incidents were symptomatic of the widespread drug use that became a matter of record in the celebrated drug trials of 1985. In the spring of that year, a federal grand jury in Pittsburg heard testimony from eleven active major league players, resulting in a May 31, 1985, indictment of seven drug dealers who associated with players from December 1979 to January 1985. The dealers had access to the clubhouse and team flights of the Pittsburgh Pirates, and in one of the more bizarre twists on baseball's already bizarre modern-day marketing, FBI agents wired the Pittsburgh mascot, the Pirate Parrot, to obtain evidence used in the indictments.

During the trials in September, seven active or former players testified under grants of immunity: Dale Berra (Yankees), Enos Cabell (L.A. Dodgers), Keith Hernandez (Mets), Jeff Leonard (S.F. Giants), John Milner (ex-Pirate), Dave Parker (Reds), and Lonnie Smith (Cardinals). All confessed to extensive drug use, and several implicated peers during their testimony. Milner, for example, indicated that former Pittsburgh teammates Parker, Berra, Lee Lacy, and Rod Scurry used cocaine during the 1981 and 1982 seasons. Parker and Berra testified that Pirate stars Bill Madlock and Willie Stargell distributed amphetamines to team players (a charge denied by the two, who were never prosecuted); Parker also said he had arranged sales of cocaine to Dusty Baker, Steve Howe, and Derrell Thomas of the Dodgers as well as Cabell and J. R. Richard of the Astros. Smith and Hernandez implicated their former Cardinal teammate Joaquin Andujar. In gripping testimony, Hernandez described cocaine as "the devil on this earth" and shocked observers by estimating that by 1980 40 percent of all major league baseball players used cocaine.

Not a single player went on trial, however. Pittsburgh juries separately convicted part-time caterer Curtis Strong of Philadelphia and Robert McCue of drug-trafficking charges. Freelance photographer Dale Shiffman of Pittsburgh and Philadelphia salesman Shelby Greer pled guilty and received sentences of twelve years, and three other Pittsburgh men entered guilty pleas.

In a 1985 interview with the *New York Times,* Montreal President John McHale flatly stated that cocaine use by eight of his players cost the Expos the National League Eastern Division race in 1982. Drug use was so widespread and casual, according to Lonnie Smith, that opposing players sometimes exchanged information on drug availability when they met at midfield during pregame warmup sprints. The extent of the involvement became pathetically clear when Montreal outfielder Tim Raines, the National League's leading base

stealer, admitted that he often slid headfirst into second base during a steal so as to protect the gram bottle of cocaine he kept in his back pocket.

And still the roll call continued. Two former Cy Young winners, LaMarr Hoyt of San Diego and Dwight Gooden of the New York Mets, became involved in drug use. Gooden underwent treatment for cocaine and missed the first six weeks of the 1987 season. Hoyt served time for drug trafficking following his release by the Padres in 1987.

Brawlers, Perverts, Felons and Fellow Travelers

From the origins of baseball until well into the 1890s, baseball players were regarded mainly as roughnecks, quick to anger, quicker to fight. Fans were rowdy, and brawls between players and the public were not unusual (a doozy occurred in Louisville in 1896, when the bellicose Cleveland Spiders, protesting the umpire's decision to call the game, sparked a riot that required police intervention—and landed all the Spiders in jail). In 1904, during a spring training exhibition game in Mobile, Alabama, the New York Giants became so enraged by the calls of a hometown umpire that they finally attacked the man and beat him unconscious. John McGraw hustled his team out of town, even as warrants were being sworn for the players' arrest.

Sometimes the violence has been more serious. In 1883, former National League pitcher Terry Larkin shot his wife Catherine after she complained about his drinking. In the game's goriest story, Marty Bergen, became baseball's first and only ax murderer in January of 1900, when he killed his wife and two children in North Brookfield, Massachusetts, before committing suicide. In 1917, in a crime with racial overtones, Milwaukee (of the American Association) manager Danny Shay shot and killed a black waiter in an Indianapolis hotel during an argument over the amount of sugar in a sugar bowl; Shay was later acquitted.

In perhaps the most celebrated shooting in baseball history, a "disturbed" nineteen-year-old woman, said to be a "fan," shot Phillie first baseman Eddie Waitkus in a Chicago hotel on June 15, 1949. Waitkus missed the rest of the 1949 season and had to undergo four operations, but he returned to play six more seasons—and to serve as a model for a similar incident in Bernard Malamud's baseball novel, *The Natural*. Cesar Cedeno of the Houston Astros was implicated in a more lethal incident. On December 11, 1973, the twenty-two-year-old outfielder was charged with voluntary manslaughter in the Dominican Republic when the body of a nineteen-year-old woman, shot to death, was found in his motel room. The charges were later changed—without much explanation—to involuntary manslaughter; Cedeno paid a small fine (about $100) and court costs. There have been no shootings between teammates, but not for lack of paranoia: Ty Cobb got along so poorly with his Detriot teammates during his early years that he retired to his railroad berth at night with a loaded pistol. Possibly the closest thing to an on-the-field homicide occurred in 1965, when San Francisco Giant pitcher Juan Marichal assaulted Los Angeles Dodger catcher John Roseboro with a bat.

In the old days, it was not uncommon for players to duke it out with their managers. One of the most savage beatings was administered in 1929 by White Sox player Art "Whattaman" Shires, a notorious drunkard and self-styled boxer. Shires cornered Chicago manager Lena Blackburne and the team's traveling secretary in a hotel room and thrashed both; it took four men, including two hotel detectives, to drag Shires off. He beat up his manager three times in one year. More recently, in 1977, Texas infielder Lenny Randle landed several punches on the face of manager Frank Lucchesi, shattering his cheekbone and requiring plastic surgery. The Rangers suspended Randle, fined him $10,000 and then released him; in court, Randle plea-bargained a felony charge down to simple battery and paid a $1,000 fine, along with medical expenses.

In the twentieth century, three figures stand out for their combativeness as well as their ability to arouse controversy over the long haul: Ty Cobb, Babe Ruth, and Billy Martin.

Ty Cobb is generally considered the meanest player ever to don spikes. Cobb had to leave his first major league spring training camp, in 1906, to attend the trial of his mother, Amanda Cobb, who was acquitted of voluntary manslaughter charges in the death of Ty's father; she had shot him in 1905, believing him to be a prowler. Cobb seemed to carry a chip on his shoulder throughout his career. Thin-skinned, bigoted, a nasty street fighter, Cobb forever blemished his reputation in 1912 when he dove into the stands in New York to silence a heckler, kicking and spiking the man. The spectator turned out to be a man with no hands. Cobb's response was "I don't care if he has no feet"; American League president Ban Johnson's response was to suspend Cobb for ten days. (His Tiger teammates, in sympathy with Cobb, launched a strike that lasted one game.) During his career, Cobb engaged in drawn-out, knock-down fights with umpires, teammates, opposing players, fans, even a hotel watchman (the latter resulted in an indictment in Cleveland in 1909 for felonious assault). A racist with a broad palette, Cobb tarred all races with his brush: he liked to refer to Honus Wagner as "Krauthead" and once refused to room with Babe Ruth, believing Ruth's dark complexion suggested black ancestry.

Ruth, on the other hand, enjoyed the reputation of a good-hearted, if adolescently rambunctious, personality; although he often indulged in scandalous behavior, he never amounted to a scandal. A man of immense and uncontrollable appetites, Ruth set new standards for eating, drinking, and whoring off the field just as he set long-ball standards on it. Particularly in the early days of his career, Ruth had little control of his temper. In 1917, as a Boston pitcher, he attacked umpire Brick Owens, and once went into the stands with a bat to chase a heckler; in the 1922 season alone, he was suspended five times, usually for swearing at umpires. He drank whiskey and ginger ale for breakfast, spent countless hours and dollars at the racetrack, partied past curfews in any time zone, frequented illegal breweries, and never wanted for liquor during Prohibition. A legendary philanderer, Ruth once bragged that he had slept with every girl in a St. Louis whorehouse, and even when his first wife Helen accompanied him on road trips, teammates facilitated Ruth's infidelities by making their rooms available for the Babe's liaisons. For all his energetic rutting, Ruth apparently contracted venereal disease more than once. A $50,000 paternity suit filed against Ruth by a Long Island woman accelerated the demise of his marriage, which was also undermined by Ruth's open affair with Claire Merritt Hodgson (she later became his second wife). Ruth's behavior struck many as reckless and often infantile, but it was rarely malicious and often perversely innocent, which is why he never lost the admiration and love of the public. That strange brew of raging hormones and American innocence is

perfectly summed up by an incident during a barnstorming trip to the Orient in the 1930s: brought to a geisha house, Ruth mistook it for a bordello and promptly started to undress.

Innocence seems lamentably absent from the adventures of infielder Billy Martin, who gave new, darker meaning to the word "scrappy." He was involved in at least five major fights on the field. He beat up one of his own pitchers, Dave Boswell, while managing the Twins in 1969 (Boswell required twenty stitches in the face); had punched out reporters (*Nevada State Journal* writer Ray Hagar in 1978) and marshmallow sales man (Joseph Cooper in 1979); got into a vicious fight with another member of his pitching staff while managing the Yankees (Ed Whitson in 1985); and brawled in a Texas strip joint (1988). He earned his reputation as "King of the Sucker Punch" in 1960 when, playing for the Reds, he sucker-punched Cub pitcher Jim Brewer after an inside pitch, shattering Brewer's cheekbone and landing him in the hospital for two weeks. No crass gesture has been too small or juvenile to be excluded from the Martin oeuvre: for his 1972 baseball card, as manager of the Detroit Tigers, Martin reverted to the classic junior high school prank of extending his middle finger in an unmistakably vulgar gesture while leaning on a bat. Although often suspected of prevarication, he spoke the absolute truth when he once referred to his boss as a "convicted felon."

Indeed, Yankee principal owner George Steinbrenner had the dubious distinction of dragging baseball down into the Watergate scandal. In 1974, a federal grand jury in Cleveland indicted Steinbrenner on fourteen felony counts for illegal corporate contributions (by his American Shipbuilding Company) to the reelection campaign of Richard Nixon as well as for obstruction of justice. Represented by famed criminal attorney Edward Bennet Williams, Steinbrenner struck a deal with Watergate special prosecutor Leon Jaworski and pled guilty to a single felony charge.

Some observers considered Steinbrenner's light sentence (a $15,000 fine; no jail term) puzzling, since the Yankee owner admitted in court to such grave offenses as causing his employees to lie to the FBI and give false testimony to a federal grand jury. Williams literally saved Steinbrenner's baseball career; Commissioner Kuhn later admitted he would have expelled Steinbrenner for life had he received a jail sentence. Instead, Kuhn suspended Steinbrenner for two years, later reduced to one season. Steinbrenner, incidentally, was not the first owner to commit a felonious offense. In 1953, St. Louis owner Fred Saigh was forced to divest his control of the Cardinals when he began a fifteen-month sentence for tax evasion; that paved the way for Saigh's sale of the team to Anheuser-Busch.

No Sex, Please; We're Heroes

As baseball became popular, so too did public interest in its practitioners extend beyond the field to the home, and sometimes right on through the bedroom door. Within the bounds of Victorian society, one of baseball's earliest sex "scandals" involved the hard-fighting Walter "Arlie" Latham, third baseman of the St. Louis Browns. Around 1885, his second wife filed for divorce on the grounds of assault, desertion, infidelity, and perversion.

Sports pages in the 1880s also carried accounts of Sam Crane, infielder for the Metropolitans and later a prominent sportswriter, who was arrested for running off with $1,500 belonging to a Scranton fruit dealer named Travenfelter—*and* with his wife Hattie. Edwin "Ned" Bligh was among the earliest of players named in a paternity suit; Bligh just missed more serious charges, since his accuser was seventeen-year-old Zella Coleman. By the end of the century, domestic problems—such as the divorces of popular players like John Montgomery Ward, Amos Rusie, and Tony Mullane—became fodder for reporters.

Probably the most tragic scandal involved minor league pitcher Edgar McNabb, who made it to the majors for one season with Baltimore in 1893. McNabb had been carrying on an affair with actress Louise Kellogg, wife of Seattle businessman R. E. Rockwell. The idyll came to an end on February 28, 1894, in a room at the Hotel Eiffel in Pittsburgh. For reasons that remain a mystery to this day, McNabb shot Kellogg twice (paralyzing her but not killing her), then turned the gun on himself and showed better control. In another romance-related suicide, Red Sox manager Chick Stahl took his life in 1907 after facing pressure from a woman who'd become pregnant by him.

On the whole, though, twentieth century sex scandals in baseball have been more elliptical than explicit. Apart from Ruth's legendary wenching, there was little to arouse prurient interest, except perhaps the vicarious experience of Joe DiMaggio's marriage to Marilyn Monroe or perhaps Bo Belinsky's dalliance with Mamie Van Doren. In 1988, Dave Winfield's bout with Ruth Roper, mother-in-law of Mike Tyson, brought VD into the courts. But in terms of vague but suggestive explanations, nothing beats the adventure of Brooklyn pitcher Van Lingle Mungo during spring training in 1941 in Havana. Authors Gene Karst and Martin J. Jones, Jr., note that the Dodger player had to be hustled hastily back to the mainland after he "became involved with a former bullfighter and his girlfriend." No further explanations offered.

But hardly a sex scandal in any field quite measures up to a wife-swapping scheme that became public in March 1973. New York Yankee pitchers Fritz Peterson and Mike Kekich pulled off one of the most daring trades in baseball history: they exchanged wives and children. In a straight-up deal, Peterson received Susanne Kekich, her two young daughters, and the Kekich family dog, in exchange for Marilyn "Chip" Peterson, her two young sons, and the Peterson family pet. If, as is often said, you cannot judge the value of a trade until five years have passed, it must be stated that neither side came out ahead on this one. Marilyn Peterson left Kekich and both pitchers were out of baseball by 1980.

## CHAPTER 16

Tragedies and Shortened Careers

Joseph M. Overfield

If, of all words of tongue and pen,
The saddest are, "It might have been,"
More sad are these we daily see:
"It is, but hadn't ought to be."

—*Bret Harte*

In the eleventh century in the reign of William the Conqueror, detailed information about the landowners of England and their assets was gathered and then recorded in what were called *Domesday Books*. Much of what is known of the demographics of early England is derived from these books.

Baseball also has its *Domesday Books,* but they are called *Encyclopedias*. They list the name, vital statistics, and records of every player who ever appeared in a major league game, beginning with the formation of the National Association in 1871. So assiduously have baseball's *Domesday Books* been corrected, refined, and updated, it is safe to say that detailed information is more readily available about ballplayers, even the most obscure, than it is for statesmen, authors, artists, poets, or captains of industry.

Informative as they are, the *Encyclopedias* still leave much unsaid. For example, why did Bert Shepard play but a single game, while Jim McGuire played for twenty-six seasons? Short careers, like Shepard's, usually mean a lack of ability or, perhaps, the failure to receive a fair opportunity; but often they are short for other reasons—death, illness, injury, accident, suicide, or even murder. It is with such tragically shortened careers that this chapter will deal. Although the subject was carefully researched, no assertion of 100 percent completeness is proffered.

Since baseball's *Domesday Books* are limited to major league players and managers, no listing will be found there for James P. Creighton of the preprofessional era, nor for minor leaguers like Bill Thomas of the 1906 Buffalo Bisons or Ralph Worrell of the 1918 Baltimore Orioles.

James Creighton was the star pitcher of the Excelsior Club, a famous Brooklyn amateur nine of the 1850s and 1860s. Before Creighton's day, it was customary for pitchers to toss the ball gently to the plate. Creighton changed all this by developing a snap throw that gave speed and spin to the ball. In addition, he was one of the most powerful hitters of his day. It is said that he completed one entire season without being put out. On October 14, 1862, the Excelsiors were playing the Union Club of Morrisania in their final match of the season. Creighton, at bat for the Excelsiors, swung mightily and sent the ball beyond the reach of the outfielders. As he crossed first base, he collapsed, obviously in great pain. Legend has it that he staggered around the bases for a home run. He was immediately taken home by his teammates. Four days

later, the twenty-one-year-old pitcher was dead. According to an account in the *Brooklyn Eagle,* headlined "Obsequies of a Celebrated Ballplayer," Creighton had ruptured his bladder with the force of his final swing and died from internal bleeding.

A. G. Spalding, in his book *Baseball, America's National Game,* devoted two pages to Creighton, with his picture and a view of the towering granite monument his teammates erected in his memory on Tulip Hill in Brooklyn's Greenwood Cemetery. The monument is embossed with crossed bats, a cap, a base, and a scorebook.

The circumstances of the death of Bill Thomas, a twenty-five-year-old Buffalo pitcher, in April 1906, are still a mystery. Thomas had been a big winner in the Pacific Coast League, and manager George Stallings of Buffalo had brought him east to test his mettle in the stronger Eastern League. He was successful in his first start at Baltimore. The Bisons then finished a series at Providence and took a train to New Bedford, Massachusetts, from which point they boarded the night boat *Richard Peck,* en route to New York City. Thomas had left word with the porter and with his roommate, pitcher Joe Galaski, that he wanted an early call so he could see the New York skyline at sunrise. In the morning, when the porter came into the stateroom, the Thomas bunk, which had been slept in, was empty. Thomas was never seen again.

In 1918 Ralph Worrell, only nineteen, won 25 games for Jack Dunn's Baltimore Orioles, but he never pitched again. Instead of becoming another Lefty Grove (also a Jack Dunn discovery), Worrell failed to survive the winter, dying in the terrible World War One flu epidemic.

The deaths of young, healthy, vigorous athletes like Creighton, Thomas, and Worrell are sad and decidedly against the odds, but in the muster rolls of major league players in baseball's *Domesday Books,* such cases are far from rare.

Fatal Illnesses of Players and Managers

Elmer White was long thought to be a brother of James "Deacon" White and Will White. The early encyclopedias listed him as playing 15 games for the Forest Cities of Cleveland in 1872, but nothing more. A trip by the writer to the village of Caton in New York's southern tier and to the cemetery behind the Methodist Church there resulted in the finding of Elmer White's grave. The inscription on the tombstone, which showed he was Jim's and Will's cousin, not a brother, told with great economy of words the story of a short life and a short baseball career: "Born December 7, 1850. Died March 17, 1873."

Of all the deaths of active major leaguers to be recounted here, significantly, only one—that of Ray Chapman, who was

killed by a Carl Mays pitch—resulted directly from activity on the diamond. Many of the deaths, especially those in the first fifty years, were from illnesses routinely controlled today. Typhoid fever, for example, killed first baseman Alex McKinnon of Pittsburgh (NL) on July 24, 1887. He played in the July 4 game, complained of not feeling well, and was taken home. He died twenty days later at the age of thirty. Less than a year later, on April 29, 1888, Charlie Ferguson, an outstanding young pitcher who had won 21, 26, 30, and 22 games for Philadelphia (NL) from 1884 through 1887 and was a strong hitter as well (.288 in four seasons), died from the same disease, twelve days after his twenty-fifth birthday.

Edward "Sy" Sutcliffe, a catcher for most of his career, had shifted to first base for Baltimore (NL) in 1892 and had done quite well, batting .279 in 66 games. In the off-season, the twenty-nine-year-old native of Wheaton, Illinois, developed Bright's disease. He died February 13, 1893.

Joe Cassidy, an infielder for the Washington Senators in 1904 and 1905, was a third victim of the deadly typhoid. He was only twenty-three when he died at his home in Chester, Pennsylvania, March 25, 1906. Just a year and four days later, March 29, 1907, Patrick Henry "Cozy" Dolan, a nine-year outfielder in the majors, most recently with Boston (NL), also died of typhoid. He took ill during Boston's spring training trip, and died in a Louisville hospital, at age thirty-four. News of his death was overshadowed in the Boston papers by the extensive coverage given to the sensational suicide of manager Chick Stahl of the other Boston club, the day before in West Baden, Indiana.

Mike Powers, who caught in the majors from 1898 to 1909, mainly with the Philadelphia Athletics, was an anomaly in those hard-bitten days of the game's history, in that he held a degree from Holy Cross College and had also attended Notre Dame Medical School. Powers, incidentally, recruited the legendary Louis "Chief" Sockalexis for both of his alma maters, as shall be seen later. Powers was not a strong hitter (.216 lifetime), but he was considered a fine defensive catcher. He was behind the plate in an early season game in 1909, when he complained of nausea and asked to be taken to a hospital. He underwent three stomach operations, and then gangrene set in. He died April 26, 1909, at the age of thirty-eight.

Alan Storke was an infielder for Pittsburgh and St. Louis (NL) from 1906 through 1909. He never made it to spring training in 1910. He was a mere twenty-five when he died in Newton, Massachusetts, March 18, 1910, following a lung operation. Less than two years later, February 1, 1912, another National League infielder, thirty-year-old Jimmy Doyle, who had batted .282 for the Cubs in 1911, died in Syracuse, New York, after an appendicitis operation.

Addie Joss pitched in the majors only eight seasons and part of a ninth, but his record was so extraordinary that he was elected to the Hall of Fame (in 1978), despite his short tenure. With Cleveland from 1902 to 1910, he won 160 games, lost 97, and compiled an ERA of 1.88 (second on the all-time list). He pitched a perfect game on October 2, 1908, defeating Big Ed Walsh, 1–0, with first place on the line. Joss had another no-hitter on April 20, 1910, also against the White Sox, just before his health began to fail.

Joss made only 13 appearances in 1910, and still felt weak when he went south in 1911. He collapsed on the bench during an exhibition game at Chattanooga, Tennessee, then became ill again when the team reached Cincinnati. Doctors said it was pleurisy and sent him home to Toledo. On April 14, 1911, two days after his team had opened the season in St. Louis, he died at the age of thirty-one. The cause of his death was given as tubercular meningitis. Famed ballplayer-preacher Billy Sunday presided at his funeral, said to have been the biggest ever seen in Toledo.

Leonard "King" Cole, a righthanded pitcher who had won 20 games for the Cubs in 1910 and 18 the following season, was, like Charlie Ferguson, to have a brilliant career nipped in the bud by a fatal illness. During the 1915 season, when Cole was with the Yankees, it was discovered that he had been suffering from tuberculosis. He returned to his home in Bay City, Michigan, where he died on January 6, 1916, at twenty-nine. He left a splendid 56–27 (.675) won–lost record.

Joe Leonard, a twenty-five-year-old infielder who began with Pittsburgh in 1914 and played for Washington in 1916, 1917, and 1919, appeared in only one game for the Senators in 1920, became ill, and was taken to George Washington Hospital. He died there on May 1, following an appendicitis operation.

In 1922, the St. Louis Cardinals lost two young ballplayers within nine months. First to go was William "Pickles" Dillhoefer, who had caught in the majors since 1917, usually in a backup role. He was twenty-seven when he died in a St. Louis hospital, February 22, 1922, of that old bugaboo, typhoid fever. Outfielder Austin McHenry had started with the Cardinals in 1918, but had not really blossomed until 1921, when he batted .350 and hit 37 doubles, 8 triples, and 17 home runs. The following year he began to have difficulties in judging fly balls. Manager Branch Rickey sent him to a doctor, who diagnosed his problem as a brain tumor. An operation proved unsuccessful, and he died at Jefferson Township, Ohio, November 27, 1922. He was twenty-seven, the same age as Dillhoefer.

The 1924 season saw the deaths of two veterans of the Cincinnati Reds within eight months. Pat Moran was a catcher in the majors from 1901 to 1914 and then a highly successful manager, first with the Phillies and then with the Reds. In nine managerial seasons, he compiled a record of 748–586 and won a pennant with each team. His 1915 Phillies lost the World Series to Boston, in five games, while his 1919 Reds won the tainted 1919 Series from the White Sox, 5–3. Moran was forty-eight when he died of Bright's disease at Orlando, Florida, March 7, 1924, while at spring training with the Reds. The second Red to die that year was Jake Daubert, a fancy-fielding first baseman who could hit (.303 in fifteen years with the Dodgers and the Reds). Although forty years old, he played 102 games for the Reds in 1924, batted .281 and fielded .990. He became ill in October and was taken to Good Samaritan Hospital in Cincinnati, where he died on October 9 following an appendicitis operation, just as Jimmy Doyle and Joe Leonard had before him.

Legendary New York Giants outfielder and future Hall of Famer Ross Youngs was at the height of his career when he was struck down by Bright's disease, diagnosed during spring training in 1926. Despite his illness, he played 95 games and batted .306. All through the season, he was accompanied by a male nurse hired by manager John McGraw. Youngs was bedridden for the entire 1927 season and died on October 22 at the age of thirty. Despite his relatively short career, nine seasons and part of another, his record was impressive enough to earn him election to the Hall of Fame in 1972. McGraw said he was the greatest outfielder he had ever seen.

Urban Shocker was an outstanding pitcher for the great

Yankee teams of the 1925–1927 period. His record was 18–6 for the 1927 Yankees, but illness kept him out of the World Series. His thirteen-year record with the St. Louis Browns and the Yankees is in Hall of Fame country—187–117 (.615)—and he never had a losing season. His health continued to fail in 1928, and he appeared in only one game before being released. On September 9, 1928, in Denver, he died of heart disease and pneumonia. He was thirty-eight.

Shocker's manager, Miller Huggins, was to survive him little more than a year. On September 20, 1929, Huggins, who had managed the Yankees since 1918 and had won six pennants and three world's championships, asked coach Art Fletcher to take over for him, so that he could check into a hospital. Five days later, he was dead of erysipelas, a streptococcal skin infection. Huggins, who was of Munchkin size at 5′6″ and 140 pounds, had been in the majors since 1904, batting a career .265, and winning 1,413 games and losing 1,134 as a manager. His showdowns with his rambunctious slugger, Babe Ruth, are part of baseball lore. Huggins was elected to the Hall of Fame in 1964.

On May 28, 1930, Hal Carlson, thirty-eight-year-old right-handed pitcher of the Chicago Cubs, and a fourteen-year veteran of the National League, called several of his teammates to his apartment in a Chicago hotel, saying that he was in severe pain. Shortly after the team physician arrived, Carlson was dead from what was described as "an internal hemorrhage." He left a three-year-old son and his wife, who was expecting another child.

Twenty-nine-year-old infielder Mickey Finn, who had played for the Dodgers from 1930 to 1932 and then for the Phillies, became ill midway through the 1933 season. Owner Gerry Nugent of the Phillies summoned his brother-in-law, Dr. H. P. Boyle, who diagnosed Finn's trouble as a duodenal ulcer. Surgery was performed in an Allentown, Pennsylvania, hospital. He seemed on the road to recovery, but unforeseen medical problems arose, leading to his death on July 7, 1933.

On August 28, 1949, Ernie Bonham, who had pitched seven seasons for the Yankees and appeared in three World Series, but who was now with the Pirates, pitched his team to an 8–2 win over the Phillies. He had complained of some discomfort during the game, and as a precaution was taken to a Pittsburgh hospital, where appendicitis was diagnosed. The normally routine operation extended for three hours when complications developed. He was very weak when manager Billy Meyer visited him a few days later. "Billy, they are hitting me all over the field, and I can't get anybody out," he mumbled. On September 15, minutes before Meyer and coach Goldie Holt arrived for another visit, he passed away. Bonham, who was thirty-six, left an impressive 103–72 record.

Perhaps the closest parallel to the death of James Creighton in the preprofessional era was the shocking and tragic passing of first baseman Harry Agganis of the Boston Red Sox, on June 27, 1955 at the age of twenty-five. Like Creighton, Agganis was young and talented, with a glorious career seemingly assured.

At 6′2″, 200 pounds, and lefthanded, Agganis was a drawing-board first baseman. "The Golden Greek," as he was called, was the most publicized athlete to come out of Boston University since Mickey Cochrane in 1923. Such were Agganis's skills as a quarterback that he was a first-round draft pick of the Cleveland Browns, who offered him $25,000 to sign. When the Boston Red Sox upped this figure by $10,000,

he chose baseball. After the 1953 season at Louisville (American Association), where he batted .281, had 23 home runs, 108 RBIs, and played in 155 games, he took over at first base for the parent club in 1954. He batted only .251 his first season. In the early going in 1955, he was over .300 when he developed pneumonia and was hospitalized for ten days. He returned to the lineup, but became ill again in Kansas City. He flew back to Boston and checked into Sancta Maria Hospital in nearby Cambridge. He was thought to be recovering nicely, when suddenly on June 27, he died. The cause of his death was given as a massive pulmonary embolism.

Agganis's body lay in state at St. George's Greek Orthodox Church in his home town of Lynn, Massachusetts. On the day before the funeral, ten thousand mourners passed the bier.

Righthanded pitcher Jim Umbricht of Houston underwent a cancer operation on March 8, 1963. By May 9 he was back in uniform, and he finished the year with a 4–3 record and an ERA of 2.61 in 35 appearances. He did not make it into the next season. The malignancy spread, and he died on April 8, 1964, at age thirty-three.

Infielder Danny Thompson, who broke in with Minnesota in 1970, had played for three years in the majors when he learned he had leukemia. He continued to play, however, and on June 1, 1976, he was involved in one of the big trades of the year, when he was bundled with pitcher Bert Blyleven and shipped to Texas for Roy Smalley, Bill Singer, Mike Cubbage, Jim Gideon, and $250,000. Thompson finished the season with Texas, but it was to be his last. Baseball's Most Courageous Performer (he was so voted in 1974) was only twenty-nine when he died December 10, 1976, at Rochester, Minnesota.

Quiet, efficient, and soft-spoken Dick Howser was an American League infielder from 1961 to 1968 with Kansas City, Cleveland, and New York. He became manager of the Yankees in 1980 and led them to 103 wins and a division title. After the Yankees lost the league championship series to Kansas City, 0–3, owner George Steinbrenner made things so uncomfortable for Howser that he resigned. He moved to Kansas City in 1981, winning a division title in 1984, then a pennant and a world's championship in 1985.

Early in the 1986 season, Howser began to suffer from headaches and to experience visual and memory problems. On July 18, he learned he had a malignant brain tumor. Operations followed, and he recovered sufficiently to return to uniform in 1987. But his health continued to deteriorate and he was forced to give up his managerial duties. He was fifty years old when he died, June 17, 1987.

Suicides and Other Violent Deaths

According to present information, five active major leaguers and one league president ended their lives by their own hands. Two others, Dan McGann and Benny Frey, killed themselves in the year after they had been sent to the minors. An eighth, Johnny Mostil, attempted suicide but recovered. There is also some intimation that the violent deaths of Len Koenecke and Ed Delahanty might have been "death wish" situations.

On February 28, 1894, Edgar McNabb, a pitcher who had won eight games for the Baltimore Orioles in 1893, checked in at the Eiffel Hotel on Smithfield Street in Pittsburgh. He told the clerk that his wife had gone to Braddock to visit her ailing parents and that he should give her the room key when she returned. Earlier that day, the McNabbs had run into a

friend, one Louis Gillen, and the three had agreed to attend the theater that evening.

When the agreed time for the meeting passed, Gillen became concerned and went to the McNabbs' room. As he stood outside the door, he heard a woman's screams. He called for help, and when the room clerk opened the door, the two were shocked and sickened by the bloody and grisly scene before them. Mrs. McNabb lay on the floor, bleeding horribly from bullet holes in her neck and head, but still breathing. Lying beside her, dead, with bullet holes in the head, was Edgar McNabb. A pistol was still in his hand.

As the story unfolded, it became more than a tragic domestic confrontation. The dying woman was not Mrs. McNabb at all. She was Mrs. E. E. Rockwell, wife of a prominent Seattle businessman who had once been president of the Pacific Northwest Baseball League. She was an actress by profession and used the stage name of Louise Kellogg.

It appeared that Miss Kellogg, who had just finished a theatrical engagement in New York, had asked McNabb to meet her in Pittsburgh. According to a newspaper account, she was planning to break off her relationship with the ballplayer. Letters found in the room indicated that she had been sending him money to tide him over the winter, and further that there had been recent disagreements between them. In the judgment of the police who investigated, an argument had developed, culminating in McNabb's shooting of Miss Kellogg and then turning the gun on himself.

Among McNabb's possessions on the scene was a copy of a message which read: IN GREAT TROUBLE, TELEGRAPH $100 IMMEDIATELY. SEE YOU IN TWO WEEKS. It was probably this message that led Edgar McNabb and Louise Kellogg to their fateful rendezvous at the Eiffel Hotel.

Even more shocking than the McNabb affair was the sad denouement of Marty Bergen, first-string catcher for Frank Selee's Boston (NL) club from 1896 to 1899.

On the morning of January 19, 1900, Marty's father, Michael Bergen, who was staying at the house of a neighbor, walked to his son's property, which was called "Snowball Farm," to get some milk. Seeing no activity around the house, he left. He returned at noon and still saw no signs of life. He walked through the unlocked kitchen door, only to be confronted by a scene of unspeakable horror. On the kitchen floor, lay the body of his six-year-old granddaughter Florence. In the adjoining room, he found the body of his daughter-in-law Harriet Bergen and next to her that of her three-year-old son Joseph. Mrs. Bergen's hands were raised as though in supplication or as though trying to ward off a blow. A bloody ax, the apparent murder weapon, was found on the scene. Bergen himself had committed suicide with a straight razor, almost severing his head from his body.

Dr. W. E. Norwood, the medical examiner, made an almost on-the-spot judgment, ruling that the crime had been committed "in a fit of insanity," and that no autopsies would be necessary. According to the account in *The Sporting Life,* the funeral service at St. Joseph's Church in North Brookfield was somber and brief, and "only a few words suitable to the occasion were spoken." The only prominent baseball people present were Connie Mack of the Milwaukee club and Billy Hamilton, a Bergen teammate.

What triggered the carnage at Snowball Farm will never be known. Bergen's manager, Frank Selee, said that he seemed, at times, to act irrationally and to be pursued by hallucinations. It was also revealed that he had sought help

from his pastor and his doctor, and that on one occasion he had accused the latter of trying to kill him. Bergen was not a drinker and apparently had no pressing money problems. He was buying the farm on the installment plan and had $2,000 in cash.

On January 12, 1903, not quite three years after the Bergen murder-suicide, the baseball world was stunned by the self-inflicted death of another prominent player. George Barclay "Win" Mercer was a versatile performer who had played every position but catcher in nine years in the majors, winning 131 games as a pitcher and batting .285. He was manager-designate for Detroit, where he had played in 1902.

Mercer was on the West Coast for a series of exhibition games between teams from the American and National leagues. A small man with striking good looks, he had a weakness for fast women and slow horses, a deadly combination that apparently was to do him in. On the fatal day, he did not appear when expected in the dining room of the San Francisco hotel where the players were staying. When the door of his room was opened, Mercer's body was found. A rubber hose was connected to a gas jet. He had died of self-inflicted asphyxiation.

Mercer left a suicide note in which he warned of the evils of women and gambling. He also left a note for his mother and one for his fiancée in East Liverpool, Ohio. Another letter was addressed to Tip O'Neill, manager of the ballplayer troupe, for which Mercer was in charge of finances. Even though Mercer had recently incurred heavy gambling losses, it was reported that his baseball accounts were in order.

Charles "Chick" Stahl had batted .307 in ten major league seasons and was considered one of the game's premier defensive outfielders. Stahl, a Marty Bergen teammate at Boston (NL) from 1897 to 1899, had been named manager of the Boston Puritans (AL) late in the 1906 season, succeeding his friend and roommate Jimmy Collins. Stahl was handsome, popular, well paid for his era, and recently married. Despite his oft-expressed distaste for managing and a recent attempt to resign, it seemed he had almost every reason to be on top of the world; but on March 28, 1907, in his room at the West Baden Hotel in West Baden, Indiana, he ingested a lethal dose of carbolic acid. As he staggered toward his bed, roommate Collins went to his assistance, just in time to hear him gasp: "Boys, I couldn't help it; it drove me to it."

For years, baseball historians pondered Stahl's cryptic words, then usually concluded it was the pressure of managing that forced him to swallow the poison. Dissenting was Harold Seymour, who, in his *Baseball, The Early Years,* strongly hints at the real reason: *cherchez la femme.* In the May 1986 issue of *Boston Magazine,* author Glenn Stout dug out the rest of the Stahl story and wrote it.

Stahl, according to Stout, although in love with a young lady named Julia Harmon of Roxbury, Massachusetts, was also attracted to other young ladies, the groupies of his day. Furthermore, according to Stout, one of his admirers, a Lulu Ortman, demanded that Stahl marry her. When he spurned her, she twice tried to shoot him but missed. Meanwhile, on November 14, 1906, Stahl had married Miss Harmon at St. Francis de Sales Church in Roxbury. It seems that he had also been involved, late in the 1906 season, with another woman, who now claimed to be preg-

nant by him. She pressured Stahl to marry her on pain of exposure. He told her that marriage was impossible, since he was already married. She persisted that spring, and it was this pressure, concludes Stout, not the pressure of managing, that led to his suicide.

A sad postscript to the Stahl suicide was the fate of his wife, Julia. Shortly after his death, she attempted suicide herself, but survived. On November 15, 1908, she was found dead in the doorway of a house in South Boston, after a night on the town. An autopsy showed that she had died of edema of the brain.

Little more than two years after the Stahl tragedy, another suicide rocked the game, but it had none of the nasty characteristics of the McNabb, Bergen, or Stahl cases.

Richard Cory, in Edwin Arlington Robinson's poem of the same name, was young, elegant, and well thought of, but one summer night he "went home and put a bullet through his head." Harry Clay Pulliam, president of the National League, was baseball's Richard Cory. On June 28, 1909, Pulliam went to his room in the New York Athletic Club and fired a shot through his head. He died the next morning. The forty-year-old bachelor left no suicide note. Presumably it was a combination of poor health (he had been on leave of absence for health reasons) and the burdens of his job that caused him to do it.

On December 13, 1910, Dennis "Dan" McGann, former captain of the New York Giants and a premier first baseman for thirteen seasons, but most recently a member of the Milwaukee club of the American Association, was found dead in a Louisville hotel room, a bullet hole in his heart and a revolver in his hand. He had been seen around the hotel during the day and had appeared to be in good spirits. One explanation was that he was depressed over the suicide of a brother the past summer.

On March 28, 1927, at the Youree Hotel in Shreveport, Louisiana, spring training headquarters of the Chicago White Sox, Johnny Mostil, the team's star center fielder, slashed both wrists and wounded himself in the chest, throat, and legs with a razor blade and a knife. Early reports, giving him little chance to survive, were wrong. He did recover, played later that same season, and two more seasons thereafter, followed by a long career in the game as a scout. The only explanation for his act seems to have been his hypochondriacal nature. He constantly worried and brooded over his health, although a physical examination that spring had revealed no serious problems.

In eight major league seasons, Cincinnati righthander Benny Frey had struggled to a 57–82 record. At the end of the 1936 season, the best of his career (he was 10–8), he was sent to Nashville to work an ailing arm back into shape. Apparently despondent over the failure of his arm to recover, Frey, on November 1, 1937, at Jackson, Michigan, sat in his car with the motor running and a rubber hose attached to the exhaust pipe. When police found the thirty-one-year-old pitcher, he was dead from carbon monoxide poisoning.

It was August 3, 1940, and the Cincinnati Reds were in Boston. Pleading illness, catcher Willard Hershberger told his roommate, Bill Baker (some accounts say it was Lew Riggs), that he would not be able to come to the ballpark until later. When he did not appear and his telephone was not answered, manager Bill McKechnie sent Dan Cohen, Hershberger's close friend, to the hotel to get him. When

the room was entered, Hershberger's body was found in the bathroom, his jugular vein severed by a razor.

Hershberger was young (just thirty), successful, and single, and there seemed no apparent reason for his act. As in the McGann case, there had been a previous suicide in the family. Hershberger's father had shot himself to death in 1928. It has been theorized that the catcher was depressed over his recent failures on the diamond. He had gone hitless in a crucial game, and on another occasion had supposedly called a wrong pitch to Harry Danning of the Giants, who then had hit a home run to beat the Reds in the ninth inning. On the other hand, it was no secret that he had been contemplating suicide. He had told manager McKechnie as much in recent weeks. Also, he had recently purchased a $500 bond, placed it in the hotel safe, and asked that it be given to his mother "if anything happens to me."

With all the obvious planning, it is curious that no suicide note was found. Suicidal tendencies notwithstanding, a hitless game and the call of a wrong pitch hardly seem sufficient to have provoked the deed. It took almost eighty years for the truth to be revealed about the Stahl suicide. Someday, perhaps, more light will be shed on the Hershberger story.

Over the years, ballplayers have died violently, other than by suicide. The bizarre death of Hall of Famer Ed Delahanty is a case in point. In 1903 he was with Washington of the American League, but wanted to be with the Giants in New York, where he felt he could earn more money. He dealt with his unhappiness by consuming generous doses of alcohol, starting with a drinking spree in Cleveland. Later, in Detroit, where he took out an accident policy in favor of his daughter, he was heard to threaten to take his own life.

On July 2, 1903, Delahanty boarded a Michigan Central train at Detroit with a ticket to Buffalo, from where, it is believed, he planned to catch another train to Washington to meet his wife. The conductor said Delahanty was "under the weather" when he got on at Detroit and that he had downed at least five shots of whiskey along the way. Not only was he boisterous, but he also threatened some passengers with a razor. At Bridgeburg, Ontario, just across the Niagara River from Buffalo, the conductor ejected him from the train. Delahanty, in the darkness, began to walk across the International Bridge, a railroad bridge connecting Bridgeburg and Buffalo. Bridge watchman Sam Kingston had just escorted a freight across the bridge and, lantern in hand, was walking back to the Canadian side when he confronted Delahanty. Words were exchanged and a scuffle ensued. It is not clear (Kingston told conflicting stories) if Delahanty fell, jumped, or was pushed into the river. Eight days later, his body was found at Niagara Falls, below the Horseshoe Falls.

Subsequently, Delahanty's widow filed suit in the Ontario courts against the Michigan Central Railroad, seeking $20,000 damages for the wrongful death of her husband. She was awarded $3,000, and her daughter received $2,000.

When Walter "Big Ed" Morris won 19 games for the last-place Boston Red Sox in 1928 and then came back with 14 wins for another cellar Boston club in 1929, he became one of the most sought-after pitchers in the league. One story had the Red Sox turning down a $100,000 offer. A sore arm slowed Morris in 1930 and 1931, and his record retrogressed to 4–9 and 5–7. Confident that his arm had

regained its strength, he prepared to go to spring training in 1932. As a going-away present, some of his buddies arranged a party for him at a tavern in Century, Florida, just across the state line from Morris's hometown of Flomaton, Alabama. Unfortunately, the party began to get out of hand, and soon the guest of honor was involved in a fight with Joe White, a gas station attendant from Brewton, Alabama. When Morris slipped to the floor, White pulled a knife and stabbed him twice, fatally. Morris was thirty-one and left a widow and two children.

Len Koenecke was an impressive-looking athlete—broad of shoulder, slim of waist, and ruggedly handsome. He was said to have been the last player personally scouted by John McGraw, who arranged for his purchase from Indianapolis (American Association) in 1931 for players valued at $75,000. The young outfielder failed to live up to his minor league billings and was farmed to Jersey City in 1932 and to Buffalo in 1933. An outstanding season for the Bisons in 1933 led to his sale to Brooklyn, where in 1934 he batted .320 and fielded a league-leading .994. But he slumped in 1935, and late that year manager Casey Stengel sent Koenecke and two other players home from St. Louis so that he could try out some young prospects.

On the flight from St. Louis to Detroit, Koenecke, who had been drinking, created a disturbance, and when the airport was reached he was ordered off the plane. Although it was late in the evening, he decided to charter a private plane and fly to Buffalo, where he had friends. The plane he chartered had an interesting past. It had once been owned by Smith Reynolds of the tobacco family and his wife, torch singer Libby Holman, who were principals in one of the most sensational murder cases of the 1930s. When Reynolds was shot to death at the family estate in Winston-Salem, North Carolina, his wife was charged with the crime but was later exonerated.

While the plane was still over Canada, Koenecke tried to take over the controls from pilot William Mulqueeny. Irwin Davis, the copilot, attempted to restrain the husky ballplayer but was pushed to the floor. Mulqueeny, while trying to guide the plane with one hand, picked up a fire extinguisher with the other and bludgeoned Koenecke until he was dead. Mulqueeny had no idea where he was until he spotted the lights of Toronto. Seeing a racetrack on the outskirts of the city, he decided to use the backstretch as an airport and brought the plane safely down. Then, to cap their night of terror, the two men were attacked by watch dogs as they left the plane. The dogs eventually backed off, and they were able to summon help.

After two hearings in Canadian courts, Mulqueeny and Davis were absolved of all blame in Koenecke's death. Blood tests had shown that the dead ballplayer was drunk. At one of the hearings, Edward J. Murphy, attorney for the pilots, alleged that Koenecke was trying to commit suicide and to do it "in a grand and glorious manner."

In the early hours of January 5, 1975, Don Wilson, star righthanded pitcher of the Houston Astros, who had won 104 games in nine major league seasons and pitched two no-hitters, drove his luxury car into the garage of his suburban Houston home and left the motor running. At one P.M. his lifeless body was found slumped in the passenger seat. The ignition was on, the battery was dead, the gas tank was empty, and there were exhaust-fume stains on the garage floor. In the room above the garage, his five-year-old son

Alexander was dead from the fumes. His wife, Bernice, and his daughter, Denise, were taken to the hospital in serious condition. Bernice Wilson also had a badly bruised jaw, which was never explained, but which could have been caused by a fall.

Mrs. Wilson and her daughter both recovered. Tests on the twenty-nine-year-old Don Wilson revealed a blood-alcohol content of .167. On February 5, 1975, the medical examiner ruled the deaths were accidental.

With Lyman Bostock, who had starred for Minnesota (in 1975–1977) and then had signed a lucrative free-agent contract with California, it was a case of being in the wrong place at the wrong time. On September 23, 1978, in Gary, Indiana, he was in a car being driven by his uncle when he was shot by a man named Leonard Smith, whose apparent target was Smith's estranged wife, seated next to Bostock in the back seat. Three hours after the assault, the twenty-seven-year-old Bostock was dead. There was whispering that something was going on between Bostock and Mrs. Smith. Actually they had met only twenty minutes before and were heading for different destinations.

Leonard Smith was twice tried for murder. The first trial, in which insanity was pleaded, ended in a hung jury. In the second trial, he was found not guilty by reason of insanity, spent six months in a mental hospital, and then was a free man. Outrage over the outcome of the two trials resulted in a change in the Indiana law, whereby an accused can now be judged both insane and guilty of a crime.

Planes, Cars, Trucks, and a Dune Buggy

When superstars Roberto Clemente and Thurman Munson lost their lives in air crashes, it was front-page news all over the country. In Clemente's case, the coverage was international in scope because of the mercy mission in which he was involved.

Clemente and Munson were not the first active major leaguers to perish in airplane accidents. There were at least six prior air fatalities—seven if Koenecke is included. Marvin Goodwin, a righthanded spitball pitcher who saw action with the Senators, Cardinals, and Reds from 1916 through 1925, was the first. In 1925, nearing the end of his career, he was pitcher-manager of Houston of the Texas League, on assignment from the Cardinals. He did so well at Houston (21–9) that Cincinnati purchased him conditionally late in the season, with the understanding that final payment on the deal would be made only if he lasted thirty days into the 1926 season. He made four September appearances for the Reds with no wins and no losses.

Goodwin had been a flying instructor in World War One and was still a lieutenant in the reserve. On October 18, 1925, he took off on a practice flight from Ellington Field, near Houston, with a mechanic on board. The engine failed at 200 feet, and the plane crashed. The mechanic miraculously survived, but Goodwin, who suffered two broken legs and internal injuries, died four days later. The fatality had a ghoulish aftermath. The following year, the Cardinals demanded full payment for Goodwin's contract. The Reds refused on the grounds that he was not on their roster thirty days into the 1926 season. The case was referred to the commissioner's office. Judge Landis, citing the terms of the contract, ruled in favor of the Reds.

Elmer Joseph Gedeon played in the outfield for the Wash-

ington Senators in 1939. He had been a track star at the University of Michigan and had given up a chance to run in the Olympic Games to go into baseball. But then World War Two came along, and Gedeon gave up baseball to become an early volunteer in the Air Corps. He died April 15, 1944, when his plane was shot down over France. (Two others who played in the majors in 1939 also died in battle. Bob Neighbors, a shortstop for seven games with the St. Louis Browns, died in North Korea in 1952, and Harry O'Neill, who caught one game for the Philadelphia Athletics, perished in the assault on Iwo Jima in 1945.)

After his graduation from Boston University in 1955, catcher Tom Gastall pocketed a $40,000 bonus from the Baltimore Orioles. He was used sparingly, playing 20 games in 1955 and 32 in 1956. On September 20, 1956, he took off in a light plane from Harbor Field, near Baltimore. He landed at Easton, from where he later took off for the return flight over the Chesapeake Bay. Five days later, his body and the wreckage of the plane were found in the water off Riviera Beach. Gastall was just twenty-four.

A little over two months later, on November 27, 1956, outfielder Charlie Peete, who had played 23 games for the St. Louis Cardinals that summer, died in a plane crash in the mountains of Venezuela, near Caracas, while en route to play winter ball. His wife and three children also perished in the crash.

Another victim of a Venezuelan air disaster was twenty-one-year-old Nestor Chavez, a San Francisco Giant farmhand who played in two games for the Giants in 1967. On March 16, 1969, the young pitcher was on his way to join the Giants' Phoenix farm club when his plane crashed, killing 155 passengers. It was one of the worst accidents in aviation history.

Ken Hubbs, playing 160 games for the Chicago Cubs in 1962, handled 148 consecutive chances without an error and was Rookie of the Year. He tailed off in 1963 but was still rated one of the game's rising young stars. At the end of the 1963 season, he began to take flying lessons. In early February 1964, shortly after he had received his license, Hubbs, who lived in Colton, California, flew to Provo, Utah, with a friend, Dennis Doyle, to visit Doyle's in-laws. On February 15, Hubbs and Doyle took off in a snowstorm for their return trip to California. Only five miles from Provo, the plane crashed into Utah Lake, killing Hubbs and Doyle.

After investigation, the Civil Aeronautics Board reported the probable cause as "Hubbs's attempt to continue visual flight into an area of adverse weather." The twenty-two-year-old Hubbs, who was not licensed for instrument flying, left a log book which showed he had flown just 71 hours, 16 minutes.

On September 30, 1972, Roberto Clemente, who had batted .317 in eighteen seasons with Pittsburgh, touched Jon Matlack of the Mets for a base hit. It was Clemente's 3,000th and last hit. On December 31, 1972, Clemente and four others were killed when a plane carrying food, clothing, and medical supplies to earthquake-stricken Nicaragua crashed moments after takeoff from San Juan, Puerto Rico.

Clemente's career had all the elements of a Horatio Alger tale. Born August 18, 1934, in Carolina, Puerto Rico, the son of a sugar plantation foreman, he was signed by Al Campanis of the Dodgers as a teenager. The Dodgers tried to cover him up on the Montreal (International League) roster, but Pittsburgh general manager Branch Rickey, who knew all about

him from his days with the Dodgers, drafted him for a piddling $4,000. It was one of the greatest bargains in baseball history. Clemente immediately became a regular and won all manner of plaudits for his hitting, fielding, and magnificent throwing arm. He was Most Valuable Player in 1966, batted .310 and .414 in two World Series (1960, 1971), and was *Sporting News*'s Gold Glove outfielder twelve times. Twice he hit three home runs in one game, and five times he led National League outfielders in assists.

Clemente was voted into the Baseball Hall of Fame in 1973 in a special election, with the usual five-year waiting period waived by a change of the voting rules.

Thurman Munson was the only New York Yankee to win both Rookie of the Year (1970) and Most Valuable Player (1976) awards. He was the regular Yankee catcher from 1970, averaging more than 140 games a year, despite aching knees, a beaning, and a foul ball in the throat. He was one of the league's top clutch hitters, with 701 RBIs and a .292 average over eleven seasons. His clashes with Reggie Jackson over which of them was the straw that stirred the Yankee drink drew national attention.

On August 2, 1979, an off-day, Munson flew his new Cessna Citation jet from New York to Canton, Ohio, to visit his family. Late in the afternoon, he was practicing takeoffs and landings at the Akron-Canton Airport when the plane crashed a thousand feet short of the runway. Munson's flying companions, David Hall and Jerry Anderson, survived and at great danger to themselves, attempted to pull Munson from the flaming wreckage. But there was no chance. Munson, who was thirty-two, left his wife, Diane, and three childrn, not to mention millions of mourning baseball fans. On August 6 of that year, 51,000 fans at Yankee Stadium participated in an impressive nine-minute salute to the Yankee captain, who, with a few more years under his belt, could well have been a good bet for the Hall of Fame.

As far as is known, the first active major leaguer to die in a vehicular accident was Norman Boeckel, a .298 hitter for the 1923 Boston Braves. The thirty-one-year-old third baseman died February 16, 1924, in a San Diego hospital, from pelvic injuries sustained the day before in a collision between his car and a truck. Earlier, Boeckel had played a fringe role in another piece of baseball history. He had submitted an affidavit to National League President John Heydler, attesting that he had heard pitcher Rube Benton boast of winning $3,200 on the 1919 World Series on a tip from Hal Chase. Benton was thrown out of baseball, but was later reinstated by Judge Landis.

Walter "Peck" Lerian, regular catcher for the Philadelphia Phillies in 1928 and 1929, was only twenty-six when he died on October 22, 1929, in a Baltimore hospital, after being hit by a truck which vaulted over the curb and pinned him against the wall of a building.

The pitching career of Bob Moose was a series of highs and lows. In ten years with the Pirates, he won 76 games and lost 71. One of his wins was a no-hitter against the New York Mets on September 20, 1969. On the other side of the coin is the wild pitch he uncorked in the final game of the 1972 league championship series that permitted Cincinnati to defeat Pittsburgh. He also made three appearances in the 1971 World Series, but had no decisions. On October 9, 1976, at Martin's Ferry, Ohio, he suffered fatal injuries in an automobile accident. It was his twenty-ninth birthday.

Righthanded pitcher Danny Frisella, who in ten years in

the majors saw action with the Mets, Braves, Padres, Cardinals, and Brewers (34–40), took a dune buggy out in the desert near Phoenix on New Year's Day, 1977. When the buggy overturned, he was killed instantly.

On Friday night, December 19, 1986, Honolulu native Joe DeSa hit four doubles to help his Ponce Lions defeat the Mayaguez Indians, 11–8, in a Puerto Rico winter league game. At four A.M. on December 20, DeSa was killed in a head-on crash on the Las Americas Expressway. DeSa, who had played for Buffalo (American Association) in 1985 and 1986 and was the team's most valuable player in the latter year, had signed with Kansas City and was due to report in the spring for his third hitch in the majors.

Bean Balls

Every time a batter steps to the plate, it is an act of courage. With pitches hurtling toward him at 90 miles per hour, he has but a fraction of a second to decide if he should swing, take, or bail out. Modern helmets with ear flaps have removed much of the peril, but not all. Prior to the 1950s, batters had no head protection at all; and before 1893 the risk was even greater, since the pitching distance was only 50 feet.

Considering the danger involved, it is somewhat of a miracle that only one batter has been killed by a pitched ball in the long history of major league baseball. No definitive statistics are available, but it is known that many have been killed at the amateur level and at least three in minor league play.

Major league baseball's only bean ball fatality, and its only diamond fatality for any reason, occurred on August 16, 1920, at the Polo Grounds, New York, in a game between the New York Yankees and the Cleveland Indians. It was the first half of the fifth inning, and shortstop Ray Chapman of the Indians was at bat, faced by Yankee submarine-baller Carl Mays. Chapman liked to crowd the plate and crouch over it. Mays, who had a mean streak, was not averse to throwing at any batter who encroached on his territory. Mays's first pitch was a strike, his second a ball, as Chapman seemed to edge even closer to the plate. Predictably the third pitch was high and inside. There was an ominous crack that was heard all over the Polo Grounds. Mays, thinking his pitch had hit Chapman's bat, fielded the ball and started to throw to Wally Pipp at first base, but then he saw Chapman slumped in the arms of catcher Muddy Ruel and he knew the batter had been hit. A doctor was summoned from the stands and Chapman was temporarily revived. Assisted by two of his teammates, he began the long walk to the clubhouse in center field, but he soon collapsed and was carried the rest of the way.

When a preliminary examination in the clubhouse showed the injury was extremely serious, he was taken to nearby St. Lawrence Hospital, where an operation was performed. He was still under ether when he died at five A.M. the following day, August 17.

The repercussions were immediate and furious. Mays, a surly sort and never popular among his peers, was strongly criticized. Detroit and Boston players demanded that he be barred for life, while those on the Washington and St. Louis clubs threatened to strike if Mays was allowed to pitch again. But Mays did have his defenders. Cleveland pitcher Ray Caldwell, a former Yankee, said it seemed to him that Chapman had turned his head right into the ball. Connie Mack, venerable skipper of the Philadelphia Athletics, while deploring the fatal accident, pleaded for sympathy for Mays. Catcher Muddy Ruel, who caught Chapman when he fell, said in later years that the pitch could have been a strike.

Mays appeared before the district attorney and, after a deposition, was cleared of any criminal charges. He said he was not trying to hit Chapman, only to pitch him tight. That spring, Mays pointed out, he had seen Yankee infielder Chick Fewster nearly killed by a pitch delivered by Jeff Pfeffer of the Dodgers, and from that time on he had been reluctant even to throw inside pitches, let alone throw at batters. He then suggested the fatality might have been averted had plate umpire Tom Connolly not refused to remove from play the scuffed ball that hit Chapman. This drew a sharp rejoinder from American League umpires Billy Evans and Bill Dinneen, who charged that Mays was one of the league's most notorious scuffers. They said further that club owners had complained to Ban Johnson, league president, that too many balls were being thrown out, and that Johnson had responded by sending out a directive, instructing umpires to keep balls in play, "except those which are dangerous."

In the *New York Times* of August 19, there was an impassioned plea for the development and use of batting helmets, but it was to be more than thirty years before this advice would be heeded.

At least three minor leaguers have been killed by pitched balls. On June 18, 1916, four years before the Chapman fatality, Johnny Dodge, infielder for Mobile of the Southern Association, was hit by Tom Rogers of Nashville and died the next day of a fractured skull. By the strangest of coincidences, Rogers and Carl Mays were briefly teammates on the 1921 Yankees.

On July 4, 1933 at Omaha, Jesse Batterson, nineteen-year-old third baseman for Springfield of the Western League, suffered a fractured skull when hit by a pitch thrown by Omaha's Floyd "Swede" Carlson. He was able to get to his feet and walk to the clubhouse, but then collapsed and was taken to a hospital. He died there following an operation, with pitcher Carlson at his bedside.

A third fatality occurred in the Alabama-Florida League on June 2, 1951. Lefty Jack Clifton of Headland hit Ottis Johnson of the Dothan Browns on the head and killed him. In his next start, Clifton, who had already hit 12 batters that season, pitched a no-hit, no-run game against Panama City. According to Ken Brooks in his book *The Last Rebel Yell,* every Panama City batter had one foot in the dugout.

In major league history there have been countless beanings. In most cases, the batters came back, but often were not the same hitters as before. Lowell Reidenbaugh, in his *Cooperstown,* writes that Hughie Jennings survived three skull fractures. His most serious injury was from a pitch delivered by Amos Rusie of New York, said to have been the swiftest pitcher of his day. The blow left Jennings near death and unconscious for four days. Some historians say it was Rusie's speed and the fear that he might kill someone that brought about the lengthening of the pitching distance in 1893 to the present 60 feet, 6 inches.

On May 25, 1937, future Hall of Famer Mickey Cochrane, player-manager of the Detroit Tigers, lost sight of a pitch by Bump Hadley of the Yankees. It hit him in the right temple and fractured his skull. He lay unconscious for ten days but eventually recovered, although he never played again. He did, however, resume his managerial duties and

also served with distinction in the Navy in World War Two.

Tony Conigliaro of the Boston Red Sox, who hit 166 home runs in six full seasons and parts of two others (all with the Red Sox, except for 74 games and 4 home runs for California in 1971), surely would have racked up more impressive numbers had he not been hit in the face and nearly killed by a Jack Hamilton (of California) pitch on August 18, 1967. He was out of the game for a year and a half, but then came back to hit 20 home runs in 1969 and 36 in 1970. On October 11, 1970, in a most controversial deal, he was traded to California, where he was to see only limited duty. He returned to Boston for 21 games in 1975 and then was out of baseball.

Dickie Thon was the All-Star National League shortstop for Houston in 1983 and also led the league in game-winning hits. In the fifth game of the 1984 season, he was hit in the eye by a Mike Torrez (Mets) fastball. Despite permanent damage to his eye, he was able to return to action, but never with his former effectiveness.

Don Zimmer, 1988 manager of the Chicago Cubs, suffered two serious beanings and still carries a metal plate in his head from the injuries. Paul Blair, center field magician of the Baltimore Orioles, Minnie Minoso of the White Sox, and Wayne Terwilliger, utility player for several clubs, were others whose careers were interrupted or affected by bean balls.

Sore Arms, Illnesses, Injuries, and Accidents

Up to this point, the subject has been (with a few exceptions) deaths off or on the diamond. But fatalities are only part of the story. Many a baseball career has aborted for reasons not resulting in death, at least, not at once.

In the old days, sore arms were usually rested. If there was any treatment at all, it was by the likes of John D. "Bonesetter" Reese, a self-trained muscle manipulator of Youngstown, Ohio. Nobody ever heard of the rotator cuff or even dreamed of such sophisticated operations as those which prolonged the careers of Tommy John, Ken Dayley, and others.

Charles "Lady" Baldwin was one old-timer who could have used a Tommy John bionic arm. In 1886 he won 42 games for Detroit (NL) and pitched 487 innings. He then developed arm trouble and dropped to 13 wins in 1887 and to 3 each in 1888 and 1890, after which he retired for good to his Michigan farm. Hall of Famer Christy Mathewson's arm went dead in 1916, but by then he was thirty-eight, had won 373 games, and had achieved immortality. Smoky Joe Wood was another sore arm victim, but he did beat the rap in a way. After winning 23 games for the Red Sox in 1911 and then 34 in 1912, including 16 in a row, he developed a sore arm the following spring. His days as an intimidating fireballer were over, although he did win 35 games for the Sox over the next three seasons. Realizing he could no longer pitch, he decided to become a sore-armed outfielder, and played that position with fair success for Cleveland through the 1922 season. Altogether he played in fourteen major league seasons and left a 116–57 pitching record and a career batting mark of .283.

Undocumented are the names of countless other pitchers of the game's early years who dropped out prematurely because of so-called dead arms. More is known of modern pitchers, like Karl Spooner. No pitcher ever made a more dazzling entrance or faded so fast. The twenty-three-year-old left-

hander was called up by Brooklyn from Fort Worth (Texas), late in the 1954 season. In his first start, he shut out New York and then whitewashed Pittsburgh in his second. In the two games, he allowed a total of 7 hits, while striking out 27. Hampered by a sore arm, he struggled to an 8–6 record in 1955, made two appearances in the World Series (0–1), then never pitched in the majors again.

In 1966 another Dodger lefthander, Hall of Famer Sandy Koufax was 27–9, with 5 shutouts and an ERA of 1.73 in 323 innings of work. Talk about going out on top! No pitcher in major league history ever matched that in a final season. He pitched against Baltimore in the 1966 World Series (0–1), but at the age of thirty his career was over. Traumatic arthritis in the left elbow, triggered by a fall on his left arm when attempting a pickoff during the 1964 season, made it impossible for him to continue. Had Koufax been able to pitch as long as, say, Warren Spahn, there is no telling what his record might have been. As it was, he left an imposing mark of 165–87 (.655) and an ERA of 2.76.

Mark Fidrych, the colorful Detroit pitcher known as "the Bird," was 19–9 in 1976 and was the starting pitcher in the All-Star game. But plagued by arm trouble, he faded to a combined 10–11 record over the next four seasons. He was only twenty-six when he pitched his final big league game in 1980. Twice he tried comebacks in the minors, but failed.

Lefty Don Gullett, the only man to pitch the opening game in successive World Series for two different teams (Cincinnati Reds, 1976; and New York Yankees, 1977), was just twenty-seven when his career ended with a bad arm after the 1978 season. He had been one of the first free agents signed by the Yankees, and was certainly one of their most expensive, costing them $2 million for his 18 wins in two seasons.

Righthander Wayne Garland of the Indians was operated on for a rotator cuff tear on May 5, 1978. He had won 33 games the two previous seasons. After the operation, he came back, hanging on until 1981, but he was never the same pitcher. And like Gullett, he was working on a lucrative long-term contract.

The previous pages have told of the surprising number of active major leaguers who succumbed to illness. Many others became ill and were forced to give up the game or see their baseball livelihoods interrupted. An early example was Jimmy Wood, who played for Chicago, Brooklyn, and Philadelphia in the National Association from 1871 to 1873. In 1873 he developed a leg abscess which he attempted to lance with a penknife. A severe infection developed, resulting in the loss of his leg. His playing days, of course, were over, but he did return as a manager in 1874 and 1875.

In 1890 first baseman Dave Orr of Brooklyn (in the Players' League) batted .373, hit 32 doubles, 13 triples, and 6 home runs, while striking out only 11 times. For a nonpitcher, this was the ultimate in final seasons. In the off-season, the thirty-one-year-old Orr suffered a stroke and never played again. He died in Brooklyn on June 3, 1915. He had been caretaker of Ebbets Field for many years.

Hall of Famer Amos Rusie won 243 games in nine seasons and part of a tenth, but saw his career shrouded by misfortune, some of his own making. The so-called "Hoosier Thunderbolt," who almost killed Hughie Jennings with a bean ball, himself took a line drive to the head which permanently damaged his hearing. He threw out his arm in 1898 and was out of the game for two years. He compounded his other problems with heavy drinking. Although he tried to come

back in 1901, he failed. At the age of thirty he was through.

The aforementioned Jennings, another Hall of Famer, had a baseball life replete with illness and adversity. In addition to the almost fatal beaning by Rusie, he suffered a nervous breakdown in 1925, after taking over as manager of the New York Giants when John McGraw became ill. Jennings died of spinal meningitis in 1928 at the age of fifty-eight.

Shortstop Charlie Hollocher, who played for the Cubs from 1918 to 1924, was constantly bedeviled by illness, real and imaginary, blunting what some observers feel could have been a Hall of Fame–level career. His tormented life came to an end on August 14, 1940, when he parked his car on a quiet Clayton, Missouri, street, then tore his throat apart with a blast from a sixteen-gauge shotgun.

Jackie Hayes, outstanding second baseman and shortstop for the Senators and the White Sox (1927–1940), was 3 for 3 in a 1940 Sox spring game; then in the shower room he noticed a cloudiness in one eye. He played 18 games that year, but by August he had lost his sight in the clouded eye. In a matter of three years, he had lost his sight in the other. Similarly, George "Specs" Toporcer, a former major league infielder, had lost his sight while managing Buffalo (International League) in 1951. Both men learned to live with their blindness and went on to lead productive lives, Hayes as the tax collector of Chilton County, Alabama, and Toporcer as a writer and lecturer.

Righthanded pitcher Monty Stratton (15–5 and 15–9 for the Chicago White Sox in 1937 and 1938) was hunting rabbits near his mother's home in Greenville, Texas, after the 1938 season, when he accidentally discharged a .22-caliber pistol. The slug lodged in his right knee, severing the main artery and necessitating amputation of the leg. Stratton did not pitch again in the majors, but he was a White Sox coach for three seasons. In 1946 he pitched for Sherman in the Class C East Texas League, where, remarkably, he won 18 games. Hollywood thought it saw a story in the courageous way he had faced his tragedy and made a much-acclaimed movie of his life, *The Stratton Story*, starring Jimmy Stewart.

He looked so indestructible that they called him "The Iron Horse." Henry Louis Gehrig, in seventeen years at first base for the New York Yankees, averaged .340, hit 535 doubles, 162 triples, and 493 home runs. He scored 1,888 runs, had 1,990 RBIs, and posted a slugging percentage of .632. His incredible record of playing in 2,130 consecutive games remains unchallenged. On May 2, 1939, Gehrig approached manager Joe McCarthy, told him he was not feeling well, thought he was hurting the team, and asked to be taken from the lineup. McCarthy, of course, complied, and so for the first time since the famous Wally Pipp headache of June 2, 1925, Gehrig missed a Yankee game. He was never to play another.

A few months later the bad news came from the Mayo Clinic. The indestructible one, "The Iron Horse," had been stricken with amyotrophic lateral sclerosis, a disease of the central nervous system for which no cure was known. On July 4, 1939, 61,000 gathered at Yankee Stadium for a gigantic Gehrig tribute. There he spoke his memorable words: "I consider myself the luckiest man on the face of the earth."

In the short time left to him, Gehrig devoted himself to public service. On June 2, 1941, exactly sixteen years from the day he replaced Pipp at first base, he died. He was thirty-seven years old. The malady that killed him is now generally referred to as Lou Gehrig's disease. Unfortunately it is almost as much a medical mystery today as it was fifty years ago when it struck him.

Catcher Bill DeLancey was a product of the St. Louis Cardinal farm system. After playing eight games for the parent club in 1932 and then spending a year at Columbus (American Association), he became a regular member of the "Gas House Gang" in 1934. In 1935 he found that he had tuberculosis and faced a long recovery period. It was not until 1940 that he made it back, and then it was just for 15 games. By then, he knew it was no use. His career was over. He died November 28, 1946, on his forty-fifth birthday.

When Don Black went to the mound for the Cleveland Indians against the St. Louis Browns on September 13, 1948, he could have looked back on an undistinguished six-year record with the Athletics and Indians (34–55). But there were two victories—one off the diamond—that he could recall with pride. The first was against the bottle; the second was a no-hit, no-run game against the Philadelphia Athletics on July 10, 1947.

In the late-season game against the Browns, upon retiring the Browns in the first two innings, Black came to bat against Bill Kennedy. After swinging mightily at the first pitch and fouling it back, he began to stagger and finally sank to his knees. Umpire Bill Summers bent over to assist Black and heard him whisper, "That last pitch to [Ed] Pellagrini did it." (He had struck out the Browns' shortstop with a curve ball to end the top of the second.) Apparently, that pitch plus the force of his swing had caused an aneurism to rupture, sending blood to his brain and spinal cord. (Shades of James Creighton, who had injured himself fatally while batting on August 14, 1862.) An eminent neurosurgeon was summoned. He ruled out surgery as too risky, but said Black had just a 50-50 chance of surviving. But Black did survive and on September 22 he was recipient of a large purse from a benefit game against the Red Sox that attracted a crowd of 76,772.

The Indians went on to win the pennant and then defeated the Boston Braves in the World Series, but without Black, who never pitched again. He died April 21, 1959 at the age of 42.

Baseball's *Domesday Books* credit lefthanded pitcher Bert Shepard with one major league appearance. What the books do not say is that this game was pitched by a one-legged man. When Shepard's call to World War Two service came, he was a promising young pitcher. The fortunes of war took him to the European front, where he was downed over Germany on his thirty-fifth mission and taken prisoner. Doctors removed his shattered right leg, after which a fellow prisoner of war fashioned him a wooden leg. After his recapture and return to the States, he was signed by the Washington Senators as a batting practice pitcher. In his one appearance in a regular game, he allowed one run in 5⅓ innings for an ERA of 1.69.

Lou Brissie, like Bert Shepard, was a victim of World War Two combat. Brissie, who joined the Army in 1942 as a teenager, was badly wounded on the Italian front and forced to undergo twenty-three operations. Despite the handicap of a steel leg brace and a leather guard, he never gave up his dream of becoming a major league pitcher. In 1947, for Savannah of the Sally League, he won 23 games and earned a late-season call-up from the Philadelphia Athletics. From 1947 to 1953, he won 44 games for the A's and the Indians, to whom he was traded in 1951. His best year was 1949, when he won 16 games and pitched in the All-Star Game. He was only twenty-nine when his career came to a close. He then became national director of the American Legion baseball program.

Herb Score was a third American League lefty to see his career abbreviated by injury. In 1955, Score won 16 games for Cleveland and struck out 245; then in 1956 he improved to 20 wins and 263 strikeouts. Along the banks of Lake Erie, he was hailed as a lefthanded Bob Feller. But it was not to be. On May 7, 1957, at Municipal Stadium in Cleveland, he was hit in the eye by a torrid line drive off the bat of Gil McDougald of the New York Yankees and seriously injured.

His recovery was slow, and he did not return to the Indians until 1958 and then only for 12 games. On April 18, 1960, he was traded to the White Sox for Barry Latman. After three seasons of limited duty for the Sox, he called it a day. He remains in baseball as the play-by-play announcer for the Indians.

Brooklyn catcher Roy Campanella was thirty-six and in the twilight of a remarkable career that had seen him win three Most Valuable Player awards, when disaster struck on a January night in 1958. He was driving to his Long Island home in the early hours of the morning when his borrowed car skidded on a slippery spot in the road and slammed into a utility pole. The two broken vertebrae he suffered doomed him to a long and excruciatingly painful period of recovery and rehabilitation, not to mention lifelong confinement to a wheelchair.

On May 7, 1959, before a crowd of 93,103 fans at the Los Angeles Coliseum, the Dodgers and the Yankees met in a mammoth benefit for the paralyzed Campanella. It was an emotional affair, rivaling similar tributes to Yankee greats Gehrig and Ruth at Yankee Stadium.

The courage Campanella displayed in his rehabilitation was an inspiration to many others who suffered severe spinal injuries. He received baseball's highest honor in 1969—election to the Hall of Fame.

Mike Pazik, a lefthander from Lynn, Mass., who appeared briefly for Minnesota in 1975, 1976, and 1977, saw his pitching career terminated when he suffered multiple fractures of both legs in a 1977 autombile accident. He returned to the game in 1980 as a coach for the White Sox. Later, he served four years as a roving pitching instructor for the Milwaukee Brewers, and then in late 1987 he was named pitching coach for Charlotte of the Double-A Southern League.

Houston righthander J. R. Richard, at 6'8" and 222 pounds, was an intimidating figure on the mound. From 1976 through 1979, his strikeout log showed 214, 214, 303, and 313, respectively, while his victories totaled 74. In 1980, even though slowed by arm and shoulder injuries, he was chosen to start for the National League in the All-Star Game at Los Angeles. But, as fate would have it, he was to pitch just two more innings for the Astros before being laid low by a stroke. The rehabilitation was painfully slow, but there always seemed to be hope that his career could be salvaged, but such hopes proved to be futile. Twice (in 1982 and 1983) he tried to pitch in the lower minors, but the illness had taken too great a toll.

Careers cut short for psychological reasons are not common, but there have been a few. Steve Blass, hero of the 1971 Pittsburgh World Series victory over Baltimore and winner of 19 games in 1972, suddenly could not throw strikes. So severe was the mental block that his baseball life ended in 1972 when he was only thirty-two. Kevin Saucier, a lefthanded relief pitcher for Detroit, had 13 saves and 4 wins in 1981; then, inexplicably, he developed the Steve Blass syndrome and could not throw strikes. In his case it was a fear of hittng and injuring a batter. He could not overcome the problem,

and at twenty-six he was out of baseball. Joe Cowley, who pitched for the Braves, Yankees, White Sox, and Phillies, and who has a no-hit game to his credit, simply could not throw strikes and was sent to the minors by the Phillies in 1987. He could not throw strikes there either and finally was sent home.

At least one career came to a premature end because of a fear of flying. Jackie Jensen, who hit 199 home runs in eleven seasons with the Yankees, Senators, and Red Sox, retired first in 1959, tried again in 1961, but then quit for good at the age of thirty-four.

Alcohol and Drugs

It is impossible to put a number on the baseball careers shortened or adversely affected by the excessive use of alcohol. In at least four cases (Delahanty, Koenecke, Morris, and Wilson), dealt with elsewhere in this chapter, fatalities resulted. Countless players of the game's early years were lushes. Liquor was readily available to them, often on the house, and there was plenty of time for carousing, especially when on the road. Some of the worst offenders were quielty blacklisted and faded from the game. Others who were heavy drinkers continued in uniform, because they were star players and the owners winked at their alcoholic escapades. Future Hall of Famer Michael "King" Kelly, for example, drank as hard as he played; yet in 1887 Boston paid an unheard of $10,000 to Chicago for his contract. Toward the end of his career, he opened a saloon in New York, which was like putting the fox in charge of the chicken coop. His performance level deteriorated rapidly, and by 1894 he was in the minors. That fall he developed pneumonia, and on November 8 he died at the age of thirty-six.

Terry Larkin, who won 29 games for Hartford in 1877, and 29 and 31, respectively, for Chicago in 1878 and 1879, was another nineteenth-century player whose career self-destructed from the ravages of strong drink. In 1883, while drunk, he shot his wife (she recovered) and then tried to commit suicide in jail. In 1886, while employed as a bartender in Brooklyn, he showed up for work with two pistols and challenged his employer to a duel. Police ware called and he was thrown into jail until he sobered up. He died in Brooklyn in 1894.

Equally melancholy is the story of James (The Troy Terrier) Egan, who pitched, caught and played the outfield for Troy (NL) in 1882 and then was blacklisted for drunkenness. Supposedly rehabilitated, he was given a chance with Brooklyn (AA) in 1884, but before he played a game he was arrested for theft and jailed. He died of what was described as "brain fever" in a New Haven, Connecticut, jail, September 26, 1884.

Few players have come to the majors with more raw talent than Louis Sockalexis, a Penobscot Indian from Old Towne, Maine. He played college baseball at both Holy Cross and Notre Dame. While at the latter school in 1897, he and a companion broke up an establishment run by a certain "Popcorn Jennie" and threw the furniture out the windows. When the good fathers who ran Notre Dame read about this caper in the *South Bend Tribune*, they promptly threw him out. Future major league catcher Mike Powers, who had been instrumental in getting Sockalexis into both Holy Cross and Notre Dame, wired the Cleveland Club, with whom the Indian had signed a contract to take effect at the end of the school year, and suggested it send someone to South Bend to

bail him out. Manager Patsy Tebeau caught the next train west, and in a few days Sockalexis was in a Cleveland uniform. He impressed with his strength, speed, and magnificent arm. In later years, both John McGraw and Hughie Jennings said he was the greatest natural talent they had ever seen. Even allowing for the hyperbole that often accompanies such reminiscence, it is apparent that he was a player of exceptional ability. But just as exceptional was his appetite for strong drink. Frequently interrupted by binges and injuries (once he jumped from a second-floor window and severely injured an ankle), his major league career was limited to 94 games in three seasons.

Sockalexis died in Burlington, Maine, on December 24, 1913, at the age of forty-two. His baseball monument is not his .313 batting average but the Cleveland Indians baseball club, which was nicknamed after him.

Hall of Famer Rube Waddell gained almost as much notoriety for his drinking as he did recognition for his pitching. Lowell Reidenbaugh, in his *Cooperstown,* tells how Waddell would come into a bar, penniless, and whisper to the bartender, "Give me a drink, and I will give you the ball I used to defeat Cy Young in twenty innings." According to Reidenbaugh, hundreds of bartenders "displayed what they considered to be the historic souvenir."

Despite the abuse he gave his body, the Rube lasted for thirteen major league seasons and won 191 games. But his indiscretions took their toll. He developed tuberculosis and died in San Antonio, Texas, on April 1, 1914, at the age of thirty-seven.

The problem of alcoholism continues in the modern game, but added to it is an affliction even more virulent—the use of illegal drugs. Careers are being shortened or interrupted by excessive drinking or the ingestion of drugs, or by a combination of both. In the old days, when a player drank too much, he was either shunted aside or his problem was swept under the rug. Now, the usual pattern is a confession of the problem, or exposure, followed by treatment, rehabilitation, sometimes suspension, but then a return to the game.

In 1983 the baseball world was rocked by the news that four players on the Kansas City Royals—Willie Wilson, Willie Aikens, Jerry Martin, and Vida Blue (no longer with the team)—had been involved with illegal drugs. All were suspended for one year by Commissioner Bowie Kuhn, although later an arbitrator reduced the suspensions, except for Blue's. Meanwhile, indictments were handed down and all were convicted and sentenced to one year in jail, with the last nine months suspended. Eventually Wilson returned to the Royals. Aikens was traded to Toronto but then went to the minors. Martin and Blue are out of baseball.

Pitcher Steve Howe of the Los Angeles Dodgers was suspended for the 1984 season for alleged drug use and did not challenge it. After at least two relapses, he was signed by the Texas Rangers and appeared for them late in the 1987 season. Atlanta pitcher Pascual Perez spent three months in a Dominican Republic jail on drug charges during the 1983–1984 off-season and was also suspended by Commissioner Kuhn. Arbitrator Richard I. Bloch, who had also ruled in the Willie Wilson et al. cases, subsequently threw out the Perez suspension because of lack of evidence.

Also in 1983, pitcher Dickie Noles of the Cubs spent time in jail after a drunken brawl in Cincinnati. Outfielder Ron LeFlore was arrested on drug and weapons charges in 1982 while with the White Sox. Although found not guilty, he was released by the Sox in April 1983.

Bob Welch, talented righthanded pitcher of the Dodgers, best remembered for his classic confrontation with Reggie Jackson of the Yankees in the 1978 World Series, revealed that he had been an alcoholic for many years. After rehabilitation and relegation to the minors, he returned to the Dodgers in 1986 and Oakland two years later. He has written a book about his experiences, *Five O'Clock Comes Early.*

A much-publicized drug trial that began in Pittsburgh on September 5, 1985, exposed the drug involvement of numerous players, including Keith Hernandez of the Mets (formerly with the Cardinals) and Dave Parker of the Reds (formerly with the Pirates). After the trial, Commissioner Peter Ueberroth meted out penalties to twenty-one players, ranging from heavy fines to be paid to drug prevention programs, orders to participate in random drug testing, and the performance of drug-related community service.

The shocking disclosures of widespread drug use that came out of the 1985 trial and the severe penalties that followed seemed to have a favorable impact on the drug problem, but did not eliminate it entirely. In 1986 San Diego pitcher LaMarr Hoyt, a Cy Young Award winner in 1983 when he was with the White Sox, was arrested three times on drug-related charges, and after the third was sentenced to forty-five days in federal prison. Hoyt's suspension from baseball was later overturned, and he was ordered reinstated with back pay, much to the dismay of the baseball hierarchy.

Hoyt then signed with his old club, the Chicago White Sox, but his troubles were far from over. He tested positive for cocaine three times in October 1987, and then on December 4 he was arrested in his Columbia, S.C. apartment and charged with intent to distribute cocaine and marijuana. He faced a long prison term if convicted.

The list has been a long one, and sad. It has included paragons and playboys, teetotalers and tosspots, the great, the near-great, and the never-were; some who self-destructed and many more who were simply the victims of the cruelest of bad luck. However classified, for each player the hypothetical question remains: Had his tragedy not occurred, what might have been?

Careers Shortened by Blacklisting or Expulsion

Listed below, but not discussed in this chapter, are players blacklisted or expelled from baseball for gambling, dishonest play (or knowledge of same), criminal activity, or, in one case—that of Ray Fisher—violation of a contract. The players involved in the 1877 Louisville and 1919 Chicago White Sox scandals, all of whom were barred for life, are grouped; the others are listed alphabetically:

1877 Louisville players Bill Craver, Jim Devlin, George Hall, Al Nichols.

1919 Chicago White Sox players Eddie Cicotte, Oscar Felsch, Chick Gandil, Joe Jackson, Fred McMullin, Swede Risberg, Buck Weaver, Claude Williams.

Others George Bechtel, Rube Benton, Paul Carter, Hal Chase, Cozy Dolan, Phil Douglas, Jean Dubuc, Ray Fisher, Joe Gedeon, Claude Hendrix, Richard Higham (umpire), Benny Kauff, Hubert Leonard, Lee Magee, Jimmy O'Connell, Eugene Paulette, Heinie Zimmerman.

## CHAPTER 17

Managers and Coaches
Fred Stein

The job [managing] then, on the face of it, seems virtually impossible to perform. Not only must a man be a strategist and tactician with sophisticated knowledge of a highly detailed game and have the capability of making snap decisions in critical moments, but he must also maintain harmony on a squad of twenty-five men of diverse social, economic, cultural, ethnic, and racial backgrounds during seven months of continuous traveling and constant pressures from within and without. He must be the soother of the delicate ego and the builder of the broken self-confidence. He must disguise his despair and disappointment, temper his elation, and maintain his optimism. He must deal daily with an inquiring press, be polite to countless strangers, and reassure his employers, who have placed the heart of a multimillion-dollar franchise in his care. He schemes and scrambles to keep it all going, to somehow get more spring into a man's legs and snap into his swing. And if he is a realist—and they all are—he knows that one day the general manager will call him into the office or appear suddenly at the hotel in the middle of a road trip and tell him that "for the best interests of the club we have decided...."

from *The Man in the Dugout,* by Donald Honig

The Baseball Manager

Baseball as we know it was established as a "gentleman's sport" by the 1840s and had attained a degree of commercial success by the end of the 1860s. Sometime within this transition from a participatory, upper-class social game to an organized professional, spectator sport for mass consumption, there developed a need for accountability. Someone had to be responsible for the team's success, both as a sporting endeavor and as a money-making enterprise.

Harry Wright was the first important baseball manager, and the functions thrust upon him in the 1860s were typical of the workload carried by many of the managers of that period. A former professional cricket player, Wright saw his first baseball game at age twenty-two, and it was love at first sight. A decade later, he helped organize the famous Cincinnati Red Stockings, the first all-salaried team, which won 84 consecutive games in 1869–1870. Wright's duties at the time included the following: field manager, center fielder, relief pitcher, team trainer, tracker of team baseballs and field equipment, disciplinarian, scheduler of games and travel arrangements, checker of gate receipts, and bursar.

Wright continued his managing career with the advent of "organized baseball" in 1871, winning four straight pennants with the Boston Red Stockings from 1872 through 1875. He managed the National League entry at Boston through 1881, then managed Providence for two seasons, and Philadelphia from 1884 through 1893. The highly moral, immensely popular Wright is credited with playing the dominant role in establishing the integrity of professional baseball in its critical, formative years.

It bothered Wright to hear that other managers felt they could do as well as he had done with his players. He felt that managing a team effectively involved handling players with proper recognition of their human frailties as well as capitalization of their physical skills. To a young hopeful, writing to ask what he had to do to become a professional player, Wright could be fatherly and helpful. He suggested to one young man that he develop the necessary skills—become a "sure catch," a good "thrower," a reliable batter, and a good runner—all by devoted practice. Wright added a wonderfully homespun touch, admonishing the young man to "... eat hearty. Roast beef rare will aid, live regularly, keep good hours, and abstain from intoxicating drinks and tobacco."

The baseball manager's role became more clearly defined in the 1870–1900 period, as increased revenues permitted clubs to hire people—"managers" akin to today's general managers—to handle such administrative functions as monitoring gate receipts, paying salaries, and supervising equipment and stadium operations. But these business managers, twenty-eight of whom have been carried in the Macmillan *Encyclopedia* as managers, never filled out a lineup card or accompanied the team on a road trip. The research of Rich Topp and Bob Tiemann has set the matter straight in this volume. Scheduling of games became the function of league offices, relieving the manager of this responsibility. Still, for economic reasons, the on-field manager (or "captain," as he was often designated) usually was expected to perform double duty—serving as a player as well as the field boss. He was also responsible for disciplining players, keeping them in condition, and, depending on circumstances, handling player transactions. The 1890s in particular featured increased emphasis on scientific baseball, and the strategies employed by managers became a matter of increased interest and importance.

Adrian "Cap" Anson was the most prominent manager and player of the 1880s and '90s. The massive (for the time) first baseman hit .334 over twenty-two National League seasons and .336 for his full twenty-seven-year career, and was the first National League player with more than 3,000 career hits. A gruff, no-nonsense type, Anson ranked high on the all-time managers list with a .578 won-and-lost percentage over twenty-one seasons as a manager. He directed Chicago to five pennants in his first eight seasons as a manager.

The outspoken, mustachioed Iowa native was a stern task-

master who ruled his club with an iron hand. He was an innovative manager—he utilized spring training for conditioning purposes, encouraged base stealing, rotated pitchers with contrasting styles, used signals, and employed the hit-and-run play. On the down side, the extremely conservative Anson played an important role in barring black players from organized baseball. The rough-hewn Anson had little of the philosophical concern for the game which characterized the gentle, high-minded Harry Wright. Yet Anson, not Wright, became the principal hero to the crowds of the era.

Ned Hanlon was an important manager in the 1890s, a prime exponent of the rough-and-ready, anything-to-win approach which was typical of the play of that decade. Hanlon's famed Baltimore Orioles won three successive pennants in 1894–1896, then finished in second place twice before Hanlon moved to the Brooklyn club, which he led to pennant wins in 1899 and 1900. The bookish-appearing Hanlon headed a Baltimore cast which included such legendary players as John McGraw, Wee Willie Keller, Wilbert Robinson, Joe Kelley, and Hugh Jennings. Even allowing for hyperbole, the club was noted for its "inside baseball" execution and rowdy antics reminiscent of the Katzenjammer Kids. Baseball scholars differ as to who invented strategies like the squeeze play, the "Baltimore chop," and judicious doctoring of the baseball diamond, but there is little doubt that the Orioles, under Hanlon's direction, perfected these techniques.

The managerial role in the 1900–1920 period was marked by continuing emphasis on scientific baseball, scratching out runs in a dead-ball era when runs were hard to come by. During these two decades, the game reached new heights of popularity, and some managers, along with star players, became national heroes.

Connie Mack and John McGraw were the towering managerial figures of the period. Mack (his name mercifully shortened from Cornelius McGillicuddy) was a journeyman catcher whose managing career began with Pittsburgh of the National League in 1894. After three seasons, he managed Milwaukee of the Western League until 1901, when he and Benjamin Shibe were awarded the Philadelphia franchise in the new American League.

Nicknamed "The Tall Tactician," Mack put together, and then took apart, two dominating teams in two different eras. Between 1910 and 1914, his Athletics won four pennants before, feeling the need for financial retrenchment, he began shedding such high-priced stars as second baseman Eddie Collins and pitchers Jack Coombs, Eddie Plank, and Chief Bender. As a result, the A's finished dead last from 1915 through 1921.

Beginning in the mid-1920s, Mack gathered several future Hall of Famers—Mickey Cochrane, Al Simmons, Jimmie Foxx, and Lefty Grove—and the A's won three straight pennants starting in 1929. However, with the Depression deepening and attendance dropping drastically, Mack again was forced to sell his stars. The rest was all downhill for the cash-poor Mack as the A's finished in the second division from 1934 through 1950, his last year as manager.

During Mack's incredible fifty-three-year managerial career, he won and lost more games (3,731 and 3,948) than any other major league pilot. In addition to his records, he is remembered for managing from the bench in street clothes and for deploying his fielders (usually with remarkable precision) with a wave of his ever-present scorecard. Many fans felt that the canny Irishman remained at the helm for too long, simply because he couldn't be fired. They pointed to the Athletics' ineffectual showing over the last seventeen years of his tenure, and his tendency in later years to nod off on the bench. Regardless, baseball men respected his shrewd judgment of player talent, his ability to manage unlettered eccentrics and college men with equal effectiveness, his skill in building great teams in both the dead- and live-ball eras, and his entrepreneurial skill in keeping his team afloat on a financial shoestring. Mack's players revered the dignified, erect, spindly old man with the pronounced New England accent—a link between them and the years when baseball was barely beyond its infancy.

John McGraw shared Connie Mack's Irish background and his managerial acumen, but they were direct opposites in most other respects. "The Little Napoleon" was a scrappy little third baseman whose .334 lifetime batting average, fielding skill, and driving aggressiveness would have justified Hall of Fame recognition if his managing career had not done so. McGraw was the field ringleader of Ned Hanlon's Baltimore Orioles of the 1890s. After moving to St. Louis of the National League in 1900, he went to the new American League, accepting Ban Johnson's offer to manage the Baltimore club in 1901.

Unable to get along with Johnson, McGraw jumped at the chance to manage the New York Giants in July 1902. The Giants became the most successful National League team for the next thirty years, with McGraw engendering high excitement and emotions. As famed sportswriter Grantland Rice wrote, "His very walk across the field in a hostile town is a challenge to the multitude." McGraw is credited with stimulating the growth of baseball during the 1900–1920 period, just before the advent of the lively-ball era.

Most experts consider McGraw the greatest manager ever. He ranks second only to Mack in major league games managed (4,845) and in games won (2,816). His teams captured ten National League pennants in thirty years with only two second-division finishes. McGraw's managerial genius produced strategic and tactical innovations, and attracted and developed many superb players. His career evoked continuous arguments, fistfights, and controversies with league presidents, owners, umpires, opposing managers and players, and off-the-field acquaintances. However, this bon vivant, raconteur, and man of varied nonbaseball interests was also famous for helping downtrodden former players.

Clark Griffith, Fred Clarke, and Frank Chance were three other prominent managers of the 1900-1920 period. Griffith had pitching credentials (240–141) which would have justified his election to the Hall of Fame as a player as well as a manager. The pocket-sized righthander, nicknamed "The Old Fox," relied upon control, guile, and uncanny skill at nicking or otherwise doctoring the ball to fool the hitters. He won at least 21 games a year from 1894 through 1899, then went 24–7 while managing the Chicago club of the new American League to the pennant in 1901.

At the request of American League President Ban Johnson, Griffith managed the New York Highlanders from 1903 through 1908. He managed Cincinnati in 1909–1911 before purchasing a 10 percent interest in the Washington Senators. During his managerial tenure with the Senators from 1912 to 1920, Griffith operated with little capital, as evidenced by only two first-division finishes during the period, both largely attributable to the superhuman efforts of speedballing Walter Johnson. Griffith gained controlling interest in the Senators in

1920 and vacated the manager's slot to become club president.

Fred Clarke, another outstanding player, was a field manager in nineteen of his twenty-one major league seasons. The compact outfielder had a .315 batting average while collecting 2,708 hits. He hit a career high .406 in 1897, stole over 30 bases in seven seasons, and was a superb left fielder.

Clarke managed Louisville from 1897 to 1899 and Pittsburgh for the next sixteen years, ranking among the top managers with 1,602 wins and a .576 winning percentage. Led by Clarke himself, all-time great shortstop Honus Wagner, and center fielder Ginger Beaumont, the Pirates won consecutive pennants in 1901–1903, then won the World Championship in 1909. The hallmarks of the energetic Clarke's teams were their excellent physical condition and tight discipline, both on and off the field.

Clubs managed by Frank Chance, along with McGraw and Clarke, won every National League pennant from 1901 through 1913. Chance is best remembered as the first baseman of the famous "Tinker to Evers to Chance" double-play combination of the Chicago Cubs, as the Cubs won three straight pennants in 1906–1908 and added another in 1910.

Chance, a smart, natural leader, took over the Cubs in midseason of 1905 from Frank Selee, himself a great but little-remembered pilot, and remained as manager through the 1912 season. During his 7½-year tenure, the "Peerless Leader's" clubs won 753 games and lost only 379, for a remarkable .665 winning percentage. Handicapped by recurring headaches attributable to several beanings, Chance withdrew from active play and later managed the New York Highlanders in 1913–1914 and the Boston Red Sox in 1923, but with none of his earlier success.

The lively ball changed major league baseball and managerial strategy after 1920. Such offensive baseball tactics as the stolen base, the sacrifice bunt in early innings, and the squeeze play were virtually ignored as the long ball came into vogue. "Big bang" baseball became the rule rather than the exception, with only occasional aberrations such as the deadened ball used by the National League in the early 1930s and the inferior baseball offensive talent during World War Two. Big-inning baseball strategies had largely replaced those of the dead-ball era, and baseball managers were forced to adapt to the changes.

Connie Mack successfully shifted his managerial focus to the new offensive game, and the Athletics won pennants in 1929–1931. John McGraw won four successive pennants in the early twenties, largely on the strength of strong, well-balanced teams rather than offensive powerhouses. After 1924 McGraw's failure to adapt to the power game prevented him from winning any more pennants before he left the game in 1932.

The powerful Yankees of the twenties, thirties, and early forties were famed for their power hitting complemented by exemplary pitching and fielding. Yankee managers Miller Huggins and Joe McCarthy were the beneficiaries of crushing offenses led by Babe Ruth, Lou Gehrig, Bob Meusel, Earle Combs, Tony Lazzeri, and Bill Dickey, then later by Joe DiMaggio, Tom Henrich, Joe Gordon and Charlie Keller.

Miller Huggins was a tiny second baseman, considered an excellent fielder but a weak hitter (.265 lifetime average with little extra-base power), whose offensive forte was drawing walks and stealing bases. The bright "Mighty Mite," a Cincinnati native and law school graduate, managed the St. Louis Cardinals in 1913–1917 with modest success. He was then hired by Yankee owner Col. Jacob Ruppert against the wishes of co-owner Col. Tillinghast Huston, who was overseas in World War One action at the time.

Huggins's masterstroke was in convincing the Yankees to purchase Babe Ruth from the financially troubled Boston Red Sox. Ruth's powerful hitting was largely responsible for the Yankees' developing dynasty, which brought Huggins six pennant wins in twelve seasons with New York. Ruth was important to Huggins in another respect: maintaining player discipline. Ruth regularly broke club rules until Huggins fined him $5,000 (a lot of money in 1925) and suspended him. The Yankees' management strongly supported Huggins, and Ruth and his fellow recalcitrants bowed to the diminutive Huggins's authority.

Huggins died unexpectedly at fifty while managing the Yankees in 1929, and Joe McCarthy took over as the Yankees' manager a year later. Another weak-hitting infielder, "Marse Joe" never made it to the major leagues as a player. After gaining recognition as one of the leading minor league managers, McCarthy managed the Chicago Cubs from 1926 to 1930, winning the National League pennant in 1929. McCarthy went on to win eight pennants and seven World Championships in fifteen full seasons as the Yankees' manager, with only one finish as low as fourth place. Under McCarthy the Yankees did not merely outshine the competition, they annihilated them, winning the 1936 flag by a record 19½ games and winning the 1932, 1938, and 1939 World Series in four games straight.

McCarthy's teams were noted for their attention to detail and their teamwork, as well as their overpowering talent. McCarthy was a strict, if undemonstrative, disciplinarian (ties and jackets were compulsory, and even pipe smoking was discouraged) and was adept at maintaining the defensive excellence which undergirded his teams' successes. McCarthy ranks first among all managers with a .614 winning percentage.

Charles Dillon "Casey" Stengel was the third in a line of great Yankee managers. Stengel was a sometimes comic journeyman outfielder (.284 career batting average) whose playing career is best remembered for his sparkling hitting in the 1923 World Series, when he won two games for the Giants against the Yankees with home runs.

The lovable "Old Perfessor" with the great sense of humor, total recall of past game situations, and singular gift of gab (he specialized in long-winded non sequiturs) began his fabled major league managerial career with Brooklyn in 1934. After three mediocre seasons with the Dodgers and one season (1937) when he was paid not to manage the Dodgers, Stengel spent six seasons managing the Boston Braves, still unable to rise above the second-division level.

After managing in the high minors from 1944 to 1948, Stengel signed with the Yankees for 1949. He managed the club to an unprecedented five consecutive pennants, finished in second place in 1954 (despite 103 wins), then won four more consecutive pennants before falling to third place in 1959. He closed out his stint with the Yankees with another pennant win in 1960, making it a phenomenal total of ten pennants and seven World Championships in twelve seasons. Dismissed by the Yankees as "too old," Stengel managed the fledgling New York Mets from 1962 to 1965, finishing in last place each season, before retiring two-thirds into the 1965 season. Stengel had a won–lost percentage of .508 for twenty-

five seasons, ranking fourth in games managed and seventh in games won.

Huggins and McCarthy were essentially orthodox, conservative managers who consistently turned out magnificent teams with magnificent players. Stengel, also gifted with great players—DiMaggio, Yogi Berra, Phil Rizzuto, Whitey Ford, Mickey Mantle—added another dimension to managing. He rose above crushing injuries to his stars and obtained high levels of performance from unexpected sources. Even more remarkable, he played the percentages and played *against* the percentages with outstanding success. In addition, he had unparalleled rapport with baseball writers, thereby helping the Yankees in the press as well as on the field. Stengel was, in his own word, "amazin'!"

Leo Durocher was another interesting, if more controversial, manager. The brash, street-smart "Lippy Leo" was a weak-hitting but great-fielding shortstop for the Yankees, Reds, "Gas House Gang" Cardinals, and Dodgers. Durocher became the Dodgers' player-manager in 1939, just as the frenetic, high-spending efforts of President Larry MacPhail were beginning to raise the club from its long-standing doldrums. In 1941, the Dodgers, with the help of such stars as Dolf Camilli, Pee Wee Reese, Pete Reiser, Billy Herman, Dixie Walker, Joe Medwick, and Whitlow Wyatt, won Brooklyn's first pennant in twenty-one years. Durocher's club just barely lost out to St. Louis in 1942 and 1946. Sparked by rookie Jackie Robinson, the Dodgers won the pennant in 1947, but Durocher was not on hand—he had been suspended for "conduct detrimental to baseball" for the entire 1947 season. Lippy Leo returned in 1948, but with the Dodgers doing poorly, he was moved in midseason to the New York Giants. It was a shocking deal for Giants' fans—their idolized Mel Ott replaced by the hated Durocher.

Durocher's revamped Giants, 13½ games off the pace in August 1951, came back to beat the Dodgers on Bobby Thomson's "Miracle at Coogan's Bluff" home run. In many respects this was Durocher's finest season, as he maneuvered the Giants to the pennant. Although Durocher's club went on to win both the pennant and the World Championship in 1954, the Polo Grounders slipped, and Durocher, never completely accepted by Giants' fans, was let out after the 1955 season. He returned to manage the Chicago Cubs from 1966 through midseason 1972 but was unable to win a pennant. His managerial career ended after he piloted Houston unsuccessfully through the 1973 season.

Durocher was recognized as a knowledgeable, aggressive manager who could inspire a team with winning potential but seemed to lose interest with lesser teams. Leo tended to find himself in unsavory company, the basic reason for his suspension in 1947. Although he was respected as a strategist and competitor, he was disliked intensely by many baseball men who resented his beanball orders and by umpires and fans offended by his rowdy tactics. Over his twenty-four-year managerial career, Durocher ranks fifth in games managed and sixth in wins.

Walter "Smokey" Alston was the antithesis of Durocher— a quiet, unassuming, stable man who at first won with power-packed teams, then with speedy clubs. A hard-hitting first baseman in the minors, the Ohio strongman had only one sip of a cup of coffee in the majors—in 1936 he struck out in his only major league at-bat. He was installed as the manager of the then-Brooklyn Dodgers in 1954 after they fired pennant-winning pilot Charlie Dressen, who wanted a multiyear con-

tract. Alston, who never received more than a single-year contract in his twenty-three Dodger seasons, responded with seven pennants and four World Championships. He led the famous "Boys of Summer" Dodgers—Pee Wee Reese, Gil Hodges, Jackie Robinson, Roy Campanella, Carl Furillo, Duke Snider, Carl Erskine—to pennant wins in 1955–1956. His 1965–1966 pennant winners were sparked by the herculean pitching of Sandy Koufax and the base-stealing heroics of Maury Wills. Only two men, Connie Mack and John McGraw, managed the same team for a longer period than Alston. He ranks fifth in games won with a .558 winning percentage.

The role (some would say the importance) of the manager has changed significantly over the past two decades, in terms of both strategy and the maintenance of discipline. The designated hitter rule has changed the game drastically, giving the manager either more or fewer options, depending on the viewpoint. Pitching strategy has shifted to a decreased emphasis on the starting pitcher going the route and an increased emphasis on a dominant relief pitcher to finish off the opposition. Play on artificial turf requires different strategies and playing styles from play on natural grass. Greater emphasis on base stealing has changed strategies. Platooning players, which has been around for at least seventy years, has been refined to an exquisite art.

Maintaining player discipline has become much more difficult over the years. Until the 1960s, the manager ruled completely. But today most players are paid more than managers, implying that a higher-paid star is more valuable to the team than the manager. As a result, fining highly paid players is a relatively ineffective disciplinary tactic. Today air travel has telescoped travel time, and players spend more time during the season away from their teammates. The resulting reduced team discipline and togetherness have made it more difficult for managers to weld their players into cohesive units.

Drug abuse presents an extremely difficult managerial problem. Excessive drinking has been a common difficulty from the early days of professional baseball. But drinking and its impact upon a player's performance are usually readily determined. However, the use of drugs is extremely difficult to detect, and its impact on performance is long term and virtually impossible to judge.

Managers have been laid off, sacrifices on the altars of second-division finishes or general fan or owner discontent, since the game began. But over the last two decades there is evidence that managers have become an increasingly endangered species. From 1970 through 1981, for example, National League managers enjoyed a mere 2.4-year average tenure, while their American League counterparts lasted only 1.9 years on the average.

On the positive side, today's manager has a multitude of helpers, a sufficient number to give his job a chairman-of-the-board aura. He now has available hitting instructors, base-stealing coaches, specialists in playing each position, pitching coaches, conditioning specialists, motivation experts, and, yes, someone to check on the inventory of baseballs. Shades of Harry Wright!

Several managers have been especially adept at dealing with these emerging changes. Some of the more prominent include Sparky Anderson, Earl Weaver, Dick Williams, and Billy Martin.

George Lee "Sparky" Anderson fits the classic pattern of the successful major league manager—a brainy, hustling,

good-field–no-hit infielder. After hitting .218 for the Phillies in his only major league season and playing several additional minor league seasons, Anderson managed in the minors from 1964 to 1968, then coached for the fledgling San Diego Padres in 1969.

Appointed to manage the Cincinnati Reds in 1970, Anderson was an immediate success, winning the pennant by 14½ games. Anderson's clubs won pennants again in 1972, 1975, and 1976, powered by catcher Johnny Bench, first baseman Tony Perez, left fielder Pete Rose, and second baseman Joe Morgan. Many experts rate his 1976 powerhouse with the great Yankee teams of 1927, 1936, and 1961. Despite Anderson's brilliant tenure at Cincinnati (four pennants and two World Championships in nine years), the Reds released him after a second-place finish in 1978. The Detroit Tigers hired him immediately, and he improved the club steadily, guiding them to a World Championship in 1984.

The garrulous Anderson is one of the most popular men in the game, frequently selected to broadcast postseason games despite his lamentable diction. Nicknamed "Captain Hook" because of his crisp yanking of struggling pitchers, Anderson is highly respected for his diligence, his ready availability to the press, and his fairness and loyalty to his players.

The inimitable Earl Weaver has been considered by many experts the top manager of the last twenty years. Another ex–minor league infielder who never made it to the major leagues as a player, Weaver managed in the minors from 1956 through 1967, then took over the managership of the Baltimore Orioles in midseason of 1968. He led the Orioles through the 1982 season, then stepped down voluntarily for the 1983–1984 campaigns. Summoned back as the Orioles faltered in 1985, Weaver managed through the 1986 season before retiring to pursue the good life in Florida.

Weaver ranks among the ten best managers statistically, with a .583 winning percentage. During his seventeen seasons, he won four pennants and one World Championship, but was remarkably consistent, finishing out of the first division only once.

Weaver's managerial style combined those of John McGraw and Casey Stengel. He was the most frequently ejected major league manager of his era, with ninety-one dismissals from games and four suspensions. The picture of his explosive debates with umpires (many precipitated by Weaver for his own strategic purposes) is unforgettable—the stocky little manager cheek to cheek with the umpire, his cap turned around to prevent contact, and his violent outbursts punctuated by vigorous hand slaps against his ever-present rule book.

The innovative Weaver set up an instruction plan in the early 1960s which is still used throughout the Orioles organization, permitting a future Eddie Murray or a Cal Ripken, Jr., to move from the lowest farm club in the system to the parent club with a minimum of adjustment. Weaver made unprecedented use of charts and computers, although he never abandoned his fundamental reliance upon three-run homers (he called them "a visit from Dr. Longball"), a relatively walk-free pitching staff, and a tight, well-disciplined defense.

Weaver was a complete realist in recognizing his players' capabilities and limitations. Accordingly he was a master in using his entire roster to maximize player strengths and minimize weaknesses. He accomplished this by extensive analysis of scouting reports and past performances of Oriole players

against individual opponents. Earl Weaver was unquestionably the supreme strategist of his time.

Dick Williams has been one of the most successful managers since the late 1960s. He was a journeyman outfielder-infielder with Brooklyn, Baltimore, Kansas City, Cleveland and Boston, hitting .260 over his injury-plagued thirteen-year playing career. After managing the Red Sox's Triple-A Toronto farm team in 1965–1966, Williams led the parent club to a pennant in 1967. Released after failing to repeat in 1968–1969, Williams was hired by Oakland owner Charles Finley to manage the Athletics in 1971.

Williams won two straight pennants and World Championships in three boisterous seasons in Oakland. He had an imposing aggregation of young players led by outfielders Reggie Jackson and Joe Rudi, third baseman Sal Bando, and pitchers Catfish Hunter, Vida Blue, and Rollie Fingers, as well as the unpredictable—and unignorable—Finley as his boss. Tiring of the meddling Finley, Williams quit after winning his second straight World Championship in 1973. He managed the California Angels in 1974–1976, but with little success, then managed the Montreal Expos from 1977 to 1981 without winning a pennant. Williams piloted the San Diego Padres from 1982 to 1985, winning the 1984 flag. He left the Padres before the 1986 season to take over the youthful Seattle Mariners.

Especially effective with younger players, Williams runs a no-nonsense, well-disciplined ship—no simple task in the game today. Among active managers, he trails only Sparky Anderson and Gene Mauch in career wins, going into the 1988 season.

Billy Martin has been the most combative figure in the game since joining the Yankees as a twenty-two-year-old second baseman in 1950. A fair fielder and an average hitter for a middle infielder (.257 lifetime average) who enhanced his value by his razor-sharp baseball instincts and aggressiveness, Martin is best known for his many brawls with other players, club officials, and miscellaneous bystanders. He attributes much of his bellicosity to a rough childhood in Berkeley, California, where, as he put it, "I awoke every morning figuring there was a damn good chance I'd be in a fistfight before the day was over."

Martin's managerial career has produced winning teams everywhere he has managed, but off-field troubles with owners and other incidents have resulted in his string of firings and resignations. He began managing at Denver in 1968 and in the majors with Minnesota in 1969, where his club won the American League's Western Division championship. Fired "for ignoring Twins policies," Martin was hired to manage Detroit in 1971. After a second-place finish, he led the Tigers to the Eastern Division title in 1972. He left the Tigers near the end of the 1973 season and finished out the season managing the Texas Rangers. Martin was fired by the Rangers on July 21, 1975, then took over as Yankees manager on August 2, 1975. Hired by Yankees owner George Steinbrenner to restore the Yankees to their former glory, Martin produced a pennant win in 1976. Reggie Jackson joined the Yankees in 1977, contributing to a World Championship in a tumultuous season remembered for a highly publicized feud (and a nationally televised dugout confrontation and near fight) between Jackson and Martin.

In 1978 Steinbrenner fired Martin in midseason. Then, in a dramatic announcement preceding the Yankees' Old-Timers' Game in July 1978, Steinbrenner promised to rehire Martin.

Billy returned in 1979 but was fired again in midseason because of an off-field incident. Martin managed Oakland in 1980 and, with the last-place club of the previous year playing spirited "Billy Ball," he lifted the Athletics to second place in 1980 and a division title in 1981. The A's deteriorated in 1982 and Martin was dismissed at the end of the season.

In a familiar scenario, Martin returned to manage the Yankees in 1983 but was replaced after finishing in third place. Incredibly he was rehired for a fourth time in 1985, but, after committing the crime of not winning the pennant, was dismissed at season's end and replaced by Lou Piniella. He had a career winning percentage of .552, five divisional championships, two pennants, and a World Championship.

Martin served the Yankees in the broadcasting booth and other capacities in 1986–1987. Then, as Steinbrenner's opinion of Piniella's managing soured (while others were recommending him as a candidate for Manager of the Year!), the by-now-monotonous announcement came over the wires: Martin would manage the Yankees again in 1988. The other shoe dropped to the floor in the early summer, as Martin was let go in favor of Piniella.

Similar to his mentor Casey Stengel, Martin's success in large part stems from his intense concentration on the game and his ability to motivate players of average ability. However, unlike Stengel, Martin's greatest problem has been with handling young players. He has also had difficulties with established players, especially stars such as Reggie Jackson and Don Baylor, who make no bones of their intense dislike for Martin. He has had tremendous success in attaining immediate improvement in team performance. However, he has tended to wear out his welcome with owners within a short time, and he is thought to have a tendency to burn out his starting pitchers, particularly evident during his tenure at Oakland.

Baseball historian David Voigt presented a masterful analysis of the role of expansion-era managers in the premiere issue of *The National Pastime*. Voigt wrote:

The role of the modern manager is that of supervisor, disciplinarian, and strategist. As supervisors, managers now delegate authority to coaches who conduct practices and instruct players; each coach contributes his bit of expertise and the manager is charged with coordinating these activities. As a disciplinarian, the manager retains enough authority to compel players to follow rules and do their duty. Indeed, some managerial discipline codes yet resemble those of closed institutions like police forces and mental asylums . . . As strategists, which is still the essence of the managerial mystique, pilots still rely on time-honored devices such as flashing signals to third-base coaches, devising defensive alignments to thwart hitters, and most important, setting a pitching rotation and knowing when to change pitchers.

In the final analysis, however, it may be that the manager's main function is to serve as scapegoat and thus preserve the jobs of others . . . [He] is answerable for a multitude of sins, few of his direct commission . . .

And with an owner like Steinbrenner intervening incessantly, going so far as to order special fundamental drills, one can only expect continuing pressure on managers. Indeed, the best relief for these besieged foremen seems to have been hit upon by Whitey Herzog. By functioning both as manager and GM, he seems to be pointing the way toward a protective adaptation for an otherwise highly endangered

species. And if he can find a way to buy his club—well, how do you think Connie Mack lasted fifty years?

Managerial Styles

As John McGraw—with simple directness—put it, "The idea [in managing] is to win." No argument there, but it is interesting to consider the widely different approaches major league managers have brought to the task.

First, there are the autocrats, the "you'll do it my way or else" types. Some prime examples are Cap Anson, John McGraw, Rogers Hornsby, Leo Durocher, Charlie Dressen, Earl Weaver, Gene Mauch, Dick Williams, and Billy Martin.

Cap Anson was a strong disciplinarian, a manager who did not allow his players to smoke cigarettes or cigars (apparently chewing tobacco was permitted) or to drink alcoholic beverages in a notably heavy-drinking era. Anson was the largest player on his team and was known to exert brute strength to carry out his edicts. On one occasion during a card game, Anson and his third baseman, Ed Williamson, got into a scuffle. It seems that Williamson, holding four aces, won a sizable pot from Anson, who had four queens. Anson accused Williamson of cheating, and Williamson responded by grabbing a water pitcher, prepared to part Anson's skull before cooler heads broke up the scrap. Williamson, probably aware that he had been spared a bloody beating by the huge player-manager, commented colloquially, "Cap, you're okay as a player, but you don't count for cornstalks as a man."

McGraw was the most notorious autocrat of them all. He demanded that his players submit to his will unconditionally. This included strict curfews and long hours of sliding, fielding, hitting, and bunting practice. In his rediscovered book, *Pitching in a Pinch*, Christy Mathewson told of games during which McGraw called every pitch. Mathewson wrote, ". . . McGraw . . . plans every move, most of the hitters going to the plate with definite instructions from him as to what to try to do. In order to make this system efficient, absolute discipline must be assured. If a player has other ideas than McGraw, . . . the invariable answer to him is 'You do what I tell you, and I'll take the responsibility if we lose.' "

McGraw's insistence on strict adherence to his instructions was illustrated one day in Pittsburgh. Giants' outfielder Red Murray came to bat in the ninth inning of a tied game with none out and a runner on second. He acknowledged McGraw's signal to bunt the runner to third base, then to McGraw's consternation drilled the next pitch for a game-winning home run. Flushed with success, Murray met with the outraged Little Napoleon after the game. "Murray, what did I tell you to do?" McGraw asked him. Murray responded, "You told me to bunt, but the pitch came in right in my gut, so I whacked it." McGraw snapped, "Well, I'm fining you one hundred dollars, and you can try putting that in your gut."

McGraw's unending signals and commands from the bench were a constant source of irritation to his players. One story tells of the spring training exhibition game where McGraw sat sunning himself in the center field bleachers instead of his usual place on the bench. Mrs. McGraw, seated in a box near the dugout, was uncertain whether her husband was going to stay for the full game. So at the end of one inning she called to Giant center fielder Fred Lindstrom to have him ask McGraw what he intended to do. Lindstrom didn't hear her, and one of the reporters seated near by yelled to get his attention, indi-

cating that Mrs. McGraw wanted to speak to him. When Lindstrom came over to the box, she said, in mock severity, "Freddy! Why don't you pay attention?" Lindstrom's eyes widened. "Good God!" he exclaimed. "Are you giving signals, too?"

The success of the stifling McGraw approach continued as long as players followed his orders without question during the first twenty of his thirty years at the Giants' helm. But Fred Lindstrom described its effect on the club in McGraw's later years. Lindstrom said, "With the advent of fellows like Bill Terry, Mel Ott, Carl Hubbell, Travis Jackson, and me, we were a different breed. We didn't need someone hitting us over the head to keep us in shape. In fact, we wouldn't take it—at least Terry and I wouldn't. I don't think McGraw was able to adapt his methods of handling . . . the more modern-style players. And after 1924 he never won another pennant."

While McGraw's players merely chafed restlessly at their boss's domineering style, manager Harry "the Hat" Walker's 1971 Houston Astros broadcast their defiance to the world. It seems that Walker was having extreme difficulty in preventing his players from drinking and chasing women. Walker's rebellious charges mocked his lectures and fines and openly parodied his moral stance by loudly singing a satirical clubhouse refrain with the following lyrics:

> *Now Harry Walker is the one*
> *   that manages this crew;*
> *He doesn't like it when we drink*
> *   and fight and smoke and screw;*
> *But when we win our game each day,*
> *Then what the fuck can Harry say?*
> *It makes a fellow proud to be an Astro.*

McGraw's postgame "meetings," which the entire team was required to sit through before showering, were noted for their length (sometimes as long as three hours) and for McGraw's vicious harangues. (Pete Reiser reported that Leo Durocher, another absolute ruler, forbade his Brooklyn Dodger players from taking off their uniforms after losing a game until the Lippy One gave his permission.)

Rogers Hornsby, a blunt, humorless man, was another imperious manager. Hall of Famer Billy Herman, who joined the Chicago Cubs as a rookie at the end of the 1931 season, later described Hornsby as follows:

He was a hard-nosed guy. He ran the clubhouse like a gestapo camp. You couldn't smoke, drink a soft drink, eat a sandwich. Couldn't read a paper. When you walked in the clubhouse, you put your uniform on and got ready to play . . . no more kidding around, no joking, no laughing . . . When you would hear from him is if you made a play he didn't think was quite up to his standards. It still burns me up just a little bit to remember some of his sarcastic remarks.

Billy Martin, at least in his earlier managerial years, acted like a Marine drill sergeant. Graig Nettles played for Martin in 1968 at Denver. In his book *Balls,* Nettles reports that Martin would scream from the dugout at an errant player as the player came in from the field. Martin held his players in contempt, thought they had not "scuffled around." So Martin put his players through "boot camp" to toughen them up. He taught them that things had to be done his way. Nettles concluded gamely that "on a Billy Martin team, there is only

one boss: Billy Martin. And if you do it his way, you'll win."

Then there are the managers who downplay their own importance in deference to their players. They have been likened to school guidance counselors. Typical members of this group include Connie Mack, Wilbert Robinson, Bill McKechnie, Miller Huggins, Bucky Harris, Eddie Sawyer, Walter Alston, Danny Murtaugh, Ralph Houk, Tom Lasorda, and Sparky Anderson.

Connie Mack, despite his historic importance as a baseball figure, was an unobtrusive figure who never upstaged his players. He preferred not to wear a uniform and, therefore, was forbidden from stepping onto the field. As a result, he did not project himself into the public eye during a game. According to Jimmy Dykes, who was associated with Mack for many years, nothing ever seemed to bother the equable Mack, who was perfectly content to yield the spotlight to his players. He was the same placid man sitting on the bench, whether his Athletics were in last place or playing a World Series game. To Dykes's knowledge, Mack never fined a player, although he was known to express his displeasure when a player violated the midnight curfew without permission.

The saintly Mack never used profanity; Dykes said that if Mack used the word "damn," he was deeply disturbed. There was one occasion, though, when Mack showed anger—using another four-letter word. His great pitcher, Robert "Lefty" Grove, had a rare off-day against the Yankees of the "Murderers' Row" game. When the dour, short-tempered Grove returned to the dugout after a difficult inning, Mack called out a quiet suggestion as to how to deal with Ruth, Gehrig, Dickey, et al. Grove looked angrily across the dugout at the patriarchal Mack, who was sitting there with his customary high, starched collar despite the 95-degree heat. "Oh, go take a shit," gritted Grove out of the side of his mouth. No one *ever* spoke that way to "Mr. Mack" (as his players called him). A visibly angered Mack put his scorecard down deliberately and walked stiff-legged the length of the dugout to where Grove sat. Moving in front of the surprised Lefty, Mack stood motionless for a moment, then delivered a curt, "*You* go take a shit, Robert." Then, while the entire team fought back giggles, the dignified Mack returned to his seat, picked up his scorecard, and focused on the game.

Eddie Sawyer was the perfect manager for the pennant-winning 1950 Philadelphia Phillies "Whiz Kids," a group of youngsters more in need of friendly encouragement and understanding than of a domineering boss. The unassuming, fatherly Sawyer made it a point to involve himself in the personal problems of his players. He played his father-confessor role to the hilt during one season when nine of his players were expectant fathers.

The low-key Sawyer had an unusual approach in getting his players to observe regular hours. Since Harry Wright's day, managers have applied an evening curfew—that is, they have required players to be in their rooms by a specified evening hour. Sawyer, in effect, applied a reverse curfew. There was no check-in time at night, but he would rout his players out unexpectedly for early-morning workouts. He deliberately refrained from telling his players when to go to sleep, feeling that they would get to bed at reasonable hours in order to make it through the strenuous early-morning exertions, whenever they occurred.

John McGraw's old Baltimore Orioles teammate, Wilbert Robinson, had a much more relaxed approach to managing

than the intense McGraw. One day while managing Brooklyn, "Uncle Robby" flashed the bunt sign to slugging future Hall of Fame outfielder Zack Wheat. But Wheat missed the sign and clubbed the next pitch out of the park, putting Brooklyn ahead. As Wheat trotted around past Robinson, who was coaching at third base, the jovial Robinson shouted out gleefully, "Way to go, Zack." Robby was not about to pull a McGraw and bawl out an erring player who was in the process of winning the game for his club.

His players loved Robinson for his down-to-earth approach to baseball and his reluctance to exaggerate his own considerable store of baseball knowledge. Hall of Fame pitcher Burleigh Grimes claimed that Robby was the man who made him a successful pitcher. Nobody had been interested in Grimes after two miserable seasons with Pittsburgh. Robinson, a recognized expert on pitching, picked up Grimes, and the tough spitballer surprised everyone with a 19–9 season. When Robby was asked what he had done, he responded, "Hell, all I did was just give him the ball." As Grimes described it, "Some managers would have filled a billboard telling all they had done for me, but not Robby. He told the truth; he just gave me the ball."

Again unlike McGraw, the lovable if not overly educated, Robinson was relaxed even when it came to making out his lineups. He had difficulty remembering names and, if he could remember them, he often was handcuffed by their proper spelling. One day he told rarely used outfielder Oscar Roettger that he was to play first base. But when it came to writing out the lineup card, the thought of dealing with a name like Roettger was too much for Robby. "Never mind," he said weakly, "[Babe] Herman will play first."

Walter Alston, a strong, silent man, had a simple philosophy of managing. "Be your own self. To me that's probably the most important part of it, more so than the strategy part. If you know yourself, you'll know your players—how to handle them, . . . which ones to pat on the back, which ones to give a kick in the ass now and then . . . the winning of the ballgame and the good of the team come first." With that simple credo, Alston lasted through twenty-three seasons as the Dodgers' manager, the classic "faceless" manager whose records did the talking for him.

Then there's the "I'm just one of the boys" managing school. This includes managers who wear their authority lightly, often treating their players as equals. Some who come readily to mind are Pie Traynor, Rabbit Maranville, Charlie Grimm, Mel Ott, Yogi Berra, Billy Herman, and Harvey Kuenn. Unfortunately, with some exceptions, this group tends to be comprised of "nice guys" who have been known to finish last.

By his own admission, Billy Herman was not a good manager in his rookie season as field boss of the Pittsburgh Pirates in 1946. As Herman put it, "I could run the game as well as anybody. But I was terrible with the men. I was too easy with them, letting them have too much latitude . . . I wanted to treat my men the way I'd always wanted to be treated, and it didn't work . . . For years you were friendly with everybody and one of the boys . . . I was determined not to change, and that's where I was wrong." The Pirates finished in a tie for last place and Herman was fired.

Mel Ott, who managed the New York Giants with indifferent success in the 1940s, was the subject of Leo Durocher's tough-guy contribution to the American idiom: "Nice guys finish last." Similar to that of Herman, Ott's appointment as

the Giants' manager was accompanied by admonitions to the little southern gentleman that he prevent his players from taking advantage of him. In response, Ott acted out of character during his first few years as manager. Self-conscious of his reputation for being easygoing, he overcompensated, notably in 1945 when he fined pitcher Bill Voiselle $500 for grooving an 0-and-2 pitch that resulted in a game-losing hit.

But Ott relaxed after that and became one of the boys. Giants' catcher Walker Cooper pulled a practical joke on Ott which showed how relaxed Master Melvin's relationship with his players had become. Time and again, with Ott deep in thought on the bench, Cooper slipped a lighted cigarette in the boss's hip pocket, seconds before Ott would reach into his pocket to draw out his lineup card. One day Ott pulled out his hip pockets for protection, but Cooper was ahead of him, having snipped off the pocket linings. When Ott stuck the batting-order cards in his pocket, they dropped down farther into his pants. For some time later, Giants players imitated an embarrassed Ott standing at the plate before 40,000 at the Polo Grounds, trying to fish down the inside of his uniform pants for the lineup cards.

Yet there have been pleasant, relaxed "one of the boys" managers who have done well. Laid-back Harvey Kuenn was the perfect leader for the pennant-winning Milwaukee Brewers in 1982, and relaxed Joe Altobelli replaced overwrought Earl Weaver in 1983 and led the Baltimore Orioles to the World Championship. Charlie Grimm was one of the most successful of the easygoing managers. "Jolly Cholly" replaced the forbidding Rogers Hornsby as manager of the Chicago Cubs in midseason of 1932 and managed the Cubs to the pennant. Grimm permitted his players to do things their own way, with no rules or curfews. He ran the club on the field, but he was a happy-go-lucky man off the field, singing and dancing in the clubhouse and playing his banjo after the games.

And then there was vest-pocket-sized Walter "Rabbit" Maranville, renowned for his basket catch and his world-class carousing. Informed of his appointment to manage the Cubs in midseason of 1925 while on a train with his teammates, the well-oiled Rabbit celebrated by waking up all hands and shouting at the top of his lungs, "There will be no sleeping on this train under Maranville management." Not surprisingly, the Maranville regime ended only fifty-three games after it started, with the Cubs resolutely on their way to a last-place finish.

Pitcher-author Jim Brosnan has identified another category of managers—those whose central goal is to weld their players into tightly knit communities. Adherents of this managerial style tend to insist on conformity to team standards and to unload nonconformists and troublemakers. Of the great managers, Brosnan lumps Joe McCarthy, Casey Stengel, and Al Lopez in this category. Bill Terry and Whitey Herzog, among others, can also be included in this group.

Joe McCarthy's skills as a builder of unified teams, well developed during his pre–New York Yankees managerial years, were honed to perfection during the 1931–1934 seasons, when he had to deal with a fractious, aging Babe Ruth. The Bambino made no bones about his goal: he wanted to replace McCarthy without even managing in the minor leagues (Ruth had turned down Colonel Jake Ruppert's offer of the managership of the Yankees' crack farm team at Triple-A Newark). McCarthy managed to keep his club in the running, and the team from splitting into pro- and anti-

Ruth factions, until the disillusioned Babe left the Bronx Bombers after the 1934 season.

McCarthy, a quiet but strict disciplinarian, attained tight control over his players by requiring model behavior both on and off the field. He traded two established regulars, right-hander Johnny Allen and outfielder Ben Chapman, whose hot tempers did not fit the classic Yankee mold. McCarthy's demands that his players dress formally led baseball men to anticipate a confrontation between McCarthy and Ted Williams when Marse Joe took over as Boston Red Sox manager in 1948. Williams was the embodiment of the nonconformist, as witness his refusal to wear a necktie. The first morning of spring training, Williams appeared at breakfast with an open-neck sport shirt. Said the surprisingly flexible Marse Joe, "Any manager who can't get along with a .400 hitter is out of his mind."

Bill Terry's New York Giants of the 1930s built their success on close teamwork and a tight defense, as Terry scratched for runs in the best early-1900s style. He frequently had Mel Ott, the club's only authentic home run threat, bunt runners along as early as the first inning of a game. Ken Smith, formerly the director of the Baseball Hall of Fame and before that a sportswriter for the (New York) *Daily Mirror,* told a story which illustrated Memphis Bill's emphasis on defense. The Giants took a tough 2–1 loss one day, and Smith and Terry were discussing it after the game. The amiable Smith, trying to comfort Terry, said, "Just another timely hit, Bill, and you'd have won it." Terry responded soberly, "Kenny, they shouldn't have scored two runs."

Terry was on good terms with the veteran Smith, but he had little use for most of the other writers, whom he referred to scornfully as "a bunch of twenty-five-dollar-a-week clerks." Terry refused to talk with them on his own time, and he discouraged his players from talking to writers, probably feeling that these contacts could well break down the tight unity among the Giant players. So there was a continuing feud between Terry and the writers. The (New York) *World-Telegram*'s Tom Meany, a sharp man with a one-liner, crossed verbal swords constantly with Terry. An example of the sarcastic dialogue: After learning that Terry, a shrewd business-man, had begun breeding cattle on his farm, Meany cracked, "I'll bet Terry is breeding white-faced cattle—that way he can count them at night!"

Whitey Herzog resembles Terry in mental toughness, the *esprit de corps* he engenders in his players, and in his reliance on defensive strength to keep his team competitive. Herzog's executive capacity and competence are also reminiscent of Terry in that both men served simultaneously and successfully as general manager and field manager. But they differ in two other respects: unlike Memphis Bill, Whitey talks to the media willingly; and there's the matter of playing ability—Herzog hit .293 in his best season with a journeyman .257 career average, while Hall of Famer Terry's best was .401 in 1930 en route to a resplendent .341 career average.

Managing a ballclub is a crazy business, mainly because the human element is so unpredictable. Many years ago, when Casey Stengel was managing in the minors, he walked into a hotel lobby with a writer and saw his star pitcher sprawled out fast asleep on a divan, mouth open and a silly, moronic look on his face. "This is what drives managers nuts," Casey growled. "As a manager, you work hard, analyze the game, study your players, learn the weaknesses of every team in the league, and think and sweat all day long. And once

every four or five days you have to trust your job and reputation to a lunkhead like that."

The Coaches

The first major league coaches were managers and players assigned to direct traffic on the base paths and to pass along signs, not the nonplaying, full-time coaches as we know them today. Another of the primary functions of the pre-1910 coaches was to distract the opposing pitcher. This was frequently accomplished by running up and down the baselines to divert his attention, a practice which was curtailed in 1887 with the establishment of coaching boxes in foul territory off first and third bases.

Many of the early-day coaches were especially adept at heckling pitchers to reduce their effectiveness. Often this was a matter of screaming obscenities or insults at the pitcher. Hall of Fame outfielder Mike "King" Kelly, coaching at third base for the Boston Beaneaters in the late 1880s, threw in a new variation. With Boston and Pittsburgh tied in the ninth inning and two Beaneaters on base, Kelly called authoritatively to the rookie Pittsburgh pitcher, "Let's see the ball, son." The young pitcher obliged guilelessly, tossing the ball to Kelly. Mike stepped aside to let the ball bounce past him, and the game-winning run scored.

Arlie Latham was the first full-time coach. John McGraw hired Latham in 1909, presumably without any illusions that Latham would be a character builder. Latham was a favorite of the more hardboiled fans, recognized as a relentless heckler who could stir opponents' ire; not for nothing was he known as "The Freshest Man Alive." A former infielder, he had been a troublemaker to his managers during his seventeen-year major league career. Moreover, Latham's private life was a disaster. His first wife had attempted suicide, and his second wife divorced him, charging "perversion, assault, desertion, and infidelity."

The employment of the mercurial Latham as a coach notwithstanding, coaching was becoming a more serious, reputable aspect of the game by the early 1900s. The Giants' great pitcher Christy Mathewson wrote in 1912 in his *Pitching in a Pinch:*

With the development of baseball, coaching has advanced until it is now an exact science. For many years the two men who stood at first and third bases were stationed there merely to bullyrag and abuse the pitchers, often using language that was a disgrace to a ballfield. When they were not busy with this part of their art, they handed helpful hints to the runners as to where the ball was . . . while the pitcher pretended to prepare to deliver it. But as rules were made which strictly forbade the use of indecent language to a pitcher, and as the old school of clowns passed, coaching developed into a science, and the sentries stationed at first and third bases found themselves occupying important jobs.

In 1911 McGraw hired the majors' second full-time coach, Wilbert Robinson. Uncle Robby was the first pitching coach, a man who aided the entire Giant pitching staff, but most particularly lefthander Rube Marquard, whom Robinson converted from a "$11,000 lemon" to a Hall of Fame pitcher. The rotund, jovial Robinson remained with the Giants until 1913, when he left the club after a quarrel with McGraw.

Nick Altrock, hired by the Washington Senators' Clark Griffith, was the best-known coach over the next twenty years. A former major league pitcher, Altrock was a competent coach, but his forte was his talent as a clown. He was a master mimic, imitating the mannerisms of players and umpires, throwing and catching baseballs in impossible positions, and acting out elaborate shadow-boxing routines. In his later years he teamed with Al Schacht, the "Clown Prince of Baseball," to entertain at a number of World Series. Altrock coached for the Senators for forty years.

Altrock was the only full-time nonplaying major league coach from 1914 until 1920, when the Giants hired former second baseman Johnny Evers and the Phillies picked up former lefthander Jesse Tannehill. By the end of the decade, most major league clubs employed at least one nonplaying coach. Just before World War Two, each major league club employed at least one full-time coach, and there were a total of forty major league coaches, an average of 2.5 per team.

The number of coaches increased after World War Two as major league baseball became more complex and increasing attendance and broadcasting revenues made it more economically feasible to hire bigger staffs. Teams routinely began to employ at least three coaches, two to coach the bases and one to oversee the bullpen. In addition, from the 1960s to the present, almost all teams have had a full-time pitching coach. Many clubs have employed batting coaches, rotating them from the parent club to the organization's farm teams.

The third base coach is the quarterback of the team. He relays signs from the manager, and he directs offensive strategy on the field. "Coaching at third base," Al Simmons, the Hall of Famer who was one of the top third base coaches, once remarked, "is the toughest job on the club. The coach on third gets all the blame when things go wrong, and he gets none of the credit when things go right. Yet a good coach can win a dozen or more games a season. A bad coach can lose that many—except, he doesn't last that long."

Two celebrated incidents involving third base coaches illustrate Simmons's point. First there was Enos "Country" Slaughter's famous World Series-winning score from first base in the 1946 fall classic. Slaughter tallied on a routine hit to left center, which was generously scored as a double. Enos, breaking into full stride even before the ball was hit, rounded second and headed for third. Standing in the coaching box, in full view of the charging Slaughter, stood Mike Gonzales. Mike raised both arms in the classic "stop" gesture, all the time screaming, *No! No! No!*" But Enos ignored Gonzales. He rounded third and slid home with the winning run in one of the most unforgettable plays of Series history. Technically the play should never have been attempted. Gonzales was right, and Slaughter was wrong—except that the determined Enos made it work.

Then there was the Mike Ferraro incident. Ferraro was the hapless Yankee third base coach who, in Game Two of the 1980 American League Championship Series, waved home a Yankee runner on a two-out hit. The runner was thrown out, and the Yankees lost to Kansas City, 3–2. George Steinbrenner, who had been unhappy with Ferraro's coaching before the incident, precipitated an ugly public argument with the late Dick Howser, the Yankees' manager. At Steinbrenner's insistence, Ferraro coached at first base in 1981, constantly bedeviled by taunts from the stands to "Send him home, Mike" when a batter approached first base on a weak hit to the outfield.

The first base coach has less burdensome duties. A runner traveling from second to third cannot see what's happening behind him and has to use the third base traffic cop as his eyes. But the hitter running toward first base has the field spread out in front of him. The responsibility of going for the extra base is his, not the coach's.

The first base coach is responsible for helping the runner avoid a pickoff play and, elementary as it may seem, being sure that the runner touches first base en route to an extra-base hit. When Bobby Thomson hit his pennant-winning home run in the 1951 playoff, the other Giants' players tumbled out of their dugout and danced joyously to home plate to mob Thomson. Even manager Leo Durocher, coaching at third base, went crazy. But first base coach Freddie Fitzsimmons maintained his cool, shouting to the deliriously happy Thomson, "Don't forget to touch all the bases." Fitz watched intently as Thomson touched first and second; then the coach raced for home plate to join the celebration.

The bullpen coach gets the relief pitchers ready to enter the game and sometimes recommends their selection to the manager. Ten minutes before Thomson's historic home run, Dodger manager Charlie Dressen phoned bullpen coach Clyde Sukeforth. "Who's got the best stuff out there, Sukey?" asked Dressen. "[Ralph] Branca," replied Sukeforth. "[Carl] Erskine's bouncing 'em in the dirt." So Dressen brought in Branca, and Thomson ended the game dramatically. When Dressen attempted to place the blame for the defeat on Sukeforth, the angry Sukey understandably quit. It was the manager's decision, not the coach's, and there was no way that Dressen could escape that basic truth.

There have been many well-publicized pitching coaches. Jim Turner was credited for much of the effectiveness of the Yankee pitching staff during the 1949–1959 period. Johnny Sain has been an independent-minded, exemplary pitching coach for six different teams over the last thirty years. Art Fowler, Billy Martin's ever-present alter ego in several major league jobs, has long been accused of teaching Martin's pitchers to throw the spitball. George Bamberger and Ray Miller were given much of the credit for the Baltimore Orioles' pitching excellence over the 1968–1985 period. And Roger Craig has been a highly respected pitching mentor, largely responsible for widespread use of the devastating split-fingered fastball.

Batting coaches have come into vogue over the last twenty years. Wally Moses, one of the first, was the hitting specialist for the Philadelphia Athletics as early as 1952. The late Charlie Lau and Walter Hriniak, both former catchers, have been the most celebrated batting coaches over the last several years. Lau developed a revolutionary style of hitting which has gained wide use throughout baseball—especially with star pupil George Brett and other players Lau has coached. Interestingly, Lau hit a mere .255 over his eleven-year career, and Hriniak hit .253 (without an extra-base hit) in 47 career games. These are two classic examples of "Do as I say, not as I do."

Over the last forty years, there has been a noticeable improvement in the quality of coaching. There was a time when most coaches were thought to be old pensioners or drinking companions of the manager. Or maybe they were, as Casey Stengel once commented, "relatives of the manager's wife." In contrast, today's coaches are primarily teachers with established expertise in specific areas.

There was one circumstance where coaches had a touch of

managing. After the Chicago Cubs finished seventh (in an eight-team league) in 1960, Cubs owner Philip K. Wrigley pondered how best to utilize his field supervisory team. He hit upon a novel idea. In 1961 he launched a grand experiment, called the "College of Coaches," in which a staff of coaches shared equally in managing, coaching, and player development. Wrigley hired no less than eight coaches to rotate as the supervisory "manager." The result: the player-poor Cubs finished seventh again in 1961 and did not rise above that level during the following four seasons while the unique arrangement remained in place. Needless to say, there has been no interest since in rotating coaches in the manager's job.

Albert "Cozy" Dolan, a New York Giants' coach from 1922 through 1924, represented the coaching profession at its worst and its best. In September 1924, Dolan left organized baseball in disgrace when Commissioner Kenesaw Mountain Landis barred him for life. Dolan reportedly had urged gullible Giants' outfielder Jimmy O'Connell to offer Philadelphia Phillies' shortstop Heinie Sand a bribe not to "bear down too hard" in an important game against the Giants. But a finer Dolan hour came earlier that season during spring training camp in Sarasota, Florida.

As Frank Graham described it in *McGraw of the Giants:*

This was the spring of 1924 and the Ku Klux Klan wielded a dreaded threat throughout the South. And so, one night, the lights on the main street were extinguished and there was a thin, eerie bugle call in the distance, and hooded Klansmen marched through the town. They marched in silence, and in silence they were watched by the crowd that lined the sidewalks. It was, for a split second, faintly frightening to most of the watchers [including Giant players and accompanying newspapermen]. Then the silence was broken.

"Give me a fungo stick," Cozy Dolan said, very loudly, "and I will lick all the bums by myself."

The ballplayers and the writers howled. The rest of the crowd, taking courage, giggled. The spell was broken. So was the spirit of the marching Klansmen. There was nothing even faintly frightening about them now. They were just a lot of fellows in ridiculous garb tramping along a darkened street.

Perhaps this is the way Cozy Dolan, major league coach, also ought to be remembered.

CHAPTER 18

Umpires

Larry R. Gerlach

Traditionally regarded as villains by fans, adversarial autocrats by players, and invisible men by the press, umpires have been, as Furman Bisher put it, "submerged in the history of baseball like idiot children in a family album." Yet the umpire is baseball's indispensable man, for the arbiter transformed baseball from a recreational activity to a competitive sport and has personified the integrity of the professional game. Since attorney William R. Wheaton officiated the first recorded "modern" game on October 6, 1845, umpires have made important contributions to the National Pastime. Indeed, the history of the umpire mirrors the distinctive eras and developments of the game itself.

From the creation of the modern game in the 1840s through the Civil War, the umpire was the personification of base ball (two words then) as an amateur sport played by gentlemen. According to the September 23, 1845, rules of the Knickerbocker Club of New York, which created modern baseball, the president of the club "shall appoint an Umpire, who shall keep the game in a book provided for that purpose, and note all violations of the Bylaws and Rules." As "match" games between clubs became more frequent, three officials were commonly used—one umpire chosen by each team and a neutral "referee" to decide the often partisan split decisions. In 1858 the National Association of Base Ball Players sanctioned a single umpire, sometimes a spectator or even a player, chosen by the home team with the consent of the rival captain. There was no dress code, but contemporary prints depict the idealized portrait of the gentleman arbiter—a distinguished-looking gentleman resplendent in top hat, Prince Albert coat, and cane, who stood, kneeled, or sat on a stool in foul territory along the first base line. Although the attire became less formal by the Civil War, the volunteer arbiters continued to receive no remuneration for their services other than the "honor" of being chosen "the sole judge of fair and unfair play."

The nationwide popularity of the game after the Civil War led to the professionalization of baseball and, in turn, to professional umpires. In 1871 the newly formed National Association of Professional Base Ball Players continued the tradition of unpaid volunteers by allowing the home team to choose the umpire from a list of five names submitted by the visiting club, but gave the arbiter greater authority by limiting appeals to decisions involving rules interpretation, not judgment. In 1878 the National League of Professional Base Ball Clubs, organized two years earlier, instructed home teams to pay umpires $5 per game, and in 1879 National League president William A. Hulbert appointed baseball's first umpire staff—a group of twenty men from which teams could chose an arbiter. The approved list and compensation

did not free the umpires from the "homer" syndrome (ruling in favor of the home team as a civic gesture) or suspicion of collusion with gamblers. Indeed, in 1882 Richard Higham of Troy, New York, former manager and National League player, was banished from the league for advising gamblers how to bet on games he umpired, thus earning the infamous distinction of being the only umpire ever judged guilty of dishonesty on the field. That same year a new professional circuit, the American Association, pioneered in the creation of an umpiring staff that was hired, paid, and assigned to games by the league itself. Paid $140 a month and $3 per diem for expenses while on the road, American Association umpires were required to wear blue flannel coats and caps while working games. The next year the National League adopted its own permanent paid and uniformed staff, thus completing the professionalization of major league "men in blue."

Despite increased status, umpiring in the major leagues was an uncertain, stressful, and even dangerous occupation through the end of the century. Frequent revisions in the rules and innovations in playing techniques made the umpire's job exceedingly difficult, while the physical and verbal abuse from fans and players alike often made an umpire's life intolerable. Umpires were routinely spiked, kicked, cursed, and spat upon by players, while fans hurled vile epithets and all manner of debris at the arbiters. Mobbings and physical assaults were frequent, so much so that police escorts were familiar and welcome sights to the men in blue. The transformation of the umpire from esteemed arbitrator to despised villain was largely deliberate. As club owners and league officials recognized that umpire baiting boosted gate receipts, they refused to support the umpires's field decisions, dismissed or paid player's fines, did little to curb rowdiness, and even joined sportswriters in depicting umpires as scoundrels and scapegoats. Occasionally umpires retaliated by hurling objects back into the stands or by punching players and reporters—and were summarily punished for so doing. But most found other jobs. In an era when "Kill the umpire!" was not mere rhetoric, there was a high turnover rate in umpires as few men were willing to endure such trials and tribulations for paltry pay and poor working conditions.

Nonetheless, baseball's tumultuous era produced several umpires of historical importance. William B. "Billy" McLean, part-time pugilist from Philadelphia, was the first professional umpire. So great was his ability and reputation for fairness that National League officials in 1876 not only agreed to his demands for the unheard of $5 per game but also sent him on a expense-paid tour of every city in the league. The most famous early exponents of the two basic styles of umpiring were Robert V. Ferguson and John H.

Gaffney. Ferguson, known during his playing days as "Robert the Great" and "Death to Flying Things," ruled as an iron-fisted autocrat, while Gaffney, dubbed "The King of the Umpires," controlled the game through tact and diplomacy. Gaffney also popularized the technique of working behind home plate until a player reached base and then moving behind the pitcher. (Before this the umpire worked either behind the batter or behind the pitcher and did not shift.) In 1888 Gaffney was the highest-paid umpire in baseball, earning $2,500 a year, plus expenses on the road. Other umpires of note include John O. "Honest John" Kelly, who appeared in more World Series (five) than any other umpire of the day; fiesty Timothy Hurst, quick and handy with curses, quips, and fists; Benjamin F. Young, killed in a railroad accident en route to a game, who in 1887 drew up a professional code of ethics for umpires as well as a ten-point proposal to improve their status; John F. Sheridan, the prototype of the modern umpire; and John A. Heydler and Thomas J. Lynch, each of whom later became president of the National League.

With the 1903 peace agreement between the National League and the new American League, major league baseball entered the modern era and brought stature and stability for umpires. Byron Bancroft "Ban" Johnson, president of the upstart American League, led in providing the strong support from league officials that was essential to the morale and effectiveness of the umpires. Noted for his backing of umpires when he had been the head of the Western League, Johnson insisted that umpires be respected and backed up his words by supporting their decisions and suspending players who were guilty of flagrant misconduct. In turn, he insisted upon tactfulness in contrast to the combativeness of the previous era. The National League followed suit, especially under ex-umps Lynch and Heydler, and by World War One, major league umpires enjoyed "unprecedented authority, dignity, and security." As umpire, manager, and baseball executive, Clarence "Pants" Rowland later remarked: "All umpires ought to tip their hats whenever Ban Johnson's name is mentioned."

Johnson also took the lead in dealing with the obvious handicaps presented by the single-umpire system. The game had long since become too fast and the players too devious for a lone arbiter to follow the action, let alone control the contest; moreover, in case of illness or injury clubs had to use a player to officiate the game. A three-umpire system, suggested in 1885 and actually used in the World Series that year, was an aberration, but a two-umpire system was much discussed in the 1880s and 1890s. Although the Players League of 1890 employed two umpires and in 1898 the two-umpire system was sanctioned in the rules, club owners continued to resist the expense of a second arbiter. After Johnson added a fifth umpire in 1906, the use of two arbiters became frequent, common, and then standard—an umpire-in-chief to call balls and strikes and a field umpire to make decisions on the bases. Again, the National League followed apace and in 1912 both leagues had ten-man staffs—two umpires per game and two replacements in reserve.

While front office support and the two-man system contributed greatly to the effectiveness of the umpire on the field, the enhanced stature of umpires was due perhaps as much to the personalities and contributions of the men who served in the first two decades of the twentieth century. That so many of the umpires who loom large in baseball history (and mythology) hail from the early decades of the century is partly the result of the extraordinary skill required to manage the game during the dead-ball era, when the bunt, stolen base, and hit-and-run were primary offensive tactics, and partly because of the media attention lavished on major league baseball at the time.

Ban Johnson, who personally selected his umpires with an exacting eye for ability and character, assembled an imposing staff for the American League. The senior umpire was John F. "Jack" Sheridan, veteran from the nineteenth century, who served as the acknowledged model for the younger men in both leagues and popularized working from a crouch position behind the plate. Another holdover was Franklin O'Loughlin, nicknamed "Silk" as a boy because of his long, curly hair, who successfully matched wits and words with players. College-educated William G. "Billy" Evans, who in 1906 became, at twenty-two, the youngest major league umpire in history, wrote nationally syndicated sports columns while working as an umpire, and went on to be a baseball executive. A fastidious dresser, Evans set the standard for the appearance of umpires on the field. English-born Thomas H. "Tommy" Connolly umpired the American League's first game in 1901 and thirty years later became the Junior Circuit's first umpire-in-chief (1941–54); patient and reserved yet firm, he established the league's tradition of ejecting players only as a last resort and once went ten years without a banishment.

The National League had its own illustrious arbiters. Outstanding were Canadian Bob Emslie, who for years umpired wearing a wig because his frazzled nerves caused premature baldness; hulking Cy Rigler, who while in the minors in 1905 started the tradition of raising his right hand on called strikes; Hank O'Day, stickler for technicalities, whose controversial Merkle decision in 1908 is a staple of baseball lore; and William J. "Lord" Byron, "The Singing Umpire," who periodically announced his decisions in melodious (if not poetical) singsong verse. But it was William G. "Bill" Klem, generally regarded as the greatest umpire in history, who dominated the league staff and set the style for Senior Circuit arbiters. Self-righteous and autocratic, Klem boasted of his scrupulous honesty and encyclopedic knowledge of the rules, intimidated players with threats of fines, and dramatically illustrated his insistence upon discipline and authority during arguments by drawing a mark in the dirt and warning antagonists, "Don't cross the line!" He also popularized the inside chest protector, the over-the-shoulder position for calling balls and strikes, emphatic arm signals for calls, and straddling the lines instead of standing in foul territory. Sharp-tongued and tough-minded, the highly publicized "Old Arbitrator," who for sixteen consecutive years worked every game behind the plate (instead of rotating with the base umpire as had become the norm) and vowed, "I never missed one [call] in my life," was for most of his thirty-six-year career the public's personification of the major league umpire. Upon retiring in 1941, Klem served as the league's first modern chief of umpires until his death in 1951.

Between World Wars One and Two, when baseball dominated the nation's sport consciousness as the National Pastime, umpiring became a career vocation instead of a limited occupational opportunity. Expanded schedules meant seven months of employment, and umpires received better salaries and more recognition. Staff stability became the norm: an umpire who passed muster the first two or three years could look forward to a long career. Umpires continued to be vexed by arguments with players, insults from fans, and occasional

flying objects, but the vicious rowdiness declined. The physical abuse was curtailed significantly because of the stiff penalties imposed for fighting and bottle tossing, while the verbal abuse abated as league officials and the press did an about-face after the infamous Black Sox Scandal by proclaiming the umpire the personification the game's integrity. To underscore their role as independent arbitrators, umpires had to make travel arrangements separate from players and patronize different bars, hotels, and restaurants.

Umpiring had become a desirable and respectable vocation, but the odds against a major league career were far greater for umpires than for players. Competition was keen, as normally only one or two of the some two dozen umpiring positions came open each year. And the low pay, primitive working conditions, wearisome travel, and vicious abuse from players and fans that characterized the life of the minor league umpire drove out those who would or could pursue other employment. Moreover, there was no prescribed system of career development. Becoming a professional umpire was a matter of chance opportunity or personal contacts; there was no systematic evaluation or supervision of minor league arbiters; and advancement, even to the major leagues, was sometimes more a matter of politics and personalities than merit or ability. Nonetheless, those who persevered as "men of the cloth" and proved their mettle in the big time enjoyed a secure and esteemed career. Where Tim Hurst justified working as an umpire by saying, "You can't beat the hours," Bill Klem would declare, "Baseball to me is not a game; it is a religion."

Still, major league umpires received far greater recognition than remuneration. The pay scales for umpires were the same in both leagues. In the early 1900s the annual salary for major league umpires ranged from $1,500 to $2,000; by 1910 the top salary in the National League was $3,000, with only four of the seven umpires earning more than $2,000. Umpires who worked the World Series received $400 until Bill Klem demanded and received $650 in 1917; the next year Klem received $1,000 for the Fall Classic, but the pay for all other umpires remained $650. In 1937 salaries ranged from $4,000 for new umpires to $10,000 for the most veteran arbiters; umpires could expect an extra $2,500 from the World Series. Five years later the pay scale rose to $5,000 and $12,000, but compensation for the Series remained the same. Although the salaries for men at the top of the pay scale seem good for a 154-game, seven-month season, umpires had to pay all their expenses except railroad fares while on the road until 1940, when they received a $750 allowance for travel, a sum that most umpires argued covered only about one-half of their expenses. Moreover, they had to buy and maintain their own clothing and equipment, including ball-strike indicators, masks, and chest protectors. Nonetheless, better pay, working conditions, and status translated into more attractive and thus longer careers; twenty years' service was not uncommon. Consequently, both major leagues established a pension plan for retired umpires, but they were restricted to those who had served more than fifteen years and limited to $100 per year with maximum lifetime benefits of $2,400.

The size of umpiring staffs was also increased. The two-umpire system was the norm during the 1920s, but it became common practice to assign one of the reserve umpires to critical games or series; by 1933 three umpires were assigned routinely to regular-season games. The four-man crew was instituted in 1952. In the World Series the two-man crew, one umpire from each league, was used until 1908, when a pair of two-man teams alternated games. In the third game of the 1909 Series, all four umpires were on the field at the same time, thus establishing the four-umpire tradition that continued through 1946; in 1947 an "alternate" umpire from each league was stationed along a foul line in the outfield, thus creating the current six-umpire crew. Four umpires worked the All-Star Game from 1933 to 1948; the following year it conformed to the World Series format in putting the alternates on the field.

Although major league umpires, save for a few short-lived experiments, wore blue serge suits and officiated according to the same rule book, subtle and not-so-subtle differences in the style and technique of umpiring developed between the two leagues. Inasmuch as league presidents from the beginning hired, assigned, and instructed their umpires, personal preferences were reflected in the umpiring staffs early in the century. Then interleague chauvinism sustained and accentuated the distinctiveness. Under Ban Johnson's leadership, the American League soon boasted an overall staff that was superior to the National League, just as the Junior Circuit had more star players, stronger teams, and more successful managers during the same period. Because Johnson believed that all of his umpires were good enough to work the World Series, the prestigious (and lucrative) assignment was rotated among his staff, whereas postseason honors in the National League went selectively to the best (or most favored) umpires. In return for backing his umpires to the hilt, Johnson demanded reserve and restraint on the field, whereas National League presidents adopted a more laissez-faire attitude toward their umpires.

As a result, arbiters in the Senior Circuit were far more colorful, pugnacious, and individualistic than their American League counterparts, just as National League players and managers were freer and higher spirited than those in the Junior Circuit. It was a volatile mix, and there were many more rhubarbs, fines, and suspensions in the National League, where arbiters had to be courageous in fending off mean-spirited players and managers. And because Johnson liked his umpires to display a strong physical presence, a preference shared by Tommy Connolly, American League umpires were generally "big" men, whereas most National League arbiters, because of the dominant role of the five-foot-seven-inch Bill Klem, were shorter and slight of build.

More important than general differences in style and appearance were the specific differences in technique between the two leagues. At first umpires in both leagues held large inflated chest protectors in front of their bodies when behind the plate. Consequently, they called balls and strikes by crouching directly behind the catcher and looking over his head. The American League continued to use the "balloon" or "mattress" as favored by Tommy Connolly, but it became *de rigueur* in the National League to follow Bill Klem's preference for wearing a more compact chest protector under his coat and calling balls and strikes by viewing the plate from just over the catcher's shoulder nearest the batter. Here, form had great effect: the American League umpires became known for calling more "high" strikes and the National League for calling more "low" strikes.

Not as well known as the flamboyant umpires of the formative years, the men who worked between the World Wars were collectively better umpires and included some of the game's greatest arbiters. Along with Emslie, Klem, O'Day, and Rig-

ler, the National League staff boasted George Barr, Lee Ballanfant, Larry Goetz, George Magerkurth, "Uncle Charley" Moran, Ralph "Babe" Pinelli, Ernie Quigley, and John "Beans" Reardon. Joining Connolly and Bill Dinneen in the American League were such illuminaries as Harry Geisel, Cal Hubbard, George Moriarty, Bill McGowan, Emmett "Red" Ormsby, and Clarence "Brick" Owens. Perhaps the best was McGowan, who for thirty years received universal praise from his peers and ranks as one of the premier umpires in history.

Sociologically, the umpires of the Golden Age represented both change and continuity. Like their predecessors, the majority hailed from the Northeast, the Midwest, and the South; and many were former athletes for whom umpiring was a way of staying in baseball. Some were ex-major leaguers— Charlie Berry, Bill Dinneen, George Hildebrand, Charlie Moran, George Moriarty, Hank O'Day, Al Orth, Babe Pinelli, George Pipgras, and Eddie Rommel. There were, however, important changes. Ethnically, the umpires reflected a pattern of cultural assimilation similar to that evident in the rosters of players. Initially umpires were overwhelmingly English in origin, but then the Irish by the 1890s and Germans by World War One became conspicuous and were followed by Jews in the 1920s and Italians and Slavs in the 1930s. And where collegian Billy Evans was unique among the mostly unlettered arbiters early in the century, college-educated (or graduated) umpires were increasingly common. Essentially, umpires between the wars had become a reasonable cross section of the white working-class American population.

Spurred by war-induced prosperity, continental expansion, and television revenue, baseball led the transformation of professional sport from a commercial business to an entertainment industry. Moreover, baseball, like all organized sport, felt the impact of the social and cultural changes that swept over America. After World War Two umpiring truly became a profession, and by the end of the 1980s major league umpires were not only far better trained and organized than ever before but also a forceful and independent voice in baseball affairs.

Umpiring, like baseball itself, was enormously popular in the days following World War Two. By 1949 some fifty-nine minor leagues provided extensive on-the-job training for an unprecedented number of aspiring arbiters, but it was the umpire training school that was responsible for postwar umpires being so much better prepared than their predecessors. George Barr of the National League opened the first umpire training school in 1935, and in 1939 Bill McGowan of the American League established a second school. In 1946 Bill McKinley, who attended both the Barr and McGowan schools, became the first graduate of a training school to reach the major leagues. By the mid-1950s training school graduates were common, and by the 1960s it was virtually impossible to become a professional umpire without attending one of several training schools.

The umpire schools had profound effects on umpiring. First, graduates of the training schools were more knowledgeable of rules and more skilled in techniques than the earlier "self-taught" umpires. Second, formal training had the predictable effect of imposing uniformity of style and personality, as students were instructed "by the book" and maverick characters were weeded out. Finally—and most significantly—the umpire school was the catalyst that transformed umpiring from vocation to profession.

The professionalization of umpiring had profound effects. Formalized instruction and systematic career development attracted more middle-class college men, as umpiring was increasingly viewed less as a way of staying in professional sport than as a desirable career choice. And, reflecting the demographic shifts that prompted continental expansion, most umpires, like players, now hailed from the Sun Belt or the Pacific Coast. The lone area in which umpires lagged far behind players in mirroring the social changes of society at large was race. It was not until 1966, twenty years after Jackie Robinson broke the color line, that Emmett Ashford joined the American League and became the first black major league umpire. (He was also the first black professional umpire, breaking in with the Southwestern International League in 1951.) In 1973 Art Williams integrated the National League. Despite the strong presence of Latino players since the 1940s, Armando Rodriguez (1974) and Rich Garcia (1975) were the first Hispanic umpires in the majors.

Umpires also adopted a more professional attitude. They candidly admitted errors and portrayed themselves not as omnipotent enforcers of the law who demanded respect but as impartial judges who deserved respect. That umpires were skilled but fallible men became clearly visible in 1956, when Ed Rommel and Frank Umont broke a long-standing taboo by wearing eyeglasses on the field. But the most important effect of growing professionalization was that umpires increasingly viewed themselves as deserving the pay and perquisites of professionals.

In contrast with the strong support from league headquarters for their actions on the field, umpires historically were unable to protect themselves from monetary and personnel injustices because they negotiated individually instead of collectively with the leagues. Umpires repeatedly were dismissed arbitrarily, and in 1953, for the first time in fifteen years, umpires received a modest salary increase—a salary range of $6,000 to $16,000 and an increase in World Series pay to $3,000. Early efforts at organizing were to no avail, and in 1945 Ernie Stewart of the American League was fired for alleged unionizing activity. But in 1963, led by Augie Donatelli, umpires in the Senior Circuit organized the National League Umpires Association, headed by Chicago labor attorney John J. Reynolds. After Reynolds's success in raising salaries, American League umpires became unionists. When Bill Valentine and Al Salerno were dismissed in 1968, allegedly for incompetence but patently for unionizing activities, an appeal to the National Labor Relations Board resulted in umpires in both leagues being organized into the Major League Umpires Association. A one-day strike of the first game of the championship playoffs on October 3, 1970, the first by umpires in major league history, prompted the league presidents to recognize the Association and negotiate a labor contract that set a minimum salary of $11,000 and raised the average salary to $21,000.

Eight years later the Umpires Association made major advances under the new leadership of Richard G. "Richie" Phillips, a Philadelphia lawyer who also represented National Basketball Association referees. A second umpire's strike on August 25, 1978, lasted only one day, owing to a court injunction against the Association, but a third strike from Opening Day to May 18, 1979, won major concessions for the union, including a salary schedule of $22,000 to $55,000, based on years of service; annual no-cut contracts; $77 per diem while traveling; and two weeks' midseason vacation. The aftermath

of the prolonged strike, which demonstrated the power of the Association and the inadequacy of replacement umpires, was marked by ill will between the union umpires and "the Class of '79"—the four "scab" umpires retained on each league's staff. A fourth strike of seven of the eight 1984 playoff games was settled by the intercession of new Commissioner Peter Ueberroth, who granted the umpires a sizable increase for playoff and World Series games as well as providing that the money go into a pool that would be distributed in part to umpires not working postseason contests. A fifth strike was adverted in 1985 when an arbitrator—former President Richard M. Nixon—awarded umpires a 40 percent pay increase for the expanded best-of-seven playoff series. Although most attention has been focused on contract negotiations, umpires have also successfully used the power of the Association to seek from league presidents and the commissioner the impositions of fines and suspensions on players, managers, and even owners for objectionable conduct and comments.

The growth and success of the umpire's union was made possible by two factors. First, with the expansion of franchises from the traditional sixteen (8 in each league) to twenty in 1961-1962, twenty-four in 1969, and twenty-six in 1977, umpires became a numerically significant force. Second—and far more important—was television, which not only brought unprecedented publicity to umpires but also generated the enormous revenue that made it possible for major league baseball to meet the monetary demands of umpires as well as players.

Finances aside, television was a mixed blessing for umpires. If heightened visibility underscored the umpire's skill and central role in the game, it also glaringly exposed errors to millions of viewers. The photographer's camera had occasionally exposed an incorrect call, but television's instant replay both emphasized mistakes and encouraged second-guessing. When slow-motion replays began to be shown on scoreboard screens, one crew in 1975 left the field and refused to return until the practice stopped. Television also affected performance and appearance. It had once been axiomatic for umpires to develop a subdued, even somber appearance, and take pride in anonymity. But in the Age of Television, arbiters began to project themselves into leading roles. From the time televised games became popular in the early 1950s, some umpires played to the camera through flamboyant, demonstrative motions when making calls. While a few like Emmett Ashford and Ron Luciano subsequently developed "showboating" to a fine art, umpires no longer shunned the spotlight of publicity; Luciano even parlayed his popularity for comedic calls on the field into a career in the telecast booth and as a writer.

The physical appearance of umpires was also tailored for the public eye. Increased emphasis was placed on size, as taller and more muscular men were in vogue—perhaps to personify the umpire's authority in an antiauthoritarian age. The American League's adoption of gray slacks in 1968 and maroon blazers in 1971 was part of an effort to project a distinctive "sporty" image, as was the case later when umpires in both leagues began wearing numerals on their sleeves and baseball caps with letters designating league affiliation. Similarly, contact lenses were favored over glasses and in 1988 obese umpires were put on weight-reduction programs.

Aside from the superficialities of cap insignia and jacket color, there was little to distinguish the two umpire staffs in appearance. Training in umpire schools and minor league supervision by the Umpire Development Program had the effect of imposing uniformity of style and technique on umpires and thus on the leagues. Moreover, by the 1970s American League arbiters had adopted the inside chest protector, while the National League mimicked the preference for "big" men. However, a reversal in league images also occurred: just as the players in the Senior Circuit were widely regarded as superior to those in the Junior, National League umpires were similarly perceived as better in the 1960s and 1970s; meanwhile, the American League, with umpires like Ashford and Luciano and fiery managers like Billy Martin and Earl Weaver, became more volatile than the now staid National League.

Despite television exposure, heightened after 1969 by intraleague championship playoffs, umpires as a group were more anonymous than before. Exceptions like Luciano notwithstanding, the individuality of umpires was submerged by the four-member crew, the numerical expansion of staffs, the frequent rotation among cities, the standardization of styles and techniques, the decline in the frequency of rhubarbs, and the attempt to project a more staid professional image. Few umpires stood out as demonstrably superior to their colleagues, partly because systematic training and preparation had increased generally the competence of all arbiters and partly because professional basketball and football now offered competition for outstanding officials. Nonetheless, there were some premier umpires in the postwar era, chief among them Nestor Chylak and John Stevens of the American and Al Barlick and Doug Harvey of the National League.

During the course of a century of major league baseball, the umpire became transformed from a despised, untrained, semiprofessional "necessary evil" to a respected, skilled professional who epitomizes the integrity of the game itself. In the process some arbiters became immortalized in record books for notable achievements and distinctions. J. L. Boake umpired the first professional league game (1871), Billy McLean the first National League game (1876), and Tommy Connolly the first American League game (1901). Hank O'Day and Connolly umpired the first modern World Series (1903), while Bill Dinneen, Bill Klem, Bill McGowan, and Cy Rigler worked the first All-Star Game (1933). Bill Klem holds the record for most seasons in the majors (thirty-seven), most World Series (eighteen) and most World Series games (one hundred-eight). Al Barlick and Bill Summers worked the most All-Star Games (seven). George Hildebrand holds the record for most consecutive games umpired (3,510), while Bill McGowan umpired 2,541 consecutive games (sixteen and a half years) without missing an inning. (Babe Pinelli has claimed that he did not miss a regulation game in his twenty-two-year career.) Emmett Ashford was the first black professional umpire in both the minor (1951) and major leagues (1966), while Armando Rodriguez (1974) was the first Hispanic umpire in the majors. Bernice Gera was the first female professional umpire (1972). Evans was the youngest (twenty-two) and Klem the oldest (sixty-eight) to umpire a major league game. Five umpires are enshrined in the Baseball Hall of Fame: Jocko Conlan (1974), Tommy Connolly (1953), Bill Klem (1953), Billy Evans (1973), and Cal Hubbard (1976).

The Highlights
of the Game

## CHAPTER 19

Streaks and Feats

Jack Kavanagh

The past of baseball is accented by feats of accomplishment. The heroics of individual players or collective efforts of teams are listed in record books as bare statistics. It is the purpose of this section to clothe these with accounts of how such records were made.

These are the achievements of mortals whom we have made into heroes by giving great value to things they have done. Deeds of baseball players are valued more highly than scholarship, skills in creative crafts, or sustaining a precarious balance of world peace. We can name more Cy Young Award winners than we can list those given the Nobel Peace Prize; we can rattle off batting champions but not name holders of the Pulitzer Prize.

It is axiomatic that "all records are made to be broken," yet it is wasteful to throw away old records which have been cherished by generations of fans and only replace them with a newly minted line of agate type. Those who have been on the top of the list, or came close to the peak, have been recognized by relying on lists which sustain enough depth to single out the most noteworthy performances in the many categories which are represented.

As the former mayor of New York City, the dapper, perceptive Jimmy Walker, once admonished Babe Ruth when he had fallen from grace in the eyes of fans, "The cheers of yesterday have a short echo."

The Streaks

Most records are, eventually, displaced by new ones. Some survive because the conditions under which they were made have been altered by changing circumstances in baseball. Some, such as the accumulation of sheer totals, are pushed higher. This is not so much a matter of accomplishment as it is of perseverance and lengthened seasons.

Longest Hitting Streaks

Joe DiMaggio's feat of hitting safely in 56 consecutive games is the type of record which is in jeopardy of being broken when each new baseball season begins. It is in jeopardy because every player has the same chance as DiMaggio to hit safely in every game he plays. Stringing enough of these games together to reach the level DiMaggio did in 1941 tests both a player's skill and his nerve.

The way baseball is played has not altered significantly since 1941. That year DiMaggio batted .357. In 1987 Wade Boggs, a current threat to topple DiMaggio's record, batted .363. He even moved into DiMaggio's class as a home run

hitter, with 24. In 1941 DiMaggio had hit 30. Boggs was also dropped from batting first or second to hitting third. Players with power have a different approach to collecting base hits than did Willie Keeler, whose nineteenth-century record of 44 consecutive games in which he hit safely was broken by Joe DiMaggio. Those with extra-base power are expected to sacrifice the string-extending single for a game-winning home run when the occasion rises. In setting his record, DiMaggio never once bunted for a base hit.

DiMaggio's streak is mind-boggling in its length, yet temptingly attainable by batters capable of hitting for high averages. And any player might get on a hot streak and sustain it long enough to challenge DiMaggio's total. However, those who have set extended streaks did it while accomplishing a high season's average. The trick is to string those games with base hits together. The more games in which a batter has hit safely, the greater the possibility these will come in succession for long stretches.

Until the New York press, wire services, and broadcast industry made Joe DiMaggio's consecutive-game hitting streak a matter of national awareness and interest, this kind of feat was not noted with a daily fanaticism. Streaks drew comment, but this was mostly reserved to be relished during the winter's Hot Stove League sessions among sport-starved fans.

Although Willie Keeler's consecutive-game string became the target for future attempts to exceed it, it might have been only one of the records made under special circumstances. Keeler's 44 consecutive games might only be unusual in retrospect because the string began on Opening Day, 1897. Had Bad Bill Dahlen not had a most peculiar bad day on August 7, 1894, even Joe DiMaggio's 56-game streak would only be a "modern record" set after 1900. As it is, Bill Dahlen appears high on the list with the 42 games in which he hit safely.

DiMaggio was stopped by stellar infield play. Bill Dahlen was stopped by his own inability to fatten his record in a game in which almost everyone else did. Dahlen's team, the Chicago Colts, had 17 hits, winning a ten-inning game from Cincinnati 13–11. Dahlen's blanking was more evident because it was sandwiched between the feats that day of his teammates, Jimmy Ryan and Walter Wilmot. Ryan, the leadoff batter, had five hits, three of them doubles, and Walter Wilmot, who followed Dahlen in the batting order, also had five hits, two of them triples.

Dahlen was at bat a half dozen times, but the Reds' pitchers, Chauncey Fisher and Tom Parrott, found him, uniquely that day, an easy out. Dahlen's feat was obscured. When Willie Keeler, a star of greater national awareness, hit safely in 44 games three years later, the eclipsed record was simply noted but not recounted in the detail which was later paid to the strings which exceeded it. Although appearing in 121

games and batting .362, Dahlen was not a regular shortstop at that time, dividing his games between short and third.

It was Keeler's feat which caught the public fancy, particularly as it began on Opening Day, April 22, 1897, and continued for 44 games into the season. He was eventually stopped on June 18. Until then, it seemed he had found an unending series of opportunities to "hit 'em where they ain't"—his simplistic explanation for his base-hit totals. Keeler's record not only stood the test of time until Joe DiMaggio broke it in 1941, it still stands as the National League record, tied only by Pete Rose in 1978.

It wasn't until 1922 that the feat of hitting successfully in successive games became a real target for seekers of new records. Keeler's streak had been regarded more as evidence of his great ability to rap out base hits than as a model of daily consistency. He was a widely admired player, the leadoff batter for the Baltimore Orioles, three times pennant winners prior to the 1897 season.

When Ty Cobb came along, the fact that he nearly equaled Keeler's mark in 1911, when he set an American League record with 40 successive games in which he got at least one hit, was also taken as a sign of his superiority, not necessarily observed as a model event.

But in 1922 the public and press were ready for new records, and they had popular heroes to set them. In 1922 both George Sisler and Rogers Hornsby created new marks in hitting safely in consecutive games. Sisler broke Cobb's American League record and Hornsby notched 33 games in a row in which he had a base hit. This was hailed as a new record for righthanded batters, at least since 1900. Dahlen's 42 had been made before the turn of the century. While such a demarcation might be a dubious distinction, it serves to create new records. (Eventually those who are insatiable for "new records" will draw a line across some point in the twentieth century and begin proclaiming new records by ignoring those which, like DiMaggio's 56-game streak, seem unbreakable.)

Consider, too, that Ty Cobb, the American League record holder, whose 1911 mark was Sisler's target, was still quite capable of breaking his own record in 1922. Although the hit which raised his final average that year to .401 was argued about, he was still a high-average batter and needed only to string enough games together to set a new mark. Hitting safely in consecutive games was a trademark for Cobb. He hit in 20 or more games in a row seven times during his career.

George Sisler was a very popular player. A college product when the campus was not a direct line to the major leagues, with superlative skills and a gentlemanly manner, he was widely admired. In addition, his team, the St. Louis Browns, was engaged in a hot pennant battle with the New York Yankees.

Sisler began his string on July 27 and continued through August and past Labor Day, getting his base hit in game after game. Then, with his targets in sight—Cobb's American League record and Keeler's major league record, set in the National League—Sisler injured his right shoulder. It was thought at first that not only might he not be able to keep his consecutive string going, but he might not be able to finish the season.

Ironically Sisler found himself at the threshhold of Cobb's record while playing against the Detroit Tigers, managed by Cobb, who patrolled center field. Sisler notched games 37 and 38 when the Tigers came to Sportsman's Park in St. Louis.

On September 11, struggling to keep his streak alive, Sisler tried for game 39, one short of Cobb's record.

Sisler had been granted a streak-extending single by a generous scorer on a fly ball which Bobby Veach had reached but couldn't hold, but in 1922 there were no message boards or public address systems to inform fans of scorer's decisions. So Cobb, playing center field, was too far away from the press box to see the scorer hold up one finger, the traditional sign of a safe hit. He didn't know Veach's muff had been ruled a hit. As far as he knew, Sisler, coming to bat in the bottom of the ninth, with two out, a runner on first, and the score 4–3 in favor of Detroit, was hitless.

Manager Cobb had a choice. He could order Sisler, the Browns' most dangerous hitter, walked. This would move the tying run into scoring position and put the winning run on base. It would have been bad baseball and worse sportsmanship to order an intentional walk. Cobb might have been tempted to deny his rival what he thought was a last chance, but he didn't. He did take the precaution of removing Bob "Fatty" Fothergill, a slow-footed fielder, and replacing him in right with a better defensive player, Ira Flagstead. Then he signaled Howard Ehmke to pitch. He did, and Sisler lined a triple between Cobb and Flagstead. He scored the game-winning run a moment later on a Marty McManus single. Cobb had lost a game he might have won by passing Sisler, and George had moved to within one game of tying Ty's record.

At this point Sisler's shoulder ached so much he couldn't play the next four games, a series against the last-place Boston Red Sox. It was one of those "might have been" situations. He might have set a new American League record then against the Red Sox. However, it was much more dramatically attained when the Yankees, a half game ahead of the Browns in a torrid pennant race's final stages, came to St. Louis for a crucial three-game series.

Sisler played. His shoulder and right arm were bandaged, and he could only swing his bat with one hand. But, he played and, in a 2–1 loss, he managed a lone hit off Bob Shawkey to tie Cobb's record. The next day, September 17, the Browns evened the series as Babe Ruth's nemesis, Hub Pruett, stopped the Yankees. Ruth did get a home run, but more importantly Sisler managed another one-handed base hit to break Cobb's record.

The final game of the series was won by the Yankees as Joe Bush gained his twenty-fifth victory and Sisler went hitless in four plate appearances, never making solid contact. The Yankees left town with an increased lead they nursed to a pennant by a one-game margin. With his team still in contention, Sisler was unable to play. He pinch-hit unsuccessfully the next day, as Walter Johnson defeated the Browns, then sat out games until he returned to action with a hit against the Athletics on September 23. He hit safely the next day, and then, in a peculiarity of the 1922 season, the whole league was idle for four days.

When the league resumed for the final Friday, Saturday, and Sunday, the Browns were unable to catch the Yankees, although George Sisler hit safely in the three final games. Leave out the pinch-hit effort against Walter Johnson, a desperate attempt by a player who, if he had been swinging with two hands, would have played the full game. Without an injured shoulder, Sisler arguably might have kept his string alive against Joe Bush. He might not have missed those four games against the pitching-poor Red Sox or the two final

games against the Senators. He might have hit safely in all of those games as well as the three he added at the season's end. If he had, he would have finished the season, with no more games to play to extend his streak, with 52 games in which he hit consecutively.

The DiMaggio Streak

Joe DiMaggio was playing poorly when his epochal feat began. He wasn't thinking about hitting in 56 straight games; he was worrying about getting a hit in the game of May 15. In spring training DiMaggio hit safely in every exhibition game, a forecast of the record-setting year ahead. His momentum carried through the first eight games of the 1941 season. Then he was thrown into a slump by a junk-ball pitcher, Lester McCrabbe of the Philadelphia Athletics.

By mid-May DiMaggio was still floundering, hitting below .300 and without his usual authority. On May 15 he managed a scratch single. It was an unimpressive handle hit off Cotton Ed Smith of the Chicago White Sox. However, it began a streak that wouldn't end until another pitcher named Smith, Al Smith, paired with Jim Bagby, Jr., held Joe hitless in a game against the Cleveland Indians.

The well-known DiMaggio batting eye that had produced batting championships the two preceding seasons, grew sharper, although in most games he made only a single hit. There were to be 34 games in which the string was kept alive with a lone hit. Not only was this a precarious way to sustain a batting streak, it did not, in its opening stages, draw attention to the feat that was under way. Fans followed Joe's rising batting average but not his successive daily contributions to it. He was thought to be in a contest with Ted Williams, not with the ghosts of record holders whose feats had been both unchallenged and unnoticed since the 1920s. He never caught Williams, who was enjoying the last season a champion would bat over .400.

As DiMaggio's string lengthened, the days of another Yankee immortal, Lou Gehrig, grew fewer. The Iron Horse, who had set another sort of consecutive streak by appearing in 2,130 games, died on June 2, as DiMaggio's skein reached 19.

As the string stretched into the twenties, reporters began digging into record books. The last time this arcane event excited interest had been in 1922, when George Sisler broke Ty Cobb's American League record but was stopped short of Willie Keeler's total. In 1938 another St. Louis Browns first baseman, George McQuinn, had run off a string of 34 games in which he had hit safely. Since McQuinn was playing in the anonymity of the second division, little attention was paid to his challenge.

Because there are two major leagues, record setters have two targets. DiMaggio was required first to set a league mark at 42 and then proceed to reach 45 and set an all-time mark by breaking Keeler's total set in the past century.

By regarding DiMaggio first as a righthanded batter, he could challenge the closer record of Rogers Hornsby, who had hit in 33 straight games in 1922. No mention was made of Bill Dahlen's record of 1894. Perhaps the reporters assumed it had been made under different playing conditions and shouldn't count. They were wrong; the pitching distance had been established at sixty feet, six inches in 1893, and bunts fouled off counted as strikes from 1894. In any case, Dahlen's 42 games was less than Keeler's total, which became the ultimate target.

When DiMaggio passed Roger Hornsby's total, the public's attention was heightened. Sisler's American League record was only a week's play away. The hype went into full swing. Les Brown's orchestra hurried a phonograph record onto the market, "Jolting Joe DiMaggio." As banal a tune as ever came from Tin Pan Alley, the song became a pep rally number as the band chanted, "Joe, Joe, DiMaggio, we want you on our side."

"Bojangles" Bill Robinson, who had tap-danced in movies with little Shirley Temple, did routines atop the Yankee's dugout while he sprinkled what he called "goofer dust" to enhance DiMaggio's luck.

Despite the distractions of people pressing their attention on the reserved, unemotional DiMaggio, he continued his consistent, game-after-game pursuit of the next milestone, Sisler's league record. At the same time, he was carrying the Yankees toward a pennant. They had lost the title in 1940 after four successive world championships under manager Joe McCarthy. They were out to recapture their league's title.

Interest in Joe DiMaggio's quest went beyond the readers of the sports pages. The wire services carried stories assuring newspaper readers that Joe had extended his string before they gave the account of the game in which he did it. Radio newscasts began with bulletins about Joe's progress.

Cynics and debunkers, who concentrated their suspicions on anything coming out of New York, particularly if it gave credit to the Yankees, watched closely for scoring decisions which would give DiMaggio a favored ruling.

Rival managers juggled pitching rotations to bring their best to the mound when DiMaggio and the Yankees came to town.

Dan Daniel, a prolific and conscientious sportswriter and editor, was the official scorer for games at Yankee Stadium in 1941, and he covered the team on the road for his paper. He has written extensively about DiMaggio's 56-game hitting streak. He saw every game.

The scorer's circumstances at Yankee Stadium, as described by Daniel, placed him in view of rabid Yankee supporters who gathered behind him to demand a base hit no matter how glaring the error which allowed DiMaggio to reach base.

Daniel wrote afterward that he had to have his home phone number changed. He also insisted both he and the other scorers around the league became hyperattentive every time DiMaggio came to bat once his string had become established as a potential record breaker.

Daniel also explained that players on the opposing teams were keyed up when DiMaggio batted, none wanting to contribute to extending the string by loafing on a ball and turning it into a hit. DiMaggio's streak lifted the quality of play, umpiring, and press coverage. Everyone, including DiMaggio, wanted him to earn a new record.

Years afterward, DiMaggio looked back on the 56 games and could only find one where he wished the play had not been as judgmental as it was. It came in the thirtieth game, when he was still short of Hornsby's record. The White Sox came to the Stadium, and Johnny Rigney was the pitcher. He had twice been DiMaggio's victim in earlier games in the streak but on this day had stopped the Yankee Clipper until the seventh inning.

Then DiMaggio hit a routine grounder to Luke Appling. The future Hall of Fame shortstop moved for the ball, but it took a bad bounce, hitting him in the shoulder. In his rush to

recover, Appling grabbed at the ball, dropped it, then threw too late. A bad-hop single? Butterfingered retrieval? The official scorer, Dan Daniel, ruled it a hit. Lucky for Joe and fortunate for legend, too, because on his last time up, in the ninth, Taft Wright made a leaping catch to snatch a home run out of the right field stands. Joe would have been blanked.

The next day DiMaggio got another streak-extending break, almost the same way. This time the ball was hard hit and Appling could only knock it down. He couldn't make a throw. Too hard to handle? Scorer Daniel ruled so and the fans relaxed. A few days later Hornsby's record for right-handed batters would be broken and DiMaggio would be headed for Sisler's mark. However, it took another break for DiMaggio to get there.

Eldon Auker, a St. Louis submarine-ball pitcher, held Joe hitless until the eighth inning at Yankee Stadium. Unless one of the first three batters kept the inning alive, Joe, due up fourth, would not bat again. The Yankees were ahead by two runs, and it did not appear as though there would be a bottom of the ninth.

Johnny Sturm popped up, but Red Rolfe drew a walk. Tommy Henrich, the next batter, had a dilemma. He could still deprive Joe of a chance to bat if he hit into a double play. With manager McCarthy's consent, Henrich bunted and moved Rolfe to second base. Now, with first base open, it was Auker who had a dilemma. He could walk DiMaggio, hit him with a pinch (a strategy as underhanded as his delivery), or pitch to him.

DiMaggio stood at the plate, unruffled. Coolly he smashed the first pitch into left field for a double. It was a close call, but now Sisler's record was in reach.

In a Sunday doubleheader with Washington at Yankee Stadium, on June 29, DiMaggio tied Sisler's record in the first game and broke it in the nightcap. The record-tying hit came off knuckleballer Dutch Leonard and was broken with a last-chance single off the unknown Arnold Anderson. DiMaggio was one game short of tying Willie Keeler's 1897 record.

The only mark left for DiMaggio to eclipse was tied in the second game of a July 1 doubleheader with the Boston Red Sox and broken the next day.

The day DiMaggio claimed the American League record was marked by two extremes of luck. It was fortunate his record-tying hit came early in the game because a downpour deluged Yankee Stadium and the game was called after five innings. It was unfortunate that during the rain delay no one kept an eye on the bat rack. A souvenir hunter reached over the dugout and pulled out a bat. He grabbed DiMaggio's favorite club.

Although he was upset, the man who rarely showed emotion quietly borrowed a bat from teammate Tommy Henrich the next day. It was an identical thirty-six-inch, thirty-six-ounce bat, and Joe used it to break Keeler's record. His record-smashing hit was a prodigeous home run off Dick Newsome, a 19-game winner for the Red Sox. It carried high over the head of his rival, Ted Williams, into the left field stands.

Joe DiMaggio did not rest on his laurels. Actually, with the pressure to produce at least one base hit each game lifted, he began pounding out hits in clusters. He passed the 50-game mark and his luck still held. In the fifty-fourth game, he again came up against Johnny Rigney of the White Sox. This time he would have been stopped except for a topped roller. A typical lusty swing sent a dribbler slowly toward third base where Bob Kennedy was playing fearfully deep, a precaution normally taken by rival third baseman against DiMaggio. It worked to Joe's advantage that day as he beat out the slowly hit ball for his only hit. However, it would work to his disadvantage a few days later in Cleveland.

Although Joe DiMaggio said after his streak had ended, "I wish it could have gone on forever," like all good things it had to come to an end. Joe had reached 56 games when the kind of luck which occasionally had sustained him, such as the topped roller against Chicago, turned around. The Yankees came into Cleveland and crowds came, divided between fans' wishes to witness the streak extended and hometeam rooters' hopes that their team could bring the mighty DiMaggio to a halt.

What could only be a matter of time happened. As a minor league star in his native San Francisco, a nineteen-year-old Joe DiMaggio had been stopped after hitting in 61 consecutive games. After the 1941 streak ended, the *San Francisco Chronicle,* which had made daily reports of DiMaggio's record-breaking games, observed that the Pacific Coast League string had been ended by the son of a former major league pitching star, Bob Walsh, whose father, Big Ed Walsh, would be elected to the Hall of Fame. It was pointed out that DiMaggio's major league string was ended, in part, by Jim Bagby, Jr. another son of a successful major leaguer, a 31-game winner for the 1920 world champion Cleveland Indians.

It wasn't so much the pitching of starter Al Smith or reliever Bagby that halted DiMaggio as the glove work on the right side of the Indians' infield. Twice Ken Keltner, playing a very deep third base, took drives down the baseline and turned them into outs. And Joe's last chance found him deserted by luck on a bad bounce. A ball headed up the middle took an erratic hop, and shortstop Lou Boudreau grabbed it and flipped to second to start a double play that closed off DiMaggio's chance to keep safely intact the stretch of games in which he had hit.

Although the DiMaggio streak had been stopped, he was still a hot hitter, and even his favorite bat was back. An embarrassed fan from Newark admitted the theft and returned the bat, and Joe used it to continue his torrid hitting. He kept pounding out hits on a daily basis until he had hit safely in 16 more consecutive games. This meant he would have reached an incredible 73 games had not Keltner and Boudreau pulled off outstanding defensive plays after game 56.

As it is, hitting safely in 72 of 73 games is almost unimaginable. Historians had to go back to the overlooked Bad Bill Dahlen to find a comparable feat for DiMaggio to eclipse almost half a century later. Back in 1894, after he had run up a string of 42 games, Dahlen ran off another stretch of 28 games in which he hit safely. He had left a neglected legacy of hitting in 70 of 71 games for DiMaggio to top with 72 in 73.

During his 56-game streak, Joe DiMaggio batted .408. Although he finished the 1941 season with a .357 average, he was second to Ted Williams's league-leading .406. However, DiMaggio had led his team to a championship and this, with the incredible feat of hitting in 56 straight games, earned him the Most Valuable Player Award by a close margin.

Those whose interest in statistics match, if not exceed, a curiosity about the drama of making them, will want to know that, in hitting .408 during the 56 games, DiMaggio scored 56

Joe DiMaggio's 1941 Hitting Streak

Game No.	Date	Club and Pitcher	AB	R	H
1	5-15	White Sox, Smith	4	0	1
2	5-16	White Sox, Lee	4	2	2
3	5-17	White Sox, Rigney	3	1	1
4	5-18	Browns, Harris, Niggeling	3	3	3
5	5-19	Browns, Galehouse	3	0	1
6	5-20	Browns, Auker	5	1	1
7	5-21	Tigers, Rowe, Benton	5	0	2
8	5-22	Tigers, McKain	4	0	1
9	5-23	Red Sox, Newsome	5	0	1
10	5-24	Red Sox, Johnson	4	2	1
11	5-25	Red Sox, Grove	4	0	1
12	5-27	Senators, Chase, Anderson, Carrasquel	5	3	4
13	5-28	Senators, Hudson	4	1	1
14	5-29	Senators, Sundra	3	1	1
15	5-30	Red Sox, Johnson	2	1	1
16	5-30	Red Sox, Harris	3	0	1
17	6-1	Indians, Milnar	4	1	1
18	6-1	Indians, Harder	4	0	1
19	6-2	Indians, Feller	4	2	2
20	6-3	Tigers, Trout	4	1	1
21	6-5	Tigers, Newhouser	5	1	1
22	6-7	Browns, Muncrief, Allen, Caster	5	2	3
23	6-8	Browns, Auker	4	3	2
24	6-8	Browns, Caster, Kramer	4	1	2
25	6-10	White Sox, Rigney	5	1	1
26	6-12	White Sox, Lee	4	1	2
27	6-14	Indians, Feller	2	0	1
28	6-15	Indians, Bagby	3	1	1
29	6-16	Indians, Milnar	5	0	1
30	6-17	White Sox, Rigney	4	1	1
31	6-18	White Sox, Lee	3	0	1
32	6-19	White Sox, Smith, Ross	3	2	3
33	6-20	Tigers, Newsom, McKain	5	3	4
34	6-21	Tigers, Trout	4	0	1
35	6-22	Tigers, Newhouser, Newsom	5	1	2
36	6-24	Browns, Muncrief	4	1	1
37	6-25	Browns, Galehouse	4	1	1
38	6-26	Browns, Auker	4	0	1
39	6-27	Athletics, Dean	3	1	2
40	6-28	Athletics, Babich, Harris	5	1	2
41	6-29	Senators, Leonard	4	1	1
42	6-29	Senators, Anderson	5	1	1
43	7-1	Red Sox, Harris, Ryba	4	0	2
44	7-1	Red Sox, Wilson	3	1	1
45	7-2	Red Sox, Newsome	5	1	1
46	7-5	Athletics, Marchildon	4	2	1
47	7-6	Athletics, Babich, Hadley	5	2	4
48	7-6	Athletics, Knott	4	0	2
49	7-10	Browns, Niggling	2	0	1
50	7-11	Browns, Harris, Kramer	5	1	4
51	7-12	Browns, Auker, Muncrief	5	1	2
52	7-13	White Sox, Lyons, Hallett	4	2	3
53	7-13	White Sox, Lee	4	0	1
54	7-14	White Sox, Rigney	3	0	1
55	7-15	White Sox, Smith	4	1	2
56	7-16	Indians, Milnar, Krakauskas	4	3	3
Totals			223	55	91

runs and batted in 55. He hit 15 home runs, half his season's total, and had 35 extra-base hits among the 91 hits he collected in 223 at-bats. He walked 21 times, was hit by a pitch twice, and struck out only 7 times.

The Yankees went on to defeat the Brooklyn Dodgers in the World Series and, as the Japanese went on to bomb Pearl Harbor and involve the United States in World War Two, Joe was asked to take a $2,500 cut in salary for 1942. He managed to get a $5,000 raise and play the 1942 season before entering military service in possession of a unique feat which still attracts its new challengers.

The Pete Rose Challenge

The year 1978 was a tremendous one for Pete Rose, whose career with the Cincinnati Reds qualified him as a potential challenger for Joe DiMaggio's record of hitting safely in 56 consecutive games. Although he did not hit for the high

averages of the other streakers who had held records—Keeler, Sisler, Hornsby, and DiMaggio—Rose batted leadoff and had amassed 10 seasons with 200 or more hits. Even more, he was the kind of player who would rise to any occasion. He loved a challenge.

Before he got around to taking a swing at DiMaggio's record, Rose had, as his first order of business, the matter of making his 3,000th career base hit. He opened the 1978 season needing 34 hits to reach a plateau only twelve others had gained. On May 5 Rose reached 3,000 with a single off Montreal pitcher Steve Rogers, before a hometown crowd at Riverfront Stadium.

"Charlie Hustle" was having an epoch-making season and, with one landmark reached, he soon found himself en route to another. Consecutive-game hitting streaks begin without signaling their advent. It is only as they grow that they attract attention.

Pete Rose was only batting .267 when he got a pair of hits against the Cubs on June 14. He kept adding hits in the games he played and, eventually, it was decided he had enough in a row to start looking for a record to be broken.

DiMaggio's 56-game streak in 1941 loomed far beyond expectation. However, the record keepers had gerrymandered Willie Keeler, holder of the National League record at 44, out of the books. There was a "modern" mark of 37, set during the wartime year of 1945, by Tommy Holmes of the Boston Braves.

Pete Rose hustled onward and, as luck would have it, came into Shea Stadium for a series with the Mets on the verge of knocking Holmes out of the record book. The patron saint of hype was on the ball, and a now sixty-one-year-old Tommy

Longest Hitting Streaks, NL

Player	Team	Year	G
Willie Keeler	BAL	1897	44
Pete Rose	CIN	1978	44
Bill Dahlen	CHI	1894	42
Tommy Holmes	BOS	1945	37
Billy Hamilton	PHI	1894	36
Fred Clarke	LOU	1895	35
George Davis	NY	1893	33
Rogers Hornsby	STL	1922	32
Ed Delahanty	PHI	1899	31
Willie Davis	LA	1969	31
Rico Carty	ATL	1970	31
Elmer Smith	CIN	1898	30
Stan Musial	STL	1950	30

Longest Hitting Streaks, AL

Player	Team	Year	G
Joe DiMaggio	NY	1941	56
George Sisler	STL	1922	41
Ty Cobb	DET	1911	40
Paul Molitor	MIL	1987	39
Ty Cobb	DET	1917	35
George Sisler	STL	1925	34
John Stone	DET	1930	34
George McQuinn	STL	1938	34
Dom DiMaggio	BOS	1949	34
Heinie Manush	WAS	1933	33
Sam Rice	WAS	1924	31
Ken Landreaux	MIN	1980	31
Tris Speaker	BOS	1912	30
Goose Goslin	DET	1934	30
Ron LeFlore	DET	1976	30
George Brett	KC	1980	30

Pete Rose's 1978 Hitting Streak

Game No.	Date	Club and Pitcher	AB	R	H
1	6-14	Cubs, Roberts	4	1	2
2	6-16	Cardinals, Denny	4	1	2
3	6-17	Cardinals, Yuckovich, Schultz	4	2	2
4	6-18	Cardinals, Martinez	4	1	1
5	6-20	Giants, Montefusco	5	2	2
6	6-21	Giants, Halicki	4	0	1
7	6-22	Giants, Knepper	4	0	1
8	6-23	Dodgers, Hooton	4	0	1
9	6-24	Dodgers, Welch	5	1	4
10	6-25	Dodgers, John	3	1	2
11	6-26	Astros, Lemongello	5	1	1
12	6-27	Astros, Niekro	4	1	1
13	6-28	Astros, Dixon	4	0	1
14	6-29	Astros, Bannister	3	0	1
15	6-30	Dodgers, Rautzhan	4	1	1
16	6-30	Dodgers, Welch, Forster, Hough	5	1	3
17	7-1	Dodgers, Rhoden	5	0	1
18	7-2	Dodgers, Rau	4	1	1
19	7-3	Astros, Bannister, McLaughlin	5	1	3
20	7-4	Astros, Richard	4	1	1
21	7-5	Astros, Niekro	4	0	1
22	7-6	Giants, Blue, Curtis	5	1	3
23	7-7	Giants, Barr	4	0	1
24	7-8	Giants, Montefusco	4	1	1
25	7-9	Giants, Halicki, Knepper	4	1	3
26	7-13	Mets, Koosman, Lockwood	5	0	2
27	7-14	Mets, Zachry	5	0	2
28	7-15	Mets, Swan	2	2	1
29	7-16	Mets, Siebert	5	1	1
30	7-17	Expos, Bahnsen	4	0	1
31	7-18	Expos, Dues	4	0	2
32	7-19	Phillies, Reed	4	1	1
33	7-20	Phillies, Kaat	5	1	1
34	7-21	Expos, Grimsley	3	1	1
35	7-22	Expos, Schatzeder	3	0	1
36	7-23	Expos, Rogers, Knowles	6	0	2
37	7-24	Mets, Zachry, Lockwood	5	2	2
38	7-25	Mets, Swan	4	1	3
39	7-26	Mets, Espinosa	3	0	1
40	7-28	Phillies, Lerch	2	1	1
41	7-28	Phillies, Carlton	4	0	1
42	7-29	Phillies, Lonborg, Kaat	4	1	3
43	7-30	Phillies, Christenson	5	0	2
44	7-31	Braves, Niekro	4	0	1
Totals			182	30	70

Willie Keeler's 1897 Hitting Streak

Game No.	Date	AB	R	H
1	April 22	5	2	2
2	April 23	4	1	2
3	April 24	4	1	2
4	April 26	4	0	1
5	April 27	5	2	2
6	April 28	5	1	3
7	April 29	4	1	2
8	April 20	4	3	3
9	May 3	4	0	1
10	May 4	4	0	2
11	May 5	4	0	1
12	May 6	5	0	3
13	May 7	6	2	1
14	May 8	3	1	1
15	May 10	4	0	1
16	May 11	5	1	2
17	May 12	5	0	3
18	May 14	6	2	2
19	May 15	6	2	2
20	May 16	6	3	3
21	May 17	4	1	2
22	May 18	6	1	1
23	May 19	4	1	1
24	May 20	4	1	3
25	May 21	3	1	2
26	May 22	4	2	2
27	May 25	5	0	1
28	May 26	5	1	2
29	May 27	5	1	3
30	May 29	6	2	2
31	May 30	4	0	1
32	May 31	4	1	1
33	May 31	5	2	1
34	June 2	5	1	4
35	June 5	5	1	1
36	June 7	4	1	1
37	June 9	5	2	2
38	June 10	4	0	2
39	June 11	4	0	2
40	June 12	5	2	2
41	June 14	5	1	2
42	June 15	3	0	1
43	June 16	5	2	1
44	June 18	4	3	3
Totals		201	49	82

Holmes was on hand to root for Rose. He was there in a dual capacity. Tommy Holmes was also the Mets' community relations director.

There was another reward in having Pete Rose break Holmes's record in front of the Mets' fans. In 1973 Pete had been *persona non grata* when he had wrestled on the ground with skinny shortstop Bud Harrelson in a League Championship Game after a takeout slide by Rose at second base. The Mets fans remembered Rose calling them "animals" as they threatened to avenge the honor of the team by challenging the wives and children of the Reds' players in field boxes behind the Cincinnati dugout. However, hype places a statute of limitations on vengeance in New York. Whipped to a frenzy of impartiality by the Mets' announcers and a record-hungry press, people filled Shea Stadium ready to cheer Rose on while trusting he'd not be so unappreciative as to make his record-extending safety a game-winning hit.

On July 24 Pete Rose equaled the record of Tommy Holmes and to chants of "Go, Pete, Go!" broke it the next night against Craig Swan. An appreciative Holmes, pleased to have been a short-term celebrity, came onto the field to shake the hand of the man who had erased him from the record books. Pete now held the "modern" National League record for hitting safely in consecutive games. In fairness, he would now try to reach Willie Keeler's mark of 44, a feat turned before the century began.

Pete continued his quest. He had the skill, the competitive instincts, and the attitude to do it. He was unruffled by press attention, accustomed to it as the consequence of being the game's most colorful player of his time. Would he break DiMaggio's seemingly unreachable mark? If anyone could, Pete Rose could do it. But first he had to lay the ghost of Willie Keeler and his 81-year-old record.

It was a struggle, as the whole streak had been, but Rose reached Keeler's mark on July 31 in Atlanta. His record-equaling hit came off the knuckleball pitching of Phil Niekro, a man whose own feats as a middle-aged ballplayer also merited recognition.

Keeler had been caught. Would he be passed? No. The next night a rookie lefthander, Larry McWilliams, held Pete Rose hitless through most of the game, and reliever Gene Garber provided the final denial. He struck Rose out.

Pete Rose is joined with Willie Keeler, linked now, regardless of the era when the feat was accomplished, as coholders of the National League record for hitting safely in consecutive games.

Consecutive Games Played

On June 1, 1925, no one thought the young substitute taking the field at first base for the New York Yankees was launching

the most extraordinary streak of durability the game would ever see. Lou Gehrig took the place of the team's star first baseman, Wally Pipp, and was off to an uncertain start toward a goal so distant it was unimaginable.

Gehrig had starred for Hartford in the Eastern League after the Yankees signed him off the campus of Columbia University. It was thought he would make the major league grade, but he had not been handed a starting job. Only when Pipp complained of a headache and was given the day off by manager Miller Huggins did Gehrig get a chance to start a game. So uncertain of the rookie's skills was management that two days later Aaron Ward pinch-hit for Gehrig and Pipp finished the game in the field.

Before June ended, Gehrig had been taken out of games three times for pinch hitters, although he continued to start games. On July 5 he wasn't even the starting first baseman. Fred Merkle, who in 1908, as a rookie himself, had failed to run to second on what appeared to be a game-winning single, started the game. Merkle, whose gaffe eventually cost the New York Giants a pennant to the Chicago Cubs, had been forever more labeled "Bonehead" by unforgiving fans. Gehrig was destined for adulation. This day he made a ninth-inning appearance, an unsuspected extension of a fledgling feat.

Of course at the time there was no suspicion that young Lou Gehrig had launched a string of consecutive-game appearances which wouldn't end until fourteen years later. He began it as a young giant in the prime of his life and ended it as a dying man, forced out of the lineup with a rare disease. From start to finish it became a matter of drama as the survival of the string became a compelling goal which Gehrig sustained despite injury, sickness, accident, and managed to avoid ending inadvertently.

Gehrig is remembered, or known to people who never saw him play, as the gentle giant who was portrayed by actor Gary Cooper in the movie The Pride of the Yankees. In reality, particularly in his early years, Gehrig was a hard-nosed, competitive player who would readily leap into argument with umpires and enemy players. He was ejected from a major league game a half dozen times without drawing a suspension which would have ended his string of games.

Durable, yes. Gehrig was well dubbed as "the Iron Horse" for his rawboned toughness. However, he never spared himself. A statistic which astonishes fans is that he stole home 15 times, risking crashing into a plate-blocking catcher. He ran the bases with surprising speed and fearless abandon. Babe Ruth and Lou Gehrig are remembered for the home runs they hit; yet they were also daring base runners.

Once Gehrig's penchant for never missing a game was established, just being in the boxscore was the goal. He could have simultaneously set records for consecutive games played at first base, while extending his string of boxscore appearances. However, while in the sixth year of his developing string, in a late-season game, the Yankees promoted a game in which Babe Ruth would pitch while Lou Gehrig took his place in the outfield. Harry Rice, an outfielder who sometimes spelled Gehrig late in one-sided games, played first base.

Gehrig's 2,130-game skein, stretched over fourteen seasons, was not simply a matter of having him go out to first base day after day. For one thing, there were times when he could hardly play. When the Iron Horse was no longer a frisky colt, he developed lumbago, and it hobbled him from time to time. In midseason of 1934, Lou was seized by an attack and, immobilized, had to be helped off the field.

There was a conscious awareness on the part of the Yankees of the consecutive games Gehrig played, and this was kept alive by the sportswriters who covered the team. Everett Scott had astonished baseball with his consecutive-game appearances at shortstop, ending a string of 1,307 in 1925, the season Gehrig, his rookie roommate, began his string. Scott had started his run of games with the Boston Red Sox, and when he was bought by the Yankees in 1923, he carried on the string without interruption. He slowed down drastically early in 1925 and was first benched, then sold to the Senators. Unlike Scott, Lou Gehrig, the Iron Horse, would never be put out to pasture. However, Scott had left a legend behind, and it served to lead Gehrig toward new standards of durability.

The day after Gehrig had been helped off the field, with his string at 1,426, and Scott's record broken, he made a contrived appearance in the lineup. Hardly able to stand, he was in the lineup of the visiting Yankees in Detroit as the leadoff batter, penciled in to play shortstop. Despite his pain, he lined out a single and, with his appearance established in the boxscore, gave way to pinch runner Red Rolfe, who finished the game at short while Gehrig took his aching back to the hotel. Jack Saltzgaver, a utility infielder who, over the years, replaced Gehrig at first base more often than any other player, filled in at first that day.

Gehrig was back in the regular lineup the next day, collecting four hits, three of them doubles. He was on his way to the only batting title he ever won and the Triple Crown for 1934. But it wasn't a pain-free future ahead for Lou. Lumbago continued to be a problem. He left games early because he was feeling ill, and he had a thumb injury in 1938 which he ignored to keep his string going.

It was during 1938 that the perpetual machine began to show signs of wearing out. For the first time he batted below .300; his stats—a .295 average, 29 home runs, and 107 runs batted in—would have pleased most players. But they were substandard for Lou, and so was his general play. Just age catching up, it was thought, just the way it had slowed Everett Scott in 1925 when Gehrig was starting out.

In spring training the next season, it was evident that something was amiss, but manager Joe McCarthy left it to Gehrig to decide when to call it quits. It was on May 2, 1939, after eight feebly played games had brought his string to 2,130, that Gehrig advised McCarthy to replace him.

The longest streak of its kind, seemingly impossible to ever exceed despite the longer seasons, ended. For fourteen years Gehrig had played despite a broken thumb, a broken toe, back spasms, frequent colds, and recurring attacks of lumbago. He had been forced from the lineup by something no one could foresee and almost no one had ever heard about. When the tests at Mayo Clinic proved that he had amyotrophic lateral sclerosis, it was so singular an affliction that it was renamed Lou Gehrig's Disease. It was incurable then and still is. Gehrig was a doomed man. He knew it, as did his wife, Eleanor. They bravely pretended to each other that Lou would regain his strength.

He continued to carry the lineup card to home plate during the 1939 pennant-winning season, as the team captain, but soon he had to surrender even that role. On July 4, 1939, a Lou Gehrig Day was arranged at Yankee Stadium. The scene was repeated in the Gary Cooper movie and is seen often in filmed highlights of baseball history.

Babe Ruth, who had broken relationships with Gehrig dur-

ing a 1934 postseason tour to the Pacific and Japan, embraced his former teammate, and the occasion came to a climax as Gehrig, a man who knew his life was nearly over, stood at a microphone, surrounded by the Yankees who had been his fellow players. He told a choked-up audience, "Today, I consider myself the luckiest man on the face of the earth." He died on June 2, 1941.

Far in the Distance

Lou Gehrig's legacy of stamina and determination reached such a length that all historians can do about the sturdy players who came after him is measure them for the role of runner-up.

As Gehrig's record was made in the American League, a separate claim can be laid to a National League record. Even so, the next longest string is Everett Scott's 1,307 made in the American League and, for many years, Joe Sewell's 1,103 was third on the list.

While the Gehrig streak was under way, Sewell, a future teammate, piled up most of his seasons of consecutive play with Cleveland during the 1920s. Like Everett Scott, Sewell's daily appearances were to keep his glove available for defense and to make steady contributions at bat. Sewell is best remembered for his avoidance of strikeouts. Twice he fanned only 4 times in a whole season. Once he went 115 games without striking out in 437 times at bat. He set his consecutive-game string with Cleveland, later moving to the Yankees where he played for three years as Lou Gehrig's teammate. He was elected to the Hall of Fame in 1977.

During the 1930s, Gus Suhr, a fine-fielding first baseman for the Pittsburgh Pirates, reached 822 consecutive games played. It was dwarfed, even as he made it, by Gehrig's still intact string, but he far exceeded earlier National League marks.

Gus Suhr's National League record was broken by Stan Musial, who played in 895 straight games, ending in 1957 at age thirty-six. This provided a target for Billy Williams when his career with the Cubs got under way in 1963 and daily appearances were part of his routine. He sailed past Musial to claim the National League record at 1,117. He stopped in 1970, and the occasional rest did him good. He led the National League in batting in 1972 and his career, with Oakland, ended in 1975. He has been elected to the Hall of Fame.

Williams's new National League record provided an attainable goal for the only player since Gehrig to have the remotest expectation of breaking the all-time record. Steve Garvey was not a realistic bet, but he exuded the strength, stamina, and willpower it would take. He just didn't get started soon enough. Gehrig was twenty-two when his streak began; Garvey was twenty-six.

Also, Garvey did not become an everyday regular with the Los Angeles Dodgers until 1975, his sixth season with the team. He had been regarded as erratic at third base but, once moved across the diamond in 1974, he delivered with consistency in the field, at the bat, with power, and refused to budge from the lineup.

He left the Dodgers with his string intact after the 1982 season and took his Iron Man act to San Diego. A hand injury took him out of the lineup on July 29, 1983. He had broken Billy Williams's record the previous year, and all told he played in 1,207 consecutive games.

A special recognition is due to Pete Rose. Had he not paused to catch his breath during the 1978 season, when he was thirty-seven years old, he would be in second place behind Gehrig. In 1978 Rose had more realistic aims than Gehrig's too distant goal. During that season he reached the 3,000-hit mark and set aim on Ty Cobb's all-time total. He also captured the headlines with his assault on Joe DiMaggio's 56-game hitting streak.

The year 1978 was also Rose's last season with the Cincinnati Reds and, in a celebrated case of free agency, he moved to Philadelphia. There he not only resumed his climb toward Cobb's hit totals, but played again on a daily basis. When he sat down for two games in 1978 with the Reds, he snapped a somewhat modest run of 678 games. When he finally left the daily lineup in Philadelphia, in 1983, he had run off an even longer string of 745 games. Add them together and it is 1,423 games, longer than anyone's stretch except Gehrig's but far, far behind it.

Most Consecutive Games Played

2,130	Lou Gehrig
1,307	Everett Scott
1,207	Steve Garvey
1,117	Billy Williams
1,103	Joe Sewell
1,068	Cal Ripken (streak active)
895	Stan Musial
829	Eddie Yost
822	Gus Suhr
798	Nellie Fox

Successive Pitching Victories

The 1912 baseball season produced a bumper crop of pitchers winning successive victories. Rube Marquard of the New York Giants topped everyone by running up a total of 19. This tied the record set by Tim Keefe, also of New York. Keefe had won his games in 1888, when the pitching distance was only fifty feet between pitcher and batter, but he had won them in a row and that is the measurement of this feat. The present distance of sixty feet, six inches (actually, this is only about 55 feet from the pitcher's point of release) was set in 1893, Keefe's last season.

Marquard's mark remains unmatched within the confines of a single season. The record for consecutive wins beginning in the midst of one season and extending into the next season is held by Carl Hubbell, whose 24 consecutive victories, starting in 1936 and continuing into 1937, tops the list.

However, 1912 produced more than just Marquard's record. It also produced a new American League record and an immediate challenger to it. Even while Rube Marquard was engaged in his run in the National League, Walter Johnson, almost concurrently, was setting the American League record at 16. And by the time he was stopped, another streak was under way, this one by Smokey Joe Wood of the Boston Red Sox.

No one could ask for a better matchup in 1912 than the one which brought Walter Johnson, the record holder, to the mound at Fenway Park to face Joe Wood the challenger. Johnson was the premier pitcher in the American League and its strikeout king. Wood had dazzled the baseball world while en route to a 34–5 season, with 10 shutouts. He won three

more games in the 1912 World Series. Then he injured his arm and never returned to his single-season pinnacle.

Walter Johnson, himself a 32-game winner in 1912, had broken the former American League record of 14 straight, set by Jack Chesbro in 1904. By winning his sixteenth straight game on August 23, he had set a new league mark and had his sights on the brand-new record of Rube Marquard. The New York lefthander had won his 19 by July 3. Johnson never caught Marquard.

Johnson was a victim of both bad luck and a scoring rule which today would not have cost him a loss. He lost a game in relief, taking over in the seventh inning of a tie game. There were two runners on base, and before Johnson could get the side out, one of them scored the winning run. Today the loss would be charged to the starting pitcher, Tom Hughes, who had allowed the runner to get on base. At that time the loss went against whoever was pitching when the winning run scored.

Even so, in 1912 the scorer's decision was denounced by the press and sympathetic fans. However, Ban Johnson, not only president of the American League but its iron-fisted founder, decreed the loss be placed against Walter Johnson's record, and there it remains forever. He had been stopped at 16.

When the 1912 penchant for pitchers winning consecutive victories identified the next challenger as Smokey Joe Wood of the pennant-bound Boston Red Sox, Johnson was called upon to stop him personally. The schedule brought the Washington Senators to Fenway Park to play the Red Sox, and the management was well aware they had a great gate attraction. Johnson was asked to pitch a day sooner so he would face Wood. He was glad to do it.

Whatever the capacity of Fenway Park in 1912, it was far exceeded when, on a weekday, over 30,000 baseball fans crowded the park. The crowd overflowed the stands. In fact, the players could not sit in their dugouts. Instead, they sat on chairs arranged in front of the throngs that stood just outside the baselines. Thousands more people stood in the outfield, behind ropes, reducing the area for the great Red Sox outfield to cover. Tris Speaker, Duffy Lewis, and Harry Hooper would not be able to roam back to catch deep fly balls. These would be automatic doubles if they reached the crowd herded behind the ropes.

Walter Johnson held the American League record, a string of 16 straight victories. Joe Wood had drawn nearer to Johnson's mark in his last start, beating New York on September 2 for his thirteenth win without a loss during the streak. Today he was after his fourteenth straight, Chesbro's old mark, and Walter Johnson didn't want him to get it. Unless Johnson himself stopped Wood, his own record, and possibly Marquard's, were in danger.

The game lived up to expectations. It was a pitcher's battle. Great defensive plays snuffed out rallies, and both pitchers stopped scoring threats with clutch strikeouts. A scoreless tie was broken in the sixth inning, when Tris Speaker hit a fly ball that reached the roped-back crowd for a ground-rule double and Duffy Lewis hit an opposite-field double down the right field foul line. It just eluded the grab of Danny Moeller and Speaker scored. And that was it. The game ended 1–0 as Walter Johnson lost another game in which his team failed to get him any runs. He lost 65 games during his career when his team was shut out.

When Wood pitched next, in Chicago, he was not in top form but held a 5–3 lead going into the bottom of the ninth.

When the first two White Sox batters reached base with hits, manager Jake Stahl replaced Wood with reliever Charles "Sea Lion" Hall. A sacrifice fly made the final score 5–4, but Hall retired the White Sox without further damage and Joe Wood was within one game of tying Walter Johnson.

The Red Sox rode on to St. Louis in Pullman cars for a game on September 15, and Joe Wood pitched another strong game, a 2–1 victory in eight innings to tie Johnson's record. Darkness caused the game to be called after Wood himself had scored the go-ahead run in the top of the eighth inning.

It all came to an end on September 20 in Detroit. Wood failed to break Walter Johnson's mark. He went the distance but mostly on the sufferance of manager Jake Stahl. Although two of the Tigers' runs were unearned, the 6–4 final score indicated Joe Wood's fastball lacked its usual smoke that day.

The Marquard Inheritance

When Rube Marquard wrote his way into the record books in 1912, with 19 consecutive victories, he established a benchmark which has been approached but never equaled, or exceeded, since that time. Although Walter Johnson's American League mark, itself never beaten, took on extra importance because of the affection and awe he inspired in baseball fans, Marquard set the standard for all others to challenge.

The Johnson-Wood confrontation excited the imagination, and other challenges have created their own temporary focus, but always there stands the record of Marquard. It is the pinnacle toward which others climb and never reach, on a single-season, starting pitcher basis. It has only been exceeded by joining the end of one season to the start of the next.

Perhaps even more than the way Walter Johnson was revered in the American League, Rube Marquard's teammate, Christy Mathewson, overshadowed everyone. Marquard's record was the sort of achievement Matty should have had. Until 1912 all the heroics on the Giants' staff had been his. Rube's emergence took everyone by surprise; he was still living down the onerous nickname of "The $11,000 Lemon."

Just a kid pitcher, only eighteen, when the Giants bought him from Indianapolis where he had won 28 games in 1908, Marquard had been a disappointment until the 1912 season. Then he began his streak with his first start of the season and, as he added to it, he began to attract favorable attention for the first time. When he won his sixth game, he exceeded any previous high; when he won the tenth game, he had won more than he had in his first two seasons combined.

Rube Marquard had been dubbed "the $11,000 Lemon" because John McGraw, with an eye to publicity value, had paid that much so it would top the $10,000 paid for Mike "King" Kelly when he was sold by Chicago to Boston in the previous century. In 1912, "the Lemon" turned it all around. He started right in on April 11 and didn't lose a game until July 8.

Actually, under the present scoring rules, Marquard's record would total 20 consecutive victories. In a game at the Polo Grounds, McGraw inserted Rube in the eighth inning of a game against the Brooklyn Dodgers which was tied at 3–3. Marquard inherited a bases-loaded situation but stopped Zach Wheat and Jake Daubert, both to become batting champions, and retired George Cutshaw, without a run being scored. The Giants won the game in the bottom of the ninth,

but the rules then gave the victory to the starting pitcher.

The Giants, in 1912, were winning the middle of three successive pennants, and Marquard joined with Christy Mathewson to lead the Giants' staff. He was called "Rube," a nickname often given to lefthanders with a superior fastball. This was a tribute to Rube Waddell and had no bucolic significance: Marquard was no innocent country boy turned loose on Broadway.

Marquard married a vaudeville headliner, Blossom Seeley, who was even more popular than he was. Her life story was later made into a motion picture which ignored Marquard in favor of Blossom's subsequent husband, song-and-dance man Benny Fields.

However, Rube had held up his end of the vaudeville act, serving as a straight man for the comedienne and added female impersonations, in which he sang and danced as well. This too is a performance unlikely to be duplicated by a modern player.

Streakers Blurred by Time

Although it is convenient to separate the "modern era" of baseball from its ancient past at 1900, the better dividing line would be 1893. That year the pitcher was moved back from fifty feet to the still-prevailing sixty feet, six inches. He had been allowed to throw overhand since 1884.

Until the 1890s, teams rarely used more than two principal pitchers. More open dates existed in the schedules, and two strong-armed men could carry the bulk of the work. A third pitcher, or a general substitute, could help out in doubleheaders. However, the regular duo met most occasions and had many more opportunities to reel off long strings of victories.

When Tim Keefe set the mark at 19 straight, he required only seven weeks to do it. Between June 23 and August 10, 1888, he won all his starts, 17 of them complete games. He alternated on the mound with Mickey Welch, himself the owner of an impressive winning streak. In 1885 Smiling Mickey had run off 17 in a row. That had been one less than the record Hoss Radbourn set in 1884. Pitchers in those years were capable of putting together long winning streaks.

Another contemporary, Jim McCormick of Chicago, won 14 in a row in 1885 and 16 straight the next year. When Keefe set his mark in 1888, the public was impressed but not stunned by its magnitude. After all, it only topped the recent mark of Radbourn's by one.

The New York Giants of 1888 were the toast of the town. They were led by Jim Mutrie, who had dubbed them, "my Giants," marveling at the magnitude of the star players. Such stalwarts as Roger Connor, Montgomery Ward, and Buck Ewing—all future Hall of Fame members—were in the lineup. Keefe and Welch, pitching in tandem, were also destined for Cooperstown and immortality. The Giants were easy pennant winners over Cap Anson's Chicago team.

Tim Keefe began his 19-game winning streak on June 23. He had lost his previous start to yet another star pitcher, John Clarkson. Also elected to the Hall of Fame, even before Keefe and Welch, Clarkson had won 13 straight in 1885.

Keefe's first win was a squeaker, 7–6, over Philadelphia. Then he marched along, and when he won his twelfth in a row, his opponent was Clarkson. During the streak Tim Keefe pitched 17 complete games. The two he failed to finish included one in which he was hit on the arm by a line drive

while leading 8–3 in the sixth inning. A replacement with a name more domineering than the record he left behind, Cannonball Eddie Crane, held on for a 9–6 victory credited to Keefe.

The other incomplete game would not have been added to his string by today's scoring rules. On July 16, while leading Chicago 9–0, Keefe was excused for the day after two innings. The practices of the time gave him the win.

Tim Keefe's string came to an end on August 14, when his defense betrayed him and two unearned runs were the difference in a 4–2 loss. Gus Krock, of the Chicago White Stockings, was a lefthanded rookie who soon disappeared from the major leagues, but he had the satisfaction of stopping Keefe at 19.

Considering the winning streaks his contemporaries had run off, it was probably thought that Keefe's record was temporary. Had it not been for the victory gained in that two-inning start, it would have been. He would have been tied with Hoss Radbourn at 18 and eclipsed when Rube Marquard reached 19 in 1912. As it is, more than a century after his feat, Tim Keefe stands beside Marquard with a total no one has surpassed.

American League Record Tied

It wasn't until 1931 that the lesser American League record of 16 consecutive pitching victories was challenged. Lefty Grove came very close to setting a new record in the American League and narrowly missed being the pitcher to break Marquard's mark of 19. Grove had a 31–4 season, figures which could have accommodated both record-breaking streaks.

However, the luck even the best must have to sustain a long streak deserted Grove at the critical point. He was luckless in the game which would have moved him past Walter Johnson and Smokey Joe Wood, coholders of the American League mark.

The 1931 Philadelphia Athletics were awesome. Connie Mack's last championship team won its third pennant in a row. Responding to Depression-related financial pressures, Mack would break up the team, selling off its stars, including Grove, who went to the Red Sox. Future Hall of Famers Jimmie Foxx, Mickey Cochrane, Al Simmons, and Grove himself were at the peak of their careers. The members of the supporting cast—Max Bishop, Jimmie Dykes, Mule Haas, Bing Miller, and others—were all excellent role players. This was a team which did not beat itself.

As the season advanced into August, the Athletics were virtually coasting to a pennant. They would win 107 games and distance the runner-up New York Yankees by 13½ games. Grove, pitching every fourth game and appearing in relief when needed, was on his personal roll. For the first time in many years, it appeared the American League record for consecutive victories could be broken by a pitcher. It was possible to project that Grove might go on and catch Marquard's record. There was enough time left.

Lefty Grove tied the American League record on August 19 and was expected to break it four days later with his seventeenth straight win. The day the record coheld by Walter Johnson and Joe Wood since 1912 was to fall was Sunday, August 23.

The St. Louis Browns, a second-division team and perennial victim, would provide only token opposition, and the

unheralded Dick Coffman would be the sacrificial pitching opponent. Grove pitched with close to his usual brilliance, limiting the Browns to six hits, allowing only one run, and striking out six.

However, Dick Coffman, on that particular day, outpitched Grove and shut out the Athletics with only three hits. Grove's streak came to an end at 16 straight victories. He had only joined Johnson and Wood at the top of the American League's list.

Lefty Grove had never been a gracious, philosophical loser. He refused to accept defeat gracefully. He blamed the loss on the absence of Al Simmons from the lineup. True, Simmons was at home, in Milwaukee, seeing a doctor, and his replacement, Jim Moore, was far from being a sure-handed defensive player. When Moore misjudged a fly ball, which became the game-winning hit, Grove fumed that Simmons would have caught the ball. Further, he complained, Simmons, the league-leading batter, would surely have knocked in a few runs as well as preventing the Browns from scoring a tainted one.

Grove complained every time he was asked about the end of his streak, and the image of Simmons idling away the afternoon, thumbing through *National Geographic*s in a doctor's waiting room, persisted. Actually, Simmons had an infected ankle and had already been out of the lineup for a week.

What made the defeat more bitter in retrospect was that Grove went on to win his next five starts. These victories would have put the record at 21, eclipsing not only the American League record but topping Marquard's all-time total of 19. (Grove won his next two starts, incidentally, with Simmons still missing from the lineup.) He did not lose until the final game of the season, on September 27.

Schoolboy Rowe's Row

It was only a few years later, in 1934, when the next assault was made on the American League record, now held by Lefty Grove as well as by Walter Johnson and Joe Wood. This time it was the colorful Schoolboy Rowe, blessed with a rural candor that the press found refreshing and the public fascinating, who made the run.

Mickey Cochrane, Grove's former battery mate, was a first-term manager, having been sold by the Athletics to Detroit. Still a great player and catcher, Cochrane had his team headed for the pennant and Schoolboy Rowe led the way. Rowe had been a pitcher of promise and Cochrane had brought about its fulfillment. Rowe had made a slow start, splitting his first eight decisions. His inauspicious beginning offered no portent that when, on June 15, he won his fifth victory, it was the start of a record-equaling skein. During the summer months Rowe shared the spotlight with Dizzy Dean of the National League. However, while Dean was garnering the victories which would eventually reach 30 for the season, he did not string them together the way Rowe did.

Rowe won his sixteenth straight game on August 26 but then ran into the barrier which had blocked other American League pitchers at that point. He joined Grove, Johnson, and Wood at the top of the list but also joined them among the frustrated who could not go past that point.

Rowe stumbled from the path toward a new record on August 29, when the Tigers met the now lowly Philadelphia Athletics in a doubleheader. Gone from Connie Mack's A's

were Lefty Grove, Mickey Cochrane, Al Simmons, George Earnshaw, and Rube Walberg. Only Jimmie Foxx remained from the recent championship teams.

It was the second game of an August 29 doubleheader, and Rowe was far off form. He was knocked out in the sixth inning. Unlike the contentious Lefty Grove, Rowe blamed no one but himself, saying without rancor that he'd just had an off-day. He refused the alibi offered by his manager, Mickey Cochrane, who contended that the demands of the press and public on the young pitcher had produced more turmoil than Schoolboy could handle. Rowe scoffed at the idea and went on to finish the season with 24 wins. He didn't face Dizzy Dean in the 1934 World Series, but he split two decisions, as the Cardinals won a seven-game series from Detroit. Another pennant year followed for Detroit, with Rowe winning 19 games. After that a chronic arm problem hindered his career, although he lasted a long while in the major leagues, winning 158 games, with a .610 winning average, over fifteen years.

Carl Hubbell's Fabulous Streak

When one adds the start of one season to the end of the preceding one, one finds a 17 game streak for Cleveland's Johnny Allen in 1936-1937 and another for Baltimore's Dave McNally in 1969-1970. But in this area Carl Hubbell claims all the records.

In the quirky way that records for consecutive victories by pitchers seem to come almost simultaneously, the same two seasons which provided Johnny Allen's 17 straight wins, also produced one of the most fabulous feats of all time. As had been the case with 1912, there was a magic about 1936–1937.

Carl Hubbell, between July 17, 1936 and May 27, 1937, won 24 games in a row. He won his last 16 decisions in 1936 and added 8 more victories before losing a game in 1937.

Carl Hubbell, and the team which would support him in his quest for a record, the New York Giants, were at their best in 1936 and 1937. They were the best in the National League at a time when their crosstown rivals, the Yankees, were dominant in the American League and also in the World Series. They beat the Giants both years despite Hubbell's presence. The Giants won only three World Series games in the two years and Hubbell won two of them.

Carl Hubbell was the ace of the Giants staff and the National League's most valuable player in 1936. He led the league in 1936 with 26 victories, an .813 winning percentage, and a 2.31 ERA. In 1937 he again topped the league in wins with 22 and percentage with .733 and added the strikeout crown with 159, his career high.

It was this kind of consistency that earned Carl Hubbell the nickname, "the Meal Ticket." His manager, Bill Terry, knew Hubbell would pitch in rotation and stop any losing streak before it gained momentum.

The Giants were off to a bad start in 1936, although Hubbell was winning two of every three decisions. The day Hubbell's winning streak began, July 17, the Giants were in fifth place, barely over .500 at 42–41 and 10½ games behind the defending champion Chicago Cubs. Hubbell had lost his last start, a tough two-hit 1–0 game, to the Cubs' Big Bill Lee. Chicago's run was unearned.

Appropriately Hubbell got the Giants back on a winning track by shutting out Pittsburgh, 6–0. The game contained a streak of another kind. In the first inning Joe Moore, Mel Ott, and Hank Leiber hit successive triples. Before the inning

Pitchers with 12 or More Straight Victories in Season

National League (36)

Year	Pitcher	Won
1888	Timothy Keefe, N.Y.	19
1912	Richard Marquard, N.Y.	19
1884	Charles Radbourn, Provi.	18
1885	Michael Welch, N.Y.	17
1890	John Luby, Chi.	17
1959	El Roy Face, Pitts.	17
1886	James McCormick, Chi.	16
1936	Carl Hubbell, N.Y.	16
1947	Ewell Blackwell, Cinn.	16
1962	John Sanford, S.F.	16
1924	Arthur Vance, Brook.	15
1968	Robert Gibson, St. L.	15
1972	Steven Carlton, Phila.	15
1885	James McCormick, Chi.	14
1886	John Flynn, Chi.	14
1904	Joseph McGinnity, N.Y.	14
1909	Edward Reulbach, Chi.	14
1984	Richard Sutcliffe, Chi.	14
1985	Dwight Gooden, N.Y.	14
1880	Lawrence Corcoran, Chi.	13
1884	Charles Buffinton, Bos.	13
1892	Denton Young, Cleve.	13
1896	Frank Dwyer, Cin.	13
1909	Chris. Mathewson, N.Y.	13
1910	Charles Phillippe, Pitts.	13
1927	Burleigh Grimes, N.Y.	13
1956	Brooks Lawrence, Cin.	13
1966	Philip Regan, L.A.	13
1971	Dock Ellis, Pitts.	13
1885	John Clarkson, Chi.	13
1886	Charles Ferguson, Phila.	12
1902	John Chesbro, Pitts.	12
1904	George Wiltse, N.Y.	12
1906	Edward Reulbach, Chi.	12
1914	Richard Rudolph, Bos.	12
1975	Burt Hooton, L.A.	12

American League (37)

Year	Pitcher	Won
1912	Walter Johnson, Wash.	16
1912	Joseph Wood, Bos.	16
1931	Robert Grove, Phila.	16
1934	Lynwood Rowe, Det.	16
1932	Alvin Crowder, Wash.	15
1937	John Allen, Cleve.	15
1969	David McNally, Balt.	15
1974	Gaylord Perry, Cleve.	15
1904	John Chesbro, N.Y.	14
1913	Walter Johnson, Wash.	14
1914	Charles Bender, Phila.	14
1928	Robert Grove, Phila.	14
1961	Edward Ford, N.Y.	14
1980	Steven Stone, Balt.	14
1986	W. Roger Clemens, Bos.	14
1924	Walter Johnson, Wash.	13
1925	Stanley Coveleski, Wash.	13
1930	Wesley Ferrell, Cleve.	13
1940	Louis Newsom, Det.	13
1949	Ellis Kinder, Bos.	13
1971	David McNally, Balt.	13
1973	James Hunter, Oak.	13
1978	Ronald Guidry, N.Y.	13
1983	D. LaMarr Hoyt, Chi.	13
1901	Denton Young, Bos.	12
1910	Russell Ford, N.Y.	12
1914	Hubert Leonard, Bos.	12
1929	Jonathan Zachary, N.Y.	12
1931	George Earnshaw, Phila.	12
1938	John Allen, Cleve.	12
1939	Atley Donald, N.Y.	12
1946	David Ferriss, Bos.	12
1961	Luis Arroyo, N.Y.	12
1963	Edward Ford, N.Y.	12
1968	David McNally, Balt.	12
1971	Patrick Dobson, Balt.	12
1985	Ronald Guidry, N.Y.	12

ended, Eddie Mayo, a utility infielder, added another triple. Not only was Hubbell off on a personal winning streak that wouldn't end until the next year, the Giants had found their own victory pace.

Oddly, considering the magnitude of Hubbell's record, the streak-starting shutout was the last one he pitched in 1936. He had a season-opening shutout the next year. However, low-run games predominated, and he produced an ERA of 1.95 for the run of 24 games.

Carl Hubbell's great rival was Dizzy Dean, and duels between the two were matchups between two titans. Hubbell's lefthanded screwball was matched against the fastball of the colorful "screwball" of the Cardinals. These confrontations were arranged as often as possible for their gate appeal, and Dean tried to head off Hubbell's march toward glory three times during the string.

Twice he failed gloriously and once ingloriously. During the 1936 portion of the skein, Dean lost 2–1 in an extra-inning game and lost another 2–1 game in the regulation nine innings. These were typical Hubbell-Dean matchups, with both pitchers rising to the occasion. Hubbell, over the years, rose higher more often.

Probably in frustration, when the streak reached 22 on May 19, 1937, Dean lost both the game and his temper when umpire George Barr called a balk against Dizzy for the third time. It gave a reprieve to the batter, Dick Bartell, who had flied out. He then hit a line drive which Pepper Martin dropped, and a flurry of runs followed.

Dean's retaliation was to throw beanballs at every Giant batter who dared step to the plate. In this pre-helmet time such tactics were not viewed kindly, and outfielder Jimmy Ripple offered to take Dean on in a one-to-one fistfight. Dean, who spent a career vainly trying to find someone he could lick, accepted the challenge. He was engulfed under Giant bodies, topped by players in Cardinal uniforms, in what turned into one of the best displays of belligerence ever seen on a ballfield. Individual fights ranged all around the diamond. There were no peacemakers among the players. Among the few who chose to be spectators was Carl Hubbell. He had better use for his arm than swinging it at someone. When order was restored, Hubbell finished pitching a one-run, seven-hit game.

Dean protested his subsequent fine and threatened to boycott the upcoming All Star Game. As usual his threat was unfulfilled. It would have been far better for him if he had stayed away. It was in the 1937 All Star Game that Dean was hit on the foot by an Earl Averill line drive. He tried to pitch while favoring a broken toe and ruined a great right arm.

The end of Hubbell's streak came on May 31 at the hands of the team which considered any victory over the Giants as compensation for an otherwise dismal season. The Brooklyn Dodgers invaded the Polo Grounds for a doubleheader which drew the second-largest crowd that had ever crammed into the Giants home field.

The Dodgers had always been a tough team for Hubbell. He had beaten them five times during his 24-game streak, twice in relief, but in the opening game of the doubleheader Brooklyn closed the door on Hubbell's feat.

Carl Hubbell took the long walk from the mound to the clubhouse in center field during the third inning. Five runs had scored. There had been seven hits and three walks. In came Dick Coffman, who had been Lefty Grove's nemesis. It would have been fitting if he had stopped the Dodgers in their tracks and the Giants had rallied to save Hubbell's streak so

he could extend it the next time. Neither happened; Brooklyn scored five more runs, the Giants only tallied three runs for the whole game.

Lost in The Crowd

By winning 24 games in a row over two seasons, Carl Hubbell obscured the feat of Roy Face in 1958 and 1959 when the forkballer won 22 consecutive games, all in relief. That stands as the best achievement for a reliever. Also in 1959, Face equaled Johnny Allen's mark of 17 consecutive wins, doing it all in one season.

Roy Face, only five-eight and weighing just 160 pounds, didn't lose his first decision in 1959 until September 11. He had entered the game in relief and gave up the winning run in the ninth inning of a game at Los Angeles when Charlie Neal hit a single. Until then, it appeared that Roy Face was destined to never lose a game. Even when his forkball wasn't working its usual magic, he won.

A modest man, Face would point to six or seven games when the Pirates' hitters bailed him out. The most extreme of these times came in a June 11 game, when the San Francisco Giants played Pittsburgh. Face came in to protect a 7–5 lead in the eighth inning. The Giants had two men on base and Willie Mays came up as a pinch hitter. He homered and the Giants led, 8–7. In the bottom of the inning, the Pirates erupted with five runs and Face had a win instead of a loss.

During his string, Face won eleven of his games in extra innings.

Consecutive Base Hits

The feat of making a dozen consecutive base hits has been accomplished only twice in all the years major league baseball has been played. The record has rested there for thirty-five years and might never see the time when a batter delivers a "baker's dozen" to provide a new record. The hitter who reaches 13 will cap a slow, gradual climb toward a peak shared by Pinky Higgins and Walt Dropo, both American Leaguers. The National League's record is 10.

The history of consecutive base hits goes back to 1897, when Ed Delahanty, whom you would expect to set such standards, and Jake Gettman, whom you wouldn't, each got ten hits in a row during the season. Delahanty, one of five major-league-playing brothers, batted .377 for Philadelphia in 129 games. Gettman, who only played one season as a regular, got his ten straight while appearing in only 36 games for Washington. He hit .315 overall. The National League record is still 10 consecutive hits, and six others have joined the original pair.

Tris Speaker was the first to top 10, getting 11 straight hits in 1920. Speaker had eclipsed Doc Johnson's American League total of 9, hit in 1919, the same season Brooklyn's Ed Konetchy had joined Delahanty and Gettman with 10.

The next year, when Speaker moved the major league record up a notch, his feat came amid such epoch record-setting as Babe Ruth's 54 home runs. This had broken Ruth's own mark of 29 set the season before. It dwarfed Speaker's rattling of 11 straight hits. In fact, Speaker's own accomplishment, leading the Cleveland Indians to a World Series victory despite the loss of shortstop Ray Chapman to a fatal beaning during the pennant chase, overshadowed his own batting

feats. This included a runner-up .388 to George Sisler's league-leading batting average of .407.

However, Speaker's 11 straight stood the test of time. During the 1920s others made a run at the record but couldn't get beyond 10 straight hits. They included Sisler in 1921 and Harry Heilmann in 1922. Kiki Cuyler in 1925 and Chick Hafey in 1929, all future Hall of Famers, got up to 10 straight in the National League. In 1936 another Hall of Famer to be, Joe Medwick, hit in 10 straight times at bat.

One outsider who edged onto the list with those headed for baseball's Hall of Fame was a reserve catcher, Harry McCurdy. A rookie with the White Sox in 1926, he only played in 33 games, but cracked out 10 straight hits while batting .326. He might have played in more games, but he had a month's vacation in August. He was claimed by the Yankees on waivers, but when New York discovered this included an obligation for the rookie's bonus of $30,000, they refused to complete the deal. The White Sox insisted they were honor-bound. As is usual in baseball, honor lost and McCurdy remained a substitute catcher with Chicago.

Speaker's record finally tumbled in 1938, when Mike "Pinky" Higgins, the Boston Red Sox third baseman, began by going 4 for 4 against the White Sox in Chicago. The next day the team was in Detroit to play a doubleheader with the Tigers. When Higgins went 4 for 4, with a walk, against Roxie Lawson in the first game, and singled his first time up in the second game, Cal Hubbard, umpiring on the bases, observed, "that makes you 5 for 5 for the day."

Higgins told Hubbard he was 9 for 9, counting the previous day in Chicago. It wasn't enough that Higgins put pressure on himself, but after he got his tenth straight hit, the field announcer at Briggs Field, Ty Tyson, made a public-address announcement that Higgins could tie Speaker's record if he got another hit the next time up.

Higgins shook off the hex and got the hit and, with everyone knowing a new record was on the line, ripped a single off Tommy Bridges, the best curveballer in the league, the next time up. It was an unlucky 13, however, as Higgins fanned his last time at bat. The catcher in both games of the doubleheader was Rudy York. It was the year the Tigers tried to find a place for him to play.

Even though he was to be described by Tom Meany as "part Indian, part first baseman," when Hank Greenberg moved to the outfield so York could play where he'd do the least damage, the one season as a catcher had been a disaster. Higgins later confided he had little trouble guessing a fastball was coming as York had become known to avoid complications by refusing to call for curveballs.

In 1952 the slugging first baseman of the Red Sox, Walt Dropo, tied Higgins's record. He had debuted in 1950 with a sensational season, hitting .322, but he never hit above .300 again. Dropo had begun the season with Boston, but in a multiplayer deal in June, he had been traded to Detroit. Going along with Dropo was Johnny Pesky, longtime shortstop for the Red Sox and, in the way of coincidences in record setting, had reached 11 straight hits, one behind Higgins's record, in 1946. Pesky was at shortstop in the games when Dropo tied him first for runner-up, a spot he now shared with Speaker. He watched as Dropo got his twelfth straight.

Like Higgins, Walt Dropo made his run in a doubleheader. He had gone 5 for 5 against the Yankees in a single game on July 14, and the next day, in Griffith Stadium, he had four straight in the first game. All the hits had been singles, but

starting off in the first inning of the nightcap, the powerful Dropo hit a triple with the bases loaded.

In the third inning he had his eleventh straight hit, another single, and Mickey Vernon, the Washington first baseman, told him he could tie the record with a hit the next time at bat. He did with a double. And he had another time at bat coming, in the seventh inning. Despite Dropo's hitting, the Tigers trailed, 7–6. He swung from the heels but only lifted a foul fly which catcher Mickey Grasso caught at the edge of the field boxes. The streak was over. Dropo added a single in the ninth

Most Consecutive Hits

American League

Player	Team	Year	H
Pinky Higgins	Bos.	1938	12
Walt Dropo	Det.	1952	12
Tris Speaker	Cleve.	1920	11
Johnny Pesky	Bos.	1946	11
George Sisler	St.L.	1921	10
Harry Heilmann	Det.	1922	10
Harry McCurdy	Chi.	1926	10
Ken Singleton	Balt.	1981	10
Kirby Puckett	Minn.	1987	10
Doc Johnston	Cleve.	1919	9
Ty Cobb	Det.	1925	9
Sam Rice	Wash.	1925	9
Hal Trosky	Cleve.	1936	9
Ted Williams	Bos.	1939	9
Tony Oliva	Minn.	1967	9
Nap Lajoie	Cleve.	1910	8
George Sisler	St.L.	1922	8
	St.L.	1927	8
Buddy Myer	Wash.	1929	8
Oscar Melillo	St.L.	1931	8
Sammy West	St.L.	1933	8
Hank Bauer	N.Y.	1952	8
Johnny Groth	Det.	1950	8
Don Baylor	Cal.	1978	8
Dan Ford	Cal.	1979	8
Jorge Orta	Cleve.	1980	8

National League

Player	Team	Year	H
Ed Delahanty	Phila.	1897	10
Jake Gettman	Wash.	1897	10
Ed Konetchy	Brook.	1919	10
Kiki Cuyler	Pitts.	1925	10
Chick Hafey	St.L.	1929	10
Joe Medwick	St.L.	1936	10
Buddy Hassett	Bos.	1940	10
Woody Williams	Cin.	1943	10
Joe Kelley	Balt.	1894	9
Rogers Hornsby	St.L.	1924	9
Taylor Douthit	St.L.	1926	9
Babe Herman	Brook.	1926	9
Bill Jurges	N.Y.	1941	9
Terry Moore	St.L.	1947	9
Dave Philley	Phila.	1958	9
	Phila.	1959	9
Felipe Alou	S.F.	1962	9
Willie Stargell	Pitts.	1966	9
Rennie Stennett	Pitts.	1975	9
Ron Cey	L.A.	1977	9
Roger Connor	St.L.	1895	8
Sammy Strang	Chi.	1900	8
Jack Fournier	Brook.	1923	8
Jimmy Johnston	Brook.	1923	8
Glenn Wright	Pitts.	1924	8
Chick Hafey	St.L.	1928	8
Lefty O'Doul	N.Y.	1933	8
Kiki Cuyler	Cin.	1936	8
Augie Galan	Brook.	1944	8
Wayne Terwilliger	Chi.	1949	8
Dick Sisler	Phila.	1950	8
Eddie Waitkus	Phila.	1950	8
Sid Gordon	Bos.	1952	8
Lee Walls	Chi.	1958	8
Curt Flood	St.L.	1964	8
Jerry Grote	N.Y.	1970	8
Billy Williams	Chi.	1972	8
Dave Winfield	S.D.	1979	8

inning but had to settle for a shared record which has stood against more recent assaults.

Ken Singleton of Baltimore got 10 in 1981, and Kirby Puckett of Minnesota reached 10 in 1987. No one in the National League has had 10 straight hits since Woody William did it in 1943, with the World War Two Cincinnati Reds.

Team Winning Streaks

The two longest winning streaks by teams had different outcomes. Twice National League clubs won 21 in a row and the pennant. When the Chicago White Stockings did it, under Cap Anson, in 1880, they were simply running away from the pack. They won the pennant by 15 games.

However, when their descendants, the Chicago Cubs, won 21 in a row in 1935, the drive capped a sensational stretch battle that caught and passed their rivals, the St. Louis Cardinals, within a few days of the season's end.

These two 21-game streaks are not the longest on record. The record of 26 games won in a row by the 1916 New York Giants stands as the most perverse record of achievement in baseball. No other team has won so many games so convincingly to such little purpose. The Giants came in fourth, despite having had another win streak the same season of 17 straight. Even more peculiarly, the 26 games in a row were all played at home. Maybe the Giants could only win at the Polo Grounds? No. The 17 straight were all won on the road.

John McGraw did a remarkable thing in 1916. He rebuilt the team well into the season, after they had won 17 in a row. The season had started dismally, and before they hit their stride, they had lost thirteen of the first fifteen games played. When they ran off a streak of wins, it only made up for seriously lost ground. Then they flattened out again. McGraw acted.

He had a flawed infield. Shortstop Art Fletcher was a gem, but the other positions were played by former stars, Fred Merkle at first and Larry Doyle at second. Bill McKechnie, the third baseman, would someday be a Hall of Famer, but as a manager.

John McGraw had a love-hate relationship with Buck Herzog. He loved him as a player, but hated him as an individual. Herzog had been a rookie with the Giants and was traded away to the Braves, then swapped back again to star on three successive pennant winners, in 1911 through 1913. Then he was exiled again.

McGraw coveted Herzog, an unrepentant infielder who could hit and play any place with superb skill. They met privately, agreed that the money and opportunity involved was more important than any blood feud, and McGraw swapped the immortal Christy Mathewson, whose fadeaway pitch had failed, to Cincinnati, where he would become manager. He sent McKechnie along and a young outfielder of promise but little playing time, Edd Roush. The next year and two years later Roush won the batting championships. McGraw never regretted his move. He had laid the groundwork for the 1917 pennant.

Even though the season was well along, McGraw shipped his former captain, Larry Doyle, to Chicago for Heinie Zimmerman. Doyle, who had shouted in boyish enthusiasm, "It's great to be young and a Giant," was no longer young and no longer a Giant.

Fred Merkle, forgiven the blunder of 1908, when he failed

to touch second as an apparent winning run scored and cost the Giants a pennant, had also grown old in McGraw's service and was shipped out so a rookie, Walter Holke, could finish the season at first base. When Zimmerman arrived, Herzog was shifted to second, and double plays began to be turned, base hits became infield outs, and the pitchers relished their new-found support. The Giants' drive began as late as September 7, when they were in fourth place, ten games out of third. Ferdie Schupp emerged as a star pitcher and won six games in the string. Pol Perritt won the first game of a doubleheader on September 9 and enjoyed it so much he came back and pitched a shutout in the second game. Regulars won, and rookies debuted and won. The Giants won, but they didn't move up.

The Giants ripped off 12 in a row and then paused for a rain-stopped tie game, 1–1, as Burleigh Grimes, who lost 13 in a row that season, managed a tie game for Pittsburgh. The streak resumed the next day and went on and on, although the Giants had been eliminated from catching Brooklyn in first place. It was the Phillies who were breathing on the necks of the Dodgers, with a chance to tie on the last day.

The Giants' streak was stopped in their last home game of the season, when they lost to the Boston Braves. They crossed the bridge to Brooklyn to close out the season on October 2, and McGraw set off wide speculation in the press by leaving the bench during the game and intimating afterward that the Giants had deliberately lost the game to ensure a Dodger pennant. Brooklyn was managed by Wilbert Robinson, once McGraw's closest crony, his coach and developer of pitchers. Some argument, some twist to the volatile McGraw temper had made them enemies. McGraw, who hated to lose, loathed losing to Brooklyn and Uncle Robbie. Maybe that's all there was to it, just another symptom of McGraw being a sore loser. Yet just ahead was the Black Sox scandal, and playing for the Giants were two non-Chicago players who were to be swept out of baseball when Judge Landis purged its suspect characters—Heinie Zimmerman and Bennie Kauff. McGraw's 1916 Giants finished in fourth place—right where they were when they began their 26-game streak!—and 7 games out of first place.

The 1935 Chicago Cubs, whose 21 straight wins carried them to a pennant, were a streaky team that year and the next year, too. In 1935 they faced a task made tougher by the schedule. The St. Louis Cardinals, the Gas House Gang world champions from 1934, not only led by 2½ games, but the indomitable Deans, Dizzy and Paul, headed the staff. Even more comforting for the Cards, the schedule called for the Cubs to play the last five games of the season at Sportsman's Park in St. Louis.

In 1935 the Cubs picked up momentum, and it took them past the Cards in the middle of the streak. They took the lead on September 14 as they won their eleventh game and were three games ahead of the crumbling Cards when they reached St. Louis for the final five games. Lon Warneke beat Paul Dean 1–0 in the opener, and Bill Lee won his twentieth game of the season, beating Dizzy Dean 6–3 to clinch the pennant. It was the first game of a doubleheader, and the Cubs reached 21 straight by taking the nightcap.

They lost the next game, a meaningless one in the pennant race, in extra innings on Joe Medwick's second home run of the game. The Cards won the season's finale, 2–1, but it was the Cubs who went on to the World Series.

The next year was also a season of streaks. Again the Cubs

got in gear with an impressive run of victories, taking 15 straight before midseason was reached. It did not lead to a pennant. Another 15-game winning streak, by the New York Giants, brought the championship to the Polo Grounds.

It was a streak that started late in the season and ran, in part, concurrently with Carl Hubbell's own string of 16 wins. While the Giants were racking up 15 straight, Hubbell appeared in ten consecutive games. He never ran out of steam, only games to win. The season ended with Hubbell experiencing a 16-game streak. He extended it by winning his first 8 decisions the next year to reach 24 straight wins over two seasons.

Other very long winning streaks in the National League that added late-season zest to pennant races were those of the 1924 Dodgers and, of course, the 1951 Giants. It was Dazzy Vance against the world in 1924 when he dominated the league and was the MVP. The Dodgers came up short, unable to catch the leading Giants, who added a fourth straight pennant in 1924, when Brooklyn's 15 straight were not enough.

In 1951 the same traditional rivals reversed roles, but not results. It was the Dodgers who were far in front when the Giants, managed by former Dodger skipper Leo Durocher, began a late-season drive. The Giants had started with the wrong kind of a streak. They lost their first 11 games and spent the season trying to catch the fast-flying Dodgers. They were 13½ games behind when they won the first of 16 straight decisions on August 12 and began to close the gap the Dodgers had opened.

The Giants slowly edged closer and into a tie with a game to play. When both teams won their final games, the Dodgers on Jackie Robinson's extra-inning heroics in Philadelphia, the stage was set for a playoff series. It was won by Bobby Thomson's dramatic home run in the last of the ninth of the third, and decisive, game.

The American League's consecutive winning streaks have been turned in mostly by powerhouse teams headed for easy pennant triumphs. However, the 1906 American League season produced long strings of wins by two teams locked in a hotly contested pennant race. The Chicago White Sox set a record, since tied by the 1947 Yankees and the 1988 Boston Red Sox, of 19 straight wins.

Dubbed "the Hitless Wonders" because of a .230 team batting average, the White Sox engaged in a dramatic scenario with the New York team, then called the Highlanders.

In early August the White Sox were in fourth place. Ahead of them were Philadelphia, New York, and Cleveland. Day after day the White Sox chipped away at the lead held by the teams ahead of them. They eventually passed Philadelphia and Cleveland.

The Highlanders proved the hardest to catch. They had benefited from a winning streak of their own, 15 in a row. However, in the final surge of the pennant race, it was the White Sox who came home in first place. New York became the only team to win 15 in a row and not win a pennant in the American League. In the National League since 1900, three teams have won at least 15 in a row and not won the pennant. The most glaring example, of course, was the 1916 Giants, winners of 26 and 17 straight. The 1936 Cubs won 15 in a row and finished second to the Giants, also winners of 15 straight. The 1907 Giants had the poorest finish. Despite 17 straight wins, they finished fourth, 25½ games out of first place.

In the main, however, if a team wants to ensure winning a

pennant, a good way to do it is rack up 15 or more consecutive victories along the way, preferably in the stretch run.

The Feats

What follows is a celebration of three of baseball's most rare and heroic feats: the triple crowns of batting and pitching, and the triple putout by one player, better known as the unassisted triple play. These feats do not rank with the central records of the game: Henry Aaron's 755 homers, Cy Young's 511 wins, Pete Rose's 4,256 hits, Ty Cobb's lifetime batting average of .367. They are not as distant in memory as a .400 hitter or a 40-game winner. But they are remarkable achievements and—unlike those mentioned above—are not evident from a perusal of the leaders tables found later in this book.

Triple Crown Winners—Batting

Baseball's first Triple Crown winner, Paul Hines, waited ninety years to be enthroned. The crown consists of three jewels: the batting, home run, and runs-batted-in titles must be won in a single season. The RBI count was a late starter among baseball stats and had to be reconstructed for earlier seasons. However, it was not for lack of the RBI distinction that Hines, of the Providence Grays, waited for belated recognition. His feat went unacknowledged until researchers turned up information which made him the true 1878 batting champion.

A special Baseball Records Committee met in 1968 and put a stamp of approval on statistics which had been in dispute or unverified from baseball's past. The new information appeared the next year when Macmillan published the first edition of *The Baseball Encyclopedia*.

Abner Dalrymple had gone to his grave in 1939, the year the Baseball Hall of Fame Museum opened in Cooperstown, New York, with one baseball honor to his name. He had won the National League batting championship in 1878. Paul Hines, who died in 1935, was remembered only as the winner of the 1879 title. New data—coming from the two tie games he played and the one for Dalrymple—have revealed that Hines was a repeat batting champion who won both the 1878 and 1879 championships, and Abner Dalrymple has been demoted into relative obscurity.

Paul Hines, who had previously been credited with making an unassisted triple play, then lost that distinction as historians and researchers perused boxscores, gained two others—and eventually will regain his unassisted triple play, but more on that soon.

With his newly acknowledged batting title, the RBI leadership which resulted from reconstructed stats and the small but clearly superior total of 4 home runs, Paul Hines had attained the first Triple Crown. In addition, when he won the batting title again in 1879, again through later research efforts, he became the first to repeat as hitting leader.

Another nineteenth-century player, Hugh Duffy, had—since 1969, when his RBI data first was published—been considered the first to wear the Triple Crown. In 1894 he had won the three necessary titles but had almost obscured his own feat by batting .438, later corrected upward to .440. This remains the highest batting average of all time and has always interested interviewers more than the Triple Crown.

Duffy's 18 home runs and 145 runs batted in led the league in these departments in 1894, but the idea of linking them as a diadem had not yet been formed. No one knew Paul Hines had done it and few cared that Hugh Duffy had. Although the RBI was known as a baseball stat as early as 1879, it was not commonly used until the 1910s, and not an official measure until 1920.

Hugh Duffy, a twinkle-eyed New Englander, told about his batting record for the fifty subsequent years that he spent in major league baseball, the last several decades as a coach for the Boston Red Sox. When a rookie named Ted Williams arrived in the big leagues in 1939, Hugh Duffy became his first mentor. Duffy proclaimed Williams as the greatest hitter he ever saw and watched while Williams won two Triple Crowns and missed a third by the closest margin possible.

The player who placed the stamp of the superstar most firmly on the concept of the Triple Crown was Nap Lajoie, who was the dominant player in the game when the American League was formed and ushered in twentieth-century baseball. The great Napoleon Lajoie had become the star of the Philadelphia Phillies as the nineteenth century closed. He was the prize recruit for the new league, remaining in Philadelphia where Connie Mack was establishing a new franchise. Lajoie put the team and the American League on the baseball map in 1901, when he provided the league-leading totals in the three prize categories. He batted .426, hit 14 home runs in the dead-ball era of the time, as later research showed, and, batted in 145 runs. It was the greatest season the immortal would ever have. He would win two more batting titles and again lead the league in RBIs. However, home runs were not his specialty.

Still, his Triple Crown brought instant respect to the new league and, together with other stars who had switched leagues, forced acceptance that the American League was a full-fledged major league and would be part of the basis of baseball's structure from then on.

Lajoie was succeeded as the American League's superstar by Ty Cobb, who also laid claim to the Triple Crown in 1909. As with Lajoie, hitting home runs was not Cobb's dominant ability, and despite twelve batting championships and four RBI titles, he wore the Triple Crown but once. He came close two other times, in 1907 and 1911, finishing second in home runs each of those years.

Cobb's great rival was the National League's Honus Wagner, who never wore the Triple Crown, although he too missed it by a close margin. In 1908 he was second in home runs, the most difficult final jewel for the superstars of the dead-ball era to achieve. Wagner's eight batting titles and four RBI championships were never accompanied by a home run leadership.

While the list of those who have won the Triple Crown is short, it is a quality list. All but two of the twentieth-century members have been elected to the Hall of Fame, and one seems likely, at this writing, to achieve this honor: Carl Yastrzemski.

In 1912 Heinie Zimmerman, one of the best major league third basemen, put together the greatest season he would ever have. Honus Wagner failed to repeat as batting champion, and his 102 RBI total was one less than Zimmerman's, according to the tabulations of Ernie Lanigan. The 14 home runs Zimmerman hit edged teammate Wildfire Schulte, who had led the league in four-baggers the two previous seasons, by one. Only in batting average, where Zimmerman's .372 far distanced the field, did he have a clear superiority, but a

Triple Crown by any measure is a rare treasure and it was Heinie's without dispute, that is until the researchers of Information Concepts, Inc., the group that compiled *The Baseball Encyclopedia,* downgraded his RBI total to 99. Later, an editor of *The Baseball Encyclopedia* fudged Zim's RBI count back up to 103 to restore his Triple Crown, but we cannot subscribe to such nonsense.

It was 1922 before the Triple Crown would again rest on a player's head, but when it did, it landed on the brow of the royally nicknamed "Rajah" Hornsby and just eluded Babe Ruth, "the Sultan of Swat."

Hornsby strung together six successive batting titles, from 1920 through 1925, and added another in 1928. Although he had home run power to go with his high averages, the title escaped him in 1921, when George Kelly outhomered him by two. It would have been the first Triple Crown for the Rajah and would have given him an eventual three, a total no one has ever achieved.

Babe Ruth, who got two legs up on the Triple Crown seven times without ever winning one, had many home run titles and frequently topped the league in RBIs. However, the competition for batting championships in the 1920s, when Cobb, Sisler, and Heilmann topped .400 and Heilmann alone accounted for four batting titles, was tough. Ruth managed one hitting title but lost the RBI leg that year, 1924, to Goose Goslin. The Babe won many honors, but the Triple Crown was not among them.

In the 1930s a quartet of superstars and future Hall of Fame members competed for the Triple Crown during most of the decade, and each took a single turn wearing it.

The American League had two great first baseman, Jimmie Foxx and Lou Gehrig. Each was a threat to claim the Crown every year, but when Foxx narrowly failed on two occasions, it was not Gehrig who stymied him. In 1932 Jimmie came frustratingly close. He was edged out of the batting title by the clumsy-fielding Dale Alexander in 1932. Called "Moose," Alexander split the season between Detroit and Boston, the first player to win a batting title while appearing with two teams. Alexander barely qualified for the championship, but his .367 topped the .364 by Foxx. The following year, 1933, Foxx won his lone Triple Crown.

Alexander was long gone back to the minor leagues before Jimmie Foxx had his second near-miss of the Triple Crown in 1938. This time it was the home run lead that eluded him. Although Foxx hit 50 home runs in 1938, while winning the batting and RBI honors, Hank Greenberg hit 58 homers to almost equal Babe Ruth's record of 60.

While Gehrig and Foxx were trying on the Triple Crown for size in the American League, two sluggers in the National League were sharing domination of their league. Chuck Klein was the league's outstanding batter during the early 1930s and Joe Medwick took over for the final half of the decade. Both wore the Triple Crown, Klein getting his in 1933 when Jimmie Foxx was doing likewise. It was the only year that each league produced a Triple Crown winner. Medwick won his in 1937.

The next to claim the Triple Crown was Ted Williams. A brash rookie when he reported to the Boston Red Sox in 1939, he had little to learn from the old guy hitting fungos in practice. Hugh Duffy took one look at Williams's swing and knew the only part he could serve was as a role model. Williams had his eye on hitting .400. When he did it, in 1941, his .406 was far short of Duffy's .440, the all-time record.

Williams was also one leg short of the Triple Crown in 1941. He added the home run title to his batting championship, but his main rival, Joe DiMaggio, had topped the RBI column. DiMaggio had piled up his runs-batted-in totals largely during his 56-game hitting streak that season.

Ted Williams won all three titles for the Triple Crown the next season, 1942, and then went off to serve in World War Two. Several wartime players won two legs of the Triple Crown: Rudy York, with the Detroit Tigers in 1943, and Bill Nicholson, a Chicago Cubs outfielder in 1943 and 1944. Both hit home runs and batted in runs at league-leading levels, but they were far outdistanced for the batting-average honors.

Ted Williams returned from the war in 1946 and finished second in each of the Triple Crown categories. Mickey Vernon beat him out for the batting title, and Hank Greenberg, who had blocked Jimmie Foxx in 1938, had his last hurrah with the Tigers, topping Williams in both home runs and runs batted in.

The next year, with Greenberg gone to the National League, Ted Williams claimed his second Triple Crown. No one was close to him in any of the three prize categories, and despite three prime seasons lost to wartime service, the Red Sox star seemed most likely to be the first to wear the Triple Crown three times. He had won in 1942 and 1947.

In 1948 his old nemesis, Joe DiMaggio, who was never to win a Triple Crown, picked off two of the crown jewels, leading the American League in home runs with 39 and in runs batted in with 155. Ted Williams was far ahead of the pack as batting champion with a .369 average.

It was 1949 that proved the greatest disappointment to Williams. DiMaggio was injured much of the season and did not compete for individual honors. However, the pennant race was tightly contested between the Yankees and Red Sox, and more interest was focused on that than on the seemingly assured third Triple Crown to be worn by Ted Williams.

As the season reached the final weekend, Boston came to New York for two games between the Red Sox and Yankees. Boston was a game ahead and needed to win only one to gain the pennant. They lost on Saturday, and the teams were tied when Sunday's game began.

The biggest threat to Ted Williams' third Triple Crown came from teammate Vern Stephens, a slugging shortstop who was tied with Ted for RBIs. Williams held a small but probably secure batting lead over George Kell of the Detroit Tigers.

However, Williams and the Red Sox were in a slump, and it cost both the team and the individual their honors. The final game of the season between the Yankees and Red Sox was one of the most exciting of all time, if you were a Yankee fan. If you were among the generations of faithful Red Sox followers who have seen their team fail in the final situation, one frustrating season after another, it was a bitter end. The Red Sox blew a lead in the bottom of the ninth as the Yankees rose to the heights with a last-ditch rally to win the pennant.

Williams had gone hitless and ended up not only missing a World Series appearance but his third Triple Crown. While Williams had sputtered in the final games, George Kell, who had missed two stretches of games with injuries, got back in the lineup for Detroit's final three games. With only a batting title at stake, Kell had two hits in his final game. When the final statistics were known, George Kell had batted .3429 and Ted Williams .3427. It was the closest any player ever came to a Triple Crown without actually winning it and the closest

anyone has come to earning the honor three times.

The year before, in the National League, Stan Musial had narrowly missed his bid for a Triple Crown, when he was one behind Johnny Mize and Ralph Kiner, who tied for the home run title with 40.

In 1953 Al Rosen had a near-miss almost as tight as Ted Williams had had in 1947. Rosen won the home run and RBI titles but was edged out, .337 to .336, for the batting championship by Mickey Vernon, who had blocked Williams's bid in that category in 1946.

Mickey Mantle hit his peak in 1956 when he put the necessary ingredients together to win a Triple Crown. He hit .353 for the only batting title he would win, had top totals in home runs with 52, and piled up 132 runs batted in.

Ten years later, in 1966, Frank Robinson reacted to being traded out of the National League by winning the Triple Crown in the American League. His .316 batting average was one of only two above .300 that year in the American League. He had switched leagues just in time. A .316 average wouldn't have made the top five in the National League in 1966. He won the home run and RBI titles comfortably.

In 1967, the year of the Red Sox "Impossible Dream," the team was driven to a surprise championship by the captain, Carl Yastrzemski, who had an astounding year. Yaz won the only home run title of his career and also the lone RBI championship he would record. He joined these with one of his three batting crowns and ended the season with what was to become an elusive honor, the Triple Crown.

He is the last player to wear the title, although a number of players have gained two legs, including Yaz's teammate, Jim Rice, who has done this twice. In the American League the inability of power hitters to achieve a high batting average has resulted in a parade of sluggers leading in home runs and runs batted in but falling short in base-hit percentage.

Harmon Killebrew, who tied with Yaz for home runs in Yastrzemski's crown-winning season, Frank Howard, Dick Allen, Reggie Jackson, George Scott, Eddie Murray, Tony Armas, and Jose Canseco have won two legs but failed the batting title.

Since Yaz won the last Triple Crown, two National Leaguers have won batting titles and the RBI championship, but failed in home runs. Joe Torre in 1971 and Al Oliver in 1982 earned two legs one way, and Johnny Bench, Willie Stargell, George Foster, Andre Dawson, and Mike Schmidt have done it with the home run and RBI crowns. Foster did it twice and Schmidt four times.

Combining a high batting average with power is a rare characteristic in contemporary baseball. Players such as Rod Carew and Wade Boggs, who have won frequent batting championships without expectation of adding the other elements of the Triple Crown, serve to reduce the likelihood that a pure power hitter will also annex a batting title, especially in the course of the same season.

Carl Yastrzemski might not be just part of a vanishing breed. He might be the last example of a breed that has already vanished.

Triple Crown Winners—Pitching

Tommy Bond, the only nineteenth-century pitcher on the list of Triple Crown Winners who is not in the Hall of Fame, has, at least, the honor of turning the feat first. When the National

Triple Crown Hitters

American League

Player	Team	Year	HR	RBI	BA
Nap Lajoie	Phila.	1901	14	125	.422
Ty Cobb	Det.	1909	9	115	.377
Jimmie Foxx	Phila.	1933	48	163	.356
Lou Gehrig	N.Y.	1934	49	165	.363
Ted Williams	Bos.	1942	36	137	.356
	Bos.	1947	32	114	.343
Mickey Mantle	N.Y.	1956	52	130	.353
Frank Robinson	Bal.	1966	49	122	.316
Carl Yastrzemski	Bos.	1967	44	121	.326

National League

Player	Team	Year	HR	RBI	BA
Paul Hines	Prov.	1878	4	50	.358
Hugh Duffy	Bos.	1894	18	145	.438
Heinie Zimmerman*	Chi.	1912	14	103	.372
Rogers Hornsby	St.L.	1922	42	152	.401
	St.L.	1925	39	143	.403
Chuck Klein	Phila.	1933	28	120	.368
Joe Medwick	St.L.	1937	31	154	.374

*Zimmerman ranked first in RBIs as calculated by Ernie Lanigan, but only third as calculated by ICI research in 1969.

League was formed in 1876, Bond was an established star in the National Association. The others who eventually won the pitchers' Triple Crown, for the most wins and strikeouts and the lowest ERA in a single season, began their careers in the National League.

Although he was only twenty-one when he won the Triple Crown in 1877, Bond had been pitching for prominent teams since he had been sixteen and joined the Athletics of Brooklyn. He entered the National League with Hartford but moved to Boston for his best seasons. He was Boston's only pitcher during 1877 and 1878 and pitched the great majority of games in 1879. He won 123 of the 204 games Boston played in those early years of short schedules.

Bond, who later coached baseball at Harvard, was celebrated for his victories and strikeouts. The measurement of earned runs was done retroactively.

As Bond's career lapsed, the next to claim the Triple Crown of pitching emerged. Old Hoss Radbourn reached the peak year that gave him his nickname for durability in 1884. He pitched the Providence Grays to the National League pennant, almost singlehandedly, after Charlie Sweeney's departure had left only Radbourn as the team's pitcher.

His 60 victories is the most ever won by a pitcher in a season. It shines brightest among all such jewels in the Triple Crowns worn by those who came after him. Radbourn won 308 games in his big league career, but the 60 he totaled in his 1884 season—including a streak of 26 wins in 27 decisions—gave him a celebrity which was recognized when he was named to the Hall of Fame in its opening year, 1939.

A Triple Crown is an exacting measurement of a pitcher's superiority at any time. However, because of the circumstance that he started so many games for the league's best team, Radbourn's win totals and strikeout numbers can largely be attributed to sheer volume. However, it is his 1.38 ERA at a time when the league mark was 2.98 that stamps Old Hoss as truly remarkable for his time.

Tim Keefe, the next pitcher to annex a Triple Crown, wore his for a season that has kept his name in the active files of modern baseball writers. Whenever a pitcher runs off a string of victories, this prompts a review of the record book, and Keefe's 19 in a row is remembered as the highest total, shared with Rube Marquard's 1912 season total of 19 straight. In all,

Tim Keefe won 35 games for the New York Giants in 1888, just edging out the man who would take the Triple Crown the next year.

John Clarkson pitched Boston to a pennant in 1889, winning the Triple Crown as the workhorse of a staff which included the worn Old Hoss Radbourn. Clarkson won 49 games and Radbourn 20.

Clarkson's career was overlapped by that of Amos Rusie, the most awesome pitcher of the 1890s. A burly farm boy, "the Hoosier Thunderbolt" was the principal reason the distance of the pitcher's box was pushed back in 1893. Rusie responded the following year by continuing to dominate the league in strikeouts, while topping all pitchers with 36 wins and an ERA of 2.78.

Probably because of the increased pitching distance, the league ERA ballooned to 5.32 and batters averaged .309 in 1894. This was the year Hugh Duffy won the batter's Triple Crown and set a still-unexcelled .440 batting record.

Rusie's career peaked in 1894. The next season one of the most oppressive men to own a big league team, Andrew Freedman, bought the Giants and began a blood feud with Rusie. Rusie sat out the 1896 season, but returned as a reluctant star for two more 20-game-winning seasons. Then he tore his arm muscles and retired. A token appearance in 1901 was the tenth season which qualified him for election to the Hall of Fame.

Just as Nap Lajoie marked the American League's inaugural in 1901 by winning a Triple Crown for batters, another established star, Cy Young, did the same for the pitchers' version. Young, in midcareer as a big league pitcher, won 33 games, a total almost dwarfed among the 511 he won in his career. This latter is a mark certain to stand permanently.

With two major leagues now offering the potential of a Triple Crown winner each year, it took only until 1905 to have both the American and National Leagues produce such winners. Christy Mathewson won the first of the two Triple Crowns he would win for the New York Giants, and the eccentric Rube Waddell had his last great year with the Philadelphia Athletics.

Matty won 31 games, struck out 206, and had an ERA of 1.43. The Rube produced 26 wins, 287 strikeouts, and an ERA of 1.48. The World Series, inaugurated in 1903 but boycotted by the Giants in 1904, was resumed in 1905. It would have provided marvelous theater for the two Triple Crown winners. The confrontation would have been the only one of its kind. Never since have two pennant winners also had pitching's Triple Crown winners. Alas, the colorful Rube Waddell injured his arm while wrestling a teammate just before the Series began.

Without Waddell to oppose him, Christy Mathewson won three games, all shutouts, and the Giants took the Series in five. Matty won the Triple Crown again in 1908 but lost his last start when the Chicago Cubs won the playoff game of a season which had ended in a tie. It was the failure of Fred Merkle to reach second as the "winning run" scored, resulting in his becoming an inning-ending force out, that deprived Matty of a second opportunity to wear his Triple Crown into a World Series.

Walter Johnson, the next to sport a Triple Crown, won three at widely spaced intervals in his long career. The first came in 1913, the next in 1918, and the last in 1924 when, in his eighteenth season, Johnson once more topped the American League in the three prize categories. This time it also brought a pennant to the Senators, the first in their history. The World Series came close to being a disappointing anticlimax for Johnson. He lost the opener to the New York Giants in extra innings, then lost again, but salvaged glory by winning the deciding seventh game in relief.

Earlier, during Walter Johnson's widely spaced crown jewels, Grover Alexander produced the most impressive reign ever enjoyed by a Triple Crown winner. Pitching for the Philadelphia Phillies, he had three successive seasons with 30 or more victories, starting with the pennant-winning 1915 season; each time he led the NL in ERA and K's as well. What stopped Alexander's run of mastery was World War One. Old Pete swapped his baseball uniform for the khaki of the Army and his Triple Crown honors for a sergeant's stripes.

While Pete was in the Army, another pitcher claimed the Triple Crown. Hippo Vaughn, who in 1917 had achieved immortality by engaging in a double no-hit game, losing in the tenth inning. In 1918, with Alexander away, Vaughn won the Triple Crown pitching for the Cubs.

Ironically Grover Alexander had served his Army hitch as a new member of the Cubs. With his battery mate, Reindeer Bill Killefer, he had been sold to Chicago after winning his third Triple Crown, in 1917. He pitched only three games in 1918 while Vaughn was in the star's role, and in 1919 the two teammates competed for the Triple Crown. Alexander led the league in ERA and Vaughn in strikeouts. Between them they won 37 games, but neither came close to topping the league.

However, in 1920 Grover Alexander again emerged as the Triple Crown winner. It was his fourth, the most ever won by a pitcher. He continued to star, despite personal and physical problems, during the 1920s without again leading in any of the categories which make up the diadem of the Triple Crown.

Next to wear the Triple Crown of pitchers was Dazzy Vance. Like Rusie, Waddell, and Johnson, Vance began with expectation of finishing each season with a league-leading total in strikeouts. In 1924 he won the Most Valuable Player Award, even though the Brooklyn Dodgers as a team could not win the pennant. To his strikeout superiority, the Dazzler added leadership in wins with 24 and an ERA of 2.16. His domination of the league can best be measured by comparing his ERA to a league total of 3.87 as the lively ball bounded off hitters' bats.

Lefty Grove of the Philadelphia Athletics won back to back Triple Crowns in 1930 and 1931, having missed one of the three legs in 1929. The A's won pennants all three of those years, and Grove was their leading pitcher. In 1929 teammate George Earnshaw topped him in wins, 24 to 20, as Grove missed getting decisions in an unusual number of games.

Another southpaw ace, Lefty Gomez, succeeded Lefty Grove as a Triple Crown winner. Like Grove, he wore the title twice, but not consecutively. He won his first Triple Crown, oddly, in a season when his team, the New York Yankees, didn't win a pennant, 1934. His next came in 1937 as the Yankees were in the midst of a run of four straight pennants.

Gomez was only a spot starter in 1939, when the Yankees met the Reds in the World Series, but Cincinnati had a converted third baseman, Bucky Walters heading their staff, the first National Leaguer to win the Triple Crown in fifteen years.

During World War Two, Hal Newhouser emerged as a superlative pitcher who might have been equally impressive against peacetime competition. He missed the Triple Crown

in 1944, winning two legs but coming in second to Detroit Tiger teammate Dizzy Trout for ERA honors. In 1945, the final wartime year, Newhouser topped the American League in the three prize categories, and winning the Triple Crown went into a long hiatus when the 1946 season resumed with the star pitchers back from service.

Despite leading the league in victories six times and in strikeouts seven, Bob Feller never won an ERA title to match up with the other components of the Triple Crown.

Warren Spahn topped the National League in victories eight times, led in strikeouts four times, and even took ERA honors three times, but he could never link them up in a single season.

Robin Roberts, like Feller, never won an ERA title, so despite leading in victories four times and strikeouts twice, the singular honor of the Triple Crown eluded him, as it did all other pitchers once baseball had returned to the normalcy of peacetime play.

It wasn't until Sandy Koufax reached stardom when the

Triple Crown Pitchers

American League

Player	Team	Year	W	L	SO	ERA
Cy Young	Bos.	1901	33	10	158	1.62
Rube Waddell	Phila.	1905	26	11	287	1.48
Walter Johnson	Wash.	1913	36	7	303	1.09
	Wash.	1918	23	13	162	1.27
	Wash.	1924	23	7	158	2.72
Lefty Grove	Phila.	1930	28	5	209	2.54
	Phila.	1931	31	4	175	2.06
Lefty Gomez	N.Y.	1934	26	5	158	2.33
	N.Y.	1937	21	11	194	2.33
Hal Newhouser	Det.	1945	25	9	212	1.81

National League

Player	Team	Year	W	L	SO	ERA
Tommy Bond	Bos.	1877	40	17	170	2.11
Old Hoss Radbourn	Prov.	1884	60	12	441	1.38
Tim Keefe	N.Y.	1888	35	12	333	1.74
John Clarkson	Bos.	1889	49	19	284	2.73
Amos Rusie	N.Y.	1894	36	13	195	2.78
Christy Mathewson	N.Y.	1905	31	8	206	1.27
	N.Y.	1908	37	11	259	1.43
Grover Alexander	Phila.	1915	31	10	241	1.22
	Phila.	1916	33	12	167	1.55
	Phila.	1917	30	13	201	1.86
Hippo Vaughn	Chi.	1918	22	10	148	1.74
Grover Alexander	Chi.	1920	27	14	173	1.91
Dazzy Vance	Brook.	1924	28	6	262	2.16
Bucky Walters	Cin.	1939	27	11	137	2.29
Sandy Koufax	L.A.	1963	25	5	306	1.88
	L.A.	1965	26	8	382	2.04
	L.A.	1966	27	9	317	1.73
Steve Carlton	Phila.	1972	27	10	310	1.97
Dwight Gooden	N.Y.	1985	24	4	268	1.53

Dodgers were transplanted to Los Angeles and notched three Triple Crown titles that the distinction was again achieved. Koufax topped the three needed categories in 1963, 1965, and 1966. Unlike any other winner of the Triple Crown, Koufax retired with the honor. An aching arthritic arm caused his early retirement, leaving a final season of 27 victories, 317 strikeouts, and an ERA of 1.73.

A Triple Crown-winning pitcher has not always meant a pennant for his team, although the two have gone together more often than not. However, in 1972 Steve Carlton took the honor despite pitching for a last-place team. There has never been such a contrast in the success of a team's best pitcher and the rest of its staff. The Phillies won 59 games, and Carlton was responsible for 27 of them. He also led, for the only time, in ERA, with 1.97, and struck out 310.

Again a drought followed, despite the presence of such star pitchers as Tom Seaver, Fergie Jenkins, Juan Marichal, Jim Palmer, Gaylord Perry, and others who led in some of the prize-earning stats. Then in 1985 Dwight Gooden took up the challenge and claimed the Triple Crown with a remarkable record: 24-4, 1.53, and 268 strikeouts. Gooden faltered the next year, but Roger Clemens came forward to just miss the honor by finishing second in strikeouts while winning the other two legs.

The Unassisted Triple Play

On May 30, 1987, family and friends of ninety-three-year-old Jimmy Cooney gathered at his home to celebrate the sixtieth anniversary of his unassisted triple play. Rare? It was the last one made in the National League. Only two have been made since that long ago Memorial Day—one, oddly, the day after Cooney's.

Letters from National League president A. Bartlett Giamatti and Dallas Green, the general manager of the Chicago Cubs, congratulated Jimmy Cooney. He had worn a Chicago Cubs uniform the day fate had decreed he be in the right place at the right time. A much-traveled infielder, he had worn six major league uniforms in seven seasons. It was a happy coincidence that he was Chicago's shortstop when he made his unassisted triple play. His father, the first Jimmy Cooney, had been Chicago's shortstop in 1890, '91, and part of '92.

Jimmy's younger brother John had logged twenty years in the big leagues as a pitcher, and after his arm went lame, he had become an outfielder and first baseman.

Jimmy Cooney was no stranger to unassisted triple plays. Two seasons earlier, when he was shortstop for the St. Louis Cardinals, he was doubled off second by the Pirate shortstop Glenn Wright, who next tagged out Rogers Hornsby coming from first base. Wright had snared a line drive off the bat of Jim Bottomley to start his triple play. He watched from the Pirates' bench the day Cooney emulated his feat in much the same manner.

Paul Waner provided the line drive to make the first out, with Cooney snaring it as he ran toward second base. Clyde Barnhart had broken for second on the pitch, and Lloyd Waner, the runner on second, had dashed for third as his brother, Paul, swung. Lloyd was doubled off second, and Cooney simply tagged the startled Barnhart, who thought the ball had gone into center field for a base hit.

There are certain similarities among eight of the nine unassisted triple plays which have been recorded. These have occurred with runners on first and second, have been made by infielders, and have required the complicity of base runners either attempting a double steal or racing away on a hit-and-run play. The ninth—which is soon to be revealed—was by an outfielder, with runners on second and third.

Even the most celebrated unassisted-triple-play feat had an explanation that almost absolved the victims, the Brooklyn Dodgers, of bonehead base running. This was the only such event to happen in a World Series, and it was turned in by Bill Wambsganss, the Cleveland Indian second baseman in 1920. Those who have examined the boxscore have questioned the tactics of Uncle Wilbert Robinson, the Brooklyn manager whose strategies often were charitably called "unusual." It was the fifth inning, and Brooklyn, behind 7–0, had the first

two runners on base. Play it safe? Not Uncle Robbie.

Despite being scoreless, the Dodgers had been hitting the Cleveland pitcher, Jim Bagby, hard. It was a game in which they made thirteen hits and scored a lone run. Bill Wambsganss, who told the story hundreds of times, explained that he chose to play very deep when Clarence Mitchell, a very good-hitting pitcher came to bat in the fifth inning. He didn't think a seven-run lead, so early in the game, was too secure the way the Dodgers had been hitting.

When Mitchell cracked the ball on a line, the batters took off, not thinking that Wamby was where the ball was going. He was and ran over and doubled Kilduff off second and turned and found a dumbfounded Otto Miller standing in the baseline. He tagged him out and, as has been the case after every unassisted triple play, trotted off the field in silence. It always takes the crowd a minute or more to realize what has happened.

In the early years of baseball, outfielder Paul Hines of the Providence Grays, had been credited with making an unassisted triple play. Later-day research indicated Hines had made an unassisted double play but had thrown to a base for the third out. But according to the rules of 1878, Hines did indeed register an unassisted triple play.

In 1928, Providence sportswriter W.D. "Bill" Perrin—who at that time had covered the Providence Grays for nearly half a century—described Hines' actions in the game played on May 8, 1878 in Providence. "The circumstances of this play have afforded more arguments than any other known play. That the play was made is not disputed, but whether Hines made the play unassisted or whether [second baseman Charles] Sweasy completed it by retiring the third man.... Here is what happened: [Jim] O'Rourke drew a base on balls and scored when Sweasy threw [Jack] Manning's drive over [Providence first baseman Tim] Murnane's head, Manning going to third on the error. Murname muffed [Ezra] Sutton's fly, Manning holding third [as Sutton took second]. [Jack] Burdock was next up and dropped the ball just over [short-stop Tom] Carey's head for what looked like a safe hit....

"The story in the *Providence Journal* of the next day thus describes the play: 'Manning and Sutton proceeded to the home plate,' meaning that both rounded third. "Hines ran in and caught the ball, and kept going to tag third. The rule then as now requires that when a base runner is forced to retrace his steps he must retouch the bases passed in reverse order. As Hines touched third with the ball in his hand, after making the catch, before either Manning or Sutton could get back, both were out automatically. It is true that Hines then on a signal from Sweasy threw the ball to second, but this was unnecessary as both runners were out at third."

To confirm Perrin's view, let's look at the playing for rules 1878, the year in which Hines made his celebrated play. Rule V, Section 1 reads: "Players running the bases must touch each base in regular order, viz., first, second, third, and home bases; and when obliged to return to bases they have occupied they must retouch them in reverse order. . . ." And Rule V, Section 15 reads: "Any base-runner failing to touch the base he runs for shall be declared out if the ball be held by a fielder, while touching said base, before the base-runner returns and touches it." Henry Chadwick's gloss on the latter rule stated: ". . . it is only necessary for a fielder to hold the ball on the base, which should have been touched, in order to put the runner out."

Eureka! The controversy of over a century is thus resolved, and in favor of Paul Hines and his unassisted triple play. Rewrite the record books!

Johnny Neun had read in the morning paper of May 31, 1927, about Jimmy Cooney's unassisted triple play in the National League. As first baseman for the Detroit Tigers, known for his fielding and base stealing, Neun was alert to all possibilities when Homer Summa's line drive landed in his glove. Charlie Jamieson was a dead duck, caught off first and easily tagged for the second out. Shortstop Jackie Tavener was jumping up and down at second base calling for the ball. Slow-footed Glen Myatt was lumbering back from third base.

Neun waved his shortstop out of the way and raced toward second base, implausibly shouting, "I'm running into the Hall of Fame."

In a nice touch of journalistic enterprise, *Sports Illustrated,* in 1987, noted that both Jimmy Cooney and Johnny Neun were still alive and arranged for them to talk on the telephone about their unique plays made sixty years earlier. They had been contemporaries but had played in different leagues and had never met.

When each had gone back to the minor leagues, they played against each other in the International League but simply passed each other without fraternal comment, despite having shared such an extremely rare experience. They had a very nice talk, and months later, when Jimmy reached his anniversary a day ahead of Johnny, it was Neun who called to extend congratulations. Jimmy's National League record has not been matched. Johnny Neun's American League record has.

On July 30, 1968, Ron Hansen, playing shortstop for the Washington Senators, made an unassisted triple play, following the process all other shortstops have used. He grabbed a line drive, off the bat of Joe Azcue, stepped on second to retire Dave Nelson, and tagged Russ Snyder coming from first. It was the first time the feat had been pulled since 1927, forty-one years earlier.

It was the most memorable event of Hansen's week, which was an unusual one in other ways as well. Following his play, he struck out six consecutive times, perhaps still stunned by the event. Then he regained his batting eye to hit a grand-slam home run. His unassisted triple play had been made on a road trip. He could expect applause when he came to bat the first time before hometown Washington fans when the team returned home. But he didn't get this. Instead, he was traded to the White Sox.

The first unassisted triple play of the twentieth century was made on July 19, 1909 by a Cleveland shortstop, Neal Ball. Overall Cleveland has been involved in five of the nine unassisted triple plays in the major leagues. Three times the event has taken place there, twice executed by Cleveland players, and in all a Cleveland player has been involved somewhere five times. It all began with Neal Ball, who snagged a liner hit by Boston's Amby McConnell and retired Charley Wagner and Jake Stahl on the basepaths.

George Burns, playing for the Boston Red Sox between stints as a member of the Indians, turned the tables for Boston and made Cleveland the victim in 1923. He caught Frank Brower's liner, tagged Rube Lutzke off first, and ran to second to get Riggs Stephenson before he could return.

Burns made his play on September 14, and on October 6 another unassisted triple play occurred, making the feat which had been so rare appear almost commonplace, for a while. This time Ernie Padgett, a redheaded shortstop for the

Boston Braves, turned the trick. Again the play was made in typical fashion—a line drive, a runner doubled off second base, and a surprised baserunner from first being tagged out.

Triple plays are rare enough; some are rapidly executed by quick-throwing infielders, and others are the result of erratic base running and convoluted attempts to advance or retreat by confused baserunners. An unassisted triple play is an event most baseball followers will never see. However, every time there are two runners on base and none out, the potential is there.

Unassisted Triple Plays

Player/Team	Date	Pos.	Opp.	Opp. Batter
Paul Hines, Prov.	May 8, 1878	OF	Bos.	Jack Burdock
Neal Ball, Cleve.	July 19, 1909	SS	Bos.	Amby McConnell
Bill Wambsganss, Clv.	October 10, 1920	2B	Brook.	Clarence Mitchell
George Burns, Bos.	September 14, 1923	1B	Cleve.	Frank Brower
Ernie Padgett, Bos.	October 6, 1923	SS	Phila.	Walter Holke
Glenn Wright, Pitts.	May 7, 1925	SS	St.L.	Jim Bottomley
Johnny Cooney, Chi.	May 30, 1927	SS	Pitts.	Paul Waner
Johnny Neun, Det.	May 31, 1927	1B	Cleve.	Homer Summa
Ron Hansen, Wash.	July 29, 1968	SS	Cleve.	Joe Azcue

The No-Hitters

What follows is the traditional honor roll of the 200-plus pitchers who have attained the no-hit heights. Also provided is a list of those handful of ugly-duckling no-hitters that didn't go nine innings, and those 32 games in which a pitcher retired 27 or more batters in succession. Concerning the last-named group, only 13 are officially recognized as perfect games—the rest were deprived of perfection by their fielding support, their stars, or like Dick Bosman, simply themselves.

No hit games, nine or more innings.

(Number to left is career total if greater than one)
(Home team is that of pitcher, unless team is in italics)

Joe Borden, Phi vs. Chi NA, 4-0; July 28, 1875.
George Bradley, StL vs. Har NL, 2-0' July 15, 1876.
Lee Richmond, Wor vs. Cle NL, 1-0; June 12, 1880 (perfect game).
Monte Ward, Pro vs. Buf NL, 5-0; June 17, 1880.
Larry Corcoran, Chi vs. Bos NL, 6-0; August 19, 1880.
Jim Galvin, Buf vs. Wor NL, 1-0; August 20, 1880.
Tony Mullane, Lou vs. Cin AA, 2-0; September 19, 1882.
Guy Hecker, Lou vs. Pit AA, 3-1; September 19, 1882
2 Larry Corcoran, Chi vs. Wor NL, 5-0; September 20, 1882
Hoss Radbourn, Pro vs. Cle NL, 8-0; July 25, 1883
Hugh (One Arm). Daily, Cle vs. Phi NL, 1-0; September 13, 1883.
Al Atkisson, Phi vs. Pit AA, 10-1; May 24, 1884.
Ed Morris, Col vs. Pit AA, 5-0; May 29, 1884.
Frank Mountain, Col vs. Was AA, 12-0; June 5, 1884.
3 Larry Corcoran, Chi vs. Pro NL, 6-0; June 27, 1884.
2 Jim Galvin, Buf vs. Det NL, 18-0; August 4, 1884.
Dick Burns, Cin vs. KC UA, 3-1; August 26, 1884.
Ed Cushman, Mil vs. Was UA, 5-0; September 28, 1884.
Sam Kimber, Bro vs. Tol AA, 0-0; October 4, 1884 (10 innings, tie).
John Clarkson, Chi vs. Pro NL, 5-0; July 27, 1885.
Charlie Ferguson, Phi vs. Pro NL, 1-0; August 29, 1885.
2 Al Atkisson, Phi vs. NY AA, 3-2; May 1, 1886.
Adonis Terry, Bro vs. StL AA, 1-0; July 24, 1886.
Matt Kilroy, Bal vs. Pit AA, 6-0; October 6, 1886.
2 Adonis Terry, Bro vs. Lou AA, 4-0; May 27, 1888.
Henry Porter, KC vs. Bal AA, 4-0; June 6, 1888.
Ed Seward, Phi vs. Cin AA, 12-2; July 26, 1888.
Gus Weyhing, Phi vs. KC AA, 4-0; July 31, 1888.
Cannonball Titcomb, Roch vs. Syr AA, 7-0; September 15, 1890.
Tom Lovett, Bro vs. NY NL, 4-0; June 22, 1891.
Amos Rusie, NY vs. Bro NL, 6-0; July 31, 1891.
Ted Breitenstein, StL vs. Lou AA, 8-0; October 4, 1891 (1st game). (first start in the major leagues).
Jack Stivetts, Bos vs. Bro NL, 11-0; August 6, 1892.
Ben Sanders, Lou vs. Bal NL, 6-2; August 22, 1892.

Bumpus Jones, Cin vs. Pit NL, 7-1; October 15, 1892. (first game in the major leagues).
Bill Hawke, Bal vs. Was NL, 5-0; August 16, 1893.
Cy Young, Cle vs. Cin NL, 6-0; September 18, 1897 (1st game).
2 Ted Breitenstein, Cin vs. Pit NL, 11-0; April 22, 1898.
Jim Hughes, Bal vs. Bos NL, 8-0; April 22, 1898.
Red Donahue, Phi vs. Bos NL, 5-0; July 8, 1898.
Walter Thornton, Chi vs. Bro NL, 2-0; August 21, 1898 (2nd game).
Deacon Phillippe, Lou vs. NY NL, 7-0; May 25, 1899.
Vic Willis, Bos vs. Was NL, 7-1; August 7, 1899.
Noodles Hahn, Cin vs. Phi NL, 4-0; July 12, 1900.
Earl Moore, Cle vs. Chi AL, 2-4; May 9, 1901 (lost on two hits in 10th).
Christy Mathewson, NY vs. StL NL, 5-0; July 15, 1901.
Jim Callahan, Chi vs. Det AL, 3-0; September 20, 1902 (1st game).
Chick Fraser, Phi vs. Chi NL, 10-0; September 18, 1903 (2nd game).
2 Cy Young, Bos vs. Phi AL, 3-0; May 5, 1904 (perfect game).
Bob Wicker, Chi vs. NY NL, 1-0; June 11, 1904. (won in 12 innings after allowing one hit in the 10th).
Jesse Tannehill, Bos vs. Chi AL, 6-0; August 17, 1904.
2 Christy Mathewson, NY vs. Chi NL, 1-0; June 13, 1905.
Weldon Henley, Phi vs. StL AL, 6-0; July 22, 1905 (1st game).
Frank Smith, Chi vs. Det AL, 15-0; September 6, 1905 (2nd game).
Bill Dinneen, Bos vs. Chi AL, 2-0; September 27, 1905 (1st game).
Johnny Lush, Phi vs. Bro NL, 6-0; May 1, 1906.
Mal Eason, Bro vs. StL NL, 2-0; July 20, 1906.
Harry McIntyre, Bro vs. Pit NL, 0-1; August 1, 1906. (lost on four hits in 13 innings after allowing first hit in 11th).
Frank (Jeff). Pfeffer, Bos vs. Cin NL, 6-0; May 8, 1907.
Nick Maddox, Pit vs. Bro NL, 2-1; September 20, 1907.
3 Cy Young, Bos vs. NY AL, 8-0; June 30, 1908.
Hooks Wiltse, NY vs. Phi NL, 1-0; July 4, 1908 (first game, ten innings).
Nap Rucker, Bro vs. Bos NL, 6-0; September 5, 1908 (2nd game).
Dusty Rhoades, Cle vs. Bos AL, 2-1; September 18, 1908.
2 Frank Smith, Chi vs. Phi AL, 1-0; September 20, 1908.
Addie Joss, Cle vs. Chi AL, 1-0; October 2, 1908 (perfect game).
Red Ames, NY vs. Bro NL, 0-3; April 15, 1909. (lost on seven hits in 13 innings after allowing first hit in 10th).
2 Addie Joss, Cle vs. Chi AL, 1-0; April 20, 1910.
Chief Bender, Phi vs. Cle AL, 4-0; May 12, 1910.
Tom L. Hughes, NY vs. Cle AL, 0-5; August 30, 1910 (2nd game). (lost on seven hits in 11 innings after allowing first hit in 10th).
Joe Wood, Bos vs. StL AL, 5-0; July 29, 1911 (1st game).
Ed Walsh, Chi vs. Bos AL, 5-0; August 27, 1911.
George Mullin, Det vs. StL AL, 7-0; July 4, 1912 (2nd game).
Earl Hamilton, StL vs. Det AL, 5-1; August 30, 1912.
Jeff Tesreau, NY vs. Phi NL, 3-0; September 6, 1912 (1st game).
Jim Scott, Chi vs. Was AL, 0-1; May 14, 1914 (lost on 2 two hits in 10th).
Joe Benz, Chi vs. Cle Al, 6-1; May 31, 1914.
George Davis, Bos vs. Phi NL, 7-0; September 9, 1914 (2nd game).
Ed Lafitte, Bro vs. KC FL, 6-2; September 19, 1914.
Rube Marquard, NY vs. Bro NL, 2-0; April 15, 1915.
Frank Allen, Pit vs. StL FL, 2-0; April 24, 1915
Claude Hendrix, Chi vs. Pit FL, 10-0; May 15, 1915.
Alex Main, KC vs. Buf FL, 5-0; August 16, 1915.
Jimmy Lavender, Chi vs. NY NL, 2-0; August 31, 1915 (1st game).
Dave Davenport, StL vs. Chi FL, 3-0; September 7, 1915.
2 Tom L. Hughes, Bos vs. Pit NL, 2-0; June 16, 1916.
Rube Foster, Bos vs. NY AL, 2-0; June 16, 1916.
Joe Bush, Phi vs. Cle AL, 5-0; August 26, 1916.
Hubert (Dutch) Leonard, Bos vs. StL AL, 4-0; August 30, 1916
Eddie Cicotte, Chi vs. StL AL, 11-0; April 14, 1917.
George Mogridge, NY vs. Bos AL, 2-1; April 24, 1917.
Fred Toney, Cin vs. Chi NL, 1-0; May 2, 1917 (10 innings).
Hippo Vaughn, Chi vs. Cin NL, 0-1; May 2, 1917. (lost on two hits in 10th; Toney pitched a no-hitter in this game).
Ernie Koob, StL vs. Chi AL, 1-0; May 5, 1917.
Bob Groom, StL vs. Chi AL, May 6, 1917 (2nd game).
Ernie Shore, Bos vs. Was AL, 3-0; June 23, 1917 (1st game). (perfect game).
    (Shore relieved Babe Ruth in the first inning after Ruth had been thrown out of the game for protesting a walk to the first batter. The runner was caught stealing and Shore retired the remaining 26 batters in order).
2 Hubert (Dutch). Leonard, Bos vs. Det AL, 5-0; June 3, 1918.
Hod Eller, Cin vs. StL NL, 6-0; May 11, 1919.
Ray Caldwell, Cle vs. NY AL, 3-0; September 10, 1919 (1st game).
Walter Johnson, Was vs. Bos AL, 1-0; July 1, 1920.
Charlie Robertson, Chi vs. Det AL, 2-0; April 30, 1922 (perfect game).
Jesse Barnes, NY vs. Phi NL, 6-0; May 7, 1922.
Sam Jones, NY vs. Phi AL, 2-0; September 4, 1923.
Howard Ehmke, Bos vs. Phi AL, 4-0; September 7, 1923.
Jesse Haines, StL vs. Bos NL, 5-0; July 17, 1924.
Dazzy Vance, Bro vs. Phi NL, 10-1; September 13, 1925 (1st game).
Ted Lyons, Chi vs. Bos AL, 6-0; August 21, 1926.
Carl Hubbell, NY vs. Pit NL, 11-0; May 8, 1929.
Wes Ferrell, Cle vs. StL AL, 9-0; April 29, 1931.
Bobby Burke, Was vs. Bos AL, 5-0; August 8, 1931.
Bobo Newsom, StL vs Bos AL, 1-2; September 18, 1934 (lost on one hit in 10th).
Paul Dean, StL vs. Bro NL, 3-0; September 21, 1934 (2nd game).
Vern Kennedy, Chi vs. Cle AL, 5-0; August 31, 1935.
Bill Dietrich, Chi vs. StL AL, 8-0; June 1, 1937.
Johnny Vander Meer, Cin vs. Bos NL, 3-0; June 11, 1938.
2 Johnny Vander Meer, Cin vs. Bro NL, 6-0; June 15, 1938 (next start after June 11).
Monte Pearson, NY vs. Cle AL, 13-0; August 27, 1938 (2nd game).
Bob Feller, Cle vs. Chi AL, 1-0; April 16, 1940 (opening day).

Tex Carleton, Bro vs. *Cin* NL, 3-0; April 30, 1940.
Lon Warneke, StL vs. *Cin* NL, 2-0; August 30, 1941.
Jim Tobin, Bos vs. Bro NL, 2-0; April 27, 1944.
Clyde Shoun, Cin vs. Bos NL, 1-0; May 15, 1944.
Dick Fowler, Phi vs. StL AL, 1-0; September 9, 1945 (2nd game).
Ed Head, Bro vs. Bos NL, 5-0; April 23, 1946.
2 Bob Feller, Cle vs. *NY* AL, 1-0; April 30, 1946.
Ewell Blackwell, Cin vs. Bos NL, 6-0; June 18, 1947.
Don Black, Cle vs. Phi AL, 3-0; July 10, 1947 (1st game).
Bill McCahan, Phi vs. Was AL, 3-0; September 3, 1947.
Bob Lemon, Cle vs. *Det* AL, 2-0; June 30, 1948.
Rex Barney, Bro vs. *NY* NL, 2-0; September 9, 1948.
Vern Bickford, Bos vs. Bro NL, 7-0; August 11, 1950.
Cliff Chambers, Pit vs. *Bos* NL, 3-0; May 6, 1951 (2nd game).
3 Bob Feller, Cle vs. Det AL, 2-1; July 1, 1951 (1st game).
Allie Reynolds, NY vs. *Cle* AL, 1-0; July 12, 1951.
2 Allie Reynolds, NY vs. Bos AL, 8-0; September 28, 1951 (1st game).
Virgil Trucks, Det vs. Was AL, 1-0; May 15, 1952.
Carl Erskine, Bro vs. Chi NL, 5-0; June 19, 1952.
2 Virgil Trucks, Det vs. *NY* AL, 1-0; August 25, 1952.
Bobo Holloman, StL vs. Phi AL, 6-0; May 6, 1953 (first start in the major leagues).
Jim Wilson, Mil vs. Phi NL, 2-0; June 12, 1954.
Sam Jones, Chi vs Pit NL, 4-0; May 12, 1955.
2 Carl Erskine, Bro vs. NY NL, 3-0; May 12, 1956.
Johnny Klippstein (7 innings), Hershell Freeman (1 inning) and Joe Black (3 innings)., Cin vs. *Mil* NL, 1-2; May 26, 1956. (lost on three hits in 11 innings after allowing first hit in 10th).
Mel Parnell, Bos vs. Chi AL, 4-0; July 14, 1956.
Sal Maglie, Bro vs. Phi NL, 5-0; September 25, 1956.
Don Larsen, NY AL vs. Bro NL, 2-0; October 8, 1956. (World Series). (perfect game).
Bob Keegan, Chi vs. Was AL, 6-0; August 20, 1957 (2nd game).
Jim Bunning, Det vs. *Bos* AL, 3-0; July 20, 1958 (1st game).
Hoyt Wilhelm, Bal vs. NY AL, 1-0; September 20, 1958.
Harvey Haddix, Pit vs. *Mil* NL, 0-1; May 26, 1959 (lost on one hit in 13 innings after pitching 12 perfect innings).
Don Cardwell, Chi vs. StL NL, 4-0; May 15, 1960 (2nd game).
Lew Burdette, Mil vs. Phi NL, 1-0; August 18, 1960.
Warren Spahn, Mil vs. Phi NL, 4-0; September 16, 1960.
2 Warren Spahn, Mil vs. SF NL, 1-0; April 28, 1961.
Bo Belinsky, LA vs. Bal AL, 2-0; May 5, 1962.
Earl Wilson, Bos vs. LA Al, 2-0; June 26, 1962.
Sandy Koufax, LA vs. NY NL, 5-0; June 30, 1962.
Bill Monbouquette, Bos vs. *Chi* AL, 1-0; August 1, 1962.
Jack Kralick, Min vs. KC AL, 1-0; August 26, 1962.
2 Sandy Koufax, LA vs. SF NL, 8-0; May 11, 1963.
Don Nottebart, Hou vs. Phi NL, 4-1; May 17, 1963.
Juan Marichal, SF vs. Hou NL, 1-0; June 15, 1963.
Ken T. Johnson, Hou vs. Cin NL, 0-1; April 23, 1964 (lost game).
3 Sandy Koufax, LA vs. *Phi* NL, 3-0; June 4, 1964.
2 Jim Bunning, Phi vs. *NY* NL, 6-0; June 21, 1964 (1st game; perfect game).
Jim Maloney, Cin vs. NY NL, 0-1; June 14, 1965 (lost on two hits in 11 innings after pitching 10 hitless innings).
Jim Maloney, Cin vs. *Chi* NL, 1-0; August 19, 1965 (1st game; 10 innings).
4 Sandy Koufax, LA vs. Chi NL, 1-0; September 9, 1965 (perfect game).
Dave Morehead, Bos vs. Cle AL, 2-0; September 16, 1965.
Sonny Siebert, Cle vs. Was AL, 2-0; June 10, 1966.
Steve D. Barber (8⅔ innings). and Stu Miller (⅓ inning) Bal vs. Det AL, 1-2; April 30, 1967 (1st game; lost game).
Don Wilson, Hou vs. Atl NL, 2-0; June 18, 1967.
Dean Chance, Min vs. *Cle* AL, 2-1; August 25, 1967 (2nd game).
Joe Horlen, Chi vs. Det AL, 6-0; September 10, 1967 (1st game).
Tom Phoebus, Bal vs. Bos AL, 6-0; April 27, 1968.
Catfish Hunter, Oak vs. Min AL, 4-0; May 8, 1968 (perfect game).
George Culver, Cin vs. *Phi* NL, 6-1; July 29, 1968 (2nd game).
Gaylord Perry, SF vs. StL NL, 1-0; July 29, 1968.
Ray Washburn, StL vs. *SF* NL, 2-0; September 18, 1968.
Bill Stoneman, Mon vs. *Phi* NL, 7-0; April 17, 1969.
3 Jim Maloney, Cin vs. Hou NL, 10-0; April 30, 1969.
2 Don Wilson, Hou vs. Cin NL, 4-0; May 1, 1969.
Jim Palmer, Bal vs. Oak AL, 8-0; August 13, 1969.
Ken Holtzman, Chi vs. Atl NL, 3-0; August 19, 1969.
Bob Moose, Pit vs. *NY* NL, 4-0; September 20, 1969.
Dock Ellis, Pit vs. *SD* NL, 2-0; June 12, 1970 (1st game).
Clyde Wright, Cal vs. Oak AL, 4-0; July 3, 1970.
Bill Singer, LA vs. Phi NL, 5-0; July 20, 1970.
Vida Blue, Oak vs. Min AL, 6-0; September 21, 1970.
2 Ken Holtzman, Chi vs. Cin NL, 1-0; June 3, 1971.
Rick Wise, Phi vs. Cin NL, 4-0; June 23, 1971.
Bob Gibson, StL vs. Pit NL, 11-0; August 14, 1971.
Burt Hooton, Chi vs. Phi NL, 4-0; April 16, 1972.
Milt Pappas, Chi vs. SD NL, 8-0; September 2, 1972.
2 Bill Stoneman, Mon vs. NY NL, 7-0; October 2, 1972 (2nd game).
Steve Busby, KC vs. *Det* AL, 3-0; April 27, 1973.
Nolan Ryan, Cal vs. *KC* AL, 3-0; May 15, 1973.
2 Nolan Ryan, Cal vs. *Det* AL, 6-0; July 15, 1973.
Jim Bibby, Tex vs. *Oak* AL, 6-0; July 30, 1973.
Phil Niekro, Atl vs. SD NL, 9-0; August 5, 1973.
2 Steve Busby, KC vs. *Mil* AL, 2-0; June 19, 1974.
Dick Bosman, Cle vs. Oak AL, 4-0; July 19, 1974.
3 Nolan Ryan, Cal vs. Min AL, 4-0; September 28, 1974.
4 Nolan Ryan, Cal vs. Bal AL, 1-0; June 1, 1975.
Ed Halicki, SF vs. NY NL, 6-0; August 24, 1975 (2nd game).

Vida Blue (5 innings), Glenn Abbott (1 inning), Paul Lindblad (1 inning), and Rollie Fingers (2 innings), Oak vs. Cal AL, 5-0; September 28, 1975.
Larry Dierker, Hou vs. Mon NL, 5-0; July 9, 1976.
Blue Moon Odom (5 innings) and Francisco Barrios (4 innings), Chi vs. *Oak* AL, 6-0; July 28, 1976.
John Candelaria, Pit vs. LA NL, 2-0; August 9, 1976.
John Montefusco, SF vs. *Atl* NL, 9-0; September 29, 1976.
Jim Colborn, KC vs. Tex AL, 6-0; May 14, 1977.
Dennis Eckersley, Cle vs. Cal AL, 1-0; May 30, 1977.
Bert Blyleven, Tex vs. *Cal* AL, 6-0; September 22, 1977.
Bob Forsch, StL vs. Phi NL, 5-0; April 16, 1978.
Tom Seaver, Cin vs. StL NL, 4-0; June 16, 1978.
Ken Forsch, Hou vs. Atl NL, 6-0; April 7, 1979.
Jerry Reuss, LA vs. *SF* NL, 8-0; June 27, 1980.
Charlie Lea, Mon vs. SF NL, 4-0; May 10, 1981 (2nd game).
Len Barker, Cle vs. Tor AL, 3-0; May 15, 1981 (perfect game).
5 Nolan Ryan, Hou vs. LA NL, 5-0; September 26, 1981.
Dave Righetti, NY vs. Bos AL, 4-0; July 4, 1983.
2 Bob Forsch, StL vs. Mon NL, 3-0; September 26, 1983.
Mike Warren, Oak vs. Chi AL, 3-0; September 29, 1983.
Jack Morris, Det vs. *Chi* AL, 4-0; April 7, 1984.
Mike Witt, Cal vs. *Tex* AL, 1-0; September 30, 1984 (perfect game).
Joe Cowley, Chi vs. *Cal* AL, 7-1; September 19, 1986.
Mike Scott, Hou vs. SF NL, 2-0; September 25, 1986.
Juan Nieves, Mil vs. Bal AL, 7-0; April 15, 1987.
Tom Browning, Cin vs. LA NL, 1-0; September 16, 1988 (perfect game).

No hit games, fewer than nine innings

(Home team is that of pitcher, unless team is in italics)

Larry McKeon, six innings, Ind vs. *Cin* AA, 0-0; May 6, 1884.
Charlie Gagus, eight innings, Was vs. Wil UA, 12-1; August 21, 1884.
Charlie Getzien, six innings, Det vs. Phi NL, 1-0; October 1, 1884.
Charlie Sweeney (3 innings) and Henry Boyle (2 innings), five innings, StL vs. StP U.A., 0-1; October 5, 1884.
Dupee Shaw, five innings, Pro vs. *Buf* NL, 4-0; October 7, 1885 (1st game).
George Van Haltren, six innings, Chi vs. Pit NL, 1-0; June 21, 1888.
Cannonball Crane, seven innings, NY vs. Was NL, 3-0; September 27, 1888.
Matt Kilroy, seven innings, Bal vs. StL AA, 0-0; July 29, 1889 (2nd game).
Silver King, eight innings, Chi vs. Bro PL, 0-1; June 21, 1890.
George Nicol, seven innings, StL vs. Phi AA, 21-2; September 23, 1890.
Hank Gastright, eight innings, Col vs. Tol AA, 6-0; October 12, 1890.
Jack Stivetts, five innings, Bos vs. *Was* NL, 6-0; October 15, 1892 (2nd game).
Icebox Chamberlain, seven innings, Cin vs. Bos NL, 6-0; September 23, 1893 (2nd game).
Ed Stein, six innings, Bro vs. Chi NL, 6-0; June 2, 1894.
Red Ames, five innings, NY vs. *StL* NL, 5-0; September 14, 1903 (2nd game).
Rube Waddell, five innings, Phi vs. StL AL, 2-0; August 20, 1905.
Jake Weimer, seven innings, Cin vs. Bro NL, 1-0; August 24, 1906 (2nd game).
Jimmy Dygert (3 innings) and Rube Waddell (2 innings), five innings, Phi vs. Chi AL, 4-3; September 24, 1906.
Stoney McGlynn, seven innings, StL vs. *Bro* NL, 1-1; September 24, 1906 (2nd game).
Lefty Leifield, six innings, Pit vs. *Phi* NL, 8-0; September 26, 1906, (2nd game).
Ed Walsh, five innings, Chi vs. NY AL, 8-1; May 26, 1907.
Ed Karger, seven perfect innings, StL vs. Bos NL, 4-0; August 11, 1907 (2nd game).
Howie Camnitz, five innings, Pit vs. *NY* NL, 1-0; August 23, 1907 (2nd game).
Rube Vickers, five perfect innings, Phi vs. *Was* AL, 4-0; October 5, 1907 (2nd game).
Johnny Lush, six innings, StL vs. *Bro* NL, 2-0; August 6, 1908.
King Cole, seven innings, Chi vs. *StL* NL, 4-0; July 31, 1910 (2nd game).
Jay Cashion, six innings, Was vs. Cle AL, 2-0; August 20, 1910 (2nd game).
Walter Johnson, seven innings, Was vs. StL Al, 2-0; August 25, 1910.
Fred Frankhouse, seven and two-thirds innings, Bro vs. Cin NL, 5-0; August 27, 1937.
John Whitehead, six innings, StL vs. Det AL, 4-0; August 5, 1940 (2nd game).
Jim Tobin, five innings, Bos vs. Phi NL, 7-0; June 22, 1944 (2nd game).
Mike McCormick, five innings, SF vs. *Phi* NL, 3-0; June 12, 1959.
Sam Jones, seven innings, SF vs. *StL* NL, 4-0; September 26, 1959.
Dean Chance, five perfect innings, Min vs. Bos AL, 2-0; August 6, 1967.
Dave Palmer, five perfect innings, Mon vs. *StL* NL, 4-0; April 21, 1984 (2nd game).
Pascual Perez, five innings, Mon vs. Phi NL, 1-0; September 24, 1988.

Perfection Plus

Year	Pitcher	Batters	Opponent	Notes
1959	Harvey Haddix	36	Pittsburgh	(12 innings)
1919	Waite Hoyt	34	Yanks	(2nd-13th inning)
1880	Pud Galvin	33	Worcester	(6 errors)
1884	Charlie Buffinton	32	Providence	(5 errors)
1971	Rick Wise	32	Chicago	(2nd-12th inning)
1908	Nap Rucker	30	Braves	(3 errors)
1885	John Clarkson	29	Providence	(3 errors, 1 DP)
1970	Bill Singer	29	Philadelphia	(2 errors, both his own)
1883	Hoss Radbourn	28	Cleveland	(1 error)
1884	Pud Galvin	28	Detroit	(1 error)
1905	Christy Mathewson	28	Cubs	(2 errors, one DP)
1910	Tom Hughes	28	Cleveland	(1 error)

1920	Walter Johnson	28	Red Sox	(1 error)
1967	Joel Horlen	28	Detroit	(1 error)
1974	Dick Bosman	28	Oakland	(1 error, his own)
1880	J. L. Richmond	27	Cleveland	
1880	J. M. Ward	27	Buffalo	
1904	Cy Young	27	Philadelphia	
1906	Lefty Leifield	27	Cubs	(8 innings, 3 errors)
1908	Addie Joss	27	White Sox	
1922	Charlie Robertson	27	Detroit	
1956	Don Larsen	27	Brooklyn	
1964	Jim Bunning	27	Mets	
1965	Sandy Koufax	27	Cubs	
1968	Catfish Hunter	27	Minnesota	
1981	Len Barker	27	Toronto	

1984	Mike Witt	27	Texas
1988	Tom Browning	27	Los Angeles
1954	Robin Roberts	27*	Cincinnati
1980	Jerry Reuss	27*	San Francisco
1981	Jim Bibby	27*	Atlanta
1917	Ernie Shore	26†	Washington

*Retired last twenty-seven batters in a row after giving up a hit to leadoff man.

†Starter Babe Ruth walked the first man and promptly slugged the umpire in the jaw and was banished. Ernie Shore rushed in from the bull pen, got the runner on a steal attempt, and retired the next twenty-six.

Note: Hooks Wiltse in 1908 and Lew Burdette in 1960 missed perfection because each hit a batter, with Wiltse hitting the *last* batter—the opposing pitcher—with an 0-2 count.

## CHAPTER 20

Awards and Honors

Bill Deane

This chapter presents the history and voting results of baseball's most prestigious awards and honors, including the complete balloting and current constituency of the Baseball Hall of Fame. This material will be of interest to the fan who wonders how a player of the past was viewed by his contemporaries. I have ventured an additional section of "what if" awards: what if the Cy Young Award had been instituted long before its actual inception in 1956, or the Rookie of the Year before its real debut in 1947, and so on. What follows is divided into six sections:

MVP Award: history and balloting.
Rookie of the Year Award: history and balloting.
Cy Young Award: history and balloting.
Hypothetical Awards: explanation and selections.
Gold Glove Award: history, discussion, and list of winners.
Hall of Fame: history of elections and balloting.

Balloting tables and lists of winners include each player's first initial, last name, and club city abbreviation (and point total, if applicable).

Most Valuable Player Award: History

The concept of most valuable player awards dates back more than a century. The first documented MVP-type honor in pro ball was bestowed upon James "Deacon" White of the 1875 Boston Red Stockings in the National Association. Catcher White sparked Boston to a remarkable 71–8 record that year, scoring 77 runs in 80 games and batting .355. An ardent Red Stockings' admirer presented Deacon with a silver tray, water pitcher, and loving cup inscribed with the words: WON BY JIM WHITE AS MOST VALUABLE PLAYER TO BOSTON TEAM, 1875.

The first official MVP honor was initiated some thirty-five years later. Prior to the 1910 season, baseball fan Hugh Chalmers, president and general manager of the Chalmers Motor Company, announced that he would present one of his company's automobiles—a Chalmers "30"—to the major league player who compiled the highest batting average. What appeared to be a harmless promotional gimmick was to soon turn into a public relations disaster.

The rules specified that players must accumulate a specific minimum number of times at bat, depending on position, to qualify for the award. For infielders and outfielders, it was a minimum of 350 at-bats; for catchers, 250 at-bats; and for pitchers, 100 at-bats. Interest in the award was tremendous from the outset. Ty Cobb, who already owned a Chalmers "30" roadster, wrote: "I am glad that something besides medals and trophies is offered for the championship in batting. I think the offer of a Chalmers "30" is simply great and I hope

to be lucky enough to own a new Chalmers next fall."

It developed into a two-man race, with Detroit's Cobb and Cleveland's Napoleon Lajoie, both American Leaguers, the only serious challengers for the coveted prize. Throughout the season there were charges and countercharges of favoritism by scorers in various cities. Furthermore, the general consensus of the press was that Cobb's selfish pursuit of this individual honor had cost his team the pennant. The controversy was capped by scandalous circumstances on the final day of the season.

Through games of September 16, Cobb held a solid lead over Lajoie, .368 to .357 (although, because of the era's sloppy record keeping, few actually knew the official figures at the time). From then through October 8, Cobb batted a torrid .532 (25 for 47) to seemingly lock up the crown with a .383 average. But Lajoie refused to surrender, going 30 for 54 (.556) in that same span to enter the final day, October 9, with a .376 mark. Cobb chose to sit out his final game, while Lajoie played the infamous doubleheader with the St. Louis Browns in which he went 8 for 8, including *seven bunt hits*—remarkable for a slow-footed slugger—to apparently edge out Cobb in the batting race. Browns' manager Jack O'Connor had instructed his rookie third baseman, Red Corriden, to play deep on Lajoie, advice with which Corriden complied. Lajoie took advantage of the strange defensive arrangement with the repeated safe bunts. Although neither Lajoie nor Corriden were implicated, there were charges of a Browns' frame-up to give the coveted batting title (and car) to the respected Lajoie over the disliked Cobb.

O'Connor lost his job due to his role in the alleged fix. Subsequently, AL President Ban Johnson announced that a "discrepancy" had been found in the official records, and that Cobb had actually won the batting crown after all (although this point is challenged by many current researchers, who have evidence that Cobb was credited wrongly for a 2 for 4 game). Meanwhile, Hugh Chalmers, attempting to divorce himself from the controversy, presented autos to both Cobb and Lajoie. It was generally acknowledged that this fiasco doomed the future of individual awards of any kind.

Hoping to salvage some goodwill out of the whole idea, Chalmers came up with a new proposal for the 1911 season. This time he would award an auto to one player in each league who "should prove himself as the most important and useful player to his club and to the league at large in point of deportment and value of services rendered." The decision for this honor was to be made by a committee of baseball writers, one writer from each club city in each league. Each writer was to make eight selections, with a first-place ballot scoring eight points, on down to an eighth-place vote counting one point. Thus was born the short-lived Chalmers Award, with Ty Cobb and Frank Schulte earning recognition in 1911. Both

Cobb and Schulte voluntarily withdrew from the competition in 1912, although the former received seventeen points anyway.

Interest in the award diminished within a few years. By 1914 the public was distracted by baseball's battles with the new Federal League and the escalation of the World War in Europe. The timing was right for the Chalmers Award to quietly disappear; it was noted that Mr. Chalmers had agreed to present vehicles for five years and that the 1914 awards marked the fifth presentations.

On July 15, 1922, the newly formed American League Trophy Committee adopted a set of rules governing the selection of an annual award-winner. The rules specified that "the purpose of the American League Trophy is to honor the baseball player who is of greatest all-round service to his club and credit to the sport during each season; to recognize and reward uncommon skill and ability when exercised by a player for the best interests of his team, and to perpetuate his memory." The rules further instructed voters to seek out the "winning ball player," reminding them that "combined offensive and defensive ability is not always indicated by any system of records."

Eight baseball writers, one from each AL city, were enfranchised, with each required to select exactly one player from each team, for a total of eight selections. Player-managers and previous winners were to be excluded from consideration. Points were distributed the same as in the Chalmers Award: eight for first place, down to one for eighth.

The intention of AL President Ban Johnson was to have a monument to baseball erected in East Potomac Park, Washington, D.C., engraved with the names of winners of the AL Award. This proposal was introduced as a congressional resolution in 1924, and passed in the House of Representatives before dying on the Senate Floor.

The AL voting rules led to growing criticism for several reasons, one of which was the limitation on the number of vote-getters from each team. For example, when the Browns' George Sisler won the first AL Award in 1922, he was named on all eight ballots—thus disqualifying his teammates from receiving any votes. As a result, fellow Brownie Ken Williams, who led the league in home runs (39), RBIs (155), and total bases (367) and became the first player ever to have 30 homers and 30 stolen bases in the same season, was shut out in the League Award voting.

Secondly, the rule prohibiting player-managers from eligibility drew fire. In 1925, when this rule eliminated five solid candidates from consideration, The New York Times wrote, "to say that it is impossible or impractical to divorce a man's managerial skill from his talents purely as a player is to reflect on the intelligence of the committee that awards the prize."

The Times further editorialized on the fallacy of assuming that no player can be the "most valuable" more than one year: "the purpose, of course, is to pass the honor around, but the effect is to pass an empty honor around." This rule became increasingly ridiculous when it eliminated Babe Ruth (and his 60 home runs) from consideration in 1927; by the following year, both Ruth and teammate Lou Gehrig, who were in the process of finishing one-two in the AL home run derby in five consecutive seasons, were ineligible for the League Award.

In 1924 the National League instituted its own award, with radical differences in the selection method: each writer voted for ten players rather than eight (ten points for first place, and so on); he was not bound to vote for a certain number of

players from each team; he was free to select a player-manager; and, later, he was allowed to consider previous winners of the award. Additionally, the NL offered a cash "present" of $1,000 to the award-winner.

At various times between 1925–51, writers were permitted to name "honorable mention" candidates, whose vote totals were listed but not counted in the balloting. Another feature of early voting reports was the listing of "cumulative vote leaders"—a forerunner to Bill James's "award shares"—over a period of years.

A number of factors led to the demise of the AL Award, including the award's loss of credibility due to the previously mentioned shortsighted voting rules. Secondly, Ban Johnson, having failed to secure the erection of his proposed monument, felt the award had fallen short of its aim. Finally, management was concerned with the efforts of award-winners to parlay their honors into substantial pay raises. The AL Award was officially voted out at a special league meeting on May 6, 1929.

The National League followed suit with the AL's decision, but agreed to continue its award through the 1929 season.

In October 1929, the Baseball Writers' Association of America (BBWAA) announced the results of an "unofficial" AL most valuable player poll, whose winner was Lew Fonseca of Cleveland. Two months later, The Sporting News (TSN) conducted a poll of the eight writers who had previously voted on the League Award, thereby reporting Al Simmons as the "unofficial" AL Award-winner. Combining the results of these two unofficial polls gives Fonseca 77 points, followed by Heinie Manush (57), Simmons (56), Tony Lazzeri (55) and Charlie Gehringer (44).

The Sporting News announced that, thereafter, they would take it upon themselves to conduct an annual poll to substitute for the defunct league awards. However, they retained the stipulation that each voter must select just one player on each team. In 1930, TSN chose Joe Cronin in the AL and Bill Terry in the NL. Earlier, the Associated Press also had a special committee of writers make an unofficial AL selection for 1930, while the BBWAA did the same for the NL (adding a check for $1,000 for the winner). The respective selections here were Cronin in the AL and Hack Wilson in the NL. Again combining the two sets of polls, the AL leaders were Cronin (100), Al Simmons (85), Lou Gehrig (68), Charlie Gehringer (67), and Ted Lyons (56). The NL pace-setters were Hack Wilson (111), Frankie Frisch (107), Bill Terry (105), Chuck Klein (57), and Floyd "Babe" Herman (52).

In an effort to standardize MVP voting, the BBWAA, in its annual winter meeting in New York on December 11, 1930, decided to appoint two committees (one in each league) to elect most valuable players, with the association to "award suitable emblems to the players selected." Thus was born what is considered the modern MVP Award, with most of the flaws of its forerunners eliminated.

TSN, however, continued to make its own selections in bitter competition with the BBWAA. Finally, beginning in 1938, TSN agreed to unify the award by abiding with BBWAA balloting, and presenting the Sporting News Trophy to the winner. Among the various prizes awarded to the winners were wristwatches and shotguns.

At a meeting during the 1944 World Series, the BBWAA decided to begin issuing its own trophy, the Kenesaw Mountain Landis Award, in honor of the ailing commissioner. Landis died a month later and the official MVP Award has born

his name ever since. A plaque engraved with the names of the winners hangs in the National Baseball Library in Cooperstown, New York.

The Sporting News went back to naming its own MVPs in 1944 and '45. Then, at the request of the new commissioner, Happy Chandler, TSN "withdrew from the field to cooperate in making the Landis Awards, provided by the major leagues, the official designations of the year." In 1948, however, TSN went back to its own awards, selecting a Player of the Year and Pitcher of the Year in each league, as they have done ever since. For some reason, TSN awards have never received the public recognition that the BBWAA honors have.

Two major changes in the MVP voting began in 1938. The BBWAA began polling three writers in each major league city, rather than just one, which remained in effect until it was reduced to two writers per city, starting in 1961. Also in 1938, the process was initiated to award fourteen points for each first-place vote, rather than ten.

"Split votes," which have since infiltrated all the major awards, first appeared in MVP Awards in 1959. The American League MVP race that year, by consensus, was between second baseman Nellie Fox and shortstop Luis Aparicio of the champion Chicago White Sox. Late in the season, the suggestion often arose that the two ought to share the award. When the votes were in, Fox had received fourteen first-place votes, Aparicio had gotten six, and four writers had split their votes between the two. Tickled with the idea of a split vote, one NL writer also resorted to this option, dividing his first-place nomination between Ernie Banks and Ed Mathews. The cop-out vote, having been allowed in '59, has since surfaced in sixteen more MVP Awards, ten Rookie of the Year, and six Cy Young Award elections. The ultimate folly of this practice was best exemplified in 1979. One NL writer split his fourth-place vote between pitching brothers Phil and Joe Niekro, evidently convinced that the two were identical twins. But the writer was still permitted to make six more selections. That meant that his fifth-, sixth-, and seventh-place selections received more points (six, five and four, respectively) than his fourth-place co-selections, who were credited with just three and a half points apiece!

There has long been debate about the consideration of pitchers for the MVP Award, the theory (by some) that a man who plays every fourth game cannot be as valuable as a man who plays every day. The debate escalated after the inception of the Cy Young Award in 1956, giving pitchers their own exclusive honor, and the increasing practice of five-man rotations in the 1970s, giving starting pitchers even less of a chance to contribute. As far as Jack Lang, current secretary-treasurer of the BBWAA, is concerned, there is no room for controversy. "The rules that are sent out to the voters on the [MVP] committee state: 'Keep in mind that all players are eligible. That includes pitchers, starters and relievers,' " says Lang. "Anybody on the committee that feels they cannot vote for a pitcher, we replace them. In my twenty-two years running the elections, only two writers have said that to me." Since 1931, pitchers have won the award ten times in the AL and nine times in the NL.

There have been twelve occasions in which one player received all of the available first-place MVP votes in his league. The AL players so honored are Ty Cobb (1911), Babe Ruth (1923), Hank Greenberg (1935), Al Rosen (1953), Mickey Mantle (1956), Frank Robinson (1966), Denny McLain (1968), Reggie Jackson (1973), and Jose Canseco (1988). The three unanimous NL selections are Carl Hubbell (1936), Orlando Cepeda (1967), and Mike Schmidt (1980). Hubbell's distinction is disputable, as two of the eight writers did not submit ballots that year and were not replaced on the selection committee.

Following are the maximum possible point totals that could have been earned by an individual receiving the first-place nomination of every writer polled:

National League		American League	
1911–14	64	1911–14	64
1924–29	80	1922–28	64
1931–37	80	1931–37	80
1938–60	336	1938–60	336
1961	224	1961–68	280
1962–68	280	1969–76	336
1969–present	336	1977–present	392

There have been numerous cases in which the MVP vote point totals did not add up to the correct figure. Reasons for this include inaccuracies in tabulation, inaccuracies in reporting, and writers who failed to vote or to complete their ballots. However, the total impact of all these errors is a small fraction of 1 percent of the total voting over the years.

Following is a complete tabulation of all the recognized MVP elections since 1911:

MVP Award
Chalmers Award, 1911–14

1911 NATIONAL
F. Schulte, CHI 29
C. Mathewson, NY. . 25
L. Doyle, NY 23
H. Wagner, PIT . . . 23
G. Alexander, PHI . . 23
M. Huggins, SL . . . 21
R. Marquard, NY . . 19
J. Daubert, BKN . . 16
J. Tinker, CHI 11
C. Meyers, NY 11
J. Sheckard, CHI . . . 9
M. Mitchell, CIN . . . 9
M. Doolan, PHI 6
B. Harmon, SL 6
J. Archer, CHI 5
H. Lobert, PHI 4
G. Gibson, PIT 4
M. Brown, CHI 4
B. Bescher, CIN 4
B. Sweeney, BOS . . . 3
O. Knabe, PHI 2

E. Konetchy, SL 2
D. Hoblitzell, CIN . . . 2
J. Walsh, PHI 2
J. Devore, NY 2
F. Luderus, PHI 1
J. Kling, BOS 1
B. Adams, PIT 1
N. Rucker, BKN 1

1911 AMERICAN
T. Cobb, DET 64
E. Walsh, CHI 35
E. Collins, PHI 32
J. Jackson, CLE . . . 28
W. Johnson, WAS . . 19
B. Cree, NY 16
T. Speaker, BOS . . . 16
I. Thomas, PHI 12
C. Milan, WAS 10
V. Gregg, CLE 9
F. Baker, PHI 8
J. Coombs, PHI 6
N. Lajoie, CLE 5

J. Knight, NY 4
S. Crawford, DET . . 4
B. Lord, PHI 4
D. Bush, DET 4
R. Ford, NY 3
J. Barry, PHI 3
J. Austin, SL 2
F. LaPorte, SL 2
S. McInnis, PHI 1
G. McBride, WAS . . . 1

1912 NATIONAL
L. Doyle, NY 48
H. Wagner, PIT . . . 43
C. Meyers, NY 25
J. Tinker, CHI 23
B. Bescher, CIN . . . 17
B. Sweeney, BOS . . 16
H. Zimmerman, CHI 16
R. Marquard, NY . . 13
O. Wilson, PIT 13
J. Daubert, BKN . . . 13
O. Knabe, PHI 10

E. Konetchy, SL 8
C. Mathewson, NY . . 8
D. Paskert, PHI 6
J. Tesreau, NY 6
R. Murray, NY 5
M. Huggins, SL 5
A. Marsans, CIN . . . 4
F. Merkle, NY 4
J. Evers, CHI 3
C. Hendrix, PIT 3
J. Archer, CHI 1
G. Alexander, PHI . . . 1

1912 AMERICAN
T. Speaker, BOS . . . 59
E. Walsh, CHI 30
W. Johnson, WAS . . 28
C. Milan, WAS 23
J. Wood, BOS 22
E. Collins, PHI 18
F. Baker, PHI 17
T. Cobb, DET 17
J. Jackson, CLE . . . 16

H. Wagner, BOS . . . 12
C. Gandil, WAS 7
B. Shotton, SL 6
D. Pratt, SL 5
E. Foster, WAS 4
L. Gardner, BOS . . . 4
S. Crawford, DET . . . 4
J. Barry, PHI 4
B. Carrigan, BOS . . . 3
G. Moriarty, DET . . . 3
J. Birmingham, CLE . 2
D. Moeller, WAS . . . 1
G. McBride, WAS . . . 1
S. McInnis, PHI 1
B. Daniels, NY 1

1913 NATIONAL
J. Daubert, BKN . . . 50
G. Cravath, PHI . . . 40
R. Maranville, BOS. . 23
C. Mathewson, NY. . 21
C. Meyers, NY 20
V. Saier, CHI 15

L. Cheney, CHI 12
D. Miller, PIT 11
H. Wagner, PIT 11
J. Evers, CHI 10
T. Seaton, PHI 9
A. Fletcher, NY 7
J. Archer, CHI 6
M. Doolan, PHI 6
B. Sweeney, BOS . . . 6
B. Viox, PIT 6
L. Doyle, NY 5
T. Shafer, NY 5
R. Murray, NY 4
H. Zimmerman, CHI . 4
O. Knabe, PHI 4
B. Adams, PIT 3
G. Cutshaw, BKN . . . 3
G. Burns, NY 2
A. Marsans, CIN . . . 2
B. Humphries, CHI . . 2
M. Brown, CIN 1

1913 AMERICAN
W. Johnson, WAS .. 54
J. Jackson, CLE ... 43
E. Collins, PHI 30
T. Speaker, BOS ... 26
F. Baker, PHI 21
C. Gandil, WAS 14
S. McInnis, PHI 12
W. Schang, PHI 11
C. Milan, WAS 8
J. Barry, PHI 8
N. Lajoie, CLE 7
D. Bush, DET 6
H. Wagner, BOS ... 6
R. Russell, CHI 5

B. Shotton, SL 5
G. McBride, WAS ... 5
J. Scott, CHI 5
G. Stovall, SL 5
S. Crawford, DET ... 5
T. Cobb, DET 3
R. Schalk, CHI 3
C. Bender, PHI 2
T. Turner, CLE 2
S. O'Neill, CLE 1
H. Hooper, BOS 1

1914 NATIONAL
J. Evers, BOS 50
R. Maranville, BOS.. 44

B. James, BOS 33
G. Burns, NY 31
J. Miller, SL 18
J. Tesreau, NY 15
D. Rudolph, BOS ... 14
S. Magee, PHI 14
Z. Wheat, BKN 10
G. Alexander, PHI .. 9
R. Bresnahan, CHI .. 6
L. Magee, SL 6
B. Doak, SL 5
J. Viox, PIT 5
A. Fletcher, NY 5
C. Mathewson, NY .. 4

V. Saier, CHI 4
B. Schmidt, BOS ... 4
J. Daubert, BKN 4
L. McCarty, BKN ... 3
H. Groh, CIN 2
T. Clark, CIN 1
G. Cravath, PHI 1

1914 AMERICAN
E. Collins, PHI 63
S. Crawford, DET .. 35
D. Bush, DET 17
J. Barry, PHI 17
F. Baker, PHI 17

J. Jackson, CLE ... 15
R. Schalk, CHI 13
E. Foster, WAS 11
B. Weaver, CHI 11
S. McInnis, PHI 11
D. Pratt, SL 10
W. Schang, PHI 10
T. Speaker, BOS ... 9
T. Walker, SL 9
T. Cobb, DET 7
E. Scott, BOS 7
J. Barry, PHI 6
D. Leonard, BOS ... 6

E. Plank, PHI 5
G. McBride, WAS ... 5
D. Lewis, BOS 4
H. Hooper, BOS 4
F. Maisel, NY 3
R. Peckinpaugh, NY .2
C. Milan, WAS 2
S. Agnew, SL 2
R. Hartzell, CLE 2
E. Cicotte, CHI 1
G. Moriarty, DET 1

(No official awards, 1915–21)

MVP Award
League Awards, 1922–29

1922 AMERICAN
G. Sisler, SL 59
E. Rommel, PHI 31
R. Schalk, CHI 26
L. Bush, NY 19
E. Collins, CHI 18
J. Bassler, DET 13
S. O'Neill, CLE 13
J. Judge, WAS 12

W. Pipp, NY 12
L. Blue, DET 11
C. Galloway, PHI ... 10
H. Heilmann, DET .. 8
D. Pratt, BOS 7
W. Schang, NY 7
B. Meusel, NY 6
E. Scott, NY 6
W. Johnson, WAS ... 5

U. Shocker, SL 5
C. Jamieson, CLE ... 4
J. Sewell, CLE 4
G. Burns, BOS 2
J. Dykes, PHI 2
B. Harris, WAS 2
R. Peckinpaugh, WAS 2
B. Wambsganss, CLE 2
G. Cutshaw, DET 1

C. Perkins, PHI 1

1923 AMERICAN
B. Ruth, NY 64
E. Collins, CHI 37
H. Heilmann, DET .. 31
W. Gerber, SL 20
J. Sewell, CLE 20
C. Jamieson, CLE .. 19

J. Bassler, DET ... 17
C. Galloway, PHI .. 13
G. Uhle, CLE 13
G. Burns, BOS 8
H. Ehmke, BOS 7
M. Ruel, WAS 7
R. Peckinpaugh,
　WAS 6
U. Shocker, SL 5

J. Judge, WAS 4
M. McManus, SL ... 4
K. Williams, SL 4
J. Harris, BOS 3
B. Harris, WAS 3
J. Hauser, PHI 1
W. Johnson, WAS ... 1
C. Perkins, PHI 1

(No National League awards, 1922–23)

1924 NATIONAL
D. Vance, BKN 74
R. Hornsby, SL 62
F. Frisch, NY 40
Z. Wheat, BKN 40
R. Youngs, NY 35
G. Kelly, NY 34
R. Maranville, PIT .. 33
K. Cuyler, PIT 25
J. Fournier, BKN ... 21
E. Roush, CIN 12
G. Wright, PIT 10
A. High, BKN 9
B. Pinelli, CIN 7
R. Bressler, CIN 6
G. Hartnett, CHI 5
B. Grimes, BKN 5
J. Bottomley, SL 4
J. Johnston, BKN ... 3
M. Carey, PIT 3
T. Jackson, NY 3
E. Yde, PIT 2
C. Williams, PHI 1
E. Rixey, CIN 1
G. Alexander, CHI ... 1
H. DeBerry, BKN 1

1924 AMERICAN
W. Johnson, WAS .. 55
E. Collins, CHI 49
C. Jamieson, CLE .. 25
H. Pennock, NY ... 24
J. Bassler, DET ... 22
H. Severeid, SL ... 17
J. Hauser, PHI 13
W. Jacobson, SL ... 11
H. Heilmann, DET .. 9
J. Sewell, CLE 9
M. Ruel, WAS 7
W. Schang, NY 7
A. Simmons, PHI ... 7
W. Pipp, NY 6
H. Ehmke, BOS 5
I. Flagstead, BOS ... 5
W. Gerber, SL 4
E. Whitehill, DET ... 4
L. Blue, DET 3
I. Boone, BOS 2
J.Harris, BOS 2
C. Galloway, PHI 1

K. Williams, SL 1

1925 NATIONAL
R. Hornsby, SL 73
K. Cuyler, PIT 61
G. Kelly, NY 52
G. Wright, PIT 43
D. Vance, BKN 42
D. Bancroft, BOS .. 41
J. Bottomley, SL ... 28
P. Traynor, PIT 27
F. Frisch, NY 13
E. Roush, CIN 12
M. Carey, PIT 11
I. Meusel, NY 6
D. Luque, CIN 5
C. Grimm, CHI 5
Z. Wheat, BKN 4
P. Donohue, CIN 4
B. Hargrave, CIN ... 3
G. Harper, PHI 3
J. Sand, PHI 3
W. Gautreau, BOS .. 2
V. Aldridge, PIT 1

1925 AMERICAN
R. Peckinpaugh,
　WAS 45
A. Simmons, PHI ... 41
J. Sewell, CLE 21
H. Heilmann, DET .. 20
H. Rice, SL 18
E. Sheely, CHI 17
I. Flagstead, BOS .. 10
W. Jacobson, SL ... 10
J. Mostil, CHI 10
O. Bluege, WAS 8
M. Cochrane, PHI .. 8
L. Blue, DET 7
S. Coveleski, WAS .. 7
W. Kamm, CHI 7
E. Rommel, PHI 7
R. Schalk, CHI 7
A. Wingo, DET 7
E. Combs, NY 6
B. Meusel, NY 6
T. Lyons, CHI 5
G. Burns, CLE 4
M. McManus, SL ... 4
H. Pennock, NY 4

B. Bengough, NY ... 2
H. Ehmke, BOS 2
L. Gehrig, NY 2
I. Boone, BOS 1
J. Dugan, NY 1
P. Todt, BOS 1

1926 NATIONAL
B. O'Farrell, SL ... 79
H. Critz, CIN 60
R. Kremer, PIT 32
T. Thevenow, SL ... 30
H. Wilson, CHI 25
L. Bell, SL 24
B. Hargrave, CIN ... 24
F. Rhem, SL 20
F. Lindstrom, NY ... 17
D. Bancroft, BOS .. 17
H. Carlson, PHI 16
P. Waner, PIT 15
P. Traynor, PIT 14
W. Pipp, CIN 12
E. Brown, BOS 10
F. Herman, BKN 8
C. Root, CHI 8
R. Hornsby, CHI 7
J. Butler, BKN 5
B. Southworth, SL .. 5
G. Alexander, SL ... 5
C. Mays, CIN 4
G. Kelly, NY 2
C. Walker, CIN 1

1926 AMERICAN
G. Burns, CLE 63
J. Mostil, CHI 33
H. Pennock, NY ... 32
S. Rice, WAS 18
H. Heilmann, DET .. 16
H. Manush, DET ... 16
A. Simmons, PHI ... 16
L. Grove, PHI 12
G. Goslin, WAS 9
L. Gehrig, NY 9
T. Lazzeri, NY 7
B. Falk, CHI 6
F. Fothergill, DET ... 6
O. Melillo, SL 6
H. Rice, SL 6

O. Bluege, WAS 5
P. Todt, BOS 5
M. Cochrane, PHI .. 4
J. Judge, WAS 4
M. McManus, SL ... 4
B. Meusel, NY 3
E. Rigney, BOS 3
I. Flagstead, BOS .. 2
W. Gerber, SL 2
T. Zachary, SL 2
W. Jacobson, BOS .. 1

1927 NATIONAL
P. Waner, PIT 72
F. Frisch, SL 66
R. Hornsby, NY ... 54
C. Root, CHI 46
T. Jackson, NY 42
L. Waner, PIT 25
P. Traynor, PIT 18
J. Haines, SL 16
R. Kremer, PIT 14
G. Hartnett, CHI ... 12
R. Lucas, CIN 10
H. Wilson, CHI 9
B. Terry, NY 6
J. Bottomley, SL ... 6
B. Hargrave, CIN ... 6
F. May, CIN 6
C. Williams, PHI 6
E. Farrell, BOS 4
B. Grimes, NY 4
M. Carey, BKN 3
R. Stephenson, CHI 3
G. Alexander, SL ... 3
C. Hill, PIT 2
J. Petty, BKN 2
F. Ulrich, PHI 2
C. Hafey, SL 1

1927 AMERICAN
L. Gehrig, NY 56
H. Heilmann, DET .. 35
T. Lyons, CHI 34
M. Cochrane, PHI .. 18
A. Simmons, PHI ... 18
G. Goslin, WAS 15
M. Ruel, WAS 15
J. Dykes, PHI 14

L. Sewell, CLE 13
J. Sewell, CLE 9
T. Lazzeri, NY 8
R. Reeves, WAS 7
F. O'Rourke, SL 6
J. Tavener, DET ... 6
H. Lisenbee, WAS .. 5
E. Miller, SL 5
A. Metzler, CHI 4
I. Flagstead, BOS .. 3
C. Jamieson, CLE .. 3
W. Schang, SL 3
F. Schulte, SL 3
W. Hudlin, CLE 2
W. Regan, BOS 2
J. Rothrock, BOS ... 2
B. Harriss, BOS 1
P. Todt, BOS 1

1928 NATIONAL
J. Bottomley, SL ... 76
F. Lindstrom, NY ... 70
B. Grimes, PIT 53
L. Benton, NY 37
H. Critz, CIN 37
P. Traynor, PIT 28
H. Wilson, CHI 21
S. Hogan, NY 17
T. Jackson, NY 16
R. Maranville, SL .. 14
D. Vance, BKN 13
C. Hafey, SL 11
R. Hornsby, BOS ... 10
G. Hartnett, CHI 6
P. Waner, PIT 6
L. Richbourg, BOS .. 5
T. Douthit, SL 5
D. Bissonette, BKN .. 3
D. Flowers, BKN ... 3
J. Wilson, SL 3
A. Whitney, PHI 3
H. Ford, CIN 2
L. Thompson, PHI .. 1

1928 AMERICAN
M. Cochrane, PHI .. 53
H. Manush, SL 51
J. Judge, WAS 27
T. Lazzeri, NY 27

W. Kamm, CHI 15
G. Goslin, WAS 13
E. Combs, NY 13
C. Gehringer, DET .. 12
C. Myer, BOS 11
W. Hoyt, NY 8
J. Foxx, PHI 7
J. Sewell, CLE 6
L. Sewell, CLE 6
I. Flagstead, BOS .. 5
E. Morris, BOS 4
H. Heilmann, DET .. 4
C. Lind, CLE 4
W. Cissell, CHI 4
A. Thomas, CHI 4
O. Carroll, DET 3
H. Rice, DET 3
L. Fonseca, CLE 2
T. Lyons, CHI 2
J. Hodapp, CLE 2
A. Metzler, CHI 1
W. Regan, BOS 1

1929 NATIONAL
R. Hornsby, CHI ... 60
L. O'Doul, PHI 54
B. Terry, NY 48
B. Grimes, PIT 35
L. Waner, PIT 30
R. Lucas, CIN 29
P. Traynor, PIT 27
H. Wilson, CHI 24
F. Herman, BKN ... 24
G. Bush, CHI 16
C. Klein, PHI 15
M. Ott, NY 15
T. Douthit, SL 14
C. Grimm, CHI 13
T. Jackson, NY 13
R. Maranville, BOS .. 8
H. Critz, CIN 5
C. Friberg, PHI 4
P. Malone, CHI 3
F. Frisch, SL 2
P. Whitney, PHI 2
J. Frederick, BKN ... 2
R. Stephenson, CHI 1
Z. Taylor, BOS-CHI .. 1

(There were no official selections for the American League in 1929 or for either league in 1930.)

MVP Award
Baseball Writers' Association of America Awards, 1931–Present

1931 NATIONAL
F. Frisch, SL......65
C. Klein, PHI.....55
B. Terry, NY.....53
W. English, CHI....30
C. Hafey, SL.....29
J. Wilson, SL.....28
T. Jackson, NY....24
C. Grimm, CHI.....21
E. Adams, SL.....18
E. Brandt, BOS....15
R. Maranville, BOS.15
K. Cuyler, CHI....14
P. Traynor, PIT....12
R. Lucas, CIN.....10
L. Waner, PIT.....8
J. Bottomley, SL....8
J. Elliott, PHI.....6
J. Quinn, BKN.....6
N. Finn, BKN.....5
W. Clark, BKN.....3
P. Derringer, SL....3
C. Root, CHI.....3
D. Bartell, PHI.....2
J. Vergez, NY.....2
F. Fitzsimmons, NY...1
L. O'Doul, BKN....1
G. Wright, BKN....1
T. Cuccinello, CIN...1
C. Gelbert, SL.....1

1931 AMERICAN
L. Grove, PHI......78
L. Gehrig, NY.....59
A. Simmons, PHI....51
E. Averill, CLE.....43
B. Ruth, NY.....40
E. Webb, BOS.....22
J. Cronin, WAS.....18
O. Melillo, SL.....17
S. West, WAS.....16
M. Cochrane, PHI..16
G. Earnshaw, PHI..12
W. Ferrell, CLE.....12
F. Marberry, WAS...11
H. Rhyne, BOS.....10
B. Chapman, NY....7
J. Stone, DET.....6
C. Gehringer, DET....4
L. Blue, DET.....4
R. Kress, SL.....3
C. Reynolds, CHI....2
W. Stewart, SL.....2
G. Goslin, SL.....2
D. MacFayden, BOS..2
T. Oliver, BOS.....2
J. Foxx, PHI.....1

1932 NATIONAL
C. Klein, PHI.....78
L. Warneke, CHI...68
L. O'Doul, PIT.....58
P. Waner, PIT.....37
R. Stephenson, CHI 32
B. Terry, NY.....25
D. Hurst, PHI.....24
P. Traynor, PIT.....17
B. Herman, CHI....16
M. Ott, NY.....15
R. Brown, BOS.....10
F. Herman, CIN.....8
L. Waner, PIT.....6
W. Berger, BOS.....6
H. Wilson, BKN.....6
E. Orsatti, SL.....6
R. Maranville, BOS..5
J. Wilson, SL.....5
T. Cuccinello, BKN....4
J. Dean, SL.....4
F. Frisch, SL.....3
R. Collins, SL.....3
A. Vaughan, PIT.....1
G. Bush, CHI.....1

1932 AMERICAN
J. Foxx, PHI.....75
L. Gehrig, NY.....55
H. Manush, WAS...41

E. Averill, CLE.....37
L. Gomez, NY.....27
J. Cronin, WAS....26
B. Ruth, NY.....26
T. Lazzeri, NY.....21
A. Simmons, PHI...13
C. Gehringer, DET..13
D. Alexander,
  DET-BOS.....10
W. Cissell, CLE....10
R. Ferrell, SL.....9
L. Grove, PHI.....8
J. Allen, NY.....8
B. Dickey, NY.....8
G. Goslin, SL.....7
M. Weaver, WAS....6
H. Davis, DET.....5
D. Harris, WAS.....5
W. Ferrell, CLE.....5
J. Levey, SL.....5
T. Lyons, CHI.....5
B. Sullivan, CHI.....3
E. McNair, PHI.....3
S. Jolley, BOS.....3
G. Crowder, WAS....2
M. McManus, BOS...2
G. Walker, DET.....1
J. Sewell, NY.....1

1933 NATIONAL
C. Hubbell, NY.....77
C. Klein, PHI.....48
W. Berger, BOS....44
B. Terry, NY.....35
P. Martin, SL.....31
G. Mancuso, NY...24
J. Dean, SL.....23
P. Traynor, PIT.....20
B. Ryan, NY.....19
A. Lopez, BKN.....18
B. Cantwell, BOS...18
H. Schumacher, NY.11
R. Maranville, BOS..11
G. Bush, CHI.....11
L. French, PIT.....10
F. Frisch, SL.....7
J. Bottomley, CIN....6
J. Medwick, SL.....5
G. Hartnett, CHI....5
L. Warneke, CHI....4
R. Lucas, CIN.....3
D. Bartell, PHI.....3
A. Vaughan, PIT.....2
R. Moore, BOS.....2
V. Davis, PHI.....1
C. Hafey, CIN.....1
D. Luque, NY.....1

1933 AMERICAN
J. Foxx, PHI.....74
J. Cronin, WAS....62
H. Manush, WAS...54
L. Gehrig, NY.....39
L. Grove, PHI.....35
C. Gehringer, DET..32
G. Crowder, WAS..28
A. Simmons, CHI...19
E. Whitehill, WAS...18
O. Melillo, SL.....12
S. West, SL.....11
R. Ferrell, BOS.....9
B. Dickey, NY.....9
T. Lazzeri, NY.....6
J. Kuhel, WAS.....5
E. Averill, CLE.....5
C. Myer, WAS.....5
M. Cochrane, PHI....5
B. Johnson, PHI.....5
B. Chapman, NY....4
M. Bishop, PHI.....1
L. Appling, CHI.....1
W. Kamm, CLE.....1

1934 NATIONAL
J. Dean, SL.....78
P. Waner, PIT.....50
J. Moore, NY.....42
T. Jackson, NY....39

M. Ott, NY.....37
J. Collins, SL.....32
B. Terry, NY.....30
C. Davis, PHI.....18
P. Dean, SL.....16
H. Schumacher, NY.16
C. Hubbell, NY.....16
W. Berger, BOS....13
L. Warneke, CHI...10
G. Hartnett, CHI....9
G. Slade, CIN.....5
K. Cuyler, CHI.....4
B. Frey, CIN.....4
F. Frankhouse, BOS..4
R. Boyle, BKN.....4
B. Herman, CHI....4
F. Frisch, SL.....4
W. Hoyt, PIT.....2
A. Lopez, BKN.....1
V. Mungo, BKN.....1
A. Vaughan, PIT.....1

1934 AMERICAN
M. Cochrane, DET..67
C. Gehringer, DET..65
L. Gomez, NY.....60
S. Rowe, DET.....59
L. Gehrig, NY.....54
H. Greenberg, DET..29
H. Trosky, CLE.....18
W. Ferrell, BOS....16
M. Owen, DET.....13
J. Foxx, PHI.....11
A. Simmons, CHI...9
W. Werber, BOS.....8
R. Johnson, BOS....8
G. Goslin, DET.....6
S. West, SL.....5
M. Harder, CLE.....4
F. Higgins, PHI.....3
E. Averill, CLE.....3
B. Knickerbocker,
  CLE.....2

1935 NATIONAL
G. Hartnett, CHI....75
J. Dean, SL.....66
A. Vaughan, PIT....45
B. Herman, CHI....38
J. Medwick, SL.....37
C. Hubbell, NY.....20
W. Berger, BOS....20
B. Terry, NY.....20
A. Galan, CHI.....18
P. Martin, SL.....16
H. Leiber, NY.....11
L. Warneke, CHI....9
E. Lombardi, CIN....8
F. Frisch, SL.....7
C. Blanton, PIT.....5
J. Moore, PHI.....5
E. Allen, PHI.....4
G. Mancuso, NY....4
P. Derringer, CIN....4
M. Ott, NY.....3
P. Dean, SL.....2
R. Collins, SL.....2
C. Davis, PHI.....2
P. Waner, PIT.....1
B. Lee, CHI.....1
T. Jackson, NY.....1
D. Camilli, PHI.....1

1935 AMERICAN
H. Greenberg, DET..80
W. Ferrell, BOS....62
J. Vosmik, CLE.....39
C. Myer, WAS.....36
L. Gehrig, NY.....29
C. Gehringer, DET..26
M. Cochrane, DET..24
F. Cramer, PHI.....18
J. Solters, SL.....16
R. Hemsley, SL.....16
J. Foxx, PHI.....11
T. Bridges, DET.....11
T. Lyons, CHI.....10
L. Grove, BOS.....8

Z. Bonura, CHI.....7
L. Appling, CHI.....7
L. Sewell, CHI.....7
C. Davis, PHI.....5
J. Allen, NY.....5
J. Whitehead, CHI....5
F. Higgins, PHI.....3
J. Marcum, PHI.....3
E. Auker, DET.....2
M. Harder, CLE.....2
L. Lary, SL.....1

1936 NATIONAL
C. Hubbell, NY.....60
J. Dean, SL.....53
B. Herman, CHI....37
J. Medwick, SL.....30
P. Waner, PIT.....29
M. Ott, NY.....28
F. Demaree, CHI...17
G. Mancuso, NY...13
D. MacFayden,
  BOS.....12
L. Durocher, SL.....8
P. Derringer, CIN....6
G. Hartnett, CHI....6
B. Whitehead, NY....6
A. Lopez, BOS.....5
V. Mungo, BKN.....5
W. Berger, BOS.....4
D. Camilli, PHI.....4
G. Phelps, BKN.....3
D. Bartell, NY.....2
E. Lombardi, CIN....1
T. Moore, SL.....1

1936 AMERICAN
L. Gehrig, NY.....73
L. Appling, CHI....65
E. Averill, CLE.....48
C. Gehringer, DET..39
B. Dickey, NY.....29
V. Kennedy, CHI....27
J. Kuhel, WAS.....27
J. DiMaggio, NY....26
T. Bridges, DET.....25
H. Trosky, CLE.....19
J. Foxx, BOS.....16
G. Walker, DET.....14
B. Bell, SL.....10
W. Moses, PHI.....7
L. Grove, BOS.....5
J. Dykes, CHI.....3
R. Radcliff, CHI.....3
S. West, SL.....3
Z. Bonura, CHI.....1
E. McNair, BOS.....1

1937 NATIONAL
J. Medwick, SL.....70
G. Hartnett, CHI....68
C. Hubbell, NY.....52
J. Turner, BOS.....30
L. Fette, BOS.....29
D. Bartell, NY.....26
M. Ott, NY.....24
P. Waner, PIT.....21
B. Herman, CHI....19
J. Mize, SL.....18
C. Melton, NY.....17
C. Root, CHI.....15
P. Whitney, PHI.....13
H. Danning, NY....10
F. Demaree, CHI....9
L. Warneke, SL.....6
B. Jurges, CHI.....4
J. Cooney, BKN.....4
B. Myers, CIN.....2
L. Grissom, CIN.....2
H. Manush, BKN....1

1937 AMERICAN
C. Gehringer, DET..78
J. DiMaggio, NY....74
H. Greenberg, DET..48
L. Gehrig, NY.....42
L. Sewell, CHI.....22
B. Dickey, NY.....22
J. Cronin, BOS.....19

R. Ruffing, NY.....18
L. Gomez, NY.....14
M. Kreevich, CHI....13
C. Travis, WAS.....12
W. Moses, PHI.....12
J. Allen, CLE.....11
H. Clift, SL.....11
R. Radcliff, CHI....10
B. Lewis, WAS.....7
L. Appling, CHI.....5
B. Bell, SL.....5
E. Averill, CLE.....5
L. Lary, CLE.....4
R. Lawson, DET.....3
G. Walker, DET.....3
R. York, DET.....1
P. Fox, DET.....1

1936 NATIONAL
C. Hubbell, NY.....60
J. Dean, SL.....53
B. Herman, CHI....37
J. Medwick, SL.....30
P. Waner, PIT.....29
M. Ott, NY.....28
F. Demaree, CHI...17
G. Mancuso, NY...13
D. MacFayden,
  BOS.....12
L. Durocher, SL.....8
P. Derringer, CIN....6
G. Hartnett, CHI....6
B. Whitehead, NY....6
A. Lopez, BOS.....5
V. Mungo, BKN.....5
W. Berger, BOS.....4
D. Camilli, PHI.....4
G. Phelps, BKN.....3
D. Bartell, NY.....2
E. Lombardi, CIN....1
T. Moore, SL.....1

1938 NATIONAL
E. Lombardi, CIN..229
B. Lee, CHI.....166
A. Vaughan, PIT...163
M. Ott, NY.....132
F. McCormick, CIN.130
J. Rizzo, PIT.....96
S. Hack, CHI.....87
P. Derringer, CIN...70
M. Brown, PIT.....62
G. Hartnett, CHI....61
J. Medwick, SL.....55
J. Mize, SL.....28
T. Cuccinello, BOS..23
P. Young, PIT.....19
C. Bryant, CHI.....16
H. Danning, NY....13
I. Goodman, CIN....11
L. VanderMeer, CIN..6
L. Durocher, BKN....6
D. Coffman, CIN....6
A. Lopez, BOS.....5
D. Garms, BOS.....5
D. Camilli, BKN.....5
C. Root, CHI.....3
J. Moore, NY.....3
J. Hudson, BKN.....3
H. Mulcahy, PHI....3
L. Handley, PIT.....2
L. Warneke, SL.....1
F. Fitzsimmons, BKN.1
H. Martin, PHI.....1

1938 AMERICAN
J. Foxx, BOS.....305
B. Dickey, NY.....196
H. Greenberg,
  DET.....162
R. Ruffing, NY.....146
B. Newsom, SL.....111
J. DiMaggio, NY...106
J. Cronin, BOS.....92
E. Averill, CLE.....34
C. Travis, WAS.....33
C. Gehringer, DET..27
J. Heath, CLE.....24
J. Gordon, NY.....23
H. Trosky, CLE.....22
K. Keltner, CLE.....16
M. Stratton, CHI....15
M. Harder, CLE.....14
B. Johnson, PHI....13
H. Clift, SL.....11
L. Gehrig, NY.....10
P. Fox, DET.....9
J. Vosmik, BOS.....7
G. McQuinn, SL.....7
L. Grove, BOS.....7
B. Lewis, WAS.....5
R. Rolfe, NY.....5
C. Myer, WAS.....5
E. Brucker, PHI.....3
J. Allen, CLE.....3
F. Crosetti, NY.....2
L. Gomez, NY.....1
D. Cramer, BOS.....1

1939 NATIONAL
B. Walters, CIN...303

J. Mize, SL.....178
P. Derringer, CIN..174
F. McCormick, CIN.159
C. Davis, SL.....106
L. Brown, SL.....99
J. Medwick, SL.....81
L. Durocher, BKN...52
H. Danning, NY....33
L. Hamlin, BKN....32
M. Ott, NY.....21
B. Jurges, NY.....20
D. Camilli, BKN....20
W. Myers, CIN.....18
S. Hack, CHI.....17
A. Galan, CHI.....15
T. Moore, SL.....15
M. Arnovich, PHI...10
L. Frey, CIN.....8
B. Lee, CHI.....8
E. Slaughter, SL.....8
W. Werber, CIN.....6
W. West, BOS.....5
G. Hartnett, CHI....5
I. Goodman, CIN....4
B. Hassett, BOS.....4
P. Coscarart, BKN...4
E. Fletcher, BOS-PIT..4
L. Lavagetto, BKN...3
R. Bowman, SL.....2
E. Miller, BOS.....1
B. Herman, CHI....1

1939 AMERICAN
J. DiMaggio, NY...280
J. Foxx, BOS.....170
B. Feller, CLE.....155
T. Williams, BOS...126
R. Ruffing, NY.....116
B. Dickey, NY.....110
B. Leonard, WAS...71
B. Johnson, PHI....52
J. Gordon, NY.....43
M. Kreevich, CHI...38
C. Brown, CHI.....34
K. Keltner, CLE.....26
G. McQuinn, SL.....24
C. Gehringer, DET..21
L. Grove, BOS.....17
J. Cronin, BOS.....15
T. Lyons, CHI.....13
H. Greenberg, DET.12
B. Newsom, DET...11
J. Rigney, CHI.....9
J. Kuhel, CHI.....8
C. Keller, NY.....7
J. Heath, CLE.....7
G. Walker, CHI.....7
F. Hayes, PHI.....7
T. Bridges, DET.....7
R. Rolfe, NY.....6
B. McCosky, DET...6
E. McNair, CHI.....5
H. Trosky, CLE.....4
G. Case, WAS.....3
M. Hoag, SL.....3
R. York, DET.....3
L. Appling, CHI.....1

1940 NATIONAL
F. McCormick, CIN.274
J. Mize, SL.....209
B. Walters, CIN....146
P. Derringer, CIN..121
F. Fitzsimmons,
  BKN.....84
D. Walker, BKN....71
H. Danning, NY....64
S. Hack, CHI.....61
E. Lombardi, CIN...38
W. Werber, CIN.....36
J. Cooney, BOS.....31
D. Camilli, BKN....30
E. Miller, BOS.....28
D. Garms, PIT.....28
A. Vaughan, PIT....27
C. Passeau, CHI.....26
J. Beggs, CIN.....19
T. Moore, SL.....18

E. Fletcher, PIT 16
B. Nicholson, CHI .. 12
K. Higbe, PHI 10
C. Rowell, BOS 10
A. Lopez, PIT 9
M. Van Robays, PIT .. 8
R. Sewell, PIT 7
P. Reese, BKN 6
M. West, BOS 6
N. Young, NY 6
W. Wyatt, BKN 3
J. Rizzo, PHI 3
P. May, PHI 3
H. Mulcahy, PHI 3
J. Martin, SL 2
F. Gustine, PIT 1

1940 AMERICAN
H. Greenberg, DET 292
B. Feller, CLE 222
J. DiMaggio, NY .. 151
B. Newsom, DET .. 120
L. Boudreau, CLE . 119
J. Foxx, BOS 110
L. Rowe, DET 62
R. York, DET 61
R. Radcliff, SL 55
L. Appling, CHI 54
R. Weatherly, CLE .. 34
D. Bartell, DET 26
J. Kuhel, CHI 18
S. Hudson, WAS ... 16
T. Williams, BOS ... 16
B. McCosky, DET .. 11
E. Bonham, NY 8
W. Judnich, SL 6
J. Babich, PHI 5
M. Tresh, CHI 4
F. Hayes, PHI 4
R. Mack, CLE 4
J. Gordon, NY 3
C. Travis, WAS 3
B. Kennedy, CHI 3
C. Gehringer, DET ... 3
R. Hemsley, CLE 2
T. Lyons, CHI 2
L. Finney, BOS 1
E. Auker, SL 1

1941 NATIONAL
D. Camilli, BKN ... 300
P. Reiser, BKN 183
W. Wyatt, BKN 151
J. Brown, SL 107
E. Riddle, CIN 98
E. White, SL 77
K. Higbe, BKN 64
J. Hopp, SL 61
J. Mize, SL 48
D. Walker, BKN 34
B. Herman, BKN 27
T. Moore, SL 26
S. Hack, CHI 26
E. Fletcher, PIT 22
J. Cooney, BOS 20
B. Nicholson, CHI .. 16
G. Mancuso, SL 14
F. Crespi, SL 13
M. Ott, NY 12
E. Slaughter, SL 12
B. Young, NY 10
V. DiMaggio, PIT ... 10
J. Tobin, BOS 10
A. Lopez, PIT 8
M. Marion, SL 8
M. Cooper, SL 8
L. Warneke, SL 7
N. Etten, PHI 6
B. Walters, CIN 6
B. Dahlgren, CHI 6
W. Werber, CIN 6
E. Crabtree, SL 5
J. Rucker, NY 4
D. Litwhiler, PHI 3
H. Danning, NY 2
C. Hubbell, NY 2
C. Lavagetto, BKN .. 2
A. Vaughan, PIT 2

1941 AMERICAN
J. DiMaggio, NY .. 291
T. Williams, BOS .. 254
B. Feller, CLE 174
T. Lee, CHI 144
C. Keller, NY 126
C. Travis, WAS 101
J. Gordon, NY 60
J. Heath, CLE 37
H. Newsome, BOS . 32
R. Cullenbine, SL ... 29
J. Cronin, BOS 26
S. Chapman, PHI ... 25
B. Dickey, NY 18
T. Henrich, NY 16
B. McCosky, DET ... 12
T. Lyons, CHI 12
D. Siebert, PHI 10
L. Boudreau, CLE .. 10
A. Benton, DET 8
P. Rizzuto, NY 7
E. Leonard, WAS 7
B. Campbell, DET ... 4
R. York, DET 3
F. Hayes, PHI 3
T. Wright, CHI 2
R. Ruffing, NY 2
E. Auker, SL 1
F. Higgins, DET 1
D. DiMaggio, BOS ... 1

1942 NATIONAL
M. Cooper, SL 263
E. Slaughter, SL ... 200
M. Ott, NY 190
A. Owen, BKN 103
J. Mize, NY 97
P. Reiser, BKN 91
M. Marion, SL 81
D. Camilli, BKN 42
R. Elliott, PIT 39
C. Passeau, CHI 33
W. Cooper, SL 28
S. Musial, SL 26
E. Lombardi, BOS .. 24
J. Beazley, SL 24
J. Brown, SL 24
W. Wyatt, BKN 22
J. Medwick, BKN ... 20
T. Moore, SL 15
B. Nicholson, CHI .. 14
S. Hack, CHI 11
J. VanderMeer, CIN . 11
T. Hughes, PHI 10
R. Starr, CIN 9
L. French, BKN 7
P. Reese, BKN 6
W. Kurowski, SL 6
R. Lamanno, CIN 4
M. West, BOS 4
L. Frey, CIN 4
F. McCormick, CIN ... 4
A. Javery, BOS 3
E. Miller, BOS 1

1942 AMERICAN
J. Gordon, NY 270
T. Williams, BOS .. 249
J. Pesky, BOS 143
V. Stephens, SL ... 140
E. Bonham, NY ... 102
T. Hughson, BOS ... 92
J. DiMaggio, NY 86
S. Spence, WAS ... 65
P. Marchildon, PHI .. 39
L. Boudreau, CLE .. 34
B. Doerr, BOS 24
T. Lyons, CHI 23
G. Case, WAS 17
K. Keltner, CLE 15
C. Keller, NY 15
W. Judnich, SL 14
B. Dickey, NY 12
D. Gutteridge, SL ... 12
P. Rizzuto, NY 9
C. Laabs, SL 9
R. Ferrell, SL 8
H. Borowy, NY 8
J. Bagby, CLE 6
T. Wright, CHI 6
T. Lupien BOS 4
L. Fleming, CLE 4
S. Chandler, NY 3
R. York, DET 3
B. McCosky, DET ... 1

1943 NATIONAL
S. Musial, SL 267
W. Cooper, SL 192
B. Nicholson, CHI . 181
B. Herman, BKN .. 140
M. Cooper, SL 130
R. Sewell, PIT 127
E. Riddle, CIN 68
R. Elliott, PIT 52
F. McCormick, CIN .. 26
C. Shoun, CIN 24
E. Miller, CIN 24
M. Witek, NY 21
M. Marion, SL 20
L. Rowe, PHI 18
W. Wyatt, BKN 15
A. Vaughan, BKN ... 15
R. Mueller, CIN 12
A. Javery, BOS 12
S. Hack, CHI 10
M. Ott, NY 9
E. Fletcher, PIT 7
A. Adams, NY 7
L. Klein, SL 6
A. Galan, BKN 5
D. Walker, BKN 5
J. Tobin, BOS 5
D. Bartell, NY 5
P. Cavaretta, CHI 4
T. Holmes, BOS 2
R. Northey, PHI 2
B. Dahlgren, PHI 2
H. Bithorn, CHI 1
B. Walters, CIN 1
L. Frey, CIN 1

1943 AMERICAN
S. Chandler, NY ... 246
L. Appling, CHI ... 215
R. York, DET 152
W. Johnson, NY ... 135
B. Johnson, WAS . 116
D. Wakefield, DET .. 72
N. Etten, NY 61
B. Dickey, NY 58
V. Stephens, SL 49
L. Boudreau, CLE .. 40
D. Trout, DET 38
G. Case, WAS 37
C. Keller, NY 31
B. Doerr, BOS 21
A. Smith, CLE 19
G. Priddy, WAS 17
O. Hockett, CLE ... 14
D. Gutteridge, SL ... 13
E. Wynn, WAS 13
J. Bagby, CLE 11
R. Cramer, DET 8
F. Higgins, DET 8
C. Laabs, SL 6
J. Early, WAS 6
J. Gordon, NY 4
R. Wolff, PHI 4
L. Newsome, BOS ... 3
J. Cronin, BOS 3
J. Flores, PHI 3
G. Maltzberger, CHI .. 3
F. Crosetti, NY 2
K. Keltner, CLE 2
P. Fox, BOS 1
R. Hodgin, CHI 1
J. Murphy, NY 1
D. Siebert, PHI 1
J. Tabor, BOS 1
H. Wagner, PHI 1

1944 NATIONAL
M. Marion, SL 190
B. Nicholson, CHI . 189
D. Walker, BKN ... 145
S. Musial, SL 136
B. Walters, CIN ... 107
B. Voiselle, NY 107
R. Mueller, CIN 85
W. Cooper, SL 72
M. Cooper, SL 63
R. Elliott, PIT 57
R. Sewell, PIT 49
B. Dahlgren, PIT ... 33
F. McCormick, CIN .. 32
P. Cavaretta, CHI ... 27
R. Sanders, SL 25
M. Ott, NY 20
J. Tobin, BOS 13
J. Hopp, SL 10
R. Northey, PHI 10
J. Medwick, NY 9
J. Barrett, PIT 8
E. Miller, CIN 7
T. Holmes, BOS 6
T. Wilks, SL 4
T. Lupien, PHI 3
S. Hack, CHI 2
M. Lanier, SL 2
C. Ryan, BOS 2
A. Galan, BKN 1
W. Kurowski, SL 1
J. Russell, PIT 1

1944 AMERICAN
H. Newhouser, DET 236
D. Trout, DET 232
V. Stephens, SL ... 193
S. Stirnweiss, NY . 129
D. Wakefield, DET . 128
L. Boudreau, CLE .. 84
B. Doerr, BOS 75
S. Spence, WAS ... 56
N. Potter, SL 52
B. Johnson, BOS .. 51
M. Christman, SL .. 27
T. Hughson, BOS ... 22
D. Cramer, DET 14
F. Hayes, PHI 13
P. Fox, BOS 12
J. Kramer, SL 9
J. Lindell, NY 8
P. Richards, DET 8
D. Gutteridge, SL 7
F. Higgins, DET 7
G. McQuinn, SL 7
G. Kell, PHI 6
R. Cullenbine, CLE .. 5
N. Etten, NY 5
R. York, DET 5
R. Hemsley, NY 4
M. Kreevich, SL 4
W. Moses, CHI 4
E. Mayo, DET 3
D. Siebert, PHI 3
H. Borowy, NY 2
F. Crosetti, NY 2
R. Hodgin, CHI 2
B. Muncrief, SL 1

1945 NATIONAL
P. Cavaretta, CHI .. 279
T. Holmes, BOS ... 175
C. Barrett, BOS-SL 151
A. Pafko, CHI 131
W. Kurowski, SL ... 90
H. Borowy, CHI 84
H. Wyse, CHI 72
M. Marion, SL 69
D. Walker, BKN 66
G. Rosen, BKN 56
S. Hack, CHI 42
H. Brecheen, SL ... 31
M. Ott, NY 22
A. Galan, BKN 18
J. Hopp, SL 17
R. Elliott, PIT 15
L. Olmo, BKN 13
B. Adams, SL 12
C. Passeau, CHI 9
J. Barrett, PIT 8
E. Heusser, CIN 7
D. Johnson, CHI 7
B. Kerr, NY 7
F. McCormick, CIN ... 6
B. Salkeld, PIT 6
P. Lowrey, CHI 5
A. Adams, NY 4
A. Karl, PHI 4
H. Gregg, BKN 2
A. Lopez, PIT 2
P. Masi, BOS 2
E. Miller, CIN 2
V. DiMaggio, PHI 1
E. Stanky, BKN 1

1945 AMERICAN
H. Newhouser, DET 236
E. Mayo, DET 164
S. Stirnweiss, NY . 161
B. Ferriss, BOS .. 148
G. Myatt, WAS 98
V. Stephens, SL 94
R. Wolff, WAS 78
L. Boudreau, CLE .. 70
G. Case, WAS 60
P. Richards, DET ... 35
M. Tresh, CHI 33
J. Kuhel, WAS 29
R. Cullenbine, DET . 26
H. Greenberg, DET . 25
N. Etten, NY 21
T. Cuccinello, CHI .. 18
D. Trout, DET 17
E. Leonard, WAS ... 16
R. Schalk, CHI 13
J. Heath, CLE 10
G. Binks, WAS 9
B. Muncrief, SL 8
A. Benton, DET 6
R. Ferrell, WAS 6
B. Johnson, BOS 6
M. Christman, SL 5
B. Estalella, PHI 5
F. Hayes, PHI-CLE ... 5
D. Cramer, DET 4
W. Moses, CHI 4
E. Lake, BOS 2
R. Christopher, PHI .. 1
L. Newsome, BOS ... 1
R. York, DET 1

1946 NATIONAL
S. Musial, SL 319
D. Walker, BKN ... 159
E. Slaughter, SL ... 144
H. Pollet, SL 116
J. Sain, BOS 95
P. Reese, BKN 79
E. Stanky, BKN 67
D. Ennis, PHI 61
P. Reiser, BKN 58
P. Cavaretta, CHI ... 49
B. Kerr, NY 37
J. Hopp, BOS 34
E. Waitkus, CHI 21
B. Edwards, BKN .. 20
K. Higbe, BKN 18
H. Brecheen, SL 14
J. Mize, NY 14
G. Hatton, CIN 12
T. Holmes, BOS 11
J. Tabor, PHI 10
E. Verban, PHI 10
H. Walker, SL 9
L. Rowe, PHI 8
P. Masi, BOS 7
J. VanderMeer, CIN .. 7
R. Schoendienst, SL . 6
B. Cox, PIT 5
F. Gustine, PIT 4
M. Marion, SL 4
R. Kiner, PIT 3
W. Kurowski, SL 3
R. Mueller, CIN 3
J. Schmitz, CHI 3
P. Lowrey, CHI 2
F. McCormick, PHI ... 2
C. Furillo, BKN 1
O. Judd, PHI 1

1946 AMERICAN
T. Williams, BOS .. 224
H. Newhouser, DET 197
B. Doerr, BOS 158
J. Pesky, BOS 141
M. Vernon, WAS .. 134
B. Feller, CLE 105
B. Ferriss, BOS ... 94
H. Greenberg, DET . 91
D. DiMaggio, BOS . 56
L. Boudreau, CLE .. 37
R. York, BOS 28
L. Appling, CHI 26
T. Hughson, BOS ... 19
E. Caldwell, CHI 18
C. Keller, NY 17
G. Kell, DET 12
S. Chandler, NY 12
A. Robinson, NY ... 12
J. DiMaggio, NY 6
B. Newsom, WAS ... 6
V. Stephens, SL 6
P. Marchildon, PHI .. 5
B. Rosar, PHI 4
S. Spence, WAS 4
J. Berardino, SL 2
T. Henrich, NY 1
H. Wagner, BOS 1

1947 NATIONAL
R. Elliott, BOS 205
E. Blackwell, CIN .. 175
J. Mize, NY 144
B. Edwards, BKN . 140
J. Robinson, BKN . 106
R. Kiner, PIT 101
L. Jansen, NY 91
P. Reese, BKN 80
W. Kurowski, SL ... 45
H. Walker, PHI 45
R. Branca, BKN 40
H. Casey, BKN 37
E. Leonard, PHI 32
E. Stanky, BKN 32
W. Spahn, BOS 26
W. Marshall, NY 20
J. Sain, BOS 20
W. Cooper, NY 19
D. Walker, BKN 14
E. Slaughter, SL 12
S. Musial, SL 12
E. Verban, PHI 9
P. Cavaretta, CHI 6
P. Lowrey, CHI 2
E. Miller, CIN 2
A. Pafko, CHI 1

1947 AMERICAN
J. DiMaggio, NY .. 202
T. Williams, BOS .. 201
L. Boudreau, CLE . 168
J. Page, NY 167
G. Kell, DET 132
G. McQuinn, NY ... 77
J. Gordon, CLE 59
B. Feller, CLE 58
P. Marchildon, PHI .. 47
L. Appling, CHI 43
E. Joost, PHI 35
B. McCosky, PHI ... 35
T. Henrich, NY 33
F. Shea, NY 23
Y. Berra, NY 18
A. Reynolds, NY ... 18
B. Dillinger, SL 13
J. Pesky, BOS 11
F. Fain, PHI 9
W. Johnson, NY 9
S. Spence, WAS 9
F. Hutchison, DET ... 8
E. Wynn, WAS 7
B. Doerr, BOS 6
B. Rosar, PHI 6
M. Christman, WAS .. 4
B. McCahan, PHI 4
D. Mitchell, CLE 4
R. Cullenbine, DET .. 3
J. Dobson, BOS 3
J. Heath, SL 1
E. Lopat, CHI 1
V. Stephens, SL 1
T. Wright, CHI 1

1948 NATIONAL
S. Musial, SL 303
J. Sain, BOS 223
A. Dark, BOS 174
S. Gordon, NY 72
H. Brecheen, SL ... 61
P. Reese, BKN 60
R. Kiner, PIT 55
E. Slaughter, SL 55
D. Murtaugh, PIT ... 52
S. Rojek, PIT 51
R. Ashburn, PHI ... 48
J. Schmitz, CHI 37
R. Elliott, BOS 33
W. Spahn, BOS 31
J. Robinson, BKN .. 30
A. Pafko, CHI 25
J. Mize, NY 22
R. Barney, BKN 15

J. VanderMeer, CIN . 13
J. Wyrostek, CIN 9
R. Branca, BKN 8
R. Campanella, BKN . 8
B. Chesnes, PIT 8
P. Cavaretta, CHI 6
E. Miller, PHI 4
D. Ennis, PHI 3
G. Hatton, CIN 3
L. Jansen, NY 2
D. Walker, PIT 2
G. Hodges, BKN 1
W. Lockman, NY 1
H. Sauer, CIN 1

1948 AMERICAN
L. Boudreau, CLE . 324
J. DiMaggio, NY . . 213
T. Williams, BOS . . 171
V. Stephens, BOS . 121
B. Lemon, CLE . . . 101
J. Gordon, CLE 63
T. Henrich, NY 63
G. Bearden, CLE . . . 52
H. Newhouser, DET . 48
E. Joost, PHI 39
H. Majeski, PHI 23
B. Tebbetts, BOS . . . 23
V. Raschi, NY 23
K. Keltner, CLE 18
G. Priddy, SL 16
G. Kell, DET 14
W. Evers, DET 13
A. Zarilla, SL 11
B. Doerr, BOS 10
B. Dillinger, SL 10
J. Hegan, CLE 10
L. Appling, CHI 8
B. Feller, CLE 6
L. Brissie, PHI 5
F. Fain, PHI 5
J. Dobson, BOS 5
B. Goodman, BOS . . . 4
B. McCosky, PHI 4
Y. Berra, NY 3
D. DiMaggio, BOS . . . 3
L. Doby, CLE 3
C. Fannin, SL 2
P. Mullin, DET 1
P. Rizzuto, NY 1

1949 NATIONAL
J. Robinson, BKN . 264
S. Musial, SL 226
E. Slaughter, SL 181
R. Kiner, PIT 133
P. Reese, BKN 118
C. Furillo, BKN 68
W. Spahn, BOS 60
D. Newcombe, BKN 55
K. Heintzelman, PHI 48
R. Schoendienst, SL 30
G. Hodges, BKN . . . 29
H. Pollet, SL 29
D. Ennis, PHI 28
B. Thomson, NY . . . 25
R. Campanella, BKN 22
P. Roe, BKN 21
G. Hamner, PHI 9
W. Lockman, NY 9
R. Meyer, PHI 8
K. Raffensberger, CIN 8
H. Sauer, CHI 8
T. Wilks, SL 8
R. Ashburn, PHI 6
J. Schmitz, CHI 6
A. Dark, BOS 3
M. Marion, SL 3
W. Jones, PHI 2
W. Marshall, NY 2
E. Torgeson, BOS . . . 2
S. Gordon, NY 1
D. Sisler, PHI 1

1949 AMERICAN
T. Williams, BOS . . 272
P. Rizzuto, NY 175
J. Page, NY 166
M. Parnell, BOS . . . 151
E. Kinder, BOS 122
T. Henrich, NY 121
V. Stephens, BOS . 100
G. Kell, DET 80
B. Lemon, CLE 57
V. Wertz, DET 51
V. Raschi, NY 19
J. DiMaggio, NY . . . 18
E. Joost, PHI 11
L. Boudreau, CLE . . . 10
Y. Berra, NY 9
D. DiMaggio, BOS . . . 7
B. Doerr, BOS 7
A. Kellner, PHI 6
E. Robinson, WAS . . . 6
R. Sievers, SL 6
B. Tebbetts, BOS 6
L. Appling, CHI 3
A. Houtteman, DET . . 3
J. Priddy, SL 3
V. Trucks, DET 3
D. Mitchell, CLE 2
A. Reynolds, NY 2

1950 NATIONAL
J. Konstanty, PHI . . 286
S. Musial, SL 158
E. Stanky, NY 144
D. Ennis, PHI 104
R. Kiner, PIT 91
G. Hamner, PHI 79
R. Roberts, PHI 68
G. Hodges, BKN 55
D. Snider, BKN 53
S. Maglie, NY 51
E. Blackwell, CIN . . . 41
A. Pafko, CHI 38
R. Campanella, BKN 29
A. Seminick, PHI 25
J. Robinson, BKN . . 23
C. Simmons, PHI . . . 22
P. Roe, BKN 15
T. Kluszewski, CIN . . 14
W. Spahn, BOS 14
D. Newcombe, BKN 14
J. Sain, BOS 12
S. Gordon, BOS 11
J. Hearn, NY 10
P. Reese, BKN 8
E. Waitkus, PHI 8
R. Elliott, BOS 8
E. Torgeson, BOS . . . 6
S. Jethroe, BOS 6
H. Sauer, CHI 5
V. Bickford, BOS 4
C. Furillo, BKN 4
W. Westrum, NY 3
D. Sisler, PHI 2
H. Thompson, NY . . . 2
L. Jansen, NY 2
W. Jones, PHI 1

1950 AMERICAN
P. Rizzuto, NY 284
B. Goodman, BOS 180
Y. Berra, NY 146
G. Kell, DET 127
B. Lemon, CLE 102
W. Dropo, BOS 75
V. Raschi, NY 63
L. Doby, CLE 57
J. DiMaggio, NY . . . 54
V. Wertz, DET 50
W. Evers, DET 38
C. Carrasquel, CHI . 21
D. Trout, DET 21
D. DiMaggio, BOS . . 17
I. Noren, WAS 16
B. Doerr, BOS 15
J. Mize, NY 11
J. Priddy, DET 11
A. Rosen, CLE 11
E. Yost, WAS 8
M. Parnell, BOS 7
W. Ford, NY 7
T. Williams, BOS 7
N. Garver, SL 6
V. Stephens, BOS . . . 6
A. Houtteman, DET . . 6
S. Lollar, SL 4
E. Lopat, NY 3
K. Wood, SL 2
S. Dente, WAS 1
D. Philley, CHI 1

1951 NATIONAL
R. Campanella, BKN 243
S. Musial, SL 191
M. Irvin, NY 166
S. Maglie, NY 153
P. Roe, BKN 138
J. Robinson, BKN . . 92
R. Ashburn, PHI 69
B. Thomson, NY 62
M. Dickson, PIT 59
R. Kiner, PIT 49
W. Spahn, BOS 45
A. Dark, NY 30
R. Roberts, PHI 27
L. Jansen, NY 26
P. Reese, BKN 15
G. Hodges, BKN 10
S. Gordon, BOS 10
K. Raffensberger, CIN 8
J. Wyrostek, CIN 6
E. Blackwell, CIN 6
C. Furillo, BKN 6
D. Newcombe, BKN . 3
P. Cavaretta, CHI 1
H. Sauer, CHI 1

1951 AMERICAN
Y. Berra, NY 184
N. Garver, SL 157
A. Reynolds, NY . . . 125
M. Minoso, CHI . . . 120
B. Feller, CLE 118
F. Fain, PHI 103
E. Kinder, BOS 66
V. Raschi, NY 64
G. McDougald, NY . . 63
B. Avila, CLE 49
P. Rizzuto, NY 47
E. Lopat, NY 44
T. Williams, BOS . . . 35
E. Joost, PHI 32
G. Kell, DET 30
E. Wynn, CLE 29
N. Fox, CHI 25
B. Goodman, BOS . . 21
D. DiMaggio, BOS . . 16
G. Zernial, CHI-PHI . 15
B. Shantz, PHI 14
M. Garcia, CLE 11
G. Coan, WAS 8
M. Parnell, BOS 7
E. Robinson, CHI 7
G. Woodling, NY 5
J. Pesky, BOS 5
I. Noren, WAS 4
D. Mitchell, CLE 4
V. Trucks, DET 2
E. Yost, WAS 2
J. Busby, CHI 2
J. Mize,. NY 2

1952 NATIONAL
H. Sauer, CHI 226
R. Roberts, PHI . . . 211
J. Black, BKN 208
H. Wilhelm, NY . . . 133
S. Musial, SL 127
E. Slaughter, SL 92
J. Robinson, BKN . . 31
P. Reese, BKN 29
D. Snider, BKN 29
R. Campanella, BKN 25
R. Schoendienst, SL 25
A. Dark, NY 24
M. Dickson, PIT 22
D. Ennis, PHI 18
W. Lockman, NY . . . 18
B. Thomson, NY . . . 17
F. Baumholtz, CHI . . 16
T. Kluszewski, CIN . . 16
G. Hodges, BKN 15
R. McMillan, CIN . . . 15
E. Mathews, BOS . . 13
B. Adams, CIN 9
B. Cox, BKN 8
W. Hacker, CHI 8
R. Kiner, PIT 8
S. Maglie, NY 8
K. Raffensberger, CIN 8
W. Spahn, BOS 8
P. Roe, BKN 7
S. Gordon, BOS 6
G. Hamner, PHI 5
S. Hemus, SL 5
M. Irvin, NY 5
G. Shuba, BKN 5
E. Yuhas, SL 5
A. Brazle, SL 3
J. Logan, BOS 3
T. Atwell, CHI 2
C. Metkovich, PIT . . . 2
W. Cooper, BOS 1

1952 AMERICAN
B. Shantz, PHI 280
A. Reynolds, NY . . 183
M. Mantle, NY 143
Y. Berra, NY 104
E. Wynn, CLE 99
F. Fain, PHI 66
N. Fox, CHI 59
B. Lemon, CLE 58
M. Garcia, CLE 52
A. Rosen, CLE 51
E. Robinson, CHI . . . 47
L. Doby, CLE 46
L. Easter, CLE 40
P. Rizzuto, NY 33
E. Joost, PHI 20
B. Goodman, BOS . . 18
J. Jensen, NY-WAS . 12
S. Paige, SL 12
V. Raschi, NY 12
D. Mitchell, CLE 11
H. Bauer, NY 10
G. Woodling, NY . . . 10
P. Runnels, WAS 8
C. Courtney, SL 7
D. Gernert, BOS 6
W. Dropo, DET 5
S. Rogovin, CHI 4
S. White, BOS 4
B. Avila, CLE 3
B. Pierce, CHI 3
J. Sain, NY 3
B. Young, SL 3
J. Collins, NY 2
C. Marrero, WAS 1
B. Porterfield, WAS . . 1

1953 NATIONAL
R. Campanella, BKN 297
E. Mathews, MIL . . 216
D. Snider, BKN . . . 157
R. Schoendienst, SL 155
W. Spahn, MIL 120
R. Roberts, PHI . . . 106
T. Kluszewski, CIN . . 69
S. Musial, SL 62
C. Erskine, BKN . . . 54
C. Furillo, BKN 54
P. Reese, BKN 27
J. Robinson, BKN . . 19
D. Ennis, PHI 14
G. Hodges, BKN . . . 13
M. Irvin, NY 11
D. O'Connell, PIT . . . 10
H. Haddix, SL 9
F. Thomas, PIT 6
R. Ashburn, PHI 5
G. Bell, CIN 3
J. Logan, MIL 3
R. Gomez, NY 2
G. Hamner, PHI 2
D. Crandall, MIL 1
H. Thompson, NY . . . 1

1953 AMERICAN
A. Rosen, CLE 336
Y. Berra, NY 167
M. Vernon, WAS . . 162
M. Minoso, CHI . . . 100
V. Trucks, CHI 81
P. Rizzuto, NY 76
B. Porterfield, WAS . 64
R. Boone, CLE-DET 59
J. Piersall, BOS 56
B. Pierce, CHI 55
E. Kinder, BOS 41
H. Bauer, NY 37
A. Reynolds, NY . . . 37
M. Parnell, BOS 27
H. Kuenn, DET 23
B. Lemon, CLE 22
E. Lopat, NY 18
G. Zernial, PHI 16
D. Philley, PHI 11
W. Ford, NY 8
B. Goodman, BOS . . . 5
M. Mantle, NY 4
G. Woodling, NY 3
E. Yost, WAS 3
B. Martin, NY 2
C. Carrasquel, CHI . . . 1
G. Kell, BOS 1
T. Williams, BOS 1

1954 NATIONAL
W. Mays, NY 283
T. Kluszewski, CIN 217
J. Antonelli, NY . . . 154
D. Snider, BKN . . . 135
A. Dark, NY 110
S. Musial, SL 97
R. Roberts, PHI 70
J. Adcock, MIL 60
P. Reese, BKN 53
G. Hodges, BKN . . . 40
W. Spahn, MIL 38
D. Mueller, NY 30
R. Schoendienst, SL 24
F. Thomas, PIT 24
H. Wilhelm, NY 17
E. Banks, CHI 14
D. Crandall, MIL 13
J. Logan, MIL 9
E. Mathews, MIL 5
G. Hamner, PHI 5
R. Ashburn, PHI 5
S. Maglie, NY 4
G. Conley, MIL 3
M. Grissom, NY 2
R. McMillan, CIN 2
D. Rhodes, NY 1
H. Sauer, CHI 1

1954 AMERICAN
Y. Berra, NY 230
L. Doby, CLE 210
B. Avila, CLE 203
M. Minoso, CHI . . . 186
B. Lemon, CLE . . . 179
E. Wynn, CLE 72
T. Williams, BOS . . . 65
H. Kuenn, DET 37
M. Vernon, WAS . . . 30
N. Fox, CHI 30
B. Grim, NY 25
J. Finigan, PHI 19
V. Trucks, CHI 19
J. Jensen, BOS 17
M. Mantle, NY 16
I. Noren, NY 16
A. Rosen, CLE 16
J. Busby, WAS 7
J. Coleman, BAL 6
B. Goodman, BOS . . . 6
M. Garcia, CLE 6
J. Hegan, CLE 5
H. Bauer, NY 4
A. Kaline, DET 4
B. Turley, BAL 4
S. Gromek, DET 1
C. Abrams, BAL 1
R. Boone, DET 1
R. Sievers, WAS 1

1955 NATIONAL
R. Campanella, BKN 226
D. Snider, BKN . . . 221
E. Banks, CHI 195
W. Mays, NY 165
R. Roberts, PHI . . . 159
T. Kluszewski, CIN 111
D. Newcombe, BKN 89
S. Musial, SL 46
H. Aaron, MIL 36
P. Reese, BKN 36
J. Logan, MIL 24
W. Post, CIN 23
D. Ennis, PHI 21
R. Ashburn, PHI 17
C. Labine, BKN 11
B. Friend, PIT 10
D. Crandall, MIL 8
E. Mathews, MIL 6
D. Long, PIT 3
J. Meyer, PHI 3
G. Baker, CHI 2
C. Furillo, BKN 2
V. Law, PIT 1
F. Thomas, PIT 1

1955 AMERICAN
Y. Berra, NY 218
A. Kaline, DET 201
A. Smith, CLE 200
T. Williams, BOS . . 143
M. Mantle, NY 113
R. Narleski, CLE . . . 90
N. Fox, CHI 84
H. Bauer, NY 64
V. Power, KC 53
J. Jensen, BOS 39
S. Lollar, CHI 37
G. McDougald, NY . 34
B. Klaus, BOS 27
T. Byrne, NY 24
W. Ford, NY 21
R. Boone, DET 16
R. Sievers, WAS 9
H. Kuenn, DET 8
B. Pierce, CHI 8
D. Philley, CLE-BAL . . 6
E. Wynn, CLE 6
E. Valo, KC 5
M. Vernon, WAS 4
B. Hoeft, DET 1
D. Mossi, CLE 1
F. Sullivan, BOS 1
G. Triandos, BAL 1
J. Valdivielso, WAS . . 1
S. White, BOS 1

1956 NATIONAL
D. Newcombe, BKN 223
S. Maglie, BKN . . . 183
H. Aaron, MIL 146
W. Spahn, MIL 126
J. Gilliam, BKN . . . 103
R. McMillan, CIN . . . 96
F. Robinson, CIN . . . 79
P. Reese, BKN 71
S. Musial, SL 62
D. Snider, BKN 55
J. Adcock, MIL 54
B. Friend, PIT 38
H. Freeman, CIN . . . 25
J. Antonelli, NY 18
T. Kluszewski, CIN . . 18
J. Robinson, BKN . . 17
W. Mays, NY 14
E. Bailey, CIN 13
B. Virdon, SL-PIT . . . 13
S. Lopata, PHI 11
C. Furillo, BKN 9
L. Burdette, MIL 8
B. Buhl, MIL 7
R. Roberts, PHI 7
B. Lawrence, CIN . . . 6
D. Long, PIT 4
W. Moon, SL 3
E. Banks, CHI 2
K. Boyer, SL 2
C. Labine, BKN 1
J. Logan, MIL 1
R. Ashburn, PHI 1

1956 AMERICAN
M. Mantle, NY 336
Y. Berra, NY 186
A. Kaline, DET 142

H. Kuenn, DET 80
B. Pierce, CHI 75
T. Williams, BOS ...70
B. Nieman,
   CHI-BAL 55
G. McDougald, NY .55
V. Wertz, CLE 45
B. Lemon, CLE 40
H. Simpson, KC ...37
W. Ford, NY 33
E. Wynn, CLE 32
J. Piersall, BOS ...28
N. Fox, CHI 28
S. Lollar, CHI 27
F. Lary, DET 24
P. Runnels, WAS ...24
H. Score, CLE 18
J. Jensen, BOS 15
M. Vernon, BOS ...14
T. Brewer, BOS ...11
H. Bauer, NY 8
C. Maxwell, DET 8
L. Aparicio, CHI 7
G. Triandos, BAL ...6
F. Bolling, DET 3
M. Minoso, CHI 3
V. Power, KC 3
J. Kucks, NY 2
R. Sievers, WAS 1

1957 NATIONAL
H. Aaron, MIL 239
S. Musial, SL 230
R. Schoendienst,
   NY-MIL 221
W. Mays, NY 174
W. Spahn, MIL 131
E. Banks, CHI 60
G. Hodges, BKN ...54
E. Mathews, MIL ...45
F. Robinson, CIN ...42
J. Sanford, PHI ...39
D. Hoak, CIN 31
D. Blasingame, SL ..26
E. Bouchee, PHI ...26
B. Buhl, MIL 15
D. Ennis, SL 13
D. Groat, PIT 13
A. Dark, SL 12
D. Snider, BKN 10
F. Thomas, PIT 8
D. Drysdale, BKN ...6
R. McMillan, CIN ...6
D. Drott, CHI 6
G. Hamner, PHI 3
L. Burdette, MIL ...2
J. Logan, MIL 1
H. Anderson, PHI ...1

1957 AMERICAN
M. Mantle, NY 233
T. Williams, BOS ..209
R. Sievers, WAS ..205
N. Fox, CHI 193
G. McDougald,
   NY 165
V. Wertz, CLE 61
F. Malzone, BOS ...58
M. Minoso, CHI ...55
A. Kaline, DET 40
B. Pierce, CHI 35
B. Gardner, BAL ...22
D. Donovan, CHI ...19
Y. Berra, NY 18
G. Woodling, CLE ..13
B. Grim, NY 9
B. Boyd, BAL 9
C. Maxwell, DET 5
W. Held, KC 4
W. Ford, NY 4
V. Power, KC 3
J. Piersall, BOS 2
B. Skowron, NY 2
H. Kuenn, DET 2
S. Lollar, CHI 2
T. Kubek, NY 1
B. Shantz, NY 1

1958 NATIONAL
E. Banks, CHI 283
W. Mays, SF 185
H. Aaron, MIL 166

F. Thomas, PIT 143
W. Spahn, MIL 108
B. Friend, PIT 98
R. Ashburn, PHI ...62
B. Mazeroski, PIT ..61
O. Cepeda, SF 57
D. Crandall, MIL ...48
L. Burdette, MIL ...47
S. Musial, SL 39
K. Boyer, SL 31
J. Temple, CIN 26
B. Skinner, PIT 18
W. Covington, MIL ..16
E. Face, PIT 8
H. Anderson, PHI ...5
J. Gilliam, LA 4
B. Purkey, CIN 4
F. Robinson, CIN ...4
J. Adcock, MIL 2
C. Furillo, LA 1

1958 AMERICAN
J. Jensen, BOS ...233
B. Turley, NY 191
R. Colavito, CLE ..181
B. Cerv, KC 164
M. Mantle, NY 127
R. Sievers, WAS ...95
T. Williams, BOS ...89
N. Fox, CHI 88
S. Lollar, CHI 57
P. Runnels, BOS ...29
G. Triandos, BAL ...27
D. Hyde, WAS 26
H. Kuenn, DET 24
C. McLish, CLE 18
V. Power, KC-CLE ..15
F. Bolling, DET 10
E. Howard, NY 9
Y. Berra, NY 6
M. Minoso, CLE 6
A. Kaline, DET 5
G. McDougald, NY ..5
R. Duren, NY 4
F. Lary, DET 3
J. Harshman, BAL ...2
D. Donovan, CHI ...1
F. Malzone, BOS ...1

1959 NATIONAL
E. Banks, CHI ...232½
E. Mathews,
   MIL 189½
H. Aaron, MIL 174
W. Moon, LA 161
S. Jones, SF 130
W. Mays, SF 85
E. Face, PIT 67
C. Neal, LA 64
F. Robinson, CIN ...52
K. Boyer, SL 37
D. Crandall, MIL ...27
L. Burdette, MIL ...14
R. Craig, LA 12
J. Cunningham, SL ..12
V. Pinson, CIN 11
J. Temple, CIN 8
D. Hoak, PIT 6
G. Hodges, LA 4
O. Cepeda, SF 3
V. Law, PIT 3
W. Spahn, MIL 3
G. Conley, PHI 1
W. McCovey, SF 1
D. Snider, LA 1

1959 AMERICAN
N. Fox, CHI 295
L. Aparicio, CHI ..255
E. Wynn, CHI 123
R. Colavito, CLE ..117
T. Francona, CLE ..102
A. Kaline, DET 84
A. Landis, CHI 66
H. Kuenn, DET 64
S. Lollar, CHI 44
J. Jensen, BOS 40
C. McLish, CLE 35
Y. Berra, NY 26
M. Minoso, CLE 26
F. Malzone, BOS ...24
H. Killebrew, WAS ..21
G. Woodling, BAL ..18

M. Mantle, NY 13
B. Richardson, NY ..11
C. Pascual, WAS 9
G. Shaw, CHI 8
G. Triandos, BAL ...8
B. Daley, KC 7
V. Power, CLE 5
B. Tuttle, KC 5
J. Lemon, WAS 4
P. Runnels, BOS ...2
T. Williams, BOS ...2
B. Allison, WAS 1
G. Staley, CHI 1

1960 NATIONAL
D. Groat, PIT 276
D. Hoak, PIT 162
W. Mays, SF 155
E. Banks, CHI 100
L. McDaniel, SL ...95
K. Boyer, SL 80
V. Law, PIT 80
R. Clemente, PIT ...62
E. Broglio, SL 58
E. Mathews, MIL ...52
H. Aaron, MIL 49
E. Face, PIT 47
D. Crandall, MIL ...31
W. Spahn, MIL 27
N. Larker, LA 21
S. Musial, SL 18
M. Wills, LA 7
V. Pinson, CIN 6
J. Adcock, MIL 5
S. Burgess, PIT 2
F. Robinson, CIN ...2
L. Sherry, LA 2
P. Herrera, PHI 1

1960 AMERICAN
R. Maris, NY 225
M. Mantle, NY ...222
B. Robinson, BAL .211
M. Minoso, CHI ..141
R. Hansen, BAL...110
A. Smith, CHI 73
R. Sievers, CHI 58
E. Battey, WAS 57
B. Skowron, NY ...56
J. Lemon, WAS 36
T. Kubek, NY 29
C. Estrada, BAL ...28
T. Williams, BOS ...25
W. Wertz, BOS 22
Y. Berra, NY 21
J. Gentile, BAL 21
P. Runnels, BOS ...18
N. Fox, CHI 11
V. Power, CLE 11
S. Barber, BAL 7
L. Aparicio, CHI 6
J. Perry, CLE 6
G. Staley, CHI 4
J. Bunning, DET 3
G. Woodling, BAL ..3
H. Kuenn, CLE 3
B. Daley, KC 3
M. Fornieles, BOS ..2
C. Maxwell, DET ...2
J. Piersall, CLE 2

1961 NATIONAL
F. Robinson, CIN ..219
O. Cepeda, SF ...117
V. Pinson, CIN ...104
R. Clemente, PIT ...81
J. Jay, CIN 74
W. Mays, SF 70
K. Boyer, SL 43
H. Aaron, MIL 39
M. Wills, LA 36
J. O'Toole, CIN 31
W. Spahn, MIL 31
S. Miller, SF 26
W. Moon, LA 22
G. Altman, CHI 9
J. Podres, LA 9
R. McMillan, MIL ...8
E. Mathews, MIL ...7
S. Koufax, LA 5
J. Roseboro, LA 4
J. Brosnan, CIN 3
J. Torre, MIL 2

L. Jackson, SL 1
J. Lynch, CIN 1
N. Malkmus, PHI ...1
D. Stuart, PIT 1

1961 AMERICAN
R. Maris, NY 202
M. Mantle, NY ...198
J. Gentile, BAL ...157
N. Cash, DET 151
W. Ford, NY 102
L. Arroyo, NY 95
F. Lary, DET 53
R. Colavito, DET ...51
A. Kaline, DET 35
E. Howard, NY 30
H. Killebrew, MIN ..29
L. Aparicio, CHI ...16
J. Piersall, CLE 12
S. Barber, BAL 7
D. Schwall, BOS 7
N. Siebern, KC 7
D. Donovan, WAS ...5
B. Phillips, CLE 5
B. Robinson, BAL ...4
C. Schilling, BOS ...4
T. Morgan, LA 3
A. Smith, CHI 3
Y. Berra, NY 2
B. Richardson, NY ...1
J. Romano, CLE 1
L. Thomas, LA 1
H. Wilhelm, BAL ...1

1962 NATIONAL
M. Wills, LA 209
W. Mays, SF 202
T. Davis, LA 175
F. Robinson, CIN ..164
D. Drysdale, LA 85
H. Aaron, MIL 72
J. Sanford, SF 62
B. Purkey, CIN 33
F. Howard, LA 32
S. Musial, SL 19
J. Pagan, SF 13
D. Demeter, PHI ...12
F. Alou, SF 10
B. White, SL 10
O. Cepeda, SF 9
D. Groat, PIT 7
R. Clemente, PIT ...6
E. Banks, CHI 5
K. Boyer, SL 5
J. Callison, PHI 5
H. Kuenn, SF 5
J. Marichal, SF 4
B. Skinner, PIT 4
J. Davenport, SF ...3
S. Koufax, LA 3
D. Crandall, MIL ...2
A. Mahaffey, PHI ...2
E. Roebuck, LA 2
J. Kasko, CIN 1
E. Mathews, MIL ...1

1962 AMERICAN
M. Mantle, NY ...234
B. Richardson,
   NY 152
H. Killebrew, MIN ..99
L. Wagner, LA 85
D. Donovan, CLE...64
A. Kaline, DET 58
N. Siebern, KC 53
R. Rollins, MIN 47
B. Robinson, BAL ..41
F. Robinson, CHI ..33
L. Thomas, LA 32
J. Tresh, NY 30
B. Moran, LA 28
R. Terry, NY 19
C. Pascual, MIN ...14
R. Colavito, DET ...13
H. Aguirre, DET ...10
J. Cunningham, CHI .9
P. Runnels, BOS 9
C. Yastrzemski,
   BOS 9
V. Power, MIN 8
D. Radatz, BOS 8
J. Bunning, DET 8
Z. Versalles, MIN ...8

J. Lumpe, KC 7
E. Bressoud, BOS ...6
B. Rodgers, LA 6
W. Ford, NY 6
R. Herbert, CHI 5
C. Hinton, WAS 5
F. Malzone, BOS ...3
N. Cash, DET 3
A. Smith, CHI 1

1963 NATIONAL
S. Koufax, LA 237
D. Groat, SL 190
H. Aaron, MIL 135
R. Perranoski, LA .130
W. Mays, SF 102
J. Gilliam, LA 62
B. White, SL 56
T. Davis, LA 41
R. Santo, CHI 41
V. Pinson, CIN 32
J. Marichal, SF 31
W. Spahn, MIL 30
K. Boyer, SL 19
R. Clemente, PIT ...12
J. Callison, PHI 11
T. Taylor, PHI 10
W. McCovey, SF 9
M. Wills, LA 9
D. Ellsworth, CHI ...7
J. Maloney, CIN 7
D. Demeter, PHI 3
D. Drysdale, LA 3
T. Gonzalez, PHI ...2
C. Flood, SL 1

1963 AMERICAN
E. Howard, NY ...248
A. Kaline, DET ...148
W. Ford, NY 125
H. Killebrew, MIN ..85
D. Radatz, BOS 84
C. Yastrzemski,
   BOS 81
E. Battey, MIN 57
G. Peters, CHI 55
P. Ward, CHI 52
B. Richardson, NY ..43
T. Tresh, NY 38
C. Pascual, MIN ...29
D. Stuart, BOS 25
A. Pearson, LA 22
B. Allison, MIN 15
J. Bouton, NY 11
M. Alvis, CLE 10
J. Pepitone, NY 10
L. Wagner, LA 9
S. Miller, BAL 9
W. Causey, KC 5
R. Rollins, MIN 5
L. Aparicio, BAL 3
B. Dailey, MIN 3
J. Fregosi, LA 3
N. Fox, CHI 2
T. Kubek, NY 1
F. Robinson, CHI ...1
N. Siebern, KC 1

1964 NATIONAL
K. Boyer, SL 243
J. Callison, PHI ...187
B. White, SL ...106½
F. Robinson, CIN ...98
J. Torre, MIL 85
W. Mays, SF 66
R. Allen, PHI 63
R. Santo, CHI 59
R. Clemente, PIT ...56
L. Brock, CHI-SL ...40
C. Flood, SL 38
L. Jackson, CHI ...26
J. Bunning, PHI ...23
H. Aaron, MIL 22
J. Marichal, SF 14
S. Ellis, CIN 13
S. Koufax, LA 7½
V. Pinson, CIN 6
J. Hart, SF 6
B. Williams, CHI ...6
H. Amaro, PHI 5
T. Davis, LA 4
B. Gibson, SL 2
C. Short, PHI 2

R. Hunt, NY 1
B. Schultz, SL 1

1964 AMERICAN
B. Robinson, BAL . 269
M. Mantle, NY ...171
E. Howard, NY ...124
T. Oliva, MIN 99
D. Chance, LA 97
P. Ward, CHI 67½
B. Freehan, DET ...44
D. Peters, CHI 44
D. Radatz, BOS 37
H. Killebrew, MIN ..31
B. Powell, BAL 28
B. Bunker, BAL 23
J. Fregosi, LA 21
A. Kaline, DET 17
F. Robinson, CHI ..14
R. Hansen, CHI ...10
B. Richardson, NY ..9
J. Wagner, CLE 8
J. Pizarro, CHI 8
H. Wilhelm, CHI ...8
J. Horlen, CHI 7
W. Ford, NY 7
B. Allison, MIN 5
R. Colavito, KC 5
M. Stottlemyre, NY ..4
R. Maris, NY 4
W. Causey, KC 4
L. Aparicio, BAL ..3½
D. Stuart, BOS 2
E. Bressoud, BOS ...2
C. Osteen, WAS 2
D. Wickersham,
   DET 2
D. Lock, WAS 1

1965 NATIONAL
W. Mays, SF 224
S. Koufax, LA 177
M. Wills, LA 164
D. Johnson, CIN ..108
D. Drysdale, LA 77
P. Rose, CIN 67
H. Aaron, MIL 58
R. Clemente, PIT ...56
J. Marichal, SF 26
W. McCovey, SF ...25
J. Torre, MIL 23
B. Williams, CHI ...21
F. Linzy, SF 16
W. Stargell, PIT 15
C. Flood, SL 13
J. Hart, SF 13
V. Law, PIT 12
F. Robinson, CIN ...11
R. Santo, CHI 11
E. Mathews, MIL ...8
L. Cardenas, CIN ...7
J. Maloney, CIN 7
L. Lefebvre, LA 7
J. Callison, PHI 6
L. Johnson, LA 6
C. Rojas, PHI 5
J. Roseboro, LA 5
R. Allen, PHI 4
T. Cloninger, MIL ...4
J. Gilliam, LA 3
J. Morgan, HOU 1

1965 AMERICAN
Z. Versalles, MIN ..275
T. Oliva, MIN 174
B. Robinson, BAL .150
E. Fisher, CHI 122
R. Colavito, CLE ...89
J. Grant, MIN 74
S. Miller, BAL 45
W. Horton, DET ...24
T. Tresh, NY 23
E. Battey, MIN 22
D. Wert, DET 22
C. Yastrzemski,
   BOS 22
J. Hall, MIN 19
M. Stottlemyre, NY .17
H. Killebrew, MIN ..15
A. Kaline, DET 15
J. Adair, BAL 7
R. Hansen, CHI 7
S. McDowell, CLE ...7

B. Richardson, NY . . . 6
V. Davalillo, CLE 5
J. Fregosi, CAL 5
F. Whitfield, CLE 5
B. Knoop, CAL 4
D. Buford, CHI 3
M. Mantle, NY 3
P. Richert, WAS 3
F. Robinson, CHI 3
B. Campaneris, KC . . 2
F. Howard, WAS 2
R. Kline, WAS 2
F. Mantilla, BOS 2
N. Cash, DET 1
T. Conigliaro, BOS . . . 1

1966 NATIONAL
R. Clemente, PIT . . 218
S. Koufax, LA 208
W. Mays, SF 111
R. Allen, PHI 107
F. Alou, ATL 83
J. Marichal, SF 74
P. Regan, LA 66
H. Aaron, ATL 57
M. Alou, PIT 36
P. Rose, CIN 31
G. Alley, PIT 24
R. Santo, CHI 23
J. Roseboro, LA . . . 22
O. Cepeda, SF-SL . . 22
W. Stargell, PIT 19
J. Torre, ATL 18
W. McCovey, SF . . . 12
J. Lefebvre, LA 8
G. Perry, SF 8
C. Flood, SL 7
M. Wills, LA 5
R. Staub, HOU 4
B. Mazeroski, PIT . . . 3
G. Beckert, CHI 3
J. Maloney, CIN 3
B. White, PHI 3
L. Brock, SL 2
B. Shaw, SF-NY 1
C. Short, PHI 1
W. Davis, LA 1

1966 AMERICAN
F. Robinson, BAL . . 280
B. Robinson, BAL . 153
B. Powell, BAL 122
H. Killebrew, MIN . . . 96
J. Kaat, MIN 84
T. Oliva, MIN 71
A. Kaline, DET 66
T. Agee, CHI 63
L. Aparicio, BAL . . . 51
B. Campaneris, KC . 36
S. Miller, BAL 27
N. Cash, DET 23
J. Aker, KC 22
E. Wilson,
BOS-DET 13
D. McLain, DET 12
B. Freehan, DET 9
A. Etchebarren, BAL . 7
B. Knoop, CAL 6
M. Mantle, NY 5
T. Tresh, NY 5
J. Sanford, CAL 4
R. Reichardt, CAL . . . 4
F. Valentine, WAS 4
W. Horton, DET 4
L. Wagner, CLE 4
P. Richert, WAS 3
J. Pepitone, NY 2
T. Conigliaro, BOS . . . 1
S. Siebert, CLE 1
C. Yastrzemski,
BOS 1
J. Fregosi, CAL 1

1967 NATIONAL
O. Cepeda, SL 280
T. McCarver, SL . . . 136
R. Clemente, PIT . . 129
R. Santo, CHI 103
H. Aaron, ATL 79
M. McCormick, SF . 73
L. Brock, SL 49
T. Perez, CIN 43
J. Javier, SL 41

P. Rose, CIN 40
J. Wynn, HOU 29
F. Jenkins, CHI 26
C. Flood, SL 24
E. Banks, CHI 22
N. Briles, SL 20
R. Staub, HOU 12
D. Hughes, SL 10
J. Hart, SF 10
R. Allen, PHI 9
T. Abernathy, CIN 8
C. Boyer, ATL 6
B. Gibson, SL 5
R. Hundley, CHI 5
J. Bunning, PHI 5
T. Seaver, NY 5
T. Davis, NY 3
G. Alley, PIT 3
T. Gonzalez, PHI 3
W. McCovey, SF 2

1967 AMERICAN
C. Yastrzemski,
BOS 275
H. Killebrew, MIN . . 161
B. Freehan, DET . . 137
J. Horlen, CHI 91
A. Kaline, DET 88
J. Lonborg, BOS . . . 82
C. Tovar, MIN 70
J. Fregosi, CAL 70
G. Peters, CHI 37
G. Scott, BOS 33
F. Robinson, BAL . . . 31
E. Wilson, DET 20
D. Chance, MIN 19
R. Hansen, CHI 13
J. Adair, CHI-BOS . . 11
P. Blair, BAL 9
R. Petrocelli, BOS . . . 7
E. Howard, NY-BOS . 7
T. Oliva, MIN 6
J. Kaat, MIN 4
P. Casanova, WAS . . . 3
D. Mincher, CAL 3
M. Lolich, DET 2
M. Rojas, CAL 1

1968 NATIONAL
B. Gibson, SL 242
P. Rose, CIN 205
W. McCovey, SF . . 135
C. Flood, SL 116
J. Marichal, SF 93
L. Brock, SL 73
M. Shannon, SL . . . 55
B. Williams, CHI 48
G. Beckert, CHI 40
F. Alou, ATL 33
M. Alou, PIT 32
H. Aaron, ATL 19
W. Mays, SF 14
E. Banks, CHI 14
J. Koosman, NY . . . 14
J. Bench, CIN 11
P. Regan, LA-CHI 7
F. Jenkins, CHI 6
T. Perez, CIN 5
N. Briles, SL 4
D. Maxvill, SL 4
S. Blass, PIT 3
T. Haller, LA 3
R. Santo, CHI 2
C. Carroll, ATL-CIN . . 1
T. Helms, CIN 1

1968 AMERICAN
D. McLain, DET . . . 280
B. Freehan, DET . . 161
K. Harrelson,
BOS 103
W. Horton, DET . . . 102
D. McNally, BAL . . . 78
L. Tiant, CLE 78
D. McAuliffe, DET . . 71
F. Howard, WAS 63
C. Yastrzemski,
BOS 50
M. Stottlemyre, NY . 43
B. Campaneris,
OAK 39
R. White, NY 17
J. Northrup, DET . . . 15

L. Aparicio, CHI 13
J. Fregosi, CAL 11
D. Buford, BAL 11
B. Robinson, BAL . . . 8
R. Jackson, OAK 8
T. Oliva, MIN 5
D. Cater, OAK 5
M. Andrews, BOS 4
B. Powell, BAL 4
N. Cash, DET 3
C. Tovar, MIN 3
M. Stanley, DET 2
W. Wood, CHI 2
T. Uhlaender, MIN . . . 1

1969 NATIONAL
W. McCovey, SF . . 265
T. Seaver, NY 243
H. Aaron, ATL 188
P. Rose, CIN 127
R. Santo, CHI 124
T. Agee, NY 89
C. Jones, NY 82
R. Clemente, PIT . . . 51
P. Niekro, ATL 47
T. Perez, CIN 28
M. Wills, MON-LA . . . 17
E. Banks, CHI 15
R. Carty, ATL 12
J. Bench, CIN 12
D. Kessinger, CHI . . . 8
T. Gonzalez,
SD-ATL 8
R. Hunt, SF 8
D. Menke, HOU 8
W. Granger, CIN 8
J. Wynn, HOU 8
W. Davis, LA 7
W. Stargell, PIT 7
J. Marichal, SF 6
B. Williams, CHI 6
J. Koosman, NY 6
J. Torre, SL 6
M. Alou, PIT 6
L. Dierker, HOU 6
T. Haller, LA 3
B. Gibson, SL 2
B. Bonds, SF 2
R. Hundley, CHI 2
L. May, CIN 2
T. Sizemore, LA 2
W. Parker, LA 2
J. Edwards, HOU 1
R. Staub, MON 1
O. Cepeda, ATL 1

1969 AMERICAN
H. Killebrew, MIN . . 294
B. Powell, BAL . . . 227
F. Robinson, BAL . . 162
F. Howard, WAS . . 115
R. Jackson, OAK . . 110
D. McLain, DET 85
R. Petrocelli, BOS . . 71
M. Cuellar, BAL 55
J. Perry, MIN 40
R. Carew, MIN 30
P. Blair, BAL 28
L. Cardenas, MIN . . . 27
R. Perranoski, MIN . 25
D. McNally, BAL . . . 25
T. Oliva, MIN 21
S. Bando, OAK 18
C. Tovar, MIN 9
M. Stottlemyre, NY . . 8
C. Yastrzemski,
BOS 8
E. Brinkman, WAS . . . 7
J. Fregosi, CAL 7
R. Smith, BOS 6
D. Unser, WAS 5
B. Robinson, BAL 5
M. Epstein, WAS 4
M. Andrews, BOS 3
D. Bosman, WAS 3
B. Freehan, DET 3
T. Harper, SEA 2
A. Messersmith,
CAL 2
R. Reese, MIN 2
K. Tatum, CAL 2
R. White, NY 2
M. Belanger, BAL . . . 2

D. Green, OAK 1
J. Northrup, DET 1
L. Piniella, KC 1

1970 NATIONAL
J. Bench, CIN 326
B. Williams, CHI . . . 218
T. Perez, CIN 149
B. Gibson, SL 110
W. Parker, LA 91
D. Giusti, PIT 72
P. Rose, CIN 54
J. Hickman, CHI . . . 52
W. McCovey, SF . . . 47
R. Carty, ATL 43
M. Sanguillen, PIT . . 36
R. Clemente, PIT . . . 33
D. Clendenon, NY . . 26
G. Perry, SF 24
W. Stargell, PIT 20
B. Tolan, CIN 17
H. Aaron, ATL 16
J. Torre, SL 15
T. Agee, NY 13
B. Harrelson, NY . . . 10
F. Jenkins, CHI 8
J. Merritt, CIN 8
D. Kessinger, CHI . . . 6
C. Gaston, SD 5
D. Johnson, PHI 4
L. Walker, PIT 4
C. Morton, MON 3
B. Robertson, PIT . . . 3
T. Seaver, NY 2
W. Granger, CIN 1

1970 AMERICAN
B. Powell, BAL . . . 234
T. Oliva, MIN 157
H. Killebrew, MIN . . 152
C. Yastrzemski,
BOS 136
F. Howard, WAS 91
T. Harper, MIL 78
B. Robinson, BAL . . 75
A. Johnson, CAL . . . 70
J. Perry, MIN 63
F. Robinson, BAL . . . 60
M. Cuellar, BAL 45
R. Perranoski, MIN . 35
J. Fregosi, CAL 35
L. Aparicio, CHI . . . 35
R. White, NY 25
D. McNally, BAL . . . 22
S. McDowell, CLE . . 22
C. Tovar, MIN 16
T. Munson, NY 15
D. Buford, BAL 12
C. Wright, CAL 8
L. McDaniel, NY 8
R. Fosse, CLE 7
B. Campaneris,
OAK 5
J. Palmer, BAL 4
R. Smith, BOS 3
S. Bando, OAK 1
T. Horton, CLE 1
B. Oliver, KC 1

1971 NATIONAL
J. Torre, SL 318
W. Stargell, PIT . . . 222
H. Aaron, ATL 180
B. Bonds, SF 139
R. Clemente, PIT . . . 87
M. Wills, LA 74
F. Jenkins, CHI 71
M. Sanguillen, PIT . . 49
T. Seaver, NY 46
A. Downing, LA 36
G. Beckert, CHI 35
L. May, CIN 28
L. Brock, SL 20
D. Giusti, PIT 16
W. McCovey, SF . . . 15
T. Simmons, SL 13
W. Davis, LA 13
J. Johnson, SF 12
W. Mays, SF 11
R. Staub, MON 11
B. Williams, CHI 10
B. Harrelson, NY 4
B. Gibson, SL 3

R. Garr, ATL 1
D. Roberts, SD 1
P. Rose, CIN 1

1971 AMERICAN
V. Blue, OAK 268
S. Bando, OAK . . . 182
F. Robinson, BAL . . 170
B. Robinson, BAL . 163
M. Lolich, DET 155
F. Patek, KC 77
B. Murcer, NY 72
A. Otis, KC 67
W. Wood, CHI 54
T. Oliva, MIN 36
D. McNally, BAL . . . 26
N. Cash, DET 21
B. Melton, CHI 18
R. Jackson, OAK . . . 15
C. Rojas, KC 15
K. Sanders, MIL . . . 13
P. Dobson, BAL 9
R. Smith, BOS 9
D. Johnson, BAL 8
M. Rettenmund,
BAL 8
H. Killebrew, MIN 5
J. Palmer, BAL 5
L. Cardenas, MIN . . . 5
M. Cuellar, BAL 4
C. Tovar, MIN 4
G. Scott, BOS 3
D. Buford, BAL 2
J. Hunter, OAK 1
G. Nettles, MIN 1

1972 NATIONAL
J. Bench, CIN 263
B. Williams, CHI . . . 211
W. Stargell, PIT . . . 201
J. Morgan, CIN . . . 197
S. Carlton, PHI . . . 124
C. Cedeno, HOU . . 112
A. Oliver, PIT 52
N. Colbert, SD 45
L. May, HOU 30
T. Simmons, SL 22
M. Marshall, MON . . 22
P. Rose, CIN 19
R. Clemente, PIT . . . 16
C. Carroll, CIN 16
L. Brock, SL 13
H. Aaron, ATL 12
M. Sanguillen, PIT . . 12
S. Blass, PIT 9
R. Garr, ATL 7
G. Clines, PIT 6
B. Tolan, CIN 6
D. Baker, ATL 5
M. Mota, LA 4
D. Kingman, SF 3
T. McGraw, NY 2
R. Staub, NY 2
T. Seaver, NY 2
J. Cardenal, CHI 1
F. Jenkins, Chl 1
C. Speier, SF 1

1972 AMERICAN
R. Allen, CHI 321
J. Rudi, OAK 164
S. Lyle, NY 158
C. Fisk, BOS 96
B. Murcer, NY 89
G. Perry, CLE 88
W. Wood, CHI 78
L. Tiant, BOS 70½
E. Brinkman, DET . . . 62
M. Lolich, DET 60
J. Hunter, OAK 57
J. Mayberry, KC 27
J. Palmer, BAL 21
B. Grich, BAL 16
R. Carew, MIN 16
B. Campaneris,
OAK 11
M. Epstein, OAK . . . 11
L. Aparicio, BOS . . 9½
R. Petrocelli, BOS . . 9
R. Jackson, OAK 9
C. May, CHI 6
G. Scott, MIL 6
D. Thompson, MIN . . 5

T. Harper, BOS 4
A. Kaline, DET 4
B. Freehan, DET 3
K. McMullen, CAL . . . 3
B. Robinson, BAL . . . 3
R. Smith, BOS 3
S. Bando, OAK 2
N. Ryan, CAL 2
A. Otis, KC 1
L. Piniella, KC 1

1973 NATIONAL
P. Rose, CIN 274
W. Stargell, PIT . . . 250
B. Bonds, SF 174
J. Morgan, CIN . . . 102
M. Marshall, MON . . 93
L. Brock, SL 65
T. Perez, CIN 59
T. Seaver, NY 57
K. Singleton, MON . 52
J. Bench, CIN 41
C. Cedeno, HOU . . . 39
H. Aaron, ATL 35
D. Johnson, ATL . . . 34
T. Simmons, SL 20
T. McGraw, NY 17
F. Millan, NY 12
W. Davis, LA 12
D. Evans, ATL 11
L. May, HOU 9
T. Fuentes, SF 8
B. Watson, HOU 7
J. Ferguson LA 7
J. Cardenal, CHI 6
J. Billingham, CIN . . . 6
A. Oliver, PIT 6
R. Hunt, MON 5
R. Bryant, SF 5
G. Maddox, SF 3
B. Harrelson, NY 2
B. Williams, CHI 2
G. Luzinski, PHI 2
B. Russell, LA 1

1973 AMERICAN
R. Jackson, OAK . . 336
J. Palmer, BAL 172
A. Otis, KC 112
R. Carew, MIN 83
J. Hiller, DET 83
S. Bando, OAK 83
J. Mayberry, KC 76
D. May, MIL 65
B. Murcer, NY 53
T. Davis, BAL 47
J. Hunter, OAK 47
T. Munson, NY 43
T. Harper, BOS 33
G. Scott, MIL 25
O. Cepeda, BOS . . . 21
F. Robinson, CAL . . . 21
N. Ryan, CAL 20
C. Fisk, BOS 16
B. Grich, BAL 9
C. Yastrzemski,
BOS 9
M. Belanger, BAL . . . 8
D. Johnson, OAK 8
J. Briggs, MIL 6
J. Coleman, DET 6
C. Rojas, KC 5
B. Blyleven, MIN 4
G. Perry, CLE 4
B. Campaneris,
OAK 4
V. Blue, OAK 3
C. May, CHI 3
W. Horton, DET 3
B. North, OAK 3
P. Blair, BAL 2
D. Nelson, TEX 2
R. Allen, CHI 1

1974 NATIONAL
S. Garvey, LA 270
L. Brock, SL 233
M. Marshall, LA . . . 146
J. Bench, CIN 141
J. Wynn, LA 137
M. Schmidt, PHI . . 136
A. Oliver, PIT 87
J. Morgan, CIN 72

R. Zisk, PIT ... 54
W. Stargell, PIT ... 43
R. Smith, SL ... 39
R. Garr, ATL ... 11
T. Simmons, SL ... 7
D. Cash, PHI ... 6
D. Concepcion, CIN ... 5
J. Billingham, CIN ... 4
C. Cedeno, HOU ... 4
A. Hrabosky, SL ... 4
A. Messersmith, LA ... 4
B. Capra, ATL ... 3
L. McGlothen, SL ... 2
B. McBride, SL ... 2
R. Hebner, PIT ... 2
R. Stennett, PIT ... 2
B. Buckner, LA ... 1
R. Cey, LA ... 1

1974 AMERICAN
J. Burroughs, TEX ... 248
J. Rudi, OAK ... 161½
S. Bando, OAK ... 143½
R. Jackson, OAK ... 119
F. Jenkins, TEX ... 118
J. Hunter, OAK ... 107
R. Carew, MIN ... 70
E. Maddox, NY ... 59
B. Grich, BAL ... 49
M. Cuellar, BAL ... 42
L. Tiant, BOS ... 41
B. Robinson, BAL ... 30
P. Blair, BAL ... 27
N. Ryan, CAL ... 24
B. Campaneris, OAK ... 23
R. Fingers, OAK ... 21
G. Perry, CLE ... 18
C. Yastrzemski, BOS ... 14
K. Henderson, CHI ... 12
J. Hiller, DET ... 11
L. Randle, TEX ... 10
B. Murcer, NY ... 10
L. Piniella, NY ... 8
R. Allen, CHI ... 8
S. Lyle, NY ... 7
T. Munson, NY ... 6
T. Davis, BAL ... 6
M. Belanger, BAL ... 6
D. Money, MIL ... 5
T. Murphy, MIL ... 3
H. McRae, KC ... 3
S. Busby, KC ... 3
G. Scott, MIL ... 2
P. Dobson, NY ... 1

1975 NATIONAL
J. Morgan, CIN ... 321½
G. Luzinski, PHI ... 154
D. Parker, PIT ... 120
J. Bench, CIN ... 117
P. Rose, CIN ... 114
T. Simmons, SL ... 103
W. Stargell, PIT ... 69
A. Hrabosky, SL ... 66
T. Seaver, NY ... 65
R. Jones, SD ... 54
S. Garvey, LA ... 50
B. Madlock, CHI ... 45
D. Cash, PHI ... 26
R. Staub, NY ... 20
T. Perez, CIN ... 18
M. Schmidt, PHI ... 16
M. Sanguillen, PIT ... 16
R. Cey, LA ... 11½
D. Kingman, NY ... 9
B. Watson, HOU ... 8
L. Brock, SL ... 6
L. Bowa, PHI ... 3
J. Reuss, PIT ... 2
A. Messersmith, LA ... 1
W. Montanez, PHI-SF ... 1

1975 AMERICAN
F. Lynn, BOS ... 326
J. Mayberry, KC ... 157
J. Rice, BOS ... 154
R. Fingers, OAK ... 129
R. Jackson, OAK ... 118
J. Palmer, BAL ... 82
T. Munson, NY ... 69
G. Scott, MIL ... 64½
R. Carew, MIN ... 54½
K. Singleton, BAL ... 44
G. Brett, KC ... 37½
J. Hunter, NY ... 31
R. Burleson, BOS ... 28
C. Washington, OAK ... 22
T. Harrah, TEX ... 16
M. Torrez, BAL ... 12
R. Gossage, CHI ... 11
P. Lindblad, OAK ... 7
G. Tenace, OAK ... 7
B. Powell, CLE ... 6½
D. Baylor, BAL ... 6
B. Campaneris, OAK ... 6
B. Lee, BOS ... 5
J. Todd, OAK ... 5
D. Doyle, BOS ... 5
R. Wise, BOS ... 4
J. Rudi, OAK ... 3
J. Kaat, CHI ... 2
L. May, BAL ... 2
B. Bonds, NY ... 1
C. Yastrzemski, BOS ... 1

1976 NATIONAL
J. Morgan, CIN ... 311
G. Foster, CIN ... 221
M. Schmidt, PHI ... 179
P. Rose, CIN ... 131
G. Maddox, PHI ... 98
B. Madlock, CHI ... 51
S. Garvey, LA ... 51
G. Luzinski, PHI ... 49
K. Griffey, CIN ... 49
R. Jones, SD ... 48
B. Watson, HOU ... 38
A. Oliver, PIT ... 30
R. Eastwick, CIN ... 26
J. Koosman, NY ... 20
S. Carlton, PHI ... 16
D. Cash, PHI ... 15
J. Richard, HOU ... 12
R. Monday, CHI ... 11
D. Kingman, NY ... 11
D. Parker, PIT ... 10
B. Robinson, PIT ... 9
D. Sutton, LA ... 7
R. Cey, LA ... 6
W. Montanez, SF-ATL ... 4
L. Brock, SL ... 3
C. Cedeno, HOU ... 3
C. Geronimo, CIN ... 3
R. Zisk, PIT ... 3
L. Bowa, PHI ... 1

1976 AMERICAN
T. Munson, NY ... 304
G. Brett, KC ... 217
M. Rivers, NY ... 179½
H. McRae, KC ... 99
C. Chambliss, NY ... 71½
R. Carew, MIN ... 71
A. Otis, KC ... 58
B. Campbell, MIN ... 56
L. May, BAL ... 51
J. Palmer, BAL ... 47
M. Fidrych, DET ... 41
J. Rudi, OAK ... 35
S. Bando, OAK ... 31
C. Yastrzemski, BOS ... 26
F. Tanana, CAL ... 19
R. Jackson, BAL ... 17
G. Nettles, NY ... 17
G. Tenace, OAK ... 13
R. Fingers, OAK ... 12
V. Blue, OAK ... 10
E. Figueroa, NY ... 9
S. Lyle, NY ... 8
R. LeFlore, DET ... 6
M. Littell, KC ... 5
R. Carty, CLE ... 5
R. White, NY ... 3
L. Tiant, BOS ... 3
J. Mayberry, KC ... 1
B. Wynegar, MIN ... 1

1977 NATIONAL
G. Foster, CIN ... 291
G. Luzinski, PHI ... 255
D. Parker, PIT ... 156
R. Smith, LA ... 112
S. Carlton, PHI ... 100
S. Garvey, LA ... 98
B. Sutter, CHI ... 68
R. Cey, LA ... 60
T. Simmons, SL ... 58
M. Schmidt, PHI ... 48
B. Robinson, PIT ... 34
T. John, LA ... 33
G. Templeton, SL ... 20
R. Fingers, SD ... 17
P. Rose, CIN ... 15
J. Burroughs, ATL ... 9
A. Oliver, PIT ... 9
J. Candelaria, PIT ... 8
R. Stennett, PIT ... 7
W. McCovey, SF ... 5
J. Bench, CIN ... 3
R. Reuschel, CHI ... 3
E. Valentine, MON ... 3
T. McGraw, PHI ... 2
L. Bowa, PHI ... 1
T. Seaver, NY-CIN ... 1

1977 AMERICAN
R. Carew, MIN ... 273
A. Cowens, KC ... 217
K. Singleton, BAL ... 200
J. Rice, BOS ... 163
G. Nettles, NY ... 112
S. Lyle, NY ... 79
T. Munson, NY ... 70
R. Jackson, NY ... 67
C. Fisk, BOS ... 67
B. Campbell, BOS ... 65
M. Rivers, NY ... 59
L. Hisle, MIN ... 54
G. Brett, KC ... 51
R. Zisk, CHI ... 34
J. Sundberg, TEX ... 30
B. Bonds, CAL ... 28
C. Yastrzemski, BOS ... 25
R. Guidry, NY ... 11
J. Palmer, BAL ... 9
R. LeFlore, DET ... 7
J. Thompson, DET ... 6
R. Burleson, BOS ... 5
B. Hobson, BOS ... 4
N. Ryan, CAL ... 3
G. Scott, BOS ... 3
H. McRae, KC ... 3
L. Bostock, MIN ... 2
T. Johnson, MIN ... 2
C. Chambliss, NY ... 1
O. Gamble, CHI ... 1
D. Leonard, KC ... 1

1978 NATIONAL
D. Parker, PIT ... 320
S. Garvey, LA ... 194
L. Bowa, PHI ... 189
R. Smith, LA ... 164
J. Clark, SF ... 107
G. Foster, CIN ... 104
G. Luzinski, PHI ... 48
G. Perry, SD ... 45
W. Stargell, PIT ... 39
D. Winfield, SD ... 37
P. Rose, CIN ... 35
V. Blue, SF ... 33
K. Tekulve, PIT ... 23
R. Fingers, SD ... 16
B. Hooton, LA ... 15
D. Lopes, LA ... 12
P. Niekro, ATL ... 8
B. Buckner, CHI ... 8
J. Burroughs, ATL ... 7
B. Sutter, CHI ... 5
G. Maddox, PHI ... 4
E. Cabell, HOU ... 2
B. Boone, PHI ... 1

1978 AMERICAN
J. Rice, BOS ... 352
R. Guidry, NY ... 291
L. Hisle, MIL ... 201
A. Otis, KC ... 90
R. Staub, DET ... 88
G. Nettles, NY ... 86
D. Baylor, CAL ... 51
E. Murray, BAL ... 50
C. Fisk, BOS ... 49
D. Porter, KC ... 48
R. Carew, MIN ... 46
M. Caldwell, MIL ... 41
R. Gossage, NY ... 39
A. Oliver, TEX ... 26½
J. Sundberg, TEX ... 24
R. LeFlore, DET ... 21
R. Jackson, NY ... 18
C. Yastrzemski, BOS ... 17
G. Brett, KC ... 14
A. Thornton, CLE ... 12½
L. Piniella, NY ... 11
T. Munson, NY ... 9
L. Bostock, CAL ... 8
L. Gura, KC ... 8
F. Lynn, BOS ... 6
M. Rivers, NY ... 6
B. Stanley, BOS ... 6
D. LaRoche, CAL ... 6
D. Money, MIL ... 5
W. Randolph, NY ... 5
D. Eckersley, BOS ... 4
H. McRae, KC ... 4
L. Roberts, SEA ... 3
R. Gale, KC ... 2
K. Singleton, BAL ... 2
R. Burleson, BOS ... 1
F. Tanana, CAL ... 1

1979 NATIONAL
W. Stargell, PIT ... 216
K. Hernandez, SL ... 216
D. Winfield, SD ... 155
L. Parrish, MON ... 128
R. Knight, CIN ... 82
J. Niekro, HOU ... 75½
B. Sutter, CHI ... 69
K. Tekulve, PIT ... 64
D. Concepcion, CIN ... 63
D. Parker, PIT ... 56
D. Kingman, CHI ... 53
G. Foster, CIN ... 34
M. Schmidt, PHI ... 32
S. Garvey, LA ... 30
O. Moreno, PIT ... 23
P. Rose, PHI ... 23
G. Carter, MON ... 15
B. Madlock, SF-PIT ... 14
J. Richard, HOU ... 12
P. Niekro, ATL ... 11½
J. Sambito, HOU ... 9
T. Seaver, CIN ... 9
J. Bench, CIN ... 7
A. Dawson, MON ... 6
G. Templeton, SL ... 5
G. Matthews, ATL ... 4
D. Collins, CIN ... 3
B. Horner, ATL ... 1

1979 AMERICAN
D. Baylor, CAL ... 347
K. Singleton, BAL ... 241
G. Brett, KC ... 226
F. Lynn, BOS ... 160½
J. Rice, BOS ... 124
M. Flanagan, BAL ... 100
G. Thomas, MIL ... 87
B. Grich, CAL ... 58
D. Porter, KC ... 52
B. Bell, TEX ... 48
E. Murray, BAL ... 25½
J. Kern, TEX ... 25
M. Marshall, MIN ... 25
B. Downing, CAL ... 24
S. Lezcano, MIL ... 18
R. Smalley, MIN ... 16
W. Wilson, KC ... 15
S. Kemp, DET ... 15
M. Clear, CAL ... 12
P. Molitor, MIL ... 8
R. Burleson, BOS ... 7
T. John, NY ... 5
C. Cooper, MIL ... 4
R. Jackson, NY ... 3
W. Horton, SEA ... 3
D. Ford, CAL ... 1
R. Guidry, NY ... 1
M. Hargrove, CLE ... 1

1980 NATIONAL
M. Schmidt, PHI ... 336
G. Carter, MON ... 193
J. Cruz, HOU ... 166
D. Baker, LA ... 138
S. Carlton, PHI ... 134
S. Garvey, LA ... 131
A. Dawson, MON ... 72
G. Hendrick, SL ... 50
B. Horner, ATL ... 42
B. McBride, PHI ... 32
K. Hernandez, SL ... 29
D. Murphy, ATL ... 23
C. Cedeno, HOU ... 14
J. Bibby, PIT ... 11
B. Buckner, CHI ... 11
T. McGraw, PHI ... 10
J. Bench, CIN ... 7
J. Clark, SF ... 6
J. Niekro, HOU ... 3
M. Easler, PIT ... 2
J. Reuss, LA ... 2
K. Griffey, CIN ... 1
R. LeFlore, MON ... 1
G. Richards, SD ... 1
R. Scott, MON ... 1

1980 AMERICAN
G. Brett, KC ... 335
R. Jackson, NY ... 234
R. Gossage, NY ... 218
W. Wilson, KC ... 169
C. Cooper, MIL ... 160
E. Murray, BAL ... 106
R. Cerone, NY ... 77
D. Quisenberry, KC ... 76½
S. Stone, BAL ... 53
R. Henderson, OAK ... 51
A. Oliver, TEX ... 31½
T. Armas, OAK ... 29
A. Bumbry, BAL ... 27
B. Oglivie, MIL ... 27
W. Randolph, NY ... 10
M. Norris, OAK ... 10
R. Yount, MIL ... 8
M. Rivers, TEX ... 7
B. Bell, TEX ... 7
A. Trammell, DET ... 6
K. Singleton, BAL ... 4
T. Perez, BOS ... 2
M. Dilone, CLE ... 2
F. Lynn, BOS ... 1
J. Wathan, KC ... 1

1981 NATIONAL
M. Schmidt, PHI ... 321
A. Dawson, MON ... 215
G. Foster, CIN ... 146
D. Concepcion, CIN ... 108
F. Valenzuela, LA ... 90
G. Carter, MON ... 77
D. Baker, LA ... 65
B. Sutter, SL ... 59
S. Carlton, PHI ... 41
T. Seaver, CIN ... 35
P. Rose, PHI ... 35
B. Buckner, CHI ... 35
G. Matthews, PHI ... 31
J. Cruz, HOU ... 25
G. Hendrick, SL ... 25
N. Ryan, HOU ... 23
B. Madlock, PIT ... 20
A. Howe, HOU ... 16
T. Raines, MON ... 15
R. Camp, ATL ... 9
K. Hernandez, SL ... 9
T. Herr, SL ... 7
G. Minton, SF ... 4
W. Cromartie, MON ... 3
S. Garvey, LA ... 1
M. May, SF ... 1

1981 AMERICAN
R. Fingers, MIL ... 319
R. Henderson, OAK ... 308
D. Evans, BOS ... 140
T. Armas, OAK ... 139
E. Murray, BAL ... 137
C. Lansford, BOS ... 109
D. Winfield, NY ... 98
C. Cooper, MIL ... 96
R. Gossage, NY ... 62
T. Paciorek, SEA ... 46
D. Murphy, OAK ... 45
K. Gibson, DET ... 40
S. McCatty, OAK ... 22
B. Grich, CAL ... 19
J. Morris, DET ... 17
A. Oliver, TEX ... 8
R. Yount, MIL ... 7
B. Bell, TEX ... 7
B. Almon, CHI ... 6
J. Mumphrey, NY ... 5
M. Hargrove, CLE ... 4
A. Trammell, DET ... 4
K. Singleton, BAL ... 3
S. Kemp, DET ... 3
D. Martinez, BAL ... 3
G. Luzinski, CHI ... 3
D. Stieb, TOR ... 1
G. Brett, KC ... 1

1982 NATIONAL
D. Murphy, ATL ... 283
L. Smith, SL ... 218
P. Guerrero, LA ... 175
A. Oliver, MON ... 175
B. Sutter, SL ... 134
M. Schmidt, PHI ... 54
J. Clark, SF ... 53
G. Minton, SF ... 44
S. Carlton, PHI ... 41
B. Buckner, CHI ... 38
B. Madlock, PIT ... 37
G. Carter, MON ... 35
O. Smith, SL ... 25
G. Hendrick, SL ... 20
T. Kennedy, SD ... 20
J. Morgan, SF ... 17
K. Hernandez, SL ... 12
J. Thompson, PIT ... 12
G. Garber, ATL ... 6
J. Andujar, SL ... 6
F. Valenzuela, LA ... 3
A. Dawson, MON ... 3
C. Chambliss, ATL ... 2
G. Matthews, PHI ... 2
R. Knight, HOU ... 1

1982 AMERICAN
R. Yount, MIL ... 385
E. Murray, BAL ... 228
D. DeCinces, CAL ... 178
H. McRae, KC ... 175
C. Cooper, MIL ... 152
R. Jackson, CAL ... 107
D. Evans, BOS ... 57
G. Thomas, MIL ... 44½
D. Quisenberry, KC ... 39
R. Henderson, OAK ... 38
D. Winfield, NY ... 33
P. Molitor, MIL ... 29½
L. Parrish, DET ... 26
B. Downing, CAL ... 22
W. Wilson, KC ... 16
R. Fingers, MIL ... 12
B. Boone, CAL ... 12
P. Vuckovich, MIL ... 11
J. Rice, BOS ... 10
T. Harrah, CLE ... 9
H. Baines, CHI ... 9
G. Brett, KC ... 9
D. Baylor, CAL ... 8
A. Thornton, CLE ... 8
B. Stanley, BOS ... 6
J. Palmer, BAL ... 5
D. Garcia, TOR ... 5
R. Carew, CAL ... 5
B. Caudill, SEA ... 4
B. Bell, TEX ... 3
C. Ripken, BAL ... 3
C. Lansford, BOS ... 1
R. Sutcliffe, CLE ... 1
G. Ward, MIN ... 1

1983 NATIONAL
D. Murphy, ATL ... 318

A. Dawson, MON .213
M. Schmidt, PHI . .191
P. Guerrero, LA ...182
T. Raines, MON ...83
J. Cruz, HOU 76
D. Thon, HOU 67
B. Madlock, PIT ...45
A. Holland, PHI 42
T. Kennedy, SD ...37
G. Hendrick, SL ...33
T. Pena, PIT 25
J. Denny, PHI.....24
M. Soto, CIN ...16
D. Evans, SF ...16
R. Ramirez, ATL ...15
J. Orosco, NY 14
L. Smith, CHI 8½
A. Oliver, MON ...3
J. Leonard, SF 2
L. Smith, SL.....1½
J. Davis, CHI 1
K. Hernandez, SL-NY.....1
B. Horner, ATL......1
O. Smith, SL 1

1983 AMERICAN
C. Ripken, BAL ...322
E. Murray, BAL ...290
C. Fisk, CHI ...209
J. Rice, BOS 150
C. Cooper, MIL ...123
D. Quisenberry, KC.........107½
D. Winfield, NY 85
L. Whitaker, DET ...84
L. Parrish, DET 66
H. Baines, CHI.....49
W. Upshaw, TOR . 41½
W. Boggs, BOS ...25
L. Hoyt, CHI 24½
L. Moseby, TOR ...21
B. Stanley, BOS .. 11½
A. Trammell, DET...11
G. Luzinski, CHI ...9
R. Yount, MIL 6
T. Simmons, MIL 4
R. Dotson, CHI ... 3½
R. Law, CHI 2
R. Guidry, NY.......2
J. Morris, DET.....2
J. Cruz, SEA-CHI...1
R. Henderson, OAK..1

G. Wright, TEX......1
T. Martinez, BAL ... ½

1984 NATIONAL
R. Sandberg, CHI .326
K. Hernadez, NY ...195
T. Gwynn, SD ...184
R. Sutcliffe, CHI ...151
G. Matthews, CHI ..70
B. Sutter, SL ...67
M. Schmidt, PHI . 55½
J. Cruz, HOU 53
D. Murphy, ATL . 52½
J. Davis, CHI 49
T. Raines, MON 41
L. Durham, CHI....38
R. Gossage, SD....34
G. Carter, MON 32
D. Gooden, NY 28
A. Wiggins, SD 14
R. Cey, CHI 6
K. McReynolds, SD ..6
B. Dernier, CHI 6
S. Garvey, SD 5
B. Brenly, SF 1
J. Samuel, PHI......1
J. Leonard, SF 1

1984 AMERICAN
W. Hernandez, DET.........306
K. Hrbek, MIN 247
D. Quisenberry, KC.........235
E. Murray, BAL ...197
D. Mattingly, NY ...113
K. Gibson, DET 96
T. Armas, BOS ... 87½
D. Winfield, NY 83
A. Trammell, DET.........76½
W. Wilson, KC....61
D. Evans, BOS 39
A. Davis, SEA 26
J. Rice, BOS 10
H. Baines, CHI.....10
D. Kingman, OAK ...10
L. Parrish, DET 8
W. Upshaw, TOR ...8
B. Downing, CAL....6
S. Balboni, KC.....5
A. Thornton, CLE ...5
J. Bell, TOR 5

B. Bell, TEX 4
D. Stieb, TOR 4
L. Moseby, TOR 4
J. Beniquez, CAL ...2
M. Boddicker, BAL ..2
D. Alexander, TOR . .1
C. Ripken, BAL 1

1985 NATIONAL
W. McGee, SL 280
D. Parker, CIN 220
P. Guerrero, LA ...208
D. Gooden, NY ...162
T. Herr, SL 119
G. Carter, NY 116
D. Murphy, ATL 63
K. Hernandez, NY ..61
J. Tudor, SL 61
J. Clark, SL 20
V. Coleman, SL 16
T. Raines, MON ...15
R. Sandberg, CHI ..14
M. Marshall, LA ...11
H. Brooks, MON ...11
O. Hershiser, LA 9
K. Moreland, CHI....8
O. Smith, SL 5
M. Scioscia, LA 5
J. Reardon, MON ...4
J. Cruz, HOU 2
B. Doran, HOU 2
M. Duncan, LA 1
T. Gwynn, SD......1
F. Valenzuela, LA ...1
G. Wilson, PHI......1

1985 AMERICAN
D. Mattingly, NY ...367
G. Brett, KC 274
R. Henderson, NY ..174
W. Boggs, BOS ...159
E. Murray, BAL ...130
D. Moore, CAL 96
J. Barfield, TOR 88
J. Bell, TOR 84
H. Baines, CHI 49
B. Saberhagen, KC .45
D. Quisenberry, KC .38
D. Winfield, NY 35
C. Fisk, CHI 29
Dr. Evans, DET 17
R. Guidry, NY......15
P. Bradley, SEA 12

C. Ripken, BAL 9
K. Gibson, DET 7
S. Balboni, KC 6
T. Henke, TOR 5
D. Lamp, TOR 5
K. Puckett, MIN 3
D. Alexander, TOR . .3
D. Garcia, TOR 2
R. Gedman, BOS...1

1986 NATIONAL
M. Schmidt, PHI . .287
G. Davis, HOU 231
G. Carter, NY 181
K. Hernandez, NY .179
D. Parker, CIN 144
T. Raines, MON ...99
K. Bass, HOU 73
H. Johnson, NY 42
D. Murphy, ATL 34
T. Gwynn, SD 34
M. Scott, HOU 33
B. Doran, HOU 32
E. Davis, CIN 21
S. Sax, LA 13
R. Knight, NY 9
M. Krukow, SF 8
T. Worrell, SL 7
R. McDowell, NY ...5
D. Smith, HOU 5
F. Valenzuela, LA ...4
L. Dykstra, NY 4
B. Ojeda, NY 2
D. Murphy, ATL 2
C. Maldonado, SF . .2

1986 AMERICAN
R. Clemens, BOS .339
D. Mattingly, NY ...258
J. Rice, BOS 241
J. Bell, TOR 125
J. Barfield, TOR ...107
K. Puckett, MIN ...105
W. Boggs, BOS 87
W. Joyner, CAL 74
J. Carter, CLE 72
D. Righetti, NY 71
D. DeCinces, CAL ..56
M. Witt, CAL 34
B. Baylor, BOS 32
T. Fernandez, TOR .17
T. Higuera, MIL 7
G. Gaetti, MIN 6

P. O'Brien, TEX 5
S. Fletcher, TEX 5
M. Barrett, BOS 5
J. Canseco, OAK 3
J. Presley, SEA 2
D. Schofield, CAL ...1

1987 NATIONAL
A. Dawson, CHI ...269
O. Smith, SL 193
J. Clark, SL 186
T. Wallach, MON ...165
W. Clark, SF 128
D. Strawberry, NY ...95
T. Raines, MON 80
T. Gwynn, SD 75
E. Davis, CIN 73
H. Johnson, NY 42
D. Murphy, ATL 34
V. Coleman, SL 20
J. Samuel, PHI.....19
M. Schmidt, PHI ...13
P. Guerrero, LA 12
S. Bedrosian, PHI ...6
M. Thompson, PHI . .4
B. Doran, HOU 1
T. Pendleton, SL 1

1987 AMERICAN
J. Bell, TOR 332
A. Trammell, DET . .311
K. Puckett, MIN ...201
Dw. Evans, BOS ...127
P. Molitor, MIL 125
M. McGwire, OAK ..109
D. Mattingly, NY 92
T. Fernandez, TOR .79
W. Boggs, BOS 64
G. Gaetti, MIN 47
J. Reardon, MIN 37
Dr. Evans, DET 21
D. Alexander, DET ..17
T. Henke, TOR 17
W. Joyner, CAL 17
K. Hrbek, MIN 11
D. Tartabull, KC 10
R. Yount, MIL 8
R. Clemens, BOS ...7
J. Morris, DET 5
K. Seitzer, KC 5
R. Sierra, TEX 5
J. Canseco, OAK 4

M. Nokes, DET 1

1988 NATIONAL
K. Gibson, LA ...272
D. Strawberry, NY .236
K. McReynolds, NY.......162
A. Van Slyke, PIT . .160
W. Clark, SF 135
O. Hershiser, LA ...111
A. Galarraga, MON 105
G. Davis, HOU 72
J. Jackson, CIN 41
D. Cone, NY 37
T. Gwynn, SD 29
J. Franco, CIN 23
E. Davis, CIN 14
B. Bonilla, PIT 7
A. Dawson, CHI.....6
R. Myers, NY 3
B. Butler, SF 2
S. Sax, LA 1

1988 AMERICAN
J. Canseco, OAK . . 392
M. Greenwell, BOS........242
K. Puckett, MIN ...219
D. Winfield, NY ...164
D. Eckersley, OAK . 156
W. Boggs, BOS ...107
A. Trammell, DET . . 62
P. Molitor, MIL 50
Dw. Evans, BOS ...49
F. Viola, MIN 39
R. Yount, MIL......34
G. Brett, KC 29
R. Henderson, OAK. 28
B. Hurst, BOS 15
D. Jones, CLE 11
J. Reardon, MIN ...11
F. McGriff, TOR 9
R. Henderson, NY . . 8
M. McGwire, OAK ...6
J. Carter, CLE 5
L. Smith, BOS 4
G. Gaetti, MIN 3
D. Plesac, MIL 3
D. Stewart, OAK 3
J. Franco, CLE 2
T. Fernandez, TOR ..1

Rookie of the Year Award: History

The Chicago chapter of the Baseball Writers' Association of America (BBWAA) established an award recognizing the major leagues' top rookie following the 1940 season, selecting Lou Boudreau for the honor. This procedure continued for six more years before going national. The subsequent winners of the Chicago chapter's award were Pete Reiser (1941), Johnny Beazley (1942), Bill Johnson (1943), Bill Voiselle (1944), Boo Ferriss (1945), and Eddie Waitkus (1946).

The Sporting News began naming its own Rookie of the Year in 1946, with the selection of Del Ennis. Their award has competed with that of the BBWAA ever since. In 1949 they began recognizing a winner from each league and in 1957 they started selecting both a rookie player and rookie pitcher of the year for each league.

In 1947 thirty-three baseball writers were asked to name five rookies in order of preference, with votes distributed on a 5-4-3-2-1 basis. Thus, Jackie Robinson became the first nationally recognized winner of the BBWAA Rookie of the Year Award, or the J. Louis Comiskey Memorial Award, as it was called. During the 1987 Hall of Fame induction ceremony, Commissioner Peter Ueberroth announced that, hereafter, the Rookie of the Year Award would be officially known as the Jackie Robinson Award.

In 1948 forty-eight writers took part in the award, this time naming only a single candidate on each ballot. In 1949 the BBWAA began the process of choosing a top rookie in each league. Three writers from each league city, the same men who decided on the MVP Awards, participated in the voting. Voters were free to use their individual judgments as to the eligibility of rookie candidates, which created some problems, especially in 1950 when Al Rosen, and his league-leading 37 homers, was ignored by Rookie of the Year voters. Apparently they felt that Rosen's 58 previous major league at-bats were tantamount to veteran status, while winner Walt Dropo's 41 previous at-bats were not.

In 1957 formal guidelines were finally established for determining rookie status. A player could not have accumulated more than 75 at-bats, 45 innings pitched, or have been on a major league roster between May 15 and September 1 of any previous season. Shortly after, the guidelines were changed to 90 at-bats, 45 innings pitched or 45 days on a major league roster before September 1. Finally, in 1971, the guidelines were set at 130 at-bats, 50 innings, or 45 days on a roster.

There were several instances, especially in the early days of the award, in which some Rookie of the Year voters didn't bother to exercise their franchise. In 1961, as with the MVP Award, the number of voters was reduced from three to two writers from each league city.

Following two tie votes in four years (1976 NL, 1979 AL), the writers adopted the system used in Cy Young Award

balloting: naming three rookies on each ballot, in order of preference, with votes distributed on a 5–3–1 basis. This system began in 1980.

The maximum possible point total available to Rookie of the Year candidates was 165 in 1947, 48 in 1948, and 24 in each league in 1949–60. In the National League, it was 16 in 1961, 20 in 1962–68, 24 in 1969–79, and 120 from 1980 to the present. In the American League, it was 20 in 1961–68,

24 in 1969–76, 28 in 1977–79, and 140 from 1980 to the present.

There have been seven unanimous Rookie of the Year selections since 1947: Frank Robinson (NL, 1956), Orlando Cepeda (NL, 1958), Willie McCovey (NL, 1959), Carlton Fisk (AL, 1972), Vince Coleman (NL, 1985), Benito Santiago (NL, 1987), and Mark McGwire (AL, 1987).

Rookie of the Year Award

1947
J. Robinson, BKN (NL) 129
L. Jansen, NY (NL) 105
F. Shea, NY (AL) 67
F. Fain, PHI (AL) 43
F. Baumholtz, CIN (NL) 42
(Rest of voting unknown)

1948
A. Dark, BOS, (NL) . 27
G. Bearden, CLE (AL) 8
R. Ashburn, PHI (NL) . 7
L. Brissie, PHI (AL) . . 3
B. Goodman, BOS (AL) 3

1949 NATIONAL
D. Newcombe, BKN 21
D. Crandall, BOS . . . 3

1949 AMERICAN
R. Sievers, SL 10
A. Kellner, PHI 5
G. Coleman, NY 4
B. Kuzava, CHI 1
J. Groth, DET 1
M. Garcia, CLE 1

1950 NATIONAL
S. Jethroe, BOS . . . 11
B. Miller, PHI 5
D. O' Connell, PIT . . . 4
E. Church, PHI 4
B. Serena, CHI 1

1950 AMERICAN
W. Dropo, BOS . . . 15
W. Ford, NY 6
C. Carrasquel, CHI . . 2

1951 NATIONAL
W. Mays, NY 18
C. Nichols, BOS 4
C. Labine, BKN 2

1951 AMERICAN
G. McDougald, NY . 13
M. Minoso, CHI 11

1952 NATIONAL
J. Black, BKN 19
H. Wilhelm, NY 3
D. Groat, PIT 1
E. Mathews, BOS . . . 1

1952 AMERICAN
H. Byrd, PHI 9
C. Courtney, SL 8
S. White, BOS 7

1953 NATIONAL
J. Gilliam, BKN 11
H. Haddix, SL 4
R. Jablonski, SL 3
R. Repulski, SL 2
B. Bruton, MIL 2
F. Baczewski, CIN . . . 1
J. Greengrass, CIN . . 1

1953 AMERICAN
H. Kuenn, DET 23
T. Umphlett, BOS . . . 1

1954 NATIONAL
W. Moon, SL 17
E. Banks, CHI 4
G. Conley, MIL 2
H. Aaron, MIL 1

1954 AMERICAN
B. Grim, NY 15
J. Finigan, PHI 8
A. Kaline, DET 1

1955 NATIONAL
B. Virdon, SL 15
J. Meyer, PHI 7
D. Bessent, BKN . . . 2

1955 AMERICAN
H. Score, CLE 18
B. Klaus, BOS 5
N. Zauchin, BOS . . . 1

1956 NATIONAL
F. Robinson, CIN . . . 24

1956 AMERICAN
L. Aparicio, CHI . . . 22
T. Francona, BAL . . . 1
R. Colavito, CLE . . . 1

1957 NATIONAL
J. Sanford, PHI 16
E. Bouchee, PHI . . . 4
D. Drott, CHI 3
B. Hazle, MIL 1

1957 AMERICAN
T. Kubek, NY 23
F. Malzone, BOS . . . 1

1958 NATIONAL
O. Cepeda, SF 21

1958 AMERICAN
A. Pearson, WAS . . . 14
R. Duren, NY 7
G. Bell, CLE 3

1959 NATIONAL
W. McCovey, SF . . . 24

1959 AMERICAN
B. Allison, WAS . . . 18
J. Perry, CLE 5
R. Snyder, KC 1

1960 NATIONAL
F. Howard, LA 12
P. Herrera, PHI 4
A. Mahaffey, PHI . . . 3
R. Santo, CHI 2
T. Davis, LA 1

1960 AMERICAN
R. Hansen, BAL 22
C. Estrada, BAL 1
J. Gentile, BAL 1

1961 NATIONAL
B. Williams, CHI . . . 10
J. Torre, MIL 5

J. Curtis, CHI 1

1961 AMERICAN
D. Schwall, BOS . . . 7
D. Howser, KC 6
Fl. Robinson, CHI . . 2
C. Schilling, BOS . . . 2
L. Thomas, LA 2
J. Wood, DET 1

1962 NATIONAL
K. Hubbs, CHI 19
D. Clendenon, PIT . . 1

1962 AMERICAN
T. Tresh, NY 13
B. Rodgers, LA 4
B. Allen, MIN 1
D. Chance, LA 1
D. Radatz, BOS 1

1963 NATIONAL
P. Rose, CIN 17
R. Hunt, NY 2
R. Culp, PHI 1

1963 AMERICAN
G. Peters, CHI 10
P. Ward, CHI 6
J. Hall, MIN 4

1964 NATIONAL
R. Allen, PHI 18
R. Carty, MIL 1
J. Hart, SF 1

1964 AMERICAN
T. Oliva, MIN 19
W. Bunker, BAL 1

1965 NATIONAL
J. Lefebvre, LA 13
J. Morgan, HOU . . . 4
F. Linzy, SF 3

1965 AMERICAN
C. Blefary, BAL 12
M. Lopez, CAL 8

1966 NATIONAL
T. Helms, CIN 12
S. Jackson, HOU . . . 3
T. Fuentes, SF 2
R. Hundley, CHI . . . 1
C. Jones, NY 1
L. Jaster, SL 1

1966 AMERICAN
T. Agee, CHI 16
J. Nash, KC 2
D. Johnson, BAL . . . 1
G. Scott, BOS 1

1967 NATIONAL
T. Seaver, NY 11
D. Hughes, SL 6
G. Nolan, CIN 3

1967 AMERICAN
R. Carew, MIN 19
R. Smith, BOS 1

1968 NATIONAL
J. Bench, CIN . . . 10½
J. Koosman, NY . . . 9½

1968 AMERICAN
S. Bahnsen, NY 17
D. Unser, WAS 3

1969 NATIONAL
T. Sizemore, LA 14
C. Laboy, MON 3
A. Oliver, PIT 3
B. Didier, ATL 2
L. Hisle, PHI 2

1969 AMERICAN
L. Piniella, KC 9
M. Nagy, BOS 6
C. May, CHI 5
K. Tatum, CAL 4

1970 NATIONAL
C. Morton, MON . . . 11
B. Carbo, CIN 8
L. Bowa, PHI 3
W. Simpson, CIN . . . 1
C. Cedeno, HOU . . . 1

1970 AMERICAN
T. Munson, NY 23
R. Foster, CLE 1

1971 NATIONAL
E. Williams, ATL . . . 18
W. Montanez, PHI . . . 6

1971 AMERICAN
C. Chambliss, CLE . . 11
B. Parsons, MIL 5
A. Mangual, OAK . . . 4
D. Griffin, BOS 3
P. Splittorff, KC 1

1972 NATIONAL
J. Matlack, NY 19
Dv. Rader, SF 4
J. Milner, NY 1

1972 AMERICAN
C. Fisk, BOS 24

1973 NATIONAL
G. Matthews, SF . . . 11
S. Rogers, MON . . 3½
B. Boone, PHI 2
E. Sosa, SF 2
D. Driessen, CIN . . . 2
R. Cey, LA 1
D. Lopes, LA 1
J. Grubb, SD 1
R. Zisk, PIT . . . . ½

1973 AMERICAN
A. Bumbry, BAL . . 13½
P. Garcia, MIL 3
D. Porter, MIL 2
S. Busby, KC 2
D. Medich, NY 2
R. Coggins, BAL . . 1½

1974 NATIONAL
B. McBride, SL . . . 16
G. Gross, HOU 7
B. Madlock CHI 1

1974 AMERICAN
M. Hargrove, TEX 16½

B. Dent, CHI 3
G. Brett, KC 2
R. Burleson, BOS . 1½
J. Sundberg, TEX . . . 1

1975 NATIONAL
J. Montefusco, SF . . 12
G. Carter, MON 9
Lr. Parrish, MON . . . 1
R. Eastwick, CIN . . . 1
M. Trillo, CHI 1

1975 AMERICAN
F. Lynn, BOS 23½
J. Rice, BOS . . . . . . ½

1976 NATIONAL
B. Metzger, SD 11
P. Zachry, CIN 11
H. Cruz, SL 2

1976 AMERICAN
M. Fidrych, DET . . . 22
B. Wynegar, MIN . . . 2

1977 NATIONAL
A. Dawson, MON . . . 10
S. Henderson, NY . . . 9
G. Richards, SD 4
F. Bannister, HOU . . . 1

1977 AMERICAN
E. Murray, BAL . . 12½
M. Page, OAK 9½
B. Wills, TEX 4
D. Rozema, DET . . . 2

1978 NATIONAL
B. Horner, ATL . . 12½
O. Smith, SD 8½
D. Robinson, PIT . . . 3

1978 AMERICAN
L. Whitaker, DET . . . 21
P. Molitor, MIL 3
C. Lansford, CAL . . . 2
R. Gale, KC 1
A. Trammell, DET . . . 1

1979 NATIONAL
R. Sutcliffe, LA . . . 20
J. Leonard, HOU . . . 3
S. Thompson, CHI . . 1

1979 AMERICAN
J. Castino, MIN 7
A. Griffin, TOR 7
M. Clear, CAL 5
R. Davis, NY 3
R. Baumgarten, CHI . 3
P. Putnam, TEX 3

1980 NATIONAL
S. Howe, LA 80
B. Gullickson, MON 53
L. Smith, PHI 49
R. Oester, CIN 16
D. Smith, HOU 13
J. Reardon, NY 2
A. Holland, SF 1
L. Durham, SL 1
B. Walk, PHI 1

1980 AMERICAN
J. Charboneau, CLE 102
D. Stapleton, BOS . . 40
D. Corbett, MIN . . . 38
D. Garcia, TOR 35
B. Burns, CHI 33
R. Peters, DET 3
R. Dotson, CHI 1

1981 NATIONAL
F. Valenzuela, LA . . 107
T. Raines, MON . . . 85
H. Brooks, NY 8½
B. Berenyi, CIN 5
J. Bonilla, SD 5
T. Pena, PIT 4
M. Wilson, NY 1½

1981 AMERICAN
D. Righetti, NY 127
R. Gedman, BOS . . . 64
B. Ojeda, BOS 36
M. Jones, KC 8
D. Engle, MIN 4½
M. Witt, CAL 4
S. Babitt, OAK 4
J. Bell, TOR 2
G. Ward, MIN 1½
B. Havens, MIN 1

1982 NATIONAL
S. Sax, LA 63
J. Ray, PIT 57
W. McGee, SL 39
C. Davis, SF 32
L. DeLeon, SD 10
R. Sandberg, CHI . . . 9
S. Bedrosian, ATL . . 4
D. LaPoint, SL 1
E. Show, SD 1

1982 AMERICAN
C. Ripken, BAL . . . 132
K. Hrbek, MIN 90
W. Boggs, BOS . . 10½
E. Vande Berg, SEA . . 9
G. Gaetti, MIN 4
D. Hostetler, TEX . . . 3
V. Hayes, CLE 2
J. Barfield, TOR . . . 1½

1983 NATIONAL
D. Strawberry, NY . 106
C. McMurtry, ATL . . 49
M. Hall, CHI 32
G. Redus, CIN 8
B. Doran, HOU 7
F. DiPino, HOU 6
G. Brock, LA 3
J. DeLeon, PIT 3
M. Thurmond, SD . . 1
L. Tunnell, PIT 1

1983 AMERICAN
R. Kittle, CHI 104
J. Franco, CLE 78
M. Boddicker, BAL . 70

1984 NATIONAL
D. Gooden, NY . . . 118
J. Samuel, PHI 67
O. Hershiser, LA . . . 15
D. Gladden, SF 9
R. Darling, NY 3

C. Martinez, SD 2
J. Stone, PHI 1
T. Pendleton, SL 1

1984 AMERICAN
A. Davis, SEA 134
M. Langston, SEA ..82
K. Puckett, MIN 23
T. Teufel, MIN 5
M. Young, BAL 3
R. Clemens, BOS ...2
M. Gubicza, KC 1
A. Nipper, BOS 1
R. Romanick, CAL...1

1985 NATIONAL
V. Coleman, SL ...120

T. Browning, CIN ...72
M. Duncan, LA 9
C. Brown, SF 7
G. Davis, HOU 3
R. McDowell, NY 2
J. Orsulak, PIT 2
J. Hesketh, MON 1

1985 AMERICAN
O. Guillen, CHI....101
T. Higuera, MIL 67
E. Riles, MIL 29
O. McDowell, TEX ...25
S. Cliburn, CAL 16
B. Fisher, NY 7
T. Henke, TOR 5
M. Salas, MIN 2

1986 NATIONAL
T. Worrell, SL 118
R. Thompson, SF ..46
K. Mitchell, NY 22
C. Kerfeld, HOU ...17
W. Clark, SF 5
Br. Bonds, PIT 4
J. Deshaies, HOU ..1
B. Larkin, CIN 1
B. Ruffin, PHI 1
J. Kruk, SD 1

1986 AMERICAN
J. Canseco, OAK ..110
W. Joyner, CAL 98
M. Eichhorn, TOR ..23
C. Snyder, CLE 16

D. Tartabull, SEA 4
R. Sierra, TEX 1

1987 NATIONAL
B. Santiago, SD ...120
M. Dunne, PIT 66
J. Magrane, SL 10
C. Candaele, MON ..9
G. Young, HOU 7
C. James, PHI 1
L. Lancaster, CHI....1
G. Mathews, SL.....1
R. Myers, NY 1

1987 AMERICAN
M. McGwire, OAK .140
K. Seitzer, KC 64

M. Nokes, DET 32
M. Greenwell, BOS ..9
D. White, CAL 5
M. Henneman, DET ..1
N. Liriano, TOR 1

1988 NATIONAL
C. Sabo, CIN 79
M. Grace, CHI 61
T. Belcher, LA 35
R. Gant, ATL 22
R. Alomar, SD 11
D. Berryhill, CHI.....3
G. Jefferies, NY 3
R. Jordan, PHI......2

1988 AMERICAN
W. Weiss, OAK ...103
B. Harvey, CAL 49
J. Reed, BOS 48
D. August, MIL 22
D. Gallagher, CHI...18
M. Perez, CHI 9
M. Schooler, SEA ..2
C. Espy, TEX 1

Cy Young Award: History

Commissioner Ford Frick, troubled by pitchers' lack of representation in MVP voting, spearheaded the 1956 effort to initiate a "most valuable pitcher" award. Cy Young, baseball's winningest pitcher, who had died the previous November, was the logical choice to name the honor after. At a special meeting on July 9, 1956, the Baseball Writers' Association of America approved, by the slim margin of 14-12, the establishment of the Cy Young Memorial Award, designed to honor the major leagues' outstanding pitcher each year beginning in '56. Ironically, the first winner, Brooklyn's Don Newcombe, also won his league's MVP Award.

One writer from each major league city participated in the balloting. In case of a tie vote, a second balloting was to be taken between the deadlocked pitchers. Hurlers were not to be eligible to win the award more than once, a rule which was evidently scrapped within two years.

Frick was adamantly opposed to the commonly voiced idea to recognize a Cy Young winner in each league but, not long after his December 1965 retirement, the idea became a reality. On March 1, 1967, Frick's successor William Eckert approved the plan for dual awards, with two writers from each league city designated to make selections.

The system of having each writer make only one selection prevailed until 1969, when Detroit's Denny McLain and Baltimore's Mike Cuellar tied for the AL Cy Young Award. Thereafter, writers were instructed to name three pitchers in each league, with 5 points allotted for each first-place vote, 3 for second, and 1 for third.

The maximum number of points available for one pitcher was 16 from 1956–60, 18 in 1961, 20 in 1962–68, 24 in 1969, 120 in 1970–76 (AL) and 1970–present (NL), and 140 in 1977–present (AL). As with every other major award, there have been a few instances in Cy Young voting where at least one writer failed to return a ballot.

Unanimous winners of the Cy Young Award are Sandy Koufax (NL, 1963, '65, and '66), Bob Gibson (NL, 1968), Denny McLain (AL, 1968), Steve Carlton (NL, 1972), Ron Guidry (AL, 1978), Rick Sutcliffe (NL, 1984), Dwight Gooden (NL, 1985), Roger Clemens (AL, 1986), and Orel Hershiser (NL, 1988).

Relief pitchers, once overlooked in Cy Young balloting, have become strong candidates in recent years. Until 1970 only one reliever — Lindy McDaniel in 1960 — had received even a single vote. The new voting system helped open opportunities for bullpen aces and in 1974 the Dodgers' Mike Marshall became the first reliever to win the Cy Young Award. He has been followed in that distinction by Sparky Lyle (AL, 1977), Bruce Sutter (NL, 1979), Rollie Fingers (AL, 1981), Willie Hernández (AL, 1984), and Steve Bedrosian (NL, 1987).

Cy Young Award

1956
D. Newcombe, BKN
(NL) 10
S. Maglie, BKN (NL) .4
W. Spahn, MIL (NL) ..1
W. Ford, NY (AL) 1

1957
W. Spahn, MIL (NL) .15
D. Donovan, CHI
(AL) 1

1958
B. Turley, NY (AL) ...5
W. Spahn, MIL (NL) ..4
B. Friend, PIT (NL) ...3
L. Burdette, MIL
(NL) 3

1959
E. Wynn, CHI (AL) ..13
S. Jones, SF (NL) ...2
B. Shaw, CHI (AL) ...1

1960
V. Law, PIT (NL) 8
W. Spahn, MIL (NL) ..4
E. Broglio, SL (NL)...1
L. McDaniel, SL (NL) .1

1961
W. Ford, NY (AL) 9
W. Spahn, MIL (NL) ..6
F. Lary, DET (AL) 2

1962
D. Drysdale, LA
(NL) 14
J. Sanford, SF (NL) ..4
B. Purkey, CIN (NL) ..1
B. Pierce, SF (NL) ...1

1963
S. Koufax, LA (NL)..20

1964
D. Chance, LA (AL) .17
L. Jackson, CHI (NL) .2
S. Koufax, LA (NL)...1

1965
S. Koufax, LA (NL)..20

1966
S. Koufax, LA (NL)..20

1967 NATIONAL
M. Mc Cormick, SF .18
F. Jenkins, CHI 1
J. Bunning, PHI 1

1967 AMERICAN
J. Lonborg, BOS ...18
J. Horlen, CHI 2

1968 NATIONAL
B. Gibson, SL 20

1968 AMERICAN
D. McLain, DET 20

1969 NATIONAL
T. Seaver, NY 23
P. Niekro, ATL 1

1969 AMERICAN
M. Cuellar, BAL 10
D. McLain, DET 10
J. Perry, MIN 3
D. McNally, BAL 1

1970 NATIONAL
B. Gibson, SL 118
G. Perry, SF 51
F. Jenkins CHI 16
D. Giusti, PIT 8
J. Merritt, CIN 8
G. Nolan, CIN 5
T. Seaver, NY 4
W. Granger, CIN 3
C. Morton, MON 2

L. Walker, PIT 1

1970 AMERICAN
J. Perry, MIN 55
D. McNally, BAL ...47
S. McDowell, CLE ..45
M. Cuellar, BAL 44
J. Palmer, BAL.....11
C. Wright, CAL 9
R. Perranoski, MIN ..5

1971 NATIONAL
F. Jenkins, CHI 97
T. Seaver, NY 61
A. Downing, LA 40
D. Ellis, PIT 9
B. Gibson, SL 3
J. Johnson, SF 2
D. Roberts, SD 2
J. Marichal, SF 1
B. Stoneman, MON ..1

1971 AMERICAN
V. Blue, OAK 98
M. Lolich, DET 85
W. Wood, CHI 23
D. McNally, BAL 8
D. Drago, KC 1
A. Messersmith,
CAL 1

1972 NATIONAL
S. Carlton, PHI ...120
S. Blass, PIT 35
F. Jenkins, CHI.....23
M. Marshall, MON ..8
G. Nolan, CIN 6
T. Seaver, NY 6
C. Carroll, CIN 6
D. Sutton, LA 6
B. Gibson, SL 3
M. Pappas, CHI 3

1972 AMERICAN
G. Perry, CLE 64
W. Wood, CHI 58
M. Lolich, DET 27
J. Hunter, OAK.....26
J. Palmer, BAL.....20
L. Tiant, BOS 16
S. Lyle, NY 3
N. Ryan, CAL 2

1973 NATIONAL
T. Seaver, NY 71
M. Marshall, MON ..54
R. Bryant, SF 50
J. Billingham, CIN ..30
D. Sutton, LA 7
F. Norman, SD-CIN ..3
D. Giusti, PIT 1

1973 AMERICAN
J. Palmer, BAL.....88
N. Ryan, CAL 62
J. Hunter, OAK.....52
J. Hiller, DET 6
W. Wood, CHI 3
J. Colborn, MIL 2
V. Blue, OAK 1
B. Blyleven, MIN 1
G. Perry, CLE.......1

1974 NATIONAL
M. Marshall, LA ...96
A. Messersmith,
LA 66
P. Niekro, ATL 15
D. Sutton, LA 12
A. Hrabosky, SL 9
J. Billingham, CIN ..8
D. Gullett, CIN 5
C. Carroll, CIN 2
D. Giusti, PIT 1
B. Capra, ATL 1
L. McGlothen, SL ...1

1974 AMERICAN
J. Hunter, OAK.....90
F. Jenkins, TEX 75
N. Ryan, CAL 28
G. Perry, CLE......8

L. Tiant, BOS......8
M. Cuellar, BAL.....6
J. Hiller, DET.......1

1975 NATIONAL
T. Seaver, NY......98
R. Jones, SD....80
A. Hrabosky, SL...33
J. Montefusco, SF...2
D. Gullett, CIN....1
A. Messersmith, LA..1
D. Sutton, LA......1

1975 AMERICAN
J. Palmer, BAL.....98
J. Hunter, NY....74
R. Fingers, OAK...25
F. Tanana, CAL.....7
J. Kaat, CHI.......7
V. Blue, OAK.....2
R. Gossage, CHI....2
R. Wise, BOS.....1

1976 NATIONAL
R. Jones, SD......96
J. Koosman, NY.69½
D. Sutton, LA..25½
S. Carlton, PHI....11
R. Eastwick, CIN...6
J. Matlack, NY....5
J. Richard, HOU...2
T. Seaver, NY......1

1976 AMERICAN
J. Palmer, BAL...108
M. Fidrych, DET...51
F. Tanana, CAL....18
E. Figueroa, NY...12
L. Tiant, BOS.....10
V. Blue, OAK......8
B. Campbell, MIN..7
R. Fingers, OAK...1
W. Garland, BAL...1

1977 NATIONAL
S. Carlton, PHI...104
T. John, LA.......54

T. Seaver, NY-CIN..18
R. Reuschel, CHI...18
J. Candelaria, PIT..17
B. Sutter, CHI.....5

1977 AMERICAN
S. Lyle, NY......56½
J. Palmer, BAL....48
N. Ryan, CAL....46
D. Leonard, KC...45
B. Campbell, BOS.........25½
D. Goltz, MIN.....19
R. Guidry, NY.......5
D. Rozema, DET....4
F. Tanana, CAL.....3

1978 NATIONAL
G. Perry, SD....116
B. Hooton, LA....38
V. Blue, SF.......17
J. Richard, HOU...13
K. Tekulve, PIT...12
P. Niekro, ATL....10
R. Grimsley, MON...7
R. Fingers, SD.....1
T. John, LA.......1
D. Robinson, PIT....1

1978 AMERICAN
R. Guidry, NY.....140
M. Caldwell, MIL...76
J. Palmer, BAL....14
D. Eckersley, BOS..10
R. Gossage, NY....4
F. Jenkins, TEX....2
E. Figueroa, NY....1
L. Gura, KC.......1
D. Leonard, KC....1
M. Marshall, MIN...1
P. Splittorff, KC....1
B. Stanley, BOS....1

1979 NATIONAL
B. Sutter, CHI....72
J. Niekro, HOU...66
J. Richard, HOU...41

T. Seaver, CIN....20
K. Tekulve, PIT...14
P. Niekro, ATL......3

1979 AMERICAN
M. Flanagan, BAL..136
T. John, NY.....51
R. Guidry, NY.....26
J. Kern, TEX....25
M. Marshall, MIN...7
J. Koosman, MIN...5
D. Eckersley, BOS...1
A. Lopez, DET......1

1980 NATIONAL
S. Carlton, PHI...118
J. Reuss, LA.....55
J. Bibby, PIT......28
J. Niekro, HOU....11
T. McGraw, PHI....1
S. Rogers, MON....1
J. Sambito, HOU...1
M. Soto, CIN.......1

1980 AMERICAN
S. Stone, BAL....100
M. Norris, OAK....91
R. Gossage, NY..37½
T. John, NY......14
D. Quisenberry, KC.........7½
L. Gura, KC.......1
S. McGregor, BAL...1

1981 NATIONAL
F. Valenzuela, LA...70
T. Seaver, CIN....67
S. Carlton, PHI....50
N. Ryan, HOU....28
B. Sutter, SL.......1

1981 AMERICAN
R. Fingers, MIL...126
S. McCatty, OAK..84½
J. Morris, DET....21
P. Vuckovich, MIL...8½
D. Martinez, BAL...3½

R. Gossage, NY.....3
R. Guidry, NY.....2½
B. Burns, CHI......2
L. Gura, KC.......1

1982 NATIONAL
S. Carlton, PHI...112
S. Rogers, MON...29
F. Valenzuela, LA.25½
B. Sutter, SL.....25
P. Niekro, ATL....18
G. Minton, SF.....4
J. Andujar, SL.....1
G. Garber, ATL......1
M. Soto, CIN......½

1982 AMERICAN
P. Vuckovich, MIL..87
J. Palmer, BAL....59
D. Quisenberry, KC.40
D. Stieb, TOR....36
R. Sutcliffe, CLE...14
G. Zahn, CAL.......7
B. Stanley, BOS....4
B. Caudill, SEA....4
D. Petry, DET.......1

1983 NATIONAL
J. Denny, PHI....103
M. Soto, CIN.....61
J. Orosco, NY.....19
S. Rogers, MON...15
L. McWilliams, PIT...7
A. Holland, PHI....4
C. McMurtry, ATL...3
B. Welch, LA......2
N. Ryan, HOU......1
L. Smith, CHI......1

1983 AMERICAN
L. Hoyt, CHI......116
D. Quisenberry, KC.81
J. Morris, DET....38
R. Dotson, CHI.....9
R. Guidry, NY......5
S. McGregor, BAL...3

1984 NATIONAL
R. Sutcliffe, CHI...120
D. Gooden, NY....45
B. Sutter, SL....33½
J. Andujar, SL...12½
R. Gossage, SD....3
M. Soto, CIN......2

1984 AMERICAN
W. Hernandez,
DET..........88
D. Quisenberry, KC.71
B. Blyleven, CLE...45
M. Boddicker, BAL.41
D. Petry, DET.......3
J. Morris, DET......1
D. Stieb, TOR......1

1985 NATIONAL
D. Gooden, NY...120
J. Tudor, SL.....65
O. Hershiser, LA...17
J. Andujar, SL......6
F. Valenzuela, LA....4
T. Browning, CIN....3
J. Reardon, MON....1

1985 AMERICAN
B. Saberhagen,
KC...........127
R. Guidry, NY.....88
B. Blyleven, MIN....9
D. Quisenberry, KC..9
C. Leibrandt, KC....7
D. Alexander, TOR...5
B. Burns, CHI......2
D. Moore, CAL.....2
D. Stieb, TOR......2
M. Moore, SEA.....1

1986 NATIONAL
M. Scott, HOU.....98
F. Valenzuela, LA..88
M. Krukow, SF.....15
B. Ojeda, NY.......9

R. Darling, NY......2
R. Rhoden, PIT.....2
D. Gooden, NY.....1
S. Fernandez, NY...1

1986 AMERICAN
R. Clemens, BOS..140
T. Higuera, MIL....42
M. Witt, CAL....35
D. Righetti, NY....20
J. Morris, DET....13
M. Eichhorn, TOR...2

1987 NATIONAL
S. Bedrosian, PHI...57
R. Sutcliffe, CHI....55
R. Reuschel, SF....54
O. Hershiser, LA...14
D. Gooden, NY....12
N. Ryan, HOU....12
M. Scott, HOU......9
B. Welch, LA.......3

1987 AMERICAN
R. Clemens, BOS..124
J. Key, TOR....64
D. Stewart, OAK...32
D. Alexander, DET...8
M. Langston, SEA...7
T. Higuera, MIL....5
F. Viola, MIN.......5
J. Reardon, MIN....4
J. Morris, DET......3

1988 NATIONAL
O. Hershisher, LA..120
D. Jackson, CIN...54
D. Cone, NY....42

1988 AMERICAN
F. Viola, MIN.....138
D. Eckersley, OAK..52
M. Gubicza, KC....26
D. Stewart, OAK...16
B. Hurst, BOS.....12
R. Clemens, BOS...8

Hypothetical Awards

As the "expert" in baseball award-voting, I have been asked to make a set of hypothetical award selections for the years no official honors were given; i.e., pre-1956 Cy Young, pre-1947 Rookie of the Year, and pre-1911 MVP Awards, along with awards for any other "missing" years.

While this assignment gave me unusual freedom, I felt a certain responsibility to make my selections consistent with the perceptions and voting trends of a particular era. For example, although there were better NL players than Cincinnati's Edd Roush in 1919, he did two things which, combined, would have virtually guaranteed him the MVP Award: he won the batting crown, which was *the* individual title in the dead-ball era; and he played on a pennant-winner, which has always been a key factor in MVP voting. Thus, I felt obliged to make Roush my hypothetical selection.

Besides my own opinions and intuitions, several sources were instrumental in my selection process, including:

1. SABR retroactive award surveys, which have been done for pre-1949 Rookie of the Year and pre-1967 Cy Young Awards. SABR (the Society for American Baseball Research) is comprised of more than six thousand hard-core fans, hundreds of whom chose to participate in these surveys. The ballots were tremendously helpful in screening candidates and the voting results were carefully compared to my own choices.

2. Linear Weights, an overall player rating system devised by Pete Palmer, first used in *The Hidden Game of Baseball* (Doubleday, 1984, 1985), and continued in *Total Baseball*.

3. MVP voting results, for comparing Cy Young and Rookie candidates. If rookie "A" receives 75 points in the MVP election, while comparable rookie "B" receives just 10, I am forced to conclude that the on-the-spot observers discerned some important difference that we can't see in the statistics and that "A" is probably the better choice. (Incidentally, the criteria used to determine rookies was a maximum of 90 at-bats or 45 innings pitched in any previous seasons.)

4. Unofficial awards, including 1940–46 Rookie and 1929–30 MVP selections.

5. Cy Young (1956–66) and Rookie of the Year (1947–48) balloting, for years in which one league had no official winner.

The resulting selections are not necessarily ones the average reader will agree with, nor even that the *writer* agrees with; rather, they are the ones which can be *best justified with the available evidence*. I am prepared to defend any of my choices.

In comparison with the Palmer system, my selections concurred 54 percent with top player selections and 59 percent with top pitcher nominations. In comparison with the SABR surveys, my selections agreed 84 percent in the Rookie of the Year Award and 79 percent in the Cy Young Award.

The big winner in the hypothetical awards is Christy Mathewson, who picks up a Rookie of the Year, two MVPs, and eight Cy Young Awards. Other pitchers capturing at least three Cy Youngs are Walter Johnson (7); Lefty Grove (6, consecutively); Warren Spahn (4, to add to the one he actually did win); Grover Alexander (4); Burleigh Grimes, Carl Hubbell, Bob Feller, Bucky Walters, Bob Lemon, and appropriately, Cy Young himself (3 each).

Notable Rookies of the Year include Grover Alexander, Babe Ruth, Rogers Hornsby, Dizzy Dean, Joe DiMaggio, and Ted Williams.

Honus Wagner cops six MVP Awards, including four in succession. Three-time MVPs are Nap Lajoie, Alexander, Ruth, and Hornsby. Ruth (once) and Hornsby (twice) also won official MVP Awards.

The following pages contain my hypothetical Cy Young (124), Rookie of the Year (97), and MVP (42) selections for this century.

Hypothetical Cy Young Award

American League Pitcher/Club	Year	American League Pitcher/Club	Year	American League Pitcher/Club	Year	National League Pitcher/Club	Year	National League Pitcher/Club	Year	National League Pitcher/Club	Year
C. Young, BOS	1901	G. Uhle, CLE	1923	D. Trout, DET	1944	J. McGinnity, BKN	1900	G. Alexander, PHI	1915	B. Lee, CHI	1938
C. Young, BOS	1902	W. Johnson, WAS	1924	H. Newhouser, DET	1945	N. Hahn, CIN	1901	G. Alexander, PHI	1916	B. Walters, CIN	1939
C. Young, BOS	1903	S. Coveleski, WAS	1925	H. Newhouser, DET	1946	J. Taylor, CHI	1902	G. Alexander, PHI	1917	B. Walters, CIN	1940
J. Chesbro, NY	1904	G. Uhle, CLE	1926	J. Page, NY	1947	C. Mathewson, NY	1903	J. Vaughn, CHI	1918	W. Wyatt, BKN	1941
R. Waddell, PHI	1905	W. Moore, NY	1927	B. Lemon, CLE	1948	J. McGinnity, NY	1904	J. Vaughn, CHI	1919	M. Cooper, SL	1942
O. Hess, CLE	1906	L. Grove, PHI	1928	M. Parnell, BOS	1949	C. Mathewson, NY	1905	G. Alexander, CHI	1920	M. Cooper, SL	1943
E. Walsh, CHI	1907	L. Grove, PHI	1929	B. Lemon, CLE	1950	M. Brown, CHI	1906	B. Grimes, BKN	1921	B. Walters, CIN	1944
E. Walsh, CHI	1908	L. Grove, PHI	1930	N. Garver, SL	1951	C. Mathewson, NY	1907	W. Cooper, PIT	1922	H. Wyse, CHI	1945
F. Smith, CHI	1909	L. Grove, PHI	1931	B. Shantz, PHI	1952	C. Mathewson, NY	1908	D. Luque, CIN	1923	H. Pollet, SL	1946
J. Coombs, PHI	1910	L. Grove, PHI	1932	B. Pierce, CHI	1953	C. Mathewson, NY	1909	D. Vance, BKN	1924	E. Blackwell, CIN	1947
W. Johnson, WAS	1911	L. Grove, PHI	1933	B. Lemon, CLE	1954	C. Mathewson, NY	1910	D. Vance, BKN	1925	J. Sain, BOS	1948
J. Wood, BOS	1912	L. Gomez, NY	1934	R. Narleski, CLE	1955	C. Mathewson, NY	1911	R. Kremer, PIT	1926	W. Spahn, BOS	1949
W. Johnson, WAS	1913	W. Ferrell, BOS	1935	B. Pierce, CHI	1956	R. Marquard, NY	1912	C. Root, CHI	1927	J. Konstanty, PHI	1950
W. Johnson, WAS	1914	T. Bridges, DET	1936	J. Bunning, DET	1957	C. Mathewson, NY	1913	B. Grimes, PIT	1928	S. Maglie, NY	1951
W. Johnson, WAS	1915	L. Gomez, NY	1937	C. Estrada, BAL	1960	B. James, BOS	1914	B. Grimes, PIT	1929	R. Roberts, PHI	1952
B. Ruth, BOS	1916	R. Ruffing, NY	1938	D. Donovan, CLE	1962			P. Malone, CHI	1930	W. Spahn, MIL	1953
E. Cicotte, CHI	1917	B. Feller, CLE	1939	W. Ford, NY	1963			E. Brandt, BOS	1931	J. Antonelli, NY	1954
W. Johnson, WAS	1918	B. Feller, CLE	1940	E. Fisher, CHI	1965			L. Warneke, CIN	1932	R. Roberts, PHI	1955
W. Johnson, WAS	1919	B. Feller, CLE	1941	J. Kaat, MIN	1966			C. Hubbell, NY	1933	W. Spahn, MIL	1958
J. Bagby, CLE	1920	T. Hughson, BOS	1942					D. Dean, SL	1934	S. Jones, SF	1959
R. Faber, CHI	1921	S. Chandler, NY	1943					D. Dean, SL	1935	W. Spahn, MIL	1961
E. Rommel, PHI	1922							C. Hubbell, NY	1936	L. Jackson, CHI	1964
								C. Hubbell, NY	1937		

Hypothetical Federal League Awards

	1914	1915
Most Valuable Player	B. Kauff, IND	D. Zwilling, CHI
Cy Young	C. Hendrix, CHI	G. McConnell, CHI
Rookie of the Year	B. Kauff, IND	E. Johnson, SL

Hypothetical Rookie of the Year Award

American League Player/Club	Year	American League Player/Club	Year	American League Player/Club	Year	National League Player/Club	Year	National League Player/Club	Year	National League Player/Club	Year
S. Seybold, PHI	1901	J. Bagby, CLE	1916	J. Allen, NY	1932	E. Scott, CIN	1900	T. Long, SL	1915	W. Berger, BOS	1930
A. Joss, CLE	1902	A. Sothoron, SL	1917	B. Johnson, PHI	1933	C. Mathewson, NY	1901	R. Hornsby, SL	1916	P. Derringer, SL	1931
C. Bender, PHI	1903	S. Perry, PHI	1918	H. Trosky, CLE	1934	H. Smoot, SL	1902	L. Cadore, BKN	1917	D. Dean, SL	1932
F. Glade, SL	1904	D. Kerr, CHI	1919	J. Powell, WAS	1935	J. Weimer, CHI	1903	H. Hollocher, CHI	1918	F. Demaree, CHI	1933
G. Stone, SL	1905	B. Meusel, NY	1920	J. DiMaggio, NY	1936	H. Lumley, BKN	1904	O. Tuero, SL	1919	C. Davis, PHI	1934
C. Rossman, CLE	1906	J. Sewell, CLE	1921	R. York, DET	1937	E. Reulbach, CHI	1905	J. Haines, SL	1920	C. Blanton, PIT	1935
S. Nicholls, PHI	1907	H. Pillette, DET	1922	K. Keltner, DET	1938	J. Pfiester, CHI	1906	R. Grimes, CHI	1921	J. Mize, SL	1936
E. Summers, DET	1908	H. Summa, CLE	1923	T. Williams, BOS	1939	N. Rucker, BKN	1907	H. Miller, CHI	1922	J. Turner, BOS	1937
F. Baker, PHI	1909	A. Simmons, PHI	1924	W. Judnich, SL	1940	G. McQuillan, PHI	1908	G. Grantham, CHI	1923	J. Rizzo, PIT	1938
R. Ford, NY	1910	E. Combs, NY	1925	R. Pizzuto, NY	1941	D. Miller, PIT	1909	K. Cuyler, PIT	1924	H. Casey, BKN	1939
V. Gregg, CLE	1911	T. Lazzeri, NY	1926	J. Pesky, BOS	1942	K. Cole, CHI	1910	J. Welsh, BOS	1925	B. Young, NY	1940
D. Pratt, SL	1912	W. Moore, NY	1927	B. Johnson, NY	1943	G. Alexander, PHI	1911	P. Waner, PIT	1926	E. Riddle, CIN	1941
R. Russell, CHI	1913	E. Morris, BOS	1928	J. Berry, PHI	1944	C. Cheney, CHI	1912	L. Waner, PIT	1927	J. Beazley, SL	1942
R. Bressler, PHI	1914	D. Alexander, DET	1929	B. Ferriss, BOS	1945	J. Viox, PIT	1913	D. Bissonette, BKN	1928	L. Klein, SL	1943
B. Ruth, BOS	1915	S. Jolley, CHI	1930	B. Lemon, CLE	1946	J. Pfeffer, BKN	1914	J. Frederick, BKN	1929	B. Voiselle, NY	1944
		J. Vosmik, CLE	1931	F. Shea, NY	1947					K. Burkhart, SL	1945
				G. Bearden, CLE	1948					D. Ennis, PHI	1946

Hypothetical Most Valuable Player Award

American League Player/Club	Year	American League Player/Club	Year	American League Player/Club	Year	National League Player/Club	Year	National League Player/Club	Year	National League Player/Club	Year
N. Lajoie, PHI	1901	T. Cobb, DET	1907	B. Ruth, BOS	1918	H. Wagner, PIT	1900	H. Wagner, PIT	1907	J. Vaughn, CHI	1918
C. Young, BOS	1902	E. Walsh, CHI	1908	J. Jackson, CHI	1919	H. Wagner, PIT	1901	C. Mathewson, NY	1908	E. Roush, CIN	1919
N. Lajoie, CLE	1903	T. Cobb, DET	1909	B. Ruth, NY	1920	H. Wagner, PIT	1902	H. Wagner, PIT	1909	R. Hornsby, SL	1920
J. Chesbro, NY	1904	J. Coombs, PHI	1910	B. Ruth, NY	1921	H. Wagner, PIT	1903	S. Magee, PHI	1910	R. Hornsby, SL	1921
R. Waddell, PHI	1905	E. Collins, CHI	1915	B. Fonseca, CLE	1929	J. McGinnity, NY	1904	G. Alexander, PHI	1915	R. Hornsby, SL	1922
N. Lajoie, CLE	1906	T. Speaker, CLE	1916	J. Cronin, WAS	1930	C. Mathewson, NY	1905	G. Alexander, PHI	1916	D. Luque, CIN	1923
		E. Cicotte, CHI	1917			H. Steinfeldt, CHI	1906	G. Alexander, PHI	1917	H. Wilson, CHI	1930

Gold Glove Award: History

In a 1956 spring training survey, Elmer A. Blasco—employed by Rawlings Sporting Goods as advertising, public relations and sales manager—found that 83 percent of the active regular major league players wore Rawlings gloves or mitts. Noting that Hillerich & Bradsby (the major leagues' leading baseball bat supplier) awarded Silver Bats to the leagues' top hitters, Blasco reasoned that Rawlings ought to sponsor some sort of fielding award. After his idea was accepted by Rawlings' management, Blasco contacted the Brown Shoe Company of St. Louis and obtained from them a hide of gold lamé-tanned leather used to make ladies' formal slippers. A glove was crafted from this hide, laced and stamped as a regular fielders glove, and attached to a metal fixture on a walnut base with an appropriate engraved plate.

Thus was born the Gold Glove Award.

The October 2, 1957, edition of *The Sporting News* featured a full-page advertisement/announcement: "Recognizing the importance of superior individual fielding performance to the advancement of baseball as America's national game, Rawlings (Sporting Goods Company) has established Annual Gold Glove Awards beginning with the 1957 season.

"Each of the nine Major League players chosen for *The Sporting News* All-Star Fielding Team will be honored with a Rawlings Gold Glove Award. Selections will be made by a Committee named by *The Sporting News*.

"Awards will be Rawlings custom-built gloves or mitts hand-crafted of special metallic gold-finished leather, each mounted on a suitable hardwood stand bearing an engraved plate."

TSN publisher J. G. Taylor Spink appointed nineteen noted sportswriters for the selection task. They included Shirley Povich, Edgar Munzel, Hy Hurwitz, Earl Lawson, Bob Broeg, Allen Lewis, and Hal Lebowitz. A contest to predict the winners, open to baseball-playing boys, was sponsored by Rawlings.

The first Gold Glove winners were announced with great pomp and circumstance in the December 18, 1957, issue of TSN. "Too long neglected, the magicians of the defense have had no real recognition," the article explained, adding that the selections were made "solely on the basis of their defensive ability."

Rawlings and TSN also joined forces that year in the establishment of the Silver Glove Award, given to the top minor league fielder at each position—based entirely on fielding averages.

In 1958 the Gold Glove selection privilege was turned over to the major league players and an All-Star Fielding Team was selected for each league (as it still is).

In 1961 the method for selecting outfielders was changed. Rather than choosing a left-, center-, and right fielder for each league, each voter was instructed to name three outfielders regardless of position (still the practice today).

In 1965 the managers and coaches of each team took over the voting responsibility, which they have retained ever since. Voters are not permitted to select players on their own teams. In 1987, 139 different managers and coaches took part in the balloting.

Perhaps because of its originality, the Gold Glove is the one *Sporting News* award that has gained universal acceptance and prestige in the baseball world. However, as with any award, the selections often draw criticism.

One complaint is that too much importance is given to fielding average. Most of us realize that FA is not always a reliable indicator of defensive ability, but how much does it influence the Gold Glove voters?

Of the 366 FA leaders at the various positions between 1957–87 (discounting pitchers and counting only one outfielder per league each year), 118 (32 percent) also won their respective Gold Glove Awards (see Table 1). We can say, then, that if a player leads his league in FA, he has about a one-in-three chance of winning the Gold Glove—not an overwhelming correlation, but about four times better than random chance.

This raises some interesting questions. Since official fielding statistics are not published until months *after* Gold Gloves are voted on, any voter relying on fielding stats would probably have to consult (or remember) the *previous* year's data. Therefore, if FA itself really does impress voters, we should expect to see many players winning a Gold Glove the year *after* they lead in FA. Do they? Well, no (see Table 2). The percentage here is 25 percent or one-in-four—again, considerably better than chance, but less of a factor than leading in FA in the current year.

And what about the influence of Gold Gloves on fielding averages? Is an official scorer less likely to charge an error against a player simply because he won a Gold Glove the previous year? Apparently not (see Table 3). The percentage of Gold Glove recipients leading in FA the following year is 23 percent.

"It is my belief that a lot more is considered than fielding percentage," says *TSN* editor Tom Barnidge, citing "range, throwing arm, the headiness of the ballplayer." Cincinnati's Pete Rose, a two-time Gold Glove winner and now a voter, concurs: "There are a lot of intangibles involved in voting for the Gold Glove. Take an outfielder. The coaches and managers watch these guys all the time. How they play the hitters, how strong their arms are, how often they hit the cutoff man, and all that is taken into consideration—things that do not show up in the statistics."

TABLE 1 Fielding Average Leaders Winning Gold Glove, 1957-87 (Maximum 61 Each Position).

POS.	NL	AL	TOT.	PCT.
C	7	7	14	23
1B	13	13	26	43
2B	14	5	19	31
3B	4	15	19	31
SS	14	12	26	43
OF	6	8	14	23
TOT.	58	60	118	32

TABLE 2 Fielding Average Leaders Winning Gold Glove in Following Season, 1956-86 (Maximum 61 Each Position).

POS.	NL	AL	TOT.	PCT.
C	7	7	14	23
1B	8	11	19	31
2B	9	6	15	25
3B	3	13	16	26
SS	11	9	20	33
OF	2	5	7	11
TOT.	40	51	91	25

TABLE 3 Fielding Average Leaders Who Won Gold Glove in Previous Season, 1958-87 (Maximum 59 Each Position).

POS.	NL	AL	TOT.	PCT.
C	3	7	10	17
1B	11	8	19	32
2B	8	2	10	17
3B	2	12	14	24
SS	10	9	19	32
OF	6	5	11	19
TOT.	40	43	83	23

Another criticism of the Gold Glove is that batting performance plays a role in the selections, contrary to the award's philosophy. As *USA Today* baseball editor Hal Bodley puts it, "A player who is outstanding on defense and respectable on offense has a much better chance of getting a Gold Glove than a counterpart whose forte is fielding alone."

Other factors can be distractions to the voters: flashiness, reputations, and the selection process itself. For insight on some of these and their effects, I consulted an expert on the Gold Glove: Wes Parker, a six-time winner of the award at first base.

Parker, it should be noted, would seem to have no reason to gripe about the award. He grasped the honor from a seven-time winner; he won it even when he batted as low as .239; and he became one of only two nonpitchers (Roberto Clemente is the other) to win the award in his final major league season.

"I would say many, if not most, coaches and managers fail to take their voting responsibility seriously," says Parker. "They don't treat it as a vital act. They are usually much more concerned with their team and the pennant race and, as a result, tend to zip through the ballots (distributed in September). So they wind up voting for the most recognizable names."

Parker brings out another rarely discussed procedural problem: "Since players [when they were voting] and coaches are forbidden to vote for anyone on their own team, they often won't vote for the guy who is contending with their team's leading candidate for the same award. That increases their teammate's chances."

On the subject of reputation, Parker asserts that it "has a lot to do with it, absolutely. In 1966, Bill White won the award (for the seventh consecutive time), although even White admitted that I probably deserved it. It takes a couple of years for your reputation to catch up with you, but that can work to your advantage at the end of your career."

"Flashiness is a factor too," continues Parker. "It puts the player's name in the forefront of the voter's minds." Wes also concurs with the theory that a player's bat can be the difference in winning this 'fielding' award.

"[Four-time Gold Glove winner Steve] Garvey is a good example of someone who won it with his bat and notoriety, a perfect example, in fact," opines Parker. "Garvey was vastly overrated defensively . . . he had no range, no arm, and no aggressiveness. He would hold the ball and allow opposing runners to take extra bases to avoid throwing errors. That's how he compiled his high [fielding] averages at first base. Remember, he was a terrible third baseman, worst I ever saw." (In 1972, Garvey's last season as a third-sacker, he led the NL with 28 errors in just 85 games, posting a woeful .902 percentage.)

"Amazingly, despite these prejudices," Parker concludes, "I think the Gold Glove choices have been excellent. At first base I think they have been perfect, with the exception of Garvey."

While the Gold Glove Award has adequately filled the need for a subjective fielding award, there is still something to be said about fielding statistics. It is fashionable to say that fielding stats are meaningless, but, as analyst Bill James says, "If a baseball statistic is meaningless to you, that is simply because you don't know what it means."

With the understanding of which fielding statistics *are* meaningful for each position, it is possible to make a pretty reliable judgment of a player's defensive skills based on stats alone. In recent years, several analysts have attempted to measure individual fielding performance on the basis of numbers.

One newer method is Linear Weights, Pete Palmer's translation of individual batting, pitching, and fielding statistics into runs gained and thus games won. The fielding portion of the system, Fielding or Defensive Wins, incorporates data (variously weighted according to position) on putouts, assists, errors, and double plays, comparing a player's totals against the league averages.

The formula first determines how many runs a player saves (or costs) his team as compared to an "average" player at the same position. Runs are then translated into wins, based on the league average of runs per win. For example, second baseman Glenn Hubbard was computed to have won about three and a half games for the Braves with his glove in 1986, the top Defensive Wins total in the majors.

Of the sixty players identified by the Palmer system as the best fielders in their leagues between 1957–86, twenty-eight also won their respective Gold Glove Awards.

Palmer has drawn criticism for comparing players with average, rather than replacement-level, players; for overemphasizing the double play; and for the use of arbitrary weighting schemes. It is particularly—and admittedly—inadequate in evaluating catchers.

Bill James has also presented a fielding measurement system, Defensive Won/Lost Percentage (DW/L%), although he hasn't used it since 1984. The formula varies from position to position, using four arbitrarily weighted components at each. These components range from readily available statistics (fielding average, assists per game, and so on) to abstruse estimations and calculations, using some data unavailable to the average researcher. The formula is not designed for cross-era comparisons.

The results of these calculations produce the DW/L%, which in turn is translated into defensive wins and losses, based on still more arbitrary assignments of defensive games at each position (ranging from 3 at first base to 11 at shortstop).

Of the thirty-two players identified by DW/L% as the best at their positions and leagues for the 1983–84 seasons, twelve (38 percent) also won their respective Gold Gloves.

The use of a series of arbitrary values is the glaring flaw of DW/L%. Criticism is also due for the complexity and lack of adaptability of the system(s).

The Elias Sports Bureau has demonstrated a simple and generally effective system for evaluating fielders: comparing the number of runs scored per nine innings while a player is on the field to the number scored when he isn't. For example, Elias calculated that the 1982–86 Cardinals averaged allowing 3.85 runs per nine innings with Ozzie Smith at shortstop, as compared to 4.04 per game with other shortstops.

There is nothing new or brilliant about this concept; the difference is that Elias has the data available to make this type of measurement, right down to thirds of an inning, at least for the last dozen years. Since they generally choose not to share this data with the public, however, it is of no value at present.

So, when all is said and done about modern statistical fielding measurements, a subjective measurement—the Gold Glove—is probably still the best tool we have available to rate fielders.

The following pages list the winners of the Gold Glove at each position since 1957. Complete balloting for Gold Glove elections is, unfortunately, neither available nor researchable.

The Gold Glove winners for 1988 were announced as this book was going to press; regrettably, time did not permit their inclusion here.

Gold Glove Award

Pitchers

Year	National League	American League
1957	(No selection)	B. Shantz, NY
1958	H. Haddix, CIN	B. Shantz, NY
1959	H. Haddix, PIT	B. Shantz, NY
1960	H. Haddix, PIT	B. Shantz, NY
1961	B. Shantz, PIT	F. Lary, DET
1962	B. Shantz, SL	J. Kaat, MIN
1963	B. Shantz, SL	J. Kaat, MIN
1964	B. Shantz, PHI	J. Kaat, MIN
1965	B. Gibson, SL	J. Kaat, MIN
1966	B. Gibson, SL	J. Kaat, MIN
1967	B. Gibson, SL	J. Kaat, MIN
1968	B. Gibson, SL	J. Kaat, MIN
1969	B. Gibson, SL	J. Kaat, MIN
1970	B. Gibson, SL	J. Kaat, MIN
1971	B. Gibson, SL	J. Kaat, MIN
1972	B. Gibson, SL	J. Kaat, MIN
1973	B. Gibson, SL	J. Kaat, MIN
1974	A. Messersmith, LA	J. Kaat, CHI
1975	A. Messersmith, LA	J. Kaat, CHI
1976	J. Kaat, PHI	J. Palmer, BAL
1977	J. Kaat, PHI	J. Palmer, BAL
1978	P. Niekro, ATL	J. Palmer, BAL
1979	P. Niekro, ATL	J. Palmer, BAL
1980	P. Niekro, ATL	M. Norris, OAK
1981	S. Carlton, PHI	M. Norris, OAK
1982	P. Niekro, ATL	R. Guidry, NY
1983	P. Niekro, ATL	R. Guidry, NY
1984	J. Andujar, SL	R. Guidry, NY
1985	R. Reuschel, PIT	R. Guidry, NY
1986	F. Valenzuela, LA	R. Guidry, NY
1987	R. Reuschel, SF	M. Langston, SEA

Catchers

Year	National League	American League
1957	(No selection)	S. Lollar, CHI
1958	D. Crandall, MIL	S. Lollar, CHI
1959	D. Crandall, MIL	S. Lollar, CHI
1960	D. Crandall, MIL	E. Battey, WAS
1961	J. Roseboro, LA	E. Battey, MIN
1962	D. Crandall, MIL	E. Battey, MIN
1963	J. Edwards, CIN	E. Howard, NY
1964	J. Edwards, CIN	E. Howard, NY
1965	J. Torre, MIL	B. Freehan, DET
1966	J. Roseboro, LA	B. Freehan, DET
1967	R. Hundley, CHI	B. Freehan, DET
1968	J. Bench, CIN	B. Freehan, DET
1969	J. Bench, CIN	B. Freehan, DET
1970	J. Bench, CIN	R. Fosse, CLE
1971	J. Bench, CIN	R. Fosse, CLE
1972	J. Bench, CIN	C. Fisk, BOS
1973	J. Bench, CIN	T. Munson, NY
1974	J. Bench, CIN	T. Munson, NY
1975	J. Bench, CIN	T. Munson, NY
1976	J. Bench, CIN	J. Sundberg, TEX
1977	J. Bench, CIN	J. Sundberg, TEX
1978	B. Boone, PHI	J. Sundberg, TEX
1979	B. Boone, PHI	J. Sundberg, TEX
1980	G. Carter, MON	J. Sundberg, TEX
1981	G. Carter, MON	J. Sundberg, TEX
1982	G. Carter, MON	B. Boone, CAL
1983	T. Pena, PIT	Lc. Parrish, DET
1984	T. Pena, PIT	Lc. Parrish, DET
1985	T. Pena, PIT	Lc. Parrish, DET
1986	J. Davis, CHI	B. Boone, CAL
1987	M. LaValliere, PIT	B. Boone, CAL

First Baseman

Year	National League	American League
1957	G. Hodges, BKN	(No selection)
1958	G. Hodges, LA	V. Power, CLE
1959	G. Hodges, LA	V. Power, CLE
1960	B. White, SL	V. Power, CLE
1961	B. White, SL	V. Power, CLE
1962	B. White, SL	V. Power, MIN
1963	B. White, SL	V. Power, MIN
1964	B. White, SL	V. Power, LA
1965	B. White, SL	J. Pepitone, NY
1966	B. White, PHI	J. Pepitone, NY
1967	W. Parker, LA	G. Scott, BOS
1968	W. Parker, LA	G. Scott, BOS
1969	W. Parker, LA	J. Pepitone, NY
1970	W. Parker, LA	J. Spencer, CAL
1971	W. Parker, LA	G. Scott, BOS
1972	W. Parker, LA	G. Scott, MIL
1973	M. Jorgenson, MON	G. Scott, MIL
1974	S. Garvey, LA	G. Scott, MIL
1975	S. Garvey, LA	G. Scott, MIL
1976	S. Garvey, LA	G. Scott, MIL
1977	S. Garvey, LA	J. Spencer, CHI
1978	K. Hernandez, SL	C. Chambliss, NY
1979	K. Hernandez, SL	C. Cooper, MIL
1980	K. Hernandez, SL	C. Cooper, MIL
1981	K. Hernandez, SL	M. Squires, CHI
1982	K. Hernandez, SL	E. Murray, BAL
1983	K. Hernandez, SL-NY	E. Murray, BAL
1984	K. Hernandez, NY	E. Murray, BAL
1985	K. Hernandez, NY	D. Mattingly, NY
1986	K. Hernandez, NY	D. Mattingly, NY
1987	K. Hernandez, NY	D. Mattingly, NY

Second Basemen

Year	National League	American League
1957	(No selection)	N. Fox, CHI
1958	B. Mazeroski, PIT	F. Bolling, DET
1959	C. Neal, LA	N. Fox, CHI
1960	B. Mazeroski, PIT	N. Fox, CHI
1961	B. Mazeroski, PIT	B. Richardson, NY
1962	K. Hubbs, CHI	B. Richardson, NY
1963	B. Mazeroski, PIT	B. Richardson, NY
1964	B. Mazeroski, PIT	B. Richardson, NY
1965	B. Mazeroski, PIT	B. Richardson, NY
1966	B. Mazeroski, PIT	B. Knoop, CAL
1967	B. Mazeroski, PIT	B. Knoop, CAL
1968	G. Beckert, CHI	B. Knoop, CAL
1969	F. Millan, ATL	D. Johnson, BAL
1970	T. Helms, CIN	D. Johnson, BAL
1971	T. Helms, CIN	D. Johnson, BAL
1972	F. Millan, ATL	D. Griffin, BOS
1973	J. Morgan, CIN	B. Grich, BAL
1974	J. Morgan, CIN	B. Grich, BAL
1975	J. Morgan, CIN	B. Grich, BAL
1976	J. Morgan, CIN	B. Grich, BAL
1977	J. Morgan, CIN	F. White, KC
1978	D. Lopes, LA	F. White, KC
1979	M. Trillo, PHI	F. White, KC
1980	D. Flynn, NY	F. White, KC
1981	M. Trillo, PHI	F. White, KC
1982	M. Trillo, PHI	F. White, KC
1983	R. Sandberg, CHI	L. Whitaker, DET
1984	R. Sandberg, CHI	L. Whitaker, DET
1985	R. Sandberg, CHI	L. Whitaker, DET
1986	R. Sandberg, CHI	F. White, KC
1987	R. Sandberg, CHI	F. White, KC

Third Basemen

Year	National League	American League
1957	(No selection)	F. Malzone, BOS
1958	K. Boyer, SL	F. Malzone, BOS
1959	K. Boyer, SL	F. Malzone, BOS
1960	K. Boyer, SL	B. Robinson, BAL
1961	K. Boyer, SL	B. Robinson, BAL
1962	J. Davenport, SF	B. Robinson, BAL
1963	K. Boyer, SL	B. Robinson, BAL
1964	R. Santo, CHI	B. Robinson, BAL
1965	R. Santo, CHI	B. Robinson, BAL
1966	R. Santo, CHI	B. Robinson, BAL
1967	R. Santo, CHI	B. Robinson, BAL
1968	R. Santo, CHI	B. Robinson, BAL
1969	C. Boyer, ATL	B. Robinson, BAL
1970	D. Rader, HOU	B. Robinson, BAL
1971	D. Rader, HOU	B. Robinson, BAL
1972	D. Rader, HOU	B. Robinson, BAL
1973	D. Rader, HOU	B. Robinson, BAL
1974	D. Rader, HOU	B. Robinson, BAL
1975	K. Reitz, SL	B. Robinson, BAL
1976	M. Schmidt, PHI	A. Rodriguez, DET
1977	M. Schmidt, PHI	G. Nettles, NY
1978	M. Schmidt, PHI	G. Nettles, NY
1979	M. Schmidt, PHI	B. Bell, TEX
1980	M. Schmidt, PHI	B. Bell, TEX
1981	M. Schmidt, PHI	B. Bell, TEX
1982	M. Schmidt, PHI	B. Bell, TEX
1983	M. Schmidt, PHI	B. Bell, TEX
1984	M. Schmidt, PHI	B. Bell, TEX
1985	T. Wallach, MON	G. Brett, KC
1986	M. Schmidt, PHI	G. Gaetti, MIN
1987	T. Pendleton, SL	G. Gaetti, MIN

Shortstops

National League	American League
R. McMillan, CIN	(No selection)
R. McMillan, CIN	L. Aparicio, CHI
R. McMillan, CIN	L. Aparicio, CHI
E. Banks, CHI	L. Aparicio, CHI
M. Wills, LA	L. Aparicio, CHI
M. Wills, LA	L. Aparicio, CHI
B. Wine, PHI	Z. Versalles, MIN
R. Amaro, PHI	L. Aparicio, BAL
L. Cardenas, CIN	Z. Versalles, MIN
G. Alley, PIT	L. Aparicio, BAL
G. Alley, PIT	J. Fregosi, CAL
D. Maxvill, SL	L. Aparicio, CHI
D. Kessinger, CHI	M. Belanger, BAL
D. Kessinger, CHI	L. Aparicio, CHI
B. Harrelson, NY	M. Belanger, BAL
L. Bowa, PHI	E. Brinkman, DET
R. Metzger, HOU	M. Belanger, BAL
D. Concepcion, CIN	M. Belanger, BAL
D. Concepcion, CIN	M. Belanger, BAL
D. Concepcion, CIN	M. Belanger, BAL
L. Bowa, PHI	M. Belanger, BAL
D. Concepcion, CIN	R. Burleson, BOS
O. Smith, SD	A. Trammell, DET
O. Smith, SD	A. Trammell, DET
O. Smith, SL	R. Yount, MIL
O. Smith, SL	A. Trammell, DET
O. Smith, SL	A. Trammell, DET
O. Smith, SL	A. Griffin, OAK
O. Smith, SL	T. Fernandez, TOR
O. Smith, SL	T. Fernandez, TOR

National League Outfielders

YEAR	PLAYERS		
1957	W. Mays, NY (CF)	(No other selections)	
1958	F. Robinson, CIN (LF)	W. Mays, SF (CF)	H. Aaron, MIL (RF)
1959	J. Brandt, SF (LF)	W. Mays, SF (CF)	H. Aaron, MIL (RF)
1960	W. Moon, LA (LF)	W. Mays, SF (CF)	H. Aaron, MIL (RF)
1961	W. Mays, SF	R. Clemente, PIT	V. Pinson, CIN
1962	W. Mays, SF	R. Clemente, PIT	B. Virdon, PIT
1963	W. Mays, SF	R. Clemente, PIT	C. Flood, SL
1964	W. Mays, SF	R. Clemente, PIT	C. Flood, SL
1965	W. Mays, SF	R. Clemente, PIT	C. Flood, SL
1966	W. Mays, SF	C. Flood, SL	R. Clemente, PIT
1967	R. Clemente, PIT	C. Flood, SL	W. Mays, SF
1968	W. Mays, SF	R. Clemente, PIT	C. Flood, SL
1969	R. Clemente, PIT	C. Flood, SL	P. Rose, CIN
1970	R. Clemente, PIT	T. Agee, NY	P. Rose, CIN
1971	R. Clemente, PIT	B. Bonds, SF	W. Davis, LA
1972	R. Clemente, PIT	C. Cedeno, HOU	W. Davis, LA
1973	B. Bonds, SF	C. Cedeno, HOU	B. Bonds, SF
1974	C. Cedeno, HOU	C. Geronimo, CIN	B. Bonds, SF
1975	C. Cedeno, HOU	C. Geronimo, CIN	G. Maddox, PHI
1976	C. Cedeno, HOU	C. Geronimo, CIN	G. Maddox, PHI
1977	C. Geronimo, CIN	G. Maddox, PHI	D. Parker, PIT
1978	G. Maddox, PHI	D. Parker, PIT	E. Valentine, MON
1979	G. Maddox, PHI	D. Parker, PIT	D. Winfield, SD
1980	A. Dawson, MON	G. Maddox, PHI	D. Winfield, SD
1981	A. Dawson, MON	G. Maddox, PHI	D. Baker, LA
1982	A. Dawson, MON	D. Murphy, ATL	G. Maddox, PHI
1983	A. Dawson, MON	D. Murphy, ATL	W. McGee, SL
1984	D. Murphy, ATL	B. Dernier, CHI	A. Dawson, MON
1985	W. McGee, SL	D. Murphy, ATL	A. Dawson, MON
1986	T. Gwynn, SD	D. Murphy, ATL	W. McGee, SL
1987	E. Davis, CIN	T. Gwynn, SD	A. Dawson, CHI

American League Outfielders

YEAR	PLAYERS		
1957	M. Minoso, CHI (LF)	A. Kaline, DET (RF)	(No other selection)
1958	N. Siebern, NY (LF)	J. Piersall, BOS (CF)	A. Kaline, DET (RF)
1959	M. Minoso, CLE (LF)	A. Kaline, DET (CF)	J. Jensen, BOS (RF)
1960	M. Minoso, CHI (LF)	J. Landis, CHI (CF)	R. Maris, NY (RF)
1961	A. Kaline, DET	J. Piersall, CLE	J. Landis, CHI
1962	J. Landis, CHI	M. Mantle, NY	A. Kaline, DET
1963	A. Kaline, DET	C. Yastrzemski, BOS	J. Landis, CHI
1964	A. Kaline, DET	J. Landis, CHI	V. Davalillo, CLE
1965	A. Kaline, DET	T. Tresh, NY	C. Yastrzemski, BOS
1966	A. Kaline, DET	T. Agee, CHI	T. Oliva, MIN
1967	C. Yastrzemski, BOS	P. Blair, BAL	A. Kaline, DET
1968	M. Stanley, DET	C. Yastrzemski, BOS	R. Smith, BOS
1969	P. Blair, BAL	M. Stanley, DET	C. Yastrzemski, BOS
1970	M. Stanley, DET	P. Blair, BAL	K. Berry, CHI
1971	P. Blair, BAL	A. Otis, KC	C. Yastrzemski, BOS
1972	P. Blair, BAL	B. Murcer, NY	K. Berry, CAL
1973	P. Blair, BAL	A. Otis, KC	M. Stanley, DET
1974	P. Blair, BAL	A. Otis, KC	J. Rudi, OAK
1975	P. Blair, BAL	J. Rudi, OAK	F. Lynn, BOS
1976	J. Rudi, OAK	Dw. Evans, BOS	R. Manning, CLE
1977	J. Beniquez, TEX	C. Yastrzemski, BOS	A. Cowens, KC
1978	F. Lynn, BOS	Dw. Evans, BOS	R. Miller, CAL
1979	Dw. Evans, BOS	S. Lezcano, MIL	F. Lynn, BOS
1980	F. Lynn, BOS	D. Murphy, OAK	W. Wilson, KC
1981	D. Murphy, OAK	Dw. Evans, BOS	R. Henderson, OAK
1982	Dw. Evans, BOS	D. Winfield, NY	D. Murphy, OAK
1983	Dw. Evans, BOS	D. Winfield, NY	D. Murphy, OAK
1984	Dw. Evans, BOS	D. Winfield, NY	D. Murphy, OAK
1985	G. Pettis, CAL	D. Winfield, NY	Dw. Evans, BOS & D. Murphy, OAK
1986	G. Pettis, CAL	J. Barfield, TOR	K. Puckett, MIN
1987	J. Barfield, TOR	K. Puckett, MIN	D. Winfield, NY

Hall of Fame Elections: History

In the 1930s plans were being made to celebrate baseball's 100th anniversary, based on the findings of the Mills Commission three decades earlier: "The first scheme for playing baseball, according to the best evidence obtainable to date, was devised by Abner Doubleday at Cooperstown, N.Y., in 1839." A small-scale baseball museum was established in Cooperstown, and a Centennial Committee composed of six baseball bigwigs ordered the first Hall of Fame election. On January 29, 1936, the results of this election were announced, with five immortals qualifying for enshrinement (although actual induction was delayed until formal opening of the Hall on June 12, 1939).

Actually, there were two elections in 1936: one a poll of 226 members of the Baseball Writers' Association of America (BBWAA), and the other held by a special veterans' committee of 78 designed to choose from among "old-timers." No specific guidelines were set as to who was eligible for consideration (several active players received strong support), nor to which committee would consider whom (resulting in Cy Young's split vote: 49 percent in the writers' election, 41 percent in the veterans'). A 75 percent majority was necessary for election by either committee, a voting feature which

has survived a half century of Hall of Fame elections.

Elections were held by both the BBWAA and an old-timers' committee for each of the next three years, resulting in a total of 26 inductees in 1939. (For a more detailed account of the early Hall of Fame election procedures, see the essay that follows, by James Vlasich.) After that, BBWAA elections were scheduled at three-year intervals, with only one player elected in 1942 and none in 1945. A decision was made to hold annual elections beginning in 1946. This continued through 1956, when it was decided to hold elections only every other year. Annual elections were resumed a decade later and continue to this day.

A nominating system was installed in 1945, providing for a "runoff" election in the case that no player received the necessary 75 percent on the first ballot. The top 20 vote-getters were to be considered in this runoff election, a system that was utilized in 1946 and 1949, before being discontinued in 1950. The system was revived from 1960–68, this time providing for reconsideration of the top 30 vote-getters, and was actually put to practice in 1964 and '67.

Currently, an eligible candidate must have played at least ten seasons in the majors and been active at some point during a period beginning twenty years and ending five years before a given election. The five-year wait rule was first implemented in 1954 (excepting candidates who had already received 100 or more votes in a previous election); a one-year wait had been in effect from 1946–53, and no wait was specified before then (due to World War II, it was sometimes unclear who was still "active"). At the other end of the span, the twenty-year rule has been in effect since 1962; the cutoff was thirty years from 1956–62, and twenty-five years from 1946–56.

Following Roberto Clemente's tragic death, a rule was passed in 1973 providing for the immediate consideration of an eligible candidate who dies while still active, or before the 5-year waiting period has elapsed. Clemente was inducted overwhelmingly (393 of 424 votes) in a special election held that March. A few months later, the new rule was amended to allow consideration at least six months after a player's death (or five years after his retirement, whichever is less).

Ten-year active and honorary members of the BBWAA are eligible to vote in the annual election (the 10-year restriction was installed in 1947). About 400 writers submit ballots each year, voting for up to ten eligible candidates apiece. At various times over the past three decades, it has been suggested that the enfranchisement be limited to a few dozen of the top baseball writers.

A candidate Screening Committee was first employed in 1968, limiting the ballot to 40 candidates. Standards were relaxed somewhat after former pitcher Milt Pappas vociferously objected to his elimination by this committee (Pappas was allowed on the ballot in 1979, receiving 5 of 432 votes). Nomination by any of the six members of the Screening Committee now ensures a candidate at least one try on the BBWAA ballot; however, if he receives less than 5 percent of the vote, he is eliminated from future consideration. (Fortunately for many, this rule has not always been existent; more than 70 current Hall of Famers received less than 5 percent of the vote in their first tries!)

The Baseball Hall of Fame Committee on Baseball Veterans was established in July 1953. Previously, special old-timers' committees had elected new members in 1936–39, 1944–46, and 1949.

The new committee was composed of 11 members. This number was increased to 12 in 1960, 18 in 1979, and 20 in 1987. Elections were held every other year at first, but have been held annually since 1961.

In most years the committee has been limited to naming no more than two new inductees per election. Exceptions occurred in the elections of 1953 (six), 1963 (four), 1964 (six), 1970 (three), 1971 (seven), and 1972–77 (three each). Voting details are not released to the public.

Individuals considered by the Veterans' Committee include managers, umpires, executives, and players no longer eligible through the BBWAA (except members of the committee). For eligibility under the former three groups, a person must have been retired five years, or six months if he has reached the age of sixty-five (a rule tailor-made for Casey Stengel's election in 1966). For players, the minimum wait is twenty-three years; previously, it was twenty-five years (1953–56, 1974–84), thirty years (1957–62), or twenty years (1963–73).

On June 10, 1971, a 9-member Baseball Hall of Fame Committee on Negro Baseball Leagues was established. Candidates were to have totaled at least ten years of service in the pre-1946 Negro Leagues and/or the major leagues, without being eligible for BBWAA election. A rule specified that the "Committee shall serve until it shall dissolve itself of its own motion or until further notice from the Board of Directors" of the Hall of Fame.

At least one new member was inducted by this committee in each year between 1971 and 1977. By 1975 the committee had only 6 remaining members, and by 1979 it had been dissolved and absorbed into the Veterans' Committee. Only two Negro League representatives have been enshrined since 1977.

As far back as 1944, it was suggested that a special "Roll of Honor," distinct from actual Hall of Fame induction, be established for distinguished baseball writers and similar contributors to the baseball world. In 1962 the J. G. Taylor Spink Award was initiated to honor individuals "for meritorious contributions to baseball writing." In 1978 the Ford C. Frick Award was established to dignify broadcasters "for major contributions to the game of Baseball." The awards are presented annually during the Hall of Fame induction ceremonies and the winners' names are engraved on a plaque hanging in the National Baseball Library (explaining references to a writers' or broadcasters' "wing" at the Hall of Fame). Through 1988 there had been 38 winners of the Spink Award, and 12 recipients of the Frick trophy.

There have been a total of 200 men inducted into the National Baseball Hall of Fame and Museum through 1988, including 154 major league players, 20 classified as pioneers or executives, 11 Negro Leaguers, 10 managers and 5 umpires (many of the latter four groups also played in the majors or minors); 74 individuals have been elected by the BBWAA, 117 by the various veterans' committees, and 9 by the Negro Leagues' Committee.

What follows is, first, a roster of the 200 members of the Hall of Fame named between 1936 and 1988; second, an index of every man (640 in all) who ever received so much as a single vote for the Hall of Fame, detailing each man's total for each year he received support; and third, the top ten finishers in the voting for each year of balloting since 1936. Men named to the Hall of Fame by special committee action, such as Alexander Cartwright or Josh Gibson, may not have received

votes in an election, but they are included in this index as well. (There have been four such committee groupings: the Centennial Commission of 1937–1938, the Old Timers Committee of 1939–1949, the Veterans Committee of 1953–present, and the Negro Leagues Committee of 1971–1977.)

Of special interest are some prominent players who were not elected or named to the Hall: Gil Hodges, who received the most votes for the Hall of Fame but remains outside it; Herman Long, who finished among the top ten vote-getters in the Veterans Ballot of 1936, which during later years pro-

duced 29 future Hall of Famers; Hank Gowdy and Tony Lazzeri, who in the 1950s experienced a fate similar to Long's; and Marty Marion, Red Schoendienst, and Allie Reynolds, other long-term vote-getters who were not able to bunch their support in a given year. And don't get White Sox fans talking about Nellie Fox and the election of 1985, when, in his final year of eligibility for the Baseball Writers Election, Fox fell only two votes short of the 297 that would have granted him enshrinement—the closest any man has ever come without making it.

Hall of Fame Roster

FIRST BASEMEN
Anson, Cap
Beckley, Jake
Bottomley, Jim
Brouthers, Dan
Chance, Frank
Connor, Roger
Foxx, Jimmie
Gehrig, Lou
Greenberg, Hank
Kelly, George
Killebrew, Harmon
McCovey, Willie
Mize, Johnny
Sisler, George
Stargell, Willie
Terry, Bill

SECOND BASEMEN
Collins, Eddie
Doerr, Bobby
Evers, Johnny
Frisch, Frankie
Gehringer, Charlie
Herman, Billy
Hornsby, Rogers
Lajoie, Nap
Robinson, Jackie

SHORTSTOPS
Aparicio, Luis
Appling, Luke
Bancroft, Dave
Banks, Ernie
Boudreau, Lou
Cronin, Joe
Jackson, Travis
Jennings, Hugh
Maranville, Rabbit

Reese, Pee Wee
Sewell, Joe
Tinker, Joe
Vaughan, Arky
Wagner, Honus
Wallace, Bobby
Ward, Monte

THIRD BASEMEN
Baker, Frank
Collins, Jimmy
Kell, George
Lindstrom, Fred
Mathews, Eddie
Robinson, Brooks
Traynor, Pie

LEFT FIELDERS
Brock, Lou
Burkett, Jesse
Clarke, Fred
Delahanty, Ed
Goslin, Goose
Hafey, Chick
Kelley, Joe
Kiner, Ralph
Manush, Heinie
Medwick, Joe
Musial, Stan
O'Rourke, Jim
Simmons, Al
Wheat, Zack
Williams, Billy
Williams, Ted

CENTER FIELDERS
Averill, Earl

Carey, Max
Cobb, Ty
Combs, Earle
DiMaggio, Joe
Duffy, Hugh
Hamilton, Billy
Mantle, Mickey
Mays, Willie
Roush, Edd
Snider, Duke
Speaker, Tris
Waner, Lloyd
Wilson, Hack

RIGHT FIELDERS
Aaron, Hank
Clemente, Roberto
Crawford, Sam
Cuyler, Kiki
Flick, Elmer
Heilmann, Harry
Hooper, Harry
Kaline, Al
Keeler, Willie
Kelly, King
Klein, Chuck
McCarthy, Tommy
Ott, Mel
Rice, Sam
Robinson, Frank
Ruth, Babe
Slaughter, Enos
Thompson, Sam
Waner, Paul
Youngs, Ross

CATCHERS
Berra, Yogi

Bresnahan, Roger
Campanella, Roy
Cochrane, Mickey
Dickey, Bill
Ewing, Buck
Ferrell, Rick
Hartnett, Gabby
Lombardi, Ernie
Schalk, Ray

PITCHERS
Alexander, Grover
Bender, Chief
Brown, Mordecai
Chesbro, Jack
Clarkson, John
Coveleski, Stan
Dean, Dizzy
Drysdale, Don
Faber, Red
Feller, Bob
Ford, Whitey
Galvin, Pud
Gibson, Bob
Gomez, Lefty
Grimes, Burleigh
Grove, Lefty
Haines, Jess
Hoyt, Waite
Hubbell, Carl
Hunter, Catfish
Johnson, Walter
Joss, Addie
Keefe, Tim
Koufax, Sandy
Lemon, Bob
Lyons, Ted
Marichal, Juan

Marquard, Rube
Mathewson, Christy
McGinnity, Joe
Nichols, Kid
Pennock, Herb
Plank, Eddie
Radbourn, Charles
Rixey, Eppa
Roberts, Robin
Ruffing, Red
Rusie, Amos
Spahn, Warren
Vance, Dazzy
Waddell, Rube
Walsh, Ed
Welch, Mickey
Wilhelm, Hoyt
Wynn, Early
Young, Cy

**FROM NEGRO
LEAGUES**
Bell, Cool Papa
Charleston, Oscar
Dandridge, Ray
Dihigo, Martin
Foster, Rube
Gibson, Josh
Irvin, Monte
Johnson, Judy
Leonard, Buck
Lloyd, John
Paige, Satchel

MANAGERS
Alston, Walter
Harris, Bucky

Huggins, Miller
Lopez, Al
Mack, Connie
McCarthy, Joe
McGraw, John
McKechnie, Bill
Robinson, Wilbert
Stengel, Casey

UMPIRES
Conlan, Jocko
Connolly, Tom
Evans, Billy
Hubbard, Cal
Klem, Bill

**PIONEERS AND
EXECUTIVES**
Barrow, Ed
Bulkeley, Morgan
Cartwright, Alexander
Chadwick, Henry
Chandler, Albert
Comiskey, Charles
Cummings, Candy
Frick, Ford
Giles, Warren
Griffith, Clark
Harridge, Will
Johnson, Ban
Landis, Kenesaw
MacPhail, Larry
Rickey, Branch
Spalding, Al
Weiss, George
Wright, George
Wright, Harry
Yawkey, Tom

Hall of Fame Balloting: Vote Totals of All Candidates

Hank Aaron
Inducted in 1982

1982 406

Babe Adams

1937 8
1938 11
1939 11
1942 11
1945 7
1946 6
1947 22
1948 4
1949 5
1950 6
1951 12
1952 9
1953 17
1954 13
1955 24

Sparky Adams

1958 1
1960 1

Bobby Adams

1966 1

Pete Alexander
Inducted in 1938

1936 55
1937 125
1938 212

Dick Allen

1983 14
1985 28
1986 41
1987 55
1988 52

Johnny Allen

1955 1

Doug Allison

1936 V 1

Felipe Alou

1980 3

Jay Alou

1985 1

Matty Alou

1980 5

Walt Alston
Inducted in 1983
Manager

1983 . . . . . . Vet. Com.

Nick Altrock

1937 3
1938 7
1939 6
1953 1
1954 2
1958 20
1960 18

Cap Anson
Inducted in 1939

1936 V 40
1939 . . . . . . O/T Com.

Luis Aparicio
Inducted in 1984

1979 120
1980 124
1981 48
1982 174
1983 252
1984 341

Luke Appling
Inducted in 1964

1953 2
1955 3
1956 14
1958 77
1960 72
1962 48
1964 142
1964 RO 189

Jimmy Archer

1937 6
1938 7
1939 3

Richie Ashburn

1968 6
1969 10
1970 11
1971 10
1972 11
1973 25
1974 56
1975 76
1976 85
1977 139
1978 158
1979 130
1980 134
1981 142
1982 126

Jimmy Austin

1958 1

Earl Averill
Inducted in 1975

1949 1
1952 2
1955 2
1956 3
1958 14
1960 11
1962 3
1975 . . . . . . Vet. Com.

Bob Bailey

1984 1

Frank Baker
Inducted in 1955

1936 1
1937 13
1938 32
1939 30
1942 39
1945 26
1946 39
1946 RO 36

1947	49
1948	4
1950	4
1951	8
1955	Vet. Com.

Dave Bancroft
Inducted in 1971

1937	3
1938	2
1939	1
1946	1
1948	4
1949	5
1950	9
1951	9
1952	11
1953	10
1954	10
1955	19
1956	15
1958	43
1960	30
1971	Vet. Com.

Sal Bando

1987	3

Ernie Banks
Inducted in 1977

1977	321

Ross Barnes

1936 V	3

Ed Barrow
Inducted in 1953
Executive

1953	Vet. Com.

Jack Barry

1938	3
1939	1

Dick Bartell

1948	1
1951	1
1958	1
1960	1

Joe Battin

1936 V	1

Hank Bauer

1967	23
1967 RO	9

Ginger Beaumont

1938	1
1942	1
1945	1
1946	1

Glenn Beckert

1981	1

Jake Beckley
Inducted in 1971

1936 V	1
1942	1
1971	Vet. Com.

Mark Belanger

1988	16

Cool Papa Bell
Inducted in 1974

1974	Neg. Com.

Chief Bender
Inducted in 1953

1936	2
1937	17
1938	33
1939	40
1942	55

1945	40
1946	39
1946 RO	35
1947	72
1948	5
1949	2
1950	6
1951	35
1952	70
1953	104
1953	Vet. Com.

Charlie Bennett

1936 V	3

Larry Benton

1958	1

Moe Berg

1958	3
1960	5

Marty Bergen

1937	2
1938	1
1939	1

Wally Berger

1956	1
1958	2

Yogi Berra
Inducted in 1972

1971	242
1972	339

Charlie Berry

1955	1
1958	3

Carson Bigbee

1948	1

Jack Billingham

1986	1

Max Bishop

1955	1
1956	1
1958	4
1960	5

Ewell Blackwell

1968	5
1969	11
1970	14

Ray Blades

1958	1
1960	1

Paul Blair

1986	8

Steve Blass

1980	2

Lu Blue

1954	1

Ossie Bluege

1948	2
1949	1
1954	1
1956	2
1958	2
1960	3

Ping Bodie

1937	2
1949	1

Joe Boley

1942	1

Tommy Bond

1936 V	1

Bobby Bonds

1987	24
1988	27

Jim Bottomley
Inducted in 1974

1948	4
1949	8
1950	8
1951	6
1952	7
1953	10
1954	16
1955	26
1956	42
1958	57
1960	89
1962	20
1974	Vet. Com.

Lou Boudreau
Inducted in 1970

1956	2
1958	64
1960	35
1962	12
1964	68
1964 RO	43
1966	115
1967	143
1967 RO	68
1968	146
1969	218
1970	232

Jim Bouton

1984	3

Clete Boyer

1978	1
1979	3

Ken Boyer

1975	9
1976	15
1977	14
1978	18
1979	20
1985	68
1986	95
1987	96
1988	109

Bill Bradley

1936	1
1937	5
1938	2
1939	1
1942	1
1946	1

Harry Brecheen

1960	7
1968	3
1969	2
1970	3
1971	7
1972	5
1973	3

Ted Breitenstein

1937	1

Roger Bresnahan
Inducted in 1945

1936	47
1937	43
1938	67
1939	67
1942	57
1945	133
1945	O/T Com.

Jim Brewer

1982	2

Tommy Bridges

1956	3
1958	11
1960	4
1962	1
1964	15
1964 RO	1
1966	16

Lou Brock
Inducted in 1985

1985	315

Dan Brouthers
Inducted in 1945

1936 V	2
1945	O/T Com.

Gates Brown

1981	1

Mordecai Brown
Inducted in 1949

1936	6
1937	31
1938	54
1939	54
1942	63
1945	46
1946	56
1946 RO	48
1949	O/T Com.

Bill Bruton

1971	1

Morgan Bulkeley
Inducted in 1937
Executive

1937	Cen. Com.

Jim Bunning

1977	146
1978	181
1979	147
1980	177
1981	164
1982	138
1983	138
1984	201
1985	214
1986	279
1987	289
1988	317

Lew Burdette

1973	12
1974	7
1975	11
1976	21
1977	85
1978	76
1979	53
1980	66
1981	48
1982	43
1983	43
1984	97
1985	82
1986	96
1987	96

Smoky Burgess

1973	1
1974	2

Jesse Burkett
Inducted in 1946

1936 V	1
1937	1
1938	2
1942	4
1945	2
1946	2

1946	O/T Com.

George J. Burns

1937	3
1938	3
1939	1
1949	1
1950	2

Guy Bush

1956	2

Joe Bush

1958	5

Donie Bush

1937	1
1939	2
1942	2
1945	1
1946	2
1953	1

Leon Cadore

1948	1

Johnny Callison

1979	1

Dolf Camilli

1948	1
1956	1
1958	4
1960	3

Howie Camnitz

1945	1

Roy Campanella
Inducted in 1969

1964	115
1964 RO	138
1966	197
1967	204
1967 RO	170
1968	205
1969	270

Jose Cardenal

1986	1

Leo Cardenas

1981	1
1982	1

Max Carey
Inducted in 1961

1937	6
1938	6
1939	7
1945	1
1948	9
1949	12
1950	14
1951	27
1952	36
1953	55
1954	55
1955	119
1956	65
1958	136
1961	Vet. Com.

Chico Carrasquel

1966	1

Bill Carrigan

1937	5
1938	4
1939	2
1945	3

Clay Carroll

1984	1

Rico Carty

1985	1

Alex Cartwright
Inducted in 1938
Pioneer

1938	Cen. Com.

George Case

1958	1
1960	1
1962	1
1964	2

Dave Cash

1986	2

Norm Cash

1980	6

Phil Cavarretta

1962	2
1964	22
1964 RO	1
1966	9
1967	15
1967 RO	4
1968	23
1969	37
1970	51
1971	83
1972	61
1973	73
1974	61
1975	129

Orlando Cepeda

1980	48
1981	77
1982	42
1983	59
1984	124
1985	114
1986	152
1987	179
1988	199

Henry Chadwick
Inducted in 1938
Pioneer

1938	Cen. Com.

Frank Chance
Inducted in 1946

1936	5
1937	49
1938	133
1939	158
1942	136
1945	179
1946	144
1946 RO	150
1946	O/T Com.

Happy Chandler
Inducted in 1982
Executive

1982	Vet. Com.

Spud Chandler

1950	2
1951	1
1956	1
1962	2
1964	6

Ben Chapman

1949	1
1952	1

Ray Chapman

1938	1

Sam Chapman

1958	1

Oscar Charleston
Inducted in 1976

1976	Neg. Com.

Hal Chase

1936	11
1937	18

Jack Chesbro
Inducted in 1946

1937	1
1938	2
1939	6
1946	1
1946	O/T Com.

Bill Cissell

1937	1

Watty Clark

1958	1

Fred Clarke
Inducted in 1945

1936 V	9
1936	1
1937	22
1938	63
1939	59
1942	58
1945	53
1945	O/T Com.

John Clarkson
Inducted in 1963

1936 V	5
1946	1
1963	Vet. Com.

Roberto Clemente
Inducted in 1973

1973	Spec. El.

Andy Coakley

1938	1

Ty Cobb
Inducted in 1936

1936	222

Mickey Cochrane
Inducted in 1947

1936	80
1939	28
1942	88
1945	125
1946	80
1946 RO	65
1947	128

Rocky Colavito

1974	2
1975	1

Eddie Collins
Inducted in 1939

1936	60
1937	115
1938	175
1939	213

Jimmy Collins
Inducted in 1945

1936 V	8
1936	58
1937	66
1938	79
1939	72
1942	68
1945	121
1945	O/T Com.

Shano Collins

1937	1

Earle Combs
Inducted in 1970

1937	4
1938	7
1939	3
1945	1
1948	6
1949	6
1950	3
1952	1
1953	3
1955	1
1956	14
1958	34
1960	43
1962	6
1970	Vet. Com.

Charlie Comiskey
Inducted in 1939
Executive

1936 V	6
1939	O/T Com.

Jocko Conlan
Inducted in 1974
Umpire

1974	Vet. Com.

Tommy Connolly
Inducted in 1953
Umpire

1953	Vet. Com.

Roger Connor
Inducted in 1976

1976	Vet. Com.

Wid Conroy

1945	1

Jack Coombs

1937	2
1938	2
1946	2
1948	2
1951	1

Mort Cooper

1956	2
1958	3
1960	1
1969	3

Walker Cooper

1968	8
1969	5
1970	9
1971	7
1972	8
1973	8
1974	9
1975	13
1976	56
1977	45

Wilbur Cooper

1938	1
1939	1
1948	2
1949	4
1951	1
1952	2
1953	9
1954	7
1955	11

Clint Courtney

1967	1

Stan Coveleski
Inducted in 1969

1938	1
1948	2
1949	3
1950	1
1958	34

1969 Vet. Com.

Billy Cox

1962	1

Doc Cramer

1956	4
1958	2
1960	1
1962	1
1964	12

Del Crandall

1976	15
1977	8
1978	6
1979	9

Doc Crandall

1938	1

Gavvy Cravath

1937	2
1938	2
1939	2
1946	1
1947	2

Sam Crawford
Inducted in 1957

1936	1
1937	5
1938	11
1939	6
1942	2
1945	4
1946	9
1957	Vet. Com.

Lou Criger

1936 V	1
1936	7
1937	16
1938	11
1939	2
1946	6

Hughie Critz

1956	2

Joe Cronin
Inducted in 1956

1947	6
1948	25
1949	33
1949 RO	16
1950	33
1951	44
1952	48
1953	69
1954	85
1955	135
1956	152

Frank Crosetti

1950	1
1952	1
1956	1
1958	5
1960	8
1968	15

Lave Cross

1939	1
1942	1

Al Crowder

1958	1
1960	1

Walt Cruise

1938	1

Tony Cuccinello

1956	1
1958	3

Candy Cummings
Inducted in 1939
Pioneer

1939	O/T Com.

Kiki Cuyler
Inducted in 1968

1948	3
1949	4
1950	11
1951	8
1952	10
1953	18
1954	20
1955	35
1956	55
1958	90
1960	72
1962	31
1968	Vet. Com.

Bill Dahlen

1936 V	1
1938	1

Ray Dandridge
Inducted in 1987

1987	Vet. Com.

Harry Danning

1958	1
1960	1

Alvin Dark

1966	17
1967	38
1967 RO	7
1968	36
1969	48
1970	55
1971	54
1972	55
1973	53
1974	54
1975	48
1976	62
1977	66
1978	60
1979	80
1980	43

Jake Daubert

1936 V	1
1937	2
1938	1
1939	1
1951	1
1955	1

Curt Davis

1958	1

Harry Davis

1945	1
1946	2

Tommy Davis

1982	5

Spud Davis

1948	1
1949	1

Dizzy Dean
Inducted in 1953

1945	17
1946	40
1946 RO	45
1947	88
1948	40
1949	88
1949 RO	81
1950	85
1951	145
1952	152
1953	209

Ed Delahanty
Inducted in 1945

1936 V	22
1936	17
1937	70
1938	132
1939	145
1942	104
1945	111
1945	O/T Com.

Jerry Denny

1936 V	6

Paul Derringer

1948	1
1950	1
1951	1
1955	1
1956	12
1958	15
1960	8

Bill Dickey
Inducted in 1954

1945	17
1946	40
1946 RO	32
1948	39
1949	65
1949 RO	39
1950	78
1951	118
1952	139
1953	179
1954	202

Martin Dihigo
Inducted in 1977

1977	Neg. Com.

Dom DiMaggio

1960	4
1962	2
1964	12
1968	8
1969	13
1970	15
1971	15
1972	36
1973	43

Joe DiMaggio
Inducted in 1955

1945	1
1953	117
1954	175
1955	223

Bill Dinneen

1938	4
1939	7
1942	1
1945	1
1946	1

Bill Doak

1958	3

Larry Doby

1966	7
1967	10
1967 RO	1

Bobby Doerr
Inducted in 1986

1953	2
1956	5
1958	25
1960	15
1962	10
1964	24
1964 RO	5
1966	30
1967	35
1967 RO	15
1968	48
1969	62

1970 75
1971 78
1986 Vet. Com.

Mike Donlin

1937	6
1938	5
1939	5
1945	1

Bill Donovan

1937	3
1938	1
1939	2
1945	3
1946	4

Red Dooin

1937	1
1938	1

Jack Doyle

1936 V	1

Larry Doyle

1937	2
1938	4
1939	1

Walt Dropo

1967	1

Don Drysdale
Inducted in 1984

1975	76
1976	114
1977	197
1978	219
1979	233
1980	238
1981	243
1982	233
1983	242
1984	316

Hugh Duffy
Inducted in 1945

1936 V	4
1937	7
1938	24
1939	34
1942	77
1945	64
1945	O/T Com.

Joe Dugan

1937	1
1938	1
1948	3
1949	2
1956	1
1958	5
1960	8

Fred Dunlap

1936 V	2

Jack Dunn

1942	1
1945	1
1946	1

Leo Durocher

1948	1
1949	1
1952	1
1956	1
1958	28
1960	10
1962	1
1964	15
1964 RO	2

Eddie Dyer

1947	1

Jimmy Dykes
1948 5
1949 7
1950 2
1951 3
1952 5
1953 5
1955 1
1956 1
1958 26
1960 27
1962 6

George Earnshaw
1948 3
1949 2
1950 2
1955 2
1956 3

Hank Edwards
1960 2

Howard Ehmke
1938 1
1949 1
1951 1
1952 1
1953 3
1954 4
1955 8
1956 8
1958 7
1960 12

Kid Elberfeld
1936 1
1937 1
1938 2
1942 1
1945 2

Jumbo Elliott
1958 1

Bob Elliott
1960 2
1962 1
1964 4

Dock Ellis
1985 1

Del Ennis
1966 3
1967 2

Jewel Ens
1950 1

Carl Erskine
1966 6
1968 9
1969 4
1970 2
1971 3
1972 4
1973 4
1974 11

Billy Evans
Inducted in 1973
Umpire
1973 . . . . . Vet. Com.

Johnny Evers
Inducted in 1946
1936 6
1937 44
1938 91
1939 107
1942 91
1945 134
1946 130
1946 RO 110
1946 . . . . . O/T Com.

Buck Ewing
Inducted in 1939
1936 V 40
1939 2
1939 . . . . . O/T Com.

Red Faber
Inducted in 1964
1937 3
1938 1
1939 3
1942 1
1948 3
1949 6
1950 9
1951 8
1952 9
1953 9
1954 12
1955 27
1956 34
1958 68
1960 83
1962 30
1964 . . . . . Vet. Com.

Elroy Face
1976 23
1977 33
1978 27
1979 35
1980 21
1981 23
1982 22
1983 32
1984 65
1985 62
1986 74
1987 78
1988 79

Ron Fairly
1985 3

Cy Falkenberg
1937 1

Bob Feller
Inducted in 1962
1962 150

Rick Ferrell
Inducted in 1984
1956 1
1958 1
1960 1
1984 . . . . . Vet. Com.

Wes Ferrell
1948 1
1949 1
1956 7
1960 8
1962 1

Fred Fitzsimmons
1948 2
1949 2
1950 1
1956 3
1958 16
1960 13
1962 1

Art Fletcher
1937 2
1938 3
1939 1
1947 3
1948 3
1949 1
1950 1
1951 4

Elmer Flick
Inducted in 1963
1938 1
1963 . . . . . Vet. Com.

Curt Flood
1977 16
1978 8
1979 14
1985 28
1986 45
1987 50
1988 48

Lew Fonseca
1948 1
1950 2
1956 2
1958 3
1960 3

Whitey Ford
Inducted in 1974
1973 255
1974 284

Eddie Foster
1938 2

Rube Foster
Inducted in 1981
Manager
1981 . . . . . Vet. Com.

Nellie Fox
1971 39
1972 64
1973 73
1974 79
1975 76
1976 174
1977 152
1978 149
1979 174
1980 161
1981 168
1982 127
1983 173
1984 246
1985 295

Jimmie Foxx
Inducted in 1951
1936 21
1946 26
1947 10
1948 50
1949 85
1949 RO 89
1950 103
1951 179

Curt Fraser
1939 1

Bill Freehan
1982 2

Jim Fregosi
1984 4

Ford Frick
Inducted in 1970
Executive
1970 . . . . . Vet. Com.

Frankie Frisch
Inducted in 1947
1936 14
1939 26
1942 84
1945 101
1946 104
1946 RO 67
1947 136

Carl Furillo
1966 2
1967 2
1970 2
1971 5
1972 2

Augie Galan
1968 2
1970 3

Jim Galvin
Inducted in 1965
1965 . . . . . Vet. Com.

Ned Garver
1967 1

Lou Gehrig
Inducted in 1939
1936 51
1939 . . . . . Spec. El.

Charlie Gehringer
Inducted in 1949
1945 10
1946 43
1946 RO 23
1947 105
1948 52
1949 102
1949 RO 159

Charlie Gelbert
1947 1
1949 2
1950 1
1951 1

Josh Gibson
Inducted in 1972
1972 . . . . . Neg. Com.

Bob Gibson
Inducted in 1981
1981 337

Warren Giles
Inducted in 1979
Executive
1979 . . . . . Vet. Com.

Dave Giusti
1983 1

Jack Glasscock
1936 V 2

Kid Gleason
1937 1
1938 1
1939 1
1945 1

Lefty Gomez
Inducted in 1972
1945 7
1946 4
1947 1
1948 16
1949 17
1950 18
1951 23
1952 29
1953 35
1954 38
1955 71
1956 89
1958 76
1960 51
1962 20
1972 . . . . . Vet. Com.

Mike Gonzales
1950 1
1952 1
1953 1
1958 3
1960 2

Joe Gordon
1945 1
1955 1
1956 4
1958 11
1960 11
1962 4
1964 30
1964 RO 1
1966 31
1967 66
1967 RO 13
1968 77
1969 97
1970 79

Goose Goslin
Inducted in 1968
1948 1
1949 4
1950 2
1954 1
1955 7
1956 26
1958 26
1960 30
1962 14
1968 . . . . . Vet. Com.

Hank Gowdy
1937 2
1938 8
1939 4
1942 8
1945 3
1947 1
1948 3
1949 10
1950 6
1951 26
1952 34
1953 58
1954 51
1955 90
1956 49
1958 45
1960 38

Eddie Grant
1938 1
1939 2
1942 3
1945 2
1946 1

George Grantham
1958 1

Hank Greenberg
Inducted in 1956
1945 3
1949 67
1949 RO 44
1950 64
1951 67
1952 75
1953 80
1954 97
1955 157
1956 164

Clark Griffith
Inducted in 1946
Executive
1937 4
1938 10
1939 20
1942 71
1945 108
1946 73
1946 RO 82
1946 . . . . . O/T Com.

Burleigh Grimes
Inducted in 1964
1937 1
1938 1
1939 1
1948 7
1949 8
1950 6
1951 5
1952 9
1953 9
1955 3
1956 25
1958 71
1960 92
1962 43
1964 . . . . . Vet. Com.

Charlie Grimm
1939 1
1945 1
1946 1
1948 6
1949 10
1950 13
1951 9
1952 6
1953 9
1958 26
1960 13
1962 2

Marv Grissom
1966 2

Dick Groat
1973 7
1974 4
1975 4
1976 7
1977 4
1978 3

Heinie Groh
1937 1
1938 3
1945 1
1948 1
1950 2
1954 1
1955 5
1960 1

Steve Gromek
1964 1

Orval Grove
1958 5
1960 7

Lefty Grove
Inducted in 1947
1936 12
1945 28
1946 71
1946 RO 61
1947 123

Frank Gustine
1958 3

Mule Haas
1955 1
1956 1
1958 1
1960 1

Stan Hack
1948 2
1949 4
1950 8
1951 3
1956 1
1958 6
1960 6

Harvey Haddix
1971 10
1972 9
1973 1
1974 8
1975 8
1976 8
1977 7
1978 7
1979 8
1985 15

Chick Hafey
Inducted in 1971

1948	1
1949	2
1950	4
1951	1
1952	1
1953	2
1954	2
1955	4
1956	16
1958	12
1960	29
1962	7
1971	Vet. Com.

Noodles Hahn

1939	1

Jesse Haines
Inducted in 1970

1939	1
1947	1
1948	2
1949	2
1950	11
1953	4
1954	6
1955	10
1956	14
1958	22
1960	20
1962	3
1970	Vet. Com.

Bill Hallahan

1948	1
1956	1
1958	1
1960	2

Billy Hamilton
Inducted in 1961

1936 V	2
1942	1
1961	Vet. Com.

Mel Harder

1949	4
1950	2
1951	1
1952	10
1953	8
1958	6
1960	12
1962	7
1964	51
1964 RO	14
1966	34
1967	52
1967 RO	14

Bubbles Hargrave

1947	1
1958	1
1960	1

Bud Harrelson

1986	1

Will Harridge
Inducted in 1972
Executive

1972	Vet. Com.

Bucky Harris
Inducted in 1975
Manager

1938	1
1939	1
1948	3
1949	11
1950	4
1951	9
1952	12
1953	21
1958	45
1960	31
1975	Vet. Com.

Gabby Hartnett
Inducted in 1955

1945	2
1946	2
1947	2
1948	33
1949	35
1949 RO	7
1950	54
1951	57
1952	77
1953	104
1954	151
1955	195

Grady Hatton

1966	4
1967	1

Jim Hearn

1966	1
1967	1

Jim Hegan

1966	5
1967	2

Harry Heilmann
Inducted in 1952

1937	10
1938	14
1939	8
1942	4
1945	5
1946	23
1947	65
1948	40
1949	59
1949 RO	52
1950	87
1951	153
1952	203

Tommy Helms

1983	1

Solly Hemus

1966	1

Tommy Henrich

1952	4
1953	10
1956	2
1958	11
1960	10
1962	3
1964	13
1968	22
1969	50
1970	62

Babe Herman

1942	1
1948	2
1949	5
1950	2
1951	1
1952	3
1953	2
1954	1
1955	5
1956	11
1958	13
1960	7

Billy Herman
Inducted in 1975

1948	1
1956	2
1958	7
1962	4
1964	26
1964 RO	9
1966	28
1967	59
1967 RO	14
1975	Vet. Com.

Buck Herzog

1938	1

Jim Hickman

1980	1

Mike Higgins

1950	2
1951	1
1958	6
1960	3

John Hiller

1986	11

Bill Hinchman

1937	1

Gil Hodges

1969	82
1970	145
1971	180
1972	161
1973	218
1974	198
1975	188
1976	233
1977	224
1978	226
1979	242
1980	230
1981	241
1982	205
1983	237

Tommy Holmes

1958	2
1960	2

Ken Holtzman

1985	4
1986	5

Harry Hooper
Inducted in 1971

1937	6
1938	4
1939	5
1948	2
1950	2
1951	3
1971	Vet. Com.

Rogers Hornsby
Inducted in 1942

1936	105
1937	53
1938	46
1939	176
1942	182

Willie Horton

1986	4

Art Houtteman

1964	2

Elston Howard

1974	19
1975	23
1976	55
1977	43
1978	41
1979	30
1980	29
1981	83
1982	40
1983	32
1984	45
1985	54
1986	51
1987	44
1988	53

Frank Howard

1979	6

Waite Hoyt
Inducted in 1969

1939	1
1942	1
1946	1
1948	7
1949	7
1950	11
1951	13
1952	12
1953	14
1954	14
1955	33
1956	37
1958	37
1960	29
1962	18
1969	Vet. Com.

Al Hrabosky

1988	1

Cal Hubbard
Inducted in 1976
Umpire

1976	Vet. Com.

Carl Hubbell
Inducted in 1947

1945	24
1946	101
1946 RO	75
1947	140

Miller Huggins
Inducted in 1964
Manager

1937	5
1938	48
1939	97
1942	111
1945	133
1946	129
1946 RO	106
1948	4
1950	2
1964	Vet. Com.

Catfish Hunter
Inducted in 1987

1985	212
1986	289
1987	315

Fred Hutchinson

1962	1
1964	10

Monte Irvin
Inducted in 1973

1973	Neg. Com.

Charlie Irwin

1938	1
1939	1

Joe Jackson

1936	2
1946	2

Sonny Jackson

1980	1

Travis Jackson
Inducted in 1982

1948	5
1949	6
1950	6
1951	4
1952	1
1953	2
1954	1
1955	5
1956	14
1958	11
1960	11
1962	1
1982	Vet. Com.

Hughie Jennings
Inducted in 1945

1936 V	11
1937	4
1938	23
1939	33
1942	64
1945	92
1945	O/T Com.

Jackie Jensen

1967	3
1968	3
1969	1
1970	1
1971	2
1972	1

Ban Johnson,
Inducted in 1937
Executive

1937	Cen. Com.

Dave Johnson

1984	3

Judy Johnson
Inducted in 1975

1975	Neg. Com.

Bob Johnson

1948	1
1956	1

Walter Johnson
Inducted in 1936

1936	189

Fielder Jones

1946	1

Sam P. Jones

1939	1
1955	1
1956	1

Tim Jordan

1951	1

Addie Joss
Inducted in 1978

1937	11
1938	18
1939	28
1942	33
1945	23
1946	14
1960	1
1978	Vet. Com.

Joe Judge

1937	1
1938	2
1949	1
1955	2
1956	2
1958	9
1960	15

Billy Jurges

1949	2
1958	1

Al Kaline
Inducted in 1980

1980	340

Willie Kamm

1958	3
1960	1

Tim Keefe
Inducted in 1964

1936 V	1
1964	Vet. Com.

Willie Keeler
Inducted in 1939

1936 V	33
1936	40
1937	115
1938	177
1939	207

George Kell
Inducted in 1983

1964	33
1964 RO	8
1966	29
1967	40
1967 RO	11
1968	47
1969	60
1970	90
1971	105
1972	115
1973	114
1974	94
1975	114
1976	129
1977	141
1983	Vet. Com.

Charlie Keller

1953	1
1956	2
1958	9
1960	7
1962	1
1964	12
1968	11
1969	14
1970	7
1971	14
1972	24

Joe Kelley
Inducted in 1971

1939	1
1942	1
1971	Vet. Com.

George Kelly
Inducted in 1973

1947	1
1948	2
1949	1
1956	2
1958	2
1960	5
1962	1
1973	Vet. Com.

Mike Kelly
Inducted in 1945

1936 V	15
1945	O/T Com.

Ken Keltner

1958	1
1960	1

Dickie Kerr

1937	1
1938	3
1939	5
1942	1
1945	1
1949	1
1951	3
1952	9
1953	13
1954	13
1955	25

Don Kessinger

1985	2

Harmon Killebrew
Inducted in 1984

1981 ... 239
1982 ... 246
1983 ... 269
1984 ... 335

Bill Killefer

1946 ... 1

Matt Kilroy

1936 V ... 1

Ellis Kinder

1964 ... 3

Ralph Kiner
Inducted in 1975

1962 ... 5
1964 ... 31
1964 RO ... 3
1966 ... 74
1967 ... 124
1967 RO ... 41
1968 ... 118
1969 ... 137
1970 ... 167
1971 ... 212
1972 ... 235
1973 ... 235
1974 ... 215
1975 ... 273

Chuck Klein
Inducted in 1980

1948 ... 3
1949 ... 9
1950 ... 14
1951 ... 15
1952 ... 19
1954 ... 11
1955 ... 25
1956 ... 44
1958 ... 36
1960 ... 37
1962 ... 18
1964 ... 56
1964 RO ... 18
1980 ... Vet. Com.

Bill Klem
Inducted in 1953
Umpire

1953 ... Vet. Com.

Johnny Kling

1936 ... 8
1937 ... 20
1938 ... 26
1939 ... 14
1942 ... 15
1945 ... 12
1946 ... 20
1948 ... 2
1953 ... 1

Ted Kluszewski

1967 ... 9
1968 ... 14
1969 ... 11
1970 ... 8
1971 ... 9
1972 ... 10
1973 ... 14
1974 ... 28
1975 ... 33
1976 ... 50
1977 ... 55
1978 ... 51
1979 ... 58
1980 ... 50
1981 ... 56

Otto Knabe

1939 ... 1
1946 ... 1

Sandy Koufax
Inducted in 1972

1972 ... 344

Ray Kremer

1948 ... 1
1958 ... 2

Red Kress

1958 ... 1
1960 ... 3

Harvey Kuenn

1977 ... 57
1978 ... 58
1979 ... 63
1980 ... 83
1981 ... 93
1982 ... 62
1983 ... 77
1984 ... 106
1985 ... 125
1986 ... 144
1987 ... 144
1988 ... 168

Joe Kuhel

1956 ... 1

Bob Kuzava

1964 ... 1

Nap Lajoie
Inducted in 1937

1936 V ... 2
1936 ... 146
1937 ... 168

Judge Landis
Inducted in 1944
Executive

1944 ... O/T Com.

Bill Lange

1936 V ... 6
1953 ... 1

Hal Lanier

1979 ... 1

Don Larsen

1974 ... 29
1975 ... 23
1976 ... 47
1977 ... 39
1978 ... 32
1979 ... 53
1980 ... 31
1981 ... 33
1982 ... 32
1983 ... 22
1984 ... 25
1985 ... 32
1986 ... 33
1987 ... 30
1988 ... 31

Arlie Latham

1936 V ... 1
1938 ... 1
1942 ... 1

Cookie Lavagetto

1958 ... 4
1960 ... 2

Vern Law

1973 ... 9
1974 ... 5
1975 ... 6
1976 ... 9
1977 ... 5
1978 ... 6
1979 ... 9

Tony Lazzeri

1945 ... 1
1947 ... 1
1948 ... 21
1949 ... 20
1949 RO ... 6
1950 ... 21
1951 ... 27
1952 ... 29
1953 ... 28
1954 ... 30
1955 ... 66
1956 ... 64
1958 ... 80
1960 ... 59
1962 ... 8

Fred Leach

1958 ... 2
1960 ... 1

Tommy Leach

1937 ... 1
1939 ... 1

Bill Lee

1988 ... 3

Sam Leever

1937 ... 1

Bob Lemon
Inducted in 1976

1964 ... 24
1964 RO ... 3
1966 ... 21
1967 ... 35
1967 RO ... 7
1968 ... 47
1969 ... 56
1970 ... 70
1971 ... 90
1972 ... 117
1973 ... 177
1974 ... 190
1975 ... 233
1976 ... 305

Buck Leonard
Inducted in 1972

1972 ... Neg. Com.

Emil Leonard

1960 ... 2
1968 ... 5
1969 ... 4
1970 ... 5
1971 ... 3
1972 ... 5
1973 ... 6

Duffy Lewis

1937 ... 3
1938 ... 5
1939 ... 6
1945 ... 1
1951 ... 2
1952 ... 11
1953 ... 20
1954 ... 20
1955 ... 34

Fred Lindstrom
Inducted in 1976

1949 ... 1
1956 ... 3
1958 ... 5
1960 ... 6
1962 ... 7
1976 ... Vet. Com.

John Henry Lloyd
Inducted in 1977

1977 ... Neg. Com.

Hans Lobert

1937 ... 2
1938 ... 1
1939 ... 2
1960 ... 1

Whitey Lockman

1966 ... 4

Mickey Lolich

1985 ... 78
1986 ... 86
1987 ... 84
1988 ... 109

Ernie Lombardi
Inducted in 1986

1950 ... 3
1951 ... 3
1956 ... 8
1958 ... 4
1960 ... 6
1962 ... 5
1964 ... 33
1964 RO ... 9
1966 ... 34
1967 ... 43
1967 RO ... 25
1986 ... Vet. Com.

Jim Lonborg

1985 ... 3
1986 ... 3

Herman Long

1936 V ... 16
1937 ... 1
1938 ... 1
1939 ... 1
1945 ... 1
1946 ... 1

Ed Lopat

1968 ... 2
1969 ... 2
1970 ... 1
1971 ... 4
1972 ... 2

Al Lopez
Inducted in 1977
Manager

1949 ... 1
1952 ... 2
1953 ... 2
1956 ... 1
1958 ... 34
1960 ... 26
1962 ... 11
1964 ... 57
1964 RO ... 34
1966 ... 109
1967 ... 114
1967 RO ... 50
1977 ... Vet. Com.

Bobby Lowe

1936 V ... 2
1942 ... 1
1945 ... 2

Red Lucas

1949 ... 2
1950 ... 1
1958 ... 1

Dolph Luque

1937 ... 1
1938 ... 1
1939 ... 1
1950 ... 1
1952 ... 1
1953 ... 1
1956 ... 1
1958 ... 15
1960 ... 4

Sparky Lyle

1988 ... 56

Ted Lyons
Inducted in 1955

1945 ... 4
1946 ... 3
1948 ... 15
1949 ... 29
1949 RO ... 14
1950 ... 42
1951 ... 71
1952 ... 101
1953 ... 139
1954 ... 170
1955 ... 217

Connie Mack
Inducted in 1937
Manager

1936 ... 1
1937 ... Cen. Com.

Larry MacPhail
Inducted in 1978
Executive

1978 ... Vet. Com.

Sherry Magee

1937 ... 2
1938 ... 2
1939 ... 1
1942 ... 1
1945 ... 1
1946 ... 1
1950 ... 1
1951 ... 2

Sal Maglie

1964 ... 13
1968 ... 11

Jim Maloney

1978 ... 2
1979 ... 2

Gus Mancuso

1958 ... 1

Mickey Mantle
Inducted in 1974

1974 ... 322

Heinie Manush
Inducted in 1964

1948 ... 1
1949 ... 1
1956 ... 13
1958 ... 22
1960 ... 20
1962 ... 15
1964 ... Vet. Com.

Rabbit Maranville
Inducted in 1954

1937 ... 25
1938 ... 73
1939 ... 82
1942 ... 66
1945 ... 51
1946 ... 50
1946 RO ... 29
1947 ... 91
1948 ... 38
1949 ... 58
1949 RO ... 39
1950 ... 66
1951 ... 110
1952 ... 133
1953 ... 164
1954 ... 209

Firpo Marberry

1938 ... 1
1950 ... 1
1958 ... 5
1960 ... 2
1962 ... 2

Juan Marichal
Inducted in 1983

1981 ... 233
1982 ... 305
1983 ... 313

Marty Marion

1956 ... 1
1960 ... 37
1962 ... 16
1964 ... 50
1964 RO ... 17
1966 ... 86
1967 ... 90
1967 RO ... 22
1968 ... 89
1969 ... 112
1970 ... 120
1971 ... 123
1972 ... 120
1973 ... 127

Roger Maris

1974 ... 78
1975 ... 70
1976 ... 87
1977 ... 72
1978 ... 83
1979 ... 127
1980 ... 111
1981 ... 94
1982 ... 69
1983 ... 69
1984 ... 107
1985 ... 128
1986 ... 177
1987 ... 176
1988 ... 184

Rube Marquard
Inducted in 1971

1936 ... 1
1937 ... 13
1938 ... 10
1939 ... 4
1946 ... 6
1947 ... 18
1948 ... 6
1949 ... 4
1951 ... 3
1952 ... 9
1953 ... 19
1954 ... 15
1955 ... 35
1971 ... Vet. Com.

Mike Marshall

1987 ... 6

Billy Martin

1967 ... 1

Pepper Martin

1942 ... 2
1945 ... 1
1946 ... 1
1948 ... 7
1949 ... 16
1950 ... 7
1951 ... 19
1952 ... 31
1953 ... 43
1956 ... 7
1958 ... 46
1960 ... 29
1962 ... 6
1964 ... 19
1964 RO ... 5

Morrie Martin

1966 ... 2

Eddie Mathews
Inducted in 1978

1974 ... 118
1975 ... 148
1976 ... 189
1977 ... 239
1978 ... 301

Christy Mathewson
Inducted in 1936

1936 205

Lee May

1988 2

Carl Mays

1958 6

Willie Mays
Inducted in 1979

1979 409

Bill Mazeroski

1978 23
1979 36
1980 33
1981 38
1982 28
1983 48
1984 74
1985 87
1986 100
1987 125
1988 143

Jim McAleer

1936 V 1

Joe McCarthy
Inducted in 1957
Manager

1939 3
1947 2
1951 1
1953 1
1958 2
1957 . . . . . Vet. Com.

Tommy McCarthy
Inducted in 1946

1936 V 1
1946 . . . . . . O/T Com.

Tim McCarver

1986 16

Frank McCormick

1956 3
1962 1
1964 6
1968 3

Willie McCovey
Inducted in 1986

1986 346

Lindy McDaniel

1981 1
1982 3

Gil McDougald

1966 5
1967 4
1968 4
1969 3
1970 1
1971 4
1972 4
1973 2
1974 3

Joe McGinnity
Inducted in 1946

1937 12
1938 36
1939 32
1942 59
1945 44
1946 53
1946 RO 47
1946 . . . . . . O/T Com.

John McGraw
Inducted in 1937

Manager
1936 V 17
1936 4
1937 35
1937 . . . . . Cen. Com.

Stuffy McInnis

1937 1
1938 4
1939 4
1948 5
1949 8
1950 1
1951 3

Bill McKechnie
Inducted in 1962
Manager

1945 2
1946 2
1950 1
1951 8
1962 . . . . . Vet. Com.

Denny McLain

1978 1
1979 3
1985 2

Larry McLean

1937 1

Don McMahon

1980 1

Marty McManus

1958 2
1960 2

Roy McMillan

1972 9
1973 5
1974 4

Dave McNally

1981 5
1982 5
1985 7
1986 12

Cal McVey

1936 V 1

Lee Meadows

1958 2

Ducky Medwick
Inducted in 1968

1948 1
1956 31
1958 50
1960 38
1962 34
1964 108
1964 RO 130
1966 187
1967 212
1967 RO 248
1968 240

Andy Messersmith

1985 3
1986 3

Bob Meusel

1937 1
1938 1
1945 1
1948 6
1949 3
1950 2
1952 1
1955 2
1956 1
1958 5
1960 10

Eddie Miksis

1964 1

Clyde Milan

1938 1
1950 1
1951 1
1952 1
1953 1
1954 3
1955 6

Felix Millan

1983 1

Bing Miller

1958 1
1960 6

Dots Miller

1948 1

Hack Miller

1937 1

Minnie Minoso

1969 6
1986 89
1987 82
1988 90

Johnny Mize
Inducted in 1981

1960 45
1962 14
1964 54
1964 RO 12
1966 81
1967 89
1967 RO 14
1968 103
1969 116
1970 126
1971 157
1972 157
1973 157
1981 . . . . . Vet. Com.

Wally Moon

1971 2

Jo-Jo Moore

1950 1

Terry Moore

1950 1
1953 1
1958 12
1960 7
1962 1
1964 14
1967 3
1968 33

Pat Moran

1937 1
1938 1
1939 1
1945 1

Wally Moses

1958 1
1960 1
1968 4
1969 4
1970 5
1971 7

Johnny Mostil

1956 1
1958 1

Manny Mota

1988 18

Hugh Mulcahy

1948 1

Van Mungo

1945 1
1948 1
1958 2
1960 2

Thurman Munson

1981 62
1982 26
1983 18
1984 29
1985 32
1986 35
1987 28
1988 32

Danny Murphy

1937 1
1945 1

Red Murray

1937 1
1938 1

Stan Musial
Inducted in 1969

1969 317

Buddy Myer

1949 1

Art Nehf

1937 3
1938 5
1939 1
1949 1
1950 2
1951 4
1952 3
1953 4
1954 7
1955 7
1958 13

Don Newcombe

1966 7
1967 18
1967 RO 2
1968 9
1969 3
1970 5
1971 8
1972 7
1973 11
1974 7
1975 11
1976 21
1977 43
1978 48
1979 52
1980 59

Hal Newhouser

1962 4
1964 26
1964 RO 3
1966 32
1967 62
1967 RO 13
1968 67
1969 82
1970 80
1971 94
1972 92
1973 79
1974 73
1975 155

Bobo Newsom

1960 6
1962 3
1964 17
1964 RO 1
1966 25
1967 19

1967 RO 6
1968 22
1969 32
1970 12
1971 17
1972 31
1973 33

Kid Nichols
Inducted in 1949

1936 V 3
1938 3
1939 7
1942 5
1945 5
1946 1
1949 . . . . . O/T Com.

Bill Nicholson

1960 1

Ron Northey

1964 1

Jim Northrup

1981 1

Lefty O'Doul

1948 4
1949 4
1950 9
1951 13
1952 19
1953 11
1956 5
1958 27
1960 45
1962 13

Joe Oeschger

1948 1

Bob O'Farrell

1950 4
1958 3
1960 3

Charlie O'Leary

1953 1
1958 1
1960 1

Tony Oliva

1982 63
1983 75
1984 124
1985 114
1986 154
1987 160
1988 202

Steve O'Neill

1948 2
1949 6
1950 1
1951 3
1952 10
1953 13
1958 10

Jim O'Rourke
Inducted in 1945

1945 . . . . . . O/T Com.

Claude Osteen

1981 2

Mel Ott
Inducted in 1951

1949 94
1949 RO 128
1950 115
1951 197

Charlie Pabor

1936 V 1

Andy Pafko

1966 2
1967 1

Satchel Paige
Inducted in 1971

1951 1
1971 . . . . . Neg. Com.

Milt Pappas

1979 5

Camilo Pascual

1977 3
1978 1

Dode Paskert

1937 1

Monte Pearson

1958 1

Roger Peckinpaugh

1937 3
1938 1
1939 1
1942 2
1949 1
1952 2
1953 2
1954 1
1955 1

Heinie Peitz

1939 1

Herb Pennock
Inducted in 1948

1937 15
1938 37
1939 40
1942 72
1945 45
1946 41
1946 RO 16
1947 86
1948 94

Hub Perdue

1938 1
1939 1

Cy Perkins

1958 2

Ron Perranoski

1979 6

Jim Perry

1981 6
1983 7

Johnny Pesky

1960 1

Rico Petrocelli

1982 3

Deacon Phillippe

1939 1
1942 1
1945 1
1946 1

Billy Pierce

1970 5
1971 7
1972 4
1973 4
1974 4

Lip Pike

1936 V 1

Vada Pinson
1981	18
1982	6
1983	12
1985	19
1986	43
1987	48
1988	67

Wally Pipp
1958	1

Eddie Plank
Inducted in 1946
1937	23
1938	38
1939	28
1942	63
1945	33
1946	34
1946	O/T Com.

Johnny Podres
1975	3
1976	2
1977	3

Bob Porterfield
1966	1

Boog Powell
1983	5

Vic Power
1971	2
1972	3

Herb Pruett
1949	1
1950	1
1951	1
1952	1
1953	1

Jack Quinn
1948	2
1958	9
1960	2

Charlie Radbourn
Inducted in 1939
1936 V	16
1939	O/T Com.

Vic Raschi
1962	1
1964	8
1968	1
1969	3
1971	2
1972	4
1973	7
1974	3
1975	37

Bugs Raymond
1937	1

Pee Wee Reese
Inducted in 1984
1964	73
1964 RO	47
1966	95
1967	89
1967 RO	16
1968	81
1969	89
1970	97
1971	127
1972	129
1973	126
1974	141
1975	154
1976	186
1977	163
1978	169
1984	Vet. Com.

Pete Reiser
1958	6
1960	8

Jack Remsen
1936 V	1

Allie Reynolds
1956	1
1960	24
1962	15
1964	35
1964 RO	6
1966	60
1967	77
1967 RO	19
1968	95
1969	98
1970	89
1971	110
1972	105
1973	93
1974	101

Del Rice
1966	2

Sam Rice
Inducted in 1963
1938	1
1948	1
1949	3
1950	1
1951	1
1952	1
1953	3
1954	9
1955	28
1956	45
1958	90
1960	143
1962	81
1963	Vet. Com.

J. R. Richard
1986	7

Hardy Richardson
1936 V	1

Bobby Richardson
1972	8
1973	2
1974	5

Branch Rickey
Inducted in 1967
Executive
1942	3
1945	2
1967	Vet. Com.

Jimmy Ring
1949	1

Claude Ritchey
1945	1

Eppa Rixey
Inducted in 1963
1937	1
1938	2
1945	1
1947	2
1948	5
1949	4
1950	6
1951	5
1952	3
1953	3
1954	5
1955	8
1956	27
1958	32
1960	142
1962	49
1963	Vet. Com.

Phil Rizzuto
1956	1
1962	44
1964	45
1964 RO	11
1966	54
1967	71
1967 RO	14
1968	74
1969	78
1970	79
1971	92
1972	103
1973	111
1974	111
1975	117
1976	149

Robin Roberts
Inducted in 1976
1973	213
1974	224
1975	263
1976	337

Dave Robertson
1953	1

Brooks Robinson
Inducted in 1983
1983	344

Frank Robinson
Inducted in 1982
1982	370

Jackie Robinson
Inducted in 1962
1962	124

Wilbert Robinson
Inducted in 1945
Manager
1936 V	6
1937	5
1938	17
1939	46
1942	89
1945	81
1945	O/T Com.

Preacher Roe
1960	1
1962	1
1968	2
1970	1
1971	3
1972	2

Red Rolfe
1950	7
1951	6
1952	4
1953	1
1956	3
1958	13
1960	10
1962	1

Eddie Rommel
1948	3
1949	2
1950	1
1951	1
1952	2
1953	1
1958	7
1960	12

Charlie Root
1945	1
1948	3
1949	1
1950	1
1958	6
1960	2

Edd Roush
Inducted in 1962
1936	2
1937	10
1938	9
1939	8
1942	1
1945	5
1946	11
1947	25
1948	17
1949	14
1950	16
1951	21
1952	24
1953	32
1954	52
1955	97
1956	91
1958	112
1960	146
1962	Vet. Com.

Schoolboy Rowe
1958	12
1960	3
1968	6
1969	17

Nap Rucker
1936	1
1937	11
1938	12
1939	13
1942	15
1945	10
1946	13

Dick Rudolph
1937	1
1951	1

Muddy Ruel
1946	1
1950	4
1951	1
1952	1
1953	8
1954	5
1955	11
1956	16
1958	10
1960	9

Red Ruffing
Inducted in 1967
1948	4
1949	22
1949 RO	4
1950	12
1951	9
1952	10
1953	24
1954	29
1955	60
1956	97
1958	99
1960	86
1962	72
1964	141
1964 RO	184
1966	208
1967	212
1967 RO	266

Amos Rusie
Inducted in 1977
1936 V	12
1937	1
1938	8
1939	6
1942	1
1945	1
1977	Vet. Com.

Babe Ruth
Inducted in 1936
1936	215

Ray Sadecki
1983	2

Johnny Sain
1962	1
1964	3
1968	7
1969	8
1970	9
1971	11
1972	21
1973	47
1974	51
1975	123

Manny Sanguillen
1986	2

Ron Santo
1980	15
1985	53
1986	64
1987	78
1988	108

Hank Sauer
1966	4

Al Schacht
1939	1
1948	2
1951	4
1956	1

Germany Schaefer
1942	1
1953	1

Ray Schalk
Inducted in 1955
1936	4
1937	24
1938	45
1939	35
1942	53
1945	33
1946	36
1947	50
1948	22
1949	24
1949 RO	17
1950	16
1951	37
1952	44
1953	52
1954	54
1955	113
1955	Vet. Com.

Wally Schang
1948	1
1950	1
1956	1
1958	8
1960	11

Red Schoendienst
1969	65
1970	97
1971	123
1972	104
1973	96
1974	110
1975	94
1976	129
1977	105
1978	130
1979	159
1980	164
1981	166
1982	135
1983	146

Ossie Schreck
1937	2
1938	2
1939	2

Frank Schulte
1937	1

Hal Schumacher
1948	1
1955	1
1956	2
1958	1
1960	11
1962	1
1964	10

Everett Scott
1937	2
1938	2
1939	1
1942	1
1947	1
1948	3
1949	3
1950	3
1951	2
1952	4
1953	5
1954	4
1955	8
1956	1

George Scott
1986	1

Jack Scott
1958	1

George Selkirk
1948	1
1949	1
1950	1
1951	2
1952	1
1953	1

Hank Severeid
1948	1

Joe Sewell
Inducted in 1977
1937	1
1948	1
1954	1
1955	1
1956	3
1958	1
1960	23
1977	Vet. Com.

Luke Sewell
1948	1
1958	3
1960	3
1962	1

Rip Sewell
1958	1
1962	1
1964	1

Cy Seymour
1945	1

Bobby Shantz
1970	7
1971	5
1972	9
1973	5
1974	3

Jim Sheckard
1938	1
1945	1
1946	1

Bill Sherdel
1948	1
1949	1
1950	1

1951 1
1953 1
1955 1
1956 1
1958 2
1960 2

Urban Shocker

1938 1
1939 1
1948 1
1949 2
1958 4

Chris Short

1979 1

Sonny Siebert

1981 1

Roy Sievers

1971 4
1972 3

Al Simmons
Inducted in 1953

1936 4
1946 1
1947 6
1948 60
1949 89
1949 RO 76
1950 90
1951 116
1952 141
1953 199

Curt Simmons

1973 5
1974 3

George Sisler
Inducted in 1939

1936 77
1937 106
1938 179
1939 235

Sibby Sisti

1960 1

Enos Slaughter
Inducted in 1985

1966 100
1967 123
1967 RO 48
1968 129
1969 128
1970 133
1971 165
1972 149
1973 145
1974 145
1975 177
1976 197
1977 222
1978 261
1979 297
1985 . . . . . Vet. Com.

Roy Smalley

1964 1

Earl Smith

1948 1
1956 1

Reggie Smith

1988 3

Sherry Smith

1948 1

Duke Snider
Inducted in 1980

1970 51

1971 89
1972 84
1973 101
1974 111
1975 129
1976 159
1977 212
1978 254
1979 308
1980 333

Billy Southworth

1945 1
1946 1
1949 7
1950 1
1951 4
1952 1
1953 2
1958 18

Warren Spahn
Inducted in 1973

1973 316

Al Spalding
Inducted in 1939
Pioneer

1936 V 4
1939 . . . . . . O/T Com.

Tully Sparks

1946 1

Tris Speaker
Inducted in 1937

1936 133
1937 165

Jake Stahl

1938 1
1939 1

Eddie Stanky

1960 3

Mickey Stanley

1984 2

Willie Stargell
Inducted in 1988

1988 352

Harry Steinfeldt

1937 1
1939 1
1942 1

Casey Stengel
Inducted in 1966
Manager

1938 2
1939 6
1945 2
1948 1
1949 3
1950 3
1951 8
1952 27
1953 61
1966 . . . . . Vet. Com.

Riggs Stephenson

1956 2
1958 1
1960 4
1962 1

Mel Stottlemyre

1980 3

Harry Stovey

1936 V 6

Gabby Street

1937 1

1938 1
1953 1

Gus Suhr

1956 1
1958 1
1960 1

Clyde Sukeforth

1958 1

Billy Sullivan

1937 1
1946 1

Bill Sweeney

1945 1

Jess Tannehill

1946 1

Birdie Tebbetts

1958 8
1960 1

Fred Tenney

1936 V 1
1937 5
1938 8
1939 1
1942 1
1946 1

Bill Terry
Inducted in 1954

1936 9
1938 7
1939 16
1942 36
1945 32
1946 31
1947 46
1948 52
1949 81
1949 RO 48
1950 105
1951 148
1952 155
1953 191
1954 195

Tommy Thevenow

1950 2

Ira Thomas

1938 1

Sam Thompson
Inducted in 1974

1974 . . . . . Vet. Com.

Bobby Thomson

1966 12
1967 10
1967 RO 1
1968 13
1969 6
1970 4
1971 4
1972 10
1973 6
1974 6
1975 10
1976 9
1977 10
1978 5
1979 11

Luis Tiant

1988 132

Joe Tinker
Inducted in 1946

1937 15
1938 16
1939 12

1942 36
1945 49
1946 55
1946 RO 45
1946 . . . . . . O/T Com.

Jim Tobin

1956 2

Fred Toney

1949 1

Earl Torgeson

1967 2

Joe Torre

1983 20
1984 45
1985 44
1986 60
1987 47
1988 60

Pie Traynor
Inducted in 1948

1936 16
1938 3
1939 10
1942 45
1945 81
1946 65
1946 RO 53
1947 119
1948 93

Dizzy Trout

1964 1

Virgil Trucks

1964 4

Jim Turner

1956 1

Terry Turner

1947 2

George Uhle

1956 1
1958 4
1960 4

Elmer Valo

1967 2

Dazzy Vance
Inducted in 1955

1936 1
1937 10
1938 10
1939 15
1942 37
1945 18
1946 31
1947 50
1948 23
1949 33
1949 RO 15
1950 52
1951 70
1952 105
1953 150
1954 158
1955 205

Johnny Vander Meer

1945 1
1956 3
1958 35
1960 31
1962 5
1964 51
1964 RO 20
1966 72
1967 87
1967 RO 35
1968 79

1969 95
1970 88
1971 98

George Vanhaltren

1936 V 1

Arky Vaughan
Inducted in 1985

1953 1
1954 2
1955 4
1956 9
1958 6
1960 10
1962 6
1964 17
1964 RO 6
1966 36
1967 46
1967 RO 19
1968 82
1985 . . . . . Vet. Com.

Bobby Veach

1937 1

Mickey Vernon

1966 20
1967 14
1967 RO 2
1968 22
1969 21
1970 10
1971 12
1972 12
1973 23
1974 27
1975 22
1976 52
1977 52
1978 66
1979 88
1980 96

Bill Virdon

1974 3
1975 1

Rube Waddell
Inducted in 1946

1936 33
1937 67
1938 148
1939 179
1942 126
1945 154
1946 122
1946 RO 87
1946 . . . . . . O/T Com.

Honus Wagner
Inducted in 1936

1936 V 5
1936 215

Rube Walberg

1958 1
1960 1

Dixie Walker

1962 1
1964 6
1968 6
1969 9

Harry Walker

1958 1

Bobby Wallace
Inducted in 1953

1936 V 1
1937 1
1938 7
1939 5
1942 2
1945 3
1953 . . . . . Vet. Com.

Ed Walsh
Inducted in 1946

1936 20
1937 56
1938 110
1939 132
1942 113
1945 137
1946 115
1946 RO 106
1946 . . . . . . O/T Com.

Bucky Walters

1950 4
1952 3
1953 10
1956 5
1958 33
1960 19
1962 5
1964 35
1964 RO 8
1966 56
1967 65
1967 RO 24
1968 67
1969 20
1970 29

Bill Wambsganss

1942 1
1950 1
1953 1
1954 4
1955 5
1956 1

Lloyd Waner
Inducted in 1967

1949 3
1950 1
1951 1
1952 2
1956 18
1958 39
1960 22
1962 5
1964 47
1964 RO 12
1967 . . . . . Vet. Com.

Paul Waner
Inducted in 1952

1946 4
1948 51
1949 73
1949 RO 63
1950 95
1951 162
1952 195

Monte Ward
Inducted in 1964

1936 V 3
1964 . . . . . Vet. Com.

Lon Warneke

1949 2
1958 2
1960 4
1962 2
1964 13

George Weiss
Inducted in 1971
Executive

1971 . . . . . Vet. Com.

Mickey Welch
Inducted in 1973

1973 . . . . . Vet. Com.

Billy Werber

1949 1
1950 1
1952 1
1958 3

Vic Wertz
1970	2
1971	2
1972	4
1973	4
1974	2
1975	5
1976	5
1977	4
1978	4

Sam West
1948	1

Wes Westrum
1964	2

Zach Wheat
Inducted in 1959
1937	5
1938	7
1939	4
1942	3
1945	2
1946	6
1947	37
1948	15
1949	15
1950	17
1951	19
1952	30
1953	32
1954	33
1955	51
1956	26
1959	Vet. Com.

Deacon White
1936 V	1

Will White
1975	7
1976	7
1977	4

Burgess Whitehead
1956	1

Earl Whitehill
1956	1
1958	2
1960	3

Hoyt Wilhelm
Inducted in 1985
1978	158
1979	168
1980	209
1981	238
1982	236
1983	243
1984	290
1985	331

Billy Williams
Inducted in 1987
1982	97
1983	153
1984	202
1985	252
1986	315
1987	354

Fred Williams
1938	1
1945	1
1948	1
1949	2
1950	9
1951	7
1952	4
1953	4
1954	4
1955	3
1956	11
1958	6
1960	11

Ken Williams
1956	1

1958	1

Ted Williams
Inducted in 1966
1966	282

Ned Williamson
1936 V	2

Maury Wills
1978	115
1979	166
1980	146
1981	163
1982	91
1983	77
1984	104
1985	93
1986	124
1987	113
1988	127

Jimmie Wilson
1948	8
1949	6
1950	4
1951	2
1952	7
1953	10
1954	8
1955	13
1956	17
1958	3
1960	6
1962	4

Jim Wilson
1964	2

Hack Wilson
Inducted in 1979
1937	1
1939	1
1942	1
1948	2

1949	24
1949 RO	12
1950	16
1951	21
1952	21
1953	43
1954	48
1955	81
1956	74
1958	94
1960	72
1962	39
1979	Vet. Com.

Whitey Witt
1949	1

Joe Wood
1937	13
1938	6
1939	2
1942	1
1946	5
1947	29
1948	5
1950	1
1951	5

Wilbur Wood
1984	14
1985	16
1986	23
1987	26
1988	30

Glenn Wright
1948	2
1949	1
1950	2
1951	1
1952	1
1953	3
1954	1
1955	4
1956	3

1958	8
1960	18
1962	1

George Wright
Inducted in 1937
Pioneer
1936 V	6
1937	Cen. Com.

Harry Wright
Inducted in 1953
Pioneer
1953	Vet. Com.

Whit Wyatt
1958	1

Early Wynn
Inducted in 1972
1969	95
1970	140
1971	240
1972	301

Tom Yawkey
Inducted in 1980
Executive
1980	Vet. Com.

Steve Yerkes
1945	1

Rudy York
1962	1
1964	10

Cy Young
Inducted in 1937
1936 V	32
1936	111
1937	153

Pep Young
1958	1

Ross Youngs
Inducted in 1972
1936	10
1937	16
1938	40
1939	34
1942	44
1945	22
1946	25
1947	36
1948	19
1949	20
1949 RO	11
1950	17
1951	34
1952	34
1953	31
1954	34
1955	48
1956	19
1972	Vet. Com.

Tom Zachary
1958	1
1960	1

Chief Zimmer
1938	1

Hall of Fame Balloting: Top Ten Candidates in Each Election

1936 Veterans
Needed to Elect: 59
Cap Anson	39.5
Buck Ewing	39.5
Willie Keeler	33.0
Cy Young	32.5
Ed Delahanty	21.5
John McGraw	17.0
Charlie Radbourn	16.0
Herman Long	15.5
Mike Kelly	15.0
Amos Rusie	11.5

1936
Needed to Elect: 170
Ty Cobb	222
Babe Ruth	215
Honus Wagner	215
C. Mathewson	205
Walter Johnson	189
Nap Lajoie	146
Tris Speaker	133
Cy Young	111
Rogers Hornsby	105
Mickey Cochrane	80

1937
Needed to Elect: 151
Nap Lajoie	168
Tris Speaker	165
Cy Young	153
Pete Alexander	125
Eddie Collins	115
Willie Keeler	115
George Sisler	106
Ed Delahanty	70
Rube Waddell	67
Jimmy Collins	66

1938
Needed to Elect: 197
Pete Alexander	212
George Sisler	179
Willie Keeler	177
Eddie Collins	175
Rube Waddell	148
Frank Chance	133
Ed Delahanty	132
Ed Walsh	110
Johnny Evers	91
Jimmy Collins	79

1939
Needed to Elect: 206
George Sisler	235
Eddie Collins	213
Willie Keeler	207
Rube Waddell	179
Rogers Hornsby	176
Frank Chance	158
Ed Delahanty	145
Ed Walsh	132
Johnny Evers	107
Miller Huggins	97

1942
Needed to Elect: 175
Rogers Hornsby	182
Frank Chance	136
Rube Waddell	126
Ed Walsh	113
Miller Huggins	111
Ed Delahanty	104
Johnny Evers	91
Wilbert Robinson	89
Mickey Cochrane	88
Frankie Frisch	84

1945
Needed to Elect: 185
Frank Chance	179
Rube Waddell	154
Ed Walsh	137
Johnny Evers	134
Roger Bresnahan	133
Miller Huggins	133
Mickey Cochrane	125
Jimmy Collins	121
Ed Delahanty	111
Clark Griffith	108

1946
Needed to Elect: 152
Frank Chance	144
Johnny Evers	130
Miller Huggins	129
Rube Waddell	122
Ed Walsh	115
Frankie Frisch	104
Carl Hubbell	101
Mickey Cochrane	80
Clark Griffith	73
Lefty Grove	71

1946 Run Off
Needed to Elect: 197
One Player Maximum
Frank Chance	150
Johnny Evers	110
Miller Huggins	106
Ed Walsh	106
Rube Waddell	87
Clark Griffith	82
Carl Hubbell	75
Frankie Frisch	67
Mickey Cochrane	65
Lefty Grove	61

1947
Needed to Elect: 121
Carl Hubbell	140
Frankie Frisch	136
Mickey Cochrane	128
Lefty Grove	123
Pie Traynor	119
Charlie Gehringer	105
Rabbit Maranville	91
Dizzy Dean	88
Herb Pennock	86
Chief Bender	72

1948
Needed to Elect: 91
Herb Pennock	94
Pie Traynor	93
Al Simmons	60
Charlie Gehringer	52
Bill Terry	52
Paul Waner	51
Jimmie Foxx	50
Dizzy Dean	40
Harry Heilmann	40
Bill Dickey	39

1949
Needed to Elect: 115
Charlie Gehringer	102
Mel Ott	94
Al Simmons	89
Dizzy Dean	88
Jimmie Foxx	85
Bill Terry	81
Paul Waner	73
Hank Greenberg	67
Bill Dickey	65
Harry Heilmann	59

1949 Run Off
Needed to Elect: 140
One Player Maximum
Charlie Gehringer	159
Mel Ott	128
Jimmie Foxx	89
Dizzy Dean	81
Al Simmons	76
Paul Waner	63
Harry Heilmann	52
Bill Terry	48
Hank Greenberg	44
Bill Dickey	39
Rabbit Maranville	39

1950
Needed to Elect: 125
Mel Ott	115
Bill Terry	105
Jimmie Foxx	103
Paul Waner	95
Al Simmons	90
Harry Heilmann	87
Dizzy Dean	85
Bill Dickey	78
Rabbit Maranville	66
Hank Greenberg	64

1951
Needed to Elect: 170
Mel Ott	197
Jimmie Foxx	179
Paul Waner	162
Harry Heilmann	153
Bill Terry	148
Dizzy Dean	145
Bill Dickey	118
Al Simmons	116
Rabbit Maranville	110
Ted Lyons	71

1952
Needed to Elect: 176
Harry Heilmann	203
Paul Waner	195
Bill Terry	155
Dizzy Dean	152
Al Simmons	141
Bill Dickey	139
Rabbit Maranville	133
Dazzy Vance	105
Ted Lyons	101
Gabby Hartnett	77

1953
Needed to Elect: 198
Dizzy Dean	209
Al Simmons	199
Bill Terry	191

Bill Dickey 179
Rabbit Maranville . 164
Dazzy Vance 150
Ted Lyons 139
Joe DiMaggio . . . 117
Chief Bender 104
Gabby Hartnett . . 104

1954
Needed to Elect: 189

Rabbit Maranville . 209
Bill Dickey 202
Bill Terry 195
Joe DiMaggio . . . 175
Ted Lyons 170
Dazzy Vance 158
Gabby Hartnett . . 151
Hank Greenberg . . . 97
Joe Cronin 85
Max Carey 55

1955
Needed to Elect: 188

Joe DiMaggio . . . 223
Ted Lyons 217
Dazzy Vance 205
Gabby Hartnett . . 195
Hank Greenberg . 157
Joe Cronin 135
Max Carey 119
Ray Schalk 113
Edd Roush 97
Hank Gowdy 90

1956
Needed to Elect: 145

Hank Greenberg . 164
Joe Cronin 152
Red Ruffing 97
Edd Roush 91
Lefty Gomez 89
Hack Wilson 74
Max Carey 65
Tony Lazzeri . . . 64
Kiki Cuyler 55
Hank Gowdy 49

1958
Needed to Elect: 200

Max Carey 136
Edd Roush 112
Red Ruffing 99
Hack Wilson 94
Kiki Cuyler 90
Sam Rice 90
Tony Lazzeri . . . 80
Luke Appling . . . 77
Lefty Gomez . . . 76
Burleigh Grimes . 71

1960
Needed to Elect: 202

Edd Roush 146
Sam Rice 143
Eppa Rixey 142
Burleigh Grimes . . 92
Jim Bottomley . . 89
Red Ruffing 86
Red Faber 83
Luke Appling . . . 72
Kiki Cuyler 72
Hack Wilson 72

1962
Needed to Elect: 120

Bob Feller 150

Jackie Robinson . . 124
Sam Rice 81
Red Ruffing 72
Eppa Rixey 49
Luke Appling . . . 48
Phil Rizzuto 44
Burleigh Grimes . . 43
Hack Wilson 39
Ducky Medwick . . . 34

1964
Needed to Elect: 151

Luke Appling . . . 142
Red Ruffing 141
Roy Campanella . 115
Ducky Medwick . . 108
Pee Wee Reese . . 73
Lou Boudreau . . . 68
Al Lopez 57
Chuck Klein 56
Johnny Mize . . . 54
Mel Harder 51
Johnny Vander Meer 51

1964 Run Off
Needed to Elect: 170
One Player Maximum

Luke Appling . . . 189
Red Ruffing 184
Roy Campanella . 138
Ducky Medwick . 130
Pee Wee Reese . . 47
Lou Boudreau . . . 43
Al Lopez 34
Johnny Vander Meer 20
Chuck Klein 18
Marty Marion . . . 17

1966
Needed to Elect: 227

Ted Williams . . . 282
Red Ruffing 208
Roy Campanella . 197
Ducky Medwick . 187
Lou Boudreau . . . 115
Al Lopez 109
Enos Slaughter . 100
Pee Wee Reese . . 95
Marty Marion . . . 86
Johnny Mize . . . 81

1967
Needed to Elect: 219

Ducky Medwick . 212
Red Ruffing 212
Roy Campanella . 204
Lou Boudreau . . . 143
Ralph Kiner . . . 124
Enos Slaughter . 123
Al Lopez 114
Marty Marion . . . 90
Johnny Mize . . . 89
Pee Wee Reese . . 89

1967 Run Off
Needed to Elect: 230
One Player Maximum

Red Ruffing 266
Ducky Medwick . 248
Roy Campanella . 170
Lou Boudreau . . . 68
Al Lopez 50
Enos Slaughter . 48
Ralph Kiner 41

Johnny Vander Meer 35
Ernie Lombardi . . . 25
Bucky Walters . . . 24

1968
Needed to Elect: 212

Ducky Medwick . . 240
Roy Campanella . 205
Lou Boudreau . . . 146
Enos Slaughter . . 129
Ralph Kiner 118
Johnny Mize . . . 103
Allie Reynolds . . 95
Marty Marion . . . 89
Arky Vaughan . . . 82
Pee Wee Reese . . 81

1969
Needed to Elect: 255

Stan Musial 317
Roy Campanella . 270
Lou Boudreau . . . 218
Ralph Kiner 137
Enos Slaughter . 128
Johnny Mize . . . 116
Marty Marion . . . 112
Allie Reynolds . . 98
Joe Gordon 97
Johnny Vander Meer 95
Early Wynn 95

1970
Needed to Elect: 225

Lou Boudreau . . . 232
Ralph Kiner 167
Gil Hodges 145
Early Wynn 140
Enos Slaughter . 133
Johnny Mize . . . 126
Marty Marion . . . 120
Pee Wee Reese . . 97
Red Schoendienst . 97
George Kell 90

1971
Needed to Elect: 270

Yogi Berra 242
Early Wynn 240
Ralph Kiner 212
Gil Hodges 180
Enos Slaughter . 165
Johnny Mize . . . 157
Pee Wee Reese . . 127
Marty Marion . . . 123
Red Schoendienst . 123
Allie Reynolds . . 110

1972
Needed to Elect: 297

Sandy Koufax . . . 344
Yogi Berra 339
Early Wynn 301
Ralph Kiner 235
Gil Hodges 161
Johnny Mize . . . 157
Enos Slaughter . 149
Pee Wee Reese . . 129
Marty Marion . . . 120
Bob Lemon 117

1973
Needed to Elect: 285

Warren Spahn . . . 316

Whitey Ford 255
Ralph Kiner 235
Gil Hodges 218
Robin Roberts . . . 213
Bob Lemon 177
Johnny Mize . . . 157
Enos Slaughter . 145
Marty Marion . . . 127
Pee Wee Reese . . 126

1974
Needed to Elect: 274

Mickey Mantle . . 322
Whitey Ford 284
Robin Roberts . . . 224
Ralph Kiner 215
Gil Hodges 198
Bob Lemon 190
Enos Slaughter . 145
Pee Wee Reese . . 141
Eddie Mathews . 118
Phil Rizzuto . . . 111
Duke Snider . . . 111

1975
Needed to Elect: 272

Ralph Kiner 273
Robin Roberts . . . 263
Bob Lemon 233
Gil Hodges 188
Enos Slaughter . 177
Hal Newhouser . . 155
Pee Wee Reese . 154
Eddie Mathews . 148
Phil Cavaretta . 129
Duke Snider . . . 129

1976
Needed to Elect: 291

Robin Roberts . . . 337
Bob Lemon 305
Gil Hodges 233
Enos Slaughter . 197
Eddie Mathews . 189
Pee Wee Reese . 186
Nellie Fox 174
Duke Snider . . . 159
Phil Rizzuto . . . 149
George Kell . . . 129
Red Schoendienst . 129

1977
Needed to Elect: 287

Ernie Banks 321
Eddie Mathews . 239
Gil Hodges 224
Enos Slaughter . 222
Duke Snider . . . 212
Don Drysdale . . 197
Pee Wee Reese . 163
Nellie Fox 152
Jim Bunning . . 146
George Kell . . . 141

1978
Needed to Elect: 284

Eddie Mathews . 301
Enos Slaughter . 261
Duke Snider . . . 254
Gil Hodges 226

Don Drysdale . . . 219
Jim Bunning . . . 181
Pee Wee Reese . . 169
Richie Ashburn . 158
Hoyt Wilhelm . . 158
Nellie Fox 149

1979
Needed to Elect: 324

Willie Mays 409
Duke Snider . . . 308
Enos Slaughter . . 297
Gil Hodges 242
Don Drysdale . . 233
Nellie Fox 174
Hoyt Wilhelm . . 168
Maury Wills . . . 166
Red Schoendienst . 159
Jim Bunning . . . 147

1980
Needed to Elect: 289

Al Kaline 340
Duke Snider . . . 333
Don Drysdale . . 238
Gil Hodges 230
Hoyt Wilhelm . . 209
Jim Bunning . . . 177
Red Schoendienst . 164
Nellie Fox 161
Maury Wills . . . 146
Richie Ashburn . 134

1981
Needed to Elect: 301

Bob Gibson 337
Don Drysdale . . 243
Gil Hodges 241
Harmon Killebrew . 239
Hoyt Wilhelm . . 238
Juan Marichal . . 233
Nellie Fox 168
Red Schoendienst . 166
Jim Bunning . . . 164
Maury Wills . . . 163

1982
Needed to Elect: 311

Hank Aaron 406
Frank Robinson . . 370
Juan Marichal . . 305
Harmon Killebrew . 246
Hoyt Wilhelm . . 236
Don Drysdale . . 233
Gil Hodges 205
Luis Aparicio . . 174
Jim Bunning . . . 138
Red Schoendienst . 135

1983
Needed to Elect: 281

Brooks Robinson . 344
Juan Marichal . . 313
Harmon Killebrew . 269
Luis Aparicio . . 252
Hoyt Wilhelm . . 243
Don Drysdale . . 242
Gil Hodges 237
Nellie Fox 173

Billy Williams . . . 153
Red Schoendienst . 146

1984
Needed to Elect: 302

Luis Aparicio . . . 341
Harmon Killebrew . 335
Don Drysdale . . 316
Hoyt Wilhelm . . 290
Nellie Fox 246
Billy Williams . . 202
Jim Bunning . . . 201
Orlando Cepeda . 124
Tony Oliva 124
Roger Maris . . . 107

1985
Needed to Elect: 297

Hoyt Wilhelm . . 331
Lou Brock 315
Nellie Fox 295
Billy Williams . . 252
Jim Bunning . . . 214
Catfish Hunter . . 212
Roger Maris . . . 128
Harvey Kuenn . . 125
Orlando Cepeda . 114
Tony Oliva 114

1986
Needed to Elect: 319

Willie McCovey . . 346
Billy Williams . . . 315
Catfish Hunter . . 289
Jim Bunning . . . 279
Roger Maris . . . 177
Tony Oliva 154
Orlando Cepeda . 152
Harvey Kuenn . . 144
Maury Wills . . . 124
Bill Mazeroski . . 100

1987
Needed to Elect: 310

Billy Williams . . . 354
Catfish Hunter . . 315
Jim Bunning . . . 289
Orlando Cepeda . 179
Roger Maris . . . 176
Tony Oliva 160
Harvey Kuenn . . 144
Bill Mazeroski . . 125
Maury Wills . . . 113
Ken Boyer 96
Lew Burdette . . . 96

1988
Needed to Elect: 320

Willie Stargell . . 352
Jim Bunning . . . 317
Tony Oliva 202
Orlando Cepeda . 199
Roger Maris . . . 184
Harvey Kuenn . . 168
Bill Mazeroski . . 143
Luis Tiant 132
Maury Wills . . . 127
Ken Boyer 109
Mickey Lolich . . 109

## CHAPTER 21

Baseball Lore

Eliot Cohen

Throughout this volume you'll find plenty of baseball history, verified down to the slightest nuance and the thousandth decimal place. But there is some history that is as important to the game's life as any pennant race or hitting streak, even though it may or may not be absolutely, positively, guaranteed true. To that end, here's a by no means complete sampling of baseball's lore.

When the Pope came to the United States, a small boy was impressed by the abundant pageantry of the papal motorcade. He stared at the big cars, the robes, the cheering throng lining the sidewalks for miles. After the pontiff had passed, the boy asked his mother, "How'd he get to be Pope?"

The cardinals selected him.

The boy pondered a moment, then mused, "You think the Giants would do something like that for Willie Mays?"

Classic baseball tales come in several flavors. One variety is passed down through generations, not only in the telling from parent to child, but in character, from Walter Johnson to Nolan Ryan, Babe Herman to Marv Throneberry. The measure of that story may be the number of characters it is (or could be) told about. Other tales revolve around the historic events of the game. A third type grows out of the outstanding personalities in the game. Certain unique figures stand out, but the folklore mirrors the transcendental nature of the game itself. If that prospect can't be the next Hank Aaron or Ty Cobb, maybe he can be the next Mickey Rivers.

> *"I only have trouble with fly balls."*
> —*Carmelo Martinez, outfielder*

It didn't take long for baseball fact to spawn baseball legend. The poem "Casey at the Bat" was written in 1888, and it became an instant classic. Its subtitle, "A Ballad of the Republic," indicates that author Ernest Lawrence Thayer was thinking big. The poem laid the foundation for much of baseball folklore to come, not only because it captured the spirit of the game and its fans, but because Casey failed to get that big hit. In baseball, failure is much more common than success, and some of the best anecdotes and quips are made in response to shortcomings.

Some fail by overreaching, such as erstwhile base stealer Ping Bodie. "He had larceny in his heart, but his feet were honest," observed sportswriter Bugs Baer. Some underachieve, like Commissioner Bowie Kuhn during the 1981 baseball strike. "If Bowie Kuhn were alive today, he'd do something about the strike," wrote Red Smith.

The great Honus Wagner had big hands to go with his bowed legs and didn't always discriminate between ground balls and other loose objects in the infield. He used to tell about when a rabbit ran past him about the same time as a two-hopper. Wagner scooped up both and fired the rabbit to first. "I got the runner by a hare," Wagner confided.

Catcher Bob Uecker took issue with the theory that the knuckler's tough to catch. "You just wait until it stops rolling, then pick it up." The catcher/broadcaster/actor proclaimed that he was proudest of his role in the Cardinals' 1964 pennant drive. His contribution? "I came down with hepatitis." How'd he catch it? "I think the trainer injected me with it."

But few players can joke about their foibles. During the 1910s, Ring Lardner invented a ballplayer named Alibi Ike, honoring a tradition that survives among players. Pitcher Billy Loes once explained missing a grounder by saying, "I lost it in the sun." Loes also cautioned pitchers, "If you win twenty games, they'll want you to do it every year," so he set a personal limit of fourteen. During the 1980s, a member of the Pirates complained, "I wish they wouldn't play that song. Every time they play it, we lose." He was talking about "The Star Spangled Banner." Upon seeing the Astrodome, Gabe Paul's first reaction was "It will revolutionize baseball. It will open a whole new area of alibis for players."

The game has a way of revealing character and exposing flaws.

Leo Durocher told the story (but it could just as well have been Connie Mack or Whitey Herzog) of a horse who asked him for a tryout after a spring training workout. Durocher obliged, sent the nag into the batting cage, and served up a fat pitch. Holding the bat between its teeth, the horse smacked the offering over the fence. The horse hit the curve the other way, got around on the hard stuff, handling the bat better than anyone Durocher had on the club.

So he sent the horse to the outfield and hit it fungoes. The horse caught the ball between its teeth and drop kicked it back to the infield. An impressed Durocher began considering the steed's potential. He called the horse in and said, "Okay, now I want to see you run."

The horse said, "If I could run, would I be here looking for a job?"

Chicago Cubs manager Charlie Grimm told about a kid who approached him at a tryout camp during World War Two, when the military draft had strapped the majors for talent. "I'm 4-F," the aspirant announced, meaning he'd been rejected by the Army, "but I can hit like Ted Williams, throw as fast as Dizzy Dean, and play the outfield like Joe DiMaggio."

"You're nuts," Grimm grumbled.

"Sure. That's why I'm 4-F."

There's a surprising range of ways to fail in baseball. Aside from imparting strategy, signs appear to be designed to give

players a chance to make mistakes, judging from all the talk of missed signs throughout history. John McGraw and Wilbert Robinson were friends for three decades, and McGraw hired Robinson as a coach for the Giants. Their relationship ended in acrimony when McGraw accused Robinson of missing a sign and costing the Giants a game. McGraw fined outfielder Red Murray for failing to obey a bunt sign with a runner on second, even though Murray had taken a high and tight serving that would have been nearly impossible to bunt and belted it for a homer.

Durocher once took refuge in the press box after being tossed from a game, then conspired with a sportswriter to give signs. The system worked until the sportswriter wiped his forehead. "What did you do that for?" Durocher blurted. "You just gave the steal sign."

First baseman Rocky Nelson missed a squeeze sign with Pee Wee Reese on third. Nelson swung away and nearly decapitated Reese. The livid shortstop and team captain demanded, "Why'd you swing?"

Nelson replied, "Why do you think they call me Rocky?"

When Frank Howard was with the Dodgers, they used verbal signals. The player's last name signaled a hit and run. So after the big man walked, first base coach Pete Reiser began giving him encouragement, "Okay, *Howard*, be on your toes. Be ready for anything, *Howard*."

Howard called time and told Reiser, "We're good friends, Pete. Call me Frank."

After the Dodgers infield of Steve Garvey at first, Dave Lopes at second, Bill Russell at short, and Ron Cey at third broke up after an unprecedented run from 1974 through 1981, Tom Lasorda tried to make do with Pedro Guerrero, whose best position is DH, at third base, revolving doors at short and first, and second baseman Steve Sax, who sought help from a hypnotist to overcome a chronic inability to make the throw to first. As only Lasorda can, he cajoled, begged, and badgered Guerrero to make him a better infielder. After one galling loss, Lasorda tried to get inside his star's head. "Okay, Pedro," Lasorda said, "the tying run's on, one out in the ninth. What are you thinking?"

Guerrero answered, "I'm thinking, don't hit the ball to me."

"C'mon, Pete," Lasorda chided, "what else are you thinking?"

"You really want to know?"

"Yes."

"I'm thinking," Guerrero said, "don't hit the ball to Sax either."

Lasorda is generally considered a teddy-bear type manager, but other skippers inspire fear in their players. Playing in Houston before the Astrodome was built, Gene Mauch's fiery temper erupted at the Phillies' constant complaints about the heat. "I'm sick and tired of you guys griping about the climate," Mauch began. "The other guys have to play in it, too. The next guy who complains about the heat gets fined a hundred bucks."

After the Phils' next turn in the field, right fielder Johnny Callison came back to the dugout and fell in a heap on the bench. "God, is it hot out there," he moaned. Then he saw Mauch out of the corner of his eye and, remembering the edict, quickly added, "Good and hot, just the way I like it."

Even the great Lou Gehrig had trouble performing on cue. He was scheduled to do a live radio spot for a cereal called Huskies. The announcer asked the slugger, "To what do you owe your strength and condition?"

"Wheaties," Gehrig told the listeners.

The makers of Huskies insisted that Gehrig's error brought them more publicity than the script would have. But Gehrig found endorsement offers rare after that.

The knuckleball can be equally elusive. Fluttering up to the plate at a half to two-thirds the speed of a fastball, the knuckler is difficult to master, an adventure to catch, and nearly impossible to hit.

After his Brooklyn Dodgers lost on a ninth-inning homer, Casey Stengel asked catcher Babe Phelps why he'd called for a fastball from famed knuckleballer Dutch Leonard. "His knuckler's tough to catch," Phelps explained.

"If his knuckler's tough to catch, don't you think it might be a little tough to hit, too?" Casey asked.

Famed batting coach Charley Lau said, "There are two theories about hitting the knuckleball. Unfortunately, neither works." Bobby Murcer observed that trying to hit flutterballer Phil Niekro was "like eating Jell-O with chopsticks."

"You can't hit what you can't see."
—Joe Tinker reviews Rube Marquard

Fastball pitchers have been a staple of baseball legends since the overhand delivery was legalized in 1884. Walter Johnson, Lefty Grove, Bob Feller, Sandy Koufax, and Nolan Ryan inherited the mantle of their respective generations as the king of the radio ball—you heard it, but you couldn't see it.

After striking out on three Johnson fastballs, no less an authority than Babe Ruth told the umpire, "You know, I didn't see any of them either, but the last one sounded kind of high to me." Writer Bugs Baer believed that Grove "could throw a lamb chop past a wolf." Manager Bucky Harris offered his Senators these instructions for facing Feller: "Go up and hit what you see. If you don't see it, come on back." Willie Stargell paid lefthander Steve Carlton a high compliment when he admitted, "Sometimes I hit him like I used to hit Koufax, and that's like drinking coffee with a fork." Reggie Jackson labeled Ryan baseball's exorcist because "he scares the devil out of you."

Walter Johnson didn't have the colorful personality to make himself a legend, just his fastball, but that was enough. Ray Chapman walked away from home plate after taking two strikes from Johnson. You've another strike coming, the umpire called. "Keep it. I don't want it," Chapman said and kept on walking.

A figure of grandfatherly kindness even as a rookie, Johnson was said to lay a fat pitch in for a needy hitter once a game was no longer in doubt. "Ol' Barney" also feared hitting batters, although his career total of 206 hit batsmen tops the all-time list.

Feller, like Koufax and Ryan to follow, was nearly as wild as he was fast. One overcast day, Yankee pitcher Lefty Gomez had to face Feller in the gloaming. Gomez, who earned the nickname Goofy, brought a book of matches to the plate, lit one, and held it over his head as he stepped into the batter's box.

"You think that match is going to help you see Feller's fast one?" the umpire snarled.

"You got it all wrong," Gomez explained. "I just want to make sure he can see me."

Gomez was quicker with this tongue than his fastball. Still,

he won nearly 65 percent of his decisions over fourteen seasons and went 6–0 in five World Series, earning his ticket to Cooperstown in 1972, attributing his success to "clean living and swift outfielders." Of the two components, only one can be confirmed.

On occasion, an outfielder, even a great one, might come up short. Rookie Joe DiMaggio, who roomed with Gomez on the road for several seasons, bragged, "I'm going to make 'em forget about Tris Speaker." He crept in to play a shallow center field like the Gray Eagle behind Gomez, and in the late innings, a drive to center outpaced DiMaggio for a triple, allowing the deciding runs to score.

At dinner with teammates after the game, DiMaggio was still saying that he was going to make the fans forget about Speaker. Gomez had had enough. "If you don't back up a little," he told the rookie, "you'll make 'em forget about Gomez."

Facing Jimmie Foxx in a tight game, Gomez shook off catcher Bill Dickey's signs for a fastball, changeup, and curve. So Dickey called time and angrily walked out to the mound. "You tell me what you want to throw," he snarled.

"Well, to tell you truth," Gomez replied, "I don't want to throw the ball at all."

Yankee second baseman Tony Lazzeri had a reputation for heady play. So, in a bases-loaded jam, Gomez snared a comebacker, whirled, and threw to Lazzeri, who was stationed on the edge of the infield grass between first and second. When Lazzeri recovered from the shock, he charged toward Gomez and screamed, "Why in hell did you throw the ball to me?"

"I'd been reading in the papers how smart you are, and how you always know what to do with the ball," Gomez cooed. "Well, I wanted to see what you'd do with that one."

Gomez's antics often infuriated straitlaced Yankee skipper Joe McCarthy. Gomez loved airplanes and would step off the mound to watch any plane passing overhead. After one particularly long break for aerial observation, McCarthy jumped all over Gomez at the end of the inning. "Keep your mind in the game," he scolded. "With you daydreaming like that, I'm surprised they didn't start knocking the ball out of the park."

"Izzatso?" Gomez replied. "I had ahold of the ball all the time I was watching the plane, didn't I? How could they knock it out of the park?" Gomez was always a firm believer in working slowly, "because as long as I have it, they can't hit it." (Fast-working Grover Cleveland Alexander took the opposite approach, reasoning, "What do you want me to do? Let 'em stand up there and think on my time?") When asked if he ever threw the spitball, Gomez demurred, "Not intentionally, but I sweat easily."

McCarthy once saw a bright red biplane doing some death-defying stunts above the ballfield and told Gomez about it over dinner. "You missed a real crackpot flier," he said. "It would have taught you a lesson. I hope you saw it."

"Well, not exactly," Gomez told the skipper. "I was in it."

McCarthy also found fault with Gomez's build, thinking he was too skinny to be a consistent winner. "If you had another fifteen or twenty pounds of meat on you, you'd make them forget every lefthander that ever tossed a ball."

Gomez followed McCarthy's advice and did add twenty pounds, but he had an uncharacteristically bad season on the mound. Near the end of the year, Gomez spoke with his manager. "You told me if I put on some weight, I'd make 'em forget every lefthander that ever pitched. Trouble is, when they start forgetting lefthanders, they're going to start with Gomez."

At the 1934 All-Star Game, catcher Gabby Hartnett reprimanded Gomez, owner of a .147 career batting average. "Are you trying to insult Mister Hubbell," Hartnett asked, "coming up here with a bat?" Gomez bragged that he once broke a bat. "I ran it over in the driveway."

Gomez inherited the flaky lefthander tradition from Rube Waddell, the first oddball player of the twentieth century. Waddell made a show of his trade, pouring water over his arm to cool it off and thus prevent his heat from burning off his catcher's mitt. Waddell liked to fish and chase fire engines, ready to spring off the mound in midgame for either. (Fortunately for his teammates, fish didn't roll past the ballpark with their alarms blaring.) At an Easter Sunday 1900 exhibition game, the lefty was pelted on the head with an egg. In response, he called in his fielders and struck out the side on nine pitches. Waddell wore out a number of managers until he bounced back to the Pacific Coast League in 1902. Connie Mack wanted him for his A's and dispatched two detectives to bring him back.

A pair of Pinkertons were hardly enough to keep Waddell under control in Philadelphia. On days when he wasn't pitching, and on some when he was supposed to be, Waddell could be found at bars, firehouses, playgrounds, the heads of parades, or under the stands shooting marbles with youngsters.

Catcher Ossee Schreckengost was Waddell's roommate and fellow carouser. The two were of similar mind on most issues, but one divisive item nearly ended their friendship. (History is unclear on the offender, but here's the better version of the story.) After a typically successful season, Waddell informed Connie Mack that he wouldn't sign his contract for the upcoming season. Mack, whose creativity had been stretched to the limits, he thought, to accommodate his southpaw, had already offered Waddell time off for fishing if he'd complete both ends of a doubleheader, had allowed him liberal visitation rights to local firehouses, and stood ready with bail money on those not infrequent occasions when the lefty required it.

So what was it Waddell wanted now? Well, in that era, players often shared beds on the road. Waddell had no problem with splitting the mattress, but objected to Schreckengost's habit of eating crackers on it. So Mack wrote in a contract provision banning the practice, and Waddell was booked for another season.

Otherwise, the battery mates got along famously. The catcher was hovering over Waddell's bandaged body when the pitcher awoke in a hospital after a huge drunk with the boys the night before. "How'd I get here?" Waddell asked.

Schreckengost explained that Waddell insisted he could fly, and when his teammates ridiculed the idea, the pitcher leaped out the second-story window, flapping his arms.

"Why didn't you stop me?" Waddell implored.

"What? And lose the hundred bucks I bet on you?"

Waddell had more success on the ground. While watching an alligator wrestler, Waddell asked for a shot at the reptile. The alligator never had a chance. In 1904, Waddell opened a five-game series against the Red Sox with a one-hitter, allowing a bunt single to the leadoff man, then retiring the next twenty-seven hitters. A cocky Waddell was scheduled to pitch the series finale and warned his opponent, "I'm going to give you the same thing." The opponent was a thirty-seven-year-old veteran named Cy Young, who responded to the challenge

by pitching a perfect game. Alligators were simpler foes.

Satchel Paige copied Waddell's stunt of calling in the outfield. But Paige had plenty of stories of his own to tell. The oldest rookie in major league history, Paige claimed he was thirty-nine (he was at least forty-two, probably closer to fifty) when he signed with the Indians in 1948. He challenged the nation to find records of him pitching before 1927. When one of his clippings from 1926 turned up, Paige explained that a billy goat had eaten his birth certificate and asked, "How old would you be if you didn't know how old you was?" Paige also noted, "Age is a question of mind over matter; if you don't mind, it don't matter."

Paige's routines included using a gum wrapper as his home plate, the hesitation pitch, and his be-ball, so named because "it's always where I want it to be." Paige also reminded white fans of his contemporaries in the Negro Leagues. Lists of the greatest fastballers of all time were no longer complete without Bullet Joe Rogan and Smokey Joe Williams. Testimony that Josh Gibson hit a ball out of Yankee Stadium became more credible. Paige was fond of telling about an offering that Gibson hit back between the pitcher's legs that sailed over the fence. That was nothing compared to Cool Papa Bell, who, according to Paige, "hit a line drive by me that hit him on the ass when he was sliding into second."

Paige also offered six rules for staying young. Considering that he last appeared in a major league game in 1965, at age fifty-nine or more, they're worth repeating:

- Avoid fried meats, which angry up the blood.
- If your stomach disputes you, lie down and pacify it with cool thoughts.
- Keep the juices flowing by jangling around gently as you move.
- Go very light on the vices, such as carrying on in society. The social ramble ain't restful.
- Avoid running at all times.
- Don't look back. Something might be gaining on you.

Dizzy Dean combined devastating stuff, a gift for malapropisms, and a dose of braggadocio when he burst on the scene with the Cardinals in 1931. "The good Lord was good to me," Dean conceded when inducted into the Hall of Fame in 1953. "He gave me a strong body, a good right arm, and a weak mind." In a doubleheader against the Dodgers, Dean pitched a three-hitter in the first game. His brother Paul pitched a no-hitter in the nightcap. "I wished I'd'a known Paul was goin' to pitch a no-hitter," Dizzy said. "I'd'a pitched one, too."

While the Deans were dominating the National League, Dizzy visited Brooklyn manager Casey Stengel between games of a doubleheader. Half in jest, Stengel asked, "Are there any more at home like you and Paul?"

"We got another brother, Elmer. He's down in Houston, burning up the league," Dizzy told Casey. "You might get him cheap."

Stengel couldn't contain his enthusiasm, and soon reporters were writing about the third Dean brother bound for Brooklyn. They stopped writing and started laughing when reports from the Texas League filtered back that Elmer was a peanut vendor at the Houston ballpark.

Dean once got caught out after curfew, along with three other Cardinals, in the midst of a pennant race. Manager Frankie Frisch fined all $200, except for Dean, whose fine was $400. When Dean complained to Frisch, the manager replied, "Why, Diz, you're not the same as those guys. You're the great Dizzy Dean. Everything about you has got to be bigger and better than anybody else. And that goes for fines, too." Dean had to agree.

Dean was fond of noting, "It ain't braggin' if you do it." Legend has it that Dean promised at a hospital ward to strike out Bill Terry, then the Giants' heavy hitter, with the bases loaded. So with runners on first and second and two out, Dean walked second baseman Hugh Critz, hardly a threat, to load the bases and bring up Terry. "I hate to do this, Bill," Dean told the slugger, "but I done promised a bunch of kids I'd fan you with the bases loaded." So Dean did, on three pitches.

In the 1934 World Series, Dean won the first and seventh games, and got beaned by a double-play relay throw while pinch-running in the fourth game. He was carried from the field, but was not seriously hurt. "The doctors X-rayed my head and found nothing," Dean proclaimed.

However, Joe Medwick upstaged Dean's antics in the '34 Series. The muscular left fielder was an exception to the happy-go-lucky Gashouse Gang that featured Dean and Pepper Martin. Medwick later became the only man in baseball history to knock out his own relief pitcher when hurler Ed Heusser passed an impertinent remark about Medwick's fielding in the dugout. But in the 1934 Series, Medwick reserved his ire for the Detroit Tigers, batting .379. In the seventh game, he slid into Detroit third baseman Marv Owen with his spikes high, business as usual for Medwick. The triple upped the Cards' advantage of 8–0 and moments later Medwick scored. When he returned to his post in left for the bottom of the sixth, Detroit fans added a barrage of garbage to their torrents of verbal abuse. As the debris rained onto the field, Commissioner Kenesaw Mountain Landis ordered Medwick off the field, the first player ever tossed for his own protection.

Dean understood public relations almost as well as pitching. When riding to the ballpark with a writer, Dean claimed he was puzzled by the science of locating gas stations. "Just how did these fellas know there was gas and oil under there?" he asked. When a reporter challenged him because he told every writer that he was born in a different place, Dean replied indignantly, "Them ain't lies, they's scoops."

A liner off the bat of Earl Averill struck Dean on the toe in the third inning of the 1937 All-Star Game. Billy Herman got the rebound and threw out Averill to end the inning, and Dean retired to the clubhouse with an aching toe. A doctor examined it and said it was fractured. "Fractured, hell," Dean moaned. "The damned thing's broke." The injury caused him to alter his delivery and hurt his arm. After helping the Cubs to a pennant in 1938 with an assortment of junk and hanging on for a couple more years, Dean had to retire when he was just thirty years old.

Dean stayed in the game as a broadcaster, to the exasperation of English teachers. When chided for his ungrammatical calls, Dean reminded his critics, "A lot of people who don't say 'ain't' ain't eating." When the St. Louis Board of Education circulated a petition against Dean's butchery of the language, Dean replied, "You learn 'em English, and I'll learn 'em baseball." With Dean at the mike, batters strode "confidentially" to the plate, players returned to their "respectable" bases, runners "slud," fielders "throwed," and "empires" made the calls. He urged listeners, "Don't fail to miss tomorrow's game."

While Dean was broadcasting for the St. Louis Browns in 1947, a team that lost 95 games, he didn't sugarcoat the

Browns' ineptitude. He'd suggested on the radio that he could do better than some of the Brown hurlers. So club president Bill DeWitt offered Dean a chance to start for the Browns, and Dean couldn't resist. So on September 28, 1947, more than six years after his last major league action, Dean went to the hill for the Browns against the White Sox. He held the Sox scoreless through four innings, but had to retire, for good, with a pulled leg muscle, suffered when he singled.

After the game, Dean beamed, "I said I could pitch as good as most of these fellows and I can. But I'll be doggoned if I'm ever going to try this stunt again. Talking's my game now, and I'm just glad that the muscle I pulled wasn't in my throat."

Catcher Moe Berg could speak a dozen languages, but couldn't hit in any of them. He went on to stardom with the U.S. intelligence service in World War Two. Dean's success as a broadcaster paved the way for other successful ex-players, some of whom approached his gift for mangling the English language. Jerry Coleman has had pitchers throwing up in the bullpen, outfielders lining up fly balls under the warning track, infielders chasing sun-blown pop-ups, runners sliding into second with stand-up doubles, and this memorable call: "There's a fly ball deep to center. Winfield is going back, back. He hits his head against the wall. It's rolling back toward second base."

Coleman's Yankee double-play partner Phil Rizzuto doesn't pay much attention to the game on the field, but has been known to take a stab at current events. When Curt Flood was holding out after his trade to Philadelphia, Rizzuto noted that he'd heard the center fielder was in Spain. "Maybe he's a matador," said Bill White, Scooter's partner in the booth. "Or maybe he's a bullfighter," Rizzuto parried.

Another Yankee teammate of Coleman's was Yogi Berra, who hit the Triple Crown when it came to folklore. He was ugly ("So what? You don't hit with your face."), he was good (a three-time MVP), and he had a gift for self-expression. Berra didn't try to be funny, as when a player's wife complimented him on looking cool on a sweltering afternoon. "Thanks, and you don't look so hot yourself," Yogi replied. When a clubhouse man asked for his cap size in spring training, Yogi shot back, "How should I know? I'm not in shape yet." In appreciation for Yogi Berra Day, he announced, "I want to thank everyone who made this day necessary." When his wife Carmen told him she'd seen (the movie) *Doctor Zhivago,* Berra shrugged, "What's the matter with you now?" When Berra played left field, he explained the shadows by saying, "It gets late early out there." When asked about a hitting slump, Berra asserted, "Slump? What slump? I just ain't hitting." Wary of the press, he warned reporters, "If you ask me something I don't know, I'm not going to answer." Berra contended, "It ain't over till it's over," and you can't argue with that.

Joe McCarthy tried to break Berra's habit of swinging at the first pitch, urging his catcher "to think when you're up there." After taking three strikes, Berra returned to the bench complaining, "How can a guy think and hit at the same time?" Another time, after fanning on three pitches way out of the strike zone, Berra wondered, "How can a pitcher that wild be in the big leagues?"

Some Yogi stories are less likely to be true, but no matter. When asked if he wanted his whole pizza in four or eight pieces, he said, "Better make it four. I don't think I can eat eight." When receiving a "Pay to Bearer" check, Yogi protested, "That's not how you spell my name." Berra was intro-

duced to Ernest Hemingway and told he was a writer. "What paper are you with, Ernie?" Berra asked. Talking about a restaurant, Berra said, "Nobody goes there anymore. It's too crowded." Similarly, he said one of his classmates in high school "was so popular, no one could stand him." Commenting on Mickey Mantle, he said that the switch-hitting slugger had equal power from both sides of the plate. "He's naturally amphibious." After seeing a Steve McQueen movie, Berra reasoned, "He must've made that one before he died."

When Berra visited the Vatican, he was quoted as greeting the Pontiff, "Hello, Pope." That follows the tradition of apocryphal greetings such as Casey Stengel's "Nice to meet you, King," to England's George V, and Babe Ruth's "Hot as hell, ain't it, Prez," to Warren Harding.

Despite his clownish reputation, Berra was a wise investor who made a great deal of money before ballplayers were millionaires. He also had a reputation for stinginess and was an inveterate borrower of locker room toiletries. Trouble came when Berra borrowed deodorant from Whitey Ford's locker after a game. Ford had discovered that a roll-on bottle was the perfect way to store a resin mixture that he used to get his fingers sticky. So when Berra used the roll-on bottle, he cemented his arms to his sides. The trainer had to cut the hair under his arms to free him.

Almost every manager tells the story of going out to the mound after his starter gives up six (give or take a couple) hits to start the game, all on the first pitch. The manager asks the catcher, "How's his stuff?"

"I'm not sure," the catcher replies. "I haven't caught any yet."

(In another version, the manager asks the catcher what pitch the batter hit for a home run. "I don't know," the catcher replies. "I haven't caught it yet.")

Cubs pitcher Bob Muncrief told about facing Ralph Kiner in 1949, when he was the most-feared slugger in the National League. Kiner took Muncrief deep, with a homer off the back wall of the Wrigley Field bleachers. Back in the dugout, manager Frankie Frisch asked what Kiner had hit. "A curveball," Muncrief told him. "He hit a good pitch."

"Well, forget about your curveball and just throw him fastballs next time up," Frisch counseled. "He won't even get a loud foul off you."

So when Kiner batted again with two mates aboard, Muncrief followed Frisch's advice and threw him a fastball. Kiner slugged it over the fence, over the bleachers, and out onto Waveland Avenue. When Muncrief got back to bench, he shouted at Frisch, "Well, brains, he hit yours a whole lot farther than he hit mine."

New York Giants reliever Don Liddle served up Vic Wertz's 425-foot smash to center in the 1954 World Series. Only Willie Mays's unbelievable catch and the Polo Grounds' huge center field dimensions prevented Wertz's clout from breaking the 2–2 tie wide open. Leo Durocher figured Liddle might not have his best stuff, so he summoned Marv Grissom to face the next hitter. As Grissom took the mound, Liddle told him, "Well, I got my guy."

When manager Pat Corrales came to get Jim Kern after a rough outing for the Ranger reliever, Kern complained, "I'm not tired."

"Yeah," Corrales concurred, "but your outfielders are."

Pitchers don't get much sympathy when they run into trouble, not even within their fraternity. In the Seattle Pilots' bullpen during a game, Skip Lockwood called to Jim Bouton

to ask, "Bouton, how do you hold your doubles?" When a young pitcher asked manager Lou Boudreau if pitching low to Ted Williams made sense, Boudreau advised, "Yeah, you can pitch him low, but as soon as you throw the ball, run and hide behind second base." Rudy May had his own method for handling George Brett: "The only way to pitch him is inside, so you force him to pull the ball. That way, the line drive won't hit you."

Carl Erskine wasn't shy about revealing his secret for handling Stan Musial. "I just throw him my best stuff, then run over to back up third base."

Sudden Sam McDowell of the Indians warned batters, "Trying to think with me is a mismatch. Hell, most of the time, I don't know where the pitch is going."

Sal "The Barber" Maglie earned his nickname for throwing at hitters he felt were getting a bit too cozy with the plate. "I don't want to get to know the other guys too well," Maglie said. "I might like them, and then I might not want to throw at them." One writer remarked that Maglie would throw at his mother if she crowded the plate. "You bet," the pitcher replied. "Mother was a hell of a hitter."

Mets pitcher Jerry Hinsley was a twenty-year-old rookie the first time he faced Willie Mays. The veterans advised him to knock down the great man. The righthander took their advice and decked Mays with his first pitch. Mays dusted himself off and clubbed Hinsley's next offering for a triple. "The problem was," Hinsley said, "they didn't tell me what to throw him on the second pitch."

Don Drysdale was another pitcher who believed in keeping batters loose. "The secret with Drysdale," confided Orlando Cepeda, "is to hit him before he hits you." Drysdale once apologized to Henry Aaron around the batting cage. "I'm sorry I hit you in the back last night, Henry. I meant to hit you in the neck."

Bob Gibson was a lean, mean competitor who worked so fast, it seemed there was a meter on the mound. He hated catchers' interruptions almost as much as he despised opposing batters. When receiver Tim McCarver came out to talk to Gibson in a tight spot, Bullet Bob stormed off the mound toward the catcher. "The only thing you know about pitching is that it's hard to hit!" Gibson screamed. "Now get out of here."

McCarver offered this Yogi-ism in tribute to the Cardinal ace: "That Bob Gibson is the luckiest pitcher ever. Whenever he pitches, the other team doesn't score." He was also the toughest. Gibson suffered a broken leg in 1967 on a drive hit back through the box; he threw the batter out and attempted to continue pitching. After his playing days, Gibson served as a coach under Cardinal teammate Joe Torre, imparting to pitchers his attitude as much as technique. "If there weren't fifteen thousand people watching," he told one staff member during a mound visit, "I'd hit you in the head."

Russ "Mad Monk" Meyer earned his nickname because of a one-in-a-million shot in his first start in Philadelphia after the Phils had traded him to the Brooklyn Dodgers. In the eighth inning of a tie game, Meyer and catcher Roy Campanella thought they'd struck out Richie Ashburn to end the inning. Campanella had rolled the ball to the mound, but umpire Augie Donatelli called the pitch a ball. Meyer went crazy, charging off the mound toward the umpire and calling him a "homer," preceded by several modifiers. So Donatelli gave Meyer the thumb, but Meyer wasn't through. He refused to leave the mound, even after manager Charlie

Dressen came out to get him, stomping and shouting. It wasn't until Donatelli threatened to fine him more money that Meyer decided he'd had enough and stalked off the mound, only to discover that he still had the resin bag clenched in his fist. So he whipped the bag into the air and kept stomping toward the dugout. Sure enough, the bag landed right in the middle of Meyer's cap and stuck there. Even Meyer had to laugh.

But by the time he got to the dugout, Meyer was mad all over again and wouldn't leave. He baited Donatelli into coming over to the dugout to get him off the field. As a parting gesture, Meyer grabbed his crotch. He didn't realize that he was a participant in one of the earliest nationally televised games, and his obscene gesture had been beamed to millions of viewers across the country. Commissioner Ford Frick was so disturbed by Meyer's display that he forbid cameras from shooting into the dugout.

When Hank Aguirre was a rookie with the Indians, his first assignment was Ted Williams. Unfamiliarity gave Aguirre an advantage over the Splendid Splinter, and he fanned Williams. After the game, Aguirre brought the strikeout ball into the Red Sox clubhouse and asked Williams to autograph it. Williams was probably too stunned to refuse.

A couple of weeks later, the Indians were facing the Red Sox again, and young Aguirre was called upon to face Williams. This time, the Thumper walloped Aguirre's first offering off the foul pole for a homer. As he rounded the bases, Williams yelled, "Get that ball, and I'll sign it, too."

Aguirre went on to be a pretty fair pitcher for the Tigers and other teams for sixteen years, but he had a career batting average of .085. But every dog has his day, or at least his at-bat, and one afternoon at Yankee Stadium, Aguirre teed off on an offering from Fritz Peterson for a triple. Peterson was beside himself, giving up a hit to a man who went 2 for 72 in 1962, and wasn't paying baserunner Aguirre the slightest mind. So Aguirre walked halfway down the line without drawing a look. On the second pitch, he got another walking lead unnoticed. Emboldened, Aguirre turned to the third base coach Tony Cuccinello and whispered, "Hey, Tony, I think I can steal home."

Cuccinello sighed and told Aguirre, "Hank, you got this far . . . don't screw it up."

Reliever Tug McGraw continued the line of flaky lefthanders during his twenty-year career. McGraw is credited with creating the 1973 Mets' battle cry, "You gotta believe." It all started when M. Donald Grant, the Mets' stodgy chairman of the board, came down to the clubhouse to give a speech that included the soon-to-be-famous war cry. Sitting in the back row like any good class clown, McGraw repeated the line, then stood up and did it again. The other players, inspired by this chance to cut Grant short, joined in.

Originally a starter and the owner of the Mets' first victory over Sandy Koufax, McGraw found his niche as a reliever. He had the perfect attitude for the job: "Some days you tame the tiger. And other days the tiger has you for lunch." McGraw, who pitched during an era of unprecedented salary escalation, once commented on a contract, "Ninety percent, I'll spend on good times, women, and Irish whiskey. The rest, I'll probably waste." When asked whether he preferred grass or artificial turf during the more innocent decade of the seventies, McGraw replied, "I don't know, I never smoked Astroturf." (Dick Allen's spin on this question was, "If a horse can't eat it, I don't want to play on it.")

Bill Lee was another flaky lefty. Since the right hemisphere of the brain controls the left side, Lee contended that "lefties are the only ones in their right minds." Lee and a handful of other Red Sox players formed the Loyal Order of Buffalo Heads, dedicated to ridiculing manager Don Zimmer. The name was suggested by Ferguson Jenkins, who believed the buffalo was the dumbest creature on earth.

When Buffalo Head Bernie Carbo was sold to Cleveland for $15,000, Lee walked away from the club for a day. He ripped the phone out of his wall at home, so club president Haywood Sullivan had to summon his lefthander back to the club by telegram. At the meeting, Lee agreed to rejoin the club, but Sullivan said he'd have to dock him a day's pay. Lee asked how much that amounted to, and Sullivan figured about $500. "Great," Lee said, "make it fifteen hundred and I'll take the whole weekend."

Warren Spahn was the winningest lefthander of all time, but he allowed two memorable home runs. In 1951, the Giants promoted a nineteen-year-old center fielder named Willie Mays. After batting .477 in Minneapolis over 35 games, Mays broke in 0 for 12 with the Giants and begged manager Leo Durocher to send him back to the minors. But Mays got a homer off Spahn for his first major league hit. "I'll never forgive myself," Spahn said. "We might have gotten rid of Willie forever if I'd only struck him out."

Thirty years later, Spahn's assignment was Luke Appling in an old-timers' All-Star Game in Washington, D.C. "Old Aches and Pains," who made his reputation with bat control, fouling off boxes of balls to get even with teams that denied free passes for his friends, collected only 45 homers among his 2,749 major league hits. But on that evening in 1981, seventy-four-year old Appling knocked Spahn's offering out of the park. This time, Spahn didn't take it quite so hard.

"I'd have to go with the immoral Babe Ruth."
—shortstop Johnny Logan selecting the greatest player ever

Babe Ruth's legend was a product of his performances on the field. That's not to say that the Babe didn't go out of his way to foster the myths around him. But his deeds were so awesome as to require neither embellishment nor wit. When he was reported dead in 1925, he didn't say, "Reports of my death are greatly exaggerated." He didn't have to.

Ruth was instantly recognizable and awesomely successful. His singularity and popularity ensured that fables would become attached to him. He shattered home run records in a way no one has before or since. He was purchased for the highest price ever paid for a player and became the highest paid, worth every penny of it. When confronted with the fact that his contract called for more money than the President of the U.S. was making, Ruth retorted, "I had a better year than him."

But the hard facts rendered Ruth legendary, hardly leaving room for invention. Myths that have arisen are mere apocrypha to the actual record. Ruth did spend his formative years chewing tobacco and stealing money from the till at his parents' saloon until they committed their seven-year-old to St. Mary's Industrial School, a combination reform school and vocational institute run by the Xaverian Brothers, where young George learned shirt making and baseball. Ruth really did start as a top-flight pitcher who twice defeated Walter Johnson 1–0 and held the World Series record for consecutive scoreless innings for longer than his home run marks. ("Ruth

made a grave mistake when he gave up pitching," Tris Speaker prematurely observed. "Working once a week, he might have lasted a long time and become a great star.") He did hit a ball through a plate-glass window across the street from Sportsman's Park. He owned a factory that manufactured Babe Ruth cigars with his mug on every wrapper (but the candy bar had been named for President Grover Cleveland's daughter). He did play ball with kids on a sandlot after a World Series game (on a day he didn't pitch for Boston). He really snacked on a half dozen hot dogs and soda pops, drove fast cars, and signed autographs for children tirelessly. He really broke a slump by staying out all night and hitting two homers the next day. Japanese soldiers in World War Two really did respond to Americans' taunts against the Emperor by screaming, "To hell with Babe Ruth!" Don Mattingly says that before he came to the Yankees, he thought Babe Ruth was a cartoon character. The guy Mattingly heard about couldn't have been human.

One of Ruth's favorite playmates was pitcher Waite Hoyt. When Hoyt checked into a hospital to dry out, the image-conscious ballclub announced that Hoyt was suffering from a case of amnesia. Ruth fired off a telegram to Hoyt: "Read about your case of Amnesia. Must be a new brand." The 1927 Yankees had a thirty-year-old rookie pitcher named Wiley Moore. Ruth bet him $300 to $100 that Moore wouldn't get three hits in the season. Moore won the bet (he managed five safeties) and invested the money in a pair of mules for his cotton farm in Oklahoma. The appreciative pitcher named the beasts Babe and Ruth.

What really happened to Ruth in 1925 remains a mystery, but his malady became known as the great American bellyache. That he overindulged his passions for food and women is well documented, and some suspect that syphilis was responsible for his illness, which eventually required abdominal surgery. The illness and a suspension after his return to action fed suspicions that Ruth was done at age thirty. His comeback in 1926 and subsequent seasons was nothing short of mythic.

The most famous legend about Babe Ruth involves the alleged called-shot home run in the 1932 World Series versus the Chicago Cubs. Ruth was thirty-seven, two seasons from the end of his career, appearing in his last World Series. The vituperative level of the encounter was heightened by the Cubs' decision to vote only a half share of postseason money to former Yankee Mark Koenig, after the shortstop had been a key contributor in Chicago's pennant drive. On the New York side stood manager Joe McCarthy, who'd been fired by the Cubs after following a pennant in 1929 with a second place finish in 1930.

The Yankees had swept the first two games of the Series in New York. In his first Wrigley Field at-bat, Ruth had smashed a three-run homer. But in the fourth inning, Ruth missed a shoestring catch as the Cubs tied the game at 4–4. As he faced Charlie Root in the fifth inning, the crowd and the Chicago dugout were all over the Bambino. Ruth held up his hand after taking the first pitch for a called strike and again after a second called strike evened the count. Then he pointed with his bat in the direction of the bleachers, but he may have been pointing toward Root, or sweeping the club toward the Cub dugout, or merely indicating that he still had one strike remaining. There was no doubt that Ruth deposited Root's two-two offering into the center field bleachers, giving the Yankees a 5–4 lead. Reporters decided Ruth had called

the shot, but only months after the fact. Ruth bragged of the feat as well, on about the same schedule. Root denied the tale, claiming that he would have knocked Ruth down if he thought the Babe was calling his shot. Lou Gehrig followed with his second homer of the game as the Yankees powered toward a four-game sweep.

The Babe Ruth Story, a movie dismissed as maudlin and excessively melodramatic upon its release, recorded Ruth's promise of a home run to a bedridden boy. There really was a sick boy named Johnny Sylvester who lived in New Jersey, and his father did wire Ruth with the boy's request for an autographed ball during the 1926 World Series. Sylvester did receive autographed balls from the Series rivals before Ruth's three-homer effort in fourth game.

The three-homer game was sensational enough on its own. Each shot traveled farther than the one before, the first two clearing the right field grandstand and the third landing in the center field bleachers at Sportsman's Park. A radio announcer had heard about the sick boy and the baseballs, and embellished the story into a Ruthian promise of a home run, delivered in triplicate. The story grew into legend within weeks (Red Grange sent Sylvester a football), so much so that the Babe was moved to make a surprise visit to little Johnny during a barnstorming tour that fall. Sylvester's tale gave rise to a second story that Ruth told later about a bedridden boy in Tampa who rose to see him parade with the Yankees through town for an exhibition game. True, false, or in between, neither story tops that three-homer game.

The Babe's reputation has outlived him by decades. When Montreal reporters in the late 1970s questioned Dick Williams's unsuccessful strategy of walking Bake McBride to pitch to Mike Schmidt, Williams snarled, "I don't care if Jesus Christ was coming up, I was going to walk Bake McBride."

"What if Babe Ruth was coming up?" asked one of the newsmen.

Williams paused before admitting, "I don't know about Babe Ruth."

Joe DiMaggio wasn't the larger-than-life figure that Babe Ruth was, but he fulfilled a different baseball myth for a different era. Like Ruth, he came from humble beginnings, but DiMaggio wasn't a wild youth from the wrong side of the tracks. His success in the great American game became a parable of assimilation into the American culture. Poppa DiMaggio, the San Francisco fisherman from Sicily, learned to appreciate his son's exploits on the ballfield and the money he earned from them. Lou Gehrig's background fit this mold from the Teutonic side, but like most other things Gehrig did, it was overshadowed. (Don Mattingly, who thought Ruth was a cartoon character, had never heard of Gehrig.) In addition to his success on the diamond, DiMaggio himself ripened from a skinny, hatchet-faced kid, to a dashing figure who married Marilyn Monroe, to a distinguished television pitchman in his golden years. When DiMaggio was named baseball's greatest living player as part of the centennial of professional baseball in 1969, baseball's graceful prince accepted the accolade with modesty. "At my age, I'm just happy to be named the greatest living anything."

Legend says that DiMaggio was discovered peering through a knothole at Seals Stadium at age seventeen in 1932. Scout Spike Hennessey, the story goes, dropped this pearl of wisdom on the youngster: "Never stand on the outside looking in, unless it's jail." Undoubtedly Hennessey had scouted DiMaggio in the sandlots (brother Vince was already a member of the Seals) and was aware of an offer made by the rival San Francisco Missions for Joe's services. Hennessey hauled DiMaggio to the office of Seals president Charles Graham, who offered the youngster passes to keep him away from the knothole and a tryout after asking, "Does Vince do all the playing in the family?"

In 1933, DiMaggio gained attention with a 61-game hitting streak in the Pacific Coast League. He also had his first brush with reporters, who generally found him aloof; in the prevailing climate, they chose to put him on a pedestal rather than nail him to a cross. But DiMaggio admits, "I can remember a reporter asking me for a quote, and I didn't know what a quote was. I thought it was some kind of soft drink."

But the most famous player in the minor leagues suffered the first of many setbacks in 1934. He injured his left knee getting out of a car on the way to Sunday dinner at his sister's house after a doubleheader. Injuries and recoveries would become a recurring theme in the legend of DiMaggio. The bad knee scared several clubs away, but the Yankees, at their minor league meetings that fall in French Lick, Indiana, decided to risk $25,000 (plus five players for the Seals) for the youngster on the recommendation of scout Bill Essick, a neighbor of the DiMaggio family. An additional year of seasoning in San Francisco, with Lefty O'Doul as his manager, readied Joltin' Joe for the big time in 1936.

The big time was ready for him. Ruth had been released at the end of the 1934 season, and the Yankees had not appeared in the World Series since 1932, their only trip to the fall classic in the last seven seasons. Even before he played in a major league game, Ruth's torch was passed to DiMaggio. He was to be the superstar who'd put the Yankees over the top. A generation later, the torch was passed relatively smoothly to Mickey Mantle. Rooting for the Yankees really was, as Red Smith put it, like rooting for U.S. Steel. Only by recognizing this history can the subsequent failures of Tom Tresh, Bobby Murcer, and others to extend the line of Yankee heroes be fully appreciated.

But even as a rookie, DiMaggio had to overcome an injury. He hurt his left foot sliding into third in an exhibition game, then burned the foot by overdoing heat therapy treatments. He wouldn't make his Yankee debut until May 4, 1936. He led the Yankees to their first pennant in four years and starred in the World Series, batting .346 and making a spectacular catch in front of the clubhouse steps at the Polo Grounds to end the second game. After watching DiMaggio in the Series, Giants manager Bill Terry said, "I've always heard that one player could make the difference between a losing team and a winner, and I never believed it. Now, I know it's true."

The Yankees kept winning with DiMaggio aboard. They won the next three World Series, losing but one postseason game. In the fourth game of the 1939 Series, DiMaggio started the play that would become known as "Schnozz's Snooze." Catcher Ernie "Schnozz" Lombardi was the slowest man ever to win a batting title, earning two hitting crowns even though he would get thrown out from right field occasionally on apparent singles. But he's better remembered for lying stunned during the tenth inning of the fourth and final game of the Series as DiMaggio crossed the plate with the Yankees' third run of the inning. The Reds had led 4–2 going into the ninth, but shortstop Billy Myers booted Bill Dickey's double-play grounder that made the score 4–3. DiMaggio, who was on first before Myers's miscue, raced home from

third on a grounder by Joe Gordon, narrowly beating a throw by third baseman Billy Werber to score the tying run.

With runners on first and third and one out in the tenth, DiMaggio laced a tie-breaking single to right. Ival Goodman couldn't handle the drive, allowing Charlie "King Kong" Keller to attempt to score from first. Goodman's one-hop throw hit Lombardi in the groin, and the onrushing Keller leveled the catcher, allowing DiMaggio to score from first. Clearly Lombardi was less at fault than his teammates for the incident, and, if the game had been played at Yankee Stadium instead of Cincinnati, the first run would have ended the contest. Instead, the Yankees had to shut down the Reds, who got their first two men on in the bottom of the tenth before succumbing.

In 1941, DiMaggio established one of the game's great records, a 56-game hitting streak. According to Lefty Gomez, DiMaggio's roommate, the Yankee Clipper remained calm throughout the streak, "But every day after forty-four [the previous record, held by Willie Keeler], I threw up my breakfast."

Myths grew around the streak. One was that Dom DiMaggio made a fantastic catch to rob Joe of a hit, nearly ending the streak at 43 games. Boxscore evidence doesn't support this story. DiMaggio denied rumors that Heinz was prepared to make a big promotional deal with the Yankee Clipper if he could extend the streak to 57, their corporate symbol.

It is true that DiMaggio and Gomez rode to the fateful fifty-seventh game in Cleveland together and their cab driver predicted the streak's end. Versions differ as to whether the cabbie said flatly that the streak would end or if he hedged a bit, saying the streak would end if DiMaggio didn't get a hit his first time up. In any case, Gomez cursed him for giving Joltin' Joe the jinx, but DiMaggio remained calm (although he may not have tipped heavily). DiMaggio went 0-for-3 with a walk in that fifty-seventh game, the first two outs recorded on brilliant plays by third baseman Ken Keltner. DiMaggio could have bunted to extend the streak, since Keltner was playing him in short left field, but DiMaggio's pride said he had to get a legitimate hit. Some historians may pooh-pooh that notion, pointing to several tainted streak-extending hits, but those blots were attributable to the official scorers, not DiMaggio.

Fans who saw him pointed to DiMaggio's effortless grace. His wide stance made his batting stroke fluid, and he rarely seemed to run hard for balls in the outfield, gliding to the spot. There's only one recorded instance of DiMaggio showing emotion on the ballfield. In the sixth game of the 1947 World Series, DiMaggio hit a drive to deep left field, ticketed for the bullpen. The two-on, two-out clout would have tied the game at eight, but Al Gionfriddo went back (" . . . back, back . . . ") to make a one hand stab over the low fence near the 415-foot sign. DiMaggio saw the catch as he approached second base, and kicked at the dirt with his toe to show his disappointment.

The public's other glimpse of DiMaggio's inner self came with his marriage to Marilyn Monroe in 1954. They were divorced later that year, leading raconteur Oscar Levant to remark, "It proves that no man can be a success in two national pastimes." After a trip to entertain troops in the Far East, Monroe returned beaming and told DiMaggio, "Oh, Joe, you've never heard such cheering."

"Yes, I have," DiMaggio answered.

DiMaggio's most fabled comeback from injury was in 1949. The previous November, he underwent surgery to re-move bone spurs on his right heel. He was still limping in spring training, missed the Yankees' opener, and was flown to Johns Hopkins Hosptial in Baltimore, where the operation had been performed, for further treatment. Speculation surfaced that the Yankee Clipper's playing days might be at an end. It wasn't until the last week of May that he was able to try out the heel in practice, not until a mid-June exhibition with the Giants that he played in a game. He returned to the regular lineup for a three-game series in Boston beginning June 28, against a hard-driving Red Sox squad that had won ten of its last eleven and was challenging the Yankees for the top spot.

After missing the first sixty-six games of the season, DiMaggio singled in his first at-bat and homered in his second. He broke up a potential double play in the fifth inning and caught Ted Williams's long drive in the ninth for the game's final out in a 5–4 Yankee win. The next day, the Yankees trailed 7–1 early when DiMaggio came up with two aboard. He slugged a three-run shot to make the score 7–4, then broke a 7–7 tie with another homer. In the final game of the series, with the Yankees clinging to a one-run lead, his three-run homer in the seventh brought some welcome insurance. In his first three games of the season, he'd gone five-for-eleven with four homers and nine RBIs. The triumphant return had put the Yankees eight games ahead of the Red Sox.

But the 1949 season wasn't over. The Yankees' rash of injuries continued throughout the summer. With a dozen games to go, a viral infection felled DiMaggio, who'd dropped fifteen pounds and weakened noticeably. The lead over Boston stood at two and a half games when DiMaggio went out. By the time the Red Sox came to New York for the season's final two games, Boston led the Yankees by a game. The opener on October 1 had been scheduled as Joe DiMaggio Day, and 69,551 fans turned out to honor their enervated hero. After the hour-long ceremonies in which he received over $35,000 worth of gifts for himself and his family, DiMaggio told manager Casey Stengel, "I'd like to give it a try." He had two hits in the Yankees' victory that tied them with the Red Sox, and tripled in the second game that brought the Yankees a pennant in their first year under Stengel.

"I had many years when I was not so successful as a ballplayer, as it is a game of skill."—Casey Stengel, testifying before the Senate Subcommittee on Antitrust and Monopoly in 1958.

In 1923, Casey Stengel was immortalized by Damon Runyon's "This is the way old Casey ran running his home run home" report of Stengel's game-winning inside-the-park shot in the World Series opener. Two decades later, Stengel was "The Ol' Perfesser," and two decades after that, still managing, he was able to proclaim, "Most people my age are dead at the present time."

Although he denigrated his skills as a player, Stengel batted .284 in his fourteen-year career as a lefthanded-hitting outfielder. He explained, "I broke in 4 for 4 and folks thought I was the next Ty Cobb. It took them about four days to get over that." Stengel was frequently platooned, a strategy he repopularized as a manager. In three World Series, he hit .393, with a pair of game-winning homers in 1923, the first two fall classic round-trippers hit at Yankee Stadium. As

Stengel would say, "You could look it up."

Stengel first became noted for his stunts on the field as a player, as well as sharing the name of the character of the famous poem. "He's a dandy ballplayer, but it's all from the neck down," observed one scout. Stengel responded, "Being a clown wasn't safe in the minors. Some of them bush league managers could hit you with a bat at fifty feet." If he somehow missed an opportunity for a prank or quip, his reputation ensured that he'd gain credit for it anyway.

During a spring training game early in his career, Stengel discovered a small hole with a metal cover in the deep outfield grass containing utility pipes. There was enough room to squeeze himself inside and still see the action on the field. When a fly ball came toward his position, teammates wondered where Casey had gone. Suddenly, he popped out of the hole holding the metal cover above his head and made the catch.

Stengel was also involved in another famous spring training episode where the catch wasn't made. In 1917, flying was still a novelty, and at the Dodgers spring training site in Daytona Beach, a pioneer woman aviator named Ruth Law flew a fragile biplane to generate publicity for the area. The Dodger players frequently flew with Law, and one lazy afternoon talk turned to the subject of how fast a ball would travel if dropped from the plane. A few years earlier, Senators catcher Gabby Street had caught a ball dropped from the Washington Monument, but the Dodgers were doubtful that a ball dropped from the airplane could be caught. That was all Dodger manager Wilbert Robinson, the catcher for the great original Orioles teams, needed to hear. "I could catch one," the fifty-one-year-old skipper contended. Egged on by doubting players, and probably fueled by some spirited wagering, it was agreed that Robinson would attempt the stunt the next afternoon.

Robinson strapped on his catcher's mitt and took his position by the mound, prepared to snag the ball dropped from a plane traveling about forty-five miles per hour, five hundred feet above the field. Some place Stengel riding shotgun on the biplane's wing, seated on a kitchen chair, but given the fragile state of aviation, that's not likely. Others say that the designated dropper forgot to bring a baseball into the air. Whatever happened, a sphere of some sort sped earthward with an overweight Robinson circling unsteadily below. The old catcher got a glove on it, but it hit him on the chest, splattered, and the impact knocked him to the ground. The object wasn't a baseball, but a grapefruit.

Feeling the juice, Robinson screamed, "Jesus, I'm killed! I'm dead! My chest's split open! I'm covered in blood!" Then he tasted the glop, realized he'd been had, and immediately blamed Stengel, who eagerly accepted credit, reasoning he'd been singled out because "I had a pretty good arm." Later, lubricated with other juices, Robinson claimed, "If it had been a baseball, I'd have caught it." In a more frank moment, Robinson admitted, "If that had been a baseball, I probably would have been killed." Stengel delighted in telling the story, claiming that he himself was in the biplane.

The true measure of a baseball tale is in its adaptation. George Plimpton used the grapefruit story as the basis for the opening of his 1987 novel, *The Curious Case of Sidd Finch*. To acclimate catcher Ronn Reynolds to handling the 168-mile-per-hour stuff of pitcher Finch, the Mets dropped him baseballs from a blimp at a thousand feet.

After Stengel left the Dodgers as a player, there was no shortage of clowns to take up the slack, although their antics were not necessarily by design. The principal character of Uncle Robbie's Daffiness Boys became Babe Herman, gifted with a thundering bat, a scattershot arm, and hands of steel.

With two on and two out and the Dodgers ahead by a run, the apparent third out of the ninth inning was a line drive toward Herman in right. But the Babe tripped, the ball rolled to the wall, and two runs scored for another Dodger defeat. As the team left the field, Robinson approached Herman and asked compassionately, "What happened?"

"When?" Herman enquired.

Fly balls were an adventure, if not a constant danger, for Herman. He denied the story that a fly ball had ever hit him on the head. "If a ball ever hit me on the head, I'd just hang up my spikes and quit," Herman told a reporter.

"What about the shoulder?" asked the reporter.

"Oh, no!" Herman exclaimed, sensing a trap. "The shoulder don't count, only the head."

Herman was wary of newsmen trying to build up his reputation as a character. He was not as careful on the basepaths, once attempting to steal second with the bases loaded. "Why do you guys always harp on me?" Herman complained. "Just because you got to have something to write about every day in the papers, why do you always make me out like a clown? Fun's fun and all that, but I'm a family man, and showing me up like a screwball don't help me in the game, and I gotta make a living same as you guys." With that, Herman reached into his vest pocket and pulled out a cigar.

The reporter, his conscience troubling him, said, "Here, let me give you a light."

"Don't bother," replied Herman, turning away in a puff of smoke. "It's already lit."

To his death, Herman denied the famous story of the three men on third, but this one was too good to have been made up. With the bases loaded, Herman drove a ball off the wall in right. Pitcher Dazzy Vance, the runner at second, turned third, but then retreated. The runner from first, Chick Fewster, made a headfirst dive into third, and Herman, head down, slid into third, meeting his two teammates. The third baseman tagged everyone in sight, and when the dust cleared, Herman had doubled into a double play.

A rookie observing the incident asked Uncle Robbie, "What kind of baseball is that?"

"Leave them be," Robinson replied. "It's the first time they've been together all season."

The incident led to the fable of the Brooklyn cabbie who picked up a fare leaving Ebbets Field before the end of the game and asked how the Dodgers were doing.

"The Dodgers are ahead, and we got three men on base," the spectator said.

"Which base?" asked the cabbie.

Robinson once called on Herman to bunt with a man on first and none out. Herman would have none of it and bunted the first two offerings foul. Then he belted the third delivery into the seats.

Fed up with the goofy antics and mounting losses, Robinson announced that the next dumb stunt would draw a fine, payable to what he called the Bonehead Club. Robinson promptly fattened the club's coffers. At the pregame meeting at home plate, Robinson submitted a laundry slip instead of a lineup card.

Stengel, however, showed that you didn't have to be a Dodger to clown. In spring training with the Phils, he put his

uniform on backwards. Manager Gavvy Cravath remarked, "You've done everything else backwards down here. You might as well wear your pants that way, too." As the Phils barnstormed toward opening day, they encountered a heckler who disparaged their abilities until the players challenged him to take the field and see if he could do any better. The heckler was Stengel, disguised in a straw hat, with overalls and a red bandana, who proceeded to smack out loud hits to the astonishment of the crowd.

Many other Stengel stories became standards. Playing for Pittsburgh in 1918, Stengel was having a bad day. He muffed a shoestring catch in right, kicking the ball toward second base but running in pursuit toward the foul line, thinking the ball had gone in that direction. Later, he was tagged out standing up on a play where the few fans in the stands thought he should have slid, and they booed him lustily. So before taking a seat in the dugout, Stengel addressed the crowd. "With the salary I'm getting, I'm so hollow and starving that if I slide, I'm liable to explode like a light bulb." Alibis for not sliding evolved through the years, but none were ever as good. In exhibition contests, Babe Ruth couldn't slide because he was carrying a fountain pen for signing autographs. Several players were accused of avoiding the dirt to preserve hip flasks of liquor. Tim Raines perfected a technique that allowed him to slide while toting vials of cocaine in his socks. Stengel found a way to improve his baseball income in the wartime economy by getting a job in the Brooklyn Navy Yard and arranging games with sailors as soon as their ships docked. "I wanted to play them before they got rid of their sea legs," he confided.

Back with the Pirates after the war, Stengel got into an argument with an umpire over an out call at first, ripped off his own shirt, and offered it to umpire, suggesting, "Why don't you play for our side for a change?" When the league office informed him of his fine by telegram the next day, Stengel pinned the yellow telegram to his uniform sleeve and wore it for the entire game.

Visiting Brooklyn, where he'd broken in, during 1919, the fans rode Stengel hard as a lefthanded pitcher made him look bad. In addition, Stengel had crashed into the wall in right center while failing to snare a game-breaking double. Between innings, Stengel visited the Brooklyn bullpen to chat with his former teammate Leon Cadore, a like-minded spirit who was a fair amateur magician. That afternoon Cadore's sleight of hand had caught a bird. Stengel knew what to do with it.

Stengel concealed the bird in his cap just before his turn at the plate. When the crowd greeted him with the expected jeers, Stengel turned, bowed, and removed his cap. The sparrow sat on his head for a moment to get its bearings, then flew away. Even the umpire laughed. A year later in Philadelphia, he found another bird in the outfield, caught it in his cap, and returned to his position. After catching a fly ball, he doffed his cap and away flew the bird. Years later, an attempt to recreate the feat a third time fell flat on its beak. The bird was spun by its tail to calm it before being put in his hat. When Stengel took off his cap, the woozy bird dropped to the ground at his feet.

When traded to the Giants in 1921, Stengel learned much of his future managerial skills from John J. McGraw, although Stengel exaggerated his escapades off the field to avoid criticism that he was the manager's pet. Stengel claimed that McGraw assigned one of his detectives to tail

him and outfielder Irish Meusel, who had been teammates on the Phils before joining the Giants. After a couple of days, the detective reported that Meusel and Stengel had stopped going out together. McGraw called Stengel into his office to discover the reasons for the friends' falling out. Stengel explained there was no problem between him and Meusel, but he had a beef with McGraw. "I don't want to share a detective," Stengel insisted. "I want one of my own."

Stengel began his managerial career in 1925 with Worcester, an Eastern League farm club of the Boston Braves, serving as player-manager with the added title of club president. At the end of the season, Stengel got an offer to manage the Toledo Mud Hens of the American Association, a more prestigious position. However, Stengel was still contractually obligated to the Braves' organization as a player. So Stengel the club president released Stengel the player, fired Stengel the manager, and then submitted his letter of resignation as president, freeing himself to take the job in Toledo. As a manager, Stengel became better known for his caustic wit, usually directed at players, and his curious rambling discourse known as Stengelese.

Stengel returned to the majors with the Dodgers in 1934, after Giants manager Bill Terry asked, "Is Brooklyn still in the league?" Stengel's Dodgers avenged the crack, knocking the Giants out of the pennant race in the final weekend. But the rest of the season had not been nearly as satisfying, as the Dodgers finished sixth. During a loss at Philadelphia, Stengel went out to get his pitcher, Walter Beck. Beck was earning the nickname "Boom-Boom" as the Phils had been tattooing the tin fence in right, exhausting right fielder Hack Wilson, who was already handicapped by a hangover—gin was his tonic, the pundits said. While Stengel visited the mound, Wilson took the opportunity to lean over, shut his eyes, and rest his aching head. Instead of handing Stengel the ball, Beck heaved it toward right field. The ball struck the fence with a boom, startling Wilson. Properly conditioned by previous shots, Wilson dashed back, retrieved the ball, and made his best throw of the season to second base.

Stengel concocted something called the precision play, a pick-off play to third with a righthanded batter. The pitcher would throw at the hitter, but yell "Look out," clearing the batter out of the box, attempting to freeze the baserunner, and giving the catcher a clear shot to pick him off. "The runner would freeze, but so would my man at third, and my left fielder would wear himself out chasing the overthrows."

Warren Spahn, a member of Stengel's Boston Braves in the 1940s and his Mets in the 1960s, noted, "I played for Stengel before and after he was a genius." Bad ballplayers with flair found their way to Stengel before and after his glory years with the Yankees. The first such character was Frenchy Bordagaray, an outfielder-third baseman who tried to bring back the gay nineties mustache in the thirties. "Go shave it off," Stengel advised, "before someone throws a ball at it and kills you." During pregame drills in the midst of a losing streak, one of Bordagaray's batting practice throws hit Stengel in the head. The Dodgers won that day, so Bordagaray suggested to his manager, "Let me hit you in the head every day." Then there was the time Bordagaray was standing on second base but the umpire called him out. Stengel was eager to argue, but Bordagaray discouraged him. "I was tapping my foot," Bordagaray explained, "and I guess he got me between taps." Stengel listened because Bordagaray wasn't in the habit of agreeing with umpires. He once spit in an arbiter's

eye and received a $500 fine and sixty-day suspension. Bordagaray responded, "The penalty is a little more than I expectorated."

Players like him sent Stengel to a postgame shave, instructing the barber, "Don't cut my throat, I may want to do it myself later." Just before the 1943 season, Stengel was hit by a car and suffered a broken leg. Pittsburgh manager Frankie Frisch, a teammate of Stengel's under McGraw, wired, "Your attempt at suicide fully understood. Deepest sympathy you didn't succeed." When Stengel took a Pacific Coast League managing job in Oakland in 1946, he was pleased with the presence of bridges. "Every manager wants to jump off a bridge sooner or later, and it's very nice for an old man to know he doesn't have to walk fifty miles to find one."

On an exhibition tour with the Boston Bees in Mexico, peasants lined the streets to greet the Bees' bus in Monterrey, throwing flowers and cheering wildly. Stengel, who owned a piece of the team, was already counting his club's share of the take from the presumed sellout. "I didn't know you people were so crazy about baseball," he told the guide assigned to the team.

"It's not the team they're cheering," the embarrassed guide replied. "They've never seen a Greyhound bus before."

Many questioned the appointment of this clown who didn't finish out of the second division as manager of the Yankees in 1949, but Stengel led the Yankees to ten pennants in a dozen seasons. Appreciating the value of having a good team to manage, Stengel summed up his good fortune, "There comes a time in every man's life at least once, and I've had plenty of them." People began to seek his opinions on managing. He suggested that the secret for success as a manager was "to keep the twenty guys who hate you away from the five guys who are undecided." He contended, "Most ballgames are lost, not won." Moreover, Stengel knew why. "Good pitching always stops good hitting. And vice versa."

Stengel found a new audience when he testified before a Senate subcommittee in July 1958 on baseball's antitrust exemption. Stengel gave them nearly an hour of convoluted, hysterical, yet shrewd monologue on the state of the game, the progress it had made, and the need for further improvements. The main feature, however, was Stengelese meandering and quaint phraseology which left the hearing room amused and bewildered. Mickey Mantle followed Stengel to the witness table and told the Senators, "My views are just about the same as Casey's."

At the start of the 1960 season, Stengel, sixty-nine years old, was hospitalized for a couple of weeks after complaining of chest pains. Upon release, he offered this medical report: "They examined all my organs. Some of them are quite remarkable and others are not so good. A lot of museums are bidding for them." The remarkable ones held up for the remainder of the season, and Stengel even managed to get in a stunt on the way to his record tenth pennant. In response to Bill Veeck's exploding scoreboard at Comiskey Park, Yankee players stood in front of their dugout and lit sparklers after one of their own homers.

The Yankees lost the 1960 World Series to the Pirates in seven games on Bill Mazeroski's homer leading off the bottom of the ninth in the final game. The Pirates had overcome a three-run Yankee lead in the eighth inning with the help of Bill Virdon's bad-hop grounder that hit Tony Kubek in the throat. But Stengel's managing came under criticism. He didn't start his best pitcher, Whitey Ford, until the third game. Ford threw a pair of shutouts in the third and sixth games, the start of his consecutive scoreless World Series inning streak that overtook Babe Ruth's record, but he wasn't available for a third start or even a relief appearance in the deciding contest. Additionally, Stengel failed to pinch-hit for pitcher Bobby Shantz in the top of the eighth with runners on second and third and two out. A single would have put the game out of reach, and Shantz had already pitched five innings in relief. Less than a week later, the Yankees decided it was time to go with a younger man, to which Stengel responded, "I'll never make the mistake of being seventy again."

A year later, during the 1961 World Series, Stengel accepted the appointment as the first manager of the Mets. The job would require more of his comedic skills than baseball acumen. Stengel showed he was equal to the task when explaining the Mets' first selection in the expansion draft, catcher Hobie Landrith, a veteran of twelve undistinguished years in the National League. "You have to have a catcher or you'll have a lot of passed balls," Stengel explained. A reporter noted that his starting outfield of Gus Bell, Frank Thomas, and Richie Ashburn had a total of twenty children. "If they produce as well on the field as off the field, we'll win the pennant," Stengel concluded wistfully.

He proclaimed his team "the Amazin' Mets," and the tag stuck. Stengel fully understood what was amazin' about the club: "I been in this game a hundred years, but I see new ways to lose I never knew existed before." At one particularly exasperating juncture in the Mets' 40–120 debut season, the worst record of the twentieth century, Stengel wondered aloud, "Can't anybody play this here game?" He would note after many home losses, "We trimmed the attendance again," meaning that they'd defrauded the public.

Even the rare victories came at a price. After sweeping a Sunday doubleheader from the Braves in Milwaukee, plane trouble and fog conspired to delay the team's arrival in Houston until eight the next morning. On his way to a few hours of sleep before that day's game, the usually voluble Stengel warned, "If any of the writers come looking for me, tell them I'm being embalmed."

On the 1962 Mets, the role of Frenchy Bordagaray was played by first baseman Marv Throneberry, who featured good power, bad hands, and shaky base-running skills. Writer Jimmy Breslin observed, "Having Marv Throneberry play for your team is like having Willie Sutton work for your bank." After clouting an apparent triple, Marvelous Marv was called out on appeal for missing first base. Stengel ran out to argue, but the second base umpire came over, hoping to chill Stengel's anger. "I hate to tell you this, Casey," the arbiter began, "but he missed second base, too." When Throneberry celebrated his twenty-ninth birthday on September 2, Stengel noted that there was no cake. "We was going to get him a birthday cake, but we figured he'd drop it."

Marvelous Marv became a folk hero. One inning, he had a particularly rough time with Frank Thomas, who was playing third base like the outfielder he was. Thomas heaved a throw past Throneberry for an error. Another grounder to Thomas, another poor throw, another error. Getting the idea, a third hitter smacked the ball to third and Thomas heaved it high above Throneberry's head. But Marvelous Marv leaped, spun in midair, and came down with the ball. Following the inning, Throneberry approached Thomas, who expected a well-deserved reproach. "What are you trying to do," Throneberry

asked, "take away my fans?"

The Mets had problems up the middle, too. Shortstop Elio Chacon didn't speak English, so he didn't understand center fielder Richie Ashburn when he called, "I got it." After several messed up pop flies, the resourceful Ashburn enlisted the help of a Spanish-speaking teammate and learned to say "*Yo lo tengo.*" A couple of days later, a fly ball was lifted into short left center. As Chacon moved back, Ashburn raced in, yelling, "*Yo lo tengo. Yo lo tengo.*" Sure enough, Chacon moved off. As Ashburn prepared to squeeze the ball, left fielder Frank Thomas ran him over. In the face of this adversity, Ashburn batted .306 and was honored as the team's most valuable player. "MVP on the worst team ever," Ashburn mused. "I wonder exactly what they mean by that."

Behind the plate, the Mets had Choo-Choo Coleman, who called everyone "Bub." In spring training 1963, third baseman Charlie Neal struck up a conversation with Coleman, who answered, "Yeah, Bub" and "No, Bub." Finally, Neal said, "You don't even know who I am. I was your roommate last season." Coleman considered the statement carefully before replying, "Yeah, Bub. You're number nine."

The Mets were the Siberia of baseball in those days, and some players took unusual routes to get there, none more so than Pumpsie Green, the first black player in the history of the Red Sox. Following a game at Yankee Stadium, the Red Sox bus was stuck in a major-league traffic jam. Green and Gene Conley, a six-foot-eight pitcher who also played basketball for the Boston Celtics, decided they could make better time on foot and left the bus. Some time later, they checked into a hotel without luggage, except for a couple of brown bags acquired at the local liquor store while the Red Sox initiated a search for them. They tired of New York after a couple of days, so Conley suggested they go to Israel. The inspiration for this idea may have been Green's real first name, Elijah. At the airport, some sharp airline employee recognized that this odd couple, traveling without passports or baggage, might be the missing pair of Red Sox. Both were fined, and Green was further punished with a trade to the Mets. He played only 17 games for the Amazin's before he was farmed out for good.

Stengel managed the Mets until the middle of the 1965 season, when a broken hip, suffered in falling off a barstool at an old-timers' celebration, forced his retirement. Many had urged Stengel to quit before that, chiding him for sleeping on the bench and failing to improve the team's dismal record. As the Yankee skipper, Stengel's skill was denigrated by those who felt anyone could have done as well; with the Mets, it was more true that anyone would have finished last, and Stengel never lost sight of how awful his clubs were. At an exhibition at West Point in early 1965, he slipped and broke his wrist. "I got this broken arm watching my team," he moaned. "All they gave me last year was a head cold." Discussing a pair of twenty-year-old prospects one spring morning, he said, "That there's Ed Kranepool. In ten years, he has a chance to be a star in this game. And over there's Greg Goosen. In ten years, he has a chance to be thirty."

After his retirement from the Mets, Stengel continued to make the rounds at spring training, Hall of Fame inductions (his election to Cooperstown in 1966 was a highlight of his life), and other baseball events. He observed, "Old-timers' weekends are like airplane landings. If you can walk away from them, they're successful."

There's a story that ought to be true concerning his final days in 1975. He was in his hospital bed watching a ballgame on television when the national anthem was played. He got out of bed and stood at attention one last time, an imaginary cap over his heart. When he died, his funeral was delayed a week, until an off-day in the playoffs, to allow baseball people to attend, a bit of ironic humor that Stengel would've appreciated.

"The toughest thing about the major leagues is explaining to your wife why she needs a penicillin shot for your kidney infection." —Mike Hegan

Stengel warned his players, "You gotta learn that if you don't get it by midnight, chances are you ain't gonna get it; and if you do, it ain't gonna be worth it." Stengel noted, "Being with a woman all night never hurt no professional baseball player. It's staying up all night looking for a woman that does 'em in."

Jim Bouton revealed a lot of players' tricks in his 1970 book, *Ball Four,* including the obsession with looking as well as touching. Beaver shooting was practiced in ballparks, bullpens, and through pilgrimages under bleacher grandstands and on the roof of the L-shaped Shoreham Hotel in Washington, baseball's greatest loss when the Senators left the nation's capital. Bouton also stated that a favorite player pastime was recording a session with a conquest, then playing it back on the team bus.

Bouton's book told the tale of Jim Gosger, who'd been secreted in a closet by a roommate anticipating a romp with a prime example of the so-called local talent. The thoughtful roommate even provided Gosger with a towel to chew on in the event of laughing. During the session, the woman cried, "I've never done it like that before."

Gosger stuck his head out, opined, "Yeah, sure," and returned to the closet.

As a member of the Yankees last dynasty teams of the early 1960s, Bouton played with Joe Pepitone, a dedicated prankster and victim as well as a highly successful womanizer. Pepitone, a devotee of toupees, is credited with legitimizing the presence of hair dryers in the clubhouse. Players enjoyed filling his dryer with powder so that it spewed all over his head and rug. Pepitone's best gag came at the expense of team trainers. He'd insert a piece of popcorn in his foreskin, then go to the trainer, saying he thought it might be cancer.

Pepitone's antics ran him afoul of many curfews, but avoiding bed checks has always been a part of the game. Even Stengel admitted covering for roommates. When the coach called his name from outside the door, Stengel would respond in his natural voice. If his roommate had gone out, Stengel would answer for him, doing his best to imitate the voice.

Then there's the autographed-ball story that has come down through the ages. Management places a plainclothes security guard in the hotel lobby with a baseball, and the guard asks all the players who arrive after curfew to autograph the ball. The next morning, the signers are fined.

Of course, these tricks haven't stopped the determined carouser. Ping Bodie, an outfielder best known for his quips, bragged that he roomed with Babe Ruth's valises. Pitcher Bob Veale was never bothered by bed checks. "My bed was always there." Many managers have lamented that the problem with bed checks is that "they disturb your best players."

Stengel had strong feelings about drinking. The team's hotel bar was off-limits to players. "That's where I do my drinking," he declared. When Stengel confronted pitcher

Mickey McDermott in a freight elevator at four A.M., the manager shook his head in disgust and said, "Drunk again."

The pitcher grinned. "Me too."

Stengel managed Mickey Mantle, Whitey Ford, and Billy Martin, three well-known "whiskey slicks," as the Ol' Perfesser called his drinkers. "Everybody who roomed with Mickey said he took five years off their careers," Ford reported. Upon turning forty-six, Mantle declared, "If I'd known I was going to live this long, I'd have taken better care of myself." Stengel believed, "The ones who drink milkshakes don't win many ballgames."

They don't get fooled like Johnny Mize did, either. When the Big Cat went into the shower after a spring workout, Giants trainer Frank Bowman soaked Mize's sweatshirt in alcohol. When Mize came out of the shower, Bowman urged Mize to lay off hard liquor.

"What are you talking about, Frank?" Mize retorted. "I was in at curfew last night, and all I had was a couple of beers."

"Don't try to kid me, John," the trainer said, striking a match and dropping it on the shirt. The shirt burst into flames. "That's alcohol you sweated out."

Mize stamped out the fire and pleaded with Bowman, "Don't say anything about this to anyone."

Cap Anson is credited with starting formal spring training by bringing his players to Hot Springs, Arkansas. Anson's purpose: "To boil out the alcohol microbes." John McGraw once locked pitcher Bugs Raymond in the clubhouse to keep him in shape to start the second game of a doubleheader. So Raymond lowered an empty bucket out of a clubhouse window, and an associate below filled it with beer.

Mike "King" Kelly, the first great star of the game back in the 1880s, continued the tradition of drinking. When asked if he drank during games, Kelly replied, "It depends on the length of the game." After his retirement, he offered advice to the struggling Reds: "When you see three balls, swing at the middle one."

Grover Cleveland Alexander, the only pitcher named for a former President and portrayed in the movies by a future one, was renowned for his drinking. It was assumed that "Ol' Pete" Alexander was badly hung over when he struck out Tony Lazzeri with two on and two out in the seventh inning of the seventh game of the 1926 World Series. After all, Alexander had worked nine innings the day before and presumably celebrated his second complete game victory of the Series hard that night. However, after the game six victory, manager Rogers Hornsby warned Alexander that he might call on him in the finale.

Don Larsen may have been celebrating his perfect game in the 1956 World Series the night before he pitched it. The righthander had a reputation for "mailing letters at three A.M.," as Stengel called it. Unable to find a convenient mailbox on foot during spring training in the retirement haven of St. Petersburg, Florida, Larsen wrapped his car around a telephone pole at five o'clock one morning. Larsen wasn't hurt, but he and the press corps wondered what kind of disciplinary action Stengel would order. The manager ended the mystery by proclaiming, "Anybody who can find something to do in St. Petersburg at five in the morning deserves a medal, not a fine."

"Say it ain't so, Joe."—Young fan to Shoeless Joe Jackson, who was banned from baseball for life with seven White

Sox teammates by Commissioner Kenesaw Mountain Landis for allegedly throwing the 1919 World Series.

The Baltimore Orioles won three straight National League titles starting in 1894. Manager Ned Hanlon's lineup included Hall of Famers John McGraw, Wee Willie Keeler, Wilbert Robinson, Hugh Jennings, Joe Kelley, and Dan Brouthers. One key to their success was their hustling style of scientific baseball. The original Orioles were credited with inventing the hit-and-run, the relay, and the backing up of throws. Less to their credit, the Orioles also refined techniques such as holding enemy baserunners up by the belt, cutting across the infield to take an extra base, and substituting mushy balls for the more dangerous variety when the opponents batted.

The Orioles' most famous play, one later attributed to Ty Cobb as well, involved spare balls which would be strategically placed in the high outfield grass in case a batted ball eluded the outfielders. The trickery kept a number of startled baserunners from advancing past first on what appeared to be sure extra-base hits. The system worked until one afternoon when a gapper was returned to second base by both the left fielder and center fielder. Upon seeing the two balls, the umpire figured out the gambit and forfeited the game to the Oriole's opponents.

Ty Cobb's father told him, when he left home to play ball, "Don't come home a failure." Cobb stories revolve around his toughness and readiness to beat you with his bat or his spikes or his fists. While Pete Rose was chasing Cobb's all-time hit record, one reporter asked Rose's opinion on what Cobb might be thinking if he was looking down on the chase. "From what I know about him," Rose answered, pointing skyward, "he's probably not up there."

There's hardly a baseball man who hasn't been credited with the "What would Ty Cobb hit today?" story—from Cobb himself to Yogi Berra. The response, no matter who gets the credit, is "Oh, about .350."

"That's not so great," says the surprised questioner. "It might not even lead the league."

"That's true, but you have to take into consideration he'd be seventy-three years old now."

Before an encounter with the Tigers, Red Sox catcher Lou Criger made the mistake of telling a reporter, "This Cobb is one of those ginks with a lot of flash, but he doesn't fool me. Watch him wilt when the going gets tough. I'll cut him down to size." Unfortunately for Criger, Cobb (unlike Rogers Hornsby, who eschewed the printed word and movies as harmful to the batting eye) read the paper. After singling his first time up, Cobb told Criger he'd be running on every pitch. And he did, stealing second, third, and home.

They say you can't steal first base, but Germany Schaefer did it in 1911. With two out in the ninth inning of a tie game between the Senators and White Sox, Schaefer was on first with speedy Clyde Milan on third. With a weak hitter at the dish, Schaefer tried to steal a run for his Senators by dashing toward second base in hopes of drawing a throw that would allow Milan to sneak home. But the White Sox were having none of it, and let Schaefer take second unchallenged. Undaunted, Schaefer had another plan. He took off for first, finishing his dash with a theatrical hook slide. The White Sox protested Schaefer's play, but the rule book didn't cover that situation so the play stood. (A rule was added to keep players from making a "travesty of the game," which prevented

Jimmy Piersall from running the bases in reverse order on his hundredth career homer; he had to settle for running backwards.) Schaefer, back on first, lit out for second again. This time, the Sox hoped to end the sham and pegged to second. Schaefer beat the throw, and Milan waltzed home with the winning run.

Schaefer had a number of other stunts. During a wet afternoon, with his team down 5–1 in the top of the fifth, he pleaded for the game to be called, but the umpires let the contest continue. So in the sixth he took his position at second base wearing a raincoat. The umpires let him patrol the keystone in his long coat. Pee Wee Reese recreated the sentiment years later when he carried an open umbrella to the on-deck circle during a misty fifth inning with the Dodgers trailing. Several decades had fouled the temper of arbiters worse than the weather. Reese was tossed, but the game went on.

Reese was also part of another famous stall. A Dodger laugher had suddenly turned tight, and manager Charlie Dressen hastily summoned Clyde King to relieve. When he got to the mound, King said he wasn't warm and asked Reese to buy him some time. So when King completed his allotted warmups, Reese called for time. He put his hand over his eye, in apparent agony, and went over to third baseman Billy Cox to help him get this imaginary speck out of his eye. Reese's act was a little too good; King came over to see if he could help his shortstop.

Managers often put in a rule for their pitching staff: never throw a strike on a no ball–two strike count. As the Giants manager in the forties, Mel Ott was a fervent believer in this rule. He once fined pitcher Bill Voiselle $500 for breaking the rule, and from then on, the rest of the staff toed the line.

A rookie reliever took the hill for the Giants with two runners on and a tough hitter at the plate. He got ahead on the count 0-2 and tried to waste one outside. But the ball curved over the plate, and the umpire rang up strike three. The rookie went into a panic, screaming, "No. That was a ball. What're you tryin' to do, ruin me?"

Players have been raging at umpires from the dawn of the game. Bill Klem was the first great umpire in the game, a small figure who declared, "I never missed one in my heart." He resigned in 1941 after thirty-six years in the majors because he found himself doubting a call he'd made in the game. When he was elected to the Hall of Fame in 1953, he told the crowd in Cooperstown, "To me, baseball was not just a sport; it was a religion." Many of the stories about the men in blue became attached to Klem over the years, just as stories about players stuck to Babe Ruth.

He was a short man with big ears and lips that spit when he made a call. The ballplayers called him "Catfish," but never to his face. He would brook no disrespect. But the Pirates pushed him to the limit in a critical 1913 series against the Giants. Klem threatened to clear the Pirate bench if he heard another peep.

In those days, the umpire announced pinch hitters to the crowd. So when the Pirates sent up a rookie pinch hitter, Klem asked for his name. The rookie mumbled, and Klem asked him for a repeat. "Boo," the rookie said. That was all Klem needed to hear. He threw out the hitter and the rest of the Pirates.

But Pirate manager Fred Clarke approached the red-hot arbiter with an explanation. The rookie wasn't trying to be fresh; his name was Everitt Booe.

A long drive down the line had Klem considering his decision carefully. The anxious batter questioned the Old Arbiter, "Well, was it fair or foul?"

An indignant Klem replied, "It ain't nothing until I call it."

A Klem call once infuriated Frankie Frisch, then manager of the Cardinals, who flew into a white rage and charged the umpire, spewing invective. Suddenly, Frisch collapsed. A crowd gathered around him, and a doctor came on the field to treat him. Klem didn't let sympathy cloud his judgment. "Frisch," he announced, "dead or alive, you're out of this game."

Klem accomplished what many considered impossible when he ejected Pie Traynor from a game. Traynor never cursed and was the most polite player around. There'd been no display of acrimony before the ejection, so a reporter asked Klem why Traynor had been tossed. Klem said he'd ejected Traynor because he wasn't feeling well. The reporter said he didn't see any sign of Traynor's illness.

"That's what he told me," Klem replied. "He came up to me like the perfect gentleman he is and said, 'Mr. Klem, I'm sick and tired of your stupid decisions.'" When a rookie pitcher complained about Klem's ball calls on his first three pitches to Rogers Hornsby, Klem chided the hurler, "Young man, when you pitch a strike, Mr. Hornsby will let you know."

A Klem contemporary, Bill Guthrie, is credited with creating another classic of the umpiring trade. When a batter called out on strikes launched his bat into the air in disgust, Guthrie eyed the bat and calmly announced to the batter, "Son, if that bat comes down, you're out of the game."

Umpire George Moriarty once got taken to the cleaners by a rookie. After taking two called strikes, the batter stepped out and asked, "Just for my information, sir, how do you spell your name?"

Moriarty was so surprised that he spelled out his name.

"That's what I thought, sir," the rookie said as he set himself back in the box. "Moriarty, with only one 'i.'"

Red Ormsby, another umpire during the twenties, was getting heckled from a female fan behind first base. "You blind bum," she shouted, "If you were my husband, I'd give you poison."

Ormsby walked toward the rail, removed his hat, and bowed to the woman, then roared, "If you were my wife, I'd take it."

George Magerkurth, one of the biggest umpires in the National League, got into an argument with Pee Wee Reese, one of league's smallest players. As the disputants went toe to toe, Magerkurth looked down at the shortstop and threatened, "Get out of here or I'll bite your head off."

"If you do," Reese answered, "you'll have more brains in your stomach than in your head."

When huge Frank Howard broke into the majors, umpires joined pitchers in increasing their insurance policies. Although Howard was a gentle giant, at 6'7", 255 pounds, no one wanted to be caught at the limits of his temperament. In his first at-bat with Marty Springstead behind the plate, Howard glowered at the umpire's call of strike one on a pitch around the knees. The next pitch came in at about the same spot. "That's two," Springstead announced.

"Two what?" Howard sneered.

"Too low, Frank, much too low," Springstead replied.

Nestor Chylak complained, "This is the only job in the world where they expect you to be perfect on opening day and improve as the season goes on."

The torrent of abuse hasn't let up on the umpires over the

years. Billy Martin (like baseball and malaria, according to Gene Mauch) keeps coming back. Martin claimed that Gaylord Perry, the legendary greaseballer, "smelled like a drugstore," and that even his doctored balls had a medicinal air. Bill Kunkel was umpiring when Martin brought him a ball that he thought reeked of tampering. Kunkel deferred, claiming, "I have allergies and a deviated septum."

Martin seethed, "I got an umpire who can't see or smell."

The Mets and Braves played a nineteen inning game at Atlanta on July 4, 1985. The contest finished 16–13 in favor of the Mets and lasted until almost four in the morning, followed by fireworks as scheduled. In the seventeenth inning, home plate umpire Terry Tata ejected Darryl Strawberry for arguing a called third strike. "The strike zone changes at three A.M.," Tata told Strawberry.

Tom Gorman was keenly aware that umpires are paid by the game, not by the hour. "Anytime I got those bang-bang plays at first, I called 'em out. It made the game shorter."

In his effort to move the game along, Gorman once called Henry Aaron out on strikes as Bad Henry slugged a home run. There were two strikes on Hammern' Hank when Gorman saw strike three heading for the low, outside corner. He called it, but Aaron's quick wrists smacked the pitch into the seats as Gorman bellowed, "Strike three." As Aaron ran rounded the bases, the catcher asked Gorman what was going on. "Just practicing," Gorman murmured.

Gorman, a former pitcher, may have been partial to his previous craft. When Bob Gibson fanned a record 17 Tigers in the opener of the 1968 World Series, Gorman contended, "Gibson only struck out ten. I struck out seven."

"I won't play for a penny less than fifteen hundred."
—Honus Wagner refusing a $2,000 salary offer.

The advent of professional baseball was no doubt followed closely by the first salary dispute. Until players escaped the reserve clause noose in 1976, management held all the cards.

Branch Rickey was as famous for penny-pinching when it came to players' salaries as anything else he did in the game. Rickey had his share of idiosyncrasies. Religious convictions kept him from attending most Sunday ballgames, but he had no qualms about collecting the Sunday gate. They called him the Mahatma for his canny and sometimes inscrutable ways, but he was years ahead of the baseball establishment in creating the farm system, not only to supply his Cardinals with a fresh stream of talent, but to generate income by selling players to other clubs. Rickey got a piece of the selling price for players in his early days and became a wealthy man. Rickey's also credited with coining the phrase "Baseball is a game of inches." Later, Rickey integrated the game by selecting Jackie Robinson as the first black major leaguer.

If Brooks Robinson played third base as if he came down from a higher league, Rickey was the fellow who negotiated salaries up there. "We were like kids going to war with a popgun," Pee Wee Reese recalled. Eddie Stanky reported, "I got a million dollars worth of advice and a very small increase." Chuck Connors said, "He had the players and the money and just didn't like to see the two of them mix." When Rickey took over Pittsburgh, Rickey told slugger Ralph Kiner, "We could have finished last without you." Rickey announced, "I don't want to sell Ralph, but if something overwhelming comes along, I'm willing to be overwhelmed."

Enos Slaughter said that Rickey "would go into the vault to get change for a nickel." The talk was that Rickey's ideal team would lose a tough battle for the pennant in the final week of the season. That way, the team would draw well for the entire season, but players couldn't seek raises for winning the pennant. "I don't know if that was true," said slugger Johnny Mize, who began his career with Rickey's Cardinals in the 1930s, "but that was the talk."

Preacher Roe went into contract talks with Rickey, and, as usual, the player was demanding a sum that the general manager found unreasonable. After negotiations narrowed the gap a bit, Rickey gave Roe a contract with the Dodgers' final offer. He suggested that Roe think it over at home, and added, "I've got two hunting dogs I'd like you to have. I know how much you like to hunt."

So Roe accepted the dogs and took them home. The dogs turned out to be fine hunters, and they softened Roe's attitude toward Rickey considerably. "So I went back home and signed the contract, and put it in the mail. A few hours later, those two dogs took off across the field, and I haven't seen 'em since."

A player once returned a contract to Hank Greenberg, then general manager of the Indians. Greenberg fired off a telegram, "In your haste to accept the terms, you forgot to sign the contract."

The player wired back, "In your haste to give me a raise, you put in the wrong figure."

Bill Veeck was a great innovator on the public side of the game. Veeck, who planted the ivy in Wrigley Field while his father was president of the Cubs, saw baseball as entertainment, and his clubs always had a carnival element. (Veeck tried to buy the Ringling Brothers circus in the 1950s.) Veeck was a kindly huckster, not unlike the Wizard of Oz. When he staged morning games during World War Two for workers coming off the graveyard shift, Veeck helped serve coffee and doughnuts in the stands. He let fans decide strategy with voting cards.

But Veeck wanted to win, too. He rigged fences so that they could be moved in and out to his team's advantage. His grounds crew would hose down the infield until it was muddy to slow down opposing baserunners. He sold mirrors to fans in the bleachers to shine in enemy batters' eyes. But Veeck's most famous coup was hiring Eddie Gaedel to play for the St. Louis Browns in 1951.

Veeck's stunt came in the second game of a doubleheader between the Browns and Tigers on August 19. Between games, Veeck staged an elaborate fiftieth-anniversary celebration for the American League, attended by Commissioner "Happy" Chandler. The celebration featured acrobats, antique cars, a band made up of Browns players, and for the finale, an anniversary cake. The three-foot-seven-inch Gaedel jumped out of the cake, wearing number ⅛ on a Browns uniform originally made for the son of former owner Bill DeWitt.

Folks thought they'd seen the last of Gaedel, but in the bottom of the first, the midget was announced as a pinch hitter for leadoff batter Frank Saucier. Gaedel came out of the dugout swinging a miniature bat. Gaedel had been signed to a legal contract days before, but Veeck held off mailing the papers to the league office until the Friday before the big day. He wired the league office that morning to add Gaedel to the roster, and St. Louis manager Zack Taylor had copies of both documents to show to stern plate umpire Ed Hurley that Gaedel was a legitimate member of the Browns.

Over the objections of Detroit manager Red Rolfe, Hurley allowed Gaedel to face lefthander Bob Cain. Hurley saw to it that the Tigers held to the letter of the law, forbidding catcher Bob Swift from sitting on the ground to provide a lower target. Gaedel, stationed in the righthanders' box, took a wide stance and crouched, leaving a miniscule strike zone. Hurley called all four of Cain's deliveries high. Before the at-bat, Veeck had warned Gaedel, "I've got a man up in the stands with a high-powered rifle, and if you swing at any pitch, he'll fire." (In Ring Lardner's story "You Could Look It Up," which Veeck claimed he'd never read, a midget was sent up to walk but, enticed by a fat pitch, grounded out.)

Gaedel trotted to first, where he was replaced by pinch runner Jim Delsing. Gaedel patted his caddy on the rump and trotted to the dugout accompanied by wild applause. "For a minute, I felt like Babe Ruth," Gaedel said in a postgame interview. Although Commissioner Chandler found the incident entertaining, American League president Will Harridge was not amused. He expunged Gaedel's name from the official records, and banned any further appearances by midgets.

"Fine," Veeck wrote back. "Let's establish what a midget is in fact. Is it three-feet-six inches? Eddie's height? Is it four-feet-six? If it's five-feet-six, that's great. We can get rid of Rizzuto."

If any owner could rival Rickey for parsimony and Veeck for showmanship, it was Charles O. Finley, who purchased the Kansas City Athletics in 1960 and held the franchise for two decades. Finley expanded ballpark giveaways, introduced colorful uniforms, installed a mechanical rabbit in a hole behind home plate that popped out to supply the umpire with baseballs, and cajoled his fellow owners into adopting the designated hitter rule and playing World Series games at night. He singlehandedly brought mustaches back into the majors when he offered players $300 to grow them in connection with a promotion. Finley also popularized mascots, hiring a mule that he named "Charlie O." after his favorite owner, and letting the mule defecate all over the press room, preferably on newsmen.

But as a businessman, Finley squeezed his players and landlords to get the most out of his franchise. He moved the A's to Oakland in 1968, prompting one Kansas City observer to remark, "Oakland is the luckiest city since Hiroshima." When third baseman Sal Bando escaped from Oakland as a free agent, someone wondered if it was difficult to leave the A's. "Was it hard to leave the *Titanic*?" Bando answered.

Finley probably became best known to the national audience when he attempted to put second baseman Mike Andrews on the disabled list during the 1973 World Series. Andrews had made a pair of errors in the eleventh inning of the second game of the Series to help the Mets to a win over the A's. After the game, Finley arranged for a doctor to examine Andrews and declare him physically unfit to play, allegedly because of a shoulder injury. Finley badgered Andrews into signing the doctor's report, then tried to substitute Manny Trillo, a much better fielder, on the A's roster. The Mets cried foul, and Commissioner Bowie Kuhn ruled that Andrews had to stay on the roster. When the Series moved to New York, Met fans gave Andrews a standing ovation.

"When I was a little boy, I wanted to be a baseball player and join the circus," recalled third baseman Graig Nettles. "With the Yankees, I've accomplished both." The focus of the reenvigorated Yankee franchise of the 1970s was principal owner George Steinbrenner, whose syndicate purchased the

team in 1973. In the words of Jim Bouton, "Steinbrenner was born on third base and thinks he hit a triple."

Nettles once observed a huge fat man waddling past the team bus in spring training and yelled out the window, "Hurry up, George, or we'll leave without you." Nettles added, "There are two things George doesn't know about, baseball and weight control." He figured, "It's a good thing Babe Ruth isn't here. If he was, George would have him bat seventh and tell him he's overweight." When the Yankees got off to a slow start one season, Nettles saw a good side of Steinbrenner's trips to observe the club on the road. "The more we lose, the more he flies in. And the more he flies, the better the chance that his plane will crash."

Nettles earned the nickname of "Poof" because he'd instigate trouble in the clubhouse, then, *poof*, he'd disappear. On a team flight, Nettles announced, "We've got a problem. Luis Tiant wants to use the bathroom, and it says 'no foreign objects in the toilet.'" When a flight made an unscheduled stop, Nettles asked, "What are we doing, getting new light bulbs for Bob Lemon's nose?" Lemon got that nose on the way to a successful career as a pitcher and manager. "I never took a tough loss home with me," he said. "I left it at a bar along the way."

Early in his reign, Steinbrenner ordered his troops to get rid of long hair. Lou Piniella objected, saying if long hair was good enough for Jesus Christ, why couldn't Steinbrenner allow it on his ballplayers. So Steinbrenner called Piniella up to his office and pointed off in the distance. "You see that swimming pool, Lou?"

"Yes."

"Well, the day you can go over there and walk across that pool, you can wear your hair any way you like."

Reggie Jackson, signed to a record free agent contract in 1977, made himself unwelcome to his Yankee teammates even before his arrival when he announced, "I'm the straw that stirs the drink." He'd also bragged that if he played in New York they'd name a candy bar after him. Sure enough, the Reggie bar, a clump of chocolate and nuts that bore an unfortunate resemblance to a cow chip, was born. Catfish Hunter thought the bar was unique, "I unwrapped it, and it told me how good it was." Hunter, who played with Jackson in both Oakland and New York, said that Reggie "would give you the shirt off his back. Of course, he'd call a press conference to announce it." Darold Knowles, a reliever with the A's in their glory days, said, "There isn't enough mustard in the world to cover Reggie."

Jackson was a bad outfielder by the time he got to the Yankees, but he made light of it. "Fielding? There are lots of guys who can catch a baseball. I make a million dollars with my bat."

Jackson's Yankee foil was Mickey Rivers, a serious character in his own right. Rivers was speedy, but you could time his walk from the on-deck circle to the plate with a sundial. He proclaimed that his goals for one season were "to hit .300, score a hundred runs, and stay injury prone." Rivers once asked, "What was the name of the dog on 'Rin-Tin-Tin'?" He referred to bewildered players as "Lost Mohicans." Rivers said a key to playing center field was sticking his finger in the air "to get the wind-chill factor." While a member of the Texas Rangers, Rivers predicted, "We'll do all right if we can capitalize on our mistakes."

But Rivers knew how to get Jackson's goat. When Jackson bragged that he had an IQ of 160, Rivers asked, "Out of

what, a thousand?" Rivers offered this succinct (sanitized) analysis of Reginald Martinez Jackson's personality problem: "No wonder you is messed up. You got a white man's first name, a Spanish middle name, and a black man's last name."

Jackson retorted, "Why do I listen to you? You can't even read or write."

"You better stop reading and start hitting," Rivers warned.

When Rivers was shipped off to Texas, he expected to return to the Yankees someday. "Oh, George understands me," Rivers said of the Yanks' principal owner. "Me and him and Billy, we're two of a kind."

Billy Martin saw it about the same way with Steinbrenner and Jackson. "One's a born liar and the other's convicted," Martin said, referring to Steinbrenner's conviction for making illegal contributions to the Nixon campaign in 1972. That remark got Martin fired from his first of five stints as Yankee manager.

Steinbrenner was fond of disparaging his players. He fell in love with Jackson, but only after Reggie was gone. When he got Dave Winfield, who suffered through a miserable World Series slump in 1981, Steinbrenner complained, "I got rid of Mr. October and got Mr. May." When Winfield set an American League record for RBIs in April 1988, he told reporters, "Now it's on to May, and you know about me and May."

Steinbrenner didn't confine his barbs to players. He called Chicago White Sox owners Eddie Einhorn and Jerry Reinsdorf, "Abbott and Costello." Reinsdorf retaliated by asking, "How can you tell when George Steinbrenner is lying? You see his lips move."

The antics of Steinbrenner and Finley emboldened other owners. When Ray Kroc bought the San Diego Padres, he took the microphone and announced to his opening day crowd, "The good news is that we've outdrawn the Dodgers. The bad news is that I've never seen such stupid ball playing in my life." Kroc had plenty of blame to distribute in his early days as the Padres' owner. He noted, "I signed Oscar Gamble on advice of my attorney. I no longer have Oscar Gamble, and I no longer have my attorney."

Other Leagues

CHAPTER 22

Black Ball

Jules Tygiel

In 1987, Major League Baseball, amidst much fanfare and publicity, celebrated the 40th anniversary of the finest moment in the history of the national pastime—Jackie Robinson's heroic shattering of the color barrier. But baseball might also have commemorated the centennial of a related, but far less auspicious event—the banishment of blacks from the International League in 1887 which ushered in six disgraceful decades of Jim Crow baseball. During this era, some of America's greatest ballplayers plied their trade on all-black teams, in Negro Leagues, on the playing fields of Latin America, and along the barnstorming frontier of the cities and towns of the United States, but never within the major and minor league realm of "organized baseball." When slowly and grudgingly given their chance in the years after 1947, blacks conclusively proved their competitive abilities on the diamond, but discrimination persisted as baseball executives continued to deny them the opportunity to display their talents in managerial and front office positions.

Scattered evidence exists of blacks playing baseball in the antebellum period, but the first recorded black teams surfaced in Northern cities in the aftermath of the Civil War. In October 1867, the Uniques of Brooklyn hosted the Excelsiors of Philadelphia in a contest billed as the "championship of colored clubs." Before a large crowd of black and white spectators, the Excelsiors marched around the field behind a fife and drum corps before defeating the Uniques, 37–24. Two months later, a second Philadelphia squad, the Pythians, dispatched a representative to the inaugural meetings of the National Association of Base Ball Players, the first organized league. The nominating committee unanimously rejected the Pythian's application, barring "any club which may be composed of one or more colored persons." Using the impeccable logic of a racist society, the committee proclaimed, "If colored clubs were admitted there would be in all probability some division of feeling, whereas, by excluding them no injury could result to anyone." The Philadelphia Pythians, however, continued their quest for interracial competition. In 1869, they became the first black team to face an all-white squad, defeating the crosstown City Items, 27–17.

In 1876, athletic entrepreneurs in the nation's metropolitan centers established the National League which quickly came to represent the pinnacle of the sport. The new entity had no written policy regarding blacks, but precluded them nonetheless through a "gentleman's agreement" among the owners. In the smaller cities and towns of America, however, where under-funded teams and fragile minor league coalitions quickly appeared and faded, individual blacks found scattered opportunities to pursue baseball careers. During the next decade, at least two dozen black ballplayers sought to earn a living in this erratic professional baseball world.

Bud Fowler ranked among the best and most persistent of these trailblazers. Born John Jackson in upstate New York in 1858 and raised, ironically, in Cooperstown, Fowler first achieved recognition as a 20-year-old pitcher for a local team in Chelsea, Massachusetts. In April 1878, Fowler defeated the National League's Boston club, which included future Hall of Famers George Wright and Jim O' Rourke, 2–1, in an exhibition game, besting 40-game winner Tommy Bond. Later that season, Fowler hurled three games for the Lynn Live Oaks of the International Association, the nation's first minor league, and another for Worcester in the New England League. For the next six years, he toiled for a variety of independent and semi-professional teams in the United States and Canada. Despite a reputation as "one of the best pitchers on the continent," he failed to catch on with any major or minor league squads. In 1884, now appearing regularly as a second baseman, as well as a pitcher, Fowler joined Stillwater, Minnesota, in the Northwestern League. Over the next seven seasons, Fowler played for fourteen teams in nine leagues, seldom batting less than .300 for a season. In 1886, he led the Western League in triples. "He is one of the best general players in the country," reported *Sporting Life* in 1885, "and if he had a white face he would be playing with the best of them. . . Those who know, say there is no better second baseman in the country."

In 1886, however, a better second baseman did appear in the form of Frank Grant, perhaps the greatest black player of the nineteenth century. The light-skinned Grant, described as a "Spaniard" in the *Buffalo Express*, batted .325 for Meridien in the Eastern League. When that squad folded he joined Buffalo in the prestigious International Association and improved his average to .340, third best in the league.

Although not as talented as Fowler and Grant, barehand-catcher Moses Fleetwood Walker achieved the highest level of play of blacks of this era. The son of an Ohio physician, Fleet Walker had studied at Oberlin College, where in 1881 he and his younger brother Welday helped launch a varsity baseball team. For the next two years, the elder Walker played for the University of Michigan and in 1883 he appeared in 60 games for the pennant-winning Toledo squad in the Northwestern League. In 1884, Toledo entered the American Association, the National League's primary rival, and Walker became the first black major leaguer. In an age in which many catchers caught barehanded and lacked chest protectors, Walker suffered frequent injuries and played little after a foul tip broke his rib in mid-July. Nonetheless, he batted .263 and pitcher Tony Mullane later called him "the best catcher I ever worked with." In July, Toledo briefly signed Walker's brother, Welday, who appeared in six games batting .182. The following year, the Toledo club dropped

from the league, ending the Walkers' major league careers.

These early black players found limited acceptance among teammates, fans, and opponents. In Ontario, in 1881, Fowler's teammates forced him off the club. Walker found that Mullane and other pitchers preferred not to pitch to him. Although he acknowledged Walker's skills, Mullane confessed, "I disliked a Negro and whenever I had to pitch to him I used anything I wanted without looking at his signals." At Louisville in 1884, insults from Kentucky fans so rattled Walker that he made five errors in a game. In Richmond, after Walker had actually left the team due to injuries, the Toledo manager received a letter from "75 determined men" threatening "to mob Walker" and cause "much bloodshed" if the black catcher appeared. Earlier, Chicago White Stockings star and manager Cap Anson had threatened to cancel an exhibition game with Toledo if Walker played. The injured catcher had not been slated to start, but Toledo manager Charlie Morton defied Anson and inserted Walker into the lineup. The game proceeded without incident.

In 1887, Walker, Fowler, Grant, Higgins, Stovey, and three other blacks converged on the International League, a newly reorganized circuit in Canada and upstate New York, one notch below the major league level. At the same time, a new six-team entity, the League of Colored Baseball Clubs, won recognition under baseball's National Agreement, a mutual pact to honor player contracts among team owners. Thus, an air of optimism pervaded the start of the season. But 1887 would prove a fateful year for the future of blacks in baseball.

On May 6, the Colored League made its debut in Pittsburgh with "a grand street parade and a brass band concert." Twelve hundred spectators watched the hometown Keystones lose to the Gorhams of New York, 11–8. Within days, however, the new league began to flounder. The Boston franchise disbanded in Louisville on May 8, stranding its players in the Southern city. Three weeks later, league-founder Walter Brown formally announced the demise of the infant circuit.

Meanwhile, in the International League, black players found their numbers growing, but their status increasingly uncertain. Six of the 10 teams fielded blacks, prompting *Sporting Life* to wonder, "How far will this mania for engaging colored players go?" In Newark, fans marveled at the "colored battery" of Fleet Walker, dubbed the "coon catcher" by one Canadian newspaper, and "headstrong" pitcher George Stovey. Stovey, one of the greatest black pitchers of the nineteenth century, won 35 games, still an International League record. Frank Grant, in his second season as the Buffalo second baseman, led the league in both batting average and home runs. Bud Fowler, one of two blacks on the Binghampton squad, compiled a .350 average through early July and stole 23 bases.

These athletes compiled their impressive statistics under the most adverse conditions. "I could not help pitying some of the poor black fellows that played in the International League," reported a white player. "Fowler used to play second base with the lower part of his legs encased in wooden guards. He knew that about every player that came down to second base on a steal had it in for him." Both Fowler and Grant, "would muff balls intentionally, so that [they] would not have to touch runners, fearing that they might injure [them]." In addition, "About half the pitchers try their best to hit these colored players when [they are] at bat." Grant, whose Buffalo teammates had refused to sit with him for a team portrait in 1886, reportedly saved himself from a "drub-

bing" at their hands in 1887, only by "the effective use of a club." In Toronto, fans chanted, "Kill the Nigger," at Grant, and a local newspaper headline declared, "THE COLORED PLAYERS DISTASTEFUL." In late June, Bud Fowler's Binghampton teammates refused to take the field unless the club removed him from the lineup. Binghampton submitted to these demands on July 7, releasing Fowler and a black teammate, a pitcher named Renfroe.

The most dramatic confrontations between black and white players occurred on the Syracuse squad, where a clique of refugees from the Southern League exacerbated racial tensions. In spring training, the club included a catcher named Dick Male, whom, rumors had it, was a light-skinned black named Richard Johnson. Male charged "that the man calling him a Negro is himself a black liar," but when released after a poor preseason performance, he returned to his old club, Zanesville in the Ohio State League, and resumed his true identity as Richard Johnson. In May, Syracuse signed 19-year-old black pitcher Robert Higgins, angering the Southern clique. On May 25, Higgins appeared in his first International League game in Toronto. "THE SYRACUSE PLOTTERS," as a *Sporting News* headline called his teammates, undermined his debut. According to one account, they "seemed to want the Toronto team to knock Higgins out of the box, and time and again they fielded so badly that the home team were enabled to secure many hits after the side had been retired." "A disgusting exhibition," admonished *The Toronto World*. "They succeeded in running Male out of the club," reported a Newark paper, "and they will do the same with Higgins." One week later, two Syracuse players refused to pose for a team picture with Higgins. When manager "Ice Water" Joe Simmons suspended pitcher Doug Crothers for this incident, Crothers slugged the manager. Higgins miraculously recovered from his early travails and lack of support to post a 20–7 record.

On July 14, as the directors of the International League discussed the racial situation in Buffalo, the Newark Eagles planned to send Stovey, their ace, to the mound in an exhibition game against the National League Chicago White Stockings. Once again manager Anson refused to field his squad if either Stovey or Walker appeared. Unlike 1884, Anson's will prevailed. On the same day, team owners, stating that "Many of the best players in the league are anxious to leave on account of the colored element," allowed current black players to remain, but voted by a six-to-four margin to reject all future contracts with blacks. The teams with black players all voted against the measure, but Binghampton, which had just released Fowler and Renfroe, swung the vote in favor of exclusion.

Events in 1887 continued to conspire against black players. On September 11, the St. Louis Browns of the American Association refused to play a scheduled contest against the all-black Cuban Giants. "We are only doing what is right," they proclaimed. In November, the Buffalo and Syracuse teams unsuccessfully attempted to lift the International League ban on blacks. The Ohio State League, which had fielded three black players, also adopted a rule barring additional contracts with blacks, prompting Welday Walker, who had appeared in the league, to protest, "The law is a disgrace to the present age. . . There should be some broader cause—such as lack of ability, behavior and intelligence—for barring a player, rather than his color."

After 1887, only a handful of blacks appeared on inte-

grated squads. Grant, Higgins, and Fleet Walker all returned to their International League teams in 1888. The following year, only Walker remained for one final season, the last black in the International League until 1946. Richard Johnson, the erstwhile Dick Male, reappeared in the Ohio State League in 1888 and in 1889 joined Springfield in the Central Interstate League, where he hit 14 triples, stole 45 bases, and scored 100 runs in 100 games. In 1890, Harrisburg in the Eastern Interstate League fielded two blacks, while Jamestown in the New York Penn League featured another. Bud Fowler and several other black players appeared in the Nebraska State League in 1892. Three years later, Adrian in the Michigan State League signed five blacks, including Fowler and pitcher George Wilson who posted a 29–4 record. Meanwhile Sol White, who later chronicled these events in his 1906 book, *The History of Colored Baseball*, played for Fort Wayne in the Western State League. In 1896, pitcher-outfielder Bert Jones joined Atchison in the Kansas State League where he played for three seasons before being forced out in 1898. Almost 50 years would pass before another black would appear on an interracial club in organized baseball.

While integrated teams grew rare, several leagues allowed entry to all black squads. In 1889, the Middle States League included the New York Gorhams and the Cuban Giants, the most famous black team of the age. The Giants posted a 55–17 record. In 1890, the alliance reorganized as the Eastern Interstate League and again included the Cuban Giants. Giants' star George Williams paced the circuit with a .391 batting average, while teammate Arthur Thomas slugged 26 doubles and 10 triples, both league-leading totals. The Eastern Interstate League folded in midseason, and in 1891 the Giants made one final minor league appearance in the Connecticut State League. When this circuit also disbanded, the brief entry of the Cuban Giants in organized baseball came to an end. In 1898, a team calling itself the Acme Colored Giants affiliated with Pennsylvania's Iron and Oil League, but won only eight of 49 games before dropping out, marking an ignoble conclusion to these early experiments in interracial play.

Overall, at least 70 blacks appeared in organized baseball in the late 19th century. About half played for all-black teams, the remainder for integrated clubs. Few lasted more than one season with the same team. By the 1890s, the pattern for black baseball that would prevail for the next half century had emerged. Blacks were relegated to "colored" teams playing most of their games on the barnstorming circuit, outside of any organized league structure. While exhibition contests allowed them to pit their skills against whites, they remained on the outskirts of baseball's mainstream, unheralded and unknown to most Americans.

As early as the 1880s and 1890s several all-black traveling squads had gained national reputations. The Cuban Giants, formed among the waiters of the Argyle Hotel to entertain guests in 1885, set the pattern and provided the recurrent nickname for these teams. Passing as Cubans, so as not to offend their white clientele, the Giants toured the East in a private railroad car playing amateur and professional opponents. In the 1890s, rivals like the Lincoln Giants from Nebraska, the Page Fence Giants from Michigan, and the Cuban X Giants in New York emerged. From the beginning these teams combined entertainment with their baseball to attract crowds. The Page Fence Giants, founded by Bud Fowler in 1895, would ride through the streets on bicycles to

attract attention. In 1899, Fowler organized the All-American Black Tourists, who would arrive in full dress suits with opera hats and silk umbrellas. Their showmanship notwithstanding, the black teams of the 1890s included some of the best players in the nation. The Page Fence Giants won 118 of 154 games in 1895, with two of their losses coming against the major league Cincinnati Reds.

During the early years of the 20th century many blacks still harbored hopes of regaining access to organized baseball. Sol White wrote in 1906 that baseball, "should be taken seriously by the colored player. An honest effort of his great ability will open the avenue in the near future wherein he may walk hand-in-hand with the opposite race in the greatest of all American games—baseball." Rube Foster, the outstanding figure in black baseball from 1910-1926, stressed excellence because "we have to be ready when the time comes for integration."

But even clandestine efforts to bring in blacks met a harsh fate. In 1901, Baltimore Orioles Manager John McGraw attempted to pass second baseman Charlie Grant of the Columbia Giants off as an Indian named Chief Tokohama, until Chicago White Sox President Charles Comiskey exposed the ruse. In 1911, the Cincinnati Reds raised black hopes by signing two light-skinned Cubans, Armando Marsans and Rafael Almeida, prompting the *New York Age* to speculate, "Now that the first shock is over it would not be surprising to see a Cuban a few shades darker. . .breaking into the professional ranks. . .it would then be easier for colored players who are citizens of this country to get into fast company." But the Reds rushed to certify that Marsans and Almeida were "genuine Caucasians," and while light-skinned Cubans became a fixture in the majors, their darker brethren remained unwelcome. Over the years, tales circulated of United States blacks passing as Indians or Cubans, but no documented cases exist.

Although most blacks lived in the South, during the first two decades of the 20th century, the great black teams and players congregated in the metropolises and industrial cities of the North. Chicago emerged as the primary center of black baseball with teams like the Leland Giants and the Chicago American Giants. In New York, the Lincoln Giants, which boasted pitching stars Smokey Joe Williams and Cannonball Dick Redding, shortstop John Henry Lloyd and catcher Louis Santop, reigned supreme. Other top clubs of the era included the Philadelphia Giants, the Hilldale Club (also of Philadelphia), the Indianapolis ABC's and the Bacharach Giants of Atlantic City. Player contracts were nonexistent or nonbinding and stars jumped frequently from team to team. "Wherever the money was," recalled John Henry Lloyd, "that's where I was."

Fans and writers often compared the great black players of this era to their white counterparts. Lloyd, one of the outstanding shortstops and hitters of that or any era, came to be known as "The Black Wagner," after his white contemporary Honus Wagner, who called it an "honor" and a "privilege" to be compared to the gangling black infielder. A St. Louis sportswriter once said when asked who was the best player in baseball history, "If you mean in organized baseball, the answer would be Babe Ruth; but if you mean in all baseball. . .the answer would have to be a colored man named John Henry Lloyd." Pitcher "Rube" Foster earned his nickname by outpitching future Hall of Famer Rube Waddell, and Cuban Jose Mendez was called "The Black Matty" after Christy Mathewson.

The talents of Foster and Mendez notwithstanding, the greatest black pitcher of the early twentieth century was 6'5" Smokey Joe Williams. Born in 1886, Williams spent a good part of his career pitching in his native Texas, unheralded until he joined the Leland Giants in 1909 at the age of 24. From 1912-1923 he won renown as a strikeout artist for Harlem's Lincoln Giants. Against major league competition Williams won six games, lost 4, and tied two, including a three-hit 1–0 victory over the National League champion Philadelphia Phillies in 1915. In 1925, he signed with the Homestead Grays and although approaching his fortieth birthday, starred for seven more seasons. A 1952 poll to name the outstanding black pitcher of the half-century, placed Williams in first place, ahead of the legendary Satchel Paige.

Oscar Charleston ranks as the greatest outfielder of the 1910s and 1920s. With tremendous speed and a strong, accurate arm, Charleston was the quintessential centerfielder. During his 15-year career starting in 1915, Charleston hit for both power and average and may have been the most popular player of the 1920s. After he retired he managed the Philadelphia Stars, Brooklyn Brown Dodgers, and other clubs.

Several major stars of this era labored outside the usual channels of black baseball. In 1914, white Kansas City promoter J. L. Wilkinson organized the All-Nations team, which included whites, blacks, Indians, Asians, and Latin Americans. Pitchers John Donaldson, Jose Mendez, and Bill Drake and outfielder Cristobel Torriente played for the All-Nations team, described by one observer as "strong enough to give any major league team a nip-and-tuck battle." A black Army team from the 25th Infantry Unit in Huachuca, Arizona, featured pitcher Bullet Joe Rogan and shortstop Dobie Moore. In 1920, when Wilkinson formed the famed Kansas City Monarchs, the players from the All-Nations and 25th Infantry teams formed the nucleus of his club. In 1921, the Monarchs challenged the minor league Kansas City Blues to a tournament for the city championship. The Blues won the series five games to three. In 1922, however, the Monarchs won five of six games to claim boasting honors in Kansas City. One week later, they swept a doubleheader from the touring Babe Ruth All-Stars.

In the years after 1910, Andrew "Rube" Foster emerged as the dominant figure in black baseball. Like many of his white contemporaries, Foster rose through the ranks of the national pastime from star player to field manager to club owner. Born in Texas in 1879, Foster accepted an invitation to pitch for Chicago's Union Giants in 1902. "If you play the best clubs in the land, white clubs as you say," he told owner Frank Leland, "it will be a case of Greek meeting Greek. I fear nobody." By 1903, he was hurling for the Cuban X Giants against the Philadelphia Giants in a series billed as the "Colored Championship of the World." His four victories in a best of nine series clinched the title. The following year, he had switched sides and registered two of three wins for the Philadelphia Giants in a similar matchup, striking out 18 batters in one game and tossing a two-hitter in another. In 1907, he rejoined the Leland Giants and, in 1910, pitched for and managed a reconstituted team of that name to a 123–6 record.

As a pitcher, Foster had ranked among the nation's best; as a manager, his skills achieved legendary proportions. A master strategist and motivator, Foster's teams specialized in the bunt, the steal, and the hit-and-run, which came to characterize black baseball. Fans came to watch him sit on the bench giving signs with a wave of his ever-present pipe. He became the friend and confidant of major league managers like John McGraw. Over the years, Foster trained a generation of black managers, like Dave Malarcher, Biz Mackey, and Oscar Charleston in the subtleties of the game.

In 1911, Foster entered the ownership ranks, uniting with white saloon keeper John Schorling (the son-in-law of White Sox owner Charles Comiskey) to form the Chicago American Giants. With Schorling's financial backing, Foster's managerial acumen, a regular home field in Chicago, and high salaries, the American Giants attracted the best black players in the nation. Throughout the decade, whether barnstorming or hosting opponents in Chicago, the American Giants came to represent the pinnacle of black baseball.

By World War One, Foster dominated black baseball in Chicago and parts of the Midwest. In most other areas, however, white booking agents controlled access to stadiums, and as one newspaperman charged in 1917, "used circus methods to drag a bunch of our best citizens out, only to undergo humiliation . . . while [they sat] back and [grew] rich off a percentage of the proceeds." In the East, Nat Strong, the part owner of the Brooklyn Royal Giants, Philadelphia Giants, Cuban Stars, Cuban Giants, New York Black Yankees, and the renowned white semi-pro team, the Bushwicks, held a stranglehold on black competition. To break this monopoly and place the game more firmly under black control, Foster created the National Association of Professional Baseball Clubs, better known as the Negro National League, in 1920.

Foster's new organization marked the third attempt of the century to meld black teams into a viable league. In 1906, the International League of Independent Baseball Clubs, which had four black and two white teams, struggled through one season characterized by shifting and collapsing franchises. Four years later, Beauregard Moseley, secretary of Chicago's Leland Giants attempted to form a National Negro Baseball League, but the association folded before a single game had been played.

The new Negro National League, which included the top teams from Chicago, St. Louis, Detroit, and other Midwestern cities, fared far better. At Foster's insistence, all clubs, with the exception of the Kansas City Monarchs, whom Foster reluctantly accepted, were controlled by blacks. J. L. Wilkinson, who owned the Monarchs, a major drawing card, had won the respect of his fellow owners and soon overcame Foster's reservations. He became the league secretary and Foster's trusted ally. Operating under the able guidance of Foster and Wilkinson, the league flourished during its early years. In 1923, it attracted 400,000 fans and accumulated $200,000 in gate receipts.

The success of the Negro National League inspired competitors. In 1923, booking agent Nat Strong formed an Eastern Colored League, with teams in New York, Brooklyn, Baltimore, New Jersey, and Philadelphia. With four of the six teams owned by whites, and Strong controlling an erratic schedule, the league had somewhat less legitimacy than Foster's circuit. Playing in larger population centers, however, the more affluent Eastern clubs successfully raided some of the top players of the Negro National League before the circuits negotiated an uneasy truce in 1924. Throughout the remainder of the decade, however, acrimony rather than harmony characterized interleague relations. A third association emerged in the South, where the stronger independent teams in major cities formed the Southern Negro League. While this group became a breeding ground for top players, the

impoverished nature of its clientele, and the inability of clubs to bolster revenues with games against white squads, rendered them unable to prevent their best players from jumping to the higher paying Northern teams.

At their best the Negro Leagues of the 1920s were haphazard affairs. Since most clubs continued to rely on barnstorming for their primary livelihood, scheduling proved difficult. Teams played uneven numbers of games and especially in the Eastern circuit skipped official contests for more lucrative nonleague matchups. Several of the stronger independent teams, like the Homestead Grays, remained unaffiliated. Umpires were often incompetent and lacked authority to control conditions. Finally, players frequently jumped from one franchise to another, peddling their services to the highest bidder. In 1926, Foster grew ill, stripping the Negro National League of his vital leadership. Two years later, the Eastern Colored League disbanded and in 1931, less than a year after Foster's death, the Negro National League departed the scene, once again leaving black baseball with no organized structure.

With the collapse of Foster's Negro National League and the onset of the Great Depression, the always-borderline economics of operating a black baseball club grew more precarious. White booking agents, like Philadelphia's Eddie Gottlieb or Abe Saperstein of the Midwest, again reigned supreme. In the early 1930s, only the stronger independent clubs like the Homestead Grays or Kansas City Monarchs, novelty acts like the Cincinnati Clowns, or those teams backed by the "numbers kings" of the black ghettos could survive.

The Kansas City Monarchs emerged as the healthiest holdover from the old Negro National League. In 1929, owner Wilkinson had commissioned an Omaha, Nebraska, company to design a portable lighting system for night games. The equipment, consisting of a 250-horsepower motor and a 100-kilowatt generator, which illuminated lights atop telescoping poles 50 feet above the field, took about two hours to assemble. To pay for the innovation, Wilkinson mortgaged everything he owned and took in Kansas City businessman Tom Baird as a partner. But the gamble paid off. The novelty of night baseball allowed the Monarchs to play two and three games a day and made them the most popular touring club in the nation.

Meanwhile, in Pittsburgh, former basketball star Cumberland Posey, Jr. had forged the Homestead Grays into one of the best teams in America. Posey, the son of one of Pittsburgh's wealthiest black businessmen, had joined the Grays, then a sandlot team, as an outfielder in 1911. By the early 1920s he owned the club and began recruiting top national players to supplement local talent. In 1925, he signed 39-year-old Smokey Joe Williams, and the following year he lured Oscar Charleston, whom many consider the top black player of that era. Over the next several seasons Posey recruited Judy Johnson, Martin Dihigo, and Cool Papa Bell. In 1930, he added a catcher from the Pittsburgh sandlots named Josh Gibson, and in 1934 brought in first baseman Buck Leonard from North Carolina. Unwilling to subject himself to outside control, Posey preferred to remain free from league affiliations. Yet for two decades, the Homestead Grays reigned as one of the strongest teams in black baseball.

In the 1930s, Posey faced competition from crosstown rival Gus Greenlee, "Mr. Big" of Pittsburgh's North Side numbers rackets. Greenlee took over the Pittsburgh Crawfords, a local team, in 1930. Greenlee spent $100,000 to build a new stadium, and wooed established ballplayers with lavish salary offers. In 1931, he landed the colorful Satchel Paige, the hottest young pitcher in the land, and the following year raided the Grays, outbidding Posey for the services of Charleston, Johnson, and Gibson. In 1934, James "Cool Papa" Bell jumped the St. Louis Stars and brought his legendary speed to the Crawfords. With five future Hall of Famers, Greenlee had assembled one of the great squads of baseball history.

The emergence of Gus Greenlee marked a new era for black baseball, the reign of the numbers men. In an age of limited opportunities for blacks, many of the most talented northern black entrepreneurs turned to gambling and other illegal operations for their livelihood. Novelist Richard Wright explained, "They would have been steel tycoons, Wall Street brokers, auto moguls, had they been white." Like the political bosses of nineteenth century urban America, numbers operators provided an informal assistance network for needy patrons in the impoverished black communities and represented a major source of capital for black businesses. In city after city, the numbers barons, seeking an element of respectability or an outlet to shield gambling profits from the Internal Revenue Service or merely the thrill of sports ownership, came to dominate black baseball. In Harlem, second-generation Cuban immigrant Alex Pompez, a powerful figure in the Dutch Schultz mob, ran the Cuban Stars, while Ed "Soldier Boy" Semler controlled the Black Yankees. Abe Manley of the Newark Eagles, Ed Bolden of the Philadelphia Stars, and Tom Wilson of the Baltimore Elite Giants all garnered their fortunes from the numbers game. Even Cum Posey, who had no connection with the rackets, had to bring in Homestead numbers banker Rufus "Sonnyman" Jackson as a partner and financier to stave off Greenlee's challenge.

In 1933, Greenlee unified the franchises owned by the numbers kings into a rejuvenated Negro National League. Under his leadership, writes Donn Rogosin, "The Negro National League meetings were enclaves of the most powerful black gangsters in the nation." This "unholy alliance" sustained black baseball in the Northeast through depression and war. Even the collapse of the Crawfords and demolition of Greenlee Stadium in 1939, failed to weaken the league which survived until the onset of integration. In 1937 a second circuit, the Negro American League was formed in the Midwest and South. Dominated by Wilkinson and the Kansas City Monarchs, the Negro American League relied less on numbers brokers, but more on white ownership for their financing.

The formation of the Negro American League encouraged the rejuvenation of an annual World Series, matching the champions of the two leagues. But the Negro League World Series never achieved the prominence of its white counterpart. The fact that league standings were often determined among teams playing uneven numbers of games, diluted the notion of a champion. Furthermore, impoverished urban blacks could not sustain attendance at a prolonged series. As a result, the Negro League World Series always took a back seat to the annual East-West All-Star Game played in Chicago. The East-West Game, originated by Greenlee in 1933, quickly emerged as the centerpiece of black baseball. Fans chose the players in polls conducted by black newspapers. By 1939, leading candidates received as many as 500,000 votes. Large crowds of blacks and whites watched the finest Negro League stars, and the revenues divided among the teams

often spelled the difference between profit and loss at the season's end.

By the 1930s and 1940s, black baseball had become an integral part of Northern ghetto life. With hundreds of employees and millions of dollars in revenue, the Negro Leagues, as Donn Rogosin notes, "may rank among the highest achievements of black enterprise during segregation." In addition, baseball provided an economic ripple effect, boosting business in hotels, cafes, restaurants and bars. In Kansas City and other towns, games became social events, as black citizens, recalls manager Buck O'Neil, "wore their finery." The Monarch Booster Club was a leading civic organization and the "Miss Monarch Bathing Beauty" pageant a popular event.

Black baseball also represented a source of pride for the black community. "The Monarchs was Kansas City's team," boasted bartender Jesse Fisher. "They made Kansas City the talk of the town all over the world." In several cities, white politicians routinely appeared at Opening Day games to curry favor with their often neglected black constituents. When Greenlee Field launched its operations in Pittsburgh, the mayor, city council, and county commissioners lined the field boxes. Negro League owners also played a role in the fight against segregation. In Newark, Effa Manley, who ran the Eagles with her husband Abe, served as treasurer of the New Jersey NAACP and belonged to the Citizen's League for Fair Play which fought for black employment opportunities. Manley sponsored a "Stop Lynching" fundraiser at one Eagles home game.

The impact of the Negro Leagues, however, ranged beyond the communities whose names the teams bore. Throughout the age of Jim Crow baseball, even in those years when a substantial league structure existed, official league games accounted for a relatively small part of the black baseball experience. Black teams would typically play over 200 games a year, only a third of which counted in the league standings. The vast majority of contests occurred on the "barnstorming" circuit, pitting black athletes against a broad array of professional and semi-professional competition, white and black, throughout the nation. In the pre-television era, traveling teams brought a higher level of baseball to fans in the towns and cities of America and allowed local talent to test their skills against the professionals. While some all-white teams, like the "House of David" also trod the barnstorming trail, itinerancy was the key to survival for black squads. The capital needed to finance a Negro League team existed primarily in Northern cities, but the overwhelming majority of blacks lived in the South.

"The schedule was a rugged one," recalled Roy Campanella of the Baltimore Elite Giants. "Rarely were we in the same city two days in a row. Mostly we played by day and traveled by night." After the Monarchs introduced night baseball, teams played both day and night appearing in two and sometimes three different ballparks on the same day. Teams traveled in buses—"our home, dressing room, dining room, and hotel"—or sandwiched into touring cars. "We had little time to waste on the road," states Quincy Trouppe, "so it was a rare treat when the cars would stop at times to let us stretch out and exercise for a few minutes." Most major hotels barred black guests, so even when the schedule allowed overnight stays, the athletes found themselves in less than comfortable accommodations. Large cities usually had better black hotels where ballplayers, entertainers, and other members of the black bourgeoisie congregated. On the road, however, Negro Leaguers more frequently were relegated to Jim Crow roadhouses, "continually under attack by bedbugs."

The black baseball experience extended beyond the confines of the United States and into Central America and the Caribbean. Negro Leaguers appeared regularly in the Cuban, Puerto Rican, Venezuelan, and Dominican winter leagues where they competed against black and white Latin stars and major leaguers as well. Some blacks, like Willie Wells and Ray Dandridge, jumped permanently to the Mexican League, where several also became successful managers of interracial teams. As Wells explained, "I am not faced by the racial problem. . . I've found freedom and democracy here, something I never found in the United States. . . In Mexico, I am a man."

In the United States, however, blacks often found themselves in more distasteful roles. To attract crowds throughout the nation and to keep fans interested in the frequently one-sided contests against amateur competition, some black clubs injected elements of clowning and showmanship into their pre-game and competitive performances. As early as the 1880s, comedy had characterized many barnstorming teams. Black baseball, even in its most serious form, tended to be flashier and less formal than white play. Against inferior teams, players often showboated and flaunted their superior skills. Pitcher Satchel Paige would call in his outfielders or guarantee to strike out the first six or nine batters to face him against semi-professional squads. In the late 1930s, Olympic star Jesse Owens traveled with the Monarchs, racing against horses in pre-game exhibitions.

Black teams, like the Tennessee Rats and Zulu Cannibals, thrived on their minstrel show reputations. The most famous of these franchises were the "Ethiopian Clowns." Originating in Miami in the 1930s, the Clowns later operated out of Cincinnati and then Indianapolis. Their antics included a "pepperball and shadowball" performance (later emulated by basketball's Harlem Globetrotters), and mid-game vaudeville routines by comics Spec Bebop, a dwarf, and King Tut. Players like Pepper Bassett, "the Rocking Chair Catcher" and "Goose" Tatum, a talented first baseman and natural comedian, enlivened the festivities. By the 1940s, the Clowns, through the effort of booking agent Syd Pollack, dominated the baseball comedy market. In 1943, their popularity won the Clowns entrance into the Negro Leagues, although other owners demanded they drop the demeaning "Ethiopian" nickname. Although never one of the better black teams, the Clowns greatly bolstered Negro League attendance.

Their popularity notwithstanding, the comedy teams reflected one of the worst elements of black baseball. The Clowns and Zulus perpetuated stereotypes drawn from Stepin Fetchit and Tarzan movies. "Negroes must realize the danger in insisting that ballplayers paint their faces and go through minstrel show revues before each ballgame," protested sportswriter Wendell Smith. Many black players resented the image that all were clowns. "Didn't nobody clown in our league but the Indianapolis Clowns," objected Piper Davis. "We played baseball."

Even without the clowning, black baseball offered a more freewheeling and, in many respects, more exciting brand of baseball than the major leagues. Since the 1920s, when Babe Ruth had revolutionized the game, the majors had pursued power strategies, emphasizing the home run above all else. Although the great sluggers of the Negro Leagues rivaled

those in the National and American Leagues, they comprised but one element in the speed-dominated universe of "tricky baseball." Black teams emphasized the bunt, the stolen base, and the hit-and-run. "We played by the 'coonsbury' rules," boasted second baseman Newt Allen. "That's just any way you think you can win, any kind of play you think you could get by on." In games between white and black all-star teams, this style of play often confounded the major leaguers. Centerfielder James "Cool Papa" Bell personified this approach. Bell was so fast, marveled rival third baseman Judy Johnson, "You couldn't play back in your regular position or you'd never throw him out." In one game against a major league All-Star squad, Bell scored from first base on a sacrifice bunt! In center field, his great speed allowed him to lurk in the shallow reaches of the outfield, ranging great distances to make spectacular catches.

Negro League pitching also took on a peculiar caste. "Anything went in the Negro League," reported catcher Roy Campanella, "Spitballs, shineballs, emery balls; pitchers used any and all of them." Since league officials could not afford to replace the balls as frequently as in organized ball, scuffed and nicked baseballs remained in the game, giving pitchers great latitude for creative efforts. "I never knew what the ball would do once it left the pitcher's hand," recalled Campanella.

Since most rosters included only 14 to 18 men, Negro League players demonstrated a wide range of versatility. Each was required to fill in at a variety of positions. Star pitchers often found themselves in the outfield when not on the mound. Some won renown at more than one position. Ted "Double-Duty" Radcliffe often pitched in the first game of a doubleheader and caught in the second. Cuban Martin Dihigo, whom many rank as the greatest player of all time, excelled at every position. In 1938, in the Mexican League he led the league's pitchers with an 18–2 record and the league's hitters with a .387 average.

The manpower shortage offered opportunities for individuals to display their all-around talents, but it also limited the competitiveness of the black teams. While on a given day a Negro League franchise, featuring one of its top pitchers, might defeat a major league squad, most teams lacked the depth to compete on a regular basis. "The big leagues were strong in every position," remarks Radcliffe. "Most of the colored teams had a few stars but they weren't strong in every position."

While black teams may not have matched the top clubs in organized baseball, the individual stars of the 1930s and 1940s clearly ranked among the best of any age. Homestead Gray teammates Josh Gibson and Buck Leonard won renown as the Babe Ruth and Lou Gehrig of the Negro Leagues. The Grays discovered Gibson in 1929 as an 18-year-old catcher on the sandlots of Pittsburgh, where he had already earned a reputation for 500-foot home runs. For 17 years, he launched prodigious blasts off pitchers in the Negro Leagues, on the barnstorming tour, and in Latin America. As talented as any major league star, Gibson died in January 1947, at age 35, just three months before Jackie Robinson joined the Brooklyn Dodgers. Leonard, four-years older than Gibson, starred in both the Negro and Mexican Leagues as a sure-handed, power-hitting first baseman. The Newark Eagles in the early 1940s, boasted the "million dollar infield" of first baseman Mule Suttles, second baseman Dick Seay, shortstop Willie Wells, and third baseman Ray Dandridge. The acrobatic

fielding skills of Seay, Wells and Dandridge led Roy Campanella to call this the greatest infield he ever saw.

Amidst the many talented Negro Leaguers of 1930s and 1940s, however, one long, lean figure came to personify black baseball to blacks and whites alike. Leroy "Satchel" Paige began his prolonged athletic odyssey in his hometown in 1924 as a 17-year-old pitcher with the semi-professional Mobile Tigers. He joined the Chattanooga Black Lookouts of the Negro Southern League in 1926. Two years later, the Lookouts sold his contract to the Birmingham Black Barons. By 1930, his explosive fastball, impeccable control, and eccentric mannerisms had made him a legend in the South. In 1932, Gus Greenlee brought Paige to the Pittsburgh Crawfords where the colorful pitcher embellished his reputation by winning 54 games in his first two years. Greenlee also began the practice of hiring out Paige to semi-professional clubs that needed a one-day box office boost.

For seven years Paige feuded with Greenlee, jumping the club when a better offer appeared, being banished "for life," and then returning. In the mid-1930s, in addition to his stints with the Crawfords, Paige won fame by boosting Bismarck, North Dakota, to the national semi-professional championships, hurling for the Dominican Republic at the behest of dictator Rafael Trujillo, in the Mexican League, and especially on the postseason barnstorming trail pitted against Dizzy Dean's Major League All-Stars. "That skinny old Satchel Paige with those long arms is my idea of the pitcher with the greatest stuff I ever saw," claimed the unusually immodest Dean.

Paige's appeal stemmed as much from his unusual persona as his pitching prowess. A born showman, Paige's lanky, lackadaisical presence evoked popular racial stereotypes of the age. "As undependable as a pair of second-hand suspenders," Paige often arrived late or failed to show. His names for his pitches (the "bee ball" which buzzed and all of a sudden, "be there"; the "jump ball"; and the "trouble ball") and his minstrel show one-liners enhanced the image. But on the mound, Paige invariably rose to the occasion against top competition or challenged inferior opponents by calling in the outfield or promising to strike out the side.

In 1938, a sore arm threatened to curtail Paige's career but the Kansas City Monarchs, hoping his reputation alone would draw fans, signed him for their traveling second team. On the road, Paige perfected a repertoire of curves and off-speed pitches, including his famous "hesitation" pitch. When his fastball returned in 1939, he became a better pitcher than ever. Promoted to the main Monarch club, Paige pitched the team to four consecutive Negro American League pennants. From 1941-1947, although officially still a Monarch, Paige spent far more time as an independent performer, hired out by Monarchs' owner J. L. Wilkinson to semi-pro and Negro League clubs. "He kept our league going," recalls Othello Renfroe. "Anytime a team got into trouble, it sent for Satchel to pitch." Paige also continued to hurl against major league All-Star teams. In the 1940s, the example of Satchel Paige, whose legend had spread into the white community, offered the most compelling argument for the desegregation of the National Pastime.

Paige's exploits against white players revealed a fundamental irony about baseball in the Jim Crow era. While organized baseball rigidly enforced its ban on black players within the major and minor leagues, opportunities abounded for black athletes to prove themselves against white competition along

the unpoliced boundaries of the national pastime. During the 1930s, Western promoters sponsored tournaments for the best semi-professional teams in the nation. These squads often featured former and future major leaguers as well as top local talent. In 1934, the *Denver Post* tourney, "the little World Series of the West," invited the Kansas City Monarchs to compete for the $7,500 first prize. The Monarchs fought their way into the finals against the House of David team (also owned by J. L. Wilkinson) only to find themselves confronted on the mound by Paige, rented out to pitch this one game. Paige outdueled Monarchs ace, Chet Brewer, 2–1. Black teams became a fixture in the Post series, emerging victorious for several consecutive years.

In 1935, the National Baseball Congress began an annual tournament in Wichita, Kansas. The competition attracted community squads heartily bankrolled by local business leaders. Neil Churchill, an auto dealer from Bismarck, North Dakota, recruited a half-dozen black stars, including Paige and Brewer, to represent the town in the Wichita competition. Bismarck naturally swept the series, and thereafter teams that were either integrated or all black routinely appeared in the National Baseball Congress invitational each year.

In an age in which the major leagues were confined to the East and Midwest, and television had yet to bring baseball into people's homes, postseason tours by big league stars offered yet another opportunity for black players to prove their equality on the diamond. Games pitting blacks against whites were popular features of the barnstorming circuit. Until the late 1920s, when Commissioner Kenesaw Mountain Landis limited postseason play to all-star squads, black teams frequently met and defeated major league clubs in postseason competition. During the next decade, matchups between the Babe Ruth or Dizzy Dean "All-Stars" and black players became frequent. In the autumns of 1934 and 1935, Dean's team traveled the nation accompanied by the "Satchel Paige All-Stars." In one memorable 1934 game, called by baseball executive Bill Veeck, "the greatest pitching battle I have ever seen," Paige bested Dean 1–0. Surviving records of interracial contests during the 1930s reveal that blacks won two-thirds of the games. "That's when we played the hardest," asserted Judy Johnson, "to let them know, and to let the public know, that we had the same talent they did and probably a little better at times."

The rivalries proved particularly keen on the West Coast where Monarchs co-owner Tom Baird organized the California Winter League, which included black teams, white major and minor league stars, and some of Mexico's top players. In 1940, pitcher Chet Brewer formed the Kansas City Royals, which each year fielded one of the best clubs on the coast. One year the Royals defeated the Hollywood Stars, who had won the Pacific Coast League championship, six straight times. In 1945, Brewer's team, including Jackie Robinson and Satchel Paige, regularly defeated major league competition.

The most famous of the interracial barnstorming tours occurred in 1946, when Cleveland Indian pitcher Bob Feller organized a major league All-Star Team, rented two Flying Tiger aircraft and hopped the nation accompanied by the Satchel Paige All-Stars. With Feller and Paige each pitching a few innings a day, the tour proved extremely lucrative for promoters and players alike and gave widespread publicity to the skills of the black athletes.

The World War Two years marked the heyday of the Negro Leagues. With black and white workers flooding into North-ern industrial centers, relatively full employment, and a scarcity of available consumer goods, attendance at all sorts of entertainment events increased dramatically. In 1942, three million fans saw Negro League teams play, while the East-West game in 1943 attracted over 51,000 fans. "Even the white folks was coming out big," recalled Satchel Paige.

But World War Two also generated forces which would challenge the foundations of Jim Crow baseball. In the armed forces, baseball teams like the Black Bluejackets of the Great Lakes Naval Station team posted outstanding records against teams featuring white major leaguers. In 1945, a well-publicized tournament of teams in the European theatre featured top black players like Leon Day, Joe Green, and Willard Brown in the championship round. More significantly, the hypocrisy of blacks fighting for their country but unable to participate in the national pastime grew steadily more apparent. As wartime manpower shortages forced major league teams to rely on a 15-year-old pitcher, over-the-hill veterans, and one-armed Pete Gray, their refusal to sign black players seemed increasingly irrational. "How do you think I felt when I saw a one-armed outfielder?" moaned Chet Brewer. Pitcher Nate Moreland protested, "I can play in Mexico, but I have to fight for America where I can't play." Pickets at Yankee Stadium carried placards asking, "If we are able to stop bullets, why not balls?"

Amidst this heightened awareness, organized baseball repeatedly walked to the precipice of integration, but always failed to take the final leap. In 1942, Moreland and All-American football star Jackie Robinson requested a tryout at a White Sox training camp in Pasadena, California. Robinson, in particular, impressed White Sox Jimmy Dykes but nothing came of the event. Brooklyn Dodger manager Leo Durocher publicly stated his willingness to sign blacks, only to receive a stinging rebuke from Commissioner Landis. Landis again short-circuited integration talk the following year. At the annual baseball meetings, black leaders led by actor Paul Robeson gained the opportunity to address major league owners on the issue, but Landis ruled all further discussion out of order.

In 1943, several minor and major league teams were rumored close to signing black players. In California, where winter league play had demonstrated the potential of black players, several clubs considered integration. The Los Angeles Angels of the Pacific Coast League announced tryouts for three black players, but pressure from other league owners doomed the plan. Oakland owner Vince DeVicenzi ordered Manager Johnny Vergez to consider pitcher Chet Brewer, the most popular black player on the West Coast, for the Oaks. Vergez refused and the issue died. Two years later, Bakersfield, a Cleveland Indian farm team in the California League, offered Brewer a position as player-coach, but the parent club vetoed the plan.

At the major league level, Washington Senators owner Clark Griffith called sluggers Josh Gibson and Buck Leonard into his office and asked if they would like to play in the major leagues. They answered affirmatively, but never heard from Griffith again. In Pittsburgh, *Daily Worker* sports editor Nat Low pressured Pirate owner William Benswanger to arrange a tryout for catcher Roy Campanella and pitcher Dave Barnhill. At the last minute, Benswanger canceled the audition, citing "unnamed pressures." The most promising situation occurred in Philadelphia where young Bill Veeck had arranged to buy the Phillies. Veeck planned to stock the team

with Negro League stars, whom he felt sure would guarantee Philadelphia the pennant. When Commissioner Landis learned of his plans, however, Veeck suddenly found his purchase blocked.

For more than two decades, the imperial Landis had reigned over baseball as an implacable foe of integration. While hypocritically denying the existence of any "rule, formal or informal, or any understanding—unwritten, subterranean, or sub-anything—against the signing of Negro players," Landis had stringently policed the color line. His death in 1944 removed a major barrier for integration advocates.

In April 1945, with World War Two entering its final months, the integration crusade gained momentum. On April 6, *People's Voice* sportswriter Joe Bostic appeared at the Brooklyn Dodger training camp at Bear Mountain, New York, with two Negro League players, Terris McDuffie and Dave "Showboat" Thomas, and demanded a tryout. An outraged, but outmaneuvered Dodger President Branch Rickey, allowed the pair to work out with the club. One week later, a more serious confrontation occurred in Boston. The Red Sox, under pressure from popular columnist Dave Egan and city councilman Isidore Muchnick, agreed to audition Sam Jethroe, the Negro League's leading hitter in 1944, second baseman Marvin Williams, and Kansas City Monarch shortstop Jackie Robinson, all top prospects in their mid-twenties. The Fenway Park tryout, however, proved little more than a formality and the players never again heard from the Red Sox.

The publicity surrounding these events, however, forced the major leagues to address the issue at its April meetings. At the urging of black sportswriter Sam Lacy, Leslie O'Connor, Landis's interim successor, established a Major League Committee on Baseball Integration in April 1945, to review the problem. In addition, the racial views of newly appointed Commissioner A. B. "Happy" Chandler came under close scrutiny. A former governor of the segregated state of Kentucky, Chandler nonetheless offered at least verbal support to the entry of blacks into organized ball. "If a black boy can make it on Okinawa and Guadalcanal, hell, he can make it in baseball," Chandler told black reporter Rick Roberts. Whether Chandler, however, unlike Landis, would reinforce his rhetoric with positive actions remained uncertain.

Unbeknownst to the integration advocates, baseball officials, and local politicians sand-dancing around the race issue, Branch Rickey, the president of the Brooklyn Dodgers, had already set in motion the events which would lead to the historic breakthrough.

Raised in rural Ohio in a strict Methodist family, Rickey, nicknamed by sportwriters "The Deacon" and "The Mahatma," had financed his way through college and law school playing and coaching baseball. His skills as a catcher merited two years in the major leagues. In 1913, he abandoned a fledgling law career to manage the St. Louis Browns, and in 1917 he began a 25-year relationship with the St. Louis Cardinals. Rickey served as the field manager of the Cardinals from 1919-1925, after which he became the club's vice-president and business manager. In the 1920s and 1930s, Rickey perfected the farm system, whereby a major league team controlled young, undeveloped players through a chain of minor league franchises. This innovation allowed the Cardinals to compete equally with richer teams in larger cities, generating pennants for the "Gas House Gang" and

allowing the team to profitably sell off surplus talent.

Although Rickey later claimed that his desire to integrate baseball dated from 1904, when an Indiana hotel had denied lodgings to a black player on his college squad, he gave no indication of any interest in the race issue during his years in St. Louis. Perhaps this stemmed from the fact that St. Louis was a Southern city with firmly entrenched segregationist traditions. Throughout Rickey's reign with the Cardinals, blacks sat in Jim Crow sections at Sportsman's Park, a policy which he never openly challenged.

Nonetheless, in 1942, when Rickey left the Cardinals and assumed control of the Brooklyn Dodgers, he informed the Dodger ownership of his intentions to recruit black players in the near future. Rickey never clearly explained the motivations for this dramatic turnaround. At times Rickey cited moral considerations, stating, "I couldn't face my God much longer knowing that His black creatures are held separate and distinct from His white creatures in the game that has given me all I own." On other occasions, he eschewed the role of "crusader," proclaiming, "My selfish objective is to win baseball games. . .The Negroes will make us winners for years to come." Some observers saw financial reasons behind Rickey's actions, citing the lure of the growing black population in Northern cities and the prospects of increased attendance. Certainly, Brooklyn offered a more congenial atmosphere for integration than St. Louis. In all probability, a combination of these factors—geographic, moral, competitive, and financial—coupled with Rickey's desire for a broader role in history, impelled him to seek black players.

From 1942-1945, Rickey, a conservative, cautious, and conspiratorial man, moved slowly, studying the philosophical and sociological ramifications of integration and taking few people into his confidence. During the spring and summer of 1945, under the guise of creating a new black baseball circuit, the United States League, Rickey's scouts combed the nation and the Caribbean for black players. Rickey sought one player who would spearhead the breakthrough and several other potential stars who would follow in his wake. By August 1945, scouting reports and Rickey's own investigations pointed to one man as the ideal candidate for the struggle ahead—Kansas City Monarch shortstop Jackie Robinson.

In Robinson, Rickey had found a rare combination of athletic ability, competitive fire, intelligence, maturity, and poise. Born in Georgia and raised in Pasadena, California, Robinson had won fame at UCLA as the nation's greatest all-around athlete, earning All-America honors in football, establishing broad-jump records, and leading his basketball conference in scoring, all in addition to his baseball exploits. In 1942, he enlisted in the army where he attended officer's candidate school and became a lieutenant. Two years later, while stationed in Texas, Robinson's refusal to move to the back of a bus resulted in a court martial and ultimate acquittal. This incident demonstrated his commitment to the cause of equal rights. After his discharge from the army, Robinson joined the Monarchs and earned a starting spot in the 1945 East-West All-Star Game. Robinson's college education, experience in interracial athletics, and army career complemented his playing talents. But his fiery pride and temper seemed a potential obstacle to his success.

On August 28, 1945, Robinson met with Rickey at the latter's Brooklyn offices. Rickey revealed his bold plan to integrate organized baseball and challenged Robinson to accept the primary role. The Mahatma flamboyantly playacted,

assuming the role of racist players, fans and hotel clerks, impressing upon Robinson the need to "turn the other cheek" in the event of racial confrontations. By the end of the session, Robinson had signed a contract to play for the Montreal Royals in the International League, the top farm team in the Brooklyn system. Rickey promised that if Robinson's performance merited it, he would be promoted to the Dodgers.

Rickey intended to announce the Robinson signing along with that of several other black players, but political pressures stemming from the New York City fall elections forced him to abandon his original plans and, on October 23, 1945, to reveal the signing of Robinson alone. The announcement sent shock waves through the baseball establishment and placed Robinson into a spotlight that he would never relinquish. Numerous sports figures, from players to executives to reporters, predicted the ultimate failure of Rickey's "great experiment."

Robinson's first test came at spring training in Florida in 1946. Thrust into the deep South where Jim Crow reigned supreme, Robinson and black pitcher John Wright, whom Rickey had recruited to room with Robinson, found themselves unable to room with their teammates and barred from playing in Jacksonville and other Florida cities. In addition, a shoulder injury hindered Robinson's performance, raising doubts about his abilities.

On April 18, 1946, at Roosevelt Stadium in Jersey City, Robinson became the first black to appear in modern Organized Baseball (excepting Jimmy Claxton, who passed as white in 1916 for the Oakland Oaks of the Pacific Coast League). In the process he staged one of the most remarkable performances under pressure in the history of the game. In Robinson's second at-bat, he hit a three-run home run. He followed this with three singles and two stolen bases, scoring a total of four runs. As the *New York Times* reported, "This would have been a big day for any man, but under the circumstances, it was a tremendous feat."

In many respects, 1946 proved a nightmare season for Robinson. Fans jeered him in Baltimore, and opposing players tormented him with insults. Pitchers made him a frequent target of brushback pitches and baserunners attempted to spike and maim him at second base. As the season drew to a close, Robinson hovered on the brink of a nervous breakdown. Through it all, however, Robinson remained a dominant force on the field. His .349 batting average and 113 runs-scored led the league and paced the Royals to the International League pennant. His presence inspired new attendance records throughout the circuit. In the Little World Series, which pitted Montreal against the Louisville Colonels of the American Association, Robinson braved the hostility of Kentucky fans and stroked game-winning hits in the final two games to give the Royals the championship.

Rickey's initiative and Robinson's dramatic success failed to inspire other team owners. In August, major league executives debated a controversial report discussing the "Race Question" which argued that integration would "lessen the value of several major league franchises." No other clubs moved to sign black players. Only four blacks, all in the Brooklyn system, joined Robinson in organized baseball in 1946. At Nashua, New Hampshire, in the New England League, the Dodger farm club fielded catcher Roy Campanella and pitcher Don Newcombe. The Nashua Dodgers won the league championship largely due to Campanella's hitting and Newcombe's hurling. In the small town of Trois

Rivières in Quebec, pitchers John Wright and Roy Partlow, both of whom had appeared briefly with Robinson at Montreal, led a third Dodger farm team to the Canadian-American league crown. Nonetheless, at the start of the 1947 season, no additional black players appeared on major or minor league rosters.

Although Robinson's performance at Montreal merited promotion to the Dodgers, Robinson remained a Royal when he reported to spring training in 1947. Rickey hoped that the Brooklyn players themselves, when exposed to Robinson's talents, would request his addition to the team. He switched Robinson to first base, a weak spot on the Dodger squad, to make his case more compelling. Robinson compiled a .519 batting average against the major leaguers, but several Dodger players, instead of demanding his promotion, rebelled. Led by "Dixie" Walker, a group of mostly Southern Dodgers circulated a petition against Robinson. Rickey moved quickly to short-circuit the dissension, threatening to trade any athletes who opposed Robinson. In addition, the refusal of Pete Reiser, "Pee Wee" Reese and other Dodger stars to support the protestors, effectively squelched the petition drive. Finally, on April 10, just five days before the start of the 1947 season, Rickey officially announced that Robinson would join the Dodgers.

Throughout the early months of the 1947 campaign Robinson stoically endured crises and challenges. The Philadelphia Phillies, led by manager Ben Chapman, unleashed a barrage of verbal abuse against Robinson which horrified Dodger players and fans. The Benjamin Franklin Hotel in Philadelphia refused lodgings for Robinson and death threats appeared among his voluminous daily mail. In early May, rumors that the St. Louis Cardinals planned to strike rather than compete against Robinson prompted National League President Ford Frick to warn the players, "If you do this you will be suspended from the league." Opposing pitchers targeted Robinson's body at a record setting pace and an early season 0 for 20 batting drought led many to question his qualifications. "But for the fact that he is the first acknowledged Negro in major league history," observed a Cincinnati sportswriter, "he would have been benched a week ago."

Yet, as the season unfolded, Robinson converted doubters and enemies into admirers. By the end of June, a 21-game hitting streak had raised his batting average to .315 and propelled the Dodgers into first place. Robinson's daring baserunning, typical of Negro League play, evoked images of an "Ebony Ty Cobb." In city after city, record crowds flocked to experience Robinson's charismatic dynamism as five teams set new all-time season attendance marks. While periodic controversies erupted over baserunners who used their spikes "to make a pincushion out of Robinson" at first base, Robinson won the acceptance and respect of teammates and opponents alike. In September, as the Dodgers coasted to the pennant, the *Sporting News* named Robinson the major league Rookie of the Year. To cap his triumphant season, Robinson became the first black player to appear in the World Series.

Robinson's success on the field and at the box office stimulated some movement on the part of other clubs to hire black players. In Cleveland Bill Veeck recruited 23-year-old Larry Doby, who jumped straight from the Negro League Newark Eagles to the Indians in July. Used sparingly, Doby batted a meager .156, casting doubts upon his future. The St. Louis Browns, seeking to boost flagging attendance, signed Willard

Brown and Hank Thompson of the Kansas City Monarchs. When the turnstiles failed to respond, the Browns released both Brown and Thompson, although the latter had established himself as a top prospect. In the National League, the Dodgers signed Dan Bankhead to bolster the club's pitching down the stretch. On August 25, Bankhead, the first black pitcher to appear in the major leagues, surrendered eight runs in three innings but also slammed a home run in his initial at bat.

In addition to the five athletes who appeared in the major leagues, a handful of blacks surfaced in the minors. Campanella succeeded Robinson at Montreal, earning accolades as "the best catcher in the business." Newcombe returned to Nashua where he won 19 games. The independent Stamford Bombers of the Colonial League fielded six black players, and two blacks, including future major leaguer Chuck Harmon, played in the Canadian-American League. Veteran Negro League hurler Nate Moreland won 20 games in California's Class C Sunset League. For the most part, however, organized baseball continued to ignore the treasure trove of black talent submerged in the Negro Leagues. A full year would pass before additional major league teams would add black players to their chains.

In 1948, the integration focus shifted from the Dodgers, where Robinson now reigned at second base, to the Cleveland Indians. In spring training, Larry Doby, who had performed so dismally in 1947, unexpectedly won a starting berth in the Cleveland outfield. After an erratic early season stretch in which Doby alternated errors and strikeouts with tape-measure home runs, he batted .301 and became a key performer for the American League champion Indians. In July, Cleveland owner Bill Veeck added the legendary Satchel Paige to the team. Amidst charges that his signing had been a publicity stunt, the 42-year-old Paige won six out of seven decisions, including back-to-back shutouts, and posted a 2.47 earned run average. Standing-room-only crowds greeted him in Washington, Chicago, Boston, and even in Cleveland's mammoth Municipal Stadium. The Indians, after defeating the Boston Red Sox in a pennant playoff, won the World Series in six games with Doby's .318 average leading the club.

In 1947, the Dodgers had integrated and reached the World Series; in 1948, the Indians had duplicated and surpassed this achievement. Both teams had set all-time attendance records. Remarkably, as the 1948 season drew to a close, no other franchise had followed their lead. In the minor leagues, Roy Campanella became the first black in the American Association, stopping at St. Paul before permanently joining Robinson on the Dodgers. Newcombe and Bankhead each won more than 20 games for Brooklyn affiliates. The Dodgers also added fleet-footed Sam Jethroe to the Montreal roster, where he batted .322. The Indians also began to stockpile black talent, signing future major leaguers Al Smith, Dave Hoskins, and Orestes "Minnie" Minoso to minor league contracts. Several other blacks, including San Diego catcher John Ritchey, who broke the Pacific Coast League color line, played for independent teams.

In the interregnum between the 1948 and 1949 seasons four more teams—the Giants, Yankees, Braves, and Cubs—signed blacks to play in their farm systems, and 1949 would herald the beginning of widespread integration in the minor leagues. Blacks starred in all three Triple A leagues. In the Pacific Coast League, Luke Easter won acclaim as the "greatest natural hitter . . . since Ted Williams," amassing 25 home runs and 92 runs-batted-in in just 80 games before succumbing to a knee injury. Oakland's Artie Wilson led the league in hits, stolen bases, and batting average. In the International League, Jethroe scored 151 runs and stole 89 bases while Montreal teammate Dan Bankhead won 20 games for the second straight year. At Jersey City, Monte Irvin batted .373. The outstanding performer in the American Association was Ray Dandridge. Considered by many the greatest third baseman of all time, the acrobatic Dandridge, now in his late 30s, thrilled Minneapolis fans with his spectacular fielding, batting .364 in the process. Former Negro Leaguers turned in equally stellar performances at lower minor league levels as well.

In the major leagues, the spotlight again returned to Jackie Robinson. For three years, Robinson had honored his pledge to Branch Rickey "to turn the other cheek" and avoid confrontations. With his position in the majors firmly established, Robinson announced, "They better be prepared to be rough this year, because I'm going to be rough on them." The more combative Robinson produced his finest year, batting .342 and earning the Most Valuable Player Award. Complemented by teammates Newcombe and Campanella, Robinson led the Dodgers to another pennant.

By the end of the 1949 season, integration had achieved spectacular success at both the major and minor league level, but most teams moved "with all deliberate speed" in signing black players. The New York Giants joined the interracial ranks in 1949 when they promoted Monte Irvin and Hank Thompson. The following year, the Boston Braves purchased Jethroe from the Dodgers for $100,000 and installed him in the starting lineup. In 1951, the Chicago White Sox acquired Minnie Minoso in a trade with Cleveland, and Bill Veeck, who had acquired the hapless St. Louis Browns, brought back Satchel Paige for another major league stint. Yet, as late as August 1953, out of sixteen major league teams only these six fielded black players. Several teams displayed an interest in signing blacks but bypassed established Negro League stars who might have jumped directly to the majors, concentrating instead on younger prospects for the minor leagues. Still others like the Red Sox, Phillies, Cardinals, and Tigers continued to pursue a whites-only policy.

This failure to hire and promote blacks occurred amidst a continuing backdrop of outstanding performances by black players. The first generation of players from the Negro Leagues proved an extraordinary group. Jackie Robinson quickly established himself as one of the dominant stars in the national pastime, compiling a .311 batting average over his 10-year career while thrilling fans with his baserunning and clutch-hitting talents. Sportswriters called him, "the most dangerous man in baseball today." Campanella won accolades as the best catcher in the National League and won the Most Valuable Player Award in 1951, 1953, and 1955. Both Campanella and Robinson later won election to the Baseball Hall of Fame. Pitcher Don Newcombe averaged better than 20 wins a season during his first five full years with the Dodgers. In addition, from 1950-1953 Negro League graduates Sam Jethroe, Willie Mays, Joe Black, and Jim Gilliam each won the National League Rookie of the Year Award.

In the American League, where integration proceeded at a slower pace, several players compiled outstanding records. Larry Doby, while never achieving the superstar status many expected, nonetheless became a steady producer, twice leading the league in home runs and five times driving in more

than 100 runs. His Cleveland teammate Luke Easter, who reached the majors in his mid-30s, slugged 86 home runs and drove in 300 runs in his brief three-season career. Satchel Paige, after a two-year stint with the Indians, joined the hapless St. Louis Browns from 1951-1953 and became one of the American League's best relief pitchers. On the Chicago White Sox, Minnie Minoso proved himself a consistent .300 hitter. Despite their relatively small numbers, teams with black players in both major leagues regularly finished high in the standings and only in 1950 did both pennant winners field all-white squads. In addition, the more aggressive stance of National League teams in recruiting black players gave that circuit a clear superiority in World Series and All-Star contests for more than two decades.

By the end of the 1953 season, the benefits of integration had grown apparent to all but the most recalcitrant of major league owners. In September, the Chicago Cubs purchased shortstop Ernie Banks from the Kansas City Monarchs and finally elevated longtime minor league standout Gene Baker. Connie Mack's Philadelphia Athletics ended their Jim Crow era by acquiring pitcher Bob Trice. At the start of the 1954 season, the Washington Senators, St. Louis Cardinals, Pittsburgh Pirates, and Cincinnati Reds all joined the interracial ranks. The sudden integration of six more clubs left only the Yankees, Tigers, Phillies, and Red Sox with all-white personnel. In addition, 1954 marked the debut of young Henry Aaron with the Braves and the return of Willie Mays, who had sparkled for the Giants in 1951, from military service.

The desegregation of organized baseball opened the way not only to blacks in the United States but to those in other parts of the Americas as well. Throughout the 20th century, baseball had imposed a curious double standard on Latin players, accepting those with light complexions but rejecting their darker countrymen. With the color barrier down, major league clubs found a wealth of talent in the Carribbean. Minnie Minoso, the "Cuban Comet" who integrated the Chicago White Sox, became the first of the great Latin stars. Over a 15-year career, Minoso compiled a .298 batting average. In 1954, slick-fielding Puerto Rican Vic Power launched his career with the Athletics. The following year, Roberto Clemente, the greatest of the Latin stars, debuted with the Pittsburgh Pirates. The proud Puerto Rican won four batting championships and amassed 3,000 hits en route to a .317 lifetime batting average. In the late 1950s, the San Francisco Giants revealed the previously ignored treasure trove that existed in the Dominican Republic. In 1958, Felipe Alou became the first of three Alou brothers to play for the Giants, and in 1960 the Giants unveiled pitcher Juan Marichal, "the Dominican Dandy," who won 243 games en route to the Hall of Fame.

Among the early Latin players were two sons of stars of the Jim Crow age. Perucho Cepeda, who had won renown as "The Bull" in his native Puerto Rico, had refused to play in the segregated Negro leagues. His son Orlando, dubbed "The Baby Bull," went on to star for the Giants and Cardinals. Luis Tiant, Sr., a standout performer in both Cuba and the Negro Leagues, lived to see Luis, Jr. win over 200 major league games and excel in the 1975 World Series.

As the major leagues moved slowly toward complete desegregation, throughout the nation blacks invaded the minor leagues. In the Northern and Western states, these athletes, a combination of youthful prospects and Negro League veterans, were greeted by a storm of insults, beanballs, and dis-

crimination. "I learned more names than I thought we had," states Piper Davis of his treatment by fans in the Pacific Coast League. At least a half-dozen blacks had to be carried off the field on stretchers after being hit by pitches between 1949 and 1951. In city after city, blacks found hotels and restaurants unwilling to serve them. "At the same time when they signed blacks and Latins," argues John Roseboro about his Dodger employers, "they should have made sure they would be welcome." But neither the Dodgers nor other clubs provided any special assistance for their black farmhands. Despite these conditions, blacks compiled remarkable records in league after league. In the early 1950s, blacks overcame adversity and dominated the lists of batting leaders at the Triple A level and in many of the lower circuits as well.

In 1952, blacks began to appear on minor league clubs in the Jim Crow South. The Dallas Eagles of the Texas League, hoping to boost sagging attendance, signed former Homestead Gray pitcher Dave Hoskins to become the "Jackie Robinson of the Texas League." Hoskins took the Lone Star State by storm, attracting record crowds en route to a 22–10 record. The black pitcher posted a 2.12 earned run average and also finished third in the league in batting with a .328 mark. By 1955, every Texas League club except Shreveport fielded black players.

Hoskins' performance inspired other teams throughout the South to scramble for black players. In 1953, 19-year-old Henry Aaron desegregated the South Atlantic League, which included clubs in Florida, Atlanta, and Georgia, while Bill White appeared in the Carolina League. Playing for Jacksonville (a city which seven years earlier had barred Jackie Robinson), Aaron "led the league in everything but hotel accommodations." By 1954, when the United States Supreme Court issued its historic *Brown* v. *Board of Education* decision ordering school desegregation, blacks had appeared in most Southern minor leagues.

The integration of the South, however, did not proceed without incidents. Black players recall these years as "an ordeal" or a "sentence" and described the South as "enemy country" or a "hellhole." In 1953, the Cotton States League barred brothers Jim and Leander Tugerson from competing. The following year, Nat Peeples broke the color line in the Southern Association, but lasted only two weeks. For the remainder of the decade, the league adhered to a whites-only policy, a strategy which contributed to the collapse of the Southern Association in 1961. As resistance to the civil rights movement mounted in the 1950s, black players found themselves in increasingly hostile territory. Even in the pioneering Texas League, teams visiting Shreveport, Louisiana, in 1956 had to leave their black players at home due to stricter segregation laws.

In the face of these obstacles, young black stars like Aaron, Curt Flood, Frank Robinson, Bill White, and Leon Wagner overcame their frustrations "by taking it out on the ball." "What had started as a chance to test my baseball ability in a professional setting," wrote Curt Flood, "had become an obligation to test myself as a man." Throughout the 1950s, blacks appeared regularly among the league leaders of the Texas, South Atlantic, Carolina, and other circuits, advancing both their own careers and the cause of integration.

As these events unfolded in the South, the major leagues completed their long overdue integration process. In 1955, the Yankees, after denying charges of racism for almost a decade, finally promoted Elston Howard to the parent club.

Two more years passed before the Phillies integrated, and not until 1958 did a black player don a Tiger uniform. Thus, at the start of the 1959 season, only the Boston Red Sox, who had yet to hire either black scouts or representatives in the Caribbean, retained their Jim Crow heritage. A storm of protest arose when the Red Sox cut black infielder Elijah "Pumpsie" Green just before Opening Day, but on July 21, 1959, 12 years and 107 days after Jackie Robinson's Dodger debut, Green won promotion to the Boston club, completing the cycle of major league integration.

While integration became a reality in organized baseball, the Negro Leagues gradually faded into oblivion. As early as 1947, Negro League attendance, especially in cities close to National League parks, dropped precipitously. "People wanted to go Brooklynites," recalls Monarch pitcher Hilton Smith. "Even if we were playing here in Kansas City, people wanted to go over to St. Louis to see Jackie." Negro League owners hoped to offset declining attendance by selling players to organized baseball, but major league teams paid what Effa Manley called "bargain basement" prices for all-star talent. In 1948, the Manleys' Newark Eagles and New York Black Yankees disbanded. The Homestead Grays severed all league connections and returned to its roots as a barnstorming unit. Without these teams, the Negro National League collapsed. A reorganized 10-team Negro American League, most of whose franchises were located in minor league cities, vowed to go on, but the spread of integration quickly thinned its ranks. By 1951, the league had dwindled to six teams. Two years later, only the Birmingham Black Barons, Memphis Red Sox, Kansas City Monarchs, and Indianapolis Clowns remained.

For several years in the early 1950s, the Negro Leagues remained a breeding ground for young black talent. The New York Giants plucked Willie Mays from the roster of the Birmingham Black Barons, while the Boston Braves discovered Hank Aaron on the Indianapolis Clowns. The Kansas City Monarchs produced more than two dozen major leaguers, including Robinson, Paige, Banks, and Howard. But for most black players, the demise of the Negro Leagues had disastrous effects. "The livelihoods, the careers, the families of 400 Negro ballplayers are in jeopardy," complained Effa Manley in 1948, "because four players were successful in getting into the major leagues." The slow pace of integration left most in a state of limbo set adrift by their former teams, but still unwelcomed in organized baseball. Some players like Buck Leonard and Cool Papa Bell were too old to be considered, while others like Ray Dandridge and Piper Davis found themselves relegated to the minor leagues, where outstanding records failed to win them promotion.

Throughout the 1950s the Negro American League struggled to survive, recruiting teenagers and second-rate talent for the modest four-team loop. In 1963, Kansas City hosted the 30th and last East-West All-Star Game and the following year the famed Monarchs ceased touring the nation. By 1965, the Indianapolis Clowns remained as a last vestige of Jim Crow baseball. Utilizing white as well as black players, the Clowns continued for another decade. "We are all show now," explained their owner, 'We clown, clown, clown."

But the legacy of the Negro Leagues remained. Robinson and other early black players introduced new elements of speed and "tricky baseball" into the major leagues, transforming and improving the quality of play. Since 1947, blacks have led the National League in stolen bases in all but two

seasons. In the American League, a black or Latin baserunner has topped the league every year since 1951 with only two exceptions. Nor did this injection of speed come at the expense of power. In the 1950s and 1960s, Hank Aaron, Willie Mays, and Frank Robinson reigned as the greatest power hitters in baseball. Thus, by the 1960s, the national pastime more closely resembled the well-balanced offensive structure of the Negro Leagues than the unidimensional power-oriented attack that had typified the all-white majors.

The demise of the Negro Leagues and the decline of segregation in the majors, however, did not end discrimination. Conditions on and off the field, in spring training and in the executive suites, repeatedly reminded the black athletes of their second-class status. In the early 1950s, all-white teams taunted their black opponents with racial insults. Blacks like Jackie and Frank Robinson, Minnie Minoso and Luke Easter repeatedly appeared among the league leaders in being hit by pitches. While black superstars like Willie Mays had little difficulty ascending to the major leagues, players of only slightly above average talent found themselves buried for years in the minors. Many observers charged that teams had imposed quotas on the number of blacks they would field at one time.

In cities like St. Louis, Washington, D. C., and, later, Baltimore, black ballplayers could not stay at hotels with their teammates. In 1954, they achieved a breakthrough of sorts when the luxury Chase Hotel in St. Louis informed Jackie Robinson and other Dodger players that they could room there, but had to refrain from using the dining room or swimming pool or loitering in the lobby. Ten years later, the hotel had removed these restrictions, but still relegated black players, according to Hank Aaron, to rooms "looking out over some old building or some green pastures or a blank wall, so nobody can see us through a window."

Blacks faced even greater discrimination each year in spring training in Florida. While all spring training sites now accepted blacks, segregation statutes and local traditions forced them to live in all-black boarding houses far from the luxury air-conditioned hotels which accommodated white players. "The whole set-up is wrong," protested Jackie Robinson. "There is no reason why we shouldn't be able to live with our teammates." When teams traveled from place to place, blacks could not join their fellow players in restaurants. Instead they had to wait on the bus until someone brought their food out to them. Some teams attempted to reduce the problems faced by blacks. Several clubs moved to Arizona, where conditions were only moderately improved. The Dodgers built a special spring training camp at Vero Beach where players could live together. Most organizations, however, did very little to assist their black employees.

By the time that Jackie Robinson retired in 1956, conditions had barely improved. "After 10 years of traveling in the South," he charged, " I don't think advances have been fast enough. It's my belief that baseball itself hasn't done all it can to remedy the problems faced by . . . players." Over the next decade, a new generation of black players militantly demanded change. Cardinal stars Bill White, Curt Flood, and Bob Gibson protested against conditions in St. Petersburg, while Aaron and other black Braves demanded changes in Bradenton. In many instances, however, significant changes awaited passage of the Civil Rights Act of 1965 barring segregation in public facilities.

By 1960, Robinson, Campanella, Doby, and the cadre of

Negro League veterans who had formed the vanguard of baseball integration had retired. In their wake, a second generation of black players, most of whom had never appeared in the Negro Leagues, made most Americans forget that Jim Crow baseball had ever existed, as they shattered longstanding "unbreakable" records. In 1962, black shortstop Maury Wills stole 104 bases, eclipsing Ty Cobb's 47-year-old stolen base mark. Twelve years later, outfielder Lou Brock stole 118 bases en route to breaking Cobb's career stolen-base record as well. In 1966, Frank Robinson, who had won the National League Most Valuable Player Award in 1961, became the first player to win that honor in both leagues when he led the Baltimore Orioles to the American League pennant. By the end of his career, Robinson had slugged 586 home runs; only Babe Ruth among players of the Jim Crow era had hit more. Both Ernie Banks and Willie McCovey also amassed more than 500 home runs during this era. On the pitcher's mound, the indomitable Bob Gibson proved himself one of the greatest strikeout pitchers in the game's history. Upon retirement, Gibson had amassed more strikeouts than anyone except Walter Johnson. Brock, Frank Robinson, Banks, McCovey, and Gibson all won election to the Hall of Fame in their first year of eligibility.

The greatness of these players notwithstanding, two other black players, Willie Mays and Hank Aaron, both of whom ironically had begun their careers in the Negro Leagues, reigned as the dominant stars of baseball in the 1950s and 1960s. Originally signed by the Birmingham Black Barons of the Negro American League, Mays had joined the New York Giants in midseason 1951, sparking their triumph in the most famous pennant race in history and winning the Rookie of the Year Award. After two years in the military, he returned in 1954 to bat a league-leading .345 and hit 41 home runs. The following year, he pounded 51 homers. A spectacular center fielder, Mays won widespread acclaim as the greatest all-around player in the history of the game. In 1969, he became only the second player in major league history to hit 600 home runs and took aim at Babe Ruth's legendary lifetime total of 714. Over the next four seasons, the aging Mays added 60 more homers before retiring short of Ruth's record.

Unlike Mays, who had begun his career amidst the glare of the New York media, Hank Aaron had spent his career first in Milwaukee and later in Atlanta, far distant from the center of national publicity. Nonetheless, he steadily compiled record-threatening statistics in almost every offensive category. In 1972, at age 38, he surpassed Mays's home run total and set his sights on Ruth. Entering the 1973 season, he needed just 41 home runs to catch the Babe. Performing under tremendous pressure and fanfare, Aaron stroked 40 homers, leaving him just one shy of the record. He tied Ruth's mark with his first swing of the 1974 season. Three days later, on April 8, 1974, a nationwide television audience watched Aaron stroke home run number 715. Babe Ruth's "unreachable" record thus fell to a man whose career had started with the Indianapolis Clowns of the Negro Leagues. When Aaron retired in 1976, he boasted 755 homeruns and held major league records for games played, at-bats, runs-batted-in and extra-base hits. He also ranked second to Ty Cobb in hits and runs scored.

By the 1970s, black players had become an accepted part of the baseball scene and regularly ranked among the most well-known symbols of the sport. Reggie Jackson, Willie Stargell, and Joe Morgan had succeeded Aaron, Mays, and the Robinsons as Hall of Fame caliber superstars. Yet three decades after Jackie Robinson had broken the color barrier, racism and discrimination remained a persistent problem for baseball. Several studies demonstrated that baseball management channeled blacks into positions thought to require less thinking and fewer leadership qualities. In 1968, blacks accounted for more than half of the major league outfielders, but only 20 percent of other position players. Black catchers were rare and fewer than one in 10 pitchers were black. By 1986, the disparity had grown greater. American-born blacks comprised 70 percent of all outfield positions but only 7 percent of all pitcher, second basemen, and third basemen positions. There were no black catchers in the major leagues at the start of the 1986 season.

While superior black players had open access to the major leagues, those of average or slightly above average skills often found their paths blocked. "The Negro player may have to be better qualified than a white player to win the same position," argued Aaron Rosenblatt in 1967. "The undistinguished Negro player is less likely to play in the major leagues than the equally undistinguished white player." Rosenblatt demonstrated that black major leaguers on the whole batted 20 points higher than whites. As batting averages dropped, so did the proportion of blacks. This trend continued into the 1980s. A 1982 study revealed that 70 percent of all black non-pitchers were everyday starters, indicating a substantial bias against blacks who filled utility or pinch-hitting roles. Statistics compiled in 1986 showed a strikingly similar pattern.

The subtle nature of this on-the-field discrimination obscured it from public controversy. The failure of baseball to provide jobs for blacks in managerial and front office positions, however, became an increasing embarrassment. In the early years of integration, baseball executives bypassed the substantial pool of experienced Negro Leaguers from consideration for managerial and coaching positions. A handful of blacks, including Sam Bankhead, Nate Moreland, Marvin Williams, and Chet Brewer managed independent, predominantly all-black teams in the minor leagues. The first generation of black major leaguers fared no better. "We bring dollars into club treasuries when we play," exclaimed Larry Doby, "but when we stop playing, our dollars stop." No major league organization hired a black pilot at any level until 1961 when the Pittsburgh Pirates placed Gene Baker at the helm of their Batavia franchise. By the mid-1960s no blacks had managed in the majors and only two had held full-time major league coaching positions. The first black umpire did not appear in the majors until 1966, when Emmett Ashford appeared in the American League.

In the final years of his life, Jackie Robinson made repeated pleas for baseball to eliminate these lingering vestiges of Jim Crow. "I'd like to live to see a black manager," he stated before a national television audience at the 1972 World Series. Nine days later he died, his dream unfulfilled. In 1975, the Cleveland Indians hired Frank Robinson to be the first black major league manager. This precedent, however, opened few new doors. Robinson lasted two-and-a-half seasons with the Indians, later managed the San Francisco Giants for four years, and in 1988 was made manager of the Baltimore Orioles. Maury Wills and Larry Doby each had brief half-season stints as managers. After four decades of integration, only these three men had received major league managerial opportunities.

A similar situation existed in major league front offices.

Only one black man, Bill Lucas of the Atlanta Braves, had served as a general manager. As late as 1982, a survey of 24 clubs (the Yankees and Red Sox refused to provide information) found that of 913 available white-collar baseball jobs, blacks held just 32 positions. Among 568 full-time major league scouts, only 15 were black. While many teams hired former players as announcers, few employed blacks in these roles. Five years later, conditions had not improved. Of the top 879 administrative positions in baseball only 17 were filled by blacks and 15 by Hispanics. Four teams in California—the Dodgers, Giants, Athletics, and Angels—accounted for almost two-thirds of the minority hiring. Ten out of 14 American League teams, and five of 12 National League franchises had no blacks in management positions.

These shortcomings came to haunt baseball in 1987. Commissioner Peter Ueberroth had dedicated the season to the commemoration of the fortieth anniversary of Jackie Robinson's major league debut. As the celebration began, Los Angeles Dodger general manager Al Campanis, who had played with Robinson at Montreal, appeared on ABC-TV's *Nightline*. When asked about the dearth of black managers, Campanis explained that blacks "may not have some of the necessities to be, let's say, a field manager or general manager." Campanis's statement, which surely reflected the thinking of many baseball executives, evoked a storm of protest, and precipitated his resignation. An embarrassed Ueberroth pledged to take action to bring more blacks into leadership positions and hired University of California sociologist Harry Edwards to facilitate the process. Fifty blacks and Latins with past or present connections to baseball created their own Minority Baseball Network to apprise blacks of employment opportunities and to lobby clubs to recruit more minorities for front office jobs.

When the controversy of 1987 had subsided, few franchises had taken significant steps to increase minority hiring. Several clubs added blacks to administrative positions, but none offered field or general manager positions to non-white candidates. (In 1988, Frank Robinson and Cookie Rojas were named managers.) Observers accused some teams of delaying managerial changes to avoid pressure to hire a black candidate. Thus, after forty years of integrated play, baseball had come full cycle. Long a symbol of racial intolerance, from the 1940s to the 1960s baseball had glowed as a beacon of America's promise. By the late 1980s, however, the national pastime once again offered a mirror on America's racial dilemma, a testament to the limits of integration and the persistence of discrimination.

## CHAPTER 23

Rival Leagues

Harold Dellinger

The history of Major League baseball is much more than the combined history of the National League and the American League. That history also includes the story of the eleven primary attempts, some successful and some not, to form leagues for whom major league status was claimed or would later be claimed. The earliest such attempt predates "the major leagues" as understood by the majority of baseball fans—that is, the 1876 founding of the National League—while the most recent such attempt triggered the expansion era that has seen the total of big league clubs expand from 16 to 26.

The National Association (1871–1875)

The "National Association of Professional Base Ball Players" was organized in New York City on March 17, 1871, by representatives of the ten leading professional clubs in the country. Among the business discussed was the adoption of a constitution similar to that of the National Association of Base Ball Players, which had ruled both professional and amateur teams and players in years prior to 1871. This new National Association is properly considered the first professional league.

The National Association elected as its first president United States Marshall James W. Kerns, the representative of the Philadelphia team. Upon payment of a $10 fee, clubs were admitted from Troy, Boston, New York, Philadelphia, Cleveland, Chicago, and Washington, plus Rockford, Illinois and Fort Wayne, Indiana. Several clubs did not join because the $10 fee, which was to be used to purchase a championship banner, seemed excessive.

League rules provided that each club was to arrange a series of five games with each other club. The club winning the most series would be declared the champion. A "championship committee" was to decide disputes between clubs. A procedure was established to decide cases involving players who signed with two or more clubs. Such players were called revolvers.

The most controversial discussions concerned the admission price. Harry Wright, the Boston representative, favored a higher rate. He said, "We must make the games worth witnessing, and there will be no fault found with the price of admission. A good game is worth 50 cents, a poor one is dear at 25 cents." In the end each club was allowed to set its own admission price, and the better clubs began demanding guarantees when playing less prosperous clubs.

The first National Association game was played at Fort Wayne on May 4, 1871, with the home team beating Cleveland 2–0. Most of the National Association teams had operated in 1870 and earlier seasons, and had nuclei of teams

signed and ready to play. Most of the veteran players in the country found spots with National Association teams. Dickey Pearce, for instance, who was already a thirteen-year professional at age thirty-five, played with New York. Joe Start, the premier first baseman of the day, joined the same club. Veterans George Wright and Harry Schafer joined Harry Wright, the architect of the famous Cincinnati team of 1869–1870, on the Boston team. Chicago veterans included Mart King, James Wood, and Joe Simmons. Levi Mayerle and Al Reach played for Philadelphia.

Among the young players destined to become professional stars were pitcher Al Spalding and second baseman Roscoe Barnes. Barnes became the most adept practitioner of the fair-foul hit whereby any batted ball, not just those beyond first and third bases, that landed fair and then went foul was considered a fair hit. Adrian Anson, whose playing career would stretch to 1897, played several positions for Rockford in 1871 before moving on to Philadelphia.

The 1871 championship season was plagued by a disturbing number of cancellations, forfeits, and controversy relating to the standings. Boston had won as many games but fewer series than Philadelphia and Chicago when the "Championship Committee" decided that the winner of the October 30 Philadelphia-Chicago game would be declared the champion. The Chicago team had lost all their equipment in the great Chicago fire, which had begun on October 8, and played the game in partial uniforms and the uniforms of several other clubs. Several players played with black dress hats instead of baseball caps. Philadelphia won the game 4–1 and claimed the championship with a 22–7 record. The Philadelphia manager, Hicks Hayhurst, asked Harry Wright if he could suggest where the championship banner should be placed. The very controlled response of Wright was that perhaps it should be displayed in the Philadelphia clubhouse instead of the saloon where it usually resided.

The Fort Wayne club had disbanded in late August with only six or seven wins in the four months. A Brooklyn club made a belated entry into the league, although it was not eligible for the championship. Brooklyn did little better than Fort Wayne and supposedly the Brooklyn fans that season began using the famous lament, "Wait until next year."

Harry Wright's Boston club won the four National Association championships from 1872 to 1875 and so dominated the league that it became known as "Harry Wright's League." In 1875 the Boston team overwhelmed the opposition with a 71–8 record. One of the tailenders, the Brooklyn team, posted only a 2–42 record. The unequal talents of National Association teams plagued the league during its entire existence. The irregular schedule also caused many problems, and even determining how many games were won and lost by the various teams became, and has remained, almost impossible. Third

baseman Robert Ferguson served as president of the National Association from 1872 through 1875.

The Boston team, of course, became the best-paid team in the league with salaries reaching levels not seen again until the mid-eighties. The players on the Boston team, however, certainly did earn their pay. Pitcher Al Spalding is credited by modern research with 207 wins in five National Association seasons, including a 57–5 mark in 1875. Only four other pitchers, including Bobby Matthews, posted as many as 100 National Association wins. Ross Barnes of Boston is listed in modern reference works as the National Association batting champion for the 1873 and 1875 seasons, and his career National Association batting average is calculated at .379. Other National Association batting champions were Levi Meyerle in 1871, Davey Force in 1872, and John McMullen in 1874. Batting averages were actually seldom compiled during the National Association era, and hitters were ranked by hits per game (HPG). Barnes's league-leading 1.79 HPG in 1875 has been translated into a league-leading .372 batting average. Barnes also became the first National League batting champion in 1876 before the fair-foul hit was abolished.

Several players, including Barnes, became so deadly with the fair-foul hit, that an unusual rule change was made before the 1874 season in an attempt to balance the defense with the offense. Because of the possibility of the fair-foul hit, the first baseman and the third baseman had to play right on the foul lines, leaving huge defensive gaps in the rest of the infield. Henry Chadwick's solution, to which "there is not a reasonable objection that can be brought against it," was to add a tenth player, called the "right stop," to be stationed between first and second bases. The experiment met considerable opposition and was discontinued before the season was finished.

The Boston and Philadelphia teams made special schedule arrangements in 1874 to allow them to play their required games and still make a midseason trip to England. They left on the steamship *Ohio* on July 16 and arrived eleven days later. Games were played between the two teams in places like London, Liverpool, Sheffield, and Manchester, with the Boston club winning eight of the fourteen matches. The hopes of big attendance were not realized and losses of $3,000 for the trip were reported, but both clubs were successful enough at home to cover the losses. The Boston and Philadelphia teams did not return to the United States until September 9.

In the 1875 National Association season, the first "sale" of baseball players occurred, involving the two Philadelphia teams in the league that season. The first Philadelphia team paid the officials of the second Philadelphia team to release their two best players, Bill Craver and George Bechtel, so that the first Philadelphia team might sign them and attempt to challenge Boston for the championship. The second Philadelphia team then disbanded.

Some twenty-three clubs played one or more seasons in the National Association. The Philadelphia, Boston, and New York clubs were charter members of the National Association and the only three clubs to play all five seasons. Chicago, a charter member, missed two seasons as a result of the great fire but played three seasons in the National Association. The other charter members—Rockford, Washington, Troy, and Cleveland—lasted only one or two seasons. In addition to the Brooklyn team that finished the 1871 season, a second Brooklyn team participated in four National Association seasons. Second and third Philadelphia teams were entered in, respectively, three and one National Association seasons. A second

Washington club played three National Association seasons. Two separate Baltimore teams played three and one seasons. Two St. Louis teams, neither very competent, were entered in 1875. A team from Hartford was entered in 1874 and 1875. Teams from Elizabeth, New Jersey; New Haven, Connecticut; Middletown, Connecticut; and Keokuk, Iowa, were entered unsuccessfully in one National Association season.

The National Association was easily supplanted by the newly formed National League after the 1875 season. The problems associated with scheduling and the unequal quality of opposition, because of the easy membership rules, made the stronger clubs seek a better way of doing business. Periodic problems with gamblers and rowdyism were also factors in the demise of the National Association. Even Harry Wright of Boston became involved in the new National League and entered his club.

The remnants of the National Association met in March 1876 to organize for another season, but the attempt was unsuccessful. The National Association quietly passed from the scene.

The International Association and the National Association (1877–1880)

The International Association and its successor organization, the National Association, survived four years of existence independent of the National League. The organization offered independent clubs of the era some protection against a common enemy—the National League—whose exclusiveness and aggressiveness offended and endangered the independent club.

The "International Association of Professional Base Ball Players" was organized February 20, 1877, in Pittsburgh. The meeting had been called by L. C. Waite, secretary of the St. Louis Red Stockings team. Waite had circulated letters urging that the fifty or so professional clubs that were not members of the National League form an organization to promote and protect their interests. Waite believed the National League was trying to monopolize baseball to the detriment of clubs not important enough or located in cities not big enough to join the National League.

Delegates from seventeen clubs attended the initial International Association meeting. A loosely formed body of outside clubs, much resembling the old National Association, was put together with features such as a $10 membership fee and a 25-cent admission price. There was no limit on the number of clubs which could enter, nor was there any standard by which the quality of the team which wished to enter could be judged. William "Candy" Cummings, a pitcher and the probable inventor of the curveball, was elected president. James A. Williams of Columbus, Ohio, became secretary-treasurer. He would hold this position for all four years that the IA/NA existed.

To compete for the championship of the International Association, teams were required to pay an extra $15 fee and schedule a set number of games against clubs similarly enrolled. Teams from London, Ontario; Columbus, Ohio; Pittsburgh, Pennsylvania; Lynn, Massachusetts; Guelph, Ontario; Manchester, New Hampshire; and Rochester, New York, paid the extra fee. Some sixteen other clubs became members of the International Association but did not compete for the championship.

Only a portion of the games played each year by International Association teams would count toward the championship. In practice, each club secretary would arrange games with each other club secretary to meet that year's championship requirement. There would also be other games with International Association teams that would not count toward the championship plus games versus other independent teams, National League teams, and other exhibition and "pickup" games. This was a preferred way of doing business for many professional clubs who felt they were better off playing clubs in their own vicinity more often and avoiding heavy travel expenses.

Clearly hoping to subvert a strong organization of outside clubs, the National League set up its own organization of independent clubs that came to be called the League Alliance. To member clubs of the League Alliance, the National League offered the protection of its players, plus certain other nebulous benefits. About thirty clubs were enrolled as members of the League Alliance in 1877.

The London, Ontario, team won the first International Association championship with a 14–4 record. Fred Goldsmith pitched every championship game for London and a good many of the nonchampionship games. International Association president Candy Cummings posted only a 1–7 record for the Lynn team. The Guelph and Lynn teams failed to finish the season.

Many other prominent players played in the International Association, including Mike Kelly, Joe Hornung, Lou Say, Pud Galvin, Ned Williamson, John M. Ward, and in later years Jack Glasscock, Jake Knowdell, and Davey Force. Several believed the International Association was better for players than the National League. Force urged his club not to join the National League because "there is nothing in it."

J. W. Whitney of Rochester, New York, was elected president of the International Association for the 1878 season. Clubs from thirteen cities enrolled for the championship— Rochester, New York; Utica, New York; London, Ontario; Pittsburgh, Pennsylvania; Manchester, New Hampshire; Lynn, Massachusetts; Buffalo, New York; Syracuse, New York; Binghamton, New York; Hornellsville, New York; New Bedford, Massachusetts; Lowell, Massachusetts; and Springfield, Massachusetts. New Bedford apparently never played a game and was replaced by New Haven, Connecticut, about May 8. On May 20 New Haven transferred to Hartford, Connecticut. On June 4 the Lynn club transferred to Worcester, Massachusetts. On June 8 the Pittsburgh club disbanded. On June 20 the Hartford club was expelled for not paying the visiting Buffalo club its share of the receipts. On July 19 the Binghamton club disbanded. On August 21 the Hornellsville and London teams disbanded. One story had the London team trying to enter the National League, but the disbandment may have been related to allegations of crooked play by some of the London players. The Rochester and Worcester teams disbanded in early October. Only six of the original thirteen International Association clubs finished the season.

Buffalo was eventually awarded the 1878 International Association championship, although not without some controversy. By one count, Syracuse had a 27–10 record and Buffalo a 32–12 record. But, as was usually done, games played against clubs that didn't finish the season where thrown out. Thus by another count Buffalo finished with a 27–10 record to 26–10 for Syracuse.

The championship Buffalo club was one of the very best minor league clubs ever put together. Every player on the team had played or would play in the major leagues, some with distinction such as Jim Galvin and Davey Force. Counting all its games, the Buffalo team compiled an 81–32 record, including a 10–7 record against National League teams. Galvin pitched 92 complete games out of 101 games started and totaled approximately 900 innings pitched. The Buffalo club was admitted into the National League for the 1879 season, where it conducted itself capably, finishing in third place. The Syracuse team was also admitted into the National League for the 1879 season.

The International Association changed its name to the "National Base-Ball Association" for the season of 1879. The name change was prompted by the fact that no Canadian clubs signed up for the new season. Nine clubs enrolled for the championship season representing Utica, New York; Worcester, Massachusetts; Manchester, New Hampshire; Springfield, Massachusetts; New Bedford, Massachusetts; Holyoke, Massachusetts; Washington, D.C.; and Albany, New York. Two clubs represented Albany. L. J. Powers of Springfield served as president.

On May 21 one of the Albany clubs transferred to Rochester, New York. The Manchester club disbanded on July 5. Utica disbanded on July 12, followed very late in the season by Springfield and Rochester. If games with disbanded teams had been thrown out, as in the previous year, Holyoke with a 19–10 record would have been tied with Albany with a 19–11 record for the championship. The number of games won, not the percentage of games won, was used to determine champions. The games against disbanded teams were not thrown out, however, and the championship was awarded to Albany with a 27–13 record over Holyoke with a 23–16 record.

For the 1880 season, the National Association enrolled clubs from only three cities—Washington, D.C.; Albany, New York; and Baltimore, Maryland. Some seventeen other independent clubs were affiliated with the National Association but were not involved in the championship race. H. W. Garfield of Albany served as the last president of the National Association.

The Baltimore club played only two or three games before disbanding. Several of the Baltimore players were shifted to Rochester, which was admitted to membership. The Albany club disbanded about July 20 and Rochester quit in early September. The Washington club had a 27–12 record, and since it was the only team remaining, it must be considered the National Association champion.

The American Association (1882–1891)

The "American Association of Base-Ball Clubs" was formally organized November 2, 1881, in meetings at Cincinnati. The National League constitution was adopted with modifications "affording more liberal conditions to cities and players." A fixed guarantee was adopted and each club was given the right to set the admission price. H. D. McKnight of Pittsburgh was elected president and James Williams of Columbus, Ohio, was elected secretary. The secretary was to be paid a fixed salary.

Clubs were admitted to the American Association from Brooklyn, Philadelphia, Cincinnati, St. Louis, Pittsburgh, and Louisville. Applicants from Boston and New York were not admitted but were encouraged to apply again when better

arrangements had been made. The Brooklyn franchise withdrew before the season began, and a team was admitted from Baltimore to fill a sixth spot. The six teams were placed in cities without major league baseball and did not challenge existing National League teams.

The American Association became known as the "Beer and Whiskey League" because it seemed most of the owners were involved in the production or sale of beer and other alcohols. Chris Von der Ahe, backer of the St. Louis franchise, was said to have become interested in baseball because he noticed that baseball fans drank a lot of beer. Von der Ahe owned a saloon near the St. Louis ballpark and had operated an independent team run on the cooperative plan in St. Louis during the 1881 season. The Baltimore team was backed by Harry Vonderhorst, a brewer. The Louisville backers included the treasurer of the Kentucky Malting Company. In the spring of 1882, the American Association abrogated an earlier temporary rule against the sale of liquor at the ballpark.

That there was room for a new league was evident to most observers. Louisville had been without professional baseball since being removed in 1877 because of financial problems. St. Louis had been without a regular-league team for the same period of time because of disputes over the sale of liquor at the ballpark. New York and Philadelphia were open because their teams had been expelled in 1876. The Cincinnati franchise had been "vacated" because of the continued sale of liquor on the grounds of the ballpark. The presence of several prime cities without professional baseball plus the greatly expanding urban population made a new league look like a promising possibility.

The National League adopted a pose of indifference toward the new league. Public statements about the American Association by the National League were not inflammatory or warlike. Teams from the two leagues even played about twenty exhibition games in the spring of 1882. Unfortunately the National League chose to be indifferent about contracts signed with American Association clubs. Sam Wise and John "Dasher" Troy had played for the Detroit National League club in 1881. Neither had been reserved for 1882. Wise signed with the Cincinnati American Association club and Troy with the Philadelphia American Association club. Then Wise and Troy signed respectively with the Boston and New York clubs of the National League and played there in 1882. The American Association took the Wise case to court but failed to achieve the restraining order they sought. In retaliation the American Association, in May of 1882, decided on a strategy of "non-intercourse" with the National League. There was to be no relationship with the National League, and National League reserve lists were to be ignored.

Despite the loss of a few players, the American Association managed to complete its schedule with Cincinnati winning the championship of the first season. The Cincinnati team attempted to engage in a postseason series with the National League champion but was stopped by President McKnight's orders enforcing the policy of "non-intercourse." During the season American Association representatives managed to sign at least thirteen National League players to options for their services in the 1883 season. The new tactic failed when most of the players failed to follow through. Detroit catcher Charlie Bennett signed such an option with Pittsburgh but signed again with Detroit for 1883. The American Association lost the case in court because an option was a preliminary agreement, not a final one.

The American Association enjoyed success in its first season. All six teams were believed to have made a profit, with Cincinnati reporting profits of $15,000. American Association clubs in New York and Columbus, Ohio, were added for the 1883 season. The National League dropped two of its weaker clubs, Troy and Worcester, and placed new clubs in Philadelphia and New York. National League clubs then challenged American Association clubs in those two important cities.

On February 17, 1883, a joint conference or "Harmony Conference" was held in New York City with representatives of the American Association, the National League, and the new Northwestern League present. The result was a "National Agreement" or "Tripartite Agreement" between the three leagues. The Tripartite Agreement provided that the three leagues would honor each other's reserve, suspension, and expulsion lists. This was the first official agreement to include provision for the reserve list. Another new feature was the creation of an arbitration committee to settle disputes between the leagues. The Northwestern League and National League endorsed the Tripartite Agreement immediately, and the American Association added its approval about a month later.

Philadelphia won the 1883 American Association championship by one game over St. Louis. The eight-club format proved very successful, and most clubs reported substantial profits. Both Philadelphia and St. Louis reported profits of over $50,000. Baltimore and Cincinnati had profits in the range of $20,000 to $30,000. Two other clubs broke even, and two lost small amounts. The "official" batting champion was Tom Mansell of the St. Louis Browns, with a .402 batting average compiled, however, in less than 30 games. Modern reference books credit Ed Swartwood of the Allegheny Club of Pittsburgh, with a .356 batting average in some 94 games, as the batting champion.

In 1884 the American Association was an active participant and loser in the war with the Union Association. Probably the most ill-advised move of the year was the expansion of the American Association into an additional four cities, namely Toledo, Indianapolis, Washington, and Brooklyn. With the National League operating eight teams and the Union Association with thirteen teams, there was great demand for players. *The Sporting Life* of Philadelphia remarked, "The ballplayer who fails to get employment . . . had better give up all idea of ever going into the business." Two of the players who finally got their chance were brothers Moses ("Fleet") and Welday Walker, who played part of the 1884 season with the Toledo American Association club. They were the first blacks to play in the major leagues and the last until Jackie Robinson in 1947.

Most American Association clubs lost substantial amounts of money. New York reported losses of $15,000 despite winning the American Association championship with a 75–32 record. Washington disbanded after the games of August 2, owing some $1,500 in unpaid player salaries. Richmond withdrew from the Eastern League and entered the American Association in its place. *The Spalding Guide* later assessed the 1884 American Association twelve-club experiment as follows:

The Association tried the experiment of a twelve-league circuit but under circumstances that insured failure from the start. . . . The clubs were so unevenly matched and so badly

managed that the failure of the experiment was a certainty.

For the 1885 season the American Association reduced back to eight clubs by dropping the franchises in Richmond, Toledo, Columbus, and Indianapolis. New trouble with the National League developed over the transfer of pitcher Tim Keefe from the New York American Association club to the New York National League club. It had been rumored that the New York clubs were both owned by the same parties.

On December 8, 1885, the American Association canceled the franchise of the New York club because of its subservient relationship to the National League. A new Washington club was admitted in its place. Unknown to the American Association owners, New York financier Erastus Wiman had just purchased the New York American Association franchise for a reported $25,000. Wiman went to court to prevent the expulsion. The New York franchise was readmitted on December 28, and the new Washington club was dropped.

The St. Louis team dominated the American Association from 1885 to 1888, winning four consecutive championships. In each of those years they engaged in a World Championship Series with the National League winner, winning one series, tying one series, and losing two.

The heart of these great St. Louis teams was a cast of steady everyday players plus talented young pitchers. The regular players included Charles Comiskey, James "Tip" O'Neill, Curt Welch, Walter Latham, A. J. "Doc" Bushong, and Thomas McCarthy. O'Neill hit an amazing "official" .492 in 1887, the only season in which a fourth strike was allowed and base on balls were counted as hits. Modern reference works list O'Neill with a .435 average, after apparently factoring out the base on balls.

The St. Louis pitchers included Robert Caruthers, who won 40, 30, and 29 games before being traded away to Brooklyn prior to the 1888 season. Nat Hudson won 25 games one season before fading to 3 the next season. David Foutz won 114 games in four seasons, including 41 in 1886. Charles "Silver" King won 112 games in three seasons, including 45 in 1888.

Prior to the 1886 season, the owner of the New York team, Erastus Wiman, donated to the American Association a trophy to be given to the league champion each year. The "Wiman Trophy" was twenty inches high, apparently silver, and featured a ballplayer about to strike. The model for the trophy was "Chief" Roseman of the New York team. St. Louis got to keep the trophy after its string of consecutive championships.

In addition to the talented players of the St. Louis team, many other stars of the Eighties and early Nineties played all or part of their careers in the American Association. Pitcher Guy Hecker of Louisville, one of the early stars of the league and a 52-game winner in 1884, played eight years in the American Association. Hall of Famer Tim Keefe pitched two seasons with New York in the American Association, winning 41 and 37 games. Pitcher Will White of Cincinnati, the first player to wear eyeglasses, twice won more than 40 games in a season. Matt Kilroy of Baltimore struck out 513 batters in 1886 and won 46 games in 1887. Pete Browning averaged better than .340 for a thirteen-year career that included eight years with Louisville of the American Association. Herman Long and Billy Hamilton were among those young players whose careers began in the American Association although reaching full flower in the National League.

The American Association experienced successful seasons through the 1888 season, with high attendance and substantial profits. In 1886 every club in the American Association showed a profit except the New York club. Some of the clubs reported profits approaching $100,000. Relationships with the National League were generally peaceful, although a few minor player disputes occurred. There were only three franchise shifts from 1886 to 1888. After the 1886 season the Pittsburgh club withdrew and entered the National League, citing a desire to engage in the better business practices of the National League. Cleveland was admitted in Pittsburgh's place. After the 1887 season the New York franchise withdrew and a club was placed in Kansas City. The Cleveland team dropped out after the 1888 season and a Columbus team was admitted in its place.

Brooklyn won the 1889 American Association championship but lost the World Championship Series to the New York National League team. Louisville managed to lose 111 games during the season and became the first professional team to lose over 100 games in a season. Considerable tensions developed within the American Association, perhaps related to schemes by Von der Ahe and others to consolidate with the National League into one twelve-club league. On another level the tensions were related to a series of disputes relating to the treatment of the members of a "combine" within the league versus the treatment of non-combine clubs. The "combine" was said to have been composed of the owners of the St. Louis, Louisville, Columbus, and Philadelphia clubs. Particularly galling was a series of rulings on forfeits and called games that went against the non-combine clubs. Henry Chadwick stated that in 1889 the American Association "saw the culmination of its career and that of its usefulness . . . the combine in its ranks . . . gave it its death blow."

When the American Association met in New York on November 13, 1889, matters had deteriorated greatly. The dispute centered on the election of the president of the American Association. Zach Phelps of Louisville was the "combine candidate." L. C. Krauthoff of Kansas City was the candidate of the other clubs. After two days and over forty ballots, the candidates remained deadlocked with four votes apiece. In disgust the Brooklyn and Cincinnati clubs resigned their American Association memberships, followed within days by the Kansas City and Baltimore clubs. Brooklyn and Cincinnati sought and secured National League franchises for 1890 while Kansas City returned to the Western Association and Baltimore to the Eastern League.

New American Association franchises were placed in Rochester, Syracuse, and Toledo, and a new club was organized in Brooklyn. The first three teams brought in their players from the previous season, but the new Brooklyn team had to start from scratch. In addition, the American Association lost the players from its 1889 Brooklyn, Cincinnati, Kansas City, and Baltimore teams, plus several others to the new Players League.

Some of the American Association players did not take transfer from league to league without question. One notable case involved infielder John Pickett of Kansas City. The Kansas City American Association club had purchased Pickett's contract from St. Paul with his approval in May 1889 for a reported $3,500. He signed with Kansas City for 1890 but when the club dropped out of the American Association, Pickett announced that since the club was now in the minor leagues, he would break the agreement. He did so by signing

with the Players League. Although he was enjoined by the courts from playing for anybody except Kansas City, he nevertheless played for Philadelphia of the Players League, where the court had no jurisdiction.

Louisville was the surprise winner of the 1890 American Association championship. The tail-end Louisville club of the previous season lost fewer men to the Players League than the other American Association clubs and, with the addition of several youngsters, managed to come out on top of the greatly weakened league. Payrolls were down from about $35,000 per club in 1889 to $20,000 per club in 1890. Brooklyn was plagued by poor attendance all season, and beginning with the games of August 27 it was replaced by Baltimore. Every team in the American Association was thought to have lost money in 1890 except perhaps Louisville. Brooklyn of the National League engaged the Louisville team in what proved to be the last of the early World Series matches. Each team won three games before the match was called because of bad weather and public indifference. Von der Ahe and others apparently attempted a consolidation with the Players League, but the effort failed.

Negotiations throughout the fall of 1890 finally produced a settlement of the Players League war. The American Association part of the agreement allowed the dropping of the Toledo, Rochester, and Syracuse franchises, replacing them with franchises in Boston and Washington. A Chicago franchise was planned but did not materialize, and a team was located in Cincinnati. All players were to return to the club that had employed them in 1889. A new National Agreement between the National League, American Association, and Western Association was signed, with provision for a National Board to rule on disputes between leagues and teams.

The peace did not last long. Louis Bierbauer and Harry Stovey had both played for Philadelphia of the American Association in 1889. Both were highly regarded, and Stovey had hit as high as .404 in 1884. Bierbauer and Stovey had played for the Brooklyn and Boston Players League teams in 1890. Under terms of the peace agreement, each would have been returned to Philadelphia for the 1891 season, but that team mistakenly failed to properly reserve them. Stovey signed with the Boston National League team and Bierbauer with the Pittsburgh National League team. The latter team became known as the "Pirates" as a result of the affair. On February 14, 1891, the newly formed National Board ruled the two players could stay with the National League clubs.

On February 17, 1891, the American Association withdrew from the National Agreement and a new war was on. Within days the National Board released all American Association players from reservation and the National League began signing American Association players. Mark Baldwin, a pitcher for Columbus in 1889, signed with Pittsburgh of the National League for 1891. He was accused by Von der Ahe of inducing St. Louis players to jump and was twice arrested on conspiracy charges. *The Spalding Guide* attributed the problems again to the American Association "combine" and stated, "The revolt . . . was simply a crime, as it was a blow against the very life of the professional organizations at large—the protective compact of the National Agreement."

As a result of the American Association resignation from the National Agreement, the Western Association and a rejuvenated Eastern Association were admitted as "major leagues" for the season of 1891. The plans were that these two leagues would eventually replace the American Association

and stand on almost equal footing with the National League. The National League, though, would always be superior. "That is to say, that the National League will stand forth as the leader in the matter of catering exclusively for the better class of professional club patrons."

The new Boston team won the 1891 American Association championship by some 8 games over St. Louis. Several American Association players jumped to the National League before the season ended, including Charles King, who ended up with Chicago. Phil Ehret and Harry Raymond of Louisville jumped to Omaha of the minor league Western Association in late July. In early August Tom Vickery and Bill Schriver joined Anson's Chicago team. Milwaukee, one of the Western Association stalwarts, replaced Cincinnati in the American Association on August 18. The Cincinnati owners, who included Von der Ahe, retained the franchise, which was only transferred to Milwaukee for the remainder of the season. The defection of Milwaukee from the Western Association to the American Association delayed peace negotiations, which had begun in July.

The American Association met in Chicago on October 22, 1891, and admitted a new Chicago club into the league. The evidence is that Von der Ahe supplied most of the money. An attempt was made to replace Louisville with a Kansas City team, but that was not accomplished.

On December 15–18, 1891, the National League and the American Association held a joint meeting in Indianapolis. Details had been worked out earlier, and after some minor hurdles were removed, an agreement was reached. A single league, to be officially called the National League and American Association of Professional Base Ball Clubs, was formed. American Association teams in Baltimore, St. Louis, Washington, and Louisville were joined with the existing eight National League clubs to form a single twelve-club league. The remaining five American Association clubs, including the new Chicago club, were bought out for a total of approximately $130,000, with the debt assumed by the new league. A new split-season plan was adopted, beginning with the 1892 season. All player contracts were to be honored in full.

The Spalding Guide emphasized the importance of the amalgamation of the leagues as follows:

"Out of evil cometh good," says Scripture, and the saying is emphasized by the eventual outcome of the revolutionary period of 1890 and '91, in the form of the establishment of a new government for the fraternity at large, in the organization of the new twelve-club League as the successor both of the old National League and the late American Association. The compensating result . . . has been the adoption of a system of professional club business on what may be regarded as true business principles, something neither of the old organizations fully enjoyed before. From this time forth we say, "Let the dead past bury its dead." Give the new era in professional baseball history a chance to show that it is an era of coming prosperity for the game at large.

The Union Association (1884)

The Union Association operated in the season of 1884 and involved itself in a spirited war with the National League and the American Association over the basic issues of the reserve rule and territorial rights.

The "Union Association of Professional Baseball Clubs" was organized in Pittsburgh on September 12, 1883. Delegates from eight cities were present, and communications from four more cities were read. H. B. Bennett of Washington, D.C., was elected president and among the most important business was the unanimous adoption of the following:

Resolved, that while we recognize the validity of all contracts made by the League and American Association, we cannot recognize any agreement whereby any number of ball-players may be reserved for any club for any time beyond the terms of their contract with such club.

The Union Association adopted, with other minor changes, the American Association constitution and chose the lively Wright and Ditson baseball for Union Association play.

"We are certain to succeed," said Union Association Secretary W. W. White. He added, "Our refusal to be bound by the eleven-man reserve rule assures us of the good will of every player in the country." Detractors pointed out that there were already two major leagues in the field and almost no large city without a major league team.

The Union Association grew out of the plans of promoter James Jackson to form a new major league in opposition to the reserve rule. "Projector" Jackson's new major league was to be called the American League. Jackson had lost control of his idea by the time of the initial Union Association meeting but was present, seeking a New York City franchise. He was not successful in that endeavor and was not further connected with the Union Association.

Leading directly to the events of 1884 was the prosperity of the baseball season of 1883. The eleven-man reserve rule and the accompanying lack of competition for players kept salaries at a tolerable level. The American Association and National League had enjoyed high attendance and thus profits were high. The inaugural season of the minor league Northwestern League had also been successful, and expectations were that the success could be duplicated in future seasons. The Northwestern League, located in medium-sized cities of what we now call the Midwest, seemed secure in its role as the only minor league in a three-way or "Tripartite Agreement" with the two major leagues. Tripartite Agreement members enjoyed rights of reserve and protection of their territory. Baseball was suddenly good business in 1883, and challenges by those who desired a piece of the business were probably inevitable.

After consideration of the financial standing of the applicants, the Union Association placed franchises in Chicago, Baltimore, Philadelphia, Boston, Cincinnati, Washington, D.C., St. Louis, and Altoona, Pennsylvania. Among the substantial backers were A. W. Henderson, who owned parts of both the Baltimore and Chicago teams. George Wright owned part of the Boston team. Officials of the Pennsylvania Railroad may have sponsored the Altoona club. Henry Lucas, a prominent young railroad man, surfaced as the backer of the St. Louis franchise and, with the Union Association annual meeting of December 18, 1883, became president of the Union Association. So important did Lucas become to Union Association affairs that he became known as "I am the Union Association Lucas."

There was heavy competition for players. Ted Sullivan was one of those who scoured the country in search of players for the Union Association. Increased salaries, two- and three-year

contracts, and the absence of the reserve rule made Union Association offers particularly interesting. A. G. Mills, president of the National League, complained, "The Unions are making efforts to debauch our players."

The National League and the American Association responded to the Union Association's attempted player acquisitions in several ways. Extra teams of players, called "reserve teams," were signed by several of the existing major league teams. The "reserve team" players' only obligations were to play a few exhibition games and be ready should the parent club need them. As a result the "reserve" players would not be available for a Union Association club. The Union Associates owners talked of forming "preserve" clubs in retaliation.

At the National League's annual meeting, held in Washington on November 21, 1883, strict legislation was proposed by John B. Day of New York to stop players from ignoring the reserve rule. The Day Resolution read:

Resolved: That no league club shall at any time employ or enter into contract with any of its reserved players who shall, while reserved to any such club, 'play with' any other club.

Although the Day Resolution would not be formally approved until the March 12, 1884, National League meeting, its policies were the operational policies of the National League from that point in time.

At its annual meeting, held in Cincinnati on December 12, 1883, the American Association surprisedly voted to expand to twelve clubs by placing new franchises in Brooklyn, Indianapolis, Toledo, and Washington, D.C. The expansion was regarded as an attempt to tie up more players and territory. Now only Altoona of the eight Union Association teams would exist without opposition from another team.

The American Association also adopted a modified Day Resolution, providing that deserters of the American Association reserve could be accepted back any time prior to the time the player actually participated in a Union Association game. Once they actually played in a Union Association game, they would be expelled and not accepted back.

Hundreds of players received Union Association offers and perhaps thirty players reserved by major league clubs agreed to Union Association terms. Many of those eventually jumped back to their original teams. Among the most celebrated "double jumpers" were star pitchers Larry Corcoran and Tony Mullane.

Corcoran had won 34 games for Al Spalding's Chicago National League team in 1883. He agreed to, but did not sign, a contract with Spalding's club for 1884. He received a better offer from the Chicago Unions and actually signed a contract. He jumped back to the Chicago National League club with an increase in pay, after being advised by Spalding that agreeing to the original contract offer was as good as signing it. It was also said that "Spalding threatened him with everything but death."

Even more complicated was the Tony "Count" Mullane case. He had pitched for St. Louis of the American Association in 1883, winning 35 games. He was reserved by them for 1884. He was offered a $1,900 salary for 1884 but refused it. In November 1883 he signed with the St. Louis Unions for $2,500. Mullane was threatened with expulsion under the terms of the Day Resolution and later signed another contract with the new Toledo American Association club, also for $2,500. The St. Louis American Association owner, Chris

Von der Ahe, agreed to the transfer to Toledo in order to keep Mullane away from the Unions. The Union Association obtained court orders restraining Mullane from pitching in the city of St. Louis but had no success regaining his services. Lucas announced that the Unions now would also go into the "contract-breaking business."

About twenty players opened the season with Union Association clubs after leaving behind the reserve of National League or American Association clubs. David Rowe, who played for Baltimore of the American Association in 1883, was among those signed by the St. Louis Unions. Hugh "One Arm" Daily had left behind the Cleveland National League team to pitch for the Chicago Unions. Fred Dunlap jumped from the same Cleveland team to sign with the St. Louis Unions. He resisted considerable pressure to return including offers of increased salary. Approximately fifteen other Union Association players on opening-day rosters had ignored the reserve or claims of minor league clubs.

The Union Association opened play April 17, 1884, with games in Philadelphia, Baltimore, and Cincinnati. The Union Association "Grand Opening" in St. Louis was delayed by rain until April 20, when St. Louis beat Chicago 7–2. The league planned a 128-game schedule with play not ending until mid-October.

The Chicago, Baltimore, Boston, Cincinnati, and Philadelphia teams opened the season with mostly experienced, if mostly unknown, players. The Washington team was composed mostly of local players, including several youngsters. Altoona opened the season with local players, only a few of whom had professional experience. Lucas, on the other hand, stocked his St. Louis team with solid major leaguers, including George "Orator" Shaffer, Lew Dickerson, and Billy Taylor, plus the previously mentioned Rowe and Dunlap.

The St. Louis team was easily the best in the Union Association. The team won its first 20 or 21 games and did not lose a game until May 24. Baltimore and Boston were the best of the other clubs in the early portion of the season.

Altoona dropped out of the Union Association after the games of May 31. Poor attendance was cited as the reason. This very unremarkable major league club won only 4 games in its six weeks of existence.

Kansas City was admitted as the replacement for Altoona. Kansas City had been one of the original Union Association applicants but was not chosen because of its "far western" location. The team began play June 7 with a collection of castoffs and reserve-team players, and fared rather poorly until strengthened by the signing of several Northwestern League players. The Kansas City franchise proved one of the leagues most successful at the box office if not on the field.

In early July, Billy Taylor of the St. Louis Unions, the leading pitcher in the Union Association with a 25–4 record, was induced to jump back to the American Association. Lucas was angered, of course, and said, "Everything is fair in baseball as in war, and I want my share of the fun while it is going on." To replace Taylor, Lucas signed suspended Providence National League pitcher Charlie Sweeney.

The Unions planned more retaliation. In August they induced star pitcher Jim McCormick, star infielder Jack Glasscock, and journeyman catcher Charlie "Fatty" Briody to jump their Cleveland National League team to join the Cincinnati Unions. They were paid a $1,000 bonus to jump and received contracts for the rest of the season and for 1885 as well. Briody spoke for the Cleveland jumpers when he said,

"It is a matter of dollars and cents." The president of the Cincinnati Unions promised that from now on, the Unions would take any player they could get. With the new players the Cincinnati Unions became one of the better teams in the league and actually played at a level almost equal to St. Louis for the remainder of the season.

The Cleveland team was badly damaged by the defections and, with its faltering attendance, required National League subsidy to finish the season. The Cleveland team nickname became "the Remnants."

After the games of August 7, the Philadelphia Union club folded. Lucas was able to convince the owners of the Wilmington Eastern League club to enter the Union Association as a replacement for the Philadelphia team. Wilmington was leading the Eastern League at the time but had lost money.

There were other towns still seeking a major league franchise. Quincy, Illinois, had one of the better teams in the Northwestern League despite losing several players to the Union Association. The Quincy ownership applied for a franchise at or about the time the Philadelphia team folded. Receiving no immediate reply to their application, they then challenged Lucas's St. Louis Unions to a game to show their quality of play was equal to that of the Unions. The game, played on August 14, resulted in a 5–1 win for St. Louis. The fielding of the Quincy players was much admired, but the team was not admitted.

The Chicago Unions were transferred to Pittsburgh beginning with the games of August 25. Attendance had dropped dramatically in Chicago, and competing with Al Spalding's Chicago National League team had become impossible.

It was also in August that first reports were heard that Henry Lucas might be interested in a National League franchise for St. Louis. Justus Thorner, owner of the Cincinnati Unions, was also said to be pursuing a National League franchise.

The Northwestern League ceased operations on September 7, with only four clubs still in at the end. The Northwestern League provided more players to the Union Association than any other, and the Northwestern League suffered more than any other in the baseball war of 1884.

After the games of September 12, the Wilmington team folded. The Wilmington owners complained that they had lost almost as much money in the Union Association as in the Eastern League. Milwaukee, a remnant of the Northwestern League, was admitted in Wilmington's place. On September 18 the Pittsburgh club folded. Omaha, Nebraska, was to replace the Pittsburgh club but then declined. St. Paul was finally admitted in its stead.

In all, thirteen cities were represented in the Union Association. Only five of the original eight teams played the entire season.

The St. Louis Unions won the Union Association championship rather easily with what is now calculated as a 94–19 record. Some 21 games back were the Cincinnati Unions with a 69–36 record. Baltimore, Boston, and short-termer Milwaukee also finished with winning records. Everybody else was a loser.

Fred Dunlap of St. Louis won the Union Association batting championship with a .412 batting average. He also led in home runs with 13. Billy Sweeney of Baltimore won 40 of the 62 games he pitched, with over 370 strikeouts. "One Arm" Daily struck out over 480 batters, including nineteen in one game against Boston on July 7. Over 260 players appeared in

one or more Union Association games.

Only Kansas City and Washington of the long-term Union Association clubs claimed to have made a profit during the season. Kansas City claimed profits of $6,000 and very much looked forward to another Union Association season. Washington claimed to have cleared $7,000. Everybody else in the Union Association lost money. Although actually breaking even with his own St. Louis team, Lucas claimed losses of $17,000 overall when funds used to keep the league going were accounted for. Boston lost $5,000. Cincinnati and Chicago were thought to have lost about $15,000 apiece.

Financial losses were also the rule in the National League and the American Association. Several National League franchises had to be subsidized by the league, including Providence and Cleveland. The American Association, greatly overexpanded at twelve teams, also had its troubles and even had to shift its Washington franchise to Richmond late in the season.

Only four Union Association teams—Milwaukee, St. Louis, Cincinnati, and Kansas City—sent delegates to the Union Association annual meeting on December 18 in St. Louis. Nevertheless plans were made for the continued operation of the Union Association in 1885. The league in 1885 was to be comprised of St. Louis, Kansas City, Milwaukee, Cincinnati, Columbus, Indianapolis, and possibly Detroit and Cleveland. Union Association teams commenced signing players, and Kansas City and Milwaukee soon had full teams signed. Henry Lucas was re-elected president.

Later in December there were "startling rumors" that Lucas was, in fact, negotiating for a National League team. Cincinnati and Washington were said to be interested in American Association franchises.

The Union Association met once more, on January 15, in Milwaukee. Lucas was not present. Only the Kansas City and Milwaukee delegates attended, and the only action taken was a vote to disband.

On April 18, 1885, the Lucas club was finally admitted into the National League. The terms of the agreement were that Lucas had to publicly admit that the reserve clause was necessary and that Lucas had to pay $6,000 in order to retain the several players he had secured from National League teams. Lucas insisted that blacklisted players be reinstated, and that was done, although several were fined up to $1,000. In addition, pitcher Tony Mullane was suspended for the entire 1885 season, even though he had been allowed to play in 1884.

The Players League (1890)

The "Players National League" was formed at meetings in New York City on November 4–7, 1889. The force behind the new league was the union representing most of the players in the National League. The union was called the Brotherhood of Professional Base Ball Players.

On the first day of the meeting, the Brotherhood issued its statement of why the players had found it necessary to seek the organization of a new league in opposition to the National League. The "Brotherhood Manifesto," addressed "To the Public," included the following:

Players have been bought, sold, and exchanged as though they were sheep instead of American citizens. "Reservation" became for them another name for property right in the player. By a combination among themselves, stronger than the strongest trust, they were able to enforce the most arbitrary measures, and the player had either to submit or get out of the profession in which he had spent years in attaining a proficiency.

The Players League was conceived on an unusual theoretical basis. The plan was never for labor to completely manage its own affairs and reap all the benefits thereof. Instead the plan was to withhold labor from the capitalists of the National League but join labor with the capital of other capitalists for the greater benefit of labor. The Brotherhood proposed "to manage their managers instead of permitting their managers to manage them."

During the summer of 1889, Pittsburgh outfielder Ned Hanlon had convinced Al Johnson, a wealthy Cleveland street-car entrepreneur, of the soundness of the plan. Johnson was extremely effective in locating additional backers for the Players League. The other backers included Colonel Edwin A. McAlpin, a New York real estate speculator, and the wealthy Wagner brothers, who were Philadelphia butchers. John Addison was a Chicago contractor. John Montgomery Ward, president of the Brotherhood of Professional Base Ball Players, was one of several players who were minority investors.

The organizers of the Players League proposed several reforms. The hated reserve clause was abolished. Two- and three-year contracts were to be offered to many players. No player would be released until the end of the season and then only by a vote of the club board of directors, which would include players. All players would receive monies at least equal to their 1889 salaries. Receipts were to be used, first, to pay club expenses. Next to be paid would be player salaries for which a guarantee fund was established. Backers would receive the next $10,000. Additional profits would be shared by players and backers on a league-wide shared basis. The arbitrary "blacklist" was not to be tolerated. Penalties, not involving blacklisting, were established for drunkenness and other offenses.

In December 1889 Edwin McAlpin was elected president of the new league. Addison was elected vice president. Frank Brunnell, a former sportswriter, served as secretary-treasurer and publicist for the Players League. Clubs were placed in Cleveland, New York, Brooklyn, Pittsburgh, Philadelphia, Boston, Chicago, and Buffalo.

The Brotherhood of Professional Base Ball Players had been organized in 1885 with primarily fraternal and charitable objectives. John Montgomery Ward of the New York club was chosen president and remained so through the entire history of the "Brotherhood." By 1887, ninety National League players were members and each league city had a chapter.

The Brotherhood became involved in several issues in the late Eighties, including opposition to the buying and selling of players and blacklisting of players who refused to accept club salary offers. The articulate Ward offered many of the more penetrating analyses on the reserve rule. For instance, in 1887 he wrote about the hated rule, "It inaugurated a species of serfdom which gave one set of men a life-estate in the labor of another, and withheld from the latter any corresponding claim." Ward illustrated his opposition to the reserve rule with the story of what happened to outfielder Charlie Foley.

When ill during the 1883 season, Foley was laid off without pay but was reserved by the Buffalo National League club that fall. He was still unable to play in the spring of 1884, but the Buffalo club again refused to pay him or release him. Later in the 1884 season Foley had recovered enough to play and, in fact, received several minor league offers. Buffalo would not release him and would not pay him or reinstate him. That fall Buffalo reserved Foley again.

The Brotherhood long opposed the practice of any player being reserved at any salary less than that received the previous season. In conferences with the National League in 1888 the Brotherhood proposed that the practice be abolished. The National League postponed action on the request until most players had signed their 1889 contracts and then refused to abolish the practice. The National League also attempted to institute the Brush classification plan, named after John T. Brush. It provided for grouping of players by skill levels and a prescribed payment for each level. The threat of the classification plan was considered most obnoxious by most National League players and led most directly to the formation of the Players League in the fall of 1889. Tim Keefe, New York pitcher and secretary of the Brotherhood, remarked at the time, "The League will not classify as many as they think."

The cause of Brotherhood members Jack Rowe and Jim "Deacon" White also caused much sympathy among National League players, and there was immediate strike talk. Rowe and White had both played for the Detroit National League team in 1888. Each was sold to Pittsburgh prior to the 1889 season. In the meantime they had purchased part of the Buffalo minor league team, planning to play there in 1889. White became president of the Buffalo club. Frederick Stearns, president of the Pittsburgh club, said, "White may have been elected president of the Buffalo club . . . but that won't allow him to play ball in Buffalo. He'll play in Pittsburgh or he'll get off the earth." Upon advice of John Ward, White and Rowe did eventually play for Pittsburgh in 1889, after becoming aware of the plans for 1890. White and Rowe became among the major backers of the Buffalo Players League club.

The players were enthusiastic about the prospect of the new league. Mike Kelly, when speaking of his former owners, three in number, of the Boston National League team, exuberantly proclaimed:

I'm one of the bosses now, and the triumvirate—well, to be frank, they are my understudies. The whirling of time brings ballplayers to their level. Next year they will be in command and the former presidents will have to drive horse cars for a living and borrow rain checks to see a game.

The baseball establishment never understood, or at least pretended never to understand, the Brotherhood members' desire for more control over their lives and careers. *The Spalding Guide* reported that the trouble arose "from the selfish greed of a small minority of the overpaid 'star' players of the National League of 1889, who thought they saw an opening for their becoming wealthy club magnates in the place of being fancy salaried players."

Brotherhood members were advised not to sign contracts with the National League for the 1890 season. Even after the formation of the Players League, attorneys assured National League owners that the reserve clause in the contract would be enough to hold the players. Ward was personally notified that he was reserved for 1890 and would be taken to court if necessary. In January 1890 the New York National League club was denied an injunction against Ward because the reserve clause in his contract lacked fairness and mutuality. Injunctions were also sought against "Buck" Ewing of the New York club and George Hallman of the Philadelphia club. The National League lost those cases also. Outfielder "Orator" O'Rourke of New York, himself a lawyer, was ecstatic: "He that hath committed inequity shall not have equity."

An almost total defection of the star players from the National League followed. By March 1890 over one hundred players had signed Players League contracts. Virtually every star player of the National League joined the Players League. Another twenty or so players deserted the American Association, including Pete Browning of Louisville and Charles King of St. Louis. Less than forty of the 1889 National League players remained loyal to the league. Al Spalding's National League team retained only first baseman/manager Adrian Anson, who was a stockholder, plus pitcher Bill Hutchison and third baseman Tom Burns. The rest of the Chicago team was eventually filled out with young players, called the "cubs" by the sportswriters. Chicago managed to finish in second place in the greatly weakened National League.

The National League attempted to get several of the players to return with offers including huge salary increases, bribes, and two– and three-year contracts. The most interesting attempt involved Mike "King" Kelly, who was offered a $10,000 bonus and a contract to be filled in with his own figures. Kelly declined, saying, "I can't go back on the boys." Players League secretary Brunnell pointed out the hypocrisy of the National League methods: "They would blacklist a man who broke a contract with them on the ground that he was unworthy of confidence, yet they brazenly offer fabulous bribes to induce our men to desert us."

Some twelve players did jump Players League contracts to return to the National League, but several of those, including Jake Beckley, eventually returned to the Players League. Perhaps they remembered the favorite Players League Bible quote from 1 Peter—chapter 2, verse 17—which advised, "Honor all men. Love the Brotherhood."

Players League managers included Brotherhood members and star players Mike Kelly at Boston, John Ward at Brooklyn, Buck Ewing at New York, Charles Comiskey at Chicago, Jack Rowe at Buffalo, and Ned Hanlon at Pittsburgh.

The Players League opened on April 19, 1890. Games were deliberately scheduled to conflict with National League games. The Players League opener in New York had an attendance of 12,000 despite chilly weather. The New York Players League team had a most familiar look for the New York fans as the entire opening-day lineup had played for the New York National League club in 1889. The Boston and Pittsburgh Players League teams drew over 10,000 apiece for their openers.

By June the Players League and in fact all of baseball was suffering poor attendance. In July each Players League club was assessed an extra $2,500 to keep the league afloat. There was, throughout the season, widespread falsification of attendance totals by both the Players League and the National League. The best guess is that the Players League outdrew the National League by about 200,000. It appears certain that the Players League and the National League totals together were less than that of the National League in the

previous season. Years later Al Spalding of the Chicago National League team said in his autobiography:

If either party of this controversy ever furnished to the press one solitary truthful statement as to the progress of the war from his standpoint; if anyone at any time during the contest made true representation of conditions in his own ranks, a monument should be erected to his memory. I have no candidates to recommend for the distinction.

The National League was considerably weakened by the war with the Players League. Both the New York and Pittsburgh clubs experienced major financial problems. The New York club had to be subsidized to the extent of $80,000 and Pittsburgh required close to the same amount. Total National League losses for the 1890 season were estimated at almost $500,000.

The Players League remained reasonably solvent until bad weather in September hampered attendance and dulled a close pennant race. After the season Players League secretary Brunnell reported losses of some $125,000. Boston won the Players League championship with a 81–48 record but was refused its offer to play in a three-way World Series with the National League and American Association winners. Chicago, Brooklyn, New York, and Philadelphia also posted winning records in the Players League. Buffalo finished last with a 36–96 record. Pete Browning of Cleveland won the batting championship with a .391 batting average. Two Chicago pitchers, Charles King and Mark Baldwin, won 32 games apiece to lead the pitchers.

By the end of the 1890 season there was a general inclination by the owners of National League franchises and backers of Players League clubs to seek a peace. The National League was perhaps frightened into the spirit of compromise when the owner of the Cincinnati National League club, Aaron Stern, sold his team to a group of Players League backers headed by Al Johnson. The National League declared the Cincinnati franchise forfeited and eventually awarded it to John T. Brush of Brush Classification Plan fame.

The first peace negotiations were held in early October of 1890. Al Spalding, chairman of the National League War Committee, said, "We had been playing two games all through—baseball and bluff. At this stage I put up the strongest play at the latter game I had ever presented." The Players League backers "greedily accepted" the terms of surrender.

Later more formal negotiations, from which the players were excluded, produced the dismantling of the Players League. In November the New York Players League backers announced that their club would be absorbed by the New York National League club. Within days, the Pittsburgh Players League club was merged with the Pittsburgh National League club. In December the Chicago Players League team was sold to Al Spalding for $18,000, despite the attempt of the Chicago players to hold up the sale.

Further negotiations provided for the merging of the opposing Brooklyn National League and Players League teams and the entry of the Boston Players League team into the American Association. The backers of the Philadelphia Players League team became the owners of the Philadelphia American Association franchise. The Buffalo and Cleveland Players League teams simply disappeared.

Johnson and Brunnell had been left out of the mergers. As a result they attempted to reorganize the remnants of the Players League into an independent eight- or ten-club league. The league would also include cities without major league baseball, such as Syracuse and Toledo, both of which had been dropped by the American Association. "Wrecker" Johnson counted heavily on Brotherhood support, even though reduced salaries would be necessary. The new league was never launched, however, because the Brotherhood members had seen enough. A popular baseball poem of 1890 had a kernel of truth in it:

> *Backward, turn backward, O Time, in thy rush,*
> *Make me a slave again, well dressed and flush,*
> *Bondage, come back from the shoeless shore,*
> *And bring me the shackles I formerly wore.*

John Ward attributed the defeat of the Players League to "stupidity, avarice, and treachery," and it was all of that. Al Spalding speculated that the defeat of the players "settled forever the theory that professional ballplayers can at the same time direct both the business and playing ends of the game."

The Second American Association (1894)

In the fall of 1894 a new "American Association of Baseball Clubs" was proposed. At an organizational meeting in Philadelphia on October 18, 1894, franchises were granted to interests in Pittsburgh, Chicago, Milwaukee, New York, Brooklyn, Philadelphia, and Washington. Applications were also reported pending from other large cities for the proposed eight-club league. Several prominent baseball men were involved, including F. C. Richter, the influential editor of *The Sporting Life* of Philadelphia, who was elected president of the new league.

Identified as prime movers behind the new league were three men who had been active in the National League during the 1894 season: A. C. Buckenberger, who had managed the Pittsburgh team, was affiliated with the new Pittsburgh club. William Barnie, who had managed the Louisville team, was an investor in the new Brooklyn team. Fred Pfeffer, the star second baseman of the Louisville team, planned to operate the new Chicago team.

Although invading several National League cities, the organizers of the new American Association publicly stated they planned no fight with the National League if it could be avoided. They planned to adopt a schedule that did not conflict with that of the National League and vowed to honor all valid contracts of players with National League clubs.

The proposed American Association reforms included allowing play on Sunday, setting the admission price at 25 cents, and prohibiting the buying and selling of player releases. The "double umpire" or two-umpire system was to be instituted. Most importantly, the oppressive reserve clause of National League contracts was to be ignored.

The American Association organizers were convinced there was ample room for two big leagues. A. W. Becannon, the backer of the New York franchise, was quoted as saying, "We only want our share of the patronage and we think we can get it." Several prominent players whose National League contracts had run out were reported considering signing with the new league.

The National League, as well as the Eastern and Western Leagues, particularly feared competition for their players and their territory. They reacted very harshly to the threat. At the National League annual meeting on November 16, 1894, a "Manifesto" was adopted which read in part:

The obligations of contracts, the rights of reserve and the territorial rights of clubs, associations, and leagues must be upheld, and shall be, at any cost.

They also announced that the penalty for "treachery to national agreement interests" would be "ineligibility and suspension for life."

Buckenberger, Barnie, and Pfeffer were suspended and given until December 31 to prove their innocence or the suspensions would be made permanent.

American Association president Richter called the threats a "tremendous bluff." Nevertheless the "bluff" worked, and little more was heard of the new organization. The new American Association died without ever adopting a schedule or signing a player.

Buckenberger was the first to ask for forgiveness. He signed an affidavit denying he had been involved in the interest of the American Association while employed by a league club. He was reinstated and later signed to manage the St. Louis team.

Barnie and Pfeffer were more of a problem. At a hearing on December 20, 1894, Barnie denied affiliating with the American Association until after his National League contract with Louisville had expired. Barnie also refused, after much "wild talk and gesticulation," to sign a letter swearing allegiance to the National Agreement. He was nevertheless reinstated because of a lack of "positive evidence" of his treachery. Barnie soon signed to manage Scranton of the Eastern League. Pfeffer forwarded his written arguments to the hearing but failed to appear personally and was blacklisted.

Pfeffer soon signed to coach the Princeton University baseball team but indicated he still desired to play. Louisville fans instituted a petition drive which collected the signatures of 10,000 persons who promised to boycott Louisville games if Pfeffer were not reinstated. Because of that pressure and the threat of a lawsuit, Pfeffer was reinstated on February 25, 1895, on the condition that he play only for Louisville, that he agree to loyalty to the National Agreement, and that he pay a fine of $500. Friends paid the fine, and Pfeffer was reinstated and went on to play parts of three more seasons in the National League.

The New American Association (1900)

The "American Association of Baseball Clubs," later to be called the "New American Association," began organization at meetings in Chicago on September 17–18, 1899. The main force behind the league seems to have been George Schaefer, a St. Louis city alderman. Several prominent baseball figures were also involved, including Adrian Anson, Chris Von der Ahe, H. D. Quinn, and Al Spinks, who claimed credit for the idea for the new league. Also involved, although not initially named, were Francis Richter of *The Sporting Life,* John McGraw, and Wilbert Robinson of the Baltimore National League team. H. D. Quinn was elected temporary president of the new league.

Franchises were proposed for St. Louis, Milwaukee, Detroit, Chicago, Baltimore, New York, Philadelphia, and Washington. Detroit and Milwaukee had existing Western League franchises, and the remainder of the cities had National League franchises in 1899. The intentions of the new league were announced as follows: "Honest competition, no syndicate baseball, no reserve rule, to respect all contracts and popular prices."

The American Association organizers felt that by not recognizing the reserve rule they could compete for the best of the baseball talent. They also believed that by charging only 25 cents admission price, instead of 50 cents as charged by the National League, they could capture their share of the baseball patronage. The American Association organizers "disclaimed any intention of going to war with the minor leagues, but they strongly intimated that it was war to the finish with the National organization."

The formation of the new league followed closely a confusing series of events during the summer of 1899. In June the National League had announced it would consider dropping four of its unprofitable clubs in order to increase the profits of the other eight. The Washington, Louisville, Baltimore, and Cleveland clubs were those so threatened. When rumors of the new league were first heard, Ban Johnson, president of the Western League, was identified by some as the backer of the new league. Later, when Johnson was invited to join his league with the new league, he declined, as did other Western League figures such as Charles Comiskey.

The National League had reigned as the only major league since 1892, but the twelve-club format had proved unpopular with fans, and attendance dropped steadily through the nineties. The existence of only one major league limited the number of cities who could offer major league baseball, and it also limited the number of would-be magnates.

The motivations of the organizers of the new league were varied. McGraw and Robinson hoped to be able to remain in Baltimore, where they were extremely popular, if the National League ousted that city. Quinn had been unable to acquire a major league franchise for Milwaukee since his club had been dropped following the amalgamation of the National League and the old American Association. Von der Ahe had been manipulated out of his National League franchise in St. Louis after the 1898 season and sought a return to his former prominence in baseball affairs. Von der Ahe even went so far as to give to the new American Association, for award to the championship team, the famous Wiman Trophy captured by his famous St. Louis Browns team for winning AA championships in 1886, 1887, and 1888.

The National League took several actions to fight the new league because "by coming into our territory the new association invites war." National League owners believed they could forbid the use of the name of the American Association because when they had absorbed the old American Association they had acquired use of the name and were legally known as the National League and American Association of Baseball Clubs.

Secondly the National League announced plans for their own American Association. This league, which became known as American Association II, would be organized as a minor league, would charge only 25 cents admission, and would play in National League parks when the major league teams were on the road. Thirdly, Ban Johnson's Western League, by then with a name change to the American

League, would be allowed or encouraged to move into Chicago and Cleveland.

Formal organization of the new American Association occurred in Chicago on February 13, 1900. Arrangements for the New York and Washington clubs had fallen through. Boston and Louisville clubs were admitted to join Baltimore, Milwaukee, Detroit, Chicago, and St. Louis clubs in signing the required agreements and posting a $1,200 bond. Philadelphia was still desired for the eighth club. In fact, Philadelphia was considered essential to the success of the new league. Anson was elected president of the new league and announced the new league would open play on April 16, 1900. Among other business, the name of the new league was changed to the New American Association.

McGraw traveled to Philadelphia after the Chicago meeting to finalize arrangements in that city. McGraw's conferences with W. J. Gilmore, reportedly the major backer, were unsatisfactory. Gilmore informed him he had experienced difficulty locating a place to play and would need three more weeks before he would decide if he would enter a team.

On February 16, 1900, President Anson announced the New American Association had collapsed and would not operate in 1900. Some of the backers attempted to reorganize for the 1901 season but were unsuccessful.

The Columbian Baseball League (1912)

The "Columbian Baseball League" was first proposed at a meeting in Chicago on January 13, 1912. The meeting was called by John T. Powers, an ex-president of the Wisconsin-Illinois League, and was attended by representatives of interests in cities of the Midwest.

At a meeting in St. Louis on February 12, 1912, the Columbian League was formally organized, with franchises awarded to Chicago, Kansas City, St. Louis, Louisville, Indianapolis, Detroit, Cleveland, and Milwaukee. All these cities had existing teams in either the American League, National League, or the minor league American Association. Powers was elected president the new league.

The baseball public was assured that good playing grounds had been located in most of these cities and that sufficient financial resources existed to operate the new league. Powers indicated the quality of play would equal that of the high minor leagues in the first season and rival that of the major leagues in following seasons.

The Columbian League did not plan to encourage contract jumping but did announce that it would ignore the reserve clause. By late February Powers was able to display letters from sixty-three players interested in playing in the new league. About forty of these had been reserved by teams within organized baseball. Several ex-big leaguers were announced as probable managers of Columbian League teams, including Danny Shay at Kansas City and Ed McKean at Cleveland.

Powers obviously anticipated strong opposition to the new league. He indicated that organized baseball would be fought under the Sherman Antitrust law if it attacked the new league. Powers added that:

We are not fighting capital with capital, and do not seek a fight with any person or combination. But we have the right to exist and compete with the "baseball trust."

Organized baseball interfered very little with the new league other than labeling it an "outlaw league" and implying that it took more than just talk to operate a successful league. That opinion proved correct. When financial backing proved insufficient, the Columbian League folded before ever playing its first game. Some of the Columbian League backers then became involved in yet another independent league, the United States League.

The United States League (1912–1913)

The "United States League of Professional Baseball Clubs" operated briefly in both the 1912 and 1913 seasons. The United States League posed itself as the "third major league" and attempted to exist peacefully and profitably, yet separately, from organized baseball.

The United States League was formally organized in New York City on January 20, 1912. Its chief organizer, William A. Witman of Reading, Pennsylvania, was elected president of the new league. Applications for franchises were reported from twelve or thirteen cities for what was projected as an eight-club league.

The United States League innovations included the absence of a reserve clause in their player contracts. However, organized baseball's own reserve clause was to be respected, as were existing contracts. United States League contracts with players were to be made for one to three years at the option of the player. At the expiration of the contract, the player was to be a free agent. The only real conflict with organized baseball was over "territorial rights."

A second attempt in 1912 to form an independent league, the Columbian League, proved unsuccessful, and in March several backers of that league switched allegiance and money to the United States League. Most prominent and wealthy of the new backers as William Nieson of Chicago.

Good and solid financing for the United States League was promised, and franchises for 1912 were ultimately located in New York; Brooklyn; Cleveland; Chicago; Washington; Cincinnati; Richmond, Virginia; and Reading, Pennsylvania. United States League cities all had existing major league franchises except Richmond and Reading. President Witman was to operate the Reading franchise. Hall of Famer "Pop" Anson attempted to buy into both the New York and Washington franchises and tried to buy the Reading franchise and move it to Buffalo. He was rebuffed in all instances, but his interest, and the overtures of other parties, indicates a belief in the viability of the new league.

The United States League planned a 126-game schedule with play to begin on May 1. Attendance was 2,000 that day in New York, but soon it dropped to an average of 300 to 400 for most United States League games. Unfortunately, much bad weather dropped attendance even further.

Several ex-major leaguers played on or managed United States League teams, including Deacon Phillippe, Bert Blue, Joe Wall, and Bugs Raymond. Most of the players, however, were unremarkable minor leaguers and semiprofessionals, plus a significant number of promising youngsters. Among the latter was New York-born Al Schacht, who pitched well (5–0 according to his autobiography) for the Cleveland team.

That the United States League lasted into late May amazed many. One rumor had it that the newly formed Professional Baseball Players Fraternity was secretly supporting

the United States League. When the Detroit Tigers of the American League staged a brief strike in support of the suspended Ty Cobb, they were reported to be jumping to the United States League. At least five of the Tigers, including Cobb, did receive offers from the United States League, but the strike was settled and the Tigers remained in place.

On May 20 the Cincinnati franchise owners announced that they would transfer games to an as yet undetermined site. On May 21 the Washington players quit because salaries had not been paid. The New York franchise was forfeited on May 28. Then in rapid succession the Richmond and Cincinnati franchises folded, and Witman filed for personal bankruptcy with his debts including $970 owed to Reading players. Witman stated his undoing was "the combination of organized baseball and political forces that had been formed to trim me."

Despite Witman's accusations there is little evidence of interference with the United States League by organized baseball. The Cincinnati Reds president August Herrmann admitted, "We have no right to object to them, no right to annoy them." Most of baseball simply ignored the United States League.

The last regularly scheduled United States League games were played on June 1, although some games were played as late as June 8. Pittsburgh, with an unofficial 23–8 record, compiled easily the best record, with Richmond in second place. On June 23 Marshall Henderson of Pittsburgh succeeded Witman as the United States League president. He attempted to reorganize the United States League into a six-club league to finish the season but was unsuccessful. All United States League teams reported heavy financial losses, with the exception of the Pittsburgh club, which showed a modest profit. The *Reach Guide* summarized the 1912 United States League experience as follows:

This organization was started, but it went the way of all "houses builded on sand," after just one month of wretched existence. The organization had neither officials, circuit, or magnates to commend themselves to the public; or players to attract or hold patronage. Furthermore, there was no baseball brain to plan and direct, no courage to combat and circumvent adverse conditions, and no capital to help the organization over the inevitable losing initial season.

The United States League surfaced again on January 5, 1913, with plans for a new eight-club league based in cities in and near the East Coast. It was hoped that reduced travel costs would make the venture more profitable. William A. Witman, his financial affairs straightened out, was again the chief organizer and was again elected president of the United States League.

For 1913 United States League franchises were awarded to Baltimore, Brooklyn, Reading, New York, Newark, Philadelphia, Washington, and Lynchburg, Virginia. Plans were also announced to eventually expand into, or at least play in, foreign countries. The players were again mostly has-beens, career minor leaguers, semiprofessionals, and promising youngsters.

The 1913 United States League season opened May 10 with four games. The next day New York refused to play, having not received the guarantee from the previous day. On May 12 Brooklyn refused to play Washington for the same reason. Washington and New York were dropped from the

league, but reorganization failed, and the last United States League game was played on May 13. Baltimore won both of its games and could be considered the unofficial league champion.

The Federal League (1913–15)

The Federal League operated in the 1913, 1914, and 1915 seasons. During the latter two seasons, the Federal League posed as severe a threat to the status quo as any league in the history of baseball.

The "Federal League of Baseball Clubs" was organized on March 8, 1913, in Indianapolis. John Powers, who in 1912 had tried to launch a Midwest-based Columbian League, was the chief organizer and was elected president of the new league. The new league was to be an independent league and not under the control of the National Commission. The Federal League did not, however, plan to tamper with players affiliated with organized baseball but planned to develop its own players. Each team to be entered into the Federal League had to post a bond with the new league of $5,000 and was further required to be capitalized to the extent of $100,000.

Franchises were awarded to interests in Chicago, Pittsburgh, Cleveland, St. Louis, Indianapolis, and Cincinnati. Two more franchises were sought, but they did not materialize, possibly because of the short time remaining until the opening of the season. In addition, preparations for the Cincinnati franchise ran into trouble, and the franchise was eventually located in Covington, Kentucky, across the river from Cincinnati. Federal League teams challenged existing major league teams in five locations and the minor league American Association in one.

The Federal League strategy for its first season was to sign a well-known manager and as many experienced free-agent players as possible and fill out the team with promising youngsters. Burt Keeley became the manager at Chicago, Deacon Phillippe at Pittsburgh, Bill Phillips at Indianapolis, Sam Leever at Covington, Jack O'Connor at St. Louis, and Cy Young at Cleveland.

The season opened May 3 with Covington and Cleveland playing a 6–6 ten-inning tie. The other teams opened three days later with surprisingly good attendance in some locations. On May 11, Indianapolis drew some 18,500 to a game—in part because of a new provision they had made for fans. Parking for automobiles was available, and over two hundred cars were accommodated. Unfortunately, attendance declined steadily through the remainder of the season.

Organized baseball ignored the Federal League at first. Then in early June Federal League teams signed three players whom they considered were free of organized-baseball ties but who were still claimed by their former teams. Elmer Knetzer, an ex-Brooklyn Dodger, had left that team because of illness in his family and had his salary reduced as a result. He signed with Pittsburgh, which was his hometown. Two other Pittsburgh boys, Jack Lewis and Tom Murray, felt they were unfairly assigned to St. Paul and left that team also to join the Pittsburgh Feds.

Within days, teams in organized baseball began raids on Federal League teams with Indianapolis losing two stars, Ben Taylor and James Scott. Several Chicago Federal League players also received offers mostly from the NL Cubs.

The Federal League also faced other difficulties. The Western Union Telegraph had refused to allow Federal League scores on its ticker service. In mid-June a representative of the Federal League, E. E. Gates of Indianapolis, appeared before the Interstate Commerce Commission and alleged that such refusal was a violation of the Hepburn Act. He stated that the Federal League had offered to pay for the ticker service privilege but had been refused. The Federal League believed organized baseball was behind the Western Union refusal. Gates also conferred with U.S. Representative Gallagher, who had introduced a resolution in Congress asking that baseball be investigated for possible antitrust violations. Gates complained about reserve clauses, blacklists, and other arbitrary actions of baseball. Gates thought the questions was "Is it possible that organized baseball, through its years of tyrannical rule and usurpation, has secured certain privileges and immunities which do not belong to other organizations in the country?" Gates thought not.

Indianapolis had the best team in the Federal League and by the end of June had a four-game lead over Chicago. Cleveland and Covington also had posted winning records, with Pittsburgh bringing up the rear. Despite its winning record, the Covington team was plagued by poor attendance and on June 26 was transferred to Kansas City.

On June 28 a conference of American Association and major league baseball leaders was held in Chicago to combat "the encroachments of the Federal League." Two Indianapolis American Association players, Ray Aschenfelder and Fred Link, had just signed with Federal League teams. That and the invasion of Kansas City was said to have "aroused all the clubs owners in the American Association to the necessity of strengthening their hold on their players and their territory." It was all-out war from that point in time.

On August 2, Powers was removed as president by the Federal League owners. He was replaced by James Gilmore of Chicago, who was able to stabilize matters in the Federal League and allow it to finish the season despite some talk of disbandment.

The Indianapolis Feds easily won the Federal League championship with a 75–45 record, some 10 games ahead of Cleveland. Pittsburgh finished last with a 49–71 record. "Biddy" Dolan of Indianapolis, a career minor leaguer, is usually considered the batting champion with a .346 batting average. Only one player in the league hit more than 5 home runs: John Kading of Chicago hit 9 to easily lead the league. Two pitchers, Pete Henning of Covington and Kansas City and Tom McGuire of Chicago, each pitched 18 wins to lead the hurlers. McGuire also led with 170 strikeouts.

The Federal League, instead of disbanding, expanded for the 1914 season. Clubs were added in Buffalo, Brooklyn, and Baltimore, and the Cleveland club was dropped. Gilmore was extremely successful at adding men with money to the Federal League owners. Charles Weeghman, owner of a chain of lunchrooms, took over the Chicago team. Phillip Ball of St. Louis invested in the St. Louis franchise. Most important for the Federal League finances, Robert Ward became the backer of the new Brooklyn team. The Federal League declared that beginning with the 1914 season, it was a major league equal to the other major leagues.

Federal League teams challenged existing major league teams in four cities. They challenged the International League in Baltimore and Buffalo and the American Association in Indianapolis and Kansas City. St. Louis and Chicago now had three "major league" teams apiece.

The Federal League, at least by the beginning of the 1914 season, was organized as a single corporation with the stock divided among the owners. It is unclear whether this had also been the arrangement in 1913. The Federal League player contract was also different. It did not contain a reserve clause but provided for an option for the players' services for the next year. The option for the next season had to be exercised by September 15, and a minimum 5 percent increase in salary was required. A player could become a free agent after ten Federal League seasons.

The Federal League jumped quickly into the fray with the signing for 1914 of three well-known National League stars as managers for their teams. George Stovall was signed to manage the Kansas City club after squabbling with the St. Louis National League owner the entire 1913 season. Mordecai "Three Finger" Brown joined the St. Louis club as manager after pitching for Cincinnati in 1913. Most irritating to the National League was the signing of Joe Tinker. Tinker, the long-time Chicago star of "Tinker to Evers to Chance" fame, had just been sold by the Cincinnati Reds to the Brooklyn Dodgers for a reported $15,000. Tinker at first agreed to the deal but then refused when offered a salary of only $7,500. He then signed with the Chicago Feds for $12,000 per year plus stock in the club.

Many other National and American League players used Federal League offers to seek and receive better contracts from their original clubs. The best-known case involved Bill Killefer, a a catcher for the Philadelphia Phillies in 1913. Killefer promised to sign again with Philadelphia for 1914 but instead signed a three-year Federal League contract for a total of $17,500. After being pressured by his former team and threatened with the blacklist, he signed with Philadelphia again for $6,500 a season. The matter ended up in the courts with Philadelphia winning because part of Killefer's 1913 salary had been designated as payment for an option on his services for 1914. At least three other players "did a Killefer" and returned to their organized-baseball club after signing with the Federal League.

National Commission rules specified a three-year suspension for reserve rule jumpers and five-year suspensions for contract breakers.

Other notable battles were fought over the ten-day clause in the standard National League and American League contract. This provision allowed a club to release a player on ten days' notice whereas a player was bound to a club for his whole career if the club chose. When pitcher Chief Johnson jumped his contract to sign with the Kansas City Feds, the matter ended up in court with the ruling eventually being that such a contract lacked mutuality. Then Hal Chase, first baseman of the Chicago White Sox, gave them a ten-day notice and jumped to the Buffalo Feds. The case ended up in court with Chase finally winning.

The 1914 Federal League pennant winner was again Indianapolis, this time with an 88–65 record, only 1½ games ahead of Chicago. Bennie Kauff, "the Ty Cobb of the Federal League," was the batting champion with a .370 batting average. Duke Kenworthy of Kansas City and Dutch Zwilling of Chicago each had 15 home runs to lead the league. Claude Hendrix of Chicago led the pitchers with 29 wins.

There were secret peace discussions following the 1914 season, but they proved futile because the Federal League wanted too much. What was requested is not clearly indi-

cated, but it is believed that the Federal League wished to continue operation as the third major league.

On January 5, 1915, the Federal League filed suit against organized baseball, charging that violations of the antitrust laws had occurred. Organized baseball was said to have been an illegal combination and monopoly which engaged in illegal acts such as farming out of players and other actions in restraint of free trade. The suit was filed in the court of Judge Kenesaw Mountain Landis, who had a reputation as a trust buster because of his famous antitrust decision against Standard Oil.

Federal League president Gilmore made several changes in preparation for a continuing Federal League in 1915. New money was located in the person of the fabulously rich Harry Sinclair, later to be implicated in the Teapot Dome Scandals. Sinclair wanted to operate a club in Newark as an entree into an eventual move into New York City. The Federal League attempted to transfer the Kansas City club to Newark, but the Kansas City investors took the matter to court. Gilmore acquiesced and allowed the club to stay in Kansas City. Eventually the Indianapolis club, the Federal League pennant winner in its first two seasons, was moved to Newark. Kauff was assigned to the Brooklyn team in order to strengthen that franchise.

The player raids began again in earnest after the breakdown of the peace talks. Several members of Connie Mack's pennant-winning Philadelphia A's were known to be negotiating with the Federal League, and Eddie Plank did jump to the Federal League. Mack sold the rest of his stars rather than lose them to the Federal League, and as a result his club finished last in 1915 and in each of the next six seasons.

Most alarming to organized baseball was the apparent defection of Washington Senator star pitcher Walter Johnson to the Chicago Federal League team. Johnson had received an offer from Washington for 1915 but found it inadequate. He then signed a three-year contract with the Chicago Federal League team and pocketed a $6,000 bonus. Washington owner Clark Griffith convinced Johnson to return to his fold with a contract calling for $12,500 per season. To his credit Johnson returned the Federal League bonus, but he never adequately explained the breaking of the Federal League contract.

Organized baseball also attempted their share of player raids. Federal League batting champion Bennie Kauff signed a three-year contract with the Brooklyn Federal League club after being transferred there from Indianapolis. He then signed with the New York Giants and played in exhibition games with them. The Boston Braves complained that Kauff had previously jumped his contract with organized baseball and was blacklisted as a contract jumper. Kauff applied for reinstatement but was refused. He then returned to the Brooklyn Federal League team.

The 1915 Federal League season was one of the closest and most interesting of all time. Six of the eight clubs were in the race until the last week of the season. The championship was not settled until the last day of the season when Chicago split a doubleheader with Pittsburgh to finish with an 86–66 record, just ahead of St. Louis at 87–67 and Pittsburgh at 86–67. Bennie Kauff again won the batting championship, this time with a .342 batting average. Hal Chase of Buffalo hit 17 home runs to lead in that category. George McConnell of Chicago lead the pitchers with 25 wins.

By one count, that of historian Harold Seymour, 264 players appeared in one or more games in the two years the Federal League was a major league. Of that total, 43 players jumped major or minor league contracts to join the Federal League, and 188 players ignored the reserve clause to join the Federal League. The remaining 33 players were free agents or had no previous professional experience.

Although aided greatly by the close pennant race, attendance was generally disappointing throughout the Federal League in 1915. Several clubs, including Kansas City and Buffalo, required league assistance to finish the season. The prevailing sentiment of Federal League owners was to push for a settlement. That sentiment was reinforced when wealthy Brooklyn Federal League owner Robert Ward died in October.

After prolonged negotiations, a peace agreement was finally reached and signed on December 22, 1915, in Cincinnati. Terms of the agreement provided that Weeghman of the Chicago Feds would be allowed to purchase the Chicago Cubs (for a reported $500,000) and that Ball would be allowed to purchase the St. Louis Browns (for $525,000). The Ward estate was to receive $400,000 to be paid in twenty payments. The owners of the Pittsburgh Feds received $50,000 and the right to bid on several major league franchises on which prices had been established. Sinclair was given $100,000 to be paid in ten payments and control of all of the Newark, Kansas City, and Buffalo players plus Benny Kauff, Lee Magee, and George Anderson of the Brooklyn team. The Baltimore owners were offered $50,000 for their settlement but did not accept. The Baltimore club eventually filed suit over the agreement, with the suit dragging on until 1922. Other Federal League owners got left behind for the most part, although initially they were promised International League franchises. The antitrust suit pending before Judge Landis and all other suits were to be dismissed.

All Federal League players were removed from the blacklist and certified as eligible to play for organized baseball clubs in 1916. All Federal League contracts were to be paid in full, and the organized baseball team that had lost them originally could not get them back unless they purchased them.

Estimates of Federal League losses ranged from $2 million to $3 million, with the losses of the National League and American League close to $2 million. It had been a costly war, and the editor of *The Spalding Guide* mused as follows:

The war is over. It is not the intention of the editor of The Guide *to enter into any new argument or refutation of false argument in connection with this episode in Base Ball. It is his intention, however, to call attention again to the fact that Organized Base Ball has once more proved to the world that it is the originator of the best and finest method to control a sport, which is called a nation's sport, of any method in the history of sport throughout the civilized world.*

The Continental League (1959–1960)

The "Continental League" was organized on July 27, 1959, in New York City. The backers, who included several men now associated with the National League or the American League, planned an eight-club league with a very important franchise to be located in New York City. Other charter members were Denver, Houston, Toronto, and the twin cities

of Minneapolis and St. Paul. The eleven other cities listed as applicants included San Juan, Puerto Rico.

New York had been abandoned after the 1957 season by both the Giants and the Dodgers. Each club cited better opportunities on the West Coast. National League president Warren Giles had even downplayed the importance of New York by quipping, "Who needs New York?"

The founders' group of the Continental League included chairman William Shea of New York, Jack Kent Cooke of Toronto, and Craig F. Cullian, Jr., of Houston.

The Continental League founders hoped to operate the new league within the structure of organized baseball. When asked why the Continental League was formed, the founders replied:

The Continental League is the result of the increasing demand of cities in this country and Canada for major league baseball. Not only New York, since losing the Giants and Dodgers, but many other cities have done everything in their power to obtain franchises in the two existing major leagues without success.

When asked what action the Continental League would take if the established major leagues opposed the new league, Shea replied, "We will go ahead anyway."

Continental League teams were to be capitalized to $2,500,000, exclusive of the cost of stadiums and other facilities. Each stadium was to have a capacity of at least 35,000. The Continental League name was one of four considered for the new league, the others being the Third League, the United States League, and the International League.

The National League and the American League were, surprisingly, not openly hostile to the new league, although several observers expressed the fear that the Continental League would weaken the minor leagues by taking several of the best minor league cities. Ford Frick, commissioner of baseball, announced that a committee which would include the presidents of the National and American Leagues would be appointed to meet with the representatives of the new league.

One of the motivating factors may have been the hearings being conducted by the House Judiciary Committee into possible antitrust violations by baseball. The chairman of that committee, Representative Emanuel Celler of Brooklyn, was a long-time critic of the big-business aspects of baseball. He said that if the new league ran into any problems with which Congress could help, "it would be duty-bound to do so in the interest of the national pastime."

Pressure to accept the new league also came from Senator Estes Kefauver of Tennessee, chairman of the Senate Antitrust and Monopoly Committee. He had introduced a bill proposing to limit to eighty the number of players a major league team could control. Kefauver said of the Continental League, "I hope we can get some legislation that will help them get started."

Branch Rickey, a seventy-seven-year-old ex-major league player, manager, and executive, was appointed president of the Continental League on August 18, 1959. An hour after his appointment. Rickey met with Ford Frick's major league committee. Rickey's statements to the committee included, "We want your cooperation, we need your cooperation, we demand your cooperation."

After some seven hours of meeting, the committee endorsed the idea of the Continental League as a major league providing that several conditions were met. The Continental League was required to play a balanced 154-game schedule; it had to adopt the major league minimum-salary agreement and join the player pension plan and agree to admit no city smaller than the smallest currently in the major leagues. Kansas City was the smallest major league city, with a population of 460,000.

Rickey and Shea were among those who had testified in front of Senator Kefauver's committee. Their joint letter to the committee read in part:

The present major league franchise owners apparently have a total lack of loyalty to the communities which support their enterprises. The major league owner today refers to the "national pastime" with great reverence. And, when it suits him, he behaves as if he were operating a quasi-public trust. But let a better "deal" be offered in another city and he reverts instantaneously to the hundred percent businessman whose only guide is the earnings statement.

In October 1959 Calvin Griffith, owner of the Washington Senators, was reportedly seriously considering moving his club to Minneapolis, and the Cincinnati Reds were considering relocating to New York. Both moves were apparently stymied by the pending legislation. Representative Celler said if the moves were made it would "prove that baseball is not a sport but a business."

By January 29, 1960, Buffalo, Atlanta, and Dallas-Ft. Worth had been admitted into the Continental League, thus completing an eight-club league. Branch Rickey found it significant that the Continental League completed its circuit sixty years to the day from the founding of the American League.

Indemnification of the minor leagues proved to be a major obstacle for the Continental League. The International League, which was to lose two cities, demanded $750,000 per city plus $100,000 relocation costs per franchise. The American Association expected $800,000 total per city lost. Although the monetary demands were later moderated, territorial issues continued to plague the Continental League with the International League proving particularly obstreperous.

The question of where the Continental League would find players was addressed in several ways. Rickey reported a number of inquiries about the possibility of playing in the Continental League. Secondly, Rickey helped form a new Class D Western Carolina League to begin operation in 1960. The Continental League was to subsidize the league with $60,000, to be divided among the eight clubs plus paying managers' salaries, training costs, and certain transportation costs. All Western Carolina League players were to train together and then were to be allocated to the various clubs. The Western Carolina League as proposed was rejected by Ford Frick, commissioner of baseball, because the player pool to be operated under Continental League sponsorship, violated, he said, a long-standing rule against major league teams controlling more than one team in a league.

Kefauver's bill to limit the control of organized baseball over players and removal of its antitrust exemption was narrowly defeated in June 1960, despite the lobbying of Senate Majority Leader Lyndon B. Johnson. With the defeat, pressure on the established major leagues was off.

On July 18, 1960, the National League voted to expand if it

developed that the Continental League idea was not practical. New York was to be a part of any expansion plan, Ford Frick assured. The American League also set up an expansion committee at about this time.

About two weeks later, on August 2, 1960, the Continental League backers submitted a formal application to organized baseball for recognition as the third major league. Instead, the immediate expansion by two clubs each of the existing major leagues was approved, with the eight Continental League backers concurring. With that action the Continental League formally expired.

A New York National League franchise was ultimately awarded to William Shea, with Houston joining at the same time. They began play in the 1962 season. The American League moved even quicker. They allowed the Washington club to move to Minneapolis-St. Paul and admitted new clubs for 1961 in Washington and Los Angeles. The rest of the Continental League cities were promised consideration when expansion occurred again. All except Denver and Buffalo eventually ended up with major league franchises, either through more expansion or the transfer of other clubs.

Afterword

In 1968 a Special Baseball Records Committee, appointed by the Commissioner of Baseball, considered the various claims made by and for leagues that they were or had been major leagues. Four of the "other major leagues"—the American Association (1882–1891), the Union Association (1884),

the Players League (1890), and the Federal League (1914–1915)—joined the National League (1876 to present) and the American League (1901 to present) as recognized major leagues. Not recognized as part of their major league histories were the 1900 American League season and the 1913 Federal League season.

The decisions of this Special Baseball Records Committee have been widely accepted by modern historians, although certain contemporaries of the Union Association and the Players League might have expressed considerable surprise in the decisions. Of the modern authorities, *The Sporting News* has continued to treat the Federal League as less than a major league in its reference books but is in agreement on the remaining leagues.

The National Association was not recognized by the committee as a major league despite the fact that it was the very first professional league and the only professional league for five years. "Erratic scheduling and procedures" were cited as reasons. Many early historians of the game had a different opinion. *Total Baseball,* alone of reference works, lists the National Association as a major league.

The claims of the other leagues that actually did operate were not accepted by the Special Baseball Records Committee and are not taken seriously by modern historians. The International Association/National Association (1877–1880) had even more erratic scheduling and procedures than the old National Association, if that is possible. The United States League (1912–1913) lasted only a little over a month over two seasons, and no one makes much of a case for it. None will be attempted here.

## CHAPTER 24

The Minor Leagues

Bob Hoie

The International Association, founded in 1877, is frequently described as the first minor league. For two major reasons it shouldn't be so regarded. First, it was barely a league. Structurally it resembled the old National Association—there was virtually no central authority, no limitation on the number or location of member teams, no set schedule, and haphazard umpire selection. The league was so loosely assembled in fact that some member teams competed at the same time for the championships of other organizations like the New England Association and the League Alliance. Second, the International Association was originally established as a rival to the National League and never officially recognized itself as being subordinate. It was generally acknowledged that several of its teams were as good as or better than some in the National League. Various off-the-field problems, administrative weaknesses, and a lack of solidarity and resolve on the part of the member clubs assured its subordinate status.

A strong case could be made for the 1879 Northwestern League as the first minor league—it had a preset schedule and had no pretensions of rivaling the National League, but the absence of league-appointed umpires led to frequent forfeits due to charges of biased "hometown" umpiring, and the league folded after only two months.

The Eastern Association was founded in 1881, but this was another loose alliance with no set schedule.

The first recognized minor league was another Northwestern League, this one organized on October 27, 1882. At that time they requested of the National League cooperation and reciprocity in protecting player contracts. This was necessary because independent clubs frequently lost their best players during the course of the season to the National League and later to the American Association clubs. In response to this request, the National League, American Association, and Northwestern League signed a "Tripartite Agreement" in March 1883. This agreement bound the clubs to honor the contracts of players on reserve lists, assured mutual recognition of expulsions and suspensions, established territorial rights, and created an arbitration committee to settle disputes. Minimum salaries were established and pegged at a higher level in the National League and American Association than in the Northwestern League or "any other parties to the agreement," thus by implication assigning a "major" and "minor" status to the leagues.

The Interstate Association was established early in 1883 and was quickly accepted as an "alliance" league by the American Association, becoming a junior partner of the Tripartite Agreement. Both the Northwestern and the Interstate opened their seasons on May 1, 1883. Each had a formal league organization, a schedule that was preset before the season opening, and a complement of umpires appointed and paid for by the league. Both leagues recognized and accepted their status as subordinate to the two "majors." In 1884 the Interstate Association reorganized as the Eastern League and became a fourth member of what now became known as the National Agreement.

In October 1885 a new National Agreement was adopted which made the National League and American Association the principal parties and removed from minor league clubs the protection of the reserve clause. Two years later the reserve clause was reinstated for the minors, but the major-minor league distinction had been formalized. Following the collapse of the American Association in 1892, another National Agreement for the first time established minor league classifications and gave major league clubs the right to draft minor league players at fixed prices.

While these events were taking place, organized baseball expanded dramatically, going from two leagues in 1883 to seventeen by 1890. Baseball was played throughout the country, of course, but organized ball was confined to the northeast quadrant of the United States in 1884; it expanded to the South in 1885, to Colorado and the upper Midwest in 1886, California in 1887, Texas in 1888, and the Pacific Northwest in 1890. So in the year that the American frontier was officially declared closed, organized baseball had extended to all corners of the country.

In 1887 an organization called the Negro Baseball League, fearing player raids by the still moderately integrated minors, sought and received protection under the National Agreement. The league was to play in eight cities that also had major league teams, but it folded in less than two weeks. This was unfortunately characteristic of the era. Many teams and leagues were underfinanced and were ultrasensitive to changes in the national or local economy. In addition, being unable or unwilling to pay the required fees for reserving their players, they lost their better ones at the close of the season— and those teams that even managed to finish the season could usually consider themselves lucky. During the nineteenth century, more than one-third of the leagues that started a season failed to finish it. There was, however, a solid core of support for minor league baseball. Regardless of how many leagues started each season—usually about fifteen but sometimes up to nineteen—ten usually finished; the rest failed. The 1890s were not a period of expansion nor of stability as throughout the decade an average of 40 percent of the leagues that started a season failed to finish it. A depression in 1892-1893 and the Spanish-American War in 1898 were significant factors, but a proliferation of "fly-by-night" operators played a role as well.

At the close of the 1900 season, the still minor American League withdrew from the National Agreement, announcing through that action its intention not to allow its players to be

drafted and not to respect the reserve clause or territorial rights any longer.

In September 1901 the National League announced its intention to abrogate the National Agreement, contending that with the American League invading its cities and raiding its players the National League could not be expected to sit back and abide by restrictions which did not hinder its rival. Essentially this meant that the National, like the American, considered the players on minor league rosters "fair game."

In immediate reaction to this, the presidents of seven minor leagues met in Chicago on September 5, 1901, and in an act of self-protection they organized the National Association of Professional Baseball Leagues. On October 25 representatives of nine minor leagues met in New York and adopted a new "National Agreement." This new agreement established league classifications, roster and salary limits, and a draft system; it recognized reserve lists and created a Board of Arbitration which was given the power to suspend players, clubs, or officials for violations of the agreement. By the beginning of the 1902 season, the National Association included fifteen member leagues.

The American and National Leagues ratified a peace agreement early in 1903, and in late August the presidents of the two major leagues and the National Association drafted a National Agreement which was initially rejected by the minors. After some concessions were made by the majors, such as a prohibition on "farming," the plan was adopted in September. The agreement formalized relations between the majors and minors and established a National Commission to serve as a Board of Arbitration.

These agreements were necessary because the majors and minors were mutually dependent on each other. The majors needed the minors as a reliable source of talent, while the minors, many of whom relied on player sales to stay in business, needed assurances from the majors that they would recognize their property rights in players.

Despite this mutual dependence there was a basic buyer-seller conflict. The majors wanted to acquire players as cheaply as possible, while the minors wanted to sell them for as much as possible. This same conflict existed within the minors as well, with the highest-classification clubs wanting to buy cheaply from the lower minors and sell at high prices to the majors. Thus the National Agreement, the major-minor agreement, and the National Association itself were uneasy alliances of clubs and leagues with competing and often conflicting objectives, and the nearly annual revisions in draft rules and prices and limits on optional player assignments were required to maintain the equilibrium necessary to keep the alliance intact.

The majors favored an unlimited draft—i.e., any player on a minor league roster could be purchased for a fixed rate. As early as 1896, when Minneapolis of the Western League was decimated through what were in effect forced sales, it became clear that some limitations were necessary, so by 1905 only one player could be drafted from a club per year. The draft prices of top-classification minor leaguers went from $750 to $1,000 in 1905 and then to $2,500 in 1911. While these prices were not particularly low for average prospects in that era, they were well below the value of the best prospects in the minors; thus the draft or the threat of it served as an incentive for minor league clubs at all levels to sell their better players to major or higher-classification minor league clubs at competitive market prices. From the players' standpoint, the draft

had the positive effect of allowing them eventually to advance to whatever levels their ability would take them. The lower-classification minor league clubs received lower draft prices for their players but seemed relatively satisfied with the system—after all, this was an era when the contracts of Tris Speaker, Rogers Hornsby, and Ty Cobb were sold to major league clubs for $400, $500, and $700 respectively.

On the other hand, many of the higher-classification minor league clubs had never really been satisfied with the draft. As early as 1908, this dissatisfaction nearly caused the two top minor leagues at that time—the American Association and the Eastern League—to go independent. Several of the top minor league clubs drew more fans annually than some major league clubs and represented substantial investments; their owners were understandably not happy with a system that forced the sale of their top players for below-market prices to the majors; in addition to the challenge to club stability and autonomy caused by the draft, the gap between the market value of the top prospects and the draft price widened throughout the 1910s.

Despite the rumblings of discontent, the establishment of the National Association ushered in a period of minor league expansion to a fairly stable core of thirty leagues. While there were still leagues that failed to finish the season, the failure rate was down to 10–15 percent. For some reason, in 1910 the minors reached a level never to be topped until the post–World War Two boom era—fifty-two leagues started the season and forty-six finished it. For the next five years more leagues folded, but each season generally closed with forty leagues operating. Then, for reasons that ranged from the automobile, movies, the war in Europe, and the Federal League War, the bottom started to drop out. Forty-four leagues started in the 1914 season, and by the end of the 1918 season only one was operating (ten leagues had started that year—one folded and eight suspended operations due to the war).

After the 1918 season, with most of the lower minors driven out of business, the National Association, for the first time dominated by the higher minors, adopted a resolution demanding that the majors relinquish the right of the draft and end the practice of "farming out" players. When the majors as expected rejected these demands, the National Association withdrew from the National Agreement. Pending a new major agreement, the majors and minors reached general agreement on property rights in players and territorial rights, and the National Commission ruled that the major league draft would be suspended. In addition the minors would not accept major league players on option, meaning that any players owned or controlled by major league clubs in excess of the active player roster limit would have to be sold or released to minor league clubs.

A. R. Tierney, president of two minor leagues and a leader in the fight to end the draft, said, "This means that the minor leagues will be able to build fences for themselves instead of for the major leagues." He predicted expansion of the minors and higher sale prices for the players. He was correct on both counts. With no players on option, the majors needed to buy more players from the minors, some of whom they had been forced to sell but now had to buy back at higher prices, and without the draft the minor league clubs could virtually name their own price. The minors expanded, as the leagues that had been driven out of business during the war now reentered the fold.

The reappearance of the low minors again shifted the balance of power within the minors. The higher minors had never been happy with the one-league, one-vote system in the National Association. Club owners were wary of having their investments affected by the vote of what they perceived as little more than "fly-by-night" operators, and on occasion they tried to change the arrangement. But just as the majors needed the minors, so the high minors needed the low minors. Thus the high minors always stopped short of enacting measures that might drive their underlings out of the Association.

As noted previously, many of the low minors needed the revenues they received from the draft to survive, and although the minor league draft still existed, it had ceased to be a dependable source of revenue as the combination of numerous prewar minor league failures and returning military veterans yielded more than enough talent to fill the higher minors' rosters. In addition, many of the low-minor clubs did not have the resources to scout for and sign enough players to remain competitive on the field and/or at the box office; thus they were dependent on receiving some players on option.

So while most of the higher minor leagues were prospering as never before under the new independence, by 1920 the low minors were ready to withdraw from the National Association if a new agreement with the majors restoring the draft was not adopted. In addition, some of the higher minor league clubs were upset that the "no-farming" rules were being circumvented by "gentleman's agreements" which enabled the major league clubs to "sell" a player to a minor league club and "buy" him back at the end of the season with little or no money actually changing hands.

On January 10, 1921, a new major-minor league agreement was signed which restored the major league draft with a top price of $5,000 but as a compromise gave individual minor leagues the right to be exempt from the draft; in addition major league clubs could option up to eight players for no more than two consecutive years, and a tax on player sales was instituted to help reduce the fake player transfers. Quickly the top three minors—the International League, Pacific Coast League, and the American Association—together with the Western and Three-I Leagues declared their exemption from the draft; this in turn prohibited them from drafting from the lower minors.

The prices the majors paid for top minor league players nearly doubled between 1919 and 1920, but they skyrocketed during the draft-exemption era. In 1921 the Giants paid $75,000 to San Francisco for Jimmy O'Connell; in 1922 the Giants paid $72,000 to Baltimore for Jack Bentley and the White Sox paid $100,000 to San Francisco for Willie Kamm. The majors clearly were not happy with this situation, and in 1922 they offered to raise the draft price to $7,500, but this failed to lure back the draft-exempt leagues. In early 1923 the majors, after considering but eventually rejecting the idea of a maximum purchase price of $25,000 for any minor league player and/or a boycott of draft-exempt leagues, declared that all players sent to the minors either by sale or option would be subject to the draft and increased the number of players who could be optioned to fifteen. Western League clubs immediately began accepting players on option under these conditions.

The prices for ballplayers remained high in 1923. Baltimore of the International League was reportedly offered $100,000 by Brooklyn for Joe Boley and sold Max Bishop to the Philadelphia A's for $50,000. Salt Lake sold Paul Strand to the A's for a reported $70,000, Louisville sold Earle Combs to the Yankees for $50,000, Toronto sold Red Wingo to the Tigers for $50,000 and Rochester sold Maurice Archdeacon to the White Sox for $50,000, but these were isolated cases. Baltimore, aided by five years of draft exemption, had built a powerhouse, but many of the higher-classification minor league clubs had not been nearly as successful and found that they needed to receive players on option to fill holes and remain competitive. Therefore at the close of the 1923 season all exempt leagues but the International agreed to the modified draft which exempted only those players who had come up through the minors. In 1924, after Baltimore sold Lefty Grove for $100,000 to the A's, the International League also fell into line.

The modified draft did nothing to reduce the prices paid for top minor league stars: Louisville sold Wayland Dean to the Giants for $72,000 in 1924, San Francisco sold Paul Waner and Hal Rhyne to Pittsburgh for $100,000 in 1925, and Baltimore continued selling star players to the majors for big prices—Tommy Thomas to the White Sox in 1925, Joe Boley to the A's in 1926, John Ogden to the Browns and George Earnshaw to the A's in 1927. In 1927 Portland (of the PCL) sold Billy Cissel to the White Sox for a package of cash and players worth over $100,000 and Oakland sold Lyn Lary and Jimmy Reese to the Yankees for $100,000. With prices like these, clubs could afford to lose a Lefty O'Doul or Hack Wilson in the modified draft.

The major-minor agreement expired at the end of the 1927 season, with the National Association members deadlocked on the issue of the draft. The majors and minors were also at an impasse, so the modified draft continued and many of the higher minor league clubs continued to prosper, both through player sales and at the gate. The Los Angeles franchise and ballpark were valued at $2 million, and in 1928 the Oakland club was sold for $500,000. But in the lower minors all was not well through the 1920s. There were generally twenty-five or thirty leagues starting each year, and an average of three or four of these would fold during the season. Leagues were operating that never should have been admitted to the National Association—one of the four leagues that not unexpectedly failed in 1924 was the West Arkansas, which included six towns within a 750-square-mile area with a combined population of 16,000.

In 1929 the rift between the high and low minors widened as the low minors, rebuffed in their efforts to nullify the modified draft agreement, now attempted to impose their own draft exemption—essentially exempting from the draft any player with fewer than two seasons of organized baseball.

Early in 1931 the majors and minors finally adopted a new National Agreement, including a provision which eliminated the modified draft and granted to major league clubs greater control of talent through revised option and draft rules. The higher minors had originally objected, but the majors told them to accept the universal draft or they would no longer have any relations with them—in other words, major league teams would not sell or option players to or buy players from the American Association, the International League, or the Pacific Coast League. While such threats had been taken relatively lightly by the minors in the early days of the draft-exempt leagues, they were now taken seriously enough that in less than a month the three recalcitrant leagues capitulated to the majors' terms. In exchange for all this and largely to secure the support of the low minors, the majors agreed to

sign only collegian amateurs, leaving all high-schoolers and sandlotters to the minors. Of course, by this time farm systems had developed to the point that most major league clubs could still sign noncollegian amateurs through their farm clubs.

Milwaukee had sold Fred Schulte to the Browns for a reported $100,000 in 1928, but this was the end of an era. There would be no more $100,000 minor leaguers; in fact there would be few if any minor leaguers sold for as much as $50,000 again. It would be more than fifty years before minor league clubs ever sold for as much as $500,000, and at the 1928 National Association Convention, president Mike Sexton wondered when the majors would own enough clubs to control the National Association. The farm system, an old idea now in the process of being perfected by Branch Rickey, had clearly begun to alter the way the minors operated, and despite the efforts of some—most notably Judge Landis—the trend couldn't be reversed.

The Great Depression caused a contraction of the minors in the early 1930s, but even though a near-record low of fourteen leagues opened the 1933 season, none of them folded. The minors then entered an era of unprecedented growth and stability, reaching forty-four leagues in 1940, with only two leagues failing to finish the season between 1933 and 1941. This can be attributed in part to the substantial involvement of the major leagues through outright ownership or regular infusions of money through working agreements, but there were obviously other factors at work. Judge Bramham, on becoming president of the National Association, instituted a number of reforms, many of which were aimed at getting rid of "fly-by-night" or "shoestring" operators. Minor league baseball was better promoted—they had established a public relations department in 1934—and the advent of night baseball was of incalculable value in generating increased attendance, which reached 20 million in 1940. Interestingly, this was a year when 54 percent of the minor league clubs were not affiliated with any major league clubs compared to just 37 percent that were operating independently in 1936.

World War Two caused the minors to drop to just ten leagues in 1944, but in the first postwar year it was up to forty-three, increasing to an all-time high of fifty-nine in 1949, and during that time no leagues folded. (In 1946 the Mexican National League, set up by organized baseball to compete with the outlaw Mexican League, is listed by the National Association as having folded during the season, but actually it only withdrew from the Association and continued to operate independently.)

According to a general consensus, it was the coming of television that caused the minors to begin to disintegrate. Between 1949 and 1963 the number of minor leagues dropped from fifty-nine to eighteen. Attendance decreased even more sharply, going from 42 million to less than 10 million over the same time period.

By 1963, the minors had become nothing more than a training ground for the majors—90 percent of the clubs were major league affiliates, and most of those that weren't were in the largely autonomous Mexican League. While TV was commonly cited as the cause of the minors' contraction, some contended it was a natural response to overexpansion. Gerry Hirn, in an April 1954 *Baseball Digest* article, contended that while the number of minor leagues had dropped from fifty-nine to thirty-six, that was still too many and the minors would be stronger and more efficient if only sixteen to twenty

leagues operated. Interestingly, in 1954 three leagues failed to finish the season, the most failures in peacetime since 1932; they remain the last U.S.-based minor leagues that failed to finish a season (the Inter-American League, which had a team in Miami but was largely based in the Caribbean, failed to finish the 1979 season—the only year it operated).

For reasons that aren't entirely clear, minor league baseball exploded in popularity in the 1980s. Attendance, which had remained stuck at 10–11 million through the 1960s and most of the 1970s, took off in the late 1970s, topping 20 million in 1987 for the first time since 1953. Louisville, which dropped out of organized ball after drawing just 116,000 in 1972, topped a million in 1983. Nashville, which dropped out in 1963 after drawing just 54,000 for the season, drew over half a million in 1980. Former weak sister Buffalo became a box-office powerhouse in 1988. The picture is not all positive: some franchises still draw very poorly, but now there always seems to be a willing buyer when the previous owner gets tired of losing money. The Louisville franchise, which didn't exist in 1981 (what became the Louisville franchise was at that time in Springfield, Illinois, drawing 120,000) sold for more than $4 million in 1987. Minor league franchises that fifteen years ago were given to anyone who would pay the outstanding debts were selling for nearly a million dollars.

The minors have been riding a roller coaster of success and failure over the past century—the Newark franchise which sold for a reported $600,000 during the depths of the Depression didn't even exist twenty years later. Louisville and Nashville have been slipping at the gate the last few years, so it is probably safe to assume the current wave of success won't last forever. Regardless of these fluctuations in popularity and economic viability, the minors have always been, and one can safely assume will continue to be, the primary training ground for major league players.

The Players

Great players have passed through the minors, their careers frequently going in opposite directions and occasionally teaming up or crossing in unlikely locations such as Easton, Maryland, where in 1924 Jimmie Foxx broke into organized baseball as a catcher and the player-manager was Home Run Baker in his last season as an active player. There were many others: Rube Waddell and Red Faber with Minneapolis in 1911, young Waite Hoyt and ancient Jesse Burkett with Hartford in 1916, Dazzy Vance and Roger Bresnahan with Toledo in 1917, Chief Bender and Lefty Grove with Baltimore in 1923, and more recently Enos Slaughter and Billy Williams with Houston in 1960.

Former Negro Leaguers, their careers going in opposite directions, Ray Dandridge and Willie Mays were teammates at Minneapolis in 1951 where another teammate was a seven-year minor league veteran, Hoyt Wilhelm. Wilhelm, a twenty-eight-year-old knuckleballer with a background that included three years in Class D ball and three more in the military service, at that time appeared to be a member of what in that era was a vast army of career minor leaguers, the best of whom held their own with the acknowledged major league greats passing through the minors, but who for a variety of reasons—some good, some not—would themselves spend the bulk of their careers in the minors.

For some of these players who were left behind, the DH rule came fifty years too late, because while they could hit

both for average and power, they generally lacked speed or had defensive shortcomings. For others it is less clear what, if any, deficiencies kept them in the minors, but from these groups a few players emerged as true minor league greats whose impact on fans in minor league cities—Buzz Arlett in Oakland, Joe Hauser in Minneapolis, and Bunny Brief in Kansas City, to name a few—was as great as that of more renowned players in major league cities.

The greatest of the minor league players is generally acknowledged to be Buzz Arlett.

Arlett started his career as a right-handed spitball pitcher with the hometown Oakland Oaks in 1918 and went on to win 108 games, twice going over 25 wins in a season. The Detroit Tigers looked at him, but without the spitball, which he wouldn't be able to use in the majors, they did not consider him a prospect. After suffering arm trouble early in 1923, Buzz switched to the outfield. Although he had been nothing more than a fair-hitting pitcher, once becoming a regular he annually averaged nearly .360 with 30 homers and 140 RBIs through the rest of the 1920s, but early in his career as an outfielder a Cardinal scout labeled him "good hit, no field," and it stuck. Finally in 1931 he was purchased by the Phillies. The thirty-two-year-old switch-hitter batted .313 with 18 homers and 73 RBIs in a season when the National League introduced a "dead ball" in reaction to the hitting orgies of 1929–1930. However, at the end of the year Arlett was sent to Baltimore, where in 1932 he hit 4 homers in a game twice within a five-week period and led the league with 54 homers for the season, but he would never return to the majors. He spent another year with Baltimore, when he again won the home run title, a little over a month with Birmingham, and nearly three years with Minneapolis, where he had another home run championship. After a few games with Syracuse in 1937, Arlett's career was over.

In addition to his 108 wins, he hit 432 homers, a minor league record that held up until Hector Espino topped it in 1977. Arlett walked a lot, didn't strike out much, ran pretty well early in his career, had a .341 lifetime batting average—.350 after he became an outfielder—and was the only player to finish in the top five in home runs and slugging percentage in his only season in the majors. In addition, modern statistical analysis, including range factors, suggests he was nowhere near the defensive liability he was portrayed as being. He was big (6-4, 230) and gave the appearance of being lackadaisical, which apparently irritated some of his managers, but the evidence is strong that Arlett, despite nearly two decades spent in the minors, was a major-league-caliber player.

Ike Boone was another player whose hitting feats were not limited to the minors. Boone was a college teammate (at the University of Alabama) of Joe Sewell and Riggs Stephenson; his lifetime major league batting average was .319, and in his only two full seasons in the majors—1924-1925 with the Boston Red Sox—he hit .333 and .330, but due to alleged defensive deficiencies most of his career was spent in the minors. In 1929 with the Missions of San Francisco, Boone probably had the finest season any player has had in the minors. On the all-time minor league list of single-season accomplishments, his 553 total bases that year are first, his 323 hits are second, his 195 runs scored are tied for third, and his 218 RBIs are fourth. On the all-time Pacific Coast League list, his .407 average is second, and his 55 home runs are tied for fourth.

Boone's greatness wasn't confined to a single season; in four of his first eight years in the minors he hit over .400 (he was on his way to perhaps his greatest season in 1930, batting .448 with 22 homers and 96 RBIs when he was sold to Brooklyn in late June). His .402 average with San Antonio in 1923 is the highest in twentieth-century Texas League history; his .389 with New Orleans in 1921 is the fifth highest in the Southern Association; he also led the International League in batting twice. His .370 lifetime average is the minor league record for players with ten or more seasons. He had an exceptional arm, but limited range in the outfield. Although he hit 77 home runs in a season and a half with the Missions, he was not generally regarded as a power hitter. He was, however, a great pure hitter; in eleven of his fourteen seasons in the minors, he hit over .350, and there is no evidence that he couldn't hit major league pitching.

Smead Jolley was an atrocious outfielder. Stories of his defensive lapses are legion, and the statistical evidence suggests those stories are more than isolated anecdotes. Like Boone, Jolley had a powerful arm but no speed; like Arlett, he was big and awkward; and like both, he could hit—majors or minors. In the equivalent of three full major league seasons with the White Sox and Red Sox, he hit .305 and averaged 15 homers and 105 RBIs. He won six minor league batting championships—leading the Pacific Coast League in hitting three times (winning the Triple Crown with San Francisco in 1928) and the International League once. Twice he had over 300 hits in a season, and twice he drove in more than 180 runs. In the thirteen minor league seasons in which he played over 100 games, he had this run: .370, .372, .346, .397, .404, .387, .360, .372, .373, .350, .309, .373, .345. Perhaps because he spent nearly six years in the low minors, the first four as a pitcher, and had a somewhat nomadic career (he was with thirteen minor league teams), he has not always been ranked in the top echelon of minor league greats, yet he may have been the finest hitter of them all.

Minor league stars generally fit two stereotypes: one-dimensional players who could hit but could do nothing else well enough to stay in the majors—justly or not, Arlett, Boone, and Jolley were consigned to this group. Then there are those who excelled in the minors but couldn't produce in the majors. Perhaps the classic example is Bunny Brief.

Brief, born Antonio Bordetski, may have been the most dominant power hitter in the minor leagues. In major league trials with the Browns, White Sox, and Pirates between 1912 and 1917, he was consistently unimpressive—in a combined 569 at-bats, he hit .223 with 5 homers, 59 RBIs, and nearly 100 strikeouts. In the minors, however, it was a different story. Although he hit 40 or more homers only twice and never had more than 42, he had eight league home run championships. Before going up to the majors, he led the Michigan State League twice; later he led the Pacific Coast League once and the American Association five times. He also led the Association in RBIs five times (four in succession), including a league-record 191 in 1921. He had a six-year stretch (1921–1926) with Kansas City and Milwaukee, where he averaged 90 extra-base hits, 151 RBIs, and a .351 average per season. Brief also drew a lot of walks. Early in his career he had excellent speed, and although he played most of his career at first base, he was the best defensive outfielder of the big minor league sluggers, with good range and an excellent arm—yet for reasons that remain unclear, Brief never played in a major league game after his twenty-fifth birthday.

Nick Cullop was another minor league great who never produced in the majors. He, like many of the great minor

league sluggers, began his career as a pitcher. In trials with the Yankees, Senators, Indians, Dodgers, and Reds between 1926 and 1931 he totaled 490 at-bats, hit 11 homers, drove in 67 runs, hit .249, and struck out 128 times. He was the first farm-system minor league star, playing 1,450 games in the Cardinal chain from 1932 to 1944. In the minors, he drove in 1,857 runs, the all-time career high, ten times exceeding 100 in a season. He hit 420 home runs, third on the all-time list.

Cullop had good speed early in his career and was a good enough outfielder to play center field into the late 1920s, but he slowed up considerably in the 1930s. While it is not clear why Brief never did well in the majors, Cullop struck out a lot even in the minors and didn't walk much—suggesting that he had holes which could be and were pitched to effectively in the majors.

Ox Eckhardt was a great football star at the University of Texas who signed with both Austin of the Texas Association and the Cleveland Indians after graduation. The resulting dispute delayed his real professional debut until he was twenty-six years old. He made up for lost time, hitting .376 with a league-leading 27 triples for Wichita and Amarillo in the Western League in 1928. That fall he played for the New York Giants of the NFL and then went to spring training with the Detroit Tigers; he didn't make it and was sent to Seattle, where he hit .354 and again led the league in triples. In the spring of 1930, he was back with the Tigers, didn't make the team and was then sent to Beaumont, where he led the Texas League with a .379 average. He was back with the Tigers in the spring of 1931, but again he didn't make the club and was sent to the Missions, where he led the PCL with a .369 average. In the spring of 1932 he was with the Boston Braves—he played 8 games at the start of the season as a pinch hitter and was then sent back to the Missions, where over the next four seasons he hit .371, .414, .378, and .399, winning the batting title three times. He went to the Dodgers in 1936, lasted 16 games batting just .182, and was sent to Indianapolis, where he hit .353 and .341 over the next two years. He hit .321 with Toledo and Beaumont in 1938, .361 with Memphis in 1939, and after hitting .293 with Dallas in 1940, he retired with a minor league career batting average of .367 and the highest career average in organized baseball— .365. (Ty Cobb's minor league record drops his overall average to .3630; Ike Boone's major league record drops his organized-baseball average to .3629.) Eckhardt has the highest single-season and career batting average in the PCL, and ten times he hit over .350.

Unlike many of the minor league stars, Eckhardt did not want for opportunities to play in the majors—counting a trial with the Indians in 1925, he had six shots, but they resulted in his playing in just 24 major league games. The reasons for his failure to make it in the majors are not obscure. Despite being an exceptional athlete with good speed early in his career, he was a poor fielder with a weak arm and no power. Although he was 6-1, 190, the lefthanded-hitting Eckhardt sliced or punched almost every hit down the left field line. Reportedly managers tried to get him to pull the ball—an idea that should certainly have advanced his career in Detroit or Brooklyn—but it only served to foul up his swing, which he would rediscover after being returned to the minors.

A few minor league greats don't fit the stereotypes: Jigger Statz was the opposite of most—his strengths were speed and defense. Joe Hauser appeared to be on his way to a successful career in the majors, broke his leg, never regained his past

form, and went to the minors, where he became the only player to have two 60-home-run seasons. Hector Espino spent virtually his entire career in Mexico, and while major league scouts believed he could hit in the majors, he apparently had no desire to leave his homeland.

Of the great minor league stars, Statz spent the most time in the majors—683 games—and the most time with one club: all of his eighteen minor league seasons were with Los Angeles. His 3,473 games in organized baseball were a record until broken by Pete Rose in 1983.

Statz was a great fielder; virtually all of his contemporaries considered him the best or one of the best they had seen. Playing very shallow, he reminded many of Tris Speaker. The statistics offer strong support for his claim to greatness. In four full seasons in the majors, he led the league in chances-per-game once and was second the other three years. Between 1922 and 1932 in the majors and minors he had a stretch of ten seasons in which he played in at least 100 games and never finished lower than second in chances-per-game. He had excellent speed, but during most of his career with the Angels they were a hard-hitting club that did not feature the running game, but that changed in the mid-1930s, and in the three seasons following his thirty-sixth birthday he stole 157 bases. His game was not just limited to speed and defense. A classic leadoff man of his era—a good contact hitter, small and fast—he hit .285 in the majors and .315 in the minors, collecting over 2,300 runs, 4,000 hits, 700 doubles, and 500 stolen bases in his organized-baseball career.

On April 7, 1925, the day of Babe Ruth's "big bellyache," Joe Hauser a twenty-six-year-old first baseman beginning his fourth season with the Athletics, broke his leg in a non-contact play while fielding during a preseason game against the Phillies at Baker Bowl. He had a .304 average for his first three major league seasons and had hit 27 homers with 115 RBIs in 1924. The injury kept him out for the entire 1925 season. In 1926 he tried to come back but hit only .192. After an excellent season with Kansas City, he went back to the majors but didn't do much in stints with the Philadelphia A's and Indians. He went back to the minors and had 4½ remarkable seasons. In 1930 with Baltimore he set a professional record with 63 homers; then he dropped to 31 in 1931 but still led the league. In 1932 he went to Minneapolis, where he led the American Association in homers with 49. In 1933 he broke his own home run record with 69, and he was off to a great start in 1934—33 homers, 88 RBIs in 82 games—when he broke his kneecap, knocking him out for the season. He continued to play until 1942 but never came close to achieving the success he had in the early 1930s.

Hauser did not hit for a high average, and it has been suggested that he took enormous advantage of short right field fences in Baltimore and Minneapolis—no one would argue that point, since 50 of his 69 homers in 1933 came at home—but many greats played in Oriole and Nicollet Parks, and none came close to Hauser's two record-breaking seasons, which remain the two highest home run seasons in the high minors.

Hector Espino holds the minor league career home run record with 484, and all but 3 of those were hit in Mexico. At the end of the 1964 Mexican League season, the twenty-five-year-old first baseman, who had led the league with 46 homers and a .371 batting average, was sold by Monterrey to the St. Louis Cardinals' Jacksonville farm club. He hit .300 with those 3 homers in 100 at-bats and was invited to spring train-

ing by the Cards for 1965, but he never reported and was eventually returned to Monterrey. In the late 1960s, the California Angels coveted Espino, who had led the Mexican League in hitting in 1966–1968, but they were never able to consummate a deal. Espino was a legend in Mexico, but it has never been clear why he never tried the majors—he has given conflicting answers. Possibly he enjoyed being a big fish in a small pond—it wasn't the money, since he never made more than $18,000 a year in Mexico. He was notorious for marching to his own drummer, occasionally leaving clubs for a midseason vacation, and perhaps he was unwilling to sacrifice that independence.

Espino could hit for power and average—he led the Mexican League in batting five times and home runs four times—and scouts said he could have done the same in the majors, but like many players he played too long. His power started a sharp decline after his thirty-third birthday, and he was virtually helpless at the plate during his last two or three seasons. Nevertheless he ranks as perhaps the greatest minor league player who never played in the majors.

Great players do not have to be distributed evenly among all positions or across all eras, but the emphasis being on great hitters, the result is a number of outfielder-first baseman-designated hitter types, most of whom played in the high-scoring 1920s and 1930s.

Ray French was perhaps the best middle infielder in the minors. He spent twenty-eight years in the minors, most of it in the Pacific Coast League. He played 2,736 games at shortstop and was a brilliant fielder. In the fourteen seasons that he played more than 100 games at short, he led the league in chances-per-game seven times. He was not an outstanding hitter, but his fielding kept him around long enough for him to collect 3,254 hits—seventh on the all-time minor league list.

The two best nineteenth-century minor leaguers were first baseman Perry Werden and pitcher Willie Mains. Werden had good speed and power. He had several good years in the majors (twice leading the league in triples), won six minor league home run titles, including two seasons when he went over 40, and his .341 lifetime average was exceptionally high for that era. Mains was the first minor league pitcher to win 300 games, reaching that figure early in 1905. A seven-time twenty-game winner, he was also an excellent hitter in an era when pitchers were frequently expected to take a shift in the outfield. Most of his career was in the New York State League, but in an interesting example of the mobility of players in the game's early years, in 1892–1893 Mains had back-to-back seasons in Portland, Oregon, and Portland, Maine.

A highly productive but not great player who deserves mention is Spencer Harris, a little lefthanded-hitting outfielder who holds the minor league career records for runs, hits, doubles, total bases, and walks. He reached those levels primarily because he kept playing until he was forty-eight years old. He did lead the American Association in homers in 1928 while at Minneapolis, but he was aided enormously by the friendly right field fence at Nicollet Park. (He averaged 17 homers a year in ten seasons with Minneapolis but only 6 a year in his sixteen other minor league seasons.) He was never thought of as the top player on his many minor league clubs—just as a good solid player of the type that formed the backbone of the minors for so many years.

There have been few minor league pitching stars of the magnitude of the great hitters. Perhaps this is because pitching is a one-dimensional skill—no pitchers were kept in the minors because they couldn't hit or field. Many of the outstanding minor league pitchers stayed there because they didn't have great stuff. Bill Thomas, who won 383 games, and Hal Turpin, who won 271 without ever getting shots at the majors, had the same statistical profile—they struck out few, walked even less, and allowed a lot of hits.

Two pitchers that didn't fit that profile, however, were Joe Martina and Dick Barrett. Martina was a power pitcher who spent most of his career with Beaumont and with his hometown New Orleans Pelicans. He held the minor league career strikeout record until ageless George Brunet broke it while toiling in the Mexican League in 1981. Martina was a workhorse, pitching over 250 innings thirteen times and was a seven-time twenty-game winner. He got his first and only big league opportunity at age thirty-five with the world champion Washington Senators in 1924.

Kewpie Dick Barrett didn't really find himself until he joined Seattle of the PCL in 1935, ten years into his professional career. A little lefthander with less than pinpoint control (he holds the minor league record for career bases on balls), he had good stuff and eight 20-win seasons.

Frank Shellenback is most frequently named as the greatest minor league pitcher. The Pacific Coast League career leader in wins with 295, Shellenback won 10 games with the White Sox as a nineteen-year-old rookie spitballer in 1918. After a poor start the following season, he was sent to Minneapolis. In February 1920 the baseball rules committee outlawed the spitball and other trick pitches. Each major league team was allowed to designate two spitball pitchers who would be able to continue using the pitch in the majors. Unfortunately for Shellenbeck, he was on the Vernon roster by this time and at age twenty-one would be consigned forever to pitching in the minors if he couldn't get by without the spitball. Throughout much of his career, articles would be written that usually declared that Shellenback would be a major league star if he was eligible to play there. He did have a great six-year stretch with Hollywood (1928–1933) when he went 142–59. He was a very popular player with the Stars as well as Vernon and a fine hitter with good power, but a review of his record suggests he was never as good as everyone thought he was—he led the PCL in wins twice but never led in another category. He had only five 20-win seasons.

Because of the spitball ban, Shellenback was viewed as a tragic figure, but he wasn't alone. Spitballer Paul Wachtel won 203 games in the Texas League after the ban, including five 20-win seasons. Rube Robinson won 145 games in the Southern Association, including two league-leading 26-win seasons. Wheeler Fuller, who never pitched in the majors, won 166 in the Eastern League after the ban.

Perhaps the greatest minor league pitcher was Tony Freitas, a little lefthander who spent all or part of fifteen seasons with Sacramento. He had great control, could get the strikeout, and had nine 20-win seasons (plus two 19-win seasons). If he hadn't lost three years to the military, he probably would have won 400 games in the minors. Freitas had an impressive major league debut, going 12–5 in less than a full season with the 1932 Philadelphia A's, but that was the last success he would have in the majors.

Four other pitchers worthy of mention are Sam Gibson, George Boehler, Bill Bailey, and George Brunet.

Gibson was an underappreciated pitcher who spent most of his career in the PCL—twelve years with San Francisco. He

didn't make his organized-baseball debut until he was twenty-three years old. After two promising seasons with Detroit, he never had much success in the majors, but he was extremely effective in the minors. He had six 20-win seasons (plus three 19-win seasons) and, pitching in a high-scoring era, he had eight seasons where his ERA was below 3.00.

Boehler was a hard-throwing workhorse who spent most of his career in the Western League. Twice he pitched over 400 innings, six times over 300. Unfortunately he was terribly inconsistent: with Tulsa in 1921–1923 his seasonal win totals were 4–38–7. He was consistently ineffective in a number of major league trials.

Bailey had seven league-leading strikeout seasons in four different leagues (International, Texas, Southern, Western) but only three 20-win seasons. After a promising September debut with the Browns in 1907, he pitched over 200 games in the majors with five teams spread over fifteen years with no success.

Brunet pitched in organized ball for thirty-three years (1953-1985), and astonishingly he was a regular-rotation pitcher for all but the last year. When he was forty-eight years old, he had a 1.94 ERA pitching regularly in the Mexican League. He never won more than 17 games in a season, had only two 200-strikeout seasons (they were twenty-one years apart), but he had a credible major league career and holds the minor league career strikeout record.

The Teams

There have been a number of debates about the greatest minor league teams. The 1937 Newark Bears, the 1934 Los Angeles Angels, the 1920-1925 Ft. Worth Panthers, and the 1919-1925 Baltimore Orioles usually draw the most support. All were dominant teams with good players.

The Bears included Charlie Keller, Joe Gordon, George McQuinn, Atley Donald, and five other players who would go to the majors the following year. They won the International League pennant by 25½ games with a 109–41 record. The Angels included Frank Demaree, Jigger Statz, Gene Lillard, and Fay Thomas, and they compiled an astounding 137–50 record. The Panthers (or Cats) won six straight pennants and five Dixie Series. They were led by the home run hitting of Big Boy Kraft and a fine pitching staff that included spit-baller Paul Wachtel and Joe Pate.

It is doubtful that any of the three could have competed successfully in the majors. It is occasionally claimed that the 1937 Newark Bears were the Yankee B team and could have

finished second in the American League, or at least in the first division. But that ignores the talent that was in the majors. The Red Sox finished fifth in 1937 with a club that included Jimmie Foxx, Joe Cronin, Lefty Grove, Pinky Higgins, Doc Cramer, Ben Chapman, Jack Wilson, and Bobo Newsom, all of whom, it is safe to say, would have started for the Bears. The same is true of the Angels, whose pitching staff chose 1934 to have career years, and of the Cats, who played well as a team but had few players that were even considered minor league standouts.

The Orioles were a different story. Thanks to the draft exemption, Jack Dunn was able to assemble a powerhouse comprised of players ready and capable of playing in the majors. The 1922 team was probably the best minor league club ever assembled. It had Jack Bentley, Max Bishop, Fritz Maisel, and Joe Boley in the infield, and Otis Lawry, Merwyn Jacobson, and Jimmy Walsh in the outfield. The catcher was Lena Styles, and the pitchers were Lefty Grove, John Ogden, Tommy Thomas, Rube Parnham, and Harry Frank with Bentley occasionally seeing action in that capacity.

Grove, Ogden, and Thomas combined for 60 wins and six years later would win a combined 56 games in the majors. Parnham, a free spirit who pitched when he wanted, was around long enough to win 16 (the following year he won 33). Frank won 22, but his career would soon be cut short by illness. Bentley hit .350 and won 13 games; he went to the Giants in 1923 as a pitcher but hit .427. Bishop and Boley, who hit .261 and .343 respectively, went on to become the double-play combo with the 1929-1930 world champion Philadelphia A's. Styles was just twenty-two years old and hit .315, but that was his peak. Maisel (.306), Walsh (.327), Jacobson (.304), and Lawry (.333) had all played briefly and/or ineffectively in the majors but would all go on to have great careers in the International League. A twenty-year-old rookie utility player on the team was Dick Porter, who hit .279 and would have seven excellent seasons with the Orioles before going on to have several good years with the Indians.

As good as the Orioles were and as good as some of their players became, it is doubtful that even they could have finished in the first division of the American or National Leagues in 1922. Yet the strongest evidence of the attraction of minor league baseball and the hold it has long held on fans who were exposed to it is that those great Oriole, Bear, and Angel teams are far better known and more fondly remembered than hundreds of more talented second-division and higher major league clubs.

Minor Leagues

Year	Leagues Started	Didn't Finish	Year	Leagues Started	Didn't Finish	Year	Leagues Started	Didn't Finish	Year	Leagues Started	Didn't Finish	Year	Leagues Started	Didn't Finish	Year	Leagues Started	Didn't Finish
1883	2		1901	14	3	1919	15	1	1937	37		1954	36	3	1971	20	
1884	7	2	1902	17	2	1920	22	1	1938	37		1955	33		1972	19	
1885	7	2	1903	20		1921	26		1939	41		1956	28		1973	18	
1886	10	1	1904	24	2	1922	30	2	1940	44	1	1957	28		1974	18	
1887	15	6	1905	31	5	1923	31	3	1941	41		1958	24		1975	18	
1888	17	7	1906	33	3	1924	29	3	1942	31	5	1959	21		1976	20	
1889	15	5	1907	37	4	1925	25	3	1943	10	1	1960	22		1977	19	
1890	17	7	1908	40	11	1926	30	4	1944	10		1961	22		1978	18	
1891	14	3	1909	35	4	1927	24		1945	11		1962	20		1979	18	1
1892	12	3	1910	52	6	1928	31	3	1946	43	1	1963	18		1980	17	
1893	7	4	1911	51	10	1929	26	2	1947	52		1964	20		1981	17	
1894	9	3	1912	47	11	1930	23	2	1948	58		1965	19		1982	17	
1895	18	8	1913	43	4	1931	19	3	1949	59		1966	19		1983	17	
1896	14	7	1914	44	6	1932	19	4	1950	58	1	1967	19		1984	17	
1897	17	7	1915	34	8	1933	14		1951	50	1	1968	20		1985	18	
1898	19	10	1916	27	6	1934	20	1	1952	43		1969	21		1986	17	
1899	14	4	1917	21	9	1935	21		1953	38		1970	21		1987	17	
1900	14	6	1918	10	9	1936	26										

Annual Overall Minor League Pitching Percentage Leader (20 or more decisions)

Year	Player	Team (League)	W–L	Pct.	Overall W–L	Overall Pct.
1900	Willie Mains	Rome (N.Y. St.)	27–5	.844		
1901	Henry Allemang	Little Rock (So. Assn.)	20–4	.833		
1902	Louis Bruce	Toronto (Eastern)	18–2	.900		
1903	Ernest Nichols	Spokane (Pac. Nat.)	20–4	.833		
1904	Ed Craig	Springfield (Mo. Valley)	19–4	.826		
1905	Fred Steele	Oskaloosa (Iowa St.)	18–3	.857		
1906	Frank Dick	Marshalltown (Iowa St.)	18–3	.857		
1907	Harley Young	Wichita (West. Assn.)	29–4	.879		
1908	Harry Gaspar	Waterloo (Cent. Assn.)	32–4	.889		
1909	Ray Fisher	Hartford (Conn.)	24–5	.828		
1910	Cyrus Dahlgren	Superior (Minn.-Wis.)	22–3	.880		
1911	Howard Northrop	Reading (Inter.-St.)	27–4	.871		
1912	Larue Kirby	Traverse City (Mich. St.)	18–3	.857		
1913	Ralph Bell	Winona (Northern)	28–6	.824		
1914	Joe Chabek	Harrisburg (Tri-St.)	28–3	.903		
1915	Booth Hopper	Minneapolis (A.A.)	18–3	.857		
1916	Howard Ehmke	Syracuse (N.Y. St.)	31–7	.816		
1917	John Verbout	Wilkes-Barre (N.Y. St.)	26–7	.788		
1918	John Beckvermit	Binghamton (Int.)	17–4	.810		
1919	C. A. (Chief) Bender	Richmond (Va.)	29–2	.935		
1920	George Carmen	London (Mich.,-Ont.)	26–2	.926		
1921	Earl Keiser	Mitchell (S.D. St.)	20–2			
		Oakland (PCL)	3–0		23–2	.920
1922	Byrd Hodges	Joplin (West. Assn.)	26–3	.897		
1923	Emil Levsen	Cedar Rapids (Miss. Val.)	19–4	.826		
1924	Carl Dunagan	Dyersburg (Kitty)	19–2	.905		
1925	Lloyd Brown	Ardmore-Western Association	17–1	.944*		
1926	Frank Tubbs	Port Huron (Mich.-Ont.)	8–1			
		Port Huron (Mich. St.)	8–0			
		Oklahoma City (Western)	9–2		25–3	.893
1927	Ben Cantwell	Jacksonville (So'east.)	25–5	.833		
1928	Paul Fittery	Carrollton (Ga.-Ala.)	21–2	.913		
1929	Andrew Bednar	McCook (Neb. St.)	21–4	.840		
1930	Jim Cameron	McCook (Neb. St.)	19–2	.905		
1931	Lyle (Bud) Tinning	Minneapolis (A.A.)	1–2			
		Des Moines (West. Assn.)	24–2		25–4	.862
1932	Marvin Duke	Erie (Central)	23–4	.852		
1933	Al Piechota	Davenport (Miss. Val.)	19–4	.826		
1934	Fay Thomas	Los Angeles (PCL)	28–4	.875		
1935	Lloyd Sterling	Winnipeg (Northern)	24–2	.923		
1936	Bill Yocke	Akron (Mid. Atl.)	1–2			
		Norfolk (Piedmont)	18–1		19–3	.864
1937	Joe Kohlman	Salisbury (E. Shore)	25–1	.962		
1938	Paige Dennis	Thomasville (N.C. St.)	28–2	.933		
1939	Charles Wensloff	Joplin (West. Assn.)	26–4	.867		
1940	Arthur Cyrolewski	Johnson City (App.)	20–3	.870		
	Mervin Hensley	La Crosse (Wis. St.)	20–3	.870		
1941	Frank Marino	Macon (Sally)	19–1	.950		
1942	Paul Minner	Elizabethton (App.)	18–2			
		Knoxville (So. Assn.)	1–0		19–2	.905
1943	Irvin Stein	Portsmouth (Piedmont)	24–6	.800		
1944	Pete Naktenis	Hartford (Eastern)	18–3	.857		
1945	Lewis Carpenter	Atlanta (So. Assn.)	22–2	.917		
1946	Bill Kennedy	Rocky Mount (C. Plain)	28–3	.903		
1947	Chris VanCuyk	Cambridge (E. Shore)	25–2	.926		
1948	Albert Tefft	Blackstone (Va.)	20–1	.952		
1949	Lynn Southworth	Thomasville (N.C. St.)	21–1	.955		
1950	Mike Hudak	Big Stone Gap (Mt. St.)	19–2	.905		
1951	Anderson Bush	Hagerstown (Int. St.)	22–3	.880		
1952	Russell Harris	Ozark (Ala-Fla.)	27–3	.900		
1953	Steve Kraly	Binghamton (Eastern)	19–2	.905		
1954	Bob Thorpe	Stockton (Calif.)	28–4	875		
1955	Jim Grant	Keokuk (I-I-I)	19–3	.864		
1956	Francisco Ramirez	Mexico City Reds (Mex.)	20–3	.870		
1957	Bob Riesner	Alexandria (Evang.)	20–0			
		New Orleans (So. Assn.)	0–2		20–2	.909
1958	Jerry Walker	Knoxville (Sally)	18–4	.818		
	Art Henriksen	St. Petersburg (Fla. St.)	17–3			
		New Orleans (So. Assn.)	0–1		18–4	.818
1959	Les Bass	Boise (Pioneer)	21–3	.875		
			0–1			
1960	Tom Haake	Grand Forkes (Northern)	0–1			
		Dubuque (Midwest)	19–3		19–4	.826
1961	David Seeman	Selma (Ala.-Fla.)	17–3			
		Burlington (Carolina)	7–0		24–3	.889
1962	Bob Schmidt	Modesto (Calif.)	0–0			
		Jamestown (NYP)	17–3		17–3	.850
1963	Bob Lee	Batavia (NYP)	20–2			
		Asheville (Sally)	1–1		21–3	.875
1964	Ed Watt	Aberdeen (Northern)	14–1			
		Elmira (Eastern)	3–1		17–2	.895**
1965	Billy MacLeod	Pittsfield (Eastern)	18–0	1000†		
1966	Bob Snow	Winston-Salem (Carolina)	20–2	.909		
1967	John Parker	Spartanburg (W. Car.)	17–3	.850		
1968	Pablo Montes De Oca	Campeche (Mex. S.E.)	21–4	.840		
1969	Don Eddy	Appleton (Northern)	18–3	.857		
1970	Jim Flynn	Albuquerque (Texas)	19–4	.826		
1971	Rich Gossage	Appleton (Midwest)	18–2	.900		
1972	Andres Ayon	Saltillo (Mexican)	22–3	.880		
1973	Silvano Quezada	Tampico (Mexican)	22–2	.917		
1974	Bob Knepper	Fresno (Calif.)	20–5	.800		
1975	Jerry Garvin	Reno (Calif.)	17–5	.773		
1976	Enrique Romo	Mexico City Reds (Mexican)	20–4	.833		
1977	Mike Chris	Lakeland (Fla. St.)	18–5	.783		
1978	Tomas Armas	Saltillo (Mexican)	22–4	.846		
1979	Miguel Solis	Saltillo (Mexican)	25–5	.833		
1980	Gene Nelson	Ft. Lauderdale (Fla. St.)	20–3	.870		
1981	Ted Power	Albuquerque (PCL)	18–3	.857		
1982	Mike Warren	Stockton-Modesto (Calif.)	19–4	.826		
1983	Alfonso Pulido	Mexico City Reds (Mexican)	17–3	.850		
1984	Mike Bielecki	Hawaii (PCL)	19–3	.864		
1985	Eleazar Beltran	Tampico (Mexican)	18–3	.857		
1986	George Ferran	Shreveport (Texas)	16–1	.941‡		
1987	Bob Faron	Springfield (Midwest)	19–2	.905		
1988	Jimmy Rodgers	Myrtle Beach (So. Atl.)	18–4	.818		

*Adding two losses to Brown's record giving him 20 decisions yields a .850 percent, better than John Schmutte, Johnstown Middie Atlantic, 19– 4, .822.

**Adding 1 loss to Watt's record, giving him 20 decisions, yields an .850 percentage, better than Dave Leonhard, Aberdeen (Northern), 16–4 .800

†Adding 2 losses to MacLeod's record, giving him 20 decisions, yields a .900 percentage, better than Dave Leonhard, Elmira (Eastern), 20–5 .800

‡Adding 3 losses to Ferran's record, giving him 20 decisions, yields an .800 percentage, better than Kevin Armstrong, Columbia (Sally), 17–5 .773

Annual Overall Minor League Batting Leader (400 or more at-bats)

Year	Player	Team (League)	G	AB	R	H	2B	3B	HR	RBI	SB	AVG.
1900	Kitty Bransfield	Worcester (Eastern)	122	501	115*	186*	—	—	—	—	40	.371*
1901	Frank Huelsman	Shreveport (So. Assn.)	121*	487	98	191*	31	10	9	—	15	.392*
1902	Emil Frisk	Denver (Western)	123	450	89	168	22	22	14*	—	20	.373*
1903	Frank Huelsman	Spokane (Pac. Int.)	98	418	89	160	35	11	6	—	14	.392*
1904	Billy Hamilton	Haverhill (New Eng.)	113	408	113*	168*	32	8	0	—	74*	.412*
1905	Charlie Hemphill	St. Paul (A. A.)	145	560	122	204*	38	12	5	—	40	.364*
1906	Mike Welday	Des Moines (Western)	129	549	93	197	—	—	—	—	31	.359
1907	Ed Householder	Aberdeen (Northwest)	127	499	64	173	30*	19	9	—	19	.347*
1908	Ward Miller	Wausau (Wis.-Ill.)	124	408	91*	156*	—	—	—	—	—	.382*
1909	Harry Welch	Omaha (Western)	151	527	81	196*	41	15	7	—	51	.372*
1910	Dave Callahan	Eau Claire (Minn.-Wis.)	126	460	92*	168*	25	17*	2	—	52	.365*
1911	Frank Huelsman	Great Falls (U.A.)	135	516	117	212	48	15	17*	125*	25	.411*
1912	Charlie Johnson	Trenton (Tri-State)	109	400	86	161	—	—	—	—	22	.403*
1913	Frank Huelsman	Salt Lake City (U.A.)	122	473	123*	200*	36*	20*	22*	126*	16	.423*
1914	Joe Harris	Bay City (So. Michigan)	139	510	135	197*	39	22*	10	—	42	.386*
1915	Big Bill Kay	Binghamton (N.Y. St.)	125	447	98*	169*	—	—	—	—	35	.378*
1916	Hank Butcher	Denver (Western)	145	541	116	204	31	20*	15	—	32	.377*
1917	Nap Lajoie	Toronto (Int.)	151	581	83	221*	39*	4	5	—	4	.380*
1918	Polly McLarry	Shreveport (Texas)	29	84	12	24	3	1	1	—	6	.286
		Binghamton (Int.)	103	335	51	129	26	7	4	—	15	.385*
											overall	.365
1919	Joe Wilhoit	Seattle (PCL)	17	67	8	11	1	0	0	—	3	.164
		Wichita (Western)	128	526	126*	222*	41	10	7	—	13	.422*
											overall	.393
1920	Merwyn Jacobson	Baltimore (Int.)	154*	581	161*	235*	35	16*	7	—	18	.404*
1921	Jack Lelivelt	Omaha (Western)	166	659	149	274*	70*	9	14	—	24	.416*
1922	Jack Schaefer	London (Mich.-Ont.)	100	407	79	167	27	21	9	—	9	.410*
1923	Moses Solomon	Hutchinson (So'west.)	134	527	143*	222*	40*	15	49*	—	12	.421*
1924	T. P. Osborne	Mt. Pleasant (E. Tex.)	101	396	93	171*	48	3	23	—	46*	.432*[1]
1925	Paul Waner	San Francisco (PCL)	174	599	167	280	75*	7	11	130	8	.401*
1926	Bill Diester	Salina (So'west.)	106	428	110*	190*	33*	4	27	—	10	.444*
		Tulsa (Western)	11	44	5	15	4	0	0	—	0	.341
											overall	.434
1927	Elton Langford	Des Moines (Western)	149	611	132	250	47	28*	8	—	31	.409*
1928	Danny Boone	High Point (Piedmont)	128	468	123	196*	40	11	38*	131*	11	.419*
1929	Ed Kallina	Midland (W. Tex.)	94	367	126	159	28	7	44*	—	16	.433*
		Sherman (Lone Star)	17	64	22	22	—	—	6	—	1	.344
											overall	.420
1930	Tony Antista	Bisbee (Arizona St.)	109*	444	127*	191*	36	16*	17	100	18	.430*
1931	Babe Phelps	Youngstown (Mid-Atl.)	115	436	71	178	29	9	15	88	9	.408*
1932	George Puccinelli	Baltimore (Int.)	133	478	102	187	34	8	28	115	2	.391*
1933	Ox Eckhardt	Mission (PCL)	189*	760	145	315*	56	16	12	143	15	.414*
1934	Frank Demaree	Los Angeles (PCL)	186	702	190*	269*	51*	4	45*	173*	41	.383*
1935	Ox Eckhardt	Mission (PCL)	172	710	149	283*	40	11	2	114	8	.399*
1936	Cal Lahman	Jamestown (Northern)	127	466	154*	182*	30	9	48*	162*	20	.391*
1937	Earl (Red) Martin	Beckley (Mt. St.)	91	360	80	144	39*	14*	8	96*	7	.400*
		Scranton (NYP)	11	41	7	10	1	0	0	4	1	.244
											overall	.384
1938	Murray Franklin	Beckley (Mt. St.)	94	385	91	169	31	13*	26*	110	13	.439*[2]
1939	Joe Schmidt	Duluth (Northern)	120	440	114*	194*	29	9	31*	133*	17	.441*
1940	Ed Schweda	Lubbock (W. Tex.-N.M.)	114	469	142	198	39	15	11	118	7	.422*
1941	Lew Flick	Elizabethton (App.)	117	502*	127*	210*	37*	13	5	116*	20	.418*
1942	Don Manno	Welch (Mt. St.)	117	457	136*	174*	32	14*	34*	122*	23	.381*
1943	George Kell	Lancaster (Inter-St.)	138	555	120*	220*	33	23*	5	79	14	.396*
1944	Roland Gladu	Hartford (Eastern)	119	417	92	155	28	14	7	102	8	.372
1945	Arden (Cotton) McCaskey	Bristol (App.)	106	437	72	164*	26*	14*	2	96	5	.375*
1946	Walt Forwood	Carbondale (N. Atl.)	111	419	98	170*	43*	7	3	101	22	.406*
1947	Jim Prince	Midland (Longhorn)	108	415	111	178	31	6	34	141	4	.429*
		Lubbock (W. Tex.-N.M.)	12	37	7	10	3	0	1	12	0	.270
											overall	.416
1948	Hershel Martin	Albuquerque (W. Tex.-N.M.)	132	447	133	190	61*	6	18	128	5	.425*
1949	Bob Montag	Pawtucket (New Eng.)	125	454	139*	192*	36	18*	21*	91	43*	.423*
1950	Oscar Sierra	Hornell (Pony)	93	358	99	151	28	2	21	114	12	.422*
		Newport News (Piedmont)	15	45	5	13	1	0	0	5	0	.289
											overall	.407
1951	D. C. (Pud) Miller	Hickory (N.C. St.)	119	426	115	181	32	1	40*	136*	2	.425*
1952	Don Stafford	Salisbury (N.C. St.)	105	392	99	160	31	3	18	90	1	.408*[3]
1953	Russ Snyder	McAlester (Sooner St.)	138	556	137	240*	32	16	2	84	74*	.432*
1954	Neal Cobb	Crestview (Ala.-Fla.)	115	435	108	188	27	8	5	124	3	.432*
1955	Tom Jordan	Artesia (Longhorn)	136	543	116	221*	69*	2	28	159*	4	.407*
1956	Len Tucker	Pampa (So'west)	140	565	181*	228	40	13	51*	181*	47*	.404*
1957	Fran Bonair	Reno (Calif.)	110	443	102	193	33	15	11	138*	4	.436*
		Pueblo (Western)	11	37	5	9	1	0	0	7	3	.243
											overall	.421
1958	Neb Wilson	Ft. Walton Beach-Pensacola (Ala.-Fla.)	119	409	102*	162	38*	3	24*	106*	3	.396*
1959	Tom Hamilton	St. Petersburg (Fla. St.)	125	401	109	155	20	3	20*	96	3	.387*
1960	Al Pinkston	Mexico City Reds (Mexican)	138	567	110	225*	41	11	26	144*	4	.397*
1961	Al Pinkston	Vera Cruz (Mexican)	109	406	79	152	26*	4	13	86	4	.374*
1962	Ramiro Caballero	Guanajuato (Mex. Center)	113	423	123	175*	25	0	59*	170	3	.414*
1963	Vinicio Garcia	Monterrey (Mexican)	122	475	107*	175	36*	5	21	88	3	.368*
1964	Ramiro Caballero	Leon (Mex. Center)	121	460	135*	175*	29	1	35*	145*	3	.380*
1965	Alfonso Peciado	Guanajuato (Mex. Center)	130	529	103	224*	48*	14*	11	147	11	.423*
1966	Heriberto Vargas	Vera Cruz (Mexican)	7	14	0	3	0	0	0	0	0	.214
		Guanajuato (Mex. Center)	127	481	168*	214	33	1	55*	174*	3	.445*
											overall	.438
1967	Hilario Pena	Campeche (Mex. S.E.)	102	404	60	159	61	3	1	49	9	.394*
1968	Jim Hicks	Tulsa (PCL)	117	407	100*	149	32	7	23	85	14	.366*
1969	Bernie Carbo	Indianapolis (A.A.)	111	404	83	145	37	2	21	76	7	.359*

Year	Player	Team (League)	G	AB	R	H	2B	3B	HR	RBI	SB	AVG.
1970	Miguel Suarez	Tampico (Mex. Center)	126	460	105	181*	37*	4	14	101	15	.393*
1971	Téolindo Acosta	Puebla (Mexican)	133	441	75	173	22	11	7	71	17	.392*
1972	Don Anderson	Jalisco (Mexican)	130	445	76	161	31	2	8	68	0	.362*
1973	Hector Espino	Tampico (Mexican)	116	422	82	159	20	2	22	107*	3	.377*
1974	Téolindo Acosta	Puebla (Mexican)	122	464	93*	170*	17	6	2	43	85*	.366*
1975	Gene Richards	Reno (Calif.)	134	501*	148*	191*	29	10	12	58	8	.381*
1976	Pat Putnam	Asheville (W. Car.)	138	538	100	194*	33*	3	24*	142*	37	.361*
1977	Rudy Law	Lodi (California)	122	451	124	174	22	5	9	88	37	.386*
1978	Champ Summers	Indianapolis (A.A.)	132	462	98	170*	25	5	34*	124*	11	.368
1979	Jimmie Collins	Chihuahua (Mexican)	124	470	95	206*	35	10	6	60	33	.438*
1980	Jimmie Collins	Chihuahua (Mex. #1)	91	346	62	131	19	13	4	52	19	.379
		Saltillo (Mex. #2)	39	137	25	52*	8	3*	2	31*	5	.380
											overall	.379
1981	Kent Hrbek	Visalia (Calif.)	121	462	119	175	25	5	27	111	12	.379*
1982	Randy Ready	El Paso (Texas)	132	475	122*	178*	33	5	20	99	13	.375*
1983	Chris Smith	Phoenix (PCL)	123	449	88	170	31	5	21	102	4	.379
1984	Jimmie Collins	Mexico City Reds-Cordoba (Mexican)	109	403	81	166	35	4	6	59	12	.412*
1985	Oswaldo Olivares	Aguas.-Campeche (Mexican)	110	441	85	175*	22	14*	5	49	20	.397*
1986	Willie Aikens	Puebla (Mexican)	129	445	134	202*	38	3	46	154*	0	.454*
1987	Orlando Sanchez	Puebla (Mexican)	123	439	95	182	34	1	25	115	6	.415*
1988	Nelson Barrera	Mexico City Reds (Mexican)	—	460	90	171	26	0	31	124*	7	.372

*Led league in category

¹If charged with 400 at-bats, Osborne's average would be .428, higher than any player with 400 or more at-bats.
(George Rhinehardt, Greenville (Sally) G: 120, AB: 495, R: 110*, H: 200*, 2B: 45*, 3B: 18, HR: 8, RBI: 92, SB: 32*, AVG: .404*)

²If charged with 400 at-bats, Franklin's average would be .423, higher than any player with 400 or more at-bats.
(Butch Moran, Rogers (Ark.-Mo.) G: 105, AB: 406, R: 107, H: 159, 2B: 43*, 3B: 12, HR: 22*, RBI: 114, SB: 8, AVG: .392*)

³If charged with 400 at-bats, Stafford's average would be .400, higher than any player with 400 or more at-bats.
(Clint McCord, Clinton (Miss. Ohio Val.) G:119, AB: 482, R: 123, H: 189*, 2B: 40, 3B: 15, HR: 15, RBI: 109, SB: 20, AVG: .392*)

Minor League Career Records

Batters	Years	G	AB	R	H	2B	3B	HR	RBI	SB	AVG
Buzz Arlett	1918–37	2390	8001	1610	2726	598	107	432	1786	200	.341
Ike Boone	1920–37	1857	6807	1362	2521	477	128	215	1334	120	.370
Bunny Brief	1910–28	2426	8945	1776	2963	594	152	340	1776	247	.331
Nick Cullop	1920–44	2484	8571	1607	2670	523	147	420	1857	154	.312
Ox Eckhardt	1925–40	1926	7563	1275	2773	455	146	66	1037	140	.367
Hector Espino	1960–84	2500	8605	1597	2898	403	49	484	1678	54	.337
Ray French	1914–41	3278	12174	1769	3254	590	129	46	1029	363	.267
Spencer Harris	1921–48	3258	11377	2287	3617	743	150	258	1769	241	.318
Joe Hauser	1918–42	1854	6426	1430	1923	340	116	399	1353	109	.299
Smead Jolley	1922–41	2231	8298	1455	3037	612	75	334	1593	61	.366
Jigger Statz	1920–42	2790	10657	1996	3356	595	137	66	1044	466	.315
Perry Werden	1884–1908	1539	6221	1214	2119	390	87	168	—	349	.341

Pitchers	Years	G	IP	W	L	H	R	ER	BB	SO	ERA
Bill Bailey	1906–25	578	3730	242	219	3452	1572	612	1565	2375	2.87
Dick Barrett	1925–53	790	4961	325	257	4572	2170	1747	2096	2512	3.34
George Boehler	1911–30	562	3711	248	202	3421	1745	874	1464	2319	3.74
George Brunet	1953–85	668	4041	244	242	3761	1832	1466	1754	3175	3.27
Tony Freitas	1928–53	736	4905	342	238	5090	2073	1694	932	2324	3.11
Sam Gibson	1923–49	661	4469	307	200	4460	1860	1413	1073	2195	3.08
Willie Mains	1887–1906	545	4014	318	179	4399	2417	—	1280	1669	
Joe Martina	1910–31	833	5417	349	277	4950	2307	1355	1868	2770	3.22
Frank Shellenback	1917–38	638	4514	315	192	4922	2110	1775	1021	1742	3.55
Bill Thomas	1926–52	1016	5995	383	347	6721	3098	2211	1230	2204	3.71
Hal Turpin	1927–46	635	4084	271	203	4512	1917	1367	807	1254	3.28

CHAPTER 25

Japanese Baseball

Yoichi Nagata and John B. Holway

Just when baseball arrived in Japan, and who introduced it, is not clear. Horace Wilson, a professor in Tokyo in the 1870s, is one of those credited with being the Abner Doubleday of Japan, teaching baseball to students who ran bases and flagged grounders in *geta,* or wooden clogs. They named it *yakyu* (yok-yoo')—field ball—or *beisu boru.* In 1909, when the University of Wisconsin team arrived for four games against Keio University, the Japanese lost three tough one-run games, then swamped the visitors 8–0 in the fourth game.

In 1913 the Chicago White Sox and New York Giants stopped in Japan on a round-the-world tour, playing three games with Japanese college teams. In 1922 a big league All-Star team, including Casey Stengel, also sailed into Tokyo harbor. And in 1928 Ty Cobb himself went over to teach the Japanese his batting secrets.

By 1930 *yakyu* began to rival *sumo* as the Japanese national pastime. The two games still tug in opposite directions at the nation's sports psyche, the one traditional and native, the other newer and outward-looking, but baseball has far outdistanced *sumo* as the nation's most popular sport.

The game thrived in schools and colleges. In fact, scholastic baseball still has a grip on the fans, like college football in America, high school basketball in Indiana, or the Final Four of the NCAA basketball tourney. Japan's annual national high school tournaments in Osaka every March and August fill huge Koshien Stadium for two weeks and command dawn-to-dusk TV coverage.

Japan's first professional team, the Nihon Undo Kyokai (Japan Athletic Association), was formed in 1920. The following year the Hankyu Railway formed a second pro club, the Takará-zuka Kyokai. A third club, somewhat like the U.S. Harlem Globetrotters, barnstormed. All three expired, victims of a lack of competition as well as of the great earthquake of 1923.

In the fall of 1931, Lou Gehrig, Lefty Grove, Frankie Frisch, and Lefty O'Doul arrived for a tour. Several black teams visited Japan in the 1920s and in 1932, with stars such as Bullet Joe Rogan and Biz Mackey, who later became Roy Campanella's mentor.

Japanese baseball reached a watershed in 1934 with the arrival of Babe Ruth, Gehrig, Jimmy Foxx, Al Simmons, Charlie Gehringer, and Lefty Gomez. Matsutaro Shoriki, owner of the Yomiuri newspapers, sponsored the tour and would become the great genius–father figure of professional baseball there, the Alexander Cartwright-Al Spalding-Harry Wright of Japan. Ruth and the others, soon to receive plaques in Cooperstown, played eighteen games and easily won seventeen of them. Ruth hit thirteen home runs and clowned in right field, holding an umbrella, while Gehrig played first base in galoshes. But they weren't clowning when a high

school boy, Eiji Sawamura, almost shut them out, whiffing Gehringer, Ruth, Gehrig, and Foxx in succession before losing 1–0. Sawamura became, and still is, a national hero, especially on his death, at twenty-six, in World War Two.

Shoriki signed a professional, Osamu Mihara (later famous as the "Magic Manager"), to his All-Japan team to oppose Ruth, although the Japanese looked down on professional sports as "unpure." The next year he formed an all-pro team, Dai-Nippon (Greater Japan), with Sawamura, Mihara, the white Russian Vic Starffin, and others. They toured the United States that year and would become the present-day Yomiuri (later Tokyo) Giants (*Kyojin*), a name hung on them by O'Doul. Shoriki urged other businesses to form pro teams and by 1936 formed the country's first professional league.

World War Two interrupted baseball. American words, such as *out* and *safe,* became *hi-ké* (withdraw) and *yoshi* (good), etc., and Japanese soldiers shouted, "To hell with Beibu Rusu." The league succumbed completely in 1945, and the Giants' proud stadium became an ammo dump.

After the war General MacArthur ordered the stadium cleared and encouraged the rebirth of the game. O'Doul, a veteran of the 1931 and 1934 tours, brought his San Francisco Seals of the PCL in 1949 and won all four games. He returned with Joe DiMaggio and other big leaguers in 1951.

The big league tours continued every other year or so, and, *mirabile dictu*, in 1953 the Americans even lost two games. In 1956 the champion Dodgers lost four games, and in 1966 they lost eight and won nine. Of course the players considered the tours as vacations for shopping and partying, but they were learning that unless they played their best, they could no longer waltz to easy victories.

In 1950 Shoriki's league split into two leagues, which now have six teams apiece. The Central League, dominated by the Giants, is by far the more popular, with the benefit of the nationwide publicity the Yomiuri empire gives its club. The Giants have drawn three million fans in a 65-game home schedule. That's over 46,000 per game, or 3.7 million for a U.S. schedule of 81 games. Even when they finished last in 1975, they drew 2.8 million. The Pacific League, struggling to break even, in 1973 instituted a split season (since abandoned) and the DH (still in effect). It now averages about 21,000 attendance per game, compared to 31,000 for the Central League. Average pay is $55,000, compared to over $200,000 in the U.S. majors. Three-time Triple Crown winner Hiromitsu Ochiai is the highest paid, at $600,000, although a few Americans in Japan—Bill Madlock, Bill Gullickson, etc.— make twice that.

Of course every Japanese kid wants to grow up to play for the Giants, leaving the other eleven clubs talent-poor. A draft system, begun in 1966, has helped give the other teams a better chance to compete. Since 1974 the Pacific League has

won eight of the fourteen Japan Series.

Every night a Japanese *sarariman* (salaried man, or wage earner) who is *kichigai* (crazy) about *yakyu* can switch on nationwide TV to watch the Giants. Where America has one weekly sports paper, *The Sporting News*, Japan has seven sports *dailies*, which concentrate mostly on baseball.

Most teams are owned by large companies and operated as advertising write-offs. For years Hiroshima was the only club owned by a city—its fans are considered as rabid as the old Brooklynites used to be—but it is now owned by the Mazda company. Ten of the twelve clubs play in the two metropolitan centers, Tokyo-Yokohama and Osaka-Kobe-Kyoto.

In the early 1950s, it was a shock for Tokyo fans when the American big leaguers arrived, standing a head taller than the Japanese. Today it is a shock for the same fan to visit a U.S. spring training camp and see visiting Japanese dressing at lockers next to the Americans: There isn't that much difference anymore. Sadaharu Oh and Hank Aaron could almost trade uniforms.

The Japanese began talking of a real World Series. Their victory over America in the 1984 Los Angeles Olympics stirred the fantasy even more.

In general, American observers say, Japanese outfielders and catchers don't have the arms of Americans and Latins. But their infielders are among the best in the world, many of their pitchers are outstanding, and their batters are beginning to hit with big league power.

Americans also say the draconian training methods leave the players burned out in the second half of the season. And especially the Japanese attitude that "the future is now" has led to sacrificing many a great young pitcher to brutal overwork until his arm is ruined forever. In 1961 Hiroshi Gondo won 35 games in 429 innings. The next year he won 30 in 362. The next year he was down to 10, then 6, then 1; then he was out. This, however, is changing, as the Japanese are beginning to adopt the American pitching rotation.

About half the teams play on artificial turf, and in 1988 Japan got its first dome, the Tokyo Dome, built on the site of historic Korakuen (Ko-ra′-kwen) Stadium, similar to Minnesota's Metrodome.

Meanwhile Japanese baseball has produced some outstanding heroes and memorable moments.

A Gallery of Stars

Tetsuharu Kawakami "The God of Batting," he has also been called "Japan's Lou Gehrig." Wearing glasses and swinging his famous red bat, Kawakami hit cleanup on the great Tokyo Giant teams of 1938–1958 and set a record with .377 in 1951. His lifetime .313 is fourth highest in Japanese annals. Against the Dodgers in 1956, he batted .364 with two home runs. His concentration was so intense, he said he could visually "stop" a pitch in midflight.

But Kawakami's hitting paled compared to his managing—11 pennants in fourteen years. He was the man at the helm as the Giants won nine straight Japan Series, a feat accomplished by no other professional team in any sport. The Negro League Homestead Grays won nine straight pennants 1937–1945, but they lost several Black World Series and one playoff.

The Grays had Josh Gibson and Buck Leonard. Kawakami had Sadaharu Oh and Shigeo Nagashima. And he did it without using a single foreign player, desiring to prove the superiority of a "pure" Japanese team with fighting spirit.

Hiroshi Oshita (O′-shta) A three-time batting champ and three-time home run leader, Oshita was the postwar hero who dueled with his blue bat against Kawakami's red bat and helped lift the nation's spirit after World War Two. He was popular with the fans and with visiting Americans, who nicknamed him "Oyster."

With a soft and graceful swing, he lofted balls that left lofty, graceful traces in the sky. His 20 homers in 1946 seem a modest total, but they were 10 percent of all the homers hit in the Japanese majors that year. He hit cleanup on the Lions' "H-Bomb Row" of the 1950s.

Futoshi Nakanishi A Japanese Hack Wilson, in Leo Durocher's phrase, Nakanishi hit the second-longest tapemeasure home run in Japanese history—530 feet—as a sophomore in 1953. He led the league in homers five out of the six years 1953–1958 and, with Oshita and pitcher Kazuhisa Inao, helped the Nishitetsu Lions win three Japan championships, all over the hated Giants.

Nakanishi helped spark the Lions to an amazing comeback in 1958, beginning from eleven games behind the Hawks. In one September stretch, they won seventeen out of eighteen games, and Nakanishi's homer vanquished the Hawks in their final meeting.

Nakanishi's career was cut short by an injury to his left hand after 244 home runs and a .307 average.

He managed the Lions to the flag in another heroic comeback starting from fourteen games behind. An eight-game winning streak in October finally put them a half game ahead, and American Tony Roig's homer clinched it on the final day.

Katsuya Nomura (Kot′-su-ya) The slugging catcher Nomura was the first home run king Oh had to catch before he could go after Ruth and Aaron. Nomura played in Japan's smallest park, with 280-foot foul lines, but he was a legitimate star, with a high of 52 homers in 150 games in 1963, when he almost batted the Hawks to the pennant over the Lions.

Nomura's lifetime homer total, 1954–1980, was 657. He led the Pacific League eight straight times—nine in all.

Nomura was the most enduring catcher of all time. His 2,918 games behind the plate are almost 1,000 more than the U.S. record, by Bob Boone. Six years Nomura played every game on the schedule. Once he caught every inning in 150 games, including 16 doubleheaders. Hard work only made him stronger. He hit a combined .235 in the first games of the doubleheaders, .339 in the second games.

Overshadowed by Oh and Nagashima of the Giants, who enjoyed a tremendous publicity advantage, Nomura called them "sunflowers" and himself "an evening primrose."

Slow afield and afoot (Americans called him "Moose"), Nomura admired Campanella, who taught him how to catch without blocking the ump's view of low pitches and how to give his pitchers more confidence. An intelligent catcher, Nomura played each game in his head, pitch by pitch, the night before. Batters swore he could read their minds.

Nomura made a reliever of strikeout king Enatsu and in 1959 caught Sugiura's magnificent 38–4 season, forming one of the finest batteries of all time.

In 1965 he won the Triple Crown, with a little help from the league's pitchers, who walked American Daryl Spencer to prevent him from winning the home run title.

Shigeo Nagashima (She-gay'-o) The most popular player ever to play in Japan, Nagashima ("long island") came to the Yomiuri Giants in 1958 and led the league in homers and RBIs his rookie year. He went on to win another HR crown, four more RBI titles, six batting crowns, and five MVPs—pretty good for a man whose main rival for all these honors was Sadaharu Oh.

In fact, Oh joined the team the year after Nagashima, and the two of them gave the Giants the dreaded "O-N Cannons" that propelled them to nine straight Japan championships. With Nagashima hitting cleanup behind Oh, pitchers couldn't pitch around Sadaharu. In the first year of Nagashima's retirement, 1975, Oh lost his HR crown after thirteen straight years as king.

Nagashima was considered the greater clutch hitter. He was nicknamed "Mr. Giant" and "the burning man" for the intensity of his play. His years of greatness coincided with Japan's dramatic economic surge, a period of national pride that he seemed to symbolize.

In 1959 Nagashima won the most famous game ever played in Japan, before the Emperor and Empress, with a ninth-inning homer. Seven years later, in 1966, his majesty attended his second game, against the L.A. Dodgers. Nagashima homered off Alan Foster in the first, singled in the fourth after a brushback pitch, and singled again in the seventh, as the Japanese won 11–3. He's the first player to receive an audience at the Imperial Palace.

At third base, Nagashima was compared to Ron Santo by Americans who saw him. Dodger G.M. Fresco Thompson said Los Angeles could have won two extra pennants with Nagashima on third.

Fans adored him. His every move on the bases, in the field, or at bat, delighted them. Even Oh admitted that Nagashima was the first Japanese to realize that the game belongs to the fans. Early on, Oh realized he would never be able to rival Nagashima in popularity and that he would have to concentrate on setting records instead.

Although the two Giants were not unfriendly, neither were they close friends. Never once, Oh says, did they meet socially off the field or even take a drink together.

Like Gehrig and Ruth, Oh was upstaged by Nagashima. In '64 Oh blasted 55 homers, a Japanese record. But that was the year Nagashima got married—the number one sports story of the year.

When Oh won a then unprecedented second straight Triple Crown in 1974, he again had to take a back seat to Nagashima, whose retirement was the biggest story of the year. In true Ted Williams fashion, Nagashima hit his 444th, and last, home run on his final day, then tearfully toured the field, while his fans wept with him and implored him not to go.

The next year Nagashima succeeded Kawakami as manager. He was officially given the appointment before thousands in Korakuen Stadium in a ceremony which author Robert Whiting called "a coronation."

In his first year at the helm, the Giants came in last, a national shock. Nagashima led the team in a formal bow of apology to the fans on the final day. But they bounced back to first the next two years.

Sadaharu Oh The world home-run king, Oh smashed 868 to pass Ruth and Aaron by more than 100 and put the record out of sight for at least the rest of the twentieth century and probably for several generations into the twenty-first. Clete Boyer, who played and coached for many years in Japan, said Oh had the strength of Aaron and the eyes of Williams. Oh's homers were the result of his samurai dedication, his mastery of the martial arts of *aikido* and *kendo* (swordsmanship), and thousands of hours of work with his devoted coach, Hiroshi Arakawa.

Sadaharu hit .161 as a Tokyo Giant rookie pitcher (!) in 1959. Then Oh and Arakawa began their search for The Way. Oh gave up late-night drinking bouts on the Ginza and studied with masters of martial arts to attain physical, mental, and spiritual mastery. From the legend of the swordsman Miyamoto Musashi, Oh learned that superior spirit conquers superior technique.

But a hitch in his swing still kept Oh back until Arakawa made him stand on one leg before the pitch. If he hitched, he'd topple over. Thus the famous dog-at-the-hydrant stance, which no one before or since has attempted. (Mel Ott's raised foot was entirely different.) The bat angle, with the barrel pointing toward the pitcher, was an integral part of the balance.

Aikido taught Oh patience at the plate. *Kendo* taught him hip action, a downward swing (the fastest path to the ball), and focusing *ki*, or energy, from the shoulders to the "sweet" part of the bat.

Oh put it together in 1962, and the home runs began to explode. For 12 of the next 13 years he hit 41–55 homers a year. True, Japanese fences are shorter, 300' down the line. But so is the Japanese season—130 games. And Oh saw a lot more junkball pitchers than American hitters do. In addition, they walked him as many as 166 times a year—he never came to bat 500 times in one year in his life. The result: home run totals that ranged up to 67 per 550 at-bats. The 67 came in 1974 with 49 homers in only 385 AB.

Some lifetime comparisons:

	AB	HR	HR/550AB
Aaron	12,364	755	34
Ruth	8,399	714	45
Oh	9,250	868	49

Some other stats on Oh:

- 15 HR titles (13 in a row)—Ruth had 12, Aaron four
- 13 straight RBI crowns
- 13 straight times leading in runs
- nine MVP's—Ruth and Aaron had one each
- five bat championships—Ruth won one, Aaron two
- two back-to-back Triple Crowns—no American has done it
- nine Gold Gloves (they call them Diamond Gloves in Japan).

Early on, Arakawa instilled in Oh the goal of catching Ruth, then Aaron, then going for 800. Aaron and Oh met face to face in 1974 in a home run contest before 50,000 fans in Tokyo. Aaron was still shaking off jet lag when his tenth homer broke a 9–9 tie. Oh was sorry to see Aaron retire—the competition had given him a goal.

Besides becoming a great hitter, Oh also became an excellent pianist. He drinks a secret blend of ginseng tea, the traditional Korean brew for energy. His bats, like Pete Rose's bats and like the sword blades used by samurai warriors, were hand made for him. Oh insisted that his bats be fashioned from a rare tree found only in northern Japan—and only from the branches of female trees.

Isao Harimoto (E′-sow) The only member of Japan's 3,000-hit club, Harimoto set the Japanese batting record with .383 in 1970, and many thought he could go on to become the country's first .400 hitter. He didn't, partly because he refused to bunt, but he did win two more titles, for a total of seven, slugged 504 home runs, and batted .319, third-highest lifetime average in Japan.

A Korean born in Hiroshima, he was being carried by his mother outside the city when the atom bomb went off. She shielded him, but a sister was killed. At the age of four, two fingers on his right hand were severely burned, making it difficult for him to swing a bat. For five years his coach, Kenjiro Matsuki (Maht′-ski), pitched 500 balls a day to him, and Harimoto took 500 one-handed swings a day until suddenly, at the age of twenty-five, he found he could get around even against Yutaka Enatsu, perhaps the fastest pitcher ever in Japan.

Harimoto used a "level-up" swing—the bat was level until it met the ball, then went sharply up on the follow-through. Like Willie Keeler, he hit to all fields, wherever "they ain't."

Harimoto was active in establishing pro ball in Korea.

Shinichi Eto (Shin-i′-chi Et-o) A husky first baseman, Eto hit 367 homers but had the misfortune to come up with the Chunichi Dragons the same year Oh joined the Giants, 1959, and in the same league. It cost Eto several home run crowns.

But he had the pleasure of costing Oh two Triple Crowns, beating him out of the batting titles in 1964 and 1965.

Koichi Tabuchi Big (six-three, 210 pounds), handsome Tabuchi is the man who ended Oh's home run reign in 1975 after thirteen straight titles. Tabuchi slugged 43 that year, in spite of playing in the country's largest park. He had done even better the year before with 45 to Oh's 49. The Japanese call him their Johnny Bench.

Japanese connoisseurs consider Tabuchi's homers even more beautiful than Oh's—long and high, with a lot of "hang time."

Yutaka Fukumoto This fleet little (five-seven) Braves outfielder is the world's stolen base champ—with 1,062 through 1987 as compared to Lou Brock's 938.

Thirteen straight times, in 1970–1982, Fukumoto led the league in steals. His high, 106 in 122 games in 1972, broke Maury Wills's then record of 104 in 148 games. Brock stole 118 in 1974, but he had many more opportunities:

Player	Year	1B	BB	OB*	SB	SB/OB
Wills	1962	150	59	209	104	.498
Brock	1974	159	61	220	118	.536
Cobb	1915	161	118	279	96	.344
Fukumoto	1972	97	65	163	106	.650

*Times reached first base

Fukumoto stole 95 more in 1973 and 94 in 1974.

In that thirteen-year span, the Braves won six pennants. No wonder they took out a half-million-dollar insurance policy on his legs.

Was he stealing on the weak arms of Japanese receivers? American Don Blasingame, who played for years in Japan, said Fukumoto could have stolen on Bench.

Fukumoto led the league in runs ten times, triples eight times, walks (+ HBP) six times, hits four times, and doubles three times, and won the MVP for his great performance in 1972.

Sachio Kinugasa (Sah′-chio Ke-nu-ga′-sa) Kinugasa passed Lou Gehrig's consecutive-game record in 1987 and topped him in lifetime homers as well, 504–493.

Breaking in with the doormat Hiroshima Carp in 1965, he teamed with college star Koji Yamamoto to lift the Carp to their first pennant in 1975. They won again in 1979 and 1980, the so-called "Red Helmet" era, like Cincinnati's "Big Red Machine"—both teams wore red helmets.

A "GI baby" (his father was black), Kinugasa played in Yamamoto's shadow, often taking practice swings in his hotel room until two A.M. It paid off in 1984, his twentieth season, when he hit .300 for the only time in his life, led in RBI, and won the MVP.

Kinugasa once confided that he would like to find his father someday. "Keep playing like that," a teammate answered, "and your father will find *you*."

Hiromitsu Ochiai (O′-che-aye) With Oh, Nomura, and the other hard hitters of the past retired, Ochiai ranks alone as the top Japanese slugger today and the only man, Japanese or American, to win three Triple Crowns in 1982 and 1985–1986. Nonchalant and outspoken, he doesn't even shrink from predicting his Triple Crowns. As Dizzy Dean said, "If you kin do it, it ain't braggin'." (Ochiai missed the Triple Crown he predicted in 1987, however.)

His 52 homers in 1985 ties him with Nomura for the Pacific League record.

Not a pull hitter, Ochiai has won two other batting titles, in addition to his Triple Crowns. However, he would probably not hit for power in the larger U.S. stadiums.

Pitchers

Eiji Sawamura A true folk hero, in 1934 the eighteen-year-old Sawamura whiffed four of America's greatest Hall of Famers in a row—Gehringer (.356, 11 home runs), Ruth (.288, 22), Gehrig (.363, 49), and Foxx (.334, 44).

The Americans had been averaging four homers and eight runs per game until they met the schoolboy with the excellent fastball and drop. The kid considered the visitors "gods" but gulped and took the mound against Earl Whitehill (14–11 for the seventh-place Senators).

With the score 0–0 going into the seventh, Ruth grounded out. (The sun got in his eyes, he said.) Next up was Gehrig, who led both majors in both batting and homers that year. Sawamura threw a strike past him. The next pitch was a high curve, which Lou slammed over the right field wall to win the game 1–0.

In the last of the seventh, the Japanese put a man on second with one out, and Shigeru Mizuhara pulled a low line drive down the right field foul line. A diving catch by Bing Miller saved one run and maybe more.

In all, the kid gave seven hits, struck out nine, and walked one. Connie Mack was so impressed, he offered the boy a contract.

The next year Eiji toured the States with Shoriki's Dai Nippon nine (later tagged the Tokyo Giants by Lefty O'Doul), playing PCL and semipro clubs. American fans crowded around for autographs, and one asked him to sign in English, not Japanese. Eiji obliged, only to discover later that he had signed a contract! It took some fast talking, and perhaps some yen, to get Sawamura out of the scout's clutches.

Sawamura went on to lead the new pro league in 1936 with a 13–3 record. In the postseason playoff against the Hanshin Tigers, he pitched all three games, holding them to a .116 batting average and an 0.19 ERA, as the Giants won, two games to one.

The next year he was 33–10.

In his brief five-year career, he pitched three no-hitters.

Sawamura was called away to military service in 1938–1939, and again in 1942 and 1944. In December 1944 his troop ship was torpedoed by a submarine off Formosa, and he went down with the ship.

Masaichi Kaneda (Masa-ichi Ka-nay'-da) Only Cy Young and Walter Johnson have surpassed Kaneda's 400 victories. Akin to Johnson's experience, he won most of his with one of the weakest teams in Japan, the Yakult Swallows, who finished in the first division only once in his fifteen years with them 1950–1964.

In 1958 the Swallows were last in homers and near last in batting. But Kaneda was 31–14 with a 1.30 ERA. The Swallows were 27–54 without him.

In all, he won 43 percent of the Swallows' victories. He won and lost more 1–0 games than anyone—21 victories, 23 defeats.

The lefthanded Kaneda was the first man to break Walter Johnson's lifetime strikeout record, as well as the first to break his scoreless innings streak. Nolan Ryan broke Kaneda's strikeout mark, 4,490, but no one has touched his mark of 64 straight shutout innings.

Kaneda whiffed the great Nagashima four straight times in Nagashima's big league debut, the only pitcher ever to do that to the great batting star.

Kaneda finally joined the Giants for five years at the end of the line. His 16–5 in 1967 at the age of thirty-four got them off to the third of their nine straight championships.

Kaneda was also the Wes Ferrell of Japan. His 36 home runs are the Japanese record for pitchers.

A Japanese-born Korean (*kane* is *Kim* in Korean), when he retired with bone chips in his elbow, his glove was donated to the U.S. Hall of Fame in Cooperstown.

Takumi Otomo (Ta-ku'-me O'-to-mo) The little submarine-baller beat the New York Giants and Hoyt Wilhelm 2–1 in 1953 in one of the ten greatest games in Japan's history. With Lefty O'Doul urging him to keep the ball high, Otomo stayed ahead in the count, then fed them bad balls until they popped up or rolled out.

He won the MVP that year with a 27–6 record, plus two wins in the Japan Series. His ERA, 1.85, was the highest he posted in a four-year period. The lowest: 1.68 in 1956.

In 1955 he was 30–6.

Kazuhisa Inao (Ka-zu-hee'-sa E-now') Until his arm finally weakened from overwork, Inao was one of the world's most amazing pitchers.

His record of pitching six Japan Series games in 1958 and winning the last four of them will probably never be done again by any pitcher in any country. He won 42 games in 1961, 35 in 1957, and 33 in 1958. He was voted best pitcher in the league five times.

A poor fisherman's son, he reported as an unknown rookie to the Nishitetsu Lions' camp, with muscles bulging from rowing his father's boat in rough seas. He threw up to 300 pitches a day, posted a 20–6 record with a 1.06 ERA, and lifted the Lions to the pennant. In 262 innings, he gave up two home runs. He won three more games in the Japan Series.

Nicknamed *"Tetsu Wan"*—Iron Arm—in 1957 Inao won a record 20 straight at the end of the year to lift the Lions from third to another pennant.

In 1961 he tied Vic Starffin's record of 42 wins and lost his bid for his forty-third, 1–0, in the first game of two on the final day. He considered coming back in Game Two and going for the record but at last decided to rest on his laurels.

Inao came back as a relief pitcher in 1965 and led the league in ERA once more, with 1.79.

His final totals: 276–137, 1.98, with 2,574 strikeouts.

Tadashi Sugiura (Su-ghee-u'-ra) One year after Inao won four straight games in the Japan Series, the bespectacled Sugiura won four straight too. But he pitched all four games and won all four!

Nagashima's teammate in college, Sugiura had spurned the Yomiuri Giants after Nankai Hawk manager Kazuto Tsuru-oka bowed to him and said, "We need you to beat the Giants."

As a rookie Sugiura was 27–12, 2.05 with the second-place Hawks, though Inao (33–10) and the Lions won their third straight flag.

Then in 1959 it was Sugiura's turn. He pitched 371 innings, held enemy hitters to a 1.40 ERA, and posted a 38–4 record. He pitched 29 games in the last eight weeks, or virtually every other day. He was 17–1 after August 1 and won his last 13 in a row. The stretch included 54 straight shutout innings, an ERA of 0.10, 95 strikeouts, and only 4 walks! His final victory clinched the flag.

Then came the Japan Series against the Giants, who had just won their fifth straight flag. The Hawks had never beaten them.

In spite of a painful elbow, Sugiura went eight innings in Game One, gave up nine hits, but won 10–7. The next day Sugiura pitched five innings of relief, gave three hits and one run, and got the victory 6-3.

After a travel day Sugiura started Game Three in Tokyo. Midway through, a corn came off his pitching hand, and catcher Nomura suddenly found himself catching a bloody ball. In the samurai spirit, however, Sugiura refused to come out. He lost a 2–1 lead on a homer in the ninth, and the Giants put two more men on second and third with one out. "My God, I'm done for," he says he thought, desperately looking into the dugout for relief. Tsuruoka kept his eyes averted, however, sending a coach out with a good luck amulet instead. Sugiura buckled down and got the last two outs and won in the tenth 3–2. He gave up only one walk.

Rain gave Sugiura a day of rest. Would the Hawks give him another in Game Four? The finger still pained him. "Can you go?" Tsuruoka asked. "I can go," Sugiura answered. He went nine more innings and shut the Giants out on five hits.

Ecstatic Hawk fans rewarded their hero with a new car, license number 38-4.

In his first three years, he had won 96 games:

Year	Rank	G	IP	BB	SO	W–L	ERA	Series	Awards
1958	2	53	299	85	215	27–12	2.05		
1959	1	69	371	46	336	38–4	1.40*	4–0	MVP
1960	2	57	333	49	317	31–11	2.05		

But then the overwork finally told. After an operation on

his arm, he fell to 20–9 in 1961. He dropped to 14–15, then 14–16, made a brief comeback in 1964 with 20–15, and then was sent to the bullpen. He was all pitched out.

His final totals: 187–106.

Tetsuya Yoneda (Tet'-su-ya Yo-nay-da)   Like Kaneda or Phil Niekro, Yoneda slaved for a doormat team, the Braves. Yet he posted the second-highest winning total in Japan—350–285, second only to Kaneda's 400 wins.

In 1966 Yoneda led the league with 25–17, while his team finished next to last. His biggest year was 1968, when he went 29–13 as the Braves won the pennant. He was voted the MVP of the league.

Yoneda is second to Kaneda in hitting too, with 33 homers to Kaneda's 36. Yoneda might have passed his rival, but the coming of the DH rule stopped his bid.

He did pass Kaneda, and everyone, including Cy Young, in one department, total games—949.

Keishi Suzuki   For six straight years, 1967–1972—eight years in all—the lefty Suzuki led the Pacific League in strike-outs. As a sophomore lefty in 1967, he was 21–13 for the last-place Kintetsu Buffaloes.

Like Robin Roberts, another fastballing control pitcher, Suzuki gave up a lot of homers—482.

He was a natural righthander, but his father had tied his right hand to force him to pitch as a lefty.

His final figures: 317–238, and 3,060 strikeouts.

Minoru Murayama   In 1959 rookie fastballer Murayama faced Japan's best player, Nagashima, in the greatest game ever played in Japan, a contest before 50,000 fans, including the Emperor himself.

Murayama, as famous for his forkball as his fastball, pitched for the Yomiuri Giants' biggest rivals, the Hanshin Tigers. An Osaka native and boyhood Tiger fan, he spurned a Giant bonus in order to stay home and pitch for the Tigers for half the amount the Giants offered.

The night before the big game, Murayama had come in in the ninth inning against the Giants and struck out the side, Nagashima included.

The next night, before their majesties, Masa-aki Koyama started for the Tigers and they took an early lead. Nagashima ripped a single and home run to tie the score. The Tigers went back into the lead, and in the seventh Nagashima struck out, but a rookie named Sadaharu Oh pumped a two-run home run to tie it again.

That brought in Murayama, who got the Giants out to end the seventh, then shut them out in the eighth, as the scoreboard clock inched toward nine-thirty, the time when the imperial couple would have to leave. They stayed in their seats, however, to see Nagashima and Murayama duel each other in the last of the ninth.

This was a classic Japanese showdown, or *shobu*. Under the unwritten rule, there could be no nibbling the corners or dirty tricks; it had to be a head-on challenge, strength against strength.

Murayama's first pitch was a forkball, for a ball. Next another forkball, for a strike. Then a fastball, which Nagashima fouled back.

Another fastball was outside, making the count 2–2. Then he uncorked still another fastball on the inside. Nagashima swung and parked it ten rows into the left field stands. To this

day Murayama insists it was foul. But Nagashima circled the bases before the royal box, to be mobbed by his teammates waiting at the plate.

Nagashima went on to win the batting championship. Murayama went on to strike out 294 men in 295 innings; he won 18 and lost 10, with a 1.19 ERA, and won the Sawamura Award.

But nothing could erase the memory of that one fateful home run. Nagashima was invited to the palace for an audience. There was no imperial audience for Murayama, however. Ever after, he waited for his revenge.

When he neared the 1,500th strikeout of his career, he announced that he would get it against Nagashima; he did. Then he announced that he was saving number 2,000 for Nagashima as well, and he delivered on that promise too.

In 1961 Murayama was 24–13; in 1962, 25–14 with a 1.20 ERA to lift the Tigers to the pennant and win another Sawamura. It was a partial revenge at least.

That fall Murayama took part of his anger out on the visiting Detroit Tigers. Murayama had been hit hard by the Americans earlier in the tour. But this day his fastball and forkball were snapping.

He struck out the first two hitters, Chico Fernandez (.249) and Bill Bruton (.278). Norm Cash (.243) walked, but Al Kaline (.304) was the third out.

For the next six innings not another Detroiter got on base. "I was keeping every ball down," Murayama said later. "My slider and forkball were working well. I was thinking no-hitter."

Former American League pitcher Tom Ferrick watched the game and repeated what he had said before: Murayama was the best pitcher in Japan; his fastballs were jamming the hitters, and he delivered both the fastball and the forkball with the same deceptive motion. "No major leaguer could have hit Murayama today," Ferrick said.

For seven innings, no major leaguer did. In the eighth Dick McAuliffe (.263) led off with a walk, the first Detroit base runner since the first inning. Murayama retired Bubba Morton (.262) and Steve Boros (.228). Then Mike Roarke (.213) lined one into left field to break up the no-hitter. Lefthanded Bobo Osborne (.230) pinch-hit and popped to second.

Murayama got Fernandez out to open the ninth. Then Bruton dropped a bunt and beat it out for the second—and last—hit. Cash walked again. But Kaline lifted a foul to shortstop, McAuliffe hit a high fly to left, and the Tigers were finished. It was the first shutout a U.S. big league team had ever suffered in Japan.

The Detroiters probably didn't know what hit them, or why. As Murayama said, "I have become what I am because of Nagashima."

His final stats: 222–147, 2.09.

Yutaka Enatsu   One of the most amazing athletes in Japanese baseball, in 1968 Enatsu struck out 401 men in 329 innings—that's eleven every nine innings. He was only twenty years old and just two years out of high school.

The lefty was one of the few pitchers who could get Nagashima and Oh out consistently. As a result his pennant-hungry managers worked him like a slave in every series against the Giants. Enatsu pitched the first and third games of a three-game series, and sometimes relieved in the middle game as well.

In 1970 he shut the Giants out twice in three days, then

pitched the final game of the season with no rest and lost it 2–1 in ten innings. The Giants won by two games.

In 1971 Enatsu had elbow trouble and won only 15 games—but six of them were against the Giants, including 34 straight scoreless innings. And in the All-Star Game that summer he pitched three innings and struck out all nine men he faced. (Three years later Suguru Egawa almost matched him. He whiffed the first eight men on thirty-seven pitches, or about 4.5 per man, then got two fastball strikes on batter number nine. He shook off a sign for another fastball and instead threw a curve, which the batter hit on the ground for the final out.)

Enatsu was a free spirit who rebelled against the strict samurai-style workouts, saying he wanted to save himself for the season—the way they worked him, he was probably right. To dramatize his revolt one spring, he lay down in the outfield and went to sleep while the other pitchers ran. The Tigers finished last that year. They fired the manager and kept Enatsu.

Another time he was suspended for accepting a watch from a gambler.

In 1973 the Tigers were making a hard run at ending the Giants' pennant streak. On August 30, with one day of rest, Enatsu tossed an eleven-inning no-hitter, winning it himself 1–0 with a home run. In September he pitched a fourteen-inning one-hitter, retiring thirty-three straight batters in a row—the equal of eleven perfect innings—then lost 1–0.

When the Giants arrived for the climactic series, Enatsu faced them with two days rest and lost. As usual manager Murayama put him in to pitch the third game. The exhausted pitcher was leading 3–1 in the seventh, when he loaded the bases on a walk, a single, and a bunt, with Oh at bat. Enatsu got two strikes on Oh, then walked him on four straight pitches. Nagashima followed with a single to win the game and, eventually, the pennant. Enatsu ended with 24–13. It was his last great year as a starter.

He became Japan's greatest relief ace and bounced to the Hawks, Carp, and Lions, fighting with most of his managers. Finally, at the age of thirty-eight, he came to America to try out with the Brewers. It was too late; his arm was gone. Fifteen years earlier, and who knows how he might have done? Red Schoendienst called him one of the greatest lefties he'd ever seen.

Enatsu's final record: 206–158, plus 193 saves. And 2,987 strikeouts.

"East is East, and west is West, and never the twain shall meet."—*Rudyard Kipling*

Gaijin—*Foreigners*

Next to trade policy, no area of U.S.-Japanese relations contains the seeds of more controversy than baseball. The two games may appear the same from the left field stands, but the two nations actually play two quite different games. This can sometimes lead to bitter misunderstanding.

According to U.S. observers, among the differences are:
Japanese managers . . .
- Conduct spring training like marine boot camp.
- Overwork their pitchers.
- Bench players in midgame for one error or one strikeout.
- Overemphasize home runs.

- Resent advice.
- Are too conservative.
- Won't let Americans excel.

Japanese players . . .
- Take half an hour batting practice every day.
- Don't miss signs.
- Don't dive for fly balls.
- Won't break up double plays.
- Don't block the plate.
- Don't backhand grounders.
- Don't chew tobacco.
- Carry their own bags.
- Shine their own shoes.

Japanese pitchers . . .
- Throw sidearm and underhand more than in the States.
- Have good curves but mediocre fastballs.
- Won't throw brushback pitches.
- Throw 300–500 pitches a day—just to stay in shape.
- Burn out early.

Japanese fans . . .
- Eat sushi instead of hotdogs at the game.
- Throw foul balls back.

According to the Japanese, among the differences are:
American players . . .
- Are overpaid, stuck up, and out of shape.
- Won't work hard.
- Don't follow orders.
- Play dirty baseball.
- Bait the umpires.
- Are quick to punch opponents.
- Look down on the Japanese.
- Won't learn the language.
- Don't like Japanese food.
- Won't carry their own bags.
- Won't shine their own shoes.

Still, like lovers having a quarrel, the two nations can't stay away from each other on the ballfield.

The Japanese have used more than 300 foreigners—in Japanese, *gaijin*, which means "outside people." There is an ambivalence toward these aliens. On the one hand, teams are tempted to use them to gain a competitive advantage (there's a cap of three per team). On the other hand, the Japanese yearn for the day that an all-Japanese team will win a *real* world series and reign as kings of the baseball world.

Although the Japanese regularly import players, they are paranoid about exporting any to the U.S. majors. America has a very favorable "balance-of-baseball" trade. And the currently devalued dollar means Japan can afford even more American shortstops—more Yanks for the yen.

In 1987 they gave Bob Horner of the Braves $1.4 million dollars. He rewarded them with six homers in his first four games and put an estimated quarter of a million more people in the park. But he spurned a $3 million offer to stay, preferring to go home to the Cards for $1 million rather than play "something like baseball."

The Japanese offered Dave Righetti a reported $8 million for two years and Reggie Jackson $2 million for one. They turned it down. But the Japanese teams landed Bill Madlock for $1 million, Bill Gullickson for $1.1 million, and Doug DeCinces for $1.5 million—this only four years after Japan's commissioner had announced a plan to ban all *gaijin*.

(Gullickson returned from Tokyo after signing his contract

to report that he saw only two English words there—Sony and Mitsubishi.)

Here are some of the best—and the worst—foreigners to play in Japan.

Vic Starffin Now that baseball is an Olympic sport, the Russians have set themselves the goal of winning a gold medal some day. A preview of what the future may hold was big (six-four) Victor Starffin, the White Russian whose parents brought him to Japan fleeing the Bolshevik Revolution. He took to baseball like Khrushchev to vodka and became the greatest Russian baseball player of all time.

Joining the Dai-Nippon team, Starffin towered over the Japanese and opened a rivalry with teammate Sawamura. Vic was 28–12 in 1937, 33–5 in 1938, 42–15 in 1939 (two-thirds of the team's wins), and 38–12 (1.01) in 1940. Those 42 wins remained the record until Inao tied it in 1961.

On the U.S. tour in 1935, Americans assumed he spoke English. He didn't, once telling a waitress, "I am a chicken." (He later learned the language.)

Excused from military service as a stateless person, Starffin served as a Russian translator at the Tokyo war crimes trials. He spent his postwar years with some tailend teams but finished at 303–177, Japan's first 300-game winner.

He was killed soon afterward when he was driving his car home while drunk and hit a train. His plaque in Japan's Hall of Fame is inscribed in both Japanese and Russian.

Henry "Bozo" Wakabayashi (Wa-ka-bigh-yah'-shee) The son of a Japanese immigrant to Hawaii, Wakabayashi first played in Japan in 1928, graduated from one of Tokyo's "Big Six" universities, and pitched for the Osaka Tigers from the beginning of pro ball in 1936. A finesse pitcher, Wakabayashi threw seven different pitches ("seven-color magic pitches"). In 1939 he was 30–7 with a 1.25 ERA. For six years in a row, 1939–1944, he had ERAs of under 1.86; his best was 1.06 in 1943.

Twice MVP, his most famous game came in the first Japan Series in 1950 at the age of forty-two, when he was the surprise starter in Game One against the Robins, who boasted a team batting average of .287. Bozo beat them 3–2.

Wakabayashi retired at 240–141 and 1.99 and remained a baseball ambassador for decades.

Bucky Harris Bucky Harris, another American (no, not the Senators' manager), was the Japanese home run king in 1938 and the first foreigner to win the MVP. A veteran catcher from the American PCL, he had a good throwing arm and repeatedly won exhibitions throwing through a barrel at second base.

He studied hard to learn the language and, given a day of honor at his retirement, replied with a *sayonara* speech in Japanese.

Wally Yonamine (Yo-na'-mi-nay) The Jackie Robinson of Japan, Yonamine introduced a slashing, running game and blazed the way for American players there. This Hawaiian-born Nisei didn't know a word of Japanese when he left the San Francisco 49ers' backfield to join the Tokyo Giants in 1951. (He'd played some baseball in the low U.S. minors; Brooklyn's Billy Loes, who pitched against him, said he was the toughest out he ever faced.)

Wally carried a double stigma. Not only was he an Ameri-can, when the wounds of the war were still fresh, he was a Nisei (son of a Japanese who chooses another country), who was regarded by the Japanese in about the same way as Americans would regard a fellow countryman who had defected to Russia.

The Giants put him in center field and batted him leadoff, and he promptly hit .354. He also ran out sacrifice bunts, which surprised the Japanese, and threw rolling blocks into second basemen on the double play, which horrified them. And he played center like his stateside contemporary, Dom DiMaggio, who also wore glasses.

A Yonamine single, a hit-and-run, and a base hit by Kawakami was the usual Giant formula. They rose from third to first in Wally's first season and won the flag every year he was with them except one. Wally and Kawakami were rivals for hitting honors, and a jealousy arose. Yonamine was much the better fielder and won three batting titles and one MVP, made seven All-Star teams, and ended with a .311 average, one of the highest in Japan. Against the Dodgers in 1956 Wally hit .347. The Japanese hailed him as the greatest lead-off man in their history, and he's probably still the biggest American star to play in Japan.

Another Nisei, Jun Hirota, caught for the Giants. When the New York Giants arrived in 1953, manager Leo Durocher, coaching at first, abandoned signals and merely told his runners to "go down on the next pitch." Hirota calmly threw them out. Leo didn't known Jun was a graduate of the University of Hawaii.

When Kawakami took over as Giant manager, he eased Wally off the team.

Yonamine got his revenge, however. As manager of the Dragons in 1974 he nipped Kawakami's Giants by one game, or .001 points, to end Kawakami's record of nine straight pennants.

Thereafter the U.S.-Japan baseball romance was a rocky one. Some Americans made a big hit. Others were big bombs.

Ugly Americans

Don Newcombe and Larry Doby The first big-name American stars in Japan, Newcombe and Doby signed with the Chunichi Dragons in 1962. Both were in retirement, and Newk especially arrived overweight and out of shape. He pitched only 4 innings but batted .262 in 81 games in the field. Larry hit .225 with 10 home runs, although some of them were eye-popping 500-footers. The Dragons, who had finished second before they came, finished third with them. The pair were not invited back.

Marshall, Logan, Stuart, Johnson, Howard Instead, in 1963 the optimistic Dragons signed Jim Marshall, a reserve first baseman for San Francisco with a .242 big league average, for $40,000, more than either Nagashima or Oh were making. Marshall stayed for three years, averaging .268 and 26 homers a year.

The thirty-seven-year-old Johnny Logan, a former star shortstop for the Milwaukee Braves, joined the Nankai Hawks in 1964. He hit .189 and set a Japanese record by going 38 straight at-bats without a hit.

Dick Stuart came well touted in 1967. He hit 33 homers his first year, but in his second fell to 17 homers and .217. They sent him home, where he signed with the California Angels, the first Japanese reject to return to play in the U.S. majors.

In 1973 Davey Johnson hit 43 homers for Atlanta, a record for big league second basemen. The next year the Tokyo Giants obtained him to replace the great Nagashima and integrate the Giants once again. It was a job no mortal man could fill, and Johnson didn't. He hit .197, as the Giants finished dead last. He did make a comeback the next year, and so did they, hitting .275 with 26 homers, as the Giants won the pennant. But Dave was happy to say *sayonara* and go home to the Phils, where he hit .321.

Big Frank Howard cost the Lions $80,000 in 1974. He hurt his knee, came to bat twice, and didn't get a hit. His salary came to $40,000 per at-bat.

Joe Pepitone In 1973 the Yakult Atoms forked over $140,000 to Pepitone, a .258-hitting former Yankee. He arrived with shoulder-length hair, got a headache from bumping his head on low hotel room doors, complained about the food and high prices, played 14 games, hit .163, developed a "bad leg," and refused to play—but discoed into the morning. He finally flew home, leaving his roommate a $2,000 phone bill, and the Japanese with a new noun, *pepitone*, meaning "a goof-off."

The Japanese players' union protested against these high-priced foreigners who were taking jobs away from Japanese and getting paid more for doing less.

Some Handsome Americans

Blasingame, Boyer, Kirkland Thank goodness Don Blasingame came to Japan in 1967 after hitting .258 for several teams in the States. He hit 20 points better for the Nankai Hawks, learned to speak good Japanese, was cheerful to his teammates, respectful to his manager, and popular with the fans.

When home run champ Katsuya Nomura took over as manager, he appointed "Blaser" as his head coach and *de facto* bench manager, while Nomura concentrated on his play in the field. They got along splendidly and won the pennant in 1973.

Clete Boyer, possibly the greatest fielding third baseman of all time, also won friends and influenced people as a gritty player for the Taiyo Whales in 1972–1975. He also enjoyed the people, spoke their language, ate their food, and showed them the same sensational play he had shown Yankee fans back home.

Willie Kirkland hit .240 with 20 homers a year for the San Francisco Giants and others before he joined the Hanshin Tigers in 1968. He gave them 37 homers his first year, stayed for six years, joked in Japanese with fans in the outfield, and thrilled them with long distance blasts—three in one game against the hated Giants. He hit .246, the same as he had in the States, and averaged 21 homers a year.

Leron and Leon Lee Leron Lee, a vet of four big league teams (.250), owns the highest lifetime batting average in Japan, .320, plus 283 homers in 11 seasons, 1977–1987. He almost won the Triple Crown in his rookie year, got an 800 percent raise, and brought his kid brother Leon over.

Leon, who never played in the majors, was almost as good, hitting .309 with 268 homers.

Both were considered "good *gaijin*," on and off the field. Leon learned Japanese well enough to act as Bob Horner's interpreter.

Xenophobia

The Japanese have not been blameless in their handling of the cross-cultural experiments. Sometimes their bias against *gaijin* is subtle, sometimes blatant.

Daryl Spencer A 33-year-old infielder with fair power and a .244 big league average, Spencer, at six-three, was a "monster" in Japanese eyes. In his first year, 1964, he hit 36 homers, second to Nomura's 41, and lifted the Hankyu Braves from last to second.

The next year Spencer was hitting .300 and leading Nomura by six homers in August, when, he said, his own coaches took him aside and told him to concentrate on the batting title and forget home runs, because Nomura usually finished strong. Spencer refused, so the Japanese pitchers sent their own message—they began walking him. At one stretch he got 16 straight balls. He even stepped into the box holding his bat upside down and still drew a walk. Of course, Nomura's Nankai Hawk pitchers were the most flagrant evaders of Spencer's strike zone. Nomura won the home run crown, 42–38, and took the batting crown too, .320 to .311. (He also won the RBI title for a Triple Crown.) The Braves fell to fourth.

A student of the game, Spencer analyzed every pitch and defensive alignment. One of his ideas: move the left field fence in ten feet to help him hit more homers. Spencer played for seven years. He told Whiting that his manager resented his advice. "I spoke my mind once too many times," Spencer told Whiting, "and I think I'm blackballed." Japanese observers, however, understood that manager Yukio Nishimoto had welcomed Spencer's help.

Other Americans felt a similar sense of discrimination. In 1968 Dave Roberts, a .239-hitting utility man with several big league clubs, hit 40 homers for the Sankei Atoms, to Oh's 49. The next year Roberts was leading for the Triple Crown, when a Giants pitcher ran into him at first base, breaking his shoulder. Dave was out for the rest of the year, and Oh and Nagashima took the three batting titles.

George Altman In 1968 the former National League outfielder (.269, fair power) started a new career in Japan at age thirty-five. He was an immediate success, hitting .320 with 34 homers and 100 RBI. In 1970 he helped pull the Lotte Orions into first place with .319 and 30 homers.

In 1969, George said, he got nothing but balls from the pitchers and nothing but strikes from the umps. He slumped to 21 homers and .269.

In 1971 Altman had his best year—39 homers and 103 RBI, and was in a race for the batting title with his teammate, Shinichi Eto. When Eto came up, he noticed, the infielders suddenly left a big hole between first and second, and Eto punched four hits through it in one game. "That," Altman told Whiting, "is when I figured my chances of winning the title were almost zero."

Randy Bass Big, bewhiskered Randy Bass played a little first base for the Padres and Rangers (batting .212) before joining the Japanese Hanshin Tigers in 1983. In 1985 he burst into stardom, winning the Triple Crown with .350, 134 RBIs, and 54 home runs.

He was just one home run short of tying Oh's Japanese record, with one game left—against the Giants, managed by

Oh. The Giant pitchers walked him all four times he came to bat.

But Bass did lead the Tigers to the pennant over the hated Giants, and his home runs won two Japan Series games as the Tigers took the Japanese championship in seven games. He became a media star, his poster advertisements appearing all over Tokyo. He even agreed to shave his beard for a razor blade company.

Some Other Gaijin Stars

Some minor leaguers have done well in Japan.

Jack Bloomfield won two batting titles in 1962 and 1963.

Pitcher Joe Stanka won an MVP, with 26–7 for the Nankai Hawks in 1964.

Gene Bacque (Bock'-ay) won a Sawamura (Cy Young) for pitching the Tigers to the 1964 pennant with a 29–9. However, his brushback pitches appalled the Japanese. When he tried one against the great Oh, the whole Giants team mobbed him. In the melee, Oh says, coach Hiroshi Arakawa, Oh's best friend and an aikido black belt, broke Gene's thumb and put him out for the rest of the season.

Clarence Jones won a home run crown in 1974.

Boomer Wells won the Triple Crown and MVP in 1984.

Richard Lancellotti was home run king in 1987 while batting .218.

Japanese in America

Mashi Murakami Many Japanese have played in the U.S. minors and one in the majors.

The big leaguer was Masanori "Mashi" Murakami, who almost caused a complete rupture in U.S.-Japan diamond relations. Murakami was one of three members of the Nankai Hawks sent over to gain experience with the San Francisco Giants' farmteams in Fresno and Magic Valley in 1964. The twenty-year-old did so well (11–7) and was so well liked (bowing to teammates who made good plays behind him) that he was promoted to the Giants. He made his debut against the last-place Mets before 50,000 fans at Shea Stadium and pitched one inning of shutout relief. That year he won one and saved one with a 1.80 ERA. He struck out 15 men in 15 innings and walked only 1.

At this point the Giants invoked the fine print in their contract—the paragraph giving them the right to buy any of the three who made the parent club. The Japanese had never anticipated this development! They said Murakami had only been on loan. Besides, they said, he was homesick and didn't want to go back to the States. The boy dutifully agreed. The Hawks even charged that the contract was a forgery, thus enraging the Giants. Who did they think Murakami was, club president Chub Feeney demanded—Christy Mathewson?

U.S. Commissioner Ford Frick threatened to break relations with Japan if they didn't honor the contract. This could have cut off all further U.S. players going there to play.

At last a compromise broke the impasse. Murakami would play one more year in the States, then would be free to choose his own destiny.

Mashi flew back to San Francisco, won 4 games, lost 1, saved 8, and struck out 85 men in 74 innings. He was a darling of the San Francisco Nisei community.

In 1966 the Hawks enticed him home with a $40,000 contract, twice what the Giants had offered. The Hawks rubbed their hands in anticipation of seeing Murakami obliterate every pitching record in the book. Alas, he never lived up to his promise. He won a total of 9 games his first two years. He had only one good year, 1968, when he was 18–4. He was the first and last Japanese to play in the U.S. majors.

The Young Lions

In a second experiment, the Nishitetsu Lions bought a U.S. minor league team in Lodi, California, and stocked it with nine of their rookies plus a coach, along with U.S. players.

But the Japanese players, like some Americans in Japan, couldn't adjust to the food and the language. After two years the Lions sold their Lodi club and brought their players home.

Undaunted, in 1982 the Seibu Lions (unrelated to Nishitetsu) signed a working agreement with the Baltimore Orioles' Class A farmteam at San Jose and each year have sent several rookies there for experience. The plan paid off big. The Lions won the pennant five of the next six years, and experts attributed it in part to their San Jose graduates. Most famous of the group was Koji Akiyama, the 1987 Japanese home run king.

The "Magic" Manager, Mihara

Two of the greatest managers in Japanese history were Osamu Mihara (Three Plains) and Shigeru Mizuhara (Water Plain). Their duels are compared to the legendary duel of the greatest swordsmen of literature, Miyamoto Mushashi and Sasaki Kojiro.

Mihara and Mizuhara attended rival high schools on Shikoku Island and went to rival colleges in the highly competitive Tokyo Big Six Conference. In 1931, before 65,000 fans, Mihara stole home against pitcher Mizuhara to lead his school to victory.

In 1934 both played on the All-Japan team against Babe Ruth's Stars. Then Mihara went into military service; Mizuhara toured the States with Dai-Nippon, sparked the Giants to several pennants (he was MVP in 1942), and then was drafted himself.

Mizuhara languished in a Soviet POW camp for four years after the war, while Mihara took over the Giants and rebuilt that once proud club into champs in 1949.

But Mihara's triumph was spoiled when Mizuhara was repatriated that same year. "I am Mizuhara," he announced. "I have returned." Mizuhara was given the manager's job and won eight pennants in ten years, 1950–1959. Mihara was kicked upstairs, where he spent his time playing go.

Then Mihara left to manage a new club, the Nishitetsu Lions, in faroff Kyushu. He lived in the dorm with his players, mostly recent high school kids like Nakanishi and Inao, and built them into champs in 1954. They won again in 1956 and beat Mizuhara's strutting Yomiuri Giants in the Japan Series. They did it again in 1957 and 1958. In the last year the Giants won the first three games, but the Lions, behind Inao, won the last four.

In 1960 Mihara moved back to the Central League with the Taiyo Whales, who had finished last for six straight years. Shades of the Mets! In Mihara's first year, he whipped the Giants for the pennant by 4½ games, then swept the Japan Series in four straight!

No wonder they called him "the Magician."

A Real World Series

Matsutaro Shoriki died in 1969 with one dream still unfulfilled—a real World Series between his Giants and the winner of the American World Series. It's a goal every Japanese fan keeps before his eyes.

In frequent series against U.S. big league teams, the Japanese have already established one thing: the Americans can still win, but they have to field strong teams and play hard to do it.

In 1966 the Giants played seven games against the NL champion Dodgers and won four of them. Overall, the Dodgers were 9–8–1 in Japan. Of course, Sandy Koufax and Don Drysdale didn't make the trip. But their number three pitcher, Claude Osteen (17–14), did and was bombed out of the box five times.

In 1968 the NL champion Cards (Bob Gibson, Lou Brock, Orlando Cepeda, etc.) arrived fresh from the World Series. Beset by jet lag, they lost two of their first three games but came back to win 12 of their last 15 for a 13–5 record overall. The Japanese might have done better if Nagashima had not missed the series with an injury. Oh hit .356 with six homers.

In 1971, after a 9–6 spring training record against U.S. teams, Kawakami announced that "the Americans have nothing more to teach us." The nation looked confidently forward to the arrival that fall of the AL champ Orioles for what the Japanese were hailing as the long awaited "world series." Bowie Kuhn even threw out the first ball.

The Japanese knocked Jim Palmer (20–9) out three times, but Pat Dobson (20–8) pitched three shutouts, including a no-hitter. The O's held Oh to a .111 average. Nagashima hit .258, and the Orioles won 12 games to two, with four ties.

But when the Americans sent subpar teams—the fifth-place Mets in 1974 and the fifth-place Orioles in 1984, the competition was closer.

There is still about a twenty-pound difference between the average U.S. and Japanese big leaguer, which means that today's Japanese player is about as big as a major leaguer of Babe Ruth's day.

Some Japanese doubt that Japan can ever catch up with the U.S. majors. They say the Olympics are a better arena for competition — Japan won the "demonstration" Olympic title in 1984, defeating the United States in the finale.

Will we ever see a *real* World Series? If so, when? In this generation? The next?

Japan's economic miracle, which surprised the world, suggests that one thing is certain—don't bet on anything.

Pennant Winners: Central League

YEAR		TEAM	WON	LOST	PCT.
1937	SPRING	YOMIURI GIANTS	41	13	.759
	FALL	HANSHIN TIGERS	39	9	.813
1938	SPRING	HANSHIN TIGERS	29	6	.829
	FALL	YOMIURI GIANTS	30	9	.769
1939		YOMIURI GIANTS	66	26	.717
1940		YOMIURI GIANTS	76	28	.731
1941		YOMIURI GIANTS	62	22	.738
1942		YOMIURI GIANTS	73	27	.730
1943		YOMIURI GIANTS	54	27	.667
1944		HANSHIN TIGERS	27	6	.818
1945		PLAY SUSPENDED			
1946		GREATRING	65	38	.631
1947		HANSHIN TIGERS	79	37	.681
1948		NANKAI	87	49	.640
1949		YOMIURI GIANTS	85	48	.639
1950		SHOCHIKU ROBINS	98	35	.737
1951		YOMIURI GIANTS	79	29	.731
1952		YOMIURI GIANTS	83	37	.692
1953		YOMIURI GIANTS	87	37	.702
1954		CHUNICHI DRAGONS	86	40	.683
1955		YOMIURI GIANTS	92	37	.713
1956		YOMIURI GIANTS	82	44	.646
1957		YOMIURI GIANTS	74	53	.581
1958		YOMIURI GIANTS	77	52	.596
1959		YOMIURI GIANTS	77	48	.612
1960		TAYIO WHALES	70	56	.554
1961		YOMIURI GIANTS	71	53	.569

YEAR	TEAM	WON	LOST	PCT.
1962	HANSHIN TIGERS	75	55	.577
1963	YOMIURI GIANTS	83	55	.601
1964	HANSHIN TIGERS	80	56	.588
1965	YOMIURI GIANTS	91	47	.659
1966	YOMIURI GIANTS	89	41	.685
1967	YOMIURI GIANTS	84	46	.646
1968	YOMIURI GIANTS	77	53	.592
1969	YOMIURI GIANTS	73	51	.589
1970	YOMIURI GIANTS	79	47	.627
1971	YOMIURI GIANTS	70	52	.574
1972	YOMIURI GIANTS	74	52	.587
1973	YOMIURI GIANTS	66	60	.524
1974	CHUNICHI DRAGONS	70	49	.588
1975	HIROSHIMA CARP	72	47	.605
1976	YOMIURI GIANTS	76	45	.628
1977	YOMIURI GIANTS	80	46	.635
1978	YAKULT SWALLOWS	68	46	.596
1979	HIROSHIMA CARP	67	73	.573
1980	HIROSHIMA CARP	73	44	.624
1981	YOMIURI GIANTS	73	48	.603
1982	CHUNICHI DRAGONS	64	47	.577
1983	YOMIURI GIANTS	72	50	.590
1984	HIROSHIMA CARP	75	45	.625
1985	HANSHIN TIGERS	74	49	.602
1986	HIROSHIMA CARP	73	46	.613
1987	YOMIURI GIANTS	76	43	.639

Pennant Winners: Pacific League

YEAR		TEAM	WON	LOST	PCT.	YEAR		TEAM	WON	LOST	PCT.
1950		MAINICHI ORIONS	81	34	.704		2nd HALF	HANKYU BRAVES	43	19	.694
1951		NANKAI HAWKS	72	24	.750	1974	1st HALF	HANKYU BRAVES	36	23	.610
1952		NANKAI HAWKS	76	44	.633		2nd HALF	*LOTTE ORIONS	38	23	.623
1953		NANKAI HAWKS	71	48	.597	1975	1st HALF	*HANKYU BRAVES	38	25	.603
1954		NISHITETSU LIONS	90	47	.657		2nd HALF	KINTETSU BUFFALOES	40	20	.667
1955		NANKAI HAWKS	99	41	.707	1976	1st HALF	KINTETSU BUFFALOES	42	21	.667
1956		NISHITETSU LIONS	96	51	.646		2nd HALF	*HANKYU BRAVES	37	24	.607
1957		NISHITETSU LIONS	83	44	.648	1977	1st HALF	*HANKYU BRAVES	35	25	.583
1958		NISHITETSU LIONS	78	47	.619		2nd HALF	LOTTE ORIONS	33	24	.579
1959		NANKAI HAWKS	88	42	.677	1978	1st HALF	HANKYU BRAVES	44	20	.688
1960		DAIMAI ORIONS	82	48	.631		2nd HALF	HANKYU BRAVES	38	19	.667
1961		NANKAI HAWKS	85	49	.629	1979	1st HALF	*KINTETSU BUFFALOES	39	19	.672
1962		TOEI FLYERS	78	52	.600		2nd HALF	HANKYU BRAVES	36	23	.610
1963		NISHITETSU LIONS	86	60	.589	1980	1st HALF	LOTTE ORIONS	33	25	.569
1964		NANKAI HAWKS	84	63	.571		2nd HALF	*KINTETSU BUFFALOES	35	26	.574
1965		NANKAI HAWKS	88	49	.642	1981	1st HALF	LOTTE ORIONS	35	26	.574
1966		NANKAI HAWKS	79	51	.608		2nd HALF	*NIPPON HAM FIGHTERS	37	23	.617
1967		HANKYU BRAVES	75	55	.577	1982	1st HALF	NISHITETSU LIONS	36	27	.571
1968		HANKYU BRAVES	80	50	.615		2nd HALF	*NIPPON HAM FIGHTERS	35	23	.603
1969		HANKYU BRAVES	76	50	.603	1983		NISHITETSU LIONS	86	40	.683
1970		LOTTE ORIONS	80	47	.630	1984		HANKYU BRAVES	75	45	.625
1971		HANKYU BRAVES	80	39	.672	1985		NISHITETSU LIONS	79	45	.637
1972		HANKYU BRAVES	80	48	.625	1986		NISHITETSU LIONS	68	49	.581
1973	1st HALF	*NANKAI HAWKS	38	26	.594	1987		NISHITETSU LIONS	71	45	.612

*playoff winner

Japan Series

YEAR	TEAM/LEAGUE	WON	TEAM/LEAGUE	WON		YEAR	TEAM/LEAGUE	WON	TEAM/LEAGUE	WON	
1950	MAINICHI ORIONS, PL	4	SCOCHIKU ROBINS, CL	2		1970	YOMIURI GIANTS, CL	4	DAIMAI ORIONS, PL	1	
1951	YOMIURI GIANTS, CL	4	NANKAI HAWKS, PL	1		1971	YOMIURI GIANTS, CL	4	HANKYU BRAVES, PL	1	
1952	YOMIURI GIANTS, CL	4	NANKAI HAWKS, PL	2		1972	YOMIURI GIANTS, CL	4	HANKYU BRAVES, PL	1	
1953	YOMIURI GIANTS, CL	4	NANKAI HAWKS, PL	2	1 TIE	1973	YOMIURI GIANTS, CL	4	NANKAI HAWKS, PL	1	
1954	CHUNICHI DRAGONS, CL	4	NISHITETSU LIONS, PL	3		1974	LOTTE ORIONS, PL	4	CHUNICHI DRAGONS, CL	2	
1955	YOMIURI GIANTS, CL	4	NANKAI HAWKS, PL	3		1975	HANKYU BRAVES, PL	4	HIROSHIMA CARP, CL	0	2 TIES
1956	NISHITETSU LIONS, PL	4	YOMIURI GIANTS, CL	2		1976	HANKYU BRAVES, PL	4	YOMIURI GIANTS, CL	3	
1957	NISHITETSU LIONS, PL	4	YOMIURI GIANTS, CL	0	1 TIE	1977	HANKYU BRAVES, PL	4	YOMIURI GIANTS, CL	1	
1958	NISHITETSU LIONS, PL	4	YOMIURI GIANTS, CL	3		1978	YAKULT SWALLOWS, CL	4	HANKYU BRAVES, PL	3	
1959	NANKAI HAWKS, PL	4	YOMIURI GIANTS, CL	0		1979	HIROSHIMA CARP, CL	4	KINTETSU BUFFALOES, PL	3	
1960	TAYIO WHALES, CL	4	DAIMAI ORIONS, PL	0		1980	HIROSHIMA CARP, CL	4	KINTETSU BUFFALOES, PL	3	
1961	YOMIURI GIANTS, CL	4	NANKAI HAWKS, PL	2		1981	YOMIURI GIANTS, CL	4	NIPPON HAM FIGHTERS, PL	2	
1962	TOKYO FLYERS, PL	4	HANSHIN TIGERS, CL	2	1 TIE						
1963	YOMIURI GIANTS, CL	4	NISHITETSU LIONS, PL	3		1982	NISHITETSU LIONS, PL	4	CHUNICHI DRAGONS, CL	2	
1964	NANKAI HAWKS, PL	4	HANSHIN TIGERS	3		1983	NISHITETSU LIONS, PL	4	YOMUIRI GIANTS, CL	3	
1965	YOMIURI GIANTS, CL	4	NANKAI HAWKS, PL	1		1984	HIROSHIMA CARP, CL	4	HANYKU BRAVES, PL	3	
1966	YOMIURI GIANTS, CL	4	NANKAI HAWKS, PL	2		1985	HANSHIN TIGERS, CL	4	NISHITETSU LIONS, PL	2	
1967	YOMIURI GIANTS, CL	4	HANKYU BRAVES, PL	2		1986	NISHITETSU LIONS, PL	4	HIROSHIMA CARP, CL	3	1 TIE
1968	YOMIURI GIANTS, CL	4	HANKYU BRAVES, PL	2		1987	NISHITETSU LIONS, PL	4	YOMIURI GIANTS, CL	2	
1969	YOMIURI GIANTS, CL	4	HANKYU BRAVES, PL	2							

U.S. Major League Batters in Japan

Name	Yrs		G	HR	BA	Titles Won	Name	Yrs		G	HR	BA	Titles Won
Adair, Jerry	1	1971	90	7	.300		Corey, Mark	1	1984	31	3	.215	
Adduci, Jim	1	1987	82	13	.268		Cosey, Ray	1	1981	120	15	.251	
Allen, Kim	2	1982-83	125	5	.265		Cromartie, Warren	4	1984-87	489	132	.315	
Alou, Matty	3	1974-76	262	14	.283		Cruz, Hector	1	1983	58	4	.240	
Altman, George	8	1968-75	935	205	.309		Cruz, Tommy	6	1980-85	712	120	.310	
Andrews, Mike	2	1975-76	123	12	.231		Dade, Paul	1	1981	37	1	.219	
Arnold, Chris	3	1978-81	330	43	.274		Davis, Dick	4	1984-87	419	110	.334	
Aspromonte, Ken	3	1964-66	295	31	.273		Davis, Willie	2	1977-78	199	43	.297	
Ault, Doug	1	1981	102	18	.307		Doby, Larry	1	1962	72	10	.225	
Barbier, Jim	1	1970	93	9	.188		Doyle, Jeff	2	1984-85	243	29	.263	
Bass, Randy	5	1983-87	592	200	.337	85-86 hr-ba-rbi	Duncan, Taylor	1	1980	64	14	.235	
Batista, Rafael	1	1975	48	3	.204		Dupree, Mike	1	1980	127	10	.266	
Baumer, Jim	5	1963-67	690	82	.251		Edwards, Mike	1	1983	53	1	.291	
Bertoia, Reno	1	1964	20	1	.175		Emery, Carvin	1	1970	94	8	.213	
Blasingame, Don	3	1967-69	366	15	.274		Essegian, Chuck	1	1964	110	15	.263	
Boisclair, Bruce	1	1980	80	1	.249		Ewing, Sam	1	1979	119	15	.286	
Boles, Carl	6	1966-71	577	117	.265		Fernandez, Chico	1	1965	52	1	.144	
Boyer, Clete	4	1972-75	419	71	.257		Gaines, Joe	1	1969	51	3	.225	
Bradford, Buddy	1	1956	56	4	.192		Gardner, Art	2	1981-82	218	32	.272	
Brant, Marshall	2	1984-85	118	25	.244		Garrett, Adrian	3	1977-79	384	102	.260	
Breedon, Hal	3	1976-78	260	79	.251		Garrett, Wayne	2	1969-70	192	28	.241	
Brewer, Tony	2	1986-87	259	55	.312		Gentile, Jim	1	1979	65	8	.256	
Briggs, John	1	1976	40	7	.227		Gonzales, Dan	1	1981	9	1	.174	
Brouhard, Mark	2	1986-87	140	23	.265		Gonzalez, Tony	1	1972	31	0	.279	
Budaska, Mark	1	1982	86	14	.222		Goodwin, Danny	1	1986	83	8	.231	
Buford, Don	4	1973-76	490	65	.270		Green, David	1	1986	67	10	.270	
Cage, Wayne	2	1981-82	252	62	.235		Grunwald, Alfred	1	1962	70	3	.211	
Chance, Bob	2	1969-70	143	22	.271		Hadley, Kent	6	1962-67	781	131	.260	
Christian, Bob	2	1971-72	232	27	.263		Hammond, Steve	1	1987	115	9	.274	
Coggins, Frank	1	1973	13	2	.125		Hampton, Ike	1	1981	72	15	.232	

Name	Yrs		G	HR	BA	Titles Won
Hansen, Jimmy	2	1977-78	232	31	.271	
Harlow, Larry	1	1982	42	4	.164	
Harris, Vic	3	1981-83	280	35	.233	
Hicks, Jim	2	1973-74	183	33	.247	
Hilton, Dave	3	1978-80	251	38	.284	
Horner, Bob	1	1987	93	31	.327	
Hopkins, Gail	3	1975-77	360	69	.289	
Hostetler, Dave	2	1986-87	254	42	.270	
Howard, Frank	1	1974	1	0	.000	
Ireland, Tom	2	1983-84	204	18	.275	
Jackson, Lou	3	1966-68	329	68	.257	
James, Skip	1	1980	111	21	.269	
Jestadt, Garry	2	1975-76	236	27	.239	
Johnson, Dave	2	1975-76	199	39	.241	
Johnson, Frank	1	1972	101	13	.232	
Johnson, Greg	1	1982	104	10	.256	
Johnson, Randall	1	1987	101	6	.319	
Johnson, Stan	1	1969	96	5	.242	
Jones, Bobby	2	1979-80	174	10	.284	
Jones, Clarence	8	1970-77	961	246	.239	75, 76 hr
Keough, Marty	1	1968	134	17	.231	
Kirkland, Willie	6	1968-73	703	126	.246	
Kostro, Frank	1	1970	37	1	.200	
Klaus, Billy	1	1963	62	3	.257	
Krsnich, Mike	5	1963-67	506	90	.265	
Lacock, Pete	1	1981	90	12	.269	
Larker, Norm	2	1965-66	224	14	.267	
Lancellotti, Rich	1	1987	121	39	.218	87 hr
Lee, Leron	10	1978-87	1315	283	.320	80 ba, 77 hr-rbi
Lefebvre, Jim	4	1973-76	330	60	.263	
Lezcano, Sixto	1	1987	20	3	.217	
Lind, Jack	1	1977	65	7	.237	
Lis, Joe	1	1978	95	6	.206	
Llenas, Wionston	1	1976	101	6	.227	
Locklear, Gene	1	1978	108	8	.240	
Logan, Johnny	1	1964	96	7	.189	
Lolich, Ron	3	1974-76	272	56	.238	
Lopez, Arturo	6	1968-73	750	116	.290	
Loman, Doug	1	1986	126	14	.291	
Lytle, Jim	7	1977-83	876	166	.285	
Macha, Ken	4	1982-85	473	82	.304	
Manuel, Charlie	6	1976-81	621	189	.303	79-80 hr, 80 rbi
Marshall, Jim	3	1963-65	408	78	.268	
Martin, Gene	6	1974-79	746	189	.272	
May, Carlos	4	1978-81	415	70	.309	
McFadden, Leon	1	1972	54	2	.283	
McGuire, Mickey	2	1973-74	207	11	.265	
McManus, Jim	2	1962-63	190	20	.236	
McNulty, Bill	1	1975	64	13	.190	
Mejias, Roman	1	1966	30	0	.288	
Millan, Felix	3	1978-80	325	12	.306	79 ba
Miller, John	3	1970-72	382	79	.245	
Mitchell, Bobby	4	1976-79	474	113	.250	78 hr
Money, Don	1	1984	29	8	.260	
Morton, Bubba	1	1970	48	3	.173	
Muser, Tony	1	1979	65	2	.196	
Nettles, Jim	1	1975	84	3	.234	
Newcombe, Don	1	1962	81	12	.262	
Nieman, Bob	1	1963	110	13	.301	
Nyman, Chris	2	1984-85	246	55	.276	
Oglivie, Ben	1	1987	110	24	.300	
Ontiveros, Steve	6	1980-85	686	82	.312	
Ortenzio, Frank	2	1979-80	149	30	.250	

Name	Yrs		G	HR	BA	Titles Won
Parker, Wes	1	1974	127	14	.301	
Patterson, Mike	1	1985	88	16	.225	
Palys, Stan	4	1964-67	446	66	.275	
Pepitone, Joe	1	1973	14	1	.163	
Perlozzo, Sam	1	1980	118	15	.281	
Peterson, Carl	3	1961-63	357	58	.272	
Pierce, Jack	1	1977	95	13	.227	
Pointer, Aaron	3	1970-72	302	40	.230	
Ponce, Carlos	2	1986-87	258	62	.320	87 rbi
Putnam, Pat	2	1986-87	243	37	.266	
Qualls, Jimmy	2	1972-73	162	15	.253	
Raines, Larry	3	1953-55	330	31	.302	54 ba, 53 sb
Rajsich, Gary	2	1986-87	216	60	.278	
Reinback, Mike	5	1976-80	565	94	.296	
Repoz, Roger	5	1973-77	526	122	.262	
Rivera, Bombo	2	1985-86	158	37	.240	
Roberts, Dave	7	1967-73	814	183	.275	
Rodgers, Andre	1	1969	49	4	.210	
Roig, Tony	6	1963-68	779	126	.255	
Rosario, Jim	2	1975-76	131	5	.215	
Scheinblum, Rich	2	1975-76	239	33	.295	
Scott, John	3	1979-81	279	48	.262	
Shirley, Bart	2	1971-72	246	15	.183	
Sipin, John	9	1972-80	1036	218	.297	
Smith, Chris	2	1984-85	68	5	.202	
Smith, Reggie	2	1983-84	186	45	.271	
Smith, Willie	2	1972-73	170	29	.259	
Solaita, Tony	4	1979-82	510	155	.268	81 hr-rbi
Sorrell, Bill	2	1972-73	183	20	.278	
Spencer, Daryl	7	1964-70	731	152	.275	
Spikes, Charlie	1	1981	26	1	.122	
Stanton, Leroy	1	1979	121	23	.225	
Stephens, Gene	1	1966	109	5	.224	
Stroughter, Steve	1	1983	28	5	.276	
Stuart, Dick	2	1967-68	208	49	.257	
Tatum, Jarvis	1	1971	31	1	.192	
Taylor, Robert	3	1973-75	358	30	.259	
Testa, Nick	1	1962	57	0	.136	
Thomas, Lee	1	1969	109	12	.263	
Thomasson, Gary	2	1981-82	167	20	.249	
Tolan, Bobby	1	1978	98	6	.267	
Tracy, Jim	2	1983-84	128	20	.301	
Tyrone, Jim	4	1979-82	435	74	.287	
Valentine, Fred	1	1970	123	11	.246	
Versalles, Zoilo	1	1972	48	4	.189	
Vidal, Jose	1	1971	39	2	.221	
Vukovich, George	2	1986-87	222	32	.256	
Walls, Lee	1	1965	108	14	.239	
Walton, Danny	1	1978	75	9	.215	
Ward, Jay	1	1966	104	14	.238	
Wells, Greg	5	1983-87	634	170	.334	84 hr-ba-rbi, 87 rbi
Werhas, Johnny	1	1971	100	8	.214	
Whitfield, Terry	3	1981-83	374	85	.289	
White, Roy	3	1979-81	362	54	.283	
Williams, Bernie	6	1975-80	718	96	.258	
Williams, Walt	2	1976-77	239	44	.277	
Wills, Bump	2	1983-84	203	16	.259	
Wilson, George	2	1963-64	225	27	.258	
Windhorn, Gordon	6	1964-69	641	86	.255	
Wolfe, Larry	1	1982	88	14	.224	
Woods, Ron	2	1975-76	192	19	.263	
Zimmer, Don	1	1966	87	9	.182	

U.S. Major League Pitchers in Japan*

Name	Yrs		Won-Lost	ERA
Alexander, Bob	1	1959	2-5	4.67
Austin, Rich	1	1974	1-1	2.33
Beene, Andy	1	1985	2-2	7.25
Burnside, Pete	2	1964-65	10-22	3.10
Castillo, Bobby	1	1987	1-1	7.84
Comstock, Keith	2	1985-86	8-10	4.47
Culver, George	1	1975	1-4	6.50
Foytack, Paul	1	1964	2-3	3.16
Gail, Rich	2	1985-86	18-18	4.42
Grunwald, Alfred	1	1962	2-8	4.50
Kekich, Mike	1	1974	no record	
Keough, Matt	1	1987	11-14	3.80
Kiely, Leo	1	1953	6-0	1.80
Krueger, Rich	1	1979	2-1	4.66
Kuhaulua, Fred	1	1978	3-4	4.32
Lesley, Brad	2	1986-87	7-5	3.00
Ley, Richard	2	1974-75	5-5	4.09
Mickens, Glenn	5	1959-63	45-51	2.50

Name	Yrs		Won-Lost	ERA
Newcombe, Don	1	1962	0-0	4.50
Paine, Phil	1	1953	4-3	1.77
Palmquist, Ed	1	1963	0-1	3.00
Rajsich, David	1	1983	0-0	3.18
Reynolds, Bob	1	1977	0-0	9.00
Sanchez, Luis	2	1986-87	4-4	2.54
Shirley, Steve	2	1983-84	5-7	4.17
Smith, Willie	1	1972	0-1	81.00
Stanka, Joe	7	1960-66	100-72	3.03
Stone, Dean	1	1964	0-0	3.75
Tillotson, Thad	1	1971	3-4	6.40
Wright, Clyde	3	1975-78	10-22	3.97
TOTALS			254-268	

* Lists compiled from Graczyk, Wayne, *Americans in Japan 1950-1986*, and Chiba, Isao, "Kiroko no Techno (Record Notes)", *Shukan Baseball* March 28, 1988 and April 4, 1988.

CHAPTER 26

Baseball in the Caribbean

Rob Ruck

Soon after the World Series marks the season's end in the United States, baseball springs back to life in and around the Caribbean. There, to the beat of *salsa* and *merengue* and against a backdrop of palm trees and seasonal labor, some of the best baseball in the world is played each winter. While most of South America follows football and the British West Indies follows cricket, the rest of the Caribbean basin plays baseball—and has for the better part of a century.

Since baseball fever first infected Cuba in the 1870s, the game has infiltrated the sporting psyches of Mexico, Nicaragua, the Dominican Republic, Venezuela, Puerto Rico, Panama, and Colombia. Although tied to major league baseball in four of these countries through a set of winter leagues and as a source of fresh talent, Caribbean baseball is not simply an appendage of the game that is played in the United States. Rather, baseball has acquired an autonomous persona as the peoples of the region have made the game into their own national pastimes.

More than simply recreation or a display of grace and competence, baseball has catalyzed national consciousness and cohesion in the Caribbean basin. A critical part of the fabric of everyday life, the sport has also influenced how these societies have come to define themselves, their relations with each other, and their ties to the United States. "It's more than a game," Dominican winter league manager Winston Llenas once remarked. "It's our passion. It's almost our way of life."

Pedro Julio Santana stands at his office window in what was once the colonial zone of Santo Domingo. A sportsman at the center of Dominican baseball's evolution earlier this century, he searches for words to describe how the game penetrated his country and the rest of the basin. Glancing below to the hulking walls of the first Catholic cathedral in the western hemisphere, Santana finds his metaphor. "It is much the same as that which happened with Christianity. Jesus could be compared to the North Americans, but the apostles were the ones that spread the faith, and the apostles of baseball were Cubans. Even though the Dominican Republic and Puerto Rico were occupied by the North Americans, the Cubans first brought baseball here, and to Mexico and Venezuela, too."

Caribbean baseball's first epicenter was Cuba, which had fallen into orbit around the United States by the late nineteenth century. Baseball arrived there last century, brought by sailors, students, and businessmen from the United States as well as by Cubans who had traveled north. The U.S. military occupations that followed the 1898 conflict with Spain stimulated baseball's expansion there and across the basin. By the time the Good Neighbor Policy had supplanted the Big Stick in the 1930s, baseball was entrenched. Moreover, Cuban baseball had become the focal point of an international network that stretched from the Caribbean basin through the Negro Leagues.

What was likely the first ballgame in Cuba with local participation occurred in June 1866, when sailors of a U.S. ship taking on sugar invited Cuban longshoremen to play. *El Club Habana* (Havana) began two years later, crushing a team from Matanzas in the first organized contest of two Cuban teams.

Havana's victory over Matanzas featured two of Cuba's sporting pioneers, Esteban Bellan and Emilio Sabourín. Bellan became the first Latino in U.S. organized baseball, playing three seasons in the National Association (1871–1873). Sabourín, the A. G. Spalding of Cuban baseball, was the motivating force behind the *Liga de Beisbol Profesional Cubana,* whose inaugural tournament was won by Sabourín's reconstituted Havana club in 1878. Sabourín proselytized for his sport as well as for the cause of Cuban independence from Spain until his contribution of baseball revenues to the independence movement incurred the wrath of Spanish officials. They imprisoned Sabourín until his death and banned baseball in parts of their colony.

While initially a game of the more affluent and those with contact with the United States, baseball soon spread to all classes of Cuban society, both urban and rural. U.S. military occupations, support by companies and businessmen, and close ties to political elites would shape its subsequent development, much as these forces would elsewhere in the basin.

The game was organized on three overlapping levels in its early years. The first was an ad hoc player-organized, self-directed network of teams. The second involved clubs sponsored by businessmen, companies, and politicians who sought the promotional advantages of such patronage. The third level was that of professional (sometimes semiprofessional) baseball, which organized championships from 1878 until 1961, with a changing cast of teams and format. In some years, no tournaments were held, while in others both a summer and winter season took place. Havana, Almendares, Santa Clara, Cienfuegos, and Marianao were the league's mainstays.

Until the 1959 Cuban Revolution and the ensuing U.S. blockade, Cuba set the standard for Caribbean baseball. It sent the most players to the major and Negro leagues while its winter and summer tournaments featured the highest caliber of Latin ball and attracted players from both the States and the basin. Cuban players, radio broadcasts, and emigrants, in turn, became baseball's emissaries to the rest of the region.

In the Dominican Republic, Cubans who had migrated to escape the turmoil of the Ten Years' War (1868–1878) were the first to form teams. Young Dominicans emulated them

and joined with compatriots who had studied in the United States to establish a self-organized matrix of teams and tournaments well in place before the U.S. Marines arrived in 1916 for their eight-year occupation. Santo Domingo's *Licey,* the oldest of the six professional Dominican clubs, formed in 1907, while the forerunners of San Pedro de Macoris's *Estrellas Orientales,* Santiago's *Aguilas Cibaeñas,* and Santo Domingo's other club, *Escogido,* took to the field soon afterward.

While Dominicans refer to these early decades as the romantic epoch of baseball, commercial forces were already at work there and across the basin. Teams occasionally recruited players with the lure of financial reward and soon began importing Cubans and Puerto Ricans for championship tournaments. Moreover, local clubs often induced talented players with payment in cash or work. North American oil companies in Venezuela, rum distilleries and tobacco manufacturers in Cuba, and sugar cane companies in Nicaragua, Puerto Rico, Cuba, and the Dominican Republic sponsored or assisted workplace teams for recreation and community entertainment, but with an industrial agenda, too — winning their workers' hearts and minds.

During these "Yankee years," between 1898 and 1933, when the Marines hit the beaches thirty-four times in ten different basin countries, they found baseball already implanted in Cuba, Puerto Rico, Nicaragua, Mexico, and the Dominican Republic. They never made it to Venezuela, but would have found baseball there, too, as early as the organization of the Caracas club in 1895. The occupations, though, helped to push the sport along. While Nicaraguans had played on their Atlantic coast since 1888, the nation's longest-running pro team, *Boer,* was founded by the U.S. consul in Managua. In the Dominican Republic, U.S. marines and sailors played ball to bolster morale; they were frequently challenged by Dominican teams, for whom these contests were both a test of sporting abilities and national character. Far more baseball was in evidence by the end of the U.S. stay on the island.

While Cubans and some other basin natives had broken into baseball in the States during the first half of the century, the center of gravity for Caribbean baseball remained a regional one. A "Have Glove—Will Travel" mentality soon took hold of basin baseball and its ablest practitioners made the rounds of national tournaments. A core of the finest black players from the States—then barred from major league play by the color line, as were most Latinos—joined them in Cuba, the Dominican Republic, Puerto Rico, Venezuela, and Mexico.

Caribbean baseball's apogee was probably reached in the summer of 1937 in the Dominican Republic during a national championship dedicated to the re-election of the then state-of-the-art dictator Rafael Trujillo. Top Dominican players were joined by the best Cuban, Puerto Rican, and Negro league talent that the Dominican peso could buy to form a three-team league. Santiago boasted the services of Martín Dihigo, Luís Tiant Sr., and Horacio Martínez; San Pedro de Macoris countered with Tetelo Vargas, Ramón Bragaña, and Cocaína García, while the eventual victor, *Ciudad Trujillo* (a merger of *Licey* and *Escogido* that represented the city Trujillo had renamed in his own honor) relied on future Hall of Famers Josh Gibson, Cool Papa Bell, and Satchel Paige, as well as Silvío García, Perucho Cepeda, and Sam Bankhead. Baseball on the island was the equal of that played anywhere that summer. These players barnstormed year-round, and many of them later played together as *Santa Clara* in Cuba and as *La Concordia* in Venezuela.

The proprietary interest taken by caudillos such as Trujillo or Nicaragua's Anastasio Somoza ensured baseball of its most-favored sport status and contributed to the growth of strong regional rivalries. Caribbean participation in the *Mundiales,* the world amateur baseball championships that began in 1938, and later the Caribbean Series of pro circuits, which started in 1949, reinforced the game's hegemony.

Latin ball was an opportunity for North American players to supplement their income and hone their skills in encounters that sometimes surpassed the caliber of major league play. However, it was also a threat to organized baseball in the States. Major league teams had played in Cuba before the turn of the century, and afterward Negro league squads as well as individual black and white pros journeyed south. The 1937 raids on the Negro leagues by Dominican teams destroyed the Pittsburgh Crawfords, and other Negro league squads frequently lost their best players and gate attractions to basin teams. From 1939 until the demise of independent black baseball a decade later, Venezuelan and Mexican franchises vied for Negro leaguers during the summer months, enticing Josh Gibson, Ray Dandridge, and other stars to jump their Negro league teams. They offered better pay and a different atmosphere. "Not only do I get more money playing here, but I live like a king," Willie Wells wrote to *Pittsburgh Courier* sportswriter Wendell Smith in 1939 to explain his switch from the Newark Eagles to Vera Cruz. "I am not faced with the racial problem. . . . I've found freedom and democracy here, something I never found in the United States. . . . Here, in Mexico, I am a man."

The major leagues were less vulnerable to such competition, but even they blanched when Mexican liquor mogul Jorge Pasquel sought major leaguers in addition to Negro leaguers to bolster the six-team summer Mexican League in 1946. Railroad workers from the States taught the game to their Mexican colleagues as early as the 1880s and a strong semipro league formed in the 1920s. In Sonora and Mexico City, the game felt the pull of baseball across the northern border, which Mexican and black teams frequently crossed. In the Yucatan, baseball pointed more toward the Caribbean, especially Cuba. Pasquel, pumping new capital into the league, persuaded Mickey Owens, Sal Maglie, and Max Lanier to desert their major league teams, prompting the latter to ban them. Pasquel also pursued Stan Musial, reportedly placing $50,000 on the bed in his spring training hotel room at a time when the Cardinals' outfielder was making but $13,000 a season. Other basin leagues also lost top players in the Mexican effort to upgrade. Pasquel's challenge, however, was blunted by organized baseball in the States, which tried to limit any competition for its players, and by the Mexican League's own logistical and financial difficulties. The challenge faded after the 1948 season. In the aftermath of the Mexican raids and with integration imminent, major league baseball began to sign accords with professional leagues throughout the basin, formalizing player movement and institutionalizing winter play.

That was especially important, for with the end of the color line in 1947 Latinos soon renewed their assault on major league ball. By the 1970s, the basin would constitute the freshest source of talent in the majors, especially important as the black community turned away from baseball as part of a general shift toward other sports in the United States. But

Latin players—black and white—had played pro ball in the United States long before Jackie Robinson's historic debut.

Colombia's Luis Castro broke ground in baseball's modern era, after the creation of the National and American Leagues, but Cubans for the most part led the way. While Castro played only part of the 1902 season, Rafael Almeida and Armando Marsans spearheaded a Cuban invasion in 1911 that left its imprimatur on the game and numbered over thirty players before integration. Another ninety or so Cubans played major league ball after that divide.

The crucial factor controlling the entry of Cubans and other basin players into the major leagues was skin color. Barnstorming their way through black communities from the early century on, Cuban teams had become a mainstay of the Negro leagues that began in 1920. Popular draws, the Cuban Stars and the New York Cubans featured Latinos too dark to pass the color line into the majors. Playing most of their contests on the road, these Caribbean squads injected talent and a tropical allure to the game. Cubans Martín Dihigo, Alejandro Oms, Luís Tiant Sr., Orestes "Minnie" Miñoso, and Silvío García were joined by Dominicans Horacio Martínez and Tetelo Vargas, Puerto Rican Peruchin Cepeda, Panamanian Pat Scantlebury, and sometimes several black North Americans who passed for Cubans, on these pan-Caribbean aggregations. A few Cubans, such as Cristóbal Torriente, a powerful outfielder, and José de la Caridad Méndez, *"El Diamante Negro,"* who took a no-hitter into the ninth inning the first time he faced the barnstorming Cincinnati Reds, became mainstays of other Negro league franchises.

Lighter-skinned Cubans from that predominantly mixed island played on the other side of sport's racial boundary in the States, in the major leagues. Perhaps the greatest pre–Jackie Robinson Cuban major leaguer was Adolfo Luque, a pitcher whose twenty big league seasons were capped by a brilliant 27–8 record in 1923 and a winning relief stint of shutout ball in the seventh game of the 1933 World Series. Following that game, Clark Griffith, whose Washington Senators had lost the Series, decided to back a scouting exhibition to Cuba. He sent Joe Cambria.

"Papa Joe," as many still refer to Cambria, stocked the Senators with Cubans. Among his first signees was Roberto Estalella, from the sugarcane milltown that Hershey Chocolate operated in Cárdenas. The *Cincinnati Enquirer* had greeted the signings of Almeida and Marsans in 1911 with relief, introducing them as "two of the purest bars of Castilian soap to ever wash upon our shores," but the darker-hued Estalella was more controversial. No one challenged this indirect breaching of the color line, although it prompted Red Smith to write his classic column in which he suspected that "there was a Senegambian somewhere in the Cuban batpile where Senatorial lumber was seasoned."

The player regarded in the Caribbean as the best Cuban ever, and arguably the finest ballplayer of all time, never played major league ball. Martín Dihigo displayed his talents in Cuba, the United States, Mexico, Venezuela, and the Dominican Republic, and is enshrined in their respective Halls of Fame. Dihigo excelled at the plate, on the mound, and as a manager, but integration came too late for him. His bust at Havana's *Estadio Latinoamericano* reads simply, *El Inmortal.*

The contradiction that some Cubans played in the majors and others in the Negro leagues was not lost upon blacks in the States or on Latin ballplayers. As early as Almeida's and Marsans' 1911 debut, the black press began to hope that black ballplayers would soon follow them into baseball's most exclusive league. And while Negro leaguers went south to adulation and greater pay, dark-skinned Latinos who came north encountered prejudice based on both skin color and nationality. As major leaguers such as Ty Cobb, Tris Speaker, and Carl Hubbell traveled south to play in winter ball, black North Americans and Latinos found that they could more than hold their own. These symbolic victories were appreciated both in the States and throughout the basin. North American blacks and the peoples of the region shared each other's athletes and appropriated each other's sporting heroes and symbols. If a proving ground was necessary to show that blacks could compete with whites, that the two could coexist on the same squad, or to dispel any other racial shibboleth, Caribbean baseball was just that.

Following integration, the more farsighted owners began scouring the islands for prospects. Soon a fresh wave of Latinos arrived in the majors, including three future Hall of Famers: Venezuela's Luís Aparicio, Puerto Rico's Roberto Clemente, and the Dominican Republic's Juan Marichal. They signaled, moreover, a shift away from Cuba as the primary spawning waters for Caribbean players.

With the 1959 Cuban Revolution and the subsequent deterioration of relations with the United States, Cuba fell out of organized baseball's system. The Havana Sugar Kings, an International League franchise affiliated with the Reds since 1954, were on their way to winning the Little World Series of the AAA minor leagues in 1959, just months after Fidel Castro came to power. The revolutionary government offered to underwrite the Sugar Kings' debts, and Castro sought to keep the franchise there, "even if I have to pitch," but the International League shipped the club to Jersey City during the 1960 season. Baseball in Cuba was cut off completely from baseball in the United States, and the movement of players and equipment halted. Cuba developed its own sporting goods industry and relied on the repatriated Dihigo, a political exile during the 1950s who had given money to Che Guevara and who now returned to help teach the game. Cuban baseball soon shed its commercial skin and sought instead to advance the social and political aims of the revolution. Cuba has remained *the* powerhouse in world amateur baseball ever since, but the island stopped producing new major leaguers. After the Zoilo Versalles, Tony Oliva, Tony Pérez generations passed out of baseball, the next set of Cubans to reach the majors were those who, while born on the island, had grown up in the United States.

The fulcrum of baseball power, meanwhile, shifted one island to the east, where the Dominican Republic shared Hispaniola with French-speaking, soccer-playing Haiti. After the star-studded 1937 season, pro ball in the Dominican Republic entered a fourteen-year hiatus. While an occasional tournament celebrated an event such as the nation's centennial, Dominican pros Horacio Martínez and Tetelo Vargas plied their trade in Cuba, Venezuela, or the United States. But several forces revitalized Dominican baseball in the 1940s, and after the reappearance of a professional league in 1951, these dynamics propelled over a hundred players to the major leagues.

The first catalyst was the birth of the *Mundial,* an international championship tournament for amateur baseball. After its inauguration in England in 1938, the *Mundial* moved to the Caribbean. Held in the basin throughout the 1940s, with

Cuba hosting five consecutive tournaments, the *Mundial* had a decidedly Latin flavor and became the most important sporting competition in which these nations competed on something approximating equal footing, both with each other and with the United States. Basin nations won every championship from 1940 through 1972, with Cuba winning eleven out of eighteen times.

National aspirations and international rivalries sometimes were injected into the *Mundial*. An irate Anastasio Somoza fired the Nicaraguan manager in the midst of one and took to the dugout to direct the team himself. Nicaraguan national honor was restored by a victory over Cuba in the final game of the 1972 series, an event still celebrated as one of the Central American nation's greatest sporting exploits. The Dominican victory in 1948, coming just months after virtually the entire national championship team perished in a plane crash by the Río Verde, captivated the Republic and lent impetus to pro ball's rebirth there.

A second factor in Dominican baseball's rejuvenation was the creation of the *Dirección General de Deportes*. Modeled in part after the comparable Cuban agency, this government body organized regional and then national tournaments for amateur baseball (often with semiprofessional overtones) that gave further purpose to local, company, and armed forces support. Many of the Dominicans that entered the majors from the late 1950s on, including Marichal, Manuel Mota, and the three Rojas Alou brothers, played on these squads.

The final catalysts to Dominican ascendancy were bananas and sugarcane, and the concentrations of baseball fervor and expertise which they fostered. While the sugarcane milltowns of the southeast produce the most prospects today, the banana region along the northwest border with Haiti was instrumental in cultivating the first contingent of pros in the late 1950s. There the Grenada Company, a United Fruit Company subsidiary, began two teams for its workers and their sons in the 1940s. The squad won three national championships, and Juan Marichal and Guayubín Olivo passed through its ranks to the majors.

Dominican sugarcane milltowns, like those in Cuba, had long spawned ballclubs. The six-month long *tiempo muerto,* or dead season, when the cane required minimal attention and most workers were unemployed, contributed to an intense sporting environment, first for cricket and ultimately for baseball. In the 1920s and '30s, *Central La Romana's Papagayo* team was an amateur powerhouse, and in the 1940s the milltowns in and around San Pedro de Macoris made their play. There the descendants of cricket-playing migrants from the British West Indies brought to cut cane and work in the mills displayed an aptitude for playing baseball and an approach to organizing the game that made San Pedro baseball's Mecca. Since Rico Carty's breakthrough in the 1960s, San Pedro has contributed about one-third of the Dominicans to play in the big leagues. The town currently sends more of its native sons to the majors on a per-capita basis than any town ever has. There is probably no other place on earth where the game is played as well and as widely.

Since the end of the color line, ballplayers from Cuba, the Dominican Republic, Venezuela, Puerto Rico, Panama, Nicaragua, Mexico, Colombia, and even the Bahamas have played major league ball. Although the Dominican Republic leads this basin contingent, substantial numbers of Puerto Ricans and Venezuelans are present, too. Mexico, despite a population that dwarfs the rest of the region combined and its

well-developed pro leagues, sends few players to the majors. Unlike the other basin leagues, Mexican teams retain first rights to sign any native amateur. A major league club, therefore, must buy the contract from a player's Mexican club, usually for more than it costs to sign a prospect elsewhere in the region. This relationship, the summer Mexican league, and perhaps cultural factors, too, persuade native ballplayers to remain in Mexico.

Cuba opted out of this network after its revolution, and Nicaragua, whose eleven-year fling with the pro winter leagues ended in 1967, followed suit after its 1979 revolution. Panama and Colombia have also tried winter ball, but financial pressures made play sporadic.

The flow of players continues to run both north and south. Minor and major leaguers from the United States still play in the winter leagues, which presently operate in Venezuela, Puerto Rico, the Dominican Republic, and Mexico. In their heyday during the 1950s and '60s, these winter leagues featured major leaguers like Tommy Lasorda, Whitey Ford, and Willie Stargell. But as a major league salaries soared in the 1970s and unfavorable rates of exchanges weakened basin economies, the winter leagues restricted the number of North American imports. Minor leaguers and inexperienced major leaguers have replaced them. For them, these leagues provide the chance to play in the winter months, developing the potential that might allow them to crack a big league roster. They also earn higher pay than they do in the minors, encounter competition from top Latino players, and are treated as demigods by the impassioned *fanáticos* of the winter game.

The winners of the winter leagues have met in a *Serie del Caribe* since 1949. Between 1949 and 1960, the pennant-winning squads of Cuba, Panama, Puerto Rico, and Venezuela played in early February to determine a champion of the Caribbean. Cuba won over half of these tournaments, but after the revolution, the series was discontinued. When it resumed in 1970, Mexico and the Dominican Republic replaced Cuba and Panama. The current round-robin format sends the teams that win their postseason tournaments to the *Serie del Caribe* along with a number of reinforcements, including North Americans, from their defeated opponents. Willie Mays, Monte Irvin, Camilo Pasqual, Rico Carty, and Vic Pellot Power are among those who have starred in these postseason celebrations.

Winter ball has descended from its zenith of the 1950s and '60s largely due to economic dynamics beyond the control of the Caribbean franchises. Rising player and fuel costs, devalued currencies, and underdevelopment pushed many into deficits, with government subsidies often vital to their continuation. Government support, long a feature of basin baseball, helps to keep current the Dominican saying that there will never be political trouble during the baseball season, only afterward. But by the middle of the 1980s, fewer of the established Latin major leaguers suited up for the October-through-January campaign. The demands of the regular season, the threat of injury, and the relatively inconsequential pay of winter ball suggest that this trend will continue. The pattern, however, has given younger Latin ballplayers the chance to play before knowledgeable fans and against competition that is often at a major league level.

While winter ball in the late 1980s is troubled and other sports are making inroads, baseball remains *el rey de deportes* (the king of sports) throughout the basin. From the rocky hillsides and arid plains of northern Mexico through the

canefields of the islands to the basin's southernmost flank in the Andes, baseball commands a fascination approaching reverence.

Baseball's significance derives from the role that it has played in the coming together of these societies in the twentieth century. Knitting a common cultural fabric, serving as a vent to social and political tensions, and offering a vehicle not only for individual mobility but collective social affirmation, baseball indeed has been more than a game. It has offered the citizens of the basin a chance to enter a ritual kinship embracing all fans and players. And while reflecting the progressive penetration of the United States in the region, baseball has been more than a cultural transmission belt for North American values. Beating each other and excelling in the major leagues and international competitions at a time when the Caribbean basin has encountered difficulties in asserting either its political or economic autonomy have been tremendous sources of pride. And that symbolic recognition has become a catalyst to national cohesion and consciousness for the region in its troubled evolution this century.

First Major Leaguers from Caribbean Basin Countries

Country	Player	Year	Team
Colombia	Luis "Jud" Castro	1902	Philadelphia Athletics
Cuba	Esteban Bellan	1871	Troy Haymakers
	Rafael Almeida	1911	Cincinnati Reds
	Armando Marsans	1911	Cincinnati Reds
Mexico	Baldomero "Mel" Almada	1933	Boston Red Sox
Venezuela	Alejandro Carrasquel	1939	Washington Senators
Puerto Rico	Hiram Bithorn	1942	Chicago Cubs
Panama	Héctor López	1955	Kansas City Athletics
	Humberto Robinson	1955	Milwaukee Braves
Dominican Republic	Osvaldo Virgil	1956	New York Giants
Nicaragua	Dennis Martínez	1976	Baltimore Orioles
Honduras	Gerald Young	1987	Houston Astros

Serie del Caribe

Series	Year	Site	Winning Team/Country	Series	Year	Site	Winning Team/Country
I	1949	Cuba	Almendares/Cuba	XVI	1973	Venezuela	Licey/Dominican Republic
II	1950	Puerto Rico	Carta Vieja/Panama	XVII	1974	Mexico	Caguas/Puerto Rico
III	1951	Venezuela	Santurce/Puerto Rico	XVIII	1975	Puerto Rico	Bayamón/Puerto Rico
IV	1952	Panama	La Habana/Cuba	XIX	1976	Dominican Republic	Hermosillo/Mexico
V	1953	Cuba	Santurce/Puerto Rico	XX	1977	Venezuela	Licey/Dominican Republic
VI	1954	Puerto Rico	Caguas/Puerto Rico	XXI	1978	Mexico	Mayagüez/Puerto Rico
VII	1955	Venezuela	Santurce/Puerto Rico	XXII	1979	Puerto Rico	Magallanes/Venezuela
VIII	1956	Panama	Cienfuegos/Cuba	XXIII	1980	Dominican Republic	Licey/Dominican Republic
IX	1957	Cuba	Marianao/Cuba		1981	Not Held	
X	1958	Puerto Rico	Marianao/Cuba	XXIV	1982	Mexico	Caracas/Venezuela
XI	1959	Venezuela	Almendares/Cuba	XXV	1983	Venezuela	Arecibo/Puerto Rico
XII	1960	Panama	Cienfuegos/Cuba	XXVI	1984	Puerto Rico	Zulia/Venezuela
	1961–69	Not Held		XXVII	1985	Mexico	Licey/Dominican Republic
XIII	1970	Venezuela	Magallanes/Venezuela	XXVIII	1986	Venezuela	Mexicali/Mexico
XIV	1971	Puerto Rico	Licey/Dominican Republic	XXIX	1987	Mexico	Caguas/Venezuela
XV	1972	Dominican Republic	Ponce/Puerto Rico	XXX	1988	Dominican Republic	Escogido/Dominican Republic

Dominican League Statistics

Year	Champion	BA Leader	HR Leader	Most Games Won
1951	Licey	Luis Villodas .346	Pedro Formental 13	Guayuabín Olivo 10
1952	Aguilas	Luis Olmo .344	Alonzo Perry 14	Terry McDuffie
1953	Licey	Tetelo Vargas .355	Alonzo Perry 11	Emilio Cueche 13
1954	Estrellas Orientales	Alonzo Perry .326	Bob Thurman 11	Carrao Bracho G. Olivo 8
1955–56	Escogido*	Bob Wilson .333	Willie Kirkland 9	Fred Waters 11
1956–57	Escogido	Osvaldo Virgil .312	Danny Kravitz 4	Pete Burnside 11
1957–58	Escogido	Alonzo Perry .332	Dick Stuart 14	Fred Kipp 11
1958–59	Licey	Felipe Alou .351	Jim McDaniels 12	Bennie Daniels 12
1959–60	Escogido	Felipe Alou .359	Frank Howard 9	Stan Williams 12
1960–61	Escogido	Manuel Mota .344	Manuel Jiménez J.V. Nicolás Victor Ramirez Felipe Alou N. Saviñón Tied with 4	Danilo Riva 13
1961–62	Incomplete Season			
1962–63	Not Held			
1963–64	Licey	Manuel Mota .379	O. McFarlane 10	G. Olivo Steve Blass 9
1964–65	Aguilas	Manuel Mota .364	O. McFarlane 8	Dick LeMay 8
1965–66	Season not organized by league			
1966–67	Aguilas	Mateo Alou .363	Bob Robertson 10	Dock Ellis 9
1967–68	Estrellas Orientales	Ricardo Carty .350	Bob Robertson 9	Silvano Quezada 11
1968–69	Escogido	Mateo Alou .390	Nate Colbert 8	Jay Ritchie 9
1969–70	Licey	Ralph Garr .387	Winston Llenas Byron Browne 9	G. Rounsaville 8
1970–71	Licey	Ralph Garr .457	César Cedeño 8	Rollie Fingers 9
1971–72	Aguilas	Ralph Garr .388	Charlie Sands 10	Gene Garber 9
1972–73	Licey	Von Joshua .358	Adrian Garrett 9	Pedro Borbón 9
1973–74	Licey	Dave Parker .345	Ricardo Carty 9	Rick Waits 8
1974–75	Aguilas	Bruce Bochte .352	Rafael Batista Bobby Darwin 8	James Richards 8
1975–76	Aguilas	Wilbur Howard .341	Wilbur Howard John Hale Gary Alexander Larry Parrish G. Thomasson Bill Nahorodny Andre Thornton Tied with 4	Nino Espinosa Tom Dettore 8
1976–77	Licey	Mario Guerrero .365	Pedro Guerrero Ike Hampton 6	Angel Torres 10
1977–78	Aguilas	Omar Moreno .345	Dick Davis 8	Odell Jones Al Holland Mickey Mahler 7
1978–79	Aguilas	Ted Cox .319	Bob Beall Dick Davis 7	Bo McLaughlin Mike Proly 9
1979–80	Licey	Tony Peña .317	A. De Freitas Alberto Lois Leon Durham Samuel Mejía Pedro Guerrero Tied with 3	Jerry Hannahs 9
1980–81	Escogido	Ken Landreaux .394	Tony Peña 7	Mario Soto M. Mahler 7
1981–82	Escogido	Pedro Hernandez .408	Dave Hostetler 9	Pasqual Pérez 10
1982–83	Licey	César Geronimo .341	Howard Johnson 8	Pasqual Pérez 9
1983–84	Licey	Miguel Diloné .343	Reggie Whittemore 12	Orel Hershiser Frank Wills 8
1984–85	Licey	Junior Noboa .327	Ralph Bryant 9	Tom Filer 8
1985–86	Aguilas	Tony Fernández .364	Tony Peña 9	Mickey Mahler 8
1986–87	Aguilas	Stanley Javier .374	Ralph Bryant 13	Gibson Alba José Nuñez Eric Plunk Tied with 5
1987–88	Escogido	Stanley Javier .363	Mark Parent 10	José Bautista 8

* First year held in winter

Cuban League Statistics

Year	Champion	BA Leader	HR Leader	Most Games Won
1878–79	Habana Undefeated			
1879–80	Habana			
1880–81	Not held			
1882	Disputed: Fe and Habana			
1882–83	Habana			
1885	Habana	Pablo Ronquilla .350		
1885–86	Habana Undefeated	Wenceslao Gálvez .345		Adolfo Luján 5–0
1887	Habana	R. Martínez .439		Adolfo Luján 5–0
1888	Fe	Antonio García .448		Francisco Hernández 10–2
1889	Habana	Francisco Salabarria .305		Adolfo Luján 10–3
1889–90	Habana	Antonio García .364		Miguel Prats 11–2
1890–91	Fe	Alfredo Crespo .375		Miguel Prats 9–4
1892	Habana	Antonio García .362		E. Hernández 4–1
1892–93	Matanzas	Antonio García .385		Francisco Hernández 4–1
1893–94	Almendares	Miguel Pratts .394		José Pastoriza 16–7
1894–95	Suspended due to War of Independence	Alfredo Arcaño .430		Enrique García 12–4
1897–98	Not finished			
1898	Habanista	Valentín González .394		José Romero 5–2
1900	San Francisco	Esteban Pratts .333		Luis Padrón 13–4
1901	Habana	Julián Castillo .454		Carlos Royer 12–3

Year	Champion	BA Leader	HR Leader	Most Games Won
1902	Habana Undefeated	Luis Padrón .463		Carlos Royer 17-0
1903	Habana	Julián Castillo .330		Cándido Fontanals 14-6
1904	Habana	Regino García .397		Carlos Royer 13-3
1905	Almendares	Regino García .305		Angel D'Meza 10-4
1905-6	Fe	Regino García .304		José Muñoz 8-1
1907	Almendares	Regino García .324		George Mack 4-2
1908	Almendares	Emilio Palomino .350		José Méndez 9-0
1908-9	Habana	Julián Castillo .315		José Méndez L. Haggerman 15-6
1910	Almendares	Emilio Palomino .408		José Méndez 7-0
1910-11	Almendares	Preston Hill .365		José Méndez 11-2
1912	Habana	Emilio Palomino .440		José Junco 6-1
1913	Fe	Armando Marsans .400		Red Redding 7-2
1913-14	Almendares	Manuel Villa .351		José Méndez 10-0
1914-15	Habana	Cristóbal Torriente .387		José Acosta 5-1
1915-16	Almendares	Eustaquio Pedrosos .413		José Acosta 8-3
1917	Orientales	Adolfo Luque .355		José Acosta 2-1
1918-19	Habana	Manuel Cueto .344		José Acosta 16-10
1919-20	Almendares	Cristóbal Torriente .360		Emilio Palmero 5-1
1920-21	Habana	Pelayo Chacon .344	Cristóbal Torriente M. González B. Jiménez M. Guerra Tied with 1	José "Cheo" Hernández 4-1
1921*	Habana	Bienvenido Jiménez .619	Manuel Cueto 1	Julio Leblanc 2-0
1922-23	Marianao	Bernardo Baró .401	Cristóbal Torriente 4	Lucas Boada 10-4
1923-24	Santa Clara	Oliver Marcells .393	Bienvenido Jiménez 4	Bill Holland 10-2
1924-25	Almendares	Manuel Cueto .364	Esteban Mantalvo 5	José Acosta 4-1
1925-26	Almendares	Johnny Wilson .430	J. H. Lloyd Jud Wilson 3	César Alvarez 10-2
1926-27	Habana	Manuel Cueto .404	J. Hernández 4	Juan Olmo 3-0
1927-28	Habana	Johnny Wilson .424	Oscar Charleston 5	Oscar Levis 7-2
1928-29	Habana	Alejandro Oms .432	Cool Papa Bell 5	Adolfo Luque 9-2
1929-30	Cienfuegos	Alejandro Oms .380	Mule Suttles 7	Heliodoro "Yoyo" Diaz 13-3
1930-31*	Not finished	O. Charleston .373	Ernest Smith José Fernández 1	Martin Dihigo 2-0
1931-32	Almendares	Rámon Cueto .400	Alejandro Oms Ismael Morales 3	Juan Eckelson 5-1
1932-33	Tie: Habana Almendares	M. González .432	R. Estalella 3	Jésus Lorenzo 3-0
1933-34	No championship held			
1934-35	Almendares	Lázaro Salazar .407	Eleven tied with 1	Lázaro Salazar 6-1
1935-36	Santa Clara	Martín Dihigo .358	Willie Wells Jacinto Roque 5	Martín Dihigo 11-2
1936-37	Marianao	Harry Williams .349	H. Andrews R. Estalella 5	Raymond Brown 21-4
1937-38	Santa Clara	Sam Bankhead .366	Willie Wells R. Estalella Raymond Brown 4	Raymond Brown 12-5
1938-39	Santa Clara	Tony Castaños .371	Josh Gibson 11	Martín Dihigo 14-2
1939-40	Almendares	Tony Castaños .340	Mule Suttles 4	Rodolfo Fernández 7-4
1940-41	Habana	Lázaro Salazar .316	A. Crespo 3	Gilberto Torres 10-3
1941-42	Almendares	Silvío García .351		Macon Mayor Agapito Mayor 6-2
1942-43	Almendares	A. Crespo .337	Roberto Ortiz Saguita Hernández 2	Cocaina García 10-3
1943-44	Habana	Roberto Ortiz .337	Saguita Hernández 4	Martín Dihigo 8-1
1944-45	Almendares	Claro Duany .340	Claro Duany 3	Oliverio Ortiz 10-4
1945-46	Cienfuegos	L. Davenport .333	Dick Sisler 9	Adrián Zabala 9-3
1946-47	Almendares	Lou Klein .330	Roberto Ortiz 11	Cocaina García 10-3
1947-48	Habana	Harry Kimbro .346	Jesús Chanquilon Díaz 7	C. Marrero 12-2
1948-49	Almendares	A. Crespo .326	Monte Irvin 10	Octavio Rubert 8-1
1949-50	Almendares	P. Formental .336	Roberto Ortiz Don Lenhardt 15	Octavio Rubert 5-1
1950-51	Habana	Silvío García .347	P. Formental, Bert Hass Ed Mierkowitz Charles Grant Tied with 8	Vincente López 7-3
1951-52	Habana	Bert Hass .323	P. Formental James Basso 9	Joe Black 15-6
1952-53	Habana	Edmundo Amorós .373	Louis Klein 16	R. Alexander 10-3
1953-54	Almendares	Rocky Nelson .352	Earl Rapp Rafael Noble 10	Cliff Fanning 13-4
1954-55	Almendares	Angel Scull .370	Rocky Nelson 13	Joe Hatten 13-5
1955-56	Cienfuegos	Forrest Jacobs .321	Ultus Alvarez 10	Pedro Ramos 13-5
1956-57	Marianao	Orestes Miñoso .312	Archie Wilson 11	Camilo Pascual 15-5
1957-58	Marianao	Milton Smith .320	Daniel Morejon Norman Laker B. Robinson Frank Herrera 9	Billy O'Dell 7-2
1958-59	Almendares	Tony Taylor .303	Jim Baxes 9	Orlando Peña 13-5
1959-60	Cienfuegos	Octavio Rojas .322		
1960-61	Cienfuegos			

* Short season

CHAPTER 27

College Baseball

Cappy Gagnon

Intercollegiate baseball has come a long way since July 1, 1859, when the first match was played between Amherst and Williams Colleges, at Pittsfield, Massachusetts. Amherst won by a 73–32 score, on a playing field unrecognizable today. The pitcher was twenty-five feet closer to the batter, and the diamond was only sixty feet on a side. In keeping more with the academic orientation of the times, the two schools engaged in a chess match on the following day. The baseball game was played under the "Massachusetts rules," which eventually gave way to "New York rules," the forerunner of the game we know today. At the time of this game, Abraham Lincoln was not yet President. After the game there were rumors of some "ringers" being used by each team. This was a problem which haunted college sports for the next six decades.

Early college baseball thus preceded the National League by seventeen years. The colleges also provided one very significant equipment innovation. It was a Harvard man named Fred W. Thayer who invented the catcher's mask. Thayer gave his homemade creation to Harry Thatcher, the Crimson backstop (though several sources credit instead Harvard's star, James Tyng). After overcoming taunts about his "babyish and cowardly" act, Thatcher adjusted to wearing the mask. A short while later, Thayer saw the potential of this invention, and on February 12, 1878, he obtained a patent for it.

From the founding of the National Association in 1871 to the present there has been a collegiate influence on the national pastime. There is little evidence that this influence has raised the level of scholarship in the dugout, but unquestionably college baseball has provided an important feeder system for the majors. Initially, this role was important because major league teams of the pre-Rickey era did not have their own farm systems and competed vigorously with each other for raw playing talent. Colleges were an additional place for youngsters to develop.

The majors became more closely aligned with the campuses beginning in the 1890s, when veteran players began to serve as coaches of college teams. Until about 1910, college teams did not have full-time baseball field coaches. During February and March of each year, teams practiced in gymnasiums until weather permitted outside play. These practices were often supervised by a big leaguer, or other pro, limbering up for his own spring training to follow. He might have been a player from the neighboring area, as when Lou Criger of Elkhart, Indiana, or Harry Arndt of South Bend coached the Notre Dame teams. Or he might have been a recent graduate of the school, as when Jesse Burkett coached Holy Cross. Such coaches usually retained an entrée with the college when his big league team was looking for prospects. Norwood

Gibson and Red Morgan followed Criger to the Red Sox, Red Murray followed Arndt to the Cardinals, and Lou Sockalexis followed Burkett to the Cleveland Spiders.

Once the intercollegiate season began, there would be little or no involvement from university staff in the conduct of play. The team captain, a player, would function as the manager. Another student, a nonplayer, would function as the athletic director, scheduling games with other colleges and with independent and professional teams. George Huff, of Illinois, was probably the first paid full-time "coacher." His knowledge of the game helped make the Illini a "western" power, while at the same time developing future pros. Huff scouted for the Cubs and recruited players from his own teams and neighboring colleges for the Southsiders. In the former group were pitchers Carl Lundgren, Big Jeff Pfeffer, and Fred Beebe. Pitcher Ed Reulbach, of Notre Dame, was an example of the latter.

With a few exceptions in California (notably St. Mary's), college baseball until after World War Two was primarily a northeastern and midwestern sport. Because of travel difficulties and the location of all sixteen major league teams within a handful of eastern and midwestern states, college baseball became dominated by the eastern athletic powers (Harvard, Yale, Princeton, and Brown). "Western" upstarts like Illinois, Michigan, Chicago, and Notre Dame were lightly regarded by them. Because intersectional play did not occur until around 1910, however, there was no way to evaluate the competing claims of superiority.

Early collegians showed their cleverness in choosing pseudonyms. The two great Columbia players were known as "Sullivan" (Eddie Collins) and "Lewis" (Lou Gehrig). John Mohardt of Notre Dame had an interesting story as a result of his baseball alias: Mohardt became "Cavanaugh" when the entire Notre Dame team went to New Hampton, Iowa, for the summer of 1920. Mohardt picked up a girlfriend during that summer. He confided to her what the "ND" on the team caps stood for (his teammates claimed they were from North Dakota), but did not divulge his real name. Later that fall, when she sent a love note to "Johnny Cavanaugh, c/o Notre Dame," it was delivered to the Reverend John Cavanaugh, C.S.C., president of the university, who was not amused.

Early "tramp athletes" went from school to school and played on semipro teams under various aliases. Some "collegiate" players were not even enrolled in the colleges they represented. Bert Daniels was one of a number of itinerant collegians. He played at Villanova, Notre Dame, and Bucknell—all under his own name, while playing minor league ball during the summers, using five different aliases. As "Ayres," at Altoona in 1910, he was called the "next Ty Cobb." Unfortunately, he was already twenty-seven years old

and had already played ten years of college and semipro football. All this had taken its toll on his legs. Daniels did make good use of his schooling, however, becoming an engineer.

Big leaguers came from virtually every college, including small and lesser-known colleges. Mathewson of Bucknell, Coombs of Colby, Plank of Gettysburg, Thorpe of Carlisle, and Beaumont of Beloit were good examples of why the majors scouted even the small schools. Although college teams played fewer than thirty games at this time, due to cold weather and travel difficulties and perhaps an occasional class or two, the top collegiate players seemed to get in sufficient playing time to impress big league scouts. Semipro, Industrial League, and town-team leagues were three of the types of ball for which a skilled collegian could pick up a little money for tuition and supporting his family.

The rise of college programs in the South and Far West came much later. The first major leaguer from the University of Southern California was Fay Thomas in 1927. Rod Dedeaux of the 1935 Dodgers was the fourth. Notre Dame had at least forty men reach the big leagues by 1920. Brown had fourteen in the majors by 1900. Georgetown was another early producer of big leaguers.

Once there was full-time college baseball, the relationship between the majors and the colleges became even more pronounced. In 1909 Connie Mack installed Jack Barry, a Holy Cross collegian as the shortstop in his $100,000 infield. During his forty years as coach of the Crusaders (1921–1961), Barry sent at least twenty-three players to the majors, including Gene Desautels and Mike Hegan. Connie Mack sent his son Earle to Niagara and Notre Dame.

According to Ellery Clark in *Red Sox Forever,* the early Bosox team featured many collegians, including two stars from St. Mary's (Duffy Lewis and Harry Hooper) who formed two-thirds of the best outfield of its day and the two best players from Vermont's 1908 team (Ray Collins and Larry Gardner).

One factor which may have encouraged many players to matriculate instead of trying out with the majors was the number of them who were multiple-sports stars. Christy Mathewson played football and basketball; Robin Roberts played basketball at Michigan State; Alvin Dark was a football star at Louisiana State University; Ted Kluszewski and Moose Skowron were football players at Indiana and Purdue respectively; Joe Adcock was a scoring star in basketball at Louisiana State University; Lou Boudreau, Frank Baumholtz, and Dick Groat were All-Americans in basketball at Illinois, Ohio, and Duke; and Jackie Robinson starred in football and track at U.C.L.A.

Many players better known for football were major leaguers too: George Halas, Ernie Nevers, Jim Thorpe, Red Badgro, Ace Parker, etc. Similarly, many collegiate baseball players achieved fame in other professional sports, like NFL quarterbacks Joe Theismann (ND) and John Elway (Stanford). The legendary George Gipp played a little baseball at Notre Dame. The Cubs allegedly offered him a contract after watching him play semipro baseball with Kiki Cuyler in Michigan.

College men were not always warmly received into the majors. Veteran players had a natural reluctance to accept anyone who was out to win a scarce job, in the days of sixteen teams and eighteen-man rosters. Secondly, the crude, often ill-educated pros were more than a little resentful of the more-cultured and better-educated collegians. Writing just before the turn of the century, sportswriter George E. Stackhouse quoted "a well-known professional catcher . . . [whose manager] . . . was beginning to get the college baseball fever." The player approached a collegian and asked him if he were thinking of becoming a professional. When the collegian said he had no idea of becoming a pro, the catcher replied, "with much warmth: 'Now that's square, old man. You know Greek, Latin, and something about the world. You can make a good living anywhere. Don't interfere with us fellows, because you don't have to.' "

Henry Edwards of the Major League Service Bureau estimated this percentage of collegians in the majors at almost one-third in 1932. This is a big jump from 1909, when only fifty-seven big leaguers—or approximately 14 percent—had college backgrounds.

Because of the harsh conditions they faced, many star baseballers took their schooling seriously and skipped the majors. Another factor is that player salaries, in an era long before Marvin Miller, were often not attractive enough to persuade a bright college man to give up a career in a profession.

According to the 1900 U.S. Census, fewer than 2 percent of twenty-three-year-old men were college graduates. The average annual earnings of a working man from 1900 through World War One ranged from a little more than $400 to a little less than $1,000. A college man stood a much better chance to earn more than his counterpart. Similarly, professional players did not earn much more than average, and their short careers and unpleasant travel conditions made it difficult to develop either a nest egg or a headstart on a post-playing career.

The Notre Dame baseball captain in 1900 was probably as good a player as Peaches O'Neill, Red Morgan, Bob Bescher, Henry Thielman, Norwood Gibson, Bert Keeley, Frank Shaughnessy, and several other of his teammates who went on to the majors. Instead, first baseman Angus MacDonald, a four-letter winner, took his business degree to New York City, where he went to work for the Southern Pacific Railroad, later becoming president of the railroad.

Despite the closer relationship, considerable hostility remained between organized ball and the colleges. An editorial in *The Sporting News* on March 14, 1946, defended major league baseball's plantation treatment of the colleges.

Referring to the case of Gale Bishop of Washington State, who was signed early and made ineligible for further collegiate play, "University authorities have complained about this and similar practices, but few have shown any disposition to give the game an adequate place in their athletic programs, because of the emphasis placed on football and basketball." The fact that Bishop had no major league career to show for the disruption of his college athletics only exacerbated the problem.

On July 2, 1947, *The Sporting News* reported that a foundation was being laid for a truce between organized ball and the colleges. Earlier, Branch Rickey, himself a college man from Ohio Wesleyan and later George Sisler's baseball coach at Michigan when he was the country's top college pitcher, said that he felt the colleges had "dirty skirts" themselves and were in no position to lecture the majors. Rickey said he would continue to scout and sign collegians because he felt that some college teams had relationships with major league teams that were akin to their being farmclubs. And we know

that Branch Rickey was not going to be "out-farmclubbed" by anyone.

One of the committee members representing organized baseball in its deliberations with the colleges was Frank "Shag" Shaughnessy, president of the International League. He said, "The player should not be compelled to wait to play professional ball if he needs the money to complete his education."

Shag was a star baseball and football player at Notre Dame who paid for his college education by playing semipro (as "Shannon") and professional ball.

Once the minor league teams were no longer able to sign and develop their own players, but were dependent upon "working agreements" with big league teams, long-term player development became a function of college baseball programs. Major league teams could avoid signing hundreds of players and maintaining ten or more minor league affiliates by simply letting the colleges do their work for them. College facilities and coaching were at least as good as the low minors. Players were "signed" to a scholarship and nurtured by the colleges. Big league scouts could watch their playing and learn something about their competitive abilities, injury history, and maturity. After two or three years, the best players would be drafted and sent to Rookie Ball or higher. Some think that a good college program might be the equivalent of Double-A baseball.

From the 1950s on, the major leagues changed their relationship with the minors dramatically, thereby thrusting the college game into an even more prominent role. Schools such as Arizona, Arizona State, and Texas began to produce big leaguers by the gross. When Dedeaux returned to his alma mater as coach, he increased their big league output dramatically while winning ten collegiate championships from 1958 to 1978.

From 1954 through 1980, there were only three years when U.S.C. did not send at least one player to the majors—forty-five players in twenty-seven years. Tom Seaver, Dave Kingman, Fred Lynn, Ron Fairly, and Don Buford were among this invasion. Commissioner Bowie Kuhn estimated in 1978 that more than two-thirds of major leaguers were college men.

There are also advantages for the collegians in this relationship. If an aspiring major leaguer's baseball apprenticeship does not work out, he can concentrate on his studies and find another vocation. He is in an environment where he has more opportunity for enrichment, for overall personal development, than would result from his being thrown into the minors at age seventeen or eighteen, as so often occurred during baseball's early days.

Great collegiate baseball teams can be evaluated in terms of two measures: the number of games won and the number of major league players produced. It is hard to argue with those who regard the University of Southern California as the greatest school on both counts. Since the inception of the Division I NCAA baseball championship in 1947, the U.S.C. Trojans have won eleven times and have finished as runner-up once. Next closest are Arizona State, with five firsts and three seconds; Texas with four firsts and one second; Arizona with three of each; and Minnesota with three titles. Oklahoma State, Cal State at Fullerton, Florida State, Brigham Young, and Miami are other schools with baseball programs that have been very strong during the past decade.

Besides Barry and Dedeaux, former big leaguers coaching these NCAA championship teams have included Bibb Falk (at Texas), Ray Fisher and Don Lund (Michigan), Dick Siebert (Minnesota), and Jerry Kindall (Arizona).

The Trojans, the Longhorns, and the Fighting Irish are the three top schools in terms of total major leaguers produced. The next echelon includes Holy Cross, Illinois, Alabama, Arizona State, Michigan, and Brown.

Texas has provided the majors with Roger Clemens, Greg Swindell, Burt Hooten, Calvin Schiraldi, and Keith Moreland among recent stars. Alabama claims Frank Lary, Riggs Stephenson, Joe Sewell, Del Pratt, and Butch Hobson. Michigan sent Charlie Gehringer, Bill Freehan, and Dick Wakefield. Brigham Young has been strong recently with Jack Morris, Wally Joyner, and Cory Snyder.

In 1973, the California Angels thought so much of the coaching of Bobby Winkles of the Arizona State Sun Devils that they hired him as their manager, the first time the majors had ever hired a college coach with no prior big league experience. Winkles managed two years each with the Angels and the A's. At Arizona State Winkles had coached Rick Monday, Reggie Jackson, and Sal Bando.

The NCAA has selected a championship Series Most Valuable Player since 1949. Winners of this award have included future big leaguers Tom Yewcic (C, Michigan State), Tom Borland (P, Oklahoma State), Cal Emery (P-1B, Penn State), Bob Garibaldi (P, Santa Clara), Sal Bando (3B, Arizona State), Steve Arlin (P, Ohio State), Jerry Tabb (1B, Tulsa), Dave Winfield (P-OF, Minnesota), Bob Horner (3B, Arizona State), Terry Francona (LF, Arizona), and Calvin Schiraldi (P, Texas).

## CHAPTER 28

Baseball and the Armed Services

Harrington E. Crissey, Jr.

It is regrettable that the average fan has little or no knowledge of the historical relationship between the military and baseball, considering that the links between the two date back to the beginning of the game's evolution in North America approximately 150 years ago. Perhaps it is because most people associate baseball with pleasure and military service with anything but that; or it may be that those who have never served in the armed forces have no appreciation of the value of baseball in relieving either the stress or boredom of military life, depending on one's circumstances. Whatever the reasons, the connections between the armed services and this truly international pastime are long and storied, and deserve our careful and devoted attention because the military has had a profound impact on the propagation of baseball worldwide and on the development of the game as a social leveler and instrument of international relations.

A story about the origin of baseball was advanced by a committee of the game's elder statesmen in 1907. The committee, led by former player and sporting goods magnate Albert G. Spalding, said that Abner Doubleday had designed the first baseball diamond at Cooperstown, New York, in 1839 while a cadet at the U.S. Military Academy. This version was quickly accepted as official by the baseball moguls and held sway for several decades, but it is now considered a myth by serious baseball historians.

Doubleday fought in the Battle of Monterey during the Mexican War; sighted the first gun in defense of Fort Sumter when it was fired on by Southerners on April 12, 1861, thus starting the Civil War; fought at Second Bull Run and Antietam; distinguished himself at Gettysburg by helping to repel Pickett's Charge, the Confederates' major attack of the battle; and eventually retired from the Army as a general in 1873. He was dead, however, by the time the committee put forth its opinion, so no one could get his views on the matter. There is nothing in his writings which suggests he invented the game, and other early commentators such as Henry Chadwick advanced different theories regarding the origin of the game. Nevertheless, the name of Abner Doubleday, a career soldier, remains inextricably linked to baseball in the popular mind.

To discover the first bona fide influence of the military on baseball, and a tremendous one at that, we must move ahead to the American Civil War (1861–1865). Baseball before the Civil War was almost exclusively a gentleman's game, with the upper classes of society participating and the true amateur spirit and British rules of sportsmanship holding sway. Most of the prominent teams were in the East, with a few, such as those in Chicago and St. Louis, in the Midwest. During the war, baseball became a sport played by people of all social classes over a wide geographical area. It was played among Union troops during their leisure hours and an unheard-of crowd of 40,000 soldiers watched a game in Hilton Head, South Carolina, on Christmas Day, 1862, between the 165th New York Volunteer Infantry (Duryea's Zouaves) and a team picked from other Union regiments. A. G. Mills, later to become president of the National League, played in that contest.

Baseball was known in the South prior to the Civil War. Soldiers were said to have played baseball during the Mexican War, the game was popular in New Orleans, and many people south of the Mason-Dixon Line subscribed to Northern periodicals which featured baseball news. Nevertheless, the growth of the sport in Dixie was greatly stimulated by Northern prisoners playing the game to relieve boredom or tension in Southern POW camps. Their guards first watched, then decided they wanted to try, and finally organized teams to play against their captives. Southern POWs returned home similarly enlightened about the game. With more than a million men under arms during the conflict, is it any wonder that the game proliferated when the veterans went home to practically every town in the nation?

The Civil War accelerated two trends that were first discernible in the late 1850s: increasingly fierce competition and with it increased commercialism. Diaries written by Union troops in the Army of the Potomac and the Army of Northern Virginia show that as the war went on and baseball became ever more popular and competitive, emphasis on skill was the great consideration. If a player was good, he got to play. Teams in Army units may have been promoted by officers or high-ranking noncoms, but the players on the field were the most skilled. In 1863 and 1864, some outfits had first and second teams based on skill levels. This idea of skill predominating over social or military rank certainly fit the competitive pattern of post–Civil War baseball, as more emphasis on winning led to keen rivalries between cities and the rise of professionalism.

In 1873, eight years after the cessation of hostilities in the United States and twenty years after American ships under Commodore Matthew Perry had succeeded in opening Japan to the West, two American missionaries named Wilson and Maget introduced baseball to the Land of the Rising Sun. The game took root in part because influential Japanese of that time, such as Kido and many former *daimyo* (feudal lords), supported its growth. They originally viewed baseball as an American version of a martial sport like Japanese *judo* or *kendo*. Practicing the sport was in their minds a way of getting at the essence of the American fighting spirit, and thus baseball was played every day, regardless of weather conditions.

As time went on, the game evolved into a high school and college sport. From 1888 until 1902, the top team in Japan was that of First High School, now known as Tokyo University. It sometimes played games against American residents in Yokohama and teams from U.S. Navy battleships. Whenever the battlewagons made port calls in Yokohama, the First High School club would challenge them and usually would win the contests. Judging from a few of the scores, the Japanese students had ample reason to feel good about their progress in the sport: in 1902, they slaughtered the U.S.S. *Kentucky*, 35–1, and the next year clobbered the same ship again, 27–0!

The United States involved itself in war with Spain and its colonial possessions in the Caribbean Sea and Pacific Ocean in 1898. The Spanish-American War was short, lasting roughly the length of the baseball season. The war didn't have a significant impact on the game at home but undoubtedly influenced its spread to Puerto Rico, and other lands which border on the Caribbean, and the Philippine Islands.

Dr. Arlie Pond was pitching for the Baltimore Orioles of the National League when the war started. He had won 16 games for the Orioles in their pennant-winning season of 1896 and followed it up with 18 victories in 1897, but at the start of hostilities he entered the Army, joined a medical unit, and went first to Cuba and then the Philippines. After the war and the Philippine Insurrection, he left active duty but stayed in the Philippines and devoted the rest of his life to combating disease there, except for World War One, when he returned to the States and became assistant surgeon general of the Army with the rank of colonel. Near the end of the war, he went with the U.S. forces to Siberia following the Russian Revolution. In 1919, he returned to the islands after again relinquishing his Army commission and died there in 1930 at the age of fifty-seven.

A year after the war, Dave Wills quit his medical studies at the University of Virginia to play first base for Louisville of the National League. After hitting only .223 in twenty-four games, he decided to join the Marines and wound up staying twenty years in the service. He served as a paymaster in the European Theater with the rank of major in World War One and was buried in Arlington National Cemetery upon his death in 1959. A little more than a decade after the Spanish-American War, Hall of Famer Oscar Charleston, a Negro League great, was first recognized for his baseball ability while serving with the Army (1911–1915) in the Philippines.

World War One began in Europe in August 1914, but the United States didn't enter the conflict until April 1917. Before the Yanks went "over there," Canadian units in the British Army took the lead in teaching many Englishmen and Australians how to play. In the fall of 1917, a series for the championship of the Canadian forces overseas was played in England. One hundred and one teams took part, with several minor league and semipro players dotting the rosters.

By the end of 1917 there were seventy-six American major league players in the service: forty-eight from the American League, including fifteen Boston Red Sox, and twenty-eight from the National League. Forty-two were in the Army, twenty-one in the Navy, and thirteen in other branches of the service.

In May 1918 there occurred the promulgation of a "work or fight" order by the provost marshal of the armed forces, General Enoch Crowder. It was designed to force all men of draft age out of nonessential work and into the Army or war-related employment in order to aid in the prosecution of the war. Baseball players were classified as nonessential while actors, opera singers, and movie stars were deemed essential. This was because the baseball magnates didn't present their case in person, as did representatives of the other specially exempted occupations.

Relatively few players left baseball, however. The great majority remained with their teams. When the July time limit set by the Crowder order was reached, various draft boards issued conflicting orders to the players, some saying their work was essential and others saying it wasn't.

Eventually the Crowder edict was enforced and organized baseball shut down its operation by the beginning of September 1918, although two additional weeks were allotted for the World Series between the Boston Red Sox and the Chicago Cubs. Despite the fact that the Crowder edict applied only to men of draft age, the owners decided not to finish the season with players younger than eighteen or older than thirty-five. The magnates made it clear to the players, however, that the reserve clause was still in effect, that the players weren't free agents, and that they would be bound to their former teams upon resumption of play.

By the end of the war in November 1918, 144 American Leaguers and 103 National Leaguers were in the military. Very few players went into war-related work. Of the 144 American Leaguers serving Uncle Sam, a considerable percentage of them were known to be overseas. At least eighty-three were in the Army and forty-one in the Navy. The Detroit Tigers led the league with twenty-five servicemen, while the team with the fewest was the St. Louis Browns with thirteen, even though the Brownies had won American League prexy Ban Johnson's $500 prize for performing best in military close-order drill (using bats as rifles) in 1917. Among the National Leaguers, the Brooklyn Dodgers and Pittsburgh Pirates tied for the lead in enlistees with eighteen apiece, while the Cincinnati Reds had only six. Boston Brave catcher Hank Gowdy was the first major leaguer to volunteer for military service. He was eventually sent to France, as were other prominent players and executives such as Cincinnati Red manager Christy Mathewson, Detroit Tiger outfielder Ty Cobb, Philadelphia Phillie pitcher Grover Cleveland Alexander, Brooklyn Dodger hurler Sherry Smith, Chicago White Sox catcher Joe Jenkins, Boston Brave executive Percy Haughton, and St. Louis Cardinal executive Branch Rickey. Haughton and Rickey received their commissions as majors and Mathewson was a captain in the Army's gas-and-flame division. Mathewson suffered gas poisoning during his service. It led to tuberculosis and his ultimate demise in 1925. Former major leaguers killed in action were infielder Eddie Grant, who had played for four teams between 1905 and 1915, in the Argonne Forest in October 1918; Robert Troy, who had been born in Germany and pitched and lost one game for the Detroit Tigers in 1912, at the Meuse in October 1918; and Alex Barr, also with one game in the big time as a New York Yankee outfielder in 1914, on his twenty-fifth birthday, November 1, 1918, a mere ten days before the armistice.

Servicemen's baseball was alive and well in Europe in both 1917 and 1918. In addition to the aforementioned Canadian championship series in England in the fall of 1917, an Anglo-American League was formed. It was composed of regular teams of American and Canadian soldiers, and was organized in London by W. E. Booker and former big leaguer Arlie Latham. The league played a regular weekend schedule in

London, the English provinces, and Scotland. Every team had four or five professional players. A benefit game between American Army and Navy teams at Chelsea, London, on July 4, 1918, drew more than forty thousand spectators, including the King of England and Allied military notables. The regular season ended on September 7, 1918, but the clubs continued to play Sunday ball until September 29.

Whereas the Canadians had initially taught baseball to the British and Australians, the Americans introduced it to the French. The game was not exactly new in Paris because Americans had occasionally played it there before the war. Once the Yanks began arriving in large numbers, games were played every Sunday in the Bois du Boulogne and other public parks. The YMCA organized an Association League in France, with thirty teams playing a fifteen-game schedule each Sunday up to the middle of September. Shortly before the armistice, French soldiers were under orders to learn baseball! Their primary teacher was erstwhile National League great Johnny Evers, who had been sent to France by the Knights of Columbus for that purpose. Where did all the equipment come from? There were three sources: the aforementioned YMCA, the Knights of Columbus and the Ball and Bat Fund, headed by Clark Griffith, manager of the Washington Senators. The fund disbursed $63,865.29 worth of baseball gear, although the supply ship *Kansan*, with its load of equipment for the American Expeditionary Force, was torpedoed and sunk by a German submarine while en route to Europe.

The top service teams of World War One (1918) included the 342nd Field Artillery, American Expeditionary Force club, which featured Grover Cleveland Alexander and several other major leaguers and beat all comers; the Second Naval District, Newport, Rhode Island, aggregation, with a handful of big leaguers on its roster; the Great Lakes, Illinois, Naval Station club, piloted by White Sox outfielder Phil Chouinard and later Senator shortstop Doc Lavan, which posted a 30–8 won-lost record and had Hall of Fame pitcher Urban "Red" Faber and pro football great George Halas; the 85th Division, Battle Creek, Michigan, nine, which lost only one game, beat the Great Lakes club, and had the Browns' Urban Shocker hurling for them; the Camp Dodge, Iowa, club, which logged 27 wins against 8 setbacks and counted six major leaguers among its players; the San Diego, California, Naval Training Camp team, with a 78–10 record to its credit; and the Kelly Field club in San Antonio, Texas, which won 42 games and lost only 8.

During and immediately after the war, baseball was played in Great Britain, France, Belgium, Italy, and the German Rhineland. There was enthusiastic talk in the *Reach* and *Spalding Baseball Guides* of the period about baseball becoming a major sport in England and France, but such a development failed to take place. Colonel Tillinghast L'Hommedieu Huston, part owner of the New York Yankees, guessed the result correctly. Upon returning to the United States from France after sixteen months in the Army, he commented that if American soldiers had been in Europe for at least another year, baseball might have taken hold, but the soldiers were returning home too fast to make a lasting impression.

The influence of the military during the period between the world wars was negligible, save for the occasional ballplayer who served a hitch in the armed forces. "Barnacle Bill" Posedel joined the Navy in 1925 while still in his teens, put in four years of active duty, later became a pitcher with the Brooklyn Dodgers and Boston Bees on the eve of World War Two, served four more years in the Navy during that conflict, and eventually became a major league pitching coach. Nemo Gaines was a star pitcher for the U.S. Naval Academy, class of 1921. Upon graduation, he received permission to take special leave and pitch for the Washington Senators. After four appearances with the Nats, he went on active duty and served until 1946, when he retired with the rank of captain. Pitcher Sig Jakucki, who was to become an important cog in the St. Louis Browns' drive to their only American League pennant in 1944, was in the Army from 1927 to 1931 and starred for the Schofield Barracks team in Hawaii as an outfielder and occasional hurler. As was customary, American servicemen brought baseball with them wherever they went. On July 29, 1937, sailors from a Navy squadron formed two teams and played a softball game in the sports stadium of the port they were visiting. The locale? Vladivostok in the Soviet Union!

Germany invaded Poland on September 1, 1939, and World War Two was on in Europe. As the war clouds drifted across the Atlantic and became more ominous over America, the United States government instituted a military draft in the autumn of 1940, the first in its history during peacetime. It required the registration of men ages twenty-one to thirty-five. The first major leaguer to get drafted was Philadelphia Phillie pitcher Hugh Mulcahy in March 1941, nine months before Pearl Harbor. The next to go was a star—Detroit Tiger slugger and 1940 American League Most Valuable Player Hank Greenberg. Hammerin' Hank had led the Tigers to the pennant the year before. After hitting two homers in a 7-4 win over the Yankees on May 6, he entered the Army the next day, the same day the Tigers officially raised their 1940 championship flag. Thus began a parade of professional ballplayers into the armed forces, a parade which would continue unabated until the Japanese surrender in August 1945.

Perhaps no other statistic better expresses the extent to which the military put its stamp on professional baseball during World War Two than the one which appeared in the *New York Times* in the spring of 1945: as of January of that year, 5,400 of the 5,800 pro baseball players in the country at the time of Pearl Harbor were in the service. With an impact of that magnitude, it would take a decent-sized book to describe in detail military baseball alone during the war years, not to mention pro and military ball combined, a task which has already been accomplished twice in recent memory. How then should one approach the topic? By emphasizing that the military is ultimately made up of people.

Over fifty professional ballplayers made the supreme sacrifice while serving in the armed forces. The majority of them died in combat. Two were ex–major leaguers who appeared briefly in the American League in 1939. Harry O'Neill, who caught one game for the Philadelphia Athletics, died on Iwo Jima in March 1945. Army Air Corps Captain Elmer Gedeon, an outfielder in 5 games for the Washington Senators in 1939, was shot down over France on April 15, 1944, his twenty-seventh birthday. The first pro player to enlist, minor league outfielder Billy Southworth, Jr., joined the Army Air Corps in December 1940. He was the son of the St. Louis Cardinals' manager and compiled quite a war record as a bomber pilot in Europe before being killed in a crash after takeoff on a routine flight from Long Island to Florida on February 15, 1945. He had attempted an emergency landing

at LaGuardia Field but plunged into Flushing Bay after over-shooting the runway. His grieving father was not alone among major league pilots. Ex-Tiger skipper Mickey Cochrane and former Cub boss Jimmie Wilson also lost sons in the war.

Several men who played major league ball were wounded in action, among them Army Air Corps fighter pilot Bert Shepard, who was shot down by antiaircraft fire over Germany in May 1944 and had his right leg amputated below the knee. After spending the better part of a year in a German POW camp, he was repatriated in a prisoner-of-war exchange and, with the help of an artificial limb, pitched in one regular-season game and several exhibitions for the Washington Senators in 1945. Others in the category of the wounded included the St. Louis Cardinals' John Grodzicki; the Philadelphia Athletics' Jack Knott, Bob Savage, and Lou Brissie; the Cleveland Indians' Gene Bearden; and the Brooklyn Dodgers' Tommy Warren—all of them pitchers.

Yet another pitcher, Phil Marchildon of the Philadelphia Athletics, spent nine months in a German prison camp while serving in the Royal Canadian Air Force. Cecil Travis, the star Washington shortstop, had his feet frozen at the Battle of the Bulge and lasted only two seasons after the war due to his limited mobility. The major league careers of hurlers Hugh Mulcahy of the Phillies and Charlie Wagner of the Red Sox were effectively curtailed by weight loss brought on by dysentery contracted in the Philippines. Two other pitchers, Johnny Rigney of the White Sox and 1942 rookie sensation Johnny Beazley of the Cardinals, threw their arms out while pitching service exhibitions. Outfielder Elmer "Red" Durrett hooked on with the Dodgers in 1944 after being discharged from the Marine Corps. He had suffered shell shock on Guadalcanal. It took a while for infielder Billy Cox and outfielder Monte Irvin to recover from the emotional effects of their Army experiences before they hit their stride again. Cardinal second baseman Frank Crespi broke his left leg in a game at Fort Riley, Kansas, in 1943. While convalescing at a military hospital, he got into a wheelchair race, slammed into a wall, and broke the leg again, thus ending whatever chance he had of returning to the Redbirds after hostilities had ceased.

There were the great ones—men like Ted Williams, Joe DiMaggio, Bob Feller, and Hank Greenberg—who lost between three and five of their prime years to the service, thus giving rise to a multitude of "what if?" questions regarding their lifetime statistics had there been no war. Then there were the legions of players who didn't stick with their former clubs because of the personnel crunch in the spring of 1946, when the mix of returning veterans and wartime holdovers was so great that many men never had a chance to get back into shape gradually and compete for jobs effectively. Although major league clubs carried thirty men rather than twenty-five on their 1946 rosters in an effort to mitigate the problem, the remedy was hardly adequate to accommodate the flood of returnees. A few players—Tony Lupien, Merrill May, Bob Harris, Bruce Campbell, Steve Sundra, and Al Niemiec—either threatened legal action or undertook it in an effort to protect their reemployment rights under the then-new GI Bill, but most of them settled out of court on the issue of pay, and none stayed with their former teams.

For every sad story, there was a courageous or heartening one. Jack Knott of the Athletics and southpaw Earl Johnson of the Red Sox won battlefield commissions after showing bravery under fire. Former first baseman Zeke Bonura won the Legion of Merit as an Army corporal for organizing and promoting sports programs for service men and women in North Africa. General Dwight D. Eisenhower personally pinned the award on him. The aforementioned Bert Shepard served as an inspiration to all disabled servicemen when he made occasional appearances on the mound for the Senators. The opportunity to gain valuable experience by playing service ball with and against seasoned professionals presented itself to people like outfielder Del Ennis, who jumped from one year in the low minors to the major leagues after discharge. For others, it served to showcase their talents as prior amateurs or semipros. Johnny Groth, an eighteen-year-old wonder fresh out of Chicago Latin High School, proceeded to win a starting berth in centerfield for the 1945 Great Lakes Naval Training Center team with which he hit .341. He was signed to a Detroit organization contract at war's end and went on to have a long and productive major league career despite key injuries along the way. Maurice "Mo" Mozzali was a Louisville area semipro who impressed his teammates while performing for submarine-base teams at Pearl Harbor and New London, Connecticut. He signed a pro contract in 1946 and rose to the level of Triple-A as an All-Star first baseman with Columbus of the American Association.

Several prominent players had triumphant returns to the major leagues after completion of their service hitches. On August 24, 1945, after forty-four months in the Navy, Bob Feller made his first start against the Tigers in Cleveland. His appearance resulted in Cleveland's biggest baseball crowd in three years (46,777 fans). Bullet Bob struck out twelve, gave up only four hits, and won easily, 4–2. In his second game versus Detroit late that summer, he one-hit the Tigers. When he pitched in Yankee Stadium on September 10, a total of 67,816 spectators were present. Hank Greenberg heralded his return to the Tigers on July 1, 1945, by hitting a home run against the Athletics before 48,000 hometown fans. On the final day of the season, his grand slam home run in the rain against the Browns clinched the American League pennant for Detroit. Tiger righthander Virgil Trucks was discharged from the Navy less than a week before the 1945 season ended. He started the Tigers' pennant-winning 6–3 victory over St. Louis and followed that up with a 4–1 complete-game win over the Chicago Cubs in the second game of the World Series.

Navy duty during the war resulted in the beginning of new professions for Max Patkin and Dusty Cooke. Patkin began his long and famous career as a baseball clown while pitching first for Aiea Hospital and then for Aiea Barracks in Hawaii in 1944. Cooke was trained as a pharmacist's mate. This training came in handy after the war. In search of a baseball job, he hooked on with former teammate Ben Chapman and the Philadelphia Phillies as club trainer and later went on to coach and even manage the team for a few days in 1948 between the departure of Chapman and the arrival of Eddie Sawyer.

At times there was an embarrassment of riches on military teams. In the first two years of the war, former heavyweight boxing champion Gene Tunney's eight-week enlisted athletic specialist training course was located at the Norfolk, Virginia Naval Training Station. Thus the Norfolk NTS manager, Gary Bodie, had his pick of the numerous professional athletes who were taking the course. In 1943 he was faced with the difficult yet wonderful prospect of choosing between two of the premier shortstops in baseball, Phil Rizzuto and Pee Wee Reese, for his ballclub. He kept Rizzuto and sent Reese

a mile down the road to Norfolk Naval Air Station, where he became part of NTS's opposition.

The Army stockpiled its talent in the Hawaiian Islands at the Seventh Army Air Force, Hickam Field, in 1944. Manager Tom Winsett, a former major league outfielder, had three top-level second basemen—Joe Gordon, Gerry Priddy, and Dario Lodigiani—at his disposal that summer. Priddy and Lodigiani were the first to arrive, with Lodigiani staying at his normal position and Priddy playing shortstop. When Priddy was transferred, Gordon replaced him.

There were also some wacky trades. After the Tunney school was shifted from Norfolk to Bainbridge, Maryland, former St. Louis Browns outfielder Red McQuillen went through the program. Norfolk NTS needed an outfielder and Bainbridge needed a life raft, so the deal was made. The raft turned out to be defective upon receipt in Bainbridge, but the deal wasn't voided and McQuillen went on to bat .367 and lead the Norfolk club in hits and triples in 1944. General William Flood, commanding officer of the aforementioned Seventh Army Air Force at Hickam Field, wanted Eddie Funk, a good pitcher with a little experience in the low minors, for his ballclub. Funk was at another facility on the island of Oahu, and his CO was anxious to keep him; however, the CO had two dogs which he loved, and they were sick. General Flood had the only veterinary service among the military stations in Hawaii, so he made a proposition to Funk's boss: you give me Funk and your two dogs will get well. The deal was consummated, and Funk went on to pitch excellent ball for the Seventh Army Air Force.

It was common for the top service teams to have past or future major leaguers at every position. Both the Army and the Navy had outstanding teams at several of their installations around the country. For instance, Navy outfits at the training centers in Norfolk, Great Lakes, Bainbridge, and Sampson, New York, were superb. The Army aggregations at the Seventh Army Air Force, Fort Riley, Kansas; New Cumberland, Pennsylvania; and the Waco, Texas, Army Flying School distinguished themselves. The Marine Corps had fine clubs at Quantico, Virginia, and Parris Island, South Carolina, and the Coast Guard teams at Curtis Bay, Maryland, and New London, Connecticut, were excellent. There was also a multiplicity of top-notch clubs on the West Coast.

Most of these teams rang up outstanding won–lost records against all types of opposition—for example, the magnificent 48–2 log achieved by the 1944 Great Lakes club. Many exhibitions were played against major and minor league teams, with the majority being won by the service clubs. Some of the scores are legendary, like the 17–4 slaughtering the Great Lakes sailors gave the Cleveland Indians in their 1944 season finale, or the pastings administered to the Boston Red Sox (20–7) and the Cleveland Indians (15–2) by the 1944 Sampson Naval Training Center nine. Were the major leaguers trying? Evidence indicates that they were, although second-line pitchers were often thrown against the service clubs and sometimes the pros played a position other than their normal one. Because big league clubs often took fewer than the normal twenty-five players on road trips during the war, it was not uncommon for players to be platooned at an unfamiliar position—as, for example, a pitcher playing in the outfield.

Service players participated in some great war-benefit games. Perhaps the most famous was the American League All-Stars–Service All-Stars contest at Municipal Stadium in Cleveland on July 7, 1942, when 62,094 fans saw a one-of-a-kind ballgame in which the American Leaguers triumphed, 5–0. The gross receipts from the spectacle totaled $143,571; $100,000 of the net went to the Bat and Ball Fund and the rest to Army and Navy Relief. A month earlier, the Norfolk NTS team had played a group of Army ballplayers in the Polo Grounds in New York. The year 1943 saw the $2 million war-bond game between the Norfolk NTS squad and the Washington Senators, won by Norfolk, 4–3, at Griffith Stadium in Washington, on May 24; the Service All-Stars–Boston Braves contest at Fenway Park, Boston, on July 12, in which the All-Stars, managed by Babe Ruth and featuring Ted Williams, nipped the Braves, 9–8; the July 28 game in Yankee Stadium between North Carolina Pre-Flight (Navy) and a combined team of New York Yankees and Cleveland Indians, called the "Yank-lands" and managed by Babe Ruth, in which North Carolina Pre-Flight triumphed, 11–5, and $30,000 was poured into the Baseball War Relief and Service Fund, Inc.; and the $800 million war-bond game at the Polo Grounds on August 26, when a combined team of Yankees, Dodgers, and Giants beat a group of Army All-Stars, 5–2, before 38,000 people. It is interesting to note that the only picture supposedly taken of Ted Williams and Babe Ruth together in uniform was snapped at that Fenway Park contest in July.

A few takeoffs on the World Series occurred. At the end of the 1943 season, the Norfolk Naval Training Station and Norfolk Naval Air Station clubs engaged in an exciting best-of-seven series, which the Training Station won, four games to three. Following the 1944 baseball campaign in Hawaii, the cream of the crop of Army and Navy ballplayers participated in the famous Service World Series. What started out as a best-of-seven affair limited to Oahu Island wound up as an eleven-game extravaganza, with the final four contests being played on the islands of Maui, Hawaii, and Kauai. The Navy, shored up at the last minute with reinforcements from the continental United States and Australia, won the first six games and finished with an 8–2–1 record for the series, the tie being a fourteen-inning 6–6 humdinger in Hoolulu Park, Hilo, Hawaii. The following fall, the Navy had its own World Series in the Hawaiian Islands, featuring the American League against the National League. The AL squad was favored, but the National Leaguers won, four games to two. As in the previous year, an additional contest was played for the benefit of service men and women, with the Americans beating the Nationals; so the final tally was Nationals four, Americans three.

Baseball was played all over the world during the Second World War. In late February 1945, twenty-eight Navy ballplayers boarded two Marine Corps planes and proceeded to make two tours of the forward areas of the Pacific, with both of them ending on Guam; then the players were dispersed among Guam, Saipan, Tinian, Peleliu, and Ulithi. Shortly afterward, Army Air Corps players did the same thing. Right after the war in Europe ended, many pro players had German and Italian POWs build fields for them and top-flight competition ensued. An Army All-Star team was formed and toured Europe, visiting cities in Germany, France, Italy, and Austria.

Perhaps the most important outgrowth of World War Two military baseball was black-white integration. A full year before Branch Rickey signed Jackie Robinson to a Brooklyn Dodger organization contract, Hal Hairston, a black pitcher formerly with the Homestead Grays of the Negro National

League, was hurling for the Army against the Navy in the Service World Series in Hawaii. A year later, Calvin Medley, another black pro, was pitching for the Fleet Marine team on Oahu Island. Two thousand miles away from the U.S. mainland, on a group of islands populated with Hawaiian natives and American, Chinese, and Japanese immigrants, racially integrated baseball could become a reality. Blacks and whites could play together on service teams and black, white, and yellow people could perform as a unit in the Honolulu semipro league. Back in the continental United States, black and white service teams would remain segregated until after the war. Thus the white Great Lakes team won 48 and lost only 2 in 1944, while the black club went 32–10 and won the championship of the Midwest Service League. Larry Doby, star shortstop on the black team and later the first man of his race to play in the American League, could not play with whites in Illinois but was welcome to play softball on Ulithi Atoll a year later with white professionals like Mickey Vernon and Billy Goodman. Negro League stars Leon Day and Willard Brown couldn't as yet crack the color barrier back home, but they could lead a team comprised almost exclusively of white semipro players to victory in Nuremberg's famous stadium, site of the massive Nazi Party rallies of the 1930s. Against the hand-picked professionals of General George Patton's Third Army club, righthanded fireballer Day led the Overseas Invasion Service Expedition (OISE) club to a 2–1 victory for the European Theater of Operations (ETO) championship before a huge crowd.

No description of military baseball during the period would be complete without mention of what transpired in Japan. The Land of the Rising Sun had been on a war footing since the Marco Polo Bridge incident in Beijing, China, on July 7, 1937. Professional ballplayers had been drafted at least from 1938 on, as evidenced by the induction that year of Eiji Sawamura, the country's most famous pitcher. In fact, Sawamura was to be taken into the Army three times: in 1938, 1941, and again in 1944. With the coming of global war following Pearl Harbor, intense Japanese nationalism and militarism manifested themselves in many ways regarding baseball. Team names on uniforms were changed to Japanese characters from Roman letters, and the traditional baseball cap took on a military look. The Tokyo Giants were renamed *Kyojin Gun* or "Giant Troop." Baseball terms imported from the foreign enemy, the United States, were changed to Japanese equivalents. "Strike" became *yoshi* ("good") and "ball" became *dame* ("bad"). "Safe" was transformed into *ikita* ("alive") and "out" to *shinda* ("dead"). A shortstop became a *yugeki* ("free-lancer").

After 1942, many outstanding players, both professionals and collegians, were drafted into the military. The two most famous collegiate baseball clubs, those of Keio and Waseda Universities, had an emotional farewell game before 30,000 students in October 1943. The presidents of both universities had negotiated successfully with the government for this contest to be held, and after it was over tears flowed freely as both players and spectators wondered if they would ever see another game. Their sadness was well founded. Among the three million Japanese, military and civilian, who died on the home islands or in the Pacific, China, and Southeast Asia were a great number of good players, including the best, Sawamura, who was killed on a troop transport in the Taiwan Strait on December 2, 1944. Today the Japanese equivalent of the Cy Young Award, given annually to the best pitcher in each of the American leagues, is named in his memory. Ironically, Japan's number two pitcher, Viktor Staffin, was spared because as a child immigrant from the Soviet Union he was exempt from conscription.

By 1944 only six clubs were competing for the professional championship and the season was only thirty-five games long. In 1945, the last year of the war, play was suspended altogether as cities were ravaged by fire bombing, the economy collapsed, and the two atomic bomb detonations hastened Japan's surrender late that summer.

When the last of the American wartime draftees was mustered out of the service and returned home during the 1946 season, it marked the beginning of a temporary halt in the influence of the military on baseball performance but not on fan interest in the United States. The strong desire of many who had been in the service to put rigorous or traumatic wartime experiences aside, to get on with one's life, to get out, relax, and enjoy a ballgame sparked a large increase in attendance at professional games and a rise in the number of minor leagues that was to peak in 1949 before the advent of television took its toll.

In defeated Japan, the victorious Allies, particularly the United States, were calling the shots, and the American military had the fate of Japanese baseball in the palm of its hand. Fortunately the resurrection of the game was in line with the aim of the occupation forces, namely to reform Japanese political, economic, and social institutions so that they would more closely reflect those of the Western democracies.

General Headquarters encouraged the revival of spectator sports, and in November 1945, just three months after the unconditional surrender, the Japanese professional baseball league was reorganized as many players returned from duty in Manchuria, China, and Southeast Asia. There were problems at first because the occupation forces controlled the ballparks, used them for their own entertainment, and made the Japanese professional and college leagues negotiate for their use; but key people in the Allied administration aided the Japanese in their negotiations and smoothed the way for ever-increasing privileges. General Douglas MacArthur, head of the occupation government, personally issued the order to clean up Korakuen Stadium, home of the Tokyo Giants, which had been used as an ammunition dump during the war.

In 1946 Japanese professional play resumed with a total of four hundred and twenty games being contested. By 1948, there were eight teams in the league, and such great progress was made that in 1950 two leagues were formed. There were fifteen teams that year, but the number eventually dropped to twelve, six teams in each league, which is the present setup.

Such was the situation on both sides of the Pacific when on June 25, 1950, North Korean forces invaded the South and the Korean War began. For the second time in a decade, the specter of large-scale military conscription and its inevitable effect on players and pennant races loomed over the American professional baseball scene.

The effect of the war was felt before the 1950 season ended. The Philadelphia Phillies "Whiz Kids" were out in front of the National League pack and aiming for their first pennant in thirty-five years when on September 10, their number two pitcher, Curt Simmons, who had already won 17 games, was called away when his Pennsylvania National Guard unit was mobilized. Simmons's loss, as well as injuries to three other key players, took the steam out of the Phillies, but they managed to hang on and win the pennant on the last day of

the season against the Brooklyn Dodgers. Simmons received a furlough to attend the World Series, but Phillie manager Eddie Sawyer decided not to put Curt back on the eligibility list because of his limited baseball activity while away. The Phillies lost the Series to the New York Yankees in four straight games.

The following spring, veteran sportswriters making their predictions about the 1951 pennant races focused in part on the possible effect of the draft. The consensus was that veteran teams like the Boston Red Sox in the American League and the St. Louis Cardinals and Boston Braves in the National League would stand better chances of winning because they would be the least likely to lose players. Comparatively young clubs like the Philadelphia Phillies would be the most vulnerable, while teams like the Brooklyn Dodgers, with a combination of veterans and rookies, might stand the best chance of all. They would do well in the first half of the race with their youngsters, then would come on strong in the second half with their veterans as Selective Service took its toll.

The entire line of reasoning proved almost meaningless because a large-scale call-up never took place. The war was limited. What happened instead was that a handful of individuals got drafted, usually one or two players per team, for a period of two years. This pattern continued throughout the decade of the 1950s, even after the Korean War ended in 1953. The only service that had a general recall of its World War Two veteran ballplayers was the Marine Corps, which took its Reserve aviators. This recall involved only two key players—Red Sox outfielder Ted Williams and Yankee second baseman Jerry Coleman.

Williams's farewell was especially poignant. Shortly after the 1952 season began, on April 30 to be exact, a Wednesday afternoon crowd of 24,764 took part in pregame festivities. The Splendid Splinter was given a Cadillac and a memory book containing 430,000 signatures. The fans held hands and sang "Auld Lang Syne." Williams didn't disappoint them. He hit a two-run homer off Detroit Tiger pitcher Dizzy Trout in the seventh inning in his final at-bat of the game to lead the Red Sox to victory. Given The Thumper's age (thirty-three), many felt they would never see him play again.

Ted's experience as a fighter pilot almost proved their thinking correct. He completed thirty-eight combat missions in Korea, was hit by antiaircraft fire three times, and almost didn't make it back on the second occasion. He was awarded an Air Medal with two Gold Stars in lieu of his second and third Air Medals before being transferred back to the United States for a nagging inner ear and nose ailment that ultimately left him partially deaf in one ear. He was discharged on July 28, 1953. After a little over a week of conditioning, Teddy Ballgame returned to major league play and hit a phenomenal .407 in 37 games, with 13 home runs and a whopping slugging percentage of .901. Seven more years of superb hitting were to follow.

While the Red Sox plunged to sixth place without Williams in 1952, other contending clubs who lost players to the service didn't fare that badly. The Yankees were so deep in talent that they won five straight pennants between 1949 and 1953 despite the loss of ace lefthander Whitey Ford (1951–1952), third baseman Bobby Brown (1952–1953), and infielder Jerry Coleman (1952–1953). They lost to the Cleveland Indians in 1954 without the services of their crack second baseman, Billy Martin, but still managed to win 105 games. Only a tremendous 111-win season by the Indians outdid them; how-

ever, Martin returned late in the 1955 campaign, in time to spark the Yankees to the top of the heap again.

The Dodgers won pennants in 1952 and 1953 without their top righthander, Don Newcombe, but lost to the Giants in 1954 when he returned. Newcombe went on to be the bellwether of the Brooklyn staff in the Dodgers' 1955 and 1956 National League championship seasons. The Giants won in a playoff with the Dodgers in 1951, Willie Mays's rookie season, but lost without him in 1952 and 1953. When the Say Hey Kid returned in 1954, they won again.

The Army got practically all of the professional ballplayers who were drafted during the Korean War, and thus it had some outstanding teams, both stateside and overseas. The 1951 Fort Myer, Virginia, club featured pitchers Johnny Antonelli (Braves) and Bob Purkey (Giants), infielder Danny O'Connell (Pirates), and catcher Sam Calderone (Giants). That same year, the Brooke Army Medical Center team in San Antonio, Texas, boasted outfielder Dick Kokos (Browns), second baseman Owen Friend (Browns), pitcher Glenn Mickens (Dodgers), and catcher Gus Triandos (Yankees). In 1953 the All-Army champions at Fort Belvoir, Virginia, had Dick Groat (Pirates) at shortstop and Tom Poholsky (Cardinals) on the mound. Fort Jackson, South Carolina, could call on outfielder Faye Throneberry (Red Sox), catchers Frank House (Tigers) and Haywood Sullivan (Red Sox), and pitcher Joe Landrum (Dodgers).

Several players wound up in the Far East Command, where the real action was. With Japan being used as a staging area for Korea, a few servicemen found themselves playing with or against Japanese professionals. In 1953, Leo Kiely of the Red Sox and Phil Paine of the Braves pitched a few games for the Mainichi Orions and Nishitetsu Lions, respectively. Two years earlier, ex–Pacific Coast League southpaw Ken Lehman of the 40th Infantry Division had been the star performer of the Far East Command, with a 14–1 record on the mound and a .408 average at the plate. Among his accomplishments during the 1951 season was defeating a group of Japanese All-Stars, 1–0, before 32,000 fans at Miyagi Stadium in Sendai. When Lefty O'Doul brought a group of topflight major leaguers to Japan for an exhibition tour after the American season ended, Lehman was invited to play with them and pitched excellent ball in two games, one a start against the Japanese Central League All-Stars. He later went on to pitch for the Dodgers, Orioles, and Phillies.

Only one ex–big leaguer lost his life in combat during the Korean War: Bob Neighbors, an Air Force major, who died in North Korea in August 1952. He had played in seven games for the St. Louis Browns in 1939 and also served his country in World War Two.

After the cessation of overt hostilities in Korea in 1953, Army baseball continued to feature a smattering of professional players who were two-year draftees; but in 1957 the All-Army championship tournament was discontinued, and the following year the level of competition was reduced to intramurals at the lowest unit level possible. Because the Navy wasn't drafting people and had not been a force to be reckoned with in baseball since the end of the Second World War, the Army's actions effectively spelled the end of topflight military hardball. Over the last quarter century, softball has been the serviceman's game.

The Vietnam War, like the Korean conflict, was limited in scope. This fact, coupled with the availability of Reserve programs which required only six months of active duty,

made the impact of the military on professional baseball slight from 1964, the year the war escalated after the Gulf of Tonkin "incident," to 1973, when the United States began to pull its forces out of Vietnam and terminate the draft.

Most players and executives who were eligible for the draft entered Reserve components of the armed forces, particularly that of the Army. They were obliged to do six months of basic training and spend six years attending one weekend meeting or four weekday meetings each month, and two weeks of active duty for training each fiscal year. The sixth year was basically inactive in the sense of the Reservist not having to attend meetings or do the two-week stint. The active duty obligations were normally performed during the off-season. Monthly attendance at drills became a problem on occasion, and a player might miss a weekend's worth of games here and there, but many Reserve units used the players in public relations roles for recruiting or image-building purposes and, as such, meetings could be staggered to suit the individual.

While pitching the Red Sox to their "Impossible Dream" pennant in 1967, Private First Class Jim Lonborg had to fly down to Atlanta and do his two-week Army Reserve duty. His fortnight began on Sunday, July 30, in the heat of the pennant race, and ended on Saturday, August 12. Fortunately, he was able to work out with the Atlanta Braves and with the aid of passes, didn't miss a start. After being shelled by the Minnesota Twins two days before his departure, he flew back to

Boston and worked $5\frac{1}{3}$ innings against the Kansas City Athletics on Tuesday, August 1, giving up three runs and eight hits but gaining his fifteenth win of the season. On Sunday, August 6, he lost to the Twins in Minnesota, 2–0, in a rain-shortened, five-inning contest. His counterpart, Dean Chance, pitched a perfect game. On Wednesday, August 9, he beat the Athletics in Kansas City, 5–1, for win number sixteen, tops in the majors. With his two-week sojourn over, he lost to the California Angels, 3–2, on the West Coast on Sunday, August 13.

While military duty may have caused Lonborg a mild inconvenience, youngsters like Al Bumbry and Garry Maddox were serving in Vietnam. They would go on to make their mark as top-quality major league outfielders in the 1970s. With the demise of the draft, future ballplayers wouldn't have to worry about such unpleasant career interruptions.

If there is another major war ahead of us, modern armaments, particularly nuclear weapons, will probably make it a short one, perhaps a year or less. The influence of the military on baseball should therefore remain minimal and not approach the high-water mark of World War Two, when both the length and the extent of the conflict had a pervasive effect on the game, both at home and abroad. As venerable and fascinating as the link between the military and baseball is, let us hope it remains low-profile in the future.

CHAPTER 29

Women in Baseball

Debra A. Shattuck

Baseball has long been considered a man's game. Traditionally the accepted place for a woman at a baseball stadium has been in the grandstand—not out on the field. This is beginning to change somewhat, as Little League baseball was officially opened up to girls in 1974, but, by and large, many still share the view of the male critic who wrote in *The Reach Official American League Guide, 1911* that the idea of women actually playing baseball was "positively repugnant." It is not surprising in today's open society that girls and women are taking up baseball. What is surprising is how many women actually played baseball at a time when many felt that a woman's place was in the home.

Many of the first female baseball players were college students. The secluded atmosphere of all-girl's schools enabled women to play the game without attracting too much attention. Students at Vassar College organized two baseball clubs as early as 1866. In 1879, according to Vassar alumna Sophia Foster Richardson, the Vassar girls organized at least seven baseball clubs. The private grounds of college campuses did not always protect female players from public criticism, however. In a speech to an alumnae association in 1896, Richardson recalled, "The public, so far as it knew of our playing, was shocked, but in our retired grounds, and protected from observation even in these grounds by sheltering trees, we continued to play in spite of a censorious public." Within a few years, however, the "censorious public" and "disapproving mothers" had succeeded in stifling the game at Vassar. But Vassar was not the only college where women tried their hand at baseball. In a letter to her former classmates at Smith College, Minnie Stephens (class of 1883) reminisced about the baseball clubs they had organized at the school in 1879. Stephens described the enthusiasm of the players and the keen competition at games. She also related how the Victorian-style clothing of the day, generally a hindrance to sporting endeavors, had actually benefited one of the players during a heated contest, "One vicious batter drove a ball directly into the belt line of her opponent, and had it not been for the rigid steel corset clasp worn in those days, she would have been knocked out completely." Like the women at Vassar, baseball players at Smith College faced opposition which eventually forced them to give up the game for a number of years.

Female baseball players were not limited to college campuses. In Springfield, Illinois, three men organized a women's baseball club in 1875. They were confident that the novelty of women playing baseball would attract large crowds and fatten their bankroll. On September 11, 1875, the club's teams, labeled the "Blondes" and "Brunettes," played their first match. Newspapers heralded the event as the "first game of

baseball ever played in public for gate money between feminine ball-tossers." The concept evidently caught on, for numerous other male entrepreneurs copied the idea and organized women's baseball teams. One group started the "Young Ladies' Baseball Club" in Philadelphia in 1883. These owners billed their team's games as entertainment spectacles, not serious competition, and they continually stressed the femininity and moral respectability of their players. A newspaper account of one of the club's first games relayed the management's claim that players were "selected with tender solicitude from 200 applicants, variety actresses and ballet girls being positively barred." Furthermore the article noted, "Only three of the lot had ever been on the stage, and they were in the strictly legitimate business."

The Young Ladies Baseball Club played its first game on August 18, 1883, at Pastime Park in Philadelphia. Despite the supposed "200 applicants," only sixteen girls were mustered to form the two teams for the contest; two young men rounded out the rosters. The game was played on a regulation-size diamond, but, as one observer wrote, it was too large for the women. "A ball thrown from pitcher to second base almost invariably fell short and was stopped on the roll. The throw from first to third base was an utter impossibility." Five hundred spectators witnessed the club's debut and were caught up in "uncontrollable laughter" much of the time. From a financial standpoint, however, the venture was a success. More than 1,500 fans turned out for the club's match at the Manhattan Athletic Club on September 23, 1883, where they "laughed themselves hungry and thirsty." Though one observer conceded that "four of the girls had become expert—for girls," it is obvious that "novelty" and not "ability" was the hallmark of women's baseball at the time.

Another novel group of female baseball players was the Bloomer Girls. Actually "Bloomer Girls" was a misnomer, since Bloomer Girls teams were composed of both men and women. Kansas City Bloomer Girls, New York Bloomer Girls, Texas Bloomer Girls, and Boston Bloomer Girls were just a few of the teams traveling from diamond to diamond in the late nineteenth and early twentieth centuries in search of fame and fortune. Despite the number of Bloomer Girl teams, they did not play each other and no formal league was set up. Instead, they journeyed from town to town, challenging men's amateur and semiprofessional teams. The Bloomer Girls teams relied on sideshow style appeal to draw fans and, not surprisingly, the bottom line was money. The manager of the Texas Bloomer Girls wrote to one prospective promoter in 1913, assuring him that the team's seven girls and four boys, "including the one-armed boy who plays center field," would draw enough fans to ensure the backer "three hundred dollars clear money" each week. A few of the male Bloomer Girls

players like "Smoky Joe" Wood and Hall of Famer Rogers Hornsby went on to become successful big league ballplayers, but the future was not as bright for the female players who could not aspire to anything higher in the baseball world.

The Bloomer Girls teams were not the only option available to baseball-playing females around the turn of the century. Women's teams and mixed teams competed occasionally in "pickup" games. One such game took place in Kearsarge, New Hampshire, on August 7, 1903. An article in the *Boston Herald* the following day noted, "The teams were made up of young ladies gowned in white and young men decked out in girls' clothes, all New Englanders, guests at the hotel." On August 31, the newspaper announced an upcoming game at Forest Hills between the "Hickey and Clover clubs," each composed of five women and four men. One year later, in Flat Rock, Indiana, a group of women organized two baseball clubs, one consisting only of married players, the other only of single players.

While some women played on all-female or coed teams, others challenged social constraints of the day by playing on otherwise all-male teams. On June 12, 1903, the *Cincinnati Enquirer* printed an article about the efforts of a local woman, Miss M. E. Phelan, to get a job as center fielder with the all-male Flora Baseball Club of Indiana. Phelan wrote to the club's manager informing him, "I have played with a number of lady ball clubs and am considered the equal of the average country player." Whether the Flora club took Phelan up on her offer to play for them for "$60 per month and expenses" is unknown, but only four years later another Ohioan, Alta Weiss, became an overnight female baseball-playing sensation and, as one article put it, "perhaps the only girl in the United States to obtain [a] college education through skill as a baseball player."

Weiss, a native of Ragersville, Ohio, became a celebrity in the Cleveland area when she made her pitching debut with the all-male, semiprofessional Vermilion Independents on September 2, 1907. More than 1,200 fans attended the game in which Weiss pitched 5 innings, giving up only 4 hits and 1 run. By the time Weiss made her second appearance on September 8, she was already being heralded as the "Girl Wonder" in the press. According to the *Vermilion News,* so many fans wanted to see Weiss play that special trains had to be run to Vermilion from Cleveland and surrounding towns.

Weiss pitched 8 games for the Independents during their 1907 season. More than 13,000 fans saw the games, including a season high of 3,182, who witnessed her debut at Cleveland's League Park on October 2, 1907. At least a dozen newspapers covered her exploits. The following year her father bought a half-interest in a men's semiprofessional team which was known thereafter as the Weiss All-Stars. It was based in Cleveland and, with Alta as a drawing card, played for large crowds throughout Ohio and Kentucky.

Though Weiss was far and away the best-known female baseball player in northern Ohio at this time, she was not the only one. On June 22, 1908, the *Cleveland Press* introduced fourteen-year-old Carita Masteller to the public. The paper reported that she had been playing baseball for eight or nine years and was as good as Weiss. That same month Weiss pitched against another female pitcher, Irma Gribble. The two dueled again in August. In another unique game, two sisters from Bellevue, Ohio, Irene and Ruth Basford, pitched for opposing men's teams.

Another well-known female baseball player who played on

men's teams was Rhode Islander Elizabeth Murphy. "Lizzie," as she liked to be called, played amateur and semiprofessional baseball from about 1915 to 1935 and was known as the "Queen of Baseball" throughout New England and eastern Canada. After playing for a number of amateur teams in Rhode Island, Murphy signed with the semiprofessional Providence Independents in 1918. A few years later she joined Ed Carr's All-Stars of Boston and earned quite a reputation for her skills as a first baseman.

In 1928, while Murphy was still impressing the fans in New England, fourteen-year-old Margaret Gisolo helped her Blanford, Indiana, American Legion men's baseball team win county, district, sectional, and state championships. In seven tournament games she had 9 hits in 21 at-bats. She scored 10 putouts and 28 assists in the field, with no errors charged against her. A protest against her participation filed by opposing teams went all the way to the American Legion's National Americanism Commission, which referred it to the major league baseball commissioner, Judge Kenesaw Mountain Landis. Landis determined that American Legion rules did not specifically ban the participation of women and disallowed the protest.

Landis had to address a similar situation three years later when the "Barnum of Baseball," Chattanooga Lookouts manager Joe Engel, signed seventeen-year-old Jackie Mitchell to a contract with his Class AA minor league team, thus making her the first female professional baseball player. Mitchell had been taught to pitch by major leaguer Dazzy Vance and had once struck out nine men in a row in an amateur game. She became an overnight celebrity on April 2, 1931, when she pitched in an exhibition game against the visiting New York Yankees—and struck out Babe Ruth and Lou Gehrig, back to back. Speculation continues as to whether Ruth and Gehrig were merely putting on a show or really trying to hit Mitchell's pitches. Mitchell contended that it was not a setup and that the only instructions to the Yankee players had been to try not to hit the ball straight through the pitcher's box. A number of Yankee players confirmed her story. Unfortunately Mitchell never had a chance to repeat her performance as a professional baseball player. A few days after her debut, Landis informed Engel that he had disallowed Mitchell's contract on the grounds that life in baseball was too strenuous for women. Organized baseball formalized the ban against women signing professional baseball contracts with men's teams on June 21, 1952; the ruling still stands.

The restriction on women playing professional baseball on men's teams did not prevent the formation of a women's professional baseball league, however. In 1943, with wartime manpower shortages threatening major league baseball, Chicago Cubs' owner Philip K. Wrigley decided to form a women's professional softball league which would play its games in the major league stadiums while the men were away at war. Within a year of its founding, the league modified its rules and the All-American Girls Professional *Baseball* League (AAGPBL) was born. The AAGPBL made its debut in 1943, when four teams—the Rockford [Illinois] Peaches, the South Bend [Indiana] Blue Sox, the Racine [Wisconsin] Belles, and the Kenosha [Wisconsin] Comets—squared off during the League's 108-game schedule. Attendance that year was 176,000 fans, which, according to one contemporary, meant that the League was "drawing a higher percentage of the population [in league cities] than major league baseball ever did in its greatest attendance years." Attendance figures con-

tinued to rise year after year, reaching a peak in 1948, when the League's ten teams drew almost 1,000,000 fans. That same year, AAGPBL teams drew more than 100,000 fans for a series of nine games in Puerto Rico.

Unlike women's teams of the past, the AAGPBL relied on players' skills, not their gender, to draw fans to the ballpark. The 500 women who played in the AAGPBL during its eleven-year existence were top-notch athletes. Many were veterans of championship school, community, or industrial softball teams, and a few had even played on boys' or men's baseball teams. In addition, many of the AAGPBL managers were experienced professional baseball players—some, like Bill Wambsganss (the only player ever to achieve an unassisted triple play in a World Series), Max Carey, Jimmie Foxx, and Dave Bancroft, were legends.

By 1954 televised major league baseball games and organi-zational problems led to the demise of the AAGPBL. But the lack of a formal league has not hindered women who still desire to play baseball. Many girls continue to play the game on an informal basis; a few play on Little League teams, and one women's team even tried to gain admission to the men's Class A Florida State League in 1984. That effort failed, but in June, 1988, baseball enthusiast, Darlene Mehrer, founded a new women's baseball league in Glenview, Illinois. Time will tell whether the new league will ever achieve the popularity of the AAGPBL. In the meantime, baseball will continue to be considered a "man's" game, but there can be no doubt that female players have enriched baseball's past and are striving to change baseball's future. And with Pam Postema umpiring at the Triple-A level and scores of women working behind the scenes in professional baseball, women bode well to influence the game at other levels, too.

The Game Off the Field

CHAPTER 30

The Business of Baseball

Steve Mann

Major league baseball, like every other professional sport, is an entertainment business. And the financial success of any top-level entertainment business rests on its ability to attract consistently large audiences. In order to meet that requirement, the business must do two things. It must assemble and maintain a group of the very best performers in their field, and it must provide pleasant accommodations for the spectators. Every other facet of the business is tied to these fundamental necessities.

In professional sports, the top performers are essentially world-class athletes. And, by definition, there is always a relatively scarce supply of such athletes. This scarcity demands constant vigilance on the part of club management in identifying and developing new talent. The task of maintaining an ample supply of highly skilled performers is difficult in any sport for the simple reason that the players have relatively short careers. But it is especially challenging in baseball because the amateur players, no matter how gifted and experienced they are, almost invariably need intensive long-term training to be able to compete at the major league level. To continue producing that level of talent, season after season, the clubs are obliged to invest heavily and continuously in scouting and player development.

Although the association between major league clubs and their towns runs deep, and one therefore tends to think that the clubs belong to their towns, major league baseball is actually a form of private enterprise. It is an industry made up of twenty-six separate, semi-independent franchises, all of which are owned by private individuals, groups, or companies. Each franchise is contractually linked to a half dozen or more minor league clubs through which it develops its big league talent. The network of those two hundred or so clubs is organized under the Office of the Commissioner of Major League Baseball.

Like any other private industry, baseball has had to depend upon income and profits for its existence. In the game's earliest days, nearly all of its revenue came from sales of tickets to spectators. As the sport grew in popularity, and as bigger and more comfortable stadiums were built to accommodate the increasing number of fans, the sale of refreshments, scorecards, pennants and other team paraphernalia became significant new sources of club revenue. The advent of radio broadcasts in the 1920s brought yet another form of income to the game: advertising revenue. Sponsors paid radio stations handsomely for promoting their products during games. And the stations, in turn, paid the clubs for the rights to carry the games. As the listening audiences grew, the charges for broadcast rights increased. When television was introduced, a generation later, a flood of new advertising money washed over the major leagues. By the mid-1980s, total industry income from radio and television rights, in-stadium advertising and promotions, and club shares of ballpark concessions exceeded gate receipts.

Then, in 1987, baseball commissioner Peter Ueberroth raised several million more dollars for the industry from an entirely new source, the national sponsor. Through this scheme, huge corporations pay large sums for the privilege of becoming the official "mega-sponsors" of baseball. Now, for example, International Business Machines and Chevrolet are the official computer and automobile manufacturers, respectively, of the major leagues.

While all of this new money was being raked in, baseball's resurgent popularity continued to soar. Attendance records were being broken year after year. In 1986, every club exceeded the 1 million mark in home attendance, a major league first. And in 1987, thanks largely to unprecedented competitive parity on the field (fifteen of the twenty-six clubs were still legitimate contenders on September 1), even more fans poured through the turnstiles. At the present time, average annual club revenue exceeds $20 million. Total annual industry income is now, therefore, greater than a half billion dollars.

The baseball business also generates revenue for publishers, sporting goods companies, T-shirt manufacturers, transportation companies, service stations, restaurants, bars, legal and illegal gambling operations, and a variety of other business interests. Consequently a major league franchise is not only a source of pride for its hometown fans but also an economic boon to the city that houses it.

Where all this money comes from, of course, is the fans. It is the fans who pay for the tickets, the fans who purchase the scorecards and yearbooks, the pennants and caps, the hotdogs and sodas that supplement the gate receipts. Furthermore it is the fans who ultimately pay for newspaper, radio, television, and in-stadium advertising, for it is they who absorb the built-in costs of advertising when they buy the sponsors' goods. And for the moment, at least, the fans seem quite willing to pay the increasing costs of their spectatorship.

Given the huge and still growing influx of income to the baseball owners' coffers, one would expect that the clubs are by now embarrassingly profitable. In truth, however, the baseball business is in trouble. The problem is that throughout the revenue bonanza of the 1980s, the rate of increase in the costs of running the clubs has far exceeded the rate of increase in income. The startling rise in costs can be attributed almost entirely to a single category of club expenses—player salaries.

On the surface, the issue is simply money. Ownership claims that it still doesn't have enough of it, and the players

seem to behave as though they can't get enough of it either. The sports news media tend to pay only sporadic attention to the dilemma, in part because cries of distress are hard to accept from either party, and in part because there is no base of popular support for either party. The fans are generally unsympathetic toward either camp. In fact, public sentiment on the subject is by and large measured in terms of resentment for one or both sides, with the players lately holding a distinct edge in unpopularity.

The financial situation is quite bleak—major league baseball actually is teetering on the brink of bankruptcy. The primary cause of baseball's paradoxical dilemma is the adversary relationship that has existed between the players and owners since 1879. It was then that the baseball owners first established a limited version of the infamous "reserve clause." This was a provision in certain players' contracts that made them captives, virtual slaves, of their owners. Within six years of its inception, the provision was extended to include all major and minor league players. The ballplayers did not obtain freedom from the reserve clause, and thus did not begin to receive a reasonable share of baseball's income, until the 1977 season.

For today's players, a century-old legacy of financial slavery and the personal animosity and political entrenchment that naturally flow from that condition are neither quickly nor easily erased. In light of the dubious practices of the clubs since the 1985 season, which include collusion in dealing with free agents, the players appear justified in maintaining their basic distrust of management.

For the owners, the eleven years since the players gained their freedom have been a horror show of fiscal ineptitude and mismanagement. They have watched their own club executives drive salaries to unthinkably high levels. In several instances they have themselves added significantly to the escalation. But while many of the baseball moguls privately blame their fellow owners and themselves for allowing the game's financial crisis to develop in the first place, their public anger is directed squarely at the players, their agents, and their union.

So contrary to popular opinion, the current standoff is not merely a case of two greedy opponents using hardball negotiating tactics to force concessions out of each other, all at the fans' expense. Rather it is a clash over rights and principles. And if greed is at all involved in baseball's internal conflict, then it is more as a manifestation of that conflict than a cause of it.

In fact, the history of the business of baseball is the history of the tension between individual rights on the one hand and the priorities and practices of businessmen on the other. Like the game itself, the story is uniquely American. In many respects it runs parallel to the history of labor-management relations in America. The story begins in 1846, with the first match game of the Knickerbocker Base Ball Club, and winds its way through the institution of the reserve clause and the many challenges to it over the years, the breaking of the color bar, transcontinental franchise shifts, rich television contracts, and league expansion. But as these events are detailed elsewhere in this volume (see the contributions by Voigt, Hailey, Tygiel, Dellinger, Cohen, and Hoie), the present essay will focus on the turbulent years since 1968, when the Players Association and the owners signed the game's first bilateral agreement.

The Storm Before the Calm: 1968–1975

When Ford Frick retired as commissioner in 1965, the owners hired an unheralded Air Force general by the name of William D. Eckert. "Spike," as he was known, was openly pleased to be a ceremonial chief. But he asumed the job just at the time the Players Association was beginning to make bold moves.

To deal with the growing strength of the opposition, owners created a Player Relations Committee in 1967. The PRC, as it is commonly called, was headed by John J. Gaherin, former president of the New York City Newspaper Publishers Association. It included the two major league presidents and three owners from each league and was supported by a legal staff. As its name implied, the Player Relations Committee's sole function was to act as a link between the Players Association and the owners, delivering information to and from both bodies and assisting in the formulation of management policy.

The first big item on the PRC's agenda was a collective-bargaining agreement, something that the association had been angling to get for some time. The purpose of the agreement was to make some inroads into the standard contract. It was not yet time to launch a frontal attack on the reserve clause.

The document which emerged from the negotiations was officially entitled the Basic Agreement. Signed in February 1968, it was the first in a still unbroken series of such accords. It established a formal grievance procedure for the players and provided for subsequent study of the reserve clause by both parties. Probably the most important feature of the first Basic Agreement was that it would take official precedence over the old major league rules wherever they were found to be in conflict. This meant that players were involved in major league policymaking for the first time.

By now the players had racked up a series of important victories, and it was clear that William Eckert's administration was overmatched. During the short period in which Eckert held office, the players hired Marvin Miller, built their Park Avenue office, and successfully negotiated the first Basic Agreement. The war was on, but General Eckert was in the wrong army. The owners fired him in December 1968.

Within three months of Eckert's removal, and with the commissioner's job still vacant, the owners were confronted with a serious crisis. Management had offered the players a contract package that was a distinct improvement over the previous deal. The Players Association had rejected the offer because they felt they deserved additional increases in health care, life insurance, and pension benefits. Both sides were angry, and neither side would yield an inch of negotiating ground. So the players refused to sign contracts and threatened to strike. Spring training was scheduled to begin in just a couple of weeks, and it appeared that the players were fully prepared to delay its start.

The PRC called on one of the National League lawyers, a big pleasant chap named Bowie Kent Kuhn, to see if he could untie the knot. Kuhn, in a style which would become his trademark, devoted most of his time to calming and soothing his irritated management colleagues. Having accomplished that not-so-easy feat, he gave the players everything they had asked for. Six months later, he was rewarded for his efforts with an eight-year term as the commissioner of baseball.

Within seven months after he assumed office, Kuhn was confronted with the Curt Flood case. Flood had been a very

fine outfielder with the Cardinals for twelve years when he was informed by a low-level club official after the 1969 season that he would be playing ball with the Phillies in 1970. The Phillies had finished 24 games behind the Cardinals, and Flood apparently didn't much like the town of Philadelphia anyway. So he wrote a letter to the commissioner requesting that he be permitted to "consider offers from other clubs before making any decisions."

Kuhn could not grant the request without simultaneously and singlehandedly overturning the reserve clause. He denied Flood's request. With the Players Association behind him, Curt Flood decided to take the issue to court. The case reached the United States Supreme Court, but, as usual, yet another player went down in defeat.

Why did it always turn out that the lawmakers and judges, many of whom were openly sympathetic to the players' cause, were unwilling to rule in the players' favor? Essentially it was because no less than the relationship between government and private industry was at stake. If Congress or the United States Supreme Court had chosen to modify or overturn the reserve clause, it would have immediately established a fundamentally different and presumably more equal balance of power between the players and the owners, but with unknown results. The uncertainty was the hangup. Whatever the effects of altering the reserve clause might be, the publicity such an action would receive would be enormous. Sports fans and politics watchers, a sizable audience to say the least, would be riveted to the issue. And if major league competition and franchise stability were indeed sacrificed through the removal or modification of the reserve clause, as the owners had been warning would happen since 1885, then the government officials responsible for the decision, either the Supreme Court justices or the members of Congress, would be held accountable. If baseball could not right itself in a reasonable amount of time or, worse, if it were to collapse, this would be especially embarrassing and possibly damaging to nothing less than a branch of the United States government.

Except in the most extreme circumstances, neither Congress nor the Supreme Court is inclined to take a potentially profound step where the outcome of its decisions is so thoroughly unpredictable. Both bodies would much prefer that basic struggles of this sort be brought to a higher level of resolution before they will bring their heavy conclusive weight to bear upon them. Not a single meaningful aspect of the reserve system had been altered yet. The real effects of altering or removing the controversial clause were still basically untested. So it is reasonable to conclude that in the eyes of Washington politicos baseball's eternal adversaries had a long way to go before the federal government would get seriously involved.

Despite the risks involved, the Supreme Court's decision to retain baseball's antitrust exemption in the case of *Flood* v. *Kuhn* was a upheld by a narrow 5–3 margin. Subsequent revelations concerning the justices who ruled on the case suggest that the issue troubled a few of them deeply and that the vote was even closer than the final tally indicated. It could have gone either way. Furthermore public opinion at the time was overwhelmingly on the side of Curt Flood.

These were definite signs that the owners were in a lonelier position than they had ever been in before. Indeed, they were cornered. And Commissioner Kuhn's previous behavior as well as the personal risks his job entailed should have been clear hints to the owners that he would be more inclined to commiserate with them than fight for them when the going got tough.

The Players Association, which had responsibly cautioned Flood against pursuing his case, was nonetheless delighted that he had chosen to disregard their advice. Flood's case would keep the reserve system in full public view.

This was just the first loud shot in what would become an unceasing legal siege on baseball management. Starting with the Flood case, the two sides have engaged in major confrontations roughly once a year ever since. Just during the time that the Flood case was being heard, the association fought a battle over the second Basic Agreement in 1970, which it followed up with a players' strike in 1972, which was in turn followed by a third Basic Agreement in 1973 that gave the players the right to outside, impartial salary arbitration.

Between these big surges, the union maintained a barrage of smaller assaults. And in what was effectively a flanking operation, they directed a flurry of attacks on the renewal clause of the uniform baseball contract. What the renewal provision said, in brief, was that a player who did not sign a new contract for the coming season at a salary set by the club would still be the property of his current club for one year—the renewal year. What it did not say was what would happen after the renewal year. Would a player be free to sell his services to any club at the conclusion of the renewal year? Thus a pivotal legal question remained unanswered, a question that shared its legal border with the reserve clause.

In 1969, pitcher Al Downing of the Yankees made a serious inquiry into the matter. He wanted to play the 1970 season without signing so that he could become a free agent the following year. After being cautioned by Marvin Miller against testing the renewal clause, Downing was told by Yankees management that if he refused to sign his 1970 contract, he might as well not bother to show up at spring training. Downing signed. He was then traded to Oakland before the 1970 season began.

In 1972 St. Louis catcher Ted Simmons came even closer to testing the renewal clause. He played unsigned for half a season before finally agreeing to a two-year contract with the Cardinals. From 1973 to 1975, seventeen more players started seasons without contracts, all of whom threatened to play out their options for a stab at becoming free agents. Two of them, pitchers Dave McNally and Andy Messersmith, carried out the threat—they never did sign.

Meanwhile, association gains were piling up. The 1970 Basic Agreement had given the players the right to arbitrate grievances. The Flood case had led to the inclusion of the "five-and-ten" rule in the 1973 Basic Agreement, by which players with ten or more years of major league service who have played for at least the last five years with one club have the right to approve a trade to another club. Though the rule affected only a very small segment of the major league population, it marked the first time that any group of players had any control over where they would ply their trade. A breach of contract by Oakland A's owner Charles O. Finley had made pitcher Catfish Hunter a free agent in 1974. That decision had been of little direct value to other players, except to grant them protection against illegally drawn contracts. But it had demonstrated the determination and the growing strength of the union.

Next on the agenda was a full test of the renewal clause by Messersmith and McNally in the fall of 1975. Both pitchers had played the entire 1975 season without contracts. The

bounds of the Basic Agreement had thus been exceeded, leaving the two pitchers in a legal no-man's-land. Would the parent clubs still own the contracts of the players after the renewal year, or would the players become free agents, thereby allowing them to sell their services to other teams? That was the multimillion-dollar question.

The case was to be heard by a three-man arbitration panel. The panel chairman was Peter Seitz, a man with twenty years of experience as an arbitrator. Marvin Miller and John Gaherin were the other panel members, so naturally their partisan votes on the case would cancel out. This meant that Seitz would, in effect, be making the most important decision in the history of baseball's labor-management relations all by himself.

Although the issue was ostensibly the renewal clause, it was really the reserve clause that was on trial. For if Seitz ruled that the two pitchers were free, then every other player in the major leagues could take the same circuitous route to freedom. It would be a cavernous loophole, but a perfectly legal one.

Seitz tried vigorously to get the two sides to work out the problem through bargaining. Like Congress and the Supreme Court, he felt that the matter was far too important to be adjudicated in any other way. He even went so far as to write a letter to management, explaining that the weight of the case was definitely on the side of the players and warning that he would not shrink from his duty to act, and act quickly, on the case. But the owners stonewalled it. They rejected Seitz's recommendation.

Two days before Christmas 1975, Mr. Seitz placed a nicely wrapped gift under the owners' tree—a sixty-one-page decision in favor of Messersmith and McNally.

The owners' first response was to fire Seitz. Then they sent their attorneys around to all of the courts that would listen, trying desperately to appeal the decision. The courts listened, but did not heed the call. Every appeal was rejected, the last one coming in March 1976. Spring training had not begun. The owners had locked the players out. Another delay in the start of a big league season was looming on the not-too-distant horizon.

Then, suddenly and very uncharacteristically, Bowie Kuhn defied the owners and opened the training camps. Recognizing the unpopularity of their position and having exhausted all of their legal options, the owners entered into negotiations with the Players Association for a new Basic Agreement. By this action, the owners had officially surrendered.

The specter of the Messersmith decision cast a pall over the management negotiators. They knew that they were going to have to yield expensive turf. The only question was how much. This was it, the big face-to-face showdown between baseball management and labor, and the culmination of an ancient quest by ballplayers for a proper share of major league revenue.

On the face of it, the Basic Agreement that emerged from the negotiations in July 1976 did not seem revolutionary. Indeed, to the astonishment of many, it retained nearly all of the elements of the original reserve clause. But there was one historic exception: a provision that any player with six or more years of major league service would now have the right to declare himself a free agent.

Was this what all of the commotion had been about—the freedom to sell one's services after six full major league seasons? The answer was a resounding "Yes!" The new provision gave the players all the freedom they would ever need. In fact, 1976 was a year of unsurpassable celebration for the union members. It marked the two-hundredth birthday of the United States of America, the one-hundredth birthday of major league baseball, and the erection of a fountain of wealth for the men who play the game.

Thus ended the first long chapter in the history of labor-management relations in major league baseball. Nearly a century of internal struggle had been devoted essentially to the revison of a single sentence in the standard player's contract, a single clause that meant the difference between economic slavery and economic freedom. Although the new 1976 version of the reserve clause still restricted that freedom, and although no one could predict what effects limited free agency would ultimately have, the players had finally built a tunnel to the outside from their financial prison. And golden rays of sunshine immediately began to pour into the cells of some of the veteran inmates.

The peculiarities of the baseball industry had produced a strange, even unique form of economic struggle. The last attempt to establish a third baseball league had been crushed sixty years before arbitrator Seitz's ruling. So the baseball players received none of the large and lasting financial boosts that the American Football League, the American Basketball Association, and the World Hockey League had generated for professional football, basketball, and hockey players. And with little more than expressions of positive sentiment on the part of the fans and the politicians, they had had to fight their salary battles in virtual isolation. The transiency of the major league labor force had made it extremely difficult for them to mount a sustained offensive. Furthermore, by paying many of the star players rather handsomely, ownership had bought most of them out of opposition. Given the ease with which the owners could remove ordinary players, who would not be terribly missed by the paying customers anyway, it was next to impossible for the players to get a grassroots movement started. Troublemakers and malcontents generally found themselves tied up in court, or quickly dispatched to the minor leagues, or dispensed with altogether. Besides, it truly was a whole lot better to be turning double plays for a living than turning sod in a field or flapjacks on a grill.

Baseball players had always been a young, hungry, competitive lot, generally unschooled in and intimidated by corporate matters. So most of them were quite content to play ball for a living, regardless of the level of pay. And they tended to look back on their major league experience, their days in the sun, not with rancor, but with understandable pride and satisfaction. What resentment the players did harbor for the barons who owned them generally lasted no longer than their careers.

Under these circumstances, and given the socioeconomic climate of America during baseball's first seventy years, all that the baseball owners had had to do to protect their dictatorial monopoly was play hard-fisted defense. They and their cadre of lawyers and bureaucrats practiced the traditional corporate techniques of stonewalling, name-calling, delaying, and postponing. Furthermore they were an integral part of the business establishment. This had given them unfettered access to and clout with the sports media. Add to those advantages the reluctance of the Congress and the courts to intervene meaningfully on the players' behalf, plus the relative indifference of the fans to the whole matter, and management had been practically invulnerable. Being as ambitious,

competitive, and self-interested as they were, management had never even attempted to accommodate the players, in any area, not even when Commissioners Kenesaw M. Landis and A. B. Chandler had advised them to do so.

The owners were The Club. And they had ruled with the club, primitively and uncompromisingly, for one hundred years. The only club the player had had was made of hickory or ash and called a bat. It was the only club he had had, that is, until the star players took up the cause.

The stars were the ones who had attracted the crowds in New York in the 1850s and 1860s and put baseball on the map. It was they who had received the game's first big paychecks and eventually prompted the restrictive methods adopted by the owners, including the oppressive reserve clause. It was the stars upon whom the hapless rival leagues had pinned their takeover attempts. And it was they to whom the established clubs had paid even higher salaries to keep them in the fold.

To the fans the stars were kings, to be envied. To the owners they were pawns, to be played against the other players and the rival leagues in the interest of minimizing salaries and maximizing profits. To the players the stars were the winners in an environment in which it was every man for himself.

Baseball's stars had let their teammates down for seventy-odd years. Ty Cobb's steely disregard for his fellow ballplayers at the Celler Committee hearings in 1952—when he spoke of the necessity for maintaining the reserve clause—was perhaps the most galling example. But in the early 1950s, the stars turned and the rest of the players gradually joined the effort. Perhaps the courage of Jackie Robinson in his fight for integration had inspired them to act. Perhaps Branch Rickey's treatment of Ralph Kiner—paying him far less than his performance warranted, simply because he played for an inferior team ("We could have finished last without you" were Rickey's immortal words)—was the pivotal event in their crusade. Perhaps it was the continuing emergence of the Roosevelt-inspired middle class, or the conclusion of the war. Probably it was all of those things, and more. But whatever their personal reasons, the commitment of stars such as Bob Feller, Allie Reynolds, Ralph Kiner, and Robin Roberts to their fellow players, a commitment that led to the very formation of the Players Association in 1954 and would require their continued attention and devotion to the cause after their own careers were over, was the key to the success of the players' revolt. Others played very significant roles. Marvin Miller, Curt Flood, Andy Messersmith, and Dave McNally are among the most obvious. Dozens of lesser-known participants made important contributions, too. But when the stars finally took action, that is when the scenery really started to change. And by 1976 the stage was set for a new period in major league history—the free-agency era.

The baseball industry had undergone another dramatic change from the late 1950s to the mid-1970s. During that time the mantle of club ownership was being gradually handed over to a new genre of proprietor, the corporate magnate.

Prior to the 1950s, one did not need excessive wealth to become a club owner. Thanks to the reserve clause, operating costs had always been relatively low. And the monopoly status of the sport had served as protection against outside competition, especially after the Federal League incursion had been quashed in 1916. Clubs were generally owned by individuals or small groups of investors. Most franchises were family-run

businesses that depended for their survival and success more upon baseball savvy and blood-and-guts determination than upon managerial sophistication or huge cash reserves. The ballclub, in most cases, was the livelihood of the owner. And his fortune normally rose and fell with the standing of his team or the general economic health of the major leagues.

Through the 1950s the motivation to own a ballclub came from the prestige that one automatically acquired, the profits that one stood a very good chance of making, and, perhaps above all, a deep devotion to the game. For without an abiding attachment to baseball, one would have succumbed to the unrelenting, undifferentiated demands of the job. The fact that the game was a cash business practically mandated that management personnel be family members or highly trusted friends. Someone, after all, always had to keep an eye on the till.

In those days, most owners assumed major responsibility for the day-to-day running of their clubs. In nearly all cases, it was they who dictated and negotiated player contracts. This gave the sport a head-to-head, man-to-man character. All were in it together—the owner, his cadre of management personnel, and the players. But the relative intimacy of ballclubs did not promote fair and equitable treatment for club employees. Most of the front-office people and their assistants fared no better than the players.

The fellowship that existed resembled the sort that is found in military organizations. There was a strict top-down chain of command, in which orders were obeyed, rights and privileges were decreed, and nonsense was not tolerated. But along with that stern order came a unity of purpose among all involved and a high level of camaraderie among the troops. Those qualities helped to keep the teams and the sport intact throughout its embattled development.

The quasi-military nature of the sport helped to foster a public perception of team loyalty and stability. That perception grew after the Black Sox scandal and flourished during the Landis regime. In the meantime, the big league clubs had become embedded in their cities. For exactly fifty years, starting in 1903, not one of the sixteen American and National League franchises left its hometown. The music had stopped and the chairs were in place. The sport and each of its teams had become seemingly permanent features of the American cultural landscape.

Then, in 1953, all of that began to change. After having won the National League pennant in 1948 with a record of 91–62, the Boston Braves began to slide. By 1952, they had fallen to seventh place with a 64–89 record. The next year, the franchise moved to Milwaukee. This was the first in a rapid shakeout of two-team cities. Towns like Milwaukee had been aching to obtain major league clubs for years. Since there were as yet no firm plans to expand the major leagues, the obvious takeover targets for the disfranchised towns were the weaker clubs in two-team cities.

The next two teams to move out were both from the American League. The St. Louis Browns became the Baltimore Orioles in 1954, and the Philadelphia A's moved to Kansas City in 1955. Both clubs had been last-place finishers the year before they pulled up stakes. And both had been distinctly weaker, competitively and economically, than their National League counterparts for a long stretch of time. As a result, these first club relocations in a half-century were rather easily accepted by the hometown fans. And the general perception of franchise stability remained unshaken.

During this brief period, the Players Association was being formed, and television had begun to expand the reach and the income of the baseball business. A decade had passed since the end of World War Two, and the jet age was just beginning. It was a new world with new frontiers. And the big leagues could not buck the momentum of change.

After the 1957 season, the baseball industry was thoroughly introduced to the magnitude of that momentum, for it was then that the New York Giants and the Brooklyn Dodgers were moved to San Francisco and Los Angeles, respectively. Both franchises had maintained huge and loyal followings. Thus the decisions by Giants' owner Horace Stoneham and Dodgers' owner Walter O'Malley to go west sent shock waves through the baseball community. It was one thing to sell a wilting franchise to an enthusiastic new owner and a hungry new town. But it was quite a different matter for an owner simply to rip a solid club away from its faithful fans. The Brooklyn fans were particularly enraged. Their team had been one of the very best in baseball for the preceding decade. In their eyes, and in the eyes of many others, mainly from the East, baseball had broken a social contract by allowing the moves to take place.

From the perspective of Stoneham and O'Malley, the uprooting was strictly a sound business decision. Both viewed California as an untapped source of practically boundless opportunity. And despite the strong base of support in New York and Brooklyn, the industrial East was stagnating. Attendance at Giant and Dodger home games, though respectable, did not match the quality of the teams, especially in the case of the Dodgers. Walter O'Malley recognized that baseball was in the midst of a transition to a more demanding, higher profile, and more lucrative entertainment industry.

The Dodgers' first year in Los Angeles was a bust on the field. The club wound up the season in seventh place, 21 games behind the pennant-winning Braves. But the club set its all-time attendance record, reaching nearly 1,850,000. Only twice before had the Dodgers drawn in the 1.8 million range, in the immediate postwar years of 1946 and 1947. And this was only the beginning. After he built his own stadium in 1962 and assumed control of all ballpark concessions, O'Malley's new vision was complete. By putting a solid baseball organization in the booming Los Angeles area and securing ownership of all related property, O'Malley constructed the most successful baseball operation in the history of the sport. For its first sixteen years, club attendance averaged slightly better than 2 million. For the last fifteen years, it has averaged close to 3 million. No other club has remotely approached that degree of success at the turnstiles.

Meanwhile, up the coast, the Giants were trying to win at the same game. The first several years, the years of Willie Mays, Juan Marichal, and Willie McCovey, were magical. Great talent continued to flow into the organization, enabling the club to be a serious contender for most of its first fourteen years in San Francisco, through the 1971 season. But attendance in the city by the bay never reached the dizzying heights attained by the Dodgers. The highest total came in 1960, the year in which the club took up residence at Candlestick Park. The number was an all-time club record 1,795,356. Average attendance held at around 1.5 million through 1967, which was well above the league average of roughly 1 million for the period.

Then, however, the A's moved from Kansas City to Oakland. The Giants' attendance plummeted overnight. By the

time the club had lost its edge on the field, in 1972, annual attendance had settled in the 700,000 range, making it one of the weakest draws in the National League. Attendance languished at that level for five more years, during which time the A's were busy winning three World Series and attracting 900,000 fans per year. It was immediately evident that the San Francisco Bay area would have difficulty supporting and sustaining two major league clubs. And Candlestick Park, with its sixtyish temperatures and its erratic, blustery winds, was becoming progressively less acceptable, both to the fans and to the new principal owner of the club, Robert Lurie. Giant attendance has bounced back to the 1.2 million range since 1978. But the club, at this writing, is actively seeking a new home outside California despite the fact that it won the 1987 Western Division championship.

By the mid-1960s, the financial stakes had become higher for the major league baseball business, and the new California teams highlighted some of the opportunities and risks involved.

The most important transformation in the character of big league club ownership started in the 1960s, when corporate interests began to replace family ownership groups. Overall baseball attendance had ebbed by then, due in part to a severe drop in run production caused by a legislated increase in the size of the strike zone, and due in larger part to the ascendancy of the National Football League. The nation was in a countercultural frenzy at that time, with drugs, sex, rock-and-roll, and the Vietnam War sharing center stage. Under the circumstances, football was hot, baseball was not. There was a growing sense among the members of the major league establishment that the national pastime would have to kick into a higher gear to keep up with the faster pace and more indulgent interests of the society. The first big corporation to get into the act was the Columbia Broadcasting System. CBS purchased the New York Yankees in 1964.

One way to meet the demands of the time was to replace old, typically small, and in some cases dilapidated, baseball parks with large new all-purpose stadiums. Nineteen of the twenty-six stadiums in use today have been built since 1960. Fifteen of those have been constructed since 1966. Yankee Stadium, one of the eight existing parks built before 1960, underwent massive reconstruction in 1974–1975. A few of the seven remaining older parks are soon to be replaced.

The new stadiums reflected the comparatively cold, artificial, plastic, hyped qualities of the new era they were ushering in. They were equipped with massive electronic scoreboards and message boards. Giant sound systems piped advertising jingles through the vast concrete terraces of plastic seats. Spectators were led in cheers, taunts, and songs by computer-graphic instructions flashed on the huge, usually garish message machines. In the Houston Astrodome, touted for its first several years of existence as the eighth manmade wonder of the world, fans were even prompted to applaud by the center field message board, where jerky animated figures of hands would suddenly appear, clapping to the synthesized beat of a high-technology organ.

By way of these innovations, several ballparks became enormous television studios, filled with all of the technical gadgetry and special accommodations needed to put on dazzling spectacles, both for the in-stadium and at-home spectators. Even the playing fields did not escape the reconstruction trend. Artificial grass was developed for the sun-starved floor of the Astrodome in 1966, and it soon spread through the big

leagues, as though it was the real thing. Ten stadiums are now paved with plastic turf.

So by the mid-1970s the surface features of baseball had been altered markedly. For the clubs that joined in the reconstruction movement, the immediate and long-term financial costs were high. The new gimmickry, by itself, was very expensive. The cost of building a stadium had become so great by the mid-1960s that practically every one of the newer stadiums was funded by a local bond issue. And even with the local populaces paying for the ballparks, the annual rent charges to the clubs had become quite costly. Club organizations needed to become more diversified to keep up with the increasing complexities of the business. More importantly, to some of the old-style owners the game was turning into a promotion-ridden circus. The days of pure unadulterated baseball entertainment were numbered. As a result, the business was being invaded by public-relations-minded corporate magnates.

And the Messersmith-McNally decision was hanging over the industry, threatening to restructure its century-old financial foundations.

The Free-Agency Era: 1976–1989

The Messersmith-McNally arbitration decision put major league salary matters on hold for a full year while labor and management worked out the details for implementing free agency. Neither side could predict what effects the new arrangement would have, so both sides were inclined to proceed slowly and cautiously in laying it out. As a result, free-agent bidding did not begin until the fall of 1976. The two sides also agreed to suspend the salary arbitration process through the 1977 season.

What emerged from the 1976 bargaining talks was a salary system made up of four basic elements: a guaranteed minimum salary of $19,000, maximum salary cuts of 20 percent in one year and 30 percent over a two-year period, the right for players with at least two years but less than six years of major league service to have their salaries determined through arbitration, and the right for players with six or more years of service to declare free agency and sell their services to any club.

The first two components, the minimum salary and the maximum permissible cuts, were the players' defensive weapons. Both had been in place for many years. Arbitration, which was first adopted after the 1973 season, was designed to allow any player dissatisfied with a club salary offer to have his dispute heard and ruled upon by an impartial arbitrator. It was intended to give the player an opportunity to raise his income to a level commensurate with other players of similar ability and experience and thereby protect him against salary gouging. Free agency was strictly an offensive instrument. It enabled the player to determine his dollar value through free-market bidding by clubs.

In theory, an ordered salary structure would emerge from the new four-part system. There would now be three mutually exclusive "classes" of players.

At the bottom of the salary pyramid would be those players with less than two years of major league service, who would have no explicit rights beyond the major league minimum. Their salaries would be unilaterally determined by management. If such players felt they were underpaid, their only recourse would be to hold out, refusing to play unless and until they received higher pay. Holding out had been the players' only real source of negotiating leverage for one hundred years. Now, just those players with less than two years of service would be forced to rely on such an extreme negotiating measure, and only on rare occasions.

In the middle would be the arbitration eligibles. If they did not want to accept a club's offer, they would be free to take the matter to an arbitrator.

The salary arbitration procedure is essentially simple and straightforward. If, in the course of negotiations, a player has reason to believe that his club will not offer him as much money as he feels he is worth, then he officially files for arbitration by a specified date in early January. If he and the club are still unable to reach an accord as of a second deadline, at the end of January, then both sides are required to submit a salary figure. Within twenty-four hours of the submissions, the player, the club, the Players Association, and the Player Relations Committee are notified of the salary amounts that the two parties have submitted. An arbitration hearing is then scheduled for a specific morning or afternoon between February 1 and February 20, the official arbitration period. If the two parties remain unable to reach a settlement before the appointed hearing, then the case is heard in a four- to six-hour session. The arbitrator then has twenty-four hours to select one of the two submissions. It is an either-or proposition; there is no middle ground. Thus if the player is seeking, say, $350,000 and the club is offering $250,000, the arbitrator must choose one or the other figure. He may not, for example, split the difference and award the player a $300,000 contract.

In its first two years of implementation, in 1974 and 1975, arbitration did not amount to much. Indeed, it could not amount to much because nearly all salaries were relatively low. The average salary was between $40,000 and $45,000; the median was between $30,000 and $35,000. In those years, arbitration battles were generally fought over differences in the $10,000 to $20,000 range.

The top salary class in the new structure would consist of the players eligible to be free agents. They would either receive enough income from their original clubs to stay with those clubs or they would declare themselves free and seek higher pay elsewhere. In either event, there would be pressure on the clubs to pay all players with six or more years of service well enough to secure their services, assuming, of course, that the clubs would uphold the letter and the spirit of the free agency rules by earnestly bidding for players.

The scheme, as a whole, follows the logic of military employment. Like the armed services, the owners would be giving the players training and instruction in the minor leagues in exchange for six years of active duty, at which point the soldiers of summer would be free to remain with their original employers or strike out on their own. Under the circumstances, this seems to have been a surprisingly fair and reasonable resolution of the players' ancient problem. Management had cornered itself, legally, in its dealings with the Players Association and with arbitrator Seitz. So they might well have been backed into a deeper hole by the players. But this final salary arrangement appeared to give the clubs plenty of financial breathing room.

When free agency was set into place in November 1976, it had immediate impact on veteran players. Their salaries took off. In that first year, the average major league salary increased by nearly 50 percent, jumping from $51,501 to

$76,066. The median increased by a similar percentage, going from around $40,000 to around $58,000. But the extra $25,000 per player was not distributed evenly. The 1976 minimum salary of $19,000 was retained in 1977, which meant that the younger players had received no boost at the bottom end. So most of the significant raises were going to players with six or more years of major league service behind them. Those veterans represented approximately 40 percent of the player population. Thus what had happened was that the six-year veterans had realized an average increase of about $50,000, while the players with less than six years of service had, as a group, made only marginal gains. This dichotomy was to have been expected. For not only did the younger players not possess the valuable right of free agency, but they also had no access to arbitration. And even if they had been able to take salary disputes to arbitration, the awards would have been limited by the fact that players of similar skill and experience were not making big salaries either.

Over the next three years, the same principles held. The result was a lopsided three-tiered salary structure, with the youngest players hovering around the minimum, the arbitration eligibles a full notch higher, and the veterans far, far ahead. And the costs of retaining the older players continued to climb steadily and dramatically, widening the gap even further.

The average salary for all players shot up to $113,500 by the end of the 1979 season. Management took on a siege mentality, with owners and executives privately and publicly predicting doom for the baseball business. But the new system created a good deal of interest in baseball's backstage politics. If anything, it contributed to a resurgence in the game's popularity—and in the owners' revenue. The American League's expansion in 1977, from twelve teams to fourteen, and increasing competitive balance on the field in both leagues provided additional boosts to club income. The dollar value of clubs began to skyrocket. More corporate owners bought into the business, and few family-owned and -operated clubs remained. With the stakes now so high, the small owner was simply unable to compete for the better players.

For the players, the last years of the 1970s were an exciting beginning. At long last some of them had started to share in the profits of the entertainment industry that they were the center of. But the huge gap between the arbitration eligibles and the free-agency eligibles kept growing. Even the star players with less than six years of major league service were unable to bridge that gap. What had happened was that the two groups had become segregated. Veterans were being compared with veterans, and younger players were being compared with younger players, due strictly to the difference in service. Consequently middling players with many years of service were generally earning quite a bit more than stars with less than six years of service.

This development kept the rate of salary inflation from getting completely out of control. It was the silver lining in the cloud that had formed over the owners. To the players and their union leaders, it was illogical and unfair that a number of over-the-hill veterans were making hundreds of thousands of dollars more per year than many outstanding young players, such as Eddie Murray, Keith Hernandez, Pete Vuckovich, and Dennis Eckersley. In their view, too much credit was being given for sheer longevity and not enough for quality of play. But under the new salary system, the only way the younger players could move toward the veteran salary range would be through arbitration. The owners certainly weren't going to elevate their salaries out of generosity.

Meanwhile, the arbitration arena was becoming an interesting sideshow feature of the big league circus. Once the combination of free agency and arbitration was permitted to function, after the 1977 season, arbitration began to take on the character of a high stakes pokerfest. The spreads between player demands and club offers were occasionally reaching six figures. Then, after the close of the 1979 season, a major showdown started to take shape. Relief pitcher Bruce Sutter of the Chicago Cubs had completed his fourth year of unsurpassed excellence on the mound. Every big league club would have loved to have Sutter in its bullpen. At the winter meetings in Toronto, in December 1979, several club executives expressed the view that Sutter was among the three or four most valuable players in the game. Some felt that he was the topmost banana in the whole bunch. December trades and purchases of players had dried up considerably as a direct result of the new salary system. As a result, much of the attention of the press and the clubs was given to arbitration, especially to the Sutter matter. The rumors floating around the headquarters hotel suggested that Sutter would be seeking more than a half million dollars for the 1980 season, while the Cubs would not be willing to spend much more than a quarter of a million for his services.

In January the arbitration filing figures came out. The Cubs were offering their relief ace $350,000, a very high amount at that time for a player with barely four years of service, but not much higher than the income he had received the previous year. Sutter's demand was $700,000, a staggering figure that, if granted, would place him near the top of the salary pyramid despite his nonveteran status. In February the case was heard. And to the astonishment of management, Sutter was declared the winner.

This was the first big crack in the wall that separated the free agents from the younger players. The decision implied that a star is a star, regardless of his prior service time, and that he should be paid accordingly. That is to say, he should earn a salary consistent with, though perhaps not quite as high as, that of a veteran with a similar qualitative performance record.

Inside the baseball establishment there was a swirl of controversy surrounding the Cubs' handling of the case. Suggestions were made that Cubs' management committed one or two key tactical blunders. Whether those claims are valid or not, the Sutter case suggested that a few weak links among the clubs with respect to the negotiation and arbitration of salaries could have impact on all other cases and clubs. The case also helped to establish a new high-paid class of player, the relief ace.

The clubs were badly shaken by the Sutter decision. A few of the owners, particularly George Steinbrenner of the Yankees, Ray Kroc of the San Diego Padres, and Brad Corbett of the Texas Rangers, had already sent the salaries of free agents into the stratosphere. Now the clubs felt that they would have to give equal attention to the growing threat of salary arbitration. For even though the Sutter decision was the act of only a single arbitrator, the full precedential impact of which would not be determined for at least a few years, it was a strong signal of danger.

How the clubs responded to their deteriorating position is mystifying. It is also of bottom-line importance to the history of the baseball business, because that response more than

anything else is what led the clubs into the deep and dire financial straits in which they are currently mired. Management's convoluted strategy proceeded more or less along the following lines.

It was obvious to all of the clubs that free agency was costing them dearly. It was equally clear that the big bidders had not reached a plateau, so there was no telling when, where, or if the veterans' spiraling salaries would stop.

By 1980 the $1 million mark had been surpassed by several players. In the meantime, the overarching priority for nearly all of the clubs was still to put the best possible team on the field. That was their business. A handful of less well-off owners refused to enter the fray and simply turned their backs on free agents. But they were too few to buck the inflationary trend. They were on their way out of the industry anyway. For the rest, the problem was not only to decide if and to what extent they would get involved in bidding for free agents. They also had to figure out how they could keep their better young players on their teams once those players reached the sixth year of service and became free agents. Front-office people throughout both leagues dreaded the prospect of having to lose players whom they had selected, trained, and groomed for eight or more years just because some other club would be willing to pay more for them in free-agent bidding. The anxiety was particularly acute among the clubs in the smaller and less profitable media markets. So a defensive contract strategy was needed.

A few clubs responded to the dilemma by entering into long-term contracts with their most prized young players. Such contracts had been virtually nonexistent prior to free agency. The reserve clause had made the player the permanent property of his club, so there had been no good reason for the clubs to guarantee anyone more than the coming year's salary. Now, however, there was a special incentive to sign players for several years at a time. The reasoning went as follows. If a club had an All-Star quality player with four years of service, then by signing that player for, say, five years the club would retain ownership of his contract through the player's ninth year of service. In other words, the club would in effect buy out three years' worth of the player's free agency rights. In practical terms, this meant that the clubs would be willing to risk wheelbarrows full of current dollars on players purely for the purpose of being able to hang on to them for an additional one, two, three years, or more.

The multiyear contract would typically be of great benefit to the player, for no matter what might happen during the term of the contract, most or all of the money would be fully guaranteed. Thus if the player's performance were to fall off, or if he were to become incapacitated through wear and tear or injury, his financial future would be secure.

There were only two risks to the player in agreeing to a multiyear deal. With salaries escalating at a wild rate, no one could know what the future dollar value of a player might be. Consequently a salary of $750,000 in year four of the contract might appear irresistible to the player upon signing, but he could actually be worth much more than that in the major league market by the time that fourth year rolled around. The other risk of entering into a long-term contract was that the player's performance might improve dramatically, again raising his relative dollar value. If both possibilities came to be, then the player might lose hundreds of thousands of dollars, or millions, by taking the multiyear offer. Though there weren't very many of them, future Hall of Famers Johnny

Bench and Tom Seaver were among the principal victims of the multiyear contract. Each of them missed out on an income bonanza by agreeing to a long-term deal early in the free agency era, before salaries went through the roof.

Having bitten the multiyear bullet, the question now facing the clubs was how exactly to design these long-term contracts. Since each player belonged to his club through year six, it seemed unnecessary to pay any player more than a fair wage for years three, four, or five. One would have expected, therefore, that the clubs would have granted modest raises prior to a player's sixth year of service, and that they would have built much larger raises into the contract for all subsequent years, raises that would make the player's pay consistent with free agents of similar ability. In fact, what the clubs started to do was to offer free-agent level salaries for each and every year of a multiyear contract.

A hypothetical example will help to illustrate this critical issue. Let's say a club had a better-than-average third baseman who had earned $100,000 in his third year of major league service in 1979. The club wanted to ensure that it would keep the player on the team for as long as reasonably possible. So it decided to offer the player a six-year deal covering the years 1980 through 1985. Comparable third basemen with less than six years of service were making between $150,000 and $250,000. Comparable free agent third basemen, however, were earning between $600,000 and $700,000 per year. With both the player and the club anticipating continued, rampant salary inflation, they might agree that the player would be worth more than $1 million by the beginning of the sixth year of the proposed contract. A fair contract, under these circumstances, might have been constructed as follows:

Calendar Yr.	Yrs. of Service	Contract Yr.	Salary
1979	3	—	$ 100,000
1980	4	1	200,000
1981	5	2	300,000
1982	6	3	700,000
1983	7	4	850,000
1984	8	5	1,000,000
1985	9	6	1,150,000
Tot. Cum. Salary			4,300,000

In the first two contract years, before the player would have reached free agent status, he would have been paid at a rate slightly higher than, but generally consistent with, the pay of other third basemen who had not accrued six years of service. Then his salary would have leaped up to the free-agent level in contract years three through six.

What the clubs in fact did in many such instances was draw up contracts that looked more like the following:

Calendar Yr.	Yrs. of Service	Contract Yr.	Salary
1979	3	—	$ 100,000
1980	4	1	500,000
1981	5	2	650,000
1982	6	3	800,000
1983	7	4	925,000
1984	8	5	1,050,000
1985	9	6	1,175,000
Tot. Cum. Salary			5,200,000

The first two years of this deal, while not quite at the free-

agent level, are roughly double what a comparable player would have been worth in normal negotiations or arbitration. And the total value of the second contract is $900,000 greater than the first, more than a 20 percent boost.

Of course, by adopting this approach major league executives cost their clubs both immediate and long-term cash. But, far more important than that, they set into motion a wave of big salary increases via the arbitration process. Why? Because the third baseman from the above example would be used as a basis of comparison by players of similar quality who had also not yet obtained free agency rights. In negotiations, a comparable young player would point to that contract and any others like it, claiming that if the other third baseman were worth $500,000 after just four years in the big leagues, then so, too, was he. And if the club didn't accept the claim, then the player would take the case to an arbitrator. More and more players did indeed take such cases to arbitration.

By the end of the 1983 season, this almost breathtaking act of fiscal self-destruction on the part of club management had become standard policy. Nearly every major league club had a few players with less than six years of service who were reaping very hefty incomes. As a result, the salaries of the arbitration eligibles, as a group, had increased by several hundred percent. Although they were still a clear notch or two behind the veterans in income, they had pulled away from the players with less than two years of service, who had no arbitration rights. Had the clubs not overplayed their new defensive strategy, which they clearly did not have to do, the arbitration eligibles might still have salaries within hailing distance of the major league minimum. It was by this time, of course, too late for the clubs to correct their grave strategic error. And the wall separating the younger players from the veterans had been reduced to an embattled trench.

To make matters worse for management, the Sutter precedent continued to exert its own upward pressure on the salaries of arbitration eligibles. That is, the players were still trying to establish the principle that a star is a star, regardless of his prior experience, and that he should be paid the full wages of a veteran star. The nub of their reasoning was that a young star has at least as much present value as an older star, and certainly greater future value to his club. The clubs continued to insist that service time is the bedrock of the salary structure, just as seniority is in other industries.

The first three years of the free agency era can be regarded as an experimental phase. No one on either side of the table knew precisely what was unfolding or how it would play itself out. As of 1980 it was evident to the clubs that free agency was producing an unchecked inflationary spiral and that arbitration would demand very serious attention.

Help for the clubs in the arbitration arena was already on the way. Talbot M. "Tal" Smith had been the president and general manager of the Houston Astros from 1975 through 1980. He was renowned in management circles as a tough but fair-minded chief executive with extraordinary skills in fiscal management. Smith had also brought the Astros from the depths of mediocrity to a division championship in his relatively brief tenure at Houston. But he and the new Astros owner, John McMullen, did not see eye to eye on a number of internal club matters, particularly the assignment of contracts. So despite his club's 1980 success on the field, Smith was fired almost immediately after the Astros lost the League Championship Series to the Eastern Division champion Phillies, three games to two.

Smith had gotten his feet wet in arbitration prior to his last season at the helm. Although he had lost both cases, his interest in the arbitration process had been piqued by the experience. He genuinely enjoyed the challenge of the specialized competition that arbitration is. So he decided to offer his personal services to a few of his front-office colleagues. The Oakland A's took him up on the offer. The club was headed toward contract battles with two of its best players, outfielder Tony Armas and pitcher Mike Norris. With Tal Smith representing them, the A's prevailed over both players in arbitration.

The victories prompted Smith to set up a business, Tal Smith Enterprises, to extend his salary services to other clubs. At the end of the 1981 season, six major league clubs retained Smith for support in salary negotiations and arbitration. Smith quickly assembled a small group of legal and statistical experts to round out his salary team. He had commented, privately, in his last months as the president of the Astros that backup catchers were now earning more than general managers. He felt strongly that the financial survival of major league baseball was in jeopardy and regarded his new role as a mission, a financial crusade, to save the game. His lament over fiscal conditions was sincere, and it was music to the ears of a lot of club executives.

Prior to the formation of Tal Smith Enterprises, the Player Relations Committee had been solely responsible for providing advice, counsel, and data support to the clubs. The PRC's executive director, Raymond Grebey, was a gruff and rather arrogant veteran of labor-management wars. He had headed the PRC since 1978, but had not scored many victories for the clubs. Instead of allying himself with Smith, Grebey seemed to view Smith as a competitor for Grebey's rightful role as management's protector. He even attempted in various ways to thwart Tal Smith's efforts. This bureaucratic pettiness exemplified management's internal divisions over policies and methods for combating the gains being racked up by the Players Association and its constituents.

Grebey notwithstanding, crusader Smith and his band of Young Turks put on a dazzling display in the 1982 arbitration campaign. Of the eight cases that went to hearings, the Smith team won seven. It was a previously unheard-of margin of victory, and it helped to quell Grebey's noisome opposition. More importantly, it sent a strong message to the players and their agents. They would have a better organized and much more formidable arbitration adversary than they had ever before encountered. A line had been drawn in the arbitration sand, giving the clubs a small but significant beachhead.

As the 1982 salary returns came in, it was plainly evident that the clubs were routinely granting enormous percentage increases to arbitration eligibles and free agents. There was a rising tide of salaries that was lifting nearly all boats. Furthermore, the clubs, inexplicably, were tendering virtually no salary cuts, even though they were empowered to do so. Equally difficult to explain was the fact that franchise sales were proceeding apace, with prices going up, way up. The last of the family owners was gone, and corporate interests were evidently still anxious to gain membership in the baseball owners' club.

Tal Smith Enterprises' accomplishments the year before led six more clubs to sign up after the 1982 season. Smith had to expand his workforce and computerize his operation to keep up with the demand for his services. The client load increased to thirteen clubs the following year and remained at

that level through 1986. Smith was, thus, representing half of the clubs in baseball.

Smith's presence no doubt tempered the submissions of a sizable percentage of players in arbitration, and it helped to slow the pace of inflation in normal negotiations carried out by his client clubs. But the Smith team compiled only a .500 record after its first splashy campaign. Inherent in the arbitration process is a tendency for the arbitrators to split their decisions, for if they come down too heavily on one side they are likely to be permanently removed from the pool of arbitrators by the opposing side. This worked against Smith, perhaps even unduly after his highly publicized rookie campaign. Moreover, even Smith's clients saw their payrolls rise at a bankrupting rate. The past practices of ill-prepared clubs had gone on too long and they were precedential. Those practices had helped to establish the micro-rules of the arbitration game, and there was little that Tal Smith or anyone else could do about it. Besides, of the more than 700 contracts that are signed each year, only 25 or so end up in hearings. And of that total, only about 60 percent, or roughly 15 cases, are handled by Smith. In other words, Smith brought too little, too late. The structural damage had already been done even before he had officially hung up his shingle. To make matters worse, by the end of the 1985 arbitration season many of the club executives and the player agents were complaining that arbitration had become a random process. Decisions were almost totally unpredictable. The term being bandied about was "crapshoot"—arbitration, many were saying, had turned into a crapshoot.

Throughout the first decade of the free agency era, labor-management relations worsened. The clubs' hiring of Smith had put an additional buffer between the players and the clubs, just as the cadre of player agents had done several years earlier. By adding such layers of representation, the ballplayers and their owners became a step more detached and alienated from each other. The more intimate love-hate relationship that had existed between the old family owners and their players, which was more akin to the relationship between troops and their generals, or between sons and their fathers, steadily gave way to an entrenched business relationship after World War Two. Meanwhile, salaries continued to rise. The labor-management war drums were beating, perhaps more loudly than ever before. But now the owners were the Indians.

More bad news greeted the besieged front offices after the 1985 season. Two years earlier, baseball had signed a six-year television contract with ABC and NBC that was worth approximately $8 million per year to each club. The $1.3 billion deal was triple the value of the prior network-TV contract. But now there was open talk that TV revenues had passed their peak. The networks were initiating an industry-wide reduction in personnel and a streamlining of their corporate structures. Accordingly, they were letting it be known that baseball can fully expect a decline in income when the next contract comes up for negotiation in 1989. The clubs also began to see their cable television income level off. And prices for tickets, parking, and concessions had all risen steadily as the players' salaries increased. Those prices were now barely, if at all, increasable. And radio and in-stadium advertising and promotions were rapidly reaching a saturation point.

To demonstrate the gravity of the situation, the owners made the unprecedented and startling decision to open the clubs' financial books in the fall of 1985. The central purposes of this action were to prove management's claims of insolvency and to obtain changes in the Basic Agreement that would reverse, or at least stem, the flow of red ink. By their accounting, the industry was losing roughly $58 million per year, or a bit more than $2 million per club. The Players Association had its own financial analysts review the data. They concluded that the clubs had actually netted $9 million in profits in 1985. According to one highly placed club executive, the financial data were so poorly organized, so incomplete, and so out of date that no one could draw reliable conclusions with respect to club costs or revenues.

Wherever the truth lay, it was clear that no more than two or three clubs were regularly showing profits. The Los Angeles Dodgers were, and still are, in their own special category at the top of the heap. The rest were fighting a losing battle. Nonetheless, between 1982 and 1985 the Detroit, Minnesota, and Cincinnati franchises were purchased—at astronomical prices. And there was talk, encouraged by the game's new commissioner, Peter V. Ueberroth, that the expansion of the major leagues to twenty-eight or thirty teams would take place in the relatively near future.

Given the extremely discouraging financial conditions of the baseball industry in the 1980s, one wonders why anyone, including the high rollers who had replaced their generally less wealthy predecessors, would want to get into the business. By 1985, every big league club was backed by at least one big corporate entity. In name, almost every club was owned by an individual or a group of individuals, but in reality the clubs belonged to large parent companies. The list included a variety of large media corporations, an international brewery, a blue-chip jeans manufacturer, a nationwide pizza franchise, a big-time law firm, a regional car dealership, and two major shipbuilding companies. What distinguished the new breed of owners from the earlier model was that the new baseball moguls were uninvolved in day-to-day club operations. Several owners meddled in important personnel and salary decisions, but club management was now essentially in the hands of front-office executives. This absentee style of ownership was a clear indication of the relative unimportance to the owners of the financial condition of their baseball franchises. It also suggested what the main motivation to own a ballclub had finally become—promotion. For whether or not a club made money, the individuals and the corporate interests that undergirded them would constantly be in the national limelight. Thus the clubs had turned into the promotional, public-relations playthings of their corporate overlords. How else can one explain the appreciation in club values in the midst of the game's financial plunge? Is the alternative view, that so many ultrawealthy parties are just slipshod businesspeople, really credible? After all, if the new owners are so terribly lacking in business acumen, how have they gotten to where they are?

Whatever their individual reasons for buying into the baseball business, the new hands-off owners relied on front-office personnel to oversee their organizations. Within the front offices there had always been a barrier between business and baseball. The baseball people—general managers, player personnel directors, farm system directors, assistants in those areas, scouts, and all the rest—had jealously protected their professional turf and the inside information upon which their jobs rested. They were also a relatively uneducated group, the bulk of whose professional experience was limited to the playing field. The finance people, stadium operations people, ticket office personnel, and so forth minded their own busi-

ness. This kind of compartmentalization of responsibility and authority was another of the quasi-military aspects of the sport. The new owners in most cases empowered their one or two top baseball executives to hire and supervise the business personnel, thereby keeping the old order intact. As a result, salary matters generally fell to people ill-equipped to deal with salary techniques and strategies.

Salary determination is inherently a blend of performance evaluation and comparative salary analysis, and a rather exacting intellectual exercise. But with the owners basically uninvolved and with the traditional organizational barrier still standing, there were very few club personnel qualified to do a creditable job in the salary arena. The rapid and broad success of Tal Smith stood as proof that the clubs could not adequately manage their own salary matters. And if there was a single area on which the current and future financial health of each franchise depended, it was undeniably the area of salaries. It is for these reasons that free agency and arbitration led to rampant inflation. To put it another way, the Messersmith-McNally decision had freed only the veterans; it was the unsupervised and fiscally deficient baseball executives who had made the rest of the major league players wealthy. In effect, they had given away the store while the owners were fishing.

The first loud signal of ownership's recognition of its managerial shortcomings came when the owners' council selected the business entrepreneur Peter Ueberroth to replace the attorney Bowie Kuhn as baseball's commissioner. Ueberroth had demonstrated his take-charge, no-nonsense, profit-oriented approach to sports when he organized the 1984 Olympic Games held in Los Angeles. The owners' appointment of Ueberroth was nothing less than a reversion to the strong-commissioner strategy that had brought Judge Landis into baseball and saved the game in the aftermath of the Black Sox scandal. It showed that they were deeply concerned about the existing state of affairs. It was also a virtual admission that when the going gets tough, the ever-divided house of owners must seek outside help.

When Ueberroth took office as the commissioner at the beginning of 1985, baseball was awash in red ink and the tide was still rising. The clubs could not unilaterally rewrite the Basic Agreement. Nor could they control the behavior of arbitrators. They had opened their books, but the players remained unconvinced that they were in trouble. How, the players asked, could the clubs possibly be insolvent and at the same time have a string of anxious buyers waiting in line to pay exorbitant and still escalating prices for those clubs? Management was becoming desperate.

The new commissioner was not the type of administrator who would simply sit back and allow a bad situation to deteriorate further. In late September of 1985, Ueberroth addressed the club owners and their representatives at a regularly scheduled quarterly meeting. After the season ended, he attended two more of management's private meetings. His broad message to the clubs at those gatherings was that they would have to exercise fiscal responsibility in order to keep their industry viable. His more specific advice to them came in the form of a negative statement that he made at the general managers' meeting at Tarpon Springs, Florida, in early November:

"It is not smart to sign long-term contracts."

Shortly after that meeting, sixty-two players filed for free agency. Though the list was long, it was perhaps the least impressive group, talentwise, since free agency was instituted. It was loaded with marginal and soon-to-retire players. One of the few exceptions, however, was All-Star outfielder Kirk Gibson. The twenty-eight-year-old Gibson had been with the Detroit Tigers for his entire professional career, and he was coming off his best season as a major leaguer. Many clubs would normally have had serious interest in obtaining a player of Gibson's caliber. But the deadline for bidding on free agents came and went, and not a single club made an offer to Gibson. In fact, practically all of the free agents had been completely ignored by the clubs. Of the group of sixty-two, only five changed clubs. And all five were players in whom their previous employers had officially indicated no interest by waiving their right to negotiate with them.

To the Players Association, it was obvious that the clubs had entered into a tacit agreement not to pursue any free agents that their most recent employers wished to retain. In their view, that amounted to a conspiracy to violate the terms of the Basic Agreement. The legal term for such behavior is collusion. So the association lodged a grievance against all twenty-six clubs, claiming that they had violated Article XVIII of the agreement, which states that "the Clubs shall not act in concert with the other Clubs" in signing free agents.

Veteran arbitrator Thomas Tuttle Roberts began hearing the case in the summer of 1986. In September the owners attempted to dismiss Roberts from the case. He had just ruled, in a separate case, that the clubs could not insert drug-testing provisions in players' contracts without the consent of the Players Association, and that had angered the owners, or so they claimed. The association felt that this was merely an excuse and that management was engaging, as it had done for more than a century, in delaying tactics. For the longer it would take to resolve the collusion case, the more opportunity the clubs would have to defy free agency and maybe even wreck it.

To the delight of management, the case dragged on through the winter of 1986–1987. This time, however, the free agent pool was one of the best on record. It included perennial All-Stars Tim Raines, Andre Dawson, Jack Morris, and Lance Parrish. But, true to form, the clubs continued the practice of the previous year. They made no bids for free agents whom their previous clubs wanted to keep. And, not surprisingly, the Players Association filed another grievance.

Then the final 1985 salary tallies came in. What those results showed was that management's initial attack on free agency had had little if any effect on salaries. The major league payroll had continued to grow at a bankrupting pace. Management was sweating bullets, and they were looking more and more ready to fight back in other ways.

Some of the provisions of the Basic Agreement had been changed through prior negotiations between the players and the clubs. The changes went into effect after the 1986 season. The most important of them dealt with arbitration rights. Players now would have to complete three full years of major league service instead of just two to become eligible for arbitration. Using the new provision to full advantage, the clubs grossly underpaid some of the game's brightest young stars, including 1986 Cy Young Award winner Roger Clemens of the Boston Red Sox. It was, as it always had been, within the clubs' rights to unilaterally assign contracts to such players. But by recent standards, the salaries tendered to Clemens and a half dozen other outstanding young players were, in each

instance, hundreds of thousands of dollars below the established scale. Several of the players threatened to hold out for the 1987 season. Clemens did hold out until shortly after the season began. In addition, the clubs took a firmer stand in arbitration than ever before. They submitted several offers that represented no raise over the previous year's salaries, and they even went so far as to try to cut a few salaries by way of arbitration. Given the almost total absence of holds and cuts in prior arbitration proceedings, these were highly risky actions.

The 1986–1987 arbitration results revealed the chaotic state into which the process had lapsed. At the bottom end of the salary scale, the clubs had cleaned up. Twenty-six players had taken their cases to arbitration and seven of them had returned without salary increases. Four of those had received cuts in pay. But at the high end, Yankee first baseman Don Mattingly received an award of $1,975,000, which was the largest arbitration award ever. Overall, the clubs won sixteen of the twenty-six cases. And the players realized the lowest percentage gain in income in the history of arbitration.

The most interesting case was that of Detroit pitcher Jack Morris. Morris had gone to arbitration four years earlier and had lost. After the 1986 season, he declared himself a free agent. But because the Tigers wanted to keep him, none of the other clubs would bid for his services. His agent, Richard Moss, decided to throw the Tigers a curveball. He advised his client to pursue a new option available to free agents, namely to withdraw his declaration of free agency and subject himself, once again, to arbitration. Detroit management was over a barrel. Morris was one of the best pitchers in the game, and he had plenty of statistical evidence to back up that assessment. So the club knew that if it were to accept the offer, it would stand a pretty good chance of getting clobbered in arbitration. On the other hand, if the club were to turn down the offer to arbitrate, it would not be permitted to negotiate with Morris until May 1, a full month into the 1987 season. The club consented to arbitrate. Jack Morris won this one, and it cost the club a whopping $1,850,000 to retain his services for the 1987 season.

When the final figures for 1987 came in at the end of November, it appeared that the array of extreme measures taken by management had at last reversed the salary inflation trend. In fact, the average major league salary had declined by a few thousand dollars. And Tal Smith Enterprises was still proudly leading the cost-reduction crusade on behalf of the ballclubs.

But it was not yet time for the owners to celebrate, because two months earlier arbitrator Tom Roberts ruled that the major league clubs had indeed acted "in concert" when they shunned the free agents after the 1985 season. This was also a clear indication that the second collusion grievance, then being heard by arbitrator George Nicolau, would also go the players' way, as it did. No one will know precisely what effect the grievance proceedings will have until the specific remedies for the Roberts and Nicolau cases are determined. In any event, though, the players will ultimately have earned more in both years than the currently tabulated figures show. So it is possible that salaries actually continued to rise.

What is certain is that the ballplayers and the major league clubs remain deeply entrenched in financial warfare. The chairman of the board, president and chief executive officer of the Philadelphia Phillies, William Y. Giles, has been a baseball executive for more than thirty years. He was one of the principal negotiators in the lucrative six-year pact signed by the television networks. And he is widely regarded as one of the "nicest guys" in the business. When asked recently by a Philadelphia reporter how labor-management relations were faring, Giles said that the animosity between the parties is "at an all-time high."

The Spoils of War

For the better part of a century, major league baseball players fought for a reasonable portion of the proceeds of their entertainment industry. However, with no viable competition from outside the baseball monopoly, the players were forced to accept whatever salaries and conditions their owners saw fit to give them. They eventually made progress, but only after they pulled together as a bargaining unit and slowly and painfully loosened the grip of the reserve clause. In the end, what they obtained was not a specified level of income but rather a system of salary determination. The system contained no financial guarantees beyond the major league minimum salary. How much money the players would ultimately receive through free agency and salary arbitration would rest entirely on the behavior of the clubs.

What the system did was create a form of free-market competition within the monopoly. In a sense, it turned a single business into twenty-six separate businesses and unleashed a self-destructive frenzy of interclub competition. To the players' amazement and joy, they saw their salaries reach heights that they could not have imagined were possible.

To most of the fans and the press, the dizzying escalation in their incomes made the players appear baldly greedy. And when filthy-rich players began to complain that they were being underpaid compared to other individuals or groups of players, the public's growing distaste for them was understandable. But greed really was not the issue. What was at stake for the carping millionaire pitcher or outfielder was not the money but rather his standing as a ballplayer. Money had become the measure of his talent, and every player wanted and still wants his money to match his skills. So when he sees that a player whom he considers himself superior to is earning more than he is, he feels underrated, cheated. That is his value system.

Unfortunately, as long as the salary system remains a chaotic hodgepodge without fixed standards of evaluation, in which the negotiating skills of agents and club executives are often more of a factor in determining the players' worth than their actual on-the-field contributions to their teams are, a good number of players will always feel cheated. And the clubs will continue to be and to feel besieged.

The system is under attack now. Management has chosen to use unethical or illegal methods to achieve its ends, as it has since 1879 when the first version of the reserve clause was introduced. The latest ploy in the owners' bottomless bag of tricks is collusion. Consequently, trust and respect between management and labor are at a low. And whatever hope the clubs might have had of smoothing out their differences with the players and their union has been all but dashed.

Meanwhile, until the next Basic Agreement is hammered out through collective bargaining, in 1989, the players will continue to earn astounding sums of money and the club owners will continue to bask in the national limelight, thereby getting plenty of public-relations bang for their otherwise

poorly managed bucks. And the fans will continue to be the ones who ultimately pay for the follies of both sides. Thus one of the key questions facing the major leagues is how long the fans will go on subsidizing the war of principle between the players and the clubs.

The answer may be forthcoming rather soon, because baseball is currently planning what may turn out to be the final insult to the baseball fan. According to Commissioner Ueberroth, the clubs need new sources of revenue to regain financial health and they are poised to impose per-game charges for watching games on cable television. What this means is that in addition to the monthly subscription fee, it may soon cost the fan a dollar or two to view each game.

Whether or not the fee-per-game plan is implemented, the recent and steady shift from free over-the-air telecasts to paid-for cable-TV telecasts is continuing. This development is taking viewing opportunities away from those people who either do not have cable access or cannot afford to pay the monthly fee. The problem is already rather acute for New York Yankee fans, because there is no cable television in the Bronx at this time and the majority of Yankee games are broadcast exclusively on the Sports Channel, a cable-TV operation.

In the long run, the shift to cable will necessarily diminish the size of the baseball viewing audience, which will erode the major league fan population and thereby reduce the future income of the sport.

The shift also raises a fundamental question concerning baseball's exemption from antitrust laws. The matter has been addressed by Charles E. Schumer, a member of the House of Representatives from New York's Tenth Congressional district. In an article for the *New York Times* written in the summer of 1987, he posed the following challenge:

If baseball is simply a "business," then why should it have a special antitrust exemption? On the other hand, if baseball enjoys protection from the nation's laws because it is a national treasure, then Americans have a right to demand reasonable access to it.

Congressman Schumer has introduced legislation which would require that the Yankees and major league baseball choose between two alternatives. They must, in his words, "either act like a business and receive no governmental protection, or behave like a great national pastime by making sure that New Yorkers can see the game on cable or free TV."

There is an eerie quality to the maelstrom in which baseball now finds itself. For none of the central issues that have haunted the game since its inception has really been resolved. The business is still a monopoly. The reserve clause, though drastically altered, remains largely in force, and the owners are trying to resurrect the rest of it by undermining free agency. Many individual players are still dissatisfied because

they do not feel that their contracts reflect their relative value as on-the-field performers. Members of Congress are beginning to consider legislation aimed, as before, at removing baseball's antitrust exemption. And baseball's un-merry-go-round, the seamier side of the industry, keeps spinning on its own goofy axis. In the words of Yogi Berra, "It seems like déjà vu all over again."

Nevertheless, the game is bringing in more spectators and more money than ever before. And the irrepressible club owners, though they are now more a clique of promotion-minded high rollers than a league of dyed-in-the-wool baseball men, seem undaunted by the growing financial threats to their industry. A recent ballclub purchase is perhaps the clearest demonstration that the barons of baseball believe their business will endure no matter what. A few months before the start of the 1987 season, Nelson Doubleday, Jr., and a group of limited partners paid $100 million to the publishing concern, Doubleday and Company, for the New York Mets franchise. Not only did the sale price set a record, but it was nearly twice the highest price ever before paid for a major league baseball club.

The Future of the Baseball Business

In 1989, as baseball's owners and players approach the final year of the current Basic Agreement, the industry faces two major threats to its well-being, one external and one internal.

The external threat comes from the fans, whose willingness to subsidize the excesses of the clubs and the players is being severely tested. Will the rising costs of attending games and viewing them on television reduce the fan base? Will spectatorship become a privilege available only to those who can afford it?

The internal threat concerns the salary system. By way of collusion, the clubs have discovered that they can beat free agency by simply abstaining from bidding for players. And even though that ploy has been officially ruled illegal, the fact remains that the clubs have learned how to use it. Does this mean that free agency is from this point forward unenforceable? If not, how then can the clubs be made to bid for players? And even if they could somehow be compelled to make bids, how could they be required to offer more money than they wish to offer? Does this mean that free agency is dead? Not if the players can figure out a way to sustain it. Does it mean that arbitration will replace free agency? Not if the owners can help it.

And the drums keep beating, and the music keeps playing, and both sides keep screaming baseball's most familiar war cry:

"Wait till next year!"

## CHAPTER 31

Baseball and the Law

Gary D. Hailey

ike many other members of our litigation-happy society, baseball players and team owners have spent their fair share of time in the courtroom. Judges have been asked to decide lawsuits involving everything from a team's liability for fan injuries from foul balls and thrown bats to the legality of the decision to resume the infamous Yankees-Royals "Pine Tar Game" nearly a month after George Brett's home run had been ruled a game-ending out.

But the most significant baseball-related court cases were a series of mostly unsuccessful challenges to organized baseball's attempts to limit competition—especially from rivals like the Players League and the Federal League—for players' services. That litigation has reached the United States Supreme Court three times, and all three times that Court has ruled that baseball is not governed by the antitrust laws. The reasoning behind this holding may have been perfectly logical when the first of those cases was decided in 1922, but it seemed bizarre and irrational when it was reiterated half a century later in *Flood* v. *Kuhn.*

From the game's earliest days, baseball owners have struggled to keep their expenses down and maintain control over the players, who often decide that the grass (and the money) is greener in someone else's ballpark. In 1870 the National Association of Base Ball Players tried to stop "revolving," or contract jumping, by adopting a rule requiring players to give 60 days' notice before leaving one club for another. Tougher controls were agreed to after word leaked that A. G. Spalding and three other Boston Red Stockings stars had signed contracts in the middle of the 1875 season to play for Chicago in 1876. In 1879 the National League secretly agreed to allow each team owner to "reserve" his five best players at the end of the season; other owners were prohibited from bidding for the services of the reserved players. The owners also agreed not to sign any player who refused to play for the team that reserved him.

The reserve rule and blacklist helped protect the National League owners from their fellows, but proved less useful against the newly formed American Association, which declared war on the NL in 1882. One of the biggest names to jump to the rival league was catcher Charles Bennett, who had played for the NL's Pittsburgh club in 1882. In August of that year, he accepted $100 in exchange for his written promise to sign a contract with Pittsburgh for the 1883 season. But before Bennett signed that contract, the Detroit AA team offered him more money. Pittsburgh got wind of what was happening and immediately filed suit in federal court, seeking an injunction ordering Bennett to sign the Pittsburgh contract.

Bennett's lawyers offered a number of legal defenses, some

rather narrow and technical. The court ruled in Bennett's favor[1] but did not issue a written opinion, so it is unclear just which of his attorneys' arguments were persuasive. The dismissal may have resulted from the court concluding that the reserve system and blacklist illegally limited Bennett's freedom to earn a living. But the court may have refused to enjoin Bennett's jump to Detroit simply because of the timing of the lawsuit. The Pittsburgh club would have suffered no real harm from Bennett's refusal to sign an 1883 contract until it had to play a game without him in the lineup. Its October 1882 lawsuit was, in a sense, premature because Bennett might have changed his mind and returned to Pittsburgh before the opening day of the 1883 season.

Shortstop Sam Wise did Bennett one better. He signed a contract with the AA's Cincinnati club but then jumped back to Boston when they upped their original offer. Cincinnati got an Ohio court to order Boston not to play Wise, but they were unable to enforce the order in other states. Wise simply stayed at home when the Boston team came to Cleveland to play.

The National League and American Association made peace in 1883 and signed the "National Agreement," which contained a strengthened reserve rule. The promoters of the Union Association hoped to capitalize on the players' resentment of the one-sided terms of their contracts with organized baseball, but the established leagues fought back hard by adopting the "Day Resolution," an agreement to blacklist any reserved player who jumped to a Union club. Star pitcher Tony Mullane, who jumped from the St. Louis Browns to the St. Louis Maroons of the new league, tried to return to the Browns after hearing about the Day Resolution. The Browns refused to welcome their prodigal back because they knew the Maroons would haul them into court if they did. The Toledo AA club wanted Mullane, but the National Agreement did not provide for player trades or sales. The Browns simply released Mullane outright, and Toledo signed him. The Union Association failed to persuade an Ohio federal judge to order Mullane back to the Maroons.[2] After the demise of the upstart league at the end of the 1884 season, Toledo agreed to send Mullane back to the Browns, but the Cincinnati AA club—in flagrant violation of the National Agreement—signed the 35-game winner to a lucrative bonus contract. The Association's powers-that-be ultimately awarded Mullane to Cincinnati, but ordered him to sit out the 1885 season and give back part of his bonus.

Once the Union Association was dead and buried, organized baseball tightened the screws a bit more by trying to establish a maximum annual player salary of $2,000. In response the players formed the National Brotherhood of Professional Base Ball Players under the leadership of John

Montgomery Ward, the New York Giants shortstop who attended Columbia University law school in the off-season. Ward claimed that the reserve clause, the blacklist, and other intimidating provisions of the standard player contract were legally unenforceable. When the owners refused to scrap the salary cap or to agree not to sell or trade players without their consent, the brotherhood went on to form the Players League, which fielded eight teams in 1890. Over 80 National League players and almost 30 from the American Association— including future Hall of Famers Dan Brouthers, John Clarkson, Hugh Duffy, "Buck" Ewing, "King" Kelly, Connie Mack, and "Old Hoss" Radbourne—signed up with the Players League.

Organized baseball used every weapon at its disposal to strike back at this new rival. The owners told fans that the players were aligned with radical unionists. Boston reportedly gave pitcher Clarkson $10,000—five times the average 1889 salary—to desert the brotherhood, while Spalding offered King Kelly a blank check to play for the White Stockings. When propaganda and bankrolls failed, the established league fielded a team of lawyers at courthouses around the country.

The reserve rule was originally adopted by the parties to the National Agreement as a sort of gentlemen's agreement not to compete for their fellow owners' players. When the National League tried to enforce the reserve clause against the Players League, it got nowhere. A federal court in New York City held that the Giants could not keep catcher Ewing from playing for their brotherhood rival because the reserve provisions in his 1889 contract were "merely a contract to make a contract" for 1890 "if the parties agree."[3] The reserve clause was valuable because it gave the Giants a "prior and exclusive" right to negotiate with Ewing that was enforceable against other clubs in organized baseball. But as a basis for an injunction preventing a player from taking the field for a Players League team, Ewing's contract was held "wholly nugatory" because it did not set forth in detail contract terms and conditions (including salary) for 1890. A party who seeks enforcement of a contract with vague or indefinite terms is really asking the court to fill in the blank spaces in that contract, which is something that courts are reluctant to do.

Other courts objected not only to the indefiniteness of player contracts but also to their one-sidedness, which they referred to as a "lack of mutuality." Owners could release players on ten days' notice, but the reserve clause purported to bind a player to one team for as long as the team wanted him. A New York state court judge expressed disgust at "the spectacle" of the Giants' attempt to enforce "a contract which binds [the player] for a series of years and [the team] for 10 days."[4] The National League spent $15,000 on lawyers' fees in New York alone fighting the Players League, but came away with nothing to show for it.

The Players League won the legal battles, but not the war—in fact, everyone lost money. Both sides agreed to Spalding's suggestion that some Players League teams be merged with existing NL and AA franchises and the rest be dissolved. After a bit of skirmishing over the rights to sign some of the returning Players League stars, the NL and AA merged their sixteen clubs into twelve after the 1891 season, and then signed a new National Agreement with the minor leagues. Players had little choice but to accept the terms offered by the "Baseball Trust," but a few rebelled. Amos Rusie won 22 games in 1895 and led the league in strikeouts, but Giants owner Andrew Freedman rewarded him by with-holding $600 in fines from his paycheck. Rusie sat out 1896 and then sued the Giants when they invoked their reserve for 1897 as well. The case was settled before trial, with all the National League owners reportedly kicking in a portion of Rusie's $5,000 claim.

As usual the next baseball war set off a spate of contract jumping and legal skirmishes. Over half of the players who suited up for the American League's first season of play were ex-National Leaguers. The older league went to court to try to wrest back a number of their players, most notably Napoleon Lajoie. Lajoie signed a contract with the Phillies in 1900, but refused to be bound by the reserve clause and jumped to the Athletics before the 1901 season. The Pennsylvania Supreme Court held that the Phillies were entitled to an injunction barring the batting champ from playing for the A's.[5] But that decision turned in part on two unusual factors. First, the Phillies' contract reserved Lajoie for only three years and stated what salary would be paid in each of those three years, so it was not simply "a contract to make a contract." Second, Lajoie was a star of the very highest order. Courts are reluctant to order someone to perform a contract for personal services, although they are not at all reluctant to order the defendant to pay monetary damages equal to the harm caused by his nonperformance. Only when the harm cannot be measured in dollars or the contract involves something unique or irreplaceable are injunctions or other nonmonetary remedies granted by a court. The Phillies may have been able to find equally talented replacements for many of their players, but Lajoie—who led the AL in hits, doubles, home runs, runs, RBIs, batting average, and slugging average in 1901— was a unique talent.

The Phillies' legal victory proved hollow. The A's quickly dealt Lajoie to Cleveland. Whenever Cleveland was scheduled to play in Philadelphia, Lajoie stayed far away. His old team's attempts to obtain an injunction from an Ohio court were not successful.

Other National League efforts to hold on to players also failed. Citing a Supreme Court case holding that a contract that could be abandoned on one year's notice was not enforceable, a federal judge dismissed Brooklyn's suit against veteran catcher Deacon McGuire because the team could terminate his contract on only ten days' notice.[6] The judge also questioned whether McGuire's talents were so "unique and peculiar" that Brooklyn could not replace him. McGuire was a fine player, but he was no Nap Lajoie. A state judge in St. Louis went further in a case involving pitcher Jack Harper. Not only was the standard NL player contract lacking in mutuality, according to the court, but it also unreasonably restrained competition in violation of the Sherman Antitrust Act.[7]

After two years of rivalry, the National League agreed to recognize the American League as an equal. The two major leagues used blacklists and boycotts to bring "outlaw" minor leagues to their knees and keep control of players who had the audacity to hold out for higher salaries. When Ty Cobb refused to accept Detroit's 1913 salary offer, the Tigers suspended him. The impasse was broken only when two Georgia congressmen called for a federal investigation. The threat of government action got Ty Cobb a raise, but the players in general benefited much more from organized baseball's war with the Federal League, which no doubt had the National and American Leagues muttering "Two's company, three's a crowd" when the 1914 season opened.

The established leagues didn't even try to use the courts to

stop reserve jumpers from playing for the Federal League, but they did seek injunctions against a number of players who jumped, even though they had signed contracts for the upcoming season. The irrepressible Hal Chase signed a 1914 contract with the White Sox, but then moved on to the new league. Teams could release players they didn't want on ten days' notice, so Chase gave Chicago ten days' warning and shuffled off to the Buffalo Federals. A New York state judge agreed with Chase's reasoning and turned down Chicago's request that he order Chase to return.[8] Not only did the contract lack mutuality, said the judge, but organized baseball placed so many limits on the freedom of players that they were left in a state of *quasi* peonage" that was "contrary to the spirit of American institutions and . . . contrary to the spirit of the Constitution of the United States." The court's opinion did contain some good news for organized baseball: it ruled that baseball did not involve interstate commerce and, therefore, did not violate the Sherman Act.

The judges who heard cases involving contract jumpers occasionally showed real distaste for the whole nasty business. Phillies catcher Bill Killefer signed with the Chicago Federal League club for a substantial increase in salary, but re-signed with the Phillies only 12 days later when they topped Chicago's offer. When the Federals asked a Michigan federal judge to order Killefer not to play for Philadelphia, they were rudely received. Citing the opinions in the Ewing, Ward, and McGuire cases, Judge Sessions noted that the right of reservation in the Phillies' 1913 contract with Killefer did not bind him for the 1914 season because it was indefinite and lacked mutuality.[9] But he refused to enforce Chicago's contract because it came into court with "unclean hands." Killefer was under a moral, although not a legal obligation to play for Philadelphia in 1914, but Chicago persuaded him to repudiate that obligation. Both teams had "acted wrongfully and in bad faith," and the judge refused to lift a finger to help either one of them. He also let Killefer know what he thought of him, calling him "a person upon whose pledged word little or no reliance can be placed, and who, for gain to himself, neither scruples nor hesitates to disregard and violate his express engagements and agreements." Chicago appealed the decision but was unsuccessful. The Sixth Circuit Court of Appeals agreed with Judge Sessions that none of the parties to these underhanded dealings was deserving of any assistance from the courts.[10]

Knowing that they could not outlast their better-financed rivals, the Federal League owners filed an antitrust suit against organized baseball in Chicago on January 5, 1915. They asked federal Judge Kenesaw Mountain Landis, who had a reputation as a committed trustbuster, to declare the National Agreement's reserve and blacklisting provisions to be unreasonable and illegal restraints on competition. The trial was completed that month, but the Federal League's hopes for a quick verdict in their favor were in vain. The future baseball commissioner pondered the evidence all through the 1915 season, which resulted in another healthy dose of red ink for team owners. After waiting almost a year for Judge Landis to make up his mind, the rival leagues cut a deal. Organized baseball bought some of the Federal League's player contracts and stadiums—in reality, they were buying peace—and the Federals dropped the antitrust suit.

The final deal satisfied everyone except AL president Ban Johnson, who preferred to fight to the death rather than pay his enemies a nickel of tribute, and the Baltimore Federal

League club, which wanted to buy an existing major league franchise and move it to Baltimore. Angered by Brooklyn owner Ebbets's scornful description of their city as "one of the worst minor league towns in this country," the Baltimore owners pledged $50,000 to finance a new antitrust suit against organized baseball and the Federal League owners who had sold the league out for a few pieces of silver. When the Department of Justice refused to investigate, Baltimore filed its complaint in federal district court in Washington, D.C., in 1917.

The testimony given at the trial, which didn't begin until March 1919, left little doubt that organized baseball's team owners had agreed to use the reserve clause and blacklisting to maintain tight control over the supply of players and paid the Federal League to go out of business in order to protect their monopoly over professional baseball. The judge's directions to the jury virtually directed a verdict for the plaintiffs. The Baltimore club won $254,000 in damages.

Organized baseball's lawyers immediately appealed the decision. They contended that baseball was not commerce because it involved "personal effort not related to [the] production" of material goods. If baseball did not involve interstate commerce, it was not subject to the Sherman Act or any other federal law. The court of appeals heard oral arguments on October 15, 1920, only three days after the final game of the World Series was played between the Cleveland Indians and the Brooklyn Dodgers. Only a few weeks later, it overturned the lower court's decision in favor of Baltimore.[11] The appellate court first noted that

The transportation in interstate commerce of the players and the paraphernalia used by them was but an incident to the main purpose of the appellants, namely the production of the game. It was for it they were in business—not for the purpose of transferring players, balls, and uniforms . . .

. . . So here, baseball is not commerce, though some of its incidents may be. Suppose a law firm in the city of Washington sends its members to points in different states to try lawsuits; they would travel, and probably carry briefs and records, in interstate commerce. Could it be correctly said that the firm, in the trial of the lawsuits, was engaged in trade and commerce? Or, take the case of a lecture bureau, which employs persons to deliver lectures before Chautauqua gatherings at points in different states. It would be necessary for the lecturers to travel in interstate commerce, in order that they might fulfill their engagements; but would it not be an unreasonable stretch of the ordinary meaning of the words to say that the bureau was engaged in trade or commerce?

The court of appeals then cited with approval cases holding that those who produce theatrical exhibitions, practice medicine, or launder clothes are not engaged in commerce.

The Baltimore club tried to persuade the United States Supreme Court to reinstate the original verdict in its favor. But Justice Oliver Wendell Holmes, writing for a unanimous Court, upheld the decision of the court of appeals.[12]

[E]xhibitions of base ball . . . are purely state affairs. It is true that, in order to attain for the exhibitions the great popularity that they have achieved, competitions must be arranged between clubs from different cities and States. But the fact that in order to give the exhibitions the League must

induce free persons to cross state lines and arrange and pay for their doing so is not enough to change the character of the business . . . [T]he transport is a mere incident, not the essential thing. That to which it is incident, the exhibition, although made for money would not be called trade or commerce in the commonly accepted use of those words. As it is put by the defendants, personal effort, not related to production, is not a subject of commerce. That which in its consummation is not commerce does not become commerce among the States because the transportation that we have mentioned takes place. To repeat the illustrations given by the Court below, a firm of lawyers sending out a member to argue a case, or the Chautauqua lecture bureau sending out lecturers, does not engage in such commerce because the lawyer or lecturer goes to another State.

Only a year later, the Court ruled that a company that presented vaudeville shows in cities around the country was, unlike major league baseball, engaged in interstate commerce.[13] Justice Holmes explained the different outcomes in the two cases by pointing to the difference in "the degree of interstate activity" in baseball games and vaudeville shows, but his reasoning is unconvincing.

The next challenge to organized baseball's hegemony came a quarter century later from Don Jorge Pasqual, the millionaire organizer of the Mexican League, who lured 18 major leaguers south of the border in 1946. In August of that year, the owners amended their Rule 15 to provide that any player who jumped to the new league would be ineligible to return to organized baseball for five years. The Cubs' general manager, who proposed the amendment, said that the prospect of being blacklisted for five years "will do a lot more to discourage Stan Musial from going to Mexico next winter than any suits we may file on the reserve clause."

The Rule 15 blacklist stemmed the southward flow of players. Commissioner A. B. "Happy" Chandler refused to reinstate the players who returned to the states in 1947. Catcher Mickey Owen was reduced to managing a semipro club in Winner, South Dakota, while several other Mexican League refugees signed with Cuban clubs.

When blacklisted outfielder Danny Gardella filed an antitrust complaint against organized baseball, a federal district judge in New York noted the "clear trend toward a broader conception of what constitutes interstate commerce" than had existed when *Federal Baseball Club of Baltimore* was decided over 25 years earlier, but felt bound to follow the Supreme Court's decision in that case.[14] But in February 1949 a federal court of appeals voted 2–1 to reverse the district court's dismissal of Gardella's complaint.[15] Judge Learned Hand distinguished *Federal Baseball* by emphasizing the importance to modern-day baseball of interstate radio and television broadcasts of major league games. Judge Frank's separate opinion strongly condemned the reserve system.

For the "reserve clause," as has been observed, results in something resembling peonage of the baseball player . . . Although many courts have refused to enforce the "reserve" clause, yet severe and practically efficacious extra-legal penalties are imposed for violation. The most extreme of these penalties is the blacklisting of the player so that no club in organized baseball will hire him . . . The violator may perhaps become a . . . bartender or a street-sweeper, but his

chances of ever playing baseball are exceedingly slim.

Gardella's victory was not a final one—it simply allowed him the opportunity to prove his allegations in a trial. Former Cardinals Fred Martin, Max Lanier, and Lou Klein filed a separate suit, and all four players asked the district court to order their immediate reinstatement pending the outcome of the trials, but the court declined to do so.[16] Faced with the prospect of spending the 1949 season in a courtroom rather than on a baseball field, the players were receptive to baseball's offer to settle the case. Commissioner Chandler later characterized his reinstatement of the four "good kids" who had "said they were sorry" for jumping their reserves as inspired by his desire to "temper justice with mercy." But the court of appeals decision—and Judge Frank's sentiments in particular—no doubt had an effect too. Gardella, who had been working as a hospital orderly after returning from Mexico, was reportedly given $60,000 to drop his case.

Subsequent litigation and congressional inquiries kept baseball's attorneys busy in the 1950s. Organized baseball was the defendant in eight pending antitrust suits when it sought relief from Congress in 1951. At its behest three separate bills that would have granted all professional sports leagues a complete exemption from the antitrust laws were introduced in the House of Representatives that year. After lengthy hearings, Congressman Emanuel Celler's Subcommittee on the Study of Monopoly Power recommended that the bills not be passed, and none of them were. The Celler Subcommittee did not favor blanket antitrust immunity, but did conclude that professional baseball could not operate successfully without some form of the reserve clause.[17]

After the Gardella decision, organized baseball's lawyers and the Subcommittee assumed that *Federal Baseball* was no longer good law. But the Supreme Court surprised them in 1953 in *Toolson* v. *New York Yankees*.[18] When Yankee farm-hand George Toolson was placed on the ineligible list for refusing to accept a demotion to a lower-classification team, he sued the Yankees. A California federal judge dismissed the case before trial on the basis of *Federal Baseball*. "If [that] case is, as Judge Frank intimates [in his *Gardella* opinion], an 'impotent zombi,'" the judge wrote, "I feel that it is not my duty to so find but that the Supreme Court should so declare."[19] The Ninth Circuit Court of Appeals agreed,[20] and the Supreme Court reaffirmed *Federal Baseball* in a one-paragraph opinion.

In Federal Baseball . . . *this Court held that . . . professional baseball . . . was not within the scope of the federal antitrust laws. Congress has had the ruling under consideration but has not seen fit to bring such business under these laws by legislation having prospective effect. . . . The present cases ask us to overrule the prior decision, and, with retrospective effect, hold the [antitrust laws] applicable. We think that if there are evils in this field which now warrant application to it of the antitrust laws it should be by legislation. Without re-examination of the underlying issues, the judgments below are affirmed on the authority of* Federal Baseball . . .

The Court's conclusion that "Congress has had the ruling under consideration but has not seen fit to bring [baseball] under [the antitrust] laws by legislation" is questionable. The Celler Subcommittee report concluded that given the *Gardella* decision and cases subsequent to *Federal Baseball*,

which took a broader view of what constituted interstate commerce, "it may be seriously doubted whether baseball should now be regarded as exempt from the antitrust laws." If Congress assumed that baseball was subject to the antitrust laws, its failure to act on bills granting an antitrust exemption was evidence that it did not intend baseball to be exempt—which was just the opposite of what the Court said in *Toolson*.

The next few years saw the Supreme Court hold that professional boxing and football did not share baseball's antitrust immunity. In *Radovich v. National Football League*,[21] the Court expressly limited the reach of the *Federal Baseball* precedent to baseball. Three justices dissented from this decision "to put baseball in a class by itself."

Another flurry of congressional activity followed. In 1957 the House Antitrust Subcommittee held fifteen days of hearings on seven different bills, some of which would have exempted all professional sports from antitrust liability. Congressman Celler introduced a bill exempting only those acts that were "reasonably necessary" to maintaining competitive balance and the integrity of sports, but the full House voted to give professional sports leagues a broader although not unlimited exemption. A Senate committee held more hearings in 1958—Casey Stengel, Mickey Mantle, Ted Williams, and Stan Musial testified the day after the All-Star Game was played in nearby Baltimore—but the full Senate never considered the bill. In a 1959 report to the membership, the Major League Baseball Players Association's lawyers said, "There does not seem any doubt that Congress will eventually pass a law concerning Baseball's right to continue its reserve clause," but Congress never came any closer to passing comprehensive sports antitrust legislation. Bills were introduced year after year—attempts to organize a third major league, franchise moves, and the CBS purchase of the Yankees inspired some of the legislative proposals—but none was enacted.

In 1972 the U.S. Supreme Court upheld *Federal Baseball* once more in *Flood v. Kuhn*.[22] When the Cardinals traded Curt Flood to the Phillies after the 1969 season, Flood refused to go. "I am [not] a piece of property to be bought and sold irrespective of my wishes," he wrote to Commissioner Bowie Kuhn. Kuhn refused to declare him a free agent, so Flood hired former Supreme Court Justice and Secretary of Labor Arthur Goldberg and filed suit. The lower court's dismissal of his case was eventually upheld by the Supreme Court. Justice Harry Blackmun's opinion noted that baseball's antitrust immunity was "an anomaly" and "an aberration," but he felt bound by history.

Remedial legislation has been introduced repeatedly in Congress but none has ever been enacted. The Court, accordingly, has concluded that Congress as yet has had no intention to subject baseball's reserve system to the reach of the antitrust statutes . . . If there is any inconsistency or illogic in all this, it is an inconsistency and illogic of long standing that is to be remedied by the Congress and not this Court.

The Court's opinion also noted that state antitrust laws could not apply to baseball. Flood's career had ended by the time the Supreme Court issued its decision. After sitting out the 1970 season, he was traded to the Senators in 1971, but retired after hitting only .200 in 13 games.

It seems unlikely that the Court would reach a different result if a similar antitrust case were presented to it today. But does baseball's antitrust exemption really matter today? The players' union has managed to win free agency, salary arbitration, and limits on trades without a player's consent through collective bargaining or arbitration. After two arbitrators' decisions that the owners violated the collective-bargaining agreement by failing to bid for free agents like Kirk Gibson and Tim Raines after the 1985 and 1986 seasons, the players seem to be in the catbird seat. But what if the baseball owners choose to hang as tough as the football owners did in the 1987 strike? The courts have held that neither labor nor management can be sued under the antitrust laws over provisions in a collective-bargaining agreement, even if those provisions are clearly anticompetitive. The football players are litigating whether the labor exemption applies after a union contract has expired. But even if they win, baseball's unique antitrust exemption might still serve as a shield for the baseball owners if the players ever file a similar suit.

Baseball's exemption might protect it from the players but not from other parties who have less connection to the on-the-field aspects of the business of baseball. For example, an anticompetitive owner conspiracy involving stadium concession or parking revenues might not be exempt.

But what if a maverick owner—say, Ted Turner or George Steinbrenner—tried to move his team to another city without the approval of his peers? Al Davis and Bob Irsay could move the Raiders and Colts to greener pastures because the antitrust laws prevent other NFL owners from agreeing to boycott them or take other punitive action. While there is some authority for the proposition that baseball's antitrust exemption is broad enough to cover that kind of situation, a court that was uncomfortable with the reasoning of *Federal Baseball* and its progeny could justify a different outcome in such a case much more easily than in a case involving free agency or other player-management disputes.

[1]*Allegheny Base-ball Club v. Bennett*, 14 Fed. 257 (C.C.W.D. Pa., 1882).
[2]*St. Louis Athletic Ass'n v. Mullane*, No. 3642 (C.C.S.D. Ohio, May 13, 1884). Reprinted in *Sporting Life*, May 21, 1884, p.2, col.1.
[3]*Metropolitan Exhibition Co. v. Ewing*, 42 Fed. 198 (C.C.S.D. N.Y. 1890).
[4]*Metropolitan Exhibition Co. v. Ward*, 24 Abb.N.C. 414 (1890).
[5]*Philadelphia Base Ball Club v. Lajoie*, 51 Atl. 973 (Pa. S. Ct. 1902).
[6]*Brooklyn Baseball Club v. McGuire*, 116 Fed. 783 (C.C.E.D. Pa. 1902).
[7]*American Base Ball & Athletic Exhibition Co. of St. Louis v. Harper*, 54 Cent. L.J. 449 (St. Louis Cir. Ct. 1902).
[8]*American League Baseball Club of Chicago v. Chase*, 86 Misc. 441, 149 N.Y. Supp. 6 (Sup. Ct. 1914).
[9]*Weeghman v. Killefer*, 214 Fed. 168 (W.D. Mich. 1914).
[10]*Weeghman v. Killefer*, 215 Fed. 289 (6th Cir. 1914).
[11]*National League of Professional Baseball Clubs v. Federal Baseball Club of Baltimore*, 269 Fed. 681 (D.C. Cir. 1921).
[12]*Federal Baseball Club of Baltimore v. National League of Professional Baseball Clubs*, 259 U.S. 200 (1922).
[13]*Hart v. Keith Vaudeville Exchange*, 262 U.S. 271 (1923).
[14]*Gardella v. Chandler*, 79 F.Supp. 260 (S.D.N.Y. 1948).
[15]*Gardella v. Chandler*, 172 F.2d 402 (2d Cir. 1949).
[16]*Martin v. Chandler*, 174 F.2d 917 (2d. Cir. 1949); *Gardella v. Chandler*, 174 F.2d 919 (2d. Cir. 1949).
[17]H.R. Rep. 2002, 82d Cong., 2d Sess. 228–32 (1952).
[18]346 U.S. 356 (1953).
[19]*Toolson v. New York Yankees*, 101 F.Supp. 93 (S.D. Cal. 1951).
[20]200 F.2d 198 (9th Cir. 1952).
[21]358 U.S. 445 (1957).
[22]407 U.S. 258 (1972).

## CHAPTER 32

Trades and Free Agency

Eliot Cohen

By the late '70s, players were following the lure of the dollars to the highest bidder. Owners lamented the detrimental effects of player movement on fan loyalty and competitive balance, unless, of course, those moves were orchestrated by the clubs via trades.

That's the 1870's, folks. Ballplayers have been changing uniforms nearly as long as they've been taking a called third strike. The National Association of Baseball Players, founded in 1858, allowed players to change teams provided they gave sixty days notice. Despite that restriction and that era's patina of "gentlemanly, amateur" competition, paid "ringers" frequently suited up for different clubs, sometimes serving one club in the morning and another in the afternoon.

Players changed teams regularly throughout the five-year history of the National Association of Professional Baseball, mainly to accommodate fluctuation in size between nine teams for the 1871 debut, as few as eight for 1873, and 13 in the loop's final season in 1875. The first National League trade on record took place in the middle of the 1879 season as catcher Lew "Blower" Brown moved from Providence to Chicago for the soon-to-be proverbial player to be named later, in this case, shortstop Johnny Peters.

Since then, players have been traded for Hall of Famers, has-beens, cash, spite, managers, equipment, announcers, and even themselves. Trades and player sales are part of baseball's lifeblood, in-season acquisitions boosting contenders' hopes and winter moves stoking hot stoves. There's hardly a pennant winner that hasn't used a trade to reach the top or a Hall of Famer who hasn't been peddled in the flesh mart.

By the 1890s, a draft system was in place for major league clubs to acquire players from minor league teams. Teams at every level could pluck players from lower classifications for a fixed fee. (Today's minor league draft every December is a remnant of this practice. Players not on a major league 40-man roster after three professional seasons may be selected by clubs at higher levels, but must be retained at the higher level or returned.) It wasn't long before John Brush, then owner of both the Cincinnati Reds and the Indianapolis entry in the Western League, realized that he could use the system to draft players from rival minor league teams for Cincinnati and move them between the clubs at will, creating a farm in Indianapolis where his prospects could grow, and a competitive edge at both outposts. Not until the 1920s, however, did Branch Rickey legitimize the farm system concept; despite opposition from Commissioner Kenesaw Mountain Landis and other traditionalists, fearing this return to "Brushism," working agreements with the majors became the key to survival in the bushes.

Other changes in the system evolved to address abuses or new situations. In 1903, to prevent clubs from fattening their rosters with stars before the first World Series, representatives of the National League's Pittsburgh entry and the American League's Boston club wrote in a line to their typed agreement prohibiting participation by any player acquired on or after September 1. The rule remains in force today for all postseason play.

Waivers and options arose in tandem with farm systems to prevent the best clubs from monopolizing talent. The amateur draft was created in 1965 to end the rich teams' monopoly on the best prospects and allow the worst teams to get the top choices. Trading between leagues required waivers until the initial interleague trading period, limited to four weeks, was declared after the 1959 season and became the principal business of the annual winter meetings in December. Today, waivers are required only for trades from August 1 to the end of the season. Options, which limit the number of times a player can be assigned to a minor league roster, were liberalized in 1985, permitting the Yankees to rev up the infamous Columbus shuttle with their top affiliate. In 1973, players won the right to veto trades, providing they had 10 years in the big leagues, the last five with their present team. Ron Santo, a 14-year fixture at third base for the Cubs, was the first player to exercise his five-and-10 veto power, canceling a deal that would have sent him to the California Angels. The Cubs accommodated his desire to stay in Chicago by shipping him to the White Sox.

Free agency, established by arbitrator Peter Seitz's ruling prior to the 1976 season, required further changes in the system of player movement. At first, teams held a re-entry draft to choose which free agents they would offer contracts. From 1981-1984, a compensation draft was held in which teams losing free agents selected a replacement player from a pool. The re-entry draft was abandoned after 1984 as well. Although the new era has given players devices to change address on their own—including the right to demand a trade or freedom after being traded in the middle of a multi-year contract, and the leverage to fill contracts with an array of no-trade clauses and other disincentives to unapproved moves—trades remain the primary vehicle for rapidly improving a team.

Mike "King" Kelly became the first big name player to be shipped out of town. After he won the 1886 National League batting title with a .388 average, the pennant winning Chicago White Stockings (who later became the Cubs) sold their star outfielder-catcher to Boston for the outrageous sum of $10,000. That record stood until the New York Giants paid $11,000 to the minor league club in Indianapolis for Hall of Fame lefthander Rube Marquard in 1908. Before farm systems were popularized by Branch Rickey's St. Louis

Cardinals in the 1920s and 1930s, ballclubs regularly purchased their players from these independent operators.

Occasionally, owners purchased players from themselves. After Christy Mathewson made an inauspicious debut with the Giants in 1900, they sent him back to the Virginia League where the Cincinnati Reds drafted him for $100. Reds' owner John Brush knew he'd soon own a piece of the New York franchise and recognized the potential of Mathewson. So Brush's Reds accepted Hall of Fame pitcher Amos Rusie, who had sat out the previous two seasons in a salary dispute with the Giants, from Brush's future club for Mathewson. Rusie retired after showing an 0–1 record in three 1901 starts for Cincinnati. Mathewson went 1–0 for Cincinnati in 1916, 372–188 for the Giants.

Dirty deals were nothing new for a franchise whose early days featured close ties with New York's infamous Tammany Hall Democratic Party machine. The original Mets, New York's American Association entry, won the 1884 championship, but their owner, John Day, happened also to own the Giants—and transferred the Mets' leading pitcher, Tim Keefe, best hitter, Dude Esterbrook, and manager Jim Mutrie to his NL entry. The Mets plummeted to eighth in the nine-team league.

Similar ethics helped the 1899 Cleveland Spiders compile the worst record ever, a shameful 20–134. Before the 1899 season, Cleveland's Robison brothers acquired control of the St. Louis Browns, a 39–111 basket case in 1898. Reasoning that the profit potential of St. Louis outweighed that of the mistake by the lake, they transferred the Spiders' entire starting lineup, including outfielder Jesse Burkett, plus Cy Young and Jack Powell, winners of 25 and 24 games respectively for the 1898 Spiders, to St. Louis. Third baseman Lave Cross, a St. Louis regular in 1898, was appointed Cleveland's manager, but 38 games into the season, he was summoned to St. Louis, as was Wee Willy Sudhoff, the Spiders' remaining respectable moundsman.

In the mid-1950s, the New York Yankees appeared to have a similar arrangement with the Kansas City Athletics. In fact, before the A's moved to the midwest from Philadelphia, the Yankees had a top farm club in Kansas City for 18 seasons. For the rest of the 1950s, the Yankees and A's acted as if nothing had changed. The Yankees shipped their tired or untried to Kansas City for pennant-drive help in deals that often smacked of lend-lease. After New York acquired Enos Slaughter in 1954, they couldn't find him playing time in 1955, so they shipped him to KC with an end-of-the-line Johnny Sain. Slaughter got about 500 at-bats with the A's before returning to the Yankees for the 1956 stretch run and World Series heroics. Pitching prospect Ralph Terry went to the A's for seasoning in 1957—Billy Martin accompanied Terry to KC as punishment for his role in the Copacabana brawl—and came back two years later, ready to win 76 games for the final phase of the dynasty, including a league-high 23 in 1962.

Other key Yankee reinforcements from Kansas City included pitchers Ryne Duren, Bobby Shantz, Art Ditmar, Murry Dickson and Duke Maas, plus outfielders Hector Lopez, lend-leaser Bob Cerv (he hit 38 homers, drove in 104 runs, and batted .305 in 1958, and followed up with a 20, 87, .285 season, so the Yanks decided to get him back), and Roger Maris. KC pried the future two-time MVP from the Indians in June 1958, and shipped him to the Yankees eighteen months later.

The most suspicious of the sixteen deals between the clubs over the last half of the quiet decade involved Clete Boyer. The A's signed the bonus-baby third baseman in 1955 and kept him on their roster for the most of the required two seasons, then shipped him to New York with Shantz and Ditmar after the 1956 season for a package of junk. The A's later admitted that they had signed Boyer on the Bombers' behalf. Commissioner Ford Frick ruled that Boyer had to complete his bonus period with the A's prior to going to New York, but otherwise neither party was punished for this shady deal.

A similar "birds-of-a-feather deal" appeared to begin in June 1983 when the Orioles shipped catcher Floyd "Sugar Bear" Rayford to the Cardinals for outfielder Tito Landrum. The following March 25, Landrum returned to the Cards for minor league hurler Jose Brito. Five days later, Rayford went back to the Orioles for $50,000, the minor league draft price that Brito would have fetched.

The Giants became the dominant team in the National League during the first part of the 20th century, largely thanks to Mathewson and John J. McGraw. The Giants got more than strong leadership when McGraw joined the New York club in July, 1902, after selling his interest in the fledgling American League's Baltimore Orioles. The Little Napoleon's withdrawal from the AL ended a stormy one and a half seasons characterized by suspensions and feuds with the league's patriarch and president, Ban Johnson. For revenge, McGraw conspired with Oriole outfielder Joe Kelley's father-in-law and Andrew Freedman, who owned the Giants in partnership with Brush, to acquire a majority stake in the Orioles. Upon taking control, Freedman released nearly half the Baltimore roster: catcher Roger Bresnahan, pitchers Joe McGinnity and Jack Cronin, first baseman Dan McGann, and outfielders Cy Williams and Kelley, who became manager of the Reds and took Williams with him to Cincinnati. The other four players joined McGraw's Giants.

As the new league warred with the senior circuit, players made the best of the opportunity to switch to the highest bidder. Big-name league jumpers included Boston third baseman Jimmy Collins and Philadelphia second baseman Napoleon Lajoie, who both moved from the NL to AL teams in the same city. The Lajoie jump wound up in the courts—so much for "the good old days when all the action was on the field". To circumvent a 1902 temporary restraining order barring Lajoie from playing with any team in Philadelphia except the NL Phillies, Ban Johnson arranged to deal Lajoie to the Cleveland Indians, owned by the league's financial angel, Charles Somers. Six Pittsburgh Pirates, most notably pitcher Jack Chesbro, agreed to become New York Highlanders for the 1903 season, while AL batting champ Big Ed Delahanty was signed by the NL Giants from the Senators. The latter move displeased officials of both leagues, since Delahanty had been property of the NL Phillies prior to jumping to the AL.

The leagues made peace after the 1902 season, accepting player jumps prior to the 1902 season and individually deciding the fates of 16 players, including Delahanty, Wee Willie Keeler, Wahoo Sam Crawford, Lajoie, and Christy Mathewson, who had signed with the AL Philadelphia A's after that date. The leagues also drafted a standard player contract that included the reserve clause. For more than 70 years, except for the brief intervention of the Federal League prior to American entry into World War One and the post-World War Two Mexican League, players would have the choice of play-

ing for the team that held their contract, accepting whatever trade that club might make for them, or finding another line of work.

The war between the leagues spotlighted baseball's reliance on the golden rule; whoever has the gold, rules. In order to stay afloat, owners of less profitable franchises have been forced to sell their major assets, star players. Twice during his half-century stewardship of the Philadelphia A's, Connie Mack faced this dilemma. In both cases, he chose to keep the franchise.

Second baseman Eddie Collins, keystone of the Athletics' $100,000 infield that won three AL flags from 1910 to 1914, was sold to the White Sox following the A's 4–0 loss to the Boston Braves in the 1914 World Series. By the middle of the 1915 season, Mack had sold off pitchers Herb Pennock and Bob Shawkey, shortstop Jack Barry and rightfielder Eddie Murphy from the defending champs. By the opening of the 1918 campaign, the last of the $100,000 infield members, first baseman Stuffy McInnis, had been traded away.

Frustration influenced Connie Mack's decision to dismantle the A's. So did the specter of the Federal League, which had already spirited away star pitchers Chief Bender and Eddie Plank. Ban Johnson, seeking to keep his league profitable, influenced Collins' destination. The Chicago Federals had signed Walter Johnson (Washington later signed him back), so President Johnson wanted an AL star in town to balance the Big Train. Similarly, Shoeless Joe Jackson was sold to Chicago by the Cleveland Indians for $30,000 and three bodies in late 1915.

Mack invested some of the nearly $200,000 his sales accumulated to purchase minor leaguers and by the late 1920s the A's were competitive again. The lineup boasted future Hall of Famers Jimmie Foxx, Lefty Grove, Al Simmons and Mickey Cochrane and made three straight trips to the Series starting in 1929. But after losing the 1931 Series and falling behind the revitalized Yankees in 1932, Mack began stripping his team. Despite the championships, Mack was losing money in a depression that showed no signs of letting up. Outfielders Al Simmons and Mule Haas were sold to the White Sox with second baseman Jimmy Dykes for $150,000. Before the 1934 season got underway, sale items included pitchers Lefty Grove, Hank McDonald, Rube Walberg, and George Earnshaw, and Hall of Fame catcher Mickey Cochrane.

The start of the Federal League may have cost Philadelphia its top stars, but it was the end of the rival league that drove the Red Sox star center fielder Tris Speaker out of Boston. When the rival circuit disbanded before the 1916 season, Red Sox owner Joseph Lannin wanted to cut Speaker's salary back to its pre-Federal League level, from $18,000 to $9,000. Speaker said he'd rather sit than accept that 50 percent cut. Loath to see one of his league's prime gate attractions on the sidelines, President Johnson arranged to deal Speaker to the Cleveland Indians for pitcher Sad Sam Jones, third baseman Fred Thomas and $55,000. Speaker threatened not to report, but Johnson persuaded Lannin to share $10,000 of the purchase price with Speaker. Jones posted 16 of his 229 major league victories for the pennant winning 1918 Sox, but Cleveland got the better of the deal. The Gray Eagle was their signature player for the next decade, leading the AL in batting in 1916, taking over as the Tribe's manager in 1919 and leading them to their first world championship in 1920.

If Bostonians were furious over the Speaker trade and glad to see Lannin sell the team after a World Series victory in 1916, the joy was short-lived. New owner Harry Frazee, a theatrical producer specializing in flops, joined Mack as a prolific vendor of talent to the rest of the league. After purchasing several of Mack's A's, the Sox were short of funds even though they won the 1918 World Series, so Frazee sold pitchers Ernie Shore, Dutch Leonard and Carl Mays, plus outfielder Duffy Lewis to the Yankees, netting over $50,000.

After the 1919 season, Frazee needed additional cash, so he dispatched Babe Ruth to the Yankees for $125,000 plus a $300,000 loan secured by Fenway Park. Although Frazee brazenly declared that the Sox would be better off without Ruth, the deal stands unchallenged as the most lopsided transaction in baseball history. For good measure, and more Yankee dollars, over the next two years Frazee sent to New York pitchers Waite Hoyt, Joe Bush, Sad Sam Jones, catcher Wally Schang, shortstop Everett Scott, and third baseman Joe Dugan. By the time the Yanks acquired pitcher Red Ruffing from Boston for outfielder Cederic Durst and $50,000 in May 1930, Frazee had established himself as chief architect of the Yankee dynasty.

The Yankees weren't alone in wooing Frazee to acquire Ruth. John McGraw put in a bid on the Sox slugger but was rebuffed. So McGraw turned his attention to the best right-handed hitter around, St. Louis Cardinal second baseman Rogers Hornsby. Reportedly, during the winter of 1919-1920 McGraw offered Branch Rickey $250,000 for his star (another report pegged the offer at five players and a more reasonable $70,000). Hornsby's six straight batting titles from 1920-1925, with triple crowns in 1922 and 1925, may have inspired Rickey's maxim, "Some of the best deals are the ones you don't make." But back in 1919, the stumbling block was a replacement second baseman. Rickey wanted Frankie Frisch, the Fordham Flash, who had batted .226 and stolen 15 bases in a 54-game rookie campaign. McGraw refused to part with his future captain and debating partner.

When the Giants faltered, the Cardinals took the world championship in 1926 with Hornsby serving as manager. The Rajah's production dropped, and his dictatorial manner had players near rebellion. But Hornsby's biggest problem was with owner Harry Breadon, whom Hornsby had cursed in full view of the Cardinal players when Breadon refused to cancel an exhibition game during the 1926 pennant race. Breadon ordered Rickey to trade the manager. So Rickey, whose gospel included "better to trade a player a year too early than a year too late," offered the 30-year old second sacker to McGraw for Frisch, who had averaged 28 steals per year but had gotten on the wrong side of his manager. The Giants sweetened the deal with pitcher Jimmy Ring and the two second basemen were swapped. Hornsby batted .361 while leading the NL in runs scored for the Giants, and Cardinal Frisch took the stolen-base crown, but neither club won the flag in 1927.

Predictably, the strong wills of McGraw and Hornsby clashed, resulting in the Rajah's exit to the Boston Braves for catcher Shanty Hogan and outfielder Jimmy Welsh following the 1927 season. After a seventh batting crown with the Braves in 1928, Boston sent him to the Cubs for five players and an irresistible $200,000. Hornsby took over for Joe McCarthy as manager of the Cubs at the end of 1930 and continued through nearly two-thirds of the 1932 campaign before angering another owner. Charlie Grimm took the reins from Hornsby and led the club to the pennant. Hornsby

began the 1933 season with the Cardinals but moved across town to the Browns as player-manager with 54 games to go and remained there through the 1937 season, never finishing in the first division. Frisch was a key member of the Cardinals' Gas House Gang, going to the World Series in 1928, 1930 and 1931. The Fordham Flash became their manager in the middle of 1933, led them to a World Series victory over the Tigers in 1934, and stayed at the helm until the tail end of the 1938 season.

The Red Sox passed into the capable hands and deep pockets of Tom Yawkey in 1933, just in time to participate in Connie Mack's final Philadelphia fire sale. That December, marginal pitcher Bob Kline, shortstop Rabbit Warstler plus $125,000 brought the Red Sox Hall of Famer Grove, plus pitcher Walberg and second baseman Max Bishop. Two Decembers later, $150,000 of Yawkey's cash, minor league catcher George Savino, and 2–10 righthander Gordon Rhodes pried Hall of Fame slugger Jimmie Foxx from Mack.

Throughout the Depression, Yawkey's cash made him a popular man with Boston fans and AL owners alike. The Red Sox bought a number of quality players, including outfielders Bing Miller and Henie Manush, and the brothers Ferrell, catcher Rick and pitcher Wes, in separate deals. (Subsequently, in the only transaction of its kind, the batterymate brothers were traded together to the Senators in 1937 for outfielder Ben Chapman and pitcher Bobo Newsom.) In another family affair, Washington owner Clark Griffith reluctantly sold his Hall of Fame shortstop and son-in-law Joe Cronin to the Sox after the 1934 season for $225,000 and shortstop Lyn Lary. Legend has it that Yawkey swayed The Old Fox by saying, "I can do more for your son-in-law than you can," and then signed Cronin to a $30,000 contract. (Lest anyone suspect the Sox have gone soft on family ties, Boston managing partner Haywood Sullivan sold his son, catcher Marc, to the Houston Astros prior to the 1988 season.) Yawkey's acquisitions improved the Red Sox—not surprisingly since they were 43–111 in 1932—but they failed to capture the AL flag until 1946.

The Cubs rivaled the Cards as the NL's best team during the Depression on the strength of the Wrigley family bank account and trades for Hornsby, Kiki Cuyler, and Chuck Klein. In 1938, they picked up Dizzy Dean, thought to be finished after breaking a toe in the 1937 All-Star Game, then hurting his arm. Dean dipsy-doodled his way to a 7–1, 1.81 season for the eventual World Series sweep victims. The Reds unseated the Cubs in 1939 on the strength of trades throughout the decade including those for pitchers Paul Derringer and Bucky Walters, outfielder Ival Goodman and second baseman Lonnie Frey. But the Reds' best deal of the 1930s was undone. They purchased Johnny Mize from the Cards in December 1934, but returned the Big Cat when he showed up with a bad knee. Mize averaged 26 homers in six seasons for the Cards, notching a pair of home run titles before going to the Giants after the 1941 season for three no-names and 50 grand. Two homer crowns later, Mize moved to the Yankees in August 1949 for $40,000, helping New York win its first of 10 pennants under skipper Casey Stengel. Mize led the AL in pinch hits three times as the Yankees made five straight trips to the World Series during his tenure in the Bronx.

Upon purchasing the Indians in June 1946, Bill Veeck hoped to stick it to the Yankees, symbols of the baseball establishment he detested. After the 1946 season, Veeck stole lefty knuckleballer Gene Bearden, 20–7 with a league-best

2.43 ERA for the Tribe's 1948 world champions, along with pitcher Al Gettel and three-toed outfielder Hal Peck, both helpful in restoring the Tribe to respectability in 1947, for catcher Sherm Lollar and second baseman Ray Mack, neither much good as Yankees. Veeck selected Bearden from a list of prospects on the advice of Casey Stengel, who had managed for Veeck's Milwaukee Brewers in the American Association. Before 1948, Veeck got outfielder Allie Clark, a .310 hitter with 38 RBI as a part-timer, for pitcher Red Embree, who had eight wins left in his major league career.

The usual show-biz flair characterized Veeck's stewardship. St. Louis Browns utility infielder Johnny Berardino refused a trade to the Senators over the winter of 1947 and announced his retirement to pursue a promising career in the movies. Veeck quickly acquired Berardino for outfielder Catfish Metkovich and $50,000 (a broken finger caused the Brownies to return Metkovich and settle for an additional $15,000), then wooed the 30-year-old actor back into baseball by offering a higher salary plus an attendance clause, a movie contract (Veeck's Cleveland investors included Bob Hope), and insuring Berardino's face for $1 million, the same amount riding on Betty Grable's legs. Berardino, who went on to stardom in the *General Hospital* soap opera, generated loads of publicity, but Veeck's pursuit had a solid baseball foundation. Detroit, second-place finishers in 1947, desperately needed a second baseman, and Veeck wanted to keep Berardino out of the Tigers' clutches.

Amid the sideshows and promotions, Veeck's key deal to make the Tribe world champions in 1948 was that most rare type, one that benefited both teams. The Indians had a magnificent shortstop in Lou Boudreau, who also served as their manager, but they needed a quality second baseman to pair with him. At the 1946 World Series, Veeck met his Yankee counterpart Lee MacPhail, an angry spectator on the prowl for pitching. He offered MacPhail 31-year-old righthander Allie Reynolds, four games over .500 after four years in the Indians' rotation. Veeck decoyed, suggesting that MacPhail trade him George "Snuffy" Stirnweiss, an infielder with two stolen base crowns and a batting title to his credit during the war years. MacPhail balked, counteroffering 31-year-old second baseman Joe Gordon with whom he'd been feuding. That was the man Veeck wanted.

With Boudreau and Gordon in the middle of the infield, the 1947 Indians turned 31 more double plays and led the league in fielding, tacking on a second fielding crown in 1948. Gordon piled up 29 homers and 93 RBI's in his first season in Cleveland and followed up with a 32-homer, 124-RBI, .280 campaign for the 1948 world champs. Reynolds went 19–8, leading the AL in winning percentage for the pennant winning 1947 Yankees, then topped the league in ERA, shutouts and strikeouts while winning 20 in 1952. A stalwart in the Yankee rotation through 1954, Reynolds finished his career at 182–107, 75 games over .500. The Indians got their world championship with Gordon, and the Yankees got six, the way things went back then. The Indians' World Series triumph over the Boston Braves in 1948 would be the last for an AL squad other than the Yankees until the Orioles swept the Dodgers in 1966.

When the Yankees didn't reach the World Series in 1954 after five straight visits, general manager George Weiss took dramatic action, engineering a record 18-player deal with the Orioles, commencing November 18, 1954 and winding up the next May when pitcher Art Schallock went to Baltimore via

the waiver wire. The Yankees got the better of the mess, largely composed of marginal players, most notably hurlers Don Larsen and Bob Turley. Larsen, 3–21 for the 1954 Birds, went 45-24 in five seasons wearing the pinstripes, adding three World Series victories including his perfect game in 1956. Turley went 17–13 for the resurgent 1955 Yankees, and took the Cy Young Award in 1958, leading the AL with 21 wins and 19 complete games. Turley also contributed from the bench as an expert pitch stealer, tipping off Mickey Mantle and others about the upcoming delivery with a whistle or clap.

The New York-Kansas City pipeline during the 1950s prompted one of baseball's best nicknames: Harry "Suitcase" Simpson. The outfielder-first baseman spent three uneventful seasons in Cleveland, batting .266 once, under .230 twice, then found himself back in the minors in 1954 at age 28. Simpson climbed back onto the Indians' roster in 1955 but after three appearances was sold to the A's on May 11 and thus his saga began. Simpson batted .300 for the A's and thought he had found a home. In 1956 he led the AL in triples with 11, hit 21 homers, drove in 105 runs, and batted .293, exploits that earned the attention of the Yankees. On June 15, 1957, Simpson and his .296 batting average went to New York with pitcher Ryne Duren and outfielder Jim Pisoni in exchange for Ralph Terry, Woodie Held, and brawling Billy Martin. Simpson finished 1957 with a .270 average and again led the league with nine triples. Exactly one year later, June 15, 1958, the Yankees sent Simpson back to Kansas City with pitcher Bob Grim for pitchers Duke Maas and Virgil Trucks. He ended the 1958 season with a .255 mark and opened the 1959 season in Kansas City, but a month into the campaign he was traded to the White Sox for third baseman Ray Boone. Fifteen weeks later, Simpson was traded to Pittsburgh with a minor league infielder for Ted Kluszewski. Pittsburgh sold Simpson back to the White Sox at the end of the season. With no frequent flyer programs to motivate him, Simpson never returned to the majors. In all, he logged six trades, five of them in 26 months, all but the finale in mid-season.

During this same era, Frank Lane served as general manager for the White Sox, Cardinals, Indians and A's. He helped construct the White Sox squad that interrupted the Yankee's stranglehold on the AL pennant, then earned the wrath of Cleveland fans by trading 1959 AL homer leader (tied at 42 with Harmon Killebrew) and local hero Rocky Colavito for Detroit's 1959 batting titlist Harvey Kuenn. The move was splashy and daring, but helped neither team unseat the Yankees. Lane may be best remembered for his mid-1960 swap of managers, acquiring Jimmy Dykes to lead his Indians and sending Joe Gordon to pilot the Tigers.

Stan Musial, the St. Louis Cardinals' finest player of the post-war era, retired after the 1963 season, having last visited a World Series in 1946. In 1964, the Cards won their first of three pennants and two world titles during the 1960s. After selling future Hall of Fame reliever Hoyt Wilhelm to Cleveland in September 1957, the Cards ran off a string of trading successes nearly unbroken for a dozen years that would have made Branch Rickey proud.

The construction of the Cardinals' championship teams of the 1960s dates from the December 5, 1957 acquisition of center fielder Curt Flood, along with outfielder Joe Taylor, from the Reds for pitchers Marty Kutyna and Ted Wieand. Before a later deal made him famous, Flood won six Gold Gloves and batted over .300 six times (under .296 once)

between 1961 and 1969. At the end of spring training in 1959, fine-fielding first baseman Bill White was acquired from the Giants, who had plenty of other lefthanded first basemen, with third baseman Ray Jablonski for another pair of pitchers, Don Choate, who never had a major league victory, and Sam Jones. At 33, this second Sad Sam topped the NL with 22 wins and a 2.83 ERA in 1959 and won 18 more games in 1960, then dropped off severely. White batted at least .283, topping .300 four times, in seven seasons with the Cards, knocked in 100 runs three times and averaged 20 homers, while collecting a Gold Glove annually. With Ken Boyer anchoring third base, St. Louis secured the remainder of the infield for their 1964 championship squad with help from Pittsburgh. Second baseman Julian Javier escaped the shadow of perennial all-star Bill Mazeroski in May 1960, and shortstop Dick Groat, NL batting champion in 1960 for the world champion Bucs, arrived in '63.

These moves made the Cardinals contenders, six games behind the Dodgers in 1963, but the Redbirds needed more help to get over the top. They got it from their long-standing rivals, the Chicago Cubs. The Cards sent pitchers Ernie Broglio and Bobby Shantz plus part-time outfielder Doug Clemens to Chicago for a couple of marginal hurlers and an outfielder three days short of his 25th birthday named Lou Brock. Broglio hurt his arm and went 7–19 in three seasons with Chicago before dropping from sight. Shantz recorded a loss during his two months in Chicago before moving to Philadelphia, his eighth and final major league team.

In his 16 years with the Cardinals, Brock picked up where Maury Wills left off in re-establishing the stolen base as an integral part of major league offenses. All but 50 of Brock's career-record 938 steals were made in a St. Louis uniform, including a then-season record 118 in 1974. Brock ranks second to Stan Musial in hits, runs, total bases, and doubles for the Cards, finishing with 3,023 hits and a ticket to Cooperstown. With Brock igniting the offense from the leadoff spot, the 1964 Cardinals squeaked past the Philadelphia Phillies in a wild pennant race and defeated the New York Yankees. The Cards won again in 1967 and lost a seventh game to Mickey Lolich and the Detroit Tigers in 1968. Brock's seven steals in both the 1967 and 1968 remain single-Series standards. In 21 October classic games, Brock batted .391, tops among participants in 20 or more Series games, and is tied with Eddie Collins for the Series career lead with 14 steals.

The Dodgers matched the Cards with three pennants in the 1960s, with trips to the Series in 1963, 1965 and 1966, aided by deals providing bullpen support for the homegrown hurlers. They shipped third baseman Don Zimmer to the Cubs for reliever Ron Perranoski, as well as third baseman John Goryl, a minor league outfielder and $25,000, just before opening day in 1960. After a year of seasoning in the minors, Perranoski became a dominant reliever, going 16–3 with a 1.67 ERA and saving 23 games for the 1963 champs. He saved the Dodgers' only 1963 World Series triumph that wasn't a complete game in their stunning sweep of the Yankees. Before the 1966 season, the Dodgers got reliever Phil "The Vulture" Regan from the Tigers for utility infielder Dick Tracewski. Regan imitated Perranoski's previous heroics, with a 14–1, 1.62 mark and league leading 21 saves for 1966 pennant winners.

The Cards kept dealing. In May 1966, they got another first baseman from the Giants, Orlando Cepeda, for lefthander Ray Sadecki, a 20-game winner in 1964 who never

again broke a dozen wins. Cepeda dubbed his new club "El Birdos," then batted .325 in 1967 with 25 homers and an NL best 111 RBI's to receive National League MVP honors. Traded to the Braves for Joe Torre during spring training in 1969, Cepeda helped Atlanta win the first NL West crown, but there's no word as to whether he called his new club "El Bravos." Roger Maris, acquired from the Yankees at the winter meetings before the 1967 season for third baseman Charley Smith, allowed the Cards to move Mike Shannon from right-field to third.

The Cincinnati Reds followed Rickey's adage about trading a player a year too soon when they sent Frank Robinson, an "old 30," according to the Reds' brain trust, to the Baltimore Orioles for pitchers Milt Pappas, Jack Baldschun, and Dick Simpson. But what a year too soon it turned out to be. Robinson won the triple crown and MVP as the Orioles collected their first-ever world championship. The O's bagged another three American League pennants and a second world title during Robinson's six seasons in Baltimore. The trio of pitchers Cincinnati received recorded a total of 31 victories for the Reds, and none of them was still in the majors when Robby hung up his spikes in 1976.

Trades helped rebuild the Reds after the Robinson disaster, adding key components to a farm system harvest that included Pete Rose, Tony Perez, Johnny Bench, and Dave Concepcion. The team was perennially short of starting pitching but picked up relievers to back Sparky Anderson's Captain Hook act and had phenomenal success trading for position players.

After the 1968 season, the Reds traded aging center-fielder Vada Pinson to the Cardinals for center-fielder Bobby Tolan, who led the NL in steals with 57 in 1970, batted .316 with 16 homers and 80 RBIs and seemed ready for greater things before a torn Achilles' tendon kept him out for the entire 1971 campaign. As if that wasn't enough, the deal also brought the Reds' reliever Wayne Granger, who paced the NL with 35 saves in 1970. In May 1971, sending pitcher Vern Geishert and shortstop Frank Duffy to San Francisco secured George Foster, winner of three consecutive RBI titles starting in 1976.

After a fourth place finish in 1971, their last sub-.500 season until 1982, the Reds sent the right side of their infield (first baseman Lee May and second baseman Tommy Helms) to the Astros with outfielder Jimmy Stewart for super center-fielder Cesar Geronimo, third baseman Dennis Menke (moving Tony Perez to a more comfortable existence at first base), pitcher Jack Billingham, who became the workhorse of the Cincinnati starting staff, reserve outfielder Ed Armbrister, and second baseman Joe Morgan, who notched MVP honors in 1975 and 1976. The trade gave the Reds classic strength up the middle, with Geronimo, Morgan, Concepcion, and Bench receiving Gold Gloves annually from 1974 to 1977.

Trades boosted other 1970s winners. Early in the decade, the Yankees acquired Graig Nettles and Chris Chambliss to anchor the corners, Lou Piniella and Oscar Gamble as platooning doctors of hitology, and stole reliever Sparky Lyle from the Red Sox for first baseman Danny Cater, who murdered Boston hurlers but few others. Center-fielder and offensive catalyst Mickey Rivers and stalwart starter Ed Figueroa were acquired for Bobby Bonds at the winter meetings of 1975, as was second baseman Willie Randolph with pitchers Ken Brett and Dock Ellis from the Pirates for Doc Medich. The Yankees also bolstered the rival Orioles by sending key

lefthanders Scott McGregor and Tippy Martinez, righties Rudy May and Dave Pagan, plus catcher Rick Dempsey to Baltimore for pitchers Ken Holtzman, Grant Jackson and Doyle Alexander, all of whom would do their best work elsewhere, and washed-up catcher Elrod Hendricks on June 15, 1976. The three-time world champion A's supplemented their fine nucleus with Holtzman, acquired before the 1972 campaign for center-fielder Rick Monday, first baseman Mike Epstein, and reliever Darold Knowles in 1971, center-fielder Billy North before the 1973 campaign, and a succession of DHs such as Orlando Cepeda, Deron Johnson, Rico Carty, and Billy Williams from NL clubs, at bargain prices since the senior circuit had less use for their single skill. The Dodgers, who provided the Reds with their most serious competition in the NL West, annually shored up their offense with used power hitters: Richie Allen for 1971; Frank Robinson and Larry Hisle for 1972; Jimmy Wynn for 1974, and Reggie Smith in 1976, along with Dusty Baker, both of whom lasted into the 1980s. They won the 1974 West title as reliever Mike Marshall, acquired from Montreal the previous winter for aged speedster Willie Davis, appeared in a record 106 games, ringing up a 15–12, 21 save log.

Three of the game's all-time great hurlers were involved in trades during the 1970s. The Mets, following their post-1969 season trade of Amos Otis to Kansas City for third base flop Joe Foy, acquired Jim Fregosi from the California Angels for a scatter-armed fireballer named Nolan Ryan and three prospects. The Phils heisted Steve Carlton from the Cards in February 1972 for Rick Wise. In June 1977, the Mets sent Tom Seaver to the Reds for outfielders Steve Henderson and Dan Norman, second baseman Doug Flynn, and pitcher Pat Zachry, a deal brought on by a contract dispute and sealed by a vendetta conducted against Seaver by columnist Dick Young on behalf of the Mets' chairman M. Donald Grant. In the aftermath of the trade, Shea Stadium became known as Grant's Tomb.

The deal with the greatest impact on the 1970s was made in October 1969, when the Cardinals tried to send Curt Flood to the Phillies in a seven-player swap. Although Flood lost his suit against the reserve clause, the challenge alerted owners to the need for concessions and brought arbitrators into the game. The arbitrator's ruling that ended the reserve system in 1975 came about in part because of lefthander Dave McNally's refusal to sign a contract for 1975 following his trade from the Orioles to Montreal. An arbitrator declared Oakland A's star pitcher Catfish Hunter a free agent following the 1974 season, because owner Charles O. Finley had reneged on paying for an annuity. Baseball owners got a taste of what was to come. After leading the AL with 25 wins, his fourth consecutive 20-plus win season, and a 2.49 ERA, Hunter was the object of lively bidding before agreeing to a five-year, $3.75 million contract with the Yankees on New Year's Eve. At the time, the average major league salary was under $45,000. Before the 1981 season, an arbitrator declared Boston catcher Carlton Fisk a free agent because the Red Sox had failed to mail him a contract on time, allowing Fisk to change to the White Sox. Arbitrators found major league owners guilty of collusion to restrain free agent movement after the 1985 and 1986 seasons, and seven Class of '85 members were granted a second chance at free agency prior to the '88 campaign. Only outfielder Kirk Gibson signed with a new club, leaving Detroit for LA and leading the Dodgers to postseason play.

The run-up to the new free agent system in 1976 featured

frantic dealing by clubs unsure of where the chips would fall. Knowing that he couldn't afford to keep all of his stars, Oakland A's owner Charles O. Finley traded Reggie Jackson, Ken Holtzman, and a minor leaguer to Baltimore (which couldn't afford them either) for Don Baylor and pitchers Mike Torrez and Paul Mitchell. Thus began the era of rent-a-player, as teams tried to get something for potential free agents they expected to lose, and receiving clubs hoped for good salary-drive seasons. Bill Veeck used this approach with some success, not to mention increased program sales, during his second stint with the White Sox from 1976 to 1980, with one-year wonders like Richie Zisk and Oscar Gamble.

Realizing he couldn't outbid rich clubs for the best players, Finley hoped to sell the remaining stars from the three-time world champion teams, just as Connie Mack did with the franchise six decades earlier. Finley sold pitcher Vida Blue to the Yankees, reportedly for $1.5 million, and outfielder Joe Rudi and reliever Rollie Fingers to the Red Sox at $1 million each. Blue never reached New York, but Fingers and Rudi reported to Boston on June 15 and donned Red Sox uniforms, but didn't play in that evening's contest.

The next day, Commissioner Bowie Kuhn barred the three players from further competition pending his review, then undid the deals. Kuhn ruled that Finley's sales would cheat the people of Oakland out of a competitive team. (Commissioner Kuhn saw things differently than attorney Kuhn, who argued in court for the Braves' right to abandon Milwaukee for Atlanta in 1965.) Finley argued that the cash would allow him to rebuild a depleted farm system, the best method for a low-income club like Oakland to compete in the age of escalating salaries. Kuhn's edict also ignored the reality that the A's and their fans would lose those free agents with no return at the end of the season, as happened with Rudi, Fingers and host of others after 1976 (Blue had been signed to a contract in anticipation of his sale). In December 1977, Finley tried to sell Blue, this time to the Reds for $1.75 million, plus minor league slugger Dave Revering. Kuhn again foiled Finley, establishing a $400,000 per transaction cash limit still in effect. Later that winter, Finley finally disposed of his prize lefty, shipping him across the bay to San Francisco for seven players and $390,000.

Management complained that the end of the reserve system would hamstring their ability to make trades, as well as upset the competitive balance. But trading continued as a major part of building winners. All that was upset was the split of revenue between players and owners. The signings of Reggie Jackson and relief ace Rich Gossage were driving forces in the Yankees' four AL East titles and a pair of world championships in the first five years of free agency. Equally important were trades for defensive specialist Paul Blair, shortstop Bucky Dent, pitcher Mike Torrez, and reliever Ron Davis. The "We Are Family" Pirates of 1979 were abetted by trades for outfielder Mike Easler, second baseman Phil Garner, pitchers Bert Blyleven and Rick Rhoden, shortstop Tim Foli, and, finally, on June 28, Bill Madlock to fill the troublesome third base slot. The deal was notable in addition to its pennant implications for including infielder Lenny Randle, who had slugged manager Frank Lucchesi while a member of the Texas Rangers in the spring of 1977, and pitcher Ed Whitson, who would slug manager Billy Martin while a member of the Yankees in 1985. Madlock never got beyond shoving his glove into umpire Jerry Crawford's face in 1980.

The Phillies, who divided NL East honors with the Pirates

between 1975 and 1980, combined a potent farm system that produced Mike Schmidt, Greg Luzinski, Larry Bowa, Bob Boone, and others, the continuing dominance of Steve Carlton, and sharp trades for pitchers Jim Lonborg and Jim Kaat, second baseman Dave Cash, center-fielder and secretary of defense Garry Maddox, and relief ace Tug McGraw. The Cardinals obtained star relievers Rollie Fingers from San Diego (with pitcher Bob Shirley and catchers Gene Tenace and Bob Geren for catchers Terry Kennedy and Steve Swisher, utility infielder Mike Phillips and four pitchers of little note), and, one day later at the winter meetings, Bruce Sutter from the Cubs (for first baseman Leon Durham, third baseman Ken Reitz, and utility man Ty Waller). The Cards then shipped Fingers to Milwaukee with pitcher Pete Vuckovich and catcher Ted Simmons for outfielders Sixto Lezcano and David Green, plus pitchers Lary Sorensen and Dave LaPoint. The deal helped bring the Cards and Brewers together for the 1982 World Series, as Fingers (1981) and Vuckovich (1982) won back-to-back Cy Young Awards, the only pitchers in the same trade to pull off that feat.

The Cards reloaded for three trips to the World Series during the 1980s with smart deals for Ozzie Smith (with two pitchers from the Padres for Garry Templeton, Sixto Lezcano, and Luis DeLeon), Lonnie Smith (in a three team trade also involving Indians and Phillies that cost St. Louis pitchers Silvio Martinez and Lary Sorensen), and Willie McGee (from the Yankees for pitcher Bob Sykes) before the 1982 world championship, John Tudor (with Brian Harper, who would have had the game winning RBI in the sixth game of the 1985 World Series but for Don Denkinger's infamous call at first base, for George Hendrick and a minor league catcher), and Jack Clark (from the Giants for David Green, Dave LaPoint, Gary Rajsich, and that ultimate player to be named later, Jose Gonzalez who became Jose Uribe).

The baseball strike of 1981 resulted in a new way to acquire players, a compensation pool from which teams losing a top-ranked free agent (as determined by a complex statistical system) could choose an unprotected player from any team. The most important picks from the short-lived pool, which ended with the Basic Agreement signed in 1985, were fireballing Toronto closer Tom Henke; reliever Donnie Moore, instrumental in the Angels' 1986 AL West title; righthander Tim Belcher, a key to the Dodgers' 1988 success, who had previously been plucked by the Oakland A's days after signing out of college with the Yankees; and the Chicago White Sox's selection of Tom Seaver in 1984 after the Mets had brought their all-time leading pitcher back with great fanfare in 1983 to restore faith in the franchise. Perhaps there was some justice in the Mets' random loss of Seaver since they acquired him through a similar stroke.

William Eckert's most meaningful act in his tenure as Commissioner involved picking a slip out of a hat, awarding Seaver to the Mets. Seaver had been drafted off the Southern Cal campus in January of that year and signed by the Atlanta Braves, but his contract was invalidated on a technicality, while the NCAA ruled him ineligible for further college competition. Threatened with a lawsuit unless the righthander was allowed to sign another pro contract immediately, Eckert offered Seaver to any club that would match the Braves $40,000 bonus. Three teams expressed interest, the Indians, Phillies, and Mets, and on April 3, Eckert pulled New York's slip out of a hat and a franchise out of the wilderness.

Today's serious consideration of salary, contract term and major league tenure that go into making deals shouldn't obscure how zany trades can be. Perhaps today's game is too sophisticated to again see a club pay its rent for spring training facilities in Little Rock with Tris Speaker, as the Red Sox did in 1908. At least the Sox were farsighted enough to retain the option to repurchase Speaker from Little Rock in the Southern Association for the $500 they owed in rent. Perhaps several decades' perspective will uncover a deal as amusing as that 1939 trade sending outfielder Gee Walker to the Senators from the White Sox for outfielder *Taffy* Wright and pitcher Pete *Apple*ton. Someday we may see a repeat of the Cardinals and Cubs exchange of outfielders Max Flack and Cliff Heathcoate between games of a May 30, 1922 doubleheader, although the modern version will likely require a preceding rain out.

Rest assured, trade history can repeat itself. The Mets obtained Harry Chiti from Cleveland on April 26, 1962, for a player to be named later. After watching Chiti hit .195 in 15 games, the Mets named Chiti as the player to be sent to the Indians. In September 1987, the Cubs sent reliever Dickie Noles to assist the Tigers' bare bullpen in their pennant drive for that PTBNL. It was rumored that Noles was the forward scout for a larger deal between the clubs, involving the Cubs' hard-hitting, harder-gloved third baseman Keith Moreland. However, in November, Chicago GM Dallas Green resigned and any contemplated deal fell apart. The clubs haggled unsuccessfully on a fair price for Noles, eventually agreeing to make him the Cubs' player to be named.

A recent trend in the market seems to be many players for one star, such as the Phillies' acquisition of Von Hayes from the Indians at the 1982 winter meetings for outfielder George Vukovich, catcher Jerry Willard, pitcher Jay Baller, and infielders Manny Trillo and Julio Franco. The Yankees got Rickey Henderson (and pitcher Bert Bradley) from the A's after the 1983 season for outfielder Stan Javier and pitchers Eric Plunk, Jose Rijo, Jay Howell, and Tim Birtsas. The Mets snatched catcher Gary Carter from the Expos after the 1984 season for infielder Hubie Brooks, outfielder Herm Winningham, pitcher Floyd Youmans, and catcher Mike Fitzgerald. In each case, the stars have outperformed the numbers. But for sheer bulk, there's still no challenger to the biggest one-for-one ever, the December 12, 1975, deal that sent Detroit pitcher Mickey Lolich to the Mets for outfielder Rusty Staub, close to 500 pounds of beef changing sides.

Even the old Yankee-Kansas City pipeline may be in the midst of a revival, rerouted through Chicago. The Yankees and White Sox made seven deals between December 1984 and November 1987, even though the Yankees' principal owner had once called White Sox partners Jerry Reinsdorf and Eddie Einhorn "Abbott and Costello." Those seven deals saw minor leaguers Mike Soper, Glen Braxton, and Scott Nielsen ping-pong between the organizations, and four of the deals included big league catcher Ron "Hand Luggage" Hassey.

If you're looking for the oddest trade ever, refer to the June 1973 deal that sent Yankee lefthander Mike Kekich to Cleveland for a pitcher named Lowell Powell. The trade came about because an earlier swap had soured, one between Kekich and fellow Yankee southpaw Fritz Peterson. They exchanged their families, wives, houses, and dogs, a scene the Yankees broke up when Kekich's relationship with the previous Mrs. Peterson deteriorated and resentment affected his pitching. (Kekich was out of the majors in 1974 and, naturally, Peterson was traded to Cleveland that year. After their major league careers, Peterson became a honcho in Baseball Chapel and Kekich, who studied medicine and pitched in Mexico, became a doctor.)

Baseball's Most One-Sided Trades

1) Babe Ruth from Boston Red Sox to New York Yankees for $125,000 and a $300,000 loan, January 3, 1920: If you're looking at the bottom line, gate receipts from a couple of World Series would have brought in more cash than the Sox got from the Yankees. If you're looking at baseball history, no one made more than George Herman Ruth.

2) Christy Mathewson to New York Giants from Cincinnati Reds for Amos Rusie, December 15, 1900: After throwing 3,748 innings in nine seasons, Rusie had 22 innings left in his arm. Mathewson had 373 victories to go. A deal this bad had to be crooked. And it was.

3) Lou Brock with pitchers Jack Spring and Paul Toth from Chicago Cubs to St. Louis Cardinals for pitchers Ernie Broglio and Bobby Shantz and outfielder Doug Clemens, June 15, 1964: Broglio went 7–19 in three season with the Cubs, Clemens batted .500 for the Cubs (.279 in 1964 and .221 in 1965), and 39-year-old Shantz lasted 20 games before finishing his career with Philadelphia later that season. With St. Louis, Hall of Famer Brock batted .297, scored 1,427 runs, stole 888 bases, and sparked the Cards to three pennants.

4) Frank Robinson to Baltimore Orioles from Cincinnati Reds for pitchers Milt Pappas and Jack Baldschun and outfielder Dick Simpson, December 9, 1965: Robinson won the triple crown, MVP, and a World Series ring in his first season with the Orioles, powering the team to four World Series in six years. Pappas and Baldschun combined for a 31–34 record with the Reds, Simpson had 34 hits for Cincinnati and none were still in the majors when Robinson, "an old 30" according to Reds at the time of the trade, retired 10 years later.

5) Mordecai "Three Finger" Brown with catcher Jack O'Neill to Chicago Cubs from St. Louis Cardinals for pitcher Jack Taylor and catcher Larry McLean, December 12, 1903: Traded after a 9–13, 2.60 rookie season, Brown went on to win 239 games, reaching 20 victories in six straight seasons, 1906-1911. He ranks among the all-time leaders with a 2.06 ERA, a .649 winning percentage and 57 shutouts, plus three more whitewashings and five complete games in nine World Series starts for the fearsome Cubs of the century's first decade. Taylor went 44–49 with St. Louis before returning to the Cubs for a 12–3 record in the 1906 pennant drive. O'Neill batted .206 in two seasons with the Cubs, 39 points better than McLean managed for the Cards before being peddled to Cincinnati.

6) Roger Maris with shortstop Joe DeMaestri and first baseman Kent Hadley to New York Yankees from Kansas City Athletics for outfielders Hank Bauer and Norm Siebern and pitcher Don Larsen, December 11, 1959: Siebern hit at least .272 in each of his four seasons at KC with a top of .308, and Bauer became the A's manager in 1961. DeMaestri went 14 for 76 with four RBIs in two seasons and Hadley hit .203 in 64 at-bats with the Yankees. So far, so good, even if Larsen was 2–10 for the A's. But Maris won back-to-back MVP awards for the Yankees and hit 203 homers in seven seasons while playing marvelously in right field.

7) Ferguson Jenkins with outfielders Adolfo Phillips and

John Herrnstein to Chicago Cubs from Philadelphia Phillies for pitchers Larry Jackson and Bob Buhl, April 21, 1966: It looked like a steal for the Phils in 1966 as Jackson won 15 and Buhl added six while Jenkins struggled to a 6–8 mark. But the Phillies' pair of pitchers were long retired when Jenkins rolled up the last of six straight 20-win seasons for Chicago. In nine-plus Cub campaigns, Jenkins tallied 167 wins, on his way to a career total of 284.

8) Grover Cleveland Alexander and catcher Bill Killefer to Chicago Cubs from Philadelphia Phillies for pitcher Iron Mike Prendergast and catcher Pickles Dillhoefer, December 11, 1917: The Phillies got the better nicknames but the Cubs got the better deal. Uncertainty over the draft status of ball-players during World War One precipitated the trade, and Alexander was lost for most of the 1918 season. He returned to log 128 wins in just over seven seasons in Chicago before moving to St. Louis. Prendergast was 13–15 in two seasons with the Phils and Dillhoefer hit .223 in five years of part-time duty.

9) Nolan Ryan with pitcher Don Rose, outfielder Leroy Stanton and catcher Francisco Estrada to California Angels from New York Mets for shortstop Jim Fregosi, December 10, 1971: The Mets acquired Fregosi to answer their perpetual problem at third base, a position Fregosi had never played in the majors: strike one. Fregosi batted .233 in 146 games for the Mets: strike two. The Mets gave up Nolan Ryan . . .

10) Ron Perranoski with third baseman John Goryl, minor league outfielder Lee Handley and $25,000 to Los Angeles Dodgers from Chicago Cubs for third baseman Don Zimmer, April 8, 1960: The Dodgers got a dominant reliever for the better part of a decade, a useful Triple A player, and mad money for Walter O'Malley. The Cubs got a third baseman who would one day manage them.

Dishonorable Mention: P Steve Carlton to Phillies from Cardinals for P Rick Wise, '72; 1B Orlando Cepeda to Cards from Giants for P Ray Sadecki, '66; CF Curt Flood with OF Joe Taylor to Cardinals from Reds for P Marty Kutyna and P Ted Wieand, '57; 2B Nellie Fox to White Sox from A's for C Joe Tipton, '49; 1B Jimmie Foxx with P Johnny Marcum to Red Sox from A's for P Gordon Rhodes, C George Salvino, and $150,000, '35; OF-INF Pedro Guerrero to Dodgers from Indians for P Bruce Ellingsen, '74; 1B Keith Hernandez to Mets from Cardinals for P Neil Allen and P Rick Ownbey, '83; C Ernie Lombardi with OF Babe Herman and 3B Wally Gilbert to Reds from Dodgers for 2B Tony Cuccinello, 3B Joe Stripp, and C Clyde Sukeforth, '32; P Sparky Lyle to Yankees from Red Sox for 1B-OF Danny Cater, '72; CF Willie McGee to Cardinals from Yankees for P Bob Sykes, '81; P Mike Marshall to Dodgers from Expos for OF Willie Davis, '73; OF George Foster to Reds from Giants for SS Frank Duffy and P Vern Geishert, '71; P Gaylord Perry with SS Frank Duffy (what's with this guy?) to Indians from Giants for P Sam McDowell, '71; P Jeff Reardon with OF Dan Norman to Expos from Mets for OF Ellis Valentine, '81; 2B Ryne Sandberg with SS Larry Bowa to Cubs from Phillies for SS Ivan DeJesus, '82; P Tom Seaver to Reds from Mets for P Pat Zachry, 2B Doug Flynn, OF Steve Henderson and OF Dan Norman, '77.

Brains for Brawn

In addition to trading for help on the field, teams sometimes seek aid in the dugout. Although the trade of Detroit's Jimmy Dykes for Cleveland's Joe Gordon in the middle of the 1960 season remains the only manager-for-manager swap, teams have gone to the trade-mart for leadership 13 times.

• Second baseman Buck Herzog traded by Giants to Reds as player-manager with catcher Grover Hartley for outfielder Bob Bescher, December 12, 1913.

• Christy Mathewson traded by Giants to Reds as manager with outfielder Edd Roush and infielder Bill McKechnie for outfielder Red Killefer and ex-manager Buck Herzog, July 20, 1916—Mathewson activated himself for a final start against old rival Three-Finger Brown.

• Shortstop Dave Brancroft traded by Giants to Boston Braves as player-manager with outfielders Casey Stengel and Bill Cunningham for pitcher Joe Oeschger and outfielder Billy Southworth, November 12, 1923.

• Player-manager Bucky Harris traded by Senators to Tigers for infielder Jack Warner to succeed George Moriarty at Detroit, December 19, 1928.

• Catcher Jimmie "Ace" Wilson traded by Cardinals to Phillies as player-manager for catcher Spud Davis and second baseman Eddie Delker, November 15, 1933.

• Catcher Mickey Cochrane traded by Athletics to Tigers as player-manager for catcher Johnny Pasek and $100,000, December 12, 1933. Black Mike led the Tigers to a pennant by seven games over the Yankees and took the Cardinals to seven games in the World Series in 1934. In 1935, he became the first traded manager to garner a world championship as the Tigers downed the Cubs in six.

• Catcher Bob O'Farrell traded by Cardinals to Reds as player-manager with pitcher Syl Johnson for pitcher Glenn Spencer, January 11, 1934.

• Second baseman Eddie Stanky by Giants to Cards as player-manager for pitcher Max Lanier (Hal's dad) and outfielder Chuck Diering, December 11, 1951.

• Second baseman Solly Hemus traded by Phillies to Cardinals as player-manager for third baseman Gene Freese, September 29, 1958.

• First baseman Gil Hodges traded by Mets to Senators as manager for outfielder Jimmy Piersall, May 23, 1963.

• Manager Gil Hodges traded by Senators to Mets for pitcher Bill Denehy and $100,000, November 27, 1968. Hodges became the first non-playing manager acquired in a trade to win a world championship with the 1969 Amazin's.

• Manager Chuck Tanner traded by A's to Pirates for catcher Manny Sanguillen and $100,000, November 5, 1976. Tanner also won a world championship for his new team. The Pirates actually kept some of the cash in the Tanner deal as the A's purchased Buc infielder Tommy Helms on the same date. Helms was returned to Pittsburgh that spring with infielder Phil Garner and pitcher Chris Batton in one of Finley's finest heists, the A's acquiring pitchers Rick Langford, Doc Medich, Doug Bair, and Dave Guisti plus outfielders Mitchell Page and Tony Armas.

• First baseman Pete Rose traded by Expos to Reds as player-manager for infielder Tom Lawless, August 16, 1984.

## CHAPTER 33

Baseball Commissioners

A. D. Suehsdorf

From the beginning, organized baseball has been controlled by the owners of the major league clubs. Acting in concert and accountable only to themselves, they have parceled out the franchises, built the grandstands, set the ticket prices, assembled the players, written the game's rules, defined league structure and operation, dominated the minor league dependencies, and, until recent times, bound their players absolutely through the reserve clause written into every contract. Virtually the only restraint on this monopoly power has been fear of alienating the fans from whom all profit flows by actions or circumstances threatening confidence in the honesty and integrity of the game. Even this, on occasion, has been put at risk.

Owner power has been matched by owner intractability. Whatever their virtues as individuals, baseball owners in the aggregate through much of their history have been quarrelsome, devious, inclined to factional fights, and to circumventing, if not subverting, the rules of their own National Agreement under which all baseball is expected to operate. In part this has resulted from their paradoxical position as cooperative competitors, in part from the entrepreneur's traditional resistance to authority.

During the quarter century of National League supremacy (1876-1900), it was of little consequence that the league presidents were figureheads and the owners' squabbles flagrant. But when Ban Johnson's American League established itself as an equal in 1901—the first and only competitor ever to do so—it became imperative to create an agency empowered to arbitrate matters between the still-touchy partners and to present a facade of unity to the outside world.

The result was the National Commission of 1903: the two league presidents, Ban Johnson of the American League and Harry Pulliam of the National, and August "Garry" Herrmann, president of the Cincinnati Reds, as unsalaried chairman. The National League's edge was more apparent than real. *Gemütlich* Garry was an old friend of Ban's and had won regard in both leagues for his efforts in mediating peace between them. Further, while Herrmann and Johnson served all seventeen years of the Commission's life, the National League had four presidents, breaks in continuity that diminished its role. And in any event the triumvirate was dominated by the dynamic Johnson, whose wit, energy, and administrative skill soon made him the acknowledged "Czar of Baseball."

Basically, the Commission's responsibility was interpretation and enforcement of the National Agreement, and punishment of violations by fines and suspensions. Neither the minor leagues nor the players were officially represented. The Commission assumed protection of their rights in grievances against individual clubs or the major leagues, although its concern was paternalistic at best. Intra-league matters were left to the appropriate president and his board of directors.

Overall, historians give the Commission marks of fair to good for its efforts. The first twelve years of its existence were prosperous, relatively harmonious, and progressive insofar as they consolidated baseball as the national pastime. The final five were a time of anger, turmoil, and disruption.

Strain was inherent, for the concept of the National Commission was fundamentally flawed. League presidents, by their nature, could not view intra- and inter-league affairs equally. The club owners of each league expected the loyalty of their Commission representative and were infuriated when justice or equity required a decision that went against them. It also was impossible to select a neutral chairman from among the owners themselves, yet the money men were never pleased to do the bidding of commissioners who had no financial stake in the game.

In external affairs the Commission did reasonably well. Dealings with the Base Ball Players Fraternity (1912-17), while accompanied by bluster and stonewalling, were on the whole conducted fairly and brought about some improvements in player contracts. It contributed to settlement of the Federal League uprising and to keeping the game going during World War I.

Internally, it lacked the heart to confront long-range baseball problems, such as gambling, which was widespread in and around ballparks, and, in consequence, an undercurrent of crooked players, bribe offers, and thrown games. Investigations were tentative, conclusions irresolute: A coat of whitewash, or passing the buck to the league or teams concerned, while sighing with relief that no one outside baseball was the wiser.

As men of their time, the Commissioners shared proprietors' beliefs in the sanctity of property and the subservience of labor, and rigorously upheld the reserve and ten-day clauses, while assiduously avoiding any legal test of their validity. Yet despite this tilt toward their employers, they showed their best side in the justice of many difficult decisions affecting the commerce in players.

Under the National Agreement players had the right to advance as far and as fast as their talents permitted. Contrarily, they were not to be "farmed" or "covered up" or otherwise hindered from pursuing this goal. The Agreement was inspired less by a regard for players than by assurance of an open market for owners, so that by offering opportunity to baseball's best prospects the clubs would enjoy a competitive balance and hold fan interest. Yet for the owners a gentleman's agreement was always more compelling than the national one. They connived with each other to diddle the draft, waiver, and option processes, and, incidentally, to limit

salaries and rosters, hold up the pay of injured players, and burden released players with the travel costs of getting wherever they were being sent. Such sharp practice and cheeseparing economies were considered shrewd business, and the Commission, when it did not agree with them, was hard put to remedy any but the most egregious injustices.

Where it was most at risk was in settling conflicting claims to players—viz., Sisler to the Browns instead of the Pirates, Quinn to the Yankees, not the White Sox. These interclub fights were bitter and the losers nursed their grievances for years. Cumulatively, they were serious enough to topple the Commission. The last straw was President Johnson's suspension of Carl Mays in mid-1919. Having gone AWOL from the Red Sox, the pitcher was traded to New York in defiance of Ban's order that no deal be made until Mays had been disciplined. This enraged both clubs, as well as long-simmering malcontents in both leagues who had had enough of Ban, whether as president, commissioner, or czar. The Yankees got the suspension overturned in court. The American League drastically reduced Ban's authority by appointing a two-owner committee to review all but the most minor fines and suspensions. And the National League, long exasperated with Herrmann for being Johnson's docile creature, forced him to resign. Johnson, having lost his customary American League backing, was powerless to keep Garry in office, although he bullheadedly blocked the election of a new Commission chairman. As rancor led to impasse, the baseball establishment drifted.

To prod the owners out of their rut, Albert D. Lasker, a prominent Chicago advertising man and a substantial stockholder in the Cubs, proposed a new commission of three distinguished, disinterested public figures with "unreviewable authority" over owners, players, and franchises. Wearied as they were of bosses from within the ranks, the magnates did not welcome supervision by outsiders as an improvement. While they maundered, the Black Sox scandal broke.

Horrified, if not surprised, by this corruption of their enterprise, the owners took dramatic action to restore public confidence in the game. Although splintered by in-house controversy and intrigue, they mustered a majority vote to scrap the National Agreement and create a new three-man commission. Shortly after a Grand Jury heard evidence of the 1919 World Series fix, they named Kenesaw Mountain Landis as their principal Commissioner.

Then 53, Landis had been a Federal district court judge for fifteen years. He was meagerly educated, narrow in vision, and simplistic in his judicial decisions, many of which were overturned on appeal. Nonetheless, with his craggy face, dramatic shock of white hair, and flamboyant manner, not to mention an easily aroused sense of outrage, he had the public image of a fierce but twinkly eyed man of rectitude. The owners were certain he saw things their way. In 1915, he had delayed action on the Federal League's antitrust suit against the majors until a negotiated settlement could be reached and the need for a decision was past, thus avoiding once again a legal test of baseball's monopoly status. To the press and public, he had the common touch of a lifelong affection for the Cubs and, to all appearances, the backbone to clean up baseball's mess.

Commissioner Landis took office in January, 1921 (although not surrendering his seat on the Federal bench for another year). His mandate was to deal as he saw fit with anything deemed "detrimental" to baseball. His powers were written into a new National Agreement and incorporated in player contracts. His decisions and penalties were to be binding. There could be no recourse to the courts and no public criticism. Even the most tentative objections were met by threats of resignation before which the owners invariably quailed.

Landis relished the free hand he had demanded and got. The appointment of associate commissioners was forgotten, and even as advisers, the two league presidents—Johnson and John A. Heydler—generally were ignored.

The eight Black Sox were first to feel the Commissioner's wrath. Whatever the courts might determine, in Judge Landis's eyes their conduct had been atrociously detrimental to baseball and he banned them all, plus Joe Gedeon, who had "guilty knowledge," for life.

Player delinquency was a continuing embarrassment. Old villainies surfaced and new ones occurred. Over the next several years six more players were expelled and many others declared ineligible for varying periods. Landis's sweeping actions often were inconsistent, arbitrary, and unfair. Some rascals escaped scrutiny. Some great stars were acquitted on their own say-so. A few culprits were severely punished for trifles. Benny Kauff, indicted for, but acquitted of, auto theft, was ruled permanently ineligible because Landis decided he was probably guilty. Ray Fisher was blacklisted without explanation, hearing, or appeal, evidently for negotiating with an "outlaw" club. Petitions for reinstatement of such sinners as Buck Weaver were refused or went unanswered.

Landis opposed all forms of gambling—horse racing especially—and tried to keep gamblers out of the ballparks, but with indifferent success. He failed to act against the known gambling connections of Charles Stoneham of the Giants; the racing stables of Frank Navin of Detroit, or the betting proclivities of such dedicated horse players as John McGraw and Rogers Hornsby.

Still, by his vehemence and persistence he sent a clear message to baseball that crooks and cheats would not be tolerated, and he persuaded Americans that he was making their game honest again.

For all his harshness, he acted to protect the rights of players and professed sympathetic interest in them. He cracked down on cover-ups and other management maneuvering that impeded players' progress, although here, too, he was ever unpredictable. In two cover-up cases six months apart, he made the Indians turn Tommy Henrich loose, while allowing them to keep Bob Feller.

Similarly, he favored an unrestricted draft and fought a losing battle against the farm system, most prominently in skirmishes with Branch Rickey, farming's principal architect. In 1938, he made free agents of 91 Cardinal farmhands unfairly sequestered, and in 1940 another 91 young Tigers. Landis's resistance to the farm system began soon after he was installed as Commissioner and it remained a central issue of his many years in office. Whether farming killed minor league ball or kept it alive, it was an idea whose time had come, and Landis alienated many owners by his efforts to stamp it out.

The Judge loved to preside at the World Series each year. As an interleague affair, it always had been a National Commission responsibility, but Landis had his own czarist inclinations and went beyond scheduling, umpires, and distribution of receipts to make the event uniquely his own. He reduced the format from nine games to seven, negotiated the first

contracts for radio broadcasting, and, as he was always in attendance with his chin on the railing of a front-row box, he usurped the umpires' authority to call a game or oust a player—most notably the removal of Ducky Medwick in 1934.

It did not take the owners long to regret their hasty and comprehensive surrender of power. By the mid-1920s they were grumbling at Landis's interference in player transactions, and by 1932 voted limits on his jurisdiction in this area. The opprobrium once reserved for Ban Johnson was now applied to Landis, but stopped short of calling his bluff about quitting. Capricious, high-handed, and profane as he was, he was also an unassailable national institution. Among his last acts was the legitimate but Draconian expulsion of owner William D. Cox for betting on his Philadelphia Phillies. Frail and ill as his term reached 24 years, the Judge still was the only logical candidate for Commissioner on the owners' horizon. He died at 78 in 1944 and was elected to baseball's Hall of Fame.

Rid of the tyrant at last, the magnates threw off a few of their shackles. They restricted the detrimental-to-baseball authority by exempting from it all their major league rules and any action taken in compliance with them. They wiped out the gag that prohibited criticizing a Commissioner's ruling, or going to court to block it. And they changed the margin for approval of an interleague action from a simple majority to three quarters of the clubs of each league.

They then chose 47-year-old Senator Albert B. "Happy" Chandler of Kentucky as Landis's successor. It was a surprise appointment engineered by Larry MacPhail, then a Yankee owner, who brought his colleagues, divided and squabbling as usual, to a decision.

A greater contrast to Landis would have been hard to find. Happy was the prototypical politico: shrewd, ebullient, folksy, and smarter than he seemed. The owners obviously wanted a glad-handing good-will ambassador for baseball and a lightweight boss for themselves. They got the first, but not the second. Although rather too exuberant and good ol' boy for the New York press, which thought him foolish and began to ride him hard, Happy was his own man. He bluntly told his new employers that they did not own baseball, that it was America's game and would remain so as long as fans did not think it "a bloody business" run by profiteers. This did not sit well in baseball's councils; nor did his efforts to improve wages and working conditions for umpires and his support of benefits for players, such as a minimum wage ($5,000!), a 25 percent limit on salary cuts, and a pension plan to be funded by a percentage of the receipts from television and radio broadcasts of the World Series.

If the owners were displeased, they knew they were in a weak position from which to object. In 1946, the upstart Mexican League was an enticing alternative to players uncertain about the level and stability of their baseball earnings. Chandler met the Mexican League threat by suspending 18 jumpers for five years (though granting amnesty in 1949, when the insurrection failed). Several of the disgruntled jumpers thereupon filed suits challenging the sacred reserve clause, which was a profound worry to the owners until the clubs involved persuaded the plaintiffs to withdraw. Still, Chandler was seen as having invited an unnecessary risk.

The most significant event of his regime was the integration of the major leagues by Brooklyn's introduction of Jackie Robinson; the most sensational was the one-year suspension of Brooklyn's manager, Leo Durocher, both in April 1947.

While not a prime mover in Robinson's arrival, Happy was openly and genuinely supportive of Branch Rickey's stunning assault on the game's long-standing color barrier. Unlike Landis, who addressed the matter only obliquely—in blocking Bill Veeck's attempt to buy the Phils and recruit Negro Leaguers for them—Chandler spoke forthrightly in favor of integration.

Durocher's suspension was brought on specifically by an unseemly confrontation between Leo and Larry MacPhail, but it appeared to stem from official exasperation with an accumulation of Durocher scrapes, altercations, dubious associations, on-field rows, and marital difficulties, all of which presumably added up to that convenient catchall, "conduct detrimental to baseball." It was the stiffest penalty ever levied against a manager.

Unfortunately, having pronounced judgment without citing the particulars on which it was based, Chandler enforced silence on all parties and refused to discuss it himself. In the confusion and controversy which followed, it was never made clear whether the suspension "year" was the duration of the baseball season or the calendar's twelve months, whether a suspended manager's contract was valid, and whether, at suspension's end, he could be rehired. Far from a salutary punishment, l'affaire Durocher made a martyr of Leo and lost face for Happy.

Throughout his term, the Commissioner was confronted by the ineradicable problems of owner manipulation of baseball rules and of inappropriate association with racing or gambling interests. In a remarkable burst of confidence, Alva Bradley of the Indians confessed blandly to generalized owner cheating, and Chandler encountered enough violations of the option process and premature signing of high school prospects to believe him.

As always, investigations of possible wrong-doing made no friends, and adverse decisions always made enemies. Hearing rumbles of dissatisfaction before the winter meetings of 1950, the penultimate year in which, by custom, reelection of the Commissioner would be considered, Happy asked for a vote of confidence. Nine were for, seven against—three short of the mandatory three quarters. Happy resigned, accepting one year's salary as severance. In 1982, he was elected to the Hall of Fame.

Ford C. Frick, 56, a one-time "gee-whiz" sportswriter and, since 1934, president of the National League, was picked to replace Happy in 1951. He was a compromise candidate maneuvered into the job by Walter O'Malley of Brooklyn, an emerging power among the magnates.

Now fully recovered from the Landis era, the owners had acquired the complacent, pliable Commissioner most to their liking. In the span of Frick's two seven-year terms, baseball underwent revolutionary changes, not one of them bearing his imprint. He busied himself with administrative detail, pursuing the struggle against gambling, punishing management infractions of baseball rules, and occasionally freeing covered-up minor leaguers. He determined that Roger Maris's 61 homers should have separate mention in the record book because they took 162 games to achieve and, like Landis and Chandler before him, he refused an appeal to reinstate old Buck Weaver of the Black Sox. Beyond that, anything the owners wanted was all right with him.

He presided over an era when commonplace air travel, widening TV markets, and beckoning tax breaks prompted

the Braves, Browns, A's, Giants, and Dodgers to shift their franchises, when talk of a potential third big league was enough to hustle the majors into expanding to 10 clubs each, and when minor leagues were dying from all these invasions of their territories. The character of club ownership was changing from the rough-and-ready old-timers to big-money businessmen or corporations. Congress conducted hearings on baseball's curious exemption from the antitrust laws (though without taking action). Some prominent players were benefiting from exorbitant signing bonuses, while others were looking for greater security and considering unionization. Commissioner Frick saw these as league matters, outside his jurisdiction. In 1965, full of years, he resigned with an election to the Hall of Fame in prospect.

The choice of William D. "Spike" Eckert as Commissioner was a mistake and an embarrassment. A retired Air Force lieutenant general with a distinguished record in World War II, he had not sought the job, but was recommended by a brother officer, Curtis LeMay, bellicose boss of the Strategic Air Command, who refused to be a candidate himself. Spike, an amiable if diffident man, had become a business consultant with fair administrative skills and no knowledge of baseball. He immediately was dubbed "the Unknown Soldier." The owners supported him with four of their number to assist in his major areas of responsibility. Yet his ineptitude was obvious. He was deferential to his owners, limp with his league presidents, and had no awareness of baseball's problems or of the direction it should be headed. He aroused national indignation by failing to cancel games after the assassinations of Martin Luther King and Robert Kennedy.

In December 1968, with an organized players' strike in prospect, he was fired. As balm, he continued to receive his salary until his death in 1971. For this uncomfortable interlude, the owners had no one to blame but themselves.

When elected in 1969, Bowie Kuhn was baseball's youngest (42), tallest (six-five), and biggest (240 pounds) Commissioner ever. He had worked the Griffith Stadium scoreboard as a youth, graduated Princeton, and was well-acquainted with baseball through his New York law firm which had the National League as a client.

Kuhn's first act was to get negotiations between the Major League Players Association and the owner's Player Relations Committee, which had stalled over the terms of a pension package, moving again. He helped bring about a successful settlement which saved the 1969 season from the disruption of a player strike.

A positive man, though in his own words a bit stiff-necked and starchy, Kuhn believed that the still-extraordinary powers of the Commissioner had been granted in order to be used. Furthermore, the owners had decided that their governance needed "restructuring," and charged him with developing a plan for more efficient administration of their business. Kuhn and an ad hoc committee of baseball executives and management experts proposed a further concentration of power in the Commissioner's office. The plan was utterly rejected. Many owners felt that, with more lines on the organization chart leading to the Commissioner, they would be surrendering control of their franchises.

With many important areas of baseball business excluded from his purview, Kuhn resumed his role as persuader, counselor, and positive influence. He was never more than that in the fierce negotiations with the MLPA and its zealous executive director, Marvin Miller. For the owners, negotiations

were conducted by the PRC, a body of their peers. It was this group, with confirmation by the owners as a whole, which made the landmark concessions to union recognition, player agents, arbitration, free agency, the resulting destruction of the reserve clause, and skyrocketing salaries. During the 50-day player strike of 1981, cries were heard for Bowie's locking both sides in a room until they emerged with a settlement. In Landis's day, maybe, but things no longer worked that way. By 1978, the owners had made the PRC a separate corporation, distinctly separate from the Commissioner's office.

Where Kuhn acted boldly—more so than any of his predecessors—was in his dealings with owners and players. He cracked down on George Steinbrenner of the Yankees (two-year suspension), Ted Turner of the Braves (one-year suspension), and went head-to-head with Charlie Finley of the Oakland A's in what seemed unfair salary wrangles with Reggie Jackson, Vida Blue, and Catfish Hunter. In 1976, believing that Finley was liquidating, not rebuilding, his club, Kuhn negated sales of three A's for $3.5 million.

He met the emerging drug problem directly, despite opposition from owners who felt that acknowledging involvement made baseball "look bad," and from the MLPA, which resisted all disciplinary measures imposed by the Commissioner. He returned the All-Star Game voting to the fans, presided over a new and lucrative television contract, and brought the 1972 strike to a speedy conclusion.

Greater furors arose from making Willie Mays and Mickey Mantle sever their association with baseball while working for gambling casinos, and from acceding to television's demand for World Series games in prime-time hours at night.

Victims of his direct actions often became unforgiving enemies. What might be good for baseball was not necessarily good for an owner's corporate interests that underwrote his baseball venture. An insurrection that threatened his re-election in 1975 was headed off by a friendly majority. But by 1983, five National League owners were unalterably disaffected. Lingering unhappiness with the costly 1981 strike and its aftermath was a burden. A proposal for more equitable sharing of broadcasting revenues among rich and poor clubs was a new and divisive problem. And there were renewed calls for "restructuring." Magnates now said they wanted a chief executive officer—a real corporate CEO with the business skills to guide them through the complexities of baseball in the contemporary world. Views on the powers he would have were mixed.

In the voting, the National League dissidents held firm. (There were three inconsequential "no" votes in the American League.) With 18 out of 26 owners on his side—a 69 percent approval rating—Kuhn failed to get the necessary three-quarters majority in each league.

For all the complaints, Bowie Kuhn was probably the most capable Commissioner the owners ever had, and after more years in office than anyone but Landis, it was not easy to find an equally qualified replacement. Kuhn overstayed his term by a year until Peter V. Ueberroth, 47 years old and fresh from a triumph as head of the Los Angeles Olympic Organizing Committee, was unanimously elected to a five-year term in October 1984.

In this trim, composed, and self-confident executive, the owners finally acquired the leadership they knew was needed to deal with the complexities of contemporary life that were engulfing the baseball business.

Ueberroth became the game's CEO. All departments and

activities reported to him, as did the two league presidents, Dr. Bobby Brown of the American and A. Bartlett Giamatti of the National. The Commissioner's authority to discipline owners was greatly increased. He could transfer or deny any club's draft choices, and the limit on club fines was upped from $5,000 to $250,000. Reelection of the Commissioner reverted to a majority vote of the clubs, with a required minimum of five votes from each league. His salary was raised to a reported $450,000, nearly twice what Kuhn was paid.

Having concentrated power in his own hands, Ueberroth then demonstrated that his management style was to delegate responsibility. Although he took unilateral actions to tidy up baseball operations that he found "in disarray," he preferred to have problems solved by the people most closely involved. Cool and controlled in demeanor, yet insistent on high levels of performance and not afraid to make unpopular decisions—he once described himself as "shy and ruthless"—Ueberroth worked first to restore fiscal "sanity" to owners' operations. Many franchises—estimates ran as high as 21 of the 26—were losing money yet continuing to offer long-term player contracts at high wages, even to veterans headed for the inactive list. Exchanges of information to control this extravagance soon brought charges of collusion from the Players Association, which complained of a suspicious absence of bidding by clubs for free agents. Two arbitrators agreed that this was indeed the case during the 1986 and 1987 seasons. Ueberroth denied the allegation but did not dispute the judgment, insisting that baseball must find ways to improve financial stability before such looming problems as expansion could be faced. Tentatively, new franchises could be awarded by 1990 and new teams take the field by 1993.

Internally, baseball felt the impact of two pervasive social problems of the 1980s: drugs and job opportunities for minorities. Each club conducted its own rehabilitation program for drug users through its medical department. The Players Association objected to testing as an invasion of privacy and Ueberroth tended to agree, even though minor leaguers and front-office personnel were tested. The Commissioner also was empowered to suspend relapsed players for one year without pay.

The hiring of blacks and other minorities, particularly those individuals with distinguished baseball careers, for positions of responsibility on or off the field remained a sensitive issue. Ueberroth contended that all clubs had accepted the obligation, although at his departure few, if any, highly visible jobs (such as manager, which minority groups say will prove the point of good faith) had gone to blacks or Latinos.

In assaults on gambling, Ueberroth worked principally behind the scenes to eliminate club-owner investment in racing stables or tracks. In one of his first public gestures he won approval by lifting Kuhn's rather farfetched ban on Mantle and Mays.

Ueberroth urged the Cubs to install lights, or face the possibility of reimbursing the leagues for lost TV revenue. And he entered negotiations with umpires and players only as a goad to keep the parties bargaining until a settlement was reached. He backed away from the designated-hitter controversy, leaving it to the clubs and players to reconcile when his own research failed to indicate a clear preference.

Like Kuhn, Ueberroth did not always find his assertiveness welcomed by the owners. They have been slow to acknowledge the realities of financial imbalance among clubs, not in regard to national TV revenues, which are split equally, but in terms of local TV markets, which reward New York's Yankees, for instance, far more liberally than Seattle's Mariners. Owners have also been at odds over the appropriate system for dealing equitably and effectively with the vexing drug problem. And they did not always react well to Ueberroth's forceful business intelligence—an outsider's voice in which they heard as much coercion as persuasion.

The CEO eventually decided to resign, even if a second term were offered, and in September 1988 National League president Bart Giamatti, 50, was unanimously elected baseball's seventh Commissioner. He signed on for five years beginning April 1, 1989, six months before the traditional October date for transfer of power.

Giamatti's background is intellectually glamorous: he has been professor of Renaissance literature and president of Yale University. His becoming Commissioner had been a possibility before Ueberroth's election, but he then kept to his commitment to Yale. In 1986, however, he accepted the National League presidency when Charles "Chub" Feeney retired.

As a baseball man, Giamatti is an ardent fan, with the New Englander's inevitable devotion to the Red Sox. He has suspended players for scuffing balls and corking bats. During the 1988 season he held firm against protests over his 30-day suspension of Reds' Manager Pete Rose for bumping an umpire, and he enforced a strict interpretation of the balk rule. He is on record as supporting "social justice" in minority hiring and for improving the atmosphere of raucous and rowdy ball parks. He is lukewarm on expansion and does not believe club owners guilty of collusion to restrict the free-agent market.

Ueberroth stayed on during the transitional months, undertaking to achieve new agreements with national TV and the evermore powerful Players Association before existing contracts expired in 1989. Three quarters of the clubs were now making money.

## CHAPTER 34

The Farm System

Bob Hoie

Farm teams are nearly as old as organized baseball. In 1884 the Boston Beaneaters of the National League owned a team called the Boston Reserves in the Massachusetts State Association. The Reserves, also called the Colts, were apparently intended to serve as a source of replacements for disabled members of the major league club. It has also been suggested that the farm team was a device to keep more players under contract and out of the hands of the Union Association that year. Whatever the origins of the idea, during the next decade a number of major league clubs operated such reserve teams, but they usually competed in local semipro leagues rather than in organized baseball and were viewed more as quick sources of replacements rather than as training grounds for players.

With John B. Day's joint ownership of the New York Gothams of the National League and the New York Metropolitans of the American Association as early as 1883 and with the proliferation of interlocking ownerships of major league clubs in the 1890s, it was only natural that some major and minor league clubs would come under joint ownership as well. The first instance of any significance, however, occurred when John T. Brush, owner of Cincinnati in the National League, entered the Indianapolis club in the newly formed Western League in 1894. While this was not the first case of joint major-minor league club ownership, Brush appears to have been the first to grasp the potential of such an arrangement. Indianapolis served as a place to develop talent that was not quite ready for the majors. The team gave Cincinnati an expanded roster as players were frequently shuffled to and from Indianapolis during the season; it also served as a source of profit because Indianapolis drew well at the gate, having become the dominant club in the Western League, with three pennants and two second-place finishes in five seasons (1895–1899). Indianapolis's success was aided in no small part by Brush's practice of drafting players from other Western League clubs and sending them to Indianapolis, thus simultaneously weakening the opposition and strenghtening the Hoosiers. Efforts were made by the other Western League club owners to control "farming" or to modify the draft rules to stop Brush, but none were successful.

Perhaps copying Brush's strategy, in 1896 several National League clubs obtained minor league affiliates: Pittsburgh had Toronto, Boston had Wilkes-Barre, and Cleveland had Ft. Wayne. Philadelphia had a Philadelphia farm club in the Pennsylvania State League, and when that league folded, they shifted the junior club to the Atlantic Association. The New York Giants had the first farm "system," with the New York Mets in the Atlantic Association and Syracuse in the Eastern League.

When the National Agreement was adopted in 1903, it banned the "farming out" of players, but "farming" as defined in the agreement referred only to those efforts by major league clubs to exceed the limits on players who could be optioned through subterfuge—"fake transfers" such as loans or sell/buy-back arrangements with minor league clubs where title to a player was never actually surrendered.

The independent minor league operators saw farming as a curse for two reasons. First, it reduced their autonomy and potential revenue by placing more players under major league ownership, thus reducing the majors' need to buy or draft players from the minors. Second, clubs accepting players from the majors, either openly through options or secretly, might gain an unfair competitive advantage on the field. So while in 1905 the New York Giants' request to establish a working agreement with Bridgeport was validated by the National Commission, most of the legislation was focused on restricting farming, normally by limiting the number of players who could be optioned and the number of times each player could be optioned. For example, in 1904 a rule was adopted which required a player sent out on option to stay with the minor league club for the remainder of that season. In 1907 the rule was relaxed so that a major league club could option a player and recall him, but only once in a season. In 1911 a team could have no more than eight players out on option at one time.

Working agreements became quite common during this period. The major league club furnished the minor league club with its surplus players—youngsters in need of more experience or veterans past their prime who could still strengthen a minor league club—and/or cash. In return the major league club could obtain promising players from the minor league club. During this era the formal working agreement between major and minor league clubs was usually of short duration—a year or two at most—suggesting that major league clubs targeted certain minor league clubs that had two or three players they might be interested in and established a working agreement in order to get first claim on those that developed satisfactorily. There were also informal working agreements, generally based on friendships between major and minor league club operators, and it was usually through such arrangements that the "fake transfers" banned by the National Agreement took place. In the early 1900s, for example, there was substantial traffic in players between the White Sox and Milwaukee of the American Association and between the Dodgers and Baltimore in the Eastern League. (Brewer manager Joe Cantillon was a long-time friend of Charles Comiskey, and Brooklyn manager Ned Hanlon was also a minority owner of the Orioles.)

The most efficient and only legal method of circumventing the rules relating to major league control of players was

through joint ownership of major and minor league clubs. By 1912 Charles W. Somers owned Cleveland and Toledo, and Charles Ebbets owned both Brooklyn and Newark. This enabled the Indians to hold title to sixty players and the Dodgers to sixty-one. In 1913 a National Commission confidential bulletin directed major league clubs to divest their interest in minor league clubs by January 1, 1914, but neither Somers nor Ebbets complied until several years later (in fact, Somers secretly acquired New Orleans in 1913). In 1921 the joint ownership of major and minor league clubs was again permitted, and the New National Agreement, although retaining option limits, dropped the antifarming provisions that had been in it since 1903.

In 1921 the Cardinals, who had already acquired an interest in Ft. Smith of the Western Association and Houston of the Texas League, acquired a half interest in Syracuse of the International League. This was the beginning of Branch Rickey's farm system, but initially it attracted little attention as it didn't appear to represent anything particularly new. Major league clubs had long been signing young talent directly off the sandlots and developing it in the minors. In 1910, for example, Cleveland signed Roger Peckinpaugh out of the Cleveland City League, gave him a brief trial, and then optioned him to New Haven and Portland in successive seasons before recalling him when he was deemed ready for the majors. This practice had developed to the point that Mike Sexton, president of the National Association, in 1921 spoke out against the fact that the majors and higher minors had preempted the low minors' traditional role of discovering and signing young talent.

As we have seen, major league clubs had occasionally owned minor league clubs, primarily to expand the number of players under their control, but these were always higher-classification clubs, where talent was refined rather than developed. Rickey's approach was original because he was the first to assemble a system of teams at various levels or classifications. This enabled him to sign young talent and, through a hierarchy of minor league clubs, to develop and retain continuous title to a large number of players, his theory being that out of quantity comes quality. It didn't take long for the system to begin producing talent—the Cards, who had never finished higher than third in this century, won the World Series in 1926 with a team that included future Hall of Famers Jim Bottomley and Chick Hafey as well as regulars Taylor Douthit, Tommy Thevenow, Les Bell, Ray Blades, Flint Rhem, and Art Reinhardt plus reserves Watty Holm, Jake Flowers, Spec Toporcher, Ernie Vick, and Bill Hallahan—all of whom were products of a farm system that was less than seven years old. In addition, Billy Southworth was acquired from the Giants for Heinie Mueller, another product of the Cardinal farm system.

During those seven years when the Cardinals were discovering, signing, and developing unprecedented quantities of players at little expense, the other major league clubs were essentially operating as they always had, signing some players out of the amateur ranks, optioning them out for seasoning, and buying top prospects from minor league clubs, even though the new draft rules were driving the prices of such players to unprecedented levels. For example, the Yankee team the Cardinals defeated in the 1926 World Series had just one home-grown player—Lou Gehrig, who was signed out of Columbia University in 1923 and optioned to Hartford until ready. Although this had been an inexpensive acquisi-

tion, the Yankees subsequently had purchased, for $50,000 each, Earle Combs from Louisville, Mark Koenig from St. Paul (with whom the Yankees had a working agreement), and Tony Lazzeri from Salt Lake. In 1925, the year the Pirates won the World Series, they acquired Paul Waner and Hal Rhyne from the San Francisco Seals for $100,000 and also signed Joe Cronin off the San Francisco sandlots for little more than train fare to his first assignment—Johnstown, Pennsylvania.

But the escalating prices of players and the success of the Cardinals finally encouraged other clubs to begin acquiring minor league clubs. Shortly after the Cardinals acquired the half interest in Syracuse in 1921, William Wrigley, owner of the Cubs, acquired Los Angeles of the Pacific Coast League, but he treated them virtually as separate investments. By 1927, however, major league acquisition of minor league clubs was causing concern in the minors. The first formal notice came late that year, when the American Association adopted a new Constitution which effectively prohibited major league ownership of its clubs (excluding Columbus, which was already owned by Cincinnati). At the National Association meeting in December 1928, Mike Sexton wondered aloud when the majors would own enough clubs to control the National Association. Early in 1929 major league clubs owned or controlled twenty-seven minor league clubs. At that point Judge Landis, who until then had been remarkably quiet on the issue of farm systems, opened fire. He began granting free agency to minor leaguers "covered up" by various major league organizations. Later in 1929, Landis denounced the farm system, and announced his intention of destroying it. In response, Sam Breadon, owner of the Cardinals, cited letters from seven minor leagues saying the farm system was beneficial to them. Interestingly, in 1921 Landis had said, "The object of organized baseball is to facilitate the development of skill among ball players." No one could seriously argue that this wasn't the purpose of the farm system, but by 1929 Landis was accusing Rickey and Breadon of "raping the minors," robbing smalltown America of its precious heritage of independent minor league baseball.

Through the 1930s Landis tried to make good on his threat to destroy the farm system, but since it was not contrary to baseball law, he had to pick at the edges—by levying fines against teams having an interest in more than one team in a minor league or by granting free agency to players who were "covered up" through violations of the option rules or "secret agreements." Attracting much attention in Landis's crusade was his granting of free agency to seventy-four Cardinal farmhands in 1938, and to ninety-one Detroit minor leaguers in 1940, but these were futile shots being fired long after the war had been lost.

More important than the fireworks that erupted between Landis and Breadon at the 1929 major league meeting was Yankees owner Jacob Ruppert's declaration at the same meetings that no ball club could afford the prices being paid for minor league players; Ruppert added that he was "going to be forced into owning minor league clubs, and so is every other major league owner in this room." At the time he spoke, the Yankees had already purchased the Chambersburg club of the Class D Blue Ridge League. In November 1931 Ruppert purchased Newark of the International League for a reported $600,000 and soon thereafter hired Baltimore general manager George Weiss to develop a farm system. Thus the farm system, a concept that had been created largely out

of necessity by Branch Rickey because the Cardinals didn't have the financial resources to compete with other clubs for top minor league prospects, had in less than a decade been embraced by the wealthiest club in baseball as being the most efficient method of acquiring talent. There would still be an occasional Joe DiMaggio or Ted Williams, signed by a minor league club and sold to the majors, but the major league club that didn't establish a farm system did so at its own peril—it cannot be coincidental that the eight teams which were the slowest to get on the bandwagon and had the thinnest farm systems in the 1930s—the Phillies, Athletics, Senators, White Sox, Giants, Cubs, Braves, and Pirates—were, aside from the Browns, the eight least successful teams in the 1940s. (The Browns and Reds established extensive farm systems in the 1930s, and overall they were the two most improved clubs of the 1940s.)

While several clubs caught on to what the Cardinals were doing, none could catch up as Rickey, taking advantage of the Depression, which had created a large pool of young men with few career options, signed players by the hundreds at tryout camps. Whereas during the 1920s the Cardinal system had only increased from three clubs to five, by 1936 it had expanded to twenty-eight teams—remarkable considering that there were only twenty-six minor leagues that year (the Cardinals had two teams each in the Nebraska State, Georgia-Florida, and Arkansas-Missouri Leagues). The Cardinal system finally topped out with thirty-three clubs in 1937—more than the two next-largest farm systems combined. Rickey's belief that out of quantity comes quality was proven on the field by the 1942 world champion Cardinals. Every player on the active roster, except for second-line pitchers Harry Gumbert and Whitey Moore, was a product of the Cardinal farm system, and Gumbert had been acquired in exchange for Cardinal farm graduate Bill McGee. In addition, the sale of players developed by the Cardinals kept the coffers full—in 1940–1941 alone, Johnny Mize, Joe Medwick, and Mickey Owen were exchanged to other clubs for $240,000 and nine players.

Thus from the perspective of the majors the farm system was a success, and the minors seemed to be flourishing—going from fourteen leagues in 1933 to forty-four by 1940. Sam Breadon, responding to another barrage of attacks by Landis in the late 1930s, claimed that the farm system had brought stability and strength to the minors, but there were other factors at work—the proliferation of night games, better promotion, and an influx of good young talent resulted in a per-club increase in attendance of 40 percent from 1937 to 1940. During that same period the portion of minor league clubs affiliated with the majors actually dropped from 61 to 46 percent. Rickey's theory that out of quantity comes quality might have had practical merit during a depression, or again immediately following World War Two when there was an influx of returning veterans. However, under normal circumstances huge farm systems were not cost-effective. While the minors were still expanding in the late 1930s, the Cardinals began pruning back their farm system of more than thirty teams; again while the minors were expanding in the late 1940s, farm systems were contracting—in 1948 there were six farm systems of twenty or more teams; by 1951 there were none. The portion of minor league teams affiliated with major league teams dropped from 62 percent in 1946 to 47 percent in 1951 as major league farm systems collectively dropped from 280 to 175 clubs and outright major league ownership of minor league clubs dropped from 125 to 75.

In 1950 there were 232 minor league teams not affiliated with the majors. This was the highest number of independent teams in organized baseball since the early teens. Nine of the fifty-eight leagues had no teams with major league affiliations, and more than a dozen others had only one or two affiliates. These leagues operated virtually outside the player-development chain, existing much as a semipro team or league does—to provide entertainment and reflect civic pride. Their only source of revenue was through the turnstiles, and just as forty years earlier automobiles and the movies helped drive out the marginal teams and leagues, now TV did the same. This can be clearly seen as the heavily populated Northeast, the first region to be heavily penetrated by television, suffered the first wave of league failures.

Over the next few years, attendance declined sharply, most of the independent clubs folded, and farm systems continued to contract. In 1956 the majors established a "stabilization fund" of $500,000 to aid clubs and leagues in lower classifications, but the free-fall of leagues, clubs, and attendance continued. In 1959 the majors discontinued the stabilization fund and established a fund of $1 million to finance a player-development and promotional program for the minors. In 1962 the majors and minors adopted the Player Development Plan that, by requiring each major league club to have five farm teams, would guarantee the operation of at least one-hundred minor league teams, which the majors felt was adequate for their player-development purposes. The plan also included the Player Development Contract under the terms of which the parent major league club became responsible for all spring training costs and all or most of the salaries of players, managers, and coaches. After major league expansion in 1969, major league clubs were only required to support four farm clubs each, but their financial support of each was increased. By 1976 there were only 106 minor league teams with major league affiliations, the lowest peacetime total since 1935. American League expansion the following year created the need for additional minor league affiliates, and in subsequent years the major league clubs have expanded their farm systems—all of them back up to a minimum of five clubs by 1984. By 1988 the number of minor league teams with major league affiliations was up to 150.

In 1928 Mike Sexton had asked how long it would be before the majors owned enough minor league clubs to control the National Association. Other than during World War Two, when the minors were severely constricted, major league clubs never have "owned" more than 28 percent of the minor league clubs; however, possibly as early as 1934, probably by 1935, and certainly by 1936, the majors through outright ownership, working agreements, or other interlocking devices "controlled" the National Association, and this situation was generally acknowledged throughout baseball by 1938.

Until about 1960 there was still some room for independent clubs and career minor league players, but since then the minors have existed almost exclusively to develop talent for the majors. While this has dismayed many minor league fans and traditionalists, it should be remembered that the principal role of the minors within organized baseball has always been to develop talent for the majors, and to receive money in exchange. The farm system, which owed its success in no small part to the greed of some minor league operators, was merely a different device by which talent moved to the majors and money moved to the minors.

Major League Farm Systems
1936–1969

	36	37	38	39	40	41	42	43	44	45	46	47	48	49	50	51	52	53	54	55	56	57	58	59	60	61	62	63	64	65	66	67	68	69
Boston, AL	9	10	7	8	6	7	6	3	5	4	12	13	15	11	8	8	6	6	6	6	5	7	7	6	6	6	6	5	5	5	6	5	6	6
Chicago, AL	5	4	10	8	6	5	5	0	0	0	17	12	15	9	8	8	6	8	6	6	5	6	6	6	6	6	6	5	5	5	6	6	6	6
Cleveland, AL	5	7	13	16	8	9	8	3	3	3	11	18	20	20	16	12	10	8	8	9	9	8	8	8	7	5	6	5	4	4	4	4	5	5
Detroit, AL	11	8	12	7	5	11	8	2	3	2	7	11	16	14	9	8	7	8	10	9	8	10	7	8	8	6	6	5	5	5	5	6	6	6
New York, AL	11	15	15	15	14	12	9	5	5	5	15	22	24	22	15	14	10	11	9	10	11	10	10	8	8	7	7	6	5	7	7	7	6	6
Phila.-K.C.-Oakland, AL	5	3	3	3	4	5	3	2	2	4	7	15	10	11	15	9	8	8	6	7	7	9	8	8	8	6	5	5	6	6	6	6	6	5
St. Louis-Baltimore, AL	3	15	16	12	11	11	6	1	3	3	11	15	20	18	13	10	12	10	12	8	9	7	7	9	6	6	7	6	6	6	6	7	8	8
Wash.-Minnesota, AL	1	5	2	8	4	6	3	1	2	2	5	7	12	9	10	6	8	7	8	7	6	8	8	7	6	7	7	7	6	8	8	8	8	8
Milwaukee-Atlanta, NL	4	6	6	6	5	4	4	1	1	2	13	15	15	11	8	8	12	11	10	10	12	15	14	12	10	9	8	7	6	5	6	7	5	4
Brklyn.-Los Angeles, NL	5	14	14	11	18	14	10	4	7	9	21	25	26	26	22	19	17	15	15	16	14	13	12	12	12	11	9	7	8	6	6	6	6	6
Chicago, NL	5	6	5	2	2	9	11	4	6	7	18	23	19	16	15	14	10	9	9	8	8	10	8	6	6	6	5	5	5	5	6	6	5	5
Cincinnati, NL	16	10	10	10	8	8	5	2	1	3	4	8	11	10	7	4	6	7	9	9	9	11	11	8	8	6	5	5	4	4	5	5	5	5
N.Y.-San Francisco, NL	2	11	4	5	6	7	7	3	5	8	16	19	22	19	18	14	13	9	9	10	10	10	12	9	8	9	8	7	7	6	6	6	6	5
Philadelphia, NL	1	2	3	3	8	3	2	1	3	5	9	11	15	14	12	11	11	9	9	8	8	9	9	7	10	8	7	6	6	6	7	7	6	6
Pittsburgh, NL	4	5	7	7	9	8	7	4	4	4	13	14	19	13	13	11	15	11	10	13	13	10	11	9	7	7	7	6	6	6	6	6	6	6
St. Louis, NL	28	33	32	28	29	25	22	6	7	18	19	22	20	21	16	15	16	22	18	15	11	14	12	9	8	6	5	5	6	6	7	7	7	7
L.A.-California, AL																										2	4	6	6	6	5	5	5	5
Washington, AL																										2	4	4	4	4	4	4	5	5
Houston, NL																											2	4	5	5	5	6	6	5
New York, NL																										3	4	5	4	4	5	6	6	5
Kansas City, AL																																		7
Seattle, AL																																		4
Montreal, NL																																		3
San Diego, NL																																		4

Minor League Clubs/Major League Affiliations

Year	Minor League Clubs	Affiliated with Majors	Owned by Majors	Year	Minor League Clubs	Affiliated with Majors	Owned by Majors	Year	Minor League Clubs	Affiliated with Majors	Owned by Majors
1936	184	115	38	1954	269	156	49	1971	155	127	45
1937	251	154	39	1955	243	155	40	1972	148	125	49
1938	267	163	48	1956	217	150	33	1973	147	117	38
1939	292	149	47	1957	209	153	32	1974	145	113	27
1940	310	143	60	1958	173	157	34	1975	137	109	26
1941	304	143	61	1959	150	132	30	1976	148	106	24
1942	206	116	46	1960	152	126	18	1977	150	113	23
1943	66	42	23	1961	147	129	21	1978	156	118	24
1944	70	57	21	1962	134	121	22	1979	155	119	
1945	85	68	33	1963	127	114	22	1980	155	125	
1946	316	197	79	1964	136	108	19	1981	152	133	
1947	406	247	103	1965	136	110	28	1982	160	136	
1948	452	280	125	1966	138	116	32	1983	162	139	
1949	461	243	116	1967	141	118	36	1984	164	140	
1950	446	210	99	1968	142	119	39	1985	168	140	
1951	373	172	75	1969	155	128	46	1986	162	143	
1952	324	166	65	1970	153	120	39	1987	168	145	
1953	292	152	50								

## CHAPTER 35

The Fans

Paul D. Adomites

Called "kranks" or "bugs" during the early days of professional baseball, the followers of the sport were allegedly given the name of "fans" by Ted Sullivan, manager of the St. Louis Browns in 1883. Although some say the word came from "fanatic," etymologist Peter Tamony has stated it probably derived from "fancier,"—i.e., one who fancies the sport.

Famous Fans

Along with heroic athletes and staunch umpires, baseball has had a large number of fans who also achieved celebrity status. In the first modern World Series in 1903, the Boston "Royal Rooters" were headed by the tall, bulky bartender Mike McGreevy, whose stature as ultimate authority on all baseball matters earned him the sobriquet of "'Nuf Ced." The Rooters sang parodies of popular songs with new lyrics uncomplimentary to Boston's opponents: "Tessie, why do I love you madly?" became "Honus [Wagner], why do you hit so badly?" for example. When Boston triumphed in the Series, at least one Pirate gave the Rooters credit. Tommy Leach noted, "It was that damn song."

'Nuf Ced and the Rooters also had an effect on the 1912 World Series, although an opposite one. When a 6–6 tie in the second game, called on account of darkness after 10 innings, sent the Series back to Boston for an additional game, the Rooters expected they would keep the rights to the seats they had for Games Two, Three, and Five. But a clerk wasn't thinking; he sold the Rooters' seats for Game Seven.

The game was nearly ready to begin when 'Nuf Ced and his gang (five hundred strong), including Boston Mayor John Fitzgerald (whose daughter would bear future President John Fitzgerald Kennedy) marched onto the field and toward their seats, only to discover other people sitting there. The Rooters took to the field in protest. Today it would have been called a riot. It took mounted police more than a half hour to clear the crowd from the field. Meanwhile, Boston starting pitcher Smokey Joe Wood, who had stopped his warmups while the police rounded up the Royal Rooters, cooled off, and was ineffective.

But before 'Nuf Ced and the Royal Rooters, many teams had fans who earned fame, usually through lung power. In the 1890s, Frank B. Wood of the grizzled countenance and loud voice became a minor celebrity at the Polo Grounds for his editorial "Well well well."

The 1940s and '50s were the era of three of the most famous female fans. One, Mary Ott of St. Louis, had a "neigh . . . known to cause stampedes in Kansas City stockyards"; Lollie Hopkins, a prim Bostonian, used a megaphone to cheer for both sides when they played well; the legendary

Hilda Chester toted two large cowbells and displayed a banner saying "Hilda is here" to make her voice heard in Ebbets Field for years.

Ebbets Field featured another famous fan in the late 1930s who did more than just root. Jack Pierce used to buy ten seats, a bottle of Scotch, balloons and the gas to blow them up, all to salute Dodgers' shortstop Cookie Lavagetto. Pierce's dedication was so complete that he continued his gaseous act even in 1942, when Cookie was in the Army.

Legendary lungs could be found in nearly every big league town. In the 1930s, the Kessler Brothers, Bull and Eddie, of Philadelphia, would sit "on opposite sides of the grandstand and conduct what practically amounted to a private conversation across the diamond." In Pittsburgh, Bruce McAllister's screeching could be heard at every game and over the radio, too. Detroit's Patsy O'Toole was hailed as the "All-American earache."

Then there were the fans of dedication, not just noise. Some fans received press mention because they routinely took road trips with their favorite team. Others made a point of never missing a World Series, spring training, or All-Star Game, thereby meriting recognition. Still others built extensive (and expensive) "museums" or libraries.

The Royal Rooters tradition of fan groups—sitting together, leading cheers, and heckling the opposition—also had counterparts in most towns. In St. Louis it was the Ice Wagon Boys, in Chicago the Stockyards Boys, and in Pittsburgh the Steel Puddlers. But group cheering was less popular during the thirties and forties until it reappeared in the form of Wrigley Field's Bleacher Bums, who have inspired their own literature, including an Off-Broadway play. Active in the 1960s, dormant in the '70s, and resuscitated in the '80s, the Bleacher Bums were described tongue-in-cheek as "almost on a par with the old Brooklyn Dodger fans, but with more taste."

Fandom once created an on-the-field star. In 1902, Bill Armour, manager of the pitching-short Cleveland team, was told by a Philadelphia ticket-taker that a talented young pitcher was in the stands. Given a quick tryout and just as quickly signed, Charlie Smith won the game and went on to a ten-year big league career.

Worthy of special mention are the Brooklyn Dodger fans of today who still cannot mention the name of Walter O'Malley without a curse, and the St. Louis Browns Fan Club, active today more than thirty years after their team's demise.

Many people who achieved celebrity status in other fields were famous fans, too. Poetess Marianne Moore's love of the game was legendary. Composer Charles Ives wrote a piano piece called "Some Southpaw Pitching." Broadway, music, and film stars, including DeWolf Hopper, Harry Ruby,

George M. Cohan, Jack White, and Pearl Bailey were avid fans, along with many politicians, especially Presidents Taft, Eisenhower, and Nixon, and Speaker of the House Uncle Joe Cannon. Of course, many pols used fandom to garner favor; it was never certain whether they attended because they truly loved the game or whether they simply loved being seen in public.

Being Rowdy

The color that fun-loving fans add to a game turns, however, when fans interfere with the on-the-field action. Baseball kranks were causing trouble from the beginning. As early as 1857, there were eight incidents of bad fan behavior altering a game's result.

In fact, in the game that many call the first great American professional game (the Cincinnati Red Stockings vs. the Brooklyn Atlantics, June 14, 1870), a Brooklyn fan is said to have jumped on the back of Red Stockings' outfielder Cal McVey as he tried to field a ball in the eleventh inning. Brooklyn won the game 8–7, ending Cincinnati's 84-game winning streak.

Through the 1890s, a fan attacking the umpire or an opposing player was considered a social gaffe, but hardly a criminal offense. There are several instances cited of umpires being mobbed, seriously injured, or two-fistedly turning on their attackers. Pop bottles were the commonest weapons for umpire abuse, and a record of a woman serving time for tossing a bottle at an ump was not described in the outraged tone one might expect.

Fans could harm the game even without maiming the umpires or attacking opponents. In the 1880s, tossing straw hats on the field to acknowledge a good play was common. However, cleaning up the skimmers often delayed the proceedings. In 1892, a Chicago crowd "cheered madly as Anson's men thrashed the whey out of Louisville." The exuberant fans demonstrated their joy by tossing a deluge of seat cushions on the field. Manager Cap Anson pleaded with them to stop, but to no avail. Chicago lost in a forfeit.

In 1911, William Phelon described a different kind of fan behavior. "Out at Kansas City, the crowd had a custom, once, that was all its own. Whenever the multitude couldn't see the wisdom of a decision, they arose, marched down onto the field, and advanced upon the umpire. They never offered harm or discourtesy to that official, but simply asked him, with all courtesy, to tell them the rules governing that one decision. The umpire would tell them, and then with a chorus of thanks, they would turn, march back to their seats, and let the game go on."

But two major factors changed the sentiment about what made a baseball outing fun. The first was the gradual elimination of ballpark gambling, which altered behavior both off and on the field. Another was the increased presence of women at the parks.

Legend has it that Ladies Day began in 1889 in Cincinnati because the women wanted to see handsome Tony Mullane pitch. However, the New York Knickerbockers had established a regular Ladies Day by 1867. The Athletics and Orioles did the same in 1883, Brooklyn in 1885. *The Sporting News* pointed out in 1886 that when women are present, the men become less excited and exercise "more choice in their selection of adjectives."

By the turn of the century, baseball was less a rowdy after-noon for gamblers and toughs, and much more of a family enterprise. The newer parks of the century were larger, too, making it harder for the fans to interfere.

But they still managed. A rain of snowballs from the stands in April 1907 led to forfeiture of the Giants' Opening Day game to the Phillies. The same year, some thought the pop-bottle hit taken by umpire Billy Evans would be fatal. (Evans did survive, though, and his teenaged assailant was fined $100.) This kind of behavior was hardly unexpected; a popular song of the teens was "Let's Get the Umpire's Goat."

On May 15, 1912, Ty Cobb leaped into the stands to beat up a fan who was harassing him—a fan described in the press as a "helpless cripple." Cobb's suspension for this act led his teammates to walk out the following day, and the locally recruited "substitutes" took a 24–2 licking from the Athletics before Cobb's reinstatement.

After Yankee center fielder Whitey Witt was struck by a pop bottle in 1922, the leagues cracked down on bottle throwing, and seriously. Ban Johnson offered a $1,000 reward to find the culprit. However, he received so many versions of what happened that he finally settled on $100 cash, railroad fare, and a World Series ticket to someone who claimed that "Witt stepped on the neck of a bottle and caused it to jump up and hit him on the head." The stricter enforcement (and public relations efforts of paper cup manufacturers) did the trick.

Fan violence was minimal in the 1920s. By the '30s, things had re-soured. In the seventh game of the 1934 World Series, Cardinal left fielder Joe Medwick slid hard into third baseman Marv Owen. When Medwick took his defensive position the next inning, the Tiger fans showered him with fruit. Four times he was forced off the field. (Allegedly the concessionaire was increasing the price of an apple each time.) Finally Commissioner Landis ordered both Medwick and Owen out of the game. Owen later admitted that he overreacted (the score was 7–0 at the time) and probably helped to incite the crowd.

In 1940 umpire George Magerkurth was attacked in Ebbets Field by a Frank Germano. The story goes that the attacker, looking toward a sentence of six months at hard labor, commented, "I'll be out in time for Opening Day."

The Cleveland Indians of 1940 earned the nickname of "Cry Babies" for their public dissatisfaction with manager Ossie Vitt. Fans demonstrated their displeasure by hurling baby bottles. The changing tables were turned, however, when Cleveland fans pelted the Detroit Tigers' Hank Greenberg with fruit in a critical series at the end of that year.

In 1941, a sportswriter, reflecting on "Fifty Years of Being a Baseball Fan," said that night baseball and broadcasting had resulted in a "marked increase in the baseball intelligence of the fans . . . Perhaps this increased knowledge is responsible for one marked change for the better I have noticed over these fifty years—the improvement in sportsmanship of the fans."

His perception held true throughout the 1950s and '60s. But the 1970s were the noisiest years of fan violence since the early days of professional baseball. Unlike the literal "Kill the umpire" cries of the 1870s and '80s, however, the violence of the 1970s was undirected and mindless. Fans turned on each other, on the players, on the fields themselves. "Celebrations" after winning playoff or World Series games became orgies of destruction that spilled out of the ballparks into city streets.

Several ballpark promotions to boost attendance resulted

in hometeam forfeits when fans got out of hand, most memorably a riot during a "10-cent Beer Night" at Cleveland in 1974. At Chicago's Comiskey Park in 1979, a "Disco Demolition" record-burning event began rowdy and got worse. The second game scheduled for that night was canceled and forfeited to Detroit.

An incident in the 1973 National League Championship Series in New York's Shea Stadium paralleled the Medwick/Owen spat. Pete Rose slid hard into Mets' shortstop Bud Harrelson; ballplayer fisticuffs resulted; the fans got into the act when Rose took his place in left field the next inning. Their garbage and abuse actually drove the Reds from the field. It took a peace delegation—Yogi Berra, Tom Seaver, Cleon Jones, Rusty Staub and Willie Mays (a legend on his last legs)—to walk to the outfield and settle the crowd.

All in all, the 1970s had nearly forty "noteworthy" examples of bad fan behavior, with 1974 and 1979 being the worst years. The nation's sportswriters were unable to offer viable reasons. One national columnist interviewed a medical nutritionist who said additives in the ballpark food were the culprit, another lay the blame at the feet of the Watergate scandal ("Richard Nixon loves baseball and used to come out to the ballpark. No more. Wonder why?").

The situation stayed consistently grim for the first few years of the 1980s. Detroit owner Jim Campbell closed the bleachers after fourteen fans were arrested for fighting during a 1980 contest. On the day that Pittsburgh paid tribute to Willie Stargell, the noble heart of its "family" team, a battery nearly struck Pirate right fielder Dave Parker, and Parker and Pittsburgh were never on speaking terms again. During a 1981 playoff game, a Yankee fan jumped from the stands and attacked umpire Mike Reilly.

Since then, baseball teams have taken strong steps to prevent the ugliness that fan rowdiness can become. Tightening of alcohol sales—smaller cups, limited quantities per sale, closing of beer sales after a specified inning—have shown success. In every park, security is emphasized. The massive troubles of the 1970s have not reoccurred.

Gambling

One of the major factors that changed baseball from crude entertainment to "the National Pastime" was the eradication of gambling from the game. In the early days, betting at ballparks was widespread, with a double effect. First, the atmosphere in the crowd was rowdy and vulgar; people with money at stake behave differently from people who are there merely for the pleasure of seeing a game well played.

The second effect was more damaging to the game's health. Ballplayers themselves were bettors, and "hippodroming," or throwing games, was common.

Despite fines and bans and the inclusion of antigambling statutes in the league bylaws, gambling remained a large part of the game. Along with the notorious Hal Chase, figures as "respectable" as John McGraw, Ty Cobb, and Tris Speaker had their names linked to game fixing. Every year the *Spalding Baseball Guide* railed against gambling evils in its introduction.

From the 1870s through the early 1900s, the baseball pools were the most popular form of gambling. Similar to today's football pools, a pool bettor simply picked the team that would win the most games or score the most or fewest runs in the week, rather than bet on a team to win a particular game.

Although certainly less harmful than direct game betting, these pools still offered the gamblers great chances to win money by "involving" players or managers.

The betting was substantial. According to Professor Harold Seymour, one such pool in Pittsburgh ranged over the entire East Coast and Canada, offering prizes of $1,000 a week. (The average per capita income annually was less than $550.) Another pool earned its managers from $30,000 to $50,000 a week. A 1911 estimate said that in the city of New Haven alone, 40,000 factory workers and boys held pool tickets costing $10,000.

Baseball understood the danger and kept responding, in fits and starts, to the problem. On August 5, 1908, the *New York Evening Telegram* said, "Efforts to stamp out gambling in baseball will immediately be made by the American League." (Interestingly, this followed by two days a spurious announcement in the *New York American*: "Bookmaking on baseball games in Chicago has not been profitable, and bookmakers announced they are going out of the business . . . 'The baseball "fan" is too wise. He knows too much about the game,' said one disgusted bookmaker.")

The effort to eliminate betting continued throughout the 1910s. *New York Times,* 1913: "Gamblers ejected from game"; 1914, "Gambling pools barred"; 1915, "Arrests for gambling." By 1919, the *Times* could state "Gambling stopped at all ball parks."

But it wasn't until 1920, the year of the Black Sox Scandal, that the action to eradicate gambling took hold. That year six people were arrested for gambling in Boston, four at the Polo Grounds, forty-seven in Chicago, five more in New York, ten at a Pacific Coast League game. The uproar over a gambling-run World Series had finally been too much for baseball and its fans to take.

Today baseball is still heavily gambled; Las Vegas estimates of legal baseball gambling place it at around thirty million dollars a year, about a third of that wagered on pro football. But with major league baseball playing 2,000 games a year and pro football one-tenth as many, the difference per game is substantial. When less is wagered, less can be won, which means less incentive for someone to attempt to "swing the odds."

Attendance

Before the National League was founded in 1876, baseball already had recorded single-game attendances as high as 40,000. In 1876, the patent of Bright's self-registering turnstile helped keep baseball body counts, although formal data were not regularly available until the turn of the century.

1880s. According to baseball historian Bill James, "Systematic data [were] not available. [But] attendance grew rapidly during this period."
- 1884. The first "bargain bill" doubleheader was held by Cleveland.
- 1889. The White Stockings drew 216,802 at home.

1890s. The average per game according to Bill James, was 2,000–3,000. He described overall attendance during this period as "Awful, and declining," reporting that "In 1890 . . . the Players' League drew 981,000 fans, the National League 814,000."
- The first promotion and advertising occurred: street-

car billing, signboards, handbills, window hangers, posters, boys on streets giving out handbills. Cincinnati ran paid ads in local papers (including the German-language one).
- Baseball cards were introduced as advertisements.
- "Children's Days" with 10¢ admission were popular, and women were admitted free on Ladies Days.
- 1891. "Base Ball Day" in Chicago let all amateur teams in uniform in free.

1900s. Total attendance was 50 million—4,058 per game.
- 1908. "Take Me Out to the Ball Game" was introduced.
- 1909. The first concrete and steel stadiums were built.
- Old Timers Days began, along with "days" to honor individual players.

1910s. Total attendance was 56 million—4,545 per game. James: "Essentially a decade of no growth." Seymour: "A prodigious $100 billion increase in national wealth brightened the first two decades of the century." The effects included suburbs with trolley lines and stadiums as the population moved from the country to the city.

Sunday baseball, which had disappeared with the demise of the American Association in 1891, was finally permitted by state and local legislatures. By 1918 it was legal in Cleveland, Detroit, and Washington. New York voted it in the following year. (Boston didn't allow it till 1929; the state of Pennsylvania, the final holdout, did not until 1933.)
- 1912. "Foreign-born spectators from seventeen different countries were observed at a game in New York." (*Spalding Baseball Guide*). Blacks also were becoming avid fans.
- 1913. In Brooklyn, the first Honor Roll Day was held.
- 1917. Scorecard winning numbers become common.
- 1917. The first "Knothole Gang" was organized in St. Louis.
- Ladies Day, which had been abolished by the National League in 1909, resurfaced eight years later.

1920s. Total attendance, 93 million—7,548 per game. The Yankees exceeded a million almost every year. Average club attendance rose 50 percent over what it had been the decade before. Seymour states that even though 1920–1930 showed the largest single-decade rise in American population ever (17 million), baseball attendance rose at an even faster rate.
- 1921. Pittsburgh, August 5. The first baseball broadcast occurred, over KDKA radio with Harold Arlin. The World Series (Giants vs. Yankees) was also broadcast that year.
- 1925. Philip K. Wrigley allowed all Cubs game to be aired every day.

1930s. Total attendance, 81 million—6,574 per game. The first night baseball game was held in 1880, at Nantasket Beach, Massachusetts. Amateur players from two local department stores performed in a promotion for the light company; the event has since been celebrated in a General Electric television commercial. Described as having "innumerable" errors because of lights, the first effort was not successful. Three years later, a game in Fort Wayne, Indiana, was.

Night baseball was first embraced on the minor league level. By 1934, fifteen of nineteen minor leagues had at least one lighted park. On May 24, 1935, Cincinnati owner Larry MacPhail hosted the first major league night game, at Crosley Field. A total of 20,422 attended, President Franklin D. Roosevelt threw the switch from the White House. Ford Frick, then the National League president, threw out the first ball, and the Reds defeated the Dodgers 2–1.

In 1938, when MacPhail moved to Brooklyn, so did lights. The first Brooklyn night game, on June 15, was Johnny Vander Meer's second successive no-hitter. The first American League team to play night games was Philadelphia, in 1939. By 1940, seventy major league night games were scheduled. The only parks without lights that year were Washington, which added them the next year; Yankee Stadium and Braves Field (which added them in 1946); Fenway Park (1947); Detroit (1948); and Chicago's Wrigley Field (1988). The first World Series game to be played at night happened on October 13, 1971, when the Pirates beat the Orioles at Three Rivers Stadium.
- 1930. Major league attendance in 1930 was 10,132,272—the highest of any season between 1901 and 1945.
- 1931. Players' numbers became official practice in the AL.
- 1935. Night baseball was introduced.
- 1939. All teams broadcast their games on radio.
- August 26, 1939. The first TV broadcast was made.

1940s. Total attendance, 135 million—10,958 per game.

James describes 1946 as "the Great Leap Forward"—1946 attendance was 18.5 million, 71 percent above the previous high. He lists as reasons the advent of night baseball, a return to economic normalcy after World War II, and great pennant races.

1950s. Total attendance, 165 million—13,392 per game.
- 1951. The first nationally televised World Series game occurred.

David Voigt says, "In the years after the war, baseball crowds became predominantly family gatherings, united by the ethic of 'togetherness' in their fun-seeking. Television pushed the trend by bombarding families with ball games in the summertime."

1960s. Total attendance, 224 million—14,050 per game.
- Bill Veeck added players' names to their uniforms in 1960.
- Major League Baseball expanded (after changing only two locations in fifty-seven years previously), adding eight new teams.

1970s. Total attendance, 330 million—16,561 per game.
- 1976. Free agency was instated by an arbitrator's decree.
- 1977. Cable television began to have an impact on viewing.

1980–1987. Total attendance 404 million—22,194 per game.
- 1981. A strike by players eliminated as many as fifty-nine games of the season for some teams.
- 1986. Bill Veeck died.

CHAPTER 36

Concessions

Paul D. Adomites

Food and beverages have been a big part of the fun at a baseball game from the beginning. In 1859, New Orleans ballclubs pitched "commodious tents for the ladies . . . under the umbrageous branches of fine old live oaks" to shelter their delicate skin from the sun as they enjoyed refreshments as well as the local baseball rivalry.

In the first decade of professional baseball, you could find an array of food: peanuts, soft drinks, crackerjacks, ice cream, cherry pie, cheese, chocolates, planked onions, and even tripe. Vendors moved through the crowd hawking sandwiches, soda water, and chewing gum. By 1871 the Olympics of Washington, D.C., had anticipated the "stadium clubs" of today's parks when they opened a first-class restaurant at the park.

Ballpark concession stands as we have come to know them can be traced to 1875, from which time we have a photo of the Boston team posed in front of their grandstand clearly showing large painted signs saying SODA and REFRESHMENTS. During his tenure as owner of the Chicago team, Albert Spalding himself encouraged concession stands, rather than hawkers moving throughout the crowd. The ChiFeds of 1914 lay claim to the earliest permanent concession *stand* in Wrigley Field.

Along with various sorts of munchies, ballparks sold beer and hard liquor, too. In his *Baseball: The Early Years,* Harold Seymour lists how many beer and whiskey glasses the typical ballpark bar stocked. But in 1880, the always image-conscious National League tried to eliminate ballpark drinking, and the result was the second major professional league, the American Association.

The four-year-old National League was trying to civilize its image, fighting the coarsening effect of gambling and promoting the calming influence of female attendance. As part of this effort, in 1880 the league passed a law forbidding gambling and the sale of alcohol at the ballparks. Unfortunately the Cincinnati team had a long tradition of beer and whiskey sales; they were averaging $3,000 a season of concession income. Breweries and distilleries were two of the largest industries in the city. So rather than face the financial damage of a no-beer ballpark, Cincinnati quit the league and was the leader in starting the Association, which detractors unsurprisingly called "The Beer and Whiskey League." The *New York World,* with perfect big city parochialism, charged that Cincinnati was a place to "watch for flying mugs . . . cheap sports and toughs" gathered behind home plate. Meanwhile, the New York Giants had a bar in full view of the field.

Although the major league American Association folded after ten years, and the attempt to eliminate gambling continued for twenty more, baseball and beer have always remained linked.

Ballpark food and drink and scorecards can be traced back to the 1850s and sixties, but it wasn't till the 1880s that one man turned these concepts into enterprise: the first professional concessionaire and the first concession empire. Harry M. Stevens, a British immigrant, went to a baseball game in Columbus, Ohio, one afternoon (so the story goes). Realizing that there was no way to identify the players, Stevens sought out the owner and for $500 obtained the right to publish and sell a program. (Scorecards predate this anecdote by twenty years, but they were usually very modest items, with little or no advertising. It took Stevens to see the potential for profits.) "Scorecard Harry" sold the programs himself, calling out the now famous slogan "You can't tell the players without a scorecard."

The scorecard idea had an intriguing spinoff. Although the ballplayers had no numbers on their uniforms, they were given numbers on the scorecards. Then, as each player came to bat, his number was placed on the scoreboard. A scandal occurred when people brought old scorecards into the park, or bought "counterfeit" ones from "illegal" scorecard vendors outside. The teams were forced to change the scorecard numbers often.

Harry M. Stevens didn't stop with scorecards. An ambitious promoter, he started selling food: hard-boiled eggs, sandwiches, even coconut custard pies. He expanded his business into Wheeling, Pittsburgh, Toledo, and Milwaukee. A conversation with New York Giants manager John Montgomery Ward in Pittsburgh in 1893 led to Harry's landing the Polo Grounds concession. Before long the Stevens empire used its New York connection to include contracts with Madison Square Garden, hotels, and racetracks.

Stevens was always the innovator. On a cold day in the Polo Grounds in 1901, ice cream wasn't selling, but Harry had an idea. He sent an assistant out for frankfurters (locally called "dachshund sausages"), which were sold in the neighborhood German groceries, heated the sausages in hot water, and put them in long buns so the fans could hold and eat them. The vendors shouted out what made these inventions so special: "Get 'em while they're hot! Get your red hots here!"

Sports cartoonist Thomas A. "Tad" Dorgan, looking for an idea that day, drew a sketch of waiters serving talking frankfurters ("You're not so hot!" "Bologna!"). Some say Dorgan couldn't remember how to spell "dachshund"; others say his spelling problem was with "frankfurter." For whatever reason, he coined the term "hot dogs" instead. Baseball food has never been the same. To this day, hot dogs, soda pop, and beer are the three biggest-selling items in every major league park.

Stevens continued to bring new ideas to his business. Realizing that fans might not purchase soda pop because raising their heads to drink might make them miss some of the game

action, Harry came up with the idea of selling the soda with a straw. Now even the most devoted fan could quench his or her thirst and never miss a single pitch.

Still largely family-owned and -operated, the Harry M. Stevens Company, one hundred years later, is one of the largest ballpark concessionaires in the nation, with sales close to $175 million overall.

During the early decades of the century, only scattered figures are available, but they mention profits of several thousand dollars a year for the average club. By 1929, *Baseball Magazine* was saying that concession "receipts at Wrigley Field soar far above $100,000 a year." The same article stated that money from gate sales created 87.6 percent of the major leagues' gross profit, and concessions 5.5 percent.

But the end of the Second World War brought a new popularity to baseball. America's return to normalcy was also a return to the ballpark. As historian David Voigt puts it, "In the years after the war, baseball crowds became predominantly family gatherings, united by the ethic of 'togetherness' in their fun-seeking . . . The new breed of fans demanded and won comforts and pleasures from promoters . . . including neatly packaged food, canned music and giveaways. Food and drink sales now rivaled ticket sales in revenue production."

Today selling food at the ballparks, stadiums, and racetracks of America is big business. Since Harry M. Stevens, many companies have entered the field. At the most basic level, professional concessionaires provide and prepare all the food for the ballgames, hire and train their employees, and then agree to pay the contractee a percentage of their gross. (The few absolute exceptions are those teams which act as their own concessionaire, subcontracting specialized stands for specific food items to outside companies—Kentucky Fried Chicken, Burger King, etc.)

The average fan spends from $4 to $6 per game (that's up from 70¢ to 90¢ a game in the 1960s), so rough figures indicate that a ball club with two million attendance will generate as much as $12 million in concessions. How much the team gets, however, depends.

The contract to provide concession services may be with the baseball team, or it may be with the stadium authority, or it may be with the city or municipality that owns the stadium. Everyone gets a share; the main contractee gets the most. For example, some concessionaires pay as much as 52 percent of their receipts back to the contractee. If the baseball team signed the contract, it could receive 47 percent of that 52 percent, and give the rest to the other partners. Or the club could receive 24 or 25 percent (which is about average).

But few baseball teams own their ballparks; most share the facility with pro football or other teams. So the football team could receive a certain percentage of the gross, the baseball team another, the stadium authority another. In certain *categories* the percentage can vary; the baseball club may get a bigger percentage of soft drink sales than the football team, which might get more for hot drink sales; the city may take the lion's share of the concessionaire income and allot only a certain percentage to the teams, or vice versa.

With only a handful of major concessionaires (Harry M. Stevens, ARA Services, Ogden Allied, Sportservice, and a few others), and with contracts that typically run for fifteen to eighteen years (some for thirty), the competition is fierce.

The growth of fast food restaurants has changed the kinds of food available in ballparks, by making certain kinds of packaging acceptable. Although hot dogs, beer and soda pop are still one-two-three in sales nearly everywhere, the changing American palate has led to some new menu items. Soft ice cream is a new favorite in Houston and Baltimore; onion rings in Cleveland; Montreal is considering adding a Chinese food section; and nachos are hot everywhere.

In addition, the modern stadiums of today are echoing the earlier days, with their "cafes" and restaurants offering more serious fare before, during, and after the game. Homer Rose, longtime employee of the Harry M. Stevens Company, and grandson of Harry himself, said, "At first it was peanuts, ice cream cones, lemonade, and bottled soft drinks. Now in the dining rooms and private boxes we're serving shrimp salads and full-course dinners." The Stevens Company alone runs restaurants at dozens of racetracks and stadiums.

On the average, a typical ballpark hot dog costs $1.25 today, 87 years after its Polo Grounds introduction. A larger version sells for about $2.00. Hamburgers run close to $2.00, pizza $1.50 or so, french fries nearly $1.25, ice cream $1.00, and popcorn anywhere from $1.00 to twice that.

One more change is becoming apparent—beer, a ballpark staple since the beginning, is again less easy to obtain. Concern about drunk driving has resulted in every team selling beer in smaller servings, allowing fewer servings to be sold to one person at one time, having special no-alcohol sections, and stopping sales after a certain time in the game. So far, no one has raised a serious voice about banning all alcohol sales at the ballpark.

## CHAPTER 37

Baseball on the Air

Paul D. Adomites

The story of broadcast baseball actually begins almost seventy years before the first game was aired. Baseball owners have always been of two minds about any fan interest that wasn't satisfied at the game itself. The common sentiment was "They'll stay home instead of coming to the game." Yet these outside sources generated extra income, and owners are businessmen first of all. As early as the 1860s, it was already clear that baseball sold newspapers, and newspapers sold baseball. Yet some owners feared "giving the game away."

The owners' schizophrenic response also occurred with telegraphy. Even though telegraph operators paid for the privilege of relaying game reports to saloons and poolrooms, a "hot debate" over whether this "free" sport was keeping people away from the parks led some owners to try to ban telegraph machines from their operations.

In 1897, each team received $300 worth of free telegrams on a league-wide contract, and some owners complained that it was hurting attendance. Sixteen years later, Western Union offered each team $17,000 a year for five years for the telegraph rights. It was hard for the owners to say no.

Even the fledgling motion picture industry got into the act, paying baseball $500 in 1910 for the rights to film and show the World Series. American League President Ban Johnson, who saw movies as competition, suggested that baseball ask for ten times as much for rights to film the 1911 Series, figuring that it would frighten the moviemen away. It didn't. However, baseball had to settle for only seven times what it had received the year before.

The point is obvious—baseball was far from being overexposed. Even though he was talking about telegraphy, John R. Tunis in 1923 pointed out the real value of broadcasting baseball. He described the World Series thrilling people in New Orleans, San Francisco, Honolulu, and even "an excited group of Mongolians in Seoul, the capital of Korea." The point is, advanced communications create fans *everywhere*, even thousands of miles from the parks.

Radio Days

The first major league game was broadcast over radio on August 5, 1921, from Pittsburgh, home of the Westinghouse Corporation, over the new Westinghouse station, KDKA. Harold Arlin, a Westinghouse foreman, announced the Pirates-Phillies contest from Forbes Field. Westinghouse was eager to make a name for itself in the new industry. The next day, Arlin broadcast the U.S. Open tennis tournament, also near Pittsburgh. Two months later he did the first football broadcast.

That same year the first World Series broadcast was aired

to a handful of fans on the East Coast. By 1922, the Series was heard "live by 5,000,000 people." Re-creations were heard by fans *on three continents*.

(Many of the early baseball broadcasts, and almost all away-game airings were re-created in a hometown radio studio, with announcers reading pitch-by-pitch information from ticker tapes, and using sound effects and canned crowd noises to simulate live action. In 1950, the Red Sox provided the first live coverage of all their away games. Within five years, major-league re-creations were antiques, as the teams were broadcasting all their games live. At the minor-league level, re-creation continued for away games into the 1960s.)

The first owner to see radio's promise to boost fan interest was the Cubs' boss Philip Wrigley. In 1925 he invited all the Chicago radio stations to carry all the Cubs' games. No charge. Sam Breadon, the Cardinals' owner, followed suit soon thereafter, in the first two attempts to develop regional followings.

In 1926 and 1927 the first great national radio networks began operation: NBC and CBS. This was the beginning of radio's golden era. Sales of radio equipment, a $60 million industry in 1922, were nearly a billion dollars in 1929.

Yet many owners were still wary. By the 1930s, the two-team cities of Boston, Philadelphia, St. Louis, and Chicago had an agreement not to broadcast away games. In other words, if the Braves were at home, you could hear *their* game on the radio, but not the Red Sox. The owners' wail ("they won't come to the park if you give the game away") seemed turned on its logical head under this arrangement, but home radio is where you ballyhoo home-game attendance, which was the concern, anyway.

The New York owners went one step further. In 1932 they agreed to ban all radio, even visitors' re-creations, from their parks.

Larry MacPhail took over the Reds in 1933 and sold a controlling interest in the club to Powel Crosley, owner of two Cincinnati radio stations. It was a match made in economic heaven: MacPhail knew that broadcasting games would promote the team (he hired southerner Red Barber as his announcer), Crosley now could boost his radio ratings. The mutuality was akin to Chris von der Ahe, the St. Louis beer garden magnate, taking over the St. Louis club in the American Association in order to sell more beer.

Then, when MacPhail moved to Brooklyn in 1938, he brought Red Barber with him, and broke the New York ban. The next year was the first year that all the teams in the major leagues broadcast their games. Prophetically, it was also the year of the first *televised* baseball game.

In 1935, Judge Landis moved in to orchestrate the radio deal to cover the World Series. All three networks were in-

volved, and baseball made $400,000. Landis, as ever, was imperious; he dismissed Ted Husing as announcer of the games, even though with five World Series under his belt, Ted was second only to the ubiquitous Graham MacNamee in Series-announcing experience.

The money for baseball broadcasting was growing. Gillette, the razor blade manufacturer, one of the first companies to realize the power of sports as an advertising vehicle, tried to flex their muscles by offering Red Barber a substantial amount to walk out on his Dodger contract to join Gillette on a new Yankees/Giants network. Barber refused. It's no wonder Gillette felt powerful; in 1946 they were rich enough to sign a ten-year deal for exclusive radio sponsorship of the World Series and All-Star Games, for $14 million.

But the World Series was the exception; otherwise, baseball remained locally dominated. However, in 1950, Gordon McLendon changed all that, when he founded a new radio network, one with daily baseball as its centerpiece: the Liberty Broadcasting System. His announcers re-created a game every day, plus extras on weekends. McLendon charged the stations $10 per game, and enrolled 300 of them. He paid his announcers $27.50 a week, netting himself a weekly profit of over $2,970.

But once again the moguls of baseball feared too much free publicity. A rule banned the Game of the Day from many areas because there were fears that it might conflict with local broadcasts within a 75-mile area.

The paradoxical result, according to Curt Smith, was "If you lived in Butte, Montana, or Amarillo, Texas, you got to hear every club in baseball," as many as ten games a week. But if you lived in a major league town (or near one), you could hear only the locals, and only when the club decided the broadcasts wouldn't "interfere" with attendance. McLendon's gold mine didn't last long: he lost a suit against baseball and folded. Yet the Mutual Broadcasting Network mimicked his strategy and succeeded.

In 1951 Liberty broadcast more than 200 games, almost 600 hours of baseball; Mutual did 145 games. That amount of time was more than quadruple the amount of total network time (via television and radio) that baseball would receive in *1984*. More importantly, the Liberty/Mutual style set a pattern for successful TV coverage years later.

TV or Not TV

Baseball on television began to take hold in the late 1950s. The Yankees were the first team to sell their TV rights (in 1946, for $75,000; in 1987 the Yankees earned 250 times as much for their TV rights). The first televised World Series was the memorable 1947 set. Harry Coyle, the NBC dean of baseball producers, was there. In Chicago, Jack Brickhouse was announcing White Sox telecasts in 1948.

By 1950 the World Series was televised as far west as Omaha; 38 million watched. The next year World Series baseball television reached the West Coast. (Radio still had strengths: the 1953 Brooklyn Dodgers Radio Network linked 117 stations, making the Bums the first "America's Team.")

The era of baseball broadcasting that began in 1953 should have opened the owners' eyes to the future, but it didn't. That year the first televised Game of the Week began (then on ABC). Naturally, it was banned from all major league cities. (Does this sound familiar?) Yet with the irrepressible Dizzy Dean at the microphone, it rolled up incredible ratings any-

way: 11.4 percent of all households with sets, 51 percent of all sets in use. That translated to 75 percent of all sets in use not in big league cities.

And there was no doubt that the colorful Diz, with his demented grammar, malapropisms, and ambling yarn-weaving, *was* the program. In 1955, a slick advertising agency move landed the Game of the Week for CBS, and Curt Smith says, "the most transforming baseball series in television's show of shows . . . was born." Two years later a group of Sunday games was added to the schedule. Baseball was on its way to becoming the *truly* national game; the owners just felt they could do it without the help of the fans in the cities where the teams played.

Television was becoming a national mania. By 1955 only four teams didn't televise (the Braves, Pirates, A's, and Indians). On the other hand, the Cubs, Dodgers, Yankees, and Giants broadcast every home game, the Cards every road game. The Reds televised all weekday afternoon home games; the Phillies showed 29 home and 27 road games; Baltimore showed 65 contests; even the Red Sox and Senators had TV on their schedule; six stations in Michigan showed 42 Tigers games; WGN televised every day game from Comiskey Park.

Then came football. The upstart NFL (and their very wise leader Pete Rozelle) realized that TV was the way to *build* fan interest. Baseball's less progressive owners still feared "giving it away," preferring local/regional efforts. As Harold Rosenthal explains, "Football fans were sold as National Football League fans—network television made them that way . . . In Appleton, Wisconsin, a guy would turn on the tube and watch the Giants play the Browns . . . Baseball fans were brought up to follow the Cardinals or Giants or Tigers . . . the local coverage mattered, the local announcer."

When the NFL signed an immense contract with TV in the early 1960s, guaranteeing coverage, with all the NFL teams sharing the wealth, baseball wanted to copy the plan. They asked for millions, but they didn't get it.

What baseball got was the ABC Game of the Week: 28 telecasts a season; each of the clubs receiving $300,000. Curt Smith explains the upshot: "By 1966, instead of watching as many as 123 games on three networks, a majority of American viewers could behold only 28 telecasts on one network." The "common good" policy was a mistake, but baseball couldn't figure this out. They changed networks, to NBC, and we got a new announcer.

"Curt Gowdy emerged for an entire generation of listeners as the national signature of baseball broadcasting. From 1966 through 1975, he called play-by-play for every All-Star Game, every World Series game, and virtually every regular season network game" (Curt Smith). And that list doesn't even include Gowdy's work on seven Super Bowls, seven Olympic Games, twelve NCAA basketball championships, 13 Rose Bowls, the Pan Am Games, and twenty years of "The American Sportsman."

But Curt couldn't bring in the ratings; his highest regular season rating was still two full points below Dizzy Dean's first year (and remember, Dizzy wasn't allowed into any major league markets), and it dropped 15 percent by 1970; Curt's World Series ratings fell by nearly 20 percent, though it was certainly no fault of his own. Solid, professional, and competent, he was just never exciting. People never talked about him as they did about Dizzy or other announcers. And he was definitely overexposed.

Meanwhile football was coming on strong. In 1969 pro

football televised three times as many games on network TV as baseball. (Three times!) By 1969 not even all the baseball postseason games were broadcast nationally. The NFL wasn't just growing; they were promoting. Their highlight films featured thrilling action, rich drama, and the golden voice of orator John Facenda.

Baseball, it was clear to everyone in the national press, was losing the battle. "Baseball is dead" was a cliché. A Lou Harris poll showed that football was now Americans' favorite sport. More importantly, another Harris poll showed how baseball's popularity paralleled the degree of its TV coverage. Where the big leagues were most heavily covered, baseball was most popular. Where fans received only network coverage, baseball ranked lowest.

But Commissioner Bowie Kuhn had something to say about the matter; he pushed for World Series night games (the first was in 1971) because they could attract a much larger audience. And while you could cynically dismiss this move as pure economics (bigger viewership means more advertising dollars), it worked.

In 1975 baseball announced a new kind of TV deal: Alternating coverage of the World Series, playoffs and All-Star Games between NBC and ABC. The networks saw the advantages: postseason baseball play was the perfect time to begin promoting the new fall TV season. The alternating feature built in an element of competition without economic overtones: to outdo the other in quality of coverage.

Then came October 21, 1975. The Boston Red Sox, unable to win a World Series since 1918, were on their way to a loss in six games to Cincinnati's "Big Red Machine." But a three-run pinch-hit homer by Bernie Carbo tied the game in the eighth, and in the twelfth (by now it was 12:34 A.M.), Carlton Fisk hit a solo shot over the Green Monster to win the game. A total of 62 million people saw it, and television couldn't have planned it better, because as Fisk hit his homer, the camera in the left field scoreboard followed *him*, not the ball, and on replay the audience saw Fisk furiously trying to wave the ball fair: the first-ever home run reaction shot.

The next night, 75,890,000 people watched the seventh game, and baseball was definitely back. In 1976, baseball received revenue from radio and television near $51 million. Lou Harris said in 1977: "For the first time since 1968, more sports fans in the country follow baseball than football." Ten years later baseball received $350 million in broadcast income.

And 1977 is also the year that cable television broadcasts began to have their impact. The situation was analogous to the Liberty/Mutual networks' Game of the Day, or the Dizzy Dean/CBS Game of the Week. Now fans all over the country could see a lot of baseball, every day. By 1982, cable TV was in 35 percent of all American homes; in 1987 it passed the 50 percent mark.

Superstations like Ted Turner's Atlanta TBS, Chicago's WGN, and New York's WWOR and WPIX, along with the all-sports network, ESPN, were giving fans more baseball on a regular basis than they had ever had before. In 1986 Cubs' games were viewed by 20 million fans. For his definitive history, *Voices of the Game,* Curt Smith interviewed Cub fans in Kodiak, Alaska; Costa Rica; and Boise, Idaho—all because of Harry Caray's calls on the Chicago superstation. A Peter Ueberroth–inspired change in the rules to make superstations give the other teams a certain amount of money per viewer passed over Ted Turner's noisy objections. Sports-only premium cable networks have failed in several places, largely due to the availability of the "free" (part of the basic cable charge) coverage.

Even though the superstation teams do not benefit directly, in cash income, from sending their games around the country, (their parent corporations do, of course . . .), they do help to promote interest in baseball as a whole. (For example, every Atlanta Braves game can be seen in 48 percent of U.S. households, yet in 1987 the Braves' broadcast rights earned them the same as the Pittsburgh Pirates, whose five-station network reached as far as Johnstown.) As Harry Caray says, "We've made the Cubs part of their lives; they have to be interested." The point is clear: baseball has not yet reached a saturation point on television. The fears of baseball owners that *too much* would keep people away haven't come true, despite 140 years of worrying.

And neither has the oft-stated fear described by noted historian Harold Seymour in 1971: "Although gate receipts are still the lifeblood of the industry, television receipts have swelled steadily in recent years . . . There are even those who go so far as to predict that eventually television income will supplant gate receipts, and the teams will perform quietly among themselves in deserted stadiums for TV audiences."

## CHAPTER 38

Baseball Betting

Phil Erwin

"That ain't gonna go, that's too high!"
"Dollar says it goes!"
"OK!"

Jonesy and Harold watched as Mantle's high fly turned into an upper-deck home run. Harold owed Jonesy another buck, but I had not kept track and could not say for sure who owed whom how much. I was eleven years old and had been fascinated for nine innings by the two men sitting in front of me. They bet on everything, all through the game, beginning by muttering to each other in the early innings, opening up so others could hear them in midgame ("Quarter the first pitch is a strike," "Dime to a nickel he doesn't hit anything out of the infield," "Bet a buck this pitcher don't last the fifth," "Quarter says he fouls this 3-2 pitch"). They were having a great time, and captured the attention of most people sitting around them, punctuating the game with verbal exchanges, predictions backed by dimes, quarters, and half-bucks. Who knows if they ever settled up or even kept track?

Betting in the stands was still common into the early 1960s, in the old major league cities, where the last remnants of the old-time "sporting crowd" still maintained their spots in Fenway, old Yankee, Comiskey, Wrigley, Shibe, Forbes, and other esteemed venues. Informal wagering in the stands is a practice that harks back to the very beginnings of baseball as a professional sports event. When players began to be paid, admission began to be charged, and owners ("magnates" in those days) quickly recognized that friendly man-to-man bets on game outcomes, scores, the number of hits, or anything else were going on inside their turnstiles. Why discourage patronage by forcing bettors out? Indeed, some of the magnates themselves enjoyed the tension accompanying a fine wager. The National Association, the first major league, formed in the robber baron 1870s era, disbanded in part because of problems associated with gambling supported by the magnates. Lee Allen, baseball historian, noted that the Brooklyn Atlantics "fostered so much open betting that one section of the grounds was known as the Gold Board, with activity that rivaled that of the stock exchange."

Person-to-person betting remained popular, but it was encumbered by the problems that arise when money and ego become entwined in personal relationships. Not everyone got along as well as Jonesy and Harold. A more organized form of betting developed, known as pool betting, centered around "pool rooms," where the pool owner held a kind of auction before games. Another type of pool involved a lottery-style ticket, probably similar to the football cards of the present. Gradually, however, the English form of "bookmaking" supplanted the pools. The bookmaker established odds, took bets on all sides, and changed the odds and propositions to (he hoped) assure himself a profit as, in essence, the broker in bets between strangers.

Baseball, horse racing, boxing, and, to a lesser extent, college football and basketball were the major betting sports in America for a long time. The invention of the "pointspread" gave football, especially professional football, the impetus to become the most popular betting sport. Baseball now ranks behind football and basketball in terms of interest to bettors. The point spread, which has only limited application to baseball, is primarily responsible for the change.

Baseball is still an odds-based betting proposition. An example is necessary to explain the odds system. Say the Mets are at home versus the Cardinals, favored by 6½ to 7½. This type of odds quote is an "Eastern line," and means that a player must risk $7.50 to win $5 if he backs the Mets, and will risk $5 to win $6.50 if he takes the Cardinals. In Las Vegas, the same proposition would be translated into a "money line," where the Mets would be −1.50 favorites, the Cards +1.30 underdogs. For every $1.50 risked on New York, a winner would profit by $1, or he could risk $1 to win $1.30 on St. Louis. Notice the 20¢ difference (1.50−1.30). This is called a "20¢ line," and is common for smaller wagers outside Nevada. The bookmaker's percentage ("vigorish," "juice") is derived from the varying payoffs. If a bookmaker has the same amount of money placed on both sides of a game, he is guaranteed a profit.

In Nevada, because of the open competition between the legal sports books for the gambling business, a 10¢ line is common. The Mets would be −1.45, and the Cardinals +1.35 in the same game. The bookmaker's percentage is somewhat lower, with a corresponding benefit to the bettor.

Odds vary from "pick 'em," where the better chooses which team will be a −1.05 favorite (−1.10 if a 20¢ line is involved) in what should be a closely contested game, up to the −3.00 range, for a champion club on a winning streak at home with its ace pitcher going against a cellar dweller on a losing streak with a sacrificial lamb taking the mound.

Bookmakers will take bets of as little as $10, or up to $10,000 or more on a single baseball game. One of the highest single baseball wagers known to this writer involved the famous publisher of a men's magazine who shopped a World Series bet of close to $500,000 around Las Vegas for a few days, before one sports book manager got permission from his casino-owner boss to take the bet. Unfortunately for the publisher, it was 1983 and he was backing the Phillies.

Another type of baseball bet involves predicting the total runs that will be scored in a game against a "totals," or "over/under" line. Normally the number is between 6 (two great pitchers throwing in a big ballpark) and 12 or even more (the

wind is blowing out at Wrigley or Fenway). In the above Met–Cardinal example, perhaps 7 would be a likely total number. The wagerer could play the over, winning if the Mets and Cardinals tallied 8 runs or more between them, or the under, with a 4–3 game tying the number for a "no bet," or "push." The player risks 1.10 to win 1.00 to choose his over or under.

Nongambling baseball fans encounter baseball odds only through the line published in daily newspapers. The odds published every day are not necessarily the actual odds being used by bookmakers, however. Newspapers get the "line" from a news service, which obtains it from handicappers paid to create it for them. Due to the need to publish early editions of today's paper (last night's early edition), the odds in today's paper were actually created yesterday afternoon, before last night's games were played. They were based on factors and starting pitcher plans as they were known then. Although the newspaper odds do have news value—they represent the educated view of a professional linemaker—bookmakers do not look in the local paper for the odds they will use.

Instead, they call a line service, which usually obtains its odds directly from the display boards in Las Vegas sports books on the morning of the game. What reasoning goes into the creation of the line? The purpose of the line is to divide the betting—the bookies want both sides in a game to get about the same amount of "action." When journalists say that an upset proved the linemaker wrong, they are mistaking the line for a prediction. It is not, except as it operates as a prediction of public betting psychology. Top teams playing at home are usually big favorites. Betting behavior, represented by the money wagered, is the biggest determinant of the odds. Other factors of importance are the starting pitcher, the perceived quality of the teams, winning or losing streaks or publicized trends. In totals betting, the ballpark site is a key factor.

The rise of "rotisserie" or fantasy leagues in recent years must be seen as a new form of wagering, as many of the participants in effect bet on them. This seems like an extension of the old betting in the stands, with the statistics of chosen players being used to settle season-long wagers between the "owners" of the rotisserie teams. Somewhere a bookie is being prosecuted by an assistant district attorney who himself has $500 staked on his own "rotisserie" team.

Hollywood treatments and occasional real-life scandals have combined to give sports betting and bookmakers an undeserved bad name. In fact, most baseball gamblers are professional people (doctors, lawyers, accountants, stockbrokers, and businessmen) who are devout fans. They are no more or no less honest than other citizens. Bookmakers gain their clientele by word-of-mouth referral, deal on a credit basis without security, and must deal honestly to keep their businesses afloat. Aside from legal problems, bookmaking can be a precarious business financially, since in order to stay in business the bookie must be able to pay winners—if he does not, he loses them as customers.

Consider the best-known baseball betting scandal, the Black Sox affair. If the "fix" had never become known, the honest gamblers and bookmakers would still have been hurt by it monetarily. Could such a scandal happen again? Baseball is probably the most honest team sport in America, and a similar fix is extremely unlikely. The players are much better paid than they were in the Black Sox days. Just as important, communication is much better. In Cincinnati in 1919, the odds changed so drastically that some suspected a fix, but bettors in the rest of the country did not know. Today, such a shift in odds would be known nationwide immediately, transmitted by long-distance telephone, computer modem, radio, and TV. Unjustified heavy betting on one team would cause bookmakers across the country to refuse bets and to demand an immediate investigation. Also, the commissioners' offices of all major sports monitor betting activity and changes in the odds.

Baseball gambling, like other baseball traditions, will continue. In recent years interest has grown, and it is possible that some states besides Nevada may legalize sports betting. Fans like to have the extra interest and tension accompanying a personal stake in baseball games, whether they are carrying stacks of currency around Las Vegas, calling the neighborhood bookie, drafting rotisserie teams, or just betting a nickel that the next pitch will be a strike.

PART TWO

PART TWO

Introduction

Part Two, the statistical section of *Total Baseball*, presents the record of major league contests played from 1871 through 1988—all 148,316 of them. It details the accomplishments of the game's 2,010 teams and 13,160 players more completely and more accurately than any other encyclopedic work; it applies to all of baseball's glorious past the "sabermetric" stats that fans have embraced in the 1980s; it introduces original measures of player performance. Yet for all its innovation, *Total Baseball* stands squarely in the tradition of baseball record keeping; it is—like each new spring of our national pastime—a link in a long, long chain. As the game of one hundred and fifty years ago lives on in the game of today, so is this volume enriched by the labors of statisticians from Henry Chadwick to Ernie Lanigan, from S. C. Thompson to David Neft to Bill James.

The Origins, 1845–1875

In fact, baseball and stats were a tandem from the outset of the game's history, as the editors of this volume first discussed in their earlier *Hidden Game of Baseball* (1984), from which portions of this introduction are adapted. The first box score appeared in the *New York Herald* on October 25, 1845, just a month after Alexander Cartwright and his Knickerbocker teammates codified the first set of rules. Why did these early players and scribes measure individual performance rather than simply count the score? In part to imitate the custom of cricket; yet the larger explanation is that the numbers served to legitimize men's concern with a boys' pastime. The pioneers of baseball reporting—William Cauldwell of the *Sunday Mercury*, William Porter of *Spirit of the Times*, the unknown annalist at the *Herald*, and later Henry Chadwick—may indeed have reflected that if they did not cloak the game in the "importance" of statistics, it might not seem worthwhile for adults to read about, let alone play. Statistics elevated baseball from other boys' field games of the 1840s and '50s to make it somehow "serious," like business; its essential simplicity was adorned with intricate detail that suited it perfectly to quantification.

In the development of baseball statistics, no man is more important than Father Chadwick. Born in England in 1824, he came to these shores at age thirteen steeped in the tradition of cricket. In his teens he played the English game and in his twenties he reported on it for a variety of newspapers, including the *Long Island Star* and the *New York Times*. In the early 1840s, before the Knickerbocker rules eliminated the practice of retiring a base runner by throwing the ball at him rather than to the base, Chadwick occasionally played baseball too, but he was not favorably impressed, having received "some hard hits in the ribs." Not until 1856, by which time he had been a cricket reporter for a decade, were Chadwick's eyes opened to the possibilities in the American game, which had improved dramatically since his youth. In 1868 he recalled, "On returning from the early close of a cricket match on Fox Hill, I chanced to go through the Elysian Fields during the progress of a contest between the noted Eagle and Gotham clubs. The game was being sharply played on both sides, and I watched it with deeper interest than any previous ball game between clubs that I had seen. It was not long before I was struck with the idea that baseball was just the game for a national sport for Americans . . . as much so as cricket in England. At the time I refer to I had been reporting cricket for years, and, in my method of taking notes of contests, I had a plan peculiarly my own. It was not long, therefore, after I had become interested in baseball, before I began to invent a method of giving detailed reports of leading contests at baseball . . ."

Thus Chadwick's cricket background was largely the impetus to his method of scoring a baseball game, the format of his early box scores, and the copious if primitive statistics that appeared in his year-end summaries in the *New York Clipper*, Beadle's *Dime Base-Ball Player*, and other publications.

Actually, cricket had begun to shape baseball statistics even before Chadwick's conversion. The first box score reported on two categories, outs and runs: outs, or "hands out," counted both unsuccessful times at bat and outs run into on the basepaths; "runs" were runs scored, not those driven in. The reason for not recording hits in the early years, when coverage of baseball matches appeared alongside that of cricket matches, was that, unlike baseball, cricket had no such category as the successful hit which did not produce a run. To reach "base" in cricket is to run to the opposite wicket, which tallies a run; if you hit the ball and do not score a run, you have been put out.

Cricket box scores were virtual play-by-plays, a fact made possible by the lesser number of possible events. This play-by-play aspect was applied to a baseball box score as early as 1856; interestingly, despite the abundance of detail, hits were not accounted, nor did they appear in Chadwick's own box scores until 1867. The batting champion as declared by Chadwick, whose computations were immediately and universally accepted as "official," was the man with the highest average of runs per game. An inverse though imprecise measure of batting quality was outs per game. After 1863, when a fair ball caught on one bounce was no longer an out, fielding leaders were those with the greatest total of fly catches, assists, and "foul bounds" (fouls caught on one bounce). Pitching effectiveness was based purely on control, with the leader recognized as the one whose delivery offered the most opportunities for outs at first base and led to the fewest passed balls.

In a sense, Chadwick's measuring of baseball as if it were

cricket can be viewed as correct in that when you strip the game to its basic elements, those that determine victory or defeat, outs and runs are all that count in the end. No individual statistic is meaningful to the team unless it relates directly to the scoring of runs. Chadwick's blind spot in his early years of baseball reporting lay in not recognizing the linear character of the game, the sequential nature whereby a string of base hits or men reaching base on error (there were no walks then) was necessary in most cases to produce a run. In cricket each successful hit must produce at least one run, while in baseball, more of a team game on offense, a successful hit may produce none.

Early player stats were of the most primitive kind, the counting kind. They'd tell you how many runs, or outs, or fly catches had occurred—later, how many hits or total bases. Counting is the most basic of all statistical processes; the next step up is averaging, and Chadwick was the first to put this into practice.

As professionalism infiltrated the game, teams began to bid for star-caliber players. Stars were known not by their stats but by their style until 1865, when Chadwick began to record in the *Clipper* a form of batting average taken from the cricket pages—runs per game. Two years later, in his newly founded baseball weekly, *The Ball Players' Chronicle,* he began to record not only average runs and outs per game, but also home runs, total bases, total bases per game—and hits per game. The averages were expressed not with decimal places but in the standard cricket format of the "average and over." Thus a batter with 23 hits in 6 games would have an average expressed not as 3.83 but as "3-5"—an average of 3 with an overage, or remainder, of 5. Another innovation was to remove from the individual accounting all bases gained through errors. Runs scored by a team, beginning in 1867, were divided between those scored after a man reached base on a clean hit and those arising from a runner's having reached base on an error. This was, of course, a precursor of today's earned run average.

In 1868, despite Chadwick's derision, the *Clipper* continued to award the prize for the batting championship to the player with the greatest average of runs per game. Actually, the old yardstick had been less preposterous a measure of batsmanship than one might imagine today, because team defense was so much poorer and the pitcher, with severe restrictions on his method of delivery, was so much less important. If you reached first base, whether by a hit or by an error, your chances of scoring were excellent; indeed, teams of the mid-1860s registered more runs than hits! By 1876, the caliber of both pitching and defense had improved to the extent that the ratio of runs to hits was about 6.5 to 10; today the ratio stands at roughly 5 to 10.

By the end of the decade Chadwick was recording total bases and home runs, but he placed little stock in either, as conscious attempts at slugging violated his cricket-bred image of "form." Just as cricket aficionados watch the game for the many opportunities for fine fielding it affords, so was baseball from its inception perceived as a fielders' sport. The original Cartwright rules of 1845, in fact, specified that a ball hit out of the field—in fair territory or foul—was a foul ball! "Long hits are showy," Chadwick wrote in the *Clipper* in 1868, "but they do not pay in the long run. Sharp grounders insuring the first-base certain, and sometimes the second-base easily are worth all the hits made for home-runs which players strive for."

Chadwick prevailed, and hits per game became the criterion for the *Clipper* batting championship and remained so until 1876, when the problem with using games as the denominator in the average at last became clear. If you were playing for a successful team, and thus were surrounded by good batters, or if your team played several weak rivals who committed many errors, the number of at-bats for each individual in that lineup would increase. The more at-bats one is granted in a game, the more hits one is likely to have. So, for example, if Player A had 10 at-bats in a game, which was not so unusual in the 1860s, he might have 4 base hits. In a more cleanly played game, Player B might bat only 6 times, and get 3 base hits. Yet Player A, with his 4-for-10, would achieve an average of 4.00; the average of Player B, who went 3-for-6, would be only 3.00. By modern standards, of course, Player A would be batting .400 while Player B would be batting .500.

In short, the batting average used in the 1860s is the same as that used today except in its denominator, with at-bats replacing games. Moreover, Chadwick created a measure in the 1860s that divided total bases by games played; change the denominator to at-bats and you have today's slugging average—which, incidentally, was not accepted by the National League as an official statistic until 1923 and by the American until 1946 (baseball was born and bred conservative).

Chadwick's "total bases average" represents the game's first attempt at a weighted average—an average in which the elements collected together in the numerator or the denominator are recognized numerically as being unequal. In this instance, a single is the unweighted unit, the double is weighted by a factor of two, the triple by three, and the home run by four. Statistically, this is a distinct leap forward from, first, counting, and next, averaging. The weighted average is in fact the cornerstone of today's statistical innovations, or "sabermetrics."

The 1870s gave rise to some new batting stats and to the first attempt to quantify thoroughly the other principal facets of the game, pitching and fielding. Although the *Clipper* recorded base hits and total bases as early as 1868, a significant wrinkle was added in 1870 when at-bats were listed as well. This was a critical introduction because it permitted the improvement of the batting average, first introduced in its current form in the Boston press on August 10, 1874, and first computed officially—that is, for the National League—in 1876. Since then the batting average has not changed, except for the aberrations of 1876, when bases on balls were figured as outs, and 1887, when they were counted as hits. *Total Baseball* counts a walk as neither an at-bat nor an out for all years since 1871.

The objections to the batting average are well known, but to date have not dislodged it from its place as the most popular measure of hitting ability. First of all, the batting average makes no distinction between the single, the double, the triple, and the home run, treating all as the same unit. This objection had been addressed in 1868 by Chadwick's total bases average.

Second, it gives no indication of the effect of that base hit—that is, its value to the team. This was the reason Chadwick clung to runs per game as the best possible batting measure. Third, the batting average does not take into account those occasions when first base is reached via a walk, hit by pitch, or error. This last point was addressed at a surprisingly early date, too, as for 1879 the National League

adopted as an official statistic a forerunner of the on-base percentage; it was called "reached first base," which included times reached by error as well as base on balls and base hits. (Being hit by a pitch did not give the batter first base until 1884 in the American Association, 1887 in the National League.)

The Flowering, 1876–1920

Ever since the Civil War, guide serials like Beadle and DeWitt and sporting columns like those in the *Clipper* had carried year-end tabulations of batting, fielding, and pitching exploits, varying from year to year with the brainstorms of Chadwick or other demon compilers like New York's M. J. Kelly or Philadelphia's Al Wright. But the year 1876 was special. It was significant not only for the founding of the National League and the official debut of the batting average in its current form, it was also the Centennial of the United States, which was marked by a giant exposition in Philadelphia celebrating the mechanical marvels of the day. American ingenuity reigned, and technology was seen as the new handmaiden of democracy. Baseball, that mirror of American life, reflected the fervor for things scientific with an explosion of statistics far more complex than those seen before, particularly in the previously neglected areas of pitching and fielding. The increasingly minute statistical examination of the game met a responsive audience, one primed to view complexity as a measure of worth.

The crossroads year of 1876 highlights how the game had changed to that point, and how it has changed since.

In that year, the number of offensive stats tabulated at season's end in any of the publications inspired by Chadwick or Spalding was six: games, at-bats, runs, hits, runs per game, and batting average. (And as with all the various guides until 1941, the stats of men who played in fewer than a specified minimum number of games were not noted.) Of these six, only runs and runs per game were common in the 1860s, while that decade's tabulation of total bases vanished. The number of offensive stats a hundred years later? Twenty. (Today the number is twenty-two, with the addition of on base percentage and the game-winning RBI.)

The number of pitching categories in 1876 was eleven, and there were some surprises, such as earned run average, hits allowed, hits per game, and opponents' batting average. Strikeouts were not recorded, for Chadwick saw them strictly as a sign of poor batting rather than good pitching (his view had such an impact that pitcher strikeouts were not kept officially until 1889). The number of pitching stats today? Twenty-four.

The number of fielding categories in 1876 was six. One hundred years later it was still six (with the exception of the catcher, who gets a seventh: passed balls), dramatizing how the game, which originated as a showcase for fielders, had changed. The fielding stats of 1876 lumped "battery errors" with fielding errors, so that wild pitches and passed balls—in some years, even walks—diminished one's fielding percentage. This practice continued until 1887, but in *Total Baseball* battery errors are not included in fielding stats. Batterymates' fielding stats were boosted by the awarding of an assist to the pitcher on strikeouts. This practice lasted until 1889, but is not reflected in *Total Baseball*.

The custom in 1876, as it is now, was to combine putouts, assists, and errors to form a "percentage of chances accepted," or what is today known as fielding average or fielding percentage. A "missing link" variant, devised by Al Wright in 1875, was to form averages by dividing the putouts by the number of games to yield a "putout average"; dividing the assists similarly to arrive at an "assist average"; and dividing putouts plus assists by games to get "fielding average." These averages took no account of errors. (Wright's "fielding average" was reborn a century later as Bill James's Range Factor.)

The public's appetite for new statistics was not sated by the outburst of 1876. New measures were introduced in dizzying profusion in the remaining years of the century. Some of these did not catch on and were soon dropped for all time, like the ridiculous "total bases run," while others fizzled only to reappear with new vigor in the twentieth century. These include (a) the above-mentioned "reached first base," which resurfaced in the early 1950s in an unofficial, improved form called on base percentage and became an official stat more than thirty years later, and (b) an 1860s stat, earned run average, which was periodically revived before dropping from sight in the 1880s, only to return triumphant to the NL in 1912 and the AL in 1913. In 1913 Ban Johnson not only proclaimed the ERA official but became so enamored with it that he also instructed American League scorers to compile *no* official won-lost records (this state of affairs lasted for seven years, 1913–1919).

Another stat that was "sent back to the minors" before its eventual adoption as an official stat in 1920 was the run batted in. Introduced by a Buffalo newspaper in 1879, the stat was picked up the following year by the *Chicago Tribune* and even became an official NL stat in 1891. Then in the late 1890s it faded as most scorers declined to account for it in their summaries. Ernie Lanigan picked up the RBI baton with his reports to the *New York Press* in 1907, but only about a third of his data has been found, and he did not figure RBIs for men who played in fewer than ten games, or club totals for traded players. For *Total Baseball* we have placed much reliance upon the source material donated by Information Concepts, Inc. (ICI) to the National Baseball Library in Cooperstown following publication of its *Baseball Encyclopedia* for Macmillan in 1969. David Neft also kindly supplied us with his unpublished RBI data for the previously missing National League seasons of 1880–1885. The John Tattersall collection of nineteenth century game accounts and box scores was valuable as well.

Other statistics introduced officially before the turn of the century were stolen bases (though not caught stealing); doubles, triples, and homers; and sacrifice bunts (though an at-bat was charged from 1889 through 1894). Pitcher strikeouts, bases on balls, and the hit-by-pitch also appeared before 1900, but hit-by-pitch stats were not kept for batters on a systematic basis until 1917 in the NL and 1920 in the AL. Through newspaper research, we have filled in HBP data from 1884 through 1916 in the National League, Players League, and American Association, and from 1909 through 1919 in the American League; research continues for the 1901–1908 period in both leagues, as well as for 1914–1915 in the Federal League. We are indebted in this area to Alex Haas, John Schwartz, John Tattersall, and Bob Davids.

Hit into double play—including line outs as well as groundouts—was recorded erratically in the nineteenth century, but separate stats for groundouts into double plays have been kept by the leagues only since 1933 in the NL and 1939 in the AL. Batters' strikeouts were reported unofficially in

1891, but not as a league stat until 1910 in the NL and 1913 in the AL. Innings pitched were not kept until 1908 in the AL and 1910 in the NL.

Stolen bases were awarded not only for clean steals but also for extra bases taken through daring, from the first year in which totals were kept, 1886, until 1898 (the Macmillan *Baseball Encyclopedia* begins its record of stolen bases with 1887). Because the figures reported in the guides were grossly inflated (such as Harry Stovey's ostensible 156 steals in 1888), the figures in *Total Baseball* reflect game-by-game research and refiguring. Caught-stealing (CS) figures are available on a very sketchy basis in some of the later years of the century, as some newspapers carried the data in the box scores of hometown games. From 1912 on, Lanigan recorded CS in box scores of the *New York Press,* but the leagues did not keep the figure officially until 1920. The AL has tabulated CS from that year to the present, excepting 1927, which members of the Society for American Baseball Research are reconstructing from newspaper box scores. National League caught-stealing data exists for 1920–1925, and for 1951 to the present.

The new century added little in the way of *new* official statistics—ERA, RBI, and slugging average are better regarded as revivals despite their respective adoption dates of 1912, 1920, and 1923. But back in 1908 there was a classic case of a statistic rushing in to fill a void, as Phillies' manager Billy Murray observed that his outfielder Sherry Magee had the happy facility of providing a long fly ball whenever presented with a situation of a man on third and fewer than two outs. Taking up the cudgels on his player's behalf, Murray protested to the National League office that it was unfair to charge Magee with an unsuccessful time at bat when he was in fact succeeding, doing precisely what the situation demanded.

Murray won his point, but baseball flip-flopped a couple of times on this stat, in some years reverting to calling it a time at bat, in other years not even crediting an RBI. The sacrifice-fly rule was in effect from 1908 through 1930, with a sacrifice being given for advancing any runner, not just to home, for the final four years of this period. The rule was revived for one year in 1939. In none of these years was a distinction made between a sacrifice bunt or fly. When the rule came back into force in 1954, there was a breakdown of each.

More recent stats that have followed from this sort of perception—that something important was occurring on the field which had no verifiable reality because it was not yet being measured—are the save and the game-winning RBI, which will be discussed later.

A signal event took place in 1912: the publication by *Baseball Magazine* editor John Lawres of *Who's Who in Baseball,* a small book that became the first to provide career statistics and personal facts for a group of players. Although thoroughly inadequate by today's standards—its only tabulations were games, batting average, and fielding average (even for pitchers, who were given no mound records!)—*Who's Who* was a groundbreaking work, giving rise to a much-expanded format in 1916 and inspiring two other significant encyclopedic works: in 1914, George Moreland's self-published opus called *Balldom* (grandiosely subtitled "The Britannica of Baseball," which it surely wasn't), and Ernest J. Lanigan's *Baseball Cyclopedia,* also sponsored by *Baseball Magazine,* which debuted in 1922 and was updated annually through 1933.

The Golden Age, 1920–1968

There have been other new statistical tabulations in this century, but generally of the counting sort: complete games (NL 1910, AL 1922), games started (AL 1926, NL 1938), games finished (NL 1920, AL 1926). And there were sacrifice bunts allowed (NL 1916, AL 1922), intentional bases on balls (only since 1955), and, in the next period, saves (1969) and game-winning RBIs (1980). The only new average since slugging average was adopted in 1923 has been the on base percentage, adopted in 1985. The ICI group computed saves for prior years. Another such stat that failed to survive, alas, was stolen bases off pitchers, which the American League recorded only in 1920–1924; it has been recorded on an unofficial basis in the 1980s by the Elias Sports Bureau and Project Scoresheet.) The only new fielding measure was team double plays, added to the AL list in 1912 and the NL in 1919. Other new and more interesting stats appeared in the 1940s and '50s but have not yet gained the official stamp of approval, such as Ted Oliver's Weighted Rating System, Alfred P. Berry's Average Bases Allowed (opponents' slugging average), and Branch Rickey and Allan Roth's Isolated Power.

This period of baseball's history may have fielded its most dazzling array of stars, but strategically and statistically it was pretty dim. There was some excitement, however, in baseball record keeping. First came *Daguerreotypes,* issued by *The Sporting News* in 1934, featuring the playing records of many retired players both celebrated and obscure; most if not all of these statistical and biographical profiles originally appeared in the pages of *TSN.* Although its number of statistical categories was fewer than one might have wished, *Daguerreotypes* was very useful and, through its several editions ably edited by Paul Mac Farlane, long-lived.

In 1940 came *The Sporting News*'s *Baseball Register,* which supplied full records for active players, managers, coaches, and umpires, plus a grab bag of former stars. Since the expansion of the major leagues from sixteen teams to twenty-six, the *Register* has only accommodated contemporary players and managers, but it remains a valuable source. One year later, *TSN* issued a notable edition of its *Official Baseball Record Book,* giving for the first time full statistical lines for all men who played in a major league game the previous year.

In 1944 a little-known man named Ted Oliver published in obscurity a booklet called *Kings of the Mound.* It introduced a new stat called the Weighted Rating System for pitchers, a stat that we have modified and continue to employ as Wins Above Team. Moved by the inadequacy of both the won-lost percentage and the ERA to reflect the value of a decent pitcher laboring for a lousy club, Oliver ingeniously subtracted the pitcher's decisions from his team's, then took the difference between the pitcher's won-lost percentage and his team's and multiplied that difference by the pitcher's number of decisions. Although his concept and his math were flawed, his principles—viewing a pitcher's record in relation to his team and weighting the result of his calculation by the number of decisions—were of unparalleled sophistication for the time. (Oliver's formula for his Weighted Rating System and its modification in *Total Baseball* are detailed in the Glossary, as are the calculations behind every statistic employed in this book.)

Then in 1951 came the first true encyclopedia of baseball,

the claims of Moreland and Lanigan notwithstanding. Compiled by Hy Turkin and S. C. Thompson, *The Official Encyclopedia of Baseball* was published by the A. S. Barnes Company. Its 620 pages contained a wealth of features such as manager and umpire rosters, historical essays, playing tips, a bibliography, and much more. But the heart of the volume and the key to its subsequent success was a register of nearly nine thousand men who played one or more games at the major league level from 1871 through 1949 (the 1950 record of players appearing in ten games or more was tacked on to the end). In this register, Turkin/Thompson also offered birth and death data and what today seems fairly limited statistical information but by previous standards was a veritable cornucopia: year, club, league, position, games, and batting average or won-lost record. A landmark volume that did much to inspire this one, *The Official Encyclopedia of Baseball* lasted through ten revised editions, the last being published in 1979, ten years after the initial appearance of Macmillan's *Baseball Encyclopedia*.

The genesis of the Turkin/Thompson opus was one day in September 1944 when musician Thompson invited his neighbor, New York *Daily News* sportswriter Turkin, to "look over his baseball collection." What Turkin saw was a massive treasure chest of data, collected and collated over twenty years. "Tommy" Thompson was a baseball nut—a figure filbert, in the parlance of the time—who researched baseball just for the love of it. He was not alone in this pursuit, although very nearly so—other baseball archeologists of the time who contributed to this encyclopedia were Frank Marcellus, Tom Shea, Lee Allen, Ralph Lin Weber, Joe Overfield, Bob McConnell, and the aforementioned Ernie Lanigan.

The Official Encyclopedia of Baseball went a long way toward making the study of baseball history and records a respectable pursuit, just as a century earlier the statistical accounting of a boys' game had helped to make baseball a sport for grown men. The researchers' ranks expanded to include such men as Bob Davids, who in 1971, aided by other experts like Cliff Kachline, Bill Haber, Ray Nemec, John Pardon, and Joe Simenic, would create SABR, the Society for American Baseball Research (pronounced "saber"). Formerly the lonely pursuit of a handful of "nuts" like S. C. Thompson, baseball research and sabermetrics—a neologism coined in honor of SABR, signifying the statistical analysis of the game's records—would become the pastime of thousands.

An article in *Life* magazine by Branch Rickey on August 2, 1954, gave further impetus to the study of baseball statistics, but not just to set the historical record straight. Indeed, this article may be viewed as the opening shot of the sabermetric assault of the 1980s. In "Goodby to Some Old Baseball Ideas," Rickey, with the aid of some new mathematical tools supplied by Dodger statistician Allan Roth, sought to puncture some long-held conceptions about how the game was divided among its elements (batting, base running, pitching, fielding), who was best at playing it, and what caused one team to win and another to lose. This is a pretty fair statement of what sabermetrics is about.

Rickey attacked the batting average and proposed in its place the on base percentage; advocated the use of Isolated Power (extra bases beyond singles, divided by at-bats) as a better measure than slugging average; introduced a "clutch" measure of run-scoring efficiency for teams, and a similar concept for pitchers (earned runs divided by baserunners allowed); reaffirmed the basic validity of the ERA; saw the strikeout as the insubstantial thing it was—and more. But the most important thing Rickey did for baseball statistics was to pull it back from the wrong path it had taken with the introduction of the batting average in 1876: to strip the game and its stats to their essentials and start again, this time remembering that individual stats came into being as an attempt to apportion the players' contributions to achieving a team victory, for that is what the game is about.

Rickey and Roth devised a formula to measure a team's efficiency in turning its offensive and defensive statistics into runs, and thus wins. They realized, and had confirmed for them by mathematicians at the Massachusetts Institute of Technology, that just as the team which scores more runs in a game gets the win, so a team which over the course of a season scores more runs than it allows should win more games than it loses—and by an extent correlated to its run differential. From this startlingly simple (or rather, seemingly simple) observation in 1954 flowed: first, the trailblazing but little noted work of George Lindsey in the 1950s and early 1960s, when he developed a model for run-scoring probability from the twenty-four combinations of outs and bases occupied; the development of "percentage baseball" stats and strategies by Earnshaw Cook in the 1960s; the play-by-play analysis of complete seasons by the Mills brothers, Eldon and Harlan, in 1969–1970; and, over the next two decades, the statistical and historical works of several sabermetricians, most notably Bill James.

The Computer Age, 1969–

Despite the death of Turkin in 1957 and Thompson ten years later, their *Official Encyclopedia of Baseball* remained the dominant book of baseball statistics, although many fans were frustrated with the fragmentary records it presented. As Frank V. Phelps wrote in the 1987 edition of *The National Pastime,* "Gaps and obvious errors in official averages, the lack of many early records, difficulty in securing the records of players who appeared in only a few games, and frustrating discrepancies among existing guides and registers had long since created a desire for an ultimate, complete, correct set of major league records. But it wasn't until the mid-1960s that the development of sophisticated computers which could absorb, retain, order, and output huge amounts of data finally made a project feasible."

Beginning in 1967, a battalion of researchers commanded by David Neft foraged through the official records and newspaper box scores to provide freshly compiled figures for those who had no ERAs, RBIs, slugging averages, saves, and all manner of wonderful things. All the material which finally appeared in the tome was entered into a data bank, and the book was the first typeset entirely by computer, now a common practice. Published in 1969, *The Baseball Encyclopedia* was a milestone in computer technology, but as indispensable as the computer were the old-fashioned scrapbooks and files of Lee Allen and John Tattersall. The result was a mammoth ledger book of the major leagues more thorough than any that had appeared before.

The Baseball Encyclopedia researchers not only found new data to correct old inaccuracies but also applied new yardsticks to men who had gone to their graves never having heard of an RBI or a save. They also raised the hackles of traditionalists with many of their findings, which prompted the formation of a Special Baseball Records Committee. Its members

ruled upon such matters as whether, for the historical record, bases on balls should be counted as hits (as they were in 1887), outs (as they were in 1876), or neither (as has been the practice in all other years); or whether "sudden-death" home runs—thirty-seven game-winning blows with men on base that they identified as having occurred in the bottom half of the ninth or extra inning—would be credited as homers or, in the practice before 1920, would count for only as many bases as needed to push across the winning run. In the latter controversy, committee members first decided to count the disputed blows as homers, but then, when complaints arose that Babe Ruth's famous total of 714 would change to 715, they reversed themselves. They decided that the National Association of 1871–1875 was not a major league, while the Federal League, Union Association, and Players League were; and they ruled on several other issues, all of which were published in the Appendix to *The Baseball Encyclopedia.*

In *Total Baseball,* we have abided by most of the committee's decisions—not to preserve Ruth's total, but because there were many more such homers before 1920 than the thirty-seven the committee identified, and the disputes surrounding some of them are now beyond settling. We have, however, treated the National Association as a major league, as Turkin/Thompson and all previous record books did, and in accordance with the views of most historians. And we have differed from the committee's ruling on awarding pitchers wins and losses in the years before 1920. Not finding any official scoring rule or practice for that time, they chose to apply 1950 guidelines to decisions awarded in 1876–1920. This well-intentioned decision produced substantial alterations in the records of such hurlers as Cy Young, Christy Mathewson, Grover Alexander, and others. In the ensuing years, the notable research of Frank Williams (reported in "All the Record Books Are Wrong," *The National Pastime,* 1982) revealed that there was indeed a pattern and a rationale for the way decisions were awarded in those days; the data in *Total Baseball* conforms with his findings.

ICI research created new stars, launching several previously underappreciated heroes of old into the Hall of Fame. Sam Thompson, Addie Joss, Roger Connor, Amos Rusie—their phenomenal level of play was hidden simply because statisticians back then were not recording the particular numbers which would show them off to best advantage. If sabermetrics consists of finding things in the existing data that were not seen before, or collecting that data which makes possible the application of new statistics to old performances, the first edition of *The Baseball Encyclopedia* was a monument in the course of sabermetrics.

However, its subsequent editions declined from that standard, dropping valuable data, jimmying figures for star players in a misguided homage to tradition, and making a shambles of individual/team balance in the totals. As Phelps wrote of the second edition, edited by Joseph L. Reichler for the Macmillan Company after the ICI group broke up and relinquished supervision:

"Players' batting statistics were changed without compensating for changes in the records of other players on the same teams or in the corresponding team and league totals. Later editions included even more unbalanced adjustments . . .

"Quite apart from the problem of record-balancing, the numerous changes in players' totals and averages has caused serious misapprehensions and confusions for fans, writers, and researchers. The records of Fred Clarke and Cy Young

differ in all six editions [to 1987] even without counting Clarke's astronomical 1899 BA [in the third edition, Clarke was credited with a batting average of .986 that boosted his lifetime mark by 15 points]. The figures for Burkett, Chesbro, Duffy, Hornsby, Walter Johnson, Radbourn, Speaker, and Waddell differ in five of the six books. The same is so in four of six for at least twenty-three other Hall of Famers, and many more less gifted players." The seventh edition was issued in 1988 and, like the five that preceded it, it remains less accurate than the classic first issue. (David Neft of ICI, along with *Baseball Encyclopedia* staff alumni Dick Cohen and Jordan Deutsch, went on to form Sport Products, Inc. Since 1974 they have issued the excellent *Sports Encyclopedia: Baseball,* which has endured as the baseball reference of choice for thousands of sophisticated fans.)

We will have more to add about accuracy and balance in the "Errors and Controversies" section of this Introduction.

There were two other interesting developments in 1969. The first and less celebrated was a research project launched by Eldon and Harlan Mills that, like the ICI encyclopedia, could not have been contemplated without the computer. The Mills brothers tracked the entire major league seasons of 1969 and 1970 on a play-by-play basis. Then they applied to that record the probabilities of winning which derived from each possible outcome of a plate appearance, as determined by a computer simulation incorporating nearly eight thousand possibilities. What, for example, was the visiting team's chance of winning the game before the first pitch was thrown? Fifty percent, if we are pitting two theoretical teams of equal or unknown ability on a neutral site. If the first man fails to get on base, the chances of the visiting team winning are reduced to 49.8 percent; should he hit a double, the visiting team's chance of victory is raised to 55.9 percent, as determined by the probabilistic simulation. Every possible situation—combining half inning, score, men on base, and men out—was tested by the simulator to arrive at "Win Points."

The Mills' purpose was to determine the clutch value of, say, hitting a homer with two men on and one man out in the bottom of the ninth, with the team trailing by two runs, the situation Bobby Thomson faced in the climactic National League game of 1951—oddly, the rookie year of the first modern computer. (It gained for him 1,472 Win Points; had it come with no one on in the eighth inning of a game in which his team led 4–0, the homer would have been worth only 12 Win Points.) What the Mills brothers were attempting to do was to evaluate not only the *what* of a performance, which traditional statistics indicate, but the *when,* or clutch factor, which no statistic to that time could provide.

This project, detailed in a small book issued in 1970 called *Player Win Averages,* proceeded from the same impulse that led to other measures of clutch performance: the game winning RBI, introduced as an official major league stat in 1980; the measure of batting performance in late-inning pressure situations first published by Seymour Siwoff, Steve Hirdt, and Peter Hirdt of the Elias Sports Bureau in 1985; and the historically complete indexes of clutch hitting and clutch pitching developed for this book.

The other noteworthy baseball event of 1969 (besides the centennial of professional baseball and the miracle of the Mets) was the adoption by the major leagues of the save, the stat associated with the most significant strategic development since the advent of the gopher ball. Now shown in the papers on a daily basis, saves were not officially recorded at all

until 1960; it was at the instigation of Jerry Holtzman of the *Chicago Sun-Times,* with the cooperation of *The Sporting News,* that this statistic was finally accepted. (Although Pat McDonough, a founding member of SABR, had developed a similar stat in 1924 which he called "games finished by relief hurlers"; its first appearance in print came in the *New York Telegram* three years later.) The need for the save arose because relievers operated at a disadvantage when it came to picking up wins. The bullpen specialists were a new breed, and as their role increased, the need arose to identify excellence, as it had long ago for batters, starting pitchers, and fielders. The save's prime statistical drawback is that there is no negative to counteract the positive, no stat for saves blown (except, all too often, a victory for the "fireman"); unofficial attempts to develop such a stat have accelerated in recent years.

August 10, 1971, marked another milestone, the founding in Cooperstown of SABR, the group in whose annual publications most of today's sabermetricians cut their analytical teeth. Its statistical analysis research committee, headed for more than a decade by Pete Palmer, has served as a sounding board for the inventive approaches of such men as Dallas Adams, Dick Cramer, Steve Mann, Craig Wright, and Bill James.

James published *The Baseball Abstract* from his home in Lawrence, Kansas, for five years to a minute if appreciative audience (its 1977 publication budget: $112.73). In 1982 Ballantine Books, recognizing the increasing sophistication of baseball fans in the computer age, assumed publication of the *Abstract,* and the audience for sabermetrics became sizable indeed, with James's annuals reaching the bestseller lists and his *Historical Baseball Abstract* becoming an essential book for anyone who viewed himself as a serious fan. James has popularized a different approach to the whole question of what baseball statistics are for—that they are not brass knuckles to beat a barroom adversary with, but a means of achieving a better understanding of the game and heightening one's pleasure in it.

Among the many valuable analytical tools he has developed are the Brock-2 System of projecting career totals, the Victory Important RBI, Offensive and Defensive Winning Percentages, Secondary Average, Range Factor, and Runs Created. The last-mentioned, perhaps because James developed it earlier in his career, is the most widely known, and we apply it in this book to all batters, in all fourteen variations of the formula, bringing in data for stolen bases, caught stealing, hit-by-pitch, and grounded into double play for those years in which it is available. (See the Glossary for the formulas.)

The 1980s also brought attention to another attempt to redefine the measure of individual performance. In 1978 Barry Codell of Chicago distributed a paper describing his new statistic, the Base-Out Percentage, to fellow statisticians and figures in the sports media. At about the same time, Tom Boswell, not a statistician by trade or inclination but rather a sportswriter for the *Washington Post,* developed a stat called Total Average. Like the Base-Out Percentage, Total Average is a gauge of offensive proficiency which takes into account not only batting but also base-running skills. As with Runs Created, Total Average is calculated for all nonpitchers in this book. (See the Glossary.)

Dallas Adams and Dick Cramer devoted themselves in the late 1970s to a discussion of average batting, pitching, and fielding skill, which more than a decade later remains a subject of intense interest and passionate disagreement. The question, roughly put, is: *How would Cy Young do against the batters of today? Or Wade Boggs against the pitchers of the 1890s? How many homers would Babe Ruth hit if he were active today? Or how many strikeouts would Nolan Ryan have registered in 1880, pitching from a fifty-foot distance?* In other words, how can we adjust the statistics of players to reflect the certainty that the average batter, pitcher, and fielder have improved over time, thus narrowing the gap between each succeeding era's peak performance and its average one? (For more on this philosophically and mathematically complex subject, we refer you to *The Hidden Game of Baseball.*)

Adams and Cramer advanced a discussion that had begun in 1976 with the first article on cross-era comparison, in which David Shoebotham proposed a new statistic called the Relative Batting Average. Shoebotham recognized that a .320 batting average in 1893, when the National League batted .280, did not represent the same level of accomplishment as that average did in 1968 when, for a number of reasons, the National League batted a measly .243. His solution? To normalize the players' averages to their respective league averages simply by dividing the player's batting average by that of his league.

In this fashion he demonstrated, for example, that Pete Rose, who led the NL with a .335 BA in 1968, had a Relative BA of 1.38; while Ed Delahanty, who led the NL with a BA of .380 in 1893, had a Relative BA of only 1.36. Another way of stating this conclusion is that Rose's .335 was 38 percent above the average batting performance in the NL of 1968, while Delahanty exceeded his league's norm by 36 percent. The inferences that might be drawn from this approach are many: that batting skill has not declined since the days of Ruth, Gehrig, Foxx, et al., but that pitching skill might have increased; that no batting average of the years around 1930 ought to be taken without a carload of salt; that some of the most notable batting performances of all time, as measured by the batting average, have occurred right under our noses, unbeknownst to us.

Normalizing a statistic to its league average is a valuable analytical tool if employed logically. A Relative Batting Average, for example, tells a good deal more, and tells it more straightforwardly, than Relative Homers or Relative Strikeouts. The relativist approach works better with ratios such as batting average, on base percentage, or slugging average—or for that matter with Runs Created or Total Average—than it does for simple counter stats.

Another worthwhile adjustment to various averages is for home-park effects. The pioneering work in this area was done by Robert Kingsley, particularly in regard to why homers flew out of Atlanta's park despite its "normal" dimensions, but Pete Palmer was first to measure the effects of home parks on run totals and then to devise a park adjustment for the records of batters and pitchers. These were discussed in depth in *The Hidden Game of Baseball,* and the data base for park factor in this book has been upgraded to include runs scored and runs allowed at home parks instead of just the latter.

In 1984 the editors of this volume introduced, in *The Hidden Game,* the Linear Weights System of assessing players' contributions to their teams—at the bat, on the basepaths, in the field, or on the mound—in terms of runs, which are the currency of the game. Its back-to-basics foundation is the same as that underlying the Rickey formula of 1954 and most

of the new statistics developed since then: that wins and losses are what the game is about; that wins and losses are proportional in some way to runs scored and runs allowed; and that runs in turn are proportional to the events which go into their making.

In the Linear Weights System, these events are expressed not in the familiar yet deceptive ratios—base hits to at-bats, wins to decisions, etc.—but in *runs themselves,* the runs contributed (by batting or base stealing) or saved (by pitching or fielding). Computer simulations of over 100,000 games produced the run values of, for example: a single (.47 runs), double (.78), triple (1.09), home run (1.40), walk (.33), steal (.30), caught stealing (−.60), out (−.25), and out made on base (−.50). Using a straightforward additive formula, one can calculate a batter or baserunner's contribution to his team in runs. These would be expressed in terms of runs contributed beyond what a league-average replacement player could contribute in his stead, and that average is defined as a baseline of zero. A team composed entirely of average performers would finish with a record of .500, as the league must—so each above-average player contributes positive runs toward a win, and each subpar player contributes negative runs.

Normalizing factors (to league average) are built into the formulas for all but base stealing, where league average is not a shaping force; these factors enable us to compute, for example, the number of runs (Batting Runs) that Jose Canseco provided in 1988 beyond those an average hitter might have produced in an equivalent number of plate appearances. And by adjusting Canseco's Batting Runs for Oakland's homepark influences, the Linear Weights comparison may be extended to how many runs he accounted for beyond what an average player might have produced in the same number of at-bats *had he too played half his games in Oakland-Alameda Stadium.*

Furthermore, having determined the number of runs above average required to transform a loss to a win in the final standings (generally around ten, historically in the range of nine to eleven; for more on the theory behind this, see the Glossary), we can convert a player's Linear Weights record—expressed as Batting Runs, Base Stealing Runs, Pitching Runs, or Fielding Runs—to the number of *wins above average* he alone contributed. What are individual statistics for if not to achieve some understanding of this? Last, by reviewing the win contributions of all a team's personnel, we may establish a solid assessment of that team's strength and weaknesses—either to predict a team's chances for success in the upcoming season or, in an encyclopedia like *Total Baseball,* to analyze how and even why it failed its reasonable statistical expectations or exceeded them.

Formulas for the Linear Weights measures for batting, base running, fielding, and pitching will be found in the Glossary.

Other developments of the decade include the previously mentioned adoption of the game-winning RBI (GWRBI) in 1980; it credits the batter who drives in a run to give his club a lead that it never relinquishes. This stat has been pilloried in the press from its introduction, with merit. In 1984 on base percentage was made official, thirty years after its introduction to the general baseball public by Branch Rickey and Allan Roth. Subsequent years brought the Quality Start, which takes note of a pitcher who gives his club six innings or more while allowing three runs or less. Under this construction, an ERA of 4.50 in a mercifully shortened outing is held

to be commendable. The editors of this book do not regard the Quality Start as a quality stat.

More interesting are the situational stats which are the specialty of the Elias Sports Bureau and Project Scoresheet—performance in day games vs. night, grass vs. artificial turf, lefty vs. righty, day game following night, bases-loaded situations, and so on. When the data is drawn from a large enough sample, these stats can be provocative and meaningful; too often, however, television announcers desperate to maintain conversation flow will burden their listeners with something like, "Over the last two seasons, he's batted .375 against this guy" (not bothering to add that the figure represents three hits in eight times at bat). Situational stats are the wave of the future in baseball, but are not yet of much use for reviewing the past—Elias has kept them systematically only since 1975.

Total Baseball

The next major event in the history of baseball record keeping may be the book you now hold. Founded upon a unique historical data base that Pete Palmer has cultivated for over twenty years—in the tradition of baseball archivists like S. C. Thompson, Bradshaw Swales, Leonard Gettelson, and John Tattersall—*Total Baseball* is the third-generation encyclopedia of the game. Just as the advent of the Macmillan/ICI encyclopedia supplanted Turkin/Thompson, the standard for two decades, *Total Baseball* has taken advantage of new technology and new research, notably by members of the Society for American Baseball Research, to present more accurate data than ever before, and more of it. There are, of course, the traditional stats one would expect in a baseball reference work; there are many of the new, more revealing stats discussed above; there are stats never published before and developed now for this book. And as you have seen in Part One, there is a recognition that baseball history and knowledge resides not only in its numbers.

But returning to the statistics and records which make up this second part of *Total Baseball,* here is a brief rundown of what's coming (full descriptions will be found in the separate introduction to each section):

- *The Annual Record:* Season-by-season standings and records for all teams since 1871, plus the top five league leaders in generally forty-eight categories per season.
- *Home-Road Statistics:* Team stats for all years of major league play, including years before 1900, plus in-depth records for twenty-seven superstars.
- *The Rosters:* A completely revised manager roster, courtesy of some splendid research into the early years by SABR's Bob Tiemann and Richard Topp; a definitive roster of the men in blue, compiled by expert Larry Gerlach; a roster of coaches, never before compiled; and a roster of all the teams of major league history, listing the starting lineups plus principal pitchers and substitutes.
- *The Player and Pitcher Registers:* The heart of this section of *Total Baseball,* presenting complete seasonal and lifetime records for every major leaguer, with twenty-seven stats for players and twenty-eight for pitchers.
- *All-Time Leaders:* The top one hundred lifetime and single-season performers in ninety-five categories, includ-

ing important conventional stats not found in other encyclopedias and dozens of the sabermetric variety.

Now that the genealogy of the more significant records and record books has been described, it's time to say a few words about the measures you'll find in the main statistical sections of *Total Baseball:* the annual record and the player/pitcher registers. We will not attempt to define the basic counting stats such as games, at-bats, wins, losses, and so on; if these are puzzling to you, you have picked up the wrong book.

Batting

Let's start with the batting statistics, and the first of these to consider will be that venerable, uncannily durable fraud, the batting average. (It consists simply of hits divided by at-bats.) We know as well as anyone else that this monument just won't topple; the best that can be hoped is that in time fans and officials will recognize it as a bit of nostalgia, a throwback to the period of its invention when power counted for naught, bases on balls were scarce, and no one wanted to place a statistical accomplishment in historical context because there wasn't much history yet.

Time has given the batting average a powerful hold on the American baseball public; everyone knows that a man who hits .300 is a good hitter while one who hits .250 is not. Everyone knows that—no matter that it is not true. You want to trade Rafael Palmeiro for Darryl Strawberry? Vance Law for Will Clark? Batting average treats all hits in an egalitarian fashion. A two-out bunt single in the ninth with no one on base and your team trailing by six runs counts the same as Bobby Thomson's "shot heard 'round the world." And what about a walk? Say you foul off four 3–2 pitches, then watch a close one go by to take your base. Where's your credit for a neat bit of offensive work? Not in this stat. And a .250 batting average may have represented a distinct accomplishment in certain years, like 1968 when the American League mean was .230. That .250 hitter stood in the same relation to an average hitter of his season as a .282 hitter did in the American League in 1988—or a *.329* hitter in the National League of 1930! If .329 and .282 and .250 all mean roughly the same thing, it raises questions about the value of the measure.

And yet, the batting champion each year is declared to be the one with the highest batting average, and this will not soon change. And the Hall of Fame is filled with .300 hitters who couldn't carry the pine tar of many who will stay forever on the outside looking in. Knowledgeable fans have long realized that the ability to reach base and to produce runs are not adequately measured by batting average, and they have looked to other measures—for example, the other two components of the Triple Crown, home runs and RBIs. Still more sophisticated fans have looked to the slugging average or on base percentage, and in the 1980s to various sabermetric measures.

The slugging average does acknowledge the role of the man whose talent is for the long ball and who may, with management's blessing, be sacrificing bat control and thus batting average in order to let'er rip. (Slugging average is the number of total bases divided by at-bats.) But the slugging average has its problems, too. It declares that a double is worth two singles, that a triple is worth one and a half doubles, and that a home run is worth four singles. All of these proportions are intuitively pleasing, for they relate to the number of bases touched on each hit, but in terms of the hits' value in generating runs, the proportions are wrong. One home run in four at-bats is not worth as much as four singles, for instance, in part because the total run potential for the team of four singles is greater, and in part because the man who hit the four singles did not also make three outs; yet the man who goes one for four at the plate, that one being a homer, has the same slugging percentage of 1.000 as a man who singles four times in four at-bats.

Moreover, it is possible to attain a high slugging percentage without being a slugger. In other words, if you have a high batting average, you must have a decent slugging percentage; it's difficult to hit .350 and have a slugging percentage of only .400. Even a bunt single boosts not only your batting average but also your slugging percentage. (The attempt to counteract this problem is a statistic called Isolated Power, which divides only extra bases by at-bats.) Other things the slugging percentage does not do are: indicate how many runs were produced by the hits; give any credit for other offensive categories, such as walks, hit-by-pitch, or steals; permit the comparison of sluggers from different eras (if Jimmie Foxx had a slugging percentage of .749 in 1932 and Mickey Mantle had one of .705 in 1957, was Fox 7 percent superior? The answer is no, and the reason is in the higher slugging average of the AL in 1932.

Well, how about on base percentage? (To calculate this stat, divide hits, walks, and hit-by-pitch by hits, at-bats, walks, hit-by-pitch, and sacrifice flies.) On base percentage has the advantage of giving credit for walks and hit-by-pitch, but it is an unweighted average and thus makes no distinction between those two events and, say, a grand-slam homer. A fellow like Eddie Yost, who, in some years when he hit under .250, drew nearly a walk a game, gets his credit with this stat as does a Gene Tenace, one of those guys whose statistical line looks puny without his walks. Similarly, players like Mickey Rivers or Omar Moreno, leadoff hitters with a lot of speed, no power, and no patience, are exposed by the OBP as distinctly marginal major leaguers, even in years when their batting averages look respectable or excellent. In short, on base percentage does tell you more about a man's ability to get on than does the batting average, and thus is a better indicator of run generation, but it's not enough by itself to separate the "good" hitters from the "average" or "poor" ones.

Not by itself, no . . . but when you add it to slugging average, you come up with a very powerful indicator of batting ability. These two one-legged men, when joined together, make for a very sturdy tandem, the infirmity of the one being almost exactly compensated by the power of the other. The virtues of on base plus slugging, a combined stat called Production, are that it is easily computed from officially issued stats and that it is the most accurate of all the newer stats except those denominated directly in runs. Its weaknesses are that because it is stated as the sum of two averages, it is—like a batting average or earned run average or any other average—a measure of the *rate* of success rather than the *amount,* and the fan needs considerable context to know what it means. Is a Production mark of .750 poor, average, or outstanding? (Answer: pretty good, because the league average figure in recent years has been in the low .700s—although in the NL of 1930 it exceeded .800.)

This second drawback may be eliminated in the same manner for all averages: by normalizing, or adjusting, each individual performance to the league average in that category for

the year in which it took place. If a batter's Production was .700 in a year when the league average was .700, he performed at a rate of 100 (his Production divided by the league's, discarding the decimal point for ease of expression). If his Production was .800, his league-adjusted mark would be 114. The meaningfulness of that performance might be further refined by adjusting it once more, to take into account the run-producing characteristics of the man's home park: a batter whose home park was a hitters' haven like Wrigley Field might have his Production adjusted downward, while another playing half his games in the Astrodome might have his adjusted upward. In *Total Baseball,* all figures adjusted for league average and park factor are denoted by "/A" following the raw figure, and the Park Factor (PF) is expressed with a baseline of 100—a hitter's park might have a factor of 110, a pitcher's park 90.

RBIs? Don't they indicate run production and clutch ability? Yes and no. The RBI does tell you something about run-producing ability, but not enough: it's a situation-dependent statistic, inextricably tied to factors which vary wildly for individuals on the same team or on others (including, importantly, the position of each player in the batting order). And the RBI makes no distinction between being hit by a pitch to drive in the twelfth run of a game that concludes 14–3 and, again for comparison, the Thomson blast. RBIs tell how many runs a batter pushed across the plate, all right, but they don't tell how many fewer he might have driven in had he batted eighth rather than fourth, or how many more he might have driven in on a team that put more men on base. They don't even tell how many more runs a batter might have driven in if he had delivered a higher proportion of his hits with men on base.

The American League kept RBI Opportunities—men on base presented to each batter—as an official stat for the first three weeks of 1918, then saw how much work was involved and ditched it. The problem remains: how to assess run productivity for batters. Pitchers are easier. Their accomplishments are directly measured in runs allowed. But batters, base runners, and fielders make their contributions in the constituent parts of runs—outs, hits, and a variety of more or less successful other events. (Even a batter who hits a solo homer contributes more than one run to his team, because he permits another player to bat who otherwise would not have, and each batter has a potential for producing further runs.)

You hear a lot in the media about the value of Runs Produced, a stat we track in *Total Baseball* in the top five section of the Annual Record. Runs Produced is simply runs scored plus runs batted in, subtracting homers because a dinger gives a batter "double credit"—a run scored plus an RBI. The editors view Runs Produced as an odd linkage of one opportunity-dependent stat with another that depends upon largely the same factors, but we offer the stat for those who like that sort of thing.

And so we come to the newly formulated game-winning RBI (GWRBI)—a noble attempt at describing the value of a hit to the team, its "clutchness," but a measure which was misconceived in its presumption that a game could be won with a hit in the first inning. A man who drives in a run in the first inning is simply doing his job, not performing an extraordinary feat; if the pitcher makes that run hold up by throwing a shutout, bully for him, but why credit the hitter? Were he to drive in the lone run of the game in the seventh inning or later, that would be different. Nonetheless, the cur-

rent formulation of the stat would give the man who drove in that first-inning run a GWRBI even if his team eventually won 22–0, since it gave the team a lead that was never relinquished.

Worse, the GWRBI is situation-dependent to an even greater degree than the RBI. You can't play for a lousy team and lead the league in GWRBIs because there aren't enough games won to go around. And it's even harder to accumulate GWRBIs from the eighth place in the batting order than it is to accumulate RBIs. Last, if you put your team ahead with an RBI in the bottom of the eighth, why should you lose your GWRBI simply because the pitcher allows the lead to be lost? Wasn't your hit "clutch"? Say the pitcher allows the score to be tied, then a teammate might pick up the GWRBI that should have been safely tucked away for you. Nicely motivated, the GWRBI, but utterly without merit and thus absent from *Total Baseball.*

We do, however, present a measure called Clutch Hitting Index, which addresses the problem of run-producing opportunities on a historical basis. We offer this with several reservations, including the classic philosophical one about whether clutch ability exists at all. Is a man who hits .280 with men on base and .240 with the sacks clear a hero in the former situation or a bum in the latter? The Clutch Hitting Index measures actual RBIs over expected RBIs, which have been calculated on the basis of a man's extra-base hits and the opportunities he could have been expected to have, based on the average RBIs per league and where he batted in the lineup and who batted above him. This is, by admission, a rough measure indeed, but we think it's an interesting one. For teams, the measure of clutch hitting is more elegant: the ratio of its actual runs to its runs as calculated by the Linear Weights method.

Previously discussed were Runs Created, Total Average, and Batting Runs. Total Average numbers will tend to look like those of Production, which measures largely the same things only in a different manner. The numerical expression of Runs Created exceeds that of Batting Runs, except that its baseline of zero defines the worst player in the league rather than the average one.

Base Stealing

Many fans understand, as a result of sabermetric findings of the 1980s, that a man with a lot of stolen bases is not necessarily the best base runner, nor even an asset to his team; he might have been caught nearly as often as he stole and thus may have cost his team many runs on balance. The game's encyclopedic reference works have in years past contained stolen base totals, even if the tabulations for the early years were suspect because of unclear standards for what differentiated a steal from clever base running. What they have not offered is the flip side of the steal—the caught-stealing numbers that make sense of the steal itself.

As mentioned above, caught stealing was recorded officially in the AL beginning in 1920, then was dropped for 1927, was resumed in 1928, and has been continuously in use ever since. In the NL, it was computed for 1920–1925, then was dropped until 1951, when it resumed on a continuous basis. We also have figures kept by Ernie Lanigan for the years 1914–1916 in the AL and for 1915–1916 in the NL. In *Total Baseball* we present, for those years in which the data exists, the raw CS data, Stolen Base Averages, and Stolen

Base Runs. This last is expressed in runs, based on the computer-derived value of .30 runs for a stolen base and −.60 runs for a thwarted steal. To make a positive contribution to his team, a base thief must be successful in more than two-thirds of his attempts.

Fielding

When, back in 1954, Rickey and Roth came up with their "efficiency formula" for run scoring and run prevention, the defensive half of the equation was divided into five segments. The first was opponents' batting average; the second was opponents' reaching base through bases on balls or hit batsmen; the third was a measure of a pitcher's clutch ability; the fourth was his strikeout capability; and the fifth was fielding, to which they assigned a mathematical value of zero. "There is nothing on earth," Rickey declared, "anyone can do with fielding." Besides, he added, good fielding might account for the critical run in a ballgame only four or five times a year.

Was Rickey right? The central weakness of the fielding average has long been known: you can't make an error on a ball you don't touch. To counter this weakness in fielding average and to credit the plays made as well as the plays not made, total chances per game is a more useful statistic—and when errors are deducted from chances, you have a fielder's Range Factor. James pointed out how absurd it had become, in a time when the best-fielding second baseman might commit ten errors a season and the worst twenty, to focus on this difference of ten rather than on the 250–300 in total chances which might separate the most agile keystoner from the exemplar of Lot's wife.

Another difficulty with the fielding average is that to understand what figure represents mean performance (and thus be able to identify inferior and superior fielders), one must adjust for position: a shortstop who fields .980 has done quite well, but a first baseman, catcher, or outfielder with that figure would have been below average. Thus the fan must bring to the fielding average a great deal of background knowledge— the mean for each fielding average for each position. This is a demand that, on first reflection, is not created by the batting average (all men stepping to the plate occupy the same position—batter). On second thought, however, the knowledgeable fan recognizes that a batting line of .267, 10 HRs, 80 RBIs will mean different things when applied to a shortstop or to a left fielder. In other words, just as any evaluation of fielding performance carries an inherent positional bias, so does batting performance.

High double-play totals are believed to indicate excellence among middle infielders, but the more double plays a club turns, as a rule, the worse the pitching. Which teams had the most double plays in major league history? In the 154-game season, the Philadelphia A's of 1949 and the Los Angeles Dodgers of 1958; in the 162-game season, Toronto and Boston of 1980 and Pittsburgh of 1966. Of these, only the last-mentioned had a team ERA better than the league average. If the pitchers are putting a lot of men on base, the team can get a lot of double plays even without a great-fielding shortstop and second baseman.

So what to do? How do we assess fielding excellence? The idea of crediting stellar fielding plays individually has been proposed occasionally ever since 1868, when Chadwick wrote: "The best player in a nine is he who makes the most good plays in a match, not the one who commits the fewest errors, and it is in the record of his good plays that we are to look for the most correct data for an estimate of his skill in the position he occupies." Father Chadwick was correct to see that fielding percentage emphasized failure rather than success, but in truth the fielding percentage was a far better measure of ability in the 1860s, when one play in four produced an error, than now, when only two plays in a hundred are flubbed.

The choice in *Total Baseball* has been to concentrate on Total Chances but not to disregard the error, as Range Factor does; nor to include it in Total Chances, as David Neft would favor; nor to subtract it from Total Chances, as Barry Codell once advocated. The error may be infrequent today but it is not insignificant; instead, it is a peculiarly damaging event, turning an out (with its computer-derived run value of −.25) to, in effect, a hit (with its run value of +.50). This is a turnaround of .75 runs, or *the equivalent of three outs;* an outfield error costs even more, because it so often produces more than one base for batter and runners both. Thus the defensive stats we employ in this book are Linear Weights formulas, expressed in runs and computed differently for the different positions (see the Glossary for formulas). However, in all cases the elements of the statistics are putouts, assists, double plays, and errors (and for catchers, passed balls).

Position players are gauged by Fielding Runs, a Linear Weights measure of the runs they saved (or allowed) through their play that an average man *at that position* would not have (second baseman are compared with other second baseman rather than, say, with left fielders—even the worst-fielding second sacker would cost his teams fewer runs at the position than the best defensive left fielder). Pitcher Defense (like Pitcher Batting) is to be found in the Pitcher Register.

Pitching

On to the pitching statistics you will see in the Annual Record and Pitcher Register. First to be reviewed are wins and losses, and won-lost percentage. Wins are a team statistic, obviously, as are losses, but we credit a win entirely to one pitcher in each game. Why not to the shortstop? Or the left fielder? Or some combination of the three? In a 13–11 game, several players may have had more to do with the win than any pitcher. No matter. We're not going to change this custom, though Ban Johnson gave it a good try when he banished it from the American League records for seven years beginning in 1913.

To win many games a pitcher generally must play for a team that wins many games. Look at Red Ruffing's won-lost record with the miserable Red Sox of the 1930s, then at his mark with the Yankees. Or at Danny Jackson, first with Kansas City, then with Cincinnati. There is an endless list of good pitchers traded to stronger offensive clubs who "emerge" as stars.

The recognition of the weakness of this statistic came early. Originally it was not computed by such men as Chadwick because most teams leaned heavily, if not exclusively, on one starter, and relievers as we know them today did not exist. As the season schedules lengthened, the need for a pitching staff became evident, and separating out the team's record on the basis of who was in the box seemed a good idea. However, it was not then nor is it now a good measure of performance, for the simple reason that one may pitch poorly and win, or pitch well and lose.

The natural corrective to this deficiency of the won-lost percentage is the earned run average—which, strangely, preceded it, gave way to it in the 1880s, and then returned in 1912. Originally, the ERA was computed as earned runs per game because pitchers almost invariably went nine innings. In this century it has been calculated as earned runs times nine, divided by innings pitched.

The purpose of the earned run average is noble: to give a pitcher credit for doing what *he* can to prevent runs from scoring, aside from his own fielding lapses and those of the men around him. It succeeds to a remarkable extent in isolating the performance of the pitcher from his situation, but objections to the statistic remain. Say a pitcher retires the first two men in an inning, then has the shortstop kick a ground ball to allow the batter to reach first base. Six runs follow before the third out is secured. How many of these runs are earned? None.

The prime difficulty with the ERA in the early days, say 1913, when one of every four runs scored was unearned, was that a pitcher got a lot of credit in his ERA for playing with a bad defensive club. The errors would serve to cover up in the ERA a good many runs which probably should not have scored. Those runs would hurt the team, but not the pitcher's record. This situation has been aggravated further by the use of newly computed ERAs for pitchers prior to 1913, the first year of its official status. Example: Bobby Mathews, sole pitcher for the New York Mutuals of 1876, allowed 7.19 runs per game, yet his ERA was only 2.86—almost a perfect illustration of the league's 40 percent proportion of earned runs.

It is not an accident that pitchers of the dead-ball era of this century (1900–1919) dominate the lifetime and seasonal leaders tables in ERA. Yes, there were circumstances away from the mound that depressed batting, but the pitchers of that period also benefited mightily in the ERA column from the high number of errors, as compared to today. How to compare the ERA of an Ed Walsh or Three Finger Brown with a Frank Viola or a Dwight Gooden? As with batting stats, normalize the ERA to league average and adjust for home park effects. A pitcher from 1908 whose Adjusted ERA was 150 can be compared to one from 1988 with the same Adjusted ERA—each stood in the same relation to his peers, that is, 50 percent better than average.

What gave rise to the ERA, and what we appreciate about it, is that like the batting average it is an attempt at an isolating stat, a measure of individual performance not dependent upon one's own team. Its principal shortcoming is that it indicates only a pitcher's *rate* of efficiency, not his actual benefit to the team. In a league with an ERA of 4.00, a starter who throws 300 innings with an ERA of 3.50 must be worth more to his team than a starter whose ERA is the same but who pitches in only half as many innings. Through the Linear Weights figures of Pitching Runs (broken out in the top-five section of the Annual Record as Starter Runs and Relief Runs), we can determine the number of runs a pitcher saved his team beyond what a pitcher performing at the league-average ERA would have allowed. A truly simple stat, it consists of nothing more than a pitcher's normalized, or league-adjusted, earned run average weighted by his innings pitched.

Because Pitching Runs has a built-in normalizing factor, when you see it in *Total Baseball* under a heading for "/A," that adjustment will be for park factor. Pitchers' park factor is calculated differently from batters' park factor, for a number of fairly complex reasons that technical-minded readers might best consult in the Glossary.

While the ERA is a far more accurate reflection of a pitcher's value than the BA is of a hitter's, it fails to a greater degree than the BA in offering an isolated measure. For a truly unalloyed individual pitching measure, we must look to the glamour statistic of strikeouts, the pitcher's mate to the home run (though home runs are highly dependent upon home park, strikeouts are to only a slight degree).

Is a strikeout artist a good pitcher? Maybe yes, maybe no; a good analogue would be to ask whether a home run slugger is a good hitter. The two stats run together: periods of high home run activity (as a percentage of all hits) invariably are accompanied by high strikeout totals. Strikeout totals, however, may soar even in the absence of overzealous swingers, say, as the result of a rules change such as the legalization of overhand pitching in 1884, the introduction of the foul strike (NL, 1901; AL, 1903), or the expanded strike zone in 1963.

Just as home run totals are a function of the era in which one plays, so are strikeouts. The great nineteenth-century totals—Matches Kilroy's 513, Toad Ramsey's 499, One Arm Daily's 483—were achieved under different rules and fashions. No one in that era fanned batters at the rate of one per inning; indeed, among regular pitchers (those with 154 innings pitched or more), only Herb Score did until 1960. In the next five years the barrier was passed by Sandy Koufax, Jim Maloney, Bob Veale, Sam McDowell, and Sonny Siebert. Walter Johnson, Rube Waddell, and Bob Feller didn't run up numbers like that. Were they slower, or easier to hit, than Sonny Siebert?

Even in today's game, which lends itself to the accumulation of, by historic standards, high strikeout totals for a good many pitchers and batters, the strikeout is, as it always has been, just another way to make an out. Yes, it is a sure way to register an out without the risk of advancing base runners and so is highly useful in a situation such as when there is a man on third with fewer than two outs; otherwise, it is a vastly overrated stat because it has nothing to do with victory or defeat—it is mere spectacle. A high strikeout total indicates raw talent and overpowering stuff, but the imperative of the pitcher is simply to retire the batter, not to crush him. What's not listed in your daily averages are strikeouts by batters—fans are not as interested in that because it's a negative measure—yet the strikeout may be a more significant stat for batters than it is for pitchers.

Bases on balls will drive a manager crazy and put lead in fielders' feet, but it is possible to survive, even to excel, without first-rate control—provided your stuff is good enough to hold down the number of hits. *Total Baseball* offers two stats that are, like strikeouts, highly interesting but ultimately of debatable value: Opponents' Batting Average and Opponents' On Base Percentage. (The same could be said of Fewest Hits Per Game and Fewest Walks Per Game, of course.) It is illuminating to compare one or the other with a pitcher's ERA or Pitching Runs, but both calculations are somewhat academic, for at the end of a game, season, or career, it doesn't matter how many men a pitcher puts on base. Theoretically he can put three men on every inning, leave the twenty-seven base runners allowed, and pitch a shutout. A man who gives up one hit over nine innings can lose 1–0; it's even possible to allow no hits and lose. Who is the better pitcher? The man with the shutout and twenty-seven base

runners allowed, or the man who allows one hit? No matter how sophisticated your measurements for pitchers, the best ones are counted in runs.

The nature of baseball at all points is one man against nine. It's the pitcher against a series of batters. With that situation prevailing, we have tended to examine batting with intricate, ingenious stats, while viewing pitching through generally much weaker, though perhaps more copious, measurements. What if the game were to be turned around so that we had a "pitching order"— nine pitchers facing one batter? Think of that for a minute. The nature of the statistics would change, too, so that your batting stats would be vastly simplified. You wouldn't care about all the individual components of the batter's performance, all combining in some obscure fashion to reveal run production. You'd care only about *runs*. Yet what each of the nine pitchers did would bear intense scrutiny, and over the course of a year each pitcher's Opponents' Batting Average, Opponents' On Base Percentage, Opponents' Slugging Average, and so forth, would be recorded and spun to come up with a sense of how many runs each pitcher had saved.

A pitching stat with an interesting history is complete games. This is your basic counter stat, but it's taken to mean more than most of those measurements by baseball people and knowledgeable fans. When everyone was completing 90–100 percent of his starts, the stat was without meaning and thus was not kept. As relief pitchers crept into the game after 1905, the percentage of completed games declined rapidly. By the 1920s it became a point of honor to complete three quarters of one's starts; today the man who completes half is quite likely to lead his league. So with these shifting standards, what do CGs tell you? About pitchers, not a lot anymore: about managers and bullpens, a great deal.

Can we say that a pitcher with 18 complete games out of 37 starts is better than one with 12 complete games in 35 starts? Not without a lot of supporting help, we can't, not without a store of knowledge about the individuals, the teams, and especially the eras involved. The more uses to which we attempt to put the stat, the weaker it becomes, the more attenuated its force. If we declare the hurler with 18 CGs "better," how are we to compare him with another pitcher from, say, fifty years earlier who completed 27 out of 30 starts? Or another pitcher of eighty years ago who completed all the games he started? (Jack W. Taylor completed every one of the 187 games he started *over five years*.) Or what about Will White, who in 1880 started 75 games and completed every blessed one of them? But the rules were different, you say, or the ball was less resilient, or they pitched from a different distance, with a different motion, or this, or that. The point is, there are limits to what a traditional, unadjusted baseball statistic can tell you about a player's performance in any given year, let alone compare his efforts to those of a player from a different era.

Of shutouts there is little to say that is not perfectly obvious, except that historical totals have been revised because (a) in 1920–1939 the American League did not count games of less than nine innings as shutouts, and (b) in those years and before, in both leagues, a pitcher was credited with a shutout even if he was pulled midway, if he had pitched enough innings of a combined whitewash. *Total Baseball* counts only complete-game shutouts.

Wins Above Team is, as discussed, a variation of Ted Oliver's stat made public in 1944, which he called the Weighted Rating System. Apart from modifying his math, we have taken Oliver's "points"—the thousands of points his formula gave to hurlers who performed well for poor teams—and by retaining the decimal that he would have discarded, we have come up with a stat that is expressed quite properly in wins.

Newly developed for this book was a Clutch Pitching Index that, like the measure for clutch hitting, could be applied to historical data. The CPI is figured by taking how many earned runs the pitcher should have allowed, based on the performance of the batters who faced him, and how many he actually allowed (see the Glossary for the formula). The Clutch Pitching Index consists of expected runs over actual runs, so marks over 100 exceed league-average performance.

For relief pitchers, we have previously discussed saves, and Relief Runs (the Linear Weights category) are figured no differently than Starter Runs, except that eligibility for the category is limited to those hurlers who averaged less than three innings per appearance. Newly developed here is Relief Ranking, which adjusts Relief Runs for the greater situational importance of each run a bullpenner saves or yields. The other elements of the formula are wins, losses, and saves, in a proportion detailed in the Glossary.

Bringing It All Together

Pitcher Batting and Pitcher Defense are recorded in the Pitcher Register as Linear Weights figures, expressed in runs. (Pitcher batting has been removed from league stats for such computations, so that the batting records of everyday players are compared only with those of their peers and pitchers' batting records are compared only with those of *their* peers. The totals are seldom of a great magnitude—and for AL pitchers since 1973, the batting figure is, of course, zero—but in earlier years a pitcher's ability to help himself and his team off the mound has occasionally counted for a great deal in a given season; spitballer Ed Walsh in 1907, the year before he won 40 games for the White Sox, accounted for an astounding 2.3 Fielding Wins. The hitting ability of a Wes Ferrell or Don Drysdale certainly counted for something in their teams' prospects for victory. In *Total Baseball* a pitcher's overall contribution is reflected in the Total Pitcher Index, converted from Runs above average to Wins, based on the Runs required to create an extra Win in that year.

For everyday position players, add Fielding Runs to Stolen Base Runs to Batting Runs, then convert those combined Runs to Wins, and you have the best measure of the complete ballplayer: the Total Player Rating. We believe, however, that a positional adjustment must be deducted from the above combination to reflect the greater skill required to play, for example, second base than left field; this adjustment is based on the average batting skill required at that position to hold a major league job. Historically, left fielders have presented the best record in Batting Runs and middle infielders the worst. In other words, a left fielder who accounted for 10 Fielding Runs should not be regarded as having the same value to a team as a shortstop who also contributed 10 Fielding Runs: Have the two men switch positions and you would soon see who made more of a defensive contribution. And because some positions—shortstop, catcher, second base, and third base—are harder to play than others, we see a relative scarcity of good hitters at these positions and an abundance at the others. Again, see the Glossary for more detail.

The ultimate stat brings together batters, pitchers, fielders,

and base runners in the Total Baseball Ranking. The equivalent of a Most Valuable Player Award and Cy Young Award wrapped into one, it reveals the best baseball player every season and the best ever. Relief pitchers and shortstops can compete on the same plane—wins contributed to their team through all their accomplishments. In 1978 the MVP question in the American League was whether to vote for Jim Rice, who had 46 homers, 139 RBIs, and 400 total bases (the first time for an American Leaguer in forty-one years), or for Ron Guidry, 25–3 with an .893 won-lost percentage that was the all-time high for a starter with 20 or more wins, and whose ERA of 1.74 was less than half the league average. Why don't you flip to the page in the Annual Record for 1978 and see for yourself who deserved the MVP Award that year.

Total Baseball also sums things up on the team level. Fielding Runs are expressed as Wins in the team stats section of the Annual Record, as are Batting Runs, Stolen Base Runs, and Pitching Runs. This enables one to see the component parts of a team's predicted success or failure—that is, the wins or losses beyond the average (a .500 season) that the players' performance could have been expected to produce. The Differential figure (DIF) in this section of the Annual Record states the spread between the team's actual won-lost record and that predicted by the Linear Weights measures of batting, base stealing, fielding, and pitching. The miracle Mets of 1969 exceeded expectations by 13 Wins—in other words, instead of finishing 87–75 as their players' performance would have warranted, they finished 100–62. Did the Dodgers also do it with mirrors in 1988? Check for yourself.

Errors and Controversies

The data ICI reported in the first edition of *The Baseball Encyclopedia* upset many people in baseball, for their numbers were different from those traditionally accepted; however, their changes were responsible ones, the product of new research that corrected errors of long standing, or in response to the rulings of the Special Baseball Records Committee. For example, much of the statistical information on Hall of Fame plaques was rendered obsolete. The result has been that through the ensuing editions, the offending data has been fudged to bring it into line with tradition—more on this in a moment.

Despite the uproar that greeted ICI's revised numbers, 1969 was hardly the first time corrections had been made to official data. In 1929 Grover Cleveland Alexander won his 373rd game, breaking Christy Mathewson's National League record, then thought to be 372. He never won another game. A number of years later, Joe Reichler found a game in which, by today's rules, Matty should have gotten the win, this game taking place on May 21, 1902. The record was changed and they were given a tie. The problem was that no one checked all of Mathewson's other games to see how many times he received a win under the old rules that wouldn't have been credited that way today. When ICI did their research in 1968, they found Matty had only 367 wins total by today's rules, while Alexander had 374. The Records Committee decided that all wins and losses should be awarded according to the present rules, so Macmillan printed the totals as such in the *Baseball Encyclopedia*. However, after the book came out, Commissioner Bowie Kuhn decided that it was better to show stats that agreed with previously published recognized sources, so all records—not only those of Mathewson and

Alexander—were supposed to be changed back in accordance with the scoring practices at the time. What happened in the next edition was that some records, especially those of the stars, were changed, while others were not; team totals and the records of other players on the same team were not; and the data base was corrupted.

Here's another celebrated example of record-book flip-flops. When the American League was formed in 1901, Nap Lajoie was credited with a .422 average, with 220 hits in 543 at-bats. After a number of years, someone noticed that if you take these at-bats and hits, the average comes out only to .405, so his average was changed. (Turkin/Thompson gave Nap a mark of .409 in its first edition.) Later in the 1950s, John Tattersall had his doubts and decided to go through his newspaper collection of box scores. He found 229 hits for Lajoie, not 220—the error had been in the figure for hits, not in the figure for batting average. Thus his average was restored to .422, which happened to be the highest in American League history. Then ICI research in this area came up with a .426 mark (232 for 544, based on newspaper accounts), which was published in the first edition, then trimmed back to .422 in subsequent editions. The .426 figure is the one this book uses.

Nap seemed to be involved in a number of controversies. ICI research found four more hits for him in 1902, raising his average from .369 to .378, passing Ed Delahanty, the only player thought to have led both leagues in batting. Later editions have changed Lajoie's stats back to the old values; we have not.

In 1910 there was a very close batting race between Cobb and Lajoie. At the end of the season, most people thought Nap had won, based on his getting seven hits in a doubleheader on the final day of the season. There was talk that the opposing Browns had let him get a number of bunts by playing back, so that the hated Cobb would lose. However, the AL office went over their figures and gave Cobb the title, .385 to .384. Nearly eighty years later, Pete Palmer discovered a critical error: a game in which Cobb had two hits in three at-bats had been entered twice. This was found because Sam Crawford had 157 games on his official sheet yet the Tigers only played 156. It turned out that Detroit played a doubleheader on September 24, but the second game inadvertently was inserted in the official sheets as being played on September 25. Later, this second game of the twenty-fourth, which appeared to have been missing, was put in the scoresheets again. The League Office discovered this mistake soon after its official announcement that Cobb had won the batting title, because the double entry was corrected for all the other Detroit players. However, Ban Johnson had made a big deal out of how carefully his people had checked the figures in order to settle the controversy, so they kept quiet about the gaffe, leaving Cobb the winner.

Appeals to Commissioner Kuhn in 1981 to set the matter straight officially were to no avail, because that would not only have changed the outcome of the 1910 batting race, it would also have altered Cobb's lifetime hit total, then being pursued to massive media attention by Pete Rose. Kuhn's statement read, in part, "The passage of 70 years, in our judgment . . . constitutes a certain statute of limitation as to recognizing any changes in the records with confidence of the accuracy of such changes. . . . Since a variety of questions have been raised through the years about the accuracy of the statistics of that period, the only way to make changes with

confidence would be for a complete and thorough review of all team and individual statistics. That is not practical." It may not have not been practical, but we have done it.

In 1912, Heinie Zimmerman got credit for a Triple Crown victory, although it wasn't called that then. Ernie Lanigan's RBI figures gave him 98, compared to 94 for Honus Wagner. However, ICI research gave Wagner 102 and Zimmerman 99. Later editions of *The Baseball Encyclopedia* changed Zimmerman up to 103—giving him back his phony Triple Crown.

The National League batting data has been pretty accurate since 1910. That was the first year that the NL kept daily game records for teams as well as players and compared the team totals to the sum for the players for that team and tried to resolve any differences. Before then, the team totals simply *were* the sum for the players. The American League had team totals all the way back to 1905, but never compared them with the sum of the players and therefore had a great many errors. The AL, however, did introduce team pitching first in 1930, while the NL followed in 1941. The AL never published league totals, so the fact that the batter hits, strikeouts, walks, etc. did not agree with the corresponding pitcher totals was somewhat academic. However, the NL did publish league totals starting in 1926, and when they first presented team pitching, the totals did not agree. In order to make this look correct, they doctored the pitching totals to agree with the batting stats. After a few years, this was no longer necessary, as they took the time to resolve and correct differences. For the AL, most team totals did not agree with the sum of the players for that team until around 1935: the at-bats, runs, hits, and extra-base hits usually checked out, but walks and strikeouts did not add up until the 1960s. The AL converted to computer in 1973, while the NL did in 1981, improving accuracy.

On the whole there have been surprisingly few errors in the National League stats. Most of the bigger ones have involved innings pitched in the years before 1930. Because no one added up the innings and compared them to putouts to check for discrepancies, in 1926 Wayland Dean brought up the rear in ERA with a 6.10 mark. It turned out that his innings pitched had been added up incorrectly, and he should have had 204, not 164. This reduced his ERA to 4.90. For a game in 1920, Jimmy Ring had his faced batsman total of 35 put in the innings pitched column, giving him 26 extra innings pitched for the game. It would seem that someone adding up innings pitched would question a figure of 35 for one game, but it slipped through. Ring was also credited for nine extra innings in 1923. But the strangest mix-up in the NL was in 1909, the year before the team totals were kept. For some strange reason, 700 putouts were dropped from the team totals, all the result of adding mistakes for catchers. Pat Moran and Red Dooin each lost 200, while Peaches Graham, Bill Bergen, and Doc Marshall lost 100 each.

The American League has had many errors of 100 or more putouts or assists over the years due to addition mistakes, as well as quite a few blunders in innings pitched. Ed Willett in 1910 lost 77 innings, showing only 147 instead of 224. The correction lowered his ERA from 3.60 to 2.36. However, this was still more than a run behind the leader, Ed Walsh. Frank Williams discovered a dozen or more errors in entering wins and losses for pitchers in the AL *every year* from 1905 through 1919. And John Tattersall, in his home run research, found over 100 official errors, about 80 percent in the AL and

most before 1920. George Sisler picked up 3 new homers, These were on April 12, 1916, September 22, 1921, and June 29, 1929, giving him 102 instead of 99.

From 1912 to 1914, the AL statistician decided not to enter anything for a player who had all zeroes for his line in any given game. Most of these were relief pitchers, but they had entries on their pitching sheets and these games were restored by the ICI researchers. There were about 600 other cases where nonpitchers had games omitted. These are included in *Total Baseball*. This kind of record keeping over the early years kept some men out of the encyclopedias altogether, like pinch runners or defensive replacements. SABR research has added several of these one-time ciphers to *The Baseball Encyclopedia* over the years, and now adds two to *Total Baseball*.

For the American League records of 1913, the official sheets disagree with the data published in the baseball guides for almost every player. The only logical explanation is that the official figures weren't ready when it came time to publish the guide, so they must have used data from another source. *Total Baseball* uses the official figures, as they have daily sheets to support the data.

An interesting quirk in the way records are kept—and another reminder, as if one needed it, that baseball record keeping remains subject to error and controversy—occurred as recently as 1981. The league rule was to round off the innings pitched at the end of the season, although the weekly reports showed thirds of innings. Baltimore's Sammy Stewart had 29 earned runs in 112⅓ innings, while Oakland's Steve McCatty had 48 in 185⅔ innings. This gave Stewart the ERA title, 2.323 to 2.327. But when the innings were rounded off, McCatty won, 2.32 to 2.33. McCatty got the title, but the next year both leagues decided to count thirds of innings.

Sources

The computer has made possible the rapid analysis of mountains of raw baseball data based upon observed games or mathematically accurate, probabilistic computer simulations. Questions once thought to be unanswerable are mysteries no longer. What is the worth, in terms of its run-producing capacity, of a single, or a walk, or a homer? How valuable is a stolen base? Who were the best clutch hitters? But as invaluable as the computer has been in producing the statistical data for *Total Baseball,* the editors owe more to the people who have contributed their time, their expertise, their love of the game, and their passion for getting things right. These individuals are listed here or in the Acknowledgments. A collective debt is owed to the Society for American Baseball Research and the National Baseball Library.

The statistics were obtained primarily from the following sources:

- John Tattersall Collection of newspaper box scores and compilations for 1876–1890 NL.
- ICI computer printouts, National Baseball Library, 1891–1902 NL, 1882–1891 AA, 1884 UA, 1890 PL, 1901–1904 AL, 1914–1915 FL.
- Official league averages, 1903–date NL, 1905–date AL.

Supplemental sources were:

- For batters hit by pitch, 1884–1899 AA/NL/PL,

1909–1916 NL, 1909–1919 AL, research from newspapers by Alex Haas, Pete Palmer, John Schwartz, Bob Davids, John Tattersall, and others. (Note: research continues for the 1900–1908 period, as well as for the 1914–1915 FL.)

- For home runs allowed by pitchers, 1876–1950 AL/NL, the Tattersall Collection, reviewed and corrected by Bob McConnell.
- For runs batted in, 1903–1919 NL, 1905–1919 AL, ICI research.
- For runs batted in, 1880–1885 NL, David Neft.
- For pitcher saves (except 1901–1919 AL) 1876–1968 NL/AA/UA/PL/AL.
- For stolen bases, 1886 NL, *Spalding Baseball Guide*.
- For wins and losses for pitchers, 1876–1900 NL/AA/PL, and for wins, losses, games started, complete games, shutouts, saves, 1900–1919 AL, and complete pitching data, 1892, research from newspapers and official sheets by Frank Williams.
- For shutouts, 1920–1939 AL, Joe Wayman.
- For biographical data, the biographical research committee of SABR, notably Richard Topp, Bill Carle.
- For caught-stealing data, 1914–1916 AL, 1915–1916 NL, Ernie Lanigan, courtesy of Bob Davids.
- For home/away data, 1876–1891 NL/AA/UA/PL, Bob McConnell.
- For game scores, 1876–1884 NL/AA/UA, Bob Tiemann.

- For game scores, 1885–1891 NL/AA/PL, Richard Topp.
- For runs and homers home/away, 1980s NL/AL, Bill Carr.

Missing data includes:

- Hit batters: 1900–1908 AL; 1914–1915 FL.
- Caught stealing: 1886–1914, 1916 (players with more than 20 steals), 1917–1919, 1926–1950 NL; 1886–1891 AA; 1890 PL; 1901–1913, 1916 (players with more than 20 steals), 1917–1919, 1927 AL; 1914–15 FL.
- Sacrifice hits: 1927–1930 (fly balls advancing runners to any base counted as sacrifice hits).
- Sacrifice flies: 1908–1930, 1939, 1940–1953.
- Runs batted in, 1882–1887, 1890 AA; 1884 UA.
- Strikeouts for batters: 1882–1888, 1890 AA; 1884 UA; 1897–1909 NL; 1901–1912 AL.

Incomplete data for those years through 1902 NL and 1904 AL are available from the ICI computer printouts at the National Baseball Library. Additional research could turn up more data. For example, in 1887, Tip O'Neill had 103 runs batted in with about 90 percent of the games covered. If your research or sharp eye should detect errors or gaps in *Total Baseball*, please write us in care of the publisher and we'll be delighted to improve our data and credit your catch in the next edition.

The Annual Record

The Annual Record

This section contains the season-by-season standings and records for all teams since 1871, plus 36 statistical categories for each team's batting and baserunning, and 20 for its pitching. In those years in which major league play consisted of more than one league, the statistics are presented in the order of the leagues' founding: that is, the National League record precedes those of all its rivals; the American Association precedes the Union Association and Players League; and the American League follows the National League but precedes the Federal League.

The figure for the leading team in a given category is displayed in boldface. Where data are unavailable, the statistical column is blank. In the case of the National Association, so much data is missing that the records for the five years of its existence, 1871–1875, are presented in a more compact format. (A research project of the Society for American Baseball Research to reconstruct all data from this period, based on original box scores and play-by-plays collected over decades by Michael Stagno of New York, is in progress. It is hoped that new, authoritative records can be developed for the next edition of *Total Baseball*.)

Also presented here are the top three to five players/pitchers in up to 48 categories per season. When fewer than 48 categories are shown, it means that official records are lacking; that data are not reconstructible at present, such as is the case for records of stolen bases before 1886; or that available data are not meaningful, such as those for Relief Runs or Relief Ranking in the early years of this century. When fewer than five individuals appear in a given category, this signifies the lack of credible standouts, such as in the case of Stolen Base Wins in most years. The criterion used for identifying pitching leaders is a minimum of one inning pitched per scheduled game; for batters the criterion employed is the one officially in place at the time or, in the absence of any known practice, 3.1 plate appearances per scheduled game.

Ties in counting stats are common, and occasionally they are so numerous that space does not permit listing all the players by name; ties for fifth place are not shown. Highly uncommon are ties in those stats based on a large array of data, as with batting averages, on base percentages, earned run averages, and sabermetric stats such as Runs Created, Total Average, or the various Linear Weights measures. Where rounding off has created the appearance of a tie, the true leader—as extra decimal places for a complete calculation would have revealed—is listed first. An example is the AL batting race of 1949, in which George Kell and Ted Williams are both shown as hitting .343; Kell in fact hit .3429 and Williams .3428. Both men are credited with batting averages of .343, but Kell, the actual leader, is listed first. (This procedure does not hold for calculated stats based on pitchers' won-lost percentages, where the narrow array of data frequently produces actual ties.)

For additional useful information about a team in a given year, we refer the reader to the Home/Road section, the Player and Pitcher registers, and the various rosters. Team abbreviations used in the Annual Record are to be found on the last page of this book.

The abbreviations employed in the team statistical reviews of the Annual Record, plus brief descriptions of what the less common statistics measure, follow. For fuller explanations, see the general introduction to Part Two, and for more technical information about formulas and computation, see the Glossary. Also included below are descriptions of statistics not computed for teams but for which league-leading players are shown in the Annual Record.

Batting and Baserunning

G	Games played
W	Wins
L	Losses
PCT	Percentage of games won
GB	Games Behind the league or division leader
R	Runs scored
OR	Opponents' Runs scored
AB	At-Bats
H	Hits
2B	Doubles
3B	Triples
HR	Home Runs
BB	Bases on Balls
SO	Strikeouts
AVG	Batting Average
OBP	On Base Percentage
SLG	Slugging Average
PRO	Production (On Base Percentage plus Slugging Average; for PRO/A, normalized and park-adjusted Production, a mark of 100 is a league-average performance.)
BR	Batting Runs (Linear Weights measure of runs contributed *beyond* what a league-average batter or team might have contributed, defined as zero.)

PF	Park Factor (Calculated separately for batters and pitchers: above 100 signifies a park favorable to hitters, below 100 signifies a park favorable to pitchers; see Home/Road section and Glossary for further data and technical information.)
/A	Adjusted (Signifies that the stat to the immediate left is here normalized to league average and adjusted for home park factor. A mark of 100 is a league-average performance. Pitcher batting is removed from all league batting statistics before normalization, for a variety of reasons expanded upon in the Glossary.)
CHI	Clutch Hitting Index (Actual RBIs over expected RBIs, adjusted for league average and position in batting order; marks above the median of 100 are superior. See Glossary for precise formula.)
RC	Runs Created (Bill James's formulation for run contribution from a variety of batting and baserunning events; many different formulas are applied, depending on data available; see Glossary.)
TA	Total Average (Tom Boswell's formulation for offensive contribution from a variety of batting and baserunning events; calculated to make use of the maximum available data.)
SB	Stolen Bases (1886 to the present.)
CS	Caught Stealing (Available 1915, 1916 for players with more than 20 steals, 1920–1925, 1951–date NL; 1914–1915, 1916 for players with more than 20 steals, 1920–1926, 1928–date AL.)
SBA	Stolen Base Average (Stolen bases divided by attempts; availability dependent upon CS, as shown above.)
SBR	Stolen Base Runs (Linear weights measure of runs contributed *beyond* what a league-average base stealer or team might have gained, defined as zero; individual SBRs are calculated on basis of 66.7 percent success rate, the rate necessary to produce benefit, while team SBRs are normalized to success rate for league in that season; availability dependent upon CS.)

Pitching and Fielding

CG	Complete Games
SHO	Shutouts (Individual and combined when calculated for teams; individual only for top five leaders.)
SV	Saves (Employing definition in force at the time, and 1969 definition for years prior to 1969.)
IP	Innings Pitched (Fractional innings given for teams; rounded-off whole innings for individuals.)

H	Hits allowed
H/G	Hits allowed per Game (Game defined as nine innings.)
HR	Home Runs allowed
BB	Bases on Balls allowed
BB/G	Bases on Balls per Game (Game defined as nine innings; league leaders calculated on basis of fewest Bases on Balls per nine innings.)
SO	Strikeouts
SO/G	Strikeouts per Game (Game defined as nine innings; league leaders calculated on basis of most strikeouts per nine innings.)
ERA	Earned Run Average (For ERA/A, normalized and park-adjusted ERA, a mark of 100 is a league-average performance, while marks over 100 are superior to league average and those below 100 indicate poor pitching performance.)
OAVG	Opponents' Batting Average
OOBA	Opponents' On Base Average (Percentage)
PR	Pitching Runs (Linear Weights measure of runs saved *beyond* what a league-average pitcher or team might have saved, defined as zero.)
/A	Adjusted (Signifies that the stat to the immediate left is here normalized to league average and adjusted for home park factor.)
PF	Park Factor (Calculated separately for batters and pitchers; above 100 signifies a park favorable to hitters, below 100 signifies a park favorable to pitchers; see Home/Road section and Glossary for further data and technical information.)
CPI	Clutch Pitching Index (Expected runs over actual runs, with 100 being a league-average performance and marks above 100 indicate better than expected results. See Glossary.)
FA	Fielding Average
E	Errors
DP	Double Plays
FW	Fielding Wins (Fielding Runs divided by the number of runs required to create an additional win beyond average; average is defined as a team record of .500 because a league won-lost average must be .500. For more technical data about Runs Per Win and Fielding Run formulas, see Glossary.)
PW	Pitching Wins (Adjusted Pitching Runs divided by the number of runs required to create an additional win beyond average; average is defined as a team record of .500 because a league won-lost average must be .500. For more technical data about Runs Per Win and Pitching Run formulas, see Glossary.)

BW   Batting Wins (Adjusted Batting Runs divided by the number of runs required to create an additional win beyond average; average is defined as a team record of .500 because a league won-lost average must be .500. For more technical data about Runs Per Win and Batting Run formulas, see Glossary.)

SBW   Stolen Base Wins (Stolen Base Runs divided by the number of runs required to create an additional win beyond average; average is defined as a team record of .500 because a league won-lost average must be .500. For more technical data about Runs Per Win and Stolen Base Run formulas, see Glossary.)

DIF   Differential (Difference between the team's actual won-lost record and that predicted by the total of its Pitching Wins, Batting Wins, Fielding Wins, and Stolen Base Wins; indicates the extent to which a team outperformed or underperformed its talent.)

Other stats carried only on an individual basis in the Annual Record portion of *Total Baseball* are as follows.

Fielding Runs: the Linear Weights measure of runs saved *beyond* what a league-average player at that position might have saved, defined as zero; calculated to take account of the particular demands of the different positions. See Glossary for formulas.

Wins Above Team: How many wins a pitcher garnered beyond those expected of an average pitcher for that team. As the editors of this volume, in their earlier *Hidden Game of Baseball*, modified Ted Oliver's Weighted Rating System, they now improve this statistic thanks to Bill Deane's corrective for its tendency to overvalue the contributions of good pitchers on awful teams. See Glossary for formulas.

Starter Runs: Identical to Pitching Runs but confined to starting pitchers, defined as pitchers who average more than three innings per appearance.

Relief Runs: Identical to Pitching Runs but confined to relief pitchers, defined as pitchers who average less than three innings per appearance.

Relief Ranking: Adjusted Relief Runs, weighted for the greater value of a bullpen "closer" who limits his opponents' scoring in the late innings; see Glossary for formula. Relief Runs will tend to benefit long and middle relievers, who are effective over many innings, while Relief Ranking will tend to benefit relievers with perhaps fewer innings but more saves and decisions.

Total Player Rating: The sum of a player's Adjusted Batting Runs, Fielding Runs, and Base Stealing Runs, minus his positional adjustment, all divided by the Runs Per Win factor for that year (generally around 10, historically in the 9–11 range).

Total Pitcher Index: The sum of a pitcher's Pitching Runs, Batting Runs (in the AL since 1973, zero), and Fielding Runs, all divided by the Runs Per Win factor for that year (generally around 10, historically in the 9–11 range).

Total Baseball Ranking: The "MVP" of statistics, this ranks pitchers and position players by the total runs contributed in all their endeavors, revealing the most valuable performers in a given year. For rare individuals like Babe Ruth in his Red Sox years or Bob Caruthers, who played a position in the field when they were not pitching, the TPR will sum up their records in both endeavors.

1871 NATIONAL ASSOCIATION

TEAM	G	W	L	PCT	R	AB	H	AVG	
ATH	29	22	7	.759	367	1331	412	**.310**	PHILADELPHIA Athletics
CHI	29	20	9	.690	302	1250	316	.253	CHICAGO White Stockings
BOS	33	22	10	.688	401	1438	424	.295	BOSTON Red Stockings
OLY	33	16	15	.516	310	1400	371	.265	WASHINGTON Olympics
TRO	31	15	15	.500	353	1302	370	.284	TROY Haymakers
MUT	35	17	18	.486	302	1428	392	.275	NEW YORK Mutuals
CLE	29	10	19	.345	249	1214	326	.269	CLEVELAND Forest City
KEK	28	7	21	.250	137	765	179	.234	FORT WAYNE Kekiongas
ROK	27	6	21	.222	231	1081	273	.253	ROCKFORD Forest City
TOT	137				2652	11209	3063	.273	

Runs		Hits		Batting Average	
Barnes-Bos	66	Meyerle-Ath	65	Meyerle-Ath	.492
Birdsall-Bos	51	McVey-Bos	65	McVey-Bos	.419
Radcliff-Ath	47	Barnes-Bos	65	King-Tro	.396
Cuthbert-Ath	47	King-Tro	57	Barnes-Bos	.378
Waterman-Oly	46	Start-Mut	56	Anson-Rok	.352

Games Pitched		Wins		Win Percentage	
Wolters-Mut	32	Spalding-Bos	20	McBride-Ath	.800
Spalding-Bos	31	McBride-Ath	20	Zettlein-Chi	.667
Brainard-Oly	30	Zettlein-Chi	18	Spalding-Bos	.667
McMullin-Tro	29	Wolters-Mut	16	Wolters-Mut	.500
Pratt-Cle	28				

1872 NATIONAL ASSOCIATION

TEAM	G	W	L	PCT	R	AB	H	AVG	
BOS	48	39	8	.830	521	2176	671	**.308**	BOSTON Red Stockings
ATH	47	30	14	.682	534	2209	659	.298	PHILADELPHIA Athletics
BAL	57	34	19	.642	597	2561	717	.280	BALTIMORE Lord Baltimores
MUT	56	34	20	.630	523	2503	681	.272	NEW YORK Mutuals
TRO	25	15	10	.600	272	1123	333	.297	TROY Haymakers
CLE	21	6	15	.286	171	957	283	.296	CLEVELAND Forest City
ATL	35	8	27	.229	220	1452	334	.230	BROOKLYN Atlantics
OLY	9	2	7	.222	54	372	93	.250	WASHINGTON Olympics
MAN	24	5	19	.208	223	1013	277	.273	MIDDLETOWN Mansfields
ECK	29	3	26	.103	151	1133	233	.205	BROOKLYN Eckfords
NAT	11	0	11	.000	80	451	108	.239	WASHINGTON Nationals
TOT	181				3346	15950	4389	.275	

Runs		Hits		Batting Average	
Eggler-Mut	95	Eggler-Mut	102	Force-Tro-Bal	.412
Wright-Bos	86	Barnes-Bos	97	Barnes-Bos	.404
Barnes-Bos	81	Force-Tro-Bal	93	Anson-Ath	.381
Cuthbert-Ath	80	Hatfield-Mut	90	Hastings-Cle-Bal	.349
Hatfield-Mut	75	Anson-Ath	88	Eggler-Mut	.346

Games Pitched		Wins		Win Percentage	
Cummings-Mut	55	Spalding-Bos	37	Spalding-Bos	.822
Spalding-Bos	48	Cummings-Mut	33	McBride-Ath	.682
McBride-Ath	46	McBride-Ath	30	Cummings-Mut	.623
Mathews-Bal	45	Mathews-Bal	25	Mathews-Bal	.610
Britt-Atl	35	Zettlein-Tro-Eck	15	Zettlein-Tro-Eck	.500

1873 NATIONAL ASSOCIATION

TEAM	G	W	L	PCT	R	AB	H	AVG	
BOS	60	43	16	.729	**739**	2878	**931**	.323	BOSTON Red Stockings
PHI	53	36	17	.679	526	2418	641	.265	PHILADELPHIA White Stockings
BAL	56	33	22	.600	624	2599	783	.301	BALTIMORE Lord Baltimores
ATH	52	28	23	.549	474	2387	671	.281	PHILADELPHIA Athletics
MUT	53	29	24	.547	424	2297	614	.267	NEW YORK Mutuals
ATL	55	17	37	.315	366	2310	583	.252	BROOKLYN Atlantics
NAT	39	8	31	.205	283	1629	406	.249	WASHINGTON Nationals
RES	23	2	21	.087	98	923	204	.221	ELIZABETH Resolutes
MAR	5	0	5	.000	16	184	26	.141	BALTIMORE Marylands
TOT	198				3550	17625	4859	.276	

Runs		Hits		Batting Average	
Barnes-Bos	126	Barnes-Bos	136	Barnes-Bos	.402
Wright-Bos	98	Wright-Bos	126	White-Bos	.382
Spalding-Bos	85	White-Bos	124	Wright-Bos	.378
Leonard-Bos	83	Spalding-Bos	105	Anson-Ath	.353
Eggler-Mut	83	O'Rourke-Bos	99	Pabor-Atl	.346

Games Pitched		Wins		Win Percentage	
Spalding-Bos	57	Spalding-Bos	41	Spalding-Bos	.732
Britt-Atl	54	Zettlein-Phi	36	Zettlein-Phi	.720
Mathews-Mut	51	Mathews-Mut	29	Cummings-Bal	.667
Zettlein-Phi	50	Cummings-Bal	28	Mathews-Mut	.569
McBride-Ath	46	McBride-Ath	25	McBride-Ath	.543

1874 NATIONAL ASSOCIATION

TEAM	G	W	L	PCT	R	AB	H	AVG	
BOS	71	52	18	.743	**735**	3155	**1033**	.327	BOSTON Red Stockings
MUT	65	42	23	.646	500	2808	708	.252	NEW YORK Mutuals
ATH	55	33	23	.689	441	2304	763	**.331**	PHILADELPHIA Athletics
PHI	58	29	29	.500	475	2537	683	.269	PHILADELPHIA White Stockings
CHI	59	28	31	.475	418	2565	674	.263	CHICAGO White Stockings
ATL	56	22	33	.400	301	2233	495	.222	BROOKLYN Atlantics
HAR	54	17	37	.315	371	2103	611	.291	HARTFORD
BAL	47	9	38	.191	227	1890	430	.228	BALTIMORE Lord Baltimores
TOT	233				3468	19595	5397	.275	

Runs		Hits		Batting Average	
McVey-Bos	90	McVey-Bos	131	McMullin-Ath	.387
Spalding-Bos	80	Spalding-Bos	121	McVey-Bos	.382
O'Rourke-Bos	80	Leonard-Bos	119	Hastings-Har	.371
Wright-Bos	75	O'Rourke-Bos	115	Meyerle-Chi	.369
White-Bos	112	Anson-Ath	367	Bond-Atl	.55

Games Pitched		Wins		Win Percentage	
Spalding-Bos	71	Spalding-Bos	52	Spalding-Bos	.743
Mathews-Mut	65	Mathews-Mut	42	Mathews-Mut	.646
Zettlein-Chi	57	McBride-Ath	33	McBride-Ath	.600
McBride-Ath	55	Cummings-Phi	28	Cummings-Phi	.519
Zettlein-Chi	27	Zettlein-Chi	.474		

1875 NATIONAL ASSOCIATION

TEAM	G	W	L	PCT	R	AB	H	AVG	
BOS	82	71	8	.899	**832**	3564	**1161**	.326	BOSTON Red Stockings
ATH	77	53	20	.726	699	3292	942	.286	PHILADELPHIA Athletics
HAR	86	54	28	.659	554	3466	863	.249	HARTFORD
STL	72	39	29	.574	385	2651	660	.249	ST.LOUIS Brown Stockings
PHI	70	37	31	.544	469	2645	683	.258	PHILADELPHIA White Stockings
CHI	69	30	37	.448	380	2832	709	.250	CHICAGO White Stockings
MUT	71	30	38	.441	328	2771	630	.227	NEW YORK Mutuals
RS	18	4	14	.222	55	670	121	.181	ST.LOUIS Red Stockings
NH	47	7	40	.149	170	1814	368	.203	NEW HAVEN
NAT	27	4	23	.148	96	990	181	.183	WASHINGTON Nationals
CEN	14	2	12	.143	70	549	125	.228	PHILADELPHIA Centennials
WES	13	1	12	.077	45	484	81	.167	KEOKUK Westerns
ATL	44	2	42	.045	132	1590	306	.192	BROOKLYN Atlantics
TOT	345				4215	27318	6830	.250	

Runs		Hits		Batting Average	
Barnes-Bos	116	Barnes-Bos	148	Barnes-Bos	.372
Wright-Bos	105	McVey-Bos	138	White-Bos	.355
O'Rourke-Bos	96	Wright-Bos	137	McVey-Bos	.352
McVey-Bos	90	White-Bos	136	Pike-StL	.342
Leonard-Bos	87	Leonard-Bos	128	Wright-Bos	.337

Games Pitched		Wins		Win Percentage	
Mathews-Mut	70	Spalding-Bos	57	Spalding-Bos	.919
Spalding-Bos	66	McBride-Ath	44	McBride-Ath	.759
McBride-Ath	60	Cummings-Har	35	Cummings-Har	.745
Bradley-StL	60	Bradley-StL	33	Zettlein-Chi-Phi	.569
Zettlein-Chi-Phi	52			Bradley-StL	.559

How to Read a Team Line

TEAM	G	W	L	PCT	GB	R	OR	AB	H	2B	3B	HR	BB	SO	AVG	OBP	SLG	PRO	/A	BR	/A	PF	CHI	RC	TA	SB	CS	SBA	SBR
EAST																													
NY	160	100	60	.625		703	532	5408	1387	251	24	152	544	842	.256	.328	.396	.724	114	95	156	90	97	717	.686	140	51	73	11
PIT	160	85	75	.531	15	651	616	5379	1327	240	45	110	553	947	.247	.321	.369	.690	104	33	47	98	98	648	.639	119	60	66	0
MON	163	81	81	.500	20	628	592	5573	1400	260	48	107	454	1053	.251	.311	.373	.684	102	12	-22	106	97	636	.628	189	89	68	3
CHI	163	77	85	.475	24	660	694	5675	1481	262	46	113	403	910	.261	.312	.383	.695	105	31	2	104	98	673	.625	120	46	72	8
STL	162	76	86	.469	25	578	633	5518	1373	207	33	71	484	827	.249	.312	.337	.649	93	-46	-71	104	98	601	.602	234	64	79	32
PHI	162	65	96	.404	35.5	597	734	5403	1294	246	31	106	489	981	.239	.308	.355	.663	96	-21	-28	101	99	599	.602	112	49	70	4
WEST																													
LA	162	94	67	.584		628	544	5431	1346	217	25	99	437	947	.248	.308	.352	.660	96	-31	-69	106	106	590	.591	131	46	74	12
CIN	161	87	74	.540	7	641	596	5426	1334	246	25	122	479	922	.246	.311	.368	.679	101	5	-28	105	102	639	.640	207	56	79	29
SD	161	83	78	.516	11	594	583	5366	1325	205	35	94	494	892	.247	.313	.351	.664	97	-18	-1	97	98	594	.599	123	50	71	7
SF	162	83	79	.512	11.5	670	626	5450	1353	227	44	113	550	1023	.248	.321	.368	.689	104	31	69	94	100	650	.635	121	78	61	-10
HOU	162	82	80	.506	12.5	617	631	5494	1338	239	31	96	474	840	.244	.308	.351	.659	95	-31	11	93	103	604	.609	198	71	74	17
ATL	160	54	106	.338	39.5	555	741	5440	1319	228	28	96	432	848	.242	.301	.348	.649	92	-55	-82	104	98	549	.564	95	69	58	-12
TOT	969					7522		65563	16277	2828	415	1279	5793	11032	.248	.313	.363	.675								1789	729	71	99

TEAM	CG	SHO	SV	IP	H	H/G	HR	BB	BB/G	SO	SO/G	ERA	/A	OAVG	OOBA	PR	/A	PF	CPI	FA	E	DP	FW	PW	BW	SBW	DIF
EAST																											
NY	31	22	46	1439.0	1253	7.8	78	404	2.5	1100	6.9	2.91	104	.234	.287	86	19	88	97	.981	115	127	.9	2.0	16.8	.3	-.0
PIT	12	11	46	1440.7	1349	8.4	108	469	2.9	790	4.9	3.47	97	.250	.306	-3	-18	97	101	.980	125	126	.4	-1.9	5.1	-.9	2.4
MON	18	12	43	1482.7	1310	8.0	122	476	2.9	923	5.6	3.08	117	.237	.297	59	88	105	105	.978	142	145	-.6	9.5	-2.4	-.6	-6.0
CHI	30	10	29	1464.3	1494	9.2	115	490	3.0	897	5.5	3.84	94	.264	.321	-64	-37	105	102	.980	125	128	.4	-4.0	.2	-.0	-.6
STL	17	14	42	1470.7	1387	8.5	91	486	3.0	881	5.4	3.47	104	.251	.307	-3	23	105	99	.981	121	131	.6	2.5	-7.7	2.6	-3.0
PHI	16	6	36	1433.0	1447	9.1	118	628	3.9	859	5.4	4.14	86	.264	.336	-110	-93	103	102	.976	145	139	-.8	-10.0	-3.0	-.5	-1.2
WEST																											
LA	32	24	49	1463.3	1291	7.9	84	473	2.9	1029	6.3	2.96	122	.237	.295	78	106	105	102	.977	142	126	-.6	11.4	-7.4	.4	9.7
CIN	24	13	43	1455.0	1271	7.9	121	504	3.1	934	5.8	3.35	108	.236	.299	16	43	105	98	.980	125	131	.4	4.6	-3.0	2.2	2.3
SD	30	9	39	1449.0	1332	8.3	112	439	2.7	885	5.5	3.28	102	.246	.299	26	11	97	102	.980	120	147	.6	1.2	-.1		.9
SF	25	13	42	1462.3	1323	8.1	99	422	2.6	875	5.4	3.39	95	.242	.293	10	-27	93	93	.980	129	145	.1	-2.9	7.4	-2.0	-.7
HOU	21	15	40	1474.7	1339	8.2	123	478	2.9	1049	6.4	3.41	95	.242	.299	6	-30	93	99	.978	138	124	-.4	-3.2	1.2	.9	2.5
ATL	14	4	25	1446.0	1481	9.2	108	524	3.3	810	5.0	4.09	90	.267	.327	-103	-64	107	100	.976	151	138	-1.1	-6.9	-8.8	-2.2	-7.0
TOT	270	153	480	17480.7		8.4			3.0		5.7	3.45		.248	.313					.979	1578	1607					

The Los Angeles Dodgers had a miracle season in 1988, winning the National League pennant and the World Series against seemingly far superior opponents, the New York Mets and the Oakland Athletics, respectively. But their first miracle was to win the National League's Western Division title after finishing 73-89 in each of the previous two seasons. How did they win the West? With mirrors, mostly, for they had below-average fielding and hitting that should have negated their outstanding pitching.

Let's just track the Dodgers' showing in some of the key categories to show how illuminating a close examination of team data in the Annual Record can be. The Dodgers' on base percentage (OBP) and slugging average (SLG) reveal them to have been a weak hitting club, and their Adjusted Production (PRO/A) is worse still, for they scored fewer runs in their park than might have been expected from the total run-scoring picture at Chavez Ravine (Park Factor 106). However, their Clutch Hitting Index (CHI) was the best in their division, testifying to their character, their good fortune, or both. Their Stolen Base Average was above average, but still only accounted for 12 extra runs over the course of the season, so this wasn't the secret of their success.

The pitching numbers are superlative—fewest runs al-lowed in the West and lowest ERA—despite the fact that Cincinnati held opponents to a lower batting average (OAVG) and San Francisco to a lower on base percentage or average (OOBA). Their West-leading Clutch Pitching Index (CPI) suggests that Dodger hurlers pulled their belts a notch tighter when men were on base, and their Home Runs allowed (HR) gives another tip that they knew how to stay away from the big inning. And maybe all those Shutouts (SHO) are indicative of the many games they won while scoring few runs themselves.

Look at their batting (which cost them 7.4 wins in the BW, or Batting Wins, column) and baserunning and fielding (which are a virtual wash at +0.4 and −0.6, respectively, in the SBW and FW columns), and notice that their pitching, good as it was, only supplied 11.4 wins beyond average (.500). On balance, then, their offense and defense combined to produce only four wins beyond average. They should have finished with a record of 85–77, or four games beyond the 81–81 league average. Instead they finished 94–67, nine wins beyond their expectations, as indicated in the Differential (DIF) column. Maybe it was manager Tommy Lasorda's doing after all.

TEAM	G	W	L	PCT	GB	R	OR	AB	H	2B	3B	HR	BB	SO	AVG	OBP	SLG	PRO	/A	BR	/A	PF	CHI	RC	TA	SB	CS	SBA	SBR
CHI	66	52	14	.788		624	257	2748	926	131	32	8	70	45	.337	.353	.417	.770	157	160	53	125	107	415	.667				
STL	64	45	19	.703	6	386	229	2478	642	73	27	2	59	63	.259	.276	.313	.589	97	-5	42	88	102	219	.454				
HAR	69	47	21	.691	6	429	261	2664	711	96	22	2	39	78	.267	.277	.322	.599	100	1	-32	108	105	244	.459				
BOS	70	39	31	.557	15	471	450	2722	723	96	24	9	58	98	.266	.281	.328	.609	104	11	32	95	110	257	.476				
LOU	69	30	36	.455	22	280	344	2570	641	68	14	6	24	98	.249	.256	.294	.550	84	-41	-56	104	80	198	.404				
NY	57	21	35	.375	26	260	412	2180	494	39	15	2	18	35	.227	.233	.261	.494	65	-75	-32	102		136	.348				
PHI	60	14	45	.237	34.5	378	534	2387	646	79	35	7	27	36	.271	.279	.342	.621	107	16	19	99	100	233	.484				
CIN	65	9	56	.138	42.5	238	579	2372	555	51	12	4	41	136	.234	.247	.271	.518	74	-62	-24	90	79	163	.376				
TOT	260					3066		20121	5338	633	181	40	336	589	.265	.277	.321	.598											

TEAM	CG	SHO	SV	IP	H	H/G	HR	BB	BB/G	SO	SO/G	ERA	/A	OAVG	OOBA	PR	/A	PF	CPI	FA	E	DP	FW	PW	BW	SBW	DIF
CHI	58	8	4	592.3	608	9.2	6	29	.4	51	.8	1.76	148	.247	.256	35	56	113	101	.899	282	33	5.6	4.9	4.7		3.8
STL	63	16	0	577.0	472	7.4	3	39	.6	103	1.6	1.22	155	.207	.221	70	42	82	66	.902	268	33	6.4	3.7	3.7		-.8
HAR	69	11	0	624.0	570	8.2	2	27	.4	114	1.6	1.67	142	.226	.234	44	48	103	70	.887	337	27	2.8	4.2	-2.8		8.8
BOS	49	3	7	632.0	732	10.4	7	104	1.5	77	1.1	2.51	87	.270	.297	-13	-23	94	109	.860	442	42	-2.7	-2.0	2.8		5.9
LOU	67	5	0	643.0	605	8.5	3	38	.5	125	1.7	1.69	145	.231	.242	43	53	106	81	.875	397	44	-.3	4.7	-4.9		-2.4
NY	56	2	0	530.0	718	12.2	8	24	.4	37	.6	2.94	73	.302	.309	-37	-46	93	115	.825	473	18	-4.3	-4.0	-2.8		4.2
PHI	53	1	2	550.0	783	12.8	2	41	.7	22	.4	3.22	75	.313	.324	-55	-48	105	115	.839	456	32	-3.4	-4.2	1.7		-9.5
CIN	57	0	0	591.0	850	12.9	9	34	.5	60	.9	3.64	64	.315	.324	-87	-87	100	105	.841	469	45	-4.1	-7.6	-2.1		-9.7
TOT	472	46	13	4739.3		10.1			.6		1.1	2.31		.265	.277					.866	3124	274					

Runs		Hits		Doubles		Triples		Home Runs		Total Bases	
Barnes-Chi	126	Barnes-Chi	138	Hines-Chi	21	Barnes-Chi	14	Hall-Phi	5	Barnes-Chi	190
Wright-Bos	72	Peters-Chi	111	Higham-Har	21	Hall-Phi	13	Jones-Cin	4	Hall-Phi	146
Peters-Chi	70	Anson-Chi	110	Barnes-Chi	21	Pike-StL	10			Anson-Chi	139
White-Chi	66	McVey-Chi	107	Pike-StL	19	Meyerle-Phi	8			Hines-Chi	134
Burdock-Har	66	White-Chi	104								

Runs Batted In		Runs Produced		Bases On Balls		Batting Average		On Base Percentage		Slugging Average	
White-Chi	60	Barnes-Chi	184	Barnes-Chi	20	Barnes-Chi	.429	Barnes-Chi	.462	Barnes-Chi	.590
Hines-Chi	59	White-Chi	125	O'Rourke-Bos	15	Hall-Phi	.366	Hall-Phi	.384	Hall-Phi	.545
Barnes-Chi	59	Anson-Chi	120	Burdock-Har	13	Anson-Chi	.356	Anson-Chi	.380	Pike-StL	.472
Anson-Chi	59	Hines-Chi	119	Glenn-Chi	12	Peters-Chi	.351	White-Chi	.358	Anson-Chi	.450
McVey-Chi	53	Peters-Chi	116	Anson-Chi	12	McVey-Chi	.347	O'Rourke-Bos	.358	Meyerle-Phi	.449

Production		Adjusted Production		Batter Runs		Adjusted Batter Runs		Clutch Hitting Index		Runs Created	
Barnes-Chi	1.052	Hall-Phi	208	Barnes-Chi	50.0	Barnes-Chi	37.0	White-Chi	165	Barnes-Chi	90
Hall-Phi	.929	Barnes-Chi	198	Hall-Phi	29.1	Hall-Phi	29.4	Hines-Chi	151	Hall-Phi	57
Anson-Chi	.830	Pike-StL	192	Anson-Chi	24.2	Pike-StL	25.1	Schafer-Bos	145	Anson-Chi	54
Pike-StL	.813	O'Rourke-Bos	167	Pike-StL	19.7	O'Rourke-Bos	21.7	Battin-StL	144	Peters-Chi	48
Meyerle-Phi	.797	Meyerle-Phi	165	O'Rourke-Bos	19.1	Meyerle-Phi	16.7	Spalding-Chi	139	O'Rourke-Bos	48

Total Average		Stolen Bases	Stolen Base Average	Stolen Base Runs	Fielding Runs		Total Player Rating	
Barnes-Chi	1.141				Somerville-Lou	27.7	Barnes-Chi	3.3
Hall-Phi	.906				Force-Phi-NY	20.4	Hall-Phi	2.5
Anson-Chi	.759				Wright-Bos	14.7	Wright-Bos	2.5
Pike-StL	.738				Battin-StL	14.3	Battin-StL	2.2
Meyerle-Phi	.698				Anson-Chi	12.4	Anson-Chi	2.0

Wins		Win Percentage		Games		Complete Games		Shutouts		Saves	
Spalding-Chi	47	Spalding-Chi	.797	Devlin-Lou	68	Devlin-Lou	66	Bradley-StL	16	Manning-Bos	5
Bradley-StL	45	Manning-Bos	.783	Bradley-StL	64	Bradley-StL	63	Spalding-Chi	8	Zettlein-Phi	2
Bond-Har	31	Bond-Har	.705	Spalding-Chi	61	Mathews-NY	55	Bond-Har	6	McVey-Chi	2
Devlin-Lou	30	Bradley-StL	.703	Mathews-NY	56	Spalding-Chi	53	Devlin-Lou	5		
Mathews-NY	21	Cummings-Har	.667	Bond-Har	45	Bond-Har	45	Cummings-Har	5		

Innings Pitched		Fewest Hits/Game		Fewest BB/Game		Strikeouts		Strikeouts/Game		Wins Above Team	
Devlin-Lou	622	Bradley-StL	7.38	Zettlein-Phi	.23	Devlin-Lou	122	Bond-Har	1.94	Bradley-StL	22.5
Bradley-StL	573	Bond-Har	7.83	Fisher-Cin	.24	Bradley-StL	103	Devlin-Lou	1.77	Devlin-Lou	15.0
Spalding-Chi	529	Devlin-Lou	8.19	Bond-Har	.29	Bond-Har	88	Bradley-StL	1.62	Mathews-NY	10.5
Mathews-NY	516	Cummings-Har	8.96	Mathews-NY	.42	Spalding-Chi	39	Borden-Bos	1.40	Spalding-Chi	8.5
Bond-Har	408	Spalding-Chi	9.22	Williams-Cin	.43	Mathews-NY	37	Fisher-Cin	1.14	Manning-Bos	7.0

Earned Run Average		Adjusted ERA		Opponents' Batting Avg.		Opponents' On Base Pct.		Starter Runs		Adjusted Starter Runs	
Bradley-StL	1.23	Davlin-Lou	157	Bradley-StL	.208	Bradley-StL	.221	Bradley-StL	69.0	Devlin-Lou	61.2
Devlin-Lou	1.56	Bradley-StL	154	Bond-Har	.218	Bond-Har	.224	Devlin-Lou	51.6	Spalding-Chi	50.6
Cummings-Har	1.67	Spalding-Chi	149	Devlin-Lou	.226	Devlin-Lou	.237	Spalding-Chi	32.7	Bradley-StL	41.8
Bond-Har	1.68	Cummings-Har	142	Cummings-Har	.242	Cummings-Har	.254	Bond-Har	28.7	Bond-Har	31.6
Spalding-Chi	1.75	Bond-Har	142	Spalding-Chi	.247	Spalding-Chi	.256	Cummings-Har	15.4	Cummings-Har	17.0

Clutch Pitching Index		Relief Runs	Adjusted Relief Runs	Relief Ranking	Total Pitcher Index		Total Baseball Ranking	
Knight-Phi	133				Devlin-Lou	7.1	Devlin-Lou	7.1
Mathews-NY	116				Spalding-Chi	6.3	Spalding-Chi	6.3
Dean-Cin	111				Bradley-StL	4.1	Bradley-StL	4.1
Manning-Bos	108				Bond-Har	3.6	Bond-Har	3.6
Borden-Bos	107				Cummings-Har	.8	Barnes-Chi	3.3

TEAM	G	W	L	PCT	GB	R	OR	AB	H	2B	3B	HR	BB	SO	AVG	OBP	SLG	PRO	/A	BR	/A	PF	CHI	RC	TA	SB	CS	SBA	SBR
BOS	61	42	18	.700		419	263	2368	700	91	37	4	65	121	.296	.314	.370	.684	118	47	17	108	104	283	.565				
LOU	61	35	25	.583	7	339	288	2355	659	75	36	9	58	140	.280	.297	.354	.651	108	19	-93	132	91	254	.525				
HAR	60	31	27	.534	10	341	311	2358	637	63	31	4	30	97	.270	.279	.328	.607	94	-16	21	89	102	222	.467				
STL	60	28	32	.467	14	284	318	2178	531	51	36	1	57	147	.244	.263	.302	.565	80	-45	-50	102	101	177	.434				
CHI	60	26	33	.441	15.5	366	375	2273	633	79	30	0	57	111	.278	.296	.340	.636	103	8	13	98	105	234	.505				
CIN	58	15	42	.263	25.5	291	485	2135	545	72	34	6	78	110	.255	.282	.329	.611	95	-10	48	82	93	203	.491				
TOT	180					2040		13667	3705	431	204	24	345	726	.271	.289	.338	.627											

TEAM	CG	SHO	SV	IP	H	H/G	HR	BB	BB/G	SO	SO/G	ERA	/A	OAVG	OOBA	PR	/A	PF	CPI	FA	E	DP	FW	PW	BW	SBW	DIF
BOS	61	7	0	548.0	557	9.1	5	38	.6	177	2.9	2.15	133	.248	.261	40	42	101	98	.894	290	36	1.0	3.7	1.5		5.8
LOU	61	4	0	559.0	617	9.9	4	41	.7	141	2.3	2.25	162	.264	.276	34	86	130	112	.904	267	37	2.1	7.7	-8.3		3.5
HAR	59	4	0	544.0	572	9.5	2	56	.9	99	1.6	2.32	105	.254	.273	30	7	87	101	.885	313	32	-.2	.6	1.9		-.3
STL	52	1	0	541.0	582	9.7	2	92	1.5	132	2.2	2.68	109	.259	.288	8	13	103	98	.892	281	29	1.4	1.2	-4.5		-.1
CHI	45	3	3	534.0	630	10.6	7	58	1.0	92	1.6	3.37	82	.277	.295	-33	-35	99	90	.883	313	43	-.2	-3.1	1.2		-1.4
CIN	48	1	1	515.0	747	13.1	4	61	1.1	85	1.5	4.21	60	.320	.337	-80	-95	90	103	.851	394	33	-4.2	-8.5	4.3		-5.2
TOT	326	20	4	3241.0		10.3			1.0		2.0	2.81		.271	.289					.885	1858	210					

Runs		Hits		Doubles		Triples		Home Runs		Total Bases	
O'Rourke-Bos	68	White-Bos	103	Anson-Chi	19	White-Bos	11	Pike-Cin	4	White-Bos	145
Wright-Bos	58	McVey-Chi	98	York-Har	16	Hall-Lou	8	Shaffer-Lou	3	McVey-Chi	121
McVey-Chi	58	O'Rourke-Bos	96	Manning-Cin	16	Brown-Bos	8	White-Bos	2	O'Rourke-Bos	118
Start-Har	55	Cassidy-Har	95	Wright-Bos	15			Snyder-Lou	2	Hall-Lou	118
Hall-Lou	53	Start-Har	90	Hall-Lou	15					Cassidy-Har	115

Runs Batted In		Runs Produced		Bases On Balls		Batting Average		On Base Percentage		Slugging Average	
White-Bos	49	White-Bos	98	O'Rourke-Bos	20	White-Bos	.387	O'Rourke-Bos	.407	White-Bos	.545
Peters-Chi	41	McVey-Chi	94	Hall-Lou	12	Cassidy-Har	.378	White-Bos	.405	Cassidy-Har	.458
Sutton-Bos	39	Wright-Bos	93	Booth-Cin	12	McVey-Chi	.368	McVey-Chi	.387	McVey-Chi	.455
York-Har	37	O'Rourke-Bos	91	Jones-Chi-Cin	11	O'Rourke-Bos	.362	Cassidy-Har	.386	O'Rourke-Bos	.445
		Peters-Chi	86	Force-StL	11	Anson-Chi	.337	Anson-Chi	.360	Hall-Lou	.439

Production		Adjusted Production		Batter Runs		Adjusted Batter Runs		Clutch Hitting Index		Runs Created	
White-Bos	.950	Cassidy-Har	184	White-Bos	28.2	White-Bos	24.9	Ferguson-Har	165	White-Bos	60
O'Rourke-Bos	.852	White-Bos	181	O'Rourke-Bos	21.2	Cassidy-Har	21.6	Croft-StL	162	O'Rourke-Bos	49
Cassidy-Har	.844	Manning-Cin	171	McVey-Chi	18.9	McVey-Chi	19.6	Bond-Bos	150	McVey-Chi	48
McVey-Chi	.842	McVey-Chi	167	Cassidy-Har	17.6	O'Rourke-Bos	17.7	Spalding-Chi	150	Cassidy-Har	45
Hall-Lou	.791	Pike-Cin	161	Hall-Lou	14.4	Manning-Cin	17.7	Sutton-Bos	146	Hall-Lou	43

Total Average		Stolen Bases		Stolen Base Average		Stolen Base Runs		Fielding Runs		Total Player Rating	
White-Bos	.939							Peters-Chi	20.9	Peters-Chi	2.4
O'Rourke-Bos	.817							Gerhardt-Lou	18.7	Jones-Chi-Cin	2.2
McVey-Chi	.768							Ferguson-Har	18.6	White-Bos	2.2
Cassidy-Har	.756							Brown-Bos	13.3	Ferguson-Har	1.7
Hall-Lou	.714							Shaffer-Lou	13.1	Anson-Chi	1.6

Wins		Win Percentage		Games		Complete Games		Shutouts		Saves	
Bond-Bos	40	Bond-Bos	.702	Devlin-Lou	61	Devlin-Lou	61	Bond-Bos	6	McVey-Chi	2
Devlin-Lou	35	Devlin-Lou	.583	Bond-Bos	58	Bond-Bos	58	Larkin-Har	4	Spalding-Chi	1
Larkin-Har	29	Larkin-Har	.537	Larkin-Har	56	Larkin-Har	55	Devlin-Lou	4	Manning-Cin	1
Nichols-StL	18	Nichols-StL	.439	Bradley-Chi	50	Nichols-StL	35	Bradley-Chi	2		
Bradley-Chi	18	Bradley-Chi	.439	Nichols-StL	42	Bradley-Chi	35				

Innings Pitched		Fewest Hits/Game		Fewest BB/Game		Strikeouts		Strikeouts/Game		Wins Above Team	
Devlin-Lou	559	Bond-Bos	9.16	Bond-Bos	.62	Bond-Bos	170	Mitchell-Cin	3.69	Devlin-Lou	17.5
Bond-Bos	521	Larkin-Har	9.16	Devlin-Lou	.66	Devlin-Lou	141	Bond-Bos	2.94	Bond-Bos	3.0
Larkin-Har	501	Nichols-StL	9.67	Cummings-Cin	.75	Larkin-Har	96	Blong-StL	2.45	Mitchell-Cin	2.4
Bradley-Chi	394	Blong-StL	9.77	Bradley-Chi	.89	Nichols-StL	80	Devlin-Lou	2.27	Larkin-Har	2.0
Nichols-StL	350	Devlin-Lou	9.93	Larkin-Har	.95	Bradley-Chi	59	Nichols-StL	2.06	Blong-StL	1.5

Earned Run Average		Adjusted ERA		Opponents' Batting Avg.		Opponents' On Base Pct.		Starter Runs		Adjusted Starter Runs	
Bond-Bos	2.11	Devlin-Lou	162	Bond-Bos	.249	Bond-Bos	.261	Bond-Bos	40.8	Devlin-Lou	86.4
Larkin-Har	2.14	Bond-Bos	135	Larkin-Har	.249	Larkin-Har	.268	Larkin-Har	37.6	Bond-Bos	43.1
Devlin-Lou	2.25	Larkin-Har	114	Nichols-StL	.259	Devlin-Lou	.277	Devlin-Lou	34.7	Larkin-Har	16.6
Nichols-StL	2.60	Nichols-StL	112	Blong-StL	.261	Nichols-StL	.285	Nichols-StL	8.4	Nichols-StL	12.1
Blong-StL	2.74	Blong-StL	106	Devlin-Lou	.264	Bradley-Chi	.288	Reis-Chi	8.3	Reis-Chi	8.1

Clutch Pitching Index		Relief Runs		Adjusted Relief Runs		Relief Ranking		Total Pitcher Index		Total Baseball Ranking	
Mathews-Cin	126							Devlin-Lou	9.2	Devlin-Lou	9.2
Devlin-Lou	112							Bond-Bos	4.0	Bond-Bos	4.0
Booth-Cin	108							Larkin-Har	1.5	Peters-Chi	2.4
Larkin-Har	102							Reis-Chi	.6	Jones-Chi-Cin	2.2
Bond-Bos	100							Blong-StL	.3	White-Bos	2.2

TEAM	G	W	L	PCT	GB	R	OR	AB	H	2B	3B	HR	BB	SO	AVG	OBP	SLG	PRO	/A	BR	/A	PF	CHI	RC	TA	SB	CS	SBA	SBR
BOS	60	41	19	.683		298	241	2220	535	75	25	2	35	154	.241	.253	.300	.553	85	-34	-57	108	109	173	.416				
CIN	61	37	23	.617	4	333	281	2281	629	67	22	5	58	141	.276	.294	.331	.625	109	21	36	95	98	227	.492				
PRO	62	33	27	.550	8	353	337	2298	604	107	30	8	50	218	.263	.279	.346	.625	109	19	26	98	104	227	.499				
CHI	61	30	30	.500	11	371	331	2333	677	91	20	0	88	157	.290	.316	.350	.666	123	56	29	108	96	265	.546				
IND	63	24	36	.400	17	293	328	2300	542	76	15	3	64	197	.236	.256	.286	.542	82	-42	1	87	104	173	.410				
MIL	61	15	45	.250	26	256	386	2212	552	65	20	2	69	214	.250	.272	.300	.572	92	-17	-37	107	87	185	.441				
TOT	184					1904		13644	3539	481	132	23	364	1081	.259	.279	.319	.598											

TEAM	CG	SHO	SV	IP	H	H/G	HR	BB	BB/G	SO	SO/G	ERA	/A	OAVG	OOBA	PR	/A	PF	CPI	FA	E	DP	FW	PW	BW	SBW	DIF
BOS	58	9	0	544.0	595	9.8	6	38	.6	184	3.0	2.32	104	.264	.276	0	5	105	102	.914	228	48	3.8	.5	-5.3		12.1
CIN	61	6	0	548.0	546	9.0	2	63	1.0	220	3.6	1.84	116	.246	.267	28	17	93	107	.900	269	37	1.5	1.6	3.4		.5
PRO	59	6	0	556.0	609	9.9	5	86	1.4	173	2.8	2.38	94	.264	.291	-4	-9	97	109	.892	311	42	-.8	-.8	2.4		2.2
CHI	61	1	0	551.0	577	9.4	4	35	.6	175	2.9	2.37	103	.256	.267	-3	4	106	88	.891	304	37	-.4	.4	2.7		-2.7
IND	59	2	1	578.0	621	9.7	3	87	1.4	182	2.8	2.32	87	.261	.287	-1	-18	88	106	.898	290	37	.4	-1.7	.0		-4.8
MIL	54	1	0	547.0	589	9.7	3	55	.9	147	2.4	2.60	101	.261	.279	-17	1	114	89	.866	376	32	-4.4	.0	-3.5		-7.2
TOT	352	25	1	3324.0		9.6			1.0		2.9	2.30		.259	.279					.893	1778	233					

Runs		Hits		Doubles		Triples		Home Runs		Total Bases	
Higham-Pro	60	Start-Chi	100	Higham-Pro	22	York-Pro	10	Hines-Pro	4	York-Pro	125
Start-Chi	58	Dalrymple-Mil	96	Brown-Pro	21	O'Rourke-Bos	7	Jones-Cin	3	Start-Chi	125
York-Pro	56	Hines-Pro	92	York-Pro	19	Jones-Cin	7	McVey-Cin	2	Hines-Pro	125
Anson-Chi	55	Ferguson-Chi	91	Shaffer-Ind	19			McKelvy-Ind	2	Shaffer-Ind	121
Dalrymple-Mil	52			O'Rourke-Bos	17					Higham-Pro	117

Runs Batted In		Runs Produced		Bases On Balls		Batting Average		On Base Percentage		Slugging Average	
Hines-Pro	50	Anson-Chi	95	Remsen-Chi	17	Hines-Pro	.358	Ferguson-Chi	.375	Hines-Pro	.486
Brown-Pro	43	Hines-Pro	88	Larkin-Chi	17	Dalrymple-Mil	.354	Anson-Chi	.372	York-Pro	.465
Anson-Chi	40	Higham-Pro	88	Shaffer-Ind	13	Ferguson-Chi	.351	Shaffer-Ind	.369	Shaffer-Ind	.455
Jones-Cin	39	Jones-Cin	86	Clapp-Ind	13	Start-Chi	.351	Dalrymple-Mil	.368	Brown-Pro	.453
Ferguson-Chi	39	Brown-Pro	86	Anson-Chi	13	Anson-Chi	.341	Hines-Pro	.363	Jones-Cin	.441

Production		Adjusted Production		Batter Runs		Adjusted Batter Runs		Clutch Hitting Index		Runs Created	
Hines-Pro	.849	Shaffer-Ind	196	Hines-Pro	20.0	Shaffer-Ind	24.7	McClellan-Chi	193	Hines-Pro	47
Shaffer-Ind	.824	Hines-Pro	181	Shaffer-Ind	19.6	Hines-Pro	20.9	Hague-Pro	166	Shaffer-Ind	46
Start-Chi	.794	York-Pro	162	Start-Chi	17.2	York-Pro	17.0	McKelvy-Ind	164	Start-Chi	46
York-Pro	.793	Brown-Pro	156	Dalrymple-Mil	16.4	Larkin-Chi	16.2	Redmond-Mil	148	Dalrymple-Mil	43
Dalrymple-Mil	.789	Jones-Cin	155	York-Pro	16.1	Jones-Cin	14.4	Harbidge-Chi	145	York-Pro	42

Total Average		Stolen Bases		Stolen Base Average		Stolen Base Runs		Fielding Runs		Total Player Rating	
Hines-Pro	.770							Burdock-Bos	20.0	Ferguson-Chi	3.2
Shaffer-Ind	.761							Hague-Pro	19.3	Shaffer-Ind	2.3
York-Pro	.715							Ferguson-Chi	18.5	Burdock-Bos	2.1
Brown-Pro	.692							Snyder-Bos	11.4	Brown-Pro	2.0
Start-Chi	.686							Wright-Bos	11.0	Hines-Pro	1.7

Wins		Win Percentage		Games		Complete Games		Shutouts		Saves	
Bond-Bos	40	Bond-Bos	.678	Bond-Bos	59	Bond-Bos	57	Bond-Bos	9	Healey-Pro-Ind	1
White-Cin	30	Ward-Pro	.629	Larkin-Chi	56	Larkin-Chi	56	Ward-Pro	6		
Larkin-Chi	29	White-Cin	.588	White-Cin	52	White-Cin	52	White-Cin	5		
Ward-Pro	22	Larkin-Chi	.527	Weaver-Mil	45	Weaver-Mil	39				
Nolan-Ind	13			Nolan-Ind	38						

Innings Pitched		Fewest Hits/Game		Fewest BB/Game		Strikeouts		Strikeouts/Game		Wins Above Team	
Bond-Bos	533	Mitchell-Cin	7.76	Weaver-Mil	.49	Bond-Bos	182	Mitchell-Cin	5.74	Larkin-Chi	11.2
Larkin-Chi	506	Ward-Pro	8.30	Larkin-Chi	.55	White-Cin	169	Wheeler-Pro	3.63	Ward-Pro	5.9
White-Cin	468	Weaver-Mil	8.72	Bond-Bos	.56	Larkin-Chi	163	White-Cin	3.25	Weaver-Mil	2.7
Weaver-Mil	383	Larkin-Chi	9.09	Nichols-Pro	.73	Nolan-Ind	125	Nolan-Ind	3.24	Wheeler-Pro	2.5
Nolan-Ind	347	White-Cin	9.17	White-Cin	.87	Ward-Pro	116	Ward-Pro	3.13	Mitchell-Cin	2.1

Earned Run Average		Adjusted ERA		Opponents' Batting Avg.		Opponents' On Base Pct.		Starter Runs		Adjusted Starter Runs	
Ward-Pro	1.51	Ward-Pro	148	Mitchell-Cin	.221	Weaver-Mil	.252	Ward-Pro	29.5	Weaver-Mil	28.6
McCormick-Ind	1.69	Weaver-Mil	134	Ward-Pro	.233	Ward-Pro	.252	White-Cin	26.8	Ward-Pro	26.8
White-Cin	1.79	McCormick-Ind	120	Weaver-Mil	.242	Larkin-Chi	.261	Weaver-Mil	15.1	Bond-Bos	20.6
Weaver-Mil	1.95	White-Cin	119	Larkin-Chi	.249	Mitchell-Cin	.263	Bond-Bos	14.5	White-Cin	17.9
Bond-Bos	2.06	Bond-Bos	117	White-Cin	.251	White-Cin	.268	McCormick-Ind	8.0	Larkin-Chi	10.9

Clutch Pitching Index		Relief Runs		Adjusted Relief Runs		Relief Ranking		Total Pitcher Index		Total Baseball Ranking	
McCormick-Ind	148							Ward-Pro	2.9	Ferguson-Chi	3.2
Healey-Pro-Ind	116							Weaver-Mil	2.8	Ward-Pro	2.9
Nichols-Pro	113							Larkin-Chi	2.2	Weaver-Mil	2.8
White-Cin	112							Bond-Bos	1.9	Shaffer-Ind	2.3
Bond-Bos	108							White-Cin	.6	Larkin-Chi	2.2

TEAM	G	W	L	PCT	GB	R	OR	AB	H	2B	3B	HR	BB	SO	AVG	OBP	SLG	PRO	/A	BR	/A	PF	CHI	RC	TA	SB	CS	SBA	SBR
PRO	85	59	25	.702		612	355	3392	1003	142	55	12	91	172	.296	.314	.381	.695	132	110	102	102	103	416	.578				
BOS	84	54	30	.643	5	562	348	3217	883	138	51	20	90	222	.274	.294	.368	.662	121	68	35	107	107	357	.545				
BUF	79	46	32	.590	10	394	365	2906	733	105	54	2	78	314	.252	.272	.328	.600	100	1	-57	114	95	265	.474				
CHI	83	46	33	.582	10.5	437	411	3116	808	167	32	3	73	294	.259	.276	.336	.612	104	14	-7	105	96	297	.486				
CIN	81	43	37	.538	14	485	464	3085	813	127	53	8	66	207	.264	.279	.347	.626	109	27	50	95	104	306	.500				
SYR	71	22	48	.314	30	276	462	2611	592	61	19	5	28	238	.227	.235	.270	.505	69	-81	-40	89	97	170	.364				
CLE	82	27	55	.329	31	322	461	2987	666	116	29	4	37	214	.223	.232	.285	.517	72	-82	-79	99	95	203	.383				
TRO	77	19	56	.253	35.5	321	543	2841	673	102	24	4	45	182	.237	.249	.294	.543	81	-53	-26	93	92	213	.406				
TOT	321					3409		24155	6171	958	317	58	508	1843	.255	.271	.329	.599											

TEAM	CG	SHO	SV	IP	H	H/G	HR	BB	BB/G	SO	SO/G	ERA	/A	OAVG	OOBA	PR	/A	PF	CPI	FA	E	DP	FW	PW	BW	SBW	DIF
PRO	73	2	2	776.0	765	8.9	9	62	.7	329	3.8	2.18	108	.241	.255	27	15	94	96	.902	382	41	1.8	1.4	9.4		4.4
BOS	79	12	1	753.0	757	9.0	9	46	.5	230	2.7	2.19	116	.244	.255	25	28	101	98	.913	319	58	4.9	2.6	3.2		1.3
BUF	78	8	0	713.0	698	8.8	3	47	.6	198	2.5	2.34	121	.239	.251	12	39	114	84	.906	331	62	2.9	3.6	-5.3		5.7
CHI	82	5	0	744.0	762	9.2	5	57	.7	211	2.6	2.46	106	.248	.261	3	12	104	91	.900	381	52	1.3	1.1	-.6		4.7
CIN	79	4	0	726.0	756	9.4	11	81	1.0	246	3.0	2.29	102	.251	.270	16	4	94	108	.877	454	48	-3.1	.4	4.6		1.1
SYR	64	5	0	649.0	775	10.7	4	52	.7	132	1.8	3.19	74	.277	.291	-49	-59	95	97	.873	398	37	-2.7	-5.4	-3.7		-1.2
CLE	79	3	0	741.0	818	9.9	4	116	1.4	287	3.5	2.65	97	.262	.288	-12	-5	103	108	.889	406	42	-.3	-.5	-7.3		-6.0
TRO	75	3	0	695.0	840	10.9	13	47	.6	210	2.7	2.80	89	.280	.291	-23	-23	100	115	.875	460	44	-4.4	-2.1	-2.4		-9.6
TOT	609	42	3	5797.0		9.6			.8		2.9	2.50		.255	.271					.892	3131	384					

Runs
Jones-Bos 85
Hines-Pro 81
Wright-Pro 79
Kelly-Cin 78
Dickerson-Cin 73

Hits
Hines-Pro 146
O'Rourke-Pro 126
Kelly-Cin 120
Jones-Bos 112
White-Cin 110

Doubles
Eden-Cle 31
York-Pro 25
Hines-Pro 25
Dalrymple-Chi 25
Houck-Bos 24

Triples
Dickerson-Cin 14
Williamson-Chi 13
Kelly-Cin 12
O'Rourke-Bos 11

Home Runs
Jones-Bos 9
O'Rourke-Bos 6
Brouthers-Tro 4
Eden-Cle 3

Total Bases
Hines-Pro 197
Jones-Bos 181
Kelly-Cin 170
O'Rourke-Pro 166
O'Rourke-Bos 165

Runs Batted In
O'Rourke-Bos 62
Jones-Bos 62
Dickerson-Cin 57
McVey-Cin 55

Runs Produced
Jones-Bos 138
Hines-Pro 131
Dickerson-Cin 128
O'Rourke-Bos 125
Kelly-Cin 123

Bases On Balls
Jones-Bos 29
Williamson-Chi 24
York-Pro 19
Richardson-Buf 16
Barnes-Cin 16

Batting Average
Hines-Pro 357
O'Rourke-Pro 348
Kelly-Cin 348
O'Rourke-Bos 341
White-Cin 330

On Base Percentage
O'Rourke-Pro 371
Hines-Pro 369
Jones-Bos 367
Kelly-Cin 363
O'Rourke-Bos 357

Slugging Average
O'Rourke-Bos 521
Jones-Bos 510
Kelly-Cin 493
Hines-Pro 482
O'Rourke-Pro 459

Production
O'Rourke-Bos 877
Jones-Bos 877
Kelly-Cin 855
Hines-Pro 851
O'Rourke-Pro 829

Adjusted Production
Kelly-Cin 189
Hines-Pro 175
Jones-Bos 173
O'Rourke-Bos 173
O'Rourke-Pro 169

Batter Runs
Jones-Bos 33.1
Hines-Pro 32.9
Kelly-Cin 28.1
O'Rourke-Bos 28.0
O'Rourke-Pro 27.2

Adjusted Batter Runs
Hines-Pro 32.0
Kelly-Cin 30.7
Jones-Bos 29.3
O'Rourke-Pro 26.4
O'Rourke-Bos 24.7

Clutch Hitting Index
Gerhardt-Cin 162
Brown-Pro-Chi 148
Morrill-Bos 145
McVey-Cin 137
White-Cin 134

Runs Created
Hines-Pro 75
Jones-Bos 68
Kelly-Cin 63
O'Rourke-Pro 63
O'Rourke-Bos 60

Total Average
Jones-Bos 864
O'Rourke-Bos 828
Kelly-Cin 791
Hines-Pro 779
O'Rourke-Pro 758

Stolen Bases

Stolen Base Average

Stolen Base Runs

Fielding Runs
Snyder-Bos 21.2
Williamson-Chi 19.6
Wright-Pro 19.5
Shaffer-Chi 19.0
Evans-Tro 16.8

Total Player Rating
Williamson-Chi 3.6
Jones-Bos 3.5
Kelly-Cin 3.2
Hines-Pro 3.1
Wright-Pro 2.9

Wins
Ward-Pro 47
White-Cin 43
Bond-Bos 43
Galvin-Buf 37
Larkin-Chi 31

Win Percentage
Ward-Pro 712
Bond-Bos 694
Hankinson-Chi 600
White-Cin 581
Galvin-Buf 578

Games
White-Cin 76
Ward-Pro 70
Galvin-Buf 66
Bond-Bos 64
McCormick-Cle 62

Complete Games
White-Cin 75
Galvin-Buf 65
McCormick-Cle 59
Bond-Bos 59
Ward-Pro 58

Shutouts
Bond-Bos 12
Galvin-Buf 6
McCormick-Syr 5
White-Cin 4

Saves
Ward-Pro 1
Mathews-Pro 1
Foley-Bos 1

Innings Pitched
White-Cin 680
Galvin-Buf 593
Ward-Pro 587
Bond-Bos 555
McCormick-Cle 546

Fewest Hits/Game
McGunnigle-Buf 8.48
Ward-Pro 8.75
Bond-Bos 8.81
Galvin-Buf 8.88
White-Cin 8.95

Fewest BB/Game
Bond-Bos 39
Galvin-Buf 47
Bradley-Tro 48
Larkin-Chi 53
Ward-Pro 55

Strikeouts
Ward-Pro 239
White-Cin 232
McCormick-Cle 197
Bond-Bos 155
Larkin-Chi 142

Strikeouts/Game
McGunnigle-Buf 4.65
Mathews-Pro 4.29
Mitchell-Cle 4.15
Ward-Pro 3.66
McCormick-Cle 3.25

Wins Above Team
White-Cin 21.5
Bond-Bos 12.0
McCormick-Syr 4.6
Ward-Pro 4.5
Salisbury-Tro 1.1

Earned Run Average
Bond-Bos 1.96
White-Cin 1.99
Ward-Pro 2.15
Salisbury-Tro 2.22
Galvin-Buf 2.28

Adjusted ERA
Bond-Bos 129
Galvin-Buf 124
White-Cin 118
Salisbury-Tro 112
Ward-Pro 110

Opponents' Batting Avg.
McGunnigle-Buf 233
Ward-Pro 239
Bond-Bos 240
Galvin-Buf 241
White-Cin 243

Opponents' On Base Pct.
Bond-Bos 248
Ward-Pro 250
Galvin-Buf 251
Larkin-Chi 255
McGunnigle-Buf 257

Starter Runs
White-Cin 38.6
Bond-Bos 32.9
Ward-Pro 22.8
Galvin-Buf 14.5
Goldsmith-Tro 6.5

Adjusted Starter Runs
Galvin-Buf 36.7
Bond-Bos 34.9
White-Cin 27.5
Ward-Pro 13.7
McCormick-Cle 9.6

Clutch Pitching Index
Salisbury-Tro 134
Bradley-Tro 114
White-Cin 112
Mathews-Pro 111
McCormick-Cle 108

Relief Runs

Adjusted Relief Runs

Relief Ranking

Total Pitcher Index
Galvin-Buf 4.5
Bond-Bos 4.2
Ward-Pro 3.3
McCormick-Cle 1.1
Foley-Bos 8

Total Baseball Ranking
Galvin-Buf 4.5
Bond-Bos 4.2
Williamson-Chi 3.6
Jones-Bos 3.5
Ward-Pro 3.3

TEAM	G	W	L	PCT	GB	R	OR	AB	H	2B	3B	HR	BB	SO	AVG	OBP	SLG	PRO	/A	BR	/A	PF	CHI	RC	TA	SB	CS	SBA	SBR
CHI	86	67	17	.798		538	317	3135	876	164	39	4	104	217	.279	.303	.360	.663	126	81	59	105	108	350	.546				
PRO	87	52	32	.619	15	419	299	3196	793	114	34	8	89	186	.248	.268	.313	.581	98	-5	11	96	101	275	.453				
CLE	85	47	37	.560	20	387	337	3002	726	130	52	7	75	241	.242	.260	.327	.587	100	0	5	99	98	262	.464				
TRO	83	41	42	.494	25.5	392	438	3007	755	114	37	5	119	261	.251	.280	.319	.599	105	14	-27	110	95	275	.478				
WOR	85	40	43	.482	26.5	412	370	3024	699	129	52	8	82	276	.231	.251	.316	.567	93	-20	-69	113	109	246	.446				
BOS	86	40	44	.476	27	416	456	3080	779	134	41	20	106	218	.253	.278	.343	.621	111	35	68	92	94	300	.505				
BUF	85	24	58	.293	42	331	502	2962	669	104	37	3	90	328	.226	.249	.289	.538	84	-47	-10	91	96	218	.413				
CIN	83	21	59	.263	44	296	472	2895	649	91	36	7	75	266	.224	.244	.288	.532	81	-53	-48	99	90	208	.404				
TOT	340					3191		24301	5946	980	328	62	740	1993	.245	.267	.320	.587											

TEAM	CG	SHO	SV	IP	H	H/G	HR	BB	BB/G	SO	SO/G	ERA	/A	OAVG	OOBA	PR	/A	PF	CPI	FA	E	DP	FW	PW	BW	SBW	DIF
CHI	80	9	3	775.0	622	7.2	8	129	1.5	367	4.3	1.93	121	.208	.241	38	34	98	82	.913	329	41	2.1	3.3	5.7		13.9
PRO	75	13	2	799.0	663	7.5	7	51	.6	286	3.2	1.64	133	.214	.226	64	48	92	86	.910	357	53	.6	4.7	1.1		3.7
CLE	83	7	1	759.7	685	8.1	4	98	1.2	289	3.4	1.90	122	.228	.252	40	34	97	102	.910	330	52	2.0	3.3	.5		-.8
TRO	81	4	0	738.0	763	9.3	8	113	1.4	173	2.1	2.74	97	.253	.280	-30	-7	112	99	.899	366	58	.1	-.7	-2.6		2.7
WOR	68	7	5	762.7	709	8.4	13	97	1.1	297	3.5	2.27	117	.233	.257	9	32	111	95	.906	355	49	.7	3.1	-6.7		1.4
BOS	70	3	0	744.7	840	10.2	2	86	1.0	187	2.3	3.08	71	.270	.290	-58	-72	93	98	.901	367	54	.0	-7.0	6.6		-1.7
BUF	72	6	1	739.0	879	10.7	10	78	.9	186	2.3	3.09	74	.281	.298	-59	-67	96	109	.891	408	55	-2.1	-6.5	-1.0		-7.4
CIN	79	3	0	713.3	785	9.9	10	88	1.1	208	2.6	2.44	102	.265	.286	-4	3	105	122	.876	437	49	-3.6	.3	-4.7		-11.0
TOT	608	52	12	6031.3		8.9			1.1		3.0	2.37		.245	.267					.901	2949	411					

Runs
Dalrymple-Chi 91
Stovey-Wor 76
Kelly-Chi 72
O'Rourke-Bos 71
Gore-Chi 70

Hits
Dalrymple-Chi 126
Anson-Chi 120
Gore-Chi 116
Hines-Pro 115
Connor-Tro 113

Doubles
Dunlap-Cle 27
Dalrymple-Chi 25
Anson-Chi 24
Gore-Chi 23
O'Rourke-Bos 22

Triples
Stovey-Wor 14
Dalrymple-Chi 12
O'Rourke-Bos 11
Hornung-Buf 11
Phillips-Cle 10

Home Runs
Stovey-Wor 6
O'Rourke-Bos 6
Jones-Bos 5
Dunlap-Cle 4

Total Bases
Dalrymple-Chi 175
Stovey-Wor 161
O'Rourke-Bos 160
Dunlap-Cle 160
Connor-Tro 156

Runs Batted In
Anson-Chi 74
Kelly-Chi 60
Gore-Chi 47
Connor-Tro 47
O'Rourke-Bos 45

Runs Produced
Kelly-Chi 131
Dalrymple-Chi 127
Anson-Chi 127
Gore-Chi 115
O'Rourke-Bos 110

Bases On Balls
Ferguson-Tro 24
O'Rourke-Bos 21
Gore-Chi 21
Clapp-Cin 21
Crowley-Buf 19

Batting Average
Gore-Chi 360
Anson-Chi 337
Connor-Tro 332
Dalrymple-Chi 330
Burns-Chi 309

On Base Percentage
Gore-Chi 399
Anson-Chi 362
Connor-Tro 357
Dalrymple-Chi 335
Burns-Chi 333

Slugging Average
Gore-Chi 463
Connor-Tro 459
Dalrymple-Chi 458
Stovey-Wor 454
O'Rourke-Bos 441

Production
Gore-Chi 862
Connor-Tro 816
Dalrymple-Chi 793
Anson-Chi 781
O'Rourke-Bos 756

Adjusted Production
Gore-Chi 182
Jones-Bos 167
O'Rourke-Bos 167
O'Rourke-Bos 161
Connor-Tro 158

Batter Runs
Gore-Chi 30.4
Connor-Tro 25.4
Dalrymple-Chi 24.5
Anson-Chi 22.9
O'Rourke-Bos 19.9

Adjusted Batter Runs
Gore-Chi 28.2
O'Rourke-Bos 23.9
Dalrymple-Chi 22.0
Connor-Tro 20.8
Anson-Chi 20.5

Clutch Hitting Index
Anson-Chi 171
Kelly-Chi 165
Richmond-Wor 153
Hanlon-Cle 146
Whitney-Wor 145

Runs Created
Gore-Chi 61
Dalrymple-Chi 60
Connor-Tro 57
Anson-Chi 55
O'Rourke-Bos 52

Total Average
Gore-Chi 825
Connor-Tro 744
Dalrymple-Chi 695
Anson-Chi 691
O'Rourke-Bos 688

Stolen Bases

Stolen Base Average

Stolen Base Runs

Fielding Runs
Irwin-Wor 31.4
Force-Buf 29.0
Clapp-Cin 20.9
Bradley-Pro 15.8
Shaffer-Cle 15.1

Total Player Rating
Clapp-Cin 3.6
Irwin-Wor 3.2
Gore-Chi 2.7
Dunlap-Cle 2.4
O'Rourke-Bos 2.3

Wins
McCormick-Cle 45
Corcoran-Chi 43
Ward-Pro 39
Welch-Tro 34
Richmond-Wor 32

Win Percentage
Goldsmith-Chi 875
Corcoran-Chi 754
Ward-Pro 619
McCormick-Cle 616
Welch-Tro 531

Games
Richmond-Wor 74
McCormick-Cle 74
Ward-Pro 70
Welch-Tro 65

Complete Games
McCormick-Cle 72
Welch-Tro 64
Ward-Pro 59
White-Cin 58

Shutouts
Ward-Pro 8
McCormick-Cle 7
Richmond-Wor 5
Galvin-Buf 5
Corcoran-Chi 5

Saves
Richmond-Wor 3
Corey-Wor 2
Corcoran-Chi 2

Innings Pitched
McCormick-Cle 658
Ward-Pro 595
Richmond-Wor 591
Welch-Tro 574
Corcoran-Chi 536

Fewest Hits/Game
Keefe-Tro 6.09
Corcoran-Chi 6.78
Bradley-Pro 7.26
Ward-Pro 7.58
Corey-Wor 7.97

Fewest BB/Game
Bradley-Pro 28
Galvin-Buf 63
Ward-Pro 68
Weidman-Buf 71
Goldsmith-Chi 77

Strikeouts
Corcoran-Chi 268
McCormick-Cle 260
Richmond-Wor 243
Ward-Pro 230
White-Cin 161

Strikeouts/Game
Corcoran-Chi 4.50
Goldsmith-Chi 3.86
Richmond-Wor 3.70
Keefe-Tro 3.69
McCormick-Cle 3.56

Wins Above Team
McCormick-Cle 19.4
Welch-Tro 8.3
Galvin-Buf 7.0
Goldsmith-Chi 5.6
White-Cin 5.3

Earned Run Average
Keefe-Tro 86
Bradley-Pro 1.38
Ward-Pro 1.74
Goldsmith-Chi 1.76
McCormick-Cle 1.85

Adjusted ERA
Keefe-Tro 309
Bradley-Pro 159
Goldsmith-Chi 133
Ward-Pro 126
McCormick-Cle 125

Opponents' Batting Avg.
Keefe-Tro 182
Corcoran-Chi 199
Bradley-Pro 209
Ward-Pro 217
Corey-Wor 225

Opponents' On Base Pct.
Bradley-Pro 216
Keefe-Tro 216
Ward-Pro 232
Corcoran-Chi 236
Goldsmith-Chi 245

Starter Runs
Ward-Pro 42.0
McCormick-Cle 38.6
Corcoran-Chi 25.4
Bradley-Pro 21.7
Keefe-Tro 17.7

Adjusted Starter Runs
McCormick-Cle 33.5
Richmond-Wor 32.7
Ward-Pro 29.6
Corcoran-Chi 23.0
Keefe-Tro 20.9

Clutch Pitching Index
White-Cin 130
Poorman-Buf-Chi 115
Galvin-Buf 113
Bond-Bos 111
Purcell-Cin 109

Relief Runs

Adjusted Relief Runs

Relief Ranking

Total Pitcher Index
McCormick-Cle 3.7
Ward-Pro 3.4
Corcoran-Chi 3.0
Richmond-Wor 2.7
Keefe-Tro 2.3

Total Baseball Ranking
McCormick-Cle 3.7
Clapp-Cin 3.6
Ward-Pro 3.4
Irwin-Wor 3.2
Corcoran-Chi 3.0

TEAM	G	W	L	PCT	GB	R	OR	AB	H	2B	3B	HR	BB	SO	AVG	OBP	SLG	PRO	/A	BR	/A	PF	CHI	RC	TA	SB	CS	SBA	SBR
CHI	84	56	28	.667		550	379	3114	918	157	36	12	140	224	.295	.325	.380	.705	124	83	47	108	105	394	.602				
PRO	85	47	37	.560	9	447	426	3077	780	144	37	11	146	214	.253	.287	.335	.622	98	-5	25	93	104	304	.512				
BUF	83	45	38	.542	10.5	440	447	3019	797	157	50	12	108	270	.264	.289	.361	.650	106	20	15	101	99	323	.539				
DET	84	41	43	.488	15	439	429	2995	780	131	53	17	136	250	.260	.293	.357	.650	107	20	-7	106	99	320	.544				
TRO	85	39	45	.464	17	399	429	3046	754	124	31	5	140	240	.248	.281	.314	.595	90	-33	-33	100	100	275	.478				
BOS	83	38	45	.458	17.5	349	410	2916	733	121	27	5	110	193	.251	.279	.317	.596	90	-32	3	91	92	264	.473				
CLE	85	36	48	.429	20	392	414	3117	796	120	39	7	132	224	.255	.286	.326	.612	95	-17	1	96	93	297	.494				
WOR	83	32	50	.390	23	410	492	3093	781	114	31	7	121	169	.253	.281	.316	.597	90	-32	-52	105	102	281	.475				
TOT	336					3426		24377	6339	1068	304	76	1033	1784	.260	.290	.338	.628											

TEAM	CG	SHO	SV	IP	H	H/G	HR	BB	BB/G	SO	SO/G	ERA	/A	OAVG	OOBA	PR	/A	PF	CPI	FA	E	DP	FW	PW	BW	SBW	DIF
CHI	81	9	0	744.7	722	8.7	14	122	1.5	228	2.8	2.43	118	.243	.273	28	36	103	97	.916	309	54	2.1	3.4	4.4		4.2
PRO	76	7	0	757.7	756	9.0	5	138	1.6	264	3.1	2.40	107	.248	.281	31	13	92	102	.896	390	66	-2.2	1.2	2.3		3.7
BUF	72	5	0	742.3	881	10.7	9	89	1.1	185	2.2	2.84	99	.282	.302	-5	-2	101	115	.892	408	48	-3.2	-.2	1.4		5.5
DET	83	10	0	744.7	785	9.5	8	137	1.7	265	3.2	2.65	111	.259	.291	10	24	106	105	.906	338	80	.5	2.2	-.7		-3.1
TRO	85	7	0	770.0	813	9.5	11	159	1.9	207	2.4	2.97	94	.259	.295	-16	-14	101	97	.917	311	70	1.9	-1.3	-3.1		-.6
BOS	72	6	3	730.7	763	9.4	9	143	1.8	199	2.5	2.72	95	.257	.291	4	-11	93	102	.909	325	54	1.2	-1.0	.3		-4.0
CLE	82	2	0	760.0	737	8.7	9	126	1.5	240	2.8	2.68	100	.243	.273	8	0	96	86	.904	348	68	-.0	.0	.0		-6.1
WOR	80	5	0	737.3	882	10.8	11	120	1.5	196	2.4	3.54	84	.284	.310	-62	-45	107	97	.903	353	50	-.3	-4.2	-4.9		.3
TOT	631	51	3	5987.3		9.5			1.6		2.7	2.78		.260	.290					.905	2782	490					

Runs
Gore-Chi............86
Kelly-Chi............84
Dalrymple-Chi........72
O'Rourke-Buf........71
Farrell-Pro............69

Hits
Anson-Chi..........137
Dalrymple-Chi......117
Dickerson-Wor......116

Doubles
Kelly-Chi............27
Hines-Pro............27
Stovey-Wor..........25
Dunlap-Cle..........25
White-Buf............24

Triples
Rowe-Buf............11
Phillips-Cle..........10

Home Runs
Brouthers-Buf........8
Bennett-Pro............7
Farrell-Pro............5
Burns-Chi............4

Total Bases
Anson-Chi..........175
Dunlap-Cle..........156
Kelly-Chi............153
Dalrymple-Chi......150
Dickerson-Wor......149

Runs Batted In
Anson-Chi............82
Bennett-Det..........64
Kelly-Chi............55

Runs Produced
Anson-Chi..........148
Kelly-Chi............137
Gore-Chi............129
Knight-Det..........118
Richardson-Buf......113

Bases On Balls
Clapp-Cle............35
York-Pro............29
Ferguson-Tro........29
Farrell-Pro............29

Batting Average
Anson-Chi..........399
Start-Pro............328
Dunlap-Cle..........325
Dalrymple-Chi......323
Kelly-Chi............323

On Base Percentage
Anson-Chi..........442
York-Pro............362
Brouthers-Buf......361
Dunlap-Cle..........358
Gore-Chi............354

Slugging Average
Brouthers-Buf......541
Anson-Chi..........510
Bennett-Det........478
Dunlap-Cle..........444
Kelly-Chi............433

Production
Anson-Chi..........952
Brouthers-Buf......902
Bennett-Det........819
Dunlap-Cle..........802
York-Pro............790

Adjusted Production
Anson-Chi..........183
Brouthers-Buf......178
York-Pro............158
Dunlap-Cle..........157
Bennett-Det........145

Batter Runs
Anson-Chi..........38.7
Brouthers-Buf......23.9
Dunlap-Cle..........19.8
Bennett-Det........18.1
Kelly-Chi............17.8

Adjusted Batter Runs
Anson-Chi..........34.7
Brouthers-Buf......23.6
Dunlap-Cle..........21.9
York-Pro............20.9
Start-Pro............15.5

Clutch Hitting Index
Anson-Chi..........169
Ward-Pro............167
White-Buf............149
Richmond-Wor......147
Radbourn-Pro......146

Runs Created
Anson-Chi............79
Dunlap-Cle..........57
Kelly-Chi............55
Brouthers-Buf......54
Dalrymple-Chi......54

Total Average
Anson-Chi..........976
Brouthers-Buf......891
Bennett-Det........770
York-Pro............745
Dunlap-Cle..........734

Stolen Bases

Stolen Base Average

Stolen Base Runs

Fielding Runs
Force-Buf..........25.3
Richardson-Buf....24.2
Ewing-Tro..........22.4
Williamson-Chi....17.2
Bushong-Wor......15.8

Total Player Rating
Richardson-Buf.....3.0
Anson-Chi............2.8
Bennett-Det........2.7
Dunlap-Cle..........2.6
Williamson-Chi.....2.0

Wins
Whitney-Bos........31
Corcoran-Chi........31
Galvin-Buf..........29
Derby-Det............29
McCormick-Cle......26

Win Percentage
Radbourn-Pro......694
Corcoran-Chi......689
Goldsmith-Chi......649
Galvin-Buf..........547
Welch-Tro..........538

Games
Whitney-Bos........66
McCormick-Cle......59
Galvin-Buf..........56
Derby-Det............56
Richmond-Wor......53

Complete Games
Whitney-Bos........57
McCormick-Cle......57
Derby-Det............55
Richmond-Wor......50
Galvin-Buf..........48

Shutouts
Derby-Det............9
Whitney-Bos........6
Goldsmith-Chi......5
Galvin-Buf..........5

Saves
Mathews-Pro-Bos....2
Morrill-Bos..........1

Innings Pitched
Whitney-Bos........552
McCormick-Cle......526
Derby-Det............495
Galvin-Buf..........474
Richmond-Wor......462

Fewest Hits/Game
McCormick-Cle.....8.28
Weidman-Det......8.45
Radbourn-Pro......8.56
Corcoran-Chi......8.61
Ward-Pro............8.89

Fewest BB/Game
Galvin-Buf..........87
Weidman-Det.......94
Goldsmith-Chi......1.20
Richmond-Wor......1.32
McCormick-Cle.....1.44

Strikeouts
Derby-Det............212
McCormick-Cle......178
Whitney-Bos........162
Richmond-Wor......156
Corcoran-Chi......150

Strikeouts/Game
Derby-Det............3.85
Corcoran-Chi......3.40
Ward-Pro............3.25
Radbourn-Pro......3.24
McCormick-Cle.....3.05

Wins Above Team
Richmond-Wor......8.7
Radbourn-Pro......7.8
Whitney-Bos........5.9
Derby-Det............5.3
McCormick-Cle......4.7

Earned Run Average
Weidman-Det......1.80
Ward-Pro............2.13
Derby-Det............2.20
Corcoran-Chi......2.31
Galvin-Buf..........2.37

Adjusted ERA
Weidman-Det......164
Derby-Det............134
Corcoran-Chi......124
Ward-Pro............120
Galvin-Buf..........118

Opponents' Batting Avg.
McCormick-Cle......234
Weidman-Det......238
Radbourn-Pro......240
Corcoran-Chi......241
Ward-Pro............247

Opponents' On Base Pct.
Weidman-Det......257
McCormick-Cle......264
Goldsmith-Chi......272
Radbourn-Pro......276
Ward-Pro............276

Starter Runs
Derby-Det............31.7
Ward-Pro............23.8
Galvin-Buf..........21.2
Corcoran-Chi......20.5
McCormick-Cle.....19.3

Adjusted Starter Runs
Derby-Det............41.2
Corcoran-Chi......24.5
Galvin-Buf..........23.0
Ward-Pro............15.9
Weidman-Det......14.7

Clutch Pitching Index
Galvin-Buf..........126
Derby-Det............115
Mathews-Pro-Bos...114
Ward-Pro............110
Weidman-Det......109

Relief Runs

Adjusted Relief Runs

Relief Ranking

Total Pitcher Index
Derby-Det............3.2
Galvin-Buf..........2.7
Corcoran-Chi......2.0
Goldsmith-Chi......1.7
Ward-Pro............1.5

Total Baseball Ranking
Derby-Det............3.2
Richardson-Buf.....3.0
Anson-Chi............2.8
Galvin-Buf..........2.7
Bennett-Det........2.7

TEAM	G	W	L	PCT	GB	R	OR	AB	H	2B	3B	HR	BB	SO	AVG	OBP	SLG	PRO	/A	BR	/A	PF	CHI	RC	TA	SB	CS	SBA	SBR
CHI	84	55	29	.655		604	353	3225	892	209	54	15	142	262	.277	.307	.389	.696	124	82	76	101	107	395	.598				
PRO	84	52	32	.619	3	463	356	3104	776	121	53	11	102	255	.250	.274	.334	.608	96	-15	-41	106	105	291	.489				
BUF	84	45	39	.536	10	500	461	3128	858	146	47	18	116	228	.274	.300	.368	.668	115	50	30	104	97	355	.559				
BOS	85	45	39	.536	10	472	414	3118	823	114	50	15	134	244	.264	.294	.347	.641	107	23	8	103	97	326	.530				
CLE	84	42	40	.512	12	402	411	3009	716	139	40	20	122	261	.238	.268	.331	.599	93	-23	22	90	95	273	.487				
DET	86	42	41	.506	12.5	407	488	3144	724	117	44	19	122	308	.230	.259	.314	.573	84	-52	-59	102	98	262	.458				
TRO	85	35	48	.422	19.5	430	522	3057	747	116	59	12	109	298	.244	.270	.333	.603	94	-19	2	95	99	282	.487				
WOR	84	18	66	.214	37	379	652	2984	689	109	57	16	113	303	.231	.259	.322	.581	87	-42	-41	100	95	255	.468				
TOT	338					3657		24769	6225	1071	404	126	960	2159	.251	.279	.342	.622											

TEAM	CG	SHO	SV	IP	H	H/G	HR	BB	BB/G	SO	SO/G	ERA	/A	OAVG	OOBA	PR	/A	PF	CPI	FA	E	DP	FW	PW	BW	SBW	DIF
CHI	83	7	0	763.7	667	7.9	13	102	1.2	279	3.3	2.22	123	.221	.247	56	43	95	90	.899	376	54	.1	3.9	6.9		2.0
PRO	80	9	1	752.0	690	8.3	12	87	1.0	273	3.3	2.27	131	.230	.251	51	58	103	95	.900	371	67	.4	5.3	-3.7		8.1
BUF	79	3	0	737.0	778	9.5	16	114	1.4	287	3.5	3.25	92	.255	.282	-29	-22	103	93	.911	315	42	3.3	-2.0	2.7		-1.0
BOS	81	4	0	749.0	738	8.9	10	77	.9	352	4.2	2.80	105	.243	.261	7	10	102	87	.910	314	37	3.3	.9	.7		-2.0
CLE	81	4	0	751.7	743	8.9	22	132	1.6	232	2.8	2.75	94	.243	.274	10	-13	90	101	.905	358	71	1.1	-1.2	2.0		-.9
DET	82	7	0	793.0	808	9.2	19	129	1.5	354	4.0	2.98	101	.249	.277	-8	1	104	96	.894	396	44	-.9	.0	-5.4		6.7
TRO	81	6	0	757.0	837	10.0	13	168	2.0	189	2.2	3.08	91	.264	.301	-16	-22	98	111	.887	432	70	-2.7	-2.0	.2		-1.9
WOR	75	0	0	738.3	964	11.8	21	151	1.8	195	2.4	3.75	82	.298	.329	-71	-54	107	119	.878	468	66	-4.6	-4.9	-3.7		-10.8
TOT	642	40	1	6041.7		9.3			1.4		3.2	2.89		.251	.279					.898	3030	451					

Runs		Hits		Doubles		Triples		Home Runs		Total Bases	
Gore-Chi	99	Brouthers-Buf	129	Kelly-Chi	37	Connor-Tro	18	Wood-Det	7	Brouthers-Buf	192
Dalrymple-Chi	96	Anson-Chi	126	Anson-Chi	29	Wood-Det	12	Muldoon-Cle	6	Connor-Tro	185
Stovey-Wor	90			Hines-Pro	28	Corey-Wor	12	Brouthers-Buf	6	Hines-Pro	177
Kelly-Chi	81			Williamson-Chi	27					Anson-Chi	174
Purcell-Buf	79			Glasscock-Cle	27					Dalrymple-Chi	167

Runs Batted In		Runs Produced		Bases On Balls		Batting Average		On Base Percentage		Slugging Average	
Anson-Chi	83	Anson-Chi	151	Gore-Chi	29	Brouthers-Buf	.368	Brouthers-Buf	.403	Brouthers-Buf	.547
Brouthers-Buf	63	Gore-Chi	147	Williamson-Chi	27	Anson-Chi	.362	Anson-Chi	.397	Connor-Tro	.530
Williamson-Chi	60	Kelly-Chi	135	Shaffer-Cle	27	Connor-Tro	.330	Whitney-Bos	.382	Whitney-Bos	.510
Richardson-Buf	57	Dalrymple-Chi	131	Hanlon-Det	26	Start-Pro	.329	Gore-Chi	.369	Anson-Chi	.500
Kelly-Chi	55	Brouthers-Buf	128			Whitney-Bos	.323	Connor-Tro	.354	Hines-Pro	.467

Production		Adjusted Production		Batter Runs		Adjusted Batter Runs		Clutch Hitting Index		Runs Created	
Brouthers-Buf	.950	Brouthers-Buf	193	Brouthers-Buf	39.1	Brouthers-Buf	36.8	Anson-Chi	167	Brouthers-Buf	79
Anson-Chi	.897	Connor-Tro	188	Anson-Chi	32.7	Anson-Chi	32.2	Pfeffer-Tro	159	Anson-Chi	71
Whitney-Bos	.892	Anson-Chi	183	Connor-Tro	29.7	Connor-Tro	32.1	Holbert-Tro	152	Connor-Tro	67
Connor-Tro	.884	Whitney-Bos	178	Whitney-Bos	23.7	Whitney-Bos	27.8	Rowen-Bos	150	Hines-Pro	59
Hines-Pro	.793	Glasscock-Cle	158	Gore-Chi	22.2	Glasscock-Cle	21.6	Williamson-Chi	142	Gore-Chi	59

Total Average		Stolen Bases		Stolen Base Average		Stolen Base Runs		Fielding Runs		Total Player Rating	
Brouthers-Buf	.959							Glasscock-Cle	19.7	Glasscock-Cle	4.4
Whitney-Bos	.894							Dunlap-Cle	16.9	Dunlap-Cle	2.8
Anson-Chi	.874							Irwin-Wor	16.3	Bennett-Det	2.6
Connor-Tro	.846							Holbert-Tro	15.4	Connor-Tro	2.2
Gore-Chi	.736							Evans-Wor	14.3	Williamson-Chi	2.2

Wins		Win Percentage		Games		Complete Games		Shutouts		Saves	
McCormick-Cle	36	Corcoran-Chi	.692	McCormick-Cle	68	McCormick-Cle	65	Welch-Tro	5	Ward-Pro	1
Radbourn-Pro	33	Radbourn-Pro	.623	Radbourn-Pro	55	Radbourn-Pro	51	Radbourn-Pro	5		
Goldsmith-Chi	28	Goldsmith-Chi	.622	Galvin-Buf	52	Galvin-Buf	48				
Galvin-Buf	28	Ward-Pro	.613	Whitney-Bos	49	Whitney-Bos	46				
Corcoran-Chi	27	Mathews-Bos	.559	Richmond-Wor	48	Goldsmith-Chi	45				

Innings Pitched		Fewest Hits/Game		Fewest BB/Game		Strikeouts		Strikeouts/Game		Wins Above Team	
McCormick-Cle	596	Corcoran-Chi	7.10	Mathews-Bos	.69	Radbourn-Pro	201	Mathews-Bos	4.83	McCormick-Cle	9.0
Radbourn-Pro	474	Radbourn-Pro	8.15	Galvin-Buf	.81	McCormick-Cle	200	Derby-Det	4.52	Richmond-Wor	5.0
Galvin-Buf	445	McCormick-Cle	8.31	Goldsmith-Chi	.84	Derby-Det	182	Corcoran-Chi	4.30	Weidman-Det	4.4
Whitney-Bos	420	Goldsmith-Chi	8.38	Weidman-Det	.85	Whitney-Bos	180	Daily-Buf	4.08	Corcoran-Chi	3.6
		Ward-Pro	8.45	Whitney-Bos	.88	Corcoran-Chi	170	Whitney-Bos	3.86	Galvin-Buf	1.8

Earned Run Average		Adjusted ERA		Opponents' Batting Avg.		Opponents' On Base Pct.		Starter Runs		Adjusted Starter Runs	
Corcoran-Chi	1.95	Radbourn-Pro	142	Corcoran-Chi	.205	Corcoran-Chi	.239	Radbourn-Pro	42.0	Radbourn-Pro	46.4
Radbourn-Pro	2.09	Corcoran-Chi	140	Radbourn-Pro	.228	Radbourn-Pro	.248	Corcoran-Chi	37.1	Corcoran-Chi	31.0
McCormick-Cle	2.37	Ward-Pro	115	McCormick-Cle	.231	Goldsmith-Chi	.250	McCormick-Cle	34.1	Weidman-Det	17.0
Goldsmith-Chi	2.42	Weidman-Det	114	Goldsmith-Chi	.233	Weidman-Det	.254	Goldsmith-Chi	20.8	McCormick-Cle	14.6
Keefe-Tro	2.50	Keefe-Tro	113	Ward-Pro	.234	Mathews-Bos	.255	Keefe-Tro	16.2	Goldsmith-Chi	13.8

Clutch Pitching Index		Relief Runs		Adjusted Relief Runs		Relief Ranking		Total Pitcher Index		Total Baseball Ranking	
Mountain-Wor	121							Radbourn-Pro	4.3	Glasscock-Cle	4.4
Corey-Wor	120							Whitney-Bos	4.1	Radbourn-Pro	4.3
Richmond-Wor	116							Corcoran-Chi	2.9	Whitney-Bos	4.1
Welch-Tro	113							Keefe-Tro	2.2	Corcoran-Chi	2.9
Egan-Tro	112							Weidman-Det	1.1	Dunlap-Cle	2.8

TEAM	G	W	L	PCT	GB	R	OR	AB	H	2B	3B	HR	BB	SO	AVG	OBP	SLG	PRO	/A	BR	/A	PF	CHI	RC	TA	SB	CS	SBA	SBR
CIN	80	55	25	.688		489	268	3007	795	95	47	5	102	204	.264	.289	.332	.621	113	38	0	109	103	295	.498				
PHI	75	41	34	.547	11.5	406	389	2707	660	89	21	4	125	164	.244	.277	.297	.574	98	-4	-50	112	103	228	.453				
LOU	80	42	38	.525	13	443	352	2806	728	110	28	9	128	193	.259	.292	.328	.620	113	37	63	94	99	275	.505				
PIT	79	39	39	.500	15	428	418	2904	730	110	58	21	90	183	.251	.274	.351	.625	114	37	49	97	94	286	.510				
STL	80	37	43	.463	18	399	496	2865	663	87	41	11	112	226	.231	.260	.302	.562	93	-19	-18	100	100	231	.444				
BAL	74	19	54	.260	32.5	273	515	2583	535	60	24	4	72	215	.207	.229	.254	.483	66	-87	-58	92	96	153	.355				
TOT	234					2438		16872	4111	551	219	54	629	1185	.244	.271	.312	.583											

TEAM	CG	SHO	SV	IP	H	H/G	HR	BB	BB/G	SO	SO/G	ERA	/A	OAVG	OOBA	PR	/A	PF	CPI	FA	E	DP	FW	PW	BW	SBW	DIF
CIN	77	11	0	721.3	609	7.6	7	125	1.6	165	2.1	1.66	161	.213	.246	82	81	100	118	.907	332	41	3.2	7.4	.0		4.3
PHI	72	2	0	663.0	682	9.3	13	99	1.3	190	2.6	2.97	100	.248	.274	-21	0	111	96	.895	361	36	1.9	.0	-4.6		6.2
LOU	73	6	0	693.3	637	8.3	6	112	1.5	240	3.1	2.03	119	.228	.258	51	29	90	112	.893	385	57	.8	2.7	5.8		-7.2
PIT	77	2	0	696.7	694	9.0	4	82	1.1	252	3.3	2.79	93	.242	.263	-7	-15	97	90	.889	397	40	.2	-1.4	4.5		-3.3
STL	75	3	1	688.3	729	9.5	7	103	1.3	225	2.9	2.92	96	.254	.280	-17	-9	104	101	.875	446	41	-2.0	-.8	-1.7		1.5
BAL	64	1	0	646.3	760	10.6	15	108	1.5	113	1.6	3.90	71	.274	.301	-86	-82	102	94	.859	490	41	-4.1	-7.5	-5.3		-.6
TOT	438	25	1	4109.0		9.0			1.4		2.6	2.69		.244	.271					.886	2411	256					

Runs
Swartwood-Pit ...86
Sommer-Cin ...82
Carpenter-Cin ...78
Browning-Lou ...67
Birchall-Phi ...65

Hits
Carpenter-Cin ...120
Browning-Lou ...109
Swartwood-Pit ...107
Sommer-Cin ...102
Gleason-StL ...100

Doubles
Swartwood-Pit ...18
Mansell-Pit ...18
Browning-Lou ...17
Taylor-Pit ...16
Cuthbert-StL ...16

Triples
Mansell-Pit ...16
Taylor-Pit ...12
Wheeler-Cin ...11
Swartwood-Pit ...11
Wolf-Lou ...8

Home Runs
Walker-StL ...7
Swartwood-Pit ...5
Browning-Lou ...5
Taylor-Pit ...4

Total Bases
Swartwood-Pit ...162
Mansell-Pit ...152
Carpenter-Cin ...148
Browning-Lou ...147
Taylor-Pit ...136

Runs Batted In

Runs Produced
Swartwood-Pit ...81
Sommer-Cin ...81
Carpenter-Cin ...77
Birchall-Phi ...65

Bases On Balls
Gleason-StL ...27
Browning-Lou ...26
Sommer-Cin ...24
Reccius-Lou ...23
Swartwood-Pit ...21

Batting Average
Browning-Lou ...378
Carpenter-Cin ...342
Swartwood-Pit ...329
O'Brien-Phi ...303
Wolf-Lou ...299

On Base Percentage
Browning-Lou ...430
Swartwood-Pit ...370
Carpenter-Cin ...360
O'Brien-Phi ...339
Sommer-Cin ...333

Slugging Average
Browning-Lou ...510
Swartwood-Pit ...498
Taylor-Pit ...455
Mansell-Pit ...438
Carpenter-Cin ...422

Production
Browning-Lou ...940
Swartwood-Pit ...868
Carpenter-Cin ...782
O'Brien-Phi ...758
Taylor-Pit ...752

Adjusted Production
Browning-Lou ...231
Swartwood-Pit ...196
Taylor-Pit ...155
Carpenter-Cin ...150
Mansell-Pit ...147

Batter Runs
Browning-Lou ...35.3
Swartwood-Pit ...30.2
Carpenter-Cin ...22.0
Taylor-Pit ...14.8
Mansell-Pit ...14.4

Adjusted Batter Runs
Browning-Lou ...38.1
Swartwood-Pit ...31.6
Carpenter-Cin ...17.5
Taylor-Pit ...16.0
Mansell-Pit ...15.9

Clutch Hitting Index

Runs Created
Browning-Lou ...65
Swartwood-Pit ...61
Carpenter-Cin ...55
Mansell-Pit ...45
Sommer-Cin ...44

Total Average
Browning-Lou ...966
Swartwood-Pit ...839
Carpenter-Cin ...684
O'Brien-Phi ...679
Taylor-Pit ...665

Stolen Bases

Stolen Base Average

Stolen Base Runs

Fielding Runs
Stricker-Phi ...20.3
Battin-Pit ...18.3
Snyder-Cin ...13.2
White-Cin ...12.5
Gleason-StL ...10.9

Total Player Rating
Browning-Lou ...4.5
Swartwood-Pit ...2.1
Gleason-StL ...1.9
Mansell-Pit ...1.5
Snyder-Cin ...1.5

Wins
White-Cin ...40
Mullane-Lou ...30
Weaver-Phi ...26
McGinnis-StL ...25
Salisbury-Pit ...20

Win Percentage
White-Cin ...769
Weaver-Phi ...634
McGinnis-StL ...595
Mullane-Lou ...556
Salisbury-Pit ...526

Games
Mullane-Lou ...55
White-Cin ...54
Landis-Phi-Bal ...44
McGinnis-StL ...44
Weaver-Phi ...42

Complete Games
White-Cin ...52
Mullane-Lou ...51
McGinnis-StL ...42
Weaver-Phi ...41
Salisbury-Pit ...38

Shutouts
White-Cin ...8
Mullane-Lou ...5
McGinnis-StL ...3
McCormick-Cin ...3
Weaver-Phi ...2

Saves
Fusselback-StL ...1

Innings Pitched
White-Cin ...480
Mullane-Lou ...460
McGinnis-StL ...379
Weaver-Phi ...371
Landis-Phi-Bal ...358

Fewest Hits/Game
Hecker-Lou ...6.49
McCormick-Cin ...7.24
Driscoll-Pit ...7.25
White-Cin ...7.71
Geis-Bal ...7.87

Fewest BB/Game
Hecker-Lou ...43
Driscoll-Pit ...54
Weaver-Phi ...85
Salisbury-Pit ...99
Landis-Phi-Bal ...1.18

Strikeouts
Mullane-Lou ...170
Salisbury-Pit ...135
McGinnis-StL ...134
White-Cin ...122
Weaver-Phi ...104

Strikeouts/Game
Salisbury-Pit ...3.63
Arundel-Pit ...3.53
Mullane-Lou ...3.33
McGinnis-StL ...3.18
Reccius-Lou ...2.94

Wins Above Team
White-Cin ...13.1
McGinnis-StL ...8.6
Weaver-Phi ...7.1
Mullane-Lou ...4.7
Driscoll-Pit ...2.6

Earned Run Average
Driscoll-Pit ...1.21
Hecker-Lou ...1.30
McCormick-Cin ...1.51
White-Cin ...1.54
Mullane-Lou ...1.88

Adjusted ERA
Driscoll-Pit ...215
Hecker-Lou ...186
McCormick-Cin ...177
White-Cin ...174
Mullane-Lou ...128

Opponents' Batting Avg.
Hecker-Lou ...188
McCormick-Cin ...206
Driscoll-Pit ...206
White-Cin ...216
Geis-Bal ...220

Opponents' On Base Pct.
Hecker-Lou ...199
Driscoll-Pit ...218
McCormick-Cin ...243
White-Cin ...244
Salisbury-Pit ...253

Starter Runs
White-Cin ...61.3
Mullane-Lou ...41.4
Driscoll-Pit ...33.0
McCormick-Cin ...28.7
Hecker-Lou ...16.1

Adjusted Starter Runs
White-Cin ...60.9
Driscoll-Pit ...31.0
McCormick-Cin ...28.5
Mullane-Lou ...27.2
McGinnis-StL ...13.7

Clutch Pitching Index
White-Cin ...125
McCormick-Cin ...121
Reccius-Lou ...119
Mullane-Lou ...119
Driscoll-Pit ...113

Relief Runs

Adjusted Relief Runs

Relief Ranking

Total Pitcher Index
White-Cin ...7.8
Mullane-Lou ...4.6
Driscoll-Pit ...2.3
McCormick-Cin ...2.2
Weaver-Phi ...1.3

Total Baseball Ranking
White-Cin ...7.8
Mullane-Lou ...4.6
Browning-Lou ...4.5
Driscoll-Pit ...2.3
Hecker-Lou ...2.2

TEAM	G	W	L	PCT	GB	R	OR	AB	H	2B	3B	HR	BB	SO	AVG	OBP	SLG	PRO	/A	BR	/A	PF	CHI	RC	TA	SB	CS	SBA	SBR
BOS	98	63	35	.643		669	456	3657	1010	209	86	34	123	423	.276	.300	.408	.708	117	68	31	106	104	459	.611				
CHI	98	59	39	.602	4	679	540	3658	1000	277	61	13	129	399	.273	.298	.393	.691	112	49	-3	109	109	439	.590				
PRO	98	58	40	.592	5	636	436	3685	1001	189	59	21	149	309	.272	.300	.372	.672	107	29	25	101	104	422	.566				
CLE	100	55	42	.567	7.5	476	443	3457	852	184	38	6	139	374	.246	.276	.329	.605	87	-52	-76	105	96	321	.489				
BUF	98	52	45	.536	10.5	614	576	3729	1058	184	59	8	147	342	.284	.311	.371	.682	110	44	44	100	97	441	.573				
NY	98	46	50	.479	16	530	577	3524	900	139	69	24	127	297	.255	.281	.354	.635	95	-17	-15	100	98	360	.524				
DET	101	40	58	.408	23	524	650	3726	931	164	48	13	166	378	.250	.282	.330	.612	89	-45	6	91	96	355	.499				
PHI	99	17	81	.173	46	437	887	3576	859	181	48	3	141	355	.240	.269	.320	.589	82	-73	-17	90	89	316	.473				
TOT	395					4565		29012	7611	1527	468	124	1121	2877	.262	.290	.360	.650											

TEAM	CG	SHO	SV	IP	H	H/G	HR	BB	BB/G	SO	SO/G	ERA	/A	OAVG	OOBA	PR	/A	PF	CPI	FA	E	DP	FW	PW	BW	SBW	DIF
BOS	89	6	3	860.0	853	8.9	11	90	.9	538	5.6	2.55	125	.243	.262	55	61	102	95	.901	409	58	3.1	5.3	2.7		2.8
CHI	91	5	1	862.0	942	9.8	21	123	1.3	299	3.1	2.78	120	.262	.286	34	54	107	113	.879	543	76	-3.5	4.7	-.3		9.0
PRO	88	4	1	871.0	827	8.5	12	111	1.1	376	3.9	2.37	128	.235	.259	74	63	96	96	.903	419	75	2.7	5.5	2.2		-1.3
CLE	92	5	2	879.0	818	8.4	7	217	2.2	402	4.1	2.22	146	.232	.276	89	100	104	111	.909	389	69	4.1	8.7	-6.6		.3
BUF	90	5	2	859.3	971	10.2	12	101	1.1	362	3.8	3.33	93	.268	.288	-18	-20	99	95	.895	445	52	1.4	-1.7	3.8		.0
NY	87	5	0	866.0	907	9.4	19	170	1.8	323	3.4	2.94	108	.253	.287	19	21	101	103	.890	468	52	.2	1.8	-1.3		-2.8
DET	89	4	2	894.3	1026	10.3	22	184	1.9	324	3.3	3.58	82	.271	.305	-44	-63	94	100	.893	470	77	.1	-5.5	.5		-4.2
PHI	91	3	0	864.7	1267	13.2	20	125	1.3	253	2.6	5.34	58	.322	.343	-211	-213	99	94	.858	639	62	-8.2	-18.6	-1.5		-3.7
TOT	717	37	11	6956.3		9.8			1.5		3.7	3.14		.262	.290					.891	3782	521					

Runs		Hits		Doubles		Triples		Home Runs		Total Bases	
Hornung-Bos	107	Brouthers-Buf	159	Williamson-Chi	49	Brouthers-Buf	17	Ewing-NY	10	Brouthers-Buf	243
Gore-Chi	105	Connor-NY	146	Brouthers-Buf	41	Morrill-Bos	16	Hornung-Bos	8	Morrill-Bos	212
O'Rourke-Buf	102	O'Rourke-Buf	143	Burns-Chi	37	Sutton-Bos	15	Denny-Pro	8	Connor-NY	207
Sutton-Bos	101	Sutton-Bos	134	Anson-Chi	36	Connor-NY	15	Ward-NY	7	Sutton-Bos	201
Hines-Pro	94	Wood-Det	133					Morrill-Bos	6	Hornung-Bos	199

Runs Batted In		Runs Produced		Bases On Balls		Batting Average		On Base Percentage		Slugging Average	
Brouthers-Buf	97	Brouthers-Buf	179	York-Cle	37	Brouthers-Buf	.374	Brouthers-Buf	.397	Brouthers-Buf	.572
Burdock-Bos	88	Sutton-Bos	171	Hanlon-Det	34	Connor-NY	.357	Connor-NY	.394	Morrill-Bos	.525
Sutton-Bos	73	Hornung-Bos	165	Powell-Det	28	Gore-Chi	.334	Gore-Chi	.377	Connor-NY	.506
Morrill-Bos	68	Burdock-Bos	163	Shaffer-Buf	27	Burdock-Bos	.330	Dunlap-Cle	.361	Sutton-Bos	.486
Anson-Chi	68			Gore-Chi	27	O'Rourke-Buf	.328	Burdock-Bos	.353	Ewing-NY	.481

Production		Adjusted Production		Batter Runs		Adjusted Batter Runs		Clutch Hitting Index		Runs Created	
Brouthers-Buf	.969	Brouthers-Buf	190	Brouthers-Buf	44.4	Brouthers-Buf	44.4	Burdock-Bos	158	Brouthers-Buf	99
Connor-NY	.900	Connor-NY	171	Connor-NY	34.6	Connor-NY	34.7	Anson-Chi	144	Connor-NY	84
Morrill-Bos	.868	Bennett-Det	162	Morrill-Bos	27.6	Whitney-Bos	29.6	Brouthers-Buf	141	Morrill-Bos	75
Gore-Chi	.849	Morrill-Bos	150	Gore-Chi	26.5	Bennett-Det	26.5	Burns-Chi	135	Sutton-Bos	72
Sutton-Bos	.836	Wood-Det	149	Sutton-Bos	24.4	Wood-Det	24.9	Start-Pro	135	Gore-Chi	72

Total Average		Stolen Bases		Stolen Base Average		Stolen Base Runs		Fielding Runs		Total Player Rating	
Brouthers-Buf	.974							Farrell-Pro	22.3	Bennett-Det	3.6
Connor-NY	.882							Richardson-Buf	20.2	Wood-Det	3.0
Morrill-Bos	.825							Shaffer-Buf	18.1	Ewing-NY	2.9
Gore-Chi	.812							Ward-NY	16.7	Richardson-Buf	2.9
Bennett-Det	.783							Williamson-Chi	16.4	Brouthers-Buf	2.8

Wins		Win Percentage		Games		Complete Games		Shutouts		Saves	
Radbourn-Pro	48	McCormick-Cle	.700	Radbourn-Pro	76	Galvin-Buf	72	Galvin-Buf	5	Whitney-Bos	2
Galvin-Buf	46	Radbourn-Pro	.658	Galvin-Buf	76	Radbourn-Pro	66	Welch-NY	4	Weidman-Det	2
Whitney-Bos	37	Buffinton-Bos	.641	Coleman-Phi	65	Coleman-Phi	59	Radbourn-Pro	4		
Corcoran-Chi	34	Whitney-Bos	.638	Whitney-Bos	62	Whitney-Bos	54	Daily-Cle	4		
McCormick-Cle	28	Corcoran-Chi	.630	Corcoran-Chi	56	Corcoran-Chi	51	Buffinton-Bos	4		

Innings Pitched		Fewest Hits/Game		Fewest BB/Game		Strikeouts		Strikeouts/Game		Wins Above Team	
Galvin-Buf	656	Sawyer-Cle	7.60	Whitney-Bos	.61	Whitney-Bos	345	Whitney-Bos	6.04	Galvin-Buf	17.6
Radbourn-Pro	632	Radbourn-Pro	8.02	Galvin-Buf	.69	Radbourn-Pro	315	Buffinton-Bos	5.08	Radbourn-Pro	15.7
Coleman-Phi	538	McCormick-Cle	8.32	Radbourn-Pro	.80	Galvin-Buf	279	Sawyer-Cle	4.85	McCormick-Cle	8.6
Whitney-Bos	514	Daily-Cle	8.55	Coleman-Phi	.80	Corcoran-Chi	216	Radbourn-Pro	4.49	Corcoran-Chi	3.8
Corcoran-Chi	474	Whitney-Bos	8.61	Goldsmith-Chi	.92	Buffinton-Bos	188	Corcoran-Chi	4.10	Welch-NY	3.6

Earned Run Average		Adjusted ERA		Opponents' Batting Avg.		Opponents' On Base Pct.		Starter Runs		Adjusted Starter Runs	
McCormick-Cle	1.84	McCormick-Cle	177	Sawyer-Cle	.215	Radbourn-Pro	.241	Radbourn-Pro	76.4	Radbourn-Pro	68.0
Radbourn-Pro	2.05	Radbourn-Pro	147	Radbourn-Pro	.225	Whitney-Bos	.250	Whitney-Bos	51.3	Whitney-Bos	54.3
Whitney-Bos	2.24	Whitney-Bos	142	McCormick-Cle	.231	Galvin-Buf	.265	McCormick-Cle	49.3	McCormick-Cle	53.7
Sawyer-Cle	2.36	Sawyer-Cle	138	Daily-Cle	.236	McCormick-Cle	.266	Corcoran-Chi	34.3	Corcoran-Chi	45.1
Daily-Cle	2.42	Corcoran-Chi	134	Whitney-Bos	.237	Ward-NY	.266	Galvin-Buf	30.8	Daily-Cle	35.1

Clutch Pitching Index		Relief Runs		Adjusted Relief Runs		Relief Ranking		Total Pitcher Index		Total Baseball Ranking	
McCormick-Cle	121							Radbourn-Pro	8.2	Radbourn-Pro	8.2
Shaw-Det	119							Whitney-Bos	7.8	Whitney-Bos	7.8
O'Neill-NY	116							McCormick-Cle	5.6	McCormick-Cle	5.6
Goldsmith-Chi	115							Corcoran-Chi	4.2	Corcoran-Chi	4.2
Burns-Det	112							Galvin-Buf	2.3	Bennett-Det	3.6

TEAM	G	W	L	PCT	GB	R	OR	AB	H	2B	3B	HR	BB	SO	AVG	OBP	SLG	PRO	/A	BR	/A	PF	CHI	RC	TA	SB	CS	SBA	SBR
PHI	98	66	32	.673		720	547	3714	972	149	50	20	194	268	.262	.298	.345	.643	110	42	26	103	114	392	.538				
STL	98	65	33	.663	1	549	409	3495	892	118	46	7	125	240	.255	.281	.321	.602	97	-11	-54	108	103	323	.479				
CIN	98	61	37	.622	5	662	413	3669	961	122	73	35	139	261	.262	.289	.364	.653	113	47	27	103	107	395	.544				
NY	97	54	42	.563	11	498	405	3534	883	111	58	6	142	259	.250	.279	.319	.598	96	-16	-57	108	93	322	.479				
LOU	98	52	45	.536	13.5	564	562	3553	891	114	66	12	140	305	.251	.279	.330	.609	99	-3	29	94	102	336	.493				
COL	97	32	65	.330	33.5	476	659	3553	854	101	78	16	134	410	.240	.268	.326	.594	94	-23	47	87	90	318	.479				
PIT	98	31	67	.316	35	525	728	3609	892	120	58	13	162	345	.247	.280	.323	.603	97	-10	26	94	94	334	.489				
BAL	96	28	68	.292	37	471	742	3534	870	125	49	5	162	331	.246	.279	.314	.593	94	-20	-58	107	88	317	.477				
TOT	390					4465		28661	7215	960	478	114	1198	2419	.252	.282	.331	.612											

TEAM	CG	SHO	SV	IP	H	H/G	HR	BB	BB/G	SO	SO/G	ERA	/A	OAVG	OOBA	PR	/A	PF	CPI	FA	E	DP	FW	PW	BW	SBW	DIF
PHI	92	1	0	873.0	921	9.5	22	95	1.0	347	3.6	2.88	114	.253	.272	41	37	99	113	.865	584	40	-3.9	3.3	2.3		15.3
STL	93	9	1	879.3	729	7.5	7	150	1.5	325	3.3	2.23	155	.211	.243	104	120	105	97	.909	388	62	4.5	10.6	-4.8		5.6
CIN	96	8	0	866.7	766	8.0	17	168	1.7	215	2.2	2.26	143	.221	.257	99	93	98	114	.906	383	57	4.8	8.2	2.4		-3.3
NY	97	6	0	874.0	749	7.7	12	123	1.3	480	4.9	2.90	120	.216	.243	38	55	105	78	.894	439	45	2.4	4.8	-5.0		3.8
LOU	96	7	0	873.7	987	10.2	7	110	1.1	269	2.8	3.51	88	.267	.288	-20	-40	94	101	.884	488	67	.3	-3.5	2.6		4.2
COL	90	4	0	840.3	980	10.5	16	211	2.3	222	2.4	3.97	76	.273	.313	-62	-89	91	105	.873	540	69	-2.0	-7.8	4.1		-10.8
PIT	82	1	1	867.7	1140	11.8	21	151	1.6	271	2.8	4.62	70	.297	.324	-126	-133	98	102	.884	506	55	-.5	-11.7	2.3		-8.1
BAL	86	1	0	844.7	943	10.0	12	190	2.0	290	3.1	4.09	91	.264	.302	-74	-33	113	93	.855	624	44	-5.6	-2.9	-5.1		-6.4
TOT	732	37	2	6919.3		9.4			1.6		3.1	3.30		.252	.282					.884	3952	439					

Runs		Hits		Doubles		Triples		Home Runs		Total Bases	
Stovey-Phi	110	Swartwood-Pit	147	Stovey-Phi	31	Smith-Col	17	Stovey-Phi	14	Stovey-Phi	212
Reilly-Cin	103	Reilly-Cin	136	Swartwood-Pit	24	Reilly-Cin	14	Jones-Cin	11	Reilly-Cin	212
Carpenter-Cin	99	Carpenter-Cin	129	Knight-Phi	23	Kuehne-Col	14	Reilly-Cin	9	Swartwood-Pit	196
Knight-Phi	98	Stovey-Phi	127	Hayes-Pit	23	Mansell-Pit	13	Fulmer-Cin	5	Jones-Cin	185
		Nelson-NY	127			Mann-Col	13	Brown-Col	5	Gleason-StL	167

Runs Batted In		Runs Produced		Bases On Balls		Batting Average		On Base Percentage		Slugging Average	
Knight-Phi	97	Knight-Phi	97	Stearns-Bal	34	Swartwood-Pit	.356	Swartwood-Pit	.391	Stovey-Phi	.504
Stovey-Phi	96	Nelson-NY	96	Nelson-NY	31	Browning-Lou	.338	Browning-Lou	.378	Reilly-Cin	.485
Carpenter-Cin	96	Carpenter-Cin	96	Moynahan-Phi	30	Clinton-Bal	.313	Clinton-Bal	.357	Swartwood-Pit	.475
Reilly-Cin	94	Reilly-Cin	94	Gleason-StL-Lou	29	Reilly-Cin	.311	Moynahan-Phi	.356	Jones-Cin	.473
Birchall-Phi	94	Clinton-Bal	94	Clinton-Bal	27	Moynahan-Phi	.308	Nelson-NY	.353	Browning-Lou	.458

Production		Adjusted Production		Batter Runs		Adjusted Batter Runs		Clutch Hitting Index		Runs Created	
Swartwood-Pit	.866	Swartwood-Pit	190	Swartwood-Pit	35.0	Swartwood-Pit	39.2			Swartwood-Pit	79
Stovey-Phi	.846	Browning-Lou	178	Stovey-Phi	31.5	Browning-Lou	30.2			Stovey-Phi	74
Browning-Lou	.836	Stovey-Phi	165	Browning-Lou	26.8	Stovey-Phi	29.7			Reilly-Cin	71
Reilly-Cin	.810	Reilly-Cin	152	Reilly-Cin	26.1	Reilly-Cin	23.9			Browning-Lou	64
Jones-Cin	.802	Jones-Cin	150	Jones-Cin	23.1	Jones-Cin	21.0			Jones-Cin	62

Total Average		Stolen Bases		Stolen Base Average		Stolen Base Runs		Fielding Runs		Total Player Rating	
Swartwood-Pit	.827							Holbert-NY	36.7	Smith-Col	3.2
Stovey-Phi	.810							Battin-Pit	28.0	Swartwood-Pit	3.1
Browning-Lou	.789							Richmond-Col	23.2	Richmond-Col	3.0
Jones-Cin	.743							Latham-StL	20.6	Holbert-NY	2.3
Reilly-Cin	.734							Gerhardt-Lou	18.6	Gerhardt-Lou	2.2

Wins		Win Percentage		Games		Complete Games		Shutouts		Saves	
White-Cin	43	Mullane-StL	.700	Keefe-NY	68	Keefe-NY	68	White-Cin	6	Mullane-StL	1
Keefe-NY	41	Mathews-Phi	.698	White-Cin	65	White-Cin	64	McGinnis-StL	6	Barr-Pit	1
Mullane-StL	35	Bradley-Phi	.696	Mountain-Col	59	Mountain-Col	57	Keefe-NY	5		
Mathews-Phi	30	White-Cin	.662	Mullane-StL	53	Mullane-StL	49	Weaver-Lou	4		
McGinnis-StL	28	McGinnis-StL	.636	Hecker-Lou	51	Hecker-Lou	49	Mountain-Col	4		

Innings Pitched		Fewest Hits/Game		Fewest BB/Game		Strikeouts		Strikeouts/Game		Wins Above Team	
Keefe-NY	619	Keefe-NY	7.07	Mathews-Phi	.73	Keefe-NY	361	Keefe-NY	5.25	Mountain-Col	9.9
White-Cin	577	Mullane-StL	7.26	Weaver-Lou	.82	Mathews-Phi	203	Mathews-Phi	4.80	Keefe-NY	8.8
Mountain-Col	503	White-Cin	7.38	Lynch-NY	.88	Mullane-StL	191	Lynch-NY	4.20	White-Cin	8.3
Mullane-StL	461	McGinnis-StL	7.64	Bradley-Phi	.93	Mountain-Col	159	Mullane-StL	3.73	Driscoll-Pit	6.0
Hecker-Lou	451	Deagle-Cin	8.27	Driscoll-Pit	1.04	Hecker-Lou	153	Henderson-Bal	3.65	Mullane-StL	5.0

Earned Run Average		Adjusted ERA		Opponents' Batting Avg.		Opponents' On Base Pct.		Starter Runs		Adjusted Starter Runs	
White-Cin	2.09	Mullane-StL	158	Keefe-NY	.202	Keefe-NY	.233	White-Cin	77.6	White-Cin	73.4
Mullane-StL	2.19	White-Cin	155	Mullane-StL	.207	Mullane-StL	.238	Keefe-NY	61.0	Keefe-NY	73.3
Deagle-Cin	2.31	McGinnis-StL	149	White-Cin	.209	White-Cin	.244	Mullane-StL	57.1	Mullane-StL	65.4
McGinnis-StL	2.33	Keefe-NY	144	McGinnis-StL	.215	McGinnis-StL	.249	McGinnis-StL	41.5	McGinnis-StL	48.4
Keefe-NY	2.41	Deagle-Cin	140	Deagle-Cin	.229	Bradley-Phi	.263	Mathews-Phi	35.8	Mathews-Phi	34.2

Clutch Pitching Index		Relief Runs		Adjusted Relief Runs		Relief Ranking		Total Pitcher Index		Total Baseball Ranking	
Mathews-Phi	127							Keefe-NY	7.6	Keefe-NY	7.6
Corey-Phi	123							White-Cin	6.7	White-Cin	6.7
McCormick-Cin	123							Mullane-StL	6.6	Mullane-StL	6.6
Valentine-Col	122							McGinnis-StL	4.0	McGinnis-StL	4.0
Deagle-Cin	118							Mathews-Phi	2.5	Smith-Col	3.2

TEAM	G	W	L	PCT	GB	R	OR	AB	H	2B	3B	HR	BB	SO	AVG	OBP	SLG	PRO	/A	BR	/A	PF	CHI	RC	TA	SB	CS	SBA	SBR
PRO	114	84	28	.750		665	388	4093	987	153	43	21	300	469	.241	.293	.315	.608	95	-17	-26	102	106	387	.512				
BOS	116	73	38	.658	10.5	684	468	4189	1063	179	60	36	207	660	.254	.289	.351	.640	104	17	30	98	104	435	.536				
BUF	114	64	47	.577	19.5	700	626	4197	1099	163	69	39	215	458	.262	.298	.361	.659	110	46	3	107	101	463	.559				
NY	116	62	50	.554	22	693	623	4124	1053	149	67	23	249	492	.255	.298	.341	.639	104	20	32	98	105	429	.539				
CHI	112	62	50	.554	22	834	647	4182	1176	162	50	142	264	469	.281	.324	.446	.770	144	201	149	108	98	619	.708				
PHI	113	39	73	.348	45	549	824	3998	934	149	39	14	209	512	.234	.272	.301	.573	84	-71	-22	92	101	335	.461				
CLE	113	35	77	.313	49	458	716	3934	934	147	49	16	170	576	.237	.269	.312	.581	86	-62	-75	102	85	338	.466				
DET	114	28	84	.250	56	445	736	3966	824	114	47	31	207	699	.208	.247	.284	.531	70	-130	-90	94	93	285	.424				
TOT	456					5028		32683	8070	1216	424	322	1821	4335	.247	.287	.340	.626											

TEAM	CG	SHO	SV	IP	H	H/G	HR	BB	BB/G	SO	SO/G	ERA	/A	OAVG	OOBA	PR	/A	PF	CPI	FA	E	DP	FW	PW	BW	SBW	DIF
PRO	107	16	2	1036.3	825	7.2	26	172	1.5	639	5.5	1.61	177	.206	.239	157	143	96	104	.918	398	50	5.1	12.8	-2.3		12.4
BOS	109	14	2	1037.0	932	8.1	30	135	1.2	742	6.4	2.47	112	.227	.251	58	35	93	85	.921	384	46	5.9	3.1	2.7		5.8
BUF	108	14	1	1001.0	1041	9.4	46	189	1.7	534	4.8	2.95	106	.253	.286	3	20	105	105	.905	462	71	1.7	1.8	.3		4.7
NY	111	4	0	1014.0	1011	9.0	28	326	2.9	567	5.0	3.12	92	.245	.301	-15	-27	97	100	.896	514	69	-1.1	-2.4	2.9		6.6
CHI	106	9	0	997.3	1028	9.3	83	231	2.1	472	4.3	3.03	103	.252	.292	-6	8	105	114	.886	595	107	-5.4	.7	13.3		-2.6
PHI	106	3	1	981.0	1090	10.0	38	254	2.3	411	3.8	3.93	74	.266	.309	-103	-111	97	92	.889	536	67	-2.3	-9.9	-2.0		-2.8
CLE	107	7	0	994.7	1046	9.5	35	269	2.4	482	4.4	3.43	93	.255	.301	-49	-24	108	96	.897	512	75	-1.0	-2.1	-6.7		-11.2
DET	109	3	0	984.7	1097	10.0	36	245	2.2	488	4.5	3.38	87	.266	.308	-44	-46	99	105	.887	549	60	-3.0	-4.1	-8.1		-12.9
TOT	863	70	6	8046.0		9.0			2.0		4.8	2.98		.247	.287					.900	3950	545					

Runs		Hits		Doubles		Triples		Home Runs		Total Bases	
Kelly-Chi	120	Sutton-Bos	162	Hines-Pro	36	Ewing-NY	20	Williamson-Chi	27	Dalrymple-Chi	263
O'Rourke-Buf	119	O'Rourke-Buf	162	O'Rourke-Buf	33	Brouthers-Buf	15	Pfeffer-Chi	25	Anson-Chi	258
Hornung-Bos	119	Dalrymple-Chi	161	Anson-Chi	30	Rowe-Buf	14	Dalrymple-Chi	22	Pfeffer-Chi	240
Dalrymple-Chi	111	Kelly-Chi	160	Manning-Phi	29	Phillips-Cle	12	Anson-Chi	21	Kelly-Chi	237
Anson-Chi	108	Anson-Chi	159			McKinnon-NY	12	Brouthers-Buf	14	Williamson-Chi	231

Runs Batted In		Runs Produced		Bases On Balls		Batting Average		On Base Percentage		Slugging Average	
Anson-Chi	102	Kelly-Chi	202	Gore-Chi	61	Kelly-Chi	.354	Kelly-Chi	.414	Brouthers-Buf	.563
Pfeffer-Chi	101	Anson-Chi	189	Kelly-Chi	46	O'Rourke-Buf	.347	Gore-Chi	.404	Williamson-Chi	.554
Kelly-Chi	95	Pfeffer-Chi	181	Hines-Pro	44	Sutton-Bos	.346	O'Rourke-Buf	.392	Anson-Chi	.543
Burns-Chi	94	O'Rourke-Buf	177	Williamson-Chi	42	Anson-Chi	.335	Sutton-Bos	.384	Kelly-Chi	.524
Williamson-Chi	84	Connor-NY	176			Brouthers-Buf	.327	Brouthers-Buf	.378	Pfeffer-Chi	.514

Production		Adjusted Production		Batter Runs		Adjusted Batter Runs		Clutch Hitting Index		Runs Created	
Brouthers-Buf	.941	Brouthers-Buf	180	Kelly-Chi	48.8	Kelly-Chi	43.1	Burns-Chi	229	Kelly-Chi	100
Kelly-Chi	.938	Kelly-Chi	179	Anson-Chi	44.6	Anson-Chi	38.8	Dorgan-NY	142	Anson-Chi	99
Anson-Chi	.916	Anson-Chi	171	Brouthers-Buf	41.2	Brouthers-Buf	37.1	Caskin-NY	140	O'Rourke-Buf	90
Williamson-Chi	.898	Sutton-Bos	166	O'Rourke-Buf	38.8	Sutton-Bos	34.8	McKinnon-NY	135	Dalrymple-Chi	88
O'Rourke-Buf	.872	Williamson-Chi	165	Williamson-Chi	36.7	O'Rourke-Buf	34.0	Morrill-Bos	135	Brouthers-Buf	87

Total Average		Stolen Bases	Stolen Base Average	Stolen Base Runs	Fielding Runs		Total Player Rating	
Kelly-Chi	.969				Pfeffer-Chi	40.4	Pfeffer-Chi	5.8
Brouthers-Buf	.959				Glasscock-Cle	27.4	Williamson-Chi	4.2
Anson-Chi	.908				Williamson-Chi	22.1	Kelly-Chi	3.7
Williamson-Chi	.907				Lillie-Buf	11.9	Ewing-NY	2.9
O'Rourke-Buf	.849				Briody-Cle	11.6	Glasscock-Cle	2.8

Wins		Win Percentage		Games		Complete Games		Shutouts		Saves	
Radbourn-Pro	60	Radbourn-Pro	.833	Radbourn-Pro	75	Radbourn-Pro	73	Galvin-Buf	12	Morrill-Bos	2
Buffinton-Bos	48	Buffinton-Bos	.750	Galvin-Buf	72	Galvin-Buf	71	Radbourn-Pro	11	Sweeney-Pro	1
Galvin-Buf	46	Sweeney-Pro	.680	Buffinton-Bos	67	Buffinton-Bos	63	Buffinton-Bos	8	Radbourn-Pro	1
Welch-NY	39	Galvin-Buf	.676	Welch-NY	65	Welch-NY	62	Corcoran-Chi	7	O'Rourke-Buf	1
Corcoran-Chi	35	Welch-NY	.650	Corcoran-Chi	60	Corcoran-Chi	57	Whitney-Bos	6	Ferguson-Phi	1

Innings Pitched		Fewest Hits/Game		Fewest BB/Game		Strikeouts		Strikeouts/Game		Wins Above Team	
Radbourn-Pro	679	Sweeney-Pro	6.23	Whitney-Bos	.72	Radbourn-Pro	441	Clarkson-Chi	7.78	Radbourn-Pro	21.0
Galvin-Buf	636	Radbourn-Pro	7.00	Galvin-Buf	.89	Buffinton-Bos	417	Whitney-Bos	7.23	Galvin-Buf	15.1
Buffinton-Bos	587	Clarkson-Chi	7.17	Buffinton-Bos	1.17	Galvin-Buf	369	Getzein-Det	6.55	Buffinton-Bos	14.9
Welch-NY	557	Getzein-Det	7.22	Sweeney-Pro	1.18	Welch-NY	345	Buffinton-Bos	6.39	Welch-NY	11.2
Corcoran-Chi	517	Whitney-Bos	7.29	Coleman-Phi	1.29	Corcoran-Chi	272	Sweeney-Pro	5.90	McCormick-Cle	6.3

Earned Run Average		Adjusted ERA		Opponents' Batting Avg.		Opponents' On Base Pct.		Starter Runs		Adjusted Starter Runs	
Radbourn-Pro	1.38	Radbourn-Pro	207	Sweeney-Pro	.185	Sweeney-Pro	.212	Radbourn-Pro	120.6	Radbourn-Pro	111.0
Sweeney-Pro	1.55	Sweeney-Pro	184	Radbourn-Pro	.203	Whitney-Bos	.225	Galvin-Buf	69.4	Galvin-Buf	80.6
Getzein-Det	1.96	Galvin-Buf	157	Clarkson-Chi	.207	Radbourn-Pro	.232	Buffinton-Bos	54.2	Buffinton-Bos	41.4
Galvin-Buf	2.00	Getzein-Det	151	Getzein-Det	.208	Getzein-Det	.241	Sweeney-Pro	35.1	Corcoran-Chi	40.7
Whitney-Bos	2.09	Clarkson-Chi	146	Whitney-Bos	.209	Galvin-Buf	.244	Whitney-Bos	33.2	Sweeney-Pro	32.0

Clutch Pitching Index		Relief Runs	Adjusted Relief Runs	Relief Ranking	Total Pitcher Index		Total Baseball Ranking	
Meinke-Det	119				Radbourn-Pro	10.7	Radbourn-Pro	10.7
Corcoran-Chi	114				Galvin-Buf	7.1	Galvin-Buf	7.1
Weidman-Det	111				Buffinton-Bos	5.5	Pfeffer-Chi	5.8
Radbourn-Pro	111				Corcoran-Chi	4.8	Buffinton-Bos	5.5
Serad-Buf	108				Sweeney-Pro	4.3	Corcoran-Chi	4.8

TEAM	G	W	L	PCT	GB	R	OR	AB	H	2B	3B	HR	BB	SO	AVG	OBP	SLG	PRO	/A	BR	/A	PF	CHI	RC	TA	SB	CS	SBA	SBR
NY	112	75	32	.701		734	423	4012	1052	155	64	21	203	315	.262	.304	.348	.652	119	82	80	100	107	435	.553				
COL	110	69	39	.639	6.5	585	459	3759	901	107	96	40	196	404	.240	.288	.351	.639	114	59	74	97	93	390	.551				
LOU	110	68	40	.630	7.5	573	425	3957	1004	152	68	18	146	408	.254	.286	.340	.626	110	41	105	89	91	395	.517				
STL	110	67	40	.626	8	658	539	3952	986	151	60	11	174	339	.249	.288	.326	.614	107	29	-29	110	106	381	.507				
CIN	112	68	41	.624	8	754	512	4090	1037	109	98	34	154	404	.254	.289	.353	.642	115	65	29	106	111	428	.540				
BAL	108	63	43	.594	11.5	636	515	3845	896	133	84	30	211	425	.233	.284	.335	.619	108	36	41	99	102	375	.530				
PHI	108	61	46	.570	14	700	546	3959	1057	167	100	26	153	425	.267	.301	.379	.680	128	113	28	114	99	463	.584				
TOL	110	46	58	.442	27.5	463	571	3712	859	153	48	8	157	541	.231	.268	.305	.573	93	-26	-45	104	88	310	.461				
RIC	46	12	30	.286	30.5	194	294	1469	325	40	33	7	53	284	.221	.260	.308	.568	91	-12	-9	99	93	120	.462				
BRO	109	40	64	.385	33.5	476	644	3763	845	112	47	16	179	417	.225	.263	.292	.555	87	-48	-33	98	92	296	.443				
WAS	63	12	51	.190	41	248	481	2166	434	61	24	5	102	377	.200	.242	.258	.500	69	-67	-29	88	96	138	.390				
PIT	110	30	78	.278	45.5	406	725	3689	777	105	50	2	143	411	.211	.248	.268	.516	74	-95	-77	97	89	251	.402				
IND	110	29	78	.271	46	462	755	3813	890	129	62	20	125	560	.233	.262	.315	.577	94	-24	-3	96	86	323	.462				
TOT	659					6889		46186	11063	1574	834	238	1996	5430	.240	.271	.325	.596											

TEAM	CG	SHO	SV	IP	H	H/G	HR	BB	BB/G	SO	SO/G	ERA	/A	OAVG	OOBA	PR	/A	PF	CPI	FA	E	DP	FW	PW	BW	SBW	DIF
NY	111	9	0	984.7	800	7.3	15	119	1.1	611	5.6	2.46	127	.210	.234	85	71	96	89	.905	450	42	2.0	6.5	7.3		5.7
COL	102	8	1	962.3	815	7.6	22	172	1.6	526	4.9	2.68	116	.217	.251	59	44	96	96	.908	433	74	2.3	4.0	6.8		1.9
LOU	101	6	0	989.7	836	7.6	9	97	.9	470	4.3	2.17	130	.216	.235	117	70	87	103	.912	426	84	2.6	6.4	9.6		-4.6
STL	99	8	0	987.0	881	8.0	16	172	1.6	477	4.3	2.67	132	.226	.258	62	93	109	103	.900	490	65	-.1	8.5	-2.6		7.8
CIN	111	11	0	983.7	956	8.7	27	181	1.7	308	2.8	3.33	100	.241	.274	-9	0	103	98	.909	430	82	2.8	.0	2.6		8.0
BAL	105	8	1	955.7	869	8.2	16	219	2.1	635	6.0	2.71	117	.229	.271	56	47	98	110	.900	459	61	.8	4.3	3.7		1.1
PHI	105	5	0	948.7	920	8.7	16	127	1.2	530	5.0	3.42	107	.241	.265	-18	25	113	89	.901	457	63	.9	2.3	2.6		1.8
TOL	103	9	1	946.0	885	8.4	12	169	1.6	501	4.8	3.07	111	.234	.267	18	35	105	96	.900	469	67	.8	3.2	-4.1		-5.9
RIC	45	1	0	370.3	402	9.8	14	52	1.3	167	4.1	4.52	73	.262	.286	-52	-49	102	84	.874	239	27	-1.5	-4.5	-.8		-2.2
BRO	105	6	0	948.7	996	9.4	21	163	1.5	378	3.6	3.79	85	.255	.285	-58	-59	94	94	.890	520	68	-1.6	-5.4	-3.0		-2.0
WAS	62	3	0	543.7	643	10.6	21	110	1.8	235	3.9	4.01	76	.279	.312	-46	-59	93	111	.858	400	40	-5.2	-5.4	-2.6		-6.2
PIT	108	4	0	943.3	1059	10.1	25	216	2.1	338	3.2	4.35	75	.268	.306	-115	-112	101	95	.889	522	71	-1.6	-10.2	-7.0		-5.1
IND	107	2	0	937.7	1001	9.6	30	199	1.9	479	4.6	4.21	77	.259	.295	-100	-100	100	92	.889	514	45	-1.2	-9.1	-.3		-13.9
TOT	1264	80	3	11501.3		8.7			1.6		4.4	3.24		.240	.271					.897	5811	789					

Runs
Stovey-Phi 124
Jones-Cin 117
Latham-StL 115
Reilly-Cin 114
Nelson-NY 114

Hits
Orr-NY 162
Reilly-Cin 152
Esterbrook-NY 150
Browning-Lou 150
Jones-Cin 148

Doubles
Barkley-Tol 39
Browning-Lou 33
Orr-NY 32
Esterbrook-NY 29
Lewis-StL 25

Triples
Stovey-Phi 23
Reilly-Cin 19
Mann-Col 18
Peltz-Ind 17
Jones-Cin 17

Home Runs
Reilly-Cin 11
Stovey-Phi 10
Orr-NY 9
Mann-Col 7
Jones-Cin 7

Total Bases
Reilly-Cin 247
Orr-NY 247
Stovey-Phi 244
Jones-Cin 222
Browning-Lou 211

Runs Batted In
Stovey-Phi 114
Latham-StL 114
Nelson-NY 113
Jones-Cin 110
Esterbrook-NY 109

Runs Produced

Bases On Balls
Nelson-NY 74
Geer-Bro 38
Jones-Cin 37
Macullar-Bal 36
Richmond-Col 35

Batting Average
Orr-NY 354
Reilly-Cin 339
Browning-Lou 336
Stovey-Phi 326
Lewis-StL 323

On Base Percentage
Jones-Cin 376
Nelson-NY 375
Stovey-Phi 368
Fennelly-Was-Cin 367
Reilly-Cin 366

Slugging Average
Reilly-Cin 551
Stovey-Phi 545
Orr-NY 539
Fennelly-Was-Cin 480
Browning-Lou 472

Production
Reilly-Cin 918
Stovey-Phi 913
Orr-NY 901
Fennelly-Was-Cin 847
Jones-Cin 846

Adjusted Production
Orr-NY 193
Browning-Lou 193
Fennelly-Was-Cin 189
Reilly-Cin 188
Stovey-Phi 173

Batter Runs
Stovey-Phi 46.2
Reilly-Cin 45.9
Orr-NY 43.5
Jones-Cin 40.4
Browning-Lou 33.0

Adjusted Batter Runs
Orr-NY 43.3
Reilly-Cin 42.1
Browning-Lou 40.2
Stovey-Phi 36.4
Jones-Cin 36.2

Clutch Hitting Index

Runs Created
Reilly-Cin 93
Stovey-Phi 92
Orr-NY 92
Jones-Cin 85
Browning-Lou 77

Total Average
Stovey-Phi 907
Reilly-Cin 899
Orr-NY 855
Jones-Cin 830
Fennelly-Was-Cin 824

Stolen Bases

Stolen Base Average

Stolen Base Runs

Fielding Runs
Latham-StL 36.5
Smith-Col 27.2
Gerhardt-Lou 25.6
Barkley-Tol 25.3
Snyder-Cin 24.8

Total Player Rating
Barkley-Tol 4.6
Latham-StL 3.8
Fennelly-Was-Cin 3.5
Jones-Cin 3.5
Smith-Col 3.5

Wins
Hecker-Lou 52
Mullane-Tol 37
Lynch-NY 37
Keefe-NY 37

Win Percentage
Morris-Col 723
Hecker-Lou 722
Foutz-StL 714
Lynch-NY 712
Keefe-NY 685

Games
Hecker-Lou 75
Mullane-Tol 68
McKeon-Ind 61
Keefe-NY 58
Terry-Bro 57

Complete Games
Hecker-Lou 72
Mullane-Tol 65
McKeon-Ind 59
Keefe-NY 57
Terry-Bro 55

Shutouts
Mullane-Tol 8
White-Cin 7
Hecker-Lou 6

Saves
O'Day-Tol 1
Mountain-Col 1
Burns-Bal 1

Innings Pitched
Hecker-Lou 671
Mullane-Tol 576
McKeon-Ind 512
Keefe-NY 492
Lynch-NY 487

Fewest Hits/Game
Morris-Col 7.01
Hecker-Lou 7.06
Keefe-NY 7.10
Mountain-Col 7.20
Foutz-StL 7.26

Fewest BB/Game
Driscoll-Lou 62
Hecker-Lou 75
Lynch-NY 78
Dugan-Ric 81
McGinnis-StL 89

Strikeouts
Hecker-Lou 385
Henderson-Bal 346
Mullane-Tol 329
Keefe-NY 323
McKeon-Ind 308

Strikeouts/Game
Henderson-Bal 7.09
Davis-StL 6.50
Morris-Col 6.32
Mathews-Phi 5.97
Keefe-NY 5.91

Wins Above Team
Hecker-Lou 18.0
Mullane-Tol 14.8
Morris-Col 8.3
Emslie-Bal 5.9
Mathews-Phi 5.0

Earned Run Average
Hecker-Lou 1.80
Foutz-StL 2.17
Morris-Col 2.18
Keefe-NY 2.29
Mountain-Col 2.44

Adjusted ERA
Foutz-StL 162
Hecker-Lou 157
Taylor-Phi 145
Morris-Col 142
Mullane-Tol 137

Opponents' Batting Avg.
Morris-Col 203
Hecker-Lou 204
Keefe-NY 205
Mountain-Col 208
Foutz-StL 209

Opponents' On Base Pct.
Hecker-Lou 221
Morris-Col 227
Lynch-NY 233
Keefe-NY 236
Foutz-StL 243

Starter Runs
Hecker-Lou 107.9
Keefe-NY 52.4
Morris-Col 51.0
Mullane-Tol 48.6
Lynch-NY 32.6

Adjusted Starter Runs
Hecker-Lou 76.0
Mullane-Tol 59.2
Keefe-NY 45.3
Morris-Col 44.2
Taylor-Phi 32.5

Clutch Pitching Index
O'Neill-StL 122
Hamill-Was 115
Foutz-StL 112
Henderson-Bal 112
White-Cin 111

Relief Runs

Adjusted Relief Runs

Relief Ranking

Total Pitcher Index
Hecker-Lou 10.7
Mullane-Tol 9.2
Keefe-NY 5.3
Morris-Col 4.4
Mountain-Col 3.8

Total Baseball Ranking
Hecker-Lou 10.7
Mullane-Tol 9.2
Keefe-NY 5.3
Barkley-Tol 4.6
Morris-Col 4.4

TEAM	G	W	L	PCT	GB	R	OR	AB	H	2B	3B	HR	BB	SO	AVG	OBP	SLG	PRO	/A	BR	/A	PF	CHI	RC	TA	SB	CS	SBA	SBR
STL	114	94	19	.832		887	429	4285	1251	259	41	30	181	542	.292	.321	.393	.714	142	180	156	104	102	553	.614				
CIN	105	69	36	.657	21	703	466	3786	1027	118	62	27	147	482	.271	.298	.357	.655	122	85	37	108	102	413	.543				
BAL	106	58	47	.552	32	662	627	3883	952	150	26	17	144	652	.245	.272	.310	.582	98	-6	-70	110	108	336	.460				
BOS	111	58	51	.532	34	636	558	3940	928	168	32	19	128	787	.236	.260	.309	.569	93	-27	-17	98	106	324	.447				
MIL	12	8	4	.667	35.5	53	34	395	88	25	0	0	20	70	.223	.260	.286	.546	86	-4	-4	100	89	30	.433				
STP	9	2	6	.250	39.5	24	57	272	49	13	1	0	7	47	.180	.201	.235	.436	48	-13	-13	100	80	13	.318				
CP	93	41	50	.451	42	438	482	3212	742	127	26	10	119	505	.231	.258	.296	.554	88	-35	-31	99	92	252	.433				
ALT	25	6	19	.240	44	90	216	899	223	30	6	2	22	130	.248	.266	.301	.567	93	-6	-7	101	66	74	.433				
WIL	18	2	16	.111	44.5	35	114	521	91	8	8	2	22	123	.175	.208	.232	.440	50	-25	-27	103	60	26	.333				
WAS	114	47	65	.420	46.5	572	679	3926	931	120	26	4	118	558	.237	.259	.284	.543	85	-58	-37	97	102	296	.412				
PHI	67	21	46	.313	50	414	545	2518	618	108	35	7	103	405	.245	.275	.324	.599	104	10	39	93	100	230	.484				
KC	82	16	63	.203	61	311	618	2802	557	102	15	8	123	529	.199	.232	.254	.486	66	-93	-34	87	87	170	.372				
TOT	428					4825		30439	7457	1228	278	126	1134	4830	.245	.272	.316	.588											

TEAM	CG	SHO	SV	IP	H	H/G	HR	BB	BB/G	SO	SO/G	ERA	/A	OAVG	OOBA	PR	/A	PF	CPI	FA	E	DP	FW	PW	BW	SBW	DIF
STL	104	8	6	993.0	838	7.6	9	110	1.0	550	5.0	1.96	151	.213	.235	116	110	98	104	.888	554	79	3.8	9.6	13.7		10.4
CIN	95	11	1	914.3	831	8.2	17	90	.9	503	5.0	2.38	133	.226	.244	64	79	105	100	.882	532	45	2.6	6.9	3.2		3.8
BAL	92	4	0	946.7	1002	9.5	24	177	1.7	628	6.0	3.20	103	.254	.286	-20	10	110	107	.873	616	53	-.8	.9	-6.1		11.6
BOS	100	5	1	953.3	885	8.4	17	110	1.0	753	7.1	2.70	109	.230	.251	33	25	98	93	.868	633	39	-.3	2.2	-1.5		3.1
MIL	12	3	0	104.0	49	4.2	1	13	1.1	139	12.0	2.25	134	.131	.160	8	8	100	11	.892	53	4	.6	.7	-.4		1.0
STP	7	1	0	71.0	72	9.1	1	27	3.4	44	5.6	3.17	95	.246	.309	-1	-1	100	115	.873	47	6	.2	-.0	-1.1		-.9
CP	86	5	0	803.7	743	8.3	12	137	1.5	679	7.6	2.18	138	.229	.260	73	73	100	121	.883	459	38	2.8	6.4	-2.7		-11.0
ALT	20	0	0	219.7	292	12.0	3	52	2.1	93	3.8	4.67	70	.299	.335	-40	-34	109	103	.862	156	4	-.6	-3.0	-.6		-2.3
WIL	15	0	0	142.0	165	10.5	4	18	1.1	113	7.2	3.04	108	.272	.293	0	3	109	124	.860	104	10	-.1	.3	-2.4		-4.8
WAS	94	5	0	953.7	992	9.4	16	168	1.6	684	6.5	3.44	86	.250	.281	-44	-50	98	94	.869	625	55	.7	-4.4	-3.2		-2.1
PHI	64	1	0	593.3	726	11.0	7	105	1.6	310	4.7	4.63	62	.282	.310	-106	-116	95	89	.842	501	36	-5.3	-10.2	3.4		-.5
KC	70	0	0	702.7	862	11.0	14	127	1.6	334	4.3	4.07	68	.283	.311	-82	-102	92	103	.861	520	51	-2.5	-8.9	-3.0		-9.1
TOT	759	43	8	7397.3		9.1			1.4		5.9	3.01		.245	.272					.872	4800	420					

Runs
Dunlap-StL 160
Shaffer-StL 130
Seery-Bal-KC 115
Robinson-Bal 101
Rowe-StL 95

Hits
Dunlap-StL 185
Shaffer-StL 168
Moore-Was 155
Seery-Bal-KC 146
Rowe-StL 142

Doubles
Shaffer-StL 40
Dunlap-StL 39
Rowe-StL 32
O'Brien-Bos 31
Gleason-StL 30

Triples
Burns-Cin 12
Rowe-StL 11
Shaffer-StL 10

Home Runs
Dunlap-StL 13
Crane-Bos 12
Levis-Bal-Was 6

Total Bases
Dunlap-StL 279
Shaffer-StL 234
Rowe-StL 205
Crane-Bos 193
Seery-Bal-KC 192

Runs Batted In

Runs Produced
Dunlap-StL 147
Shaffer-StL 128
Seery-Bal-KC 113
Robinson-Bal 99
Rowe-StL 92

Bases On Balls
Robinson-Bal 37
Shaffer-StL 30
Dunlap-StL 29
Harbidge-Cin 25
Gleason-StL 23

Batting Average
Dunlap-StL 412
Hoover-Phi 364
Shaffer-StL 360
Moore-Was 336
Gleason-StL 324

On Base Percentage
Dunlap-StL 448
Shaffer-StL 398
Hoover-Phi 390
Moore-Was 363
Gleason-StL 361

Slugging Average
Dunlap-StL 621
Shaffer-StL 501
Hoover-Phi 495
Burns-Cin 457
Crane-Bos 451

Production
Dunlap-StL 1.069
Shaffer-StL 899
Hoover-Phi 885
Gleason-StL 794
Moore-Was 777

Adjusted Production
Dunlap-StL 249
Hoover-Phi 213
Shaffer-StL 195
Moore-Was 168
Gleason-StL 162

Batter Runs
Dunlap-StL 72.5
Shaffer-StL 49.1
Moore-Was 28.9
Gleason-StL 27.4
Hoover-Phi 27.0

Adjusted Batter Runs
Dunlap-StL 69.9
Shaffer-StL 46.5
Moore-Was 31.3
Hoover-Phi 30.3
Gleason-StL 25.2

Clutch Hitting Index

Runs Created
Dunlap-StL 128
Shaffer-StL 96
Moore-Was 71
Seery-Bal-KC 67
Rowe-StL 65

Total Average
Dunlap-StL 1.167
Shaffer-StL 883
Hoover-Phi 846
Gleason-StL 727
Moore-Was 686

Stolen Bases

Stolen Base Average

Stolen Base Runs

Fielding Runs
Dunlap-StL 24.5
Fusselback-Bal . . . 15.9
Robinson-Bal 13.9
Wise-Was 13.2
Krieg-CP 11.2

Total Player Rating
Dunlap-StL 7.6
Shaffer-StL 3.7
Hoover-Phi 2.7
Moore-Was 2.2
Glasscock-Cin 2.0

Wins
Sweeney-Bal 40
Daily-CP -Was 28
Taylor-StL 25
Bradley-Cin 25
Sweeney-StL 24

Win Percentage
McCormick-Cin 875
Taylor-StL 862
Boyle-StL 833
Sweeney-StL 774
Sweeney-Bal 656

Games
Sweeney-Bal 62
Daily-CP -Was 58
Wise-Was 50
Bakely-Phi-Wil 41
Bradley-Cin 41

Complete Games
Sweeney-Bal 58
Daily-CP -Was 56
Bakely-Phi-Wil 40
Bradley-Cin 36
Shaw-Bos 35

Shutouts
McCormick-Cin 7
Shaw-Bos 5
Daily-CP -Was 4
Wise-Was 4
Sweeney-Bal 4

Saves
Taylor-StL 4
Sylvester-Cin 1
Dunlap-StL 1
Brown-Bos 1
Boyle-StL 1

Innings Pitched
Sweeney-Bal 538
Daily-CP -Was 501
Wise-Was 364
Bakely-Phi-Wil 362
Bradley-Cin 342

Fewest Hits/Game
Shaw-Bos 6.47
McCormick-Cin . . . 6.47
Sweeney-StL 6.87
Boyle-StL 7.08
Werden-StL 7.21

Fewest BB/Game
Sweeney-StL 43
McCormick-Cin 60
Boyle-StL 60
Bradley-Cin 61
Murphy-Wil-Alt 62

Strikeouts
Daily-CP -Was 483
Sweeney-StL 374
Shaw-Bos 309
Wise-Was 268
Burke-Bos 255

Strikeouts/Game
Shaw-Bos 8.80
Daily-CP -Was 8.68
Geggus-Was 7.93
Robinson-Bal 7.32
Burke-Bos 7.13

Wins Above Team
Sweeney-Bal 12.7
McCormick-Cin 8.3
Wise-Was 6.9
Daily-CP -Was 5.4
Werden-StL 3.7

Earned Run Average
McCormick-Cin 1.54
Taylor-StL 1.68
Boyle-StL 1.74
Shaw-Bos 1.77
Sweeney-StL 1.83

Adjusted ERA
McCormick-Cin 205
Taylor-StL 176
Boyle-StL 170
Shaw-Bos 166
Sweeney-StL 162

Opponents' Batting Avg.
Shaw-Bos 188
McCormick-Cin 188
Sweeney-StL 197
Boyle-StL 202
Werden-StL 205

Opponents' On Base Pct.
McCormick-Cin 202
Sweeney-StL 207
Shaw-Bos 212
Boyle-StL 215
Werden-StL 236

Starter Runs
Daily-CP -Was 60.7
Shaw-Bos 43.8
Taylor-StL 39.0
Sweeney-StL 35.7
McCormick-Cin . . . 34.3

Adjusted Starter Runs
Daily-CP -Was 59.7
Sweeney-Bal 42.7
Shaw-Bos 41.1
McCormick-Cin . . . 37.7
Taylor-StL 37.4

Clutch Pitching Index
Hodnett-StL 139
Robinson-Bal 131
Daily-CP -Was 127
Taylor-StL 127
Sweeney-Bal 109

Relief Runs

Adjusted Relief Runs

Relief Ranking

Total Pitcher Index
Taylor-StL 5.7
Daily-CP -Was 5.4
Sweeney-StL 5.1
Burns-Cin 4.8
Sweeney-Bal 3.9

Total Baseball Ranking
Dunlap-StL 7.5
Taylor-StL 5.7
Daily-CP -Was 5.4
Sweeney-StL 5.1
Burns-Cin 4.8

TEAM	G	W	L	PCT	GB	R	OR	AB	H	2B	3B	HR	BB	SO	AVG	OBP	SLG	PRO	/A	BR	/A	PF	CHI	RC	TA	SB	CS	SBA	SBR
CHI	113	87	25	.777		834	470	4093	1079	184	75	54	340	429	.264	.320	.385	.705	132	143	62	114	113	517	.635				
NY	112	85	27	.759	2	691	370	4029	1085	150	83	15	221	312	.269	.307	.359	.666	120	81	27	109	106	455	.566				
PHI	111	56	54	.509	30	513	511	3893	891	156	35	20	0		.229	.229	.302	.531	74	-113	-133	104	114	169	.346				
PRO	110	53	57	.482	33	442	531	3727	820	114	30	6	265	430	.220	.272	.272	.544	80	-73	-26	91	96	282	.439				
BOS	113	46	66	.411	41	528	589	3950	915	144	53	22	190	522	.232	.267	.312	.579	91	-40	-4	94	103	337	.468				
DET	108	41	67	.380	44	514	582	3773	917	149	65	26	216	451	.243	.284	.338	.622	105	18	31	97	93	371	.522				
BUF	112	38	74	.339	49	495	761	3900	980	149	50	23	179	380	.251	.284	.333	.617	103	11	15	99	89	378	.506				
STL	111	36	72	.333	49	390	593	3758	829	121	21	8	214	412	.221	.263	.270	.533	76	-91	-50	92	88	273	.420				
TOT	445					4407		31123	7516	1167	412	174	1625	2936	.241	.284	.322	.606											

TEAM	CG	SHO	SV	IP	H	H/G	HR	BB	BB/G	SO	SO/G	ERA	/A	OAVG	OOBA	PR	/A	PF	CPI	FA	E	DP	FW	PW	BW	SBW	DIF
CHI	108	14	4	1015.7	868	7.7	37	202	1.8	458	4.1	2.23	133	.220	.258	66	83	106	106	.904	496	80	-2.8	7.8	5.8		20.2
NY	109	16	1	992.0	755	6.8	11	266	2.4	519	4.7	1.72	167	.200	.253	120	126	102	110	.929	331	85	5.8	11.9	2.5		8.8
PHI	108	9	0	976.0	860	7.9	18	218	2.0	378	3.5	2.39	122	.225	.267	46	57	104	101	.906	447	66	-.3	5.4	-12.5		8.4
PRO	108	8	0	960.7	912	8.5	18	235	2.2	371	3.5	2.71	97	.238	.282	11	-8	93	104	.903	459	70	-.9	-.8	-2.4		2.1
BOS	111	10	0	981.0	1045	9.6	26	188	1.7	480	4.4	3.03	88	.260	.293	-22	-38	95	109	.901	478	79	-1.9	-3.6	-.4		-4.2
DET	105	6	1	954.3	966	9.1	18	224	2.1	475	4.5	2.88	97	.250	.291	-6	-10	99	108	.901	463	61	-1.1	-.9	2.9		-13.9
BUF	107	3	1	956.0	1175	11.1	31	234	2.2	320	3.0	4.30	69	.288	.327	-157	-142	105	100	.901	464	65	-1.1	-13.4	1.4		-4.9
STL	107	4	0	965.3	935	8.7	15	278	2.6	337	3.1	3.37	81	.242	.293	-58	-67	97	90	.916	398	67	2.3	-6.3	-4.7		-9.3
TOT	863	70	7	7801.0		8.7			2.1		3.9	2.82		.241	.284					.908	3536	573					

Runs		Hits		Doubles		Triples		Home Runs		Total Bases	
Kelly-Chi	124	Connor-NY	169	Anson-Chi	35	O'Rourke-NY	16	Dalrymple-Chi	11	Connor-NY	225
O'Rourke-NY	119	Brouthers-Buf	146	Brouthers-Buf	32	Connor-NY	15	Kelly-Chi	9	Brouthers-Buf	221
Gore-Chi	115	Anson-Chi	144	Rowe-Buf	28	Gore-Chi	13			Dalrymple-Chi	219
Dalrymple-Chi	109	Sutton-Bos	143	Dalrymple-Chi	27	Bennett-Det	13			Anson-Chi	214
Connor-NY	102	O'Rourke-NY	143	Mulvey-Phi	25					O'Rourke-NY	211

Runs Batted In		Runs Produced		Bases On Balls		Batting Average		On Base Percentage		Slugging Average	
Anson-Chi	108	Anson-Chi	201	Williamson-Chi	75	Connor-NY	.371	Connor-NY	.435	Brouthers-Buf	.543
Kelly-Chi	75	Kelly-Chi	190	Gore-Chi	68	Brouthers-Buf	.359	Brouthers-Buf	.408	Connor-NY	.495
Pfeffer-Chi	73	Gore-Chi	167	Morrill-Bos	64	Dorgan-NY	.326	Gore-Chi	.405	Ewing-NY	.471
Burns-Chi	71	Connor-NY	166	Connor-NY	51	Richardson-Buf	.319	Hanlon-Det	.372	Anson-Chi	.461
		Dalrymple-Chi	159			Gore-Chi	.313	Anson-Chi	.357	Richardson-Buf	.458

Production		Adjusted Production		Batter Runs		Adjusted Batter Runs		Clutch Hitting Index		Runs Created	
Brouthers-Buf	.951	Brouthers-Buf	207	Connor-NY	51.7	Brouthers-Buf	47.3	Williamson-Chi	170	Connor-NY	100
Connor-NY	.929	Connor-NY	183	Brouthers-Buf	46.8	Connor-NY	45.3	Anson-Chi	169	Brouthers-Buf	92
Gore-Chi	.858	Bennett-Det	165	Gore-Chi	40.6	Gore-Chi	31.3	Pfeffer-Chi	159	Gore-Chi	83
Anson-Chi	.819	Richardson-Buf	161	Anson-Chi	31.7	Richardson-Buf	27.2	Gerhardt-NY	150	Anson-Chi	78
Bennett-Det	.812	Gore-Chi	156	O'Rourke-NY	29.5	Bennett-Det	25.9	White-Buf	140	O'Rourke-NY	77

Total Average		Stolen Bases		Stolen Base Average		Stolen Base Runs		Fielding Runs		Total Player Rating	
Brouthers-Buf	.977							Dunlap-StL	20.3	Dunlap-StL	4.2
Connor-NY	.965							Pfeffer-Chi	20.2	Richardson-Buf	3.7
Gore-Chi	.884							Fogarty-Phi	19.4	Bennett-Det	3.3
Bennett-Det	.808							McGuire-Det	17.7	Wise-Bos	3.0
Anson-Chi	.775							Glasscock-StL	12.0	Glasscock-StL	2.8

Wins		Win Percentage		Games		Complete Games		Shutouts		Saves	
Clarkson-Chi	53	Welch-NY	.800	Clarkson-Chi	70	Clarkson-Chi	68	Clarkson-Chi	10	Williamson-Chi	2
Welch-NY	44	Clarkson-Chi	.768	Welch-NY	56	Welch-NY	55	Welch-NY	7	Pfeffer-Chi	2
Keefe-NY	32	McCormick-Pro-Chi	.750	Whitney-Bos	51	Whitney-Bos	50	Keefe-NY	7	Welch-NY	1
Radbourn-Pro	28	Keefe-NY	.711	Buffinton-Bos	51			Shaw-Pro	6	Galvin-Buf	1
		Radbourn-Pro	.571	Daily-Phi	50			Buffinton-Bos	6	Baldwin-Det	1

Innings Pitched		Fewest Hits/Game		Fewest BB/Game		Strikeouts		Strikeouts/Game		Wins Above Team	
Clarkson-Chi	623	Keefe-NY	6.72	Whitney-Bos	.76	Clarkson-Chi	308	Baldwin-Det	6.79	Welch-NY	7.9
Welch-NY	492	Welch-NY	6.80	Galvin-Buf	1.17	Welch-NY	258	Keefe-NY	5.20	Radbourn-Pro	6.7
Radbourn-Pro	446	Baldwin-Det	6.89	Clarkson-Chi	1.40	Buffinton-Bos	242	Buffinton-Bos	5.02	Ferguson-Phi	4.2
Whitney-Bos	441	Clarkson-Chi	7.18	Baldwin-Det	1.41	Keefe-NY	230	Welch-NY	4.72	Baldwin-Det	3.2
Daily-Phi	440	Daily-Phi	7.57	Sweeney-StL	1.64	Whitney-Bos	200	Clarkson-Chi	4.45	Boyle-StL	3.0

Earned Run Average		Adjusted ERA		Opponents' Batting Avg.		Opponents' On Base Pct.		Starter Runs		Adjusted Starter Runs	
Keefe-NY	1.58	Keefe-NY	182	Keefe-NY	.198	Baldwin-Det	.233	Clarkson-Chi	67.1	Clarkson-Chi	77.8
Welch-NY	1.66	Welch-NY	173	Welch-NY	.200	Clarkson-Chi	.240	Welch-NY	63.1	Welch-NY	66.2
Clarkson-Chi	1.85	Clarkson-Chi	161	Baldwin-Det	.202	Keefe-NY	.249	Keefe-NY	54.6	Keefe-NY	57.1
Baldwin-Det	1.86	Baldwin-Det	150	Clarkson-Chi	.209	Welch-NY	.253	Radbourn-Pro	30.7	Daily-Phi	34.8
Radbourn-Pro	2.20	Daily-Phi	132	Daily-Phi	.217	Daily-Phi	.257	Daily-Phi	29.8	Ferguson-Phi	31.4

Clutch Pitching Index		Relief Runs		Adjusted Relief Runs		Relief Ranking		Total Pitcher Index		Total Baseball Ranking	
Getzein-Det	121							Clarkson-Chi	9.1	Clarkson-Chi	9.1
Radbourn-Pro	117							Welch-NY	6.1	Welch-NY	6.1
Keefe-NY	115							Keefe-NY	5.6	Keefe-NY	5.6
Whitney-Bos	115							Ferguson-Phi	5.3	Ferguson-Phi	5.3
Welch-NY	110							Radbourn-Pro	3.6	Dunlap-StL	4.2

TEAM	G	W	L	PCT	GB	R	OR	AB	H	2B	3B	HR	BB	SO	AVG	OBP	SLG	PRO	/A	BR	/A	PF	CHI	RC	TA	SB	CS	SBA	SBR
STL	112	79	33	.705		677	**461**	3972	979	132	57	14	234	**282**	.246	.297	.319	.616	102	11	52	93	**107**	385	.518				
CIN	112	63	49	.563	16	642	575	4050	1046	108	77	25	153	420	.258	.294	.341	.635	107	31	7	104	98	416	.528				
PIT	111	56	55	.505	22.5	547	539	3975	955	123	79	5	189	537	.240	.282	.315	.597	95	-18	-57	106	92	362	.491				
PHI	113	55	57	.491	24	**764**	691	4142	**1099**	169	77	**29**	223	410	.265	.310	**.364**	**.674**	120	90	68	103	104	479	**.584**				
LOU	112	53	59	.473	26	564	598	3969	986	126	**83**	19	152	448	.248	.281	.336	.617	101	3	-11	102	93	384	.507				
BRO	112	53	59	.473	26	624	650	3943	966	121	65	14	238	324	.245	.295	.319	.614	101	9	-14	104	100	381	.517				
NY	108	44	64	.407	33	526	688	3731	921	123	58	20	217	428	.247	.295	.327	.622	103	16	109	84	88	368	.524				
BAL	110	41	68	.376	36.5	541	683	3820	837	124	59	17	**279**	529	.219	.280	.296	.576	89	-39	-74	106	96	324	.486				
TOT	445					4885		31602	7789	1026	555	143	1685	3378	.246	.285	.328	.612											

TEAM	CG	SHO	SV	IP	H	H/G	HR	BB	BB/G	SO	SO/G	ERA	/A	OAVG	OOBA	PR	/A	PF	CPI	FA	E	DP	FW	PW	BW	SBW	DIF
STL	**111**	**11**	0	1002.0	**879**	7.9	12	**168**	1.5	378	3.4	**2.44**	118	.225	.257	89	48	89	99	.920	381	64	2.9	4.3	4.7		11.1
CIN	102	7	1	999.3	998	9.0	24	250	2.3	330	3.0	3.26	102	.249	.293	-1	7	103	103	.910	426	**86**	.6	.6	.6		5.1
PIT	104	7	0	1011.0	918	8.2	14	201	1.8	454	4.0	2.93	118	.231	.269	35	59	107	92	.912	426	77	.6	5.3	-5.1		-.3
PHI	105	5	0	1003.3	1038	9.3	11	212	1.9	**506**	**4.5**	3.25	102	.255	.292	0	8	102	102	.901	483	79	-2.4	.7	6.1		-5.5
LOU	109	3	1	1002.0	927	8.3	13	217	1.9	462	4.1	2.68	**125**	.235	.275	63	75	103	105	.904	466	75	-1.5	6.8	-1.0		-7.3
BRO	110	3	1	991.7	955	8.7	27	211	1.9	436	4.0	3.46	98	.242	.281	-23	-6	105	90	.908	447	56	-.5	-.5	-1.3		-.7
NY	103	2	0	937.0	1015	9.7	36	204	2.0	408	3.9	4.15	67	.264	.301	-93	-140	86	92	.901	452	62	-.8	-12.6	**9.8**		-6.5
BAL	104	2	4	971.0	1059	9.8	12	222	2.1	395	3.7	3.90	91	.266	.304	-70	-38	109	94	.910	419	71	1.0	-3.4	-6.7		-4.4
TOT	848	40	7	7917.3		8.9			1.9		3.25			.246	.285					.908	3500	570					

Batting Leaders

Runs	Hits	Doubles	Triples	Home Runs	Total Bases
Stovey-Phi 130	Browning-Lou 174	Larkin-Phi 37	Orr-NY 21	Stovey-Phi 13	Browning-Lou 255
Larkin-Phi 114	Jones-Cin 157	Browning-Lou 34	Kuehne-Pit 19	Fennelly-Cin 10	Orr-NY 241
Jones-Cin 108	Stovey-Phi 153	Orr-NY 29	Wolf-Lou 17	Browning-Lou 9	Larkin-Phi 238
Nelson-NY 98	Orr-NY 152	Stovey-Phi 27	Jones-Cin 17	Larkin-Phi 8	Stovey-Phi 237
Browning-Lou 98	Larkin-Phi 149		Fennelly-Cin 17	Orr-NY 6	Jones-Cin 222

Runs Batted In	Runs Produced	Bases On Balls	Batting Average	On Base Percentage	Slugging Average
Stovey-Phi 117		Nelson-NY 61	Browning-Lou .362	Browning-Lou .393	Orr-NY .543
Larkin-Phi 106		Macullar-Bal 49	Orr-NY .342	Larkin-Phi .372	Browning-Lou .530
Jones-Cin 104		Hotaling-Bro 49	Larkin-Phi .329	Stovey-Phi .371	Larkin-Phi .525
Nelson-NY 97		Stovey-Phi 39	Jones-Cin .322	Brown-Pit .366	Stovey-Phi .488
Browning-Lou 89			Stovey-Phi .315	Phillips-Bro .364	Jones-Cin .456

Production	Adjusted Production	Batter Runs	Adjusted Batter Runs	Clutch Hitting Index	Runs Created
Browning-Lou .923	Orr-NY 220	Browning-Lou 48.5	Orr-NY 50.2		Browning-Lou 103
Orr-NY .901	Browning-Lou 189	Larkin-Phi 41.7	Browning-Lou 46.7		Larkin-Phi 91
Larkin-Phi .897	Larkin-Phi 178	Stovey-Phi 39.5	Larkin-Phi 39.3		Stovey-Phi 90
Stovey-Phi .858	Stovey-Phi 167	Orr-NY 39.5	Stovey-Phi 36.9		Orr-NY 88
Jones-Cin .818	Roseman-NY 162	Jones-Cin 32.1	Jones-Cin 29.3		Jones-Cin 82

Total Average	Stolen Bases	Stolen Base Average	Stolen Base Runs	Fielding Runs	Total Player Rating
Browning-Lou .912				Smith-Bro 36.7	Browning-Lou 3.9
Larkin-Phi .885				Smith-Pit 31.2	Larkin-Phi 3.7
Orr-NY .863				Houck-Phi 20.8	Orr-NY 3.4
Stovey-Phi .841				Hankinson-NY 17.9	Smith-Bro 3.4
Jones-Cin .764				Corkhill-Cin 15.6	Jones-Cin 3.2

Pitching Leaders

Wins	Win Percentage	Games	Complete Games	Shutouts	Saves
Caruthers-StL 40	Caruthers-StL .755	Morris-Pit 63	Morris-Pit 63	Morris-Pit 6	Burns-Bal 3
Morris-Pit 39	Foutz-StL .702	Henderson-Bal 61	Henderson-Bal 59	Caruthers-StL 6	Terry-Bro 1
Porter-Bro 33	Mathews-Phi .638	Porter-Bro 54	Porter-Bro 53	McGinnis-StL 3	Sommer-Bal 1
Foutz-StL 33	Morris-Pit .619	Hecker-Lou 53	Caruthers-StL 53		Reccius-Lou 1
	Porter-Bro .611	Caruthers-StL 53	Hecker-Lou 51		Corkhill-Cin 1

Innings Pitched	Fewest Hits/Game	Fewest BB/Game	Strikeouts	Strikeouts/Game	Wins Above Team
Morris-Pit 581	Morris-Pit 7.11	Lynch-NY 1.00	Morris-Pit 298	Mathews-Phi 6.10	Morris-Pit 12.9
Henderson-Bal 539	Mays-Lou 7.74	Hecker-Lou 1.01	Mathews-Phi 286	Cushman-Phi-NY 5.50	Porter-Bro 11.0
Porter-Bro 482	Foutz-StL 7.74	Caruthers-StL 1.06	Henderson-Bal 263	Morris-Pit 4.62	Mathews-Phi 9.7
Caruthers-StL 482	McGinnis-StL 7.87	Mathews-Phi 1.22	Hecker-Lou 209	Henderson-Bal 4.39	Hecker-Lou 7.7
Hecker-Lou 480	Porter-Bro 7.97	McGinnis-StL 1.53	Porter-Bro 197	Harkins-Bro 4.33	Caruthers-StL 7.3

Earned Run Average	Adjusted ERA	Opponents' Batting Avg.	Opponents' On Base Pct.	Starter Runs	Adjusted Starter Runs
Caruthers-StL 2.07	Hecker-Lou 154	Morris-Pit .208	Morris-Pit .243	Caruthers-StL 62.9	Morris-Pit 71.3
Hecker-Lou 2.17	Morris-Pit 147	Mays-Lou .222	Caruthers-StL .251	Morris-Pit 57.7	Hecker-Lou 62.9
Morris-Pit 2.35	Caruthers-StL 139	Foutz-StL .222	McGinnis-StL .258	Hecker-Lou 57.2	Caruthers-StL 43.1
Mathews-Phi 2.43	Mathews-Phi 137	McGinnis-StL .225	Hecker-Lou .260	Mathews-Phi 38.3	Mathews-Phi 41.6
Foutz-StL 2.63	Porter-Bro 122	Porter-Bro .228	Mathews-Phi .262	Foutz-StL 28.2	Porter-Bro 33.1

Clutch Pitching Index	Relief Runs	Adjusted Relief Runs	Relief Ranking	Total Pitcher Index	Total Baseball Ranking
Hecker-Lou 120				Hecker-Lou 7.8	Hecker-Lou 7.8
Caruthers-StL 112				Morris-Pit 6.1	Morris-Pit 6.1
Mathews-Phi 107				Caruthers-StL 4.8	Caruthers-StL 4.8
Mountjoy-Cin-Bal 105				Mathews-Phi 3.3	Browning-Lou 3.9
Henderson-Bal 100				Porter-Bro 3.1	Larkin-Phi 3.7

TEAM	G	W	L	PCT	GB	R	OR	AB	H	2B	3B	HR	BB	SO	AVG	OBP	SLG	PRO	/A	BR	/A	PF	CHI	RC	TA	SB	CS	SBA	SBR
CHI	126	90	34	.726		900	555	4378	1223	198	87	53	460	513	.279	.348	.401	.749	133	176	64	116	103	701	.769	213			
DET	126	87	36	.707	2.5	829	538	4501	1260	176	81	53	374	426	.280	.335	.390	.725	126	137	76	109	99	670	.717	194			
NY	124	75	44	.630	12.5	692	558	4298	1156	175	68	21	237	410	.269	.307	.356	.663	107	29	103	89	102	531	.612	155			
PHI	119	71	43	.623	14	621	498	4072	976	145	66	26	282	516	.240	.289	.327	.616	92	-36	-24	98	106	461	.594	226			
BOS	118	56	61	.479	30.5	657	661	4180	1085	151	59	24	250	537	.260	.301	.341	.642	100	0	17	97	104	489	.592	156			
STL	126	43	79	.352	46	547	712	4250	1001	183	46	30	235	656	.236	.276	.321	.597	86	-70	-36	95	96	430	.541	156			
KC	123	30	91	.248	58.5	494	872	4236	967	177	48	19	269	608	.228	.274	.306	.580	81	-91	-132	107	89	392	.508	96			
WAS	122	28	92	.233	60	445	791	4082	856	135	51	23	265	582	.210	.258	.285	.543	69	-142	-102	94	93	345	.487	143			
TOT	492					5185		33997	8524	1340	506	249	2372	4248	.251	.300	.342	.641								1339			

TEAM	CG	SHO	SV	IP	H	H/G	HR	BB	BB/G	SO	SO/G	ERA	/A	OAVG	OOBA	PR	/A	PF	CPI	FA	E	DP	FW	PW	BW	SBW	DIF
CHI	116	8	3	1097.7	988	8.1	49	262	2.1	647	5.3	2.54	143	.230	.274	92	132	110	109	.912	475	82	-2.4	11.9	5.8		12.7
DET	122	8	0	1103.7	995	8.1	20	270	2.2	592	4.8	2.86	119	.230	.276	54	67	103	91	.928	373	82	3.2	6.1	6.9		9.4
NY	119	3	1	1067.0	1028	8.7	23	278	2.3	582	4.9	2.85	99	.242	.289	53	-3	85	105	.929	359	70	3.9	-.3	9.3		2.5
PHI	110	10	2	1045.7	923	7.9	29	264	2.3	540	4.6	2.45	129	.227	.274	98	82	96	106	.921	393	46	2.1	7.4	-2.2		6.7
BOS	116	3	0	1029.0	1049	9.2	33	298	2.6	511	4.5	3.24	99	.253	.303	6	-4	97	106	.906	457	63	-1.4	-.4	1.5		-2.3
STL	118	6	0	1032.3	1050	9.2	34	392	3.4	501	4.4	3.36	96	.253	.317	-6	-14	98	109	.912	452	92	-1.1	-1.3	-3.3		-12.3
KC	117	4	0	1066.7	1345	11.3	27	246	2.1	442	3.7	4.85	78	.295	.331	-183	-128	114	91	.910	482	79	-2.8	-11.6	-11.9		-4.2
WAS	116	4	0	1041.0	1147	9.9	34	379	3.3	500	4.3	4.31	77	.268	.328	-116	-115	100	94	.910	458	69	-1.5	-10.4	-9.2		-10.9
TOT	934	46	6	8483.0		9.0			2.5		4.6	3.30		.251	.300					.916	3449	583					

Runs
Kelly-Chi 155
Gore-Chi 150
Brouthers-Det 139
Richardson-Det 125
Anson-Chi 117

Hits
Richardson-Det 189
Anson-Chi 187
Brouthers-Det 181
Kelly-Chi 175
Connor-NY 172

Doubles
Brouthers-Det 40
Anson-Chi 35
Kelly-Chi 32
Hines-Was 30

Triples
Connor-NY 20
Wood-Phi 15
Brouthers-Det 15
Thompson-Det 13

Home Runs
Richardson-Det 11
Brouthers-Det 11
Anson-Chi 10
Hines-Was 9
Denny-StL 9

Total Bases
Brouthers-Det 284
Anson-Chi 274
Richardson-Det 271
Connor-NY 262
Kelly-Chi 241

Runs Batted In
Anson-Chi 147
Pfeffer-Chi 95
Thompson-Det 89
Rowe-Det 87
Ward-NY 81

Runs Produced
Anson-Chi 254
Kelly-Chi 230
Gore-Chi 207
Brouthers-Det 200
Thompson-Det 182

Bases On Balls
Gore-Chi 102
Kelly-Chi 83
Williamson-Chi 80
Brouthers-Det 66
Radford-KC 58

Batting Average
Kelly-Chi 388
Anson-Chi 371
Brouthers-Det 370
Connor-NY 355
Richardson-Det 351

On Base Percentage
Kelly-Chi 483
Brouthers-Det 445
Gore-Chi 434
Anson-Chi 433
Connor-NY 405

Slugging Average
Brouthers-Det 581
Anson-Chi 544
Connor-NY 540
Kelly-Chi 534
Richardson-Det 504

Production
Brouthers-Det 1.026
Kelly-Chi 1.018
Anson-Chi 977
Connor-NY 945
Richardson-Det 906

Adjusted Production
Connor-NY 209
Brouthers-Det 193
Kelly-Chi 180
Anson-Chi 168
Richardson-Det 160

Batter Runs
Brouthers-Det 65.9
Kelly-Chi 64.3
Anson-Chi 58.2
Connor-NY 48.7
Richardson-Det 47.4

Adjusted Batter Runs
Brouthers-Det 59.0
Connor-NY 57.3
Kelly-Chi 52.0
Anson-Chi 45.4
Richardson-Det 40.2

Clutch Hitting Index
Pfeffer-Chi 164
Dorgan-NY 162
Anson-Chi 151
White-Det 148
Ward-NY 147

Runs Created
Kelly-Chi 146
Brouthers-Det 139
Anson-Chi 134
Richardson-Det 129
Connor-NY 116

Total Average
Kelly-Chi 1.366
Brouthers-Det 1.205
Anson-Chi 1.129
Gore-Chi 1.042
Richardson-Det 1.029

Stolen Bases
Andrews-Phi 56
Kelly-Chi 53
Hanlon-Det 50
Richardson-Det 42
Radford-KC 39

Stolen Base Average

Stolen Base Runs

Fielding Runs
Denny-StL 26.9
Knowles-Was 24.0
Glasscock-StL 20.9
Dunlap-StL-Det . . . 19.5
Johnston-Bos 15.1

Total Player Rating
Kelly-Chi 4.7
Glasscock-StL 4.3
Richardson-Det 4.0
Connor-NY 4.0
Dunlap-StL-Det 3.1

Wins
Keefe-NY 42
Baldwin-Det 42
Clarkson-Chi 36
Welch-NY 33
McCormick-Chi 31

Win Percentage
Flynn-Chi 793
Ferguson-Phi 769
Baldwin-Det 764
McCormick-Chi 738
Getzein-Det 732

Games
Keefe-NY 64
Welch-NY 59
Radbourn-Bos 58
Baldwin-Det 56
Clarkson-Chi 55

Complete Games
Keefe-NY 62
Radbourn-Bos 57
Welch-NY 56
Baldwin-Det 55
Clarkson-Chi 50

Shutouts
Baldwin-Det 7
Ferguson-Phi 4
Casey-Phi 4

Saves
Ferguson-Phi 2
Williamson-Chi 1
Ryan-Chi 1
Flynn-Chi 1
Devlin-NY 1

Innings Pitched
Keefe-NY 540
Radbourn-Bos 509
Welch-NY 500
Baldwin-Det 487
Clarkson-Chi 467

Fewest Hits/Game
Baldwin-Det 6.86
Ferguson-Phi 7.20
Flynn-Chi 7.25
Stemmeyer-Bos 7.74
Casey-Phi 7.95

Fewest BB/Game
Whitney-KC 1.26
Ferguson-Phi 1.57
Clarkson-Chi 1.66
Keefe-NY 1.67
Baldwin-Det 1.85

Strikeouts
Baldwin-Det 323
Clarkson-Chi 313
Keefe-NY 291
Welch-NY 272
Stemmeyer-Bos 239

Strikeouts/Game
Stemmeyer-Bos 6.16
Clarkson-Chi 6.03
Baldwin-Det 5.97
Boyle-StL 5.51
Healy-StL 5.42

Wins Above Team
Ferguson-Phi 9.6
Baldwin-Det 8.3
Keefe-NY 7.3
Flynn-Chi 4.3
Stemmeyer-Bos 3.9

Earned Run Average
Ferguson-Phi 1.98
Baldwin-Det 2.24
Boyle-StL 2.24
Flynn-Chi 2.24
Clarkson-Chi 2.41

Adjusted ERA
Flynn-Chi 162
Ferguson-Phi 160
Baldwin-Det 152
Clarkson-Chi 151
Boyle-StL 144

Opponents' Batting Avg.
Baldwin-Det 202
Ferguson-Phi 210
Flynn-Chi 211
Stemmeyer-Bos 223
Casey-Phi 227

Opponents' On Base Pct.
Baldwin-Det 244
Ferguson-Phi 245
Flynn-Chi 259
Keefe-NY 263
Clarkson-Chi 265

Starter Runs
Ferguson-Phi 58.4
Baldwin-Det 57.8
Clarkson-Chi 46.4
Keefe-NY 46.2
Casey-Phi 36.5

Adjusted Starter Runs
Baldwin-Det 63.5
Clarkson-Chi 63.2
Ferguson-Phi 52.3
Flynn-Chi 39.6
McCormick-Chi 31.3

Clutch Pitching Index
Boyle-StL 171
McCormick-Chi 120
Welch-NY 118
Kirby-StL 112
Casey-Phi 109

Relief Runs

Adjusted Relief Runs

Relief Ranking

Total Pitcher Index
Ferguson-Phi 7.2
Clarkson-Chi 6.8
Baldwin-Det 6.7
Flynn-Chi 4.4
McCormick-Chi 3.5

Total Baseball Ranking
Ferguson-Phi 7.2
Clarkson-Chi 6.8
Baldwin-Det 6.7
Kelly-Chi 4.7
Flynn-Chi 4.4

TEAM	G	W	L	PCT	GB	R	OR	AB	H	2B	3B	HR	BB	SO	AVG	OBP	SLG	PRO	/A	BR	/A	PF	CHI	RC	TA	SB	CS	SBASBR
STL	139	93	46	.669		944	592	5009	1365	206	85	20	400	425	.273	.333	.360	.693	123	127	34	111	100	729	.710	336		
PIT	140	80	57	.584	12	810	647	4854	1171	187	96	15	478	713	.241	.314	.329	.643	107	43	103	93	95	597	.644	260		
BRO	141	76	61	.555	16	832	832	5053	1261	196	80	16	433	523	.250	.311	.330	.641	106	35	32	100	97	610	.623	248		
LOU	138	66	70	.485	25.5	833	805	4921	1294	182	88	20	410	558	.263	.323	.348	.671	116	86	22	108	94	634	.648	202		
CIN	141	65	73	.471	27.5	883	865	4915	1224	145	97	40	374	633	.249	.311	.342	.653	110	53	84	96	103	595	.625	185		
PHI	139	63	72	.467	28	772	942	4856	1142	192	82	21	378	697	.235	.296	.321	.617	98	-8	-8	100	99	560	.617	284		
NY	137	53	82	.393	38	628	766	4683	1047	108	72	18	330	578	.224	.279	.289	.568	83	-88	-114	104	94	422	.505	120		
BAL	139	48	83	.366	41	625	878	4639	945	124	51	8	379	603	.204	.269	.258	.527	70	-150	-78	91	103	404	.509	269		
TOT	557					6327		38930	9449	1340	651	158	3182	4730	.243	.300	.323	.623								1904		

TEAM	CG	SHO	SV	IP	H	H/G	HR	BB	BB/G	SO	SO/G	ERA	/A	OAVG	OOBA	PR	/A	PF	CPI	FA	E	DP	FW	PW	BW	SBW	DIF
STL	134	14	2	1229.3	1087	8.0	13	329	2.4	583	4.3	2.52	145	.226	.276	127	155	106	109	.915	494	96	3.4	13.6	3.0		3.5
PIT	137	15	1	1226.0	1130	8.3	10	299	2.2	515	3.8	2.83	110	.233	.278	84	37	90	100	.917	487	90	3.8	3.2	9.0		-4.6
BRO	138	6	0	1234.7	1202	8.8	17	464	3.4	540	3.9	3.42	101	.243	.308	4	5	100	103	.900	611	87	-2.5	.4	2.8		6.8
LOU	131	5	2	1209.7	1109	8.3	16	432	3.2	720	5.4	3.07	121	.232	.296	50	86	108	103	.901	593	89	-1.6	7.6	1.9		-9.9
CIN	129	3	0	1247.7	1267	9.1	25	481	3.5	495	3.6	4.19	79	.251	.316	-102	-123	96	91	.904	588	122	-1.3	-10.8	7.4		.8
PHI	134	4	0	1218.7	1308	9.7	35	388	2.9	513	3.8	3.98	89	.262	.315	-71	-58	103	100	.894	637	99	-3.8	-5.1	-.7		5.1
NY	134	5	0	1186.3	1148	8.7	23	386	2.9	559	4.2	3.50	104	.242	.299	-7	19	106	96	.907	546	81	.8	1.7	-10.0		-6.9
BAL	134	5	0	1206.7	1197	8.9	25	403	3.0	805	6.0	4.09	79	.247	.305	-85	-113	94	87	.908	536	59	1.3	-9.9	-6.8		-2.0
TOT	1071	57	5	9759.0		8.7			2.9		4.4	3.45		.243	.300					.906	4492	723					

Runs
Latham-StL 152
McPhee-Cin 139
Larkin-Phi 133
McClellan-Bro 131
Pinkney-Bro 119

Hits
Orr-NY 193
O'Neill-StL 190
Larkin-Phi 180
Latham-StL 174
Phillips-Bro 160

Doubles
McClellan 36
McClellan-Bro 33
Barkley-Pit 32
Welch-StL 31
Browning-Lou 29

Triples
Orr-NY 31
Coleman-Phi-Pit 17
Kuehne-Pit 17
Fennelly-Cin 17
Larkin-Phi 16

Home Runs
Stovey-Phi 7
Orr-NY 7
McPhee-Cin 7
Fennelly-Cin 6

Total Bases
Orr-NY 301
O'Neill-StL 255
Larkin-Phi 254
Welch-StL 221
McPhee-Cin 217

Runs Batted In

Runs Produced
Latham-StL 151
McPhee-Cin 132
Larkin-Phi 131
McClellan-Bro 130
Pinkney-Bro 119

Bases On Balls
Swartwood-Bro 70
Pinkney-Bro 70
Mack-Lou 68
Kerins-Lou 66

Batting Average
Browning-Lou 340
Orr-NY 338
O'Neill-StL 328
Larkin-Phi 319
Latham-StL 301

On Base Percentage
Larkin-Phi 390
Browning-Lou 389
O'Neill-StL 385
Stovey-Phi 377
Swartwood-Bro 377

Slugging Average
Orr-NY 527
Larkin-Phi 450
Browning-Lou 441
O'Neill-StL 440
Stovey-Phi 440

Production
Orr-NY 890
Larkin-Phi 839
Browning-Lou 830
O'Neill-StL 826
Stovey-Phi 817

Adjusted Production
Orr-NY 174
Larkin-Phi 165
Carroll-Pit 159
Stovey-Phi 158
Browning-Lou 150

Batter Runs
Orr-NY 47.3
Larkin-Phi 42.7
Caruthers-StL 42.1
O'Neill-StL 40.0
Stovey-Phi 33.4

Adjusted Batter Runs
Caruthers-StL 51.3
Orr-NY 44.2
Larkin-Phi 42.6
Hecker-Lou 36.7
Stovey-Phi 33.3

Clutch Hitting Index

Runs Created
Orr-NY 118
Larkin-Phi 114
Stovey-Phi 109
O'Neill-StL 104
Latham-StL 104

Total Average
Stovey-Phi 1.009
Larkin-Phi 914
Robinson-StL 903
Orr-NY 897
Browning-Lou 873

Stolen Bases
Stovey-Phi 68
Latham-StL 60
Welch-StL 59
Robinson-StL 51
McClellan-Bro 43

Stolen Base Average

Stolen Base Runs

Fielding Runs
Kerins-Lou 37.7
McPhee-Cin 31.5
Hankinson-NY 24.0
Holbert-NY 17.7
Smith-Pit 15.3

Total Player Rating
McPhee-Cin 4.7
Kerins-Lou 4.5
Carroll-Pit 4.3
Fennelly-Cin 3.7
Larkin-Phi 3.5

Wins
Morris-Pit 41
Foutz-StL 41
Ramsey-Lou 38
Mullane-Cin 33
Caruthers-StL 30

Win Percentage
Foutz-StL 719
Caruthers-StL 682
Morris-Pit 672
Hudson-StL 615
Atkinson-Phi 595

Games
Kilroy-Bal 68
Ramsey-Lou 67
Morris-Pit 64
Mullane-Cin 63
Foutz-StL 59

Complete Games
Ramsey-Lou 66
Kilroy-Bal 66
Morris-Pit 63
Mullane-Cin 55
Foutz-StL 55

Shutouts
Morris-Pit 12
Foutz-StL 11
Terry-Bro 5
Kilroy-Bal 5
Ramsey-Lou 3

Saves
Strauss-Lou-Bro 1
Morris-Pit 1
Hudson-StL 1
Foutz-StL 1
Ely-Lou 1

Innings Pitched
Ramsey-Lou 589
Kilroy-Bal 583
Morris-Pit 555
Mullane-Cin 530
Foutz-StL 504

Fewest Hits/Game
Ramsey-Lou 6.83
Kilroy-Bal 7.35
Morris-Pit 7.38
Foutz-StL 7.46
Caruthers-StL 7.51

Fewest BB/Game
Galvin-Pit 1.55
Morris-Pit 1.91
Caruthers-StL 2.00
McGinnis-StL-Bal . . . 2.27
Atkinson-Phi 2.29

Strikeouts
Kilroy-Bal 513
Ramsey-Lou 499
Morris-Pit 326
Foutz-StL 283
Mullane-Cin 250

Strikeouts/Game
Kilroy-Bal 7.92
Ramsey-Lou 7.62
Morris-Pit 5.29
Miller-Phi 5.24
Terry-Bro 5.06

Wins Above Team
Ramsey-Lou 10.2
Morris-Pit 10.0
Kilroy-Bal 7.9
Mullane-Cin 7.1
Foutz-StL 6.6

Earned Run Average
Foutz-StL 2.11
Caruthers-StL 2.33
Morris-Pit 2.45
Ramsey-Lou 2.46
Galvin-Pit 2.67

Adjusted ERA
Foutz-StL 173
Caruthers-StL 157
Ramsey-Lou 151
Hecker-Lou 130
Morris-Pit 127

Opponents' Batting Avg.
Ramsey-Lou 201
Kilroy-Bal 213
Morris-Pit 213
Foutz-StL 215
Caruthers-StL 216

Opponents' On Base Pct.
Morris-Pit 255
Caruthers-StL 259
Ramsey-Lou 269
Foutz-StL 270
Kilroy-Bal 272

Starter Runs
Foutz-StL 75.2
Ramsey-Lou 64.8
Morris-Pit 61.8
Caruthers-StL 48.4
Galvin-Pit 37.8

Adjusted Starter Runs
Foutz-StL 86.6
Ramsey-Lou 82.2
Caruthers-StL 57.1
Morris-Pit 40.1
Hecker-Lou 39.8

Clutch Pitching Index
Galvin-Pit 123
Foutz-StL 119
McGinnis-StL-Bal 116
Hart-Phi 115
Miller-Phi 114

Relief Runs

Adjusted Relief Runs

Relief Ranking

Total Pitcher Index
Caruthers-StL 10.5
Foutz-StL 10.3
Hecker-Lou 7.3
Ramsey-Lou 7.3
Morris-Pit 2.9

Total Baseball Ranking
Caruthers-StL 10.5
Foutz-StL 10.3
Hecker-Lou 7.3
Ramsey-Lou 7.3
McPhee-Cin 4.7

TEAM	G	W	L	PCT	GB	R	OR	AB	H	2B	3B	HR	BB	SO	AVG	OBP	SLG	PRO	/A	BR	/A	PF	CHI	RC	TA	SB	CS	SBA	SBR
DET	127	79	45	.637		969	714	4689	1404	213	126	55	352	258	.299	.353	.434	.787	124	146	133	102	101	833	.819	267			
PHI	128	75	48	.610	3.5	901	702	4630	1269	213	89	47	385	346	.274	.337	.389	.726	107	48	74	97	105	744	.771	355			
CHI	127	71	50	.587	6.5	813	716	4350	1177	178	98	80	407	400	.271	.336	.412	.748	113	75	-48	116	97	748	.819	382			
NY	129	68	55	.553	10.5	816	723	4516	1259	167	93	48	361	326	.279	.339	.389	.728	108	50	-6	107	98	753	.792	415			
BOS	127	61	60	.504	16.5	831	792	4531	1255	185	94	53	340	392	.277	.333	.394	.727	107	44	61	98	101	736	.774	373			
PIT	125	55	69	.444	24	621	750	4414	1141	183	78	20	319	381	.258	.314	.349	.663	90	-55	-4	93	88	567	.647	221			
WAS	126	46	76	.377	32	601	818	4414	1069	149	63	47	269	339	.242	.292	.336	.628	79	-116	-81	95	94	544	.636	334			
IND	127	37	89	.294	43	628	965	4368	1080	162	70	33	300	379	.247	.302	.339	.641	83	-91	-59	96	95	562	.657	334			
TOT	508					6180		35912	9654	1450	711	383	2733	2821	.269	.321	.381	.701								2681			

TEAM	CG	SHO	SV	IP	H	H/G	HR	BB	BB/G	SO	SO/G	ERA	/A	OAVG	OOBA	PR	/A	PF	CPI	FA	E	DP	FW	PW	BW	SBW	DIF
DET	122	3	1	1116.3	1172	9.4	52	344	2.8	337	2.7	3.95	100	.261	.314	12	-1	97	96	.926	394	92	3.3	-.0	11.3		2.5
PHI	119	7	1	1132.7	1173	9.3	48	305	2.4	435	3.5	3.47	109	.259	.306	72	40	94	103	.913	471	76	-.6	3.4	6.3		4.4
CHI	117	4	3	1126.0	1156	9.2	55	338	2.7	510	4.1	3.47	135	.257	.309	72	149	115	106	.915	472	19	-.6	12.6	-4.1		2.6
NY	123	5	1	1113.7	1115	9.0	27	373	3.0	412	3.3	3.60	119	.252	.311	56	83	106	96	.921	431	83	1.4	7.0	-.5		-1.5
BOS	123	3	1	1100.7	1226	10.0	55	396	3.2	254	2.1	4.41	89	.273	.332	-43	-58	97	97	.905	522	94	-3.1	-4.9	5.2		3.4
PIT	123	3	0	1108.7	1287	10.4	39	246	2.0	248	2.0	4.12	94	.281	.318	-8	-30	96	98	.921	425	70	1.7	-2.5	-.3		-5.9
WAS	124	4	0	1090.3	1216	10.0	47	299	2.5	396	3.3	4.19	95	.273	.319	-17	-23	99	95	.910	483	77	-1.2	-1.9	-6.9		-5.0
IND	118	4	1	1088.0	1289	10.7	60	431	3.6	245	2.0	5.25	78	.285	.348	-145	-138	101	91	.912	479	105	-1.0	-11.7	-5.0		-8.3
TOT	969	34	8	8876.3		9.8			2.8		2.9	4.05		.269	.321					.915	3677	616					

Runs
Brouthers-Det 153
Rowe-Det 135
Richardson-Det 131
Kelly-Bos 120

Hits
Thompson-Det 203
Ward-NY 184
Richardson-Det 178
Rowe-Det 171
Brouthers-Det 169

Doubles
Brouthers-Det 36
Kelly-Bos 34
Denny-Ind 34
Anson-Chi 33

Triples
Thompson-Det 23
Connor-NY 22
Johnston-Bos 20
Brouthers-Det 20
Wood-Phi 19

Home Runs
O'Brien-Was 19
Connor-NY 17
Pfeffer-Chi 16
Wood-Phi 14

Total Bases
Thompson-Det 311
Brouthers-Det 281
Richardson-Det 263
Denny-Ind 256
Connor-NY 255

Runs Batted In
Thompson-Det 166
Connor-NY 104
Anson-Chi 102
Brouthers-Det 101
Denny-Ind 97

Runs Produced
Thompson-Det 273
Brouthers-Det 242
Rowe-Det 225
Richardson-Det 217
Anson-Chi 202

Bases On Balls
Fogarty-Phi 82
Connor-NY 75
Williamson-Chi 73
Seery-Ind 71
Brouthers-Det 71

Batting Average
Thompson-Det 372
Anson-Chi 347
Brouthers-Det 338
Ward-NY 338
Wise-Bos 334

On Base Percentage
Brouthers-Det 426
Anson-Chi 422
Thompson-Det 416
Schomberg-Ind 397
Kelly-Bos 393

Slugging Average
Thompson-Det 571
Brouthers-Det 562
Connor-NY 541
Wise-Bos 522
Anson-Chi 517

Production
Brouthers-Det 988
Thompson-Det 987
Anson-Chi 939
Connor-NY 933
Wise-Bos 913

Adjusted Production
Brouthers-Det 172
Thompson-Det 171
Wise-Bos 157
Carroll-Pit 156
Kelly-Bos 149

Batter Runs
Thompson-Det 52.6
Brouthers-Det 51.9
Anson-Chi 40.6
Connor-NY 38.5
Wise-Bos 33.0

Adjusted Batter Runs
Thompson-Det 51.2
Brouthers-Det 50.5
Wise-Bos 34.8
Connor-NY 32.2
Kelly-Bos 32.1

Clutch Hitting Index
O'Rourke-NY 167
Thompson-Det 143
Mulvey-Phi 141
McGeachey-Ind 132
Donnelly-Was 129

Runs Created
Thompson-Det 142
Brouthers-Det 138
Kelly-Bos 129
Ward-NY 125
Connor-NY 120

Total Average
Brouthers-Det 1.184
Kelly-Bos 1.146
Connor-NY 1.131
Thompson-Det 1.094
Fogarty-Phi 1.085

Stolen Bases
Ward-NY 111
Fogarty-Phi 102
Kelly-Bos 84
Hanlon-Det 69
Glasscock-Ind 62

Stolen Base Average

Stolen Base Runs

Fielding Runs
Glasscock-Ind 34.6
Fogarty-Phi 28.6
Ward-NY 27.4
Sutton-Bos 24.2
Johnston-Bos 22.8

Total Player Rating
Thompson-Det 4.5
Fogarty-Phi 4.1
Richardson-Det 3.4
Denny-Ind 3.3
Glasscock-Ind 3.1

Wins
Clarkson-Chi 38
Keefe-NY 35
Getzien-Det 29
Galvin-Pit 28
Casey-Phi 28

Win Percentage
Getzien-Det 690
Ferguson-Phi 688
Casey-Phi 683
Keefe-NY 648
Clarkson-Chi 644

Games
Clarkson-Chi 60
Keefe-NY 56
Radbourn-Bos 50
Galvin-Pit 49
Whitney-Was 47

Complete Games
Clarkson-Chi 56
Keefe-NY 54
Radbourn-Bos 48
Galvin-Pit 47
Whitney-Was 46

Shutouts
Casey-Phi 4
Whitney-Was 3
Madden-Bos 3
Healy-Ind 3

Saves

Innings Pitched
Clarkson-Chi 523
Keefe-NY 479
Galvin-Pit 441
Radbourn-Bos 425
Whitney-Was 405

Fewest Hits/Game
Conway-Det 8.14
Keefe-NY 8.40
Casey-Phi 8.70
Welch-NY 8.82
Clarkson-Chi 8.83

Fewest BB/Game
Whitney-Was 93
Galvin-Pit 1.37
Ferguson-Phi 1.42
Clarkson-Chi 1.58
Boyle-Ind 1.89

Strikeouts
Clarkson-Chi 237
Keefe-NY 186
Baldwin-Chi 164
Buffinton-Phi 160
Whitney-Was 146

Strikeouts/Game
Baldwin-Chi 4.42
Gilmore-Was 4.37
Buffinton-Phi 4.34
VanHaltren-Chi 4.25
Clarkson-Chi 4.08

Wins Above Team
Keefe-NY 8.8
Galvin-Pit 8.1
Whitney-Was 7.8
Clarkson-Chi 7.1
Casey-Phi 5.3

Earned Run Average
Casey-Phi 2.86
Conway-Det 2.90
Ferguson-Phi 3.00
Clarkson-Chi 3.08
Keefe-NY 3.10

Adjusted ERA
Clarkson-Chi 152
Keefe-NY 138
Baldwin-Chi 137
Conway-Det 136
Casey-Phi 133

Opponents' Batting Avg.
Conway-Det 234
Ferguson-Phi 240
Casey-Phi 246
Welch-NY 249
Clarkson-Chi 249

Opponents' On Base Pct.
Clarkson-Chi 281
Ferguson-Phi 281
Keefe-NY 281
Whitney-Was 283
Conway-Det 293

Starter Runs
Clarkson-Chi 56.4
Casey-Phi 51.6
Keefe-NY 50.6
Galvin-Pit 37.5
Whitney-Was 37.3

Adjusted Starter Runs
Clarkson-Chi 92.2
Keefe-NY 62.5
Baldwin-Chi 47.2
Casey-Phi 40.5
Welch-NY 35.3

Clutch Pitching Index
Casey-Phi 114
VanHaltren-Chi 111
Baldwin-Chi 111
Galvin-Pit 107
Ferguson-Phi 103

Relief Runs

Adjusted Relief Runs

Relief Ranking

Total Pitcher Index
Clarkson-Chi 9.8
Keefe-NY 6.2
Ferguson-Phi 5.1
Whitney-Was 4.3
Baldwin-Chi 3.7

Total Baseball Ranking
Clarkson-Chi 9.8
Keefe-NY 6.2
Ferguson-Phi 5.1
Thompson-Det 4.5
Whitney-Was 4.3

TEAM	G	W	L	PCT	GB	R	OR	AB	H	2B	3B	HR	BB	SO	AVG	OBP	SLG	PRO	/A	BR	/A	PF	CHI	RC	TA	SB	CS	SBA SBR
STL	138	95	40	.704		**1131**	761	5048	**1550**	261	78	**39**	442	340	**.307**	**.371**	**.413**	**.784**	125	168	78	110	101	1012	**.907**	**581**		
CIN	136	81	54	.600	14	892	**745**	4797	1285	179	**102**	37	382	366	.268	.329	.371	.700	101	5	-69	108	99	778	.781	527		
BAL	141	77	58	.570	18	975	861	4825	1337	202	100	31	**469**	**334**	.277	.349	.380	.729	109	67	**102**	96	99	852	.835	545		
LOU	139	76	60	.559	19.5	956	854	4916	1420	195	98	26	436	356	.289	.352	.384	.736	111	77	13	107	96	849	.810	466		
PHI	137	64	69	.481	30	893	890	4954	1370	231	84	29	321	388	.277	.327	.375	.702	101	4	9	99	98	782	.754	476		
BRO	138	60	74	.448	34.5	904	918	4913	1281	200	82	25	456	365	.261	.330	.350	.680	95	-22	-8	99	100	720	.726	409		
NY	138	44	89	.331	50	754	1093	4820	1197	193	66	20	439	463	.248	.318	.328	.646	86	-81	29	88	92	614	.656	305		
CLE	133	39	92	.298	54	729	1112	4649	1170	178	77	14	375	463	.252	.314	.332	.646	86	-82	-60	98	93	611	.667	355		
TOT	550					7234		38922	10610	1639	687	221	3320	3075	.273	.330	.367	.697								3664		

TEAM	CG	SHO	SV	IP	H	H/G	HR	BB	BB/G	SO	SO/G	ERA	/A	OAVG	OOBA	PR	/A	PF	CPI	FA	E	DP	FW	PW	BW	SBW	DIF
STL	132	6	2	1199.3	1254	9.4	19	**323**	2.4	334	2.5	3.77	119	**.259**	**.306**	69	95	105	94	**.916**	485	86	**3.4**	7.7	6.3		10.1
CIN	129	**11**	1	1182.7	**1202**	**9.1**	28	396	3.0	330	2.5	**3.60**	**127**	**.254**	.311	**91**	**127**	106	101	.915	488	**106**	3.3	**10.3**	-5.6		5.5
BAL	132	8	0	1220.0	1288	9.5	**16**	418	3.1	470	3.5	3.87	105	.261	.319	58	25	94	97	.906	558	66	-.2	2.0	**8.3**		-.6
LOU	**133**	3	1	1205.7	1274	9.5	31	357	2.7	**544**	**4.1**	3.82	119	.261	.312	63	96	106	98	.903	576	83	-1.1	7.8	1.1		.3
PHI	131	5	1	1186.3	1227	9.3	29	433	3.3	417	3.2	4.61	93	.257	.319	-41	-44	100	82	.907	528	95	1.3	-3.6	.7		-.9
BRO	132	3	**3**	1185.3	1348	10.2	27	454	3.4	332	2.5	4.47	95	.276	.337	-22	-30	99	98	.904	565	88	-.5	-2.4	-.6		-3.4
NY	132	1	0	1180.3	1545	11.8	39	406	3.1	316	2.4	5.29	75	.305	.356	-130	-175	92	98	.892	643	102	-4.4	-14.2	2.3		-6.3
CLE	127	2	1	1136.0	1472	11.7	34	533	4.2	332	2.6	5.01	88	.302	.371	-89	-75	103	**109**	.897	589	97	-1.7	-6.1	-4.9		-13.8
TOT	1048	39	9	9495.7		10.1			3.1		2.9	4.30		.273	.330					.905	4432	723					

Runs	Hits	Doubles	Triples	Home Runs	Total Bases
O'Neill-StL 167	O'Neill-StL 225	O'Neill-StL 52		O'Neill-StL 14	O'Neill-StL 357
Latham-StL 163	Browning-Lou 220	Lyons-Phi 43		Reilly-Cin 10	Browning-Lou 299
Griffin-Bal 142	Lyons-Phi 209	Reilly-Cin 35		Burns-Bal 9	Lyons-Phi 298
Poorman-Phi 140	Latham-StL 198	Latham-StL 35			Burns-Bal 286
Comiskey-StL 139	Burns-Bal 188	Browning-Lou 35			Reilly-Cin 263

Runs Batted In	Runs Produced	Bases On Balls	Batting Average	On Base Percentage	Slugging Average
Latham-StL 161	O'Neill-StL 210	Radford-NY 106	O'Neill-StL 435	O'Neill-StL 490	O'Neill-StL 691
O'Neill-StL 153	Browning-Lou 172	Robinson-StL 92	Browning-Lou 402	Browning-Lou 464	Caruthers-StL 547
Griffin-Bal 139	Burns-Bal 168	Nicol-Cin 86	Lyons-Phi 367	Caruthers-StL 463	Browning-Lou 547
Poorman-Phi 136	Caruthers-StL 168	Mack-Lou 83	Caruthers-StL 357	Robinson-StL 445	Lyons-Phi 523
	Lyons-Phi 166	Fennelly-Cin 82	Foutz-StL 357	Lyons-Phi 421	Burns-Bal 519

Production	Adjusted Production	Batter Runs	Adjusted Batter Runs	Clutch Hitting Index	Runs Created
O'Neill-StL 1.180	O'Neill-StL 210	O'Neill-StL 87.9	O'Neill-StL 78.7		O'Neill-StL 194
Browning-Lou 1.011	Browning-Lou 172	Browning-Lou 62.5	Browning-Lou 55.4		Browning-Lou 191
Caruthers-StL 1.010	Burns-Bal 168	Lyons-Phi 48.5	Burns-Bal 49.6		Lyons-Phi 160
Lyons-Phi......... .943	Caruthers-StL 168	Burns-Bal 45.6	Lyons-Phi 49.1		Burns-Bal 146
Burns-Bal .... .933	Lyons-Phi 166	Caruthers-StL 44.0	Caruthers-StL 37.0		Latham-StL 146

Total Average	Stolen Bases	Stolen Base Average	Stolen Base Runs	Fielding Runs	Total Player Rating
O'Neill-StL 1.514	Nicol-Cin 138			Smith-Bro 31.6	O'Neill-StL 5.2
Browning-Lou 1.422	Latham-StL 129			McPhee-Cin ... 24.9	Caruthers-StL 4.0
Caruthers-StL 1.368	Comiskey-StL 117			White-Lou 23.5	Browning-Lou 3.6
Robinson-StL 1.197	Browning-Lou 103			Kerins-Lou 23.2	Lyons-Phi 2.9
Lyons-Phi........ 1.175	McPhee-Cin 95			Snyder-Cle 21.4	Smith-Bro 2.8

Wins	Win Percentage	Games	Complete Games	Shutouts	Saves
Kilroy-Bal 46	Caruthers-StL 763	Kilroy-Bal 69	Kilroy-Bal 66	Mullane-Cin 6	Terry-Bro 3
Ramsey-Lou.........37	King-StL 727	Ramsey-Lou 65	Ramsey-Lou 61	Kilroy-Bal 6	
Smith-Cin 34	Kilroy-Bal 708	Smith-Bal 58	Smith-Bal 54	Smith-Cin 3	
King-StL 32	Foutz-StL 676	Weyhing-Phi 55	Weyhing-Phi 53	Seward-Phi 3	
Mullane-Cin 31	Smith-Cin 667	Seward-Phi 55	Seward-Phi 52		

Innings Pitched	Fewest Hits/Game	Fewest BB/Game	Strikeouts	Strikeouts/Game	Wins Above Team
Kilroy-Bal 589	Smith-Cin 8.05	Hecker-Lou 1.58	Ramsey-Lou 355	Ramsey-Lou 5.70	Kilroy-Bal 15.4
Ramsey-Lou........561	Seward-Phi 8.50	Caruthers-StL ... 1.61	Kilroy-Bal 217	Morrison-Cle 4.49	Smith-Cin 6.2
Smith-Bal 491	Toole-Bro 8.63	Lynch-NY 1.73	Smith-Bal 206	Terry-Bro 3.91	Caruthers-StL 4.9
Seward-Phi 471	Ramsey-Lou 8.73	Foutz-StL 2.39	Weyhing-Phi 193	Smith-Bal 3.78	Mullane-Cin 4.0
Weyhing-Phi 466	Caruthers-StL 8.89	Kilroy-Bal 2.40	Smith-Cin 176	Weyhing-Phi 3.73	Toole-Bro 3.4

Earned Run Average	Adjusted ERA	Opponents' Batting Avg.	Opponents' On Base Pct.	Starter Runs	Adjusted Starter Runs
Smith-Cin 2.94	Smith-Cin 156	Smith-Cin 231	Caruthers-StL 281	Kilroy-Bal 80.3	Smith-Cin 81.1
Kilroy-Bal 3.07	Mullane-Cin 141	Seward-Phi 241	Smith-Cin 283	Smith-Cin 67.5	Ramsey-Lou 69.2
Mullane-Cin 3.25	Caruthers-StL 136	Toole-Bro 243	Seward-Phi 294	Ramsey-Lou 53.9	Kilroy-Bal 64.3
Caruthers-StL 3.30	Ramsey-Lou 132	Ramsey-Lou 245	Kilroy-Bal 297	Mullane-Cin 48.7	Mullane-Cin 61.4
Ramsey-Lou 3.43	Kilroy-Bal 132	Caruthers-StL 249	Ramsey-Lou 298	Caruthers-StL 37.9	Caruthers-StL 45.2

Clutch Pitching Index	Relief Runs	Adjusted Relief Runs	Relief Ranking	Total Pitcher Index	Total Baseball Ranking
Daily-Cle 132				Kilroy-Bal 6.9	Caruthers-StL 7.8
Crowell-Cle 114				Smith-Cin 6.9	Kilroy-Bal 6.9
Morrison-Cle 113				Mullane-Cin 5.3	Smith-Cin 6.9
Chamberlin-Lou 111				Ramsey-Lou 4.5	Mullane-Cin 5.3
Porter-Bro 106				Caruthers-StL 3.8	O'Neill-StL 5.2

TEAM	G	W	L	PCT	GB	R	OR	AB	H	2B	3B	HR	BB	SO	AVG	OBP	SLG	PRO	/A	BR	/A	PF	CHI	RC	TA	SB	CS	SBA	SBR
NY	137	84	47	.641		659	479	4747	1149	130	76	55	270	456	.242	.287	.336	.623	106	33	79	93	100	562	.614	314			
CHI	135	77	58	.570	9	734	659	4616	1201	147	95	77	290	563	.260	.308	.383	.691	128	139	96	107	97	649	.695	287			
PHI	131	69	61	.531	14.5	535	509	4528	1021	151	46	16	268	485	.225	.276	.290	.566	88	-49	-130	114	97	441	.535	246			
BOS	137	70	64	.522	15.5	669	619	4834	1183	167	89	56	282	524	.245	.291	.351	.642	112	63	26	106	95	593	.631	293			
DET	134	68	63	.519	16	721	629	4849	1275	177	72	51	307	396	.263	.313	.361	.674	123	122	132	98	94	623	.642	193			
PIT	138	66	68	.493	19.5	534	580	4713	1070	150	49	14	194	583	.227	.264	.289	.553	84	-79	-45	95	99	446	.518	287			
IND	136	50	85	.370	36	603	731	4623	1100	180	33	33	236	492	.238	.281	.313	.594	97	-11	18	95	101	518	.589	350			
WAS	136	48	86	.358	37.5	482	731	4546	944	98	49	31	246	499	.208	.255	.271	.526	75	-115	-91	96	99	409	.514	331			
TOT	542					4937		37456	8943	1200	509	333	2093	3998	.239	.279	.325	.604								2301			

TEAM	CG	SHO	SV	IP	H	H/G	HR	BB	BB/G	SO	SO/G	ERA	/A	OAVG	OOBA	PR	/A	PF	CPI	FA	E	DP	FW	PW	BW	SBW	DIF
NY	136	19	1	1208.0	906	6.7	27	308	2.3	724	5.4	1.96	128	.200	.251	117	74	89	105	.924	432	76	.9	7.3	7.8		2.6
CHI	123	13	1	1186.3	1139	8.6	63	308	2.3	588	4.5	2.96	101	.243	.290	-16	4	106	105	.927	417	112	1.7	.4	9.4		-2.0
PHI	125	9	3	1167.0	1072	8.3	26	196	1.5	519	4.0	2.38	135	.235	.266	58	106	113	101	.924	424	70	1.3	10.4	-12.8		5.1
BOS	134	7	0	1225.3	1104	8.1	36	269	2.0	484	3.6	2.61	114	.231	.273	30	49	105	97	.917	494	91	-2.4	4.8	2.6		-2.0
DET	130	9	1	1199.0	1115	8.4	44	183	1.4	522	3.9	2.74	100	.237	.266	12	0	97	93	.919	463	83	-.8	.0	13.0		-9.7
PIT	135	13	0	1203.3	1190	8.9	23	223	1.7	367	2.7	2.67	101	.248	.282	21	3	95	104	.927	416	88	1.7	.3	-4.4		1.4
IND	132	6	0	1187.7	1260	9.5	64	308	2.3	388	2.9	3.82	72	.262	.306	-130	-139	98	95	.922	449	84	-.0	-13.7	1.8		-5.6
WAS	133	6	0	1179.3	1157	8.8	50	298	2.3	406	3.1	3.56	80	.247	.292	-94	-91	101	88	.913	494	69	-2.4	-9.0	-9.0		1.3
TOT	1048	82	6	9556.0		8.4			2.0		3.8	2.83		.239	.279					.922	3589	673					

Runs
Brouthers-Det 118
Ryan-Chi 115
Johnston-Bos 102
Anson-Chi 101
Connor-NY 98

Hits
Ryan-Chi 182
Anson-Chi 177
Johnston-Bos 173
Brouthers-Det 160
White-Det 157

Doubles
Ryan-Chi 33
Brouthers-Det 33
Johnston-Bos 31
Denny-Ind 27
Hines-Ind 26

Triples
Johnston-Bos 18
Connor-NY 17
Nash-Bos 15
Ewing-NY 15

Home Runs
Ryan-Chi 16
Connor-NY 14
Johnston-Bos 12
Denny-Ind 12
Anson-Chi 12

Total Bases
Ryan-Chi 283
Johnston-Bos 276
Anson-Chi 257
Brouthers-Det 242
Connor-NY 231

Runs Batted In
Anson-Chi 84
Nash-Bos 75
Rowe-Det 74
Williamson-Chi 73

Runs Produced
Brouthers-Det 175
Anson-Chi 173
Ryan-Chi 163
Johnston-Bos 158
Connor-NY 155

Bases On Balls
Connor-NY 73
Hoy-Was 69
Brouthers-Det 68
Williamson-Chi 65
Seery-Ind 64

Batting Average
Anson-Chi .... .344
Ryan-Chi .... .332
Kelly-Bos .... .318
Brouthers-Det .... .307
Ewing-NY .... .306

On Base Percentage
Anson-Chi .... .400
Brouthers-Det .... .399
Connor-NY .... .389
Ryan-Chi .... .377
Hoy-Was .... .374

Slugging Average
Ryan-Chi .... .515
Anson-Chi .... .499
Connor-NY .... .480
Kelly-Bos .... .480
Johnston-Bos ..... .472

Production
Anson-Chi .... .899
Ryan-Chi .... .892
Connor-NY .... .869
Brouthers-Det .... .862
Kelly-Bos .... .848

Adjusted Production
Connor-NY 193
Brouthers-Det 180
Anson-Chi 176
Ryan-Chi 173
Ewing-NY 173

Batter Runs
Ryan-Chi 50.7
Anson-Chi 50.5
Brouthers-Det 47.9
Connor-NY 44.9
Kelly-Bos 34.5

Adjusted Batter Runs
Connor-NY 50.1
Brouthers-Det 49.1
Anson-Chi 45.7
Ryan-Chi 45.7
Tiernan-NY 32.2

Clutch Hitting Index
Burns-Chi 163
Rowe-Det 148
Bassett-Ind 148
Williamson-Chi 140
Smith-Pit 139

Runs Created
Ryan-Chi 133
Anson-Chi 117
Brouthers-Det 113
Connor-NY 103
Kelly-Bos 101

Total Average
Ryan-Chi 1.044
Kelly-Bos 1.007
Anson-Chi .... .985
Brouthers-Det .... .983
Connor-NY .... .982

Stolen Bases
Hoy-Was 82
Seery-Ind 80
Sunday-Pit 71
Pfeffer-Chi 64
Ryan-Chi 60

Stolen Base Average

Stolen Base Runs

Fielding Runs
Pfeffer-Chi 37.4
Daly-Chi 16.2
Sunday-Pit 15.4
Nash-Bos 14.8
Mack-Was 14.2

Total Player Rating
Ryan-Chi 4.5
Pfeffer-Chi 4.5
Anson-Chi 4.0
Nash-Bos 3.8
Ewing-NY 3.8

Wins
Keefe-NY 35
Clarkson-Bos 33
Conway-Det 30
Morris-Pit 29
Buffinton-Phi 28

Win Percentage
Keefe-NY .... .745
Conway-Det .... .682
Sanders-Phi ...... .655
Krock-Chi .... .641
Clarkson-Bos ..... .623

Games
Morris-Pit 55
Clarkson-Bos 54
Keefe-NY 51
Galvin-Pit 50
Welch-NY 47

Complete Games
Morris-Pit 54
Clarkson-Bos 53
Keefe-NY 51
Galvin-Pit 49
Welch-NY 47

Shutouts
Keefe-NY 8
Galvin-Pit 6
Welch-NY 5
Morris-Pit 5

Saves
Wood-Phi 2
VanHaltren-Chi 1
Tyng-Phi 1
Twitchell-Det 1
Crane-NY 1

Innings Pitched
Clarkson-Bos 483
Morris-Pit 480
Galvin-Pit 437
Keefe-NY 434
Welch-NY 425

Fewest Hits/Game
Keefe-NY 6.55
Titcomb-NY 6.81
Welch-NY 6.95
Conway-Det 7.25
Buffinton-Phi 7.29

Fewest BB/Game
Sanders-Phi 1.08
Galvin-Pit 1.09
Krock-Chi 1.19
Getzein-Det 1.20
Madden-Bos 1.31

Strikeouts
Keefe-NY 333
Clarkson-Bos 223
Getzein-Det 202
Buffinton-Phi 199
O'Day-Was 186

Strikeouts/Game
Keefe-NY 6.91
Titcomb-NY 5.89
Baldwin-Chi 5.63
VanHaltren-Chi ... 5.09
Getzein-Det 4.50

Wins Above Team
Conway-Det 9.6
Keefe-NY 9.1
Clarkson-Bos 8.1
Buffinton-Phi 6.1
Morris-Pit 5.0

Earned Run Average
Keefe-NY 1.74
Sanders-Phi 1.90
Buffinton-Phi 1.91
Welch-NY 1.93
Sowders-Bos 2.07

Adjusted ERA
Sanders-Phi 169
Buffinton-Phi 168
Keefe-NY 144
Sowders-Bos 143
Welch-NY 130

Opponents' Batting Avg.
Keefe-NY .... .196
Titcomb-NY .... .202
Welch-NY .... .206
Conway-Det .... .213
Buffinton-Phi .... .214

Opponents' On Base Pct.
Keefe-NY .... .239
Conway-Det .... .242
Buffinton-Phi .... .243
Gruber-Det .... .249
Titcomb-NY .... .249

Starter Runs
Keefe-NY 52.7
Welch-NY 42.8
Buffinton-Phi 41.0
Sanders-Phi 28.6
Morris-Pit 28.1

Adjusted Starter Runs
Buffinton-Phi 57.6
Sanders-Phi 40.0
Keefe-NY 37.1
Sowders-Bos 31.7
Welch-NY 27.6

Clutch Pitching Index
Baldwin-Chi 125
Gleason-Phi 117
Morris-Pit 114
Burdick-Ind 112
Sowders-Bos 110

Relief Runs

Adjusted Relief Runs

Relief Ranking

Total Pitcher Index
Buffinton-Phi 7.1
Sanders-Phi 5.6
Conway-Det 3.8
Keefe-NY 3.2
Sowders-Bos 2.9

Total Baseball Ranking
Buffinton-Phi 7.1
Sanders-Phi 5.6
Pfeffer-Chi 4.5
Ryan-Chi 4.4
Anson-Chi 4.0

TEAM	G	W	L	PCT	GB	R	OR	AB	H	2B	3B	HR	BB	SO	AVG	OBP	SLG	PRO	/A	BR	/A	PF	CHI	RC	TA	SB	CS	SBA	SBR
STL	137	92	43	.681		789	501	4755	1189	149	47	36	410	521	.250	.316	.324	.640	113	74	-4	111	99	651	.692	468			
BRO	143	88	52	.629	6.5	758	584	4871	1177	172	70	25	353	439	.242	.300	.321	.621	106	37	2	105	98	584	.625	334			
PHI	136	81	52	.609	10	827	594	4828	1209	183	89	31	303	473	.250	.305	.344	.649	115	80	74	101	103	656	.684	434			
CIN	137	80	54	.597	11.5	745	628	4801	1161	132	82	32	345	555	.242	.301	.323	.624	107	41	34	101	97	623	.667	469			
BAL	137	57	80	.416	36	653	779	4656	1068	162	70	18	298	479	.229	.284	.306	.590	96	-17	10	96	96	510	.587	326			
CLE	135	50	82	.379	40.5	651	839	4603	1076	128	59	12	315	559	.234	.294	.295	.589	96	-12	5	97	95	516	.597	353			
LOU	139	48	87	.356	44	689	870	4881	1177	183	67	14	322	604	.241	.297	.315	.612	103	21	88	91	91	565	.606	318			
KC	132	43	89	.326	47.5	579	896	4588	999	142	61	17	288	604	.218	.272	.286	.558	85	-66	-109	106	93	439	.534	257			
TOT	548					5691		37983	9056	1251	545	185	2634	4234	.238	.288	.315	.602								2959			

TEAM	CG	SHO	SV	IP	H	H/G	HR	BB	BB/G	SO	SO/G	ERA	/A	OAVG	OOBA	PR	/A	PF	CPI	FA	E	DP	FW	PW	BW	SBW	DIF
STL	132	12	0	1212.7	939	7.0	19	225	1.7	517	3.8	2.09	155	.206	.243	130	156	106	89	.924	430	73	3.5	14.4	-.4		7.0
BRO	138	9	0	1286.3	1059	7.4	15	285	2.0	577	4.0	2.33	134	.216	.259	104	112	102	93	.917	507	88	-.8	10.3	.2		8.3
PHI	133	13	0	1208.7	988	7.4	14	324	2.4	596	4.4	2.41	123	.215	.266	87	74	97	94	.918	477	73	.9	6.8	6.8		-.0
CIN	132	10	2	1237.7	1103	8.0	19	310	2.3	539	3.9	2.73	111	.230	.276	45	42	99	96	.923	458	100	1.9	3.9	3.1		4.0
BAL	130	3	0	1200.3	1162	8.7	24	419	3.1	525	3.9	3.78	79	.245	.306	-95	-104	98	88	.920	461	88	1.8	-9.6	.9		-4.6
CLE	131	6	1	1171.0	1235	9.5	38	389	3.0	500	3.8	3.74	82	.261	.317	-87	-86	100	101	.915	490	87	.1	-7.9	.5		-8.7
LOU	133	6	0	1231.3	1264	9.2	28	281	2.1	599	4.4	3.25	88	.256	.296	-25	-53	93	101	.900	611	75	-6.6	-4.9	8.1		-16.1
KC	128	4	0	1157.7	1306	10.2	32	401	3.1	381	3.0	4.30	80	.274	.330	-159	-112	112	97	.915	507	95	-.8	-10.3	-10.1		-1.8
TOT	1057	63	3	9705.7		8.4			2.4		3.9	3.06		.238	.288					.916	3941	679					

Runs	Hits	Doubles	Triples	Home Runs	Total Bases
Pinkney-Bro 134	O'Neill-StL 177	Collins-Lou-Bro 31	Stovey-Phi 20	Reilly-Cin 13	Reilly-Cin 264
Collins-Lou-Bro 133	Reilly-Cin 169	Wolf-Lou 28	Burns-Bal-Bro 15	Stovey-Phi 9	Stovey-Phi 244
Stovey-Phi 127	McKean-Cle 164	Reilly-Cin 28	McKean-Cle 15	Larkin-Phi 7	O'Neill-StL 236
Welch-Phi 125	Collins-Lou-Bro 162	Larkin-Phi 28	Reilly-Cin 14		McKean-Cle 233
Latham-StL 119	Corkhill-Cin-Bro 160		Foutz-Bro 13		Burns-Bal-Bro 230

Runs Batted In	Runs Produced	Bases On Balls	Batting Average	On Base Percentage	Slugging Average
Reilly-Cin 103	Reilly-Cin 202	Robinson-StL 116	O'Neill-StL 335	Robinson-StL 400	Reilly-Cin 501
Larkin-Phi 101	O'Neill-StL 189	Fennelly-Cin-Phi 72	Reilly-Cin 321	O'Neill-StL 390	Stovey-Phi 460
Foutz-Bro 99	Foutz-Bro 187	Nicol-Cin 67	Browning-Lou 313	Browning-Lou 380	O'Neill-StL 446
O'Neill-StL 98	Larkin-Phi 186	McTamany-KC 67	Collins-Lou-Bro 307	Collins-Lou-Bro 373	Browning-Lou 436
Corkhill-Cin-Bro 93	Welch-Phi 185	Pinkney-Bro 66	McKean-Cle 299	Stovey-Phi 365	Burns-Bal-Bro 435

Production	Adjusted Production	Batter Runs	Adjusted Batter Runs	Clutch Hitting Index	Runs Created
Reilly-Cin 864	Browning-Lou 182	Reilly-Cin 43.8	Reilly-Cin 43.1	Gleason-Phi 153	Reilly-Cin 129
O'Neill-StL 836	Reilly-Cin 178	O'Neill-StL 41.7	Collins-Lou-Bro . . .41.1	Smith-Bro 151	Stovey-Phi 124
Stovey-Phi 825	Collins-Lou-Bro 172	Stovey-Phi 40.0	Stovey-Phi 39.3	Fennelly-Cin-Phi 149	Collins-Lou-Bro 112
Browning-Lou 816	Stovey-Phi 166	Collins-Lou-Bro . . .34.7	Browning-Lou 33.3	Gilks-Cle 144	Welch-Phi 106
Collins-Lou-Bro 796	O'Neill-StL 155	Burns-Bal-Bro 29.8	O'Neill-StL 33.0	Lyons-StL 142	O'Neill-StL 105

Total Average	Stolen Bases	Stolen Base Average	Stolen Base Runs	Fielding Runs	Total Player Rating
Reilly-Cin 1.064	Latham-StL 109			Shindle-Bal 35.9	Collins-Lou-Bro 4.8
Stovey-Phi 1.048	Nicol-Cin 103			McPhee-Cin 31.0	McPhee-Cin 3.7
Collins-Lou-Bro 956	Welch-Phi 95			McCarthy-StL 30.7	Stovey-Phi 3.3
Robinson-StL 934	McCarthy-StL 93			Davis-KC 29.9	Reilly-Cin 3.1
Browning-Lou 928	Stovey-Phi 87			Robinson-Phi 24.9	Davis-KC 3.0

Wins	Win Percentage	Games	Complete Games	Shutouts	Saves
King-StL 45	Hudson-StL 714	King-StL 66	King-StL 64	Seward-Phi 6	Corkhill-Cin-Bro 1
Seward-Phi 35	Chamberlin-Lou-StL .694	Bakely-Cle 61	Bakely-Cle 60	King-StL 6	Mullane-Cin 1
Caruthers-Bro 29	King-StL 682	Seward-Phi 57	Seward-Phi 57	Smith-Cin 5	Gilks-Cle 1
Weyhing-Phi 28	Caruthers-Bro 659	Porter-KC 55	Porter-KC 53	Hudson-StL 5	
Viau-Cin 27	Viau-Cin 659	Cunningham-Bal 51	Cunningham-Bal 50		

Innings Pitched	Fewest Hits/Game	Fewest BB/Game	Strikeouts	Strikeouts/Game	Wins Above Team
King-StL 586	Terry-Bro 6.69	King-StL 1.17	Seward-Phi 272	Terry-Bro 6.37	Chamberlin-Lou-StL . 8.5
Bakely-Cle 533	King-StL 6.71	Caruthers-Bro 1.22	King-StL 258	Ramsey-Lou 6.00	Seward-Phi 4.3
Seward-Phi 519	Seward-Phi 6.73	Hudson-StL 1.59	Ramsey-Lou 228	Chamberlin-Lou-StL 5.14	Viau-Cin 4.2
Porter-KC 474	Chamberlin-Lou-StL 6.95	Ewing-Lou 1.60	Bakely-Cle 212	Smith-Bal-StL 4.90	Bakely-Cle 4.1
Cunningham-Bal . . .453	Hughes-Bro 6.97	Hecker-Lou 1.74	Weyhing-Phi 204	Seward-Phi 4.72	Caruthers-Bro 2.5

Earned Run Average	Adjusted ERA	Opponents' Batting Avg.	Opponents' On Base Pct.	Starter Runs	Adjusted Starter Runs
King-StL 1.64	King-StL 198	Terry-Bro 200	King-StL 227	King-StL 92.3	King-StL 104.9
Seward-Phi 2.01	Terry-Bro 153	King-StL 200	Seward-Phi 250	Seward-Phi 60.5	Seward-Phi 55.2
Terry-Bro 2.03	Seward-Phi 148	Seward-Phi 201	Caruthers-Bro 250	Hughes-Bro 37.5	Hughes-Bro 39.7
Hughes-Bro 2.13	Hughes-Bro 146	Chamberlin-Lou-StL .206	Hudson-StL 256	Weyhing-Phi 36.4	Weyhing-Phi 32.3
Chamberlin-Lou-StL 2.19	Chamberlin-Lou-StL .135	Hughes-Bro 206	Foutz-Bro 257	Chamberlin-Lou-StL 29.8	Caruthers-Bro 31.7

Clutch Pitching Index	Relief Runs	Adjusted Relief Runs	Relief Ranking	Total Pitcher Index	Total Baseball Ranking
Hecker-Lou 108				King-StL 11.9	King-StL 11.9
Sullivan-KC 105				Seward-Phi 5.3	Seward-Phi 5.3
Ramsey-Lou 104				Weyhing-Phi 3.6	Collins-Lou-Bro 4.8
Terry-Bro 104				Hudson-StL 3.5	Caruthers-Bro 4.1
Bakely-Cle 104				Hughes-Bro 3.2	McPhee-Cin 3.7

TEAM	G	W	L	PCT	GB	R	OR	AB	H	2B	3B	HR	BB	SO	AVG	OBP	SLG	PRO	/A	BR	/A	PF	CHI	RC	TA	SB	CS	SBA SBR
NY	131	83	43	.659		935	708	4671	1319	208	77	52	538	386	.282	.360	.393	.753	119	120	80	105	103	785	.804	292		
BOS	133	83	45	.648	1	826	626	4628	1251	196	54	42	471	450	.270	.343	.363	.706	105	38	24	102	102	707	.747	331		
CHI	136	67	65	.508	19	867	814	4849	1274	184	66	79	518	516	.263	.338	.377	.715	108	48	56	99	101	716	.732	243		
PHI	130	63	64	.496	20.5	742	748	4695	1248	215	52	44	393	353	.266	.327	.362	.689	100	0	-32	104	96	660	.695	269		
PIT	134	61	71	.462	25	726	801	4748	1202	209	65	42	420	467	.253	.320	.351	.671	95	-31	54	89	96	622	.666	231		
CLE	136	61	72	.459	25.5	656	720	4673	1167	131	59	25	429	417	.250	.318	.319	.637	85	-80	-103	103	95	563	.626	237		
IND	135	59	75	.440	28	819	894	4879	1356	228	35	62	377	447	.278	.335	.377	.712	107	39	-29	109	98	719	.713	252		
WAS	127	41	83	.331	41	632	892	4395	1105	151	57	25	466	456	.251	.329	.329	.658	92	-37	23	92	90	566	.664	232		
TOT	531					6203		37538	9922	1522	465	371	3612	3492	.264	.329	.359	.688								2087		

TEAM	CG	SHO	SV	IP	H	H/G	HR	BB	BB/G	SO	SO/G	ERA	/A	OAVG	OOBA	PR	/A	PF	CPI	FA	E	DP	FW	PW	BW	SBW	DIF
NY	118	6	3	1151.0	1064	8.3	38	542	4.1	542	4.2	3.47	117	.237	.317	71	77	101	97	.920	437	90	-.2	6.7	6.9		6.6
BOS	121	10	4	1166.0	1152	8.9	41	413	3.2	497	3.8	3.36	118	.249	.311	86	78	98	102	.926	413	105	1.0	6.8	2.1		9.1
CHI	123	6	2	1237.0	1313	9.6	71	408	3.0	434	3.2	3.73	106	.263	.319	40	30	98	104	.923	463	91	-1.5	2.6	4.9		-4.9
PHI	106	4	2	1153.3	1288	10.1	33	428	3.3	443	3.5	4.00	106	.273	.333	3	28	105	101	.915	466	92	-1.7	2.4	-2.8		1.5
PIT	125	5	1	1130.7	1296	10.3	42	374	3.0	345	2.7	4.51	80	.278	.332	-60	-112	90	92	.929	385	94	2.5	-9.7	4.7		-2.4
CLE	132	6	1	1191.7	1182	8.9	36	519	3.9	435	3.3	3.66	115	.250	.324	48	71	104	99	.936	365	108	3.5	6.1	-8.9		-6.2
IND	109	3	2	1174.3	1365	10.5	73	420	3.2	408	3.1	4.87	91	.281	.338	-110	-57	110	92	.926	420	102	.7	-4.9	-2.5		-1.2
WAS	113	1	0	1103.0	1261	10.3	37	527	4.3	388	3.2	4.68	82	.278	.353	-79	-101	96	97	.905	519	91	-4.3	-8.7	2.0		-9.9
TOT	947	41	15	9307.0		9.6			3.5		3.4	4.03		.264	.329					.923	3468	773					

Runs	Hits	Doubles	Triples	Home Runs	Total Bases
Tiernan-NY 147	Glasscock-Ind 205	Kelly-Bos 41	Wilmot-Was 19	Thompson-Phi 20	Ryan-Chi 287
Duffy-Chi 144	Brouthers-Bos 181	Glasscock-Ind 40	Fogarty-Phi 17	Denny-Ind 18	Glasscock-Ind 272
Ryan-Chi 140	Ryan-Chi 177	Thompson-Phi 36	Connor-NY 17	Ryan-Chi 17	Thompson-Phi 262
Gore-NY 132	Duffy-Chi 172	O'Rourke-NY 36	Tiernan-NY 14	Connor-NY 13	Connor-NY 262
Glasscock-Ind 128	VanHaltren-Chi 168	Richardson-Bos 33	Ryan-Chi 14	Duffy-Chi 12	Tiernan-NY 248

Runs Batted In	Runs Produced	Bases On Balls	Batting Average	On Base Percentage	Slugging Average
Connor-NY 130	Connor-NY 234	Tiernan-NY 96	Brouthers-Bos 373	Carroll-Pit 486	Connor-NY 528
Brouthers-Bos 118	Duffy-Chi 221	Connor-NY 93	Glasscock-Ind 352	Brouthers-Bos 462	Brouthers-Bos 507
Anson-Chi 117	Brouthers-Bos 216	Radford-Cle 91	Tiernan-NY 335	Tiernan-NY 447	Ryan-Chi 498
Denny-Ind 112	Tiernan-NY 210	Anson-Chi 86	Carroll-Pit 330	Connor-NY 426	Tiernan-NY 497
Thompson-Phi 111	Anson-Chi 210	Carroll-Pit 85	Ewing-NY 327	Gore-NY 416	Thompson-Phi 492

Production	Adjusted Production	Batter Runs	Adjusted Batter Runs	Clutch Hitting Index	Runs Created
Carroll-Pit 970	Carroll-Pit 195	Brouthers-Bos . . . 50.7	Brouthers-Bos 49.2	Quinn-Bos 144	Ryan-Chi 132
Brouthers-Bos 969	Brouthers-Bos 170	Tiernan-NY 48.3	Tiernan-NY 45.5	Dunlap-Pit 144	Glasscock-Ind 132
Connor-NY 955	Connor-NY 160	Connor-NY 47.3	Tiernan-NY 43.8	Richardson-NY 144	Tiernan-NY 129
Tiernan-NY 944	Tiernan-NY 158	Carroll-Pit 38.7	Connor-NY 42.9	Whitney-NY 144	Brouthers-Bos 127
Ryan-Chi 886	Wilmot-Was 151	Ryan-Chi 36.7	Ryan-Chi 37.8	Nash-Bos 138	Connor-NY 124

Total Average	Stolen Bases	Stolen Base Average	Stolen Base Runs	Fielding Runs	Total Player Rating
Carroll-Pit 1.263	Fogarty-Phi 99			Glasscock-Ind 30.6	Glasscock-Ind 4.9
Tiernan-NY 1.151	Kelly-Bos 68			Pfeffer-Chi 17.7	Ryan-Chi 4.0
Brouthers-Bos 1.145	Brown-Bos 63			Fogarty-Phi 17.3	Brouthers-Bos 3.4
Connor-NY 1.115	Ward-NY 62			Wilmot-Was 14.7	Carroll-Pit 3.4
Ryan-Chi 1.023	Glasscock-Ind 57			Ewing-NY 14.3	Wilmot-Was 3.2

Wins	Win Percentage	Games	Complete Games	Shutouts	Saves
Clarkson-Bos 49	Clarkson-Bos 721	Clarkson-Bos 73	Clarkson-Bos 68	Clarkson-Bos 8	Sowders-Bos-Pit 2
Keefe-NY 28	Welch-NY 692	Staley-Pit 49	Staley-Pit 46	Galvin-Pit 4	Welch-NY 2
Buffinton-Phi 28	Keefe-NY 683	Keefe-NY 47	Welch-NY 39		Bishop-Chi 2
Welch-NY 27	Radbourn-Bos 645	Buffinton-Phi 47	O'Brien-Cle 39		
Galvin-Pit 23	Buffinton-Phi 636	Boyle-Ind 46			

Innings Pitched	Fewest Hits/Game	Fewest BB/Game	Strikeouts	Strikeouts/Game	Wins Above Team
Clarkson-Bos 620	Keefe-NY 7.66	Galvin-Pit 2.06	Clarkson-Bos 284	Keefe-NY 5.17	Clarkson-Bos 12.1
Staley-Pit 420	Welch-NY 8.16	Boyle-Ind 2.26	Keefe-NY 209	Crane-NY 5.09	Buffinton-Phi 8.2
Buffinton-Phi 380	Clarkson-Bos 8.55	Radbourn-Bos 2.34	Staley-Pit 159	Rusie-Ind 4.36	Galvin-Pit 6.0
Boyle-Ind 379	Crane-NY 8.65	Dwyer-Chi 2.35	Buffinton-Phi 153	Healy-Was-Chi 4.35	Ferson-Was 5.4
Welch-NY 375	Hutchinson-Chi 8.66	Sanders-Phi 2.47	Getzein-Ind 139	Clarkson-Bos 4.12	O'Brien-Cle 5.0

Earned Run Average	Adjusted ERA	Opponents' Batting Avg.	Opponents' On Base Pct.	Starter Runs	Adjusted Starter Runs
Clarkson-Bos 2.73	Clarkson-Bos 145	Keefe-NY 223	Keefe-NY 299	Clarkson-Bos 89.5	Clarkson-Bos 85.1
Bakely-Cle 2.96	Bakely-Cle 142	Welch-NY 234	Clarkson-Bos 301	Welch-NY 41.9	Welch-NY 43.9
Welch-NY 3.02	Welch-NY 135	Clarkson-Bos 243	Radbourn-Bos 301	Bakely-Cle 36.1	Bakely-Cle 41.9
Buffinton-Phi 3.24	Buffinton-Phi 130	Crane-NY 245	Welch-NY 305	Buffinton-Phi 33.1	Buffinton-Phi 41.4
Keefe-NY 3.31	Keefe-NY 123	Hutchinson-Chi 245	Staley-Pit 306	Keefe-NY 28.9	Keefe-NY 30.9

Clutch Pitching Index	Relief Runs	Adjusted Relief Runs	Relief Ranking	Total Pitcher Index	Total Baseball Ranking
Casey-Phi 114				Clarkson-Bos 9.0	Clarkson-Bos 9.0
Clarkson-Bos 113				Bakely-Cle 3.9	Glasscock-Ind 4.9
Sanders-Phi 112				Buffinton-Phi 3.8	Ryan-Chi 4.0
Bakely-Cle 111				Welch-NY 3.5	Bakely-Cle 3.9
Crane-NY 109				Sanders-Phi 2.9	Buffinton-Phi 3.8

TEAM	G	W	L	PCT	GB	R	OR	AB	H	2B	3B	HR	BB	SO	AVG	OBP	SLG	PRO	/A	BR	/A	PF	CHI	RC	TA	SB	CS	SBA	SBR
BRO	140	93	44	.679		995	706	4815	1266	188	79	48	550	401	.263	.344	.365	.709	109	62	96	96	108	757	.773	389			
STL	141	90	45	.667	2	957	680	4939	1312	211	64	58	493	477	.266	.339	.370	.709	108	55	-50	112	104	751	.747	336			
PHI	138	75	58	.564	16	880	787	4868	1339	239	65	43	534	496	.275	.354	.377	.731	115	102	122	98	91	758	.761	252			
CIN	141	76	63	.547	18	897	769	4844	1307	197	96	52	452	511	.270	.340	.382	.722	112	74	32	105	97	806	.799	462			
BAL	139	70	65	.519	22	791	795	4756	1209	155	68	20	418	536	.254	.325	.328	.653	92	-38	-33	100	100	624	.668	311			
COL	140	60	78	.435	33.5	779	924	4816	1247	171	95	36	507	609	.259	.335	.356	.691	103	26	103	91	89	693	.720	304			
KC	139	55	82	.401	38	852	1031	4947	1256	162	77	17	440	626	.254	.322	.328	.650	91	-47	-96	106	105	691	.702	472			
LOU	140	27	111	.196	66.5	632	1091	4955	1249	170	75	22	320	521	.252	.303	.330	.633	86	-90	-54	96	84	571	.593	203			
TOT	559					6783		38940	10185	1493	619	296	3704	4177	.262	.326	.355	.680								2729			

TEAM	CG	SHO	SV	IP	H	H/G	HR	BB	BB/G	SO	SO/G	ERA	/A	OAVG	OOBA	PR	/A	PF	CPI	FA	E	DP	FW	PW	BW	SBW	DIF
BRO	120	10	1	1212.7	1205	8.9	33	400	3.0	471	3.5	3.61	98	.251	.308	31	-11	92	91	.928	421	92	4.3	-.9	8.1		13.0
STL	121	7	3	1237.7	1166	8.5	39	413	3.0	617	4.5	3.00	139	.241	.301	116	161	109	102	.925	438	100	3.4	13.6	-4.2		9.7
PHI	130	9	1	1199.3	1200	9.0	35	509	3.8	479	3.6	3.53	105	.252	.324	42	23	96	102	.920	465	120	1.9	1.9	10.3		-5.7
CIN	114	3	8	1243.0	1270	9.2	35	475	3.4	562	4.1	3.50	113	.256	.321	47	64	103	102	.926	440	121	3.3	5.4	2.7		-4.9
BAL	128	10	1	1192.0	1168	8.8	27	424	3.2	540	4.1	3.56	107	.248	.310	37	34	99	91	.907	536	104	-2.1	2.9	-2.8		4.5
COL	114	9	4	1199.0	1274	9.6	33	551	4.1	610	4.6	4.41	81	.264	.339	-75	-114	92	90	.915	497	92	.1	-9.6	8.7		-8.2
KC	128	0	2	1204.3	1373	10.3	51	457	3.4	447	3.3	4.36	96	.278	.339	-68	-23	109	98	.899	611	109	-6.2	-1.9	-8.1		2.8
LOU	127	2	1	1226.3	1529	11.2	43	475	3.5	451	3.3	4.81	82	.296	.355	-131	-120	102	99	.906	584	117	-4.7	-10.2	-4.6		-22.5
TOT	982	50	21	9714.3		9.4			3.4		3.9	3.85		.262	.326					.916	3992	855					

Runs	Hits	Doubles	Triples	Home Runs	Total Bases
Stovey-Phi ...152	Tucker-Bal ...196	Welch-Phi ...39	Marr-Col ...15	Stovey-Phi ...19	Stovey-Phi ...292
Griffin-Bal ...152	Orr-Col ...183	Stovey-Phi ...38	Griffin-Bal ...14	Holliday-Cin ...19	Holliday-Cin ...280
O'Brien-Bro ...146	Holliday-Cin ...181	Lyons-Phi ...36	Beard-Cin ...14	Duffee-StL ...15	Tucker-Bal ...255
Hamilton-KC ...144	O'Neill-StL ...179	O'Neill-StL ...33		Milligan-StL ...12	O'Neill-StL ...255
Collins-Bro ...139	Shindle-Bal ...178	Long-KC ...32			Orr-Col ...250

Runs Batted In	Runs Produced	Bases On Balls	Batting Average	On Base Percentage	Slugging Average
Stovey-Phi ...119	Stovey-Phi ...252	Robinson-StL ...118	Tucker-Bal ...372	Tucker-Bal ...450	Stovey-Phi ...525
Foutz-Bro ...113	O'Neill-StL ...224	McTamany-Col ...116	O'Neill-StL ...335	Larkin-Phi ...428	Holliday-Cin ...497
O'Neill-StL ...110	Foutz-Bro ...224	Griffin-Bal ...91	Lyons-Phi ...329	Lyons-Phi ...426	Tucker-Bal ...484
Bierbauer-Phi ...105	O'Brien-Bro ...221	Marr-Col ...87	Orr-Col ...327	O'Neill-StL ...419	O'Neill-StL ...478
Holliday-Cin ...104	Hamilton-KC ...218	Hamilton-KC ...87	Holliday-Cin ...321	Hamilton-KC ...413	Lyons-Phi ...469

Production	Adjusted Production	Batter Runs	Adjusted Batter Runs	Clutch Hitting Index	Runs Created
Tucker-Bal ...934	Tucker-Bal ...169	Tucker-Bal ...49.8	Tucker-Bal ...50.3	Hornung-Bal ...149	Tucker-Bal ...147
Stovey-Phi ...918	Stovey-Phi ...167	Stovey-Phi ...44.5	Stovey-Phi ...46.9	Robinson-StL ...144	Stovey-Phi ...143
O'Neill-StL ...897	Lyons-Phi ...161	O'Neill-StL ...41.6	Lyons-Phi ...43.3	Mack-Bal ...141	Hamilton-KC ...136
Lyons-Phi ...895	Marr-Col ...150	Lyons-Phi ...41.0	Marr-Col ...38.9	Manning-KC ...136	O'Brien-Bro ...129
Holliday-Cin ...869	Larkin-Phi ...150	Larkin-Phi ...36.0	Larkin-Phi ...38.3	Foutz-Bro ...135	Holliday-Cin ...124

Total Average	Stolen Bases	Stolen Base Average	Stolen Base Runs	Fielding Runs	Total Player Rating
Tucker-Bal ...1.187	Hamilton-KC ...111			Long-KC ...45.1	Stovey-Phi ...4.9
Hamilton-KC ...1.134	O'Brien-Bro ...91			McPhee-Cin ...38.3	Long-KC ...4.7
Stovey-Phi ...1.125	Long-KC ...89			Bierbauer-Phi ...36.2	Bierbauer-Phi ...4.3
O'Brien-Bro ...1.020	Nicol-Cin ...80			Beard-Cin ...34.4	Lyons-Phi ...4.3
O'Neill-StL ...1.014	Latham-StL ...69			Easterday-Col ...20.2	Marr-Col ...3.9

Wins	Win Percentage	Games	Complete Games	Shutouts	Saves
Caruthers-Bro ...40	Caruthers-Bro ...784	Baldwin-Col ...63	Kilroy-Bal ...55	Caruthers-Bro ...7	Mullane-Cin ...5
King-StL ...35	King-StL ...686	Kilroy-Bal ...59	Baldwin-Col ...54	Baldwin-Col ...6	
Duryea-Cin ...32	Chamberlin-StL ...681	King-StL ...56	Weyhing-Phi ...50	Kilroy-Bal ...5	
Chamberlin-StL ...32	Lovett-Bro ...630	Caruthers-Bro ...56	King-StL ...47	Foreman-Bal ...5	
Weyhing-Phi ...30	Duryea-Cin ...627	Weyhing-Phi ...54	Caruthers-Bro ...46	Weyhing-Phi ...4	

Innings Pitched	Fewest Hits/Game	Fewest BB/Game	Strikeouts	Strikeouts/Game	Wins Above Team
Baldwin-Col ...514	Stivetts-StL ...7.17	Caruthers-Bro ...2.10	Baldwin-Col ...368	Stivetts-StL ...6.70	Caruthers-Bro ...11.2
Kilroy-Bal ...481	Weyhing-Phi ...7.66	Conway-KC ...2.42	Kilroy-Bal ...217	Baldwin-Col ...6.44	Duryea-Cin ...6.5
King-StL ...458	Terry-Bro ...7.87	King-StL ...2.46	Weyhing-Phi ...213	Terry-Bro ...5.13	Conway-KC ...4.1
Weyhing-Phi ...449	Foreman-Bal ...7.91	Lovett-Bro ...2.55	Chamberlin-StL ...202	Sowders-KC ...5.06	Mays-Col ...2.5
Caruthers-Bro ...445	Chamberlin-StL ...8.02	Swartzel-KC ...2.57	King-StL ...188	Gastright-Col ...4.64	King-StL ...2.3

Earned Run Average	Adjusted ERA	Opponents' Batting Avg.	Opponents' On Base Pct.	Starter Runs	Adjusted Starter Runs
Stivetts-StL ...2.25	Stivetts-StL ...186	Stivetts-StL ...212	Stivetts-StL ...280	Duryea-Cin ...57.4	Duryea-Cin ...63.1
Duryea-Cin ...2.56	Duryea-Cin ...155	Weyhing-Phi ...223	Foreman-Bal ...290	Kilroy-Bal ...52.6	Chamberlin-StL ...56.7
Kilroy-Bal ...2.86	Chamberlin-StL ...141	Terry-Bro ...228	Caruthers-Bro ...294	Weyhing-Phi ...45.0	King-StL ...52.4
Weyhing-Phi ...2.95	Kilroy-Bal ...134	Foreman-Bal ...229	Duryea-Cin ...296	Chamberlin-StL ...41.4	Kilroy-Bal ...51.4
Chamberlin-StL ...2.96	Mullane-Cin ...133	Chamberlin-StL ...231	Terry-Bro ...299	King-StL ...35.8	Stivetts-StL ...41.1

Clutch Pitching Index	Relief Runs	Adjusted Relief Runs	Relief Ranking	Total Pitcher Index	Total Baseball Ranking
Mullane-Cin ...114				Kilroy-Bal ...6.5	Kilroy-Bal ...6.5
Duryea-Cin ...112				Duryea-Cin ...6.3	Duryea-Cin ...6.3
Hughes-Bro ...108				King-StL ...5.1	King-StL ...5.1
Kilroy-Bal ...107				Chamberlin-StL ...4.8	Stovey-Phi ...4.9
Smith-Cin ...107				Mullane-Cin ...3.8	Chamberlin-StL ...4.8

TEAM	G	W	L	PCT	GB	R	OR	AB	H	2B	3B	HR	BB	SO	AVG	OBP	SLG	PRO	/A	BR	/A	PF	CHI	RC	TA	SB	CS	SBA	SBR
BRO	129	86	43	.667		884	620	4419	1166	184	75	43	517	361	.264	.346	.369	.715	115	90	87	100	109	702	.780	349			
CHI	139	84	53	.613	6	847	692	4891	1271	147	59	67	516	514	.260	.336	.355	.691	108	54	-17	109	101	712	.726	329			
PHI	133	78	54	.591	9.5	823	707	4707	1267	220	78	23	522	403	.269	.350	.364	.714	115	96	35	108	96	735	.765	335			
CIN	134	77	55	.583	10.5	753	633	4644	1204	150	120	27	433	377	.259	.329	.361	.690	108	42	-15	108	96	670	.718	312			
BOS	134	76	57	.571	12	763	593	4722	1220	175	62	31	530	515	.258	.342	.341	.683	106	46	-35	111	94	665	.713	285			
NY	135	63	68	.481	24	713	698	4832	1250	208	89	25	350	478	.259	.315	.354	.669	101	1	39	95	94	647	.670	289			
CLE	136	44	88	.333	43.5	630	832	4633	1073	132	59	21	497	474	.232	.312	.299	.611	84	-79	-32	94	94	491	.583	152			
PIT	138	23	113	.169	66.5	597	1235	4739	1088	160	43	20	408	458	.230	.300	.294	.594	79	-116	-23	88	94	492	.569	208			
TOT	539					6010		37587	9539	1376	585	257	3773	3580	.254	.322	.342	.664								2259			

TEAM	CG	SHO	SV	IP	H	H/G	HR	BB	BB/G	SO	SO/G	ERA	/A	OAVG	OOBA	PR	/A	PF	CPI	FA	E	DP	FW	PW	BW	SBW	DIF
BRO	115	6	2	1145.0	1102	8.7	27	401	3.2	403	3.2	3.07	112	.245	.307	63	46	96	100	.938	320	92	5.4	4.1	7.7		4.3
CHI	126	6	3	1237.3	1103	8.0	41	481	3.5	504	3.7	3.24	117	.231	.302	43	76	107	89	.939	344	89	3.9	6.8	-1.5		6.3
PHI	122	8	2	1194.7	1210	9.1	22	486	3.7	507	3.8	3.32	115	.255	.324	31	64	107	103	.929	398	122	.6	5.7	3.1		2.6
CIN	124	9	1	1190.7	1097	8.3	42	407	3.1	488	3.7	2.79	136	.237	.299	102	131	106	105	.933	382	106	1.6	11.6	-1.3		-.9
BOS	132	13	1	1189.0	1131	8.6	27	354	2.7	506	3.8	2.93	131	.243	.297	83	120	108	98	.933	359	77	3.0	10.7	-3.1		-1.1
NY	115	6	1	1177.0	1029	7.9	14	607	4.6	612	4.7	3.06	110	.228	.319	65	39	94	98	.919	449	104	-2.5	3.5	3.5		-6.9
CLE	129	2	0	1184.3	1322	10.0	32	462	3.5	306	2.3	4.14	84	.274	.337	-76	-89	97	96	.930	405	108	.2	-7.9	-2.8		-11.4
PIT	119	3	0	1176.3	1520	11.6	52	573	4.4	381	2.9	5.97	57	.304	.375	-314	-339	95	88	.897	607	94	-12.2	-30.1	-2.0		-.6
TOT	982	53	10	9494.3		9.0			3.6		3.5	3.56		.254	.322					.927	3264	792					

Runs
Collins-Bro 148
Carroll-Chi 134
Hamilton-Phi 133
Tiernan-NY 132
McPhee-Cin 125

Hits
Thompson-Phi 172
Glasscock-NY 172
Tiernan-NY 168
Reilly-Cin 166
Carroll-Chi 166

Doubles
Thompson-Phi 41
Glasscock-NY 32
Collins-Bro 32
Myers-Phi 29
O'Brien-Bro 28

Triples
Reilly-Cin 26
McPhee-Cin 22
Tiernan-NY 21
Beard-Cin 15

Home Runs
Wilmot-Chi 13
Tiernan-NY 13
Burns-Bro 13
Long-Bos 8

Total Bases
Tiernan-NY 274
Reilly-Cin 261
Thompson-Phi 243
Wilmot-Chi 237
Glasscock-NY 225

Runs Batted In
Burns-Bro 128
Anson-Chi 107
Thompson-Phi 102
Wilmot-Chi 99
Foutz-Bro 98

Runs Produced
Burns-Bro 217
Thompson-Phi 214
Collins-Bro 214
Wilmot-Chi 200
Foutz-Bro 199

Bases On Balls
Anson-Chi 113
McKean-Cle 87
Allen-Phi 87
Collins-Bro 85
Hamilton-Phi 83

Batting Average
Glasscock-NY 336
Hamilton-Phi 325
Clements-Phi 315
Thompson-Phi 313
Knight-Cin 312

On Base Percentage
Anson-Chi 443
Hamilton-Phi 430
Pinkney-Bro 411
McKean-Cle 401
Glasscock-NY 395

Slugging Average
Tiernan-NY 495
Clements-Phi 472
Reilly-Cin 472
Burns-Bro 464
Burkett-NY 461

Production
Tiernan-NY 880
Clements-Phi 864
Anson-Chi 844
Pinkney-Bro 842
Glasscock-NY 834

Adjusted Production
Tiernan-NY 167
Glasscock-NY 153
Burkett-NY 151
McKean-Cle 150
Pinkney-Bro 148

Batter Runs
Tiernan-NY 39.8
Anson-Chi 39.3
Hamilton-Phi 33.3
Pinkney-Bro 32.5
McKean-Cle 30.8

Adjusted Batter Runs
Tiernan-NY 44.4
McKean-Cle 36.3
Glasscock-NY 33.3
Pinkney-Bro 32.1
Anson-Chi 31.2

Clutch Hitting Index
Hines-Pit-Bos 146
Burns-Bro 144
Mayer-Phi 142
Anson-Chi 139
Hornung-NY 139

Runs Created
Hamilton-Phi 132
Tiernan-NY 130
Wilmot-Chi 113
Glasscock-NY 113
Collins-Bro 111

Total Average
Hamilton-Phi 1.170
Tiernan-NY 1.047
Pinkney-Bro 1.015
Anson-Chi 1.009
Collins-Bro 1.005

Stolen Bases
Hamilton-Phi 102
Collins-Bro 85
Sunday-Pit-Phi 84
Wilmot-Chi 76
Tiernan-NY 56

Stolen Base Average

Stolen Base Runs

Fielding Runs
Allen-Phi 32.9
McPhee-Cin 25.6
Zimmer-Cle 18.7
Smalley-Cle 16.5
Sunday-Pit-Phi 15.9

Total Player Rating
Glasscock-NY 4.0
McPhee-Cin 3.4
Miller-Pit 2.7
Allen-Phi 2.5
Clements-Phi 2.4

Wins
Hutchinson-Chi 42
Gleason-Phi 38
Lovett-Bro 30
Rusie-NY 29
Rhines-Cin 28

Win Percentage
Lovett-Bro 732
Gleason-Phi 691
Luby-Chi 690
Caruthers-Bro 676
Hutchinson-Chi 627

Games
Hutchinson-Chi 71
Rusie-NY 67
Gleason-Phi 60
Beatin-Cle 54
Nichols-Bos 48

Complete Games
Hutchinson-Chi 65
Rusie-NY 56
Gleason-Phi 54
Beatin-Cle 53
Nichols-Bos 47

Shutouts
Nichols-Bos 7
Rhines-Cin 6
Gleason-Phi 6
Hutchinson-Chi 5

Saves
Hutchinson-Chi 2
Gleason-Phi 2
Foutz-Bro 2

Innings Pitched
Hutchinson-Chi 603
Rusie-NY 549
Gleason-Phi 506
Beatin-Cle 474
Nichols-Bos 427

Fewest Hits/Game
Rusie-NY 7.15
Mullane-Cin 7.54
Hutchinson-Chi 7.54
Rhines-Cin 7.56
Luby-Chi 7.59

Fewest BB/Game
Young-Cle 1.82
Duryea-Cin 1.97
Getzein-Bos 2.11
Nichols-Bos 2.36
Rhines-Cin 2.54

Strikeouts
Rusie-NY 341
Hutchinson-Chi 289
Nichols-Bos 222
Gleason-Phi 222
Terry-Bro 185

Strikeouts/Game
Rusie-NY 5.59
Nichols-Bos 4.68
Terry-Bro 4.50
Hutchinson-Chi 4.31
Sharrott-NY 4.11

Wins Above Team
Gleason-Phi 9.8
Lovett-Bro 5.4
Beatin-Cle 5.0
Luby-Chi 3.5
Young-Cle 3.2

Earned Run Average
Rhines-Cin 1.95
Nichols-Bos 2.21
Mullane-Cin 2.24
Rusie-NY 2.56
Gleason-Phi 2.63

Adjusted ERA
Rhines-Cin 194
Nichols-Bos 174
Mullane-Cin 169
Gleason-Phi 145
Hutchinson-Chi 141

Opponents' Batting Avg.
Rusie-NY 212
Mullane-Cin 221
Hutchinson-Chi 221
Rhines-Cin 221
Luby-Chi 222

Opponents' On Base Pct.
Rhines-Cin 275
Nichols-Bos 278
Hutchinson-Chi 283
Young-Cle 286
Luby-Chi 288

Starter Runs
Rhines-Cin 71.7
Nichols-Bos 64.0
Rusie-NY 61.3
Hutchinson-Chi 57.7
Gleason-Phi 52.3

Adjusted Starter Runs
Rhines-Cin 81.4
Nichols-Bos 77.2
Hutchinson-Chi 73.7
Gleason-Phi 66.1
Rusie-NY 49.1

Clutch Pitching Index
Mullane-Cin 126
Vickery-Phi 113
Rhines-Cin 113
Gleason-Phi 109
Nichols-Bos 106

Relief Runs

Adjusted Relief Runs

Relief Ranking

Total Pitcher Index
Nichols-Bos 7.7
Rhines-Cin 7.5
Hutchinson-Chi 7.1
Rusie-NY 6.1
Gleason-Phi 5.7

Total Baseball Ranking
Nichols-Bos 7.7
Rhines-Cin 7.5
Hutchinson-Chi 7.1
Rusie-NY 6.1
Gleason-Phi 5.7

TEAM	G	W	L	PCT	GB	R	OR	AB	H	2B	3B	HR	BB	SO	AVG	OBP	SLG	PRO	/A	BR	/A	PF	CHI	RC	TA	SB	CS	SBASBR
LOU	136	88	44	.667		819	588	4687	1310	156	65	15	410	460	.279	.344	.350	.694	113	71	17	107	99	698	.722	341		
COL	140	79	55	.590	10	831	617	4741	1225	159	78	15	545	557	.258	.340	.334	.674	106	48	55	99	100	676	.719	353		
STL	139	78	58	.574	12	870	736	4800	1308	178	72	49	474	490	.273	.349	.370	.719	120	120	-5	116	95	746	.759	307		
TOL	134	68	64	.515	20	739	689	4575	1152	152	108	24	486	558	.252	.331	.348	.679	108	45	24	103	92	683	.746	421		
ROC	133	63	63	.500	22	709	711	4553	1088	131	64	31	446	538	.239	.314	.316	.630	93	-33	22	93	100	564	.649	310		
SYR	128	55	72	.433	30.5	698	831	4469	1158	151	59	14	457	482	.259	.332	.329	.661	102	18	87	90	93	600	.680	292		
PHI	136	54	78	.409	34	702	945	4490	1057	181	51	24	475	540	.235	.320	.314	.634	94	-22	-1	97	97	563	.662	305		
BB	134	41	92	.308	47.5	674	925	4688	1047	150	62	16	453	608	.223	.299	.292	.591	81	-100	-100	100	101	507	.594	283		
TOT	540					6042		37003	9345	1258	559	188	3746	4233	.253	.321	.332	.653								2612		

TEAM	CG	SHO	SV	IP	H	H/G	HR	BB	BB/G	SO	SO/G	ERA	/A	OAVG	OOBA	PR	/A	PF	CPI	FA	E	DP	FW	PW	BW	SBW	DIF
LOU	114	13	7	1206.0	1120	8.4	18	293	2.2	587	4.4	2.57	156	.238	.283	173	193	104	113	.934	380	79	2.7	17.0	1.5		.8
COL	120	14	3	1214.7	976	7.2	20	471	3.5	624	4.6	2.99	124	.213	.287	118	97	96	90	.931	401	101	1.6	8.5	4.8		-3.0
STL	118	4	1	1195.3	1127	8.5	38	447	3.4	733	5.5	3.67	120	.241	.308	25	99	115	94	.916	478	93	-2.3	8.7	-.4		4.1
TOL	122	4	2	1159.3	1122	8.7	23	429	3.3	533	4.1	3.56	111	.246	.311	39	49	102	98	.925	419	75	.7	4.3	2.1		-5.1
ROC	122	5	2	1161.7	1115	8.6	19	530	4.1	477	3.7	3.58	99	.245	.323	37	-2	92	102	.926	416	95	.8	-.2	1.9		-2.6
SYR	115	5	0	1089.7	1158	9.6	28	518	4.3	454	3.7	4.98	71	.264	.342	-134	-172	92	86	.925	391	90	2.1	-15.1	7.7		-3.2
PHI	119	3	2	1132.0	1405	11.2	17	514	4.1	461	3.7	5.23	75	.295	.364	-171	-164	101	96	.918	452	93	-1.0	-14.4	-.0		3.5
BB	132	1	0	1194.3	1318	9.9	24	544	4.1	364	2.7	4.52	88	.271	.345	-86	-74	103	97	.912	522	113	-4.6	-6.5	-8.8		-5.6
TOT	962	49	17	9353.0		9.0			3.6		4.1	3.87		.253	.321					.923	3459	739					

Runs
McTamany-Col 140
McCarthy-StL 137
Fuller-StL 118
Sneed-Tol-Col 117
Welch-Phi-BB 116

Hits
Wolf-Lou 197
McCarthy-StL 192
Johnson-Col 186
Childs-Syr 170
Taylor-Lou 169

Doubles
Childs-Syr 33
Wolf-Lou 29
Lyons-Phi 29

Triples
Werden-Tol 20
Johnson-Col 18
Alvord-Tol 16
Sneed-Tol-Col 15

Home Runs
Campau-StL 10
Cartwright-StL 8
Stivetts-StL 7
Lyons-Phi 7

Total Bases
Wolf-Lou 260
McCarthy-StL 256
Johnson-Col 248
Childs-Syr 237
Werden-Tol 227

Runs Batted In

Runs Produced
McTamany-Col 139
McCarthy-StL 131
Fuller-StL 117
Sneed-Tol-Col 115
Taylor-Lou 115

Bases On Balls
McTamany-Col 112
Crooks-Col 96
Swartwood-Tol 80
Werden-Tol 78
Scheffler-Roc 78

Batting Average
Wolf-Lou 363
McCarthy-StL 350
Johnson-Col 346
Childs-Syr 345
Swartwood-Tol 327

On Base Percentage
Swartwood-Tol 442
Childs-Syr 434
McCarthy-StL 430
Wright-Syr 427
Wolf-Lou 419

Slugging Average
Childs-Syr 481
Wolf-Lou 479
McCarthy-StL 467
Johnson-Col 461
Werden-Tol 456

Production
Childs-Syr 915
Wolf-Lou 898
McCarthy-StL 898
Swartwood-Tol 885
Johnson-Col 870

Adjusted Production
Childs-Syr 191
Johnson-Col 161
Swartwood-Tol 160
Wolf-Lou 157
Griffin-Roc 156

Batter Runs
McCarthy-StL 47.6
Childs-Syr 46.5
Wolf-Lou 44.6
Lyons-Phi 42.0
Swartwood-Tol 41.7

Adjusted Batter Runs
Childs-Syr 54.6
Lyons-Phi 43.7
Johnson-Col 40.0
Swartwood-Tol 39.5
Wolf-Lou 38.4

Clutch Hitting Index

Runs Created
McCarthy-StL 150
Wolf-Lou 132
Childs-Syr 130
Johnson-Col 122
Werden-Tol 118

Total Average
McCarthy-StL 1.169
Childs-Syr 1.149
Swartwood-Tol 1.135
Werden-Tol 1.071
Wolf-Lou 1.038

Stolen Bases
McCarthy-StL 83
Scheffler-Roc 77
VanDyke-Tol 73
Welch-Phi-BB 72

Stolen Base Average

Stolen Base Runs

Fielding Runs
Gerhardt-BB -StL . . . 33.9
Reilly-Col 24.8
Ely-Syr 19.1
Tomney-Lou 17.8
Robinson-Phi-BB . . . 14.8

Total Player Rating
Childs-Syr 6.1
Lyons-Phi 4.5
Swartwood-Tol 3.3
McGuire-Roc 2.9
McCarthy-StL 2.7

Wins
McMahon-Phi-BB 36
Stratton-Lou 34
Gastright-Col 30
Barr-Roc 28
Stivetts-StL 27

Win Percentage
Stratton-Lou 708
Chamberlin-StL-Col . .682
Gastright-Col 682
Ehret-Lou 641
McMahon-Phi-BB . . .632

Games
McMahon-Phi-BB 60
Barr-Roc 57
Stivetts-StL 54
Stratton-Lou 50
Gastright-Col 48

Complete Games
McMahon-Phi-BB 55
Barr-Roc 52
Stratton-Lou 44
Healy-Tol 44

Shutouts
Chamberlin-StL-Col . . .6
Stratton-Lou 4
Gastright-Col 4
Ehret-Lou 4

Saves
Goodall-Lou 4
Knauss-Col 2
Ehret-Lou 2

Innings Pitched
McMahon-Phi-BB . . .509
Barr-Roc 493
Stratton-Lou 431
Stivetts-StL 419
Gastright-Col 401

Fewest Hits/Game
Knauss-Col 6.72
Gastright-Col 7.00
Easton-Col 7.49
Chamberlin-StL-Col . .7.50
Healy-Tol 7.54

Fewest BB/Game
Stratton-Lou 1.27
Ehret-Lou 1.98
Ramsey-StL 2.63
Smith-Tol 2.83
McMahon-Phi-BB . . .2.94

Strikeouts
McMahon-Phi-BB . . .291
Stivetts-StL 289
Ramsey-StL 257
Healy-Tol 225
Barr-Roc 209

Strikeouts/Game
Ramsey-StL 6.63
Stivetts-StL 6.21
Meakim-Lou 5.77
Chamberlin-StL-Col . .5.49
Healy-Tol 5.21

Wins Above Team
McMahon-Phi-BB . . 13.6
Gastright-Col 6.6
Stratton-Lou 4.4
Smith-Tol 3.3
Barr-Roc 3.2

Earned Run Average
Stratton-Lou 2.36
Ehret-Lou 2.53
Knauss-Col 2.80
Chamberlin-StL-Col . .2.83
Healy-Tol 2.89

Adjusted ERA
Stratton-Lou 170
Ehret-Lou 159
Meakim-Lou 138
Healy-Tol 136
Chamberlin-StL-Col . .136

Opponents' Batting Avg.
Knauss-Col 202
Gastright-Col 208
Easton-Col 220
Chamberlin-StL-Col . .220
Healy-Tol 221

Opponents' On Base Pct.
Stratton-Lou 265
Gastright-Col 274
Knauss-Col 277
Healy-Tol 283
Ehret-Lou 288

Starter Runs
Stratton-Lou 72.2
Ehret-Lou 53.2
Healy-Tol 42.1
Gastright-Col 41.3
Barr-Roc 33.8

Adjusted Starter Runs
Stratton-Lou 79.4
Ehret-Lou 59.2
Healy-Tol 45.6
Stivetts-StL 42.1
Gastright-Col 34.2

Clutch Pitching Index
Ehret-Lou 121
Titcomb-Roc 114
Stratton-Lou 107
Daily-BB -Lou 107
Chamberlin-StL-Col . .107

Relief Runs

Adjusted Relief Runs

Relief Ranking

Total Pitcher Index
Stratton-Lou 10.1
Stivetts-StL 6.5
Ehret-Lou 5.2
Healy-Tol 4.9
McMahon-Phi-BB . . . 3.6

Total Baseball Ranking
Stratton-Lou 10.1
Stivetts-StL 6.5
Childs-Syr 6.1
Ehret-Lou 5.2
Healy-Tol 4.9

TEAM	G	W	L	PCT	GB	R	OR	AB	H	2B	3B	HR	BB	SO	AVG	OBP	SLG	PRO	/A	BR	/A	PF	CHI	RC	TA	SB	CS	SBA	SBR
BOS	130	81	48	.628		992	767	4626	1306	223	77	51	652	435	.282	.376	.397	.773	114	103	42	107	98	867	.886	412			
BRO	133	76	56	.576	6.5	964	893	4887	1354	186	93	34	502	369	.277	.349	.374	.723	100	5	-50	106	104	752	.748	272			
NY	132	74	57	.565	8	1018	875	4913	1393	204	97	64	486	364	.284	.352	.404	.756	109	54	-26	109	104	798	.776	231			
CHI	138	75	62	.547	10	886	770	4968	1311	200	96	30	431	410	.264	.335	.361	.696	93	-48	-86	104	100	711	.712	276			
PHI	132	68	63	.519	14	941	855	4855	1348	187	113	49	431	321	.278	.343	.393	.736	103	16	-4	102	102	742	.739	203			
PIT	128	60	68	.469	20.5	835	892	4577	1192	168	113	36	569	375	.260	.349	.370	.719	99	1	72	92	94	695	.758	249			
CLE	131	55	75	.423	26.5	849	1027	4804	1373	213	94	27	509	345	.286	.360	.386	.746	106	48	122	92	88	751	.756	180			
BUF	134	36	96	.273	46.5	793	1199	4795	1249	180	64	20	541	367	.260	.347	.337	.684	90	-51	25	92	91	632	.681	160			
TOT	529					7278		38425	10526	1561	747	311	4182	2986	.274	.345	.378	.723								1983			

TEAM	CG	SHO	SV	IP	H	H/G	HR	BB	BB/G	SO	SO/G	ERA	/A	OAVG	OOBA	PR	/A	PF	CPI	FA	E	DP	FW	PW	BW	SBW	DIF
BOS	105	6	2	1137.3	1291	10.2	49	467	3.7	345	2.7	3.80	116	.273	.339	54	75	104	107	.918	460	109	2.2	6.0	3.4		5.0
BRO	111	4	7	1184.0	1334	10.1	26	570	4.3	377	2.9	3.95	113	.272	.348	37	67	105	103	.909	531	114	-2.0	5.3	-4.0		10.6
NY	111	3	6	1172.3	1219	9.4	37	569	4.4	449	3.4	4.17	109	.256	.336	8	48	107	89	.921	450	94	2.8	3.8	-2.1		4.0
CHI	124	5	2	1219.3	1238	9.1	27	503	3.7	460	3.4	3.39	128	.252	.321	114	129	103	98	.918	492	107	.3	10.3	-6.9		2.8
PHI	118	4	2	1154.3	1292	10.1	33	495	3.9	361	2.8	4.06	105	.271	.339	21	27	101	97	.910	510	118	-.7	2.2	-.3		1.4
PIT	121	7	0	1116.7	1267	10.2	36	334	2.7	318	2.6	4.22	93	.273	.322	2	-38	92	87	.907	512	80	-.9	-3.0	5.7		-5.9
CLE	115	1	1	1143.7	1386	10.9	45	571	4.5	325	2.6	4.23	94	.287	.362	0	-32	94	110	.907	533	103	-2.1	-2.6	9.7		-15.1
BUF	125	2	0	1141.0	1499	11.8	67	673	5.3	351	2.8	6.12	67	.303	.387	-239	-256	97	91	.914	491	116	.4	-20.4	2.0		-11.9
TOT	930	32	20	9268.7		10.2			4.1		2.9	4.23		.274	.345					.913	3979	841					

Runs
Duffy-Chi 161
Brown-Bos 146
Stovey-Bos 142
Ward-Bro 134
Connor-NY 133

Hits
Duffy-Chi 191
Ward-Bro 189
Shindle-Phi 188
Browning-Cle 184
Richardson-Bos 181

Doubles
Browning-Cle 40
Beckley-Pit 38
O'Rourke-NY 37
Duffy-Chi 36
Brouthers-Bos 36

Triples
Visner-Pit 22
Beckley-Pit 22
Shindle-Phi 21
Fields-Pit 20
Joyce-Bro 18

Home Runs
Connor-NY 13
Stovey-Bos 11
Richardson-Bos 11

Total Bases
Shindle-Phi 281
Duffy-Chi 280
Beckley-Pit 279
Richardson-Bos 268
Connor-NY 262

Runs Batted In
Richardson-Bos 143
Orr-Bro 124
Beckley-Pit 120
O'Rourke-NY 115
Larkin-Cle 112

Runs Produced
Richardson-Bos 258
Duffy-Chi 236
Connor-NY 223
Bierbauer-Bro 220
Beckley-Pit 219

Bases On Balls
Joyce-Bro 123
Robinson-Pit 101
Brouthers-Bos 99
Hoy-Buf 94

Batting Average
Browning-Cle 373
Orr-Bro 373
O'Rourke-NY 360
Connor-NY 349
Ryan-Chi 340

On Base Percentage
Brouthers-Bos 466
Browning-Cle 459
Connor-NY 450
Robinson-Pit 434
Gore-NY 432

Slugging Average
Connor-NY 541
Beckley-Pit 541
Orr-Bro 537
Browning-Cle 517
O'Rourke-NY 515

Production
Connor-NY 992
Browning-Cle 976
Orr-Bro 952
Gore-NY 931
O'Rourke-NY 925

Adjusted Production
Browning-Cle 177
Beckley-Pit 160
Larkin-Cle 156
Connor-NY 153
Orr-Bro 147

Batter Runs
Connor-NY 48.2
Browning-Cle 46.7
Brouthers-Bos 39.7
Orr-Bro 34.4
Larkin-Cle 32.7

Adjusted Batter Runs
Browning-Cle 54.6
Larkin-Cle 40.7
Connor-NY 39.7
Beckley-Pit 38.7
Brouthers-Bos 33.1

Clutch Hitting Index
Nash-Bos 130
McGeachey-Bro 129
Rowe-Buf 127
Richardson-Bos 125
Farrell-Chi 125

Runs Created
Duffy-Chi 141
Browning-Cle 136
Stovey-Bos 133
Connor-NY 131
Shindle-Phi 126

Total Average
Stovey-Bos 1.207
Browning-Cle 1.191
Connor-NY 1.184
Brouthers-Bos 1.149
Gore-NY 1.129

Stolen Bases
Stovey-Bos 97
Brown-Bos 79
Duffy-Chi 78
Hanlon-Pit 65
Ward-Bro 63

Stolen Base Average

Stolen Base Runs

Fielding Runs
Pfeffer-Chi 22.0
Bierbauer-Bro 21.1
Farrell-Chi 18.2
White-Buf 17.8
Nash-Bos 16.2

Total Player Rating
Browning-Cle 4.2
Connor-NY 3.0
Ward-Bro 2.6
Ewing-NY 2.5
Tebeau-Cle 2.5

Wins
Baldwin-Chi 34
Weyhing-Bro 30
King-Chi 30
Radbourn-Bos 27
Gumbert-Bos 23

Win Percentage
Daley-Bos 720
Radbourn-Bos 692
Knell-Phi 667
Gumbert-Bos 657
Weyhing-Bro 652

Games
Baldwin-Chi 59
King-Chi 56
Weyhing-Bro 49
Gruber-Cle 48
Staley-Pit 46

Complete Games
Baldwin-Chi 54
King-Chi 48
Staley-Pit 44
Gruber-Cle 39
Weyhing-Bro 38

Shutouts
King-Chi 4
Weyhing-Bro 3
Staley-Pit 3

Saves
Hemming-Cle-Bro 3
O'Day-NY 3

Innings Pitched
Baldwin-Chi 501
King-Chi 461
Weyhing-Bro 390
Staley-Pit 388
Gruber-Cle 383

Fewest Hits/Game
King-Chi 8.20
Crane-NY 8.81
Hemming-Cle-Bro . . 8.88
Baldwin-Chi 8.95
Keefe-NY 8.96

Fewest BB/Game
Staley-Pit 1.72
Sanders-Phi 1.79
Galvin-Pit 2.03
Morris-Pit 2.19
Radbourn-Bos 2.62

Strikeouts
Baldwin-Chi 211
King-Chi 185
Weyhing-Bro 177
Staley-Pit 145
Ewing-NY 145

Strikeouts/Game
Ewing-NY 4.89
Daley-Bos 4.21
Weyhing-Bro 4.08
McGill-Cle 4.01
Haddock-Buf 3.80

Wins Above Team
Knell-Phi 6.1
Weyhing-Bro 5.8
Radbourn-Bos 4.5
Baldwin-Chi 4.1
Daley-Bos 3.6

Earned Run Average
King-Chi 2.69
Staley-Pit 3.22
Baldwin-Chi 3.31
Radbourn-Bos 3.31
Keefe-NY 3.38

Adjusted ERA
King-Chi 161
Keefe-NY 134
Radbourn-Bos 133
Baldwin-Chi 131
Weyhing-Bro 124

Opponents' Batting Avg.
King-Chi 232
Crane-NY 245
Hemming-Cle-Bro . . .247
Baldwin-Chi 248
Keefe-NY 249

Opponents' On Base Pct.
Staley-Pit 285
King-Chi 296
Radbourn-Bos 304
Keefe-NY 312
Sanders-Phi 315

Starter Runs
King-Chi 78.8
Baldwin-Chi 51.6
Staley-Pit 43.5
Radbourn-Bos 35.3
Weyhing-Bro 27.4

Adjusted Starter Runs
King-Chi 84.4
Baldwin-Chi 57.7
Radbourn-Bos 41.6
Weyhing-Bro 37.3
Keefe-NY 29.6

Clutch Pitching Index
Daley-Bos 121
O'Brien-Cle 119
Gruber-Cle 111
Sowders-Bro 111
McGill-Cle 111

Relief Runs

Adjusted Relief Runs

Relief Ranking

Total Pitcher Index
King-Chi 7.4
Baldwin-Chi 5.4
Radbourn-Bos 3.9
Sanders-Phi 2.9
Staley-Pit 2.3

Total Baseball Ranking
King-Chi 7.4
Baldwin-Chi 5.4
Browning-Cle 4.2
Radbourn-Bos 3.9
Connor-NY 3.0

TEAM	G	W	L	PCT	GB	R	OR	AB	H	2B	3B	HR	BB	SO	AVG	OBP	SLG	PRO	/A	BR	/A	PF	CHI	RC	TA	SB	CS	SBA	SBR
BOS	140	87	51	.630		847	658	4956	1264	181	80	54	532	538	.255	.337	.357	.694	110	68	-24	112	98	711	.723	289			
CHI	137	82	53	.607	3.5	832	730	4873	1233	159	88	60	526	457	.253	.332	.359	.691	109	58	9	106	100	676	.704	238			
NY	136	71	61	.538	13	754	711	4833	1271	189	72	47	438	394	.263	.329	.361	.690	109	50	97	94	94	664	.686	224			
PHI	138	68	69	.496	18.5	756	773	4929	1244	180	51	21	482	412	.252	.326	.322	.648	96	-11	26	95	99	609	.641	232			
CLE	141	65	74	.468	22.5	835	888	5074	1294	183	88	22	519	464	.255	.330	.339	.669	103	22	-17	105	101	663	.668	242			
BRO	137	61	76	.445	25.5	765	820	4748	1233	200	69	23	464	435	.260	.345	.345	.675	104	30	51	97	99	669	.705	337			
PIT	137	55	80	.407	30.5	679	744	4794	1148	148	71	28	427	503	.239	.308	.317	.625	89	-57	-66	101	98	546	.604	205			
CIN	138	56	81	.409	30.5	646	790	4791	1158	148	90	40	414	439	.242	.308	.335	.643	95	-32	34	91	90	584	.635	244			
TOT	552					6114		38998	9845	1388	609	295	3802	3642	.252	.319	.342	.661								2011			

TEAM	CG	SHO	SV	IP	H	H/G	HR	BB	BB/G	SO	SO/G	ERA	/A	OAVG	OOBA	PR	/A	PF	CPI	FA	E	DP	FW	PW	BW	SBW	DIF
BOS	126	9	6	1241.7	1223	8.9	51	364	2.6	525	3.8	2.76	132	.247	.299	80	122	109	106	.938	358	96	4.3	10.9	-2.1		5.0
CHI	114	6	3	1220.7	1207	8.9	53	475	3.5	477	3.5	3.47	101	.248	.315	-17	4	105	93	.933	397	119	1.7	.4	.8		11.6
NY	117	11	3	1204.0	1098	8.2	27	593	4.4	651	4.9	2.99	104	.233	.319	47	15	93	100	.933	384	104	2.6	1.3	8.7		-7.6
PHI	105	3	5	1229.3	1280	9.4	29	505	3.7	343	2.5	3.73	86	.258	.327	-52	-73	95	91	.925	443	108	-1.3	-6.5	2.3		5.0
CLE	118	1	3	1244.0	1371	9.9	24	466	3.4	400	2.9	3.51	101	.269	.330	-22	4	106	102	.920	485	86	-4.1	.4	-1.5		.7
BRO	121	8	3	1204.7	1272	9.5	40	459	3.4	407	3.0	3.86	85	.261	.324	-68	-77	98	90	.924	432	73	-.6	-6.9	4.6		-4.6
PIT	122	7	2	1197.7	1160	8.7	31	465	3.5	446	3.4	2.89	118	.244	.312	60	70	102	104	.918	475	76	-3.4	6.3	-5.9		-9.4
CIN	125	6	1	1218.7	1234	9.1	40	465	3.4	393	3.5	3.55	88	.253	.318	-27	-58	93	91	.931	409	101	.9	-5.2	3.0		-11.3
TOT	948	51	26	9760.7		9.1			3.5		3.4	3.35		.252	.319					.928	3383	763					

Runs
Hamilton-Phi 141
Long-Bos 129
Childs-Cle 120
Latham-Cin 119
Stovey-Bos 118

Hits
Hamilton-Phi 179
McKean-Cle 170
Tiernan-NY 166
Davis-Cle 165
O'Rourke-NY 164

Doubles
Griffin-Bro 36
Davis-Cle 35
Stovey-Bos 31
Tiernan-NY 30

Triples
Stovey-Bos 20
Beckley-Pit 19
McPhee-Cin 16
Ryan-Chi 15
Virtue-Cle 14

Home Runs
Tiernan-NY 16
Stovey-Bos 16
Wilmot-Chi 11

Total Bases
Stovey-Bos 271
Tiernan-NY 268
Long-Bos 236
Davis-Cle 233
Beckley-Pit 232

Runs Batted In
Anson-Chi 120
Stovey-Bos 95
O'Rourke-NY 95
Nash-Bos 95
Connor-NY 94

Runs Produced
Davis-Cle 201
Childs-Cle 201
Hamilton-Phi 199
Connor-NY 199
Stovey-Bos 197

Bases On Balls
Hamilton-Phi 102
Childs-Cle 97
Connor-NY 83
Long-Bos 80
Pfeffer-Chi 79

Batting Average
Hamilton-Phi 340
Holliday-Cin 319
Browning-Pit-Cin 317
Clements-Phi 310
Tiernan-NY 306

On Base Percentage
Hamilton-Phi 453
Connor-NY 399
Childs-Cle 395
Browning-Pit-Cin 395
Tiernan-NY 388

Slugging Average
Stovey-Bos 498
Tiernan-NY 494
Holliday-Cin 473
Connor-NY 449
Ryan-Chi 434

Production
Tiernan-NY 882
Hamilton-Phi 874
Stovey-Bos 870
Holliday-Cin 848
Connor-NY 848

Adjusted Production
Tiernan-NY 169
Hamilton-Phi 166
Holliday-Cin 163
Connor-NY 159
Browning-Pit-Cin . . . 148

Batter Runs
Hamilton-Phi 45.7
Tiernan-NY 39.5
Stovey-Bos 36.7
Connor-NY 32.2
Holliday-Cin 25.7

Adjusted Batter Runs
Hamilton-Phi 50.1
Tiernan-NY 44.9
Connor-NY 37.3
Holliday-Cin 31.8
Stovey-Bos 26.4

Clutch Hitting Index
Anson-Chi 151
Brodie-Bos 139
Nash-Bos 133
Myers-NY 132
Zimmer-Cle 129

Runs Created
Hamilton-Phi 155
Tiernan-NY 128
Stovey-Bos 125
Long-Bos 115
Latham-Cin 112

Total Average
Hamilton-Phi 1.270
Tiernan-NY 1.045
Stovey-Bos 1.041
Latham-Cin 974
Connor-NY 968

Stolen Bases
Hamilton-Phi 111
Latham-Cin 87
Griffin-Bro 65
Long-Bos 60

Stolen Base Average

Stolen Base Runs

Fielding Runs
Richardson-NY 43.6
Pfeffer-Chi 22.9
Griffin-Bro 22.6
McPhee-Cin 21.7
Thompson-Phi 19.3

Total Player Rating
Latham-Cin 4.2
Hamilton-Phi 4.2
Richardson-NY 4.1
McPhee-Cin 3.7
Thompson-Phi 3.1

Wins
Hutchinson-Chi 44
Rusie-NY 33
Clarkson-Bos 33
Nichols-Bos 30
Young-Cle 27

Win Percentage
Ewing-NY 724
Hutchinson-Chi 698
Staley-Pit-Bos 649
Nichols-Bos 638
Clarkson-Bos 635

Games
Hutchinson-Chi 66
Rusie-NY 61
Young-Cle 55
Clarkson-Bos 55

Complete Games
Hutchinson-Chi 56
Rusie-NY 52
Baldwin-Pit 48
Clarkson-Bos 47
Nichols-Bos 45

Shutouts
Rusie-NY 6
Nichols-Bos 5
Ewing-NY 5
Hutchinson-Chi 4

Saves
Nichols-Bos 3
Clarkson-Bos 3
Young-Cle 2
Thornton-Phi 2

Innings Pitched
Hutchinson-Chi 561
Rusie-NY 500
Clarkson-Bos 461
Baldwin-Pit 438

Fewest Hits/Game
Rusie-NY 7.04
Baldwin-Pit 7.91
Ewing-NY 7.93
Hutchinson-Chi 8.15
Mullane-Cin 8.24

Fewest BB/Game
Nichols-Bos 2.18
Staley-Pit-Bos 2.22
Galvin-Pit 2.26
Radbourn-Cin 2.56
Hutchinson-Chi 2.86

Strikeouts
Rusie-NY 337
Hutchinson-Chi 261
Nichols-Bos 240
Baldwin-Pit 197
King-Pit 160

Strikeouts/Game
Rusie-NY 6.07
Nichols-Bos 5.07
Ewing-NY 4.62
Hutchinson-Chi 4.19
Baldwin-Pit 4.05

Wins Above Team
Hutchinson-Chi 11.4
Rusie-NY 7.2
Ewing-NY 6.7
Young-Cle 5.5
Lovett-Bro 5.2

Earned Run Average
Ewing-NY 2.28
Nichols-Bos 2.39
Rusie-NY 2.56
Staley-Pit-Bos 2.58
Baldwin-Pit 2.77

Adjusted ERA
Nichols-Bos 153
Staley-Pit-Bos 139
Ewing-NY 137
Clarkson-Bos 131
Hutchinson-Chi 125

Opponents' Batting Avg.
Rusie-NY 207
Baldwin-Pit 227
Ewing-NY 228
Hutchinson-Chi 233
Mullane-Cin 235

Opponents' On Base Pct.
Nichols-Bos 289
Staley-Pit-Bos 289
Hutchinson-Chi 290
Ewing-NY 299
Clarkson-Bos 300

Starter Runs
Nichols-Bos 45.4
Rusie-NY 44.0
Hutchinson-Chi 33.6
Ewing-NY 32.0
Clarkson-Bos 28.4

Adjusted Starter Runs
Nichols-Bos 59.7
Clarkson-Bos 43.9
Hutchinson-Chi 43.4
Staley-Pit-Bos 36.3
Young-Cle 33.0

Clutch Pitching Index
Viau-Cle 113
Caruthers-Bro 112
Nichols-Bos 112
Ewing-NY 107
Galvin-Pit 106

Relief Runs

Adjusted Relief Runs

Relief Ranking

Total Pitcher Index
Nichols-Bos 6.2
Clarkson-Bos 5.2
Hutchinson-Chi 3.9
Staley-Pit-Bos 3.4
Rusie-NY 3.4

Total Baseball Ranking
Nichols-Bos 6.2
Clarkson-Bos 5.2
Latham-Cin 4.2
Hamilton-Phi 4.2
Richardson-NY 4.1

TEAM	G	W	L	PCT	GB	R	OR	AB	H	2B	3B	HR	BB	SO	AVG	OBP	SLG	PRO	/A	BR	/A	PF	CHI	RC	TA	SB	CS	SBA SBR
BOS	139	93	42	.689		1028	675	4889	1341	163	100	51	651	499	.274	.367	.380	.747	122	148	160	99	103	867	.851	447		
STL	139	85	51	.625	8.5	976	753	5005	1330	169	51	58	625	440	.266	.357	.355	.712	112	89	-32	114	102	753	.754	283		
PHI	143	73	66	.525	22	817	794	5039	1301	182	123	55	447	548	.258	.328	.376	.704	109	46	20	103	92	686	.686	149		
BAL	139	71	64	.526	22	850	798	4771	1217	142	99	30	551	553	.255	.346	.345	.691	106	45	36	101	98	705	.746	342		
CM	138	64	72	.471	29.5	776	799	4845	1170	163	73	40	535	499	.241	.325	.330	.655	95	-25	-120	112	97	604	.656	211		
COL	138	61	76	.445	33	702	777	4697	1113	154	61	20	529	530	.237	.319	.308	.627	87	-69	14	89	97	565	.640	280		
LOU	139	54	83	.394	40	713	890	4833	1247	130	69	17	443	473	.258	.329	.324	.653	94	-28	49	90	92	606	.644	230		
WAS	139	44	91	.326	49	691	1067	4715	1183	147	84	19	468	485	.251	.328	.330	.658	96	-19	17	95	89	597	.656	219		
TOT	557					6553		38794	9902	1250	660	290	4249	4027	.255	.329	.344	.673								2161		

TEAM	CG	SHO	SV	IP	H	H/G	HR	BB	BB/G	SO	SO/G	ERA	/A	OAVG	OOBA	PR	/A	PF	CPI	FA	E	DP	FW	PW	BW	SBW	DIF
BOS	108	9	8	1219.7	1158	8.5	42	497	3.7	524	3.9	3.03	115	.242	.313	94	63	94	105	.934	392	115	4.0	5.4	13.8		2.2
STL	103	8	5	1222.7	1106	8.1	50	576	4.2	621	4.6	3.27	127	.233	.316	61	119	112	97	.920	468	91	-.5	10.3	-2.8		10.0
PHI	135	3	0	1233.7	1274	9.3	35	520	3.8	533	3.9	4.02	95	.257	.328	-40	-27	103	89	.933	389	109	4.2	-2.3	1.7		-.1
BAL	118	6	2	1217.0	1238	9.2	33	472	3.5	408	3.0	3.43	109	.255	.321	39	41	100	99	.915	503	103	-2.5	3.5	3.1		-.6
CM	121	5	1	1211.7	1212	9.0	26	566	4.2	468	3.5	3.19	131	.251	.330	70	133	113	109	.915	505	88	-2.6	11.5	-10.3		-2.5
COL	118	6	0	1213.3	1141	8.5	29	588	4.4	502	3.7	3.75	89	.240	.324	-4	-54	90	87	.935	379	126	4.8	-4.7	1.2		-8.9
LOU	128	9	1	1226.0	1353	9.9	33	464	3.4	485	3.6	4.27	80	.270	.332	-75	-113	92	89	.922	458	113	.1	-9.7	4.2		-9.1
WAS	123	2	2	1181.0	1420	10.8	44	566	4.3	486	3.7	4.83	77	.288	.361	-145	-143	101	96	.900	589	95	-7.6	-12.3	1.5		-5.0
TOT	954	48	19	9725.0		9.2			3.9		3.7	3.72		.255	.329					.922	3683	840					

Runs
Brown-Bos 177
VanHaltren-Bal 136
Hoy-StL 136
Duffy-Bos 134
McCarthy-StL 127

Hits
Brown-Bos 189
VanHaltren-Bal 180
Duffy-Bos 180
McCarthy-StL 179
Brouthers-Bos 170

Doubles
Milligan-Phi 35
Brown-Bos 30
O'Neill-StL 28
Duffee-Col 28
Larkin-Phi 27

Triples
Brown-Bos 21
Brouthers-Bos 19
Werden-Bal 18
Canavan-CM 18

Home Runs
Farrell-Bos 12
Milligan-Phi 11
Lyons-StL 11

Total Bases
Brown-Bos 276
VanHaltren-Bal 251
Brouthers-Bos 249
Duffy-Bos 240
McCarthy-StL 236

Runs Batted In
Farrell-Bos 110
Duffy-Bos 108
Brouthers-Bos 108
Milligan-Phi 106
Werden-Bal 104

Runs Produced
Brown-Bos 243
Duffy-Bos 234
Brouthers-Bos 220
McCarthy-StL 214
VanHaltren-Bal 210

Bases On Balls
Hoy-StL 119
Crooks-Col 103
McTamany-Col-Phi . .101
Radford-Bos 96
Johnson-Bal 89

Batting Average
Brouthers-Bos 350
Duffy-Bos 336
Brown-Bos 321
O'Neill-StL 321
VanHaltren-Bal 318

On Base Percentage
Brouthers-Bos 471
Lyons-StL 445
Hoy-StL 424
Seery-CM 423
Duffy-Bos 408

Slugging Average
Brouthers-Bos 512
Milligan-Phi 505
Farrell-Bos 474
Brown-Bos 469
Cross-Phi 458

Production
Brouthers-Bos 983
Milligan-Phi 903
Lyons-StL 900
Brown-Bos 865
Farrell-Bos 858

Adjusted Production
Brouthers-Bos 188
Milligan-Phi 157
Brown-Bos 153
Farrell-Bos 151
Duffy-Bos 150

Batter Runs
Brouthers-Bos 59.2
Lyons-StL 41.3
Brown-Bos 37.9
Milligan-Phi 35.5
Duffy-Bos 33.6

Adjusted Batter Runs
Brouthers-Bos 60.5
Brown-Bos 39.4
Duffy-Bos 35.0
Milligan-Phi 33.1
VanHaltren-Bal 31.5

Clutch Hitting Index
Comiskey-StL 144
Wolf-Lou 143
Radford-Bos 138
Johnson-Bal 132
Farrell-Bos 130

Runs Created
Brown-Bos 155
Duffy-Bos 136
Brouthers-Bos 135
VanHaltren-Bal 133
Hoy-StL 114

Total Average
Brouthers-Bos 1.237
Brown-Bos 1.140
Duffy-Bos 1.096
VanHaltren-Bal . . . 1.039
Lyons-StL 1.036

Stolen Bases
Brown-Bos 106
Duffy-Bos 85
VanHaltren-Bal 75
Hoy-StL 59
Radford-Bos 55

Stolen Base Average

Stolen Base Runs

Fielding Runs
Stricker-Bos 26.8
Crooks-Col 21.6
Wheelock-Col 17.4
Alvord-Was 15.3
Andrews-CM 14.8

Total Player Rating
Crooks-Col 4.3
Milligan-Phi 4.2
Brouthers-Bos 3.9
Farrell-Bos 3.6
McGuire-Was 2.7

Wins
McMahon-Bal 34
Haddock-Bos 34
Stivetts-StL 33
Weyhing-Phi 31
Buffinton-Bos 29

Win Percentage
Buffinton-Bos 763
Haddock-Bos 756
Weyhing-Phi 608
Stivetts-StL 600
McMahon-Bal 586

Games
Stivetts-StL 64
McMahon-Bal 61
Knell-Col 58
Carsey-Was 54
Weyhing-Phi 52

Complete Games
McMahon-Bal 53
Weyhing-Phi 51
Knell-Col 47
Carsey-Was 46
Chamberlin-Phi 44

Shutouts
McMahon-Bal 5
Knell-Col 5
Haddock-Bos 5

Saves
Buffinton-Bos 3
Daley-Bos 2

Innings Pitched
McMahon-Bal 503
Knell-Col 462
Weyhing-Phi 450
Stivetts-StL 440
Carsey-Was 415

Fewest Hits/Game
Knell-Col 7.07
Stivetts-StL 7.30
Buffinton-Bos 7.49
Crane-CM 7.78
Haddock-Bos 7.82

Fewest BB/Game
Stratton-Lou 1.78
Sanders-Phi 2.30
McMahon-Bal 2.67
Ehret-Lou 2.85
Griffith-StL-Bos 2.91

Strikeouts
Stivetts-StL 259
Knell-Col 228
Weyhing-Phi 219
McMahon-Bal 219
Chamberlin-Phi 204

Strikeouts/Game
Meekin-Lou 5.68
Stivetts-StL 5.30
McGill-CM-StL 4.96
Chamberlin-Phi 4.52
Knell-Col 4.44

Wins Above Team
Haddock-Bos 6.5
Weyhing-Phi 6.4
McMahon-Bal 5.9
Buffinton-Bos 5.8
Foreman-Was 5.1

Earned Run Average
Crane-CM 2.45
Haddock-Bos 2.49
Buffinton-Bos 2.55
McMahon-Bal 2.81
Stivetts-StL 2.86

Adjusted ERA
Crane-CM 171
Stivetts-StL 145
Haddock-Bos 140
Buffinton-Bos 137
Mains-CM 136

Opponents' Batting Avg.
Knell-Col 209
Stivetts-StL 215
Buffinton-Bos 219
Crane-CM 225
Haddock-Bos 226

Opponents' On Base Pct.
Buffinton-Bos 281
Haddock-Bos 293
Knell-Col 300
McMahon-Bal 301
Weyhing-Phi 306

Starter Runs
Haddock-Bos 52.1
McMahon-Bal 51.0
Buffinton-Bos 47.5
Stivetts-StL 41.9
Knell-Col 41.0

Adjusted Starter Runs
Stivetts-StL 62.8
McMahon-Bal 51.8
Crane-CM 48.3
Haddock-Bos 42.4
Buffinton-Bos 38.2

Clutch Pitching Index
Crane-CM 122
O'Brien-Bos 117
Mains-CM 117
McMahon-Bal 105
Foreman-Was 103

Relief Runs

Adjusted Relief Runs

Relief Ranking

Total Pitcher Index
Stivetts-StL 7.9
Haddock-Bos 5.1
McMahon-Bal 4.8
Crane-CM 4.0
Buffinton-Bos 3.8

Total Baseball Ranking
Stivetts-StL 7.9
Haddock-Bos 5.1
McMahon-Bal 4.8
Crooks-Col 4.3
Milligan-Phi 4.2

TEAM	G	W	L	PCT	GB	R	OR	AB	H	2B	3B	HR	BB	SO	AVG	OBP	SLG	PRO	/A	BR	/A	PF	CHI	RC	TA	SB	CS	SBA	SBR
BOS	152	102	48	.680		862	649	5301	1324	203	51	34	526	488	.250	.325	.327	.652	104	32	-69	113	105	689	.668	338			
CLE	153	93	56	.624	8.5	855	613	5412	1375	196	96	26	552	536	.254	.328	.340	.668	109	62	35	103	99	694	.658	225			
BRO	158	95	59	.617	9	935	733	5485	1439	183	105	30	629	506	.262	.344	.350	.694	117	124	112	101	99	822	.745	409			
PHI	155	87	66	.569	16.5	860	690	5413	1420	225	95	50	528	515	.262	.334	.367	.701	119	121	85	104	93	753	.697	216			
CIN	155	82	68	.547	20	766	731	5349	1288	155	75	44	503	474	.241	.311	.322	.633	98	-8	-33	103	98	635	.624	270			
PIT	155	80	73	.523	23.5	802	796	5469	1288	143	108	38	435	453	.236	.297	.322	.619	94	-43	7	94	107	604	.589	222			
CHI	147	70	76	.479	30	635	735	5063	1188	149	92	26	427	482	.235	.299	.316	.615	93	-45	10	92	92	561	.592	233			
NY	153	71	80	.470	31.5	811	826	5291	1326	173	85	39	510	469	.251	.320	.338	.658	106	39	54	98	99	686	.664	301			
LOU	154	63	89	.414	40	649	804	5334	1208	133	61	18	433	508	.226	.290	.284	.574	80	-119	-57	99	93	533	.550	275			
WAS	151	58	93	.384	44.5	731	869	5204	1245	149	78	37	529	553	.239	.314	.319	.633	98	-3	-38	105	95	624	.633	276			
STL	155	56	94	.373	46	703	922	5259	1187	138	53	45	607	491	.226	.312	.298	.610	91	-39	0	95	94	568	.598	209			
BAL	152	46	101	.313	54.5	779	1020	5296	1342	160	111	30	499	480	.253	.325	.343	.668	109	58	59	100	93	680	.658	227			
TOT	920					9388		63876	15630	2007	1010	417	6178	5955	.245	.311	.327	.639								3201			

TEAM	CG	SHO	SV	IP	H	H/G	HR	BB	BB/G	SO	SO/G	ERA	/A	OAVG	OOBA	PR	/A	PF	CPI	FA	E	DP	FW	PW	BW	SBW	DIF
BOS	143	15	1	1336.0	1156	7.8	41	460	3.1	509	3.4	2.86	128	.224	.287	63	116	111	91	.929	454	127	.6	10.7	-6.4		22.0
CLE	140	11	2	1336.0	1178	7.9	28	413	2.8	472	3.2	2.41	137	.227	.284	129	133	101	104	.935	407	95	3.4	12.3	3.2		-.4
BRO	132	12	5	1405.7	1285	8.2	26	600	3.8	597	3.8	3.25	101	.233	.309	6	3	99	92	.940	398	98	3.9	.3	10.4		3.5
PHI	131	10	5	1379.0	1297	8.5	24	492	3.2	502	3.3	2.93	115	.238	.302	54	68	103	99	.939	393	128	4.2	6.3	7.9		-7.9
CIN	131	8	2	1377.3	1327	8.7	39	535	3.5	437	2.9	3.18	107	.243	.310	16	31	103	100	.939	402	140	3.7	2.9	-3.1		3.5
PIT	130	3	1	1347.3	1300	8.7	29	537	3.6	455	3.0	3.10	99	.243	.312	28	-3	94	102	.927	483	113	-1.0	-.3	.6		4.2
CHI	133	6	1	1298.0	1269	8.8	35	424	2.9	518	3.6	3.16	97	.246	.303	18	-13	93	97	.932	424	85	2.4	-1.2	.9		-5.1
NY	139	5	1	1322.7	1165	7.9	32	635	4.3	641	4.4	3.29	98	.227	.312	0	-9	98	91	.912	565	97	-5.8	-.8	5.0		-2.9
LOU	147	9	0	1346.0	1358	9.1	26	447	3.0	430	2.9	3.34	92	.251	.309	-7	-40	93	96	.928	471	133	-.3	-3.7	-5.3		-3.7
WAS	129	5	3	1315.3	1293	8.8	39	556	3.8	479	3.3	3.47	101	.247	.319	-26	2	106	98	.916	547	122	-4.8	.2	-3.5		-9.4
STL	139	4	1	1344.7	1466	9.8	47	543	3.6	478	3.2	4.21	76	.266	.332	-137	-151	97	93	.929	452	100	.8	-14.0	.0		-5.8
BAL	131	2	1	1298.7	1537	10.7	51	536	3.7	437	3.0	4.29	78	.283	.347	-144	-133	102	103	.910	584	100	-6.9	-12.3	5.5		-13.7
TOT	1625	90	23	16106.7		8.7			3.5		3.3	3.29		.245	.311					.928	5580	1338					

Split Season: First-half Winner BOS (52-22); Second-half Winner CLE (53-23)

Runs
Childs-Cle 136
Hamilton-Phi 132
Duffy-Bos 125
Connor-Phi 123
Brouthers-Bro 121

Hits
Brouthers-Bro 197
Thompson-Phi 186
Duffy-Bos 184
Hamilton-Phi 183
Long-Bos 181

Doubles
Connor-Phi 37
Long-Bos 33
Delahanty-Phi 30
Brouthers-Bro 30
Zimmer-Cle 29

Triples
Delahanty-Phi 21
Virtue-Cle 20
Brouthers-Bro 20
Dahlen-Chi 19
Beckley-Pit 19

Home Runs
Holliday-Cin 13
Connor-Phi 12
Ryan-Chi 10
Beckley-Pit 10
Thompson-Phi 9

Total Bases
Brouthers-Bro 282
Holliday-Cin 270
Thompson-Phi 263
Connor-Phi 261
Duffy-Bos 251

Runs Batted In
Brouthers-Bro 124
Thompson-Phi 104
Larkin-Was 96
Burns-Bro 96
Beckley-Pit 96

Runs Produced
Brouthers-Bro 240
Thompson-Phi 204
Duffy-Bos 201
Holliday-Cin 192

Bases On Balls
Crooks-StL 136
Childs-Cle 117
Connor-Phi 116
McCarthy-Bos 93

Batting Average
Brouthers-Bro 335
Hamilton-Phi 330
Childs-Cle 317
Burns-Bro 315
Delahanty-Phi 306

On Base Percentage
Childs-Cle 443
Brouthers-Bro 432
Hamilton-Phi 423
Connor-Phi 420
Crooks-StL 400

Slugging Average
Delahanty-Phi 495
Brouthers-Bro 480
Connor-Phi 463
Burns-Bro 454
Holliday-Cin 449

Production
Brouthers-Bro 911
Connor-Phi 883
Delahanty-Phi 855
Burns-Bro 849
Childs-Cle 841

Adjusted Production
Brouthers-Bro 175
Connor-Phi 162
Ryan-Chi 160
Burns-Bro 156
Delahanty-Phi 153

Batter Runs
Brouthers-Bro 58.4
Connor-Phi 52.1
Childs-Cle 47.0
Hamilton-Phi 40.4
Burns-Bro 38.8

Adjusted Batter Runs
Brouthers-Bro 57.1
Connor-Phi 48.1
Childs-Cle 44.0
Burns-Bro 37.6
Hamilton-Phi 36.6

Clutch Hitting Index
McKean-Cle 159
Nash-Bos 158
Larkin-Was 152
Corcoran-Bro 138
Comiskey-Cin 137

Runs Created
Brouthers-Bro 138
Hamilton-Phi 123
Connor-Phi 122
VanHaltren-Bal-Pit . .117
Holliday-Cin 114

Total Average
Brouthers-Bro . . . 1.056
Connor-Phi 1.018
Hamilton-Phi 1.005
Childs-Cle 982
Burns-Bro 943

Stolen Bases
Ward-Bro 88
Brown-Lou 78
Latham-Cin 66
Hoy-Was 60
Dahlen-Chi 60

Stolen Base Average

Stolen Base Runs

Fielding Runs
Richardson-Was . . . 49.4
Shindle-Bal 35.9
McPhee-Cin 25.4
Dahlen-Chi 24.2
Nash-Bos 22.3

Total Player Rating
Dahlen-Chi 5.5
Brouthers-Bro 5.1
McPhee-Cin 4.1
Hamilton-Phi 4.1
Shindle-Bal 3.9

Wins
Hutchinson-Chi 37
Young-Cle 36
Stivetts-Bos 35
Nichols-Bos 35
Weyhing-Phi 32

Win Percentage
Young-Cle 750
Haddock-Bro 690
Staley-Bos 688
Stivetts-Bos 686
Nichols-Bos 686

Games
Hutchinson-Chi 75
Rusie-NY 64
Killen-Was 60
Weyhing-Phi 59
Baldwin-Pit 56

Complete Games
Hutchinson-Chi 67
Rusie-NY 58
Nichols-Bos 50
Young-Cle 48

Shutouts
Young-Cle 9
Weyhing-Phi 6
Stein-Bro 6

Saves
Weyhing-Phi 3
Duryea-Cin-Was 2

Innings Pitched
Hutchinson-Chi 627
Rusie-NY 532
Weyhing-Phi 470
Killen-Was 460
Nichols-Bos 454

Fewest Hits/Game
Mullane-Cin 6.77
Rusie-NY 6.85
Terry-Bal-Pit 6.94
Young-Cle 7.21
Duryea-Cin-Was 7.25

Fewest BB/Game
Stratton-Lou 1.79
Dwyer-StL-Cin 2.03
Sanders-Lou 2.08
Young-Cle 2.34
Ehret-Pit 2.36

Strikeouts
Hutchinson-Chi 316
Rusie-NY 288
Weyhing-Phi 202
Stein-Bro 190
Nichols-Bos 187

Strikeouts/Game
Kennedy-Bro 5.09
Rusie-NY 4.87
Hutchinson-Chi 4.54
Stein-Bro 4.54
Crane-NY 4.30

Wins Above Team
Young-Cle 10.2
Killen-Was 8.9
McMahon-Bal 5.7
Haddock-Bro 5.2
Terry-Bal-Pit 4.8

Earned Run Average
Young-Cle 1.93
Keefe-Phi 2.36
Clarkson-Bos-Cle . . . 2.48
Cuppy-Cle 2.51
Terry-Bal-Pit 2.57

Adjusted ERA
Young-Cle 172
Keefe-Phi 143
Clarkson-Bos-Cle 140
Cuppy-Cle 132
Mullane-Cin 131

Opponents' Batting Avg.
Mullane-Cin 201
Rusie-NY 203
Terry-Bal-Pit 205
Young-Cle 211
Duryea-Cin-Was 212

Opponents' On Base Pct.
Young-Cle 262
Nichols-Bos 279
Keefe-Phi 280
Duryea-Cin-Was 281
Stratton-Lou 281

Starter Runs
Young-Cle 68.5
Hutchinson-Chi 38.0
Clarkson-Bos-Cle . . . 35.1
Weyhing-Phi 32.7
Cuppy-Cle 32.3

Adjusted Starter Runs
Young-Cle 69.8
Clarkson-Bos-Cle . . 42.8
Nichols-Bos 40.7
Weyhing-Phi 37.3
Keefe-Phi 35.4

Clutch Pitching Index
Sullivan-Cin 132
Galvin-Pit-StL 120
Luby-Chi 114
McMahon-Bal 113
Vickery-Bal 112

Relief Runs

Adjusted Relief Runs

Relief Ranking

Total Pitcher Index
Young-Cle 7.1
Stivetts-Bos 5.8
Nichols-Bos 4.6
Clarkson-Bos-Cle . . . 3.8
Cuppy-Cle 3.8

Total Baseball Ranking
Young-Cle 7.1
Stivetts-Bos 5.8
Dahlen-Chi 5.5
Brouthers-Bro 5.1
Nichols-Bos 4.6

TEAM	G	W	L	PCT	GB	R	OR	AB	H	2B	3B	HR	BB	SO	AVG	OBP	SLG	PRO	/A	BR	/A	PF	CHI	RC	TA	SB	CS	SBA	SBR
BOS	131	86	43	.667		1008	795	4678	1358	178	50	65	561	292	.290	.372	.391	.763	109	70	46	103	108	790	.808	243			
PIT	131	81	48	.628	5	970	766	4834	1447	176	127	37	537	273	.299	.377	.411	.788	116	113	56	106	97	848	.826	210			
CLE	129	73	55	.570	12.5	976	839	4747	1425	222	98	32	532	229	.300	.374	.408	.782	114	100	66	104	101	841	.829	252			
PHI	133	72	57	.558	14	1011	841	5151	1553	246	90	80	468	335	.301	.368	.431	.799	119	125	127	100	96	912	.823	202			
NY	136	68	64	.515	19.5	941	845	4858	1424	182	101	61	504	279	.293	.366	.410	.776	113	85	54	104	97	860	.830	299			
CIN	131	65	63	.508	20.5	759	814	4617	1195	161	65	29	532	256	.259	.342	.341	.683	88	-71	-82	101	98	634	.699	238			
BRO	130	65	63	.508	20.5	775	845	4511	1200	173	83	45	473	296	.266	.341	.371	.712	95	-29	48	91	98	659	.725	213			
BAL	130	60	70	.462	26.5	820	893	4651	1281	164	86	27	537	323	.275	.359	.365	.724	99	3	-54	107	95	711	.753	233			
CHI	128	56	71	.441	29	829	844	4664	1299	186	93	32	465	262	.279	.348	.379	.727	99	-3	-32	104	99	722	.750	255			
STL	135	57	75	.432	30.5	745	829	4879	1288	152	98	10	524	251	.264	.343	.341	.684	88	-71	-63	99	91	674	.697	250			
LOU	126	50	75	.400	34	759	942	4566	1185	178	73	19	485	306	.260	.338	.343	.681	87	-76	-45	96	101	612	.683	203			
WAS	130	40	89	.310	46	722	1032	4742	1260	180	83	23	524	237	.266	.347	.353	.700	92	-43	47	90	88	650	.694	154			
TOT	785					10315		56898	15915	2198	1047	460	6142	3339	.280	.350	.379	.729								2752			

TEAM	CG	SHO	SV	IP	H	H/G	HR	BB	BB/G	SO	SO/G	ERA	/A	OAVG	OOBA	PR	/A	PF	CPI	FA	E	DP	FW	PW	BW	SBW	DIF
BOS	115	2	2	1163.7	1314	10.2	67	402	3.1	253	2.0	4.43	106	.276	.332	31	36	101	99	.936	353	118	1.6	3.0	3.8		13.2
PIT	104	8	1	1167.0	1232	9.5	28	504	3.9	280	2.2	4.09	120	.263	.334	76	104	105	98	.938	347	112	1.9	8.5	4.6		1.5
CLE	110	2	2	1140.3	1361	10.7	35	356	2.8	242	1.9	4.21	114	.287	.337	59	75	103	104	.929	395	92	-.7	6.1	5.4		-1.8
PHI	107	4	2	1189.0	1359	10.3	31	521	3.9	283	2.1	4.68	98	.278	.348	0	-12	98	95	.944	318	121	3.5	-1.0	10.4		-5.5
NY	111	6	4	1211.3	1271	9.4	34	581	4.3	395	2.9	4.32	111	.261	.340	47	65	103	95	.927	432	95	-2.8	5.3	4.4		-5.0
CIN	97	4	5	1172.0	1305	10.0	38	549	4.2	258	2.0	4.61	103	.273	.348	9	20	102	96	.943	321	138	3.4	1.6	-6.7		2.7
BRO	109	3	3	1154.0	1262	9.8	40	547	4.3	297	2.3	4.55	94	.270	.346	15	-37	91	96	.930	385	88	-.2	-3.0	3.9		.3
BAL	104	1	2	1123.7	1325	10.6	28	534	4.3	275	2.2	4.98	101	.285	.358	-37	5	108	95	.929	384	113	-.1	.4	-4.4		-.9
CHI	101	4	5	1117.3	1278	10.3	26	553	4.5	273	2.2	4.83	101	.278	.356	-19	5	104	95	.922	421	92	-2.2	.4	-2.6		-3.1
STL	114	3	4	1207.0	1292	9.6	38	542	4.0	301	2.2	4.07	115	.265	.339	81	80	100	102	.930	398	110	-.9	6.6	-5.2		-9.5
LOU	114	4	1	1080.0	1431	11.9	37	479	4.0	190	1.6	5.95	77	.309	.374	-152	-163	98	92	.937	330	111	2.9	-13.4	-3.7		1.7
WAS	110	2	0	1139.0	1485	11.7	54	574	4.5	292	2.3	5.57	77	.306	.379	-112	-162	92	101	.912	497	96	-6.4	-13.3	3.9		-8.7
TOT	1296	43	31	13864.3		10.3			4.0		2.2	4.68		.280	.350					.931	4581	1268					

Runs
Long-Bos ... 149
Duffy-Bos ... 147
Delahanty-Phi ... 145
Childs-Cle ... 145
Burkett-Cle ... 145

Hits
Thompson-Phi ... 222
Delahanty-Phi ... 219
Duffy-Bos ... 203
Davis-NY ... 195
Ward-NY ... 193

Doubles
Thompson-Phi ... 37
Delahanty-Phi ... 35
Tebeau-Cle ... 32
Beckley-Pit ... 32

Triples
Werden-StL ... 29
Davis-NY ... 27
McKean-Cle ... 24
Smith-Pit ... 23
Beckley-Pit ... 19

Home Runs
Delahanty-Phi ... 19
Clements-Phi ... 17
Tiernan-NY ... 14
Lowe-Bos ... 14

Total Bases
Delahanty-Phi ... 347
Thompson-Phi ... 318
Davis-NY ... 304
Smith-Pit ... 272

Runs Batted In
Delahanty-Phi ... 146
McKean-Cle ... 133
Thompson-Phi ... 126
Nash-Bos ... 123
Ewing-Cle ... 122

Runs Produced
Delahanty-Phi ... 272
Duffy-Bos ... 259
Thompson-Phi ... 245
Ewing-Cle ... 233
McKean-Cle ... 232

Bases On Balls
Crooks-StL ... 121
Childs-Cle ... 120
Radford-Was ... 105
McGraw-Bal ... 101
Burkett-Cle ... 98

Batting Average
Hamilton-Phi ... .380
Thompson-Phi ... .370
Delahanty-Phi ... .368
Duffy-Bos ... .363
Davis-NY ... .355

On Base Percentage
Hamilton-Phi ... .490
Childs-Cle ... .463
Burkett-Cle ... .459
McGraw-Bal ... .454
Smith-Pit ... .435

Slugging Average
Delahanty-Phi ... .583
Davis-NY ... .554
Thompson-Phi ... .530
Smith-Pit ... .525
Hamilton-Phi ... .524

Production
Hamilton-Phi ... 1.014
Delahanty-Phi ... 1.007
Davis-NY ... .964
Smith-Pit ... .960
Thompson-Phi ... .954

Adjusted Production
Hamilton-Phi ... 172
Delahanty-Phi ... 169
Thompson-Phi ... 155
Davis-NY ... 152
Burkett-Cle ... 149

Batter Runs
Delahanty-Phi ... 54.6
Burkett-Cle ... 45.3
Thompson-Phi ... 45.2
Smith-Pit ... 43.1
Davis-NY ... 41.8

Adjusted Batter Runs
Delahanty-Phi ... 54.9
Thompson-Phi ... 45.6
Burkett-Cle ... 41.4
Hamilton-Phi ... 41.2
Davis-NY ... 38.4

Clutch Hitting Index
Anson-Chi ... 172
Vaughn-Cin ... 172
Nash-Bos ... 149
McCarthy-Bos ... 140
Lyons-Pit ... 139

Runs Created
Delahanty-Phi ... 167
Thompson-Phi ... 146
Davis-NY ... 143
Burkett-Cle ... 137
Smith-Pit ... 133

Total Average
Hamilton-Phi ... 1.386
Burkett-Cle ... 1.186
Delahanty-Phi ... 1.173
Smith-Pit ... 1.121
Davis-NY ... 1.107

Stolen Bases
T.Brown-Lou ... 66
Dowd-StL ... 59
Latham-Cin ... 57
Burke-NY ... 54
Brodie-StL-Bal ... 49

Stolen Base Average

Stolen Base Runs

Fielding Runs
McPhee-Cin ... 32.5
T.Brown-Lou ... 26.9
Delahanty-Phi ... 26.7
Farrell-Was ... 21.1
Smith-Cin ... 18.5

Total Player Rating
Delahanty-Phi ... 6.2
McPhee-Cin ... 3.3
Wise-Was ... 3.3
Hamilton-Phi ... 3.2
Davis-NY ... 3.1

Wins
Young-Cle ... 34
Nichols-Bos ... 34
Killen-Pit ... 34
Rusie-NY ... 33
Kennedy-Bro ... 25

Win Percentage
Gastright-Pit-Bos ... .750
Nichols-Bos ... .708
Killen-Pit ... .708
Young-Cle ... .680
Staley-Bos ... .643

Games
Rusie-NY ... 56
Killen-Pit ... 55
Young-Cle ... 53
Nichols-Bos ... 52
Mullane-Cin-Bal ... 49

Complete Games
Rusie-NY ... 50
Nichols-Bos ... 44
Young-Cle ... 42
Kennedy-Bro ... 40

Shutouts
Rusie-NY ... 4
Ehret-Pit ... 4

Saves
Mullane-Cin-Bal ... 2
Baldwin-Pit-NY ... 2
Dwyer-Cin ... 2
Donnelly-Chi ... 2

Innings Pitched
Rusie-NY ... 482
Nichols-Bos ... 425
Young-Cle ... 423
Killen-Pit ... 415

Fewest Hits/Game
Rusie-NY ... 8.42
Breitenstein-StL ... 8.44
Killen-Pit ... 8.70
Kennedy-Bro ... 8.84
Stein-Bro ... 8.88

Fewest BB/Game
Young-Cle ... 2.19
Nichols-Bos ... 2.50
Cuppy-Cle ... 2.77
Staley-Bos ... 2.77
Stratton-Lou ... 2.89

Strikeouts
Rusie-NY ... 208
Kennedy-Bro ... 107
Young-Cle ... 102
Breitenstein-StL ... 102
Weyhing-Phi ... 101

Strikeouts/Game
Rusie-NY ... 3.88
Meekin-Was ... 3.34
Hawley-StL ... 2.89
Terry-Pit ... 2.75
Hawke-StL-Bal ... 2.74

Wins Above Team
Young-Cle ... 9.0
Rusie-NY ... 8.0
Killen-Pit ... 7.3
McMahon-Bal ... 5.1
Nichols-Bos ... 4.4

Earned Run Average
Breitenstein-StL ... 3.20
Rusie-NY ... 3.23
Young-Cle ... 3.36
Ehret-Pit ... 3.44
Clarkson-StL ... 3.48

Adjusted ERA
Rusie-NY ... 149
Breitenstein-StL ... 146
Young-Cle ... 143
Ehret-Pit ... 142
Killen-Pit ... 134

Opponents' Batting Avg.
Rusie-NY ... .240
Breitenstein-StL ... .241
Killen-Pit ... .246
Kennedy-Bro ... .249
Stein-Bro ... .250

Opponents' On Base Pct.
Nichols-Bos ... .302
Young-Cle ... .304
Killen-Pit ... .306
Breitenstein-StL ... .313
Stein-Bro ... .319

Starter Runs
Rusie-NY ... 77.6
Breitenstein-StL ... 63.1
Young-Cle ... 61.9
Nichols-Bos ... 54.9
Killen-Pit ... 47.7

Adjusted Starter Runs
Rusie-NY ... 84.6
Young-Cle ... 67.8
Breitenstein-StL ... 62.9
Killen-Pit ... 57.6
Nichols-Bos ... 56.5

Clutch Pitching Index
Esper-Was ... 118
Clarkson-StL ... 112
McNabb-Bal ... 110
Rusie-NY ... 108
Dwyer-Cin ... 108

Relief Runs

Adjusted Relief Runs

Relief Ranking

Total Pitcher Index
Rusie-NY ... 8.1
Killen-Pit ... 6.4
Young-Cle ... 6.0
Breitenstein-StL ... 5.3
Nichols-Bos ... 4.8

Total Baseball Ranking
Rusie-NY ... 8.1
Killen-Pit ... 6.4
Delahanty-Phi ... 6.2
Young-Cle ... 6.0
Breitenstein-StL ... 5.3

TEAM	G	W	L	PCT	GB	R	OR	AB	H	2B	3B	HR	BB	SO	AVG	OBP	SLG	PRO	/A	BR	/A	PF	CHI	RC	TA	SB	CS	SBA	SBR
BAL	129	89	39	.695		1171	820	4799	1647	271	150	33	516	200	.343	.418	.483	.901	123	188	194	99	98	1131	1.033	324			
NY	137	88	44	.667	3	940	789	4806	1446	197	96	43	476	217	.301	.368	.409	.777	93	-51	-47	100	101	860	.831	241			
BOS	133	83	49	.629	8	1222	1002	5011	1658	272	93	103	535	261	.331	.401	.484	.885	119	150	15	113	103	1094	.969	241			
PHI	131	71	57	.555	18	1143	966	4967	1732	252	131	40	496	245	.349	.414	.476	.890	121	172	221	95	96	1120	.987	273			
BRO	134	70	61	.534	20.5	1021	1007	4816	1507	228	130	42	466	294	.313	.378	.440	.818	103	20	75	94	102	930	.877	282			
CLE	130	68	61	.527	21.5	932	947	4764	1442	241	90	37	471	301	.303	.368	.414	.782	94	-40	-145	111	100	828	.809	220			
PIT	132	65	65	.500	25	955	972	4676	1458	222	124	48	434	208	.312	.379	.443	.822	104	26	81	94	97	903	.879	256			
CHI	135	57	75	.432	34	1041	1066	4960	1555	265	86	65	496	298	.314	.380	.441	.821	103	28	-47	108	100	979	.895	327			
STL	133	56	76	.424	35	771	954	4610	1320	171	113	54	442	289	.286	.354	.408	.762	99	-84	-95	101	90	750	.775	190			
CIN	132	55	75	.423	35	910	1085	4671	1374	224	67	61	508	252	.294	.368	.410	.778	93	-45	-44	100	99	804	.813	215			
WAS	132	45	87	.341	46	882	1122	4581	1317	218	118	59	617	375	.287	.381	.425	.806	100	9	30	98	90	857	.884	249			
LOU	130	36	94	.277	54	692	1001	4482	1206	173	88	42	350	364	.269	.330	.375	.705	75	-183	-76	88	96	641	.703	217			
TOT	794					11680		57143	17662	2734	1286	627	5807	3304	.309	.373	.435	.808								3113			

TEAM	CG	SHO	SV	IP	H	H/G	HR	BB	BB/G	SO	SO/G	ERA	/A	OAVG	OOBA	PR	/A	PF	CPI	FA	E	DP	FW	PW	BW	SBW	DIF
BAL	97	1	11	1116.3	1371	11.1	32	472	3.8	275	2.2	5.01	102	.299	.364	39	15	96	95	.944	293	105	6.1	1.2	14.9		2.9
NY	111	5	5	1212.0	1292	9.6	37	539	4.0	395	2.9	3.83	137	.270	.344	202	190	98	105	.924	443	101	-2.4	14.6	-3.6		13.4
BOS	108	3	1	1166.0	1529	11.8	89	411	3.2	262	2.0	5.42	109	.313	.366	-10	66	111	99	.925	415	120	-.8	5.1	1.2		11.6
PHI	102	3	4	1125.7	1482	11.8	62	469	3.7	262	2.1	5.64	88	.314	.376	-38	-81	94	96	.935	338	111	3.5	-6.2	16.9		-7.3
BRO	105	3	5	1162.3	1447	11.2	41	555	4.3	285	2.2	5.52	91	.302	.374	-24	-64	94	92	.928	390	85	.6	-4.9	5.8		3.1
CLE	107	6	1	1124.3	1390	11.1	53	435	3.5	254	2.0	4.99	118	.300	.360	43	113	111	98	.935	344	107	3.2	8.7	-11.1		2.8
PIT	106	2	0	1164.7	1552	12.0	39	457	3.5	304	2.3	5.68	89	.316	.374	-44	-82	95	93	.936	354	106	2.6	-6.3	6.2		-2.5
CHI	117	0	0	1148.0	1561	12.2	43	557	4.4	281	2.2	5.69	101	.321	.390	-45	8	108	100	.918	452	113	-2.9	.6	-3.6		-3.1
STL	114	2	0	1161.0	1418	11.0	48	500	3.9	319	2.5	5.29	104	.298	.364	5	24	103	92	.923	426	109	-1.4	1.8	-7.3		-3.1
CIN	110	4	3	1147.3	1585	12.4	85	491	3.9	219	1.7	6.02	90	.324	.386	-87	-76	102	98	.925	423	119	-1.3	-5.8	-3.4		.5
WAS	102	1	4	1107.0	1573	12.8	59	446	3.6	190	1.5	5.53	96	.330	.388	-23	-25	100	107	.908	499	81	-5.6	-1.9	2.3		-15.8
LOU	113	2	1	1096.7	1462	12.0	39	475	3.9	258	2.1	5.46	88	.316	.380	-15	-76	91	99	.920	428	130	-1.6	-5.8	-5.8		-15.8
TOT	1292	32	35	13731.3		11.6			3.8		2.2	5.33		.309	.373					.927	4805	1287					

Runs		Hits		Doubles		Triples		Home Runs		Total Bases	
Hamilton-Phi	192	Duffy-Bos	237	Duffy-Bos	51	Reitz-Bal	31	Duffy-Bos	18	Duffy-Bos	372
Kelley-Bal	165	Hamilton-Phi	220	Kelley-Bal	48	Thompson-Phi	27	Lowe-Bos	17	Lowe-Bos	319
Keeler-Bal	165	Keeler-Bal	219	Wilmot-Chi	45	Treadway-Bro	26	Joyce-Was	17	Kelley-Bal	305
Duffy-Bos	161	Lowe-Bos	212			Connor-NY-StL	25	Dahlen-Chi	15	Keeler-Bal	305
Lowe-Bos	158	Brodie-Bal	210			Brouthers-Bal	23			Stenzel-Pit	303

Runs Batted In		Runs Produced		Bases On Balls		Batting Average		On Base Percentage		Slugging Average	
Duffy-Bos	145	Duffy-Bos	288	Hamilton-Phi	126	Duffy-Bos	.440	Hamilton-Phi	.523	Duffy-Bos	.690
Thompson-Phi	141	Hamilton-Phi	275	Kelley-Bal	107	Thompson-Phi	.407	Kelley-Bal	.502	Thompson-Phi	.686
Delahanty-Phi	131	Delahanty-Phi	274	Childs-Cle	107	Delahanty-Phi	.407	Duffy-Bos	.502	Joyce-Was	.648
Wilmot-Chi	130	Kelley-Bal	270	Nash-Bos	91	Hamilton-Phi	.404	Joyce-Was	.496	Kelley-Bal	.602
		Wilmot-Chi	259	McGraw-Bal	91	Kelley-Bal	.393	Delahanty-Phi	.478	Delahanty-Phi	.585

Production		Adjusted Production		Batter Runs		Adjusted Batter Runs		Clutch Hitting Index		Runs Created	
Duffy-Bos	1.192	Thompson-Phi	184	Duffy-Bos	76.6	Hamilton-Phi	67.6	Robinson-Bal	152	Duffy-Bos	216
Thompson-Phi	1.145	Joyce-Was	180	Kelley-Bal	61.8	Kelley-Bal	62.5	Shindle-Bro	137	Hamilton-Phi	206
Joyce-Was	1.143	Kelley-Bal	169	Hamilton-Phi	61.5	Duffy-Bos	62.0	Decker-Chi	136	Kelley-Bal	181
Kelley-Bal	1.104	Duffy-Bos	165	Thompson-Phi	50.6	Thompson-Phi	54.9	Ward-NY	136	Stenzel-Pit	165
Delahanty-Phi	1.063	Delahanty-Phi	165	Joyce-Was	48.3	Delahanty-Phi	52.7	Bierbauer-Pit	136	Thompson-Phi	152

Total Average		Stolen Bases		Stolen Base Average	Stolen Base Runs	Fielding Runs		Total Player Rating	
Duffy-Bos	1.613	Hamilton-Phi	98			Dahlen-Chi	32.2	Dahlen-Chi	4.8
Hamilton-Phi	1.605	McGraw-Bal	78			Jennings-Bal	31.5	Delahanty-Phi	4.7
Joyce-Was	1.528	Wilmot-Chi	74			McPhee-Cin	27.8	Hamilton-Phi	4.7
Kelley-Bal	1.503	Brown-Lou	66			Cross-Phi	23.8	Duffy-Bos	4.3
Thompson-Phi	1.409	Lange-Chi	65			Quinn-StL	20.9	Kelley-Bal	4.0

Wins		Win Percentage		Games		Complete Games		Shutouts		Saves	
Rusie-NY	36	Meekin-NY	.786	Breitenstein-StL	56	Breitenstein-StL	46	Rusie-NY	3	Mullane-Bal-Cle	4
Meekin-NY	33	McMahon-Bal	.758	Rusie-NY	54	Rusie-NY	45	Nichols-Bos	3	Mercer-Was	3
Nichols-Bos	32	Rusie-NY	.735	Hawley-StL	53	Young-Cle	44	Cuppy-Cle	3	Hawke-Bal	3
Stein-Bro	27	Nichols-Bos	.711	Young-Cle	52	Nichols-Bos	40				
Breitenstein-StL	27	Stein-Bro	.659	Meekin-NY	52	Meekin-NY	40				

Innings Pitched		Fewest Hits/Game		Fewest BB/Game		Strikeouts		Strikeouts/Game		Wins Above Team	
Breitenstein-StL	447	Rusie-NY	8.64	Young-Cle	2.33	Rusie-NY	195	Rusie-NY	3.95	Rusie-NY	9.4
Rusie-NY	444	Meekin-NY	8.89	Menefee-Lou-Pit	2.47	Breitenstein-StL	140	Hawke-Bal	2.99	Breitenstein-StL	7.2
Young-Cle	409	Stein-Bro	9.93	Gleason-StL-Bal	2.54	Meekin-NY	133	Wadsworth-Lou	2.97	Rusie-NY	7.1
Meekin-NY	409	Breitenstein-StL	10.01	Staley-Bos	2.63	Hawley-StL	120	Meekin-NY	2.93	Stein-Bro	7.1
Nichols-Bos	407	Clarkson-Cle	10.31	Nichols-Bos	2.68	Nichols-Bos	113	Chamberlin-Cin	2.88	Nichols-Bos	6.8

Earned Run Average		Adjusted ERA		Opponents' Batting Avg.		Opponents' On Base Pct.		Starter Runs		Adjusted Starter Runs	
Rusie-NY	2.78	Rusie-NY	189	Rusie-NY	.250	Meekin-NY	.328	Rusie-NY	126.1	Rusie-NY	121.7
Meekin-NY	3.70	Young-Cle	150	Meekin-NY	.256	Rusie-NY	.329	Meekin-NY	74.4	Young-Cle	89.1
Mercer-Was	3.76	Meekin-NY	142	Stein-Bro	.277	Clarkson-Cle	.335	Young-Cle	63.4	Meekin-NY	70.3
Young-Cle	3.94	Mercer-Was	142	Breitenstein-StL	.279	Young-Cle	.336	Mercer-Was	58.4	Mercer-Was	57.8
Taylor-Phi	4.08	Clarkson-Cle	134	Clarkson-Cle	.285	Taylor-Phi	.341	Taylor-Phi	41.6	Nichols-Bos	53.2

Clutch Pitching Index		Relief Runs	Adjusted Relief Runs	Relief Ranking	Total Pitcher Index		Total Baseball Ranking	
Mercer-Was	133				Rusie-NY	11.1	Rusie-NY	11.1
Rusie-NY	124				Young-Cle	7.3	Young-Cle	7.3
Hemming-Lou-Bal	110				Meekin-NY	6.0	Meekin-NY	6.0
Terry-Pit-Chi	110				Mercer-Was	5.0	Mercer-Was	5.0
Killen-Pit	110				Nichols-Bos	4.8	Nichols-Bos	4.8

TEAM	G	W	L	PCT	GB	R	OR	AB	H	2B	3B	HR	BB	SO	AVG	OBP	SLG	PRO	/A	BR	/A	PF	CHI	RC	TA	SB	CS	SBA	SBR
BAL	132	87	43	.669		1009	646	4725	1530	235	89	25	355	243	.324	.384	.427	.811	115	109	47	107	102	916	.873	310			
CLE	131	84	46	.646	3	917	720	4658	1423	194	67	29	472	361	.305	.375	.395	.770	105	43	71	97	100	779	.787	187			
PHI	133	78	53	.595	9.5	1068	957	5037	1664	272	73	61	463	262	.330	.394	.450	.844	124	178	188	99	95	1027	.911	276			
CHI	133	72	58	.554	15	866	854	4708	1401	171	85	55	422	344	.298	.361	.405	.766	103	23	-4	103	97	801	.796	260			
BRO	133	71	60	.542	16.5	867	834	4717	1330	189	77	39	397	318	.282	.346	.379	.725	92	-48	4	94	105	699	.718	183			
BOS	132	71	60	.542	16.5	907	826	4715	1369	197	57	54	500	236	.290	.365	.391	.756	95	13	-11	103	100	763	.775	199			
PIT	134	71	61	.538	17	811	787	4645	1349	190	89	26	376	299	.290	.352	.386	.738	96	-23	6	97	97	740	.756	257			
CIN	132	66	64	.508	21	903	854	4684	1395	235	106	36	414	249	.298	.359	.416	.775	105	36	-29	108	100	838	.829	326			
NY	132	66	65	.504	21.5	852	834	4605	1324	191	90	32	454	292	.288	.355	.389	.744	97	-11	35	95	100	759	.782	292			
WAS	132	43	85	.336	43	837	1048	4577	1314	207	101	55	518	396	.287	.366	.412	.778	106	48	20	103	91	797	.826	237			
STL	135	39	92	.298	48.5	747	1032	4781	1344	155	87	38	384	279	.281	.338	.374	.712	89	-76	-73	100	93	690	.699	205			
LOU	133	35	96	.267	52.5	698	1090	4724	1320	171	73	34	346	323	.279	.339	.368	.707	88	-81	-38	95	88	658	.681	156			
TOT	796					10482		56576	16763	2407	994	484	5101	3602	.296	.354	.400	.754								2888			

TEAM	CG	SHO	SV	IP	H	H/G	HR	BB	BB/G	SO	SO/G	ERA	/A	OAVG	OOBA	PR	/A	PF	CPI	FA	E	DP	FW	PW	BW	SBW	DIF
BAL	104	10	4	1134.3	1216	9.6	31	430	3.4	244	1.9	3.81	130	.270	.333	123	146	104	102	.946	288	108	5.3	11.8	3.8		1.0
CLE	108	6	3	1143.7	1272	10.0	33	346	2.7	326	2.6	3.91	116	.277	.328	111	78	95	99	.936	348	77	2.0	6.3	5.8		4.9
PHI	106	2	7	1161.0	1467	11.4	36	485	3.8	330	2.6	5.47	86	.303	.367	-87	-99	98	91	.933	369	93	.8	-8.0	15.2		4.5
CHI	119	3	1	1150.7	1422	11.1	38	432	3.4	297	2.3	4.67	106	.299	.357	15	34	103	101	.928	401	113	-1.0	2.8	-.5		5.5
BRO	103	5	6	1150.7	1360	10.6	41	395	3.1	216	1.7	4.96	90	.289	.345	-21	-61	94	89	.941	325	96	3.3	-4.9	.3		6.8
BOS	115	4	4	1175.3	1364	10.4	56	363	2.8	370	2.8	4.27	114	.286	.336	67	80	102	100	.934	364	104	1.1	6.5	-.9		-1.2
PIT	106	4	6	1171.7	1263	9.7	17	500	3.8	382	2.9	4.08	113	.271	.342	92	68	96	97	.930	392	95	-.5	5.5	.5		-.5
CIN	97	2	6	1147.3	1451	11.4	39	362	2.8	245	1.9	4.82	107	.304	.353	-3	41	107	98	.931	377	112	.4	3.3	-2.3		-.4
NY	115	6	1	1147.3	1359	10.7	34	415	3.3	409	3.2	4.53	100	.290	.348	32	-1	94	97	.922	438	106	-3.0	-.0	2.8		.8
WAS	99	0	5	1101.7	1507	12.3	55	465	3.8	258	2.1	5.29	95	.320	.382	-61	-29	105	107	.917	447	96	-3.5	-2.3	1.6		-16.8
STL	105	1	1	1152.3	1562	12.2	64	439	3.4	280	2.2	5.80	85	.318	.374	-128	-113	102	95	.930	380	104	.2	-9.2	-5.9		-11.6
LOU	104	3	1	1117.3	1520	12.2	40	470	3.8	245	2.0	5.93	80	.319	.380	-141	-149	99	93	.913	477	104	-5.2	-12.1	-3.1		-10.2
TOT	1281	46	45	13753.3		11.0			3.3		2.4	4.79		.296	.354					.930	4606	1198					

Runs		Hits		Doubles		Triples		Home Runs		Total Bases	
Hamilton-Phi	166	Burkett-Cle	225	Delahanty-Phi	49	Selbach-Was	22	Thompson-Phi	18	Thompson-Phi	352
Keeler-Bal	162	Keeler-Bal	213	Thompson-Phi	45	Tiernan-NY	21	Joyce-Was	17	Delahanty-Phi	296
Jennings-Bal	159	Thompson-Phi	211	Jennings-Bal	41	Thompson-Phi	21	Clements-Phi	13	Burkett-Cle	288
Burkett-Cle	153	Jennings-Bal	204	Stenzel-Pit	38	Cooley-StL	20	Delahanty-Phi	11	McKean-Cle	283
Delahanty-Phi	149	Hamilton-Phi	201	Griffin-Bro	38					Kelley-Bal	283

Runs Batted In		Runs Produced		Bases On Balls		Batting Average		On Base Percentage		Slugging Average	
Thompson-Phi	165	Jennings-Bal	280	Joyce-Was	96	Burkett-Cle	.409	Delahanty-Phi	.500	Thompson-Phi	.654
Kelley-Bal	134	Thompson-Phi	278	Hamilton-Phi	96	Delahanty-Phi	.404	Hamilton-Phi	.490	Delahanty-Phi	.617
Brodie-Bal	134	Kelley-Bal	272	Griffin-Bro	93	Thompson-Phi	.392	Burkett-Cle	.486	Lange-Chi	.575
Jennings-Bal	125	Delahanty-Phi	244	Delahanty-Phi	86	Lange-Chi	.389	McGraw-Bal	.459	Kelley-Bal	.546
McKean-Cle	119	McKean-Cle	242	Kelley-Bal	77	Hamilton-Phi	.389	Lange-Chi	.456	Stenzel-Pit	.539

Production		Adjusted Production		Batter Runs		Adjusted Batter Runs		Clutch Hitting Index		Runs Created	
Delahanty-Phi	1.117	Delahanty-Phi	192	Delahanty-Phi	67.9	Delahanty-Phi	69.0	Brodie-Bal	163	Hamilton-Phi	177
Thompson-Phi	1.085	Thompson-Phi	182	Thompson-Phi	58.7	Thompson-Phi	59.8	Cross-Phi	149	Delahanty-Phi	175
Lange-Chi	1.032	Burkett-Cle	168	Burkett-Cle	56.0	Burkett-Cle	59.5	Childs-Cle	136	Thompson-Phi	167
Burkett-Cle	1.009	Lange-Chi	162	Hamilton-Phi	51.3	Hamilton-Phi	52.5	McCarthy-Bos	135	Burkett-Cle	164
Kelley-Bal	1.003	Stenzel-Pit	161	Kelley-Bal	49.0	Stenzel-Pit	47.2	Nash-Bos	132	Lange-Chi	160

Total Average		Stolen Bases		Stolen Base Average		Stolen Base Runs		Fielding Runs		Total Player Rating	
Delahanty-Phi	1.517	Hamilton-Phi	97					Jennings-Bal	30.4	Jennings-Bal	5.8
Hamilton-Phi	1.443	Lange-Chi	67					Dahlen-Chi	29.1	Delahanty-Phi	5.5
Lange-Chi	1.373	McGraw-Bal	61					Fuller-NY	28.8	Thompson-Phi	4.8
Kelley-Bal	1.289	Kelley-Bal	54					Cross-Phi	28.3	McGuire-Was	3.9
Thompson-Phi	1.269							McGuire-Was	22.9	Lange-Chi	3.5

Wins		Win Percentage		Games		Complete Games		Shutouts		Saves	
Young-Cle	35	Hoffer-Bal	.838	Hawley-Pit	56	Breitenstein-StL	46	Young-Cle	4	Parrott-Cin	3
Hoffer-Bal	31	Young-Cle	.778	Breitenstein-StL	54	Hawley-Pit	44	Rusie-NY	4	Nichols-Bos	3
Hawley-Pit	31	Rhines-Cin	.655	Rusie-NY	49	Rusie-NY	42	McMahon-Bal	4	Beam-Phi	3
				Nichols-Bos	48	Nichols-Bos	42	Hoffer-Bal	4		
						Griffith-Chi	39	Hawley-Pit	4		

Innings Pitched		Fewest Hits/Game		Fewest BB/Game		Strikeouts		Strikeouts/Game		Wins Above Team	
Hawley-Pit	444	Foreman-Pit	8.42	Young-Cle	1.82	Rusie-NY	201	Rusie-NY	4.60	Hoffer-Bal	11.0
Breitenstein-StL	430	Hoffer-Bal	8.48	Clark-NY	1.91	Hawley-Pit	142	McGill-Phi	4.32	Young-Cle	10.7
Rusie-NY	393	Rusie-NY	8.79	Nichols-Bos	2.04	Nichols-Bos	140	Foreman-Pit	3.47	Griffith-Chi	5.7
Nichols-Bos	380	Young-Cle	8.83	Staley-StL	2.21	Breitenstein-StL	127	Stivetts-Bos	3.43	Rhines-Cin	5.1
Young-Cle	370	Maul-Was	9.00	Taylor-Phi	2.23	Young-Cle	121	Nichols-Bos	3.32	Nichols-Bos	4.8

Earned Run Average		Adjusted ERA		Opponents' Batting Avg.		Opponents' On Base Pct.		Starter Runs		Adjusted Starter Runs	
Maul-Was	2.45	Maul-Was	206	Foreman-Pit	.244	Young-Cle	.290	Hawley-Pit	79.3	Hawley-Pit	70.4
Hawley-Pit	3.18	Hoffer-Bal	155	Hoffer-Bal	.246	Maul-Was	.305	Young-Cle	64.0	Nichols-Bos	62.5
Hoffer-Bal	3.21	Hawley-Pit	145	Rusie-NY	.252	Hawley-Pit	.308	Nichols-Bos	58.3	Hoffer-Bal	61.3
Foreman-Pit	3.21	Nichols-Bos	143	Young-Cle	.253	Nichols-Bos	.314	Hoffer-Bal	55.1	Young-Cle	53.3
Young-Cle	3.24	Foreman-Pit	143	Maul-Was	.257	Hoffer-Bal	.316	Cuppy-Cle	48.9	Griffith-Chi	39.7

Clutch Pitching Index		Relief Runs		Adjusted Relief Runs		Relief Ranking		Total Pitcher Index		Total Baseball Ranking	
Maul-Was	135							Hawley-Pit	7.3	Hawley-Pit	7.3
Mercer-Was	122							Nichols-Bos	5.2	Jennings-Bal	5.8
Clark-NY	117							Young-Cle	5.0	Delahanty-Phi	5.5
Foreman-Cin	112							Hoffer-Bal	4.8	Nichols-Bos	5.2
Griffith-Chi	111							Cuppy-Cle	4.4	Young-Cle	5.0

TEAM	G	W	L	PCT	GB	R	OR	AB	H	2B	3B	HR	BB	SO	AVG	OBP	SLG	PRO	/A	BR	/A	PF	CHI	RC	TA	SB	CS	SBA	SBR
BAL	132	90	39	.698		995	662	4719	1548	207	100	23	386	201	.328	.393	.429	.822	124	167	150	102	101	993	.937	441			
CLE	135	80	48	.625	9.5	840	650	4856	1463	207	72	28	436	316	.301	.363	.391	.754	105	43	-37	110	95	772	.750	175			
CIN	128	77	50	.606	12	783	620	4360	1283	205	73	20	382	226	.294	.357	.389	.746	103	22	-14	105	101	748	.802	350			
BOS	132	74	57	.565	17	860	761	4717	1416	175	74	36	414	274	.300	.363	.392	.755	106	43	-19	108	100	777	.773	241			
CHI	132	71	57	.555	18.5	815	799	4582	1311	182	97	34	409	290	.286	.349	.390	.739	101	10	-55	108	102	759	.784	332			
PIT	131	66	63	.512	24	787	741	4701	1371	169	94	27	387	286	.292	.353	.385	.738	101	9	63	93	96	733	.742	217			
NY	133	64	67	.489	27	829	821	4661	1383	159	87	40	439	271	.297	.364	.394	.758	107	49	60	99	96	787	.794	274			
PHI	131	62	68	.477	28.5	890	891	4680	1382	234	84	49	438	297	.295	.363	.413	.776	111	74	58	102	100	790	.794	191			
WAS	133	58	73	.443	33	818	920	4639	1328	179	79	45	516	365	.286	.365	.388	.753	105	46	85	95	94	770	.796	258			
BRO	133	58	73	.443	33	692	764	4548	1292	174	87	28	344	269	.284	.340	.379	.719	96	-27	70	87	92	669	.708	198			
STL	131	40	90	.308	50.5	593	929	4520	1162	134	78	37	332	300	.257	.313	.346	.659	79	-131	-92	95	93	561	.630	185			
LOU	133	38	93	.290	53	653	997	4588	1197	142	80	37	371	427	.261	.322	.351	.673	83	-105	-89	98	96	596	.655	195			
TOT	792					9555		55571	16136	2167	1005	404	4854	3522	.290	.347	.387	.735								3057			

TEAM	CG	SHO	SV	IP	H	H/G	HR	BB	BB/G	SO	SO/G	ERA	/A	OAVG	OOBA	PR	/A	PF	CPI	FA	E	DP	FW	PW	BW	SBW	DIF
BAL	115	9	1	1168.3	1281	9.9	22	339	2.6	302	2.3	3.69	117	.276	.326	87	79	99	98	.945	296	114	2.6	6.7	12.7		3.4
CLE	113	9	5	1195.7	1363	10.3	27	280	2.1	336	2.5	3.46	136	.284	.324	120	164	108	107	.949	288	117	3.1	13.9	-3.1		2.1
CIN	105	12	4	1108.0	1240	10.1	27	310	2.5	219	1.8	3.68	122	.280	.328	84	101	103	101	.951	252	107	5.3	8.6	-1.2		.8
BOS	110	6	3	1155.7	1254	9.8	57	397	3.1	277	2.2	3.78	123	.274	.332	74	112	107	104	.934	368	94	-1.7	9.5	-1.6		2.3
CHI	118	2	1	1161.0	1302	10.1	30	467	3.6	353	2.7	4.43	107	.281	.347	-8	37	108	92	.934	366	115	-1.6	3.1	-4.7		10.1
PIT	108	8	1	1159.3	1286	10.0	18	439	3.4	362	2.8	4.31	94	.279	.341	7	-33	93	90	.942	317	103	1.4	-2.8	5.3		-2.4
NY	104	1	2	1136.7	1303	10.3	33	403	3.2	312	2.5	4.56	94	.285	.343	-24	-32	99	90	.933	365	90	-1.5	-2.7	5.1		-2.4
PHI	107	3	3	1117.0	1473	11.9	39	387	3.1	243	2.0	5.21	86	.315	.367	-105	-93	102	96	.941	313	112	1.6	-7.9	4.9		-1.6
WAS	106	2	3	1136.7	1435	11.4	24	435	3.4	292	2.3	4.62	91	.305	.364	-31	-53	96	102	.928	398	94	-3.5	-4.5	7.2		-6.7
BRO	97	3	1	1144.0	1353	10.6	40	400	3.1	259	2.0	4.26	90	.292	.348	14	-52	88	102	.945	297	104	2.6	-4.4	5.9		-11.6
STL	115	1	1	1130.7	1448	11.5	40	456	3.6	279	2.2	5.33	80	.308	.370	-121	-130	98	93	.937	345	73	-.3	-11.0	-7.8		-5.9
LOU	108	1	4	1148.7	1398	11.0	47	541	4.2	288	2.3	5.13	86	.298	.370	-97	-88	102	95	.916	475	110	-8.1	-7.5	-7.6		-4.4
TOT	1306	57	28	13761.7		10.6			3.2		2.3	4.37		.290	.347					.938	4080	1238					

Runs
Burkett-Cle 160
Keeler-Bal 153
Hamilton-Bos 152
Kelley-Bal 148
Dahlen-Chi 137

Hits
Burkett-Cle 240
Keeler-Bal 210
Jennings-Bal 209
Delahanty-Phi 198
VanHaltren-NY 197

Doubles
Delahanty-Phi 44
Miller-Cin 38
Kelley-Bal 31
Dahlen-Chi 30

Triples
VanHaltren-NY 21
McCreery-Lou 21
Kelley-Bal 19
Dahlen-Chi 19
Clarke-Lou 18

Home Runs
Joyce-Was-NY 14
Delahanty-Phi 13
Thompson-Phi 12
Connor-StL 11

Total Bases
Burkett-Cle 317
Delahanty-Phi 315
Kelley-Bal 282
VanHaltren-NY 272
Keeler-Bal 270

Runs Batted In
Delahanty-Phi 126
Jennings-Bal 121
McKean-Cle 112
Duffy-Bos 112

Runs Produced
Jennings-Bal 246
Delahanty-Phi 244
Kelley-Bal 240
Keeler-Bal 231
Burkett-Cle 226

Bases On Balls
Hamilton-Bos 110
Joyce-Was-NY 101
Childs-Cle 100
Kelley-Bal 91
Tiernan-NY 77

Batting Average
Burkett-Cle 410
Jennings-Bal 401
Delahanty-Phi 397
Keeler-Bal 386
Tiernan-NY 369

On Base Percentage
Hamilton-Bos 477
Jennings-Bal 472
Delahanty-Phi 472
Joyce-Was-NY 470
Kelley-Bal 469

Slugging Average
Delahanty-Phi 631
Dahlen-Chi 553
McCreery-Lou 546
Kelley-Bal 543
Burkett-Cle 541

Production
Delahanty-Phi 1.103
Kelley-Bal 1.013
Burkett-Cle 1.002
Joyce-Was-NY 994
Dahlen-Chi 990

Adjusted Production
Delahanty-Phi 188
Joyce-Was-NY 170
Smith-Pit 167
Kelley-Bal 166
Tiernan-NY 159

Batter Runs
Delahanty-Phi 66.3
Kelley-Bal 56.4
Burkett-Cle 56.3
Joyce-Was-NY 51.0
Hamilton-Bos 46.5

Adjusted Batter Runs
Delahanty-Phi 64.6
Kelley-Bal 54.4
Joyce-Was-NY 54.4
Smith-Pit 48.1
Tiernan-NY 47.0

Clutch Hitting Index
Reitz-Bal 176
Anson-Chi 165
McPhee-Cin 156
Duffy-Bos 155
Cross-Phi 150

Runs Created
Kelley-Bal 178
Delahanty-Phi 170
Burkett-Cle 166
Hamilton-Bos 159
Jennings-Bal 157

Total Average
Kelley-Bal 1.430
Delahanty-Phi 1.405
Hamilton-Bos 1.316
Joyce-Was-NY . . . 1.315
Jennings-Bal 1.263

Stolen Bases
Kelley-Bal 87
Lange-Chi 84
Hamilton-Bos 83
Miller-Cin 76
Doyle-Bal 73

Stolen Base Average

Stolen Base Runs

Fielding Runs
Childs-Cle 41.9
Jennings-Bal 30.2
Lowe-Bos 22.7
Dahlen-Chi 21.3
Corcoran-Bro 20.4

Total Player Rating
Childs-Cle 6.2
Jennings-Bal 6.2
Delahanty-Phi 6.1
Dahlen-Chi 4.8
Joyce-Was-NY 4.5

Wins
Nichols-Bos 30
Killen-Pit 30
Young-Cle 28
Meekin-NY 26

Win Percentage
Hoffer-Bal 781
Hemming-Bal 714
Foreman-Cin 714
Dwyer-Cin 686
Nichols-Bos 682

Games
Killen-Pit 52
Young-Cle 51
Nichols-Bos 49
Hawley-Pit 49
Clark-NY 48

Complete Games
Killen-Pit 44
Young-Cle 42
Mercer-Was 38

Shutouts
Young-Cle 5
Killen-Pit 5

Saves
Young-Cle 3
Hill-Lou 2
Fisher-Cin 2

Innings Pitched
Killen-Pit 432
Young-Cle 414
Hawley-Pit 378
Nichols-Bos 372
Mercer-Was 366

Fewest Hits/Game
Rhines-Cin 8.06
Hawley-Pit 9.10
Sullivan-NY 9.15
Friend-Chi 9.22
Hoffer-Bal 9.23

Fewest BB/Game
Young-Cle 1.35
Clark-NY 1.54
Dwyer-Cin 1.87
Cuppy-Cle 1.89
Griffith-Chi 1.98

Strikeouts
Young-Cle 140
Hawley-Pit 137
Killen-Pit 134
Breitenstein-StL 114
Meekin-NY 110

Strikeouts/Game
Briggs-Chi 3.90
Pond-Bal 3.36
McJames-Was 3.31
Hawley-Pit 3.26
Young-Cle 3.04

Wins Above Team
Meekin-NY 8.0
Nichols-Bos 7.8
Killen-Pit 7.8
Mercer-Was 7.1
Griffith-Chi 5.8

Earned Run Average
Rhines-Cin 2.45
Nichols-Bos 2.83
Cuppy-Cle 3.12
Dwyer-Cin 3.15
Young-Cle 3.24

Adjusted ERA
Rhines-Cin 184
Nichols-Bos 165
Cuppy-Cle 151
Young-Cle 145
Dwyer-Cin 143

Opponents' Batting Avg.
Rhines-Cin 238
Hawley-Pit 261
Sullivan-NY 262
Friend-Chi 263
Hoffer-Bal 264

Opponents' On Base Pct.
Rhines-Cin 300
Cuppy-Cle 311
Young-Cle 312
Nichols-Bos 314
Dwyer-Cin 315

Starter Runs
Nichols-Bos 63.5
Young-Cle 51.9
Cuppy-Cle 49.7
Killen-Pit 45.6
Dwyer-Cin 39.2

Adjusted Starter Runs
Nichols-Bos 75.8
Young-Cle 67.3
Cuppy-Cle 63.1
Dwyer-Cin 43.7
Griffith-Chi 41.9

Clutch Pitching Index
Nichols-Bos 121
Wallace-Cle 119
Payne-Bro 113
Dwyer-Cin 112
Mercer-Was 109

Relief Runs

Adjusted Relief Runs

Relief Ranking

Total Pitcher Index
Young-Cle 7.7
Cuppy-Cle 6.8
Nichols-Bos 6.8
Griffith-Chi 4.2
Dwyer-Cin 4.2

Total Baseball Ranking
Young-Cle 7.7
Cuppy-Cle 6.8
Nichols-Bos 6.8
Childs-Cle 6.2
Jennings-Bal 6.2

TEAM	G	W	L	PCT	GB	R	OR	AB	H	2B	3B	HR	BB	SO	AVG	OBP	SLG	PRO	/A	BR	/A	PF	CHI	RC	TA	SB	CS	SBA	SBR
BOS	135	93	39	.705		1025	665	4937	1574	230	83	45	423	262	.319	.378	.426	.804	119	137	78	107	105	906	.835	233			
BAL	136	90	40	.692	2	964	674	4872	1584	243	66	20	437	256	.325	.394	.414	.808	121	158	199	95	97	977	.904	401			
NY	137	83	48	.634	9.5	895	695	4844	1449	188	84	31	404	201	.290	.352	.392	.753	106	44	57	98	104	824	.794	328			
CIN	134	76	56	.576	17	763	705	4524	1311	219	69	22	380	218	.290	.352	.383	.735	101	10	-44	107	98	696	.736	194			
CLE	132	69	62	.527	23.5	773	680	4604	1374	192	88	16	435	344	.298	.364	.389	.753	106	44	-38	111	93	735	.757	181			
WAS	135	61	71	.462	32	781	793	4636	1376	194	77	36	374	348	.297	.357	.395	.752	105	37	26	101	95	746	.758	208			
BRO	136	61	71	.462	32	802	845	4810	1343	202	72	22	351	255	.279	.335	.365	.700	91	-56	-68	102	107	667	.677	187			
PIT	135	60	71	.458	32.5	676	835	4590	1266	140	108	25	359	334	.276	.337	.370	.707	93	-43	-29	98	93	644	.688	170			
CHI	138	59	73	.447	34	832	894	4803	1356	189	97	38	430	317	.282	.347	.386	.733	100	3	2	100	102	754	.753	264			
PHI	134	55	77	.417	38	752	792	4756	1392	213	83	40	399	299	.293	.352	.398	.750	105	31	65	96	90	742	.741	163			
LOU	134	52	78	.400	40	669	859	4520	1197	160	70	40	370	453	.265	.329	.358	.687	88	-74	-38	95	97	612	.676	195			
STL	132	29	102	.221	63.5	588	1083	4642	1277	149	67	31	354	314	.275	.336	.356	.692	89	-64	-12	93	82	629	.669	172			
TOT	809					9520		56538	16499	2319	964	366	4716	3727	.292	.346	.386	.733								2696			

TEAM	CG	SHO	SV	IP	H	H/G	HR	BB	BB/G	SO	SO/G	ERA	/A	OAVG	OOBA	PR	/A	PF	CPI	FA	E	DP	FW	PW	BW	SBW	DIF
BOS	115	8	7	1194.3	1273	9.6	39	393	3.0	329	2.5	3.66	122	.271	.327	86	106	103	99	.951	272	80	3.8	9.1	6.7		7.5
BAL	118	3	0	1197.7	1296	9.7	18	382	2.9	361	2.7	3.56	111	.274	.328	100	54	92	99	.951	277	110	3.5	4.6	17.0		-.1
NY	118	8	3	1187.3	1214	9.2	26	456	3.7	456	3.5	3.48	120	.262	.333	110	89	96	102	.930	397	109	-3.7	7.6	4.9		8.7
CIN	100	4	2	1156.7	1375	10.7	18	329	2.6	270	2.1	4.09	113	.293	.339	29	66	107	97	.949	273	100	3.7	5.7	-3.8		4.4
CLE	111	6	0	1119.3	1297	10.4	32	289	2.3	277	2.2	3.96	120	.287	.330	44	96	110	98	.950	261	74	4.4	8.2	-3.3		-5.9
WAS	103	7	5	1148.0	1383	10.8	27	400	3.1	348	2.7	4.02	109	.295	.351	37	45	102	107	.933	369	103	-2.1	3.9	2.2		-9.0
BRO	114	4	2	1194.7	1417	10.7	34	410	3.1	256	1.9	4.62	95	.292	.347	-39	-27	102	92	.936	364	99	-1.8	-2.3	-5.8		4.9
PIT	112	2	2	1153.3	1397	10.9	22	318	2.5	342	2.7	4.67	92	.297	.341	-45	-46	100	88	.936	346	70	-.7	-3.9	-2.5		1.6
CHI	131	2	1	1197.0	1485	11.2	30	433	3.3	361	2.7	4.55	96	.302	.358	-30	-26	101	100	.932	393	111	-3.5	-2.2	.2		-1.4
PHI	115	4	2	1155.3	1415	11.0	28	364	2.8	253	2.0	4.61	90	.299	.349	-37	-59	96	93	.944	296	72	2.3	-5.1	5.6		-13.8
LOU	114	2	0	1138.0	1363	10.8	39	459	3.6	267	2.1	4.44	95	.294	.358	-15	-29	97	101	.929	395	84	-3.6	-2.5	-3.3		-3.6
STL	109	1	1	1127.3	1584	12.6	54	453	3.6	207	1.7	6.24	68	.328	.386	-240	-248	99	90	.933	375	84	-2.4	-21.2	-1.0		-11.8
TOT	1360	51	25	13969.0		10.6			3.0		2.4	4.32		.292	.346					.939	4018	1096					

Runs		Hits		Doubles		Triples		Home Runs		Total Bases	
Hamilton-Bos	152	Keeler-Bal	239	Stenzel-Bal	43	Davis-Pit	28	Duffy-Bos	11	Lajoie-Phi	310
Keeler-Bal	145	Clarke-Lou	202	Lajoie-Phi	40	Lajoie-Phi	23	Davis-NY	10	Keeler-Bal	307
Griffin-Bro	136	Delahanty-Phi	200	Delahanty-Phi	40	Wallace-Cle	21	Lajoie-Phi	9	Delahanty-Phi	285
Jones-Bro	134	Burkett-Cle	198	Wallace-Cle	33	Keeler-Bal	19	Beckley-NY -Cin	8	Clarke-Lou	276
Jennings-Bal	133	Lajoie-Phi	197	Ryan-Chi	33					Duffy-Bos	265

Runs Batted In		Runs Produced		Bases On Balls		Batting Average		On Base Percentage		Slugging Average	
Davis-NY	134	Duffy-Bos	248	Hamilton-Bos	105	Keeler-Bal	.424	McGraw-Bal	.471	Lajoie-Phi	.569
Collins-Bos	132	Davis-NY	236	McGraw-Bal	99	Clarke-Lou	.390	Burkett-Cle	.468	Keeler-Bal	.544
Duffy-Bos	129	Collins-Bos	229	Griffin-Bro	81	Burkett-Cle	.383	Keeler-Bal	.464	Delahanty-Phi	.538
Lajoie-Phi	127	Kelley-Bal	226	Selbach-Was	80	Delahanty-Phi	.377	Jennings-Bal	.463	Clarke-Lou	.533
Kelley-Bal	118	Lajoie-Phi	225	Joyce-NY	78	Kelley-Bal	.362	Hamilton-Bos	.461	Davis-NY	.509

Production		Adjusted Production		Batter Runs		Adjusted Batter Runs		Clutch Hitting Index		Runs Created	
Keeler-Bal	1.008	Keeler-Bal	177	Keeler-Bal	55.1	Keeler-Bal	59.7	Gleason-NY	163	Keeler-Bal	176
Clarke-Lou	.994	Clarke-Lou	173	Clarke-Lou	50.1	Clarke-Lou	54.4	Shindle-Bro	151	Clarke-Lou	157
Delahanty-Phi	.982	Delahanty-Phi	169	Delahanty-Phi	47.4	Delahanty-Phi	51.4	Lowe-Bos	147	Delahanty-Phi	142
Lajoie-Phi	.959	Lajoie-Phi	161	Burkett-Cle	44.0	Kelley-Bal	43.7	Collins-Bos	144	Davis-NY	137
Burkett-Cle	.944	Kelley-Bal	158	Kelley-Bal	39.2	Lajoie-Phi	41.6	Anson-Chi	143	Stenzel-Bal	137

Total Average		Stolen Bases		Stolen Base Average		Stolen Base Runs		Fielding Runs		Total Player Rating	
Keeler-Bal	1.271	Lange-Chi	73					Dahlen-Chi	27.7	Jennings-Bal	5.8
Clarke-Lou	1.269	Stenzel-Bal	69					Clingman-Lou	27.2	Davis-NY	4.6
Jennings-Bal	1.251	Hamilton-Bos	66					Jennings-Bal	26.4	Clarke-Lou	4.2
Hamilton-Bos	1.162	Davis-NY	65					Cross-StL	25.4	Delahanty-Phi	4.1
Kelley-Bal	1.143	Keeler-Bal	64					Collins-Bos	20.4	Keeler-Bal	4.0

Wins		Win Percentage		Games		Complete Games		Shutouts		Saves	
Nichols-Bos	31	Klobedanz-Bos	.788	Young-Cle	46	Killen-Pit	38	Mercer-Was	3	Nichols-Bos	3
Rusie-NY	28	Nops-Bal	.769	Nichols-Bos	46	Griffith-Chi	38	McJames-Was	3		
Klobedanz-Bos	26	Corbett-Bal	.750	Donahue-StL	46	Donahue-StL	38				
Corbett-Bal	24	Nichols-Bos	.738	Mercer-Was	45	Nichols-Bos	37				
Breitenstein-Cin	23	Rusie-NY	.737			Kennedy-Bro	36				

Innings Pitched		Fewest Hits/Game		Fewest BB/Game		Strikeouts		Strikeouts/Game		Wins Above Team	
Nichols-Bos	368	Seymour-NY	8.22	Young-Cle	1.32	McJames-Was	156	Seymour-NY	4.82	Rusie-NY	6.8
Donahue-StL	348	Rusie-NY	8.78	Tannehill-Pit	1.52	Seymour-NY	149	McJames-Was	4.33	Klobedanz-Bos	5.7
Griffith-Chi	344	Nichols-Bos	8.85	Nichols-Bos	1.66	Corbett-Bal	149	Corbett-Bal	4.28	Griffith-Chi	4.3
Kennedy-Bro	343	Hill-Lou	9.45	Cuppy-Cle	1.68	Rusie-NY	135	Rusie-NY	3.77	Breitenstein-Cin	4.3
Killen-Pit	337	Corbett-Bal	9.49	Killen-Pit	2.03	Nichols-Bos	127	Nichols-Bos	3.11	Nops-Bal	3.8

Earned Run Average		Adjusted ERA		Opponents' Batting Avg.		Opponents' On Base Pct.		Starter Runs		Adjusted Starter Runs	
Rusie-NY	2.54	Nichols-Bos	169	Seymour-NY	.242	Nichols-Bos	.290	Nichols-Bos	68.5	Nichols-Bos	74.5
Nichols-Bos	2.64	Rusie-NY	164	Rusie-NY	.254	Rusie-NY	.303	Rusie-NY	63.4	Rusie-NY	57.9
Nops-Bal	2.81	Powell-Cle	150	Nichols-Bos	.256	Cuppy-Cle	.306	Corbett-Bal	42.1	Mercer-Was	41.6
Corbett-Bal	3.11	Cuppy-Cle	149	Hill-Lou	.268	Nops-Bal	.312	Mercer-Was	39.2	Powell-Cle	39.4
Powell-Cle	3.16	Nops-Bal	141	Corbett-Bal	.269	Young-Cle	.314	Nops-Bal	37.0	Young-Cle	35.3

Clutch Pitching Index		Relief Runs		Adjusted Relief Runs		Relief Ranking		Total Pitcher Index		Total Baseball Ranking	
Mercer-Was	124							Nichols-Bos	7.3	Nichols-Bos	7.3
Nops-Bal	117							Rusie-NY	5.8	Rusie-NY	5.8
Rusie-NY	114							Mercer-Was	4.5	Jennings-Bal	5.8
Dwyer-Cin	113							Breitenstein-Cin	3.6	Davis-NY	4.6
McJames-Was	112							Powell-Cle	3.3	Mercer-Was	4.5

TEAM	G	W	L	PCT	GB	R	OR	AB	H	2B	3B	HR	BB	SO	AVG	OBP	SLG	PRO	/A	BR	/A	PF	CHI	RC	TA	SB	CS	SBA	SBR
BOS	152	102	47	.685		872	**614**	5276	1531	190	55	53	405	303	.290	.344	**.377**	.721	114	92	63	104	102	762	.693	172			
BAL	154	96	53	.644	6	**933**	623	5242	**1584**	154	77	12	519	316	.302	.381	.368	**.749**	123	177	154	103	96	852	.779	250			
CIN	157	92	60	.605	11.5	831	740	5334	1448	207	101	19	455	**300**	.271	.332	.359	.691	106	36	-24	108	102	707	.659	165			
CHI	152	85	65	.567	17.5	828	679	5219	1431	175	83	19	476	394	.274	.342	.350	.692	106	50	26	103	101	719	.684	220			
CLE	156	81	68	.544	21	730	683	5246	1379	162	56	18	**545**	306	.263	.337	.325	.662	97	0	34	96	93	622	.617	93			
PHI	150	78	71	.523	24	823	784	5118	1431	**238**	81	33	472	382	.280	.345	**.377**	.722	115	97	138	95	97	748	.712	182			
NY	157	77	73	.513	25.5	837	800	5349	1422	190	86	33	428	372	.266	.328	.352	.680	102	17	58	95	**105**	705	.660	214			
PIT	152	72	76	.486	29.5	634	694	5087	1313	140	88	14	336	343	.258	.312	.328	.640	90	-59	-40	98	94	568	.576	107			
LOU	154	70	81	.464	30	728	833	5193	1389	150	71	32	375	429	.267	.324	.342	.666	98	-9	17	96	98	668	.643	235			
BRO	149	54	91	.372	46	638	811	5126	1314	156	66	17	328	314	.256	.309	.322	.631	88	-74	-33	95	96	565	.571	130			
WAS	155	51	101	.336	52.5	704	939	5257	1423	177	81	35	370	386	.271	.327	.355	.682	103	17	2	102	90	692	.653	197			
STL	154	39	111	.260	63.5	571	929	5214	1290	149	55	13	383	402	.247	.309	.305	.614	83	-103	-146	106	87	536	.550	104			
TOT	921					9129		62661	16955	2088	900	298	5092	4247	.271	.325	.347	.672								2069			

TEAM	CG	SHO	SV	IP	H	H/G	HR	BB	BB/G	SO	SO/G	ERA	/A	OAVG	OOBA	PR	/A	PF	CPI	FA	E	DP	FW	PW	BW	SBW	DIF
BOS	127	9	7	1340.0	**1186**	8.0	37	470	3.2	432	2.9	2.98	122	**.236**	**.301**	93	99	101	93	.950	310	102	3.2	9.3	5.9		9.1
BAL	138	12	0	1323.0	1236	8.4	17	400	2.7	422	2.9	2.90	124	.245	**.301**	104	101	100	95	.947	326	105	2.3	9.4	14.4		-4.6
CIN	131	10	2	1385.3	1484	9.6	16	449	2.9	294	1.9	3.50	110	.272	.327	16	54	107	99	.950	325	128	2.4	5.0	-2.2		10.8
CHI	137	**13**	0	1342.7	1357	9.1	17	364	2.4	323	2.2	**2.83**	130	.260	.309	116	125	102	107	.936	412	**149**	-2.7	11.7	2.4		-1.4
CLE	**142**	9	0	1334.0	1429	9.6	26	**309**	2.1	339	2.3	3.20	107	.272	.312	59	31	95	102	**.952**	301	95	3.8	2.9	3.2		-3.3
PHI	129	10	0	1288.3	1440	10.1	23	399	2.8	325	2.3	3.72	91	.280	.332	-16	-47	94	100	.937	379	102	-.8	-4.4	12.9		-4.2
NY	141	9	1	1353.7	1359	9.0	21	587	3.9	**558**	3.7	3.44	99	.259	.334	25	-6	94	101	.932	447	113	-4.7	-.6	5.4		1.9
PIT	131	10	3	1323.7	1400	9.5	**14**	346	2.4	330	2.2	3.41	104	.269	.315	29	19	98	95	.946	340	105	1.5	1.8	-3.7		-1.5
LOU	137	4	0	1334.0	1457	9.8	33	470	3.2	271	1.8	4.25	83	.276	.335	-95	-108	98	88	.939	382	114	-1.0	-10.1	1.6		4.0
BRO	134	1	0	1298.7	1446	10.0	34	476	3.3	294	2.0	4.03	86	.279	.340	-60	-79	96	97	.947	334	125	1.8	-7.4	-3.1		-9.9
WAS	129	0	1	1307.0	1577	10.9	29	450	3.1	371	2.6	4.52	83	.296	.351	-133	-109	105	94	.929	443	119	-4.5	-10.2	.2		-10.5
STL	133	0	2	1324.3	1584	10.8	32	372	2.5	288	2.0	4.55	87	.294	.340	-138	-87	110	89	.939	388	97	-1.3	-8.1	-13.6		-12.9
TOT	1609	87	16	15954.7		9.6		2.9		2.4		3.61		.271	.325					.942	4387	1354					

Runs
McGraw-Bal 143
Jennings-Bal 135
VanHaltren-NY 129
Keeler-Bal 126
Cooley-Phi 123

Hits
Keeler-Bal 216
Burkett-Cle 213
VanHaltren-NY 204
Lajoie-Phi 197

Doubles
Lajoie-Phi 43
Delahanty-Phi 36
Dahlen-Chi 35
Collins-Bos 35
Ryan-Chi 32

Triples
Anderson-Was-Bro . . .22
Hoy-Lou 16
VanHaltren-NY 16

Home Runs
Collins-Bos 15
Wagner-Lou 10
Joyce-NY 10

Total Bases
Collins-Bos 286
Lajoie-Phi 280
VanHaltren-NY 270
Anderson-Was-Bro . . .257
Cooley-Phi 256

Runs Batted In
Lajoie-Phi 127
Collins-Bos 111
Kelley-Bal 110
Duffy-Bos 108
McGann-Bal 106

Runs Produced
Lajoie-Phi 234
Jennings-Bal 221
Delahanty-Phi 203
Collins-Bos 203
McGann-Bal 200

Bases On Balls
McGraw-Bal 112
Joyce-NY 88
Hamilton-Bos 87
Flick-Phi 86
Jennings-Bal 78

Batting Average
Keeler-Bal 385
Hamilton-Bos 369
McGraw-Bal 342
Smith-Cin 342
Burkett-Cle 341

On Base Percentage
Hamilton-Bos 480
McGraw-Bal 474
Jennings-Bal 451
Flick-Phi 424
Smith-Cin 423

Slugging Average
Anderson-Was-Bro . .494
Collins-Bos 479
Lajoie-Phi 461
Delahanty-Phi 454
Hamilton-Bos 453

Production
Hamilton-Bos 933
Delahanty-Phi 877
Flick-Phi 873
Jennings-Bal 872
McGraw-Bal 871

Adjusted Production
Hamilton-Bos 165
Delahanty-Phi 163
Flick-Phi 162
Jennings-Bal 149
McGraw-Bal 149

Batter Runs
McGraw-Bal 47.0
Jennings-Bal 45.2
Hamilton-Bos 45.1
Delahanty-Phi 41.3
Ryan-Chi 36.1

Adjusted Batter Runs
Delahanty-Phi 45.9
McGraw-Bal 44.5
Jennings-Bal 42.7
Hamilton-Bos 42.6
Flick-Phi 39.6

Clutch Hitting Index
Kelley-Bal 169
Hartman-NY 157
McGann-Bal 151
Duffy-Bos 147
Connor-Chi 147

Runs Created
Delahanty-Phi 133
McGraw-Bal 120
Hamilton-Bos 120
Ryan-Chi 118
Jennings-Bal 117

Total Average
Hamilton-Bos 1.262
McGraw-Bal 1.112
Delahanty-Phi 1.071
Jennings-Bal 1.039
Flick-Phi 1.019

Stolen Bases
Delahanty-Phi 58
Hamilton-Bos 54
DeMontrevil-Bal 49
Dexter-Lou 44
McGraw-Bal 43

Stolen Base Average

Stolen Base Runs

Fielding Runs
Davis-NY 32.9
Gleason-NY 20.3
Selbach-Was 17.6
Cross-StL 16.6
Wallace-Cle 15.9

Total Player Rating
Davis-NY 4.5
Jennings-Bal 4.5
Collins-Bos 4.3
Delahanty-Phi 3.7
Flick-Phi 3.5

Wins
Nichols-Bos 31
Cunningham-Lou 28
McJames-Bal 27
Hawley-Cin 27
Lewis-Bos 26

Win Percentage
Lewis-Bos 765
Maul-Bal 741
Nichols-Bos 721
Hawley-Cin 711
Griffith-Chi 706

Games
Taylor-StL 50
Nichols-Bos 50
Young-Cle 46

Complete Games
Taylor-StL 42
Cunningham-Lou 41
Young-Cle 40
Nichols-Bos 40
McJames-Bal 40

Shutouts
Powell-Cle 6
Piatt-Phi 6
Tannehill-Pit 5
Nichols-Bos 5
Hughes-Bal 5

Saves
Nichols-Bos 3
Tannehill-Pit 2
Lewis-Bos 2
Hickman-Bos 2
Damman-Cin 2

Innings Pitched
Taylor-StL 397
Nichols-Bos 388
Young-Cle 378
McJames-Bal 374
Cunningham-Lou 362

Fewest Hits/Game
Nichols-Bos 7.33
Willis-Bos 7.64
Lewis-Bos 7.68
Maul-Bal 7.76
McJames-Bal 7.87

Fewest BB/Game
Young-Cle 98
Dwyer-Cin 1.58
Cunningham-Lou . . . 1.62
Tannehill-Pit 1.73
Griffith-Chi 1.77

Strikeouts
Seymour-NY 239
McJames-Bal 178
Willis-Bos 160
Nichols-Bos 138
Piatt-Phi 121

Strikeouts/Game
Seymour-NY 6.03
Willis-Bos 4.63
McJames-Bal 4.28
Doheny-NY 4.06
Piatt-Phi 3.56

Wins Above Team
Cunningham-Lou . . . 9.2
Tannehill-Pit 7.7
Griffith-Chi 6.5
Hawley-Cin 6.2
Young-Cle 5.9

Earned Run Average
Griffith-Chi 1.88
Maul-Bal 2.10
Nichols-Bos 2.13
McJames-Bal 2.36
Callahan-Chi 2.46

Adjusted ERA
Griffith-Chi 195
Maul-Bal 171
Nichols-Bos 171
McJames-Bal 152
Callahan-Chi 149

Opponents' Batting Avg.
Nichols-Bos 221
Willis-Bos 229
Lewis-Bos 229
Maul-Bal 231
McJames-Bal 234

Opponents' On Base Pct.
Nichols-Bos 265
Maul-Bal 271
Griffith-Chi 283
Young-Cle 283
McJames-Bal 291

Starter Runs
Nichols-Bos 63.5
Griffith-Chi 62.6
McJames-Bal 51.9
Young-Cle 45.5
Maul-Bal 40.2

Adjusted Starter Runs
Nichols-Bos 65.0
Griffith-Chi 64.8
McJames-Bal 51.1
Maul-Bal 39.7
Young-Cle 37.6

Clutch Pitching Index
Griffith-Chi 127
Orth-Phi 118
Damman-Cin 115
Callahan-Chi 113
Doheny-NY 111

Relief Runs

Adjusted Relief Runs

Relief Ranking

Total Pitcher Index
Nichols-Bos 6.7
Griffith-Chi 6.7
Young-Cle 4.9
Callahan-Chi 4.4
McJames-Bal 4.4

Total Baseball Ranking
Nichols-Bos 6.7
Griffith-Chi 6.7
Young-Cle 4.9
Davis-NY 4.5
Jennings-Bal 4.5

TEAM	G	W	L	PCT	GB	R	OR	AB	H	2B	3B	HR	BB	SO	AVG	OBP	SLG	PRO	/A	BR	/A	PF	CHI	RC	TA	SB	CS	SBA	SBR
BRO	150	101	47	.682		892	658	4937	1436	178	97	26	477	263	.291	.362	.382	.744	112	91	55	105	103	800	.773	271			
BOS	153	95	57	.625	8	858	645	5290	1517	178	89	40	431	269	.287	.345	.377	.722	106	43	2	105	100	770	.702	185			
PHI	154	94	58	.618	9	916	743	5353	1613	241	84	30	441	341	.301	.361	.395	.756	116	114	138	108	93	861	.756	212			
BAL	152	86	62	.581	15	827	691	5073	1509	204	71	17	418	383	.297	.365	.376	.741	112	89	28	108	93	849	.788	364			
STL	155	84	67	.556	18.5	819	739	5304	1514	172	89	46	468	262	.285	.347	.377	.724	107	50	-13	108	94	787	.716	210			
CIN	156	83	67	.553	19	856	770	5225	1439	194	105	13	485	295	.275	.340	.360	.700	100	7	-39	106	104	736	.693	228			
PIT	154	76	73	.510	25.5	834	765	5450	1574	196	121	27	384	345	.289	.342	.384	.726	107	47	58	99	95	796	.699	179			
CHI	152	75	73	.507	26	812	763	5148	1428	173	82	27	406	342	.277	.337	.359	.696	99	-5	25	96	103	723	.687	247			
LOU	155	75	77	.493	28	827	775	5307	1484	192	68	40	436	375	.280	.342	.360	.706	101	-11	-11	99	98	759	.698	233			
NY	152	60	90	.400	42	734	863	5092	1431	161	65	23	387	360	.281	.336	.352	.688	96	-18	2	97	96	698	.669	234			
WAS	155	54	98	.355	49	743	983	5256	1429	162	87	47	350	341	.272	.327	.363	.690	97	-23	11	96	95	698	.656	176			
CLE	154	20	134	.130	84	529	1252	5279	1333	142	50	12	289	280	.253	.298	.305	.603	72	-187	-102	89	87	532	.528	127			
TOT	921					9647		62714	17707	2193	1008	348	4972	3856	.282	.335	.366	.701								2666			

TEAM	CG	SHO	SV	IP	H	H/G	HR	BB	BB/G	SO	SO/G	ERA	/A	OAVG	OOBA	PR	/A	PF	CPI	FA	E	DP	FW	PW	BW	SBW	DIF
BRO	121	9	9	1269.3	1320	9.4	32	463	3.3	331	2.3	3.25	121	.268	.330	84	97	102	108	.948	314	125	3.3	8.8	5.0		9.9
BOS	138	13	4	1348.0	1273	8.5	44	432	2.9	385	2.6	3.27	121	.249	.308	87	102	103	91	.952	303	124	3.9	9.2	.2		5.6
PHI	129	15	4	1333.3	1398	9.4	17	370	2.5	281	1.9	3.47	106	.269	.318	56	30	95	93	.940	379	110	-.5	2.7	12.5		3.3
BAL	133	9	4	1304.3	1403	9.7	13	349	2.4	294	2.0	3.31	124	.274	.321	78	113	106	100	.949	308	96	3.6	10.2	2.5		-4.4
STL	134	7	1	1340.7	1476	9.9	41	321	2.2	331	2.2	3.36	123	.279	.320	74	113	107	104	.940	397	117	-1.5	10.2	-1.2		1.0
CIN	130	8	5	1361.0	1484	9.8	26	370	2.4	360	2.4	3.60	109	.277	.324	22	53	105	93	.947	339	111	1.8	4.8	-3.5		4.9
PIT	117	9	4	1364.0	1464	9.7	27	437	2.9	334	2.2	3.60	105	.274	.329	39	27	98	98	.945	361	98	.6	2.4	5.3		-6.8
CHI	147	8	1	1331.3	1433	9.7	20	330	2.2	313	2.1	3.38	109	.274	.317	70	45	96	97	.935	428	145	-3.3	4.1	2.3		-2.0
LOU	134	5	2	1351.7	1509	10.0	33	323	2.2	287	1.9	3.46	114	.282	.323	59	74	103	102	.940	394	101	-1.4	6.7	-1.0		-5.3
NY	138	4	0	1278.3	1454	10.2	19	628	4.4	397	2.8	4.29	89	.285	.364	-62	-69	99	99	.932	433	140	-3.6	-6.3	.2		-5.3
WAS	131	3	0	1300.3	1649	11.4	35	422	2.9	328	2.3	4.93	77	.308	.359	-156	-166	98	92	.935	403	99	-1.9	-15.0	1.0		-6.1
CLE	138	0	0	1264.0	1844	13.1	43	527	3.8	215	1.5	6.38	58	.339	.397	-354	-376	96	91	.937	388	121	-1.0	-34.1	-9.2		-12.7
TOT	1590	90	32	15846.3		10.1			2.8		2.2	3.85		.282	.335					.942	4447	1387					

Runs
McGraw-Bal 140
Keeler-Bro 140
Thomas-Phi 137
Delahanty-Phi 135
Williams-Pit 126

Hits
Delahanty-Phi 238
Burkett-StL 221
Williams-Pit 219
Keeler-Bro 216
Tenney-Bos 209

Doubles
Delahanty-Phi 55
Wagner-Lou 43
Holmes-Bal 31
Long-Bos 30
Duffy-Bos 29

Triples
Williams-Pit 27
Freeman-Was 25
Stahl-Bos 18
Tenney-Bos 17
McCarthy-Pit 17

Home Runs
Freeman-Was 25
Wallace-StL 12
Williams-Pit 9
Mertes-Chi 9
Delahanty-Phi 9

Total Bases
Delahanty-Phi 338
Freeman-Was 331
Williams-Pit 328
Stahl-Bos 285
Wagner-Lou 282

Runs Batted In
Delahanty-Phi 137
Freeman-Was 122
Williams-Pit 116
Wagner-Lou 113
Wallace-StL 108

Runs Produced
Delahanty-Phi 263
Williams-Pit 233
Wagner-Lou 204
Freeman-Was 204

Bases On Balls
McGraw-Bal 124
Thomas-Phi 115
VanHaltren-NY 74
Childs-StL 74

Batting Average
Delahanty-Phi 410
Burkett-StL 396
McGraw-Bal 391
Keeler-Bro 379
Williams-Pit 355

On Base Percentage
McGraw-Bal 547
Delahanty-Phi 463
Burkett-StL 463
Thomas-Phi 455
Stahl-Bos 426

Slugging Average
Delahanty-Phi 582
Freeman-Was 563
Williams-Pit 532
Burkett-StL 500
Stahl-Bos 495

Production
Delahanty-Phi 1.045
McGraw-Bal 994
Burkett-StL 963
Williams-Pit 947
Freeman-Was 924

Adjusted Production
Delahanty-Phi 195
McGraw-Bal 165
Williams-Pit 164
Freeman-Was 161
Burkett-StL 155

Batter Runs
Delahanty-Phi 69.8
McGraw-Bal 58.4
Burkett-StL 53.7
Williams-Pit 50.9
Stahl-Bos 44.9

Adjusted Batter Runs
Delahanty-Phi 72.5
McGraw-Bal 52.6
Williams-Pit 52.2
Burkett-StL 46.8
Freeman-Was 42.2

Clutch Hitting Index
Corcoran-Cin 149
Flick-Phi 143
Duffy-Bos 140
Lauder-Phi 139
Lowe-Bos 138

Runs Created
Delahanty-Phi 175
Williams-Pit 151
Burkett-StL 144
McGraw-Bal 141
Stahl-Bos 139

Total Average
McGraw-Bal 1.601
Delahanty-Phi 1.242
Burkett-StL 1.107
Stahl-Bos 1.053
Williams-Pit 1.050

Stolen Bases
Sheckard-Bal 77
McGraw-Bal 73
Heidrick-StL 55
Holmes-Bal 50
Clarke-Lou 49

Stolen Base Average

Stolen Base Runs

Fielding Runs
Davis-NY 43.3
Wallace-StL 34.0
Cross-Cle-StL 29.9
Gleason-NY 23.5
Sheckard-Bal 20.7

Total Player Rating
Davis-NY 5.9
Delahanty-Phi 5.3
Williams-Pit 5.1
McGraw-Bal 4.8
Lajoie-Phi 4.6

Wins
McGinnity-Bal 28
Hughes-Bro 28
Willis-Bos 27
Young-StL 26
Tannehill-Pit 24

Win Percentage
Hughes-Bro 824
Willis-Bos 771
Hahn-Cin 742
Donahue-Phi 724
Kennedy-Bro 710

Games
Leever-Pit 51
Powell-StL 48
McGinnity-Bal 48
Young-StL 44
Carrick-NY 44

Complete Games
Young-StL 40
Powell-StL 40
Carrick-NY 40
Taylor-Chi 39
McGinnity-Bal 38

Shutouts
Willis-Bos 5

Saves
Leever-Pit 3

Innings Pitched
Leever-Pit 379
Powell-StL 373
Young-StL 369
McGinnity-Bal 366
Carrick-NY 362

Fewest Hits/Game
Willis-Bos 7.27
Hughes-Bro 7.71
Hahn-Cin 8.16
Seymour-NY 8.29
Leever-Pit 8.38

Fewest BB/Game
Young-StL 1.07
Cuppy-StL 1.36
Tannehill-Pit 1.47
Woods-Lou 1.79
Phillippe-Lou 1.79

Strikeouts
Hahn-Cin 145
Seymour-NY 142
Leever-Pit 121
Willis-Bos 120
Doheny-NY 115

Strikeouts/Game
Seymour-NY 4.77
Hahn-Cin 4.22
Doheny-NY 3.91
McJames-Bro 3.44
Willis-Bos 3.15

Wins Above Team
Hughes-Bro 8.7
Willis-Bos 7.9
Hahn-Cin 7.4
Tannehill-Pit 5.8
Callahan-Chi 5.2

Earned Run Average
Willis-Bos 2.49
Young-StL 2.59
Hahn-Cin 2.68
McGinnity-Bal 2.68
Hughes-Bro 2.68

Adjusted ERA
Young-StL 159
Willis-Bos 159
McGinnity-Bal 153
Hahn-Cin 151
Kitson-Bal 149

Opponents' Batting Avg.
Willis-Bos 221
Hughes-Bro 232
Hahn-Cin 242
Seymour-NY 245
Leever-Pit 247

Opponents' On Base Pct.
Young-StL 282
Hahn-Cin 284
Willis-Bos 288
Nichols-Bos 295
Kitson-Bal 296

Starter Runs
Young-StL 52.0
Willis-Bos 51.9
McGinnity-Bal 47.7
Hahn-Cin 40.3
Kitson-Bal 40.3

Adjusted Starter Runs
Young-StL 62.9
McGinnity-Bal 57.6
Willis-Bos 55.9
Kitson-Bal 49.2
Hahn-Cin 47.2

Clutch Pitching Index
Kennedy-Bro 129
Tannehill-Pit 121
Dowling-Lou 119
Woods-Lou 116
Callahan-Chi 115

Relief Runs

Adjusted Relief Runs

Relief Ranking

Total Pitcher Index
Young-StL 6.7
Willis-Bos 5.3
McGinnity-Bal 5.2
Hughes-Bro 4.7
Kitson-Bal 4.5

Total Baseball Ranking
Young-StL 6.7
Davis-NY 5.9
Delahanty-Phi 5.3
Willis-Bos 5.3
McGinnity-Bal 5.2

TEAM	G	W	L	PCT	GB	R	OR	AB	H	2B	3B	HR	BB	SO	AVG	OBP	SLG	PRO	/A	BR	/A	PF	CHI	RC	TA	SB	CS	SBA	SBR
BRO	142	82	54	.603		816	722	4860	1423	199	81	26	421	272	.293	.349	.383	.732	110	67	11	108	100	764	.744	274			
PIT	140	79	60	.568	4.5	733	612	4817	1312	185	100	25	327	321	.272	.319	.368	.687	97	-24	-44	103	104	636	.649	174			
PHI	141	75	63	.543	8	810	792	4969	1439	187	82	29	440	374	.290	.347	.378	.725	108	56	71	98	99	741	.714	205			
BOS	142	66	72	.478	17	778	739	4952	1403	163	68	48	395	278	.283	.336	.373	.709	103	22	-129	120	100	699	.683	182			
STL	142	65	75	.464	19	744	748	4877	1420	141	81	36	406	318	.291	.346	.375	.721	107	47	97	93	94	735	.717	243			
CHI	146	65	75	.464	19	635	751	4907	1276	202	51	33	343	383	.260	.308	.342	.650	86	-86	-31	93	97	590	.609	189			
CIN	144	62	77	.446	21.5	703	745	5026	1335	178	83	33	333	408	.266	.311	.354	.665	91	-64	-2	92	101	626	.622	183			
NY	141	60	78	.435	23	713	823	4724	1317	177	61	23	369	343	.279	.331	.357	.688	97	-13	5	97	101	652	.672	236			
TOT	569					5932		39132	10925	1432	607	253	3034	2697	.279	.331	.366	.697								1686			

TEAM	CG	SHO	SV	IP	H	H/G	HR	BB	BB/G	SO	SO/G	ERA	/A	OAVG	OOBA	PR	/A	PF	CPI	FA	E	DP	FW	PW	BW	SBW	DIF
BRO	104	8	4	1225.7	1370	10.1	30	405	3.0	300	2.2	3.89	101	.282	.337	-26	3	106	99	.948	303	102	2.6	.3	1.0		10.2
PIT	114	11	1	1229.0	1232	9.0	24	295	2.2	415	3.0	3.06	122	.260	.303	87	91	101	97	.945	322	106	1.4	8.3	-4.0		3.8
PHI	116	7	3	1248.7	1506	10.9	29	402	2.9	284	2.0	4.13	88	.297	.349	-59	-71	98	103	.945	330	125	.9	-6.5	6.5		5.1
BOS	116	8	2	1240.3	1263	9.2	59	463	3.4	340	2.5	3.73	119	.263	.328	-4	97	120	98	.953	273	86	4.4	8.9	-11.8		-4.5
STL	117	12	0	1217.3	1373	10.2	32	299	2.2	325	2.4	3.77	91	.283	.325	-9	-43	93	97	.943	331	73	.8	-3.9	8.9		-10.8
CHI	137	9	1	1271.0	1375	9.7	21	324	2.3	357	2.5	3.23	108	.275	.319	66	37	94	105	.933	418	98	-4.5	3.4	-2.8		-1.0
CIN	118	9	1	1274.7	1383	9.8	28	404	2.9	399	2.8	3.83	90	.276	.330	-18	-56	93	94	.945	341	120	.2	-5.1	-.2		-2.4
NY	114	4	0	1207.3	1423	10.6	26	442	3.3	277	2.1	3.97	93	.292	.351	-35	-39	99	106	.928	439	124	-5.8	-3.6	.5		-.0
TOT	936	68	12	9914.0		9.9			2.8		2.4	3.70		.279	.331					.942	2757	834					

Runs
Thomas-Phi 132
Slagle-Phi 115
VanHaltren-NY 114
Barrett-Cin 114
Wagner-Pit 107

Hits
Keeler-Bro 204
Burkett-StL 203
Wagner-Pit 201
Flick-Phi 200
Beckley-Cin 190

Doubles
Wagner-Pit 45
Lajoie-Phi 33
Flick-Phi 32
Delahanty-Phi 32
VanHaltren-NY 30

Triples
Wagner-Pit 22
Kelley-Bro 17
Hickman-NY 17
Stahl-Bos 16
Flick-Phi 16

Home Runs
Long-Bos 12
Flick-Phi 11
Donlin-StL 10
Hickman-NY 9
Sullivan-Bos 8

Total Bases
Wagner-Pit 302
Flick-Phi 297
Burkett-StL 265
Keeler-Bro 253
Beckley-Cin 242

Runs Batted In
Flick-Phi 110
Delahanty-Phi 109
Wagner-Pit 100
Collins-Bos 95
Beckley-Cin 94

Runs Produced
Flick-Phi 205
Wagner-Pit 203
Collins-Bos 193
Beckley-Cin 190
Delahanty-Phi 189

Bases On Balls
Thomas-Phi 115
Hamilton-Bos 107
McGraw-StL 85
Dahlen-Bro 73

Batting Average
Wagner-Pit 381
Flick-Phi 367
Burkett-StL 363
Keeler-Bro 362
Beckley-Cin 341

On Base Percentage
Hamilton-Bos 447
Thomas-Phi 438
Burkett-StL 427
Wagner-Pit 426
Flick-Phi 426

Slugging Average
Wagner-Pit 573
Flick-Phi 545
Lajoie-Phi 510
Kelley-Bro 485
Hickman-NY 482

Production
Wagner-Pit 999
Flick-Phi 971
Burkett-StL 901
Selbach-NY 878
Kelley-Bro 875

Adjusted Production
Flick-Phi 173
Wagner-Pit 172
Burkett-StL 162
Selbach-NY 149
Lajoie-Phi 141

Batter Runs
Wagner-Pit 52.7
Flick-Phi 50.7
Burkett-StL 40.2
Selbach-NY 33.9
Hamilton-Bos 33.4

Adjusted Batter Runs
Flick-Phi 52.4
Wagner-Pit 50.4
Burkett-StL 46.1
Selbach-NY 36.1
McGraw-StL 34.2

Clutch Hitting Index
Cross-Phi 153
Jennings-Bro 146
Delahanty-Phi 138
Dahlen-Bro 135
Lowe-Bos 132

Runs Created
Wagner-Pit 148
Flick-Phi 145
Burkett-StL 130
Keeler-Bro 119
Selbach-NY 118

Total Average
Wagner-Pit 1.169
Flick-Phi 1.125
Burkett-StL 1.008
Selbach-NY 1.006
Hamilton-Bos 994

Stolen Bases
VanHaltren-NY 45
Donovan-StL 45
Barrett-Cin 44
Keeler-Bro 41

Stolen Base Average

Stolen Base Runs

Fielding Runs
Steinfeldt-Cin 33.0
Lajoie-Phi 27.2
Davis-NY 20.9
Dahlen-Bro 18.2
Heidrick-StL 14.9

Total Player Rating
Lajoie-Phi 4.8
Flick-Phi 4.2
Davis-NY 4.0
Wagner-Pit 3.6
Burkett-StL 3.2

Wins
McGinnity-Bro 28
Tannehill-Pit 20
Phillippe-Pit 20
Kennedy-Bro 20
Dinneen-Bos 20

Win Percentage
McGinnity-Bro 778
Tannehill-Pit 769
Fraser-Phi 625
Phillippe-Pit 606
Kennedy-Bro 606

Games
Carrick-NY 45
McGinnity-Bro 44
Scott-Cin 43
Kennedy-Bro 42

Complete Games
Hawley-NY 34
Dinneen-Bos 33

Shutouts
Young-StL 4
Nichols-Bos 4
Hahn-Cin 4
Griffith-Chi 4

Saves
Kitson-Bro 4
Bernhard-Phi 2

Innings Pitched
McGinnity-Bro 343
Carrick-NY 342
Hawley-NY 329
Scott-Cin 323

Fewest Hits/Game
Waddell-Pit 7.58
Garvin-Chi 8.23
Nichols-Bos 8.38
Dinneen-Bos 8.52
Hahn-Cin 8.79

Fewest BB/Game
Young-StL 1.01
Phillippe-Pit 1.35
Tannehill-Pit 1.65
Scott-Cin 1.84
Griffith-Chi 1.85

Strikeouts
Waddell-Pit 130
Hahn-Cin 127
Young-StL 115
Garvin-Chi 107
Dinneen-Bos 107

Strikeouts/Game
Waddell-Pit 5.60
Garvin-Chi 3.91
Hahn-Cin 3.77
Newton-Cin 3.37
Leever-Pit 3.24

Wins Above Team
McGinnity-Bro 9.3
Tannehill-Pit 6.7
Dinneen-Bos 4.4
Menefee-Chi 2.9
Hawley-NY 2.7

Earned Run Average
Waddell-Pit 2.37
Garvin-Chi 2.41
Taylor-Chi 2.55
Leever-Pit 2.70
Phillippe-Pit 2.84

Adjusted ERA
Waddell-Pit 157
Garvin-Chi 145
Nichols-Bos 144
Dinneen-Bos 141
Leever-Pit 138

Opponents' Batting Avg.
Waddell-Pit 228
Garvin-Chi 243
Nichols-Bos 246
Dinneen-Bos 250
Hahn-Cin 256

Opponents' On Base Pct.
Waddell-Pit 280
Phillippe-Pit 285
Young-StL 290
Garvin-Chi 292
Griffith-Chi 296

Starter Runs
Garvin-Chi 35.1
Waddell-Pit 30.9
McGinnity-Bro 29.0
Taylor-Chi 28.3
Phillippe-Pit 26.7

Adjusted Starter Runs
Dinneen-Bos 46.4
McGinnity-Bro 37.3
Nichols-Bos 35.0
Waddell-Pit 31.6
Garvin-Chi 29.5

Clutch Pitching Index
Fraser-Phi 132
Taylor-Chi 122
Carrick-NY 116
Donahue-Phi 115
McGinnity-Bro 112

Relief Runs

Adjusted Relief Runs

Relief Ranking

Total Pitcher Index
Dinneen-Bos 5.2
Nichols-Bos 3.3
McGinnity-Bro 3.0
Tannehill-Pit 3.0
Waddell-Pit 2.8

Total Baseball Ranking
Dinneen-Bos 5.2
Lajoie-Phi 4.8
Flick-Phi 4.2
Davis-NY 4.0
Wagner-Pit 3.7

TEAM	G	W	L	PCT	GB	R	OR	AB	H	2B	3B	HR	BB	SO	AVG	OBP	SLG	PRO	/A	BR	/A	PF	CHI	RC	TA	SB	CS	SBA	SBR
PIT	140	90	49	.647		776	534	4913	1407	182	92	28	386	493	.286	.338	.378	.716	116	98	94	101	102	714	.698	203			
PHI	140	83	57	.593	7.5	668	543	4793	1275	194	58	24	430	549	.266	.326	.346	.672	103	25	7	103	98	621	.650	199			
BRO	137	79	57	.581	9.5	744	600	4879	1399	206	93	32	312	449	.287	.330	.387	.717	116	89	50	106	101	698	.683	178			
STL	142	76	64	.543	14.5	792	689	5039	1430	187	94	39	314	540	.284	.326	.381	.707	113	75	97	97	106	705	.672	190			
BOS	140	69	69	.500	20.5	531	556	4746	1180	135	36	28	303	519	.249	.294	.310	.604	83	-97	-170	112	99	490	.542	158			
NY	141	52	85	.380	37	544	755	4839	1225	167	46	19	303	575	.253	.297	.318	.615	86	-80	-24	91	96	510	.547	133			
CHI	140	53	86	.381	37	578	699	4844	1250	153	61	18	314	532	.258	.303	.326	.629	90	-56	-56	100	98	554	.583	204			
CIN	142	52	87	.374	38	561	818	4914	1232	173	70	38	323	584	.251	.297	.338	.635	92	-52	-18	95	93	547	.576	137			
TOT	561					5194		38967	10398	1397	550	226	2685	4241	.267	.314	.348	.663								1402			

TEAM	CG	SHO	SV	IP	H	H/G	HR	BB	BB/G	SO	SO/G	ERA	/A	OAVG	OOBA	PR	/A	PF	CPI	FA	E	DP	FW	PW	BW	SBW	DIF
PIT	119	15	4	1242.7	1198	8.7	20	244	1.8	505	3.7	2.58	123	.251	.288	102	83	96	104	.950	287	97	1.2	8.1	9.2		2.0
PHI	125	15	2	1244.7	1221	8.8	19	259	1.9	480	3.5	2.87	116	.254	.293	61	62	100	97	.954	262	65	2.7	6.1	.7		3.5
BRO	111	7	5	1212.0	1244	9.2	18	435	3.2	583	4.3	3.14	109	.263	.325	23	37	103	109	.950	281	99	1.6	3.6	4.9		.9
STL	118	5	5	1269.3	1333	9.5	39	332	2.4	445	3.2	3.68	85	.268	.313	-50	-75	95	92	.949	305	108	.1	-7.3	9.5		3.7
BOS	128	11	2	1261.7	1196	8.5	29	349	2.5	558	4.0	2.90	128	.248	.299	58	115	112	99	.952	282	89	1.5	11.3	-16.7		3.9
NY	118	11	1	1230.3	1389	10.2	24	377	2.8	542	4.0	3.87	82	.282	.333	-75	-97	95	99	.941	348	81	-2.5	-9.5	-2.4		-2.2
CHI	131	2	0	1241.3	1348	9.8	27	324	2.3	586	4.2	3.33	102	.274	.319	-1	10	103	105	.943	336	87	-1.8	1.0	-5.5		-10.2
CIN	126	4	0	1263.7	1469	10.5	51	365	2.6	542	3.9	4.17	79	.288	.336	-119	-120	100	98	.940	355	102	-2.9	-11.8	-1.8		-1.1
TOT	976	70	19	9965.7		9.4			2.4		3.8	3.32		.267	.314					.947	2456	728					

Runs
Burkett-StL 142
Keeler-Bro 123
Beaumont-Pit 120
Clarke-Pit 118
Sheckard-Bro 116

Hits
Burkett-StL 226
Keeler-Bro 202
Sheckard-Bro 196
Wagner-Pit 194
Delahanty-Phi 192

Doubles
Delahanty-Phi 38
Daly-Bro 38
Wagner-Pit 37
Beckley-Cin 36
Wallace-StL 34

Triples
Sheckard-Bro 19
Flick-Phi 17

Home Runs
Crawford-Cin 16
Sheckard-Bro 11
Burkett-StL 10

Total Bases
Burkett-StL 306
Sheckard-Bro 296
Delahanty-Phi 286
Wagner-Pit 271

Runs Batted In
Wagner-Pit 126
Delahanty-Phi 108
Sheckard-Bro 104
Crawford-Cin 104

Runs Produced
Wagner-Pit 221
Sheckard-Bro 209
Burkett-StL 207
Delahanty-Phi 206
Flick-Phi 192

Bases On Balls
Thomas-Phi 100
Hartsel-Chi 74
Davis-Bro-Pit 66
Delahanty-Phi 65
Hamilton-Bos 64

Batting Average
Burkett-StL 376
Delahanty-Phi 354
Sheckard-Bro 354
Wagner-Pit 353
Keeler-Bro 339

On Base Percentage
Burkett-StL 432
Thomas-Phi 428
Delahanty-Phi 423
Hartsel-Chi 413
Wagner-Pit 410

Slugging Average
Sheckard-Bro 534
Delahanty-Phi 528
Crawford-Cin 524
Burkett-StL 509
Flick-Phi 500

Production
Delahanty-Phi 951
Burkett-StL 941
Sheckard-Bro 939
Wagner-Pit 904
Crawford-Cin 899

Adjusted Production
Burkett-StL 181
Delahanty-Phi 173
Crawford-Cin 170
Sheckard-Bro 164
Wagner-Pit 163

Batter Runs
Burkett-StL 57.4
Delahanty-Phi 53.7
Sheckard-Bro 49.9
Wagner-Pit 44.4
Hartsel-Chi 44.0

Adjusted Batter Runs
Burkett-StL 60.2
Delahanty-Phi 51.7
Sheckard-Bro 45.5
Wagner-Pit 44.1
Hartsel-Chi 44.0

Clutch Hitting Index
Ganzel-NY 162
Dexter-Phi 158
Wagner-Pit 155
Long-Bos 154
Dahlen-Bro 149

Runs Created
Burkett-StL 147
Sheckard-Bro 137
Delahanty-Phi 137
Wagner-Pit 135
Hartsel-Chi 130

Total Average
Delahanty-Phi 1.086
Sheckard-Bro 1.056
Wagner-Pit 1.051
Burkett-StL 1.045
Hartsel-Chi 1.024

Stolen Bases
Wagner-Pit 49
Hartsel-Chi 41
Strang-NY 40
Harley-Cin 37
Beaumont-Pit 36

Stolen Base Average

Stolen Base Runs

Fielding Runs
Wallace-StL 25.0
Flick-Phi 16.9
Daly-Bro 14.1
Davis-NY 12.2
Childs-Chi 11.7

Total Player Rating
Wallace-StL 5.2
Wagner-Pit 4.5
Burkett-StL 4.5
Delahanty-Phi 4.2
Daly-Bro 4.1

Wins
Donovan-Bro 25
Harper-StL 23
Phillippe-Pit 22
Hahn-Cin 22

Win Percentage
Chesbro-Pit 677
Phillippe-Pit 647
Tannehill-Pit 643
Harper-StL 639
Kitson-Bro 633

Games
Taylor-NY 45
Powell-StL 45
Donovan-Bro 45
Hahn-Cin 42
Mathewson-NY 40

Complete Games
Hahn-Cin 41
Taylor-NY 37
Mathewson-NY 36
Donovan-Bro 36
Donahue-Phi 34

Shutouts
Willis-Bos 6
Orth-Phi 6
Chesbro-Pit 6

Saves
Powell-StL 3
Donovan-Bro 3

Innings Pitched
Hahn-Cin 375
Taylor-NY 353
Donovan-Bro 351
Powell-StL 338
Mathewson-NY 336

Fewest Hits/Game
Townsend-Phi 7.38
Mathewson-NY 7.71
Willis-Bos 7.73
Orth-Phi 7.98
Chesbro-Pit 8.16

Fewest BB/Game
Orth-Phi 1.02
Phillippe-Pit 1.16
Tannehill-Pit 1.29
Duggleby-Phi 1.30
Powell-StL 1.33

Strikeouts
Hahn-Cin 239
Donovan-Bro 226
Hughes-Chi 225
Mathewson-NY 221
Waddell-Pit-Chi 172

Strikeouts/Game
Hughes-Chi 6.57
Waddell-Pit-Chi 6.14
Mathewson-NY 5.92
Donovan-Bro 5.79
Hahn-Cin 5.74

Wins Above Team
Hahn-Cin 6.8
Mathewson-NY 6.0
Harper-StL 4.7
Nichols-Bos 3.2
Donovan-Bro 2.9

Earned Run Average
Tannehill-Pit 2.18
Phillippe-Pit 2.22
Orth-Phi 2.27
Willis-Bos 2.36
Chesbro-Pit 2.38

Adjusted ERA
Willis-Bos 158
Orth-Phi 147
Tannehill-Pit 146
Phillippe-Pit 143
Chesbro-Pit 134

Opponents' Batting Avg.
Townsend-Phi 222
Mathewson-NY 230
Willis-Bos 231
Orth-Phi 236
Chesbro-Pit 240

Opponents' On Base Pct.
Orth-Phi 264
Phillippe-Pit 275
Chesbro-Pit 282
Tannehill-Pit 283
Willis-Bos 286

Starter Runs
Phillippe-Pit 36.2
Mathewson-NY 33.9
Orth-Phi 33.0
Willis-Bos 32.5
Tannehill-Pit 31.9

Adjusted Starter Runs
Willis-Bos 46.2
Orth-Phi 33.2
Phillippe-Pit 31.7
Tannehill-Pit 28.1
Mathewson-NY 28.0

Clutch Pitching Index
Kitson-Bro 125
Taylor-Chi 120
Hughes-Bro 117
Taylor-NY 116
Tannehill-Pit 114

Relief Runs

Adjusted Relief Runs

Relief Ranking

Total Pitcher Index
Willis-Bos 4.7
Orth-Phi 4.4
Mathewson-NY 3.6
Phillippe-Pit 3.5
Nichols-Bos 3.5

Total Baseball Ranking
Wallace-StL 5.2
Willis-Bos 4.7
Wagner-Pit 4.5
Burkett-StL 4.5
Orth-Phi 4.4

TEAM	G	W	L	PCT	GB	R	OR	AB	H	2B	3B	HR	BB	SO	AVG	OBP	SLG	PRO	/A	BR	/A	PF	CHI	RC	TA	SB	CS	SBA	SBR
CHI	137	83	53	.610		819	631	4725	1303	173	89	32	475	337	.276	.342	.370	.712	105	37	42	99	104	711	.732	280			
BOS	138	79	57	.581	4	759	608	4866	1353	183	104	37	331	282	.278	.324	.381	.705	102	10	32	97	100	668	.667	157			
DET	136	74	61	.548	8.5	741	694	4676	1303	180	80	29	380	346	.279	.333	.370	.703	102	14	-59	110	100	660	.686	204			
PHI	137	74	62	.544	9	805	761	4882	1409	239	87	35	301	344	.289	.330	.395	.725	108	42	39	100	102	710	.691	173			
BAL	135	68	65	.511	13.5	760	750	4589	1348	179	111	24	369	377	.294	.346	.397	.743	113	79	31	107	96	720	.740	207			
WAS	137	61	73	.455	21	678	767	4772	1282	191	83	33	356	340	.269	.319	.364	.683	96	-23	-14	99	95	611	.636	127			
CLE	137	55	82	.401	28.5	663	827	4833	1311	197	68	12	243	326	.271	.306	.348	.654	88	-79	-39	95	102	566	.581	125			
MIL	139	48	89	.350	35.5	641	828	4795	1250	192	66	26	325	384	.261	.308	.345	.653	87	-78	-42	95	97	576	.607	176			
TOT	548					5866		38138	10559	1534	688	228	2780	2736	.277	.326	.371	.697								1449			

TEAM	CG	SHO	SV	IP	H	H/G	HR	BB	BB/G	SO	SO/G	ERA	/A	OAVG	OOBA	PR	/A	PF	CPI	FA	E	DP	FW	PW	BW	SBW	DIF
CHI	110	11	2	1217.7	1250	9.2	27	312	2.3	394	2.9	2.98	118	.262	.307	92	72	96	106	.941	345	100	.9	6.5	3.8		3.8
BOS	123	7	1	1216.3	1178	8.7	33	294	2.2	396	2.9	3.04	114	.251	.295	83	55	94	94	.943	337	104	1.4	5.0	2.9		1.8
DET	118	8	2	1186.7	1326	10.1	22	313	2.4	307	2.3	3.30	121	.279	.323	47	93	109	109	.930	410	127	-3.1	8.4	-5.3		6.6
PHI	124	6	1	1200.0	1346	10.1	20	374	2.8	350	2.6	4.00	91	.279	.331	-44	-46	100	94	.942	337	93	1.4	-4.2	3.5		5.2
BAL	115	4	3	1157.3	1313	10.2	21	344	2.7	271	2.1	3.73	105	.282	.331	-9	22	107	101	.926	401	76	-2.6	2.0	2.8		-.7
WAS	118	8	2	1180.7	1396	10.6	51	284	2.2	308	2.3	4.09	90	.290	.330	-56	-54	100	99	.943	323	97	2.3	-4.9	-1.3		-2.1
CLE	122	7	4	1181.0	1365	10.4	22	464	3.5	334	2.5	4.12	87	.285	.349	-60	-72	97	101	.942	329	99	1.9	-6.5	-3.5		-5.4
MIL	107	3	4	1216.7	1383	10.2	32	395	2.9	376	2.8	4.06	88	.282	.336	-53	-63	98	97	.934	393	106	-2.1	-5.7	-3.8		-8.9
TOT	937	54	19	9556.3		9.9		2.6		2.6	3.66		.277	.326					.938	2875	802				

Runs
Lajoie-Phi	145
Jones-Chi	120
Williams-Bal	113
Hoy-Chi	112
Barrett-Det	110

Hits
Lajoie-Phi	232
Anderson-Mil	190
Collins-Bos	187
Waldron-Mil-Was	186
Dungan-Was	179

Doubles
Lajoie-Phi	48
Anderson-Mil	46
Collins-Bos	42
Farrell-Was	32

Triples
Williams-Bal	21
Keister-Bal	21
Mertes-Chi	17
Stahl-Bos	16
Collins-Bos	16

Home Runs
Lajoie-Phi	14
Freeman-Bos	12
Grady-Was	9

Total Bases
Lajoie-Phi	350
Collins-Bos	279
Anderson-Mil	274
Freeman-Bos	255
Williams-Bal	248

Runs Batted In
Lajoie-Phi	125
Freeman-Bos	114
Anderson-Mil	99
Mertes-Chi	98
Williams-Bal	96

Runs Produced
Lajoie-Phi	256
Williams-Bal	202
Collins-Bos	196
Freeman-Bos	190
Mertes-Chi	187

Bases On Balls
Hoy-Chi	86
Jones-Chi	84
Barrett-Det	76
McFarland-Chi	75
McGraw-Bal	61

Batting Average
Lajoie-Phi	.426
Donlin-Bal	.340
Freeman-Bos	.339
Seybold-Phi	.334
Collins-Bos	.332

On Base Percentage
Lajoie-Phi	.451
Jones-Chi	.407
Donlin-Bal	.406
Freeman-Bos	.393
Hoy-Chi	.393

Slugging Average
Lajoie-Phi	.643
Freeman-Bos	.520
Seybold-Phi	.503
Williams-Bal	.495
Collins-Bos	.495

Production
Lajoie-Phi	1.094
Freeman-Bos	.914
Seybold-Phi	.892
Donlin-Bal	.881
Williams-Bal	.881

Adjusted Production
Lajoie-Phi	203
Freeman-Bos	159
Seybold-Phi	148
Collins-Bos	145
Anderson-Mil	138

Batter Runs
Lajoie-Phi	71.6
Freeman-Bos	34.6
Donlin-Bal	30.4
Williams-Bal	30.3
Collins-Bos	28.5

Adjusted Batter Runs
Lajoie-Phi	71.3
Freeman-Bos	36.9
Collins-Bos	31.0
Seybold-Phi	28.1
Anderson-Mil	26.2

Clutch Hitting Index
Keister-Bal	142
Hartman-Chi	140
Freeman-Bos	131
Elberfeld-Det	131
Mertes-Chi	129

Runs Created
Lajoie-Phi	174
Anderson-Mil	113
Collins-Bos	113
Freeman-Bos	110
Donlin-Bal	108

Total Average
Lajoie-Phi	1.285
Donlin-Bal	.994
Freeman-Bos	.975
Williams-Bal	.950
Seybold-Phi	.940

Stolen Bases
Isbell-Chi	52
Mertes-Chi	46
Seymour-Bal	38
Jones-Chi	38

Stolen Base Average

Stolen Base Runs

Fielding Runs
Elberfeld-Det	22.6
Pickering-Cle	20.9
Clingman-Was	18.4
Lajoie-Phi	17.2
Seymour-Bal	14.9

Total Player Rating
Lajoie-Phi	7.4
Collins-Bos	3.7
Elberfeld-Det	3.6
Pickering-Cle	3.0
Seybold-Phi	2.5

Wins
Young-Bos	33
McGinnity-Bal	26
Griffith-Chi	24
Miller-Det	23
Fraser-Phi	22

Win Percentage
Griffith-Chi	.774
Young-Bos	.767
Callahan-Chi	.652
Patten-Was	.643
Miller-Det	.639

Games
McGinnity-Bal	48
Dowling-Mil-Cle	43
Young-Bos	43
Carrick-Was	42
Patterson-Chi	41

Complete Games
McGinnity-Bal	39
Young-Bos	38
Miller-Det	35
Fraser-Phi	35
Carrick-Was	34

Shutouts
Young-Bos	5
Griffith-Chi	5
Patterson-Chi	4
Patten-Was	4
Moore-Cle	4

Saves
Hoffer-Cle	3
Garvin-Mil	2

Innings Pitched
McGinnity-Bal	382
Young-Bos	371
Miller-Det	332
Fraser-Phi	331
Carrick-Was	324

Fewest Hits/Game
Young-Bos	7.86
Callahan-Chi	8.16
Moore-Cle	8.39
Lewis-Bos	8.52
Winter-Bos	8.74

Fewest BB/Game
Young-Bos	.90
Gear-Was	1.21
Lee-Was	1.55
Griffith-Chi	1.69
Cronin-Det	1.72

Strikeouts
Young-Bos	158
Patterson-Chi	127
Dowling-Mil-Cle	124
Garvin-Mil	122
Fraser-Phi	110

Strikeouts/Game
Garvin-Mil	4.27
Patten-Was	3.86
Young-Bos	3.83
Patterson-Chi	3.66
Dowling-Mil-Cle	3.65

Wins Above Team
Young-Bos	11.6
Griffith-Chi	7.5
Patten-Was	5.6
Miller-Det	4.6
Moore-Cle	4.0

Earned Run Average
Young-Bos	1.63
Callahan-Chi	2.43
Yeager-Det	2.61
Griffith-Chi	2.66
Winter-Bos	2.80

Adjusted ERA
Young-Bos	212
Yeager-Det	154
Callahan-Chi	145
Miller-Det	136
Griffith-Chi	132

Opponents' Batting Avg.
Young-Bos	.232
Callahan-Chi	.239
Moore-Cle	.244
Lewis-Bos	.247
Winter-Bos	.252

Opponents' On Base Pct.
Young-Bos	.252
Callahan-Chi	.283
Griffith-Chi	.297
Plank-Phi	.299
Lewis-Bos	.300

Starter Runs
Young-Bos	84.0
Griffith-Chi	29.7
Callahan-Chi	29.5
Miller-Det	26.1
Yeager-Det	23.4

Adjusted Starter Runs
Young-Bos	75.4
Miller-Det	38.8
Yeager-Det	31.0
Callahan-Chi	26.0
Griffith-Chi	25.3

Clutch Pitching Index
Katoll-Chi	125
Yeager-Det	121
Young-Bos	117
Siever-Det	117
Sparks-Mil	114

Relief Runs

Adjusted Relief Runs

Relief Ranking

Total Pitcher Index
Young-Bos	7.5
Callahan-Chi	4.3
Miller-Det	4.1
Yeager-Det	4.0
Griffith-Chi	3.6

Total Baseball Ranking
Young-Bos	7.5
Lajoie-Phi	7.4
Callahan-Chi	4.3
Miller-Det	4.1
Yeager-Det	4.0

TEAM	G	W	L	PCT	GB	R	OR	AB	H	2B	3B	HR	BB	SO	AVG	OBP	SLG	PRO	/A	BR	/A	PF	CHI	RC	TA	SB	CS	SBA	SBR
PIT	142	103	36	.741		775	440	4926	1410	189	94	19	372	446	.286	.336	.374	.710	127	147	115	105	106	714	.695	228			
BRO	141	75	63	.543	27.5	564	519	4845	1242	147	49	19	319	489	.256	.302	.319	.621	99	-7	22	95	100	523	.557	145			
BOS	142	73	64	.533	29	572	516	4728	1178	142	39	14	398	481	.249	.307	.305	.612	96	-14	11	95	104	513	.571	189			
CIN	141	70	70	.500	33.5	633	566	4908	1383	188	77	18	297	465	.282	.323	.362	.685	119	97	40	110	94	632	.626	131			
CHI	141	68	69	.496	34	530	501	4802	1200	131	40	6	353	565	.250	.301	.298	.599	92	-39	-15	96	100	510	.556	222			
STL	140	56	78	.418	44.5	517	695	4751	1226	116	37	10	273	438	.258	.298	.304	.602	93	-38	-10	95	100	491	.532	158			
PHI	138	56	81	.409	46	484	649	4615	1139	110	43	5	356	481	.247	.301	.293	.594	90	-45	-73	105	96	449	.522	108			
NY	139	48	88	.353	53.5	401	590	4571	1088	147	34	8	252	530	.238	.278	.290	.568	82	-94	-92	100	92	431	.507	187			
TOT	562					4476		38146	9866	1170	413	99	2620	3895	.259	.306	.319	.625								1368			

TEAM	CG	SHO	SV	IP	H	H/G	HR	BB	BB/G	SO	SO/G	ERA	/A	OAVG	OOBA	PR	/A	PF	CPI	FA	E	DP	FW	PW	BW	SBW	DIF
PIT	131	21	3	1263.3	1142	8.1	4	250	1.8	564	4.0	2.30	118	.241	.279	66	59	98	92	.958	247	87	3.2	6.2	12.1		12.0
BRO	132	14	3	1255.0	1113	8.0	10	363	2.6	536	3.8	2.69	97	.237	.292	12	-12	94	87	.952	275	79	1.4	-1.3	2.3		3.5
BOS	124	14	4	1258.3	1233	8.8	16	372	2.7	523	3.7	2.61	100	.256	.309	23	0	94	108	.959	240	90	3.6	.0	1.2		-.3
CIN	130	9	1	1237.3	1228	8.9	15	352	2.6	430	3.1	2.67	113	.258	.309	14	46	108	107	.945	322	118	-1.5	4.8	4.2		-7.6
CHI	132	16	2	1274.3	1235	8.7	9	279	2.0	437	3.1	2.21	120	.254	.294	80	62	95	114	.945	327	111	-1.8	6.5	-1.6		-3.6
STL	112	7	4	1225.7	1399	10.3	16	338	2.5	400	2.9	3.47	79	.286	.332	-94	-98	99	102	.944	336	107	-2.4	-10.3	-1.1		2.8
PHI	118	8	3	1209.3	1323	9.8	12	334	2.5	504	3.8	3.50	87	.277	.325	-96	-62	109	94	.946	305	81	-.5	-6.5	-7.7		2.2
NY	118	11	1	1225.0	1193	8.8	16	332	2.4	501	3.7	2.82	103	.255	.304	-5	9	104	97	.943	330	104	-2.0	.9	-9.7		-9.2
TOT	997	100	21	9948.3		8.9			2.4		3.5	2.78		.259	.306					.949	2382	777					

Runs
Wagner-Pit 105
Clarke-Pit 103
Beaumont-Pit 100
Leach-Pit 97
Crawford-Cin 92

Hits
Beaumont-Pit 193
Keeler-Bro 186
Crawford-Cin 185
Wagner-Pit 176
Beckley-Cin 175

Doubles
Wagner-Pit 30
Clarke-Pit 27
Cooley-Bos 26
Dahlen-Bro 25
Beckley-Cin 23

Triples
Leach-Pit 22
Crawford-Cin 22
Wagner-Pit 16
Clarke-Pit 14
Gremminger-Bos 12

Home Runs
Leach-Pit 6
Beckley-Cin 5
Sheckard-Bro 4
McCreery-Bro 4

Total Bases
Crawford-Cin 256
Wagner-Pit 247
Beckley-Cin 227
Beaumont-Pit 226
Leach-Pit 219

Runs Batted In
Wagner-Pit 91
Leach-Pit 85
Crawford-Cin 78
Dahlen-Bro 74

Runs Produced
Wagner-Pit 193
Leach-Pit 176
Crawford-Cin 167
Beaumont-Pit 167
Clarke-Pit 154

Bases On Balls
Thomas-Phi 107
Lush-Bos 76
Tenney-Bos 73
Sheckard-Bro 57

Batting Average
Beaumont-Pit 357
Crawford-Cin 333
Keeler-Bro 333
Wagner-Pit 330
Beckley-Cin 330

On Base Percentage
Thomas-Phi 412
Tenney-Bos 404
Beaumont-Pit 400
Slagle-Chi 387
Crawford-Cin 385

Slugging Average
Wagner-Pit 463
Crawford-Cin 461
Clarke-Pit 449
Beckley-Cin 427
Leach-Pit 426

Production
Crawford-Cin 847
Wagner-Pit 842
Clarke-Pit 833
Beaumont-Pit 818
Beckley-Cin 797

Adjusted Production
Wagner-Pit 154
Clarke-Pit 151
Tenney-Bos 150
Crawford-Cin 149
Beaumont-Pit 147

Batter Runs
Crawford-Cin 39.9
Wagner-Pit 37.1
Beaumont-Pit 34.3
Clarke-Pit 31.9
Tenney-Bos 28.6

Adjusted Batter Runs
Wagner-Pit 33.7
Crawford-Cin 33.4
Tenney-Bos 31.4
Beaumont-Pit 30.9
Clarke-Pit 28.8

Clutch Hitting Index
McCreery-Bro 144
Dahlen-Bro 141
Kling-Chi 141
Ritchey-Pit 140
Carney-Bos 134

Runs Created
Wagner-Pit 112
Crawford-Cin 107
Beaumont-Pit 106
Clarke-Pit 93
Beckley-Cin 92

Total Average
Wagner-Pit 927
Clarke-Pit 911
Crawford-Cin 862
Beaumont-Pit 856
Tenney-Bos 830

Stolen Bases
Wagner-Pit 42
Slagle-Chi 40
Donovan-StL 34
Beaumont-Pit 33
Smith-NY 32

Fielding Runs
Farrell-StL 22.7
Steinfeldt-Cin 21.0
Lowe-Chi 18.0
Long-Bos 17.5
Leach-Pit 13.2

Total Player Rating
Wagner-Pit 4.0
Tenney-Bos 4.0
Leach-Pit 3.8
Crawford-Cin 2.9
Farrell-StL 2.7

Wins
Chesbro-Pit 28
Willis-Bos 27
Pittinger-Bos 27
Taylor-Chi 23
Hahn-Cin 23

Win Percentage
Chesbro-Pit 824
Doheny-Pit 800
Tannehill-Pit 769
Leever-Pit 696
Phillippe-Pit 690

Games
Willis-Bos 51
Pittinger-Bos 46
Yerkes-StL 39

Complete Games
Willis-Bos 45
Pittinger-Bos 36
Hahn-Cin 35
White-Phi 34
Taylor-Chi 33

Shutouts
Mathewson-NY 8
Chesbro-Pit 8
Taylor-Chi 7
Pittinger-Bos 7
Hahn-Cin 6

Saves
Willis-Bos 3
O'Neill-StL 2
Newton-Bro 2
Leever-Pit 2

Innings Pitched
Willis-Bos 410
Pittinger-Bos 389
Taylor-Chi 325
Hahn-Cin 321
White-Phi 306

Fewest Hits/Game
Newton-Bro 7.09
McGinnity-NY 7.18
Taylor-Chi 7.50
Donovan-Bro 7.55
Chesbro-Pit 7.62

Fewest BB/Game
Phillippe-Pit 86
Tannehill-Pit 97
Menefee-Chi 1.19
Taylor-Chi 1.19
Leever-Pit 1.26

Strikeouts
Willis-Bos 225
White-Phi 185
Pittinger-Bos 174
Donovan-Bro 170
Mathewson-NY 159

Strikeouts/Game
White-Phi 5.44
Mathewson-NY 5.17
Donovan-Bro 5.13
Willis-Bos 4.94
Wicker-StL 4.62

Wins Above Team
Taylor-Chi 7.2
Hahn-Cin 6.6
Chesbro-Pit 6.5
Pittinger-Bos 6.5
Poole-Pit-Cin 4.2

Earned Run Average
Taylor-Chi 1.33
Hahn-Cin 1.77
Tannehill-Pit 1.95
Lundgren-Chi 1.97
Phillippe-Pit 2.05

Adjusted ERA
Taylor-Chi 199
Hahn-Cin 170
Poole-Pit-Cin 143
McGinnity-NY 141
Tannehill-Pit 140

Opponents' Batting Avg.
Newton-Bro 217
McGinnity-NY 219
Taylor-Chi 227
Donovan-Bro 228
Chesbro-Pit 229

Opponents' On Base Pct.
Taylor-Chi 260
Tannehill-Pit 266
McGinnity-NY 271
Phillippe-Pit 275
Hahn-Cin 276

Starter Runs
Taylor-Chi 52.3
Hahn-Cin 36.1
Willis-Bos 26.5
Phillippe-Pit 21.9
Tannehill-Pit 21.3

Adjusted Starter Runs
Taylor-Chi 47.7
Hahn-Cin 44.3
Mathewson-NY 24.1
Phillippe-Pit 20.3
Tannehill-Pit 19.9

Clutch Pitching Index
Lundgren-Chi 150
Eason-Chi-Bos 139
Poole-Pit-Cin 137
Taylor-Chi 129
Taylor-NY 126

Total Pitcher Index
Taylor-Chi 6.0
Hahn-Cin 4.7
Tannehill-Pit 3.6
Phillips-Cin 3.2
Mathewson-NY 3.1

Total Baseball Ranking
Taylor-Chi 6.0
Hahn-Cin 4.7
Wagner-Pit 4.2
Tenney-Bos 4.0
Leach-Pit 3.8

TEAM	G	W	L	PCT	GB	R	OR	AB	H	2B	3B	HR	BB	SO	AVG	OBP	SLG	PRO	/A	BR	/A	PF	CHI	RC	TA	SB	CS	SBASBR
PHI	137	83	53	.610		775	636	4762	1369	235	67	38	343	293	.287	.335	.389	.724	109	51	-5	108	106	706	.706	201		
STL	140	78	58	.574	5	619	607	4736	1254	208	61	29	373	327	.265	.318	.353	.671	94	-36	-50	102	96	590	.626	137		
BOS	138	77	60	.562	6.5	664	600	4875	1356	195	95	42	275	375	.278	.317	.383	.700	101	1	5	99	97	649	.646	132		
CHI	138	74	60	.552	8	675	602	4654	1248	170	50	14	411	381	.268	.328	.335	.663	92	-40	-9	95	106	613	.656	265		
CLE	137	69	67	.507	14	686	667	4840	1401	248	68	33	308	356	.289	.332	.389	.721	108	43	65	97	94	689	.678	140		
WAS	138	61	75	.449	22	707	790	4734	1338	262	66	47	329	296	.283	.329	.396	.725	109	47	57	99	98	673	.684	121		
DET	137	52	83	.385	30.5	566	657	4644	1167	141	55	22	359	287	.251	.305	.320	.625	81	-111	-103	99	102	505	.567	130		
BAL	141	50	88	.362	34	715	848	4760	1318	202	107	33	417	429	.277	.335	.385	.720	107	47	33	102	97	695	.709	189		
TOT	553					5407		38005	10451	1661	569	258	2815	2744	.275	.325	.369	.694								1315		

TEAM	CG	SHO	SV	IP	H	H/G	HR	BB	BB/G	SO	SO/G	ERA	/A	OAVG	OOBA	PR	/A	PF	CPI	FA	E	DP	FW	PW	BW	SBW	DIF
PHI	114	5	2	1215.3	1292	9.6	33	368	2.7	455	3.4	3.29	115	.273	.325	37	67	106	108	.953	270	75	1.5	6.4	-.5		7.6
STL	120	7	2	1242.7	1273	9.2	36	343	2.5	348	2.5	3.34	109	.265	.314	31	41	102	99	.953	274	122	1.3	3.9	-4.7		9.6
BOS	123	6	1	1236.7	1217	8.9	27	326	2.4	431	3.1	3.02	116	.258	.306	75	66	98	100	.955	263	101	2.0	6.3	.5		-.2
CHI	116	11	0	1219.7	1269	9.4	30	331	2.4	346	2.6	3.41	98	.268	.316	21	-7	94	98	.955	257	125	2.3	-.7	-.9		6.2
CLE	116	16	3	1203.0	1199	9.0	26	411	3.1	361	2.7	3.28	105	.260	.321	39	19	96	101	.950	287	96	.5	1.8	6.2		-7.4
WAS	130	2	1	1225.7	1403	10.3	56	312	2.3	300	2.2	4.36	82	.288	.330	-107	-107	100	91	.946	316	70	-1.3	-10.2	5.4		-.9
DET	116	9	3	1188.7	1267	9.6	20	370	2.8	245	1.9	3.56	101	.273	.327	1	3	101	99	.943	332	111	-2.3	.3	-9.8		-3.7
BAL	119	3	1	1207.3	1531	11.4	30	354	2.6	258	1.9	4.31	86	.309	.355	-99	-78	104	105	.938	357	109	-3.9	-7.4	3.1		-10.8
TOT	954	59	13	9739.0		9.7			2.6		2.5	3.57		.275	.325					.949	2356	809					

Runs
Hartsel-Phi 109
Fultz-Phi 109
Strang-Chi 108
Bradley-Cle 104
Delahanty-Was 103

Hits
Hickman-Bos-Cle 193
L.Cross-Phi 191
Bradley-Cle 187
Delahanty-Was 178
Freeman-Bos 174

Doubles
Delahanty-Was 43
Davis-Phi 43
L.Cross-Phi 39
Bradley-Cle 39
Freeman-Bos 38

Triples
Williams-Bal 21
Freeman-Bos 19
Ferris-Bos 14
Delahanty-Was 14
Hickman-Bos-Cle 13

Home Runs
Seybold-Phi 16
Hickman-Bos-Cle 11
Freeman-Bos 11
Bradley-Cle 11
Delahanty-Was 10

Total Bases
Hickman-Bos-Cle 289
Freeman-Bos 283
Bradley-Cle 283
Delahanty-Was 279
Seybold-Phi 264

Runs Batted In
Freeman-Bos 121
Hickman-Bos-Cle 110
L.Cross-Phi 108
Seybold-Phi 97

Runs Produced
L.Cross-Phi 198
Delahanty-Was 186
Freeman-Bos 185
Davis-Phi 175

Bases On Balls
Hartsel-Phi 87
Strang-Chi 76
Barrett-Det 74
Burkett-StL 71
Davis-Chi 65

Batting Average
Delahanty-Was 376
Hickman-Bos-Cle 361
Dougherty-Bos 342
L.Cross-Phi 342
Bradley-Cle 340

On Base Percentage
Delahanty-Was 449
Dougherty-Bos 400
Barrett-Det 391
Selbach-Bal 390
Jones-Chi 387

Slugging Average
Delahanty-Was 590
Hickman-Bos-Cle 541
Bradley-Cle 515
Seybold-Phi 506
Freeman-Bos 502

Production
Delahanty-Was 1.038
Hickman-Bos-Cle 920
Bradley-Cle 885
Seybold-Phi 874
Williams-Bal 860

Adjusted Production
Delahanty-Was 191
Hickman-Bos-Cle 159
Bradley-Cle 150
Williams-Bal 136
Freeman-Bos 135

Batter Runs
Delahanty-Was 56.9
Hickman-Bos-Cle . . . 35.8
Lajoie-Phi-Cle 31.5
Bradley-Cle 30.9
Seybold-Phi 28.0

Adjusted Batter Runs
Delahanty-Was 57.9
Hickman-Bos-Cle . . . 37.7
Bradley-Cle 33.4
Lajoie-Phi-Cle 33.0
Freeman-Bos 23.8

Clutch Hitting Index
Davis-Chi 159
Mertes-Chi 151
L.Cross-Phi 139
Daly-Chi 131
Keister-Was 126

Runs Created
Delahanty-Was 136
Hickman-Bos-Cle 116
Bradley-Cle 112
Freeman-Bos 106
L.Cross-Phi 103

Total Average
Delahanty-Was 1.210
Hickman-Bos-Cle 918
Hartsel-Phi 887
Bradley-Cle 884
Seybold-Phi 877

Stolen Bases
Hartsel-Phi 47
Mertes-Chi 46
Fultz-Phi 44

Stolen Base Average

Stolen Base Runs

Fielding Runs
Ferris-Bos 25.0
Jones-Chi 12.9
Schreck-Cle-Phi 12.6
Bradley-Cle 12.3
M.Cross-Phi 11.8

Total Player Rating
Lajoie-Phi-Cle 4.4
Delahanty-Was 4.0
Bradley-Cle 3.9
Hickman-Bos-Cle . . . 2.8
Davis-Chi 2.5

Wins
Young-Bos 32
Waddell-Phi 24
Powell-StL 22
Donahue-StL 22
Dinneen-Bos 21

Win Percentage
Bernhard-Phi-Cle 783
Waddell-Phi 774
Young-Bos 744
Donahue-StL 667
Griffith-Chi 625

Games
Young-Bos 45
Powell-StL 42
Dinneen-Bos 42
Wiltse-Phi-Bal 38
Orth-Was 38

Complete Games
Young-Bos 41
Dinneen-Bos 39
Powell-StL 36
Orth-Was 36

Shutouts
Joss-Cle 5
Siever-Det 4
Moore-Cle 4
Mercer-Det 4

Saves
Powell-StL 2

Innings Pitched
Young-Bos 385
Dinneen-Bos 371
Powell-StL 328
Orth-Was 324
Donahue-StL 316

Fewest Hits/Game
Bernhard-Phi-Cle . . . 7.01
Waddell-Phi 7.30
Joss-Cle 7.53
Siever-Det 7.95
Winter-Bos 7.98

Fewest BB/Game
Orth-Was 1.11
Young-Bos 1.24
Bernhard-Phi-Cle . . . 1.47
Siever-Det 1.53
Plank-Phi 1.83

Strikeouts
Waddell-Phi 210
Young-Bos 160
Powell-StL 137
Dinneen-Bos 136
Plank-Phi 107

Strikeouts/Game
Waddell-Phi 6.85
Powell-StL 3.76
Young-Bos 3.74
Joss-Cle 3.55
Piatt-Chi 3.51

Wins Above Team
Young-Bos 10.9
Waddell-Phi 7.5
Bernhard-Phi-Cle . . . 6.9
Donahue-StL 4.4
McGinnity-Bal 4.1

Earned Run Average
Siever-Det 1.91
Waddell-Phi 2.05
Bernhard-Phi-Cle . . . 2.15
Young-Bos 2.15
Garvin-Chi 2.21

Adjusted ERA
Siever-Det 187
Waddell-Phi 184
Young-Bos 163
Bernhard-Phi-Cle 160
Garvin-Chi 152

Opponents' Batting Avg.
Bernhard-Phi-Cle 216
Waddell-Phi 223
Joss-Cle 228
Siever-Det 238
Winter-Bos 239

Opponents' On Base Pc'.
Bernhard-Phi-Cle 250
Waddell-Phi 269
Young-Bos 270
Siever-Det 271
Joss-Cle 283

Starter Runs
Young-Bos 60.7
Waddell-Phi 46.4
Bernhard-Phi-Cle . . . 35.6
Siever-Det 34.6
Donahue-StL 28.3

Adjusted Starter Runs
Young-Bos 57.9
Waddell-Phi 53.2
Siever-Det 34.9
Bernhard-Phi-Cle . . . 32.5
Donahue-StL 30.7

Clutch Pitching Index
Garvin-Chi 128
Shields-Bal-StL 125
Moore-Cle 120
Husting-Bos-Phi 119
Donahue-StL 110

Relief Runs

Adjusted Relief Runs

Relief Ranking

Total Pitcher Index
Waddell-Phi 6.4
Young-Bos 5.3
Donahue-StL 3.8
Bernhard-Phi-Cle . . . 3.3
Siever-Det 3.1

Total Baseball Ranking
Waddell-Phi 6.4
Young-Bos 5.3
Lajoie-Phi-Cle 4.4
Delahanty-Was 4.0
Bradley-Cle 3.9

TEAM	G	W	L	PCT	GB	R	OR	AB	H	2B	3B	HR	BB	SO	AVG	OBP	SLG	PRO	/A	BR	/A	PF	CHI	RC	TA	SB	CS	SBA	SBR
PIT	141	91	49	.650		793	613	4991	1430	208	110	34	364		.287	.335	.393	.728	116	90	57	105	100	744	.701	172			
NY	142	84	55	.604	6.5	729	567	4741	1290	181	49	20	379		.272	.326	.344	.670	99	-3	-46	106	108	652	.658	264			
CHI	139	82	56	.594	8	695	599	4733	1300	191	62	9	422		.275	.334	.347	.681	103	19	50	95	100	664	.677	259			
CIN	141	74	65	.532	16.5	765	656	4857	1399	228	92	28	403		.288	.343	.390	.733	118	102	40	109	97	726	.706	144			
BRO	139	70	66	.515	19	667	682	4534	1201	177	56	15	522		.265	.341	.339	.680	102	26	17	101	97	647	.699	273			
BOS	140	58	80	.420	32	578	699	4682	1145	176	47	25	398		.245	.304	.318	.622	85	-84	-58	96	100	524	.579	159			
PHI	139	49	86	.363	39.5	617	738	4781	1283	186	62	12	338		.268	.317	.341	.658	96	-28	-24	92	96	584	.597	120			
STL	139	43	94	.314	46.5	505	795	4689	1176	138	65	8	277		.251	.293	.313	.606	80	-118	-94	96	96	501	.545	171			
TOT	560					5349		38008	10224	1485	543	151	3103	3767	.269	.324	.349	.673								1562			

TEAM	CG	SHO	SV	IP	H	H/G	HR	BB	BB/G	SO	SO/G	ERA	/A	OAVG	OOBA	PR	/A	PF	CPI	FA	E	DP	FW	PW	BW	SBW	DIF
PIT	117	15	5	1251.0	1215	8.7	9	384	2.8	454	3.3	2.91	114	.255	.310	50	56	101	97	.951	295	100	1.4	5.4	5.5		8.7
NY	115	8	8	1267.3	1257	8.9	20	371	2.6	628	4.5	2.95	115	.259	.311	45	60	103	100	.951	287	87	2.0	5.7	-4.4		11.2
CHI	117	6	6	1231.0	1182	8.6	14	354	2.6	451	3.3	2.77	110	.252	.305	68	39	94	99	.942	338	78	-1.5	3.7	4.8		5.9
CIN	126	11	1	1229.0	1277	9.4	14	378	2.8	480	3.5	3.07	114	.268	.321	27	58	107	104	.946	312	84	.3	5.6	3.8		-5.2
BRO	118	11	4	1212.0	1276	9.5	18	377	2.8	438	3.3	3.44	97	.270	.324	-22	-15	102	96	.951	284	98	2.2	-1.4	1.6		-.4
BOS	125	5	1	1190.7	1310	9.9	30	460	3.5	516	3.9	3.34	96	.279	.343	-9	-16	98	114	.937	361	89	-3.0	-1.5	-5.6		-.9
PHI	126	5	3	1205.0	1347	10.1	21	425	3.2	381	2.8	3.97	78	.282	.341	-94	-118	94	94	.947	300	76	1.1	-11.3	2.3		-10.6
STL	111	4	2	1211.3	1353	10.1	25	430	3.2	419	3.1	3.76	88	.282	.341	-65	-58	102	101	.940	354	111	-2.5	-5.6	-9.0		-8.4
TOT	955	65	30	9797.3		9.4			2.9		3.5	3.27		.269	.324					.946	2531	723					

Runs	Hits	Doubles	Triples	Home Runs	Total Bases
Beaumont-Pit 137	Beaumont-Pit 209	Steinfeldt-Cin 32	Wagner-Pit 19	Sheckard-Bro 9	Beaumont-Pit 272
Donlin-Cin 110	Seymour-Cin 191	Mertes-NY 32	Donlin-Cin 18		Seymour-Cin 267
Browne-NY 105	Browne-NY 185	Clarke-Pit 32	Leach-Pit 17		Wagner-Pit 265
Slagle-Chi 104	Wagner-Pit 182				Donlin-Cin 256
Strang-Bro 101	Donlin-Cin 174				Sheckard-Bro 245

Runs Batted In	Runs Produced	Bases On Balls	Batting Average	On Base Percentage	Slugging Average
Mertes-NY 104	Beaumont-Pit 198	Thomas-Phi 107	Wagner-Pit 355	Thomas-Phi 450	Clarke-Pit 532
Wagner-Pit 101	Mertes-NY 197	Dahlen-Bro 82	Clarke-Pit 351	Bresnahan-NY 435	Wagner-Pit 518
Doyle-Bro 91	Wagner-Pit 193	Slagle-Chi 81	Donlin-Cin 351	Chance-Chi 428	Donlin-Cin 516
Leach-Pit 87	Leach-Pit 177	Chance-Chi 78	Bresnahan-NY 350	Sheckard-Bro 417	Bresnahan-NY 493
Steinfeldt-Cin 83	Doyle-Bro 175		Seymour-Cin 342	Donlin-Cin 417	Steinfeldt-Cin 481

Production	Adjusted Production	Batter Runs	Adjusted Batter Runs	Clutch Hitting Index	Runs Created
Clarke-Pit 940	Clarke-Pit 162	Donlin-Cin 43.2	Sheckard-Bro 38.6	Corcoran-Cin 158	Sheckard-Bro 133
Donlin-Cin 933	Wagner-Pit 158	Wagner-Pit 41.5	Wagner-Pit 38.2	Doyle-Bro 139	Wagner-Pit 130
Bresnahan-NY 927	Chance-Chi 157	Sheckard-Bro 39.6	Donlin-Cin 36.8	Chance-Chi 138	Donlin-Cin 120
Wagner-Pit 924	Bresnahan-NY 157	Clarke-Pit 37.1	Thomas-Phi 36.7	Dahlen-Bro 132	Beaumont-Pit 116
Sheckard-Bro 893	Sheckard-Bro 155	Bresnahan-NY 36.9	Chance-Chi 35.4	Beckley-Cin 131	Chance-Chi 114

Total Average	Stolen Bases	Stolen Base Average	Stolen Base Runs	Fielding Runs	Total Player Rating
Chance-Chi 1.141	Sheckard-Bro 67			Sheckard-Bro 30.0	Sheckard-Bro 5.7
Sheckard-Bro 1.125	Chance-Chi 67			Gremminger-Bos . . . 20.0	Wagner-Pit 5.4
Bresnahan-NY 1.117	Wagner-Pit 46			Farrell-StL 17.2	Donlin-Cin 4.0
Wagner-Pit 1.076	Strang-Bro 46			Dahlen-Bro 16.7	Bresnahan-NY 3.4
Donlin-Cin 1.050	Mertes-NY 45			Slagle-Chi 15.8	Dahlen-Bro 2.9

Wins	Win Percentage	Games	Complete Games	Shutouts	Saves
McGinnity-NY 31	Leever-Pit 781	McGinnity-NY 55	McGinnity-NY 44	Leever-Pit 7	Miller-NY 3
Mathewson-NY 30	Phillippe-Pit 735	Mathewson-NY 45	Mathewson-NY 37	Schmidt-Bro 5	Lundgren-Chi 3
Phillippe-Pit 25	Weimer-Chi 714	Pittinger-Bos 44	Pittinger-Bos 35	Hahn-Cin 5	
Leever-Pit 25	Mathewson-NY 698	Schmidt-Bro 40	Hahn-Cin 34	Phillippe-Pit 4	
	Wicker-StL-Chi 690		Taylor-Chi 33	Jones-Bro 4	

Innings Pitched	Fewest Hits/Game	Fewest BB/Game	Strikeouts	Strikeouts/Game	Wins Above Team
McGinnity-NY 434	Weimer-Chi 7.69	Phillippe-Pit 90	Mathewson-NY 267	Mathewson-NY 6.57	Leever-Pit 7.0
Mathewson-NY 366	Mathewson-NY 7.89	Hahn-Cin 1.43	McGinnity-NY 171	Piatt-Bos 4.97	Mathewson-NY 6.6
Pittinger-Bos 352	Taylor-Chi 7.99	Taylor-Chi 1.64	Garvin-Bro 154	Garvin-Bro 4.65	Hahn-Cin 5.1
Jones-Bro 324	Leever-Pit 8.08	McFarland-StL 1.89	Pittinger-Bos 140	Weimer-Chi 4.09	Schmidt-Bro 5.1
Taylor-Chi 312	McGinnity-NY 8.11	Leever-Pit 1.90	Weimer-Chi 128	Willis-Bos 4.05	Phillippe-Pit 5.1

Earned Run Average	Adjusted ERA	Opponents' Batting Avg.	Opponents' On Base Pct.	Starter Runs	Adjusted Starter Runs
Leever-Pit 2.06	Leever-Pit 161	Weimer-Chi 232	Phillippe-Pit 269	Mathewson-NY 41.0	McGinnity-NY 45.9
Mathewson-NY 2.26	Mathewson-NY 149	Mathewson-NY 236	Taylor-Chi 277	McGinnity-NY 40.7	Mathewson-NY 45.4
Weimer-Chi 2.30	McGinnity-NY 139	Taylor-Chi 238	Leever-Pit 284	Leever-Pit 38.2	Leever-Pit 39.5
McGinnity-NY 2.43	Hahn-Cin 139	Leever-Pit 240	Mathewson-NY 293	Weimer-Chi 30.5	Hahn-Cin 32.1
Phillippe-Pit 2.43	Phillippe-Pit 136	McGinnity-NY 241	Hahn-Cin 295	Taylor-Chi 28.4	Phillippe-Pit 28.4

Clutch Pitching Index	Relief Runs	Adjusted Relief Runs	Relief Ranking	Total Pitcher Index	Total Baseball Ranking
Brown-StL 152				Mathewson-NY 5.1	Sheckard-Bro 5.7
Pittinger-Bos 121				McGinnity-NY 4.1	Wagner-Pit 5.4
Malarkey-Bos 118				Leever-Pit 3.9	Mathewson-NY 5.1
Piatt-Bos 117				Hahn-Cin 3.1	McGinnity-NY 4.1
Ewing-Cin 113				Phillippe-Pit 2.6	Donlin-Cin 4.0

TEAM	G	W	L	PCT	GB	R	OR	AB	H	2B	3B	HR	BB	SO	AVG	OBP	SLG	PRO	/A	BR	/A	PF	CHI	RC	TA	SB	CS	SBA	SBR
BOS	141	91	47	.659		708	504	4919	1336	222	113	48	262	561	.272	.308	.392	.700	117	92	21	112	103	654	.651	141			
PHI	137	75	60	.556	14.5	597	519	4673	1236	228	68	31	268	513	.264	.304	.362	.666	107	38	17	104	98	577	.616	157			
CLE	140	77	63	.550	15	639	579	4773	1265	231	95	31	259	595	.265	.303	.373	.676	110	51	71	96	101	607	.631	175			
NY	136	72	62	.537	17	579	573	4565	1136	193	62	18	332	465	.249	.300	.330	.630	97	-13	-13	100	105	512	.583	160			
DET	137	65	71	.478	25	567	539	4582	1229	162	91	12	292	526	.268	.312	.351	.663	107	37	54	97	95	556	.605	128			
STL	139	65	74	.468	26.5	500	525	4639	1133	166	68	12	271	539	.244	.286	.317	.603	88	-61	-32	95	99	461	.526	101			
CHI	138	60	77	.438	30.5	516	613	4670	1152	176	49	14	325	537	.247	.296	.314	.610	91	-45	0	92	97	499	.561	180			
WAS	140	43	94	.314	47.5	437	691	4613	1066	172	71	17	257	463	.231	.272	.310	.582	81	-97	-127	105	94	435	.513	131			
TOT	554					4543		37434	9553	1550	617	183	2266	4199	.255	.298	.344	.642								1173			

TEAM	CG	SHO	SV	IP	H	H/G	HR	BB	BB/G	SO	SO/G	ERA	/A	OAVG	OOBA	PR	/A	PF	CPI	FA	E	DP	FW	PW	BW	SBW	DIF
BOS	123	20	4	1253.7	1142	8.2	22	269	1.9	579	4.2	2.56	124	.242	.282	54	85	108	100	.959	239	86	1.9	8.8	2.2		9.1
PHI	112	10	1	1206.0	1124	8.4	20	315	2.4	728	5.4	2.98	101	.246	.294	-3	4	102	94	.960	217	66	3.3	.4	1.8		2.0
CLE	125	20	1	1243.3	1161	8.4	16	271	2.0	521	3.8	2.66	106	.246	.287	40	21	95	100	.946	322	99	-3.4	2.2	7.4		.9
NY	111	7	2	1200.7	1171	8.8	19	245	1.8	463	3.5	3.08	96	.254	.292	-17	-17	100	92	.953	264	87	.3	-1.8	-1.3		7.8
DET	123	15	2	1195.3	1169	8.8	19	336	2.5	554	4.2	2.75	103	.255	.306	27	11	96	112	.950	281	82	-.8	1.1	5.6		-8.9
STL	124	12	3	1220.7	1220	9.0	26	237	1.7	511	3.8	2.77	102	.259	.295	24	6	96	100	.953	268	94	.0	.6	-3.3		-1.8
CHI	114	9	4	1234.7	1233	9.0	24	287	2.1	391	2.9	3.02	92	.259	.301	-8	-33	94	102	.949	297	85	-1.8	-3.4	.0		-3.2
WAS	122	6	3	1222.7	1333	9.8	38	306	2.3	452	3.3	3.82	86	.276	.319	-117	-72	111	96	.954	260	86	.5	-7.5	-13.2		-5.4
TOT	954	99	20	9777.0		8.8			2.1		3.9	2.95		.255	.298					.953	2148	685					

Runs
Dougherty-Bos 106
Bradley-Cle 101
Keeler-NY 95
Barrett-Det 95
Bay-Cle 94

Hits
Dougherty-Bos 195
Crawford-Det 184
Parent-Bos 170
Bay-Cle 169
Bradley-Cle 168

Doubles
Seybold-Phi 45
Lajoie-Cle 41
Freeman-Bos 39
Bradley-Cle 36
Anderson-StL........34

Triples
Crawford-Det 25
Bradley-Cle 22
Freeman-Bos 20
Parent-Bos 17
Collins-Bos 17

Home Runs
Freeman-Bos 13
Hickman-Cle.........12
Ferris-Bos 9
Seybold-Phi 8

Total Bases
Freeman-Bos 281
Crawford-Det 269
Bradley-Cle 266
Lajoie-Cle 251
Dougherty-Bos 250

Runs Batted In
Freeman-Bos 104
Hickman-Cle........97
Lajoie-Cle 93
L.Cross-Phi 90
Crawford-Det 89

Runs Produced
Lajoie-Cle 176
Crawford-Det 173
Freeman-Bos 165
Bradley-Cle 163
Dougherty-Bos 161

Bases On Balls
Barrett-Det 74
Lush-Det 70
Pickering-Phi 53
Burkett-StL 52
Flick-Cle 51

Batting Average
Lajoie-Cle 344
Crawford-Det 335
Dougherty-Bos 331
Barrett-Det 315
Bradley-Cle 313

On Base Percentage
Barrett-Det 401
Lush-Det 377
Lajoie-Cle 375
Green-Chi 368
Dougherty-Bos 366

Slugging Average
Lajoie-Cle 518
Bradley-Cle 496
Freeman-Bos 496
Crawford-Det 489
Hickman-Cle........466

Production
Lajoie-Cle 893
Crawford-Det 853
Bradley-Cle 840
Freeman-Bos 819
Seybold-Phi 808

Adjusted Production
Lajoie-Cle 174
Crawford-Det 161
Bradley-Cle 157
Green-Chi 151
Barrett-Det 145

Batter Runs
Lajoie-Cle 37.8
Crawford-Det 35.3
Bradley-Cle 31.3
Barrett-Det 29.1
Hartsel-Phi 29.0

Adjusted Batter Runs
Lajoie-Cle 39.9
Crawford-Det 37.3
Bradley-Cle 33.6
Barrett-Det 31.2
Green-Chi 29.4

Clutch Hitting Index
Gochnauer-Cle 168
L.Cross-Phi 152
Williams-NY 152
Ganzel-NY 143
Lajoie-Cle 130

Runs Created
Crawford-Det 107
Dougherty-Bos 107
Lajoie-Cle 105
Bradley-Cle 101
Freeman-Bos 95

Total Average
Lajoie-Cle 931
Barrett-Det 856
Crawford-Det 852
Bradley-Cle 848
Green-Chi 835

Stolen Bases
Bay-Cle 45
Pickering-Phi 40
Holmes-Was-Chi 35
Dougherty-Bos 35
Conroy-NY 33

Stolen Base Average

Stolen Base Runs

Fielding Runs
Lajoie-Cle 36.7
Wallace-StL 17.2
Williams-NY 14.2
Ferris-Bos 13.6
Selbach-Was 13.1

Total Player Rating
Lajoie-Cle 7.9
Bradley-Cle 4.5
Crawford-Det 4.2
Barrett-Det 2.7
Williams-NY 2.6

Wins
Young-Bos 28
Plank-Phi 23

Win Percentage
Young-Bos 757
Hughes-Bos 741
Moore-Cle 679
Dinneen-Bos 618
Plank-Phi 590

Games
Plank-Phi 43
Mullin-Det 41
Young-Bos 40
Flaherty-Chi 40
Chesbro-NY 40

Complete Games
Young-Bos 34
Waddell-Phi 34
Donovan-Det 34

Shutouts
Young-Bos 7
Mullin-Det 6
Dinneen-Bos 6
Sudhoff-StL 5
Hughes-Bos 5

Saves
Young-Bos 2
Powell-StL 2
Orth-Was 2
Mullin-Det 2
Dinneen-Bos 2

Innings Pitched
Young-Bos 342
Plank-Phi 336
Chesbro-NY 325
Waddell-Phi 324
Mullin-Det 321

Fewest Hits/Game
Moore-Cle 7.11
Donovan-Det 7.24
Joss-Cle 7.35
Waddell-Phi 7.61
Dinneen-Bos 7.68

Fewest BB/Game
Young-Bos 97
Bernhard-Cle 1.14
Donahue-StL-Cle ..1.14
Joss-Cle 1.17
Tannehill-NY 1.28

Strikeouts
Waddell-Phi 302
Donovan-Det 187
Young-Bos 176
Plank-Phi 176
Mullin-Det 170

Strikeouts/Game
Waddell-Phi 8.39
Donovan-Det 5.48
Moore-Cle 5.37
Powell-StL 4.97
Mullin-Det 4.77

Wins Above Team
Young-Bos 6.5
Sudhoff-StL 4.9
Moore-Cle 4.7
Hughes-Bos 3.8
Bernhard-Cle 3.7

Earned Run Average
Moore-Cle 1.74
Young-Bos 2.08
Bernhard-Cle 2.11
White-Chi 2.13
Joss-Cle 2.19

Adjusted ERA
Moore-Cle 161
Young-Bos 153
Dinneen-Bos 141
Bernhard-Cle 133
White-Chi 130

Opponents' Batting Avg.
Moore-Cle 217
Donovan-Det 220
Joss-Cle 223
Waddell-Phi 229
Dinneen-Bos 230

Opponents' On Base Pct.
Joss-Cle 249
Young-Bos 253
Bernhard-Cle 267
Moore-Cle 267
Dinneen-Bos 274

Starter Runs
Moore-Cle 33.4
Young-Bos 33.2
White-Chi 27.4
Mullin-Det 25.3
Joss-Cle 24.2

Adjusted Starter Runs
Young-Bos 41.6
Dinneen-Bos 30.5
Moore-Cle 29.9
Plank-Phi 23.5
White-Chi 21.5

Clutch Pitching Index
Kitson-Det 128
Mullin-Det 121
Donahue-StL-Cle ...119
Plank-Phi 111
Moore-Cle 110

Relief Runs

Adjusted Relief Runs

Relief Ranking

Total Pitcher Index
Young-Bos 5.8
Mullin-Det 3.8
White-Chi 3.2
Dinneen-Bos 3.1
Moore-Cle 2.9

Total Baseball Ranking
Lajoie-Cle 7.9
Young-Bos 5.8
Bradley-Cle 4.5
Crawford-Det 4.2
Mullin-Det 3.8

TEAM	G	W	L	PCT	GB	R	OR	AB	H	2B	3B	HR	BB	SO	AVG	OBP	SLG	PRO	/A	BR	/A	PF	CHI	RC	TA	SB	CS	SBA	SBR
NY	158	106	47	.693		744	476	5150	1347	201	66	31	434		.262	.319	.344	.663	113	78	46	105	106	691	.655	283			
CHI	156	93	60	.608	13	599	517	5210	1294	157	62	22	298		.248	.289	.315	.604	94	-37	-40	101	104	569	.553	227			
CIN	157	88	65	.575	18	695	547	5231	1332	189	92	21	399		.255	.307	.338	.645	107	43	-46	114	104	630	.602	179			
PIT	156	87	66	.569	19	675	592	5160	1333	164	102	15	391		.258	.311	.338	.649	109	49	53	99	101	627	.605	178			
STL	155	75	79	.487	31.5	602	595	5104	1292	175	66	24	343		.253	.300	.327	.627	102	8	14	99	98	590	.581	199			
BRO	154	56	97	.366	50	497	614	4917	1142	159	53	15	411		.232	.291	.295	.586	89	-54	-26	95	92	511	.548	205			
BOS	155	55	98	.359	51	491	749	5135	1217	153	50	24	316		.237	.281	.300	.581	87	-75	-53	97	93	498	.511	143			
PHI	155	52	100	.342	53.5	571	784	5103	1268	170	54	23	377		.248	.300	.316	.616	98	-7	37	93	95	560	.561	159			
TOT	623					4874		41010	10225	1368	545	175	2969	4277	.249	.300	.322	.622								1573			

TEAM	CG	SHO	SV	IP	H	H/G	HR	BB	BB/G	SO	SO/G	ERA	/A	OAVG	OOBA	PR	/A	PF	CPI	FA	E	DP	FW	PW	BW	SBW	DIF
NY	127	21	15	1392.0	1151	7.4	36	349	2.3	707	4.6	2.17	125	.226	.275	86	84	100	100	.956	294	93	1.9	8.9	4.9		13.9
CHI	139	18	6	1380.0	1150	7.5	15	402	2.6	618	4.0	2.30	117	.227	.284	65	59	99	96	.954	298	89	1.7	6.2	-4.2		12.8
CIN	142	12	2	1387.0	1256	8.1	14	343	2.2	502	3.3	2.35	129	.242	.289	58	106	111	104	.954	301	81	1.5	11.2	-4.9		3.7
PIT	133	14	1	1347.7	1273	8.5	13	379	2.5	455	3.0	2.89	92	.250	.302	-24	-34	98	94	.955	291	93	2.1	-3.6	5.6		6.4
STL	146	7	2	1359.7	1286	8.5	23	319	2.1	529	3.5	2.64	102	.250	.294	13	7	99	100	.952	307	83	1.1	.7	1.5		-5.3
BRO	135	12	2	1331.7	1281	8.7	27	414	2.8	453	3.1	2.70	99	.253	.310	3	-5	98	110	.945	343	87	-1.2	-.5	-2.7		-16.0
BOS	136	13	0	1340.0	1405	9.4	25	500	3.4	544	3.7	3.43	81	.270	.334	-104	-97	102	104	.945	353	91	-1.9	-10.2	-5.6		-3.8
PHI	131	10	2	1334.0	1418	9.6	22	425	2.9	469	3.2	3.39	78	.272	.327	-97	-110	97	102	.936	403	93	-5.1	-11.6	3.9		-11.2
TOT	1089	107	30	10872.0		8.5			2.6			3.5	2.73	.249	.300					.950	2590	710					

Runs
Browne-NY 99
Wagner-Pit 97
Beaumont-Pit 97
Huggins-Cin 96

Hits
Beaumont-Pit 185
Beckley-StL 179
Wagner-Pit 171
Browne-NY 169
Seymour-Cin 166

Doubles
Wagner-Pit 44
Mertes-NY 28
Delahanty-Bos 27
Seymour-Cin 26
Dahlen-NY 26

Triples
Lumley-Bro 18
Wagner-Pit 14
Tinker-Chi 13
Seymour-Cin 13
Kelley-Cin 13

Home Runs
Lumley-Bro 9
Brain-StL 7

Total Bases
Wagner-Pit 255
Lumley-Bro 247
Seymour-Cin 233
Beaumont-Pit 230
Beckley-StL 222

Runs Batted In
Dahlen-NY 80
Mertes-NY 78
Lumley-Bro 78
Wagner-Pit 75
Corcoran-Cin 74

Runs Produced
Wagner-Pit 168
Mertes-NY 157
Lumley-Bro 148
Dahlen-NY 148
Beaumont-Pit 148

Bases On Balls
Thomas-Phi 102
Huggins-Cin 88
Devlin-NY 62
Wagner-Pit 59
Ritchey-Pit 59

Batting Average
Wagner-Pit 349
Beckley-StL 325
Seymour-Cin 313
Chance-Chi 310
Beaumont-Pit 301

On Base Percentage
Wagner-Pit 419
Thomas-Phi 411
Huggins-Cin 375
Beckley-StL 365
Devlin-NY 364

Slugging Average
Wagner-Pit 520
Seymour-Cin 439
Chance-Chi 430
Lumley-Bro 428
Brain-StL 408

Production
Wagner-Pit 939
Chance-Chi 792
Seymour-Cin 787
Beckley-StL 768
Thomas-Phi 756

Adjusted Production
Wagner-Pit 193
Thomas-Phi 148
Chance-Chi 146
Lumley-Bro 141
Titus-Phi 141

Batter Runs
Wagner-Pit 52.8
Thomas-Phi 28.3
Seymour-Cin 25.5
Donlin-Cin-NY 24.4
Beckley-StL 24.4

Adjusted Batter Runs
Wagner-Pit 53.2
Thomas-Phi 33.1
Beckley-StL 25.1
Lumley-Bro 24.4
Grady-StL 23.6

Clutch Hitting Index
Dahlen-NY 170
Corcoran-Cin 159
Bransfield-Pit 154
Kelley-Cin 141
Gilbert-NY 138

Runs Created
Wagner-Pit 132
Lumley-Bro 93
Mertes-NY 90
Beckley-StL 89
Beaumont-Pit 89

Total Average
Wagner-Pit 1.150
Chance-Chi 875
Thomas-Phi 855
Mertes-NY 805
Devlin-NY 771

Stolen Bases
Wagner-Pit 53
Mertes-NY 47
Dahlen-NY 47
McGann-NY 42
Chance-Chi 42

Stolen Base Average

Stolen Base Runs

Fielding Runs
Leach-Pit 32.2
Evers-Chi 31.1
Dahlen-NY 24.3
Odwell-Cin 18.7
Farrell-StL 16.8

Total Player Rating
Wagner-Pit 4.9
Leach-Pit 4.1
Thomas-Phi 3.9
Evers-Chi 3.1
Titus-Phi 2.9

Wins
McGinnity-NY 35
Mathewson-NY 33
Harper-Cin 23
Taylor-NY 21
Nichols-StL 21

Win Percentage
McGinnity-NY 814
Mathewson-NY 733
Harper-Cin 719
Flaherty-Pit 679

Games
McGinnity-NY 51
Mathewson-NY 48
Jones-Bro 46
Willis-Bos 43
Fraser-Phi 42

Complete Games
Willis-Bos 39
Taylor-StL 39
McGinnity-NY 38
Jones-Bro 38

Shutouts
McGinnity-NY 9
Harper-Cin 6

Saves
McGinnity-NY 5
Wiltse-NY 3
Briggs-Chi 3
Ames-NY 3

Innings Pitched
McGinnity-NY 408
Jones-Bro 377
Mathewson-NY 368
Taylor-NY 352
Willis-Bos 350

Fewest Hits/Game
Brown-Chi 6.58
Weimer-Chi 6.71
McGinnity-NY 6.77
Garvin-Bro 6.97
Taylor-NY 7.02

Fewest BB/Game
Hahn-Cin 1.06
Phillippe-Pit 1.40
Nichols-StL 1.42
Kellum-Cin 1.84
McFarland-StL 1.87

Strikeouts
Mathewson-NY 212
Willis-Bos 196
Weimer-Chi 177
Pittinger-Bos 146
McGinnity-NY 144

Strikeouts/Game
Wiltse-NY 5.73
Weimer-Chi 5.19
Mathewson-NY 5.18
Willis-Bos 5.04
Phillippe-Pit 4.42

Wins Above Team
McGinnity-NY 10.2
Harper-Cin 6.3
Nichols-StL 5.2
Flaherty-Pit 4.1
Mathewson-NY 4.0

Earned Run Average
McGinnity-NY 1.61
Garvin-Bro 1.68
Brown-Chi 1.87
Weimer-Chi 1.91
Nichols-StL 2.02

Adjusted ERA
McGinnity-NY 169
Garvin-Bro 159
Hahn-Cin 148
Brown-Chi 144
Weimer-Chi 141

Opponents' Batting Avg.
Brown-Chi 205
Weimer-Chi 209
McGinnity-NY 210
Garvin-Bro 215
Taylor-NY 216

Opponents' On Base Pct.
McGinnity-NY 260
Brown-Chi 260
Hahn-Cin 262
Nichols-StL 265
Mathewson-NY 271

Starter Runs
McGinnity-NY 50.7
Mathewson-NY 28.6
Weimer-Chi 28.1
Nichols-StL 25.1
Hahn-Cin 22.3

Adjusted Starter Runs
McGinnity-NY 50.2
Hahn-Cin 32.6
Mathewson-NY 28.1
Weimer-Chi 26.9
Nichols-StL 23.9

Clutch Pitching Index
Garvin-Bro 153
O'Neill-StL 146
Briggs-Chi 127
Walker-Cin 118
Willis-Bos 118

Relief Runs

Adjusted Relief Runs

Relief Ranking

Total Pitcher Index
McGinnity-NY 5.9
Mathewson-NY 3.7
Hahn-Cin 3.6
Weimer-Chi 3.2
Garvin-Bro 2.6

Total Baseball Ranking
McGinnity-NY 5.9
Wagner-Pit 4.9
Leach-Pit 4.1
Thomas-Phi 3.9
Mathewson-NY 3.7

TEAM	G	W	L	PCT	GB	R	OR	AB	H	2B	3B	HR	BB	SO	AVG	OBP	SLG	PRO	/A	BR	/A	PF	CHI	RC	TA	SB	CS	SBA	SBR
BOS	157	95	59	.617		608	466	5231	1294	194	105	26	347	570	.247	.294	.340	.634	108	41	14	105	101	566	.565	101			
NY	155	92	59	.609	1.5	598	526	5220	1354	195	91	27	312	548	.259	.301	.347	.648	112	66	-2	112	96	610	.592	163			
CHI	156	89	65	.578	6	600	482	5027	1217	193	68	14	373	586	.242	.294	.316	.610	100	5	9	99	109	544	.571	216			
CLE	154	86	65	.570	7.5	647	482	5152	1340	225	90	27	307	714	.260	.302	.354	.656	115	78	69	102	103	620	.606	178			
PHI	155	81	70	.536	12.5	557	503	5088	1266	197	77	31	313	605	.249	.292	.336	.628	106	30	20	102	97	553	.565	137			
STL	156	65	87	.428	29	481	604	5291	1266	153	53	10	332	609	.239	.284	.294	.578	90	-54	-25	95	94	497	.506	150			
DET	162	62	90	.408	32	505	627	5321	1231	154	69	11	344	635	.231	.278	.292	.570	87	-69	-43	96	100	475	.492	112			
WAS	157	38	113	.252	55.5	437	743	5149	1170	171	57	10	283	759	.227	.267	.288	.555	82	-96	-55	93	97	448	.482	150			
TOT	626					4433		41479	10138	1482	610	156	2611	5026	.244	.289	.321	.610								1207			

TEAM	CG	SHO	SV	IP	H	H/G	HR	BB	BB/G	SO	SO/G	ERA	/A	OAVG	OOBA	PR	/A	PF	CPI	FA	E	DP	FW	PW	BW	SBW	DIF
BOS	148	21	1	1405.7	1208	7.7	31	233	1.5	612	3.9	2.12	124	.232	.265	74	80	101	103	.962	242	83	1.5	8.9	1.6		6.0
NY	123	15	1	1380.3	1180	7.7	29	311	2.0	684	4.5	2.57	112	.232	.276	4	46	111	90	.958	275	90	-.7	5.1	-.2		12.3
CHI	134	26	3	1378.7	1161	7.6	13	303	2.0	550	3.6	2.30	109	.229	.272	45	31	97	94	.964	238	95	1.7	3.5	1.0		5.8
CLE	141	20	0	1355.3	1273	8.5	10	285	1.9	627	4.2	2.22	115	.249	.288	57	48	98	117	.959	255	86	.6	5.4	7.7		-3.2
PHI	137	26	0	1360.0	1149	7.6	13	366	2.4	887	5.9	2.35	111	.229	.282	37	40	101	98	.959	250	67	.9	4.5	2.2		-2.1
STL	135	13	1	1408.3	1335	8.5	25	333	2.1	577	3.7	2.83	90	.250	.295	-36	-46	98	99	.960	267	78	-.2	-5.1	-2.8		-2.9
DET	143	15	2	1429.3	1345	8.5	16	433	2.7	556	3.5	2.77	92	.249	.305	-27	-35	98	104	.959	273	92	-.6	-3.9	-4.8		-4.7
WAS	137	7	4	1359.0	1487	9.8	19	347	2.3	533	3.5	3.62	71	.278	.322	-154	-158	99	98	.951	314	97	-3.3	-17.7	-6.1		-10.4
TOT	1098	143	12	11076.7		8.2			2.1		4.1	2.60		.244	.289					.959	2114	688					

Runs
Dougherty-Bos-NY . .113
Flick-Cle 97
Bradley-Cle 94
Lajoie-Cle 92

Hits
Lajoie-Cle 208
Keeler-NY 186
Bradley-Cle 183
Dougherty-Bos-NY . .181
Flick-Cle 177

Doubles
Lajoie-Cle 49
Collins-Bos 33
Bradley-Cle 32

Triples
Stahl-Bos 19
Freeman-Bos 19
Cassidy-Was 19
Murphy-Phi 17
Flick-Cle 17

Home Runs
Davis-Phi 10
Murphy-Phi 7
Freeman-Bos 7
Bradley-Cle 246

Total Bases
Lajoie-Cle 305
Flick-Cle 260
Freeman-Bos 246

Runs Batted In
Lajoie-Cle 102
Freeman-Bos 84
Bradley-Cle 83
Anderson-NY 82

Runs Produced
Lajoie-Cle 188
Bradley-Cle 172
Parent-Bos 156
Collins-Bos 149
Murphy-Phi 148

Bases On Balls
Barrett-Det 79
Burkett-StL 78
Hartsel-Phi 75
Selbach-Was-Bos . . .72
Lush-Cle 72

Batting Average
Lajoie-Cle 376
Keeler-NY 343
Flick-Cle 306
Bradley-Cle 300
Seybold-Phi 292

On Base Percentage
Lajoie-Cle 405
Keeler-NY 382
Flick-Cle 362
Stahl-Bos 359
Burkett-StL 358

Slugging Average
Lajoie-Cle 552
Flick-Cle 449
Murphy-Phi 440
Hickman-Cle-Det . . .437
Stahl-Bos 416

Production
Lajoie-Cle 957
Flick-Cle 811
Keeler-NY 791
Stahl-Bos 775
Murphy-Phi 754

Adjusted Production
Lajoie-Cle 201
Flick-Cle 156
Stahl-Bos 141
Hickman-Cle-Det . . .137
Murphy-Phi 137

Batter Runs
Lajoie-Cle 61.3
Flick-Cle 37.5
Stahl-Bos 32.2
Keeler-NY 31.9
Davis-Phi 27.9

Adjusted Batter Runs
Lajoie-Cle 60.4
Flick-Cle 36.5
Stahl-Bos 29.1
Davis-Phi 27.2
Keeler-NY 24.7

Clutch Hitting Index
Anderson-NY 145
Tannehill-Chi 140
Callahan-Chi 140
Jones-StL 135
Ferris-Bos 132

Runs Created
Lajoie-Cle 139
Flick-Cle 111
Keeler-NY 95
Stahl-Bos 94
Bradley-Cle 91

Total Average
Lajoie-Cle 1.046
Flick-Cle 868
Keeler-NY 779
Stahl-Bos 765
Murphy-Phi 728

Stolen Bases
Flick-Cle 38
Bay-Cle 38
Heidrick-StL 35
Davis-Chi 32
Conroy-NY 30

Stolen Base Average

Stolen Base Runs

Fielding Runs
Tannehill-Chi 25.4
Davis-Chi 17.2
Williams-NY 16.2
Murphy-Phi 10.8
Barrett-Det 10.6

Total Player Rating
Lajoie-Cle 7.3
Flick-Cle 4.0
Bradley-Cle 3.7
Murphy-Phi 3.6
Davis-Phi 2.9

Wins
Chesbro-NY 41
Young-Bos 26
Plank-Phi 26
Waddell-Phi 25

Win Percentage
Chesbro-NY 774
Tannehill-Bos 656
Smith-Chi 640
Bernhard-Cle 639
Dinneen-Bos 622

Games
Chesbro-NY 55
Powell-NY 47
Waddell-Phi 46
Patten-Was 45
Mullin-Det 45

Complete Games
Chesbro-NY 48
Mullin-Det 42
Young-Bos 40
Waddell-Phi 39
Powell-NY 38

Shutouts
Young-Bos 10
Waddell-Phi 8
White-Chi 7
Plank-Phi 7
Mullin-Det 7

Saves
Patten-Was 3

Innings Pitched
Chesbro-NY 455
Powell-NY 390
Waddell-Phi 383
Mullin-Det 382
Young-Bos 380

Fewest Hits/Game
Chesbro-NY 6.69
Owen-Chi 6.94
Smith-Chi 7.00
Gibson-Bos 7.12
Waddell-Phi 7.21

Fewest BB/Game
Young-Bos 69
Tannehill-Bos 1.05
Patterson-Chi 1.31
Joss-Cle 1.41
Altrock-Chi 1.41

Strikeouts
Waddell-Phi 349
Chesbro-NY 239
Powell-NY 202
Plank-Phi 201
Young-Bos 200

Strikeouts/Game
Waddell-Phi 8.20
Bender-Phi 6.57
Moore-Cle 5.49
Plank-Phi 5.07
Glade-StL 4.86

Wins Above Team
Chesbro-NY 14.0
Plank-Phi 4.9
Glade-StL 4.1
Patten-Was 3.9
Donovan-Det 3.6

Earned Run Average
Joss-Cle 1.59
Waddell-Phi 1.62
White-Chi 1.78
Chesbro-NY 1.82
Owen-Chi 1.94

Adjusted ERA
Waddell-Phi 161
Joss-Cle 159
Chesbro-NY 158
White-Chi 141
Young-Bos 134

Opponents' Batting Avg.
Chesbro-NY 208
Owen-Chi 214
Smith-Chi 215
Gibson-Bos 219
Waddell-Phi 221

Opponents' On Base Pct.
Chesbro-NY 249
Young-Bos 249
Owen-Chi 254
Joss-Cle 259
Tannehill-Bos 266

Starter Runs
Waddell-Phi 41.5
Chesbro-NY 39.3
Young-Bos 26.6
Owen-Chi 22.9
Joss-Cle 21.4

Adjusted Starter Runs
Chesbro-NY 53.3
Waddell-Phi 42.3
Young-Bos 28.2
Joss-Cle 20.2
Owen-Chi 19.7

Clutch Pitching Index
White-Chi 152
Siever-StL 136
Bernhard-Cle 133
Waddell-Phi 125
Donahue-Cle 120

Relief Runs

Adjusted Relief Runs

Relief Ranking

Total Pitcher Index
Chesbro-NY 7.0
Waddell-Phi 5.2
Mullin-Det 3.1
Tannehill-Bos 3.0
Owen-Chi 3.0

Total Baseball Ranking
Lajoie-Cle 7.3
Chesbro-NY 7.0
Waddell-Phi 5.2
Flick-Cle 4.0
Bradley-Cle 3.7

TEAM	G	W	L	PCT	GB	R	OR	AB	H	2B	3B	HR	BB	SO	AVG	OBP	SLG	PRO	/A	BR	/A	PF	CHI	RC	TA	SB	CS	SBA	SBR
NY	155	105	48	.686		778	505	5094	1392	191	88	39	517		.273	.340	.368	.708	121	131	123	101	100	772	.725	291			
PIT	155	96	57	.627	9	692	570	5213	1385	190	91	22	382		.266	.316	.350	.666	108	43	17	104	100	674	.629	202			
CHI	155	92	61	.601	13	667	442	5108	1249	157	82	12	448		.245	.305	.314	.619	93	-31	-60	105	109	609	.601	267			
PHI	155	83	69	.546	21.5	708	602	5243	1362	187	82	16	406		.260	.313	.336	.649	103	16	-11	104	106	644	.605	180			
CIN	155	79	74	.516	26	735	698	5205	1401	160	101	27	434		.269	.325	.354	.679	112	74	53	103	101	696	.646	181			
STL	154	58	96	.377	47.5	535	734	5066	1254	140	85	20	391		.248	.301	.321	.622	94	-32	-22	91	90	565	.571	162			
BOS	156	51	103	.331	54.5	468	731	5190	1217	148	52	17	302		.234	.277	.293	.570	78	-134	-114	97	95	479	.492	132			
BRO	155	48	104	.316	56.5	506	807	5100	1255	154	60	29	327		.246	.292	.317	.609	90	-62	-35	96	90	554	.554	186			
TOT	620					5089		41219	10515	1327	641	182	3207	4462	.255	.309	.332	.641								1601			

TEAM	CG	SHO	SV	IP	H	H/G	HR	BB	BB/G	SO	SO/G	ERA	/A	OAVG	OOBA	PR	/A	PF	CPI	FA	E	DP	FW	PW	BW	SBW	DIF
NY	117	18	15	1367.7	1160	7.6	25	364	2.4	760	5.0	2.39	120	.232	.284	91	72	96	100	.960	258	93	2.3	7.5	12.8		6.0
PIT	113	12	6	1372.3	1270	8.3	11	389	2.6	512	3.4	2.86	106	.248	.301	20	27	102	96	.961	255	112	2.5	2.8	1.8		12.4
CHI	133	23	2	1402.7	1135	7.3	15	385	2.5	627	4.0	2.04	147	.224	.278	148	148	100	106	.962	248	99	2.9	15.4	-6.2		3.4
PHI	119	12	5	1389.0	1303	8.4	21	411	2.7	516	3.3	2.81	109	.250	.305	27	37	102	103	.953	275	99	1.2	3.8	-1.1		3.1
CIN	119	10	2	1361.7	1409	9.3	22	439	2.9	547	3.6	3.01	102	.269	.326	-2	9	103	115	.953	310	122	-1.0	.9	5.5		-2.9
STL	135	10	2	1347.3	1431	9.6	28	367	2.5	411	2.7	3.59	79	.274	.322	-89	-111	95	97	.957	274	83	1.3	-11.5	2.3		-11.0
BOS	139	13	0	1378.3	1390	9.1	36	433	2.8	533	3.5	3.52	87	.264	.320	-80	-71	102	96	.951	325	89	-2.0	-7.4	-11.8		-4.8
BRO	125	7	3	1342.7	1416	9.5	24	476	3.2	556	3.7	3.76	81	.273	.334	-114	-107	102	97	.937	408	101	-7.3	-11.1	-3.6		-6.0
TOT	1000	105	35	10961.7		8.6			2.7		3.7	2.99		.255	.309					.954	2353	798					

Runs
Donlin-NY	124
Thomas-Phi	118
Huggins-Cin	117
Wagner-Pit	114

Hits
Seymour-Cin	219
Donlin-NY	216
Wagner-Pit	199
Barry-Chi-Cin	182
Magee-Phi	180

Doubles
Seymour-Cin	40
Titus-Phi	36
Wagner-Pit	32
Donlin-NY	31
Ritchey-Pit	29

Triples
Seymour-Cin	21
Mertes-NY	17
Magee-Phi	17
Smoot-StL	16
Donlin-NY	16

Home Runs
Odwell-Cin	9
Seymour-Cin	8
Lumley-Bro	7
Donlin-NY	7
Dahlen-NY	7

Total Bases
Seymour-Cin	325
Donlin-NY	300
Wagner-Pit	277
Magee-Phi	253
Titus-Phi	239

Runs Batted In
Seymour-Cin	121
Mertes-NY	108
Wagner-Pit	101
Magee-Phi	98
Titus-Phi	89

Runs Produced
Wagner-Pit	209
Seymour-Cin	208
Donlin-NY	197
Magee-Phi	193
Titus-Phi	186

Bases On Balls
Huggins-Cin	103
Slagle-Chi	97
Thomas-Phi	93
Chance-Chi	78
Titus-Phi	69

Batting Average
Seymour-Cin	.377
Wagner-Pit	.363
Donlin-NY	.356
Thomas-Phi	.317
Smoot-StL	.311

On Base Percentage
Seymour-Cin	.427
Wagner-Pit	.420
Thomas-Phi	.414
Donlin-NY	.411
Titus-Phi	.386

Slugging Average
Seymour-Cin	.559
Wagner-Pit	.505
Donlin-NY	.495
Titus-Phi	.436
McGann-NY	.434

Production
Seymour-Cin	.987
Wagner-Pit	.926
Donlin-NY	.906
Titus-Phi	.822
McGann-NY	.804

Adjusted Production
Seymour-Cin	190
Wagner-Pit	171
Donlin-NY	170
Smoot-StL	148
Titus-Phi	141

Batter Runs
Seymour-Cin	65.8
Donlin-NY	52.5
Wagner-Pit	51.7
Chance-Chi	33.2
Titus-Phi	32.7

Adjusted Batter Runs
Seymour-Cin	63.6
Donlin-NY	51.7
Wagner-Pit	49.0
Chance-Chi	30.8
Titus-Phi	29.7

Clutch Hitting Index
Mertes-NY	162
Dahlen-NY	152
Wolverton-Bos	140
Corcoran-Cin	139
Tinker-Chi	134

Runs Created
Seymour-Cin	152
Wagner-Pit	144
Donlin-NY	140
Magee-Phi	107
Mertes-NY	100

Total Average
Wagner-Pit	1.112
Seymour-Cin	1.097
Donlin-NY	.997
Mertes-NY	.851
McGann-NY	.843

Stolen Bases
Maloney-Chi	59
Devlin-NY	59
Wagner-Pit	57
Mertes-NY	52
Magee-Phi	48

Stolen Base Average

Stolen Base Runs

Fielding Runs
Huggins-Cin	36.1
Sheckard-Bro	25.0
Tenney-Bos	20.3
Corcoran-Cin	18.7
Wagner-Pit	17.6

Total Player Rating
Wagner-Pit	7.0
Seymour-Cin	6.0
Huggins-Cin	6.0
Sheckard-Bro	3.9
Chance-Chi	2.7

Wins
Mathewson-NY	31
Pittinger-Phi	23
Ames-NY	22
McGinnity-NY	21

Win Percentage
Leever-Pit	.800
Mathewson-NY	.795
Ames-NY	.733
Wiltse-NY	.714
Lynch-Pit	.680

Games
Pittinger-Phi	46
McGinnity-NY	46
Young-Bos	43
Mathewson-NY	43
Overall-Cin	42

Complete Games
Young-Bos	41
Willis-Bos	36
Fraser-Bos	35
Taylor-StL	34

Shutouts
Mathewson-NY	8
Young-Bos	6
Reulbach-Chi	5
Phillippe-Pit	5
Briggs-Chi	5

Saves
Elliott-NY	6
Wiltse-NY	4
McGinnity-NY	3

Innings Pitched
Young-Bos	378
Willis-Bos	342
Mathewson-NY	339
Pittinger-Phi	337
Fraser-Bos	334

Fewest Hits/Game
Reulbach-Chi	6.41
Mathewson-NY	6.69
Wicker-Chi	7.03
Lundgren-Chi	7.03
Wiltse-NY	7.22

Fewest BB/Game
Phillippe-Pit	1.55
Brown-Chi	1.59
Young-Bos	1.69
Mathewson-NY	1.70
McGinnity-NY	2.00

Strikeouts
Mathewson-NY	206
Ames-NY	198
Overall-Cin	173
Ewing-Cin	164
Young-Bos	156

Strikeouts/Game
Ames-NY	6.78
Wiltse-NY	5.48
Mathewson-NY	5.47
Overall-Cin	4.90
Scanlan-Bro	4.86

Wins Above Team
Mathewson-NY	8.1
Leever-Pit	6.3
Young-Bos	6.0
Ewing-Cin	4.8
Scanlan-Bro	4.8

Earned Run Average
Mathewson-NY	1.27
Reulbach-Chi	1.42
Wicker-Chi	2.02
Briggs-Chi	2.14
Brown-Chi	2.17

Adjusted ERA
Mathewson-NY	225
Reulbach-Chi	211
Wicker-Chi	148
Sparks-Phi	140
Briggs-Chi	140

Opponents' Batting Avg.
Reulbach-Chi	.203
Mathewson-NY	.210
Wicker-Chi	.218
Lundgren-Chi	.218
Wiltse-NY	.223

Opponents' On Base Pct.
Mathewson-NY	.250
Reulbach-Chi	.268
Phillippe-Pit	.273
Wicker-Chi	.273
Brown-Chi	.275

Starter Runs
Mathewson-NY	64.7
Reulbach-Chi	51.0
Phillippe-Pit	24.7
Sparks-Phi	23.4
Brown-Chi	22.8

Adjusted Starter Runs
Mathewson-NY	59.9
Reulbach-Chi	51.0
Phillippe-Pit	26.2
Sparks-Phi	25.3
Brown-Chi	22.8

Clutch Pitching Index
Chech-Cin	134
Duggleby-Phi	127
Mathewson-NY	126
Reulbach-Chi	124
Case-Pit	117

Relief Runs

Adjusted Relief Runs

Relief Ranking

Total Pitcher Index
Mathewson-NY	7.6
Reulbach-Chi	5.7
Phillippe-Pit	2.7
Brown-Chi	2.4
Sparks-Phi	2.1

Total Baseball Ranking
Mathewson-NY	7.6
Wagner-Pit	7.0
Seymour-Cin	6.0
Huggins-Cin	6.0
Reulbach-Chi	5.7

TEAM	G	W	L	PCT	GB	R	OR	AB	H	2B	3B	HR	BB	SO	AVG	OBP	SLG	PRO	/A	BR	/A	PF	CHI	RC	TA	SB	CS	SBA	SBR
PHI	152	92	56	.622		623	492	5107	1300	256	51	24	376		.255	.306	.339	.645	113	66	12	109	97	601	.603	189			
CHI	158	92	60	.605	2	612	451	5109	1212	200	55	11	439		.237	.298	.304	.602	99	-1	18	97	105	533	.561	194			
DET	154	79	74	.516	15.5	512	602	4968	1208	191	54	13	375		.243	.296	.311	.607	100	4	14	98	90	509	.545	129			
BOS	153	78	74	.513	16	579	564	5031	1177	165	69	29	486		.234	.301	.311	.612	102	20	18	100	96	525	.567	131			
CLE	155	76	78	.494	19	567	587	5130	1309	211	72	18	286		.255	.294	.335	.629	107	33	34	100	94	575	.574	188			
NY	152	71	78	.477	21.5	586	622	4957	1228	163	61	23	360		.248	.299	.319	.618	104	20	10	102	101	546	.574	200			
WAS	154	64	87	.424	29.5	559	623	5009	1117	193	68	22	298		.223	.267	.302	.569	87	-72	-95	104	115	459	.508	169			
STL	156	54	99	.353	40.5	511	608	5204	1205	153	49	16	362		.232	.282	.289	.571	88	-63	-12	91	98	472	.499	130			
TOT	617					4549		40515	9756	1532	479	156	2982	5107	.241	.293	.314	.606								1330			

TEAM	CG	SHO	SV	IP	H	H/G	HR	BB	BB/G	SO	SO/G	ERA	/A	OAVG	OOBA	PR	/A	PF	CPI	FA	E	DP	FW	PW	BW	SBW	DIF
PHI	117	19	0	1427.0	1137	7.2	21	409	2.6	895	5.6	2.19	129	.221	.278	72	99	106	102	.958	264	64	.5	10.9	1.3		5.3
CHI	131	17	0	1415.7	1163	7.4	11	329	2.1	613	3.9	1.99	124	.226	.273	103	74	93	108	.968	217	95	3.7	8.1	2.0		2.2
DET	124	17	1	1336.3	1226	8.3	11	474	3.2	578	3.9	2.83	94	.246	.312	-27	-26	100	105	.957	265	80	.5	-2.9	1.5		3.4
BOS	124	15	1	1344.0	1198	8.0	33	292	2.0	652	4.4	2.84	93	.241	.283	-28	-29	100	91	.953	294	75	-1.5	-3.2	2.0		4.7
CLE	140	16	0	1363.0	1251	8.3	23	334	2.2	555	3.7	2.85	93	.246	.293	-31	-30	100	96	.963	229	84	2.9	-3.3	3.7		-4.3
NY	88	19	4	1348.0	1235	8.2	26	396	2.6	642	4.3	2.92	93	.246	.301	-40	-30	103	99	.952	293	88	-1.4	-3.3	1.1		.1
WAS	118	12	1	1358.7	1250	8.3	12	385	2.6	539	3.6	2.87	97	.247	.300	-33	-11	106	97	.951	318	76	-3.1	-1.2	-10.4		3.2
STL	134	11	2	1378.3	1245	8.1	19	389	2.5	633	4.1	2.74	90	.243	.297	-14	-41	93	100	.955	295	78	-1.5	-4.5	-1.3		-15.1
TOT	976	126	9	10971.0		8.0			2.5		4.2	2.65		.241	.293					.957	2175	640					

Runs
Davis-Phi 92
Jones-Chi 91
Bay-Cle 90
Hartsel-Phi 87
Keeler-NY 81

Hits
Stone-StL 187
Davis-Phi 171
Crawford-Det 171
Keeler-NY 169
Bay-Cle 166

Doubles
Davis-Phi 47
Crawford-Det 38
Hickman-Det-Was 37
Seybold-Phi 37

Triples
Flick-Cle 18
Ferris-Bos 16
Turner-Cle 14
Stone-StL 13
Burkett-Bos 13

Home Runs
Davis-Phi 8
Stone-StL 7

Total Bases
Stone-StL 259
Davis-Phi 254
Crawford-Det 247
Hickman-Det-Was . .232
Flick-Cle 231

Runs Batted In
Davis-Phi 83
L.Cross-Phi 77
Donahue-Chi 76
Crawford-Det 75
Turner-Cle 72

Runs Produced
Davis-Phi 167
Donahue-Chi 146
L.Cross-Phi 145
Crawford-Det 142
Murphy-Phi 136

Bases On Balls
Hartsel-Phi 121
Jones-Chi 73
Selbach-Bos 67
Burkett-Bos 67
Davis-Chi 60

Batting Average
Flick-Cle 308
Keeler-NY 302
Bay-Cle 301
Crawford-Det 297
Stone-StL 296

On Base Percentage
Hartsel-Phi 410
Flick-Cle 374
Crawford-Det 354
Keeler-NY 352
Selbach-Bos 351

Slugging Average
Flick-Cle 462
Crawford-Det 430
Davis-Phi 422
Stone-StL 410
Hickman-Det-Was . . .405

Production
Flick-Cle 836
Crawford-Det 783
Hartsel-Phi 757
Davis-Phi 754
Stone-StL 752

Adjusted Production
Flick-Cle 168
Stone-StL 154
Crawford-Det 153
Hartsel-Phi 131
Bay-Cle 129

Batter Runs
Flick-Cle 37.5
Hartsel-Phi 34.6
Crawford-Det 31.7
Stone-StL 27.2
Davis-Phi 25.8

Adjusted Batter Runs
Flick-Cle 37.7
Stone-StL 33.3
Crawford-Det 32.9
Hartsel-Phi 28.2
Davis-Phi 19.6

Clutch Hitting Index
Donahue-Chi 152
Gleason-StL 145
L.Cross-Phi 136
Jones-StL 128
Stahl-Was 124

Runs Created
Flick-Cle 102
Stone-StL 100
Davis-Phi 99
Crawford-Det 97
Hartsel-Phi 93

Total Average
Flick-Cle 922
Hartsel-Phi 886
Crawford-Det 790
Davis-Phi 773
Stone-StL 739

Stolen Bases
Hoffman-Phi 46
Fultz-NY 44
Stahl-Was 41

Stolen Base Average

Stolen Base Runs

Fielding Runs
Cassidy-Was 35.7
Tannehill-Chi 27.0
Wallace-StL 21.3
Howell-StL 17.8
McIntyre-Det 15.5

Total Player Rating
Wallace-StL 4.5
Crawford-Det 3.9
Davis-Chi 3.8
Flick-Cle 3.0
Collins-Bos 2.7

Wins
Waddell-Phi 27
Plank-Phi 24
Killian-Det 23
Altrock-Chi 23
Tannehill-Bos 22

Win Percentage
Waddell-Phi 730
Tannehill-Bos 710
Coakley-Phi 692
Plank-Phi 667
Altrock-Chi 657

Games
Waddell-Phi 46
Mullin-Det 44
Patten-Was 42
Owen-Chi 42

Complete Games
Plank-Phi 35
Mullin-Det 35
Howell-StL 35
Killian-Det 33
Owen-Chi 32

Shutouts
Killian-Det 8
Waddell-Phi 7
Tannehill-Bos 6
Orth-NY 6
Hughes-Was 6

Saves
Buchanan-StL 2

Innings Pitched
Mullin-Det 348
Plank-Phi 347
Owen-Chi 334
Waddell-Phi 329
Howell-StL 323

Fewest Hits/Game
Waddell-Phi 6.32
Smith-Chi 6.63
Young-Bos 6.95
Howell-StL 7.02
White-Chi 7.06

Fewest BB/Game
Young-Bos 84
Joss-Cle 1.45
Owen-Chi 1.51
Bernhard-Cle 1.76
Altrock-Chi 1.79

Strikeouts
Waddell-Phi 287
Young-Bos 210
Plank-Phi 210
Howell-StL 198
Smith-Chi 171

Strikeouts/Game
Waddell-Phi 7.85
Young-Bos 5.89
Bender-Phi 5.58
Howell-StL 5.52
Hogg-NY 5.49

Wins Above Team
Tannehill-Bos 7.1
Waddell-Phi 6.4
Killian-Det 5.0
Joss-Cle 4.9
Rhoads-Cle 4.1

Earned Run Average
Waddell-Phi 1.48
White-Chi 1.77
Young-Bos 1.82
Coakley-Phi 1.84
Altrock-Chi 1.88

Adjusted ERA
Waddell-Phi 190
Coakley-Phi 153
Young-Bos 145
White-Chi 140
Joss-Cle 132

Opponents' Batting Avg.
Waddell-Phi 200
Smith-Chi 208
Young-Bos 216
Howell-StL 218
White-Chi 219

Opponents' On Base Pct.
Young-Bos 236
Waddell-Phi 258
Owen-Chi 262
White-Chi 264
Joss-Cle 267

Starter Runs
Waddell-Phi 42.7
Young-Bos 29.4
Altrock-Chi 26.9
White-Chi 25.5
Howell-StL 24.0

Adjusted Starter Runs
Waddell-Phi 48.8
Young-Bos 29.3
Coakley-Phi 27.7
Plank-Phi 21.5
Altrock-Chi 20.5

Clutch Pitching Index
Coakley-Phi 144
Altrock-Chi 122
Waddell-Phi 117
Mullin-Det 115
Townsend-Was 113

Relief Runs

Adjusted Relief Runs

Relief Ranking

Total Pitcher Index
Waddell-Phi 5.8
Howell-StL 4.4
Altrock-Chi 3.4
Young-Bos 3.2
Coakley-Phi 3.0

Total Baseball Ranking
Waddell-Phi 5.8
Wallace-StL 4.5
Howell-StL 4.4
Crawford-Det 3.9
Davis-Chi 3.8

TEAM	G	W	L	PCT	GB	R	OR	AB	H	2B	3B	HR	BB	SO	AVG	OBP	SLG	PRO	/A	BR	/A	PF	CHI	RC	TA	SB	CS	SBA	SBR
CHI	155	116	36	.763		705	381	5018	1316	181	71	20	448		.262	.323	.339	.662	116	84	46	107	108	683	.656	283			
NY	153	96	56	.632	20	625	510	4768	1217	162	53	15	563		.255	.334	.321	.655	113	84	84	100	99	642	.671	288			
PIT	154	93	60	.608	23.5	623	470	5030	1313	164	67	12	424		.261	.318	.327	.645	110	57	33	104	101	615	.601	162			
PHI	154	71	82	.464	45.5	528	564	4911	1183	197	47	12	432		.241	.302	.307	.609	98	-5	39	92	98	542	.569	180			
BRO	153	66	86	.434	50	496	625	4897	1156	141	68	25	388		.236	.292	.308	.600	95	-27	45	87	96	523	.554	175			
CIN	155	64	87	.424	51.5	470	582	5025	1198	140	71	16	395		.238	.294	.304	.598	95	-30	-112	115	101	532	.547	170			
STL	154	52	98	.347	63	470	607	5075	1195	137	69	10	361		.235	.286	.296	.582	90	-61	-64	101	95	490	.508	110			
BOS	152	49	102	.325	66.5	408	649	4925	1115	136	43	16	356		.226	.279	.281	.560	82	-96	-96	100	93	437	.481	93			
TOT	615					4388		39649	9693	1258	489	126	3367	4537	.244	.304	.310	.614								1461			

TEAM	CG	SHO	SV	IP	H	H/G	HR	BB	BB/G	SO	SO/G	ERA	/A	OAVG	OOBA	PR	/A	PF	CPI	FA	E	DP	FW	PW	BW	SBW	DIF
CHI	125	30	10	1386.7	1018	6.6	12	446	2.9	702	4.6	1.76	148	.208	.275	134	130	99	103	.969	194	100	4.4	14.4	5.1		16.1
NY	105	18	18	1329.3	1207	8.2	13	394	2.7	639	4.3	2.49	103	.246	.302	20	10	97	105	.963	233	84	1.8	1.1	9.3		7.8
PIT	116	27	2	1364.0	1234	8.1	13	309	2.0	532	3.5	2.21	120	.245	.289	63	66	101	108	.964	228	109	2.1	7.3	3.7		3.4
PHI	108	20	5	1339.3	1201	8.1	18	436	2.9	500	3.4	2.58	95	.243	.305	7	-20	93	103	.956	271	83	-.7	-2.2	4.3		-6.9
BRO	119	22	11	1344.3	1255	8.4	15	453	3.0	476	3.2	3.13	75	.251	.313	-75	-116	90	91	.955	283	73	-1.5	-12.8	5.0		-.6
CIN	126	12	5	1359.3	1248	8.3	14	470	3.1	567	3.8	2.69	114	.248	.312	-8	55	116	104	.959	262	97	-.1	6.1	-12.4		-5.1
STL	118	4	2	1317.3	1246	8.5	17	479	3.3	559	3.8	3.04	90	.253	.319	-60	-45	104	99	.957	272	92	-.8	-5.0	-7.1		-10.1
BOS	137	10	0	1325.0	1291	8.8	24	436	3.0	562	3.8	3.18	87	.259	.318	-80	-58	106	97	.947	337	102	-5.1	-6.4	-10.6		-4.3
TOT	954	143	53	10765.3		8.1			2.9		3.8	2.63		.244	.304					.959	2080	740					

Runs
Wagner-Pit 103
Chance-Chi 103
Sheckard-Chi 90
Nealon-Pit 82

Hits
Steinfeldt-Chi 176
Wagner-Pit 175
Seymour-Cin-NY 165
Magee-Phi 159
Huggins-Cin 159

Doubles
Wagner-Pit 38
Magee-Phi 36
Bransfield-Phi 28
Steinfeldt-Chi 27
Sheckard-Chi 27

Triples
Schulte-Chi 13
Clarke-Pit 13
Nealon-Pit 12
Lumley-Bro 12

Home Runs
Jordan-Bro 12
Lumley-Bro 9
Seymour-Cin-NY 8
Schulte-Chi 7

Total Bases
Wagner-Pit 237
Steinfeldt-Chi 232
Lumley-Bro 231
Magee-Phi 229
Schulte-Chi 223

Runs Batted In
Steinfeldt-Chi 83
Nealon-Pit 83
Seymour-Cin-NY 80
Jordan-Bro 78

Runs Produced
Wagner-Pit 172
Chance-Chi 171
Nealon-Pit 162
Steinfeldt-Chi 161
Seymour-Cin-NY 142

Bases On Balls
Thomas-Phi 107
Bresnahan-NY 81
Titus-Phi 78
Dahlen-NY 76
Devlin-NY 74

Batting Average
Wagner-Pit 339
Steinfeldt-Chi 327
Lumley-Bro 324
Chance-Chi 319
Devlin-NY 299

On Base Percentage
Chance-Chi 406
Wagner-Pit 406
Bresnahan-NY 401
Devlin-NY 390
Thomas-Phi 387

Slugging Average
Lumley-Bro 477
Wagner-Pit 459
Steinfeldt-Chi 430
Chance-Chi 430
Jordan-Bro 422

Production
Wagner-Pit 865
Lumley-Bro 863
Chance-Chi 837
Steinfeldt-Chi 811
Devlin-NY 779

Adjusted Production
Lumley-Bro 198
Wagner-Pit 165
Jordan-Bro 164
Chance-Chi 153
Magee-Phi 148

Batter Runs
Wagner-Pit 43.0
Lumley-Bro 38.3
Chance-Chi 36.7
Steinfeldt-Chi 33.3
Devlin-NY 28.7

Adjusted Batter Runs
Lumley-Bro 45.4
Wagner-Pit 40.6
Chance-Chi 33.1
Steinfeldt-Chi 29.4
Devlin-NY 28.7

Clutch Hitting Index
Tinker-Chi 161
Nealon-Pit 156
Ritchey-Pit 138
Mertes-NY -StL 135
Kelley-Cin 134

Runs Created
Wagner-Pit 121
Chance-Chi 109
Lumley-Bro 105
Steinfeldt-Chi 102
Magee-Phi 100

Total Average
Chance-Chi 1.025
Wagner-Pit 1.021
Lumley-Bro 960
Devlin-NY 923
Bresnahan-NY 859

Stolen Bases
Chance-Chi 57
Magee-Phi 55
Devlin-NY 54
Wagner-Pit 53
Evers-Chi 49

Stolen Base Average

Stolen Base Runs

Fielding Runs
Devlin-NY 27.6
Brain-Bos 20.8
Huggins-Cin 20.5
Gilbert-NY 19.0
Kelley-Cin 15.3

Total Player Rating
Wagner-Pit 6.6
Devlin-NY 5.5
Lumley-Bro 4.2
Strang-NY 4.0
Huggins-Cin 3.2

Wins
McGinnity-NY 27
Brown-Chi 26
Willis-Pit 23
Mathewson-NY 22
Leever-Pit 22

Win Percentage
Reulbach-Chi 826
Brown-Chi 813
Leever-Pit 759
Lundgren-Chi 739
Pfiester-Chi 714

Games
McGinnity-NY 45
Young-Bos 43
Sparks-Phi 42
Duggleby-Phi 42

Complete Games
Young-Bos 37
Pfeffer-Bos 33

Shutouts
Brown-Chi 9
Leifield-Pit 8

Saves
Ferguson-NY 7
Wiltse-NY 6
Stricklett-Bro 5

Innings Pitched
Young-Bos 358
McGinnity-NY 340
Willis-Pit 322
Sparks-Phi 317
Lindaman-Bos 307

Fewest Hits/Game
Reulbach-Chi 5.33
Brown-Chi 6.43
Pfiester-Chi 6.43
Beebe-Chi-StL 6.66
Lundgren-Chi 6.92

Fewest BB/Game
Phillippe-Pit 1.07
Leever-Pit 1.66
Sparks-Phi 1.76
Ewing-Cin 1.87
McGinnity-NY 1.88

Strikeouts
Beebe-Chi-StL 171
Pfeffer-Bos 158
Ames-NY 156
Pfiester-Chi 153

Strikeouts/Game
Ames-NY 6.92
Beebe-Chi-StL 6.66
Pfiester-Chi 5.69
Overall-Cin-Chi 5.06
Lush-Phi 4.84

Wins Above Team
Leever-Pit 6.3
Weimer-Cin 5.8
Scanlan-Bro 4.7
McGinnity-NY 4.1
Brown-Chi 4.0

Earned Run Average
Brown-Chi 1.04
Pfiester-Chi 1.56
Reulbach-Chi 1.65
Willis-Pit 1.73
Leifield-Pit 1.86

Adjusted ERA
Brown-Chi 251
Pfiester-Chi 167
Reulbach-Chi 158
Willis-Pit 153
Leifield-Pit 142

Opponents' Batting Avg.
Reulbach-Chi 175
Brown-Chi 204
Pfiester-Chi 204
Beebe-Chi-StL 210
Lundgren-Chi 217

Opponents' On Base Pct.
Brown-Chi 254
Sparks-Phi 264
Pfiester-Chi 270
Reulbach-Chi 278
Ewing-Cin 279

Starter Runs
Brown-Chi 48.9
Willis-Pit 32.1
Pfiester-Chi 28.7
Reulbach-Chi 23.7
Leifield-Pit 21.8

Adjusted Starter Runs
Brown-Chi 48.2
Willis-Pit 32.7
Weimer-Cin 28.4
Pfiester-Chi 28.1
Reulbach-Chi 23.1

Clutch Pitching Index
Willis-Pit 141
Brown-Chi 139
Lush-Phi 130
Lindaman-Bos 128
Leifield-Pit 125

Relief Runs
Ferguson-NY 2

Adjusted Relief Runs

Relief Ranking

Total Pitcher Index
Brown-Chi 6.1
Willis-Pit 4.5
Weimer-Cin 3.3
Pfiester-Chi 3.3
Reulbach-Chi 3.1

Total Baseball Ranking
Wagner-Pit 6.6
Brown-Chi 6.1
Devlin-NY 5.5
Willis-Pit 4.5
Lumley-Bro 4.2

TEAM	G	W	L	PCT	GB	R	OR	AB	H	2B	3B	HR	BB	SO	AVG	OBP	SLG	PRO	/A	BR	/A	PF	CHI	RC	TA	SB	CS	SBA	SBR
CHI	154	93	58	.616		570	460	4921	1132	152	52	6	453		.230	.295	.286	.581	89	-48	-2	92	111	490	.547	214			
NY	155	90	61	.596	3	644	543	5095	1354	166	77	17	331		.266	.311	.339	.650	111	58	-55	120	103	610	.601	192			
CLE	157	89	64	.582	5	663	482	5414	1511	240	73	11	330		.279	.321	.356	.677	120	112	93	103	93	701	.631	203			
PHI	149	78	67	.538	12	561	542	4883	1206	213	49	31	385		.247	.302	.330	.632	105	29	64	94	97	550	.588	166			
STL	154	76	73	.510	16	558	498	5053	1250	145	60	20	366		.247	.298	.312	.610	98	-7	4	98	100	549	.569	222			
DET	151	71	78	.477	21	518	599	4927	1194	154	64	10	333		.242	.290	.306	.596	94	-32	-77	108	100	509	.548	205			
WAS	151	55	95	.367	37.5	518	664	4966	1181	144	65	26	306		.238	.282	.309	.591	92	-46	2	91	103	511	.547	233			
BOS	155	49	105	.318	45.5	462	706	5168	1223	160	75	13	298		.237	.278	.304	.582	89	-63	-52	98	91	477	.499	99			
TOT	613					4494		40427	10051	1374	515	134	2802	4561	.249	.297	.318	.616								1534		

TEAM	CG	SHO	SV	IP	H	H/G	HR	BB	BB/G	SO	SO/G	ERA	/A	OAVG	OOBA	PR	/A	PF	CPI	FA	E	DP	FW	PW	BW	SBW	DIF
CHI	117	32	3	1377.7	1212	7.9	11	255	1.7	543	3.5	2.13	112	.239	.275	85	40	89	104	.963	243	80	1.7	4.4	-.2		11.6
NY	99	18	5	1356.7	1236	8.2	21	351	2.3	605	4.0	2.78	114	.245	.294	-13	60	118	95	.957	272	69	-.1	6.6	-6.0		14.1
CLE	133	27	4	1414.0	1197	7.6	16	365	2.3	530	3.4	2.09	128	.232	.283	94	91	99	110	.967	216	111	3.4	10.0	10.2		-11.2
PHI	107	19	4	1315.3	1135	7.8	9	425	2.9	749	5.1	2.60	96	.235	.297	12	-14	93	97	.957	267	86	.2	-1.5	7.0		-.2
STL	133	17	5	1358.3	1132	7.5	14	314	2.1	558	3.7	2.23	116	.229	.275	68	54	97	96	.954	290	80	-1.3	5.9	.4		-3.6
DET	128	7	4	1338.0	1398	9.4	14	389	2.6	469	3.2	3.06	97	.271	.323	-55	-13	110	109	.959	260	86	.7	-1.4	-8.5		5.7
WAS	115	13	1	1326.3	1331	9.0	15	451	3.1	558	3.8	3.25	78	.263	.324	-82	-105	94	101	.955	279	78	-.6	-11.5	.2		-8.1
BOS	124	6	6	1369.7	1360	8.9	37	285	1.9	549	3.6	3.41	82	.261	.300	-109	-95	104	88	.949	335	84	-4.1	-10.4	-5.7		-7.7
TOT	956	139	32	10856.0		8.3			2.4		3.8	2.69		.249	.297					.958	2162	674					

Runs		Hits		Doubles		Triples		Home Runs		Total Bases	
Flick-Cle	98	Lajoie-Cle	214	Lajoie-Cle	48	Flick-Cle	22	Davis-Phi	12	Stone-StL	291
Keeler-NY	96	Stone-StL	208	Davis-Phi	40	Stone-StL	20	Hickman-Was	9	Lajoie-Cle	280
Hartsel-Phi	96	Flick-Cle	194	Flick-Cle	33	Crawford-Det	16	Stone-StL	6	Flick-Cle	274
Davis-Phi	94	Chase-NY	193	Turner-Cle	27	Ferris-Bos	13	Seybold-Phi	5	Davis-Phi	253
Stone-StL	91	Keeler-NY	180	Davis-Chi	26					Chase-NY	236

Runs Batted In		Runs Produced		Bases On Balls		Batting Average		On Base Percentage		Slugging Average	
Davis-Phi	96	Lajoie-Cle	179	Hartsel-Phi	88	Stone-StL	.358	Stone-StL	.411	Stone-StL	.501
Lajoie-Cle	91	Davis-Phi	178	Jones-Chi	83	Lajoie-Cle	.355	Lajoie-Cle	.386	Lajoie-Cle	.465
Davis-Chi	80	Chase-NY	160	Hahn-NY -Chi	72	Chase-NY	.323	Flick-Cle	.366	Davis-Phi	.459
Williams-NY	77	Flick-Cle	159	Wallace-StL	58	Flick-Cle	.311	Hartsel-Phi	.361	Flick-Cle	.439
Chase-NY	76	Stone-StL	156	McIntyre-Det	56	Keeler-NY	.304	Davis-Phi	.350	Crawford-Det	.407

Production		Adjusted Production		Batter Runs		Adjusted Batter Runs		Clutch Hitting Index		Runs Created	
Stone-StL	.912	Stone-StL	191	Stone-StL	57.1	Stone-StL	58.5	Davis-Phi	179	Stone-StL	137
Lajoie-Cle	.851	Davis-Phi	165	Lajoie-Cle	44.5	Lajoie-Cle	42.5	Wallace-StL	152	Lajoie-Cle	119
Davis-Phi	.809	Lajoie-Cle	163	Flick-Cle	37.6	Davis-Phi	37.1	Williams-NY	151	Flick-Cle	117
Flick-Cle	.805	Flick-Cle	149	Davis-Phi	33.1	Flick-Cle	35.4	Coughlin-Det	145	Davis-Phi	99
Crawford-Det	.746	Hemphill-StL	130	Crawford-Det	21.5	Seybold-Phi	24.2	Stahl-Was	143	Chase-NY	91

Total Average		Stolen Bases		Stolen Base Average		Stolen Base Runs		Fielding Runs		Total Player Rating	
Stone-StL	1.013	Flick-Cle	39					Tannehill-Chi	27.2	Lajoie-Cle	6.8
Flick-Cle	.853	Anderson-Was	39					Lajoie-Cle	23.1	Stone-StL	6.2
Lajoie-Cle	.851	Isbell-Chi	37					Turner-Cle	21.7	Turner-Cle	3.8
Davis-Phi	.833	Altizer-Was	37					Schlafly-Was	15.4	Davis-Phi	3.5
Hartsel-Phi	.748	Donahue-Chi	36					Hahn-NY -Chi	14.4	Flick-Cle	3.1

Wins		Win Percentage		Games		Complete Games		Shutouts		Saves	
Orth-NY	27	Plank-Phi	.760	Chesbro-NY	49	Orth-NY	36	Walsh-Chi	10	Hess-Cle	3
Chesbro-NY	23	White-Chi	.750	Orth-NY	45	Mullin-Det	35	Joss-Cle	9	Bender-Phi	3
Rhoads-Cle	22	Joss-Cle	.700	Waddell-Phi	43	Hess-Cle	33	Waddell-Phi	8		
Owen-Chi	22	Rhoads-Cle	.688	Hess-Cle	43	Rhoads-Cle	31				
		Owen-Chi	.629	Owen-Chi	42						

Innings Pitched		Fewest Hits/Game		Fewest BB/Game		Strikeouts		Strikeouts/Game		Wins Above Team	
Orth-NY	339	Pelty-StL	6.52	Young-Bos	.78	Waddell-Phi	196	Waddell-Phi	6.46	Plank-Phi	6.6
Hess-Cle	334	White-Chi	6.58	Altrock-Chi	1.31	Falkenberg-Was	178	Bender-Phi	6.01	Patten-Was	5.9
Mullin-Det	330	Walsh-Chi	6.96	Joss-Cle	1.37	Walsh-Chi	171	Walsh-Chi	5.54	Joss-Cle	4.9
Chesbro-NY	325	Joss-Cle	7.02	White-Chi	1.56	Hess-Cle	167	Falkenberg-Was	5.36	Rhoads-Cle	4.8
Rhoads-Cle	315	Powell-StL	7.23	Jacobson-StL	1.57	Bender-Phi	159	Powell-StL	4.87	White-Chi	4.7

Earned Run Average		Adjusted ERA		Opponents' Batting Avg.		Opponents' On Base Pct.		Starter Runs		Adjusted Starter Runs	
White-Chi	1.52	Pelty-StL	164	Pelty-StL	.206	White-Chi	.244	Pelty-StL	32.0	Orth-NY	31.7
Pelty-StL	1.59	White-Chi	158	White-Chi	.207	Joss-Cle	.250	Hess-Cle	31.8	Hess-Cle	31.0
Joss-Cle	1.72	Joss-Cle	155	Walsh-Chi	.217	Pelty-StL	.254	Rhoads-Cle	31.1	Rhoads-Cle	30.3
Powell-StL	1.77	Rhoads-Cle	148	Joss-Cle	.218	Walsh-Chi	.260	Joss-Cle	30.2	Joss-Cle	29.6
Rhoads-Cle	1.80	Powell-StL	147	Powell-StL	.223	Glade-StL	.268	White-Chi	28.4	Pelty-StL	29.2

Clutch Pitching Index		Relief Runs		Adjusted Relief Runs		Relief Ranking		Total Pitcher Index		Total Baseball Ranking	
Rhoads-Cle	128							Orth-NY	4.5	Lajoie-Cle	6.8
Siever-Det	124							Pelty-StL	4.0	Stone-StL	6.2
Smith-Was	120							Joss-Cle	3.8	Orth-NY	4.5
Donahue-Det	120							Hess-Cle	3.4	Pelty-StL	4.0
Owen-Chi	119							Rhoads-Cle	3.3	Turner-Cle	3.8

TEAM	G	W	L	PCT	GB	R	OR	AB	H	2B	3B	HR	BB	SO	AVG	OBP	SLG	PRO	/A	BR	/A	PF	CHI	RC	TA	SB	CS	SBA	SBR
CHI	155	107	45	.704		572	390	4892	1224	162	48	13	435		.250	.311	.311	.622	104	25	-8	106	103	585	.597	235			
PIT	157	91	63	.591	17	634	510	4957	1261	133	78	19	469		.254	.319	.324	.643	111	62	34	105	106	633	.633	264			
PHI	149	83	64	.565	21.5	512	476	4725	1113	162	65	12	424		.236	.299	.305	.604	98	-8	-27	104	103	504	.559	154			
NY	155	82	71	.536	25.5	574	510	4874	1222	160	48	23	516		.251	.322	.317	.639	110	61	32	105	95	601	.621	205			
BRO	153	65	83	.439	40	446	522	4895	1135	142	63	18	336		.232	.281	.298	.579	90	-59	-30	94	97	478	.509	121			
CIN	156	66	87	.431	41.5	526	519	4966	1226	126	90	15	372		.247	.299	.318	.617	102	8	32	95	98	556	.563	158			
BOS	152	58	90	.392	47	502	652	5020	1222	142	61	22	413		.243	.301	.309	.610	100	0	25	95	94	532	.548	118			
STL	155	52	101	.340	55.5	419	606	5008	1163	121	51	19	312		.232	.277	.288	.565	85	-84	-62	96	95	464	.489	125			
TOT	616					4185		39337	9566	1148	504	141	3277	4217	.243	.301	.309	.610								1380			

TEAM	CG	SHO	SV	IP	H	H/G	HR	BB	BB/G	SO	SO/G	ERA	/A	OAVG	OOBA	PR	/A	PF	CPI	FA	E	DP	FW	PW	BW	SBW	DIF
CHI	113	32	8	1372.0	1054	6.9	11	402	2.6	586	3.8	1.73	145	.217	.277	111	118	102	105	.967	211	110	3.0	13.4	-.9		15.5
PIT	111	24	5	1359.3	1207	8.0	12	368	2.4	497	3.3	2.30	110	.243	.295	24	33	102	102	.959	256	75	-.1	3.7	3.9		6.5
PHI	110	21	4	1295.7	1095	7.6	13	422	2.9	499	3.5	2.43	104	.234	.297	4	15	103	94	.957	256	104	-.1	1.7	-3.1		11.0
NY	109	22	13	1363.0	1219	8.0	25	369	2.4	655	4.3	2.45	104	.244	.296	1	16	104	100	.963	232	75	1.5	1.8	3.6		-1.5
BRO	125	20	1	1350.3	1218	8.1	16	463	3.1	479	3.2	2.38	99	.246	.310	12	-1	96	111	.959	262	94	-.5	-.1	-3.4		-4.9
CIN	118	10	2	1347.7	1223	8.2	16	444	3.0	481	3.2	2.41	97	.247	.309	7	-10	95	109	.963	227	118	1.9	-1.1	3.6		-14.9
BOS	121	9	2	1332.0	1324	8.9	28	458	3.1	426	2.9	3.34	73	.264	.326	-128	-133	99	95	.961	249	128	.4	-15.1	2.8		-4.1
STL	126	20	2	1359.3	1212	8.0	20	500	3.3	594	3.9	2.69	92	.244	.313	-34	-33	100	99	.948	340	105	-5.9	-3.7	-7.0		-7.8
TOT	933	158	37	10779.3		8.0			2.9		3.5	2.46		.243	.301					.960	2033	809					

Runs
Shannon-NY 104
Leach-Pit 102
Wagner-Pit 98
Clarke-Pit 97
Tenney-Bos 83

Hits
Beaumont-Bos 187
Wagner-Pit 180
Leach-Pit 166
Magee-Phi 165
Mitchell-Cin 163

Doubles
Wagner-Pit 38
Magee-Phi 28
Steinfeldt-Chi 25
Seymour-NY 25
Brain-Bos 24

Triples
Ganzel-Cin 16
Alperman-Bro 16
Wagner-Pit 14
Beaumont-Bos 14
Clarke-Pit 13

Home Runs
Brain-Bos 10
Lumley-Bro 9
Murray-StL 7
Wagner-Pit 6
Browne-NY 5

Total Bases
Wagner-Pit 264
Beaumont-Bos 246
Magee-Phi 229
Leach-Pit 221
Brain-Bos 214

Runs Batted In
Magee-Phi 85
Wagner-Pit 82
Abbaticchio-Pit 82
Seymour-NY 75
Steinfeldt-Chi 70

Runs Produced
Wagner-Pit 174
Magee-Phi 156
Clarke-Pit 154
Abbaticchio-Pit 143
Leach-Pit 141

Bases On Balls
Thomas-Phi 83
Huggins-Cin 83
Tenney-Bos 82
Shannon-NY 82
Anderson-Pit 80

Batting Average
Wagner-Pit 350
Magee-Phi 328
Beaumont-Bos 322
Leach-Pit 303
Seymour-NY 294

On Base Percentage
Wagner-Pit 403
Magee-Phi 392
Clarke-Pit 374
Jordan-Bro 370
Thomas-Phi 369

Slugging Average
Wagner-Pit 513
Magee-Phi 455
Lumley-Bro 425
Beaumont-Bos 424
Brain-Bos 420

Production
Wagner-Pit 915
Magee-Phi 847
Beaumont-Bos 787
Clarke-Pit 764
Leach-Pit 755

Adjusted Production
Wagner-Pit 180
Magee-Phi 162
Beaumont-Bos 156
Lumley-Bro 141
Brain-Bos 140

Batter Runs
Wagner-Pit 50.4
Magee-Phi 38.6
Beaumont-Bos 30.2
Clarke-Pit 25.5
Leach-Pit 22.7

Adjusted Batter Runs
Wagner-Pit 47.6
Magee-Phi 36.5
Beaumont-Bos 33.0
Jordan-Bro 23.4
Clarke-Pit 22.7

Clutch Hitting Index
Abbaticchio-Pit 194
Seymour-NY 152
Steinfeldt-Chi 152
Devlin-NY 134
Ganzel-Cin 129

Runs Created
Wagner-Pit 134
Magee-Phi 111
Beaumont-Bos 101
Leach-Pit 95
Clarke-Pit 89

Total Average
Wagner-Pit 1.107
Magee-Phi 970
Clarke-Pit 843
Leach-Pit 798
Beaumont-Bos 784

Stolen Bases
Wagner-Pit 61
Magee-Phi 46
Evers-Chi 46
Leach-Pit 43
Devlin-NY 38

Stolen Base Average

Stolen Base Runs

Fielding Runs
Evers-Chi 28.2
Byrne-StL 22.0
Brain-Bos 20.8
Alperman-Bro 17.6
Mitchell-Cin 16.2

Total Player Rating
Wagner-Pit 5.8
Brain-Bos 4.4
Beaumont-Bos 3.9
Magee-Phi 3.6
Mitchell-Cin 3.2

Wins
Mathewson-NY 24
Overall-Chi 23
Sparks-Phi 22
Willis-Pit 21

Win Percentage
Reulbach-Chi 810
Brown-Chi 769
Overall-Chi 767
Sparks-Phi 733
Lundgren-Chi 720

Games
McGinnity-NY 47
McGlynn-StL 45
Mathewson-NY 41
Ewing-Cin 41

Complete Games
McGlynn-StL 33
Ewing-Cin 32
Mathewson-NY 31
Karger-StL 28
Willis-Pit 27

Shutouts
Overall-Chi 8
Mathewson-NY 8
Lundgren-Chi 7

Saves
McGinnity-NY 4
Overall-Chi 3
Brown-Chi 3

Innings Pitched
McGlynn-StL 352
Ewing-Cin 333
Mathewson-NY 315
McGinnity-NY 310
Karger-StL 310

Fewest Hits/Game
Lundgren-Chi 5.65
Pfiester-Chi 6.60
Camnitz-Pit 6.75
Overall-Chi 6.76
Reulbach-Chi 6.89

Fewest BB/Game
Phillippe-Pit 1.51
Mathewson-NY 1.51
Brown-Chi 1.55
McGinnity-NY 1.68
Sparks-Phi 1.73

Strikeouts
Mathewson-NY 178
Ewing-Cin 147
Ames-NY 146
Beebe-StL 141
Overall-Chi 139

Strikeouts/Game
Ames-NY 5.64
Beebe-StL 5.33
Mathewson-NY 5.09
Overall-Chi 4.72
Reulbach-Chi 4.50

Wins Above Team
Sparks-Phi 6.6
Mathewson-NY 6.1
Reulbach-Chi 4.1
Pastorius-Bro 3.9
Overall-Chi 3.8

Earned Run Average
Pfiester-Chi 1.15
Lundgren-Chi 1.17
Brown-Chi 1.39
Leever-Pit 1.66
Reulbach-Chi 1.69

Adjusted ERA
Pfiester-Chi 217
Lundgren-Chi 214
Brown-Chi 180
Leever-Pit 152
Reulbach-Chi 149

Opponents' Batting Avg.
Lundgren-Chi 185
Pfiester-Chi 210
Camnitz-Pit 214
Overall-Chi 214
Reulbach-Chi 217

Opponents' On Base Pct.
Mathewson-NY 260
Brown-Chi 260
Pfiester-Chi 267
Karger-StL 275

Starter Runs
Lundgren-Chi 29.6
Pfiester-Chi 28.3
Brown-Chi 27.7
Ewing-Cin 27.1
Overall-Chi 22.5

Adjusted Starter Runs
Lundgren-Chi 30.7
Pfiester-Chi 29.4
Brown-Chi 29.0
Overall-Chi 23.9
Ewing-Cin 22.6

Clutch Pitching Index
Pfiester-Chi 135
Pastorius-Bro 131
Coakley-Cin 131
Lundgren-Chi 129
Leever-Pit 125

Relief Runs

Adjusted Relief Runs

Relief Ranking

Total Pitcher Index
Brown-Chi 4.0
Lundgren-Chi 3.7
Pfiester-Chi 3.3
Overall-Chi 3.0
Mathewson-NY 2.4

Total Baseball Ranking
Wagner-Pit 5.8
Brain-Bos 4.4
Brown-Chi 4.0
Beaumont-Bos 3.9
Lundgren-Chi 3.7

TEAM	G	W	L	PCT	GB	R	OR	AB	H	2B	3B	HR	BB	SO	AVG	OBP	SLG	PRO	/A	BR	/A	PF	CHI	RC	TA	SB	CS	SBASBR
DET	153	92	58	.613		694	532	5168	1382	179	75	11	315		.267	.310	.337	.647	114	71	62	102	109	614	.595	192		
PHI	150	88	57	.607	1.5	582	511	5002	1277	220	45	22	384		.255	.308	.330	.638	111	60	26	106	94	566	.584	138		
CHI	157	87	64	.576	5.5	588	474	5079	1205	147	34	5	421		.237	.296	.283	.579	92	-38	-58	104	111	488	.524	175		
CLE	158	85	67	.559	8	530	525	5068	1221	182	68	11	335		.241	.288	.310	.598	98	-14	23	93	97	521	.546	193		
NY	152	70	78	.473	21	605	665	5042	1257	150	67	14	304		.249	.292	.314	.606	100	-2	-49	109	110	535	.553	206		
STL	155	69	83	.454	24	542	555	5224	1324	154	64	9	370		.253	.303	.313	.616	104	20	32	98	90	552	.551	144		
BOS	155	59	90	.396	32.5	464	548	5238	1223	155	48	18	305		.233	.276	.292	.568	92	-72	-77	101	92	487	.487	124		
WAS	154	49	102	.325	43.5	506	691	5105	1243	137	57	12	390		.243	.297	.300	.597	97	-10	-46	90	90	534	.555	223		
TOT	617					4511		40926	10132	1324	458	102	2824	4476	.248	.296	.309	.605								1395		

TEAM	CG	SHO	SV	IP	H	H/G	HR	BB	BB/G	SO	SO/G	ERA	/A	OAVG	OOBA	PR	/A	PF	CPI	FA	E	DP	FW	PW	BW	SBW	DIF
DET	120	15	7	1366.7	1281	8.4	7	380	2.5	512	3.4	2.33	107	.250	.302	31	24	98	113	.959	260	79	1.1	2.6	6.8		6.4
PHI	106	27	6	1353.7	1106	7.4	13	378	2.5	789	5.2	2.35	113	.225	.281	29	46	104	89	.958	263	67	.9	5.1	2.9		6.7
CHI	112	17	9	1404.3	1279	8.2	13	305	2.0	604	3.9	2.22	116	.245	.287	50	54	101	107	.966	233	101	3.0	6.0	-6.4		8.9
CLE	127	20	5	1388.0	1253	8.1	8	362	2.3	513	3.3	2.26	104	.243	.293	43	15	93	107	.960	264	137	.8	1.7	2.5		4.0
NY	94	10	5	1320.3	1327	9.0	13	428	2.9	511	3.5	3.03	92	.264	.321	-72	-35	110	103	.947	334	74	-4.1	-3.9	-5.4		9.4
STL	129	15	9	1377.3	1254	8.2	17	352	2.3	463	3.0	2.61	96	.245	.293	-10	-17	98	96	.959	266	97	.7	-1.9	3.5		-9.3
BOS	100	17	7	1399.0	1222	7.9	22	337	2.2	517	3.3	2.45	107	.237	.284	14	26	103	94	.959	274	100	.1	2.9	-8.5		-10.0
WAS	106	12	5	1381.3	1381	9.0	10	341	2.2	567	3.7	3.11	77	.262	.307	-86	-110	94	93	.952	311	69	-2.5	-12.1	5.1		-16.9
TOT	894	133	53	10990.7		8.3			2.4		3.7	2.54		.248	.296					.958	2205	729					

Runs
Crawford-Det 102
Jones-Det 101
Cobb-Det 97
Hartsel-Phi 93
Hahn-Chi 87

Hits
Cobb-Det 212
Stone-StL 191
Crawford-Det 188
Ganley-Was 167
Flick-Cle 166

Doubles
Davis-Phi 37
Crawford-Det 34
Lajoie-Cle 30
Collins-Bos-Phi 29
Seybold-Phi 29

Triples
Flick-Cle 18
Crawford-Det 17
Cobb-Det 14
Unglaub-Bos 13

Home Runs
Davis-Phi 8
Seybold-Phi 5
Hoffman-NY 5
Cobb-Det 5

Total Bases
Cobb-Det 283
Crawford-Det 268
Stone-StL 238
Davis-Phi 232
Flick-Cle 226

Runs Batted In
Cobb-Det 119
Seybold-Phi 92
Davis-Phi 87
Crawford-Det 81
Wallace-StL 70

Runs Produced
Cobb-Det 211
Crawford-Det 179
Davis-Phi 163
Seybold-Phi 145
Donahue-Chi 143

Bases On Balls
Hartsel-Phi 106
Hahn-Chi 84
Jones-Chi 67
Flick-Cle 64
Jones-Det 60

Batting Average
Cobb-Det 350
Crawford-Det 323
Stone-StL 320
Flick-Cle 302
Nicholls-Phi 302

On Base Percentage
Hartsel-Phi 405
Stone-StL 382
Flick-Cle 375
Cobb-Det 375
Crawford-Det 363

Slugging Average
Cobb-Det 468
Crawford-Det 460
Flick-Cle 412
Stone-StL 399
Davis-Phi 399

Production
Cobb-Det 843
Crawford-Det 824
Flick-Cle 787
Stone-StL 781
Hartsel-Phi 771

Adjusted Production
Cobb-Det 168
Flick-Cle 164
Crawford-Det 162
Stone-StL 155
Lajoie-Cle 145

Batter Runs
Cobb-Det 44.2
Crawford-Det 39.5
Stone-StL 35.1
Hartsel-Phi 34.4
Flick-Cle 33.7

Adjusted Batter Runs
Cobb-Det 43.2
Crawford-Det 38.6
Flick-Cle 38.0
Stone-StL 36.6
Hartsel-Phi 30.6

Clutch Hitting Index
Wallace-StL 154
Davis-Chi 144
Seybold-Phi 144
Rohe-Chi 141
Cobb-Det 137

Runs Created
Cobb-Det 128
Crawford-Det 107
Flick-Cle 103
Stone-StL 102
Hartsel-Phi 85

Total Average
Cobb-Det 906
Flick-Cle 864
Hartsel-Phi 855
Crawford-Det 820
Stone-StL 790

Stolen Bases
Cobb-Det 49
Flick-Cle 41
Conroy-NY 41
Ganley-Was 40
Altizer-Was 38

Stolen Base Average

Stolen Base Runs

Fielding Runs
Lajoie-Cle 39.3
Walsh-Chi 21.5
Donahue-Chi 20.8
Ganley-Was 19.7
Jones-Det 19.0

Total Player Rating
Lajoie-Cle 6.5
Cobb-Det 5.2
Flick-Cle 3.5
Crawford-Det 3.3
Ganley-Was 2.8

Wins
White-Chi 27
Joss-Cle 27
Killian-Det 25
Donovan-Det 25

Win Percentage
Donovan-Det 862
Dygert-Phi 724
Joss-Cle 711
Smith-Chi 697
White-Chi 675

Games
Walsh-Chi 56
White-Chi 46
Mullin-Det 46
Waddell-Phi 44

Complete Games
Walsh-Chi 37
Mullin-Det 35
Joss-Cle 34
Young-Bos 33
Plank-Phi 33

Shutouts
Plank-Phi 8
Waddell-Phi 7
Young-Bos 6
White-Chi 6
Joss-Cle 6

Saves
Dinneen-Bos-StL 4
Walsh-Chi 4
Hughes-Was 4

Innings Pitched
Walsh-Chi 422
Mullin-Det 357
Plank-Phi 344
Young-Bos 343
Joss-Cle 339

Fewest Hits/Game
Dygert-Phi 6.87
Winter-Bos 6.93
Walsh-Chi 7.27
Howell-StL 7.35
Donovan-Det 7.37

Fewest BB/Game
White-Chi 1.18
Altrock-Chi 1.30
Young-Bos 1.34
Bender-Phi 1.40
Joss-Cle 1.43

Strikeouts
Waddell-Phi 232
Walsh-Chi 206
Plank-Phi 183
Dygert-Phi 151
Young-Bos 147

Strikeouts/Game
Waddell-Phi 7.33
Dygert-Phi 5.19
Plank-Phi 4.79
Bender-Phi 4.60
Walsh-Chi 4.39

Wins Above Team
Donovan-Det 10.0
Joss-Cle 7.8
Young-Bos 6.7
White-Chi 5.9
Smith-Chi 5.6

Earned Run Average
Walsh-Chi 1.60
Killian-Det 1.78
Joss-Cle 1.83
Howell-StL 1.94
Young-Bos 1.99

Adjusted ERA
Walsh-Chi 160
Killian-Det 140
Young-Bos 131
Bender-Phi 129
Joss-Cle 129

Opponents' Batting Avg.
Dygert-Phi 214
Winter-Bos 216
Walsh-Chi 224
Howell-StL 226
Donovan-Det 226

Opponents' On Base Pct.
Joss-Cle 260
Young-Bos 260
Bender-Phi 263
Winter-Bos 265
Walsh-Chi 266

Starter Runs
Walsh-Chi 44.2
Joss-Cle 26.7
Killian-Det 26.7
Howell-StL 21.2
Young-Bos 20.9

Adjusted Starter Runs
Walsh-Chi 45.4
Killian-Det 24.9
Young-Bos 23.9
Joss-Cle 19.9
Howell-StL 19.5

Clutch Pitching Index
Killian-Det 143
Hogg-NY 125
Liebhardt-Cle 124
Rhoads-Cle 117
Walsh-Chi 114

Relief Runs

Adjusted Relief Runs

Relief Ranking

Total Pitcher Index
Walsh-Chi 8.1
Killian-Det 4.0
Howell-StL 3.9
Joss-Cle 3.3
White-Chi 2.1

Total Baseball Ranking
Walsh-Chi 8.1
Lajoie-Cle 6.5
Cobb-Det 5.2
Killian-Det 4.0
Howell-StL 3.9

TEAM	G	W	L	PCT	GB	R	OR	AB	H	2B	3B	HR	BB	SO	AVG	OBP	SLG	PRO	/A	BR	/A	PF	CHI	RC	TA	SB	CS	SBA	SBR
CHI	158	99	55	.643		624	461	5085	1267	196	56	19	418		.249	.306	.321	.627	109	51	18	106	106	574	.592	212			
PIT	155	98	56	.636	1	585	469	5109	1263	162	98	25	420		.247	.304	.332	.636	112	65	91	95	98	572	.599	186			
NY	157	98	56	.636	1	652	456	5006	1339	182	43	20	494		.267	.333	.333	.666	122	128	105	104	98	627	.639	181			
PHI	155	83	71	.539	16	504	445	5012	1223	194	68	11	334		.244	.291	.316	.607	102	10	11	100	96	522	.560	200			
CIN	155	73	81	.474	26	489	544	4879	1108	129	77	14	372		.227	.282	.294	.576	92	-39	-51	103	104	463	.531	196			
BOS	156	63	91	.409	36	537	622	5131	1228	137	43	17	414		.239	.296	.293	.589	97	-13	-32	104	103	489	.525	134			
BRO	154	53	101	.344	46	377	516	4897	1044	110	60	28	323		.213	.262	.277	.539	80	-105	-80	95	95	385	.466	113			
STL	154	49	105	.318	50	371	626	4959	1105	134	57	17	282		.223	.265	.283	.548	83	-94	-61	94	91	409	.476	150			
TOT	622					4139		40078	9577	1244	502	151	3057	4180	.239	.293	.306	.599								1372			

TEAM	CG	SHO	SV	IP	H	H/G	HR	BB	BB/G	SO	SO/G	ERA	/A	OAVG	OOBA	PR	/A	PF	CPI	FA	E	DP	FW	PW	BW	SBW	DIF
CHI	108	29	12	1430.7	1137	7.2	20	437	2.7	668	4.2	2.14	112	.223	.285	32	40	102	98	.969	205	76	3.4	4.6	2.1		11.9
PIT	100	24	9	1400.3	1142	7.3	16	406	2.6	468	3.0	2.12	102	.228	.286	34	6	92	100	.964	226	74	1.9	.7	10.5		7.9
NY	95	25	18	1406.7	1214	7.8	27	288	1.8	656	4.2	2.14	109	.238	.279	32	31	100	102	.962	250	79	.2	3.6	12.1		5.1
PHI	116	22	6	1385.7	1167	7.6	8	379	2.5	476	3.1	2.10	110	.234	.288	37	31	98	103	.963	238	75	1.1	3.6	1.3		.0
CIN	110	18	8	1361.7	1218	8.1	19	415	2.7	433	2.9	2.37	103	.245	.303	-4	9	104	108	.959	255	72	-.2	1.0	-5.9		1.0
BOS	92	14	1	1385.7	1262	8.2	29	423	2.7	416	2.7	2.79	89	.248	.306	-69	-48	106	97	.962	253	90	-.0	-5.6	-3.7		-4.7
BRO	118	20	4	1358.3	1165	7.7	17	444	2.9	535	3.5	2.47	93	.237	.300	-19	-24	99	99	.961	247	66	.4	-2.8	-9.3		-12.4
STL	97	13	4	1346.3	1217	8.1	16	430	2.9	528	3.5	2.64	88	.247	.307	-44	-45	100	100	.946	348	68	-6.8	-5.2	-7.1		-8.9
TOT	836	165	62	11075.3		7.7			2.6		3.4	2.34		.239	.293					.961	2022	600					

Runs
Tenney-NY 101
Wagner-Pit 100
Leach-Pit 93
Evers-Chi 83
Clarke-Pit 83

Hits
Wagner-Pit 201
Donlin-NY 198
Murray-StL 167
Lobert-Cin 167
Bransfield-Phi 160

Doubles
Wagner-Pit 39
Magee-Phi 30
Chance-Chi 27
Knabe-Phi 26
Donlin-NY 26

Triples
Wagner-Pit 19
Lobert-Cin 18
Magee-Phi 16
Leach-Pit 16

Home Runs
Jordan-Bro 12
Wagner-Pit 10
Murray-StL 7
Tinker-Chi 6
Donlin-NY 6

Total Bases
Wagner-Pit 308
Donlin-NY 268
Murray-StL 237
Lobert-Cin 232
Leach-Pit 222

Runs Batted In
Wagner-Pit 109
Donlin-NY 106
Seymour-NY 92
Bransfield-Phi 71
Tinker-Chi 68

Runs Produced
Wagner-Pit 199
Donlin-NY 171
Tenney-NY 148
Seymour-NY 147

Bases On Balls
Bresnahan-NY 83
Tenney-NY 72
Evers-Chi 66
Clarke-Pit 65

Batting Average
Wagner-Pit 354
Donlin-NY 334
Bransfield-Phi 304
Evers-Chi 300
Lobert-Cin 293

On Base Percentage
Wagner-Pit 410
Evers-Chi 396
Bresnahan-NY 395
Donlin-NY 359
Bridwell-NY 356

Slugging Average
Wagner-Pit 542
Donlin-NY 452
Magee-Phi 417
Lobert-Cin 407
Murray-StL 400

Production
Wagner-Pit 952
Donlin-NY 811
Evers-Chi 771
Magee-Phi 764
Bresnahan-NY 753

Adjusted Production
Wagner-Pit 217
Donlin-NY 154
Magee-Phi 146
Murray-StL 142
Evers-Chi 141

Batter Runs
Wagner-Pit 65.2
Donlin-NY 36.6
Bresnahan-NY 26.5
Evers-Chi 26.0
Lobert-Cin 25.9

Adjusted Batter Runs
Wagner-Pit 68.1
Donlin-NY 34.2
Magee-Phi 25.5
Lobert-Cin 24.5
Bresnahan-NY 24.3

Clutch Hitting Index
Seymour-NY 175
Donlin-NY 151
Steinfeldt-Chi 150
McGann-Bos 150
Abbaticchio-Pit ...148

Runs Created
Wagner-Pit 145
Donlin-NY 104
Lobert-Cin 94
Murray-StL 89
Magee-Phi 85

Total Average
Wagner-Pit 1.131
Evers-Chi 887
Magee-Phi 827
Donlin-NY 813
Lobert-Cin 806

Stolen Bases
Wagner-Pit 53
Murray-StL 48
Lobert-Cin 47
Magee-Phi 40
Evers-Chi 36

Stolen Base Average

Stolen Base Runs

Fielding Runs
Tinker-Chi 32.2
Burch-Bro 28.0
Hummel-Bro 21.4
Seymour-NY 20.5
Murray-StL 19.5

Total Player Rating
Wagner-Pit 6.8
Murray-StL 4.7
Tinker-Chi 4.5
Donlin-NY 3.0
Burch-Bro 2.7

Wins
Mathewson-NY 37
Brown-Chi 29
Reulbach-Chi 24

Win Percentage
Reulbach-Chi 774
Mathewson-NY 771
Brown-Chi 763
Maddox-Pit 742
Leever-Pit 682

Games
Mathewson-NY 56
Raymond-StL 48
McQuillan-Phi 48
Reulbach-Chi 46

Complete Games
Mathewson-NY 34
Wilhelm-Bro 33
McQuillan-Phi 32
Wiltse-NY 30
Rucker-Bro 30

Shutouts
Mathewson-NY 11
Brown-Chi 9

Saves
McGinnity-NY 5
Mathewson-NY 5
Brown-Chi 5
Overall-Chi 4
Ewing-Cin 3

Innings Pitched
Mathewson-NY 391
McQuillan-Phi 360
Rucker-Bro 333
Wilhelm-Bro 332
Wiltse-NY 330

Fewest Hits/Game
Brown-Chi 6.17
Raymond-StL 6.56
Mathewson-NY 6.56
McQuillan-Phi 6.58
Overall-Chi 6.60

Fewest BB/Game
Mathewson-NY 97
Brown-Chi 1.41
Ewing-Cin 1.74
Sparks-Phi 1.75
McGinnity-NY 1.79

Strikeouts
Mathewson-NY 259
Rucker-Bro 199
Overall-Chi 167
Raymond-StL 145
Reulbach-Chi 133

Strikeouts/Game
Overall-Chi 6.68
Mathewson-NY 5.96
Rucker-Bro 5.38
Camnitz-Pit 4.48
Ferguson-Bos 4.24

Wins Above Team
Mathewson-NY 11.0
Brown-Chi 7.7
Reulbach-Chi 6.5
Maddox-Pit 5.3
Rucker-Bro 4.3

Earned Run Average
Mathewson-NY 1.43
Brown-Chi 1.47
McQuillan-Phi 1.52
Camnitz-Pit 1.56
Coakley-Cin-Chi .. 1.79

Adjusted ERA
Mathewson-NY 164
Brown-Chi 163
McQuillan-Phi 151
Camnitz-Pit 139
Coakley-Cin-Chi ..134

Opponents' Batting Avg.
Brown-Chi 199
Raymond-StL 209
Mathewson-NY 209
McQuillan-Phi 210
Overall-Chi 210

Opponents' On Base Pct.
Mathewson-NY 235
Brown-Chi 238
McQuillan-Phi 266
Willis-Pit 272
Ewing-Cin 276

Starter Runs
Mathewson-NY 39.8
McQuillan-Phi 32.7
Brown-Chi 30.2
Camnitz-Pit 20.7
Wilhelm-Bro 17.5

Adjusted Starter Runs
Mathewson-NY 39.5
Brown-Chi 32.0
McQuillan-Phi 31.1
Coakley-Cin-Chi .. 17.9
Wilhelm-Bro 16.2

Clutch Pitching Index
McGinnity-NY 144
Coakley-Cin-Chi ..138
Camnitz-Pit 132
Fraser-Chi 124
Leever-Pit 119

Relief Runs

Adjusted Relief Runs

Relief Ranking

Total Pitcher Index
Mathewson-NY 6.1
Brown-Chi 3.8
McQuillan-Phi 3.5
Wilhelm-Bro 2.2
Camnitz-Pit 1.8

Total Baseball Ranking
Wagner-Pit 6.8
Mathewson-NY 6.1
Murray-StL 4.7
Tinker-Chi 4.5
Brown-Chi 3.8

TEAM	G	W	L	PCT	GB	R	OR	AB	H	2B	3B	HR	BB	SO	AVG	OBP	SLG	PRO	/A	BR	/A	PF	CHI	RC	TA	SB	CS	SBA	SBR
DET	154	90	63	.588		647	547	5109	1347	199	86	19	320		.264	.307	.347	.654	121	105	99	101	100	573	.601	165			
CLE	157	90	64	.584	0.5	568	457	5108	1221	188	58	18	364		.239	.290	.309	.599	102	12	-20	106	102	486	.543	169			
CHI	156	88	64	.579	1.5	537	470	5027	1127	145	41	3	463		.224	.290	.271	.561	90	-41	-10	94	107	437	.522	209			
STL	155	83	69	.546	6.5	544	483	5152	1261	173	56	20	343		.245	.292	.312	.604	104	20	2	103	96	485	.533	126			
BOS	155	75	79	.487	15.5	564	513	5047	1243	116	88	14	289		.246	.287	.312	.599	102	9	17	98	105	480	.535	168			
PHI	157	68	85	.444	22	486	562	5064	1131	183	49	21	368		.223	.276	.291	.567	92	-41	-81	108	98	420	.498	116			
WAS	155	67	85	.441	22.5	479	539	5040	1185	131	74	8	368		.235	.287	.295	.582	97	-13	11	95	91	456	.526	170			
NY	155	51	103	.331	39.5	459	713	5036	1187	142	51	12	288		.236	.277	.291	.568	92	-43	-18	95	95	449	.516	230			
TOT	622					4284		40583	9702	1277	503	115	2803	4928	.239	.288	.304	.592								1353			

TEAM	CG	SHO	SV	IP	H	H/G	HR	BB	BB/G	SO	SO/G	ERA	/A	OAVG	OOBA	PR	/A	PF	CPI	FA	E	DP	FW	PW	BW	SBW	DIF
DET	119	15	5	1379.0	1313	8.6	12	318	2.1	553	3.6	2.40	98	.254	.297	-2	-6	99	112	.953	305	95	-2.0	-.7	11.3		4.9
CLE	108	18	5	1418.3	1172	7.4	16	328	2.1	548	3.5	2.02	122	.228	.274	57	70	103	103	.962	257	95	1.4	8.0	-2.3		6.0
CHI	107	23	10	1412.7	1170	7.5	10	284	1.8	623	4.0	2.22	100	.228	.269	26	-1	93	89	.966	232	82	3.1	-.1	-1.1		10.2
STL	107	15	5	1393.3	1151	7.4	7	387	2.5	607	3.9	2.15	113	.228	.283	36	42	102	101	.964	237	97	2.7	4.8	.2		-.7
BOS	102	12	7	1378.3	1200	7.8	18	364	2.4	624	4.1	2.27	102	.237	.289	17	6	97	106	.955	297	71	-1.4	.7	1.9		-3.2
PHI	102	23	4	1388.3	1186	7.7	10	409	2.7	740	4.8	2.57	102	.234	.291	-27	6	110	92	.957	272	68	.3	.7	-9.2		-.3
WAS	105	15	7	1376.0	1238	8.1	16	347	2.3	649	4.2	2.34	99	.243	.292	6	-5	97	107	.958	275	89	.1	-.6	1.3		-9.8
NY	91	11	3	1326.0	1286	8.7	26	457	3.1	584	4.0	3.16	76	.258	.320	-114	-110	101	100	.947	337	78	-4.2	-12.5	-2.0		-7.3
TOT	841	132	46	11072.0		7.9			2.4		4.0	2.39		.239	.288					.958	2212	675					

Runs
McIntyre-Det 105
Crawford-Det 102
Schaefer-Det 96
Jones-Chi 92
Stone-StL 89

Hits
Cobb-Det 188
Crawford-Det 184
McIntyre-Det 168
Lajoie-Cle 168
Stone-StL 165

Doubles
Cobb-Det 36
Rossman-Det 33
Crawford-Det 33
Lajoie-Cle 32
Stovall-Cle 29

Triples
Cobb-Det 20
Stahl-NY -Bos 16
Crawford-Det 16
Gessler-Bos 14

Home Runs
Crawford-Det 7
Hinchman-Cle 6
Niles-NY -Bos 5
Stone-StL 5
Davis-Phi 5

Total Bases
Cobb-Det 276
Crawford-Det 270
Rossman-Det 219
McIntyre-Det 218
Lajoie-Cle 218

Runs Batted In
Cobb-Det 108
Crawford-Det 80
Lajoie-Cle 74
Ferris-StL 74
Rossman-Det 71

Runs Produced
Cobb-Det 192
Crawford-Det 175
Lajoie-Cle 149
Schaefer-Det 145
Jones-Chi 141

Bases On Balls
Hartsel-Phi 93
Jones-Chi 86
McIntyre-Det 83
Clarke-Cle 76
Davis-Phi 61

Batting Average
Cobb-Det 324
Crawford-Det 311
Gessler-Bos 308
Hemphill-NY 297
McIntyre-Det 295

On Base Percentage
McIntyre-Det 385
Gessler-Bos 381
Hartsel-Phi 371
Hemphill-NY 371
Cobb-Det 361

Slugging Average
Cobb-Det 475
Crawford-Det 457
Gessler-Bos 423
Rossman-Det 418
McIntyre-Det 383

Production
Cobb-Det 836
Crawford-Det 809
Gessler-Bos 804
McIntyre-Det 768
Rossman-Det 746

Adjusted Production
Cobb-Det 172
Gessler-Bos 167
Crawford-Det 163
McIntyre-Det 151
Hemphill-NY 146

Batter Runs
Cobb-Det 43.6
Crawford-Det 39.1
McIntyre-Det 36.0
Gessler-Bos 31.1
Hemphill-NY 23.5

Adjusted Batter Runs
Cobb-Det 43.0
Crawford-Det 38.4
McIntyre-Det 35.2
Gessler-Bos 31.9
Hemphill-NY 26.1

Clutch Hitting Index
Wallace-StL 148
Ferris-StL 146
Cobb-Det 135
Gessler-Bos 130
Murphy-Phi 128

Runs Created
Cobb-Det 110
Crawford-Det 97
McIntyre-Det 90
Hemphill-NY 80
Stone-StL 79

Total Average
Cobb-Det 888
Gessler-Bos 844
McIntyre-Det 800
Hemphill-NY 792
Crawford-Det 791

Stolen Bases
Dougherty-Chi 47
Hemphill-NY 42
Schaefer-Det 40
Cobb-Det 39
Clarke-Cle 37

Stolen Base Average

Stolen Base Runs

Fielding Runs
Lajoie-Cle 46.7
McBride-Was 31.5
Wagner-Bos 29.5
Tannehill-Chi 20.4
Conroy-NY 18.1

Total Player Rating
Lajoie-Cle 6.8
Cobb-Det 4.5
McIntyre-Det 4.5
McBride-Was 3.4
Wagner-Bos 3.2

Wins
Walsh-Chi 40
Summers-Det 24
Joss-Cle 24
Young-Bos 21
Waddell-StL 19

Win Percentage
Walsh-Chi 727
Donovan-Det 720
Joss-Cle 686
Summers-Det 667
Young-Bos 656

Games
Walsh-Chi 66
Vickers-Phi 53
Chesbro-NY 45
Waddell-StL 43
Hughes-Was 43

Complete Games
Walsh-Chi 42
Young-Bos 30
Joss-Cle 29
Howell-StL 27
Mullin-Det 26

Shutouts
Walsh-Chi 11
Joss-Cle 9
Vickers-Phi 6
Johnson-Was 6
Donovan-Det 6

Saves
Walsh-Chi 6
Hughes-Was 4
Waddell-StL 3

Innings Pitched
Walsh-Chi 464
Joss-Cle 325
Howell-StL 324
Vickers-Phi 317
Summers-Det 301

Fewest Hits/Game
Joss-Cle 6.42
Smith-Chi 6.43
Walsh-Chi 6.65
Johnson-Was 6.79
Berger-Cle 6.87

Fewest BB/Game
Joss-Cle 83
Burns-Was 98
Walsh-Chi 1.09
Young-Bos 1.11
Summers-Det 1.64

Strikeouts
Walsh-Chi 269
Waddell-StL 232
Hughes-Was 165
Dygert-Phi 164
Johnson-Was 160

Strikeouts/Game
Waddell-StL 7.30
Dygert-Phi 6.18
Johnson-Was 5.60
Hughes-Was 5.38
Donovan-Det 5.22

Wins Above Team
Walsh-Chi 12.7
Young-Bos 6.1
Joss-Cle 5.2
Donovan-Det 4.5
Summers-Det 4.2

Earned Run Average
Joss-Cle 1.16
Young-Bos 1.26
Walsh-Chi 1.42
Summers-Det 1.64
Johnson-Was 1.65

Adjusted ERA
Joss-Cle 212
Young-Bos 183
Walsh-Chi 156
Summers-Det 143
Chech-Cle 142

Opponents' Batting Avg.
Joss-Cle 197
Smith-Chi 203
Walsh-Chi 203
Johnson-Was 211
Young-Bos 213

Opponents' On Base Pct.
Joss-Cle 218
Walsh-Chi 232
Young-Bos 240
Smith-Chi 256
Burns-Was 257

Starter Runs
Walsh-Chi 50.0
Joss-Cle 44.2
Young-Bos 37.3
Summers-Det 24.8
Johnson-Was 21.1

Adjusted Starter Runs
Joss-Cle 47.1
Walsh-Chi 40.8
Young-Bos 35.0
Summers-Det 23.8
Rhoads-Cle 21.0

Clutch Pitching Index
Summers-Det 148
Willett-Det 143
Rhoads-Cle 142
Howell-StL 127
Chech-Cle 125

Relief Runs

Adjusted Relief Runs

Relief Ranking

Total Pitcher Index
Walsh-Chi 6.6
Joss-Cle 6.2
Young-Bos 3.5
Rhoads-Cle 2.7
Summers-Det 2.7

Total Baseball Ranking
Lajoie-Cle 6.8
Walsh-Chi 6.6
Joss-Cle 6.2
Cobb-Det 4.5
McIntyre-Det 4.5

TEAM	G	W	L	PCT	GB	R	OR	AB	H	2B	3B	HR	BB	SO	AVG	OBP	SLG	PRO	/A	BR	/A	PF	CHI	RC	TA	SB	CS	SBA	SBR
PIT	153	110	42	.724		699	447	5129	1332	218	92	25	479		.260	.327	.353	.680	118	100	72	105	103	656	.661	185			
CHI	155	104	49	.680	6.5	635	390	4999	1227	203	60	20	420		.245	.308	.322	.630	102	7	4	101	111	562	.596	187			
NY	158	92	61	.601	18.5	623	546	5218	1327	173	68	26	530		.254	.329	.328	.657	111	70	41	105	94	632	.644	210			
CIN	156	77	76	.503	33.5	606	599	5088	1273	159	72	22	478		.250	.319	.323	.642	106	35	69	94	99	618	.639	280			
PHI	154	74	79	.484	36.5	516	518	5034	1228	185	53	12	370		.244	.303	.309	.612	96	-25	-60	106	96	534	.569	185			
BRO	155	55	98	.359	55.5	444	627	5056	1157	176	59	16	330		.229	.279	.296	.575	84	-97	-90	98	98	456	.510	141			
STL	154	54	98	.355	56	583	731	5108	1242	148	56	15	568		.243	.326	.303	.629	102	25	46	96	96	556	.605	161			
BOS	155	45	108	.294	65.5	435	683	5017	1121	124	43	15	400		.223	.285	.274	.559	79	-115	-93	96	98	450	.512	190			
TOT	620					4541		40649	9907	1386	503	151	3575	4397	.244	.310	.314	.624								1539			

TEAM	CG	SHO	SV	IP	H	H/G	HR	BB	BB/G	SO	SO/G	ERA	/A	OAVG	OOBA	PR	/A	PF	CPI	FA	E	DP	FW	PW	BW	SBW	DIF
PIT	93	20	11	1400.3	1174	7.5	12	320	2.1	490	3.1	2.07	124	.232	.278	80	77	99	95	.964	228	100	3.7	8.5	8.0		13.8
CHI	111	31	11	1408.0	1094	7.0	6	364	2.3	680	4.3	1.75	140	.219	.272	130	110	95	97	.962	244	95	2.6	12.2	.4		12.2
NY	105	17	15	1435.3	1248	7.8	29	397	2.5	695	4.4	2.27	118	.239	.293	50	63	103	103	.954	307	99	-1.5	7.0	4.5		5.5
CIN	91	10	8	1400.3	1233	7.9	5	510	3.3	477	3.1	2.52	96	.241	.310	10	-14	94	99	.952	309	120	-1.6	-1.6	7.6		-4.0
PHI	89	17	6	1380.7	1190	7.8	22	472	3.1	612	4.0	2.44	113	.237	.303	23	48	106	100	.962	241	97	2.8	5.3	-6.6		-4.0
BRO	126	17	3	1370.3	1277	8.4	32	528	3.5	594	3.9	3.10	86	.252	.322	-77	-66	103	96	.955	282	86	.2	-7.3	-10.0		-4.4
STL	84	5	4	1372.7	1368	9.0	23	483	3.2	435	2.9	3.41	75	.265	.328	-125	-127	99	92	.950	322	90	-2.5	-14.1	5.1		-10.6
BOS	98	12	6	1366.0	1329	8.8	23	543	3.6	414	2.7	3.20	82	.260	.331	-93	-86	102	99	.948	342	101	-3.8	-9.5	-10.3		-7.9
TOT	797	129	64	11133.7		8.0			2.9		3.6	2.59		.244	.310					.956	2275	788					

Runs
Leach-Pit 126
Clarke-Pit 97
Byrne-StL-Pit 92
Wagner-Pit 92

Hits
Doyle-NY 172
Grant-Phi 170
Wagner-Pit 168
Konetchy-StL 165
Burch-Bro 163

Doubles
Wagner-Pit 39
Magee-Phi 33
Miller-Pit 31
Sheckard-Chi 29
Leach-Pit 29

Triples
Mitchell-Cin 17
Magee-Phi 14
Konetchy-StL 14
Miller-Pit 13

Home Runs
Murray-NY 7
Leach-Pit 6
Doyle-NY 6
Becker-Bos 6
Wagner-Pit 5

Total Bases
Wagner-Pit 242
Doyle-NY 239
Konetchy-StL 228
Mitchell-Cin 225
Miller-Pit 222

Runs Batted In
Wagner-Pit 100
Murray-NY 91
Miller-Pit 87
Mitchell-Cin 86
Konetchy-StL 80

Runs Produced
Wagner-Pit 187
Mitchell-Cin 165
Konetchy-StL 164
Leach-Pit 163
Clarke-Pit 162

Bases On Balls
Clarke-Pit 80
Byrne-StL-Pit 78
Evers-Chi 73
Sheckard-Chi 72
Bridwell-NY 67

Batting Average
Wagner-Pit .... .339
Mitchell-Cin ...... .310
Hoblitzel-Cin ..... .308
Doyle-NY .... .302
Bridwell-NY .... .294

On Base Percentage
Wagner-Pit .... .420
Bridwell-NY .... .386
Clarke-Pit .... .384
Mitchell-Cin ...... .378
Evers-Chi .... .369

Slugging Average
Wagner-Pit .... .489
Mitchell-Cin ...... .430
Doyle-NY .... .419
Hoblitzel-Cin ..... .418
Magee-Phi .... .398

Production
Wagner-Pit .... .909
Mitchell-Cin ...... .808
Hoblitzel-Cin ..... .782
Doyle-NY .... .779
Konetchy-StL ...... .762

Adjusted Production
Wagner-Pit 173
Mitchell-Cin 160
Hoblitzel-Cin 152
Konetchy-StL 141
Doyle-NY 135

Batter Runs
Wagner-Pit 48.1
Mitchell-Cin 30.3
Doyle-NY 26.2
Clarke-Pit 25.3
Konetchy-StL 24.9

Adjusted Batter Runs
Wagner-Pit 45.4
Mitchell-Cin 33.8
Hoblitzel-Cin 27.7
Konetchy-StL 27.2
Doyle-NY 23.3

Clutch Hitting Index
Murray-NY 152
Wagner-Pit 150
Lobert-Cin 146
Abstein-Pit 145
Mitchell-Cin 140

Runs Created
Wagner-Pit 114
Mitchell-Cin 97
Doyle-NY 95
Konetchy-StL 90
Clarke-Pit 89

Total Average
Wagner-Pit 1.058
Mitchell-Cin ...... .884
Clarke-Pit .... .821
Doyle-NY .... .809
Konetchy-StL ...... .791

Stolen Bases
Bescher-Cin 54
Murray-NY 48
Egan-Cin 39
Magee-Phi 38
Burch-Bro 38

Stolen Base Average

Stolen Base Runs

Fielding Runs
Egan-Cin 21.5
Doolan-Phi 19.0
Tinker-Chi 17.3
Bergen-Bro 15.5
Devlin-NY 15.0

Total Player Rating
Wagner-Pit 6.2
Mitchell-Cin 3.3
Konetchy-StL 3.1
Clarke-Pit 3.1
Devlin-NY 3.0

Wins
Brown-Chi 27
Mathewson-NY 25
Camnitz-Pit 25
Willis-Pit 22

Win Percentage
Mathewson-NY ...... .806
Camnitz-Pit .... .806
Brown-Chi .... .750
Pfiester-Chi ...... .739
Leifield-Pit ...... .704

Games
Brown-Chi 50
Mattern-Bos 47
Gaspar-Cin 44
Beebe-StL 44

Complete Games
Brown-Chi 32
Bell-Bro 29
Rucker-Bro 28
Mathewson-NY 26

Shutouts
Overall-Chi 9
Mathewson-NY 8
Brown-Chi 8

Saves
Brown-Chi 7
Crandall-NY 6

Innings Pitched
Brown-Chi 343
Mattern-Bos 316
Rucker-Bro 309
Moore-Phi 300
Willis-Pit 290

Fewest Hits/Game
Mathewson-NY 6.28
Fromme-Cin 6.29
Overall-Chi 6.44
Brown-Chi 6.45
Camnitz-Pit 6.58

Fewest BB/Game
Mathewson-NY 1.18
Brown-Chi 1.39
Wiltse-NY 1.71
Maddox-Pit 1.73
McQuillan-Phi 1.96

Strikeouts
Overall-Chi 205
Rucker-Bro 201
Moore-Phi 173
Brown-Chi 172
Ames-NY 156

Strikeouts/Game
Overall-Chi 6.47
Rucker-Bro 5.85
Ames-NY 5.75
Marquard-NY 5.67
Moore-Phi 5.19

Wins Above Team
Mathewson-NY 8.8
Camnitz-Pit 5.4
Brown-Chi 4.8
Gaspar-Cin 4.6
Bell-Bro 4.5

Earned Run Average
Mathewson-NY 1.15
Brown-Chi 1.31
Overall-Chi 1.42
Camnitz-Pit 1.62
Reulbach-Chi 1.78

Adjusted ERA
Mathewson-NY 233
Brown-Chi 187
Overall-Chi 173
Camnitz-Pit 158
Reulbach-Chi 138

Opponents' Batting Avg.
Overall-Chi .... .198
Mathewson-NY ...... .200
Fromme-Cin .... .201
Brown-Chi .... .202
Moore-Phi .... .210

Opponents' On Base Pct.
Mathewson-NY ...... .228
Brown-Chi .... .239
Overall-Chi .... .262
Camnitz-Pit .... .267
McQuillan-Phi ..... .271

Starter Runs
Brown-Chi 48.6
Mathewson-NY 44.1
Overall-Chi 37.0
Camnitz-Pit 30.4
Reulbach-Chi 23.6

Adjusted Starter Runs
Mathewson-NY 46.5
Brown-Chi 43.7
Overall-Chi 32.9
Camnitz-Pit 29.7
Moore-Phi 21.8

Clutch Pitching Index
Richie-Phi-Bos 126
Corridon-Phi 123
Sallee-StL 119
Wilhelm-Bro 117
Marquard-NY 117

Relief Runs

Adjusted Relief Runs

Relief Ranking

Total Pitcher Index
Mathewson-NY 6.5
Brown-Chi 5.1
Overall-Chi 3.9
Camnitz-Pit 3.2
Reulbach-Chi 2.8

Total Baseball Ranking
Mathewson-NY 6.5
Wagner-Pit 6.2
Brown-Chi 5.1
Overall-Chi 3.9
Mitchell-Cin 3.3

TEAM	G	W	L	PCT	GB	R	OR	AB	H	2B	3B	HR	BB	SO	AVG	OBP	SLG	PRO	/A	BR	/A	PF	CHI	RC	TA	SB	CS	SBA	SBR
DET	158	98	54	.645		666	493	5095	1630	209	58	19	397		.320	.374	.395	.769	151	282	227	110	80	834	.787	280			
PHI	153	95	58	.621	3.5	605	408	4905	1259	186	87	22	403		.257	.321	.344	.665	117	93	82	102	97	587	.646	205			
BOS	152	88	63	.583	9.5	597	550	4964	1306	151	69	20	348		.263	.321	.333	.654	114	75	26	109	98	580	.627	215			
CHI	159	78	74	.513	20	492	463	5017	1110	145	56	4	441		.221	.292	.275	.567	86	-71	-55	97	104	446	.534	211			
NY	153	74	77	.490	23.5	590	587	4981	1234	143	61	16	407		.248	.313	.311	.624	104	25	28	99	105	523	.588	187			
CLE	155	71	82	.464	27.5	493	532	5044	1214	173	81	10	283		.241	.287	.313	.600	96	-39	-39	102	98	485	.546	183			
STL	154	61	89	.407	36	441	575	4964	1152	116	45	10	331		.232	.287	.280	.567	85	-77	-32	92	98	419	.500	136			
WAS	156	42	110	.276	56	380	656	4982	1112	148	41	9	321		.223	.276	.275	.551	80	-108	-54	90	90	397	.483	136			
TOT	620					4264		39952	10017	1271	498	110	2931	4921	.251	.303	.309	.611								1553			

TEAM	CG	SHO	SV	IP	H	H/G	HR	BB	BB/G	SO	SO/G	ERA	/A	OAVG	OOBA	PR	/A	PF	CPI	FA	E	DP	FW	PW	BW	SBW	DIF
DET	117	17	12	1423.7	1254	7.9	16	359	2.3	528	3.3	2.26	116	.244	.293	33	58	106	97	.959	276	87	.0	6.6	25.8		-10.4
PHI	110	27	3	1381.7	1069	7.0	9	386	2.5	728	4.7	1.92	125	.221	.279	84	73	97	89	.961	245	92	2.0	8.3	9.3		-1.1
BOS	75	11	15	1359.0	1214	8.0	18	384	2.5	555	3.7	2.60	103	.247	.301	-19	10	108	90	.955	292	95	-1.0	1.1	3.0		9.4
CHI	115	26	4	1428.0	1190	7.5	8	341	2.1	671	4.2	2.04	117	.234	.282	67	54	97	92	.964	246	101	1.9	6.1	-6.2		.2
NY	94	18	7	1338.0	1223	8.2	21	422	2.8	597	4.0	2.68	92	.251	.311	-30	-33	99	96	.948	329	94	-3.4	-3.7	3.2		2.4
CLE	110	15	3	1355.7	1211	8.0	9	349	2.3	569	3.8	2.39	106	.247	.297	12	23	103	93	.957	275	110	.0	2.6	-4.4		-3.8
STL	105	21	4	1348.3	1287	8.6	16	383	2.6	620	4.1	2.88	81	.259	.312	-60	-81	95	92	.958	267	107	.6	-9.2	-3.6		-1.8
WAS	99	11	2	1367.7	1288	8.5	12	424	2.8	653	4.3	3.04	78	.257	.315	-86	-101	96	86	.957	280	100	-.2	-11.5	-6.1		-16.2
TOT	825	146	50	11002.0		8.0			2.5		4.0	2.47		.251	.303					.957	2210	786					

Runs
Cobb-Det 116
Bush-Det 114
Collins-Phi 104
Lord-Bos 86
Crawford-Det 83

Hits
Cobb-Det 216
Collins-Phi 198
Crawford-Det 185
Speaker-Bos 168
Lord-Bos 166

Doubles
Crawford-Det 35
Lajoie-Cle 33
Cobb-Det 33
Collins-Phi 30
Murphy-Phi 28

Triples
Baker-Phi 19
Murphy-Det 14
Crawford-Det 14

Home Runs
Orth-NY 9
Cobb-Det 9
Speaker-Bos 7
Stahl-Bos 6
Crawford-Det 6

Total Bases
Cobb-Det 296
Crawford-Det 266
Collins-Phi 257
Baker-Phi 242
Speaker-Bos 241

Runs Batted In
Cobb-Det 107
Crawford-Det 97
Baker-Phi 85
Speaker-Bos 77
Davis-Phi 75

Runs Produced
Cobb-Det 214
Crawford-Det 174
Collins-Phi 157
Baker-Phi 154
Bush-Det 147

Bases On Balls
Bush-Det 88
Collins-Phi 62
Demmitt-NY 55
McIntyre-Det 54

Batting Average
Cobb-Det 377
Collins-Phi 346
Lajoie-Cle 324
Crawford-Det 314
Lord-Bos 311

On Base Percentage
Cobb-Det 431
Collins-Phi 416
Bush-Det 380
Lajoie-Cle 378
Stahl-Bos 377

Slugging Average
Cobb-Det 517
Crawford-Det 452
Collins-Phi 449
Baker-Phi 447
Speaker-Bos 443

Production
Cobb-Det 947
Collins-Phi 865
Crawford-Det 817
Stahl-Bos 812
Lajoie-Cle 809

Adjusted Production
Cobb-Det 181
Collins-Phi 170
Lajoie-Cle 152
Baker-Phi 146
Crawford-Det 143

Batter Runs
Cobb-Det 63.3
Collins-Phi 48.9
Crawford-Det 36.7
Speaker-Bos 31.5
Lajoie-Cle 28.8

Adjusted Batter Runs
Cobb-Det 57.1
Collins-Phi 47.7
Crawford-Det 30.4
Lajoie-Cle 27.8
Speaker-Bos 26.2

Clutch Hitting Index
Engle-NY 157
Davis-Phi 146
Gessler-Bos-Was 140
Ferris-StL 138
Baker-Phi 137

Runs Created
Cobb-Det 157
Collins-Phi 132
Crawford-Det 105
Speaker-Bos 97
Baker-Phi 87

Total Average
Cobb-Det 1.193
Collins-Phi 1.048
Stahl-Bos 857
Speaker-Bos 854
Crawford-Det 851

Stolen Bases
Cobb-Det 76
Collins-Phi 67
Bush-Det 53
Lord-Bos 36
Dougherty-Chi 36

Stolen Base Average

Stolen Base Runs

Fielding Runs
Lajoie-Cle 23.1
Speaker-Bos . . . 20.0
Demmitt-NY 15.2
Parent-Chi 14.2
Hoffman-StL 13.1

Total Player Rating
Cobb-Det 6.9
Collins-Phi 5.6
Lajoie-Cle 5.3
Speaker-Bos 4.5
Baker-Phi 3.0

Wins
Mullin-Det 29
Smith-Chi 25
Willett-Det 21

Win Percentage
Mullin-Det 784
Krause-Phi 692
Bender-Phi 692
Summers-Det 679
Willett-Det 677

Games
Smith-Chi 51
Arellanes-Bos 45
Groom-Was 44
Willett-Det 41

Complete Games
Smith-Chi 37
Young-Cle 30
Mullin-Det 29
Johnson-Was 27
Morgan-Bos-Phi 26

Shutouts
Walsh-Chi 8
Smith-Chi 7
Krause-Phi 7
Coombs-Phi 6

Saves
Arellanes-Bos 8
Powell-StL 3

Innings Pitched
Smith-Chi 365
Mullin-Det 304
Johnson-Was 297
Young-Cle 295
Morgan-Bos-Phi 294

Fewest Hits/Game
Morgan-Bos-Phi . . . 6.24
Krause-Phi 6.38
Walsh-Chi 6.50
Cicotte-Bos 6.58
Wood-Bos 6.76

Fewest BB/Game
Joss-Cle 1.15
White-Chi 1.57
Powell-StL 1.58
Bender-Phi 1.62
Summers-Det 1.66

Strikeouts
Smith-Chi 177
Johnson-Was 164
Berger-Cle 162
Bender-Phi 161
Waddell-StL 141

Strikeouts/Game
Berger-Cle 5.90
Krause-Phi 5.87
Bender-Phi 5.80
Waddell-StL 5.77
Bailey-StL 5.16

Wins Above Team
Mullin-Det 8.5
Smith-Chi 4.6
Young-Cle 3.7
Cicotte-Bos 3.3

Earned Run Average
Krause-Phi 1.39
Walsh-Chi 1.41
Bender-Phi 1.66
Joss-Cle 1.70
Killian-Det 1.72

Adjusted ERA
Krause-Phi 172
Walsh-Chi 169
Killian-Det 153
Joss-Cle 149
Bender-Phi 145

Opponents' Batting Avg.
Morgan-Bos-Phi 202
Walsh-Chi 203
Krause-Phi 204
Wood-Bos 209
Cicotte-Bos 210

Opponents' On Base Pct.
Walsh-Chi 253
Bender-Phi 254
Joss-Cle 255
Smith-Chi 257
Krause-Phi 266

Starter Runs
Smith-Chi 27.2
Walsh-Chi 27.1
Krause-Phi 25.5
Bender-Phi 22.6
Morgan-Bos-Phi . . . 21.7

Adjusted Starter Runs
Walsh-Chi 24.9
Krause-Phi 23.8
Smith-Chi 23.7
Joss-Cle 22.7
Morgan-Bos-Phi . . . 21.6

Clutch Pitching Index
Burns-Was-Chi 133
Brockett-NY 124
Killian-Det 121
Waddell-StL 118
Bailey-StL 111

Relief Runs

Adjusted Relief Runs

Relief Ranking

Total Pitcher Index
Smith-Chi 4.6
Walsh-Chi 3.9
Joss-Cle 2.7
Bender-Phi 2.7
Morgan-Bos-Phi 2.7

Total Baseball Ranking
Cobb-Det 6.9
Collins-Phi 5.6
Lajoie-Cle 5.3
Smith-Chi 4.6
Speaker-Bos 4.5

TEAM	G	W	L	PCT	GB	R	OR	AB	H	2B	3B	HR	BB	SO	AVG	OBP	SLG	PRO	/A	BR	/A	PF	CHI	RC	TA	SB	CS	SBA	SBR
CHI	154	104	50	.675		712	499	4977	1333	219	84	34	542	501	.268	.344	.366	.710	113	82	78	101	100	696	.707	173			
NY	155	91	63	.591	13	715	567	5061	1391	204	83	31	562	489	.275	.354	.366	.720	116	106	135	95	96	759	.751	282			
PIT	154	86	67	.562	17.5	655	576	5125	1364	214	83	33	437	524	.266	.328	.360	.688	107	31	-41	112	100	655	.655	148			
PHI	157	78	75	.510	25.5	674	639	5171	1319	223	71	22	506	559	.255	.327	.338	.665	100	-2	24	96	106	641	.648	199			
CIN	156	75	79	.487	29	620	684	5121	1326	150	70	23	529	515	.259	.332	.329	.661	99	-4	-10	101	98	663	.673	310			
BRO	156	64	90	.416	40	497	623	5125	1174	166	73	25	434	706	.229	.294	.305	.599	80	-131	-101	95	101	506	.553	151			
STL	153	63	90	.412	40.5	639	718	4912	1217	167	70	15	655	581	.248	.345	.319	.664	100	19	72	92	99	609	.671	179			
BOS	157	53	100	.346	50.5	495	701	5123	1260	173	49	31	359	540	.246	.301	.317	.618	86	-97	-182	114	95	536	.565	152			
TOT	621					5007		40615	10384	1516	583	214	4024	4415	.256	.328	.337	.666								1594			

TEAM	CG	SHO	SV	IP	H	H/G	HR	BB	BB/G	SO	SO/G	ERA	/A	OAVG	OOBA	PR	/A	PF	CPI	FA	E	DP	FW	PW	BW	SBW	DIF
CHI	100	28	13	1372.0	1171	7.7	18	474	3.1	609	4.0	2.51	116	.238	.304	78	61	96	96	.963	230	110	2.2	6.4	8.2		10.2
NY	96	9	10	1393.7	1290	8.3	30	397	2.6	717	4.6	2.68	104	.253	.307	53	17	92	99	.955	291	117	-1.7	1.8	14.2		-.3
PIT	73	13	12	1371.7	1254	8.2	20	392	2.6	479	3.1	2.83	118	.250	.305	30	76	110	90	.961	245	102	1.2	8.0	-4.3		4.6
PHI	84	19	9	1409.7	1297	8.3	36	547	3.5	657	4.2	3.05	94	.251	.323	-4	-26	95	97	.960	258	132	.4	-2.7	2.5		1.3
CIN	86	18	11	1381.0	1334	8.7	28	528	3.4	497	3.2	3.08	101	.261	.330	-8	2	102	102	.955	291	103	-1.7	.2	-1.1		.5
BRO	103	15	5	1412.7	1331	8.5	17	545	3.5	555	3.5	3.07	96	.256	.327	-7	-17	98	96	.964	235	125	1.9	-1.8	-10.6		-2.5
STL	81	5	14	1337.3	1396	9.4	30	541	3.6	466	3.1	3.78	74	.276	.346	-112	-144	93	95	.959	261	109	.2	-15.1	7.6		-6.2
BOS	72	12	9	1386.7	1328	8.6	36	599	3.9	531	3.4	3.22	111	.259	.337	-29	55	118	102	.954	305	137	-2.6	5.8	-19.1		-7.6
TOT	695	119	83	11064.7		8.5			3.3		3.7	3.03		.256	.328					.959	2116	935					

Runs
Magee-Phi 110
Huggins-StL 101
Byrne-Pit 101
Doyle-NY 97
Bescher-Cin 95

Hits
Wagner-Pit 178
Byrne-Pit 178
Wheat-Bro 172
Magee-Phi 172
Hoblitzel-Cin 170

Doubles
Byrne-Pit 43
Magee-Phi 39
Wheat-Bro 36
Merkle-NY 35
Wagner-Pit 34

Triples
Mitchell-Cin 18
Magee-Phi 17
Konetchy-StL 16
Hofman-Chi 16

Home Runs
Schulte-Chi 10
Beck-Bos 10
Doyle-NY 8
Daubert-Bro 8

Total Bases
Magee-Phi 263
Schulte-Chi 257
Byrne-Pit 251
Wheat-Bro 244
Wagner-Pit 240

Runs Batted In
Magee-Phi 123
Mitchell-Cin 88
Murray-NY 87
Hofman-Chi 86
Wagner-Pit 81

Runs Produced
Magee-Phi 227
Wagner-Pit 167
Hofman-Chi 166
Mitchell-Cin 162
Konetchy-StL 162

Bases On Balls
Huggins-StL 116
Evers-Chi 108
Magee-Phi 94
Titus-Phi 93
Sheckard-Chi 83

Batting Average
Magee-Phi 331
Hofman-Chi 325
Snodgrass-NY 321
Wagner-Pit 320
Bates-Phi 305

On Base Percentage
Magee-Phi 445
Snodgrass-NY 440
Evers-Chi 413
Hofman-Chi 406
Huggins-StL 399

Slugging Average
Magee-Phi 507
Hofman-Chi 461
Schulte-Chi 460
Merkle-NY 441
Snodgrass-NY 432

Production
Magee-Phi 952
Snodgrass-NY 871
Hofman-Chi 867
Konetchy-StL 822
Wagner-Pit 822

Adjusted Production
Magee-Phi 185
Snodgrass-NY 162
Konetchy-StL 153
Hofman-Chi 152
Bates-Phi 140

Batter Runs
Magee-Phi 54.9
Hofman-Chi 32.4
Snodgrass-NY 31.9
Konetchy-StL 28.0
Wagner-Pit 27.9

Adjusted Batter Runs
Magee-Phi 57.7
Snodgrass-NY 34.4
Konetchy-StL 33.6
Hofman-Chi 32.0
Bates-Phi 25.1

Clutch Hitting Index
Magee-Phi 162
Evans-StL 158
Murray-NY 146
Steinfeldt-Chi 145
Devlin-NY 143

Runs Created
Magee-Phi 139
Byrne-Pit 104
Wagner-Pit 103
Hofman-Chi 102
Doyle-NY 101

Total Average
Magee-Phi 1.205
Snodgrass-NY 1.071
Hofman-Chi 975
Konetchy-StL 884
Paskert-Cin 884

Stolen Bases
Bescher-Cin 70
Murray-NY 57
Paskert-Cin 51
Magee-Phi 49
Devore-NY 43

Stolen Base Average

Stolen Base Runs

Fielding Runs
Shean-Bos 42.2
Knabe-Phi 17.4
Doolan-Phi 16.4
Mowrey-StL 13.9
Sheckard-Chi 12.7

Total Player Rating
Magee-Phi 4.7
Konetchy-StL 4.0
Mowrey-StL 3.3
Hofman-Chi 3.1
Wagner-Pit 2.8

Wins
Mathewson-NY 27
Brown-Chi 25
Moore-Phi 22
Suggs-Cin 20
Cole-Chi 20

Win Percentage
Cole-Chi 833
Crandall-NY 810
Mathewson-NY 750
Adams-Pit 667
Brown-Chi 641

Games
Mattern-Bos 51
Gaspar-Cin 48

Complete Games
Rucker-Bro 27
Mathewson-NY 27
Brown-Chi 27
Bell-Bro 25
Barger-Bro 25

Shutouts
Brown-Chi 8
Moore-Phi 7
Rucker-Bro 6
Mattern-Bos 6

Saves
Gaspar-Cin 7
Brown-Chi 7
Crandall-NY 5
Richie-Bos-Chi 4
Phillippe-Pit 4

Innings Pitched
Rucker-Bro 320
Mathewson-NY 318
Bell-Bro 310
Mattern-Bos 305
Brown-Chi 295

Fewest Hits/Game
Cole-Chi 6.53
Moore-Phi 7.25
Scanlan-Bro 7.26
Drucke-NY 7.28
Ames-NY 7.63

Fewest BB/Game
Suggs-Cin 1.62
Mathewson-NY 1.70
Crandall-NY 1.86
Brown-Chi 1.95
Wiltse-NY 1.99

Strikeouts
Moore-Phi 185
Mathewson-NY 184
Frock-Pit-Bos 171
Drucke-NY 151
Rucker-Bro 147

Strikeouts/Game
Drucke-NY 6.32
Frock-Pit-Bos 5.99
Moore-Phi 5.88
Mathewson-NY 5.21
Ames-NY 4.45

Wins Above Team
Mathewson-NY 8.2
Cole-Chi 6.3
Crandall-NY 6.0
Phillippe-Pit 5.9
Suggs-Cin 5.1

Earned Run Average
Cole-Chi 1.80
Brown-Chi 1.86
Mathewson-NY 1.90
Ames-NY 2.23
Adams-Pit 2.24

Adjusted ERA
Cole-Chi 162
Brown-Chi 157
Adams-Pit 149
Mathewson-NY 147
Brown-Bos 134

Opponents' Batting Avg.
Cole-Chi 211
Drucke-NY 228
Moore-Phi 228
Brown-Chi 232
Scanlan-Bro 234

Opponents' On Base Pct.
Brown-Chi 277
Mathewson-NY 286
Crandall-NY 289
Adams-Pit 291
Bell-Bro 296

Starter Runs
Mathewson-NY 39.9
Brown-Chi 38.2
Cole-Chi 32.7
McQuillan-Phi 24.1
Adams-Pit 21.4

Adjusted Starter Runs
Brown-Chi 34.5
Mathewson-NY 31.8
Cole-Chi 29.7
Adams-Pit 29.7
Brown-Bos 26.6

Clutch Pitching Index
Cole-Chi 136
Brown-Bos 122
Barger-Bro 122
Mathewson-NY 117
Curtis-Bos 116

Relief Runs

Adjusted Relief Runs

Relief Ranking

Total Pitcher Index
Mathewson-NY 5.2
Brown-Chi 4.0
Cole-Chi 3.4
Brown-Bos 3.1
Adams-Pit 2.9

Total Baseball Ranking
Mathewson-NY 5.2
Magee-Phi 4.7
Brown-Chi 4.0
Konetchy-StL 3.9
Cole-Chi 3.4

TEAM	G	W	L	PCT	GB	R	OR	AB	H	2B	3B	HR	BB	SO	AVG	OBP	SLG	PRO	/A	BR	/A	PF	CHI	RC	TA	SB	CS	SBA SBR
PHI	155	102	48	.680		673	441	5167	1376	194	106	19	409		.266	.326	.356	.682	120	106	93	102	98	667	.660	207		
NY	156	88	63	.583	14.5	626	557	5050	1252	163	75	20	464		.248	.320	.322	.642	107	42	0	107	102	613	.645	289		
DET	155	86	68	.558	18	679	582	5048	1319	192	73	26	459		.261	.329	.344	.673	117	94	83	102	655	.669	249			
BOS	158	81	72	.529	22.5	638	564	5205	1350	175	87	43	430		.259	.323	.351	.674	117	93	98	99	93	656	.651	194		
CLE	161	71	81	.467	32	548	657	5359	1310	185	63	9	366		.244	.297	.308	.605	95	-36	-33	100	99	546	.553	189		
CHI	156	68	85	.444	35.5	457	479	5028	1062	115	58	7	403		.211	.276	.261	.537	73	-147	-118	95	111	413	.490	183		
WAS	157	66	85	.437	36.5	501	550	4983	1175	145	46	9	449		.236	.309	.289	.598	93	-30	-34	101	94	508	.568	192		
STL	158	47	107	.305	57	451	743	5077	1115	131	60	12	415		.220	.283	.276	.559	80	-109	-76	94	99	444	.510	169		
TOT	628					4573		40917	9959	1300	568	145	3395	5276	.243	.308	.313	.621								1672		

TEAM	CG	SHO	SV	IP	H	H/G	HR	BB	BB/G	SO	SO/G	ERA	/A	OAVG	OOBA	PR	/A	PF	CPI	FA	E	DP	FW	PW	BW	SBW	DIF
PHI	123	24	5	1417.7	1103	7.0	8	450	2.9	789	5.0	1.78	137	.220	.284	115	103	97	104	.965	230	117	4.1	11.4	10.3		1.2
NY	110	14	8	1383.3	1238	8.1	16	364	2.4	654	4.3	2.59	103	.244	.295	-11	10	106	90	.956	284	95	.4	1.1	.0		11.0
DET	108	17	5	1389.0	1257	8.1	34	460	3.0	532	3.4	2.84	88	.247	.309	-50	-51	100	94	.956	288	79	.0	-5.6	9.2		5.4
BOS	100	12	6	1427.0	1236	7.8	30	414	2.6	670	4.2	2.46	99	.238	.295	8	-1	97	95	.954	309	80	-1.4	-.1	10.9		-4.9
CLE	92	13	5	1428.7	1386	8.7	10	487	3.1	614	3.9	2.89	89	.260	.322	-60	-52	102	99	.964	247	112	2.9	-5.8	-3.7		1.5
CHI	103	23	7	1413.0	1130	7.2	15	381	2.4	785	5.0	2.01	119	.224	.279	78	59	95	93	.954	314	100	-1.7	6.5	-13.1		-.2
WAS	119	19	3	1376.3	1223	8.0	19	374	2.4	675	4.4	2.45	104	.243	.296	9	16	102	95	.959	264	99	1.7	1.8	-3.8		-9.2
STL	100	9	3	1388.0	1356	8.8	15	532	3.4	557	3.6	3.09	82	.261	.330	-89	-87	101	99	.944	377	113	-6.1	-9.6	-8.4		-5.9
TOT	855	131	42	11223.0		8.0			2.8		4.2	2.51		.243	.308					.956	2313	795					

Runs
Cobb-Det 106
Speaker-Bos 92
Lajoie-Cle 92
Bush-Det 90
Milan-Was 89

Hits
Lajoie-Cle 227
Cobb-Det 194
Collins-Phi 188
Speaker-Bos 183
Crawford-Det 170

Doubles
Lajoie-Cle 51
Cobb-Det 35
Lewis-Bos 29
Murphy-Phi 28
Oldring-Phi 27

Triples
Crawford-Det 19
Lord-Cle-Phi 18
Murphy-Phi 18
Stahl-Bos 16
Cree-NY 16

Home Runs
Stahl-Bos 10
Lewis-Bos 8
Cobb-Det 8
Speaker-Bos 7
Crawford-Det 5

Total Bases
Lajoie-Cle 304
Cobb-Det 279
Speaker-Bos 252
Crawford-Det 249
Murphy-Phi 244

Runs Batted In
Crawford-Det 120
Cobb-Det 91
Collins-Phi 81
Stahl-Bos 77
Lajoie-Cle 76

Runs Produced
Crawford-Det 198
Cobb-Det 189
Lajoie-Cle 164
Collins-Phi 159
Baker-Phi 155

Bases On Balls
Bush-Det 78
Milan-Was 71
Wolter-NY 66
Cobb-Det 64

Batting Average
Lajoie-Cle 384
Cobb-Det 383
Speaker-Bos 340
Collins-Phi 322
Oldring-Phi 308

On Base Percentage
Cobb-Det 456
Lajoie-Cle 445
Speaker-Bos 404
Collins-Phi 381
Milan-Was 379

Slugging Average
Cobb-Det 551
Lajoie-Cle 514
Speaker-Bos 468
Murphy-Phi 436
Oldring-Phi 430

Production
Cobb-Det 1.008
Lajoie-Cle 960
Speaker-Bos 873
Collins-Phi 798
Cree-NY 775

Adjusted Production
Cobb-Det 211
Lajoie-Cle 201
Speaker-Bos 175
Collins-Phi 147
Murphy-Phi 139

Batter Runs
Lajoie-Cle 68.2
Cobb-Det 67.9
Speaker-Bos 44.9
Collins-Phi 33.0
Murphy-Phi 23.6

Adjusted Batter Runs
Lajoie-Cle 68.5
Cobb-Det 66.8
Speaker-Bos 45.5
Collins-Phi 31.6
Murphy-Phi 22.3

Clutch Hitting Index
Crawford-Det 178
LaPorte-NY 166
McBride-Was 143
Moriarty-Det 137
Purtell-Chi-Bos 133

Runs Created
Cobb-Det 156
Lajoie-Cle 147
Collins-Phi 122
Speaker-Bos 115
Crawford-Det 89

Total Average
Cobb-Det 1.321
Lajoie-Cle 1.088
Speaker-Bos 972
Collins-Phi 959
Cree-NY 820

Stolen Bases
Collins-Phi 81
Cobb-Det 65
Zeider-Chi 49
Bush-Det 49
Milan-Was 44

Stolen Base Average

Stolen Base Runs

Fielding Runs
Collins-Phi 33.0
Lajoie-Cle 24.1
McBride-Was 22.7
Lewis-Bos 13.9
Wallace-StL 12.3

Total Player Rating
Lajoie-Cle 8.9
Cobb-Det 6.3
Collins-Phi 5.9
Speaker-Bos 5.0
Oldring-Phi 2.6

Wins
Coombs-Phi 31
Ford-NY 26
Johnson-Was 25
Bender-Phi 23
Mullin-Det 21

Win Percentage
Bender-Phi 821
Ford-NY 813
Coombs-Phi 775
Donovan-Det 708
Mullin-Det 636

Games
Walsh-Chi 45
Johnson-Was 45
Coombs-Phi 45
Scott-Chi 41

Complete Games
Johnson-Was 38
Coombs-Phi 35
Walsh-Chi 33
Ford-NY 29
Mullin-Det 27

Shutouts
Coombs-Phi 13
Johnson-Was 8
Ford-NY 8
Walsh-Chi 7

Saves
Walsh-Chi 5
Browning-Det 3

Innings Pitched
Johnson-Was 374
Walsh-Chi 370
Coombs-Phi 353
Ford-NY 300
Morgan-Phi 291

Fewest Hits/Game
Ford-NY 5.82
Walsh-Chi 5.89
Coombs-Phi 6.32
Johnson-Was 6.47
Smith-Chi-Bos 6.48

Fewest BB/Game
Walsh-Chi 1.48
Young-Cle 1.49
Collins-Bos 1.51
Bender-Phi 1.69
Johnson-Was 1.83

Strikeouts
Johnson-Was 313
Walsh-Chi 258
Coombs-Phi 224
Ford-NY 209
Bender-Phi 155

Strikeouts/Game
Johnson-Was 7.53
Wood-Bos 6.56
Walsh-Chi 6.28
Ford-NY 6.27
Coombs-Phi 5.71

Wins Above Team
Ford-NY 9.7
Johnson-Was 7.4
Coombs-Phi 7.3
Bender-Phi 6.9
Donovan-Det 4.5

Earned Run Average
Walsh-Chi 1.26
Coombs-Phi 1.30
Johnson-Was 1.35
Morgan-Phi 1.55
Bender-Phi 1.58

Adjusted ERA
Johnson-Was 190
Walsh-Chi 189
Coombs-Phi 187
Ford-NY 161
Morgan-Phi 158

Opponents' Batting Avg.
Walsh-Chi 187
Ford-NY 188
Coombs-Phi 201
Hall-Bos 207
Bender-Phi 207

Opponents' On Base Pct.
Walsh-Chi 226
Ford-NY 245
Bender-Phi 255
Johnson-Was 262
Collins-Bos 264

Starter Runs
Walsh-Chi 51.3
Johnson-Was 48.4
Coombs-Phi 47.5
Morgan-Phi 31.2
Ford-NY 28.7

Adjusted Starter Runs
Johnson-Was 50.3
Walsh-Chi 46.3
Coombs-Phi 44.6
Ford-NY 33.7
Morgan-Phi 28.8

Clutch Pitching Index
Morgan-Phi 142
Olmstead-Chi 141
Vaughn-NY 121
Wood-Bos 117
Coombs-Phi 113

Relief Runs

Adjusted Relief Runs

Relief Ranking

Total Pitcher Index
Walsh-Chi 7.2
Johnson-Was 5.9
Coombs-Phi 5.0
Ford-NY 4.2
Bender-Phi 4.0

Total Baseball Ranking
Lajoie-Cle 8.9
Walsh-Chi 7.2
Cobb-Det 6.3
Johnson-Was 5.9
Collins-Phi 5.9

TEAM	G	W	L	PCT	GB	R	OR	AB	H	2B	3B	HR	BB	SO	AVG	OBP	SLG	PRO	/A	BR	/A	PF	CHI	RC	TA	SB	CS	SBA	SBR
NY	154	99	54	.647		756	542	5006	1399	225	105	39	530	506	.279	.358	.390	.748	116	108	91	102	96	820	.808	347			
CHI	157	92	62	.597	7.5	757	607	5130	1335	218	101	54	585	617	.260	.341	.374	.715	107	44	68	97	102	729	.727	214			
PIT	155	85	69	.552	14.5	744	557	5137	1345	206	106	48	525	583	.262	.336	.371	.707	105	27	21	101	103	697	.697	160			
PHI	153	79	73	.520	19.5	658	669	5044	1307	214	56	60	490	588	.259	.328	.359	.687	99	-10	-60	108	99	647	.666	153			
STL	158	75	74	.503	22	671	745	5132	1295	199	85	27	592	650	.252	.337	.340	.677	96	-16	-22	101	98	652	.672	175			
CIN	159	70	83	.458	29	682	706	5291	1379	180	105	21	578	594	.261	.337	.346	.683	98	-9	49	92	97	716	.699	289			
BRO	154	64	86	.427	33.5	539	659	5059	1198	151	71	28	425	683	.237	.301	.311	.612	77	-151	-130	97	105	528	.576	184			
BOS	156	44	107	.291	54	699	1021	5308	1417	249	54	37	554	577	.267	.340	.355	.695	101	9	-14	103	97	696	.678	169			
TOT	623					5506		41107	10675	1642	683	314	4279	4798	.260	.335	.356	.691								1691			

TEAM	CG	SHO	SV	IP	H	H/G	HR	BB	BB/G	SO	SO/G	ERA	/A	OAVG	OOBA	PR	/A	PF	CPI	FA	E	DP	FW	PW	BW	SBW	DIF
NY	95	19	13	1365.0	1267	8.4	34	369	2.4	771	5.1	2.69	124	.252	.303	106	98	99	103	.959	256	86	.6	9.8	9.1		3.0
CHI	85	12	16	1405.7	1270	8.1	27	525	3.4	582	3.7	2.90	110	.247	.317	76	43	94	99	.960	260	114	.3	4.3	6.8		3.5
PIT	91	13	11	1374.0	1249	8.2	36	375	2.5	605	4.0	2.84	116	.248	.300	83	69	97	94	.963	232	131	2.1	6.9	2.1		-3.1
PHI	90	21	10	1369.3	1285	8.4	42	598	3.9	697	4.6	3.30	111	.254	.333	13	53	108	101	.963	242	113	2.2	5.3	-6.0		1.5
STL	88	6	10	1396.0	1296	8.4	39	701	4.5	561	3.6	3.68	94	.252	.342	-44	-32	102	93	.960	261	106	.3	-3.2	-2.2		5.6
CIN	77	4	12	1420.0	1410	8.9	36	476	3.0	557	3.5	3.26	96	.265	.325	21	-21	92	100	.955	295	108	-1.9	-2.1	4.9		-7.4
BRO	81	14	10	1366.7	1310	8.6	26	566	3.7	533	3.5	3.39	99	.258	.332	0	-4	99	96	.962	241	112	1.5	-.4	-13.0		.9
BOS	73	5	7	1370.3	1570	10.3	76	672	4.4	486	3.2	5.08	73	.294	.373	-256	-209	109	93	.947	347	110	-5.1	-21.0	-1.4		-4.0
TOT	680	94	89	11067.0		8.7			3.5		3.9	3.39		.260	.335					.958	2123	880					

Runs
Sheckard-Chi 121
Huggins-StL 106
Bescher-Cin 106
Schulte-Chi 105
Doyle-NY 102

Hits
Miller-Bos 192
Hoblitzel-Cin 180
Daubert-Bro 176
Schulte-Chi 173
Luderus-Phi 166

Doubles
Konetchy-StL 38
Miller-Bos 36
Wilson-Pit 34
Herzog-Bos-NY 33
Sweeney-Bos 33

Triples
Doyle-NY 25
Mitchell-Cin 22
Schulte-Chi 21
Zimmerman-Chi 17
Byrne-Pit 17

Home Runs
Schulte-Chi 21
Luderus-Phi 16
Magee-Phi 15
Doyle-NY 13

Total Bases
Schulte-Chi 308
Doyle-NY 277
Luderus-Phi 260
Hoblitzel-Cin 258
Wilson-Pit 257

Runs Batted In
Wilson-Pit 107
Schulte-Chi 107
Luderus-Phi 99
Magee-Phi 94

Runs Produced
Schulte-Chi 191
Konetchy-StL 172
Wilson-Pit 167
Wagner-Pit 167
Sheckard-Chi 167

Bases On Balls
Sheckard-Chi 147
Bates-Cin 103
Bescher-Cin 102
Huggins-StL 96
Knabe-Phi 94

Batting Average
Wagner-Pit 334
Miller-Bos 333
Sweeney-Bos 314
Doyle-NY 310
Daubert-Bro 307

On Base Percentage
Sheckard-Chi 434
Wagner-Pit 423
Bates-Cin 415
Sweeney-Bos 404
Doyle-NY 397

Slugging Average
Schulte-Chi 534
Doyle-NY 527
Wagner-Pit 507
Magee-Phi 483
Wilson-Pit 472

Production
Wagner-Pit 930
Doyle-NY 924
Schulte-Chi 918
Magee-Phi 849
Wilson-Pit 826

Adjusted Production
Schulte-Chi 161
Wagner-Pit 159
Doyle-NY 154
Bates-Cin 138
Sheckard-Chi 135

Batter Runs
Schulte-Chi 40.5
Doyle-NY 39.3
Wagner-Pit 38.8
Sheckard-Chi 31.7
Clarke-Pit 26.9

Adjusted Batter Runs
Schulte-Chi 43.4
Wagner-Pit 38.3
Doyle-NY 37.5
Sheckard-Chi 34.6
Bates-Cin 30.2

Clutch Hitting Index
Hofman-Chi 155
Miller-Pit 138
Grant-Cin 136
Mitchell-Cin 130
Magee-Phi 129

Runs Created
Schulte-Chi 127
Doyle-NY 124
Bescher-Cin 115
Wagner-Pit 109
Miller-Bos 107

Total Average
Doyle-NY 1.077
Wagner-Pit 1.057
Schulte-Chi 1.015
Sheckard-Chi 1.003
Bates-Cin 943

Stolen Bases
Bescher-Cin 81
Devore-NY 61
Snodgrass-NY 51
Merkle-NY 49

Stolen Base Average

Stolen Base Runs

Fielding Runs
Tinker-Chi 22.2
Doolan-Phi 18.5
Sheckard-Chi 18.3
Egan-Cin 14.4
Merkle-NY 13.1

Total Player Rating
Sheckard-Chi 4.7
Wagner-Pit 3.8
Sweeney-Bos 3.0
Schulte-Chi 3.0
Tinker-Chi 2.8

Wins
Alexander-Phi 28
Mathewson-NY 26
Marquard-NY 24
Harmon-StL 23

Win Percentage
Marquard-NY 774
Crandall-NY 750
Cole-Chi 720
Alexander-Phi 683
Mathewson-NY 667

Games
Brown-Chi 53
Harmon-StL 51
Rucker-Bro 48
Alexander-Phi 48

Complete Games
Alexander-Phi 31
Mathewson-NY 29
Harmon-StL 28
Leifield-Pit 26
Adams-Pit 24

Shutouts
Alexander-Phi 7
Adams-Pit 6

Saves
Brown-Chi 13
Crandall-NY 5

Innings Pitched
Alexander-Phi 367
Harmon-StL 348
Leifield-Pit 318
Rucker-Bro 316
Moore-Phi 308

Fewest Hits/Game
Alexander-Phi 6.99
Marquard-NY 7.15
Rucker-Bro 7.26
Ames-NY 7.46
Harmon-StL 7.50

Fewest BB/Game
Mathewson-NY 1.11
Adams-Pit 1.29
Steele-Pit-Bro 1.71
Brown-Chi 1.83
Wiltse-NY 1.88

Strikeouts
Marquard-NY 237
Alexander-Phi 227
Rucker-Bro 190
Moore-Phi 174
Harmon-StL 144

Strikeouts/Game
Marquard-NY 7.67
Alexander-Phi 5.57
Rucker-Bro 5.41
Ames-NY 5.18
Moore-Phi 5.08

Wins Above Team
Alexander-Phi 8.5
Marquard-NY 6.4
Rucker-Bro 5.4
Adams-Pit 4.4
Harmon-StL 4.3

Earned Run Average
Mathewson-NY 1.99
Richie-Chi 2.31
Adams-Pit 2.33
Marquard-NY 2.49
Alexander-Phi 2.57

Adjusted ERA
Mathewson-NY 168
Alexander-Phi 142
Adams-Pit 141
Moore-Phi 139
Richie-Chi 138

Opponents' Batting Avg.
Alexander-Phi 219
Marquard-NY 219
Ames-NY 223
Rucker-Bro 226
Keefe-Cin 229

Opponents' On Base Pct.
Adams-Pit 271
Ames-NY 277
Mathewson-NY 283
Wiltse-NY 292
Alexander-Phi 293

Starter Runs
Mathewson-NY 47.7
Adams-Pit 34.4
Alexander-Phi 33.3
Richie-Chi 30.3
Marquard-NY 27.7

Adjusted Starter Runs
Mathewson-NY 45.9
Alexander-Phi 43.9
Moore-Phi 35.0
Adams-Pit 31.4
Marquard-NY 26.2

Clutch Pitching Index
Moore-Phi 130
Mathewson-NY 122
Richie-Chi 119
Leifield-Pit 117
Crandall-NY 116

Relief Runs
Richter-Chi 1.7

Adjusted Relief Runs
Richter-Chi 4

Relief Ranking
Richter-Chi 3

Total Pitcher Index
Mathewson-NY 5.7
Alexander-Phi 4.5
Leifield-Pit 3.0
Adams-Pit 2.9
Moore-Phi 2.7

Total Baseball Ranking
Mathewson-NY 5.7
Sheckard-Chi 4.7
Alexander-Phi 4.5
Wagner-Pit 3.8
Leifield-Pit 3.0

TEAM	G	W	L	PCT	GB	R	OR	AB	H	2B	3B	HR	BB	SO	AVG	OBP	SLG	PRO	/A	BR	/A	PF	CHI	RC	TA	SB	CS	SBA SBR
PHI	152	101	50	.669		861	601	5199	1540	233	93	35	424		.296	.357	.397	.754	117	107	157	93	104	820	.759	226		
DET	154	89	65	.578	13.5	831	776	5293	1544	230	96	30	471		.292	.355	.388	.743	113	92	33	108	101	825	.761	276		
CLE	156	80	73	.523	22	691	712	5314	1500	238	81	20	354		.282	.333	.369	.702	102	2	-18	103	96	717	.675	209		
CHI	154	77	74	.510	24	719	624	5210	1399	179	92	20	385		.269	.325	.350	.675	94	-46	-22	97	108	660	.644	201		
BOS	153	78	75	.510	24	680	643	5024	1379	203	66	35	506		.274	.350	.362	.712	105	37	43	99	91	709	.710	190		
NY	153	76	76	.500	25.5	684	724	5056	1375	190	96	25	493		.272	.344	.362	.706	103	24	-50	111	94	724	.722	270		
WAS	154	64	90	.416	38.5	625	766	5062	1307	159	53	16	466		.258	.330	.320	.650	87	-74	-50	97	100	606	.634	215		
STL	152	45	107	.296	56.5	567	812	5005	1192	187	63	17	460		.238	.307	.311	.618	78	-143	-110	95	104	514	.570	125		
TOT	614					5658		41163	11236	1619	640	198	3559	5093	.273	.338	.358	.696								1712		

TEAM	CG	SHO	SV	IP	H	H/G	HR	BB	BB/G	SO	SO/G	ERA	/A	OAVG	OOBA	PR	/A	PF	CPI	FA	E	DP	FW	PW	BW	SBW	DIF
PHI	97	13	13	1426.0	1343	8.5	17	487	3.1	739	4.7	3.01	98	.256	.319	52	-9	88	94	.965	225	100	4.9	-.9	15.5		6.0
DET	108	8	3	1381.0	1514	9.9	28	460	3.0	538	3.5	3.73	96	.286	.343	-59	-22	107	97	.951	318	78	-1.1	-2.2	3.2		12.0
CLE	93	6	6	1389.0	1376	8.9	16	550	3.6	673	4.4	3.37	102	.266	.337	-4	12	103	95	.954	302	108	-.0	1.2	-1.8		4.1
CHI	87	17	11	1384.0	1349	8.8	22	384	2.5	752	4.9	3.02	105	.263	.314	49	24	95	94	.961	252	98	3.2	2.4	-2.2		-1.9
BOS	87	10	8	1349.0	1314	8.8	20	475	3.2	713	4.8	2.73	121	.263	.327	91	84	99	111	.949	323	93	-1.4	8.3	4.2		-9.6
NY	91	5	3	1364.7	1404	9.3	26	406	2.7	667	4.4	3.54	105	.273	.327	-30	26	111	90	.949	328	99	-1.7	2.6	-4.9		4.1
WAS	106	13	3	1349.0	1471	9.8	39	410	2.7	628	4.2	3.52	94	.285	.338	-27	-31	99	102	.953	305	90	-.2	-3.1	-4.9		-4.8
STL	92	8	1	1329.3	1465	9.9	29	463	3.1	383	2.6	3.83	87	.287	.347	-72	-74	100	97	.945	358	104	-3.7	-7.3	-10.8		-9.2
TOT	761	80	48	10972.0		9.2			3.0		4.2	3.34		.273	.338					.953	2411	770					

Runs		Hits		Doubles		Triples		Home Runs		Total Bases	
Cobb-Det	147	Cobb-Det	248	Cobb-Det	47	Cobb-Det	24	Baker-Phi	11	Cobb-Det	367
Jackson-Cle	126	Jackson-Cle	233	Jackson-Cle	45	Cree-NY	22	Speaker-Bos	8	Jackson-Cle	337
Bush-Det	126	Crawford-Det	217	Baker-Phi	40	Jackson-Cle	19	Cobb-Det	8	Crawford-Det	302
Milan-Was	109	Baker-Phi	198	LaPorte-StL	37	Lord-Chi	18			Baker-Phi	299
Crawford-Det	109	Milan-Was	194			Wolter-NY	15			Cree-NY	267

Runs Batted In		Runs Produced		Bases On Balls		Batting Average		On Base Percentage		Slugging Average	
Cobb-Det	127	Cobb-Det	266	Bush-Det	98	Cobb-Det	.420	Jackson-Cle	.468	Cobb-Det	.621
Crawford-Det	115	Crawford-Det	217	Milan-Was	74	Jackson-Cle	.408	Cobb-Det	.467	Jackson-Cle	.590
Baker-Phi	115	Jackson-Cle	202	Gessler-Was	74	Crawford-Det	.378	Collins-Phi	.451	Crawford-Det	.526
Bodie-Chi	97	Baker-Phi	200	Hooper-Bos	73	Collins-Phi	.365	Crawford-Det	.438	Cree-NY	.513
Delahanty-Det	94			Austin-StL	69	Cree-NY	.348	Cree-NY	.415	Baker-Phi	.505

Production		Adjusted Production		Batter Runs		Adjusted Batter Runs		Clutch Hitting Index		Runs Created	
Cobb-Det	1.088	Jackson-Cle	189	Cobb-Det	78.4	Cobb-Det	72.1	Stovall-Cle	176	Cobb-Det	207
Jackson-Cle	1.058	Cobb-Det	187	Jackson-Cle	71.8	Jackson-Cle	69.5	Hartzell-NY	153	Jackson-Cle	175
Crawford-Det	.964	Collins-Phi	172	Crawford-Det	52.4	Collins-Phi	48.0	Bodie-Chi	147	Crawford-Det	147
Collins-Phi	.932	Baker-Phi	160	Collins-Phi	43.0	Crawford-Det	46.1	McBride-Was	141	Baker-Phi	130
Cree-NY	.928	Crawford-Det	156	Cree-NY	40.0	Baker-Phi	41.6	Gessler-Was	141	Cree-NY	129

Total Average		Stolen Bases		Stolen Base Average		Stolen Base Runs		Fielding Runs		Total Player Rating	
Cobb-Det	1.464	Cobb-Det	83					Tannehill-Chi	29.6	Jackson-Cle	6.5
Jackson-Cle	1.308	Milan-Was	58					McBride-Was	25.0	Cobb-Det	6.5
Collins-Phi	1.125	Cree-NY	48					Austin-StL	18.4	Collins-Phi	4.2
Crawford-Det	1.120	Callahan-Chi	45					Hogan-Phi-StL	15.5	Baker-Phi	3.3
Cree-NY	1.103	Lord-Chi	43					Bush-Det	15.1	Speaker-Bos	2.7

Wins		Win Percentage		Games		Complete Games		Shutouts		Saves	
Coombs-Phi	28	Bender-Phi	.773	Walsh-Chi	56	Johnson-Was	36	Plank-Phi	6	Walsh-Chi	4
Walsh-Chi	27	Gregg-Cle	.767	Coombs-Phi	47	Walsh-Chi	33	Johnson-Was	6	Plank-Phi	4
Johnson-Was	25	Plank-Phi	.742	Wood-Bos	44	Ford-NY	26	Wood-Bos	5	Hall-Bos	4
		Coombs-Phi	.700	Caldwell-NY	41	Coombs-Phi	26	Walsh-Chi	5	Wood-Bos	3
		Morgan-Phi	.682					Gregg-Cle	5	Bender-Phi	3

Innings Pitched		Fewest Hits/Game		Fewest BB/Game		Strikeouts		Strikeouts/Game		Wins Above Team	
Walsh-Chi	369	Gregg-Cle	6.32	White-Chi	1.47	Walsh-Chi	255	Wood-Bos	7.53	Johnson-Was	9.2
Coombs-Phi	337	Wood-Bos	7.37	Lake-StL	1.67	Wood-Bos	231	Walsh-Chi	6.22	Gregg-Cle	8.5
Johnson-Was	323	Krapp-Cle	7.62	Walsh-Chi	1.76	Johnson-Was	207	Lange-Cle	5.78	Ford-NY	6.4
Ford-NY	281	Morgan-Phi	7.81	Warhop-NY	1.89	Coombs-Phi	185	Johnson-Was	5.77	Walsh-Chi	5.5
Wood-Bos	276	Scott-Chi	7.91	Powell-StL	1.90	Ford-NY	158	Kahler-Cle	5.67	Plank-Phi	4.1

Earned Run Average		Adjusted ERA		Opponents' Batting Avg.		Opponents' On Base Pct.		Starter Runs		Adjusted Starter Runs	
Gregg-Cle	1.80	Gregg-Cle	192	Gregg-Cle	.205	Walsh-Chi	.280	Johnson-Was	51.9	Johnson-Was	50.8
Johnson-Was	1.89	Johnson-Was	175	Wood-Bos	.223	Johnson-Was	.283	Walsh-Chi	46.0	Ford-NY	45.0
Wood-Bos	2.02	Ford-NY	163	Krapp-Cle	.232	Wood-Bos	.284	Gregg-Cle	41.9	Gregg-Cle	44.9
Plank-Phi	2.10	Wood-Bos	163	Ford-NY	.237	Gregg-Cle	.286	Wood-Bos	40.5	Walsh-Chi	39.1
Bender-Phi	2.17	Walsh-Chi	143	Johnson-Was	.238	Ford-NY	.291	Plank-Phi	35.4	Wood-Bos	38.9

Clutch Pitching Index		Relief Runs		Adjusted Relief Runs		Relief Ranking		Total Pitcher Index		Total Baseball Ranking	
Plank-Phi	133							Johnson-Was	6.1	Jackson-Cle	6.5
Pape-Bos	130							Walsh-Chi	5.6	Cobb-Det	6.5
Cicotte-Bos	122							Wood-Bos	5.1	Johnson-Was	6.1
Bender-Phi	117							Ford-NY	4.5	Walsh-Chi	5.6
Willett-Det	111							Gregg-Cle	4.4	Wood-Bos	5.1

TEAM	G	W	L	PCT	GB	R	OR	AB	H	2B	3B	HR	BB	SO	AVG	OBP	SLG	PRO	/A	BR	/A	PF	CHI	RC	TA	SB	CS	SBA	SBR
NY	154	103	48	.682		823	571	5067	1451	231	88	48	514	497	.286	.360	.395	.755	113	90	64	104	103	830	.803	319			
PIT	152	93	58	.616	10	751	565	5252	1493	222	129	39	420	514	.284	.340	.398	.738	108	44	53	99	99	767	.722	177			
CHI	152	91	59	.607	11.5	756	668	5048	1398	245	91	42	560	615	.277	.354	.386	.740	109	62	36	104	98	750	.744	164			
CIN	155	75	78	.490	29	656	722	5115	1310	183	91	19	479	492	.256	.323	.339	.662	87	-90	-35	92	107	638	.653	248			
PHI	152	73	79	.480	30.5	670	688	5077	1354	245	68	42	464	615	.267	.332	.367	.699	97	-23	-25	100	99	671	.676	159			
STL	153	63	90	.412	41	659	830	5092	1366	190	77	27	508	620	.268	.340	.352	.692	95	-26	-22	100	97	675	.681	193			
BRO	153	58	95	.379	46	651	754	5141	1377	220	73	32	490	584	.268	.335	.358	.694	96	-27	6	95	95	677	.677	179			
BOS	155	52	101	.340	52	693	861	5361	1465	227	68	35	454	693	.273	.335	.361	.696	96	-27	-78	107	98	693	.660	137			
TOT	613					5659		41153	11214	1763	685	284	3889	4630	.272	.340	.370	.710								1576			

TEAM	CG	SHO	SV	IP	H	H/G	HR	BB	BB/G	SO	SO/G	ERA	/A	OAVG	OOBA	PR	/A	PF	CPI	FA	E	DP	FW	PW	BW	SBW	DIF
NY	93	9	15	1366.7	1352	8.9	36	338	2.2	652	4.3	2.58	131	.264	.310	123	119	99	109	.956	280	123	-2.2	11.7	6.3		11.8
PIT	94	18	7	1381.0	1268	8.3	29	497	3.2	664	4.3	2.85	114	.250	.317	84	59	95	96	.972	169	125	6.2	5.8	5.2		.3
CHI	80	15	9	1352.0	1307	8.7	34	493	3.3	554	3.7	3.42	101	.260	.326	-3	6	102	88	.960	249	125	.1	.6	3.5		11.8
CIN	86	13	10	1372.0	1455	9.5	28	452	3.0	561	3.7	3.42	93	.278	.336	-3	-37	93	98	.960	249	102	.1	-3.6	-3.4		5.5
PHI	82	10	9	1350.7	1381	9.2	43	515	3.4	616	4.1	3.25	105	.271	.338	21	24	101	104	.963	231	98	1.5	2.4	-2.5		-4.4
STL	62	6	12	1358.3	1466	9.7	31	560	3.7	487	3.2	3.85	90	.282	.352	-68	-55	103	96	.957	274	113	-1.8	-5.4	-2.2		-4.2
BRO	71	10	8	1349.0	1399	9.3	45	510	3.4	553	3.7	3.64	91	.274	.340	-36	-51	97	95	.959	255	96	-.3	-5.0	.6		-13.7
BOS	92	6	5	1378.0	1544	10.1	43	521	3.4	542	3.5	4.17	90	.289	.353	-117	-65	110	93	.954	297	129	-3.5	-6.4	-7.7		-6.9
TOT	660	87	75	10907.7		9.2			3.2		3.8	3.40		.272	.340					.960	2004	911					

Runs
Bescher-Cin 120
Carey-Pit 114
Paskert-Phi 102
Campbell-Bos 102

Hits
Zimmerman-Chi 207
Sweeney-Bos 204
Campbell-Bos 185
Doyle-NY 184
Wagner-Pit 181

Doubles
Zimmerman-Chi 41
Paskert-Phi 37
Wagner-Pit 35
Miller-Pit 33
Doyle-NY 33

Triples
Wilson-Pit 36
Wagner-Pit 20
Murray-NY 20
Daubert-Bro 16

Home Runs
Zimmerman-Chi 14
Schulte-Chi 13
Wilson-Pit 11
Merkle-NY 11
Cravath-Phi 11

Total Bases
Zimmerman-Chi 318
Wilson-Pit 299
Wagner-Pit 277
Sweeney-Bos 264
Doyle-NY 263

Runs Batted In
Wagner-Pit 102
Sweeney-Bos 100
Zimmerman-Chi 99
Wilson-Pit 95
Murray-NY 92

Runs Produced
Wagner-Pit 186
Sweeney-Bos 183
Zimmerman-Chi 180
Doyle-NY 178
Carey-Pit 175

Bases On Balls
Sheckard-Chi 122
Paskert-Phi 91
Huggins-StL 87
Bescher-Cin 83
Titus-Phi-Bos 82

Batting Average
Zimmerman-Chi 372
Sweeney-Bos 344
Evers-Chi 341
Doyle-NY 330
Wagner-Pit 324

On Base Percentage
Evers-Chi 431
Huggins-StL 422
Paskert-Phi 420
Zimmerman-Chi 418
Sweeney-Bos 416

Slugging Average
Zimmerman-Chi 571
Wilson-Pit 513
Wagner-Pit 496
Doyle-NY 471
Cravath-Phi 470

Production
Zimmerman-Chi 989
Wagner-Pit 891
Evers-Chi 873
Doyle-NY 864
Titus-Phi-Bos 862

Adjusted Production
Zimmerman-Chi 163
Wagner-Pit 145
Evers-Chi 134
Wilson-Pit 134
Konetchy-StL 131

Batter Runs
Zimmerman-Chi . . . 49.8
Wagner-Pit 32.1
Sweeney-Bos 30.9
Evers-Chi 29.1
Meyers-NY 28.2

Adjusted Batter Runs
Zimmerman-Chi . . . 47.1
Wagner-Pit 33.1
Evers-Chi 26.6
Meyers-NY 26.3
Paskert-Phi 25.5

Clutch Hitting Index
Murray-NY 139
Miller-Pit 131
Mitchell-Cin 126
Tinker-Chi 126
Mowrey-StL 123

Runs Created
Zimmerman-Chi 141
Sweeney-Bos 123
Wagner-Pit 118
Doyle-NY 116
Paskert-Phi 108

Total Average
Zimmerman-Chi . . . 1.100
Wagner-Pit 976
Paskert-Phi 965
Evers-Chi 962
Doyle-NY 955

Stolen Bases
Bescher-Cin 67
Carey-Pit 45
Snodgrass-NY 43
Murray-NY 38

Stolen Base Average

Stolen Base Runs

Fielding Runs
Sweeney-Bos 26.1
Tinker-Chi 25.5
Wagner-Pit 18.8
Sheckard-Chi 12.6
Miller-Bro 12.1

Total Player Rating
Wagner-Pit 6.3
Zimmerman-Chi 4.5
Sweeney-Bos 4.4
Evers-Chi 2.6
Tinker-Chi 2.5

Wins
Marquard-NY 26
Cheney-Chi 26
Hendrix-Pit 24
Mathewson-NY 23
Camnitz-Pit 22

Win Percentage
Hendrix-Pit 727
Cheney-Chi 722
Tesreau-NY 708
Marquard-NY 703
Richie-Chi 667

Games
Benton-Cin 50
Sallee-StL 48
Alexander-Phi 46
Rucker-Bro 45
Seaton-Phi 44

Complete Games
Cheney-Chi 28
Mathewson-NY 27
Alexander-Phi 26
Suggs-Cin 25
Hendrix-Pit 25

Shutouts
Rucker-Bro 6
Suggs-Cin 5
O'Toole-Pit 5

Saves
Sallee-StL 6
Rucker-Bro 4
Reulbach-Chi 4
Mathewson-NY 4

Innings Pitched
Mathewson-NY 310
Alexander-Phi 310
Suggs-Cin 303
Cheney-Chi 303
Benton-Cin 302

Fewest Hits/Game
Tesreau-NY 6.56
Robinson-Pit 7.51
O'Toole-Pit 7.76
Cheney-Chi 7.78
Brown-Bos 7.82

Fewest BB/Game
Mathewson-NY 99
Robinson-Pit 1.54
Suggs-Cin 1.66
Ames-NY 1.76
Adams-Pit 1.85

Strikeouts
Alexander-Phi 195
Hendrix-Pit 176
Marquard-NY 175
Benton-Cin 162
Rucker-Bro 151

Strikeouts/Game
Alexander-Phi 5.66
Hendrix-Pit 5.48
Marquard-NY 5.34
Tyler-Bos 5.06
O'Toole-Pit 4.91

Wins Above Team
Cheney-Chi 6.4
Hendrix-Pit 5.7
Harmon-StL 3.4
Rucker-Bro 3.3
Seaton-Phi 2.9

Earned Run Average
Tesreau-NY 1.96
Mathewson-NY 2.12
Rucker-Bro 2.20
Robinson-Pit 2.26
Ames-NY 2.46

Adjusted ERA
Tesreau-NY 172
Mathewson-NY 159
Rucker-Bro 150
Robinson-Pit 143
Ames-NY 137

Opponents' Batting Avg.
Tesreau-NY 199
Cheney-Chi 228
Brown-Bos 228
Robinson-Pit 230
O'Toole-Pit 235

Opponents' On Base Pct.
Mathewson-NY 275
Robinson-Pit 276
Rucker-Bro 289
Tesreau-NY 292
Adams-Pit 294

Starter Runs
Mathewson-NY 44.0
Rucker-Bro 39.5
Tesreau-NY 38.7
Marquard-NY 27.3
Hendrix-Pit 26.1

Adjusted Starter Runs
Mathewson-NY 43.1
Tesreau-NY 38.0
Rucker-Bro 36.2
Sallee-StL 28.7
Marquard-NY 26.5

Clutch Pitching Index
Ames-NY 117
Geyer-StL 112
Benton-Cin 108
Yingling-Bro 107
O'Toole-Pit 106

Relief Runs

Adjusted Relief Runs

Relief Ranking

Total Pitcher Index
Mathewson-NY 5.0
Hendrix-Pit 4.2
Rucker-Bro 4.1
Tesreau-NY 3.8
Marquard-NY 2.5

Total Baseball Ranking
Wagner-Pit 6.3
Mathewson-NY 5.0
Zimmerman-Chi 4.5
Sweeney-Bos 4.4
Hendrix-Pit 4.2

TEAM	G	W	L	PCT	GB	R	OR	AB	H	2B	3B	HR	BB	SO	AVG	OBP	SLG	PRO	/A	BR	/A	PF	CHI	RC	TA	SB	CS	SBA	SBR
BOS	154	105	47	.691		799	544	5071	1404	269	84	29	565		.277	.355	.380	.735	116	104	56	107	100	752	.743	185			
WAS	154	91	61	.599	14	698	581	5074	1298	202	86	20	472		.256	.324	.341	.665	95	-31	-25	99	108	645	.666	274			
PHI	153	90	62	.592	15	779	658	5111	1442	204	108	22	485		.282	.349	.377	.726	113	83	87	99	100	763	.738	258			
CHI	158	78	76	.506	28	638	646	5181	1321	174	80	17	423		.255	.317	.329	.646	90	-67	-59	99	99	610	.618	205			
CLE	155	75	78	.490	30.5	676	680	5134	1403	218	77	10	407		.273	.333	.352	.685	101	3	-5	101	98	668	.659	194			
DET	154	69	84	.451	36.5	720	777	5141	1375	189	86	19	530		.267	.343	.349	.692	103	26	62	95	99	705	.704	270			
STL	157	53	101	.344	53	552	764	5081	1263	166	71	19	449		.249	.315	.320	.635	87	-85	-76	99	93	565	.601	176			
NY	153	50	102	.329	55	630	842	5095	1320	168	79	18	463		.259	.329	.334	.663	95	-31	-40	101	96	638	.656	247			
TOT	619					5492		40888	10826	1590	671	154	3794	5150	.265	.333	.348	.681								1809			

TEAM	CG	SHO	SV	IP	H	H/G	HR	BB	BB/G	SO	SO/G	ERA	/A	OAVG	OOBA	PR	/A	PF	CPI	FA	E	DP	FW	PW	BW	SBW	DIF
BOS	108	18	6	1369.7	1243	8.2	18	385	2.5	712	4.7	2.76	124	.249	.303	88	99	102	97	.957	267	88	2.4	9.9	5.6		11.1
WAS	98	11	7	1387.0	1219	7.9	24	525	3.4	828	5.4	2.69	120	.243	.315	99	84	97	105	.954	297	92	.6	8.4	-2.5		8.5
PHI	95	11	9	1366.7	1273	8.4	12	518	3.4	601	4.0	3.32	98	.254	.324	3	-10	97	91	.959	263	115	2.6	-1.0	8.7		3.7
CHI	85	14	16	1416.3	1397	8.9	26	426	2.7	697	4.4	3.06	108	.265	.320	43	39	99	103	.956	291	102	1.0	3.9	-5.9		2.0
CLE	94	7	7	1357.7	1367	9.1	15	523	3.5	622	4.1	3.30	103	.269	.337	6	12	101	104	.954	287	124	1.2	1.2	-.5		-3.4
DET	107	7	5	1379.0	1424	9.3	16	517	3.4	506	3.3	3.78	85	.274	.339	-67	-88	96	94	.950	338	91	-1.7	-8.8	6.2		-3.2
STL	85	8	5	1372.3	1433	9.4	17	442	2.9	547	3.6	3.71	92	.276	.333	-56	-42	103	93	.947	341	127	-1.9	-4.2	-7.6		-10.3
NY	105	5	3	1347.0	1448	9.7	28	436	2.9	637	4.3	4.13	85	.282	.338	-117	-91	105	89	.940	382	77	-4.2	-9.1	-4.0		-8.7
TOT	777	81	58	10995.7		8.8			3.1		4.2	3.34		.265	.333					.952	2466	816					

Runs
Collins-Phi 137
Speaker-Bos 136
Jackson-Cle 121
Cobb-Det 119
Baker-Phi 116

Hits
Cobb-Det 227
Jackson-Cle 226
Speaker-Bos 222
Baker-Phi 200

Doubles
Speaker-Bos 53
Jackson-Cle 44
Baker-Phi 40
Lewis-Bos 36

Triples
Jackson-Cle 26
Cobb-Det 23
Crawford-Det 21
Baker-Phi 21
Gardner-Bos 18

Home Runs
Speaker-Bos 10
Baker-Phi 10
Cobb-Det 7

Total Bases
Jackson-Cle 331
Speaker-Bos 329
Cobb-Det 324
Baker-Phi 312
Crawford-Det 273

Runs Batted In
Baker-Phi 130
Lewis-Bos 109
Crawford-Det 109
McInnis-Phi 101

Runs Produced
Baker-Phi 236
Speaker-Bos 216
Jackson-Cle 208
Collins-Phi 201
Cobb-Det 195

Bases On Balls
Bush-Det 117
Collins-Phi 101
Rath-Chi 95
Shotton-StL 86
Speaker-Bos 82

Batting Average
Cobb-Det 410
Jackson-Cle 395
Speaker-Bos 383
Lajoie-Cle 368
Collins-Phi 348

On Base Percentage
Speaker-Bos 464
Jackson-Cle 458
Cobb-Det 458
Collins-Phi 450
Lajoie-Cle 414

Slugging Average
Cobb-Det 586
Jackson-Cle 579
Speaker-Bos 567
Baker-Phi 541
Crawford-Det 470

Production
Cobb-Det 1.043
Jackson-Cle 1.036
Speaker-Bos 1.031
Baker-Phi 945
Collins-Phi 885

Adjusted Production
Cobb-Det 209
Jackson-Cle 193
Speaker-Bos 182
Baker-Phi 171
Collins-Phi 154

Batter Runs
Speaker-Bos 72.8
Jackson-Cle 70.3
Cobb-Det 67.9
Baker-Phi 49.2
Collins-Phi 43.7

Adjusted Batter Runs
Cobb-Det 71.6
Jackson-Cle 69.4
Speaker-Bos 67.3
Baker-Phi 49.7
Collins-Phi 44.2

Clutch Hitting Index
Lewis-Bos 151
Gandil-Was 145
McInnis-Phi 140
Lajoie-Cle 139
Crawford-Det 135

Runs Created
Speaker-Bos 175
Cobb-Det 174
Jackson-Cle 166
Baker-Phi 140
Collins-Phi 136

Total Average
Cobb-Det 1.328
Speaker-Bos 1.310
Jackson-Cle 1.249
Collins-Phi 1.130
Baker-Phi 1.082

Stolen Bases
Milan-Was 88
Collins-Phi 63
Cobb-Det 61
Speaker-Bos 52
Zeider-Chi 47

Stolen Base Average

Stolen Base Runs

Fielding Runs
McBride-Was 29.4
Bush-Det 28.1
Rath-Chi 17.8
Speaker-Bos 16.6
Collins-Phi 15.0

Total Player Rating
Speaker-Bos 7.3
Jackson-Cle 6.9
Cobb-Det 5.7
Collins-Phi 5.6
Baker-Phi 5.4

Wins
Wood-Bos 34
Johnson-Was 33
Walsh-Chi 27
Plank-Phi 26
Groom-Was 24

Win Percentage
Wood-Bos 872
Plank-Phi 813
Johnson-Was 733
Bedient-Bos 690
Coombs-Phi 677

Games
Walsh-Chi 62
Johnson-Was 50
Wood-Bos 43
Groom-Was 43
Benz-Chi 42

Complete Games
Wood-Bos 35
Johnson-Was 34
Walsh-Chi 32
Ford-NY 30

Shutouts
Wood-Bos 10
Johnson-Was 7
Walsh-Chi 6
Plank-Phi 5
Collins-Bos 4

Saves
Walsh-Chi 10
Warhop-NY 3
Mogridge-Chi 3
Lange-Chi 3
Dubuc-Det 3

Innings Pitched
Walsh-Chi 393
Johnson-Was 368
Wood-Bos 344
Groom-Was 316
Ford-NY 292

Fewest Hits/Game
Johnson-Was 6.33
Wood-Bos 6.99
Houck-Phi 7.36
Walsh-Chi 7.60
O'Brien-Bos 7.73

Fewest BB/Game
Bender-Phi 1.74
Johnson-Was 1.86
Collins-Bos 1.90
Powell-StL 1.99
Warhop-NY 2.06

Strikeouts
Johnson-Was 303
Wood-Bos 258
Walsh-Chi 254
Gregg-Cle 184
Groom-Was 179

Strikeouts/Game
Johnson-Was 7.41
Wood-Bos 6.75
Gregg-Cle 6.11
Walsh-Chi 5.82
Lange-Chi 5.24

Wins Above Team
Wood-Bos 12.8
Plank-Phi 9.6
Johnson-Was 9.4
Walsh-Chi 6.2
Dubuc-Det 5.0

Earned Run Average
Johnson-Was 1.39
Wood-Bos 1.91
Walsh-Chi 2.15
Plank-Phi 2.22
Collins-Bos 2.53

Adjusted ERA
Johnson-Was 233
Wood-Bos 179
Walsh-Chi 154
Plank-Phi 147
Collins-Bos 135

Opponents' Batting Avg.
Johnson-Was 196
Wood-Bos 216
Walsh-Chi 231
Houck-Phi 234
Dubuc-Det 235

Opponents' On Base Pct.
Johnson-Was 248
Wood-Bos 272
Walsh-Chi 279
Bedient-Bos 288
Collins-Bos 297

Starter Runs
Johnson-Was 79.6
Wood-Bos 54.7
Walsh-Chi 51.9
Plank-Phi 32.5
Groom-Was 25.3

Adjusted Starter Runs
Johnson-Was 75.7
Wood-Bos 57.4
Walsh-Chi 50.6
Plank-Phi 29.8
O'Brien-Bos 25.6

Clutch Pitching Index
Hughes-Was 129
McConnell-NY 121
Cashion-Was 120
Kahler-Cle 120
Plank-Phi 120

Relief Runs

Adjusted Relief Runs

Relief Ranking

Total Pitcher Index
Johnson-Was 9.5
Wood-Bos 8.5
Walsh-Chi 6.1
Plank-Phi 2.9
McConnell-NY 2.8

Total Baseball Ranking
Johnson-Was 9.5
Wood-Bos 8.5
Speaker-Bos 7.3
Jackson-Cle 6.9
Walsh-Chi 6.1

TEAM	G	W	L	PCT	GB	R	OR	AB	H	2B	3B	HR	BB	SO	AVG	OBP	SLG	PRO	/A	BR	/A	PF	CHI	RC	TA	SB	CS	SBA	SBR
NY	156	101	51	.664		684	515	5218	1427	226	70	31	444	501	.273	.338	.361	.699	106	43	24	103	99	708	.709	296			
PHI	159	88	63	.583	12.5	693	636	5400	1433	257	78	73	383	578	.265	.318	.382	.700	106	28	-51	112	100	695	.665	156			
CHI	155	88	65	.575	13.5	720	625	5022	1289	195	96	59	554	634	.257	.335	.369	.704	107	52	60	99	104	683	.704	181			
PIT	155	78	71	.523	21.5	673	585	5252	1383	210	86	35	391	545	.263	.319	.356	.675	99	-13	13	96	106	641	.640	181			
BOS	154	69	82	.457	31.5	641	690	5145	1318	191	60	32	488	640	.256	.326	.335	.661	95	-25	9	95	103	619	.636	177			
BRO	152	65	84	.436	34.5	595	613	5165	1394	193	86	39	361	555	.270	.321	.363	.684	101	3	-24	104	93	646	.651	188			
CIN	156	64	89	.418	37.5	607	717	5132	1339	170	96	27	458	579	.261	.325	.347	.672	98	-19		102	96	639	.658	226			
STL	153	51	99	.340	49	523	755	4967	1229	152	72	15	451	573	.247	.316	.316	.632	86	-77	-30	93	95	550	.598	171			
TOT	620					5136		41301	10812	1594	644	311	3530	4605	.262	.325	.354	.679								1576			

TEAM	CG	SHO	SV	IP	H	H/G	HR	BB	BB/G	SO	SO/G	ERA	/A	OAVG	OOBA	PR	/A	PF	CPI	FA	E	DP	FW	PW	BW	SBW	DIF
NY	82	12	11	1417.7	1276	8.1	35	315	2.0	651	4.1	2.43	131	.246	.283	120	118	100	101	.961	254	107	-.7	12.3	2.5		11.0
PHI	77	22	11	1453.0	1407	8.7	40	512	3.2	667	4.1	3.16	112	.260	.317	6	62	111	101	.968	214	112	1.8	6.4	-5.3		9.5
CHI	89	12	15	1372.0	1330	8.7	39	478	3.1	556	3.6	3.13	99	.260	.316	10	-4	97	102	.959	260	106	-1.1	-.4	6.2		6.8
PIT	74	9	7	1398.7	1344	8.6	26	434	2.8	590	3.8	2.90	104	.259	.307	46	17	94	102	.964	226	94	1.1	1.8	1.4		-.7
BOS	105	12	9	1370.0	1343	8.8	37	419	2.8	597	3.9	3.19	96	.263	.309	1	-20	96	97	.957	273	82	-1.9	-2.1	.9		-3.4
BRO	70	9	7	1368.3	1287	8.5	33	439	2.9	548	3.6	3.13	107	.255	.306	10	33	105	94	.961	243	125	-.0	3.4	-2.5		-10.4
CIN	71	10	10	1372.0	1398	9.2	40	456	3.0	522	3.4	3.46	96	.270	.319	-39	-21	104	98	.961	251	104	-.5	-2.2	-2.0		-7.8
STL	74	6	11	1351.3	1423	9.5	57	476	3.2	464	3.1	4.24	73	.277	.328	-156	-170	97	88	.965	219	113	1.5	-17.7	-3.1		-4.7
TOT	642	92	75	11103.0		8.8			2.9		3.7	3.20		.262	.325					.962	1940	843					

Runs
Leach-Chi 99
Carey-Pit 99
Lobert-Phi 98
Saier-Chi 94
Magee-Phi 92

Hits
Cravath-Phi 179
Daubert-Bro 178
Burns-NY 173
Lobert-Phi 172
Carey-Pit 172

Doubles
Smith-Bro 40
Burns-NY 37
Magee-Phi 36
Cravath-Phi 34

Triples
Saier-Chi 21
Miller-Pit 20
Konetchy-StL 17
Wilson-Pit 14
Cravath-Phi 14

Home Runs
Cravath-Phi 19
Luderus-Phi 18
Saier-Chi 14
Magee-Phi 11
Wilson-Pit 10

Total Bases
Cravath-Phi 298
Luderus-Phi 254
Saier-Chi 249
Miller-Pit 243
Lobert-Phi 243

Runs Batted In
Cravath-Phi 128
Zimmerman-Chi 95
Saier-Chi 92
Miller-Pit 90
Luderus-Phi 86

Runs Produced
Cravath-Phi 187
Saier-Chi 172
Miller-Pit 158
Zimmerman-Chi 155
Magee-Phi 151

Bases On Balls
Bescher-Cin 94
Huggins-StL 92
Leach-Chi 77
Bridwell-Chi 74

Batting Average
Daubert-Bro 350
Cravath-Phi 341
Viox-Pit 317
Zimmerman-Chi 313
Magee-Phi 306

On Base Percentage
Huggins-StL 432
Cravath-Phi 407
Daubert-Bro 405
Viox-Pit 399
Leach-Chi 391

Slugging Average
Cravath-Phi 568
Zimmerman-Chi 490
Saier-Chi 480
Magee-Phi 479
Smith-Bro 441

Production
Cravath-Phi 974
Zimmerman-Chi 868
Saier-Chi 850
Magee-Phi 848
Daubert-Bro 829

Adjusted Production
Cravath-Phi 157
Zimmerman-Chi 149
Saier-Chi 143
Viox-Pit 141
Leach-Chi 134

Batter Runs
Cravath-Phi 50.4
Saier-Chi 27.5
Zimmerman-Chi 26.3
Daubert-Bro 25.2
Viox-Pit 24.8

Adjusted Batter Runs
Cravath-Phi 42.5
Saier-Chi 28.4
Viox-Pit 27.4
Zimmerman-Chi 27.0
Daubert-Bro 22.4

Clutch Hitting Index
Zimmerman-Chi 143
Doyle-NY 139
Cravath-Phi 134
Miller-Pit 131
Murray-NY 123

Runs Created
Cravath-Phi 124
Saier-Chi 100
Lobert-Phi 94
Daubert-Bro 94
Smith-Bro 91

Total Average
Cravath-Phi 1.058
Saier-Chi 927
Zimmerman-Chi 925
Magee-Phi 905
Leach-Chi 895

Stolen Bases
Carey-Pit 61
Myers-Bos 57
Lobert-Phi 41
Burns-NY 40
Cutshaw-Bro 39

Stolen Base Average

Stolen Base Runs

Fielding Runs
Mowrey-StL 31.8
Carey-Pit 21.7
Evers-Chi 20.4
Cutshaw-Bro 17.8
Maranville-Bos 14.0

Total Player Rating
Tinker-Cin 3.1
Cravath-Phi 3.1
Mowrey-StL 3.1
Zimmerman-Chi 2.7
Evers-Chi 2.5

Wins
Seaton-Phi 27
Mathewson-NY 25
Marquard-NY 23
Tesreau-NY 22
Alexander-Phi 22

Win Percentage
Humphries-Chi 800
Alexander-Phi 733
Marquard-NY 697
Mathewson-NY 694
Seaton-Phi 692

Games
Cheney-Chi 54
Seaton-Phi 52
Sallee-StL 50
Alexander-Phi 47
Camnitz-Pit-Phi 45

Complete Games
Tyler-Bos 28
Mathewson-NY 25
Cheney-Chi 25
Adams-Pit 24
Alexander-Phi 23

Shutouts
Alexander-Phi 9
Seaton-Phi 6

Saves
Cheney-Chi 11
Brown-Cin 6
Sallee-StL 5

Innings Pitched
Seaton-Phi 322
Adams-Pit 314
Mathewson-NY 306
Alexander-Phi 306
Cheney-Chi 305

Fewest Hits/Game
Tesreau-NY 7.09
Seaton-Phi 7.32
Allen-Bro 7.41
Pearce-Chi 7.56
Tyler-Bos 7.60

Fewest BB/Game
Mathewson-NY 62
Humphries-Chi 1.19
Adams-Pit 1.40
Marquard-NY 1.53
Suggs-Cin 1.58

Strikeouts
Seaton-Phi 168
Tesreau-NY 167
Alexander-Phi 159
Marquard-NY 151
Adams-Pit 144

Strikeouts/Game
Tesreau-NY 5.33
Hendrix-Pit 5.15
Marquard-NY 4.72
Seaton-Phi 4.70
Alexander-Phi 4.68

Wins Above Team
Sallee-StL 6.6
Seaton-Phi 6.3
Alexander-Phi 6.2
Adams-Pit 5.8
Humphries-Chi 5.6

Earned Run Average
Mathewson-NY 2.06
Adams-Pit 2.15
Tesreau-NY 2.17
Demaree-NY 2.21
Pearce-Chi 2.32

Adjusted ERA
Mathewson-NY 155
Brennan-Phi 148
Tesreau-NY 147
Demaree-NY 144
Adams-Pit 140

Opponents' Batting Avg.
Tesreau-NY 220
Seaton-Phi 226
Allen-Bro 231
Pearce-Chi 234
Tyler-Bos 235

Opponents' On Base Pct.
Adams-Pit 261
Mathewson-NY 261
Marquard-NY 267
Humphries-Chi 273
Perdue-Bos 278

Starter Runs
Mathewson-NY 38.8
Adams-Pit 36.6
Tesreau-NY 32.2
Marquard-NY 22.4
Demaree-NY 22.1

Adjusted Starter Runs
Mathewson-NY 38.2
Seaton-Phi 33.8
Tesreau-NY 31.7
Adams-Pit 30.1
Brennan-Phi 26.5

Clutch Pitching Index
Brennan-Phi 128
Packard-Cin 127
Brown-Cin 119
Ames-NY -Cin 119
Pearce-Chi 112

Relief Runs

Adjusted Relief Runs

Relief Ranking

Total Pitcher Index
Mathewson-NY 4.6
Adams-Pit 4.0
Tesreau-NY 3.8
Seaton-Phi 3.3
Brennan-Phi 2.7

Total Baseball Ranking
Mathewson-NY 4.6
Adams-Pit 4.0
Tesreau-NY 3.8
Seaton-Phi 3.3
Tinker-Cin 3.1

TEAM	G	W	L	PCT	GB	R	OR	AB	H	2B	3B	HR	BB	SO	AVG	OBP	SLG	PRO	/A	BR	/A	PF	CHI	RC	TA	SB	CS	SBA	SBR
PHI	153	96	57	.627		794	592	5044	1412	223	80	33	534	547	.280	.356	.375	.731	121	135	156	97	105	747	.747	221			
WAS	155	90	64	.584	6.5	596	561	5074	1281	156	80	20	440	595	.252	.317	.327	.644	95	-33	-67	106	104	594	.641	291			
CLE	155	86	66	.566	9.5	633	536	5030	1348	205	74	16	405	557	.268	.329	.348	.677	105	24	-11	106	100	631	.651	191			
BOS	151	79	71	.527	15.5	631	610	4965	1334	220	101	17	466	534	.269	.336	.364	.700	112	66	47	103	94	664	.689	189			
CHI	153	78	74	.513	17.5	488	498	4822	1139	157	66	23	398	550	.236	.299	.310	.609	84	-94	-64	95	100	496	.567	156			
DET	153	66	87	.431	30	624	716	5064	1344	180	101	24	496	501	.265	.336	.355	.691	109	55	62	99	93	669	.688	218			
NY	153	57	94	.377	38	529	668	4880	1157	154	45	9	534	617	.237	.320	.293	.613	86	-74	-78	101	101	525	.597	203			
STL	155	57	96	.373	39	528	642	5031	1193	179	73	18	459	769	.237	.306	.312	.618	87	-78	-49	95	100	539	.595	209			
TOT	614					4823		39910	10208	1474	620	160	3732	4670	.256	.325	.336	.661								1678			

TEAM	CG	SHO	SV	IP	H	H/G	HR	BB	BB/G	SO	SO/G	ERA	/A	OAVG	OOBA	PR	/A	PF	CPI	FA	E	DP	FW	PW	BW	SBW	DIF
PHI	69	17	22	1349.3	1200	8.0	24	532	3.5	630	4.2	3.20	85	.246	.320	-40	-73	93	87	.966	212	108	3.3	-7.8	16.6		7.4
WAS	78	23	20	1397.3	1175	7.6	35	465	3.0	757	4.9	2.72	113	.236	.301	32	54	105	89	.960	261	122	.1	5.7	-7.1		14.3
CLE	93	18	5	1381.7	1278	8.3	19	502	3.3	689	4.5	2.52	121	.253	.321	62	79	104	112	.962	242	124	1.3	8.4	-1.2		1.4
BOS	83	12	11	1350.3	1318	8.8	6	441	2.9	709	4.7	2.93	103	.264	.323	0	11	103	99	.961	237	84	1.6	1.2	5.0		-3.8
CHI	84	17	8	1357.7	1189	7.9	10	438	2.9	602	4.0	2.33	120	.243	.305	90	69	104	104	.960	255	104	.5	7.3	-6.8		1.0
DET	90	4	7	1358.7	1359	9.0	13	504	3.3	468	3.1	3.41	86	.268	.335	-72	-70	101	94	.954	300	105	-2.4	-7.4	6.6		-7.2
NY	75	8	7	1347.7	1318	8.8	31	455	3.0	530	3.5	3.27	93	.264	.325	-51	-35	104	95	.954	293	94	-2.0	-3.7	-8.3		-4.5
STL	104	14	5	1377.0	1369	8.9	21	454	3.0	476	3.1	3.06	93	.267	.327	-19	-30	98	101	.954	301	125	-2.5	-3.2	-5.2		-8.6
TOT	676	113	85	10919.7		8.4			3.1		4.0	2.93		.256	.325					.959	2101	866					

Runs		Hits		Doubles		Triples		Home Runs		Total Bases	
Collins-Phi	125	Jackson-Cle	197	Jackson-Cle	39	Crawford-Det	23	Baker-Phi	12	Crawford-Det	298
Baker-Phi	116	Crawford-Det	193	Speaker-Bos	35	Speaker-Bos	22	Crawford-Det	9	Jackson-Cle	291
Jackson-Cle	109	Baker-Phi	190	Baker-Phi	34	Jackson-Cle	17	Bodie-Chi	8	Baker-Phi	278
Shotton-StL	105	Speaker-Bos	189	Crawford-Det	32	Williams-StL	16	Jackson-Cle	7	Speaker-Bos	277
Murphy-Phi	105	Collins-Phi	184			Cobb-Det	16			Collins-Phi	242

Runs Batted In		Runs Produced		Bases On Balls		Batting Average		On Base Percentage		Slugging Average	
Baker-Phi	117	Baker-Phi	221	Shotton-StL	99	Cobb-Det	.390	Cobb-Det	.467	Jackson-Cle	.551
McInnis-Phi	90	Collins-Phi	195	Collins-Phi	85	Jackson-Cle	.373	Jackson-Cle	.460	Cobb-Det	.535
Lewis-Bos	90	Jackson-Cle	173	Wolter-NY	80	Speaker-Bos	.363	Collins-Phi	.441	Speaker-Bos	.533
Pratt-StL	87	Oldring-Phi	167	Jackson-Cle	80	Collins-Phi	.345	Speaker-Bos	.441	Baker-Phi	.493
Barry-Phi	85	McInnis-Phi	165	Bush-Det	80	Baker-Phi	.337	Baker-Phi	.413	Crawford-Det	.489

Production		Adjusted Production		Batter Runs		Adjusted Batter Runs		Clutch Hitting Index		Runs Created	
Jackson-Cle	1.011	Cobb-Det	195	Jackson-Cle	65.5	Jackson-Cle	61.7	Barry-Phi	176	Jackson-Cle	144
Cobb-Det	1.002	Jackson-Cle	185	Speaker-Bos	55.9	Speaker-Bos	53.9	Lewis-Bos	155	Speaker-Bos	135
Speaker-Bos	.974	Speaker-Bos	179	Cobb-Det	51.8	Cobb-Det	52.5	McInnis-Phi	142	Collins-Phi	125
Baker-Phi	.906	Baker-Phi	171	Baker-Phi	45.9	Baker-Phi	48.3	Turner-Cle	142	Baker-Phi	125
Collins-Phi	.894	Collins-Phi	167	Collins-Phi	45.7	Collins-Phi	48.1	Baker-Phi	140	Cobb-Det	122

Total Average		Stolen Bases		Stolen Base Average		Stolen Base Runs		Fielding Runs		Total Player Rating	
Cobb-Det	1.314	Milan-Was	74					Weaver-Chi	36.4	Speaker-Bos	7.1
Jackson-Cle	1.215	Moeller-Was	62					Speaker-Bos	22.3	Baker-Phi	6.1
Speaker-Bos	1.193	Collins-Phi	54					Lajoie-Cle	17.7	Collins-Phi	5.9
Collins-Phi	1.109	Cobb-Det	52					Collins-Phi	12.7	Jackson-Cle	5.2
Baker-Phi	1.029	Speaker-Bos	46					Shotton-StL	11.9	Cobb-Det	5.0

Wins		Win Percentage		Games		Complete Games		Shutouts		Saves	
Johnson-Was	36	Johnson-Was	.837	Russell-Chi	52	Johnson-Was	29	Johnson-Was	11	Bender-Phi	13
Falkenberg-Cle	23	Bush-Phi	.714	Scott-Chi	48	Russell-Chi	26	Russell-Chi	8	Hughes-Was	6
Russell-Chi	22	Boehling-Was	.708	Johnson-Was	48	Scott-Chi	25	Plank-Phi	7	Bedient-Bos	5
Bender-Phi	21	Collins-Bos	.704	Bender-Phi	48			Falkenberg-Cle	6		
		Falkenberg-Cle	.697	Gregg-Cle	44						

Innings Pitched		Fewest Hits/Game		Fewest BB/Game		Strikeouts		Strikeouts/Game		Wins Above Team	
Johnson-Was	346	Johnson-Was	6.03	Johnson-Was	.99	Johnson-Was	243	Johnson-Was	6.32	Johnson-Was	14.7
Russell-Chi	317	Mitchell-Cle	6.35	Collins-Bos	1.35	Gregg-Cle	166	Mitchell-Cle	5.85	Falkenberg-Cle	5.9
Scott-Chi	312	Engel-Was	6.76	Mitchell-StL	1.73	Falkenberg-Cle	166	Plank-Phi	5.59	Collins-Bos	5.7
Gregg-Cle	286	Leverenz-StL	7.05	Plank-Phi	2.11	Scott-Chi	158	Falkenberg-Cle	5.41	Boehling-Was	4.0
Falkenberg-Cle	276	Russell-Chi	7.10	Weilman-StL	2.14	Groom-Was	156	Groom-Was	5.32	Hamilton-StL	3.4

Earned Run Average		Adjusted ERA		Opponents' Batting Avg.		Opponents' On Base Pct.		Starter Runs		Adjusted Starter Runs	
Johnson-Was	1.14	Johnson-Was	268	Johnson-Was	.187	Johnson-Was	.217	Johnson-Was	68.6	Johnson-Was	74.1
Cicotte-Chi	1.58	Cicotte-Chi	177	Mitchell-Cle	.199	Russell-Chi	.273	Cicotte-Chi	40.2	Cicotte-Chi	36.0
Russell-Chi	1.90	Mitchell-Cle	159	Engel-Was	.207	Bender-Phi	.277	Russell-Chi	36.1	Russell-Chi	31.2
Scott-Chi	1.90	Russell-Chi	147	Houck-Phi	.214	Cicotte-Chi	.281	Scott-Chi	35.5	Scott-Chi	30.6
Mitchell-Cle	1.91	Scott-Chi	146	Russell-Chi	.219	Scott-Chi	.281	Mitchell-Cle	24.6	Mitchell-Cle	27.3

Clutch Pitching Index		Relief Runs		Adjusted Relief Runs		Relief Ranking		Total Pitcher Index		Total Baseball Ranking	
Blanding-Cle	141							Johnson-Was	8.8	Johnson-Was	8.8
Gregg-Cle	130							Cicotte-Chi	4.9	Speaker-Bos	7.1
Ford-NY	123							Scott-Chi	3.3	Baker-Phi	6.1
Baumgardner-StL	118							Boehling-Was	2.9	Collins-Phi	5.9
Cicotte-Chi	114							Russell-Chi	2.8	Jackson-Cle	5.2

TEAM	G	W	L	PCT	GB	R	OR	AB	H	2B	3B	HR	BB	SO	AVG	OBP	SLG	PRO	/A	BR	/A	PF	CHI	RC	TA	SB	CS	SBA	SBR
BOS	158	94	59	.614		657	548	5206	1307	213	60	35	502	617	.251	.323	.335	.658	102	17	-9	104	102	618	.625	139			
NY	156	84	70	.545	10.5	672	576	5146	1363	222	59	30	447	479	.265	.330	.348	.678	108	53	80	96	102	655	.670	239			
STL	157	81	72	.529	13	558	540	5046	1249	203	65	33	445	618	.248	.314	.333	.647	99	-8	-31	104	99	585	.625	204			
CHI	156	78	76	.506	16.5	605	638	5050	1229	199	74	41	501	577	.243	.317	.336	.653	101	5	15	98	99	594	.630	164			
BRO	154	75	79	.487	19.5	622	618	5152	1386	172	90	31	376	559	.269	.323	.355	.678	108	43	37	101	97	636	.641	173			
PHI	154	74	80	.481	20.5	651	687	5110	1345	211	52	62	472	570	.263	.329	.361	.690	112	69	68	100	97	654	.661	145			
PIT	158	69	85	.448	25.5	503	540	5145	1197	148	79	18	416	608	.233	.295	.303	.598	84	-100	-54	92	101	503	.546	147			
CIN	157	60	94	.390	34.5	530	651	4991	1178	142	64	16	441	627	.236	.305	.300	.605	86	-78	-105	105	104	517	.581	224			
TOT	625					4798		40846	10254	1510	543	266	3600	4655	.251	.317	.334	.651								1435			

TEAM	CG	SHO	SV	IP	H	H/G	HR	BB	BB/G	SO	SO/G	ERA	/A	OAVG	OOBA	PR	/A	PF	CPI	FA	E	DP	FW	PW	BW	SBW	DIF
BOS	104	19	5	1420.7	1272	8.1	38	477	3.0	606	3.8	2.74	103	.246	.303	6	14	102	96	.963	246	143	1.6	1.5	-1.0		15.4
NY	88	20	9	1388.3	1298	8.4	47	367	2.4	563	3.6	2.94	89	.254	.295	-24	-51	94	91	.961	254	119	1.1	-5.5	8.6		2.8
STL	84	16	12	1423.7	1279	8.1	26	422	2.7	531	3.4	2.38	121	.246	.291	64	79	104	104	.964	239	109	2.1	8.5	-3.3		-2.7
CHI	70	14	11	1383.3	1169	7.6	37	528	3.4	651	4.2	2.71	101	.235	.299	11	5	99	93	.951	310	87	-2.7	.5	1.6		1.6
BRO	80	11	11	1370.7	1282	8.4	36	466	3.1	605	4.0	2.82	100	.254	.308	-4	-1	101	101	.961	248	112	1.5	-.1	4.0		-7.3
PHI	85	14	7	1373.3	1403	9.2	26	452	3.0	650	4.3	3.06	92	.271	.320	-42	-38	101	104	.950	324	81	-3.7	-4.1	7.3		-2.6
PIT	86	10	11	1403.7	1272	8.2	27	392	2.5	488	3.1	2.70	96	.248	.291	13	-17	93	92	.966	223	96	3.1	-1.8	-5.8		-3.5
CIN	74	15	15	1385.7	1259	8.2	30	489	3.2	607	3.9	2.94	102	.248	.304	-24	7	107	92	.952	314	113	-3.0	.8	-11.3		-3.5
TOT	671	119	81	11149.3		8.3			2.9		3.8	2.78		.251	.317					.958	2158	860					

Runs		Hits		Doubles		Triples		Home Runs		Total Bases	
Burns-NY	100	Magee-Phi	171	Magee-Phi	39	Carey-Pit	17	Cravath-Phi	19	Magee-Phi	277
Magee-Phi	96	Wheat-Bro	170	Zimmerman-Chi	36	Zimmerman-Chi	12	Saier-Chi	18	Cravath-Phi	249
Daubert-Bro	89	Burns-NY	170	Burns-NY	35	Wilson-StL	12	Magee-Phi	15	Wheat-Bro	241
Saier-Chi	87	Zimmerman-Chi	167	Connolly-Bos	28	Cutshaw-Bro	12	Luderus-Phi	12	Zimmerman-Chi	239
Doyle-NY	87	Becker-Phi	167							Burns-NY	234

Runs Batted In		Runs Produced		Bases On Balls		Batting Average		On Base Percentage		Slugging Average	
Magee-Phi	103	Magee-Phi	184	Huggins-StL	105	Daubert-Bro	.329	Stengel-Bro	.404	Magee-Phi	.509
Cravath-Phi	100	Zimmerman-Chi	158	Saier-Chi	94	Becker-Phi	.325	Burns-NY	.403	Cravath-Phi	.499
Wheat-Bro	89	Cravath-Phi	157	Burns-NY	89	Dalton-Bro	.319	Cravath-Phi	.402	Wheat-Bro	.452
Miller-StL	88	Burns-NY	157	Evers-Bos	87	Wheat-Bro	.319	Huggins-StL	.396	Becker-Phi	.446
Zimmerman-Chi	87	Miller-StL	151	Cravath-Phi	83	Stengel-Bro	.316	Dalton-Bro	.396	Daubert-Bro	.432

Production		Adjusted Production		Batter Runs		Adjusted Batter Runs		Clutch Hitting Index		Runs Created	
Cravath-Phi	.901	Cravath-Phi	167	Cravath-Phi	42.7	Cravath-Phi	42.6	Fletcher-NY	151	Burns-NY	113
Magee-Phi	.890	Magee-Phi	163	Magee-Phi	40.6	Magee-Phi	40.6	Maranville-Bos	148	Magee-Phi	111
Wheat-Bro	.830	Burns-NY	151	Burns-NY	33.9	Burns-NY	37.1	Cutshaw-Bro	144	Cravath-Phi	108
Stengel-Bro	.829	Stengel-Bro	145	Connolly-Bos	31.0	Connolly-Bos	29.0	Miller-StL	143	Wheat-Bro	96
Burns-NY	.820	Wheat-Bro	145	Wheat-Bro	29.3	Wheat-Bro	28.7	Schmidt-Bos	141	Saier-Chi	89

Total Average		Stolen Bases		Stolen Base Average		Stolen Base Runs		Fielding Runs		Total Player Rating	
Burns-NY	.997	Burns-NY	62					Maranville-Bos	49.5	Maranville-Bos	4.5
Cravath-Phi	.997	Herzog-Cin	46					Herzog-Cin	30.5	Cravath-Phi	4.2
Magee-Phi	.965	Dolan-StL	42					Cutshaw-Bro	26.4	Burns-NY	4.0
Stengel-Bro	.904	Carey-Pit	38					Smith-Bro-Bos	17.9	Herzog-Cin	3.9
Wheat-Bro	.857							Wilson-StL	16.9	Smith-Bro-Bos	3.8

Wins		Win Percentage		Games		Complete Games		Shutouts		Saves	
Rudolph-Bos	27	James-Bos	.788	Cheney-Chi	50	Alexander-Phi	32	Tesreau-NY	8	Sallee-StL	6
Alexander-Phi	27	Doak-StL	.760	Mayer-Phi	48	Rudolph-Bos	31	Doak-StL	7	Ames-Cin	6
Tesreau-NY	26	Rudolph-Bos	.730	Ames-Cin	47	James-Bos	30	Rudolph-Bos	6	Cheney-Chi	5
James-Bos	26	Tesreau-NY	.722			Mathewson-NY	29	Cheney-Chi	6	Pfeffer-Bro	4
Mathewson-NY	24	Pfeffer-Bro	.657			Pfeffer-Bro	27	Alexander-Phi	6	McQuillan-Pit	4

Innings Pitched		Fewest Hits/Game		Fewest BB/Game		Strikeouts		Strikeouts/Game		Wins Above Team	
Alexander-Phi	355	Tesreau-NY	6.65	Mathewson-NY	.66	Alexander-Phi	214	Alexander-Phi	5.43	James-Bos	8.4
Rudolph-Bos	336	Doak-StL	6.79	Adams-Pit	1.24	Tesreau-NY	189	Tesreau-NY	5.28	Tesreau-NY	8.2
James-Bos	332	Cheney-Chi	6.92	Marquard-NY	1.58	Vaughn-Chi	165	Vaughn-Chi	5.05	Alexander-Phi	8.1
Tesreau-NY	322	Douglas-Cin	7.00	Rudolph-Bos	1.63	Cheney-Chi	157	Tyler-Bos	4.65	Pfeffer-Bro	6.8
Mayer-Phi	321	James-Bos	7.08	Alexander-Phi	1.93	James-Bos	156	Ragan-Bro	4.59	Doak-StL	6.7

Earned Run Average		Adjusted ERA		Opponents' Batting Avg.		Opponents' On Base Pct.		Starter Runs		Adjusted Starter Runs	
Doak-StL	1.72	Doak-StL	167	Tesreau-NY	.209	Adams-Pit	.268	James-Bos	32.7	James-Bos	34.7
James-Bos	1.90	James-Bos	150	Cheney-Chi	.215	Mathewson-NY	.271	Doak-StL	30.2	Doak-StL	33.0
Pfeffer-Bro	1.97	Pfeffer-Bro	142	Doak-StL	.216	Rudolph-Bos	.271	Pfeffer-Bro	28.5	Pfeffer-Bro	29.3
Vaughn-Chi	2.05	Sallee-StL	137	Vaughn-Chi	.222	Doak-StL	.282	Vaughn-Chi	24.0	Sallee-StL	24.3
Sallee-StL	2.11	Vaughn-Chi	134	Douglas-Cin	.223	Alexander-Phi	.284	Sallee-StL	21.3	Vaughn-Chi	22.9

Clutch Pitching Index		Relief Runs		Adjusted Relief Runs		Relief Ranking		Total Pitcher Index		Total Baseball Ranking	
Cooper-Pit	126							James-Bos	4.3	Maranville-Bos	4.5
James-Bos	121							Doak-StL	4.0	James-Bos	4.3
Crutcher-Bos	120							Pfeffer-Bro	2.8	Cravath-Phi	4.2
Perritt-StL	116							Sallee-StL	2.8	Burns-NY	4.0
Sallee-StL	116							Alexander-Phi	2.7	Doak-StL	4.0

TEAM	G	W	L	PCT	GB	R	OR	AB	H	2B	3B	HR	BB	SO	AVG	OBP	SLG	PRO	/A	BR	/A	PF	CHI	RC	TA	SB	CS	SBA SBR
PHI	158	99	53	.651		749	529	5126	1392	165	80	29	545	517	.272	.348	.352	.700	118	112	127	97	106	662	.671	231	188	55-43
BOS	159	91	62	.595	8.5	588	511	5117	1278	226	85	18	490	549	.250	.320	.338	.658	105	25	38	98	97	567	.606	177	176	50 -52
WAS	158	81	73	.526	19	572	519	5108	1245	176	81	18	470	640	.244	.313	.320	.633	97	-17	-22	101	102	544	.589	220	163	57 -31
DET	157	80	73	.523	19.5	615	618	5102	1318	195	84	25	557	537	.258	.336	.344	.680	112	75	63	102	92	630	.652	211	154	58 -28
STL	159	71	82	.464	28.5	523	614	5101	1241	185	75	17	423	863	.243	.306	.319	.625	95	-38	-24	98	98	516	.572	233	189	55 -43
NY	157	70	84	.455	30	538	550	4992	1144	149	52	12	577	711	.229	.315	.287	.602	88	-59	-58	100	104	484	.571	251	191	57 -38
CHI	157	70	84	.455	30	487	560	5050	1205	161	71	19	408	609	.239	.301	.310	.611	90	-60	-78	103	96	496	.547	167	152	52 -40
CLE	157	51	102	.333	48.5	538	709	5157	1262	178	70	10	450	685	.245	.310	.312	.622	94	-38	-51	102	100	517	.559	167	157	52 -43
TOT	631					4610		40753	10085	1435	598	148	3920	5111	.247	.319	.323	.642								1657	1370	55 -324

TEAM	CG	SHO	SV	IP	H	H/G	HR	BB	BB/G	SO	SO/G	ERA	/A	OAVG	OOBA	PR	/A	PF	CPI	FA	E	DP	FW	PW	BW	SBW	DIF
PHI	89	24	17	1401.0	1264	8.1	18	521	3.3	720	4.6	2.78	91	.248	.318	-7	-38	93	98	.966	213	116	3.4	-4.2	14.0	-.3	10.0
BOS	88	24	8	1424.3	1212	7.7	18	397	2.5	605	3.8	2.35	112	.237	.292	60	43	96	94	.963	242	99	1.6	4.7	4.2	-1.3	5.2
WAS	75	25	20	1417.0	1170	7.4	20	520	3.3	784	5.0	2.54	107	.232	.304	30	29	100	92	.961	254	116	.9	3.2	-2.4	1.1	1.3
DET	81	14	12	1406.7	1285	8.2	17	498	3.2	567	3.6	2.86	97	.250	.317	-19	-11	102	95	.958	286	101	-1.1	-1.2	7.0	1.4	-2.6
STL	81	15	11	1414.3	1309	8.3	20	540	3.4	553	3.5	2.84	96	.253	.323	-16	-18	100	102	.952	317	114	-3.0	-2.0	-2.6	-.3	2.4
NY	98	9	5	1394.7	1277	8.2	30	390	2.5	563	3.6	2.82	97	.251	.304	-13	-12	100	92	.963	238	93	1.9	-1.3	-6.4	.3	-1.4
CHI	74	17	11	1395.0	1207	7.8	15	401	2.6	660	4.3	2.48	116	.240	.296	39	60	105	93	.955	299	90	-1.9	6.6	-8.6	.0	-3.2
CLE	69	9	3	1380.0	1365	8.9	10	666	4.3	688	4.5	3.20	90	.265	.350	-72	-47	106	107	.953	300	119	-1.9	-5.2	-5.6	-.3	-12.5
TOT	655	137	87	11233.0		8.1			3.2		4.1	2.73		.247	.319					.959	2149	848					

Runs	Hits	Doubles	Triples	Home Runs	Total Bases
Collins-Phi 122	Speaker-Bos 193	Speaker-Bos 46	Crawford-Det 26	Baker-Phi 9	Speaker-Bos 287
Murphy-Phi 101	Crawford-Det 183	Lewis-Bos 37	Gardner-Bos 19	Crawford-Det 8	Crawford-Det 281
Speaker-Bos 100	Baker-Phi 182	Pratt-StL 34	Speaker-Bos 18	Walker-StL 6	Baker-Phi 252
Bush-Det 97	McInnis-Phi 181	Collins-Chi 34	Walker-StL 16	Fournier-Chi 6	Pratt-StL 240
	Collins-Phi 181	Leary-StL 28	Hooper-Bos 15		Collins-Phi 238

Runs Batted In	Runs Produced	Bases On Balls	Batting Average	On Base Percentage	Slugging Average
Crawford-Det 104	Collins-Phi 205	Bush-Det 112	Collins-Phi 344	Collins-Phi 452	Speaker-Bos 503
McInnis-Phi 95	Speaker-Bos 186	Collins-Phi 97	Speaker-Bos 338	Speaker-Bos 423	Crawford-Det 483
Speaker-Bos 90	Crawford-Det 170	Murphy-Phi 87	Jackson-Cle 338	Jackson-Cle 399	Jackson-Cle 464
Baker-Phi 89	McInnis-Phi 168	Speaker-Bos 77	Baker-Phi 319	Crawford-Det 388	Collins-Phi 452
Collins-Phi 85	Baker-Phi 164	Maisel-NY 76	Crawford-Det 314	Baker-Phi 380	Baker-Phi 442

Production	Adjusted Production	Batter Runs	Adjusted Batter Runs	Clutch Hitting Index	Runs Created
Speaker-Bos 926	Speaker-Bos 182	Speaker-Bos 54.9	Speaker-Bos 56.5	McInnis-Phi 176	Speaker-Bos 124
Collins-Phi 904	Collins-Phi 177	Collins-Phi 51.6	Collins-Phi 53.4	Lewis-Bos 150	Collins-Phi 120
Crawford-Det 871	Crawford-Det 159	Cobb-Det 42.3	Cobb-Det 41.5	Veach-Det.........138	Crawford-Det 113
Jackson-Cle 862	Jackson-Cle 156	Crawford-Det 42.1	Crawford-Det 40.8	Shanks-Was 138	Baker-Phi 95
Baker-Phi 822	Baker-Phi 151	Jackson-Cle 31.6	Baker-Phi 32.9	Gandil-Was 135	Walker-StL 87

Total Average	Stolen Bases	Stolen Base Average	Stolen Base Runs	Fielding Runs	Total Player Rating
Collins-Phi 1.064	Maisel-NY 74	Maisel-NY 81.3	Maisel-NY 12.0	Bush-Det 33.2	Speaker-Bos 7.0
Speaker-Bos 1.015	Collins-Phi 58	Sweeney-NY 76.0	Sweeney-NY 2.1	Speaker-Bos 22.8	Collins-Phi 5.8
Crawford-Det 906	Speaker-Bos 42	Chapman-Cle 72.7	Kopf-Phi 1.8	Walker-StL 21.7	Bush-Det 5.2
Jackson-Cle 883	Lewis-Bos 41	Moriarty-Det 69.4	Chapman-Cle 1.8	Gandil-Was 21.4	Walker-StL 4.1
Walker-StL 821	Shotton-StL 40	Peckinpaugh-NY ...69.1		Moriarty-Det 15.4	Baker-Phi 4.1

Wins	Win Percentage	Games	Complete Games	Shutouts	Saves
Johnson-Was 28	Bender-Phi 850	Johnson-Was 51	Johnson-Was 33	Johnson-Was 9	Shaw-Was 4
Coveleski-Det 22	Leonard-Bos 792	Ayers-Was 49	Coveleski-Det......23	Leonard-Bos 7	Mitchell-StL 4
Collins-Bos 20	Plank-Phi 682	Shaw-Was 48	Dauss-Det 22	Bender-Phi 7	Faber-Chi 4
Leonard-Bos 19	Shawkey-Phi 667	Benz-Chi 48	Caldwell-NY 22	Collins-Bos 6	Dauss-Det 4
	Caldwell-NY 654				Bentley-Was 4

Innings Pitched	Fewest Hits/Game	Fewest BB/Game	Strikeouts	Strikeouts/Game	Wins Above Team
Johnson-Was 372	Leonard-Bos 5.56	McHale-NY 1.55	Johnson-Was 225	Leonard-Bos 7.04	Leonard-Bos 6.3
Coveleski-Det......303	Caldwell-NY 6.46	Russell-Chi........ 1.78	Mitchell-Cle 179	Mitchell-Cle 6.27	Bender-Phi 6.0
Hamilton-StL 302	Shaw-Was 6.93	Johnson-Was 1.79	Leonard-Bos 176	Shaw-Was 5.74	Johnson-Was 5.3
Dauss-Det 302	Johnson-Was 6.94	Warhop-NY 1.82	Shaw-Was 164	Johnson-Was 5.44	Caldwell-NY 5.3
Weilman-StL.......299	Foster-Bos 6.96	Ayers-Was 1.83	Dauss-Det 150	Bender-Phi 5.38	Coveleski-Det...... 5.3

Earned Run Average	Adjusted ERA	Opponents' Batting Avg.	Opponents' On Base Pct.	Starter Runs	Adjusted Starter Runs
Leonard-Bos .... .96	Leonard-Bos 273	Leonard-Bos 180	Leonard-Bos 246	Leonard-Bos 44.3	Johnson-Was 41.7
Foster-Bos 1.70	Johnson-Was 159	Caldwell-NY 205	Caldwell-NY 260	Johnson-Was 41.9	Leonard-Bos 41.6
Johnson-Was 1.72	Foster-Bos 154	Shaw-Was 216	Johnson-Was 265	Foster-Bos 24.4	Cicotte-Chi 24.7
Caldwell-NY 1.94	Caldwell-NY 141	Johnson-Was 217	Foster-Bos 274	Weilman-StL 21.8	Foster-Bos 21.8
Cicotte-Chi 2.04	Cicotte-Chi 140	Foster-Bos 218	Benz-Chi 282	Cicotte-Chi 20.7	Weilman-StL 21.4

Clutch Pitching Index	Relief Runs	Adjusted Relief Runs	Relief Ranking	Total Pitcher Index	Total Baseball Ranking
Hagerman-Cle 126				Johnson-Was 6.3	Speaker-Bos 7.0
Steen-Cle 123				Leonard-Bos 4.6	Johnson-Was 6.3
Shawkey-Phi 109				Cicotte-Chi 3.6	Collins-Phi 5.8
James-StL 106				Benz-Chi 2.9	Bush-Det 5.2
Bender-Phi 106				Weilman-StL 2.5	Leonard-Bos 4.6

TEAM	G	W	L	PCT	GB	R	OR	AB	H	2B	3B	HR	BB	SO	AVG	OBP	SLG	PRO	/A	BR	/A	PF	CHI	RC	TA	SB	CS	SBA	SBR
IND	157	88	65	.575		762	622	5176	1474	230	90	33	470	668	.285	.344	.383	.727	114	94	23	111	101	750	.736	273			
CHI	157	87	67	.565	1.5	621	517	5098	1314	227	50	51	520	645	.258	.326	.352	.678	100	6	63	91	95	639	.657	171			
BAL	160	84	70	.545	4.5	645	628	5120	1374	222	67	32	487	589	.268	.332	.357	.689	103	24	29	99	96	655	.658	152			
BUF	155	80	71	.530	7	620	602	5064	1264	177	74	38	430	761	.250	.308	.336	.644	90	-61	-87	104	109	578	.621	228			
BRO	157	77	77	.500	11.5	662	677	5221	1402	225	85	42	404	665	.269	.321	.368	.689	103	15	10	101	100	665	.667	220			
KC	154	67	84	.444	20	644	683	5127	1369	226	77	39	399	621	.267	.320	.364	.684	102	6	37	95	100	638	.648	171			
PIT	154	64	86	.427	22.5	605	698	5114	1339	180	90	34	410	575	.262	.317	.352	.669	97	-19	17	94	97	612	.626	153			
STL	154	62	89	.411	25	565	697	5078	1254	193	65	26	503	662	.247	.315	.326	.641	89	-61	-97	106	97	566	.594	113			
TOT	624					5124		40998	10790	1680	598	295	3623	5186	.263	.323	.355	.678								1481			

TEAM	CG	SHO	SV	IP	H	H/G	HR	BB	BB/G	SO	SO/G	ERA	/A	OAVG	OOBA	PR	/A	PF	CPI	FA	E	DP	FW	PW	BW	SBW	DIF
IND	104	15	9	1396.3	1352	8.7	29	476	3.1	664	4.3	3.06	113	.261	.324	22	62	108	103	.958	274	118	-.7	6.4	2.4		3.3
CHI	93	17	8	1419.0	1204	7.6	42	393	2.5	650	4.1	2.44	117	.237	.291	120	64	89	101	.962	250	120	.7	6.7	6.5		-3.9
BAL	88	15	13	1390.0	1389	9.0	34	392	2.5	732	4.7	3.13	101	.268	.319	12	6	99	102	.960	265	106	-.1	.6	3.0		3.5
BUF	89	15	16	1385.0	1249	8.1	45	505	3.3	662	4.3	3.16	106	.248	.316	7	26	104	95	.962	243	107	1.2	2.7	-9.0		9.7
BRO	91	11	9	1383.7	1375	8.9	31	559	3.6	636	4.1	3.33	97	.266	.338	-19	-14	101	105	.957	273	112	-.6	-1.5	1.0		1.0
KC	82	10	12	1360.3	1387	9.2	37	445	2.9	600	4.0	3.41	90	.271	.330	-30	-50	96	101	.959	266	135	-.2	-5.2	3.8		-7.0
PIT	97	9	6	1368.3	1416	9.3	39	444	2.9	510	3.4	3.56	86	.274	.332	-53	-73	96	99	.960	254	100	.5	-7.6	1.8		-5.7
STL	97	9	6	1366.0	1418	9.3	38	409	2.7	661	4.4	3.59	97	.275	.328	-58	-18	108	96	.956	277	92	-.8	-1.9	-10.1		-.7
TOT	741	101	79	11068.7		8.8			2.9		4.2	3.21		.263	.323					.959	2102	890					

Runs
Kauff-Ind 120
McKechnie-Ind 107
Duncan-Bal 99
Kenworthy-KC 93
Evans-Bro 93

Hits
Kauff-Ind 211
Zwilling-Chi 185
Evans-Bro 179
Oakes-Pit 178
Hanford-Buf 174

Doubles
Kauff-Ind 44
Evans-Bro 41
Kenworthy-KC 40
Zwilling-Chi 38

Triples
Evans-Bro 15
Esmond-Ind 15
Kenworthy-KC 14

Home Runs
Zwilling-Chi 15
Kenworthy-KC 15
Hanford-Buf 13
Evans-Bro 12

Total Bases
Kauff-Ind 305
Kenworthy-KC 286
Evans-Bro 286
Zwilling-Chi 284
Hanford-Buf 267

Runs Batted In
LaPorte-Ind 107
Evans-Bro 96
Zwilling-Chi 95
Kauff-Ind 95
Kenworthy-KC 91

Runs Produced
Kauff-Ind 207
LaPorte-Ind 189
Evans-Bro 177
Zwilling-Chi 171
Kenworthy-KC 169

Bases On Balls
Wickland-Chi 81
Agler-Buf 77
Kauff-Ind 72

Batting Average
Kauff-Ind 370
Evans-Bro 348
Campbell-Ind 318
Kenworthy-KC 317
Louden-Buf 313

On Base Percentage
Kauff-Ind 440
Lennox-Pit 409
Evans-Bro 406
Meyer-Bal 391
Wilson-Chi 388

Slugging Average
Evans-Bro 556
Kauff-Ind 534
Kenworthy-KC 525
Lennox-Pit 493
Zwilling-Chi 480

Production
Kauff-Ind 974
Evans-Bro 962
Lennox-Pit 902
Kenworthy-KC 884
Wilson-Chi 854

Adjusted Production
Evans-Bro 173
Lennox-Pit 167
Kauff-Ind 161
Kenworthy-KC 159
Wilson-Chi 158

Batter Runs
Kauff-Ind 59.1
Evans-Bro 47.6
Lennox-Pit 33.9
Kenworthy-KC 32.9
Zwilling-Chi 28.4

Adjusted Batter Runs
Kauff-Ind 51.2
Evans-Bro 47.2
Lennox-Pit 37.2
Kenworthy-KC 36.2
Zwilling-Chi 34.9

Clutch Hitting Index
LaPorte-Ind 176
Swacina-Bal 160
Wisterzil-Bro 139
Stovall-KC 138
Hofman-Bro 135

Runs Created
Kauff-Ind 153
Evans-Bro 120
Kenworthy-KC 108
Zwilling-Chi 107
Lennox-Pit 94

Total Average
Kauff-Ind 1.256
Evans-Bro 1.057
Lennox-Pit 1.020
Kenworthy-KC 965
Wilson-Chi 923

Stolen Bases
Kauff-Ind 75
McKechnie-Ind 47
Myers-Bro 43
Chadbourne-KC 42

Stolen Base Average

Stolen Base Runs

Fielding Runs
Kenworthy-KC 24.4
Doolan-Bal 22.9
McKechnie-Ind 22.2
Knabe-Bal 15.2
Farrell-Chi 15.2

Total Player Rating
Kenworthy-KC 6.3
Kauff-Ind 4.9
Wilson-Chi 4.4
Evans-Bro 3.4
McKechnie-Ind 2.7

Wins
Hendrix-Chi 29
Quinn-Bal 26
Seaton-Bro 25
Falkenberg-Ind 25
Suggs-Bal 24

Win Percentage
Ford-Buf 778
Hendrix-Chi 744
Quinn-Bal 650
Seaton-Bro 641
Suggs-Bal 632

Games
Hendrix-Chi 49
Falkenberg-Ind 49
Wilhelm-Bal 47
Suggs-Bal 46
Quinn-Bal 46

Complete Games
Hendrix-Chi 34
Falkenberg-Ind 33
Moseley-Ind 29
Quinn-Bal 27

Shutouts
Falkenberg-Ind 9
Seaton-Bro 7
Suggs-Bal 6
Hendrix-Chi 6

Saves
Ford-Buf 6
Wilhelm-Bal 5
Packard-KC 5
Hendrix-Chi 5

Innings Pitched
Falkenberg-Ind 377
Hendrix-Chi 362
Quinn-Bal 343
Suggs-Bal 319
Moseley-Ind 317

Fewest Hits/Game
Hendrix-Chi 6.51
Ford-Buf 6.92
Krapp-Buf 7.04
Fiske-Chi 7.32
Watson-Chi-StL 7.34

Fewest BB/Game
Ford-Buf 1.49
Suggs-Bal 1.61
Quinn-Bal 1.71
Hendrix-Chi 1.91
Keupper-StL 2.07

Strikeouts
Falkenberg-Ind 236
Moseley-Ind 205
Hendrix-Chi 189
Seaton-Bro 172
Groom-StL 167

Strikeouts/Game
Davenport-StL 5.92
Moseley-Ind 5.82
Falkenberg-Ind 5.63
Groom-StL 5.35
Seaton-Bro 5.11

Wins Above Team
Hendrix-Chi 9.4
Ford-Buf 7.8
Seaton-Bro 6.7
Knetzer-Pit 6.4
Quinn-Bal 5.7

Earned Run Average
Hendrix-Chi 1.69
Ford-Buf 1.82
Watson-Chi-StL 2.01
Falkenberg-Ind 2.22
Lange-Chi 2.23

Adjusted ERA
Ford-Buf 183
Hendrix-Chi 169
Falkenberg-Ind 156
Watson-Chi-StL 152
Krapp-Buf 134

Opponents' Batting Avg.
Hendrix-Chi 203
Krapp-Buf 210
Ford-Buf 214
Cullop-KC 215
Lange-Chi 224

Opponents' On Base Pct.
Hendrix-Chi 251
Ford-Buf 254
Cullop-KC 275
Lange-Chi 282
Falkenberg-Ind 284

Starter Runs
Hendrix-Chi 60.9
Falkenberg-Ind 41.3
Ford-Buf 38.0
Watson-Chi-StL 30.2
Cullop-KC 28.4

Adjusted Starter Runs
Falkenberg-Ind 52.1
Hendrix-Chi 46.7
Ford-Buf 41.5
Watson-Chi-StL 26.3
Cullop-KC 24.0

Clutch Pitching Index
Dickson-Pit 132
Mullin-Ind 131
Lafitte-Bro 125
Watson-Chi-StL 114
Kaiserling-Ind 112

Relief Runs

Adjusted Relief Runs

Relief Ranking

Total Pitcher Index
Hendrix-Chi 6.7
Falkenberg-Ind 6.2
Ford-Buf 4.7
Quinn-Bal 3.8
Krapp-Buf 3.3

Total Baseball Ranking
Hendrix-Chi 6.7
Kenworthy-KC 6.3
Falkenberg-Ind 6.2
Kauff-Ind 4.9
Ford-Buf 4.7

TEAM	G	W	L	PCT	GB	R	OR	AB	H	2B	3B	HR	BB	SO	AVG	OBP	SLG	PRO	/A	BR	/A	PF	CHI	RC	TA	SB	CS	SBA	SBR
PHI	153	90	62	.592		589	**463**	4916	1216	202	39	**58**	460	600	.247	.316	.340	**.656**	105	31	-9	107	101	550	**.599**	121	113	52	-31
BOS	157	83	69	.546	7	582	545	5070	1219	**231**	57	17	**549**	620	.240	**.321**	.319	.640	100	15	25	98	98	554	.593	121	98	55	-22
BRO	154	80	72	.526	10	536	560	5120	1268	165	75	14	313	**496**	.248	.295	.317	.612	91	-56	-63	101	107	496	.527	131	126	51	-35
CHI	156	73	80	.477	17.5	570	620	5114	1246	212	66	53	393	639	.244	.303	.334	.643	101	4	-7	102	100	555	.588	166	124	57	-24
PIT	156	73	81	.474	18	557	520	5113	1259	197	91	24	419	656	.246	.309	.334	.643	101	8	15	99	97	563	.595	**182**	111	**62**	**-11**
STL	157	72	81	.471	18.5	**590**	601	5106	1297	159	**92**	20	457	658	**.254**	.320	.333	.653	104	30	**28**	100	98	**568**	.597	162	144	53	-37
CIN	160	71	83	.461	20	516	585	5231	**1323**	194	84	15	360	512	.253	.300	.331	.639	100	-4	-18	99	90	553	.568	156	142	52	-37
NY	155	69	83	.454	21	582	628	5218	1312	195	68	24	315	547	.251	.300	.329	.629	97	-26	22	91	**108**	526	.552	155	137	53	-35
TOT	624					4522		40888	10140	1555	572	225	3266	4728	.248	.309	.331	.640								1194	995	55	-238

TEAM	CG	SHO	SV	IP	H	H/G	HR	BB	BB/G	SO	SO/G	ERA	/A	OAVG	OOBA	PR	/A	PF	CPI	FA	E	DP	FW	PW	BW	SBW	DIF
PHI	98	20	8	1369.7	**1161**	7.6	26	342	2.2	652	**4.3**	2.17	132	**.234**	**.276**	87	105	104	102	**.966**	216	99	1.1	**11.7**	-1.0	-.1	2.3
BOS	95	17	**13**	1401.3	1257	8.1	23	366	2.4	630	4.0	2.57	104	.245	.287	26	15	97	96	**.966**	**213**	115	**1.3**	1.7	2.8	.9	.4
BRO	87	16	8	1386.7	1252	8.1	29	473	3.1	499	3.2	2.65	106	.246	.301	14	22	102	**104**	.963	238	96	-.4	2.4	-7.0	-.6	9.5
CHI	71	18	8	1395.0	1272	8.2	28	480	3.1	**657**	4.2	3.11	91	.248	.302	-56	-43	103	90	.958	268	94	-2.4	-4.8	-.8	.6	3.8
PIT	91	18	11	1377.3	1229	8.0	**21**	384	2.5	544	3.6	2.60	103	.244	.288	21	12	98	96	**.966**	214	100	**1.3**	1.3	1.7	**2.1**	-10.3
STL	79	12	9	1396.7	1320	8.5	30	402	2.6	538	3.5	2.88	96	.255	.297	-21	-19	101	98	.964	235	109	-.2	-2.1	**3.1**	-.8	-4.6
CIN	80	19	12	1429.7	1304	8.2	28	497	3.1	572	3.6	2.84	101	.248	.303	-15	2	104	99	**.966**	222	**148**	.7	.2	-2.0	-.8	-4.2
NY	78	15	9	1383.7	1350	8.8	40	**325**	2.1	637	4.1	3.11	81	.261	.295	-56	-88	92	93	.960	256	119	-1.6	-9.8	2.4	-.6	2.5
TOT	679	135	78	11140.0		8.2			2.6		3.8	2.74		.248	.309					.964	1862	880					

Runs		Hits		Doubles		Triples		Home Runs		Total Bases	
Cravath-Phi	89	Doyle-NY	189	Doyle-NY	40	Long-StL	25	Cravath-Phi	24	Cravath-Phi	266
Doyle-NY	86	Griffith-Cin	179	Luderus-Phi	36	Wagner-Pit	17	Williams-Chi	13	Doyle-NY	261
Bancroft-Phi	85	Hinchman-Pit	177	Saier-Chi	35	Griffith-Cin	16	Schulte-Chi	12	Griffith-Cin	254
Burns-NY	83	Groh-Cin	170	Smith-Bos	34	Hinchman-Pit	14	Saier-Chi	11	Hinchman-Pit	253
O'Mara-Bro	77	Burns-NY	169	Magee-Bos	34	Burns-NY	14	Becker-Phi	11	Wagner-Pit	239

Runs Batted In		Runs Produced		Bases On Balls		Batting Average		On Base Percentage		Slugging Average	
Cravath-Phi	115	Cravath-Phi	180	Cravath-Phi	86	Doyle-NY	.320	Cravath-Phi	.393	Cravath-Phi	.510
Magee-Bos	87	Magee-Bos	157	Bancroft-Phi	77	Luderus-Phi	.315	Luderus-Phi	.376	Luderus-Phi	.457
Griffith-Cin	85	Doyle-NY	152	Viox-Pit	75	Griffith-Cin	.307	Daubert-Bro	.369	Long-StL	.446
Wagner-Pit	78	Hinchman-Pit	144	Huggins-StL	74	Hinchman-Pit	.307	Hinchman-Pit	.368	Saier-Chi	.445
Hinchman-Pit	77	Miller-StL	143	Smith-Bos	67	Daubert-Bro	.301	Doyle-NY	.358	Doyle-NY	.442

Production		Adjusted Production		Batter Runs		Adjusted Batter Runs		Clutch Hitting Index		Runs Created	
Cravath-Phi	.902	Cravath-Phi	160	Cravath-Phi	46.8	Cravath-Phi	42.3	Fletcher-NY	156	Cravath-Phi	105
Luderus-Phi	.833	Doyle-NY	155	Luderus-Phi	30.3	Doyle-NY	32.5	Magee-Bos	153	Doyle-NY	94
Hinchman-Pit	.807	Hinchman-Pit	145	Hinchman-Pit	29.7	Hinchman-Pit	30.5	Miller-StL	149	Hinchman-Pit	94
Doyle-NY	.799	Luderus-Phi	141	Doyle-NY	27.1	Luderus-Phi	26.2	Schmidt-Bos	145	Luderus-Phi	87
Saier-Chi	.795	Saier-Chi	137	Griffith-Cin	25.3	Griffith-Cin	23.7	Cutshaw-Bro	143	Griffith-Cin	85

Total Average		Stolen Bases		Stolen Base Average		Stolen Base Runs		Fielding Runs		Total Player Rating	
Cravath-Phi	.966	Carey-Pit	36	Bresnahan-Chi	86.4	Bresnahan-Chi	3.9	Fletcher-NY	33.0	Cravath-Phi	4.1
Saier-Chi	.843	Herzog-Cin	35	Saier-Chi	76.3	Saier-Chi	3.3	Herzog-Cin	30.9	Snyder-StL	3.3
Luderus-Phi	.819	Saier-Chi	29	Baird-Pit	70.7	Costello-Pit	1.5	Myers-Bro	17.8	Luderus-Phi	3.3
Hinchman-Pit	.782	Baird-Pit	29	Robertson-NY	68.8	Baird-Pit	1.5	Maranville-Bos	17.8	Herzog-Cin	3.2
Doyle-NY	.757	Cutshaw-Bro	28	Herzog-Cin	68.6	Gerber-Pit	1.2	Carey-Pit	17.3	Groh-Cin	2.9

Wins		Win Percentage		Games		Complete Games		Shutouts		Saves	
Alexander-Phi	31	Alexander-Phi	.756	Hughes-Bos	50	Alexander-Phi	36	Alexander-Phi	12	Hughes-Bos	9
Rudolph-Bos	22	Toney-Cin	.739	Dale-Cin	49	Rudolph-Bos	30	Tesreau-NY	8	Benton-Cin-NY	5
Mayer-Phi	21	Mamaux-Pit	.724	Alexander-Phi	49	Pfeffer-Bro	26	Mamaux-Pit	8	Lavender-Chi	4
Mamaux-Pit	21	Vaughn-Chi	.625	Schneider-Cin	48	Harmon-Pit	25	Toney-Cin	6	Cooper-Pit	4
Vaughn-Chi	20	Coombs-Bro	.600	Sallee-StL	46	Tesreau-NY	24	Pfeffer-Bro	6		

Innings Pitched		Fewest Hits/Game		Fewest BB/Game		Strikeouts		Strikeouts/Game		Wins Above Team	
Alexander-Phi	376	Alexander-Phi	6.06	Mathewson-NY	.97	Alexander-Phi	241	Alexander-Phi	5.77	Alexander-Phi	9.8
Rudolph-Bos	341	Toney-Cin	6.46	Humphries-Chi	1.20	Tesreau-NY	176	Hughes-Bos	5.50	Mamaux-Pit	7.7
Tesreau-NY	306	Mamaux-Pit	6.50	Adams-Pit	1.25	Hughes-Bos	171	Mamaux-Pit	5.43	Toney-Cin	6.4
Dale-Cin	297	Hughes-Bos	6.69	Alexander-Phi	1.53	Mamaux-Pit	152	Tesreau-NY	5.18	Vaughn-Chi	5.3
Pfeffer-Bro	292	Zabel-Chi	6.85	Rudolph-Bos	1.69	Vaughn-Chi	148	Douglas-Cin-Bro	5.05	Tesreau-NY	3.5

Earned Run Average		Adjusted ERA		Opponents' Batting Avg.		Opponents' On Base Pct.		Starter Runs		Adjusted Starter Runs	
Alexander-Phi	1.22	Alexander-Phi	235	Alexander-Phi	.191	Alexander-Phi	.228	Alexander-Phi	63.6	Alexander-Phi	68.6
Toney-Cin	1.57	Toney-Cin	181	Toney-Cin	.207	Hughes-Bos	.259	Toney-Cin	28.9	Toney-Cin	31.7
Mamaux-Pit	2.04	Pfeffer-Bro	133	Mamaux-Pit	.208	Tesreau-NY	.263	Pfeffer-Bro	21.0	Pfeffer-Bro	22.7
Pfeffer-Bro	2.10	Mamaux-Pit	132	Hughes-Bos	.213	Toney-Cin	.269	Mamaux-Pit	19.8	Mamaux-Pit	18.2
Hughes-Bos	2.12	Hughes-Bos	126	Tesreau-NY	.215	Sallee-StL	.270	Hughes-Bos	19.3	Hughes-Bos	17.1

Clutch Pitching Index		Relief Runs	Adjusted Relief Runs	Relief Ranking	Total Pitcher Index		Total Baseball Ranking	
Humphries-Chi	140				Alexander-Phi	9.3	Alexander-Phi	9.3
Perritt-NY	121				Toney-Cin	3.3	Cravath-Phi	4.1
Schneider-Cin	121				Pfeffer-Bro	2.6	Snyder-StL	3.3
Rixey-Phi	120				Mayer-Phi	2.4	Luderus-Phi	3.3
Stroud-NY	118				Schneider-Cin	1.9	Toney-Cin	3.3

TEAM	G	W	L	PCT	GB	R	OR	AB	H	2B	3B	HR	BB	SO	AVG	OBP	SLG	PRO	/A	BR	/A	PF	CHI	RC	TA	SB	CS	SBA	SBR
BOS	155	101	50	.669		668	499	5024	1308	202	76	14	527	476	.260	.336	.339	.675	107	46	50	99	100	610	.625	118	121	49	-36
DET	156	100	54	.649	2.5	778	597	5128	1372	207	94	23	681	527	.268	.357	.358	.715	120	131	77	108	100	711	.716	241	146	62	-14
CHI	155	93	61	.604	9.5	717	509	4918	1269	163	102	25	583	575	.258	.345	.348	.693	113	81	95	98	102	637	.678	233	183	56	-39
WAS	155	85	68	.556	17	569	491	5029	1225	152	79	12	458	541	.244	.312	.312	.624	92	-51	-57	101	102	535	.578	186	106	64	-7
NY	154	69	83	.454	32.5	584	588	4982	1162	167	50	31	570	668	.233	.317	.305	.622	91	-46	-36	98	103	523	.590	198	133	60	-19
STL	159	63	91	.409	39.5	521	679	5112	1255	166	65	19	472	765	.246	.315	.315	.630	94	-44	-17	96	91	535	.579	202	160	56	-34
CLE	154	57	95	.375	44.5	539	670	5030	1210	169	79	20	490	681	.241	.313	.317	.630	94	-42	-63	104	95	527	.575	138	117	54	-28
PHI	154	43	109	.283	58.5	545	888	5081	1204	183	72	16	440	634	.237	.305	.311	.616	89	-72	-48	96	102	508	.555	127	89	59	-14
TOT	621					4921		40304	10005	1409	617	160	4221	4867	.248	.325	.326	.651								1443	1055	58	-199

TEAM	CG	SHO	SV	IP	H	H/G	HR	BB	BB/G	SO	SO/G	ERA	/A	OAVG	OOBA	PR	/A	PF	CPI	FA	E	DP	FW	PW	BW	SBW	DIF
BOS	81	19	15	1395.3	1164	7.5	18	446	2.9	634	4.1	2.39	118	.233	.297	85	66	96	97	.964	226	95	2.4	7.0	5.3	-1.2	11.9
DET	86	10	19	1409.3	1259	8.0	14	489	3.1	550	3.5	2.86	108	.246	.312	12	34	105	94	.961	258	107	.3	3.6	8.2	1.2	9.7
CHI	91	16	9	1399.3	1242	8.0	14	350	2.3	635	4.1	2.43	113	.245	.294	79	49	94	98	.965	222	95	2.7	5.2	10.1	-1.5	-.5
WAS	87	21	13	1394.7	1161	7.5	12	455	2.9	715	4.6	2.30	127	.233	.297	100	96	99	100	.964	230	101	2.2	10.2	-6.1	1.9	.3
NY	101	12	2	1381.7	1272	8.3	41	517	3.4	559	3.6	3.09	94	.252	.321	-22	-28	99	99	.966	217	118	3.0	-3.0	-3.8	.6	-3.9
STL	76	6	7	1395.0	1256	8.1	21	612	3.9	566	3.7	3.07	95	.247	.329	-19	-24	99	98	.949	336	144	-4.7	-2.5	-1.8	-1.0	-4.0
CLE	62	11	10	1372.0	1287	8.4	18	518	3.4	610	4.0	3.13	100	.255	.325	-28	0	106	96	.957	280	82	-1.1	.0	-6.7	-.3	-10.9
PHI	78	6	2	1348.0	1358	9.1	22	827	5.5	588	3.9	4.33	70	.269	.372	-208	-195	103	93	.947	338	118	-4.9	-20.7	-5.1	1.2	-3.5
TOT	662	101	77	11095.3		8.1			3.4		3.9	2.94		.248	.325					.959	2107	860					

Runs
Cobb-Det 144
E.Collins-Chi ...118
Vitt-Det ...116
Speaker-Bos ...108
Chapman-Cle ...101

Hits
Cobb-Det 208
Crawford-Det ...183
Veach-Det ...178
Speaker-Bos ...176
Pratt-StL ...175

Doubles
Veach-Det 40
Pratt-StL ...31
Lewis-Bos ...31
Crawford-Det ...31
Cobb-Det ...31

Triples
Crawford-Det 19
Fournier-Chi ...18
Roth-Chi-Cle ...17
J.Collins-Chi ...17
Chapman-Cle ...17

Home Runs
Roth-Chi-Cle 7
Oldring-Phi ...6

Total Bases
Cobb-Det 274
Crawford-Det ...267
Veach-Det ...247
Pratt-StL ...237
E.Collins-Chi ...227

Runs Batted In
Veach-Det 112
Crawford-Det ...112
Cobb-Det ...99
J.Collins-Chi ...85
Jackson-Cle-Chi ...81

Runs Produced
Cobb-Det 240
E.Collins-Chi ...191
Veach-Det ...190
Crawford-Det ...188
Speaker-Bos ...177

Bases On Balls
E.Collins-Chi ...119
Shotton-StL ...118
Fournier-Chi ...118
Bush-Det ...118
Hooper-Bos ...89

Batting Average
Cobb-Det 369
E.Collins-Chi ...332
Fournier-Chi ...322
Speaker-Bos ...322
McInnis-Phi ...314

On Base Percentage
Cobb-Det 486
E.Collins-Chi ...460
Fournier-Chi ...429
Speaker-Bos ...416
Shotton-StL ...409

Slugging Average
Fournier-Chi 491
Cobb-Det ...487
Jackson-Cle-Chi ...445
Crawford-Det ...436
E.Collins-Chi ...436

Production
Cobb-Det 973
Fournier-Chi ...920
E.Collins-Chi ...896
Jackson-Cle-Chi ...830
Speaker-Bos ...827

Adjusted Production
Fournier-Chi ...179
Cobb-Det ...176
E.Collins-Chi ...172
Speaker-Bos ...148
Jackson-Cle-Chi ...146

Batter Runs
Cobb-Det 71.6
E.Collins-Chi ...51.9
Fournier-Chi ...40.9
Speaker-Bos ...35.0
Veach-Det ...32.3

Adjusted Batter Runs
Cobb-Det 65.4
E.Collins-Chi ...53.5
Fournier-Chi ...42.1
Speaker-Bos ...35.5
Shotton-StL ...30.4

Clutch Hitting Index
Veach-Det 158
J.Collins-Chi ...140
Gardner-Bos ...133
Schalk-Chi ...133
Jackson-Cle-Chi ...133

Runs Created
Cobb-Det 155
E.Collins-Chi ...116
Crawford-Det ...102
Speaker-Bos ...97
Veach-Det ...97

Total Average
Cobb-Det ...1.267
E.Collins-Chi ...1.050
Fournier-Chi ...1.017
Speaker-Bos ...864
Shotton-StL ...841

Stolen Bases
Cobb-Det 96
Maisel-NY ...51
E.Collins-Chi ...46
Shotton-StL ...43
Milan-Was ...40

Stolen Base Average
Schang-Phi 85.7
Maisel-NY ...81.0
Foster-Was ...76.9
Moeller-Was ...76.2
Roth-Chi-Cle ...72.2

Stolen Base Runs
Maisel-NY 8.1
Cobb-Det ...6.0
Schang-Phi ...3.6
Moeller-Was ...3.6
Williams-StL ...2.7

Fielding Runs
Boone-NY 19.5
O'Neill-Cle ...17.0
Strunk-Phi ...16.4
Vitt-Det ...14.2
Leibold-Cle-Chi ...13.1

Total Player Rating
E.Collins-Chi ...6.3
Cobb-Det ...5.9
Fournier-Chi ...3.7
Chapman-Cle ...3.5
Speaker-Bos ...3.4

Wins
Johnson-Was ...27
Scott-Chi ...24
Faber-Chi ...24
Dauss-Det ...24
Coveleski-Det ...22

Win Percentage
Wood-Bos 750
Shore-Bos ...704
Foster-Bos ...704
Ruth-Bos ...692
Scott-Chi ...686

Games
Faber-Chi 50
Coveleski-Det ...50
Scott-Chi ...48
Jones-Cle ...48

Complete Games
Johnson-Was ...35
Caldwell-NY ...31
Dauss-Det ...27
Scott-Chi ...23
Dubuc-Det ...22

Shutouts
Scott-Chi 7
Johnson-Was ...7
Morton-Cle ...6
Foster-Bos ...5
Dubuc-Det ...5

Saves
Mays-Bos 7

Innings Pitched
Johnson-Was ...337
Coveleski-Det ...313
Dauss-Det ...310
Caldwell-NY ...305
Faber-Chi ...300

Fewest Hits/Game
Leonard-Bos ...6.39
Ruth-Bos ...6.85
Wood-Bos ...6.88
Johnson-Was ...6.89
Morton-Cle ...7.09

Fewest BB/Game
Johnson-Was ...1.50
Ayers-Was ...1.62
Benz-Was ...1.63
Russell-Chi ...1.85
Cicotte-Chi ...1.94

Strikeouts
Johnson-Was ...203
Faber-Chi ...182
Wyckoff-Phi ...157
Coveleski-Det ...150
Mitchell-Cle ...149

Strikeouts/Game
Leonard-Bos ...5.70
Mitchell-Cle ...5.68
Faber-Chi ...5.46
Johnson-Was ...5.42
Lowdermilk-StL-Det ...5.33

Wins Above Team
Johnson-Was ...6.6
Fisher-NY ...5.1
Scott-Chi ...4.4
Morton-Cle ...4.2
Caldwell-NY ...3.5

Earned Run Average
Wood-Bos ...1.49
Johnson-Was ...1.55
Shore-Bos ...1.64
Scott-Chi ...2.04
Fisher-NY ...2.10

Adjusted ERA
Wood-Bos ...189
Johnson-Was ...189
Shore-Bos ...172
Morton-Cle ...146
Fisher-NY ...138

Opponents' Batting Avg.
Leonard-Bos ...208
Ruth-Bos ...212
Johnson-Was ...214
Morton-Cle ...216
Wood-Bos ...216

Opponents' On Base Pct.
Johnson-Was ...260
Morton-Cle ...268
Wood-Bos ...275
Benz-Chi ...276
Ayers-Was ...276

Starter Runs
Johnson-Was ...52.2
Shore-Bos ...35.8
Scott-Chi ...29.8
Wood-Bos ...25.4
Foster-Bos ...23.4

Adjusted Starter Runs
Johnson-Was ...51.5
Shore-Bos ...32.4
Morton-Cle ...26.4
Scott-Chi ...23.5
Wood-Bos ...23.2

Clutch Pitching Index
Hamilton-StL ...126
Shore-Bos ...123
Foster-Bos ...121
Fisher-NY ...119
Wood-Bos ...118

Relief Runs

Adjusted Relief Runs

Relief Ranking

Total Pitcher Index
Johnson-Was ...6.9
Shore-Bos ...3.7
Dauss-Det ...3.4
Wood-Bos ...3.2
Foster-Bos ...3.0

Total Baseball Ranking
Johnson-Was ...6.9
E.Collins-Chi ...6.3
Cobb-Det ...5.9
Shore-Bos ...3.7
Fournier-Chi ...3.7

TEAM	G	W	L	PCT	GB	R	OR	AB	H	2B	3B	HR	BB	SO	AVG	OBP	SLG	PRO	/A	BR	/A	PF	CHI	RC	TA	SB	CS	SBA	SBR
STL	159	87	67	.565		634	527	5145	1344	199	81	23	576	502	.261	.336	.345	.681	108	56	26	105	93	689	.670	195			
CHI	155	86	66	.566		640	538	5133	1320	185	77	50	444	590	.257	.316	.341	.663	103	19	36	97	103	643	.633	161			
PIT	156	86	67	.562	0.5	592	524	5040	1318	180	80	20	448	561	.262	.322	.341	.663	102	13	-10	104	97	646	.642	224			
KC	153	81	72	.529	5.5	547	551	4937	1206	200	66	28	368	503	.244	.297	.329	.626	91	-61	-41	97	106	547	.572	144			
NEW	155	80	72	.526	6	585	562	5097	1283	210	80	17	438	550	.252	.311	.334	.645	97	-21	13	94	101	609	.610	184			
BUF	153	74	78	.487	12	574	634	5065	1261	193	68	40	420	587	.249	.306	.338	.644	96	-26	-24	100	102	590	.608	184			
BRO	153	70	82	.461	16	647	673	5035	1348	205	75	36	473	654	.268	.331	.360	.691	110	62	76	98	98	692	.687	249			
BAL	154	47	107	.305	40	550	760	5060	1235	196	53	36	470	641	.244	.308	.325	.633	93	-39	-80	107	98	569	.586	128			
TOT	619					4769		40512	10315	1568	580	250	3637	4588	.255	.316	.340	.657								1469			

TEAM	CG	SHO	SV	IP	H	H/G	HR	BB	BB/G	SO	SO/G	ERA	/A	OAVG	OOBA	PR	/A	PF	CPI	FA	E	DP	FW	PW	BW	SBW	DIF
STL	94	24	9	1424.3	1267	8.0	22	396	2.5	698	4.4	2.73	114	.245	.299	47	59	102	96	.967	218	112	1.2	6.3	2.8		-.4
CHI	97	21	10	1396.3	1232	7.9	33	402	2.6	576	3.7	2.64	109	.243	.299	60	36	95	101	.963	238	103	.0	3.9	3.9		2.2
PIT	88	16	12	1382.0	1273	8.3	37	441	2.9	517	3.4	2.79	111	.251	.311	37	48	102	106	.972	173	101	3.9	5.2	-1.1		1.5
KC	95	16	11	1357.0	1210	8.0	29	390	2.6	526	3.5	2.82	104	.245	.301	31	16	97	95	.961	252	99	-.8	1.7	-4.4		8.0
NEW	100	16	7	1406.0	1308	8.4	15	453	2.9	581	3.7	2.60	109	.253	.314	67	38	94	112	.963	241	127	-.1	4.1	1.4		-1.3
BUF	79	13	11	1359.7	1271	8.4	34	553	3.7	594	3.9	3.38	91	.254	.329	-53	-48	101	97	.964	229	105	.6	-5.2	-2.6		5.2
BRO	78	10	16	1355.7	1299	8.6	27	536	3.6	467	3.1	3.37	88	.259	.331	-51	-59	98	98	.955	291	105	-3.1	-6.3	8.2		-4.7
BAL	85	5	7	1360.0	1455	9.6	53	466	3.1	570	3.8	3.96	85	.281	.340	-140	-87	111	98	.958	266	143	-1.6	-9.4	-8.6		-10.4
TOT	716	121	83	11041.0		8.4			3.0		3.7	3.03		.255	.316					.963	1908	895					

Runs
Borton-StL	97
Berghammer-Pit	96
Evans-Bro-Bal	94
Tobin-StL	92
Kauff-Bro	92

Hits
Tobin-StL	184
Konetchy-Pit	181
Evans-Bro-Bal	171
Kauff-Bro	165
Chase-Buf	165

Doubles
Evans-Bro-Bal	34
Zwilling-Chi	32
Konetchy-Pit	31
Chase-Buf	31

Triples
Mann-Chi	19
Konetchy-Pit	18
Kelly-Pit	17
Gilmore-KC	15

Home Runs
Chase-Buf	17
Zwilling-Chi	13
Kauff-Bro	12
Konetchy-Pit	10
Walsh-Bal-StL	9

Total Bases
Konetchy-Pit	278
Chase-Buf	267
Tobin-StL	254
Kauff-Bro	246
Zwilling-Chi	242

Runs Batted In
Zwilling-Chi	94
Konetchy-Pit	93
Chase-Buf	89
Kauff-Bro	83
Borton-StL	83

Runs Produced
Borton-StL	177
Kauff-Bro	163
Konetchy-Pit	162
Evans-Bro-Bal	157
Chase-Buf	157

Bases On Balls
Borton-StL	92
Kauff-Bro	85
Berghammer-Pit	83
Miller-StL	79

Batting Average
Kauff-Bro	.342
Magee-Bro	.323
Konetchy-Pit	.314
Flack-Chi	.314
Campbell-New	.310

On Base Percentage
Kauff-Bro	.440
Miller-StL	.395
Borton-StL	.388
Cooper-Bro	.384
Evans-Bro-Bal	.378

Slugging Average
Kauff-Bro	.509
Konetchy-Pit	.483
Chase-Buf	.471
Zwilling-Chi	.442
Mann-Chi	.438

Production
Kauff-Bro	.949
Konetchy-Pit	.842
Zwilling-Chi	.806
Evans-Bro-Bal	.804
Mann-Chi	.794

Adjusted Production
Kauff-Bro	185
Konetchy-Pit	143
Zwilling-Chi	142
Mann-Chi	138
Magee-Bro	136

Batter Runs
Kauff-Bro	51.6
Konetchy-Pit	31.7
Evans-Bro-Bal	26.6
Zwilling-Chi	25.7
Borton-StL	24.5

Adjusted Batter Runs
Kauff-Bro	53.0
Konetchy-Pit	29.1
Zwilling-Chi	27.6
Wilson-Chi	25.4
Cooper-Bro	25.1

Clutch Hitting Index
Oakes-Pit	146
Borton-StL	142
Engle-Buf	140
Smith-Buf-Bro	134
Zwilling-Chi	128

Runs Created
Kauff-Bro	130
Konetchy-Pit	110
Tobin-StL	105
Zwilling-Chi	98
Miller-StL	96

Total Average
Kauff-Bro	1.214
Konetchy-Pit	.876
Cooper-Bro	.858
Zwilling-Chi	.852
Miller-StL	.849

Stolen Bases
Kauff-Bro	55
Mowrey-Pit	40
Kelly-Pit	38
Flack-Chi	37
Magee-Bro	34

Stolen Base Average

Stolen Base Runs

Fielding Runs
Rariden-New	23.5
Doolan-Bal-Chi	22.7
Johnson-StL	19.1
Esmond-New	17.9
Cooper-Bro	16.8

Total Player Rating
Kauff-Bro	6.3
Rariden-New	4.2
Cooper-Bro	3.9
Esmond-New	3.7
Konetchy-Pit	3.5

Wins
McConnell-Chi	25
Allen-Pit	23
Davenport-StL	22
Cullop-KC	22

Win Percentage
McConnell-Chi	.714
Brown-Chi	.680
Reulbach-New	.677
Cullop-KC	.667
Plank-StL	.656

Games
Davenport-StL	55
Bedient-Buf	53
Crandall-StL	51
Johnson-KC	46

Complete Games
Davenport-StL	30
Hendrix-Chi	26
Schulz-Buf	25
Allen-Pit	24

Shutouts
Davenport-StL	10
Plank-StL	6
Allen-Pit	6

Saves
Bedient-Buf	10
Barger-Pit	5
Wiltse-Bro	5
Upham-Bro	5

Innings Pitched
Davenport-StL	393
Crandall-StL	313
Schulz-Buf	310
McConnell-Chi	303
Cullop-KC	302

Fewest Hits/Game
Davenport-StL	6.87
Main-KC	7.08
Plank-StL	7.12
Anderson-Buf	7.20
Brown-Chi	7.21

Fewest BB/Game
Plank-StL	1.81
Bender-Bal	1.87
Hearn-Pit	1.89
Cullop-KC	2.00
Quinn-Bal	2.07

Strikeouts
Davenport-StL	229
Schulz-Buf	160
McConnell-Chi	151
Plank-StL	147

Strikeouts/Game
Anderson-Buf	5.33
Davenport-StL	5.24
Plank-StL	4.94
Bailey-Bal-Chi	4.92
Groom-StL	4.78

Wins Above Team
McConnell-Chi	7.1
Reulbach-New	5.7
Cullop-KC	5.7
Schulz-Buf	4.7
Plank-StL	4.0

Earned Run Average
Moseley-New	1.91
Plank-StL	2.08
Brown-Chi	2.10
McConnell-Chi	2.20
Davenport-StL	2.20

Adjusted ERA
Plank-StL	149
Moseley-New	149
Davenport-StL	141
Brown-Chi	137
McConnell-Chi	131

Opponents' Batting Avg.
Davenport-StL	.215
Plank-StL	.218
Brown-Chi	.220
Main-KC	.222
Anderson-Buf	.222

Opponents' On Base Pct.
Plank-StL	.262
Davenport-StL	.268
Brown-Chi	.279
Anderson-Buf	.285
Reulbach-New	.287

Starter Runs
Davenport-StL	36.3
Moseley-New	33.2
Plank-StL	28.2
McConnell-Chi	28.0
Brown-Chi	24.5

Adjusted Starter Runs
Davenport-StL	39.5
Plank-StL	30.4
Moseley-New	27.7
McConnell-Chi	22.9
Brown-Chi	20.5

Clutch Pitching Index
Moran-New	132
Kaiserling-New	130
Rogge-Pit	129
Moseley-New	125
Suggs-Bal	120

Relief Runs

Adjusted Relief Runs

Relief Ranking

Total Pitcher Index
Crandall-StL	4.1
Plank-StL	4.0
McConnell-Chi	4.0
Brown-Chi	3.5
Davenport-StL	3.1

Total Baseball Ranking
Kauff-Bro	6.3
Rariden-New	4.2
Crandall-StL	4.1
Plank-StL	4.0
McConnell-Chi	4.0

TEAM	G	W	L	PCT	GB	R	OR	AB	H	2B	3B	HR	BB	SO	AVG	OBP	SLG	PRO	/A	BR	/A	PF	CHI	RC	TA	SB	CS	SBA	SBR
BRO	156	94	60	.610		585	471	5234	1366	195	80	28	355	550	.261	.313	.345	.658	108	46	29	103	98	645	.617	187			
PHI	154	91	62	.595	2.5	581	489	4985	1244	223	53	42	399	571	.250	.310	.341	.651	106	33	55	96	104	593	.610	149			
BOS	158	89	63	.586	4	542	453	5075	1181	166	73	22	437	646	.233	.299	.307	.606	92	-37	1	93	107	535	.561	141			
NY	155	86	66	.566	7	597	504	5152	1305	188	74	42	356	558	.253	.307	.343	.650	106	31	53	96	105	617	.617	206			
CHI	156	67	86	.438	26.5	520	541	5179	1237	194	56	46	399	662	.239	.298	.325	.623	97	-17	-108	117	99	559	.570	133			
PIT	157	65	89	.422	29	484	586	5181	1246	147	91	20	372	618	.240	.298	.316	.614	95	-31	-55	105	94	556	.567	173			
STL	153	60	93	.392	33.5	476	629	5030	1223	155	74	25	335	651	.243	.295	.318	.613	94	-34	-15	97	98	535	.565	182			
CIN	155	60	93	.392	33.5	505	617	5254	1336	187	88	14	362	573	.254	.307	.331	.638	102	12	22	98	91	596	.587	157			
TOT	622					4290		41090	10138	1455	589	239	3015	4829	.247	.303	.328	.632						1328					

TEAM	CG	SHO	SV	IP	H	H/G	HR	BB	BB/G	SO	SO/G	ERA	/A	OAVG	OOBA	PR	/A	PF	CPI	FA	E	DP	FW	PW	BW	SBW	DIF
BRO	96	22	9	1419.7	1201	7.6	24	372	2.4	634	4.0	2.12	124	.234	.278	78	79	100	103	.965	224	90	1.2	9.0	3.3		3.4
PHI	97	24	9	1380.0	1238	8.1	28	295	1.9	601	3.9	2.36	104	.244	.278	38	13	94	98	.963	234	119	.4	1.5	6.3		6.3
BOS	97	22	11	1414.3	1206	7.7	24	325	2.1	644	4.1	2.19	108	.235	.274	66	29	91	97	.967	212	124	2.2	3.3	.1		7.4
NY	88	22	12	1394.7	1267	8.2	41	310	2.0	638	4.1	2.60	94	.247	.283	1	-24	94	95	.966	217	108	1.6	-2.7	6.1		5.1
CHI	72	17	13	1413.0	1265	8.1	32	365	2.3	616	3.9	2.65	116	.244	.284	-5	65	117	93	.957	286	104	-2.6	7.4	-12.3		-2.0
PIT	88	11	7	1417.0	1277	8.1	24	443	2.8	596	3.8	2.76	101	.245	.294	-23	5	107	94	.959	260	97	-.9	.6	-6.3		-5.4
STL	58	14	15	1349.7	1331	8.9	31	445	3.0	529	3.7	3.14	83	.262	.312	-79	-78	100	99	.957	278	124	-2.4	-8.9	-1.7		-3.5
CIN	86	7	6	1402.3	1356	8.7	35	458	2.9	569	3.7	3.10	85	.259	.309	-75	-73	101	97	.965	228	126	.9	-8.3	2.5		-11.6
TOT	682	139	82	11190.7		8.2			2.4		3.9	2.61		.247	.303					.963	1939	892					

Runs
Burns-NY 105
Carey-Pit 90
Robertson-NY 88
Groh-Cin 85
Paskert-Phi 82

Hits
Chase-Cin 184
Robertson-NY 180
Wheat-Bro 177
Hinchman-Pit 175
Burns-NY 174

Doubles
Niehoff-Phi 42
Wheat-Bro 32
Paskert-Phi 30

Triples
Hinchman-Pit 16
Roush-NY -Cin 15
Kauff-NY 15
Hornsby-StL 15

Home Runs
Williams-Chi 12
Robertson-NY 12
Cravath-Phi 11
Wheat-Bro 9
Kauff-NY 9

Total Bases
Wheat-Bro 262
Robertson-NY 250
Chase-Cin 249
Hinchman-Pit 237
Burns-NY 229

Runs Batted In
Zimmerman-Chi-NY . . .83
Chase-Cin 82
Hinchman-Pit 76
Kauff-NY 74
Wheat-Bro 73

Runs Produced
Zimmerman-Chi-NY . . 153
Robertson-NY 145
Chase-Cin 144
Konetchy-Bos 143
Burns-NY 141

Bases On Balls
Groh-Cin 84
Saier-Chi 79
Bancroft-Phi 74
Kauff-NY 68
Cravath-Phi 64

Batting Average
Chase-Cin 339
Daubert-Bro 316
Hinchman-Pit 315
Hornsby-StL 313
Wheat-Bro 312

On Base Percentage
Cravath-Phi 379
Hinchman-Pit 378
Williams-Chi 372
Daubert-Bro 371
Groh-Cin 370

Slugging Average
Wheat-Bro 461
Chase-Cin 459
Williams-Chi 459
Hornsby-StL 444
Cravath-Phi 440

Production
Williams-Chi 831
Wheat-Bro 828
Chase-Cin 822
Cravath-Phi 819
Hornsby-StL 814

Adjusted Production
Cravath-Phi 158
Chase-Cin 155
Hornsby-StL 155
Wheat-Bro 149
Hinchman-Pit 140

Batter Runs
Wheat-Bro 34.5
Hinchman-Pit 31.1
Chase-Cin 30.2
Cravath-Phi 28.7
Hornsby-StL 28.2

Adjusted Batter Runs
Wheat-Bro 32.7
Chase-Cin 31.3
Cravath-Phi 30.8
Hornsby-StL 30.0
Hinchman-Pit 28.4

Clutch Hitting Index
Mowrey-Bro 157
Magee-Bos 156
Zimmerman-Chi-NY . .139
Fletcher-NY 139
Cutshaw-Bro 138

Runs Created
Wheat-Bro 103
Hinchman-Pit 96
Chase-Cin 93
Hornsby-StL 88
Carey-Pit 87

Total Average
Williams-Chi 863
Cravath-Phi 857
Wheat-Bro 844
Hornsby-StL 826
Hinchman-Pit 797

Stolen Bases
Carey-Pit 63
Kauff-NY 40
Bescher-StL 39
Burns-NY 37
Herzog-Cin-NY 34

Stolen Base Average
Carey-Pit 76.8
Bescher-StL 76.5
Daubert-Bro 75.0
Maranville-Bos 68.1
Chase-Cin 66.7

Stolen Base Runs
Carey-Pit 7.5
Bescher-StL 4.5
Daubert-Bro 2.1
Maranville-Bos 6

Fielding Runs
Carey-Pit 23.8
Bancroft-Phi 22.4
Fletcher-NY 21.4
Maranville-Bos 20.1
Betzel-StL 19.0

Total Player Rating
Fletcher-NY 4.3
Groh-Cin 4.3
Carey-Pit 4.1
Wheat-Bro 4.0
Doyle-NY -Chi 3.4

Wins
Alexander-Phi 33
Pfeffer-Bro 25
Rixey-Phi 22
Mamaux-Pit 21

Win Percentage
Hughes-Bos 842
Alexander-Phi 733
Pfeffer-Bro 694
Rixey-Phi 688
Benton-NY 667

Games
Meadows-StL 51
Alexander-Phi 48
Mamaux-Pit 45
Ames-StL 45

Complete Games
Alexander-Phi 38
Pfeffer-Bro 30
Rudolph-Bos 27
Mamaux-Pit 26
Demaree-Phi 25

Shutouts
Alexander-Phi 16
Tyler-Bos 6
Pfeffer-Bro 6

Saves
Ames-StL 8
Packard-Chi 5
Marquard-Bro 5
Hughes-Bos 5

Innings Pitched
Alexander-Phi 389
Pfeffer-Bro 329
Rudolph-Bos 312
Mamaux-Pit 310
Toney-Cin 300

Fewest Hits/Game
Cheney-Bro 6.33
Hughes-Bos 6.76
Cooper-Pit 6.91
Miller-Pit 7.02
Ragan-Bos 7.07

Fewest BB/Game
Rudolph-Bos 1.10
Alexander-Phi 1.16
Demaree-Phi 1.52
Sallee-StL-NY 1.63
Marquard-Bro 1.67

Strikeouts
Alexander-Phi 167
Cheney-Bro 166
Mamaux-Pit 163
Toney-Cin 146
Vaughn-Chi 144

Strikeouts/Game
Cheney-Bro 5.91
Hughes-Bos 5.42
Hendrix-Chi 4.83
Mamaux-Pit 4.73
Marquard-Bro 4.70

Wins Above Team
Alexander-Phi 9.5
Hughes-Bos 6.2
Mamaux-Pit 6.0
Pfeffer-Bro 4.8
Rixey-Phi 4.4

Earned Run Average
Alexander-Phi 1.55
Marquard-Bro 1.58
Rixey-Phi 1.85
Cooper-Pit 1.87
Pfeffer-Bro 1.91

Adjusted ERA
Marquard-Bro 166
Alexander-Phi 158
Cooper-Pit 150
Vaughn-Chi 139
Pfeffer-Bro 137

Opponents' Batting Avg.
Cheney-Bro 198
Cooper-Pit 215
Hughes-Bos 215
Ragan-Bos 218
McConnell-Chi 223

Opponents' On Base Pct.
Rudolph-Bos 255
Alexander-Phi 255
McConnell-Chi 260
Marquard-Bro 261
Ragan-Bos 265

Starter Runs
Alexander-Phi 45.9
Schupp-NY 26.6
Pfeffer-Bro 25.5
Rixey-Phi 24.3
Marquard-Bro 23.5

Adjusted Starter Runs
Alexander-Phi 38.8
Vaughn-Chi 28.2
Pfeffer-Bro 25.9
Cooper-Pit 25.5
Schupp-NY 24.0

Clutch Pitching Index
Dell-Bro 124
Sallee-StL-NY 117
Meadows-StL 116
Schulz-Cin 114
Alexander-Phi 114

Relief Runs

Adjusted Relief Runs

Relief Ranking

Total Pitcher Index
Alexander-Phi 5.9
Pfeffer-Bro 3.5
Vaughn-Chi 3.1
Cooper-Pit 3.0
Rixey-Phi 2.4

Total Baseball Ranking
Alexander-Phi 5.9
Fletcher-NY 4.3
Groh-Cin 4.3
Carey-Pit 4.1
Wheat-Bro 4.0

TEAM	G	W	L	PCT	GB	R	OR	AB	H	2B	3B	HR	BB	SO	AVG	OBP	SLG	PRO	/A	BR	/A	PF	CHI	RC	TA	SB	CS	SBA	SBR
BOS	156	91	63	.591		550	480	5017	1245	196	56	14	464	482	.248	.317	.318	.635	97	-20	15	94	100	579	.590	129			
CHI	155	89	65	.578	2	601	497	5081	1277	194	100	17	447	591	.251	.319	.339	.658	104	18	-28	108	101	638	.638	197			
DET	155	87	67	.565	4	670	595	5193	1371	202	96	17	545	529	.264	.337	.350	.687	113	78	51	105	100	700	.675	190			
NY	156	80	74	.519	11	577	561	5200	1277	194	59	35	516	632	.246	.318	.326	.644	100	-4	-12	101	99	612	.618	179			
STL	158	79	75	.513	12	588	545	5159	1262	181	50	14	627	610	.245	.331	.322	.638	98	2	30	95	99	620	.638	234			
CLE	157	77	77	.500	14	630	602	5064	1264	133	66	16	522	605	.250	.324	.311	.635	97	-13	-11	100	111	594	.603	160			
WAS	159	76	77	.497	14.5	536	543	5113	1239	170	60	12	535	597	.242	.320	.306	.626	94	-28	-27	100	97	579	.603	185			
PHI	154	36	117	.235	54.5	447	776	5010	1212	169	65	19	406	631	.242	.303	.313	.616	91	-60	-48	98	90	538	.567	151			
TOT	625					4599		40837	10147	1439	552	144	4062	4677	.248	.321	.324	.645								1425			

TEAM	CG	SHO	SV	IP	H	H/G	HR	BB	BB/G	SO	SO/G	ERA	/A	OAVG	OOBA	PR	/A	PF	CPI	FA	E	DP	FW	PW	BW	SBW	DIF
BOS	76	24	16	1406.7	1221	7.8	10	463	3.0	584	3.7	2.47	105	.241	.305	55	20	92	99	.972	183	108	3.0	2.2	1.7		7.1
CHI	73	20	15	1411.7	1189	7.6	14	405	2.6	644	4.1	2.36	127	.236	.293	72	98	106	95	.968	205	134	1.5	10.8	-3.1		2.7
DET	81	8	13	1405.7	1254	8.0	11	578	3.7	531	3.4	2.97	98	.246	.323	-23	-10	103	94	.968	211	110	1.2	-1.1	5.6		4.3
NY	84	12	17	1426.0	1249	7.9	37	476	3.0	616	3.9	2.77	103	.243	.307	8	13	101	96	.967	219	119	.7	1.4	-1.3		2.2
STL	74	9	13	1444.3	1292	8.1	15	478	3.0	505	3.1	2.58	103	.247	.310	39	12	94	101	.963	248	120	-.9	1.3	3.3		-1.7
CLE	65	9	16	1411.0	1292	8.8	17	467	3.0	537	3.4	2.99	94	.264	.325	-26	-29	99	102	.965	232	120	.0	-3.2	-1.2		4.4
WAS	85	11	7	1425.3	1271	8.0	14	540	3.4	706	4.5	2.66	106	.246	.318	26	26	100	103	.964	232	119	.2	2.9	-3.0		-.6
PHI	94	11	3	1339.7	1311	8.8	26	715	4.8	575	3.9	3.84	77	.264	.357	-151	-129	105	95	.951	314	126	-5.5	-14.3	-5.3		-15.4
TOT	632	104	100	11270.3		8.1			3.3		3.8	2.82		.248	.321					.965	1844	966					

Runs
Cobb-Det 113
Graney-Cle 106
Speaker-Cle 102
Shotton-StL 97
Veach-Det 92

Hits
Speaker-Cle 211
Jackson-Chi 202
Cobb-Det 201
Sisler-StL 177
Shotton-StL 174

Doubles
Speaker-Cle 41
Graney-Cle 41
Jackson-Chi 40
Pratt-StL 35
Veach-Det 33

Triples
Jackson-Chi 21
E.Collins-Chi 17
Witt-Phi 15
Veach-Det 15

Home Runs
Pipp-NY 12
Baker-NY 10
Schang-Phi 7
Felsch-Chi 7

Total Bases
Jackson-Chi 293
Speaker-Cle 274
Cobb-Det 267
Veach-Det 245

Runs Batted In
Pratt-StL 103
Pipp-NY 93
Veach-Det 91
Speaker-Cle 79
Jackson-Chi 78

Runs Produced
Veach-Det 180
Speaker-Cle 179
Cobb-Det 176
Jackson-Chi 166
Pratt-StL 162

Bases On Balls
Shotton-StL 111
Graney-Cle 102
E.Collins-Chi 86
Speaker-Cle 82
Hooper-Bos 80

Batting Average
Speaker-Cle 386
Cobb-Det 371
Jackson-Chi 341
Strunk-Phi 316
Gardner-Bos 308

On Base Percentage
Speaker-Cle 470
Cobb-Det 452
E.Collins-Chi 405
Jackson-Chi 393
Strunk-Phi 393

Slugging Average
Speaker-Cle 502
Jackson-Chi 495
Cobb-Det 493
Veach-Det 433
Felsch-Chi 427

Production
Speaker-Cle 972
Cobb-Det 944
Jackson-Chi 888
Strunk-Phi 814
E.Collins-Chi 802

Adjusted Production
Speaker-Cle 192
Cobb-Det 176
Jackson-Chi 154
Strunk-Phi 147
Gardner-Bos 137

Batter Runs
Speaker-Cle 64.6
Cobb-Det 57.5
Jackson-Chi 44.9
E.Collins-Chi . . . 30.5
Strunk-Phi 30.2

Adjusted Batter Runs
Speaker-Cle 64.7
Cobb-Det 54.7
Jackson-Chi 39.7
Strunk-Phi 31.5
E.Collins-Chi . . . 25.2

Clutch Hitting Index
Pratt-StL 157
Gandil-Cle 150
Marsans-StL 142
Heilmann-Det 137
Burns-Det 136

Runs Created
Cobb-Det 136
Speaker-Cle 132
Jackson-Chi 119
E.Collins-Chi 99
Veach-Det 94

Total Average
Cobb-Det 1.137
Speaker-Cle 1.091
Jackson-Chi 911
E.Collins-Chi 867
Strunk-Phi 808

Stolen Bases
Cobb-Det 68
Marsans-StL 46
Shotton-StL 41
E.Collins-Chi 40
Speaker-Cle 35

Stolen Base Average
Cobb-Det 73.9
Hooper-Bos 71.1
Schalk-Chi 69.8
Roth-Cle 67.4
Shanks-Was 65.7

Stolen Base Runs
Cobb-Det 6.0
Hooper-Bos 1.5
Schalk-Chi 1.2
Roth-Cle 3

Fielding Runs
Vitt-Det 26.5
Pratt-StL 22.7
Lavan-StL 19.3
Schalk-Chi 16.8
Milan-Was 12.3

Total Player Rating
Cobb-Det 6.6
Speaker-Cle 6.0
Pratt-StL 4.1
Jackson-Chi 3.0
Nunamaker-NY 2.7

Wins
Johnson-Was 25
Shawkey-NY 24
Ruth-Bos 23
Coveleski-Det 21
Dauss-Det 19

Win Percentage
Cicotte-Chi 682
Ruth-Bos 657
Coveleski-Det 656
Faber-Chi 654
Shawkey-NY 632

Games
Davenport-StL 59
Russell-Chi 56
Shawkey-NY 53
Gallia-Was 49

Complete Games
Johnson-Was 36
Myers-Phi 31
Bush-Phi 25
Ruth-Bos 23
Coveleski-Det 22

Shutouts
Ruth-Bos 9
Bush-Phi 8
Leonard-Bos 6
Russell-Chi 5

Saves
Shawkey-NY 8
Russell-NY 6
Leonard-Bos 6
Cicotte-Chi 5
Bagby-Cle 5

Innings Pitched
Johnson-Was 371
Ruth-Bos 324
Coveleski-Det 324
Myers-Phi 315
Davenport-StL 291

Fewest Hits/Game
Ruth-Bos 6.39
Shawkey-NY 6.63
Cicotte-Chi 6.64
Bush-Phi 6.96
Johnson-Was 7.04

Fewest BB/Game
Russell-Chi 1.43
Cullop-NY 1.72
Coveleski-Det 1.75
Shore-Bos 1.95
Johnson-Was 1.99

Strikeouts
Johnson-Was 228
Myers-Phi 182
Ruth-Bos 170
Bush-Phi 157
Harper-Was 149

Strikeouts/Game
Williams-Chi 5.54
Johnson-Was 5.53
Russell-NY 5.47
Harper-Was 5.36
Myers-Phi 5.20

Wins Above Team
Shawkey-NY 5.5
Bush-Phi 4.8
Myers-Phi 4.3
Coveleski-Det 4.0
Johnson-Was 3.6

Earned Run Average
Ruth-Bos 1.75
Cicotte-Chi 1.78
Johnson-Was 1.89
Coveleski-Det 1.97
Faber-Chi 2.02

Adjusted ERA
Cicotte-Chi 168
Johnson-Was 149
Ruth-Bos 149
Faber-Chi 148
Coveleski-Det 147

Opponents' Batting Avg.
Ruth-Bos 201
Shawkey-NY 209
Cicotte-Chi 218
Bush-Phi 219
Johnson-Was 220

Opponents' On Base Pct.
Russell-Chi 254
Johnson-Was 270
Shawkey-NY 273
Ruth-Bos 280
Coveleski-Det 282

Starter Runs
Ruth-Bos 38.6
Johnson-Was 38.4
Coveleski-Det 30.6
Cicotte-Chi 21.7
Weilman-StL 20.6

Adjusted Starter Runs
Johnson-Was 38.5
Coveleski-Det 33.5
Ruth-Bos 30.6
Cicotte-Chi 25.1
Faber-Chi 22.0

Clutch Pitching Index
Cicotte-Chi 117
Gallia-Was 117
Mogridge-NY 114
Fisher-NY 113
Weilman-StL 113

Relief Runs

Adjusted Relief Runs

Relief Ranking

Total Pitcher Index
Ruth-Bos 5.3
Johnson-Was 4.8
Coveleski-Det 4.6
Cicotte-Chi 3.2
Mays-Bos 2.5

Total Baseball Ranking
Cobb-Det 6.6
Speaker-Cle 6.0
Ruth-Bos 5.3
Johnson-Was 4.8
Coveleski-Det 4.6

TEAM	G	W	L	PCT	GB	R	OR	AB	H	2B	3B	HR	BB	SO	AVG	OBP	SLG	PRO	/A	BR	/A	PF	CHI	RC	TA	SB	CS	SBA	SBR
NY	158	98	56	.636		635	457	5211	1360	170	71	39	373	533	.261	.317	.343	.660	109	50	66	97	105	610	.617	162			
PHI	154	87	65	.572	10	578	500	5084	1262	225	60	38	435	533	.248	.310	.339	.649	105	29	-12	108	100	573	.598	109			
STL	154	82	70	.539	15	531	567	5083	1271	159	93	26	359	652	.250	.303	.333	.636	101	2	-6	102	98	552	.587	159			
CIN	157	78	76	.506	20	601	611	5251	1385	196	100	26	312	477	.264	.309	.354	.663	109	48	90	92	100	607	.610	153			
CHI	157	74	80	.481	24	552	567	5135	1229	194	67	17	415	599	.239	.299	.313	.612	93	-34	-58	105	106	524	.556	127			
BOS	157	72	81	.471	25.5	536	552	5201	1280	169	75	22	427	587	.246	.309	.320	.629	99	-1	20	96	95	563	.585	155			
BRO	156	70	81	.464	26.5	511	559	5251	1299	159	78	25	334	527	.247	.296	.322	.618	95	-31	-50	104	97	534	.552	130			
PIT	157	51	103	.331	47	464	595	5169	1230	160	61	9	399	580	.238	.298	.298	.596	89	-60	-57	100	93	506	.542	150			
TOT	625					4408		41385	10316	1432	605	202	3054	4488	.249	.305	.328	.633								1145			

TEAM	CG	SHO	SV	IP	H	H/G	HR	BB	BB/G	SO	SO/G	ERA	/A	OAVG	OOBA	PR	/A	PF	CPI	FA	E	DP	FW	PW	BW	SBW	DIF
NY	92	18	14	1424.7	1221	7.7	29	327	2.1	551	3.5	2.27	111	.236	.274	68	38	93	98	.968	208	122	1.6	4.3	7.5		7.6
PHI	102	22	5	1387.0	1258	8.2	25	327	2.1	617	4.0	2.46	116	.247	.285	37	60	106	101	.967	212	112	1.4	6.8	-1.4		4.2
STL	66	16	10	1388.7	1257	8.1	29	421	2.7	502	3.3	3.03	91	.246	.296	-51	-41	102	88	.967	221	153	.8	-4.6	-.7		10.5
CIN	94	12	6	1395.3	1363	8.8	20	404	2.6	492	3.2	2.66	94	.261	.304	6	-24	93	111	.962	247	120	-.8	-2.7	10.2		-5.7
CHI	79	15	9	1397.7	1303	8.4	34	374	2.4	654	4.2	2.62	108	.252	.293	12	32	105	105	.959	267	121	-2.0	3.6	-6.5		2.0
BOS	105	22	9	1416.7	1309	8.3	19	371	2.4	593	3.8	2.77	94	.250	.290	-11	-25	97	94	.966	224	122	.6	-2.8	2.3		-4.6
BRO	99	8	9	1416.7	1288	8.2	32	405	2.6	582	3.7	2.78	102	.247	.292	-13	7	105	96	.962	245	102	-.7	.8	-5.6		.0
PIT	84	17	6	1414.7	1318	8.4	14	432	2.7	509	3.2	3.01	92	.252	.298	-48	-38	103	91	.961	251	119	-1.0	-4.3	-6.4		-14.2
TOT	721	130	62	11241.3		8.3			2.5		3.6	2.70		.249	.305					.964	1875	971					

Runs
Burns-NY 103
Groh-Cin 91
Kauff-NY 89
Hornsby-StL 86

Hits
Groh-Cin 182
Burns-NY 180
Roush-Cin 178
Zimmerman-NY 174
Carey-Pit 174

Doubles
Groh-Cin 39
Merkle-Bro-Chi 31
Smith-Bos 31
Cravath-Phi 29
Chase-Cin 28

Triples
Hornsby-StL 17
Cravath-Phi 16
Chase-Cin 15
Roush-Cin 14
Long-StL 14

Home Runs
Robertson-NY 12
Cravath-Phi 12
Hornsby-StL 8

Total Bases
Hornsby-StL 253
Groh-Cin 246
Burns-NY 246
Cravath-Phi 238

Runs Batted In
Zimmerman-NY 102
Chase-Cin 86
Cravath-Phi 83
Stengel-Bro 73
Luderus-Phi 72

Runs Produced
Zimmerman-NY 158
Chase-Cin 153
Kauff-NY 152
Roush-Cin 145
Hornsby-StL 144

Bases On Balls
Burns-NY 75
Groh-Cin 71
Cravath-Phi 70
Luderus-Phi 65
Paskert-Phi 62

Batting Average
Roush-Cin 341
Hornsby-StL 327
Kauff-NY 308
Groh-Cin 304
Burns-NY 302

On Base Percentage
Groh-Cin 385
Hornsby-StL 385
Burns-NY 380
Roush-Cin 379
Kauff-NY 379

Slugging Average
Hornsby-StL 484
Cravath-Phi 473
Roush-Cin 454
Burns-NY 412
Groh-Cin 411

Production
Hornsby-StL 868
Cravath-Phi 842
Roush-Cin 833
Groh-Cin 796
Burns-NY 792

Adjusted Production
Roush-Cin 168
Hornsby-StL 163
Groh-Cin 156
Burns-NY 147
Cravath-Phi 146

Batter Runs
Hornsby-StL 39.6
Cravath-Phi 34.6
Groh-Cin 33.4
Roush-Cin 32.3
Burns-NY 32.2

Adjusted Batter Runs
Hornsby-StL 38.7
Groh-Cin 38.5
Roush-Cin 36.5
Burns-NY 34.1
Cravath-Phi 30.3

Clutch Hitting Index
Zimmerman-NY 171
Ward-Pit 143
Luderus-Phi 143
Deal-Chi 141
Chase-Cin 141

Runs Created
Burns-NY 105
Groh-Cin 102
Hornsby-StL 102
Carey-Pit 94
Roush-Cin 93

Total Average
Hornsby-StL 906
Cravath-Phi 870
Burns-NY 868
Roush-Cin 843
Groh-Cin 815

Stolen Bases
Carey-Pit 46
Burns-NY 40
Kauff-NY 30
Maranville-Bos 27
Baird-Pit-StL 26

Stolen Base Average

Stolen Base Runs

Fielding Runs
Bancroft-Phi 27.3
Fletcher-NY 24.9
Carey-Pit 21.8
Miller-StL 19.1
Maranville-Bos 17.8

Total Player Rating
Hornsby-StL 6.2
Groh-Cin 4.5
Carey-Pit 4.3
Burns-NY 3.8
Roush-Cin 3.4

Wins
Alexander-Phi 30
Toney-Cin 24
Vaughn-Chi 23
Schupp-NY 21
Schneider-Cin 20

Win Percentage
Schupp-NY 750
Sallee-NY 720
Perritt-NY 708
Alexander-Phi 698
Nehf-Bos 680

Games
Douglas-Chi 51
Barnes-Bos 50
Schneider-Cin 46
Alexander-Phi 45
Doak-StL 44

Complete Games
Alexander-Phi 34
Toney-Cin 31
Vaughn-Chi 27
Barnes-Bos 27
Schupp-NY 25

Shutouts
Alexander-Phi 8
Toney-Cin 7
Cooper-Pit 7
Schupp-NY 6

Saves
Sallee-NY 4

Innings Pitched
Alexander-Phi 388
Toney-Cin 340
Schneider-Cin 334
Cooper-Pit 298
Vaughn-Chi 296

Fewest Hits/Game
Schupp-NY 6.68
Anderson-NY 6.78
Nehf-Bos 7.61
Pfeffer-Bro 7.61
Tyler-Bos 7.64

Fewest BB/Game
Alexander-Phi 1.30
Sallee-NY 1.42
Nehf-Bos 1.51
Barnes-Bos 1.53
Douglas-Chi 1.54

Strikeouts
Alexander-Phi 200
Vaughn-Chi 195
Douglas-Chi 151
Schupp-NY 147
Schneider-Cin 138

Strikeouts/Game
Vaughn-Chi 5.93
Schupp-NY 4.86
Alexander-Phi 4.64
Douglas-Chi 4.64
Marquard-Bro 4.52

Wins Above Team
Alexander-Phi 7.9
Vaughn-Chi 6.6
Cooper-Pit 6.5
Nehf-Bos 5.5
Marquard-Bro 5.1

Earned Run Average
Anderson-NY 1.44
Alexander-Phi 1.83
Perritt-NY 1.88
Schupp-NY 1.95
Vaughn-Chi 2.01

Adjusted ERA
Anderson-NY 174
Alexander-Phi 156
Vaughn-Chi 141
Perritt-NY 133
Schupp-NY 129

Opponents' Batting Avg.
Schupp-NY 209
Anderson-NY 209
Nehf-Bos 231
Marquard-Bro 232
Pfeffer-Bro 234

Opponents' On Base Pct.
Anderson-NY 250
Schupp-NY 259
Alexander-Phi 260
Nehf-Bos 263
Barnes-Bos 269

Starter Runs
Alexander-Phi 37.4
Vaughn-Chi 22.8
Anderson-NY 22.6
Schupp-NY 22.6
Schneider-Cin 22.2

Adjusted Starter Runs
Alexander-Phi 44.0
Vaughn-Chi 27.1
Anderson-NY 19.2
Rixey-Phi 18.1
Pfeffer-Bro 17.6

Clutch Pitching Index
Schneider-Cin 145
Vaughn-Chi 119
Perritt-NY 117
Hendrix-Chi 116
Mayer-Phi 114

Relief Runs

Adjusted Relief Runs

Relief Ranking

Total Pitcher Index
Alexander-Phi 6.3
Vaughn-Chi 3.6
Rixey-Phi 2.4
Anderson-NY 1.8
Nehf-Bos 1.8

Total Baseball Ranking
Alexander-Phi 6.3
Hornsby-StL 6.2
Groh-Cin 4.5
Carey-Pit 4.3
Burns-NY 3.8

TEAM	G	W	L	PCT	GB	R	OR	AB	H	2B	3B	HR	BB	SO	AVG	OBP	SLG	PRO	/A	BR	/A	PF	CHI	RC	TA	SB	CS	SBA	SBR
CHI	156	100	54	.649		656	464	5057	1281	152	81	18	522	479	.253	.329	.326	.655	105	36	49	98	108	615	.645	219			
BOS	157	90	62	.592	9	555	454	5048	1243	188	64	14	466	473	.246	.314	.317	.631	98	-12	-58	108	99	555	.580	105			
CLE	156	88	66	.571	12	584	543	4994	1224	218	64	13	549	596	.245	.324	.322	.646	103	21	-60	114	98	595	.637	210			
DET	154	78	75	.510	21.5	639	577	5093	1317	204	76	26	483	476	.259	.328	.344	.672	111	61	74	98	101	631	.647	163			
WAS	157	74	79	.484	25.5	543	566	5142	1238	173	70	4	500	574	.241	.313	.304	.617	93	-34	10	92	101	548	.582	166			
NY	155	71	82	.464	28.5	558	558	5136	1226	173	52	27	496	535	.239	.310	.308	.618	94	-33	-71	107	97	545	.576	136			
STL	155	57	97	.370	43	510	687	5090	1249	183	63	15	405	540	.245	.305	.315	.620	94	-38	-8	95	98	535	.572	157			
PHI	154	55	98	.359	44.5	529	691	5111	1296	177	62	17	435	519	.254	.316	.322	.638	100	-1	35	94	94	565	.584	112			
TOT	622					4540		40671	10074	1468	532	134	3856	4192	.248	.318	.320	.638								1268			

TEAM	CG	SHO	SV	IP	H	H/G	HR	BB	BB/G	SO	SO/G	ERA	/A	OAVG	OOBA	PR	/A	PF	CPI	FA	E	DP	FW	PW	BW	SBW	DIF
CHI	78	22	21	1417.7	1236	7.8	10	413	2.6	517	3.3	2.16	115	.242	.298	79	51	93	105	.967	204	117	2.2	5.7	5.4		9.7
BOS	115	16	7	1422.0	1197	7.6	13	413	2.6	509	3.2	2.20	128	.235	.293	72	97	106	97	.972	183	116	3.7	10.8	-6.4		6.0
CLE	73	20	22	1412.7	1270	8.1	17	438	2.8	451	2.9	2.52	120	.247	.307	22	77	113	99	.964	242	136	-.6	8.6	-6.7		9.7
DET	78	20	15	1395.3	1209	7.8	12	504	3.3	516	3.3	2.56	100	.241	.310	16	0	96	96	.964	234	95	.0	.0	8.2		-6.7
WAS	84	21	10	1415.3	1228	7.8	12	536	3.4	637	4.1	2.77	89	.241	.313	-17	-47	93	90	.961	251	127	-1.2	-5.2	1.1		2.9
NY	87	10	6	1410.3	1280	8.2	29	427	2.7	571	3.6	2.66	108	.249	.307	0	31	107	97	.965	225	129	.6	3.4	-7.9		-1.7
STL	66	12	12	1377.0	1280	8.2	19	537	3.5	429	2.8	3.20	82	.260	.330	-82	-88	98	95	.957	281	139	-3.4	-9.8	-.9		-5.9
PHI	80	8	8	1364.7	1310	8.6	22	562	3.7	516	3.4	3.27	79	.260	.334	-92	-104	97	95	.961	251	106	-1.2	-11.6	3.9		-12.6
TOT	661	129	101	11215.0		8.1			3.1		3.3	2.66		.248	.318					.964	1871	965					

Runs
Bush-Det 112
Cobb-Det 107
Chapman-Cle 98
Jackson-Chi 91
E.Collins-Chi 91

Hits
Cobb-Det 225
Sisler-StL 190
Speaker-Cle 184
Veach-Det 182

Doubles
Cobb-Det 44
Speaker-Cle 42
Veach-Det 31
Sisler-StL 30
Roth-Cle 30

Triples
Cobb-Det 23
Jackson-Chi 17
Judge-Was 15
Chapman-Cle 13

Home Runs
Pipp-NY 9
Veach-Det 8
Cobb-Det 7
Bodie-Phi 7

Total Bases
Cobb-Det 336
Veach-Det 261
Speaker-Cle 254
Sisler-StL 244
Bodie-Phi 233

Runs Batted In
Veach-Det 103
Felsch-Chi 102
Cobb-Det 102
Heilmann-Det 86
Jackson-Chi 75

Runs Produced
Cobb-Det 202
Veach-Det 174
Felsch-Chi 171
Jackson-Chi 161
E.Collins-Chi 158

Bases On Balls
Graney-Cle 94
E.Collins-Chi 89
Hooper-Bos 80
Bush-Det 80
Leibold-Chi 74

Batting Average
Cobb-Det 383
Sisler-StL 353
Speaker-Cle 352
Veach-Det 319
Felsch-Chi 308

On Base Percentage
Cobb-Det 444
Speaker-Cle 432
Veach-Det 393
Sisler-StL 390
E.Collins-Chi 389

Slugging Average
Cobb-Det 571
Speaker-Cle 486
Veach-Det 457
Sisler-StL 453
Jackson-Chi 429

Production
Cobb-Det 1.016
Speaker-Cle 918
Veach-Det 850
Sisler-StL 843
Jackson-Chi 805

Adjusted Production
Cobb-Det 215
Sisler-StL 166
Veach-Det 163
Speaker-Cle 157
Jackson-Chi 149

Batter Runs
Cobb-Det 74.7
Speaker-Cle 51.2
Veach-Det 40.0
Sisler-StL 34.0
Jackson-Chi 28.7

Adjusted Batter Runs
Cobb-Det 76.3
Speaker-Cle 42.7
Veach-Det 41.6
Sisler-StL 37.1
Jackson-Chi 30.2

Clutch Hitting Index
Bates-Phi 156
Felsch-Chi 155
Heilmann-Det 142
Schalk-Chi 141
Roth-Cle 135

Runs Created
Cobb-Det 162
Speaker-Cle 120
Veach-Det 110
Sisler-StL 102
Chapman-Cle 98

Total Average
Cobb-Det 1.256
Speaker-Cle 1.056
Veach-Det 905
Sisler-StL 900
E.Collins-Chi 873

Stolen Bases
Cobb-Det 55
E.Collins-Chi 53
Chapman-Cle 52
Roth-Cle 51
Sisler-StL 37

Stolen Base Average

Stolen Base Runs

Fielding Runs
Chapman-Cle 24.1
Wambsganss-Cle 16.7
Felsch-Chi 15.8
Pratt-StL 14.9
Baker-NY 11.1

Total Player Rating
Cobb-Det 7.9
Chapman-Cle 4.9
Veach-Det 4.3
Speaker-Cle 4.2
Sisler-StL 4.0

Wins
Cicotte-Chi 28
Ruth-Bos 24
Johnson-Was 23
Bagby-Cle 23
Mays-Bos 22

Win Percentage
Russell-Chi 750
Mays-Bos 710
Cicotte-Chi 700
Williams-Chi 680
Ruth-Bos 649

Games
Danforth-Chi 50
Cicotte-Chi 49
Bagby-Cle 49
Sothoron-StL 48

Complete Games
Ruth-Bos 35
Johnson-Was 30
Cicotte-Chi 29
Mays-Bos 27

Shutouts
Coveleski-Cle 9
Johnson-Was 8
Bagby-Cle 8
Cicotte-Chi 7

Saves
Danforth-Chi 9
Bagby-Cle 7
Boland-Det 6
Coumbe-Cle 5

Innings Pitched
Cicotte-Chi 347
Johnson-Was 328
Ruth-Bos 326
Bagby-Cle 321
Coveleski-Cle 298

Fewest Hits/Game
Coveleski-Cle 6.10
Cicotte-Chi 6.38
Ruth-Bos 6.74
Johnson-Was 7.11
Mays-Bos 7.16

Fewest BB/Game
Russell-Chi 1.52
Mogridge-NY 1.79
Cicotte-Chi 1.82
Johnson-Was 1.84
Bagby-Cle 2.05

Strikeouts
Johnson-Was 188
Cicotte-Chi 150
Leonard-Bos 144
Coveleski-Cle 133
Ruth-Bos 128

Strikeouts/Game
Johnson-Was 5.16
Harper-Was 4.98
Bush-Phi 4.67
Leonard-Bos 4.41
Danforth-Chi 4.11

Wins Above Team
Mays-Bos 5.2
Johnson-Was 5.0
Klepfer-Cle 4.6
Davenport-StL 4.2
Cicotte-Chi 3.7

Earned Run Average
Cicotte-Chi 1.53
Mays-Bos 1.74
Coveleski-Cle 1.81
Faber-Chi 1.92
Russell-Chi 1.95

Adjusted ERA
Coveleski-Cle 167
Cicotte-Chi 163
Mays-Bos 162
Bagby-Cle 154
Ruth-Bos 140

Opponents' Batting Avg.
Coveleski-Cle 194
Cicotte-Chi 203
Ruth-Bos 211
Johnson-Was 220
Mays-Bos 221

Opponents' On Base Pct.
Cicotte-Chi 248
Coveleski-Cle 261
Johnson-Was 270
Russell-Chi 279
Mays-Bos 282

Starter Runs
Cicotte-Chi 43.7
Mays-Bos 29.6
Coveleski-Cle 28.2
Bagby-Cle 25.0
Ruth-Bos 23.5

Adjusted Starter Runs
Coveleski-Cle 40.0
Bagby-Cle 37.7
Cicotte-Chi 36.9
Mays-Bos 34.5
Ruth-Bos 29.1

Clutch Pitching Index
Faber-Chi 136
Ayers-Was 128
James-Det 127
Morton-Cle 117
Mitchell-Det 116

Relief Runs

Adjusted Relief Runs

Relief Ranking

Total Pitcher Index
Mays-Bos 6.0
Ruth-Bos 5.8
Bagby-Cle 4.5
Cicotte-Chi 4.3
Coveleski-Cle 3.8

Total Baseball Ranking
Cobb-Det 7.9
Mays-Bos 6.0
Ruth-Bos 5.8
Chapman-Cle 4.9
Bagby-Cle 4.5

TEAM	G	W	L	PCT	GB	R	OR	AB	H	2B	3B	HR	BB	SO	AVG	OBP	SLG	PRO	/A	BR	/A	PF	CHI	RC	TA	SB	CS	SBA	SBR
CHI	131	84	45	.651		538	393	4325	1147	164	54	20	358	343	.265	.325	.342	.667	109	47	36	102	102	527	.637	159			
NY	124	71	53	.573	10.5	480	415	4164	1081	150	53	13	271	365	.260	.310	.330	.640	101	1	11	98	106	459	.587	130			
CIN	129	68	60	.531	15.5	530	496	4265	1185	165	84	15	304	303	.278	.330	.366	.696	118	86	99	97	96	551	.658	128			
PIT	126	65	60	.520	17	466	412	4091	1016	107	72	15	371	285	.248	.315	.321	.636	99	1	-26	106	102	467	.620	200			
BRO	126	57	69	.452	25.5	360	463	4212	1052	121	62	10	212	326	.250	.291	.315	.606	90	-52	-58	101	91	411	.534	113			
PHI	125	55	68	.447	26	430	507	4192	1022	158	28	25	346	400	.244	.305	.313	.618	94	-28	-69	109	100	432	.560	97			
BOS	124	53	71	.427	28.5	424	469	4162	1014	107	59	13	350	438	.244	.307	.307	.614	93	-31	-2	94	99	426	.552	83			
STL	131	51	78	.395	33	454	527	4369	1066	147	64	27	329	461	.244	.301	.325	.626	96	-20	11	93	99	461	.573	119			
TOT	508					3682		33780	8583	1119	476	138	2541	2921	.254	.311	.328	.638								1029			

TEAM	CG	SHO	SV	IP	H	H/G	HR	BB	BB/G	SO	SO/G	ERA	/A	OAVG	OOBA	PR	/A	PF	CPI	FA	E	DP	FW	PW	BW	SBW	DIF
CHI	92	25	8	1197.0	1050	7.9	13	296	2.2	472	3.5	2.18	124	.241	.281	77	70	98	105	.966	188	91	.1	7.8	4.0		7.6
NY	74	18	11	1112.7	1002	8.1	20	228	1.8	330	2.7	2.64	100	.246	.278	15	1	96	89	.971	152	78	2.4	.1	1.2		5.2
CIN	84	14	6	1142.7	1136	8.9	19	381	3.0	321	2.5	3.00	89	.265	.315	-30	-43	96	105	.964	192	127	-.1	-4.8	11.0		-2.1
PIT	85	12	7	1143.7	1005	7.9	13	299	2.4	367	2.9	2.48	117	.242	.283	35	52	105	94	.966	179	108	.7	5.8	-2.9		-1.1
BRO	85	17	2	1127.0	1024	8.2	22	320	2.6	395	3.2	2.81	102	.248	.293	-6	7	104	93	.963	193	74	-.2	.8	-6.5		-.1
PHI	78	10	6	1137.0	1086	8.6	22	312	2.5	312	2.5	3.15	98	.257	.306	-49	-9	111	94	.961	211	91	-1.3	-1.0	-7.7		3.6
BOS	96	13	0	1116.3	1111	9.0	14	277	2.2	340	2.7	2.90	90	.265	.302	-17	-34	95	99	.965	184	89	.4	-3.8	-.2		-5.4
STL	72	3	5	1192.7	1148	8.7	16	352	2.7	361	2.7	2.96	89	.259	.304	-25	-43	95	97	.962	220	116	-1.9	-4.8	1.2		-8.0
TOT	666	112	45	9169.0		8.4			2.5		2.8	2.76		.254	.311					.965	1519	774					

Runs
Groh-Cin 86
Burns-NY 80
Flack-Chi 74
Hollocher-Chi 72

Hits
Hollocher-Chi 161
Groh-Cin 158
Roush-Cin 145
Youngs-NY 143
Merkle-Chi 143

Doubles
Groh-Cin 28
Mann-Chi 27
Cravath-Phi 27
Meusel-Phi 25
Merkle-Chi 25

Triples
Daubert-Bro 15
Wickland-Bos 13
S.Magee-Cin 13
L.Magee-Cin 13

Home Runs
Cravath-Phi 8
Williams-Phi 6
Cruise-StL 6

Total Bases
Hollocher-Chi 202
Roush-Cin 198
Groh-Cin 195
Mann-Chi 188
Merkle-Chi 187

Runs Batted In
S.Magee-Cin 76
Cutshaw-Pit 68
Luderus-Phi 67
Smith-Bos 65
Merkle-Chi 65

Runs Produced
Burns-NY 127
Paskert-Chi 126
Mann-Chi 122
Groh-Cin 122
S.Magee-Cin 120

Bases On Balls
Carey-Pit 62
Flack-Chi 56
Groh-Cin 54
Cravath-Phi 54
Bancroft-Phi 54

Batting Average
Wheat-Bro 335
Roush-Cin 333
Groh-Cin 320
Hollocher-Chi 316
Daubert-Bro 308

On Base Percentage
Groh-Cin 395
Hollocher-Chi 379
Smith-Bos 373
S.Magee-Cin 370
Wheat-Bro 369

Slugging Average
Roush-Cin 455
Daubert-Bro 429
Hornsby-StL 416
S.Magee-Cin 415
Wickland-Bos 398

Production
Roush-Cin 823
Groh-Cin 791
Daubert-Bro 789
S.Magee-Cin 785
Hollocher-Chi 775

Adjusted Production
Roush-Cin 155
Groh-Cin 146
S.Magee-Cin 143
Hornsby-StL 142
Wickland-Bos 142

Batter Runs
Groh-Cin 26.4
Roush-Cin 24.3
Hollocher-Chi 22.9
S.Magee-Cin 19.2
Daubert-Bro 18.2

Adjusted Batter Runs
Groh-Cin 28.1
Roush-Cin 25.8
Hollocher-Chi 21.7
S.Magee-Cin 20.5
Hornsby-StL 18.9

Clutch Hitting Index
S.Magee-Cin 170
Konetchy-Bos 160
Smith-Bos 157
Paulette-StL 142
Luderus-Phi 140

Runs Created
Hollocher-Chi 84
Groh-Cin 83
Roush-Cin 77
Carey-Pit 74
Burns-NY 73

Total Average
Roush-Cin 848
Carey-Pit 844
Wickland-Bos 812
Burns-NY 809
S.Magee-Cin 804

Stolen Bases
Carey-Pit 58
Burns-NY 40
Hollocher-Chi 26
Cutshaw-Pit 25
Baird-StL 25

Stolen Base Average

Stolen Base Runs

Fielding Runs
Fletcher-NY 21.8
Bancroft-Phi 17.6
Carey-Pit 14.9
Fisher-StL 11.0
Myers-Bro 9.8

Total Player Rating
Groh-Cin 3.5
Hornsby-StL 3.2
Fisher-StL 2.7
Smith-Bos 2.7
Roush-Cin 2.6

Wins
Vaughn-Chi 22
Hendrix-Chi 20
Tyler-Chi 19
Grimes-Bro 19
Cooper-Pit 19

Win Percentage
Hendrix-Chi 741
Tyler-Chi 704
Mayer-Phi-Pit 696
Vaughn-Chi 688
Grimes-Bro 679

Games
Grimes-Bro 40
Cooper-Pit 38
Eller-Cin 37

Complete Games
Nehf-Bos 28
Vaughn-Chi 27
Cooper-Pit 26
Tyler-Chi 22
Hendrix-Chi 21

Shutouts
Vaughn-Chi 8
Tyler-Chi 8
Grimes-Bro 7
Perritt-NY 6

Saves
Toney-Cin-NY 3
Oeschger-Phi 3
Cooper-Pit 3
Anderson-NY 3

Innings Pitched
Vaughn-Chi 290
Nehf-Bos 284
Cooper-Pit 273
Grimes-Bro 270
Tyler-Chi 269

Fewest Hits/Game
Vaughn-Chi 6.70
Grimes-Bro 7.00
Cooper-Pit 7.22
Tyler-Chi 7.29
Oeschger-Phi 7.78

Fewest BB/Game
Sallee-NY 82
Perritt-NY 1.47
Toney-Cin-NY 1.54
Demaree-NY 1.58
Packard-StL 1.63

Strikeouts
Vaughn-Chi 148
Cooper-Pit 117
Grimes-Bro 113
Tyler-Chi 102
Nehf-Bos 96

Strikeouts/Game
Vaughn-Chi 4.59
Cooper-Pit 3.86
Grimes-Bro 3.77
Cheney-Bro 3.72
May-StL 3.59

Wins Above Team
Grimes-Bro 6.6
Mayer-Phi-Pit 5.0
Hendrix-Chi 4.1
Hamilton-Pit 3.0
Cooper-Pit 2.5

Earned Run Average
Vaughn-Chi 1.74
Tyler-Chi 2.01
Cooper-Pit 2.11
Douglas-Chi 2.12
Grimes-Bro 2.13

Adjusted ERA
Vaughn-Chi 156
Cooper-Pit 137
Tyler-Chi 135
Grimes-Bro 135
Douglas-Chi 128

Opponents' Batting Avg.
Vaughn-Chi 208
Grimes-Bro 216
Cooper-Pit 223
Tyler-Chi 226
Oeschger-Phi 238

Opponents' On Base Pct.
Sallee-NY 252
Vaughn-Chi 261
Grimes-Bro 269
Perritt-NY 270
Tyler-Chi 272

Starter Runs
Vaughn-Chi 33.0
Tyler-Chi 22.6
Cooper-Pit 19.8
Grimes-Bro 18.9
Hamilton-Pit 11.6

Adjusted Starter Runs
Vaughn-Chi 31.4
Cooper-Pit 23.6
Grimes-Bro 22.2
Tyler-Chi 21.1
Hogg-Phi 13.9

Clutch Pitching Index
Bressler-Cin 123
Mayer-Phi-Pit 117
Schneider-Cin 113
Eller-Cin 113
Demaree-NY 112

Relief Runs

Adjusted Relief Runs
Davis-Phi 0

Relief Ranking
Davis-Phi 0

Total Pitcher Index
Vaughn-Chi 4.2
Grimes-Bro 3.0
Tyler-Chi 3.0
Cooper-Pit 2.9
Hogg-Phi 2.3

Total Baseball Ranking
Vaughn-Chi 4.2
Groh-Cin 3.5
Hornsby-StL 3.2
Grimes-Bro 3.0
Tyler-Chi 3.0

TEAM	G	W	L	PCT	GB	R	OR	AB	H	2B	3B	HR	BB	SO	AVG	OBP	SLG	PRO	/A	BR	/A	PF	CHI	RC	TA	SB	CS	SBA	SBR
BOS	126	75	51	.595		474	380	3982	990	159	54	15	406	324	.249	.322	.327	.649	101	5	25	95	105	465	.617	110			
CLE	129	73	54	.575	2.5	504	447	4166	1084	176	67	9	492	386	.260	.344	.341	.685	112	68	29	108	93	552	.688	165			
WAS	130	72	56	.563	4	461	412	4472	1144	156	48	5	376	361	.256	.318	.316	.634	96	-20	-40	104	99	493	.589	137			
NY	126	60	63	.488	13.5	493	475	4224	1085	160	45	20	367	370	.257	.320	.330	.651	101	2	27	95	105	482	.597	88			
STL	123	58	64	.475	15	426	448	4019	1040	152	40	5	397	340	.259	.331	.320	.651	102	11	14	99	92	476	.623	138			
CHI	124	57	67	.460	17	457	446	4132	1057	136	54	9	375	358	.256	.322	.321	.643	99	-4	-6	101	101	470	.600	116			
DET	128	55	71	.437	20	476	557	4262	1063	141	56	13	452	380	.249	.325	.318	.643	99	-1	14	97	101	488	.610	123			
PHI	130	52	76	.406	24	412	538	4278	1039	124	44	22	343	485	.243	.303	.308	.611	89	-58	-76	104	101	431	.546	83			
TOT	508					3703		33535	8502	1204	408	98	3208	3004	.254	.323	.323	.646								960			

TEAM	CG	SHO	SV	IP	H	H/G	HR	BB	BB/G	SO	SO/G	ERA	/A	OAVG	OOBA	PR	/A	PF	CPI	FA	E	DP	FW	PW	BW	SBW	DIF
BOS	105	26	2	1123.7	931	7.5	9	380	3.0	392	3.1	2.31	111	.233	.300	57	32	93	94	.971	152	89	2.6	3.6	2.8		3.1
CLE	78	5	13	1158.0	1126	8.8	9	343	2.7	364	2.8	2.64	112	.263	.317	16	39	107	105	.962	207	82	-.9	4.3	3.2		2.8
WAS	75	19	8	1228.3	1021	7.5	10	395	2.9	505	3.7	2.14	133	.234	.297	85	97	103	100	.960	226	95	-2.1	10.8	-4.5		3.7
NY	59	8	13	1156.0	1103	8.6	25	463	3.6	369	2.9	3.03	86	.259	.332	-33	-54	94	101	.970	161	137	2.0	-6.0	3.0		-.5
STL	67	8	8	1112.3	993	8.0	11	402	3.3	346	2.8	2.75	101	.247	.315	2	1	100	94	.963	190	86	.2	.1	1.6		-4.9
CHI	76	9	8	1118.7	1092	8.8	9	300	2.4	349	2.8	2.69	103	.264	.313	10	10	100	100	.967	169	81	1.5	1.1	-.7		-7.0
DET	74	8	7	1151.7	1130	8.8	10	437	3.4	371	2.9	3.40	80	.265	.333	-80	-85	99	90	.960	212	77	-1.2	-9.5	1.6		1.1
PHI	80	13	9	1152.3	1105	8.6	13	479	3.7	279	2.2	3.22	93	.260	.335	-57	-29	108	95	.959	228	136	-2.2	-3.2	-8.5		1.9
TOT	614	96	68	9201.0		8.3			3.1		2.9	2.77		.254	.323					.964	1545	800					

Runs
Chapman-Cle	84
Cobb-Det	83
Hooper-Bos	81
Bush-Det	74
Speaker-Cle	73

Hits
Burns-Phi	178
Cobb-Det	161
Sisler-StL	154
Baker-NY	154
Speaker-Cle	150

Doubles
Speaker-Cle	33
Ruth-Bos	26
Hooper-Bos	26
Baker-NY	24

Triples
Cobb-Det	14
Veach-Det	13
Hooper-Bos	13
Roth-Cle	12

Home Runs
Walker-Phi	11
Ruth-Bos	11
Burns-Phi	6
Baker-NY	6

Total Bases
Burns-Phi	236
Cobb-Det	217
Baker-NY	206
Speaker-Cle	205
Sisler-StL	199

Runs Batted In
Veach-Det	78
Burns-Phi	70
Wood-Cle	66
Ruth-Bos	66
Cobb-Det	64

Runs Produced
Cobb-Det	144
Veach-Det	134
Speaker-Cle	134
Burns-Phi	125
Hooper-Bos	124

Bases On Balls
Chapman-Cle	84
Bush-Det	79
Hooper-Bos	75
E.Collins-Chi	73
Shotton-Was	67

Batting Average
Cobb-Det	.382
Burns-Phi	.352
Sisler-StL	.341
Speaker-Cle	.318
Baker-NY	.306

On Base Percentage
Cobb-Det	.440
E.Collins-Chi	.407
Speaker-Cle	.403
Sisler-StL	.400
Hooper-Bos	.391

Slugging Average
Cobb-Det	.515
Burns-Phi	.467
Sisler-StL	.440
Speaker-Cle	.435
Walker-Phi	.423

Production
Cobb-Det	.955
Burns-Phi	.857
Sisler-StL	.841
Speaker-Cle	.839
Hooper-Bos	.796

Adjusted Production
Cobb-Det	195
Sisler-StL	155
Burns-Phi	152
Hooper-Bos	147
Speaker-Cle	141

Batter Runs
Cobb-Det	44.0
Ruth-Bos	34.8
Burns-Phi	32.8
Speaker-Cle	31.3
Sisler-StL	28.8

Adjusted Batter Runs
Cobb-Det	45.5
Ruth-Bos	36.5
Burns-Phi	30.7
Sisler-StL	29.2
Hooper-Bos	27.7

Clutch Hitting Index
McInnis-Bos	159
Demmitt-StL	148
Gandil-Chi	146
Roth-Cle	145
Shanks-Was	144

Runs Created
Cobb-Det	104
Burns-Phi	93
Speaker-Cle	92
Sisler-StL	90
Hooper-Bos	85

Total Average
Cobb-Det	1.131
Sisler-StL	.970
Speaker-Cle	.931
Roth-Cle	.929
Hooper-Bos	.875

Stolen Bases
Sisler-StL	45
Roth-Cle	35
Cobb-Det	34
Chapman-Cle	30
Speaker-Cle	27

Stolen Base Average

Stolen Base Runs

Fielding Runs
Peckinpaugh-NY	26.8
Scott-Bos	16.0
Gedeon-StL	15.6
McAvoy-Phi	14.3
Pratt-NY	12.6

Total Player Rating
Cobb-Det	3.9
Ruth-Bos	3.8
Sisler-StL	3.4
Baker-NY	3.4
Burns-Phi	3.1

Wins
Johnson-Was	23
Coveleski-Cle	22
Mays-Bos	21
Perry-Phi	20
Bagby-Cle	17

Win Percentage
Jones-Bos	.762
Johnson-Was	.639
Coveleski-Cle	.629
Mays-Bos	.618
Shaw-Was	.571

Games
Mogridge-NY	45
Bagby-Cle	45
Perry-Phi	44
Shaw-Was	41
Ayers-Was	40

Complete Games
Perry-Phi	30
Mays-Bos	30
Johnson-Was	29
Bush-Bos	26
Coveleski-Cle	25

Shutouts
Mays-Bos	8
Johnson-Was	8
Bush-Bos	7
Jones-Bos	5

Saves
Mogridge-NY	7
Bagby-Cle	6
Russell-NY	4
Geary-Phi	4

Innings Pitched
Perry-Phi	332
Johnson-Was	325
Coveleski-Cle	311
Mays-Bos	293
Bush-Bos	273

Fewest Hits/Game
Sothoron-StL	6.55
Johnson-Was	6.67
Harper-Was	6.71
Ruth-Bos	6.78
Mays-Bos	7.06

Fewest BB/Game
Cicotte-Chi	1.35
Mogridge-NY	1.62
Benz-Chi	1.64
Enzmann-Cle	1.91
Johnson-Was	1.94

Strikeouts
Johnson-Was	162
Shaw-Was	129
Bush-Bos	125
Morton-Cle	123
Mays-Bos	114

Strikeouts/Game
Morton-Cle	5.15
Shaw-Was	4.82
Johnson-Was	4.49
Bush-Bos	4.12
Love-NY	3.73

Wins Above Team
Jones-Bos	4.8
Perry-Phi	4.7
Johnson-Was	4.1
Boland-Det	3.6
Wright-StL	3.2

Earned Run Average
Johnson-Was	1.27
Coveleski-Cle	1.82
Sothoron-StL	1.94
Perry-Phi	1.98
Bush-Bos	2.11

Adjusted ERA
Johnson-Was	224
Coveleski-Cle	162
Perry-Phi	151
Sothoron-StL	143
Harper-Was	131

Opponents' Batting Avg.
Sothoron-StL	.205
Johnson-Was	.210
Harper-Was	.212
Ruth-Bos	.214
Mays-Bos	.221

Opponents' On Base Pct.
Johnson-Was	.253
Ruth-Bos	.267
Sothoron-StL	.267
Coveleski-Cle	.272
Mays-Bos	.277

Starter Runs
Johnson-Was	54.0
Coveleski-Cle	32.7
Perry-Phi	29.1
Bush-Bos	20.0
Sothoron-StL	19.3

Adjusted Starter Runs
Johnson-Was	57.0
Coveleski-Cle	39.0
Perry-Phi	37.1
Sothoron-StL	19.2
Harper-Was	18.3

Clutch Pitching Index
Perry-Phi	124
Mogridge-NY	122
Coumbe-Cle	119
Russell-NY	118
Shellenback-Chi	116

Relief Runs
Houck-StL	3.1

Adjusted Relief Runs
Houck-StL	3.1

Relief Ranking
Houck-StL	2.5

Total Pitcher Index
Johnson-Was	8.3
Coveleski-Cle	4.4
Perry-Phi	3.8
Mays-Bos	3.5
Bush-Bos	2.7

Total Baseball Ranking
Johnson-Was	8.3
Ruth-Bos	4.6
Coveleski-Cle	4.4
Cobb-Det	3.9
Perry-Phi	3.8

TEAM	G	W	L	PCT	GB	R	OR	AB	H	2B	3B	HR	BB	SO	AVG	OBP	SLG	PRO	/A	BR	/A	PF	CHI	RC	TA	SB	CS	SBA	SBR
CIN	140	96	44	.686		577	401	4577	1204	135	84	19	405	368	.263	.327	.342	.669	107	43	15	105	103	560	.636	143			
NY	140	87	53	.621	9	605	470	4664	1254	204	64	40	328	408	.269	.322	.366	.688	112	64	65	100	105	587	.653	157			
CHI	140	75	65	.536	21	454	407	4581	1174	166	58	21	298	350	.256	.308	.332	.640	98	-13	-15	100	93	505	.590	150			
PIT	139	71	68	.511	24.5	472	466	4538	1132	130	82	17	344	381	.249	.306	.325	.631	95	-24	-48	105	99	498	.599	196			
BRO	141	69	71	.493	27	525	513	4844	1272	167	66	25	258	304	.263	.304	.340	.644	99	-12	20	94	103	525	.572	112			
BOS	140	57	82	.410	38.5	465	563	4746	1201	142	62	24	355	481	.253	.311	.324	.635	96	-16	-4	98	91	520	.587	145			
STL	138	54	83	.394	40.5	463	552	4588	1175	163	52	18	304	415	.256	.305	.326	.631	95	-27	0	94	98	491	.576	148			
PHI	138	47	90	.343	47.5	510	699	4746	1191	208	50	42	323	469	.251	.303	.342	.645	99	-8	-27	104	100	521	.588	114			
TOT	558					4071		37284	9603	1315	518	206	2615	3277	.258	.311	.337	.648								1165		

TEAM	CG	SHO	SV	IP	H	H/G	HR	BB	BB/G	SO	SO/G	ERA	/A	OAVG	OOBA	PR	/A	PF	CPI	FA	E	DP	FW	PW	BW	SBW	DIF
CIN	89	23	9	1271.3	1104	7.8	21	298	2.1	407	2.9	2.23	132	.239	.279	96	100	101	104	.974	151	98	2.6	11.1	1.7		10.6
NY	72	11	13	1255.7	1153	8.3	34	305	2.2	340	2.4	2.70	104	.250	.288	29	14	96	99	.964	216	96	-1.1	1.6	7.2		9.3
CHI	80	21	5	1263.0	1127	8.0	14	294	2.1	495	3.5	2.21	131	.244	.282	98	95	99	108	.969	185	87	.7	10.6	-1.7		-4.6
PIT	91	17	4	1248.7	1113	8.0	23	263	1.9	391	2.8	2.88	106	.244	.276	4	24	105	82	.970	165	89	1.8	2.7	-5.3		2.3
BRO	98	12	1	1279.7	1256	8.8	21	292	2.1	476	3.3	2.73	100	.262	.296	26	0	94	104	.963	219	84	-1.3	.0	2.2		-1.9
BOS	79	5	9	1269.0	1313	9.3	29	337	2.4	374	2.7	3.17	92	.273	.310	-36	-35	100	103	.966	204	111	-.4	-3.9	-.4		-7.7
STL	55	6	8	1215.3	1146	8.5	25	415	3.1	414	3.1	3.23	87	.255	.308	-42	-56	97	93	.963	214	112	-1.0	-6.2	.0		-7.3
PHI	93	6	2	1251.0	1391	10.0	40	408	2.9	397	2.9	4.17	76	.287	.331	-175	-140	109	93	.963	218	112	-1.2	-15.6	-3.0		-1.7
TOT	657	101	51	10053.7		8.6			2.3		2.9	2.91		.258	.311					.967	1572	789					

Runs
Burns-NY	86
Groh-Cin	79
Daubert-Cin	79
Rath-Cin	77

Hits
Olson-Bro	164
Hornsby-StL	163
Roush-Cin	162
Burns-NY	162

Doubles
Youngs-NY	31
Luderus-Phi	30
Burns-NY	30
Kauff-NY	27
Meusel-Phi	26

Triples
Southworth-Pit	14
Myers-Bro	14
Roush-Cin	13

Home Runs
Cravath-Phi	12
Kauff-NY	10
Williams-Phi	9
Hornsby-StL	8
Doyle-NY	7

Total Bases
Myers-Bro	223
Hornsby-StL	220
Wheat-Bro	219
Roush-Cin	216
Burns-NY	216

Runs Batted In
Myers-Bro	73
Roush-Cin	71
Hornsby-StL	71
Kauff-NY	67
Groh-Cin	63

Runs Produced
Roush-Cin	141
Groh-Cin	137
Hornsby-StL	131

Bases On Balls
Burns-NY	82
Rath-Cin	64
Groh-Cin	56
Luderus-Phi	54
Boeckel-Pit-Bos	53

Batting Average
Roush-Cin	.321
Hornsby-StL	.318
Youngs-NY	.311
Groh-Cin	.310
Stock-StL	.307

On Base Percentage
Burns-NY	.396
Groh-Cin	.392
Hornsby-StL	.384
Youngs-NY	.384
Roush-Cin	.380

Slugging Average
Myers-Bro	.436
Groh-Cin	.431
Hornsby-StL	.430
Roush-Cin	.429
Kauff-NY	.422

Production
Groh-Cin	.823
Hornsby-StL	.814
Roush-Cin	.809
Burns-NY	.801
Youngs-NY	.799

Adjusted Production
Hornsby-StL	153
Burns-NY	141
Myers-Bro	141
Youngs-NY	141
Groh-Cin	140

Batter Runs
Cravath-Phi	32.2
Burns-NY	30.0
Hornsby-StL	28.5
Groh-Cin	27.4
Roush-Cin	26.6

Adjusted Batter Runs
Hornsby-StL	31.7
Cravath-Phi	31.2
Burns-NY	30.2
Youngs-NY	25.4
Groh-Cin	24.6

Clutch Hitting Index
Kopf-Cin	146
Zimmerman-NY	141
Merkle-Chi	139
Neale-Cin	138
Deal-Chi	127

Runs Created
Burns-NY	98
Hornsby-StL	90
Roush-Cin	88
Youngs-NY	85
Groh-Cin	83

Total Average
Burns-NY	.909
Groh-Cin	.887
Youngs-NY	.846
Hornsby-StL	.837
Roush-Cin	.830

Stolen Bases
Burns-NY	40
Cutshaw-Pit	36
Bigbee-Pit	31
Smith-StL	30

Stolen Base Average

Stolen Base Runs

Fielding Runs
Maranville-Bos	29.0
Fletcher-NY	26.8
Rath-Cin	13.4
Bigbee-Pit	10.8
Blackburne-Bos-Phi	10.1

Total Player Rating
Maranville-Bos	4.3
Hornsby-StL	4.3
Groh-Cin	3.3
Fletcher-NY	3.1
Stock-StL	3.0

Wins
Barnes-NY	25
Vaughn-Chi	21
Sallee-Cin	21

Win Percentage
Ruether-Cin	.760
Sallee-Cin	.750
Barnes-NY	.735
Eller-Cin	.679
Adams-Pit	.630

Games
Tuero-StL	45
Meadows-StL-Phi	40
Vaughn-Chi	38
Eller-Cin	38
Barnes-NY	38

Complete Games
Cooper-Pit	27
Pfeffer-Bro	26
Vaughn-Chi	25
Rudolph-Bos	24

Shutouts
Alexander-Chi	9
Eller-Cin	7
Adams-Pit	6
Fisher-Cin	5

Saves
Tuero-StL	4

Innings Pitched
Vaughn-Chi	307
Barnes-NY	296
Cooper-Pit	287
Rudolph-Bos	274
Nehf-Bos-NY	271

Fewest Hits/Game
Alexander-Chi	6.89
Cooper-Pit	7.18
Ruether-Cin	7.22
Carlson-Pit	7.28
Adams-Pit	7.29

Fewest BB/Game
Adams-Pit	.79
Sallee-Cin	.79
Barnes-NY	1.06
Cadore-Bro	1.40
Alexander-Chi	1.46

Strikeouts
Vaughn-Chi	141
Eller-Cin	137
Alexander-Chi	121
Meadows-StL-Phi	116
Cooper-Pit	106

Strikeouts/Game
Eller-Cin	4.97
Alexander-Chi	4.63
Meadows-StL-Phi	4.18
Vaughn-Chi	4.13
Grimes-Bro	4.08

Wins Above Team
Barnes-NY	6.2
Nehf-Bos-NY	4.0
Adams-Pit	3.8
Ruether-Cin	3.4
Sallee-Cin	3.4

Earned Run Average
Alexander-Chi	1.72
Vaughn-Chi	1.79
Ruether-Cin	1.81
Toney-NY	1.84
Adams-Pit	1.98

Adjusted ERA
Alexander-Chi	168
Ruether-Cin	162
Vaughn-Chi	162
Adams-Pit	154
Toney-NY	153

Opponents' Batting Avg.
Alexander-Chi	.211
Adams-Pit	.220
Ruether-Cin	.223
Cooper-Pit	.225
Nehf-Bos-NY	.225

Opponents' On Base Pct.
Adams-Pit	.235
Alexander-Chi	.241
Barnes-NY	.255
Miller-Pit	.263
Fisher-Cin	.264

Starter Runs
Vaughn-Chi	38.3
Alexander-Chi	31.0
Ruether-Cin	29.6
Adams-Pit	27.1
Rudolph-Bos	22.7

Adjusted Starter Runs
Vaughn-Chi	37.5
Adams-Pit	31.4
Ruether-Cin	30.5
Alexander-Chi	30.4
Rudolph-Bos	22.7

Clutch Pitching Index
Rudolph-Bos	142
Smith-Bro	141
Martin-Chi	123
Jacobs-Phi-StL	122
Toney-NY	121

Relief Runs

Adjusted Relief Runs

Relief Ranking

Total Pitcher Index
Alexander-Chi	4.3
Vaughn-Chi	4.1
Ruether-Cin	3.9
Adams-Pit	3.2
Rudolph-Bos	3.0

Total Baseball Ranking
Maranville-Bos	4.3
Hornsby-StL	4.3
Alexander-Chi	4.3
Vaughn-Chi	4.1
Ruether-Cin	3.9

TEAM	G	W	L	PCT	GB	R	OR	AB	H	2B	3B	HR	BB	SO	AVG	OBP	SLG	PRO	/A	BR	/A	PF	CHI	RC	TA	SB	CS	SBA	SBR
CHI	140	88	52	.629		667	534	4675	1343	218	70	25	427	358	.287	.351	.380	.731	111	69	41	105	103	674	.716	150			
CLE	139	84	55	.604	3.5	636	537	4565	1268	254	71	25	498	367	.278	.354	.381	.735	112	78	40	107	97	667	.724	113			
NY	141	80	59	.576	7.5	578	506	4775	1275	193	49	45	386	429	.267	.326	.356	.682	97	-20	-51	106	103	590	.634	101			
DET	140	80	60	.571	8	618	578	4665	1319	222	84	23	391	427	.283	.346	.353	.679	110	60	97	97	97	572	.703	121			
STL	140	67	72	.482	20.5	533	567	4671	1234	176	73	31	391	443	.264	.326	.353	.679	96	-24	-6	97	97	572	.625	74			
BOS	138	66	71	.482	20.5	564	552	4548	1188	181	49	33	471	411	.261	.336	.344	.680	97	-10	38	91	101	577	.652	108			
WAS	142	56	84	.400	32	533	570	4757	1238	177	63	24	416	511	.260	.325	.339	.664	92	-46	-34	98	99	571	.628	142			
PHI	140	36	104	.257	52	457	742	4730	1156	171	71	35	349	565	.244	.300	.333	.633	83	-109	-141	106	100	503	.575	103			
TOT	560					4586		37386	10021	1592	530	241	3367	3511	.268	.333	.359	.692								912			

TEAM	CG	SHO	SV	IP	H	H/G	HR	BB	BB/G	SO	SO/G	ERA	/A	OAVG	OOBA	PR	/A	PF	CPI	FA	E	DP	FW	PW	BW	SBW	DIF
CHI	88	14	3	1263.7	1245	8.9	25	342	2.4	468	3.3	3.04	108	.265	.315	24	32	102	94	.969	176	116	1.7	3.3	4.3		8.7
CLE	80	10	10	1239.7	1242	9.0	19	362	2.6	432	3.1	2.92	115	.268	.321	40	60	104	102	.965	201	102	.0	6.3	4.2		4.0
NY	85	14	7	1287.7	1143	8.0	47	433	3.0	500	3.5	2.78	120	.245	.309	61	80	104	96	.968	193	108	.6	8.4	-5.3		6.9
DET	85	10	4	1260.3	1254	9.0	35	431	3.1	428	3.1	3.30	90	.267	.328	-12	-46	92	96	.964	205	81	-.2	-4.8	10.1		4.9
STL	78	14	4	1252.7	1255	9.0	35	421	3.0	415	3.0	3.13	100	.268	.329	11	0	98	102	.963	215	98	-.9	.0	-.6		-1.0
BOS	89	15	8	1220.3	1251	9.2	16	420	3.1	380	2.8	3.30	89	.273	.334	-11	-49	91	97	.975	140	118	4.0	-5.1	4.0		-5.4
WAS	68	13	10	1274.3	1237	8.7	20	451	3.2	536	3.8	3.01	106	.262	.326	28	23	99	99	.960	227	86	-1.6	2.4	-3.6		-11.2
PHI	72	1	3	1234.0	1371	10.0	44	503	3.7	417	3.0	4.26	85	.289	.357	-143	-90	112	94	.956	257	96	-3.6	-9.4	-14.7		-6.2
TOT	645	91	49	10032.7		9.0			3.0		3.2	3.21		.268	.333					.965	1614	805					

Runs
Ruth-Bos 103
Sisler-StL 96
Cobb-Det 92
Weaver-Chi 89
Peckinpaugh-NY 89

Hits
Veach-Det 191
Cobb-Det 191
Jackson-Chi 181
Sisler-StL 180
Rice-Was 179

Doubles
Veach-Det 45
Speaker-Cle 38
Cobb-Det 36
O'Neill-Cle 35

Triples
Veach-Det 17
Sisler-StL 15
Heilmann-Det 15
Jackson-Chi 14
Cobb-Det 13

Home Runs
Ruth-Bos 29
Walker-Phi 10
Sisler-StL 10
Baker-NY 10
Smith-Cle 9

Total Bases
Ruth-Bos 284
Veach-Det 279
Sisler-StL 271
Jackson-Chi 261

Runs Batted In
Ruth-Bos 114
Veach-Det 101
Jackson-Chi 96
Heilmann-Det 93
Lewis-NY 89

Runs Produced
Ruth-Bos 188
Veach-Det 185
Sisler-StL 169
Jackson-Chi 168
E.Collins-Chi 163

Bases On Balls
Graney-Cle 105
Ruth-Bos 101
Judge-Was 81
Hooper-Bos 79
Bush-Det 75

Batting Average
Cobb-Det .... .384
Veach-Det .... .355
Sisler-StL .... .352
Jackson-Chi ...... .351
Tobin-StL .... .327

On Base Percentage
Ruth-Bos .... .456
Cobb-Det .... .429
Jackson-Chi ...... .422
Leibold-Chi ...... .404
E.Collins-Chi .... .400

Slugging Average
Ruth-Bos .... .657
Sisler-StL .... .530
Veach-Det .... .519
Cobb-Det .... .515
Jackson-Chi ...... .506

Production
Ruth-Bos 1.114
Cobb-Det .... .944
Jackson-Chi ..... .928
Sisler-StL ...... .921
Veach-Det .... .916

Adjusted Production
Ruth-Bos 231
Cobb-Det 176
Veach-Det 167
Sisler-StL 162
Jackson-Chi 153

Batter Runs
Ruth-Bos 66.5
Jackson-Chi 41.7
Cobb-Det 41.6
Veach-Det 37.7
Sisler-StL 35.8

Adjusted Batter Runs
Ruth-Bos 71.5
Cobb-Det 45.5
Veach-Det 41.9
Jackson-Chi 38.6
Sisler-StL 37.6

Clutch Hitting Index
Lewis-NY 152
Gardner-Cle 143
Jones-Det 141
Felsch-Chi 140
Veach-Det 135

Runs Created
Ruth-Bos 138
Cobb-Det 115
Jackson-Chi 115
Veach-Det 114
Sisler-StL 110

Total Average
Ruth-Bos 1.358
Cobb-Det 1.056
Sisler-StL 1.000
Jackson-Chi ..... .997
Veach-Det .... .968

Stolen Bases
E.Collins-Chi 33
Sisler-StL 28
Cobb-Det 28
Rice-Was 26

Stolen Base Average

Stolen Base Runs

Fielding Runs
Pratt-NY 27.3
Peckinpaugh-NY .. 26.1
Felsch-Chi 19.4
Vitt-Bos 18.9
Speaker-Cle 15.3

Total Player Rating
Peckinpaugh-NY ... 7.1
Ruth-Bos 7.1
Peckinpaugh-NY ... 4.9
Cobb-Det 4.7
Pratt-NY 4.1
Sisler-StL 4.0

Wins
Cicotte-Chi 29
Coveleski-Cle 24
Williams-Chi 23
Dauss-Det 21

Win Percentage
Cicotte-Chi ..... .806
Dauss-Det .... .700
Williams-Chi .... .676
Pennock-Bos ..... .667
Coveleski-Cle ... .667

Games
Shaw-Was 45
Russell-NY -Bos ... 44
Kinney-Phi 43
Coveleski-Cle 43

Complete Games
Cicotte-Chi 30
Williams-Chi 27
Johnson-Was 27
Mays-Bos-NY 26
Coveleski-Cle 24

Shutouts
Johnson-Was 7

Saves
Russell-NY -Bos 5
Shawkey-NY 5
Shaw-Was 5
Coveleski-Cle 4

Innings Pitched
Shaw-Was 307
Cicotte-Chi 307
Williams-Chi 297
Johnson-Was 290
Coveleski-Cle 286

Fewest Hits/Game
Johnson-Was 7.29
Thormahlen-NY ... 7.38
Cicotte-Chi 7.50
Shawkey-NY 7.52
Mays-Bos-NY 7.68

Fewest BB/Game
Cicotte-Chi 1.44
Johnson-Was 1.58
Bagby-Cle 1.64
Williams-Chi 1.76
Coveleski-Cle ... 1.89

Strikeouts
Johnson-Was 147
Shaw-Was 128
Williams-Chi 125
Shawkey-NY 122
Coveleski-Cle 118

Strikeouts/Game
Erickson-Det-Was .. 5.51
Russell-NY -Bos ... 4.80
Johnson-Was 4.56
Kinney-Phi 4.30
Leonard-Det 4.23

Wins Above Team
Cicotte-Chi 9.9
Johnson-Was 6.4
Dauss-Det 5.3
Pennock-Bos 4.8
Sothoron-StL 4.8

Earned Run Average
Johnson-Was 1.49
Cicotte-Chi 1.82
Weilman-StL 2.07
Mays-Bos-NY 2.10
Sothoron-StL 2.20

Adjusted ERA
Johnson-Was 213
Cicotte-Chi 180
Weilman-StL 152
Mays-Bos-NY 149
Sothoron-StL 143

Opponents' Batting Avg.
Johnson-Was ..... .219
Cicotte-Chi ..... .228
Thormahlen-NY ... .228
Shawkey-NY ...... .231
Mays-Bos-NY ..... .233

Opponents' On Base Pct.
Johnson-Was ..... .259
Cicotte-Chi ..... .261
Williams-Chi .... .289
Morton-Cle ...... .293
Quinn-NY .... .295

Starter Runs
Johnson-Was 55.5
Cicotte-Chi 47.6
Mays-Bos-NY 33.0
Sothoron-StL 30.4
Coveleski-Cle ... 19.1

Adjusted Starter Runs
Johnson-Was 54.4
Cicotte-Chi 49.7
Mays-Bos-NY 30.2
Sothoron-StL 28.1
Coveleski-Cle ... 23.6

Clutch Pitching Index
Weilman-StL 118
Ehmke-Det 113
Sothoron-StL 113
Harper-Was 107
Pennock-Bos 106

Relief Runs
Phillips-Cle 1.6

Adjusted Relief Runs
Phillips-Cle 2.5

Relief Ranking
Phillips-Cle 2.0

Total Pitcher Index
Johnson-Was 6.6
Cicotte-Chi 5.2
Mays-Bos-NY 3.9
Coveleski-Cle 3.3
Quinn-NY 2.5

Total Baseball Ranking
Ruth-Bos 7.0
Johnson-Was 6.6
Cicotte-Chi 5.2
Peckinpaugh-NY ... 4.9
Cobb-Det 4.7

TEAM	G	W	L	PCT	GB	R	OR	AB	H	2B	3B	HR	BB	SO	AVG	OBP	SLG	PRO	/A	BR	/A	PF	CHI	RC	TA	SB	CS	SBA	SBR
BRO	155	93	61	.604		660	528	5399	1493	205	99	28	359	391	.277	.324	.367	.691	103	19	-50	111	102	637	.609	70	80	47	-26
NY	155	86	68	.558	7	682	543	5309	1627	210	76	46	432	545	.306	.362	.401	.763	125	165	168	100	87	764	.716	131	113	54	-28
CIN	154	82	71	.536	10.5	639	569	5176	1432	169	76	18	382	367	.277	.332	.349	.681	101	11	73	90	103	602	.618	158	128	55	-28
PIT	155	79	75	.513	14	530	552	5219	1342	162	90	16	374	405	.257	.310	.332	.642	89	-66	-71	101	98	544	.580	181	61	61	-15
STL	155	75	79	.487	18	675	682	5495	1589	238	96	32	373	484	.289	.337	.385	.722	112	83	97	98	94	704	.657	126	114	53	-30
CHI	154	75	79	.487	18	619	635	5117	1350	223	67	34	428	421	.264	.326	.354	.680	100	7	13	99	100	589	.616	115	129	47	-42
BOS	153	62	90	.408	30	523	670	5218	1385	186	86	23	385	488	.265	.315	.339	.654	93	-44	-22	96	93	557	.574	88	98	47	-31
PHI	153	62	91	.405	30.5	565	714	5264	1385	229	54	64	283	531	.263	.305	.364	.669	97	-29	-80	109	99	577	.589	100	83	55	-19
TOT	617					4893		42197	11576	1604	644	261	3016	3632	.274	.322	.357	.679								969	862	53	-226

TEAM	CG	SHO	SV	IP	H	H/G	HR	BB	BB/G	SO	SO/G	ERA	/A	OAVG	OOBA	PR	/A	PF	CPI	FA	E	DP	FW	PW	BW	SBW	DIF
BRO	89	17	10	1425.7	1381	8.7	25	327	2.1	553	3.5	2.62	129	.261	.296	80	121	108	99	.966	226	118	-.3	13.0	-5.4	.2	8.4
NY	86	20	9	1410.7	1379	8.8	44	297	1.9	380	2.4	2.80	108	.263	.294	50	34	97	96	.969	210	137	.7	3.6	18.0	.0	-13.4
CIN	90	13	9	1393.7	1327	8.6	26	393	2.5	435	2.8	2.84	97	.258	.302	43	-12	88	94	.968	200	125	1.3	-1.3	7.8	.0	-2.4
PIT	92	17	10	1413.3	1389	8.8	25	280	1.8	444	2.8	2.89	110	.264	.293	36	43	101	89	.971	186	119	2.2	4.6	-7.6	1.4	1.4
STL	72	9	12	1425.7	1488	9.4	30	529	3.3	529	3.3	3.43	89	.276	.325	-47	-58	98	96	.961	256	136	-2.1	-6.2	10.4	-.2	-3.9
CHI	95	13	9	1387.7	1459	9.5	37	382	2.5	508	3.3	3.27	95	.278	.317	-22	-26	99	98	.965	225	112	-.2	-2.8	1.4	-1.5	1.1
BOS	93	14	6	1387.7	1464	9.5	39	415	2.7	368	2.4	3.54	88	.278	.320	-64	-67	99	93	.964	239	125	-1.0	-7.2	-2.4	-.3	-3.1
PHI	77	9	11	1375.7	1480	9.7	35	444	2.9	419	2.7	3.63	96	.282	.326	-77	-20	112	95	.964	232	135	-.6	-2.1	-8.6	1.0	-4.2
TOT	694	112	76	11220.0		9.1			2.4		2.9	3.13		.274	.322					.966	1774	1007					

Runs
Burns-NY 115
Bancroft-Phi-NY 102
Daubert-Cin 97
Hornsby-StL 96
Youngs-NY 92

Hits
Hornsby-StL 218
Youngs-NY 204
Stock-StL 204
Roush-Cin 196
Williams-Phi 192

Doubles
Hornsby-StL 44
Bancroft-Phi-NY 36
Williams-Phi 36
Myers-Bro 36
Burns-NY 35

Triples
Myers-Bro 22
Hornsby-StL 20
Roush-Cin 16
Maranville-Bos 15
Bigbee-Pit 15

Home Runs
Williams-Phi 15
Meusel-Phi 14
Kelly-NY 11
Robertson-Chi 10
McHenry-StL 10

Total Bases
Hornsby-StL 329
Williams-Phi 293
Youngs-NY 277
Wheat-Bro 270
Myers-Bro 269

Runs Batted In
Kelly-NY 94
Hornsby-StL 94
Roush-Cin 90
Duncan-Cin 83
Myers-Bro 80

Runs Produced
Hornsby-StL 181
Roush-Cin 167
Youngs-NY 164
Stock-StL 161
Myers-Bro 159

Bases On Balls
Burns-NY 76
Youngs-NY 75
Paskert-Chi 64
Hornsby-StL 60
Groh-Cin 60

Batting Average
Hornsby-StL 370
Youngs-NY 351
Roush-Cin 339
Wheat-Bro 328
Williams-Phi 325

On Base Percentage
Hornsby-StL 431
Youngs-NY 427
Roush-Cin 386
Wheat-Bro 385
Groh-Cin 375

Slugging Average
Hornsby-StL 559
Williams-Phi 497
Youngs-NY 477
Meusel-Phi 473
Wheat-Bro 463

Production
Hornsby-StL 990
Youngs-NY 904
Williams-Phi 861
Wheat-Bro 848
Roush-Cin 839

Adjusted Production
Hornsby-StL 187
Youngs-NY 160
Roush-Cin 156
Daubert-Cin 139
Groh-Cin 135

Batter Runs
Hornsby-StL 62.6
Youngs-NY 47.1
Williams-Phi 32.1
Wheat-Bro 31.9
Roush-Cin 29.7

Adjusted Batter Runs
Hornsby-StL 64.2
Youngs-NY 47.4
Roush-Cin 36.7
Williams-Phi 26.3
Wheat-Bro 24.4

Clutch Hitting Index
Whitted-Pit 178
Kopf-Cin 174
Duncan-Cin 155
Kelly-NY 144
Paskert-Chi 140

Runs Created
Hornsby-StL 138
Youngs-NY 118
Williams-Phi 103
Wheat-Bro 102
Roush-Cin 98

Total Average
Hornsby-StL 1.047
Youngs-NY 942
Williams-Phi 846
Roush-Cin 843
Wheat-Bro 826

Stolen Bases
Carey-Pit 52
Roush-Cin 36
Frisch-NY 34
Bigbee-Pit 31
Neale-Cin 29

Stolen Base Average
Carey-Pit 83.9
Frisch-NY 75.6
Neale-Cin 70.7
Bigbee-Pit 67.4
Meusel-Phi 60.7

Stolen Base Runs
Carey-Pit 9.6
Frisch-NY 3.6
Neale-Cin 1.5
Tragesser-Phi 1.2
Gowdy-Bos 1.2

Fielding Runs
Bancroft-Phi-NY 28.8
Fletcher-NY -Phi 19.6
Hornsby-StL 15.5
O'Neil-Bos 15.2
Maranville-Bos 15.1

Total Player Rating
Hornsby-StL 8.0
Bancroft-Phi-NY 4.0
Roush-Cin 3.9
Youngs-NY 3.6
Hollocher-Chi 2.6

Wins
Alexander-Chi 27
Cooper-Pit 24
Grimes-Bro 23
Toney-NY 21
Nehf-NY 21

Win Percentage
Grimes-Bro 676
Alexander-Chi 659
Toney-NY 656
Pfeffer-Bro 640
Nehf-NY 636

Games
Haines-StL 47
Douglas-NY 46
Alexander-Chi 46
Scott-StL 44
Cooper-Pit 44

Complete Games
Alexander-Chi 33
Cooper-Pit 28
Rixey-Phi 25
Grimes-Bro 25
Vaughn-Chi 24

Shutouts
Adams-Pit 8
Alexander-Chi 7

Saves
Sherdel-StL 6
McQuillan-Bos 5
Alexander-Chi 5
Hubbell-NY -Phi 4
Mamaux-Bro 4

Innings Pitched
Alexander-Chi 363
Cooper-Pit 327
Grimes-Bro 304
Haines-StL 302
Vaughn-Chi 301

Fewest Hits/Game
Luque-Cin 7.27
Ruether-Cin 7.95
Grimes-Bro 8.02
Mamaux-Bro 8.10
Adams-Pit 8.21

Fewest BB/Game
Adams-Pit 62
Cooper-Pit 1.43
Nehf-NY 1.44
Benton-NY 1.45
Marquard-Bro 1.66

Strikeouts
Alexander-Chi 173
Vaughn-Chi 131
Grimes-Bro 131
Haines-StL 120
Schupp-StL 119

Strikeouts/Game
Mamaux-Bro 4.76
Alexander-Chi 4.29
Schupp-StL 4.27
Marquard-Bro 4.22
Sherdel-StL 3.92

Wins Above Team
Alexander-Chi 8.3
Cooper-Pit 5.1
Doak-StL 5.1
Toney-NY 4.2
Meadows-Phi 3.8

Earned Run Average
Alexander-Chi 1.91
Adams-Pit 2.16
Grimes-Bro 2.22
Cooper-Pit 2.39
Ruether-Cin 2.47

Adjusted ERA
Alexander-Chi 162
Grimes-Bro 153
Adams-Pit 147
Cooper-Pit 132
Cadore-Bro 129

Opponents' Batting Avg.
Luque-Cin 225
Grimes-Bro 238
Adams-Pit 244
Ponder-Pit 246
Ruether-Cin 247

Opponents' On Base Pct.
Adams-Pit 250
Grimes-Bro 274
Barnes-NY 277
Marquard-Bro 279
Ponder-Pit 279

Starter Runs
Alexander-Chi 49.0
Grimes-Bro 30.6
Adams-Pit 28.3
Cooper-Pit 26.5
Vaughn-Chi 19.5

Adjusted Starter Runs
Alexander-Chi 48.0
Grimes-Bro 39.4
Adams-Pit 29.6
Cooper-Pit 28.1
Smith-Bro 23.2

Clutch Pitching Index
Meadows-Phi 116
Vaughn-Chi 114
Fillingim-Bos 114
Alexander-Chi 112
Sherdel-StL 111

Relief Runs

Adjusted Relief Runs

Relief Ranking

Total Pitcher Index
Alexander-Chi 6.3
Grimes-Bro 6.2
Smith-Bro 3.5
Cadore-Bro 2.9
Cooper-Pit 2.8

Total Baseball Ranking
Hornsby-StL 8.0
Alexander-Chi 6.3
Grimes-Bro 6.2
Bancroft-Phi-NY 4.0
Roush-Cin 3.9

TEAM	G	W	L	PCT	GB	R	OR	AB	H	2B	3B	HR	BB	SO	AVG	OBP	SLG	PRO	/A	BR	/A	PF	CHI	RC	TA	SB	CS	SBA	SBR
CLE	154	98	56	.636		857	642	5196	1574	300	95	35	576	379	.303	.376	.417	.793	116	125	98	104	98	827	.768	73	92	44	-32
CHI	154	96	58	.623	2	794	665	5330	1569	267	92	36	473	355	.294	.356	.399	.755	106	42	72	96	101	763	.713	111	96	54	-23
NY	154	95	59	.617	3	838	629	5176	1448	268	71	115	539	626	.280	.350	.426	.776	111	71	55	102	105	773	.742	64	82	44	-29
STL	154	76	77	.497	21.5	797	766	5358	1651	279	83	50	427	339	.308	.363	.419	.782	113	93	9	111	95	822	.747	118	79	60	-11
BOS	154	72	81	.471	25.5	650	698	5199	1397	216	71	22	533	429	.269	.342	.350	.692	89	-70	-40	96	97	637	.638	98	111	47	-36
WAS	153	68	84	.447	29	723	802	5251	1526	233	81	36	433	543	.291	.351	.386	.737	101	7	43	95	98	718	.697	161	114	59	-19
DET	155	61	93	.396	37	652	833	5215	1408	228	72	30	479	391	.270	.334	.359	.693	89	-79	-100	103	100	640	.631	76	66	54	-16
PHI	156	48	106	.312	50	558	834	5258	1326	219	49	46	356	594	.252	.305	.339	.644	75	-184	-140	94	104	546	.558	50	67	43	-24
TOT	617					5869		41983	11899	2010	614	370	3816	3656	.283	.347	.387	.734								751	707	52	-198

TEAM	CG	SHO	SV	IP	H	H/G	HR	BB	BB/G	SO	SO/G	ERA	/A	OAVG	OOBA	PR	/A	PF	CPI	FA	E	DP	FW	PW	BW	SBW	DIF
CLE	94	11	7	1377.3	1448	9.5	31	401	2.6	466	3.0	3.41	111	.277	.329	57	57	100	97	.971	184	124	2.2	5.5	9.5	-.7	4.5
CHI	109	9	10	1382.0	1467	9.6	45	405	2.6	438	2.9	3.59	99	.279	.331	30	-6	94	96	.968	198	142	1.2	-.6	7.0	.2	11.3
NY	88	15	11	1368.7	1414	9.3	48	420	2.8	480	3.2	3.31	113	.274	.329	72	65	99	102	.969	194	129	1.5	6.3	5.3	-.4	5.3
STL	84	9	14	1371.0	1481	9.7	53	578	3.8	444	2.9	4.03	104	.283	.354	-37	26	111	98	.963	233	119	-1.3	2.5	.9	1.3	-4.0
BOS	92	11	6	1391.7	1481	9.6	39	461	3.0	481	3.1	3.83	96	.280	.338	-6	-25	97	93	.972	183	131	2.2	-2.4	-3.9	-1.1	.7
WAS	81	10	10	1363.3	1521	10.0	51	520	3.4	418	2.8	4.17	88	.289	.353	-58	-78	96	96	.963	232	95	-1.2	-7.6	4.2	.6	-4.0
DET	74	9	7	1380.7	1487	9.7	46	561	3.7	483	3.1	4.04	99	.282	.351	-38	-3	106	95	.964	230	95	-1.1	-.3	-9.7	.9	-5.8
PHI	79	6	2	1375.0	1612	10.6	56	461	3.0	423	2.8	3.92	95	.300	.355	-20	-27	99	107	.960	265	126	-3.5	-2.6	-13.6	.0	-9.4
TOT	701	80	67	11009.7		9.7			3.1		3.0	3.79		.283	.347					.966	1719	961					

Runs
Ruth-NY 158
Speaker-Cle 137
Sisler-StL 137
E.Collins-Chi 115

Hits
Sisler-StL 257
E.Collins-Chi 222
Jackson-Chi 218
Jacobson-StL 216
Speaker-Cle 214

Doubles
Speaker-Cle 50
Sisler-StL 49
Jackson-Chi 42

Triples
Jackson-Chi 20
Sisler-StL 18
Hooper-Bos 17

Home Runs
Ruth-NY 54
Sisler-StL 19
Walker-Phi 17
Felsch-Chi 14

Total Bases
Sisler-StL 399
Ruth-NY 388
Jackson-Chi 336
Speaker-Cle 310
Jacobson-StL 305

Runs Batted In
Ruth-NY 137
Sisler-StL 122
Jacobson-StL 122
Jackson-Chi 121
Gardner-Cle 118

Runs Produced
Ruth-NY 241
Sisler-StL 240
Speaker-Cle 236
Jackson-Chi 214
Jacobson-StL 210

Bases On Balls
Ruth-NY 148
Speaker-Cle 97
Hooper-Bos 88
Young-Det 85
Roth-Was 75

Batting Average
Sisler-StL 407
Speaker-Cle 388
Jackson-Chi 382
Ruth-NY 376
E.Collins-Chi 369

On Base Percentage
Ruth-NY 530
Speaker-Cle 483
Sisler-StL 449
Jackson-Chi 444
E.Collins-Chi 436

Slugging Average
Ruth-NY 847
Sisler-StL 632
Jackson-Chi 589
Speaker-Cle 562
Felsch-Chi 540

Production
Ruth-NY 1.378
Sisler-StL 1.082
Speaker-Cle 1.045
Jackson-Chi 1.033
E.Collins-Chi 925

Adjusted Production
Ruth-NY 255
Jackson-Chi 179
Speaker-Cle 170
Sisler-StL 166
E.Collins-Chi 151

Batter Runs
Ruth-NY 113.2
Sisler-StL 73.2
Speaker-Cle 65.7
Jackson-Chi 58.3
E.Collins-Chi 40.8

Adjusted Batter Runs
Ruth-NY 111.5
Sisler-StL 63.6
Speaker-Cle 62.7
Jackson-Chi 61.6
E.Collins-Chi 44.3

Clutch Hitting Index
Gardner-Cle 171
Roth-Was 144
Pratt-NY 140
Jacobson-StL 137
Smith-Cle 135

Runs Created
Ruth-NY 211
Sisler-StL 176
Speaker-Cle 152
Jackson-Chi 145
E.Collins-Chi 132

Total Average
Ruth-NY 1.843
Sisler-StL 1.251
Speaker-Cle 1.202
Jackson-Chi 1.121
E.Collins-Chi 992

Stolen Bases
Rice-Was 63
Sisler-StL 42
Roth-Was 24
Menosky-Bos 23
Tobin-StL 21

Stolen Base Average
Sisler-StL 71.2
E.Collins-Chi 70.4
Williams-StL 69.2
Rice-Was 67.7
Roth-Was 66.7

Stolen Base Runs
Sisler-StL 2.4
Burns-Phi-Cle 1.5
Smith-StL 9
Rice-Was 9
E.Collins-Chi 9

Fielding Runs
Rice-Was 15.8
Scott-Bos 15.8
Sisler-StL 15.1
Perkins-Phi 14.0
Felsch-Chi 13.6

Total Player Rating
Ruth-NY 8.8
Sisler-StL 7.7
E.Collins-Chi 5.5
Speaker-Cle 4.7
Jackson-Chi 4.4

Wins
Bagby-Cle 31
Mays-NY 26
Coveleski-Cle 24
Faber-Chi 23
Williams-Chi 22

Win Percentage
Bagby-Cle 721
Mays-NY 703
Kerr-Chi 700
Cicotte-Chi 677

Games
Bagby-Cle 48
Ayers-Det 46
Mays-NY 45
Kerr-Chi 45
Zachary-Was 44

Complete Games
Bagby-Cle 30
Faber-Chi 28
Cicotte-Chi 28
Mays-NY 26
Coveleski-Cle 26

Shutouts
Mays-NY 6
Shocker-StL 5
Shawkey-NY 5

Saves
Shocker-StL 5
Kerr-Chi 5
Burwell-StL 4

Innings Pitched
Bagby-Cle 340
Faber-Chi 319
Coveleski-Cle 315
Mays-NY 312
Cicotte-Chi 303

Fewest Hits/Game
Coveleski-Cle 8.11
Shocker-StL 8.20
Collins-NY 8.23
Shawkey-NY 8.26
Davis-StL 8.36

Fewest BB/Game
Quinn-NY 1.71
Coveleski-Cle 1.86
Bagby-Cle 2.09
Cicotte-Chi 2.20
Perry-Phi 2.22

Strikeouts
Coveleski-Cle 133
Williams-Chi 128
Shawkey-NY 126
Faber-Chi 108
Shocker-StL 107

Strikeouts/Game
Ayers-Det 4.44
Shawkey-NY 4.23
Harper-Bos 3.92
Shocker-StL 3.91
Williams-Chi 3.85

Wins Above Team
Bagby-Cle 6.4
Shocker-StL 5.8
Mays-NY 5.1
Davis-StL 3.6
Kerr-Chi 3.6

Earned Run Average
Shawkey-NY 2.45
Coveleski-Cle 2.49
Shocker-StL 2.71
Rommel-Phi 2.84
Bagby-Cle 2.89

Adjusted ERA
Shocker-StL 155
Shawkey-NY 152
Coveleski-Cle 152
Davis-StL 132
Rommel-Phi 131

Opponents' Batting Avg.
Coveleski-Cle 243
Collins-NY 247
Shawkey-NY 248
Shocker-StL 248
Ehmke-Det 253

Opponents' On Base Pct.
Coveleski-Cle 285
Shocker-StL 305
Shawkey-NY 308
Quinn-NY 308
Rommel-Phi 309

Starter Runs
Coveleski-Cle 45.6
Shawkey-NY 39.8
Bagby-Cle 34.1
Shocker-StL 29.5
Faber-Chi 28.2

Adjusted Starter Runs
Coveleski-Cle 45.6
Shocker-StL 40.9
Shawkey-NY 38.3
Bagby-Cle 34.1
Davis-StL 30.7

Clutch Pitching Index
Naylor-Phi 130
Harper-Bos 128
Davis-StL 117
Oldham-Det 116
Perry-Phi 113

Relief Runs

Adjusted Relief Runs

Relief Ranking

Total Pitcher Index
Coveleski-Cle 5.4
Shocker-StL 4.4
Shawkey-NY 3.6
Bagby-Cle 3.3
Mays-NY 3.2

Total Baseball Ranking
Ruth-NY 8.8
Sisler-StL 7.7
E.Collins-Chi 5.5
Coveleski-Cle 5.4
Speaker-Cle 4.7

TEAM	G	W	L	PCT	GB	R	OR	AB	H	2B	3B	HR	BB	SO	AVG	OBP	SLG	PRO	/A	BR	/A	PF	CHI	RC	TA	SB	CS	SBA	SBR
NY	153	94	59	.614		840	637	5278	1575	237	93	75	469	390	.298	.359	.421	.780	112	94	111	98	104	795	.750	137	114	55	-26
PIT	154	90	63	.588	4	692	595	5379	1533	231	104	37	341	371	.285	.330	.387	.717	95	-37	-60	103	102	684	.655	134	93	59	-15
STL	154	87	66	.569	7	809	681	5309	1635	260	88	83	382	452	.308	.358	.437	.795	116	113	149	95	98	816	.750	94	94	50	-27
BOS	153	79	74	.516	15	721	697	5385	1561	209	100	61	377	470	.290	.339	.400	.739	101	5	55	93	99	718	.674	94	100	48	-31
BRO	152	77	75	.507	16.5	667	681	5263	1476	209	85	59	325	400	.280	.325	.386	.711	93	-51	-82	105	103	655	.640	91	73	55	-16
CIN	153	70	83	.458	24	618	649	5112	1421	221	94	20	375	308	.278	.333	.370	.703	92	-55	-60	101	97	623	.637	117	120	49	-36
CHI	153	64	89	.418	30	668	773	5385	1553	234	56	37	343	343	.292	.339	.378	.717	95	-31	-77	107	98	671	.636	70	97	42	-36
PHI	154	51	103	.331	43.5	617	919	5329	1512	238	50	88	294	615	.284	.324	.397	.721	96	-36	-47	102	94	668	.641	66	80	45	-36
TOT	613					5632		42376	12266	1839	670	460	2906	3380	.289	.339	.397	.736								803	771	51	-221

TEAM	CG	SHO	SV	IP	H	H/G	HR	BB	BB/G	SO	SO/G	ERA	/A	OAVG	OOBA	PR	/A	PF	CPI	FA	E	DP	FW	PW	BW	SBW	DIF
NY	71	9	18	1370.3	1497	9.8	79	295	1.9	357	2.3	3.56	100	.284	.312	33	-1	94	100	.971	187	155	1.3	-.0	11.0	.2	5.2
PIT	88	10	10	1413.7	1448	9.2	37	322	2.0	500	3.2	3.16	121	.271	.303	97	106	102	96	.973	172	129	2.2	10.5	-5.9	1.3	5.5
STL	70	12	16	1369.3	1486	9.8	61	399	2.6	464	3.0	3.62	97	.283	.324	23	-19	93	101	.965	219	130	-.7	-1.9	14.7	.0	-1.7
BOS	74	11	12	1385.7	1488	9.7	54	420	2.7	382	2.5	3.90	90	.281	.325	-18	-62	92	92	.969	199	122	.5	-6.1	5.4	-.3	3.0
BRO	82	9	12	1362.3	1556	10.3	46	361	2.4	471	3.1	3.70	107	.293	.328	11	39	105	102	.964	232	142	-1.5	3.8	-8.1	1.2	5.6
CIN	83	7	9	1360.7	1500	9.9	37	305	2.0	408	2.7	3.46	111	.286	.315	48	56	101	99	.969	193	139	.9	5.5	-5.9	-.8	-6.2
CHI	73	8	7	1360.0	1605	10.6	67	409	2.7	441	2.9	4.39	93	.300	.339	-92	-44	108	95	.974	166	129	2.6	-4.3	-7.6	-.8	-2.3
PHI	82	5	8	1346.7	1665	11.1	79	371	2.5	333	2.2	4.48	90	.310	.342	-104	-65	107	100	.955	295	127	-5.3	-6.4	-4.6	.0	-9.7
TOT	623	71	92	10968.7		10.0			2.4		2.8	3.78		.289	.339					.967	1663	1073					

Runs
Hornsby-StL 131
Frisch-NY 121
Bancroft-NY 121
Powell-Bos 114
Burns-NY 111

Hits
Hornsby-StL 235
Frisch-NY 211
Bigbee-Pit 204
Johnston-Bro 203

Doubles
Hornsby-StL 44
Kelly-NY 42
Johnston-Bro 41
Grimes-Chi 38
McHenry-StL 37

Triples
Powell-Bos 18
Hornsby-StL 18
Grimm-Pit 17
Frisch-NY 17
Bigbee-Pit 17

Home Runs
Kelly-NY 23
Hornsby-StL 21
Williams-Phi 18
McHenry-StL 17
Fournier-StL 16

Total Bases
Hornsby-StL 378
Kelly-NY 310
McHenry-StL 305
Meusel-Phi-NY 302
Frisch-NY 300

Runs Batted In
Hornsby-StL 126
Kelly-NY 122
Youngs-NY 102
McHenry-StL 102
Frisch-NY 100

Runs Produced
Hornsby-StL 236
Kelly-NY 213
Frisch-NY 194
Youngs-NY 189
Bancroft-NY 182

Bases On Balls
Burns-NY 80
Youngs-NY 71
Grimes-Chi 70
Carey-Pit 70
Bancroft-NY 66

Batting Average
Hornsby-StL 397
McHenry-StL 350
Fournier-StL 343
Meusel-Phi-NY 343
Frisch-NY 341

On Base Percentage
Hornsby-StL 458
Youngs-NY 411
Fournier-StL 409
Grimes-Chi 406
Carey-Pit 395

Slugging Average
Hornsby-StL 639
McHenry-StL 531
Kelly-NY 528
Meusel-Phi-NY 515
Fournier-StL 505

Production
Hornsby-StL 1.097
McHenry-StL 924
Fournier-StL 914
Meusel-Phi-NY 895
Kelly-NY 884

Adjusted Production
Hornsby-StL 197
McHenry-StL 150
Fournier-StL 148
Meusel-Phi-NY 135
Kelly-NY 134

Batter Runs
Hornsby-StL 74.4
Fournier-StL 34.4
McHenry-StL 33.4
Meusel-Phi-NY 27.5
Frisch-NY 24.8

Adjusted Batter Runs
Hornsby-StL 78.6
Fournier-StL 38.6
McHenry-StL 37.3
Cruise-Bos 27.8
Meusel-Phi-NY 27.6

Clutch Hitting Index
Youngs-NY 166
Lavan-StL 152
Barnhart-Pit 133
Konetchy-Bro-Phi . . . 130
Myers-Bro 130

Runs Created
Hornsby-StL 169
Frisch-NY 118
Fournier-StL 114
McHenry-StL 111
Meusel-Phi-NY 110

Total Average
Hornsby-StL 1.238
Fournier-StL 937
Frisch-NY 933
Youngs-NY 907
McHenry-StL 903

Stolen Bases
Frisch-NY 49
Carey-Pit 37
Johnston-Bro 28
Bohne-Cin 26
Maranville-Pit 25

Stolen Base Average
Frisch-NY 79.0
Carey-Pit 75.5
Maisel-Chi 70.8
Maranville-Pit 67.6
Johnston-Bro 63.6

Stolen Base Runs
Frisch-NY 6.9
Carey-Pit 3.9
Stock-StL 1.5
Cutshaw-Pit 1.2

Fielding Runs
Lavan-StL 18.4
Bancroft-NY 17.5
Bigbee-Pit 16.7
Rawlings-Phi-NY 12.7
Frisch-NY 11.8

Total Player Rating
Hornsby-StL 7.2
Bancroft-NY 5.0
Frisch-NY 4.5
Kelly-NY 2.7
Fournier-StL 2.3

Wins
Grimes-Bro 22
Cooper-Pit 22
Oeschger-Bos 20
Nehf-NY 20
Rixey-Cin 19

Win Percentage
Doak-StL 714
Nehf-NY 667
Grimes-Bro 629
Barnes-NY 625
Toney-NY 621

Games
Scott-Bos 47
Oeschger-Bos 46
McQuillan-Bos 45
Watson-Bos 44
Fillingim-Bos 44

Complete Games
Grimes-Bro 30
Cooper-Pit 29
Luque-Cin 25

Shutouts

Saves
North-StL 7
Barnes-NY 6
McQuillan-Bos 5

Innings Pitched
Cooper-Pit 327
Luque-Cin 304
Grimes-Bro 302
Rixey-Cin 301
Oeschger-Bos 299

Fewest Hits/Game
Glazner-Pit 8.23
Adams-Pit 8.72
Oeschger-Bos 9.12
Nehf-NY 9.17
Pertica-StL 9.17

Fewest BB/Game
Adams-Pit 1.01
Alexander-Chi 1.18
Barnes-NY 1.53
Hubbell-Phi 1.55
Doak-StL 1.59

Strikeouts
Grimes-Bro 136
Cooper-Pit 134
Luque-Cin 102
McQuillan-Bos 94

Strikeouts/Game
Grimes-Bro 4.05
Cooper-Pit 3.69
Doak-StL 3.57
Martin-Chi 3.57
Glazner-Pit 3.38

Wins Above Team
Grimes-Bro 5.2
Doak-StL 3.9
Glazner-Pit 3.7
Adams-Pit 3.7
Alexander-Chi 3.3

Earned Run Average
Doak-StL 2.58
Adams-Pit 2.64
Glazner-Pit 2.77
Rixey-Cin 2.78
Grimes-Bro 2.83

Adjusted ERA
Adams-Pit 145
Grimes-Bro 140
Glazner-Pit 138
Rixey-Cin 138
Mitchell-Bro 137

Opponents' Batting Avg.
Glazner-Pit 250
Adams-Pit 251
Pertica-StL 267
Watson-Bos 270
Nehf-NY 271

Opponents' On Base Pct.
Adams-Pit 268
Glazner-Pit 299
Nehf-NY 303
Watson-Bos 304
Luque-Cin 304

Starter Runs
Rixey-Cin 33.4
Grimes-Bro 31.8
Doak-StL 27.7
Glazner-Pit 26.2
Adams-Pit 20.2

Adjusted Starter Runs
Grimes-Bro 37.9
Rixey-Cin 35.1
Glazner-Pit 27.7
Mitchell-Bro 22.6
Cooper-Pit 21.3

Clutch Pitching Index
Barnes-NY 124
Mitchell-Bro 118
Doak-StL 116
Rixey-Cin 113
Grimes-Bro 112

Relief Runs
North-StL 2.1
Sallee-NY 1.3

Adjusted Relief Runs

Relief Ranking

Total Pitcher Index
Grimes-Bro 4.7
Rixey-Cin 3.4
Mitchell-Bro 3.1
Alexander-Chi 2.6
Adams-Pit 2.4

Total Baseball Ranking
Hornsby-StL 7.2
Bancroft-NY 5.0
Grimes-Bro 4.7
Frisch-NY 4.5
Rixey-Cin 3.4

TEAM	G	W	L	PCT	GB	R	OR	AB	H	2B	3B	HR	BB	SO	AVG	OBP	SLG	PRO	/A	BR	/A	PF	CHI	RC	TA	SB	CS	SBA	SBR
NY	153	98	55	.641		948	708	5249	1576	285	87	134	588	569	.300	.375	.464	.839	119	142	119	103	102	929	.844	89	64	58	-11
CLE	154	94	60	.610	4.5	925	712	5383	1656	355	90	42	623	376	.308	.383	.430	.813	113	112	117	99	100	916	.803	50	42	54	-9
STL	154	81	73	.526	17.5	835	845	5442	1655	246	106	66	413	407	.304	.357	.425	.782	104	27	20	101	102	826	.739	92	71	56	-14
WAS	154	80	73	.523	18	704	738	5294	1468	240	96	42	462	472	.277	.342	.383	.725	90	-79	-68	99	100	712	.683	111	66	63	-5
BOS	154	75	79	.487	23.5	668	696	5206	1440	248	69	17	456	344	.277	.335	.361	.695	82	-132	-130	100	106	642	.631	83	65	56	-13
DET	154	71	82	.464	27	883	852	5461	1724	268	100	58	582	376	.316	.385	.433	.818	114	120	151	96	94	921	.803	95	89	52	-24
CHI	154	62	92	.403	36.5	683	858	5329	1509	242	82	35	445	474	.283	.343	.379	.722	89	-85	-79	99	98	696	.664	97	93	51	-26
PHI	155	53	100	.346	45	657	894	5465	1497	256	64	83	424	565	.274	.331	.390	.721	88	-100	-125	103	95	711	.662	68	55	55	-12
TOT	616					6303		42829	12525	2140	694	477	3965	3583	.292	.357	.408	.765								685	545	56	-121

TEAM	CG	SHO	SV	IP	H	H/G	HR	BB	BB/G	SO	SO/G	ERA	/A	OAVG	OOBA	PR	/A	PF	CPI	FA	E	DP	FW	PW	BW	SBW	DIF
NY	92	8	15	1363.3	1461	9.6	51	470	3.1	481	3.2	3.79	112	.280	.331	73	68	99	100	.965	222	138	-.2	6.4	11.1	.4	3.8
CLE	81	11	14	1377.7	1534	10.0	43	431	2.8	475	3.1	3.90	105	.288	.329	57	31	96	99	.967	204	124	.8	2.9	10.9	.6	1.8
STL	77	9	9	1377.3	1543	10.1	71	557	3.6	478	3.1	4.61	94	.289	.345	-51	-45	101	93	.964	224	127	-.3	-4.2	1.9	.1	6.5
WAS	80	10	10	1384.0	1568	10.2	51	442	2.9	452	2.9	3.97	107	.291	.335	47	42	99	101	.963	235	153	-.9	3.9	-6.4	1.0	5.9
BOS	88	9	5	1365.3	1521	10.0	53	452	3.0	446	2.9	3.99	107	.288	.332	43	45	100	100	.975	157	151	3.5	4.2	-12.2	.2	2.2
DET	73	4	16	1387.0	1634	10.6	71	495	3.2	452	2.9	4.40	93	.299	.347	-18	-47	96	101	.963	232	107	-.8	-4.4	14.1	-.8	-13.6
CHI	84	7	9	1363.7	1603	10.6	52	549	3.6	392	2.6	4.94	88	.299	.351	-100	-87	102	91	.969	200	155	1.1	-8.1	-7.4	-1.0	.5
PHI	75	2	7	1400.0	1645	10.6	85	548	3.5	431	2.8	4.61	99	.299	.350	-51	-4	107	100	.958	274	144	-3.2	-.4	-11.7	.3	-8.6
TOT	650	60	85	11018.3		10.2			3.2		2.9	4.28		.292	.357					.965	1748	1099					

Runs		Hits		Doubles		Triples		Home Runs		Total Bases	
Ruth-NY	177	Heilmann-Det	237	Speaker-Cle	52	Shanks-Was	19	Ruth-NY	59	Ruth-NY	457
Tobin-StL	132	Tobin-StL	236	Ruth-NY	44	Tobin-StL	18	Williams-StL	24	Heilmann-Det	365
Peckinpaugh-NY	128	Sisler-StL	216	Veach-Det	43	Sisler-StL	18	Meusel-NY	24	Meusel-NY	334
Sisler-StL	125	Jacobson-StL	211	Heilmann-Det	43			Walker-Phi	23	Tobin-StL	327
Cobb-Det	124	Veach-Det	207	Meusel-NY	40			Heilmann-Det	19	Veach-Det	324

Runs Batted In		Runs Produced		Bases On Balls		Batting Average		On Base Percentage		Slugging Average	
Ruth-NY	171	Ruth-NY	289	Ruth-NY	144	Heilmann-Det	.394	Ruth-NY	.512	Ruth-NY	.846
Heilmann-Det	139	Heilmann-Det	234	Blue-Det	103	Cobb-Det	.389	Cobb-Det	.452	Heilmann-Det	.606
Meusel-NY	135	Veach-Det	222	Peckinpaugh-NY	84	Ruth-NY	.378	Heilmann-Det	.444	Cobb-Det	.596
Veach-Det	128	Sisler-StL	218	Sewell-Cle	80	Sisler-StL	.371	Speaker-Cle	.439	Williams-StL	.561
Gardner-Cle	120	Gardner-Cle	218	Schang-NY	78	Speaker-Cle	.362	Williams-StL	.429	Meusel-NY	.559

Production		Adjusted Production		Batter Runs		Adjusted Batter Runs		Clutch Hitting Index		Runs Created	
Ruth-NY	1.358	Ruth-NY	234	Ruth-NY	119.2	Ruth-NY	116.6	Gardner-Cle	164	Ruth-NY	238
Heilmann-Det	1.051	Heilmann-Det	172	Heilmann-Det	58.4	Heilmann-Det	61.8	Pratt-Bos	145	Heilmann-Det	159
Cobb-Det	1.048	Cobb-Det	172	Cobb-Det	50.2	Cobb-Det	53.2	Severeid-StL	132	Cobb-Det	134
Williams-StL	.990	Williams-StL	149	Williams-StL	42.4	Williams-StL	41.8	Pipp-NY	128	Sisler-StL	132
Speaker-Cle	.977	Speaker-Cle	149	Speaker-Cle	38.2	Speaker-Cle	38.7	Sewell-Cle	127	Williams-StL	130

Total Average		Stolen Bases		Stolen Base Average		Stolen Base Runs		Fielding Runs		Total Player Rating	
Ruth-NY	1.782	Sisler-StL	35	Judge-Was	77.8	Sisler-StL	3.9	Scott-Bos	37.7	Ruth-NY	9.9
Cobb-Det	1.178	Harris-Was	29	Harris-Was	76.3	Harris-Was	3.3	Collins-Chi	29.7	Cobb-Det	5.5
Heilmann-Det	1.137	Rice-Was	25	Sisler-StL	76.1	Judge-Was	2.7	Dykes-Phi	25.6	Sisler-StL	4.4
Williams-StL	1.083	Johnson-Chi	22	Meusel-NY	73.9	Welch-Phi	1.8	Johnson-Chi	24.6	Collins-Chi	4.2
Sisler-StL	1.053	Cobb-Det	22	Rice-Was	67.6			Cobb-Det	19.7	Williams-StL	3.2

Wins		Win Percentage		Games		Complete Games		Shutouts		Saves	
Shocker-StL	27	Mays-NY	.750	Mays-NY	49	Faber-Chi	32	Jones-Bos	5	Middleton-Det	7
Mays-NY	27	Shocker-StL	.692	Shocker-StL	47	Shocker-StL	30	Shocker-StL	4	Mays-NY	7
Faber-Chi	25	Bush-Bos	.640	Bayne-StL	47	Mays-NY	30	Mogridge-Was	4		
Jones-Bos	23	Coveleski-Cle	.639	Rommel-Phi	46	Coveleski-Cle	28	Faber-Chi	4		
Coveleski-Cle	23	Faber-Chi	.625								

Innings Pitched		Fewest Hits/Game		Fewest BB/Game		Strikeouts		Strikeouts/Game		Wins Above Team	
Mays-NY	337	Faber-Chi	7.97	Hasty-Phi	2.01	Johnson-Was	143	Johnson-Was	4.88	Faber-Chi	8.9
Faber-Chi	331	Bush-Bos	8.65	Mays-NY	2.03	Shocker-StL	132	Shawkey-NY	4.63	Shocker-StL	8.2
Shocker-StL	327	Mays-NY	8.87	Bagby-Cle	2.06	Shawkey-NY	126	Bayne-StL	4.50	Mays-NY	6.6
Coveleski-Cle	315	Shawkey-NY	9.00	Mogridge-Was	2.06	Faber-Chi	124	Leonard-Det	4.41	Jones-Bos	4.9
Kerr-Chi	309	Johnson-Was	9.03	Zachary-Was	2.12	Leonard-Det	120	Mails-Cle	4.04	Kerr-Chi	4.6

Earned Run Average		Adjusted ERA		Opponents' Batting Avg.		Opponents' On Base Pct.		Starter Runs		Adjusted Starter Runs	
Faber-Chi	2.47	Faber-Chi	176	Faber-Chi	.242	Faber-Chi	.287	Faber-Chi	66.3	Faber-Chi	69.6
Mogridge-Was	3.00	Mogridge-Was	141	Mays-NY	.257	Mays-NY	.298	Mays-NY	46.1	Mays-NY	44.7
Mays-NY	3.04	Mays-NY	139	Bush-Bos	.260	Mogridge-Was	.307	Mogridge-Was	40.9	Mogridge-Was	39.8
Hoyt-NY	3.10	Hoyt-NY	137	Shawkey-NY	.263	Shocker-StL	.312	Hoyt-NY	37.0	Hoyt-NY	35.8
Jones-Bos	3.22	Jones-Bos	133	Johnson-Was	.263	Coveleski-Cle	.316	Jones-Bos	35.1	Jones-Bos	35.4

Clutch Pitching Index		Relief Runs	Adjusted Relief Runs	Relief Ranking	Total Pitcher Index		Total Baseball Ranking	
Russell-Bos	122				Faber-Chi	6.8	Ruth-NY	9.5
Zachary-Was	118				Mays-NY	5.8	Faber-Chi	6.8
Keefe-Phi	114				Jones-Bos	3.5	Mays-NY	5.8
Uhle-Cle	108				Shocker-StL	3.5	Cobb-Det	5.5
Hoyt-NY	107				Mogridge-Was	3.4	Sisler-StL	4.4

TEAM	G	W	L	PCT	GB	R	OR	AB	H	2B	3B	HR	BB	SO	AVG	OBP	SLG	PRO	/A	BR	/A	PF	CHI	RC	TA	SB	CS	SBA	SBR
NY	156	93	61	.604	—	852	658	5454	1661	253	90	80	448	421	.305	.363	.428	.791	110	77	49	104	98	848	.760	116	83	58	-14
CIN	156	86	68	.558	7	766	677	5282	1561	226	99	45	436	381	.296	.353	.401	.754	100	8	40	96	99	737	.706	130	136	49	-42
STL	154	85	69	.552	8	863	819	5425	1634	280	88	107	447	425	.301	.357	.444	.801	112	91	82	101	99	860	.768	73	63	54	-15
PIT	155	85	69	.552	8	865	736	5521	1698	239	110	52	423	326	.308	.360	.419	.779	107	56	28	104	102	848	.750	145	59	71	8
CHI	156	80	74	.519	13	771	808	5335	1564	248	71	42	525	447	.293	.359	.390	.749	99	7	46	95	97	752	.704	97	108	47	-35
BRO	155	76	78	.494	17	743	754	5413	1569	235	76	56	339	318	.290	.335	.392	.727	93	-57	-19	95	104	709	.658	79	60	57	-11
PHI	154	57	96	.373	35.5	738	920	5459	1537	268	55	116	450	611	.282	.341	.415	.756	101	-2	-106	113	94	771	.703	48	60	44	-21
BOS	154	53	100	.346	39.5	596	822	5161	1355	162	73	32	387	451	.263	.317	.341	.658	75	-178	-134	94	106	566	.579	67	65	51	-18
TOT	620					6194		43050	12579	1911	662	530	3455	3380	.292	.348	.404	.753								755	634	54	-153

TEAM	CG	SHO	SV	IP	H	H/G	HR	BB	BB/G	SO	SO/G	ERA	/A	OAVG	OOBA	PR	/A	PF	CPI	FA	E	DP	FW	PW	BW	SBW	DIF
NY	76	8	15	1393.7	1454	9.4	71	393	2.5	388	2.5	3.45	119	.274	.316	100	102	100	101	.970	194	145	1.0	9.6	4.6	.5	.2
CIN	88	8	3	1384.0	1481	9.6	49	326	2.1	357	2.3	3.53	109	.279	.312	86	50	94	95	.968	205	147	.3	4.7	3.8	-2.1	2.4
STL	60	8	12	1362.7	1609	10.6	61	447	3.0	465	3.1	4.44	93	.299	.342	-51	-49	100	96	.961	239	122	-1.9	-4.6	7.7	.4	6.4
PIT	88	15	7	1386.3	1613	10.5	52	358	2.3	490	3.2	3.98	104	.296	.329	17	26	101	98	.970	187	126	1.5	2.5	2.6	2.6	-1.2
CHI	74	8	12	1394.3	1579	10.2	77	475	3.1	402	2.6	4.34	90	.290	.338	-37	-65	96	95	.968	204	154	.4	-6.1	4.3	-1.5	5.9
BRO	82	13	8	1383.3	1568	10.2	74	490	3.2	499	3.2	4.04	97	.290	.338	8	-21	95	103	.967	208	139	.1	-2.0	-1.8	.8	1.9
PHI	73	6	5	1377.3	1692	11.1	89	460	3.0	394	2.6	4.64	103	.307	.350	-83	20	117	100	.965	225	152	-1.0	1.9	-10.0	-.2	-10.2
BOS	63	7	6	1346.0	1565	10.5	57	489	3.3	360	2.4	4.37	92	.296	.344	-41	-55	98	97	.965	215	121	-.4	-5.2	-12.6	.1	-5.4
TOT	604	73	68	11027.7		10.3			2.8		2.7	4.10		.292	.348					.967	1677	1106					

Runs
Hornsby-StL 141
Carey-Pit 140
Smith-StL 117
Bancroft-NY 117
Maranville-Pit 115

Hits
Hornsby-StL 250
Bigbee-Pit 215
Bancroft-NY 209
Carey-Pit 207
Daubert-Cin 205

Doubles
Hornsby-StL 46
Grimes-Chi 45
Duncan-Cin 44
Bancroft-NY 41
Hollocher-Chi 37

Triples
Daubert-Cin 22
Meusel-NY 17
Maranville-Pit 15
Bigbee-Pit 15

Home Runs
Hornsby-StL 42
Williams-Phi 26
Lee-Phi 17
Kelly-NY 17

Total Bases
Hornsby-StL 450
Meusel-NY 314
Wheat-Bro 302
Williams-Phi 300
Daubert-Cin 300

Runs Batted In
Hornsby-StL 152
Meusel-NY 132
Wheat-Bro 112
Kelly-NY 107

Runs Produced
Hornsby-StL 251
Meusel-NY 216
Bigbee-Pit 207
Carey-Pit 200
Wheat-Bro 188

Bases On Balls
Carey-Pit 80
O'Farrell-Chi 79
Bancroft-NY 79
Burns-Cin 78
Grimes-Chi 75

Batting Average
Hornsby-StL 401
Grimes-Chi 354
Miller-Chi 352
Bigbee-Pit 350
Tierney-Pit 345

On Base Percentage
Hornsby-StL 459
Grimes-Chi 442
O'Farrell-Chi 439
Carey-Pit 408
Bigbee-Pit 405

Slugging Average
Hornsby-StL 722
Grimes-Chi 572
Tierney-Pit 515
Williams-Phi 514
Miller-Chi 511

Production
Hornsby-StL 1.181
Grimes-Chi 1.014
Williams-Phi 905
Miller-Chi 899
Walker-Phi 899

Adjusted Production
Hornsby-StL 198
Grimes-Chi 168
Miller-Chi 137
Wheat-Bro 135
O'Farrell-Chi 134

Batter Runs
Hornsby-StL 90.0
Grimes-Chi 47.1
Williams-Phi 27.5
Walker-Phi 26.3
Daubert-Cin 24.7

Adjusted Batter Runs
Hornsby-StL 89.0
Grimes-Chi 51.0
Daubert-Cin 28.5
Wheat-Bro 28.4
O'Farrell-Chi 23.8

Clutch Hitting Index
Terry-Chi 146
Meusel-NY 135
Traynor-Pit 133
Pinelli-Cin 125
Tierney-Pit 124

Runs Created
Hornsby-StL 200
Carey-Pit 131
Grimes-Chi 130
Walker-Phi 118
Bigbee-Pit 116

Total Average
Hornsby-StL 1.384
Grimes-Chi 1.128
Carey-Pit 1.000
O'Farrell-Chi 963
Williams-Phi 935

Stolen Bases
Carey-Pit 51
Frisch-NY 31
Burns-Cin 30
Maranville-Pit 24
Bigbee-Pit 24

Stolen Base Average
Carey-Pit 96.2
Traynor-Pit 85.0
Smith-StL 72.0
Johnston-Bro 66.7
Youngs-NY 65.4

Stolen Base Runs
Carey-Pit 14.1
Traynor-Pit 3.3
Kelly-NY 1.8
Griffith-Bro 1.5
Smith-StL 1.2

Fielding Runs
Parkinson-Phi 28.0
Bancroft-NY 21.9
Pinelli-Cin 20.9
Bigbee-Pit 14.4
O'Farrell-Chi 14.4

Total Player Rating
Hornsby-StL 7.2
Grimes-Chi 4.1
Carey-Pit 3.9
Bancroft-NY 3.7
O'Farrell-Chi 3.6

Wins
Rixey-Cin 25
Cooper-Pit 23
Ruether-Bro 21
Pfeffer-StL 19
Nehf-NY 19

Win Percentage
Donohue-Cin 667
Rixey-Cin 658
Couch-Cin 640
Ruether-Bro 636
Cooper-Pit 622

Games
North-StL 53
Sherdel-StL 47
Ryan-NY 46
Oeschger-Bos 46
Morrison-Pit 45

Complete Games
Cooper-Pit 27
Ruether-Bro 26
Rixey-Cin 26

Shutouts
Vance-Bro 6
Morrison-Pit 5
Cooper-Pit 4
Adams-Pit 4

Saves
Jonnard-NY 5
North-StL 4

Innings Pitched
Rixey-Cin 313
Cooper-Pit 295
Morrison-Pit 286
Nehf-NY 268
Ruether-Bro 267

Fewest Hits/Game
Douglas-NY 8.77
Osborne-Chi 8.95
Ryan-NY 9.09
Luque-Cin 9.17
Vance-Bro 9.48

Fewest BB/Game
Adams-Pit 79
Alexander-Chi 1.24
Rixey-Cin 1.29
Donohue-Cin 1.60
Barnes-NY 1.61

Strikeouts
Vance-Bro 134
Cooper-Pit 129
Ring-Phi 116
Morrison-Pit 104
Grimes-Bro 99

Strikeouts/Game
Vance-Bro 4.90
Ring-Phi 4.19
Osborne-Chi 3.96
Cooper-Pit 3.94
Doak-StL 3.65

Wins Above Team
Ruether-Bro 5.5
Rixey-Cin 5.3
Donohue-Cin 3.8
Vance-Bro 3.7
Cooper-Pit 3.6

Earned Run Average
Douglas-NY 2.62
Ryan-NY 3.00
Donohue-Cin 3.12
Cooper-Pit 3.17
Nehf-NY 3.29

Adjusted ERA
Douglas-NY 157
Weinert-Phi 141
Ryan-NY 137
Cooper-Pit 131
Nehf-NY 125

Opponents' Batting Avg.
Douglas-NY 257
Luque-Cin 268
Ryan-NY 269
Osborne-Chi 271
Rixey-Cin 275

Opponents' On Base Pct.
Douglas-NY 296
Rixey-Cin 296
Adams-Pit 297
Donohue-Cin 304
Barnes-NY 306

Starter Runs
Cooper-Pit 30.3
Donohue-Cin 26.1
Douglas-NY 25.9
Nehf-NY 24.0
Ryan-NY 23.4

Adjusted Starter Runs
Cooper-Pit 32.1
Douglas-NY 26.2
Weinert-Phi 25.5
Nehf-NY 24.5
Ryan-NY 23.7

Clutch Pitching Index
Weinert-Phi 130
Ryan-NY 116
Cooper-Pit 113
Morrison-Pit 110
McQuillan-Bos-NY . . .110

Relief Runs
McNamara-Bos 13.3
Causey-NY 7.3
Braxton-Bos 5.5
Mamaux-Bro 4.1
Barnes-NY 3.7

Adjusted Relief Runs
McNamara-Bos 12.6
Causey-NY 7.4
Braxton-Bos 4.8
Barnes-NY 3.8
Jonnard-NY 2.9

Relief Ranking
McNamara-Bos 11.2
Causey-NY 6.8
Jonnard-NY 2.2
Braxton-Bos 1.9
Mamaux-Bro 1.3

Total Pitcher Index
Cooper-Pit 3.9
Meadows-Phi 2.8
Douglas-NY 2.7
Nehf-NY 2.7
Weinert-Phi 2.5

Total Baseball Ranking
Hornsby-StL 7.2
Grimes-Chi 4.1
Cooper-Pit 3.9
Carey-Pit 3.9
Bancroft-NY 3.7

TEAM	G	W	L	PCT	GB	R	OR	AB	H	2B	3B	HR	BB	SO	AVG	OBP	SLG	PRO	/A	BR	/A	PF	CHI	RC	TA	SB	CS	SBA	SBR
NY	154	94	60	.610		758	618	5245	1504	220	75	95	497	532	.287	.353	.412	.765	105	36	25	102	98	774	.726	62	59	51	-16
STL	154	93	61	.604	1	867	643	5416	1693	291	94	97	473	381	.313	.372	.455	.827	121	156	114	106	95	923	.818	132	73	64	-3
DET	155	79	75	.513	15	828	791	5360	1641	250	87	54	530	378	.306	.372	.415	.787	111	94	110	98	97	848	.760	78	61	56	-12
CLE	155	78	76	.506	16	768	817	5293	1544	320	73	32	554	331	.292	.364	.398	.762	105	42	29	102	97	792	.734	89	58	61	-7
CHI	155	77	77	.500	17	691	691	5267	1463	243	62	45	482	463	.278	.343	.373	.716	92	-51	-58	101	100	690	.668	106	84	56	-18
WAS	154	69	85	.448	25	650	706	5201	1395	229	76	45	458	442	.268	.334	.367	.701	88	-83	-24	92	102	659	.653	94	54	64	-3
PHI	155	65	89	.422	29	705	830	5241	1409	229	63	111	497	591	.269	.329	.400	.729	95	-43	-73	104	104	694	.675	60	63	49	-19
BOS	154	61	93	.396	33	598	769	5288	1392	250	55	45	366	455	.263	.316	.357	.673	81	-148	-120	96	105	600	.595	60	63	49	-19
TOT	618					5865		42311	12041	2032	585	524	3797	3573	.285	.348	.398	.746								681	515	57	-104

TEAM	CG	SHO	SV	IP	H	H/G	HR	BB	BB/G	SO	SO/G	ERA	/A	OAVG	OOBA	PR	/A	PF	CPI	FA	E	DP	FW	PW	BW	SBW	DIF
NY	100	7	14	1387.7	1402	9.1	73	423	2.7	458	3.0	3.39	118	.269	.315	98	92	99	102	.975	157	124	2.1	8.9	2.4	-.3	3.9
STL	79	8	22	1389.3	1412	9.1	71	419	2.7	534	3.5	3.38	122	.270	.315	100	112	102	103	.968	201	158	-.5	10.9	11.1	1.0	-6.4
DET	67	7	15	1385.0	1554	10.1	62	473	3.1	461	3.0	4.27	92	.290	.337	-36	-53	97	95	.970	191	133	.0	-5.1	10.7	.1	-3.7
CLE	76	14	7	1380.3	1605	10.5	58	464	3.0	489	3.2	4.60	90	.297	.342	-87	-71	103	92	.968	202	147	-.5	-6.9	2.8	.6	5.0
CHI	86	13	8	1395.0	1472	9.5	57	529	3.4	484	3.1	3.93	104	.277	.331	16	22	101	97	.975	155	143	2.2	2.1	-5.6	-.5	1.8
WAS	84	13	10	1360.0	1485	9.8	49	500	3.1	422	2.8	3.81	98	.284	.335	33	-11	93	103	.969	196	168	-.2	-1.1	-2.3	1.0	-5.4
PHI	73	4	6	1359.0	1573	10.4	107	469	3.1	373	2.5	4.59	94	.296	.341	-84	-45	106	98	.966	215	118	-1.3	-4.4	-7.1	-.6	1.3
BOS	71	10	6	1372.0	1508	9.9	48	503	3.3	359	2.4	4.30	93	.285	.334	-41	-46	99	92	.965	224	145	-1.8	-4.5	-11.6	-.6	2.5
TOT	636	76	88	11028.3		9.8			3.1		2.9	4.03		.285	.348					.969	1541	1136					

Runs		Hits		Doubles		Triples		Home Runs		Total Bases	
Sisler-StL	134	Sisler-StL	246	Speaker-Cle	48	Sisler-StL	18	Williams-StL	39	Williams-StL	367
Blue-Det	131	Cobb-Det	211	Pratt-Bos	44	Jacobson-StL	16	Walker-Phi	37	Sisler-StL	348
Williams-StL	128	Tobin-StL	207	Sisler-StL	42	Cobb-Det	16	Ruth-NY	35	Walker-Phi	310
Tobin-StL	122	Veach-Det	202	Cobb-Det	42	Judge-Was	15	Miller-Phi	21	Cobb-Det	297
						Mostil-Chi	14	Heilmann-Det	21	Tobin-StL	296

Runs Batted In		Runs Produced		Bases On Balls		Batting Average		On Base Percentage		Slugging Average	
Williams-StL	155	Williams-StL	244	Witt-NY	89	Sisler-StL	.420	Speaker-Cle	.474	Ruth-NY	.672
Veach-Det	126	Sisler-StL	231	Ruth-NY	84	Cobb-Det	.401	Sisler-StL	.467	Williams-StL	.627
McManus-StL	109	Veach-Det	213	Blue-Det	82	Speaker-Cle	.378	Cobb-Det	.462	Speaker-Cle	.606
Sisler-StL	105	Cobb-Det	194	Speaker-Cle	77	Heilmann-Det	.356	Ruth-NY	.434	Heilmann-Det	.598
Jacobson-StL	102	McManus-StL	186	Williams-StL	74	Miller-Phi	.335	Heilmann-Det	.432	Sisler-StL	.594

Production		Adjusted Production		Batter Runs		Adjusted Batter Runs		Clutch Hitting Index		Runs Created	
Ruth-NY	1.106	Ruth-NY	182	Sisler-StL	64.4	Sisler-StL	59.9	Sewell-Cle	142	Sisler-StL	162
Speaker-Cle	1.080	Speaker-Cle	177	Williams-StL	56.1	Cobb-Det	54.0	O'Neill-Cle	138	Williams-StL	150
Sisler-StL	1.061	Cobb-Det	170	Speaker-Cle	52.8	Speaker-Cle	51.7	Veach-Det	137	Cobb-Det	133
Williams-StL	1.040	Heilmann-Det	170	Cobb-Det	52.4	Williams-StL	51.4	Jacobson-StL	136	Speaker-Cle	127
Heilmann-Det	1.030	Sisler-StL	166	Ruth-NY	50.5	Ruth-NY	49.6	Wood-Cle	136	Ruth-NY	120

Total Average		Stolen Bases		Stolen Base Average		Stolen Base Runs		Fielding Runs		Total Player Rating	
Speaker-Cle	1.284	Sisler-StL	51	Jacobson-StL	76.0	Sisler-StL	3.9	Harris-Was	26.4	Sisler-StL	5.9
Ruth-NY	1.268	Williams-StL	37	Sisler-StL	72.9	Veach-Det	2.1	Scott-NY	18.8	Williams-StL	5.0
Sisler-StL	1.256	Harris-Was	25	Rigney-Det	70.4	Jacobson-StL	2.1	Peckinpaugh-Was	16.3	Speaker-Cle	4.7
Williams-StL	1.183	Johnson-Chi	21	Harris-Was	69.4	Evans-Cle	2.1	Schalk-Chi	15.2	Ruth-NY	3.9
Heilmann-Det	1.148			Rice-Was	69.0	Shanks-Was	1.8	Williams-StL	13.4	Cobb-Det	3.6

Wins		Win Percentage		Games		Complete Games		Shutouts		Saves	
Rommel-Phi	27	Bush-NY	.788	Rommel-Phi	51	Faber-Chi	31	Uhle-Cle	5	Jones-NY	8
Bush-NY	26	Rommel-Phi	.675	Uhle-Cle	50	Shocker-StL	29			Pruett-StL	7
Shocker-StL	24	Shawkey-NY	.625	Shocker-StL	48	Uhle-Cle	23			Wright-StL	5
Uhle-Cle	22	Pillette-Det	.613	Harriss-Phi	47	Johnson-Was	23				
Faber-Chi	21	Hoyt-NY	.613								

Innings Pitched		Fewest Hits/Game		Fewest BB/Game		Strikeouts		Strikeouts/Game		Wins Above Team	
Faber-Chi	352	Davis-StL	8.38	Shocker-StL	1.47	Shocker-StL	149	Morton-Cle	4.52	Rommel-Phi	10.3
Shocker-StL	348	Bush-NY	8.47	Vangilder-StL	1.76	Faber-Chi	148	Harriss-Phi	3.99	Bush-NY	8.5
Shawkey-NY	300	Faber-Chi	8.54	Mays-NY	1.88	Shawkey-NY	130	Shawkey-NY	3.90	Mogridge-Was	4.4
Rommel-Phi	294	Shawkey-NY	8.58	Kolp-StL	1.91	Ehmke-Det	108	Shocker-StL	3.85	Kolp-StL	4.2
Uhle-Cle	287	Wright-StL	8.65	Hasty-Phi	1.92	Johnson-Was	105	Faber-Chi	3.78	Zachary-Was	3.9

Earned Run Average		Adjusted ERA		Opponents' Batting Avg.		Opponents' On Base Pct.		Starter Runs		Adjusted Starter Runs	
Faber-Chi	2.81	Faber-Chi	145	Davis-StL	.250	Faber-Chi	.289	Faber-Chi	47.7	Faber-Chi	49.3
Pillette-Det	2.85	Wright-StL	141	Bush-NY	.252	Shocker-StL	.296	Shocker-StL	40.9	Shocker-StL	43.9
Shawkey-NY	2.91	Shocker-StL	138	Faber-Chi	.252	Quinn-Bos	.297	Shawkey-NY	37.4	Shawkey-NY	36.1
Wright-StL	2.92	Pillette-Det	138	Shawkey-NY	.256	Rommel-Phi	.301	Pillette-Det	36.2	Rommel-Phi	33.2
Shocker-StL	2.97	Shawkey-NY	137	Pillette-Det	.258	Vangilder-StL	.303	Johnson-Was	32.5	Pillette-Det	32.8

Clutch Pitching Index		Relief Runs		Adjusted Relief Runs		Relief Ranking		Total Pitcher Index		Total Baseball Ranking	
Mogridge-Was	125	Murray-NY	5	Murray-NY	3	Murray-NY	3	Faber-Chi	4.9	Sisler-StL	5.9
Wright-StL	118							Shocker-StL	4.4	Williams-StL	5.0
Johnson-Was	114							Rommel-Phi	3.4	Faber-Chi	4.9
Pillette-Det	111							Shawkey-NY	3.4	Speaker-Cle	4.7
Shawkey-NY	109							Pillette-Det	3.3	Shocker-StL	4.4

TEAM	G	W	L	PCT	GB	R	OR	AB	H	2B	3B	HR	BB	SO	AVG	OBP	SLG	PRO	/A	BR	/A	PF	CHI	RC	TA	SB	CS	SBA	SBR
NY	153	95	58	.621		854	679	5452	1610	248	76	85	487	406	.295	.356	.415	.771	109	71	60	101	103	816	.738	106	70	60	-9
CIN	154	91	63	.591	4.5	708	629	5278	1506	237	95	45	439	367	.285	.344	.392	.736	100	-1	15	98	95	707	.680	96	105	48	-33
PIT	154	87	67	.565	8.5	786	696	5405	1592	224	111	49	407	362	.295	.347	.404	.751	104	26	49	97	102	766	.713	154	75	67	1
CHI	154	83	71	.539	12.5	756	704	5259	1516	243	52	90	455	485	.288	.348	.406	.754	104	32	0	104	98	735	.721	181	143	56	-31
STL	154	79	74	.516	16	746	732	5526	1582	274	76	63	438	446	.286	.343	.398	.741	101	5	80	90	96	761	.690	89	61	59	-9
BRO	155	76	78	.494	19.5	753	741	5476	1559	214	81	62	425	382	.285	.340	.387	.727	97	-20	-2	98	102	730	.668	71	50	59	-8
BOS	155	54	100	.351	41.5	636	798	5329	1455	213	58	32	429	404	.273	.331	.353	.684	86	-99	-96	100	98	625	.606	57	80	42	-30
PHI	155	50	104	.325	45.5	748	1008	5491	1528	259	39	112	414	556	.278	.333	.401	.734	99	-14	-116	114	101	729	.675	70	73	49	-22
TOT	617					5987		43216	12348	1912	588	538	3494	3408	.286	.343	.395	.738								824	657	56	-146

TEAM	CG	SHO	SV	IP	H	H/G	HR	BB	BB/G	SO	SO/G	ERA	/A	OAVG	OOBA	PR	/A	PF	CPI	FA	E	DP	FW	PW	BW	SBW	DIF
NY	62	10	18	1377.0	1440	9.4	82	424	2.8	453	3.0	3.90	101	.272	.319	13	4	99	93	.972	176	141	2.5	.4	5.8	.9	9.0
CIN	88	11	9	1389.0	1465	9.5	29	359	2.3	450	2.9	3.21	120	.274	.312	120	98	96	101	.969	202	144	.9	9.4	1.4	-1.4	3.6
PIT	92	5	9	1374.0	1313	8.6	53	402	2.6	414	2.7	3.87	98	.254	.301	17	-10	95	77	.971	179	157	2.3	-1.0	4.7	1.9	2.1
CHI	80	8	11	1364.0	1419	9.4	86	435	2.9	408	2.7	3.82	108	.271	.320	25	45	103	96	.967	208	144	.5	4.3	.0	-1.2	2.3
STL	77	10	7	1398.7	1539	9.9	70	456	2.9	398	2.6	3.87	93	.282	.329	18	-44	90	100	.963	232	141	-.9	-4.2	7.7	-.9	-1.0
BRO	94	8	5	1396.0	1522	9.8	54	477	3.1	549	3.5	3.73	104	.280	.331	39	24	98	101	.955	293	137	-4.6	2.3	-.2	1.0	.5
BOS	54	13	7	1382.7	1662	10.8	64	394	2.6	351	2.3	4.22	97	.300	.339	-35	-20	102	100	.964	230	157	-.8	-1.9	-9.2	-1.1	-10.0
PHI	68	3	8	1374.3	1801	11.8	100	549	3.6	384	2.5	5.30	89	.319	.371	-200	-91	118	100	.966	217	172	.0	-8.7	-11.1	-.3	-6.8
TOT	615	68	74	11055.7		9.9		2.8		2.8		3.99		.286	.343					.966	1737	1193					

Runs
Youngs-NY	121
Carey-Pit	120
Frisch-NY	116
Johnston-Bro	111
Statz-Chi	110

Hits
Frisch-NY	223
Statz-Chi	209
Traynor-Pit	208
Johnston-Bro	203
Youngs-NY	200

Doubles
Roush-Cin	41
Tierney-Pit-Phi	36
Grantham-Chi	36
Bottomley-StL	34

Triples
Traynor-Pit	19
Carey-Pit	19
Roush-Cin	18
Southworth-Bos	16

Home Runs
Williams-Phi	41
Fournier-Bro	22
Miller-Chi	20
Meusel-NY	19
Hornsby-StL	17

Total Bases
Frisch-NY	311
Williams-Phi	308
Fournier-Bro	303
Traynor-Pit	301
Statz-Chi	288

Runs Batted In
Meusel-NY	125
Williams-Phi	114
Frisch-NY	111
Kelly-NY	103
Fournier-Bro	102

Runs Produced
Frisch-NY	215
Meusel-NY	208
Youngs-NY	205
Traynor-Pit	197
Carey-Pit	177

Bases On Balls
Burns-Cin	101
Sand-Phi	82
Youngs-NY	73
Carey-Pit	73
Grantham-Chi	71

Batting Average
Hornsby-StL	.384
Bottomley-StL	.371
Fournier-Bro	.351
Roush-Cin	.351
Frisch-NY	.348

On Base Percentage
Hornsby-StL	.459
Bottomley-StL	.425
Youngs-NY	.412
Fournier-Bro	.411
O'Farrell-Chi	.408

Slugging Average
Hornsby-StL	.627
Fournier-Bro	.588
Williams-Phi	.576
Bottomley-StL	.535
Roush-Cin	.531

Production
Hornsby-StL	1.086
Fournier-Bro	.999
Bottomley-StL	.960
Williams-Phi	.947
Roush-Cin	.938

Adjusted Production
Hornsby-StL	204
Bottomley-StL	168
Fournier-Bro	165
Roush-Cin	149
Grimm-Pit	132

Batter Runs
Hornsby-StL	52.0
Fournier-Bro	43.7
Bottomley-StL	39.1
Roush-Cin	34.0
Williams-Phi	33.2

Adjusted Batter Runs
Hornsby-StL	58.0
Bottomley-StL	46.4
Fournier-Bro	45.4
Roush-Cin	35.7
Hargrave-Cin	28.0

Clutch Hitting Index
Stock-StL	159
McInnis-Bos	145
Meusel-NY	137
Kelly-NY	123
Grimm-Pit	122

Runs Created
Fournier-Bro	125
Frisch-NY	123
Hornsby-StL	120
Bottomley-StL	117
Carey-Pit	117

Total Average
Hornsby-StL	1.220
Fournier-Bro	1.083
Bottomley-StL	.994
Williams-Phi	.992
Roush-Cin	.950

Stolen Bases
Carey-Pit	51
Grantham-Chi	43
Smith-StL	32
Heathcote-Chi	32

Stolen Base Average
Carey-Pit	86.4
Smith-StL	74.4
Frisch-NY	70.7
Traynor-Pit	68.3
Heathcote-Chi	65.3

Stolen Base Runs
Carey-Pit	10.5
Smith-StL	3.0
Rawlings-Pit	2.7

Fielding Runs
Carey-Pit	16.0
Statz-Chi	14.6
Bohne-Cin	13.6
Neis-Bro	13.5
Nixon-Bos	13.3

Total Player Rating
Carey-Pit	4.2
Fournier-Bro	4.1
Hornsby-StL	3.9
Traynor-Pit	3.6
Frisch-NY	3.3

Wins
Luque-Cin	27
Morrison-Pit	25
Alexander-Chi	22
Grimes-Bro	21
Donohue-Cin	21

Win Percentage
Luque-Cin	.771
Ryan-NY	.762
Scott-NY	.696
Morrison-Pit	.658
Alexander-Chi	.647

Games
Ryan-NY	45
Jonnard-NY	45
Oeschger-Bos	44
Barnes-NY -Bos	43
Genewich-Bos	43

Complete Games
Grimes-Bro	33
Luque-Cin	28
Morrison-Pit	27
Cooper-Pit	26
Alexander-Chi	26

Shutouts
Luque-Cin	6
Barnes-NY -Bos	5
McQuillan-NY	5

Saves
Jonnard-NY	5
Ryan-NY	4

Innings Pitched
Grimes-Bro	327
Luque-Cin	322
Rixey-Cin	309
Alexander-Chi	305
Ring-Phi	304

Fewest Hits/Game
Luque-Cin	7.80
Vance-Bro	8.45
Morrison-Pit	8.55
Keen-Chi	8.59
Aldridge-Chi	8.67

Fewest BB/Game
Alexander-Chi	.89
Adams-Pit	1.42
Genewich-Bos	1.82
Rixey-Cin	1.89
Meadows-Phi-Pit	2.15

Strikeouts
Vance-Bro	197
Luque-Cin	151
Grimes-Bro	119
Morrison-Pit	114
Ring-Phi	112

Strikeouts/Game
Vance-Bro	6.33
Luque-Cin	4.22
Bentley-NY	3.93
Osborne-Chi	3.45
Morrison-Pit	3.40

Wins Above Team
Luque-Cin	8.8
Ring-Phi	6.1
Morrison-Pit	5.0
Alexander-Chi	4.8
Ryan-NY	4.3

Earned Run Average
Luque-Cin	1.93
Rixey-Cin	2.80
Keen-Chi	3.00
Kaufmann-Chi	3.10
Haines-StL	3.11

Adjusted ERA
Luque-Cin	199
Rixey-Cin	137
Keen-Chi	137
Kaufmann-Chi	133
Alexander-Chi	129

Opponents' Batting Avg.
Luque-Cin	.235
Vance-Bro	.250
Aldridge-Chi	.251
Morrison-Pit	.253
Osborne-Chi	.255

Opponents' On Base Pct.
Alexander-Chi	.271
Luque-Cin	.286
Ryan-NY	.300
Aldridge-Chi	.303
McQuillan-NY	.307

Starter Runs
Luque-Cin	73.7
Rixey-Cin	40.9
Alexander-Chi	27.2
Haines-StL	25.9
Kaufmann-Chi	20.3

Adjusted Starter Runs
Luque-Cin	68.5
Rixey-Cin	36.0
Alexander-Chi	31.7
Ring-Phi	27.7
Kaufmann-Chi	23.4

Clutch Pitching Index
Kaufmann-Chi	117
Rixey-Cin	116
Genewich-Bos	115
Doak-StL	115
Luque-Cin	115

Relief Runs
Decatur-Bro	15.4
Jonnard-NY	7.5
Keck-Cin	2.6
Barnes-NY	.5

Adjusted Relief Runs
Decatur-Bro	14.3
Jonnard-NY	6.9
Keck-Cin	1.2
Barnes-NY	.1

Relief Ranking
Decatur-Bro	8.9
Jonnard-NY	5.3
Keck-Cin	1.1
Barnes-NY	.1

Total Pitcher Index
Luque-Cin	7.4
Alexander-Chi	3.6
Rixey-Cin	3.2
Kaufmann-Chi	2.5
Ring-Phi	2.2

Total Baseball Ranking
Luque-Cin	7.4
Carey-Pit	4.2
Fournier-Bro	4.1
Hornsby-StL	3.9
Alexander-Chi	3.6

TEAM	G	W	L	PCT	GB	R	OR	AB	H	2B	3B	HR	BB	SO	AVG	OBP	SLG	PRO	/A	BR	/A	PF	CHI	RC	TA	SB	CS	SBA	SBR
NY	152	98	54	.645		823	622	5347	1554	231	79	105	521	516	.291	.357	.422	.779	110	73	41	104	101	811	.745	69	74	48	-23
DET	155	83	71	.539	16	831	741	5266	1579	270	69	41	596	385	.300	.377	.401	.778	111	90	115	97	98	827	.760	87	62	58	-10
CLE	153	82	71	.536	16.5	888	746	5290	1594	301	75	59	633	384	.301	.381	.420	.801	117	134	125	101	99	869	.791	79	77	51	-22
WAS	155	75	78	.490	23.5	720	747	5244	1436	224	93	26	532	448	.274	.346	.367	.713	93	-45	-4	95	103	693	.672	102	67	60	-9
STL	154	74	78	.487	24	688	720	5298	1489	248	62	82	442	423	.281	.339	.398	.737	99	-15	-44	104	96	724	.683	64	54	54	-12
PHI	153	69	83	.454	29	661	761	5196	1407	229	65	52	445	517	.271	.333	.370	.703	90	-74	-76	100	102	653	.644	72	62	54	-15
CHI	156	69	85	.448	30	692	741	5246	1463	254	57	42	532	458	.279	.350	.373	.723	96	-26	-13	98	96	706	.697	191	119	62	-13
BOS	154	61	91	.401	37	584	809	5181	1354	253	54	34	391	480	.261	.318	.351	.669	81	-142	-153	102	103	578	.594	77	91	46	-31
TOT	616					5887		42068	11876	2010	554	441	4092	3611	.282	.351	.388	.739								741	606	55	-140

TEAM	CG	SHO	SV	IP	H	H/G	HR	BB	BB/G	SO	SO/G	ERA	/A	OAVG	OOBA	PR	/A	PF	CPI	FA	E	DP	FW	PW	BW	SBW	DIF
NY	101	9	10	1382.0	1365	8.9	68	491	3.2	506	3.3	3.66	110	.264	.320	50	55	101	95	.977	144	131	3.4	5.3	4.0	-.5	9.8
DET	61	9	12	1375.3	1502	9.8	58	449	2.9	447	2.9	4.09	99	.284	.330	-15	-45	95	94	.968	200	103	.0	-4.4	11.1	.7	-1.5
CLE	77	10	11	1368.0	1517	10.0	36	466	3.1	407	2.7	3.91	101	.287	.334	11	4	99	99	.964	226	143	-1.6	.4	12.1	-.4	-5.0
WAS	71	8	16	1382.3	1531	10.0	56	559	3.6	474	3.1	3.99	95	.287	.343	0	-31	95	104	.966	216	182	-1.0	-3.0	-.4	.8	-5.0
STL	83	10	10	1373.0	1430	9.4	59	528	3.5	488	3.2	3.93	106	.275	.331	8	36	105	96	.971	177	145	1.4	3.5	-4.3	.5	-3.2
PHI	65	7	12	1360.0	1465	9.7	68	550	3.6	400	2.6	4.08	100	.281	.337	-14	-1	102	99	.965	221	127	-1.3	-.0	-7.3	.3	1.5
CHI	74	5	11	1399.3	1512	9.7	49	534	3.4	467	3.0	4.03	98	.282	.334	-7	-12	99	97	.971	184	138	1.0	-1.2	-1.3	.5	-7.0
BOS	77	3	11	1368.0	1534	10.1	48	520	3.4	412	2.7	4.20	100	.290	.341	-32	1	106	98	.963	232	126	-2.0	.0	-14.8	-1.3	2.9
TOT	609	61	93	11008.0		9.7			3.3		2.9	3.99		.282	.351					.968	1600	1095					

Runs
Ruth-NY 151
Speaker-Cle 133
Jamieson-Cle 130
Heilmann-Det 121
Rice-Was 117

Hits
Jamieson-Cle 222
Speaker-Cle 218
Heilmann-Det 211
Ruth-NY 205
Tobin-StL 202

Doubles
Speaker-Cle 59
Burns-Bos 47
Ruth-NY 45
Heilmann-Det 44
Sewell-Cle 41

Triples
Rice-Was 18
Goslin-Was 18
Tobin-StL 15
Mostil-Chi 15

Home Runs
Ruth-NY 41
Williams-StL 29
Heilmann-Det 18
Speaker-Cle 17
Hauser-Phi 17

Total Bases
Ruth-NY 399
Speaker-Cle 350
Williams-StL 346
Heilmann-Det 331
Tobin-StL 303

Runs Batted In
Speaker-Cle 130
Ruth-NY 130
Heilmann-Det 115
Sewell-Cle 109
Pipp-NY 108

Runs Produced
Speaker-Cle 246
Ruth-NY 240
Heilmann-Det 218
Sewell-Cle 204
Rice-Was 189

Bases On Balls
Ruth-NY 170
Sewell-Cle 98
Blue-Det 96
Speaker-Cle 93
Collins-Chi 84

Batting Average
Heilmann-Det 403
Ruth-NY 393
Speaker-Cle 380
Collins-Chi 360
Williams-StL 357

On Base Percentage
Ruth-NY 545
Heilmann-Det 481
Speaker-Cle 469
Sewell-Cle 456
Collins-Chi 455

Slugging Average
Ruth-NY 764
Heilmann-Det 632
Williams-StL 623
Speaker-Cle 610
Harris-Bos 520

Production
Ruth-NY 1.309
Heilmann-Det 1.113
Speaker-Cle 1.079
Williams-StL 1.062
Sewell-Cle 935

Adjusted Production
Ruth-NY 232
Heilmann-Det 198
Speaker-Cle 180
Williams-StL 171
Sewell-Cle 145

Batter Runs
Ruth-NY 119.1
Speaker-Cle 70.9
Heilmann-Det 70.7
Williams-StL 61.2
Sewell-Cle 42.7

Adjusted Batter Runs
Ruth-NY 115.4
Heilmann-Det 73.3
Speaker-Cle 69.9
Williams-StL 58.0
Sewell-Cle 41.8

Clutch Hitting Index
Pipp-NY 160
Sewell-Cle 144
Sheely-Chi 142
Rigney-Det 134
Judge-Was 130

Runs Created
Ruth-NY 223
Speaker-Cle 166
Heilmann-Det 159
Williams-StL 148
Sewell-Cle 128

Total Average
Ruth-NY 1.746
Heilmann-Det 1.306
Speaker-Cle 1.252
Williams-StL 1.190
Sewell-Cle 1.041

Stolen Bases
Collins-Chi 49
Mostil-Chi 41
Harris-Was 23
Rice-Was 20
Jamieson-Cle 19

Stolen Base Average
Rice-Was 71.4
Mostil-Chi 70.7
Collins-Chi 62.8
Jamieson-Cle 61.3
Harris-Was 59.0

Stolen Base Runs
Mostil-Chi 2.1
Barrett-Cle 1.8
Veach-Det 1.2
Rice-Was 1.2

Fielding Runs
Peckinpaugh-Was . . 23.0
Lutzke-Cle 21.1
Ruel-Was 19.9
Flagstead-Det-Bos . . 19.1
Harris-Was 17.6

Total Player Rating
Ruth-NY 9.0
Sewell-Cle 5.7
Speaker-Cle 5.6
Heilmann-Det 5.6
Williams-StL 4.9

Wins
Uhle-Cle 26
Jones-NY 21
Dauss-Det 21
Shocker-StL 20
Ehmke-Bos 20

Win Percentage
Pennock-NY 760
Jones-NY 724
Hoyt-NY 654
Shocker-StL 625
Uhle-Cle 619

Games
Rommel-Phi 56
Uhle-Cle 54
Russell-Was 52
Cole-Det 52
Dauss-Det 50

Complete Games
Uhle-Cle 29
Ehmke-Bos 28
Shocker-StL 24
Dauss-Det 22
Bush-NY 22

Shutouts
Coveleski-Cle 5
Vangilder-StL 4
Dauss-Det 4

Saves
Russell-Was 9
Quinn-Bos 7
Harriss-Phi 6

Innings Pitched
Uhle-Cle 358
Ehmke-Bos 317
Dauss-Det 316
Rommel-Phi 298
Vangilder-StL 282

Fewest Hits/Game
Shawkey-NY 8.06
Hoyt-NY 8.55
Bush-NY 8.58
Danforth-StL 8.80
Russell-Was 8.80

Fewest BB/Game
Shocker-StL 1.59
Coveleski-Cle 1.66
Thurston-StL-Chi 1.74
Quinn-Bos 1.96
Dauss-Det 2.22

Strikeouts
Johnson-Was 130
Shawkey-NY 125
Bush-NY 125
Ehmke-Bos 121

Strikeouts/Game
Johnson-Det 4.76
Johnson-Was 4.48
Shawkey-NY 4.34
Bush-NY 4.08
Harriss-Phi 3.83

Wins Above Team
Ehmke-Bos 5.3
Shocker-StL 5.1
Uhle-Cle 4.9
Pennock-NY 4.6
Cole-Det 3.8

Earned Run Average
Coveleski-Cle 2.76
Hoyt-NY 3.01
Russell-Was 3.03
Vangilder-StL 3.06
Mogridge-Was 3.11

Adjusted ERA
Coveleski-Cle 142
Vangilder-StL 136
Hoyt-NY 133
Pennock-NY 128
Thurston-StL-Chi 127

Opponents' Batting Avg.
Shawkey-NY 246
Hoyt-NY 253
Jones-NY 257
Faber-Chi 259
Bush-NY 260

Opponents' On Base Pct.
Shocker-StL 298
Hoyt-NY 299
Faber-Chi 301
Jones-NY 306
Pennock-NY 308

Starter Runs
Coveleski-Cle 31.0
Vangilder-StL 28.9
Hoyt-NY 25.9
Rommel-Phi 24.0
Pennock-NY 22.4

Adjusted Starter Runs
Vangilder-StL 34.7
Coveleski-Cle 29.7
Rommel-Phi 26.8
Hoyt-NY 26.7
Shocker-StL 23.3

Clutch Pitching Index
Thurston-StL-Chi 139
Russell-Was 128
Mogridge-Was 122
Vangilder-StL 121
Coveleski-Cle 121

Relief Runs

Adjusted Relief Runs

Relief Ranking

Total Pitcher Index
Rommel-Phi 3.4
Vangilder-StL 3.2
Bush-NY 2.7
Coveleski-Cle 2.5
Pennock-NY 2.4

Total Baseball Ranking
Ruth-NY 9.0
Sewell-Cle 5.7
Speaker-Cle 5.6
Heilmann-Det 5.6
Williams-StL 4.9

TEAM	G	W	L	PCT	GB	R	OR	AB	H	2B	3B	HR	BB	SO	AVG	OBP	SLG	PRO	/A	BR	/A	PF	CHI	RC	TA	SB	CS	SBA	SBR
NY	154	93	60	.608		857	641	5445	1634	269	81	95	467	479	.300	.358	.432	.790	117	124	186	91	101	849	.758	82	53	61	-6
BRO	154	92	62	.597	1.5	717	675	5339	1534	227	54	72	447	357	.287	.345	.391	.736	102	19	26	99	98	725	.672	34	46	43	-16
PIT	153	90	63	.588	3	724	588	5288	1517	222	122	43	366	396	.287	.336	.399	.735	102	11	-32	106	102	714	.696	181	92	66	0
CIN	153	83	70	.542	10	649	579	5301	1539	236	111	36	349	334	.290	.337	.397	.734	101	9	5	101	92	698	.669	103	98	51	-27
CHI	154	81	72	.529	12	698	699	5134	1419	207	59	66	469	521	.276	.340	.378	.718	97	-9	-15	101	102	652	.667	137	149	48	-47
STL	154	65	89	.422	28.5	740	750	5349	1552	270	87	67	382	418	.290	.341	.411	.752	106	42	24	103	99	740	.695	86	86	50	-25
PHI	152	55	96	.364	37	676	849	5306	1459	256	56	94	382	452	.275	.328	.397	.725	99	-11	-63	108	98	687	.660	57	67	46	-22
BOS	154	53	100	.346	40	520	800	5283	1355	194	52	25	354	451	.256	.306	.327	.633	74	-180	-137	94	103	532	.546	74	68	52	-18
TOT	614					5581		42445	12009	1881	622	498	3216	3408	.283	.337	.392	.728								754	659	53	-168

TEAM	CG	SHO	SV	IP	H	H/G	HR	BB	BB/G	SO	SO/G	ERA	/A	OAVG	OOBA	PR	/A	PF	CPI	FA	E	DP	FW	PW	BW	SBW	DIF
NY	71	4	21	1376.7	1464	9.6	77	392	2.6	406	2.7	3.62	93	.277	.321	37	-36	88	103	.971	186	160	.3	-3.6	18.5	1.5	-.2
BRO	97	10	5	1375.3	1432	9.4	58	403	2.6	638	4.2	3.64	104	.273	.318	34	24	98	97	.968	196	121	-.3	2.4	2.6	.5	9.8
PIT	85	15	5	1382.7	1387	9.0	42	323	2.1	364	2.4	3.27	123	.265	.300	91	114	104	94	.971	183	161	.5	11.3	-3.2	2.1	2.8
CIN	77	14	9	1377.0	1408	9.2	30	293	1.9	451	2.9	3.12	123	.269	.300	114	109	99	98	.966	217	142	-1.4	10.8	.5	-.6	-2.8
CHI	85	4	6	1380.3	1459	9.5	89	438	2.9	416	2.7	3.83	102	.276	.324	5	11	101	100	.966	218	153	-1.5	1.1	-1.5	-2.6	8.9
STL	79	7	6	1362.3	1528	10.1	69	486	3.2	393	2.6	4.15	96	.288	.339	-42	-26	103	101	.969	188	162	.2	-2.6	2.4	-.4	-11.6
PHI	59	7	10	1359.0	1689	11.2	84	469	3.1	349	2.3	4.87	88	.309	.355	-151	-89	111	99	.972	175	168	-.8	-8.8	-6.3	-.0	-6.2
BOS	66	10	4	1376.3	1607	10.5	49	402	2.6	364	2.4	4.46	86	.296	.334	-90	-97	99	92	.973	168	154	1.3	-9.6	-13.6	.3	-1.9
TOT	619	71	66	10989.7		9.8			2.6		2.8	3.87		.283	.337					.970	1531	1221					

Runs
Hornsby-StL 121
Frisch-NY 121
Carey-Pit 113
Youngs-NY 112
Williams-Phi 101

Hits
Hornsby-StL 227
Wheat-Bro 212
Frisch-NY 198
High-NY 191
Fournier-Bro 188

Doubles
Hornsby-StL 43
Wheat-Bro 41
Kelly-NY 37

Triples
Roush-Cin 21
Maranville-Pit 20
Wright-Pit 18
Cuyler-Pit 16
Frisch-NY 15

Home Runs
Fournier-Bro 27
Hornsby-StL 25
Williams-Phi 24
Kelly-NY 21

Total Bases
Hornsby-StL 373
Wheat-Bro 311
Williams-Phi 308
Kelly-NY 303
Fournier-Bro 302

Runs Batted In
Kelly-NY 136
Fournier-Bro 116
Wright-Pit 111
Bottomley-StL 111
Meusel-NY 102

Runs Produced
Kelly-NY 206
Hornsby-StL 190
Wright-Pit 184
Bottomley-StL 184
Frisch-NY 183

Bases On Balls
Hornsby-StL 89
Fournier-Bro 83
Youngs-NY 77
Williams-Phi 67
Friberg-Chi 66

Batting Average
Hornsby-StL 424
Wheat-Bro 375
Youngs-NY 356
Cuyler-Pit 354
Roush-Cin 348

On Base Percentage
Hornsby-StL 507
Youngs-NY 441
Fournier-Bro 428
Wheat-Bro 428
Williams-Phi 403

Slugging Average
Hornsby-StL 696
Williams-Phi 552
Wheat-Bro 549
Cuyler-Pit 539
Fournier-Bro 536

Production
Hornsby-StL 1.203
Wheat-Bro 978
Fournier-Bro 965
Youngs-NY 962
Williams-Phi 955

Adjusted Production
Hornsby-StL 214
Youngs-NY 172
Wheat-Bro 162
Fournier-Bro 159
Kelly-NY 152

Batter Runs
Hornsby-StL 94.1
Wheat-Bro 48.2
Fournier-Bro 48.1
Youngs-NY 45.3
Williams-Phi 42.1

Adjusted Batter Runs
Hornsby-StL 92.2
Youngs-NY 51.6
Wheat-Bro 49.0
Fournier-Bro 49.0
Williams-Phi 36.4

Clutch Hitting Index
Friberg-Chi 164
Meusel-NY 158
Wright-Pit 152
Griffith-Bro 145
Brown-Bro 145

Runs Created
Hornsby-StL 186
Fournier-Bro 133
Wheat-Bro 132
Youngs-NY 123
Williams-Phi 121

Total Average
Hornsby-StL 1.461
Fournier-Bro 1.058
Youngs-NY 1.049
Cuyler-Pit 1.026
Wheat-Bro 1.025

Stolen Bases
Carey-Pit 49
Cuyler-Pit 32
Heathcote-Chi 26
Traynor-Pit 24
Smith-StL 24

Stolen Base Average
Carey-Pit 79.0
Cuyler-Pit 74.4
Frisch-NY 71.0
Critz-Cin 63.3
Smith-StL 60.0

Stolen Base Runs
Carey-Pit 6.9
Cuyler-Pit 3.0
Hartnett-Chi 1.8

Fielding Runs
Frisch-NY 25.7
Pinelli-Cin 25.5
Statz-Chi 13.1
O'Neil-Bos 12.9
Smith-StL 11.3

Total Player Rating
Hornsby-StL 6.8
Frisch-NY 4.9
Wheat-Bro 4.8
Fournier-Bro 4.7
Youngs-NY 4.1

Wins
Vance-Bro 28
Grimes-Bro 22
Mays-Cin 20
Cooper-Pit 20
Kremer-Pit 18

Win Percentage
Yde-Pit 842
Vance-Bro 824
Bentley-NY 762
Mays-Cin 690
Kremer-Pit 643

Games
Morrison-Pit 41
Kremer-Pit 41
Keen-Chi 40
Sheehan-Cin 39

Complete Games
Vance-Bro 30
Grimes-Bro 30
Cooper-Pit 25
Barnes-Bos 21
Aldridge-Chi 20

Shutouts

Saves
May-Cin 6
Ryan-NY 5
Jonnard-NY 5

Innings Pitched
Grimes-Bro 311
Vance-Bro 309
Cooper-Pit 269
Barnes-Bos 268
Kremer-Pit 259

Fewest Hits/Game
Vance-Bro 6.93
Yde-Pit 7.93
Morrison-Pit 8.05
Doak-StL-Bro 8.16
Rixey-Cin 8.28

Fewest BB/Game
Benton-Cin 1.33
Alexander-Chi 1.33
Cooper-Pit 1.34
Mays-Cin 1.43
Donohue-Cin 1.46

Strikeouts
Vance-Bro 262
Grimes-Bro 135
Luque-Cin 86
Morrison-Pit 85
Kaufmann-Chi 79

Strikeouts/Game
Vance-Bro 7.63
Grimes-Bro 3.91
Nehf-NY 3.77
Luque-Cin 3.53
Kaufmann-Chi 3.42

Wins Above Team
Vance-Bro 10.6
Yde-Pit 6.2
Mays-Cin 5.4
Bentley-NY 4.5
Nehf-NY 4.2

Earned Run Average
Vance-Bro 2.16
McQuillan-NY 2.69
Rixey-Cin 2.76
Benton-Cin 2.76
Yde-Pit 2.83

Adjusted ERA
Vance-Bro 176
Yde-Pit 142
Rixey-Cin 139
Benton-Cin 139
Alexander-Chi 129

Opponents' Batting Avg.
Vance-Bro 213
Yde-Pit 244
Morrison-Pit 245
Rixey-Cin 246
Doak-StL-Bro 249

Opponents' On Base Pct.
Vance-Bro 265
Rixey-Cin 277
Benton-Cin 289
Alexander-Chi 295
Morrison-Pit 296

Starter Runs
Vance-Bro 58.7
Rixey-Cin 29.2
McQuillan-NY 24.0
Yde-Pit 22.3
Barnes-NY 20.4

Adjusted Starter Runs
Vance-Bro 56.4
Rixey-Cin 28.4
Yde-Pit 25.5
Kremer-Pit 23.5
Cooper-Pit 21.9

Clutch Pitching Index
Sherdel-StL 117
Sothoron-StL 115
Ring-Phi 113
McQuillan-NY 113
Aldridge-Chi 110

Relief Runs
Jonnard-NY 14.7
May-Cin 9.5
Stone-Pit 6.5

Adjusted Relief Runs
Jonnard-NY 9.8
May-Cin 9.2
Stone-Pit 7.5

Relief Ranking
Jonnard-NY 10.1
Stone-Pit 6.4
May-Cin 6.3

Total Pitcher Index
Vance-Bro 5.9
Mays-Cin 3.3
Yde-Pit 3.0
Rixey-Cin 3.0
Cooper-Pit 2.8

Total Baseball Ranking
Hornsby-StL 6.8
Vance-Bro 5.9
Frisch-NY 4.9
Wheat-Bro 4.8
Fournier-Bro 4.7

TEAM	G	W	L	PCT	GB	R	OR	AB	H	2B	3B	HR	BB	SO	AVG	OBP	SLG	PRO	/A	BR	/A	PF	CHI	RC	TA	SB	CS	SBA	SBR
WAS	156	92	62	.597		755	613	5304	1558	255	88	22	513	392	.294	.361	.387	.748	98	-7	5	98	98	761	.713	115	87	57	-17
NY	153	89	63	.586	2	798	667	5240	1516	248	86	97	478	420	.289	.352	.425	.777	105	28	34	99	101	789	.740	69	64	52	-17
DET	156	86	68	.558	6	849	796	5389	1604	315	76	35	607	400	.298	.377	.404	.781	107	64	68	100	98	863	.773	100	41	71	5
STL	153	74	78	.487	17	769	809	5196	1528	265	62	67	461	349	.294	.355	.408	.763	102	8	-45	107	101	755	.719	85	84	50	-24
PHI	152	71	81	.467	20	685	778	5184	1459	251	59	63	374	482	.281	.334	.389	.723	91	-76	-70	99	104	675	.661	79	66	54	-15
CLE	153	67	86	.438	24.5	755	814	5332	1580	306	59	40	492	371	.296	.361	.398	.759	101	7	33	97	97	785	.722	84	51	62	-4
BOS	157	67	87	.435	25	737	806	5300	1468	300	61	30	598	413	.277	.355	.374	.729	93	-44	-72	104	99	733	.694	79	61	56	-12
CHI	154	66	87	.431	25.5	793	858	5255	1512	254	58	41	604	418	.288	.365	.382	.747	98	-5	19	97	102	763	.726	138	86	62	-9
TOT	617					6141		42200	12225	2194	549	395	4127	3245	.290	.358	.397	.755								749	540	58	-98

TEAM	CG	SHO	SV	IP	H	H/G	HR	BB	BB/G	SO	SO/G	ERA	/A	OAVG	OOBA	PR	/A	PF	CPI	FA	E	DP	FW	PW	BW	SBW	DIF
WAS	74	13	25	1384.0	1329	8.6	34	505	3.3	469	3.0	3.34	122	.259	.314	136	110	96	96	.972	171	149	1.2	10.4	.5	-.4	3.4
NY	76	13	13	1358.0	1483	9.8	59	522	3.5	487	3.2	3.86	106	.284	.340	56	36	97	106	.974	156	131	2.1	3.4	3.2	-.4	4.7
DET	60	5	20	1396.7	1582	10.2	55	465	3.0	439	2.8	4.20	99	.292	.336	4	-4	99	98	.971	187	142	.2	-.4	6.4	1.6	1.1
STL	65	11	7	1342.0	1511	10.1	68	517	3.5	386	2.6	4.58	100	.290	.343	-51	-3	108	94	.969	183	141	.4	-.3	-4.2	-1.1	3.2
PHI	68	8	10	1346.3	1527	10.2	43	597	4.0	371	2.5	4.39	97	.292	.353	-23	-18	101	99	.971	180	157	.6	-1.7	-6.6	-.2	3.2
CLE	87	7	7	1345.7	1603	10.7	43	503	3.4	312	2.1	4.40	94	.302	.352	-25	-41	97	101	.967	205	130	-.9	-3.9	3.1	.8	-8.6
BOS	73	8	16	1380.3	1563	10.2	43	523	3.4	414	2.7	4.35	102	.292	.342	-17	13	105	96	.967	210	124	-1.2	1.2	-6.8	.0	-3.2
CHI	76	1	11	1369.0	1635	10.7	52	512	3.4	360	2.4	4.75	87	.303	.350	-79	-92	98	95	.963	229	136	-2.4	-8.7	1.8	.3	-1.5
TOT	579	66	109	10922.0		10.1			3.4		2.7	4.23		.290	.358					.969	1521	1110					

Runs	Hits	Doubles	Triples	Home Runs	Total Bases
Ruth-NY ...143	Rice-Was ...216	J.Sewell-Cle ...45	Pipp-NY ...19	Ruth-NY ...46	Ruth-NY ...391
Cobb-Det ...115	Jamieson-Cle ...213	Heilmann-Det ...45	Goslin-Was ...17	Hauser-Phi ...27	Jacobson-StL ...306
Collins-Chi ...108	Cobb-Det ...211	Wambsganss-Bos ...41	Heilmann-Det ...16	Jacobson-StL ...19	Heilmann-Det ...304
Hooper-Chi ...107	Ruth-NY ...200	Jacobson-StL ...41	Rice-Was ...14	Williams-StL ...18	Goslin-Was ...299
Heilmann-Det ...107	Goslin-Was ...199	Meusel-NY ...40	Jacobson-StL ...12	Boone-Bos ...13	Hauser-Phi ...290

Runs Batted In	Runs Produced	Bases On Balls	Batting Average	On Base Percentage	Slugging Average
Goslin-Was ...129	Ruth-NY ...218	Ruth-NY ...142	Ruth-NY ...378	Ruth-NY ...513	Ruth-NY ...739
Ruth-NY ...121	Goslin-Was ...217	Rigney-Det ...102	Jamieson-Cle ...359	Collins-Chi ...441	Heilmann-Det ...533
Meusel-NY ...120	Heilmann-Det ...210	Sheely-Chi ...95	Falk-Chi ...352	Speaker-Cle ...432	Williams-StL ...533
Hauser-Phi ...115	Meusel-NY ...201	Collins-Chi ...89	Collins-Chi ...349	Heilmann-Det ...428	Jacobson-StL ...528
	J.Sewell-Cle ...199	Cobb-Det ...85	Heilmann-Det ...346	Sheely-Chi ...426	Goslin-Was ...516

Production	Adjusted Production	Batter Runs	Adjusted Batter Runs	Clutch Hitting Index	Runs Created
Ruth-NY ...1.252	Ruth-NY ...222	Ruth-NY ...100.8	Ruth-NY ...101.5	Kamm-Chi ...149	Ruth-NY ...205
Heilmann-Det ...961	Speaker-Cle ...148	Heilmann-Det ...40.4	Heilmann-Det ...40.8	Pratt-Det ...146	Heilmann-Det ...134
Williams-StL ...958	Heilmann-Det ...148	Goslin-Was ...35.5	Goslin-Was ...36.9	Rigney-Det ...146	Goslin-Was ...126
Speaker-Cle ...943	Goslin-Was ...143	Speaker-Cle ...32.4	Speaker-Cle ...35.0	Sheely-Chi ...143	Cobb-Det ...121
Goslin-Was ...937	Williams-StL ...136	Collins-Chi ...30.5	Collins-Chi ...33.1	Veach-Bos ...141	Collins-Chi ...119

Total Average	Stolen Bases	Stolen Base Average	Stolen Base Runs	Fielding Runs	Total Player Rating
Ruth-NY ...1.596	Collins-Chi ...42	Collins-Chi ...71.2	Collins-Chi ...2.4	J.Sewell-Cle ...20.7	Ruth-NY ...8.3
Williams-StL ...1.079	Meusel-NY ...26	Jamieson-Cle ...65.6		Wambsganss-Bos ...15.4	J.Sewell-Cle ...4.6
Heilmann-Det ...1.056	Rice-Was ...24	Harris-Was ...65.5		Lutzke-Cle ...14.9	Heilmann-Det ...3.2
Collins-Chi ...1.021	Cobb-Det ...23	Meusel-NY ...65.0		Jacobson-StL ...12.9	Collins-Chi ...3.0
Speaker-Cle ...1.009	Jamieson-Cle ...21	Rice-Was ...64.9		Crouse-Chi ...10.1	Rigney-Det ...3.0

Wins	Win Percentage	Games	Complete Games	Shutouts	Saves
Johnson-Was ...23	Johnson-Was ...767	Marberry-Was ...50	Thurston-Chi ...28	Johnson-Was ...6	Marberry-Was ...15
Pennock-NY ...21	Pennock-NY ...700	Holloway-Det ...49	Ehmke-Bos ...26	Davis-StL ...5	Russell-Was ...8
Thurston-Chi ...20	Whitehill-Det ...654	Shaute-Cle ...46	Pennock-NY ...25	Shocker-StL ...4	Quinn-Bos ...7
Shaute-Cle ...20	Zachary-Was ...625	Hoyt-NY ...46	Shaute-Cle ...21	Pennock-NY ...4	Dauss-Det ...6
Ehmke-Bos ...19		Ehmke-Bos ...45	Rommel-Phi ...21	Ehmke-Bos ...4	Connally-Chi ...6

Innings Pitched	Fewest Hits/Game	Fewest BB/Game	Strikeouts	Strikeouts/Game	Wins Above Team
Ehmke-Bos ...315	Johnson-Was ...7.54	Smith-Cle ...1.52	Johnson-Was ...158	Johnson-Was ...5.12	Johnson-Was ...7.1
Thurston-Chi ...291	Collins-Det ...8.29	Thurston-Chi ...1.86	Ehmke-Bos ...119	Shawkey-NY ...4.93	Thurston-Chi ...5.6
Pennock-NY ...286	Marberry-Was ...8.77	Shocker-StL ...1.90	Shawkey-NY ...114	Ehmke-Bos ...3.40	Pennock-NY ...4.8
Shaute-Cle ...283	Zachary-Was ...8.78	Pennock-NY ...2.01	Pennock-NY ...101	Shocker-StL ...3.22	Shaute-Cle ...4.2
	Wingard-StL ...8.88	Quinn-Bos ...2.04	Shocker-StL ...88	Pennock-NY ...3.18	Baumgartner-Phi ...4.2

Earned Run Average	Adjusted ERA	Opponents' Batting Avg.	Opponents' On Base Pct.	Starter Runs	Adjusted Starter Runs
Johnson-Was ...2.72	Johnson-Was ...149	Johnson-Was ...224	Johnson-Was ...279	Johnson-Was ...46.7	Johnson-Was ...41.5
Zachary-Was ...2.75	Baumgartner-Phi ...148	Collins-Det ...249	Collins-Det ...298	Pennock-NY ...44.5	Pennock-NY ...40.3
Pennock-NY ...2.83	Zachary-Was ...148	Marberry-Was ...262	Smith-Cle ...304	Smith-Cle ...33.6	Ehmke-Bos ...34.4
Baumgartner-Phi ...2.88	Pennock-NY ...145	Wingard-StL ...262	Pennock-NY ...306	Zachary-Was ...33.5	Smith-Cle ...30.6
Smith-Cle ...3.01	Smith-Cle ...137	Davis-StL ...263	Shocker-StL ...307	Ehmke-Bos ...27.1	Quinn-Bos ...30.0

Clutch Pitching Index	Relief Runs	Adjusted Relief Runs	Relief Ranking	Total Pitcher Index	Total Baseball Ranking
Baumgartner-Phi ...132	Speece-Was ...9.4	Speece-Was ...8.4	Speece-Was ...4.2	Johnson-Was ...4.6	Ruth-NY ...8.3
Pennock-NY ...117				Pennock-NY ...3.7	Johnson-Was ...4.6
Zachary-Was ...113				Zachary-Was ...3.4	J.Sewell-Cle ...4.6
Ferguson-Bos ...113				Ehmke-Bos ...3.3	Pennock-NY ...3.7
Hoyt-NY ...111				Smith-Cle ...3.1	Zachary-Was ...3.4

TEAM	G	W	L	PCT	GB	R	OR	AB	H	2B	3B	HR	BB	SO	AVG	OBP	SLG	PRO	/A	BR	/A	PF	CHI	RC	TA	SB	CS	SBA	SBR
PIT	153	95	58	.621		912	715	5372	1651	316	105	77	499	363	.307	.369	.448	.817	114	115	100	102	101	908	.818	159	63	72	10
NY	152	86	66	.566	8.5	736	702	5327	1507	239	61	114	411	494	.283	.337	.415	.752	97	-25	-16	99	99	742	.701	79	65	55	-14
CIN	153	80	73	.523	15	690	643	5233	1490	221	90	44	409	327	.285	.339	.387	.726	91	-65	-45	97	99	680	.666	108	107	50	-31
STL	153	77	76	.503	18	828	764	5329	1592	292	80	109	446	414	.299	.356	.445	.801	110	72	56	102	98	846	.769	70	51	58	-9
BOS	153	70	83	.458	25	708	802	5365	1567	260	70	41	405	380	.292	.345	.390	.735	93	-47	2	94	97	722	.672	77	72	52	-19
PHI	153	68	85	.444	27	812	930	5412	1598	288	58	100	456	542	.295	.354	.425	.779	104	35	48	116	99	814	.733	48	59	45	-20
BRO	153	68	85	.444	27	786	866	5468	1617	250	58	60	437	383	.296	.351	.406	.757	99	-5	44	94	100	787	.701	37	30	55	-6
CHI	154	68	86	.442	27.5	723	773	5353	1473	254	70	85	397	470	.275	.329	.396	.725	90	-77	-56	97	104	699	.670	94	70	57	-13
TOT	612					6195		42859	12495	2120	614	634	3460	3373	.292	.348	.414	.762								672	517	57	-108

TEAM	CG	SHO	SV	IP	H	H/G	HR	BB	BB/G	SO	SO/G	ERA	/A	OAVG	OOBA	PR	/A	PF	CPI	FA	E	DP	FW	PW	BW	SBW	DIF
PIT	77	2	13	1354.7	1526	10.1	81	387	2.6	386	2.6	3.87	109	.287	.328	59	50	99	103	.964	224	171	-.9	4.7	9.4	2.2	3.2
NY	80	6	8	1359.3	1532	10.1	73	408	2.7	446	3.0	3.94	106	.287	.329	49	38	98	102	.968	199	129	.6	3.6	-1.5	-.0	7.4
CIN	92	11	12	1374.0	1447	9.5	35	324	2.1	437	2.9	3.38	122	.273	.309	135	112	97	96	.968	203	161	.3	10.5	-4.2	-1.6	-1.5
STL	82	8	7	1333.0	1480	10.0	86	470	3.2	428	2.9	4.36	99	.284	.336	-14	-7	101	95	.964	204	156	.3	-.7	5.2	.4	-4.8
BOS	77	6	4	1367.0	1567	10.3	67	458	3.0	351	2.3	4.39	92	.290	.336	-19	-50	95	95	.964	221	145	-.7	-4.7	.2	-.5	-.8
PHI	69	8	9	1349.7	1753	11.7	117	444	3.0	371	2.5	5.02	100	.317	.359	-113	0	118	103	.966	211	147	-.1	.0	-8.1	-.6	.4
BRO	82	4	4	1347.7	1608	10.7	75	477	3.2	518	3.5	4.77	85	.298	.346	-75	-107	95	94	.966	210	130	-.0	-10.0	4.1	.7	-3.2
CHI	75	5	10	1368.7	1575	10.5	102	485	3.2	435	2.9	4.41	95	.291	.343	-22	-33	98	100	.969	198	161	.6	-3.1	-5.2	.0	-1.4
TOT	634	50	67	10854.0		10.4			2.9		2.8	4.27		.292	.348					.966	1670	1200					

Runs		Hits		Doubles		Triples		Home Runs		Total Bases	
Cuyler-Pit	144	Bottomley-StL	227	Bottomley-StL	44	Cuyler-Pit	26	Hornsby-StL	39	Hornsby-StL	381
Hornsby-StL	133	Wheat-Bro	221	Cuyler-Pit	43	Walker-Cin	16	Hartnett-Chi	24	Cuyler-Pit	369
Wheat-Bro	125	Cuyler-Pit	220	Wheat-Bro	42	Roush-Cin	16	Fournier-Bro	22	Bottomley-StL	358
Traynor-Pit	114	Hornsby-StL	203	Hornsby-StL	41	Fournier-Bro	16	Meusel-NY	21	Wheat-Bro	333
Blades-StL	112	Stock-Bro	202	Burrus-Bos	41			Bottomley-StL	21	Fournier-Bro	310

Runs Batted In		Runs Produced		Bases On Balls		Batting Average		On Base Percentage		Slugging Average	
Hornsby-StL	143	Hornsby-StL	237	Fournier-Bro	86	Hornsby-StL	.403	Hornsby-StL	.489	Hornsby-StL	.756
Fournier-Bro	130	Cuyler-Pit	228	Hornsby-StL	83	Bottomley-StL	.367	Fournier-Bro	.446	Cuyler-Pit	.598
Bottomley-StL	128	Wheat-Bro	214	Moore-Pit	73	Wheat-Bro	.359	Blades-StL	.423	Bottomley-StL	.578
Wright-Pit	121	Traynor-Pit	214	Youngs-NY	66	Cuyler-Pit	.357	Cuyler-Pit	.423	Fournier-Bro	.569
Barnhart-Pit	114	Fournier-Bro	207	Carey-Pit	66	Fournier-Bro	.350	Carey-Pit	.418	Harper-Phi	.558

Production		Adjusted Production		Batter Runs		Adjusted Batter Runs		Clutch Hitting Index		Runs Created	
Hornsby-StL	1.245	Hornsby-StL	209	Hornsby-StL	87.1	Hornsby-StL	85.5	Barnhart-Pit	170	Hornsby-StL	187
Cuyler-Pit	1.021	Fournier-Bro	168	Cuyler-Pit	53.1	Fournier-Bro	55.5	Traynor-Pit	137	Cuyler-Pit	158
Fournier-Bro	1.015	Cuyler-Pit	155	Fournier-Bro	50.1	Cuyler-Pit	51.5	Brown-Bro	133	Bottomley-StL	145
Bottomley-StL	.992	Wheat-Bro	148	Bottomley-StL	45.5	Bottomley-StL	43.7	Wright-Pit	131	Fournier-Bro	141
Blades-StL	.958	Bottomley-StL	147	Wheat-Bro	34.9	Wheat-Bro	40.4	Fournier-Bro	130	Wheat-Bro	134

Total Average		Stolen Bases		Stolen Base Average		Stolen Base Runs		Fielding Runs		Total Player Rating	
Hornsby-StL	1.549	Carey-Pit	46	Smith-StL	90.9	Carey-Pit	7.2	Adams-Chi	25.1	Hornsby-StL	5.8
Cuyler-Pit	1.173	Cuyler-Pit	41	Carey-Pit	80.7	Smith-StL	4.8	Traynor-Pit	20.8	Cuyler-Pit	5.3
Fournier-Bro	1.133	Adams-Chi	26	Cuyler-Pit	75.9	Cuyler-Pit	4.5	Pinelli-Cin	18.7	Fournier-Bro	3.8
Carey-Pit	1.041	Roush-Cin	22	Moore-Pit	73.1	Stock-Bro	1.8	Critz-Cin	18.2	Traynor-Pit	3.7
Bottomley-StL	1.035	Frisch-NY	21	Adams-Chi	68.4	Grantham-Pit	1.8	Kelly-NY	14.9	Bancroft-Bos	3.5

Wins		Win Percentage		Games		Complete Games		Shutouts		Saves	
Vance-Bro	22	Sherdel-StL	.714	Morrison-Pit	44	Donohue-Cin	27	Vance-Bro	4	Morrison-Pit	4
Rixey-Cin	21	Vance-Bro	.710	Donohue-Cin	42	Vance-Bro	26	Luque-Cin	4	Bush-Chi	4
Donohue-Cin	21	Aldridge-Pit	.682	Bush-Chi	42	Rixey-Cin	22	Carlson-Phi	4		
Meadows-Pit	19	Kremer-Pit	.680	Osborne-Bro	41	Luque-Cin	22	Donohue-Cin	3		
		Rixey-Cin	.656	Kremer-Pit	40	Ring-Phi	21				

Innings Pitched		Fewest Hits/Game		Fewest BB/Game		Strikeouts		Strikeouts/Game		Wins Above Team	
Donohue-Cin	301	Luque-Cin	8.13	Alexander-Chi	1.11	Vance-Bro	221	Vance-Bro	7.51	Vance-Bro	8.3
Luque-Cin	291	Benton-Bos	8.36	Donohue-Cin	1.47	Luque-Cin	140	Luque-Cin	4.33	Rixey-Cin	5.3
Rixey-Cin	287	Vance-Bro	8.39	Rixey-Cin	1.47	Ring-Phi	93	Sothoron-StL	3.87	Sherdel-StL	4.8
Ring-Phi	270	Aldridge-Pit	9.21	Cooney-Bos	1.83	Blake-Chi	93	Bush-Chi	3.76	Benton-Bos	4.4
Vance-Bro	265	Donohue-Cin	9.27	Sherdel-StL	1.89	Aldridge-Pit	88	Aldridge-Pit	3.72	Alexander-Chi	3.6

Earned Run Average		Adjusted ERA		Opponents' Batting Avg.		Opponents' On Base Pct.		Starter Runs		Adjusted Starter Runs	
Luque-Cin	2.63	Luque-Cin	157	Luque-Cin	.239	Luque-Cin	.287	Luque-Cin	52.9	Luque-Cin	48.1
Rixey-Cin	2.89	Rixey-Cin	143	Benton-Bos	.249	Donohue-Cin	.293	Rixey-Cin	44.0	Rixey-Cin	39.3
Donohue-Cin	3.08	Sherdel-StL	139	Vance-Bro	.250	Vance-Bro	.297	Donohue-Cin	39.7	Donohue-Cin	34.7
Benton-Bos	3.10	Donohue-Cin	134	Donohue-Cin	.268	Rixey-Cin	.300	Scott-NY	29.8	Scott-NY	27.8
Sherdel-StL	3.11	Scott-NY	133	Scott-NY	.269	Scott-NY	.305	Sherdel-StL	25.8	Sherdel-StL	26.8

Clutch Pitching Index		Relief Runs		Adjusted Relief Runs		Relief Ranking		Total Pitcher Index		Total Baseball Ranking	
Nehf-NY	122	Huntzinger-NY	5.3	Huntzinger-NY	4.8	Huntzinger-NY	4.1	Luque-Cin	5.8	Hornsby-StL	5.8
Yde-Pit	117							Donohue-Cin	3.8	Luque-Cin	5.8
Sherdel-StL	109							Rixey-Cin	3.5	Cuyler-Pit	5.3
Rixey-Cin	108							Scott-NY	3.4	Donohue-Cin	3.8
Morrison-Pit	107							Sherdel-StL	2.7	Fournier-Bro	3.8

TEAM	G	W	L	PCT	GB	R	OR	AB	H	2B	3B	HR	BB	SO	AVG	OBP	SLG	PRO	/A	BR	/A	PF	CHI	RC	TA	SB	CS	SBA	SBR
WAS	152	96	55	.636		829	670	5206	1577	251	71	56	533	427	.303	.373	.411	.784	104	39	56	98	100	816	.767	134	88	60	-12
PHI	153	88	64	.579	8.5	831	713	5399	1659	298	79	76	453	432	.307	.364	.434	.798	108	53	29	103	97	857	.762	67	59	53	-14
STL	154	82	71	.536	15	900	906	5440	1620	304	68	110	498	375	.298	.360	.439	.799	108	52	-9	108	105	859	.770	85	78	52	-20
DET	156	81	73	.526	16.5	903	829	5371	1621	277	84	50	640	386	.302	.379	.413	.792	107	63	70	99	101	872	.783	97	63	61	-8
CHI	154	79	75	.513	18.5	811	770	5224	1482	299	59	38	524	405	.284	.370	.385	.755	97	-6	30	96	100	781	.745	129	88	59	-13
CLE	155	70	84	.455	27.5	782	817	5436	1613	285	58	52	520	379	.297	.361	.399	.760	98	-11	-62	106	97	795	.720	90	76	54	-18
NY	156	69	85	.448	28.5	706	774	5353	1471	247	74	110	470	482	.275	.336	.410	.746	94	-60	-29	96	96	738	.697	67	73	48	-23
BOS	152	47	105	.309	49.5	639	922	5166	1375	257	64	41	513	422	.266	.336	.364	.700	83	-130	-90	95	99	647	.642	42	56	43	-20
TOT	616					6401		42595	12418	2218	557	533	4289	3308	.292	.360	.408	.768								711	581	55	-134

TEAM	CG	SHO	SV	IP	H	H/G	HR	BB	BB/G	SO	SO/G	ERA	/A	OAVG	OOBA	PR	/A	PF	CPI	FA	E	DP	FW	PW	BW	SBW	DIF
WAS	69	10	21	1356.3	1426	9.5	49	543	3.6	464	3.1	3.67	114	.276	.336	108	76	95	105	.972	170	166	2.0	7.0	5.2	.5	5.9
PHI	61	8	18	1380.3	1468	9.6	60	544	3.5	495	3.2	3.89	114	.278	.337	76	83	101	101	.966	211	148	-.5	7.7	2.7	.3	1.9
STL	67	7	10	1377.3	1598	10.4	99	675	4.4	419	2.7	4.85	98	.296	.361	-70	-18	108	101	.964	226	164	-1.4	-1.7	-.8	-.3	9.7
DET	66	2	18	1382.7	1582	10.3	70	556	3.6	419	2.7	4.61	93	.293	.348	-33	-47	98	96	.972	173	143	1.8	-4.4	6.5	.8	-.7
CHI	71	12	13	1384.0	1583	10.3	69	493	3.2	375	2.4	4.34	96	.293	.342	8	-25	95	99	.968	200	162	.2	-2.3	2.8	.4	1.0
CLE	93	6	9	1377.0	1604	10.5	41	493	3.2	345	2.3	4.49	104	.295	.345	-15	30	107	95	.967	210	146	-.4	2.8	-5.7	-.1	-3.5
NY	80	8	13	1387.3	1560	10.1	78	505	3.3	492	3.2	4.33	99	.290	.342	9	-9	97	99	.974	160	150	2.6	-.8	-2.7	-.6	-6.5
BOS	68	6	6	1326.3	1615	11.0	67	510	3.5	310	2.1	4.96	88	.306	.353	-83	-87	99	96	.957	271	150	-4.1	-8.1	-8.3	-.3	-8.2
TOT	575	59	108	10971.3		10.2			3.5		2.7	4.39		.292	.360					.968	1621	1229					

Runs
Mostil-Chi 135
Simmons-Phi 122
Combs-NY 117
Goslin-Was 116
Rice-Was 111

Hits
Simmons-Phi 253
Rice-Was 227
Heilmann-Det 225
Sisler-StL 224
J.Sewell-Cle 204

Doubles
McManus-StL 44
Simmons-Phi 43
Sheely-Chi 43
Burns-Cle 41

Triples
Goslin-Was 20
Mostil-Chi 16
Sisler-StL 15

Home Runs
Meusel-NY 33
Williams-StL 25
Ruth-NY 25
Simmons-Phi 24
Gehrig-NY 20

Total Bases
Simmons-Phi 392
Meusel-NY 338
Goslin-Was 329
Heilmann-Det 326
Sisler-StL 311

Runs Batted In
Meusel-NY 138
Heilmann-Det 134
Simmons-Phi 129
Goslin-Was 113
Sheely-Chi 111

Runs Produced
Simmons-Phi 227
Heilmann-Det 218
Goslin-Was 211
Meusel-NY 206
Rice-Was 197

Bases On Balls
Mostil-Chi 90
Kamm-Chi 90
Collins-Chi 87
Bishop-Phi 87
Blue-Det 83

Batting Average
Heilmann-Det 393
Speaker-Cle 389
Simmons-Phi 387
Cobb-Det 378
Wingo-Det 370

On Base Percentage
Speaker-Cle 479
Cobb-Det 468
Collins-Chi 461
Heilmann-Det 457
Wingo-Det 456

Slugging Average
Simmons-Phi 599
Cobb-Det 598
Speaker-Cle 578
Heilmann-Det 569
Goslin-Was 547

Production
Cobb-Det 1.066
Speaker-Cle 1.057
Heilmann-Det 1.026
Simmons-Phi 1.018
Wingo-Det 983

Adjusted Production
Cobb-Det 170
Heilmann-Det 160
Speaker-Cle 157
Simmons-Phi 152
Wingo-Det 150

Batter Runs
Heilmann-Det 52.4
Simmons-Phi 51.4
Speaker-Cle 47.0
Cobb-Det 45.3
Wingo-Det 35.2

Adjusted Batter Runs
Heilmann-Det 53.2
Simmons-Phi 48.7
Cobb-Det 45.9
Speaker-Cle 42.7
Wingo-Det 35.9

Clutch Hitting Index
Galloway-Phi 155
Blue-Det 148
Collins-Chi 144
Falk-Chi 136
J.Sewell-Cle 133

Runs Created
Simmons-Phi 155
Heilmann-Det 149
Goslin-Was 131
Speaker-Cle 123
Cobb-Det 118

Total Average
Cobb-Det 1.240
Speaker-Cle 1.239
Heilmann-Det 1.130
Wingo-Det 1.086
Collins-Chi 1.049

Stolen Bases
Mostil-Chi 43
Rice-Was 26
Goslin-Was 26

Stolen Base Average
Blue-Det 79.2
Goslin-Was 76.5
Collins-Chi 76.0
Rice-Was 70.3
Mostil-Chi 67.2

Stolen Base Runs
Goslin-Was 3.0
Haney-Det 2.7
Blue-Det 2.7
Collins-Chi 2.1
Peckinpaugh-Was . . . 1.5

Fielding Runs
J.Sewell-Cle 15.8
O'Rourke-Det 15.3
Flagstead-Bos 13.6
Rice-Was 10.3
Wingo-Det 10.0

Total Player Rating
J.Sewell-Cle 3.9
Speaker-Cle 3.6
Wingo-Det 2.9
Cobb-Det 2.5
Heilmann-Det 2.5

Wins
Rommel-Phi 21
Lyons-Chi 21
Johnson-Was 20
Coveleski-Was 20
Harriss-Phi 19

Win Percentage
Coveleski-Was 800
Johnson-Was 741
Ruether-Was 720
Blankenship-Chi 680
Rommel-Phi 677

Games
Marberry-Was 55
Walberg-Phi 53
Vangilder-StL 52
Rommel-Phi 52
Pennock-NY 47

Complete Games
Smith-Cle 22
Ehmke-Bos 22
Pennock-NY 21
Lyons-Chi 19
Wingfield-Bos 18

Shutouts
Lyons-Chi 5
Gray-Phi 4
Giard-StL 4

Saves
Marberry-Was 15
Doyle-Det 8
Connally-Chi 8
Walberg-Phi 7

Innings Pitched
Pennock-NY 277
Lyons-Chi 263
Rommel-Phi 261
Ehmke-Bos 261
Wingfield-Bos 254

Fewest Hits/Game
Johnson-Was 8.29
Blankenship-Chi . . . 8.46
Coveleski-Was 8.59
Pennock-NY 8.68
Gray-Phi 8.78

Fewest BB/Game
Smith-Cle 1.82
Quinn-Bos-Phi 1.84
Shocker-NY 2.14
Faber-Chi 2.23
Pennock-NY 2.31

Strikeouts
Grove-Phi 116
Johnson-Was 108
Harriss-Phi 95
Ehmke-Bos 95
Jones-NY 92

Strikeouts/Game
Grove-Phi 5.30
Johnson-Was 4.24
Shawkey-NY 3.92
Walberg-Phi 3.84
Gray-Phi 3.53

Wins Above Team
Coveleski-Was 6.2
Lyons-Chi 5.5
Blankenship-Chi . . . 4.8
Holloway-Det 4.5
Johnson-Was 4.5

Earned Run Average
Coveleski-Was 2.84
Pennock-NY 2.96
Blankenship-Chi . . . 3.03
Johnson-Was 3.07
Dauss-Det 3.16

Adjusted ERA
Coveleski-Was 147
Pennock-NY 144
Miller-Cle 141
Blankenship-Chi . . . 138
Johnson-Was 136

Opponents' Batting Avg.
Johnson-Was 243
Blankenship-Chi 253
Pennock-NY 254
Coveleski-Was 255
Gray-Phi 260

Opponents' On Base Pct.
Pennock-NY 297
Blankenship-Chi 301
Johnson-Was 306
Coveleski-Was 307
Gray-Phi 311

Starter Runs
Pennock-NY 44.1
Coveleski-Was 41.6
Blankenship-Chi . . . 35.2
Johnson-Was 33.7
Lyons-Chi 33.3

Adjusted Starter Runs
Pennock-NY 40.2
Coveleski-Was 35.9
Blankenship-Chi . . . 29.5
Dauss-Det 29.0
Miller-Cle 29.0

Clutch Pitching Index
Dauss-Det 119
Shocker-NY 114
Zachary-Was 113
Lyons-Chi 111
Shawkey-NY 110

Relief Runs
Marberry-Was 9.4
Gregg-Was 2.1

Adjusted Relief Runs
Marberry-Was 7.2
Gregg-Was 4

Relief Ranking
Marberry-Was 12.3
Gregg-Was 2

Total Pitcher Index
Johnson-Was 3.9
Pennock-NY 3.2
Dauss-Det 2.8
Harriss-Phi 2.7
Coveleski-Was 2.7

Total Baseball Ranking
Johnson-Was 3.9
J.Sewell-Cle 3.9
Speaker-Cle 3.6
Pennock-NY 3.2
Wingo-Det 2.9

TEAM	G	W	L	PCT	GB	R	OR	AB	H	2B	3B	HR	BB	SO	AVG	OBP	SLG	PRO	/A	BR	/A	PF	CHI	RC	TA	SB	CS	SBA	SBR
STL	156	89	65	.578		817	678	5381	1541	259	82	90	478	518	.286	.348	.415	.763	111	76	59	102	101	770	.736	83			
CIN	157	87	67	.565	2	747	651	5320	1541	242	120	35	454	333	.290	.349	.400	.749	107	52	87	95	96	738	.706	51			
PIT	157	84	69	.549	4.5	769	689	5312	1514	243	106	44	434	350	.285	.343	.396	.739	104	28	-59	112	104	713	.700	91			
CHI	155	82	72	.532	7	682	602	5229	1453	291	49	66	445	447	.278	.338	.390	.728	101	7	-35	106	96	685	.688	85			
NY	151	74	77	.490	13.5	663	668	5167	1435	214	58	73	339	420	.278	.325	.384	.709	96	-36	-21	98	103	631	.654	94			
BRO	155	71	82	.464	17.5	623	705	5130	1348	246	62	40	475	464	.263	.329	.358	.687	90	-64	-59	99	99	607	.639	76			
BOS	153	66	86	.434	22	624	719	5216	1444	209	62	16	426	348	.277	.335	.350	.685	90	-65	30	86	98	612	.626	81			
PHI	152	58	93	.384	29.5	687	900	5254	1479	244	50	75	422	479	.281	.337	.390	.727	101	5	-17	103	98	683	.673	47			
TOT	618					5612		42009	11755	1948	589	439	3473	3359	.280	.338	.386	.724								608			

TEAM	CG	SHO	SV	IP	H	H/G	HR	BB	BB/G	SO	SO/G	ERA	/A	OAVG	OOBA	PR	/A	PF	CPI	FA	E	DP	FW	PW	BW	SBW	DIF
STL	90	10	6	1397.0	1423	9.2	76	397	2.6	365	2.4	3.67	104	.269	.311	23	22	100	96	.969	198	141	.2	2.2	5.8		3.8
CIN	88	14	8	1408.3	1449	9.3	40	324	2.1	424	2.7	3.42	104	.271	.303	63	22	93	94	.972	183	160	1.1	2.2	8.6		-1.8
PIT	83	12	18	1381.3	1422	9.3	50	455	3.0	387	2.5	3.67	116	.271	.319	24	88	111	97	.965	220	161	-1.1	8.7	-5.8		5.7
CHI	77	13	14	1377.7	1407	9.2	39	486	3.2	508	3.3	3.26	123	.270	.322	86	113	105	108	.974	162	174	2.3	11.2	-3.5		-5.0
NY	61	4	15	1341.7	1370	9.2	70	427	2.9	419	2.8	3.77	99	.270	.318	8	-3	98	96	.970	186	150	.9	-.3	-2.1		-.0
BRO	83	6	9	1361.7	1440	9.5	50	472	3.1	517	3.4	3.82	101	.277	.324	0	4	101	98	.963	209	95	-1.6	.4	-5.8		1.6
BOS	60	9	9	1363.7	1536	10.1	46	455	3.0	408	2.7	4.01	83	.289	.332	-28	-100	88	101	.967	208	150	-.4	-9.9	3.0		-2.7
PHI	68	5	5	1331.3	1699	11.5	68	454	3.1	331	2.2	5.03	81	.316	.358	-178	-138	107	98	.964	224	153	-1.3	-13.6	-1.7		-.9
TOT	610	73	84	10962.7		9.6			2.8		2.8	3.82		.280	.338					.968	1610	1184					

Runs
Cuyler-Pit 113
P.Waner-Pit 101
Southworth-NY-StL ...99
Sand-Phi 99

Hits
Brown-Bos 201
Cuyler-Pit 197
Adams-Chi 193
Bell-StL 189

Doubles
Bottomley-StL 40
Roush-Cin 37
Wilson-Chi 36

Triples
P.Waner-Pit 22
Walker-Cin 20
Traynor-Pit 17

Home Runs
Wilson-Chi 21
Bottomley-StL 19
Williams-Phi 18
Bell-StL 17
Southworth-NY-StL ..16

Total Bases
Bottomley-StL 305
Bell-StL 301
Wilson-Chi 285
P.Waner-Pit 283
Cuyler-Pit 282

Runs Batted In
Bottomley-StL 120
Wilson-Chi 109
Bell-StL 100
Southworth-NY-StL ...99
Pipp-Cin 99

Runs Produced
Bottomley-StL 199
Cuyler-Pit 197
Wilson-Chi 185
Southworth-NY-StL ..182
Hornsby-StL 178

Bases On Balls
Wilson-Chi 69
P.Waner-Pit 66
Sand-Phi 66
Bancroft-Bos 64
Blades-StL 62

Batting Average
P.Waner-Pit 336
Leach-Phi 329
Brown-Bos 328
Bell-StL 325
Roush-Cin 323

On Base Percentage
P.Waner-Pit 413
Blades-StL 409
Wilson-Chi 406
Grantham-Pit 400
Bancroft-Bos 399

Slugging Average
Wilson-Chi 539
P.Waner-Pit 528
Bell-StL 518
Bottomley-StL 506
Herman-Bro 500

Production
Wilson-Chi 944
P.Waner-Pit 941
Bell-StL 901
Grantham-Pit 890
Herman-Bro 875

Adjusted Production
Wilson-Chi 144
Bell-StL 137
P.Waner-Pit 135
Herman-Bro 135
Blades-StL 131

Batter Runs
P.Waner-Pit 39.5
Wilson-Chi 39.2
Bell-StL 31.5
Williams-Phi 29.8
Bottomley-StL 25.2

Adjusted Batter Runs
Wilson-Chi 34.8
P.Waner-Pit 30.4
Bell-StL 29.7
Williams-Phi 28.2
Hargrave-Cin 24.0

Clutch Hitting Index
Pipp-Cin 142
Butler-Bro 135
Traynor-Pit 130
Burrus-Bos 125
Critz-Cin 124

Runs Created
P.Waner-Pit 115
Wilson-Chi 115
Bell-StL 112
Bottomley-StL 109
Cuyler-Pit 105

Total Average
Wilson-Chi 1.031
P.Waner-Pit 1.022
Grantham-Pit 938
Blades-StL 938
Bell-StL 929

Stolen Bases
Cuyler-Pit 35
Adams-Chi 27
Frisch-NY 23
Douthit-StL 23
Youngs-NY 21

Stolen Base Average

Stolen Base Runs

Fielding Runs
Adams-Chi 24.1
Critz-Cin 23.2
Friberg-Phi 19.3
Dressen-Cin 18.8
Thevenow-StL 17.4

Total Player Rating
P.Waner-Pit 3.1
Wilson-Chi 2.8
Adams-Chi 2.7
Bancroft-Bos 2.5
O'Farrell-StL 2.5

Wins
Rhem-StL 20
Meadows-Pit 20
Kremer-Pit 20
Donohue-Cin 20
Mays-Cin 19

Win Percentage
Kremer-Pit 769
Rhem-StL 741
Meadows-Pit 690
Mays-Cin 613
Donohue-Cin 588

Games
Scott-NY 50
Willoughby-Phi 47
Donohue-Cin 47
Ulrich-Phi 45
May-Cin 45

Complete Games
Mays-Cin 24
Petty-Bro 23
Root-Chi 21
Rhem-StL 20
Carlson-Phi 20

Shutouts
Donohue-Cin 5
Smith-Bos 4
Blake-Chi 4

Saves
Davies-NY 6
Scott-NY 5
Kremer-Pit 5
Ehrhardt-Bro 4

Innings Pitched
Donohue-Cin 286
Mays-Cin 281
Petty-Bro 276
Root-Chi 271
Carlson-Phi 267

Fewest Hits/Game
Petty-Bro 8.02
Greenfield-NY 8.31
Rhem-StL 8.41
Jones-Chi 8.49
Bush-Chi 8.54

Fewest BB/Game
Donohue-Cin 1.23
Alexander-Chi-StL . 1.39
Carlson-Phi 1.58
Mays-Cin 1.70
Lucas-Cin 1.75

Strikeouts
Vance-Bro 140
Root-Chi 127
May-Cin 103
Benton-Bos 103
Petty-Bro 101

Strikeouts/Game
Vance-Bro 7.46
May-Cin 5.52
Jones-Chi 4.50
Blake-Chi 4.32
Root-Chi 4.22

Wins Above Team
Kremer-Pit 7.0
Rhem-StL 5.8
Carlson-Phi 5.5
Meadows-Pit 5.2
Haines-StL 4.0

Earned Run Average
Kremer-Pit 2.61
Root-Chi 2.82
Petty-Bro 2.84
Bush-Chi 2.87
Barnes-NY 2.87

Adjusted ERA
Kremer-Pit 162
Root-Chi 142
Bush-Chi 140
Petty-Bro 136
Kaufmann-Chi 133

Opponents' Batting Avg.
Petty-Bro 240
Alexander-Chi-StL ..250
Rhem-StL 250
Greenfield-NY 251
Kremer-Pit 252

Opponents' On Base Pct.
Alexander-Chi-StL ..275
Petty-Bro 285
Kremer-Pit 289
Donohue-Cin 291
Mays-Cin 296

Starter Runs
Kremer-Pit 31.2
Petty-Bro 30.3
Root-Chi 30.2
Fitzsimmons-NY ... 23.1
Mays-Cin 21.4

Adjusted Starter Runs
Kremer-Pit 41.9
Root-Chi 35.5
Petty-Bro 31.1
Carlson-Phi 25.5
Fitzsimmons-NY ... 21.1

Clutch Pitching Index
Jones-Chi 122
Blake-Chi 119
Fitzsimmons-NY 118
Wertz-Bos 117
Root-Chi 111

Relief Runs

Adjusted Relief Runs

Relief Ranking

Total Pitcher Index
Kremer-Pit 4.4
Root-Chi 3.1
Carlson-Phi 2.6
Mays-Cin 2.6
Petty-Bro 2.4

Total Baseball Ranking
Kremer-Pit 4.4
P.Waner-Pit 3.1
Root-Chi 3.1
Wilson-Chi 2.8
Adams-Chi 2.7

TEAM	G	W	L	PCT	GB	R	OR	AB	H	2B	3B	HR	BB	SO	AVG	OBP	SLG	PRO	/A	BR	/A	PF	CHI	RC	TA	SB	CS	SBA	SBR
NY	155	91	63	.591		847	713	5221	1508	262	75	121	642	580	.289	.369	.437	.806	117	123	128	99	97	866	.802	79	60	57	-11
CLE	154	88	66	.571	3	738	612	5293	1529	333	49	27	455	331	.289	.349	.386	.735	98	-16	-12	100	103	735	.688	88	44	67	0
PHI	150	83	67	.553	6	677	570	5046	1359	259	65	61	523	449	.269	.341	.383	.724	95	-38	-162	118	100	680	.679	56	49	53	-12
WAS	152	81	69	.540	8	802	761	5223	1525	244	97	43	555	369	.292	.364	.401	.765	106	48	63	98	102	780	.741	122	89	58	-16
CHI	155	81	72	.529	9.5	730	665	5220	1508	314	60	32	556	381	.289	.361	.390	.751	102	24	85	92	96	761	.726	121	77	61	-9
DET	157	79	75	.513	12	793	830	5315	1547	281	90	36	599	423	.291	.367	.398	.765	96	52	75	97	98	800	.739	88	72	55	-16
STL	155	62	92	.403	29	682	845	5259	1449	253	78	72	437	465	.276	.335	.394	.729	96	-37	-41	101	99	698	.672	62	71	47	-23
BOS	154	46	107	.301	44.5	562	835	5185	1325	249	54	32	465	450	.256	.321	.343	.664	79	-155	-162	101	101	586	.594	48	51	48	-15
TOT	616					5831		41762	11750	2195	568	424	4232	3448	.281	.351	.392	.743								664	513	56	-108

TEAM	CG	SHO	SV	IP	H	H/G	HR	BB	BB/G	SO	SO/G	ERA	/A	OAVG	OOBA	PR	/A	PF	CPI	FA	E	DP	FW	PW	BW	SBW	DIF
NY	63	4	20	1371.0	1442	9.5	56	478	3.1	486	3.2	3.86	101	.277	.326	23	5	97	97	.966	210	117	-1.2	.5	12.4	.2	2.0
CLE	96	11	4	1377.0	1412	9.2	49	450	2.9	381	2.5	3.40	115	.271	.319	94	78	97	103	.972	173	153	1.1	7.6	-1.2	1.3	2.2
PHI	62	10	16	1345.0	1362	9.1	38	451	3.0	571	3.8	3.00	155	.269	.318	152	245	116	114	.972	171	131	1.2	23.7	-15.7	.2	-1.4
WAS	65	5	26	1348.3	1489	9.9	45	566	3.8	418	2.8	4.34	90	.286	.344	-48	-64	97	96	.969	184	129	.4	-6.2	6.1	-.2	-5.8
CHI	85	11	12	1374.3	1426	9.3	47	506	3.3	458	3.0	3.74	97	.274	.328	42	-16	90	98	.973	165	122	1.5	-1.5	8.2	.4	-4.2
DET	57	10	18	1395.3	1570	10.1	58	555	3.6	469	3.0	4.41	89	.290	.345	-61	-76	98	97	.969	193	151	-.2	-7.4	7.3	-.2	2.5
STL	64	5	9	1364.7	1549	10.2	86	654	4.3	337	2.2	4.66	89	.292	.354	-97	-77	103	101	.963	235	167	-2.7	-7.5	-4.0	-.9	.0
BOS	53	6	5	1359.0	1520	10.1	45	546	3.6	336	2.2	4.72	90	.289	.339	-106	-71	106	88	.970	193	143	-.2	-6.9	-15.7	-.1	-7.6
TOT	545	62	110	10934.7		9.7			3.5		2.8	4.02		.281	.351					.969	1524	1113					

Runs		Hits		Doubles		Triples		Home Runs		Total Bases	
Ruth-NY	139	Rice-Was	216	Burns-Cle	64	Gehrig-NY	20	Ruth-NY	47	Ruth-NY	365
Gehrig-NY	135	Burns-Cle	216	Simmons-Phi	53	Gehringer-Det	17	Simmons-Phi	19	Simmons-Phi	329
Mostil-Chi	120	Goslin-Was	201	Speaker-Cle	52	Mostil-Chi	15	Lazzeri-NY	18	Gehrig-NY	314
Combs-NY	113	Simmons-Phi	199	Jacobson-StL-Bos	51	Goslin-Was	15	Williams-StL	17	Goslin-Was	308
Goslin-Was	105	Mostil-Chi	197	Gehrig-NY	47			Goslin-Was	17	Burns-Cle	298

Runs Batted In		Runs Produced		Bases On Balls		Batting Average		On Base Percentage		Slugging Average	
Ruth-NY	146	Ruth-NY	238	Ruth-NY	144	Manush-Det	.378	Ruth-NY	.516	Ruth-NY	.737
Lazzeri-NY	114	Gehrig-NY	226	Bishop-Phi	116	Ruth-NY	.372	Heilmann-Det	.445	Simmons-Phi	.564
Burns-Cle	114	Burns-Cle	207	Rigney-Bos	108	Heilmann-Det	.367	Bishop-Phi	.431	Manush-Det	.564
Simmons-Phi	109	Goslin-Was	196	Gehrig-NY	105	Burns-Cle	.358	Goslin-Was	.425	Gehrig-NY	.549
		Falk-Chi	186	Speaker-Cle	94	Goslin-Was	.354	Manush-Det	.421	Goslin-Was	.542

Production		Adjusted Production		Batter Runs		Adjusted Batter Runs		Clutch Hitting Index		Runs Created	
Ruth-NY	1.253	Ruth-NY	226	Ruth-NY	97.4	Ruth-NY	98.0	Judge-Was	144	Ruth-NY	196
Manush-Det	.985	Manush-Det	160	Gehrig-NY	44.2	Gehrig-NY	44.8	Haney-Bos	138	Gehrig-NY	137
Heilmann-Det	.979	Heilmann-Det	159	Goslin-Was	42.3	Heilmann-Det	44.0	Dugan-NY	136	Goslin-Was	131
Gehrig-NY	.969	Goslin-Was	154	Heilmann-Det	41.7	Goslin-Was	43.9	Sheely-Chi	135	Simmons-Phi	127
Goslin-Was	.967	Gehrig-NY	152	Manush-Det	38.2	Manush-Det	40.3	Burns-Cle	132	Mostil-Chi	122

Total Average		Stolen Bases		Stolen Base Average		Stolen Base Runs		Fielding Runs		Total Player Rating	
Ruth-NY	1.634	Mostil-Chi	35	McNeely-Was	75.0	Mostil-Chi	2.1	Rigney-Bos	17.9	Ruth-NY	7.8
Gehrig-NY	1.070	Rice-Was	25	Hunnefield-Chi	72.7	McNeely-Was	1.8	Regan-Bos	13.2	Kamm-Chi	3.7
Heilmann-Det	1.062	Hunnefield-Chi	24	Mostil-Chi	71.4	Kamm-Chi	1.8	Kamm-Chi	12.7	Mostil-Chi	3.7
Manush-Det	1.044	McNeely-Was	18	J.Sewell-Cle	70.8	Hunnefield-Chi	1.8	Mostil-Chi	12.2	Goslin-Was	3.6
Goslin-Was	1.029	J.Sewell-Cle	17	Lazzeri-NY	69.6	Speaker-Cle	1.2	Rice-Was	12.2	Manush-Det	3.3

Wins		Win Percentage		Games		Complete Games		Shutouts		Saves	
Uhle-Cle	27	Uhle-Cle	.711	Marberry-Was	64	Uhle-Cle	32	Wells-Det	4	Marberry-Was	22
Pennock-NY	23	Pennock-NY	.676	Pate-Phi	47	Lyons-Chi	24			Dauss-Det	9
Shocker-NY	19	Shocker-NY	.633	Grove-Phi	45	Johnson-Was	22			Pate-Phi	6
Lyons-Chi	18	Faber-Chi	.625	Thomas-Chi	44	Grove-Phi	20			Grove-Phi	6
		Hoyt-NY	.571			Pennock-NY	19			Jones-NY	5

Innings Pitched		Fewest Hits/Game		Fewest BB/Game		Strikeouts		Strikeouts/Game		Wins Above Team	
Uhle-Cle	318	Grove-Phi	7.92	Pennock-NY	1.45	Grove-Phi	194	Grove-Phi	6.77	Uhle-Cle	7.4
Lyons-Chi	284	Thomas-Chi	8.13	Smith-Cle	1.48	Uhle-Cle	159	Thomas-Chi	4.59	Pate-Phi	4.5
Pennock-NY	266	Uhle-Cle	8.49	Quinn-Phi	1.98	Thomas-Chi	127	Uhle-Cle	4.50	Pennock-NY	4.3
Johnson-Was	262	Lyons-Chi	8.49	Rommel-Phi	2.22	Johnson-Was	125	Johnson-Was	4.29	Dauss-Det	3.1
		Buckeye-Cle	8.67	Wingfield-Bos	2.36	Whitehill-Det	109	Whitehill-Det	3.89	Faber-Chi	2.8

Earned Run Average		Adjusted ERA		Opponents' Batting Avg.		Opponents' On Base Pct.		Starter Runs		Adjusted Starter Runs	
Grove-Phi	2.51	Grove-Phi	185	Thomas-Chi	.244	Pennock-NY	.303	Grove-Phi	43.2	Grove-Phi	61.0
Uhle-Cle	2.83	Rommel-Phi	151	Grove-Phi	.244	Rommel-Phi	.303	Uhle-Cle	41.9	Uhle-Cle	38.1
Lyons-Chi	3.01	Uhle-Cle	138	Lyons-Chi	.252	Hoyt-NY	.306	Lyons-Chi	31.8	Rommel-Phi	37.9
Rommel-Phi	3.08	Quinn-Phi	136	Uhle-Cle	.253	Johnson-Was	.306	Coveleski-Was	24.4	Walberg-Phi	30.9
Buckeye-Cle	3.09	Buckeye-Cle	126	Levsen-Cle	.261	Lyons-Chi	.310	Rommel-Phi	22.8	Quinn-Phi	22.6

Clutch Pitching Index		Relief Runs		Adjusted Relief Runs		Relief Ranking		Total Pitcher Index		Total Baseball Ranking	
Wingard-StL	128	Pate-Phi	16.4	Pate-Phi	24.3	Marberry-Was	22.3	Grove-Phi	5.8	Ruth-NY	7.8
Zachary-StL	122	Marberry-Was	15.6	Marberry-Was	13.9	Pate-Phi	20.3	Uhle-Cle	4.2	Grove-Phi	5.8
Grove-Phi	119	Braxton-NY	9.9	Braxton-NY	9.0	Braxton-NY	7.9	Rommel-Phi	3.8	Uhle-Cle	4.2
Coveleski-Was	117	Russell-Bos	4.7	Russell-Bos	7.3	Russell-Bos	3.3	Walberg-Phi	2.8	Rommel-Phi	3.8
Buckeye-Cle	115							Pate-Phi	2.8	Kamm-Chi	3.7

TEAM	G	W	L	PCT	GB	R	OR	AB	H	2B	3B	HR	BB	SO	AVG	OBP	SLG	PRO	/A	BR	/A	PF	CHI	RC	TA	SB	CS	SBA	SBR
PIT	156	94	60	.610		817	659	5397	1648	257	78	54	437	355	.305	.361	.412	.773	113	98	84	102	99	790	.735	65			
STL	153	92	61	.601	1.5	754	665	5207	1450	264	79	84	484	511	.278	.343	.408	.751	107	47	-2	107	100	723	.730	110			
NY	155	92	62	.597	2	817	720	5372	1594	251	62	109	461	462	.297	.356	.427	.783	116	113	115	100	98	805	.758	73			
CHI	153	85	68	.556	8.5	750	661	5303	1505	266	63	74	481	492	.284	.346	.400	.746	106	43	42	100	98	730	.709	65			
CIN	153	75	78	.490	18.5	643	653	5185	1439	222	77	29	402	332	.278	.332	.367	.699	93	-47	-45	100	99	628	.637	62			
BRO	154	65	88	.425	28.5	541	619	5193	1314	195	74	39	368	494	.253	.306	.342	.648	79	-151	-168	103	101	539	.586	106			
BOS	155	60	94	.390	34	651	771	5370	1498	216	61	37	346	363	.279	.326	.363	.689	90	-72	-23	93	102	626	.625	100			
PHI	155	51	103	.331	43	678	903	5317	1487	216	46	57	434	482	.280	.337	.370	.707	95	-29	-3	96	99	660	.652	68			
TOT	617					5651		42344	11935	1887	540	483	3413	3491	.282	.339	.386	.725								649			

TEAM	CG	SHO	SV	IP	H	H/G	HR	BB	BB/G	SO	SO/G	ERA	/A	OAVG	OOBA	PR	/A	PF	CPI	FA	E	DP	FW	PW	BW	SBW	DIF
PIT	90	10	10	1384.0	1400	9.1	58	418	2.7	435	2.8	3.66	106	.267	.310	38	33	99	94	.969	187	130	.5	3.3	8.3		5.0
STL	89	14	11	1367.7	1416	9.3	72	363	2.4	394	2.6	3.57	116	.272	.311	51	84	106	99	.966	213	170	-.9	8.3	-.2		8.3
NY	65	7	16	1382.3	1520	9.9	77	453	2.9	442	2.9	3.97	97	.284	.331	-9	-21	98	102	.969	195	160	.0	-2.1	11.3		5.7
CHI	75	11	5	1384.0	1439	9.4	50	514	3.3	465	3.0	3.65	106	.273	.328	40	32	99	103	.971	181	152	.8	3.2	4.1		.4
CIN	87	12	12	1367.3	1472	9.7	36	316	2.1	407	2.7	3.54	110	.280	.310	56	56	100	98	.973	165	160	1.7	5.5	-4.4		-4.3
BRO	74	7	10	1371.7	1382	9.1	63	418	2.7	574	3.8	3.36	121	.267	.310	84	108	104	103	.963	229	117	-1.8	10.7	-16.6		-3.8
BOS	52	4	11	1390.3	1602	10.4	43	468	3.0	402	2.6	4.22	88	.294	.336	-47	-75	95	99	.963	231	130	-1.9	-7.4	-2.3		-5.4
PHI	81	5	6	1351.7	1710	11.4	84	462	3.1	377	2.5	5.35	73	.313	.354	-215	-214	100	93	.972	169	152	1.5	-21.1	-.3		-6.1
TOT	613	70	81	10999.0		9.8			2.8		2.9	3.91		.282	.339					.969	1570	1171					

Runs
L.Waner-Pit 133
Hornsby-NY 133
Wilson-Chi 119
P.Waner-Pit 113
Frisch-StL 112

Hits
P.Waner-Pit 237
L.Waner-Pit 223
Frisch-StL 208
Hornsby-NY 205
Stephenson-Chi 199

Doubles
Stephenson-Chi 46
P.Waner-Pit 40
Lindstrom-NY 36
Dressen-Cin 36
Brown-Bos 35

Triples
P.Waner-Pit 17
Bottomley-StL 15
Thompson-Phi 14
Terry-NY 13
Wilson-Chi 12

Home Runs
Wilson-Chi 30
Williams-Phi 30
Hornsby-NY 26
Terry-NY 20
Bottomley-StL 19

Total Bases
P.Waner-Pit 338
Hornsby-NY 333
Wilson-Chi 319
Terry-NY 307
Bottomley-StL 292

Runs Batted In
P.Waner-Pit 131
Wilson-Chi 129
Hornsby-NY 125
Bottomley-StL 124
Terry-NY 121

Runs Produced
P.Waner-Pit 235
Hornsby-NY 232
Wilson-Chi 218
Terry-NY 202
Bottomley-StL 200

Bases On Balls
Hornsby-NY 86
Harper-NY 84
Grantham-Pit 74
Bottomley-StL 74

Batting Average
P.Waner-Pit 380
Hornsby-NY 361
L.Waner-Pit 355
Stephenson-Chi 344
Traynor-Pit 342

On Base Percentage
Hornsby-NY 448
P.Waner-Pit 437
Harper-NY 435
Stephenson-Chi 415
Harris-Pit 402

Slugging Average
Hornsby-NY 586
Wilson-Chi 579
P.Waner-Pit 543
Terry-NY 529
Bottomley-StL 509

Production
Hornsby-NY 1.035
Wilson-Chi 980
P.Waner-Pit 980
Harper-NY 930
Terry-NY 907

Adjusted Production
Hornsby-NY 176
Wilson-Chi 160
P.Waner-Pit 158
Harper-NY 149
Stephenson-Chi 142

Batter Runs
Hornsby-NY 62.5
P.Waner-Pit 54.4
Wilson-Chi 45.7
Harper-NY 37.0
Stephenson-Chi 35.7

Adjusted Batter Runs
Hornsby-NY 62.7
P.Waner-Pit 52.8
Wilson-Chi 45.6
Harper-NY 37.2
Stephenson-Chi 35.6

Clutch Hitting Index
Wright-Pit 157
Bressler-Cin 155
Traynor-Pit 142
Farrell-NY -Bos 141
Felix-Bro 131

Runs Created
P.Waner-Pit 148
Wilson-Chi 144
Hornsby-NY 126
Stephenson-Chi 117
Bottomley-StL 112

Total Average
Hornsby-NY 1.190
Wilson-Chi 1.088
P.Waner-Pit 1.052
Harper-NY 1.037
Stephenson-Chi 955

Stolen Bases
Frisch-StL 48
Carey-Bro 32
Hendrick-Bro 29
Adams-Chi 26
Richbourg-Bos 24

Stolen Base Average

Stolen Base Runs

Fielding Runs
Frisch-StL 48.8
Jackson-NY 21.6
Friberg-Phi 14.6
Dressen-Cin 13.6
Hartnett-Chi 13.4

Total Player Rating
Frisch-StL 6.3
Hornsby-NY 6.1
P.Waner-Pit 5.3
Jackson-NY 4.7
Wilson-Chi 3.3

Wins
Root-Chi 26
Haines-StL 24
Hill-Pit 22
Alexander-StL 21

Win Percentage
Benton-Bos-NY 708
Haines-StL 706
Kremer-Pit 704
Grimes-NY 704
Alexander-StL 677

Games
Scott-Phi 48
Root-Chi 48
Ehrhardt-Bro 46
Henry-NY 45
May-Cin 44

Complete Games
Vance-Bro 25
Meadows-Pit 25
Haines-StL 25
Hill-Pit 22
Alexander-StL 22

Shutouts
Haines-StL 6
Root-Chi 4
Lucas-Cin 4
Kremer-Pit 3

Saves
Sherdel-StL 6
Nehf-Cin-Chi 5
Mogridge-Bos 5
Henry-NY 4

Innings Pitched
Root-Chi 309
Haines-StL 301
Meadows-Pit 299
Hill-Pit 278
Vance-Bro 273

Fewest Hits/Game
Vance-Bro 7.98
Haines-StL 8.16
Kremer-Pit 8.16
Bush-Chi 8.25
Hill-Pit 8.42

Fewest BB/Game
Alexander-StL 1.28
Lucas-Cin 1.46
Donohue-Cin 1.51
Carlson-Phi-Chi 1.63
Henry-NY 1.70

Strikeouts
Vance-Bro 184
Root-Chi 145
May-Cin 121
Grimes-NY 102
Petty-Bro 101

Strikeouts/Game
Vance-Bro 6.07
Elliott-Bro 4.74
May-Cin 4.61
Pruett-Phi 4.35
Root-Chi 4.22

Wins Above Team
Haines-StL 5.3
Root-Chi 4.7
Benton-Bos-NY 4.4
Lucas-Cin 4.3
Grimes-NY 4.1

Earned Run Average
Kremer-Pit 2.47
Alexander-StL 2.52
Vance-Bro 2.70
Haines-StL 2.72
Petty-Bro 2.98

Adjusted ERA
Alexander-StL 164
Kremer-Pit 157
Haines-StL 152
Vance-Bro 151
Petty-Bro 137

Opponents' Batting Avg.
Vance-Bro 239
Kremer-Pit 244
Haines-StL 245
Hill-Pit 249
Bush-Chi 250

Opponents' On Base Pct.
Lucas-Cin 277
Alexander-StL 277
Kremer-Pit 278
Petty-Bro 281
Vance-Bro 282

Starter Runs
Alexander-StL 41.5
Haines-StL 39.9
Vance-Bro 36.7
Kremer-Pit 36.3
Petty-Bro 28.3

Adjusted Starter Runs
Alexander-StL 48.0
Haines-StL 47.2
Vance-Bro 41.4
Kremer-Pit 35.4
Petty-Bro 33.0

Clutch Pitching Index
Blake-Chi 117
McWeeny-Bro 116
Smith-Bos 114
Donohue-Cin 112
Alexander-StL 109

Relief Runs
Clark-Bro 13.2
Ehrhardt-Bro 3.7
Cvengros-Pit 3.5
Songer-Pit-NY 1.9

Adjusted Relief Runs
Clark-Bro 14.5
Ehrhardt-Bro 5.4
Cvengros-Pit 3.3
Songer-Pit-NY 1.5
Bell-StL 1.2

Relief Ranking
Clark-Bro 16.7
Ehrhardt-Bro 5.3
Songer-Pit-NY 2.1
Cvengros-Pit 1.8
Bell-StL 7

Total Pitcher Index
Alexander-StL 5.6
Haines-StL 4.9
Vance-Bro 4.0
Kremer-Pit 3.3
Luque-Cin 2.4

Total Baseball Ranking
Frisch-StL 6.3
Hornsby-NY 6.1
Alexander-StL 5.6
P.Waner-Pit 5.3
Haines-StL 4.9

TEAM	G	W	L	PCT	GB	R	OR	AB	H	2B	3B	HR	BB	SO	AVG	OBP	SLG	PRO	/A	BR	/A	PF	CHI	RC	TA	SB	CS	SBA	SBR
NY	155	110	44	.714		975	599	5347	1644	291	103	158	635	605	.307	.383	.489	.872	131	235	236	100	95	993	.908	90			
PHI	155	91	63	.591	19	841	726	5296	1606	281	70	56	551	326	.303	.372	.414	.786	109	79	105	97	98	816	.779	98			
WAS	157	85	69	.552	25	782	730	5389	1549	268	87	29	498	359	.287	.351	.386	.737	96	-24	0	97	104	729	.714	133			
DET	156	82	71	.536	27.5	845	805	5299	1533	282	100	51	587	420	.289	.363	.409	.772	106	47	-15	108	102	789	.775	141			
CHI	153	70	83	.458	39.5	662	708	5157	1433	285	61	36	493	389	.278	.344	.378	.722	92	-53	-68	102	94	673	.687	90			
CLE	153	66	87	.431	43.5	668	766	5202	1471	321	52	26	381	366	.283	.337	.379	.716	91	-69	-46	97	99	660	.661	63			
STL	155	59	94	.386	50.5	724	904	5220	1440	262	59	55	443	420	.276	.338	.380	.718	91	-67	-111	106	106	668	.678	91			
BOS	154	51	103	.331	59	597	856	5207	1348	271	78	28	430	456	.259	.320	.357	.677	80	-148	-107	95	100	596	.625	82			
TOT	619					6094		42117	12024	2261	610	439	4018	3341	.285	.352	.399	.751								788			

TEAM	CG	SHO	SV	IP	H	H/G	HR	BB	BB/G	SO	SO/G	ERA	/A	OAVG	OOBA	PR	/A	PF	CPI	FA	E	DP	FW	PW	BW	SBW	DIF
NY	82	11	20	1388.0	1403	9.1	42	409	2.7	431	2.8	3.20	121	.269	.312	94	105			.969	195	123	.6	9.7	22.4		.3
PHI	66	8	25	1384.0	1467	9.5	65	442	2.9	553	3.6	3.95	99	.279	.324	27	-5	95	97	.970	190	124	.9	-.5	10.0		3.6
WAS	62	10	23	1400.3	1444	9.3	53	491	3.2	497	3.2	3.95	100	.273	.324	27	1	96	93	.969	195	125	.6	.0	.0		7.3
DET	75	5	17	1385.0	1542	10.0	52	577	3.7	421	2.7	4.13	107	.289	.345	0	46	107	104	.968	206	173	-.0	4.4	-1.4		2.6
CHI	85	10	8	1364.7	1467	9.7	55	440	2.9	365	2.4	3.91	108	.281	.326	32	50	103	98	.971	178	131	1.7	4.7	-6.5		-6.4
CLE	72	5	8	1352.7	1542	10.3	37	508	3.4	366	2.4	4.27	95	.293	.343	-21	-29	99	99	.968	201	146	.3	-2.8	-4.4		-3.6
STL	80	4	8	1350.3	1592	10.6	79	604	4.0	385	2.6	4.95	91	.300	.359	-123	-67	109	98	.960	248	166	-2.6	-6.4	-10.5		2.0
BOS	63	6	7	1362.7	1603	10.6	56	558	3.7	381	2.5	4.68	87	.300	.351	-84	-91	99	98	.964	228	167	-1.4	-8.6	-10.2		-5.8
TOT	585	59	116	10987.7		9.9			3.3		2.8	4.13		.285	.352					.967	1641	1155					

Runs		Hits		Doubles		Triples		Home Runs		Total Bases	
Ruth-NY	158	Combs-NY	231	Gehrig-NY	52	Combs-NY	23	Ruth-NY	60	Gehrig-NY	447
Gehrig-NY	149	Gehrig-NY	218	Burns-Cle	51	Manush-Det	18	Gehrig-NY	47	Ruth-NY	417
Combs-NY	137	Sisler-StL	201	Heilmann-Det	50	Gehrig-NY	18	Lazzeri-NY	18	Combs-NY	331
Gehringer-Det	110	Heilmann-Det	201	J.Sewell-Cle	48	Goslin-Was	15	Williams-StL	17	Heilmann-Det	311
Heilmann-Det	106	Goslin-Was	194	Meusel-NY	47	Rice-Was	14	Simmons-Phi	15	Goslin-Was	300

Runs Batted In		Runs Produced		Bases On Balls		Batting Average		On Base Percentage		Slugging Average	
Gehrig-NY	175	Gehrig-NY	277	Ruth-NY	138	Heilmann-Det	.398	Ruth-NY	.487	Ruth-NY	.772
Ruth-NY	164	Ruth-NY	262	Gehrig-NY	109	Gehrig-NY	.373	Heilmann-Det	.475	Gehrig-NY	.765
Heilmann-Det	120	Heilmann-Det	212	Bishop-Phi	105	Fothergill-Det	.359	Gehrig-NY	.474	Heilmann-Det	.616
Goslin-Was	120	Goslin-Was	203	Heilmann-Det	72	Cobb-Phi	.357	Bishop-Phi	.442	Williams-StL	.525
Fothergill-Det	114	Fothergill-Det	198	Blue-Det	71	Combs-NY	.356	Cobb-Phi	.440	Goslin-Was	.516

Production		Adjusted Production		Batter Runs		Adjusted Batter Runs		Clutch Hitting Index		Runs Created	
Ruth-NY	1.259	Ruth-NY	223	Gehrig-NY	100.8	Gehrig-NY	101.0	J.Sewell-Cle	133	Gehrig-NY	208
Gehrig-NY	1.240	Gehrig-NY	218	Ruth-NY	100.7	Ruth-NY	100.8	Cobb-Phi	131	Ruth-NY	204
Heilmann-Det	1.091	Heilmann-Det	168	Heilmann-Det	62.3	Heilmann-Det	56.3	Fothergill-Det	129	Heilmann-Det	145
Fothergill-Det	.929	Cobb-Phi	144	Simmons-Phi	44.1	Simmons-Phi	46.1	Hale-Phi	126	Combs-NY	134
Williams-StL	.928	Combs-NY	139	Combs-NY	37.1	Combs-NY	37.3	Barrett-Chi	124	Goslin-Was	114

Total Average		Stolen Bases		Stolen Base Average		Stolen Base Runs		Fielding Runs		Total Player Rating	
Ruth-NY	1.615	Sisler-StL	27					Falk-Chi	21.5	Ruth-NY	8.5
Gehrig-NY	1.555	Meusel-NY	24					Gehringer-Det	16.0	Gehrig-NY	8.2
Heilmann-Det	1.303	Neun-Det	22					Metzler-Chi	14.2	Simmons-Phi	3.6
Cobb-Phi	1.048	Lazzeri-NY	22					Bluege-Was	13.5	Lazzeri-NY	3.3
Williams-StL	1.007	Cobb-Phi	22					Koenig-NY	12.6	Heilmann-Det	3.2

Wins		Win Percentage		Games		Complete Games		Shutouts		Saves	
Lyons-Chi	22	Hoyt-NY	.759	Braxton-Was	58	Lyons-Chi	30	Lisenbee-Was	4	Moore-NY	13
Hoyt-NY	22	Shocker-NY	.750	Marberry-Was	56	Thomas-Chi	24			Braxton-Was	13
Grove-Phi	20	Moore-NY	.731	Grove-Phi	51	Hoyt-NY	23			Marberry-Was	9
		Pennock-NY	.704	Moore-NY	50	Gaston-StL	21			Grove-Phi	9
		Lisenbee-Was	.667	Walberg-Phi	46						

Innings Pitched		Fewest Hits/Game		Fewest BB/Game		Strikeouts		Strikeouts/Game		Wins Above Team	
Thomas-Chi	308	Moore-NY	7.82	Quinn-Phi	1.66	Grove-Phi	174	Grove-Phi	5.98	Lyons-Chi	6.1
Lyons-Chi	308	Thomas-Chi	7.92	Shocker-NY	1.85	Walberg-Phi	136	Braxton-Was	5.57	Hudlin-Cle	5.2
Hudlin-Cle	265	Hadley-Was	8.01	Hoyt-NY	1.90	Thomas-Chi	107	Walberg-Phi	4.92	Lisenbee-Was	4.0
Grove-Phi	262	Pipgras-NY	8.02	Braxton-Was	1.92	Lisenbee-Was	105	Pipgras-NY	4.39	Hadley-Was	3.6
Hoyt-NY	256	Lisenbee-Was	8.22	Lyons-Chi	1.96	Braxton-Was	96	Ruffing-Bos	4.39	Rommel-Phi	3.5

Earned Run Average		Adjusted ERA		Opponents' Batting Avg.		Opponents' On Base Pct.		Starter Runs		Adjusted Starter Runs	
Moore-NY	2.28	Moore-NY	169	Moore-NY	.234	Braxton-Was	.281	Lyons-Chi	44.3	Lyons-Chi	48.2
Hoyt-NY	2.64	Lyons-Chi	150	Thomas-Chi	.244	Moore-NY	.282	Moore-NY	43.7	Thomas-Chi	43.2
Lyons-Chi	2.83	Hoyt-NY	147	Hadley-Was	.244	Lyons-Chi	.284	Hoyt-NY	42.4	Moore-NY	37.5
Shocker-NY	2.84	Thomas-Chi	142	Lisenbee-Was	.245	Hoyt-NY	.287	Thomas-Chi	39.3	Hoyt-NY	35.0
Hadley-Was	2.85	Hadley-Was	139	Braxton-Was	.246	Thomas-Chi	.292	Shocker-NY	28.7	Whitehill-Det	28.2

Clutch Pitching Index		Relief Runs		Adjusted Relief Runs		Relief Ranking		Total Pitcher Index		Total Baseball Ranking	
Ruether-NY	120	Braxton-Was	20.1	Braxton-Was	17.2	Braxton-Was	22.3	Lyons-Chi	5.5	Ruth-NY	8.5
Gibson-Det	119	Burke-Was	1.9	Smith-Det	4.0	Smith-Det	2.5	Moore-NY	3.9	Gehrig-NY	8.2
Pennock-NY	118	Smith-Det	1.6	Burke-Was	.0	Burke-Was	.0	Thomas-Chi	3.4	Lyons-Chi	5.5
Zachary-StL-Was	114							Hoyt-NY	3.4	Moore-NY	3.9
Stoner-Det	114							Hadley-Was	2.6	Simmons-Phi	3.6

TEAM	G	W	L	PCT	GB	R	OR	AB	H	2B	3B	HR	BB	SO	AVG	OBP	SLG	PRO	/A	BR	/A	PF	CHI	RC	TA	SB	CS	SBA	SBR
STL	154	95	59	.617		807	636	5357	1505	292	70	113	568	438	.281	.353	.425	.778	110	73	73	100	99	802	.768	82			
NY	155	93	61	.604	2	807	653	5459	1600	276	59	118	444	376	.293	.349	.430	.779	110	68	54	102	100	805	.747	62			
CHI	154	91	63	.591	4	714	615	5260	1460	251	64	92	508	517	.278	.345	.402	.747	102	11	50	95	97	728	.720	83			
PIT	152	85	67	.559	9	837	704	5371	1659	246	100	52	435	352	.309	.364	.421	.785	112	89	39	107	102	809	.751	64			
CIN	153	78	74	.513	16	648	686	5184	1449	229	67	32	386	330	.280	.333	.368	.701	90	-76	-48	96	103	630	.643	83			
BRO	155	77	76	.503	17.5	665	640	5243	1393	229	70	66	557	510	.266	.340	.374	.714	93	-45	-37	99	98	673	.683	81			
BOS	153	50	103	.327	44.5	631	878	5228	1439	241	41	52	447	377	.275	.335	.367	.702	90	-70	-50	97	98	643	.647	60			
PHI	152	43	109	.283	51	660	957	5234	1396	257	47	85	503	510	.267	.333	.382	.715	93	-49	-78	104	99	667	.672	53			
TOT	614					5769		42336	11901	2021	518	610	3848	3410	.281	.344	.397	.741								568			

TEAM	CG	SHO	SV	IP	H	H/G	HR	BB	BB/G	SO	SO/G	ERA	/A	OAVG	OOBA	PR	/A	PF	CPI	FA	E	DP	FW	PW	BW	SBW	DIF
STL	83	4	21	1416.0	1470	9.3	86	399	2.5	422	2.7	3.38	114	.273	.314	94	75	97	105	.974	160	134	1.3	7.3	7.1		2.3
NY	79	7	16	1393.3	1454	9.4	77	399	2.6	399	2.6	3.66	108	.274	.316	49	44	99	98	.972	178	175	.2	4.3	5.3		6.2
CHI	75	12	14	1380.3	1383	9.0	56	508	3.3	531	3.5	3.39	109	.266	.322	90	45	93	102	.975	156	176	1.5	4.4	4.9		3.2
PIT	82	8	11	1353.0	1422	9.5	66	446	3.0	385	2.6	3.95	105	.275	.321	4	31	105	93	.967	201	123	-1.2	3.0	3.8		3.4
CIN	68	11	11	1370.7	1516	10.0	58	410	2.7	355	2.3	3.94	98	.285	.325	6	-13	97	97	.974	162	194	1.2	-1.3	-4.7		6.8
BRO	75	16	15	1395.3	1378	8.9	59	468	3.0	551	3.6	3.25	121	.263	.312	113	103	99	102	.965	217	113	-2.2	10.1	-3.6		-3.8
BOS	54	1	6	1359.0	1596	10.6	100	524	3.5	343	2.3	4.83	84	.298	.349	-127	-119	101	96	.969	193	141	-.7	-11.6	-4.9		-9.3
PHI	42	4	11	1344.7	1654	11.1	108	671	4.5	403	2.7	5.52	79	.307	.371	-230	-175	109	96	.971	181	171	.0	-17.1	-7.6		-8.3
TOT	558	63	105	11012.3		9.7			3.1		2.8	3.98		.281	.344					.971	1448	1227					

Runs
P.Waner-Pit	142
Bottomley-StL	123
L.Waner-Pit	121
Douthit-StL	111
Frisch-StL	107

Hits
Lindstrom-NY	231
P.Waner-Pit	223
L.Waner-Pit	221
Richbourg-Bos	206
Traynor-Pit	192

Doubles
P.Waner-Pit	50
Hafey-StL	46
Hornsby-Bos	42
Bottomley-StL	42
Lindstrom-NY	39

Triples
Bottomley-StL	20
P.Waner-Pit	19
L.Waner-Pit	14
Bressler-Bro	13
Bissonette-Bro	13

Home Runs
Wilson-Chi	31
Bottomley-StL	31
Hafey-StL	27
Bissonette-Bro	25
Hornsby-Bos	21

Total Bases
Bottomley-StL	362
Lindstrom-NY	330
P.Waner-Pit	329
Bissonette-Bro	319
Hafey-StL	314

Runs Batted In
Bottomley-StL	136
Traynor-Pit	124
Wilson-Chi	120
Hafey-StL	111
Lindstrom-NY	107

Runs Produced
Bottomley-StL	228
P.Waner-Pit	222
Traynor-Pit	212
Lindstrom-NY	192
Hafey-StL	185

Bases On Balls
Hornsby-Bos	107
Douthit-StL	84
Bressler-Bro	80
Wilson-Chi	77
P.Waner-Pit	77

Batting Average
Hornsby-Bos	.387
P.Waner-Pit	.370
Lindstrom-NY	.358
Sisler-Bos	.340
Herman-Bro	.340

On Base Percentage
Hornsby-Bos	.498
P.Waner-Pit	.446
Grantham-Pit	.408
Stephenson-Chi	.407
Wilson-Chi	.404

Slugging Average
Hornsby-Bos	.632
Bottomley-StL	.628
Hafey-StL	.604
Wilson-Chi	.588
P.Waner-Pit	.547

Production
Hornsby-Bos	1.130
Bottomley-StL	1.030
Wilson-Chi	.992
P.Waner-Pit	.992
Hafey-StL	.990

Adjusted Production
Hornsby-Bos	199
Bottomley-StL	166
Wilson-Chi	165
Hafey-StL	155
P.Waner-Pit	148

Batter Runs
Hornsby-Bos	72.4
P.Waner-Pit	53.3
Bottomley-StL	52.4
Wilson-Chi	42.1
Hafey-StL	38.5

Adjusted Batter Runs
Hornsby-Bos	74.5
Bottomley-StL	52.5
P.Waner-Pit	47.6
Wilson-Chi	46.2
Hafey-StL	38.5

Clutch Hitting Index
Traynor-Pit	172
Walker-Cin	137
Whitney-Phi	134
Ford-Cin	133
Wilson-Phi-StL	128

Runs Created
Hornsby-Bos	154
P.Waner-Pit	145
Bottomley-StL	142
Bissonette-Bro	125
Wilson-Chi	122

Total Average
Hornsby-Bos	1.409
Bottomley-StL	1.147
P.Waner-Pit	1.100
Wilson-Chi	1.090
Hafey-StL	1.055

Stolen Bases
Cuyler-Chi	37
Frisch-StL	29
Walker-Cin	19
Thompson-Phi	19

Stolen Base Average

Stolen Base Runs

Fielding Runs
Maguire-Chi	48.2
Jackson-NY	27.6
Douthit-StL	21.2
Ford-Cin	16.3
Lindstrom-NY	14.8

Total Player Rating
Hornsby-Bos	4.8
Hartnett-Chi	4.5
P.Waner-Pit	4.4
Jackson-NY	4.4
Lindstrom-NY	4.1

Wins
Grimes-Pit	25
Benton-NY	25
Vance-Bro	22
Sherdel-StL	21

Win Percentage
Benton-NY	.735
Haines-StL	.714
Bush-Chi	.714
Fitzsimmons-NY	.690
Vance-Bro	.688

Games
Grimes-Pit	48
Kolp-Cin	44
Rixey-Cin	43

Complete Games
Grimes-Pit	28
Benton-NY	28
Vance-Bro	24
Sherdel-StL	20
Haines-StL	20

Shutouts
Vance-Bro	4
McWeeny-Bro	4
Lucas-Cin	4
Grimes-Pit	4
Blake-Chi	4

Saves
Sherdel-StL	5
Haid-StL	5
Carlson-Chi	4
Benton-NY	4

Innings Pitched
Grimes-Pit	331
Benton-NY	310
Rixey-Cin	291
Vance-Bro	280
Fitzsimmons-NY	261

Fewest Hits/Game
Vance-Bro	7.26
Blake-Chi	7.80
Malone-Chi	7.82
McWeeny-Bro	8.04
Root-Chi	8.13

Fewest BB/Game
Alexander-StL	1.36
Sherdel-StL	2.02
Benton-NY	2.06
Rixey-Cin	2.07
Grimes-Pit	2.09

Strikeouts
Vance-Bro	200
Malone-Chi	155
Root-Chi	122
Grimes-Pit	97
Benton-NY	90

Strikeouts/Game
Vance-Bro	6.43
Malone-Chi	5.56
Root-Chi	4.63
Clark-Bro	3.92
Ring-Phi	3.75

Wins Above Team
Vance-Bro	6.8
Benton-NY	6.6
Grimes-Pit	4.6
Haines-StL	4.1
Fitzsimmons-NY	3.7

Earned Run Average
Vance-Bro	2.09
Blake-Chi	2.46
Nehf-Chi	2.64
Clark-Bro	2.68
Benton-NY	2.73

Adjusted ERA
Vance-Bro	188
Blake-Chi	150
Clark-Bro	146
Benton-NY	145
Nehf-Chi	140

Opponents' Batting Avg.
Vance-Bro	.221
McWeeny-Bro	.235
Malone-Chi	.236
Blake-Chi	.240
Root-Chi	.242

Opponents' On Base Pct.
Vance-Bro	.271
Grimes-Pit	.288
Benton-NY	.293
Clark-Bro	.294
Root-Chi	.296

Starter Runs
Vance-Bro	58.9
Benton-NY	43.1
Blake-Chi	40.6
Grimes-Pit	36.4
Malone-Chi	32.0

Adjusted Starter Runs
Vance-Bro	57.0
Grimes-Pit	43.1
Benton-NY	42.2
Blake-Chi	32.8
Sherdel-StL	27.8

Clutch Pitching Index
Nehf-Chi	133
Bush-Chi	117
Blake-Chi	115
Kolp-Cin	114
Rhem-StL	114

Relief Runs

Adjusted Relief Runs

Relief Ranking

Total Pitcher Index
Vance-Bro	6.4
Grimes-Pit	6.3
Benton-NY	4.0
Blake-Chi	3.1
Sherdel-StL	2.8

Total Baseball Ranking
Vance-Bro	6.4
Grimes-Pit	6.3
Hornsby-Bos	4.8
Hartnett-Chi	4.5
P.Waner-Pit	4.4

TEAM	G	W	L	PCT	GB	R	OR	AB	H	2B	3B	HR	BB	SO	AVG	OBP	SLG	PRO	/A	BR	/A	PF	CHI	RC	TA	SB	CS	SBA	SBR
NY	154	101	53	.656		894	685	5337	1578	269	79	133	562	544	.296	.365	.450	.815	120	146	205	92	99	888	.798	51	51	50	-14
PHI	153	98	55	.641	2.5	829	615	5226	1540	323	75	89	533	442	.295	.363	.436	.799	115	115	95	103	97	843	.777	59	48	55	-10
STL	154	82	72	.532	19	772	742	5217	1431	276	76	63	548	479	.274	.346	.393	.739	100	1	-24	104	104	736	.705	76	43	64	-2
WAS	155	75	79	.487	26	718	705	5320	1510	277	93	40	469	390	.284	.346	.393	.739	100	1	-10	102	96	743	.701	110	59	65	-1
CHI	155	72	82	.468	29	656	725	5207	1405	231	77	24	469	488	.270	.334	.358	.692	87	-87	-79	99	102	641	.644	139	82	63	-7
DET	154	68	86	.442	33	744	804	5292	1476	265	97	62	469	438	.279	.340	.401	.741	100	-1	4	99	101	730	.701	113	77	59	-11
CLE	155	62	92	.403	39	674	830	5386	1535	299	61	34	377	426	.285	.335	.382	.717	94	-48	-90	106	97	696	.646	50	45	53	-11
BOS	154	57	96	.373	43.5	589	770	5132	1356	260	62	38	389	512	.264	.319	.361	.680	84	-118	-105	98	99	602	.615	99	64	61	-8
TOT	617					5876		42117	11831	2200	620	483	3828	3719	.281	.344	.397	.741								697	469	60	-71

TEAM	CG	SHO	SV	IP	H	H/G	HR	BB	BB/G	SO	SO/G	ERA	/A	OAVG	OOBA	PR	/A	PF	CPI	FA	E	DP	FW	PW	BW	SBW	DIF
NY	82	13	21	1375.7	1466	9.6	59	452	3.0	487	3.2	3.74	96	.278	.326	45	-25	89	103	.968	194	136	-.0	-2.4	19.8	-.5	7.1
PHI	81	16	15	1367.0	1349	8.9	66	424	2.8	607	4.0	3.36	119	.263	.311	103	96	99	102	.970	181	124	.7	9.3	9.2	-.0	2.4
STL	80	6	15	1373.7	1487	9.7	93	454	3.0	456	3.0	4.17	100	.281	.327	-19	-1	103	99	.969	189	146	.2	-.0	-2.3	.7	6.5
WAS	77	15	10	1380.7	1420	9.3	40	466	3.0	462	3.0	3.88	105	.271	.320	24	32	101	92	.972	178	146	.9	3.1	-1.0	.8	-5.8
CHI	88	6	11	1373.7	1516	9.9	66	501	3.3	418	2.7	3.98	102	.285	.336	9	10	100	105	.970	186	149	.4	1.0	-7.6	.2	1.0
DET	65	6	15	1369.3	1481	9.7	58	567	3.7	451	3.0	4.32	94	.281	.339	-42	-41	100	96	.965	140	140	-1.5	-4.0	.4	-.2	-3.7
CLE	71	4	15	1374.7	1615	10.6	52	511	3.3	416	2.7	4.47	98	.298	.346	-66	-14	108	100	.965	221	187	-1.7	-1.4	-8.7	-.2	-3.1
BOS	70	5	9	1349.0	1492	10.0	49	452	3.0	407	2.7	4.39	93	.285	.331	-52	-45	101	92	.971	178	139	.9	-4.3	-10.1	.1	-6.0
TOT	614	69	113	10963.7		9.7			3.1		3.0	4.04		.281	.344					.969	1545	1167					

Runs
Ruth-NY 163
Gehrig-NY 139
Combs-NY 118
Blue-StL 116
Gehringer-Det 108

Hits
Manush-StL 241
Gehrig-NY 210
Rice-Was 202
Combs-NY 194
Gehringer-Det 193

Doubles
Manush-StL 47
Gehrig-NY 47
Meusel-NY 45
Schulte-StL 44
Lind-Cle 42

Triples
Combs-NY 21
Manush-StL 20
Gehringer-Det 16

Home Runs
Ruth-NY 54
Gehrig-NY 27
Goslin-Was 17
Hauser-Phi 16
Simmons-Phi 15

Total Bases
Ruth-NY 380
Manush-StL 367
Gehrig-NY 364
Combs-NY 290
Heilmann-Det 283

Runs Batted In
Ruth-NY 142
Gehrig-NY 142
Meusel-NY 113
Manush-StL 108

Runs Produced
Gehrig-NY 254
Ruth-NY 251
Manush-StL 199
Blue-StL 182
Meusel-NY 179

Bases On Balls
Ruth-NY 135
Blue-StL 105
Bishop-Phi 97
Gehrig-NY 95
Judge-Was 80

Batting Average
Goslin-Was 379
Manush-StL 378
Gehrig-NY 374
Simmons-Phi 351
Miller-Phi 329

On Base Percentage
Gehrig-NY 467
Ruth-NY 461
Goslin-Was 442
Bishop-Phi 435
Manush-StL 414

Slugging Average
Ruth-NY 709
Gehrig-NY 648
Goslin-Was 614
Manush-StL 575
Simmons-Phi 558

Production
Ruth-NY 1.170
Gehrig-NY 1.115
Goslin-Was 1.056
Manush-StL 989
Simmons-Phi 954

Adjusted Production
Ruth-NY 221
Gehrig-NY 207
Goslin-Was 172
Manush-StL 152
Simmons-Phi 144

Batter Runs
Ruth-NY 83.9
Gehrig-NY 76.0
Manush-StL 50.3
Goslin-Was 49.0
Foxx-Phi 30.4

Adjusted Batter Runs
Ruth-NY 90.7
Gehrig-NY 82.6
Goslin-Was 48.0
Manush-StL 47.3
Lazzeri-NY 29.0

Clutch Hitting Index
Meusel-NY 149
Judge-Was 144
Cissell-Chi 141
Kress-StL 136
Kamm-Chi 133

Runs Created
Ruth-NY 182
Gehrig-NY 169
Manush-StL 150
Goslin-Was 125
Combs-NY 114

Total Average
Ruth-NY 1.418
Gehrig-NY 1.287
Goslin-Was 1.213
Manush-StL 1.052
Simmons-Phi 964

Stolen Bases
Myer-Bos 30
Mostil-Chi 23
Rice-Det 20
Cissell-Chi 18
Bluege-Was 18

Stolen Base Average
Rice-Was 84.2
Goslin-Was 84.2
Judge-Was 80.0
Manush-StL 77.3

Stolen Base Runs
Rice-Was 3.0
Goslin-Was 3.0
Reynolds-Chi 2.7
Judge-Was 2.4
Manush-StL 2.1

Fielding Runs
J.Sewell-Cle 23.3
L.Sewell-Cle 14.5
Gerber-StL-Bos 12.5
Bluege-Was 11.5
Schulte-StL 10.7

Total Player Rating
Ruth-NY 7.0
Gehrig-NY 5.7
Goslin-Was 4.6
J.Sewell-Cle 4.3
Manush-StL 4.2

Wins
Pipgras-NY 24
Grove-Phi 24
Hoyt-NY 23
Crowder-StL 21
Gray-StL 20

Win Percentage
Crowder-StL 808
Hoyt-NY 767
Grove-Phi 750
Pennock-NY 739
Quinn-Phi 720

Games
Marberry-Was 48
Morris-Bos 47
Pipgras-NY 46
Rommel-Phi 43

Complete Games
Ruffing-Bos 25
Thomas-Chi 24
Grove-Phi 24
Pipgras-NY 22

Shutouts
Pennock-NY 5
Quinn-Phi 4
Pipgras-NY 4
Jones-Was 4
Grove-Phi 4

Saves
Hoyt-NY 8
Hudlin-Cle 7
Lyons-Chi 6
Braxton-Was 6

Innings Pitched
Pipgras-NY 301
Ruffing-Bos 289
Thomas-Chi 283
Hoyt-NY 273
Gray-StL 263

Fewest Hits/Game
Braxton-Was 7.31
Grove-Phi 7.83
Earnshaw-Phi 8.15
Jones-Was 8.36
Johnson-NY 8.50

Fewest BB/Game
Rommel-Phi 1.34
Quinn-Phi 1.45
Pennock-NY 1.71
Braxton-Was 1.82
Russell-Bos 1.84

Strikeouts
Grove-Phi 183
Pipgras-NY 139
Thomas-Chi 129
Ruffing-Bos 118
Earnshaw-Phi 117

Strikeouts/Game
Earnshaw-Phi 6.66
Grove-Phi 6.29
Johnson-NY 4.97
Walberg-Phi 4.27
Whitehill-Det 4.27

Wins Above Team
Crowder-StL 8.2
Morris-Bos 6.0
Grove-Phi 5.7
Jones-Was 5.7
Hoyt-NY 5.6

Earned Run Average
Braxton-Was 2.52
Pennock-NY 2.56
Grove-Phi 2.58
Jones-Was 2.84
Quinn-Phi 2.90

Adjusted ERA
Braxton-Was 162
Grove-Phi 155
Jones-Was 144
Pennock-NY 140
Quinn-Phi 138

Opponents' Batting Avg.
Braxton-Was 222
Grove-Phi 229
Earnshaw-Phi 240
Johnson-NY 250
Jones-Was 252

Opponents' On Base Pct.
Grove-Phi 258
Grove-Phi 275
Rommel-Phi 289
Pennock-NY 296
Thomas-Chi 303

Starter Runs
Grove-Phi 42.5
Braxton-Was 36.8
Pennock-NY 34.6
Thomas-Chi 29.9
Jones-Was 29.9

Adjusted Starter Runs
Grove-Phi 41.2
Braxton-Was 38.1
Jones-Was 31.2
Thomas-Chi 30.2
Gray-StL 28.5

Clutch Pitching Index
Miller-Cle 119
Quinn-Phi 119
Blankenship-Chi 114
Adkins-Chi 113
Pennock-NY 113

Relief Runs

Adjusted Relief Runs
Simmons-Bos 4

Relief Ranking
Simmons-Bos 1

Total Pitcher Index
Grove-Phi 4.0
Jones-Was 3.9
Braxton-Was 3.5
Gray-StL 3.1
Thomas-Chi 3.0

Total Baseball Ranking
Ruth-NY 7.0
Gehrig-NY 5.7
Goslin-Was 4.6
J.Sewell-Cle 4.3
Manush-StL 4.2

TEAM	G	W	L	PCT	GB	R	OR	AB	H	2B	3B	HR	BB	SO	AVG	OBP	SLG	PRO	/A	BR	/A	PF	CHI	RC	TA	SB	CS	SBA	SBR
CHI	156	98	54	.645		982	758	5471	1655	310	45	140	589	567	.303	.373	.452	.825	111	92	81	101	104	917	.838	103			
PIT	154	88	65	.575	10.5	904	780	5490	1663	285	116	60	503	335	.303	.364	.430	.794	103	28	0	103	103	850	.780	94			
NY	152	84	67	.556	13.5	897	709	5388	1594	251	47	136	482	405	.296	.358	.436	.794	103	18	21	100	106	827	.778	85			
STL	154	78	74	.513	20	831	806	5364	1569	310	84	100	490	455	.293	.354	.438	.792	102	12	25	98	99	819	.772	72			
PHI	154	71	82	.464	27.5	897	1032	5484	1693	305	51	153	573	470	.309	.377	.467	.844	115	125	43	110	92	951	.848	59			
BRO	153	70	83	.458	28.5	755	888	5273	1535	282	69	99	504	454	.291	.355	.427	.782	100	-1	45	94	93	792	.765	80			
CIN	155	66	88	.429	33	586	760	5269	1478	258	79	34	412	347	.281	.336	.379	.715	83	-132	-127	99	102	664	.677	134			
BOS	154	56	98	.364	43	657	876	5291	1481	252	78	32	408	432	.280	.335	.375	.710	82	-142	-92	94	98	658	.652	65			
TOT	616					6609		43030	12668	2253	569	754	3961	3465	.294	.357	.426	.783						692					

TEAM	CG	SHO	SV	IP	H	H/G	HR	BB	BB/G	SO	SO/G	ERA	/A	OAVG	OOBA	PR	/A	PF	CPI	FA	E	DP	FW	PW	BW	SBW	DIF
CHI	79	14	21	1396.7	1542	9.9	77	564	3.6	548	3.5	4.16	111	.284	.344	85	69	98	105	.975	154	169	1.3	6.3	7.4		7.0
PIT	79	5	13	1378.3	1530	10.0	96	439	2.9	409	2.7	4.36	110	.285	.330	53	64	102	98	.975	181	136	-.2	5.8	.0		5.9
NY	68	9	13	1372.3	1536	10.1	102	387	2.5	431	2.8	3.97	115	.287	.325	113	90	97	108	.975	158	163	1.1	8.2	1.9		-2.7
STL	83	6	8	1357.7	1604	10.6	101	474	3.1	453	3.0	4.66	99	.298	.347	7	-6	98	102	.971	174	149	.2	-.5	2.3		.1
PHI	45	5	24	1346.7	1743	11.6	122	369	2.5	369	2.5	6.13	86	.317	.375	-212	-130	112	94	.969	191	153	-.8	-11.8	3.9		3.2
BRO	59	8	16	1356.7	1553	10.3	92	549	3.6	549	3.6	4.92	92	.291	.347	-31	-58	96	95	.968	192	113	-.9	-5.3	4.1		-4.5
CIN	75	5	8	1367.7	1558	10.3	61	413	2.7	347	2.3	4.41	107	.290	.331	45	49	101	95	.974	162	148	.9	4.5	-11.5		-4.8
BOS	78	4	12	1351.7	1604	10.7	103	530	3.5	366	2.4	5.12	89	.299	.351	-61	-81	97	96	.967	204	146	-1.5	-7.4	-8.4		-3.7
TOT	566	56	115	10927.7		10.4			3.3		2.9	4.71		.294	.357					.971	1416	1177					

Runs
Hornsby-Chi 156
O'Doul-Phi 152
Ott-NY 138
Wilson-Chi 135
L.Waner-Pit 134

Hits
O'Doul-Phi 254
L.Waner-Pit 234
Hornsby-Chi 229
Terry-NY 226
Klein-Phi 219

Doubles
Frederick-Bro 52
Hornsby-Chi 47
Hafey-StL 47
Klein-Phi 45
Kelly-Cin 45

Triples
L.Waner-Pit 20
P.Waner-Pit 15
Walker-Cin 15
Whitney-Phi 14

Home Runs
Klein-Phi 43
Ott-NY 42
Wilson-Chi 39
Hornsby-Chi 39
O'Doul-Phi 32

Total Bases
Hornsby-Chi 409
Klein-Phi 405
O'Doul-Phi 397
Wilson-Chi 355
Herman-Bro 348

Runs Batted In
Wilson-Chi 159
Ott-NY 151
Hornsby-Chi 149
Klein-Phi 145
Bottomley-StL 137

Runs Produced
Hornsby-Chi 266
Wilson-Chi 255
Ott-NY 247
O'Doul-Phi 242
Klein-Phi 228

Bases On Balls
Ott-NY 113
Grantham-Pit 93
P.Waner-Pit 89
Hornsby-Chi 87
Walker-Cin 85

Batting Average
O'Doul-Phi 398
Herman-Bro 381
Hornsby-Chi 380
Terry-NY 372
Stephenson-Chi 362

On Base Percentage
O'Doul-Phi 465
Hornsby-Chi 459
Ott-NY 449
Stephenson-Chi 445
Cuyler-Chi 438

Slugging Average
Hornsby-Chi 679
Klein-Phi 657
Ott-NY 635
Hafey-StL 632
O'Doul-Phi 622

Production
Hornsby-Chi 1.139
O'Doul-Phi 1.087
Ott-NY 1.084
Klein-Phi 1.065
Herman-Bro 1.047

Adjusted Production
Hornsby-Chi 176
Herman-Bro 166
Ott-NY 166
Wilson-Chi 153
O'Doul-Phi 152

Batter Runs
Hornsby-Chi 74.1
O'Doul-Phi 68.4
Ott-NY 58.4
Klein-Phi 53.2
Herman-Bro 49.6

Adjusted Batter Runs
Hornsby-Chi 72.9
O'Doul-Phi 58.9
Ott-NY 58.7
Herman-Bro 54.5
Wilson-Chi 47.9

Clutch Hitting Index
Sheely-Pit 148
Comorosky-Pit 144
Kelly-Cin 143
Grimm-Chi 137
Traynor-Pit 133

Runs Created
Hornsby-Chi 183
O'Doul-Phi 180
Klein-Phi 158
Ott-NY 157
Wilson-Chi 148

Total Average
Hornsby-Chi 1.338
Ott-NY 1.287
O'Doul-Phi 1.247
Herman-Bro 1.205
Cuyler-Chi 1.181

Stolen Bases
Cuyler-Chi 43
Swanson-Cin 33
Frisch-StL 24
Herman-Bro 21
Allen-Cin 21

Stolen Base Average

Stolen Base Runs

Fielding Runs
Whitney-Phi 21.3
Jackson-NY 18.8
Maranville-Bos 18.7
English-Chi 16.7
Ott-NY 15.7

Total Player Rating
Hornsby-Chi 7.0
Ott-NY 5.4
Jackson-NY 4.2
O'Doul-Phi 3.9
Whitney-Phi 3.4

Wins
Malone-Chi 22
Root-Chi 19
Lucas-Cin 19

Win Percentage
Root-Chi 760
Bush-Chi 720
Grimes-Pit 708
Malone-Chi 688
Kremer-Pit 643

Games
Bush-Chi 50
Willoughby-Phi 49
Sweetland-Phi 43
Root-Chi 43
Collins-Phi 43

Complete Games
Lucas-Cin 28

Shutouts
Malone-Chi 5
Root-Chi 4
Fitzsimmons-NY . . . 4

Saves
Morrison-Bro 8
Bush-Chi 8
Koupal-Bro-Phi 6

Innings Pitched
Clark-Bro 279
Root-Chi 272
Bush-Chi 271
Lucas-Cin 270
Hubbell-NY 268

Fewest Hits/Game
Lucas-Cin 8.90
Kremer-Pit 9.16
Hubbell-NY 9.17
Johnson-StL 9.20
Bush-Chi 9.20

Fewest BB/Game
Vance-Bro 1.83
Lucas-Cin 1.93
Petty-Pit 2.05
Hubbell-NY 2.25
Clark-Bro 2.29

Strikeouts
Malone-Chi 166
Clark-Bro 140
Vance-Bro 126
Root-Chi 124
Hubbell-NY 106

Strikeouts/Game
Malone-Chi 5.60
Vance-Bro 4.91
Clark-Bro 4.52
May-Cin 4.16
Root-Chi 4.10

Wins Above Team
Lucas-Cin 5.8
Root-Chi 4.6
Grimes-Pit 4.2
Morrison-Bro 3.9
Moss-Bro 3.2

Earned Run Average
Walker-NY 3.08
Grimes-Pit 3.13
Root-Chi 3.47
Malone-Chi 3.57
Lucas-Cin 3.60

Adjusted ERA
Grimes-Pit 153
Walker-NY 148
Root-Chi 133
Lucas-Cin 132
Malone-Chi 129

Opponents' Batting Avg.
Lucas-Cin 257
Johnson-StL 265
Hubbell-NY 265
Bush-Chi 265
Grimes-Pit 269

Opponents' On Base Pct.
Lucas-Cin 290
Petty-Pit 305
Hubbell-NY 306
Vance-Bro 307
Kremer-Pit 309

Starter Runs
Grimes-Pit 41.0
Root-Chi 37.4
Malone-Chi 33.8
Lucas-Cin 33.3
Walker-NY 32.2

Adjusted Starter Runs
Grimes-Pit 42.8
Root-Chi 34.4
Lucas-Cin 34.0
Malone-Chi 30.8
Walker-NY 29.2

Clutch Pitching Index
Walker-NY 129
Mitchell-StL 129
Sweetland-Phi 116
Grimes-Pit 116
Malone-Chi 115

Relief Runs
Hill-Pit-StL 3.1
Cvengros-Chi 5

Adjusted Relief Runs
Hill-Pit-StL 4.4

Relief Ranking
Hill-Pit-StL 2.6

Total Pitcher Index
Grimes-Pit 5.1
Lucas-Cin 3.3
Root-Chi 2.8
Malone-Chi 2.7
Bush-Chi 2.3

Total Baseball Ranking
Hornsby-Chi 7.0
Ott-NY 5.4
Grimes-Pit 5.1
Jackson-NY 4.2
O'Doul-Phi 3.9

TEAM	G	W	L	PCT	GB	R	OR	AB	H	2B	3B	HR	BB	SO	AVG	OBP	SLG	PRO	/A	BR	/A	PF	CHI	RC	TA	SB	CS	SBA	SBR
PHI	151	104	46	.693		901	615	5204	1539	288	76	122	543	440	.296	.365	.451	.816	115	112	44	109	102	875	.804	61	38	62	-4
NY	154	88	66	.571	18	899	775	5379	1587	262	74	142	554	518	.295	.364	.450	.814	115	110	120	99	100	892	.796	51	44	54	-10
CLE	152	81	71	.533	24	717	736	5187	1525	294	79	62	453	363	.294	.353	.417	.770	103	23	21	100	92	759	.722	75	85	47	-28
STL	154	79	73	.520	26	733	713	5174	1426	276	63	47	589	431	.276	.352	.381	.733	94	-33	-32	100	99	723	.699	72	46	61	-5
WAS	153	71	81	.467	34	730	776	5237	1445	244	66	48	556	400	.276	.347	.375	.722	91	-55	-51	100	102	706	.681	86	61	59	-10
DET	155	70	84	.455	36	926	928	5592	1671	339	97	110	521	496	.299	.360	.453	.813	114	109	130	97	101	914	.793	95	72	57	-14
CHI	152	59	93	.388	46	627	792	5248	1406	240	74	37	425	436	.268	.325	.363	.688	82	-133	-93	100	101	631	.629	106	67	61	-7
BOS	155	58	96	.377	48	605	803	5160	1377	285	69	28	413	494	.267	.325	.365	.690	83	-130	-142	102	98	616	.624	85	80	52	-22
TOT	613					6138		42181	11976	2228	598	596	4054	3578	.284	.349	.408	.757								631	493	56	-106

TEAM	CG	SHO	SV	IP	H	H/G	HR	BB	BB/G	SO	SO/G	ERA	/A	OAVG	OOBA	PR	/A	PF	CPI	FA	E	DP	FW	PW	BW	SBW	DIF
PHI	70	9	24	1356.0	1371	9.1	73	487	3.2	573	3.8	3.44	128	.267	.323	120	146	104	108	.975	146	117	2.7	13.8	4.1	.9	7.5
NY	64	12	18	1366.3	1475	9.7	83	485	3.2	484	3.2	4.18	98	.280	.332	8	-12	97	98	.971	178	152	.8	-1.1	11.3	.3	-.2
CLE	80	8	10	1349.7	1570	10.5	56	488	3.3	389	2.6	4.05	105	.295	.345	28	31	101	109	.968	198	162	-.5	2.9	2.0	-1.4	2.0
STL	83	15	10	1369.7	1474	9.7	100	462	3.0	415	2.7	4.08	103	.279	.328	23	20	100	101	.975	156	148	2.1	1.9	-3.0	.8	1.2
WAS	62	3	17	1353.7	1429	9.5	48	496	3.3	494	3.3	4.34	98	.275	.329	-15	-13	100	88	.968	195	156	-.3	-1.2	-4.8	.3	1.0
DET	82	5	9	1388.0	1641	10.6	73	646	4.2	467	3.0	4.96	83	.299	.360	-111	-129	97	98	.961	242	149	-3.2	-12.2	12.3	-.0	-3.8
CHI	78	5	7	1355.0	1481	9.8	84	505	3.4	328	2.2	4.41	94	.282	.334	-25	-41	98	96	.970	188	153	.1	-3.9	-8.8	.6	-5.1
BOS	84	9	5	1364.0	1537	10.1	78	496	3.3	416	2.7	4.43	101	.289	.338	-28	3	105	98	.965	218	159	-1.7	.3	-13.4	-.8	-3.3
TOT	603	66	100	10902.3		9.9			3.4		2.9	4.24		.284	.349					.969	1521	1196					

Runs
Gehringer-Det 131
Johnson-Det 128
Gehrig-NY 127
Foxx-Phi 123
Ruth-NY 121

Hits
Gehringer-Det ...215
Alexander-Det ...215
Simmons-Phi ...212
Fonseca-Cle ...209
Manush-StL 204

Doubles
Manush-StL 45
Johnson-Det 45
Gehringer-Det 45
Fonseca-Cle 44

Triples
Gehringer-Det 19
Scarritt-Bos 17
Miller-Phi 16

Home Runs
Ruth-NY 46
Gehrig-NY 35
Simmons-Phi 34
Foxx-Phi 33
Alexander-Det 25

Total Bases
Simmons-Phi 373
Alexander-Det 363
Ruth-NY 348
Gehringer-Det 337

Runs Batted In
Simmons-Phi 157
Ruth-NY 154
Alexander-Det ...137
Gehrig-NY ...126
Heilmann-Det ...120

Runs Produced
Simmons-Phi ...237
Ruth-NY ...229
Gehringer-Det ...224
Alexander-Det ...222
Gehrig-NY ...218

Bases On Balls
Bishop-Phi 128
Blue-StL 126
Gehrig-NY 122
Foxx-Phi 103
Cronin-Was 85

Batting Average
Fonseca-Cle ...369
Simmons-Phi ...365
Manush-StL ...355
Lazzeri-NY ...354
Foxx-Phi ...354

On Base Percentage
Foxx-Phi 463
Gehrig-NY 431
Ruth-NY 430
Lazzeri-NY 429
Fonseca-Cle 426

Slugging Average
Ruth-NY 697
Simmons-Phi 642
Foxx-Phi 625
Gehrig-NY 584
Alexander-Det 580

Production
Ruth-NY 1.128
Foxx-Phi 1.088
Simmons-Phi 1.040
Gehrig-NY 1.015
Lazzeri-NY 991

Adjusted Production
Ruth-NY 188
Foxx-Phi 163
Gehrig-NY 161
Lazzeri-NY 155
Heilmann-Det 153

Batter Runs
Foxx-Phi 63.1
Ruth-NY 61.8
Gehrig-NY 51.5
Simmons-Phi 50.2
Lazzeri-NY 43.8

Adjusted Batter Runs
Ruth-NY 62.8
Foxx-Phi 55.9
Gehrig-NY 52.6
Alexander-Det 45.0
Lazzeri-NY 44.9

Clutch Hitting Index
Kress-StL 144
West-Was 141
Heilmann-Det 139
Schulte-StL 136
Cochrane-Phi 130

Runs Created
Foxx-Phi 154
Ruth-NY 150
Gehrig-NY 146
Simmons-Phi 145
Alexander-Det 140

Total Average
Ruth-NY 1.297
Foxx-Phi 1.282
Gehrig-NY 1.161
Simmons-Phi 1.102
Lazzeri-NY 1.069

Stolen Bases
Gehringer-Det 27
Cissell-Chi 26
Miller-Phi 24
Rothrock-Bos 23
Johnson-Det 20

Stolen Base Average
Gehringer-Det ...75.0
Miller-Phi ...72.7
Myer-Was ...72.0
Reynolds-Chi ...67.9
Rice-Was ...66.7

Stolen Base Runs
Gehringer-Det 2.7
Miller-Phi 1.8
Myer-Was 1.2
Kamm-Chi 1.2
Goslin-Was 1.2

Fielding Runs
Johnson-Det 18.7
Gardner-Cle 18.3
Melillo-StL 17.9
Simmons-Phi 16.6
Tavener-Cle 16.5

Total Player Rating
Simmons-Phi 5.0
Ruth-NY 4.1
Gehringer-Det 3.9
Lazzeri-NY 3.9
Foxx-Phi 2.8

Wins
Earnshaw-Phi 24
Ferrell-Cle 21
Grove-Phi 20
Marberry-Was 19

Win Percentage
Grove-Phi 769
Earnshaw-Phi 750
Ferrell-Cle 677
Walberg-Phi 621
Marberry-Was 613

Games
Marberry-Was 49
Earnshaw-Phi 44
Gray-StL 43
Ferrell-Cle 43

Complete Games
Thomas-Chi 24
Uhle-Det 23
Gray-StL 23
Hudlin-Cle 22
Lyons-Chi 21

Shutouts
MacFayden-Bos 4
Gray-StL 4
Crowder-StL 4
Blaeholder-StL 4

Saves
Marberry-Was 11
Moore-NY 8
Shores-Phi 7
Ferrell-Cle 5

Innings Pitched
Gray-StL 305
Hudlin-Cle 280
Grove-Phi 275
Walberg-Phi 268
Crowder-StL 267

Fewest Hits/Game
Earnshaw-Phi ...8.22
Wells-NY 8.35
Marberry-Was ...8.39
Walberg-Phi 8.60
Shores-Phi 8.82

Fewest BB/Game
Russell-Bos 1.59
Pennock-NY 1.61
Thomas-Chi 2.08
Uhle-Det 2.10
Quinn-Phi 2.18

Strikeouts
Grove-Phi 170
Earnshaw-Phi 149
Pipgras-NY 125
Marberry-Was 121

Strikeouts/Game
Grove-Phi 5.56
Earnshaw-Phi 5.26
Pipgras-NY 5.00
Hadley-Was 4.52
Marberry-Was 4.36

Wins Above Team
Zachary-NY 6.0
Ferrell-Cle 5.6
Marberry-Was 5.0
Rommel-Phi 3.9
Grove-Phi 3.7

Earned Run Average
Grove-Phi 2.81
Marberry-Was 3.06
Thomas-Chi 3.18
Earnshaw-Phi 3.28
Hudlin-Cle 3.34

Adjusted ERA
Grove-Phi 157
Marberry-Was 139
Earnshaw-Phi 134
Thomas-Chi 130
Hudlin-Cle 127

Opponents' Batting Avg.
Earnshaw-Phi 241
Wells-NY 248
Marberry-Was 252
Walberg-Phi 254
Grove-Phi 262

Opponents' On Base Pct.
Marberry-Was 300
Thomas-Chi 302
Grove-Phi 310
Hudlin-Cle 311
Walberg-Phi 312

Starter Runs
Grove-Phi 43.5
Marberry-Was 32.7
Thomas-Chi 30.4
Hudlin-Cle 27.9
Earnshaw-Phi 27.1

Adjusted Starter Runs
Grove-Phi 48.7
Marberry-Was 33.1
Earnshaw-Phi 31.9
Hudlin-Cle 28.5
Thomas-Chi 27.4

Clutch Pitching Index
McKain-Chi 130
Gaston-Bos 117
Shaute-Cle 116
Ferrell-Cle.........116
Collins-StL 113

Relief Runs
Moore-NY 7

Adjusted Relief Runs

Relief Ranking

Total Pitcher Index
Grove-Phi 4.6
Hudlin-Cle 3.2
Marberry-Was 3.1
Thomas-Chi 2.6
Earnshaw-Phi 2.6

Total Baseball Ranking
Simmons-Phi 5.0
Grove-Phi 4.6
Ruth-NY 4.1
Gehringer-Det 3.9
Lazzeri-NY 3.9

TEAM	G	W	L	PCT	GB	R	OR	AB	H	2B	3B	HR	BB	SO	AVG	OBP	SLG	PRO	/A	BR	/A	PF	CHI	RC	TA	SB	CS	SBA	SBR
STL	154	92	62	.597		1004	784	5512	1732	373	89	104	479	496	.314	.372	.471	.843	108	72	29	105	104	944	.840	72			
CHI	156	90	64	.584	2	998	870	5581	1722	305	72	171	588	635	.309	.378	.481	.859	112	110	64	105	97	1001	.876	70			
NY	154	87	67	.565	5	959	814	5553	1769	264	83	143	422	382	.319	.369	.473	.842	108	67	87	98	100	941	.827	59			
BRO	154	86	68	.558	6	871	738	5433	1654	303	73	122	481	541	.304	.364	.454	.818	102	21	16	101	97	881	.802	53			
PIT	154	80	74	.519	12	891	928	5346	1622	285	119	86	494	449	.303	.365	.449	.814	101	15	41	97	100	862	.804	76			
BOS	154	70	84	.455	22	693	835	5356	1503	246	78	66	332	397	.281	.326	.393	.719	78	-185	-159	97	105	669	.657	69			
CIN	154	59	95	.383	33	665	857	5245	1475	265	67	74	445	489	.281	.339	.400	.739	83	-134	-52	90	93	703	.691	48			
PHI	156	52	102	.338	40	944	1199	5667	1783	345	44	126	450	459	.315	.367	.458	.825	104	37	-15	106	100	929	.798	34			
TOT	618					7025		43693	13260	2386	625	892	3691	3848	.303	.360	.448	.808								481			

TEAM	CG	SHO	SV	IP	H	H/G	HR	BB	BB/G	SO	SO/G	ERA	/A	OAVG	OOBA	PR	/A	PF	CPI	FA	E	DP	FW	PW	BW	SBW	DIF
STL	63	5	21	1379.0	1595	10.4	87	477	3.1	641	4.2	4.40	115	.293	.342	87	100	102	103	.970	183	176	.2	8.8	2.6		3.5
CHI	67	7	12	1404.7	1642	10.5	111	528	3.4	601	3.9	4.80	107	.296	.349	26	51	103	100	.973	170	167	.9	4.5	5.6		1.9
NY	64	6	19	1362.7	1546	10.2	117	439	2.9	522	3.4	4.60	103	.289	.336	56	24	96	98	.974	164	144	1.3	2.1	7.7		-1.1
BRO	74	13	15	1371.7	1480	9.7	115	394	2.6	526	3.5	4.03	122	.279	.321	143	132	99	103	.972	174	167	.7	11.7	1.4		-4.7
PIT	80	5	13	1361.0	1730	11.4	128	438	2.9	393	2.6	5.24	93	.313	.353	-40	-59	98	101	.965	216	164	-1.8	-5.2	3.6		6.4
BOS	71	6	11	1360.7	1624	10.7	117	475	3.1	424	2.8	4.91	100	.300	.345	9	2	99	100	.971	178	167	.4	.2	-14.0		6.4
CIN	61	6	11	1335.3	1650	11.1	75	394	2.7	361	2.4	5.08	91	.307	.344	-16	-67	93	93	.973	161	164	1.4	-5.9	-4.6		-8.9
PHI	54	8	7	1374.7	1993	13.0	142	543	3.6	384	2.5	6.71	81	.342	.386	-265	-194	109	96	.962	239	169	-3.1	-17.1	-1.3		-3.4
TOT	534	51	109	10949.7		10.9			3.0		3.2	4.97		.303	.360					.970	1485	1318					

Runs
Klein-Phi 158
Cuyler-Chi 155
English-Chi 152
Wilson-Chi 146
Herman-Bro 143

Hits
Terry-NY 254
Klein-Phi 250
Herman-Bro 241
Lindstrom-NY 231
Cuyler-Chi 228

Doubles
Klein-Phi 59
Cuyler-Chi 50
Herman-Bro 48
Comorosky-Pit 47
Frisch-StL 46

Triples
Comorosky-Pit 23
P.Waner-Pit 18
English-Chi 17
Cuyler-Chi 17
Terry-NY 15

Home Runs
Wilson-Chi 56
Klein-Phi 40
Berger-Bos 38
Hartnett-Chi 37
Herman-Bro 35

Total Bases
Klein-Phi 445
Wilson-Chi 423
Herman-Bro 416
Terry-NY 392
Cuyler-Chi 351

Runs Batted In
Wilson-Chi 190
Klein-Phi 170
Cuyler-Chi 134
Herman-Bro 130
Terry-NY 129

Runs Produced
Klein-Phi 288
Wilson-Chi 280
Cuyler-Chi 276
Terry-NY 245
Herman-Bro 238

Bases On Balls
Wilson-Chi 105
Ott-NY 103
English-Chi 100
Grantham-Pit 81
Suhr-Pit 80

Batting Average
Terry-NY 401
Herman-Bro 393
Klein-Phi 386
O'Doul-Phi 383
Lindstrom-NY 379

On Base Percentage
Ott-NY 458
Herman-Bro 455
Wilson-Chi 454
O'Doul-Phi 453
Terry-NY 452

Slugging Average
Wilson-Chi 723
Klein-Phi 687
Herman-Bro 678
Hafey-StL 652
Hartnett-Chi 630

Production
Wilson-Chi 1.177
Herman-Bro 1.132
Klein-Phi 1.123
Terry-NY 1.071
Hafey-StL 1.059

Adjusted Production
Wilson-Chi 170
Herman-Bro 168
Terry-NY 159
Klein-Phi 157
Ott-NY 152

Batter Runs
Wilson-Chi 75.4
Herman-Bro 68.6
Klein-Phi 67.3
Terry-NY 57.6
O'Doul-Phi 46.9

Adjusted Batter Runs
Wilson-Chi 70.3
Herman-Bro 68.1
Klein-Phi 61.3
Terry-NY 60.0
Ott-NY 47.5

Clutch Hitting Index
Traynor-Pit 155
Thevenow-Phi 144
Whitney-Phi 140
Wright-Bro 130
Grimm-Chi 121

Runs Created
Wilson-Chi 189
Klein-Phi 186
Herman-Bro 183
Terry-NY 170
Cuyler-Chi 148

Total Average
Wilson-Chi 1.411
Herman-Bro 1.351
Klein-Phi 1.274
Ott-NY 1.224
Terry-NY 1.208

Stolen Bases
Cuyler-Chi 37
P.Waner-Pit 18
Herman-Bro 18

Stolen Base Average

Stolen Base Runs

Fielding Runs
Klein-Phi 33.0
Frisch-StL 22.9
Whitney-Phi 20.7
Terry-NY 12.5
Gilbert-Bro 10.3

Total Player Rating
Klein-Phi 7.2
Terry-NY 5.7
Wilson-Chi 5.4
Frisch-StL 4.6
Lindstrom-NY 4.2

Wins
Malone-Chi 20
Kremer-Pit 20
Fitzsimmons-NY 19

Win Percentage
Fitzsimmons-NY 731
Malone-Chi 690
Brame-Pit 680
Kremer-Pit 625
Hallahan-StL 625

Games
Elliott-Phi 48
Collins-Phi 47
Bush-Chi 46
Pruett-NY 45
Malone-Chi 45

Complete Games
Malone-Chi 22
Brame-Pit 22
French-Pit 21
Vance-Bro 20
Seibold-Bos 20

Shutouts
Vance-Bro 4
Root-Chi 4
Hubbell-NY 3
French-Pit 3

Saves
Bell-StL 8
Heving-NY 6
Clark-Bro 6

Innings Pitched
Kremer-Pit 276
French-Pit 275
Malone-Chi 272
Vance-Bro 259
Seibold-Bos 251

Fewest Hits/Game
Vance-Bro 8.37
Hallahan-StL 8.85
Fitzsimmons-NY . . . 9.24
Elliott-Bro 9.27
Clark-Bro 9.41

Fewest BB/Game
Clark-Bro 1.71
Johnson-StL 1.82
Kolp-Cin 1.82
Lucas-Cin 1.88
Vance-Bro 1.91

Strikeouts
Hallahan-StL 177
Vance-Bro 173
Malone-Chi 142
Root-Chi 124
Hubbell-NY 117

Strikeouts/Game
Hallahan-StL 6.72
Vance-Bro 6.01
Root-Chi 5.07
Malone-Chi 4.70
Johnson-StL 4.40

Wins Above Team
Collins-Phi 5.8
Fitzsimmons-NY . . . 5.5
Brame-Pit 4.7
Malone-Chi 4.3
Kremer-Pit 4.2

Earned Run Average
Vance-Bro 2.61
Hubbell-NY 3.87
Walker-NY 3.93
Malone-Chi 3.94
Elliott-Bro 3.95

Adjusted ERA
Vance-Bro 188
Malone-Chi 130
Elliott-Bro 124
Hubbell-NY 123
Grimes-Bos-StL 123

Opponents' Batting Avg.
Kolp-Cin 240
Vance-Bro 246
Hallahan-StL 260
Fitzsimmons-NY 266
Walker-NY 268

Opponents' On Base Pct.
Kolp-Cin 265
Vance-Bro 284
Clark-Bro 299
Fitzsimmons-NY 307
Hubbell-NY 320

Starter Runs
Vance-Bro 68.0
Malone-Chi 31.2
Hubbell-NY 29.6
Walker-NY 28.3
Seibold-Bos 23.6

Adjusted Starter Runs
Vance-Bro 65.9
Malone-Chi 36.0
Hubbell-NY 23.9
Walker-NY 22.5
Seibold-Bos 22.3

Clutch Pitching Index
Grimes-Bos-StL 119
Smith-Bos 117
Haines-StL 109
Vance-Bro 108
Phelps-Bro 107

Relief Runs
Bell-StL 13.5
Lindsey-StL 6.5
Johnson-Cin 0

Adjusted Relief Runs
Bell-StL 14.6
Lindsey-StL 7.5
Nelson-Chi 2

Relief Ranking
Bell-StL 10.3
Lindsey-StL 8.5
Nelson-Chi 0

Total Pitcher Index
Vance-Bro 5.7
Malone-Chi 3.5
Grimes-Bos-StL 2.2
Fitzsimmons-NY 2.1
Root-Chi 1.9

Total Baseball Ranking
Klein-Phi 7.2
Vance-Bro 5.7
Terry-NY 5.7
Wilson-Chi 5.4
Frisch-StL 4.6

TEAM	G	W	L	PCT	GB	R	OR	AB	H	2B	3B	HR	BB	SO	AVG	OBP	SLG	PRO	/A	BR	/A	PF	CHI	RC	TA	SB	CS	SBA	SBR
PHI	154	102	52	.662		951	751	5345	1573	319	74	125	599	531	.294	.369	.452	.821	113	101	106	99	100	913	.813	48	33	59	-4
WAS	154	94	60	.610	8	892	689	5370	1620	300	98	57	537	438	.302	.369	.426	.795	106	58	47	101	98	860	.776	101	67	60	-9
NY	154	86	68	.558	16	1062	898	5448	1683	298	110	152	644	569	.309	.384	.488	.872	125	206	296	90	99	1035	.892	91	60	60	-8
CLE	154	81	73	.526	21	890	915	5439	1654	358	59	72	490	461	.304	.364	.431	.795	106	54	12	105	98	863	.760	51	47	52	-12
DET	154	75	79	.487	27	783	833	5297	1504	298	90	82	461	508	.284	.344	.421	.765	98	-18	-57	105	97	771	.728	98	70	58	-12
STL	154	64	90	.416	38	751	886	5278	1415	289	67	75	497	550	.268	.333	.391	.724	88	-95	-160	108	103	696	.678	93	71	57	-14
CHI	154	62	92	.403	40	729	884	5419	1496	256	90	63	389	479	.276	.328	.391	.719	86	-110	-132	103	101	705	.660	74	40	65	-1
BOS	154	52	102	.338	50	612	814	5286	1393	257	68	47	358	552	.264	.313	.365	.678	76	-191	-134	93	100	608	.598	42	35	55	-7
TOT	616					6670		42882	12338	2375	656	673	3975	4088	.288	.351	.421	.772								598	423	59	-73

TEAM	CG	SHO	SV	IP	H	H/G	HR	BB	BB/G	SO	SO/G	ERA	/A	OAVG	OOBA	PR	/A	PF	CPI	FA	E	DP	FW	PW	BW	SBW	DIF
PHI	72	8	21	1369.0	1457	9.6	84	488	3.2	672	4.4	4.28	105	.275	.328	55	29	96	99	.975	145	121	3.0	2.6	9.6	.5	9.3
WAS	78	6	14	1369.3	1367	9.0	52	504	3.3	524	3.4	3.96	115	.262	.320	104	90	98	95	.974	157	150	2.3	8.1	4.2	.0	2.3
NY	65	7	15	1364.3	1586	10.5	93	524	3.5	572	3.8	4.88	83	.293	.347	-35	-124	87	99	.965	207	132	-.7	-11.2	26.8	.1	-5.9
CLE	68	5	14	1359.7	1663	11.0	85	528	3.5	441	2.9	4.88	100	.303	.354	-34	2	105	105	.962	237	156	-2.6	.2	1.1	-.2	5.5
DET	68	4	17	1349.3	1507	10.1	86	570	3.8	574	3.8	4.70	104	.285	.345	-8	31	106	100	.967	192	156	.2	2.8	-5.2	-.2	.4
STL	68	5	10	1371.3	1639	10.8	124	449	2.9	470	3.1	5.07	101	.299	.342	-64	6	110	99	.970	188	152	.4	.5	-14.5	-.4	.9
CHI	63	2	10	1360.7	1629	10.8	74	407	2.7	471	3.1	4.71	104	.299	.337	-9	25	105	100	.962	235	136	-2.4	2.3	-11.9	.8	-3.6
BOS	78	4	5	1360.3	1505	10.0	75	488	3.2	356	2.4	4.70	95	.283	.332	-7	-36	96	94	.968	196	161	-.0	-3.3	-12.1	.2	-9.8
TOT	560	41	106	10904.0		10.2			3.3		3.4	4.65		.288	.351					.968	1557	1164					

Runs
Simmons-Phi 152
Ruth-NY 150
Gehringer-Det 144
Gehrig-NY 143
Combs-NY 129

Hits
Hodapp-Cle 225
Gehrig-NY 220
Simmons-Phi 211
Rice-Was 207
Morgan-Cle 204

Doubles
Hodapp-Cle 51
Manush-StL-Was 49
Morgan-Cle 47
Gehringer-Det 47

Triples
Combs-NY 22
Reynolds-Chi 18
Gehrig-NY 17
Simmons-Phi 16

Home Runs
Ruth-NY 49
Gehrig-NY 41
Goslin-Was-StL 37
Foxx-Phi 37
Simmons-Phi 36

Total Bases
Gehrig-NY 419
Simmons-Phi 392
Ruth-NY 379
Foxx-Phi 358

Runs Batted In
Gehrig-NY 174
Simmons-Phi 165
Foxx-Phi 156
Ruth-NY 153
Goslin-Was-StL 138

Runs Produced
Simmons-Phi 281
Gehrig-NY 276
Ruth-NY 254
Foxx-Phi 246
Cronin-Was 240

Bases On Balls
Ruth-NY 136
Bishop-Phi 128
Gehrig-NY 101
Foxx-Phi 93
Blue-StL 81

Batting Average
Simmons-Phi 381
Gehrig-NY 379
Ruth-NY 359
Reynolds-Chi 359
Cochrane-Phi 357

On Base Percentage
Ruth-NY 493
Gehrig-NY 473
Foxx-Phi 429
Bishop-Phi 426
Combs-NY 424

Slugging Average
Ruth-NY 732
Gehrig-NY 721
Simmons-Phi 708
Foxx-Phi 637

Production
Ruth-NY 1.225
Gehrig-NY 1.194
Simmons-Phi 1.130
Foxx-Phi 1.066
Morgan-Cle 1.014

Adjusted Production
Ruth-NY 230
Gehrig-NY 221
Simmons-Phi 182
Foxx-Phi 167
Combs-NY 155

Batter Runs
Ruth-NY 89.5
Gehrig-NY 88.3
Simmons-Phi 64.1
Foxx-Phi 57.0
Morgan-Cle 46.3

Adjusted Batter Runs
Ruth-NY 99.2
Gehrig-NY 98.4
Simmons-Phi 64.6
Foxx-Phi 57.5
Combs-NY 41.9

Clutch Hitting Index
Lazzeri-NY 146
Rice-Det-NY 142
Cronin-Was 130
Alexander-Det 130
Hodapp-Cle 123

Runs Created
Ruth-NY 195
Gehrig-NY 191
Simmons-Phi 163
Foxx-Phi 154
Morgan-Cle 144

Total Average
Ruth-NY 1.538
Gehrig-NY 1.427
Simmons-Phi 1.278
Foxx-Phi 1.202
Morgan-Cle 1.099

Stolen Bases
McManus-Det 23
Gehringer-Det 19
Goslin-Was-StL 17
Johnson-Det 17
Cronin-Was 17

Stolen Base Average
Reynolds-Chi 80.0
McManus-Det 74.2
Cissell-Chi 64.0
Johnson-Det 63.0
Cronin-Was 63.0

Stolen Base Runs
Lary-NY 3.0
Reynolds-Chi 2.4
McManus-Det 2.1

Fielding Runs
Melillo-StL 26.7
Cronin-Was 25.7
Kamm-Chi 14.2
Hodapp-Cle 13.2
Goldman-Cle 9.6

Total Player Rating
Ruth-NY 7.7
Gehrig-NY 6.8
Cronin-Was 6.5
Simmons-Phi 5.8
Cochrane-Phi 3.3

Wins
Grove-Phi 28
Ferrell-Cle 25
Lyons-Chi 22
Earnshaw-Phi 22
Stewart-StL 20

Win Percentage
Grove-Phi 848
Marberry-Was 750
Jones-Was 682
Ferrell-Cle 658
Ruffing-Bos-NY 652

Games
Grove-Phi 50
Earnshaw-Phi 49
Pipgras-NY 44
Johnson-NY 44
Ferrell-Cle 43

Complete Games
Lyons-Chi 29
Crowder-StL-Was 25
Ferrell-Cle 25
Stewart-StL 23
Grove-Phi 22

Shutouts
Pipgras-NY 3
Earnshaw-Phi 3
Brown-Cle 3

Saves
Grove-Phi 9
Braxton-Was-Chi 6
Quinn-Phi 6
Sullivan-Det 5
McKain-Chi 5

Innings Pitched
Lyons-Chi 298
Ferrell-Cle 297
Earnshaw-Phi 296
Grove-Phi 291
Crowder-StL-Was 279

Fewest Hits/Game
Hadley-Was 8.38
Grove-Phi 8.44
Collins-StL 8.79
Crowder-StL-Was 8.90
Gaston-Bos 8.97

Fewest BB/Game
Pennock-NY 1.15
Lyons-Chi 1.72
Grove-Phi 1.86
Russell-Bos 2.07
Brown-Cle 2.14

Strikeouts
Grove-Phi 209
Earnshaw-Phi 193
Hadley-Was 162
Ferrell-Cle 143
Ruffing-Bos-NY 131

Strikeouts/Game
Grove-Phi 6.46
Johnson-NY 5.91
Earnshaw-Phi 5.87
Hadley-Was 5.61
Ruffing-Bos-NY 5.31

Wins Above Team
Grove-Phi 10.1
Lyons-Chi 7.1
Stewart-StL 6.6
Ferrell-Cle 6.4
Wells-NY 4.3

Earned Run Average
Grove-Phi 2.54
Ferrell-Cle 3.30
Stewart-StL 3.45
Uhle-Det 3.65
Hadley-Was 3.74

Adjusted ERA
Grove-Phi 176
Ferrell-Cle 148
Stewart-StL 148
Uhle-Det 134
Lyons-Chi 129

Opponents' Batting Avg.
Grove-Phi 247
Hadley-Was 247
Crowder-StL-Was 259
Collins-StL 259
Gaston-Bos 259

Opponents' On Base Pct.
Grove-Phi 284
Stewart-StL 309
Lyons-Chi 310
Caraway-Chi 313
Marberry-Was 314

Starter Runs
Grove-Phi 68.3
Ferrell-Cle 44.4
Stewart-StL 35.9
Lyons-Chi 28.9
Uhle-Det 26.4

Adjusted Starter Runs
Grove-Phi 62.7
Ferrell-Cle 52.5
Stewart-StL 50.1
Lyons-Chi 36.6
Uhle-Det 33.5

Clutch Pitching Index
Henry-Chi 122
Harder-Cle 115
Sorrell-Det 115
Hoyt-NY -Det 113
Ferrell-Cle 113

Relief Runs
Quinn-Phi 2.5

Adjusted Relief Runs
Quinn-Phi 8

Relief Ranking
Quinn-Phi 1.3

Total Pitcher Index
Grove-Phi 6.0
Ferrell-Cle 5.7
Stewart-StL 5.2
Lyons-Chi 4.5
Uhle-Det 3.7

Total Baseball Ranking
Ruth-NY 7.8
Gehrig-NY 6.8
Cronin-Was 6.5
Grove-Phi 6.0
Simmons-Phi 5.8

TEAM	G	W	L	PCT	GB	R	OR	AB	H	2B	3B	HR	BB	SO	AVG	OBP	SLG	PRO	/A	BR	/A	PF	CHI	RC	TA	SB	CS	SBA	SBR
STL	154	101	53	.656		815	614	5435	1554	353	74	60	432	475	.286	.342	.411	.753	109	61	14	107	107	787	.725	114			
NY	153	87	65	.572	13	768	599	5372	1554	251	64	101	383	395	.289	.340	.416	.756	109	61	84	97	103	776	.715	83			
CHI	156	84	70	.545	17	828	710	5451	1578	340	67	83	577	641	.289	.360	.422	.782	117	130	160	96	97	865	.762	49			
BRO	153	79	73	.520	21	681	673	5309	1464	240	77	71	409	512	.276	.331	.390	.721	100	-3	-11	101	100	705	.664	45			
PIT	155	75	79	.487	26	636	691	5360	1425	243	70	41	493	454	.266	.330	.360	.690	92	-53	-56	101	98	667	.635	59			
PHI	155	66	88	.429	35	684	828	5375	1502	299	52	81	437	492	.279	.336	.400	.736	104	26	-16	106	95	745	.684	42			
BOS	156	64	90	.416	37	533	680	5296	1367	221	59	34	368	430	.258	.309	.341	.650	81	-136	-129	99	98	580	.571	46			
CIN	154	58	96	.377	43	592	742	5343	1439	241	70	21	403	463	.269	.323	.352	.675	88	-84	-51	95	98	631	.597	24			
TOT	618					5537		42941	11883	2188	533	492	3502	3862	.277	.334	.387	.721								462			

TEAM	CG	SHO	SV	IP	H	H/G	HR	BB	BB/G	SO	SO/G	ERA	/A	OAVG	OOBA	PR	/A	PF	CPI	FA	E	DP	FW	PW	BW	SBW	DIF
STL	80	17	20	1383.3	1470	9.6	65	449	2.9	626	4.1	3.45	116	.272	.324	63	82	103	108	.974	160	169	1.0	8.2	1.4		13.5
NY	90	17	12	1358.7	1341	8.9	71	422	2.8	570	3.7	3.30	109	.258	.310	85	46	93	102	.974	159	126	1.0	4.6	8.4		-3.0
CHI	80	8	8	1385.3	1448	9.4	54	524	3.4	541	3.5	3.97	91	.269	.329	-16	-53	94	94	.973	169	141	.5	-5.3	15.9		-4.1
BRO	64	10	18	1355.7	1520	10.1	56	351	2.3	546	3.6	3.84	102	.283	.322	3	10	101	99	.969	187	154	-.6	1.0	-1.1		3.7
PIT	89	9	5	1388.3	1489	9.7	55	442	2.9	345	2.2	2.66	107	.274	.323	30	39	102	101	.968	194	167	-1.0	3.9	-5.6		.7
PHI	60	6	16	1360.3	1603	10.6	75	511	3.4	499	3.3	4.58	92	.293	.348	-108	-56	109	99	.966	210	149	-2.0	-5.6	-1.6		-1.9
BOS	78	12	9	1379.7	1465	9.6	66	406	2.6	419	2.7	3.90	101	.272	.317	-5	4	102	94	.973	170	141	.4	.4	-12.8		-1.0
CIN	70	7	6	1345.0	1545	10.3	51	399	2.7	317	2.1	4.22	89	.288	.329	-53	-66	98	95	.973	165	194	.7	-6.6	-5.1		-8.1
TOT	611	86	94	10956.3		9.8			2.9		3.2	3.86		.277	.334					.971	1414	1241					

Runs
Terry-NY 121
Klein-Phi 121
English-Chi 117
Ott-NY 104
Cuyler-Chi 100

Hits
L.Waner-Pit 214
Terry-NY 213
English-Chi 202
Cuyler-Chi 202
Klein-Phi 200

Doubles
Adams-StL 46
Berger-Bos 44
Terry-NY 43
Herman-Bro 43
Bartell-Phi 43

Triples
Terry-NY 20
Herman-Bro 16
Traynor-Pit 15
Bissonette-Bro 14

Home Runs
Klein-Phi 31
Ott-NY 29
Berger-Bos 19
Herman-Bro 18
Arlett-Phi 18

Total Bases
Klein-Phi 347
Terry-NY 323
Herman-Bro 320
Berger-Bos 316
Cuyler-Chi 290

Runs Batted In
Klein-Phi 121
Ott-NY 115
Terry-NY 112
Traynor-Pit 103
Herman-Bro 97

Runs Produced
Terry-NY 224
Klein-Phi 211
Ott-NY 190
Traynor-Pit 182
Cuyler-Chi 179

Bases On Balls
Ott-NY 80
P.Waner-Pit 73
Cuyler-Chi 72
Grantham-Pit 71
English-Chi 68

Batting Average
Hafey-StL 349
Terry-NY 349
Klein-Phi 337
O'Doul-Bro 336
Grimm-Chi 331

On Base Percentage
Hafey-StL 404
Cuyler-Chi 404
P.Waner-Pit 404
Grantham-Pit 400
Klein-Phi 398

Slugging Average
Klein-Phi 584
Hafey-StL 569
Ott-NY 545
Terry-NY 529
Herman-Bro 525

Production
Klein-Phi 982
Hafey-StL 973
Ott-NY 937
Terry-NY 926
Berger-Bos 892

Adjusted Production
Ott-NY 155
Terry-NY 152
Klein-Phi 151
Hafey-StL 149
Cuyler-Chi 141

Batter Runs
Klein-Phi 48.9
Terry-NY 39.0
Hafey-StL 36.2
Ott-NY 35.0
Hornsby-Chi 33.5

Adjusted Batter Runs
Klein-Phi 44.2
Terry-NY 41.7
Ott-NY 37.4
Cuyler-Chi 35.6
Hornsby-Chi 35.5

Clutch Hitting Index
Sheely-Bos 163
Traynor-Pit 148
Frisch-StL 143
Cuccinello-Cin 138
Gelbert-StL 127

Runs Created
Klein-Phi 140
Terry-NY 130
Cuyler-Chi 122
Berger-Bos 122
Herman-Bro 118

Total Average
Hafey-StL 1.055
Klein-Phi 1.051
Ott-NY 1.031
Terry-NY 955
Cuyler-Chi 925

Stolen Bases
Frisch-StL 28
Herman-Bro 17
Martin-StL 16
Adams-StL 16
Watkins-StL 15

Stolen Base Average

Stolen Base Runs

Fielding Runs
P.Waner-Pit 19.8
Frisch-StL 14.6
Crabtree-Cin 12.7
Heathcote-Cin 12.6
L.Waner-Pit 11.4

Total Player Rating
Terry-NY 3.8
Hornsby-Chi 3.7
P.Waner-Pit 3.7
Klein-Phi 3.1
English-Chi 3.1

Wins
Meine-Pit 19
Hallahan-StL 19
Elliott-Phi 19

Win Percentage
Derringer-StL 692
Hallahan-StL 679
Bush-Chi 667
Grimes-StL 654

Games
Elliott-Phi 52
Johnson-Cin 42
Collins-Phi 42

Complete Games
Lucas-Cin 24
Brandt-Bos 23
Meine-Pit 22
Hubbell-NY 21
French-Pit 20

Shutouts
Walker-NY 6
Hubbell-NY 4
Fitzsimmons-NY 4
Derringer-StL 4

Saves
Quinn-Bro 15
Lindsey-StL 7
Elliott-Phi 5
Hallahan-StL 4
Collins-Phi 4

Innings Pitched
Meine-Pit 284
French-Pit 276
Johnson-Cin 262
Fitzsimmons-NY 254
Root-Chi 251

Fewest Hits/Game
Hubbell-NY 7.66
Walker-NY 7.98
Brandt-Bos 8.21
Fitzsimmons-NY 8.57
Root-Chi 8.61

Fewest BB/Game
Johnson-StL 1.40
Lucas-Cin 1.47
Cantwell-Bos 1.96
Clark-Bro 2.01
Zachary-Bos 2.08

Strikeouts
Hallahan-StL 159
Hubbell-NY 155
Vance-Bro 150
Derringer-StL 134
Root-Chi 131

Strikeouts/Game
Vance-Bro 6.16
Hallahan-StL 5.75
Derringer-StL 5.69
Hubbell-NY 5.63
Root-Chi 4.70

Wins Above Team
Brandt-Bos 5.8
Elliott-Phi 5.1
Meine-Pit 4.0
Bush-Chi 3.6
Lucas-Cin 3.6

Earned Run Average
Walker-NY 2.26
Hubbell-NY 2.65
Brandt-Bos 2.92
Meine-Pit 2.98
Johnson-StL 3.00

Adjusted ERA
Walker-NY 160
Hubbell-NY 136
Brandt-Bos 135
Johnson-StL 133
Benge-Phi 133

Opponents' Batting Avg.
Hubbell-NY 227
Walker-NY 231
Brandt-Bos 244
Fitzsimmons-NY 251
Root-Chi 252

Opponents' On Base Pct.
Hubbell-NY 279
Walker-NY 282
Johnson-StL 283
Fitzsimmons-NY 291
Cantwell-Bos 294

Starter Runs
Walker-NY 42.6
Hubbell-NY 33.5
Meine-Pit 27.9
Brandt-Bos 26.3
Fitzsimmons-NY 23.0

Adjusted Starter Runs
Walker-NY 35.8
Meine-Pit 29.7
Benge-Phi 28.4
Brandt-Bos 28.1
Hubbell-NY 26.4

Clutch Pitching Index
Benton-Cin 125
Dudley-Phi 120
Grimes-StL 114
Hallahan-StL 113
Derringer-StL 112

Relief Runs
Lindsey-StL 9.2
Quinn-Bro 8.5
Moore-Bro 6

Adjusted Relief Runs
Lindsey-StL 10.2
Quinn-Bro 8.8
Moore-Bro 9

Relief Ranking
Quinn-Bro 15.8
Lindsey-StL 14.4
Moore-Bro 4

Total Pitcher Index
Brandt-Bos 3.8
Fitzsimmons-NY 3.3
Hubbell-NY 2.9
Meine-Pit 2.8
Walker-NY 2.6

Total Baseball Ranking
Terry-NY 3.8
Brandt-Bos 3.8
Hornsby-Chi 3.7
P.Waner-Pit 3.7
Fitzsimmons-NY 3.3

TEAM	G	W	L	PCT	GB	R	OR	AB	H	2B	3B	HR	BB	SO	AVG	OBP	SLG	PRO	/A	BR	/A	PF	CHI	RC	TA	SB	CS	SBA	SBR
PHI	153	107	45	.704		858	626	5377	1544	311	64	118	526	543	.287	.354	.435	.789	113	92	53	105	97	843	.759	27	23	54	-5
NY	155	94	59	.614	13.5	1067	760	5608	1667	277	78	155	748	554	.297	.383	.457	.840	127	219	235	98	1016	.868	138	68	67	1
WAS	156	92	62	.597	16	843	691	5576	1588	308	93	49	481	459	.285	.345	.400	.745	101	8	3	101	103	774	.694	72	64	53	-16
CLE	155	78	76	.506	30	885	833	5445	1612	321	69	71	481	433	.296	.363	.419	.782	111	91	40	106	99	840	.751	63	60	51	-16
STL	154	63	91	.409	45	722	870	5374	1455	287	62	76	488	580	.271	.333	.390	.723	95	-39	-57	102	98	696	.667	73	80	48	-25
BOS	153	62	90	.408	45	625	800	5379	1409	289	34	37	405	565	.262	.315	.349	.664	80	-153	-104	94	102	596	.582	42	43	49	-12
DET	154	61	93	.396	47	651	836	5430	1456	292	69	43	480	468	.268	.330	.371	.701	90	-78	-106	104	92	675	.650	117	75	61	-9
CHI	156	56	97	.366	51.5	704	939	5481	1423	238	69	27	483	445	.260	.323	.343	.666	81	-145	-83	92	108	632	.607	94	39	71	5
TOT	618					6355		43670	12154	2323	538	576	4166	4047	.278	.344	.396	.740								626	452	58	-82

TEAM	CG	SHO	SV	IP	H	H/G	HR	BB	BB/G	SO	SO/G	ERA	/A	OAVG	OOBA	PR	/A	PF	CPI	FA	E	DP	FW	PW	BW	SBW	DIF
PHI	97	12	16	1365.0	1342	8.8	73	457	3.0	574	3.8	3.47	128	.258	.315	138	145	101	107	.976	141	151	3.2	13.5	4.9	.5	8.8
NY	78	4	17	1408.7	1461	9.3	67	543	3.5	686	4.4	4.20	97	.263	.327	27	-16	94	94	.972	169	131	1.6	-1.5	21.9	1.1	-5.6
WAS	60	7	24	1394.0	1434	9.3	73	498	3.2	582	3.8	3.76	114	.264	.323	95	83	98	104	.976	142	148	3.2	7.7	.3	-.5	4.3
CLE	76	6	9	1354.0	1577	10.5	64	561	3.7	470	3.1	4.63	100	.286	.351	-37	0	106	100	.963	232	143	-2.1	.0	3.7	-.5	-.0
STL	65	4	10	1363.0	1623	10.7	84	444	2.9	436	2.9	4.75	97	.292	.344	-56	-23	105	99	.963	232	160	-2.1	-2.1	-5.3	-1.4	-3.1
BOS	61	5	10	1366.3	1559	10.3	54	473	3.1	365	2.4	4.60	92	.284	.339	-32	-56	97	95	.970	188	127	.5	-5.2	-9.7	-.1	.6
DET	86	5	6	1384.7	1549	10.1	79	597	3.9	511	3.3	4.59	102	.282	.349	-31	13	107	102	.964	220	139	-1.4	1.2	-9.9	.1	-6.1
CHI	54	6	10	1387.3	1611	10.5	82	588	3.8	420	2.7	5.05	83	.287	.353	-102	-131	96	96	.961	245	131	-2.9	-12.2	-7.7	1.4	.9
TOT	577	49	102	11023.0		9.9			3.4		3.3	4.38		.278	.344					.968	1569	1130					

Runs
Gehrig-NY 163
Ruth-NY 149
Averill-Cle 140
Combs-NY 120
Chapman-NY 120

Hits
Gehrig-NY 211
Averill-Cle 209
Simmons-Phi 200
Ruth-NY 199
Webb-Bos 196

Doubles
Webb-Bos 67
Alexander-Det 47
Kress-StL 46
Cronin-Was 44

Triples
Johnson-Det 19
Gehrig-NY 15
Blue-Chi 15
Vosmik-Cle 14
Reynolds-Chi 14

Home Runs
Ruth-NY 46
Gehrig-NY 46
Averill-Cle 32
Foxx-Phi 30
Goslin-StL 24

Total Bases
Gehrig-NY 410
Ruth-NY 374
Averill-Cle 361
Simmons-Phi 329
Goslin-StL 328

Runs Batted In
Gehrig-NY 184
Ruth-NY 163
Averill-Cle 143
Simmons-Phi 128
Cronin-Was 126

Runs Produced
Gehrig-NY 301
Ruth-NY 266
Averill-Cle 251
Chapman-NY 225
Cronin-Was 217

Bases On Balls
Ruth-NY 128
Blue-Chi 127
Gehrig-NY 117
Bishop-Phi 112
Lary-NY 88

Batting Average
Simmons-Phi 390
Ruth-NY 373
Morgan-Cle 351
Cochrane-Phi 349
Gehrig-NY 341

On Base Percentage
Ruth-NY 495
Morgan-Cle 451
Gehrig-NY 446
Simmons-Phi 444
Blue-Chi 430

Slugging Average
Ruth-NY 700
Gehrig-NY 662
Simmons-Phi 641
Averill-Cle 576
Foxx-Phi 567

Production
Ruth-NY 1.195
Gehrig-NY 1.108
Simmons-Phi 1.085
Averill-Cle 979
Cochrane-Phi 976

Adjusted Production
Ruth-NY 215
Gehrig-NY 191
Simmons-Phi 174
Webb-Bos 153
Goslin-StL 148

Batter Runs
Ruth-NY 91.5
Gehrig-NY 79.9
Simmons-Phi 59.6
Averill-Cle 48.2
Goslin-StL 44.7

Adjusted Batter Runs
Ruth-NY 93.2
Gehrig-NY 81.7
Simmons-Phi 55.9
Goslin-StL 42.6
Averill-Cle 42.4

Clutch Hitting Index
Kamm-Chi-Cle 139
Vosmik-Cle 139
Bluege-Was 136
Cronin-Was 134
Lary-NY 132

Runs Created
Ruth-NY 192
Gehrig-NY 185
Simmons-Phi 145
Averill-Cle 144
Goslin-StL 137

Total Average
Ruth-NY 1.499
Gehrig-NY 1.295
Simmons-Phi 1.209
Morgan-Cle 1.062
Goslin-StL 1.045

Stolen Bases
Chapman-NY 61
Johnson-Det 33
Burns-StL 19
Lazzeri-NY 18
Cissell-Chi 18

Stolen Base Average
Cissell-Chi 75.0
Reynolds-Chi 73.9
Chapman-NY 72.6
Lazzeri-NY 66.7
Bluege-Was 61.5

Stolen Base Runs
Chapman-NY 4.5
Walker-Det 2.4
Blue-Chi 2.1
Cissell-Chi 1.8

Fielding Runs
Melillo-StL 33.7
Burns-StL 17.9
Johnson-Det 16.7
West-Was 15.4
Rhyne-Bos 15.0

Total Player Rating
Ruth-NY 6.4
Gehrig-NY 5.0
Simmons-Phi 4.9
Cronin-Was 4.5
Cochrane-Phi 3.3

Wins
Grove-Phi 31
Ferrell-Cle 22
Gomez-NY 21
Earnshaw-Phi 21
Walberg-Phi 20

Win Percentage
Grove-Phi 886
Marberry-Was 800
Mahaffey-Phi 789
Earnshaw-Phi 750
Gomez-NY 700

Games
Hadley-Was 55
Moore-Bos 53
Caraway-Chi 51
Frasier-Chi 46
Fischer-Was 46

Complete Games
Grove-Phi 27
Ferrell-Cle 27
Earnshaw-Phi 23
Whitehill-Det 22
Stewart-StL 20

Shutouts
Grove-Phi 4
Earnshaw-Phi 3

Saves
Moore-Bos 10
Hadley-Was 8
Marberry-Was 7
Kimsey-StL 7
Earnshaw-Phi 6

Innings Pitched
Walberg-Phi 291
Grove-Phi 289
Earnshaw-Phi 282
Ferrell-Cle 276
Whitehill-Det 271

Fewest Hits/Game
Hadley-Was 7.25
Gomez-NY 7.63
Grove-Phi 7.75
Johnson-NY 8.08
Earnshaw-Phi 8.14

Fewest BB/Game
Pennock-NY 1.43
Gray-StL 1.88
Grove-Phi 1.93
Brown-Cle 2.12
Blaeholder-StL 2.23

Strikeouts
Grove-Phi 175
Earnshaw-Phi 152
Gomez-NY 150
Ruffing-NY 132
Hadley-Was 124

Strikeouts/Game
Hadley-Was 6.20
Gomez-NY 5.56
Bridges-Det 5.46
Grove-Phi 5.45
Ruffing-NY 5.01

Wins Above Team
Grove-Phi 11.8
Ferrell-Cle 5.8
Marberry-Was 5.4
MacFayden-Bos 4.5
Gomez-NY 3.9

Earned Run Average
Grove-Phi 2.06
Gomez-NY 2.67
Hadley-Was 3.05
Brown-Was 3.20
Marberry-Was 3.45

Adjusted ERA
Grove-Phi 216
Gomez-NY 154
Hadley-Was 141
Brown-Was 135
Uhle-Det 134

Opponents' Batting Avg.
Hadley-Was 218
Grove-Phi 229
Johnson-NY 234
Earnshaw-Phi 236
Coffman-StL 241

Opponents' On Base Pct.
Grove-Phi 269
Earnshaw-Phi 284
Coffman-StL 294
Uhle-Det 301
Marberry-Was 303

Starter Runs
Grove-Phi 74.7
Gomez-NY 46.3
Brown-Was 34.1
Hadley-Was 26.6
Marberry-Was ... 22.6

Adjusted Starter Runs
Grove-Phi 76.2
Gomez-NY 38.6
Brown-Was 31.8
Ferrell-Cle 26.9
Uhle-Det 25.2

Clutch Pitching Index
Gomez-NY 141
Mahaffey-Phi 118
Grove-Phi 118
Faber-Chi 116
Whitehill-Det 115

Relief Runs

Adjusted Relief Runs
Kimsey-StL 2.0
Appleton-Cle 1

Relief Ranking
Kimsey-StL 2.3
Appleton-Cle 1

Total Pitcher Index
Grove-Phi 7.4
Ferrell-Cle 5.0
Brown-Was 3.4
Gomez-NY 3.3
Earnshaw-Phi 3.0

Total Baseball Ranking
Grove-Phi 7.4
Ruth-NY 6.4
Gehrig-NY 5.0
Ferrell-Cle 5.0
Simmons-Phi 4.9

TEAM	G	W	L	PCT	GB	R	OR	AB	H	2B	3B	HR	BB	SO	AVG	OBP	SLG	PRO	/A	BR	/A	PF	CHI	RC	TA	SB	CS	SBA	SBR
CHI	154	90	64	.584		720	633	5462	1519	296	60	69	398	514	.278	.330	.392	.722	100	0	-29	104	101	728	.663	48			
PIT	154	86	68	.558	4	701	711	5421	1543	274	90	47	358	385	.285	.333	.394	.727	101	8	12	99	98	728	.670	71			
BRO	154	81	73	.526	9	752	747	5433	1538	296	59	109	388	574	.283	.334	.419	.753	108	54	82	96	99	777	.707	61			
PHI	154	78	76	.506	12	844	796	5510	1608	330	67	122	446	547	.292	.348	.442	.790	118	131	44	112	98	870	.764	71			
BOS	155	77	77	.500	13	649	655	5506	1460	262	53	63	347	496	.265	.311	.366	.677	87	-93	-45	93	105	643	.598	36			
STL	156	72	82	.468	18	684	717	5458	1467	307	51	76	420	514	.269	.324	.385	.709	96	-26	-26	100	100	702	.662	92			
NY	154	72	82	.468	18	755	706	5530	1527	263	54	116	348	391	.263	.322	.406	.728	101	1	10	99	106	735	.662	31			
CIN	155	60	94	.390	30	575	715	5443	1429	265	68	47	436	436	.263	.320	.362	.682	89	-76	-49	96	90	654	.613	35			
TOT	618					5680		43763	12091	2293	502	649	3141	3857	.276	.328	.396	.724								445			

TEAM	CG	SHO	SV	IP	H	H/G	HR	BB	BB/G	SO	SO/G	ERA	/A	OAVG	OOBA	PR	/A	PF	CPI	FA	E	DP	FW	PW	BW	SBW	DIF
CHI	79	9	7	1399.7	1444	9.3	68	409	2.6	527	3.4	3.44	116	.265	.313	68	84	103	102	.973	173	146	.4	8.3	-2.9		7.2
PIT	71	12	12	1377.0	1472	9.6	86	338	2.2	377	2.5	3.75	103	.272	.311	19	17	100	98	.969	185	124	-.4	1.7	1.2		6.5
BRO	61	7	16	1383.7	1538	10.0	72	403	2.6	497	3.2	4.27	87	.280	.324	-59	-84	96	92	.971	183	169	-.3	-8.3	8.1		4.5
PHI	59	4	17	1383.0	1589	10.3	107	450	2.9	459	3.0	4.47	97	.287	.336	-90	-23	111	99	.968	194	133	-.9	-2.3	4.4		-.2
BOS	72	8	8	1411.7	1483	9.5	61	440	2.7	440	2.8	3.53	102	.269	.314	54	13	93	101	.976	152	145	1.6	1.3	-4.5		1.5
STL	70	14	8	1397.0	1533	9.9	76	455	2.9	681	4.4	3.97	98	.278	.327	-13	-9	101	100	.971	175	155	.2	-.9	-2.6		-1.8
NY	57	3	16	1375.3	1533	10.0	112	387	2.5	506	3.3	3.83	99	.281	.323	7	-5	98	108	.969	191	143	-.7	-.5	1.0		-4.8
CIN	83	6	6	1393.3	1505	9.7	69	276	1.8	359	2.3	3.79	101	.274	.304	13	6	99	92	.971	178	129	.0	.6	-4.8		-12.8
TOT	552	63	91	11120.7		9.8			2.5		3.1	3.88		.276	.328					.971	1431	1144					

Runs
Klein-Phi 152
Terry-NY 124
O'Doul-Bro 120
Ott-NY 119
Bartell-Phi 118

Hits
Klein-Phi 226
Terry-NY 225
O'Doul-Bro 219
P.Waner-Pit 215
Herman-Chi 206

Doubles
P.Waner-Pit 62
Klein-Phi 50
Stephenson-Chi 49
Bartell-Phi 48

Triples
Herman-Cin 19
Suhr-Pit 16
Klein-Phi 15

Home Runs
Ott-NY 38
Klein-Phi 38
Terry-NY 28
Hurst-Phi 24
Wilson-Bro 23

Total Bases
Klein-Phi 420
Terry-NY 373
Ott-NY 340
O'Doul-Bro 330
P.Waner-Pit 321

Runs Batted In
Hurst-Phi 143
Klein-Phi 137
Whitney-Phi 124
Wilson-Bro 123
Ott-NY 123

Runs Produced
Klein-Phi 251
Hurst-Phi 228
Terry-NY 213
Whitney-Phi 204
Ott-NY 204

Bases On Balls
Ott-NY 100
Hurst-Phi 65
Bartell-Phi 64
Suhr-Pit 63

Batting Average
O'Doul-Bro 368
Terry-NY 350
Klein-Phi 348
P.Waner-Pit 341
Hurst-Phi 339

On Base Percentage
Ott-NY 424
O'Doul-Bro 423
Hurst-Phi 412
Klein-Phi 404
P.Waner-Pit 397

Slugging Average
Klein-Phi 646
Ott-NY 601
Terry-NY 580
O'Doul-Bro 555
Hurst-Phi 547

Production
Klein-Phi 1.050
Ott-NY 1.025
O'Doul-Bro 978
Terry-NY 962
Hurst-Phi 959

Adjusted Production
Ott-NY 174
O'Doul-Bro 167
Klein-Phi 158
Terry-NY 156
Herman-Cin 153

Batter Runs
Klein-Phi 68.1
Ott-NY 59.8
O'Doul-Bro 51.1
Terry-NY 46.4
Hurst-Phi 46.1

Adjusted Batter Runs
Ott-NY 60.9
Klein-Phi 58.1
O'Doul-Bro 54.3
Terry-NY 47.5
Herman-Cin 40.7

Clutch Hitting Index
Whitney-Phi 153
Hurst-Phi 145
Wilson-Bro 142
Hogan-NY 134
Piet-Pit 132

Runs Created
Klein-Phi 171
Ott-NY 151
O'Doul-Bro 142
Terry-NY 142
Hurst-Phi 134

Total Average
Klein-Phi 1.182
Ott-NY 1.166
O'Doul-Bro 1.059
Hurst-Phi 1.042
Terry-NY 981

Stolen Bases
Klein-Phi 20
Piet-Pit 19
Watkins-StL 18
Frisch-StL 18
Davis-Phi 16

Stolen Base Average

Stolen Base Runs

Fielding Runs
Jurges-Chi 26.0
Herman-Chi 19.0
Cuccinello-Bro 19.0
Stripp-Bro 15.7
Reese-StL 15.2

Total Player Rating
Klein-Phi 5.3
Terry-NY 5.1
Ott-NY 4.9
Herman-Cin 4.4
Cuccinello-Bro 3.3

Wins
Warneke-Chi 22
Clark-Bro 20
Bush-Chi 19

Win Percentage
Warneke-Chi 786
Bush-Chi 633
Rhem-StL-Phi 625
Clark-Bro 625
Hubbell-NY 621

Games
French-Pit 47
J.Dean-StL 46
Carleton-StL 44
Collins-Phi 43

Complete Games
Lucas-Cin 28
Warneke-Chi 25
Hubbell-NY 22

Shutouts
Warneke-Chi 4
Swetonic-Pit 4
J.Dean-StL 4

Saves
Quinn-Bro 8
Benge-Phi 6
Luque-NY 5
Cantwell-Bos 5

Innings Pitched
J.Dean-StL 286
Hubbell-NY 284
Warneke-Chi 277
French-Pit 274
Clark-Bro 273

Fewest Hits/Game
Swift-Pit 7.40
Brown-Bos 7.90
Warneke-Chi 8.03
Hubbell-NY 8.24
Malone-Chi 8.43

Fewest BB/Game
Swift-Pit 1.09
Lucas-Cin 1.17
Hubbell-NY 1.27
Benton-Cin 1.35
Betts-Bos 1.42

Strikeouts
J.Dean-StL 191
Hubbell-NY 137
Malone-Chi 120
Carleton-StL 113
Brown-Bos 110

Strikeouts/Game
J.Dean-StL 6.01
Hallahan-StL 5.52
Vance-Bro 5.27
Carleton-StL 5.19
Brown-Bos 4.65

Wins Above Team
Warneke-Chi 7.5
Hubbell-NY 4.8
Clark-Bro 4.0
Brown-Bos 3.9
Rhem-StL-Phi 3.3

Earned Run Average
Warneke-Chi 2.37
Hubbell-NY 2.50
Betts-Bos 2.80
Swetonic-Pit 2.82
Lucas-Cin 2.94

Adjusted ERA
Warneke-Chi 168
Hubbell-NY 151
Swetonic-Pit 137
Lucas-Cin 130
Betts-Bos 129

Opponents' Batting Avg.
Swetonic-Pit 221
Warneke-Chi 237
Hubbell-NY 238
Brown-Bos 238
Malone-Chi 244

Opponents' On Base Pct.
Hubbell-NY 264
Lucas-Cin 269
Swift-Pit 269
Warneke-Chi 280
Swetonic-Pit 283

Starter Runs
Warneke-Chi 46.4
Hubbell-NY 43.4
Lucas-Cin 28.0
Betts-Bos 26.7
French-Pit 26.1

Adjusted Starter Runs
Warneke-Chi 49.5
Hubbell-NY 40.6
Lucas-Cin 26.6
French-Pit 25.6
Bush-Chi 20.7

Clutch Pitching Index
Bush-Chi 123
French-Pit 123
Zachary-Bos 117
Hallahan-StL 113
Derringer-StL 113

Relief Runs
Quinn-Bro 5.5
Frankhouse-Bos 4.0

Adjusted Relief Runs
Quinn-Bro 3.9
Frankhouse-Bos 8

Relief Ranking
Quinn-Bro 4.9
Frankhouse-Bos 7

Total Pitcher Index
Hubbell-NY 5.4
Warneke-Chi 5.3
Lucas-Cin 2.8
J.Dean-StL 2.3
French-Pit 2.3

Total Baseball Ranking
Hubbell-NY 5.4
Klein-Phi 5.3
Warneke-Chi 5.3
Terry-NY 5.1
Ott-NY 4.9

TEAM	G	W	L	PCT	GB	R	OR	AB	H	2B	3B	HR	BB	SO	AVG	OBP	SLG	PRO	/A	BR	/A	PF	CHI	RC	TA	SB	CS	SBA	SBR
NY	156	107	47	.695		1002	724	5477	1564	279	82	160	766	527	.286	.376	.454	.830	121	172	210	95	99	961	.843	77	66	54	-16
PHI	154	94	60	.610	13	981	752	5537	1606	303	51	173	647	640	.290	.366	.457	.823	119	148	31	114	100	951	.818	38	23	62	-1
WAS	154	93	61	.604	14	840	716	5515	1565	303	100	61	505	442	.284	.347	.408	.755	101	8	11	100	102	793	.714	70	47	60	-6
CLE	153	87	65	.572	19	845	747	5412	1544	310	74	78	556	454	.285	.355	.413	.768	105	41	-26	108	99	808	.734	52	54	49	-16
DET	153	76	75	.503	29.5	799	787	5409	1479	291	80	80	486	523	.273	.335	.401	.736	96	-35	-49	102	105	741	.697	103	49	68	2
STL	154	63	91	.409	44	736	898	5449	1502	274	69	67	507	528	.276	.339	.388	.727	94	-44	-44	100	97	726	.676	69	62	53	-16
CHI	152	49	102	.325	56.5	667	897	5336	1426	274	56	36	459	386	.267	.327	.360	.687	84	-121	-21	87	101	642	.627	89	58	61	-7
BOS	154	43	111	.279	64	566	915	5295	1331	253	57	53	469	539	.251	.314	.351	.665	78	-170	-146	97	93	593	.595	46	46	50	-13
TOT	615					6436		43430	12017	2287	569	708	4395	4039	.277	.346	.405	.750								544	405	57	-79

TEAM	CG	SHO	SV	IP	H	H/G	HR	BB	BB/G	SO	SO/G	ERA	/A	OAVG	OOBA	PR	/A	PF	CPI	FA	E	DP	FW	PW	BW	SBW	DIF
NY	96	11	15	1409.0	1425	9.1	93	561	3.6	780	5.0	3.98	103	.260	.326	78	15	91	101	.969	188	124	-.0	1.4	19.4	-.6	9.8
PHI	95	10	10	1386.7	1477	9.6	112	511	3.3	591	3.8	4.45	111	.271	.331	4	76	111	98	.979	124	142	3.8	7.0	2.9	.8	2.5
WAS	66	11	22	1383.7	1463	9.5	73	526	3.4	437	2.8	4.16	105	.271	.332	49	33	98	100	.979	125	157	3.7	3.1	1.0	.4	7.9
CLE	94	6	8	1377.0	1506	9.8	70	446	2.9	439	2.9	4.12	116	.273	.325	55	102	107	99	.969	191	129	-.2	9.4	-2.4	-.6	4.7
DET	67	9	17	1362.7	1421	9.4	89	592	3.9	521	3.4	4.30	106	.268	.339	27	37	102	102	.969	187	154	-.0	3.4	-4.5	1.1	.5
STL	63	7	11	1376.7	1592	10.4	103	574	3.8	496	3.2	5.01	92	.289	.353	-80	-63	103	100	.969	188	156	-.0	-5.8	-4.1	-.6	-3.5
CHI	50	2	12	1348.7	1551	10.4	88	580	3.9	379	2.5	4.82	84	.287	.353	-51	-113	91	101	.958	264	170	-4.5	-10.4	-1.9	.3	-9.9
BOS	42	3	7	1362.0	1574	10.4	79	612	4.0	365	2.4	5.02	91	.289	.357	-81	-64	102	99	.963	233	165	-2.7	-5.9	-13.5	-.3	-11.6
TOT	573	59	102	11006.3		9.8			3.6		3.3	4.48		.277	.346					.969	1500	1197					

Runs		Hits		Doubles		Triples		Home Runs		Total Bases	
Foxx-Phi	151	Simmons-Phi	216	McNair-Phi	47	Cronin-Was	18	Foxx-Phi	58	Foxx-Phi	438
Simmons-Phi	144	Manush-Was	214	Gehringer-Det	44	Myer-Was	16	Ruth-NY	41	Gehrig-NY	370
Combs-NY	143	Foxx-Phi	213	Cronin-Was	43	Lazzeri-NY	16	Simmons-Phi	35	Simmons-Phi	367
Gehrig-NY	138	Gehrig-NY	208			Chapman-NY	15	Gehrig-NY	34	Averill-Cle	359
Manush-Was	121	Averill-Cle	198					Averill-Cle	32	Manush-Was	325

Runs Batted In		Runs Produced		Bases On Balls		Batting Average		On Base Percentage		Slugging Average	
Foxx-Phi	169	Foxx-Phi	262	Ruth-NY	130	Foxx-Phi	.364	Ruth-NY	.489	Foxx-Phi	.749
Simmons-Phi	151	Simmons-Phi	260	Foxx-Phi	116	Gehrig-NY	.349	Foxx-Phi	.469	Ruth-NY	.661
Gehrig-NY	151	Gehrig-NY	255	Bishop-Phi	110	Manush-Was	.342	Gehrig-NY	.451	Gehrig-NY	.621
Ruth-NY	137	Manush-Was	223	Gehrig-NY	108	Ruth-NY	.341	Bishop-Phi	.412	Averill-Cle	.569
Averill-Cle	124	Ruth-NY	216	Cochrane-Phi	100	Walker-Det	.323	Cochrane-Phi	.412	Simmons-Phi	.548

Production		Adjusted Production		Batter Runs		Adjusted Batter Runs		Clutch Hitting Index		Runs Created	
Foxx-Phi	1.218	Ruth-NY	204	Foxx-Phi	96.7	Foxx-Phi	83.8	Cronin-Was	141	Foxx-Phi	207
Ruth-NY	1.150	Foxx-Phi	185	Ruth-NY	71.2	Ruth-NY	74.8	Dykes-Phi	134	Gehrig-NY	168
Gehrig-NY	1.072	Gehrig-NY	183	Gehrig-NY	68.6	Gehrig-NY	72.9	Kamm-Cle	129	Ruth-NY	157
Averill-Cle	.961	Lazzeri-NY	139	Averill-Cle	41.1	Averill-Cle	33.2	Lazzeri-NY	127	Averill-Cle	140
Cochrane-Phi	.921	Averill-Cle	135	Alexander-Det-Bos	31.8	Alexander-Det-Bos	33.2	Cissell-Chi-Cle	126	Simmons-Phi	134

Total Average		Stolen Bases		Stolen Base Average		Stolen Base Runs		Fielding Runs		Total Player Rating	
Foxx-Phi	1.470	Chapman-NY	38	Walker-Det	83.3	Walker-Det	5.4	Warstler-Bos	20.0	Foxx-Phi	5.7
Ruth-NY	1.439	Walker-Det	30	Johnson-Det-Bos	76.9	Johnson-Det-Bos	2.4	Averill-Cle	15.8	Ruth-NY	5.5
Gehrig-NY	1.216	Johnson-Det-Bos	20	Blue-Chi	73.9	Blue-Chi	1.5	West-Was	13.8	Gehrig-NY	4.1
Averill-Cle	1.009	Cissell-Chi-Cle	18	Chapman-NY	67.9			Rogell-Det	12.4	Cronin-Was	3.7
Cochrane-Phi	1.003			Burns-StL	60.7			Melillo-StL	11.9	Averill-Cle	3.6

Wins		Win Percentage		Games		Complete Games		Shutouts		Saves	
Crowder-Was	26	Allen-NY	.810	Marberry-Was	54	Grove-Phi	27	Grove-Phi	4	Marberry-Was	13
Grove-Phi	25	Gomez-NY	.774	Gray-StL	52	Ferrell-Cle	26	Bridges-Det	4	Moore-Bos-NY	8
Gomez-NY	24	Ruffing-NY	.720	Crowder-Was	50	Ruffing-NY	22			Hogsett-Det	7
Ferrell-Cle	23	Grove-Phi	.714							Grove-Phi	7
Weaver-Was	22	Weaver-Was	.688							Faber-Chi	6

Innings Pitched		Fewest Hits/Game		Fewest BB/Game		Strikeouts		Strikeouts/Game		Wins Above Team	
Crowder-Was	327	Allen-NY	7.59	Brown-Cle	1.71	Ruffing-NY	190	Ruffing-NY	6.60	Grove-Phi	5.6
Grove-Phi	292	Ruffing-NY	7.61	Crowder-Was	2.12	Grove-Phi	188	Gomez-NY	5.98	Gomez-NY	4.7
Ferrell-Cle	288	Bridges-Det	7.79	Gray-StL	2.30	Gomez-NY	176	Grove-Phi	5.79	Allen-NY	4.3
Walberg-Phi	272	Grove-Phi	8.29	Harder-Cle	2.40	Hadley-Chi-StL	145	Hadley-Chi-StL	5.24	Weaver-Was	4.0
Gomez-NY	265	Crowder-Was	8.78	Grove-Phi	2.43	Pipgras-NY	111	Allen-NY	5.11	Crowder-Was	3.9

Earned Run Average		Adjusted ERA		Opponents' Batting Avg.		Opponents' On Base Pct.		Starter Runs		Adjusted Starter Runs	
Grove-Phi	2.84	Grove-Phi	175	Ruffing-NY	.226	Grove-Phi	.289	Grove-Phi	53.3	Grove-Phi	68.6
Ruffing-NY	3.09	Bridges-Det	135	Allen-NY	.228	Crowder-Was	.292	Crowder-Was	41.7	Crowder-Was	37.8
Lyons-Chi	3.27	Ruffing-NY	132	Bridges-Det	.233	Allen-NY	.302	Gomez-NY	39.9	Ferrell-Cle	36.2
Crowder-Was	3.33	Crowder-Was	131	Grove-Phi	.241	Ruffing-NY	.307	Lyons-Chi	31.0	Harder-Cle	29.6
Bridges-Det	3.36	Ferrell-Cle	131	Crowder-Was	.252	Brown-Cle	.310	Ferrell-Cle	26.3	Ruffing-NY	28.4

Clutch Pitching Index		Relief Runs		Adjusted Relief Runs		Relief Ranking		Total Pitcher Index		Total Baseball Ranking	
Hogsett-Det	129	Faber-Chi	8.7	Kimsey-StL-Chi	5.8	Kimsey-StL-Chi	5.4	Grove-Phi	6.6	Grove-Phi	6.6
Lyons-Chi	121	Kimsey-StL-Chi	6.3	Faber-Chi	3.9	Faber-Chi	4.8	Ferrell-Cle	4.2	Foxx-Phi	5.7
Weiland-Bos	117			Krausse-Phi	2.3	Krausse-Phi	1.8	Ruffing-NY	3.7	Ruth-NY	5.5
Bridges-Det	116							Crowder-Was	3.4	Ferrell-Cle	4.2
Gaston-Chi	115							Harder-Cle	3.2	Gehrig-NY	4.1

TEAM	G	W	L	PCT	GB	R	OR	AB	H	2B	3B	HR	BB	SO	AVG	OBP	SLG	PRO	/A	BR	/A	PF	CHI	RC	TA	SB	CS	SBA	SBR
NY	156	91	61	.599		636	515	5461	1437	204	41	82	377	477	.263	.312	.361	.673	98	-14	-5	99	104	667	.594	31			
PIT	154	87	67	.565	5	667	619	5429	1548	249	84	39	366	334	.285	.333	.383	.716	111	71	103	95	95	750	.645	34			
CHI	154	86	68	.558	6	646	536	5255	1422	256	51	72	392	475	.271	.325	.380	.705	107	47	64	97	98	705	.644	52			
BOS	156	83	71	.539	9	552	531	5243	1320	217	56	54	326	428	.252	.299	.345	.644	90	-69	-47	96	103	588	.557	25			
STL	154	82	71	.536	9.5	687	609	5387	1486	256	61	57	391	528	.276	.329	.378	.707	108	53	40	102	101	726	.655	99			
BRO	157	65	88	.425	26.5	617	695	5367	1413	224	51	62	397	453	.263	.316	.359	.675	99	-7	14	97	101	662	.613	82			
PHI	152	60	92	.395	31	607	760	5261	1439	240	41	60	381	479	.274	.326	.369	.695	105	32	-75	118	94	689	.630	55			
CIN	153	58	94	.382	33	496	643	5156	1267	208	37	34	349	354	.246	.298	.320	.618	82	-109	-100	99	102	540	.531	30			
TOT	618					4908		42559	11332	1854	422	460	2979	3528	.266	.317	.362	.679								408			

TEAM	CG	SHO	SV	IP	H	H/G	HR	BB	BB/G	SO	SO/G	ERA	/A	OAVG	OOBA	PR	/A	PF	CPI	FA	E	DP	FW	PW	BW	SBW	DIF
NY	75	24	15	1408.0	1280	8.2	61	400	2.6	555	3.5	2.71	118	.242	.290	98	77	96	101	.973	178	156	-.6	8.2	-.5		8.0
PIT	70	16	12	1372.7	1417	9.3	54	313	2.1	401	2.6	3.27	96	.266	.302	9	-21	94	96	.972	166	133	.2	-2.2	10.9		1.1
CHI	95	16	9	1363.0	1308	8.6	51	415	2.7	491	3.2	2.93	108	.252	.302	61	35	95	102	.973	168	163	.0	3.7	6.8		-1.5
BOS	85	14	16	1398.3	1391	9.0	54	355	2.3	383	2.5	2.96	108	.259	.298	58	36	96	103	.978	138	148	2.0	3.8	-5.0		5.2
STL	73	11	16	1382.7	1391	9.1	55	452	2.9	635	4.1	3.37	99	.261	.314	-5	-3	100	98	.973	162	119	.4	-.3	4.2		1.2
BRO	71	9	10	1386.3	1502	9.8	51	374	2.4	415	2.7	3.73	88	.276	.315	-60	-70	98	94	.971	177	120	-.5	-7.4	1.5		-5.0
PHI	52	11	13	1336.7	1563	10.5	87	410	2.8	341	2.3	4.34	93	.291	.335	-149	-45	121	98	.970	183	156	-.9	-4.8	-7.9		-2.4
CIN	74	13	8	1350.0	1470	9.8	47	257	1.7	310	2.1	3.42	99	.277	.303	-12	-4	102	96	.971	177	139	-.5	-.4	-10.6		-6.4
TOT	595	114	99	10997.7		9.3			2.4		2.9	3.34		.266	.317					.973	1349	1134					

Runs
Martin-StL 122
P.Waner-Pit 101
Klein-Phi 101
Ott-NY 98
Medwick-StL 92

Hits
Klein-Phi 223
Fullis-Phi 200
P.Waner-Pit 191
Traynor-Pit 190
Martin-StL 189

Doubles
Klein-Phi 44
Medwick-StL 40
Lindstrom-Pit 39
P.Waner-Pit 38
Berger-Bos 37

Triples
Vaughan-Pit 19
P.Waner-Pit 16
Martin-StL 12
Herman-Chi 12

Home Runs
Klein-Phi 28
Berger-Bos 27
Ott-NY 23
Medwick-StL 18

Total Bases
Klein-Phi 365
Berger-Bos 299
Medwick-StL 296
P.Waner-Pit 282
Vaughan-Pit 274

Runs Batted In
Klein-Phi 120
Berger-Bos 106
Ott-NY 103
Medwick-StL 98
Vaughan-Pit 97

Runs Produced
Klein-Phi 193
Ott-NY 178
Vaughan-Pit 173
Medwick-StL 172
Martin-StL 171

Bases On Balls
Ott-NY 75
Suhr-Pit 72
Martin-StL 67
Vaughan-Pit 64
P.Waner-Pit 60

Batting Average
Klein-Phi 368
Davis-Phi 349
Terry-NY 322
Schulmerich-Bs-Phi .318
Martin-StL 316

On Base Percentage
Klein-Phi 422
Davis-Phi 395
Vaughan-Pit 388
Martin-StL 387
Terry-NY 375

Slugging Average
Klein-Phi 602
Berger-Bos 566
Herman-Chi 502
Medwick-StL 497
Vaughan-Pit 478

Production
Klein-Phi 1.025
Berger-Bos 932
Davis-Phi 867
Vaughan-Pit 866
Herman-Chi 855

Adjusted Production
Berger-Bos 169
Klein-Phi 161
Vaughan-Pit 154
Herman-Chi 146
P.Waner-Pit 143

Batter Runs
Klein-Phi 69.1
Berger-Bos 40.4
Vaughan-Pit 35.2
Martin-StL 32.3
Davis-Phi 29.8

Adjusted Batter Runs
Klein-Phi 56.7
Berger-Bos 42.6
Vaughan-Pit 38.8
P.Waner-Pit 32.4
Martin-StL 30.9

Clutch Hitting Index
Traynor-Pit 139
Hartnett-Chi 130
Bottomley-Cin 129
Vaughan-Pit 128
Hurst-Phi 127

Runs Created
Klein-Phi 162
Berger-Bos 113
Vaughan-Pit 112
Martin-StL 111
P.Waner-Pit 109

Total Average
Klein-Phi 1.132
Berger-Bos 935
Martin-StL 881
Vaughan-Pit 861
Herman-Chi 827

Stolen Bases
Martin-StL 26
Fullis-Phi 18
Frisch-StL 18
Klein-Phi 15
Orsatti-StL 14

Stolen Base Average

Stolen Base Runs

Fielding Runs
Critz-NY 40.4
Herman-Chi 29.3
Jurges-Chi 20.8
Ryan-NY 17.4
Allen-StL 9.1

Total Player Rating
Klein-Phi 5.8
Vaughan-Pit 4.0
Herman-Chi 3.9
Berger-Bos 3.7
Martin-StL 3.3

Wins
Hubbell-NY 23
J.Dean-StL 20
Cantwell-Bos 20
Bush-Chi 20
Schumacher-NY 19

Win Percentage
Cantwell-Bos 667
Hubbell-NY 657
Meine-Pit 652
Bush-Chi 625
Schumacher-NY 613

Games
J.Dean-StL 48
French-Pit 47
Liska-Phi 45
Hubbell-NY 45
Carleton-StL 44

Complete Games
Warneke-Chi 26
J.Dean-StL 26
Brandt-Bos 23
Hubbell-NY 22

Shutouts
Hubbell-NY 10
Schumacher-NY 7
French-Pit 5

Saves
Collins-Phi 6
Hubbell-NY 5
Harris-Pit 5
Bell-NY 5

Innings Pitched
Hubbell-NY 309
J.Dean-StL 293
French-Pit 291
Brandt-Bos 288
Warneke-Chi 287

Fewest Hits/Game
Schumacher-NY 6.92
Hubbell-NY 7.46
Parmelee-NY 7.89
Brandt-Bos 8.00
Mungo-Bro 8.09

Fewest BB/Game
Lucas-Cin 74
Hubbell-NY 1.37
Swift-Pit 1.49
Hansen-Phi 1.61
French-Pit 1.70

Strikeouts
J.Dean-StL 199
Hubbell-NY 156
Carleton-StL 147
Warneke-Chi 133
Parmelee-NY 132

Strikeouts/Game
J.Dean-StL 6.11
Parmelee-NY 5.45
Carleton-StL 4.78
Hubbell-NY 4.54
Warneke-Chi 4.17

Wins Above Team
Cantwell-Bos 4.8
Hubbell-NY 3.2
Tinning-Chi 3.0
Mungo-Bro 3.0
Bush-Chi 2.9

Earned Run Average
Hubbell-NY 1.66
Warneke-Chi 2.01
Schumacher-NY 2.15
Brandt-Bos 2.59
Root-Chi 2.60

Adjusted ERA
Hubbell-NY 193
Warneke-Chi 158
Schumacher-NY 149
Brandt-Bos 123
Cantwell-Bos 122

Opponents' Batting Avg.
Schumacher-NY 214
Hubbell-NY 227
Parmelee-NY 232
Mungo-Bro 236
Warneke-Chi 244

Opponents' On Base Pct.
Hubbell-NY 254
Schumacher-NY 276
Swift-Pit 279
Betts-Bos 284
Cantwell-Bos 286

Starter Runs
Hubbell-NY 57.6
Warneke-Chi 42.4
Schumacher-NY 34.0
Brandt-Bos 23.8
Cantwell-Bos 20.6

Adjusted Starter Runs
Hubbell-NY 53.1
Warneke-Chi 37.0
Schumacher-NY 30.3
Brandt-Bos 19.3
Cantwell-Bos 16.6

Clutch Pitching Index
Fitzsimmons-NY 154
Warneke-Chi 130
Root-Chi 120
Walker-StL 117
Holley-Phi 116

Relief Runs
Bell-NY 14.9
Luque-NY 5.7
Harris-Pit 9

Adjusted Relief Runs
Bell-NY 13.4
Luque-NY 4.5

Relief Ranking
Bell-NY 14.1
Luque-NY 5.6

Total Pitcher Index
Hubbell-NY 7.1
Warneke-Chi 5.8
Schumacher-NY 3.0
Brandt-Bos 3.0
Cantwell-Bos 2.1

Total Baseball Ranking
Hubbell-NY 7.1
Klein-Phi 5.8
Warneke-Chi 5.8
Vaughan-Pit 4.0
Herman-Chi 3.9

TEAM	G	W	L	PCT	GB	R	OR	AB	H	2B	3B	HR	BB	SO	AVG	OBP	SLG	PRO	/A	BR	/A	PF	CHI	RC	TA	SB	CS	SBA	SBR
WAS	153	99	53	.651		850	665	5524	1586	281	86	60	539	395	.287	.353	.402	.755	106	46	77	96	102	798	.713	65	50	57	-10
NY	152	91	59	.607	7	927	768	5274	1495	241	75	144	700	506	.283	.369	.440	.809	121	155	224	91	100	880	.810	74	59	56	-12
PHI	152	79	72	.523	19.5	875	853	5330	1519	297	56	140	625	618	.285	.362	.441	.803	119	136	198	92	96	868	.786	33	34	49	-10
CLE	151	75	76	.497	23.5	654	669	5240	1366	218	77	50	448	426	.261	.321	.360	.681	86	-102	-135	105	103	616	.610	36	40	47	-12
DET	155	75	79	.487	25	722	733	5502	1479	283	78	57	475	523	.269	.329	.380	.709	94	-53	-103	107	100	698	.651	68	50	58	-9
CHI	151	67	83	.447	31	683	814	5318	1448	231	53	43	539	416	.272	.342	.360	.702	92	-49	-55	100	96	644	.644	43	46	48	-14
BOS	149	63	86	.423	34.5	700	758	5201	1407	294	56	50	519	464	.271	.338	.377	.715	95	-30	-38	101	98	685	.668	62	37	63	-3
STL	153	55	96	.364	43.5	669	820	5285	1337	244	64	64	520	556	.253	.322	.360	.682	86	-101	-211	115	103	625	.625	70	60	54	-14
TOT	608					6080		42674	11637	2089	545	608	4365	3904	.273	.342	.390	.732								451	376	55	-89

TEAM	CG	SHO	SV	IP	H	H/G	HR	BB	BB/G	SO	SO/G	ERA	/A	OAVG	OOBA	PR	/A	PF	CPI	FA	E	DP	FW	PW	BW	SBW	DIF
WAS	68	5	26	1390.3	1415	9.2	64	452	2.9	447	2.9	3.82	104	.263	.318	71	26	93	98	.979	131	149	2.5	2.5	7.3	.1	10.6
NY	70	8	22	1355.0	1426	9.5	66	612	4.1	711	4.7	4.36	87	.267	.339	-12	-87	88	96	.972	165	122	.4	-8.2	21.2	-.0	2.7
PHI	69	6	14	1343.7	1523	10.2	77	644	4.3	423	2.8	4.81	81	.282	.354	-78	-133	92	99	.966	203	121	-1.9	-12.6	18.7	.1	-.8
CLE	74	12	7	1350.0	1382	9.2	60	465	3.1	437	2.9	3.71	121	.263	.320	86	117	105	102	.974	156	127	1.0	11.1	-12.8	-.0	.3
DET	69	6	17	1398.0	1415	9.1	84	561	3.6	575	3.7	3.95	116	.263	.329	51	96	107	103	.971	178	167	-.4	9.1	-9.8	.2	-1.2
CHI	53	8	13	1371.0	1505	9.9	85	519	3.4	423	2.8	4.45	99	.277	.337	-25	-5	103	99	.970	186	143	-.9	-.5	-5.2	-.3	-1.2
BOS	60	4	14	1327.7	1396	9.5	75	591	4.0	467	3.2	4.35	100	.270	.341	-10	2	102	101	.966	204	133	-2.0	.2	-3.6	.8	-6.9
STL	55	7	10	1360.7	1574	10.4	96	531	3.5	426	2.8	4.82	104	.289	.348	-81	30	117	100	.976	149	162	1.4	2.8	-20.0	-.3	-4.5
TOT	518	56	123	10896.3		9.6			3.6		3.2	4.28		.273	.342					.972	1372	1124					

Runs
Gehrig-NY 138
Foxx-Phi 125
Manush-Was 115
Chapman-NY 112
Cramer-Phi 109

Hits
Manush-Was 221
Gehringer-Det 204
Foxx-Phi 204
Simmons-Chi 200
Gehrig-NY 198

Doubles
Cronin-Was 45
Johnson-Phi 44
Burns-StL 43
Rogell-Det 42
Gehringer-Det 42

Triples
Manush-Was 17
Combs-NY 16
Averill-Cle 16
Myer-Was 15
Reynolds-StL 14

Home Runs
Foxx-Phi 48
Ruth-NY 34
Gehrig-NY 32
Johnson-Phi 21
Lazzeri-NY 18

Total Bases
Foxx-Phi 403
Gehrig-NY 359
Manush-Was 302
Gehringer-Det 294
Simmons-Chi 291

Runs Batted In
Foxx-Phi 163
Gehrig-NY 139
Simmons-Chi 119
Cronin-Was 118
Kuhel-Was 107

Runs Produced
Gehrig-NY 245
Foxx-Phi 240
Manush-Was 205
Cronin-Was 202
Chapman-NY 201

Bases On Balls
Ruth-NY 114
Cochrane-Phi 106
Bishop-Phi 106
Foxx-Phi 96
Swanson-Chi 93

Batting Average
Foxx-Phi 356
Manush-Was 336
Gehrig-NY 334
Simmons-Chi 331
Gehringer-Det 325

On Base Percentage
Cochrane-Phi 459
Foxx-Phi 449
Bishop-Phi 446
Ruth-NY 442
Gehrig-NY 424

Slugging Average
Foxx-Phi 703
Gehrig-NY 605
Ruth-NY 582
Cochrane-Phi 515
Johnson-Phi 505

Production
Foxx-Phi 1.153
Gehrig-NY 1.030
Ruth-NY 1.023
Cochrane-Phi 974
Johnson-Phi 892

Adjusted Production
Foxx-Phi 219
Gehrig-NY 187
Ruth-NY 186
Cochrane-Phi 172
Johnson-Phi 147

Batter Runs
Foxx-Phi 82.7
Gehrig-NY 59.5
Ruth-NY 49.5
Cochrane-Phi 41.6
Johnson-Phi 26.8

Adjusted Batter Runs
Foxx-Phi 89.7
Gehrig-NY 67.3
Ruth-NY 56.1
Cochrane-Phi 47.3
Johnson-Phi 33.3

Clutch Hitting Index
Cronin-Was 147
Melillo-StL 136
Ferrell-StL-Bos 134
Bluege-Was 133
R.Johnson-Bos 127

Runs Created
Foxx-Phi 184
Gehrig-NY 151
Ruth-NY 124
Gehringer-Det 117
Manush-Was 111

Total Average
Foxx-Phi 1.353
Ruth-NY 1.187
Cochrane-Phi 1.138
Gehrig-NY 1.130
Johnson-Phi 948

Stolen Bases
Chapman-NY 27
Walker-Det 26
Swanson-Chi 19
Kuhel-Was 17

Stolen Base Average
Walker-Det 74.3
Kuhel-Was 68.0
Swanson-Chi 63.3
Chapman-NY 60.0

Stolen Base Runs
Walker-Det 2.4
Werber-NY-Bos 1.5
Stumpf-Bos 1.2

Fielding Runs
Rogell-Det 19.4
Melillo-StL 15.6
Ferrell-StL-Bos 14.4
Scharein-StL 13.3
Hayes-Chi 12.5

Total Player Rating
Foxx-Phi 7.6
Cochrane-Phi 4.8
Gehrig-NY 4.4
Cronin-Was 4.2
Ruth-NY 3.9

Wins
Grove-Phi 24
Crowder-Was 24
Whitehill-Was 22

Win Percentage
Grove-Phi 750
Whitehill-Was 733
Stewart-Was 714
Allen-NY 682

Games
Crowder-Was 52
Russell-Was 50
Welch-Bos 47
Kline-Bos 46

Complete Games
Grove-Phi 21
Whitehill-Was 19
Hadley-StL 19
Ruffing-NY 18

Shutouts
Hildebrand-Cle 6
Gomez-NY 4
Blaeholder-StL 3

Saves
Russell-Was 13
Hogsett-Det 9
Moore-NY 8
Heving-Chi 6
Grove-Phi 6

Innings Pitched
Hadley-StL 317
Crowder-Was 299
Grove-Phi 275
Whitehill-Was 270
Blaeholder-StL 256

Fewest Hits/Game
Bridges-Det 7.42
Weiland-Bos 8.21
Allen-NY 8.32
Gomez-NY 8.35
Hildebrand-Cle 8.39

Fewest BB/Game
Brown-Cle 1.65
Marberry-Det 2.31
Stewart-Was 2.34
Harder-Cle 2.38
Blaeholder-StL 2.43

Strikeouts
Gomez-NY 163
Hadley-StL 149
Ruffing-NY 122
Bridges-Det 120
Allen-NY 119

Strikeouts/Game
Gomez-NY 6.24
Allen-NY 5.79
Ruffing-NY 4.67
Bridges-Det 4.64
Fischer-Det 4.57

Wins Above Team
Grove-Phi 8.6
Whitehill-Was 4.2
Marberry-Det 3.2
VanAtta-NY 3.1
Hildebrand-Cle 3.0

Earned Run Average
Harder-Cle 2.95
Bridges-Det 3.09
Gomez-NY 3.18
Grove-Phi 3.21
Weaver-Was 3.26

Adjusted ERA
Harder-Cle 152
Bridges-Det 148
Marberry-Det 139
Brown-Cle 132
Jones-Chi 132

Opponents' Batting Avg.
Bridges-Det 226
Gomez-NY 240
Allen-NY 242
Weiland-Bos 244
Hildebrand-Cle 245

Opponents' On Base Pct.
Marberry-Det 297
Stewart-Was 301
Harder-Cle 302
Brown-Cle 304
Crowder-Was 312

Starter Runs
Harder-Cle 37.3
Grove-Phi 32.8
Bridges-Det 30.8
Pearson-Cle 29.2
Gomez-NY 28.8

Adjusted Starter Runs
Harder-Cle 43.2
Hadley-StL 39.0
Bridges-Det 38.3
Marberry-Det 33.8
Pearson-Cle 32.4

Clutch Pitching Index
Cain-Phi 125
Jones-Chi 124
Harder-Cle 115
Whitehill-Was 112
Grove-Phi 111

Relief Runs
Russell-Was 22.0
Heving-Chi 21.1
Faber-Chi 7.9
Burke-Was 7.4
Herring-Det 3.0

Adjusted Relief Runs
Heving-Chi 22.9
Russell-Was 18.0
Gray-StL 11.5
Faber-Chi 9.2
Burke-Was 5.4

Relief Ranking
Russell-Was 27.7
Heving-Chi 23.5
Gray-StL 11.1
Faber-Chi 7.9
Burke-Was 5.3

Total Pitcher Index
Harder-Cle 5.1
Bridges-Det 4.2
Pearson-Cle 3.4
Hadley-StL 3.3
Marberry-Det 2.5

Total Baseball Ranking
Foxx-Phi 7.6
Harder-Cle 5.1
Cochrane-Phi 4.8
Gehrig-NY 4.4
Cronin-Was 4.2

TEAM	G	W	L	PCT	GB	R	OR	AB	H	2B	3B	HR	BB	SO	AVG	OBP	SLG	PRO	/A	BR	/A	PF	CHI	RC	TA	SB	CS	SBA	SBR
STL	154	95	58	.621		799	656	5502	1582	294	75	104	392	535	.288	.337	.425	.762	109	63	-35	114	101	796	.698	69			
NY	153	93	60	.608	2	760	583	5396	1485	240	41	126	406	526	.275	.329	.405	.734	102	8	22	98	104	736	.656	19			
CHI	152	86	65	.570	8	705	639	5347	1494	263	44	101	375	630	.279	.330	.402	.732	101	5	21	98	99	719	.658	59			
BOS	152	78	73	.517	16	683	714	5370	1460	233	44	83	375	440	.272	.323	.378	.701	93	-51	50	86	103	660	.610	30			
PIT	151	74	76	.493	19.5	735	713	5361	1541	281	77	52	440	398	.287	.344	.398	.742	104	34	-2	105	98	742	.667	44			
BRO	153	71	81	.467	23.5	748	795	5427	1526	284	52	79	548	555	.281	.344	.396	.746	106	50	89	95	95	782	.692	55			
PHI	149	56	93	.376	37	675	794	5218	1480	286	35	56	398	534	.284	.338	.384	.722	99	-3	-61	108	97	685	.642	52			
CIN	152	52	99	.344	42	590	801	5361	1428	227	65	55	313	532	.266	.311	.364	.675	86	-105	-110	101	99	603	.573	34			
TOT	608					5695		42982	11996	2108	433	656	3247	4150	.279	.333	.394	.727								362			

TEAM	CG	SHO	SV	IP	H	H/G	HR	BB	BB/G	SO	SO/G	ERA	/A	OAVG	OOBA	PR	/A	PF	CPI	FA	E	DP	FW	PW	BW	SBW	DIF
STL	78	15	16	1386.0	1463	9.5	77	411	2.7	689	4.5	3.69	122	.269	.316	57	127	111	100	.972	166	141	.2	12.4	-3.4		9.3
NY	68	13	30	1369.0	1384	9.1	75	351	2.3	499	3.3	3.19	121	.260	.302	133	100	95	105	.972	179	141	-.6	9.7	2.1		5.2
CHI	73	11	9	1361.7	1432	9.5	80	417	2.8	633	4.2	3.76	104	.268	.316	45	24	97	99	.977	137	135	1.9	2.3	2.0		4.2
BOS	62	13	20	1358.0	1512	10.0	78	405	2.7	462	3.1	4.11	85	.279	.325	-6	-91	86	97	.972	169	120	.0	-8.9	4.9		6.5
PIT	63	8	8	1327.7	1523	10.3	78	354	2.4	487	3.3	4.20	101	.285	.325	-20	8	105	97	.975	145	118	1.4	.8	-.2		-3.0
BRO	66	6	12	1353.3	1540	10.2	81	475	3.2	520	3.5	4.48	86	.284	.337	-63	-91	95	96	.970	180	141	-.6	-8.9	8.7		-4.2
PHI	52	8	15	1299.7	1501	10.4	126	437	3.0	416	2.9	4.76	95	.287	.336	-100	-37	111	97	.966	197	140	-1.6	-3.6	-5.9		-7.3
CIN	51	3	19	1347.3	1645	11.0	61	389	2.6	438	2.9	4.37	97	.298	.339	-45	-17	105	101	.970	181	136	-.7	-1.7	-10.7		-10.4
TOT	513	77	129	10802.7		10.0			2.7		3.5	4.06		.279	.333					.972	1354	1072					

Runs
P.Waner-Pit 122
Ott-NY 119
Collins-StL 116
Vaughan-Pit 115
Medwick-StL 110

Hits
P.Waner-Pit 217
Terry-NY 213
Collins-StL 200
Medwick-StL 198

Doubles
Cuyler-Chi 42
Allen-Phi 42
Vaughan-Pit 41
Medwick-StL 40
Collins-StL 40

Triples
Medwick-StL 18
P.Waner-Pit 16
Suhr-Pit 13
Collins-StL 12

Home Runs
Ott-NY 35
Collins-StL 35
Berger-Bos 34
Hartnett-Chi 22
Klein-Chi 20

Total Bases
Collins-StL 369
Ott-NY 344
Berger-Bos 336
Medwick-StL 328
P.Waner-Pit 323

Runs Batted In
Ott-NY 135
Collins-StL 128
Berger-Bos 121
Medwick-StL 106
Suhr-Pit 103

Runs Produced
Ott-NY 219
Collins-StL 209
P.Waner-Pit 198
Medwick-StL 198
Vaughan-Pit 197

Bases On Balls
Vaughan-Pit 94
Ott-NY 85
Koenecke-Bro 70
Leslie-Bro 69
P.Waner-Pit 68

Batting Average
P.Waner-Pit 362
Terry-NY 354
Cuyler-Chi 338
Vaughan-Pit 333
Collins-StL 333

On Base Percentage
Vaughan-Pit 431
P.Waner-Pit 429
Ott-NY 415
Terry-NY 414
Koenecke-Bro 411

Slugging Average
Collins-StL 615
Ott-NY 591
Berger-Bos 546
P.Waner-Pit 539
Medwick-StL 529

Production
Collins-StL 1.008
Ott-NY 1.006
P.Waner-Pit 968
Vaughan-Pit 942
Koenecke-Bro 919

Adjusted Production
Ott-NY 169
Berger-Bos 160
Koenecke-Bro 153
P.Waner-Pit 150
Collins-StL 146

Batter Runs
Ott-NY 55.2
Collins-StL 53.3
P.Waner-Pit 50.2
Vaughan-Pit 44.3
Terry-NY 31.5

Adjusted Batter Runs
Ott-NY 56.8
P.Waner-Pit 46.0
Collins-StL 42.4
Berger-Bos 40.8
Vaughan-Pit 40.2

Clutch Hitting Index
Thevenow-NY 138
Durocher-StL 137
Leslie-Bro 136
Jackson-NY 135
Cuccinello-Bro 134

Runs Created
Ott-NY 150
Collins-StL 148
P.Waner-Pit 142
Vaughan-Pit 135
Terry-NY 122

Total Average
Ott-NY 1.075
Collins-StL 1.046
Vaughan-Pit 1.043
P.Waner-Pit 1.010
Koenecke-Bro 981

Stolen Bases
Martin-StL 23
Cuyler-Chi 15
Bartell-Phi 13
Taylor-Bro 12

Stolen Base Average

Stolen Base Runs

Fielding Runs
Critz-NY 26.6
G.Davis-StL-Phi 16.3
Hack-Chi 14.5
Bartell-Phi 13.4
Ryan-NY 12.9

Total Player Rating
P.Waner-Pit 4.3
Vaughan-Pit 4.2
Ott-NY 3.8
Collins-StL 3.6
Berger-Bos 2.9

Wins
J.Dean-StL 30
Schumacher-NY 23
Warneke-Chi 22
Hubbell-NY 21

Win Percentage
J.Dean-StL 811
Hoyt-Pit 714
Schumacher-NY 697
Warneke-Chi 688
Frankhouse-Bos 654

Games
C.Davis-Phi 51
Hansen-Phi 50
J.Dean-StL 50
Hubbell-NY 49
French-Pit 49

Complete Games
Hubbell-NY 25
J.Dean-StL 24
Warneke-Chi 23
Mungo-Bro 22
Brandt-Bos 20

Shutouts
J.Dean-StL 7
Hubbell-NY 5
P.Dean-StL 5
Lee-Chi 4

Saves
Hubbell-NY 8
Luque-NY 7
J.Dean-StL 7
Bell-NY 6

Innings Pitched
Mungo-Bro 315
Hubbell-NY 313
J.Dean-StL 312
Schumacher-NY 297
Warneke-Chi 291

Fewest Hits/Game
Parmelee-NY 7.88
Hubbell-NY 8.22
J.Dean-StL 8.31
Warneke-Chi 8.44
Mungo-Bro 8.57

Fewest BB/Game
Hubbell-NY 1.06
Freitas-Cin 1.47
Frey-Cin 1.54
Leonard-Bro 1.61
Fitzsimmons-NY 1.75

Strikeouts
J.Dean-StL 195
Mungo-Bro 184
P.Dean-StL 150
Warneke-Chi 143
Derringer-Cin 122

Strikeouts/Game
P.Dean-StL 5.79
J.Dean-StL 5.63
Weaver-Chi 5.55
Mungo-Bro 5.26
Malone-Chi 5.23

Wins Above Team
J.Dean-StL 10.5
C.Davis-Phi 5.4
Warneke-Chi 5.2
Hoyt-Pit 5.0
Schumacher-NY 4.5

Earned Run Average
Hubbell-NY 2.30
J.Dean-StL 2.65
Hoyt-Pit 2.92
C.Davis-Phi 2.96
Fitzsimmons-NY 3.05

Adjusted ERA
J.Dean-StL 170
Hubbell-NY 167
C.Davis-Phi 152
Hoyt-Pit 146
Walker-StL 145

Opponents' Batting Avg.
Parmelee-NY 238
Hubbell-NY 239
J.Dean-StL 241
Warneke-Chi 244
Hoyt-Pit 248

Opponents' On Base Pct.
Hubbell-NY 259
Warneke-Chi 285
J.Dean-StL 286
P.Dean-StL 290
Hoyt-Pit 292

Starter Runs
Hubbell-NY 61.3
J.Dean-StL 48.9
C.Davis-Phi 33.7
Fitzsimmons-NY 29.7
Schumacher-NY 29.1

Adjusted Starter Runs
J.Dean-StL 64.5
Hubbell-NY 54.0
C.Davis-Phi 46.9
Hoyt-Pit 28.5
P.Dean-StL 27.9

Clutch Pitching Index
Walker-StL 137
Leonard-Bro 121
C.Davis-Phi 120
Freitas-Cin 111
Frankhouse-Bos 111

Relief Runs
Haines-StL 5.6
Bell-NY 2.4
Brennan-Cin 2.2

Adjusted Relief Runs
Haines-StL 10.1
Brennan-Cin 3.8
Bell-NY 1.1

Relief Ranking
Haines-StL 8.4
Brennan-Cin 3.3
Bell-NY 1.6

Total Pitcher Index
J.Dean-StL 7.0
Hubbell-NY 5.9
C.Davis-Phi 5.8
Schumacher-NY 3.4
Fitzsimmons-NY 3.3

Total Baseball Ranking
J.Dean-StL 7.0
Hubbell-NY 5.9
C.Davis-Phi 5.8
P.Waner-Pit 4.3
Vaughan-Pit 4.2

TEAM	G	W	L	PCT	GB	R	OR	AB	H	2B	3B	HR	BB	SO	AVG	OBP	SLG	PRO	/A	BR	/A	PF	CHI	RC	TA	SB	CS	SBA	SBR
DET	154	101	53	.656		958	708	5475	1644	349	53	74	639	528	.300	.376	.424	.800	113	112	132	98	103	905	.800	124	55	69	4
NY	154	94	60	.610	7	842	669	5368	1494	226	61	135	700	597	.278	.364	.419	.783	109	70	105	96	96	848	.775	71	46	61	-5
CLE	154	85	69	.552	16	814	763	5396	1550	340	46	100	526	433	.287	.353	.423	.776	107	44	40	101	98	820	.742	52	32	62	-3
BOS	153	76	76	.500	24	820	775	5339	1465	287	70	51	610	535	.274	.350	.383	.733	96	-26	-72	106	107	748	.710	116	47	71	7
PHI	153	68	82	.453	31	764	838	5317	1491	236	50	144	491	584	.280	.343	.425	.768	104	20	41	97	96	785	.730	57	35	62	-3
STL	154	67	85	.441	33	674	800	5288	1417	252	59	62	514	631	.268	.335	.373	.708	89	-83	-113	104	98	680	.653	42	31	58	-5
WAS	155	66	86	.434	34	729	806	5448	1512	278	70	51	567	447	.278	.348	.382	.730	95	-35	-43	101	95	746	.684	49	42	54	-10
CHI	153	53	99	.349	47	704	946	5301	1395	237	40	71	565	524	.263	.336	.363	.699	87	-96	-90	99	103	672	.647	36	27	57	-4
TOT	615					6305		42932	11968	2205	449	688	4612	4279	.279	.351	.399	.750								547	315	63	-24

TEAM	CG	SHO	SV	IP	H	H/G	HR	BB	BB/G	SO	SO/G	ERA	/A	OAVG	OOBA	PR	/A	PF	CPI	FA	E	DP	FW	PW	BW	SBW	DIF
DET	74	13	14	1370.7	1467	9.6	86	488	3.2	640	4.2	4.06	104	.273	.331	66	23	94	102	.974	159	150	1.1	2.1	12.3	.7	7.8
NY	83	13	10	1382.7	1349	8.8	71	542	3.5	656	4.3	3.76	111	.254	.320	113	63	93	97	.973	157	151	1.2	5.9	9.8	-.2	.4
CLE	72	8	19	1366.7	1476	9.7	70	582	3.8	554	3.6	4.28	105	.275	.343	32	30	100	101	.972	172	164	.4	2.8	3.7	.0	1.1
BOS	68	9	9	1360.0	1527	10.1	70	543	3.6	538	3.6	4.32	109	.282	.344	26	61	105	103	.969	188	141	-.5	5.7	-6.7	.9	.6
PHI	68	8	8	1337.0	1429	9.6	84	693	4.7	480	3.2	5.01	88	.275	.356	-76	-87	98	94	.967	196	166	-1.0	-8.1	3.8	.0	-1.8
STL	50	6	20	1350.0	1499	10.0	94	632	4.2	499	3.3	4.49	106	.283	.355	0	41	106	107	.969	187	160	-.5	3.8	-10.5	-.2	-1.7
WAS	61	4	12	1382.0	1622	10.6	74	503	3.3	412	2.7	4.68	98	.294	.347	-27	-11	102	101	.974	162	167	.9	-1.0	-4.0	-.6	-5.3
CHI	72	5	8	1355.7	1599	10.6	139	628	4.2	506	3.4	5.40	86	.291	.360	-136	-114	103	97	.966	207	126	-1.6	-10.6	-8.4	-.0	-2.4
TOT	548	66	100	10904.7		9.9			3.8		3.5	4.50		.279	.351					.970	1428	1225					

Runs
Gehringer-Det 134
Werber-Bos 129
Gehrig-NY 128
Averill-Cle........128
Foxx-Phi 120

Hits
Gehringer-Det 214
Gehrig-NY 210
Trosky-Cle 206
Cramer-Phi.........202
Greenberg-Det 201

Doubles
Greenberg-Det 63
Gehringer-Det 50
Averill-Cle........48
Trosky-Cle 45
Hale-Cle 44

Triples
Chapman-NY 13
Manush-Was 11

Home Runs
Gehrig-NY 49
Foxx-Phi 44
Trosky-Cle 35
Johnson-Phi.........34
Averill-Cle 31

Total Bases
Gehrig-NY 409
Trosky-Cle 374
Greenberg-Det 356
Foxx-Phi 352
Averill-Cle 340

Runs Batted In
Gehrig-NY 165
Trosky-Cle 142
Greenberg-Det 139
Foxx-Phi.........130
Gehringer-Det 127

Runs Produced
Gehringer-Det 250
Gehrig-NY 244
Greenberg-Det 231
Trosky-Cle 224
Rogell-Det 211

Bases On Balls
Foxx-Phi..........111
Gehrig-NY 109
Ruth-NY 103
Myer-Was 102

Batting Average
Gehrig-NY 363
Gehringer-Det 356
Manush-Was 349
Simmons-Chi 344
Greenberg-Det 339

On Base Percentage
Gehrig-NY 465
Gehringer-Det 450
Foxx-Phi 449
Cochrane-Det......428
Myer-Was 419

Slugging Average
Gehrig-NY 706
Foxx-Phi 653
Greenberg-Det 600
Trosky-Cle 598
Averill-Cle 569

Production
Gehrig-NY 1.172
Foxx-Phi 1.102
Greenberg-Det 1.005
Trosky-Cle 987
Averill-Cle 982

Adjusted Production
Gehrig-NY 208
Foxx-Phi 186
Greenberg-Det 160
Gehringer-Det 153
Trosky-Cle 151

Batter Runs
Gehrig-NY 85.6
Foxx-Phi 66.4
Gehringer-Det 47.8
Greenberg-Det 46.7
Averill-Cle 45.6

Adjusted Batter Runs
Gehrig-NY 89.6
Foxx-Phi 68.8
Gehringer-Det 50.1
Greenberg-Det 48.9
Averill-Cle 45.2

Clutch Hitting Index
Cronin-Was 153
Dykes-Chi.........148
Rogell-Det 147
R.Johnson-Bos 147
Morgan-Bos 143

Runs Created
Gehrig-NY 195
Foxx-Phi 165
Averill-Cle 145
Trosky-Cle 145
Gehringer-Det 144

Total Average
Gehrig-NY 1.414
Foxx-Phi 1.316
Greenberg-Det 1.083
Averill-Cle 1.080
Gehringer-Det 1.073

Stolen Bases
Werber-Bos 40
White-Det 28
Chapman-NY 26
Fox-Det 25
Walker-Det 20

Stolen Base Average
White-Det 82.4
Werber-Bos 72.7
Fox-Det 71.4
Walker-Det 69.0
Chapman-NY 61.9

Stolen Base Runs
Werber-Bos 4.8
White-Det 3.0
Lazzeri-NY 2.7
Cronin-Was 2.4

Fielding Runs
Hale-Cle 22.6
Werber-Bos 21.4
Cronin-Was 16.4
Hemsley-StL 14.3
Melillo-StL 11.4

Total Player Rating
Gehrig-NY 5.8
Gehringer-Det 5.8
Foxx-Phi........... 4.6
Averill-Cle 4.4
Werber-Bos 3.9

Wins
Gomez-NY 26
Rowe-Det 24
Bridges-Det 22
Harder-Cle 20
Ruffing-NY 19

Win Percentage
Gomez-NY 839
Rowe-Det 750
Marberry-Det 750
Auker-Det 682
Bridges-Det 667

Games
Russell-Was 54
Newsom-StL 47
Rowe-Det 45
Knott-StL 45

Complete Games
Gomez-NY 25
Bridges-Det 23
Lyons-Chi 21
Rowe-Det 20

Shutouts
Harder-Cle 6
Gomez-NY 6
Ruffing-NY 5
Dietrich-Phi 4

Saves
Russell-Was 7
Brown-Cle 6
Newsom-StL 5

Innings Pitched
Gomez-NY 282
Bridges-Det 275
Rowe-Det 266
Newsom-StL 262
Ruffing-NY 256

Fewest Hits/Game
Gomez-NY 7.12
Bridges-Det 8.15
Ruffing-NY 8.16
Burke-Was 8.30
Murphy-NY 8.35

Fewest BB/Game
W.Ferrell-Bos 2.44
Auker-Det 2.46
Blaeholder-StL 2.62
Rowe-Det 2.74
Weaver-Was 2.77

Strikeouts
Gomez-NY 158
Bridges-Det 151
Ruffing-NY 149
Rowe-Det 149
Pearson-Cle 140

Strikeouts/Game
Ruffing-NY 5.24
Gomez-NY 5.04
Rowe-Det 5.04
Bridges-Det 4.94
Pearson-Cle 4.94

Wins Above Team
Gomez-NY 9.9
Rowe-Det 5.2
W.Ferrell-Bos 4.8
Earnshaw-Chi 4.6
Knott-StL 4.0

Earned Run Average
Gomez-NY 2.33
Harder-Cle 2.61
Murphy-NY 3.12
Burke-Was 3.21
Auker-Det 3.42

Adjusted ERA
Gomez-NY 179
Harder-Cle 172
Burke-Was 143
Ostermueller-Bos 136
Murphy-NY 134

Opponents' Batting Avg.
Gomez-NY 215
Ruffing-NY 236
Bridges-Det 241
Burke-Was 245
Benton-Phi 249

Opponents' On Base Pct.
Gomez-NY 279
Ruffing-NY 306
Rowe-Det 307
Bridges-Det 309
Harder-Cle 312

Starter Runs
Gomez-NY 67.9
Harder-Cle 53.4
Murphy-NY 31.9
Rowe-Det 30.9
Bridges-Det 25.4

Adjusted Starter Runs
Gomez-NY 57.6
Harder-Cle 53.0
Ostermueller-Bos 27.6
Burke-Was 25.9
Murphy-NY 24.3

Clutch Pitching Index
Harder-Cle 126
Auker-Det 123
Ostermueller-Bos 116
Murphy-NY 113
Coffman-StL 109

Relief Runs
Pennock-Bos 10.0
McColl-Was 8.0
Russell-Was 6.0
Bean-Cle 3.5

Adjusted Relief Runs
Pennock-Bos 11.6
McColl-Was 9.3
Russell-Was 7.8
Bean-Cle 3.4

Relief Ranking
Russell-Was 7.4
McColl-Was 5.4
Pennock-Bos 3.8
Bean-Cle 3.6

Total Pitcher Index
Harder-Cle 5.3
Gomez-NY 5.1
Rowe-Det 3.2
W.Ferrell-Bos 2.9
Ostermueller-Bos 2.8

Total Baseball Ranking
Gehrig-NY 5.8
Gehringer-Det 5.8
Harder-Cle 5.3
Gomez-NY 5.1
Foxx-Phi 4.6

TEAM	G	W	L	PCT	GB	R	OR	AB	H	2B	3B	HR	BB	SO	AVG	OBP	SLG	PRO	/A	BR	/A	PF	CHI	RC	TA	SB	CS	SBA	SBR
CHI	154	100	54	.649		847	597	5486	1581	303	62	88	464	471	.288	.347	.414	.761	111	81	86	99	102	812	.705	66			
STL	154	96	58	.623	4	829	625	5457	1548	286	59	86	404	521	.284	.335	.405	.740	105	33	4	104	108	759	.674	71			
NY	156	91	62	.595	8.5	770	675	5623	1608	248	56	123	392	479	.286	.336	.416	.752	108	54	81	96	95	797	.676	32			
PIT	153	86	67	.562	13.5	743	647	5415	1543	255	90	66	457	437	.285	.343	.402	.745	106	49	-1	107	95	758	.671	30			
BRO	154	70	83	.458	29.5	711	767	5410	1496	235	62	59	430	520	.277	.333	.376	.709	97	-20	24	94	101	691	.632	60			
CIN	154	68	85	.444	31.5	646	772	5296	1403	244	68	73	392	547	.265	.319	.378	.697	93	-50	-3	93	98	658	.626	72			
PHI	156	64	89	.418	35.5	685	871	5442	1466	249	32	92	392	661	.269	.322	.378	.700	94	-46	-145	114	101	681	.621	52			
BOS	153	38	115	.248	61.5	575	852	5309	1396	233	33	75	353	436	.263	.311	.362	.673	86	-97	-65	96	95	596	.571	20			
TOT	617					5806		43438	12041	2053	462	662	3284	4072	.277	.331	.391	.722								403			

TEAM	CG	SHO	SV	IP	H	H/G	HR	BB	BB/G	SO	SO/G	ERA	/A	OAVG	OOBA	PR	/A	PF	CPI	FA	E	DP	FW	PW	BW	SBW	DIF
CHI	81	12	14	1393.3	1417	9.2	85	400	2.6	589	3.8	3.26	117	.262	.308	117	85	95	108	.970	186	163	.3	8.3	8.4		6.1
STL	73	10	18	1385.7	1447	9.4	68	382	2.5	594	3.9	3.54	114	.267	.311	74	76	100	100	.972	164	133	1.6	7.4	.4		9.7
NY	76	10	11	1403.7	1433	9.2	106	411	2.6	524	3.4	3.78	101	.262	.309	37	3	95	97	.972	174	129	1.0	.3	7.9		5.3
PIT	76	15	11	1364.7	1428	9.4	63	312	2.1	549	3.6	3.42	124	.267	.303	90	123	105	99	.968	190	94	.0	12.0	-.0		-2.4
BRO	62	11	20	1358.7	1519	10.1	88	438	2.9	480	3.2	4.22	90	.280	.329	-29	-61	95	99	.969	188	146	.2	-5.9	2.3		-3.1
CIN	59	9	13	1355.0	1490	9.9	65	438	2.9	500	3.3	4.30	89	.277	.325	-41	-70	95	92	.966	204	139	-.7	-6.8	-.3		-.7
PHI	53	8	15	1373.7	1652	10.8	106	505	3.3	475	3.1	4.76	99	.295	.348	-113	-8	117	101	.963	228	145	-2.1	-.8	-14.1		4.5
BOS	54	6	5	1330.3	1645	11.1	81	404	2.7	355	2.4	4.93	82	.301	.342	-134	-133	100	95	.967	197	101	-.3	-12.9	-6.3		-18.9
TOT	534	81	107	10965.0		9.9			2.7		3.3	4.02		.277	.331					.968	1531	1050					

Runs
Galan-Chi 133
Medwick-StL 132
Martin-StL 121
Ott-NY 113
Herman-Chi 113

Hits
Herman-Chi 227
Medwick-StL 224

Doubles
Herman-Chi 57
Medwick-StL 46
Allen-Phi 46
Martin-StL 41
Galan-Chi 41

Triples
Goodman-Cin 18
L.Waner-Pit 14
Medwick-StL 13

Home Runs
Berger-Bos 34
Ott-NY 31
Camilli-Phi 25
Medwick-StL 23
Collins-StL 23

Total Bases
Medwick-StL 365
Ott-NY 329
Berger-Bos 323
Herman-Chi 317
Leiber-NY 314

Runs Batted In
Berger-Bos 130
Medwick-StL 126
Collins-StL 122
Ott-NY 114
Leiber-NY 107

Runs Produced
Medwick-StL 235
Collins-StL 208
Galan-Chi 200
Ott-NY 196
Leiber-NY 195

Bases On Balls
Vaughan-Pit 97
Galan-Chi 87
Ott-NY 82
Suhr-Pit 70
Frey-Bro 66

Batting Average
Vaughan-Pit ..... .385
Medwick-StL ..... .353
Herman-Chi ...... .341
Terry-NY .... .341
Leiber-NY .... .331

On Base Percentage
Vaughan-Pit ..... .491
Ott-NY .... .407
Hack-Chi .... .406
Galan-Chi .... .399
P.Waner-Pit ..... .392

Slugging Average
Vaughan-Pit ..... .607
Medwick-StL ..... .576
Ott-NY .... .555
Berger-Bos ...... .548
Collins-StL ..... .529

Production
Vaughan-Pit 1.098
Medwick-StL ..... .962
Ott-NY .... .962
Collins-StL ..... .915
Berger-Bos ...... .903

Adjusted Production
Vaughan-Pit 181
Ott-NY 162
Medwick-StL 149
Leiber-NY 145
Berger-Bos 145

Batter Runs
Vaughan-Pit 71.9
Ott-NY 47.6
Medwick-StL 46.0
Collins-StL 35.0
Leiber-NY 34.3

Adjusted Batter Runs
Vaughan-Pit 66.8
Ott-NY 50.7
Medwick-StL 42.8
Leiber-NY 37.3
Berger-Bos 33.3

Clutch Hitting Index
Leslie-Bro 146
Young-Pit 138
Jurges-Chi 131
Durocher-StL 130
Collins-StL 124

Runs Created
Vaughan-Pit 163
Ott-NY 144
Medwick-StL 139
Galan-Chi 133
Collins-StL 125

Total Average
Vaughan-Pit 1.317
Ott-NY 1.037
Medwick-StL ..... .948
Galan-Chi .... .937
Collins-StL ..... .930

Stolen Bases
Galan-Chi 22
Martin-StL 20
Bordagaray-Bro 18
Hack-Chi 14
Goodman-Cin 14

Stolen Base Average

Stolen Base Runs

Fielding Runs
Jurges-Chi 27.7
Herman-Chi 19.0
Allen-Phi 13.1
Moore-StL 12.3
Bartell-NY 10.9

Total Player Rating
Vaughan-Pit 5.9
Herman-Chi 5.6
Ott-NY 4.7
Medwick-StL 3.4
Berger-Bos 3.2

Wins
J.Dean-StL 28
Hubbell-NY 23
Derringer-Cin 22
Warneke-Chi 20
Lee-Chi 20

Win Percentage
Lee-Chi .... .769
Castleman-NY .... .714
J.Dean-StL ...... .700
Schumacher-NY ... .679
Hubbell-NY ...... .657

Games
Jorgens-Phi 53
J.Dean-StL 50
Bivin-Phi 47
Smith-Bos 46
P.Dean-StL 46

Complete Games
J.Dean-StL 29
Hubbell-NY 24
Blanton-Pit 23
Warneke-Chi 20
Derringer-Cin 20

Shutouts
Weaver-Pit 4
Mungo-Bro 4
French-Chi 4
Fitzsimmons-NY 4
Blanton-Pit 4

Saves
Leonard-Bro 8
Johnson-Phi 6
Hoyt-Pit 6

Innings Pitched
J.Dean-StL 324
Hubbell-NY 303
Derringer-Cin 277
P.Dean-StL 270

Fewest Hits/Game
Blanton-Pit 7.80
Schumacher-NY ... 8.07
Swift-Pit 8.51
Parmelee-NY 8.52
Hollingswort-Cin 8.58

Fewest BB/Game
Clark-Bro 1.22
Hubbell-NY 1.46
Hoyt-Pit 1.48
Derringer-Cin ... 1.59
Johnson-Phi 1.59

Strikeouts
J.Dean-StL 182
Hubbell-NY 150
Mungo-Bro 143
P.Dean-StL 143
Blanton-Pit 142

Strikeouts/Game
Mungo-Bro 6.01
J.Dean-StL 5.06
Blanton-Pit 5.03
P.Dean-StL 4.77
Hollingswort-Cin 4.63

Wins Above Team
Derringer-Cin 6.8
J.Dean-StL 5.1
Lee-Chi 5.0
Mungo-Bro 4.3
Davis-Phi 3.5

Earned Run Average
Blanton-Pit 2.59
Swift-Pit 2.69
Schumacher-NY ... 2.89
French-Chi 2.96
Lee-Chi 2.96

Adjusted ERA
Blanton-Pit 164
Swift-Pit 157
Johnson-Phi 133
Schumacher-NY 132
J.Dean-StL 130

Opponents' Batting Avg.
Blanton-Pit ..... .229
Schumacher-NY ... .238
Hollingswort-Cin .243
Swift-Pit .... .247
P.Dean-StL ...... .249

Opponents' On Base Pct.
Blanton-Pit ..... .266
Swift-Pit .... .278
Clark-Bro .... .286
Schumacher-NY ... .289
P.Dean-StL ...... .289

Starter Runs
Blanton-Pit 40.5
Schumacher-NY ... 33.1
J.Dean-StL 32.8
Swift-Pit 30.1
Lee-Chi 29.6

Adjusted Starter Runs
Blanton-Pit 46.5
Swift-Pit 35.0
J.Dean-StL 33.3
Davis-Phi 26.9
Schumacher-NY ... 26.9

Clutch Pitching Index
French-Chi 126
Zachary-Bro 121
Walker-StL 116
Lee-Chi 111
Hallahan-StL 111

Relief Runs

Adjusted Relief Runs

Relief Ranking

Total Pitcher Index
Blanton-Pit 4.6
Schumacher-NY 3.6
Swift-Pit 3.4
J.Dean-StL 3.3
Davis-Phi 2.9

Total Baseball Ranking
Vaughan-Pit 5.9
Herman-Chi 5.6
Ott-NY 4.7
Blanton-Pit 4.6
Schumacher-NY 3.6

TEAM	G	W	L	PCT	GB	R	OR	AB	H	2B	3B	HR	BB	SO	AVG	OBP	SLG	PRO	/A	BR	/A	PF	CHI	RC	TA	SB	CS	SBA	SBR
DET	152	93	58	.616		919	665	5423	1573	301	83	106	627	456	.290	.366	.435	.801	112	95	121	97	103	885	.789	70	45	61	-5
NY	149	89	60	.597	3	818	632	5214	1462	255	70	104	604	469	.280	.358	.416	.774	105	42	95	93	102	799	.755	68	46	60	-6
CLE	156	82	71	.536	12	776	739	5534	1573	324	77	93	460	567	.284	.341	.421	.762	102	3	7	99	98	796	.715	63	54	54	-13
BOS	154	78	75	.510	16	718	732	5288	1458	281	63	69	609	470	.276	.353	.424	.745	98	-10	-73	108	93	757	.718	89	59	60	-8
CHI	153	74	78	.487	19.5	738	750	5314	1460	262	42	74	580	405	.275	.348	.382	.730	94	-40	-108	109	100	733	.689	46	28	62	-2
WAS	154	67	86	.438	27	823	903	5592	1591	255	95	32	595	406	.285	.357	.381	.738	96	-18	50	92	104	787	.697	54	37	59	-5
STL	155	65	87	.428	28.5	718	930	5365	1446	291	51	73	593	561	.270	.344	.384	.728	94	-48	-98	107	97	735	.687	45	25	64	-1
PHI	149	58	91	.389	34	710	869	5269	1470	243	44	112	475	602	.279	.341	.406	.747	98	-22	-20	100	97	738	.697	42	35	55	-7
TOT	611					6220		42999	12033	2212	525	663	4543	3936	.280	.351	.402	.753								477	329	59	-53

TEAM	CG	SHO	SV	IP	H	H/G	HR	BB	BB/G	SO	SO/G	ERA	/A	OAVG	OOBA	PR	/A	PF	CPI	FA	E	DP	FW	PW	BW	SBW	DIF
DET	87	16	11	1364.0	1440	9.5	78	522	3.4	584	3.9	3.82	108	.270	.335	96	45	93	107	.978	128	154	2.3	4.2	11.3	.2	-.5
NY	76	12	13	1331.0	1276	8.6	91	516	3.5	594	4.0	3.60	111	.250	.316	125	60	90	101	.974	151	114	1.0	5.6	8.9	.0	-1.1
CLE	67	13	21	1396.0	1527	9.8	68	457	2.9	498	3.2	4.15	106	.277	.328	47	38	99	97	.972	177	147	-.5	3.6	.7	-.6	2.4
BOS	82	6	11	1376.0	1520	9.9	67	520	3.4	470	3.1	4.05	119	.280	.339	62	119	108	106	.969	194	136	-1.5	11.1	-6.8	-.1	-1.2
CHI	80	8	8	1360.7	1443	9.5	105	574	3.8	436	2.9	4.38	111	.272	.340	11	73	109	100	.976	146	133	1.3	6.8	-10.1	.4	-.4
WAS	67	5	12	1378.7	1672	10.9	89	613	4.0	456	3.0	5.25	79	.301	.367	-121	-172	93	99	.972	171	186	-.2	-16.1	4.7	.2	1.9
STL	42	4	15	1380.3	1667	10.9	92	640	4.2	435	2.8	5.26	93	.297	.365	-123	-56	110	97	.970	187	138	-1.1	-5.2	-9.2	.5	4.0
PHI	58	7	10	1326.3	1486	10.1	73	704	4.8	469	3.2	5.12	89	.284	.364	-97	-81	102	96	.968	190	150	-1.3	-7.6	-1.9	-.0	-5.8
TOT	559	71	101	10913.0		9.9			3.7		3.3	4.46		.280	.351					.972	1344	1158					

Runs
Gehrig-NY 125
Gehringer-Det 123
Greenberg-Det 121
Foxx-Phi 118
Chapman-NY 118

Hits
Vosmik-Cle 216
Myer-Was 215
Cramer-Phi 214
Greenberg-Det 203

Doubles
Vosmik-Cle 47
Greenberg-Det 46
Solters-Bos-StL 45
Fox-Det 38
Chapman-NY 38

Triples
Vosmik-Cle 20
Stone-Was 18
Greenberg-Det 16
Cronin-Bos 14
Averill-Cle 13

Home Runs
Greenberg-Det 36
Foxx-Phi 36
Gehrig-NY 30
Johnson-Phi 28
Trosky-Cle 26

Total Bases
Greenberg-Det 389
Foxx-Phi 340
Vosmik-Cle 333
Solters-Bos-StL 314
Gehrig-NY 312

Runs Batted In
Greenberg-Det 170
Gehrig-NY 119
Foxx-Phi 115
Trosky-Cle 113
Solters-Bos-StL 112

Runs Produced
Greenberg-Det 255
Gehrig-NY 214
Gehringer-Det 212
Myer-Was 210
Foxx-Phi 197

Bases On Balls
Gehrig-NY 132
Appling-Chi 122
Foxx-Phi 114
Myer-Was 96
Cochrane-Det 96

Batting Average
Myer-Was 349
Vosmik-Cle 348
Foxx-Phi 346
Cramer-Phi 332
Gehringer-Det 330

On Base Percentage
Gehrig-NY 466
Foxx-Phi 461
Cochrane-Det 452
Myer-Was 440
Appling-Chi 437

Slugging Average
Foxx-Phi 636
Greenberg-Det 628
Gehrig-NY 583
Vosmik-Cle 537
Fox-Det 513

Production
Foxx-Phi 1.096
Gehrig-NY 1.049
Greenberg-Det 1.039
Vosmik-Cle 946
Gehringer-Det 911

Adjusted Production
Gehrig-NY 183
Foxx-Phi 181
Greenberg-Det 171
Myer-Was 147
Vosmik-Cle 144

Batter Runs
Foxx-Phi 67.2
Gehrig-NY 61.6
Greenberg-Det 57.5
Vosmik-Cle 38.3
Myer-Was 36.5

Adjusted Batter Runs
Gehrig-NY 67.6
Foxx-Phi 67.4
Greenberg-Det 60.6
Myer-Was 44.4
Vosmik-Cle 38.8

Clutch Hitting Index
Goslin-Det 144
Owen-Det 139
Powell-Was 134
Dykes-Chi 126
Stone-Was 125

Runs Created
Foxx-Phi 163
Greenberg-Det 161
Gehrig-NY 154
Vosmik-Cle 137
Myer-Was 132

Total Average
Foxx-Phi 1.299
Gehrig-NY 1.249
Greenberg-Det 1.146
Cochrane-Det 1.018
Vosmik-Cle 983

Stolen Bases
Werber-Bos 29
Lary-Was-StL 28
Almada-Bos 20
White-Det 19
Chapman-NY 17

Stolen Base Average
Lary-Was-StL 87.5
Werber-Bos 80.6
Almada-Bos 69.0
White-Det 65.5
Chapman-NY 63.0

Stolen Base Runs
Lary-Was-StL 6.0
Werber-Bos 4.5
Solters-Bos-StL 2.1
Hughes-Cle 2.1

Fielding Runs
Appling-Chi 21.3
Travis-Was 21.0
Solters-Bos-StL 20.6
Werber-Bos 16.4
Chapman-NY 13.5

Total Player Rating
Foxx-Phi 5.5
Myer-Was 5.2
Gehrig-NY 4.7
Greenberg-Det 4.6
Gehringer-Det 4.3

Wins
W.Ferrell-Bos 25
Harder-Cle 22
Bridges-Det 21
Grove-Bos 20
Rowe-Det 19

Win Percentage
Auker-Det 720
Broaca-NY 682
Bridges-Det 677
Harder-Cle 667
Lyons-Chi 652

Games
VanAtta-NY -StL 58
Walkup-StL 55
Andrews-StL 50
Thomas-StL 49
Knott-StL 48

Complete Games
W.Ferrell-Bos 31
Grove-Bos 23
Bridges-Det 23
Rowe-Det 21

Shutouts
Rowe-Det 6
Harder-Cle 4
Bridges-Det 4

Saves
Knott-StL 7

Innings Pitched
W.Ferrell-Bos 322
Harder-Cle 287
Whitehill-Was 279
Rowe-Det 276
Bridges-Det 274

Fewest Hits/Game
Allen-NY 8.03
Ruffing-NY 8.15
Gomez-NY 8.16
Whitehead-Chi 8.47
Grove-Bos 8.87

Fewest BB/Game
Harder-Cle 1.66
Grove-Bos 2.14
Rowe-Det 2.22
Andrews-StL 2.24
Hudlin-Cle 2.37

Strikeouts
Bridges-Det 163
Rowe-Det 140
Gomez-NY 138
Grove-Bos 121
Allen-NY 113

Strikeouts/Game
Allen-NY 6.09
Bridges-Det 5.35
Gomez-NY 5.05
VanAtta-NY -StL 4.63
Rowe-Det 4.57

Wins Above Team
W.Ferrell-Bos 6.4
Harder-Cle 5.5
Marcum-Phi 5.4
Grove-Bos 4.5
Andrews-StL 4.2

Earned Run Average
Grove-Bos 2.70
Lyons-Chi 3.02
Ruffing-NY 3.12
Gomez-NY 3.18
Harder-Cle 3.29

Adjusted ERA
Grove-Bos 179
Lyons-Chi 161
Andrews-StL 138
W.Ferrell-Bos 137
Harder-Cle 134

Opponents' Batting Avg.
Allen-NY 238
Ruffing-NY 239
Gomez-NY 242
Whitehead-Chi 250
Broaca-NY 254

Opponents' On Base Pct.
Grove-Bos 296
Rowe-Det 298
Ruffing-NY 301
Gomez-NY 302
Allen-NY 305

Starter Runs
Grove-Bos 53.1
Harder-Cle 37.1
Gomez-NY 34.8
W.Ferrell-Bos 33.4
Ruffing-NY 32.9

Adjusted Starter Runs
Grove-Bos 64.5
W.Ferrell-Bos 46.8
Lyons-Chi 39.2
Harder-Cle 35.2
Andrews-StL 31.8

Clutch Pitching Index
Lyons-Chi 125
Harder-Cle 119
Bridges-Det 113
Auker-Det 112
Grove-Bos 112

Relief Runs
Brown-Cle 11.4
Hogsett-Det 10.0
DeShong-NY 9.2
Murphy-NY 4.9
Wilson-Bos 1.7

Adjusted Relief Runs
Brown-Cle 10.6
Hogsett-Det 6.4
DeShong-NY 5.8
Wilson-Bos 4.3

Relief Ranking
Brown-Cle 12.5
Hogsett-Det 7.9
Wilson-Bos 4.4
DeShong-NY 4.3

Total Pitcher Index
W.Ferrell-Bos 7.4
Grove-Bos 6.3
Lyons-Chi 3.9
Harder-Cle 3.8
Ruffing-NY 3.1

Total Baseball Ranking
W.Ferrell-Bos 7.4
Grove-Bos 6.3
Foxx-Phi 5.5
Myer-Was 5.2
Gehrig-NY 4.7

TEAM	G	W	L	PCT	GB	R	OR	AB	H	2B	3B	HR	BB	SO	AVG	OBP	SLG	PRO	/A	BR	/A	PF	CHI	RC	TA	SB	CS	SBA SBR
NY	154	92	62	.597		742	621	5449	1529	237	48	97	431	452	.281	.337	.395	.732	103	19	16	100	99	744	.657	31		
STL	155	87	67	.565	5	795	794	5537	1554	332	60	88	442	577	.281	.336	.410	.746	106	40	80	94	103	772	.681	69		
CHI	154	87	67	.565	5	755	603	5409	1545	275	36	76	491	462	.286	.349	.392	.741	105	44	8	105	97	757	.677	68		
PIT	156	84	70	.545	8	804	718	5586	1596	283	80	60	517	502	.286	.349	.397	.746	107	56	73	98	99	798	.681	37		
CIN	154	74	80	.481	18	722	760	5393	1476	224	73	82	410	584	.274	.329	.388	.717	98	-13	11	97	103	699	.645	68		
BOS	157	71	83	.461	21	631	715	5478	1450	207	44	68	433	582	.265	.322	.356	.678	88	-85	-47	95	98	635	.584	23		
BRO	156	67	87	.435	25	662	752	5574	1518	263	43	33	390	458	.272	.323	.353	.676	88	-91	-126	105	103	649	.584	55		
PHI	154	54	100	.351	38	726	874	5465	1538	250	46	103	451	586	.281	.339	.401	.740	105	32	-26	108	95	757	.670	50		
TOT	620					5837		43891	12206	2071	430	607	3565	4203	.278	.335	.386	.722								401		

TEAM	CG	SHO	SV	IP	H	H/G	HR	BB	BB/G	SO	SO/G	ERA	/A	OAVG	OOBA	PR	/A	PF	CPI	FA	E	DP	FW	PW	BW	SBW	DIF
NY	60	12	22	1384.7	1458	9.5	75	401	2.6	500	3.2	3.46	114	.269	.315	85	75	98	105	.974	168	164	1.2	7.3	1.6		4.9
STL	65	6	24	1396.7	1610	10.4	89	434	2.8	559	3.6	4.47	85	.287	.332	-71	-105	95	95	.974	156	134	1.9	-10.2	7.8		10.6
CHI	77	17	10	1382.3	1413	9.2	77	434	2.8	597	3.9	3.53	116	.263	.314	74	87	102	101	.976	146	156	2.4	8.5	.8		-1.7
PIT	67	5	12	1395.3	1475	9.5	74	379	2.4	559	3.6	3.89	99	.270	.312	19	-4	96	93	.967	199	113	-.6	-.4	7.1		.9
CIN	50	5	23	1366.7	1576	10.4	51	418	2.8	459	3.0	4.22	92	.287	.332	-31	-49	97	96	.969	191	150	-.1	-4.8	1.1		.8
BOS	61	7	13	1412.7	1566	10.0	69	451	2.9	421	2.7	3.94	98	.279	.328	12	-11	96	100	.971	189	175	-.0	-1.1	-4.6		-.3
BRO	59	7	18	1400.7	1466	9.4	84	528	3.4	651	4.2	3.98	107	.268	.327	5	46	107	98	.966	208	107	-1.1	4.5	-12.3		-1.1
PHI	51	7	14	1364.0	1630	10.8	87	515	3.4	454	3.0	4.64	96	.295	.350	-94	-29	111	100	.959	252	144	-3.6	-2.8	-2.5		-14.0
TOT	490	66	136	11103.0		9.9			2.9		3.4	4.01		.278	.335					.969	1509	1143					

Runs
Vaughan-Pit 122
Martin-StL 121
Ott-NY 120
Medwick-StL 115
Suhr-Pit 111

Hits
Medwick-StL 223
P.Waner-Pit 218
Demaree-Chi 212
Herman-Chi 211
Moore-NY 205

Doubles
Medwick-StL 64
Herman-Chi 57
P.Waner-Pit 53
Moore-StL 39
Moore-Bos 38

Triples
Goodman-Cin 14
Medwick-StL 13
Camilli-Phi 13

Home Runs
Ott-NY 33
Camilli-Phi 28
Klein-Chi-Phi 25
Berger-Bos 25
Mize-StL 19

Total Bases
Medwick-StL 367
Ott-NY 314
Klein-Chi-Phi 308
Camilli-Phi 306
P.Waner-Pit 304

Runs Batted In
Medwick-StL 138
Ott-NY 135
Suhr-Pit 118
Klein-Chi-Phi 104

Runs Produced
Medwick-StL 235
Ott-NY 222
Suhr-Pit 218
P.Waner-Pit 196
Vaughan-Pit 191

Bases On Balls
Vaughan-Pit 118
Camilli-Phi 116
Ott-NY 111
Suhr-Pit 95
Hack-Chi 89

Batting Average
P.Waner-Pit 373
Medwick-StL 351
Demaree-Chi 350
Vaughan-Pit 335
Herman-Chi 334

On Base Percentage
Vaughan-Pit 453
Ott-NY 448
P.Waner-Pit 446
Camilli-Phi 441
Suhr-Pit 410

Slugging Average
Ott-NY 588
Camilli-Phi 577
Medwick-StL 577
P.Waner-Pit 520
Klein-Chi-Phi 512

Production
Ott-NY 1.036
Camilli-Phi 1.018
P.Waner-Pit 965
Medwick-StL 964
Vaughan-Pit 927

Adjusted Production
Ott-NY 176
Medwick-StL 166
P.Waner-Pit 163
Camilli-Phi 159
Vaughan-Pit 153

Batter Runs
Ott-NY 61.9
Camilli-Phi 57.9
P.Waner-Pit 51.4
Vaughan-Pit 47.2
Medwick-StL 46.9

Adjusted Batter Runs
Ott-NY 61.6
P.Waner-Pit 53.3
Camilli-Phi 51.6
Medwick-StL 51.4
Vaughan-Pit 49.3

Clutch Hitting Index
Brubaker-Pit 160
Suhr-Pit 145
Young-Pit 141
Cuccinello-Bos 130
Galan-Chi 130

Runs Created
Ott-NY 153
Camilli-Phi 148
Medwick-StL 141
P.Waner-Pit 140
Vaughan-Pit 137

Total Average
Ott-NY 1.188
Camilli-Phi 1.162
Vaughan-Pit 1.034
P.Waner-Pit 1.016
Medwick-StL 956

Stolen Bases
Martin-StL 23
Martin-StL 17
Hack-Chi 17
Chiozza-Phi 17

Stolen Base Average

Stolen Base Runs

Fielding Runs
Bartell-NY 43.4
Whitehead-NY 28.4
Cuccinello-Bos 21.5
Moore-StL 17.4
Herman-Chi 15.0

Total Player Rating
Medwick-StL 5.5
Bartell-NY 5.4
P.Waner-Pit 5.2
Ott-NY 4.8
Herman-Chi 4.7

Wins
Hubbell-NY 26
Dean-StL 24
Derringer-Cin 19

Win Percentage
Hubbell-NY 813
Lucas-Pit 789
French-Chi 667
Dean-StL 649
Lee-Chi 621

Games
Derringer-Cin 51
Dean-StL 51
Passeau-Phi 49
Brown-Pit 47

Complete Games
Dean-StL 28
Hubbell-NY 25
Mungo-Bro 22
MacFayden-Bos 21
Lee-Chi 20

Shutouts

Saves
Dean-StL 11
Brennan-Cin 9
Smith-Bos 8
Johnson-Phi 7
Coffman-NY 7

Innings Pitched
Dean-StL 315
Mungo-Bro 312
Hubbell-NY 304
Derringer-Cin 282
MacFayden-Bos 267

Fewest Hits/Game
Hubbell-NY 7.85
Mungo-Bro 7.93
Lee-Chi 8.27
Dean-StL 8.86
Blanton-Pit 8.96

Fewest BB/Game
Lucas-Pit 1.33
Derringer-Cin 1.34
Dean-StL 1.51
Hubbell-NY 1.69
Gabler-NY 1.89

Strikeouts
Mungo-Bro 238
Dean-StL 195
Blanton-Pit 127
Hubbell-NY 123
Derringer-Cin 121

Strikeouts/Game
Mungo-Bro 6.87
Dean-StL 5.57
Blanton-Pit 4.84
Weaver-Phi 4.30
Warneke-Chi 4.24

Wins Above Team
Hubbell-NY 9.5
Lucas-Pit 5.4
Dean-StL 4.4
French-Chi 3.6
MacFayden-Bos 3.5

Earned Run Average
Hubbell-NY 2.31
MacFayden-Bos . . .2.87
Gabler-NY 3.11
Lucas-Pit 3.17
Dean-StL 3.17

Adjusted ERA
Hubbell-NY 171
MacFayden-Bos 135
Mungo-Bro 128
Passeau-Phi 128
Gabler-NY 127

Opponents' Batting Avg.
Mungo-Bro 234
Hubbell-NY 236
Lee-Chi 246
Dean-StL 253
Blanton-Pit 257

Opponents' On Base Pct.
Hubbell-NY 272
Dean-StL 281
Lucas-Pit 284
Blanton-Pit 295
Mungo-Bro 302

Starter Runs
Hubbell-NY 57.6
MacFayden-Bos . . .34.1
Dean-StL 29.5
Mungo-Bro 23.2
Lee-Chi 20.5

Adjusted Starter Runs
Hubbell-NY 55.3
Mungo-Bro 32.2
MacFayden-Bos . . .29.6
Passeau-Phi 23.1
Lee-Chi 22.9

Clutch Pitching Index
Schumacher-NY 120
Gabler-NY 120
Chaplin-Bos 111
Smith-NY 109
Carleton-Chi 108

Relief Runs
Bryant-Chi 4.4
Coffman-NY 1.5

Adjusted Relief Runs
Bryant-Chi 5.0
Johnson-Phi 1.8
Coffman-NY 7

Relief Ranking
Bryant-Chi 2.3
Johnson-Phi 2.0
Coffman-NY 9

Total Pitcher Index
Hubbell-NY 5.9
Mungo-Bro 3.0
Passeau-Phi 2.9
MacFayden-Bos . . .2.8
Lee-Chi 2.1

Total Baseball Ranking
Hubbell-NY 5.9
Medwick-StL 5.5
Bartell-NY 5.4
P.Waner-Pit 5.2
Ott-NY 4.8

TEAM	G	W	L	PCT	GB	R	OR	AB	H	2B	3B	HR	BB	SO	AVG	OBP	SLG	PRO	/A	BR	/A	PF	CHI	RC	TA	SB	CS	SBA	SBR
NY	155	102	51	.667		1065	731	5591	1676	315	83	182	700	594	.300	.381	.483	.864	120	162	210	95	99	1056	.888	76	40	66	0
DET	154	83	71	.539	19.5	921	871	5464	1638	326	55	94	640	462	.300	.377	.431	.808	106	57	97	95	98	912	.801	72	49	60	-7
WAS	153	82	71	.536	20	889	799	5433	1601	293	84	62	576	398	.295	.365	.414	.779	99	-6	15	98	103	847	.762	103	42	71	6
CHI	153	81	70	.536	20	920	873	5466	1597	282	56	60	684	417	.292	.374	.397	.771	97	-8	-1	99	104	851	.756	66	29	69	2
CLE	157	80	74	.519	22.5	921	862	5646	1715	357	82	123	514	470	.304	.364	.461	.825	110	70	21	106	96	948	.803	66	53	55	-11
BOS	155	74	80	.481	28.5	753	764	5383	1485	288	62	86	584	465	.276	.349	.400	.749	91	-71	-122	106	97	773	.714	54	44	55	-9
STL	155	57	95	.375	44.5	804	1064	5391	1502	299	66	79	625	627	.279	.356	.403	.759	94	-50	-77	103	98	804	.736	62	20	76	7
PHI	154	53	100	.346	49	714	1045	5373	1443	240	60	72	524	590	.269	.336	.376	.712	82	-150	-154	101	102	694	.660	59	43	58	-7
TOT	618					7009		43747	12657	2400	548	758	4847	4023	.289	.363	.421	.784								558	320	64	-24

TEAM	CG	SHO	SV	IP	H	H/G	HR	BB	BB/G	SO	SO/G	ERA	/A	OAVG	OOBA	PR	/A	PF	CPI	FA	E	DP	FW	PW	BW	SBW	DIF
NY	77	6	21	1400.3	1474	9.5	84	663	4.3	624	4.0	4.17	109	.270	.346	134	55	90	108	.973	163	148	.7	4.9	18.5	.3	1.1
DET	76	13	13	1360.0	1568	10.4	100	562	3.7	526	3.5	5.00	95	.289	.353	6	-34	95	100	.975	153	159	1.3	-3.0	8.6	-.3	-.5
WAS	78	8	14	1345.7	1484	9.9	73	588	3.9	462	3.1	4.58	106	.279	.349	68	39	96	101	.970	182	163	-.3	3.4	1.3	.8	.3
CHI	80	5	8	1365.0	1603	10.6	104	578	3.8	414	2.7	5.06	98	.293	.358	-3	-14	99	102	.973	168	174	.4	-1.2	-.0	.4	5.0
CLE	74	6	12	1389.3	1604	10.4	73	607	3.9	619	4.0	4.83	109	.289	.357	31	68	105	102	.971	178	154	-.1	6.0	1.9	-.7	-4.0
BOS	78	11	9	1373.0	1501	9.8	78	552	3.6	584	3.8	4.39	122	.276	.340	99	144	106	102	.972	165	139	.6	12.7	-10.8	-.5	-5.0
STL	54	3	13	1348.3	1776	11.9	115	609	4.1	399	2.7	6.24	86	.314	.381	-180	-127	107	95	.969	188	143	-.7	-11.2	-6.8	.9	-1.2
PHI	68	3	12	1352.3	1645	10.9	131	696	4.6	405	2.7	6.08	87	.299	.375	-156	-116	105	94	.965	209	152	-1.9	-10.2	-13.6	-.3	2.5
TOT	585	55	102	10934.0		10.4			4.0		3.3	5.04		.289	.363					.971	1406	1232					

Runs
Gehrig-NY 167
Clift-StL 145
Gehringer-Det . . . 144
Crosetti-NY 137
Averill-Cle 136

Hits
Averill-Cle 232
Gehringer-Det 227
Trosky-Cle 216
Bell-StL 212
Radcliff-Chi 207

Doubles
Gehringer-Det 60
Walker-Det 55
Chapman-NY -Was . 50
Hale-Cle 50

Triples
Rolfe-NY 15
DiMaggio-NY 15
Averill-Cle 15
Johnson-Phi 14

Home Runs
Gehrig-NY 49
Trosky-Cle 42
Foxx-Bos 41
DiMaggio-NY 29
Averill-Cle 28

Total Bases
Trosky-Cle 405
Gehrig-NY 403
Averill-Cle 385
Foxx-Bos 369
DiMaggio-NY 367

Runs Batted In
Trosky-Cle 162
Gehrig-NY 152
Foxx-Bos 143
Bonura-Chi 138
Solters-StL 134

Runs Produced
Gehrig-NY 270
Bonura-Chi 246
Gehringer-Det 245
Trosky-Cle 244
Averill-Cle 234

Bases On Balls
Gehrig-NY 130
Lary-StL 117
Clift-StL 115
Foxx-Bos 105
Lazzeri-NY 97

Batting Average
Appling-Chi 388
Averill-Cle 378
Gehringer-Det 354
Gehrig-NY 354
Walker-Det 353

On Base Percentage
Gehrig-NY 478
Appling-Chi 474
Foxx-Bos 440
Averill-Cle 438
Gehringer-Det 431

Slugging Average
Gehrig-NY 696
Trosky-Cle 644
Foxx-Bos 631
Averill-Cle 627
DiMaggio-NY 576

Production
Gehrig-NY 1.174
Foxx-Bos 1.071
Averill-Cle 1.065
Trosky-Cle 1.026
Gehringer-Det 987

Adjusted Production
Gehrig-NY 197
Foxx-Bos 152
Averill-Cle 152
Gehringer-Det 149
Appling-Chi 143

Batter Runs
Gehrig-NY 82.2
Foxx-Bos 56.9
Averill-Cle 56.4
Gehringer-Det 43.1
Trosky-Cle 41.9

Adjusted Batter Runs
Gehrig-NY 87.6
Averill-Cle 51.1
Foxx-Bos 51.1
Gehringer-Det 47.8
Appling-Chi 41.1

Clutch Hitting Index
Appling-Chi 154
Bonura-Chi 148
Sewell-Chi 137
Owen-Det 137
Vosmik-Cle 135

Runs Created
Gehrig-NY 199
Averill-Cle 168
Foxx-Bos 168
Gehringer-Det 157
Trosky-Cle 150

Total Average
Gehrig-NY 1.437
Foxx-Bos 1.248
Averill-Cle 1.179
Appling-Chi 1.107
Gehringer-Det . . . 1.077

Stolen Bases
Lary-StL 37
Powell-Was-NY . . . 26
Werber-Bos 23
Chapman-NY -Was . 20
Hughes-Cle 20

Stolen Base Average
Lary-StL 80.4
Crosetti-NY 72.0
Powell-Was-NY . . . 70.3
Chapman-NY -Was . 69.0
Hughes-Cle 69.0

Stolen Base Runs
Hale-Was 5.7
Hill-Was 3.3
Stone-Was 2.4
Sewell-Chi 2.1

Fielding Runs
Hale-Chi 16.3
Hayes-Chi 16.3
Appling-Chi 15.9
Gehringer-Det 15.7
Sewell-Chi 12.6

Total Player Rating
Gehringer-Det 6.4
Gehrig-NY 5.7
Appling-Chi 5.7
Dickey-NY 3.5
Averill-Cle 3.3

Wins
Bridges-Det 23
Kennedy-Chi 21
Ruffing-NY 20
Ferrell-Bos 20
Allen-Cle 20

Win Percentage
Pearson-NY 731
Kennedy-Chi 700
Bridges-Det 676
Allen-Cle 667
Rowe-Det 655

Games
VanAtta-StL 52
Knott-StL 47

Complete Games
Ferrell-Bos 28
Bridges-Det 26
Ruffing-NY 25
Newsom-Was 24
Grove-Bos 22

Shutouts
Grove-Bos 6
Bridges-Det 5
Rowe-Det 4
Newsom-Was 4
Allen-Cle 4

Saves
Malone-NY 9
Knott-StL 6
Murphy-NY 5
Brown-Chi 5
Hildebrand-Cle 4

Innings Pitched
Ferrell-Bos 301
Bridges-Det 295
Newsom-Was 286
Kennedy-Chi 274
Ruffing-NY 271

Fewest Hits/Game
Pearson-NY 7.71
Grove-Bos 8.43
Allen-Cle 8.67
Gomez-NY 8.76
Bridges-Det 8.82

Fewest BB/Game
Lyons-Chi 2.23
Grove-Bos 2.31
Rowe-Det 2.35
Andrews-StL 2.36
Marcum-Bos 2.69

Strikeouts
Bridges-Det 175
Allen-Cle 165
Newsom-Was 156
Grove-Bos 130
Pearson-NY 118

Strikeouts/Game
Allen-Cle 6.11
Bridges-Det 5.34
Gomez-NY 5.00
Newsom-Was 4.91
Pearson-NY 4.76

Wins Above Team
Kennedy-Chi 6.1
Bridges-Det 6.0
Allen-Cle 5.3
Kelley-Phi 4.9
Rowe-Det 4.3

Earned Run Average
Grove-Bos 2.81
Allen-Cle 3.44
Appleton-Was 3.52
Bridges-Det 3.60
Pearson-NY 3.71

Adjusted ERA
Grove-Bos 190
Allen-Cle 153
Appleton-Was 138
Kelley-Phi 137
Bridges-Det 133

Opponents' Batting Avg.
Pearson-NY 233
Grove-Bos 246
Gomez-NY 254
Appleton-Was 254
Bridges-Det 255

Opponents' On Base Pct.
Grove-Bos 292
Rowe-Det 317
Ruffing-NY 319
Appleton-Was 321
Bridges-Det 322

Starter Runs
Grove-Bos 62.6
Bridges-Det 47.1
Allen-Cle 43.0
Ruffing-NY 35.7
Appleton-Was 34.1

Adjusted Starter Runs
Grove-Bos 70.8
Allen-Cle 49.5
Bridges-Det 38.4
Ferrell-Bos 38.2
Kelley-Phi 37.4

Clutch Pitching Index
Hadley-NY 116
Kelley-Phi 115
Grove-Bos 115
Bridges-Det 109
Thomas-StL 108

Relief Runs
Lee-Cle 2.1
Gumpert-Phi 1.7
Kimsey-Det 1.1
Brown-Chi 5

Adjusted Relief Runs
Lee-Cle 5.5
Gumpert-Phi 3.5

Relief Ranking
Lee-Cle 3.4
Gumpert-Phi 1.8

Total Pitcher Index
Grove-Bos 6.7
Allen-Cle 4.6
Ferrell-Bos 4.5
Bridges-Det 3.7
Ruffing-NY 3.3

Total Baseball Ranking
Grove-Bos 6.7
Gehringer-Det 6.4
Gehrig-NY 5.7
Appling-Chi 5.7
Allen-Cle 4.6

TEAM	G	W	L	PCT	GB	R	OR	AB	H	2B	3B	HR	BB	SO	AVG	OBP	SLG	PRO	/A	BR	/A	PF	CHI	RC	TA	SB	CS	SBA	SBR
NY	152	95	57	.625		732	602	5329	1484	251	41	111	412	492	.278	.334	.403	.737	106	39	39	100	100	734	.667	45			
CHI	154	93	61	.604	3	811	682	5349	1537	253	74	96	538	496	.287	.355	.416	.771	116	116	98	103	98	816	.727	71			
PIT	154	86	68	.558	10	704	646	5433	1550	223	86	47	463	480	.285	.343	.384	.727	104	30	13	102	95	734	.648	32			
STL	157	81	73	.526	15	789	733	5476	1543	264	67	94	385	569	.282	.331	.406	.737	106	35	31	101	106	744	.667	78			
BOS	152	79	73	.520	16	579	556	5124	1265	200	41	63	485	707	.247	.314	.339	.653	83	-108	-43	90	101	565	.574	45			
BRO	155	62	91	.405	33.5	616	772	5295	1401	258	53	37	469	583	.265	.327	.354	.681	91	-57	-86	104	96	629	.605	69			
PHI	155	61	92	.399	34.5	724	869	5424	1482	258	37	103	478	640	.273	.334	.391	.725	103	21	-36	108	99	730	.662	66			
CIN	155	56	98	.364	40	612	707	5230	1329	215	59	73	437	586	.254	.315	.360	.675	89	-77	-17	91	101	599	.594	53			
TOT	617					5567		42660	11591	1922	458	624	3667	4553	.272	.332	.382	.714								459			

TEAM	CG	SHO	SV	IP	H	H/G	HR	BB	BB/G	SO	SO/G	ERA	/A	OAVG	OOBA	PR	/A	PF	CPI	FA	E	DP	FW	PW	BW	SBW	DIF
NY	67	11	17	1361.0	1341	8.9	85	404	2.7	653	4.3	3.43	111	.257	.305	72	58	100	100		159	143	1.0	5.8	3.9		8.3
CHI	73	11	13	1380.7	1434	9.3	91	502	3.3	596	3.9	3.98	98	.267	.326	-10	-9	100	98	.975	151	141	1.5	-.9	9.7		5.7
PIT	67	14	17	1366.3	1398	9.2	71	428	2.8	643	4.2	3.56	111	.264	.315	54	61	101	101	.970	181	135	-.2	6.0	1.3		1.9
STL	81	10	4	1390.0	1546	10.0	95	448	2.9	571	3.7	3.98	98	.281	.329	-10	-13	100	105	.973	164	127	.8	-1.3	3.1		1.4
BOS	85	16	10	1359.7	1344	8.9	60	372	2.5	387	2.6	3.22	109	.258	.302	105	45	90	101	.975	157	128	1.2	4.5	-4.3		1.6
BRO	63	5	8	1363.0	1470	9.7	68	476	3.1	592	3.9	4.13	102	.275	.328	-32	9	107	96	.964	217	127	-2.2	.9	-8.5		-4.6
PHI	59	6	15	1366.0	1629	10.7	116	501	3.3	529	3.5	5.06	86	.295	.349	-174	-111	111	96	.970	184	157	-.4	-11.0	-3.6		-.6
CIN	64	10	18	1358.0	1428	9.5	38	533	3.5	581	3.9	3.94	92	.270	.331	-4	-45	93	96	.966	208	139	-1.7	-4.5	-1.7		-13.1
TOT	559	83	102	10944.7		9.5			3.0		3.7	3.91		.272	.332					.971	1421	1097					

Runs
Medwick-StL 111
Herman-Chi 106
Hack-Chi 106
Galan-Chi 104
Demaree-Chi 104

Hits
Medwick-StL 237
P.Waner-Pit 219
Mize-StL 204
Demaree-Chi 199
Herman-Chi 189

Doubles
Medwick-StL 56
Mize-StL 40
Bartell-NY 38
Phelps-Bro 37
Moore-NY 37

Triples
Vaughan-Pit 17
Suhr-Pit 14
Handley-Pit 12
Goodman-Cin 12
Herman-Chi 11

Home Runs
Ott-NY 31
Medwick-StL 31
Camilli-Phi 27
Mize-StL 25
Galan-Chi 18

Total Bases
Medwick-StL 406
Mize-StL 333
Demaree-Chi 298
Ott-NY 285
Camilli-Phi 279

Runs Batted In
Medwick-StL 154
Demaree-Chi 115
Mize-StL 113
Suhr-Pit 97
Ott-NY 95

Runs Produced
Medwick-StL 234
Demaree-Chi 202
Mize-StL 191
Hack-Chi 167
P.Waner-Pit 166

Bases On Balls
Ott-NY 102
Camilli-Phi 90
Suhr-Pit 83
Hack-Chi 83
Galan-Chi 79

Batting Average
Medwick-StL 374
Mize-StL 364
P.Waner-Pit 354
Whitney-Phi 341
Camilli-Phi 339

On Base Percentage
Camilli-Phi 446
Mize-StL 427
Medwick-StL 414
P.Waner-Pit 413
Ott-NY 408

Slugging Average
Medwick-StL 641
Mize-StL 595
Camilli-Phi 587
Ott-NY 523
Demaree-Chi 485

Production
Medwick-StL 1.056
Camilli-Phi 1.034
Mize-StL 1.021
Ott-NY 931
Herman-Chi 875

Adjusted Production
Medwick-StL 182
Mize-StL 174
Camilli-Phi 165
Ott-NY 151
Herman-Chi 133

Batter Runs
Medwick-StL 68.8
Mize-StL 57.4
Camilli-Phi 54.9
Ott-NY 41.2
Hartnett-Chi 31.0

Adjusted Batter Runs
Medwick-StL 68.4
Mize-StL 57.0
Camilli-Phi 49.4
Ott-NY 41.2
Hartnett-Chi 29.8

Clutch Hitting Index
Suhr-Pit 151
Durocher-StL 144
Scharein-Phi 142
Jurges-Chi 134
Todd-Pit 130

Runs Created
Medwick-StL 170
Mize-StL 150
Camilli-Phi 137
Ott-NY 128
P.Waner-Pit 118

Total Average
Camilli-Phi 1.189
Medwick-StL 1.113
Mize-StL 1.097
Ott-NY 1.021
Vaughan-Pit 864

Stolen Bases
Galan-Chi 23
Hack-Chi 16

Stolen Base Average

Stolen Base Runs

Fielding Runs
Bartell-NY 36.7
Whitehead-NY 25.9
Herman-Chi 19.3
Riggs-Cin 16.6
Martin-StL 11.8

Total Player Rating
Bartell-NY 6.2
Medwick-StL 6.0
Herman-Chi 5.1
Camilli-Phi 4.6
Ott-NY 3.9

Wins
Hubbell-NY 22
Turner-Bos 20
Melton-NY 20
Fette-Bos 20
Warneke-StL 18

Win Percentage
Hubbell-NY 733
Melton-NY 690
Fette-Bos 667
Carleton-Chi 667
Turner-Bos 645

Games
Mulcahy-Phi 56
Jorgens-Phi 52

Complete Games
Turner-Bos 24
Fette-Bos 23
Weiland-StL 21

Shutouts
Turner-Bos 5
Grissom-Cin 5
Fette-Bos 5

Saves
Melton-NY 7
Brown-Pit 7
Grissom-Cin 6
Root-Chi 5
Hollingswort-Cin 5

Innings Pitched
Passeau-Phi 292
Lee-Chi 272
Weiland-StL 264
Hubbell-NY 262
Fette-Bos 259

Fewest Hits/Game
Mungo-Bro 7.60
Grissom-Cin 7.75
Melton-NY 7.84
Carleton-Chi 7.92
Turner-Bos 7.98

Fewest BB/Game
Dean-StL 1.51
Root-Chi 1.61
Hoyt-Pit-Bro 1.66
Turner-Bos 1.82
Castleman-NY 1.86

Strikeouts
Hubbell-NY 159
Grissom-Cin 149
Blanton-Pit 143
Melton-NY 142

Strikeouts/Game
Mungo-Bro 6.82
Grissom-Cin 5.99
Henshaw-Bro 5.65
Bauers-Pit 5.65
LaMaster-Phi 5.52

Wins Above Team
Fette-Bos 5.3
Hubbell-NY 5.0
Turner-Bos 4.8
Warneke-StL 3.4
Melton-NY 3.0

Earned Run Average
Turner-Bos 2.38
Melton-NY 2.61
Dean-StL 2.70
Bauers-Pit 2.87
Fette-Bos 2.88

Adjusted ERA
Turner-Bos 148
Melton-NY 146
Dean-StL 144
Mungo-Bro 144
Bauers-Pit 138

Opponents' Batting Avg.
Mungo-Bro 229
Grissom-Cin 232
Melton-NY 233
Turner-Bos 235
Carleton-Chi 236

Opponents' On Base Pct.
Turner-Bos 272
Melton-NY 276
Castleman-NY 283
Root-Chi 287
Dean-StL 287

Starter Runs
Turner-Bos 43.7
Melton-NY 35.8
Fette-Bos 29.6
MacFayden-Bos 27.0
Dean-StL 26.7

Adjusted Starter Runs
Melton-NY 33.2
Turner-Bos 32.5
Dean-StL 26.2
Mungo-Bro 23.0
Bauers-Pit 22.8

Clutch Pitching Index
Johnson-StL 128
Brandt-Pit 124
Weiland-StL 115
Frankhouse-Bro 113
MacFayden-Bos 112

Relief Runs
Coffman-NY 7.8
Hutchinson-Bos 2.0

Adjusted Relief Runs
Coffman-NY 7.0

Relief Ranking
Coffman-NY 9.2

Total Pitcher Index
Turner-Bos 3.7
Melton-NY 3.3
Mungo-Bro 3.0
Bauers-Pit 2.7
Dean-StL 2.6

Total Baseball Ranking
Bartell-NY 6.2
Medwick-StL 6.0
Herman-Chi 5.1
Camilli-Phi 4.6
Ott-NY 3.9

TEAM	G	W	L	PCT	GB	R	OR	AB	H	2B	3B	HR	BB	SO	AVG	OBP	SLG	PRO	/A	BR	/A	PF	CHI	RC	TA	SB	CS	SBA	SBR
NY	157	102	52	.662		979	671	5487	1554	282	73	174	709	607	.283	.369	.456	.825	114	112	96	102	103	952	.833	60	36	63	-3
DET	155	89	65	.578	13	935	841	5516	1611	309	62	150	656	711	.292	.370	.452	.822	113	106	31	109	99	947	.826	89	45	66	0
CHI	154	86	68	.558	16	780	730	5277	1478	280	76	67	549	447	.280	.350	.400	.750	95	-37	-57	103	103	763	.717	70	34	67	1
CLE	156	83	71	.539	19	817	768	5353	1499	304	76	103	570	551	.280	.352	.423	.775	101	4	24	98	101	812	.751	76	51	60	-7
BOS	154	80	72	.526	21	821	775	5354	1506	269	64	100	601	557	.281	.357	.411	.768	100	0	-25	103	101	804	.744	79	61	56	-12
WAS	158	73	80	.477	28.5	757	841	5578	1559	245	84	47	591	503	.279	.351	.379	.730	90	-73	-25	94	99	767	.688	61	35	64	-2
PHI	154	54	97	.358	46.5	699	854	5228	1398	278	60	94	583	557	.267	.341	.397	.738	92	-63	-14	94	97	732	.712	95	48	66	0
STL	156	46	108	.299	56	715	1023	5510	1573	327	44	71	514	510	.285	.348	.399	.747	94	-46	-35	99	93	780	.696	30	27	53	-6
TOT	622					6503		43303	12178	2294	539	806	4773	4443	.281	.355	.415	.770								560	337	62	-33

TEAM	CG	SHO	SV	IP	H	H/G	HR	BB	BB/G	SO	SO/G	ERA	/A	OAVG	OOBA	PR	/A	PF	CPI	FA	E	DP	FW	PW	BW	SBW	DIF
NY	82	15	21	1396.0	1417	9.1	92	506	3.3	652	4.2	3.65	123	.261	.321	150	130	97	103	.972	170	134	.0	11.9	8.8	.1	4.1
DET	70	6	11	1378.0	1521	9.9	102	635	4.1	485	3.2	4.87	102	.279	.352	-38	15	108	95	.976	147	149	1.4	1.4	2.8	.4	6.0
CHI	70	15	21	1351.3	1435	9.6	115	532	3.5	533	3.5	4.17	113	.272	.336	67	80	102	104	.971	174	173	-.2	7.3	-5.2	.5	6.6
CLE	64	4	15	1364.7	1529	10.1	61	566	3.7	630	4.2	4.39	102	.285	.350	34	10	97	102	.974	159	153	.7	.9	2.2	-.3	2.4
BOS	74	6	14	1366.3	1520	10.0	92	597	3.9	682	4.5	4.48	106	.279	.347	21	37	102	100	.970	177	139	-.4	3.4	-2.3	-.7	4.0
WAS	75	5	14	1398.7	1498	9.6	96	671	4.3	524	3.4	4.58	96	.274	.352	7	-25	96	99	.972	170	181	.0	-2.3	-2.3	.2	.8
PHI	65	6	9	1335.0	1490	10.0	105	613	4.1	469	3.2	4.85	92	.280	.351	-34	-60	96	97	.967	198	150	-1.6	-5.5	-1.3	.4	-13.5
STL	55	2	8	1363.0	1768	11.7	143	653	4.3	468	3.1	6.00	80	.315	.383	-209	-185	103	100	.972	173	166	-.1	-17.0	-3.2	-.2	-10.5
TOT	555	59	113	10953.0		10.0			3.9		3.7	4.62		.281	.355					.972	1368	1245					

Runs		Hits		Doubles		Triples		Home Runs		Total Bases	
DiMaggio-NY	151	Bell-StL	218	Bell-StL	51	Walker-Chi	16	DiMaggio-NY	46	DiMaggio-NY	418
Rolfe-NY	143	DiMaggio-NY	215	Greenberg-Det	49	Kreevich-Chi	16	Greenberg-Det	40	Greenberg-Det	397
Gehrig-NY	138	Walker-Det	213	Moses-Phi	48	Stone-Was	15	Gehrig-NY	37	Gehrig-NY	366
Greenberg-Det	137	Lewis-Was	210	Vosmik-StL	47	DiMaggio-NY	15	Foxx-Bos	36	Moses-Phi	357
Gehringer-Det	133	Gehringer-Det	209	Lary-Cle	46	Greenberg-Det	14	York-Det	35	Trosky-Cle	329

Runs Batted In		Runs Produced		Bases On Balls		Batting Average		On Base Percentage		Slugging Average	
Greenberg-Det	183	Greenberg-Det	280	Gehrig-NY	127	Gehringer-Det	.371	Gehrig-NY	.473	DiMaggio-NY	.673
DiMaggio-NY	167	DiMaggio-NY	272	Greenberg-Det	102	Gehrig-NY	.351	Gehringer-Det	.458	Greenberg-Det	.668
Gehrig-NY	159	Gehrig-NY	260	Foxx-Bos	99	DiMaggio-NY	.346	Greenberg-Det	.436	Gehrig-NY	.643
Dickey-NY	133	Gehringer-Det	215	Johnson-Phi	98	Bonura-Chi	.345	Johnson-Phi	.425	Bonura-Chi	.573
Trosky-Cle	128	Foxx-Bos	202	Clift-StL	98	Travis-Was	.344	Dickey-NY	.417	Dickey-NY	.570

Production		Adjusted Production		Batter Runs		Adjusted Batter Runs		Clutch Hitting Index		Runs Created	
Gehrig-NY	1.116	Gehrig-NY	175	Gehrig-NY	73.3	Gehrig-NY	71.6	Hayes-Chi	146	Gehrig-NY	181
Greenberg-Det	1.105	DiMaggio-NY	166	Greenberg-Det	67.2	Greenberg-Det	59.6	Higgins-Bos	138	Greenberg-Det	178
DiMaggio-NY	1.085	Greenberg-Det	160	DiMaggio-NY	61.3	Greenberg-Det	58.8	Myer-Was	135	DiMaggio-NY	173
Dickey-NY	.987	Johnson-Phi	155	Gehringer-Det	44.0	Johnson-Phi	39.8	Greenberg-Det	128	Gehringer-Det	140
Bonura-Chi	.984	Dickey-NY	144	Dickey-NY	37.5	Clift-StL	37.1	Hale-Cle	127	Clift-StL	134

Total Average		Stolen Bases		Stolen Base Average		Stolen Base Runs		Fielding Runs		Total Player Rating	
Gehrig-NY	1.347	Chapman-Was-Bos	35	Hill-Was-Phi	81.8	Clift-StL	3.3	Clift-StL	40.1	Clift-StL	7.1
Greenberg-Det	1.285	Werber-Phi	35	Walker-Det	76.7	Hill-Was-Phi	3.0	Hayes-Chi	23.4	DiMaggio-NY	5.5
DiMaggio-NY	1.207	Walker-Det	23	Pytlak-Cle	76.2	Werber-Phi	2.7	Hale-Cle	16.2	Gehringer-Det	4.5
Johnson-Phi	1.104			Chapman-Was-Bos	74.5	Walker-Det	2.7	Appling-Chi	13.6	Dickey-NY	4.2
Gehringer-Det	1.100			Werber-Phi	72.9	Kreevich-Chi	2.4	Johnson-Phi	9.7	Gehrig-NY	4.2

Wins		Win Percentage		Games		Complete Games		Shutouts		Saves	
Gomez-NY	21	Allen-Cle	.938	Brown-Chi	53	Ferrell-Bos-Was	26	Gomez-NY	6	Brown-Chi	18
Ruffing-NY	20	Stratton-Chi	.750	Wilson-Bos	51	Gomez-NY	25	Stratton-Chi	5	Murphy-NY	10
Lawson-Det	18	Ruffing-NY	.741	Newsom-Was-Bos	41	Ruffing-NY	22	Whitehead-Chi	4	Wilson-Bos	7
Grove-Bos	17	Lawson-Det	.720	Kelley-Phi	41	Grove-Bos	21	Ruffing-NY	4	Malone-NY	6
Auker-Det	17	Gomez-NY	.656	Heving-Cle	40	DeShong-Was	20	Appleton-Was	4		

Innings Pitched		Fewest Hits/Game		Fewest BB/Game		Strikeouts		Strikeouts/Game		Wins Above Team	
Ferrell-Bos-Was	281	Gomez-NY	7.54	Stratton-Chi	2.02	Gomez-NY	194	Gomez-NY	6.28	Allen-Cle	7.0
Gomez-NY	278	Stratton-Chi	7.75	Hudlin-Cle	2.20	Newsom-Was-Bos	166	Wilson-Bos	5.58	Lawson-Det	4.7
Newsom-Was-Bos	276	Smith-Phi	8.13	Marcum-Bos	2.30	Grove-Bos	153	Newsom-Was-Bos	5.41	Stratton-Chi	4.7
DeShong-Was	264	Allen-Cle	8.17	Ruffing-NY	2.39	Feller-Cle	150	Grove-Bos	5.26	Grove-Bos	4.0
Grove-Bos	262	Ruffing-NY	8.51	Lyons-Chi	2.40	Bridges-Det	138	Bridges-Det	5.07	Ruffing-NY	3.6

Earned Run Average		Adjusted ERA		Opponents' Batting Avg.		Opponents' On Base Pct.		Starter Runs		Adjusted Starter Runs	
Gomez-NY	2.33	Stratton-Chi	196	Gomez-NY	.223	Stratton-Chi	.278	Gomez-NY	70.7	Gomez-NY	66.7
Stratton-Chi	2.40	Gomez-NY	193	Stratton-Chi	.234	Gomez-NY	.285	Grove-Bos	46.5	Grove-Bos	49.6
Allen-Cle	2.55	Allen-Cle	175	Smith-Phi	.242	Ruffing-NY	.294	Ruffing-NY	46.4	Ruffing-NY	42.8
Ruffing-NY	2.99	Grove-Bos	156	Allen-Cle	.244	Lee-Chi	.308	Stratton-Chi	40.7	Stratton-Chi	42.2
Grove-Bos	3.02	Ruffing-NY	150	Ruffing-NY	.247	Allen-Cle	.311	Allen-Cle	39.8	Allen-Cle	36.8

Clutch Pitching Index		Relief Runs		Adjusted Relief Runs		Relief Ranking		Total Pitcher Index		Total Baseball Ranking	
Allen-Cle	120	Brown-Chi	13.3	Brown-Chi	14.3	Brown-Chi	23.8	Gomez-NY	6.3	Clift-StL	7.1
Whitehead-Chi	120	Cohen-Was	9.2	Cohen-Was	8.0	Cohen-Was	9.1	Grove-Bos	4.6	Gomez-NY	6.3
Wilson-Bos	115	Murphy-NY	5.5	Murphy-NY	3.9	Murphy-NY	6.2	Stratton-Chi	4.3	DiMaggio-NY	5.5
Knott-StL	112	Fink-Phi	5.1	Fink-Phi	3.5	Fink-Phi	1.3	Ruffing-NY	4.0	Grove-Bos	4.6
Grove-Bos	111	Wyatt-Cle	1.5	Wyatt-Cle	.2	Wyatt-Cle	.1	Auker-Det	3.9	Gehringer-Det	4.5

TEAM	G	W	L	PCT	GB	R	OR	AB	H	2B	3B	HR	BB	SO	AVG	OBP	SLG	PRO	/A	BR	/A	PF	CHI	RC	TA	SB	CS	SBA SBR
CHI	154	89	63	.586		713	598	5333	1435	242	70	65	522	476	.269	.338	.377	.715	103	25	-8	105	100	689	.644	49		
PIT	152	86	64	.573	2	707	630	5422	1511	265	66	65	485	409	.279	.340	.388	.728	107	48	47	100	96	727	.655	47		
NY	152	83	67	.553	5	705	637	5255	1424	210	36	125	465	528	.271	.334	.396	.730	107	46	23	103	98	715	.662	31		
CIN	151	82	68	.547	6	723	634	5391	1495	251	57	110	366	518	.277	.327	.406	.733	107	43	59	98	101	720	.648	19		
BOS	153	77	75	.507	12	561	618	5250	1311	199	39	54	424	548	.250	.309	.333	.642	82	-118	-38	88	103	549	.551	49		
STL	156	71	80	.470	17.5	725	721	5528	1542	288	74	91	412	492	.279	.331	.407	.738	109	56	-21	111	97	752	.665	55		
BRO	151	69	80	.463	18.5	704	710	5142	1322	225	79	61	611	615	.257	.338	.367	.705	100	13	42	96	103	671	.656	66		
PHI	151	45	105	.300	43	550	840	5192	1318	233	29	40	423	507	.254	.312	.333	.645	83	-110	-111	100	101	549	.550	38		
TOT	610					5388		42513	11358	1913	450	611	3708	4093	.267	.329	.376	.705								354		

TEAM	CG	SHO	SV	IP	H	H/G	HR	BB	BB/G	SO	SO/G	ERA	/A	OAVG	OOBA	PR	/A	PF	CPI	FA	E	DP	FW	PW	BW	SBW	DIF
CHI	67	16	18	1388.0	1414	9.2	71	454	2.9	583	3.8	3.38	115	.262	.316	62	78	103	105	.978	135	151	2.1	7.8	-.8		3.8
PIT	57	9	15	1379.7	1406	9.2	71	432	2.8	557	3.6	3.46	108	.262	.312	50	41	99	102	.974	163	168	.5	4.1	4.7		1.7
NY	59	9	18	1347.7	1370	9.1	87	389	2.6	497	3.3	3.62	107	.262	.309	24	35	102	98	.973	168	147	.2	3.5	2.3		2.0
CIN	72	11	16	1361.7	1329	8.8	75	463	3.1	542	3.6	3.62	100	.254	.310	24	0	96	94	.971	172	133	-.0	.0	5.9		1.1
BOS	83	15	12	1377.7	1375	9.0	66	465	3.0	413	2.7	3.40	99	.258	.313	59	-5	89	102	.972	173	136	-.1	-.5	-3.8		5.4
STL	58	10	16	1385.0	1482	9.6	77	474	3.1	534	3.5	3.84	109	.272	.325	-8	55	111	101	.967	199	145	-1.7	5.5	-2.1		-6.3
BRO	56	13	14	1330.7	1464	9.9	88	446	3.0	469	3.2	4.07	89	.277	.329	-42	-66	96	100	.973	157	148	.8	-6.6	4.2		-3.9
PHI	68	3	6	1328.3	1516	10.3	76	582	3.9	492	3.3	4.93	81	.285	.351	-169	-137	106	91	.966	201	135	-1.8	-13.8	-11.2		-3.3
TOT	520	86	115	10898.7		9.4			3.1		3.4	3.78		.267	.329					.972	1368	1163					

Runs
Ott-NY 116
Hack-Chi 109
Camilli-Bro 106
Goodman-Cin 103
Medwick-StL 100

Hits
McCormick-Cin 209
Hack-Chi 195
L.Waner-Pit 194
Medwick-StL 190
Mize-StL 179

Doubles
Medwick-StL 47
McCormick-Cin 40
Young-Pit 36
Martin-Phi 36

Triples
Mize-StL 16
Gutteridge-StL 15
Suhr-Pit 14
Riggs-Cin 13
Koy-Bro 13

Home Runs
Ott-NY 36
Goodman-Cin 30
Mize-StL 27
Camilli-Bro 24
Rizzo-Pit 23

Total Bases
Mize-StL 326
Medwick-StL 316
Ott-NY 307
Goodman-Cin 303
Rizzo-Pit 285

Runs Batted In
Medwick-StL 122
Ott-NY 116
Rizzo-Pit 111
McCormick-Cin 106
Mize-StL 102

Runs Produced
Medwick-StL 201
Ott-NY 196
McCormick-Cin 190
Rizzo-Pit 185
Camilli-Bro 182

Bases On Balls
Camilli-Bro 119
Ott-NY 118
Vaughan-Pit 104
Hack-Chi 94
Suhr-Pit 87

Batting Average
Lombardi-Cin 342
Mize-StL 337
McCormick-Cin 327
Medwick-StL 322
Vaughan-Pit 322

On Base Percentage
Ott-NY 442
Vaughan-Pit 433
Mize-StL 422
Hack-Chi 411
Suhr-Pit 394

Slugging Average
Mize-StL 614
Ott-NY 583
Medwick-StL 536
Goodman-Cin 533
Lombardi-Cin 524

Production
Mize-StL 1.036
Ott-NY 1.024
Lombardi-Cin 915
Medwick-StL 905
Goodman-Cin 901

Adjusted Production
Ott-NY 174
Mize-StL 163
Lombardi-Cin 153
Goodman-Cin 149
Camilli-Bro 147

Batter Runs
Ott-NY 61.9
Mize-StL 59.2
Vaughan-Pit 36.4
Medwick-StL 34.4
Goodman-Cin 33.5

Adjusted Batter Runs
Ott-NY 59.5
Mize-StL 51.4
Vaughan-Pit 36.3
Goodman-Cin 35.3
Camilli-Bro 34.7

Clutch Hitting Index
Durocher-Bro 146
Arnovich-Phi 139
Lavagetto-Bro 135
Todd-Pit 132
Young-Pit 129

Runs Created
Ott-NY 149
Mize-StL 141
Hack-Chi 119
Goodman-Cin 116
Vaughan-Pit 115

Total Average
Ott-NY 1.164
Mize-StL 1.104
Camilli-Bro 964
Vaughan-Pit 960
Goodman-Cin 908

Stolen Bases
Hack-Chi 16
Lavagetto-Bro 15
Koy-Bro 15
Vaughan-Pit 14
Gutteridge-StL 14

Stolen Base Average

Stolen Base Runs

Fielding Runs
Young-Pit 32.2
Herman-Chi 24.8
Bartell-NY 23.3
Vaughan-Pit 18.7
Arnovich-Phi 18.5

Total Player Rating
Vaughan-Pit 6.4
Ott-NY 5.4
Young-Pit 3.7
Mize-StL 3.7
Goodman-Cin 3.6

Wins
Lee-Chi 22
Derringer-Cin 21
Bryant-Chi 19
Weiland-StL 16

Win Percentage
Lee-Chi 710
Bryant-Chi 633
Brown-Pit 625
VanderMeer-Cin 600
Derringer-Cin 600

Games
Coffman-NY 51
Brown-Pit 51
McGee-StL 47
Mulcahy-Phi 46

Complete Games
Derringer-Cin 26
Turner-Bos 22
Walters-Phi-Cin 20
MacFayden-Bos 19
Lee-Chi 19

Shutouts
Lee-Chi 9
MacFayden-Bos 5
Warneke-StL 4
Schumacher-NY 4
Derringer-Cin 4

Saves
Coffman-NY 12
Root-Chi 8
Hamlin-Bro 6
Errickson-Bos 6

Innings Pitched
Derringer-Cin 307
Lee-Chi 291
Bryant-Chi 270
Turner-Bos 268
Mulcahy-Phi 267

Fewest Hits/Game
VanderMeer-Cin 7.08
Bauers-Pit 7.67
Bryant-Chi 7.83
MacFayden-Bos 8.51
Hubbell-NY 8.60

Fewest BB/Game
Davis-StL 1.40
Derringer-Cin 1.44
Hubbell-NY 1.66
Root-Chi 1.68
Turner-Bos 1.81

Strikeouts
Bryant-Chi 135
Derringer-Cin 132
VanderMeer-Cin 125
Lee-Chi 121

Strikeouts/Game
Hubbell-NY 5.23
VanderMeer-Cin 5.00
Weiland-StL 4.62
Bryant-Chi 4.50

Wins Above Team
Lee-Chi 5.4
Tamulis-Bro 3.7
Weiland-StL 3.6
Warneke-StL 3.3
Klinger-Pit 2.9

Earned Run Average
Lee-Chi 2.66
Root-Chi 2.85
Derringer-Cin 2.93
MacFayden-Bos 2.95
Klinger-Pit 3.00

Adjusted ERA
Lee-Chi 146
Root-Chi 136
McGee-StL 131
Hubbell-NY 126
Bryant-Chi 125

Opponents' Batting Avg.
VanderMeer-Cin 213
Bauers-Pit 233
Bryant-Chi 235
MacFayden-Bos 247
Schumacher-NY 248

Opponents' On Base Pct.
Hubbell-NY 281
Derringer-Cin 288
Root-Chi 290
Lohrman-NY 293
Turner-Bos 294

Starter Runs
Lee-Chi 36.3
Derringer-Cin 29.1
Bryant-Chi 20.5
MacFayden-Bos 20.5
Bauers-Pit 19.2

Adjusted Starter Runs
Lee-Chi 39.6
McGee-StL 23.9
Derringer-Cin 23.8
Bryant-Chi 23.6
Root-Chi 18.5

Clutch Pitching Index
Lee-Chi 119
Pressnell-Bro 111
Blanton-Pit 111
Tamulis-Bro 110
Fette-Bos 110

Relief Runs
Brown-NY 19.8
Russell-Chi 4.9
Coffman-NY 3.7

Adjusted Relief Runs
Brown-NY 20.6
Russell-Chi 6.0
Coffman-NY 4.6
Shoun-StL 6

Relief Ranking
Brown-NY 19.0
Coffman-NY 5.6
Russell-Chi 4.1
Shoun-StL 6

Total Pitcher Index
Lee-Chi 4.4
Bryant-Chi 2.6
McGee-StL 2.5
Derringer-Cin 2.2
Brown-NY 2.0

Total Baseball Ranking
Vaughan-Pit 6.4
Ott-NY 5.4
Lee-Chi 4.4
Young-Pit 3.7
Mize-StL 3.7

TEAM	G	W	L	PCT	GB	R	OR	AB	H	2B	3B	HR	BB	SO	AVG	OBP	SLG	PRO	/A	BR	/A	PF	CHI	RC	TA	SB	CS	SBA	SBR
NY	157	99	53	.651		966	710	5410	1480	283	63	174	749	616	.274	.366	.446	.812	110	77	31	105	103	926	.831	91	28	76	11
BOS	150	88	61	.591	9.5	902	751	5230	1566	298	56	98	650	463	.299	.378	.434	.812	110	87	67	102	99	881	.804	55	51	52	-13
CLE	153	86	66	.566	13	847	782	5356	1506	300	89	113	550	605	.281	.350	.434	.784	102	9	19	99	102	832	.765	83	36	70	3
DET	155	84	70	.545	16	862	795	5270	1434	219	52	137	695	581	.272	.359	.411	.770	99	0	-1	100	104	813	.764	76	41	65	-1
WAS	152	75	76	.497	23.5	814	873	5474	1602	278	72	85	573	379	.293	.362	.416	.778	101	12	55	95	95	845	.751	65	37	64	-2
CHI	149	65	83	.439	32	709	752	5199	1439	239	55	67	514	489	.277	.343	.383	.726	88	-90	-71	98	101	700	.677	56	39	59	-6
STL	156	55	97	.362	44	755	962	5333	1498	273	36	92	590	528	.281	.355	.397	.752	95	-37	-37	100	95	774	.717	51	40	56	-8
PHI	154	53	99	.349	46	726	956	5229	1410	243	62	98	605	590	.270	.348	.396	.744	93	-56	-64	101	96	741	.714	65	53	55	-11
TOT	613					6581		42501	11935	2133	485	864	4926	4251	.281	.358	.415	.773								542	325	63	-31

TEAM	CG	SHO	SV	IP	H	H/G	HR	BB	BB/G	SO	SO/G	ERA	/A	OAVG	OOBA	PR	/A	PF	CPI	FA	E	DP	FW	PW	BW	SBW	DIF
NY	91	11	13	1382.0	1436	9.4	85	566	3.7	567	3.7	3.91	124	.267	.334	134	145	102	106	.973	169	177	.2	13.1	2.8	1.4	5.5
BOS	67	10	15	1316.3	1472	10.2	102	528	3.6	484	3.3	4.46	108	.281	.344	48	49	100	103	.968	190	172	-1.0	4.4	6.1	-.8	4.8
CLE	68	5	17	1353.0	1416	9.4	100	681	4.5	717	4.8	4.60	102	.268	.351	29	12	98	99	.974	151	145	1.2	1.1	1.7	.6	5.3
DET	75	3	11	1348.3	1532	10.2	110	608	4.1	435	2.9	4.79	99	.286	.355	0	-5	99	103	.976	147	172	1.5	-.5	-.0	.3	5.8
WAS	59	6	11	1360.3	1472	9.7	92	655	4.1	515	3.4	4.94	94	.275	.352	-22	-53	96	94	.970	180	179	-.4	-4.8	5.0	.2	-.5
CHI	83	5	9	1316.3	1449	9.9	101	550	3.8	432	3.0	4.36	108	.279	.344	62	51	98	106	.967	196	155	-1.3	4.6	-6.4	-.2	-5.7
STL	71	3	7	1344.7	1584	10.6	132	737	4.9	632	4.2	5.80	85	.294	.377	-151	-129	103	96	.975	145	163	1.6	-11.7	-3.3	-.4	-7.2
PHI	56	4	12	1324.0	1573	10.7	142	599	4.1	473	3.2	5.48	91	.291	.359	-101	-69	105	96	.965	206	119	-1.9	-6.2	-5.8	-.6	-8.5
TOT	570	47	95	10745.0		10.0			4.1		3.6	4.79		.281	.358					.971	1384	1282					

Runs
Greenberg-Det 144
Foxx-Bos 139
Gehringer-Det 133
Rolfe-NY 132
DiMaggio-NY 129

Hits
Vosmik-Bos 201
Cramer-Bos 198
Almada-Was-StL 197
Foxx-Bos 197
Rolfe-NY 196

Doubles
Cronin-Bos 51
McQuinn-StL 42
Trosky-Cle 40
Chapman-Bos 40
Vosmik-Bos 37

Triples
Heath-Cle 18
Averill-Cle 15
DiMaggio-NY 13

Home Runs
Greenberg-Det 58
Foxx-Bos 50
Clift-StL 34
York-Det 33
DiMaggio-NY 32

Total Bases
Foxx-Bos 398
Greenberg-Det 380
DiMaggio-NY 348
Johnson-Phi 311
Heath-Cle 302

Runs Batted In
Foxx-Bos 175
Greenberg-Det 146
DiMaggio-NY 140
York-Det 127
Clift-StL 118

Runs Produced
Foxx-Bos 264
DiMaggio-NY 237
Greenberg-Det 232
Gehringer-Det 220
Clift-StL 203

Bases On Balls
Greenberg-Det 119
Foxx-Bos 119
Clift-StL 118
Gehringer-Det 113
Gehrig-NY 107

Batting Average
Foxx-Bos 349
Heath-Cle 343
Chapman-Bos 340
Myer-Was 336
Travis-Was 335

On Base Percentage
Foxx-Bos 462
Myer-Was 454
Greenberg-Det 438
Averill-Cle 429
Cronin-Bos 428

Slugging Average
Foxx-Bos 704
Greenberg-Det 683
Heath-Cle 602
DiMaggio-NY 581
York-Det 579

Production
Foxx-Bos 1.166
Greenberg-Det . . . 1.122
York-Det 995
Heath-Cle 985
Dickey-NY 981

Adjusted Production
Foxx-Bos 184
Greenberg-Det 176
York-Det 146
Heath-Cle 145
Clift-StL 143

Batter Runs
Foxx-Bos 78.1
Greenberg-Det 66.0
Clift-StL 37.6
Cronin-Bos 34.8
York-Det 33.9

Adjusted Batter Runs
Foxx-Bos 75.9
Greenberg-Det 65.8
Clift-StL 37.6
York-Det 33.8
Averill-Cle 32.7

Clutch Hitting Index
Higgins-Bos 166
Heffner-StL 152
Doerr-Bos 127
Radcliff-Chi 126
R.Ferrell-Was 123

Runs Created
Foxx-Bos 189
Greenberg-Det 172
DiMaggio-NY 136
Clift-StL 133
Gehrig-NY 131

Total Average
Foxx-Bos 1.403
Greenberg-Det . . . 1.319
Clift-StL 1.117
York-Det 1.110
Dickey-NY 1.083

Stolen Bases
Crosetti-NY 27
Lary-Cle 23
Werber-Phi 19
Lewis-Was 17
Fox-Det 16

Stolen Base Average
Lary-Cle 79.3
Fox-Det 69.6
Crosetti-NY 69.2
Lewis-Was 65.4
Werber-Phi 55.9

Stolen Base Runs
Gehringer-Det 3.6
Rolfe-NY 3.3
Lary-Cle 3.3
Hale-Cle 1.8

Fielding Runs
Crosetti-NY 17.7
Gordon-NY 16.9
Clift-StL 14.4
Doerr-Bos 8.4
Sullivan-StL 8.2

Total Player Rating
Foxx-Bos 5.3
Clift-StL 5.0
Greenberg-Det 4.4
Cronin-Bos 4.2
Gehringer-Det 3.5

Wins
Ruffing-NY 21
Newsom-StL 20
Gomez-NY 18
Harder-Cle 17
Feller-Cle 17

Win Percentage
Ruffing-NY 750
Pearson-NY 696
Harder-Cle 630
Stratton-Chi 625
Feller-Cle 607

Games
Humphries-Cle 45
Newsom-StL 44
Smith-Phi 43
Bagby-Bos 43
Appleton-Was 43

Complete Games
Newsom-StL 31
Ruffing-NY 22
Gomez-NY 20
Feller-Cle 20
Caster-Phi 20

Shutouts
Gomez-NY 4
Wilson-Bos 3
Ruffing-NY 3
Leonard-Was 3

Saves
Murphy-NY 11
McKain-Bos 6
Humphries-Cle 6
Potter-Phi 5
Appleton-Was 5

Innings Pitched
Newsom-StL 330
Caster-Phi 281
Feller-Cle 278
Ruffing-NY 247
Lee-Chi 245

Fewest Hits/Game
Feller-Cle 7.28
Allen-Cle 8.51
Pearson-NY 8.82
Rigney-Chi 8.84
Hadley-NY 8.89

Fewest BB/Game
Leonard-Was 2.14
Harder-Cle 2.33
Lyons-Chi 2.40
Chandler-NY 2.46
Thomas-Phi 2.63

Strikeouts
Feller-Cle 240
Newsom-StL 226
H.Mills-StL 134
Gomez-NY 129
Ruffing-NY 127

Strikeouts/Game
Feller-Cle 7.77
Newsom-StL 6.16
H.Mills-StL 5.74
Grove-Bos 5.43
Allen-Cle 5.04

Wins Above Team
Newsom-StL 6.5
Ruffing-NY 4.6
Stratton-Chi 4.5
Grove-Bos 4.4
Caster-Phi 3.3

Earned Run Average
Grove-Bos 3.07
Ruffing-NY 3.32
Gomez-NY 3.35
Leonard-Was 3.43
Lee-Chi 3.49

Adjusted ERA
Grove-Bos 156
Ruffing-NY 147
Gomez-NY 145
Lee-Chi 135
Hadley-NY 135

Opponents' Batting Avg.
Feller-Cle 220
Allen-Cle 246
Hadley-NY 254
Stratton-Chi 255
Rigney-Chi 256

Opponents' On Base Pct.
Leonard-Was 299
Stratton-Chi 312
Grove-Bos 314
Ruffing-NY 314
Chandler-NY 315

Starter Runs
Ruffing-NY 40.4
Gomez-NY 38.2
Lee-Chi 35.4
Leonard-Was 33.7
Grove-Bos 31.3

Adjusted Starter Runs
Ruffing-NY 42.4
Gomez-NY 40.1
Lee-Chi 33.3
Grove-Bos 31.4
Leonard-Was 28.6

Clutch Pitching Index
Lyons-Chi 125
Gill-Det 119
Grove-Bos 118
Rigney-Chi 117
Ruffing-NY 110

Relief Runs
Murphy-NY 5.4
McKain-Bos 3.2

Adjusted Relief Runs
Murphy-NY 6.2
McKain-Bos 3.3

Relief Ranking
Murphy-NY 7.8
McKain-Bos 3.1

Total Pitcher Index
Ruffing-NY 4.8
Gomez-NY 3.8
Lee-Chi 3.6
Leonard-Was 2.9
Grove-Bos 2.9

Total Baseball Ranking
Foxx-Bos 5.3
Clift-StL 5.0
Ruffing-NY 4.8
Greenberg-Det 4.4
Cronin-Bos 4.2

TEAM	G	W	L	PCT	GB	R	OR	AB	H	2B	3B	HR	BB	SO	AVG	OBP	SLG	PRO	/A	BR	/A	PF	CHI	RC	TA	SB	CS	SBA	SBR
CIN	156	97	57	.630		767	595	5378	1493	269	60	98	500	538	.278	.343	.405	.748	107	50	28	103	101	759	.690	46			
STL	155	92	61	.601	4.5	779	633	5447	1601	332	62	98	475	566	.294	.354	.432	.786	117	122	86	105	94	834	.731	44			
BRO	157	84	69	.549	12.5	708	645	5350	1420	265	57	78	564	631	.265	.338	.380	.718	99	0	-50	107	101	697	.661	59			
CHI	156	84	70	.545	13	724	678	5293	1407	263	62	91	523	553	.266	.336	.391	.727	101	9	3	101	101	702	.670	61			
NY	151	77	74	.510	18.5	703	685	5129	1395	211	38	116	498	499	.272	.340	.396	.736	104	28	34	99	101	683	.665	26			
PIT	153	68	85	.444	28.5	666	721	5269	1453	261	60	63	477	420	.276	.338	.384	.722	100	3	5	100	97	687	.650	44			
BOS	152	64	88	.417	32.5	572	659	5286	1395	199	39	56	366	494	.264	.314	.348	.662	84	-116	-60	92	103	575	.566	41			
PHI	152	45	106	.298	50.5	553	856	5133	1341	232	40	49	421	486	.261	.318	.351	.669	86	-97	-57	94	98	570	.580	47			
TOT	616					5472		42285	11505	2032	418	649	3824	4187	.272	.335	.386	.722								368			

TEAM	CG	SHO	SV	IP	H	H/G	HR	BB	BB/G	SO	SO/G	ERA	/A	OAVG	OOBA	PR	/A	PF	CPI	FA	E	DP	FW	PW	BW	SBW	DIF
CIN	86	13	9	1403.7	1340	8.6	81	499	3.2	637	4.1	3.27	120	.253	.310	100	100	100	104	.974	162	170	.5	10.0	2.8		6.7
STL	45	18	32	1383.3	1377	9.0	76	498	3.2	603	3.9	3.59	112	.261	.318	49	65	103	100	.971	177	140	-.3	6.5	8.6		.7
BRO	69	9	13	1410.3	1431	9.1	93	399	2.5	528	3.4	3.64	114	.265	.308	43	81	106	98	.972	176	157	-.2	8.1	-5.0		4.6
CHI	72	8	13	1391.7	1504	9.7	74	430	2.8	584	3.8	3.80	103	.277	.323	17	17	100	101	.970	186	126	-.7	1.7	.3		5.7
NY	55	7	20	1321.3	1412	9.6	86	477	3.2	505	3.4	4.07	95	.275	.330	-23	-31	99	99	.975	153	151	1.0	-3.1	3.4		.2
PIT	53	10	15	1349.7	1537	10.2	70	423	2.8	464	3.1	4.15	95	.288	.331	-34	-30	101	100	.972	168	153	.2	-3.0	.5		-6.2
BOS	68	11	15	1358.0	1400	9.3	63	513	3.4	430	2.8	3.71	98	.268	.324	30	-9	93	101	.971	181	178	-.5	-.9	-6.0		-5.1
PHI	67	3	12	1328.0	1502	10.2	106	579	3.9	447	3.0	5.17	75	.286	.347	-185	-188	99	90	.970	171	136	.0	-18.8	-5.7		-6.0
TOT	515	79	129	10946.0		9.5			3.1		3.5	3.92		.272	.335					.972	1374	1211					

Runs
Werber-Cin 115
Hack-Chi 112
Herman-Chi 111
Camilli-Bro 105

Hits
McCormick-Cin 209
Medwick-StL 201
Mize-StL 197
Slaughter-StL 193
Brown-StL 192

Doubles
Slaughter-StL 52
Medwick-StL 48
Mize-StL 44
McCormick-Cin 41

Triples
Herman-Chi 18
Goodman-Cin 16
Mize-StL 14
Camilli-Bro 12

Home Runs
Mize-StL 28
Ott-NY 27
Camilli-Bro 26
Leiber-Chi 24
Lombardi-Cin 20

Total Bases
Mize-StL 353
McCormick-Cin 312
Medwick-StL 307
Camilli-Bro 296
Slaughter-StL 291

Runs Batted In
McCormick-Cin 128
Medwick-StL 117
Mize-StL 108
Camilli-Bro 104
Leiber-Chi 88

Runs Produced
McCormick-Cin 209
Medwick-StL 201
Mize-StL 184
Camilli-Bro 183
Herman-Chi 174

Bases On Balls
Camilli-Bro 110
Ott-NY 100
Mize-StL 92
Werber-Cin 91
Lavagetto-Bro 78

Batting Average
Mize-StL 349
McCormick-Cin 332
Medwick-StL 332
P.Waner-Pit 328
Arnovich-Phi 324

On Base Percentage
Ott-NY 449
Mize-StL 444
Camilli-Bro 409
Goodman-Cin 401
Arnovich-Phi 397

Slugging Average
Mize-StL 626
Ott-NY 581
Camilli-Bro 524
Goodman-Cin 515
Medwick-StL 507

Production
Mize-StL 1.070
Ott-NY 1.030
Camilli-Bro 933
Goodman-Cin 916
Medwick-StL 886

Adjusted Production
Ott-NY 176
Mize-StL 176
West-Bos 141
Goodman-Cin 140
Camilli-Bro 139

Batter Runs
Mize-StL 68.6
Ott-NY 45.9
Camilli-Bro 41.8
Leiber-Chi 30.4
Goodman-Cin 29.8

Adjusted Batter Runs
Mize-StL 64.7
Ott-NY 46.5
Camilli-Bro 36.1
Leiber-Chi 30.1
Goodman-Cin 27.9

Clutch Hitting Index
McCormick-Cin 136
Bonura-NY 132
May-Phi 130
Medwick-StL 130
Russell-Chi 125

Runs Created
Mize-StL 162
Camilli-Bro 128
Medwick-StL 114
Ott-NY 112
McCormick-Cin 110

Total Average
Mize-StL 1.194
Ott-NY 1.194
Camilli-Bro 995
Goodman-Cin 941
Frey-Cin 860

Stolen Bases
Handley-Pit 17
Hack-Chi 17
Werber-Cin 15
Lavagetto-Bro 14
Hassett-Bos 13

Stolen Base Average

Stolen Base Runs

Fielding Runs
Danning-NY 18.0
Jurges-NY 17.7
Whitehead-NY 17.5
Slaughter-StL 15.1
Majeski-Bos 13.0

Total Player Rating
Mize-StL 4.2
Ott-NY 3.9
Danning-NY 3.8
Vaughan-Pit 3.4
Frey-Cin 3.3

Wins
Walters-Cin 27
Derringer-Cin 25
Davis-StL 22
Hamlin-Bro 20
Lee-Chi 19

Win Percentage
Derringer-Cin 781
Walters-Cin 711
French-Chi 652
Gumbert-NY 621
Hamlin-Bro 606

Games
Shoun-StL 53
Sewell-Pit 52
Bowman-StL 51
Davis-StL 49
Brown-Pit 47

Complete Games
Walters-Cin 31
Derringer-Cin 28
Lee-Chi 20
Hamlin-Bro 19
Posedel-Bos 18

Shutouts
Fette-Bos 6
Posedel-Bos 5
Derringer-Cin 5
McGee-StL 4

Saves
Shoun-StL 9
Bowman-StL 9
Davis-StL 7
Brown-NY 7
Brown-Pit 7

Innings Pitched
Walters-Cin 319
Derringer-Cin 301
Lee-Chi 282
Passeau-Phi-Chi 274
Hamlin-Bro 270

Fewest Hits/Game
Walters-Cin 7.05
Bowman-StL 7.51
Moore-Cin 8.47
Grissom-Cin 8.47
Hamlin-Bro 8.50

Fewest BB/Game
Derringer-Cin 1.05
Hubbell-NY 1.40
Davis-StL 1.74
Hamlin-Bro 1.80
Root-Chi 1.83

Strikeouts
Passeau-Phi-Chi 137
Walters-Cin 137
Cooper-StL 130
Derringer-Cin 128
Lee-Chi 105

Strikeouts/Game
Cooper-StL 5.55
Tamulis-Bro 4.70
French-Chi 4.55
Passeau-Phi-Chi 4.50
Bowman-StL 4.15

Wins Above Team
Derringer-Cin 7.5
Walters-Cin 5.1
Gumbert-NY 3.8
Posedel-Bos 3.3
French-Chi 3.0

Earned Run Average
Walters-Cin 2.29
Bowman-StL 2.61
Hubbell-NY 2.75
Derringer-Cin 2.93
Casey-Bro 2.93

Adjusted ERA
Walters-Cin 171
Bowman-StL 154
Casey-Bro 142
Hubbell-NY 141
Derringer-Cin 134

Opponents' Batting Avg.
Walters-Cin 220
Bowman-StL 232
Hamlin-Bro 248
Hubbell-NY 249
Grissom-Cin 249

Opponents' On Base Pct.
Hubbell-NY 275
Hamlin-Bro 281
Walters-Cin 284
Derringer-Cin 288
Bowman-StL 292

Starter Runs
Walters-Cin 57.8
Derringer-Cin 33.0
Casey-Bro 24.8
Bowman-StL 24.5
Thompson-Cin 23.1

Adjusted Starter Runs
Walters-Cin 57.7
Derringer-Cin 32.8
Casey-Bro 30.8
Bowman-StL 26.4
Thompson-Cin 23.1

Clutch Pitching Index
Brown-Pit 120
Shoffner-Bos-Cin 115
Casey-Bro 113
Cooper-StL 113
Moore-Cin 113

Relief Runs
Russell-Chi 2.0
Shoun-StL 1.8

Adjusted Relief Runs
Shoun-StL 3.0
Russell-Chi 2.0

Relief Ranking
Russell-Chi 2.0
Shoun-StL 1.6

Total Pitcher Index
Walters-Cin 8.4
Casey-Bro 3.5
Derringer-Cin 3.1
Davis-StL 2.6
Wyatt-Bro 2.5

Total Baseball Ranking
Walters-Cin 8.4
Mize-StL 4.2
Ott-NY 3.9
Danning-NY 3.8
Casey-Bro 3.5

TEAM	G	W	L	PCT	GB	R	OR	AB	H	2B	3B	HR	BB	SO	AVG	OBP	SLG	PRO	/A	BR	/A	PF	CHI	RC	TA	SB	CS	SBA	SBR
NY	152	106	45	.702		967	556	5300	1521	259	55	166	701	543	.287	.374	.451	.825	117	134	203	91	102	923	.817	72	37	66	0
BOS	152	89	62	.589	17	890	795	5308	1543	287	57	124	591	505	.291	.363	.436	.799	110	78	11	108	101	831	.749	42	44	49	-13
CLE	154	87	67	.565	20.5	797	700	5316	1490	291	79	85	557	574	.280	.350	.413	.763	101	4	22	98	99	715	.712	72	46	61	-5
CHI	155	85	69	.552	22.5	755	737	5279	1451	220	56	64	579	502	.275	.349	.374	.723	91	-61	-112	107	102	708	.673	113	61	65	-2
DET	155	81	73	.526	26.5	849	762	5326	1487	277	67	124	620	592	.279	.356	.426	.782	106	43	-46	111	99	821	.748	88	38	70	4
WAS	153	65	87	.428	41.5	702	797	5334	1483	249	79	44	547	460	.278	.346	.379	.725	91	-61	17	90	95	718	.669	94	47	67	0
PHI	153	55	97	.362	51.5	711	1022	5309	1438	282	55	98	503	532	.271	.336	.400	.736	94	-55	-33	97	96	713	.671	60	34	64	-1
STL	156	43	111	.279	64.5	733	1035	5422	1453	242	50	91	559	606	.268	.339	.381	.720	90	-79	-82	100	100	706	.653	48	38	56	-7
TOT	615					6404		42594	11866	2107	498	796	4657	4314	.279	.352	.408	.759								589	345	63	-29

TEAM	CG	SHO	SV	IP	H	H/G	HR	BB	BB/G	SO	SO/G	ERA	/A	OAVG	OOBA	PR	/A	PF	CPI	FA	E	DP	FW	PW	BW	SBW	DIF
NY	87	15	26	1348.7	1208	8.1	85	567	3.8	565	3.8	3.31	119	.240	.313	196	94	85	107	.978	126	159	3.0	8.7	18.7	.3	-.2
BOS	52	4	20	1350.7	1533	10.2	77	543	3.6	539	3.6	4.56	108	.286	.347	9	55	107	102	.970	180	147	.2	5.1	1.0	-.8	8.1
CLE	69	10	13	1364.7	1394	9.2	75	602	4.0	614	4.0	4.08	109	.266	.336	81	55	96	103	.970	180	148	.2	5.1	2.0	-.1	2.9
CHI	62	5	21	1377.0	1470	9.6	99	454	3.0	535	3.5	4.31	114	.274	.325	47	92	106	98	.972	167	140	.8	8.5	-10.3	.2	8.8
DET	64	6	16	1367.3	1430	9.4	104	574	3.8	633	4.2	4.29	118	.267	.334	49	117	110	100	.967	198	147	-.8	10.8	-4.2	.7	-2.5
WAS	72	4	10	1354.7	1420	9.4	75	602	4.0	521	3.5	4.60	92	.270	.339	2	-57	91	94	.966	205	167	-1.1	-5.3	1.6	.3	-6.5
PHI	50	6	12	1342.7	1687	11.3	148	579	3.9	397	2.7	5.79	81	.306	.365	-174	-160	102	99	.964	210	131	-1.4	-14.7	-3.0	.3	-2.1
STL	56	3	3	1371.3	1724	11.3	133	739	4.8	516	3.4	6.01	81	.309	.384	-212	-177	105	100	.968	199	144	-.8	-16.3	-7.6	-.3	-9.0
TOT	512	53	121	10877.0		9.8			3.9		3.6	4.62		.279	.352					.969	1465	1183					

Runs
Rolfe-NY 139
Williams-Bos 131
Foxx-Bos 130
McCosky-Det 120
Johnson-Phi 115

Hits
Rolfe-NY 213
McQuinn-StL 195
Keltner-Cle 191
McCosky-Det 190
Williams-Bos 185

Doubles
Rolfe-NY 46
Williams-Bos 44
Greenberg-Det 42
McQuinn-StL 37
Keltner-Cle 35

Triples
Lewis-Was 16
McCosky-Det 14
McQuinn-StL 13
Campbell-Cle 13

Home Runs
Foxx-Bos 35
Greenberg-Det 33
Williams-Bos 31
DiMaggio-NY 30
Gordon-NY 28

Total Bases
Williams-Bos 344
Foxx-Bos 324
Rolfe-NY 321
McQuinn-StL 318
Greenberg-Det 311

Runs Batted In
Williams-Bos 145
DiMaggio-NY 126
Johnson-Phi 114
Greenberg-Det 112

Runs Produced
Williams-Bos 245
Johnson-Phi 206
Rolfe-NY 205
DiMaggio-NY 204
Foxx-Bos 200

Bases On Balls
Clift-StL 111
Williams-Bos 107
Appling-Chi 105
Selkirk-NY 103
Johnson-Phi 99

Batting Average
DiMaggio-NY 381
Foxx-Bos 360
Johnson-Phi 338
Trosky-Cle 335
Keller-NY 334

On Base Percentage
Foxx-Bos 464
Selkirk-NY 452
DiMaggio-NY 448
Keller-NY 447
Johnson-Phi 440

Slugging Average
Foxx-Bos 694
DiMaggio-NY 671
Greenberg-Det 622
Williams-Bos 609
Trosky-Cle 589

Production
Foxx-Bos 1.158
DiMaggio-NY 1.119
Williams-Bos 1.045
Greenberg-Det 1.042
Trosky-Cle 994

Adjusted Production
DiMaggio-NY 199
Foxx-Bos 177
Selkirk-NY 161
Johnson-Phi 157
Keller-NY 155

Batter Runs
Foxx-Bos 66.1
Williams-Bos 56.3
DiMaggio-NY 56.0
Greenberg-Det 47.3
Johnson-Phi 45.7

Adjusted Batter Runs
DiMaggio-NY 62.0
Foxx-Bos 59.9
Williams-Bos 48.9
Johnson-Phi 48.0
Selkirk-NY 41.2

Clutch Hitting Index
Wright-Was 140
Walker-Chi 131
Keller-NY 128
Vosmik-Bos 127
McNair-Chi 126

Runs Created
Williams-Bos 157
Foxx-Bos 150
DiMaggio-NY 139
Johnson-Phi 138
Greenberg-Det 136

Total Average
Foxx-Bos 1.313
DiMaggio-NY 1.242
Williams-Bos 1.164
Greenberg-Det . . . 1.161
Selkirk-NY 1.138

Stolen Bases
Case-Was 51
Kreevich-Chi 23
Fox-Det 23
McCosky-Det 20

Stolen Base Average
McCosky-Det 83.3
Kuhel-Chi 78.3
Chapman-Cle 75.0
Case-Was 75.0
Walker-Chi 73.9

Stolen Base Runs
Case-Was 5.1
McCosky-Det 3.6
Welaj-Was 2.7
Kuhel-Chi 2.4
Henrich-NY 2.1

Fielding Runs
Doerr-Bos 27.0
Clift-StL 12.4
Kreevich-Chi 11.6
Lewis-Was 10.3
Johnson-Phi 9.9

Total Player Rating
DiMaggio-NY 5.7
Johnson-Phi 5.0
Foxx-Bos 4.6
Williams-Bos 3.8
Dickey-NY 3.7

Wins
Feller-Cle 24
Ruffing-NY 21
Newsom-StL-Det 20
Leonard-Was 20
Bridges-Det 17

Win Percentage
Grove-Bos 789
Ruffing-NY 750
Feller-Cle 727
Leonard-Was 714
Bridges-Det 708

Games
Brown-Chi 61
Dean-Phi 54
Dickman-Bos 48
Heving-Bos 46

Complete Games
Newsom-StL-Det 24
Feller-Cle 24
Ruffing-NY 22
Leonard-Was 21
Grove-Bos 17

Shutouts
Ruffing-NY 5
Feller-Cle 4

Saves
Murphy-NY 19
Brown-Chi 18
Heving-Bos 7
Dean-Phi 7
Appleton-Was 6

Innings Pitched
Feller-Cle 297
Newsom-StL-Det 292
Leonard-Was 269
Lee-Chi 235
Ruffing-NY 233

Fewest Hits/Game
Feller-Cle 6.88
Hadley-NY 7.71
Gomez-NY 7.86
Ruffing-NY 8.15
Chase-Was 8.34

Fewest BB/Game
Lyons-Chi 1.35
Leonard-Was 1.97
Beckmann-Phi 2.38
Lee-Chi 2.68
Grove-Bos 2.73

Strikeouts
Feller-Cle 246
Newsom-StL-Det 192
Bridges-Det 129
Rigney-Chi 119
Chase-Was 118

Strikeouts/Game
Feller-Cle 7.45
Newsom-StL-Det 5.92
Bridges-Det 5.86
Rigney-Chi 4.89
Gomez-NY 4.64

Wins Above Team
Leonard-Was 7.7
Feller-Cle 7.1
Bridges-Det 5.1
Grove-Bos 4.9
Newsom-StL-Det 4.7

Earned Run Average
Grove-Bos 2.54
Lyons-Chi 2.76
Feller-Cle 2.85
Ruffing-NY 2.94
Hadley-NY 2.98

Adjusted ERA
Grove-Bos 194
Lyons-Chi 178
Feller-Cle 156
Bridges-Det 145
Trout-Det 140

Opponents' Batting Avg.
Feller-Cle 210
Gomez-NY 235
Hadley-NY 237
Ruffing-NY 240
Bridges-Det 243

Opponents' On Base Pct.
Lyons-Chi 269
Leonard-Was 297
Ruffing-NY 298
Feller-Cle 299
Grove-Bos 299

Starter Runs
Feller-Cle 58.4
Grove-Bos 44.0
Ruffing-NY 43.6
Lyons-Chi 35.8
Newsom-StL-Det 33.9

Adjusted Starter Runs
Feller-Cle 52.8
Grove-Bos 50.6
Newsom-StL-Det 46.2
Lyons-Chi 41.4
Bridges-Det 34.4

Clutch Pitching Index
Hadley-NY 132
Grove-Bos 126
Trout-Det 116
Harder-Cle 116
Milnar-Cle 110

Relief Runs
Heving-Bos 10.9
Brown-Chi 9.6
Dickman-Bos 2.5
Murphy-NY 1.3
Appleton-Was 9

Adjusted Relief Runs
Heving-Bos 14.6
Brown-Chi 13.4
Dickman-Bos 6.4

Relief Ranking
Brown-Chi 26.0
Heving-Bos 19.3
Dickman-Bos 6.2

Total Pitcher Index
Feller-Cle 5.7
Grove-Bos 4.7
Lyons-Chi 4.5
Newsom-StL-Det 4.1
Bridges-Det 3.4

Total Baseball Ranking
DiMaggio-NY 5.7
Feller-Cle 5.7
Johnson-Phi 5.0
Grove-Bos 4.7
Foxx-Bos 4.6

TEAM	G	W	L	PCT	GB	R	OR	AB	H	2B	3B	HR	BB	SO	AVG	OBP	SLG	PRO	/A	BR	/A	PF	CHI	RC	TA	SB	CS	SBA	SBR
CIN	155	100	53	.654		707	528	5372	1427	264	38	89	453	503	.266	.327	.379	.706	101	6	0	101	102	672	.640	72			
BRO	156	88	65	.575	12	697	621	5470	1421	256	70	93	522	570	.260	.327	.383	.710	102	14	-40	108	98	692	.647	56			
STL	156	84	69	.549	16	747	699	5499	1514	266	61	119	479	610	.275	.336	.411	.747	112	83	68	102	96	764	.699	97			
PIT	156	78	76	.506	22.5	809	783	5466	1511	276	68	76	553	494	.276	.346	.394	.740	111	83	115	95	103	757	.689	69			
CHI	154	75	79	.487	25.5	681	636	5389	1441	272	48	86	482	566	.267	.331	.384	.715	104	25	28	100	96	691	.651	63			
NY	152	72	80	.474	27.5	663	659	5324	1423	201	46	91	453	478	.267	.329	.374	.703	100	3	1	100	98	653	.626	45			
BOS	152	65	87	.428	34.5	623	745	5329	1366	219	50	59	453	581	.256	.311	.349	.660	88	-82	-74	99	107	581	.573	48			
PHI	153	50	103	.327	50	494	750	5137	1225	180	35	75	435	527	.238	.300	.331	.631	80	-133	-114	97	96	512	.540	25			
TOT	617					5421		42986	11328	1934	416	688	3779	4329	.264	.326	.376	.702								475			

TEAM	CG	SHO	SV	IP	H	H/G	HR	BB	BB/G	SO	SO/G	ERA	/A	OAVG	OOBA	PR	/A	PF	CPI	FA	E	DP	FW	PW	BW	SBW	DIF
CIN	91	10	11	1407.7	1263	8.1	73	445	2.8	557	3.6	3.05	123	.239	.294	125	110	98	100	.981	117	158	2.8	11.1	.0		9.6
BRO	65	17	14	1431.7	1366	8.6	101	393	2.5	639	4.0	3.50	117	.250	.296	55	94	106	96	.970	183	110	-.4	9.5	-4.0		6.5
STL	71	10	14	1394.7	1457	9.4	83	488	3.1	550	3.5	3.83	102	.267	.323	2	9	101	102	.971	174	134	.0	.9	6.9		-.3
PIT	49	9	24	1388.3	1569	10.2	72	491	3.2	491	3.2	4.36	84	.283	.337	-79	-110	95	98	.966	217	161	-2.1	-11.1	11.6		2.6
CHI	69	12	14	1392.0	1418	9.2	74	430	2.8	564	3.6	3.54	107	.263	.311	47	39	99	102	.968	199	143	-1.2	3.9	2.8		-7.6
NY	57	12	18	1360.3	1383	9.1	110	473	3.1	606	4.0	3.79	102	.262	.319	8	9	100	104	.977	139	132	1.7	.9	.1		-6.7
BOS	76	9	12	1358.3	1444	9.6	83	573	3.8	435	2.9	4.36	89	.271	.337	-76	-71	101	97	.970	184	169	-.5	-7.2	-7.5		4.1
PHI	66	5	8	1358.0	1429	9.5	92	475	3.1	485	3.2	4.40	89	.269	.324	-83	-72	102	91	.970	181	136	-.3	-7.3	-11.5		-7.4
TOT	544	84	115	11091.0		9.2			3.1		3.5	3.85		.264	.326					.972	1394	1143					

Runs		Hits		Doubles		Triples		Home Runs		Total Bases	
Vaughan-Pit	113	F.McCormick-Cin	191	F.McCormick-Cin	44	Vaughan-Pit	15	Mize-StL	43	Mize-StL	368
Mize-StL	111	Hack-Chi	191	Vaughan-Pit	40	Ross-Bos	14	Nicholson-Chi	25	F.McCormick-Cin	298
Werber-Cin	105	Mize-StL	182	Gleeson-Chi	39	Slaughter-StL	13	Rizzo-Pit-Cin-Phi	24	Medwick-StL-Bro	280
Frey-Cin	102	Vaughan-Pit	178	Hack-Chi	38	Mize-StL	13	Camilli-Bro	23	Camilli-Bro	271
Hack-Chi	101	Medwick-StL-Bro	175	Walker-Bro	37	Camilli-Bro	13			Vaughan-Pit	269

Runs Batted In		Runs Produced		Bases On Balls		Batting Average		On Base Percentage		Slugging Average	
Mize-StL	137	Mize-StL	205	Fletcher-Pit	119	Hack-Chi	.317	Fletcher-Pit	.418	Mize-StL	.636
F.McCormick-Cin	127	Vaughan-Pit	201	Ott-NY	100	Mize-StL	.314	Ott-NY	.407	Nicholson-Chi	.534
VanRobays-Pit	116	F.McCormick-Cin	201	Camilli-Bro	89	Gleeson-Chi	.313	Mize-StL	.404	Camilli-Bro	.529
Fletcher-Pit	104	VanRobays-Pit	187	Vaughan-Pit	88	F.McCormick-Cin	.309	Camilli-Bro	.397	Slaughter-StL	.504
Young-NY	101	Fletcher-Pit	182	Mize-StL	82	Walker-Bro	.308	Hack-Chi	.395	F.McCormick-Cin	.482

Production		Adjusted Production		Batter Runs		Adjusted Batter Runs		Clutch Hitting Index		Runs Created	
Mize-StL	1.039	Mize-StL	179	Mize-StL	63.9	Mize-StL	62.3	VanRobays-Pit	167	Mize-StL	152
Camilli-Bro	.926	Nicholson-Chi	146	Camilli-Bro	38.7	Fletcher-Pit	35.2	Fletcher-Pit	151	Camilli-Bro	114
Nicholson-Chi	.899	Fletcher-Pit	143	Fletcher-Pit	31.7	Camilli-Bro	33.2	F.McCormick-Cin	141	Vaughan-Pit	113
Slaughter-StL	.874	Camilli-Bro	142	Ott-NY	31.6	Vaughan-Pit	32.4	Young-NY	134	Hack-Chi	112
Ott-NY	.864	Vaughan-Pit	139	Vaughan-Pit	28.7	Ott-NY	31.5	West-Bos	131	Ott-NY	107

Total Average		Stolen Bases		Stolen Base Average		Stolen Base Runs		Fielding Runs		Total Player Rating	
Mize-StL	1.135	Frey-Cin	22					Danning-NY	20.9	Vaughan-Pit	5.5
Camilli-Bro	1.005	Hack-Chi	21					Frey-Cin	17.8	Mize-StL	4.2
Fletcher-Pit	.930	Moore-StL	18					Herman-Chi	15.5	Danning-NY	3.9
Ott-NY	.915	Werber-Cin	16					Moore-StL	15.3	Hack-Chi	3.6
Nicholson-Chi	.901	Reese-Bro	15					Miller-Bos	14.7	Miller-Bos	3.3

Wins		Win Percentage		Games		Complete Games		Shutouts		Saves	
Walters-Cin	22	Fitzsimmons-Bro	.889	Shoun-StL	54	Walters-Cin	29	Wyatt-Bro	5	Brown-NY	7
Passeau-Chi	20	Sewell-Pit	.762	Brown-Pit	48	Derringer-Cin	26	Salvo-Bos	5	Brown-Pit	7
Derringer-Cin	20	Walters-Cin	.688	Passeau-Chi	46	Mulcahy-Phi	21	Lohrman-NY	5	Beggs-Cin	7
		Thompson-Cin	.640	Casey-Bro	44	Passeau-Chi	20			Shoun-StL	5
		Derringer-Cin	.625	Raffensberge-Chi	43	Higbe-Phi	20			Passeau-Chi	5

Innings Pitched		Fewest Hits/Game		Fewest BB/Game		Strikeouts		Strikeouts/Game		Wins Above Team	
Walters-Cin	305	Walters-Cin	7.11	Derringer-Cin	1.45	Higbe-Phi	137	Melton-NY	4.90	Fitzsimmons-Bro	6.9
Derringer-Cin	297	Higbe-Phi	7.70	Turner-Cin	1.54	Wyatt-Bro	124	Schumacher-NY	4.88	Sewell-Pit	5.8
Higbe-Phi	283	Thompson-Cin	7.88	Hamlin-Bro	1.68	Passeau-Chi	124	Wyatt-Bro	4.67	Passeau-Chi	4.6
Passeau-Chi	281	Casey-Bro	7.95	Davis-StL-Bro	1.79	Schumacher-NY	123	Hamlin-Bro	4.50	Beggs-Cin	3.4
Mulcahy-Phi	280	Sullivan-Bos	7.98	Warneke-StL	1.82			Higbe-Phi	4.36	Higbe-Phi	2.9

Earned Run Average		Adjusted ERA		Opponents' Batting Avg.		Opponents' On Base Pct.		Starter Runs		Adjusted Starter Runs	
Walters-Cin	2.48	Passeau-Chi	152	Walters-Cin	.220	Derringer-Cin	.272	Walters-Cin	46.5	Walters-Cin	43.3
Passeau-Chi	2.50	Walters-Cin	152	Higbe-Phi	.232	Passeau-Chi	.275	Passeau-Chi	42.2	Passeau-Chi	40.6
Sewell-Pit	2.79	Hamlin-Bro	134	Thompson-Cin	.233	Walters-Cin	.280	Derringer-Cin	26.0	Derringer-Cin	23.0
Turner-Cin	2.89	Tamulis-Bro	132	Passeau-Chi	.237	Tamulis-Bro	.286	Sewell-Pit	22.3	Hamlin-Bro	20.8
Olsen-Chi	2.97	Sewell-Pit	131	Casey-Bro	.237	Hamlin-Bro	.289	Turner-Cin	20.0	Warneke-StL	19.4

Clutch Pitching Index		Relief Runs		Adjusted Relief Runs		Relief Ranking		Total Pitcher Index		Total Baseball Ranking	
Errickson-Bos	124	Beggs-Cin	15.9	Beggs-Cin	15.1	Beggs-Cin	29.7	Passeau-Chi	5.1	Vaughan-Pit	5.5
Olsen-Chi	119	Russell-StL	8.1	Russell-StL	8.4	Russell-StL	10.1	Walters-Cin	4.9	Passeau-Chi	5.1
Schumacher-NY	114	Raffensberge-Chi	6.2	Raffensberge-Chi	5.5	Raffensberge-Chi	7.3	Warneke-StL	2.4	Walters-Cin	4.9
Turner-Cin	113	MacFayden-Pit	2.9	Pressnell-Bro	2.9	Pressnell-Bro	4.5	Olsen-Chi	2.4	Mize-StL	4.2
Hamlin-Bro	111	Joiner-NY	2.7	Joiner-NY	2.7	Brown-NY	3.2	Schumacher-NY	2.3	Danning-NY	3.9

TEAM	G	W	L	PCT	GB	R	OR	AB	H	2B	3B	HR	BB	SO	AVG	OBP	SLG	PRO	/A	BR	/A	PF	CHI	RC	TA	SB	CS	SBA	SBR
DET	155	90	64	.584		888	717	5418	1549	312	65	134	664	556	.286	.366	.442	.808	115	124	35	111	97	913	.783	66	39	63	-3
CLE	155	89	65	.578	1	710	637	5361	1422	287	61	101	519	597	.265	.332	.398	.730	95	-43	9	93	99	724	.666	53	36	60	-5
NY	155	88	66	.571	2	817	671	5286	1371	243	66	155	648	606	.259	.344	.418	.762	103	25	36	99	102	789	.725	59	35	63	-2
CHI	155	82	72	.532	8	735	672	5386	1499	238	63	73	496	569	.278	.340	.387	.727	94	-41	-69	104	104	713	.649	52	60	46	-19
BOS	154	82	72	.532	8	872	825	5481	1566	301	80	145	590	597	.286	.356	.449	.805	114	109	103	101	97	889	.762	55	49	53	-12
STL	156	67	87	.435	23	757	882	5416	1423	278	58	118	556	642	.263	.333	.374	.705	88	-34	-78	106	102	744	.675	51	40	56	-8
WAS	154	64	90	.416	26	665	811	5365	1453	266	67	52	468	504	.271	.331	.374	.705	88	-84	-30	93	99	690	.639	94	40	70	4
PHI	154	54	100	.351	36	703	932	5304	1391	242	53	105	556	656	.262	.334	.387	.721	93	-53	-18	96	99	704	.657	48	33	59	-4
TOT	619					6147		43017	11674	2167	513	883	4497	4727	.271	.342	.407	.750								478	332	59	-55

TEAM	CG	SHO	SV	IP	H	H/G	HR	BB	BB/G	SO	SO/G	ERA	/A	OAVG	OOBA	PR	/A	PF	CPI	FA	E	DP	FW	PW	BW	SBW	DIF
DET	59	10	23	1375.3	1425	9.3	102	570	3.7	752	4.9	4.01	119	.265	.334	56	114	109	105	.968	194	116	-.7	10.8	3.3	.4	-.7
CLE	72	13	22	1375.0	1328	8.7	86	512	3.4	686	4.5	3.63	111	.254	.320	114	59	92	102	.975	149	164	1.7	5.6	.8	.2	3.7
NY	76	10	14	1373.0	1389	9.1	119	511	3.3	559	3.7	3.89	108	.261	.324	75	48	96	104	.975	152	158	1.5	4.5	3.4	.5	1.1
CHI	83	10	18	1386.7	1335	8.7	111	480	3.1	574	3.7	3.74	120	.249	.309	99	116	103	96	.969	185	125	-.2	11.0	-6.5	-1.1	1.9
BOS	51	4	16	1379.7	1568	10.2	124	625	4.1	613	4.0	4.89	90	.283	.355	-77	-77	100	101	.972	173	156	.4	-7.3	9.7	-.5	2.6
STL	64	4	9	1373.3	1592	10.4	113	646	4.2	439	2.9	5.12	92	.290	.362	-113	-60	108	100	.974	158	179	1.2	-5.7	-7.4	-.0	1.9
WAS	74	6	7	1350.0	1494	10.0	93	618	4.1	618	4.1	4.59	91	.281	.352	-31	-63	95	103	.968	194	144	-.7	-5.9	-2.8	1.0	-4.5
PHI	72	4	12	1345.0	1543	10.3	135	534	3.6	488	3.3	5.22	83	.282	.343	-124	-131	99	91	.960	238	131	-3.1	-12.4	-1.7	.3	-6.2
TOT	551	61	121	10958.0		9.6			3.7		3.9	4.38		.271	.342					.970	1443	1195					

Runs
Williams-Bos 134
Greenberg-Det 129
McCosky-Det 123
Gordon-NY 112
Kuhel-Chi 111

Hits
Radcliff-StL 200
McCosky-Det 200
Cramer-Bos 200
Appling-Chi 197
Wright-Chi 196

Doubles
Greenberg-Det 50
York-Det 46
Boudreau-Cle 46
Williams-Bos 43
Moses-Phi 41

Triples
McCosky-Det 19
Keller-NY 15
Finney-Bos 15
Williams-Bos 14
Appling-Chi 13

Home Runs
Greenberg-Det 41
Foxx-Bos 36
York-Det 33
Johnson-Phi 31
DiMaggio-NY 31

Total Bases
Greenberg-Det 384
York-Det 343
Williams-Bos 333
DiMaggio-NY 318
Gordon-NY 315

Runs Batted In
Greenberg-Det 150
York-Det 134
DiMaggio-NY 133
Foxx-Bos 119
Williams-Bos 113

Runs Produced
Greenberg-Det 238
Williams-Bos 224
York-Det 206
DiMaggio-NY 195
Cronin-Bos 191

Bases On Balls
Keller-NY 106
Clift-StL 104
Gehringer-Det 101
Foxx-Bos 101
Williams-Bos 96

Batting Average
DiMaggio-NY 352
Appling-Chi 348
Williams-Bos 344
Radcliff-StL 342
Greenberg-Det 340

On Base Percentage
Williams-Bos 442
Greenberg-Det 433
Gehringer-Det 428
DiMaggio-NY 425
Appling-Chi 420

Slugging Average
Greenberg-Det 670
DiMaggio-NY 626
Williams-Bos 594
York-Det 583
Foxx-Bos 581

Production
Greenberg-Det 1.103
DiMaggio-NY 1.051
Williams-Bos 1.036
York-Det 993
Foxx-Bos 993

Adjusted Production
DiMaggio-NY 171
Williams-Bos 165
Greenberg-Det ...163
Foxx-Bos 153
Trosky-Cle 146

Batter Runs
Greenberg-Det 68.8
Williams-Bos 57.1
DiMaggio-NY 50.8
York-Det 47.3
Foxx-Bos 42.6

Adjusted Batter Runs
Greenberg-Det 59.1
Williams-Bos 56.5
DiMaggio-NY 51.9
Foxx-Bos 42.0
York-Det 37.4

Clutch Hitting Index
Tresh-Cle 142
Heffner-StL 127
Bloodworth-Was ...125
DiMaggio-NY 124
Bell-Cle 123

Runs Created
Greenberg-Det 171
Williams-Bos 154
York-Det 147
DiMaggio-NY 135
Foxx-Bos 124

Total Average
Greenberg-Det 1.222
Williams-Bos 1.132
DiMaggio-NY 1.104
York-Det 1.055
Foxx-Bos 1.044

Stolen Bases
Case-Was 35
Walker-Was 21
Gordon-NY 18
Lewis-Was 15
Kreevich-Chi 15

Stolen Base Average
Walker-Was 84.0
Case-Was 77.8
Gordon-NY 69.2

Stolen Base Runs
Case-Was 4.5
Walker-Was 3.9
Gehringer-Det 3.0
Bartell-Det 2.4
Rosar-NY 1.5

Fielding Runs
Heffner-StL 17.4
Doerr-Bos 16.9
Bartell-Det 14.1
Gordon-NY 14.0
Boudreau-Cle 12.2

Total Player Rating
Greenberg-Det 4.6
Williams-Bos 4.3
Boudreau-Cle 3.9
Cronin-Bos 3.7
DiMaggio-NY 3.7

Wins
Feller-Cle 27
Newsom-Det 21
Milnar-Cle 18
Hudson-Was 17

Win Percentage
Rowe-Det 842
Newsom-Det 808
Feller-Cle 711
Smith-Cle 682
Milnar-Cle 643

Games
Feller-Cle 43
Benton-Det 42
Wilson-Bos 41
Heusser-Phi 41
Dobson-Cle 40

Complete Games
Feller-Cle 31
Lee-Chi 24
Leonard-Was 23

Shutouts
Milnar-Cle 4
Lyons-Chi 4
Feller-Cle 4

Saves
Benton-Det 17
Brown-Chi 10
Murphy-NY 9

Innings Pitched
Feller-Cle 320
Leonard-Was 289
Rigney-Chi 281
Newsom-Det 264
Auker-StL 264

Fewest Hits/Game
Feller-Cle 6.89
Rigney-Chi 7.69
Bridges-Det 7.77
Smith-Chi 7.78
Newsom-Det 8.01

Fewest BB/Game
Lyons-Chi 1.79
Lee-Chi 2.21
Rowe-Det 2.29
Leonard-Was 2.43
Russo-NY 2.62

Strikeouts
Feller-Cle 261
Newsom-Det 164
Rigney-Chi 141
Bridges-Det 133
Chase-Was 129

Strikeouts/Game
Feller-Cle 7.34
Bridges-Det 6.05
Wilson-Bos 5.81
Newsom-Det 5.59
Smith-Chi 5.17

Wins Above Team
Newsom-Det 7.6
Feller-Cle 7.2
Rowe-Det 6.2
Auker-StL 4.3
Babich-Phi 4.0

Earned Run Average
Feller-Cle 2.62
Newsom-Det 2.83
Rigney-Chi 3.11
Smith-Chi 3.22
Chase-Was 3.23

Adjusted ERA
Newsom-Det 168
Feller-Cle 154
Rigney-Chi 145
Bridges-Det 142
Smith-Chi 140

Opponents' Batting Avg.
Feller-Cle 210
Smith-Chi 228
Bridges-Det 229
Rigney-Chi 230
Newsom-Det 238

Opponents' On Base Pct.
Feller-Cle 282
Lyons-Chi 285
Rigney-Chi 288
Lee-Chi 296
Russo-NY 302

Starter Runs
Feller-Cle 62.9
Newsom-Det 45.6
Rigney-Chi 39.9
Chase-Was 33.6
Milnar-Cle 29.9

Adjusted Starter Runs
Newsom-Det 56.6
Feller-Cle 50.1
Rigney-Chi 43.4
Bridges-Det 30.7
Smith-Chi 29.4

Clutch Pitching Index
Chase-Was 134
Leonard-Was 122
Newsom-Det 119
Smith-Cle 117
Milnar-Cle 115

Relief Runs
Eisenstat-Cle 10.1
Trotter-StL 6.7
Brown-Chi 5.1
Murphy-NY 4.7

Adjusted Relief Runs
Trotter-StL 10.5
Eisenstat-Cle 7.2
Brown-Chi 6.0
Murphy-NY 3.5
Benton-Det 2.8

Relief Ranking
Trotter-StL 13.0
Brown-Chi 10.2
Murphy-NY 7.0
Benton-Det 6.4
Eisenstat-Cle 5.4

Total Pitcher Index
Newsom-Det 5.5
Feller-Cle 4.7
Rigney-Chi 4.3
Smith-Chi 3.1
Rowe-Det 3.0

Total Baseball Ranking
Newsom-Det 5.5
Feller-Cle 4.7
Greenberg-Det 4.6
Williams-Bos 4.3
Rigney-Chi 4.3

TEAM	G	W	L	PCT	GB	R	OR	AB	H	2B	3B	HR	BB	SO	AVG	OBP	SLG	PRO	/A	BR	/A	PF	CHI	RC	TA	SB	CS	SBA	SBR
BRO	157	100	54	.649		800	581	5485	1494	286	69	101	600	535	.272	.347	.405	.752	118	128	105	103	98	792	.704	36			
STL	155	97	56	.634	2.5	734	589	5457	1482	254	56	70	540	543	.272	.340	.377	.717	109	62	-5	110	99	719	.656	47			
CIN	154	88	66	.571	12	616	564	5218	1288	213	33	64	477	428	.247	.313	.337	.650	89	-71	-63	99	108	556	.574	68			
PIT	156	81	73	.526	19	690	643	5297	1417	233	65	56	547	516	.268	.338	.368	.706	105	39	21	103	99	670	.642	59			
NY	156	74	79	.484	25.5	667	706	5395	1401	248	35	95	504	518	.260	.326	.371	.697	103	14	-6	103	98	659	.624	36			
CHI	155	70	84	.455	30	666	670	5230	1323	239	25	99	559	670	.253	.327	.365	.692	101	8	49	94	101	642	.629	39			
BOS	156	62	92	.403	38	592	720	5414	1357	231	38	48	471	608	.251	.312	.334	.646	86	-81	-35	93	102	568	.563	61			
PHI	155	43	111	.279	57	501	793	5233	1277	188	38	64	451	596	.244	.307	.331	.638	86	-96	-77	97	92	528	.554	65			
TOT	622					5266		42729	11039	1892	359	597	4149	4414	.258	.326	.361	.688								411			

TEAM	CG	SHO	SV	IP	H	H/G	HR	BB	BB/G	SO	SO/G	ERA	/A	OAVG	OOBA	PR	/A	PF	CPI	FA	E	DP	FW	PW	BW	SBW	DIF
BRO	66	17	22	1421.0	1236	7.8	81	495	3.1	603	3.8	3.14	115	.233	.295	77	72	99	93	.974	162	125	.7	7.4	10.8		4.1
STL	64	15	20	1416.7	1289	8.2	85	502	3.2	659	4.2	3.19	122	.241	.302	69	110	107	100	.973	172	146	.2	11.3	-.5		9.5
CIN	89	19	10	1386.7	1300	8.4	61	510	3.3	627	4.1	3.17	112	.247	.308	71	59	98	102	.975	152	147	1.3	6.1	-6.5		10.1
PIT	71	9	12	1373.0	1392	9.1	66	492	3.2	410	2.7	3.48	106	.262	.320	23	31	102	104	.968	196	130	-1.2	3.2	2.2		-.1
NY	55	12	18	1392.0	1455	9.4	90	539	3.5	566	3.7	3.94	96	.268	.328	-47	-25	104	101	.974	160	144	.9	-2.6	-.6		-.2
CHI	74	8	9	1363.0	1431	9.4	60	449	3.0	548	3.6	3.72	91	.269	.320	-12	-48	94	99	.970	180	139	-.3	-4.9	5.0		-6.8
BOS	62	10	9	1386.7	1440	9.3	75	554	3.6	446	2.9	3.95	88	.266	.329	-49	-74	96	98	.969	191	174	-.9	-7.6	-3.6		-2.9
PHI	35	4	9	1372.3	1499	9.8	79	606	4.0	552	3.6	4.50	83	.276	.343	-132	-117	103	96	.969	187	147	-.7	-12.0	-7.9		-13.4
TOT	516	94	109	11111.3		8.9			3.4		3.6	3.63		.258	.326					.972	1400	1152					

Runs
Reiser-Bro	117
Hack-Chi	111
Medwick-Bro	100
Rucker-NY	95
Fletcher-Pit	95

Hits
Hack-Chi	186
Reiser-Bro	184
Litwhiler-Phi	180
Rucker-NY	179
Medwick-Bro	171

Doubles
Reiser-Bro	39
Mize-StL	39
Rucker-NY	38
Dallessandro-Chi	36

Triples
Reiser-Bro	17
Fletcher-Pit	13
Hopp-StL	11
Medwick-Bro	10
Elliott-Pit	10

Home Runs
Camilli-Bro	34
Ott-NY	27
Nicholson-Chi	26
Young-NY	25
Dahlgren-Bos-Chi	23

Total Bases
Reiser-Bro	299
Camilli-Bro	294
Medwick-Bro	278
Litwhiler-Phi	275
Young-NY	265

Runs Batted In
Camilli-Bro	120
Young-NY	104
Mize-StL	100
DiMaggio-Pit	100
Nicholson-Chi	98

Runs Produced
Reiser-Bro	179
Camilli-Bro	178
Medwick-Bro	170
Young-NY	169
Fletcher-Pit	158

Bases On Balls
Fletcher-Pit	118
Camilli-Bro	104
Ott-NY	100
Hack-Chi	99

Batting Average
Reiser-Bro	.343
Medwick-Bro	.318
Hack-Chi	.317
Mize-StL	.317
Etten-Phi	.311

On Base Percentage
Fletcher-Pit	.421
Hack-Chi	.417
Camilli-Bro	.407
Reiser-Bro	.406
Mize-StL	.406

Slugging Average
Reiser-Bro	.558
Camilli-Bro	.556
Mize-StL	.535
Medwick-Bro	.517
Slaughter-StL	.496

Production
Reiser-Bro	.964
Camilli-Bro	.962
Mize-StL	.941
Ott-NY	.898
Slaughter-StL	.886

Adjusted Production
Reiser-Bro	164
Camilli-Bro	164
Mize-StL	149
Ott-NY	147
Hack-Chi	147

Batter Runs
Camilli-Bro	50.1
Reiser-Bro	47.9
Mize-StL	40.2
Ott-NY	38.7
Fletcher-Pit	38.2

Adjusted Batter Runs
Camilli-Bro	47.8
Reiser-Bro	45.8
Hack-Chi	38.8
Ott-NY	36.5
Fletcher-Pit	36.3

Clutch Hitting Index
Lavagetto-Bro	173
VanRobays-Pit	154
Dallessandro-Chi	150
Elliott-Pit	141
Bragan-Phi	134

Runs Created
Camilli-Bro	128
Reiser-Bro	124
Ott-NY	115
Hack-Chi	114
Fletcher-Pit	111

Total Average
Camilli-Bro	1.057
Reiser-Bro	1.006
Mize-StL	.991
Ott-NY	.976
Fletcher-Pit	.965

Stolen Bases
Murtaugh-Phi	18
Benjamin-Phi	17
Handley-Pit	16
Frey-Cin	16
Hopp-StL	15

Stolen Base Average

Stolen Base Runs

Fielding Runs
May-Phi	21.6
Danning-NY	20.6
Stringer-Chi	17.1
Miller-Bos	11.6
Brown-StL	10.1

Total Player Rating
Reiser-Bro	4.7
Walker-Bro	2.9
Ott-NY	2.9
Camilli-Bro	2.9
Hack-Chi	2.6

Wins
Wyatt-Bro	22
Higbe-Bro	22
Walters-Cin	19
Riddle-Cin	19

Win Percentage
Riddle-Cin	.826
Higbe-Bro	.710
White-StL	.708
Wyatt-Bro	.688
Warneke-StL	.654

Games
Higbe-Bro	48
Pearson-Phi	46
Casey-Bro	45
Hutchings-Cin-Bos	44
Johnson-Bos	43

Complete Games
Walters-Cin	27
Wyatt-Bro	23
Tobin-Bos	20
Passeau-Chi	20

Shutouts
Wyatt-Bro	7
VanderMeer-Cin	6
Walters-Cin	5
Davis-Bro	5

Saves
Brown-NY	8
Crouch-Phi-StL	7
Casey-Bro	7
Pearson-Phi	6

Innings Pitched
Walters-Cin	302
Higbe-Bro	298
Wyatt-Bro	288
Sewell-Pit	249
Warneke-StL	246

Fewest Hits/Game
VanderMeer-Cin	6.85
Wyatt-Bro	6.97
White-StL	7.24
Higbe-Bro	7.37
Riddle-Cin	7.47

Fewest BB/Game
Passeau-Chi	2.03
Derringer-Cin	2.13
Lohrman-NY	2.26
Tobin-Bos	2.27
Lee-Chi	2.32

Strikeouts
VanderMeer-Cin	202
Wyatt-Bro	176
Walters-Cin	129
Higbe-Bro	121
Cooper-StL	118

Strikeouts/Game
VanderMeer-Cin	8.04
Cooper-StL	5.68
Wyatt-Bro	5.50
White-StL	5.01
Melton-NY	4.64

Wins Above Team
Riddle-Cin	7.3
Krist-StL	5.0
Higbe-Bro	3.2
Carpenter-NY	2.9
White-StL	2.8

Earned Run Average
Riddle-Cin	2.24
Wyatt-Bro	2.34
White-StL	2.40
VanderMeer-Cin	2.83
Walters-Cin	2.83

Adjusted ERA
White-StL	162
Riddle-Cin	159
Wyatt-Bro	154
Gumbert-NY -StL	126
VanderMeer-Cin	126

Opponents' Batting Avg.
Wyatt-Bro	.212
VanderMeer-Cin	.214
White-StL	.217
Higbe-Bro	.220
Riddle-Cin	.224

Opponents' On Base Pct.
Wyatt-Bro	.268
Riddle-Cin	.276
White-StL	.283
Tobin-Bos	.295
Sewell-Pit	.296

Starter Runs
Wyatt-Bro	41.2
Riddle-Cin	33.6
White-StL	28.7
Walters-Cin	26.9
VanderMeer-Cin	20.2

Adjusted Starter Runs
Wyatt-Bro	40.3
White-StL	34.8
Riddle-Cin	31.6
Walters-Cin	24.2
Warneke-StL	20.3

Clutch Pitching Index
Olsen-Chi	120
Heintzelman-Pit	117
Butcher-Pit	112
Johnson-Bos	111
Walters-Cin	111

Relief Runs
Pressnell-Chi	4.2
Brown-NY	2.0
Pearson-Phi	.9

Adjusted Relief Runs
Brown-NY	2.9
Pressnell-Chi	2.4
Pearson-Phi	2.4

Relief Ranking
Brown-NY	3.7
Pearson-Phi	3.1
Pressnell-Chi	2.6

Total Pitcher Index
Wyatt-Bro	5.1
Riddle-Cin	3.7
White-StL	3.5
Walters-Cin	3.1
Gumbert-NY -StL	2.8

Total Baseball Ranking
Wyatt-Bro	5.1
Reiser-Bro	4.7
Riddle-Cin	3.7
White-StL	3.5
Walters-Cin	3.1

TEAM	G	W	L	PCT	GB	R	OR	AB	H	2B	3B	HR	BB	SO	AVG	OBP	SLG	PRO	/A	BR	/A	PF	CHI	RC	TA	SB	CS	SBA	SBR
NY	156	101	53	.656		830	631	5444	1464	243	60	151	616	565	.269	.346	.419	.765	109	64	78	98	102	822	.723	51	33	61	-4
BOS	155	84	70	.545	17	865	750	5359	1517	304	55	124	683	567	.283	.366	.430	.796	118	136	113	103	97	872	.765	67	50	57	-9
CHI	156	77	77	.500	24	638	649	5404	1376	245	47	47	510	476	.255	.322	.343	.665	83	-127	-79	94	105	612	.589	91	54	63	-4
DET	155	75	79	.487	26	686	743	5370	1412	247	55	81	602	584	.263	.340	.375	.715	96	-26	-71	106	94	713	.653	43	28	61	-3
CLE	155	75	79	.487	26	677	668	5283	1350	249	84	103	512	605	.256	.323	.393	.716	96	-39	-43	101	99	691	.655	63	47	57	-8
WAS	156	70	84	.455	31	728	798	5521	1502	257	80	52	490	488	.272	.331	.376	.707	94	-52	-34	98	106	702	.632	79	36	69	2
STL	157	70	84	.455	31	765	823	5408	1440	281	58	91	775	552	.266	.360	.390	.750	106	56	56	100	93	804	.715	50	39	56	-7
PHI	154	64	90	.416	37	713	840	5336	1431	240	69	85	574	588	.268	.340	.387	.727	99	-6	-11	101	98	711	.655	27	36	43	-13
TOT	622					5902		43125	11492	2066	508	734	4742	4425	.266	.341	.389	.730								471	323	59	-52

TEAM	CG	SHO	SV	IP	H	H/G	HR	BB	BB/G	SO	SO/G	ERA	/A	OAVG	OOBA	PR	/A	PF	CPI	FA	E	DP	FW	PW	BW	SBW	DIF
NY	75	13	26	1396.3	1309	8.4	81	598	3.9	589	3.8	3.53	111	.247	.321	96	62	95	102	.973	165	196	.4	6.0	7.6	.2	9.7
BOS	70	8	11	1372.0	1453	9.5	88	611	4.0	574	3.8	4.19	100	.269	.341	-5	1	101	102	.972	172	139	.0	.0	11.0	-.2	-3.9
CHI	106	14	4	1416.0	1362	8.7	89	521	3.3	564	3.6	3.52	110	.251	.315	98	57	94	102	.971	180	145	-.4	5.5	-7.7	.2	2.3
DET	52	8	16	1381.7	1399	9.1	80	645	4.2	697	4.5	4.18	107	.259	.335	-4	42	107	96	.969	186	129	-.7	4.1	-6.9	.3	1.2
CLE	68	10	19	1377.0	1366	8.9	71	660	4.3	617	4.0	3.90	107	.259	.340	38	41	101	103	.976	142	158	1.7	4.0	-4.2	-.1	-3.4
WAS	69	8	7	1389.3	1524	9.9	69	603	3.9	544	3.5	4.35	94	.279	.347	-31	-39	99	101	.969	187	169	-.8	-3.8	-3.3	.8	.0
STL	65	7	10	1389.0	1563	10.1	120	549	3.6	454	2.9	4.72	89	.283	.346	-87	-81	101	99	.975	151	156	1.2	-7.9	5.4	-.0	-5.8
PHI	64	3	18	1365.3	1516	10.0	136	557	3.7	386	2.5	4.83	88	.279	.343	-103	-84	103	97	.967	200	150	-1.5	-8.1	-1.1	-.6	-1.7
TOT	569	71	111	11086.7		9.3			3.9		3.6	4.15		.266	.341					.972	1383	1242					

Runs
Williams-Bos 135
DiMaggio-NY 122
DiMaggio-Bos 117
Clift-StL 108

Hits
Travis-Was 218
Heath-Cle 199
DiMaggio-NY 193
Appling-Chi 186
Williams-Bos 185

Doubles
Boudreau-Cle 45
DiMaggio-NY 43
Judnich-StL 40
Travis-Was 39
Kuhel-Chi 39

Triples
Heath-Cle 20
Travis-Was 19
Keltner-Cle 13

Home Runs
Williams-Bos 37
Keller-NY 33
Henrich-NY 31
DiMaggio-NY 30
York-Det 27

Total Bases
DiMaggio-NY 348
Heath-Cle 343
Williams-Bos 335
Travis-Was 316
Chapman-Phi 300

Runs Batted In
DiMaggio-NY 125
Heath-Cle 123
Keller-NY 122
Williams-Bos 120
York-Det 111

Runs Produced
Williams-Bos 218
DiMaggio-NY 217
Travis-Was 200
Keller-NY 191
Heath-Cle 188

Bases On Balls
Williams-Bos 145
Cullenbine-StL 121
Clift-StL 113
Keller-NY 102

Batting Average
Williams-Bos 406
Travis-Was 359
DiMaggio-NY 357
Heath-Cle 340
Siebert-Phi 334

On Base Percentage
Williams-Bos 551
Cullenbine-StL 452
DiMaggio-NY 440
Keller-NY 416
Foxx-Bos 412

Slugging Average
Williams-Bos 735
DiMaggio-NY 643
Heath-Cle 586
Keller-NY 580
Chapman-Phi 543

Production
Williams-Bos 1.286
DiMaggio-NY 1.083
Keller-NY 996
Heath-Cle 982
Travis-Was 930

Adjusted Production
Williams-Bos 231
DiMaggio-NY 187
Keller-NY 164
Heath-Cle 156
Travis-Was 148

Batter Runs
Williams-Bos 102.0
DiMaggio-NY 64.3
Keller-NY 45.7
Heath-Cle 44.8
Cullenbine-StL 38.3

Adjusted Batter Runs
Williams-Bos 99.8
DiMaggio-NY 65.8
Keller-NY 47.2
Heath-Cle 44.3
Travis-Was 40.0

Clutch Hitting Index
Berardino-StL 165
Cullenbine-StL 136
Tabor-Bos 135
Wright-Chi 135
Vernon-Was 133

Runs Created
Williams-Bos 202
DiMaggio-NY 162
Heath-Cle 138
Keller-NY 134
Travis-Was 131

Total Average
Williams-Bos 1.702
DiMaggio-NY 1.213
Keller-NY 1.110
Cullenbine-StL 1.034
Heath-Cle 1.030

Stolen Bases
Case-Was 33
Kuhel-Chi 20
Lewis-Was 18
Tabor-Bos 17
Kreevich-Chi 17

Stolen Base Average
Kuhel-Chi 80.0
Case-Was 78.6
Kreevich-Chi 77.3
Tabor-Bos 65.4
Heath-Cle 60.0

Stolen Base Runs
Case-Was 4.5
Kuhel-Chi 3.0
Kreevich-Chi 2.1
Fox-Bos 1.5

Fielding Runs
Keltner-Cle 22.0
Bloodworth-Was 21.9
Rizzuto-NY 17.2
Boudreau-Cle 14.8
Case-Was 14.2

Total Player Rating
Williams-Bos 8.0
DiMaggio-NY 6.0
Keller-NY 4.0
Travis-Was 3.8
Keltner-Cle 3.5

Wins
Feller-Cle 25
Lee-Chi 22
Newsome-Bos 19
Leonard-Was 18

Win Percentage
Gomez-NY 750
Ruffing-NY 714
Benton-Det 714
Lee-Chi 667
Feller-Cle 658

Games
Feller-Cle 44
Newsom-Det 43
Brown-Cle 41
Ryba-Bos 40
Benton-Det 38

Complete Games
Lee-Chi 30
Feller-Cle 28
Smith-Chi 21
Lyons-Chi 19
Leonard-Was 19

Shutouts
Feller-Cle 6
Leonard-Was 4
Humphries-Chi 4
Chandler-NY 4

Saves
Murphy-NY 15
Ferrick-Phi 7
Benton-Det 7
Ryba-Bos 6

Innings Pitched
Feller-Cle 343
Lee-Chi 300
Smith-Chi 263
Leonard-Was 256

Fewest Hits/Game
Benton-Det 7.41
Feller-Cle 7.45
Lee-Chi 7.74
Donald-NY 7.98
Chandler-NY 8.01

Fewest BB/Game
Lyons-Chi 1.78
Leonard-Was 1.90
Muncrief-StL 2.23
Ruffing-NY 2.61
Lee-Chi 2.76

Strikeouts
Feller-Cle 260
Newsom-Det 175
Lee-Chi 130
Rigney-Chi 119

Strikeouts/Game
Feller-Cle 6.82
Newsom-Det 6.30
Newhouser-Det 5.51
Harris-Bos 5.15
Rigney-Chi 4.52

Wins Above Team
Feller-Cle 7.6
Lee-Chi 6.4
Benton-Det 5.0
Leonard-Was 4.2
Newsome-Bos 4.1

Earned Run Average
Lee-Chi 2.37
Benton-Det 2.96
Wagner-Bos 3.08
Russo-NY 3.09
Feller-Cle 3.15

Adjusted ERA
Lee-Chi 164
Benton-Det 150
Wagner-Bos 136
Feller-Cle 132
Harris-Bos 129

Opponents' Batting Avg.
Benton-Det 221
Feller-Cle 226
Lee-Chi 232
Donald-NY 237
Chandler-NY 239

Opponents' On Base Pct.
Lee-Chi 289
Benton-Det 299
Ruffing-NY 301
Lyons-Chi 302
Chandler-NY 302

Starter Runs
Lee-Chi 59.2
Feller-Cle 38.1
Smith-Chi 28.2
Russo-NY 24.8
Wagner-Bos 22.2

Adjusted Starter Runs
Lee-Chi 50.5
Feller-Cle 38.9
Benton-Det 26.1
Wagner-Bos 23.1
Smith-Chi 20.6

Clutch Pitching Index
Lee-Chi 122
Wagner-Bos 120
Gomez-NY 114
Marchildon-Phi 114
Smith-Chi 112

Relief Runs
Murphy-NY 18.5
Heving-Cle 14.7
Carrasquel-Was 7.7
Brown-Cle 7.1

Adjusted Relief Runs
Murphy-NY 16.6
Heving-Cle 14.9
Brown-Cle 7.3
Carrasquel-Was 7.2
Thomas-Det 2.1

Relief Ranking
Murphy-NY 28.6
Heving-Cle 15.6
Brown-Cle 6.4
Carrasquel-Was 5.6
Thomas-Det 1.2

Total Pitcher Index
Lee-Chi 5.7
Feller-Cle 3.9
Smith-Chi 2.5
Russo-NY 2.3
Wagner-Bos 2.2

Total Baseball Ranking
Williams-Bos 8.0
DiMaggio-NY 6.0
Lee-Chi 5.7
Keller-NY 4.0
Feller-Cle 3.9

TEAM	G	W	L	PCT	GB	R	OR	AB	H	2B	3B	HR	BB	SO	AVG	OBP	SLG	PRO	/A	BR	/A	PF	CHI	RC	TA	SB	CS	SBA	SBR
STL	156	106	48	.688		755	482	5421	1454	282	69	60	551	507	.268	.338	.379	.717	117	108	57	108	102	718	.665	71			
BRO	155	104	50	.675	2	742	510	5285	1398	263	34	62	572	484	.265	.338	.362	.700	112	79	67	102	107	671	.648	79			
NY	155	85	67	.559	20	675	600	5210	1323	162	35	109	558	511	.254	.330	.361	.691	109	59	43	103	102	627	.624	39			
CIN	154	76	76	.500	29	527	545	5260	1216	198	39	66	483	549	.231	.299	.321	.620	88	-80	-86	101	101	519	.541	42			
PIT	149	66	81	.449	36.5	585	631	5104	1250	173	49	54	537	536	.245	.320	.330	.650	97	-15	-19	101	102	556	.578	41			
CHI	155	68	86	.442	38	591	665	5352	1360	224	41	75	509	607	.254	.321	.353	.674	104	23	46	96	93	619	.605	61			
BOS	151	59	89	.399	44	515	645	5077	1216	210	19	68	474	507	.240	.307	.329	.636	92	-48	-21	95	97	520	.556	49			
PHI	151	42	109	.278	62.5	394	706	5060	1174	168	37	44	392	488	.232	.289	.306	.595	80	-124	-91	94	88	451	.499	37			
TOT	613					4784		41769	10391	1680	323	538	4076	4189	.249	.318	.343	.661								419			

TEAM	CG	SHO	SV	IP	H	H/G	HR	BB	BB/G	SO	SO/G	ERA	/A	OAVG	OOBA	PR	/A	PF	CPI	FA	E	DP	FW	PW	BW	SBW	DIF
STL	70	18	15	1410.0	1192	7.6	49	473	3.0	651	4.2	2.55	133	.228	.291	120	133	103	103	.972	169	137	-.3	14.3	6.1		8.9
BRO	67	17	24	1398.0	1205	7.8	73	493	3.2	612	3.9	2.85	113	.232	.298	72	57	97	102	.977	138	150	1.5	6.1	7.2		12.1
NY	70	12	13	1369.7	1299	8.5	94	493	3.2	497	3.3	3.31	101	.249	.310	0	6	101	104	.977	138	128	1.5	.6	4.6		2.2
CIN	80	12	8	1412.3	1213	7.7	47	526	3.4	616	3.9	2.82	119	.231	.299	78	85	101	99	.971	177	158	-.8	9.1	-9.2		.9
PIT	64	13	11	1351.0	1376	9.2	62	435	2.9	426	3.3	3.58	94	.263	.315	-40	-31	102	98	.969	184	128	-1.2	-3.3	-2.0		-.9
CHI	71	11	14	1400.7	1447	9.3	70	525	3.4	507	3.3	3.60	90	.266	.327	-44	-56	98	105	.973	170	136	-.4	-6.0	4.9		-7.6
BOS	68	10	8	1334.0	1326	8.9	82	518	3.5	414	2.8	3.76	86	.258	.324	-65	-75	98	99	.976	142	138	1.3	-8.0	-2.3		-6.0
PHI	51	2	6	1340.0	1328	8.9	61	605	4.1	472	3.2	4.12	81	.258	.332	-120	-115	101	91	.968	194	147	-1.8	-12.3	-9.8		-9.6
TOT	541	95	99	11015.7		8.5			3.3		3.4	3.31		.249	.318					.973	1312	1122					

Runs
Ott-NY 118
Slaughter-StL 100
Mize-NY 97
Hack-Chi 91

Hits
Slaughter-StL 188
Nicholson-Chi 173
Medwick-Bro 166
Hack-Chi 166
Elliott-Pit 166

Doubles
Marion-StL 38
Medwick-Bro 37
Hack-Chi 36
Herman-Bro 34
Reiser-Bro 33

Triples
Slaughter-StL 17
Nicholson-Chi 11
Musial-StL 10
Litwhiler-Phi 9

Home Runs
Ott-NY 30
Mize-NY 26
Camilli-Bro 26
Nicholson-Chi 21
West-Bos 16

Total Bases
Slaughter-StL 292
Mize-NY 282
Nicholson-Chi 280
Ott-NY 273
Camilli-Bro 247

Runs Batted In
Mize-NY 110
Camilli-Bro 109
Slaughter-StL 98
Medwick-Bro 96
Ott-NY 93

Runs Produced
Slaughter-StL 185
Ott-NY 181
Mize-NY 181
Camilli-Bro 172
Medwick-Bro 161

Bases On Balls
Ott-NY 109
Fletcher-Pit 105
Camilli-Bro 97
Hack-Chi 94
Slaughter-StL 88

Batting Average
Slaughter-StL 318
Musial-StL 315
Reiser-Bro 310
Mize-NY 305
Novikoff-Chi 300

On Base Percentage
Fletcher-Pit 417
Ott-NY 415
Slaughter-StL 412
Hack-Chi 402
Musial-StL 397

Slugging Average
Mize-NY 521
Ott-NY 497
Slaughter-StL 494
Musial-StL 490
Nicholson-Chi 476

Production
Ott-NY 912
Slaughter-StL 906
Mize-NY 901
Musial-StL 888
Nicholson-Chi 859

Adjusted Production
Ott-NY 162
Mize-NY 158
Nicholson-Chi 156
Slaughter-StL 152
Musial-StL 147

Batter Runs
Slaughter-StL 49.8
Ott-NY 49.3
Mize-NY 40.7
Nicholson-Chi 37.6
Musial-StL 35.0

Adjusted Batter Runs
Ott-NY 47.5
Slaughter-StL 44.1
Nicholson-Chi 40.3
Mize-NY 39.1
Hack-Chi 32.4

Clutch Hitting Index
Medwick-Bro 154
McCormick-Cin 135
Elliott-Pit 134
Camilli-Bro 127
Herman-Bro 125

Runs Created
Slaughter-StL 128
Ott-NY 122
Nicholson-Chi 112
Mize-NY 110
Hack-Chi 100

Total Average
Ott-NY 990
Slaughter-StL 966
Musial-StL 926
Mize-NY 911
Camilli-Bro 888

Stolen Bases
Reiser-Bro 20
Reese-Bro 15
Fernandez-Bos 15
Merullo-Chi 14
Hopp-StL 14

Stolen Base Average

Stolen Base Runs

Fielding Runs
Reese-Bro 18.0
Glossop-Phi 14.0
DiMaggio-Pit 13.8
Murtaugh-Phi 13.6
Frey-Cin 11.8

Total Player Rating
Nicholson-Chi 4.9
Slaughter-StL 4.5
Ott-NY 4.4
Frey-Cin 3.4
Reese-Bro 3.1

Wins
M.Cooper-StL 22
Beazley-StL 21
Wyatt-Bro 19
Passeau-Chi 19
VanderMeer-Cin 18

Win Percentage
French-Bro 789
Beazley-StL 778
M.Cooper-StL 759
Wyatt-Bro 731
Davis-Bro 714

Games
Adams-NY 61
Casey-Bro 50
Podgajny-Phi 43
Beazley-StL 43

Complete Games
Tobin-Bos 28
Passeau-Chi 24
M.Cooper-StL 22
Walters-Cin 21
VanderMeer-Cin 21

Shutouts
M.Cooper-StL 10
Sewell-Pit 5
Javery-Bos 5
Davis-Bro 5

Saves
Casey-Bro 13
Adams-NY 11
Beggs-Cin 8
Sain-Bos 6
Gumbert-StL 5

Innings Pitched
Tobin-Bos 288
M.Cooper-StL 279
Passeau-Chi 278
Starr-Cin 277
Javery-Bos 261

Fewest Hits/Game
M.Cooper-StL 6.68
VanderMeer-Cin 6.93
Higbe-Bro 7.30
Starr-Cin 7.41
Beazley-StL 7.58

Fewest BB/Game
Warneke-StL-Chi 1.79
Lohrman-StL-NY 1.84
Hubbell-NY 1.95
Derringer-Cin 2.11
M.Cooper-StL 2.19

Strikeouts
VanderMeer-Cin 186
M.Cooper-StL 152
Higbe-Bro 115
Walters-Cin 109
Melton-Phi 107

Strikeouts/Game
VanderMeer-Cin 6.86
Lanier-StL 5.20
M.Cooper-StL 4.90
Higbe-Bro 4.66
Melton-Phi 4.61

Wins Above Team
Passeau-Chi 4.7
Beazley-StL 4.4
Lohrman-StL-NY 4.0
M.Cooper-StL 3.8
French-Bro 3.6

Earned Run Average
M.Cooper-StL 1.77
Beazley-StL 2.13
Davis-Bro 2.36
VanderMeer-Cin 2.43
Lohrman-StL-NY 2.47

Adjusted ERA
M.Cooper-StL 191
Beazley-StL 159
VanderMeer-Cin 138
Davis-Bro 136
Lohrman-StL-NY 136

Opponents' Batting Avg.
M.Cooper-StL 204
VanderMeer-Cin 208
Higbe-Bro 223
Wyatt-Bro 225
Starr-Cin 226

Opponents' On Base Pct.
M.Cooper-StL 255
Lohrman-StL-NY 276
Davis-Bro 282
Warneke-StL-Chi 283
Wyatt-Bro 283

Starter Runs
M.Cooper-StL 47.7
Beazley-StL 28.2
French-Bro 24.5
VanderMeer-Cin 23.8
Davis-Bro 21.8

Adjusted Starter Runs
M.Cooper-StL 50.3
Beazley-StL 30.1
VanderMeer-Cin 25.2
French-Bro 22.9
Starr-Cin 21.5

Clutch Pitching Index
Bithorn-Chi 130
Passeau-Chi 121
Beazley-StL 114
Schumacher-NY 113
Carpenter-NY 112

Relief Runs
Adams-NY 14.4
Casey-Bro 13.2
Beggs-Cin 11.8
Shoun-StL-Cin 9.2
Webber-Bro 2.1

Adjusted Relief Runs
Adams-NY 14.8
Beggs-Cin 12.3
Casey-Bro 12.0
Shoun-StL-Cin 9.7
Webber-Bro 1.6

Relief Ranking
Adams-NY 20.8
Beggs-Cin 16.1
Casey-Bro 11.8
Shoun-StL-Cin 4.7
Webber-Bro 1.4

Total Pitcher Index
M.Cooper-StL 5.5
Beazley-StL 3.4
Walters-Cin 3.2
French-Bro 2.9
VanderMeer-Cin 2.9

Total Baseball Ranking
M.Cooper-StL 5.5
Nicholson-Chi 4.9
Slaughter-StL 4.5
Ott-NY 4.4
Beazley-StL 3.4

TEAM	G	W	L	PCT	GB	R	OR	AB	H	2B	3B	HR	BB	SO	AVG	OBP	SLG	PRO	/A	BR	/A	PF	CHI	RC	TA	SB	CS	SBA	SBR
NY	154	103	51	.669		801	507	5305	1429	223	57	108	591	556	.269	.346	.394	.740	116	104	107	99	104	759	.693	69	33	68	1
BOS	152	93	59	.612	9	761	594	5248	1451	244	55	103	591	508	.276	.352	.403	.755	120	132	108	104	95	774	.707	68	61	53	-15
STL	151	82	69	.543	19.5	730	637	5229	1354	239	62	98	609	607	.259	.338	.385	.723	111	68	41	104	100	703	.663	37	38	49	-11
CLE	156	75	79	.487	28	590	659	5317	1344	223	58	50	500	544	.253	.320	.345	.665	94	-42	13	92	96	596	.584	69	74	48	-23
DET	156	73	81	.474	30	589	587	5327	1313	217	37	76	509	476	.246	.314	.344	.659	92	-57	-139	113	98	582	.572	39	40	49	-11
CHI	148	66	82	.446	34	538	609	4949	1215	214	36	25	497	427	.246	.316	.318	.634	85	-87	-79	99	102	520	.564	114	70	62	-7
WAS	151	62	89	.411	39.5	653	817	5295	1364	224	49	40	581	536	.258	.333	.341	.674	97	-14	15	96	101	641	.616	98	29	77	12
PHI	154	55	99	.357	48	549	801	5285	1315	213	46	33	440	490	.249	.309	.325	.634	85	-101	-77	96	101	536	.537	44	45	49	-13
TOT	611					5211		41955	10785	1797	400	533	4318	4144	.257	.329	.357	.686								538	390	58	-72

TEAM	CG	SHO	SV	IP	H	H/G	HR	BB	BB/G	SO	SO/G	ERA	/A	OAVG	OOBA	PR	/A	PF	CPI	FA	E	DP	FW	PW	BW	SBW	DIF
NY	88	18	17	1375.0	1259	8.2	71	431	2.8	558	3.7	2.91	118	.244	.301	114	80	94	108	.976	142	190	1.9	8.2	11.0	1.0	3.9
BOS	84	11	17	1359.0	1260	8.3	65	553	3.7	500	3.3	3.44	107	.246	.317	32	34	100	99	.974	157	156	1.0	3.5	11.1	-.6	2.0
STL	68	12	13	1363.0	1387	9.2	63	505	3.3	488	3.2	3.59	104	.262	.324	9	22	102	103	.972	167	143	.5	2.3	4.2	-.2	-.2
CLE	61	12	11	1402.7	1353	8.7	61	560	3.6	448	2.9	3.59	94	.253	.322	9	-31	93	99	.974	163	175	.7	-3.2	1.3	-1.4	.6
DET	65	12	14	1399.3	1321	8.5	60	598	3.8	671	4.3	3.13	132	.247	.321	81	154	113	111	.969	194	142	-1.0	15.8	-14.2	-.2	-4.3
CHI	86	8	8	1314.3	1304	8.9	74	473	3.2	432	3.0	3.58	102	.257	.319	11	12	100	102	.970	173	144	.2	1.2	-8.1	.2	-1.5
WAS	68	12	11	1346.7	1496	10.0	50	558	3.7	496	3.3	4.58	79	.279	.343	-138	-146	99	91	.962	222	133	-2.6	-15.0	1.5	2.2	.3
PHI	67	5	9	1374.7	1404	9.2	89	639	4.2	546	3.6	4.45	83	.263	.338	-120	-114	101	93	.969	188	124	-.7	-11.7	-7.9	-.4	-1.3
TOT	587	90	100	10934.7		8.9			3.6		3.4	3.66		.257	.329					.971	1406	1207					

Runs
Williams-Bos 141
DiMaggio-NY 123
DiMaggio-Bos 110
Clift-StL 108
Keller-NY 106

Hits
Pesky-Bos 205
Spence-Was 203
Williams-Bos 186
DiMaggio-NY 186
Keltner-Cle 179

Doubles
Kolloway-Chi 40
Clift-StL 39
Heath-Cle 37
DiMaggio-Bos 36

Triples
Spence-Was 15
Heath-Cle 13
DiMaggio-NY 13
McQuillen-StL 12

Home Runs
Williams-Bos 36
Laabs-StL 27
Keller-NY 26
York-Det 21
DiMaggio-NY 21

Total Bases
Williams-Bos 338
DiMaggio-NY 304
Keller-NY 279
Spence-Was 272
DiMaggio-Bos 272

Runs Batted In
Williams-Bos 137
DiMaggio-NY 114
Keller-NY 108
Gordon-NY 103
Doerr-Bos 102

Runs Produced
Williams-Bos 242
DiMaggio-NY 216
Keller-NY 188
Gordon-NY 173
Spence-Was 169

Bases On Balls
Williams-Bos 145
Keller-NY 114
Fleming-Cle 106
Clift-StL 106
Laabs-StL 88

Batting Average
Williams-Bos 356
Pesky-Bos 331
Spence-Was 323
Gordon-NY 322
Case-Was 320

On Base Percentage
Williams-Bos 499
Keller-NY 417
Judnich-StL 413
Fleming-Cle 412
Gordon-NY 409

Slugging Average
Williams-Bos 648
Keller-NY 513
Judnich-StL 499
DiMaggio-NY 498
Laabs-StL 498

Production
Williams-Bos 1.147
Keller-NY 930
Judnich-StL 912
Gordon-NY 900
Laabs-StL 878

Adjusted Production
Williams-Bos 213
Keller-NY 161
Gordon-NY 153
Fleming-Cle 150
Judnich-StL 150

Batter Runs
Williams-Bos 92.6
Keller-NY 46.9
Gordon-NY 38.5
Judnich-StL 35.3
DiMaggio-NY 34.4

Adjusted Batter Runs
Williams-Bos 89.9
Keller-NY 47.3
Gordon-NY 39.0
Fleming-Cle 38.2
DiMaggio-NY 34.9

Clutch Hitting Index
Lupien-Bos 135
Siebert-Phi 132
Kuhel-Chi 130
Doerr-Bos 130
Tabor-Bos 121

Runs Created
Williams-Bos 185
Keller-NY 131
DiMaggio-NY 120
Spence-Was 111
Gordon-NY 108

Total Average
Williams-Bos 1.400
Keller-NY 1.043
Judnich-StL 957
Gordon-NY 906
Laabs-StL 885

Stolen Bases
Case-Was 44
Vernon-Was 25
Rizzuto-NY 22
Kuhel-Chi 22

Stolen Base Average
Case-Was 88.0
Vernon-Was 80.6
Rizzuto-NY 78.6
Appling-Chi 77.3
Kuhel-Chi 71.0

Stolen Base Runs
Case-Was 9.6
Vernon-Was 3.9
Rizzuto-NY 3.0
Keller-NY 3.0
Appling-Chi 2.1

Fielding Runs
Rizzuto-NY 28.6
Pesky-Bos 18.6
Keltner-Cle 16.1
York-Det 15.9
DiMaggio-Bos 15.1

Total Player Rating
Williams-Bos 8.3
Gordon-NY 5.2
Keller-NY 4.1
Rizzuto-NY 4.0
Pesky-Bos 4.0

Wins
Hughson-Bos 22
Bonham-NY 21
Marchildon-Phi 17
Bagby-Cle 17
Chandler-NY 16

Win Percentage
Bonham-NY 808
Borowy-NY 789
Hughson-Bos 786
Chandler-NY 762
Bagby-Cle 654

Games
Haynes-Chi 40
Caster-StL 39

Complete Games
Hughson-Bos 22
Bonham-NY 22
Lyons-Chi 20
Hudson-Was 19

Shutouts
Bonham-NY 6

Saves
Murphy-NY 11
Haynes-Chi 6
Brown-Bos 6
Newhouser-Det 5
Caster-StL 5

Innings Pitched
Hughson-Bos 281
Bagby-Cle 271
Auker-StL 249
Marchildon-Phi 244
Hudson-Was 239

Fewest Hits/Game
Newhouser-Det 6.70
Niggeling-StL 7.56
Dobson-Bos 7.62
Trucks-Det 7.88
Chandler-NY 7.88

Fewest BB/Game
Bonham-NY 96
Lyons-Chi 1.30
Ruffing-NY 1.90
Breuer-NY 2.03
Bagby-Cle 2.13

Strikeouts
Newsom-Was 113
Hughson-Bos 113
Marchildon-Phi 110
Benton-Det 110
Niggeling-StL 107

Strikeouts/Game
Newhouser-Det 5.04
Bridges-Det 5.02
Trucks-Det 4.88
Newsom-Was 4.75
Niggeling-StL 4.67

Wins Above Team
Hughson-Bos 7.0
Bonham-NY 6.0
Marchildon-Phi 5.4
Lyons-Chi 4.9
Bagby-Cle 4.8

Earned Run Average
Lyons-Chi 2.10
Bonham-NY 2.27
Chandler-NY 2.37
Newhouser-Det 2.45
Borowy-NY 2.53

Adjusted ERA
Lyons-Chi 174
Newhouser-Det 169
Bonham-NY 151
Trucks-Det 151
Bridges-Det 150

Opponents' Batting Avg.
Newhouser-Det 207
Niggeling-StL 226
Dobson-Bos 231
Trucks-Det 231
Borowy-NY 233

Opponents' On Base Pct.
Bonham-NY 257
Lyons-Chi 271
Ruffing-NY 290
Hughson-Bos 290
Breuer-NY 292

Starter Runs
Bonham-NY 34.8
Hughson-Bos 33.2
Lyons-Chi 31.1
Chandler-NY 28.7
Newhouser-Det 24.8

Adjusted Starter Runs
Newhouser-Det 34.3
Hughson-Bos 33.6
Lyons-Chi 31.3
Benton-Det 31.0
White-Det 29.5

Clutch Pitching Index
Chandler-NY 136
Lyons-Chi 131
Hollingswort-StL 123
Humphries-Chi 121
Niggeling-StL 118

Relief Runs
Ferrick-Cle 14.9
Haynes-Chi 11.9
Caster-StL 7.5
Murphy-NY 1.6
Brown-Bos 1.4

Adjusted Relief Runs
Ferrick-Cle 12.5
Haynes-Chi 11.9
Caster-StL 8.2
Brown-Bos 1.5
Henshaw-Det 4

Relief Ranking
Haynes-Chi 15.1
Caster-StL 10.4
Ferrick-Cle 8.0
Brown-Bos 3.0
Henshaw-Det 4

Total Pitcher Index
Lyons-Chi 4.1
Newhouser-Det 3.9
Hughson-Bos 3.9
Chandler-NY 3.3
White-Det 3.1

Total Baseball Ranking
Williams-Bos 8.3
Gordon-NY 5.2
Keller-NY 4.1
Lyons-Chi 4.1
Rizzuto-NY 4.0

TEAM	G	W	L	PCT	GB	R	OR	AB	H	2B	3B	HR	BB	SO	AVG	OBP	SLG	PRO	/A	BR	/A	PF	CHI	RC	TA	SB	CS	SBA	SBR
STL	157	105	49	.682		679	475	5438	1515	259	72	70	428	438	.279	.333	.391	.724	115	93	64	105	94	720	.651	40			
CIN	155	87	67	.565	18	608	543	5329	1362	229	47	43	445	476	.256	.315	.340	.655	95	-34	-29	99	99	581	.571	49			
BRO	153	81	72	.529	23.5	716	674	5309	1444	263	35	39	580	422	.272	.346	.357	.703	110	70	72	100	103	675	.641	58			
PIT	157	80	74	.519	25	669	605	5353	1401	240	73	42	573	566	.262	.335	.357	.692	106	45	18	104	100	657	.631	64			
CHI	154	74	79	.484	30.5	632	600	5279	1380	207	56	52	574	522	.261	.336	.351	.687	105	38	45	99	96	641	.623	53			
BOS	153	68	85	.444	36.5	465	612	5196	1213	202	36	39	469	609	.233	.299	.309	.608	81	-120	-152	106	97	491	.525	56			
PHI	157	64	90	.416	41	571	676	5297	1321	186	36	66	499	556	.249	.316	.335	.651	94	-37	2	94	99	565	.565	29			
NY	156	55	98	.359	49.5	558	713	5290	1309	153	33	81	480	470	.247	.313	.335	.648	93	-47	-22	96	99	552	.559	35			
TOT	621					4898		42491	10945	1739	388	432	4048	4059	.258	.324	.347	.671								384			

TEAM	CG	SHO	SV	IP	H	H/G	HR	BB	BB/G	SO	SO/G	ERA	/A	OAVG	OOBA	PR	/A	PF	CPI	FA	E	DP	FW	PW	BW	SBW	DIF
STL	94	21	15	1426.0	1241	7.8	33	477	3.0	639	4.0	2.57	132	.235	.296	129	131	100	103	.976	151	183	.7	14.0	6.8		6.4
CIN	78	18	17	1403.0	1298	8.3	38	579	3.7	498	3.2	3.14	106	.246	.316	38	28	98	100	.980	125	193	2.2	3.0	-3.1		7.9
BRO	50	14	22	1371.7	1230	8.1	59	637	4.2	588	3.9	3.88	86	.240	.323	-75	-80	99	85	.972	168	137	-.2	-8.5	7.7		5.6
PIT	74	11	12	1399.7	1424	9.2	44	422	2.7	396	2.5	3.09	113	.264	.314	45	60	103	108	.973	170	159	-.3	6.4	1.9		-5.0
CHI	67	13	14	1385.3	1378	9.0	53	394	2.6	513	3.3	3.31	100	.260	.308	11	1	98	98	.973	168	138	-.2	.1	4.8		-7.2
BOS	87	13	4	1397.3	1361	8.8	66	441	2.8	409	2.6	3.25	113	.256	.310	20	66	109	101	.972	176	139	-.7	7.0	-16.2		1.4
PHI	66	10	14	1393.7	1430	9.2	59	451	2.9	431	2.8	3.78	86	.266	.318	-61	-84	96	93	.969	189	143	-1.4	-9.0	.2		-2.8
NY	35	6	19	1393.3	1473	9.5	80	626	4.0	588	3.8	4.08	82	.272	.343	-107	-113	99	102	.973	166	140	-.1	-12.1	-2.3		-7.0
TOT	551	106	117	11170.0		8.7			3.2		3.3	3.38		.258	.324					.974	1313	1232					

Runs
Vaughan-Bro 112
Musial-StL 108
Nicholson-Chi 95
Cavaretta-Chi 93
Stanky-Chi 92

Hits
Musial-StL 220
Witek-NY 195
Herman-Bro 193
Nicholson-Chi 188
Vaughan-Bro 186

Doubles
Musial-StL 48
Herman-Bro 41
DiMaggio-Pit 41
Vaughan-Bro 39
Holmes-Bos 33

Triples
Musial-StL 20
Klein-StL 14
Lowrey-Chi 12
Elliott-Pit 12

Home Runs
Nicholson-Chi 29
Ott-NY 18
Northey-Phi 16
Triplett-StL-Phi 15
DiMaggio-Pit 15

Total Bases
Musial-StL 347
Nicholson-Chi 323
Elliott-Pit 258
Klein-StL 257

Runs Batted In
Nicholson-Chi 128
Elliott-Pit 101
Herman-Bro 100
DiMaggio-Pit 88

Runs Produced
Nicholson-Chi 194
Musial-StL 176
Elliott-Pit 176
Herman-Bro 174
Vaughan-Bro 173

Bases On Balls
Galan-Bro 103
Ott-NY 95
Fletcher-Pit 95
Stanky-Chi 92
Tipton-Cin 85

Batting Average
Musial-StL 357
Herman-Bro 330
Elliott-Pit 315
Witek-NY 314
Nicholson-Chi 309

On Base Percentage
Musial-StL 425
Galan-Bro 412
Herman-Bro 398
Fletcher-Pit 395
Tipton-Cin 395

Slugging Average
Musial-StL 562
Nicholson-Chi 531
Elliott-Pit 444
Kurowski-StL 439
Northey-Phi 430

Production
Musial-StL 988
Nicholson-Chi 917
Elliott-Pit 820
Tipton-Cin 819
Galan-Bro 818

Adjusted Production
Musial-StL 176
Nicholson-Chi 166
Ott-NY 140
Tipton-Cin 137
Galan-Bro 137

Batter Runs
Musial-StL 65.5
Nicholson-Chi 47.8
Galan-Bro 28.5
Herman-Bro 28.0
Elliott-Pit 26.5

Adjusted Batter Runs
Musial-StL 62.2
Nicholson-Chi 48.6
Galan-Bro 28.7
Herman-Bro 28.3
Tipton-Cin 26.3

Clutch Hitting Index
Herman-Bro 153
Miller-Cin 149
Elliott-Pit 133
Wasdell-Pit-Phi 130
Stanky-Chi 127

Runs Created
Musial-StL 147
Nicholson-Chi 129
Herman-Bro 97
Vaughan-Bro 96
Elliott-Pit 96

Total Average
Musial-StL 1.039
Nicholson-Chi 944
Ott-NY 895
Galan-Bro 876
Tipton-Cin 825

Stolen Bases
Vaughan-Bro 20
Lowrey-Chi 13
Workman-Bos 12
Russell-Pit 12
Gustine-Pit 12

Stolen Base Average

Stolen Base Runs

Fielding Runs
Miller-Cin 24.9
Wietelmann-Bos 19.2
Stanky-Chi 18.0
Witek-NY 13.7
Frey-Cin 13.5

Total Player Rating
Musial-StL 5.5
Nicholson-Chi 4.9
Galan-Bro 3.1
Witek-NY 3.0
Klein-StL 2.8

Wins
Sewell-Pit 21
Riddle-Cin 21
M.Cooper-StL 21
Bithorn-Chi 18
Javery-Bos 17

Win Percentage
M.Cooper-StL 724
Sewell-Pit 700
Lanier-StL 682
Riddle-Cin 656
Bithorn-Chi 600

Games
Adams-NY 70
Webber-Bro 54
Head-Bro 47
Shoun-Cin 45
Mungo-NY 45

Complete Games
Sewell-Pit 25
Tobin-Bos 24
M.Cooper-StL 24
Andrews-Bos 23

Shutouts
Bithorn-Chi 7
M.Cooper-StL 6

Saves
Webber-Bro 10
Adams-NY 9
Shoun-Cin 7
Head-Bro 6
Beggs-Cin 6

Innings Pitched
Javery-Bos 303
VanderMeer-Cin 289
Andrews-Bos 284
M.Cooper-StL 274
Sewell-Pit 265

Fewest Hits/Game
Wyatt-Bro 6.91
VanderMeer-Cin 7.10
M.Cooper-StL 7.49
Krist-StL 7.74
Barrett-Chi-Phi 7.95

Fewest BB/Game
Rowe-Phi 1.31
Wyse-StL 1.96
Derringer-Chi 2.02
Wyatt-Bro 2.14
Davis-Bro 2.14

Strikeouts
VanderMeer-Cin 174
M.Cooper-StL 141
Javery-Bos 134
Lanier-StL 123
Higbe-Bro 108

Strikeouts/Game
VanderMeer-Cin 5.42
Higbe-Bro 5.25
Lanier-StL 5.20
M.Cooper-StL 4.63
Head-Bro 4.39

Wins Above Team
Sewell-Pit 6.4
Rowe-Phi 4.6
Wyatt-Bro 4.5
Shoun-Cin 4.1
Riddle-Cin 4.0

Earned Run Average
Lanier-StL 1.90
M.Cooper-StL 2.30
Wyatt-Bro 2.49
Sewell-Pit 2.55
Andrews-Bos 2.57

Adjusted ERA
Lanier-StL 179
M.Cooper-StL 148
Andrews-Bos 143
Tobin-Bos 138
Sewell-Pit 137

Opponents' Batting Avg.
Wyatt-Bro 207
VanderMeer-Cin 224
M.Cooper-StL 226
Krist-StL 233
Barrett-Chi-Phi 237

Opponents' On Base Pct.
Wyatt-Bro 253
Rowe-Phi 274
M.Cooper-StL 281
Andrews-Bos 286
Bithorn-Chi 287

Starter Runs
Lanier-StL 35.1
M.Cooper-StL 33.1
Andrews-Bos 25.8
Sewell-Pit 24.7
Bithorn-Chi 22.0

Adjusted Starter Runs
Lanier-StL 35.4
Andrews-Bos 35.1
M.Cooper-StL 33.5
Tobin-Bos 28.2
Sewell-Pit 27.6

Clutch Pitching Index
Lanier-StL 151
Butcher-Pit 122
Sewell-Pit 121
Riddle-Cin 117
Tobin-Bos 113

Relief Runs
Beggs-Cin 13.3
Adams-NY 8.7
Prim-Chi 5.6
Brandt-Pit 1.4

Adjusted Relief Runs
Beggs-Cin 12.4
Adams-NY 8.1
Prim-Chi 5.2
Brandt-Pit 2.1

Relief Ranking
Beggs-Cin 14.1
Adams-NY 10.6
Prim-Chi 5.6
Brandt-Pit 1.6

Total Pitcher Index
Tobin-Bos 4.4
Andrews-Bos 4.2
Sewell-Pit 3.9
Lanier-StL 3.8
M.Cooper-StL 3.4

Total Baseball Ranking
Musial-StL 5.5
Nicholson-Chi 4.9
Tobin-Bos 4.4
Andrews-Bos 4.2
Sewell-Pit 3.9

TEAM	G	W	L	PCT	GB	R	OR	AB	H	2B	3B	HR	BB	SO	AVG	OBP	SLG	PRO	/A	BR	/A	PF	CHI	RC	TA	SB	CS	SBA	SBR
NY	155	98	56	.636		669	542	5282	1350	218	59	100	624	562	.256	.337	.376	.713	115	96	117	96	95	683	.650	46	60	43	-21
WAS	153	84	69	.549	13.5	666	595	5233	1328	245	50	47	605	579	.254	.336	.347	.683	106	45	22	104	102	656	.641	142	55	72	10
CLE	153	82	71	.536	15.5	600	577	5265	1344	246	45	55	567	521	.255	.329	.350	.679	105	32	91	90	94	626	.604	47	58	45	-20
CHI	155	82	72	.532	16	573	594	5252	1297	193	46	33	561	581	.247	.322	.320	.642	94	-31	-36	101	101	570	.587	173	87	67	0
DET	155	78	76	.506	20	632	560	5364	1401	200	47	77	483	553	.261	.324	.349	.683	106	31	-2	106	99	620	.591	40	43	48	-13
STL	153	72	80	.474	25	596	604	5175	1269	229	36	78	569	646	.245	.322	.349	.671	102	13	10	100	98	603	.598	37	43	46	-14
BOS	155	68	84	.447	29	563	607	5392	1314	223	42	57	486	591	.244	.308	.332	.640	93	-48	-69	104	100	570	.562	86	61	59	-10
PHI	155	49	105	.318	49	497	717	5244	1219	174	44	26	430	465	.232	.294	.297	.591	78	-137	-144	101	110	466	.494	55	42	57	-8
TOT	617					4796		42207	10522	1728	369	473	4325	4498	.249	.322	.341	.663								626	449	58	-81

TEAM	CG	SHO	SV	IP	H	H/G	HR	BB	BB/G	SO	SO/G	ERA	/A	OAVG	OOBA	PR	/A	PF	CPI	FA	E	DP	FW	PW	BW	SBW	DIF
NY	83	14	13	1415.3	1229	7.8	60	489	3.1	653	4.2	2.93	106	.233	.295	58	25	94	95	.974	160	166	.2	2.7	12.7	-1.2	6.6
WAS	61	16	21	1388.0	1293	8.4	48	540	3.5	495	3.2	3.18	106	.246	.313	17	28	102	99	.971	179	145	-.9	3.0	2.4	2.2	.8
CLE	64	14	20	1406.3	1293	7.9	52	606	3.9	585	3.7	3.15	94	.239	.316	22	-31	90	100	.975	157	183	.4	-3.4	9.8	-1.1	-.3
CHI	70	12	19	1400.3	1352	8.7	54	501	3.2	476	3.1	3.20	104	.254	.318	14	21	101	105	.973	166	167	-.2	2.3	-3.9	1.1	5.7
DET	67	18	20	1411.7	1226	7.8	51	549	3.5	706	4.5	3.00	114	.233	.303	45	66	104	95	.971	177	130	-.8	7.1	-.2	-.3	-4.8
STL	64	10	14	1384.7	1397	9.1	74	488	3.2	572	3.7	3.41	98	.262	.321	-17	-14	101	106	.975	152	127	.6	-1.5	1.1	-.4	-3.8
BOS	62	13	16	1426.3	1369	8.6	61	615	3.9	513	3.2	3.45	100	.256	.328	-24	-1	104	105	.976	153	179	.6	-.1	-7.5	.0	-1.0
PHI	73	5	13	1394.0	1421	9.2	73	536	3.5	503	3.2	4.05	86	.265	.329	-116	-86	106	94	.973	162	148	.0	-9.3	-15.6	.2	-3.4
TOT	544	102	136	11226.7		8.4			3.5		3.6	3.30		.249	.322					.973	1306	1245					

Runs		Hits		Doubles		Triples		Home Runs		Total Bases	
Case-Was	102	Wakefield-Det	200	Wakefield-Det	38	Moses-Chi	12	York-Det	34	York-Det	301
Keller-NY	97	Appling-Chi	192	Case-Was	36	Lindell-NY	12	Keller-NY	31	Wakefield-Det	275
Wakefield-Det	91	Cramer-Det	182	Gutteridge-StL	35	York-Det	11	Stephens-StL	22	Keller-NY	269
York-Det	90	Case-Was	180	Etten-NY	35	Keller-NY	11	Heath-Cle	18	Doerr-Bos	249
Vernon-Was	89					Spence-Was	10			Stephens-StL	247

Runs Batted In		Runs Produced		Bases On Balls		Batting Average		On Base Percentage		Slugging Average	
York-Det	118	York-Det	174	Keller-NY	106	Appling-Chi	.328	Appling-Chi	.419	York-Det	.527
Etten-NY	107	Etten-NY	171	Gordon-NY	98	Wakefield-Det	.316	Cullenbine-Cle	.407	Keller-NY	.525
Johnson-NY	94	Wakefield-Det	163	Cullenbine-Cle	96	Cramer-Det	.300	Keller-NY	.396	Stephens-StL	.482
Stephens-StL	91	Johnson-NY	159	Boudreau-Cle	90	Case-Was	.294	Boudreau-Cle	.388	Heath-Cle	.481
Spence-Was	88	Case-Was	153	Appling-Chi	90	Curtwright-Chi	.291	Curtwright-Chi	.382	Wakefield-Det	.434

Production		Adjusted Production		Batter Runs		Adjusted Batter Runs		Clutch Hitting Index		Runs Created	
Keller-NY	.922	Keller-NY	175	Keller-NY	45.7	Keller-NY	48.0	Sullivan-Was	175	Keller-NY	116
York-Det	.893	Heath-Cle	164	York-Det	41.0	York-Det	37.3	Johnson-NY	157	Appling-Chi	109
Heath-Cle	.850	Cullenbine-Cle	152	Appling-Chi	35.0	Appling-Chi	34.4	Siebert-Phi	150	York-Det	108
Stephens-StL	.839	York-Det	151	Wakefield-Det	28.8	Cullenbine-Cle	33.4	Etten-NY	144	Wakefield-Det	101
Appling-Chi	.825	Stephens-StL	144	Cullenbine-Cle	27.4	Heath-Cle	29.9	Higgins-Det	143	Spence-Was	93

Total Average		Stolen Bases		Stolen Base Average		Stolen Base Runs		Fielding Runs		Total Player Rating	
Keller-NY	.992	Case-Was	61	Case-Was	81.3	Case-Was	9.9	Boudreau-Cle	27.6	Boudreau-Cle	5.7
York-Det	.883	Moses-Chi	56	Moses-Chi	80.0	Moses-Chi	8.4	Gordon-NY	24.7	Gordon-NY	5.4
Appling-Chi	.860	Tucker-Chi	29	Appling-Chi	77.1	Culberson-Bos	4.2	York-Det	18.3	York-Det	5.3
Heath-Cle	.853	Appling-Chi	27	Vernon-Was	75.0	Appling-Chi	3.3	Doerr-Bos	14.5	Appling-Chi	4.9
Cullenbine-Cle	.827	Vernon-Was	24	Fox-Bos	73.3	Vernon-Was	2.4	Clift-StL-Was	13.1	Keller-NY	4.9

Wins		Win Percentage		Games		Complete Games		Shutouts		Saves	
Trout-Det	20	Chandler-NY	.833	Brown-Bos	49	Hughson-Bos	20	Trout-Det	5	Maltzberger-Chi	14
Chandler-NY	20	Smith-Cle	.708	Trout-Det	44	Chandler-NY	20	Chandler-NY	5	Heving-Cle	9
Wynn-Was	18	Bonham-NY	.652	Wolff-Phi	41	Wensloff-NY	18	Hughson-Bos	4	Brown-Bos	9
Smith-Cle	17	Trout-Det	.625	Ryba-Bos	40	Trout-Det	18	Bonham-NY	4	Murphy-NY	8
Bagby-Cle	17	Grove-Chi	.625	Carrasquel-Was	39	Grove-Chi	18			Caster-StL	8

Innings Pitched		Fewest Hits/Game		Fewest BB/Game		Strikeouts		Strikeouts/Game		Wins Above Team	
Bagby-Cle	273	Reynolds-Cle	6.33	Leonard-Was	1.88	Reynolds-Cle	151	Reynolds-Cle	6.83	Chandler-NY	7.0
Hughson-Bos	266	Niggeling-StL-Was	6.67	Chandler-NY	1.92	Newhouser-Det	144	Newhouser-Det	6.61	Smith-Cle	4.9
Wynn-Was	257	Haefner-Was	6.87	Bonham-NY	2.07	Chandler-NY	134	Bridges-Det	5.81	Trout-Det	4.6
Chandler-NY	253	Chandler-NY	7.01	Muncrief-StL	2.11	Bridges-Det	124	Trucks-Det	5.23	Judd-Bos	3.3
Trout-Det	247	Wensloff-NY	7.22	Trucks-Det	2.31	Trucks-Det	118	Chandler-NY	4.77	Trucks-Det	3.3

Earned Run Average		Adjusted ERA		Opponents' Batting Avg.		Opponents' On Base Pct.		Starter Runs		Adjusted Starter Runs	
Chandler-NY	1.64	Chandler-NY	189	Reynolds-Cle	.202	Chandler-NY	.258	Chandler-NY	46.6	Chandler-NY	40.8
Bonham-NY	2.27	Haefner-Was	147	Niggeling-StL-Was	.204	Trucks-Det	.273	Bonham-NY	25.8	Trout-Det	26.1
Haefner-Was	2.29	Bridges-Det	143	Haefner-Was	.208	Wensloff-NY	.276	Trout-Det	22.4	Hughson-Bos	23.7
Bridges-Det	2.39	Trout-Det	138	Chandler-NY	.215	Bonham-NY	.277	Hughson-Bos	19.4	Bridges-Det	22.1
Trout-Det	2.48	Bonham-NY	136	Wensloff-NY	.219	Niggeling-StL-Was	.278	Bridges-Det	19.3	Bonham-NY	20.5

Clutch Pitching Index		Relief Runs		Adjusted Relief Runs		Relief Ranking		Total Pitcher Index		Total Baseball Ranking	
Hughson-Bos	124	Brown-Bos	12.1	Brown-Bos	13.6	Caster-StL	18.9	Chandler-NY	6.1	Chandler-NY	6.1
Muncrief-StL	120	Caster-StL	9.8	Caster-StL	10.0	Brown-Bos	18.7	Trout-Det	3.8	Boudreau-Cle	5.7
Bonham-NY	116	Maltzberger-Chi	9.3	Maltzberger-Chi	9.8	Maltzberger-Chi	12.9	Bridges-Det	2.8	Gordon-NY	5.4
Galehouse-StL	115	Naymick-Cle	7.1	Naymick-Cle	4.6	Murphy-NY	10.3	Hughson-Bos	2.4	York-Det	5.3
Candini-Was	115	Murphy-NY	5.9	Murphy-NY	4.3	Naymick-Cle	5.6	Haefner-Was	2.2	Appling-Chi	4.9

TEAM	G	W	L	PCT	GB	R	OR	AB	H	2B	3B	HR	BB	SO	AVG	OBP	SLG	PRO	/A	BR	/A	PF	CHI	RC	TA	SB	CS	SBA	SBR
STL	157	105	49	.682		772	490	5475	1507	274	59	100	544	473	.275	.344	.402	.746	116	110	105	101	97	775	.691	37			
PIT	158	90	63	.588	14.5	744	662	5428	1441	248	80	70	573	616	.265	.338	.379	.717	108	57	22	105	101	707	.666	87			
CIN	155	89	65	.578	16	573	537	5271	1340	229	31	51	423	391	.254	.313	.338	.651	89	-73	-42	95	100	558	.563	51			
CHI	157	75	79	.487	30	702	669	5462	1425	236	46	71	520	521	.261	.328	.360	.688	100	-1	-5	101	104	658	.618	53			
NY	155	67	87	.435	38	682	773	5306	1398	191	47	93	542	480	.263	.331	.370	.701	103	22	-1	104	100	656	.628	38			
BOS	155	65	89	.422	40	593	674	5282	1299	250	39	79	456	509	.246	.308	.353	.661	92	-60	-24	95	100	586	.583	37			
BRO	155	63	91	.409	42	690	832	5393	1450	255	51	56	486	451	.269	.331	.366	.697	102	16	21	99	101	664	.622	43			
PHI	154	61	92	.399	43.5	539	658	5301	1331	199	42	55	470	500	.251	.316	.336	.652	89	-70	-71	100	92	571	.566	32			
TOT	623					5295		42918	11191	1882	395	575	3984	3941	.261	.326	.363	.689								378			

TEAM	CG	SHO	SV	IP	H	H/G	HR	BB	BB/G	SO	SO/G	ERA	/A	OAVG	OOBA	PR	/A	PF	CPI	FA	E	DP	FW	PW	BW	SBW	DIF
STL	89	26	12	1426.0	1228	7.8	55	468	3.0	637	4.0	2.68	129	.233	.294	148	121	95	103	.982	112	162	3.6	12.4	10.8		1.2
PIT	77	10	19	1416.0	1466	9.3	65	435	2.8	452	2.9	3.43	109	.265	.314	28	48	104	103	.970	191	122	-1.3	4.9	2.3		7.6
CIN	93	17	12	1398.0	1292	8.3	60	390	2.5	369	2.4	2.97	115	.245	.295	98	68	95	99	.978	137	153	2.0	7.0	-4.3		7.3
CHI	70	11	13	1400.7	1484	9.5	75	458	2.9	545	3.5	3.59	101	.273	.325	4	4	100	108	.970	186	151	-1.0	.4	-.5		-.9
NY	47	4	21	1365.0	1413	9.3	116	587	3.9	499	3.3	4.29	89	.265	.335	-102	-73	105	98	.971	179	128	-.5	-7.5	-.1		-1.9
BOS	70	14	12	1386.7	1430	9.3	80	527	3.4	454	2.9	3.67	94	.267	.329	-9	-31	96	106	.971	182	160	-.7	-3.2	-2.5		-5.6
BRO	50	4	13	1366.0	1471	9.7	75	660	4.3	487	3.2	4.68	78	.273	.349	-162	-152	102	93	.966	197	112	-1.7	-15.6	2.2		1.1
PHI	66	12	6	1393.3	1407	9.1	49	459	3.0	496	3.2	3.64	102	.260	.314	-4	9	103	93	.972	177	138	-.4	.9	-7.3		-8.7
TOT	562	98	108	11151.7		9.0			3.2		3.2	3.61		.261	.326					.972	1361	1126					

Runs
Nicholson-Chi 116
Musial-StL 112
Russell-Pit 109
Hopp-StL 106
Cavaretta-Chi 106

Hits
Musial-StL 197
Cavaretta-Chi 197
Holmes-Bos 195
Walker-Bro 191
Russell-Pit 181

Doubles
Musial-StL 51
Galan-Bro 43
Holmes-Bos 42

Triples
Barrett-Pit 19
Elliott-Pit 16
Cavaretta-Chi 15
Russell-Pit 14
Musial-StL 14

Home Runs
Nicholson-Chi 33
Ott-NY 26
Northey-Phi 22
McCormick-Cin 20
Kurowski-StL 20

Total Bases
Nicholson-Chi 317
Musial-StL 312
Holmes-Bos 288
Walker-Bro 283
Northey-Phi 283

Runs Batted In
Nicholson-Chi 122
Elliott-Pit 108
Northey-Phi 104
Sanders-StL 102
McCormick-Cin 102

Runs Produced
Nicholson-Chi 205
Musial-StL 194
Elliott-Pit 183
Cavaretta-Chi 183

Bases On Balls
Galan-Bro 101
Nicholson-Chi 93
Ott-NY 90
Musial-StL 90
Barrett-Pit 86

Batting Average
Walker-Bro 357
Musial-StL 347
Medwick-NY 337
Hopp-StL 336
Cavaretta-Chi 321

On Base Percentage
Musial-StL 440
Walker-Bro 434
Galan-Bro 426
Ott-NY 423
Hopp-StL 404

Slugging Average
Musial-StL 549
Nicholson-Chi 545
Ott-NY 544
Walker-Bro 529
Hopp-StL 499

Production
Musial-StL 990
Ott-NY 967
Walker-Bro 963
Nicholson-Chi 935
Galan-Bro 922

Adjusted Production
Musial-StL 176
Walker-Bro 172
Ott-NY 165
Galan-Bro 160
Nicholson-Chi 160

Batter Runs
Musial-StL 60.9
Walker-Bro 51.2
Nicholson-Chi 47.4
Galan-Bro 46.5
Ott-NY 40.4

Adjusted Batter Runs
Musial-StL 60.5
Walker-Bro 51.8
Galan-Bro 47.1
Nicholson-Chi 46.9
Ott-NY 38.5

Clutch Hitting Index
Elliott-Pit 146
Olmo-Bro 143
Medwick-NY 136
Dahlgren-Pit 129
Sanders-StL 129

Runs Created
Musial-StL 145
Nicholson-Chi 132
Walker-Bro 128
Galan-Bro 123
Russell-Pit 112

Total Average
Musial-StL 1.095
Ott-NY 1.087
Walker-Bro 1.034
Nicholson-Chi 1.002
Galan-Bro 992

Stolen Bases
Barrett-Pit 28
Lupien-Phi 18
Hughes-Chi 16
Hopp-StL 15
Kerr-NY 14

Stolen Base Average

Stolen Base Runs

Fielding Runs
Kerr-NY 15.7
Williams-Cin 14.4
Miller-Cin 12.7
Russell-Pit 12.3
McCormick-Cin 12.3

Total Player Rating
Musial-StL 4.4
Walker-Bro 3.8
Galan-Bro 3.8
Nicholson-Chi 3.5
Elliott-Pit 3.5

Wins
Walters-Cin 23
M.Cooper-StL 22
Voiselle-NY 21
Sewell-Pit 21
Tobin-Bos 18

Win Percentage
Wilks-StL 810
Brecheen-StL 762
M.Cooper-StL 759
Walters-Cin 742
Sewell-Pit 636

Games
Adams-NY 65
Webber-Bro 48
Rescigno-Pit 48
Voiselle-NY 43
Tobin-Bos 43

Complete Games
Tobin-Bos 28
Walters-Cin 27
Voiselle-NY 25
Sewell-Pit 24
M.Cooper-StL 22

Shutouts
M.Cooper-StL 7
Walters-Cin 6
Tobin-Bos 5
Lanier-StL 5
Butcher-Pit 5

Saves
Adams-NY 13
Schmidt-StL 5
Rescigno-Pit 5
Davis-Bro 4
Cuccurullo-Pit 4

Innings Pitched
Voiselle-NY 313
Tobin-Bos 299
Sewell-Pit 286
Walters-Cin 285
Raffensberge-Phi 259

Fewest Hits/Game
Walters-Cin 7.36
Wilks-StL 7.49
Heusser-Cin 7.69
Lanier-StL 7.71
Voiselle-NY 7.94

Fewest BB/Game
Raffensberge-Phi . . 1.56
Strincevich-Pit 1.75
Davis-Bro 1.81
Shoun-Cin 1.86
Derringer-Chi 1.95

Strikeouts
Voiselle-NY 161
Lanier-StL 141
Javery-Bos 137
Raffensberge-Phi 136

Strikeouts/Game
Lanier-StL 5.67
Javery-Bos 4.85
Raffensberge-Phi . . . 4.73
Voiselle-NY 4.63
Melton-Bro 4.38

Wins Above Team
Walters-Cin 6.9
Voiselle-NY 5.3
Wilks-StL 4.6
M.Cooper-StL 4.1
Passeau-Chi 3.6

Earned Run Average
Heusser-Cin 2.38
Walters-Cin 2.40
M.Cooper-StL 2.46
Wilks-StL 2.64
Lanier-StL 2.65

Adjusted ERA
Heusser-Cin 144
Walters-Cin 142
M.Cooper-StL 140
Ostermueller-Br-Pit . .132
Wilks-StL 130

Opponents' Batting Avg.
Walters-Cin 219
Wilks-StL 227
Heusser-Cin 231
Voiselle-NY 232
Lanier-StL 234

Opponents' On Base Pct.
Heusser-Cin 270
Wilks-StL 272
Raffensberge-Phi 279
Walters-Cin 279
De LaCruz-Cin 281

Starter Runs
Walters-Cin 38.4
M.Cooper-StL 32.1
Munger-StL 30.6
Heusser-Cin 26.4
Lanier-StL 23.9

Adjusted Starter Runs
Walters-Cin 32.2
Munger-StL 28.3
M.Cooper-StL 27.4
Voiselle-NY 27.3
Ostermueller-Br-Pt. . . 24.9

Clutch Pitching Index
Fleming-Chi 121
Ostermueller-Br-Pit . .121
Chipman-Bro-Chi 119
Wyse-Chi 113
Javery-Bos 111

Relief Runs
Karl-Phi 12.7
Donnelly-StL 12.5

Adjusted Relief Runs
Karl-Phi 13.6
Donnelly-StL 11.1

Relief Ranking
Karl-Phi 7.6
Donnelly-StL 4.6

Total Pitcher Index
Walters-Cin 4.4
Munger-StL 3.2
Tobin-Bos 3.0
Voiselle-NY 2.8
Ostermueller-Br-Pit . . 2.8

Total Baseball Ranking
Musial-StL 4.4
Walters-Cin 4.4
Walker-Bro 3.8
Galan-Bro 3.8
Nicholson-Chi 3.5

TEAM	G	W	L	PCT	GB	R	OR	AB	H	2B	3B	HR	BB	SO	AVG	OBP	SLG	PRO	/A	BR	/A	PF	CHI	RC	TA	SB	CS	SBA	SBR
STL	154	89	65	.578		684	587	5269	1328	223	45	72	531	604	.252	.323	.352	.675	99	-3	-14	102	**109**	629	.603	44	33	57	-6
DET	156	88	66	.571	1	658	**581**	5344	1405	220	44	60	532	500	.263	.332	.354	.686	102	21	-11	105	99	641	.608	61	55	53	-14
NY	154	83	71	.539	6	674	617	5331	1410	216	**74**	**96**	523	627	.264	.333	**.387**	**.720**	**112**	75	35	106	95	707	**.661**	91	31	**75**	**9**
BOS	156	77	77	.500	12	**739**	676	5400	1456	**277**	56	69	522	505	**.270**	**.336**	.380	.716	111	73	**87**	98	103	**710**	.647	60	40	60	-5
PHI	155	72	82	.468	17	525	594	5312	1364	169	47	36	422	490	.257	.314	.327	.641	89	-72	-77	101	95	547	.537	42	32	57	-6
CLE	155	72	82	.468	17	643	677	5481	**1458**	270	50	70	512	593	.266	.331	.372	.703	107	46	46	100	92	684	.623	48	42	53	-10
CHI	154	71	83	.461	18	543	662	5292	1307	210	55	23	439	**448**	.247	.307	.320	.627	85	-96	-95	100	104	533	.536	66	47	58	-7
WAS	154	64	90	.416	25	592	664	5319	1386	186	42	33	470	477	.261	.324	.330	.654	93	-40	25	90	100	594	.580	**127**	59	68	3
TOT	619					5058		42748	11114	1771	413	459	3951	4244	.260	.325	.353	.678								539	339	61	-41

TEAM	CG	SHO	SV	IP	H	H/G	HR	BB	BB/G	SO	SO/G	ERA	/A	OAVG	OOBA	PR	/A	PF	CPI	FA	E	DP	FW	PW	BW	SBW	DIF
STL	71	16	17	1396.7	1392	9.0	58	469	3.0	**581**	**3.7**	3.17	108	.258	.314	40	39	100	**105**	.972	171	142	.5	4.1	-1.5	-.0	9.0
DET	**87**	**20**	8	1400.0	1373	8.8	**39**	452	2.9	568	**3.7**	**3.09**	115	.257	.312	53	72	104	103	.970	190	184	-.7	**7.6**	-1.2	-.9	6.2
NY	78	9	13	1390.3	1351	**8.7**	82	532	3.4	529	3.4	3.39	107	.256	.320	6	35	105	105	**.974**	156	170	**1.3**	3.7	3.7	**1.5**	-4.2
BOS	58	7	17	1394.3	1404	9.1	66	592	3.8	524	3.4	3.82	87	.262	.333	-60	-78	97	98	.972	171	154	.5	-8.2	**9.1**	.0	-1.4
PHI	72	10	14	1398.3	**1345**	**8.7**	58	**390**	**2.5**	534	3.4	3.26	108	**.251**	**.301**	26	38	102	93	.971	176	127	.2	4.0	-8.1	-.0	-1.0
CLE	48	7	**18**	1419.3	1428	9.1	40	621	3.9	524	3.3	3.65	95	.264	.337	-35	-31	101	102	**.974**	165	**192**	.8	-3.3	4.8	-.5	-6.9
CHI	64	5	17	1391.7	1411	9.1	68	420	2.7	481	3.1	3.58	98	.264	.313	-22	-10	102	97	.970	183	154	-.2	-1.1	-10.0	-.2	5.5
WAS	83	13	11	1381.0	1410	9.2	48	475	3.1	503	3.3	3.49	89	.264	.321	-9	-59	91	99	.964	218	156	-2.3	-6.2	2.6	.9	-8.0
TOT	561	87	115	11171.7		9.0			3.2		3.4	3.43		.260	.325					.971	1430	1279					

Runs
Stirnweiss-NY 125
Johnson-Bos 106
Cullenbine-Cle 98
Doerr-Bos 95
Metkovich-Bos 94

Hits
Stirnweiss-NY 205
Boudreau-Cle 191
Spence-Was 187
Lindell-NY 178
Rocco-Cle 174

Doubles
Boudreau-Cle 45
Keltner-Cle 41
Johnson-Bos 40
Fox-Det 37
Stirnweiss-NY 35

Triples
Stirnweiss-NY 16
Lindell-NY 16
Gutteridge-StL 11
Doerr-Bos 10

Home Runs
Etten-NY 22
Stephens-StL 20
York-Det 18
Spence-Was 18
Lindell-NY 18

Total Bases
Lindell-NY 297
Stirnweiss-NY 296
Spence-Was 288
Johnson-Bos 277

Runs Batted In
Stephens-StL 109
Johnson-Bos 106
Lindell-NY 103
Spence-Was 100
York-Det 98

Runs Produced
Johnson-Bos 195
Stephens-StL 180
Lindell-NY 176
Spence-Was 165
Cullenbine-Cle 162

Bases On Balls
Etten-NY 97
Johnson-Bos 95
Cullenbine-Cle 87
McQuinn-StL 85
Higgins-Det 81

Batting Average
Boudreau-Cle 327
Doerr-Bos 325
Johnson-Bos 324
Stirnweiss-NY 319
Spence-Was 316

On Base Percentage
Johnson-Bos 431
Boudreau-Cle 406
Doerr-Bos 399
Etten-NY 399
Byrnes-StL 396

Slugging Average
Doerr-Bos 528
Johnson-Bos 528
Lindell-NY 500
Spence-Was 486

Production
Johnson-Bos 959
Doerr-Bos 927
Spence-Was 877
Etten-NY 865
Lindell-NY 851

Adjusted Production
Johnson-Bos 177
Spence-Was 167
Doerr-Bos 167
Boudreau-Cle 141
Etten-NY 138

Batter Runs
Johnson-Bos 52.8
Spence-Was 38.1
Doerr-Bos 37.9
Etten-NY 37.2
Wakefield-Det 36.7

Adjusted Batter Runs
Johnson-Bos 54.3
Spence-Was 45.6
Doerr-Bos 39.2
Wakefield-Det 35.0
Boudreau-Cle 33.1

Clutch Hitting Index
Christman-StL 145
Carnett-Chi 133
Stephens-StL 131
Torres-Was 124
Trosky-Chi 124

Runs Created
Stirnweiss-NY 128
Johnson-Bos 124
Spence-Was 118
Etten-NY 114
Boudreau-Cle 112

Total Average
Johnson-Bos 1.005
Doerr-Bos 951
Stirnweiss-NY 934
Etten-NY 884
Spence-Was 873

Stolen Bases
Stirnweiss-NY 55
Case-Was 49
Myatt-Was 26
Moses-Chi 21
Gutteridge-StL 20

Stolen Base Average
Stirnweiss-NY 83.3
Moses-Chi 75.0
Case-Was 73.1
Myatt-Was 72.2
Gutteridge-StL 71.4

Stolen Base Runs
Stirnweiss-NY 9.9
Case-Was 3.9
Moses-Chi 2.1
Myatt-Was 1.8
Grimes-NY 1.8

Fielding Runs
Mayo-Det 24.5
Boudreau-Cle 23.4
Stirnweiss-NY 18.9
Rocco-Cle 16.8
Spence-Was 16.4

Total Player Rating
Boudreau-Cle 6.8
Stirnweiss-NY 6.6
Spence-Was 5.5
Johnson-Bos 5.4
Doerr-Bos 4.5

Wins
Newhouser-Det 29
Trout-Det 27
Potter-StL 19
Hughson-Bos 18

Win Percentage
Hughson-Bos 783
Newhouser-Det 763
Potter-StL 731
Trout-Det 659
Borowy-NY 586

Games
Heving-Cle 63
Berry-Phi 53
Trout-Det 49
Newhouser-Det 47
Klieman-Cle 47

Complete Games
Trout-Det 33
Newhouser-Det 25

Shutouts
Trout-Det 7
Newhouser-Det 6
Jakucki-StL 4

Saves
Maltzberger-Chi 12
Caster-StL 12
Berry-Phi 12
Heving-Cle 10
Barrett-Bos 8

Innings Pitched
Trout-Det 352
Newhouser-Det 312
Newsom-Phi 265
Kramer-StL 257
Borowy-NY 253

Fewest Hits/Game
Gromek-Cle 7.06
Niggeling-Was 7.17
Newhouser-Det 7.62
Hughson-Bos 7.63
Borowy-NY 7.97

Fewest BB/Game
Harris-Phi 1.34
Leonard-Was 1.45
Bonham-NY 1.72
Gorsica-Det 1.78
Hamlin-Phi 1.80

Strikeouts
Newhouser-Det 187
Trout-Det 144
Newsom-Phi 142
Kramer-StL 124
Niggeling-Was 121

Strikeouts/Game
Newhouser-Det 5.39
Niggeling-Was 5.29
Gromek-Cle 5.07
Hughson-Bos 4.97
Newsom-Phi 4.82

Wins Above Team
Newhouser-Det 9.8
Hughson-Bos 7.0
Trout-Det 5.3
Potter-StL 5.3
Maltzberger-Chi 3.0

Earned Run Average
Trout-Det 2.12
Newhouser-Det 2.22
Hughson-Bos 2.26
Niggeling-Was 2.32
Kramer-StL 2.49

Adjusted ERA
Trout-Det 167
Newhouser-Det 160
Hughson-Bos 147
Kramer-StL 138
Borowy-NY 137

Opponents' Batting Avg.
Gromek-Cle 219
Niggeling-Was 221
Hughson-Bos 225
Newhouser-Det 230
Borowy-NY 236

Opponents' On Base Pct.
Hughson-Bos 264
Leonard-Was 280
Trout-Det 282
Gromek-Cle 284
Newhouser-Det 289

Starter Runs
Trout-Det 51.2
Newhouser-Det 41.9
Kramer-StL 27.0
Hughson-Bos 26.4
Niggeling-Was 25.5

Adjusted Starter Runs
Trout-Det 55.9
Newhouser-Det 46.1
Borowy-NY 27.5
Kramer-StL 26.9
Hughson-Bos 23.7

Clutch Pitching Index
Donald-NY 129
Woods-Bos 122
Smith-Cle 116
Haynes-Chi 116
Bonham-NY 115

Relief Runs
Heving-Cle 19.7
Berry-Phi 18.3
Caster-StL 8.9
Maltzberger-Chi 4.7

Adjusted Relief Runs
Heving-Cle 20.1
Berry-Phi 19.2
Caster-StL 8.8
Maltzberger-Chi 5.5

Relief Ranking
Berry-Phi 32.8
Heving-Cle 20.3
Caster-StL 14.7
Maltzberger-Chi 9.8

Total Pitcher Index
Trout-Det 8.8
Newhouser-Det 5.9
Kramer-StL 3.6
Borowy-NY 2.8
Hughson-Bos 2.5

Total Baseball Ranking
Trout-Det 8.8
Boudreau-Cle 6.8
Stirnweiss-NY 6.6
Newhouser-Det 5.9
Spence-Was 5.5

TEAM	G	W	L	PCT	GB	R	OR	AB	H	2B	3B	HR	BB	SO	AVG	OBP	SLG	PRO	/A	BR	/A	PF	CHI	RC	TA	SB	CS	SBA	SBR
CHI	155	98	56	.636		735	532	5298	1465	229	52	57	554	462	.277	.349	.372	.721	107	53	61	99	98	714	.668	69			
STL	155	95	59	.617	3	756	583	5487	1498	256	44	64	515	488	.273	.338	.371	.709	104	25	24	100	103	716	.647	55			
BRO	155	87	67	.565	11	795	724	5418	1468	257	71	57	629	434	.271	.349	.376	.725	108	66	95	96	102	746	.685	75			
PIT	155	82	72	.532	16	753	686	5343	1425	259	56	72	590	480	.267	.342	.377	.719	106	45	21	103	102	701	.668	81			
NY	154	78	74	.513	19	668	700	5350	1439	175	35	114	501	457	.269	.336	.379	.715	105	33	35	100	92	692	.648	38			
BOS	154	67	85	.441	30	721	728	5441	1453	229	25	101	520	510	.267	.334	.374	.708	103	20	-66	112	100	692	.650	82			
CIN	154	61	93	.396	37	536	694	5283	1317	221	26	56	392	532	.249	.304	.333	.637	83	-121	-82	94	98	537	.551	71			
PHI	154	46	108	.299	52	548	865	5203	1278	197	27	56	449	501	.246	.307	.326	.633	82	-121	-97	96	101	527	.549	54			
TOT	618					5512		42823	11343	1823	336	577	4150	3864	.265	.333	.364	.696								525			

TEAM	CG	SHO	SV	IP	H	H/G	HR	BB	BB/G	SO	SO/G	ERA	/A	OAVG	OOBA	PR	/A	PF	CPI	FA	E	DP	FW	PW	BW	SBW	DIF
CHI	86	17	14	1366.0	1301	8.6	57	385	2.5	541	3.6	2.98	121	.249	.299	124	96	95	102	.980	121	124	3.3	9.6	6.1		2.0
STL	77	18	9	1408.7	1351	8.6	70	497	3.2	510	3.3	3.24	114	.253	.314	87	70	97	106	.977	137	150	2.3	7.0	2.4		6.3
BRO	61	8	18	1391.0	1357	8.8	74	586	3.8	557	3.6	3.71	97	.253	.325	14	-17	95	98	.962	230	144	-3.3	-1.7	9.5		5.5
PIT	73	8	16	1386.0	1477	9.6	61	455	3.0	518	3.4	3.77	103	.272	.325	5	18	102	100	.971	178	141	-.1	1.8	5.1		1.2
NY	53	13	21	1374.7	1401	9.2	85	528	3.5	530	3.5	4.06	94	.262	.325	-39	-38	100	95	.973	166	112	.6	-3.8	3.5		1.7
BOS	57	7	13	1390.7	1474	9.5	99	557	3.6	404	2.6	4.04	106	.271	.335	-36	37	113	104	.969	193	160	-1.1	3.7	-6.6		-5.0
CIN	77	11	6	1367.3	1438	9.5	70	534	3.5	372	2.4	4.00	92	.270	.333	-29	-46	97	100	.976	146	138	1.8	-4.6	-8.2		-5.0
PHI	31	4	26	1349.0	1544	10.3	61	608	4.1	432	2.9	4.65	84	.285	.353	-127	-114	102	97	.962	234	150	-3.5	-11.4	-9.7		-6.3
TOT	515	86	123	11033.3		9.3			3.4		3.2	3.80		.265	.333					.971	1405	1119					

Runs		Hits		Doubles		Triples		Home Runs		Total Bases	
Stanky-Bro	128	Holmes-Bos	224	Holmes-Bos	47	Olmo-Bro	13	Holmes-Bos	28	Holmes-Bos	367
Rosen-Bro	126	Rosen-Bro	197	Walker-Bro	42	Pafko-Chi	12	Workman-Bos	25	Adams-Phi-StL	279
Holmes-Bos	125	Hack-Chi	193	Galan-Bro	36	Rucker-NY	11	Adams-Phi-StL	22	Rosen-Bro	279
Galan-Bro	114	Clay-Cin	184	Elliott-Pit	36	Rosen-Bro	11	Ott-NY	21	Walker-Bro	266
Hack-Chi	110			Cavaretta-Chi	34	Cavaretta-Chi	10	Kurowski-StL	21	Kurowski-StL	261

Runs Batted In		Runs Produced		Bases On Balls		Batting Average		On Base Percentage		Slugging Average	
Walker-Bro	124	Walker-Bro	218	Stanky-Bro	148	Cavaretta-Chi	.355	Cavaretta-Chi	.449	Holmes-Bos	.577
Holmes-Bos	117	Holmes-Bos	214	Galan-Bro	114	Holmes-Bos	.352	Galan-Bro	.423	Kurowski-StL	.511
Pafko-Chi	110	Galan-Bro	197	Hack-Chi	99	Rosen-Bro	.325	Hack-Chi	.420	Cavaretta-Chi	.500
Olmo-Bro	110	Adams-Phi-StL	191	Nicholson-Chi	92	Hack-Chi	.323	Holmes-Bos	.420	Ott-NY	.499
Adams-Phi-StL	109	Rosen-Bro	189	Sanders-StL	83	Kurowski-StL	.323	Stanky-Bro	.417	Olmo-Bro	.462

Production		Adjusted Production		Batter Runs		Adjusted Batter Runs		Clutch Hitting Index		Runs Created	
Holmes-Bos	.997	Cavaretta-Chi	166	Holmes-Bos	62.9	Holmes-Bos	52.7	Walker-Bro	157	Holmes-Bos	156
Cavaretta-Chi	.949	Holmes-Bos	156	Cavaretta-Chi	46.4	Cavaretta-Chi	47.2	Elliott-Pit	157	Cavaretta-Chi	119
Ott-NY	.910	Ott-NY	153	Galan-Bro	36.8	Galan-Bro	40.1	Pafko-Chi	145	Galan-Bro	116
Kurowski-StL	.894	Kurowski-StL	147	Ott-NY	33.4	Ott-NY	33.7	Lowrey-Chi	139	Hack-Chi	111
Galan-Bro	.864	Galan-Bro	147	Kurowski-StL	30.7	Kurowski-StL	30.6	Olmo-Bro	136	Rosen-Bro	110

Total Average		Stolen Bases		Stolen Base Average		Stolen Base Runs		Fielding Runs		Total Player Rating	
Holmes-Bos	1.078	Schoendienst-StL	26					Kerr-NY	28.3	Holmes-Bos	4.5
Cavaretta-Chi	1.037	Barrett-Pit	25					Gillenwater-Bos	19.4	Stanky-Bro	4.3
Ott-NY	.959	Clay-Cin	19					Hack-Chi	15.7	Hack-Chi	4.3
Galan-Bro	.936							Masi-Bos	13.7	Cavaretta-Chi	3.8
Kurowski-StL	.876							Coscarart-Pit	11.1	Walker-Bro	3.0

Wins		Win Percentage		Games		Complete Games		Shutouts		Saves	
Barrett-Bos-StL	23	Brecheen-StL	.789	Karl-Phi	67	Barrett-Bos-StL	24	Passeau-Chi	5	Karl-Phi	15
Wyse-Chi	22	Burkhart-StL	.692	Adams-NY	65	Wyse-Chi	23	Voiselle-NY	4	Adams-NY	15
Gregg-Bro	18	Wyse-Chi	.688	Hutchings-Bos	57	Passeau-Chi	19	Heusser-Cin	4	Rescigno-Pit	9
Burkhart-StL	18	Barrett-Bos-StL	.657	Barrett-Bos-StL	45	Strincevich-Pit	18	Donnelly-StL	4		
Passeau-Chi	17	Passeau-Chi	.654	Fox-Cin	45	Heusser-Cin	18	Burkhart-StL	4		

Innings Pitched		Fewest Hits/Game		Fewest BB/Game		Strikeouts		Strikeouts/Game		Wins Above Team	
Barrett-Bos-StL	285	Prim-Chi	7.75	Prim-Chi	1.25	Roe-Pit	148	Roe-Pit	5.67	Brecheen-StL	4.6
Wyse-Chi	278	Brecheen-StL	7.80	Barrett-Bos-StL	1.71	Gregg-Bro	139	Mungo-NY	4.97	Borowy-Chi	3.9
Gregg-Bro	254	Gregg-Bro	7.83	Roe-Pit	1.76	Voiselle-NY	115	Gregg-Bro	4.93	Barrett-Bos-StL	3.7
Roe-Pit	235	Mungo-NY	7.92	Wyse-Chi	1.78	Mungo-NY	101	Hutchings-Bos	4.82	Mungo-NY	3.7
Voiselle-NY	232	Passeau-Chi	8.13	Strincevich-Pit	1.93	Hutchings-Bos	99	Prim-Chi	4.80	Cooper-StL-Bos	3.0

Earned Run Average		Adjusted ERA		Opponents' Batting Avg.		Opponents' On Base Pct.		Starter Runs		Adjusted Starter Runs	
Prim-Chi	2.40	Prim-Chi	151	Prim-Chi	.228	Prim-Chi	.253	Wyse-Chi	34.4	Passeau-Chi	29.2
Passeau-Chi	2.46	Passeau-Chi	147	Gregg-Bro	.232	Passeau-Chi	.285	Passeau-Chi	33.9	Wyse-Chi	28.7
Brecheen-StL	2.52	Brecheen-StL	146	Brecheen-StL	.238	Wyse-Chi	.291	Prim-Chi	25.7	Roe-Pit	26.4
Walters-Cin	2.68	Walters-Cin	138	Mungo-NY	.238	Barrett-Bos-StL	.292	Barrett-Bos-StL	25.4	Barrett-Bos-StL	24.3
Wyse-Chi	2.69	Roe-Pit	135	Passeau-Chi	.238	Roe-Pit	.294	Roe-Pit	24.3	Logan-Bos	22.9

Clutch Pitching Index		Relief Runs		Adjusted Relief Runs		Relief Ranking		Total Pitcher Index		Total Baseball Ranking	
Logan-Bos	124	Karl-Phi	16.4	Karl-Phi	18.1	Karl-Phi	17.8	Passeau-Chi	3.5	Holmes-Bos	4.5
Butcher-Pit	124	Buker-Bro	4.7	Adams-NY	4.8	Adams-NY	9.1	Wyse-Chi	2.9	Stanky-Bro	4.3
Walters-Cin	124	Adams-NY	4.7	Buker-Bro	2.8	Buker-Bro	2.9	Logan-Bos	2.5	Hack-Chi	4.3
Lee-Phi-Bos	123	Chipman-Chi	2.4	Chipman-Chi	.9	Chipman-Chi	1.0	Walters-Cin	2.5	Cavaretta-Chi	3.8
Wyse-Chi	117							Roe-Pit	2.5	Passeau-Chi	3.5

TEAM	G	W	L	PCT	GB	R	OR	AB	H	2B	3B	HR	BB	SO	AVG	OBP	SLG	PRO	/A	BR	/A	PF	CHI	RC	TA	SB	CS	SBA	SBR
DET	155	88	65	.575		633	565	5257	1345	**227**	47	77	517	533	.256	.324	.361	.685	104	20	-16	106	101	627	.609	60	54	53	-13
WAS	156	87	67	.565	1.5	622	562	5326	1375	197	63	27	545	489	.258	.330	.664	.685	98	-7	35	93	102	612	.595	110	65	63	-5
STL	154	81	70	.536	6	597	548	5227	1302	215	37	63	500	555	.249	.316	.341	.657	96	-28	-119	115	104	584	.572	25	31	45	-10
NY	152	81	71	.533	6.5	676	606	5176	1343	189	61	93	618	567	.259	**.343**	**.373**	.716	113	90	47	107	97	698	**.666**	64	43	60	-6
CLE	147	73	72	.503	11	557	548	4898	1249	216	48	65	505	578	.255	.326	.359	.685	104	23	31	99	94	588	.604	19	31	38	-12
CHI	150	71	78	.477	15	596	633	5077	1330	204	55	22	470	467	**.262**	.326	.337	.663	98	-12	15	95	**105**	571	.579	78	54	59	-8
BOS	157	71	83	.461	17.5	599	674	5367	**1393**	225	44	50	541	534	.260	.330	.346	.676	102	12	43	95	95	634	.602	72	50	59	-7
PHI	153	52	98	.347	34.5	494	638	5296	1297	201	37	33	449	**463**	.245	.306	.316	.622	86	-95	-56	94	98	523	.522	25	45	36	-19
TOT	612					4774		41624	10634	1674	392	430	4145	4186	.255	.325	.346	.671								453	373	55	-87

TEAM	CG	SHO	SV	IP	H	H/G	HR	BB	BB/G	SO	SO/G	ERA	/A	OAVG	OOBA	PR	/A	PF	CPI	FA	E	DP	FW	PW	BW	SBW	DIF
DET	78	**19**	16	1393.7	1305	8.4	48	538	3.5	**588**	**3.8**	2.99	118	.249	.316	58	81	105	**108**	.975	158	173	.3	8.7	-1.7	-.2	4.5
WAS	82	**19**	11	1412.3	1307	**8.3**	42	**440**	2.8	550	3.5	**2.92**	106	**.241**	**.296**	68	26	92	93	.970	183	124	-1.1	2.8	3.7	**.6**	4.0
STL	**91**	10	8	1382.7	1307	8.5	59	506	3.3	570	3.7	3.14	**122**	.249	.310	33	**107**	114	101	.976	143	123	1.1	**11.5**	-12.7	.1	5.6
NY	78	9	14	1355.0	1277	8.5	66	485	3.2	474	3.1	3.45	103	.249	.310	-13	15	106	93	.971	175	170	-.7	1.6	**5.0**	.5	-1.5
CLE	76	14	12	1302.3	**1269**	8.8	**39**	501	3.5	497	3.4	3.31	100	.257	.322	7	0	98	102	**.977**	**126**	149	2.1	.0	3.3	-.1	-4.8
CHI	84	13	13	1330.7	1400	9.5	63	448	3.0	486	3.3	3.69	87	.270	.326	-48	-68	96	96	.970	180	139	-1.0	-7.3	1.6	.3	2.8
BOS	71	15	13	1391.0	1389	9.0	58	656	4.2	490	3.2	3.80	85	.263	.341	-66	-86	96	102	.973	169	**198**	-.4	-9.2	4.6	.4	-1.5
PHI	65	11	8	1381.0	1380	9.0	55	571	3.7	531	3.5	3.62	90	.262	.330	-39	-58	96	101	.973	168	160	-.3	-6.2	-6.0	-.9	-9.6
TOT	625	110	95	10948.7		8.7			3.4		3.4	3.36		.255	.325					.973	1302	1236					

Runs		Hits		Doubles		Triples		Home Runs		Total Bases	
Stirnweiss-NY	107	Stirnweiss-NY	195	Moses-Chi	35	Stirnweiss-NY	22	Stephens-StL	24	Stirnweiss-NY	301
Stephens-StL	90	Moses-Chi	168	Stirnweiss-NY	32	Moses-Chi	15	Cullenbine-Cle-Det	18	Stephens-StL	270
Cullenbine-Cle-Det	83	Stephens-StL	165	Binks-Was	32	Kuhel-Was	13	York-Det	18	Etten-NY	247
		Hall-Phi	161	McQuinn-StL	31	Dickshot-Chi	10	Etten-NY	18	York-Det	246
		Etten-NY	161			Peck-Phi	9	Heath-Cle	15	Moses-Chi	239

Runs Batted In		Runs Produced		Bases On Balls		Batting Average		On Base Percentage		Slugging Average	
Etten-NY	111	Etten-NY	170	Cullenbine-Cle-Det	113	Stirnweiss-NY	.309	Lake-Bos	.412	Stirnweiss-NY	.476
Cullenbine-Cle-Det	93	Stirnweiss-NY	161	Lake-Bos	106	Dickshot-Chi	.302	Cullenbine-Cle-Det	.402	Stephens-StL	.473
Stephens-StL	89	Cullenbine-Cle-Det	158	Grimes-NY	97	Estalella-Phi	.299	Estalella-Phi	.399	Cullenbine-Cle-Det	.444
York-Det	87	Stephens-StL	155	Etten-NY	90	Myatt-Was	.296	Grimes-NY	.395	Etten-NY	.437
Binks-Was	81	Kuhel-Was	146	Kuhel-Was	79	Moses-Chi	.295	Etten-NY	.387	Estalella-Phi	.435

Production		Adjusted Production		Batter Runs		Adjusted Batter Runs		Clutch Hitting Index		Runs Created	
Stirnweiss-NY	.862	Estalella-Phi	152	Stirnweiss-NY	39.1	Stirnweiss-NY	33.9	Schalk-Chi	158	Stirnweiss-NY	121
Cullenbine-Cle-Det	.846	Lake-Bos	146	Cullenbine-Cle-Det	35.0	Lake-Bos	31.8	Michaels-Chi	143	Cullenbine-Cle-Det	106
Estalella-Phi	.834	Stirnweiss-NY	139	Etten-NY	29.9	Cullenbine-Cle-Det	31.3	Etten-NY	141	Etten-NY	98
Stephens-StL	.825	Cullenbine-Cle-Det	138	Heath-Cle	29.4	Heath-Cle	30.1	Tresh-Chi	135	Stephens-StL	98
Etten-NY	.824	Moses-Chi	136	Lake-Bos	28.7	Estalella-Phi	29.7	Kuhel-Was	131	Moses-Chi	97

Total Average		Stolen Bases		Stolen Base Average		Stolen Base Runs		Fielding Runs		Total Player Rating	
Stirnweiss-NY	.892	Stirnweiss-NY	33	Dickshot-Chi	85.7	Dickshot-Chi	3.6	Lake-Bos	26.7	Lake-Bos	6.5
Cullenbine-Cle-Det	.888	Myatt-Was	30	Metkovich-Bos	76.0	Myatt-Was	2.4	Stirnweiss-NY	25.6	Stirnweiss-NY	6.4
Lake-Bos	.868	Case-Was	30	Myatt-Was	73.2	Metkovich-Bos	2.1	Hall-Phi	24.8	Cullenbine-Cle-Det	3.7
Estalella-Phi	.807	Metkovich-Bos	19	Stirnweiss-NY	66.0	Crosetti-NY	1.5	Mayo-Det	19.7	Mayo-Det	2.8
Etten-NY	.801	Dickshot-Chi	18	Case-Was	65.2	Richards-Det	1.2	Kell-Phi	19.6	Moses-Chi	2.6

Wins		Win Percentage		Games		Complete Games		Shutouts		Saves	
Newhouser-Det	25	Newhouser-Det	.735	Berry-Phi	52	Newhouser-Det	29	Newhouser-Det	8	Turner-NY	10
Ferriss-Bos	21	Leonard-Was	.708	Reynolds-Cle	44	Ferriss-Bos	26	Ferriss-Bos	5	Berry-Phi	5
Wolff-Was	20	Gromek-Cle	.679	Pieretti-Was	44	Wolff-Was	21	Benton-Det	5		
Gromek-Cle	19	Ferriss-Bos	.677	Trout-Det	41	Potter-StL	21				
		Wolff-Was	.667	Newhouser-Det	40	Gromek-Cle	21				

Innings Pitched		Fewest Hits/Game		Fewest BB/Game		Strikeouts		Strikeouts/Game		Wins Above Team	
Newhouser-Det	313	Newhouser-Det	6.87	Bonham-NY	1.09	Newhouser-Det	212	Newhouser-Det	6.10	Newhouser-Det	7.4
Ferriss-Bos	265	Wolff-Was	7.20	Leonard-Was	1.46	Kramer-StL	129	Kramer-StL	4.62	Ferriss-Bos	7.1
Newsom-Phi	257	Potter-StL	7.48	Wolff-Was	1.91	Newsom-Phi	127	Niggeling-Was	4.58	Gromek-Cle	5.6
Potter-StL	255	Niggeling-Was	8.19	Overmire-Det	2.33	Reynolds-Cle	112	Potter-StL	4.55	Muncrief-StL	4.4
Gromek-Cle	251	Gettel-NY	8.19	Gromek-Cle	2.37			Newsom-Phi	4.45	Leonard-Was	4.4

Earned Run Average		Adjusted ERA		Opponents' Batting Avg.		Opponents' On Base Pct.		Starter Runs		Adjusted Starter Runs	
Newhouser-Det	1.81	Newhouser-Det	194	Newhouser-Det	.211	Wolff-Was	.254	Newhouser-Det	54.0	Newhouser-Det	59.4
Benton-Det	2.02	Benton-Det	175	Wolff-Was	.215	Potter-StL	.273	Wolff-Was	34.5	Potter-StL	39.0
Wolff-Was	2.12	Potter-StL	156	Potter-StL	.226	Newhouser-Det	.277	Leonard-Was	29.7	Benton-Det	32.1
Leonard-Was	2.13	Wolff-Was	146	Niggeling-Was	.240	Leonard-Was	.277	Benton-Det	28.8	Wolff-Was	26.9
Lee-Chi	2.45	Leonard-Was	146	Benton-Det	.241	Bonham-NY	.284	Potter-StL	25.3	Leonard-Was	23.2

Clutch Pitching Index		Relief Runs		Adjusted Relief Runs		Relief Ranking		Total Pitcher Index		Total Baseball Ranking	
Benton-Det	139	Berry-Phi	14.6	Berry-Phi	12.8	Berry-Phi	14.5	Newhouser-Det	8.1	Newhouser-Det	8.1
Lee-Chi	121	Holcombe-NY	9.6	Holcombe-NY	10.8	Holcombe-NY	10.6	Potter-StL	5.0	Lake-Bos	6.5
Shirley-StL	117	Barrett-Bos	7.1	Barrett-Bos	5.9	Barrett-Bos	4.8	Benton-Det	3.2	Stirnweiss-NY	6.4
Hollingswort-StL	116	Zoldak-StL	.2	Zoldak-StL	3.9	Zoldak-StL	2.5	Hollingswort-StL	2.8	Potter-StL	5.0
Ferriss-Bos	114							Ferriss-Bos	2.7	Cullenbine-Cle-Det	3.7

TEAM	G	W	L	PCT	GB	R	OR	AB	H	2B	3B	HR	BB	SO	AVG	OBP	SLG	PRO	/A	BR	/A	PF	CHI	RC	TA	SB	CS	SBA	SBR
STL	156	98	58	.628		712	545	5372	1426	265	56	81	530	537	.265	.334	.381	.715	109	53	12	107	105	702	.658	58			
BRO	157	96	60	.615	2	701	570	5285	1376	233	66	55	691	575	.260	.348	.361	.709	107	59	42	103	101	699	.676	100			
CHI	155	82	71	.536	14.5	626	581	5298	1344	223	50	56	586	599	.254	.331	.346	.677	98	-8	28	94	101	622	.609	43			
BOS	154	81	72	.529	15.5	630	592	5225	1377	238	48	44	558	468	.264	.337	.353	.690	102	16	49	95	100	641	.627	60			
PHI	155	69	85	.448	28	560	705	5233	1351	209	40	80	417	590	.258	.315	.359	.674	97	-29	1	95	98	598	.592	41			
CIN	156	67	87	.435	30	523	570	5291	1262	206	33	65	493	604	.239	.307	.327	.634	85	-100	-123	104	101	546	.565	82			
PIT	155	63	91	.409	34	552	668	5199	1300	202	52	60	592	555	.250	.328	.344	.672	96	-18	-37	103	93	602	.607	48			
NY	154	61	93	.396	36	612	685	5191	1326	176	37	121	532	546	.255	.328	.374	.702	105	26	16	102	97	644	.638	46			
TOT	621					4916		42094	10762	1752	382	562	4399	4474	.256	.329	.356	.684								478			

TEAM	CG	SHO	SV	IP	H	H/G	HR	BB	BB/G	SO	SO/G	ERA	/A	OAVG	OOBA	PR	/A	PF	CPI	FA	E	DP	FW	PW	BW	SBW	DIF
STL	75	18	15	1398.0	1326	8.5	63	493	3.2	607	3.9	3.01	117	.253	.315	62	79	103	107	.980	124	167	2.0	8.4	1.3		8.3
BRO	52	16	28	1416.3	1280	8.1	58	671	4.3	647	4.1	3.05	112	.243	.323	56	56	100	107	.972	174	154	-1.0	5.9	4.5		8.6
CHI	59	15	11	1401.0	1370	8.8	58	527	3.4	619	4.0	3.22	99	.256	.319	29	-7	93	102	.976	146	119	.7	-.7	3.0		2.6
BOS	73	9	12	1372.3	1291	8.5	76	478	3.1	566	3.7	3.34	96	.248	.308	10	-22	94	93	.972	169	129	-.7	-2.3	5.2		2.3
PHI	55	12	23	1367.0	1442	9.5	73	542	3.6	490	3.2	4.00	83	.272	.337	-88	-100	98	97	.975	148	144	.6	-10.6	.1		2.0
CIN	69	20	11	1412.0	1334	8.5	70	467	3.0	506	3.2	3.08	116	.251	.308	52	78	105	101	.975	155	192	.1	8.3	-13.1		-5.4
PIT	61	10	6	1370.7	1406	9.2	50	561	3.7	458	3.0	3.72	97	.268	.334	-46	-17	106	99	.970	184	127	-1.6	-1.8	-3.9		-6.7
NY	47	8	13	1352.7	1313	8.7	114	660	4.4	581	3.9	3.92	90	.256	.336	-76	-60	103	100	.973	159	121	-.0	-6.4	1.7		-11.2
TOT	491	108	119	11090.0		8.7			3.6		3.6	3.41		.256	.329					.974	1259	1153					

Runs
Musial-StL 124
Slaughter-StL 100
Stanky-Bro 98
Schoendienst-StL 94
Cavaretta-Chi 89

Hits
Musial-StL 228
Walker-Bro 184
Slaughter-StL 183
Holmes-Bos 176
Schoendienst-StL 170

Doubles
Musial-StL 50
Holmes-Bos 35
Kurowski-StL 32
Herman-Bro-Bos 31

Triples
Musial-StL 20
Reese-Bro 10
Cavaretta-Chi 10
Walker-Bro 9

Home Runs
Kiner-Pit 23
Mize-NY 22
Slaughter-StL 18
Ennis-Phi 17

Total Bases
Musial-StL 366
Slaughter-StL 283
Ennis-Phi 262
Walker-Bro 258
Holmes-Bos 241

Runs Batted In
Slaughter-StL 130
Walker-Bro 116
Musial-StL 103
Kurowski-StL 89
Kiner-Pit 81

Runs Produced
Slaughter-StL 212
Musial-StL 211
Walker-Bro 187
Cavaretta-Chi 159
Holmes-Bos 153

Bases On Balls
Stanky-Bro 137
Fletcher-Pit 111
Cavaretta-Chi 88
Reese-Bro 87
Hack-Chi 83

Batting Average
Musial-StL 365
Hopp-Bos 333
Walker-Bro 319
Ennis-Phi 313
Holmes-Bos 310

On Base Percentage
Stanky-Bro 436
Musial-StL 434
Cavaretta-Chi 401
Herman-Bro-Bos 395
Walker-Bro 391

Slugging Average
Musial-StL 587
Ennis-Phi 485
Slaughter-StL 465
Kurowski-StL 462
Walker-Bro 448

Production
Musial-StL 1.021
Kurowski-StL 853
Ennis-Phi 849
Walker-Bro 839
Slaughter-StL 838

Adjusted Production
Musial-StL 177
Ennis-Phi 147
Cavaretta-Chi 145
Hopp-Bos 142
Holmes-Bos 134

Batter Runs
Musial-StL 70.8
Mize-NY 43.5
Kurowski-StL 29.1
Walker-Bro 28.8
Slaughter-StL 28.5

Adjusted Batter Runs
Musial-StL 66.1
Mize-NY 42.8
Cavaretta-Chi 31.3
Ennis-Phi 28.4
Walker-Bro 27.1

Clutch Hitting Index
Walker-Bro 161
Slaughter-StL 152
Elliott-Pit 137
Reiser-Bro 130
Cavaretta-Chi 125

Runs Created
Musial-StL 164
Slaughter-StL 110
Walker-Bro 104
Kurowski-StL 97
Ennis-Phi 96

Total Average
Musial-StL 1.114
Stanky-Bro 890
Reiser-Bro 877
Kurowski-StL 855
Walker-Bro 848

Stolen Bases
Reiser-Bro 34
Haas-Cin 22
Hopp-Bos 21
Adams-Cin 16
Walker-Bro 14

Stolen Base Average

Stolen Base Runs

Fielding Runs
Marion-StL 22.0
Adams-Cin 18.3
Seminick-Phi 17.3
Frey-Cin 13.9
Pafko-Chi 13.5

Total Player Rating
Musial-StL 5.8
Ennis-Phi 4.0
Mize-NY 3.6
Cavaretta-Chi 3.1
Seminick-Phi 2.9

Wins
Pollet-StL 21
Sain-Bos 20
Higbe-Bro 17
Dickson-StL 15
Brecheen-StL 15

Win Percentage
Dickson-StL 714
Higbe-Bro 680
Pollet-StL 677
Sain-Bos 588
Brecheen-StL 500

Games
Trinkle-NY 48
Dickson-StL 47
Behrman-Bro 47
Casey-Bro 46

Complete Games
Sain-Bos 24
Pollet-StL 22
Koslo-NY 17
Ostermueller-Pit 16
Cooper-Bos 15

Shutouts
Blackwell-Cin 6
VanderMeer-Cin 5
Brecheen-StL 5
Pollet-StL 4

Saves
Raffensberge-Phi 6
Pollet-StL 5
Karl-Phi 5
Herring-Bro 5
Casey-Bro 5

Innings Pitched
Pollet-StL 266
Sain-Bos 265
Koslo-NY 265
Brecheen-StL 231
Schmitz-Chi 224

Fewest Hits/Game
Kennedy-NY 7.36
Schmitz-Chi 7.39
Blackwell-Cin 7.42
Higbe-Bro 7.59
Sain-Bos 7.64

Fewest BB/Game
Cooper-Bos 1.76
Raffensberge-Phi 1.79
Beggs-Cin 1.85
Heusser-Cin 2.09
Strincevich-Pit 2.25

Strikeouts
Schmitz-Chi 135
Higbe-Bro 134
Sain-Bos 129
Koslo-NY 121
Brecheen-StL 117

Strikeouts/Game
Higbe-Bro 5.72
Schmitz-Chi 5.42
Blackwell-Cin 4.64
Brecheen-StL 4.56
Voiselle-NY 4.50

Wins Above Team
Rowe-Phi 4.1
Wilks-StL 4.0
Kush-Chi 3.4
Ostermueller-Pit 3.4
Lanier-StL 3.0

Earned Run Average
Pollet-StL 2.10
Sain-Bos 2.21
Beggs-Cin 2.32
Blackwell-Cin 2.46
Brecheen-StL 2.49

Adjusted ERA
Pollet-StL 168
Beggs-Cin 154
Blackwell-Cin 146
Sain-Bos 145
Brecheen-StL 141

Opponents' Batting Avg.
Schmitz-Chi 221
Kennedy-NY 224
Blackwell-Cin 226
Higbe-Bro 229
Sain-Bos 230

Opponents' On Base Pct.
Cooper-Bos 273
Beggs-Cin 283
Sain-Bos 289
Dickson-StL 291
Pollet-StL 295

Starter Runs
Pollet-StL 38.8
Sain-Bos 35.5
Brecheen-StL 23.6
Beggs-Cin 23.0
Blackwell-Cin 20.5

Adjusted Starter Runs
Pollet-StL 42.0
Sain-Bos 29.1
Beggs-Cin 26.6
Brecheen-StL 26.3
Blackwell-Cin 24.1

Clutch Pitching Index
Hatten-Bro 129
Pollet-StL 127
Beggs-Cin 124
Wyse-Chi 116
Heintzelman-Pit 110

Relief Runs
Casey-Bro 15.9
Thompson-NY 14.9
Malloy-Cin 5.3
Budnick-NY 2.4
Herring-Bro 6

Adjusted Relief Runs
Casey-Bro 15.9
Thompson-NY 15.6
Malloy-Cin 6.6
Budnick-NY 3.4
Wilks-StL 1.1

Relief Ranking
Casey-Bro 24.7
Thompson-NY 24.5
Malloy-Cin 6.2
Budnick-NY 2.0
Wilks-StL 9

Total Pitcher Index
Pollet-StL 4.9
Sain-Bos 4.3
Beggs-Cin 3.3
Blackwell-Cin 2.8
Brecheen-StL 2.7

Total Baseball Ranking
Musial-StL 5.8
Pollet-StL 4.9
Sain-Bos 4.3
Ennis-Phi 4.0
Mize-NY 3.6

TEAM	G	W	L	PCT	GB	R	OR	AB	H	2B	3B	HR	BB	SO	AVG	OBP	SLG	PRO	/A	BR	/A	PF	CHI	RC	TA	SB	CS	SBA	SBR
BOS	156	104	50	.675		792	594	5318	1441	268	50	109	687	661	.271	.356	.402	.758	119	136	42	114	100	790	.713	45	36	56	-7
DET	155	92	62	.597	12	704	567	5318	1373	212	41	108	622	616	.258	.337	.374	.711	105	42	-10	108	102	698	.655	65	41	61	-4
NY	154	87	67	.565	17	684	547	5139	1275	208	50	136	627	706	.248	.334	.387	.721	108	54	52	100	100	695	.674	48	35	58	-6
WAS	155	76	78	.494	28	608	706	5337	1388	260	63	60	511	641	.260	.327	.366	.693	100	1	51	92	96	653	.617	51	50	50	-14
CHI	155	74	80	.481	30	562	595	5312	1364	206	44	37	501	600	.257	.323	.333	.669	93	-63	-42	97	99	579	.571	78	64	55	-14
CLE	156	68	86	.442	36	537	638	5242	1285	233	56	79	506	697	.245	.313	.356	.669	93	-49	22	89	93	596	.593	57	49	54	-11
STL	156	66	88	.429	38	621	710	5373	1350	220	46	84	465	713	.251	.313	.356	.669	93	-52	-38	98	107	601	.578	23	35	40	-13
PHI	155	49	105	.318	55	529	680	5200	1317	220	51	40	482	594	.253	.318	.338	.656	90	-67	-93	104	96	574	.568	39	30	57	-5
TOT	621					5037		42239	10793	1827	401	653	4401	5228	.256	.328	.364	.692								406	340	54	-81

TEAM	CG	SHO	SV	IP	H	H/G	HR	BB	BB/G	SO	SO/G	ERA	/A	OAVG	OOBA	PR	/A	PF	CPI	FA	E	DP	FW	PW	BW	SBW	DIF
BOS	79	15	20	1396.7	1359	8.8	89	501	3.2	667	4.3	3.38	115	.253	.314	18	76	111	100	.977	139	163	1.4	8.0	4.4	.3	12.9
DET	94	18	15	1402.0	1277	8.2	97	497	3.2	896	5.8	3.22	115	.240	.303	44	74	106	95	.974	155	138	.5	7.8	-1.0	.7	7.2
NY	68	17	17	1361.0	1232	8.1	66	552	3.7	653	4.3	3.13	109	.242	.313	55	43	98	100	.975	150	174	.8	4.5	5.4	.4	-1.2
WAS	71	8	10	1396.3	1459	9.4	81	547	3.5	537	3.5	3.74	88	.268	.334	-36	-68	94	103	.966	211	162	-2.8	-7.1	5.3	-.4	4.0
CHI	62	9	16	1392.7	1348	8.7	80	508	3.3	550	3.6	3.10	110	.254	.317	63	48	97	110	.972	175	170	-.7	5.0	-4.4	-.4	-2.5
CLE	63	16	13	1388.7	1282	8.3	84	649	4.2	789	5.1	3.62	88	.245	.325	-17	-69	90	96	.975	147	147	.9	-7.2	2.3	-.0	-4.9
STL	63	13	12	1382.3	1465	9.5	73	573	3.7	574	3.7	3.95	88	.272	.337	-68	-70	100	99	.974	159	157	.2	-7.3	-4.0	-.3	.4
PHI	61	10	5	1342.7	1371	9.2	83	577	3.9	562	3.8	3.90	96	.263	.334	-59	-20	107	98	.971	167	141	-.2	-2.1	-9.7	.6	-16.5
TOT	561	106	108	11062.3		8.8			3.6		4.3	3.50		.256	.328					.973	1303	1252					

Runs
Williams-Bos 142
Pesky-Bos 115
Lake-Det 105
Keller-NY 98
Doerr-Bos 95

Hits
Pesky-Bos 208
Vernon-Was 207
Appling-Chi 180
Williams-Bos 176
Lewis-Was 170

Doubles
Vernon-Was 51
Spence-Was 50
Pesky-Bos 43
Williams-Bos 37
Doerr-Bos 34

Triples
Edwards-Cle 16
Lewis-Was 13
Kell-Phi-Det 10
Spence-Was 10
Keller-NY 10

Home Runs
Greenberg-Det 44
Williams-Bos 38
Keller-NY 30
Seerey-Cle 26
DiMaggio-NY 25

Total Bases
Williams-Bos 343
Greenberg-Det 316
Vernon-Was 298
Spence-Was 287
Keller-NY 287

Runs Batted In
Greenberg-Det 127
Williams-Bos 123
York-Bos 119
Doerr-Bos 116
Keller-NY 101

Runs Produced
Williams-Bos 227
Doerr-Bos 193
York-Bos 180
Greenberg-Det 174
Keller-NY 169

Bases On Balls
Williams-Bos 156
Keller-NY 113
Lake-Det 103
Cullenbine-Det 88
Henrich-NY 87

Batting Average
Vernon-Was 353
Williams-Bos 342
Pesky-Bos 335
Kell-Phi-Det 322
DiMaggio-Bos 316

On Base Percentage
Williams-Bos 497
Keller-NY 405
Vernon-Was 403
Pesky-Bos 401
DiMaggio-Bos 393

Slugging Average
Williams-Bos 667
Greenberg-Det 604
Keller-NY 533
DiMaggio-NY 511
Edwards-Cle 509

Production
Williams-Bos 1.164
Greenberg-Det 977
Keller-NY 938
Vernon-Was 910
DiMaggio-NY 878

Adjusted Production
Williams-Bos 195
Vernon-Was 166
Keller-NY 160
Edwards-Cle 159
Greenberg-Det 157

Batter Runs
Williams-Bos 94.2
Greenberg-Det 46.1
Keller-NY 45.9
Cullenbine-Det 42.2
Vernon-Was 40.3

Adjusted Batter Runs
Williams-Bos 83.9
Vernon-Was 45.7
Keller-NY 45.7
Greenberg-Det 40.8
Cullenbine-Det 38.5

Clutch Hitting Index
York-Bos 158
Doerr-Bos 147
Travis-Was 141
Berardino-StL 123
Heath-Was-StL 123

Runs Created
Williams-Bos 188
Keller-NY 127
Vernon-Was 120
Greenberg-Det 119
Pesky-Bos 111

Total Average
Williams-Bos 1.431
Keller-NY 1.015
Greenberg-Det 1.013
Vernon-Was 898
DiMaggio-NY 862

Stolen Bases
Case-Cle 28
Stirnweiss-NY 18
Lake-Det 15

Stolen Base Average
Stirnweiss-NY 75.0
Case-Cle 71.8

Stolen Base Runs
Stirnweiss-NY 1.8
Dillinger-StL 1.8
Case-Cle 1.8
Philley-Chi 1.5
Evers-Det 1.5

Fielding Runs
Doerr-Bos 28.5
Boudreau-Cle 14.8
Gordon-NY 13.9
Rosar-Phi 13.8
Rizzuto-NY 12.7

Total Player Rating
Williams-Bos 7.7
Doerr-Bos 4.5
Greenberg-Det 3.8
Keller-NY 3.5
Vernon-Was 3.4

Wins
Newhouser-Det 26
Feller-Cle 26
Ferriss-Bos 25
Hughson-Bos 20
Chandler-NY 20

Win Percentage
Ferriss-Bos 806
Newhouser-Det 743
Chandler-NY 714
Harris-Bos 654
Hughson-Bos 645

Games
Feller-Cle 48
Savage-Phi 40
Ferriss-Bos 40
Hughson-Bos 39
Caldwell-Chi 39

Complete Games
Feller-Cle 36
Newhouser-Det 29
Ferriss-Bos 26
Trout-Det 23
Hughson-Bos 21

Shutouts
Feller-Cle 10
Newhouser-Det 6
Hughson-Bos 6
Ferriss-Bos 6
Chandler-NY 6

Saves
Klinger-Bos 9
Caldwell-Chi 8
Murphy-NY 7
Ferrick-Cle-StL 6

Innings Pitched
Feller-Cle 371
Newhouser-Det 293
Hughson-Bos 278
Trout-Det 276
Ferriss-Bos 274

Fewest Hits/Game
Newhouser-Det 6.60
Feller-Cle 6.72
Chandler-NY 7.00
Embree-Cle 7.65
Bevens-NY 7.67

Fewest BB/Game
Hughson-Bos 1.65
Lopat-Chi 1.87
Leonard-Was 2.00
Flores-Phi 2.21
Ferriss-Bos 2.33

Strikeouts
Feller-Cle 348
Newhouser-Det 275
Hughson-Bos 172
Trucks-Det 161
Trout-Det 151

Strikeouts/Game
Newhouser-Det 8.45
Feller-Cle 8.44
Trucks-Det 6.11
Hutchinson-Det 6.00
Hughson-Bos 5.57

Wins Above Team
Feller-Cle 8.6
Newhouser-Det 7.4
Ferriss-Bos 7.1
Chandler-NY 5.5
Caldwell-Chi 4.9

Earned Run Average
Newhouser-Det . . . 1.94
Chandler-NY 2.10
Feller-Cle 2.18
Bevens-NY 2.23
Flores-Phi 2.32

Adjusted ERA
Newhouser-Det 191
Chandler-NY 163
Flores-Phi 162
Trout-Det 157
Bevens-NY 153

Opponents' Batting Avg.
Newhouser-Det 201
Feller-Cle 208
Chandler-NY 218
Embree-Cle 227
Bevens-NY 232

Opponents' On Base Pct.
Newhouser-Det 267
Hughson-Bos 270
Chandler-NY 283
Lopat-Chi 284
Feller-Cle 286

Starter Runs
Newhouser-Det 54.4
Feller-Cle 51.0
Chandler-NY 40.0
Trout-Det 35.4
Bevens-NY 35.3

Adjusted Starter Runs
Newhouser-Det 57.3
Trout-Det 41.3
Feller-Cle 40.5
Chandler-NY 37.6
Hughson-Bos 34.8

Clutch Pitching Index
Grove-Chi 126
Flores-Phi 121
Trout-Det 119
Haynes-Chi 117
Bevens-NY 115

Relief Runs
Caldwell-Chi 14.4
Lemon-Cle 10.6
Klinger-Bos 7.2
Kinder-StL 1.9

Adjusted Relief Runs
Caldwell-Chi 13.5
Klinger-Bos 9.6
Lemon-Cle 7.1
Kinder-StL 1.8
Johnson-Bos 1.5

Relief Ranking
Caldwell-Chi 25.4
Klinger-Bos 10.9
Lemon-Cle 6.3
Johnson-Bos 1.6
Kinder-StL 1.1

Total Pitcher Index
Newhouser-Det 6.8
Trout-Det 5.6
Chandler-NY 4.7
Feller-Cle 4.0
Hughson-Bos 3.4

Total Baseball Ranking
Williams-Bos 7.7
Newhouser-Det 6.8
Trout-Det 5.6
Chandler-NY 4.7
Doerr-Bos 4.5

TEAM	G	W	L	PCT	GB	R	OR	AB	H	2B	3B	HR	BB	SO	AVG	OBP	SLG	PRO	/A	BR	/A	PF	CHI	RC	TA	SB	CS	SBA	SBR
BRO	155	94	60	.610		774	668	5249	1428	241	50	83	732	561	.272	.364	.384	.748	106	62	28	105	98	781	.734	88			
STL	156	89	65	.578	5	780	634	5422	1462	235	65	115	612	511	.270	.347	.401	.748	102	40	-5	106	101	762	.694	28			
BOS	154	86	68	.558	8	701	622	5253	1444	265	42	85	558	500	.275	.346	.390	.736	102	18	40	97	96	717	.680	58			
NY	155	81	73	.526	13	830	761	5343	1446	220	48	221	494	568	.271	.335	.454	.789	115	95	90	101	104	809	.741	29			
CIN	154	73	81	.474	21	681	755	5299	1372	242	43	95	539	530	.259	.330	.375	.705	94	-47	17	91	103	672	.644	46			
CHI	155	69	85	.448	25	567	722	5305	1373	231	48	71	471	578	.259	.321	.361	.682	87	-92	-98	101	94	620	.600	22			
PIT	156	62	92	.403	32	744	817	5307	1385	216	44	156	607	687	.261	.340	.406	.746	104	30	23	101	100	738	.694	30			
PHI	155	62	92	.403	32	589	687	5256	1354	210	52	60	464	594	.258	.321	.352	.673	85	-108	-108	100	101	597	.596	60			
TOT	620					5666		42434	11264	1860	392	886	4477	4529	.265	.338	.391	.729								361			

TEAM	CG	SHO	SV	IP	H	H/G	HR	BB	BB/G	SO	SO/G	ERA	/A	OAVG	OOBA	PR	/A	PF	CPI	FA	E	DP	FW	PW	BW	SBW	DIF
BRO	47	14	34	1375.7	1299	8.5	104	626	4.1	592	3.9	3.81	109	.251	.330	37	54	103	100	.978	129	169	.9	5.3	2.8		8.0
STL	65	12	20	1397.7	1417	9.1	106	495	3.2	642	4.1	3.53	119	.265	.326	82	105	104	110	.979	128	169	1.0	10.3	-.5		1.2
BOS	74	14	13	1362.3	1342	8.9	93	453	3.0	494	3.3	3.62	107	.255	.312	66	37	95	95	.974	153	124	-.5	3.6	3.9		2.0
NY	58	6	14	1363.7	1428	9.4	122	590	3.9	553	3.6	4.44	91	.266	.336	-57	-61	99	94	.974	155	136	-.7	-6.0	8.9		1.8
CIN	54	13	13	1365.3	1442	9.5	102	589	3.9	633	4.2	4.41	85	.273	.343	-53	-101	92	98	.977	138	134	.4	-9.9	1.7		3.9
CHI	46	8	15	1367.7	1449	9.5	106	618	4.1	571	3.8	4.03	104	.274	.346	4	26	104	109	.975	150	159	-.4	2.6	-9.6		-.6
PIT	44	9	13	1373.0	1488	9.8	155	592	3.9	530	3.5	4.69	88	.277	.347	-95	-82	102	101	.975	149	131	-.3	-8.1	2.3		-8.9
PHI	70	8	14	1362.0	1399	9.2	98	513	3.4	514	3.4	3.96	104	.276	.340	15	26	102	108	.974	152	140	-.5	2.6	-10.6		-6.5
TOT	458	84	136	10967.3		9.2			3.7		3.7	4.06		.265	.338					.976	1154	1162					

Runs
Mize-NY 137
Robinson-Bro 125
Kiner-Pit 118
Musial-StL 113
Kurowski-StL 108

Hits
Holmes-Bos 191
Walker-StL-Phi 186
Musial-StL 183
Gustine-Pit 183
Baumholtz-Cin 182

Doubles
Miller-Cin 38
Elliott-Bos 35
Ryan-Bos 33
Holmes-Bos 33
Baumholtz-Cin 32

Triples
Walker-StL-Phi 16
Slaughter-StL 13
Musial-StL 13
Schoendienst-StL 9
Baumholtz-Cin 9

Home Runs
Mize-NY 51
Kiner-Pit 51
Marshall-NY 36
Cooper-NY 35
Thomson-NY 29

Total Bases
Kiner-Pit 361
Mize-NY 360
Marshall-NY 310
Cooper-NY 302
Musial-StL 296

Runs Batted In
Mize-NY 138
Kiner-Pit 127
Cooper-NY 122
Elliott-Bos 113
Marshall-NY 107

Runs Produced
Mize-NY 224
Kiner-Pit 194
Musial-StL 189
Kurowski-StL 185
Elliott-Bos 184

Bases On Balls
Reese-Bro 104
Greenberg-Pit 104
Stanky-Bro 103
Kiner-Pit 98
Walker-Bro 97

Batting Average
Walker-StL-Phi 363
Elliott-Bos 317
Galan-Cin 314
Cavaretta-Chi 314
Kiner-Pit 313

On Base Percentage
Galan-Cin 449
Walker-StL-Phi 436
Kurowski-StL 420
Kiner-Pit 417
Walker-Bro 415

Slugging Average
Kiner-Pit 639
Mize-NY 614
Cooper-NY 586
Kurowski-StL 544
Marshall-NY 528

Production
Kiner-Pit 1.055
Mize-NY 998
Kurowski-StL 964
Elliott-Bos 927
Cooper-NY 926

Adjusted Production
Kiner-Pit 175
Mize-NY 160
Elliott-Bos 149
Kurowski-StL 145
Walker-StL-Phi 144

Batter Runs
Kiner-Pit 61.3
Mize-NY 48.2
Kurowski-StL 41.7
Elliott-Bos 36.7
Walker-StL-Phi 35.4

Adjusted Batter Runs
Kiner-Pit 60.6
Mize-NY 47.7
Elliott-Bos 39.1
Kurowski-StL 37.2
Walker-StL-Phi 35.1

Clutch Hitting Index
Walker-Bro 146
Marion-StL 138
Haas-Cin 135
Edwards-Bro 135
Cavaretta-Chi 131

Runs Created
Kiner-Pit 154
Mize-NY 143
Elliott-Bos 120
Kurowski-StL 118
Musial-StL 118

Total Average
Kiner-Pit 1.155
Mize-NY 1.060
Kurowski-StL 1.019
Walker-StL-Phi 979
Torgeson-Bos 973

Stolen Bases
Robinson-Bro 29
Reiser-Bro 14
Walker-StL-Phi 13
Hopp-Bos 13
Torgeson-Bos 11

Stolen Base Average

Stolen Base Runs

Fielding Runs
Marion-StL 16.8
Verban-Phi 14.9
Gustine-Pit 14.7
Stanky-Bro 11.9
Lowrey-Chi 11.0

Total Player Rating
Kiner-Pit 6.2
Mize-NY 4.5
Walker-StL-Phi 3.5
Reese-Bro 3.1
Elliott-Bos 3.0

Wins
Blackwell-Cin 22
Spahn-Bos 21
Sain-Bos 21
Jansen-NY 21
Branca-Bro 21

Win Percentage
Jansen-NY 808
Munger-StL 762
Blackwell-Cin 733
Hatten-Bro 680
Spahn-Bos 677

Games
Trinkle-NY 62
Higbe-Bro-Pit 50
Behrman-Pit-Bro 48
Kush-Chi 47
Dickson-StL 47

Complete Games
Blackwell-Cin 23
Spahn-Bos 22
Sain-Bos 22
Jansen-NY 20
Leonard-Phi 19

Shutouts
Spahn-Bos 7
Munger-StL 6
Blackwell-Cin 6
Dickson-StL 4
Branca-Bro 4

Saves
Casey-Bro 18
Trinkle-NY 10
Gumbert-Cin 10
Behrman-Pit-Bro 8

Innings Pitched
Spahn-Bos 290
Branca-Bro 280
Blackwell-Cin 273
Sain-Bos 266
Jansen-NY 248

Fewest Hits/Game
Taylor-Bro 7.22
Blackwell-Cin 7.48
Spahn-Bos 7.60
Lombardi-Bro 8.02
Branca-Bro 8.07

Fewest BB/Game
Rowe-Phi 2.07
Jansen-NY 2.07
Leonard-Phi 2.18
Barrett-Bos 2.26
Brazle-StL 2.57

Strikeouts
Blackwell-Cin 193
Branca-Bro 148
Sain-Bos 132
Spahn-Bos 123
Munger-StL 123

Strikeouts/Game
Blackwell-Cin 6.36
Munger-StL 4.94
Branca-Bro 4.76
Brazle-StL 4.55
Sain-Bos 4.47

Wins Above Team
Jansen-NY 8.3
Blackwell-Cin 8.2
Leonard-Phi 5.1
Munger-StL 5.0
Spahn-Bos 4.9

Earned Run Average
Spahn-Bos 2.33
Blackwell-Cin 2.47
Branca-Bro 2.67
Leonard-Phi 2.68
Brazle-StL 2.84

Adjusted ERA
Spahn-Bos 166
Branca-Bro 156
Leonard-Phi 154
Blackwell-Cin 151
Brazle-StL 148

Opponents' Batting Avg.
Taylor-Bro 225
Spahn-Bos 226
Blackwell-Cin 234
Branca-Bro 240
Lombardi-Bro 241

Opponents' On Base Pct.
Spahn-Bos 281
Barrett-Bos 289
Leonard-Phi 300
Blackwell-Cin 300
Jansen-NY 304

Starter Runs
Spahn-Bos 55.8
Blackwell-Cin 48.2
Branca-Bro 43.3
Leonard-Phi 36.0
Dickson-StL 25.7

Adjusted Starter Runs
Spahn-Bos 49.7
Branca-Bro 46.7
Blackwell-Cin 38.4
Leonard-Phi 37.9
Dickson-StL 29.4

Clutch Pitching Index
Brazle-StL 139
Leonard-Phi 123
Branca-Bro 122
Blackwell-Cin 115
Jansen-NY 114

Relief Runs
Lanfranconi-Bos 7.9
Kush-Chi 7.1
Trinkle-NY 3.4
Gumbert-Cin 1.6
Casey-Bro 7

Adjusted Relief Runs
Kush-Chi 8.6
Lanfranconi-Bos 6.5
Trinkle-NY 3.2
Casey-Bro 1.7

Relief Ranking
Kush-Chi 10.4
Lanfranconi-Bos 7.6
Trinkle-NY 4.4
Casey-Bro 3.6

Total Pitcher Index
Spahn-Bos 5.0
Leonard-Phi 4.2
Branca-Bro 4.2
Blackwell-Cin 4.0
Dickson-StL 3.2

Total Baseball Ranking
Kiner-Pit 6.2
Spahn-Bos 5.0
Mize-NY 4.5
Leonard-Phi 4.2
Branca-Bro 4.2

TEAM	G	W	L	PCT	GB	R	OR	AB	H	2B	3B	HR	BB	SO	AVG	OBP	SLG	PRO	/A	BR	/A	PF	CHI	RC	TA	SB	CS	SBA	SBR
NY	155	97	57	.630		794	568	5308	1439	230	72	115	610	581	.271	.349	.407	.756	116	109	131	97	104	780	.703	27	23	54	-5
DET	158	85	69	.552	12	714	642	5276	1363	234	42	103	762	565	.258	.353	.377	.730	109	76	48	104	96	735	.687	52	60	46	-19
BOS	157	83	71	.539	14	720	669	5322	1412	206	54	103	666	590	.265	.349	.382	.731	109	70	19	108	98	734	.675	41	35	54	-5
CLE	157	80	74	.519	17	687	588	5367	1392	234	51	112	502	609	.259	.324	.385	.709	103	8	33	96	104	687	.635	29	25	54	-5
PHI	156	78	76	.506	19	633	614	5198	1311	218	52	105	605	563	.252	.333	.349	.682	96	-23	-24	100	101	635	.615	37	33	53	-8
CHI	155	70	84	.455	27	553	661	5274	1350	211	41	53	492	527	.256	.321	.342	.663	90	-69	-47	97	98	584	.582	91	57	61	-6
WAS	154	64	90	.416	33	496	675	5112	1234	186	48	42	525	534	.241	.313	.321	.634	82	-117	-97	97	98	523	.549	53	51	51	-14
STL	154	59	95	.383	38	564	744	5145	1238	189	52	90	583	664	.241	.320	.350	.670	92	-54	-66	102	97	596	.606	69	49	58	-8
TOT	623					5161		42002	10739	1708	412	679	4745	4633	.256	.333	.365	.698								399	333	55	-79

TEAM	CG	SHO	SV	IP	H	H/G	HR	BB	BB/G	SO	SO/G	ERA	/A	OAVG	OOBA	PR	/A	PF	CPI	FA	E	DP	FW	PW	BW	SBW	DIF
NY	73	14	21	1374.3	1221	8.0	95	628	4.1	691	4.5	3.39	101	.237	.318	47	3	92	100	.981	109	151	1.5	.3	13.6	.5	4.1
DET	77	15	18	1398.7	1382	8.9	79	531	3.4	648	4.2	3.57	107	.257	.321	20	36	103	100	.975	155	142	-1.2	3.7	5.0	-.9	1.4
BOS	64	13	19	1391.3	1383	8.9	84	575	3.7	586	3.8	3.81	104	.261	.330	-16	23	107	100	.977	137	172	-.1	2.4	2.0	.2	1.6
CLE	55	13	29	1402.3	1244	8.0	94	628	4.0	590	3.8	3.44	101	.240	.320	41	7	94	100	.983	104	178	1.8	.7	3.4	.5	-3.4
PHI	70	12	15	1391.3	1291	8.4	85	597	3.9	493	3.2	3.51	105	.247	.323	29	29	100	99	.976	143	161	-.5	3.0	-2.5	.2	.7
CHI	47	11	27	1391.0	1384	9.0	76	603	3.9	522	3.4	3.64	104	.261	.332	10	3	99	105	.975	155	180	-1.2	.3	-4.9	.4	-1.8
WAS	67	15	12	1362.0	1408	9.3	63	579	3.8	551	3.6	3.97	94	.267	.336	-40	-37	101	100	.976	143	151	-.5	-3.8	-10.0	-.4	1.8
STL	50	7	13	1365.0	1426	9.4	103	604	4.0	552	3.6	4.33	90	.271	.341	-94	-63	106	98	.977	134	169	.0	-6.5	-6.8	.2	-4.9
TOT	503	100	154	11076.0		8.7			3.9		3.8	3.71		.256	.333					.977	1080	1304					

Runs
Williams-Bos 125
Henrich-NY 109
Pesky-Bos 106
Stirnweiss-NY 102
DiMaggio-NY 97

Hits
Pesky-Bos 207
Kell-Det 188
Williams-Bos 181
McCosky-Phi 179

Doubles
Boudreau-Cle 45
Williams-Bos 40
Henrich-NY 35
DiMaggio-NY 31

Triples
Henrich-NY 13
Vernon-Was 12
Philley-Chi 11

Home Runs
Williams-Bos 32
Gordon-Cle 29
Heath-StL 27
Cullenbine-Det 24
York-Bos-Chi 21

Total Bases
Williams-Bos 335
Gordon-Cle 279
DiMaggio-NY 279
Henrich-NY 267
Pesky-Bos 250

Runs Batted In
Williams-Bos 114
Henrich-NY 98
DiMaggio-NY 97
Jones-Chi-Bos 96

Runs Produced
Williams-Bos 207
Henrich-NY 191
DiMaggio-NY 174
Kell-Det 163
Doerr-Bos 157

Bases On Balls
Williams-Bos 162
Cullenbine-Det 137
Lake-Det 120
Joost-Phi 114
Fain-Phi 95

Batting Average
Williams-Bos .... .343
McCosky-Phi .... .328
Pesky-Bos .... .324
Kell-Det .... .320
Mitchell-Cle .... .316

On Base Percentage
Williams-Bos .... .499
Fain-Phi .... .414
Cullenbine-Det .... .401
McCosky-Phi .... .395
McQuinn-NY .... .395

Slugging Average
Williams-Bos .... .634
DiMaggio-NY .... .522
Gordon-Cle .... .496
Henrich-NY .... .485
Heath-StL .... .485

Production
Williams-Bos 1.133
DiMaggio-NY .... .913
Henrich-NY .... .857
Heath-StL .... .850
Gordon-Cle .... .842

Adjusted Production
Williams-Bos 198
DiMaggio-NY 158
Henrich-NY 142
Gordon-Cle 138
McQuinn-NY 136

Batter Runs
Williams-Bos 91.0
DiMaggio-NY 36.4
Henrich-NY 26.4
Fain-Phi 24.7
Cullenbine-Det 23.8

Adjusted Batter Runs
Williams-Bos 85.2
DiMaggio-NY 38.7
Henrich-NY 28.7
McQuinn-NY 25.5
Fain-Phi 24.5

Clutch Hitting Index
Johnson-NY 151
Kell-Det 141
Vernon-Was 130
Jones-Chi-Bos 129
Chapman-Phi 129

Runs Created
Williams-Bos 186
DiMaggio-NY 112
Henrich-NY 104
Pesky-Bos 103
McQuinn-NY 97

Total Average
Williams-Bos 1.394
DiMaggio-NY .... .918
Cullenbine-Det .... .903
Heath-StL .... .859
Henrich-NY .... .854

Stolen Bases
Dillinger-StL 34
Philley-Chi 21
Vernon-Was 12
Pesky-Bos 12

Stolen Base Average
Dillinger-StL 72.3
Philley-Chi 56.8

Stolen Base Runs
Dillinger-StL 2.4
Valo-Phi 1.5
Binks-Phi 1.2

Fielding Runs
Doerr-Bos 21.5
Kell-Det 16.2
Boudreau-Cle 15.1
Rosar-Phi 15.0
DiMaggio-Bos 14.5

Total Player Rating
Williams-Bos 8.1
Boudreau-Cle 3.8
DiMaggio-NY 3.5
Kell-Det 3.2
Cullenbine-Det 3.1

Wins
Feller-Cle 20
Reynolds-NY 19
Marchildon-Phi 19
Hutchinson-Det 18
Dobson-Bos 18

Win Percentage
Reynolds-NY .... .704
Dobson-Bos .... .692
Marchildon-Phi .... .679
Feller-Cle .... .645
Hutchinson-Det .... .643

Games
Klieman-Cle 58
Page-NY 56
Johnson-Bos 45
Savage-Phi 44
Christopher-Phi 44

Complete Games
Newhouser-Det 24
Wynn-Was 22
Lopat-Chi 22
Marchildon-Phi 21
Feller-Cle 20

Shutouts
Feller-Cle 5
Reynolds-NY 4
Masterson-Was 4
Haefner-Was 4

Saves
Page-NY 17
Klieman-Cle 17
Christopher-Phi 12
Ferrick-Was 9

Innings Pitched
Feller-Cle 299
Newhouser-Det 285
Marchildon-Phi 277
Masterson-Was 253
Lopat-Chi 253

Fewest Hits/Game
Shea-NY 6.39
Feller-Cle 6.92
Marchildon-Phi 7.41
Embree-Cle 7.56
Masterson-Was 7.65

Fewest BB/Game
Galehouse-StL-Bos 2.49
Hutchinson-Det 2.50
Lopat-Chi 2.60
Muncrief-StL 2.61
Dobson-Bos 2.87

Strikeouts
Feller-Cle 196
Newhouser-Det 176
Masterson-Was 135
Reynolds-NY 129
Marchildon-Phi 128

Strikeouts/Game
Feller-Cle 5.90
Hughson-Bos 5.67
Newhouser-Det 5.56
Trucks-Det 5.37
Kinder-StL 5.10

Wins Above Team
Marchildon-Phi 5.5
Dobson-Bos 4.9
Haynes-Chi 4.8
Feller-Cle 4.8
Wynn-Was 3.8

Earned Run Average
Haynes-Chi 2.42
Feller-Cle 2.68
Lopat-Chi 2.81
Fowler-Phi 2.81
Newhouser-Det 2.87

Adjusted ERA
Haynes-Chi 151
Dobson-Bos 134
Newhouser-Det 133
Fowler-Phi 131
Lopat-Chi 130

Opponents' Batting Avg.
Shea-NY .... .200
Feller-Cle .... .215
Marchildon-Phi .... .224
Reynolds-NY .... .227
Embree-Cle .... .233

Opponents' On Base Pct.
Dobson-Bos .... .296
Feller-Cle .... .296
Shea-NY .... .300
Hutchinson-Det .... .301
Lopat-Chi .... .302

Starter Runs
Feller-Cle 34.1
Newhouser-Det 26.3
Haynes-Chi 25.9
Lopat-Chi 25.2
Fowler-Phi 22.5

Adjusted Starter Runs
Newhouser-Det 29.6
Feller-Cle 26.8
Dobson-Bos 25.8
Haynes-Chi 25.0
Lopat-Chi 23.9

Clutch Pitching Index
Haynes-Chi 124
Fowler-Phi 118
Lopat-Chi 117
Ferriss-Bos 114
Newsom-Was-NY 112

Relief Runs
Page-NY 19.0
Christopher-Phi 7.3
Klieman-Cle 6.9
Murphy-Bos 5.6
Ferrick-Was 3.7

Adjusted Relief Runs
Page-NY 14.5
Christopher-Phi 7.3
Murphy-Bos 7.2
Klieman-Cle 4.6
Ferrick-Was 3.8

Relief Ranking
Page-NY 24.3
Christopher-Phi 16.3
Klieman-Cle 6.0
Ferrick-Was 5.9
White-Det 2.0

Total Pitcher Index
Newhouser-Det 3.8
Hutchinson-Det 3.6
Feller-Cle 3.2
Haynes-Chi 3.0
Dobson-Bos 2.8

Total Baseball Ranking
Williams-Bos 8.1
Newhouser-Det 3.8
Boudreau-Cle 3.8
Hutchinson-Det 3.6
DiMaggio-NY 3.5

TEAM	G	W	L	PCT	GB	R	OR	AB	H	2B	3B	HR	BB	SO	AVG	OBP	SLG	PRO	/A	BR	/A	PF	CHI	RC	TA	SB	CS	SBA	SBR
BOS	154	91	62	.595		739	584	5297	1458	272	49	95	671	536	.275	.359	.399	.758	112	95	84	102	92	784	.719	43			
STL	155	85	69	.552	6.5	742	646	5302	1396	238	58	105	594	521	.263	.340	.389	.729	104	30	26	101	102	713	.671	24			
BRO	155	84	70	.545	7.5	744	667	5328	1393	256	54	91	601	684	.261	.338	.381	.719	101	12	-17	104	104	709	.685	114			
PIT	156	83	71	.539	8.5	706	699	5286	1388	191	54	108	580	578	.263	.338	.380	.718	101	10	-20	104	101	698	.670	68			
NY	155	78	76	.506	13.5	780	704	5277	1352	210	49	164	599	648	.256	.334	.408	.742	107	46	48	100	106	731	.699	51			
PHI	155	66	88	.429	25.5	591	729	5287	1367	227	39	91	440	598	.259	.318	.368	.686	92	-62	-22	94	96	625	.616	68			
CIN	153	64	89	.418	27	588	752	5127	1266	221	37	104	478	586	.247	.313	.365	.678	89	-75	-96	103	100	587	.605	42			
CHI	155	64	90	.416	27.5	597	706	5352	1402	225	44	87	443	578	.262	.322	.369	.691	93	-52	-4	93	94	641	.613	39			
TOT	619					5487		42256	11022	1840	384	845	4406	4729	.261	.333	.383	.716								449			

TEAM	CG	SHO	SV	IP	H	H/G	HR	BB	BB/G	SO	SO/G	ERA	/A	OAVG	OOBA	PR	/A	PF	CPI	FA	E	DP	FW	PW	BW	SBW	DIF
BOS	70	10	17	1389.3	1354	8.8	93	430	2.8	579	3.8	3.38	116	.249	.302	89	81	99	96	.976	143	132	.7	8.1	8.4		-2.7
STL	60	14	18	1368.7	1392	9.2	103	476	3.1	625	4.1	3.91	100	.261	.319	7	0	99	97	.980	119	138	2.0	.0	2.6		3.4
BRO	52	9	22	1392.0	1328	8.6	119	633	4.1	670	4.3	3.76	108	.253	.333	31	47	103	107	.973	161	151	-.2	4.7	-1.7		4.2
PIT	65	5	19	1371.0	1373	9.0	120	564	3.7	543	3.5	4.15	99	.260	.330	-29	-3	104	98	.977	137	150	1.1	-.3	-2.0		7.2
NY	54	16	21	1369.7	1425	9.4	122	556	3.7	527	3.5	3.94	99	.269	.336	3	-6	98	109	.974	156	134	.0	-.6	4.8		-3.2
PHI	61	6	15	1362.3	1385	9.1	95	556	3.7	550	3.6	4.08	94	.262	.329	-17	-38	97	97	.964	210	126	-2.8	-3.8	-2.2		-2.2
CIN	40	8	20	1340.0	1410	9.5	104	572	3.8	599	4.0	4.48	94	.269	.338	-77	-40	106	95	.973	158	135	-.0	-4.0	-9.6		1.1
CHI	51	7	10	1355.7	1355	9.0	89	619	4.1	636	4.2	4.00	94	.261	.336	-6	-37	95	101	.972	172	152	-.8	-3.7	-.4		-8.1
TOT	453	75	142	10948.7		9.1			3.6		3.9	3.96		.261	.333					.974	1256	1118					

Runs
Musial-StL 135
Lockman-NY 117
Mize-NY 110
Robinson-Bro 108
Kiner-Pit 104

Hits
Musial-StL 230
Holmes-Bos 190
Rojek-Pit 186
Slaughter-StL 176
Dark-Bos 175

Doubles
Musial-StL 46
Ennis-Phi 40
Dark-Bos 39
Robinson-Bro 38
Holmes-Bos 35

Triples
Musial-StL 18
Hopp-Pit 12
Slaughter-StL 11
Waitkus-Chi 10
Lockman-NY 10

Home Runs
Mize-NY 40
Kiner-Pit 40
Musial-StL 39
Sauer-Cin 35

Total Bases
Musial-StL 429
Mize-NY 316
Ennis-Phi 309
Kiner-Pit 296
Pafko-Chi 283

Runs Batted In
Musial-StL 131
Mize-NY 125
Kiner-Pit 123
Gordon-NY 107
Pafko-Chi 101

Runs Produced
Musial-StL 227
Mize-NY 195
Kiner-Pit 187
Robinson-Bro 181
Gordon-NY 177

Bases On Balls
Elliott-Bos 131
Kiner-Pit 112
Mize-NY 94

Batting Average
Musial-StL 376
Ashburn-Phi 333
Holmes-Bos 325
Dark-Bos 322
Slaughter-StL 321

On Base Percentage
Musial-StL 450
Elliott-Bos 423
Ashburn-Phi 410
Slaughter-StL 409
Mize-NY 395

Slugging Average
Musial-StL 702
Mize-NY 564
Gordon-NY 537
Kiner-Pit 533
Ennis-Phi 525

Production
Musial-StL ... 1.152
Mize-NY 959
Gordon-NY 927
Kiner-Pit 924
Elliott-Bos 897

Adjusted Production
Musial-StL 207
Mize-NY 157
Pafko-Chi 149
Gordon-NY 149
Kiner-Pit 142

Batter Runs
Musial-StL 90.2
Mize-NY 44.6
Kiner-Pit 38.5
Elliott-Bos 37.8
Gordon-NY 35.0

Adjusted Batter Runs
Musial-StL 89.8
Mize-NY 44.8
Elliott-Bos 36.6
Gordon-NY 35.2
Kiner-Pit 35.1

Clutch Hitting Index
Murtaugh-Pit 146
Jones-StL 140
Stallcup-Cin 139
Lowrey-Chi 128
Marshall-NY 128

Runs Created
Musial-StL 191
Mize-NY 131
Kiner-Pit 120
Elliott-Bos 117
Slaughter-StL 110

Total Average
Musial-StL ... 1.298
Mize-NY ... 1.032
Elliott-Bos 980
Kiner-Pit 974
Gordon-NY 953

Stolen Bases
Ashburn-Phi 32
Reese-Bro 25
Rojek-Pit 24
Robinson-Bro 22
Torgeson-Bos 19

Stolen Base Average

Stolen Base Runs

Fielding Runs
Ashburn-Phi 12.7
Gustine-Pit 11.9
Smalley-Chi 11.8
Marion-StL 11.5
Reese-Bro 10.6

Total Player Rating
Musial-StL 8.1
Mize-NY 4.6
Pafko-Chi 3.8
Reese-Bro 2.8
Ashburn-Phi 2.3

Wins
Sain-Bos 24
Brecheen-StL 20
Schmitz-Chi 18
Jansen-NY 18
VanderMeer-Cin 17

Win Percentage
Brecheen-StL 741
Jones-NY 667
Sain-Bos 615
Jansen-NY 600
Schmitz-Chi 581

Games
Gumbert-Cin 61
Wilks-StL 57
Higbe-Pit 56
Jones-NY 55
Dobernic-Chi 54

Complete Games
Sain-Bos 28
Brecheen-StL 21
Schmitz-Chi 18
Spahn-Bos 16
Leonard-Phi 16

Shutouts
Brecheen-StL 7
Sain-Bos 4
Raffensberge-Cin 4
Jansen-NY 4
Barney-Bro..........4

Saves
Gumbert-Cin 17
Wilks-StL 13
Higbe-Pit 10
Trinkle-NY 7
Behrman-Bro 7

Innings Pitched
Sain-Bos 315
Jansen-NY 277
Spahn-Bos 257
Dickson-StL 252
Barney-Bro 247

Fewest Hits/Game
Schmitz-Chi 6.92
Barney-Bro 7.03
Brecheen-StL 7.45
Branca-Bro 7.87
Roe-Bro 7.89

Fewest BB/Game
Roe-Bro 1.67
Jansen-NY 1.75
Raffensberge-Cin 1.85
Brecheen-StL 1.89
Leonard-Phi 2.15

Strikeouts
Brecheen-StL 149
Barney-Bro 138
Sain-Bos 137
Jansen-NY 126
Branca-Bro 122

Strikeouts/Game
Brecheen-StL 5.76
Branca-Bro 5.08
Barney-Bro 5.03
Higbe-Pit 4.90
Meyer-Chi 4.85

Wins Above Team
Brecheen-StL 6.3
Schmitz-Chi 5.1
Sewell-Pit 5.0
Jones-NY 4.4
VanderMeer-Cin 4.1

Earned Run Average
Brecheen-StL 2.24
Leonard-Phi 2.51
Sain-Bos 2.60
Roe-Bro 2.63
Schmitz-Chi 2.64

Adjusted ERA
Brecheen-StL 175
Roe-Bro 155
Leonard-Phi 152
Sain-Bos 150
Schmitz-Chi 142

Opponents' Batting Avg.
Schmitz-Chi 215
Barney-Bro 217
Brecheen-StL 222
Branca-Bro 232
Roe-Bro 233

Opponents' On Base Pct.
Brecheen-StL 262
Roe-Bro 268
Schmitz-Chi 289
Raffensberge-Cin 291
Sain-Bos 293

Starter Runs
Sain-Bos 47.5
Brecheen-StL 44.4
Leonard-Phi 36.4
Schmitz-Chi 35.4
Roe-Bro 26.3

Adjusted Starter Runs
Sain-Bos 45.7
Brecheen-StL 43.2
Leonard-Phi 33.0
Schmitz-Chi 30.0
Roe-Bro 28.4

Clutch Pitching Index
Leonard-Phi 135
Jones-NY 125
Hatten-Bro 124
Voiselle-Bos 120
Sain-Bos 115

Relief Runs
Wilks-StL 19.6
Hansen-NY 11.0
Minner-Bro 10.7
Higbe-Pit 10.5
Dobernic-Chi 7.8

Adjusted Relief Runs
Wilks-StL 18.9
Higbe-Pit 13.5
Minner-Bro 11.4
Hansen-NY 10.3
Gumbert-Cin 8.5

Relief Ranking
Wilks-StL 19.8
Gumbert-Cin 16.1
Higbe-Pit 13.4
Minner-Bro 11.9
Trinkle-NY 7.8

Total Pitcher Index
Sain-Bos 4.9
Brecheen-StL 4.7
Leonard-Phi 3.6
Schmitz-Chi 3.4
Roe-Bro 2.7

Total Baseball Ranking
Musial-StL 8.1
Sain-Bos 4.9
Brecheen-StL 4.7
Mize-NY 4.6
Pafko-Chi 3.8

TEAM	G	W	L	PCT	GB	R	OR	AB	H	2B	3B	HR	BB	SO	AVG	OBP	SLG	PRO	/A	BR	/A	PF	CHI	RC	TA	SB	CS	SBA	SBR
CLE	156	97	58	.626		840	568	5446	1534	242	54	155	646	575	.282	.360	.431	.791	116	111	122	99	97	868	.752	54	44	55	-9
BOS	155	96	59	.619	1	907	720	5363	1471	277	40	121	823	552	.274	.374	.409	.783	114	115	113	100	103	869	.761	38	17	69	1
NY	154	94	60	.610	2.5	857	633	5324	1480	251	75	139	623	478	.278	.356	.432	.788	115	98	97	100	103	838	.741	24	24	50	-6
PHI	154	84	70	.545	12.5	729	735	5181	1345	231	47	68	726	523	.260	.353	.362	.715	96	-20	-30	102	102	699	.665	40	56	56	-6
DET	154	78	76	.506	18.5	700	726	5235	1396	219	58	78	671	504	.267	.353	.375	.728	99	0	26	96	95	723	.670	22	32	41	-12
STL	155	59	94	.386	37	578	849	5303	1438	251	62	63	578	572	.271	.345	.386	.723	98	-20	-62	106	94	711	.659	63	44	59	-7
WAS	154	56	97	.366	40	578	796	5111	1245	203	75	31	568	572	.244	.322	.331	.653	79	-151	-172	103	105	566	.583	76	48	61	-5
CHI	154	51	101	.336	44.5	559	814	5192	1303	172	39	55	595	528	.251	.329	.331	.660	81	-133	-100	95	96	588	.585	46	47	49	-13
TOT	618					5841		42155	11212	1846	450	710	5230	4304	.266	.350	.382	.731								363	288	56	-63

TEAM	CG	SHO	SV	IP	H	H/G	HR	BB	BB/G	SO	SO/G	ERA	/A	OAVG	OOBA	PR	/A	PF	CPI	FA	E	DP	FW	PW	BW	SBW	DIF
CLE	66	26	30	1409.3	1246	8.0	82	628	4.0	595	3.8	3.22	125	.239	.319	166	125	94	108	.982	114	183	1.3	12.1	11.8	-.0	-5.6
BOS	70	11	13	1380.3	1445	9.4	83	592	3.9	513	3.3	4.26	98	.269	.340	4	-14	97	99	.981	116	174	1.2	-1.4	11.0	.9	6.9
NY	62	16	24	1365.7	1289	8.5	94	641	4.2	654	4.3	3.75	110	.250	.331	81	57	96	104	.979	120	161	.9	5.5	9.4	.2	.9
PHI	74	7	18	1369.7	1456	9.6	86	638	4.2	486	3.2	4.42	98	.275	.348	-20	-10	102	101	.981	113	180	1.3	-1.0	-2.9	.2	9.4
DET	60	5	22	1377.0	1367	8.9	92	589	3.8	678	4.4	4.15	100	.258	.328	21	0	97	95	.974	155	143	-.9	.0	2.5	-.4	-.2
STL	35	4	20	1373.3	1513	9.9	103	737	4.8	531	3.5	5.01	93	.281	.366	-109	-50	109	99	.972	168	190	-1.6	-4.8	-6.0	.0	-5.1
WAS	42	4	22	1357.3	1439	9.5	81	734	4.9	446	3.0	4.65	99	.272	.358	-55	-9	107	99	.974	154	144	-.9	-.9	-16.7	.3	-2.4
CHI	35	2	23	1346.0	1454	9.7	89	673	4.5	403	2.7	4.89	87	.279	.358	-89	-91	100	97	.974	160	176	-1.2	-8.8	-9.7	-.5	-4.8
TOT	444	75	172	10978.7		9.2			4.3		3.5	4.29		.266	.350					.977	1100	1351					

Runs
Henrich-NY.........138
DiMaggio-Bos.......127
Williams-Bos.......124
Pesky-Bos..........124
Boudreau-Cle.......116

Hits
Dillinger-StL......207
Mitchell-Cle.......204
Boudreau-Cle.......199
DiMaggio-NY........190
Williams-Bos.......188

Doubles
Williams-Bos.......44
Henrich-NY.........42
Majeski-Phi........41
Priddy-StL.........40
DiMaggio-Bos.......40

Triples
Henrich-NY.........14
Stewart-NY -Was....13
Yost-Was...........11
Mullin-Det.........11
DiMaggio-NY........11

Home Runs
DiMaggio-NY........39
Gordon-Cle.........32
Keltner-Cle........31
Stephens-Bos.......29
Doerr-Bos..........27

Total Bases
DiMaggio-NY........355
Henrich-NY.........326
Williams-Bos.......313
Stephens-Bos.......299
Boudreau-Cle.......299

Runs Batted In
DiMaggio-NY........155
Stephens-Bos.......137
Williams-Bos.......127
Gordon-Cle.........124
Majeski-Phi........120

Runs Produced
Williams-Bos.......226
DiMaggio-NY........226
Stephens-Bos.......222
Henrich-NY.........213
DiMaggio-Bos.......205

Bases On Balls
Williams-Bos.......126
Joost-Phi..........119
Fain-Phi...........113
DiMaggio-Bos.......101
Pesky-Bos..........99

Batting Average
Williams-Bos.......369
Boudreau-Cle.......355
Mitchell-Cle.......336
Zarilla-StL........329
McCosky-Phi........326

On Base Percentage
Williams-Bos.......497
Boudreau-Cle.......453
Appling-Chi........423
Goodman-Bos........414
Fain-Phi...........412

Slugging Average
Williams-Bos.......615
DiMaggio-NY........598
Henrich-NY.........554
Boudreau-Cle.......534
Keltner-Cle........522

Production
Williams-Bos.....1.112
DiMaggio-NY........994
Boudreau-Cle.......987
Henrich-NY.........945
Keltner-Cle........917

Adjusted Production
Williams-Bos.......194
Boudreau-Cle.......164
DiMaggio-NY........162
Henrich-NY.........149
Keltner-Cle........145

Batter Runs
Williams-Bos.......75.6
Boudreau-Cle.......52.6
DiMaggio-NY........48.5
Henrich-NY.........38.8
Keltner-Cle........32.9

Adjusted Batter Runs
Williams-Bos.......75.4
Boudreau-Cle.......53.9
DiMaggio-NY........48.5
Henrich-NY.........38.7
Keltner-Cle........34.1

Clutch Hitting Index
Majeski-Phi........141
Fain-Phi...........139
Platt-StL..........136
Evers-Det..........134
Goodman-Bos........130

Runs Created
Williams-Bos.......172
Boudreau-Cle.......143
DiMaggio-NY........140
Henrich-NY.........130
Keltner-Cle........116

Total Average
Williams-Bos.....1.347
Boudreau-Cle.....1.063
DiMaggio-NY......1.014
Henrich-NY.........962
Keltner-Cle........921

Stolen Bases
Dillinger-StL......28
Coan-Was...........23
Vernon-Was.........15
Mitchell-Cle.......13

Stolen Base Average
Coan-Was...........71.9
Dillinger-StL......71.8

Stolen Base Runs
Robertson-Was......2.4
Tucker-Cle.........2.1
DiMaggio-Bos.......1.8
Dillinger-StL......1.8

Fielding Runs
Priddy-StL.........22.8
Appling-Chi........13.4
Kolloway-Chi.......13.1
Baker-Chi..........12.4
Coan-Was...........10.8

Total Player Rating
Williams-Bos.......6.6
Boudreau-Cle.......6.1
DiMaggio-NY........3.9
Priddy-StL.........3.7
Doerr-Bos..........3.6

Wins
Newhouser-Det......21
Lemon-Cle..........20
Bearden-Cle........20
Raschi-NY..........19
Feller-Cle.........19

Win Percentage
Kramer-Bos.........783
Bearden-Cle........741
Raschi-NY..........704
Reynolds-NY........696

Games
Page-NY............55
Widmar-StL.........49
Biscan-StL.........47
Thompson-Was.......46

Complete Games
Lemon-Cle..........20
Newhouser-Det......19
Raschi-NY..........18
Feller-Cle.........18

Shutouts
Lemon-Cle..........10
Raschi-NY..........6
Bearden-Cle........6
Dobson-Bos.........5

Saves
Christopher-Cle....17
Page-NY............16
Houtteman-Det......10
Ferrick-Was........10
Judson-Chi.........8

Innings Pitched
Lemon-Cle..........294
Feller-Cle.........280
Newhouser-Det......272
Dobson-Bos.........245
Reynolds-NY........236

Fewest Hits/Game
Shea-NY............6.75
Lemon-Cle..........7.07
Bearden-Cle........7.32
Trucks-Det.........8.07
Scarborough-Was....8.08

Fewest BB/Game
Hutchinson-Det.....1.95
Zoldak-StL-Cle.....2.42
Lopat-NY...........2.62
Kramer-Bos.........2.81
Houtteman-Det......2.85

Strikeouts
Feller-Cle.........164
Lemon-Cle..........147
Newhouser-Det......143
Brissie-Phi........127
Raschi-NY..........124

Strikeouts/Game
Brissie-Phi........5.89
Feller-Cle.........5.27
Trucks-Det.........5.22
Raschi-NY..........5.00
Newhouser-Det......4.73

Wins Above Team
Scarborough-Was....5.7
Kramer-Bos.........5.4
Newhouser-Det......5.2
Bearden-Cle........4.7
Raschi-NY..........3.7

Earned Run Average
Bearden-Cle........2.43
Lemon-Cle..........2.82
Scarborough-Was....2.82
Newhouser-Det......3.01
Parnell-Bos........3.14

Adjusted ERA
Bearden-Cle........166
Scarborough-Was....163
Lemon-Cle..........143
Newhouser-Det......138
Garver-StL.........137

Opponents' Batting Avg.
Shea-NY............208
Lemon-Cle..........216
Bearden-Cle........229
Scarborough-Was....233
Trucks-Det.........240

Opponents' On Base Pct.
Hutchinson-Det.....294
Lemon-Cle..........299
Newhouser-Det......305
Scarborough-Was....305
Raschi-NY..........307

Starter Runs
Lemon-Cle..........48.1
Bearden-Cle........47.6
Newhouser-Det......38.6
Scarborough-Was....30.2
Parnell-Bos........27.0

Adjusted Starter Runs
Bearden-Cle........40.9
Lemon-Cle..........39.6
Scarborough-Was....36.3
Newhouser-Det......34.5
Garver-StL.........27.9

Clutch Pitching Index
Bearden-Cle........133
Garver-StL.........129
Fowler-Phi.........119
Lopat-NY...........118
Scheib-Phi.........117

Relief Runs
Klieman-Cle........15.1
Christopher-Cle....9.1
Thompson-Was.......6.4
Harris-Phi.........1.8
Hiller-NY..........1.5

Adjusted Relief Runs
Klieman-Cle........12.8
Thompson-Was.......10.8
Christopher-Cle....7.4
Ferrick-Was........3.7
Harris-Phi.........2.5

Relief Ranking
Thompson-Was.......12.6
Christopher-Cle....10.4
Klieman-Cle........8.6
Ferrick-Was........4.3
Harris-Phi.........1.9

Total Pitcher Index
Lemon-Cle..........6.3
Bearden-Cle........5.1
Scarborough-Was....3.9
Newhouser-Det......3.8
Garver-StL.........3.4

Total Baseball Ranking
Williams-Bos.......6.6
Lemon-Cle..........6.3
Boudreau-Cle.......6.1
Bearden-Cle........5.1
DiMaggio-NY........3.9

TEAM	G	W	L	PCT	GB	R	OR	AB	H	2B	3B	HR	BB	SO	AVG	OBP	SLG	PRO	/A	BR	/A	PF	CHI	RC	TA	SB	CS	SBA	SBR
BRO	156	97	57	.630		879	651	5400	1477	236	47	152	638	570	.274	.354	.419	.773	114	103	92	102	105	815	.753	117			
STL	157	96	58	.623	1	766	616	5463	1513	281	54	102	569	482	.277	.348	.404	.752	108	61	-14	110	97	777	.692	17			
PHI	155	81	73	.526	16	662	668	5307	1349	232	55	122	528	670	.254	.325	.388	.713	97	-26	-29	101	98	674	.648	27			
BOS	157	75	79	.487	22	706	719	5336	1376	245	33	104	684	656	.258	.345	.375	.720	100	7	31	97	96	710	.668	28			
NY	157	73	81	.474	24	736	693	5308	1383	203	52	147	613	523	.261	.340	.401	.741	105	36	25	102	99	735	.694	43			
PIT	154	71	83	.461	26	681	760	5214	1350	191	41	126	548	554	.259	.332	.384	.716	98	-13	-18	101	100	682	.661	48			
CIN	156	62	92	.403	35	627	770	5469	1423	264	35	86	429	559	.260	.316	.368	.684	89	-83	-52	96	100	636	.599	31			
CHI	154	61	93	.396	36	593	773	5214	1336	212	53	97	396	573	.256	.312	.373	.685	89	-82	-42	94	100	601	.605	53			
TOT	623					5650		42711	11207	1864	370	936	4405	4587	.262	.334	.389	.723								364			

TEAM	CG	SHO	SV	IP	H	H/G	HR	BB	BB/G	SO	SO/G	ERA	/A	OAVG	OOBA	PR	/A	PF	CPI	FA	E	DP	FW	PW	BW	SBW	DIF
BRO	62	15	17	1407.7	1306	8.3	132	582	3.7	743	4.8	3.80	104	.246	.320	36	21	98	99	.980	122	162	1.5	2.1	9.1		7.3
STL	64	13	19	1407.7	1356	8.7	87	507	3.2	606	3.9	3.44	126	.252	.314	93	142	108	101	.976	146	149	.1	14.1	-1.4		6.2
PHI	58	13	15	1393.0	1389	9.0	104	502	3.2	495	3.2	3.89	104	.267	.329	23	27	101	105	.974	156	141	-.4	2.7	-2.9		4.6
BOS	68	12	11	1400.0	1466	9.4	110	520	3.3	589	3.8	3.99	98	.267	.328	8	-11	97	102	.976	148	144	.0	-1.1	3.1		-4.0
NY	68	10	9	1374.3	1328	8.7	113	544	3.6	516	3.4	3.82	106	.248	.318	32	37	101	97	.973	161	134	-.7	3.7	2.5		-9.5
PIT	53	9	15	1356.0	1452	9.6	142	535	3.6	556	3.7	4.57	90	.273	.339	-79	-65	102	99	.978	132	173	.9	-6.4	-1.8		1.3
CIN	55	10	6	1402.3	1423	9.1	124	640	4.1	538	3.5	4.34	91	.263	.340	-46	-58	98	99	.977	138	150	.6	-5.7	-5.2		-4.7
CHI	44	8	17	1358.0	1487	9.9	104	575	3.8	544	3.6	4.50	87	.278	.345	-69	-85	97	100	.970	186	160	-2.1	-8.4	-4.2		-1.3
TOT	472	90	109	11099.0		9.1			3.6		3.7	4.04		.262	.334					.975	1189	1213					

Runs
Reese-Bro	132
Musial-StL	128
Robinson-Bro	122
Kiner-Pit	116
Schoendienst-StL	102

Hits
Musial-StL	207
Robinson-Bro	203
Thomson-NY	198
Slaughter-StL	191
Schoendienst-StL	190

Doubles
Musial-StL	41
Ennis-Phi	39
Robinson-Bro	38
Hatton-Cin	38

Triples
Slaughter-StL	13
Musial-StL	13
Robinson-Bro	12
Ennis-Phi	11
Ashburn-Phi	11

Home Runs
Kiner-Pit	54
Musial-StL	36
Sauer-Cin-Chi	31
Thomson-NY	27
Gordon-NY	26

Total Bases
Musial-StL	382
Kiner-Pit	361
Thomson-NY	332
Ennis-Phi	320
Robinson-Bro	313

Runs Batted In
Kiner-Pit	127
Robinson-Bro	124
Musial-StL	123
Hodges-Bro	115
Ennis-Phi	110

Runs Produced
Robinson-Bro	230
Musial-StL	215
Reese-Bro	189
Kiner-Pit	189
Hodges-Bro	186

Bases On Balls
Kiner-Pit	117
Reese-Bro	116
Stanky-Bos	113
Musial-StL	107
Gordon-NY	95

Batting Average
Robinson-Bro	.342
Musial-StL	.338
Slaughter-StL	.336
Furillo-Bro	.322
Kiner-Pit	.310

On Base Percentage
Musial-StL	.438
Robinson-Bro	.432
Kiner-Pit	.432
Slaughter-StL	.418
Stanky-Bos	.417

Slugging Average
Kiner-Pit	.658
Musial-StL	.624
Robinson-Bro	.528
Ennis-Phi	.525
Thomson-NY	.518

Production
Kiner-Pit	1.089
Musial-StL	1.062
Robinson-Bro	.960
Slaughter-StL	.929
Gordon-NY	.909

Adjusted Production
Kiner-Pit	187
Musial-StL	165
Robinson-Bro	154
Gordon-NY	140
Ennis-Phi	136

Batter Runs
Musial-StL	72.4
Kiner-Pit	70.0
Robinson-Bro	49.9
Slaughter-StL	40.1
Gordon-NY	31.6

Adjusted Batter Runs
Kiner-Pit	69.4
Musial-StL	63.6
Robinson-Bro	48.6
Slaughter-StL	32.1
Gordon-NY	30.5

Clutch Hitting Index
Marion-StL	136
Hodges-Bro	135
Robinson-Bro	124
Cooper-NY -Cin	124
Furillo-Bro	123

Runs Created
Musial-StL	173
Kiner-Pit	163
Robinson-Bro	135
Slaughter-StL	127
Ennis-Phi	118

Total Average
Kiner-Pit	1.247
Musial-StL	1.185
Robinson-Bro	1.078
Slaughter-StL	.971
Gordon-NY	.925

Stolen Bases
Robinson-Bro	37
Reese-Bro	26

Stolen Base Average

Stolen Base Runs

Fielding Runs
Schoendienst-StL	23.0
Ashburn-Phi	17.5
Smalley-Chi	15.8
Thomson-NY	12.6
Reich-Chi	12.1

Total Player Rating
Kiner-Pit	5.6
Robinson-Bro	5.1
Musial-StL	5.0
Elliott-Bos	3.8
Reese-Bro	3.6

Wins
Spahn-Bos	21
Pollet-StL	20
Raffensberge-Cin	18

Win Percentage
Roe-Bro	.714
Pollet-StL	.690
Newcombe-Bro	.680
Meyer-Phi	.680
Munger-StL	.652

Games
Wilks-StL	59
Konstanty-Phi	53
Palica-Bro	49
Banta-Bro	48
Muncrief-Pit-Chi	47

Complete Games
Spahn-Bos	25
Raffensberge-Cin	20
Newcombe-Bro	19
Pollet-StL	17
Jansen-NY	17

Shutouts
Raffensberge-Cin	5
Pollet-StL	5
Newcombe-Bro	5
Heintzelman-Phi	5

Saves
Wilks-StL	9
Potter-Bos	7
Konstanty-Phi	7
Staley-StL	6
Palica-Bro	6

Innings Pitched
Spahn-Bos	302
Raffensberge-Cin	284
Jansen-NY	260
Heintzelman-Phi	250
Newcombe-Bro	244

Fewest Hits/Game
Staley-StL	8.11
Koslo-NY	8.19
Newcombe-Bro	8.23
Kennedy-NY	8.39
Meyer-Phi	8.41

Fewest BB/Game
Koslo-NY	1.83
Roe-Bro	1.86
Werle-Pit	2.08
Jansen-NY	2.15
Leonard-Chi	2.15

Strikeouts
Spahn-Bos	151
Newcombe-Bro	149
Jansen-NY	113
Roe-Bro	109
Branca-Bro	109

Strikeouts/Game
Newcombe-Bro	5.50
Branca-Bro	5.25
Chambers-Pit	4.73
Roe-Bro	4.61
Spahn-Bos	4.50

Wins Above Team
Spahn-Bos	4.7
Meyer-Phi	4.6
Raffensberge-Cin	4.0
Chambers-Pit	3.8
Heintzelman-Phi	3.4

Earned Run Average
Koslo-NY	2.50
Staley-StL	2.74
Pollet-StL	2.77
Roe-Bro	2.79
Heintzelman-Phi	3.02

Adjusted ERA
Koslo-NY	163
Staley-StL	159
Pollet-StL	157
Roe-Bro	141
Brazle-StL	136

Opponents' Batting Avg.
Staley-StL	.238
Koslo-NY	.239
Kennedy-NY	.242
Newcombe-Bro	.243
Spahn-Bos	.245

Opponents' On Base Pct.
Koslo-NY	.276
Staley-StL	.283
Roe-Bro	.290
Spahn-Bos	.296
Newcombe-Bro	.298

Starter Runs
Koslo-NY	36.2
Pollet-StL	32.7
Spahn-Bos	32.6
Roe-Bro	29.6
Heintzelman-Phi	28.2

Adjusted Starter Runs
Pollet-StL	40.7
Koslo-NY	36.9
Staley-StL	30.7
Heintzelman-Phi	28.9
Spahn-Bos	28.2

Clutch Pitching Index
Roe-Bro	126
Heintzelman-Phi	123
Brazle-StL	121
Jones-NY	115
Dickson-Pit	113

Relief Runs
Erautt-Cin	8.7
Konstanty-Phi	8.5
Hogue-Bos	7.3
Palica-Bro	4.5
Wilks-StL	4.0

Adjusted Relief Runs
Konstanty-Phi	8.8
Wilks-StL	8.0
Erautt-Cin	7.8
Hogue-Bos	6.3
Palica-Bro	3.5

Relief Ranking
Konstanty-Phi	12.9
Erautt-Cin	9.4
Wilks-StL	9.4
Palica-Bro	5.9
Hogue-Bos	3.7

Total Pitcher Index
Pollet-StL	4.3
Koslo-NY	4.0
Staley-StL	3.5
Brecheen-StL	2.9
Dickson-Pit	2.7

Total Baseball Ranking
Kiner-Pit	5.6
Robinson-Bro	5.1
Musial-StL	5.0
Pollet-StL	4.3
Koslo-NY	4.0

TEAM	G	W	L	PCT	GB	R	OR	AB	H	2B	3B	HR	BB	SO	AVG	OBP	SLG	PRO	/A	BR	/A	PF	CHI	RC	TA	SB	CS	SBA	SBR
NY	155	97	57	.630		829	637	5196	1396	215	60	115	731	539	.269	.362	.400	.762	108	58	55	100	105	790	.730	58	30	66	0
BOS	155	96	58	.623	1	896	667	5320	1500	272	36	131	835	510	.282	.381	.420	.801	119	147	94	107	100	890	.780	43	25	63	-1
CLE	154	89	65	.578	8	675	574	5221	1358	194	58	112	601	534	.260	.339	.384	.723	97	-30	-13	98	98	696	.661	44	40	52	-10
DET	155	87	67	.565	10	751	655	5259	1405	215	51	88	751	502	.267	.361	.378	.739	102	20	-35	108	94	739	.688	39	52	43	-19
PHI	154	81	73	.526	16	726	725	5123	1331	214	49	82	783	493	.260	.361	.369	.730	100	6	15	99	99	719	.687	36	25	59	-3
CHI	154	63	91	.409	34	648	737	5204	1340	207	66	43	702	596	.257	.347	.347	.694	90	-65	-49	98	99	637	.637	62	55	53	-13
STL	155	53	101	.344	44	667	913	5112	1301	213	30	117	631	700	.254	.339	.377	.716	96	-40	-38	100	100	670	.656	38	39	49	-11
WAS	154	50	104	.325	47	584	868	5234	1330	207	41	81	593	495	.254	.333	.356	.689	88	-92	-30	91	94	640	.620	46	33	58	-5
TOT	618					5776		41669	10961	1737	391	769	5627	4369	.263	.353	.379	.732								366	299	55	-69

TEAM	CG	SHO	SV	IP	H	H/G	HR	BB	BB/G	SO	SO/G	ERA	/A	OAVG	OOBA	PR	/A	PF	CPI	FA	E	DP	FW	PW	BW	SBW	DIF
NY	59	12	36	1371.3	1231	8.1	98	812	5.3	671	4.4	3.69	110	.242	.346	76	58	97	107	.977	138	195	-.0	5.6	5.4	.8	8.2
BOS	84	16	16	1377.0	1375	9.0	82	661	4.3	598	3.9	3.97	109	.262	.343	34	55	103	101	.980	120	207	1.0	5.4	9.1	.7	2.7
CLE	65	10	19	1383.7	1275	8.3	82	594	3.9	611	4.0	3.36	120	.247	.321	129	102	96	103	.983	103	192	2.1	9.9	-1.3	-.1	1.4
DET	70	19	12	1393.7	1338	8.6	102	628	4.1	631	4.1	3.77	118	.253	.330	66	104	106	104	.978	131	174	.4	10.1	-3.4	-1.0	3.4
PHI	85	9	11	1365.0	1359	9.0	105	758	5.0	490	3.2	4.23	99	.263	.355	-5	-13	99	103	.976	140	217	-.1	-1.3	1.5	.6	3.4
CHI	57	10	17	1363.3	1362	9.0	108	693	4.6	502	3.3	4.30	97	.264	.346	-15	-18	99	99	.977	141	180	-.2	-1.8	-4.8	-.4	-6.9
STL	43	3	16	1341.3	1583	10.6	113	685	4.6	432	2.9	5.21	84	.294	.370	-151	-126	104	98	.971	166	154	-1.7	-12.3	-3.7	-.2	-6.1
WAS	44	10	9	1345.7	1438	9.6	79	779	5.2	451	3.0	5.10	79	.276	.365	-134	-157	96	91	.973	161	168	-1.4	-15.3	-2.9	.4	-7.8
TOT	507	89	136	10941.0		9.0			4.6		3.6	4.20		.263	.353					.977	1100	1487					

Runs
Williams-Bos	150
Joost-Phi	128
DiMaggio-Bos	126
Stephens-Bos	113
Pesky-Bos	111

Hits
Mitchell-Cle	203
Williams-Bos	194
DiMaggio-Bos	186
Wertz-Det	185
Pesky-Bos	185

Doubles
Williams-Bos	39
Kell-Det	38
DiMaggio-Bos	34
Zarilla-StL-Bos	33
Stephens-Bos	31

Triples
Mitchell-Cle	23
Dillinger-StL	13
Valo-Phi	12

Home Runs
Williams-Bos	43
Stephens-Bos	39

Total Bases
Williams-Bos	368
Stephens-Bos	329
Wertz-Det	283
Mitchell-Cle	274
Doerr-Bos	269

Runs Batted In
Williams-Bos	159
Stephens-Bos	159
Wertz-Det	133
Doerr-Bos	109
Chapman-Phi	108

Runs Produced
Williams-Bos	266
Stephens-Bos	233
Wertz-Det	209
Joost-Phi	186
Doerr-Bos	182

Bases On Balls
Williams-Bos	162
Joost-Phi	149
Fain-Phi	136
Appling-Chi	121
Valo-Phi	119

Batting Average
Kell-Det	.343
Williams-Bos	.343
Dillinger-StL	.324
Mitchell-Cle	.317
Doerr-Bos	.309

On Base Percentage
Williams-Bos	.490
Appling-Chi	.439
Joost-Phi	.429
Kell-Det	.424
Michaels-Chi	.417

Slugging Average
Williams-Bos	.650
Stephens-Bos	.539
Henrich-NY	.526
Doerr-Bos	.497
Sievers-StL	.471

Production
Williams-Bos	1.141
Henrich-NY	.942
Stephens-Bos	.930
Kell-Det	.892
Doerr-Bos	.890

Adjusted Production
Williams-Bos	187
Henrich-NY	148
Stephens-Bos	135
Joost-Phi	135
Robinson-Was	133

Batter Runs
Williams-Bos	88.8
Stephens-Bos	36.9
Joost-Phi	31.8
DiMaggio-NY	31.7
Henrich-NY	29.7

Adjusted Batter Runs
Williams-Bos	82.7
Joost-Phi	32.9
DiMaggio-NY	31.5
Stephens-Bos	31.0
Henrich-NY	29.4

Clutch Hitting Index
Wertz-Det	141
Fain-Phi	137
Lipon-Det	134
Stephens-Bos	129
Doerr-Bos	123

Runs Created
Williams-Bos	193
Stephens-Bos	132
Joost-Phi	119
DiMaggio-Bos	110
Wertz-Det	110

Total Average
Williams-Bos	1.349
Henrich-NY	1.023
Joost-Phi	.997
Stephens-Bos	.952
Kell-Det	.890

Stolen Bases
Dillinger-StL	20
Rizzuto-NY	18
Valo-Phi	14
Philley-Chi	13

Stolen Base Average
Rizzuto-NY	75.0
Dillinger-StL	58.8

Stolen Base Runs
Tebbetts-Bos	1.8
Rizzuto-NY	1.8
Mapes-NY	1.8
Fain-Phi	1.8
Philley-Chi	1.5

Fielding Runs
Doerr-Bos	22.4
Pesky-Bos	19.9
Vernon-Cle	18.5
Baker-Chi	11.2
Michaels-Chi	11.1

Total Player Rating
Williams-Bos	7.5
Doerr-Bos	4.2
Joost-Phi	3.9
Stephens-Bos	3.4
Michaels-Chi	3.2

Wins
Parnell-Bos	25
Kinder-Bos	23
Lemon-Cle	22
Raschi-NY	21
Kellner-Phi	20

Win Percentage
Kinder-Bos	.793
Parnell-Bos	.781
Reynolds-NY	.739
Lemon-Cle	.688

Games
Page-NY	60
Welteroth-Was	52
Ferrick-StL	50
Kennedy-StL	48
Surkont-Chi	44

Complete Games
Parnell-Bos	27
Newhouser-Det	22
Lemon-Cle	22
Raschi-NY	21

Shutouts
Trucks-Det	6
Kinder-Bos	6
Garcia-Cle	5

Saves
Page-NY	27
Benton-Cle	10
Ferrick-StL	6
Paige-Cle	5

Innings Pitched
Parnell-Bos	295
Newhouser-Det	292
Lemon-Cle	280
Trucks-Det	275
Raschi-NY	275

Fewest Hits/Game
Byrne-NY	5.74
Lemon-Cle	6.78
Trucks-Det	6.84
Gray-Det	7.52
Pierce-Chi	7.59

Fewest BB/Game
Hutchinson-Det	2.48
Houtteman-Det	2.60
Lopat-NY	2.89
Garcia-Cle	3.07
Wynn-Cle	3.11

Strikeouts
Trucks-Det	153
Newhouser-Det	144
Lemon-Cle	138
Kinder-Bos	138
Byrne-NY	129

Strikeouts/Game
Byrne-NY	5.92
Trucks-Det	5.01
Pierce-Chi	4.97
Kinder-Bos	4.93
Garcia-Cle	4.81

Wins Above Team
Parnell-Bos	7.6
Kinder-Bos	7.3
Lemon-Cle	4.9
Scarborough-Was	4.3
Kellner-Phi	4.0

Earned Run Average
Garcia-Cle	2.35
Parnell-Bos	2.78
Trucks-Det	2.81
Hutchinson-Det	2.95
Lemon-Cle	2.99

Adjusted ERA
Garcia-Cle	171
Trucks-Det	158
Parnell-Bos	156
Hutchinson-Det	151
Lemon-Cle	135

Opponents' Batting Avg.
Byrne-NY	.183
Lemon-Cle	.211
Trucks-Det	.211
Gray-Det	.227
Pierce-Chi	.228

Opponents' On Base Pct.
Hutchinson-Det	.289
Trucks-Det	.297
Garcia-Cle	.301
Lemon-Cle	.305
Gumpert-Chi	.313

Starter Runs
Parnell-Bos	46.6
Trucks-Det	42.3
Lemon-Cle	37.6
Garcia-Cle	36.1
Benton-Cle	31.4

Adjusted Starter Runs
Parnell-Bos	51.1
Trucks-Det	49.8
Newhouser-Det	35.2
Garcia-Cle	32.7
Lemon-Cle	32.2

Clutch Pitching Index
Garcia-Cle	124
Lopat-NY	122
Wight-Chi	118
Houtteman-Det	115
Kinder-Bos	114

Relief Runs
Page-NY	24.0
Paige-Cle	10.7
Papish-Cle	6.9
Ferrick-StL	3.5

Adjusted Relief Runs
Page-NY	22.1
Paige-Cle	9.1
Papish-Cle	5.7
Ferrick-StL	5.4
Starr-StL	.3

Relief Ranking
Page-NY	41.0
Paige-Cle	12.1
Ferrick-StL	5.4
Papish-Cle	1.0
Starr-StL	.2

Total Pitcher Index
Parnell-Bos	5.6
Lemon-Cle	5.6
Trucks-Det	4.1
Newhouser-Det	4.0
Hutchinson-Det	3.9

Total Baseball Ranking
Williams-Bos	7.5
Parnell-Bos	5.6
Lemon-Cle	5.6
Doerr-Bos	4.2
Trucks-Det	4.1

TEAM	G	W	L	PCT	GB	R	OR	AB	H	2B	3B	HR	BB	SO	AVG	OBP	SLG	PRO	/A	BR	/A	PF	CHI	RC	TA	SB	CS	SBA	SBR
PHI	157	91	63	.591		722	624	5426	1440	225	55	125	535	569	.265	.334	.396	.730	98	-13	5	97	100	714	.664	33			
BRO	155	89	65	.578	2	847	724	5364	1461	247	46	194	607	632	.272	.349	.444	.793	115	107	59	107	100	833	.765	77			
NY	154	86	68	.558	5	735	643	5238	1352	204	50	133	627	629	.258	.342	.392	.734	100	3	15	98	101	726	.693	42			
BOS	156	83	71	.539	8	785	736	5363	1411	246	36	148	615	616	.263	.342	.405	.747	103	23	124	86	103	750	.706	71			
STL	153	78	75	.510	12.5	693	670	5215	1353	255	50	102	606	604	.259	.339	.386	.725	97	-14	-35	103	98	696	.669	23			
CIN	153	66	87	.431	24.5	654	734	5253	1366	257	27	99	504	497	.260	.327	.376	.703	91	-65	-96	105	105	643	.629	37			
CHI	154	64	89	.418	26.5	643	772	5230	1298	224	47	161	479	767	.248	.315	.401	.716	94	-52	-85	105	99	658	.655	46			
PIT	154	57	96	.373	33.5	681	857	5327	1404	227	59	138	564	693	.264	.338	.406	.744	102	13	-5	103	92	729	.689	43			
TOT	618					5760		42416	11085	1885	370	1100	4537	5007	.261	.336	.401	.737								372			

TEAM	CG	SHO	SV	IP	H	H/G	HR	BB	BB/G	SO	SO/G	ERA	/A	OAVG	OOBA	PR	/A	PF	CPI	FA	E	DP	FW	PW	BW	SBW	DIF
PHI	57	13	27	1405.3	1324	8.5	122	530	3.4	620	4.0	3.50	113	.250	.316	100	72	96	105	.975	151	155	-.0	7.0	.5		6.5
BRO	62	10	21	1389.7	1397	9.0	163	591	3.8	772	5.0	4.28	101	.262	.336	-21	6	104	102	.979	127	183	1.3	.6	5.8		4.3
NY	70	20	15	1374.7	1268	8.3	140	536	3.5	596	3.9	3.71	108	.245	.316	65	44	97	100	.977	137	181	.8	4.3	1.5		2.5
BOS	88	7	10	1385.0	1411	9.2	129	564	3.6	615	4.0	4.14	85	.263	.331	0	-94	85	99	.977	182	146	-1.8	-9.2	12.1		4.8
STL	57	11	14	1355.3	1398	9.3	119	535	3.6	603	4.0	3.97	107	.267	.333	25	42	103	105	.978	130	172	1.2	4.1	-3.4		-.3
CIN	67	7	13	1355.7	1363	9.0	145	582	3.9	686	4.6	4.32	102	.259	.334	-27	10	106	97	.976	140	132	.6	1.0	-9.4		-2.7
CHI	55	9	19	1373.0	1452	9.5	130	593	3.9	559	3.7	4.27	104	.271	.342	-20	24	107	103	.968	201	169	-2.8	2.3	-8.3		-3.7
PIT	42	6	16	1367.7	1472	9.7	152	616	4.1	556	3.7	4.96	88	.274	.348	-124	-89	106	95	.977	136	165	.8	-8.7	-.5		-11.1
TOT	498	83	135	11006.3		9.1			3.7		4.1	4.14		.261	.336					.975	1204	1303					

Runs
Torgeson-Bos	120
Stanky-NY	115
Kiner-Pit	112
Snider-Bro	109
Musial-StL	105

Hits
Snider-Bro	199
Musial-StL	192
Furillo-Bro	189
Ennis-Phi	185
Waitkus-Phi	182

Doubles
Schoendienst-StL	43
Musial-StL	41
Robinson-Bro	39
Kluszewski-Cin	37
Dark-NY	36

Triples
Ashburn-Phi	14
Bell-Pit	11
Snider-Bro	10
Smalley-Chi	9
Schoendienst-StL	9

Home Runs
Kiner-Pit	47
Pafko-Chi	36
Sauer-Chi	32
Hodges-Bro	32

Total Bases
Snider-Bro	343
Musial-StL	331
Ennis-Phi	328
Kiner-Pit	323
Pafko-Chi	304

Runs Batted In
Ennis-Phi	126
Kiner-Pit	118
Hodges-Bro	113
Kluszewski-Cin	111
Musial-StL	109

Runs Produced
Furillo-Bro	187
Ennis-Phi	187
Musial-StL	186
Snider-Bro	185
Torgeson-Bos	184

Bases On Balls
Stanky-NY	144
Kiner-Pit	122
Torgeson-Bos	119
Westrum-NY	92
Reese-Bro	91

Batting Average
Musial-StL	.346
Robinson-Bro	.328
Snider-Bro	.321
Ennis-Phi	.311
Kluszewski-Cin	.307

On Base Percentage
Stanky-NY	.460
Musial-StL	.437
Robinson-Bro	.423
Glaviano-StL	.421
Torgeson-Bos	.412

Slugging Average
Musial-StL	.596
Pafko-Chi	.591
Kiner-Pit	.590
Gordon-Bos	.557
Snider-Bro	.553

Production
Musial-StL	1.034
Kiner-Pit	.998
Pafko-Chi	.989
Gordon-Bos	.960
Snider-Bro	.932

Adjusted Production
Gordon-Bos	174
Musial-StL	164
Elliott-Bos	156
Kiner-Pit	155
Torgeson-Bos	153

Batter Runs
Musial-StL	57.3
Kiner-Pit	48.7
Pafko-Chi	41.5
Snider-Bro	35.6
Gordon-Bos	35.3

Adjusted Batter Runs
Musial-StL	54.9
Kiner-Pit	46.7
Gordon-Bos	44.7
Torgeson-Bos	42.9
Pafko-Chi	38.0

Clutch Hitting Index
Slaughter-StL	158
Mueller-NY	149
Wyrostek-Cin	131
Kluszewski-Cin	129
Furillo-Bro	128

Runs Created
Musial-StL	149
Kiner-Pit	133
Snider-Bro	131
Pafko-Chi	124
Torgeson-Bos	121

Total Average
Musial-StL	1.139
Kiner-Pit	1.071
Pafko-Chi	1.057
Stanky-NY	1.013
Gordon-Bos	1.003

Stolen Bases
Jethroe-Bos	35
Reese-Bro	17
Snider-Bro	16
Torgeson-Bos	15
Ashburn-Phi	14

Stolen Base Average

Stolen Base Runs

Fielding Runs
Smalley-Chi	21.3
Cox-Bro	15.7
Robinson-Bro	12.5
Lockman-NY	12.2
Marion-StL	9.3

Total Player Rating
Gordon-Bos	4.5
Stanky-NY	4.5
Robinson-Bro	4.4
Musial-StL	3.9
Kiner-Pit	3.9

Wins
Spahn-Bos	21
Sain-Bos	20
Roberts-Phi	20

Win Percentage
Maglie-NY	.818
Konstanty-Phi	.696
Simmons-Phi	.680
Roberts-Phi	.645

Games
Konstanty-Phi	74
Dickson-Pit	51
Werle-Pit	48
Maglie-NY	47
Brazle-StL	46

Complete Games
Bickford-Bos	27
Spahn-Bos	25
Sain-Bos	25
Roberts-Phi	21
Jansen-NY	21

Shutouts
Hearn-StL-NY	5
Roberts-Phi	5
Maglie-NY	5
Jansen-NY	5

Saves
Konstanty-Phi	22
Werle-Pit	8
Hogue-Bos	7
Branca-Bro	7

Innings Pitched
Bickford-Bos	312
Roberts-Phi	304
Spahn-Bos	293
Sain-Bos	278
Jansen-NY	275

Fewest Hits/Game
Blackwell-Cin	7.00
Maglie-NY	7.38
Simmons-Phi	7.45
Spahn-Bos	7.62
Jansen-NY	7.79

Fewest BB/Game
Raffensberger-Cin	1.51
Jansen-NY	1.80
Sain-Bos	2.27
Roberts-Phi	2.28
Roe-Bro	2.37

Strikeouts
Spahn-Bos	191
Blackwell-Cin	188
Jansen-NY	161
Simmons-Phi	146
Roberts-Phi	146

Strikeouts/Game
Blackwell-Cin	6.48
Simmons-Phi	6.11
Spahn-Bos	5.87
Palica-Bro	5.87
Jansen-NY	5.27

Wins Above Team
Maglie-NY	6.9
Hiller-Chi	4.5
Hearn-StL-NY	3.4
Blackwell-Cin	3.4
Konstanty-Phi	3.3

Earned Run Average
Maglie-NY	2.71
Blackwell-Cin	2.97
Jansen-NY	3.01
Roberts-Phi	3.02
Lanier-StL	3.13

Adjusted ERA
Blackwell-Cin	148
Maglie-NY	148
Lanier-StL	136
Jansen-NY	133
Roberts-Phi	131

Opponents' Batting Avg.
Blackwell-Cin	.210
Simmons-Phi	.223
Maglie-NY	.226
Spahn-Bos	.227
Jansen-NY	.232

Opponents' On Base Pct.
Jansen-NY	.269
Roberts-Phi	.294
Brecheen-StL	.295
Spahn-Bos	.296
Blackwell-Cin	.298

Starter Runs
Roberts-Phi	37.9
Jansen-NY	34.6
Blackwell-Cin	34.1
Maglie-NY	32.8
Spahn-Bos	31.9

Adjusted Starter Runs
Blackwell-Cin	41.3
Roberts-Phi	31.8
Jansen-NY	30.3
Maglie-NY	29.6
Roe-Bro	28.6

Clutch Pitching Index
Brazle-StL	125
Roe-Bro	118
Maglie-NY	116
Ramsdell-Bro-Cin	115
Minner-Chi	113

Relief Runs
Konstanty-Phi	25.0
Kramer-NY	6.0
VanderMeer-Chi	3.1
Leonard-Chi	3.1
Smith-Cin	2.9

Adjusted Relief Runs
Konstanty-Phi	21.9
VanderMeer-Chi	5.5
Leonard-Chi	5.5
Smith-Cin	5.4
Kramer-NY	4.7

Relief Ranking
Konstanty-Phi	36.9
Smith-Cin	5.2
Leonard-Chi	5.0
VanderMeer-Chi	4.8
Kramer-NY	4.5

Total Pitcher Index
Blackwell-Cin	4.2
Jansen-NY	3.2
Maglie-NY	3.2
Roberts-Phi	2.8
Newcombe-Bro	2.5

Total Baseball Ranking
Gordon-Bos	4.5
Stanky-NY	4.5
Robinson-Bro	4.4
Blackwell-Cin	4.2
Musial-StL	3.9

TEAM	G	W	L	PCT	GB	R	OR	AB	H	2B	3B	HR	BB	SO	AVG	OBP	SLG	PRO	/A	BR	/A	PF	CHI	RC	TA	SB	CS	SBA	SBR
NY	155	98	56	.636		914	691	5361	1511	234	70	159	687	463	.282	.367	.441	.808	113	92	96	99	103	902	.780	41	28	59	-4
DET	157	95	59	.617	3	837	713	5381	1518	285	50	114	722	480	.282	.369	.417	.786	107	61	88	97	97	846	.740	23	40	37	-16
BOS	154	94	60	.610	4	1027	804	5516	1665	287	61	161	719	582	.302	.385	.464	.849	123	185	68	114	103	1014	.829	32	17	65	0
CLE	155	92	62	.597	6	806	654	5263	1417	222	46	164	693	624	.269	.358	.422	.780	105	39	55	98	98	820	.744	40	34	54	-7
WAS	155	67	87	.435	31	690	813	5251	1365	190	53	76	671	606	.260	.347	.360	.707	87	-92	-85	99	101	690	.651	42	25	63	-1
CHI	155	60	94	.390	38	625	749	5260	1368	172	47	93	551	566	.260	.333	.360	.697	84	-124	-101	97	97	648	.617	19	22	46	-7
STL	154	58	96	.377	40	684	916	5163	1269	235	43	106	690	744	.246	.337	.370	.707	87	-101	-154	107	102	667	.653	39	40	49	-11
PHI	154	52	102	.338	46	670	913	5212	1361	204	53	100	685	493	.261	.349	.378	.727	92	-55	24	90	93	708	.673	42	25	63	-1
TOT	620					6253		42407	11474	1829	423	973	5418	4558	.271	.356	.402	.759								278	231	55	-54

TEAM	CG	SHO	SV	IP	H	H/G	HR	BB	BB/G	SO	SO/G	ERA	/A	OAVG	OOBA	PR	/A	PF	CPI	FA	E	DP	FW	PW	BW	SBW	DIF
NY	66	12	31	1372.7	1322	8.7	118	708	4.6	712	4.7	4.15	106	.254	.344	65	36	96	102	.980	119	188	1.3	3.4	9.0	.3	7.1
DET	72	9	20	1407.3	1444	9.2	141	553	3.5	576	3.7	4.12	105	.267	.333	70	32	95	105	.981	120	194	1.2	3.0	8.2	-.9	6.4
BOS	66	6	28	1362.3	1413	9.3	121	748	4.9	630	4.2	4.88	104	.270	.358	-45	31	111	97	.981	111	181	1.7	2.9	6.4	.6	5.4
CLE	69	11	16	1378.7	1289	8.4	120	647	4.2	674	4.4	3.75	116	.247	.328	126	94	95	103	.978	129	160	.7	8.8	5.1	.0	.3
WAS	59	7	18	1364.7	1479	9.8	99	648	4.3	486	3.2	4.66	99	.277	.352	-11	-4	101	99	.972	167	181	-1.4	-.4	-8.0	.6	-.8
CHI	62	7	9	1365.7	1370	9.0	107	734	4.8	566	3.7	4.41	103	.262	.350	25	19	99	100	.977	140	181	.1	1.8	-9.5	.0	-9.4
STL	56	7	14	1365.3	1629	10.7	129	651	4.3	448	3.0	5.20	98	.294	.367	-94	-19	111	100	.967	196	155	-3.0	-1.8	-14.4	-.4	.6
PHI	50	3	18	1346.3	1528	10.2	138	729	4.9	466	3.1	5.49	78	.287	.370	-136	-181	93	96	.974	208	155	-.7	-16.9	2.2	.6	-10.1
TOT	500	62	154	10963.0		9.4			4.4		3.7	5.58		.271	.356					.976	1137	1448					

Runs
DiMaggio-Bos 131
Stephens-Bos 125
Rizzuto-NY 125
Berra-NY 116

Hits
Kell-Det 218
Rizzuto-NY 200
DiMaggio-Bos 193
Berra-NY 192
Stephens-Bos 185

Doubles
Kell-Det 56
Wertz-Det 37
Rizzuto-NY 36
Evers-Det 35
Stephens-Bos 34

Triples
Evers-Det 11
Doerr-Bos 11
DiMaggio-Bos 11

Home Runs
Rosen-Cle 37
Dropo-Bos 34
DiMaggio-NY 32
Stephens-Bos 30
Zernial-Chi 29

Total Bases
Dropo-Bos 326
Stephens-Bos 321
Berra-NY 318
Kell-Det 310
DiMaggio-NY 307

Runs Batted In
Stephens-Bos 144
Dropo-Bos 144
Berra-NY 124
Wertz-Det 123
DiMaggio-NY 122

Runs Produced
Stephens-Bos 239
Berra-NY 212
Dropo-Bos 211
Kell-Det 207
DiMaggio-NY 204

Bases On Balls
Yost-Was 141
Fain-Phi 133
Pesky-Bos 104
Joost-Phi 103
Rosen-Cle 100

Batting Average
Goodman-Bos 354
Kell-Det 340
DiMaggio-Bos 328
Doby-Cle 326
Zarilla-Bos 325

On Base Percentage
Doby-Cle 442
Yost-Was 440
Pesky-Bos 437
Fain-Phi 430
Goodman-Bos 427

Slugging Average
DiMaggio-NY 585
Dropo-Bos 583
Evers-Det 551
Doby-Cle 545
Rosen-Cle 543

Production
Doby-Cle 986
DiMaggio-NY 979
Dropo-Bos 961
Evers-Det 959
Rosen-Cle 948

Adjusted Production
Doby-Cle 155
DiMaggio-NY 149
Evers-Det 149
Wertz-Det 144
Rosen-Cle 144

Batter Runs
Doby-Cle 41.7
Williams-Bos 40.9
DiMaggio-NY 35.5
Rosen-Cle 34.3
Evers-Det 33.5

Adjusted Batter Runs
Doby-Cle 43.4
Evers-Det 36.3
Wertz-Det 36.2
Rosen-Cle 36.1
DiMaggio-NY 35.9

Clutch Hitting Index
Vernon-Cle-Was 136
Mele-Was 135
Stephens-Bos 128
Fain-Phi 126
Dropo-Bos 123

Runs Created
Doby-Cle 130
Wertz-Det 128
DiMaggio-NY 125
Berra-NY 125
Rizzuto-NY 124

Total Average
Doby-Cle 1.090
DiMaggio-NY 1.018
Wertz-Det 980
Rosen-Cle 970
Evers-Det 969

Stolen Bases
DiMaggio-Bos 15
Valo-Phi 12
Rizzuto-NY 12
Coan-Was 10
Lipon-Det 9

Stolen Base Average

Stolen Base Runs
DiMaggio-Bos 2.1
Vernon-Cle-Was 1.8
Collins-NY 1.5
Avila-Cle 1.5
Jensen-NY 1.2

Fielding Runs
Priddy-Det 32.6
Pesky-Bos 14.1
Noren-Was 13.6
Woodling-NY 10.6
Lipon-Det 9.1

Total Player Rating
Priddy-Det 4.0
Evers-Det 3.6
Rizzuto-NY 3.4
Berra-NY 3.3
DiMaggio-NY 2.9

Wins
Lemon-Cle 23
Raschi-NY 21
Houtteman-Det 19

Win Percentage
Raschi-NY 724
Wynn-Cle 692
Lopat-NY 692
Hutchinson-Det 680
Lemon-Cle 676

Games
Harris-Was 53
Kinder-Bos 48
Ferrick-StL-NY 46
Judson-Chi 46
Brissie-Phi 46

Complete Games
Lemon-Cle 22
Garver-StL 22
Parnell-Bos 21
Houtteman-Det 21

Shutouts
Houtteman-Det 4

Saves
Harris-Was 15
Page-NY 13
Ferrick-StL-NY 11
Kinder-Bos 9
Brissie-Phi 8

Innings Pitched
Lemon-Cle 288
Houtteman-Det 275
Garver-StL 260
Raschi-NY 257
Parnell-Bos 249

Fewest Hits/Game
Wynn-Cle 6.98
Pierce-Chi 7.77
Cain-Chi 8.01
Reynolds-NY 8.03
Raschi-NY 8.12

Fewest BB/Game
Hutchinson-Det 1.86
Lopat-NY 2.48
Overmire-StL 2.52
Trout-Det 3.11
Houtteman-Det 3.24

Strikeouts
Lemon-Cle 170
Reynolds-NY 160
Raschi-NY 155
Wynn-Cle 143
Feller-Cle 119

Strikeouts/Game
Wynn-Cle 6.01
Reynolds-NY 5.98
Raschi-NY 5.43
Lemon-Cle 5.31
Byrne-NY 5.23

Wins Above Team
Hooper-Phi 5.5
Raschi-NY 4.1
Lemon-Cle 4.1
Ford-NY 3.7
Wynn-Cle 3.5

Earned Run Average
Wynn-Cle 3.20
Garver-StL 3.39
Feller-Cle 3.43
Lopat-NY 3.47
Houtteman-Det 3.53

Adjusted ERA
Garver-StL 150
Parnell-Bos 141
Wynn-Cle 137
Feller-Cle 128
Wight-Chi 127

Opponents' Batting Avg.
Wynn-Cle 212
Pierce-Chi 228
Reynolds-NY 242
Raschi-NY 243
Cain-Chi 244

Opponents' On Base Pct.
Wynn-Cle 300
Lopat-NY 313
Houtteman-Det 317
Feller-Cle 320
Kinder-Bos 322

Starter Runs
Garver-StL 34.3
Wynn-Cle 32.9
Houtteman-Det 31.9
Feller-Cle 31.7
Lopat-NY 29.1

Adjusted Starter Runs
Garver-StL 48.5
Parnell-Bos 40.9
Wynn-Cle 27.9
Feller-Cle 25.9
Houtteman-Det 24.3

Clutch Pitching Index
Garver-StL 119
Hudson-Was 113
Lemon-Cle 111
Houtteman-Det 110
Parnell-Bos 110

Relief Runs
Judson-Chi 8.0
Aloma-Chi 7.8
Ferrick-StL-NY 7.2
Benton-Cle 7.0
Flores-Cle 5.0

Adjusted Relief Runs
Judson-Chi 7.5
Aloma-Chi 7.4
Ferrick-StL-NY 6.9
Benton-Cle 5.6
Flores-Cle 3.7

Relief Ranking
Ferrick-StL-NY 14.3
Aloma-Chi 7.5
Benton-Cle 5.6
Flores-Cle 4.4
Zoldak-Cle 3.0

Total Pitcher Index
Garver-StL 5.8
Parnell-Bos 4.5
Lemon-Cle 3.6
Wynn-Cle 3.4
Lopat-NY 3.1

Total Baseball Ranking
Garver-StL 5.8
Parnell-Bos 4.5
Priddy-Det 4.0
Lemon-Cle 3.6
Evers-Det 3.6

TEAM	G	W	L	PCT	GB	R	OR	AB	H	2B	3B	HR	BB	SO	AVG	OBP	SLG	PRO	/A	BR	/A	PF	CHI	RC	TA	SB	CS	SBA	SBR
NY	157	98	59	.624		781	641	5360	1396	201	53	179	671	624	.260	.347	.418	.765	112	91	78	102	97	812	.731	55	34	62	-3
BRO	158	97	60	.618	1	855	672	5492	1511	249	37	184	603	649	.275	.352	.434	.786	118	130	145	98	100	843	.744	89	70	56	-14
STL	155	81	73	.526	15.5	683	671	5317	1404	230	57	95	569	492	.264	.339	.382	.721	100	7	0	101	97	705	.653	30	30	50	-8
BOS	155	76	78	.494	20.5	723	662	5293	1385	234	37	130	565	617	.262	.336	.394	.730	102	19	32	98	101	719	.676	80	34	70	4
PHI	154	73	81	.474	23.5	648	644	5332	1384	199	47	108	505	525	.260	.326	.375	.701	95	-38	-17	97	99	676	.634	63	28	69	2
CIN	155	68	86	.442	28.5	559	667	5285	1309	215	33	88	415	577	.248	.304	.351	.655	82	-134	-138	101	104	562	.561	44	40	52	-10
PIT	155	64	90	.416	32.5	689	845	5318	1372	218	56	137	557	615	.258	.331	.397	.728	102	11	-34	107	97	712	.663	29	27	52	-7
CHI	155	62	92	.403	34.5	614	750	5307	1327	200	47	103	477	647	.250	.315	.364	.679	88	-86	-67	97	103	613	.601	63	30	68	1
TOT	622					5552		42704	11088	1746	367	1024	4362	4746	.260	.331	.390	.721								453	293	61	-39

TEAM	CG	SHO	SV	IP	H	H/G	HR	BB	BB/G	SO	SO/G	ERA	/A	OAVG	OOBA	PR	/A	PF	CPI	FA	E	DP	FW	PW	BW	SBW	DIF
NY	64	9	18	1412.7	1334	8.5	148	482	3.1	625	4.0	3.48	113	.248	.308	75	70	99	104	.972	171	175	-1.1	7.0	7.8	.2	5.6
BRO	64	10	13	1423.3	1360	8.6	150	549	3.5	693	4.4	3.88	97	.253	.322	13	-19	95	101	.979	129	192	1.1	-1.9	14.5	-.9	5.7
STL	58	9	23	1387.3	1391	9.0	119	568	3.7	546	3.5	3.95	101	.263	.333	1	6	101	103	.980	125	187	1.3	.6	.0	-.3	2.4
BOS	73	16	12	1389.0	1378	8.9	96	595	3.9	604	3.9	3.75	102	.259	.333	33	14	97	104	.976	145	157	.3	1.4	3.2	.9	-6.8
PHI	57	19	15	1384.3	1373	8.9	110	497	3.2	570	3.7	3.81	101	.258	.320	23	4	97	98	.977	138	146	.6	.4	-1.7	.7	-4.0
CIN	55	14	23	1390.7	1357	8.8	119	490	3.2	584	3.8	3.70	110	.254	.318	39	55	103	100	.977	140	141	.5	5.5	-13.8	-.5	-.7
PIT	40	9	22	1379.3	1479	9.7	157	609	4.0	580	3.8	4.80	90	.273	.345	-128	-70	110	97	.972	170	178	-1.1	-7.0	-3.4	-.2	-1.3
CHI	48	10	10	1385.7	1416	9.2	125	572	3.7	544	3.5	4.34	91	.265	.334	-58	-59	100	96	.971	181	161	-1.7	-5.9	-6.7	.6	-1.3
TOT	459	96	136	11152.3		8.9			3.5		3.8	3.96		.260	.331					.975	1199	1337					

Runs
Musial-StL 124
Kiner-Pit 124
Hodges-Bro 118
Dark-NY 114
Robinson-Bro 106

Hits
Ashburn-Phi 221
Musial-StL 205
Furillo-Bro 197
Dark-NY 196
Robinson-Bro 185

Doubles
Dark-NY 41
Kluszewski-Cin 35
Robinson-Bro 33
Campanella-Bro 33

Triples
Musial-StL 12
Bell-Pit 12
Irvin-NY 11
Jethroe-Bos 10
Baumholtz-Chi 10

Home Runs
Kiner-Pit 42
Hodges-Bro 40
Campanella-Bro 33
Thomson-NY 32
Musial-StL 32

Total Bases
Musial-StL 355
Kiner-Pit 333
Hodges-Bro 307
Campanella-Bro 298

Runs Batted In
Irvin-NY 121
Kiner-Pit 109
Gordon-Bos 109
Musial-StL 108
Campanella-Bro 108

Runs Produced
Musial-StL 200
Kiner-Pit 191
Irvin-NY 191
Hodges-Bro 181
Gordon-Bos 176

Bases On Balls
Kiner-Pit 137
Stanky-NY 127
Westrum-NY 104
Torgeson-Bos 102
Musial-StL 98

Batting Average
Musial-StL 355
Ashburn-Phi 344
Robinson-Bro 338
Campanella-Bro 325
Irvin-NY 312

On Base Percentage
Kiner-Pit 452
Musial-StL 449
Robinson-Bro 429
Irvin-NY 415
Stanky-NY 401

Slugging Average
Kiner-Pit 627
Musial-StL 614
Campanella-Bro 590
Thomson-NY 562
Hodges-Bro 527

Production
Kiner-Pit 1.079
Musial-StL 1.063
Campanella-Bro 983
Robinson-Bro 957
Thomson-NY 947

Adjusted Production
Musial-StL 181
Kiner-Pit 176
Campanella-Bro 164
Robinson-Bro 159
Thomson-NY 149

Batter Runs
Kiner-Pit 70.7
Musial-StL 70.0
Robinson-Bro 45.7
Campanella-Bro 41.7
Irvin-NY 40.6

Adjusted Batter Runs
Musial-StL 69.3
Kiner-Pit 65.6
Robinson-Bro 47.3
Campanella-Bro 43.0
Irvin-NY 39.3

Clutch Hitting Index
Slaughter-StL 147
Irvin-NY 138
Gordon-Bos 123
Westlake-Pit-StL 121
Hamner-Phi 118

Runs Created
Musial-StL 169
Kiner-Pit 165
Robinson-Bro 133
Irvin-NY 127
Hodges-Bro 119

Total Average
Kiner-Pit 1.254
Musial-StL 1.193
Robinson-Bro 1.055
Irvin-NY 990
Campanella-Bro 983

Stolen Bases
Jethroe-Bos 35
Ashburn-Phi 29
Robinson-Bro 25
Torgeson-Bos 20
Reese-Bro 20

Stolen Base Average
Jethroe-Bos 87.5
Ashburn-Phi 82.9
Robinson-Bro 75.8
Torgeson-Bos 64.5
Reese-Bro 58.8

Stolen Base Runs
Jethroe-Bos 7.5
Ashburn-Phi 5.1
Robinson-Bro 2.7
Jackson-Chi 2.4
Irvin-NY 2.4

Fielding Runs
Ashburn-Phi 25.5
Robinson-Bro 21.3
Furillo-Bro 13.2
Schoendienst-StL . . .13.1
Hemus-StL 12.7

Total Player Rating
Robinson-Bro 7.5
Musial-StL 7.0
Kiner-Pit 5.8
Campanella-Bro 5.0
Ashburn-Phi 4.7

Wins
Maglie-NY 23
Jansen-NY 23
Spahn-Bos 22
Roe-Bro 22
Roberts-Phi 21

Win Percentage
Roe-Bro 880
Maglie-NY 793
Newcombe-Bro 690
Jansen-NY 676
Hearn-NY 654

Games
Wilks-StL-Pit 65
Werle-Pit 59
Konstanty-Phi 58
Spencer-NY 57
Brazle-StL 56

Complete Games
Spahn-Bos 26
Roberts-Phi 22
Maglie-NY 22
Roe-Bro 19
Dickson-Pit 19

Shutouts
Spahn-Bos 7
Roberts-Phi 6
Raffensberge-Cin 5

Saves
Wilks-StL-Pit 13
Smith-Cin 11
Konstanty-Phi 9
Brazle-StL 7

Innings Pitched
Roberts-Phi 315
Spahn-Bos 311
Maglie-NY 298
Dickson-Pit 289
Jansen-NY 279

Fewest Hits/Game
Maglie-NY 7.67
Newcombe-Bro 7.78
Blackwell-Cin 7.88
Branca-Bro 7.94
Bickford-Bos 7.96

Fewest BB/Game
Raffensberge-Cin 1.37
Jansen-NY 1.81
Roberts-Phi 1.83
Roe-Bro 2.23
Sain-Bos 2.53

Strikeouts
Spahn-Bos 164
Newcombe-Bro 164
Maglie-NY 146
Jansen-NY 145
Rush-Chi 129

Strikeouts/Game
Queen-Pit 6.59
Rush-Chi 5.50
Newcombe-Bro 5.43
Branca-Bro 5.21
Spahn-Bos 4.75

Wins Above Team
Roe-Bro 9.0
Maglie-NY 7.3
Dickson-Pit 5.2
Spahn-Bos 5.1
Roberts-Phi 4.6

Earned Run Average
Nichols-Bos 2.88
Maglie-NY 2.93
Spahn-Bos 2.98
Roberts-Phi 3.03
Jansen-NY 3.03

Adjusted ERA
Maglie-NY 134
Nichols-Bos 133
Jansen-NY 130
Spahn-Bos 129
Roberts-Phi 127

Opponents' Batting Avg.
Maglie-NY 230
Newcombe-Bro 230
Blackwell-Cin 233
Queen-Pit 233
Branca-Bro 237

Opponents' On Base Pct.
Raffensberge-Cin 274
Roberts-Phi 276
Jansen-NY 276
Maglie-NY 286
Newcombe-Bro 295

Starter Runs
Maglie-NY 34.1
Spahn-Bos 33.8
Roberts-Phi 32.6
Jansen-NY 28.8
Roe-Bro 26.5

Adjusted Starter Runs
Maglie-NY 33.1
Spahn-Bos 29.6
Roberts-Phi 28.4
Jansen-NY 27.8
Roe-Bro 20.5

Clutch Pitching Index
Roe-Bro 122
Sain-Bos 113
Nichols-Bos 112
Minner-Chi 111
Bickford-Bos 108

Relief Runs
Brazle-StL 14.8
Kennedy-NY 12.9
Perkowski-Cin 12.9
Wilks-StL-Pit 12.4
Leonard-Chi 12.1

Adjusted Relief Runs
Wilks-StL-Pit 16.0
Brazle-StL 15.3
Perkowski-Cin 14.0
Kennedy-NY 12.7
Leonard-Chi 12.0

Relief Ranking
Leonard-Chi 22.1
Wilks-StL-Pit 16.0
Perkowski-Cin 11.5
Brazle-StL 11.4
Smith-Cin 11.0

Total Pitcher Index
Maglie-NY 3.3
Spahn-Bos 3.3
Roberts-Phi 3.2
Jansen-NY 2.7
Blackwell-Cin 2.5

Total Baseball Ranking
Robinson-Bro 7.5
Musial-StL 7.0
Kiner-Pit 5.8
Campanella-Bro 5.0
Ashburn-Phi 4.7

TEAM	G	W	L	PCT	GB	R	OR	AB	H	2B	3B	HR	BB	SO	AVG	OBP	SLG	PRO	/A	BR	/A	PF	CHI	RC	TA	SB	CS	SBA	SBR
NY	154	98	56	.636		798	621	5194	1395	208	48	**140**	605	547	.269	.349	**.408**	**.757**	109	62	**121**	92	**104**	762	**.714**	78	39	67	0
CLE	155	93	61	.604	5	696	**594**	5250	1346	208	35	**140**	606	632	.256	.336	.389	.725	100	0	38	95	98	710	.672	52	35	60	-4
BOS	154	87	67	.565	11	804	725	5378	1428	233	32	127	**756**	594	.266	**.358**	.392	.750	108	63	6	108	100	**778**	.700	20	21	49	-6
CHI	155	81	73	.526	17	714	644	5378	**1453**	229	64	86	596	524	**.270**	.349	.385	.734	103	23	47	97	95	745	.684	**99**	70	59	-11
DET	154	73	81	.474	25	685	741	5336	1413	231	35	104	568	525	.265	.338	.380	.718	99	-14	-53	106	97	697	.647	37	34	52	-8
PHI	154	70	84	.455	28	736	745	5277	1381	**262**	43	102	677	565	.262	.349	.386	.735	103	29	-13	106	98	745	.690	47	36	57	-7
WAS	154	62	92	.403	36	672	764	5329	1399	242	45	54	560	**515**	.263	.336	.355	.691	91	-59	-25	95	103	648	.614	45	38	54	-8
STL	154	52	102	.338	46	611	882	5219	1288	223	47	86	521	693	.247	.317	.357	.674	86	-102	-133	105	103	592	.591	35	38	48	-11
TOT	617					5716		42361	11103	1836	349	839	4889	4595	.262	.342	.381	.723								413	311	57	-62

TEAM	CG	SHO	SV	IP	H	H/G	HR	BB	BB/G	SO	SO/G	ERA	/A	OAVG	OOBA	PR	/A	PF	CPI	FA	E	DP	FW	PW	BW	SBW	DIF
NY	66	**24**	22	1367.0	1290	8.5	92	562	3.7	**664**	4.4	3.56	102	.250	.323	84	11	88	103	.975	144	190	.3	1.1	**11.9**	**.8**	6.9
CLE	**76**	10	19	1391.3	**1287**	8.3	86	577	3.7	642	4.2	**3.38**	113	**.245**	**.317**	**114**	66	93	103	**.978**	**134**	151	.9	6.5	3.7	.4	4.5
BOS	46	7	**24**	1399.0	1413	9.1	100	599	3.9	658	4.2	4.14	106	.264	.337	-2	38	106	100	.977	141	184	.5	3.7	.6	.2	5.0
CHI	74	11	14	1418.3	1353	8.6	109	**549**	3.5	572	3.6	3.50	112	.251	.318	97	**68**	96	105	.975	151	176	-.0	**6.7**	4.6	-.3	-7.0
DET	51	8	17	1384.0	1385	9.0	102	602	3.9	597	3.9	4.29	102	.261	.336	-26	15	107	96	.973	163	166	-.7	1.5	-5.2	-.0	.4
PHI	52	7	22	1358.0	1421	9.4	109	569	3.8	437	2.9	4.47	98	.272	.343	-52	-14	106	98	**.978**	136	**204**	.8	-1.4	-1.3	.0	-5.2
WAS	58	6	13	1366.3	1429	9.4	110	630	4.1	475	3.1	4.49	89	.268	.344	-55	-74	97	97	.973	160	148	-.5	-7.3	-2.5	-.0	-4.7
STL	56	5	9	1370.3	1525	10.0	131	801	5.3	550	3.6	5.18	87	.282	.374	-160	-101	109	101	.971	172	179	-1.2	-9.9	-13.1	-.3	-.5
TOT	479	78	140	11054.3		9.0			4.0		3.7	4.12		.262	.342					.975	1201	1398					

Runs
DiMaggio-Bos 113
Minoso-Cle-Chi 112
Yost-Was 109
Williams-Bos 109
Joost-Phi 107

Hits
Kell-Det 191
Fox-Chi 189
DiMaggio-Bos 189
Minoso-Cle-Chi 173
Williams-Bos 169

Doubles
Yost-Was 36
Mele-Was 36
Kell-Det 36

Triples
Minoso-Cle-Chi 14
Coleman-StL-Chi ...12
Fox-Chi 12
Young-StL 9

Home Runs
Zernial-Chi-Phi 33
Williams-Bos 30
Robinson-Chi 29

Total Bases
Williams-Bos 295
Zernial-Chi-Phi 292
Robinson-Chi 279
Berra-NY 269
DiMaggio-Bos 267

Runs Batted In
Zernial-Chi-Phi 129
Williams-Bos 126
Robinson-Chi 117
Easter-Cle 103
Rosen-Cle 102

Runs Produced
Williams-Bos 205
Zernial-Chi-Phi 188
Minoso-Cle-Chi 178
Robinson-Chi 173
DiMaggio-Bos 173

Bases On Balls
Williams-Bos 144
Yost-Was 126
Joost-Phi 106
Doby-Cle 101
Rosen-Cle 85

Batting Average
Fain-Phi 344
Minoso-Cle-Chi 326
Kell-Det 319
Williams-Bos 318
Fox-Chi 313

On Base Percentage
Williams-Bos 464
Fain-Phi 451
Doby-Cle 428
Yost-Was 423
Minoso-Cle-Chi 422

Slugging Average
Williams-Bos 556
Doby-Cle 512
Zernial-Chi-Phi 511
Wertz-Det 511
Minoso-Cle-Chi 500

Production
Williams-Bos 1.019
Doby-Cle 941
Minoso-Cle-Chi 922
Fain-Phi 921
Wertz-Det 894

Adjusted Production
Doby-Cle 162
Williams-Bos 162
Minoso-Cle-Chi 154
Fain-Phi 141
Berra-NY 137

Batter Runs
Williams-Bos 62.8
Minoso-Cle-Chi ... 38.1
Doby-Cle 37.0
Fain-Phi 33.7
Joost-Phi 30.4

Adjusted Batter Runs
Williams-Bos 56.6
Minoso-Cle-Chi ... 40.6
Doby-Cle 40.6
Yost-Was 34.1
Fain-Phi 30.2

Clutch Hitting Index
Mele-Was 147
Noren-Was 140
Busby-Chi 132
Vernon-Was 128
Zernial-Chi-Phi ...125

Runs Created
Williams-Bos 152
Minoso-Cle-Chi 120
Yost-Was 117
Joost-Phi 115
Doby-Cle 108

Total Average
Williams-Bos 1.180
Doby-Cle 1.034
Minoso-Cle-Chi ... 1.013
Fain-Phi 969
Joost-Phi 926

Stolen Bases
Minoso-Cle-Chi 31
Busby-Chi 26
Rizzuto-NY 18

Stolen Base Average
Rizzuto-NY 85.7
Minoso-Cle-Chi ... 75.6
Busby-Chi 70.3

Stolen Base Runs
Rizzuto-NY 3.6
Minoso-Cle-Chi ... 3.3
Carrasquel-Chi 1.8

Fielding Runs
Coan-Was 24.4
Stephens-Bos 19.9
Carrasquel-Chi ... 16.3
Noren-Was 15.7
Zernial-Chi-Phi ... 13.4

Total Player Rating
Williams-Bos 5.5
Berra-NY 4.1
Joost-Phi 3.7
Fain-Phi 3.4
Pesky-Bos 2.9

Wins
Feller-Cle 22
Raschi-NY 21
Lopat-NY 21

Win Percentage
Feller-Cle 733
Lopat-NY 700
Reynolds-NY 680
Raschi-NY 677
Shantz-Phi 643

Games
Kinder-Bos 63
Brissie-Phi-Cle 56
Garcia-Cle 47
Scheib-Phi 46

Complete Games
Garver-StL 24
Wynn-Cle 21
Lopat-NY 20
Pierce-Chi 18

Shutouts
Reynolds-NY 7
Raschi-NY 4
Lopat-NY 4
Feller-Cle 4

Saves
Kinder-Bos 14
Scheib-Phi 10
Brissie-Phi-Cle 9
Reynolds-NY 7
Garcia-Cle 6

Innings Pitched
Wynn-Cle 274
Lemon-Cle 263
Raschi-NY 258
Garcia-Cle 254
Feller-Cle 250

Fewest Hits/Game
Reynolds-NY 6.96
McDermott-Bos 7.38
Wynn-Cle 7.46
Rogovin-Det-Chi ... 7.84
Lopat-NY 8.00

Fewest BB/Game
Hutchinson-Det 1.29
Lopat-NY 2.72
Pierce-Chi 2.74
Hooper-Phi 2.90
Garcia-Cle 2.91

Strikeouts
Raschi-NY 164
Wynn-Cle 133
Lemon-Cle 132
Gray-Det 131
McDermott-Bos 127

Strikeouts/Game
McDermott-Bos 6.65
Gray-Det 5.98
Raschi-NY 5.72
Trucks-Det 5.20
Reynolds-NY 5.13

Wins Above Team
Garver-StL 7.9
Feller-Cle 5.6
Shantz-Phi 5.5
Kinder-Bos 4.3
Martin-Phi 4.0

Earned Run Average
Rogovin-Det-Chi ... 2.78
Lopat-NY 2.91
Wynn-Cle 3.02
Pierce-Chi 3.04
Reynolds-NY 3.05

Adjusted ERA
Rogovin-Det-Chi 143
Parnell-Bos 135
McDermott-Bos 131
Pierce-Chi 130
Wynn-Cle 126

Opponents' Batting Avg.
Reynolds-NY 213
Wynn-Cle 225
McDermott-Bos 226
Rogovin-Det-Chi ...235
Lopat-NY 239

Opponents' On Base Pct.
Lopat-NY 293
Wynn-Cle 296
Rogovin-Det-Chi ...297
Hutchinson-Det 298
Reynolds-NY 302

Starter Runs
Wynn-Cle 33.5
Rogovin-Det-Chi ... 32.4
Lopat-NY 31.6
Pierce-Chi 28.9
Garcia-Cle 27.3

Adjusted Starter Runs
Rogovin-Det-Chi ... 29.0
Parnell-Bos 27.7
Wynn-Cle 24.2
Pierce-Chi 24.0
Garver-StL 21.2

Clutch Pitching Index
Parnell-Bos 119
Pierce-Chi 113
Rogovin-Det-Chi ...111
Feller-Cle 109
Raschi-NY 108

Relief Runs
Kinder-Bos 22.2
Aloma-Chi 17.6
Brissie-Phi-Cle 7.2
Ostrowski-NY 6.5
Masterson-Bos 5.0

Adjusted Relief Runs
Kinder-Bos 25.9
Aloma-Chi 16.2
Masterson-Bos 6.7
Brissie-Phi-Cle 3.8
Ferrick-NY -Was 2.7

Relief Ranking
Kinder-Bos 30.3
Aloma-Chi 14.2
Masterson-Bos 3.6
Brissie-Phi-Cle 3.1
Harris-Was 2.5

Total Pitcher Index
Parnell-Bos 3.4
Garver-StL 3.2
Rogovin-Det-Chi ... 3.1
McDermott-Bos 2.4
Wynn-Cle 2.4

Total Baseball Ranking
Williams-Bos 5.5
Berra-NY 4.1
Joost-Phi 3.7
Parnell-Bos 3.4
Fain-Phi 3.4

TEAM	G	W	L	PCT	GB	R	OR	AB	H	2B	3B	HR	BB	SO	AVG	OBP	SLG	PRO	/A	BR	/A	PF	CHI	RC	TA	SB	CS	SBA	SBR
BRO	155	96	57	.627		775	603	5266	1380	199	32	153	663	699	.262	.348	.399	.747	114	107	96	102	100	754	.707	90	49	65	-1
NY	154	92	62	.597	4.5	722	639	5229	1337	186	56	151	536	672	.256	.329	.399	.728	108	56	40	102	102	712	.670	30	31	49	-9
STL	154	88	66	.571	8.5	677	630	5200	1386	237	54	93	537	479	.267	.340	.391	.731	110	68	81	98	95	708	.667	33	32	51	-8
PHI	154	87	67	.565	9.5	657	552	5205	1353	237	45	93	540	534	.260	.332	.376	.708	103	25	18	101	97	671	.644	60	41	59	-6
CHI	155	77	77	.500	19.5	628	631	5330	1408	223	45	107	422	712	.264	.321	.383	.704	102	5	-16	103	97	652	.619	50	40	56	-8
CIN	154	69	85	.448	27.5	615	659	5234	1303	212	45	104	480	709	.249	.314	.366	.680	95	-35	-31	100	102	610	.599	32	42	43	-15
BOS	155	64	89	.418	32	569	651	5221	1214	187	31	110	483	711	.233	.301	.343	.644	85	-101	-68	95	105	555	.569	58	34	63	-2
PIT	155	42	112	.273	54.5	515	793	5193	1201	181	30	92	486	724	.231	.300	.331	.631	81	-124	-122	100	100	530	.549	43	41	51	-11
TOT	618					5158		41878	10582	1672	338	907	4147	5240	.253	.323	.374	.697								396	310	56	-66

TEAM	CG	SHO	SV	IP	H	H/G	HR	BB	BB/G	SO	SO/G	ERA	/A	OAVG	OOBA	PR	/A	PF	CPI	FA	E	DP	FW	PW	BW	SBW	DIF
BRO	45	11	24	1399.0	1295	8.3	121	544	3.5	773	5.0	3.53	104	.246	.317	31	20	98	103	.982	106	169	2.0	2.1	9.9	.8	4.8
NY	49	12	31	1371.0	1282	8.4	121	538	3.5	655	4.3	3.59	105	.247	.318	21	26	101	103	.974	158	175	-.8	2.7	4.1	-.0	9.0
STL	49	13	27	1361.3	1274	8.4	119	501	3.3	712	4.7	3.66	99	.246	.312	10	-6	97	98	.977	141	159	.1	-.6	8.4	.0	3.1
PHI	80	17	16	1386.7	1306	8.5	95	373	2.4	609	4.0	3.07	120	.248	.296	102	95	99	104	.975	150	145	-.4	9.8	1.9	.2	-1.6
CHI	59	15	15	1386.3	1265	8.2	101	534	3.5	661	4.3	3.58	108	.240	.309	22	41	103	94	.976	146	123	-.2	4.2	-1.7	-.0	-2.5
CIN	56	11	12	1363.3	1377	9.1	111	517	3.4	579	3.8	4.01	93	.266	.332	-42	-40	100	103	.982	107	145	1.9	-4.1	-3.2	-.7	-1.9
BOS	63	11	13	1396.0	1388	8.9	106	525	3.4	687	4.4	3.78	95	.259	.324	-7	-27	97	102	.975	154	143	-.6	-2.8	-7.0	.7	-2.8
PIT	43	5	8	1363.7	1395	9.2	133	615	4.1	564	3.7	4.65	84	.265	.339	-138	-109	105	94	.970	182	167	-2.1	-11.3	-12.6	-.3	-8.8
TOT	444	95	146	11027.3		8.6			3.4		4.3	3.73		.253	.323					.976	1144	1226					

Runs
Musial-StL ... 105
Hemus-StL ... 105
Robinson-Bro ... 104
Lockman-NY ... 99
Reese-Bro ... 94

Hits
Musial-StL ... 194
Schoendienst-StL ... 188
Adams-Cin ... 180
Dark-NY ... 177
Lockman-NY ... 176

Doubles
Musial-StL ... 42
Schoendienst-StL ... 40
McMillan-Cin ... 32
Sauer-Chi ... 31
Ashburn-Phi ... 31

Triples
Thomson-NY ... 14
Slaughter-StL ... 12
Kluszewski-Cin ... 11
Ennis-Phi ... 10

Home Runs
Sauer-Chi ... 37
Kiner-Pit ... 37
Hodges-Bro ... 32
Mathews-Bos ... 25
Gordon-Bos ... 25

Total Bases
Musial-StL ... 311
Sauer-Chi ... 301
Thomson-NY ... 293
Ennis-Phi ... 281
Snider-Bro ... 264

Runs Batted In
Sauer-Chi ... 121
Thomson-NY ... 108
Ennis-Phi ... 107
Hodges-Bro ... 102
Slaughter-StL ... 101

Runs Produced
Ennis-Phi ... 177
Musial-StL ... 175
Thomson-NY ... 173
Sauer-Chi ... 173
Slaughter-StL ... 163

Bases On Balls
Kiner-Pit ... 110
Hodges-Bro ... 107
Robinson-Bro ... 106
Musial-StL ... 96
Hemus-StL ... 96

Batting Average
Musial-StL ... .336
Kluszewski-Cin ... .320
Robinson-Bro ... .308
Snider-Bro ... .303
Schoendienst-StL ... .303

On Base Percentage
Robinson-Bro ... .440
Musial-StL ... .432
Hemus-StL ... .392
Hodges-Bro ... .386
Slaughter-StL ... .386

Slugging Average
Musial-StL ... .538
Kluszewski-Cin ... .531
Kiner-Pit ... .500
Hodges-Bro ... .500

Production
Musial-StL ... .970
Robinson-Bro ... .904
Kluszewski-Cin ... .892
Sauer-Chi ... .892
Hodges-Bro ... .886

Adjusted Production
Musial-StL ... 171
Robinson-Bro ... 149
Gordon-Bos ... 146
Kluszewski-Cin ... 146
Kiner-Pit ... 144

Batter Runs
Musial-StL ... 55.7
Robinson-Bro ... 41.9
Sauer-Chi ... 32.8
Kiner-Pit ... 32.7
Hodges-Bro ... 32.3

Adjusted Batter Runs
Musial-StL ... 57.2
Robinson-Bro ... 40.8
Kiner-Pit ... 32.9
Gordon-Bos ... 31.8
Hodges-Bro ... 31.3

Clutch Hitting Index
Slaughter-StL ... 161
Hatton-Cin ... 140
Campanella-Bro ... 139
Ennis-Phi ... 130
Thomson-NY ... 122

Runs Created
Musial-StL ... 141
Robinson-Bro ... 116
Sauer-Chi ... 111
Kiner-Pit ... 111
Hodges-Bro ... 106

Total Average
Musial-StL ... 1.035
Robinson-Bro ... 1.013
Kiner-Pit ... .955
Hodges-Bro ... .931
Sauer-Chi ... .891

Stolen Bases
Reese-Bro ... 30
Jethroe-Bos ... 28
Robinson-Bro ... 24
Ashburn-Phi ... 16

Stolen Base Average
Reese-Bro ... 85.7
Robinson-Bro ... 77.4
Jethroe-Bos ... 75.7
Ashburn-Phi ... 59.3

Stolen Base Runs
Reese-Bro ... 6.0
Robinson-Bro ... 3.0
Jethroe-Bos ... 3.0
Davis-Pit ... 1.5
Slaughter-StL ... 1.2

Fielding Runs
Schoendienst-StL ... 27.7
Jeffcoat-Chi ... 14.6
Ashburn-Phi ... 13.3
Wyrostek-Cin-Phi ... 12.5
Groat-Pit ... 12.1

Total Player Rating
Robinson-Bro ... 6.1
Schoendienst-StL ... 4.5
Musial-StL ... 4.5
Sauer-Chi ... 3.8
Hemus-StL ... 3.3

Wins
Roberts-Phi ... 28
Maglie-NY ... 18
Staley-StL ... 17
Rush-Chi ... 17
Raffensberge-Cin ... 17

Win Percentage
Wilhelm-NY ... .833
Roberts-Phi ... .800
Black-Bro ... .789
Maglie-NY ... .692
Hacker-Chi ... .625

Games
Wilhelm-NY ... 71
Black-Bro ... 56
Yuhas-StL ... 54
Smith-Chi ... 53
Main-Pit ... 48

Complete Games
Roberts-Phi ... 30
Dickson-Pit ... 21
Spahn-Bos ... 19
Raffensberge-Cin ... 18
Rush-Chi ... 17

Shutouts
Simmons-Phi ... 6
Raffensberge-Cin ... 6

Saves
Brazle-StL ... 16
Black-Bro ... 15
Wilhelm-NY ... 11
Leonard-Chi ... 11

Innings Pitched
Roberts-Phi ... 330
Spahn-Bos ... 290
Dickson-Pit ... 278
Rush-Chi ... 250
Raffensberge-Cin ... 247

Fewest Hits/Game
Hacker-Chi ... 7.01
Wilhelm-NY ... 7.19
Erskine-Bro ... 7.26
Rush-Chi ... 7.38
Loes-Bro ... 7.41

Fewest BB/Game
Roberts-Phi ... 1.23
Hacker-Chi ... 1.51
Raffensberge-Cin ... 1.64
Staley-StL ... 1.95
Drews-Phi ... 2.04

Strikeouts
Spahn-Bos ... 183
Rush-Chi ... 157
Roberts-Phi ... 148
Mizell-StL ... 146
Simmons-Phi ... 141

Strikeouts/Game
Mizell-StL ... 6.92
Simmons-Phi ... 6.31
Wilhelm-NY ... 6.11
Wade-Bro ... 5.90
Erskine-Bro ... 5.70

Wins Above Team
Roberts-Phi ... 10.6
Wilhelm-NY ... 5.5
Yuhas-StL ... 4.8
Black-Bro ... 4.4
Roe-Bro ... 4.0

Earned Run Average
Wilhelm-NY ... 2.43
Hacker-Chi ... 2.58
Roberts-Phi ... 2.59
Loes-Bro ... 2.70
Erskine-Bro ... 2.70

Adjusted ERA
Wilhelm-NY ... 155
Hacker-Chi ... 150
Rush-Chi ... 143
Roberts-Phi ... 142
Drews-Phi ... 136

Opponents' Batting Avg.
Hacker-Chi ... .212
Rush-Chi ... .216
Wilhelm-NY ... .220
Erskine-Bro ... .220
Loes-Bro ... .224

Opponents' On Base Pct.
Hacker-Chi ... .244
Roberts-Phi ... .261
Rush-Chi ... .280
Erskine-Bro ... .287
Spahn-Bos ... .287

Starter Runs
Roberts-Phi ... 41.8
Rush-Chi ... 28.7
Drews-Phi ... 26.0
Raffensberger-Cin ... 25.4
Spahn-Bos ... 24.3

Adjusted Starter Runs
Roberts-Phi ... 40.3
Rush-Chi ... 32.1
Hacker-Chi ... 26.3
Raffensberger-Cin ... 25.7
Drews-Phi ... 24.9

Clutch Pitching Index
Roe-Bro ... 128
Church-Phi-Cin ... 119
Wilhelm-NY ... 119
Raffensberge-Cin ... 117
Maglie-NY ... 116

Relief Runs
Black-Bro ... 24.9
Wilhelm-NY ... 22.9
Brazle-StL ... 12.2
Leonard-Chi ... 11.8
Yuhas-StL ... 11.1

Adjusted Relief Runs
Black-Bro ... 23.8
Wilhelm-NY ... 23.5
Leonard-Chi ... 12.7
Brazle-StL ... 10.8
Yuhas-StL ... 9.8

Relief Ranking
Black-Bro ... 34.4
Wilhelm-NY ... 27.6
Brazle-StL ... 18.8
Yuhas-StL ... 13.8
Leonard-Chi ... 11.5

Total Pitcher Index
Rush-Chi ... 4.7
Roberts-Phi ... 4.3
Erskine-Bro ... 2.6
Wilhelm-NY ... 2.5
Spahn-Bos ... 2.5

Total Baseball Ranking
Robinson-Bro ... 6.1
Rush-Chi ... 4.7
Schoendienst-StL ... 4.5
Musial-StL ... 4.5
Roberts-Phi ... 4.3

TEAM	G	W	L	PCT	GB	R	OR	AB	H	2B	3B	HR	BB	SO	AVG	OBP	SLG	PRO	/A	BR	/A	PF	CHI	RC	TA	SB	CS	SBA	SBR
NY	154	95	59	.617		727	557	5294	1411	221	56	129	566	652	.267	.341	.403	.744	114	89	102	98	98	758	.693	52	42	55	-9
CLE	155	93	61	.604	2	763	606	5330	1399	211	49	148	626	749	.262	.342	.404	.746	114	95	156	91	101	759	.695	46	39	54	-9
CHI	156	81	73	.526	14	610	568	5316	1337	199	38	80	541	521	.252	.327	.348	.675	94	-34	-32	100	98	633	.607	61	38	62	-4
PHI	155	79	75	.513	16	664	723	5163	1305	212	35	89	683	561	.253	.343	.359	.702	102	26	-43	111	98	659	.645	52	43	55	-9
WAS	157	78	76	.506	17	598	608	5357	1282	225	44	50	580	607	.239	.317	.326	.643	85	-97	-97	100	107	572	.566	48	37	56	-7
BOS	154	76	78	.494	19	668	658	5246	1338	233	34	113	542	739	.255	.328	.377	.705	103	14	-29	107	102	659	.638	59	47	56	-10
STL	155	64	90	.416	31	604	733	5353	1340	225	46	82	540	720	.250	.322	.356	.678	95	-38	-19	97	98	631	.600	30	34	47	-10
DET	156	50	104	.325	45	557	738	5258	1278	190	37	103	553	605	.243	.318	.352	.670	93	-51	-45	99	94	594	.589	27	38	42	-14
TOT	621					5191		42317	10690	1716	339	794	4631	5154	.253	.330	.365	.695								375	318	54	-77

TEAM	CG	SHO	SV	IP	H	H/G	HR	BB	BB/G	SO	SO/G	ERA	/A	OAVG	OOBA	PR	/A	PF	CPI	FA	E	DP	FW	PW	BW	SBW	DIF
NY	72	21	27	1381.0	1240	8.1	94	581	3.8	666	4.3	3.14	111	.242	.319	81	51	95	110	.979	127	199	.8	5.3	10.6	.0	1.2
CLE	80	19	18	1407.0	1278	8.2	94	556	3.6	671	4.3	3.32	97	.241	.311	55	-14	88	99	.975	155	141	-.8	-1.5	16.2	.0	2.0
CHI	53	15	28	1416.7	1251	7.9	86	578	3.7	774	4.9	3.25	112	.237	.310	66	60	99	98	.980	123	158	1.0	6.2	-3.3	.6	-.6
PHI	73	11	16	1384.3	1402	9.1	113	526	3.4	562	3.7	4.15	99	.262	.328	-73	-5	112	94	.977	140	148	.0	-.5	-4.5	.0	6.8
WAS	75	10	15	1429.7	1405	8.8	78	577	3.6	574	3.6	3.37	109	.257	.328	47	49	100	108	.978	132	152	.5	5.1	-10.1	.3	5.2
BOS	53	7	24	1372.3	1332	8.7	107	623	4.1	624	4.1	3.80	103	.256	.334	-19	19	107	104	.976	145	181	-.2	2.0	-3.0	-.0	.3
STL	48	6	18	1399.0	1388	8.9	111	598	3.8	581	3.7	4.12	89	.259	.333	-68	-71	100	97	.974	155	176	-.8	-7.4	-2.0	-.0	-2.8
DET	51	10	14	1388.0	1394	9.0	111	591	3.8	702	4.6	4.25	89	.261	.332	-89	-74	103	94	.975	152	145	-.6	-7.7	-4.7	-.4	-13.6
TOT	505	99	160	11178.0		8.6			3.7		4.1	3.67		.253	.330					.977	1129	1300					

Runs
Doby-Cle	104
Avila-Cle	102
Rosen-Cle	101
Berra-NY	97
Minoso-Chi	96

Hits
Fox-Chi	192
Avila-Cle	179
Robinson-Chi	176
Fain-Phi	176

Doubles
Fain-Phi	43
Mantle-NY	37
Vernon-Was	33
Robinson-Chi	33

Triples
Avila-Cle	11
Simpson-Cle	10
Rizzuto-NY	10
Fox-Chi	10

Home Runs
Doby-Cle	32
Easter-Cle	31
Berra-NY	30
Dropo-Bos-Det	29
Zernial-Phi	29

Total Bases
Rosen-Cle	297
Mantle-NY	291
Dropo-Bos-Det	282
Doby-Cle	281
Robinson-Chi	277

Runs Batted In
Rosen-Cle	105
Robinson-Chi	104
Doby-Cle	104
Zernial-Phi	100
Berra-NY	98

Runs Produced
Rosen-Cle	178
Doby-Cle	176
Berra-NY	165
Robinson-Chi	161
Mantle-NY	158

Bases On Balls
Yost-Was	129
Joost-Phi	122
Fain-Phi	105
Valo-Phi	101
Doby-Cle	90

Batting Average
Fain-Phi	.327
Mitchell-Cle	.323
Mantle-NY	.311
Kell-Det-Bos	.311
Goodman-Bos	.306

On Base Percentage
Fain-Phi	.438
Valo-Phi	.432
Mantle-NY	.394
Joost-Phi	.388
Rosen-Cle	.387

Slugging Average
Doby-Cle	.541
Mantle-NY	.530
Rosen-Cle	.524
Easter-Cle	.513
Wertz-Det-StL	.506

Production
Mantle-NY	.924
Doby-Cle	.924
Rosen-Cle	.911
Wertz-Det-StL	.887
Fain-Phi	.867

Adjusted Production
Doby-Cle	171
Rosen-Cle	167
Mantle-NY	159
Easter-Cle	148
Wertz-Det-StL	148

Batter Runs
Mantle-NY	40.3
Rosen-Cle	38.6
Doby-Cle	37.9
Fain-Phi	36.3
Robinson-Chi	28.3

Adjusted Batter Runs
Rosen-Cle	45.1
Doby-Cle	44.0
Mantle-NY	41.7
Fain-Phi	28.8
Robinson-Chi	28.4

Clutch Hitting Index
Runnels-Was	130
McDougald-NY	125
Vernon-Was	125
Robinson-Chi	120
Zernial-Phi	118

Runs Created
Mantle-NY	123
Doby-Cle	116
Rosen-Cle	115
Robinson-Chi	113
Fain-Phi	107

Total Average
Doby-Cle	.979
Mantle-NY	.964
Rosen-Cle	.914
Wertz-Det-StL	.912
Valo-Phi	.910

Stolen Bases
Minoso-Chi	22
Rivera-StL-Chi	21
Jensen-NY-Was	18
Rizzuto-NY	17
Throneberry-Bos	16

Stolen Base Average
Jensen-NY-Was	75.0
Rizzuto-NY	73.9
Rivera-StL-Chi	70.0
Throneberry-Bos	69.6
Minoso-Chi	57.9

Stolen Base Runs
Jensen-NY-Was	1.8
Rizzuto-NY	1.5
Michaels-StL-Phi	1.2
Porter-StL	1.2
Goodman-Bos	1.2

Fielding Runs
Rizzuto-NY	19.9
Goodman-Bos	18.4
McDougald-NY	18.2
Fain-Phi	16.0
Rodriguez-Chi	11.7

Total Player Rating
Doby-Cle	4.5
Fain-Phi	3.5
Mantle-NY	3.3
Berra-NY	3.3
Goodman-Bos	2.8

Wins
Shantz-Phi	24
Wynn-Cle	23
Lemon-Cle	22
Garcia-Cle	22
Reynolds-NY	20

Win Percentage
Shantz-Phi	.774
Raschi-NY	.727
Reynolds-NY	.714
Lemon-Cle	.667
Garcia-Cle	.667

Games
Kennedy-Chi	47
Paige-StL	46
Garcia-Cle	46
Hooper-Phi	43

Complete Games
Lemon-Cle	28
Shantz-Phi	27
Reynolds-NY	24
Wynn-Cle	19
Garcia-Cle	19

Shutouts
Reynolds-NY	6
Garcia-Cle	6
Shantz-Phi	5
Lemon-Cle	5

Saves
Dorish-Chi	11
Paige-StL	10
Sain-NY	7

Innings Pitched
Lemon-Cle	310
Garcia-Cle	292
Wynn-Cle	286
Shantz-Phi	280
Pierce-Chi	255

Fewest Hits/Game
Lemon-Cle	6.85
Raschi-NY	7.02
Reynolds-NY	7.16
Dobson-Chi	7.34
Shantz-Phi	7.39

Fewest BB/Game
Shantz-Phi	2.03
Pillette-StL	2.41
Marrero-Was	2.59
Houtteman-Det	2.65
Garcia-Cle	2.68

Strikeouts
Reynolds-NY	160
Wynn-Cle	153
Shantz-Phi	152
Pierce-Chi	144
Garcia-Cle	143

Strikeouts/Game
McDermott-Bos	6.50
Reynolds-NY	5.90
Trucks-Det	5.89
Gray-Det	5.54
Grissom-Chi	5.26

Wins Above Team
Shantz-Phi	9.2
Reynolds-NY	4.1
Raschi-NY	3.5
Lemon-Cle	3.2
Garcia-Cle	3.2

Earned Run Average
Reynolds-NY	2.07
Garcia-Cle	2.37
Shantz-Phi	2.48
Lemon-Cle	2.50
Dobson-Chi	2.51

Adjusted ERA
Reynolds-NY	168
Shantz-Phi	166
Dobson-Chi	145
Pierce-Chi	141
Garcia-Cle	136

Opponents' Batting Avg.
Lemon-Cle	.208
Raschi-NY	.216
Reynolds-NY	.218
Dobson-Chi	.222
Shantz-Phi	.225

Opponents' On Base Pct.
Shantz-Phi	.269
Lemon-Cle	.277
Dobson-Chi	.278
Pierce-Chi	.284
Raschi-NY	.297

Starter Runs
Reynolds-NY	43.6
Garcia-Cle	42.2
Lemon-Cle	40.6
Shantz-Phi	37.3
Pierce-Chi	31.1

Adjusted Starter Runs
Shantz-Phi	51.0
Reynolds-NY	38.2
Pierce-Chi	30.1
Garcia-Cle	27.7
Dobson-Chi	25.2

Clutch Pitching Index
Garcia-Cle	127
Byrd-Phi	125
Reynolds-NY	125
Porterfield-Was	120
Hudson-Was-Bos	117

Relief Runs
Dorish-Chi	12.2
Kennedy-Chi	7.0
Consuegra-Was	5.2
Brissie-Cle	1.9
Littlefield-Det-S	1.4

Adjusted Relief Runs
Dorish-Chi	11.8
Kennedy-Chi	6.7
Consuegra-Was	5.3
Newsom-Was-Phi	1.3
Littlefield-Det-S	1.1

Relief Ranking
Dorish-Chi	17.2
Consuegra-Was	4.7
Kennedy-Chi	4.5
Newsom-Was-Phi	1.6
Littlefield-Det-S	.9

Total Pitcher Index
Shantz-Phi	6.3
Lemon-Cle	4.0
Reynolds-NY	4.0
Pierce-Chi	3.3
Garcia-Cle	2.9

Total Baseball Ranking
Shantz-Phi	6.3
Doby-Cle	4.5
Lemon-Cle	4.0
Reynolds-NY	4.0
Fain-Phi	3.5

TEAM	G	W	L	PCT	GB	R	OR	AB	H	2B	3B	HR	BB	SO	AVG	OBP	SLG	PRO	/A	BR	/A	PF	CHI	RC	TA	SB	CS	SBA	SBR
BRO	155	105	49	.682		955	689	5373	1529	274	59	208	655	686	.285	.366	.474	.840	124	187	158	104	100	963	.830	90	47	66	0
MIL	157	92	62	.597	13	738	589	5349	1422	227	52	156	439	637	.266	.325	.415	.740	98	-22	20	94	104	727	.671	46	27	63	-1
STL	157	83	71	.539	22	768	713	5397	1474	281	56	140	574	617	.273	.347	.424	.771	107	53	41	102	95	806	.714	18	22	45	-7
PHI	156	83	71	.539	22	716	666	5290	1400	228	62	115	530	597	.265	.335	.396	.731	96	-25	-16	99	100	727	.671	42	21	67	0
NY	155	70	84	.455	35	768	747	5362	1452	195	45	176	499	608	.271	.336	.422	.758	103	19	33	98	101	771	.695	31	21	60	-2
CIN	155	68	86	.442	37	714	788	5343	1396	190	34	166	485	701	.261	.325	.403	.728	95	-42	-34	99	103	711	.656	25	20	56	-4
CHI	155	65	89	.422	40	633	835	5272	1372	204	57	137	514	746	.260	.328	.399	.727	95	-40	-61	103	91	697	.659	49	21	70	2
PIT	154	50	104	.325	55	622	887	5253	1297	178	49	99	524	715	.247	.319	.356	.675	82	-129	-142	102	103	614	.601	41	39	51	-10
TOT	622					5914		42639	11342	1777	414	1197	4220	5307	.266	.335	.412	.747								342	218	61	-27

TEAM	CG	SHO	SV	IP	H	H/G	HR	BB	BB/G	SO	SO/G	ERA	/A	OAVG	OOBA	PR	/A	PF	CPI	FA	E	DP	FW	PW	BW	SBW	DIF
BRO	51	11	29	1380.7	1337	8.7	169	509	3.3	817	5.3	4.10	104	.252	.317	28	25	100	97	.980	118	161	1.7	2.4	15.2	.3	8.4
MIL	72	14	15	1387.0	1282	8.3	107	539	3.5	738	4.8	3.30	119	.244	.314	152	97	92	106	.976	143	169	.3	9.3	1.9	.2	3.2
STL	51	11	36	1386.7	1406	9.1	139	533	3.5	732	4.8	4.23	102	.261	.328	9	13	101	98	.977	138	161	.5	1.3	3.9	-.3	.6
PHI	76	13	15	1369.0	1410	9.3	138	410	2.7	637	4.2	3.80	110	.264	.316	73	60	98	104	.975	147	161	.0	5.8	-1.5	.3	1.4
NY	46	10	20	1365.7	1403	9.2	146	610	4.0	647	4.3	4.25	99	.264	.338	5	-9	98	103	.975	151	151	-.2	-.9	3.2	.1	-9.3
CIN	47	7	15	1364.7	1484	9.8	179	488	3.2	506	3.3	4.64	93	.278	.338	-53	-51	100	102	.978	129	176	1.1	-4.9	-3.3	-.0	-1.8
CHI	38	3	22	1359.7	1491	9.9	151	554	3.7	623	4.1	4.79	95	.275	.342	-75	-34	106	97	.967	193	141	-2.5	-3.3	-5.9	.5	-.8
PIT	49	4	10	1358.0	1529	10.1	168	577	3.8	607	4.0	5.22	87	.284	.351	-141	-100	106	96	.973	163	139	-.9	-9.6	-13.7	-.6	-2.2
TOT	430	73	162	10971.3		9.3			3.5		4.4	4.29		.266	.335					.975	1182	1259					

Runs
Snider-Bro 132
Musial-StL 127
Dark-NY 126
Gilliam-Bro 125

Hits
Ashburn-Phi 205
Musial-StL 200
Snider-Bro 198
Dark-NY 194
Schoendienst-StL . . . 193

Doubles
Musial-StL 53
Dark-NY 41
Snider-Bro 38
Furillo-Bro 38
Bell-Cin 37

Triples
Gilliam-Bro 17
Bruton-Mil 14
Hemus-StL 11
Fondy-Chi 11

Home Runs
Mathews-Mil 47
Snider-Bro 42
Campanella-Cin 41
Kluszewski-Cin 40
Kiner-Pit-Chi 35

Total Bases
Snider-Bro 370
Mathews-Mil 363
Musial-StL 361
Kluszewski-Cin 325
Bell-Cin 320

Runs Batted In
Campanella-Bro 142
Mathews-Mil 135
Snider-Bro 126
Ennis-Phi 125
Hodges-Bro 122

Runs Produced
Snider-Bro 216
Musial-StL 210
Campanella-Bro 204
Mathews-Mil 198

Bases On Balls
Musial-StL 105
Kiner-Pit-Chi 100
Gilliam-Bro 100
Mathews-Mil 99
Hemus-StL 86

Batting Average
Furillo-Bro 344
Schoendienst-StL . . .342
Musial-StL 337
Snider-Bro 336
Mueller-NY 333

On Base Percentage
Musial-StL 437
Robinson-Bro 425
Snider-Bro 419
Irvin-NY 406
Mathews-Mil 406

Slugging Average
Snider-Bro 627
Mathews-Mil 627
Campanella-Bro 611
Musial-StL 609
Furillo-Bro 580

Production
Snider-Bro 1.046
Musial-StL 1.046
Mathews-Mil 1.033
Campanella-Bro . . . 1.006
Furillo-Bro 973

Adjusted Production
Mathews-Mil 174
Musial-StL 166
Snider-Bro 162
Campanella-Bro 151
Irvin-NY 147

Batter Runs
Musial-StL 62.7
Snider-Bro 59.2
Mathews-Mil 54.9
Campanella-Bro . . . 42.8
Kluszewski-Cin 34.9

Adjusted Batter Runs
Musial-StL 61.4
Mathews-Mil 59.8
Snider-Bro 56.0
Campanella-Bro . . . 40.1
Kluszewski-Cin 35.7

Clutch Hitting Index
Slaughter-StL 153
Ennis-Phi 141
Jablonski-StL 139
Robinson-Bro 135
Campanella-Bro 128

Runs Created
Musial-StL 166
Snider-Bro 161
Mathews-Mil 157
Campanella-Bro 128
Kluszewski-Cin 126

Total Average
Musial-StL 1.152
Snider-Bro 1.152
Mathews-Mil 1.126
Campanella-Bro . . . 1.054
Robinson-Bro 1.000

Stolen Bases
Bruton-Mil 26
Reese-Bro 22
Gilliam-Bro 21
Robinson-Bro 17
Snider-Bro 16

Stolen Base Average
Robinson-Bro 81.0
Reese-Bro 78.6
Bruton-Mil 70.3
Snider-Bro 69.6
Gilliam-Bro 60.0

Stolen Base Runs
Reese-Bro 3.0
Robinson-Bro 2.7
Torgeson-Phi 1.5
Miksis-Chi 1.5
Jeffcoat-Chi 1.5

Fielding Runs
Logan-Mil 24.3
Schoendienst-StL . . 23.6
Ashburn-Phi 21.5
Hemus-StL 15.7
McMillan-Cin 13.0

Total Player Rating
Schoendienst-StL . . . 5.4
Mathews-Mil 5.4
Campanella-Bro 5.3
Musial-StL 4.8
Snider-Bro 4.1

Wins
Spahn-Mil 23
Roberts-Phi 23
Haddix-StL 20
Erskine-Bro 20
Staley-StL 18

Win Percentage
Erskine-Bro 769
Spahn-Mil 767
Meyer-Bro 750
Burdette-Mil 750
Haddix-StL 690

Games
Wilhelm-NY 68
Brazle-StL 60
Hetki-Pit 54
Smith-Cin 50

Complete Games
Roberts-Phi 33
Spahn-Mil 24
Simmons-Phi 19
Haddix-StL 19
Erskine-Bro 16

Shutouts
Haddix-StL 6
Spahn-Mil 5
Roberts-Phi 5
Simmons-Phi 4
Erskine-Bro 4

Saves
Brazle-StL 18
Wilhelm-NY 15
Hughes-Bro 9
Leonard-Chi 8
Burdette-Mil 8

Innings Pitched
Roberts-Phi 347
Spahn-Mil 266
Haddix-StL 253
Erskine-Bro 247
Simmons-Phi 238

Fewest Hits/Game
Spahn-Mil 7.14
Gomez-NY 7.32
Mizell-StL 7.75
Erskine-Bro 7.76
Haddix-StL 7.83

Fewest BB/Game
Roberts-Phi 1.58
Raffensberge-Cin . . . 1.71
Minner-Chi 1.79
Staley-StL 2.11
Hacker-Chi 2.19

Strikeouts
Roberts-Phi 198
Erskine-Bro 187
Mizell-StL 173
Haddix-StL 163
Spahn-Mil 148

Strikeouts/Game
Mizell-StL 6.95
Erskine-Bro 6.81
Antonelli-Mil 6.74
Klippstein-Chi 6.05
Haddix-StL 5.80

Wins Above Team
Spahn-Mil 7.1
Haddix-StL 5.4
Staley-StL 4.3
Burdette-Mil 4.1
Baczewski-Chi-Cin . . 4.1

Earned Run Average
Spahn-Mil 2.10
Roberts-Phi 2.75
Haddix-StL 3.06
Antonelli-Mil 3.19
Simmons-Phi 3.21

Adjusted ERA
Spahn-Mil 187
Roberts-Phi 153
Haddix-StL 141
Simmons-Phi 131
Mizell-StL 123

Opponents' Batting Avg.
Spahn-Mil 217
Gomez-NY 218
Mizell-StL 227
Erskine-Bro 230
Haddix-StL 232

Opponents' On Base Pct.
Spahn-Mil 267
Roberts-Phi 274
Haddix-StL 284
Hacker-Chi 295
Simmons-Phi 298

Starter Runs
Spahn-Mil 64.7
Roberts-Phi 59.3
Haddix-StL 34.5
Simmons-Phi 28.3
Buhl-Mil 22.3

Adjusted Starter Runs
Roberts-Phi 55.8
Spahn-Mil 54.0
Haddix-StL 35.2
Simmons-Phi 26.0
Mizell-StL 20.3

Clutch Pitching Index
Raffensberge-Cin 115
Dickson-Pit 113
Drews-Phi 111
Burdette-Mil 110
Roe-Bro 108

Relief Runs
Wilhelm-NY 20.1
Labine-Bro 18.4
Johnson-Mil 14.6
White-StL 12.5
Hughes-Bro 8.0

Adjusted Relief Runs
Wilhelm-NY 18.5
Labine-Bro 18.1
White-StL 12.7
Johnson-Mil 11.3
Hughes-Bro 7.8

Relief Ranking
Labine-Bro 27.8
Wilhelm-NY 21.5
White-StL 17.2
Johnson-Mil 8.8
Hughes-Bro 7.5

Total Pitcher Index
Spahn-Mil 6.3
Roberts-Phi 5.8
Haddix-StL 4.7
Simmons-Phi 2.0
Erskine-Bro 1.8

Total Baseball Ranking
Spahn-Mil 6.3
Roberts-Phi 5.8
Schoendienst-StL . . . 5.4
Mathews-Mil 5.4
Campanella-Bro 5.3

TEAM	G	W	L	PCT	GB	R	OR	AB	H	2B	3B	HR	BB	SO	AVG	OBP	SLG	PRO	/A	BR	/A	PF	CHI	RC	TA	SB	CS	SBA	SBR
NY	151	99	52	.656		801	547	5194	1420	226	52	139	656	644	.273	.359	.417	.776	115	113	163	93	100	809	.737	34	44	44	-15
CLE	155	92	62	.597	8.5	770	627	5285	1426	201	29	160	609	683	.270	.349	.410	.759	111	76	108	95	99	780	.708	33	29	53	-7
CHI	156	89	65	.578	11.5	716	592	5212	1345	226	53	74	601	530	.258	.341	.364	.705	96	-17	-57	106	106	666	.646	73	55	57	-10
BOS	153	84	69	.549	16	656	632	5246	1385	255	37	101	496	601	.264	.332	.384	.716	99	-10	-69	109	98	683	.644	33	45	42	-16
WAS	152	76	76	.500	23.5	687	614	5149	1354	230	53	69	596	604	.263	.343	.368	.711	98	-6	31	94	102	675	.653	65	36	64	-1
DET	158	60	94	.390	40.5	695	923	5553	1479	259	44	108	506	603	.266	.331	.408	.718	99	-9	8	98	99	716	.639	30	35	46	-11
PHI	157	59	95	.383	41.5	632	799	5455	1398	205	38	116	498	602	.256	.321	.372	.693	92	-60	-75	102	99	658	.613	41	24	63	-1
STL	154	54	100	.351	46.5	555	778	5264	1310	214	25	112	507	644	.249	.317	.363	.680	89	-83	-127	107	93	606	.593	17	34	33	-14
TOT	618					5512		42358	11117	1816	331	879	4469	4911	.262	.337	.383	.720								326	302	52	-82

TEAM	CG	SHO	SV	IP	H	H/G	HR	BB	BB/G	SO	SO/G	ERA	/A	OAVG	OOBA	PR	/A	PF	CPI	FA	E	DP	FW	PW	BW	SBW	DIF
NY	50	18	39	1358.3	1286	8.5	94	500	3.3	604	4.0	3.20	110	.250	.317	119	48	88	110	.979	126	182	.4	4.8	16.3	-.5	2.4
CLE	81	11	15	1373.0	1311	8.6	92	519	3.4	586	3.8	3.64	102	.253	.321	53	8	93	99	.979	127	197	.4	.8	10.8	.3	2.7
CHI	57	17	33	1403.7	1299	8.3	113	583	3.7	714	4.6	3.41	121	.245	.319	91	112	104	105	.980	125	144	.5	11.2	-5.7	.0	6.0
BOS	41	15	37	1373.0	1333	8.7	92	584	3.8	642	4.2	3.58	121	.254	.327	63	113	108	104	.975	148	173	-.8	11.3	-6.9	-.6	4.5
WAS	76	16	10	1344.7	1313	8.8	112	478	3.2	515	3.4	3.66	102	.257	.319	49	8	93	103	.979	120	173	.8	.8	3.1	.9	-5.6
DET	50	2	16	1415.0	1633	10.4	154	585	3.7	645	4.1	5.25	77	.291	.355	-197	-188	102	96	.978	135	149	-.0	-18.8	.8	-.0	1.2
PHI	51	7	11	1408.7	1475	9.4	121	594	3.8	566	3.6	4.67	90	.270	.343	-105	-73	105	93	.977	137	161	-.2	-7.3	-7.5	.9	-3.9
STL	28	10	24	1383.7	1467	9.5	101	626	4.1	639	4.2	4.48	99	.272	.346	-73	-8	111	97	.974	152	165	-1.0	-.8	-12.7	-.4	-8.1
TOT	434	96	185	11060.0		9.0			3.6		4.0	3.99		.262	.337					.978	1070	1344					

Runs
Rosen-Cle 115
Yost-Was 107
Mantle-NY 105
Minoso-Chi 104
Vernon-Was 101

Hits
Kuenn-Det 209
Vernon-Was 205
Rosen-Cle 201
Philley-Phi 188
Busby-Was 183

Doubles
Vernon-Was 43
Kell-Bos 41
White-Bos 34
Kuenn-Det 33
Goodman-Bos 33

Triples
Rivera-Chi 16
Vernon-Was 11
Piersall-Bos 9
Philley-Phi 9

Home Runs
Rosen-Cle 43
Zernial-Phi 42
Doby-Cle 29
Berra-NY 27
Boone-Cle-Det 26

Total Bases
Rosen-Cle 367
Vernon-Was 315
Zernial-Phi 311
Philley-Phi 263
Berra-NY 263

Runs Batted In
Rosen-Cle 145
Vernon-Was 115
Boone-Cle-Det 114
Zernial-Phi 108
Berra-NY 108

Runs Produced
Rosen-Cle 217
Vernon-Was 201
Minoso-Chi 193
Boone-Cle-Det 182
Mantle-NY 176

Bases On Balls
Yost-Was 123
Fain-Chi 108
Doby-Cle 96
Gernert-Bos 88
Rosen-Cle 85

Batting Average
Vernon-Was 337
Rosen-Cle 336
Goodman-Bos 313
Minoso-Chi 313
Busby-Was 312

On Base Percentage
Woodling-NY 429
Rosen-Cle 422
Minoso-Chi 410
Fain-Chi 405
Yost-Was 403

Slugging Average
Rosen-Cle 613
Zernial-Phi 559
Berra-NY 523
Boone-Cle-Det 519
Vernon-Was 518

Production
Rosen-Cle 1.034
Vernon-Was 921
Zernial-Phi 914
Boone-Cle-Det 909
Woodling-NY 898

Adjusted Production
Rosen-Cle 185
Vernon-Was 156
Woodling-NY 153
Mantle-NY 151
Boone-Cle-Det 148

Batter Runs
Rosen-Cle 63.3
Vernon-Was 39.6
Minoso-Chi 30.5
Boone-Cle-Det 30.4
Zernial-Phi 30.4

Adjusted Batter Runs
Rosen-Cle 67.0
Vernon-Was 44.0
Boone-Cle-Det 32.4
Mantle-NY 31.8
Woodling-NY 31.2

Clutch Hitting Index
Dropo-Det 143
Minoso-Chi 134
Boone-Cle-Det 133
Rizzuto-NY 132
Jensen-Was 129

Runs Created
Rosen-Cle 155
Vernon-Was 127
Zernial-Phi 113
Boone-Cle-Det 106
Minoso-Chi 106

Total Average
Rosen-Cle 1.094
Mantle-NY 955
Boone-Cle-Det 934
Woodling-NY 922
Doby-Cle 917

Stolen Bases
Minoso-Chi 25
Rivera-Chi 22
Jensen-Was 18
Philley-Phi 13
Busby-Was 13

Stolen Base Average
Jensen-Was 69.2
Minoso-Chi 61.0
Rivera-Chi 59.5

Stolen Base Runs
Michaels-Phi 2.1
Coan-Was 2.1
Zernial-Phi 1.2
Souchock-Det 9
Philley-Phi 9

Fielding Runs
Hunter-StL 17.3
Piersall-Bos 16.1
Avila-Cle 15.3
Astroth-Phi 14.7
Murray-Phi 14.2

Total Player Rating
Rosen-Cle 5.7
Boone-Cle-Det 3.8
Vernon-Was 3.5
Zernial-Phi 3.3
Berra-NY 2.6

Wins
Porterfield-Was 22
Parnell-Bos 21
Lemon-Cle 21
Trucks-StL-Chi 20

Win Percentage
Lopat-NY 800
Ford-NY 750
Parnell-Bos 724
Porterfield-Was 688

Games
Kinder-Bos 69
Stuart-StL.........60
Martin-StL 58
Paige-StL 57
Dorish-Chi 55

Complete Games
Porterfield-Was 24
Lemon-Cle 23
Garcia-Cle 21
Pierce-Chi 19
Trucks-StL-Chi 17

Shutouts
Porterfield-Was 9
Pierce-Chi 7
Trucks-StL-Chi 5
Parnell-Bos 5
Lemon-Cle 5

Saves
Kinder-Bos 27
Dorish-Chi 18
Reynolds-NY 13
Paige-StL 11
Sain-NY 9

Innings Pitched
Lemon-Cle 287
Garcia-Cle 272
Pierce-Chi 271
Trucks-StL-Chi 264
Porterfield-Was 255

Fewest Hits/Game
Pierce-Chi 7.17
McDermott-Bos 7.38
Raschi-NY 7.46
Masterson-Was 7.86
Trucks-StL-Chi 7.98

Fewest BB/Game
Lopat-NY 1.62
Sain-NY 2.14
Kellner-Phi 2.27
Porterfield-Was 2.58
Hoeft-Det 2.64

Strikeouts
Pierce-Chi 186
Trucks-StL-Chi 149
Wynn-Cle 138
Parnell-Bos 136
Garcia-Cle 134

Strikeouts/Game
Pierce-Chi 6.18
Gray-Det 5.88
Masterson-Was 5.15
Trucks-StL-Chi 5.08
Parnell-Bos 5.08

Wins Above Team
Porterfield-Was 6.9
Parnell-Bos 6.4
Trucks-StL-Chi 5.2
Lopat-NY 4.5
Ford-NY 3.7

Earned Run Average
Lopat-NY 2.43
Pierce-Chi 2.72
Trucks-StL-Chi 2.93
Sain-NY 3.00
Ford-NY 3.00

Adjusted ERA
Pierce-Chi 152
Lopat-NY 145
McDermott-Bos 143
Trucks-StL-Chi 142
Parnell-Bos 141

Opponents' Batting Avg.
Pierce-Chi 218
McDermott-Bos ..... .224
Raschi-NY 224
Masterson-Was 232
Trucks-StL-Chi 238

Opponents' On Base Pct.
Raschi-NY 279
Lopat-NY 285
Pierce-Chi 288
Masterson-Was 301
Garcia-Cle 304

Starter Runs
Pierce-Chi 38.3
Trucks-StL-Chi ... 31.2
Lopat-NY 31.0
Parnell-Bos 25.0
Ford-NY 22.9

Adjusted Starter Runs
Pierce-Chi 42.5
Trucks-StL-Chi 36.4
Parnell-Bos 33.7
McDermott-Bos 29.9
Lopat-NY 21.7

Clutch Pitching Index
Ford-NY 127
Lopat-NY 122
Sain-NY 118
Lemon-Cle 113
Parnell-Bos 112

Relief Runs
Kinder-Bos 25.5
Dorish-Chi 9.8
Kuzava-NY 6.8
Bearden-Chi 6.7
Paige-StL 5.9

Adjusted Relief Runs
Kinder-Bos 29.4
Dorish-Chi 12.1
Paige-StL 11.4
Bearden-Chi 7.6
Stuart-StL 6.0

Relief Ranking
Kinder-Bos 56.2
Dorish-Chi 15.3
Paige-StL 13.0
Bearden-Chi 7.1
Stuart-StL.........5.5

Total Pitcher Index
McDermott-Bos 4.1
Trucks-StL-Chi 4.0
Pierce-Chi 3.8
Parnell-Bos 3.5
Kinder-Bos 3.4

Total Baseball Ranking
Rosen-Cle 5.7
McDermott-Bos 4.1
Trucks-StL-Chi 4.0
Pierce-Chi 3.8
Boone-Cle-Det 3.8

TEAM	G	W	L	PCT	GB	R	OR	AB	H	2B	3B	HR	BB	SO	AVG	OBP	SLG	PRO	/A	BR	/A	PF	CHI	RC	TA	SB	CS	SBA	SBR
NY	154	97	57	.630		732	550	5245	1386	194	42	186	522	561	.264	.335	.424	.759	103	17	-17	105	102	747	.703	30	23	57	-4
BRO	154	92	62	.597	5	778	740	5251	1418	246	56	186	634	625	.270	.353	.444	.797	113	99	90	101	95	821	.761	46	39	54	-9
MIL	154	89	65	.578	8	670	556	5261	1395	217	41	139	471	619	.265	.330	.401	.731	96	-32	14	93	100	697	.666	54	31	64	-1
PHI	154	75	79	.487	22	659	614	5184	1384	243	58	102	604	620	.267	.345	.395	.740	99	-1	9	99	94	707	.678	30	27	53	-6
CIN	154	74	80	.481	23	729	763	5234	1369	221	46	147	557	645	.262	.336	.406	.742	99	-7	-33	104	104	726	.689	47	30	61	-3
STL	154	72	82	.468	25	799	790	5405	1518	285	58	119	582	586	.281	.354	.421	.775	108	65	62	100	101	807	.727	63	46	58	-8
CHI	154	64	90	.416	33	700	766	5359	1412	229	45	159	478	693	.263	.327	.412	.739	98	-20	-23	101	102	717	.675	46	31	60	-4
PIT	154	53	101	.344	44	557	845	5088	1260	181	57	76	566	737	.248	.326	.350	.676	82	-118	-94	97	97	596	.604	21	13	62	-1
TOT	616					5624		42027	11142	1816	403	1114	4414	5086	.265	.338	.407	.745								337	240	58	-42

TEAM	CG	SHO	SV	IP	H	H/G	HR	BB	BB/G	SO	SO/G	ERA	/A	OAVG	OOBA	PR	/A	PF	CPI	FA	E	DP	FW	PW	BW	SBW	DIF
NY	45	19	33	1390.0	1258	8.1	113	613	4.0	692	4.5	3.09	134	.243	.321	150	161	102	113	.975	154	172	-.5	15.9	-1.7	.1	6.1
BRO	39	8	36	1393.7	1399	9.0	164	533	3.4	762	4.9	4.31	95	.261	.323	-36	-33	101	93	.978	129	138	.8	-3.3	8.9	-.4	8.9
MIL	63	13	21	1394.7	1296	8.4	106	553	3.6	698	4.5	3.19	117	.250	.319	137	82	91	110	.981	116	171	1.5	8.1	1.4	.4	.5
PHI	78	14	12	1365.3	1329	8.8	133	450	3.0	570	3.8	3.59	111	.256	.310	72	58	98	100	.975	145	133	-.0	5.7	.9	-.0	-8.5
CIN	34	8	27	1367.7	1491	9.8	169	547	3.6	537	3.5	4.50	94	.282	.346	-65	-38	104	105	.977	137	194	.4	-3.8	-3.3	.2	3.4
STL	40	11	18	1390.3	1484	9.6	170	535	3.5	680	4.4	4.50	91	.275	.338	-65	-64	100	100	.976	146	178	-.0	-6.3	6.1	-.3	-4.4
CHI	41	6	19	1374.3	1375	9.0	131	619	4.1	622	4.1	4.51	92	.263	.335	-66	-55	102	92	.974	154	164	-.5	-5.4	-2.3	.1	-4.9
PIT	37	4	15	1346.0	1510	10.1	128	564	3.8	525	3.5	4.92	84	.287	.348	-126	-116	102	95	.971	173	136	-1.6	-11.5	-9.3	.4	-2.1
TOT	377	83	181	11022.0		9.1			3.6		4.2	4.07		.265	.338					.976	1154	1286					

Runs
Snider-Bro 120
Musial-StL 120
Mays-NY 119
Ashburn-Phi 111
Gilliam-Bro 107

Hits
Mueller-NY 212
Snider-Bro 199
Musial-StL 195
Mays-NY 195
Moon-StL 193

Doubles
Musial-StL 41
Snider-Bro 39
Repulski-StL 39
Hamner-Phi 39

Triples
Mays-NY 13
Hamner-Phi 11
Snider-Bro 10

Home Runs
Kluszewski-Cin 49
Hodges-Bro 42
Sauer-Chi 41
Mays-NY 41

Total Bases
Snider-Bro 378
Mays-NY 377
Kluszewski-Cin 368
Musial-StL 359
Hodges-Bro 335

Runs Batted In
Kluszewski-Cin 141
Snider-Bro 130
Hodges-Bro 130
Musial-StL 126
Ennis-Phi 119

Runs Produced
Musial-StL 211
Snider-Bro 210
Kluszewski-Cin 196
Hodges-Bro 194

Bases On Balls
Ashburn-Phi 125
Mathews-Mil 113
Musial-StL 103
Thompson-NY 90
Reese-Bro 90

Batting Average
Mays-NY 345
Mueller-NY 342
Snider-Bro 341
Musial-StL 330
Kluszewski-Cin 326

On Base Percentage
Ashburn-Phi 442
Musial-StL 433
Mathews-Mil 428
Snider-Bro 427
Mays-NY 415

Slugging Average
Mays-NY 667
Snider-Bro 647
Kluszewski-Cin 642
Musial-StL 607
Mathews-Mil 603

Production
Mays-NY 1.083
Snider-Bro 1.074
Kluszewski-Cin ..1.052
Musial-StL 1.040
Mathews-Mil 1.031

Adjusted Production
Mathews-Mil 177
Snider-Bro 173
Mays-NY 168
Musial-StL 167
Kluszewski-Cin 163

Batter Runs
Snider-Bro 64.5
Mays-NY 61.7
Musial-StL 60.7
Kluszewski-Cin ...57.1
Mathews-Mil 48.6

Adjusted Batter Runs
Snider-Bro 63.6
Musial-StL 60.4
Mays-NY 58.0
Kluszewski-Cin ...54.2
Mathews-Mil 53.3

Clutch Hitting Index
Ennis-Phi 154
Jablonski-StL 148
Post-Cin 131
Furillo-Bro 128
Hodges-Bro 118

Runs Created
Snider-Bro 161
Mays-NY 155
Musial-StL 153
Kluszewski-Cin 151
Mathews-Mil 131

Total Average
Mathews-Mil 1.177
Snider-Bro 1.171
Mays-NY 1.171
Kluszewski-Cin ..1.122
Musial-StL 1.104

Stolen Bases
Bruton-Mil 34
Temple-Cin 21
Fondy-Chi 20
Moon-StL 18
Ashburn-Phi 11

Stolen Base Average
Fondy-Chi 80.0
Temple-Cin 75.0
Bruton-Mil 72.3
Moon-StL 64.3

Stolen Base Runs
Fondy-Chi 3.0
Bruton-Mil 2.4
Temple-Cin 2.1
Torgeson-Phi 1.5

Fielding Runs
Schoendienst-StL ..30.0
Grammas-StL 21.1
Logan-Mil 15.2
Ashburn-Phi 13.1
Mays-NY 12.4

Total Player Rating
Mays-NY 6.2
Mathews-Mil 5.4
Musial-StL 4.8
Snider-Bro 4.6
Schoendienst-StL ..4.4

Wins
Roberts-Phi 23
Spahn-Mil 21
Antonelli-NY 21
Haddix-StL 18
Erskine-Bro 18

Win Percentage
Antonelli-NY 750
Lawrence-StL 714
Gomez-NY 654
Spahn-Mil 636
Roberts-Phi 605

Games
Hughes-Bro 60
Hetki-Pit 58
Brazle-StL 58
Wilhelm-NY 57
Grissom-NY 56

Complete Games
Roberts-Phi 29
Spahn-Mil 23
Simmons-Phi 21
Antonelli-NY 18

Shutouts
Antonelli-NY 6

Saves
Hughes-Bro 24
Smith-Cin 20
Grissom-NY 19
Jolly-Mil 10
Hetki-Pit 9

Innings Pitched
Roberts-Phi 337
Spahn-Mil 283
Haddix-StL 260
Erskine-Bro 260
Antonelli-NY 259

Fewest Hits/Game
Antonelli-NY 7.26
Roberts-Phi 7.72
Conley-Mil 7.93
Lawrence-StL 7.98
Wehmeier-Cin-Phi .8.01

Fewest BB/Game
Roberts-Phi 1.50
Minner-Chi 2.06
Hacker-Chi 2.09
Burdette-Mil 2.34
Meyer-Bro 2.45

Strikeouts
Roberts-Phi 185
Haddix-StL 184
Erskine-Bro 166
Antonelli-NY 152
Spahn-Mil 136

Strikeouts/Game
Haddix-StL 6.37
Erskine-Bro 5.75
Littlefield-Pit 5.34
Antonelli-NY 5.28
Conley-Mil 5.24

Wins Above Team
Roberts-Phi 5.4
Lawrence-StL 5.3
Antonelli-NY 5.2
Nuxhall-Cin 3.9
Haddix-StL 3.9

Earned Run Average
Antonelli-NY 2.29
Burdette-Mil 2.76
Simmons-Phi 2.81
Gomez-NY 2.88
Roberts-Phi 2.96

Adjusted ERA
Antonelli-NY 181
Gomez-NY 144
Simmons-Phi 142
Burdette-Mil 135
Roberts-Phi 134

Opponents' Batting Avg.
Antonelli-NY 219
Roberts-Phi 231
Simmons-Phi 239
Littlefield-Pit 239
Wehmeier-Cin-Phi ..239

Opponents' On Base Pct.
Roberts-Phi 263
Antonelli-NY 288
Hacker-Chi 296
Spahn-Mil 297
Burdette-Mil 298

Starter Runs
Antonelli-NY 51.2
Roberts-Phi 41.5
Simmons-Phi 35.5
Burdette-Mil 34.7
Gomez-NY 29.4

Adjusted Starter Runs
Antonelli-NY 53.2
Roberts-Phi 38.0
Simmons-Phi 32.8
Gomez-NY 31.2
Burdette-Mil 25.3

Clutch Pitching Index
Gomez-NY 130
Dickson-Phi 123
Fowler-Cin 116
Antonelli-NY 116
Nuxhall-Cin 115

Relief Runs
Wilhelm-NY 24.2
Grissom-NY 23.2
Jolly-Mil 20.2
Johnson-Mil 13.8
Smith-Cin 12.6

Adjusted Relief Runs
Wilhelm-NY 25.1
Grissom-NY 24.1
Jolly-Mil 15.9
Smith-Cin 14.2
Johnson-Mil 9.9

Relief Ranking
Grissom-NY 38.7
Wilhelm-NY 36.1
Smith-Cin 28.5
Jolly-Mil 25.1
Hughes-Bro 15.9

Total Pitcher Index
Antonelli-NY 5.9
Gomez-NY 3.3
Roberts-Phi 3.2
Simmons-Phi 2.9
Wilhelm-NY 2.4

Total Baseball Ranking
Mays-NY 6.2
Antonelli-NY 5.9
Mathews-Mil 5.4
Musial-StL 4.8
Snider-Bro 4.6

TEAM	G	W	L	PCT	GB	R	OR	AB	H	2B	3B	HR	BB	SO	AVG	OBP	SLG	PRO	/A	BR	/A	PF	CHI	RC	TA	SB	CS	SBA	SBR
CLE	156	111	43	.721		746	**504**	5222	1368	188	39	**156**	637	668	.262	.345	.403	.748	111	76	36	106	101	739	.698	30	33	48	-10
NY	155	103	51	.669	8	**805**	563	5226	1400	215	59	133	650	632	**.268**	**.351**	**.408**	**.759**	**114**	**101**	**108**	99	**106**	**768**	**.716**	34	41	45	-13
CHI	155	94	60	.610	17	711	521	5168	1382	203	47	94	604	**536**	.267	.350	.379	.729	106	51	28	104	101	700	.683	**98**	58	63	-4
BOS	156	69	85	.448	42	700	728	5399	**1436**	**244**	41	123	**654**	660	.266	.348	.395	.743	110	73	71	100	93	749	.690	51	30	63	-2
DET	155	68	86	.442	43	584	664	5233	1351	215	41	90	492	603	.258	.324	.367	.691	95	-36	-34	100	96	609	.608	48	44	52	-11
WAS	155	66	88	.429	45	632	680	5249	1292	188	**69**	81	610	719	.246	.328	.355	.683	93	-43	-31	98	103	631	.620	37	21	**64**	-1
BAL	154	54	100	.351	57	483	668	5206	1309	195	49	52	468	634	.251	.316	.338	.654	85	-103	-73	95	90	553	.561	30	31	49	-9
PHI	156	51	103	.331	60	542	875	5206	1228	191	41	94	504	677	.236	.307	.342	.649	84	-116	-105	98	104	553	.570	30	29	51	-7
TOT	621					5203		41909	10766	1639	386	823	4619	5129	.257	.334	.373	.707								358	287	56	-64

TEAM	CG	SHO	SV	IP	H	H/G	HR	BB	BB/G	SO	SO/G	ERA	/A	OAVG	OOBA	PR	/A	PF	CPI	FA	E	DP	FW	PW	BW	SBW	DIF
CLE	**77**	12	36	1419.3	**1220**	**7.7**	89	**486**	**3.1**	678	4.3	**2.78**	**135**	**.232**	**.293**	**148**	**155**	101	100	.979	128	148	.7	**16.0**	3.7	-.2	13.8
NY	51	16	**37**	1379.3	1284	8.4	86	552	3.6	655	4.3	3.26	108	.251	.320	70	38	94	**107**	.979	126	**198**	.8	3.9	**11.2**	-.5	10.6
CHI	60	**23**	33	1383.0	1255	8.2	94	517	3.4	701	**4.6**	3.05	122	.243	.308	103	101	100	105	**.982**	**108**	149	**1.8**	10.4	2.9	.4	1.5
BOS	41	10	22	1412.3	1434	9.1	118	612	3.9	**707**	4.5	4.01	93	.265	.336	-45	-41	101	101	.972	176	163	-2.0	-4.2	7.3	.6	-9.7
DET	58	13	13	1383.0	1375	8.9	138	506	3.3	603	3.9	3.81	99	.261	.322	-12	-5	101	103	.978	129	131	.6	-.5	-3.5	-.3	-5.3
WAS	69	10	7	1383.3	1396	9.1	79	573	3.7	562	3.7	3.84	96	.265	.332	-17	-22	99	99	.977	137	172	.2	-2.3	-3.2	**.7**	-6.4
BAL	58	6	8	1373.3	1279	8.4	**78**	688	4.5	668	4.4	3.88	95	.249	.332	-23	-30	99	94	.975	147	152	-.4	-3.1	-7.5	-.0	-11.9
PHI	49	3	13	1371.3	1523	10.0	141	685	4.5	555	3.6	5.18	75	.284	.361	-221	-195	105	95	.972	169	163	-1.6	-20.1	-10.8	.1	6.5
TOT	463	93	169	11105.0		8.7			3.7		4.2	3.72		.257	.334					.977	1120	1276					

Runs
Mantle-NY 129
Minoso-Chi.........119
Avila-Cle 112
Fox-Chi............111
Carrasquel-Chi......106

Hits
Kuenn-Det 201
Fox-Chi............201
Avila-Cle 189
Busby-Was..........187
Minoso-Chi..........182

Doubles
Vernon-Was 33
Smith-Cle 29
Minoso-Chi...........29

Triples
Minoso-Chi...........18
Runnels-Was 15
Vernon-Was 14
Mantle-NY 12
Tuttle-Det 11

Home Runs
Doby-Cle 32
Williams-Bos 29
Mantle-NY 27
Jensen-Bos 25

Total Bases
Minoso-Chi.........304
Vernon-Was 294
Mantle-NY 285
Berra-NY 285
Doby-Cle 279

Runs Batted In
Doby-Cle 126
Berra-NY 125
Jensen-Bos 117
Minoso-Chi.........116

Runs Produced
Minoso-Chi.........216
Mantle-NY 204
Berra-NY 191
Doby-Cle 188
Jensen-Bos 184

Bases On Balls
Williams-Bos 136
Yost-Was 131
Mantle-NY 102
Smith-Cle 88

Batting Average
Williams-Bos 345
Avila-Cle 341
Minoso-Chi.........320
Noren-NY 319
Fox-Chi............319

On Base Percentage
Williams-Bos 516
Minoso-Chi.........416
Rosen-Cle 412
Mantle-NY 411
Yost-Was 406

Slugging Average
Williams-Bos 635
Minoso-Chi.........535
Mantle-NY 525
Rosen-Cle 506
Vernon-Was 492

Production
Williams-Bos 1.151
Minoso-Chi.........951
Mantle-NY 936
Rosen-Cle 918
Avila-Cle 882

Adjusted Production
Williams-Bos 213
Mantle-NY 157
Minoso-Chi.........154
Rosen-Cle 142
Noren-NY 137

Batter Runs
Williams-Bos 70.9
Minoso-Chi........ 47.3
Mantle-NY 42.7
Rosen-Cle 34.2
Avila-Cle 31.5

Adjusted Batter Runs
Williams-Bos 70.8
Minoso-Chi........ 44.7
Mantle-NY 43.5
Rosen-Cle 30.5
Avila-Cle 27.3

Clutch Hitting Index
Berra-NY 143
Sievers-Was 136
Doby-Cle 135
Jensen-Bos 135
Rosen-Cle 128

Runs Created
Williams-Bos 139
Mantle-NY 127
Minoso-Chi.........125
Avila-Cle 109
Doby-Cle 108

Total Average
Williams-Bos 1.452
Minoso-Chi....... 1.018
Mantle-NY 995
Rosen-Cle 965
Avila-Cle 874

Stolen Bases
Jensen-Bos 22
Rivera-Chi 18
Minoso-Chi...........18
Jacobs-Phi 17
Busby-Was...........17

Stolen Base Average
Busby-Was.......... 89.5
Jacobs-Phi 85.0
Jensen-Bos 75.9
Rivera-Chi 64.3
Fox-Chi........... 64.0

Stolen Base Runs
Busby-Was........... 3.9
Jacobs-Phi 3.3
Jensen-Bos 2.4
Cavaretta-Chi........ 1.2

Fielding Runs
Power-Phi......... 15.4
Carey-NY 14.2
Avila-Cle 13.9
Minoso-Chi........ 12.6
Lepcio-Bos........ 12.5

Total Player Rating
Williams-Bos 6.1
Minoso-Chi........... 5.3
Avila-Cle 4.7
Berra-NY 3.9
Mantle-NY 3.7

Wins
Wynn-Cle 23
Lemon-Cle 23
Grim-NY 20
Trucks-Chi 19
Garcia-Cle 19

Win Percentage
Consuegra-Chi.....842
Grim-NY 769
Lemon-Cle 767
Garcia-Cle 704
Houtteman-Cle.....682

Games
Dixon-Was-Phi 54
Martin-Phi-Chi 48
Pascual-Was 48
Kinder-Bos 48

Complete Games
Porterfield-Was 21
Lemon-Cle 21
Wynn-Cle 20
Gromek-Det 17

Shutouts
Trucks-Chi 5
Garcia-Cle 5

Saves
Sain-NY 22
Kinder-Bos 15
Narleski-Cle 13

Innings Pitched
Wynn-Cle 271
Trucks-Chi 265
Garcia-Cle 259
Lemon-Cle 258
Gromek-Det 253

Fewest Hits/Game
Turley-Bal 6.49
Ford-NY 7.25
Wynn-Cle 7.47
Coleman-Bal 7.49
Trucks-Chi 7.61

Fewest BB/Game
Lopat-NY 1.75
Gromek-Det 2.03
Garver-Det 2.27
Garcia-Cle 2.47
Zuverink-Det 2.75

Strikeouts
Turley-Bal 185
Wynn-Cle 155
Trucks-Chi 152
Pierce-Chi 148
Harshman-Chi 134

Strikeouts/Game
Pierce-Chi 7.05
Harshman-Chi 6.81
Turley-Bal 6.74
Hoeft-Det 5.86
Reynolds-NY 5.73

Wins Above Team
Consuegra-Chi...... 5.9
Grim-NY 4.5
Turley-Bal 3.5
Gromek-Det 3.3
Sullivan-Bos 3.1

Earned Run Average
Garcia-Cle 2.64
Lemon-Cle 2.72
Wynn-Cle 2.72
Gromek-Det 2.74
Trucks-Chi 2.78

Adjusted ERA
Garcia-Cle 143
Lemon-Cle 138
Wynn-Cle 138
Gromek-Det 138
Garver-Det 134

Opponents' Batting Avg.
Turley-Bal 203
Wynn-Cle 225
Ford-NY 227
Trucks-Chi 228
Garcia-Cle 229

Opponents' On Base Pct.
Garcia-Cle 278
Wynn-Cle 279
Garver-Det 281
Gromek-Det 291
Trucks-Chi 294

Starter Runs
Garcia-Cle 31.1
Wynn-Cle 30.1
Lemon-Cle 28.7
Gromek-Det 27.7
Trucks-Chi 27.6

Adjusted Starter Runs
Garcia-Cle 32.4
Wynn-Cle 31.5
Lemon-Cle 30.0
Gromek-Det 29.0
Trucks-Chi 27.3

Clutch Pitching Index
Keegan-Chi 126
Gromek-Det 116
Houtteman-Cle......114
Lopat-NY 114
Harshman-Chi 114

Relief Runs
Mossi-Cle 18.5
Narleski-Cle 14.8
Dorish-Chi 12.1
Miller-Det 10.0
Sain-NY 4.9

Adjusted Relief Runs
Mossi-Cle 18.9
Narleski-Cle 15.3
Dorish-Chi 12.0
Miller-Det 10.3
Sain-NY 3.1

Relief Ranking
Mossi-Cle 16.0
Narleski-Cle 14.3
Dorish-Chi 11.4
Sain-NY 6.3
Chakales-Cle-Bal 3.2

Total Pitcher Index
Lemon-Cle 4.3
Garcia-Cle 3.3
Wynn-Cle 3.2
Garver-Det 2.9
Gromek-Det 2.9

Total Baseball Ranking
Williams-Bos 6.1
Minoso-Chi........... 5.3
Avila-Cle 4.7
Lemon-Cle 4.3
Berra-NY 3.9

TEAM	G	W	L	PCT	GB	R	OR	AB	H	2B	3B	HR	BB	SO	AVG	OBP	SLG	PRO	/A	BR	/A	PF	CHI	RC	TA	SB	CS	SBA	SBR
BRO	154	98	55	.641		857	650	5193	1406	230	44	201	674	718	.271	.359	.448	.807	119	142	110	104	100	834	.785	79	56	59	-9
MIL	154	85	69	.552	13.5	743	668	5277	1377	219	55	182	504	735	.261	.329	.427	.756	104	26	75	93	102	733	.700	42	27	61	-3
NY	154	80	74	.519	18.5	702	673	5288	1377	173	34	169	497	581	.260	.328	.402	.730	98	-15	-4	99	102	699	.667	38	22	63	-1
PHI	154	77	77	.500	21.5	675	666	5092	1300	214	50	132	652	673	.255	.343	.395	.738	101	13	0	102	95	692	.689	44	32	58	-5
CIN	154	75	79	.487	23.5	761	684	5270	1424	216	28	181	556	657	.270	.344	.425	.769	108	62	22	106	98	773	.722	51	36	59	-5
CHI	154	72	81	.471	26	626	713	5214	1287	187	55	164	428	806	.247	.307	.398	.705	91	-74	-72	100	102	623	.630	37	35	51	-9
STL	154	68	86	.442	30.5	654	757	5266	1375	228	36	143	458	597	.261	.324	.400	.724	96	-30	-33	101	98	662	.653	64	59	52	-15
PIT	154	60	94	.390	38.5	560	767	5173	1262	210	60	91	471	652	.244	.310	.361	.671	82	-126	-105	97	100	567	.585	22	22	50	-6
TOT	616					5578		41773	10808	1677	362	1263	4240	5419	.259	.331	.407	.738								377	289	57	-59

TEAM	CG	SHO	SV	IP	H	H/G	HR	BB	BB/G	SO	SO/G	ERA	/A	OAVG	OOBA	PR	/A	PF	CPI	FA	E	DP	FW	PW	BW	SBW	DIF
BRO	46	11	37	1378.0	1296	8.5	168	483	3.2	773	5.0	3.68	110	.248	.310	54	59	101	100	.978	133	156	.5	5.9	10.9	-.1	4.4
MIL	61	5	12	1383.0	1339	8.7	138	591	3.8	654	4.3	3.85	96	.255	.326	29	-23	92	102	.975	152	155	-.6	-2.3	7.4	.5	3.0
NY	52	6	14	1386.7	1347	8.7	155	560	3.6	721	4.7	3.77	105	.256	.327	41	28	98	107	.976	142	165	.0	2.8	-.4	.6	-.0
PHI	58	11	21	1356.7	1291	8.6	161	477	3.2	657	4.4	3.93	105	.251	.311	16	28	102	96	.981	110	117	1.8	2.8	.0	.3	-4.8
CIN	38	12	22	1362.7	1373	9.1	161	443	2.9	576	3.8	3.95	107	.263	.318	13	39	104	102	.977	139	169	.2	3.9	2.2	.3	-8.5
CHI	47	10	23	1378.3	1306	8.5	153	601	3.9	686	4.5	4.17	98	.251	.325	-20	-11	101	95	.975	147	147	-.3	-1.1	-7.1	-.1	4.2
STL	42	10	15	1377.0	1376	9.0	185	549	3.6	730	4.8	4.56	91	.261	.330	-80	-66	102	95	.975	146	152	-.2	-6.5	-3.3	-.7	1.8
PIT	41	5	16	1362.3	1480	9.8	142	536	3.5	622	4.1	4.39	93	.280	.342	-53	-49	101	104	.972	166	175	-1.4	-4.9	-10.4	.2	-.5
TOT	385	70	160	10984.7		8.9			3.5		4.4	4.04		.259	.331					.976	1135	1236					

Runs		Hits		Doubles		Triples		Home Runs		Total Bases	
Snider-Bro	126	Kluszewski-Cin	192	Logan-Mil	37	Mays-NY	13	Mays-NY	51	Mays-NY	382
Mays-NY	123	Aaron-Mil	189	Aaron-Mil	37	Long-Pit	13	Kluszewski-Cin	47	Kluszewski-Cin	358
Post-Cin	116	Bell-Cin	188	Snider-Bro	34	Bruton-Mil	12	Banks-Chi	44	Banks-Chi	355
Kluszewski-Cin	116	Post-Cin	186	Post-Cin	33	Clemente-Pit	11	Snider-Bro	42	Post-Cin	345
Gilliam-Bro	110			Ashburn-Phi	32			Mathews-Mil	41	Snider-Bro	338

Runs Batted In		Runs Produced		Bases On Balls		Batting Average		On Base Percentage		Slugging Average	
Snider-Bro	136	Snider-Bro	220	Mathews-Mil	109	Ashburn-Phi	.338	Ashburn-Phi	.449	Mays-NY	.659
Mays-NY	127	Mays-NY	199	Ashburn-Phi	105	Mays-NY	.319	Snider-Bro	.421	Snider-Bro	.628
Ennis-Phi	120	Post-Cin	185	Snider-Bro	104	Musial-StL	.319	Mathews-Mil	.417	Mathews-Mil	.601
Banks-Chi	117	Aaron-Mil	184	Thompson-NY	84	Campanella-Bro	.318	Musial-StL	.411	Banks-Chi	.596
Kluszewski-Cin	113	Kluszewski-Cin	182			Aaron-Mil	.314	Mays-NY	.404	Kluszewski-Cin	.585

Production		Adjusted Production		Batter Runs		Adjusted Batter Runs		Clutch Hitting Index		Runs Created	
Mays-NY	1.063	Mathews-Mil	179	Mays-NY	62.2	Mays-NY	63.4	Jones-Phi	136	Mays-NY	157
Snider-Bro	1.050	Mays-NY	179	Snider-Bro	58.9	Snider-Bro	55.5	Mueller-NY	136	Snider-Bro	145
Mathews-Mil	1.018	Snider-Bro	166	Mathews-Mil	49.9	Mathews-Mil	55.1	Ennis-Phi	136	Kluszewski-Cin	136
Campanella-Bro	.985	Musial-StL	155	Musial-StL	46.4	Musial-StL	46.0	Snider-Bro	126	Musial-StL	131
Musial-StL	.977	Campanella-Bro	150	Kluszewski-Cin	44.8	Kluszewski-Cin	40.3	Campanella-Bro	124	Mathews-Mil	131

Total Average		Stolen Bases		Stolen Base Average		Stolen Base Runs		Fielding Runs		Total Player Rating	
Mays-NY	1.190	Bruton-Mil	25	Mays-NY	85.7	Mays-NY	4.8	McMillan-Cin	16.2	Mays-NY	7.8
Snider-Bro	1.165	Mays-NY	24	Temple-Cin	82.6	Temple-Cin	3.3	Groat-Pit	15.5	Mathews-Mil	4.6
Mathews-Mil	1.135	Boyer-StL	22	Bruton-Mil	69.4	Robinson-Bro	1.8	Mays-NY	15.3	Snider-Bro	4.5
Musial-StL	1.030	Temple-Cin	19	Boyer-StL	56.4	Blaylock-Phi	1.2	O'Connell-Mil	14.2	Banks-Chi	4.4
Campanella-Bro	1.009	Gilliam-Bro	15					Hoak-Bro	13.9	Aaron-Mil	4.0

Wins		Win Percentage		Games		Complete Games		Shutouts		Saves	
Roberts-Phi	23	Newcombe-Bro	.800	Labine-Bro	60	Roberts-Phi	26	Nuxhall-Cin	5	Meyer-Phi	16
Newcombe-Bro	20	Roberts-Phi	.622	Wilhelm-NY	59	Newcombe-Bro	17	Jones-Chi	4	Roebuck-Bro	12
Spahn-Mil	17	Nuxhall-Cin	.586	LaPalme-StL	56	Spahn-Mil	16	Dickson-Phi	4	Labine-Bro	11
Nuxhall-Cin	17	Spahn-Mil	.548	Grissom-NY	55					Freeman-Cin	11
				Freeman-Cin	52					Grissom-NY	8

Innings Pitched		Fewest Hits/Game		Fewest BB/Game		Strikeouts		Strikeouts/Game		Wins Above Team	
Roberts-Phi	305	Jones-Chi	6.51	Newcombe-Bro	1.46	Jones-Chi	198	Jones-Chi	7.36	Newcombe-Bro	6.1
Nuxhall-Cin	257	Buhl-Mil	7.49	Roberts-Phi	1.56	Roberts-Phi	160	Haddix-StL	6.49	Roberts-Phi	5.5
Spahn-Mil	246	Rush-Chi	7.85	Hacker-Chi	1.82	Haddix-StL	150	Podres-Bro	6.45	Friend-Pit	4.6
Jones-Chi	242	Antonelli-NY	7.89	Friend-Pit	2.34	Newcombe-Bro	143	Conley-Mil	6.09	Nuxhall-Cin	3.3
Antonelli-NY	235	Dickson-Phi	7.92	Spahn-Mil	2.38	Antonelli-NY	143	Newcombe-Bro	5.50	Bessent-Bro	3.2

Earned Run Average		Adjusted ERA		Opponents' Batting Avg.		Opponents' On Base Pct.		Starter Runs		Adjusted Starter Runs	
Friend-Pit	2.84	Friend-Pit	143	Jones-Chi	.206	Roberts-Phi	.276	Friend-Pit	26.7	Roberts-Phi	28.4
Newcombe-Bro	3.19	Newcombe-Bro	127	Buhl-Mil	.227	Newcombe-Bro	.277	Roberts-Phi	25.8	Friend-Pit	27.4
Buhl-Mil	3.21	Roberts-Phi	126	Rush-Chi	.234	Hacker-Chi	.279	Newcombe-Bro	22.0	Newcombe-Bro	22.8
Spahn-Mil	3.26	Nuxhall-Cin	121	Antonelli-NY	.234	Friend-Pit	.285	Spahn-Mil	21.4	Nuxhall-Cin	21.3
Roberts-Phi	3.28	Antonelli-NY	119	Dickson-Phi	.238	Rush-Chi	.291	Buhl-Mil	18.6	Schmidt-StL	19.7

Clutch Pitching Index		Relief Runs		Adjusted Relief Runs		Relief Ranking		Total Pitcher Index		Total Baseball Ranking	
Minner-Chi	122	Freeman-Cin	19.3	Freeman-Cin	21.0	Freeman-Cin	28.3	Newcombe-Bro	4.4	Mays-NY	7.8
Spahn-Mil	115	Miller-Phi	16.4	Miller-Phi	17.1	Miller-Phi	21.0	Roberts-Phi	3.9	Mathews-Mil	4.6
Jackson-StL	112	LaPalme-StL	13.3	LaPalme-StL	14.2	Jeffcoat-Chi	17.9	Friend-Pit	3.0	Snider-Bro	4.5
Law-Pit	110	Labine-Bro	12.6	Labine-Bro	13.1	Labine-Bro	17.0	Nuxhall-Cin	2.4	Newcombe-Bro	4.4
Friend-Pit	109	Jeffcoat-Chi	12.3	Jeffcoat-Chi	12.9	Meyer-Phi	14.2	Freeman-Cin	2.3	Banks-Chi	4.4

TEAM	G	W	L	PCT	GB	R	OR	AB	H	2B	3B	HR	BB	SO	AVG	OBP	SLG	PRO	/A	BR	/A	PF	CHI	RC	TA	SB	CS	SBA	SBR
NY	154	96	58	.623		762	569	5161	1342	179	55	175	609	658	.260	.343	.418	.761	111	71	85	98	101	759	.727	55	25	69	2
CLE	154	93	61	.604	3	698	601	5146	1325	195	31	148	723	715	.257	.353	.394	.747	108	59	31	104	92	741	.711	28	24	54	-5
CHI	155	91	63	.591	5	725	557	5220	1401	204	36	116	567	595	.268	.347	.388	.735	104	30	24	101	100	712	.683	69	45	61	-5
BOS	154	84	70	.545	12	755	652	5273	1392	241	39	137	707	733	.264	.354	.402	.756	110	77	-93	124	96	773	.721	43	17	72	3
DET	154	79	75	.513	17	775	658	5283	1407	211	38	130	641	583	.266	.348	.394	.742	106	46	68	97	104	736	.692	41	22	65	0
KC	155	63	91	.409	33	638	911	5335	1395	189	46	121	463	725	.261	.323	.382	.705	96	-40	-48	101	99	637	.618	22	36	38	-14
BAL	156	57	97	.370	39	540	754	5257	1263	177	39	54	560	742	.240	.316	.320	.636	77	-159	-88	90	103	532	.550	34	46	43	-16
WAS	154	53	101	.344	43	598	789	5142	1277	178	54	80	538	654	.248	.324	.351	.675	88	-85	-24	91	102	586	.597	25	32	44	-11
TOT	618					5491		41817	10802	1574	338	961	4808	5405	.258	.339	.381	.720								317	247	56	-52

TEAM	CG	SHO	SV	IP	H	H/G	HR	BB	BB/G	SO	SO/G	ERA	/A	OAVG	OOBA	PR	/A	PF	CPI	FA	E	DP	FW	PW	BW	SBW	DIF
NY	52	19	33	1372.3	1163	7.6	108	689	4.5	731	4.8	3.23	115	.231	.322	110	75	94	107	.978	128	180	.5	7.5	8.5	.9	1.6
CLE	45	15	36	1386.3	1285	8.3	111	557	3.6	877	5.7	3.39	119	.245	.315	88	100	102	101	.981	108	152	1.7	10.0	3.1	.2	1.1
CHI	55	20	23	1378.0	1301	8.5	111	497	3.2	720	4.7	3.37	115	.250	.312	90	76	98	103	.981	111	147	1.5	7.6	2.4	.2	2.3
BOS	44	9	34	1384.3	1283	8.7	128	582	3.8	674	4.4	3.72	130	.253	.325	37	173	122	102	.977	136	140	.0	17.3	-9.3	1.0	-2.0
DET	66	16	12	1380.7	1381	9.0	126	517	3.4	629	4.1	3.79	99	.260	.324	25	-6	95	102	.976	139	159	-.2	-.6	6.8	.7	-4.7
KC	29	9	22	1382.0	1486	9.7	175	707	4.6	572	3.7	5.35	79	.278	.358	-213	-176	106	94	.976	146	174	-.6	-17.6	-4.8	-.7	9.8
BAL	35	10	20	1388.7	1403	9.1	103	625	4.1	595	3.9	4.21	88	.266	.338	-38	-78	94	98	.972	167	159	-1.8	-7.8	-8.8	-.9	-.6
WAS	37	10	16	1354.7	1450	9.6	99	634	4.2	607	4.0	4.62	81	.278	.352	-99	-134	94	98	.974	154	170	-1.0	-13.4	-2.4	-.4	-6.7
TOT	363	108	196	11027.0		8.8		3.9		4.4	3.96		.258	.339					.977	1089	1281					

Runs
Smith-Cle 123
Mantle-NY 121
Kaline-Det 121
Tuttle-Det 102
Kuenn-Det 101

Hits
Kaline-Det 200
Fox-Chi 198
Power-KC 190
Kuenn-Det 190
Smith-Cle 186

Doubles
Kuenn-Det 38
Power-KC 34
Goodman-Bos 31
White-Bos 30
Finigan-KC 30

Triples
Mantle-NY 11
Carey-NY 11
Power-KC...........10

Home Runs
Mantle-NY 37
Zernial-KC 30
Williams-Bos 28

Total Bases
Kaline-Det 321
Mantle-NY 316
Power-KC 301
Smith-Cle 287
Jensen-Bos 275

Runs Batted In
Jensen-Bos 116
Boone-Det 116
Berra-NY 108
Sievers-Was 106
Kaline-Det 102

Runs Produced
Kaline-Det 196
Jensen-Bos 185
Mantle-NY 183
Smith-Cle 178
Tuttle-Det 166

Bases On Balls
Mantle-NY 113
Goodman-Bos 99
Yost-Was 99
Fain-Det-Cle 94
Smith-Cle 93

Batting Average
Kaline-Det .... .340
Power-KC 319
Kell-Chi 312
Fox-Chi 311
Kuenn-Det 306

On Base Percentage
Mantle-NY .... .433
Kaline-Det .... .425
Smith-Cle .... .411
Yost-Was .... .410
Goodman-Bos ...... .397

Slugging Average
Mantle-NY .... .611
Kaline-Det .... .546
Doby-Cle .... .505
Power-KC........... .505
Sievers-Was .... .489

Production
Mantle-NY 1.044
Kaline-Det 971
Smith-Cle 884
Doby-Cle 877
Power-KC 862

Adjusted Production
Mantle-NY 182
Kaline-Det 165
Sievers-Was 141
Vernon-Was 138
Smith-Cle 132

Batter Runs
Williams-Bos 59.3
Mantle-NY 59.0
Kaline-Det 50.1
Smith-Cle 34.6
Valo-KC 24.8

Adjusted Batter Runs
Mantle-NY 60.6
Kaline-Det 52.6
Williams-Bos 47.7
Smith-Cle 31.4
Vernon-Was 26.7

Clutch Hitting Index
Kell-Chi 148
Boone-Det 148
Jensen-Bos 130
Sievers-Was 129
Berra-NY 127

Runs Created
Mantle-NY 148
Kaline-Det 135
Smith-Cle 128
Power-KC 103
Jensen-Bos 102

Total Average
Mantle-NY 1.209
Kaline-Det 1.012
Smith-Cle 942
Doby-Cle 884
Jensen-Bos 865

Stolen Bases
Rivera-Chi 25
Minoso-Chi.........19
Jensen-Bos 16
Busby-Was-Chi 12
Smith-Cle 11

Stolen Base Average
Minoso-Chi 70.4
Jensen-Bos 69.6
Rivera-Chi 61.0

Stolen Base Runs
Torgeson-Det 2.7
Busby-Was-Chi 1.8
Mantle-NY 1.8
Klaus-Bos 1.8

Fielding Runs
Fox-Chi...........28.9
Miranda-Bal....... 18.9
McDougald-NY 16.9
Rivera-Chi 14.3
Power-KC 13.7

Total Player Rating
Mantle-NY 5.7
Kaline-Det 4.5
Fox-Chi............. 4.0
Williams-Bos 3.9
McDougald-NY 3.1

Wins
Sullivan-Bos 18
Lemon-Cle 18
Ford-NY 18
Wynn-Cle 17
Turley-NY 17

Win Percentage
Byrne-NY .... .762
Ford-NY .... .720
Hoeft-Det 696
Lemon-Cle 643
Donovan-Chi ...... .625

Games
Narleski-Cle 60
Mossi-Cle 57
Gorman-KC 57
Dorish-Chi-Bal 48
Moore-Bal 46

Complete Games
Ford-NY 18
Hoeft-Det 17

Shutouts
Hoeft-Det 7
Wynn-Cle 6
Turley-NY 6
Pierce-Chi 6

Saves
Narleski-Cle 19
Kinder-Bos 18
Gorman-KC 18
Konstanty-NY........11
Morgan-NY 10

Innings Pitched
Sullivan-Bos 260
Ford-NY 254
Turley-NY 247
Wilson-Bal 235
Lary-Det 235

Fewest Hits/Game
Turley-NY 6.12
Score-Cle 6.26
Ford-NY 6.66
Pierce-Chi 7.08
Harshman-Chi 7.24

Fewest BB/Game
Gromek-Det 1.84
Donovan-Chi 2.31
Garcia-Cle 2.39
Garver-Det 2.61
Porterfield-Was 2.73

Strikeouts
Score-Cle 245
Turley-NY 210
Pierce-Chi 157
Ford-NY 137
Hoeft-Det 133

Strikeouts/Game
Score-Cle 9.71
Turley-NY 7.65
Pierce-Chi 6.86
Harshman-Chi 5.83
Hoeft-Det 5.44

Wins Above Team
Hoeft-Det 4.8
Byrne-NY 4.2
Narleski-Cle 3.8
Ford-NY 3.6
Kellner-KC 3.0

Earned Run Average
Pierce-Chi 1.97
Ford-NY 2.62
Wynn-Cle 2.82
Score-Cle 2.85
Sullivan-Bos 2.91

Adjusted ERA
Pierce-Chi 197
Sullivan-Bos 167
Wynn-Cle 144
Ford-NY 142
Score-Cle 142

Opponents' Batting Avg.
Turley-NY 193
Score-Cle 194
Ford-NY 208
Pierce-Chi 213
Harshman-Chi 224

Opponents' On Base Pct.
Pierce-Chi 274
Wilson-Bal 294
Ford-NY 294
Hoeft-Det 295
Wynn-Cle 301

Starter Runs
Pierce-Chi 45.7
Ford-NY 37.8
Sullivan-Bos 30.4
Wynn-Cle 29.2
Score-Cle 27.9

Adjusted Starter Runs
Sullivan-Bos 55.9
Pierce-Chi 43.6
Wynn-Cle 31.3
Ford-NY 31.3
Score-Cle 30.0

Clutch Pitching Index
Pierce-Chi 120
Byrne-NY 119
Sullivan-Bos 116
Lary-Det 115
Schmitz-Was 115

Relief Runs
Consuegra-Chi 18.5
Mossi-Cle 14.1
Konstanty-NY 13.6
Kiely-Bos 11.6
Dorish-Chi-Bal 10.5

Adjusted Relief Runs
Kiely-Bos 20.4
Consuegra-Chi 17.2
Hurd-Bos 16.6
Kinder-Bos 15.1
Mossi-Cle 14.8

Relief Ranking
Kinder-Bos 29.3
Hurd-Bos 28.1
Konstanty-NY 16.7
Consuegra-Chi 15.6
Kiely-Bos 15.3

Total Pitcher Index
Sullivan-Bos 5.8
Pierce-Chi 4.5
Ford-NY 3.4
Wynn-Cle 3.2
Susce-Bos 2.8

Total Baseball Ranking
Sullivan-Bos 5.8
Mantle-NY 5.7
Pierce-Chi 4.5
Kaline-Det 4.5
Fox-Chi............. 4.0

TEAM	G	W	L	PCT	GB	R	OR	AB	H	2B	3B	HR	BB	SO	AVG	OBP	SLG	PRO	/A	BR	/A	PF	CHI	RC	TA	SB	CS	SBA	SBR
BRO	154	93	61	.604		720	601	5098	1315	212	36	179	649	738	.258	.344	.419	.763	111	81	63	103	97	728	.723	65	37	64	-2
MIL	155	92	62	.597	1	709	569	5207	1350	212	54	177	486	714	.259	.325	.423	.748	106	38	45	99	101	714	.688	29	20	59	-2
CIN	155	91	63	.591	2	775	658	5291	1406	201	32	221	528	760	.266	.338	.441	.779	114	103	47	108	99	789	.736	45	22	67	0
STL	156	76	78	.494	17	678	698	5378	1443	234	49	124	503	622	.268	.335	.399	.734	103	24	31	99	97	707	.665	41	35	54	-8
PHI	154	71	83	.461	22	668	738	5204	1313	207	49	121	585	673	.252	.331	.381	.712	97	-12	26	94	102	658	.652	45	23	66	0
NY	154	67	87	.435	26	540	650	5190	1268	192	45	145	402	659	.244	.301	.382	.683	88	-84	-66	97	96	586	.608	67	34	66	0
PIT	157	66	88	.429	27	588	653	5221	1340	199	57	110	383	752	.257	.310	.380	.690	91	-70	-83	102	102	594	.596	24	33	42	-12
CHI	157	60	94	.390	33	597	708	5260	1281	202	50	142	446	776	.244	.304	.382	.686	89	-79	-69	99	103	606	.613	55	38	59	-5
TOT	621					5275		41849	10716	1659	372	1219	3982	5694	.256	.324	.401	.725								371	242	61	-33

TEAM	CG	SHO	SV	IP	H	H/G	HR	BB	BB/G	SO	SO/G	ERA	/A	OAVG	OOBA	PR	/A	PF	CPI	FA	E	DP	FW	PW	BW	SBW	DIF
BRO	46	12	30	1368.7	1251	8.2	171	441	2.9	772	5.1	3.57	106	.244	.301	30	32	100	97	.981	111	149	1.5	3.3	6.5	.2	4.6
MIL	64	12	27	1393.3	1295	8.4	133	467	3.0	639	4.1	3.11	116	.246	.306	101	79	96	107	.979	130	159	.3	8.1	4.6	.2	1.8
CIN	47	4	29	1389.0	1406	9.1	141	458	3.0	653	4.2	3.85	104	.265	.320	-11	22	106	101	.981	113	147	1.3	2.3	4.8	.4	5.2
STL	41	12	30	1388.7	1339	8.7	155	546	3.5	709	4.6	3.97	94	.256	.322	-30	-34	99	98	.978	134	172	.0	-3.5	3.2	-.4	-.4
PHI	57	4	15	1377.3	1407	9.2	172	437	2.9	750	4.9	4.20	86	.265	.317	-65	-92	95	95	.975	144	140	-.5	-9.4	2.7	.4	.9
NY	31	9	28	1378.0	1287	8.4	144	551	3.6	765	5.0	3.78	99	.249	.317	0	-4	99	98	.976	144	143	-.5	-.4	-6.8	.4	-2.7
PIT	37	8	24	1376.3	1406	9.2	142	469	3.1	662	4.3	3.74	104	.266	.321	4	23	103	105	.973	162	140	-1.6	2.4	-8.5	-.8	-2.4
CHI	37	6	17	1391.7	1325	8.6	161	613	4.0	744	4.8	3.96	96	.252	.327	-28	-25	101	100	.976	144	141	-.5	-2.6	-7.1	-.0	-6.8
TOT	360	67	200	11063.0		8.7			3.2		4.6	3.77		.256	.324					.977	1082	1191					

Runs
Robinson-Cin 122
Snider-Bro 112
Aaron-Mil 106
Mathews-Mil 103
Gilliam-Bro 102

Hits
Aaron-Mil 200
Ashburn-Phi 190
Virdon-StL-Pit 185
Musial-StL 184
Boyer-StL 182

Doubles
Aaron-Mil 34
Snider-Bro 33
Musial-StL 33
Lopata-Phi 33
Bell-Cin 31

Triples
Bruton-Mil 15
Aaron-Mil 14
Walls-Pit 11
Moon-StL 11
Virdon-StL-Pit 10

Home Runs
Snider-Bro 43
Robinson-Cin 38
Adcock-Mil 38
Mathews-Mil 37

Total Bases
Aaron-Mil 340
Snider-Bro 324
Mays-NY 322
Robinson-Cin 319
Musial-StL 310

Runs Batted In
Musial-StL 109
Adcock-Mil 103
Kluszewski-Cin 102
Snider-Bro 101
Boyer-StL 98

Runs Produced
Aaron-Mil 172
Snider-Bro 170
Musial-StL 169
Robinson-Cin 167
Boyer-StL 163

Bases On Balls
Snider-Bro 99
Gilliam-Bro 95
Jones-Phi 92
Mathews-Mil 91
Moon-StL 80

Batting Average
Aaron-Mil 328
Virdon-StL-Pit 319
Clemente-Pit 311
Musial-StL 310
Boyer-StL 306

On Base Percentage
Snider-Bro 402
Gilliam-Bro 400
Musial-StL 390
Moon-StL 390
Jones-Phi 387

Slugging Average
Snider-Bro 598
Adcock-Mil 597
Aaron-Mil 558
Robinson-Cin 558
Mays-NY 557

Production
Snider-Bro 1.000
Robinson-Cin 939
Adcock-Mil 936
Mays-NY 928
Aaron-Mil 927

Adjusted Production
Snider-Bro 160
Mays-NY 149
Adcock-Mil 147
Aaron-Mil 146
Lopata-Phi 144

Batter Runs
Snider-Bro 50.4
Robinson-Cin 39.1
Aaron-Mil 36.3
Musial-StL 36.2
Mays-NY 35.9

Adjusted Batter Runs
Snider-Bro 48.4
Mays-NY 37.9
Aaron-Mil 37.1
Musial-StL 37.1
Robinson-Cin 32.9

Clutch Hitting Index
McMillan-Cin 151
Thomson-Mil 128
Jones-Phi 127
Musial-StL 125
Long-Pit 118

Runs Created
Snider-Bro 128
Robinson-Cin 121
Musial-StL 119
Mays-NY 118
Aaron-Mil 115

Total Average
Snider-Bro 1.060
Mays-NY 995
Robinson-Cin 969
Mathews-Mil 946
Adcock-Mil 916

Stolen Bases
Mays-NY 40
Gilliam-Bro 21
White-NY 15
Temple-Cin 14
Reese-Bro 13

Stolen Base Average
Mays-NY 80.0
Gilliam-Bro 70.0

Stolen Base Runs
Mays-NY 6.0
Ashburn-Phi 2.4
Temple-Cin 1.8
Post-Cin 1.8
Mathews-Mil 1.8

Fielding Runs
McMillan-Cin 29.6
Ashburn-Phi 21.0
Jackson-Bro 19.8
Robinson-Bro 16.1
Baker-Chi 15.1

Total Player Rating
Mays-NY 4.7
Aaron-Mil 3.9
Snider-Bro 3.8
Bailey-Cin 3.6
Gilliam-Bro 3.5

Wins
Newcombe-Bro 27
Spahn-Mil 20
Antonelli-NY 20

Win Percentage
Newcombe-Bro 794
Buhl-Mil 692
Lawrence-Cin 655
Burdette-Mil 655
Spahn-Mil 645

Games
Face-Pit 68
Wilhelm-NY 64
Freeman-Cin 64
Labine-Bro 62
Lown-Chi 61

Complete Games
Roberts-Phi 22
Spahn-Mil 20
Friend-Pit 19
Newcombe-Bro 18
Burdette-Mil 16

Shutouts
Burdette-Mil 6
Newcombe-Bro 5
Antonelli-NY 5
Friend-Pit 4

Saves
Labine-Bro 19
Freeman-Cin 18
Lown-Chi 13
Jackson-StL 9
Bessent-Bro 9

Innings Pitched
Friend-Pit 314
Roberts-Phi 297
Spahn-Mil 281
Newcombe-Bro 268
Kline-Pit 264

Fewest Hits/Game
Maglie-Bro 7.26
Newcombe-Bro 7.35
Jones-Chi 7.38
Mizell-StL 7.41
Craig-Bro 7.64

Fewest BB/Game
Roberts-Phi 1.21
Newcombe-Bro 1.54
Spahn-Mil 1.67
Fowler-Cin 1.77
Burdette-Mil 1.83

Strikeouts
Jones-Chi 176
Haddix-StL-Phi ...170
Friend-Pit 166
Roberts-Phi 157
Mizell-StL 153

Strikeouts/Game
Jones-Chi 8.38
Haddix-StL-Phi ...6.62
Mizell-StL 6.59
Nuxhall-Cin 5.37
Worthington-NY ...5.15

Wins Above Team
Newcombe-Bro 9.2
Antonelli-NY 5.9
Rush-Chi 3.7
Freeman-Cin 3.7
Simmons-Phi 3.7

Earned Run Average
Burdette-Mil 2.71
Spahn-Mil 2.79
Antonelli-NY 2.86
Maglie-Bro 2.87
Newcombe-Bro 3.06

Adjusted ERA
Burdette-Mil 134
Maglie-Bro 132
Antonelli-NY 131
Spahn-Mil 130
Newcombe-Bro 124

Opponents' Batting Avg.
Newcombe-Bro 221
Jones-Chi 221
Mizell-StL 222
Maglie-Bro 222
Craig-Bro 231

Opponents' On Base Pct.
Newcombe-Bro 255
Spahn-Mil 273
Rush-Chi 277
Maglie-Bro 278
Burdette-Mil 279

Starter Runs
Spahn-Mil 30.8
Burdette-Mil 30.3
Antonelli-NY 26.1
Newcombe-Bro 21.3
Maglie-Bro 19.0

Adjusted Starter Runs
Spahn-Mil 26.2
Burdette-Mil 26.1
Antonelli-NY 25.5
Newcombe-Bro 21.8
Maglie-Bro 19.4

Clutch Pitching Index
Conley-Mil 127
Klippstein-Cin ...111
Kline-Pit 110
Poholsky-StL 108
Jeffcoat-Cin 105

Relief Runs
Grissom-NY 19.9
Acker-Cin 13.2
Bessent-Bro 11.1
R.Miller-Phi 7.1
Labine-Bro 5.6

Adjusted Relief Runs
Grissom-NY 19.7
Acker-Cin 15.3
Bessent-Bro 11.2
Freeman-Cin 7.4
Labine-Bro 5.8

Relief Ranking
Freeman-Cin 14.4
Acker-Cin 11.9
Bessent-Bro 11.8
Face-Pit 9.6
Labine-Bro 9.3

Total Pitcher Index
Newcombe-Bro 3.4
Spahn-Mil 3.2
Antonelli-NY 3.0
Burdette-Mil 2.9
Dickson-Phi-StL ..2.1

Total Baseball Ranking
Mays-NY 4.7
Aaron-Mil 3.9
Snider-Bro 3.8
Bailey-Cin 3.6
Gilliam-Bro 3.5

TEAM	G	W	L	PCT	GB	R	OR	AB	H	2B	3B	HR	BB	SO	AVG	OBP	SLG	PRO	/A	BR	/A	PF	CHI	RC	TA	SB	CS	SBA	SBR
NY	154	97	57	.630		857	631	5312	1433	193	55	190	615	755	.270	.349	.434	.783	112	80	90	99	106	814	.747	51	37	58	-6
CLE	155	88	66	.571	9	712	581	5148	1256	199	23	153	681	764	.244	.337	.381	.718	95	-35	-43	101	104	681	.675	40	32	56	-6
CHI	154	85	69	.552	12	776	634	5286	1412	218	43	128	619	660	.267	.352	.397	.749	103	29	-1	104	102	756	.709	70	33	68	1
BOS	155	84	70	.545	13	780	751	5349	1473	261	45	139	727	687	.275	.365	.419	.784	113	100	81	103	92	826	.746	28	19	60	-2
DET	155	82	72	.532	15	789	699	5364	1494	209	50	150	644	618	.279	.359	.420	.779	111	84	108	97	96	816	.737	43	26	62	-2
BAL	154	69	85	.448	28	571	705	5090	1242	198	34	91	563	725	.244	.322	.350	.672	83	-122	-81	94	100	572	.598	39	42	48	-13
WAS	155	59	95	.383	38	652	924	5202	1302	198	62	112	690	877	.250	.343	.377	.720	96	-26	-39	102	93	681	.669	37	34	52	-8
KC	154	52	102	.338	45	619	831	5256	1325	204	41	112	480	727	.252	.317	.370	.687	86	-107	-113	101	104	610	.608	40	30	57	-5
TOT	618					5756		42007	10937	1680	353	1075	5019	5813	.260	.343	.394	.737								348	253	58	-46

TEAM	CG	SHO	SV	IP	H	H/G	HR	BB	BB/G	SO	SO/G	ERA	/A	OAVG	OOBA	PR	/A	PF	CPI	FA	E	DP	FW	PW	BW	SBW	DIF
NY	50	10	35	1381.7	1285	8.4	114	652	4.2	732	4.8	3.63	109	.248	.332	81	48	95	105	.977	136	214	.6	4.7	8.8	.0	5.9
CLE	67	17	24	1384.0	1233	8.0	116	564	3.7	845	5.5	3.32	124	.238	.310	128	121	99	100	.978	129	130	.9	11.8	-4.2	.0	2.4
CHI	65	11	13	1389.0	1351	8.8	118	524	3.4	722	4.7	3.73	114	.255	.319	66	77	102	99	.979	122	160	1.3	7.5	-.0	.7	-1.5
BOS	50	8	20	1398.0	1354	8.7	130	668	4.3	712	4.6	4.17	102	.253	.335	0	11	102	96	.972	169	168	-1.3	1.1	7.9	.4	-1.1
DET	62	10	15	1379.0	1389	9.1	140	655	4.3	788	5.1	4.06	97	.264	.343	15	-15	95	108	.976	140	151	.3	-1.5	10.6	.4	-4.8
BAL	38	10	24	1360.7	1362	9.0	99	547	3.6	715	4.7	4.20	96	.263	.328	-6	-28	97	93	.977	137	142	.5	-2.7	-7.9	-.7	2.9
WAS	36	1	18	1368.7	1539	10.1	171	730	4.8	663	4.4	5.33	83	.287	.367	-178	-137	107	99	.972	171	173	-1.4	-13.4	-3.8	-.2	.8
KC	30	3	18	1370.3	1424	9.4	187	679	4.5	636	4.2	4.86	90	.271	.352	-106	-77	105	101	.973	166	187	-1.1	-7.5	-11.1	.0	-5.4
TOT	398	70	167	11031.3		8.9			4.1		4.7	4.16		.260	.343					.975	1170	1325					

Runs
Mantle-NY 132
Fox-Chi 109
Minoso-Chi 106

Hits
Kuenn-Det 196
Kaline-Det 194
Fox-Chi 192
Mantle-NY 188
Jensen-Bos 182

Doubles
Piersall-Bos 40
Kuenn-Det 32
Kaline-Det 32

Triples
Simpson-KC 11
Minoso-Chi 11
Lemon-Was 11
Jensen-Bos 11

Home Runs
Mantle-NY 52
Wertz-Cle 32
Berra-NY 30
Sievers-Was 29
Maxwell-Det 28

Total Bases
Mantle-NY 376
Kaline-Det 327
Jensen-Bos 287
Minoso-Chi 286

Runs Batted In
Mantle-NY 130
Kaline-Det 128
Wertz-Cle 106
Simpson-KC 105
Berra-NY 105

Runs Produced
Mantle-NY 210
Kaline-Det 197
Minoso-Chi 173
Kuenn-Det 172
Berra-NY 168

Bases On Balls
Yost-Was 151
Mantle-NY 112
Williams-Bos 102
Doby-Chi 102
Sievers-Was 100

Batting Average
Mantle-NY 353
Williams-Bos 345
Kuenn-Det 332
Maxwell-Det 326
Nieman-Chi-Bal 320

On Base Percentage
Williams-Bos 479
Mantle-NY 467
Nieman-Chi-Bal 438
Minoso-Chi 430
Maxwell-Det 420

Slugging Average
Mantle-NY 705
Williams-Bos 605
Maxwell-Det 534
Berra-NY 534
Kaline-Det 530

Production
Mantle-NY 1.172
Williams-Bos 1.084
Minoso-Chi 954
Maxwell-Det 954
Nieman-Chi-Bal 934

Adjusted Production
Mantle-NY 208
Williams-Bos 180
Maxwell-Det 156
Nieman-Chi-Bal 153
Boone-Det 147

Batter Runs
Mantle-NY 83.3
Williams-Bos 54.1
Minoso-Chi 43.2
Maxwell-Det 37.5
Kaline-Det 33.4

Adjusted Batter Runs
Mantle-NY 84.3
Williams-Bos 52.6
Maxwell-Det 39.9
Minoso-Chi 39.9
Kaline-Det 36.2

Clutch Hitting Index
Doby-Chi 131
Simpson-KC 126
Triandos-Bal 123
Lollar-Chi 122
Wertz-Cle 118

Runs Created
Mantle-NY 188
Minoso-Chi 130
Kaline-Det 129
Williams-Bos 121
Maxwell-Det 118

Total Average
Mantle-NY 1.429
Williams-Bos 1.255
Minoso-Chi 1.046
Maxwell-Det 1.017
Nieman-Chi-Bal 974

Stolen Bases
Aparicio-Chi 21
Rivera-Chi 20
Avila-Cle 17
Minoso-Chi 12

Stolen Base Average
Aparicio-Chi 84.0
Avila-Cle 81.0
Rivera-Chi 69.0

Stolen Base Runs
Aparicio-Chi 3.9
Avila-Cle 2.7
Mantle-NY 2.4

Fielding Runs
Kaline-Det 17.5
Berra-NY 12.7
McDougald-NY 11.3
Yost-Was 10.7
Lopez-KC 10.3

Total Player Rating
Mantle-NY 7.6
Berra-NY 4.6
Kaline-Det 4.2
Maxwell-Det 3.8
Williams-Bos 3.7

Wins
Lary-Det 21

Win Percentage
Ford-NY 760
Wynn-Cle 690
Score-Cle 690
Pierce-Chi 690
Brewer-Bos 679

Games
Zuverink-Bal 62
Crimian-KC 54
Gorman-KC 52
Mossi-Cle 48
Delock-Bos 48

Complete Games
Pierce-Chi 21
Lemon-Cle 21
Lary-Det 20

Shutouts
Score-Cle 5

Saves
Zuverink-Bal 16
Mossi-Cle 11
Morgan-NY 11
Shantz-KC 9
Delock-Bos 9

Innings Pitched
Lary-Det 294
Wynn-Cle 278
Pierce-Chi 276
Foytack-Det 256
Lemon-Cle 255

Fewest Hits/Game
Score-Cle 5.86
Larsen-NY 6.65
Harshman-Chi 7.26
Brewer-Bos 7.38
Foytack-Det 7.42

Fewest BB/Game
Stobbs-Was 2.03
Donovan-Chi 2.26
Kucks-NY 2.89
Wynn-Cle 2.95
Sturdivant-NY 2.96

Strikeouts
Score-Cle 263
Pierce-Chi 192
Foytack-Det 184
Hoeft-Det 172
Lary-Det 165

Strikeouts/Game
Score-Cle 9.51
Pascual-Was 7.71
Foytack-Det 6.47
Sturdivant-NY 6.27
Pierce-Chi 6.26

Wins Above Team
Pierce-Chi 5.1
Ford-NY 4.9
Brewer-Bos 4.7
Wynn-Cle 4.6
Score-Cle 4.6

Earned Run Average
Ford-NY 2.47
Score-Cle 2.53
Wynn-Cle 2.72
Lemon-Cle 3.04
Harshman-Chi 3.09

Adjusted ERA
Score-Cle 163
Ford-NY 160
Wynn-Cle 151
Harshman-Chi 137
Lemon-Cle 136

Opponents' Batting Avg.
Score-Cle 186
Larsen-NY 204
Brewer-Bos 220
Harshman-Chi 221
Sturdivant-NY 224

Opponents' On Base Pct.
Score-Cle 287
Donovan-Chi 287
Wynn-Cle 288
Sturdivant-NY 290
Ford-NY 299

Starter Runs
Score-Cle 45.1
Wynn-Cle 44.5
Ford-NY 42.4
Lary-Det 32.9
Lemon-Cle 31.8

Adjusted Starter Runs
Score-Cle 43.8
Wynn-Cle 43.1
Ford-NY 37.0
Lemon-Cle 30.5
Harshman-Chi 28.7

Clutch Pitching Index
Lary-Det 117
Sullivan-Bos 116
Hoeft-Det 116
Ford-NY 115
Stobbs-Was 114

Relief Runs
Narleski-Cle 17.3
Grim-NY 11.7
Byrne-NY 9.8
Byerly-Was 7.0
Mossi-Cle 5.7

Adjusted Relief Runs
Narleski-Cle 17.0
Grim-NY 9.9
Byerly-Was 8.6
Byrne-NY 7.2
Mossi-Cle 5.2

Relief Ranking
Narleski-Cle 15.5
Byerly-Was 10.4
Grim-NY 9.8
Mossi-Cle 7.3
Byrne-NY 6.8

Total Pitcher Index
Wynn-Cle 5.0
Ford-NY 4.6
Score-Cle 4.3
Lemon-Cle 4.1
Harshman-Chi 3.3

Total Baseball Ranking
Mantle-NY 7.6
Wynn-Cle 5.0
Ford-NY 4.6
Kaline-Det 4.6
Score-Cle 4.3

TEAM	G	W	L	PCT	GB	R	OR	AB	H	2B	3B	HR	BB	SO	AVG	OBP	SLG	PRO	/A	BR	/A	PF	CHI	RC	TA	SB	CS	SBA	SBR
MIL	155	95	59	.617		**772**	613	5458	1469	221	**62**	199	461	729	.269	.329	.442	.771	112	82	**148**	90	100	787	.714	35	16	**69**	1
STL	154	87	67	.565	8	737	666	5472	**1497**	235	43	132	493	672	**.274**	.336	.405	.741	105	35	30	101	101	731	.673	58	44	57	-8
BRO	154	84	70	.545	11	690	**591**	5242	1325	188	38	147	**550**	848	.253	.341	.432	.715	98	-10	-120	113	664	.655	60	34	64	-1
CIN	154	80	74	.519	15	747	781	5389	1452	**251**	33	187	546	752	.269	**.341**	.432	**.773**	**113**	97	59	105	94	**794**	**.726**	51	36	59	-5
PHI	156	77	77	.500	18	623	656	5241	1311	213	44	117	534	758	.250	.325	.375	.700	94	-38	-25	98	98	635	.634	57	26	**69**	2
NY	154	69	85	.448	26	643	701	5346	1349	171	54	157	447	**669**	.252	.313	.393	.706	95	-41	-55	102	102	646	.635	**64**	38	63	-3
PIT	155	62	92	.403	33	586	696	5402	1447	231	60	92	374	733	.268	.318	.384	.702	94	-45	-3	94	93	649	.614	46	35	57	-6
CHI	156	62	92	.403	33	628	722	5369	1312	223	31	147	461	989	.244	.307	.380	.687	90	-77	-51	96	**105**	623	.610	28	25	53	-6
TOT	619					5426		42919	11162	1733	365	1178	3866	6150	.260	.325	.400	.725								399	254	61	-32

TEAM	CG	SHO	SV	IP	H	H/G	HR	BB	BB/G	SO	SO/G	ERA	/A	OAVG	OOBA	PR	/A	PF	CPI	FA	E	DP	FW	PW	BW	SBW	DIF
MIL	60	9	24	1411.0	1347	8.6	**124**	570	3.6	693	4.4	3.47	98	.253	.321	64	-10	88	**107**	.981	120	173	1.0	-1.0	**15.0**	-.1	2.5
STL	46	11	**29**	1413.3	1385	8.8	140	506	3.2	778	5.0	3.78	102	.256	.319	16	11	99	100	.979	131	168	.4	1.1	3.1	-.4	5.9
BRO	44	**18**	29	1399.3	**1285**	**8.3**	144	456	2.9	**891**	**5.7**	3.35	**132**	**.243**	**.302**	82	**168**	114	101	.979	127	136	.6	**17.1**	-12.2	.3	1.2
CIN	40	5	29	1395.7	1486	9.6	179	429	2.8	707	4.6	4.62	89	.274	.326	-115	-78	106	95	**.982**	**107**	139	**1.7**	-7.9	6.0	-.0	3.4
PHI	54	9	23	1401.0	1363	8.8	139	**412**	**2.6**	858	5.5	3.80	101	.254	.304	12	6	99	92	.976	130	117	.0	.6	-2.5	**.6**	1.2
NY	35	9	20	1398.7	1436	9.2	150	471	3.0	701	4.5	4.01	100	.266	.323	-20	0	103	101	.974	161	**180**	-1.3	.0	-5.6	.1	-1.2
PIT	47	9	15	1395.0	1463	9.4	158	421	2.7	663	4.3	3.88	96	.269	.319	0	-24	96	105	.972	170	143	-1.8	-2.4	-.3	-.2	-10.3
CHI	30	5	26	1403.3	1397	9.0	144	601	3.9	859	5.5	4.13	92	.260	.332	-39	-51	98	100	.975	149	140	-.6	-5.2	-5.2	-.2	-3.8
TOT	356	75	195	11217.3		9.0		3.1		4.9	3.88			.260	.325					.977	1101	1196					

Runs		Hits		Doubles		Triples		Home Runs		Total Bases	
Aaron-Mil	118	Schoendienst-NY-Mil	.200	Hoak-Cin	39	Mays-NY	20	Aaron-Mil	44	Aaron-Mil	369
Banks-Chi	113	Aaron-Mil	198	Musial-StL	38	Virdon-Pit	11	Banks-Chi	43	Mays-NY	366
Mays-NY	112	Robinson-Cin	197	Bouchee-Phi	35	Mathews-Mil	9	Snider-Bro	40	Banks-Chi	344
Mathews-Mil	109	Mays-NY	195	Banks-Chi	34	Bruton-Mil	9	Mays-NY	35	Robinson-Cin	323
Blasingame-StL	108	Ashburn-Phi	186	Moryn-Chi	33			Mathews-Mil	32	Mathews-Mil	309

Runs Batted In		Runs Produced		Bases On Balls		Batting Average		On Base Percentage		Slugging Average	
Aaron-Mil	132	Aaron-Mil	206	Temple-Cin	94	Musial-StL	.351	Musial-StL	.428	Mays-NY	.626
Ennis-StL	105	Mays-NY	174	Ashburn-Phi	94	Mays-NY	.333	Mays-NY	.411	Musial-StL	.612
Musial-StL	102	Banks-Chi	172	Mathews-Mil	90	Robinson-Cin	.322	Bouchee-Phi	.396	Aaron-Mil	.600
Banks-Chi	102	Mathews-Mil	171	Bouchee-Phi	84	Aaron-Mil	.322	Ashburn-Phi	.392	Snider-Bro	.587
Hodges-Bro	98	Hodges-Bro	165	Snider-Bro	77	Groat-Pit	.315	Temple-Cin	.391	Banks-Chi	.579

Production		Adjusted Production		Batter Runs		Adjusted Batter Runs		Clutch Hitting Index		Runs Created	
Musial-StL	1.040	Aaron-Mil	175	Mays-NY	60.5	Mays-NY	58.9	Ennis-StL	141	Mays-NY	145
Mays-NY	1.037	Musial-StL	174	Musial-StL	54.1	Aaron-Mil	55.7	McMillan-Cin	140	Aaron-Mil	136
Aaron-Mil	.979	Mays-NY	170	Aaron-Mil	48.2	Musial-StL	53.7	Hamner-Phi	134	Musial-StL	129
Snider-Bro	.957	Mathews-Mil	162	Banks-Chi	38.6	Mathews-Mil	45.6	Moryn-Chi	124	Mathews-Mil	126
Banks-Chi	.942	Banks-Chi	154	Mathews-Mil	38.2	Banks-Chi	41.5	Hoak-Cin	121	Banks-Chi	123

Total Average		Stolen Bases		Stolen Base Average		Stolen Base Runs		Fielding Runs		Total Player Rating	
Mays-NY	1.137	Mays-NY	38	Temple-Cin	79.2	Temple-Cin	2.7	Ashburn-Phi	27.3	Mays-NY	5.9
Musial-StL	1.106	Gilliam-Bro	26	Fernandez-Phi	78.3	Fernandez-Phi	2.4	Blasingame-StL	25.5	Aaron-Mil	5.9
Aaron-Mil	.991	Blasingame-StL	21	Gilliam-Bro	72.2	Robinson-Cin	1.8	Logan-Mil	22.2	Mathews-Mil	4.9
Mathews-Mil	.976	Temple-Cin	19	Blasingame-StL	70.0	Gilliam-Bro	1.8	Robinson-Cin	17.0	Robinson-Cin	4.3
Snider-Bro	.972	Fernandez-Phi	18	Mays-NY	66.7			Clemente-Pit	12.7	Musial-StL	4.1

Wins		Win Percentage		Games		Complete Games		Shutouts		Saves	
Spahn-Mil	21	Buhl-Mil	.720	Lown-Chi	67	Spahn-Mil	18	Podres-Bro	6	Labine-Bro	17
Sanford-Phi	19	Sanford-Phi	.704	Face-Pit	59	Friend-Pit	17	Spahn-Mil	4	Grissom-NY	14
Buhl-Mil	18	Spahn-Mil	.656	Labine-Bro	58	Gomez-NY	16	Newcombe-Bro	4	Lown-Chi	12
Drysdale-Bro	17	Drysdale-Bro	.654	Worthington-NY	55	Sanford-Phi	15	Drysdale-Bro	4	Wilhelm-StL	11
Burdette-Mil	17	Burdette-Mil	.654	Grissom-NY	55						

Innings Pitched		Fewest Hits/Game		Fewest BB/Game		Strikeouts		Strikeouts/Game		Wins Above Team	
Friend-Pit	277	Sanford-Phi	7.37	Newcombe-Bro	1.49	Sanford-Phi	188	Jones-StL	7.57	Sanford-Phi	6.1
Spahn-Mil	271	Podres-Bro	7.71	Roberts-Phi	1.55	Drott-Chi	170	Haddix-Phi	7.16	Drott-Chi	4.3
Burdette-Mil	257	Drott-Chi	7.86	Law-Pit	1.66	Drabowsky-Chi	170	Sanford-Phi	7.14	Farrell-Phi	4.1
Roberts-Phi	250	Buhl-Mil	7.92	Purkey-Pit	1.90	Jones-StL	154	Drott-Chi	6.68	Buhl-Mil	3.8
Lawrence-Cin	250	Worthington-NY	7.97	Jeffcoat-Cin	2.00	Drysdale-Bro	148	Drabowsky-Chi	6.38	Drysdale-Bro	3.6

Earned Run Average		Adjusted ERA		Opponents' Batting Avg.		Opponents' On Base Pct.		Starter Runs		Adjusted Starter Runs	
Podres-Bro	2.66	Podres-Bro	166	Sanford-Phi	.221	Podres-Bro	.272	Spahn-Mil	35.8	Drysdale-Bro	42.9
Drysdale-Bro	2.69	Drysdale-Bro	165	Podres-Bro	.230	Roberts-Phi	.281	Drysdale-Bro	29.2	Podres-Bro	38.5
Spahn-Mil	2.69	Law-Pit	130	Drott-Chi	.234	Newcombe-Bro	.286	Buhl-Mil	27.5	Spahn-Mil	21.4
Buhl-Mil	2.74	Newcombe-Bro	127	Drysdale-Bro	.236	Law-Pit	.288	Podres-Bro	26.5	Newcombe-Bro	21.0
Law-Pit	2.86	Spahn-Mil	126	Spahn-Mil	.237	Spahn-Mil	.289	Sanford-Phi	21.1	Sanford-Phi	20.0

Clutch Pitching Index		Relief Runs		Adjusted Relief Runs		Relief Ranking		Total Pitcher Index		Total Baseball Ranking	
Buhl-Mil	135	Farrell-Phi	13.8	Roebuck-Bro	18.3	Farrell-Phi	21.0	Drysdale-Bro	5.4	Mays-NY	5.9
Barclay-NY	117	Roebuck-Bro	12.4	Farrell-Phi	13.4	Roebuck-Bro	20.6	Podres-Bro	4.3	Aaron-Mil	5.9
Law-Pit	113	Grissom-NY	11.8	Grissom-NY	13.0	Labine-Bro	16.3	Newcombe-Bro	3.0	Drysdale-Bro	5.4
Spahn-Mil	109	Face-Pit	8.5	Labine-Bro	11.7	Grissom-NY	16.2	Roebuck-Bro	2.5	Mathews-Mil	4.9
Antonelli-NY	108	Miller-Phi	7.9	Miller-Phi	7.6	Miller-Phi	9.7	Spahn-Mil	2.3	Podres-Bro	4.3

TEAM	G	W	L	PCT	GB	R	OR	AB	H	2B	3B	HR	BB	SO	AVG	OBP	SLG	PRO	/A	BR	/A	PF	CHI	RC	TA	SB	CS	SBA	SBR
NY	154	98	56	.636		723	534	5271	1412	200	54	145	562	709	.268	.341	.409	.750	111	75	116	94	98	729	.693	49	38	56	-7
CHI	155	90	64	.584	8	707	566	5265	1369	208	41	106	633	745	.260	.347	.375	.722	104	39	44	99	100	709	.686	109	48	69	4
BOS	154	82	72	.532	16	721	668	5267	1380	231	32	153	624	739	.262	.343	.405	.748	110	76	10	110	98	725	.692	29	21	58	-3
DET	154	78	76	.506	20	614	614	5348	1376	224	37	116	504	684	.257	.324	.378	.702	98	-17	-64	107	95	644	.624	36	47	43	-16
BAL	154	76	76	.500	21	597	588	5264	1326	191	39	87	504	699	.252	.321	.353	.674	90	-66	-20	93	101	600	.598	57	35	62	-3
CLE	153	76	77	.497	21.5	682	722	5171	1304	199	26	140	591	786	.252	.332	.382	.714	101	10	0	102	103	661	.654	40	47	46	-15
KC	154	59	94	.386	38.5	563	710	5170	1262	195	40	166	364	760	.244	.297	.394	.691	93	-59	-50	99	100	578	.604	35	27	56	-5
WAS	154	55	99	.357	43	603	808	5231	1274	215	38	111	527	733	.244	.318	.363	.681	92	-55	-40	98	101	592	.601	13	38	25	-18
TOT	616					5210		41987	10703	1663	307	1024	4309	5814	.255	.328	.383	.711								368	301	55	-69

TEAM	CG	SHO	SV	IP	H	H/G	HR	BB	BB/G	SO	SO/G	ERA	/A	OAVG	OOBA	PR	/A	PF	CPI	FA	E	DP	FW	PW	BW	SBW	DIF
NY	41	13	42	1395.3	1198	7.7	110	580	3.7	810	5.2	3.00	114	.234	.312	122	64	90	109	.980	123	183	.2	6.6	12.0	.2	2.0
CHI	59	16	27	1401.7	1305	8.4	124	470	3.0	665	4.3	3.35	109	.248	.307	68	48	97	102	.982	107	169	1.1	5.0	4.5	1.3	1.1
BOS	55	9	23	1376.7	1391	9.1	116	498	3.3	692	4.5	3.88	106	.263	.325	-13	37	109	100	.976	149	179	-1.2	3.8	1.0	.6	.7
DET	52	9	21	1417.3	1330	8.4	147	505	3.2	756	4.8	3.56	114	.250	.312	36	80	107	104	.980	121	151	.3	8.3	-6.6	-.7	-.2
BAL	44	13	25	1408.0	1272	8.1	95	493	3.2	767	4.9	3.46	101	.243	.305	50	7	93	92	.981	112	159	.8	.7	-2.1	.6	-.0
CLE	46	7	23	1380.7	1381	9.0	130	618	4.0	807	5.3	4.06	95	.260	.336	-41	-28	102	101	.974	153	154	-1.4	-2.9	.0	-.6	4.4
KC	26	6	19	1369.7	1344	8.8	153	565	3.7	626	4.1	4.19	92	.260	.329	-60	-51	102	99	.979	125	162	.1	-5.3	-5.2	.4	-7.6
WAS	31	5	16	1377.0	1482	9.7	149	580	3.8	691	4.5	4.85	79	.277	.344	-162	-153	102	95	.979	128	159	-.0	-15.8	-4.1	-1.0	-1.1
TOT	354	78	196	11126.3		8.7			3.5		4.7	3.79		.255	.328					.979	1018	1316					

Runs
Mantle-NY	121
Fox-Chi	110
Piersall-Bos	103
Sievers-Was	99

Hits
Fox-Chi	196
Malzone-Bos	185
Minoso-Chi	176
Mantle-NY	173
Kuenn-Det	173

Doubles
Minoso-Chi	36
Gardner-Bal	36
Malzone-Bos	31
Kuenn-Det	30

Triples
Simpson-KC -NY	9
McDougald-NY	9
Bauer-NY	9
Fox-Chi	8
Boyd-Bal	8

Home Runs
Sievers-Was	42
Williams-Bos	38
Mantle-NY	34
Wertz-Cle	28
Zernial-KC	27

Total Bases
Sievers-Was	331
Mantle-NY	315
Williams-Bos	307
Kaline-Det	276
Malzone-Bos	271

Runs Batted In
Sievers-Was	114
Wertz-Cle	105
Minoso-Chi	103
Malzone-Bos	103
Jensen-Bos	103

Runs Produced
Minoso-Chi	187
Mantle-NY	181
Sievers-Was	171
Malzone-Bos	170
Fox-Chi	165

Bases On Balls
Mantle-NY	146
Williams-Bos	119
Smith-Cle	79
Minoso-Chi	79
Wertz-Cle	78

Batting Average
Williams-Bos	.388
Mantle-NY	.365
Woodling-Cle	.321
Boyd-Bal	.318
Fox-Chi	.317

On Base Percentage
Williams-Bos	.528
Mantle-NY	.515
Minoso-Chi	.413
Woodling-Cle	.412
Fox-Chi	.404

Slugging Average
Williams-Bos	.731
Mantle-NY	.665
Sievers-Was	.579
Woodling-Cle	.521
Wertz-Cle	.485

Production
Williams-Bos	1.259
Mantle-NY	1.179
Sievers-Was	.968
Woodling-Cle	.933
Minoso-Chi	.867

Adjusted Production
Mantle-NY	234
Williams-Bos	219
Sievers-Was	165
Woodling-Cle	151
Minoso-Chi	138

Batter Runs
Williams-Bos	89.9
Mantle-NY	88.8
Sievers-Was	47.2
Woodling-Cle	33.0
Minoso-Chi	32.6

Adjusted Batter Runs
Mantle-NY	93.1
Williams-Bos	83.9
Sievers-Was	48.8
Minoso-Chi	33.2
Woodling-Cle	32.1

Clutch Hitting Index
Minoso-Chi	147
Malzone-Bos	136
Doby-Chi	135
Skowron-NY	133
Jensen-Bos	133

Runs Created
Mantle-NY	178
Williams-Bos	167
Sievers-Was	131
Fox-Chi	109
Minoso-Chi	106

Total Average
Williams-Bos	1.602
Mantle-NY	1.544
Sievers-Was	1.012
Woodling-Cle	.960
Minoso-Chi	.883

Stolen Bases
Aparicio-Chi	28
Rivera-Chi	18
Minoso-Chi	18
Mantle-NY	16

Stolen Base Average
Rivera-Chi	90.0
Mantle-NY	84.2
Aparicio-Chi	77.8
Minoso-Chi	54.5

Stolen Base Runs
Rivera-Chi	4.2
Aparicio-Chi	3.6
Mantle-NY	3.0
Landis-Chi	1.8
Martin-NY -KC	1.5

Fielding Runs
Fox-Chi	20.7
McDougald-NY	18.8
Klaus-Bos	17.0
Phillips-Chi	16.6
Malzone-Bos	14.1

Total Player Rating
Mantle-NY	8.1
Williams-Bos	6.7
Fox-Chi	5.3
McDougald-NY	4.6
Sievers-Was	4.1

Wins
Pierce-Chi	20
Bunning-Det	20
Sturdivant-NY	16
Donovan-Chi	16
Brewer-Bos	16

Win Percentage
Sturdivant-NY	.727
Donovan-Chi	.727
Bunning-Det	.714
Wilson-Chi	.652
Pierce-Chi	.625

Games
Zuverink-Bal	56
Hyde-Was	52
Clevenger-Was	52
Delock-Bos	49
Trucks-KC	48

Complete Games
Pierce-Chi	16
Donovan-Chi	16
Brewer-Bos	15

Shutouts
Wilson-Chi	5
Turley-NY	4
Pierce-Chi	4

Saves
Grim-NY	19
Narleski-Cle	16
Delock-Bos	11
Zuverink-Bal	9
Clevenger-Was	8

Innings Pitched
Bunning-Det	267
Wynn-Cle	263
Pierce-Chi	257
Johnson-Bal	242
Sullivan-Bos	241

Fewest Hits/Game
Turley-NY	6.14
Bunning-Det	7.21
Foytack-Det	7.43
Sturdivant-NY	7.57
Sullivan-Bos	7.69

Fewest BB/Game
Sullivan-Bos	1.79
Donovan-Chi	1.83
Shantz-NY	2.08
Loes-Bal	2.15
Bunning-Det	2.43

Strikeouts
Wynn-Cle	184
Bunning-Det	182
Johnson-Bal	177
Pierce-Chi	171
Turley-NY	152

Strikeouts/Game
Turley-NY	7.77
Johnson-Bal	6.58
Wynn-Cle	6.30
Bunning-Det	6.13
Pierce-Chi	5.99

Wins Above Team
Bunning-Det	6.6
Donovan-Chi	4.2
Narleski-Cle	3.2
Sturdivant-NY	3.1
Loes-Bal	2.8

Earned Run Average
Shantz-NY	2.45
Sturdivant-NY	2.54
Bunning-Det	2.70
Turley-NY	2.71
Sullivan-Bos	2.73

Adjusted ERA
Sullivan-Bos	151
Bunning-Det	151
Shantz-NY	140
Sturdivant-NY	134
Donovan-Chi	132

Opponents' Batting Avg.
Turley-NY	.194
Bunning-Det	.218
Foytack-Det	.226
Sullivan-Bos	.230
Sturdivant-NY	.232

Opponents' On Base Pct.
Sullivan-Bos	.272
Bunning-Det	.275
Pierce-Chi	.282
Johnson-Bal	.285
Donovan-Chi	.287

Starter Runs
Bunning-Det	32.4
Sullivan-Bos	28.4
Sturdivant-NY	28.0
Shantz-NY	25.8
Donovan-Chi	25.0

Adjusted Starter Runs
Bunning-Det	40.6
Sullivan-Bos	37.5
Donovan-Chi	21.8
Foytack-Det	21.7
Sturdivant-NY	19.6

Clutch Pitching Index
Shantz-NY	131
Sturdivant-NY	121
Narleski-Cle	111
Kemmerer-Bos-Was	110
Donovan-Chi	108

Relief Runs
Staley-Chi	20.2
Zuverink-Bal	16.6
Trucks-KC	9.8
Grim-NY	9.3
Lehman-Bal	7.6

Adjusted Relief Runs
Staley-Chi	18.6
Zuverink-Bal	13.1
Trucks-KC	10.6
Byerly-Was	7.6
Grim-NY	6.3

Relief Ranking
Grim-NY	19.5
Zuverink-Bal	19.1
Trucks-KC	14.5
Staley-Chi	12.4
Byerly-Was	9.8

Total Pitcher Index
Sullivan-Bos	4.3
Bunning-Det	4.2
Shantz-NY	2.9
Donovan-Chi	2.6
McLish-Cle	2.3

Total Baseball Ranking
Mantle-NY	8.1
Williams-Bos	6.7
Fox-Chi	5.3
McDougald-NY	4.6
Sullivan-Bos	4.3

TEAM	G	W	L	PCT	GB	R	OR	AB	H	2B	3B	HR	BB	SO	AVG	OBP	SLG	PRO	/A	BR	/A	PF	CHI	RC	TA	SB	CS	SBA	SBR
MIL	154	92	62	.597		675	541	5225	1388	221	21	167	478	646	.266	.331	.412	.743	102	13	84	89	98	705	.677	26	8	76	3
PIT	154	84	70	.545	8	662	607	5247	1386	229	68	134	396	753	.264	.319	.410	.729	98	-20	13	95	103	669	.651	30	15	67	0
SF	154	80	74	.519	12	727	698	5318	1399	250	42	170	531	817	.263	.334	.422	.756	105	37	36	100	100	747	.706	64	29	69	2
CIN	154	76	78	.494	16	695	621	5273	1359	242	40	123	572	765	.258	.333	.389	.722	97	-19	-69	107	104	690	.666	61	38	62	-4
STL	154	72	82	.468	20	619	704	5255	1371	216	39	111	533	637	.261	.331	.380	.711	94	-37	-80	106	97	638	.634	44	43	51	-12
CHI	154	72	82	.468	20	709	725	5289	1402	207	49	182	487	853	.265	.332	.426	.758	106	39	35	101	99	737	.699	39	23	63	-1
LA	154	71	83	.461	21	705	715	5173	1297	166	50	172	495	850	.251	.319	.402	.721	96	-32	-62	105	105	650	.659	73	47	61	-5
PHI	154	69	85	.448	23	664	762	5363	1424	238	56	124	573	871	.266	.341	.400	.741	102	19	31	98	92	729	.684	51	33	61	-4
TOT	616					5419		42143	11026	1769	365	1183	4065	6192	.262	.330	.405	.736								388	236	62	-24

TEAM	CG	SHO	SV	IP	H	H/G	HR	BB	BB/G	SO	SO/G	ERA	/A	OAVG	OOBA	PR	/A	PF	CPI	FA	E	DP	FW	PW	BW	SBW	DIF
MIL	72	16	17	1376.0	1261	8.2	125	426	2.8	773	5.1	3.21	107	.243	.300	113	32	87	99	.980	120	152	.8	3.2	8.5	.6	1.9
PIT	43	10	41	1367.0	1344	8.8	123	470	3.1	679	4.5	3.56	104	.260	.318	59	22	94	105	.978	133	173	.1	2.2	1.3	.3	3.0
SF	38	7	25	1389.3	1400	9.1	166	512	3.3	775	5.0	3.98	99	.262	.325	-3	-7	100	103	.975	152	156	-.9	-.7	3.6	.5	.5
CIN	50	7	20	1385.3	1422	9.2	148	419	2.7	705	4.6	3.73	112	.267	.318	34	70	106	105	.983	100	148	1.9	7.1	-7.0	-.0	-2.9
STL	45	6	25	1381.7	1398	9.1	158	567	3.7	822	5.4	4.12	104	.263	.333	-25	-23	108	102	.974	153	163	-.9	2.3	-8.1	-.9	2.6
CHI	27	5	24	1361.0	1322	8.7	142	619	4.1	805	5.3	4.22	94	.254	.332	-40	-35	101	94	.975	150	161	-.8	-3.5	3.5	.2	-4.4
LA	30	7	31	1368.3	1399	9.2	173	606	4.0	855	5.6	4.47	94	.266	.340	-79	-41	106	100	.975	146	198	-.6	-4.1	-6.3	-.2	5.1
PHI	51	6	15	1397.0	1480	9.5	148	446	2.9	778	5.0	4.32	91	.271	.322	-57	-57	100	93	.978	129	136	.3	-5.7	3.1	-.0	-5.6
TOT	356	64	198	11025.7		9.0			3.3		5.1	3.95		.262	.330					.977	1083	1287					

Runs		Hits		Doubles		Triples		Home Runs		Total Bases	
Mays-SF	121	Ashburn-Phi	215	Cepeda-SF	38	Ashburn-Phi	13	Banks-Chi	47	Banks-Chi	379
Banks-Chi	119	Mays-SF	208	Groat-Pit	36	Virdon-Pit	11	Thomas-Pit	35	Mays-SF	350
Aaron-Mil	109	Aaron-Mil	196	Musial-StL	35	Mays-SF	11	Robinson-Cin	31	Aaron-Mil	328
Boyer-StL	101	Banks-Chi	193	Anderson-Phi	34	Banks-Chi	11	Mathews-Mil	31	Cepeda-SF	309
Ashburn-Phi	98	Cepeda-SF	188	Aaron-Mil	34			Aaron-Mil	30	Thomas-Pit	297

Runs Batted In		Runs Produced		Bases On Balls		Batting Average		On Base Percentage		Slugging Average	
Banks-Chi	129	Banks-Chi	201	Ashburn-Phi	97	Ashburn-Phi	.350	Ashburn-Phi	.441	Banks-Chi	.614
Thomas-Pit	109	Mays-SF	188	Temple-Cin	91	Mays-SF	.347	Musial-StL	.426	Mays-SF	.583
Anderson-Phi	97	Aaron-Mil	174	Mathews-Mil	85	Musial-StL	.337	Mays-SF	.423	Aaron-Mil	.546
Mays-SF	96	Boyer-StL	168	Cunningham-StL	82	Aaron-Mil	.326	Temple-Cin	.406	Thomas-Pit	.528
Cepeda-SF	96	Thomas-Pit	163			Skinner-Pit	.321	Skinner-Pit	.390	Musial-StL	.528

Production		Adjusted Production		Batter Runs		Adjusted Batter Runs		Clutch Hitting Index		Runs Created	
Mays-SF	1.006	Mays-SF	163	Mays-SF	55.2	Mays-SF	55.2	Anderson-Phi	121	Mays-SF	152
Banks-Chi	.984	Aaron-Mil	161	Banks-Chi	45.6	Banks-Chi	45.3	Spencer-SF	120	Banks-Chi	135
Musial-StL	.953	Banks-Chi	154	Aaron-Mil	36.9	Aaron-Mil	45.1	Thomas-Pit	119	Ashburn-Phi	129
Aaron-Mil	.933	Musial-StL	141	Musial-StL	36.6	Ashburn-Phi	37.9	Groat-Pit	117	Aaron-Mil	121
Anderson-Phi	.900	Skinner-Pit	138	Ashburn-Phi	36.4	Musial-StL	32.6	Fernandez-Phi	115	Skinner-Pit	102

Total Average		Stolen Bases		Stolen Base Average		Stolen Base Runs		Fielding Runs		Total Player Rating	
Mays-SF	1.125	Mays-SF	31	Mays-SF	83.8	Mays-SF	5.7	Clemente-Pit	22.0	Mays-SF	6.4
Banks-Chi	.993	Ashburn-Phi	30	Blasingame-StL	80.0	Zimmer-LA	3.0	Boyer-StL	21.7	Banks-Chi	5.2
Musial-StL	.970	Taylor-Chi	21	Taylor-Chi	77.8	Blasingame-StL	3.0	Zimmer-LA	20.3	Ashburn-Phi	4.9
Ashburn-Phi	.957	Blasingame-StL	20	Ashburn-Phi	71.4	Taylor-Chi	2.7	Mazeroski-Pit	19.0	Aaron-Mil	4.6
Aaron-Mil	.918	Gilliam-LA	18	Gilliam-LA	62.1	Robinson-Cin	2.4	Ashburn-Phi	14.3	Boyer-StL	3.7

Wins		Win Percentage		Games		Complete Games		Shutouts		Saves	
Spahn-Mil	22	Spahn-Mil	.667	Elston-Chi	69	Spahn-Mil	23	Willey-Mil	4	Face-Pit	20
Friend-Pit	22	Burdette-Mil	.667	Klippstein-Cin-LA	57	Roberts-Phi	21	Witt-Pit	3	Labine-LA	14
Burdette-Mil	20	Friend-Pit	.611	Face-Pit	57	Burdette-Mil	19	Purkey-Cin	3	Farrell-Phi	11
Roberts-Phi	17	Purkey-Cin	.607	Hobbie-Chi	55	Purkey-Cin	17	Jay-Mil	3		
Purkey-Cin	17	Antonelli-SF	.552			Friend-Pit	16	Burdette-Mil	3		

Innings Pitched		Fewest Hits/Game		Fewest BB/Game		Strikeouts		Strikeouts/Game		Wins Above Team	
Spahn-Mil	290	Jones-StL	7.34	Burdette-Mil	1.64	Jones-StL	225	Jones-StL	8.10	Purkey-Cin	3.7
Burdette-Mil	275	Koufax-LA	7.47	Roberts-Phi	1.70	Spahn-Mil	150	Koufax-LA	7.42	Spahn-Mil	3.5
Friend-Pit	274	Miller-SF	7.91	Law-Pit	1.74	Podres-LA	143	Drott-Chi	6.84	Witt-Pit	3.4
Roberts-Phi	270	Spahn-Mil	7.98	Purkey-Cin	1.76	Antonelli-SF	143	Podres-LA	6.13	Roberts-Phi	3.4
		Brosnan-Chi-StL	7.98	Newcombe-LA-Cin	1.94	Friend-Pit	135	Miller-SF	5.88	Friend-Pit	3.3

Earned Run Average		Adjusted ERA		Opponents' Batting Avg.		Opponents' On Base Pct.		Starter Runs		Adjusted Starter Runs	
Miller-SF	2.47	Miller-SF	159	Koufax-LA	.220	Miller-SF	.284	Burdette-Mil	31.7	Jones-StL	38.5
Jones-StL	2.88	Jones-StL	148	Jones-StL	.223	Spahn-Mil	.285	Miller-SF	29.9	Miller-SF	29.5
Burdette-Mil	2.91	Mizell-StL	125	Miller-SF	.233	Roberts-Phi	.289	Jones-StL	29.8	Witt-Pit	24.7
Spahn-Mil	3.07	Brosnan-Chi-StL	125	Spahn-Mil	.237	Burdette-Mil	.298	Spahn-Mil	28.3	Roberts-Phi	21.5
Roberts-Phi	3.23	Roberts-Phi	122	Antonelli-SF	.239	Purkey-Cin	.300	Witt-Pit	27.5	Mizell-StL	18.1

Clutch Pitching Index		Relief Runs		Adjusted Relief Runs		Relief Ranking		Total Pitcher Index		Total Baseball Ranking	
Haddix-Cin	116	Elston-Chi	11.6	Elston-Chi	11.9	Elston-Chi	21.6	Jones-StL	3.5	Mays-SF	6.4
Newcombe-LA-Cin	115	Face-Pit	9.9	Schmidt-Cin	10.1	Farrell-Phi	11.9	Miller-SF	3.2	Banks-Chi	5.2
Mizell-StL	114	Henry-Chi	9.6	Henry-Chi	7.8	Henry-Chi	11.5	Spahn-Mil	3.2	Ashburn-Phi	4.9
Miller-SF	110	Schmidt-Cin	8.3	Face-Pit	7.6	Schmidt-Cin	10.5	Burdette-Mil	2.6	Aaron-Mil	4.6
Podres-LA	109	Porterfield-Pit	6.6	Farrell-Phi	6.3	Face-Pit	9.8	Witt-Pit	2.5	Boyer-StL	3.7

TEAM	G	W	L	PCT	GB	R	OR	AB	H	2B	3B	HR	BB	SO	AVG	OBP	SLG	PRO	/A	BR	/A	PF	CHI	RC	TA	SB	CS	SBA	SBR
NY	155	92	62	.597		759	577	5294	1418	212	39	164	537	822	.268	.338	.416	.754	113	88	69	103	101	746	.700	48	32	60	-4
CHI	155	82	72	.532	10	634	615	5249	1348	191	42	101	518	669	.257	.329	.367	.696	97	-12	0	98	98	647	.640	101	33	75	11
BOS	155	79	75	.513	13	697	691	5218	1335	229	30	109	638	820	.256	.340	.400	.740	106	70	37	105	95	708	.686	29	22	57	-4
CLE	153	77	76	.503	14.5	694	635	5201	1340	210	31	161	494	819	.258	.327	.403	.730	106	38	74	94	101	677	.666	50	49	51	-13
DET	154	77	77	.500	15	659	606	5194	1384	229	41	109	463	678	.266	.329	.389	.718	103	20	-4	104	99	657	.644	48	32	60	-4
BAL	154	74	79	.484	17.5	521	575	5111	1233	195	19	108	483	731	.241	.310	.350	.660	87	-84	-46	94	95	546	.577	33	35	49	-10
KC	156	73	81	.474	19	642	713	5261	1297	196	50	138	452	747	.247	.309	.381	.690	95	-39	-74	106	106	601	.606	22	36	38	-14
WAS	156	61	93	.396	31	553	747	5156	1240	161	38	121	477	751	.240	.309	.357	.666	89	-77	-55	97	99	555	.580	22	41	35	-17
TOT	619					5159		41684	10595	1623	290	1057	4062	6037	.254	.324	.383	.707								353	280	56	-61

TEAM	CG	SHO	SV	IP	H	H/G	HR	BB	BB/G	SO	SO/G	ERA	/A	OAVG	OOBA	PR	/A	PF	CPI	FA	E	DP	FW	PW	BW	SBW	DIF
NY	53	21	33	1379.0	1201	7.8	116	557	3.6	796	5.2	3.22	116	.234	.311	84	79	99	103	.978	128	182	-.2	8.2	7.1	.4	-.5
CHI	55	15	25	1389.7	1296	8.4	152	515	3.3	751	4.9	3.61	102	.249	.313	25	11	98	104	.981	114	160	.6	1.1	.0	1.9	1.3
BOS	44	5	28	1380.0	1396	9.1	121	521	3.4	695	4.5	3.92	101	.264	.327	-23	4	105	102	.976	145	172	-1.1	.4	3.8	.4	-1.5
CLE	51	2	20	1373.3	1423	9.3	124	604	4.0	766	5.0	3.73	94	.248	.324	6	-32	93	101	.974	152	171	-1.5	-3.3	7.6	-.5	-1.8
DET	59	8	19	1357.3	1294	8.6	133	437	2.9	797	5.3	3.59	108	.252	.310	26	42	103	101	.982	106	140	1.1	4.3	-.4	.4	-5.4
BAL	55	15	28	1369.7	1277	8.4	106	403	2.6	749	4.9	3.40	106	.249	.301	56	28	95	97	.980	114	159	.6	2.9	-4.8	-.2	-1.0
KC	42	9	25	1398.3	1405	9.0	150	467	3.0	721	4.6	4.15	97	.261	.319	-59	-18	107	95	.979	125	166	.0	-1.9	-7.6	-.6	6.1
WAS	28	6	28	1376.7	1443	9.4	156	558	3.6	762	5.0	4.53	84	.271	.337	-116	-114	100	98	.980	118	163	.4	-11.8	-5.7	-1.0	2.0
TOT	387	81	206	11024.0		8.6			3.3		4.9	3.77		.254	.324					.979	1002	1313					

Runs
Mantle-NY 127
Runnels-Bos 103
Power-KC -Cle 98
Minoso-Cle 94
Cerv-KC 93

Hits
Fox-Chi 187
Malzone-Bos 185
Power-KC -Cle 184
Runnels-Bos 183
Kuenn-Det 179

Doubles
Kuenn-Det 39
Power-KC -Cle 37
Kaline-Det 34
Runnels-Bos 32
Jensen-Bos 31

Triples
Power-KC -Cle 10
Tuttle-KC 9
Lemon-Was 9
Aparicio-Chi 9
Harris-Det 8

Home Runs
Mantle-NY 42
Colavito-Cle 41
Sievers-Was 39
Cerv-KC 38
Jensen-Bos 35

Total Bases
Mantle-NY 307
Cerv-KC 305
Colavito-Cle 303
Sievers-Was 299
Jensen-Bos 293

Runs Batted In
Jensen-Bos 122
Colavito-Cle 113
Sievers-Was 108
Cerv-KC 104
Mantle-NY 97

Runs Produced
Mantle-NY 182
Jensen-Bos 170
Power-KC -Cle 162
Cerv-KC 159

Bases On Balls
Mantle-NY 129
Jensen-Bos 99
Williams-Bos 98
Runnels-Bos 87
Colavito-Cle 84

Batting Average
Williams-Bos 328
Runnels-Bos 322
Kuenn-Det 319
Kaline-Det 313
Power-KC -Cle 312

On Base Percentage
Williams-Bos 462
Mantle-NY 445
Runnels-Bos 418
Colavito-Cle 407
Jensen-Bos 398

Slugging Average
Colavito-Cle 620
Cerv-KC 592
Mantle-NY 592
Williams-Bos 584
Sievers-Was 544

Production
Williams-Bos 1.046
Mantle-NY 1.036
Colavito-Cle 1.027
Cerv-KC 964
Jensen-Bos 933

Adjusted Production
Colavito-Cle 189
Mantle-NY 177
Williams-Bos 177
Cerv-KC 152
Sievers-Was 150

Batter Runs
Mantle-NY 64.2
Williams-Bos 53.6
Colavito-Cle 52.8
Jensen-Bos 42.6
Cerv-KC 40.7

Adjusted Batter Runs
Mantle-NY 62.2
Colavito-Cle 56.3
Williams-Bos 50.8
Jensen-Bos 39.1
Cerv-KC 37.2

Clutch Hitting Index
Courtney-Was 142
Lollar-Chi 137
Jensen-Bos 130
Skowron-NY 125
Harris-Det 120

Runs Created
Mantle-NY 147
Colavito-Cle 122
Jensen-Bos 120
Williams-Bos 112
Runnels-Bos 107

Total Average
Mantle-NY 1.216
Williams-Bos 1.163
Colavito-Cle 1.084
Jensen-Bos 990
Cerv-KC 955

Stolen Bases
Aparicio-Chi 29
Rivera-Chi 21
Landis-Chi 19
Mantle-NY 18
Minoso-Cle 14

Stolen Base Average
Rivera-Chi 87.5
Mantle-NY 85.7
Aparicio-Chi 82.9
Landis-Chi 73.1

Stolen Base Runs
Aparicio-Chi 5.1
Rivera-Chi 4.5
Mantle-NY 3.6
Wilson-Det 3.0

Fielding Runs
Kaline-Det 22.8
Kubek-NY 20.3
Malzone-Bos 16.4
Aparicio-Chi 14.1
Buddin-Bos 13.6

Total Player Rating
Colavito-Cle 5.3
Mantle-NY 5.1
Runnels-Bos 3.9
Kaline-Det 3.8
Jensen-Bos 3.4

Wins
Turley-NY 21
Pierce-Chi 17
McLish-Cle 16
Lary-Det 16

Win Percentage
Turley-NY 750
McLish-Cle 667
Pierce-Chi 607
Portocarrero-Bal 577
Foytack-Det 536

Games
Clevenger-Was 55
Tomanek-Cle-KC 54
Hyde-Was 53
Wall-Bos 52

Complete Games
Turley-NY 19
Pierce-Chi 19
Lary-Det 19
Harshman-Bal 17

Shutouts
Ford-NY 7
Turley-NY 6
Wynn-Chi 4
Ramos-Was 4
Donovan-Chi 4

Saves
Duren-NY 20
Hyde-Was 18
Kiely-Bos 12
Wall-Bos 10

Innings Pitched
Lary-Det 260
Ramos-Was 259
Donovan-Chi 248
Turley-NY 245
Pierce-Chi 245

Fewest Hits/Game
Turley-NY 6.54
Bell-Cle 6.97
Ford-NY 7.15
Pierce-Chi 7.49
Portocarrero-Bal 7.60

Fewest BB/Game
Donovan-Chi 1.92
O'Dell-Bal 2.08
Sullivan-Bos 2.22
Lary-Det 2.35
Pierce-Chi 2.42

Strikeouts
Wynn-Chi 179
Bunning-Det 177
Turley-NY 168
Harshman-Bal 161
Pascual-Was 146

Strikeouts/Game
Pascual-Was 7.42
Bunning-Det 7.24
Wynn-Chi 6.71
Turley-NY 6.17
Harshman-Bal 6.14

Wins Above Team
Turley-NY 6.0
McLish-Cle 4.4
Hyde-Was 4.2
Delock-Bos 3.1
Portocarrero-Bal 2.7

Earned Run Average
Ford-NY 2.01
Pierce-Chi 2.68
Harshman-Bal 2.90
Lary-Det 2.91
O'Dell-Bal 2.97

Adjusted ERA
Ford-NY 186
Bell-Cle 137
Lary-Det 133
Turley-NY 126
Harshman-Bal 124

Opponents' Batting Avg.
Turley-NY 206
Bell-Cle 213
Ford-NY 217
Pierce-Chi 227
Grant-Cle 228

Opponents' On Base Pct.
Ford-NY 274
Pierce-Chi 276
O'Dell-Bal 280
Portocarrero-Bal 282
Harshman-Bal 289

Starter Runs
Ford-NY 42.7
Pierce-Chi 29.6
Lary-Det 24.9
Harshman-Bal 22.8
Turley-NY 21.6

Adjusted Starter Runs
Ford-NY 42.0
Lary-Det 28.0
Pierce-Chi 27.2
Turley-NY 20.8
Donovan-Chi 18.5

Clutch Pitching Index
McLish-Cle 121
Ford-NY 117
Pierce-Chi 114
Lary-Det 113
Wilson-Chi 110

Relief Runs
Hyde-Was 23.1
Duren-NY 14.8
Kiely-Bos 6.9
Staley-Chi 5.6
Morgan-Det 4.4

Adjusted Relief Runs
Hyde-Was 23.3
Duren-NY 14.6
Kiely-Bos 8.6
Daley-KC 5.8
Gorman-KC 5.3

Relief Ranking
Hyde-Was 35.6
Duren-NY 25.9
Kiely-Bos 9.5
Wall-Bos 6.2
Staley-Chi 5.6

Total Pitcher Index
Ford-NY 5.1
Harshman-Bal 3.1
Lary-Det 2.9
Pierce-Chi 2.8
Hyde-Was 2.5

Total Baseball Ranking
Colavito-Cle 5.5
Mantle-NY 5.1
Ford-NY 5.1
Runnels-Bos 3.9
Kaline-Det 3.8

TEAM	G	W	L	PCT	GB	R	OR	AB	H	2B	3B	HR	BB	SO	AVG	OBP	SLG	PRO	/A	BR	/A	PF	CHI	RC	TA	SB	CS	SBA	SBR
LA	156	88	68	.564		705	670	5282	1360	196	46	148	591	891	.257	.335	.396	.731	101	16	4	102	99	706	.684	84	51	62	-4
MIL	157	86	70	.551	2	724	623	5388	1426	216	36	177	488	765	.265	.329	.417	.746	105	31	66	95	100	729	.682	41	14	75	4
SF	154	83	71	.539	4	705	613	5281	1377	239	35	167	473	875	.261	.324	.414	.738	102	15	46	95	101	711	.686	81	34	70	4
PIT	155	78	76	.506	9	651	680	5369	1414	230	42	112	442	715	.263	.322	.384	.706	94	-40	-61	103	100	653	.624	32	26	55	-5
CIN	154	74	80	.481	13	764	738	5288	1448	258	34	161	499	763	.274	.340	.427	.767	111	75	53	103	100	764	.715	65	28	70	3
CHI	155	74	80	.481	13	673	688	5296	1321	209	44	163	498	911	.249	.319	.398	.717	97	-23	-12	98	101	673	.654	32	19	63	-1
STL	154	71	83	.461	16	641	725	5317	1432	244	49	118	485	747	.269	.333	.400	.733	102	13	-18	105	92	699	.667	65	53	55	-11
PHI	155	64	90	.416	23	599	725	5109	1237	196	48	113	498	858	.242	.314	.362	.676	86	-92	-88	99	105	574	.600	39	46	46	-15
TOT	620					5462		42330	11015	1788	324	1159	3974	6525	.260	.327	.400	.728								439	271	62	-30

TEAM	CG	SHO	SV	IP	H	H/G	HR	BB	BB/G	SO	SO/G	ERA	/A	OAVG	OOBA	PR	/A	PF	CPI	FA	E	DP	FW	PW	BW	SBW	DIF
LA	43	14	26	1411.7	1317	8.4	157	614	3.9	1077	6.9	3.79	105	.247	.325	24	30	103	101	.981	114	154	1.4	3.0	.4	-.0	5.2
MIL	69	18	18	1400.7	1406	9.0	128	429	2.8	775	5.0	3.51	105	.260	.312	68	25	93	104	.979	127	138	.7	2.5	6.6	.8	-2.6
SF	52	12	23	1376.3	1279	8.4	139	500	3.3	873	5.7	3.47	106	.245	.309	73	34	94	103	.974	152	118	-.7	3.4	4.6	.8	-2.1
PIT	48	7	17	1393.3	1432	9.2	134	418	2.7	730	4.7	3.90	105	.267	.315	7	29	104	100	.975	154	165	-.8	2.9	-6.1	-.1	5.2
CIN	44	7	26	1357.3	1460	9.7	162	456	3.0	690	4.3	4.31	94	.275	.331	-54	-38	103	102	.978	126	157	.7	-3.8	5.3	.7	-5.9
CHI	30	11	25	1391.0	1337	8.7	152	519	3.4	765	4.9	4.01	97	.253	.317	-9	-17	99	96	.977	140	142	-.0	-1.7	-1.2	.3	-.3
STL	36	8	21	1363.0	1427	9.4	137	564	3.7	846	5.6	4.34	97	.270	.337	-59	-21	106	100	.975	146	158	-.4	-2.1	-1.8	-.7	-1.0
PHI	54	8	15	1354.0	1357	9.0	150	474	3.2	769	5.1	4.27	94	.261	.319	-49	-38	102	93	.973	154	132	-.8	-3.8	-8.8	-1.1	1.6
TOT	376	85	171	11047.3		9.0			3.2		5.3	3.95		.260	.327					.977	1113	1164					

Runs
Pinson-Cin 131
Mays-SF 125
Mathews-Mil 118
Aaron-Mil 116
Robinson-Cin 106

Hits
Aaron-Mil 223
Pinson-Cin 205
Cepeda-SF 192
Temple-Cin 186
Mathews-Mil 182

Doubles
Pinson-Cin 47
Aaron-Mil 46
Mays-SF 43
Cimoli-StL 40

Triples
Neal-LA 11
Moon-LA 11
White-StL 9
Pinson-Cin 9
Dark-Chi 9

Home Runs
Mathews-Mil 46
Banks-Chi 45
Aaron-Mil 39
Robinson-Cin 36
Mays-SF 34

Total Bases
Aaron-Mil 400
Mathews-Mil 352
Banks-Chi 351
Mays-SF 335
Pinson-Cin 330

Runs Batted In
Banks-Chi 143
Robinson-Cin 125
Aaron-Mil 123
Bell-Cin 115
Mathews-Mil 114

Runs Produced
Aaron-Mil 200
Robinson-Cin 195
Pinson-Cin 195
Mays-SF 195
Banks-Chi 195

Bases On Balls
Gilliam-LA 96
Cunningham-StL 88
Moon-LA 81
Mathews-Mil 80
Ashburn-Phi 79

Batting Average
Aaron-Mil 355
Cunningham-StL 345
Cepeda-SF 317
Pinson-Cin 316
Mays-SF 313

On Base Percentage
Cunningham-StL 456
Aaron-Mil 406
Robinson-Cin 397
Moon-LA 396
Mathews-Mil 391

Slugging Average
Aaron-Mil 636
Banks-Chi 596
Mathews-Mil 593
Robinson-Cin 583
Mays-SF 583

Production
Aaron-Mil 1.042
Mathews-Mil 984
Robinson-Cin 980
Banks-Chi 975
Mays-SF 967

Adjusted Production
Aaron-Mil 181
Mathews-Mil 166
Mays-SF 160
Banks-Chi 157
Robinson-Cin 152

Batter Runs
Aaron-Mil 62.7
Mathews-Mil 48.2
Banks-Chi 44.3
Robinson-Cin 43.9
Mays-SF 42.4

Adjusted Batter Runs
Aaron-Mil 66.7
Mathews-Mil 52.2
Mays-SF 46.0
Banks-Chi 45.5
Robinson-Cin 41.7

Clutch Hitting Index
Bell-Cin 156
Post-Phi 138
Mazeroski-Pit 129
Robinson-Cin 127
Banks-Chi 126

Runs Created
Aaron-Mil 156
Mathews-Mil 143
Mays-SF 131
Banks-Chi 126
Pinson-Cin 124

Total Average
Aaron-Mil 1.089
Mays-SF 1.046
Mathews-Mil 1.043
Robinson-Cin 1.035
Cunningham-StL 997

Stolen Bases
Mays-SF 27
A.Taylor-Chi 23
Gilliam-LA 23
Cepeda-SF 23
Pinson-Cin 21

Stolen Base Average
Mays-SF 87.1
Pinson-Cin 77.8
Neal-LA 73.9
A.Taylor-Chi 71.9
Cepeda-SF 71.9

Stolen Base Runs
Mays-SF 5.7
Pinson-Cin 2.7
Temple-Cin 2.4
Aaron-Mil 2.4
Cimoli-StL 2.1

Fielding Runs
Crandall-Mil 24.8
Neal-LA 18.5
Bailey-Cin 18.4
Blasingame-StL 18.2
Virdon-Pit 17.0

Total Player Rating
Aaron-Mil 6.3
Banks-Chi 5.3
Mathews-Mil 5.0
Mays-SF 4.9
Neal-LA 3.8

Wins
Spahn-Mil 21
Jones-SF 21
Burdette-Mil 21
Antonelli-SF 19

Win Percentage
Face-Pit 947
Law-Pit 667
Antonelli-SF 655
Buhl-Mil 625

Games
Henry-Chi 65
Elston-Chi 65
McDaniel-StL 62
McMahon-Mil 60
Miller-SF 59

Complete Games
Spahn-Mil 21
Law-Pit 20
Burdette-Mil 20
Roberts-Phi 19

Shutouts
7 tied with 4

Saves
McMahon-Mil 15
McDaniel-StL 15
Elston-Chi 13
Henry-Chi 12

Innings Pitched
Spahn-Mil 292
Burdette-Mil 290
Antonelli-SF 282
Jones-SF 271
Drysdale-LA 271

Fewest Hits/Game
Haddix-Pit 7.59
Jones-SF 7.70
Hobbie-Chi 7.85
Drysdale-LA 7.87
Antonelli-SF 7.88

Fewest BB/Game
Newcombe-Cin 1.09
Burdette-Mil 1.18
Roberts-Phi 1.23
Purkey-Cin 1.78
Law-Pit 1.79

Strikeouts
Drysdale-LA 242
Jones-SF 209
Koufax-LA 173
Antonelli-SF 165
McCormick-SF 151

Strikeouts/Game
Drysdale-LA 8.04
Jones-SF 6.94
Podres-LA 6.69
Broglio-StL 6.61
McCormick-SF 6.01

Wins Above Team
Face-Pit 8.6
Law-Pit 5.0
Antonelli-SF 4.3
Conley-Phi 3.8
Newcombe-Cin 3.1

Earned Run Average
Jones-SF 2.82
Miller-SF 2.84
Buhl-Mil 2.86
Spahn-Mil 2.96
Law-Pit 2.98

Adjusted ERA
Law-Pit 137
Conley-Phi 134
Jones-SF 131
Haddix-Pit 130
Miller-SF 130

Opponents' Batting Avg.
Jones-SF 228
Haddix-Pit 228
Antonelli-SF 233
Drysdale-LA 233
Conley-Phi 235

Opponents' On Base Pct.
Haddix-Pit 268
Newcombe-Cin 276
Law-Pit 278
Conley-Phi 278
Antonelli-SF 283

Starter Runs
Jones-SF 33.9
Craig-LA 32.1
Spahn-Mil 32.1
Law-Pit 28.7
Antonelli-SF 26.7

Adjusted Starter Runs
Law-Pit 32.9
Craig-LA 32.8
Jones-SF 26.1
Jackson-StL 25.3
Haddix-Pit 23.8

Clutch Pitching Index
Miller-SF 135
Buhl-Mil 120
Spahn-Mil 105
Jones-SF 104
Jackson-StL 104

Relief Runs
Miller-SF 20.7
Henry-Chi 18.8
Face-Pit 12.8
McMahon-Mil 12.5
Elston-Chi 7.0

Adjusted Relief Runs
Henry-Chi 18.0
Miller-SF 15.9
Face-Pit 14.3
McMahon-Mil 10.0
Meyer-Phi 7.0

Relief Ranking
Face-Pit 29.7
Henry-Chi 24.2
Miller-SF 14.5
McMahon-Mil 13.1
Elston-Chi 12.5

Total Pitcher Index
Law-Pit 3.7
Craig-LA 3.0
Spahn-Mil 2.9
Haddix-Pit 2.5
Conley-Phi 2.4

Total Baseball Ranking
Aaron-Mil 6.3
Banks-Chi 5.3
Mathews-Mil 5.0
Mays-SF 4.9
Neal-LA 3.8

TEAM	G	W	L	PCT	GB	R	OR	AB	H	2B	3B	HR	BB	SO	AVG	OBP	SLG	PRO	/A	BR	/A	PF	CHI	RC	TA	SB	CS	SBA	SBR
CHI	156	94	60	.610		669	588	5297	1325	220	46	97	580	634	.250	.330	.364	.694	96	-19	3	97	99	653	.646	113	53	68	2
CLE	154	89	65	.578	5	745	646	5288	1390	216	25	167	433	721	.263	.323	.408	.731	106	32	55	97	106	682	.657	33	36	48	-11
NY	155	79	75	.513	15	687	647	5379	1397	224	40	153	457	828	.260	.321	.402	.723	103	17	67	93	98	695	.656	45	22	67	0
DET	154	76	78	.494	18	713	732	5211	1346	196	30	160	580	737	.258	.338	.400	.738	108	57	-16	111	97	720	.688	34	17	67	0
BOS	154	75	79	.487	19	726	696	5225	1335	248	28	125	626	810	.256	.338	.385	.723	104	36	-2	106	101	697	.677	68	25	73	5
BAL	155	74	80	.481	20	551	621	5208	1240	182	23	109	536	690	.238	.312	.345	.657	86	-95	-74	97	95	563	.580	36	24	60	-3
KC	154	66	88	.429	28	681	760	5264	1383	231	43	117	481	780	.263	.328	.390	.718	102	15	6	101	99	669	.645	34	24	59	-3
WAS	154	63	91	.409	31	619	701	5092	1205	173	32	163	517	881	.237	.310	.379	.689	94	-42	-42	100	101	594	.624	51	33	61	-4
TOT	618					5391		41964	10621	1690	267	1091	4210	6081	.253	.325	.384	.709								414	234	64	-15

TEAM	CG	SHO	SV	IP	H	H/G	HR	BB	BB/G	SO	SO/G	ERA	/A	OAVG	OOBA	PR	/A	PF	CPI	FA	E	DP	FW	PW	BW	SBW	DIF
CHI	44	13	36	1425.3	1297	8.2	129	525	3.3	761	4.8	3.29	112	.242	.307	90	61	95	106	.979	130	141	.5	6.2	.3	.4	9.6
CLE	58	7	23	1383.7	1230	8.0	148	635	4.1	799	5.2	3.75	98	.239	.318	17	-13	95	101	.978	127	138	.7	-1.3	5.6	-.9	8.0
NY	38	15	28	1399.0	1281	8.2	120	594	3.8	836	5.4	3.60	98	.244	.318	40	-8	92	102	.978	131	160	.5	-.8	6.8	.2	-4.6
DET	53	9	24	1360.0	1327	8.8	177	432	2.9	829	5.5	4.20	102	.253	.311	-51	13	111	94	.978	124	131	.9	1.3	-1.6	.2	-1.8
BOS	38	9	25	1364.0	1386	9.1	135	589	3.9	724	4.8	4.17	97	.265	.336	-46	-16	105	104	.978	131	167	.5	-1.6	-.2	.7	-1.4
BAL	45	15	30	1400.3	1290	8.3	111	476	3.1	735	4.7	3.56	107	.246	.306	46	36	98	96	.976	146	163	-.4	3.6	-7.5	-.0	1.4
KC	44	8	21	1361.0	1452	9.6	148	492	3.3	703	4.6	4.35	91	.273	.333	-74	-58	103	102	.973	160	156	-1.2	-5.9	.6	-.0	-4.4
WAS	46	10	21	1360.0	1358	9.0	123	467	3.1	694	4.6	4.01	98	.259	.317	-22	-13	102	96	.973	162	140	-1.4	-1.3	-4.3	-.2	-6.9
TOT	366	86	208	11053.3		8.6			3.4		5.0	3.86		.253	.325					.977	1111	1196					

Runs
Yost-Det 115
Mantle-NY 104
Power-Cle 102
Jensen-Bos 101
Kuenn-Det 99

Hits
Kuenn-Det 198
Fox-Chi 191
Runnels-Bos 176
Power-Cle 172
Minoso-Cle 172

Doubles
Kuenn-Det 42
Malzone-Bos 34
Fox-Chi 34
Williams-KC 33
Runnels-Bos 33

Triples
Allison-Was 9
McDougald-NY 8

Home Runs
Killebrew-Was 42
Colavito-Cle 42
Lemon-Was 33
Maxwell-Det 31
Mantle-NY 31

Total Bases
Colavito-Cle 301
Killebrew-Was 282
Kuenn-Det 281
Mantle-NY 278
Allison-Was 275

Runs Batted In
Jensen-Bos 112
Colavito-Cle 111
Killebrew-Was 105
Lemon-Was 100
Maxwell-Det 95

Runs Produced
Jensen-Bos 185
Minoso-Cle 163
Malzone-Bos 163
Kuenn-Det 161
Killebrew-Was 161

Bases On Balls
Yost-Det 135
Runnels-Bos 95
Mantle-NY 94
Buddin-Bos 92
Killebrew-Was 90

Batting Average
Kuenn-Det 353
Kaline-Det 327
Runnels-Bos 314
Fox-Chi 306
Minoso-Cle 302

On Base Percentage
Yost-Det 437
Runnels-Bos 415
Kaline-Det 414
Woodling-Bal 405
Kuenn-Det 405

Slugging Average
Kaline-Det 530
Killebrew-Was 516
Mantle-NY 514
Colavito-Cle 512
Lemon-Was 510

Production
Kaline-Det 944
Mantle-NY 906
Kuenn-Det 906
Yost-Det 873
Killebrew-Was 873

Adjusted Production
Mantle-NY 158
Kaline-Det 142
Woodling-Bal 140
Killebrew-Was 136
Minoso-Cle 136

Batter Runs
Kaline-Det 41.6
Yost-Det 37.8
Francona-Cle 36.6
Mantle-NY 36.3
Kuenn-Det 36.2

Adjusted Batter Runs
Mantle-NY 41.7
Francona-Cle 38.4
Kaline-Det 34.3
Yost-Det 29.5
Kuenn-Det 28.6

Clutch Hitting Index
Strickland-Cle 136
Jensen-Bos 135
Woodling-Bal 125
Cerv-KC 124
Williams-KC 120

Runs Created
Mantle-NY 118
Kuenn-Det 117
Yost-Det 115
Kaline-Det 114
Killebrew-Was 103

Total Average
Yost-Det 997
Mantle-NY 995
Kaline-Det 994
Kuenn-Det 908
Jensen-Bos 900

Stolen Bases
Aparicio-Chi 56
Mantle-NY 21
Landis-Chi 20
Jensen-Bos 20
Allison-Was 13

Stolen Base Average
Mantle-NY 87.5
Aparicio-Chi 81.2
Jensen-Bos 80.0
Landis-Chi 69.0

Stolen Base Runs
Aparicio-Chi 9.0
Mantle-NY 4.5
Jensen-Bos 3.0
Malzone-Bos 1.8
Yost-Det 1.5

Fielding Runs
Gardner-Bal 15.4
Minoso-Cle 11.8
Jensen-Bos 11.1
Landis-Chi 8.9
Malzone-Bos 8.0

Total Player Rating
Mantle-NY 4.1
Francona-Cle 4.0
Runnels-Bos 3.5
Kaline-Det 3.2
Jensen-Bos 3.1

Wins
Wynn-Chi 22
McLish-Cle 19
Shaw-Chi 18

Win Percentage
Shaw-Chi 750
McLish-Cle 704
Wynn-Chi 688
Mossi-Det 654

Games
Staley-Chi 67
Lown-Chi 60
Clevenger-Was 50
Shaw-Chi 47

Complete Games
Pascual-Was 17
Pappas-Bal 15
Mossi-Det 15
Wynn-Chi 14
Bunning-Det 14

Shutouts
Pascual-Was 6
Wynn-Chi 5
Pappas-Bal 4

Saves
Lown-Chi 15
Staley-Chi 14
Loes-Bal 14
Duren-NY 14
Fornieles-Bos 11

Innings Pitched
Wynn-Chi 256
Bunning-Det 250
Foytack-Det 240
Pascual-Was 239
McLish-Cle 235

Fewest Hits/Game
Score-Cle 6.88
Ditmar-NY 6.95
Wilhelm-Bal 7.09
Wynn-Chi 7.10
O'Dell-Bal 7.37

Fewest BB/Game
Brown-Bal 1.76
Lary-Det 1.86
Garver-KC 1.88
Mossi-Det 1.93
Ramos-Was 2.00

Strikeouts
Bunning-Det 201
Pascual-Was 185
Wynn-Chi 179
Score-Cle 147
Wilhelm-Bal 139

Strikeouts/Game
Score-Cle 8.22
Bunning-Det 7.24
Pascual-Was 6.97
Turley-NY 6.49
Wynn-Chi 6.29

Wins Above Team
Pascual-Was 5.7
Shaw-Chi 4.8
Mossi-Det 4.7
McLish-Cle 4.6
Lary-Det 4.2

Earned Run Average
Wilhelm-Bal 2.19
Pascual-Was 2.64
Shaw-Chi 2.69
Ditmar-NY 2.90
Walker-Bal 2.92

Adjusted ERA
Wilhelm-Bal 173
Pascual-Was 149
Shaw-Chi 137
Walker-Bal 130
O'Dell-Bal 129

Opponents' Batting Avg.
Score-Cle 210
Ditmar-NY 211
Wynn-Chi 216
O'Dell-Bal 220
Wilhelm-Bal 224

Opponents' On Base Pct.
Ditmar-NY 267
Pascual-Was 278
O'Dell-Bal 280
Mossi-Det 283
Brown-Bal 283

Starter Runs
Wilhelm-Bal 42.0
Pascual-Was 32.5
Shaw-Chi 30.1
Ditmar-NY 21.7
Perry-Cle 20.6

Adjusted Starter Runs
Wilhelm-Bal 40.3
Pascual-Was 34.2
Shaw-Chi 25.3
Mossi-Det 23.7
Daley-KC 19.2

Clutch Pitching Index
Wilhelm-Bal 132
Daley-KC 122
Ford-NY 119
Shaw-Chi 115
McLish-Cle 114

Relief Runs
Staley-Chi 20.8
Duren-NY 17.0
Shantz-NY 15.8
Coates-NY 10.9
Lown-Chi 9.9

Adjusted Relief Runs
Staley-Chi 18.4
Duren-NY 14.4
Shantz-NY 12.5
Stobbs-Was 9.7
Fornieles-Bos 9.0

Relief Ranking
Staley-Chi 23.5
Duren-NY 21.0
Shantz-NY 12.7
Lown-Chi 11.4
Fornieles-Bos 10.6

Total Pitcher Index
Pascual-Was 5.0
Wilhelm-Bal 3.6
Mossi-Det 2.6
Shaw-Chi 2.5
Daley-KC 2.5

Total Baseball Ranking
Pascual-Was 5.0
Mantle-NY 4.1
Francona-Cle 4.0
Wilhelm-Bal 3.6
Runnels-Bos 3.5

TEAM	G	W	L	PCT	GB	R	OR	AB	H	2B	3B	HR	BB	SO	AVG	OBP	SLG	PRO	/A	BR	/A	PF	CHI	RC	TA	SB	CS	SBA	SBR
PIT	155	95	59	.617		734	593	5406	1493	236	56	120	486	747	.276	.338	.407	.745	110	72	76	99	98	737	.676	34	24	59	-3
MIL	154	88	66	.571	7	724	658	5263	1393	198	48	170	463	793	.265	.327	.417	.744	109	59	119	91	101	714	.687	69	37	65	-1
STL	155	86	68	.558	9	639	616	5187	1317	213	48	138	501	792	.254	.323	.393	.716	102	13	-39	108	97	652	.651	48	35	58	-6
LA	154	82	72	.532	13	662	593	5227	1333	216	38	126	529	837	.255	.327	.383	.710	100	5	-95	115	99	659	.655	95	53	64	-2
SF	156	79	75	.513	16	671	631	5324	1357	220	62	130	467	846	.255	.319	.393	.712	100	0	68	90	101	663	.650	86	45	66	0
CIN	154	67	87	.435	28	640	692	5289	1324	230	40	140	512	858	.250	.320	.388	.708	99	-1	10	98	97	661	.650	73	37	66	0
CHI	156	60	94	.390	35	634	776	5311	1293	213	48	119	531	897	.243	.314	.369	.683	93	-48	-34	98	103	617	.615	51	34	60	-4
PHI	154	59	95	.383	36	546	691	5169	1235	196	44	99	448	1054	.239	.304	.351	.655	85	-101	-147	107	101	546	.573	45	48	48	-14
TOT	619					5250		42176	10745	1722	384	1042	3937	6824	.255	.322	.388	.710								501	313	62	-37

TEAM	CG	SHO	SV	IP	H	H/G	HR	BB	BB/G	SO	SO/G	ERA	/A	OAVG	OOBA	PR	/A	PF	CPI	FA	E	DP	FW	PW	BW	SBW	DIF
PIT	47	11	33	1399.7	1363	8.8	105	386	2.5	811	5.2	3.49	104	.257	.303	42	22	97	99	.979	128	163	.7	2.3	7.8	.2	7.1
MIL	55	13	28	1387.3	1327	8.6	130	518	3.4	807	5.2	3.76	89	.251	.316	0	-62	89	99	.976	141	137	-.0	-6.4	12.2	.4	4.8
STL	37	11	30	1371.0	1316	8.6	127	511	3.4	906	5.9	3.64	111	.253	.316	18	62	108	103	.976	141	152	-.0	6.4	-4.0	-.1	6.8
LA	46	13	20	1398.0	1218	7.8	154	564	3.6	1122	7.2	3.40	126	.233	.308	56	137	114	103	.979	125	142	.9	14.1	-9.8	.3	-.5
SF	55	16	26	1396.0	1288	8.3	107	512	3.3	897	5.8	3.44	97	.245	.308	49	-16	89	99	.972	166	117	-1.4	-1.6	7.0	.5	-2.4
CIN	33	8	35	1390.3	1417	9.2	134	442	2.9	740	4.8	4.00	93	.267	.321	-36	-41	99	101	.979	125	155	.9	-4.2	1.0	.5	-8.1
CHI	36	6	25	1402.7	1393	8.9	152	565	3.6	805	5.2	4.35	87	.260	.329	-91	-88	101	96	.977	143	133	-.1	-9.1	-3.5	.0	-4.4
PHI	45	6	16	1375.3	1423	9.3	133	439	2.9	736	4.8	4.01	103	.269	.320	-38	20	110	101	.974	155	129	-.8	2.1	-15.1	-1.0	-3.2
TOT	354	84	213	11120.3		8.7			3.2		5.5	3.76		.255	.322					.977	1124	1128					

Runs
Bruton-Mil 112
Mathews-Mil 108
Pinson-Cin 107
Mays-SF 107
Aaron-Mil 102

Hits
Mays-SF 190
Pinson-Cin 187
Groat-Pit 186
Bruton-Mil 180
Clemente-Pit 179

Doubles
Pinson-Cin 37
Cepeda-SF 36
Skinner-Pit 33
Robinson-Cin 33
Banks-Chi 32

Triples
Bruton-Mil 13
Pinson-Cin 12
Mays-SF 12
Aaron-Mil 11

Home Runs
Banks-Chi 41
Aaron-Mil 40
Mathews-Mil 39
Boyer-StL 32
Robinson-Cin 31

Total Bases
Aaron-Mil 334
Banks-Chi 331
Mays-SF 330
Boyer-StL 310
Pinson-Cin 308

Runs Batted In
Aaron-Mil 126
Mathews-Mil 124
Banks-Chi 117
Mays-SF 103
Boyer-StL 97

Runs Produced
Mathews-Mil 193
Aaron-Mil 188
Mays-SF 181
Banks-Chi 170
Clemente-Pit 167

Bases On Balls
Ashburn-Chi 116
Mathews-Mil 111
Gilliam-LA 96
Robinson-Cin 82
Spencer-StL 81

Batting Average
Groat-Pit 325
Larker-LA 323
Mays-SF 319
Clemente-Pit 314
Boyer-StL 304

On Base Percentage
Ashburn-Chi 416
Robinson-Cin 413
Mathews-Mil 401
Moon-LA 387
Mays-SF 386

Slugging Average
Robinson-Cin 595
Aaron-Mil 566
Boyer-StL 562
Mays-SF 555
Banks-Chi 554

Production
Robinson-Cin 1.007
Mathews-Mil 952
Mays-SF 941
Boyer-StL 934
Aaron-Mil 925

Adjusted Production
Robinson-Cin 175
Mathews-Mil 173
Mays-SF 172
Aaron-Mil 164
Banks-Chi 147

Batter Runs
Robinson-Cin 47.8
Mathews-Mil 46.0
Mays-SF 43.4
Boyer-StL 37.8
Aaron-Mil 37.3

Adjusted Batter Runs
Mathews-Mil 52.9
Mays-SF 51.2
Robinson-Cin 48.9
Aaron-Mil 44.2
Banks-Chi 35.8

Clutch Hitting Index
Larker-LA 155
Clemente-Pit 131
Skinner-Pit 127
Bailey-Cin 125
Stuart-Pit 123

Runs Created
Mathews-Mil 128
Mays-SF 124
Aaron-Mil 119
Banks-Chi 113
Robinson-Cin 113

Total Average
Robinson-Cin 1.086
Mathews-Mil 1.037
Mays-SF 977
Aaron-Mil 952
Boyer-StL 936

Stolen Bases
Wills-LA 50
Pinson-Cin 32
Taylor-Chi-Phi 26
Mays-SF 25
Bruton-Mil 22

Stolen Base Average
Javier-StL 82.6
Wills-LA 80.6
Ashburn-Chi 80.0
Pinson-Cin 72.7
Mays-SF 71.4

Stolen Base Runs
Wills-LA 7.8
Javier-StL 3.3
Blasingame-SF 3.0
Pinson-Cin 2.4
Ashburn-Chi 2.4

Fielding Runs
Mazeroski-Pit 25.7
Wills-LA 24.0
Crandall-Mil 22.7
Boyer-StL 16.2
Groat-Pit 14.5

Total Player Rating
Mays-SF 5.6
Banks-Chi 5.3
Robinson-Cin 5.2
Aaron-Mil 5.0
Boyer-StL 4.5

Wins
Spahn-Mil 21
Broglio-StL 21
Law-Pit 20
Burdette-Mil 19

Win Percentage
Broglio-StL 700
Law-Pit 690
Spahn-Mil 677
Buhl-Mil 640
Purkey-Cin 607

Games
Face-Pit 68
McDaniel-StL 65
Elston-Chi 60
Farrell-Phi 59
Roebuck-LA 58

Complete Games
Spahn-Mil 18
Law-Pit 18
Burdette-Mil 18
Hobbie-Chi 16
Friend-Pit 16

Shutouts
Sanford-SF 6
Drysdale-LA 5

Saves
McDaniel-StL 26
Face-Pit 24
Henry-Cin 17
Brosnan-Cin 12

Innings Pitched
Jackson-StL 282
Friend-Pit 276
Burdette-Mil 276
Law-Pit 272
Drysdale-LA 269

Fewest Hits/Game
Koufax-LA 6.84
Broglio-StL 6.85
Williams-LA 7.04
Drysdale-LA 7.16
Buhl-Mil 7.61

Fewest BB/Game
Burdette-Mil 1.14
Roberts-Phi 1.29
Law-Pit 1.32
Friend-Pit 1.47
Haddix-Pit 1.99

Strikeouts
Drysdale-LA 246
Koufax-LA 197
Jones-SF 190
Broglio-StL 188
Friend-Pit 183

Strikeouts/Game
Koufax-LA 10.13
Drysdale-LA 8.23
Williams-LA 7.61
Broglio-StL 7.49
Jones-SF 7.31

Wins Above Team
Broglio-StL 5.5
Purkey-Cin 4.9
Spahn-Mil 4.5
McDaniel-StL 3.7
Farrell-Phi 3.3

Earned Run Average
McCormick-SF 2.70
Broglio-StL 2.75
Drysdale-LA 2.84
Williams-LA 3.00
Friend-Pit 3.00

Adjusted ERA
Drysdale-LA 151
Broglio-StL 148
Williams-LA 143
Podres-LA 139
Simmons-Phi-StL 133

Opponents' Batting Avg.
Koufax-LA 207
Williams-LA 210
Broglio-StL 213
Drysdale-LA 215
Buhl-Mil 229

Opponents' On Base Pct.
Drysdale-LA 273
Friend-Pit 278
Williams-LA 279
Burdette-Mil 284
Law-Pit 284

Starter Runs
McCormick-SF 29.8
Drysdale-LA 27.5
Broglio-StL 25.5
Friend-Pit 23.4
Law-Pit 20.7

Adjusted Starter Runs
Drysdale-LA 43.0
Broglio-StL 32.9
Podres-LA 30.5
Williams-LA 29.5
Friend-Pit 19.5

Clutch Pitching Index
Simmons-Phi-StL 121
Podres-LA 117
O'Dell-SF 110
Sadecki-StL 109
Buhl-Mil 108

Relief Runs
McDaniel-StL 21.5
Brosnan-Cin 15.4
Roebuck-LA 12.9
Farrell-Phi 12.1
Face-Pit 11.1

Adjusted Relief Runs
McDaniel-StL 25.3
Roebuck-LA 19.7
Farrell-Phi 16.5
Brosnan-Cin 15.1
Face-Pit 9.4

Relief Ranking
McDaniel-StL 44.1
Farrell-Phi 27.0
Roebuck-LA 19.7
Face-Pit 17.7
Brosnan-Cin 16.4

Total Pitcher Index
Drysdale-LA 5.5
Broglio-StL 4.0
Williams-LA 3.3
Podres-LA 3.0
McDaniel-StL 2.9

Total Baseball Ranking
Mays-SF 5.6
Drysdale-LA 5.5
Banks-Chi 5.3
Robinson-Cin 5.2
Aaron-Mil 5.0

TEAM	G	W	L	PCT	GB	R	OR	AB	H	2B	3B	HR	BB	SO	AVG	OBP	SLG	PRO	/A	BR	/A	PF	CHI	RC	TA	SB	CS	SBA	SBR
NY	155	97	57	.630		**746**	627	5290	1377	215	40	**193**	537	818	.260	.332	**.426**	**.758**	110	63	101	94	100	**747**	**.705**	37	23	62	-2
BAL	154	89	65	.578	8	682	**606**	5170	1307	206	33	123	596	801	.253	.334	.377	.711	98	-7	-20	102	102	659	.652	37	24	61	-2
CHI	154	87	67	.565	10	741	617	5191	1402	**242**	38	112	567	648	**.270**	.348	.396	.744	107	57	48	101	100	726	**.705**	**122**	48	**72**	**8**
CLE	154	76	78	.494	21	667	693	5296	**1415**	218	20	127	444	**573**	.267	.328	.388	.716	99	-10	-4	98	100	673	.644	58	15	70	2
WAS	154	73	81	.474	24	672	696	5248	1283	205	**43**	147	584	883	.244	.326	.384	.710	95	-17	-29	102	100	656	.652	52	43	55	-9
DET	154	71	83	.461	26	633	644	5202	1243	188	34	150	**636**	728	.239	.326	.375	.701	95	-31	-41	102	97	651	.653	66	32	67	1
BOS	154	65	89	.422	32	658	775	5215	1359	234	32	124	570	798	.261	.336	.389	.725	102	16	-5	103	95	674	.658	34	28	55	-6
KC	155	58	96	.377	39	615	756	5226	1303	212	34	110	513	744	.249	.318	.366	.684	91	-68	-59	99	102	598	.600	16	11	59	-1
TOT	617					5414		41838	10689	1720	274	1086	4447	5993	.255	.331	.388	.719								422	234	64	-13

TEAM	CG	SHO	SV	IP	H	H/G	HR	BB	BB/G	SO	SO/G	ERA	/A	OAVG	OOBA	PR	/A	PF	CPI	FA	E	DP	FW	PW	BW	SBW	DIF
NY	38	**16**	**42**	1398.0	1225	7.9	123	609	3.9	712	4.6	**3.52**	102	**.237**	.315	55	8	92	98	.979	129	162	.1	.8	**10.2**	-.0	8.9
BAL	**48**	11	22	1375.7	**1222**	8.0	**117**	552	3.6	785	5.1	**3.52**	**111**	.241	.313	53	**57**	101	98	**.982**	**108**	172	1.4	**5.8**	-2.0	-.0	6.9
CHI	42	11	26	1381.0	1338	8.7	127	533	3.5	695	4.5	3.60	106	.257	.321	41	34	99	**106**	**.982**	109	175	1.4	3.4	4.9	**1.0**	-.6
CLE	32	10	30	1382.3	1308	8.5	161	636	4.1	771	5.0	3.95	96	.251	.329	-12	-22	98	103	.978	128	165	.2	-2.2	.4	.4	.3
WAS	34	10	35	1405.3	1392	8.9	130	538	3.4	775	5.0	3.77	105	.259	.325	15	29	102	103	.973	165	159	-2.1	2.9	-2.9	-.7	-1.1
DET	40	7	25	1405.7	1336	8.6	141	**474**	**3.0**	**824**	**5.3**	3.64	108	.250	**.311**	36	47	102	99	.977	138	138	-.5	4.8	-4.1	.3	-6.4
BOS	34	6	23	1361.0	1440	9.5	127	580	3.8	767	5.1	4.62	88	.272	.341	-113	-81	105	94	.976	141	156	-.6	-8.2	-.5	-.4	-2.2
KC	**44**	4	14	1374.0	1428	9.4	160	525	3.4	664	4.3	4.38	90	.271	.332	-76	-68	101	100	.979	127	149	.2	-6.9	-6.0	.0	-6.5
TOT	312	75	217	11083.0		8.7			3.6		4.9	3.87		.255	.331					.978	1045	1276					

Runs		Hits		Doubles		Triples		Home Runs		Total Bases	
Mantle-NY	119	Minoso-Chi	184	Francona-Cle	36	Fox-Chi	10	Mantle-NY	40	Mantle-NY	294
Maris-NY	98	Robinson-Bal	175	Skowron-NY	34	Robinson-Bal	9	Maris-NY	39	Maris-NY	290
Minoso-Chi	89	Fox-Chi	175	Minoso-Chi	32			Lemon-Was	38	Skowron-NY	284
Landis-Chi	89	Smith-Chi	169	Freese-Chi	32			Colavito-Det	35	Minoso-Chi	284
Sievers-Chi	87	Runnels-Bos	169					Killebrew-Was	31	Lemon-Was	268

Runs Batted In		Runs Produced		Bases On Balls		Batting Average		On Base Percentage		Slugging Average	
Maris-NY	112	Minoso-Chi	174	Yost-Det	125	Runnels-Bos	.320	Yost-Det	.416	Maris-NY	.581
Minoso-Chi	105	Mantle-NY	173	Mantle-NY	111	Smith-Chi	.315	Woodling-Bal	.403	Mantle-NY	.558
Wertz-Bos	103	Maris-NY	171	Allison-Was	92	Minoso-Chi	.311	Runnels-Bos	.403	Killebrew-Was	.534
Lemon-Was	100	Sievers-Chi	152	Woodling-Bal	84	Skowron-NY	.309	Mantle-NY	.402	Sievers-Chi	.534
Gentile-Bal	98	Robinson-Bal	148	Landis-Chi	80	Kuenn-Cle	.308	Sievers-Chi	.399	Skowron-NY	.528

Production		Adjusted Production		Batter Runs		Adjusted Batter Runs		Clutch Hitting Index		Runs Created	
Mantle-NY	.960	Mantle-NY	166	Mantle-NY	43.8	Mantle-NY	47.9	Wertz-Bos	155	Mantle-NY	125
Maris-NY	.955	Maris-NY	163	Williams-Bos	43.5	Williams-Bos	42.0	Power-Cle	135	Maris-NY	111
Sievers-Chi	.933	Sievers-Chi	148	Maris-NY	36.5	Maris-NY	40.2	Minoso-Chi	127	Minoso-Chi	104
Killebrew-Was	.911	Skowron-NY	144	Sievers-Chi	32.1	Sievers-Chi	31.4	Robinson-Bal	120	Lemon-Was	99
Skowron-NY	.884	Killebrew-Was	141	Killebrew-Was	26.8	Skowron-NY	28.2	Aparicio-Chi	119	Francona-Cle	96

Total Average		Stolen Bases		Stolen Base Average		Stolen Base Runs		Fielding Runs		Total Player Rating	
Mantle-NY	1.061	Aparicio-Chi	51	Aparicio-Chi	86.4	Aparicio-Chi	10.5	Aparicio-Chi	31.3	Aparicio-Chi	3.7
Maris-NY	.997	Landis-Chi	23	Kaline-Det	82.6	Landis-Chi	3.3	Power-Cle	20.7	Mantle-NY	3.6
Sievers-Chi	.963	Green-Was	21	Landis-Chi	79.3	Kaline-Det	3.3	Boyer-NY	14.9	Maris-NY	3.6
Killebrew-Was	.936	Kaline-Det	19	Piersall-Cle	78.3	Piersall-Cle	2.4	Fox-Chi	13.6	Williams-Bos	3.4
Yost-Det	.877	Piersall-Cle	18	Green-Was	72.4	Mantle-NY	2.4	Robinson-Bal	12.6	Runnels-Bos	2.6

Wins		Win Percentage		Games		Complete Games		Shutouts		Saves	
Perry-Cle	18	Perry-Cle	.643	Fornieles-Bos	70	Lary-Det	15	Wynn-Chi	4	Klippstein-Chi	14
Estrada-Bal	18	Ditmar-NY	.625	Staley-Chi	64	Ramos-Was	14	Perry-Cle	4	Fornieles-Bos	14
Daley-KC	16	Estrada-Bal	.621	Clevenger-Was	53	Herbert-KC	14	Ford-NY	4	Moore-Chi-Was	13
		Pappas-Bal	.577	Moore-Chi-Was	51	Wynn-Chi	13			Shantz-NY	11
				Kutyna-KC	51	Daley-KC	13				

Innings Pitched		Fewest Hits/Game		Fewest BB/Game		Strikeouts		Strikeouts/Game		Wins Above Team	
Ramos-Was	274	Estrada-Bal	6.98	Brown-Bal	1.25	Bunning-Det	201	Bunning-Det	7.18	Perry-Cle	4.7
Lary-Det	274	Turley-NY	7.18	Mossi-Det	1.82	Ramos-Was	160	Bell-Cle	6.33	Coates-NY	4.2
Perry-Cle	261	Barber-Bal	7.32	Hall-KC	1.88	Wynn-Chi	158	Estrada-Bal	6.20	Daley-KC	3.8
Herbert-KC	253	Bunning-Det	7.75	Lary-Det	2.04	Lary-Det	149	Wynn-Chi	6.00	Monbouquette-Bos	3.4
Bunning-Det	252	Ford-NY	7.83	Pierce-Chi	2.11	Estrada-Bal	144	Sullivan-Bos	5.73	Fornieles-Bos	3.4

Earned Run Average		Adjusted ERA		Opponents' Batting Avg.		Opponents' On Base Pct.		Starter Runs		Adjusted Starter Runs	
Baumann-Chi	2.68	Baumann-Chi	143	Estrada-Bal	.218	Brown-Bal	.280	Bunning-Det	30.4	Bunning-Det	32.3
Bunning-Det	2.79	Bunning-Det	141	Turley-NY	.222	Bunning-Det	.285	Baumann-Chi	24.6	Baumann-Chi	23.7
Brown-Bal	3.06	Brown-Bal	127	Barber-Bal	.226	Mossi-Det	.289	Ditmar-NY	18.0	Herbert-KC	18.4
Ditmar-NY	3.06	Barber-Bal	121	Ford-NY	.235	Ford-NY	.294	Ford-NY	17.0	Pascual-Was	15.9
Ford-NY	3.08	Herbert-KC	120	Bunning-Det	.236	Hall-KC	.296	Herbert-KC	16.8	Ramos-Was	15.6

Clutch Pitching Index		Relief Runs		Adjusted Relief Runs		Relief Ranking		Total Pitcher Index		Total Baseball Ranking	
Ditmar-NY	121	Staley-Chi	18.5	Staley-Chi	17.9	Staley-Chi	33.0	Bunning-Det	3.0	Aparicio-Chi	3.7
Lee-Was	113	Fornieles-Bos	14.9	Fornieles-Bos	17.4	Fornieles-Bos	26.6	Baumann-Chi	2.3	Mantle-NY	3.6
Perry-Cle	113	Sisler-Det	12.4	Sisler-Det	13.7	Sisler-Det	19.7	Herbert-KC	2.3	Maris-NY	3.6
Baumann-Chi	112	Aguirre-Det	10.9	Aguirre-Det	11.6	Stobbs-Was	12.3	Staley-Chi	2.2	Williams-Bos	3.4
Herbert-KC	111	Shantz-NY	8.3	Stobbs-Was	8.4	Klippstein-Cle	12.0	Fornieles-Bos	2.0	Bunning-Det	3.0

TEAM	G	W	L	PCT	GB	R	OR	AB	H	2B	3B	HR	BB	SO	AVG	OBP	SLG	PRO	/A	BR	/A	PF	CHI	RC	TA	SB	CS	SBA	SBR
CIN	154	93	61	.604		710	653	5243	1414	**247**	35	158	423	761	.270	.328	.421	.749	103	19	-7	104	100	713	.687	70	33	**68**	1
LA	154	89	65	.578	4	735	697	5189	1358	193	40	157	**596**	796	.262	**.340**	.405	.745	103	29	13	102	100	722	**.703**	**86**	45	66	0
SF	155	85	69	.552	8	**773**	655	5233	1379	219	32	183	506	764	.264	.332	**.423**	**.755**	**105**	34	45	98	**105**	719	.701	79	54	59	-8
MIL	155	83	71	.539	10	712	656	5288	1365	199	34	**188**	534	880	.258	.330	.415	.745	103	19	**75**	92	98	714	.691	70	43	62	-4
STL	155	80	74	.519	13	703	668	5307	1436	236	51	103	494	745	.271	.336	.393	.729	99	-3	-94	113	100	702	.663	46	28	62	-2
PIT	154	75	79	.487	18	694	675	5311	**1448**	232	**57**	128	428	**721**	**.273**	.330	.410	.740	101	8	12	99	98	694	.659	26	30	46	-9
CHI	156	64	90	.416	29	689	800	5344	1364	238	51	176	539	1027	.255	.327	.418	.745	102	15	15	100	94	**726**	.689	35	25	58	-4
PHI	155	47	107	.305	46	584	796	5213	1265	185	50	106	475	928	.243	.311	.357	.668	82	-122	-78	94	101	577	.593	56	30	65	0
TOT	619					5600		42128	11029	1749	350	1196	3995	6622	.262	.329	.405	.735								468	288	62	-31

TEAM	CG	SHO	SV	IP	H	H/G	HR	BB	BB/G	SO	SO/G	ERA	/A	OAVG	OOBA	PR	/A	PF	CPI	FA	E	DP	FW	PW	BW	SBW	DIF
CIN	46	12	40	1370.0	**1300**	8.5	147	500	3.3	829	5.4	3.78	110	.250	.314	37	54	103	98	.977	134	124	.7	5.4	-.7	**.5**	10.2
LA	40	10	35	1378.3	1346	8.8	167	544	3.6	**1105**	7.2	4.04	101	.255	.325	-1	7	102	101	.975	144	162	.1	.7	1.3	.4	9.5
SF	39	9	30	1388.0	1306	**8.5**	152	502	3.3	924	6.0	3.77	103	**.248**	**.312**	39	16	96	98	.977	133	126	.7	1.6	4.5	-.4	1.6
MIL	**57**	8	16	1391.3	1357	8.8	153	493	3.2	652	4.2	3.89	94	.257	.317	21	-34	91	101	**.982**	111	152	**2.0**	-3.4	7.4	.0	-.0
STL	49	10	24	1368.7	1334	8.8	136	570	3.7	823	5.4	**3.74**	**121**	.256	.326	44	**120**	113	**106**	.972	166	165	-1.1	**11.9**	-9.3	.2	1.3
PIT	34	9	29	1362.0	1442	9.5	**121**	**400**	**2.6**	759	5.0	3.92	102	.274	.322	17	10	99	102	.975	150	**187**	-.2	1.2	1.2	-.5	-3.5
CHI	34	6	25	1385.0	1492	9.7	165	465	3.0	755	4.9	4.48	92	.276	.330	-69	-57	102	99	.970	183	175	-2.1	-5.7	1.5	.0	-6.8
PHI	29	9	13	1383.3	1452	9.4	155	521	3.4	775	5.0	4.61	85	.273	.335	-88	-103	98	96	.976	146	179	.0	-10.2	-7.7	.4	-12.4
TOT	328	73	212	11026.7		9.0			3.3		5.4	4.03		.262	.329					.976	1167	1270					

Runs
Mays-SF 129
Robinson-Cin 117
Aaron-Mil 115
Boyer-StL 109

Hits
Pinson-Cin 208
Clemente-Pit 201
Aaron-Mil 197
Boyer-StL 194
Cepeda-SF 182

Doubles
Aaron-Mil 39
Pinson-Cin 34
Santo-Chi 32
Robinson-Cin 32
Mays-SF 32

Triples
Altman-Chi 12
White-StL 11
Callison-Phi 11
Boyer-StL 11

Home Runs
Cepeda-SF 46
Mays-SF 40
Robinson-Cin 37
Stuart-Pit 35
Adcock-Mil 35

Total Bases
Aaron-Mil 358
Cepeda-SF 356
Mays-SF 334
Robinson-Cin 333
Clemente-Pit 320

Runs Batted In
Cepeda-SF 142
Robinson-Cin 124
Mays-SF 123
Aaron-Mil 120
Stuart-Pit 117

Runs Produced
Mays-SF 212
Robinson-Cin 204
Cepeda-SF 201
Aaron-Mil 201
Boyer-StL 180

Bases On Balls
Mathews-Mil 93
Moon-LA 89
Mays-SF 81
Gilliam-LA 79

Batting Average
Clemente-Pit 351
Pinson-Cin 343
Boyer-StL 329
Moon-LA 328
Aaron-Mil 327

On Base Percentage
Moon-LA 438
Robinson-Cin 411
Mathews-Mil 405
Boyer-StL 400
Mays-SF 395

Slugging Average
Robinson-Cin 611
Cepeda-SF 609
Aaron-Mil 594
Mays-SF 584
Stuart-Pit 581

Production
Robinson-Cin 1.022
Aaron-Mil 979
Mays-SF 979
Cepeda-SF 972
Clemente-Pit 951

Adjusted Production
Aaron-Mil 168
Robinson-Cin 160
Mathews-Mil 159
Mays-SF 158
Cepeda-SF 154

Batter Runs
Robinson-Cin 52.4
Aaron-Mil 45.9
Mays-SF 45.7
Cepeda-SF 40.7
Mathews-Mil 40.3

Adjusted Batter Runs
Aaron-Mil 52.3
Robinson-Cin 49.5
Mays-SF 47.0
Mathews-Mil 46.7
Cepeda-SF 42.0

Clutch Hitting Index
Moon-LA 132
Cepeda-SF 123
Stuart-Pit 121
Robinson-Cin 119
Mays-SF 116

Runs Created
Robinson-Cin 137
Aaron-Mil 132
Mays-SF 130
Mathews-Mil 128
Boyer-StL 126

Total Average
Robinson-Cin 1.127
Mays-SF 1.038
Moon-LA 1.018
Aaron-Mil 1.014
Mathews-Mil 998

Stolen Bases
Wills-LA 35
Pinson-Cin 23
Robinson-Cin 22
Aaron-Mil 21
Mays-SF 18

Stolen Base Average
Robinson-Cin 88.0
Wills-LA 70.0
Aaron-Mil 70.0
Pinson-Cin 69.7
Mays-SF 66.7

Stolen Base Runs
Robinson-Cin 4.8
Maye-Mil 2.4
Williams-Chi 1.8
Wills-LA 1.5
Gonzalez-Phi 1.5

Fielding Runs
Mazeroski-Pit 31.5
Torre-Mil 16.7
Clemente-Pit 13.8
Groat-Pit 13.1
Boyer-StL 12.5

Total Player Rating
Robinson-Cin 5.3
Clemente-Pit 4.4
Aaron-Mil 4.2
Mays-SF 4.0
Banks-Chi 3.4

Wins
Spahn-Mil 21
Jay-Cin 21
O'Toole-Cin 19

Win Percentage
Podres-LA 783
O'Toole-Cin 679
Jay-Cin 677
Burdette-Mil 621
Spahn-Mil 618

Games
Baldschun-Phi 65
Miller-SF 63
Face-Pit 62
Elston-Chi 58
Anderson-Chi 57

Complete Games
Spahn-Mil 21
Koufax-LA 15
Jay-Cin 14
Burdette-Mil 14

Shutouts
Spahn-Mil 4
Jay-Cin 4

Saves
Miller-SF 17
Face-Pit 17
Henry-Cin 16
Brosnan-Cin 16
Sherry-LA 15

Innings Pitched
Burdette-Mil 272
Spahn-Mil 263
Cardwell-Chi 259
Koufax-LA 256
O'Toole-Cin 253

Fewest Hits/Game
Koufax-LA 7.45
Jay-Cin 7.91
Sadecki-StL 7.91
Gibson-StL 7.93
Spahn-Mil 8.08

Fewest BB/Game
Burdette-Mil 1.09
Friend-Pit 1.72
Purkey-Cin 1.87
Spahn-Mil 2.19
Ellsworth-Chi 2.31

Strikeouts
Koufax-LA 269
Williams-LA 205
Drysdale-LA 182
O'Toole-Cin 178
Gibson-StL 166

Strikeouts/Game
Koufax-LA 9.46
Williams-LA 7.85
Gibson-StL 7.08
Drysdale-LA 6.71
Gibbon-Pit 6.69

Wins Above Team
Podres-LA 6.0
Miller-SF 4.2
Spahn-Mil 3.6
Jay-Cin 3.4
O'Toole-Cin 3.1

Earned Run Average
Spahn-Mil 3.01
O'Toole-Cin 3.09
Simmons-StL 3.12
McCormick-SF 3.20
Gibson-StL 3.24

Adjusted ERA
Simmons-StL 145
Gibson-StL 140
O'Toole-Cin 134
Sadecki-StL 122
Spahn-Mil 122

Opponents' Batting Avg.
Koufax-LA 222
Jay-Cin 236
Sadecki-StL 238
Gibson-StL 239
O'Toole-Cin 240

Opponents' On Base Pct.
Spahn-Mil 286
Koufax-LA 291
Purkey-Cin 293
Burdette-Mil 294
Jackson-StL 299

Starter Runs
Spahn-Mil 29.8
O'Toole-Cin 26.3
McCormick-SF 23.0
Simmons-StL 19.8
Gibson-StL 18.5

Adjusted Starter Runs
Simmons-StL 30.8
Gibson-StL 30.3
O'Toole-Cin 29.5
Sadecki-StL 20.4
Spahn-Mil 19.2

Clutch Pitching Index
Simmons-StL 122
Ellsworth-Chi 121
Podres-LA 116
McCormick-SF 115
Gibson-StL 114

Relief Runs
Miller-SF 18.6
Perranoski-LA 14.2
McMahon-Mil 12.2
Henry-Cin 10.7
Schultz-Chi 10.0

Adjusted Relief Runs
Miller-SF 16.6
Perranoski-LA 14.8
Henry-Cin 11.4
Schultz-Chi 10.6
Brosnan-Cin 9.8

Relief Ranking
Miller-SF 28.4
Schultz-Chi 21.0
Brosnan-Cin 19.9
Perranoski-LA 19.6
Henry-Cin 13.6

Total Pitcher Index
Simmons-StL 3.9
Gibson-StL 3.5
Spahn-Mil 3.2
O'Toole-Cin 2.9
Jackson-StL 2.1

Total Baseball Ranking
Robinson-Cin 5.3
Clemente-Pit 4.4
Aaron-Mil 4.2
Mays-SF 4.0
Simmons-StL 3.9

TEAM	G	W	L	PCT	GB	R	OR	AB	H	2B	3B	HR	BB	SO	AVG	OBP	SLG	PRO	/A	BR	/A	PF	CHI	RC	TA	SB	CS	SBA	SBR
NY	163	109	53	.673		827	612	5559	1461	194	40	**240**	543	785	.263	.332	**.442**	**.774**	**112**	81	108	96	101	811	.723	28	18	61	-1
DET	163	101	61	.623	8	**841**	671	5561	1481	215	**53**	180	673	867	**.266**	**.349**	.421	.770	**112**	**95**	**125**	96	99	**835**	**.743**	98	36	73	**8**
BAL	163	95	67	.586	14	691	**588**	5481	1393	227	36	149	581	902	.254	.328	.390	.718	98	-16	3	97	96	699	.653	39	30	57	-5
CHI	163	86	76	.531	23	765	726	5556	1475	216	46	138	550	**612**	.265	.338	.395	.733	102	17	23	99	100	754	.685	**100**	40	71	6
CLE	161	78	83	.484	30.5	737	752	5609	**1493**	**257**	39	150	492	720	**.266**	.328	.406	.734	102	9	36	96	98	743	.665	34	11	**76**	4
BOS	163	76	86	.469	33	729	792	5508	1401	251	37	112	647	847	.254	.336	.374	.710	96	-21	-33	102	100	704	.654	56	36	61	-4
MIN	161	70	90	.438	38	707	778	5417	1353	215	40	167	597	840	.250	.328	.397	.725	99	-5	-49	106	98	698	.665	47	43	52	-11
LA	162	70	91	.435	38.5	744	784	5424	1331	218	22	189	**681**	1068	.245	.333	.398	.731	101	11	-72	111	99	734	.686	37	28	57	-5
WAS	161	61	100	.379	47.5	618	776	5366	1307	217	44	119	558	917	.244	.317	.367	.684	89	-82	-46	95	97	625	.621	81	47	63	-3
KC	162	61	100	.379	47.5	683	863	5423	1342	216	47	90	580	772	.247	.323	.354	.677	87	-89	-102	102	**107**	642	.614	58	22	73	4
TOT	811					7342		54904	14037	2226	404	1534	5902	8330	.256	.332	.395	.726								578	311	65	-12

TEAM	CG	SHO	SV	IP	H	H/G	HR	BB	BB/G	SO	SO/G	ERA	/A	OAVG	OOBA	PR	/A	PF	CPI	FA	E	DP	FW	PW	BW	SBW	DIF
NY	47	14	**39**	1451.0	1288	8.0	137	542	3.4	866	5.4	3.46	108	.239	.307	90	47	93	99	**.980**	**124**	**180**	**1.6**	4.7	10.7	.0	11.0
DET	**62**	12	30	1459.3	1404	8.7	170	**469**	**2.9**	836	5.2	3.55	106	.252	.308	77	36	94	**106**	.976	146	147	.3	3.6	**12.4**	**.9**	2.8
BAL	54	**21**	33	1471.3	**1226**	**7.5**	**109**	617	3.8	926	5.7	**3.22**	**120**	**.227**	**.304**	**131**	**104**	96	97	**.980**	128	173	1.3	**10.3**	.3	-.4	2.4
CHI	39	3	33	1448.7	1491	9.3	158	498	3.1	814	5.1	4.06	98	.267	.320	-5	-14	99	102	**.980**	128	138	1.3	-1.4	2.3	.7	2.1
CLE	35	12	23	1443.7	1426	8.9	178	599	3.7	801	5.0	4.15	94	.257	.328	-19	-42	97	102	.977	139	142	.7	-4.2	3.6	.5	-3.1
BOS	35	6	30	1442.7	1472	9.2	167	679	4.2	831	5.2	4.29	96	.265	.340	-42	-26	103	105	.977	144	170	.4	-2.6	-3.3	-.3	.7
MIN	49	14	23	1432.3	1415	8.9	163	570	3.6	914	5.7	4.28	101	.256	.325	-40	5	107	95	.971	174	150	-1.4	.5	-4.9	-1.0	-3.3
LA	25	5	34	1438.0	1391	8.7	180	713	4.5	**973**	**6.1**	4.31	105	.253	.337	-46	31	112	101	.969	192	154	-2.4	3.1	-7.1	-.4	-3.6
WAS	39	8	21	1425.0	1405	8.9	131	586	3.7	666	4.2	4.23	93	.260	.328	-32	-50	97	96	.975	156	171	-.3	-5.0	-4.6	-.2	-9.5
KC	32	5	23	1415.0	1519	9.7	141	629	4.0	703	4.5	4.74	88	.275	.347	-113	-86	104	97	.972	175	160	-1.4	-8.5	-10.1	.5	.0
TOT	417	100	289	14427.0		8.8			3.7		5.2	4.02		.256	.332					.976	1506	1585					

Runs
Maris-NY ... 132
Mantle-NY ... 132
Colavito-Det ... 129
Cash-Det ... 119
Kaline-Det ... 116

Hits
Cash-Det ... 193
Robinson-Bal ... 192
Kaline-Det ... 190
Francona-Cle ... 178
Richardson-NY ... 173

Doubles
Kaline-Det ... 41
Robinson-Bal ... 38
Kubek-NY ... 38
Siebern-KC ... 36
Power-Cle ... 34

Triples
Wood-Det ... 14
Lumpe-KC ... 9
Keough-Was ... 9

Home Runs
Maris-NY ... 61
Mantle-NY ... 54
Killebrew-Min ... 46
Gentile-Bal ... 46
Colavito-Det ... 45

Total Bases
Maris-NY ... 366
Cash-Det ... 354
Mantle-NY ... 353
Colavito-Det ... 338
Killebrew-Min ... 328

Runs Batted In
Maris-NY ... 142
Gentile-Bal ... 141
Colavito-Det ... 140
Cash-Det ... 132
Mantle-NY ... 128

Runs Produced
Colavito-Det ... 224
Maris-NY ... 213
Cash-Det ... 210
Mantle-NY ... 206
Gentile-Bal ... 191

Bases On Balls
Mantle-NY ... 126
Cash-Det ... 124
Colavito-Det ... 113
Killebrew-Min ... 107
Allison-Min ... 103

Batting Average
Cash-Det ... .361
Kaline-Det ... .324
Piersall-Cle ... .322
Mantle-NY ... .317
Gentile-Bal ... .302

On Base Percentage
Cash-Det ... .488
Mantle-NY ... .452
Gentile-Bal ... .428
Pearson-LA ... .422
Killebrew-Min ... .409

Slugging Average
Mantle-NY ... .687
Cash-Det ... .662
Gentile-Bal ... .646
Maris-NY ... .620
Killebrew-Min ... .606

Production
Cash-Det ... 1.150
Mantle-NY ... 1.138
Gentile-Bal ... 1.074
Killebrew-Min ... 1.015
Maris-NY ... .997

Adjusted Production
Cash-Det ... 213
Mantle-NY ... 207
Gentile-Bal ... 188
Maris-NY ... 167
Colavito-Det ... 167

Batter Runs
Cash-Det ... 86.0
Mantle-NY ... 76.2
Gentile-Bal ... 59.0
Killebrew-Min ... 52.9
Colavito-Det ... 51.5

Adjusted Batter Runs
Cash-Det ... 89.3
Mantle-NY ... 79.0
Gentile-Bal ... 61.0
Colavito-Det ... 54.9
Maris-NY ... 52.5

Clutch Hitting Index
Malzone-Bos ... 134
Allison-Min ... 129
Siebern-KC ... 127
Minoso-Chi ... 126
Yastrzemski-Bos ... 126

Runs Created
Cash-Det ... 178
Mantle-NY ... 174
Colavito-Det ... 141
Gentile-Bal ... 138
Maris-NY ... 138

Total Average
Mantle-NY ... 1.387
Cash-Det ... 1.372
Gentile-Bal ... 1.199
Killebrew-Min ... 1.103
Colavito-Det ... 1.056

Stolen Bases
Aparicio-Chi ... 53
Howser-KC ... 37
Wood-Det ... 30
Hinton-Was ... 22
Bruton-Det ... 22

Stolen Base Average
Hinton-Was ... 81.5
Howser-KC ... 80.4
Aparicio-Chi ... 80.3
Geiger-Bos ... 80.0
Landis-Chi ... 79.2

Stolen Base Runs
Aparicio-Chi ... 8.1
Howser-KC ... 5.7
Wood-Det ... 3.6
Kaline-Det ... 3.6
Hinton-Was ... 3.6

Fielding Runs
Boyer-NY ... 31.5
Kaline-Det ... 18.5
Kubek-NY ... 17.5
Schilling-Bos ... 17.0
Lumpe-KC ... 16.2

Total Player Rating
Cash-Det ... 7.6
Mantle-NY ... 7.0
Colavito-Det ... 5.4
Kaline-Det ... 5.3
Gentile-Bal ... 4.9

Wins
Ford-NY ... 25
Lary-Det ... 23
Barber-Bal ... 18
Bunning-Det ... 17
Terry-NY ... 16

Win Percentage
Ford-NY ... .862
Terry-NY ... .842
Arroyo-NY ... .750
Lary-Det ... .719

Games
Arroyo-NY ... 65
Morgan-LA ... 59
Lown-Chi ... 59
Kunkel-KC ... 58
Fornieles-Bos ... 57

Complete Games
Lary-Det ... 22
Pascual-Min ... 15
Barber-Bal ... 14

Shutouts
Pascual-Min ... 8
Barber-Bal ... 8
Pappas-Bal ... 4
Lary-Det ... 4
Bunning-Det ... 4

Saves
Arroyo-NY ... 29
Wilhelm-Bal ... 18
Fornieles-Bos ... 15
Moore-Min ... 14
Fox-Det ... 12

Innings Pitched
Ford-NY ... 283
Lary-Det ... 275
Bunning-Det ... 268
Ramos-Min ... 264
Pascual-Min ... 252

Fewest Hits/Game
Estrada-Bal ... 6.75
Pappas-Bal ... 6.78
Barber-Bal ... 7.04
Pascual-Min ... 7.32
Donovan-Was ... 7.35

Fewest BB/Game
Mossi-Det ... 1.76
Brown-Bal ... 1.78
Donovan-Was ... 1.86
Terry-NY ... 2.01
McClain-Was ... 2.04

Strikeouts
Pascual-Min ... 221
Ford-NY ... 209
Bunning-Det ... 194
Pizarro-Chi ... 188
McBride-LA ... 180

Strikeouts/Game
Pizarro-Chi ... 8.68
Pascual-Min ... 7.89
Estrada-Bal ... 6.79
McBride-LA ... 6.69
Ford-NY ... 6.65

Wins Above Team
Ford-NY ... 9.1
Terry-NY ... 5.2
Schwall-Bos ... 4.8
Lary-Det ... 4.7
Latman-Cle ... 4.4

Earned Run Average
Donovan-Was ... 2.40
Stafford-NY ... 2.68
Mossi-Det ... 2.96
Pappas-Bal ... 3.03
Pizarro-Chi ... 3.05

Adjusted ERA
Donovan-Was ... 163
Stafford-NY ... 140
Archer-KC ... 131
Pizarro-Chi ... 130
Schwall-Bos ... 128

Opponents' Batting Avg.
Estrada-Bal ... .207
Pappas-Bal ... .208
Pascual-Min ... .217
Barber-Bal ... .218
Donovan-Was ... .224

Opponents' On Base Pct.
Donovan-Was ... .262
Terry-NY ... .273
Brown-Bal ... .280
Bunning-Det ... .281
Lary-Det ... .287

Starter Runs
Hoeft-Bal ... 30.7
Donovan-Was ... 30.6
Stafford-NY ... 29.2
Mossi-Det ... 28.3
Ford-NY ... 25.5

Adjusted Starter Runs
Donovan-Was ... 28.5
Hoeft-Bal ... 28.2
Pascual-Min ... 23.8
Stafford-NY ... 23.4
McBride-LA ... 23.3

Clutch Pitching Index
Schwall-Bos ... 131
Mossi-Det ... 119
Shaw-Chi-KC ... 115
Monbouquette-Bos ... 114
McBride-LA ... 112

Relief Runs
Arroyo-NY ... 24.2
Wilhelm-Bal ... 21.2
Morgan-LA ... 17.1
Fox-Det ... 16.5
Lown-Chi ... 14.2

Adjusted Relief Runs
Morgan-LA ... 22.1
Arroyo-NY ... 20.6
Wilhelm-Bal ... 19.2
Fox-Det ... 14.9
Lown-Chi ... 13.5

Relief Ranking
Arroyo-NY ... 42.5
Wilhelm-Bal ... 32.2
Morgan-LA ... 27.0
Fox-Det ... 23.5
Lown-Chi ... 17.8

Total Pitcher Index
Donovan-Was ... 3.2
Hoeft-Bal ... 3.1
Pascual-Min ... 2.5
Lary-Det ... 2.5
Pizarro-Chi ... 2.4

Total Baseball Ranking
Cash-Det ... 7.6
Mantle-NY ... 7.0
Colavito-Det ... 5.4
Kaline-Det ... 5.3
Gentile-Bal ... 4.9

TEAM	G	W	L	PCT	GB	R	OR	AB	H	2B	3B	HR	BB	SO	AVG	OBP	SLG	PRO	/A	BR	/A	PF	CHI	RC	TA	SB	CS	SBA	SBR
SF	165	103	62	.624		**878**	690	5588	**1552**	235	32	**204**	523	822	**.278**	**.344**	**.441**	**.785**	**117**	**122**	**114**	101	102	**838**	**.737**	73	50	59	-7
LA	165	102	63	.618	1	842	697	5628	1510	192	**65**	140	572	886	.268	.339	.400	.739	105	40	94	93	**107**	783	.712	**198**	43	**82**	**34**
CIN	162	98	64	.605	3.5	802	685	5645	1523	**252**	40	167	498	903	.270	.333	.417	.750	107	53	39	102	101	779	.693	66	39	63	-3
PIT	161	93	68	.578	8	706	**626**	5483	1468	240	**65**	108	432	836	.268	.323	.394	.717	98	-14	-30	102	101	682	.637	50	39	56	-7
MIL	162	86	76	.531	15.5	730	665	5458	1376	204	38	181	581	975	.252	.328	.403	.731	102	15	22	99	99	720	.677	57	27	68	1
STL	163	84	78	.519	17.5	774	664	5643	1528	221	31	137	515	846	.271	.337	.394	.731	103	21	-41	109	101	747	.669	86	41	68	1
PHI	161	81	80	.503	20	705	759	5420	1410	199	39	142	531	923	.260	.332	.390	.722	100	3	41	95	97	705	.665	79	42	65	-1
HOU	162	64	96	.400	36.5	592	717	5558	1370	170	47	105	493	**806**	.246	.312	.351	.663	84	-116	-63	93	97	605	.580	42	30	58	-4
CHI	162	59	103	.364	42.5	632	827	5534	1398	196	56	126	504	1044	.253	.319	.377	.696	93	-53	-94	106	94	657	.627	78	50	61	-6
NY	161	40	120	.250	60.5	617	948	5492	1318	166	40	139	**616**	991	.240	.320	.361	.681	89	-75	-102	104	94	640	.619	59	48	55	-10
TOT	812					7278		55449	14453	2075	453	1449	5265	9032	.261	.329	.393	.722								788	409	66	-8

TEAM	CG	SHO	SV	IP	H	H/G	HR	BB	BB/G	SO	SO/G	ERA	/A	OAVG	OOBA	PR	/A	PF	CPI	FA	E	DP	FW	PW	BW	SBW	DIF
SF	**62**	10	39	1461.7	1399	8.6	148	503	3.1	886	5.5	3.79	102	.250	**.310**	24	14	99	95	.977	142	153	.8	1.4	**11.4**	-.6	7.5
LA	44	8	**46**	1488.7	**1386**	**8.4**	115	588	3.6	**1104**	**6.7**	3.62	99	**.244**	.314	53	-6	91	94	.970	193	144	-2.2	-.6	9.4	**3.5**	9.5
CIN	51	13	35	1460.7	1397	8.6	149	567	3.5	964	5.9	3.75	105	.254	.322	30	32	100	104	.977	145	144	.6	3.2	3.9	-.2	9.5
PIT	40	13	41	1432.3	1433	9.0	118	466	2.9	897	5.6	**3.37**	118	.261	.316	**90**	97	101	**110**	.976	152	**177**	.2	9.7	-3.0	-.6	6.2
MIL	59	10	24	1434.7	1443	9.1	151	**407**	**2.6**	802	5.0	3.68	105	.262	.311	42	30	98	103	**.980**	**124**	154	**1.9**	3.0	2.2	.2	-2.3
STL	53	**17**	25	1463.3	1394	8.6	149	517	3.2	914	5.6	3.55	**119**	.251	.314	63	**107**	107	104	.979	132	170	1.4	**10.7**	-4.1	.2	-5.2
PHI	43	7	24	1426.7	1469	9.3	155	574	3.6	863	5.4	4.28	88	.268	.337	-53	-82	95	102	.977	138	167	1.0	-8.2	4.1	.0	3.6
HOU	34	9	19	1453.7	1446	9.0	**113**	471	2.9	1047	6.5	3.83	97	.259	.315	18	-15	95	95	.973	173	149	-1.0	-1.5	-6.3	-.3	-6.9
CHI	29	4	26	1438.3	1509	9.4	159	601	3.8	783	4.9	4.54	94	.272	.341	-95	-41	109	99	.977	146	171	.6	-4.1	-9.4	-.5	-8.6
NY	43	4	10	1430.0	1577	9.9	192	571	3.6	772	4.9	5.04	85	.280	.345	-174	-122	108	96	.967	210	167	-3.3	-12.2	-10.2	-.9	-13.5
TOT	458	95	289	14490.0		9.0			3.3		5.6	3.94		.261	.329					.975	1555	1596					

Runs
Robinson-Cin 134
Wills-LA 130
Mays-SF 130
H.Aaron-Mil 127
T.Davis-LA 120

Hits
T.Davis-LA 230
Wills-LA 208
Robinson-Cin 208
White-StL 199
Groat-Pit 199

Doubles
Robinson-Cin 51
Mays-SF 36
Groat-Pit 34

Triples
Wills-LA 10
Virdon-Pit 10
W.Davis-LA 10
Callison-Phi 10

Home Runs
Mays-SF 49
H.Aaron-Mil 45
Robinson-Cin 39
Banks-Chi 37
Cepeda-SF 35

Total Bases
Mays-SF 382
Robinson-Cin 380
H.Aaron-Mil 366
T.Davis-LA 356
Cepeda-SF 324

Runs Batted In
T.Davis-LA 153
Mays-SF 141
Robinson-Cin 136
H.Aaron-Mil 128
Howard-LA 119

Runs Produced
T.Davis-LA 246
Robinson-Cin 231
Mays-SF 222
H.Aaron-Mil 210

Bases On Balls
Mathews-Mil 101
Gilliam-LA 93
Ashburn-NY 81
Mays-SF 78

Batting Average
T.Davis-LA .346
Robinson-Cin .342
Musial-StL .330
White-StL .324
H.Aaron-Mil .323

On Base Percentage
Robinson-Cin .424
Musial-StL .420
Skinner-Pit .397
Altman-Chi .394
H.Aaron-Mil .393

Slugging Average
Robinson-Cin .624
H.Aaron-Mil .618
Mays-SF .615
Howard-LA .560
T.Davis-LA .535

Production
Robinson-Cin 1.048
H.Aaron-Mil 1.012
Mays-SF 1.001
Musial-StL .928
T.Davis-LA .914

Adjusted Production
Robinson-Cin 174
H.Aaron-Mil 168
Mays-SF 162
T.Davis-LA 153
Howard-LA 150

Batter Runs
Robinson-Cin 66.6
Mays-SF 54.0
H.Aaron-Mil 53.9
T.Davis-LA 37.1
Altman-Chi 31.4

Adjusted Batter Runs
Robinson-Cin 65.1
H.Aaron-Mil 54.7
Mays-SF 53.1
T.Davis-LA 43.1
Howard-LA 29.4

Clutch Hitting Index
T.Davis-LA 146
Santo-Chi 130
Howard-LA 127
White-StL 120
Kuenn-SF 118

Runs Created
Robinson-Cin 160
Mays-SF 146
H.Aaron-Mil 140
T.Davis-LA 129
White-StL 114

Total Average
Robinson-Cin 1.147
H.Aaron-Mil 1.066
Mays-SF 1.064
Altman-Chi .947
Skinner-Pit .940

Stolen Bases
Wills-LA 104
W.Davis-LA 32
Pinson-Cin 26
Javier-StL 26
Taylor-Phi 20

Stolen Base Average
Mays-SF 90.0
Wills-LA 88.9
W.Davis-LA 82.1
Clendenon-Pit 80.0
Pinson-Cin 76.5

Stolen Base Runs
Wills-LA 23.4
W.Davis-LA 5.4
Mays-SF 4.2
Pinson-Cin 3.0

Fielding Runs
Mazeroski-Pit 40.7
Callison-Phi 25.8
Edwards-Cin 24.7
Crandall-Mil 14.7
H.Aaron-Mil 14.0

Total Player Rating
Robinson-Cin 6.3
H.Aaron-Mil 5.9
Mays-SF 5.4
Mazeroski-Pit 4.6
Callison-Phi 4.4

Wins
Drysdale-LA 25
Sanford-SF 24
Purkey-Cin 23
Jay-Cin 21

Win Percentage
Purkey-Cin .821
Sanford-SF .774
Drysdale-LA .735
Pierce-SF .727
Shaw-Mil .625

Games
Perranoski-LA 70
Baldschun-Phi 67
Roebuck-LA 64
Face-Pit 63
Olivo-Pit 62

Complete Games
Spahn-Mil 22
O'Dell-SF 20
Mahaffey-Phi 20
Drysdale-LA 19

Shutouts
Gibson-StL 5
Friend-Pit 5

Saves
Face-Pit 28
Perranoski-LA 20
Miller-SF 19
McDaniel-StL 14

Innings Pitched
Drysdale-LA 314
Purkey-Cin 288
O'Dell-SF 281
Mahaffey-Phi 274
Jay-Cin 273

Fewest Hits/Game
Koufax-LA 6.55
Gibson-StL 6.69
Bennett-Phi 7.41
Drysdale-LA 7.80
Farrell-Hou 7.81

Fewest BB/Game
Shaw-Mil 1.76
Friend-Pit 1.82
Spahn-Mil 1.84
Pierce-SF 1.94
Purkey-Cin 2.00

Strikeouts
Drysdale-LA 232
Koufax-LA 216
Gibson-StL 208
Farrell-Hou 203
O'Dell-SF 195

Strikeouts/Game
Koufax-LA 10.57
Johnson-Hou 8.13
Gibson-StL 8.00
Bennett-Phi 7.66
Farrell-Hou 7.55

Wins Above Team
Purkey-Cin 8.3
Sanford-SF 7.0
Drysdale-LA 6.1
Roebuck-LA 3.5
Pierce-SF 3.3

Earned Run Average
Koufax-LA 2.54
Shaw-Mil 2.80
Purkey-Cin 2.81
Drysdale-LA 2.84
Gibson-StL 2.85

Adjusted ERA
Gibson-StL 148
Purkey-Cin 141
Koufax-LA 141
Broglio-StL 140
Shaw-Mil 138

Opponents' Batting Avg.
Koufax-LA .197
Gibson-StL .204
Bennett-Phi .224
Drysdale-LA .230
Farrell-Hou .233

Opponents' On Base Pct.
Koufax-LA .259
Farrell-Hou .275
Drysdale-LA .280
Spahn-Mil .281
Pierce-SF .282

Starter Runs
Drysdale-LA 38.5
Purkey-Cin 36.1
Koufax-LA 28.6
Shaw-Mil 28.5
Gibson-StL 28.5

Adjusted Starter Runs
Purkey-Cin 36.5
Gibson-StL 35.5
Broglio-StL 29.9
Friend-Pit 27.1
Shaw-Mil 26.7

Clutch Pitching Index
Shaw-Mil 123
Friend-Pit 119
Broglio-StL 116
McBean-Pit 114
Koonce-Chi 111

Relief Runs
Face-Pit 20.8
McMahon-Mil-Hou 20.0
Shantz-Hou-StL 17.6
Umbricht-Hou 14.3
Perranoski-LA 12.9

Adjusted Relief Runs
Face-Pit 21.3
Shantz-Hou-StL 18.7
McMahon-Mil-Hou 18.2
Elston-Chi 13.4
Umbricht-Hou 12.8

Relief Ranking
Face-Pit 46.4
McMahon-Mil-Hou 26.6
Elston-Chi 25.5
Shantz-Hou-StL 23.4
Baldschun-Phi 18.1

Total Pitcher Index
Gibson-StL 4.7
Purkey-Cin 3.9
Drysdale-LA 3.1
Spahn-Mil 3.1
Broglio-StL 3.1

Total Baseball Ranking
Robinson-Cin 6.3
H.Aaron-Mil 5.9
Mays-SF 5.4
Gibson-StL 4.7
Mazeroski-Pit 4.6

TEAM	G	W	L	PCT	GB	R	OR	AB	H	2B	3B	HR	BB	SO	AVG	OBP	SLG	PRO	/A	BR	/A	PF	CHI	RC	TA	SB	CS	SBA	SBR
NY	162	96	66	.593		817	680	5644	1509	240	29	199	584	842	.267	.339	.426	.765	112	87	134	94	99	816	.714	42	29	59	-4
MIN	163	91	71	.562	5	798	713	5561	1445	215	39	185	649	823	.260	.340	.412	.752	108	67	32	105	99	789	.705	33	20	62	-1
LA	162	86	76	.531	10	718	706	5499	1377	232	35	137	602	917	.250	.328	.380	.708	97	-22	-37	102	102	698	.650	46	27	63	-1
DET	161	85	76	.528	10.5	758	692	5456	1352	191	36	209	651	894	.248	.332	.411	.743	106	41	-38	111	99	757	.705	69	21	77	8
CHI	162	85	77	.525	11	707	658	5514	1415	250	56	92	620	674	.257	.336	.372	.708	97	-13	23	95	99	701	.653	76	40	66	0
CLE	80	82	82	.494	16	682	745	5484	1341	202	22	180	502	939	.245	.314	.388	.702	94	-46	-29	98	103	671	.636	35	16	69	1
BAL	162	77	85	.475	19	652	680	5491	1363	225	34	156	516	931	.248	.316	.387	.703	95	-41	-2	95	97	665	.633	45	32	58	-5
BOS	160	76	84	.475	19	707	756	5530	1429	257	53	146	525	923	.258	.326	.403	.729	102	9	-6	102	98	716	.662	39	33	54	-7
KC	162	72	90	.444	24	745	837	5576	1467	220	58	116	556	803	.263	.334	.386	.720	100	3	2	100	102	738	.667	76	21	78	10
WAS	162	60	101	.373	35.5	599	716	5484	1370	206	38	132	466	789	.250	.310	.373	.683	89	-81	-85	101	96	623	.611	99	53	65	-1
TOT	809					7183		55239	14068	2238	400	1552	5671	8535	.255	.328	.394	.722								560	292	66	-6

TEAM	CG	SHO	SV	IP	H	H/G	HR	BB	BB/G	SO	SO/G	ERA	/A	OAVG	OOBA	PR	/A	PF	CPI	FA	E	DP	FW	PW	BW	SBW	DIF
NY	33	10	42	1470.3	1375	8.4	146	499	3.1	838	5.1	3.70	98	.247	.307	43	-10	92	96	.979	131	151	.3	-1.0	13.5	-.3	2.6
MIN	53	11	27	1462.3	1400	8.6	166	493	3.0	948	5.8	3.90	106	.253	.313	12	35	104	99	.980	129	173	.4	3.5	3.2	-.0	2.9
LA	23	15	47	1466.0	1412	8.7	118	616	3.8	858	5.3	3.70	109	.252	.325	44	57	102	104	.972	175	153	-2.2	5.7	-3.7	-.0	5.2
DET	46	8	35	1443.7	1452	9.1	169	503	3.1	873	5.4	3.81	115	.258	.317	25	91	110	105	.974	156	114	-1.1	9.1	-3.8	.9	-.6
CHI	50	13	28	1451.7	1380	8.6	123	537	3.3	821	5.1	3.73	99	.250	.314	38	1	94	97	.982	110	153	1.5	.1	2.3	.0	.0
CLE	45	12	31	1441.0	1410	8.8	174	594	3.7	780	4.9	4.14	95	.257	.328	-27	-36	99	102	.977	139	168	-.1	-3.6	-2.9	.2	5.5
BAL	32	8	33	1462.3	1373	8.5	147	549	3.4	898	5.5	3.69	102	.248	.314	45	12	95	101	.980	122	152	.8	1.2	-.2	-.4	-5.4
BOS	34	12	40	1437.7	1416	8.9	159	632	4.0	923	5.8	4.22	97	.258	.332	-39	-21	103	101	.979	131	152	.3	-2.1	-.6	-.6	-1.0
KC	32	4	33	1434.0	1450	9.1	199	655	4.1	825	5.2	4.79	84	.263	.339	-131	-123	101	97	.979	142	131	.3	-12.4	.2	1.1	1.8
WAS	38	11	13	1445.0	1400	8.7	151	593	3.7	771	4.8	4.04	100	.255	.323	-11	3	102	100	.978	139	160	-.1	.3	-8.5	-.0	-12.1
TOT	386	104	329	14514.0		8.7			3.5		5.3	3.97		.255	.328					.978	1364	1507					

Runs		Hits		Doubles		Triples		Home Runs		Total Bases	
Pearson-LA	115	Richardson-NY	209	Robinson-Chi	45	Cimoli-KC	15	Killebrew-Min	48	Colavito-Det	309
Siebern-KC	114	Lumpe-KC	193	Yastrzemski-Bos	43	Robinson-Chi	10	Cash-Det	39	Robinson-Bal	308
Allison-Min	102	Robinson-Bal	192	Bressoud-Bos	40	Lumpe-KC	10	Wagner-LA	37	Wagner-LA	306
Yastrzemski-Bos	99	Yastrzemski-Bos	191	Richardson-NY	38	Clinton-Bos	10	Colavito-Det	37	Yastrzemski-Bos	303
Richardson-NY	99	Robinson-Chi	187							Killebrew-Min	301

Runs Batted In		Runs Produced		Bases On Balls		Batting Average		On Base Percentage		Slugging Average	
Killebrew-Min	126	Siebern-KC	206	Mantle-NY	122	Runnels-Bos	.326	Mantle-NY	.488	Mantle-NY	.605
Siebern-KC	117	Robinson-Chi	187	Siebern-KC	110	Mantle-NY	.321	Siebern-KC	.416	Killebrew-Min	.545
Colavito-Det	112	Rollins-Min	176	Killebrew-Min	106	Robinson-Chi	.312	Cunningham-Chi	.415	Colavito-Det	.514
Robinson-Chi	109	Allison-Min	175	Cash-Det	104	Hinton-Was	.310	Runnels-Bos	.411	Cash-Det	.513
Wagner-LA	107	Yastrzemski-Bos	174	Cunningham-Chi	101	Siebern-KC	.308	Robinson-Chi	.387	Allison-Min	.511

Production		Adjusted Production		Batter Runs		Adjusted Batter Runs		Clutch Hitting Index		Runs Created	
Mantle-NY	1.093	Mantle-NY	205	Mantle-NY	57.3	Mantle-NY	61.0	Robinson-Chi	144	Siebern-KC	129
Killebrew-Min	.914	Siebern-KC	144	Siebern-KC	41.1	Siebern-KC	41.1	Howard-NY	124	Mantle-NY	126
Siebern-KC	.911	Robinson-Chi	138	Killebrew-Min	33.1	Killebrew-Min	30.8	Malzone-Bos	122	Colavito-Det	117
Cash-Det	.897	Killebrew-Min	136	Colavito-Det	31.4	Cunningham-Chi	29.5	Thomas-LA	120	Killebrew-Min	113
Colavito-Det	.889	Cunningham-Chi	134	Kaline-Det	30.7	Cunningham-Chi	29.1	Siebern-KC	120	Robinson-Chi	113

Total Average		Stolen Bases		Stolen Base Average		Stolen Base Runs		Fielding Runs		Total Player Rating	
Siebern-KC	.958	Aparicio-Chi	31	Howser-KC	90.5	Wood-Det	5.4	Boyer-NY	35.5	Mantle-NY	5.4
Cash-Det	.957	Hinton-Was	28	Wood-Det	88.9	Howser-KC	4.5	Versalles-Min	34.1	Boyer-NY	4.1
Killebrew-Min	.949	Wood-Det	24	Charles-KC	83.3	Charles-KC	3.6	Moran-LA	22.3	Romano-Cle	3.9
Allison-Min	.914	Charles-KC	20	Tartabull-KC	79.2	Tartabull-KC	2.7	Kindall-Cle	21.2	Siebern-KC	3.4
Colavito-Det	.899			Hinton-Was	73.7	Mantle-NY	2.7	Bressoud-Bos	21.0	Kaline-Det	3.2

Wins		Win Percentage		Games		Complete Games		Shutouts		Saves	
Terry-NY	23	Herbert-Chi	.690	Radatz-Bos	62	Pascual-Min	18	Pascual-Min	5	Radatz-Bos	24
Pascual-Min	20	Ford-NY	.680	Wyatt-KC	59	Kaat-Min	16	Kaat-Min	5	Bridges-NY	18
Herbert-Chi	20	Donovan-Cle	.667			Donovan-Cle	16	Donovan-Cle	5	Fox-Det	16
Donovan-Cle	20	Aguirre-Det	.667			Terry-NY	14	Monbouquette-Bos	4	Wilhelm-Bal	15
Bunning-Det	19	Terry-NY	.657					McBride-LA	4	Bell-Cle	12

Innings Pitched		Fewest Hits/Game		Fewest BB/Game		Strikeouts		Strikeouts/Game		Wins Above Team	
Terry-NY	299	Aguirre-Det	6.75	Donovan-Cle	1.69	Pascual-Min	206	Pizarro-Chi	7.67	Donovan-Cle	5.8
Kaat-Min	269	Cheney-Was	6.97	Terry-NY	1.72	Bunning-Det	184	Cheney-Was	7.65	Herbert-Chi	5.7
Pascual-Min	258	Belinsky-LA	7.17	Mossi-Det	1.80	Terry-NY	176	Pascual-Min	7.19	Bunning-Det	4.5
Ford-NY	258	Wilson-Bos	7.68	Roberts-Bal	1.93	Pizarro-Chi	173	Belinsky-LA	6.98	Wickersham-KC	4.1
Bunning-Det	258	Stenhouse-Was	7.72	Pascual-Min	2.06	Kaat-Min	173	Estrada-Bal	6.66	Aguirre-Det	3.9

Earned Run Average		Adjusted ERA		Opponents' Batting Avg.		Opponents' On Base Pct.		Starter Runs		Adjusted Starter Runs	
Aguirre-Det	2.21	Aguirre-Det	198	Aguirre-Det	.205	Aguirre-Det	.265	Aguirre-Det	42.3	Aguirre-Det	52.1
Roberts-Bal	2.78	Chance-LA	137	Cheney-Was	.213	Terry-NY	.266	Ford-NY	30.8	Kaat-Min	28.9
Ford-NY	2.90	Roberts-Bal	136	Belinsky-LA	.216	Pascual-Min	.282	Terry-NY	25.9	Chance-LA	25.1
Chance-LA	2.96	Kaat-Min	131	Terry-NY	.231	Roberts-Bal	.286	Roberts-Bal	25.3	Pascual-Min	22.9
Fisher-Chi	3.10	Cheney-Was	128	Wilson-Bos	.231	Fisher-Chi	.288	Kaat-Min	24.7	Bunning-Det	22.5

Clutch Pitching Index		Relief Runs		Adjusted Relief Runs		Relief Ranking		Total Pitcher Index		Total Baseball Ranking	
Chance-LA	114	Radatz-Bos	24.1	Radatz-Bos	25.7	Radatz-Bos	38.9	Aguirre-Det	4.4	Mantle-NY	5.4
Roberts-Bal	111	Hall-Bal	22.1	Hall-Bal	19.4	Wilhelm-Bal	38.0	Kaat-Min	4.1	Aguirre-Det	4.4
Ford-NY	110	Wilhelm-Bal	21.0	Wilhelm-Bal	18.9	Fox-Det	21.4	Pascual-Min	3.4	Boyer-NY	4.1
Ramos-Cle	110	Fox-Det	14.6	Fox-Det	17.2	Hall-Bal	20.0	Ford-NY	2.6	Kaat-Min	4.1
Perry-Cle	110	Fowler-LA	10.0	Fowler-LA	10.6	Morgan-LA	10.6	Roberts-Bal	2.3	Romano-Cle	3.9

TEAM	G	W	L	PCT	GB	R	OR	AB	H	2B	3B	HR	BB	SO	AVG	OBP	SLG	PRO	/A	BR	/A	PF	CHI	RC	TA	SB	CS	SBA	SBR
LA	163	99	63	.611		640	550	5428	1361	178	34	110	453	867	.251	.311	.357	.668	99	-2	28	95	104	596	.597	124	70	64	-4
STL	162	93	69	.574	6	747	628	5678	1540	231	66	128	458	915	.271	.328	.403	.731	117	119	72	107	98	751	.666	77	42	65	-1
SF	162	88	74	.543	11	725	641	5579	1442	206	35	197	441	889	.258	.318	.414	.732	117	138	63	107	99	661	.661	55	49	53	-12
PHI	162	87	75	.537	12	642	578	5524	1390	228	54	126	403	955	.252	.308	.381	.689	105	28	11	103	99	640	.610	56	39	59	-6
CIN	162	86	76	.531	13	648	594	5416	1333	225	44	122	474	960	.246	.312	.371	.683	103	25	0	104	101	630	.620	92	58	61	-6
MIL	163	84	78	.519	15	677	603	5518	1345	204	39	139	525	954	.244	.314	.370	.684	104	30	24	101	102	643	.620	75	52	59	-8
CHI	162	82	80	.506	17	570	578	5404	1286	205	44	127	439	1049	.238	.300	.363	.663	97	-20	-51	105	96	573	.583	68	60	53	-15
PIT	162	74	88	.457	25	567	595	5536	1385	181	49	108	454	940	.250	.310	.359	.669	99	-1	7	99	91	603	.584	57	41	58	-7
HOU	162	66	96	.407	33	464	640	5384	1184	170	39	62	456	938	.220	.284	.301	.585	75	-159	-111	92	103	461	.493	39	30	57	-5
NY	162	51	111	.315	48	501	774	5336	1168	156	35	99	457	1078	.219	.286	.315	.601	80	-128	-124	99	105	477	.515	41	52	44	-18
TOT	811					6181		54803	13434	1984	439	1215	4560	9545	.245	.308	.364	.671								684	493	58	-90

TEAM	CG	SHO	SV	IP	H	H/G	HR	BB	BB/G	SO	SO/G	ERA	/A	OAVG	OOBA	PR	/A	PF	CPI	FA	E	DP	FW	PW	BW	SBW	DIF
LA	51	24	29	1469.7	1329	8.1	111	402	2.5	1095	6.7	2.85	108	.239	.289	70	36	94	103	.975	159	129	-.0	3.9	3.0	.5	10.6
STL	45	17	32	1463.3	1329	8.2	124	463	2.8	978	6.0	3.32	105	.241	.300	-5	24	106	97	.976	147	136	.6	2.6	7.8	.9	.0
SF	46	9	30	1469.0	1380	8.5	126	464	2.8	954	5.8	3.35	93	.245	.302	-9	-40	94	99	.975	156	113	.1	-4.3	15.0	-.3	-3.4
PHI	45	12	31	1457.3	1262	7.8	113	553	3.4	1052	6.5	3.09	108	.235	.305	32	41	102	104	.978	142	147	.9	4.4	1.2	.3	-.9
CIN	55	22	36	1439.7	1307	8.2	117	425	2.7	1048	6.6	3.29	105	.242	.296	-1	15	103	96	.978	135	127	1.3	1.6	.0	.3	1.7
MIL	56	18	25	1472.0	1327	8.1	149	489	3.0	924	5.6	3.26	100	.241	.300	3	2	100	103	.980	129	161	1.7	.2	2.6	.1	-1.6
CHI	45	15	28	1457.0	1357	8.4	119	400	2.5	851	5.3	3.08	113	.248	.296	34	62	105	105	.976	155	172	.2	6.7	-5.5	-.6	.3
PIT	34	16	33	1448.0	1350	8.4	99	457	2.8	900	5.6	3.10	105	.249	.306	31	26	99	107	.972	182	195	-1.4	-.8	.8	.2	-9.4
HOU	36	16	20	1450.3	1341	8.3	95	378	2.3	937	5.8	3.44	91	.244	.290	-24	-51	95	87	.974	162	100	-.3	-5.5	-12.0	-1.0	2.4
NY	42	5	12	1427.3	1452	9.2	162	529	3.3	806	5.1	4.12	83	.262	.326	-132	-112	104	100	.967	210	151	-3.1	-12.2	-13.5	-1.0	-.3
TOT	459	154	276	14553.7		8.3			2.8		5.9	3.29		.245	.308					.975	1577	1431					

Runs
Aaron-Mil 121
Mays-SF 115
Flood-StL 112
White-StL 106
McCovey-SF 103

Hits
Pinson-Cin 204
Groat-StL 201
Aaron-Mil 201
White-StL 200
Flood-StL 200

Doubles
Groat-StL 43
Pinson-Cin 37
Williams-Chi 36
Gonzalez-Phi 36
Callison-Phi 36

Triples
Pinson-Cin 14
Gonzalez-Phi 12
Groat-StL 11
Callison-Phi 11
Brock-Chi 11

Home Runs
McCovey-SF 44
Aaron-Mil 44
Mays-SF 38
Cepeda-SF 34
Howard-LA 28

Total Bases
Aaron-Mil 370
Mays-SF 347
Pinson-Cin 335
Cepeda-SF 326
White-StL 323

Runs Batted In
Aaron-Mil 130
Boyer-StL 111
White-StL 109
Pinson-Cin 106
Mays-SF 103

Runs Produced
Aaron-Mil 207
White-StL 188
Pinson-Cin 180
Mays-SF 180
Boyer-StL 173

Bases On Balls
Mathews-Mil 124
Robinson-Cin 81
Aaron-Mil 78
Boyer-StL 70
Schofield-Pit 69

Batting Average
T.Davis-LA 326
Clemente-Pit 320
Groat-StL 319
Aaron-Mil 319
Cepeda-SF 316

On Base Percentage
Mathews-Mil 400
Aaron-Mil 394
Mays-SF 384
Robinson-Cin 381
Groat-StL 380

Slugging Average
Aaron-Mil 586
Mays-SF 582
McCovey-SF 566
Cepeda-SF 563
Pinson-Cin 514

Production
Aaron-Mil 980
Mays-SF 966
Cepeda-SF 930
McCovey-SF 916
Pinson-Cin 864

Adjusted Production
Mays-SF 182
Aaron-Mil 176
Cepeda-SF 171
McCovey-SF 166
Mathews-Mil 144

Batter Runs
Aaron-Mil 62.9
Mays-SF 55.8
Cepeda-SF 45.4
McCovey-SF 41.0
Mathews-Mil 37.4

Adjusted Batter Runs
Aaron-Mil 62.3
Mays-SF 58.8
Cepeda-SF 48.2
McCovey-SF 43.8
Mathews-Mil 36.7

Clutch Hitting Index
Robinson-Cin 147
Fairly-LA 146
Sievers-Phi 141
Boyer-StL 140
Edwards-Cin 130

Runs Created
Aaron-Mil 149
Mays-SF 131
White-StL 117
Cepeda-SF 113
Pinson-Cin 113

Total Average
Aaron-Mil 1.074
Mays-SF 991
McCovey-SF 914
Cepeda-SF 914
Mathews-Mil 904

Stolen Bases
Wills-LA 40
Aaron-Mil 31
Pinson-Cin 27
Robinson-Cin 26
W.Davis-LA 25

Stolen Base Average
Aaron-Mil 86.1
Gilliam-LA 79.2
Pinson-Cin 77.1
Robinson-Cin 72.2
Taylor-Phi 71.9

Stolen Base Runs
Aaron-Mil 6.3
Pinson-Cin 3.3
Maye-Mil 3.0
Harper-Cin 3.0
Gilliam-LA 2.7

Fielding Runs
Mazeroski-Pit 46.6
Hubbs-Chi 23.5
Schofield-Pit 17.8
Edwards-Cin 16.6
Menke-Mil 14.4

Total Player Rating
Aaron-Mil 6.2
Mays-SF 5.9
Mathews-Mil 4.7
Mazeroski-Pit 4.6
Cepeda-SF 4.1

Wins
Marichal-SF 25
Koufax-LA 25
Spahn-Mil 23
Maloney-Cin 23
Ellsworth-Chi 22

Win Percentage
Perranoski-LA 842
Koufax-LA 833
Spahn-Mil 767
Maloney-Cin 767
Marichal-SF 758

Games
Perranoski-LA 69
Baldschun-Phi 65
Bearnarth-NY 58
Sisk-Pit 57
McDaniel-Chi 57

Complete Games
Spahn-Mil 22
Koufax-LA 20
Ellsworth-Chi 19
Marichal-SF 18
Drysdale-LA 17

Shutouts
Koufax-LA 11
Spahn-Mil 7
Simmons-StL 6
Maloney-Cin 6

Saves
McDaniel-Chi 22
Perranoski-LA 21
Face-Pit 16
Baldschun-Phi 16
Henry-Cin 14

Innings Pitched
Marichal-SF 321
Drysdale-LA 315
Koufax-LA 311
Ellsworth-Chi 291
Sanford-SF 284

Fewest Hits/Game
Koufax-LA 6.19
Culp-Phi 6.56
Maloney-Cin 6.59
Ellsworth-Chi 6.90
Farrell-Hou 7.17

Fewest BB/Game
Friend-Pit 1.47
Farrell-Hou 1.56
Nuxhall-Cin 1.62
Drysdale-LA 1.63
Koufax-LA 1.68

Strikeouts
Koufax-LA 306
Maloney-Cin 265
Drysdale-LA 251
Marichal-SF 248
Gibson-StL 204

Strikeouts/Game
Maloney-Cin 9.54
Koufax-LA 8.86
Culp-Phi 7.80
Short-Phi 7.27
Lemaster-Mil 7.22

Wins Above Team
Koufax-LA 9.3
Marichal-SF 8.7
Spahn-Mil 8.5
Maloney-Cin 8.3
Ellsworth-Chi 6.7

Earned Run Average
Koufax-LA 1.88
Ellsworth-Chi 2.10
Friend-Pit 2.34
Marichal-SF 2.41
Simmons-StL 2.47

Adjusted ERA
Ellsworth-Chi 165
Koufax-LA 163
Simmons-StL 140
Friend-Pit 139
Jackson-Chi 136

Opponents' Batting Avg.
Koufax-LA 189
Maloney-Cin 202
Culp-Phi 206
Ellsworth-Chi 210
Broglio-StL 216

Opponents' On Base Pct.
Koufax-LA 227
Farrell-Hou 250
Marichal-SF 254
Ellsworth-Chi 259
Friend-Pit 264

Starter Runs
Koufax-LA 48.6
Ellsworth-Chi 38.3
Marichal-SF 31.3
Friend-Pit 28.3
Drysdale-LA 23.1

Adjusted Starter Runs
Ellsworth-Chi 43.9
Koufax-LA 41.2
Jackson-Chi 27.8
Friend-Pit 27.4
Simmons-StL 25.9

Clutch Pitching Index
Schwall-Pit 118
Spahn-Mil 115
Short-Phi 111
Cardwell-Pit 110
Buhl-Chi 109

Relief Runs
Perranoski-LA 23.1
Veale-Pit 19.5
Klippstein-Phi 16.9
Woodeshick-Hou 16.6
Baldschun-Phi 12.6

Adjusted Relief Runs
Perranoski-LA 20.1
Veale-Pit 19.2
Klippstein-Phi 17.6
Woodeshick-Hou . . . 14.5
Baldschun-Phi 13.4

Relief Ranking
Perranoski-LA 33.9
Woodeshick-Hou . . . 25.8
Baldschun-Phi . . . 23.2
Klippstein-Phi 18.4
Veale-Pit 17.2

Total Pitcher Index
Ellsworth-Chi 5.2
Jackson-Chi 3.8
Koufax-LA 3.8
Spahn-Mil 3.3
Simmons-StL 2.7

Total Baseball Ranking
Aaron-Mil 6.2
Mays-SF 5.9
Ellsworth-Chi 5.2
Mathews-Mil 4.7
Mazeroski-Pit 4.6

TEAM	G	W	L	PCT	GB	R	OR	AB	H	2B	3B	HR	BB	SO	AVG	OBP	SLG	PRO	/A	BR	/A	PF	CHI	RC	TA	SB	CS	SBA	SBR
NY	161	104	57	.646		714	547	5506	1387	197	35	188	434	808	.252	.310	.403	.713	105	27	23	101	105	686	.643	42	26	62	-2
CHI	162	94	68	.580	10.5	683	544	5508	1379	208	40	114	571	896	.250	.325	.365	.690	99	3	-26	104	101	675	.631	64	28	70	2
MIN	161	91	70	.565	13	767	602	5531	1408	223	35	225	547	912	.255	.326	.430	.756	117	116	113	100	97	777	.704	32	14	70	1
BAL	162	86	76	.531	18.5	644	621	5448	1359	207	32	146	469	940	.249	.312	.380	.692	99	-6	34	94	100	645	.628	97	34	74	9
DET	162	79	83	.488	25.5	700	703	5500	1388	195	36	148	592	908	.252	.329	.382	.711	105	43	19	104	98	699	.656	73	32	70	3
CLE	162	79	83	.488	25.5	653	702	5496	1314	214	29	169	469	1102	.239	.304	.385	.685	97	-25	-3	97	100	634	.616	59	36	62	-3
BOS	161	76	85	.472	28	666	704	5575	1403	247	34	171	475	954	.252	.313	.400	.713	105	31	-7	106	96	684	.638	27	16	63	-1
KC	162	73	89	.451	31.5	615	704	5495	1356	225	38	95	529	829	.247	.316	.353	.669	93	-40	-89	108	98	616	.593	47	26	64	-1
LA	161	70	91	.435	34	597	660	5506	1378	208	38	95	448	916	.250	.312	.354	.666	92	-52	4	91	98	608	.581	43	30	59	-4
WAS	162	56	106	.346	48.5	578	812	5446	1237	190	35	138	497	963	.227	.295	.351	.646	86	-95	-79	98	103	569	.576	68	28	71	4
TOT	808					6599		55011	13609	2114	352	1489	5031	9228	.247	.314	.380	.694								552	270	67	4

TEAM	CG	SHO	SV	IP	H	H/G	HR	BB	BB/G	SO	SO/G	ERA	/A	OAVG	OOBA	PR	/A	PF	CPI	FA	E	DP	FW	PW	BW	SBW	DIF
NY	59	19	31	1449.3	1239	7.7	115	476	3.0	965	6.0	3.07	116	.231	.292	89	78	98	98	.982	110	162	1.4	8.2	2.4	-.2	11.7
CHI	49	21	39	1469.0	1311	8.0	100	440	2.7	932	5.7	2.97	125	.238	.294	107	120	102	102	.979	131	163	.2	12.6	-2.7	.2	2.7
MIN	58	13	30	1446.3	1322	8.2	162	459	2.9	941	5.9	3.28	108	.241	.298	56	43	98	105	.976	144	140	-.5	4.5	11.9	.0	-5.4
BAL	35	8	43	1452.0	1353	8.4	137	507	3.1	913	5.7	3.45	98	.248	.309	28	-10	93	104	.984	99	157	2.0	-1.1	3.6	.9	-.5
DET	42	7	28	1456.3	1407	8.7	195	477	2.9	930	5.7	3.90	94	.252	.311	-43	-22	104	102	.982	113	142	1.2	-2.3	2.0	.3	-3.2
CLE	40	14	25	1469.0	1390	8.5	176	478	2.9	1018	6.2	3.79	94	.248	.305	-26	-40	98	98	.977	143	129	-.5	-4.2	-.3	-.4	3.3
BOS	29	7	32	1449.7	1367	8.5	152	539	3.3	1009	6.3	3.97	97	.247	.311	-55	-17	107	93	.978	135	119	-.0	-1.8	-.7	-.1	-1.8
KC	35	11	29	1458.0	1417	8.7	156	540	3.3	887	5.5	3.92	101	.255	.320	-46	4	109	100	.980	127	131	.4	.4	-9.3	-.1	.6
LA	30	13	31	1455.3	1317	8.1	120	578	3.6	889	5.5	3.52	95	.241	.314	16	-27	92	100	.974	163	155	-1.6	-2.8	-.4	-.5	-6.0
WAS	29	8	25	1447.3	1486	9.2	176	537	3.3	744	4.6	4.42	83	.265	.327	-126	-119	101	98	.971	182	165	-2.7	-12.5	-8.3	.4	-1.9
TOT	406	121	313	14552.0		8.4			3.1		5.7	3.63		.247	.314					.978	1347	1445					

Runs	**Hits**	**Doubles**	**Triples**	**Home Runs**	**Total Bases**
Allison-Min 99	Yastrzemski-Bos 183	Yastrzemski-Bos 40	Versalles-Min 13	Killebrew-Min 45	Stuart-Bos 319
Pearson-LA 92	Ward-Chi 177	Ward-Chi 34	Hinton-Was 12	Stuart-Bos 42	Ward-Chi 289
Yastrzemski-Bos 91	Pearson-LA 176	Torres-LA 32	Fregosi-LA 12	Allison-Min 35	Killebrew-Min 286
Tresh-NY 91	Kaline-Det 172	Causey-KC 32	Cimoli-KC 11	Hall-Min 33	Kaline-Det 283
Colavito-Det 91	Fregosi-LA 170	Alvis-Cle 32		Howard-NY 28	Allison-Min 281

Runs Batted In	**Runs Produced**	**Bases On Balls**	**Batting Average**	**On Base Percentage**	**Slugging Average**
Stuart-Bos 118	Kaline-Det 163	Yastrzemski-Bos 95	Yastrzemski-Bos ... .321	Yastrzemski-Bos .... .419	Killebrew-Min ..... .555
Kaline-Det 101	Colavito-Det 160	Pearson-LA 92	Kaline-Det .... .312	Pearson-LA .... .403	Allison-Min ...... .533
Killebrew-Min 96	Stuart-Bos 157	Allison-Min 90	Rollins-Min ...... .307	Cash-Det .... .388	Howard-NY .... .528
Colavito-Det 91	Allison-Min 155	Cash-Det 89	Pearson-LA .... .304	Allison-Min .... .381	Stuart-Bos .... .521
Allison-Min 91	Siebern-KC 147	Colavito-Det 84	Ward-Chi .... .295	Kaline-Det .... .378	Hall-Min .... .521

Production	**Adjusted Production**	**Batter Runs**	**Adjusted Batter Runs**	**Clutch Hitting Index**	**Runs Created**
Allison-Min .... .914	Allison-Min 152	Yastrzemski-Bos ... 42.0	Allison-Min 38.3	Hansen-Chi 137	Yastrzemski-Bos 118
Killebrew-Min ..... .908	Killebrew-Min 149	Allison-Min 38.6	Yastrzemski-Bos ... 37.8	Siebern-KC 133	Allison-Min 113
Yastrzemski-Bos ... .894	Kaline-Det 142	Kaline-Det 34.3	Killebrew-Min 33.3	Charles-KC 124	Kaline-Det 105
Kaline-Det .... .891	Yastrzemski-Bos ... 142	Killebrew-Min 33.4	Kaline-Det 32.0	Colavito-Det 123	Ward-Chi 104
Howard-NY .... .871	Howard-NY 139	Cash-Det 28.6	Pearson-LA 30.3	Kaline-Det 123	Pearson-LA 100

Total Average	**Stolen Bases**	**Stolen Base Average**	**Stolen Base Runs**	**Fielding Runs**	**Total Player Rating**
Allison-Min .... .969	Aparicio-Bal 40	Tartabull-KC 94.1	Aparicio-Bal 8.4	Hansen-Chi 27.2	Yastrzemski-Bos 4.2
Yastrzemski-Bos ... .928	Hinton-Was 25	Aparicio-Bal 87.0	Tartabull-KC 4.2	Boyer-NY 18.4	Howard-NY 3.9
Killebrew-Min ..... .907	Wood-Det 18	Wood-Det 78.3	Weis-Chi 3.9	Moran-LA 17.5	Allison-Min 3.4
Tresh-NY .... .886	Snyder-Bal 18	Snyder-Bal 78.3	Richardson-NY 3.9	Kubek-NY 12.5	Hall-Min 3.2
Cash-Det .... .884	Pearson-LA 17	Hinton-Was 73.5	Smith-Bal 2.7	Hall-Min 12.4	Hansen-Chi 2.9

Wins	**Win Percentage**	**Games**	**Complete Games**	**Shutouts**	**Saves**
Ford-NY 24	Ford-NY .... .774	Miller-Bal 71	Terry-NY 18	Herbert-Chi 7	Miller-Bal 27
Pascual-Min 21	Bouton-NY .... .750	Radatz-Bos 66	Pascual-Min 18	Bouton-NY 6	Radatz-Bos 25
Bouton-NY 21	Radatz-Bos .... .714	Dailey-Min 66	Stigman-Min 15		Wyatt-KC 21
Monbouquette-Bos ... 20	Peters-Chi .... .704	Lamabe-Bos 65	Herbert-Chi 14		Wilhelm-Chi 21
Barber-Bal 20	Pascual-Min .... .700	Wyatt-KC 63	Aguirre-Det 14		Dailey-Min 21

Innings Pitched	**Fewest Hits/Game**	**Fewest BB/Game**	**Strikeouts**	**Strikeouts/Game**	**Wins Above Team**
Ford-NY 269	Downing-NY 5.83	Donovan-Cle 1.22	Pascual-Min 202	Downing-NY 8.74	Ford-NY 6.4
Terry-NY 268	Bouton-NY 6.90	Terry-NY 1.31	Bunning-Det 196	Ramos-Cle 8.22	Monbouquette-Bos ... 6.3
Monbouquette-Bos ... 267	Drabowsky-KC 6.98	Herbert-Chi 1.40	Stigman-Min 193	Pascual-Min 7.33	Pascual-Min 5.3
Barber-Bal 259	Morehead-Bos 7.05	Monbouquette-Bos .. 1.42	Peters-Chi 189	Stigman-Min 7.21	Radatz-Bos 5.2
	McBride-LA 7.10	Roberts-Bal 1.43	Ford-NY 189	Bunning-Det 7.11	Bouton-NY 4.7

Earned Run Average	**Adjusted ERA**	**Opponents' Batting Avg.**	**Opponents' On Base Pct.**	**Starter Runs**	**Adjusted Starter Runs**
Peters-Chi 2.33	Peters-Chi 159	Downing-NY .... .184	Ramos-Cle .... .269	Peters-Chi 35.0	Peters-Chi 37.2
Pizarro-Chi 2.39	Pizarro-Chi 155	Morehead-Bos ..... .211	Terry-NY .... .269	Pascual-Min 32.0	Pizarro-Chi 31.6
Pascual-Min 2.47	Pascual-Min 144	Bouton-NY .... .212	Roberts-Bal ...... .269	Bouton-NY 30.4	Pascual-Min 29.8
Bouton-NY 2.53	Bouton-NY 141	Drabowsky-KC ..... .214	Peters-Chi .... .274	Pizarro-Chi 29.7	Bouton-NY 28.5
Downing-NY 2.56	Downing-NY 139	Peters-Chi .... .216	Downing-NY ...... .274	Ford-NY 26.5	Ford-NY 24.4

Clutch Pitching Index	**Relief Runs**	**Adjusted Relief Runs**	**Relief Ranking**	**Total Pitcher Index**	**Total Baseball Ranking**
Barber-Bal 127	Radatz-Bos 24.2	Radatz-Bos 27.7	Radatz-Bos 51.5	Peters-Chi 5.1	Peters-Chi 5.1
Stange-Min 121	Dailey-Min 20.0	Dailey-Min 19.0	Miller-Bal 22.4	Pascual-Min 4.0	Yastrzemski-Bos ... 4.2
Osteen-Was 120	Miller-Bal 17.2	Wilhelm-Chi 16.1	Dailey-Min 22.3	Pizarro-Chi 3.5	Pascual-Min 4.0
Segui-KC 115	Wilhelm-Chi 14.9	Miller-Bal 14.1	Wilhelm-Chi 19.4	Radatz-Bos 2.6	Howard-NY 3.9
Pascual-Min 115	Fowler-LA 11.9	Lamabe-Bos 11.9	Kline-Was 13.6	Ford-NY 2.6	Pizarro-Chi 3.5

TEAM	G	W	L	PCT	GB	R	OR	AB	H	2B	3B	HR	BB	SO	AVG	OBP	SLG	PRO	/A	BR	/A	PF	CHI	RC	TA	SB	CS	SBA	SBR
STL	162	93	69	.574		715	652	5625	**1531**	240	53	109	427	925	**.272**	.326	.392	.718	109	62	-18	112	99	711	.642	73	51	59	-8
PHI	162	92	70	.568	1	693	632	5493	1415	241	51	130	440	924	.258	.317	.391	.708	106	41	48	99	100	672	.630	30	35	46	-11
CIN	163	92	70	.568	1	660	**566**	5561	1383	220	38	130	457	974	.249	.310	.372	.682	99	-10	-30	103	102	642	.613	90	36	**71**	5
SF	162	90	72	.556	3	656	587	5535	1360	185	38	**165**	**505**	900	.246	.313	.382	.695	102	16	15	100	97	657	.628	64	35	65	-1
MIL	162	88	74	.543	5	**803**	744	5591	1522	**274**	32	159	486	**825**	**.272**	**.335**	**.418**	**.753**	**119**	**132**	**153**	97	101	**764**	**.687**	53	41	56	-8
PIT	162	80	82	.494	13	663	636	5566	1469	225	**54**	121	408	970	.264	.317	.389	.706	105	35	28	101	96	668	.619	39	33	54	-7
LA	164	80	82	.494	13	614	572	5499	1375	180	39	79	438	893	.250	.308	.340	.648	89	-69	-16	92	105	581	.575	**141**	60	70	**6**
CHI	162	76	86	.469	17	649	724	5545	1391	239	50	145	499	1041	.251	.316	.390	.706	105	37	2	105	93	679	.641	70	49	59	-7
HOU	162	66	96	.407	27	495	628	5303	1214	162	41	70	381	872	.229	.287	.315	.602	76	-158	-134	96	**106**	469	.503	40	48	45	-16
NY	163	53	109	.327	40	569	776	5566	1372	195	31	103	353	932	.246	.297	.348	.645	88	-83	-52	95	101	552	.543	36	31	54	-7
TOT	812					6517		55284	14032	2161	427	1211	4394	9256	.254	.313	.374	.687								636	419	60	-60

TEAM	CG	SHO	SV	IP	H	H/G	HR	BB	BB/G	SO	SO/G	ERA	/A	OAVG	OOBA	PR	/A	PF	CPI	FA	E	DP	FW	PW	BW	SBW	DIF
STL	47	10	38	1445.0	1405	8.8	133	410	2.6	877	5.5	3.43	115	.254	.303	16	80	111	104	.973	172	147	-.7	8.4	-1.9	-.2	6.4
PHI	37	17	**41**	1460.3	1402	8.6	129	440	2.7	1009	6.2	3.36	103	.252	.307	27	15	98	**106**	.975	157	150	.0	1.6	5.1	-.5	4.8
CIN	54	14	35	1467.0	1306	8.0	112	436	2.7	**1122**	**6.9**	3.07	**117**	.238	.292	75	**84**	102	100	**.979**	**130**	137	**1.5**	**8.9**	-3.2	1.2	2.6
SF	48	17	30	1476.0	1348	8.2	118	480	2.9	1023	6.2	3.19	110	.241	.300	56	51	99	102	.975	159	136	-.0	5.4	1.6	.5	1.5
MIL	45	14	39	1434.7	1411	8.9	160	452	2.8	906	5.7	4.12	82	.257	.310	-92	-114	96	94	.977	143	139	.8	-12.0	**16.1**	-.2	2.2
PIT	42	14	29	1443.7	1429	8.9	92	476	3.0	951	5.9	3.52	101	.259	.316	2	5	101	103	.972	177	**179**	-1.0	.5	3.0	-.0	-3.4
LA	47	**19**	27	1483.7	**1289**	**7.8**	**88**	458	2.8	1062	6.4	**2.95**	109	**.231**	**.288**	**95**	45	91	95	.973	170	126	-.6	4.7	-1.7	**1.3**	-4.7
CHI	**58**	11	19	1445.0	1510	9.4	144	423	2.6	737	4.6	4.08	92	.269	.317	-87	-50	106	98	.975	162	147	-.2	-5.3	.2	-.0	.3
HOU	30	9	31	1428.0	1421	9.0	105	**353**	**2.2**	852	5.4	3.41	102	.260	.300	19	10	98	102	.976	149	124	.5	1.1	-14.1	-1.0	-1.4
NY	40	10	15	1438.7	1511	9.5	130	466	2.9	717	4.5	4.25	82	.272	.327	-114	-124	98	98	.974	167	154	-.5	-13.1	-5.5	-.0	-8.9
TOT	448	135	304	14522.0		8.7			2.7		5.7	3.54		.254	.313					.975	1586	1439					

Runs
Allen-Phi 125
Mays-SF 121
Brock-Chi-StL 111
Robinson-Cin 103
Aaron-Mil 103

Hits
Flood-StL 211
Clemente-Pit 211
Williams-Chi 201
Allen-Phi 201
Brock-Chi-StL 200

Doubles
Maye-Mil 44
Clemente-Pit 40
Williams-Chi 39
Robinson-Cin 38
Allen-Phi 38

Triples
Santo-Chi 13
Allen-Phi 13
Brock-Chi-StL 11
Pinson-Cin 11

Home Runs
Mays-SF 47
Williams-Chi 33
Hart-SF 31
Cepeda-SF 31
Callison-Phi 31

Total Bases
Allen-Phi 352
Mays-SF 351
Williams-Chi 343
Santo-Chi 334
Callison-Phi 322

Runs Batted In
Boyer-StL 119
Santo-Chi 114
Mays-SF 111
Torre-Mil 109
Callison-Phi 104

Runs Produced
Boyer-StL 195
Allen-Phi 187
Mays-SF 185
Santo-Chi 178
Torre-Mil 176

Bases On Balls
Santo-Chi 86
Mathews-Mil 85
Mays-SF 82
Robinson-Cin 79
Boyer-StL 70

Batting Average
Clemente-Pit .339
Carty-Mil .330
Aaron-Mil .328
Torre-Mil .321
Allen-Phi .318

On Base Percentage
Santo-Chi .401
Robinson-Cin .399
Aaron-Mil .394
Carty-Mil .391
Clemente-Pit .391

Slugging Average
Mays-SF .607
Santo-Chi .564
Allen-Phi .557
Carty-Mil .554
Robinson-Cin .548

Production
Mays-SF .992
Santo-Chi .966
Robinson-Cin .947
Carty-Mil .945
Allen-Phi .940

Adjusted Production
Mays-SF 174
Carty-Mil 168
Allen-Phi 163
Santo-Chi 160
Robinson-Cin 159

Batter Runs
Mays-SF 56.5
Santo-Chi 55.0
Allen-Phi 50.4
Robinson-Cin 49.5
Williams-Chi 42.4

Adjusted Batter Runs
Mays-SF 56.4
Allen-Phi 51.3
Santo-Chi 51.2
Robinson-Cin 47.3
Aaron-Mil 43.0

Clutch Hitting Index
Fairly-LA 148
Boyer-StL 136
T.Davis-LA 135
Torre-Mil 132
Bond-Hou 128

Runs Created
Mays-SF 136
Santo-Chi 135
Allen-Phi 135
Robinson-Cin 127
Williams-Chi 125

Total Average
Mays-SF 1.071
Robinson-Cin 1.024
Santo-Chi 1.007
Allen-Phi .953
Aaron-Mil .922

Stolen Bases
Wills-LA 53
Brock-Chi-StL 43
W.Davis-LA 42
Harper-Cin 24
Robinson-Cin 23

Stolen Base Average
Harper-Cin 88.9
Aaron-Mil 84.6
Robinson-Cin 82.1
Mays-SF 79.2
W.Davis-LA 76.4

Stolen Base Runs
Wills-LA 5.7
Harper-Cin 5.4
W.Davis-LA 4.8
Aaron-Mil 4.2
Robinson-Cin 3.9

Fielding Runs
Mazeroski-Pit 33.5
W.Davis-LA 18.6
Callison-Phi 18.3
Santo-Chi 16.8
Schofield-Pit 16.0

Total Player Rating
Mays-SF 6.4
Santo-Chi 5.9
Aaron-Mil 5.8
Menke-Mil 5.4
Robinson-Cin 5.4

Wins
Jackson-Chi 24
Marichal-SF 21
Sadecki-StL 20

Win Percentage
Koufax-LA .792
Marichal-SF .724
O'Toole-Cin .708
Bunning-Phi .704
Jackson-Chi .686

Games
Miller-LA 74
Perranoski-LA 72
Baldschun-Phi 71
Taylor-StL 63
McDaniel-Chi 63

Complete Games
Marichal-SF 22
Drysdale-LA 21
Jackson-Chi 19
Gibson-StL 17
Ellsworth-Chi 16

Shutouts
Koufax-LA 7
Law-Pit 5
Fischer-Mil 5
Drysdale-LA 5
Bunning-Phi 5

Saves
Woodeshick-Hou 23
McBean-Pit 22
Baldschun-Phi 21
McDaniel-Chi 15

Innings Pitched
Drysdale-LA 321
Jackson-Chi 298
Gibson-StL 287
Bunning-Phi 284
Veale-Pit 280

Fewest Hits/Game
Koufax-LA 6.22
Drysdale-LA 6.79
Short-Phi 7.09
Veale-Pit 7.14
Maloney-Cin 7.29

Fewest BB/Game
Bunning-Phi 1.46
Bruce-Hou 1.47
Law-Pit 1.50
Marichal-SF 1.74
Jackson-Chi 1.75

Strikeouts
Veale-Pit 250
Gibson-StL 245
Drysdale-LA 237
Koufax-LA 223
Bunning-Phi 219

Strikeouts/Game
Koufax-LA 9.00
Maloney-Cin 8.92
Veale-Pit 8.04
Gibson-StL 7.68
Lemaster-Mil 7.53

Wins Above Team
Jackson-Chi 8.2
Koufax-LA 7.5
Marichal-SF 6.2
Bruce-Hou 4.9
Bunning-Phi 4.8

Earned Run Average
Koufax-LA 1.74
Drysdale-LA 2.19
Short-Phi 2.20
Marichal-SF 2.48
Bunning-Phi 2.63

Adjusted ERA
Koufax-LA 186
Short-Phi 157
Drysdale-LA 148
Marichal-SF 142
O'Toole-Cin 135

Opponents' Batting Avg.
Koufax-LA .191
Drysdale-LA .207
Veale-Pit .217
Short-Phi .217
Bolin-SF .220

Opponents' On Base Pct.
Koufax-LA .238
Drysdale-LA .253
Short-Phi .264
Bunning-Phi .269
Marichal-SF .270

Starter Runs
Drysdale-LA 48.1
Koufax-LA 44.6
Short-Phi 32.8
Marichal-SF 31.7
Bunning-Phi 28.6

Adjusted Starter Runs
Drysdale-LA 37.3
Koufax-LA 37.1
Short-Phi 31.0
Marichal-SF 30.7
Gibson-StL 29.4

Clutch Pitching Index
Craig-StL 122
Bennett-Phi 119
Farrell-Hou 115
Tsitouris-Cin 114
Hendley-SF 110

Relief Runs
McBean-Pit 16.4
Miller-LA 14.2
Ellis-Cin 12.9
Roebuck-Phi 11.2
McCool-Cin 11.0

Adjusted Relief Runs
McBean-Pit 16.6
Ellis-Cin 13.7
McCool-Cin 11.5
Roebuck-Phi 10.6
Miller-LA 9.6

Relief Ranking
McBean-Pit 27.3
Ellis-Cin 16.7
McCool-Cin 14.9
Roebuck-Phi 13.6
Woodeshick-Hou 11.8

Total Pitcher Index
Drysdale-LA 4.8
Koufax-LA 3.6
Marichal-SF 3.4
Gibson-StL 3.3
Short-Phi 3.2

Total Baseball Ranking
Mays-SF 6.4
Santo-Chi 5.9
Aaron-Mil 5.8
Menke-Mil 5.4
Robinson-Cin 5.4

TEAM	G	W	L	PCT	GB	R	OR	AB	H	2B	3B	HR	BB	SO	AVG	OBP	SLG	PRO	/A	BR	/A	PF	CHI	RC	TA	SB	CS	SBA	SBR
NY	164	99	63	.611		730	577	5705	1442	208	35	162	520	976	.253	.319	.387	.706	102	13	-8	103	105	705	.639	54	18	75	5
CHI	162	98	64	.605	1	642	501	5491	1356	184	40	106	562	902	.247	.323	.353	.676	94	-31	0	96	100	643	.615	75	39	66	0
BAL	163	97	65	.599	2	679	567	5463	1357	229	20	162	537	1019	.248	.319	.387	.706	102	14	-20	105	101	671	.645	78	38	67	1
DET	163	85	77	.525	14	699	678	5513	1394	199	57	157	517	912	.253	.321	.395	.716	105	35	64	96	100	707	.657	60	27	69	2
LA	162	82	80	.506	17	544	551	5362	1297	186	27	102	472	920	.242	.306	.344	.650	87	-88	-15	89	98	552	.562	49	39	56	-8
MIN	163	79	83	.488	20	737	678	5610	1413	227	46	221	553	1019	.252	.324	.427	.751	114	98	92	101	95	775	.700	46	22	68	1
CLE	164	79	83	.488	20	689	693	5603	1386	208	22	164	500	1063	.247	.315	.380	.695	99	-8	-26	103	104	666	.630	79	51	61	-6
BOS	162	72	90	.444	27	688	793	5513	1425	253	29	186	504	917	.258	.324	.416	.740	111	76	64	102	94	725	.669	18	16	53	-3
WAS	162	62	100	.383	37	578	733	5396	1246	199	28	125	504	1124	.231	.301	.348	.649	86	-94	-99	101	104	566	.573	47	30	61	-3
KC	163	57	105	.352	42	621	836	5524	1321	216	29	166	548	1104	.239	.313	.379	.692	98	-13	-42	105	95	645	.621	34	20	63	-1
TOT	814					6607		55180	13637	2109	333	1551	5227	9956	.247	.317	.382	.698								540	300	64	-17

TEAM	CG	SHO	SV	IP	H	H/G	HR	BB	BB/G	SO	SO/G	ERA	/A	OAVG	OOBA	PR	/A	PF	CPI	FA	E	DP	FW	PW	BW	SBW	DIF
NY	46	18	45	1506.7	1312	7.8	129	504	3.0	989	5.9	3.15	116	.234	.294	78	83	101	97	.983	109	158	1.0	8.7	-.8	.7	8.4
CHI	44	20	45	1467.7	1216	7.5	124	401	2.5	955	5.9	2.72	124	.225	.278	147	106	93	100	.981	122	164	.2	11.1	.0	.2	5.4
BAL	44	17	41	1458.7	1292	8.0	129	456	2.8	939	5.8	3.16	119	.238	.297	75	95	103	100	.985	95	159	1.9	10.0	-2.1	.3	6.0
DET	35	11	35	1453.0	1343	8.3	164	536	3.3	993	6.2	3.84	90	.243	.312	-34	-62	95	95	.982	111	137	.9	-6.5	6.7	.4	2.5
LA	30	28	41	1450.7	1273	7.9	100	530	3.3	965	6.0	2.91	111	.235	.305	115	49	89	107	.978	138	168	-.7	5.2	-1.6	-.7	-1.2
MIN	47	4	29	1478.3	1361	8.3	181	545	3.3	1099	6.7	3.57	101	.243	.308	8	7	100	100	.977	145	131	-1.1	.7	9.7	.3	-11.6
CLE	37	16	37	1487.7	1443	8.7	154	565	3.4	1162	7.0	3.75	99	.254	.320	-20	-3	103	103	.981	118	149	.5	-.3	-2.7	-.4	1.0
BOS	21	9	38	1422.0	1464	9.3	178	571	3.6	1094	6.9	4.50	83	.266	.331	-138	-118	103	103	.977	138	123	-.7	-12.4	6.7	-.1	-4.5
WAS	27	5	26	1435.3	1417	8.9	172	505	3.2	794	5.0	3.98	94	.258	.318	-56	-37	103	103	.979	127	145	-.0	-3.9	-10.4	-.1	-4.5
KC	18	6	27	1455.7	1516	9.4	220	614	3.8	966	6.0	4.71	83	.268	.339	-174	-129	108	101	.974	158	152	-1.9	-13.6	-4.4	.0	-4.2
TOT	349	134	364	14615.7		8.4			3.2		6.1	3.63		.247	.317					.980	1261	1486					

Runs
Oliva-Min	109
Howser-Cle	101
Killebrew-Min	95
Wagner-Cle	94
Versalles-Min	94

Hits
Oliva-Min	217
Robinson-Bal	194
Richardson-NY	181
Howard-NY	172
Versalles-Min	171

Doubles
Oliva-Min	43
Bressoud-Bos	41
Robinson-Bal	35
Versalles-Min	33

Triples
Versalles-Min	10
Rollins-Min	10
Yastrzemski-Bos	9
Oliva-Min	9
Fregosi-LA	9

Home Runs
Killebrew-Min	49
Powell-Bal	39
Mantle-NY	35
Colavito-KC	34
Stuart-Bos	33

Total Bases
Oliva-Min	374
Robinson-Bal	319
Killebrew-Min	316
Colavito-KC	298
Stuart-Bos	296

Runs Batted In
Robinson-Bal	118
Stuart-Bos	114
Mantle-NY	111
Killebrew-Min	111
Colavito-KC	102

Runs Produced
Robinson-Bal	172
Oliva-Min	171
Mantle-NY	168
Wagner-Cle	163

Bases On Balls
Siebern-Bal	106
Mantle-NY	99
Killebrew-Min	93
Allison-Min	92
Causey-KC	88

Batting Average
Oliva-Min	.323
Robinson-Bal	.317
Howard-NY	.313
Mantle-NY	.303
Robinson-Chi	.301

On Base Percentage
Mantle-NY	.426
Allison-Min	.406
Powell-Bal	.400
Robinson-Chi	.388
Kaline-Det	.385

Slugging Average
Powell-Bal	.606
Mantle-NY	.591
Oliva-Min	.557
Allison-Min	.553
Killebrew-Min	.548

Production
Mantle-NY	1.017
Powell-Bal	1.007
Allison-Min	.959
Killebrew-Min	.927
Oliva-Min	.918

Adjusted Production
Mantle-NY	174
Powell-Bal	167
Allison-Min	162
Killebrew-Min	153
Oliva-Min	150

Batter Runs
Mantle-NY	53.0
Allison-Min	44.9
Powell-Bal	44.1
Killebrew-Min	43.1
Oliva-Min	43.0

Adjusted Batter Runs
Mantle-NY	51.1
Allison-Min	44.4
Killebrew-Min	42.5
Oliva-Min	42.3
Powell-Bal	41.3

Clutch Hitting Index
Rodgers-LA	135
Robinson-Bal	131
Ward-Chi	130
Stuart-Bos	130
Pepitone-NY	127

Runs Created
Oliva-Min	132
Killebrew-Min	122
Mantle-NY	121
Allison-Min	119
Robinson-Bal	115

Total Average
Mantle-NY	1.131
Powell-Bal	1.081
Allison-Min	1.061
Killebrew-Min	.956
Oliva-Min	.906

Stolen Bases
Aparicio-Bal	57
Weis-Chi	22
Davalillo-Cle	21
Howser-Cle	20
Hinton-Was	17

Stolen Base Average
Aparicio-Bal	77.0
Weis-Chi	75.9
Howser-Cle	74.1
Hinton-Was	73.9
Davalillo-Cle	65.6

Stolen Base Runs
Aparicio-Bal	6.9
Tresh-NY	3.9
Wagner-Cle	3.0
Weis-Chi	2.4
Allison-Min	2.4

Fielding Runs
Knoop-LA	36.6
Freehan-Det	23.5
Rodgers-LA	20.4
Howard-NY	19.8
Boyer-NY	17.9

Total Player Rating
Freehan-Det	5.1
Howard-NY	4.6
Allison-Min	4.5
Oliva-Min	4.4
Fregosi-LA	4.3

Wins
Peters-Chi	20
Chance-LA	20
Wickersham-Det	19
Pizarro-Chi	19
Bunker-Bal	19

Win Percentage
Bunker-Bal	.792
Ford-NY	.739
Peters-Chi	.714
Pappas-Bal	.696
Chance-LA	.690

Games
Wyatt-KC	81
Radatz-Bos	79
Wilhelm-Chi	73
McMahon-Cle	70
Miller-Bal	66

Complete Games
Chance-LA	15
Pascual-Min	14
Pappas-Bal	13
Osteen-Was	13
Kaat-Min	13

Shutouts
Chance-LA	11
Ford-NY	8
Pappas-Bal	7
Lolich-Det	6
Monbouquette-Bos	5

Saves
Radatz-Bos	29
Wilhelm-Chi	27
Miller-Bal	23
Wyatt-KC	20
Lee-LA	19

Innings Pitched
Chance-LA	278
Peters-Chi	274
Bouton-NY	271
Pascual-Min	267
Osteen-Was	257

Fewest Hits/Game
Horlen-Chi	6.06
Chance-LA	6.28
Bunker-Bal	6.77
Peters-Chi	7.13
Pizarro-Chi	7.27

Fewest BB/Game
Monbouquette-Bos	1.54
Pappas-Bal	1.71
Newman-LA	1.85
Bouton-NY	1.99
Pizarro-Chi	2.07

Strikeouts
Downing-NY	217
Pascual-Min	213
Chance-LA	207
Peters-Chi	205
Lolich-Det	192

Strikeouts/Game
McDowell-Cle	9.21
Downing-NY	8.00
Pena-KC	7.56
Stigman-Min	7.53
Morehead-Bos	7.49

Wins Above Team
Bunker-Bal	6.3
Chance-LA	6.1
Radatz-Bos	4.9
Lolich-Det	4.6
Peters-Chi	4.4

Earned Run Average
Chance-LA	1.65
Horlen-Chi	1.88
Ford-NY	2.13
Peters-Chi	2.50
Pizarro-Chi	2.56

Adjusted ERA
Chance-LA	195
Horlen-Chi	180
Ford-NY	171
Bunker-Bal	139
McDowell-Cle	138

Opponents' Batting Avg.
Horlen-Chi	.190
Chance-LA	.195
Bunker-Bal	.207
Peters-Chi	.219
Pizarro-Chi	.219

Opponents' On Base Pct.
Horlen-Chi	.247
Chance-LA	.258
Pizarro-Chi	.264
Bunker-Bal	.266
Bouton-NY	.270

Starter Runs
Chance-LA	61.0
Horlen-Chi	41.0
Ford-NY	40.7
Peters-Chi	34.4
Pizarro-Chi	28.3

Adjusted Starter Runs
Chance-LA	48.4
Ford-NY	41.4
Horlen-Chi	35.2
Peters-Chi	26.9
Bunker-Bal	25.1

Clutch Pitching Index
McDowell-Cle	122
Roberts-Bal	121
Kralick-Cle	119
Grant-Cle-Min	112
Peters-Chi	111

Relief Runs
Lee-LA	32.2
Wilhelm-Chi	23.8
Radatz-Bos	23.2
Worthington-Min	18.0
Hall-Bal	17.4

Adjusted Relief Runs
Lee-LA	26.0
Radatz-Bos	25.4
Stock-Bal-KC	20.2
Wilhelm-Chi	20.2
Hall-Bal	18.7

Relief Ranking
Radatz-Bos	46.9
Wilhelm-Chi	38.5
Worthington-Min	32.6
Kline-Was	28.9
Lee-LA	26.9

Total Pitcher Index
Ford-NY	5.0
Chance-LA	4.5
Horlen-Chi	4.2
Peters-Chi	3.8
Pizarro-Chi	2.7

Total Baseball Ranking
Freehan-Det	5.1
Ford-NY	5.0
Howard-NY	4.6
Chance-LA	4.5
Allison-Min	4.5

TEAM	G	W	L	PCT	GB	R	OR	AB	H	2B	3B	HR	BB	SO	AVG	OBP	SLG	PRO	/A	BR	/A	PF	CHI	RC	TA	SB	CS	SBA	SBR
LA	162	97	65	.599		608	521	5425	1329	193	32	78	492	891	.245	.314	.335	.649	90	-61	-5	91	103	593	.596	172	77	69	5
SF	163	95	67	.586	2	682	593	5495	1384	169	43	159	476	844	.252	.315	.385	.700	104	24	-45	111	100	649	.623	47	27	64	-1
PIT	163	90	72	.556	7	675	580	5686	1506	217	57	111	419	1008	.265	.319	.382	.701	104	27	28	100	97	671	.614	51	38	57	-7
CIN	162	89	73	.549	8	825	704	5658	1544	268	61	183	538	1003	.273	.341	.439	.780	126	188	162	104	95	842	.738	82	40	67	1
MIL	162	86	76	.531	11	708	633	5542	1419	243	28	196	408	976	.256	.311	.416	.727	111	66	39	104	99	699	.658	64	37	63	-2
PHI	162	85	76	.528	11.5	654	667	5528	1380	205	53	144	494	1091	.250	.315	.384	.699	103	23	58	96	95	665	.628	46	32	59	-4
STL	162	80	81	.497	16.5	707	674	5579	1415	234	46	109	477	882	.254	.316	.371	.687	100	2	-40	107	106	659	.621	100	52	66	0
CHI	164	72	90	.444	25	635	723	5540	1316	202	33	134	532	948	.238	.309	.358	.667	94	-33	-44	102	101	613	.599	65	47	58	-8
HOU	164	65	97	.401	32	569	711	5483	1299	188	42	97	502	877	.237	.306	.340	.646	89	-73	0	89	98	574	.575	90	37	71	5
NY	164	50	112	.309	47	495	752	5441	1202	203	27	107	492	1129	.221	.278	.327	.605	76	-163	-163	100	104	480	.509	28	42	40	-16
TOT	813					6558		55377	13794	2122	422	1318	4730	9649	.249	.313	.374	.687								745	429	63	-33

TEAM	CG	SHO	SV	IP	H	H/G	HR	BB	BB/G	SO	SO/G	ERA	/A	OAVG	OOBA	PR	/A	PF	CPI	FA	E	DP	FW	PW	BW	SBW	DIF
LA	58	23	34	1476.0	1223	7.5	127	425	2.6	1079	6.6	2.81	113	.224	.279	119	61	90	99	.979	134	135	.8	6.4	-.5	.9	8.4
SF	42	17	42	1465.3	1325	8.1	137	408	2.5	1060	6.5	3.20	121	.238	.290	55	108	109	98	.976	148	124	.0	11.4	-4.8	.3	7.1
PIT	49	17	27	1479.0	1324	8.1	89	469	2.9	882	5.4	3.01	115	.240	.300	86	76	98	103	.977	152	189	-.2	8.0	3.0	-.4	-1.4
CIN	43	9	34	1457.3	1355	8.4	136	587	3.6	1113	6.9	3.88	93	.246	.319	-55	-45	102	96	.981	117	142	1.8	-4.8	17.1	.5	-6.6
MIL	43	4	38	1448.3	1336	8.3	123	541	3.4	966	6.0	3.52	104	.246	.312	3	20	103	101	.978	140	145	.5	2.1	4.1	.1	-1.9
PHI	50	18	21	1468.7	1426	8.7	116	466	2.9	1071	6.6	3.53	95	.256	.313	1	-28	95	104	.975	157	153	-.5	-3.0	6.1	-.0	1.9
STL	40	11	35	1461.3	1414	8.7	166	467	2.9	916	5.6	3.77	100	.254	.311	-37	-2	106	102	.979	130	152	1.1	-.2	-4.2	.4	2.5
CHI	33	9	35	1472.0	1470	9.0	154	481	2.9	855	5.2	3.78	97	.260	.315	-39	-20	103	104	.974	171	166	-1.3	-2.1	-4.6	-.5	-5.2
HOU	29	7	26	1461.3	1459	9.0	123	388	2.4	931	5.7	3.84	84	.259	.306	-49	-101	91	94	.974	166	130	-1.0	-10.7	.0	-.9	-5.2
NY	29	11	14	1454.7	1462	9.0	147	498	3.1	776	4.8	4.06	91	.262	.322	-84	-61	104	99	.974	171	153	-1.3	-6.4	-17.2	-1.3	-4.7
TOT	416	126	306	14644.0		8.5			2.9		5.9	3.54		.249	.313					.977	1486	1489					

Runs		Hits		Doubles		Triples		Home Runs		Total Bases	
Harper-Cin	126	Rose-Cin	209	Aaron-Mil	40	Callison-Phi	16	Mays-SF	52	Mays-SF	360
Mays-SF	118	Pinson-Cin	204	Williams-Chi	39	Clendenon-Pit	14	McCovey-SF	39	Williams-Chi	356
Rose-Cin	117	Williams-Chi	203	Rose-Cin	35	Clemente-Pit	14	Williams-Chi	34	Pinson-Cin	324
Williams-Chi	115	Clemente-Pit	194	Brock-StL	35	Allen-Phi	14	Santo-Chi	33	Aaron-Mil	319
		Flood-StL	191	Pinson-Cin	34	Morgan-Hou	12	Robinson-Cin	33	Johnson-Cin	317

Runs Batted In		Runs Produced		Bases On Balls		Batting Average		On Base Percentage		Slugging Average	
Johnson-Cin	130	Johnson-Cin	190	Morgan-Hou	97	Clemente-Pit	.329	Mays-SF	.399	Mays-SF	.645
Robinson-Cin	113	Williams-Chi	189	Santo-Chi	88	Aaron-Mil	.318	Robinson-Cin	.388	Aaron-Mil	.560
Mays-SF	112	Robinson-Cin	189	McCovey-SF	88	Mays-SF	.317	Aaron-Mil	.384	Williams-Chi	.552
Williams-Chi	108	Rose-Cin	187	Wynn-Hou	84	Williams-Chi	.315	McCovey-SF	.383	Robinson-Cin	.540
Stargell-Pit	107	Mays-SF	178	Harper-Cin	78	Rose-Cin	.312	Rose-Cin	.383	McCovey-SF	.539

Production		Adjusted Production		Batter Runs		Adjusted Batter Runs		Clutch Hitting Index		Runs Created	
Mays-SF	1.044	Mays-SF	171	Mays-SF	64.7	Mays-SF	57.5	Johnson-Cin	138	Mays-SF	143
Aaron-Mil	.943	Williams-Chi	156	Williams-Chi	49.3	Williams-Chi	47.9	Boyer-StL	138	Williams-Chi	132
Williams-Chi	.932	Aaron-Mil	155	Aaron-Mil	45.9	Robinson-Cin	43.2	Fairly-LA	130	Aaron-Mil	122
Robinson-Cin	.928	Wynn-Hou	153	Robinson-Cin	45.8	Aaron-Mil	43.1	Stargell-Pit	130	Santo-Chi	121
McCovey-SF	.922	Robinson-Cin	152	McCovey-SF	41.8	Allen-Phi	40.4	Banks-Chi	129	Robinson-Cin	120

Total Average		Stolen Bases		Stolen Base Average		Stolen Base Runs		Fielding Runs		Total Player Rating	
Mays-SF	1.124	Wills-LA	94	Wynn-Hou	91.5	Wynn-Hou	10.5	Mazeroski-Pit	30.6	Mays-SF	6.3
Aaron-Mil	.990	Brock-StL	63	Aaron-Mil	85.7	Wills-LA	9.6	Wills-LA	21.4	Wynn-Hou	5.4
Robinson-Cin	.958	Wynn-Hou	43	Harper-Cin	85.4	Harper-Cin	6.9	Alley-Pit	20.1	Santo-Chi	5.2
McCovey-SF	.955	Harper-Cin	35	Wills-LA	75.2	Aaron-Mil	4.8	Santo-Chi	18.5	Williams-Chi	4.9
Williams-Chi	.937	W.Davis-LA	25	W.Davis-LA	73.5	Allen-Phi	3.3	Beckert-Chi	13.4	Wills-LA	4.6

Wins		Win Percentage		Games		Complete Games		Shutouts		Saves	
Koufax-LA	26	Koufax-LA	.765	Abernathy-Chi	84	Koufax-LA	27	Marichal-SF	10	Abernathy-Chi	31
Cloninger-Mil	24	Maloney-Cin	.690	Woodeshick-Hou-StL	78	Marichal-SF	24	Koufax-LA	8	McCool-Cin	21
Drysdale-LA	23	Ellis-Cin	.688	McDaniel-Chi	71	Gibson-StL	20	Veale-Pit	7	Linzy-SF	21
Marichal-SF	22	Cloninger-Mil	.686	Baldschun-Phi	65	Drysdale-LA	20	Drysdale-LA	7		
Ellis-Cin	22	Bunning-Phi	.679			Cloninger-Mil	16	Bunning-Phi	7		

Innings Pitched		Fewest Hits/Game		Fewest BB/Game		Strikeouts		Strikeouts/Game		Wins Above Team	
Koufax-LA	336	Koufax-LA	5.79	Marichal-SF	1.40	Koufax-LA	382	Koufax-LA	10.23	Koufax-LA	8.0
Drysdale-LA	308	Maloney-Cin	6.67	Law-Pit	1.45	Veale-Pit	276	Veale-Pit	9.34	Cloninger-Mil	6.8
Gibson-StL	299	Marichal-SF	6.83	Bruce-Hou	1.49	Gibson-StL	270	Maloney-Cin	8.61	Ellis-Cin	5.7
Short-Phi	297	Bolin-SF	6.90	Farrell-Hou	1.51	Bunning-Phi	268	Bunning-Phi	8.29	Maloney-Cin	5.1
Marichal-SF	295	Gibson-StL	7.31	Johnson-Hou-Mil	1.86	Maloney-Cin	244	Gibson-StL	8.13	Bunning-Phi	5.1

Earned Run Average		Adjusted ERA		Opponents' Batting Avg.		Opponents' On Base Pct.		Starter Runs		Adjusted Starter Runs	
Koufax-LA	2.04	Marichal-SF	181	Koufax-LA	.179	Koufax-LA	.225	Koufax-LA	56.1	Marichal-SF	56.7
Marichal-SF	2.14	Law-Pit	161	Marichal-SF	.205	Marichal-SF	.238	Marichal-SF	46.0	Koufax-LA	42.9
Law-Pit	2.16	Koufax-LA	156	Maloney-Cin	.206	Law-Pit	.260	Law-Pit	33.3	Shaw-SF	31.9
Maloney-Cin	2.54	Shaw-SF	146	Bolin-SF	.214	Bunning-Phi	.275	Bunning-Phi	30.4	Law-Pit	31.8
Bunning-Phi	2.60	Maloney-Cin	142	Gibson-StL	.222	Drysdale-LA	.276	Maloney-Cin	28.3	Maloney-Cin	30.2

Clutch Pitching Index		Relief Runs		Adjusted Relief Runs		Relief Ranking		Total Pitcher Index		Total Baseball Ranking	
Law-Pit	115	Linzy-SF	19.2	Linzy-SF	22.2	Linzy-SF	42.0	Marichal-SF	6.7	Marichal-SF	6.7
Koonce-Chi	112	O'Dell-Mil	16.6	O'Dell-Mil	18.0	O'Dell-Mil	29.8	Koufax-LA	5.0	Mays-SF	6.3
Spahn-NY-SF	108	McBean-Pit	15.8	Abernathy-Chi	16.2	Woodeshick-Hou-StL	21.3	Law-Pit	4.2	Wynn-Hou	5.4
Culp-Phi	108	Perranoski-LA	15.3	McDaniel-Chi	15.3	McBean-Pit	19.6	Maloney-Cin	4.2	Santo-Chi	5.2
Buhl-Chi	107	Abernathy-Chi	14.5	McBean-Pit	15.0	Abernathy-Chi	19.0	Drysdale-LA	3.7	Koufax-LA	5.0

TEAM	G	W	L	PCT	GB	R	OR	AB	H	2B	3B	HR	BB	SO	AVG	OBP	SLG	PRO	/A	BR	/A	PF	CHI	RC	TA	SB	CS	SBA	SBR
MIN	162	102	60	.630		**774**	600	5488	**1396**	**257**	42	150	554	969	**.254**	.327	.399	.726	112	84	**76**	101	**105**	**730**	**.680**	92	33	**74**	**8**
CHI	162	95	67	.586	7	647	**555**	5509	1354	200	38	125	533	916	.246	.317	.364	.681	100	1	53	92	99	636	.610	50	33	60	-4
BAL	162	94	68	.580	8	641	578	5450	1299	227	38	125	529	907	.238	.309	.363	.672	97	-20	-19	100	103	607	.602	67	31	68	2
DET	162	89	73	.549	13	680	602	5368	1278	190	27	162	554	952	.238	.314	.374	.688	102	10	-24	105	**105**	628	.625	57	41	58	-7
CLE	162	87	75	.537	15	663	613	5469	1367	198	21	156	506	**857**	.250	.317	.379	.696	104	26	37	98	99	667	.641	109	46	70	5
NY	162	77	85	.475	25	611	604	5470	1286	196	31	149	489	951	.235	.300	.364	.664	94	-41	-47	101	102	593	.586	35	20	64	-1
CAL	162	75	87	.463	27	527	569	5354	1279	200	36	92	443	973	.239	.300	.341	.641	88	-80	-65	98	97	549	.567	107	59	64	-2
WAS	162	70	92	.432	32	591	721	5374	1227	179	33	136	570	1125	.228	.306	.350	.656	93	-46	-46	100	100	586	.588	30	19	61	-1
BOS	162	62	100	.383	40	669	791	5487	1378	244	40	**165**	**607**	964	.251	**.329**	**.400**	**.729**	**113**	**95**	47	107	89	715	.672	47	24	66	0
KC	162	59	103	.364	43	585	755	5393	1294	186	**59**	110	521	1020	.240	.311	.358	.669	96	-24	-4	97	96	604	.607	**110**	51	68	2
TOT	810					6388		54362	13158	2077	365	1370	5306	9634	.242	.313	.369	.682								704	357	66	-2

TEAM	CG	SHO	SV	IP	H	H/G	HR	BB	BB/G	SO	SO/G	ERA	/A	OAVG	OOBA	PR	/A	PF	CPI	FA	E	DP	FW	PW	BW	SBW	DIF
MIN	32	12	45	1457.3	1278	7.9	166	503	3.1	934	5.8	3.14	108	.234	.297	52	43	98	**107**	.973	172	158	-2.3	4.6	**8.1**	**.9**	9.7
CHI	21	14	**53**	1481.7	1261	**7.7**	122	**460**	**2.8**	946	5.7	2.99	105	**.230**	**.288**	76	22	91	98	.980	127	156	.6	2.3	5.7	-.4	5.8
BAL	32	**15**	41	1477.7	1268	**7.7**	120	510	3.1	939	5.7	**2.98**	**115**	.233	.296	**77**	**71**	99	104	.980	126	152	.6	**7.6**	-2.0	.2	6.6
DET	**45**	14	31	1455.0	1283	7.9	137	509	3.1	1069	6.6	3.35	107	.236	.301	17	40	104	99	**.981**	116	126	1.3	4.3	-2.6	-.7	5.8
CLE	41	13	41	1458.3	**1254**	**7.7**	129	500	3.1	**1156**	**7.1**	3.30	102	.231	.294	26	11	97	94	**.981**	**114**	127	**1.4**	1.2	3.9	.6	-1.1
NY	41	11	31	1459.7	1337	8.2	126	511	3.2	1001	6.2	3.28	106	.244	.306	28	34	101	104	.978	137	**166**	-.0	3.6	-5.0	-.0	-2.5
CAL	39	14	33	1441.7	1259	7.9	**91**	563	3.5	847	5.3	3.17	107	.237	.307	45	36	98	100	**.981**	123	149	.8	3.8	-6.9	-.2	-3.5
WAS	21	8	40	1435.7	1376	8.6	160	633	4.0	867	5.4	3.93	90	.254	.329	-75	-64	102	105	.977	143	148	-.4	-6.8	-4.9	-.0	1.3
BOS	33	9	25	1439.3	1443	9.0	158	543	3.4	993	6.2	4.24	89	.259	.322	-124	-74	109	95	.974	162	129	-1.6	-7.9	5.0	.0	-14.5
KC	18	7	32	1433.0	1399	8.8	161	574	3.6	882	5.5	4.24	81	.256	.324	-124	-127	100	96	.977	139	142	-.2	-13.5	-.4	.2	-8.1
TOT	323	117	372	14539.3		8.1			3.3		6.0	3.46		.242	.313					.978	1359	1453					

Runs
Versalles-Min 126
Oliva-Min 107
Tresh-NY 94
Buford-Chi 93
Colavito-Cle 92

Hits
Oliva-Min 185
Versalles-Min 182
Colavito-Cle 170
Tresh-NY 168
Fregosi-Cal 167

Doubles
Yastrzemski-Bos 45
Versalles-Min 45
Oliva-Min 40
Tresh-NY 29
Richardson-NY 28

Triples
Versalles-Min 12
Campaneris-KC 12
Aparicio-Bal 10
Smith-Cal 9

Home Runs
Conigliaro-Bos 32
Cash-Det 30
Horton-Det 29
Wagner-Cle 28

Total Bases
Versalles-Min 308
Tresh-NY 287
Oliva-Min 283
Colavito-Cle 277
Conigliaro-Bos 267

Runs Batted In
Colavito-Cle 108
Horton-Det 104
Oliva-Min 98
Mantilla-Bos 92
Whitfield-Cle 90

Runs Produced
Oliva-Min 189
Versalles-Min 184
Colavito-Cle 174
Hall-Min 147
Horton-Det 144

Bases On Balls
Colavito-Cle 93
Blefary-Bal 88
Mantilla-Bos 79
Cash-Det 77
Robinson-Chi 76

Batting Average
Oliva-Min .321
Yastrzemski-Bos .312
Davalillo-Cle .301
Robinson-Bal .297
Wagner-Cle .294

On Base Percentage
Yastrzemski-Bos .398
Colavito-Cle .387
Oliva-Min .384
Blefary-Bal .382
Mantilla-Bos .377

Slugging Average
Yastrzemski-Bos .536
Conigliaro-Bos .512
Cash-Det .512
Wagner-Cle .495
Oliva-Min .491

Production
Yastrzemski-Bos .935
Cash-Det .886
Oliva-Min .876
Wagner-Cle .866
Colavito-Cle .855

Adjusted Production
Yastrzemski-Bos 152
Wagner-Cle 146
Oliva-Min 145
Colavito-Cle 144
Cash-Det 141

Batter Runs
Yastrzemski-Bos 41.6
Oliva-Min 35.3
Colavito-Cle 34.6
Cash-Det 31.0
Wagner-Cle 29.6

Adjusted Batter Runs
Yastrzemski-Bos 37.2
Colavito-Cle 35.9
Oliva-Min 34.6
Wagner-Cle 30.7
Cash-Det 27.9

Clutch Hitting Index
Mantilla-Bos 146
Colavito-Cle 134
Horton-Det 130
Oliva-Min 130
Powell-Bal 125

Runs Created
Colavito-Cle 110
Oliva-Min 109
Yastrzemski-Bos 102
Versalles-Min 102
Tresh-NY 101

Total Average
Yastrzemski-Bos .948
Cash-Det .911
Wagner-Cle .887
Oliva-Min .885
Blefary-Bal .881

Stolen Bases
Campaneris-KC 51
Cardenal-Cal 37
Versalles-Min 27
Davalillo-Cle 26
Aparicio-Bal 26

Stolen Base Average
Hinton-Cle 85.0
Versalles-Min 84.4
Howser-Cle 81.0
Davalillo-Cle 78.8
Aparicio-Bal 78.8

Stolen Base Runs
Versalles-Min 5.1
Campaneris-KC 3.9
Davalillo-Cle 3.6
Aparicio-Bal 3.6
Hinton-Cle 3.3

Fielding Runs
Boyer-NY 27.5
Knoop-Cal 18.8
Buford-Chi 18.4
Hansen-Chi 18.3
Freehan-Det 16.4

Total Player Rating
Buford-Chi 4.6
Oliva-Min 3.8
Yastrzemski-Bos 3.7
Colavito-Cle 3.3
Boyer-NY 3.3

Wins
Grant-Min 21
Stottlemyre-NY 20
Kaat-Min 18
McDowell-Cle 17

Win Percentage
Grant-Min .750
McLain-Det .727
Stottlemyre-NY .690
Fisher-Chi .682
Siebert-Cle .667

Games
Fisher-Chi 82
Kline-Was 74
Lee-Cal 69
Dickson-KC 68
Miller-Bal 67

Complete Games
Stottlemyre-NY 18
McDowell-Cle 14
Grant-Min 14
McLain-Det 13

Shutouts
Grant-Min 6
Stottlemyre-NY 4
McLain-Det 4
Horlen-Chi 4
Chance-Cal 4

Saves
Kline-Was 29
Miller-Bal 24
Fisher-Chi 24
Lee-Cal 23
Radatz-Bos 22

Innings Pitched
Stottlemyre-NY 291
McDowell-Cle 273
Grant-Min 270
Kaat-Min 264
Newman-Cal 261

Fewest Hits/Game
McDowell-Cle 5.87
Fisher-Chi 6.44
Siebert-Cle 6.62
Richert-Was 6.77
Brunet-Cal 6.81

Fewest BB/Game
Terry-Cle 1.25
Monbouquette-Bos 1.57
Horlen-Chi 1.60
Ford-NY 1.84
Grant-Min 2.03

Strikeouts
McDowell-Cle 325
Lolich-Det 226
McLain-Det 192
Siebert-Cle 191
Downing-NY 179

Strikeouts/Game
McDowell-Cle 10.71
Siebert-Cle 9.10
Lolich-Det 8.34
McLain-Det 7.85
Morehead-Bos 7.60

Wins Above Team
Stottlemyre-NY 6.6
Grant-Min 5.2
McLain-Det 4.7
Siebert-Cle 3.8
Chance-Cal 3.6

Earned Run Average
McDowell-Cle 2.18
Fisher-Chi 2.40
Siebert-Cle 2.43
Brunet-Cal 2.56
Richert-Was 2.60

Adjusted ERA
McDowell-Cle 155
Siebert-Cle 139
McLain-Det 138
Richert-Was 136
Brunet-Cal 133

Opponents' Batting Avg.
McDowell-Cle .185
Fisher-Chi .205
Siebert-Cle .206
Brunet-Cal .209
Richert-Was .210

Opponents' On Base Pct.
Fisher-Chi .252
Siebert-Cle .256
Terry-Cle .266
McLain-Det .270
Horlen-Chi .275

Starter Runs
McDowell-Cle 38.9
Stottlemyre-NY 26.8
Siebert-Cle 21.6
Pappas-Bal 20.9
McLain-Det 20.5

Adjusted Starter Runs
McDowell-Cle 36.2
Stottlemyre-NY 27.9
McLain-Det 24.1
Richert-Was 20.0
Pappas-Bal 20.0

Clutch Pitching Index
Kaat-Min 122
Perry-Min 117
Peters-Chi 113
Richert-Was 110
Pappas-Bal 110

Relief Runs
Wilhelm-Chi 26.3
Lee-Cal 22.3
Miller-Bal 20.7
Fisher-Chi 19.4
Hamilton-NY 13.3

Adjusted Relief Runs
Lee-Cal 21.5
Wilhelm-Chi 21.1
Miller-Bal 20.2
Hamilton-NY 13.5
Fisher-Chi 13.4

Relief Ranking
Miller-Bal 41.3
Lee-Cal 32.1
Worthington-Min 28.2
Wilhelm-Chi 25.0
Fisher-Chi 20.4

Total Pitcher Index
McDowell-Cle 3.9
Stottlemyre-NY 3.9
Kaat-Min 3.0
Newman-Cal 2.3
Lee-Cal 2.3

Total Baseball Ranking
Buford-Chi 4.6
McDowell-Cle 3.9
Stottlemyre-NY 3.9
Oliva-Min 3.8
Yastrzemski-Bos 3.7

TEAM	G	W	L	PCT	GB	R	OR	AB	H	2B	3B	HR	BB	SO	AVG	OBP	SLG	PRO	/A	BR	/A	PF	CHI	RC	TA	SB	CS	SBA	SBR
LA	162	95	67	.586		606	490	5471	1399	201	27	108	430	830	.256	.316	.362	.678	94	-37	-16	97	97	615	.600	94	64	59	-9
SF	161	93	68	.578	1.5	675	626	5539	1373	195	31	181	414	860	.248	.304	.392	.696	98	-14	3	97	104	633	.610	29	30	49	-8
PIT	162	92	70	.568	3	759	641	5676	1586	238	66	158	405	1011	.279	.331	.428	.759	116	116	111	101	96	779	.689	64	60	52	-16
PHI	162	87	75	.537	8	696	640	5607	1448	224	49	117	510	969	.258	.323	.378	.701	101	11	2	101	101	683	.630	56	42	57	-7
ATL	163	85	77	.525	10	782	683	5617	1476	220	32	207	512	913	.263	.329	.424	.753	115	115	114	99	99	775	.697	59	47	56	-10
STL	162	83	79	.512	12	571	577	5480	1377	196	61	108	345	977	.251	.300	.368	.668	91	-66	-64	100	98	592	.594	144	61	70	7
CIN	160	76	84	.475	18	692	702	5521	1434	232	33	149	394	877	.260	.311	.395	.706	101	6	-84	114	104	658	.626	70	50	58	-8
HOU	163	72	90	.444	23	612	695	5511	1405	203	35	112	491	885	.255	.320	.365	.685	96	-19	-1	97	94	640	.614	90	47	66	0
NY	161	66	95	.410	28.5	587	761	5371	1286	187	35	98	446	992	.239	.303	.342	.645	85	-99	-61	94	107	546	.559	55	46	54	-10
CHI	162	59	103	.364	36	644	809	5592	1418	203	43	140	457	998	.254	.315	.380	.695	99	-6	-7	100	96	665	.625	76	47	62	-4
TOT	809					6624		55385	14202	2099	412	1378	4404	9312	.256	.316	.384	.700								737	494	60	-74

TEAM	CG	SHO	SV	IP	H	H/G	HR	BB	BB/G	SO	SO/G	ERA	/A	OAVG	OOBA	PR	/A	PF	CPI	FA	E	DP	FW	PW	BW	SBW	DIF
LA	52	20	35	1458.0	1287	7.9	84	356	2.2	1084	6.7	2.62	159	.237	.281	130		95	102	.979	133	128	.8	13.6	-1.7	-.2	1.4
SF	52	14	27	1476.5	1370	8.4	140	359	2.2	973	5.9	3.24	108	.244	.288	60	41	97	96	.974	168	131	-1.2	4.3	.3	-.0	9.1
PIT	35	12	43	1463.3	1445	8.9	125	463	2.8	898	5.5	3.52	101	.260	.317	13	6	99	105	.978	141	215	.4	.6	11.6	-.9	-.7
PHI	52	15	23	1459.7	1439	8.9	137	412	2.5	928	5.7	3.57	101	.258	.311	5	8	100	102	.982	113	147	1.9	.8	.2	-.0	3.0
ATL	37	10	36	1469.3	1430	8.8	129	485	3.0	884	5.4	3.68	95	.256	.313	-12	-28	97	98	.976	154	139	-.4	-2.9	11.9	-.3	-4.4
STL	47	19	32	1459.7	1345	8.3	130	448	2.8	892	5.5	3.11	116	.246	.301	79	79	100	107	.977	145	166	.1	8.3	-6.7	1.5	-1.2
CIN	28	10	35	1436.0	1408	8.8	153	490	3.1	1043	6.5	4.08	88	.257	.317	-75	5	114	94	.980	122	133	1.4	.5	-8.8	-.0	2.9
HOU	34	13	26	1443.7	1468	9.2	130	391	2.4	929	5.8	3.76	95	.262	.309	-24	-32	99	96	.972	174	126	-1.5	-.4	-4.8	-.3	4.1
NY	37	9	22	1427.0	1497	9.4	166	521	3.3	773	4.9	4.17	84	.271	.332	-89	-108	97	104	.975	159	171	-.6	-11.3	-6.4	-.3	4.1
CHI	28	6	24	1458.0	1513	9.3	184	479	3.0	908	5.6	4.33	85	.267	.321	-117	-102	103	97	.974	166	132	-1.0	-10.7	-.7	.4	-9.9
TOT	402	128	303	14551.0		8.8			2.7		5.8	3.61		.256	.316					.977	1475	1488					

Runs
Alou-Atl 122
Aaron-Atl 117
Allen-Phi 112
Clemente-Pit 105
Williams-Chi 100

Hits
Alou-Atl 218
Rose-Cin 205
Clemente-Pit 202
Beckert-Chi 188

Doubles
Callison-Phi 40
Rose-Cin 38
Pinson-Cin 35
Alou-Atl 32

Triples
McCarver-StL 13
Brock-StL 12
Clemente-Pit 11

Home Runs
Aaron-Atl 44
Allen-Phi 40
Mays-SF 37
Torre-Atl 36
McCovey-SF 36

Total Bases
Alou-Atl 355
Clemente-Pit 342
Allen-Phi 331
Aaron-Atl 325
Mays-SF 307

Runs Batted In
Aaron-Atl 127
Clemente-Pit 119
Allen-Phi 110
White-Phi 103
Mays-SF 103

Runs Produced
Aaron-Atl 200
Clemente-Pit 195
Allen-Phi 182
White-Phi 166

Bases On Balls
Santo-Chi 95
Morgan-Hou 89
McCovey-SF 76
Aaron-Atl 76
Menke-Atl 71

Batting Average
Alou-Pit 342
Alou-Atl 327
Carty-Atl 326
Allen-Phi 317
Clemente-Pit 317

On Base Percentage
Santo-Chi 417
Morgan-Hou 412
Allen-Phi 398
Carty-Atl 396
McCovey-SF 394

Slugging Average
Allen-Phi 632
McCovey-SF 586
Stargell-Pit 581
Torre-Atl 560
Mays-SF 556

Production
Allen-Phi 1.030
McCovey-SF 979
Stargell-Pit 965
Santo-Chi 955
Torre-Atl 945

Adjusted Production
Allen-Phi 179
McCovey-SF 172
Santo-Chi 163
Stargell-Pit 163
Torre-Atl 161

Batter Runs
Allen-Phi 56.7
Santo-Chi 51.1
McCovey-SF 46.8
Torre-Atl 42.9
Stargell-Pit 41.1

Adjusted Batter Runs
Allen-Phi 56.0
Santo-Chi 51.0
McCovey-SF 48.5
Torre-Atl 43.9
Mays-SF 41.0

Clutch Hitting Index
White-Phi 135
Staub-Hou 135
Flood-StL 135
Aaron-Atl 124
Woodward-Atl 121

Runs Created
Allen-Phi 131
Santo-Chi 127
Alou-Atl 123
McCovey-SF 119
Clemente-Pit 119

Total Average
Allen-Phi 1.105
McCovey-SF 1.041
Santo-Chi 1.000
Stargell-Pit 988
Mays-SF 943

Stolen Bases
Brock-StL 74
Jackson-Hou 49
Wills-LA 38
Phillips-Phi-Chi 32
Harper-Cin 29

Stolen Base Average
Aaron-Atl 87.5
Brock-StL 80.4
Jackson-Hou 77.8
Harper-Cin 74.4
White-Phi 72.7

Stolen Base Runs
Brock-StL 11.4
Jackson-Hou 6.3
Aaron-Atl 4.5
Harper-Cin 2.7

Fielding Runs
Mazeroski-Pit 40.9
Santo-Chi 27.1
Hundley-Chi 18.5
Groat-Phi 18.2
Alley-Pit 15.6

Total Player Rating
Santo-Chi 7.6
Torre-Atl 5.6
Aaron-Atl 5.2
Allen-Phi 4.9
Mazeroski-Pit 4.3

Wins
Koufax-LA 27
Marichal-SF 25
Perry-SF 21
Gibson-StL 21
Short-Phi 20

Win Percentage
Marichal-SF 806
Koufax-LA 750
Perry-SF 724
Short-Phi 667
Maloney-Cin 667

Games
Carroll-Atl 73
Mikkelsen-Pit 71
Knowles-Phi 69
Regan-LA 65
McDaniel-SF 64

Complete Games
Koufax-LA 27
Marichal-SF 25
Gibson-StL 20
Short-Phi 19
Bunning-Phi 16

Shutouts
6 tied with 5

Saves
Regan-LA 21
McCool-Cin 18
Face-Pit 18
Raymond-Hou 16
Linzy-SF 16

Innings Pitched
Koufax-LA 323
Bunning-Phi 314
Marichal-SF 307
Gibson-StL 280
Drysdale-LA 274

Fewest Hits/Game
Marichal-SF 6.68
Koufax-LA 6.72
Gibson-StL 6.75
Maloney-Cin 6.96
Bolin-SF 6.99

Fewest BB/Game
Marichal-SF 1.06
Law-Pit 1.21
Perry-SF 1.41
Drysdale-LA 1.48
Bunning-Phi 1.58

Strikeouts
Koufax-LA 317
Bunning-Phi 252
Veale-Pit 229
Gibson-StL 225
Marichal-SF 222

Strikeouts/Game
Koufax-LA 8.83
Maloney-Cin 8.64
Sutton-LA 8.32
Veale-Pit 7.69
Jenkins-Phi-Chi 7.34

Wins Above Team
Marichal-SF 9.2
Koufax-LA 8.2
Regan-LA 6.4
Perry-SF 5.7
Gibson-StL 4.9

Earned Run Average
Koufax-LA 1.73
Cuellar-Hou 2.22
Marichal-SF 2.23
Bunning-Phi 2.41
Gibson-StL 2.44

Adjusted ERA
Koufax-LA 199
Cuellar-Hou 160
Marichal-SF 157
Bunning-Phi 150
Gibson-StL 147

Opponents' Batting Avg.
Marichal-SF 202
Koufax-LA 205
Gibson-StL 207
Bolin-SF 211
Maloney-Cin 214

Opponents' On Base Pct.
Marichal-SF 228
Koufax-LA 250
Gibson-StL 262
Bunning-Phi 266
Cuellar-Hou 268

Starter Runs
Koufax-LA 67.4
Marichal-SF 47.0
Bunning-Phi 41.8
Gibson-StL 36.2
Cuellar-Hou 35.0

Adjusted Starter Runs
Koufax-LA 61.1
Marichal-SF 43.0
Bunning-Phi 42.3
Gibson-StL 36.1
Cuellar-Hou 33.7

Clutch Pitching Index
Jackson-StL 117
Jackson-Chi-Phi ...110
Johnson-Atl 108
Ellsworth-Chi 108
Osteen-LA 107

Relief Runs
Regan-LA 25.9
Carroll-Atl 19.7
Hoerner-StL 17.5
McCool-Cin 13.1
Woodeshick-StL ...13.1

Adjusted Relief Runs
Regan-LA 23.6
McCool-Cin 19.0
Carroll-Atl 18.1
Hoerner-StL 17.4
Woodeshick-StL ...13.0

Relief Ranking
Regan-LA 36.7
McCool-Cin 33.4
Carroll-Atl 20.1
Hoerner-StL 19.1
Face-Pit 14.3

Total Pitcher Index
Koufax-LA 5.9
Marichal-SF 5.7
Bunning-Phi 4.4
Gibson-StL 4.2
Maloney-Cin 4.1

Total Baseball Ranking
Santo-Chi 7.6
Koufax-LA 5.9
Marichal-SF 5.7
Torre-Atl 5.6
Aaron-Atl 5.2

TEAM	G	W	L	PCT	GB	R	OR	AB	H	2B	3B	HR	BB	SO	AVG	OBP	SLG	PRO	/A	BR	/A	PF	CHI	RC	TA	SB	CS	SBA	SBR
BAL	160	97	63	.606		755	601	5529	1426	243	35	175	514	926	.258	.325	.409	.734	117	114	108	101	99	727	.673	55	43	56	-8
MIN	162	89	73	.549	9	663	581	5390	1341	219	33	144	513	844	.249	.319	.382	.701	107	49	-21	111	98	643	.633	67	42	61	-4
DET	162	88	74	.543	10	719	698	5507	1383	224	45	179	551	987	.251	.323	.406	.729	115	102	87	102	96	714	.667	41	34	55	-7
CHI	163	83	79	.512	15	574	517	5348	1235	193	40	87	476	872	.231	.299	.331	.630	87	-82	-46	94	105	539	.570	153	78	66	0
CLE	162	81	81	.500	17	574	586	5474	1300	156	25	155	450	914	.237	.299	.360	.659	95	-37	-45	101	97	579	.578	53	41	56	-8
CAL	162	80	82	.494	18	604	643	5360	1244	179	54	122	525	1062	.232	.305	.354	.659	95	-28	-21	99	100	582	.594	80	54	60	-7
KC	160	74	86	.463	23	564	648	5328	1259	212	56	70	421	982	.236	.295	.337	.632	87	-82	-46	94	106	535	.562	132	50	73	10
WAS	159	71	88	.447	25.5	557	659	5318	1245	185	40	126	450	1069	.234	.296	.355	.651	93	-49	-16	95	98	569	.569	53	37	59	-5
BOS	162	72	90	.444	26	655	731	5498	1318	228	44	145	542	1020	.240	.312	.376	.688	103	24	-34	109	98	640	.618	35	24	59	-3
NY	160	70	89	.440	26.5	611	612	5330	1254	182	36	162	485	817	.235	.302	.374	.676	100	-4	35	94	99	598	.605	49	29	63	-2
TOT	806					6276		54082	13005	2021	408	1365	4927	9493	.240	.308	.369	.676								718	432	62	-43

TEAM	CG	SHO	SV	IP	H	H/G	HR	BB	BB/G	SO	SO/G	ERA	/A	OAVG	OOBA	PR	/A	PF	CPI	FA	E	DP	FW	PW	BW	SBW	DIF
BAL	23	13	51	1466.3	1267	7.8	127	514	3.2	1070	6.6	3.32	102	.233	.298	18	10	99	97	.981	115	142	1.4	1.1	11.6	-.4	3.4
MIN	52	11	28	1438.7	1246	7.8	139	392	2.5	1015	6.3	3.13	121	.231	.282	48	103	110	97	.977	139	118	-.0	11.1	-2.3	.0	-.8
DET	36	11	38	1454.3	1356	8.4	185	520	3.2	1026	6.3	3.85	91	.247	.311	-66	-56	102	102	.980	120	142	1.1	-6.0	9.3	-.3	2.9
CHI	38	22	34	1475.3	1229	7.5	101	403	2.5	896	5.5	2.68	123	.225	.278	123	84	93	100	.976	159	149	-1.2	9.0	-4.9	.5	-1.4
CLE	49	15	28	1467.3	1260	7.7	129	489	3.0	1111	6.8	3.23	108	.232	.293	34	43	102	98	.978	138	132	.0	4.6	-4.8	-.4	.6
CAL	31	12	40	1457.3	1364	8.4	136	511	3.2	836	5.2	3.56	96	.251	.313	-20	-22	100	105	.979	136	186	.1	-2.4	-2.3	-.3	3.8
KC	19	11	47	1435.7	1281	8.0	106	630	3.9	854	5.4	3.55	92	.240	.319	-18	-44	95	100	.977	139	154	-.0	-4.7	-4.9	1.5	2.2
WAS	25	6	35	1419.0	1282	8.1	154	448	2.8	866	5.5	3.70	89	.241	.298	-42	-62	96	95	.977	142	139	-.2	-6.7	-1.7	-.0	.1
BOS	32	10	31	1463.7	1402	8.6	164	577	3.5	977	6.0	3.92	97	.252	.320	-78	-20	110	103	.975	155	153	-1.0	-2.1	-3.7	.1	-2.4
NY	29	7	32	1415.0	1318	8.4	124	443	2.8	842	5.4	3.42	94	.247	.301	3	-31	94	102	.977	142	142	-.2	-3.3	3.8	.3	-10.0
TOT	334	118	364	14492.7		8.1		3.1		5.9	3.44		.240	.308					.978	1385	1457						

Runs
F.Robinson-Bal......122
Oliva-Min..........99
Cash-Det..........98
Agee-Chi..........98

Hits
Oliva-Min...........191
F.Robinson-Bal......182
Aparicio-Bal......182
Agee-Chi..........172
Cash-Det..........168

Doubles
Yastrzemski-Bos.....39
B.Robinson-Bal.....35
F.Robinson-Bal.....34
Oliva-Min..........32
Fregosi-Cal........32

Triples
Knoop-Cal.........11
Campaneris-KC.....10
Brinkman-Was........9

Home Runs
F.Robinson-Bal......49
Killebrew-Min......39
Powell-Bal........34
Cash-Det..........32
Pepitone-NY........31

Total Bases
F.Robinson-Bal......367
Oliva-Min..........312
Killebrew-Min......306
Cash-Det..........288
Agee-Chi..........281

Runs Batted In
F.Robinson-Bal......122
Killebrew-Min......110
Powell-Bal........109
B.Robinson-Bal....100
Horton-Det........100

Runs Produced
F.Robinson-Bal......195
B.Robinson-Bal....168
Agee-Chi..........162
Oliva-Min..........161
Killebrew-Min......160

Bases On Balls
Killebrew-Min......103
Foy-Bos...........91
F.Robinson-Bal.....87
Tresh-NY..........86
Yastrzemski-Bos.....84

Batting Average
F.Robinson-Bal.....316
Oliva-Min.........307
Kaline-Det........288
Powell-Bal........287
Killebrew-Min.....281

On Base Percentage
F.Robinson-Bal.....415
Kaline-Det........396
Killebrew-Min.....393
McAuliffe-Det.....375
Powell-Bal........374

Slugging Average
F.Robinson-Bal.....637
Killebrew-Min.....538
Kaline-Det........534
Powell-Bal........532
McAuliffe-Det.....509

Production
F.Robinson-Bal....1.052
Killebrew-Min.....931
Kaline-Det........931
Powell-Bal........905
McAuliffe-Det.....884

Adjusted Production
F.Robinson-Bal......196
Kaline-Det........161
Powell-Bal........155
McAuliffe-Det.....148
Killebrew-Min.....148

Batter Runs
F.Robinson-Bal....73.6
Killebrew-Min....49.9
Kaline-Det.......42.1
Powell-Bal.......36.3
Oliva-Min........33.2

Adjusted Batter Runs
F.Robinson-Bal.....73.0
Killebrew-Min....41.9
Kaline-Det.......40.8
Powell-Bal.......35.8
Mantle-NY........31.4

Clutch Hitting Index
Hershberger-KC.....134
Wert-Det.........130
B.Robinson-Bal...129
Powell-Bal.......129
Horton-Det.......128

Runs Created
F.Robinson-Bal......146
Killebrew-Min.....122
Oliva-Min........106
Kaline-Det.......105
Cash-Det.........101

Total Average
F.Robinson-Bal....1.116
Kaline-Det........983
Killebrew-Min.....972
Powell-Bal........909
Oliva-Min.........819

Stolen Bases
Campaneris-KC.....52
Buford-Chi........51
Agee-Chi..........44
Aparicio-Bal......25
Cardenal-Cal......24

Stolen Base Average
Campaneris-KC.....83.9
Tartabull-KC-Bos...82.6
Tovar-Min........72.7
Agee-Chi.........71.0
Buford-Chi.......69.9

Stolen Base Runs
Campaneris-KC.....9.6
Tartabull-KC-Bos...3.3
Salmon-Cle.......2.4
Agee-Chi.........2.4

Fielding Runs
Freehan-Det......23.4
Knoop-Cal........23.3
Fregosi-Cal......19.1
Boyer-NY.........18.8
Howard-NY........16.3

Total Player Rating
F.Robinson-Bal......6.5
Kaline-Det........4.7
Fregosi-Cal.......3.6
Oliva-Min........3.5
McAuliffe-Det.....3.4

Wins
Kaat-Min..........25
McLain-Det........20
Wilson-Bos-Det.....18
Siebert-Cle.......16
Palmer-Bal........15

Win Percentage
Siebert-Cle.......667
Kaat-Min.........658
Wilson-Bos-Det....621
Palmer-Bal.......600
McLain-Det.......588

Games
Fisher-Chi-Bal......67
Cox-Was...........66
Aker-KC...........66
Worthington-Min....65
Kline-Was.........63

Complete Games
Kaat-Min..........19
McLain-Det........14
Wilson-Bos-Det.....13
Bell-Cle..........12

Shutouts
Tiant-Cle...........5
McDowell-Cle........5
John-Chi............5

Saves
Aker-KC...........32
Kline-Was.........23
Sherry-Det........20
Fisher-Chi-Bal.....19
Miller-Bal........18

Innings Pitched
Kaat-Min..........305
Wilson-Bos-Det....264
McLain-Det.......264
Chance-Cal.......260
Bell-Cle.........254

Fewest Hits/Game
McDowell-Cle......6.03
Boswell-Min......6.39
Peters-Chi.......6.85
McLain-Det.......6.99
Chance-Cal.......7.13

Fewest BB/Game
Kaat-Min.........1.62
Peterson-NY......1.67
Grant-Min........1.77
Peters-Chi.......1.98
Hargan-Cle.......2.11

Strikeouts
McDowell-Cle......225
Kaat-Min.........205
Wilson-Bos-Det....200
Richert-Was......195
Bell-Cle.........194

Strikeouts/Game
McDowell-Cle.....10.44
Boswell-Min......9.21
Lolich-Det.......7.63
Richert-Was......7.13
Bell-Cle.........6.87

Wins Above Team
Nash-KC...........5.6
Kaat-Min.........5.6
Siebert-Cle......4.4
Wilson-Bos-Det....3.7
Krausse-KC.......3.5

Earned Run Average
Peters-Chi.......1.98
Horlen-Chi.......2.43
Hargan-Cle.......2.48
Perry-Min........2.54
John-Chi.........2.62

Adjusted ERA
Peters-Chi........162
Perry-Min........149
Hargan-Cle.......140
Kaat-Min.........138
Horlen-Chi.......132

Opponents' Batting Avg.
McDowell-Cle......188
Boswell-Min......197
Peters-Chi.......212
McLain-Det.......214
Richert-Was......215

Opponents' On Base Pct.
Peters-Chi........255
Richert-Was......268
Kaat-Min.........268
Peterson-NY......272
Ortega-Was.......272

Starter Runs
Peters-Chi.......33.3
Horlen-Chi.......23.5
Kaat-Min.........23.4
Hargan-Cle.......20.3
John-Chi.........20.1

Adjusted Starter Runs
Kaat-Min.........35.2
Peters-Chi.......27.9
Perry-Min........25.3
Hargan-Cle.......21.5
Siebert-Cle......18.5

Clutch Pitching Index
McNally-Bal.......118
Horlen-Chi.......114
Brunet-Cal.......114
Perry-Min........112
Hargan-Cle.......110

Relief Runs
Aker-KC..........18.1
Wilhelm-Chi......15.9
Miller-Bal.......12.1
Fisher-Chi-Bal...10.8
Lines-Was........10.7

Adjusted Relief Runs
Aker-KC..........16.1
Wilhelm-Chi......13.8
Worthington-Min...13.2
Miller-Bal.......11.6
McMahon-Cle-Bos...10.5

Relief Ranking
Aker-KC..........25.7
McMahon-Cle-Bos...20.5
Miller-Bal.......19.8
Worthington-Min...17.0
Locker-Chi.......14.8

Total Pitcher Index
Kaat-Min..........4.6
Peters-Chi.......4.0
Wilson-Bos-Det....3.4
Perry-Min........3.3
Horlen-Chi.......2.3

Total Baseball Ranking
F.Robinson-Bal......6.5
Kaline-Det........4.7
Kaat-Min.........4.6
Peters-Chi.......4.0
Fregosi-Cal......3.6

TEAM	G	W	L	PCT	GB	R	OR	AB	H	2B	3B	HR	BB	SO	AVG	OBP	SLG	PRO	/A	BR	/A	PF	CHI	RC	TA	SB	CS	SBA	SBR
STL	161	101	60	.627		695	557	5566	1462	225	40	115	443	919	.263	.322	.379	.701	107	51	43	101	102	676	.634	102	54	65	-1
SF	162	91	71	.562	10.5	652	551	5524	1354	201	39	140	520	978	.245	.315	.372	.687	103	23	17	101	99	641	.610	22	30	42	-10
CHI	162	87	74	.540	14	702	624	5463	1373	211	49	128	509	912	.251	.319	.378	.697	106	43	33	102	105	654	.628	63	50	56	-10
CIN	162	87	75	.537	14.5	604	563	5519	1366	251	54	109	372	969	.248	.299	.372	.671	98	-20	-75	109	102	592	.589	92	63	59	-9
PHI	162	82	80	.506	19.5	612	581	5401	1306	221	47	103	545	1033	.242	.314	.357	.671	99	-1	-28	104	98	604	.605	79	62	56	-13
PIT	163	81	81	.500	20.5	679	693	5724	1585	193	62	91	387	914	.277	.327	.380	.707	109	62	62	100	97	693	.622	79	37	68	2
ATL	162	77	85	.475	24.5	631	640	5450	1307	191	29	158	512	947	.240	.309	.372	.681	101	10	-16	104	100	615	.609	55	45	55	-10
LA	162	73	89	.451	28.5	519	595	5456	1285	203	38	82	485	881	.236	.303	.332	.635	88	-73	0	88	94	541	.550	56	47	54	-10
HOU	162	69	93	.426	32.5	626	742	5506	1372	259	46	93	537	934	.249	.319	.364	.683	102	19	59	94	96	640	.618	88	38	70	4
NY	162	61	101	.377	40.5	498	672	5417	1288	178	23	83	362	981	.238	.290	.325	.615	82	-118	-111	99	102	500	.517	58	44	57	-8
TOT	810					6218		55026	13698	2133	427	1102	4672	9468	.249	.312	.364	.675								694	470	60	-73

TEAM	CG	SHO	SV	IP	H	H/G	HR	BB	BB/G	SO	SO/G	ERA	/A	OAVG	OOBA	PR	/A	PF	CPI	FA	E	DP	FW	PW	BW	SBW	DIF
STL	44	17	45	1465.0	1313	8.1	97	431	2.6	956	5.9	3.05	110	.239	.293	53	48	99	98	.978	140	127	.0	5.2	4.7	.7	9.9
SF	64	17	25	1474.7	1283	7.8	113	453	2.8	990	6.0	2.92	115	.233	.290	75	70	99	101	.979	134	149	.4	7.6	1.8	-.3	.5
CHI	47	7	28	1457.0	1352	8.4	142	463	2.9	888	5.5	3.48	97	.245	.302	-17	-16	100	99	.981	121	143	1.1	-1.7	3.6	-.3	3.8
CIN	34	18	39	1468.0	1328	8.1	101	498	3.1	1065	6.5	3.05	120	.240	.303	53	100	109	104	.980	121	124	1.1	10.8	-8.1	-.2	2.3
PHI	46	17	23	1453.3	1372	8.5	86	403	2.5	967	6.0	3.10	113	.249	.300	44	65	104	102	.978	137	174	.2	7.0	-3.0	-.6	-2.6
PIT	35	5	35	1458.3	1439	8.9	108	561	3.5	820	5.1	3.74	90	.260	.326	-58	-57	100	103	.978	141	186	-.0	-6.2	6.7	1.0	-1.5
ATL	35	5	32	1454.0	1377	8.5	118	449	2.8	862	5.3	3.47	102	.251	.306	-15	9	105	100	.978	138	148	.2	1.0	-1.7	-.3	-3.1
LA	41	17	24	1473.0	1421	8.7	93	393	2.4	967	5.9	3.21	94	.254	.301	26	-33	89	102	.975	160	144	-1.1	-3.6	.0	-.3	-3.0
HOU	35	8	21	1445.7	1444	9.0	120	485	3.0	1060	6.6	4.03	80	.259	.317	-104	-130	95	93	.974	159	120	-1.0	-14.1	6.4	1.2	-4.5
NY	36	10	19	1433.7	1369	8.6	124	536	3.4	893	5.6	3.73	92	.252	.316	-56	-46	102	99	.975	157	147	-.9	-5.0	-12.0	-.0	-2.0
TOT	417	121	291	14582.7		8.5			2.9		5.8	3.38		.249	.312					.978	1408	1462					

Runs		Hits		Doubles		Triples		Home Runs		Total Bases	
Brock-StL	113	Clemente-Pit	209	Staub-Hou	44	Pinson-Cin	13	Aaron-Atl	39	Aaron-Atl	344
Aaron-Atl	113	Brock-StL	206	Cepeda-StL	37	Williams-Chi	12	Wynn-Hou	37	Brock-StL	325
Santo-Chi	107	Pinson-Cin	187	Aaron-Atl	37	Brock-StL	12	Santo-Chi	31	Clemente-Pit	324
Clemente-Pit	103	Wills-Pit	186			Morgan-Hou	11	McCovey-SF	31	Williams-Chi	305
Wynn-Hou	102	Alou-Pit	186					Hart-SF	29	Santo-Chi	300

Runs Batted In		Runs Produced		Bases On Balls		Batting Average		On Base Percentage		Slugging Average	
Cepeda-StL	111	Clemente-Pit	190	Santo-Chi	96	Clemente-Pit	.357	Allen-Phi	.404	Aaron-Atl	.573
Clemente-Pit	110	Aaron-Atl	183	Morgan-Hou	81	Gonzalez-Phi	.339	Cepeda-StL	.403	Allen-Phi	.566
Aaron-Atl	109	Cepeda-StL	177	Phillips-Chi	80	Alou-Pit	.338	Staub-Hou	.402	Clemente-Pit	.554
Wynn-Hou	107	Santo-Chi	174	Hart-SF	77	Flood-StL	.335	Clemente-Pit	.402	McCovey-SF	.535
Perez-Cin	102	Wynn-Hou	172	Allen-Phi	75	Staub-Hou	.333	Santo-Chi	.401	Cepeda-StL	.524

Production		Adjusted Production		Batter Runs		Adjusted Batter Runs		Clutch Hitting Index		Runs Created	
Allen-Phi	.970	Clemente-Pit	171	Clemente-Pit	52.1	Clemente-Pit	52.1	Shannon-StL	152	Clemente-Pit	126
Clemente-Pit	.956	Allen-Phi	167	Aaron-Atl	50.0	Aaron-Atl	47.1	Mazeroski-Pit	134	Aaron-Atl	126
Aaron-Atl	.946	Cepeda-StL	161	Santo-Chi	47.8	Santo-Chi	46.7	Cepeda-StL	132	Santo-Chi	120
Cepeda-StL	.927	Aaron-Atl	160	Cepeda-StL	47.2	Cepeda-StL	46.4	Lanier-SF	130	Cepeda-StL	118
McCovey-SF	.916	Staub-Hou	160	Allen-Phi	46.0	Allen-Phi	43.6	Boyer-Atl	127	Hart-SF	111

Total Average		Stolen Bases		Stolen Base Average		Stolen Base Runs		Fielding Runs		Total Player Rating	
Allen-Phi	1.069	Brock-StL	52	Morgan-Hou	85.3	Morgan-Hou	5.7	Santo-Chi	31.1	Santo-Chi	7.0
Aaron-Atl	.979	Wills-Pit	29	Wynn-Hou	80.0	Brock-StL	4.8	Mazeroski-Pit	17.4	Clemente-Pit	4.8
Clemente-Pit	.962	Morgan-Hou	29	Allen-Phi	80.0	Pinson-Cin	3.0	McCarver-StL	16.4	McCarver-StL	4.6
Cepeda-StL	.955	Pinson-Cin	26	Davis-LA	76.9	Allen-Phi	3.0	Lanier-SF	16.2	Aaron-Atl	4.5
McCovey-SF	.950	Phillips-Chi	24	Pinson-Cin	76.5	Wills-Pit	2.7	Hundley-Chi	14.8	Cepeda-StL	4.3

Wins		Win Percentage		Games		Complete Games		Shutouts		Saves	
McCormick-SF	22	Hughes-StL	.727	Perranoski-LA	70	Jenkins-Chi	20	Bunning-Phi	6	Abernathy-Cin	28
Jenkins-Chi	20	McCormick-SF	.688	Abernathy-Cin	70	Seaver-NY	18	Osteen-LA	5	Linzy-SF	17
Osteen-LA	17	Veale-Pit	.667	Willis-StL	65	Perry-SF	18	Nolan-Cin	5	Face-Pit	17
Bunning-Phi	17	Jenkins-Chi	.606	Face-Pit	61	Marichal-SF	18	McCormick-SF	5	Perranoski-LA	16
		Jarvis-Atl	.600					Jackson-Phi	4	Hoerner-StL	15

Innings Pitched		Fewest Hits/Game		Fewest BB/Game		Strikeouts		Strikeouts/Game		Wins Above Team	
Bunning-Phi	302	Hughes-StL	6.65	Pappas-Cin	1.57	Bunning-Phi	253	Nolan-Cin	8.17	McCormick-SF	5.3
Perry-SF	293	Wilson-Hou	6.90	Osteen-LA	1.62	Jenkins-Chi	236	Veale-Pit	7.94	Seaver-NY	4.7
Jenkins-Chi	289	Perry-SF	7.10	Johnson-Atl	1.63	Perry-SF	230	Carlton-StL	7.83	Holtzman-Chi	4.5
Osteen-LA	288	Queen-Cin	7.12	Niekro-Chi	1.69	Nolan-Cin	206	Wilson-Hou	7.78	Cuellar-Hou	4.4
Drysdale-LA	282	Niekro-Atl	7.13	Jackson-Phi	1.85	Cuellar-Hou	203	Gibson-StL	7.56	Veale-Pit	4.4

Earned Run Average		Adjusted ERA		Opponents' Batting Avg.		Opponents' On Base Pct.		Starter Runs		Adjusted Starter Runs	
Niekro-Atl	1.87	Niekro-Atl	189	Hughes-StL	.203	Hughes-StL	.249	Bunning-Phi	36.3	Bunning-Phi	40.7
Bunning-Phi	2.29	Bunning-Phi	153	Wilson-Hou	.209	Bunning-Phi	.269	Niekro-Atl	34.6	Niekro-Atl	38.2
Short-Phi	2.40	Short-Phi	146	Perry-SF	.214	Queen-Cin	.270	Perry-SF	24.9	Nolan-Cin	27.4
Nolan-Cin	2.58	Nolan-Cin	142	Queen-Cin	.215	Perry-SF	.271	Short-Phi	21.6	Short-Phi	24.6
Perry-SF	2.61	Queen-Cin	133	Bunning-Phi	.217	Niekro-Atl	.273	Nolan-Cin	20.1	Perry-SF	24.0

Clutch Pitching Index		Relief Runs		Adjusted Relief Runs		Relief Ranking		Total Pitcher Index		Total Baseball Ranking	
Ellis-Cin	123	Abernathy-Cin	24.8	Abernathy-Cin	28.1	Abernathy-Cin	38.2	Bunning-Phi	4.7	Santo-Chi	7.0
Niekro-Atl	121	Linzy-SF	20.0	Linzy-SF	19.7	Linzy-SF	33.7	Niekro-Atl	4.4	Clemente-Pit	4.8
Seaver-NY	114	Nottebart-Cin	12.6	Nottebart-Cin	15.2	Hall-Phi	26.2	Abernathy-Cin	3.2	Bunning-Phi	4.7
Marichal-SF	114	McBean-Pit	12.1	Farrell-Hou-Phi	13.1	Farrell-Hou-Phi	21.5	Perry-SF	3.0	McCarver-StL	4.6
Short-Phi	113	Farrell-Hou-Phi	12.0	Hall-Phi	12.5	Face-Pit	15.4	Nolan-Cin	2.9	Aaron-Atl	4.5

TEAM	G	W	L	PCT	GB	R	OR	AB	H	2B	3B	HR	BB	SO	AVG	OBP	SLG	PRO	/A	BR	/A	PF	CHI	RC	TA	SB	CS	SBA	SBR
BOS	162	92	70	.568		722	614	5471	1394	216	39	158	522	1020	.255	.323	.395	.718	118	118	29	115	99	694	.657	68	59	54	-14
MIN	164	91	71	.562	1	671	590	5458	1309	216	48	131	512	976	.240	.310	.369	.679	107	43	1	107	103	625	.611	55	37	60	-5
DET	163	91	71	.562	1	683	587	5410	1315	192	36	152	626	994	.243	.327	.376	.703	114	100	103	99	95	681	.650	37	21	64	-1
CHI	162	89	73	.549	3	531	491	5383	1209	181	34	89	480	849	.225	.293	.320	.613	87	-80	-43	94	103	504	.543	124	82	60	-11
CAL	161	84	77	.522	7.5	567	587	5307	1265	170	37	114	453	1021	.238	.302	.349	.651	98	-12	13	96	99	553	.567	40	36	53	-9
WAS	161	76	85	.472	15.5	550	637	5441	1211	168	25	115	472	1037	.223	.289	.326	.615	88	-80	-93	102	106	512	.533	53	37	59	-5
BAL	161	76	85	.472	15.5	654	592	5456	1312	215	44	138	531	1002	.240	.313	.372	.685	108	54	87	95	98	639	.620	54	37	59	-5
CLE	162	75	87	.463	17	559	613	5441	1282	213	35	131	413	984	.235	.295	.359	.654	99	-14	-15	100	96	563	.569	53	65	45	-22
NY	163	72	90	.444	20	522	621	5443	1225	166	17	100	532	1043	.225	.298	.317	.615	88	-74	-38	94	98	522	.538	63	37	63	-2
KC	161	62	99	.385	29.5	533	660	5349	1244	212	50	69	452	1019	.233	.297	.330	.627	91	-54	-51	100	100	539	.563	132	59	69	4
TOT	810					5992		54179	12766	1949	365	1197	4993	9945	.236	.305	.352	.656								679	470	59	-77

TEAM	CG	SHO	SV	IP	H	H/G	HR	BB	BB/G	SO	SO/G	ERA	/A	OAVG	OOBA	PR	/A	PF	CPI	FA	E	DP	FW	PW	BW	SBW	DIF
BOS	41	9	44	1459.3	1307	8.1	142	477	2.9	1010	6.2	3.36	108	.238	.300	-21	45	113	101	.977	142	142	-.6	5.0	3.2	-.7	4.1
MIN	58	18	24	1461.0	1336	8.2	115	396	2.4	1089	6.7	3.14	109	.242	.292	15	44	106	101	.978	132	123	.0	4.9	.1	.3	4.7
DET	46	17	40	1443.7	1230	7.7	151	472	2.9	1038	6.5	3.32	95	.230	.291	-13	-24	98	97	.978	132	126	-2.6	11.4	.8		.5
CHI	36	24	39	1490.3	1197	7.2	87	465	2.8	927	5.6	2.45	123	.219	.283	128	92	93	106	.979	138	149	-.3	10.2	-4.7	-.3	3.3
CAL	19	14	46	1430.3	1246	7.8	118	525	3.3	892	5.6	3.19	97	.236	.304	6	-14	96	105	.982	111	135	1.3	-1.5	1.4	-.1	2.4
WAS	24	14	39	1473.3	1334	8.1	113	495	3.0	878	5.4	3.38	99	.242	.303	-25	-5	104	98	.978	144	167	-.7	-.6	-10.3	.3	6.7
BAL	29	17	36	1457.3	1218	7.5	116	566	3.5	1034	6.4	3.32	91	.227	.300	-14	-48	94	95	.980	124	144	.5	-5.3	9.6	.3	-9.6
CLE	49	14	27	1477.7	1258	7.7	120	559	3.4	1189	7.2	3.25	101	.231	.300	-2	3	101	99	.981	116	138	1.0	.3	-1.7	-1.6	-4.1
NY	37	16	27	1480.7	1375	8.4	110	480	2.9	898	5.5	3.24	95	.248	.305	-1	-24	96	106	.976	154	144	-1.3	-2.6	-4.2	.6	-1.5
KC	26	10	34	1428.3	1265	8.0	125	558	3.5	990	6.2	3.68	89	.237	.309	-71	-62	102	94	.978	132	120	.0	-6.8	-5.6	1.3	-7.4
TOT	365	153	356	14602.0		7.9			3.1		6.1	3.23		.236	.305					.979	1325	1388					

Runs
Yastrzemski-Bos 112
Killebrew-Min 105
Tovar-Min 98
Kaline-Det 94
McAuliffe-Det 92

Hits
Yastrzemski-Bos 189
Tovar-Min 173
Scott-Bos 171
Fregosi-Cal 171
B.Robinson-Bal 164

Doubles
Oliva-Min 34
Tovar-Min 32
Yastrzemski-Bos 31
Johnson-Bal 30
Campaneris-KC 29

Triples
Blair-Bal 12
Buford-Chi 9

Home Runs
Yastrzemski-Bos 44
Killebrew-Min 44
Howard-Was 36
F.Robinson-Bal 30

Total Bases
Yastrzemski-Bos 360
Killebrew-Min 305
F.Robinson-Bal 276
B.Robinson-Bal 265
Howard-Was 265

Runs Batted In
Yastrzemski-Bos 121
Killebrew-Min 113
F.Robinson-Bal 94
Howard-Was 89
Oliva-Min 83

Runs Produced
Yastrzemski-Bos 189
F.Robinson-Bal 174
Kaline-Det 147
F.Robinson-Bal 147
B.Robinson-Bal 143

Bases On Balls
Killebrew-Min 131
Mantle-NY 107
McAuliffe-Det 105
Yastrzemski-Bos 91
Kaline-Det 83

Batting Average
Yastrzemski-Bos 326
F.Robinson-Bal 311
Kaline-Det 308
Scott-Bos 303
Blair-Bal 293

On Base Percentage
Yastrzemski-Bos 421
Kaline-Det 415
Killebrew-Min 413
F.Robinson-Bal 408
Mantle-NY 394

Slugging Average
Yastrzemski-Bos 622
F.Robinson-Bal 576
Killebrew-Min 558
Kaline-Det 541
Howard-Was 511

Production
Yastrzemski-Bos ...1.043
F.Robinson-Bal 984
Killebrew-Min 970
Kaline-Det 957
Mincher-Cal 855

Adjusted Production
F.Robinson-Bal 198
Kaline-Det 182
Yastrzemski-Bos 178
Killebrew-Min 172
Mincher-Cal 157

Batter Runs
Yastrzemski-Bos 76.4
Killebrew-Min 62.3
F.Robinson-Bal 53.3
Kaline-Det 48.3
Scott-Bos 33.8

Adjusted Batter Runs
Yastrzemski-Bos 66.6
Killebrew-Min 57.6
F.Robinson-Bal 56.3
Kaline-Det 48.7
Freehan-Det 33.9

Clutch Hitting Index
Hershberger-KC 134
Pepitone-NY 124
Johnson-Bal 123
Blefary-Bal 121
Oliva-Min 119

Runs Created
Yastrzemski-Bos 155
Killebrew-Min 131
F.Robinson-Bal 113
Kaline-Det 104
Scott-Bos 97

Total Average
Yastrzemski-Bos ...1.154
Killebrew-Min 1.058
F.Robinson-Bal 1.038
Kaline-Det 1.015
Mantle-NY 877

Stolen Bases
Campaneris-KC 55
Buford-Chi 34
Agee-Chi 28
McCraw-Chi 24
Clarke-NY 21

Stolen Base Average
Valentine-Was 85.0
Clarke-NY 84.0
Aparicio-Bal 78.3
Campaneris-KC 77.5
Agee-Chi 73.7

Stolen Base Runs
Campaneris-KC 6.9
Clarke-NY 3.9
Valentine-Was 3.3

Fielding Runs
B.Robinson-Bal 30.0
Casanova-Was 22.8
Gibbs-NY 18.4
Blair-Bal 15.8
McMullen-Was 12.1

Total Player Rating
Yastrzemski-Bos 7.2
B.Robinson-Bal 5.7
Kaline-Det 5.6
Freehan-Det 5.4
F.Robinson-Bal 5.1

Wins
Wilson-Det 22
Lonborg-Bos 22
Chance-Min 20
Horlen-Chi 19
McLain-Det 17

Win Percentage
Horlen-Chi 731
Lonborg-Bos 710
Wilson-Det 667
Sparma-Det 640
Peters-Chi 593

Games
Locker-Chi 77
Rojas-Cal 72
Kelso-Cal 69
Womack-NY 65
McMahon-Bos-Chi 63

Complete Games
Chance-Min 18
Lonborg-Bos 15
Hargan-Cle 15

Shutouts
McGlothlin-Cal 6
Lolich-Det 6
John-Chi 6
Horlen-Chi 6
Hargan-Cle 6

Saves
Rojas-Cal 27
Wyatt-Bos 20
Locker-Chi 20
Womack-NY 18
Worthington-Min 16

Innings Pitched
Chance-Min 284
Lonborg-Bos 273
Wilson-Det 264
Kaat-Min 263

Fewest Hits/Game
Peters-Chi 6.47
Boswell-Min 6.54
Horlen-Chi 6.56
Siebert-Cle 6.62
Downing-NY 7.04

Fewest BB/Game
Merritt-Min 1.18
Kaat-Min 1.44
Stange-Bos 1.58
Horlen-Chi 2.02
Peterson-NY 2.14

Strikeouts
Lonborg-Bos 246
McDowell-Cle 236
Chance-Min 220
Tiant-Cle 219
Peters-Chi 215

Strikeouts/Game
Tiant-Cle 9.21
McDowell-Cle 9.00
Boswell-Min 8.23
Lonborg-Bos 8.11
Phoebus-Bal 7.75

Wins Above Team
Lonborg-Bos 5.8
Horlen-Chi 5.8
Wilson-Det 4.7
Santiago-Bos 3.6
Downing-NY 3.4

Earned Run Average
Horlen-Chi 2.06
Peters-Chi 2.28
Siebert-Cle 2.38
John-Chi 2.48
Merritt-Min 2.53

Adjusted ERA
Horlen-Chi 146
Siebert-Cle 137
Merritt-Min 135
Peters-Chi 132
Stange-Bos 132

Opponents' Batting Avg.
Peters-Chi 199
Boswell-Min 202
Siebert-Cle 202
Horlen-Chi 203
Downing-NY 217

Opponents' On Base Pct.
Horlen-Chi 251
Merritt-Min 256
Siebert-Cle 264
Peters-Chi 273
John-Chi 273

Starter Runs
Horlen-Chi 33.6
Peters-Chi 27.3
Merritt-Min 17.8
Siebert-Cle 17.4
Chance-Min 15.9

Adjusted Starter Runs
Horlen-Chi 27.2
Merritt-Min 22.3
Chance-Min 21.5
Peters-Chi 20.9
Siebert-Cle 18.2

Clutch Pitching Index
Clark-Cal 121
Stottlemyre-NY 117
Kaat-Min 108
Tiant-Cle 107
Stange-Bos 106

Relief Runs
Wilhelm-Chi 18.9
Drabowsky-Bal 17.1
Locker-Chi 15.9
McMahon-Bos-Chi 15.5
Baldwin-Was 11.8

Adjusted Relief Runs
Wilhelm-Chi 16.7
Drabowsky-Bal 14.9
McMahon-Bos-Chi 14.1
Locker-Chi 12.8
Baldwin-Was 12.7

Relief Ranking
Wilhelm-Chi 23.7
Wyatt-Bos 22.7
Drabowsky-Bal 21.2
Rojas-Cal 16.4
Locker-Chi 15.6

Total Pitcher Index
Horlen-Chi 3.5
Peters-Chi 3.4
Merritt-Min 2.5
Hargan-Cle 2.2
Siebert-Cle 2.0

Total Baseball Ranking
Yastrzemski-Bos 7.2
B.Robinson-Bal 5.7
Kaline-Det 5.6
Freehan-Det 5.4
F.Robinson-Bal 5.1

TEAM	G	W	L	PCT	GB	R	OR	AB	H	2B	3B	HR	BB	SO	AVG	OBP	SLG	PRO	/A	BR	/A	PF	CHI	RC	TA	SB	CS	SBA	SBR
STL	162	97	65	.599		583	472	5561	1383	227	48	73	378	897	.249	.300	.346	.646	101	2	28	95	104	581	.567	110	45	71	6
SF	163	88	74	.543	9	599	529	5441	1301	162	33	108	508	904	.239	.310	.341	.651	103	20	32	98	102	577	.572	50	37	57	-6
CHI	163	84	78	.519	13	612	611	5458	1319	203	43	130	415	854	.242	.300	.366	.666	107	36	-31	112	103	593	.583	41	30	58	-5
CIN	163	83	79	.512	14	690	673	5767	1575	281	36	106	379	938	.273	.322	.389	.711	121	130	64	111	97	688	.619	59	55	52	-14
ATL	163	81	81	.500	16	514	549	5552	1399	179	31	80	414	782	.252	.308	.339	.647	101	9	-8	101	90	564	.556	83	44	65	-1
PIT	163	80	82	.494	17	583	532	5569	1404	180	44	80	422	953	.252	.309	.343	.652	103	18	12	101	99	556	.573	130	59	69	4
PHI	162	76	86	.469	21	543	615	5372	1253	178	30	100	462	1003	.233	.297	.333	.630	96	-23	-8	97	103	527	.546	58	51	53	-12
LA	76	86	.469	21		470	509	5354	1232	202	36	67	439	980	.230	.291	.319	.610	90	-60	-48	91	96	501	.523	72	43	57	-8
NY	163	73	89	.451	24	473	499	5503	1252	178	30	81	379	1203	.228	.283	.315	.598	86	-90	-101	102	102	486	.506	72	45	62	-4
HOU	162	72	90	.444	25	510	588	5336	1233	205	28	66	479	988	.231	.300	.317	.617	92	-40	-34	99	99	505	.530	44	51	46	-16
TOT	813					5577		54913	13351	1995	359	891	4275	9502	.243	.302	.341	.643								704	460	60	-64

TEAM	CG	SHO	SV	IP	H	H/G	HR	BB	BB/G	SO	SO/G	ERA	/A	OAVG	OOBA	PR	/A	PF	CPI	FA	E	DP	FW	PW	BW	SBW	DIF
STL	63	30	32	1479.0	1282	7.8	82	375	2.3	971	5.9	2.49	112	.233	.280	81	48	93	105	.978	140	135	-.0	5.5	3.2	1.4	5.9
SF	77	20	16	1468.7	1302	8.0	86	344	2.1	942	5.8	2.71	106	.235	.278	45	27	96	96	.975	162	125	-1.3	3.1	3.7	.0	1.5
CHI	46	12	32	1453.3	1399	8.7	138	392	2.4	894	5.5	3.41	98	.253	.300	-68	-9	112	100	.981	119	149	1.2	-1.0	-3.6	.2	6.3
CIN	24	16	38	1490.3	1399	8.4	114	573	3.5	963	5.8	3.56	93	.249	.317	-95	-42	111	100	.978	144	144	-.3	-4.8	7.3	-.9	.6
ATL	44	16	29	1474.3	1326	8.1	87	362	2.2	871	5.3	2.92	96	.241	.285	11	-20	94	98	.980	125	139	.8	-2.3	5.5	.6	-4.7
PIT	42	19	30	1487.3	1322	8.0	73	485	2.9	897	5.4	2.74	109	.239	.300	40	40	100	107	.979	139	162	.0	4.6	1.4	1.2	-8.2
PHI	42	12	27	1448.0	1416	8.8	91	421	2.6	935	5.8	3.36	88	.257	.309	-60	-66	99	100	.980	127	163	.7	-7.6	-.9	-.6	3.4
LA	38	23	31	1449.3	1293	8.0	65	414	2.6	994	6.2	2.69	101	.240	.293	6	5	91	104	.977	144	144	-.3	.6	-.9	-.2	-4.2
NY	45	25	32	1483.3	1250	7.6	87	430	2.6	1014	6.2	2.72	112	.229	.286	43	55	103	98	.979	133	142	.3	6.3	-11.6	.3	-3.4
HOU	50	12	23	1447.0	1362	8.5	68	479	3.0	1021	6.4	3.26	92	.248	.306	-43	-42	100	96	.975	156	129	-1.0	-4.8	-3.9	-1.1	1.8
TOT	471	185	290	14680.7		8.2			2.6		5.8	2.99		.243	.302					.978	1389	1432					

Runs
Beckert-Chi ... 98
Rose-Cin ... 94
Perez-Cin ... 93
Brock-StL ... 92
Williams-Chi ... 91

Hits
Rose-Cin ... 210
Alou-Atl ... 210
Beckert-Chi ... 189
Johnson-Cin ... 188
Flood-StL ... 186

Doubles
Brock-StL ... 46
Rose-Cin ... 42
Bench-Cin ... 40
Staub-Hou ... 37
Alou-Atl ... 37

Triples
Brock-StL ... 14
Clemente-Pit ... 12
Davis-LA ... 10
Allen-Phi ... 9
Williams-Chi ... 8

Home Runs
McCovey-SF ... 36
Allen-Phi ... 33
Banks-Chi ... 32
Williams-Chi ... 30
Aaron-Atl ... 29

Total Bases
Williams-Chi ... 321
Aaron-Atl ... 302
Rose-Cin ... 294
Alou-Atl ... 290
McCovey-SF ... 285

Runs Batted In
McCovey-SF ... 105
Williams-Chi ... 98
Santo-Chi ... 98
Perez-Cin ... 92
Allen-Phi ... 90

Runs Produced
Perez-Cin ... 167
Williams-Chi ... 159
Santo-Chi ... 158
McCovey-SF ... 150
Allen-Phi ... 144

Bases On Balls
Santo-Chi ... 96
Wynn-Hou ... 90
Hunt-SF ... 78
Allen-Phi ... 74
Staub-Hou ... 73

Batting Average
Rose-Cin ... .335
Alou-Pit ... .332
Alou-Atl ... .317
Johnson-Cin ... .312
Flood-StL ... .301

On Base Percentage
Rose-Cin ... .394
McCovey-SF ... .383
Wynn-Hou ... .378
Mays-SF ... .376
Staub-Hou ... .376

Slugging Average
McCovey-SF ... .545
Allen-Phi ... .520
Williams-Chi ... .500
Aaron-Atl ... .498
Mays-SF ... .488

Production
McCovey-SF ... .928
Allen-Phi ... .876
Mays-SF ... .864
Rose-Cin ... .863
Aaron-Atl ... .855

Adjusted Production
McCovey-SF ... 180
Aaron-Atl ... 166
Allen-Phi ... 165
Mays-SF ... 161
Wynn-Hou ... 156

Batter Runs
McCovey-SF ... 48.8
Rose-Cin ... 44.5
Aaron-Atl ... 39.0
Wynn-Hou ... 38.4
Allen-Phi ... 38.0

Adjusted Batter Runs
McCovey-SF ... 50.1
Aaron-Atl ... 43.3
Allen-Phi ... 39.4
Wynn-Hou ... 39.0
Rose-Cin ... 37.3

Clutch Hitting Index
Hundley-Chi ... 145
Santo-Chi ... 136
Clendenon-Pit ... 132
Perez-Cin ... 127
Swoboda-NY ... 126

Runs Created
Rose-Cin ... 113
McCovey-SF ... 110
Williams-Chi ... 107
Aaron-Atl ... 104
Alou-Atl ... 103

Total Average
McCovey-SF ... .958
Aaron-Atl ... .887
Mays-SF ... .869
Wynn-Hou ... .866
Allen-Phi ... .862

Stolen Bases
Brock-StL ... 62
Wills-Pit ... 52
Davis-LA ... 36
Aaron-Atl ... 28
Jones-NY ... 23

Stolen Base Average
Aaron-Atl ... 84.8
Brock-StL ... 83.8
Taylor-Phi ... 81.5
Davis-LA ... 78.3

Stolen Base Runs
Brock-StL ... 11.4
Aaron-Atl ... 5.4
Davis-LA ... 4.8
Taylor-Phi ... 3.6
Wills-Pit ... 3.0

Fielding Runs
Mazeroski-Pit ... 23.5
Kessinger-Chi ... 19.7
Wynn-Hou ... 18.7
Alley-Pit ... 17.5
Santo-Chi ... 16.5

Total Player Rating
Aaron-Atl ... 6.1
McCovey-SF ... 5.1
Wynn-Hou ... 4.8
Rose-Cin ... 4.2
Santo-Chi ... 3.7

Wins
Marichal-SF ... 26
Gibson-StL ... 22
Jenkins-Chi ... 20

Win Percentage
Blass-StL ... .750
Marichal-SF ... .743
Gibson-StL ... .710
Briles-StL ... .633

Games
Abernathy-SF ... 78
Regan-LA-Chi ... 73
Carroll-Atl-Cin ... 68
Taylor-NY ... 58
Linzy-SF ... 57

Complete Games
Marichal-SF ... 30
Gibson-StL ... 28
Jenkins-Chi ... 20
Perry-SF ... 19
Koosman-NY ... 17

Shutouts
Gibson-StL ... 13
Drysdale-LA ... 8
Koosman-NY ... 7
Blass-Pit ... 7

Saves
Regan-LA-Chi ... 25
Carroll-Atl-Cin ... 17
Hoerner-StL ... 17
Brewer-LA ... 14

Innings Pitched
Marichal-SF ... 326
Jenkins-Chi ... 308
Gibson-StL ... 305
Perry-SF ... 291
Seaver-NY ... 278

Fewest Hits/Game
Gibson-StL ... 5.84
Bolin-SF ... 6.51
Veale-Pit ... 6.87
Jarvis-Atl ... 7.10
Moose-Pit ... 7.16

Fewest BB/Game
Hands-Chi ... 1.25
Marichal-SF ... 1.27
Seaver-NY ... 1.55
Pappas-Cin-Atl ... 1.57
Niekro-Atl ... 1.58

Strikeouts
Gibson-StL ... 268
Jenkins-Chi ... 260
Singer-LA ... 227
Marichal-SF ... 218
Sadecki-SF ... 206

Strikeouts/Game
Singer-LA ... 7.98
Gibson-StL ... 7.91
Maloney-Cin ... 7.87
Jenkins-Chi ... 7.60
Wilson-Hou ... 7.54

Wins Above Team
Marichal-SF ... 8.7
Blass-Pit ... 6.6
Koosman-NY ... 5.3
Gibson-StL ... 5.0
Short-Phi ... 4.4

Earned Run Average
Gibson-StL ... 1.12
Bolin-SF ... 1.98
Veale-Pit ... 2.06
Koosman-NY ... 2.08
Blass-Pit ... 2.13

Adjusted ERA
Gibson-StL ... 248
Koosman-NY ... 147
Bolin-SF ... 145
Veale-Pit ... 145
Blass-Pit ... 140

Opponents' Batting Avg.
Gibson-StL ... .184
Bolin-SF ... .200
Veale-Pit ... .211
Jarvis-Atl ... .214
Moose-Pit ... .218

Opponents' On Base Pct.
Gibson-StL ... .230
Jarvis-Atl ... .250
Bolin-SF ... .256
Seaver-NY ... .257
Hands-Chi ... .260

Starter Runs
Gibson-StL ... 63.2
Koosman-NY ... 26.6
Veale-Pit ... 25.3
Seaver-NY ... 24.2
Drysdale-LA ... 22.3

Adjusted Starter Runs
Gibson-StL ... 56.3
Koosman-NY ... 28.9
Seaver-NY ... 26.6
Veale-Pit ... 25.3
Jenkins-Chi ... 24.7

Clutch Pitching Index
Blass-Pit ... 125
Briles-StL ... 124
Koosman-NY ... 123
Lemaster-Hou ... 122
Drysdale-LA ... 117

Relief Runs
Kline-Pit ... 16.5
Regan-LA-Chi ... 10.8
Linzy-SF ... 9.5
Grant-LA ... 9.5
Abernathy-Cin ... 7.8

Adjusted Relief Runs
Kline-Pit ... 16.5
Regan-LA-Chi ... 15.7
Abernathy-Cin ... 12.6
Carroll-Atl-Cin ... 8.6
Linzy-SF ... 8.4

Relief Ranking
Kline-Pit ... 24.6
Regan-LA-Chi ... 24.3
Abernathy-Cin ... 17.0
Linzy-SF ... 15.9
Carroll-Atl-Cin ... 10.4

Total Pitcher Index
Gibson-StL ... 7.5
Seaver-NY ... 3.5
Jenkins-Chi ... 3.2
Koosman-NY ... 3.0
Veale-Pit ... 2.6

Total Baseball Ranking
Gibson-StL ... 7.5
Aaron-Atl ... 6.1
McCovey-SF ... 5.1
Wynn-Hou ... 4.8
Rose-Cin ... 4.2

TEAM	G	W	L	PCT	GB	R	OR	AB	H	2B	3B	HR	BB	SO	AVG	OBP	SLG	PRO	/A	BR	/A	PF	CHI	RC	TA	SB	CS	SBA	SBR
DET	164	103	59	.636		671	492	5490	1292	190	39	185	521	964	.235	.309	.385	.694	117	102	65	106	100	646	.625	26	32	45	-10
BAL	162	91	71	.562	12	579	497	5275	1187	215	28	133	570	1019	.225	.306	.352	.658	106	41	28	102	97	585	.605	78	32	71	4
CLE	162	86	75	.534	16.5	516	504	5416	1266	210	36	75	427	858	.234	.294	.327	.621	95	-33	-37	101	99	525	.547	115	61	65	-1
BOS	162	86	76	.531	17	614	611	5303	1253	207	17	125	582	974	.236	.316	.352	.668	109	63	60	101	99	590	.605	76	62	55	-13
NY	164	83	79	.512	20	536	531	5310	1137	154	34	109	566	958	.214	.293	.318	.611	92	-45	-51	101	105	507	.549	90	50	64	-2
OAK	163	82	80	.506	21	569	544	5406	1300	192	40	94	472	1022	.240	.306	.343	.649	103	19	28	98	99	580	.590	147	61	71	8
MIN	162	79	83	.488	24	562	546	5373	1274	207	41	105	445	966	.237	.301	.350	.651	104	20	-13	106	98	564	.580	98	54	64	-2
CAL	162	67	95	.414	36	498	615	5331	1209	170	33	83	447	1080	.227	.293	.318	.611	92	-50	-17	94	100	498	.527	62	50	55	-10
CHI	162	67	95	.414	36	463	527	5405	1233	169	33	71	397	840	.228	.286	.311	.597	87	-80	-84	101	98	480	.510	90	50	64	-2
WAS	161	65	96	.404	37.5	524	665	5400	1208	160	37	124	454	960	.224	.289	.336	.625	96	-30	17	91	100	518	.539	29	19	60	-2
TOT	812					5532		53709	12359	1874	338	1104	4881	9641	.230	.299	.339	.639								811	471	63	-38

TEAM	CG	SHO	SV	IP	H	H/G	HR	BB	BB/G	SO	SO/G	ERA	/A	OAVG	OOBA	PR	/A	PF	CPI	FA	E	DP	FW	PW	BW	SBW	DIF
DET	59	19	29	1489.7	1180	7.1	129	486	2.9	1115	6.7	2.71	113	.217	.280	44	59	103	100	.983	105	133	1.9	6.8	7.5	-.7	6.5
BAL	53	16	31	1451.0	1111	6.9	101	502	3.1	1044	6.5	2.66	113	.212	.282	51	54	101	96	.981	120	131	1.0	6.2	3.2	.9	-1.3
CLE	48	23	32	1464.3	1087	6.7	98	540	3.3	1157	7.1	2.66	113	.206	.281	52	55	101	93	.979	127	130	.6	6.3	-4.2	.3	2.5
BOS	55	17	31	1447.0	1303	8.1	115	523	3.3	972	6.0	3.33	90	.240	.308	-57	-54	101	100	.979	128	147	.6	-6.2	6.9	-1.0	4.8
NY	45	14	27	1467.3	1308	8.0	99	424	2.6	831	5.1	2.79	108	.240	.292	30	35	101	108	.979	139	142	-.1	4.0	-5.8	.2	3.7
OAK	45	18	29	1455.7	1220	7.5	124	505	3.1	997	6.2	2.94	99	.226	.292	5	-5	98	101	.976	136	136	-.5	-.6	3.2	1.4	-2.5
MIN	46	14	29	1433.3	1224	7.7	92	414	2.6	996	6.3	2.89	109	.229	.284	13	40	106	94	.972	170	117	-2.0	4.6	-1.5	.2	-3.4
CAL	29	11	31	1437.0	1234	7.7	131	519	3.3	869	5.4	3.43	83	.233	.299	-72	-90	96	94	.977	140	156	-.2	-10.3	-1.9	-.7	-.9
CHI	20	11	40	1468.0	1290	7.9	97	451	2.8	834	5.1	2.75	111	.236	.297	37	47	102	110	.977	151	152	-.8	5.4	-9.6	.2	-9.2
WAS	26	11	28	1440.0	1402	8.8	118	517	3.2	826	5.2	3.64	77	.258	.319	-106	-135	94	104	.976	148	144	-.6	-15.5	1.9	.2	-1.5
TOT	426	154	307	14553.3		7.6			3.0		6.0	2.98		.230	.299					.978	1373	1388					

Runs		Hits		Doubles		Triples		Home Runs		Total Bases	
McAuliffe-Det	95	Campaneris-Oak	177	Smith-Bos	37	Fregosi-Cal	13	Howard-Was	44	Howard-Was	330
Yastrzemski-Bos	90	Tovar-Min	167	B.Robinson-Bal	36	McCraw-Chi	12	Horton-Det	36	Horton-Det	278
White-NY	89	Howard-Was	164	Yastrzemski-Bos	32	Stroud-Was	10	Harrelson-Bos	35	Harrelson-Bos	277
Tovar-Min	89	Aparicio-Chi	164	Tovar-Min	31	McAuliffe-Det	10	Jackson-Oak	29	Yastrzemski-Bos	267
Stanley-Det	88	Yastrzemski-Bos	162			Campaneris-Oak	9			Northrup-Det	259

Runs Batted In		Runs Produced		Bases On Balls		Batting Average		On Base Percentage		Slugging Average	
Harrelson-Bos	109	Harrelson-Bos	153	Yastrzemski-Bos	119	Yastrzemski-Bos	.301	Yastrzemski-Bos	.429	Howard-Was	.552
Howard-Was	106	Northrup-Det	145	Mantle-NY	106	Cater-Oak	.290	F.Robinson-Bal	.391	Horton-Det	.543
Northrup-Det	90	Yastrzemski-Bos	141	Foy-Bos	84	Oliva-Min	.289	Mantle-NY	.387	Harrelson-Bos	.518
Powell-Bal	85	Howard-Was	141	McAuliffe-Det	82	Horton-Det	.285	Monday-Oak	.373	Yastrzemski-Bos	.495
Horton-Det	85	Stanley-Det	137	Andrews-Bos	81	Uhlaender-Min	.283	Andrews-Bos	.369	Oliva-Min	.477

Production		Adjusted Production		Batter Runs		Adjusted Batter Runs		Clutch Hitting Index		Runs Created	
Yastrzemski-Bos	.924	Howard-Was	183	Yastrzemski-Bos	57.5	Yastrzemski-Bos	57.2	Foy-Bos	137	Yastrzemski-Bos	121
Horton-Det	.900	Yastrzemski-Bos	178	Howard-Was	45.1	Howard-Was	50.3	Powell-Bal	132	Howard-Was	110
Howard-Was	.892	Harrelson-Bos	163	Horton-Det	41.1	Harrelson-Bos	39.9	Harrelson-Bos	129	Horton-Det	95
Harrelson-Bos	.877	Horton-Det	159	Harrelson-Bos	40.2	Horton-Det	37.7	Northrup-Det	127	Harrelson-Bos	94
Oliva-Min	.837	F.Robinson-Bal	149	Freehan-Det	32.7	F.Robinson-Bal	28.9	Bando-Oak	126	Freehan-Det	94

Total Average		Stolen Bases		Stolen Base Average		Stolen Base Runs		Fielding Runs		Total Player Rating	
Yastrzemski-Bos	1.015	Campaneris-Oak	62	McCraw-Chi	80.0	Campaneris-Oak	5.4	Clarke-NY	30.3	Yastrzemski-Bos	7.0
Horton-Det	.875	Cardenal-Cle	40	Nelson-Cle	76.7	McCraw-Chi	3.0	Aparicio-Chi	28.1	Howard-Was	4.7
Howard-Was	.872	Tovar-Min	35	Foy-Bos	76.5	Foy-Bos	3.0	B.Robinson-Bal	16.1	Freehan-Det	4.7
F.Robinson-Bal	.871	Buford-Bal	27	Clarke-NY	74.1	Tovar-Min	2.7	Josephson-Chi	16.1	Harrelson-Bos	4.0
Harrelson-Bos	.850	Foy-Bos	26	Campaneris-Oak	73.8	Nelson-Cle	2.7	Unser-Was	14.6	Aparicio-Chi	3.5

Wins		Win Percentage		Games		Complete Games		Shutouts		Saves	
McLain-Det	31	McLain-Det	.838	Wood-Chi	88	McLain-Det	28	Tiant-Cle	9	Worthington-Min	18
McNally-Bal	22	Culp-Bos	.727	Wilhelm-Chi	72	Tiant-Cle	19			Wood-Chi	16
Tiant-Cle	21	Tiant-Cle	.700	Locker-Chi	70	Stottlemyre-NY	19			Higgins-Was	13
Stottlemyre-NY	21	Ellsworth-Bos	.696	Perranoski-Min	66	McNally-Bal	18				
Hardin-Bal	18	McNally-Bal	.688			Hardin-Bal	16				

Innings Pitched		Fewest Hits/Game		Fewest BB/Game		Strikeouts		Strikeouts/Game		Wins Above Team	
McLain-Det	336	Tiant-Cle	5.30	Peterson-NY	1.23	McDowell-Cle	283	McDowell-Cle	9.47	McLain-Det	11.4
Chance-Min	292	McNally-Bal	5.77	McLain-Det	1.69	McLain-Det	280	Tiant-Cle	9.21	Tiant-Cle	6.1
Stottlemyre-NY	279	McDowell-Cle	6.06	Ellsworth-Bos	1.70	Tiant-Cle	264	Lolich-Det	8.06	McNally-Bal	5.3
McNally-Bal	273	Siebert-Cle	6.33	Kaat-Min	1.73	Chance-Min	234	Culp-Bos	7.92	Culp-Bos	5.0
McDowell-Cle	269	McLain-Det	6.46	McNally-Bal	1.81	McNally-Bal	202	McLain-Det	7.50	Stottlemyre-NY	4.9

Earned Run Average		Adjusted ERA		Opponents' Batting Avg.		Opponents' On Base Pct.		Starter Runs		Adjusted Starter Runs	
Tiant-Cle	1.60	Tiant-Cle	187	Tiant-Cle	.168	McNally-Bal	.231	Tiant-Cle	39.4	McLain-Det	41.8
McDowell-Cle	1.81	McDowell-Cle	166	McNally-Bal	.182	Tiant-Cle	.232	McLain-Det	38.2	Tiant-Cle	39.9
McNally-Bal	1.95	McLain-Det	157	McDowell-Cle	.189	McLain-Det	.241	McDowell-Cle	35.0	McDowell-Cle	35.6
McLain-Det	1.96	McNally-Bal	154	Siebert-Cle	.198	Chance-Min	.256	McNally-Bal	31.4	McNally-Bal	32.0
John-Chi	1.98	John-Chi	153	McLain-Det	.200	Peterson-NY	.264	Bahnsen-NY	27.4	Bahnsen-NY	28.3

Clutch Pitching Index		Relief Runs		Adjusted Relief Runs		Relief Ranking		Total Pitcher Index		Total Baseball Ranking	
Horlen-Chi	133	Wood-Chi	19.6	Wood-Chi	20.7	Wood-Chi	33.9	McLain-Det	5.3	Yastrzemski-Bos	7.0
John-Chi	119	Wilhelm-Chi	13.1	Wilhelm-Chi	13.7	Romo-Cle	15.1	McDowell-Cle	4.3	McLain-Det	5.3
Fisher-Chi	117	Romo-Cle	12.5	Romo-Cle	12.6	Wilhelm-Chi	14.5	Tiant-Cle	4.1	Howard-Was	4.7
McDowell-Cle	113	McMahon-Chi-Det	9.1	McMahon-Chi-Det	9.7	Drabowsky-Bal	10.5	McNally-Bal	4.0	Freehan-Det	4.7
Bahnsen-NY	111	Drabowsky-Bal	7.2	Locker-Chi	7.4	Watt-Bal	9.2	John-Chi	3.6	McDowell-Cle	4.3

TEAM	G	W	L	PCT	GB	R	OR	AB	H	2B	3B	HR	BB	SO	AVG	OBP	SLG	PRO	/A	BR	/A	PF	CHI	RC	TA	SB	CS	SBA	SBR
EAST																													
NY	162	100	62	.617		632	541	5427	1311	184	41	109	527	1089	.242	.313	.351	.664	93	-51	-53	100	**105**	601	.593	66	43	61	-5
CHI	163	92	70	.568	8	720	611	5530	1400	215	40	142	559	928	.253	.326	.384	.710	106	37	-6	107	102	693	.643	30	32	48	-9
PIT	162	88	74	.543	12	725	652	5626	1557	220	**52**	119	454	944	**.277**	.336	.398	.734	112	84	119	95	96	742	.665	74	34	**69**	2
STL	162	87	75	.537	13	595	**540**	5536	1403	**228**	44	90	503	876	.253	.318	.359	.677	96	-25	-22	100	94	632	.606	87	49	64	-2
PHI	162	63	99	.389	37	645	745	5408	1304	227	35	137	549	1130	.241	.314	.372	.686	99	-11	0	98	101	629	.623	73	49	60	-7
MON	162	52	110	.321	48	582	791	5419	1300	202	33	125	529	962	.240	.312	.359	.671	94	-39	-41	100	95	596	.595	52	52	50	-15
WEST																													
ATL	162	93	69	.574		691	631	5460	1411	195	22	141	485	**665**	.258	.323	.380	.703	104	20	-3	104	102	655	.627	59	48	55	-10
SF	162	90	72	.556	3	713	636	5474	1325	187	28	136	**711**	1054	.242	.336	.361	.697	102	32	24	101	100	690	.656	71	32	**69**	2
CIN	163	89	73	.549	4	**798**	768	5634	1558	224	42	**171**	474	1042	**.277**	.338	**.422**	**.760**	120	132	140	99	99	**791**	**.701**	79	56	59	-9
LA	162	85	77	.525	8	645	561	5532	1405	185	**52**	97	484	823	.254	.316	.359	.675	96	-31	-21	99	102	626	.599	80	51	61	-6
HOU	162	81	81	.500	12	676	668	5348	1284	208	40	104	699	972	.240	.332	.352	.684	99	6	-3	102	101	649	.644	101	58	64	-4
SD	162	52	110	.321	41	468	746	5357	1203	180	42	99	423	1143	.225	.286	.329	.615	78	-153	-132	97	98	491	.525	45	44	51	-12
TOT	973					7890		65751	16461	2455	471	1470	6397	11628	.250	.321	.369	.690								817	548	60	-83

TEAM	CG	SHO	SV	IP	H	H/G	HR	BB	BB/G	SO	SO/G	ERA	/A	OAVG	OOBA	PR	/A	PF	CPI	FA	E	DP	FW	PW	BW	SBW	DIF
EAST																											
NY	51	**28**	35	1468.3	**1217**	7.5	119	517	3.2	1012	6.2	2.99	120	**.226**	**.292**	99	95	99	99	.980	122	146	1.4	10.0	-5.6	.2	13.0
CHI	58	22	27	1454.3	1366	8.5	118	475	2.9	1017	6.3	3.34	113	.248	.306	40	70	105	101	.979	136	149	.6	7.3	-.6	-.2	3.9
PIT	39	9	33	1445.7	1348	8.4	**96**	553	3.4	1124	7.0	3.61	93	.248	.316	-2	-38	94	95	.975	155	169	-.5	-4.0	12.5	.9	-2.0
STL	63	12	26	1460.3	1289	7.9	99	511	3.1	1004	6.2	**2.94**	121	.237	.301	105	99	99	105	.978	138	144	.5	10.4	-2.3	.5	-3.1
PHI	47	14	21	1434.0	1494	9.4	134	570	3.6	921	5.8	4.14	86	.269	.335	-87	-90	100	102	.978	137	157	.5	-9.4	-.0	-.9	-9.1
MON	26	8	21	1426.0	1429	9.0	145	702	4.4	973	6.1	4.33	86	.263	.345	-116	-99	103	102	.971	184	179	-2.1	-10.4	-4.3	-.8	-11.3
WEST																											
ATL	38	7	42	1445.0	1334	8.3	144	438	2.7	893	5.6	3.53	105	.244	.297	10	26	103	95	**.981**	115	114	1.8	2.7	-.3	-.3	8.1
SF	**71**	15	17	1473.7	1381	8.4	120	461	2.8	906	5.5	3.26	111	.247	.303	55	56	100	102	.974	169	155	-1.3	5.9	2.5	.9	.9
CIN	23	11	**44**	1465.0	1478	9.1	149	611	3.8	818	5.0	4.11	86	.261	.333	-84	-92	99	102	.974	167	158	-1.2	-9.7	**14.7**	-.2	4.3
LA	47	20	31	1457.0	1324	8.2	122	**420**	2.6	975	6.0	3.08	114	.242	.295	82	67	97	102	.980	126	130	1.2	7.0	-2.2	.1	-2.1
HOU	52	11	34	1435.7	1347	8.4	111	547	3.4	**1221**	7.7	3.60	101	.246	.314	0	7	101	96	.975	153	136	-.4	.7	-.3	-.3	-.4
SD	16	9	25	1422.3	1454	9.2	113	592	3.7	764	4.8	4.24	85	.266	.335	-102	-101	100	97	.975	156	140	-.5	-10.6	-13.9	-.5	-3.5
TOT	531	166	356	17387.3		8.5			3.3		6.0	3.59		.250	.321					.977	1758	1777					

Runs		Hits		Doubles		Triples		Home Runs		Total Bases	
Rose-Cin	120	Alou-Pit	231	Alou-Pit	41	Clemente-Pit	12	McCovey-SF	45	Aaron-Atl	332
Bonds-SF	120	Rose-Cin	218	Kessinger-Chi	38	Rose-Cin	11	Aaron-Atl	44	Perez-Cin	331
Wynn-Hou	113	Brock-StL	195	Williams-Chi	33	Williams-Chi	10	May-Cin	38	McCovey-SF	322
Kessinger-Chi	109	Tolan-Cin	194	Rose-Cin	33	Tolan-Cin	10	Perez-Cin	37	Rose-Cin	321
Alou-Pit	105	Williams-Chi	188	Brock-StL	33	Brock-StL	10	Wynn-Hou	33	May-Cin	321

Runs Batted In		Runs Produced		Bases On Balls		Batting Average		On Base Percentage		Slugging Average	
McCovey-SF	126	Santo-Chi	191	Wynn-Hou	148	Rose-Cin	.348	McCovey-SF	.458	McCovey-SF	.656
Santo-Chi	123	Perez-Cin	188	McCovey-SF	121	Clemente-Pit	.345	Wynn-Hou	.440	Aaron-Atl	.607
Perez-Cin	122	Rose-Cin	186	Staub-Mon	110	Jones-NY	.340	Rose-Cin	.432	Allen-Phi	.573
May-Cin	110	McCovey-SF	182	Morgan-Hou	110	Alou-Pit	.331	Staub-Mon	.427	Stargell-Pit	.556
Banks-Chi	106	Bonds-SF	178	Santo-Chi	96	McCovey-SF	.320	Jones-NY	.424	Clemente-Pit	.544

Production		Adjusted Production		Batter Runs		Adjusted Batter Runs		Clutch Hitting Index		Runs Created	
McCovey-SF	1.114	McCovey-SF	206	McCovey-SF	76.1	McCovey-SF	75.3	Menke-Hou	157	McCovey-SF	151
Aaron-Atl	1.005	Clemente-Pit	175	Aaron-Atl	56.3	Rose-Cin	56.9	Rader-Hou	143	Rose-Cin	138
Clemente-Pit	.958	Aaron-Atl	172	Rose-Cin	55.9	Aaron-Atl	53.8	Santo-Chi	143	Staub-Mon	128
Staub-Mon	.953	Stargell-Pit	170	Staub-Mon	52.6	Staub-Mon	52.3	Banks-Chi	143	Aaron-Atl	128
Allen-Phi	.952	Allen-Phi	166	Wynn-Hou	50.9	Wynn-Hou	49.9	Pinson-StL	135	Wynn-Hou	126

Total Average		Stolen Bases		Stolen Base Average		Stolen Base Runs		Fielding Runs		Total Player Rating	
McCovey-SF	1.296	Brock-StL	53	Bonds-SF	91.8	Bonds-SF	11.1	Kessinger-Chi	25.2	McCovey-SF	5.9
Wynn-Hou	1.136	Morgan-Hou	49	Brock-StL	79.1	Brock-StL	7.5	Lanier-SF	19.8	Rose-Cin	5.4
Aaron-Atl	1.057	Bonds-SF	45	Morgan-Hou	77.8	Morgan-Hou	6.3	Money-Phi	17.0	Wynn-Hou	5.1
Staub-Mon	1.028	Wills-Mon-LA	40	Wynn-Hou	76.7	Wynn-Hou	2.7	Callison-Phi	15.1	Aaron-Atl	5.0
Allen-Phi	.997	Tolan-Cin	26	Alou-Pit	73.3	Millan-Atl	2.4	Mazeroski-Pit	14.5	Staub-Mon	5.0

Wins		Win Percentage		Games		Complete Games		Shutouts		Saves	
Seaver-NY	25	Seaver-NY	.781	Granger-Cin	90	Gibson-StL	28	Marichal-SF	8	Gladding-Hou	29
Niekro-Atl	23	Marichal-SF	.656	McGinn-Mon	74	Marichal-SF	27	Osteen-LA	7	Upshaw-Atl	27
Marichal-SF	21	Merritt-Cin	.654	Regan-Chi	71	Perry-SF	26	Jenkins-Chi	7	Granger-Cin	27
Jenkins-Chi	21	Koosman-NY	.654	Carroll-Cin	71	Jenkins-Chi	23	Koosman-NY	6	Brewer-LA	20
		Reed-Atl	.643	Reberger-SD	67	Niekro-Atl	21	Holtzman-Chi	6	Regan-Chi	17

Innings Pitched		Fewest Hits/Game		Fewest BB/Game		Strikeouts		Strikeouts/Game		Wins Above Team	
Perry-SF	325	Seaver-NY	6.66	Marichal-SF	1.62	Jenkins-Chi	273	Griffin-Hou	9.57	Seaver-NY	7.7
Osteen-LA	321	Maloney-Cin	6.79	Niekro-Atl	1.81	Gibson-StL	269	Wilson-Hou	9.40	Moose-Pit	5.4
Singer-LA	316	Singer-LA	6.95	Jenkins-Chi	2.05	Singer-LA	247	Moose-Pit	8.74	Marichal-SF	4.3
Gibson-StL	314	Koosman-NY	6.98	Osteen-LA	2.07	Wilson-Hou	235	Selma-SD -Chi	8.53	Dierker-Hou	4.2
Jenkins-Chi	311	Carlton-StL	7.06	Niekro-Chi-SD	2.08	Perry-SF	233	Veale-Pit	8.48	Singer-LA	4.0

Earned Run Average		Adjusted ERA		Opponents' Batting Avg.		Opponents' On Base Pct.		Starter Runs		Adjusted Starter Runs	
Marichal-SF	2.10	Marichal-SF	171	Seaver-NY	.207	Marichal-SF	.259	Marichal-SF	49.8	Marichal-SF	50.0
Carlton-StL	2.17	Carlton-StL	163	Maloney-Cin	.208	Dierker-Hou	.259	Gibson-StL	49.3	Gibson-StL	48.0
Gibson-StL	2.18	Gibson-StL	163	Singer-LA	.210	Singer-LA	.260	Singer-LA	44.1	Dierker-Hou	44.5
Seaver-NY	2.21	Seaver-NY	162	Dierker-Hou	.214	Niekro-Atl	.260	Dierker-Hou	42.8	Hands-Chi	43.0
Koosman-NY	2.28	Koosman-NY	157	Carlton-StL	.216	Seaver-NY	.267	Seaver-NY	42.0	Seaver-NY	41.2

Clutch Pitching Index		Relief Runs		Adjusted Relief Runs		Relief Ranking		Total Pitcher Index		Total Baseball Ranking	
Carlton-StL	122	McGraw-NY	14.9	McGraw-NY	14.6	McGraw-NY	19.8	Gibson-StL	6.3	Gibson-StL	6.3
Perry-SF	117	Granger-Cin	12.9	Granger-Cin	12.0	Brewer-LA	17.0	Marichal-SF	6.1	Marichal-SF	6.1
Veale-Pit	114	Brewer-LA	10.1	Brewer-LA	9.2	Granger-Cin	16.2	Seaver-NY	5.0	McCovey-SF	5.9
Robertson-Mon	113	Gibbon-SF -Pit	9.3	Upshaw-Atl	9.1	Taylor-NY	13.7	Dierker-Hou	4.8	Rose-Cin	5.4
Hands-Chi	111	DiLauro-NY	8.5	DiLauro-NY	8.4	Gibbon-SF -Pit	13.2	Perry-SF	4.7	Wynn-Hou	5.1

TEAM	G	W	L	PCT	GB	R	OR	AB	H	2B	3B	HR	BB	SO	AVG	OBP	SLG	PRO	/A	BR	/A	PF	CHI	RC	TA	SB	CS	SBA	SBR
EAST																													
BAL	162	109	53	.673		779	**517**	5518	1465	234	29	175	634	**806**	.265	**.346**	.414	**.760**	**119**	**134**	**109**	104	95	791	**.718**	82	45	65	-1
DET	162	90	72	.556	19	701	601	5441	1316	188	29	182	578	922	.242	.318	.387	.705	103	17	-4	103	103	674	.645	35	28	56	-5
BOS	162	87	75	.537	22	743	736	5494	1381	234	37	**197**	**658**	923	.251	.335	**.415**	.750	116	109	76	105	94	761	.703	41	47	47	-15
WAS	162	86	76	.531	23	694	644	5447	1365	171	40	148	630	900	.251	.332	.378	.710	105	38	58	97	98	675	.648	52	40	57	-7
NY	162	80	81	.497	28.5	562	587	5308	1247	210	**44**	94	565	840	.235	.310	.344	.654	89	-73	-43	95	98	572	.596	119	74	62	-8
CLE	161	62	99	.385	46.5	573	717	5365	1272	173	24	119	535	906	.237	.309	.345	.654	89	-76	-39	94	100	568	.583	85	37	70	3
WEST																													
MIN	162	97	65	.599		**790**	618	5677	**1520**	**246**	32	163	599	906	**.268**	.342	.408	.750	116	118	104	102	97	**794**	.709	115	70	62	-7
OAK	162	88	74	.543	9	740	678	5614	1400	210	28	148	617	953	.249	.330	.376	.706	104	31	85	92	103	712	.660	100	39	72	7
CAL	163	71	91	.438	26	528	652	5316	1221	151	29	88	516	929	.230	.302	.319	.621	80	-137	-133	99	**104**	518	.542	54	39	58	-6
KC	163	69	93	.426	28	586	688	5462	1311	179	32	98	522	901	.240	.311	.338	.649	88	-83	-100	103	102	577	.585	129	70	65	-2
CHI	162	68	94	.420	29	625	723	5450	1346	210	27	112	552	844	.247	.322	.357	.679	96	-24	-79	108	98	638	.613	54	22	71	3
SEA	163	64	98	.395	33	639	799	5444	1276	179	27	125	626	1015	.234	.317	.346	.663	92	-52	-40	98	**104**	622	.625	**167**	59	**74**	**15**
TOT	973					7960		65536	16120	2385	378	1649	7032	10845	.246	.323	.369	.693								1033	570	64	-31

TEAM	CG	SHO	SV	IP	H	H/G	HR	BB	BB/G	SO	SO/G	ERA	/A	OAVG	OOBA	PR	/A	PF	CPI	FA	E	DP	FW	PW	BW	SBW	DIF
EAST																											
BAL	50	**20**	36	1473.7	**1194**	**7.3**	**117**	**498**	**3.0**	897	5.5	**2.83**	**128**	**.222**	**.287**	**130**	**131**	100	97	**.984**	**101**	145	**2.2**	**13.7**	**11.4**	.2	.5
DET	**55**	**20**	28	1455.3	1250	7.7	128	586	3.6	**1032**	**6.4**	3.31	111	.232	.306	49	61	102	98	.979	130	130	.5	6.4	-.4	-.2	2.7
BOS	30	7	41	1466.7	1423	8.7	155	685	4.2	935	5.7	3.92	97	.256	.337	-48	-20	105	106	.975	157	**178**	-1.0	-2.1	8.0	-1.3	2.4
WAS	28	10	41	1447.3	1310	8.1	135	656	4.1	835	5.2	3.49	100	.243	.323	21	0	96	**107**	.978	140	159	-.0	.0	6.1	-.5	-.6
NY	53	13	20	1440.7	1258	7.9	118	522	3.3	801	5.0	3.23	107	.235	.300	62	37	96	97	.979	131	158	.5	3.9	-4.5	-.6	.2
CLE	35	8	22	1437.0	1330	8.3	134	681	4.3	1000	6.3	3.94	88	.248	.330	-50	-72	96	99	.976	145	153	-.3	-7.5	-4.1	.6	-7.1
WEST																											
MIN	41	8	**43**	1497.7	1388	8.3	119	524	3.1	906	5.4	3.24	112	.246	.309	63	63	100	104	.977	150	177	-.6	6.6	10.9	-.5	-.4
OAK	42	14	36	1480.7	1356	8.2	163	586	3.6	887	5.4	3.71	89	.245	.317	-15	-66	91	100	.979	136	162	.2	-6.9	8.9	1.0	3.8
CAL	25	9	39	1438.3	1294	8.1	126	517	3.2	885	5.5	3.54	103	.241	.310	12	18	101	96	.978	136	164	.2	1.9	-13.9	-.3	2.2
KC	42	10	25	1464.7	1357	8.3	136	560	3.4	894	5.5	3.72	101	.246	.312	-15	8	104	95	.975	157	114	-1.0	.8	-10.5	.0	-1.4
CHI	29	9	25	1437.7	1470	9.2	146	564	3.5	810	5.1	4.21	94	.267	.333	-93	-37	110	99	.981	122	163	1.0	-3.9	-8.3	.6	-2.4
SEA	21	6	33	1463.7	1490	9.2	172	653	4.0	963	5.9	4.35	84	.263	.339	-117	-116	100	101	.974	167	149	-1.6	-12.2	-4.2	**1.9**	-.9
TOT	451	134	389	17503.3		8.3			3.6		5.6	3.62		.246	.323					.978	1672	1852					

Runs
Jackson-Oak 123
F.Robinson-Bal 111
Howard-Was 111
Killebrew-Min 106
Bando-Oak 106

Hits
Oliva-Min 197
Clarke-NY 183
Blair-Bal 178
Howard-Was 175
Horton-Cle 174

Doubles
Oliva-Min 39
Jackson-Oak 36
Johnson-Bal 34
Petrocelli-Bos 32
Blair-Bal 32

Triples
Unser-Was 8
Smith-Bos 7
Clarke-NY 7

Home Runs
Killebrew-Min 49
Howard-Was 48
Jackson-Oak 47
Yastrzemski-Bos 40
Petrocelli-Bos 40

Total Bases
Howard-Was 340
Jackson-Oak 334
Killebrew-Min 324
Oliva-Min 316
Petrocelli-Bos 315

Runs Batted In
Killebrew-Min 140
Powell-Bal 121
Jackson-Oak 118
Bando-Oak 113

Runs Produced
Killebrew-Min 197
Jackson-Oak 194
Bando-Oak 188
F.Robinson-Bal 179

Bases On Balls
Killebrew-Min 145
Jackson-Oak 114
Bando-Oak 111
Howard-Was 102
Yastrzemski-Bos 101

Batting Average
Carew-Min 332
Smith-Bos 309
Oliva-Min 309
F.Robinson-Bal 308
Powell-Bal 304

On Base Percentage
Killebrew-Min 430
F.Robinson-Bal 417
Jackson-Oak 410
Petrocelli-Bos 407
Howard-Was 403

Slugging Average
Jackson-Oak 608
Petrocelli-Bos 589
Killebrew-Min 584
Howard-Was 574
Powell-Bal 559

Production
Jackson-Oak 1.019
Killebrew-Min 1.014
Petrocelli-Bos 996
Howard-Was 978
F.Robinson-Bal 957

Adjusted Production
Jackson-Oak 197
Killebrew-Min 177
Howard-Was 176
Petrocelli-Bos 167
F.Robinson-Bal 160

Batter Runs
Killebrew-Min 65.5
Jackson-Oak 61.9
Howard-Was 56.7
Petrocelli-Bos 54.7
F.Robinson-Bal 49.8

Adjusted Batter Runs
Jackson-Oak 67.7
Killebrew-Min 64.0
Howard-Was 59.1
Petrocelli-Bos 51.4
Bando-Oak 47.5

Clutch Hitting Index
White-NY 148
Foy-KC 134
Reichardt-Cal 130
Cater-Oak 129
Killebrew-Min 126

Runs Created
Killebrew-Min 146
Jackson-Oak 144
Howard-Was 132
Petrocelli-Bos 129
F.Robinson-Bal 126

Total Average
Jackson-Oak 1.151
Killebrew-Min 1.148
Petrocelli-Bos 1.061
F.Robinson-Bal 1.034
Howard-Was 1.004

Stolen Bases
Harper-Sea 73
Campaneris-Oak 62
Tovar-Min 45
Kelly-KC 40
Foy-KC 37

Stolen Base Average
Campaneris-Oak 88.6
Alomar-Chi-Cal 87.0
Cardenal-Cle 85.7
Aparicio-Chi 85.7
Davis-Sea 82.6

Stolen Base Runs
Campaneris-Oak . . . 13.8
Harper-Sea 11.1
Cardenal-Cle 7.2
Tovar-Min 6.3
Aparicio-Chi 4.8

Fielding Runs
Cardenas-Min 31.2
Aparicio-Chi 30.3
B.Robinson-Bal 19.0
Knoop-Cal-Chi 18.2
Blair-Bal 17.2

Total Player Rating
Jackson-Oak 6.9
Petrocelli-Bos 6.1
Killebrew-Min 5.2
Cardenas-Min 4.4
F.Robinson-Bal 4.1

Wins
McLain-Det 24
Cuellar-Bal 23

Win Percentage
Palmer-Bal 800
Perry-Min 769
McNally-Bal 741
McLain-Det 727
Odom-Oak 714

Games
Wood-Chi 76
Perranoski-Min 75
Lyle-Bos 71
Locker-Chi-Sea 68
Segui-Sea 66

Complete Games
Stottlemyre-NY 24
McLain-Det 23
McDowell-Cle 18
Cuellar-Bal 18
Peterson-NY 16

Shutouts
McLain-Det 9
Palmer-Bal 6
Cuellar-Bal 5

Saves
Perranoski-Min 31
Tatum-Cal 22
Lyle-Bos 17
Watt-Bal 16
Higgins-Was 16

Innings Pitched
McLain-Det 325
Stottlemyre-NY 303
Cuellar-Bal 291
McDowell-Cle 285
Lolich-Det 281

Fewest Hits/Game
Messersmith-Cal . . . 6.08
Palmer-Bal 6.51
Cuellar-Bal 6.59
Lolich-Det 6.85
Odom-Oak 6.97

Fewest BB/Game
Peterson-NY 1.42
Bosman-Was 1.82
McLain-Det 1.86
Perry-Min 2.27
Cuellar-Bal 2.44

Strikeouts
McDowell-Cle 279
Lolich-Det 271
Messersmith-Cal 211
Boswell-Min 190

Strikeouts/Game
McDowell-Cle 8.81
Lolich-Det 8.68
Messersmith-Cal . . . 7.60
Butler-KC 7.24
Williams-Cle 7.03

Wins Above Team
McLain-Det 7.3
Perry-Min 6.1
McDowell-Cle 5.4
Nagy-Bos 5.0
Bosman-Was 4.5

Earned Run Average
Bosman-Was 2.19
Palmer-Bal 2.34
Cuellar-Bal 2.38
Messersmith-Cal . . . 2.52
Peterson-NY 2.55

Adjusted ERA
Bosman-Was 159
Palmer-Bal 155
Cuellar-Bal 153
Messersmith-Cal 145
Peterson-NY 136

Opponents' Batting Avg.
Messersmith-Cal 190
Palmer-Bal 200
Cuellar-Bal 204
Lolich-Det 210
McDowell-Cle 213

Opponents' On Base Pct.
Peterson-NY 257
Cuellar-Bal 258
Bosman-Was 259
Palmer-Bal 271
Messersmith-Cal 272

Starter Runs
Cuellar-Bal 40.1
Peterson-NY 32.5
Bosman-Was 30.7
Messersmith-Cal . . . 30.6
McLain-Det 29.8

Adjusted Starter Runs
Cuellar-Bal 40.5
McLain-Det 32.4
Messersmith-Cal . . . 31.6
Bosman-Was 27.7
Peterson-NY 27.7

Clutch Pitching Index
Cox-Was 129
Nagy-Bos 119
Tiant-Cle 118
John-Chi 114
Wilson-Det 112

Relief Runs
Tatum-Cal 21.6
Perranoski-Min 20.3
Watt-Bal 15.6
Roland-Oak 13.6
Knowles-Was 12.8

Adjusted Relief Runs
Tatum-Cal 22.0
Perranoski-Min 20.3
Watt-Bal 15.7
Lyle-Bos 14.4
Wood-Chi 13.0

Relief Ranking
Perranoski-Min 40.6
Tatum-Cal 33.3
Wood-Chi 24.1
Watt-Bal 21.8
Richert-Bal 19.9

Total Pitcher Index
Cuellar-Bal 4.2
Stottlemyre-NY 3.7
Messersmith-Cal 3.5
Peterson-NY 3.2
Bosman-Was 3.0

Total Baseball Ranking
Jackson-Oak 6.9
Petrocelli-Bos 6.1
Killebrew-Min 5.2
Cardenas-Min 4.4
Cuellar-Bal 4.2

TEAM	G	W	L	PCT	GB	R	OR	AB	H	2B	3B	HR	BB	SO	AVG	OBP	SLG	PRO	/A	BR	/A	PF	CHI	RC	TA	SB	CS	SBA	SBR
EAST																													
PIT	162	89	73	.549		729	664	5637	**1522**	235	**70**	130	444	871	**.270**	.328	.406	.734	102	12	36	97	98	740	.666	66	34	66	0
CHI	162	84	78	.519	5	806	679	5491	1424	228	44	179	607	844	.259	.335	.415	.750	107	49	-96	120	**103**	773	.702	39	16	71	2
NY	162	83	79	.512	6	695	**630**	5443	1358	211	42	120	684	1062	.249	.336	.370	.706	96	-22	-50	104	97	689	.664	54	69	3	
STL	162	76	86	.469	13	744	747	5689	1497	218	51	113	569	961	.263	.333	.379	.712	97	-19	-65	106	102	719	.655	117	47	71	7
PHI	161	73	88	.453	15.5	594	730	5456	1299	224	58	101	519	1066	.238	.307	.356	.663	83	-124	-96	96	100	582	.588	72	64	53	-16
MON	162	73	89	.451	16	687	807	5411	1284	211	35	136	659	972	.237	.324	.365	.689	91	-61	-61	100	102	658	.640	65	45	59	-7
WEST																													
CIN	162	102	60	.630		775	681	5540	1498	253	45	**191**	547	984	**.270**	.339	**.436**	**.775**	113	94	63	104	94	814	**.737**	115	52	69	3
LA	161	87	74	.540	14.5	749	684	5606	1515	233	67	87	541	841	**.270**	.337	.382	.719	99	-3	73	90	102	730	.668	**138**	57	71	7
SF	162	86	76	.531	16	831	826	5578	1460	257	35	165	**729**	1005	.262	.353	.409	.762	111	91	123	96	98	821	.735	83	27	**75**	9
HOU	162	79	83	.488	23	744	763	5574	1446	250	47	129	598	911	.259	.334	.391	.725	100	4	51	94	100	728	.676	114	41	74	**10**
ATL	162	76	86	.469	26	736	772	5546	1495	215	24	160	522	**736**	**.270**	.337	.404	.741	105	31	0	104	97	742	.676	58	34	63	-2
SD	162	63	99	.389	39	681	788	5494	1353	208	36	172	500	1164	.246	.314	.391	.705	94	-48	-13	95	101	669	.640	60	45	57	-8
TOT	971					8771		66465	17151	2743	554	1683	6919	11417	.258	.332	.392	.724								1045	516	67	4

TEAM	CG	SHO	SV	IP	H	H/G	HR	BB	BB/G	SO	SO/G	ERA	/A	OAVG	OOBA	PR	/A	PF	CPI	FA	E	DP	FW	PW	BW	SBW	DIF
EAST																											
PIT	36	13	43	1453.7	1386	8.6	106	625	3.9	990	6.1	3.70	105	.254	.330	56	30	96	**106**	.979	137	**195**	.2	3.0	3.6	-.0	1.2
CHI	**59**	9	25	1435.0	1402	8.8	143	**475**	3.0	1000	6.3	3.76	**128**	.255	.312	46	**165**	119	101	.978	137	146	.2	**16.4**	-9.6	.2	-4.3
NY	47	10	32	1459.7	**1260**	**7.8**	135	575	3.5	**1064**	6.6	3.45	121	**.232**	**.303**	97	117	103	98	.979	124	136	1.0	11.7	-5.0	.3	-5.9
STL	51	11	20	1475.7	1483	9.0	**102**	632	3.9	960	5.9	4.06	106	.263	.332	-1	38	106	100	.977	150	159	-.5	3.8	-6.5	.7	-2.5
PHI	24	8	36	1461.0	1483	9.1	132	538	3.3	1047	6.4	4.17	95	.265	.326	-20	-35	98	98	**.981**	114	134	**1.5**	-3.5	-9.6	-1.6	5.1
MON	29	10	32	1438.7	1434	9.0	162	716	4.5	914	5.7	4.50	91	.260	.346	-73	-63	102	101	.977	141	193	.0	-6.3	-6.1	-.7	5.1
WEST																											
CIN	32	15	**60**	1444.7	1370	8.5	118	592	3.7	843	5.3	3.69	113	.250	.321	57	77	103	102	.976	151	173	-.5	7.7	6.3	.3	7.3
LA	37	**17**	42	1458.7	1394	8.6	164	496	3.1	880	5.4	3.82	94	.250	.310	36	-35	89	99	.978	135	135	.4	-3.5	7.3	.7	1.7
SF	50	7	30	1457.7	1514	9.3	156	604	3.7	931	5.7	4.50	86	.267	.335	-73	-102	96	98	.973	170	153	-1.6	-10.2	**12.3**	.9	3.6
HOU	36	6	35	1456.0	1491	9.2	131	577	3.6	942	5.8	4.23	90	.265	.332	-30	-71	94	99	.978	140	144	.0	-7.1	5.1	**1.0**	-1.1
ATL	45	9	24	1430.7	1451	9.1	185	478	**3.0**	960	6.0	4.33	98	.260	.317	-44	-14	105	96	.977	141	118	-.0	-1.4	.0	-.2	-3.4
SD	24	9	32	1440.3	1483	9.3	149	611	3.8	886	5.5	4.36	90	.267	.337	-49	-72	97	102	.975	158	159	-.9	-7.2	-1.3	-.8	-7.8
TOT	470	124	411	17411.7		8.9			3.6		5.9	4.05		.258	.332					.977	1698	1845					

Runs	Hits	Doubles	Triples	Home Runs	Total Bases
Williams-Chi 137	Williams-Chi 205	Parker-LA 47	Davis-LA 16	Bench-Cin 45	Williams-Chi 373
Bonds-SF 134	Rose-Cin 205	McCovey-SF 39	Kessinger-Chi 14	Williams-Chi 42	Bench-Cin 355
Rose-Cin 120	Torre-StL 203	Rose-Cin 37	Clemente-Pit 10	Perez-Cin 40	Perez-Cin 346
Brock-StL 114	Brock-StL 202	Dietz-SF 36	Bonds-SF 10	McCovey-SF 39	Bonds-SF 334
Tolan-Cin 112	Alou-Pit 201	Bonds-SF 36			Gaston-SD 317

Runs Batted In	Runs Produced	Bases On Balls	Batting Average	On Base Percentage	Slugging Average
Bench-Cin 148	Williams-Chi 224	McCovey-SF 137	Carty-Atl 366	Carty-Atl 456	McCovey-SF 612
Williams-Chi 129	Bench-Cin 200	Staub-Mon 112	Torre-StL 325	McCovey-SF 446	Perez-Cin 589
Perez-Cin 129	Perez-Cin 196	Dietz-SF 109	Sanguillen-Pit 325	Dietz-SF 430	Bench-Cin 587
McCovey-SF 126	Bonds-SF 186	Wynn-Hou 106	Williams-Chi 322	Hickman-Chi 421	Williams-Chi 586
Aaron-Atl 118		Morgan-Hou 102	Parker-LA 319	Perez-Cin 405	Carty-Atl 584

Production	Adjusted Production	Batter Runs	Adjusted Batter Runs	Clutch Hitting Index	Runs Created
McCovey-SF 1.058	McCovey-SF 188	McCovey-SF 62.0	McCovey-SF 65.2	Parker-LA 147	Williams-Chi 147
Carty-Atl 1.040	Carty-Atl 169	Carty-Atl 54.4	Carty-Atl 51.6	Santo-Chi 137	McCovey-SF 140
Hickman-Chi 1.003	Dietz-SF 159	Perez-Cin 52.1	Perez-Cin 48.7	Davis-LA 135	Perez-Cin 140
Perez-Cin 994	Perez-Cin 156	Williams-Chi 51.1	Dietz-SF 43.9	Dietz-SF 132	Bonds-SF 134
Williams-Chi 979	Aaron-Atl 148	Hickman-Chi 49.5	Carbo-Cin 38.1	Menke-Hou 132	Hickman-Chi 129

Total Average	Stolen Bases	Stolen Base Average	Stolen Base Runs	Fielding Runs	Total Player Rating
McCovey-SF 1.214	Tolan-Cin 57	Henderson-SF 87.0	Bonds-SF 8.4	Maxvill-StL 29.3	McCovey-SF 6.1
Carty-Atl 1.108	Brock-StL 51	Harrelson-NY 85.2	Brock-StL 6.3	Alley-Pit 27.3	Dietz-SF 5.8
Hickman-Chi 1.083	Bonds-SF 48	Wynn-Hou 82.8	Tolan-Cin 5.1	Rader-Hou 22.2	Morgan-Hou 5.0
Perez-Cin 1.053	Morgan-Hou 42	Bonds-SF 82.8	Morgan-Hou 4.8	Campbell-SD 20.5	Bonds-SF 4.7
Williams-Chi 1.020	Davis-LA 38	Cedeno-Hou 81.0	Harrelson-NY 4.5	Mazeroski-Pit 19.3	Wynn-Hou 4.2

Wins	Win Percentage	Games	Complete Games	Shutouts	Saves
Perry-SF 23	Gibson-StL 767	Herbel-SD -NY 76	Jenkins-Chi 24	Perry-SF 5	Granger-Cin 35
Gibson-StL 23	Nolan-Cin 720	Selma-Phi 73	Perry-SF 23	Sutton-LA 4	Giusti-Pit 26
Jenkins-Chi 22	Walker-Pit 714	Linzy-SF -StL 67	Gibson-StL 23	Osteen-LA 4	Brewer-LA 24
Merritt-Cin 20	Perry-SF 639	Granger-Cin 67	Seaver-NY 19	Morton-Mon 4	Raymond-Mon 23
	Merritt-Cin 625	Giusti-Pit 66	Dierker-Hou 17	Ellis-Pit 4	Selma-Phi 22

Innings Pitched	Fewest Hits/Game	Fewest BB/Game	Strikeouts	Strikeouts/Game	Wins Above Team
Perry-SF 329	Simpson-Cin 6.39	Jenkins-Chi 1.73	Seaver-NY 283	Seaver-NY 8.75	Gibson-StL 9.2
Jenkins-Chi 313	Seaver-NY 7.11	Marichal-SF 1.78	Jenkins-Chi 274	Gibson-StL 8.39	Morton-Mon 5.1
Gibson-StL 294	Walker-Pit 7.12	Osteen-LA 1.81	Gibson-StL 274	Veale-Pit 7.93	Perry-SF 5.0
Seaver-NY 291	Gentry-NY 7.42	McAndrew-NY 1.86	Perry-SF 214	Jenkins-Chi 7.88	Simpson-Cin 4.7
Holtzman-Chi 288	Jenkins-Chi 7.62	Merritt-Cin 2.04	Holtzman-Chi 202	Stoneman-Mon 7.62	Walker-Pit 4.2

Earned Run Average	Adjusted ERA	Opponents' Batting Avg.	Opponents' On Base Pct.	Starter Runs	Adjusted Starter Runs
Seaver-NY 2.81	Seaver-NY 148	Simpson-Cin 198	Jenkins-Chi 262	Seaver-NY 39.8	Jenkins-Chi 48.7
Simpson-Cin 3.02	Holtzman-Chi 142	Seaver-NY 214	Seaver-NY 270	Perry-SF 30.9	Holtzman-Chi 45.4
Walker-Pit 3.04	Jenkins-Chi 141	Walker-Pit 219	McAndrew-NY 277	Gibson-StL 30.2	Seaver-NY 43.9
Gibson-StL 3.12	Pappas-Atl-Chi 141	Jenkins-Chi 224	Perry-SF 287	Jenkins-Chi 22.7	Gibson-StL 38.2
Koosman-NY 3.14	Simpson-Cin 138	Gentry-NY 224	Gibson-StL 292	Nolan-Cin 21.8	Hands-Chi 32.2

Clutch Pitching Index	Relief Runs	Adjusted Relief Runs	Relief Ranking	Total Pitcher Index	Total Baseball Ranking
Ellis-Pit 119	Selma-Phi 19.2	Carroll-Cin 18.2	Granger-Cin 30.1	Seaver-NY 5.4	McCovey-SF 6.1
Morton-Mon 118	Carroll-Cin 16.8	Selma-Phi 17.9	Selma-Phi 27.0	Gibson-StL 5.3	Dietz-SF 5.8
Coombs-SD 113	Gullett-Cin 14.1	Taylor-StL 16.1	Carroll-Cin 26.8	Holtzman-Chi 5.2	Seaver-NY 5.4
Pappas-Atl-Chi 110	Granger-Cin 13.2	Gullett-Cin 15.1	Hoerner-Phi 21.4	Jenkins-Chi 4.9	Gibson-StL 5.3
Dobson-SD 108	Taylor-StL 12.7	Granger-Cin 14.4	Taylor-StL 17.6	Hands-Chi 3.7	Holtzman-Chi 5.2

TEAM	G	W	L	PCT	GB	R	OR	AB	H	2B	3B	HR	BB	SO	AVG	OBP	SLG	PRO	/A	BR	/A	PF	CHI	RC	TA	SB	CS	SBA	SBR
EAST																													
BAL	162	108	54	.667		**792**	**574**	5545	1424	213	25	179	**717**	952	.257	**.346**	.401	.747	113	101	**123**	97	98	**795**	**.719**	84	39	68	2
NY	163	93	69	.574	15	680	612	5492	1381	208	**41**	111	588	**808**	.251	.327	.365	.692	97	-17	35	92	102	662	.635	105	61	63	-4
BOS	162	87	75	.537	21	786	722	5535	**1450**	**252**	28	**203**	594	855	**.262**	.338	**.428**	**.766**	**117**	**119**	46	111	98	786	.715	50	48	51	-13
DET	162	79	83	.488	29	666	731	5377	1282	207	38	148	656	825	.238	.325	.374	.699	99	-3	-23	103	98	658	.641	29	30	49	-8
CLE	162	76	86	.469	32	649	675	5463	1358	197	23	183	503	909	.249	.316	.394	.710	101	3	-95	115	96	670	.637	25	36	41	-13
WAS	162	70	92	.432	38	626	689	5460	1302	184	28	138	635	989	.238	.323	.358	.681	94	-35	-9	96	97	638	.625	72	42	63	-3
WEST																													
MIN	162	98	64	.605		744	605	5483	1438	230	**41**	153	501	905	**.262**	.329	.403	.732	108	50	61	98	103	709	.664	57	52	52	-13
OAK	162	89	73	.549	9	678	593	5376	1338	208	24	171	584	977	.249	.327	.392	.719	104	28	50	97	97	689	.676	**131**	68	66	-1
CAL	162	86	76	.531	12	631	630	5532	1391	197	40	114	447	922	.251	.311	.363	.674	92	-63	-6	92	104	622	.596	69	27	**72**	**5**
MIL	163	65	97	.401	33	613	751	5395	1305	202	24	126	592	985	.242	.321	.358	.679	93	-41	-28	98	96	618	.617	91	73	55	-16
KC	162	65	97	.401	33	611	705	5503	1341	202	**41**	97	514	958	.244	.311	.348	.659	88	-88	-77	98	**105**	593	.587	97	53	65	-2
CHI	162	56	106	.346	42	633	822	5514	1394	192	20	123	477	872	.253	.317	.362	.679	93	-49	-86	106	101	627	.599	53	33	62	-3
TOT	973					8109		65675	16404	2492	373	1746	6808	10957	.250	.324	.379	.703								863	562	61	-77

TEAM	CG	SHO	SV	IP	H	H/G	HR	BB	BB/G	SO	SO/G	ERA	/A	OAVG	OOBA	PR	/A	PF	CPI	FA	E	DP	FW	PW	BW	SBW	DIF
EAST																											
BAL	**60**	12	31	1478.7	1317	8.0	139	469	2.9	941	5.7	**3.15**	**111**	.239	**.296**	**93**	57	94	102	.981	117	148	**1.1**	5.9	**12.8**	.9	6.4
NY	36	6	49	1471.7	1386	8.5	**130**	**451**	**2.8**	777	4.8	3.24	105	.249	.303	77	25	91	**103**	.980	130	146	.3	2.6	3.6	.3	5.2
BOS	38	8	44	1446.3	1391	8.7	156	594	3.7	1003	6.2	3.87	105	.251	.324	-25	33	110	100	.974	156	131	-1.2	3.4	4.8	-.7	-.4
DET	33	9	39	1447.3	1443	9.0	153	623	3.9	1045	6.5	4.09	94	.259	.332	-60	-37	104	100	.978	133	142	.2	-3.8	-2.4	-.2	4.2
CLE	34	8	35	1451.3	1333	8.3	163	689	4.3	**1076**	**6.7**	3.91	109	.247	.331	-31	**59**	115	**103**	.979	133	168	.2	**6.1**	-9.9	-.7	-.8
WAS	20	11	40	1457.7	1375	8.5	139	611	3.8	823	5.1	3.80	95	.251	.324	-13	-31	97	100	**.982**	**116**	173	**1.1**	-3.2	-.9	.4	-8.4
WEST																											
MIN	26	12	**58**	1448.3	1329	8.3	**130**	486	3.0	940	5.8	3.23	**111**	.243	.305	77	57	97	**103**	.980	123	130	.7	5.9	6.3	-.7	4.7
OAK	33	**15**	40	1442.7	**1253**	**7.8**	134	542	3.4	858	5.4	3.30	108	**.233**	.303	66	40	96	98	.977	141	152	-.3	4.1	5.2	.6	-1.6
CAL	21	10	49	1462.3	1280	7.9	154	559	3.4	922	5.7	3.48	98	.236	.308	37	-13	92	99	.980	127	169	.5	-1.3	-.6	**1.2**	5.3
MIL	31	2	27	1446.7	1397	8.7	146	587	3.7	895	5.6	4.21	88	.255	.325	-78	-79	100	93	.978	136	142	-.0	-8.2	-2.9	-1.0	-3.9
KC	30	11	25	1463.7	1346	8.3	138	641	3.9	915	5.6	3.78	98	.247	.323	-10	-13	100	99	.976	152	162	-.9	-1.3	-8.0	.5	-6.2
CHI	20	6	30	1430.3	1554	9.8	164	556	3.5	762	4.8	4.54	88	.279	.343	-131	-85	108	101	.975	165	**187**	-1.7	-8.8	-8.9	.4	-5.9
TOT	382	110	467	17447.0		8.5			3.5		5.7	3.71		.250	.324					.978	1629	1850					

Runs
Yastrzemski-Bos 125
Tovar-Min 120
White-NY 109
Smith-Bos 109
Harper-Mil 104

Hits
Oliva-Min 204
Johnson-Cal 202
Tovar-Min 195
Yastrzemski-Bos 186
White-NY 180

Doubles
Tovar-Min 36
Otis-KC 36
Oliva-Min 36
Harper-Mil 35
Cardenas-Min 34

Triples
Tovar-Min 13
Stanley-Det 11
Otis-KC 9

Home Runs
Howard-Was 44
Killebrew-Min 41
Yastrzemski-Bos 40
A.Conigliaro-Bos 36
Powell-Bal 35

Total Bases
Yastrzemski-Bos 335
Oliva-Min 323
Harper-Mil 315
Howard-Was 309
Powell-Bal 289

Runs Batted In
Howard-Was 126
A.Conigliaro-Bos 116
Powell-Bal 114
Killebrew-Min 113
Oliva-Min 107

Runs Produced
Yastrzemski-Bos 187
White-NY 181
Oliva-Min 180
Howard-Was 172
A.Conigliaro-Bos 169

Bases On Balls
Howard-Was 132
Yastrzemski-Bos 128
Killebrew-Min 128
Bando-Oak 118
Buford-Bal 109

Batting Average
Johnson-Cal 329
Yastrzemski-Bos 329
Oliva-Min 325
Aparicio-Chi 313
F.Robinson-Bal 306

On Base Percentage
Yastrzemski-Bos 453
Howard-Was 420
Powell-Bal 417
Killebrew-Min 416
Buford-Bal 409

Slugging Average
Yastrzemski-Bos 592
Powell-Bal 549
Killebrew-Min 546
Howard-Was 546
Harper-Mil 522

Production
Yastrzemski-Bos . . 1.045
Powell-Bal 967
Howard-Was 966
Killebrew-Min 962
F.Robinson-Bal 922

Adjusted Production
Howard-Was 171
Powell-Bal 170
Yastrzemski-Bos 168
Killebrew-Min 166
F.Robinson-Bal 157

Batter Runs
Yastrzemski-Bos . . . 71.7
Howard-Was 54.1
Killebrew-Min 49.5
Powell-Bal 49.1
Harper-Mil 37.5

Adjusted Batter Runs
Yastrzemski-Bos . . . 63.7
Howard-Was 57.0
Powell-Bal 51.4
Killebrew-Min 50.7
Harper-Mil 38.8

Clutch Hitting Index
Piniella-KC 138
A.Conigliaro-Bos 128
Cater-NY 127
McMullen-Was-Cal . . . 125
B.Robinson-Bal 123

Runs Created
Yastrzemski-Bos 157
Howard-Was 130
Powell-Bal 123
Harper-Mil 122
Killebrew-Min 116

Total Average
Yastrzemski-Bos . . 1.202
Powell-Bal 1.036
Howard-Was 1.030
Killebrew-Min 1.007
Harper-Mil 967

Stolen Bases
Campaneris-Oak 42
Harper-Mil 38
Alomar-Cal 35
Kelly-KC 34
Otis-KC 33

Stolen Base Average
Otis-KC 94.3
Johnson-Cal 89.5
Campaneris-Oak . . . 80.8
Stroud-Was 78.4
Kenney-NY 76.9

Stolen Base Runs
Otis-KC 8.7
Campaneris-Oak 6.6
Stroud-Was 3.9
Johnson-Cal 3.9
Alomar-Cal 3.3

Fielding Runs
Brinkman-Was 31.5
Nettles-Cle 25.0
Knoop-Chi 22.8
Aparicio-Chi 21.7
Fosse-Cle 18.7

Total Player Rating
Yastrzemski-Bos 5.6
Harper-Mil 5.0
Oliva-Min 4.5
Aparicio-Chi 4.4
Powell-Bal 4.0

Wins
Perry-Min 24
McNally-Bal 24
Cuellar-Bal 24
Wright-Cal 22

Win Percentage
Cuellar-Bal 750
McNally-Bal 727
Perry-Min 667
Palmer-Bal 667
Siebert-Bos 652

Games
Wood-Chi 77
Grant-Oak 72
Knowles-Was 71
Williams-Min 68

Complete Games
Cuellar-Bal 21
McDowell-Cle 19
Palmer-Bal 17
McNally-Bal 16
Culp-Bos 15

Shutouts
Palmer-Bal 5
Dobson-Oak 5
Peters-Bos 4
Perry-Min 4
Cuellar-Bal 4

Saves
Perranoski-Min 34
McDaniel-NY 29
Timmermann-Det 27
Knowles-Was 27
Grant-Oak 24

Innings Pitched
Palmer-Bal 305
McDowell-Cle 305
Cuellar-Bal 298
McNally-Bal 296
Perry-Min 279

Fewest Hits/Game
Messersmith-Cal . . . 6.65
McDowell-Cle 6.96
Segui-Oak 7.22
Johnson-KC 7.49
Culp-Bos 7.57

Fewest BB/Game
Peterson-NY 1.38
Perry-Min 1.84
Cox-Was 2.06
Cuellar-Bal 2.08
Horlen-Chi 2.15

Strikeouts
McDowell-Cle 304
Lolich-Det 230
Johnson-KC 206
Palmer-Bal 199
Culp-Bos 197

Strikeouts/Game
McDowell-Cle 8.97
Johnson-KC 8.66
Cain-Det 7.76
Lolich-Det 7.58
Messersmith-Cal . . . 7.48

Wins Above Team
McDowell-Cle 5.5
Wright-Cal 5.0
Cuellar-Bal 4.7
Hargan-Cle 4.3
Williams-Min 4.3

Earned Run Average
Segui-Oak 2.56
Palmer-Bal 2.71
Wright-Cal 2.83
Peterson-NY 2.91
McDowell-Cle 2.92

Adjusted ERA
McDowell-Cle 146
Segui-Oak 139
Culp-Bos 134
Palmer-Bal 129
John-Chi 122

Opponents' Batting Avg.
Messersmith-Cal 205
McDowell-Cle 213
Segui-Oak 222
Culp-Bos 224
Johnson-KC 228

Opponents' On Base Pct.
Peterson-NY 276
Cuellar-Bal 283
Perry-Min 284
Blyleven-Min 284
Messersmith-Cal 287

Starter Runs
Palmer-Bal 33.9
McDowell-Cle 26.9
Wright-Cal 25.7
Peterson-NY 23.3
Perry-Min 21.1

Adjusted Starter Runs
McDowell-Cle 45.9
Culp-Bos 28.8
Palmer-Bal 26.4
Hargan-Cle 21.9
John-Chi 21.7

Clutch Pitching Index
Stottlemyre-NY 113
Kaat-Min 111
Bahnsen-NY 109
Segui-Oak 108
Wright-Cal 108

Relief Runs
Grant-Oak 25.8
Knowles-Was 22.1
Williams-Min 21.6
McDaniel-NY 21.2
Sanders-Mil 20.0

Adjusted Relief Runs
Grant-Oak 23.5
Knowles-Was 20.6
Williams-Min 20.0
Sanders-Mil 19.9
Hall-Min 17.8

Relief Ranking
Knowles-Was 35.5
Wood-Chi 32.7
McDaniel-NY 29.4
Perranoski-Min 27.2
Grant-Oak 24.1

Total Pitcher Index
McDowell-Cle 4.5
John-Chi 3.0
Grant-Oak 2.7
Palmer-Bal 2.7
Culp-Bos 2.7

Total Baseball Ranking
Yastrzemski-Bos 5.6
Harper-Mil 5.0
McDowell-Cle 4.5
Oliva-Min 4.5
Aparicio-Chi 4.4

TEAM	G	W	L	PCT	GB	R	OR	AB	H	2B	3B	HR	BB	SO	AVG	OBP	SLG	PRO	/A	BR	/A	PF	CHI	RC	TA	SB	CS	SBA	SBR
EAST																													
PIT	162	97	65	.599		**788**	599	5674	**1555**	223	**61**	**154**	469	919	.274	.333	**.416**	**.749**	**118**	**121**	**126**	99	102	**776**	**.685**	65	31	68	1
STL	163	90	72	.556	7	739	699	5610	1542	225	54	95	543	757	**.275**	**.342**	.385	.727	112	91	87	101	99	736	.669	**124**	53	70	5
NY	162	83	79	.512	14	588	**550**	5477	1365	203	29	98	547	958	.249	.321	.351	.672	97	-20	2	96	95	614	.601	89	43	67	1
CHI	162	83	79	.512	14	637	648	5438	1401	202	34	128	527	772	.258	.327	.378	.705	106	41	-19	110	94	663	.631	44	32	58	-5
MON	162	71	90	.441	25.5	622	729	5335	1312	197	29	88	543	800	.246	.325	.343	.668	96	-20	-12	99	102	598	.596	51	43	54	-10
PHI	162	67	95	.414	30	558	688	5538	1289	209	35	123	499	1031	.233	.300	.350	.650	90	-73	-90	103	99	586	.578	63	39	62	-4
WEST																													
SF	162	90	72	.556		706	644	5461	1348	224	36	140	**654**	1042	.247	.331	.378	.709	107	57	59	100	100	699	.668	101	36	**74**	**9**
LA	162	89	73	.549	1	663	587	5523	1469	213	38	95	489	755	.266	.328	.370	.698	104	28	36	99	100	661	.621	76	40	66	0
ATL	162	82	80	.506	8	643	699	5575	1434	192	30	153	434	**747**	.257	.314	.385	.699	104	18	-44	110	98	658	.619	57	46	55	-10
HOU	162	79	83	.488	11	585	567	5492	1319	**230**	52	71	478	888	.240	.304	.340	.644	88	-80	-32	93	**106**	573	.571	101	51	66	0
CIN	162	79	83	.488	11	586	581	5414	1306	203	28	138	438	907	.241	.301	.366	.667	94	-44	-21	96	102	580	.585	59	33	64	-1
SD	161	61	100	.379	28.5	486	610	5366	1250	184	31	96	438	966	.233	.294	.332	.626	83	-116	-92	96	98	513	.539	70	45	61	-5
TOT	972					7601		65903	16590	2505	457	1379	6059	10542	.252	.319	.366	.685								900	492	65	-24

TEAM	CG	SHO	SV	IP	H	H/G	HR	BB	BB/G	SO	SO/G	ERA	/A	OAVG	OOBA	PR	/A	PF	CPI	FA	E	DP	FW	PW	BW	SBW	DIF
EAST																											
PIT	43	15	**48**	1461.0	1426	8.8	108	470	2.9	813	5.0	3.31	101	.256	.312	25	7	97	105	.979	133	164	.0	.8	**13.5**	.3	1.3
STL	56	14	22	1467.0	1482	9.1	104	576	3.5	911	5.6	3.85	90	.263	.329	-63	-62	100	99	.978	142	155	-.4	-6.6	9.3	.8	6.0
NY	42	13	22	1466.3	**1227**	**7.5**	100	529	3.2	**1157**	**7.1**	**2.99**	**111**	**.226**	**.295**	**77**	**54**	96	94	.981	114	135	1.2	**5.8**	.2	.3	-5.5
CHI	**75**	17	13	1444.0	1458	9.1	132	411	2.6	900	5.6	3.61	105	.262	.310	-22	31	110	101	.980	126	150	.5	3.3	-2.0	-.3	.5
MON	49	8	25	1434.3	1418	8.9	133	658	4.1	829	5.2	4.12	84	.260	.338	-103	-103	100	100	.976	150	164	-.9	-11.0	-1.3	-.8	4.6
PHI	31	10	25	1470.7	1396	8.5	132	525	3.2	838	5.1	3.71	98	.253	.315	-40	-14	105	98	.981	122	158	.7	-1.5	-9.6	-.2	-3.4
WEST																											
SF	45	14	30	1454.7	1324	8.2	128	471	2.9	831	5.1	3.32	103	.242	.299	24	17	99	97	.972	179	153	-2.6	1.8	6.3	**1.2**	2.2
LA	48	**18**	33	1449.7	1363	8.5	110	**399**	**2.5**	853	5.3	3.23	105	.250	.297	37	24	98	98	.979	131	159	.2	2.6	3.9	.2	1.1
ATL	40	11	31	1474.7	1529	9.3	152	485	3.0	823	5.0	3.75	102	.269	.323	-46	14	111	**108**	.977	146	**180**	-.7	1.5	-4.7	-.8	5.7
HOU	43	10	25	1471.3	1318	8.1	**75**	475	2.9	914	5.6	3.13	102	.240	.302	54	10	92	95	.983	106	152	1.6	1.1	-3.4	.2	-1.5
CIN	27	11	38	1444.0	1298	8.1	112	501	3.1	750	4.7	3.35	99	.243	.304	18	-3	96	97	**.984**	**103**	174	**1.8**	-.3	-2.3	.1	-1.4
SD	47	10	17	1438.0	1351	8.5	93	559	3.5	923	5.8	3.22	105	.249	.316	38	27	98	106	.974	161	144	-1.5	2.9	-9.9	-.3	-10.7
TOT	546	151	329	17475.7		8.5			3.1		5.4	3.47		.252	.319					.979	1613	1888					

Runs
Brock-StL 126
Bonds-SF 110
Stargell-Pit 104
Garr-Atl 101
Torre-StL 97

Hits
Torre-StL 230
Garr-Atl 219
Brock-StL 200
Davis-LA 198

Doubles
Cedeno-Hou 40
Brock-StL 37
Torre-StL 34
Staub-Mon 34
Davis-LA 33

Triples
Morgan-Hou 11
Metzger-Hou 11
Davis-LA 10
Gaston-SD 9

Home Runs
Stargell-Pit 48
Aaron-Atl 47
May-Cin 39
Johnson-Phi 34

Total Bases
Torre-StL 352
Aaron-Atl 331
Stargell-Pit 321
Bonds-SF 317
Williams-Chi 300

Runs Batted In
Torre-StL 137
Stargell-Pit 125
Aaron-Atl 118
Bonds-SF 102
Montanez-Phi 99

Runs Produced
Torre-StL 210
Stargell-Pit 181
Brock-StL 180
Bonds-SF 179
Staub-Mon 172

Bases On Balls
Mays-SF 112
Dietz-SF 97
Bailey-Mon 97
Allen-LA 93
Morgan-Hou 88

Batting Average
Torre-StL 363
Garr-Atl 343
Beckert-Chi 342
Clemente-Pit 341
Aaron-Atl 327

On Base Percentage
Mays-SF 429
Torre-StL 424
Aaron-Atl 414
Hunt-Mon 403
Stargell-Pit 401

Slugging Average
Aaron-Atl 669
Stargell-Pit 628
Torre-StL 555
May-Cin 532
Bonds-SF 512

Production
Aaron-Atl 1.082
Stargell-Pit 1.029
Torre-StL 979
Mays-SF 911
Williams-Chi 889

Adjusted Production
Stargell-Pit 189
Aaron-Atl 184
Torre-StL 174
Mays-SF 158
Staub-Mon 149

Batter Runs
Aaron-Atl 65.2
Torre-StL 62.4
Stargell-Pit 58.7
Williams-Chi 39.3
Staub-Mon 38.5

Adjusted Batter Runs
Torre-StL 62.0
Aaron-Atl 59.4
Stargell-Pit 59.2
Staub-Mon 39.3
Mays-SF 37.8

Clutch Hitting Index
Bailey-Mon 143
Simmons-StL 140
Torre-StL 139
Sanguillen-Pit 136
Fairly-Mon 134

Runs Created
Torre-StL 145
Aaron-Atl 137
Stargell-Pit 131
Bonds-SF 115
Brock-StL 114

Total Average
Aaron-Atl 1.181
Stargell-Pit 1.117
Mays-SF 1.076
Torre-StL 1.000
Bonds-SF 893

Stolen Bases
Brock-StL 64
Morgan-Hou 40
Garr-Atl 30

Stolen Base Average
Mays-SF 88.5
Henderson-SF 85.7
Morgan-Hou 83.3
Agee-NY 82.4
Hernandez-SD 80.8

Stolen Base Runs
Brock-StL 7.8
Morgan-Hou 7.2
Mays-SF 5.1
Agee-NY 4.8
Harrelson-NY 4.2

Fielding Runs
Maxvill-StL 18.4
Sanguillen-Pit 17.5
Helms-Cin 14.0
Perez-Cin 11.6
Harrelson-NY 10.6

Total Player Rating
Stargell-Pit 5.2
Torre-StL 4.8
Aaron-Atl 4.8
Bonds-SF 4.0
Staub-Mon 3.8

Wins
Jenkins-Chi 24
Seaver-NY 20
Downing-LA 20
Carlton-StL 20
Ellis-Pit 19

Win Percentage
Gullett-Cin 727
Downing-LA 690
Carlton-StL 690
Ellis-Pit 679
Seaver-NY 667

Games
Granger-Cin 70
Johnson-SF 67
Marshall-Mon 66
McMahon-SF 61
Carroll-Cin 61

Complete Games
Jenkins-Chi 30
Seaver-NY 21
Stoneman-Mon 20
Gibson-StL 20

Shutouts
Pappas-Chi 5
Gibson-StL 5
Downing-LA 5
Blass-Pit 5

Saves
Giusti-Pit 30
Marshall-Mon 23
Brewer-LA 22
Johnson-SF 18
Upshaw-Atl 17

Innings Pitched
Jenkins-Chi 325
Stoneman-Mon 295
Seaver-NY 286
Perry-SF 280
Marichal-SF 279

Fewest Hits/Game
Wilson-Hou 6.55
Seaver-NY 6.61
Kirby-SD 7.18
Gentry-NY 7.40
Stoneman-Mon 7.41

Fewest BB/Game
Jenkins-Chi 1.02
Marichal-SF 1.81
Stone-Atl 1.82
Hands-Chi 1.86
Sutton-LA 1.87

Strikeouts
Seaver-NY 289
Jenkins-Chi 263
Stoneman-Mon 251
Kirby-SD 231
Sutton-LA 194

Strikeouts/Game
Seaver-NY 9.09
Kirby-SD 7.79
Stoneman-Mon 7.66
Jenkins-Chi 7.28
Gentry-NY 6.87

Wins Above Team
Jenkins-Chi 6.2
Gullett-Cin 5.5
Seaver-NY 5.4
Downing-LA 5.1
Carlton-StL 5.0

Earned Run Average
Seaver-NY 1.76
Roberts-SD 2.10
Wilson-Hou 2.45
Forsch-Hou 2.54
Sutton-LA 2.55

Adjusted ERA
Seaver-NY 189
Roberts-SD 162
Jenkins-Chi 137
Sutton-LA 133
Wilson-Hou 130

Opponents' Batting Avg.
Wilson-Hou 202
Seaver-NY 206
Kirby-SD 216
Cumberland-SF 223
Gentry-NY 224

Opponents' On Base Pct.
Seaver-NY 249
Wilson-Hou 263
Jenkins-Chi 266
Marichal-SF 270
Nolan-Cin 271

Starter Runs
Seaver-NY 54.1
Roberts-SD 41.0
Wilson-Hou 30.2
Sutton-LA 27.1
Jenkins-Chi 25.2

Adjusted Starter Runs
Seaver-NY 49.6
Roberts-SD 38.8
Jenkins-Chi 37.4
Niekro-Atl 25.6
Sutton-LA 24.7

Clutch Pitching Index
Roberts-SD 120
Downing-LA 115
Short-Phi 115
Johnson-Pit 112
Wise-Phi 111

Relief Runs
McGraw-NY 21.7
Miller-SD -Pit 21.4
Frisella-NY 15.0
Ray-Hou 14.7
Brewer-LA 14.2

Adjusted Relief Runs
Miller-SD -Pit 20.2
McGraw-NY 20.0
Frisella-NY 13.6
Brewer-LA 13.5
Hoerner-Phi 13.4

Relief Ranking
Miller-SD -Pit 30.6
McGraw-NY 27.6
Brewer-LA 24.7
Frisella-NY 21.5
Miller-Chi-SD 19.5

Total Pitcher Index
Seaver-NY 6.5
Jenkins-Chi 6.2
Roberts-SD 4.7
Wise-Phi 3.7
Sutton-LA 3.0

Total Baseball Ranking
Seaver-NY 6.5
Jenkins-Chi 6.2
Stargell-Pit 5.2
Torre-StL 4.8
Aaron-Atl 4.8

TEAM	G	W	L	PCT	GB	R	OR	AB	H	2B	3B	HR	BB	SO	AVG	OBP	SLG	PRO	/A	BR	/A	PF	CHI	RC	TA	SB	CS	SBA	SBR
EAST																													
BAL	158	101	57	.639		**742**	**530**	5303	1382	207	25	158	**672**	844	**.261**	**.349**	.398	**.747**	**119**	**133**	114	103	97	**750**	**.709**	66	38	63	-2
DET	162	91	71	.562	12	701	645	5502	1399	214	38	**179**	540	854	.254	.327	**.405**	.732	114	88	**115**	96	96	715	.668	35	43	45	-14
BOS	162	85	77	.525	18	691	667	5401	1360	**246**	28	161	552	871	.252	.325	.397	.722	111	68	33	106	99	686	.659	51	34	60	-4
NY	162	82	80	.506	21	648	641	5413	1377	195	**43**	97	581	**717**	.254	.331	.360	.691	102	22	41	97	99	643	.624	75	55	58	-10
WAS	159	63	96	.396	38.5	537	660	5290	1219	189	30	86	575	956	.230	.309	.326	.635	86	-85	-38	92	101	538	.565	68	45	60	-6
CLE	162	60	102	.370	43	543	747	5467	1303	200	20	109	467	868	.238	.302	.342	.644	88	-82	-116	106	100	558	.560	57	37	61	-4
WEST																													
OAK	161	101	60	.627		691	564	5494	1383	195	25	160	542	1018	.252	.323	.384	.707	107	42	38	101	102	681	.647	80	53	60	-7
KC	161	85	76	.528	16	603	566	5295	1323	225	40	80	490	819	.250	.316	.353	.669	96	-27	-19	99	**104**	594	.606	**130**	46	**74**	**11**
CHI	162	79	83	.488	22.5	617	597	5382	1346	185	30	138	562	870	.250	.327	.373	.700	105	33	48	98	93	661	.642	83	65	56	-13
CAL	162	76	86	.469	25.5	511	576	5495	1271	213	18	96	441	827	.231	.292	.329	.621	82	-130	-120	99	103	518	.534	72	34	68	1
MIN	160	74	86	.463	26.5	654	670	5414	**1406**	197	31	116	512	846	.260	.326	.372	.698	104	28	3	104	100	641	.621	66	44	60	-6
MIL	161	69	92	.429	32	534	609	5185	1188	160	23	104	543	924	.229	.306	.329	.635	86	-87	-105	103	103	534	.569	82	53	61	-6
TOT	966					7472		64641	15957	2426	351	1484	6477	10414	.247	.320	.364	.684								865	547	61	-68

TEAM	CG	SHO	SV	IP	H	H/G	HR	BB	BB/G	SO	SO/G	ERA	/A	OAVG	OOBA	PR	/A	PF	CPI	FA	E	DP	FW	PW	BW	SBW	DIF
EAST																											
BAL	**71**	15	22	1415.3	1257	8.0	125	**416**	**2.6**	793	5.0	**2.99**	**116**	.238	**.291**	**74**	**74**	100	101	.981	112	148	.8	**8.0**	12.3	.4	.6
DET	53	11	32	1468.3	1355	8.3	126	609	3.7	**1000**	**6.1**	3.63	90	.246	.321	-28	-57	95	99	**.983**	**106**	156	**1.2**	-6.1	**12.4**	-.9	3.5
BOS	44	11	35	1443.0	1424	8.9	136	535	3.3	871	5.4	3.80	96	.258	.323	-55	-26	105	100	.981	116	149	.6	-2.8	3.5	.2	2.5
NY	67	15	12	1452.0	1382	8.6	126	423	**2.6**	707	4.4	3.43	98	.251	.302	4	-13	97	97	.981	125	159	.0	-1.4	4.4	-.5	-1.6
WAS	30	10	26	1418.7	1376	8.7	132	554	3.5	762	4.8	3.70	88	.258	.326	-37	-70	94	105	.977	141	170	-.9	-7.5	-4.1	-.0	-4.0
CLE	21	7	32	1440.0	1352	8.4	154	770	4.8	937	5.9	4.28	88	.251	.343	-130	-83	108	99	.981	116	159	.6	-8.9	-12.5	.2	-.4
WEST																											
OAK	57	18	36	1469.3	**1229**	**7.5**	131	501	3.1	999	**6.1**	3.05	112	**.228**	.292	67	60	99	97	.981	117	157	.5	6.5	4.1	-.1	9.6
KC	34	15	**44**	1420.3	1301	8.2	**84**	496	3.1	775	4.9	3.25	105	.246	.309	33	23	98	98	.979	132	**178**	-.4	2.5	-2.0	**1.8**	2.6
CHI	46	19	32	1450.3	1348	8.4	100	468	2.9	976	**6.1**	3.12	108	.246	.303	54	39	97	101	.975	160	128	-2.0	4.2	5.2	-.8	-8.6
CAL	39	11	32	1481.0	1246	7.6	101	607	3.7	904	5.5	3.10	111	.230	.306	59	56	99	98	.980	131	159	-.3	6.0	-12.9	.7	1.5
MIN	43	9	25	1416.7	1384	8.8	139	529	3.4	895	5.7	3.81	95	.257	.321	-55	-32	104	100	.980	118	134	.5	-3.4	.3	-.0	-3.3
MIL	32	**23**	32	1416.3	1303	8.3	130	569	3.6	795	5.1	3.38	107	.247	.317	12	35	104	**106**	.977	138	152	-.7	3.8	-11.3	-.0	-3.2
TOT	537	164	360	17291.3		8.3			3.4		5.4	3.46		.247	.320					.980	1512	1849					

Runs
Buford-Bal 99
Tovar-Min 94
Murcer-NY 94
Carew-Min 88
Jackson-Oak 87

Hits
Tovar-Min 204
Alomar-Cal 179
Carew-Min 177
Smith-Bos 175
Murcer-NY 175

Doubles
Smith-Bos 33
Schaal-KC 31
Rodriguez-Det 30
Oliva-Min 30

Triples
Patek-KC 11
Carew-Min 10
Blair-Bal 8

Home Runs
Melton-Chi 33
Jackson-Oak 32
Cash-Det 32
Smith-Bos 30

Total Bases
Smith-Bos 302
Jackson-Oak 288
Murcer-NY 287
Melton-Chi 267
Oliva-Min 266

Runs Batted In
Killebrew-Min 119
F.Robinson-Bal 99
Smith-Bos 96
Murcer-NY 94
Bando-Oak 94

Runs Produced
Murcer-NY 163
F.Robinson-Bal 153
Killebrew-Min 152
White-NY 151
Smith-Bos 151

Bases On Balls
Killebrew-Min 114
Yastrzemski-Bos 106
Schaal-KC 103
Petrocelli-Bos 91
Murcer-NY 91

Batting Average
Oliva-Min 337
Murcer-NY 331
Rettenmund-Bal 318
Tovar-Min 311
Carew-Min 307

On Base Percentage
Murcer-NY 429
Rettenmund-Bal 424
Kaline-Det 421
Buford-Bal 415
White-NY 399

Slugging Average
Oliva-Min 546
Murcer-NY 543
Cash-Det 531
F.Robinson-Bal 510
Jackson-Oak 508

Production
Murcer-NY 972
Oliva-Min 918
Cash-Det 905
F.Robinson-Bal 900
Buford-Bal 891

Adjusted Production
Murcer-NY 179
Cash-Det 161
Kaline-Det 157
Oliva-Min 151
White-NY 150

Batter Runs
Murcer-NY 53.7
Rettenmund-Bal 34.8
Buford-Bal 34.5
White-NY 33.7
Oliva-Min 33.6

Adjusted Batter Runs
Murcer-NY 55.7
White-NY 35.7
Cash-Det 33.9
Rettenmund-Bal 33.0
Kaline-Det 32.9

Clutch Hitting Index
Killebrew-Min 163
Powell-Bal 148
Alou-Oak-NY 133
B.Robinson-Bal 131
F.Robinson-Bal 130

Runs Created
Murcer-NY 126
Smith-Bos 106
Jackson-Oak 103
White-NY 103
Rettenmund-Bal 99

Total Average
Murcer-NY 1.057
Buford-Bal 991
Cash-Det 933
Rettenmund-Bal 921
White-NY 910

Stolen Bases
Otis-KC 52
Patek-KC 49
Alomar-Cal 39
Campaneris-Oak 34

Stolen Base Average
Harper-Mil 89.3
Otis-KC 86.7
Campaneris-Oak . . . 82.9
Pinson-Cle 80.6
Alomar-Cal 79.6

Stolen Base Runs
Otis-KC 10.8
Patek-KC 6.3
Campaneris-Oak 6.0
Harper-Mil 5.7
Alomar-Cal 5.7

Fielding Runs
Nettles-Cle 39.6
Melton-Chi 24.3
Michael-NY 21.6
Alomar-Cal 17.5
Patek-KC 15.5

Total Player Rating
Nettles-Cle 5.0
Melton-Chi 4.8
Murcer-NY 4.5
Rettenmund-Bal 3.9
Otis-KC 3.9

Wins
Lolich-Det 25
Blue-Oak 24
Wood-Chi 22
McNally-Bal 21
Hunter-Oak 21

Win Percentage
McNally-Bal 808
Dobson-Oak 750
Blue-Oak 750
Dobson-Bal 714

Games
Sanders-Mil 83
Scherman-Det 69
Burgmeier-KC 67
Abernathy-KC 63

Complete Games
Lolich-Det 29
Blue-Oak 24
Wood-Chi 22
Cuellar-Bal 21
Palmer-Bal 20

Shutouts
Blue-Oak 8
Wood-Chi 7
Stottlemyre-NY 7
Bradley-Chi 6

Saves
Sanders-Mil 31
Abernathy-KC 23
Scherman-Det 20
Fingers-Oak 17
Burgmeier-KC 17

Innings Pitched
Lolich-Det 376
Wood-Chi 334
Blue-Oak 312
Cuellar-Bal 292

Fewest Hits/Game
Blue-Oak 6.03
McDowell-Cle 6.70
May-Cal 6.92
Messersmith-Cal . . . 7.28
Wright-Cal 7.31

Fewest BB/Game
Peterson-NY 1.38
Kline-NY 1.50
Kaat-Min 1.63
Wood-Chi 1.67
Drago-KC 1.72

Strikeouts
Lolich-Det 308
Blue-Oak 301
Coleman-Det 236
Blyleven-Min 224
Wood-Chi 210

Strikeouts/Game
Blue-Oak 8.68
McDowell-Cle 8.04
Johnson-Chi 7.74
Coleman-Det 7.43
Lolich-Det 7.37

Wins Above Team
McNally-Bal 6.7
Blue-Oak 6.1
Wood-Chi 5.7
Messersmith-Cal 5.0
Coleman-Det 4.8

Earned Run Average
Blue-Oak 1.82
Wood-Chi 1.91
Palmer-Bal 2.68
Hedlund-KC 2.71
Blyleven-Min 2.82

Adjusted ERA
Blue-Oak 188
Wood-Chi 176
Palmer-Bal 129
Blyleven-Min 128
Hedlund-KC 125

Opponents' Batting Avg.
Blue-Oak 189
McDowell-Cle 207
May-Cal 213
Messersmith-Cal 218
Palmer-Bal 221

Opponents' On Base Pct.
Blue-Oak 249
Wood-Chi 259
Kline-NY 274
Dobson-Bal 276
Hunter-Oak 279

Starter Runs
Wood-Chi 57.5
Blue-Oak 57.0
Palmer-Bal 24.5
Lolich-Det 22.6
Blyleven-Min 19.9

Adjusted Starter Runs
Blue-Oak 55.6
Wood-Chi 54.0
Palmer-Bal 24.6
Blyleven-Min 24.4
Siebert-Bos 19.1

Clutch Pitching Index
Drago-KC 119
Krausse-Mil 118
Johnson-Chi 117
Bosman-Was 112
Wood-Chi 112

Relief Runs
Sanders-Mil 23.3
Burgmeier-KC 16.8
Mingori-Cle 12.9
Queen-Cal 12.4
Grzenda-Was 11.9

Adjusted Relief Runs
Sanders-Mil 25.4
Burgmeier-KC 16.2
Mingori-Cle 14.8
Queen-Cal 12.2
Grzenda-Was 10.3

Relief Ranking
Sanders-Mil 45.0
Burgmeier-KC 33.6
Fisher-Cal 13.5
Abernathy-KC 13.3
Allen-Cal 13.1

Total Pitcher Index
Wood-Chi 6.0
Blue-Oak 5.7
Siebert-Bos 3.5
Palmer-Bal 3.0
Sanders-Mil 2.9

Total Baseball Ranking
Wood-Chi 6.0
Blue-Oak 5.7
Nettles-Cle 5.0
Melton-Chi 4.8
Murcer-NY 4.5

TEAM	G	W	L	PCT	GB	R	OR	AB	H	2B	3B	HR	BB	SO	AVG	OBP	SLG	PRO	/A	BR	/A	PF	CHI	RC	TA	SB	CS	SBA	SBR
EAST																													
PIT	155	96	59	.619		691	**512**	5490	**1505**	**251**	**47**	110	404	871	**.274**	.327	**.397**	**.724**	**112**	74	57	103	99	**701**	.644	49	30	62	-2
CHI	156	85	70	.548	11	685	567	5247	1346	206	40	133	565	815	.257	.332	.387	.719	111	74	-10	114	100	670	.661	69	47	59	-7
NY	156	83	73	.532	13.5	528	578	5135	1154	175	31	105	589	990	.225	.309	.332	.641	88	-67	-38	95	98	530	.571	41	41	50	-11
STL	156	75	81	.481	21.5	568	600	5326	1383	214	42	70	437	793	.260	.319	.355	.674	98	-13	-43	105	96	591	.595	104	48	68	2
MON	156	70	86	.449	26.5	513	609	5156	1205	156	22	91	474	828	.234	.304	.325	.629	85	-91	-105	102	101	513	.552	68	66	51	-18
PHI	156	59	97	.378	37.5	503	635	5248	1240	200	36	98	487	930	.236	.304	.344	.648	90	-64	-45	97	93	545	.566	42	50	46	-16
WEST																													
CIN	154	95	59	.617		707	557	5241	1317	214	44	124	**606**	914	.251	**.333**	.380	.713	109	67	**108**	93	103	676	**.677**	**140**	63	69	4
HOU	153	84	69	.549	10.5	**708**	636	5267	1359	233	38	134	524	907	.258	.329	.393	.722	**112**	**75**	37	106	103	686	.674	111	56	66	0
LA	155	85	70	.548	10.5	584	527	5270	1349	178	39	98	480	786	.256	.321	.360	.681	100	1	38	94	96	610	.609	82	39	68	1
ATL	155	70	84	.455	25	628	730	5278	1363	186	17	144	532	**770**	.258	.330	.382	.712	109	60	31	105	93	661	.644	47	35	57	-6
SF	155	69	86	.445	26.5	662	649	5245	1281	211	36	**150**	480	964	.244	.311	.384	.695	103	17	18	100	**107**	630	.643	123	45	**73**	**10**
SD	153	58	95	.379	36.5	488	665	5213	1181	168	38	102	407	976	.227	.284	.332	.616	81	-130	-60	88	106	489	.534	78	46	63	-3
TOT	930					7265		63116	15683	2392	430	1359	5985	10544	.248	.317	.365	.682								954	566	63	-52

TEAM	CG	SHO	SV	IP	H	H/G	HR	BB	BB/G	SO	SO/G	ERA	/A	OAVG	OOBA	PR	/A	PF	CPI	FA	E	DP	FW	PW	BW	SBW	DIF
EAST																											
PIT	39	15	48	1414.3	1282	8.2	90	433	2.8	838	5.3	2.81	**123**	.242	.298	101	**102**	100	**108**	.978	136	**171**	-.0	**11.0**	6.1	.3	1.2
CHI	54	19	32	1398.7	1329	8.6	112	**421**	**2.7**	824	5.3	3.22	121	.251	.305	36	**102**	112	105	.979	132	148	.2	**11.0**	-1.1	-.3	-2.3
NY	32	12	41	1414.7	1263	8.0	118	486	3.1	**1059**	**6.7**	3.26	101	.240	.301	29	7	96	99	.980	116	122	1.0	.8	-4.1	-.7	8.0
STL	**64**	13	13	1399.7	1290	8.3	87	531	3.4	912	5.9	3.42	106	.246	.312	5	34	105	97	.977	141	146	-.3	3.7	-4.6	.7	-2.4
MON	39	11	23	1401.3	1281	8.2	103	579	3.7	888	5.7	3.59	100	.245	.318	-21	-1	104	97	.978	134	141	.0	-.1	-11.3	-1.5	4.8
PHI	43	13	15	1400.0	1318	8.5	117	536	3.4	927	6.0	3.66	93	.251	.317	-32	-39	99	99	.981	116	142	1.0	-4.2	-4.8	-1.2	-9.8
WEST																											
CIN	25	15	**60**	1412.7	1313	8.4	129	435	2.8	806	5.1	3.21	98	.247	.301	38	-9	91	104	**.982**	**110**	143	**1.4**	-1.0	**11.6**	.9	5.1
HOU	38	14	31	1385.3	1340	8.7	114	498	3.2	971	6.3	3.77	96	.255	.318	-48	-20	105	98	.980	116	151	1.0	-2.2	4.0	.5	4.2
LA	50	**23**	29	1403.0	**1196**	**7.7**	**83**	429	2.8	856	5.5	**2.78**	115	**.229**	**.286**	**104**	66	93	96	.974	162	145	-1.5	7.1	4.1	.6	-2.8
ATL	40	4	27	1377.0	1412	9.2	155	512	3.3	732	4.8	4.27	86	.265	.326	-125	-93	106	97	.974	156	130	-1.1	-10.0	3.3	-.2	1.0
SF	44	8	23	1386.3	1309	8.5	130	507	3.3	771	5.0	3.69	93	.250	.313	-37	-39	100	98	.974	156	121	-1.1	-4.2	1.9	**1.6**	-6.6
SD	39	17	19	1403.7	1350	8.7	121	618	4.0	960	6.2	3.78	83	.254	.329	-50	-99	91	103	.976	144	146	-.5	-10.6	-6.5	.2	-1.1
TOT	507	164	361	16796.7		8.4			3.2		5.6	3.45		.248	.317					.978	1619	1706					

Runs
Morgan-Cin 122
Bonds-SF 118
Wynn-Hou 117
Rose-Cin 107
Cedeno-Hou 103

Hits
Rose-Cin 198
Brock-StL 193
Williams-Chi 191
Simmons-StL 180
Garr-Atl 180

Doubles
Montanez-Phi 39
Cedeno-Hou 39
Simmons-StL 36
Williams-Chi 34

Triples
Bowa-Phi 13
Rose-Cin 11
Sanguillen-Pit 8
Cedeno-Hou 8
Brock-StL 8

Home Runs
Bench-Cin 40
Colbert-SD 38
Williams-Chi 37
Aaron-Atl 34
Stargell-Pit 33

Total Bases
Williams-Chi 348
Cedeno-Hou 300
Bench-Cin 291
May-Hou 290
Colbert-SD 286

Runs Batted In
Bench-Cin 125
Williams-Chi 122
Stargell-Pit 112
Colbert-SD 111
May-Hou 98

Runs Produced
Wynn-Hou 183
Williams-Chi 180
Morgan-Cin 179
Bonds-SF 172
Bench-Cin 172

Bases On Balls
Morgan-Cin 115
Wynn-Hou 103
Bench-Cin 100
Aaron-Atl 92
Evans-Atl 90

Batting Average
Williams-Chi 333
Garr-Atl 325
Baker-Atl 321
Cedeno-Hou 320
Watson-Hou 312

On Base Percentage
Morgan-Cin 419
Williams-Chi 403
Santo-Chi 397
Aaron-Atl 391
Wynn-Hou 391

Slugging Average
Williams-Chi 606
Stargell-Pit 558
Bench-Cin 541
Cedeno-Hou 537
Aaron-Atl 514

Production
Williams-Chi 1.010
Stargell-Pit 935
Bench-Cin 927
Cedeno-Hou 924
Aaron-Atl 906

Adjusted Production
Bench-Cin 172
Williams-Chi 161
Stargell-Pit 158
Colbert-SD 155
Morgan-Cin 153

Batter Runs
Williams-Chi 61.1
Bench-Cin 44.0
Cedeno-Hou 42.9
Stargell-Pit 39.6
Morgan-Cin 37.2

Adjusted Batter Runs
Williams-Chi 51.8
Bench-Cin 48.6
Morgan-Cin 41.9
Cedeno-Hou 38.9
Stargell-Pit 38.0

Clutch Hitting Index
Parker-LA 152
Oliver-Pit 137
Torre-StL 135
Evans-Atl 133
Bench-Cin 132

Runs Created
Williams-Chi 137
Morgan-Cin 117
Cedeno-Hou 115
Bench-Cin 110
Rose-Cin 109

Total Average
Williams-Chi 1.053
Morgan-Cin 1.015
Cedeno-Hou 1.010
Stargell-Pit 961
Bench-Cin 957

Stolen Bases
Brock-StL 63
Morgan-Cin 58
Cedeno-Hou 55
Bonds-SF 44
Tolan-Cin 42

Stolen Base Average
Hernandez-SD 88.9
Bonds-SF 88.0
Davis-LA 87.0
Brock-StL 77.8
Morgan-Cin 77.3

Stolen Base Runs
Bonds-SF 9.6
Brock-StL 8.1
Morgan-Cin 7.2
Hernandez-SD 5.4
Davis-LA 4.2

Fielding Runs
Cash-Pit 26.9
Helms-Hou 25.2
Dyer-NY 22.1
Money-Phi 21.0
Beckert-Chi 20.7

Total Player Rating
Bench-Cin 6.0
Morgan-Cin 5.8
Cedeno-Hou 4.4
Simmons-StL 4.1
Williams-Chi 4.0

Wins
Carlton-Phi 27
Seaver-NY 21
Osteen-LA 20
Jenkins-Chi 20

Win Percentage
Nolan-Cin 750
Carlton-Phi 730
Pappas-Chi 708
Blass-Pit 704
Ellis-Pit 682

Games
Marshall-Mon 65
Carroll-Cin 65
Borbon-Cin 62
Ross-SD 60

Complete Games
Carlton-Phi 30
Jenkins-Chi 23
Gibson-StL 23
Wise-StL 20
Sutton-LA 18

Shutouts
Sutton-LA 9
Carlton-Phi 8
Norman-SD 6
Jenkins-Chi 5
Dierker-Hou 5

Saves
Carroll-Cin 37
McGraw-NY 27
Giusti-Pit 22
Marshall-Mon 18

Innings Pitched
Carlton-Phi 346
Jenkins-Chi 289
Niekro-Atl 282
Gibson-StL 278
Sutton-LA 273

Fewest Hits/Game
Sutton-LA 6.13
Carlton-Phi 6.68
Gibson-StL 7.32
Seaver-NY 7.39
Bryant-SF 7.40

Fewest BB/Game
Pappas-Chi 1.34
Nolan-Cin 1.53
Niekro-Atl 1.69
Ellis-Pit 1.82
Moose-Pit 1.87

Strikeouts
Carlton-Phi 310
Seaver-NY 249
Gibson-StL 208
Sutton-LA 207
Jenkins-Chi 184

Strikeouts/Game
Seaver-NY 8.55
Reuss-Hou 8.16
Koosman-NY 8.12
Carlton-Phi 8.06
Norman-SD 7.09

Wins Above Team
Carlton-Phi 11.7
Gibson-StL 5.1
Pappas-Chi 4.7
Sutton-LA 4.6
Bryant-SF 4.6

Earned Run Average
Carlton-Phi 1.98
Nolan-Cin 1.99
Sutton-LA 2.08
Matlack-NY 2.32
Gibson-StL 2.46

Adjusted ERA
Carlton-Phi 172
Nolan-Cin 158
Sutton-LA 154
Gibson-StL 148
Matlack-NY 143

Opponents' Batting Avg.
Sutton-LA 189
Carlton-Phi 206
Gibson-StL 224
Seaver-NY 224
Bryant-SF 224

Opponents' On Base Pct.
Sutton-LA 238
Carlton-Phi 255
Nolan-Cin 258
Niekro-Atl 271
McAndrew-NY 274

Starter Runs
Carlton-Phi 56.8
Sutton-LA 41.8
Gibson-StL 30.7
Matlack-NY 30.6
Nolan-Cin 28.5

Adjusted Starter Runs
Carlton-Phi 55.0
Gibson-StL 36.4
Sutton-LA 34.3
Blass-Pit 27.1
Matlack-NY 26.8

Clutch Pitching Index
Blass-Pit 132
Nolan-Cin 115
Matlack-NY 115
Downing-LA 115
Hooton-Chi 115

Relief Runs
Marshall-Mon 21.5
McGraw-NY 20.7
Brewer-LA 18.9
Hernandez-Pit 13.9
Carroll-Cin 12.8

Adjusted Relief Runs
Marshall-Mon 23.2
McGraw-NY 19.0
Brewer-LA 16.8
Hernandez-Pit 13.9
Giusti-Pit 12.8

Relief Ranking
Marshall-Mon 47.6
Brewer-LA 37.3
McGraw-NY 33.5
Giusti-Pit 25.4
Carroll-Cin 17.3

Total Pitcher Index
Carlton-Phi 6.8
Gibson-StL 5.2
Sutton-LA 3.7
Blass-Pit 3.4
Jenkins-Chi 3.1

Total Baseball Ranking
Carlton-Phi 6.8
Bench-Cin 6.0
Morgan-Cin 5.8
Gibson-StL 5.2
Cedeno-Hou 4.4

TEAM	G	W	L	PCT	GB	R	OR	AB	H	2B	3B	HR	BB	SO	AVG	OBP	SLG	PRO	/A	BR	/A	PF	CHI	RC	TA	SB	CS	SBA	SBR
EAST																													
DET	156	86	70	.551		558	514	5099	1206	179	32	122	483	793	.237	.306	.356	.662	103	17	-52	113	101	549	.581	17	21	45	-7
BOS	155	85	70	.548	0.5	**640**	620	5208	1289	**229**	34	124	522	858	.248	.320	**.376**	**.696**	113	83	54	105	101	**634**	**.636**	66	30	**69**	2
BAL	154	80	74	.519	5	519	**430**	5028	1153	193	29	100	507	935	.229	.304	.339	.643	97	-12	1	98	100	523	.577	78	41	66	0
NY	155	79	76	.510	6.5	557	527	5168	1288	201	24	103	493	**689**	.249	.318	.357	.675	107	45	**86**	92	95	588	.604	71	42	63	-3
CLE	156	72	84	.462	14	472	519	5207	1220	187	18	91	420	762	.234	.295	.330	.625	92	-53	-91	107	97	495	.533	49	53	48	-16
MIL	156	65	91	.417	21	493	595	5124	1204	167	22	88	472	868	.235	.303	.328	.631	94	-35	-9	95	98	495	.545	64	57	53	-14
WEST																													
OAK	155	93	62	.600		604	457	5200	1248	195	29	**134**	463	886	.240	.308	.366	.674	107	36	53	97	104	584	.608	87	48	64	-2
CHI	154	87	67	.565	5.5	566	538	5083	1208	170	28	108	511	991	.238	.311	.346	.657	102	13	-19	106	103	550	.595	100	52	66	0
MIN	154	77	77	.500	15.5	537	535	5234	1277	182	31	93	478	905	.244	.311	.346	.655	101	9	-29	107	96	554	.573	53	41	56	-8
KC	154	76	78	.494	16.5	580	545	5167	**1317**	220	26	78	**534**	711	**.255**	**.329**	.353	.682	110	64	62	100	95	601	.615	85	44	66	0
CAL	155	75	80	.484	18	454	533	5165	1249	171	26	78	358	850	.242	.294	.330	.624	92	-55	5	88	96	487	.526	57	37	61	-4
TEX	154	54	100	.351	38.5	461	628	5029	1092	166	17	56	503	926	.217	.292	.290	.582	79	-115	-84	94	**111**	438	.516	**126**	73	63	-5
TOT	929					6441		61712	14751	2260	316	1175	5742	10174	.239	.308	.343	.651								853	539	61	-67

TEAM	CG	SHO	SV	IP	H	H/G	HR	BB	BB/G	SO	SO/G	ERA	/A	OAVG	OOBA	PR	/A	PF	CPI	FA	E	DP	FW	PW	BW	SBW	DIF
EAST																											
DET	46	11	33	1388.3	1212	7.9	101	465	3.0	952	6.2	2.96	**116**	.236	.299	15	**73**	112	102	**.984**	96	137	**1.8**	**8.3**	-5.9	-.2	3.9
BOS	48	20	25	1382.7	1309	8.5	101	512	3.3	918	6.0	3.47	93	.251	.316	-62	-39	105	100	.978	130	141	-.1	-4.4	6.1	.9	5.0
BAL	**62**	20	21	1371.7	1116	7.3	**85**	395	2.6	788	5.2	**2.53**	116	.223	**.277**	80	62	96	97	.983	100	150	1.6	7.0	.1	.6	-6.4
NY	35	19	39	1373.3	1306	8.6	87	419	2.7	625	4.1	3.05	92	.252	.306	2	-36	92	105	.978	134	**179**	-.4	-4.1	9.8	.3	-4.1
CLE	47	13	24	1410.0	1232	7.9	123	534	3.4	846	5.4	2.92	113	.237	.307	22	60	108	**112**	.981	116	157	.7	6.8	-10.3	-1.2	-2.0
MIL	37	14	32	1391.7	1289	8.3	116	486	3.1	740	4.8	3.45	-60	.246	.308	-60	-76	97	97	.977	139	145	-.6	-8.6	-1.0	-1.0	-1.7
WEST																											
OAK	42	**23**	**43**	1417.7	1170	7.4	96	418	2.7	862	5.5	2.58	112	.225	.281	76	49	95	99	.979	130	146	-.1	5.6	6.0	.4	3.6
CHI	36	14	42	1385.3	1269	8.2	94	431	2.8	936	6.1	3.12	104	.245	.300	-8	18	106	99	.977	135	136	-.4	2.0	-2.2	.6	9.9
MIN	37	17	34	1399.3	1188	7.6	105	444	2.9	838	5.4	2.84	**116**	.230	.290	34	68	107	99	.974	159	133	-1.8	7.7	-3.3	-.3	-2.4
KC	44	16	29	1381.3	1293	8.4	**85**	405	2.6	801	5.2	3.24	94	.250	.303	-27	-28	100	97	.981	116	164	.7	-3.2	7.0	.6	-6.2
CAL	57	18	16	1377.7	**1109**	**7.2**	90	620	4.1	**1000**	**6.5**	3.06	89	**.222**	.305	0	-49	90	96	.981	114	135	.8	-5.6	.6	.2	1.5
TEX	11	8	34	1374.7	1258	8.2	92	613	4.0	868	5.7	3.53	84	.245	.324	-71	-85	97	99	.972	166	147	-2.2	-9.7	-9.6	.0	-1.7
TOT	502	193	372	16653.7		8.0			3.1		5.5	3.06		.239	.308					.979	1535	1770					

Runs		Hits		Doubles		Triples		Home Runs		Total Bases	
Murcer-NY	102	Rudi-Oak	181	Piniella-KC	33	Rudi-Oak	9	Allen-Chi	37	Murcer-NY	314
Rudi-Oak	94	Piniella-KC	179	Rudi-Oak	32	Fisk-Bos	9	Murcer-NY	33	Allen-Chi	305
Harper-Bos	92	Murcer-NY	171	Murcer-NY	30	Blair-Bal	8	Killebrew-Min	26	Rudi-Oak	288
Allen-Chi	90	Carew-Min	170	White-NY	29	Murcer-NY	7	Epstein-Oak	26	Mayberry-KC	255
Tovar-Min	86	May-Chi	161	Harper-Bos	29	Kelly-Chi	7			Piniella-KC	253

Runs Batted In		Runs Produced		Bases On Balls		Batting Average		On Base Percentage		Slugging Average	
Allen-Chi	113	Allen-Chi	166	White-NY	99	Carew-Min	.318	Allen-Chi	.422	Allen-Chi	.603
Mayberry-KC	100	Murcer-NY	165	Allen-Chi	99	Piniella-KC	.312	May-Chi	.408	Fisk-Bos	.538
Murcer-NY	96	Rudi-Oak	150	Killebrew-Min	94	Allen-Chi	.308	Mayberry-KC	.396	Murcer-NY	.537
Scott-Mil	88	Mayberry-KC	140	May-Chi	79	May-Chi	.308	White-NY	.385	Mayberry-KC	.507
Powell-Bal	81					Rudi-Oak	.305	Scheinblum-KC	.385	Epstein-Oak	.490

Production		Adjusted Production		Batter Runs		Adjusted Batter Runs		Clutch Hitting Index		Runs Created	
Allen-Chi	1.025	Allen-Chi	191	Allen-Chi	66.0	Allen-Chi	62.5	Billings-Tex	149	Allen-Chi	131
Fisk-Bos	.909	Murcer-NY	179	Murcer-NY	44.9	Murcer-NY	49.5	Petrocelli-Bos	142	Murcer-NY	114
Mayberry-KC	.903	Mayberry-KC	167	Mayberry-KC	42.9	Mayberry-KC	42.7	Bando-Oak	141	Mayberry-KC	101
Murcer-NY	.900	Epstein-Oak	162	Fisk-Bos	37.1	Epstein-Oak	34.7	Yastrzemski-Bos	141	May-Chi	96
Epstein-Oak	.868	Fisk-Bos	160	May-Chi	36.6	Fisk-Bos	34.6	Rojas-KC	133	Rudi-Oak	95

Total Average		Stolen Bases		Stolen Base Average		Stolen Base Runs		Fielding Runs		Total Player Rating	
Allen-Chi	1.143	Campaneris-Oak	52	Baylor-Bal	92.3	Campaneris-Oak	7.2	Patek-KC	27.6	Fisk-Bos	5.9
Mayberry-KC	.916	Nelson-Tex	51	Patek-KC	82.5	Baylor-Bal	6.0	Rodriguez-Det	24.0	Murcer-NY	5.1
Fisk-Bos	.914	Patek-KC	33	Scott-Mil	80.0	Patek-KC	5.7	Michael-NY	22.8	Allen-Chi	5.1
Murcer-NY	.909	Kelly-Chi	32	Campaneris-Oak	78.8	Nelson-Tex	5.1	Munson-NY	18.4	Grich-Bal	3.4
Epstein-Oak	.888	Otis-KC	28	Harper-Bos	78.1	Kelly-Chi	4.2	Fisk-Bos	17.4	White-NY	3.3

Wins		Win Percentage		Games		Complete Games		Shutouts		Saves	
Wood-Chi	24	Hunter-Oak	.750	Lindblad-Tex	66	Perry-Cle	29	Ryan-Cal	9	Lyle-NY	35
Perry-Cle	24	Tiant-Bos	.714	Fingers-Oak	65	Lolich-Det	23	Wood-Chi	8	Forster-Chi	29
Lolich-Det	22	Odom-Oak	.714	Granger-Min	63	Wood-Chi	20	Stottlemyre-NY	7	Fingers-Oak	21
		Palmer-Bal	.677			Ryan-Cal	20			Granger-Min	19
		Kline-NY	.640			Palmer-Bal	18			Sanders-Mil	17

Innings Pitched		Fewest Hits/Game		Fewest BB/Game		Strikeouts		Strikeouts/Game		Wins Above Team	
Wood-Chi	377	Ryan-Cal	5.26	Peterson-NY	1.58	Ryan-Cal	329	Ryan-Cal	10.43	Perry-Cle	6.4
Perry-Cle	343	Hunter-Oak	6.10	Nelson-KC	1.61	Lolich-Det	250	Messersmith-Cal	7.52	Hunter-Oak	5.9
Lolich-Det	327	Nelson-KC	6.24	Kline-NY	1.68	Perry-Cle	234	May-Cal	7.42	Palmer-Bal	5.9
Hunter-Oak	295	Tiant-Bos	6.44	Holtzman-Oak	1.77	Blyleven-Min	228	Bradley-Chi	7.23	Wright-Cal	4.5
Blyleven-Min	287	Messersmith-Cal	6.62	Wood-Chi	1.77	Coleman-Det	222	Blyleven-Min	7.15	Tiant-Bos	4.2

Earned Run Average		Adjusted ERA		Opponents' Batting Avg.		Opponents' On Base Pct.		Starter Runs		Adjusted Starter Runs	
Tiant-Bos	1.91	Perry-Cle	172	Ryan-Cal	.171	Nelson-KC	.233	Perry-Cle	43.7	Perry-Cle	52.9
Perry-Cle	1.92	Tiant-Bos	168	Hunter-Oak	.189	Hunter-Oak	.238	Hunter-Oak	33.3	Lolich-Det	33.9
Hunter-Oak	2.04	Nelson-KC	147	Nelson-KC	.196	Perry-Cle	.258	Palmer-Bal	30.2	Wood-Chi	30.8
Palmer-Bal	2.07	Palmer-Bal	142	Tiant-Bos	.202	Palmer-Bal	.265	Ryan-Cal	24.6	Hunter-Oak	27.8
Nelson-KC	2.08	Hunter-Oak	142	Perry-Cle	.205	Tiant-Bos	.271	Wood-Chi	23.2	Palmer-Bal	26.6

Clutch Pitching Index		Relief Runs		Adjusted Relief Runs		Relief Ranking		Total Pitcher Index		Total Baseball Ranking	
Paul-Tex	128	Lyle-NY	13.7	Knowles-Oak	11.2	Lyle-NY	20.3	Perry-Cle	7.2	Perry-Cle	7.2
Odom-Oak	123	Knowles-Oak	12.4	Forster-Chi	11.0	Forster-Chi	18.1	Wood-Chi	3.8	Fisk-Bos	5.9
Wilcox-Cle	119	Bell-Mil	11.1	Lyle-NY	10.7	Knowles-Oak	13.4	Palmer-Bal	3.6	Murcer-NY	5.1
Lonborg-Mil	112	Forster-Chi	9.0	Bell-Mil	10.4	Seelbach-Det	11.2	Lolich-Det	3.6	Allen-Chi	5.1
Lolich-Det	111	Abernathy-KC	8.7	Abernathy-KC	8.7	Abernathy-KC	11.1	Hunter-Oak	3.3	Wood-Chi	3.8

TEAM	G	W	L	PCT	GB	R	OR	AB	H	2B	3B	HR	BB	SO	AVG	OBP	SLG	PRO	/A	BR	/A	PF	CHI	RC	TA	SB	CS	SBA	SBR
EAST																													
NY	161	82	79	.509		608	588	5457	1345	198	24	85	540	805	.246	.317	.338	.655	88	-80	-83	101	103	583	.569	27	22	55	-4
STL	162	81	81	.500	1.5	643	603	5478	1418	240	35	75	531	796	.259	.328	.357	.685	96	-23	39	91	99	635	.614	100	46	68	2
PIT	162	80	82	.494	2.5	704	693	5608	1465	**257**	44	154	432	842	.261	.317	.405	.722	106	30	84	92	100	697	.640	23	30	43	-10
MON	162	79	83	.488	3.5	668	702	5369	1345	190	23	125	**695**	**777**	.251	**.341**	.364	.705	102	30	2	104	94	672	.654	77	68	53	-17
CHI	161	77	84	.478	5	614	655	5363	1322	201	21	117	575	855	.247	.322	.357	.679	94	-34	-88	108	98	605	.607	65	58	53	-14
PHI	162	71	91	.438	11.5	642	717	5546	1381	218	29	134	476	979	.249	.312	.371	.683	95	-39	-91	108	102	641	.609	51	47	52	-12
WEST																													
CIN	162	99	63	.611		741	621	5505	1398	232	34	137	639	947	.254	.335	.383	.718	105	43	**90**	93	101	724	.684	**148**	55	**73**	**11**
LA	162	95	66	.590	3.5	675	**565**	5604	1473	219	29	110	497	795	.263	.326	.371	.697	99	-4	-6	100	99	676	.631	109	50	69	3
SF	162	88	74	.543	11	739	702	5537	1452	212	**52**	161	590	913	.262	.337	.407	.744	112	87	54	105	96	765	.703	112	52	68	2
HOU	162	82	80	.506	17	681	672	5532	1391	216	35	134	469	962	.251	.314	.376	.690	97	-27	7	95	**106**	639	.618	92	48	66	0
ATL	162	76	85	.472	22.5	**799**	774	5631	**1497**	219	34	**206**	608	870	**.266**	**.341**	**.427**	**.768**	**119**	**134**	44	113	96	**826**	**.730**	84	40	68	1
SD	162	60	102	.370	39	548	770	5457	1330	198	26	112	401	966	.244	.298	.351	.649	85	-109	-70	94	101	566	.567	88	36	71	5
TOT	971					8062		66087	16817	2600	386	1550	6453	10507	.254	.324	.376	.700								976	552	64	-37

TEAM	CG	SHO	SV	IP	H	H/G	HR	BB	BB/G	SO	SO/G	ERA	/A	OAVG	OOBA	PR	/A	PF	CPI	FA	E	DP	FW	PW	BW	SBW	DIF
EAST																											
NY	47	15	40	1465.0	1345	8.3	127	490	3.0	**1027**	**6.3**	3.26	112	.244	.303	64	66	100	101	.980	126	140	1.1	6.9	-8.6	-.0	2.3
STL	42	14	36	1460.7	1366	8.4	**105**	486	3.0	867	5.3	3.25	101	.247	.306	66	6	90	100	.975	159	149	-.8	.6	4.1	.5	-4.5
PIT	26	11	**44**	1450.7	1426	8.8	110	564	3.5	839	5.2	3.73	90	.258	.325	-11	-60	92	100	.976	151	156	-.3	-6.2	8.7	-.7	-2.5
MON	26	6	38	1451.7	1356	8.4	128	681	4.2	866	5.4	3.71	103	.249	.329	-8	18	105	103	.974	163	156	-1.0	1.9	.2	-1.4	-1.6
CHI	27	13	40	1437.7	1471	9.2	128	**438**	**2.7**	885	5.5	3.66	109	.267	.318	0	52	109	104	.975	157	155	-.7	5.4	-9.2	-1.1	2.0
PHI	**49**	11	22	1447.3	1435	8.9	131	632	3.9	919	5.7	3.99	100	.263	.336	-53	-1	109	103	.979	134	**179**	.6	-.1	-9.5	-.9	-.2
WEST																											
CIN	39	**17**	43	1473.0	1389	8.5	135	518	3.2	801	4.9	3.40	99	.251	.312	42	-8	92	**105**	**.982**	**115**	162	**1.7**	-.8	**9.4**	**1.5**	6.3
LA	45	15	38	1491.0	**1270**	**7.7**	129	461	2.8	961	5.8	**3.00**	**121**	**.230**	**.288**	**109**	**102**	99	97	.981	125	166	1.2	**10.6**	-.6	.6	2.7
SF	33	8	**44**	1452.3	1442	8.9	145	485	3.0	787	4.9	3.79	101	.257	.314	-21	4	104	97	.974	163	138	-1.0	.4	5.6	.5	1.4
HOU	45	14	26	1460.7	1389	8.6	111	575	3.5	907	5.6	3.75	93	.251	.319	-13	-44	95	95	.981	116	140	**1.7**	-4.6	.7	.3	2.9
ATL	34	9	35	1462.0	1467	9.0	144	575	3.5	803	4.9	4.25	97	.263	.328	-95	-19	113	95	.974	166	142	-1.2	-2.0	4.6	.4	-6.4
SD	34	10	23	1430.0	1461	9.2	157	548	3.4	845	5.3	4.16	85	.266	.328	-79	-97	97	100	.973	170	152	-1.4	-10.1	-7.3	.9	-3.1
TOT	447	143	429	17482.0		8.7			3.3		5.4	3.66		.254	.324					.977	1745	1835					

Runs
Bonds-SF 131
Morgan-Cin 116
Rose-Cin 115
Evans-Atl 114
Brock-StL 110

Hits
Rose-Cin 230
Garr-Atl 200
Brock-StL 193
Simmons-StL 192
Oliver-Pit 191

Doubles
Stargell-Pit 43
Oliver-Pit 38
Staub-NY 36
Simmons-StL 36
Rose-Cin 36

Triples
Metzger-Hou 14
Matthews-SF 10
Maddox-SF 10
Davis-LA 9

Home Runs
Stargell-Pit 44
Johnson-Atl 43
Evans-Atl 41
Aaron-Atl 40
Bonds-SF 39

Total Bases
Bonds-SF 341
Stargell-Pit 337
Evans-Atl 331
Johnson-Atl 305
Oliver-Pit 303

Runs Batted In
Stargell-Pit 119
May-Hou 105
Evans-Atl 104
Bench-Cin 104
Singleton-Mon 103

Runs Produced
Bonds-SF 188
Stargell-Pit 181
Singleton-Mon 180
Baker-Atl 179
Evans-Atl 177

Bases On Balls
Evans-Atl 124
Singleton-Mon 123
Morgan-Cin 111
McCovey-SF 105
Monday-Chi 92

Batting Average
Rose-Cin .... .338
Cedeno-Hou .... .320
Maddox-SF .... .319
Perez-Cin .... .314
Watson-Hou .... .312

On Base Percentage
Singleton-Mon .... .429
Fairly-Mon .... .422
Morgan-Cin .... .408
Evans-Atl .... .407
Watson-Hou .... .405

Slugging Average
Stargell-Pit .... .646
Evans-Atl .... .556
Johnson-Atl .... .546
Cedeno-Hou .... .537
Bonds-SF .... .530

Production
Stargell-Pit 1.041
Evans-Atl .... .964
Perez-Cin .... .923
Johnson-Atl .... .917
Cedeno-Hou .... .914

Adjusted Production
Stargell-Pit 200
Perez-Cin 165
Morgan-Cin 160
Cedeno-Hou 159
Evans-Atl 146

Batter Runs
Stargell-Pit 57.8
Evans-Atl 54.8
Aaron-Atl 45.5
Singleton-Mon 44.8
Morgan-Cin 41.6

Adjusted Batter Runs
Stargell-Pit 63.1
Morgan-Cin 46.8
Perez-Cin 46.1
Evans-Atl 44.5
Singleton-Mon 41.8

Clutch Hitting Index
Bench-Cin 141
Cey-LA 137
Watson-Hou 131
Singleton-Mon 130
Speier-SF 129

Runs Created
Evans-Atl 143
Stargell-Pit 136
Bonds-SF 130
Morgan-Cin 128
Rose-Cin 119

Total Average
Stargell-Pit 1.129
Morgan-Cin 1.069
Evans-Atl 1.055
Cedeno-Hou .... .987
Bonds-SF .... .977

Stolen Bases
Brock-StL 70
Morgan-Cin 67
Cedeno-Hou 56
Bonds-SF 43
Lopes-LA 36

Stolen Base Average
Baker-Atl 88.9
Morgan-Cin 81.7
Concepcion-Cin 81.5
Cedeno-Hou 78.9
Brock-StL 77.8

Stolen Base Runs
Morgan-Cin 11.1
Brock-StL 9.0
Cedeno-Hou 7.8
Baker-Atl 5.4
Garr-Atl 3.9

Fielding Runs
Cey-LA 21.6
Simmons-StL 20.0
Kessinger-Chi 17.8
Boone-Phi 16.9
Foli-Mon 15.0

Total Player Rating
Morgan-Cin 6.2
Stargell-Pit 5.8
Simmons-StL 5.7
Cedeno-Hou 5.0
Evans-Atl 4.8

Wins
Bryant-SF 24
Seaver-NY 19
Billingham-Cin 19
Sutton-LA 18
Gullett-Cin 18

Win Percentage
John-LA .... .696
Gullett-Cin .... .692
Bryant-SF .... .667
Seaver-NY .... .655
Billingham-Cin .... .655

Games
Marshall-Mon 92
Borbon-Cin 80
Sosa-SF 71
Giusti-Pit 67
Segui-StL 65

Complete Games
Seaver-NY 18
Carlton-Phi 18
Billingham-Cin 16

Shutouts
Billingham-Cin 7
Roberts-Hou 6
Wise-StL 5
Twitchell-Phi 5

Saves
Marshall-Mon 31
McGraw-NY 25
Giusti-Pit 20
Brewer-LA 20

Innings Pitched
Carlton-Phi 293
Billingham-Cin 293
Seaver-NY 290
Reuss-Hou 279
Jenkins-Chi 271

Fewest Hits/Game
Seaver-NY 6.80
Sutton-LA 6.89
Twitchell-Phi 6.94
Wilson-Hou 7.04
Messersmith-LA 7.06

Fewest BB/Game
Marichal-SF 1.61
Jenkins-Chi 1.89
Barr-SF 1.91
Sutton-LA 1.97
Seaver-NY 1.99

Strikeouts
Seaver-NY 251
Carlton-Phi 223
Matlack-NY 205
Sutton-LA 200

Strikeouts/Game
Seaver-NY 7.79
Moore-Mon 7.72
Matlack-NY 7.62
Sutton-LA 7.03
Carlton-Phi 6.85

Wins Above Team
Bryant-SF 5.8
Seaver-NY 4.9
Stone-NY 4.6
Giusti-Pit 3.6
Morton-Atl 3.4

Earned Run Average
Seaver-NY 2.08
Sutton-LA 2.43
Twitchell-Phi 2.50
Marshall-Mon 2.66
Messersmith-LA 2.70

Adjusted ERA
Seaver-NY 176
Twitchell-Phi 159
Sutton-LA 149
Marshall-Mon 144
Renko-Mon 136

Opponents' Batting Avg.
Seaver-NY .... .206
Sutton-LA .... .209
Wilson-Hou .... .211
Messersmith-LA .... .214
Renko-Mon .... .218

Opponents' On Base Pct.
Seaver-NY .... .250
Sutton-LA .... .255
Messersmith-LA .... .275
Gibson-StL .... .277
Briles-Pit .... .283

Starter Runs
Seaver-NY 51.0
Sutton-LA 35.1
Rogers-Mon 31.5
Twitchell-Phi 28.7
Messersmith-LA 26.7

Adjusted Starter Runs
Seaver-NY 51.2
Twitchell-Phi 36.7
Sutton-LA 34.0
Rogers-Mon 34.0
Renko-Mon 28.3

Clutch Pitching Index
Marshall-Mon 134
Roberts-Hou 122
Twitchell-Phi 121
Grimsley-Cin 116
Moose-Pit 113

Relief Runs
Borbon-Cin 20.2
Marshall-Mon 19.8
Giusti-Pit 14.3
Moffitt-SF 13.7
Locker-Chi 13.1

Adjusted Relief Runs
Marshall-Mon 23.1
Locker-Chi 16.9
Borbon-Cin 16.1
Moffitt-SF 15.4
Scarce-Phi 12.4

Relief Ranking
Marshall-Mon 38.0
Locker-Chi 29.4
Borbon-Cin 22.1
Scarce-Phi 18.9
Moffitt-SF 16.0

Total Pitcher Index
Seaver-NY 6.2
Rogers-Mon 4.1
Renko-Mon 3.9
Sutton-LA 3.5
Twitchell-Phi 3.3

Total Baseball Ranking
Seaver-NY 6.2
Morgan-Cin 6.2
Stargell-Pit 5.8
Simmons-StL 5.7
Cedeno-Hou 5.0

TEAM	G	W	L	PCT	GB	R	OR	AB	H	2B	3B	HR	BB	SO	AVG	OBP	SLG	PRO	/A	BR	/A	PF	CHI	RC	TA	SB	CS	SBA	SBR
EAST																													
BAL	162	97	65	.599		754	**561**	5537	1474	229	48	119	648	752	.266	**.348**	.389	.737	107	61	9	107	98	**765**	.704	**146**	64	70	5
BOS	162	89	73	.549	8	738	647	5513	1472	235	30	147	581	799	.267	.340	**.401**	**.741**	**108**	58	16	106	97	751	.694	114	45	**72**	7
DET	162	85	77	.525	12	642	674	5508	1400	213	32	157	509	722	.254	.322	.390	.712	100	-8	-14	101	94	674	.636	28	30	48	-9
NY	162	80	82	.494	17	641	610	5492	1435	212	17	131	489	**680**	.261	.324	.378	.702	97	-24	-28	101	98	655	.620	47	43	52	-11
MIL	162	74	88	.457	23	708	731	5526	1399	229	40	145	563	793	.253	.327	.388	.715	101	2	30	96	101	702	.664	110	66	63	-6
CLE	162	71	91	.438	26	680	826	5592	1429	205	29	**158**	471	793	.256	.317	.387	.704	97	-26	-6	97	102	666	.626	60	68	47	-22
WEST																													
OAK	162	94	68	.580		**758**	615	5507	1431	216	28	147	595	919	.260	.336	.389	.725	104	28	**118**	87	**104**	730	.683	128	57	69	4
KC	162	88	74	.543	6	755	752	5508	1440	239	40	114	644	696	.261	.342	.381	.723	103	31	-32	109	103	720	.673	105	69	60	-9
MIN	162	81	81	.500	13	738	692	5625	**1521**	240	44	120	598	954	**.270**	.344	.393	.737	107	56	29	104	96	756	.681	87	46	65	-1
CAL	162	79	83	.488	15	629	657	5505	1395	183	29	93	509	816	.253	.320	.348	.668	88	-83	-55	96	**104**	609	.587	59	47	56	-10
CHI	162	77	85	.475	17	652	705	5475	1400	228	38	111	537	952	.256	.326	.372	.698	96	-27	-42	102	99	647	.626	83	73	53	-18
TEX	162	57	105	.352	37	619	844	5488	1397	195	29	110	503	791	.255	.320	.361	.681	91	-62	-42	97	99	629	.608	91	53	63	-4
TOT	972					8314		66276	17193	2624	404	1552	6647	9851	.259	.331	.381	.712								1058	661	62	-78

TEAM	CG	SHO	SV	IP	H	H/G	HR	BB	BB/G	SO	SO/G	ERA	/A	OAVG	OOBA	PR	/A	PF	CPI	FA	E	DP	FW	PW	BW	SBW	DIF
EAST																											
BAL	67	14	26	1461.7	**1297**	8.0	124	475	**2.9**	715	4.4	**3.07**	131	**.239**	**.299**	121	152	105	102	.981	119	184	1.3	**15.5**	.9	1.2	-2.9
BOS	67	10	33	1440.3	1417	8.9	158	499	3.1	808	5.0	3.65	110	.259	.319	26	55	105	**106**	.979	127	162	.8	5.6	1.6	**1.4**	-1.5
DET	39	11	**46**	1447.7	1468	9.1	154	493	3.1	911	5.7	3.90	99	.264	.323	-13	-5	101	101	**.982**	112	144	**1.7**	-.5	-1.4	-.2	4.5
NY	47	16	19	1427.7	1379	8.7	109	**457**	2.9	708	4.5	3.34	114	.254	.310	75	76	100	100	.978	156	172	-.8	7.8	-2.9	-.5	-4.7
MIL	50	11	28	1454.0	1476	9.1	119	623	3.8	671	4.2	3.98	92	.264	.337	-26	-50	96	101	.977	145	167	-.2	-5.1	3.1	.0	-4.8
CLE	55	9	21	1464.7	1532	9.4	172	602	3.7	883	5.4	4.58	82	.270	.340	-124	-131	99	96	.978	139	174	.2	-13.4	-.6	-1.6	5.4
WEST																											
OAK	46	16	41	1457.3	1311	8.1	143	494	3.1	797	4.9	3.29	99	.240	.303	85	-3	86	100	.978	137	170	.3	-.3	**12.1**	1.1	-.1
KC	40	7	41	1449.3	1521	9.4	114	617	3.8	790	4.9	4.19	99	.272	.343	-60	-4	109	100	.974	167	**192**	-1.4	-.4	-3.3	-.2	12.3
MIN	48	**18**	34	1451.7	1443	8.9	115	519	3.2	879	5.4	3.77	104	.254	.321	7	26	103	97	.978	139	147	.2	2.7	3.0	.6	-6.4
CAL	**72**	13	19	1456.3	1351	8.3	104	614	3.8	**1010**	**6.2**	3.53	104	.245	.320	46	23	96	98	.975	156	153	-.8	2.4	-5.6	-.3	2.4
CHI	48	15	35	1456.0	1484	9.2	110	574	3.5	848	5.2	3.86	102	.265	.333	-7	10	103	101	.977	144	165	-.1	1.0	-4.3	-1.2	.6
TEX	35	10	27	1430.0	1514	9.5	130	680	4.3	831	5.2	4.64	82	.273	.351	-130	-132	100	96	.974	161	164	-1.1	-13.5	-4.3	.3	-5.4
TOT	614	150	390	17396.7		8.9			3.4		5.1	3.82		.259	.331					.977	1702	1994					

Runs		Hits		Doubles		Triples		Home Runs		Total Bases	
Jackson-Oak	99	Carew-Min	203	Garcia-Mil	32	Carew-Min	11	Jackson-Oak	32	Scott-Mil	295
Scott-Mil	98	May-Mil	189	Bando-Oak	32	Bumbry-Bal	11	Robinson-Cal	30	May-Mil	295
North-Oak	98	Murcer-NY	187	Scott-Mil	30	Orta-Chi	10	Burroughs-Tex	30	Bando-Oak	295
Carew-Min	98	Scott-Mil	185	Chambliss-Cle	30	Coggins-Bal	9	Bando-Oak	29	Murcer-NY	286
Bando-Oak	97	Johnson-Tex	179	Carew-Min	30	Coluccio-Mil	8			Jackson-Oak	286

Runs Batted In		Runs Produced		Bases On Balls		Batting Average		On Base Percentage		Slugging Average	
Jackson-Oak	117	Jackson-Oak	184	Mayberry-KC	122	Carew-Min	.350	Mayberry-KC	.420	Jackson-Oak	.531
Scott-Mil	107	Scott-Mil	181	Grich-Bal	107	Scott-Mil	.306	Carew-Min	.415	Bando-Oak	.498
Mayberry-KC	100	Bando-Oak	166	Yastrzemski-Bos	105	Davis-Bal	.306	Yastrzemski-Bos	.411	Robinson-Cal	.489
Bando-Oak	98	May-Mil	164	Tenace-Oak	101	Murcer-NY	.304	Tenace-Oak	.391	Scott-Mil	.488
Robinson-Cal	97	Mayberry-KC	161	Briggs-Mil	87	May-Mil	.303	Jackson-Oak	.387	Munson-NY	.487

Production		Adjusted Production		Batter Runs		Adjusted Batter Runs		Clutch Hitting Index		Runs Created	
Jackson-Oak	.918	Jackson-Oak	179	Mayberry-KC	41.0	Jackson-Oak	49.6	Davis-Bal	156	Bando-Oak	113
Mayberry-KC	.898	Bando-Oak	166	Jackson-Oak	40.5	Bando-Oak	45.4	May-Chi	139	Carew-Min	113
Carew-Min	.885	Tenace-Oak	154	Carew-Min	38.9	Tenace-Oak	36.4	Darwin-Min	137	Mayberry-KC	113
Bando-Oak	.876	Robinson-Cal	147	Yastrzemski-Bos	36.8	Carew-Min	36.1	Oliva-Min	136	Jackson-Oak	112
Yastrzemski-Bos	.874	Scott-Mil	147	Bando-Oak	35.5	Scott-Mil	34.6	Robinson-Bal	134	Scott-Mil	106

Total Average		Stolen Bases		Stolen Base Average		Stolen Base Runs		Fielding Runs		Total Player Rating	
Mayberry-KC	.995	Harper-Bos	54	Rojas-KC	81.8	Harper-Bos	7.8	Patek-KC	34.5	Carew-Min	5.9
Jackson-Oak	.973	North-Oak	53	Money-Mil	81.5	Campaneris-Oak	4.2	Nettles-NY	26.0	Jackson-Oak	4.7
Carew-Min	.924	Nelson-Tex	43	Harper-Bos	79.4	Baylor-Bal	4.2	Bell-Cle	23.9	Munson-NY	4.6
Yastrzemski-Bos	.897	Carew-Min	41	Baylor-Bal	78.0	North-Oak	3.9	Grich-Bal	22.0	Grich-Bal	3.8
Bando-Oak	.881	Patek-KC	36	Campaneris-Oak	77.3	Money-Mil	3.6	Munson-NY	20.6	Patek-KC	3.6

Wins		Win Percentage		Games		Complete Games		Shutouts		Saves	
Wood-Chi	24	Hunter-Oak	.808	Hiller-Det	65	Perry-Cle	29	Blyleven-Min	9	Hiller-Det	38
Coleman-Det	23	Palmer-Bal	.710	Fingers-Oak	62	Ryan-Cal	26	Perry-Cle	7	Lyle-NY	27
Palmer-Bal	22	Blue-Oak	.690	Bird-KC	54	Blyleven-Min	25	Palmer-Bal	6	Fingers-Oak	22
		Splittorff-KC	.645	Knowles-Oak	52	Tiant-Bos	23			Bird-KC	20
		Colborn-Mil	.625			Colborn-Mil	22			Acosta-Chi	18

Innings Pitched		Fewest Hits/Game		Fewest BB/Game		Strikeouts		Strikeouts/Game		Wins Above Team	
Wood-Chi	359	Bibby-Tex	6.05	Kaat-Min-Chi	1.72	Ryan-Cal	383	Ryan-Cal	10.57	Hunter-Oak	7.6
Perry-Cle	344	Ryan-Cal	6.57	Blyleven-Min	1.86	Blyleven-Min	258	Bibby-Tex	7.75	Colborn-Mil	5.7
Ryan-Cal	326	Palmer-Bal	6.84	Holtzman-Oak	2.00	Singer-Cal	241	Blyleven-Min	7.14	Moret-Bos	5.4
Blyleven-Min	325	Tiant-Bos	7.18	Wood-Chi	2.28	Perry-Cle	238	Stone-Chi	7.06	Palmer-Bal	5.0
Singer-Cal	316	Blue-Oak	7.30	Lolich-Det	2.30	Lolich-Det	214	Singer-Cal	6.86	Blue-Oak	4.4

Earned Run Average		Adjusted ERA		Opponents' Batting Avg.		Opponents' On Base Pct.		Starter Runs		Adjusted Starter Runs	
Palmer-Bal	2.40	Palmer-Bal	167	Bibby-Tex	.192	Tiant-Bos	.276	Blyleven-Min	46.8	Palmer-Bal	52.8
Blyleven-Min	2.52	Blyleven-Min	156	Ryan-Cal	.203	Hunter-Oak	.281	Palmer-Bal	46.5	Blyleven-Min	51.1
Lee-Bos	2.75	Lee-Bos	146	Palmer-Bal	.211	Blyleven-Min	.282	Ryan-Cal	34.2	Lee-Bos	39.6
Ryan-Cal	2.87	Medich-NY	130	Tiant-Bos	.219	Holtzman-Oak	.285	Lee-Bos	33.8	Ryan-Cal	29.1
Medich-NY	2.95	Ryan-Cal	128	Blue-Oak	.224	Palmer-Bal	.287	Holtzman-Oak	27.9	McNally-Bal	23.4

Clutch Pitching Index		Relief Runs		Adjusted Relief Runs		Relief Ranking		Total Pitcher Index		Total Baseball Ranking	
Lee-Bos	120	Hiller-Det	33.0	Hiller-Det	33.7	Hiller-Det	59.4	Palmer-Bal	5.7	Carew-Min	5.9
Forster-Chi	117	Fingers-Oak	26.8	Reynolds-Bal	25.4	Acosta-Chi	34.9	Blyleven-Min	5.5	Palmer-Bal	5.7
Drago-KC	112	Reynolds-Bal	23.1	Fingers-Oak	19.0	Reynolds-Bal	29.4	Lee-Bos	4.5	Blyleven-Min	5.5
Curtis-Bos	112	Acosta-Chi	17.1	Jackson-Bal	18.6	Fingers-Oak	27.7	Hiller-Det	3.6	Jackson-Oak	4.7
Bahnsen-Chi	112	Jackson-Bal	16.9	Acosta-Chi	18.4	Lyle-NY	27.0	Ryan-Cal	2.9	Munson-NY	4.6

TEAM	G	W	L	PCT	GB	R	OR	AB	H	2B	3B	HR	BB	SO	AVG	OBP	SLG	PRO	/A	BR	/A	PF	CHI	RC	TA	SB	CS	SBA	SBR
EAST																													
PIT	162	88	74	.543		751	657	5702	**1560**	238	46	114	514	828	**.274**	.338	.391	.729	110	66	82	98	99	745	.658	55	31	64	-1
STL	161	86	75	.534	1.5	677	643	5620	1492	216	46	83	531	752	.265	.334	.365	.699	101	9	-14	104	98	687	.645	**172**	62	74	**14**
PHI	162	80	82	.494	8	676	701	5494	1434	233	**50**	95	469	822	.261	.322	.373	.695	100	-6	-27	103	**103**	658	.629	115	58	66	0
MON	161	79	82	.491	8.5	662	657	5343	1355	201	29	86	652	812	.254	.338	.350	.688	98	1	-28	104	99	657	.644	124	49	72	8
NY	162	71	91	.438	17	572	646	5468	1286	183	22	96	597	**735**	.235	.314	.329	.643	85	-98	-93	99	99	571	.567	43	23	65	0
CHI	162	66	96	.407	22	669	826	5574	1397	221	42	110	621	857	.251	.329	.365	.694	100	0	0	100	97	668	.631	78	73	52	-19
WEST																													
LA	162	102	60	.630		**798**	**561**	5557	1511	231	34	**139**	597	820	.272	**.346**	**.401**	**.747**	**115**	**103**	**152**	93	101	774	.708	149	75	67	0
CIN	163	98	64	.605	4	776	631	5535	1437	**271**	35	135	**693**	940	.260	.345	.394	.739	112	95	108	98	99	**776**	**.715**	146	49	**75**	**14**
ATL	163	88	74	.543	14	661	563	5533	1375	202	37	120	571	772	.249	.321	.363	.684	97	-22	-53	105	101	649	.619	72	44	62	-4
HOU	162	81	81	.500	21	653	632	5489	1441	222	41	110	471	864	.263	.324	.378	.702	102	5	18	98	98	663	.633	108	65	62	-6
SF	162	72	90	.444	30	634	723	5482	1380	228	38	93	548	869	.252	.323	.358	.681	96	-27	-78	108	99	642	.621	107	51	68	2
SD	162	60	102	.370	42	541	830	5415	1239	196	27	99	564	900	.229	.304	.330	.634	83	-122	-77	93	100	555	.567	85	45	65	-1
TOT	972					8070		66212	16907	2642	447	1280	6828	9971	.255	.328	.367	.695								1254	625	67	1

TEAM	CG	SHO	SV	IP	H	H/G	HR	BB	BB/G	SO	SO/G	ERA	/A	OAVG	OOBA	PR	/A	PF	CPI	FA	E	DP	FW	PW	BW	SBW	DIF
EAST																											
PIT	**51**	9	17	1466.0	1428	8.8	93	543	3.3	721	4.4	3.49	100	.256	.319	21	0	97	100	.975	162	154	-.5	.0	8.5	-.1	-1.0
STL	37	13	20	1473.3	1399	8.5	97	616	3.8	794	4.9	3.48	107	.253	.324	22	40	103	**104**	.977	147	**192**	.4	4.2	-1.5	**1.4**	.9
PHI	46	4	19	1447.3	1394	8.7	111	682	4.2	892	5.5	3.91	96	.257	.336	-47	-26	104	101	.976	148	168	.4	-2.7	-2.8	-.0	4.2
MON	35	8	**27**	1429.0	1340	8.4	99	544	3.4	822	5.2	3.60	105	.248	.316	3	28	104	94	.976	153	157	.0	2.9	-2.9	.8	-2.4
NY	46	15	14	1470.3	1433	8.8	99	504	3.1	908	5.6	3.42	106	.257	.315	32	35	100	102	.975	158	150	-.2	3.6	-9.7	-.0	-3.7
CHI	23	6	26	1466.3	1593	9.8	122	576	3.5	895	5.5	4.28	86	.277	.338	-107	-95	102	100	.969	199	141	-2.6	-9.9	.0	-2.0	-.5
WEST																											
LA	33	19	23	1465.3	**1272**	**7.8**	112	**464**	**2.8**	**943**	**5.8**	**2.97**	109	**.232**	**.290**	**104**	44	90	96	.975	157	122	-.2	4.6	**15.8**	-.0	.8
CIN	34	11	**27**	1466.3	1364	8.4	126	536	3.3	875	5.4	3.41	102	.247	.309	33	10	96	100	.979	134	151	1.2	1.0	11.2	**1.4**	2.1
ATL	46	**21**	22	1474.3	1343	8.2	97	488	3.0	772	4.7	3.05	**123**	.244	.302	92	**113**	104	102	.979	132	161	1.3	**11.8**	-5.5	-.4	-.1
HOU	36	18	18	1450.7	1396	8.7	**84**	601	3.7	738	4.6	3.46	102	.255	.326	25	11	98	**104**	**.982**	**113**	161	**2.4**	1.1	1.9	-.6	-4.8
SF	27	11	25	1439.0	1409	8.8	116	559	3.5	756	4.7	3.78	104	.256	.320	-25	25	109	97	.972	175	153	-1.2	2.6	-8.1	.2	-2.5
SD	25	7	19	1445.7	1536	9.6	124	715	4.5	855	5.3	4.58	76	.274	.353	-154	-173	97	99	.973	170	126	-.9	-18.0	-8.0	-.1	6.1
TOT	439	142	257	17493.7		8.7			3.5		5.1	3.62		.255	.328					.976	1848	1836					

Runs
Rose-Cin 110
Schmidt-Phi 108
Bench-Cin 108
Morgan-Cin 107
Brock-StL 105

Hits
Garr-Atl 214
Cash-Phi 206
Garvey-LA 200
Oliver-Pit 198
Stennett-Pit 196

Doubles
Rose-Cin 45
Oliver-Pit 38
Bench-Cin 38
Stargell-Pit 37

Triples
Garr-Atl 17
Oliver-Pit 12
Cash-Phi 11
Metzger-Hou 10
Bowa-Phi 10

Home Runs
Schmidt-Phi 36
Bench-Cin 33
Wynn-LA 32
Perez-Cin 28
Cedeno-Hou 26

Total Bases
Bench-Cin 315
Schmidt-Phi 310
Garr-Atl 305
Garvey-LA 301
Oliver-Pit 293

Runs Batted In
Bench-Cin 129
Schmidt-Phi 116
Garvey-LA 111
Wynn-LA 108
Simmons-StL 103

Runs Produced
Bench-Cin 204
Schmidt-Phi 188
Garvey-LA 185
Wynn-LA 180
Cedeno-Hou 171

Bases On Balls
Evans-Atl 126
Morgan-Cin 120
Wynn-LA 108
Schmidt-Phi 106
Rose-Cin 106

Batting Average
Garr-Atl .... .353
Oliver-Pit .... .321
Gross-Hou .... .314
Buckner-LA .... .314
Madlock-Chi .... .313

On Base Percentage
Morgan-Cin .... .430
Stargell-Pit .... .409
Bailey-Mon .... .400
Schmidt-Phi .... .398
Smith-StL .... .394

Slugging Average
Schmidt-Phi .... .546
Stargell-Pit .... .537
Smith-StL .... .528
Bench-Cin .... .507
Garr-Atl .... .503

Production
Stargell-Pit .... .947
Schmidt-Phi .... .944
Morgan-Cin .... .924
Smith-StL .... .922
Wynn-LA .... .891

Adjusted Production
Stargell-Pit 167
Morgan-Cin 161
Wynn-LA 160
Schmidt-Phi 157
Smith-StL 151

Batter Runs
Schmidt-Phi 48.3
Morgan-Cin 45.1
Stargell-Pit 44.4
Smith-StL 38.5
Wynn-LA 36.3

Adjusted Batter Runs
Morgan-Cin 46.5
Stargell-Pit 45.9
Schmidt-Phi 45.9
Wynn-LA 41.5
Smith-StL 36.2

Clutch Hitting Index
Cey-LA 140
Singleton-Mon 133
Montanez-Phi 131
Zisk-Pit 129
Simmons-StL 128

Runs Created
Schmidt-Phi 130
Morgan-Cin 125
Stargell-Pit 115
Bench-Cin 114
Garr-Atl 113

Total Average
Morgan-Cin 1.139
Schmidt-Phi 1.045
Stargell-Pit 1.003
Wynn-LA .... .951
Smith-StL .... .928

Stolen Bases
Brock-StL 118
Lopes-LA 59
Morgan-Cin 58
Cedeno-Hou 57
Lintz-Mon 50

Stolen Base Average
Lintz-Mon 87.7
Concepcion-Cin 87.2
Morgan-Cin 82.9
Bonds-SF 78.8
Hernandez-SD 78.7

Stolen Base Runs
Brock-StL 15.6
Lintz-Mon 10.8
Morgan-Cin 10.2
Concepcion-Cin 8.7

Fielding Runs
Cash-Phi 29.9
Schmidt-Phi 26.1
Harrelson-NY 17.5
Foli-Mon 17.5
Cey-LA 17.2

Total Player Rating
Schmidt-Phi 7.0
Morgan-Cin 5.9
Concepcion-Cin 4.4
Cash-Phi 4.2
Stargell-Pit 3.8

Wins
Niekro-Atl 20
Messersmith-LA 20
Sutton-LA 19
Billingham-Cin 19

Win Percentage
Messersmith-LA .... .769
Sutton-LA .... .679
Capra-Atl .... .667
Torrez-Mon .... .652
Billingham-Cin .... .633

Games
Marshall-LA 106
Hardy-SD 76
Borbon-Cin 73
Forsch-Hou 70
Sosa-SF 68

Complete Games
Niekro-Atl 18
Carlton-Phi 17
Lonborg-Phi 16
Rooker-Pit 15

Shutouts
Matlack-NY 7
Niekro-Atl 6

Saves
Marshall-LA 21
Moffitt-SF 15
Borbon-Cin 14
Giusti-Pit 12

Innings Pitched
Niekro-Atl 302
Messersmith-LA 292
Carlton-Phi 291
Lonborg-Phi 283
Sutton-LA 276

Fewest Hits/Game
Capra-Atl 6.76
Messersmith-LA 7.00
Niekro-Atl 7.42
Gullett-Cin 7.44
Wilson-Hou 7.46

Fewest BB/Game
Barr-SF 1.76
Reed-Atl 1.98
Ellis-Pit 2.08
Lonborg-Phi 2.23
Marshall-LA 2.42

Strikeouts
Carlton-Phi 240
Messersmith-LA 221
Seaver-NY 201
Niekro-Atl 195
Matlack-NY 195

Strikeouts/Game
Seaver-NY 7.67
Carlton-Phi 7.42
Bonham-Chi 7.07
D'Acquisto-SF 6.99
Norman-Cin 6.82

Wins Above Team
Messersmith-LA 5.4
Caldwell-SF 5.3
John-LA 4.2
Torrez-Mon 4.0
Koosman-NY 3.7

Earned Run Average
Capra-Atl 2.28
Niekro-Atl 2.38
Matlack-NY 2.41
Marshall-LA 2.42
Messersmith-LA 2.59

Adjusted ERA
Capra-Atl 164
Niekro-Atl 157
Matlack-NY 151
Barr-SF 144
McGlothen-StL 138

Opponents' Batting Avg.
Capra-Atl .... .208
Messersmith-LA .... .212
Gullett-Cin .... .222
Niekro-Atl .... .225
Matlack-NY .... .226

Opponents' On Base Pct.
Messersmith-LA .... .275
Matlack-NY .... .281
Niekro-Atl .... .281
Capra-Atl .... .282
Reed-Atl .... .283

Starter Runs
Niekro-Atl 41.4
Matlack-NY 35.5
Messersmith-LA 33.4
Capra-Atl 32.2
Rooker-Pit 24.7

Adjusted Starter Runs
Niekro-Atl 45.6
Matlack-NY 35.9
Capra-Atl 35.3
Barr-SF 32.0
McGlothen-StL 27.2

Clutch Pitching Index
Morton-Atl 117
Caldwell-SF 117
Marshall-LA 116
Schueler-Phi 113
McGlothen-StL 112

Relief Runs
Marshall-LA 27.6
Murray-Mon 20.1
House-Atl 19.4
Taylor-Mon 17.4
Carroll-Cin 16.6

Adjusted Relief Runs
Murray-Mon 21.4
House-Atl 20.8
Taylor-Mon 19.3
Marshall-LA 19.1
Carroll-Cin 15.1

Relief Ranking
Marshall-LA 26.6
Carroll-Cin 24.8
House-Atl 19.6
Taylor-Mon 17.3
Leon-Atl 13.0

Total Pitcher Index
Niekro-Atl 5.2
Barr-SF 4.1
Capra-Atl 3.6
Matlack-NY 3.5
Rooker-Pit 3.5

Total Baseball Ranking
Schmidt-Phi 7.0
Morgan-Cin 5.9
Niekro-Atl 5.2
Concepcion-Cin 4.4
Cash-Phi 4.2

TEAM	G	W	L	PCT	GB	R	OR	AB	H	2B	3B	HR	BB	SO	AVG	OBP	SLG	PRO	/A	BR	/A	PF	CHI	RC	TA	SB	CS	SBA	SBR
EAST																													
BAL	162	91	71	.562		659	612	5535	1418	226	27	116	509	770	.256	.325	.370	.695	100	-1	48	93	98	671	.642	145	58	71	9
NY	162	89	73	.549	2	671	623	5524	1451	220	30	101	515	690	.263	.328	.368	.696	100	1	29	96	100	666	.620	53	35	60	-4
BOS	162	84	78	.519	7	696	661	5499	1449	236	31	109	569	811	.264	.336	.377	.713	105	39	-4	107	98	699	.656	104	54	64	-3
CLE	162	77	85	.475	14	662	694	5474	1395	201	19	131	432	756	.255	.312	.370	.682	96	-35	-39	101	107	610	.599	79	68	54	-16
MIL	162	76	86	.469	15	647	660	5472	1335	228	49	120	500	909	.244	.310	.366	.679	95	-40	-55	102	104	622	.615	106	75	59	-12
DET	162	72	90	.444	19	620	768	5568	1375	200	35	131	436	784	.247	.304	.366	.670	92	-63	-101	106	104	607	.588	67	38	64	-2
WEST																													
OAK	162	90	72	.556		689	551	5331	1315	205	37	132	568	876	.247	.324	.373	.697	100	1		100	105	648	.654	164	93	64	-6
TEX	161	84	76	.525	5	690	698	5449	1482	198	39	99	508	710	.272	.338	.377	.715	105	42	69	96	98	677	.646	113	80	59	-13
MIN	163	82	80	.506	8	673	669	5632	1530	190	37	111	520	791	.272	.338	.378	.716	106	44	37	101	92	707	.643	74	45	62	-4
CHI	163	80	80	.500	9	684	721	5577	1492	225	23	135	519	858	.268	.333	.389	.722	107	49	37	102	94	701	.647	64	53	55	-12
KC	162	77	85	.475	13	667	662	5582	1448	232	42	89	550	768	.259	.329	.364	.693	99	-1	-43	106	98	668	.635	144	76	66	-1
CAL	163	68	94	.420	22	618	657	5401	1372	203	31	95	509	801	.254	.323	.356	.679	95	-29	20	92	98	615	.612	119	79	60	-11
TOT	973					7976		66044	17062	2564	400	1369	6135	9524	.258	.325	.371	.697								1234	758	62	-84

TEAM	CG	SHO	SV	IP	H	H/G	HR	BB	BB/G	SO	SO/G	ERA	/A	OAVG	OOBA	PR	/A	PF	CPI	FA	E	DP	FW	PW	BW	SBW	DIF
EAST																											
BAL	57	16	25	1474.0	1393	8.5	101	480	2.9	701	4.3	3.27	102	.253	.309	56	10	92	102	.980	128	174	1.0	1.0	5.0	1.7	1.2
NY	53	13	24	1455.3	1402	8.7	104	528	3.3	829	5.1	3.31	104	.255	.319	49	21	95	106	.977	142	158	.2	2.2	3.0	.3	2.2
BOS	71	12	18	1455.3	1462	9.0	126	463	2.9	751	4.6	3.72	103	.262	.317	-16	19	106	99	.977	145	156	.0	2.0	-.4	.4	1.0
CLE	45	9	27	1445.7	1419	8.8	138	479	3.0	650	4.0	3.80	96	.259	.316	-29	-23	101	98	.977	146	157	-.0	-2.4	-4.1	-.9	3.4
MIL	43	11	24	1457.7	1476	9.1	126	493	3.0	621	3.8	3.76	99	.265	.323	-23	-7	103	102	.980	127	168	1.1	-.7	-5.8	-.5	.9
DET	54	7	15	1455.7	1443	8.9	148	621	3.8	869	5.4	4.16	94	.262	.334	-87	-42	108	99	.975	158	155	-.7	-4.4	-10.6	.5	6.1
WEST																											
OAK	49	12	28	1439.7	1322	8.3	90	430	2.7	755	4.7	2.95	121	.246	.299	106	98	99	103	.977	141	154	.3	10.2	-.1	.1	-1.5
TEX	62	16	12	1433.7	1423	8.9	126	449	2.8	871	5.5	3.82	91	.259	.315	-32	-55	96	95	.974	163	164	-1.0	-5.8	7.2	-.6	4.2
MIN	43	11	29	1455.3	1436	8.9	115	513	3.2	934	5.8	3.64	100	.259	.321	-4	-1	101	100	.977	151	164	-.3	.1	3.9	.3	-3.0
CHI	55	11	29	1465.7	1470	9.0	103	548	3.4	826	5.1	3.94	94	.263	.328	-51	-38	102	96	.977	147	188	-.0	-4.0	3.9	-.5	.7
KC	54	13	17	1471.7	1477	9.0	91	482	2.9	731	4.5	3.51	109	.262	.317	17	54	106	100	.976	152	166	-.4	5.6	-4.5	.6	-5.4
CAL	64	13	12	1439.0	1339	8.4	101	649	4.1	986	6.2	3.52	95	.248	.328	15	-26	93	102	.976	147	150	-.0	-2.7	2.1	-.4	-11.9
TOT	650	144	260	17448.7		8.8			3.2		4.9	3.62		.258	.325					.977	1747	1954					

Runs		Hits		Doubles		Triples		Home Runs		Total Bases	
Yastrzemski-Bos	93	Carew-Min	218	Rudi-Oak	39	Rivers-Cal	11	Allen-Chi	32	Rudi-Oak	287
Grich-Bal	92	Davis-Bal	181	Scott-Mil	36	Otis-KC	9	Jackson-Oak	29	Henderson-Chi	281
Jackson-Oak	90	Money-Mil	178	McRae-KC	36			Tenace-Oak	26	Burroughs-Tex	279
Otis-KC	87	Henderson-Chi	176	Henderson-Chi	35			Darwin-Min	25	Carew-Min	267
Carew-Min	86	Rudi-Oak	174	Burroughs-Tex	33			Burroughs-Tex	25		

Runs Batted In		Runs Produced		Bases On Balls		Batting Average		On Base Percentage		Slugging Average	
Burroughs-Tex	118	Burroughs-Tex	177	Tenace-Oak	110	Carew-Min	.364	Carew-Min	.435	Allen-Chi	.563
Bando-Oak	103	Bando-Oak	165	Yastrzemski-Bos	104	Orta-Chi	.316	Yastrzemski-Bos	.421	Jackson-Oak	.514
Rudi-Oak	99	Yastrzemski-Bos	157	Burroughs-Tex	91	McRae-KC	.310	Burroughs-Tex	.405	Burroughs-Tex	.504
Henderson-Chi	95	Grich-Bal	155	Grich-Bal	90	Piniella-NY	.305	Maddox-NY	.397	Rudi-Oak	.484
Darwin-Min	94	Jackson-Oak	154			Maddox-NY	.303	Jackson-Oak	.396	Freehan-Det	.479

Production		Adjusted Production		Batter Runs		Adjusted Batter Runs		Clutch Hitting Index		Runs Created	
Allen-Chi	.942	Burroughs-Tex	167	Burroughs-Tex	45.3	Burroughs-Tex	48.2	Bando-Oak	154	Carew-Min	118
Jackson-Oak	.910	Allen-Chi	165	Carew-Min	44.7	Carew-Min	44.0	Davis-Bal	130	Burroughs-Tex	113
Burroughs-Tex	.908	Jackson-Oak	159	Jackson-Oak	41.0	Jackson-Oak	40.7	Petrocelli-Bos	129	Jackson-Oak	109
Carew-Min	.880	Carew-Min	152	Allen-Chi	39.3	Allen-Chi	38.3	Murcer-NY	128	Yastrzemski-Bos	102
Yastrzemski-Bos	.866	Robinson-Cal-Cle	146	Yastrzemski-Bos	38.1	Grich-Bal	33.7	Burroughs-Tex	126	Henderson-Chi	100

Total Average		Stolen Bases		Stolen Base Average		Stolen Base Runs		Fielding Runs		Total Player Rating	
Jackson-Oak	1.005	North-Oak	54	Jackson-Oak	83.3	Jackson-Oak	4.5	Robinson-Bal	22.8	Carew-Min	7.1
Allen-Chi	.956	Carew-Min	38	Coggins-Bal	81.3	Coggins-Bal	4.2	Rodriguez-Det	21.9	Jackson-Oak	5.1
Burroughs-Tex	.926	Lowenstein-Cle	36	Pinson-KC	80.8	Pinson-KC	3.3	Munson-NY	17.8	Grich-Bal	5.0
Yastrzemski-Bos	.918	Campaneris-Oak	34	Otis-KC	78.3	Miller-Bos	2.7	Carew-Min	17.0	Robinson-Bal	4.0
Carew-Min	.918	Patek-KC	33	Money-Mil	76.0	Blair-Bal	2.7	Nettles-NY	16.8	Burroughs-Tex	3.4

Wins		Win Percentage		Games		Complete Games		Shutouts		Saves	
Jenkins-Tex	25	Cuellar-Bal	.688	Fingers-Oak	76	Jenkins-Tex	29	Tiant-Bos	7	Forster-Chi	24
Hunter-Oak	25	Jenkins-Tex	.676	Murphy-Mil	70	G.Perry-Cle	28	Jenkins-Tex	6	Murphy-Mil	20
		Hunter-Oak	.676	Foucault-Tex	69	Lolich-Det	27	Hunter-Oak	6	Campbell-Min	19
		Tiant-Bos	.629	Lyle-NY	66	Ryan-Cal	26	Cuellar-Bal	5	Buskey-NY -Cle	18
				Campbell-Min	63	Tiant-Bos	25	Bibby-Tex	5	Fingers-Oak	18

Innings Pitched		Fewest Hits/Game		Fewest BB/Game		Strikeouts		Strikeouts/Game		Wins Above Team	
Ryan-Cal	333	Ryan-Cal	5.97	Jenkins-Tex	1.23	Ryan-Cal	367	Ryan-Cal	9.92	Jenkins-Tex	7.0
Jenkins-Tex	328	G.Perry-Cle	6.43	Hunter-Oak	1.30	Blyleven-Min	249	Blyleven-Min	7.98	Ryan-Cal	6.3
G.Perry-Cle	322	DalCanton-KC	6.94	Holtzman-Oak	1.80	Jenkins-Tex	225	Jenkins-Tex	6.17	Hunter-Oak	6.0
Wood-Chi	320	Hassler-Cal	7.33	Kaat-Chi	2.05	G.Perry-Cle	216	Busby-KC	6.10	Busby-KC	5.6
Hunter-Oak	318	Hunter-Oak	7.58	Wright-Mil	2.09	Lolich-Det	202	G.Perry-Cle	6.04	G.Perry-Cle	5.4

Earned Run Average		Adjusted ERA		Opponents' Batting Avg.		Opponents' On Base Pct.		Starter Runs		Adjusted Starter Runs	
Hunter-Oak	2.49	G.Perry-Cle	145	Ryan-Cal	.190	Hunter-Oak	.256	Hunter-Oak	39.8	G.Perry-Cle	40.8
G.Perry-Cle	2.52	Hunter-Oak	143	G.Perry-Cle	.204	Jenkins-Tex	.260	G.Perry-Cle	39.4	Hunter-Oak	38.0
Hassler-Cal	2.61	Fitzmorris-KC	137	DalCanton-KC	.211	G.Perry-Cle	.265	Blyleven-Min	29.9	Tiant-Bos	31.6
Blyleven-Min	2.66	Blyleven-Min	137	Hassler-Cal	.225	Blyleven-Min	.287	Jenkins-Tex	28.8	Blyleven-Min	31.0
Fitzmorris-KC	2.79	Tiant-Bos	131	Hunter-Oak	.229	Grimsley-Bal	.289	Ryan-Cal	26.8	Kaat-Chi	23.8

Clutch Pitching Index		Relief Runs		Adjusted Relief Runs		Relief Ranking		Total Pitcher Index		Total Baseball Ranking	
Goltz-Min	123	Lyle-NY	24.8	Murphy-Mil	24.7	Murphy-Mil	45.2	G.Perry-Cle	4.7	Carew-Min	7.1
Hassler-Cal	121	Murphy-Mil	23.4	Lyle-NY	22.6	Hiller-Det	43.0	Hunter-Oak	3.8	Jackson-Oak	5.1
Lee-Bos	119	Foucault-Tex	21.9	Hiller-Det	20.9	Lyle-NY	28.1	Blyleven-Min	3.4	Grich-Bal	5.0
Fitzmorris-KC	116	Lindblad-Oak	17.6	Foucault-Tex	19.6	Foucault-Tex	24.5	Tiant-Bos	3.2	G.Perry-Cle	4.7
Tanana-Cal	113	Hiller-Det	16.3	Lindblad-Oak	17.0	Campbell-Min	20.2	Murphy-Mil	2.9	Robinson-Bal	4.0

TEAM	G	W	L	PCT	GB	R	OR	AB	H	2B	3B	HR	BB	SO	AVG	OBP	SLG	PRO	/A	BR	/A	PF	CHI	RC	TA	SB	CS	SBA	SBR
EAST																													
PIT	161	92	69	.571		712	565	5489	1444	255	47	**138**	468	832	.263	.325	**.402**	.727	108	43	46	99	102	709	.658	49	28	64	-1
PHI	162	86	76	.531	6.5	735	694	5592	1506	**283**	42	125	610	960	.269	.344	.402	.746	113	97	87	101	94	785	.708	126	57	69	4
NY	162	82	80	.506	10.5	646	625	5587	1430	217	34	101	501	805	.256	.321	.361	.682	95	-35	-2	95	102	639	.598	32	26	55	-5
STL	163	82	80	.506	10.5	662	689	5597	**1527**	239	46	81	444	**649**	**.273**	.329	.375	.704	101	7	-13	103	98	683	.632	116	49	70	5
MON	162	75	87	.463	17.5	601	690	5518	1346	216	31	98	579	954	.244	.319	.348	.667	91	-63	-117	108	98	623	.606	108	58	65	-1
CHI	162	75	87	.463	17.5	712	827	5470	1419	229	41	95	650	802	.259	.341	.368	.709	98	32	5	104	100	702	.655	67	55	55	-12
WEST																													
CIN	162	108	54	.667		**840**	586	5581	1515	278	37	124	**691**	916	.271	**.355**	.401	**.756**	116	127	96	104	103	829	.742	**168**	36	82	29
LA	162	88	74	.543	20	648	534	5453	1355	217	31	118	611	825	.248	.328	.365	.693	98	-9	26	95	98	667	.648	138	52	73	10
SF	161	80	81	.497	27.5	659	671	5447	1412	235	45	84	604	775	.259	.336	.365	.701	101	10	0	102	97	673	.643	99	47	68	2
SD	162	71	91	.438	37	552	683	5429	1324	215	22	78	506	754	.244	.313	.335	.648	86	-100	-97	100	98	571	.571	85	50	63	-4
ATL	161	67	94	.416	40.5	583	739	5424	1323	179	28	107	543	759	.244	.315	.346	.661	89	-74	-42	95	100	587	.583	55	38	59	-5
HOU	162	64	97	.398	43.5	664	711	5515	1401	218	**54**	84	523	762	.254	.322	.359	.681	95	-36	1	94	**105**	643	.621	133	62	68	3
TOT	971					8014		66102	17002	2781	458	1233	6730	9793	.257	.329	.369	.699								1176	558	68	18

TEAM	CG	SHO	SV	IP	H	H/G	HR	BB	BB/G	SO	SO/G	ERA	/A	OAVG	OOBA	PR	/A	PF	CPI	FA	E	DP	FW	PW	BW	SBW	DIF
EAST																											
PIT	43	14	31	1437.3	1302	8.2	**79**	551	3.5	768	4.8	3.01	117	.242	.308	98	**83**	98	103	.976	151	147	.2	**8.7**	4.8	-.3	-1.9
PHI	33	11	30	1455.0	1353	8.4	111	546	3.4	897	5.5	3.82	96	.248	.313	-32	-27	101	89	.976	152	156	.2	-2.8	9.1	.3	-1.7
NY	40	14	31	1466.0	1344	8.3	99	580	3.6	**989**	**6.1**	3.39	101	.245	.314	37	7	95	98	.976	151	144	.2	.7	-.2	-.7	.9
STL	33	13	36	1454.7	1452	9.0	98	571	3.5	824	5.1	3.57	105	.259	.324	8	28	103	102	.973	171	140	-.9	2.9	-1.4	-.4	-.0
MON	30	12	25	1480.0	1448	8.8	102	665	4.0	831	5.1	3.72	106	.258	.334	-16	38	109	103	.973	180	**179**	-1.4	4.0	-12.2	-.3	3.9
CHI	27	8	33	1443.3	1587	9.9	130	551	3.4	850	5.3	4.49	85	.281	.341	-139	-109	105	98	.972	179	152	-1.3	-11.4	.5	-1.4	7.6
WEST																											
CIN	22	8	**50**	1459.0	1422	8.8	112	487	3.0	663	4.1	3.37	109	.257	.314	40	48	101	105	**.984**	102	173	**3.0**	5.0	10.0	2.9	6.2
LA	**51**	**18**	21	1469.7	**1215**	7.4	104	**448**	2.7	894	5.5	**2.92**	116	**.224**	**.281**	114	74	93	88	.979	127	106	1.6	7.7	2.7	.9	-5.9
SF	37	9	24	1432.7	1406	8.8	92	612	3.8	856	5.4	3.74	99	.259	.331	-18	-8	102	101	.976	164	164	.5	-.8	.0	-.0	-.2
SD	40	12	20	1463.3	1494	9.2	99	521	3.2	713	4.4	3.48	105	.266	.322	22	29	101	**107**	.971	188	163	-1.8	3.0	-10.1	-.6	-.5
ATL	32	4	24	1430.0	1543	9.7	101	519	3.3	669	4.2	3.91	90	.277	.335	-46	-63	97	105	.972	175	147	-1.1	-6.6	-4.4	-.7	-.7
HOU	39	6	25	1458.3	1436	8.9	106	679	4.2	839	5.2	4.04	85	.261	.339	-67	-97	95	99	.979	137	166	1.0	-10.1	.1	.2	-7.6
TOT	427	129	350	17450.3		8.8			3.5		5.1	3.62		.257	.329					.976	1859	1837					

Runs		Hits		Doubles		Triples		Home Runs		Total Bases	
Rose-Cin	112	Cash-Phi	213	Rose-Cin	47	Garr-Atl	11	Schmidt-Phi	38	Luzinski-Phi	322
Cash-Phi	111	Rose-Cin	210	Cash-Phi	40	Parker-Pit	10	Kingman-NY	36	Garvey-LA	314
Lopes-LA	108	Garvey-LA	210	Oliver-Pit	39	Kessinger-Chi	10	Luzinski-Phi	34	Parker-Pit	302
Morgan-Cin	107	Simmons-StL	193	Bench-Cin	39	Joshua-SF	10	Bench-Cin	28	Schmidt-Phi	294
Thomas-SF	99	Millan-NY	191	Garvey-LA	38	Gross-Hou	10			Rose-Cin	286

Runs Batted In		Runs Produced		Bases On Balls		Batting Average		On Base Percentage		Slugging Average	
Luzinski-Phi	120	Morgan-Cin	184	Morgan-Cin	132	Madlock-Chi	.354	Morgan-Cin	.471	Parker-Pit	.541
Bench-Cin	110	Staub-NY	179	Wynn-LA	110	Simmons-StL	.332	Wynn-LA	.407	Luzinski-Phi	.540
Perez-Cin	109	Rose-Cin	179	Evans-Atl	105	Sanguillen-Pit	.328	Rose-Cin	.407	Schmidt-Phi	.523
Staub-NY	105	Luzinski-Phi	171	Schmidt-Phi	101	Morgan-Cin	.327	Madlock-Chi	.406	Bench-Cin	.519
		Bench-Cin	165			Watson-Hou	.324	Murcer-SF	.404	Foster-Cin	.518

Production		Adjusted Production		Batter Runs		Adjusted Batter Runs		Clutch Hitting Index		Runs Created	
Morgan-Cin	.979	Morgan-Cin	164	Morgan-Cin	57.1	Morgan-Cin	54.1	Montanez-Phi-SF	148	Morgan-Cin	145
Luzinski-Phi	.939	Luzinski-Phi	156	Luzinski-Phi	47.4	Luzinski-Phi	46.3	Perez-Cin	144	Luzinski-Phi	128
Parker-Pit	.899	Watson-Hou	149	Simmons-StL	35.7	Simmons-StL	33.5	Morales-Chi	144	Rose-Cin	120
Stargell-Pit	.894	Parker-Pit	148	Thornton-Chi	35.4	Thornton-Chi	33.4	Murcer-SF	143	Schmidt-Phi	113
Schmidt-Phi	.890	Stargell-Pit	147	Schmidt-Phi	33.6	Schmidt-Phi	32.6	Trillo-Chi	143	Simmons-StL	108

Total Average		Stolen Bases		Stolen Base Average		Stolen Base Runs		Fielding Runs		Total Player Rating	
Morgan-Cin	1.307	Lopes-LA	77	Morgan-Cin	87.0	Lopes-LA	15.9	Schmidt-Phi	26.2	Morgan-Cin	8.0
Schmidt-Phi	.971	Morgan-Cin	67	Lopes-LA	86.5	Morgan-Cin	14.1	Evans-Atl	23.4	Schmidt-Phi	6.2
Luzinski-Phi	.970	Brock-StL	56	Maddox-SF -Phi	86.2	Brock-StL	7.2	Maddox-SF -Phi	19.2	Evans-Atl	4.1
Wynn-LA	.903	Cedeno-Hou	50	Winfield-SD	85.2	Concepcion-Cin	6.3	Trillo-Chi	19.1	Parker-Pit	3.3
Bench-Cin	.901	Cardenal-Chi	34	Concepcion-Cin	84.6	Maddox-SF -Phi	5.1	Concepcion-Cin	16.9	Thornton-Chi	3.3

Wins		Win Percentage		Games		Complete Games		Shutouts		Saves	
Seaver-NY	22	Gullett-Cin	.789	Garber-Phi	71	Messersmith-LA	19	Messersmith-LA	7	Hrabosky-StL	22
Jones-SD	20	Seaver-NY	.710	McEnaney-Cin	70	Jones-SD	18	Reuss-Pit	6	Eastwick-Cin	22
Messersmith-LA	19	Hooton-Chi-LA	.667	Tomlin-SD	67	Seaver-NY	15	Jones-SD	6	Giusti-Pit	17
Hooton-Chi-LA	18	Murray-Mon	.652	Borbon-Cin	67	Reuss-Pit	15	Seaver-NY	5	McEnaney-Cin	15
Reuss-Pit	18			Garman-StL	66					Knowles-Chi	15

Innings Pitched		Fewest Hits/Game		Fewest BB/Game		Strikeouts		Strikeouts/Game		Wins Above Team	
Messersmith-LA	322	Messersmith-LA	6.82	Nolan-Cin	1.24	Seaver-NY	243	Montefusco-SF	7.93	Seaver-NY	7.2
Jones-SD	285	Warthen-Mon	6.96	Jones-SD	1.77	Montefusco-SF	215	Seaver-NY	7.81	Jones-SD	6.1
Seaver-NY	280	Seaver-NY	6.98	Reed-Atl-StL	1.90	Messersmith-LA	213	Richard-Hou	7.80	Hrabosky-StL	5.2
Morton-Atl	278	Sutton-LA	7.16	Rau-LA	2.13	Carlton-Phi	192	Warthen-Mon	6.86	Murray-Mon	4.5
Niekro-Atl	276	Hooton-Chi-LA	7.28	Barr-SF	2.14	Richard-Hou	176	Carlton-Phi	6.78	Hooton-Chi-LA	4.4

Earned Run Average		Adjusted ERA		Opponents' Batting Avg.		Opponents' On Base Pct.		Starter Runs		Adjusted Starter Runs	
Jones-SD	2.24	Jones-SD	163	Messersmith-LA	.213	Sutton-LA	.259	Messersmith-LA	47.5	Jones-SD	45.0
Messersmith-LA	2.29	Messersmith-LA	147	Sutton-LA	.213	Jones-SD	.265	Jones-SD	43.7	Messersmith-LA	38.7
Seaver-NY	2.38	Seaver-NY	144	Seaver-NY	.214	Messersmith-LA	.270	Seaver-NY	38.6	Seaver-NY	32.8
Reuss-Pit	2.54	Reuss-Pit	139	Warthen-Mon	.217	Hooton-Chi-LA	.272	Reuss-Pit	28.3	Reuss-Pit	26.0
Forsch-StL	2.86	Forsch-StL	131	Hooton-Chi-LA	.219	Nolan-Cin	.272	Gullett-Cin	21.4	Forsch-StL	22.7

Clutch Pitching Index		Relief Runs		Adjusted Relief Runs		Relief Ranking		Total Pitcher Index		Total Baseball Ranking	
Reuss-Pit	122	Hrabosky-StL	21.0	Hrabosky-StL	22.3	Hrabosky-StL	44.6	Jones-SD	5.5	Morgan-Cin	8.0
Niekro-Atl	122	Apodaca-NY	20.2	Apodaca-NY	18.4	Apodaca-NY	20.0	Messersmith-LA	4.2	Schmidt-Phi	6.2
Blair-Mon	114	Hilgendorf-Phi	16.4	Hilgendorf-Phi	16.4	Garman-StL	18.2	Seaver-NY	4.1	Jones-SD	5.5
Koosman-NY	114	McEnaney-Cin	11.6	McEnaney-Cin	12.1	Hilgendorf-Phi	15.2	Forsch-StL	3.8	Messersmith-LA	4.2
Barr-SF	110	Garman-StL	10.8	Garman-StL	11.9	Eastwick-Cin	14.4	Reuss-Pit	3.3	Seaver-NY	4.1

TEAM	G	W	L	PCT	GB	R	OR	AB	H	2B	3B	HR	BB	SO	AVG	OBP	SLG	PRO	/A	BR	/A	PF	CHI	RC	TA	SB	CS	SBA	SBR
EAST
BOS	160	95	65	.594		796	709	5448	**1500**	284	44	134	565	741	.275	.347	**.417**	**.764**	115	**108**	47	109	99	776	**.709**	66	58	53	-14
BAL	159	90	69	.566	4.5	682	**553**	5474	1382	224	33	124	580	834	.252	.328	.373	.701	98	-13	52	91	99	680	.649	104	55	65	-1
NY	160	83	77	.519	12	681	588	5415	1430	230	39	110	486	710	.264	.328	.382	.710	100	-2	6	99	100	665	.642	102	59	63	-4
CLE	159	79	80	.497	15.5	688	703	5404	1409	201	25	**153**	525	**667**	.261	.329	.392	.721	103	17	20	100	98	672	.656	106	89	54	-21
MIL	162	68	94	.420	28	675	792	5378	1343	242	34	146	553	922	.250	.323	.389	.712	100	-1	-1	100	99	663	.647	65	64	50	-18
DET	159	57	102	.358	37.5	570	786	5366	1338	171	39	125	383	872	.249	.303	.366	.669	88	-93	-117	104	101	573	.579	63	57	53	-14
WEST
OAK	162	98	64	.605		758	606	5415	1376	220	33	151	609	846	.254	.335	.391	.726	105	34	**82**	93	104	725	**.700**	183	82	**69**	6
KC	162	91	71	.562	7	710	649	5491	1431	263	**58**	118	591	675	.261	.336	.394	.730	106	40	27	102	96	736	.693	155	75	67	2
TEX	162	79	83	.488	19	714	733	5599	1431	208	17	134	**613**	863	.256	.332	.371	.703	98	-9	-5	100	101	693	.646	102	62	62	-6
MIN	159	76	83	.478	20.5	724	736	5514	1497	215	28	121	563	746	.271	.343	.386	.729	106	46	-3	107	97	732	.672	81	48	63	-4
CHI	161	75	86	.466	22.5	655	703	5490	1400	209	38	94	611	800	.255	.334	.358	.692	96	-23	-46	103	96	659	.633	101	54	65	-1
CAL	161	72	89	.447	25.5	628	723	5377	1324	195	41	55	593	811	.246	.324	.328	.652	85	-98	-60	95	**106**	596	.612	**220**	108	67	1
TOT	963					8281		65371	16861	2662	429	1465	6672	9487	.258	.330	.379	.709								1348	811	62	-81

TEAM	CG	SHO	SV	IP	H	H/G	HR	BB	BB/G	SO	SO/G	ERA	/A	OAVG	OOBA	PR	/A	PF	CPI	FA	E	DP	FW	PW	BW	SBW	DIF
EAST
BOS	62	11	31	1436.7	1463	9.2	145	**490**	**3.1**	720	4.5	3.98	102	.265	.321	-32	12	108	99	.977	139	142	.9	1.2	4.8	-.7	8.8
BAL	**70**	**19**	21	1451.0	1285	8.0	110	500	**3.1**	717	4.4	**3.17**	106	.241	**.302**	98	31	89	100	**.983**	**107**	175	2.7	3.2	5.3	.6	-1.3
NY	**70**	11	20	1424.0	1325	8.4	104	502	3.2	809	5.1	3.29	**112**	.249	.311	77	**62**	94	103	.978	135	148	1.1	**6.3**	.6	.3	-5.3
CLE	37	6	33	1435.3	1395	8.7	136	599	3.8	800	5.0	3.84	98	.257	.329	-10	-12	100	103	.978	134	156	1.2	-1.2	2.0	-1.4	-1.0
MIL	36	10	34	1431.7	1496	9.4	133	624	3.9	643	4.0	4.34	88	.270	.344	-89	-80	101	100	.971	180	162	-1.5	-8.2	-.1	-1.1	-2.1
DET	52	10	17	1396.0	1496	9.6	137	533	3.4	787	5.1	4.27	94	.274	.336	-76	-39	106	100	.972	173	141	-1.1	-4.0	-11.9	-.7	-4.8
WEST
OAK	36	10	**44**	1448.0	**1267**	**7.9**	102	523	3.3	784	4.9	3.27	105	**.236**	**.302**	81	27	91	94	.977	143	140	.6	2.8	**8.4**	1.3	3.9
KC	52	11	25	1456.7	1422	8.8	108	498	**3.1**	815	5.0	3.47	110	.257	.316	50	57	101	102	.976	155	151	-.0	5.8	2.8	.9	.6
TEX	60	16	17	1465.7	1456	8.9	123	518	3.2	792	4.9	3.86	98	.261	.322	-13	-15	100	98	.971	191	173	-2.1	-1.5	-.5	.0	-2.0
MIN	57	7	22	1423.0	1381	8.7	137	617	3.9	846	5.4	4.05	100	.256	.330	-42	0	107	98	.973	170	147	-.9	-.0	-.3	.3	-2.6
CHI	34	7	39	1452.3	1489	9.2	107	655	4.1	799	5.0	3.93	100	.268	.343	-24	0	104	**105**	.978	140	155	.8	.0	-4.7	.6	-2.2
CAL	59	**19**	16	1453.3	1386	8.6	123	613	3.8	**975**	**6.0**	3.89	93	.253	.326	-17	-43	96	97	.971	184	164	-1.7	-4.4	-6.1	.8	2.9
TOT	625	137	319	17273.7		8.8			3.5		4.9	3.78		.258	.330					.975	1851	1854					

Runs		Hits		Doubles		Triples		Home Runs		Total Bases	
Lynn-Bos	103	Brett-KC	195	Lynn-Bos	47	Rivers-Cal	13	Scott-Mil	36	Scott-Mil	318
Mayberry-KC	95	Carew-Min	192	Jackson-Oak	39	Brett-KC	13	Jackson-Oak	36	Mayberry-KC	303
Bonds-NY	93	Munson-NY	190	McRae-KC	38	Orta-Chi	10	Mayberry-KC	34	Jackson-Oak	303
Rice-Bos	92	Washington-Oak	182	Mayberry-KC	38	Cowens-KC	8	Bonds-NY	32	Lynn-Bos	299
				Chambliss-NY	38					Brett-KC	289

Runs Batted In		Runs Produced		Bases On Balls		Batting Average		On Base Percentage		Slugging Average	
Scott-Mil	109	Lynn-Bos	187	Mayberry-KC	119	Carew-Min	.359	Carew-Min	.428	Lynn-Bos	.566
Mayberry-KC	106	Munson-NY	173	Singleton-Bal	118	Lynn-Bos	.331	Mayberry-KC	.419	Mayberry-KC	.547
Lynn-Bos	105	Rice-Bos	172	Grich-Bal	107	Munson-NY	.318	Singleton-Bal	.418	Powell-Cle	.524
Jackson-Oak	104	Mayberry-KC	167	Tenace-Oak	106	Rice-Bos	.309	Harrah-Tex	.406	Scott-Mil	.515
		Brett-KC	162	Washington-Oak	98	Washington-Oak	.308	Lynn-Bos	.405	Bonds-NY	.512

Production		Adjusted Production		Batter Runs		Adjusted Batter Runs		Clutch Hitting Index		Runs Created	
Lynn-Bos	.971	Mayberry-KC	168	Mayberry-KC	56.0	Mayberry-KC	54.6	Munson-NY	142	Mayberry-KC	135
Mayberry-KC	.966	Singleton-Bal	162	Lynn-Bos	49.4	Singleton-Bal	48.8	Stanton-Cal	140	Lynn-Bos	120
Carew-Min	.926	Lynn-Bos	158	Carew-Min	44.4	Lynn-Bos	43.5	Robinson-Bal	136	Singleton-Bal	118
Powell-Cle	.906	Powell-Cle	155	Singleton-Bal	41.3	Carew-Min	39.5	May-Bal	132	Carew-Min	118
Bonds-NY	.891	Tenace-Oak	154	Bonds-NY	35.4	Tenace-Oak	37.3	McRae-KC	127	Harrah-Tex	105

Total Average		Stolen Bases		Stolen Base Average		Stolen Base Runs		Fielding Runs		Total Player Rating	
Mayberry-KC	1.067	Rivers-Cal	70	Hisle-Min	85.0	Rivers-Cal	12.6	Belanger-Bal	29.4	Harrah-Tex	6.2
Lynn-Bos	1.014	Washington-Oak	40	Bumbry-Bal	84.2	Patek-KC	5.4	Dent-Chi	29.2	Carew-Min	5.8
Carew-Min	1.011	Otis-KC	39	Rivers-Cal	83.3	Otis-KC	5.1	Grich-Bal	25.4	Grich-Bal	5.7
Bonds-NY	.952	Carew-Min	35	Alomar-NY	82.4	Carew-Min	5.1	Munson-NY	22.9	Mayberry-KC	5.1
Harrah-Tex	.938	Remy-Cal	34	Patek-KC	82.1	Alomar-NY	4.8	Downing-Chi	18.4	Munson-NY	4.7

Wins		Win Percentage		Games		Complete Games		Shutouts		Saves	
Palmer-Bal	23	Torrez-Bal	.690	Fingers-Oak	75	Hunter-NY	30	Palmer-Bal	10	Gossage-Chi	26
Hunter-NY	23	Leonard-KC	.682	Lindblad-Oak	68	Perry-Cle-Tex	25	Hunter-NY	7	Fingers-Oak	24
Blue-Oak	22	Palmer-Bal	.676	Gossage-Chi	62	Palmer-Bal	25			Murphy-Mil	20
Torrez-Bal	20	Blue-Oak	.667	LaRoche-Cle	61	Jenkins-Tex	22			LaRoche-Cle	17
Kaat-Chi	20	Lee-Bos	.654	Foucault-Tex	59	Blyleven-Min	20			Drago-Bos	15

Innings Pitched		Fewest Hits/Game		Fewest BB/Game		Strikeouts		Strikeouts/Game		Wins Above Team	
Hunter-NY	328	Hunter-NY	6.80	Jenkins-Tex	1.87	Tanana-Cal	269	Tanana-Cal	9.42	Palmer-Bal	5.1
Palmer-Bal	323	Ryan-Cal	6.91	Perry-Cle-Tex	2.06	Perry-Cle-Tex	233	Ryan-Cal	8.45	Moret-Bos	5.0
Perry-Cle-Tex	306	Palmer-Bal	7.05	Grimsley-Bal	2.15	Blyleven-Min	233	Blyleven-Min	7.60	Tanana-Cal	4.8
Kaat-Chi	304	Eckersley-Cle	7.07	Palmer-Bal	2.23	Palmer-Bal	193	Eckersley-Cle	7.32	Hunter-NY	4.8
Wood-Chi	291	Blyleven-Min	7.14	Hunter-NY	2.28	Blue-Oak	189	Perry-Cle-Tex	6.85	Torrez-Bal	4.8

Earned Run Average		Adjusted ERA		Opponents' Batting Avg.		Opponents' On Base Pct.		Starter Runs		Adjusted Starter Runs	
Palmer-Bal	2.09	Palmer-Bal	161	Hunter-NY	.208	Hunter-NY	.260	Palmer-Bal	60.6	Palmer-Bal	45.8
Hunter-NY	2.58	Eckersley-Cle	145	Ryan-Cal	.213	Palmer-Bal	.264	Hunter-NY	43.7	Hunter-NY	40.2
Eckersley-Cle	2.60	Hunter-NY	143	Eckersley-Cle	.215	Blyleven-Min	.278	Tanana-Cal	32.9	Blyleven-Min	32.2
Tanana-Cal	2.63	Tanana-Cal	138	Palmer-Bal	.216	Perry-Cle-Tex	.281	Eckersley-Cle	24.5	Tanana-Cal	28.4
Figueroa-Cal	2.90	Blyleven-Min	135	Blyleven-Min	.219	Tanana-Cal	.283	Blyleven-Min	23.9	Kaat-Chi	27.6

Clutch Pitching Index		Relief Runs		Adjusted Relief Runs		Relief Ranking		Total Pitcher Index		Total Baseball Ranking	
Kaat-Chi	119	Gossage-Chi	30.6	Gossage-Chi	32.9	Gossage-Chi	49.1	Palmer-Bal	5.3	Harrah-Tex	6.2
Eckersley-Cle	116	Todd-Oak	20.2	Todd-Oak	15.7	LaRoche-Cle	19.3	Hunter-NY	3.9	Carew-Min	5.8
Torrez-Bal	111	LaRoche-Cle	14.4	Hiller-Det	14.7	Todd-Oak	16.2	Blyleven-Min	3.8	Grich-Bal	5.7
Osteen-Chi	110	Lindblad-Oak	14.2	LaRoche-Cle	14.3	Hiller-Det	15.9	Gossage-Chi	3.6	Palmer-Bal	5.3
Leonard-KC	108	Hiller-Det	12.8	Buskey-Cle	10.2	Burgmeier-Min	15.3	Tanana-Cal	3.4	Mayberry-KC	5.1

TEAM	G	W	L	PCT	GB	R	OR	AB	H	2B	3B	HR	BB	SO	AVG	OBP	SLG	PRO	/A	BR	/A	PF	CHI	RC	TA	SB	CS	SBA	SBR
EAST																													
PHI	162	101	61	.623		770	557	5528	1505	259	45	110	542	793	.272	.342	.395	.737	115	106	58	107	101	746	.687	127	70	64	-3
PIT	162	92	70	.568	9	708	630	5604	1499	249	56	110	433	807	.267	.323	.391	.714	108	50	48	100	101	700	.650	130	45	74	12
NY	162	86	76	.531	15	615	538	5415	1334	198	34	102	561	797	.246	.320	.352	.672	97	-19	34	92	98	608	.600	66	58	53	-14
CHI	162	75	87	.463	26	611	728	5519	1386	216	24	105	490	834	.251	.316	.356	.672	96	-26	-85	109	98	605	.591	74	74	50	-21
STL	162	72	90	.444	29	629	671	5516	1432	243	57	63	512	860	.260	.325	.359	.684	100	1	-24	104	97	644	.618	123	55	69	4
MON	162	55	107	.340	46	531	734	5428	1275	224	32	94	433	841	.235	.293	.340	.633	85	-108	-109	100	102	539	.553	86	44	66	0
WEST																													
CIN	162	102	60	.630		857	633	5702	1599	271	63	141	681	902	.280	.360	.424	.784	129	214	194	103	95	907	.783	210	57	79	29
LA	162	92	70	.568	10	608	543	5472	1371	200	34	91	486	744	.251	.315	.349	.664	94	-39	-36	100	100	604	.600	144	55	72	10
HOU	162	80	82	.494	22	625	657	5464	1401	195	50	66	530	719	.256	.325	.347	.672	97	-19	68	86	100	622	.611	150	57	72	11
SF	162	74	88	.457	28	595	686	5452	1340	211	37	85	518	778	.246	.314	.345	.659	93	-48	-67	103	100	591	.585	88	55	62	-6
SD	162	73	89	.451	29	570	662	5369	1327	216	37	64	488	716	.247	.313	.337	.650	90	-64	8	89	100	570	.573	92	46	67	0
ATL	162	70	92	.432	32	620	700	5345	1309	170	30	82	589	811	.245	.322	.334	.656	92	-43	-114	111	103	579	.583	74	61	55	-13
TOT	972					7739		65814	16778	2652	499	1113	6263	9602	.255	.323	.361	.684								1364	677	67	3

TEAM	CG	SHO	SV	IP	H	H/G	HR	BB	BB/G	SO	SO/G	ERA	/A	OAVG	OOBA	PR	/A	PF	CPI	FA	E	DP	FW	PW	BW	SBW	DIF
EAST																											
PHI	34	9	44	1459.0	1377	8.5	98	397	2.4	918	5.7	3.08	119	.249	.297	68	94	105	102	.981	115	148	1.7	10.0	6.2	-.3	2.5
PIT	45	12	35	1466.3	1402	8.6	95	460	2.8	762	4.7	3.36	103	.253	.305	22	18	99	99	.975	163	142	-1.0	1.9	5.1	1.2	3.8
NY	53	18	25	1449.0	1248	7.8	97	419	2.6	1025	6.4	2.94	108	.233	.286	90	37	91	95	.979	131	116	.8	3.9	3.6	-1.5	-1.8
CHI	27	12	33	1471.3	1511	9.2	123	490	3.0	850	5.2	3.93	99	.268	.322	-70	-8	111	100	.978	140	145	.3	-.8	-9.0	-2.3	5.8
STL	35	15	26	1453.7	1416	8.8	91	581	3.6	731	4.5	3.60	102	.258	.325	-16	9	105	103	.973	174	163	-1.7	1.0	-2.5	.4	-6.1
MON	26	10	21	1440.0	1442	9.0	89	659	4.1	783	4.9	3.99	90	.265	.341	-78	-61	103	102	.976	155	179	-.6	-6.5	-11.6	-.0	-7.4
WEST																											
CIN	33	12	45	1471.0	1436	8.8	100	491	3.0	790	4.8	3.51	100	.258	.314	0	0	100	101	.984	102	157	2.5	.0	20.6	3.1	-5.1
LA	47	17	28	1470.7	1330	8.1	97	479	2.9	747	4.6	3.02	115	.243	.301	79	71	99	104	.980	128	154	1.0	7.5	-3.8	1.0	5.3
HOU	42	17	29	1444.3	1349	8.4	82	662	4.1	780	4.9	3.56	85	.249	.327	-9	-84	87	101	.978	140	155	.3	-8.9	7.2	1.1	-.7
SF	27	18	31	1461.7	1464	9.0	68	518	3.2	746	4.6	3.53	103	.262	.320	-4	19	104	100	.971	186	153	-2.4	2.0	-7.1	-.7	1.1
SD	47	11	18	1432.3	1368	8.6	87	543	3.4	652	4.1	3.65	86	.253	.317	-23	-81	90	95	.978	141	148	.2	-8.6	.8	-.0	-.5
ATL	33	13	27	1438.0	1435	9.0	86	564	3.5	818	5.1	3.86	102	.261	.327	-57	10	112	97	.973	167	151	-1.3	1.1	-12.1	-1.4	2.7
TOT	449	164	362	17457.3		8.6			3.2		5.0	3.50		.255	.323					.977	1742	1811					

Runs
Rose-Cin 130
Morgan-Cin 113
Schmidt-Phi 112
Griffey-Cin 111
Monday-Chi 107

Hits
Rose-Cin 215
Montanez-SF-Atl 206
Garvey-LA 200
Buckner-LA 193

Doubles
Rose-Cin 42
Johnstone-Phi 38
Maddox-Phi 37
Garvey-LA 37

Triples
Cash-Phi 12
Geronimo-Cin 11
Parker-Pit 10
Davis-SD 10

Home Runs
Schmidt-Phi 38
Kingman-NY 37
Monday-Chi 32
Foster-Cin 29
Morgan-Cin 27

Total Bases
Schmidt-Phi 306
Rose-Cin 299
Foster-Cin 298
Garvey-LA 284

Runs Batted In
Foster-Cin 121
Morgan-Cin 111
Schmidt-Phi 107
Watson-Hou 102
Luzinski-Phi 95

Runs Produced
Morgan-Cin 197
Rose-Cin 183
Schmidt-Phi 181
Griffey-Cin 179
Foster-Cin 178

Bases On Balls
Wynn-Atl 127
Morgan-Cin 114
Schmidt-Phi 100
Cey-LA 89
Rose-Cin 86

Batting Average
Madlock-Chi .339
Griffey-Cin .336
Maddox-Phi .330
Rose-Cin .323
Morgan-Cin .320

On Base Percentage
Morgan-Cin .453
Madlock-Chi .415
Rose-Cin .406
Griffey-Cin .403
Cey-LA .389

Slugging Average
Morgan-Cin .576
Foster-Cin .530
Schmidt-Phi .524
Monday-Chi .507
Kingman-NY .506

Production
Morgan-Cin 1.029
Madlock-Chi .915
Schmidt-Phi .904
Foster-Cin .899
Rose-Cin .855

Adjusted Production
Morgan-Cin 185
Watson-Hou 160
Cedeno-Hou 150
Foster-Cin 149
Madlock-Chi 145

Batter Runs
Morgan-Cin 61.4
Schmidt-Phi 42.6
Madlock-Chi 40.6
Rose-Cin 39.6
Foster-Cin 36.7

Adjusted Batter Runs
Morgan-Cin 59.5
Watson-Hou 38.7
Rose-Cin 37.3
Schmidt-Phi 37.2
Madlock-Chi 34.9

Clutch Hitting Index
Simmons-StL 133
Watson-Hou 132
Cruz-StL 128
Brock-StL 127
Milner-NY 126

Runs Created
Morgan-Cin 144
Rose-Cin 123
Schmidt-Phi 121
Foster-Cin 111
Griffey-Cin 109

Total Average
Morgan-Cin 1.346
Schmidt-Phi .964
Foster-Cin .918
Madlock-Chi .911
Griffey-Cin .904

Stolen Bases
Lopes-LA 63
Morgan-Cin 60
Taveras-Pit 58
Cedeno-Hou 58
Brock-StL 56

Stolen Base Average
Morgan-Cin 87.0
Lopes-LA 86.3
Foster-Cin 85.0
Taveras-Pit 84.1
Geronimo-Cin 81.5

Stolen Base Runs
Lopes-LA 12.9
Morgan-Cin 12.6
Taveras-Pit 10.8
Cedeno-Hou 8.4
Cabell-Hou 5.7

Fielding Runs
Schmidt-Phi 24.7
Stennett-Pit 18.6
Maddox-Phi 17.4
Trillo-Chi 16.7
Concepcion-Cin 15.1

Total Player Rating
Schmidt-Phi 6.1
Morgan-Cin 5.8
Foster-Cin 4.3
Cedeno-Hou 3.9
Winfield-SD 3.8

Wins
Jones-SD 22
Sutton-LA 21
Koosman-NY 21
Richard-Hou 20
Carlton-Phi 20

Win Percentage
Carlton-Phi .741
Candelaria-Pit .696
Sutton-LA .677
Koosman-NY .677
Rooker-Pit .652

Games
Murray-Mon 81
Metzger-SD 77
Hough-LA 77
Eastwick-Cin 71
Borbon-Cin 69

Complete Games
Jones-SD 25
Koosman-NY 17
Matlack-NY 16
Sutton-LA 15
Richard-Hou 14

Shutouts
Montefusco-SF 6
Matlack-NY 6
Seaver-NY 5
Jones-SD 5

Saves
Eastwick-Cin 26
Lockwood-NY 19
Forsch-Hou 19
Hough-LA 18
Metzger-SD 16

Innings Pitched
Jones-SD 315
Richard-Hou 291
Seaver-NY 271
Niekro-Atl 271
Sutton-LA 268

Fewest Hits/Game
Richard-Hou 6.84
Seaver-NY 7.01
Candelaria-Pit 7.08
Messersmith-Atl 7.22
Falcone-StL 7.34

Fewest BB/Game
Nolan-Cin 1.02
Kaat-Phi 1.26
Jones-SD 1.43
Matlack-NY 1.96
Lonborg-Phi 2.03

Strikeouts
Seaver-NY 235
Richard-Hou 214
Koosman-NY 200
Carlton-Phi 195
Niekro-Atl 173

Strikeouts/Game
Seaver-NY 7.80
Koosman-NY 7.29
Carlton-Phi 6.94
Richard-Hou 6.62
Zachry-Cin 6.31

Wins Above Team
Jones-SD 6.2
Koosman-NY 5.6
Niekro-Atl 4.9
Carlton-Phi 4.7
Sutton-LA 4.6

Earned Run Average
Denny-StL 2.52
Rau-LA 2.57
Seaver-NY 2.59
Koosman-NY 2.70
Zachry-Cin 2.74

Adjusted ERA
Denny-StL 145
Rau-LA 134
Messersmith-Atl 129
Montefusco-SF 128
Zachry-Cin 128

Opponents' Batting Avg.
Richard-Hou .212
Seaver-NY .213
Candelaria-Pit .216
Messersmith-Atl .219
Falcone-StL .222

Opponents' On Base Pct.
Jones-SD .262
Candelaria-Pit .267
Seaver-NY .271
Nolan-Cin .273
Koosman-NY .274

Starter Runs
Seaver-NY 27.4
Jones-SD 26.6
Richard-Hou 24.2
Rau-LA 23.9
Denny-StL 22.5

Adjusted Starter Runs
Denny-StL 26.2
Rau-LA 22.7
Montefusco-SF 22.6
Burris-Chi 21.4
Barr-SF 21.2

Clutch Pitching Index
Rau-LA 139
Denny-StL 129
Burris-Chi 118
Christenson-Phi 112
Fryman-Mon 111

Relief Runs
Hough-LA 20.6
Eastwick-Cin 17.0
Reed-Phi 14.8
Moffitt-SF 14.1
Forsch-Hou 13.8

Adjusted Relief Runs
Hough-LA 19.9
Reed-Phi 17.1
Eastwick-Cin 17.0
Moffitt-SF 15.8
Twitchell-Phi 13.2

Relief Ranking
Eastwick-Cin 31.9
Hough-LA 30.7
Reed-Phi 22.2
Moffitt-SF 21.3
McGraw-Phi 18.2

Total Pitcher Index
Denny-StL 3.4
Barr-SF 3.0
Rau-LA 2.6
Messersmith-Atl 2.5
Niekro-Atl 2.4

Total Baseball Ranking
Schmidt-Phi 6.1
Morgan-Cin 5.8
Foster-Cin 4.3
Cedeno-Hou 3.9
Winfield-SD 3.8

TEAM	G	W	L	PCT	GB	R	OR	AB	H	2B	3B	HR	BB	SO	AVG	OBP	SLG	PRO	/A	BR	/A	PF	CHI	RC	TA	SB	CS	SBA	SBR
EAST																												
NY	159	97	62	.610		730	**575**	5555	1496	231	36	120	470	**616**	.269	.330	.389	.719	110	64	67	99	102	723	.670	163	65	71	10
BAL	162	88	74	.543	10.5	619	598	5457	1326	213	28	119	519	883	.243	.311	.358	.669	96	-32	-16	98	101	612	.613	150	61	71	8
BOS	162	83	79	.512	15.5	716	660	5511	1448	257	53	134	500	832	.263	.327	**.402**	**.729**	113	**80**	12	110	98	709	.666	95	70	58	-13
CLE	159	81	78	.509	16	615	615	5412	1423	189	38	85	479	631	.263	.324	.359	.683	100	-1	1	100	97	611	.597	75	69	52	-18
DET	161	74	87	.460	24	609	709	5441	1401	207	38	101	450	730	.257	.318	.365	.683	100	-6	-28	104	97	611	.605	107	59	64	-2
MIL	161	66	95	.410	32	570	655	5396	1326	170	38	88	511	909	.246	.314	.340	.654	91	-56	-49	99	98	575	.573	62	61	50	-17
WEST																												
KC	162	90	72	.556		713	611	5540	1490	**259**	57	65	484	650	.269	.331	.371	.702	105	37	38	100	103	687	.655	218	106	67	2
OAK	161	87	74	.540	2.5	686	598	5353	1319	208	33	113	**592**	818	.246	.327	.361	.688	101	13	15	100	104	663	**.685**	341	123	73	29
MIN	162	85	77	.525	5	**743**	704	5574	**1526**	222	51	81	550	714	**.274**	**.343**	.375	.718	110	78	**89**	98	100	**727**	.667	146	75	66	0
TEX	162	76	86	.469	14	616	652	5555	1390	213	26	80	568	809	.250	.323	.341	.664	95	-31	-44	102	97	616	.593	87	45	66	0
CAL	162	76	86	.469	14	550	631	5385	1265	210	23	63	534	812	.235	.309	.318	.627	84	-104	-51	92	102	531	.557	126	80	61	-9
CHI	161	64	97	.398	25.5	586	745	5532	1410	209	46	73	471	739	.255	.317	.349	.666	95	-35	-29	99	95	622	.597	120	53	69	4
TOT	967					7753		65711	16820	2588	467	1122	6128	9143	.256	.323	.361	.684								1690	867	66	-12

TEAM	CG	SHO	SV	IP	H	H/G	HR	BB	BB/G	SO	SO/G	ERA	/A	OAVG	OOBA	PR	/A	PF	CPI	FA	E	DP	FW	PW	BW	SBW	DIF
EAST																										
NY	62	15	37	1455.0	**1300**	8.0	97	448	2.8	674	4.2	**3.19**	107	**.269**	**.327**	52	37	97	122	.980	126	141	1.0	3.9	7.1	1.2	4.3
BAL	59	16	23	1468.7	1396	8.6	**80**	489	3.0	678	4.2	3.32	103	.289	.348	33	18	97	131	**.982**	**118**	157	1.4	1.9	-1.7	1.0	4.4
BOS	49	13	27	1458.0	1495	9.2	109	**409**	**2.5**	673	4.2	3.52	110	.269	.345	-1	54	110	127	.978	141	148	.1	**5.7**	1.3	-1.3	-3.9
CLE	30	**17**	**46**	1432.0	1361	8.6	**80**	533	3.3	928	5.8	3.47	101	.292	.361	7	5	100	127	.980	121	159	1.3	.5	.1	1.8	1.4
DET	55	12	20	1431.3	1426	9.0	101	550	3.5	738	4.6	3.87	95	.302	.370	-55	-29	105	128	.974	168	161	-1.4	-3.1	-3.0	-.0	1.1
MIL	45	10	27	1435.3	1406	8.8	99	567	3.6	677	4.2	3.64	97	.300	.371	-19	-19	100	**135**	.975	152	160	-.5	-2.0	-5.2	-1.7	-5.1
WEST																										
KC	41	12	35	1472.3	1356	8.3	83	493	3.0	735	4.5	3.21	108	.278	.341	50	41	99	129	.978	139	147	.2	4.4	4.0	.3	.0
OAK	39	15	29	1459.3	1412	8.7	96	415	2.6	711	4.4	3.26	106	.284	.335	42	33	98	128	.977	144	130	-.0	3.5	1.6	**3.2**	-1.7
MIN	29	11	23	1459.0	1421	8.8	89	610	3.8	762	4.7	3.69	93	.300	.377	-28	-41	98	133	.973	172	182	-1.7	-4.4	9.4	.1	.4
TEX	63	15	15	1472.0	1464	9.0	106	461	2.8	773	4.7	3.45	104	.295	.350	10	24	103	132	.976	156	142	-.7	2.5	-4.7	.1	-2.3
CAL	**64**	15	17	1477.3	1323	8.1	95	553	3.4	**992**	**6.0**	3.36	97	.277	.349	26	-13	93	128	.977	150	139	-.4	-1.4	-5.4	-.8	3.0
CHI	54	10	22	1448.0	1460	9.1	87	600	3.7	802	5.0	4.25	84	.308	.381	-118	-110	101	120	.979	130	155	.7	-11.7	-3.1	.5	-3.0
TOT	590	161	321	17468.3		8.7			3.2		4.7	3.52		.256	.323					.977	1717	1821					

Runs		Hits		Doubles		Triples		Home Runs		Total Bases	
White-NY	104	Brett-KC	215	Otis-KC	40	Brett-KC	14	Nettles-NY	32	Brett-KC	298
Carew-Min	97	Carew-Min	200	McRae-KC	34	Garner-Oak	12	Jackson-Bal	27	Chambliss-NY	283
Rivers-NY	95	Chambliss-NY	188	Evans-Bos	34	Carew-Min	12	Bando-Oak	27	Rice-Bos	280
Brett-KC	94	Munson-NY	186	Carty-Cle	34	Poquette-KC	10			Carew-Min	280
		Rivers-NY	184	Brett-KC	34	Bostock-Min	9			Nettles-NY	277

Runs Batted In		Runs Produced		Bases On Balls		Batting Average		On Base Percentage		Slugging Average	
L.May-Bal	109	Carew-Min	178	Hargrove-Tex	97	Brett-KC	.333	McRae-KC	.412	Jackson-Bal	.502
Munson-NY	105	Munson-NY	167	Harrah-Tex	91	McRae-KC	.332	Hargrove-Tex	.401	Rice-Bos	.482
Yastrzemski-Bos	102	Hisle-Min	163	Grich-Bal	86	Carew-Min	.331	Carew-Min	.398	Nettles-NY	.475
		Otis-KC	161	White-NY	83	Bostock-Min	.323	Staub-Det	.392	Lynn-Bos	.467
				Staub-Det	83	LeFlore-Det	.316	Carty-Cle	.384	Carew-Min	.463

Production		Adjusted Production		Batter Runs		Adjusted Batter Runs		Clutch Hitting Index		Runs Created	
McRae-KC	.873	McRae-KC	156	Carew-Min	40.0	Carew-Min	41.2	Mayberry-KC	160	Brett-KC	114
Carew-Min	.861	Carew-Min	154	McRae-KC	38.8	McRae-KC	38.9	Rudi-Oak	152	Carew-Min	111
Jackson-Bal	.855	Jackson-Bal	152	Brett-KC	36.2	Brett-KC	36.4	Hisle-Min	144	McRae-KC	101
Brett-KC	.843	Brett-KC	146	Staub-Det	33.2	Staub-Det	30.7	Randle-Tex	138	Staub-Det	99
Lynn-Bos	.842	Tenace-Oak	144	Carty-Cle	29.8	Jackson-Bal	30.2	L.May-Bal	137	White-NY	98

Total Average		Stolen Bases		Stolen Base Average		Stolen Base Runs		Fielding Runs		Total Player Rating	
Carew-Min	.904	North-Oak	75	Rivers-NY	86.0	Campaneris-Oak	9.0	Fisk-Bos	18.2	Nettles-NY	4.1
McRae-KC	.894	LeFlore-Det	58	Campaneris-Oak	81.8	Rivers-NY	8.7	Belanger-Bal	16.9	Brett-KC	4.0
Jackson-Bal	.875	Campaneris-Oak	54	Baylor-Oak	81.3	Baylor-Oak	8.4	Sundberg-Tex	16.7	Carew-Min	3.9
Tenace-Oak	.867	Baylor-Oak	52	Bumbry-Bal	80.8	Bumbry-Bal	6.6	Nettles-NY	16.5	McRae-KC	3.8
LeFlore-Det	.827	Patek-KC	51	Jackson-Bal	80.0	Patek-KC	6.3	Rodriguez-Det	15.9	Jackson-Bal	3.6

Wins		Win Percentage		Games		Complete Games		Shutouts		Saves	
Palmer-Bal	22	Campbell-Min	.773	Fidrych-Det	78	Fidrych-Det	24	Ryan-Cal	7	Lyle-NY	23
Tiant-Bos	21	Garland-Bal	.741	Fingers-Oak	70	Tanana-Cal	23	Blyleven-Min-Tex	6	LaRoche-Cle	21
Garland-Bal	20	Ellis-NY	.680	Lindblad-Oak	65	Palmer-Bal	23	Palmer-Bal	6	Fingers-Oak	20
		Fidrych-Det	.679	Lyle-NY	64			Blue-Oak	6	Campbell-Min	20
				LaRoche-Cle	61					Littell-KC	16

Innings Pitched		Fewest Hits/Game		Fewest BB/Game		Strikeouts		Strikeouts/Game		Wins Above Team	
Palmer-Bal	315	Ryan-Cal	6.12	Bird-KC	1.41	Ryan-Cal	327	Ryan-Cal	10.36	Garland-Bal	6.4
Hunter-NY	299	Tanana-Cal	6.63	Jenkins-Bos	1.85	Tanana-Cal	261	Eckersley-Cle	9.05	Fidrych-Det	6.3
Blue-Oak	298	Eckersley-Cle	7.01	Perry-Tex	1.87	Blyleven-Min-Tex	219	Tanana-Cal	8.16	Campbell-Min	6.1
Blyleven-Min-Tex	297	Palmer-Bal	7.29	Blue-Oak	1.90	Eckersley-Cle	200	Blyleven-Min-Tex	6.64	Tanana-Cal	5.7
Slaton-Mil	293	Brett-NY-Chi	7.67	Fidrych-Det	1.91	Hunter-NY	173	Campbell-Min	6.16	Tiant-Bos	4.9

Earned Run Average		Adjusted ERA		Opponents' Batting Avg.		Opponents' On Base Pct.		Starter Runs		Adjusted Starter Runs	
Fidrych-Det	2.34	Fidrych-Det	157	Ryan-Cal	.195	Tanana-Cal	.257	Blue-Oak	38.5	Fidrych-Det	37.3
Blue-Oak	2.36	Blue-Oak	147	Tanana-Cal	.203	Fidrych-Det	.274	Palmer-Bal	35.1	Blue-Oak	36.6
Tanana-Cal	2.44	Torrez-Oak	138	Eckersley-Cle	.214	Blue-Oak	.276	Tanana-Cal	34.6	Palmer-Bal	31.9
Torrez-Oak	2.50	Palmer-Bal	136	Palmer-Bal	.224	Palmer-Bal	.276	Fidrych-Det	32.7	Torrez-Oak	28.3
Palmer-Bal	2.51	Tanana-Cal	134	Brett-NY-Chi	.233	Bird-KC	.278	Torrez-Oak	30.0	Tanana-Cal	26.7

Clutch Pitching Index		Relief Runs		Adjusted Relief Runs		Relief Ranking		Total Pitcher Index		Total Baseball Ranking	
Hartzell-Cal	124	Littell-KC	16.7	Hiller-Det	17.5	Hiller-Det	30.3	Fidrych-Det	4.9	Fidrych-Det	4.9
Travers-Mil	120	Fingers-Oak	15.8	Littell-KC	16.0	Fingers-Oak	28.9	Blue-Oak	3.8	Nettles-NY	4.1
Umbarger-Tex	117	Hiller-Det	15.3	Kern-Cle	14.9	Lyle-NY	24.4	Palmer-Bal	3.7	Brett-KC	4.0
Garland-Bal	116	Kern-Cle	15.1	Fingers-Oak	14.9	Kern-Cle	23.6	Tanana-Cal	3.2	Carew-Min	3.9
Torrez-Oak	115	Lyle-NY	14.7	Thomas-Cle	14.3	Littell-KC	22.2	Torrez-Oak	3.1	McRae-KC	3.8

TEAM	G	W	L	PCT	GB	R	OR	AB	H	2B	3B	HR	BB	SO	AVG	OBP	SLG	PRO	/A	BR	/A	PF	CHI	RC	TA	SB	CS	SBA	SBR
EAST																													
PHI	162	101	61	.623		**847**	668	5546	1548	266	56	186	573	806	.279	.351	.448	.799	119	143	140	100	98	865	.771	135	68	67	0
PIT	162	96	66	.593	5	734	665	5662	1550	278	57	133	474	878	.274	.334	.413	.747	105	36	17	103	97	776	.718	260	120	68	6
STL	162	83	79	.512	18	737	688	5527	1490	252	56	96	489	823	.270	.332	.388	.720	98	-12	18	96	106	690	.655	134	112	54	-26
CHI	162	81	81	.500	20	692	739	5604	1489	271	37	111	534	796	.266	.333	.387	.720	98	-11	-110	114	97	709	.649	64	45	59	-7
MON	162	75	87	.463	26	665	736	5675	1474	294	50	138	478	877	.260	.320	.402	.722	98	-20	-7	98	95	715	.656	88	50	64	-3
NY	162	64	98	.395	37	587	663	5410	1319	227	30	88	529	887	.244	.315	.346	.661	83	-124	-96	96	103	577	.587	98	81	55	-18
WEST																													
LA	162	98	64	.605		769	**582**	5589	1484	223	28	**191**	588	896	.266	.338	.418	.756	108	58	58	100	98	794	.717	114	62	65	-2
CIN	162	88	74	.543	10	802	725	5524	1513	269	42	181	600	911	.274	.348	.436	.784	115	115	115	100	96	847	.765	170	64	**73**	13
HOU	162	81	81	.500	17	680	650	5530	1405	263	**60**	114	515	839	.254	.322	.385	.707	95	-40	13	93	101	697	.669	187	72	72	13
SF	162	75	87	.463	24	673	711	5497	1392	227	41	134	568	842	.253	.326	.383	.709	95	-35	-65	104	99	683	.650	90	59	60	-7
SD	162	69	93	.426	29	692	834	5602	1397	245	49	120	**602**	1057	.249	.325	.375	.700	93	-49	40	88	102	700	.656	133	57	70	6
ATL	162	61	101	.377	37	678	895	5534	1404	218	20	139	537	876	.254	.322	.376	.698	92	-58	-148	113	104	660	.629	82	53	61	-6
TOT	972					8556		66700	17465	3033	526	1631	6487	10488	.262	.330	.397	.727								1555	843	65	-38

TEAM	CG	SHO	SV	IP	H	H/G	HR	BB	BB/G	SO	SO/G	ERA	/A	OAVG	OOBA	PR	/A	PF	CPI	FA	E	DP	FW	PW	BW	SBW	DIF
EAST																											
PHI	31	7	47	1455.7	1451	9.0	134	482	3.0	856	5.3	3.71	104	.262	.319	32	21	98	103	.981	120	168	1.3	2.1	**14.2**	.3	2.1
PIT	25	**15**	39	1481.7	1406	8.5	149	485	2.9	890	5.4	3.61	110	.251	.307	49	61	102	99	.977	145	137	-.0	6.2	1.7	.9	6.2
STL	26	10	31	1446.0	1420	8.8	139	532	3.3	768	4.8	3.81	98	.260	.322	16	-14	95	102	.978	139	**174**	.3	-1.4	1.8	-2.3	3.6
CHI	16	10	44	1468.0	1500	9.2	128	489	3.0	**942**	5.8	4.01	112	.265	.321	-16	76	115	96	.977	153	147	-.5	7.7	-11.1	-.4	4.3
MON	31	11	33	1481.0	1426	8.7	135	579	3.5	856	5.2	4.01	97	.254	.320	-16	-21	99	94	.980	129	128	.8	-2.1	-.7	.0	-4.0
NY	27	12	28	1433.7	**1378**	8.7	118	490	3.1	911	5.7	3.77	100	.253	.313	21	1	97	94	.978	134	132	.5	.1	-9.7	-1.5	-6.4
WEST																											
LA	34	13	39	1475.3	1393	8.5	119	**438**	2.7	930	5.7	**3.22**	119	.251	**.303**	112	**98**	98	104	.981	124	160	1.1	**9.9**	5.9	.1	.0
CIN	33	12	32	1437.3	1469	9.2	156	544	3.4	868	5.4	4.21	92	.267	.330	-48	-54	99	100	**.984**	154	95	**2.7**	-5.5	11.6	**1.6**	-3.5
HOU	**37**	11	28	1465.7	1384	8.5	110	545	3.3	871	5.3	3.54	102	**.250**	.315	60	10	92	95	.978	146	136	.0	1.0	1.3	**1.6**	-4.1
SF	27	10	33	1459.0	1501	9.3	114	529	3.3	854	5.3	3.75	109	.267	.327	25	56	105	104	.972	179	136	-2.0	5.7	-6.6	-.4	-2.7
SD	6	5	44	1466.3	1556	9.6	160	673	4.1	827	5.1	4.43	79	.275	.348	-85	-153	89	**105**	.971	189	142	-2.5	-15.5	4.0	.9	1.0
ATL	28	5	31	1445.3	1581	9.8	169	701	4.4	915	5.7	4.85	93	.279	.355	-151	-54	115	101	.972	175	127	-1.7	-5.5	-15.0	-.3	2.5
TOT	321	121	429	17515.0		9.0			3.3		5.4	3.91		.262	.330					.977	1724	1741					

Runs		Hits		Doubles		Triples		Home Runs		Total Bases	
Foster-Cin	124	Parker-Pit	215	Parker-Pit	44	Templeton-StL	18	Foster-Cin	52	Foster-Cin	388
Griffey-Cin	117	Rose-Cin	204	Cash-Mon	42	Schmidt-Phi	11	Burroughs-Atl	41	Parker-Pit	338
Schmidt-Phi	114	Templeton-StL	200	Hernandez-StL	41	Richards-SD	11	Luzinski-Phi	39	Luzinski-Phi	329
Morgan-Cin	113	Foster-Cin	197	Cromartie-Mon	41	Almon-SD	11	Schmidt-Phi	38	Garvey-LA	322
Parker-Pit	107	Garvey-LA	192					Garvey-LA	33	Schmidt-Phi	312

Runs Batted In		Runs Produced		Bases On Balls		Batting Average		On Base Percentage		Slugging Average	
Foster-Cin	149	Foster-Cin	221	Tenace-SD	125	Parker-Pit	.338	Smith-LA	.432	Foster-Cin	.631
Luzinski-Phi	130	Luzinski-Phi	190	Morgan-Cin	117	Templeton-StL	.322	Morgan-Cin	.420	Luzinski-Phi	.594
Garvey-LA	115	Schmidt-Phi	177	Smith-LA	104	Foster-Cin	.320	Tenace-SD	.417	Smith-LA	.576
Burroughs-Atl	114	Parker-Pit	174	Schmidt-Phi	104	Griffey-Cin	.318	Simmons-StL	.410	Schmidt-Phi	.574
		Garvey-LA	173	Cey-LA	93	Simmons-StL	.318	Parker-Pit	.399	Bench-Cin	.540

Production		Adjusted Production		Batter Runs		Adjusted Batter Runs		Clutch Hitting Index		Runs Created	
Foster-Cin	1.017	Foster-Cin	168	Foster-Cin	56.0	Foster-Cin	56.1	Cey-LA	136	Foster-Cin	144
Smith-LA	1.008	Smith-LA	168	Smith-LA	50.3	Smith-LA	50.3	Watson-Hou	131	Luzinski-Phi	132
Luzinski-Phi	.993	Luzinski-Phi	162	Luzinski-Phi	48.5	Luzinski-Phi	48.2	Bench-Cin	124	Parker-Pit	130
Schmidt-Phi	.972	Schmidt-Phi	157	Schmidt-Phi	45.7	Schmidt-Phi	45.4	Luzinski-Phi	124	Schmidt-Phi	129
Parker-Pit	.929	Hendrick-SD	151	Parker-Pit	41.9	Parker-Pit	39.8	Robinson-Pit	123	Smith-LA	129

Total Average		Stolen Bases		Stolen Base Average		Stolen Base Runs		Fielding Runs		Total Player Rating	
Smith-LA	1.135	Taveras-Pit	70	Bowa-Phi	91.4	Taveras-Pit	10.2	DeJesus-Chi	36.1	Schmidt-Phi	7.2
Morgan-Cin	1.080	Cedeno-Hou	61	McBride-StL-Phi	83.7	Cedeno-Hou	9.9	Trillo-Chi	35.9	Foster-Cin	6.2
Schmidt-Phi	1.065	Richards-SD	56	Morgan-Cin	83.1	Richards-SD	9.6	Parker-Pit	30.0	Parker-Pit	5.8
Luzinski-Phi	1.048	Moreno-Pit	53	Richards-SD	82.4	Morgan-Cin	8.7	Schmidt-Phi	28.5	Morgan-Cin	4.4
Foster-Cin	1.048	Morgan-Cin	49	Cedeno-Hou	81.3	Bowa-Phi	7.8	Tyson-StL	19.4	Lopes-LA	4.0

Wins		Win Percentage		Games		Complete Games		Shutouts		Saves	
Carlton-Phi	23	Candelaria-Pit	.800	Fingers-SD	78	Niekro-Atl	20	Seaver-NY-Cin	7	Fingers-SD	35
Seaver-NY-Cin	21	Seaver-NY-Cin	.778	Tomlin-SD	76	Seaver-NY-Cin	19	Rogers-Mon	4	Sutter-Chi	31
		Christenson-Phi	.760	Spillner-SD	76	Rogers-Mon	17	R.Reuschel-Chi	4	Gossage-Pit	26
		John-LA	.741	Metzger-SD-StL	75	Carlton-Phi	17			Hough-LA	22
		Forsch-StL	.741			Richard-Hou	13				

Innings Pitched		Fewest Hits/Game		Fewest BB/Game		Strikeouts		Strikeouts/Game		Wins Above Team	
Niekro-Atl	330	Seaver-NY-Cin	6.86	Candelaria-Pit	1.95	Niekro-Atl	262	Koosman-NY	7.61	Seaver-NY-Cin	8.0
Rogers-Mon	302	Richard-Hou	7.15	John-LA	2.05	Richard-Hou	214	Richard-Hou	7.21	Forsch-StL	6.9
Carlton-Phi	283	Carlton-Phi	7.28	Rau-SF	2.08	Rogers-Mon	206	Niekro-Atl	7.15	Candelaria-Pit	6.9
Richard-Hou	267	Hooton-LA	7.43	Barr-SF	2.15	Carlton-Phi	198	Seaver-NY-Cin	6.76	R.Reuschel-Chi	5.7
Seaver-NY-Cin	261	Candelaria-Pit	7.68	Lemongello-Hou	2.18	Seaver-NY-Cin	196	Matlack-NY	6.55	John-LA	5.2

Earned Run Average		Adjusted ERA		Opponents' Batting Avg.		Opponents' On Base Pct.		Starter Runs		Adjusted Starter Runs	
Candelaria-Pit	2.34	Candelaria-Pit	170	Seaver-NY-Cin	.209	Seaver-NY-Cin	.257	Candelaria-Pit	40.3	R.Reuschel-Chi	47.3
Seaver-NY-Cin	2.59	R.Reuschel-Chi	161	Richard-Hou	.218	Candelaria-Pit	.272	Carlton-Phi	39.9	Candelaria-Pit	42.1
Hooton-LA	2.62	Seaver-NY-Cin	148	Carlton-Phi	.223	Hooton-LA	.275	Seaver-NY-Cin	38.4	Carlton-Phi	37.8
Carlton-Phi	2.64	Hooton-LA	146	Hooton-LA	.225	Carlton-Phi	.284	Hooton-LA	31.9	Seaver-NY-Cin	36.0
John-LA	2.78	Carlton-Phi	146	Koosman-NY	.232	Sutton-LA	.285	R.Reuschel-Chi	31.4	Hooton-LA	29.7

Clutch Pitching Index		Relief Runs		Adjusted Relief Runs		Relief Ranking		Total Pitcher Index		Total Baseball Ranking	
Candelaria-Pit	126	Gossage-Pit	33.8	Sutter-Chi	37.2	Gossage-Pit	62.4	R.Reuschel-Chi	5.9	Schmidt-Phi	7.2
John-LA	120	Sutter-Chi	30.5	Gossage-Pit	34.8	Sutter-Chi	55.6	Carlton-Phi	5.2	Foster-Cin	6.2
Rooker-Pit	118	Lavelle-SF	24.2	Lavelle-SF	26.7	Lavelle-SF	38.7	Candelaria-Pit	4.9	R.Reuschel-Chi	5.9
Lemongello-Hou	116	Garber-Pit	17.7	Hernandez-Chi	17.7	Garber-Pit	27.8	Seaver-NY-Cin	4.3	Parker-Pit	5.8
Rau-LA	114	Reed-Phi	15.9	Heaverlo-SF	17.1	Hernandez-Chi	23.2	Sutter-Chi	4.0	Carlton-Phi	5.2

TEAM	G	W	L	PCT	GB	R	OR	AB	H	2B	3B	HR	BB	SO	AVG	OBP	SLG	PRO	/A	BR	/A	PF	CHI	RC	TA	SB	CS	SBA	SBR
EAST																													
NY	162	100	62	.617		831	**651**	5605	1576	267	47	184	533	681	.281	.347	.444	.791	114	104	**115**	99	98	853	.748	93	57	62	-5
BAL	161	97	64	.602	2.5	719	653	5494	1433	231	25	148	560	945	.261	.332	.393	.725	97	-22	28	93	101	711	.667	90	51	64	-3
BOS	161	97	64	.602	2.5	859	712	5510	1551	258	56	**213**	528	905	.281	.349	**.465**	**.814**	**120**	**144**	16	117	98	**875**	**.772**	66	47	58	-7
DET	162	74	88	.457	26	714	751	5604	1480	228	45	166	452	764	.264	.321	.410	.731	98	-24	-57	105	101	717	.657	60	46	57	-9
CLE	161	71	90	.441	28.5	676	739	5491	1476	221	46	100	531	688	.269	.337	.380	.717	95	-30	-12	98	96	682	.644	87	87	50	-25
MIL	162	67	95	.414	33	639	765	5517	1425	255	46	125	443	862	.258	.316	.389	.705	91	-72	-37	95	98	660	.630	85	67	56	-14
TOR	161	54	107	.335	45.5	605	822	5418	1367	230	41	100	499	819	.252	.318	.365	.683	86	-105	-123	103	98	610	.602	65	55	54	-13
WEST																													
KC	162	102	60	.630		822	**651**	5594	1549	**299**	**77**	146	522	687	.277	.343	.436	.779	111	82	79	100	99	835	.750	170	87	**66**	**0**
TEX	162	94	68	.580	8	767	657	5541	1497	265	39	135	**596**	904	.270	.345	.405	.750	104	34	0	105	97	780	.714	154	85	64	-4
CHI	162	90	72	.556	12	844	771	5633	1568	254	52	192	559	**666**	.278	.347	.444	.791	114	107	111	99	98	858	.742	42	44	49	-13
MIN	161	84	77	.522	17.5	**867**	776	5639	**1588**	273	60	123	563	754	**.282**	**.351**	.417	.768	108	71	49	103	104	827	.723	105	65	62	-7
CAL	162	74	88	.457	28	675	695	5410	1380	233	40	131	542	880	.255	.327	.386	.713	93	-46	-6	95	99	681	.667	159	89	64	-5
SEA	162	64	98	.395	38	624	855	5460	1398	218	33	133	426	769	.256	.314	.381	.695	88	-90	-62	96	99	643	.625	110	67	62	-6
OAK	161	63	98	.391	38.5	605	749	5358	1284	176	37	117	516	910	.240	.311	.352	.663	80	-144	-109	95	**106**	589	.611	**176**	89	**66**	**0**
TOT	1131					10247		77274	20572	3408	644	2013	7270	11234	.266	.333	.405	.738								1462	936	61	-122

TEAM	CG	SHO	SV	IP	H	H/G	HR	BB	BB/G	SO	SO/G	ERA	/A	OAVG	OOBA	PR	/A	PF	CPI	FA	E	DP	FW	PW	BW	SBW	DIF
EAST																											
NY	52	16	34	1449.3	1395	8.7	139	486	3.0	758	4.7	3.61	109	.254	.312	72	50	97	101	.979	132	151	.6	5.0	**11.4**	.4	1.7
BAL	**65**	11	23	1451.0	1414	8.8	124	494	3.1	737	4.6	3.74	100	.260	.319	51	1	92	101	**.983**	**106**	**189**	**2.0**	.0	2.8	.6	11.0
BOS	40	13	40	1428.0	1555	9.8	158	**378**	**2.4**	758	4.8	4.11	115	.278	.322	-8	94	116	102	.978	133	162	.5	9.3	1.6	.2	4.9
DET	44	3	23	1457.0	1526	9.4	162	470	2.9	784	4.8	4.13	103	.270	.323	-11	21	105	100	.978	142	153	.0	2.1	-5.7	-.0	-3.4
CLE	45	8	30	1452.3	1441	8.9	136	550	3.4	876	5.4	4.10	97	.261	.324	-6	-17	98	96	.979	130	145	.7	-1.7	-1.2	-1.6	-5.7
MIL	38	6	25	1431.0	1461	9.2	136	566	3.6	719	4.5	4.32	91	.268	.333	-41	-64	97	97	.978	139	165	.2	-6.4	-3.7	-.5	-3.6
TOR	40	3	20	1428.3	1538	9.7	152	623	3.9	771	4.9	4.57	93	.278	.346	-80	-50	105	101	.974	164	133	-1.2	-5.0	-12.2	-.4	-7.6
WEST																											
KC	41	15	**42**	1460.7	**1377**	**8.5**	**110**	499	3.1	850	5.2	**3.52**	114	**.251**	.311	**87**	79	99	98	.978	137	145	.3	7.8	7.8	**.9**	4.2
TEX	49	**17**	31	1472.3	1412	8.6	134	471	2.9	864	5.3	3.56	**118**	.254	**.310**	80	**104**	104	101	.982	117	156	1.4	**10.3**	.0	.5	.8
CHI	34	3	40	1444.7	1557	9.7	136	516	3.2	842	5.2	4.25	94	.276	.334	-30	-39	99	101	.974	159	125	-1.0	-3.9	11.0	-.4	3.2
MIN	35	4	25	1442.0	1546	9.6	151	507	3.2	737	4.6	4.36	95	.278	.336	-47	-34	102	101	.978	143	184	-.0	-3.4	4.9	.2	1.9
CAL	53	13	26	1437.7	1383	8.7	136	572	3.6	**965**	**6.0**	3.72	103	.256	.325	54	20	95	**105**	.976	147	137	-.3	2.0	-.6	.4	-8.5
SEA	18	1	31	1433.0	1508	9.5	194	578	3.6	785	4.9	4.83	83	.271	.341	-122	-133	98	96	.976	147	162	-.3	-13.2	-6.2	.3	2.4
OAK	32	4	26	1436.7	1459	9.1	145	560	3.5	788	4.9	4.04	97	.265	.329	2	-19	97	102	.970	190	136	-2.7	-1.9	-10.8	**.9**	-2.9
TOT	586	117	416	20224.0		9.2			3.2		5.0	4.06		.266	.333					.977	1986	2143					

Runs
Carew-Min 128
Fisk-Bos 106
Brett-KC 105

Hits
Carew-Min 239
LeFlore-Det 212
Rice-Bos 206
Bostock-Min 199
Burleson-Bos 194

Doubles
McRae-KC 54
Jackson-NY 39
Lemon-Chi 38
Carew-Min 38

Triples
Carew-Min 16
Rice-Bos 15
Cowens-KC 14
Brett-KC 13
Bostock-Min 12

Home Runs
Rice-Bos 39
Nettles-NY 37
Bonds-Cal 37
Scott-Bos 33
Jackson-NY 32

Total Bases
Rice-Bos 382
Carew-Min 351
McRae-KC 330
Cowens-KC 318
LeFlore-Det 310

Runs Batted In
Hisle-Min 119
Bonds-Cal 115
Rice-Bos 114
Hobson-Bos 112
Cowens-KC 112

Runs Produced
Carew-Min 214
Cowens-KC 187
Hisle-Min 186
Fisk-Bos 182
Bonds-Cal 181

Bases On Balls
Harrah-Tex 109
Singleton-Bal 107
Hargrove-Tex 103
Gross-Oak 86
Mayberry-KC 83

Batting Average
Carew-Min 388
Bostock-Min 336
Singleton-Bal 328
Rivers-NY 326
LeFlore-Det 325

On Base Percentage
Carew-Min 452
Singleton-Bal 442
Hargrove-Tex 424
Fisk-Bos 408
Page-Oak 407

Slugging Average
Rice-Bos 593
Carew-Min 570
Jackson-NY 550
Hisle-Min 533
Brett-KC 532

Production
Carew-Min 1.022
Rice-Bos 972
Singleton-Bal 949
Fisk-Bos 929
Page-Oak 928

Adjusted Production
Carew-Min 171
Singleton-Bal 170
Page-Oak 159
Jackson-NY 151
Thornton-Cle 147

Batter Runs
Carew-Min 67.0
Rice-Bos 51.4
Singleton-Bal 48.5
Fisk-Bos 39.9
Hargrove-Tex 37.8

Adjusted Batter Runs
Carew-Min 64.6
Singleton-Bal 53.8
Page-Oak 40.8
Rice-Bos 36.8
Jackson-NY 36.7

Clutch Hitting Index
Wynegar-Min 141
Hisle-Min 133
Doyle-Bos 133
Sundberg-Tex 133
Carty-Cle 133

Runs Created
Carew-Min 160
Rice-Bos 136
Singleton-Bal 124
McRae-KC 119
Page-Oak 117

Total Average
Carew-Min 1.126
Page-Oak 1.078
Singleton-Bal 1.013
Jackson-NY 1.005
Harrah-Tex 976

Stolen Bases
Patek-KC 53
Page-Oak 42
Remy-Cal 41
Bonds-Cal 41
LeFlore-Det 39

Stolen Base Average
Page-Oak 89.4
Jackson-NY 85.0
Harrah-Tex 84.4
White-KC 82.1
Patek-KC 80.3

Stolen Base Runs
Page-Oak 9.6
Patek-KC 8.1
Harrah-Tex 5.1
White-KC 3.9

Fielding Runs
Belanger-Bal 30.7
Lemon-Chi 26.5
Campaneris-Tex 24.1
Smalley-Min 21.6
Brett-KC 20.0

Total Player Rating
Carew-Min 5.9
Page-Oak 4.8
Brett-KC 4.6
Fisk-Bos 4.4
Singleton-Bal 4.1

Wins
Palmer-Bal 20
Leonard-KC 20
Goltz-Min 20
Ryan-Cal 19

Win Percentage
Splittorff-KC 727
Johnson-Min 696
Guidry-NY 696
Rozema-Det 682

Games
Lyle-NY 72
Johnson-Min 71
Campbell-Bos 69
McClure-Mil 68
LaGrow-Chi 66

Complete Games
Ryan-Cal 22
Palmer-Bal 22
Leonard-KC 21
Garland-Cle 21
Tanana-Cal 20

Shutouts
Tanana-Cal 7
Leonard-KC 5
Guidry-NY 5
Blyleven-Tex 5

Saves
Campbell-Bos 31
Lyle-NY 26
LaGrow-Chi 25
Kern-Cle 18
LaRoche-Cle-Cal 17

Innings Pitched
Palmer-Bal 319
Goltz-Min 303
Ryan-Cal 299
Leonard-KC 293
Garland-Cle 283

Fewest Hits/Game
Ryan-Cal 5.96
Blyleven-Tex 6.93
Palmer-Bal 7.42
Guidry-NY 7.42
Tanana-Cal 7.51

Fewest BB/Game
Rozema-Det 1.40
Jenkins-Bos 1.68
Hartzell-Cal 1.81
Eckersley-Cle 1.97
Cleveland-Bos 2.04

Strikeouts
Ryan-Cal 341
Leonard-KC 244
Tanana-Cal 205
Palmer-Bal 193
Eckersley-Cle 191

Strikeouts/Game
Ryan-Cal 10.26
Tanana-Cal 7.66
Guidry-NY 7.51
Leonard-KC 7.49
Blyleven-Tex 6.97

Wins Above Team
Rozema-Det 5.0
Goltz-Min 4.7
Johnson-Min 4.6
Medich-Oak-Sea 4.3
Tanana-Cal 4.1

Earned Run Average
Tanana-Cal 2.54
Blyleven-Tex 2.72
Ryan-Cal 2.77
Guidry-NY 2.82
Palmer-Bal 2.91

Adjusted ERA
Blyleven-Tex 154
Tanana-Cal 151
Guidry-NY 139
Ryan-Cal 139
Rozema-Det 138

Opponents' Batting Avg.
Ryan-Cal 193
Blyleven-Tex 214
Guidry-NY 224
Tanana-Cal 227
Leonard-KC 227

Opponents' On Base Pct.
Eckersley-Cle 273
Blyleven-Tex 275
Leonard-KC 281
Guidry-NY 281
Tanana-Cal 282

Starter Runs
Ryan-Cal 42.8
Palmer-Bal 40.8
Tanana-Cal 40.7
Blyleven-Tex 35.0
Leonard-KC 33.1

Adjusted Starter Runs
Blyleven-Tex 38.7
Ryan-Cal 35.8
Tanana-Cal 35.0
Leonard-KC 31.5
Palmer-Bal 29.9

Clutch Pitching Index
Slaton-Mil 118
Rozema-Det 116
Grimsley-Bal 110
Splittorff-KC 108
Tanana-Cal 106

Relief Runs
Lyle-NY 28.8
Torrealba-Oak 18.8
LaGrow-Chi 17.6
Campbell-Bos 17.1
Coleman-Oak 15.7

Adjusted Relief Runs
Campbell-Bos 27.2
Lyle-NY 26.7
LaGrow-Chi 17.1
Torrealba-Oak 16.9
Johnson-Min 16.6

Relief Ranking
Campbell-Bos 52.1
Lyle-NY 43.0
Johnson-Min 27.2
Romo-Sea 25.3
LaGrow-Chi 25.2

Total Pitcher Index
Blyleven-Tex 4.2
Tanana-Cal 3.9
Ryan-Cal 3.8
Palmer-Bal 3.1
Leonard-KC 3.1

Total Baseball Ranking
Carew-Min 5.9
Page-Oak 4.8
Brett-KC 4.6
Fisk-Bos 4.4
Blyleven-Tex 4.2

TEAM	G	W	L	PCT	GB	R	OR	AB	H	2B	3B	HR	BB	SO	AVG	OBP	SLG	PRO	/A	BR	/A	PF	CHI	RC	TA	SB	CS	SBA	SBR
EAST																													
PHI	162	90	72	.556		708	586	5448	1404	248	32	133	552	866	.258	.331	.388	.719	107	49	13	105	101	715	.682	152	58	72	11
PIT	161	88	73	.547	1.5	684	637	5406	1390	239	54	115	480	874	.257	.323	.385	.708	104	21	-12	105	103	676	.671	213	90	70	10
CHI	162	79	83	.488	11	664	724	5532	1461	224	48	72	562	746	.264	.334	.361	.695	101	11	-56	110	98	673	.632	110	58	65	-1
MON	162	76	86	.469	14	633	611	5530	1404	269	31	121	396	881	.254	.308	.379	.687	97	-27	0	96	103	629	.608	80	42	66	0
STL	162	69	93	.426	21	600	657	5415	1351	263	44	79	420	713	.249	.306	.358	.664	91	-65	-33	95	106	583	.585	97	42	70	4
NY	162	66	96	.407	24	607	690	5433	1332	227	47	86	549	829	.245	.317	.352	.669	93	-46	-34	98	100	600	.600	100	77	56	-15
WEST																													
LA	162	95	67	.586		727	573	5437	1435	251	27	149	610	818	.264	.340	.402	.742	113	98	104	99	96	763	.711	137	52	72	-10
CIN	161	92	69	.571	2.5	710	688	5392	1378	270	32	136	636	899	.256	.337	.385	.730	110	75	57	103	97	730	.698	137	58	70	6
SF	162	89	73	.549	6	613	594	5364	1331	240	41	117	554	814	.248	.320	.374	.694	100	-1	53	92	95	647	.635	87	54	62	-5
SD	162	84	78	.519	11	591	598	5360	1349	208	42	75	536	848	.252	.323	.348	.671	94	-36	12	93	97	624	.621	152	70	68	4
HOU	162	74	88	.457	21	605	634	5458	1408	231	45	70	434	743	.258	.315	.355	.670	93	-48	-13	95	102	608	.606	178	59	75	18
ATL	162	69	93	.426	26	600	750	5381	1313	191	39	123	550	874	.244	.317	.363	.680	96	-27	-102	112	97	608	.613	90	65	58	-11
TOT	971					7742		65156	16556	2861	482	1276	6279	9905	.254	.323	.372	.694								1533	725	68	25

TEAM	CG	SHO	SV	IP	H	H/G	HR	BB	BB/G	SO	SO/G	ERA	/A	OAVG	OOBA	PR	/A	PF	CPI	FA	E	DP	FW	PW	BW	SBW	DIF
EAST																											
PHI	38	9	29	1436.3	1343	8.4	118	393	2.5	813	5.1	3.33	111	.250	.299	38	60	104	99	.983	104	156	2.0	6.3	1.4	.9	-1.6
PIT	30	13	44	1444.7	1366	8.5	103	499	3.1	880	5.5	3.41	110	.248	.309	25	52	105	98	.973	167	133	-1.4	5.5	-1.3	.8	3.9
CHI	24	7	38	1455.3	1475	9.1	125	539	3.3	768	4.7	4.05	98	.264	.326	-76	-12	111	98	.978	144	154	-.2	-1.3	-5.9	-.3	5.7
MON	42	13	32	1446.0	1332	8.3	117	572	3.6	740	4.6	3.42	100	.249	.318	24	-1	96	106	.979	134	150	.3	-.1	.0	-.2	-5.0
STL	32	13	22	1437.7	1300	8.1	94	600	3.8	859	5.4	3.58	96	.245	.318	0	-25	96	97	.978	136	155	.2	-2.6	-3.5	.2	-6.3
NY	21	7	26	1455.3	1447	8.9	114	531	3.3	775	4.8	3.87	92	.265	.325	-47	-51	99	101	.979	132	160	.4	-5.4	-3.6	-1.8	-4.6
WEST																											
LA	46	16	38	1440.3	1362	8.5	107	440	2.7	800	5.0	3.12	111	.250	.303	73	55	97	106	.978	140	138	.0	5.8	11.0	.8	-3.7
CIN	16	10	46	1448.3	1437	8.9	122	567	3.5	908	5.6	3.81	96	.260	.324	-37	-23	102	102	.978	134	120	.3	-2.4	6.0	.4	7.2
SF	42	17	24	1455.0	1377	8.5	84	453	2.8	840	5.2	3.30	99	.251	.304	43	-7	91	98	.977	146	118	-.3	-.7	5.6	-.7	4.2
SD	21	10	55	1433.7	1385	8.7	74	483	3.0	744	4.7	3.28	101	.257	.313	47	4	93	104	.975	160	171	-1.1	.4	1.3	.2	2.2
HOU	48	17	23	1440.3	1328	8.3	86	578	3.6	930	5.8	3.63	93	.246	.315	-8	-38	95	94	.978	133	109	.4	-4.0	-1.4	1.7	-3.7
ATL	29	12	32	1440.3	1404	8.8	132	624	3.9	848	5.3	4.08	100	.256	.330	-80	-1	114	98	.975	153	126	-.7	-.1	-10.8	-1.4	1.0
TOT	389	144	414	17333.3		8.6			3.3		5.1	3.57		.254	.323					.978	1683	1690					

Runs		Hits		Doubles		Triples		Home Runs		Total Bases	
DeJesus-Chi	104	Garvey-LA	202	Rose-Cin	51	Templeton-StL	13	Foster-Cin	40	Parker-Pit	340
Rose-Cin	103	Rose-Cin	198	Clark-SF	46	Richards-SD	12	Luzinski-Phi	35	Foster-Cin	330
Parker-Pit	102	Cabell-Hou	195	Simmons-StL	40	Parker-Pit	12	Parker-Pit	30	Garvey-LA	319
Foster-Cin	97	Parker-Pit	194	Parrish-Mon	39			Garvey-LA	29	Clark-SF	318
Moreno-Pit	95	Bowa-Phi	192	Perez-Mon	38			Smith-LA	29	Winfield-SD	293

Runs Batted In		Runs Produced		Bases On Balls		Batting Average		On Base Percentage		Slugging Average	
Foster-Cin	120	Parker-Pit	189	Burroughs-Atl	117	Parker-Pit	.334	Burroughs-Atl	.436	Parker-Pit	.585
Parker-Pit	117	Garvey-LA	181	Evans-SF	105	Garvey-LA	.316	Parker-Pit	.395	Smith-LA	.559
Garvey-LA	113	Foster-Cin	177	Tenace-SD	101	Cruz-Hou	.315	Tenace-SD	.394	Foster-Cin	.546
Luzinski-Phi	101	Clark-SF	163	Luzinski-Phi	100	Madlock-SF	.309	Smith-LA	.392	Clark-SF	.537
Clark-SF	98	Winfield-SD	161	Cey-LA	96	Winfield-SD	.308	Luzinski-Phi	.390	Burroughs-Atl	.529

Production		Adjusted Production		Batter Runs		Adjusted Batter Runs		Clutch Hitting Index		Runs Created	
Parker-Pit	.981	Smith-LA	165	Parker-Pit	52.9	Parker-Pit	49.3	Morgan-Cin	145	Parker-Pit	134
Burroughs-Atl	.965	Clark-SF	162	Burroughs-Atl	50.0	Burroughs-Atl	42.4	Montanez-NY	139	Burroughs-Atl	116
Smith-LA	.951	Parker-Pit	162	Luzinski-Phi	40.9	Clark-SF	41.7	W.Robinson-Pit	136	Foster-Cin	115
Luzinski-Phi	.916	Simmons-StL	156	Foster-Cin	39.2	Smith-LA	38.3	Reitz-StL	136	Luzinski-Phi	114
Foster-Cin	.909	Winfield-SD	152	Smith-LA	37.7	Foster-Cin	37.2	Watson-Hou	128	Clark-SF	109

Total Average		Stolen Bases		Stolen Base Average		Stolen Base Runs		Fielding Runs		Total Player Rating	
Burroughs-Atl	1.047	Moreno-Pit	71	Cedeno-Hou	92.0	Lopes-LA	11.1	Trillo-Chi	33.9	Parker-Pit	5.2
Parker-Pit	1.042	Taveras-Pit	46	Lopes-LA	91.8	Moreno-Pit	8.1	Smith-SD	32.7	Clark-SF	4.6
Smith-LA	1.025	Lopes-LA	45	McBride-Phi	90.3	McBride-Phi	6.6	Templeton-StL	27.2	Simmons-StL	4.4
Luzinski-Phi	.973	DeJesus-Chi	41	Sexton-Hou	88.9			Carter-Mon	25.0	Stearns-NY	4.3
Foster-Cin	.901	Smith-SD	40	Bowa-Phi	84.4			Stearns-NY	23.9	Carter-Mon	4.0

Wins		Win Percentage		Games		Complete Games		Shutouts		Saves	
Perry-SD	21	Perry-SD	.778	Tekulve-Pit	91	Niekro-Atl	22	Knepper-SF	6	Fingers-SD	37
Grimsley-Mon	20	Hooton-LA	.655	Littell-StL	72	Grimsley-Mon	19	Niekro-Atl	4	Tekulve-Pit	31
Niekro-Atl	19	Grimsley-Mon	.645	Moore-Chi	71	Richard-Hou	16	Halicki-SF	4	Bair-Cin	28
Hooton-LA	19	Blue-SF	.643	Moffitt-SF	70	Knepper-SF	16	Blyleven-Pit	4	Sutter-Chi	27
		John-LA	.630	Bair-Cin	70			Blue-SF	4	Garber-Phi-Atl	25

Innings Pitched		Fewest Hits/Game		Fewest BB/Game		Strikeouts		Strikeouts/Game		Wins Above Team	
Niekro-Atl	334	Richard-Hou	6.28	Christenson-Phi	1.86	Richard-Hou	303	Richard-Hou	9.92	Perry-SD	7.9
Richard-Hou	275	Swan-NY	7.13	Barr-SF	1.93	Niekro-Atl	248	Seaver-Cin	7.82	Grimsley-Mon	5.9
Grimsley-Mon	263	Hooton-LA	7.47	Reuschel-Chi	2.00	Seaver-Cin	226	Vuckovich-StL	6.77	Richard-Hou	5.0
Perry-SD	261	Halicki-SF	7.51	Halicki-SF	2.04	Blyleven-Pit	182	Blyleven-Pit	6.71	Tomlin-Chi	3.9
				Sutton-LA	2.04	Montefusco-SF	177	Niekro-Atl	6.68	D.Robinson-Pit	3.7

Earned Run Average		Adjusted ERA		Opponents' Batting Avg.		Opponents' On Base Pct.		Starter Runs		Adjusted Starter Runs	
Swan-NY	2.43	Swan-NY	146	Richard-Hou	.196	Halicki-SF	.266	Knepper-SF	27.3	Niekro-Atl	44.1
Rogers-Mon	2.47	Niekro-Atl	141	Swan-NY	.219	Hooton-LA	.273	Rogers-Mon	27.0	Swan-NY	25.6
Vuckovich-StL	2.55	Rogers-Mon	138	Halicki-SF	.221	Swan-NY	.274	Swan-NY	26.2	Carlton-Phi	23.9
Knepper-SF	2.63	Vuckovich-StL	134	Hooton-LA	.226	Christenson-Phi	.278	Niekro-Atl	25.7	Rogers-Mon	23.1
Hooton-LA	2.71	Carlton-Phi	131	Seaver-Cin	.227	D.Robinson-Pit	.281	Perry-SD	24.7	Seaver-Cin	22.8

Clutch Pitching Index		Relief Runs		Adjusted Relief Runs		Relief Ranking		Total Pitcher Index		Total Baseball Ranking	
Rau-LA	134	Tekulve-Pit	18.6	Garber-Phi-Atl	23.6	Bair-Cin	33.6	Niekro-Atl	6.0	Niekro-Atl	6.0
Vuckovich-StL	123	Garber-Phi-Atl	18.5	Tekulve-Pit	21.1	Tekulve-Pit	32.1	Carlton-Phi	3.6	Parker-Pit	5.2
Carlton-Phi	121	Bair-Cin	17.7	Bair-Cin	18.7	Garber-Phi-Atl	31.4	Swan-NY	2.9	Clark-SF	4.6
Jones-SD	114	Reed-Phi	16.3	Reed-Phi	18.0	Forster-LA	22.2	Garber-Phi-Atl	2.6	Simmons-StL	4.4
Rogers-Mon	113	D'Acquisto-SD	14.9	Brusstar-Phi	13.7	Fingers-SD	22.1	Tekulve-Pit	2.5	Stearns-NY	4.3

TEAM	G	W	L	PCT	GB	R	OR	AB	H	2B	3B	HR	BB	SO	AVG	OBP	SLG	PRO	/A	BR	/A	PF	CHI	RC	TA	SB	CS	SBA	SBR
EAST																													
NY	163	100	63	.613		735	582	5583	1489	228	38	125	505	695	.267	.332	.388	.720	102	14	22	99	104	720	.660	98	42	70	4
BOS	163	99	64	.607	1	796	657	5587	1493	270	46	172	582	835	.267	.339	.424	.763	113	96	44	107	100	793	.713	74	51	59	-7
MIL	162	93	69	.574	6.5	804	650	5536	1530	265	38	173	520	805	.276	.342	.432	.774	116	114	75	106	100	822	.731	95	53	64	-2
BAL	161	90	71	.559	9	659	633	5422	1397	248	19	154	552	864	.258	.329	.396	.725	103	18	79	91	95	691	.662	75	61	55	-13
DET	162	86	76	.531	13.5	714	653	5601	1520	218	34	129	563	695	.271	.341	.392	.733	106	45	-8	108	96	748	.675	90	38	70	4
CLE	159	69	90	.434	29	639	694	5365	1400	223	45	106	488	698	.261	.321	.379	.705	98	-19	26	93	98	649	.628	64	63	50	-18
TOR	161	59	102	.366	40	590	775	5430	1358	217	39	98	448	645	.250	.310	.359	.669	88	-92	-92	100	102	587	.576	28	52	35	-22
WEST																													
KC	162	92	70	.568		743	634	5474	1469	305	59	98	498	644	.268	.333	.399	.732	105	34	19	102	104	739	.700	216	84	72	14
TEX	162	87	75	.537	5	692	632	5347	1353	216	36	132	624	779	.253	.335	.381	.716	101	11	36	96	100	696	.688	196	91	68	4
CAL	162	87	75	.537	5	691	666	5472	1417	226	28	108	539	682	.259	.333	.370	.703	97	-13	-23	102	102	669	.638	89	69	56	-14
MIN	162	73	89	.451	19	666	678	5522	1472	259	47	82	604	684	.267	.342	.375	.717	101	20	59	94	92	715	.661	99	56	64	-3
CHI	161	71	90	.441	20.5	634	731	5393	1423	221	41	106	409	625	.264	.320	.379	.699	96	-34	-39	101	101	635	.618	83	68	55	-15
OAK	162	69	93	.426	23	532	690	5321	1304	200	31	100	433	800	.245	.305	.351	.656	84	-116	-121	101	98	552	.582	144	117	55	-26
SEA	160	56	104	.350	35	614	834	5358	1327	229	37	97	522	702	.248	.317	.359	.676	90	-72	-84	102	103	620	.618	123	47	72	9
TOT	1131					9509		76411	19952	3325	538	1680	7287	10153	.261	.329	.385	.714								1474	892	62	-92

TEAM	CG	SHO	SV	IP	H	H/G	HR	BB	BB/G	SO	SO/G	ERA	/A	OAVG	OOBA	PR	/A	PF	CPI	FA	E	DP	FW	PW	BW	SBW	DIF
EAST																											
NY	39	16	36	1460.7	1321	8.1	111	478	2.9	817	5.0	3.18	115	.243	.301	94	77	97	99	.982	113	134	1.4	7.9	2.3	1.1	5.8
BOS	57	15	26	1472.7	1530	9.4	137	464	2.8	706	4.3	3.54	113	.269	.323	36	73	106	111	.977	146	171	-.4	7.4	4.5	-.0	5.9
MIL	62	19	24	1436.0	1442	9.0	109	398	2.5	577	3.6	3.65	107	.261	.310	17	42	104	95	.977	150	144	-.7	4.3	7.7	.5	4.2
BAL	65	16	33	1429.0	1340	8.4	107	509	3.2	754	4.7	3.56	96	.250	.312	31	-25	91	95	.982	110	166	1.6	-2.6	8.1	-.7	3.0
DET	60	12	21	1455.7	1441	8.9	135	503	3.1	684	4.2	3.64	111	.262	.321	19	62	107	106	.981	118	177	1.2	6.4	-.8	1.1	-2.8
CLE	36	6	28	1407.3	1397	8.9	100	568	3.6	739	4.7	3.97	89	.261	.328	-32	-70	94	95	.980	123	142	.9	-7.2	2.7	-1.2	-5.7
TOR	35	5	23	1429.3	1529	9.6	149	614	3.9	758	4.8	4.54	85	.278	.346	-123	-110	102	100	.979	131	163	.4	-11.3	-9.5	-1.6	.5
WEST																											
KC	53	14	33	1439.0	1350	8.4	108	478	3.0	657	4.1	3.44	110	.250	.308	51	57	101	98	.976	150	153	-.7	5.9	2.0	2.1	1.7
TEX	54	12	25	1456.3	1431	8.8	108	421	2.6	776	4.8	3.36	107	.259	.308	65	39	96	102	.976	153	140	-.8	4.0	3.7	1.1	-2.0
CAL	44	13	33	1455.7	1382	8.5	125	599	3.7	892	5.5	3.65	105	.252	.323	18	26	101	102	.978	136	136	.1	2.7	-2.4	-.8	6.3
MIN	48	9	26	1459.7	1468	9.1	102	520	3.2	703	4.3	3.69	96	.265	.325	11	-22	94	102	.977	146	171	-.4	-2.3	6.1	.4	-11.7
CHI	38	9	33	1409.3	1380	8.8	128	586	3.7	710	4.5	4.21	94	.259	.330	-70	-59	102	94	.977	139	130	-.0	-6.1	-4.0	-.9	1.5
OAK	26	11	29	1433.3	1401	8.8	106	582	3.7	750	4.7	3.62	106	.258	.325	22	37	103	103	.971	179	145	-2.3	3.8	-12.5	-2.0	1.0
SEA	28	4	20	1419.3	1540	9.8	155	567	3.6	630	4.0	4.67	84	.280	.344	-143	-118	104	98	.977	141	174	-.2	-12.2	-8.6	1.6	-4.7
TOT	645	161	390	20163.3		8.9			3.3		4.5	3.76		.261	.329					.978	1935	2146					

Runs
LeFlore-Det 126
Rice-Bos 121
Baylor-Cal 103
Thornton-Cle 97
Hisle-Mil 96

Hits
Rice-Bos 213
LeFlore-Det 198
Carew-Min 188
Munson-NY 183
Staub-Det 175

Doubles
Brett-KC 45
McRae-KC 39
Fisk-Bos 39
DeCinces-Bal 37
Ford-Min 36

Triples
Rice-Bos 15
Ford-Min 10
Carew-Min 10
Yount-Mil 9
Garr-Chi 9

Home Runs
Rice-Bos 46
Hisle-Mil 34
Baylor-Cal 34
Thornton-Cle 33
Thomas-Mil 32

Total Bases
Rice-Bos 406
Murray-Bal 293
Staub-Det 279
Baylor-Cal 279
Thompson-Det 278

Runs Batted In
Rice-Bos 139
Staub-Det 121
Hisle-Mil 115
Thornton-Cle 105

Runs Produced
Rice-Bos 214
Hisle-Mil 177
LeFlore-Det 176
Staub-Det 172
Thornton-Cle 169

Bases On Balls
Hargrove-Tex 107
Singleton-Bal 98
Kemp-Det 97
Thornton-Cle 93
Smalley-Min 85

Batting Average
Carew-Min 333
Oliver-Tex 324
Rice-Bos 315
Piniella-NY 314
Oglivie-Mil 303

On Base Percentage
Carew-Min 415
Singleton-Bal 410
Hargrove-Tex 391
Otis-KC 387
Randolph-NY 385

Slugging Average
Rice-Bos 600
Hisle-Mil 533
DeCinces-Bal 526
Otis-KC 525
Thornton-Cle 516

Production
Rice-Bos 973
Otis-KC 911
Hisle-Mil 909
Thornton-Cle 898
Roberts-Sea 881

Adjusted Production
Thornton-Cle 161
Singleton-Bal 160
Rice-Bos 158
DeCinces-Bal 157
Otis-KC 151

Batter Runs
Rice-Bos 58.6
Hisle-Mil 36.3
Thornton-Cle 35.5
Otis-KC 35.2
Singleton-Bal 34.0

Adjusted Batter Runs
Rice-Bos 52.5
Singleton-Bal 40.2
Thornton-Cle 40.2
Carew-Min 38.0
Murray-Bal 34.2

Clutch Hitting Index
Johnson-Chi 137
Chambliss-NY 137
Staub-Det 131
Bostock-Cal 129
Whitaker-Det 128

Runs Created
Rice-Bos 147
LeFlore-Det 105
Carew-Min 105
Thompson-Det 104
Murray-Bal 104

Total Average
Otis-KC 994
Rice-Bos 983
Hisle-Mil 923
Thornton-Cle 915
Singleton-Bal 900

Stolen Bases
LeFlore-Det 68
Cruz-Sea 59
Wills-Tex 52
Dilone-Oak 50
Wilson-KC 46

Stolen Base Average
Cruz-Sea 85.5
Campaneris-Tex 84.6
Lowenstein-Tex 84.2
Randolph-NY 83.7
Rivers-NY 83.3

Stolen Base Runs
Cruz-Sea 11.7
LeFlore-Det 10.8
Wills-Tex 7.2
Wilson-KC 6.6
Randolph-NY 6.6

Fielding Runs
Belanger-Bal 26.1
Bell-Cle 24.6
Wills-Tex 24.2
Cruz-Sea 22.9
Whitaker-Det 21.5

Total Player Rating
Rice-Bos 5.5
Smalley-Min 5.2
Fisk-Bos 4.4
DeCinces-Bal 4.2
Carew-Min 4.0

Wins
Guidry-NY 25
Caldwell-Mil 22
Palmer-Bal 21
Leonard-KC 21

Win Percentage
Guidry-NY 893
Stanley-Bos 882
Gura-KC 800
Eckersley-Bos 714
Caldwell-Mil 710

Games
Lacey-Oak 74
Heaverlo-Oak 69
Sosa-Oak 68
Gossage-NY 63

Complete Games
Caldwell-Mil 23
Leonard-KC 20
Palmer-Bal 19
Matlack-Tex 18

Shutouts
Guidry-NY 9
Palmer-Bal 6
Caldwell-Mil 6
Tiant-Bos 5

Saves
Gossage-NY 27
LaRoche-Cal 25
Stanhouse-Bal 24
Marshall-Min 21
Hrabosky-KC 20

Innings Pitched
Palmer-Bal 296
Leonard-KC 295
Caldwell-Mil 293
Sorensen-Mil 281
Flanagan-Bal 281

Fewest Hits/Game
Guidry-NY 6.14
Ryan-Cal 7.01
Gura-KC 7.42
Palmer-Bal 7.48
Tiant-Bos 7.85

Fewest BB/Game
Jenkins-Tex 1.48
Sorensen-Mil 1.60
Caldwell-Mil 1.66
Matlack-Tex 1.70
Rozema-Det 1.77

Strikeouts
Ryan-Cal 260
Guidry-NY 248
Leonard-KC 183
Flanagan-Bal 167
Eckersley-Bos 162

Strikeouts/Game
Ryan-Cal 9.96
Guidry-NY 8.15
Kravec-Chi 6.83
Underwood-Tor 6.32
Knapp-Cal 6.03

Wins Above Team
Guidry-NY 10.6
Stanley-Bos 6.1
Gura-KC 5.7
Caldwell-Mil 5.7
Jenkins-Tex 4.9

Earned Run Average
Guidry-NY 1.74
Matlack-Tex 2.27
Caldwell-Mil 2.37
Palmer-Bal 2.46
Goltz-Min 2.50

Adjusted ERA
Guidry-NY 210
Ryan-Cal 166
Matlack-Tex 159
Goltz-Min 142
Gura-KC 140

Opponents' Batting Avg.
Guidry-NY 193
Ryan-Cal 220
Palmer-Bal 227
Gura-KC 229
Tiant-Bos 234

Opponents' On Base Pct.
Guidry-NY 246
Caldwell-Mil 271
Jenkins-Tex 275
Gura-KC 278
Matlack-Tex 280

Starter Runs
Guidry-NY 61.6
Caldwell-Mil 45.5
Matlack-Tex 44.9
Palmer-Bal 42.8
Goltz-Min 31.0

Adjusted Starter Runs
Guidry-NY 58.2
Caldwell-Mil 50.5
Matlack-Tex 39.9
Palmer-Bal 31.0
Eckersley-Bos 29.8

Clutch Pitching Index
Lee-Bos 130
Zahn-Min 129
Goltz-Min 125
Gale-KC 115
Eckersley-Bos 115

Relief Runs
Gossage-NY 26.0
Stanley-Bos 18.4
Hiller-Det 14.5
Marshall-Min 14.4
Sosa-Oak 13.6

Adjusted Relief Runs
Gossage-NY 24.4
Stanley-Bos 21.9
Hiller-Det 17.2
Sosa-Oak 14.7
Marshall-Min 12.1

Relief Ranking
Gossage-NY 45.5
Marshall-Min 29.9
Hiller-Det 28.2
Stanley-Bos 27.1
LaRoche-Cal 25.2

Total Pitcher Index
Guidry-NY 6.9
Caldwell-Mil 5.8
Matlack-Tex 4.5
Palmer-Bal 3.4
Gura-KC 3.1

Total Baseball Ranking
Guidry-NY 6.9
Caldwell-Mil 5.8
Rice-Bos 5.5
Smalley-Min 5.2
Matlack-Tex 4.5

TEAM	G	W	L	PCT	GB	R	OR	AB	H	2B	3B	HR	BB	SO	AVG	OBP	SLG	PRO	/A	BR	/A	PF	CHI	RC	TA	SB	CS	SBA	SBR
EAST																													
PIT	163	98	64	.605	—	**775**	643	5661	1541	264	52	148	483	855	.272	.333	**.416**	**.749**	110	68	28	106	101	**781**	**.709**	180	66	**73**	14
MON	160	95	65	.594	2	701	**581**	5465	1445	273	42	143	432	890	.264	.321	.408	.729	104	23	7	102	101	701	.669	121	56	68	3
STL	163	86	76	.531	12	731	693	5734	**1594**	279	**63**	100	460	838	**.278**	.335	.401	.736	107	46	13	105	94	757	.671	116	69	63	-6
PHI	163	84	78	.519	14	683	718	5463	1453	250	53	119	602	764	.266	**.343**	.396	.739	108	63	**84**	97	91	743	.697	128	76	63	-6
CHI	162	80	82	.494	18	706	707	5550	1494	250	43	135	478	762	.269	.331	.403	.734	106	40	-43	112	97	726	.666	73	52	58	-8
NY	163	63	99	.389	35	593	706	5591	1399	255	41	74	498	817	.250	.315	.350	.665	87	-90	-54	95	99	615	.598	135	79	63	-6
WEST																													
CIN	161	90	71	.559	—	731	644	5477	1445	266	31	132	**614**	902	.264	.340	.396	.736	107	55	72	97	98	741	.690	99	47	68	2
HOU	162	89	73	.549	1.5	583	582	5394	1382	224	52	49	461	**745**	.256	.317	.344	.661	86	-92	-28	90	101	591	.601	**190**	**95**	67	0
LA	162	79	83	.488	11.5	739	717	5490	1443	220	24	**183**	556	834	.263	.333	.412	.745	109	62	64	100	99	743	.695	106	46	70	4
SF	162	71	91	.438	19.5	672	751	5395	1328	192	36	125	580	925	.246	.322	.365	.687	93	-45	6	92	**106**	644	.638	140	73	66	-1
SD	161	68	93	.422	22	603	681	5446	1316	193	53	93	534	777	.242	.313	.348	.661	86	-66	-70	96	103	600	.596	100	58	63	-4
ATL	160	66	94	.413	23.5	669	763	5422	1389	220	28	126	490	818	.256	.320	.377	.697	96	-30	-91	109	105	654	.633	98	50	66	0
TOT	971					8186		66088	17229	2886	518	1427	6188	9920	.261	.327	.385	.712								1486	767	66	-13

TEAM	CG	SHO	SV	IP	H	H/G	HR	BB	BB/G	SO	SO/G	ERA	/A	OAVG	OOBA	PR	/A	PF	CPI	FA	E	DP	FW	PW	BW	SBW	DIF
EAST																											
PIT	24	7	**52**	1493.3	1424	8.6	125	504	3.0	904	5.4	3.41	114	.253	.312	53	77	104	103	.979	134	163	.3	7.9	2.9	**1.6**	4.3
MON	33	18	39	1447.3	1379	8.6	116	**450**	2.8	813	5.1	**3.14**	120	.252	.306	**94**	**99**	101	**107**	.979	131	123	.5	**10.2**	.7	.4	3.1
STL	38	10	25	1486.7	1449	8.8	127	501	3.0	788	4.8	3.72	104	.258	.314	1	27	104	94	.980	132	166	.4	2.8	1.3	-.5	.9
PHI	33	14	29	1441.3	1455	9.1	135	477	3.0	787	4.9	4.16	87	.266	.322	-68	-84	97	94	**.983**	106	148	**2.0**	-8.7	**8.7**	-.5	1.5
CHI	20	11	44	1446.7	1500	9.3	127	521	3.2	**933**	5.8	3.88	108	.270	.331	-24	49	112	105	.975	159	163	-1.2	5.1	-4.4	-.7	.3
NY	16	10	36	1482.7	1486	9.0	120	607	3.7	819	5.0	3.84	94	.266	.333	-18	-41	96	105	.978	140	**168**	-.0	-4.2	-5.6	-.5	-7.6
WEST																											
CIN	27	10	40	1440.3	1415	8.8	103	485	3.0	773	4.8	3.58	100	.259	.315	24	1	96	99	.980	124	152	.9	.1	7.4	.3	.7
HOU	**55**	**19**	31	1447.7	**1278**	**7.9**	**90**	504	3.1	854	5.3	3.20	105	**.237**	**.300**	86	27	90	93	.978	138	146	.0	2.8	-2.9	.1	7.9
LA	30	6	34	1444.0	1425	8.9	101	555	3.5	811	5.1	3.83	97	.260	.323	-15	-18	99	99	.981	118	123	1.3	-1.9	6.6	-.5	-8.5
SF	25	6	34	1436.0	1484	9.3	143	577	3.6	880	5.5	4.16	84	.268	.333	-68	-108	93	101	.974	163	138	-1.4	-11.1	.6	.0	1.9
SD	29	7	25	1453.0	1438	8.9	108	513	3.2	779	4.8	3.69	98	.262	.320	6	-9	97	101	.978	141	154	-.1	-.9	-7.2	-.3	-3.9
ATL	32	3	34	1407.7	1496	9.6	132	494	3.2	779	5.0	4.18	98	.272	.330	-70	-10	110	99	.970	183	139	-2.6	-1.0	-9.4	.1	-1.1
TOT	362	121	423	17426.7		8.9			3.2		5.1	3.73		.261	.327					.978	1669	1783					

Runs
Hernandez-StL.....116
Moreno-Pit......110
Schmidt-Phi.....109
Parker-Pit......109
Lopes-LA.......109

Hits
Templeton-StL.....211
Hernandez-StL.....210
Rose-Phi......208
Garvey-LA......204
Moreno-Pit.....196

Doubles
Hernandez-StL......48
Cromartie-Mon......46
Parker-Pit.......45
Reitz-StL.......41
Rose-Phi.......40

Triples
Templeton-StL.....19
Moreno-Pit......12
McBride-Phi.....12
Winfield-SD.....12
Dawson-Mon......12

Home Runs
Kingman-Chi.......48
Schmidt-Phi......45
Winfield-SD......34
Horner-Atl.......33
Stargell-Pit......32

Total Bases
Winfield-SD......333
Parker-Pit......327
Kingman-Chi......326
Garvey-LA......322
Matthews-Atl......317

Runs Batted In
Winfield-SD......118
Kingman-Chi......115
Schmidt-Phi......114
Garvey-LA......110
Hernandez-StL.....105

Runs Produced
Hernandez-StL......210
Winfield-SD......181
Schmidt-Phi......178
Parker-Pit......178
Garvey-LA......174

Bases On Balls
Schmidt-Phi......120
Tenace-SD......105
Lopes-LA.......97
North-SF.......96
Rose-Phi.......95

Batting Average
Hernandez-StL....344
Rose-Phi.......331
Knight-Cin......318
Garvey-LA......315
Horner-Atl......314

On Base Percentage
Hernandez-StL......421
Rose-Phi......421
Tenace-SD......407
Mazzilli-NY......397
Winfield-SD......396

Slugging Average
Kingman-Chi.......613
Schmidt-Phi......564
Foster-Cin......561
Winfield-SD......558
Horner-Atl......552

Production
Kingman-Chi......960
Schmidt-Phi......955
Winfield-SD......954
Foster-Cin......950
Hernandez-StL.....934

Adjusted Production
Winfield-SD......163
Schmidt-Phi......162
Foster-Cin......160
Hernandez-StL.....147
Cey-LA.......142

Batter Runs
Winfield-SD......47.4
Hernandez-StL......47.1
Schmidt-Phi......44.8
Parker-Pit......39.2
Kingman-Chi......37.8

Adjusted Batter Runs
Winfield-SD......50.2
Schmidt-Phi......47.1
Hernandez-StL......43.4
Rose-Phi......35.4
Foster-Cin......35.1

Clutch Hitting Index
Foli-NY-Pit.....148
Hebner-NY......148
Luzinski-Phi......132
Flynn-NY......129
Hernandez-StL......127

Runs Created
Hernandez-StL......135
Winfield-SD......132
Parker-Pit......131
Schmidt-Phi......123
Matthews-Atl......118

Total Average
Schmidt-Phi......1.036
Winfield-SD......1.009
Kingman-Chi......977
Hernandez-StL.....976
Foster-Cin......966

Stolen Bases
Moreno-Pit......77
North-SF.......58
Taveras-Pit-NY....44
Lopes-LA.......44
Scott-Mon.......39

Stolen Base Average
Lopes-LA......91.7
Parker-Pit......83.3
Morgan-Cin......82.4
Royster-Atl......81.4
Smith-SD......80.0

Stolen Base Runs
Lopes-LA......10.8
Moreno-Pit......10.5
Royster-Atl......5.7
Morgan-Cin......4.8

Fielding Runs
Templeton-StL......26.2
Smith-SD......23.9
Sizemore-Chi......23.4
Carter-Mon......21.6
Evans-SF......20.2

Total Player Rating
Schmidt-Phi......6.1
Winfield-SD......5.7
Hernandez-StL......5.4
Templeton-StL......5.0
Concepcion-Cin......4.6

Wins
Niekro-Atl.......21
Niekro-Hou......21
Richard-Hou......18
Reuschel-Chi......18
Carlton-Phi......18

Win Percentage
Seaver-Cin......727
Niekro-Hou......656
Martinez-StL......652
Sutcliffe-LA......630
Carlton-Phi......621

Games
Tekulve-Pit......94
Romo-Pit......84
Jackson-Pit......72
Lavelle-SF......70
Garber-Atl......68

Complete Games
Niekro-Atl......23
Richard-Hou......19
Rogers-Mon......13
Carlton-Phi......13
Hooton-LA......12

Shutouts
Seaver-Cin......5
Rogers-Mon......5
Niekro-Hou......5
Richard-Hou......4
Carlton-Phi......4

Saves
Sutter-Chi......37
Tekulve-Pit......31
Garber-Atl......25
Sambito-Hou......22
Lavelle-SF......20

Innings Pitched
Niekro-Atl......342
Richard-Hou......292
Niekro-Hou......264
Jones-SD......263

Fewest Hits/Game
Richard-Hou......6.78
Carlton-Phi......7.24
Niekro-Hou......7.53
Schatzeder-Mon......7.56
Andujar-Hou......7.79

Fewest BB/Game
Forsch-Hou......1.77
Candelaria-Pit......1.78
Hume-Cin......1.82
Lee-Mon......1.86
Swan-NY......2.04

Strikeouts
Richard-Hou......313
Carlton-Phi......213
Niekro-Atl......208
Blyleven-Pit......172
McGlothen-Chi......147

Strikeouts/Game
Richard-Hou......9.65
Carlton-Phi......7.64
Sanderson-Mon......7.39
Blyleven-Pit......6.53
Krukow-Chi......6.49

Wins Above Team
Seaver-Cin......4.6
Niekro-Hou......4.5
Niekro-Atl......4.4
Sutcliffe-LA......4.3
Reuschel-Chi......3.7

Earned Run Average
Richard-Hou......2.71
Hume-Cin......2.76
Schatzeder-Mon...2.83
Hooton-LA......2.97
Niekro-Hou......3.00

Adjusted ERA
Schatzeder-Mon....133
Hume-Cin......130
Rogers-Mon......125
Hooton-LA......125
Richard-Hou......124

Opponents' Batting Avg.
Richard-Hou......209
Carlton-Phi......219
Schatzeder-Mon......225
Niekro-Hou......228
Andujar-Hou......233

Opponents' On Base Pct.
Forsch-Hou......271
Richard-Hou......273
Sutton-LA......284
Seaver-Cin......286
Carlton-Phi......288

Starter Runs
Richard-Hou......33.0
Niekro-Hou......21.4
Rogers-Mon......20.2
Fulgham-StL......19.5
Hooton-LA......17.9

Adjusted Starter Runs
Niekro-Atl......27.4
Fulgham-StL......22.1
Richard-Hou......21.3
Rogers-Mon......21.0
Lee-Mon......17.8

Clutch Pitching Index
Hume-Cin......117
Lamp-Chi......114
Kobel-NY......113
Lee-Mon......113
Blyleven-Pit......112

Relief Runs
Sambito-Hou......19.7
Sosa-Mon......19.2
Hume-Cin......17.6
Minton-SF......17.2
Sutter-Chi......16.9

Adjusted Relief Runs
Sutter-Chi......22.0
Sosa-Mon......19.5
Tidrow-Chi......16.9
Tekulve-Pit......16.8
Sambito-Hou......16.1

Relief Ranking
Sutter-Chi......41.7
Sosa-Mon......35.3
Sambito-Hou......32.6
Tekulve-Pit......29.0
Littell-StL......27.5

Total Pitcher Index
Niekro-Atl......3.6
Rogers-Mon......2.6
Sutter-Chi......2.5
Fulgham-StL......2.3
Reuschel-Chi......2.3

Total Baseball Ranking
Schmidt-Phi......6.1
Winfield-SD......5.7
Hernandez-StL......5.4
Templeton-StL......5.0
Concepcion-Cin......4.6

TEAM	G	W	L	PCT	GB	R	OR	AB	H	2B	3B	HR	BB	SO	AVG	OBP	SLG	PRO	/A	BR	/A	PF	CHI	RC	TA	SB	CS	SBA	SBR
EAST																													
BAL	159	102	57	.642		757	582	5371	1401	258	24	181	608	847	.261	.339	.419	.758	103	25	44	97	98	758	.718	99	49	67	0
MIL	161	95	66	.590	8	807	722	5536	1552	291	41	185	549	745	.280	.347	.448	.795	113	95	95	100	94	850	.756	100	53	65	-1
BOS	160	91	69	.569	11.5	841	711	5538	1567	310	34	194	512	708	.283	.347	.456	.803	114	108	53	107	97	848	.751	60	43	58	-7
NY	160	89	71	.556	13.5	734	672	5421	1443	226	40	150	509	590	.266	.331	.406	.737	98	-20	13	96	101	708	.669	65	46	59	-7
DET	161	85	76	.528	18	770	738	5375	1446	221	35	164	575	814	.269	.342	.415	.757	103	24	50	96	100	754	.723	176	86	67	1
CLE	161	81	80	.503	22	760	805	5376	1388	206	29	138	657	786	.258	.344	.384	.728	96	-20	-63	106	103	720	.692	143	90	61	-10
TOR	162	53	109	.327	50.5	613	862	5423	1362	253	34	95	448	663	.251	.313	.363	.676	82	-141	-165	103	103	602	.595	75	56	57	-10
WEST																													
CAL	162	88	74	.543		866	768	5550	1563	242	43	164	589	843	.282	.354	.429	.783	110	83	140	93	101	842	.744	100	53	65	-1
KC	162	85	77	.525	3	851	816	5653	1596	286	79	116	528	675	.282	.347	.422	.769	106	51	9	105	103	836	.744	207	76	73	17
TEX	162	83	79	.512	5	750	698	5562	1549	252	26	140	461	607	.278	.337	.409	.746	100	0	1	100	99	750	.678	79	51	61	-6
MIN	162	82	80	.506	6	764	725	5544	1544	256	46	112	526	693	.278	.344	.402	.746	100	-7	-58	109	98	770	.685	66	45	59	-6
CHI	160	73	87	.456	14	730	748	5463	1505	290	33	127	454	668	.275	.335	.410	.745	100	-3	-20	102	99	726	.678	97	62	61	-7
SEA	162	67	95	.414	21	711	820	5544	1490	250	52	132	515	725	.269	.334	.404	.738	98	-16	-16	100	95	733	.682	126	52	71	7
OAK	162	54	108	.333	34	573	860	5348	1276	188	32	108	482	751	.239	.304	.346	.650	75	-188	-104	89	105	552	.575	104	69	60	-9
TOT	1128					10527		76704	20682	3529	548	2006	7413	10115	.270	.337	.408	.746								1497	831	64	-49

TEAM	CG	SHO	SV	IP	H	H/G	HR	BB	BB/G	SO	SO/G	ERA	/A	OAVG	OOBA	PR	/A	PF	CPI	FA	E	DP	FW	PW	BW	SBW	DIF
EAST																											
BAL	52	12	30	1434.3	1279	8.0	133	467	2.9	786	4.9	3.26	124	.240	.298	151	123	96	100	.980	125	161	.9	12.0	4.3	.3	5.0
MIL	61	12	23	1439.7	1563	9.8	162	381	2.4	580	3.6	4.03	104	.279	.321	29	24	99	105	.980	127	163	.7	2.3	9.3	.2	1.9
BOS	47	11	29	1431.3	1487	9.4	133	463	2.9	731	4.6	4.03	111	.269	.324	29	69	106	100	.977	142	166	-.1	6.7	5.2	-.3	-.5
NY	43	10	37	1432.3	1446	9.1	123	455	2.9	731	4.6	3.83	104	.267	.319	60	26	95	102	.981	122	183	1.0	2.5	1.3	-.3	4.5
DET	25	5	37	1423.3	1420	9.0	167	547	3.5	802	5.1	4.27	95	.265	.331	-9	-35	96	101	.981	120	181	1.1	-3.4	4.9	-.4	1.5
CLE	28	7	32	1431.7	1502	9.4	138	570	3.6	781	4.9	4.57	98	.272	.335	-56	-14	100	94	.978	134	149	.3	-1.4	-6.1	-.6	8.3
TOR	44	7	11	1417.0	1537	9.8	165	594	3.8	613	3.9	4.82	92	.281	.349	-95	-57	106	100	.975	159	187	-1.1	-5.6	-16.1	-.6	-4.6
WEST																											
CAL	46	9	33	1436.0	1463	9.2	131	573	3.6	820	5.1	4.34	89	.266	.333	-19	-75	92	96	.979	135	172	.3	-7.3	13.7	.2	.1
KC	42	7	27	1448.3	1477	9.2	165	536	3.3	640	4.0	4.45	99	.266	.326	-37	-3	105	95	.977	146	160	-.3	-.3	.9	2.0	1.7
TEX	26	10	42	1437.0	1371	8.6	135	532	3.3	773	4.8	3.86	108	.253	.316	56	51	99	97	.979	130	151	.6	5.0	.0	-.2	-3.4
MIN	31	6	33	1444.3	1590	9.9	128	452	2.8	721	4.5	4.13	110	.285	.334	13	68	108	106	.979	134	203	.3	6.6	-5.7	-.2	.0
CHI	28	9	37	1409.0	1365	8.7	114	618	3.9	675	4.3	4.10	105	.255	.330	18	34	103	96	.972	173	142	-1.9	3.3	-2.0	-.3	-6.2
SEA	37	7	26	1438.0	1567	9.8	165	571	3.6	736	4.6	4.58	93	.280	.343	-57	-49	101	103	.978	141	170	-.0	-4.8	-1.6	1.0	-8.6
OAK	41	4	20	1429.3	1606	10.1	147	654	4.1	726	4.6	4.75	81	.287	.358	-84	-143	91	105	.972	174	137	-1.9	-14.0	-10.1	-.5	-.5
TOT	551	116	417	20051.7		9.3			3.3		4.5	4.22		.270	.337					.978	1962	2318					

Runs		Hits		Doubles		Triples		Home Runs		Total Bases	
Baylor-Cal	120	Brett-KC	212	Lemon-Chi	44	Brett-KC	20	Thomas-Mil	45	Rice-Bos	369
Brett-KC	119	Rice-Bos	201	Cooper-Mil	44	Molitor-Mil	16	Rice-Bos	39	Brett-KC	363
Rice-Bos	117	Bell-Tex	200	Lynn-Bos	42	Wilson-KC	13	Lynn-Bos	39	Lynn-Bos	338
Lynn-Bos	116	Molitor-Mil	188	Brett-KC	42	Randolph-NY	13	Baylor-Cal	36	Baylor-Cal	333
Lansford-Cal	114	Lansford-Cal	188	Bell-Tex	42			Singleton-Bal	35	Singleton-Bal	304

Runs Batted In		Runs Produced		Bases On Balls		Batting Average		On Base Percentage		Slugging Average	
Baylor-Cal	139	Baylor-Cal	223	Porter-KC	121	Lynn-Bos	.333	Porter-KC	.429	Lynn-Bos	.637
Rice-Bos	130	Rice-Bos	208	Singleton-Bal	109	Brett-KC	.329	Lynn-Bos	.426	Rice-Bos	.596
Thomas-Mil	123	Brett-KC	203	Thomas-Mil	98	Downing-Cal	.326	Downing-Cal	.420	Lezcano-Mil	.573
Lynn-Bos	122	Lynn-Bos	199	Randolph-NY	95	Rice-Bos	.325	Lezcano-Mil	.420	Brett-KC	.563
Porter-KC	112	Porter-KC	193	Thornton-Cle	90	Oliver-Tex	.323	Singleton-Bal	.409	Jackson-NY	.544

Production		Adjusted Production		Batter Runs		Adjusted Batter Runs		Clutch Hitting Index		Runs Created	
Lynn-Bos	1.063	Lynn-Bos	170	Lynn-Bos	62.1	Lynn-Bos	56.6	Porter-KC	143	Lynn-Bos	147
Lezcano-Mil	.992	Lezcano-Mil	165	Rice-Bos	50.2	Singleton-Bal	46.5	Bochte-Sea	127	Rice-Bos	138
Rice-Bos	.981	Kemp-Det	158	Lezcano-Mil	44.6	Lezcano-Mil	44.6	Cerone-Tor	127	Brett-KC	134
Kemp-Det	.946	Singleton-Bal	156	Singleton-Bal	44.3	Rice-Bos	44.1	Ford-Cle	126	Singleton-Bal	127
Singleton-Bal	.942	Jackson-NY	154	Brett-KC	42.8	Baylor-Cal	43.1	Sundberg-Tex	125	Baylor-Cal	126

Total Average		Stolen Bases		Stolen Base Average		Stolen Base Runs		Fielding Runs		Total Player Rating	
Lynn-Bos	1.167	Wilson-KC	83	Wilson-KC	87.4	Wilson-KC	17.7	Smalley-Min	32.9	Smalley-Min	5.4
Lezcano-Mil	1.060	LeFlore-Det	78	Otis-KC	85.7	LeFlore-Det	15.0	Dent-NY	30.9	Brett-KC	5.3
Rice-Bos	1.002	Cruz-Sea	49	LeFlore-Det	84.8	Cruz-Sea	9.3	Burleson-Bos	26.4	Lynn-Bos	4.9
Singleton-Bal	.995	Bumbry-Bal	37	Cruz-Sea	84.5	Otis-KC	6.0	Wilfong-Min	18.5	Porter-KC	4.9
Porter-KC	.992	Wills-Tex	35	Lowenstein-Bal	80.0	Manning-Cle	4.2	Bell-Tex	17.0	Grich-Cal	4.3

Wins		Win Percentage		Games		Complete Games		Shutouts		Saves	
Flanagan-Bal	23	Caldwell-Mil	.727	Marshall-Min	90	D.Martinez-Bal	18	Ryan-Cal	5	Marshall-Min	32
John-NY	21	Flanagan-Bal	.719	Monge-Cle	76	Ryan-Cal	17	Leonard-KC	5	Kern-Tex	29
Koosman-Min	20	Morris-Det	.708	Kern-Tex	71	John-NY	17	Flanagan-Bal	5	Stanhouse-Bal	21
Guidry-NY	18	John-NY	.700	Lyle-Tex	67	Eckersley-Bos	17	Stanley-Bos	4	Lopez-Det	21
		Guidry-NY	.692	Heaverlo-Oak	62			Caldwell-Mil	4	Monge-Cle	19

Innings Pitched		Fewest Hits/Game		Fewest BB/Game		Strikeouts		Strikeouts/Game		Wins Above Team	
D.Martinez-Bal	292	Ryan-Cal	6.82	McGregor-Bal	1.18	Ryan-Cal	223	Ryan-Cal	9.00	Davis-NY	5.9
John-NY	276	Kravec-Chi	7.49	Caldwell-Mil	1.49	Guidry-NY	201	Guidry-NY	7.67	John-NY	5.6
Flanagan-Bal	266	Guidry-NY	7.74	Sorensen-Mil	1.61	Flanagan-Bal	190	Flanagan-Bal	6.43	Morris-Det	5.1
Koosman-Min	264	Morris-Det	8.14	Stanley-Bos	1.82	Jenkins-Tex	164	Jenkins-Tex	5.70	Guidry-NY	4.5
Jenkins-Tex	259	Baumgarten-Chi	8.25	John-NY	2.12	Koosman-Min	157	Bannister-Sea	5.69	Kern-Tex	4.1

Earned Run Average		Adjusted ERA		Opponents' Batting Avg.		Opponents' On Base Pct.		Starter Runs		Adjusted Starter Runs	
Guidry-NY	2.78	Eckersley-Bos	150	Ryan-Cal	.212	McGregor-Bal	.269	John-NY	38.3	Eckersley-Bos	40.6
John-NY	2.97	Guidry-NY	144	Kravec-Chi	.233	Guidry-NY	.290	Guidry-NY	37.6	Koosman-Min	34.7
Eckersley-Bos	2.99	Koosman-Min	135	Guidry-NY	.236	Flanagan-Bal	.293	Eckersley-Bos	33.7	Guidry-NY	31.9
Flanagan-Bal	3.08	John-NY	135	Baumgarten-Chi	.243	Eckersley-Bos	.294	Flanagan-Bal	33.6	John-NY	31.7
Morris-Det	3.27	Flanagan-Bal	131	Morris-Det	.244	Leonard-KC	.294	Koosman-Min	24.7	Flanagan-Bal	28.2

Clutch Pitching Index		Relief Runs		Adjusted Relief Runs		Relief Ranking		Total Pitcher Index		Total Baseball Ranking	
Eckersley-Bos	115	Kern-Tex	42.0	Kern-Tex	41.5	Kern-Tex	66.0	Eckersley-Bos	4.3	Smalley-Min	5.4
Keough-Oak	114	Monge-Cle	26.4	Marshall-Min	30.4	Marshall-Min	63.2	Kern-Tex	4.1	Brett-KC	5.3
McCatty-Oak	114	Lopez-Det	25.5	Monge-Cle	30.2	Monge-Cle	55.4	Koosman-Min	3.8	Lynn-Bos	4.9
Travers-Mil	113	Marshall-Min	25.0	Lopez-Det	23.2	Lopez-Det	33.3	John-NY	3.4	Porter-KC	4.9
Koosman-Min	113	Stoddard-Bal	16.2	Burgmeier-Bos	17.2	Drago-Bos	27.6	Marshall-Min	3.3	Grich-Cal	4.3

TEAM	G	W	L	PCT	GB	R	OR	AB	H	2B	3B	HR	BB	SO	AVG	OBP	SLG	PRO	/A	BR	/A	PF	CHI	RC	TA	SB	CS	SBA	SBR
EAST																													
PHI	162	91	71	.562		728	639	5625	1517	272	54	117	472	**708**	.270	.330	**.400**	.730	109	60	10	107	100	736	.674	140	62	69	5
MON	162	90	72	.556	1	694	629	5465	1407	250	61	114	547	865	.257	.327	.388	.715	105	35	40	99	100	709	**.690**	237	82	74	22
PIT	162	83	79	.512	8	666	646	5517	1469	249	38	116	452	760	.266	.325	.388	.713	104	26	5	103	98	686	.664	209	102	67	2
STL	162	74	88	.457	17	**738**	710	5608	**1541**	**300**	49	101	451	781	.275	**.331**	**.400**	**.731**	109	63	45	103	102	724	.664	117	54	68	3
NY	162	67	95	.414	24	611	702	5478	1407	218	41	61	501	840	.257	.322	.345	.667	92	-51	-24	96	101	601	.599	158	99	61	-11
CHI	162	64	98	.395	27	614	728	5619	1411	251	35	107	471	912	.251	.311	.365	.676	94	-46	-86	106	100	627	.600	93	64	59	-10
WEST																													
HOU	163	93	70	.571		637	**589**	5566	1455	231	**67**	75	540	755	.261	.328	.367	.695	100	2	17	98	95	688	.652	194	74	72	14
LA	163	92	71	.564	1	663	591	5566	1455	209	24	138	492	846	.263	.325	.388	.713	104	29	50	97	96	699	.654	123	72	63	-5
CIN	163	89	73	.549	3.5	707	670	5516	1445	256	45	113	537	852	.262	.330	.386	.716	105	39	27	102	101	716	.673	156	43	**78**	21
ATL	161	81	80	.503	11	630	660	5402	1352	226	22	144	434	899	.250	.308	.380	.688	97	-26	-32	101	**103**	616	.611	73	52	58	-8
SF	161	75	86	.466	17	573	634	5368	1310	199	44	80	509	840	.244	.311	.342	.653	88	-81	-52	96	102	571	.580	100	58	63	-4
SD	163	73	89	.451	19.5	591	654	5540	1410	195	43	67	563	791	.255	.326	.342	.668	92	-47	-47	93	96	641	.629	**239**	73	77	**28**
TOT	973					7852		66272	17186	2856	523	1243	5969	9849	.259	.323	.375	.697								1839	835	69	51

TEAM	CG	SHO	SV	IP	H	H/G	HR	BB	BB/G	SO	SO/G	ERA	/A	OAVG	OOBA	PR	/A	PF	CPI	FA	E	DP	FW	PW	BW	SBW	DIF
EAST																											
PHI	25	8	40	1480.0	1419	8.6	87	530	3.2	889	5.4	3.43	112	.254	.314	28	65	106	100	.979	136	136	.2	**6.9**	1.1	.0	1.7
MON	33	15	36	1456.7	1447	8.9	100	460	**2.8**	823	5.1	3.48	102	.260	.313	19	9	98	102	.977	144	126	-.2	1.0	4.2	1.9	2.1
PIT	25	8	**43**	1458.3	1422	8.8	110	**451**	**2.8**	832	5.1	3.58	104	.258	.311	3	21	103	99	.978	137	154	.2	2.2	.5	-.2	-.7
STL	**34**	9	27	1447.0	1454	9.0	90	495	3.1	664	4.1	3.93	94	.265	.322	-53	-39	102	94	.981	122	**174**	1.0	-4.1	4.8	-.1	-8.5
NY	17	9	33	1451.3	1473	9.1	140	510	3.2	886	5.5	3.85	91	.266	.323	-40	-57	97	104	.975	154	132	-.7	-6.0	-2.5	-1.6	-3.1
CHI	13	6	35	1479.0	1525	9.3	109	589	3.6	923	**5.6**	3.89	100	.271	.334	-47	-2	108	**106**	.974	174	149	-1.7	-.2	-9.1	-1.5	-4.5
WEST																											
HOU	31	18	41	1482.7	1367	**8.3**	69	466	**2.8**	929	5.6	3.10	113	**.245**	**.301**	82	64	96	96	.978	140	145	.0	6.8	1.8	1.0	1.9
LA	24	**19**	42	1472.7	**1358**	**8.3**	105	480	2.9	835	5.1	3.25	106	.246	.302	58	33	96	100	.981	123	149	.9	3.5	**5.3**	-1.0	1.8
CIN	30	12	37	1459.3	1404	8.7	113	506	3.1	833	5.1	3.85	95	.254	.313	-40	-33	101	92	**.983**	106	144	**1.8**	-.3	2.9	1.8	5.0
ATL	29	9	37	1428.0	1397	8.8	131	454	2.9	696	4.4	3.77	97	.257	.311	-26	-18	101	101	.975	162	156	-1.1	-1.9	-3.4	-1.3	8.2
SF	27	10	35	1448.3	1446	9.0	92	492	3.1	811	5.0	3.46	100	.261	.318	23	2	96	104	.975	159	124	-1.0	.2	-5.5	-.9	1.6
SD	19	9	39	1466.3	1474	9.0	97	536	3.3	728	4.5	3.65	92	.266	.325	-8	-44	94	105	.980	132	157	.5	-4.6	-.1	**2.5**	-6.2
TOT	307	132	445	17529.7		8.8		3.1			5.1	3.60		.259	.323					.978	1689	1746					

Runs
Hernandez-StL......111
Schmidt-Phi........104
Murphy-Atl.........98
Dawson-Mon.........96

Hits
Garvey-LA..........200
Richards-SD........193
Hernandez-StL......191
Buckner-Chi........187

Doubles
Rose-Phi...........42
Dawson-Mon.........41
Buckner-Chi........41
Knight-Cin.........39
Hernandez-StL......39

Triples
Scott-Mon..........13
Moreno-Pit.........13
LeFlore-Mon........11
Herndon-SF.........11

Home Runs
Schmidt-Phi........48
Horner-Atl.........35
Murphy-Atl.........33
Carter-Mon.........29
Baker-LA...........29

Total Bases
Schmidt-Phi........342
Garvey-LA..........307
Hernandez-StL......294
Baker-LA...........291
Murphy-Atl.........290

Runs Batted In
Schmidt-Phi........121
Hendrick-StL.......109
Garvey-LA..........106
Carter-Mon.........101
Hernandez-StL......99

Runs Produced
Hernandez-StL......194
Schmidt-Phi........177
Dawson-Mon.........166
Simmons-StL........161
Griffey-Cin........161

Bases On Balls
Morgan-Hou.........93
Driessen-Cin.......93
Tenace-SD..........92
Schmidt-Phi........89
Hernandez-StL......86

Batting Average
Buckner-Chi........324
Hernandez-StL......321
Templeton-StL......319
McBride-Phi........309
Cedeno-Hou.........309

On Base Percentage
Hernandez-StL......410
Cedeno-Hou.........390
Clark-SF...........390
Schmidt-Phi........388
Driessen-Cin.......382

Slugging Average
Schmidt-Phi........624
Clark-SF...........517
Murphy-Atl.........510
Simmons-StL........505
Baker-LA...........503

Production
Schmidt-Phi........1.012
Clark-SF...........907
Hernandez-StL......904
Simmons-StL........885
Murphy-Atl.........859

Adjusted Production
Schmidt-Phi........166
Clark-SF...........158
Hernandez-StL......147
Simmons-StL........141
Cedeno-Hou.........141

Batter Runs
Schmidt-Phi........56.5
Hernandez-StL......43.3
Easler-Pit.........37.2
Clark-SF...........31.1
Simmons-StL........29.6

Adjusted Batter Runs
Schmidt-Phi........51.3
Hernandez-StL......41.3
Easler-Pit.........35.7
Clark-SF...........33.5
Simmons-StL........28.0

Clutch Hitting Index
Concepcion-Cin.....135
Montanez-SD -Mon...135
McBride-Phi........131
Cruz-Hou...........130
Youngblood-NY......127

Runs Created
Schmidt-Phi........137
Hernandez-StL......122
Dawson-Mon.........105
Murphy-Atl.........101
Griffey-Cin........99

Total Average
Schmidt-Phi........1.107
Hernandez-StL......934
Cedeno-Hou.........930
Clark-SF...........921
Dawson-Mon.........882

Stolen Bases
LeFlore-Mon........97
Moreno-Pit.........96
Collins-Cin........79
Scott-Mon..........63
Richards-SD........61

Stolen Base Average
Griffey-Cin........95.8
Mumphrey-SD........91.2
LeFlore-Mon........83.6
Maddox-Phi.........83.3
Scott-Mon..........82.9

Stolen Base Runs
LeFlore-Mon........17.7
Mumphrey-SD........12.6
Scott-Mon..........11.1
Collins-Cin........11.1
Moreno-Pit.........9.0

Fielding Runs
Smith-SD...........42.8
Templeton-StL......31.2
Carter-Mon.........23.7
Schmidt-Phi........20.9
Youngblood-NY......20.5

Total Player Rating
Schmidt-Phi........7.4
Templeton-StL......5.0
Smith-SD...........5.0
Carter-Mon.........4.7
Hernandez-StL......4.0

Wins
Carlton-Phi........24
Niekro-Hou.........20
Bibby-Pit..........19
Reuss-LA...........18
Ruthven-Phi........17

Win Percentage
Bibby-Pit..........760
Reuss-LA...........750
Carlton-Phi........727
Ruthven-Phi........630
Niekro-Hou.........625

Games
Tidrow-Chi.........84
Tekulve-Pit........78
Hume-Cin...........78
Camp-Atl...........77
Romo-Pit...........74

Complete Games
Rogers-Mon.........14
Carlton-Phi........13
Niekro-Atl.........11
Niekro-Hou.........11

Shutouts
Reuss-LA...........6
Rogers-Mon.........4
Richard-Hou........4

Saves
Sutter-Chi.........28
Hume-Cin...........25
Fingers-SD.........23
Camp-Atl...........22
Allen-NY...........22

Innings Pitched
Carlton-Phi........304
Rogers-Mon.........281
Niekro-Atl.........275
Reuschel-Chi.......257
Niekro-Hou.........256

Fewest Hits/Game
Soto-Cin...........5.97
Sutton-LA..........6.92
Carlton-Phi........7.19
Seaver-Cin.........7.50
Reuss-LA...........7.59

Fewest BB/Game
Forsch-StL.........1.38
Reuss-LA...........1.57
Forsch-Hou.........1.66
Candelaria-Pit.....1.93
Sutton-LA..........2.00

Strikeouts
Carlton-Phi........286
Ryan-Hou...........200
Soto-Cin...........182
Niekro-Atl.........176
Blyleven-Pit.......168

Strikeouts/Game
Soto-Cin...........8.62
Carlton-Phi........8.47
Ryan-Hou...........7.69
Blyleven-Pit.......6.97
Welch-LA...........5.93

Wins Above Team
Carlton-Phi........7.1
Bibby-Pit..........6.9
Reuss-LA...........5.6
Ruhle-Hou..........3.5
Sutton-LA..........3.5

Earned Run Average
Sutton-LA..........2.21
Carlton-Phi........2.34
Reuss-LA...........2.52
Blue-SF............2.97
Rogers-Mon.........2.98

Adjusted ERA
Carlton-Phi........164
Sutton-LA..........156
Reuss-LA...........137
Rogers-Mon.........119
Soto-Cin...........118

Opponents' Batting Avg.
Soto-Cin...........187
Sutton-LA..........211
Carlton-Phi........218
Seaver-Cin.........225
Reuss-LA...........227

Opponents' On Base Pct.
Sutton-LA..........255
Reuss-LA...........257
Carlton-Phi........273
Soto-Cin...........273
Pastore-Cin........273

Starter Runs
Carlton-Phi........42.6
Sutton-LA..........32.8
Reuss-LA...........27.6
Ruhle-Hou..........21.6
Richard-Hou........21.6

Adjusted Starter Runs
Carlton-Phi........50.3
Sutton-LA..........29.3
Reuss-LA...........23.8
Richard-Hou........20.2
Ruhle-Hou..........19.7

Clutch Pitching Index
Reuschel-Chi.......119
Bomback-NY.........117
Zachry-NY..........114
Ruthven-Phi........111
Sanderson-Mon......111

Relief Runs
McGraw-Phi.........21.8
Caudill-Chi........20.2
Camp-Atl...........20.2
Smith-Hou..........19.2
Holland-SF.........16.8

Adjusted Relief Runs
McGraw-Phi.........24.1
Caudill-Chi........24.1
Camp-Atl...........20.8
Smith-Hou..........18.0
Hume-Cin...........16.5

Relief Ranking
McGraw-Phi.........33.0
Hume-Cin...........27.3
Camp-Atl...........26.9
Sutter-Chi.........24.5
Smith-Hou..........22.8

Total Pitcher Index
Carlton-Phi........5.7
Sutton-LA..........2.8
McGraw-Phi.........2.7
Camp-Atl...........2.6
Reuss-LA...........2.6

Total Baseball Ranking
Schmidt-Phi........7.4
Carlton-Phi........5.7
Templeton-StL......5.0
Smith-SD...........5.0
Carter-Mon.........4.7

TEAM	G	W	L	PCT	GB	R	OR	AB	H	2B	3B	HR	BB	SO	AVG	OBP	SLG	PRO	/A	BR	/A	PF	CHI	RC	TA	SB	CS	SBA	SBR
EAST																													
NY	162	103	59	.636		820	662	5553	1484	239	34	189	643	739	.267	.346	.425	.771	110	79	84	99	100	820	.734	86	36	70	4
BAL	162	100	62	.617	3	805	**640**	5585	1523	258	29	156	587	766	.273	.344	.413	.757	106	52	46	101	102	788	.711	111	38	74	11
MIL	162	86	76	.531	17	811	682	5653	1555	**298**	36	**203**	455	745	.275	.332	**.448**	**.780**	**112**	78	**118**	95	100	**834**	**.740**	131	56	70	6
DET	163	84	78	.519	19	**830**	757	5648	1543	232	53	143	**645**	844	.273	.351	.409	.760	107	66	25	105	101	804	.710	75	68	52	-17
BOS	160	83	77	.519	19	757	767	5603	1588	297	36	162	475	720	.283	.343	.436	.779	**112**	**86**	72	102	93	810	.719	79	48	62	-4
CLE	160	79	81	.494	23	738	807	5470	1517	221	40	89	617	625	.277	**.355**	.381	.736	102	26	9	102	97	739	.684	118	58	67	1
TOR	162	67	95	.414	36	624	762	5571	1398	249	53	126	448	813	.251	.310	.383	.693	89	-91	-89	100	99	640	.614	67	72	48	-22
WEST																													
KC	162	97	65	.599		809	694	5714	**1633**	266	**59**	115	508	709	**.286**	.348	.413	.761	108	62	73	98	100	826	.724	**185**	43	**81**	**30**
OAK	162	83	79	.512	14	686	642	5495	1424	212	35	137	506	824	.259	.324	.385	.709	93	-50	-10	95	102	680	.659	175	82	68	3
MIN	161	77	84	.478	19.5	670	724	5530	1468	252	46	99	436	703	.265	.322	.381	.703	92	-64	-125	109	102	655	.617	62	46	57	-8
TEX	163	76	85	.472	20.5	756	752	5690	1616	263	27	124	480	**589**	.284	.342	.405	.747	104	30	27	100	98	768	.677	91	49	65	-1
CHI	162	70	90	.438	26	587	722	5444	1408	255	38	91	399	670	.259	.314	.370	.684	87	-103	-79	97	97	608	.595	68	54	56	-11
CAL	160	65	95	.406	31	698	797	5443	1442	236	32	106	539	889	.265	.335	.378	.713	95	-32	-1	96	101	681	.647	91	63	59	-10
SEA	163	59	103	.364	38	610	793	5489	1359	211	35	104	483	727	.248	.311	.356	.667	82	-135	-157	103	**104**	598	.594	116	62	65	-1
TOT	1132					10201		77888	20958	3489	553	1844	7221	10363	.269	.334	.399	.733								1455	775	65	-28

TEAM	CG	SHO	SV	IP	H	H/G	HR	BB	BB/G	SO	SO/G	ERA	/A	OAVG	OOBA	PR	/A	PF	CPI	FA	E	DP	FW	PW	BW	SBW	DIF
EAST																											
NY	29	**15**	**50**	1464.3	1433	8.8	**102**	463	2.8	845	5.2	3.58	110	.259	.312	73	58	98	98	.978	138	160	-.0	5.8	8.4	.6	7.3
BAL	42	10	41	1460.0	1438	8.9	134	507	3.1	789	4.9	3.64	110	.260	.320	63	57	99	104	**.985**	**95**	178	**2.4**	5.7	4.6	1.3	5.0
MIL	48	14	30	1450.0	1530	9.5	137	**420**	**2.6**	575	3.6	3.71	101	.272	.320	52	8	93	**107**	.977	147	189	-.6	.8	**11.8**	.8	-7.8
DET	40	9	30	1467.3	1505	9.2	152	558	3.4	741	4.5	4.25	99	.267	.329	-35	-4	105	98	.979	133	165	.2	-.4	2.5	-1.5	2.2
BOS	30	8	43	1441.3	1557	9.7	129	481	3.0	696	4.3	4.38	94	.279	.334	-55	-42	102	97	.977	149	**206**	-.7	-4.2	7.2	-.2	.9
CLE	35	8	32	1428.0	1519	9.6	137	552	3.5	843	5.3	4.68	89	.274	.338	-103	-83	103	92	.983	105	143	1.8	-8.3	.9	.3	4.3
TOR	39	9	23	1466.0	1523	9.3	135	635	3.9	705	4.3	4.19	97	.273	.343	-25	-18	101	105	.979	133	**206**	.2	-1.8	-8.9	-2.0	-1.6
WEST																											
KC	37	10	42	1459.3	1496	9.2	129	465	2.9	614	3.8	3.83	102	.266	.319	33	15	97	100	.978	141	150	-.2	1.5	7.3	**3.2**	4.2
OAK	**94**	9	13	1471.7	**1347**	**8.2**	142	521	3.2	769	4.7	**3.46**	110	**.243**	**.307**	**93**	53	94	99	.979	130	115	.4	5.3	-1.0	.5	-3.2
MIN	35	9	30	1451.0	1502	9.3	120	468	2.9	744	4.6	3.93	**112**	.271	.324	16	**76**	109	100	.977	148	192	-.6	**7.6**	-12.5	-.6	2.6
TEX	35	6	25	1451.7	1561	9.7	119	519	3.2	**890**	**5.5**	4.02	101	.277	.335	1	3	100	104	.977	147	169	-.6	.3	2.7	.1	-7.0
CHI	32	12	42	1435.3	1434	9.0	108	563	3.5	724	4.5	3.92	101	.263	.328	18	5	98	99	.973	171	162	-1.9	.5	-7.9	-.9	.2
CAL	22	6	30	1428.3	1548	9.8	141	529	3.3	725	4.6	4.52	86	.278	.338	-76	-97	97	97	.978	134	144	.2	-9.7	-.0	-.8	-4.6
SEA	31	7	26	1457.3	1565	9.7	159	540	3.3	703	4.3	4.38	97	.277	.336	-55	-23	105	101	.977	149	189	-.7	-2.3	-15.7	.1	-3.5
TOT	549	132	457	20331.7		9.3			3.2		4.6	4.03		.269	.334					.978	1920	2368					

Runs
Wilson-KC 133
Yount-Mil 121
Bumbry-Bal 118
Henderson-Oak 111
Trammell-Det 107

Hits
Wilson-KC 230
Cooper-Mil 219
Rivers-Tex 210
Oliver-Tex 209
Bumbry-Bal 205

Doubles
Yount-Mil 49
Oliver-Tex 43
Morrison-Chi 40
McRae-KC 39
Evans-Bos 37

Triples
Wilson-KC 15
Griffin-Tor 15
Washington-KC 11
Landreaux-Min 11
Yount-Mil 10

Home Runs
Oglivie-Mil 41
Jackson-NY 41
Thomas-Mil 38
Armas-Oak 35
Murray-Bal 32

Total Bases
Cooper-Mil 335
Oglivie-Mil 333
Murray-Bal 322
Yount-Mil 317
Oliver-Tex 315

Runs Batted In
Cooper-Mil 122
Oglivie-Mil 118
Brett-KC 118
Oliver-Tex 117
Murray-Bal 116

Runs Produced
Oliver-Tex 194
Cooper-Mil 193
Yount-Mil 185
Murray-Bal 184
Brett-KC 181

Bases On Balls
Randolph-NY 119
Henderson-Oak 117
Hargrove-Cle 111
Murphy-Oak 102
Harrah-Cle 98

Batting Average
Brett-KC 390
Cooper-Mil 352
Dilone-Cle 341
Rivers-Tex 333
Carew-Cal 331

On Base Percentage
Brett-KC 461
Randolph-NY 429
Henderson-Oak 422
Hargrove-Cle 421
Thompson-Det-Cal . .402

Slugging Average
Brett-KC 664
Jackson-NY 597
Oglivie-Mil 563
Cooper-Mil 539
Yount-Mil 519

Production
Brett-KC 1.124
Jackson-NY .... .996
Cooper-Mil .... .931
Oglivie-Mil .... .930
Singleton-Bal ...... .885

Adjusted Production
Brett-KC 207
Jackson-NY 170
Cooper-Mil 161
Oglivie-Mil 160
Thompson-Det-Cal . .142

Batter Runs
Brett-KC 64.8
Jackson-NY 49.1
Cooper-Mil 42.9
Oglivie-Mil 39.2
Singleton-Bal 35.4

Adjusted Batter Runs
Brett-KC 65.7
Jackson-NY 49.6
Cooper-Mil 47.3
Oglivie-Mil 43.4
Singleton-Bal 34.8

Clutch Hitting Index
Kemp-Det 137
Manning-Cle 135
Aikens-KC 132
Brett-KC 132
Oliver-Tex 130

Runs Created
Brett-KC 135
Cooper-Mil 126
Jackson-NY 125
Oglivie-Mil 121
Henderson-Oak 120

Total Average
Brett-KC 1.278
Jackson-NY 1.065
Randolph-NY .... .965
Oglivie-Mil .... .946
Cooper-Mil .... .925

Stolen Bases
Henderson-Oak 100
Wilson-KC 79
Dilone-Cle 61
Cruz-Sea 45
Bumbry-Bal 44

Stolen Base Average
Otis-KC 94.1
Harrah-Cle 89.5
Kelly-Bal 88.9
Wilson-KC 88.8
Cruz-Sea 86.5

Stolen Base Runs
Wilson-KC 17.7
Henderson-Oak 14.4
Cruz-Sea 9.3
Dilone-Cle 7.5
Bumbry-Bal 6.6

Fielding Runs
Burleson-Bos 31.0
Smalley-Min 25.8
DeCinces-Bal 23.4
Castino-Min 22.5
Garcia-Tor 19.7

Total Player Rating
Brett-KC 6.7
Henderson-Oak 6.1
Oglivie-Mil 5.3
Cooper-Mil 4.2
Bell-Tex 3.9

Wins
Stone-Bal 25
Norris-Oak 22
John-NY 22
McGregor-Bal 20
Leonard-KC 20

Win Percentage
Stone-Bal 781
May-NY 750
McGregor-Bal 714
Norris-Oak 710
John-NY 710

Games
Quisenberry-KC 75
Corbett-Min 73
Monge-Cle 67
Lopez-Det 67

Complete Games
Langford-Oak 28
Norris-Oak 24
Keough-Oak 20
John-NY 16
Gura-KC 16

Shutouts
John-NY 6
Zahn-Min 5
Stieb-Tor 4
McGregor-Bal 4
Gura-KC 4

Saves
Quisenberry-KC 33
Gossage-NY 33
Farmer-Chi 30
Stoddard-Bal 26
Burgmeier-Bos 24

Innings Pitched
Langford-Oak 290
Norris-Oak 284
Gura-KC 283
Leonard-KC 280
John-NY 265

Fewest Hits/Game
Norris-Oak 6.81
May-NY 7.41
Clancy-Tor 7.78
Underwood-NY 7.84
Keough-Oak 7.85

Fewest BB/Game
Matlack-Tex 1.84
Splittorff-KC 1.90
John-NY 1.90
Tanana-Cal 1.99
Langford-Oak 1.99

Strikeouts
Barker-Cle 187
Norris-Oak 180
Guidry-NY 166
Leonard-KC 155
Bannister-Sea 155

Strikeouts/Game
Barker-Cle 6.84
May-NY 6.84
Guidry-NY 6.79
Bannister-Sea 6.40
Perry-Tex-NY 5.90

Wins Above Team
Stone-Bal 7.7
Norris-Oak 7.1
Darwin-Tex 4.9
Barker-Cle 4.3
McGregor-Bal 4.1

Earned Run Average
May-NY 2.47
Norris-Oak 2.54
Burns-Chi 2.84
Keough-Oak 2.92
Gura-KC 2.96

Adjusted ERA
May-NY 160
Norris-Oak 150
Burns-Chi 139
Erickson-Min 136
Gura-KC 133

Opponents' Batting Avg.
Norris-Oak 209
May-NY 224
Clancy-Tor 233
Keough-Oak 236
Underwood-NY 237

Opponents' On Base Pct.
May-NY 265
Norris-Oak 268
Eckersley-Bos 286
Burns-Chi 289
Bannister-Sea 292

Starter Runs
Norris-Oak 47.3
Gura-KC 33.8
Burns-Chi 31.7
Keough-Oak 31.0
May-NY 30.4

Adjusted Starter Runs
Norris-Oak 39.6
Gura-KC 30.4
Burns-Chi 29.5
May-NY 28.6
Erickson-Min 24.6

Clutch Pitching Index
Sorensen-Mil 126
Stanley-Bos 117
Trout-Chi 113
Keough-Oak 113
Perry-Tex-NY 112

Relief Runs
Corbett-Min 31.0
Burgmeier-Bos 22.4
Gossage-NY 19.4
Darwin-Tex 17.3
Garvin-Tor 16.2

Adjusted Relief Runs
Corbett-Min 36.6
Burgmeier-Bos 23.3
Gossage-NY 18.3
Darwin-Tex 17.4
Garvin-Tor 16.6

Relief Ranking
Corbett-Min 47.9
Burgmeier-Bos 31.7
Darwin-Tex 27.1
Gossage-NY 27.1
Garvin-Tor 23.5

Total Pitcher Index
Norris-Oak 4.6
Corbett-Min 4.1
Gura-KC 3.3
Burns-Chi 3.0
May-NY 3.0

Total Baseball Ranking
Brett-KC 6.7
Henderson-Oak 6.1
Oglivie-Mil 5.3
Norris-Oak 4.6
Cooper-Mil 4.2

TEAM	G	W	L	PCT	GB	R	OR	AB	H	2B	3B	HR	BB	SO	AVG	OBP	SLG	PRO	/A	BR	/A	PF	CHI	RC	TA	SB	CS	SBA	SBR
EAST Split Season: First-half Winner PHI (34-21); Second-half Winner MON (30-23)																													
STL	103	59	43	.578		464	417	3537	936	158	**45**	50	379	495	.265	.339	.377	.716	109	42	34	102	102	454	.666	88	45	66	0
MON	108	60	48	.556	2	443	394	3591	883	146	28	81	368	498	.246	.319	.370	.689	101	2	7	99	**105**	435	.656	**138**	40	**78**	**17**
PHI	107	59	48	.551	2.5	**491**	472	3665	**1002**	165	25	69	372	**432**	**.273**	**.344**	**.389**	**.733**	**114**	**66**	14	112	99	**495**	**.689**	103	46	69	3
PIT	103	46	56	.451	13	407	425	3576	920	176	30	55	278	494	.257	.314	.369	.683	99	-8	9	96	102	417	.627	122	52	70	5
NY	105	41	62	.398	18.5	348	432	3493	868	136	35	57	304	603	.248	.311	.356	.667	94	-25	-27	101	93	387	.607	103	42	71	6
CHI	106	38	65	.369	21.5	370	483	3546	838	138	29	57	342	611	.236	.306	.340	.646	88	-51	-66	104	103	368	.577	72	41	64	-2
WEST Split Season: First-half Winner LA (36-21); Second-half Winner HOU (33-20)																													
CIN	108	66	42	.611		464	440	3637	972	**190**	24	64	375	553	.267	.339	.385	.724	111	53	**49**	101	97	469	.662	58	37	61	-4
LA	110	63	47	.573	4	450	356	3751	984	133	20	**82**	331	550	.262	.325	.374	.699	104	16	25	98	100	450	.630	73	46	61	-5
HOU	110	61	49	.555	6	394	**331**	3693	948	160	35	45	340	488	.257	.321	.356	.677	97	-11	38	88	94	425	.610	81	43	65	-1
SF	111	56	55	.505	11.5	427	414	3766	941	161	26	63	**386**	543	.250	.322	.357	.679	98	-7	-29	105	99	431	.618	89	50	64	-2
ATL	107	50	56	.472	15	395	416	3642	886	148	22	64	321	540	.243	.308	.349	.657	92	-40	-37	100	104	391	.593	98	39	72	6
SD	110	41	69	.373	26	382	455	3757	963	170	35	32	311	525	.256	.316	.346	.662	93	-32	-2	93	96	400	.580	83	62	57	-11
TOT	644					5035		43654	11141	1881	354	719	4107	6332	.255	.322	.364	.686								1108	543	67	7

TEAM	CG	SHO	SV	IP	H	H/G	HR	BB	BB/G	SO	SO/G	ERA	/A	OAVG	OOBA	PR	/A	PF	CPI	FA	E	DP	FW	PW	BW	SBW	DIF
EAST																											
STL	11	5	**33**	943.0	902	8.6	52	290	2.8	388	3.7	3.63	97	.254	.308	-14	-11	101	91	**.981**	82	108	.6	-1.2	3.7	-.0	5.0
MON	20	12	23	975.0	902	8.3	58	**268**	**2.5**	520	4.8	3.30	104	.246	.296	21	13	98	92	.980	81	88	**.7**	1.4	.8	**1.8**	1.4
PHI	19	5	23	960.3	967	9.1	72	347	3.3	580	5.4	4.05	96	.266	.325	-59	-15	112	97	.980	86	90	.4	-1.6	1.5	.3	4.9
PIT	11	5	29	942.0	953	9.1	60	346	3.3	492	4.7	3.56	94	.266	.326	-7	-21	96	107	.979	86	106	.4	-2.3	1.0	.5	-4.6
NY	7	3	24	926.3	906	8.8	74	336	3.3	490	4.8	3.55	101	.258	.317	-5	3	103	105	.968	130	89	-1.7	.3	-2.9	.6	-6.8
CHI	6	2	20	956.7	983	9.2	59	388	3.7	532	5.0	4.01	93	.269	.334	-55	-31	106	101	.974	113	103	-.9	-3.3	-7.1	-.3	-1.9
WEST																											
CIN	25	14	20	965.7	863	8.0	67	393	3.7	593	**5.5**	3.73	94	.241	.311	-25	-23	101	90	**.981**	**80**	99	**.7**	-2.5	**5.3**	-.5	9.0
LA	**26**	**19**	24	997.0	904	8.2	54	302	2.7	603	5.4	3.01	111	.244	.297	53	38	96	100	.980	87	101	.4	4.1	2.7	-.6	1.4
HOU	23	**19**	25	990.0	**842**	**7.7**	**40**	300	2.7	**610**	**5.5**	**2.66**	**114**	**.231**	**.285**	**90**	39	87	96	.980	87	81	.4	4.2	4.1	-.2	-2.5
SF	8	9	**33**	1009.3	970	8.6	57	393	3.5	561	5.0	3.28	112	.255	.322	23	**42**	105	**109**	.977	102	102	-.4	**4.5**	-3.1	-.3	-.3
ATL	11	4	24	968.0	936	8.7	62	330	3.1	471	4.4	3.45	101	.257	.313	4	3	100	102	.976	102	93	-.4	.3	-4.0	.6	.4
SD	9	6	23	1002.0	1013	9.1	64	414	3.7	492	4.4	3.72	89	.268	.336	-25	-46	95	108	.977	102	**117**	-.4	-4.9	-.2	-1.2	-7.2
TOT	176	103	301	11635.3		8.6			3.2		4.9	3.49		.255	.322					.978	1138	1177					

Runs
Schmidt-Phi 78
Rose-Phi 73
Dawson-Mon 71
Hendrick-StL 67

Hits
Rose-Phi 140
Buckner-Chi 131
Concepcion-Cin 129
Baker-LA 128
Griffey-Cin 123

Doubles
Buckner-Chi 35
Jones-SD 34
Concepcion-Cin 28
Hernandez-StL 27
Chambliss-Atl 25

Triples
Richards-SD 12
Reynolds-Hou 12
Herr-StL 9

Home Runs
Schmidt-Phi 31
Dawson-Mon 24
Kingman-NY 22
Foster-Cin 22
Hendrick-StL 18

Total Bases
Schmidt-Phi 228
Dawson-Mon 218
Foster-Cin 215
Buckner-Chi 202
Hendrick-StL 191

Runs Batted In
Schmidt-Phi 91
Foster-Cin 90
Buckner-Chi 75
Carter-Mon 68

Runs Produced
Schmidt-Phi 138
Foster-Cin 132
Matthews-Phi 120
Concepcion-Cin 119
Garvey-LA 117

Bases On Balls
Schmidt-Phi 73
Morgan-SF 66
Hernandez-StL 61
Thompson-Pit 59
Matthews-Phi 59

Batting Average
Rose-Phi 325
Baker-LA 320
Schmidt-Phi 316
Buckner-Chi 311
Griffey-Cin 311

On Base Percentage
Schmidt-Phi 439
Hernandez-StL......405
Matthews-Phi 404
Raines-Mon 394
Rose-Phi 394

Slugging Average
Schmidt-Phi 644
Dawson-Mon 553
Foster-Cin 519
Hendrick-StL 485
Buckner-Chi 480

Production
Schmidt-Phi 1.083
Dawson-Mon 923
Foster-Cin 895
Hernandez-StL 868
Matthews-Phi 855

Adjusted Production
Schmidt-Phi 182
Dawson-Mon 161
Foster-Cin 150
Hernandez-StL 143
Cey-LA 142

Batter Runs
Schmidt-Phi 50.1
Dawson-Mon 28.7
Foster-Cin 27.6
Hernandez-StL 24.6
Madlock-Pit 22.0

Adjusted Batter Runs
Schmidt-Phi 44.7
Dawson-Mon 29.3
Foster-Cin 27.2
Hernandez-StL 23.8
Madlock-Pit 23.4

Clutch Hitting Index
Matthews-Phi 147
Concepcion-Cin 135
Buckner-Chi 134
Carter-Mon 132
Scott-Mon 129

Runs Created
Schmidt-Phi 102
Dawson-Mon 83
Foster-Cin 81
Hernandez-StL 73
Matthews-Phi 71

Total Average
Schmidt-Phi 1.243
Raines-Mon 1.081
Dawson-Mon 1.004
Matthews-Phi.......916
Hernandez-StL......905

Stolen Bases
Raines-Mon 71
Moreno-Pit 39
Scott-Mon 30

Stolen Base Average
Lopes-LA 90.9
Lacy-Pit 88.9
Dawson-Mon 86.7
Raines-Mon 86.6
Puhl-Hou 84.6

Stolen Base Runs
Raines-Mon 14.7
Lacy-Pit 5.4
Dawson-Mon 5.4
Scott-Mon 4.8
Lopes-LA 4.8

Fielding Runs
Smith-SD 27.8
Schmidt-Phi 22.4
Templeton-StL 13.7
Dawson-Mon 12.4
Benedict-Atl 11.3

Total Player Rating
Schmidt-Phi 6.6
Dawson-Mon 4.6
Foster-Cin 3.1
Raines-Mon 2.9
Hernandez-StL 2.8

Wins
Seaver-Cin 14
Valenzuela-LA 13
Carlton-Phi 13

Win Percentage

Games
Lucas-SD 57
Minton-SF 55
Tidrow-Chi 51
Hume-Cin 51
Sambito-Hou 49

Complete Games
Valenzuela-LA 11
Soto-Cin 10
Carlton-Phi 10
Reuss-LA 8
Rogers-Mon 7

Shutouts
Valenzuela-LA 8
Knepper-Hou 5
Hooton-LA 4

Saves
Sutter-StL............25
Minton-SF 21
Allen-NY 18
Camp-Atl 17

Innings Pitched
Valenzuela-LA 192
Carlton-Phi 190
Soto-Cin 175
Seaver-Cin 166
Niekro-Hou..........166

Fewest Hits/Game
Ryan-Hou 5.98
Seaver-Cin 6.51
Valenzuela-LA 6.56
Berenyi-Cin 6.93
Blue-SF 6.98

Fewest BB/Game
Perry-Atl 1.43
Reuss-LA 1.59
Sutton-Hou 1.64
Sorensen-StL....... 1.67
Solomon-Pit 1.91

Strikeouts
Valenzuela-LA 180
Carlton-Phi 179
Soto-Cin 151
Ryan-Hou 140
Gullickson-Mon 115

Strikeouts/Game
Carlton-Phi 8.48
Ryan-Hou 8.46
Valenzuela-LA 8.44
Soto-Cin 7.77
Berenyi-Cin 7.57

Wins Above Team
Seaver-Cin 5.7
Carlton-Phi 4.4
Camp-Atl 3.3
Rhoden-Pit 3.1
Ryan-Hou 2.7

Earned Run Average
Ryan-Hou 1.69
Knepper-Hou 2.18
Hooton-LA 2.28
Reuss-LA 2.29
Carlton-Phi 2.42

Adjusted ERA
Ryan-Hou 179
Carlton-Phi 162
Blue-SF 150
Hooton-LA 147
Reuss-LA 146

Opponents' Batting Avg.
Ryan-Hou 188
Valenzuela-LA 205
Seaver-Cin 205
Berenyi-Cin 211
Blue-SF 217

Opponents' On Base Pct.
Sutton-Hou 260
Valenzuela-LA 266
Sanderson-Mon 275
Knepper-Hou 276
Forsch-StL 277

Starter Runs
Ryan-Hou 29.8
Knepper-Hou 22.9
Carlton-Phi 22.7
Valenzuela-LA 21.5
Reuss-LA 20.3

Adjusted Starter Runs
Carlton-Phi 31.4
Ryan-Hou 22.1
Valenzuela-LA 18.5
Reuss-LA 18.0
Seaver-Cin 17.7

Clutch Pitching Index
Solomon-Pit 124
Mahler-Atl 124
Alexander-SF 122
Blue-SF 113
Zachry-NY 111

Relief Runs
Lucas-SD 14.9
Camp-Atl 14.5
Holland-SF 12.2
Sambito-Hou 11.8
Reardon-NY -Mon .. 10.5

Adjusted Relief Runs
Camp-Atl 14.4
Holland-SF 14.1
Lucas-SD 13.1
Falcone-NY 10.8
Reardon-NY -Mon .. 10.3

Relief Ranking
Camp-Atl 27.8
Lucas-SD 22.5
Holland-SF 17.3
Sambito-Hou 15.0
Fryman-Mon 14.9

Total Pitcher Index
Carlton-Phi 3.5
Ryan-Hou 2.8
Valenzuela-LA 2.6
Blue-SF 2.4
Reuss-LA 2.4

Total Baseball Ranking
Schmidt-Phi 6.6
Dawson-Mon 4.6
Carlton-Phi 3.5
Foster-Cin 3.1
Raines-Mon 2.9

TEAM	G	W	L	PCT	GB	R	OR	AB	H	2B	3B	HR	BB	SO	AVG	OBP	SLG	PRO	/A	BR	/A	PF	CHI	RC	TA	SB	CS	SBA	SBR
EAST Split Season: First-half Winner NY (34-22); Second-half Winner MIL (31-22)																													
MIL	109	62	47	.569		493	459	3743	961	173	20	96	300	461	.257	.317	.391	.708	103	9	27	96	108	451	.631	39	36	52	-9
BAL	105	59	46	.562	1	429	437	3516	883	165	11	88	404	454	.251	.331	.379	.710	104	22	26	99	95	431	.646	41	34	55	-7
NY	107	59	48	.551	2	421	343	3529	889	148	22	100	391	434	.252	.328	.391	.719	106	29	27	100	91	445	.659	47	30	61	-3
DET	109	60	49	.550	2	427	404	3600	922	148	29	65	404	500	.256	.334	.368	.702	102	14	-8	105	93	442	.642	61	37	62	-3
BOS	108	59	49	.546	2.5	519	481	3820	1052	168	17	90	378	520	.275	.343	.399	.742	113	65	36	106	98	514	.672	32	31	51	-8
CLE	103	52	51	.505	7	431	442	3507	922	150	21	39	343	379	.263	.331	.351	.682	97	-10	18	93	103	414	.629	119	37	76	14
TOR	106	37	69	.349	23.5	329	466	3521	797	137	23	61	284	556	.226	.288	.330	.618	78	-102	-147	111	104	326	.537	66	57	54	-13
WEST Split Season: First-half Winner OAK (37-23); Second-half Winner KC (30-23)																													
OAK	109	64	45	.587		458	403	3677	910	119	26	104	342	647	.247	.314	.379	.693	99	-7	11	96	105	438	.640	98	47	68	1
TEX	105	57	48	.543	5	452	389	3581	968	178	15	49	295	396	.270	.329	.369	.698	101	5	43	91	104	425	.615	46	41	53	-10
CHI	106	54	52	.509	8.5	476	423	3615	982	155	27	76	322	518	.272	.338	.387	.725	108	41	42	100	99	471	.669	86	44	66	0
KC	103	50	53	.485	11	397	405	3560	952	169	29	61	301	419	.267	.327	.383	.710	104	17	22	99	90	437	.648	100	53	65	-1
CAL	110	51	59	.464	13.5	476	453	3688	944	134	16	97	393	571	.256	.332	.380	.712	105	26	7	104	99	463	.650	44	33	57	-6
SEA	110	44	65	.404	20	426	521	3780	950	148	13	89	329	553	.251	.316	.368	.684	97	-18	-16	100	98	441	.626	100	50	67	0
MIN	110	41	68	.376	23	378	486	3676	884	147	36	47	275	497	.240	.295	.338	.633	82	-86	-106	105	109	355	.537	34	27	56	-5
TOT	750					6112		50813	13016	2119	305	1062	4761	6905	.256	.323	.373	.696								913	557	62	-59

TEAM	CG	SHO	SV	IP	H	H/G	HR	BB	BB/G	SO	SO/G	ERA	/A	OAVG	OOBA	PR	/A	PF	CPI	FA	E	DP	FW	PW	BW	SBW	DIF
EAST																											
MIL	11	4	35	986.0	994	9.1	72	352	3.2	448	4.1	3.91	89	.265	.324	-27	-46	95	99	.982	79	135	.2	-4.8	2.8	-.5	9.7
BAL	25	10	23	940.0	923	8.8	83	347	3.3	489	4.7	3.70	98	.260	.323	-3	-7	99	104	.983	68	114	.9	-.7	2.7	-.3	3.9
NY	16	13	30	948.0	827	7.9	64	287	2.7	606	5.8	2.90	125	.235	.290	80	76	99	99	.982	72	100	.7	8.0	2.8	.1	-6.1
DET	33	13	22	969.3	840	7.8	83	373	3.5	476	4.4	3.53	109	.235	.307	13	32	105	94	.984	67	109	.9	3.4	-.4	.1	1.9
BOS	19	4	24	987.3	983	9.0	90	354	3.2	536	4.9	3.81	101	.261	.323	-16	5	106	103	.979	91	108	-.4	.5	3.8	-.4	1.5
CLE	33	10	13	931.0	989	9.6	67	311	3.0	569	5.5	3.88	88	.273	.327	-22	-47	93	102	.978	87	91	-.2	-4.9	1.9	1.9	1.8
TOR	20	4	18	953.3	908	8.6	72	377	3.6	451	4.3	3.81	108	.252	.323	-16	33	113	97	.975	105	102	-1.3	3.5	-15.4	-.9	-1.9
WEST																											
OAK	60	11	10	993.0	883	8.0	80	370	3.4	505	4.6	3.30	105	.239	.307	39	19	95	101	.980	81	74	.1	2.0	1.2	.6	5.7
TEX	23	13	18	940.3	851	8.1	67	322	3.1	488	4.7	3.40	97	.243	.304	27	-11	90	95	.984	69	102	.8	-1.2	4.5	-.6	.9
CHI	20	8	23	940.7	891	8.5	73	336	3.2	529	5.1	3.47	104	.251	.315	19	14	99	102	.979	87	113	-.2	1.5	4.4	-.5	-5.1
KC	24	8	24	922.3	909	8.9	75	273	2.7	404	3.9	3.56	102	.259	.309	9	6	99	101	.982	72	94	.7	.6	2.3	.3	-5.4
CAL	27	8	19	971.3	958	8.9	81	323	3.0	426	3.9	3.70	103	.260	.318	-4	10	104	102	.977	101	120	-1.0	1.0	.7	-.2	-4.6
SEA	10	5	23	997.3	1039	9.4	76	360	3.2	478	4.3	4.23	87	.271	.331	-63	-59	101	95	.979	91	122	-.4	-6.2	-1.7	.5	-2.6
MIN	13	6	22	979.7	1021	9.4	79	376	3.5	500	4.6	3.98	98	.271	.334	-34	-8	107	104	.978	96	103	-.7	-.8	-11.1	-.0	-.7
TOT	334	117	304	13459.7		8.7			3.2		4.6	3.66		.256	.323					.980	1166	1487					

Runs
Henderson-Oak 89
Evans-Bos 84
Cooper-Mil 70
Harrah-Cle 64
Rivers-Tex 62

Hits
Henderson-Oak 135
Lansford-Bos 134
Wilson-KC 133
Cooper-Mil 133
Paciorek-Sea 132

Doubles
Cooper-Mil 35
Oliver-Tex 29
Paciorek-Sea 28
Dauer-Bal 27
Brett-KC 27

Triples
Castino-Min 9
Wilson-KC 7
Henderson-Oak 7
Brett-KC 7
Baines-Chi 7

Home Runs
Murray-Bal 22
Grich-Cal 22
Evans-Bos 22
Armas-Oak 22

Total Bases
Evans-Bos 215
Armas-Oak 211
Paciorek-Sea 206
Cooper-Mil 206
Murray-Bal 202

Runs Batted In
Murray-Bal 78
Armas-Oak 76
Oglivie-Mil 72
Evans-Bos 71
Winfield-NY 68

Runs Produced
Evans-Bos 133
Henderson-Oak 118
Cooper-Mil 118
Murray-Bal 113
Oglivie-Mil 111

Bases On Balls
Evans-Bos 85
Murphy-Oak 73
Kemp-Det 70
Henderson-Oak 64
Aikens-KC 62

Batting Average
Lansford-Bos 336
Paciorek-Sea 326
Cooper-Mil 320
Henderson-Oak 319
Hargrove-Cle 317

On Base Percentage
Hargrove-Cle 432
Evans-Bos 418
Henderson-Oak 411
Kemp-Det 393
Lansford-Bos 391

Slugging Average
Grich-Cal 543
Murray-Bal 534
Evans-Bos 522
Paciorek-Sea 509
Cooper-Mil 495

Production
Evans-Bos 940
Grich-Cal 924
Murray-Bal 897
Paciorek-Sea 894
Lemon-Chi 879

Adjusted Production
Evans-Bos 159
Murray-Bal 157
Grich-Cal 157
Paciorek-Sea 156
Cooper-Mil 153

Batter Runs
Evans-Bos 39.8
Paciorek-Sea 28.4
Grich-Cal 28.3
Henderson-Oak 26.9
Murray-Bal 25.9

Adjusted Batter Runs
Evans-Bos 36.5
Henderson-Oak 29.1
Paciorek-Sea 28.5
Grich-Cal 26.5
Murray-Bal 26.4

Clutch Hitting Index
Hargrove-Cle 150
Yastrzemski-Bos 150
Oglivie-Mil 149
Bell-Tex 144
Simmons-Mil 137

Runs Created
Evans-Bos 95
Henderson-Oak 81
Paciorek-Sea 76
Grich-Cal 73
Murray-Bal 70

Total Average
Evans-Bos 1.013
Henderson-Oak 968
Grich-Cal 933
Paciorek-Sea 881
Murray-Bal 875

Stolen Bases
Henderson-Oak 56
Cruz-Sea 43
LeFlore-Chi 36
Wilson-KC 34
Dilone-Cle 29

Stolen Base Average
Manning-Cle 89.3
Bannister-Cle 88.9
Cruz-Sea 84.3
Wilson-KC 81.0
Gibson-Det 77.3

Stolen Base Runs
Cruz-Sea 8.1
Manning-Cle 5.7
Wilson-KC 5.4
LeFlore-Chi 4.2

Fielding Runs
Bell-Tex 27.1
Yount-Mil 25.3
Wills-Tex 23.9
Burleson-Cal 22.6
Wilson-KC 22.4

Total Player Rating
Henderson-Oak 5.0
Bell-Tex 4.6
Yount-Mil 3.9
Grich-Cal 3.9
Burleson-Cal 3.4

Wins
Vuckovich-Mil 14
Morris-Det 14
McCatty-Oak 14
D.Martinez-Bal 14

Win Percentage

Games
Corbett-Min 54
Fingers-Mil 47
Rawley-Sea 46
Easterly-Mil 44

Complete Games
Langford-Oak 18
McCatty-Oak 16
Morris-Det 15
Norris-Oak 12
Gura-KC 12

Shutouts
Medich-Tex 4
McCatty-Oak 4
Forsch-Cal 4
Dotson-Chi 4

Saves
Fingers-Mil 28
Gossage-NY 20
Quisenberry-KC 18
Corbett-Min 17
Saucier-Det 13

Innings Pitched
Leonard-KC 202
Morris-Det 198
Langford-Oak 195
McCatty-Oak 186
Stieb-Tor 184

Fewest Hits/Game
McCatty-Oak 6.77
Morris-Det 6.95
Guidry-NY 7.09
Darwin-Tex 7.09
Stewart-Bal 7.15

Fewest BB/Game
Honeycutt-Tex 1.20
Forsch-Cal 1.59
Leonard-KC 1.83
Gura-KC 1.83
Guidry-NY 1.84

Strikeouts
Barker-Cle 127
Burns-Chi 108
Leonard-KC 107
Blyleven-Cle 107
Guidry-NY 104

Strikeouts/Game
Barker-Cle 7.42
Guidry-NY 7.37
Bannister-Sea 6.32
Burns-Chi 6.19
Blyleven-Cle 6.06

Wins Above Team
Vuckovich-Mil 4.8
D.Martinez-Bal 4.3
McGregor-Bal 3.7
Torrez-Bos 3.4
Stieb-Tor 3.3

Earned Run Average
McCatty-Oak 2.32
Stewart-Bal 2.33
Lamp-Chi 2.41
John-NY 2.64
Burns-Chi 2.64

Adjusted ERA
Stewart-Bal 156
Lamp-Chi 150
McCatty-Oak 150
John-NY 137
Burns-Chi 137

Opponents' Batting Avg.
McCatty-Oak 211
Guidry-NY 214
Darwin-Tex 218
Morris-Det 218
Lamp-Chi 222

Opponents' On Base Pct.
Guidry-NY 256
Gura-KC 262
Honeycutt-Tex 269
McCatty-Oak 274
Forsch-Cal 282

Starter Runs
McCatty-Oak 27.6
Righetti-NY 18.7
Gura-KC 17.9
Burns-Chi 17.8
Lamp-Chi 17.6

Adjusted Starter Runs
McCatty-Oak 23.8
Stieb-Tor 19.5
Righetti-NY 18.2
Morris-Det 17.3
Gura-KC 17.2

Clutch Pitching Index
Stewart-Bal 144
John-NY 128
Burns-Chi 121
Denny-Cle 119
McGregor-Bal 116

Relief Runs
Fingers-Mil 22.7
Gossage-NY 15.1
Quisenberry-KC 13.2
Saucier-Det 10.9
Corbett-Min 10.8

Adjusted Relief Runs
Fingers-Mil 21.2
Gossage-NY 14.9
Corbett-Min 13.1
Quisenberry-KC 12.9
Saucier-Det 11.9

Relief Ranking
Fingers-Mil 39.2
Gossage-NY 28.5
Saucier-Det 20.2
Quisenberry-KC 17.9
Corbett-Min 16.4

Total Pitcher Index
McCatty-Oak 2.6
Stieb-Tor 2.4
Fingers-Mil 2.3
Gura-KC 1.9
Lamp-Chi 1.9

Total Baseball Ranking
Henderson-Oak 5.0
Bell-Tex 4.6
Yount-Mil 3.9
Grich-Cal 3.9
Burleson-Cal 3.4

TEAM	G	W	L	PCT	GB	R	OR	AB	H	2B	3B	HR	BB	SO	AVG	OBP	SLG	PRO	/A	BR	/A	PF	CHI	RC	TA	SB	CS	SBA	SBR
EAST																													
STL	162	92	70	.568		685	**609**	5455	1439	239	**52**	67	569	805	.264	**.337**	.364	.701	102	24	1	103	99	682	.660	**200**	91	69	5
PHI	162	89	73	.549	3	664	654	5454	1417	245	25	112	506	831	.260	.325	.376	.701	102	13	54	94	99	654	.637	128	76	63	-6
MON	162	86	76	.531	6	697	616	5557	1454	270	38	133	503	816	.262	.327	.396	.723	108	52	16	105	96	725	.678	156	56	**74**	**13**
PIT	162	84	78	.519	8	724	696	5614	**1535**	**272**	40	134	447	862	**.273**	.330	**.408**	**.738**	**112**	**80**	11	110	96	**745**	**.685**	161	75	68	3
CHI	162	73	89	.451	19	676	709	5531	1436	239	46	102	460	869	.260	.319	.375	.694	100	-3	-24	103	103	662	.631	132	70	65	-1
NY	162	65	97	.401	27	609	723	5510	1361	227	26	97	456	1005	.247	.307	.350	.657	89	-74	-64	99	104	595	.590	137	58	70	6
WEST																													
ATL	162	89	73	.549		**739**	702	5507	1411	215	22	**146**	554	869	.256	.327	.383	.710	104	33	-14	107	105	697	.665	151	77	66	0
LA	162	88	74	.543	1	691	612	5642	1487	222	32	138	528	**804**	.264	.330	.388	.718	107	47	**84**	95	94	735	.672	151	56	73	12
SF	162	87	75	.537	2	673	687	5499	1393	213	30	133	**607**	915	.253	.329	.376	.705	103	27	69	94	96	685	.657	130	56	70	5
SD	162	81	81	.500	8	675	658	5575	1435	217	**52**	81	429	877	.257	.313	.359	.672	94	-48	6	92	**110**	626	.606	165	77	68	3
HOU	162	77	85	.475	12	569	620	5440	1342	236	48	74	435	830	.247	.305	.349	.654	88	-83	-76	99	101	578	.584	140	61	70	5
CIN	162	61	101	.377	28	545	661	5479	1375	228	34	82	470	817	.251	.313	.350	.663	91	-62	-77	102	92	588	.588	131	69	66	-1
TOT	972					7947		66263	17085	2823	445	1299	5964	10300	.258	.322	.373	.695								1782	822	68	41

TEAM	CG	SHO	SV	IP	H	H/G	HR	BB	BB/G	SO	SO/G	ERA	/A	OAVG	OOBA	PR	/A	PF	CPI	FA	E	DP	FW	PW	BW	SBW	DIF
EAST																											
STL	25	10	47	1465.3	1420	8.7	94	502	3.1	689	4.2	3.37	109	.257	.316	37	51	102	105	**.981**	124	169	.9	5.4	.1	.2	4.4
PHI	**38**	13	33	1456.3	1395	8.6	86	472	2.9	**1002**	**6.2**	3.61	93	.254	.310	-1	-39	94	93	**.981**	**121**	138	**1.1**	-4.1	5.7	-1.0	6.3
MON	34	10	43	1460.7	1371	8.4	110	**448**	**2.8**	936	5.8	3.31	**113**	.249	.302	46	**70**	104	99	.980	122	117	**1.1**	**7.4**	1.7	**1.0**	-6.1
PIT	19	7	39	1466.7	1434	8.8	118	521	3.2	933	5.7	3.81	104	.257	.317	-34	23	110	96	.977	145	133	-.3	2.4	1.2	-.0	-.3
CHI	9	7	43	1447.3	1510	9.4	125	452	**2.8**	764	4.8	3.92	95	.272	.322	-50	-29	104	102	.979	132	110	.5	-3.0	-2.5	-.5	-2.4
NY	15	5	37	1447.3	1508	9.4	119	582	3.6	759	4.7	3.88	93	.272	.335	-44	-45	100	**109**	.972	175	134	-2.0	-4.7	-6.7	.3	-2.8
WEST																											
ATL	15	11	**51**	1463.0	1484	9.1	126	502	3.1	813	5.0	3.82	100	.267	.323	-35	2	107	103	.979	137	**186**	.2	.2	-1.5	-.4	9.4
LA	37	**16**	28	1488.3	1356	**8.2**	**81**	468	**2.8**	932	5.6	**3.26**	103	**.243**	**.298**	**56**	17	94	92	.979	139	131	.0	1.8	**8.8**	.9	-4.6
SF	18	4	45	1465.3	1507	9.3	109	466	2.9	810	5.0	3.64	93	.269	.320	-5	-42	94	106	.973	173	125	-1.9	-4.4	7.2	.2	4.9
SD	20	11	41	1476.0	1348	**8.2**	139	502	3.1	765	4.7	3.52	93	**.243**	.302	12	-37	92	96	.976	152	142	-.7	-3.9	.6	-.0	4.0
HOU	37	**16**	31	1446.7	**1338**	8.3	87	479	3.0	899	5.6	3.42	105	.246	.306	29	27	100	94	.978	136	154	.3	2.8	-8.0	.2	.7
CIN	22	7	31	1460.3	1414	8.7	105	570	3.5	998	**6.2**	3.66	102	.257	.323	-9	12	104	102	.980	128	158	.7	1.3	-8.1	-.5	-13.4
TOT	289	117	469	17543.3		8.8			3.1		5.3	3.60		.258	.322					.978	1684	1697					

Runs
L.Smith-StL 120
Murphy-Atl 113
Schmidt-Phi 108
Dawson-Mon 107
Sandberg-Chi 103

Hits
Oliver-Mon 204
Buckner-Chi 201
Dawson-Mon 183
L.Smith-StL 182
Ray-Pit 182

Doubles
Oliver-Mon 43
Kennedy-SD 42
Dawson-Mon 37
Knight-Hou 36

Triples
Thon-Hou 10
Wilson-NY 9
Puhl-Hou 9
Moreno-Pit 9

Home Runs
Kingman-NY 37
Murphy-Atl 36
Schmidt-Phi 35
Horner-Atl 32
Guerrero-LA 32

Total Bases
Oliver-Mon 317
Guerrero-LA 308
Murphy-Atl 303
Dawson-Mon 303
Buckner-Chi 290

Runs Batted In
Oliver-Mon 109
Murphy-Atl 109
Buckner-Chi 105
Hendrick-StL 104
Clark-SF 103

Runs Produced
Murphy-Atl 186
Buckner-Chi 183
L.Smith-StL 181
Oliver-Mon 177
Madlock-Pit 168

Bases On Balls
Schmidt-Phi 107
Thompson-Pit 101
Hernandez-StL 100
Murphy-Atl 93
Clark-SF 90

Batting Average
Oliver-Mon 331
Madlock-Pit 319
Durham-Chi 312
L.Smith-StL 307
Buckner-Chi 306

On Base Percentage
Schmidt-Phi 407
Hernandez-StL 404
Morgan-SF 402
Thompson-Pit 397
Oliver-Mon 394

Slugging Average
Schmidt-Phi 547
Guerrero-LA 536
Durham-Chi 521
Oliver-Mon 514
Thompson-Pit 511

Production
Schmidt-Phi 954
Guerrero-LA 915
Durham-Chi 910
Oliver-Mon 908
Thompson-Pit 908

Adjusted Production
Schmidt-Phi 176
Guerrero-LA 162
Lezcano-SD 153
Durham-Chi 148
Clark-SF 147

Batter Runs
Schmidt-Phi 47.2
Oliver-Mon 42.7
Thompson-Pit 40.7
Guerrero-LA 40.3
Murphy-Atl 37.8

Adjusted Batter Runs
Schmidt-Phi 51.5
Guerrero-LA 44.1
Oliver-Mon 38.8
Durham-Chi 35.6
Clark-SF 34.1

Clutch Hitting Index
Hernandez-StL 150
Hendrick-StL 149
DeJesus-Phi 133
Lezcano-SD 124
Salazar-SD 124

Runs Created
Oliver-Mon 125
Guerrero-LA 120
Murphy-Atl 118
Schmidt-Phi 118
Thompson-Pit 117

Total Average
Schmidt-Phi 1.044
Guerrero-LA 971
Durham-Chi 952
Thompson-Pit 951
Murphy-Atl 936

Stolen Bases
Raines-Mon 78
L.Smith-StL 68
Moreno-Pit 60
Wilson-NY 58
Sax-LA 49

Stolen Base Average
Bailor-NY 87.0
Morgan-SF 85.7
Wiggins-SD 84.6
Matthews-Phi 84.0
O.Smith-StL 83.3

Stolen Base Runs
Raines-Mon 13.8
Wilson-NY 7.8
Wiggins-SD 6.3
Thon-Hou 6.3
Dawson-Mon 5.7

Fielding Runs
O.Smith-StL 33.9
Hubbard-Atl 23.0
Carter-Mon 21.1
Ramirez-Atl 18.5
Schmidt-Phi 18.1

Total Player Rating
Schmidt-Phi 6.8
Carter-Mon 5.5
Guerrero-LA 5.4
Lezcano-SD 4.4
O.Smith-StL 4.0

Wins
Carlton-Phi 23
Valenzuela-LA 19
Rogers-Mon 19
Reuss-LA 18

Win Percentage
Niekro-Atl 810
Rogers-Mon 704
Carlton-Phi 676
Lollar-SD 640
Forsch-StL 625

Games
Tekulve-Pit 85
Minton-SF 78
Scurry-Pit 76
Reardon-Mon 75
Hernandez-Chi 75

Complete Games
Carlton-Phi 19
Valenzuela-LA 18
Niekro-Hou 16
Rogers-Mon 14
Soto-Cin 13

Shutouts
Carlton-Phi 6
Niekro-Hou 5
Andujar-StL 5

Saves
Sutter-StL 36
Minton-SF 30
Garber-Atl 30
Reardon-Mon 26
Tekulve-Pit 20

Innings Pitched
Carlton-Phi 296
Valenzuela-LA 285
Rogers-Mon 277
Niekro-Hou 270
Andujar-StL 266

Fewest Hits/Game
Soto-Cin 7.05
Ryan-Hou 7.06
Lea-Mon 7.33
Lollar-SD 7.42
Niekro-Hou 7.47

Fewest BB/Game
Bird-Chi 1.41
Hammaker-SF 1.44
Andujar-StL 1.69
Reuss-LA 1.76
Candelaria-Pit 1.90

Strikeouts
Carlton-Phi 286
Soto-Cin 274
Ryan-Hou 245
Valenzuela-LA 199
Rogers-Mon 179

Strikeouts/Game
Soto-Cin 9.56
Ryan-Hou 8.82
Carlton-Phi 8.70
Candelaria-Pit 6.84
Welch-LA 6.71

Wins Above Team
Niekro-Atl 6.4
Carlton-Phi 5.6
Rogers-Mon 5.6
Lollar-SD 3.9
Niekro-Hou 3.6

Earned Run Average
Rogers-Mon 2.40
Niekro-Hou 2.47
Andujar-StL 2.47
Soto-Cin 2.79
Valenzuela-LA 2.87

Adjusted ERA
Rogers-Mon 156
Andujar-StL 149
Niekro-Hou 145
Candelaria-Pit 135
Soto-Cin 134

Opponents' Batting Avg.
Ryan-Hou 213
Soto-Cin 215
Lea-Mon 222
Lollar-SD 224
Niekro-Hou 229

Opponents' On Base Pct.
Soto-Cin 268
Reuss-LA 274
Niekro-Hou 275
Sutton-Hou 276
Lea-Mon 278

Starter Runs
Rogers-Mon 36.8
Niekro-Hou 34.0
Andujar-StL 33.4
Soto-Cin 23.2
Valenzuela-LA 23.0

Adjusted Starter Runs
Rogers-Mon 41.5
Andujar-StL 36.0
Niekro-Hou 33.6
Soto-Cin 27.1
Candelaria-Pit 19.9

Clutch Pitching Index
Camp-Atl 124
Jenkins-Chi 120
Krukow-Phi 120
Gale-SF 114
Mura-StL 110

Relief Runs
Minton-SF 24.2
Scurry-Pit 21.6
Reardon-Mon 18.6
Bedrosian-Atl 18.2
DeLeon-SD 17.8

Adjusted Relief Runs
Scurry-Pit 25.7
Bedrosian-Atl 21.9
Minton-SF 21.1
Reardon-Mon 20.4
Garber-Atl 19.8

Relief Ranking
Garber-Atl 38.1
Minton-SF 33.2
Reardon-Mon 29.5
Scurry-Pit 27.8
Tekulve-Pit 27.4

Total Pitcher Index
Rogers-Mon 4.7
Andujar-StL 4.1
Niekro-Hou 3.2
Soto-Cin 3.0
Scurry-Pit 2.8

Total Baseball Ranking
Schmidt-Phi 6.8
Carter-Mon 5.5
Guerrero-LA 5.4
Rogers-Mon 4.7
Lezcano-SD 4.4

TEAM	G	W	L	PCT	GB	R	OR	AB	H	2B	3B	HR	BB	SO	AVG	OBP	SLG	PRO	/A	BR	/A	PF	CHI	RC	TA	SB	CS	SBA	SBR
EAST																													
MIL	163	95	67	.586		**891**	717	5733	1599	277	41	**216**	484	714	.279	.337	**.455**	**.792**	**115**	**109**	**153**	94	104	**865**	**.744**	84	52	62	-5
BAL	163	94	68	.580	1	774	687	5557	1478	259	27	179	634	796	.266	.344	.419	.763	108	67	68	100	96	795	.713	49	38	56	-7
BOS	162	89	73	.549	6	753	713	5596	1536	271	31	136	547	736	.274	.342	.407	.749	105	39	-35	110	97	755	.678	42	39	52	-10
DET	162	83	79	.512	12	729	685	5590	1489	237	40	177	470	807	.266	.326	.418	.744	103	15	12	100	99	752	.686	93	66	58	-11
NY	162	79	83	.488	16	709	716	5526	1417	225	37	161	590	719	.256	.331	.398	.729	99	-4	22	96	97	716	.669	69	45	61	-5
TOR	162	78	84	.481	17	651	701	5526	1447	262	45	106	415	749	.262	.317	.383	.700	91	-70	-130	109	101	655	.628	118	81	59	-12
CLE	162	78	84	.481	17	683	748	5559	1458	225	32	109	**651**	**626**	.262	.343	.373	.716	97	-12	-13	100	93	723	.675	151	68	69	5
WEST																													
CAL	162	93	69	.574		814	**670**	5532	1518	268	26	186	613	760	.274	**.350**	.433	.783	114	108	106	100	95	834	.738	55	53	51	-14
KC	162	90	72	.556	3	784	717	5629	**1603**	**295**	**58**	132	442	758	**.285**	.340	.428	.768	109	67	66	100	99	802	.714	133	48	**73**	11
CHI	162	87	75	.537	6	786	710	5575	1523	266	52	136	533	866	.273	.340	.413	.753	106	43	61	97	101	784	.710	136	58	70	6
SEA	162	76	86	.469	17	651	712	5626	1431	259	33	130	456	806	.254	.313	.381	.694	89	-83	-150	109	101	657	.628	131	82	62	-9
OAK	162	68	94	.420	25	691	819	5448	1286	211	27	149	582	948	.236	.312	.367	.679	86	-105	-70	95	**112**	644	.652	**232**	87	**73**	**17**
TEX	162	64	98	.395	29	590	749	5445	1354	204	26	115	447	750	.249	.309	.359	.668	83	-127	-76	93	102	593	.585	63	45	58	-7
MIN	162	60	102	.370	33	657	819	5544	1427	234	44	148	474	887	.257	.319	.396	.715	95	-42	-43	100	97	676	.635	38	33	54	-7
TOT	1135					10163		77886	20566	3493	519	2080	7338	10922	.264	.330	.402	.733								1394	795	64	-58

TEAM	CG	SHO	SV	IP	H	H/G	HR	BB	BB/G	SO	SO/G	ERA	/A	OAVG	OOBA	PR	/A	PF	CPI	FA	E	DP	FW	PW	BW	SBW	DIF
EAST																											
MIL	34	6	**47**	1467.3	1514	9.3	152	511	3.1	717	4.4	3.98	94	.269	.327	15	-36	92	106	.980	125	**185**	.0	-3.6	**15.3**	-.0	2.3
BAL	38	8	34	1462.3	1436	8.8	147	488	3.0	719	4.4	3.99	101	.257	**.314**	13	7	99	95	**.984**	**101**	140	**1.4**	.7	6.8	-.3	4.4
BOS	23	11	33	1453.0	1557	9.6	155	478	3.0	816	5.1	4.03	111	.275	.331	6	71	110	**108**	.981	121	172	.3	7.1	-3.5	-.6	4.7
DET	**45**	5	27	1451.0	**1371**	**8.5**	172	554	3.4	741	4.6	**3.80**	107	**.251**	.318	**43**	43	100	104	.981	117	165	.5	4.3	1.2	-.7	-3.3
NY	24	8	39	1459.0	1471	9.1	113	491	3.0	939	5.8	3.99	98	.263	.318	13	-9	97	95	.979	128	158	-.0	-.9	2.2	-.0	-3.1
TOR	41	**13**	25	1443.7	1428	8.9	147	493	3.1	776	4.8	3.95	113	.257	.316	20	79	109	97	.978	136	146	-.5	7.9	-13.0	-.8	3.4
CLE	31	9	30	1468.3	1433	8.8	122	589	3.6	882	5.4	4.11	100	.257	.324	-5	0	101	94	.980	123	129	.2	.0	-1.3	.9	-2.8
WEST																											
CAL	40	10	27	1464.0	1436	8.8	124	482	3.0	728	4.5	3.82	105	.258	.318	41	32	99	98	.983	108	171	1.0	3.2	10.6	-1.0	-1.8
KC	16	12	45	1431.0	1443	9.1	163	471	3.0	650	4.1	4.08	99	.261	.317	-1	-4	100	98	.979	127	140	-.0	-.4	6.6	1.5	1.3
CHI	30	10	41	1439.0	1502	9.4	**99**	**460**	**2.9**	753	4.7	3.87	102	.269	.323	33	11	97	100	.976	154	173	-1.5	1.1	6.1	1.0	-.7
SEA	23	11	39	1476.3	1431	8.7	173	547	3.3	**1002**	**6.1**	3.88	**115**	.256	.320	32	**98**	110	104	.978	139	158	-.7	**9.8**	-15.0	-.5	1.4
OAK	42	6	22	1456.0	1506	9.3	177	648	4.0	697	4.3	4.54	86	.267	.339	-76	-99	96	100	.974	160	140	-1.8	-9.9	-7.0	**2.1**	3.6
TEX	32	5	24	1431.0	1554	9.8	128	483	3.0	690	4.3	4.28	90	.280	.335	-33	-70	94	102	.981	121	169	.3	-7.0	-7.6	-.3	-2.4
MIN	26	7	30	1433.0	1484	9.3	208	643	4.0	812	5.1	4.72	88	.269	.341	-103	-91	102	101	.982	108	162	1.0	-9.1	-4.3	-.3	-8.3
TOT	445	121	463	20335.0		9.1			3.2		4.8	4.07		.264	.330					.980	1768	2208					

Runs
Molitor-Mil 136
Yount-Mil 129
Evans-Bos 122
Henderson-Oak 119
Downing-Cal 109

Hits
Yount-Mil 210
Cooper-Mil 205
Molitor-Mil 201
Wilson-KC 194
McRae-KC 189

Doubles
Yount-Mil 46
McRae-KC 46
White-KC 45
DeCinces-Cal 42
Cowens-Sea 39

Triples
Wilson-KC 15
Herndon-Det 13
Yount-Mil 12
Mumphrey-NY 10

Home Runs
Thomas-Mil 39
Jackson-Cal 39
Winfield-NY 37
Oglivie-Mil 34

Total Bases
Yount-Mil 367
Cooper-Mil 345
McRae-KC 332
Evans-Bos 325
DeCinces-Cal 315

Runs Batted In
McRae-KC 133
Cooper-Mil 121
Thornton-Cle 116
Yount-Mil 114
Thomas-Mil 112

Runs Produced
Yount-Mil 214
McRae-KC 197
Cooper-Mil 193
Molitor-Mil 188
Evans-Bos 188

Bases On Balls
Henderson-Oak 116
Evans-Bos 112
Thornton-Cle 109
Hargrove-Cle 101
Murphy-Oak 94

Batting Average
Wilson-KC .... .332
Yount-Mil .... .331
Carew-Cal .... .319
Murray-Bal .... .316
Cooper-Mil .... .313

On Base Percentage
Evans-Bos .... .403
Harrah-Cle .... .400
Henderson-Oak ..... .399
Carew-Cal .... .399
Murray-Bal .... .395

Slugging Average
Yount-Mil .... .578
Winfield-NY .... .560
Murray-Bal .... .549
DeCinces-Cal .... .548
McRae-KC .... .542

Production
Yount-Mil .... .962
Murray-Bal .... .944
Evans-Bos .... .937
DeCinces-Cal .... .922
McRae-KC .... .912

Adjusted Production
Yount-Mil 170
Murray-Bal 156
DeCinces-Cal 149
McRae-KC 146
Jackson-Cal 146

Batter Runs
Yount-Mil 50.3
Evans-Bos 48.5
Murray-Bal 42.5
DeCinces-Cal 38.1
Harrah-Cle 37.9

Adjusted Batter Runs
Yount-Mil 55.2
Murray-Bal 42.6
Evans-Bos 39.8
DeCinces-Cal 38.0
McRae-KC 37.8

Clutch Hitting Index
Otis-KC 160
Foli-Cal 143
Wathan-KC 138
McRae-KC 136
Luzinski-Chi 136

Runs Created
Yount-Mil 136
Evans-Bos 134
Harrah-Cle 123
McRae-KC 123
Cooper-Mil 118

Total Average
Evans-Bos .... .980
Yount-Mil .... .975
Murray-Bal .... .962
Henderson-Oak ..... .938
Jackson-Cal .... .935

Stolen Bases
Henderson-Oak 130
Garcia-Tor 54
J.Cruz-Sea 46
Molitor-Mil 41
Wilson-KC 37

Stolen Base Average
Sexton-Oak 100.0
Fisk-Chi 89.5
Dilone-Cle 86.8
Harrah-Cle 85.0
Brown-Sea 82.4

Stolen Base Runs
Henderson-Oak 13.8
Molitor-Mil 6.9
Dilone-Cle 6.9
J.Cruz-Sea 6.0
Wathan-KC 5.4

Fielding Runs
Bell-Tex 37.0
Bernazard-Chi 27.6
DeCinces-Cal 23.9
Grich-Cal 20.2
Sundberg-Tex 20.1

Total Player Rating
Yount-Mil 6.6
DeCinces-Cal 5.7
Bell-Tex 5.5
Grich-Cal 4.5
Bernazard-Chi 4.1

Wins
Hoyt-Chi 19
Zahn-Cal 18
Vuckovich-Mil 18
Gura-KC 18

Win Percentage
Vuckovich-Mil ...... .750
Palmer-Bal .... .750
Zahn-Cal .... .692
Petry-Det .... .625
Gura-KC .... .600

Games
VandeBerg-Sea 78
T.Martinez-Bal 76
Quisenberry-KC 72
Caudill-Sea 70
Spillner-Cle 65

Complete Games
Stieb-Tor 19
Morris-Det 17
Langford-Oak 15
Hoyt-Chi 14

Shutouts
Stieb-Tor 5
Zahn-Cal 4
Forsch-Cal 4

Saves
Quisenberry-KC 35
Gossage-NY 30
Fingers-Mil 29
Caudill-Sea 26
Davis-Min 22

Innings Pitched
Stieb-Tor 288
Clancy-Tor 267
Morris-Det 266
Caldwell-Mil 258
D.Martinez-Bal 252

Fewest Hits/Game
Sutcliffe-Cle 7.25
Ujdur-Det 7.58
Righetti-NY 7.62
Palmer-Bal 7.73
Barker-Cle 7.75

Fewest BB/Game
John-NY -Cal 1.58
Eckersley-Bos 1.73
Hoyt-Chi 1.80
Haas-Mil 1.82
Langford-Oak 1.86

Strikeouts
Bannister-Sea 209
Barker-Cle 187
Righetti-NY 163
Guidry-NY 162
Tudor-Bos 146

Strikeouts/Game
Righetti-NY 8.02
Bannister-Sea 7.62
Beattie-Sea 7.33
Barker-Cle 6.87
Tudor-Bos 6.70

Wins Above Team
Vuckovich-Mil 5.2
Palmer-Bal 4.4
Hough-Tex 4.3
Zahn-Cal 4.1
Burns-Chi 3.9

Earned Run Average
Sutcliffe-Cle 2.96
Stanley-Bos 3.11
Palmer-Bal 3.13
Petry-Det 3.22
Stieb-Tor 3.25

Adjusted ERA
Stanley-Bos 144
Sutcliffe-Cle 139
Stieb-Tor 137
Beattie-Sea 134
Bannister-Sea 131

Opponents' Batting Avg.
Sutcliffe-Cle .... .226
Righetti-NY .... .229
Ujdur-Det .... .230
Palmer-Bal .... .231
Barker-Cle .... .232

Opponents' On Base Pct.
Palmer-Bal .... .285
Eckersley-Bos ...... .295
Stieb-Tor .... .296
Barker-Cle .... .296
Bannister-Sea ...... .298

Starter Runs
Sutcliffe-Cle 26.8
Stieb-Tor 26.3
Palmer-Bal 23.7
Petry-Det 23.3
Vuckovich-Mil 18.4

Adjusted Starter Runs
Stieb-Tor 38.1
Bannister-Sea 28.9
Sutcliffe-Cle 27.5
Stanley-Bos 25.6
Petry-Det 23.2

Clutch Pitching Index
Vuckovich-Mil 131
Tudor-Bos 121
Dotson-Chi 118
Wilcox-Det 113
Sutcliffe-Cle 110

Relief Runs
Spillner-Cle 23.6
Quisenberry-KC 23.0
Burgmeier-Bos 20.2
Gossage-NY 19.1
Caudill-Sea 18.4

Adjusted Relief Runs
Burgmeier-Bos 24.7
Spillner-Cle 24.1
Caudill-Sea 22.7
Quisenberry-KC 22.7
VandeBerg-Sea 17.8

Relief Ranking
Caudill-Sea 58.6
Spillner-Cle 44.2
Clear-Bos 39.1
Quisenberry-KC 36.9
VandeBerg-Sea 30.0

Total Pitcher Index
Stieb-Tor 4.5
Stanley-Bos 3.1
Sutcliffe-Cle 3.0
Bannister-Sea 3.0
Quisenberry-KC 2.9

Total Baseball Ranking
Yount-Mil 6.6
DeCinces-Cal 5.7
Bell-Tex 5.5
Grich-Cal 4.5
Stieb-Tor 4.5

TEAM	G	W	L	PCT	GB	R	OR	AB	H	2B	3B	HR	BB	SO	AVG	OBP	SLG	PRO	/A	BR	/A	PF	CHI	RC	TA	SB	CS	SBA	SBR
EAST																													
PHI	163	90	72	.556		696	635	5426	1352	209	45	125	640	906	.249	.331	.373	.704	101	16	9	101	101	676	.662	143	75	66	-1
PIT	162	84	78	.519	6	659	648	5531	1460	238	29	121	497	873	.264	.327	.383	.710	103	17	-2	103	96	682	.646	124	77	62	-8
MON	163	82	80	.506	8	677	646	5611	1482	297	41	102	509	733	.264	.329	.386	.715	104	30	19	102	95	716	.662	138	44	76	15
STL	162	79	83	.488	11	679	710	5550	1496	262	63	83	543	879	.270	.337	.384	.721	106	47	61	98	94	725	.682	207	89	70	9
CHI	162	71	91	.438	19	701	699	5512	1436	272	42	140	470	868	.261	.322	.401	.723	106	35	29	101	100	707	.661	84	40	68	1
NY	162	68	94	.420	22	575	680	5444	1314	172	26	112	436	1031	.241	.301	.344	.645	84	-112	-102	99	106	562	.576	141	64	69	4
WEST																													
LA	163	91	71	.562		654	609	5440	1358	197	34	146	541	925	.250	.331	.379	.699	99	-5	-5	100	99	663	.653	166	76	69	4
ATL	162	88	74	.543	3	746	640	5472	1489	218	45	130	582	847	.272	.344	.400	.744	112	91	53	106	98	744	.698	146	88	62	-8
HOU	162	85	77	.525	6	643	646	5502	1412	239	60	97	517	869	.257	.323	.375	.698	99	-6	60	90	97	673	.648	164	95	63	-7
SD	163	81	81	.500	10	653	653	5527	1384	207	34	93	482	822	.250	.313	.351	.664	90	-73	-67	99	110	609	.605	179	67	73	14
SF	162	79	83	.488	12	687	697	5369	1324	206	30	142	619	990	.247	.328	.375	.703	101	10	4	101	102	662	.659	140	78	64	-4
CIN	162	74	88	.457	17	623	710	5333	1274	236	35	107	588	1006	.239	.317	.356	.673	92	-48	-65	103	102	606	.625	154	77	67	0
TOT	974					7993		65717	16781	2753	484	1398	6424	10749	.255	.324	.376	.700								1786	870	67	14

TEAM	CG	SHO	SV	IP	H	H/G	HR	BB	BB/G	SO	SO/G	ERA	/A	OAVG	OOBA	PR	/A	PF	CPI	FA	E	DP	FW	PW	BW	SBW	DIF
EAST																											
PHI	20	10	41	1461.7	1429	8.8	111	464	2.9	1092	6.7	3.34	109	.256	.310	46	47	100	103	.976	152	117	-.8	4.9	.9	-.2	4.2
PIT	25	14	41	1462.3	1378	8.5	109	563	3.5	1061	6.5	3.55	105	.251	.317	12	28	103	99	.982	115	165	1.4	2.9	-.2	-1.0	-.2
MON	38	15	34	1471.0	1406	8.6	120	478	2.9	899	5.5	3.58	103	.254	.311	7	14	101	98	.981	116	130	1.4	1.5	2.0	1.4	-5.3
STL	22	10	27	1456.7	1479	9.1	115	525	3.2	709	4.4	3.80	94	.266	.325	-28	-38	98	102	.976	152	173	-.8	-4.0	6.4	.4	-4.4
CHI	9	10	42	1428.7	1496	9.4	117	498	3.1	807	5.1	4.08	90	.273	.330	-71	-64	101	100	.982	115	164	1.4	-6.7	3.0	-.0	-7.8
NY	18	7	33	1451.0	1384	8.6	97	615	3.8	717	4.4	3.68	98	.255	.326	-8	-8	100	100	.976	151	171	-.7	-.8	-10.7	.3	-1.1
WEST																											
LA	27	12	40	1464.0	1336	8.2	97	495	3.0	1000	6.1	3.10	116	.244	.301	84	81	100	101	.974	168	132	-1.7	8.5	-.5	.3	3.5
ATL	18	4	48	1444.7	1412	8.8	132	540	3.4	895	5.6	3.66	103	.259	.323	-5	19	104	105	.978	137	176	.1	2.0	5.5	-1.0	.3
HOU	22	14	48	1466.3	1276	7.8	94	570	3.5	904	5.5	3.45	95	.236	.306	28	-30	90	90	.977	147	165	-.5	-3.1	6.3	-.9	2.2
SD	23	5	44	1467.7	1389	8.5	144	528	3.2	850	5.2	3.62	99	.253	.314	1	-3	99	102	.979	129	135	.6	-.3	-7.0	1.3	5.4
SF	20	9	47	1445.7	1431	8.9	127	520	3.2	881	5.5	3.70	99	.259	.319	-11	-6	101	101	.973	171	109	-1.9	-.6	.4	-.5	.7
CIN	34	5	29	1441.3	1365	8.5	135	627	3.9	934	5.8	3.98	94	.252	.326	-57	-35	104	97	.981	114	121	1.5	-3.7	-6.8	-.1	2.1
TOT	276	115	474	17461.0		8.6			3.3		5.5	3.63		.255	.324					.978	1667	1758					

Runs		Hits		Doubles		Triples		Home Runs		Total Bases	
Raines-Mon	133	Dawson-Mon	189	Ray-Pit	38	Butler-Atl	13	Schmidt-Phi	40	Dawson-Mon	341
Murphy-Atl	131	Cruz-Hou	189	Oliver-Mon	38	Moreno-Hou	11	Murphy-Atl	36	Murphy-Atl	318
Schmidt-Phi	104	Ramirez-Atl	185	Buckner-Chi	38	Green-StL	10	Guerrero-LA	32	Guerrero-LA	310
Dawson-Mon	104	Oliver-Mon	184	Carter-Mon	37	Dawson-Mon	10	Dawson-Mon	32	Thon-Hou	283
		Raines-Mon	183					Evans-SF	30	Schmidt-Phi	280

Runs Batted In		Runs Produced		Bases On Balls		Batting Average		On Base Percentage		Slugging Average	
Murphy-Atl	121	Murphy-Atl	216	Schmidt-Phi	128	Madlock-Pit	.323	Schmidt-Phi	.402	Murphy-Atl	.540
Dawson-Mon	113	Raines-Mon	193	Thompson-Pit	99	L.Smith-StL	.321	Hernandez-StL-NY	.398	Dawson-Mon	.539
Schmidt-Phi	109	Dawson-Mon	185	Raines-Mon	97	Cruz-Hou	.318	Murphy-Atl	.396	Guerrero-LA	.531
Guerrero-LA	103	Schmidt-Phi	173	Murphy-Atl	90	Hendrick-StL	.318	Raines-Mon	.395	Schmidt-Phi	.524
Kennedy-SD	98	Cruz-Hou	163	Morgan-Phi	89	Knight-Hou	.304	Madlock-Pit	.389	Evans-SF	.516

Production		Adjusted Production		Batter Runs		Adjusted Batter Runs		Clutch Hitting Index		Runs Created	
Murphy-Atl	.936	Schmidt-Phi	153	Murphy-Atl	46.2	Schmidt-Phi	42.6	Kennedy-SD	142	Murphy-Atl	131
Schmidt-Phi	.926	Cruz-Hou	149	Schmidt-Phi	43.2	Murphy-Atl	42.0	Garner-Hou	134	Raines-Mon	120
Guerrero-LA	.908	Guerrero-LA	149	Guerrero-LA	37.7	Guerrero-LA	37.7	McGee-StL	131	Guerrero-LA	118
Evans-SF	.896	Murphy-Atl	149	Evans-SF	32.9	Cruz-Hou	35.3	Concepcion-Cin	130	Schmidt-Phi	117
Dawson-Mon	.886	Evans-SF	145	Dawson-Mon	32.3	Evans-SF	32.4	Oliver-Mon	128	Dawson-Mon	113

Total Average		Stolen Bases		Stolen Base Average		Stolen Base Runs		Fielding Runs		Total Player Rating	
Murphy-Atl	1.023	Raines-Mon	90	Morgan-Phi	90.0	Raines-Mon	18.6	Sandberg-Chi	40.5	Schmidt-Phi	5.7
Schmidt-Phi	1.005	Wiggins-SD	66	Murphy-Atl	88.2	Wiggins-SD	12.0	Carter-Mon	28.7	Raines-Mon	5.6
Raines-Mon	.989	Sax-LA	56	Raines-Mon	86.5	McGee-StL	6.9	Bowa-Chi	21.3	Thon-Hou	5.6
Guerrero-LA	.951	Wilson-NY	54	Bailor-NY	85.7	Wilson-NY	6.6	Schmidt-Phi	21.1	Guerrero-LA	4.5
Evans-SF	.923	L.Smith-StL	43	Wiggins-SD	83.5	Murphy-Atl	6.6	Hubbard-Atl	20.7	Carter-Mon	4.4

Wins		Win Percentage		Games		Complete Games		Shutouts		Saves	
Denny-Phi	19	Denny-Phi	.760	Campbell-Chi	82	Soto-Cin	18	Rogers-Mon	5	Smith-Chi	29
Soto-Cin	17	Perez-Atl	.652	Tekulve-Pit	76	Rogers-Mon	13	Valenzuela-LA	4	Holland-Phi	25
Rogers-Mon	17	McWilliams-Pit	.652	Hernandez-Chi-Phi	74	Gullickson-Mon	10	McWilliams-Pit	4	Minton-SF	22
Gullickson-Mon	17	Candelaria-Pit	.652	Scherrer-Cin	73			Lea-Mon	4	Sutter-StL	21
Lea-Mon	16	McMurtry-Atl	.625	Minton-SF	73					Reardon-Mon	21

Innings Pitched		Fewest Hits/Game		Fewest BB/Game		Strikeouts		Strikeouts/Game		Wins Above Team	
Carlton-Phi	284	Ryan-Hou	6.15	Hammaker-SF	1.67	Carlton-Phi	275	Carlton-Phi	8.71	Denny-Phi	6.3
Soto-Cin	274	Soto-Cin	6.80	Ruthven-Phi-Chi	1.87	Soto-Cin	242	Ryan-Hou	8.40	Orosco-NY	4.3
Rogers-Mon	273	Welch-LA	7.24	Denny-Phi	1.96	McWilliams-Pit	199	Soto-Cin	7.95	Reed-Phi	3.9
Niekro-Hou	264	Hammaker-SF	7.69	Reuss-LA	2.02	Valenzuela-LA	189	McWilliams-Pit	7.53	Monge-Phi-SD	3.6
Valenzuela-LA	257	Pena-LA	7.73	Candelaria-Pit	2.05	Ryan-Hou	183	Berenyi-Cin	7.31	Soto-Cin	3.6

Earned Run Average		Adjusted ERA		Opponents' Batting Avg.		Opponents' On Base Pct.		Starter Runs		Adjusted Starter Runs	
Hammaker-SF	2.25	Hammaker-SF	163	Ryan-Hou	.195	Hammaker-SF	.262	Denny-Phi	33.9	Denny-Phi	34.0
Denny-Phi	2.37	Denny-Phi	153	Soto-Cin	.208	Soto-Cin	.276	Soto-Cin	28.4	Soto-Cin	32.6
Welch-LA	2.65	Soto-Cin	140	Welch-LA	.222	Pena-LA	.279	Hammaker-SF	26.3	Hammaker-SF	26.9
Soto-Cin	2.69	Welch-LA	136	Hammaker-SF	.228	Welch-LA	.289	Welch-LA	22.2	Welch-LA	21.8
Pena-LA	2.75	Pena-LA	131	Pena-LA	.229	Denny-Phi	.291	Smith-Mon	19.5	Smith-Mon	20.2

Clutch Pitching Index		Relief Runs		Adjusted Relief Runs		Relief Ranking		Total Pitcher Index		Total Baseball Ranking	
Rhoden-Pit	119	Orosco-NY	26.3	Orosco-NY	26.3	Orosco-NY	52.1	Denny-Phi	4.0	Schmidt-Phi	5.7
Niekro-Atl	117	Smith-Chi	22.5	Smith-Chi	23.0	Smith-Chi	42.6	Soto-Cin	3.2	Raines-Mon	5.6
Denny-Phi	116	Tekulve-Pit	21.9	Tekulve-Pit	23.0	Tekulve-Pit	34.5	Orosco-NY	3.0	Thon-Hou	5.6
Reuss-LA	115	Niedenfuer-LA	18.3	Niedenfuer-LA	18.1	Howe-LA	33.7	Hammaker-SF	2.9	Guerrero-LA	4.5
Knepper-Hou	111	Howe-LA	16.8	Howe-LA	16.7	Holland-Phi	25.2	Reuss-LA	2.8	Carter-Mon	4.4

TEAM	G	W	L	PCT	GB	R	OR	AB	H	2B	3B	HR	BB	SO	AVG	OBP	SLG	PRO	/A	BR	/A	PF	CHI	RC	TA	SB	CS	SBA	SBR
EAST																													
BAL	162	98	64	.605		799	652	5546	1492	283	27	**168**	601	800	.269	**.343**	.421	.764	109	70	68	100	99	794	.713	61	33	65	-1
DET	162	92	70	.568	6	789	679	5592	1530	283	53	156	508	831	.274	.338	.427	.765	109	67	99	96	98	799	.714	93	53	64	-3
NY	162	91	71	.562	7	770	703	5631	1535	269	40	153	533	686	.273	.339	.416	.755	106	52	62	99	97	783	.699	84	42	67	0
TOR	162	89	73	.549	9	795	726	5581	1546	268	**58**	167	510	810	**.277**	.341	**.436**	**.777**	**112**	**89**	27	108	97	**818**	**.735**	131	72	65	-3
MIL	162	87	75	.537	11	764	708	5620	**1556**	281	57	132	475	**665**	**.277**	.336	.418	.754	106	44	**105**	92	98	774	.694	101	49	67	1
BOS	162	78	84	.481	20	724	775	5590	1512	**287**	32	142	536	758	.270	.337	.409	.746	104	35	26	101	94	749	.674	30	26	54	-6
CLE	162	70	92	.432	28	704	785	5476	1451	249	31	86	**605**	691	.265	.341	.369	.710	95	-22	-59	105	99	687	.651	109	71	61	-9
WEST																													
CHI	162	99	63	.611		**800**	650	5484	1439	270	42	157	527	888	.262	.332	.413	.745	104	26	3	103	**106**	762	.713	165	50	77	20
KC	163	79	83	.488	20	696	767	5598	1515	273	54	109	397	722	.271	.322	.397	.719	97	-30	-39	101	101	711	.664	182	47	**79**	**26**
TEX	163	77	85	.475	22	639	**609**	5610	1429	242	33	106	442	767	.255	.312	.366	.678	86	-107	-115	101	103	633	.606	119	60	66	0
OAK	162	74	88	.457	25	708	782	5516	1447	237	28	121	524	872	.262	.330	.381	.711	95	-33	-1	96	102	694	.674	**235**	98	71	12
CAL	162	70	92	.432	29	722	779	5640	1467	241	22	154	509	835	.260	.325	.393	.718	97	-28	3	96	101	702	.641	41	39	51	-10
MIN	162	70	92	.432	29	709	822	5601	1463	280	41	141	467	802	.261	.321	.401	.722	97	-22	-58	105	100	701	.646	44	29	60	-3
SEA	162	60	102	.370	39	558	740	5336	1280	247	31	111	460	840	.240	.303	.360	.663	82	-134	-130	100	99	574	.600	144	80	64	-4
TOT	1135					10177		77821	20662	3710	549	1903	7094	10967	.266	.330	.401	.731								1539	749	67	12

TEAM	CG	SHO	SV	IP	H	H/G	HR	BB	BB/G	SO	SO/G	ERA	/A	OAVG	OOBA	PR	/A	PF	CPI	FA	E	DP	FW	PW	BW	SBW	DIF
EAST																											
BAL	36	**15**	38	1452.3	1451	9.0	130	452	**2.8**	774	4.8	3.63	111	.261	.313	70	62	99	104	.981	121	159	.5	6.2	6.8	-.2	3.7
DET	42	9	28	1451.0	**1318**	**8.2**	170	522	3.2	875	5.4	3.80	101	**.241**	.307	41	5	95	96	.980	125	142	.3	.5	9.9	-.4	.7
NY	**47**	12	32	1456.7	1449	9.0	116	455	**2.8**	892	5.5	3.86	103	.259	.312	33	19	98	95	.978	139	157	-.5	1.9	6.2	-.0	2.5
TOR	43	8	32	1445.3	1434	8.9	145	517	3.2	835	5.2	4.12	106	.259	.322	-9	40	108	97	.981	115	148	.9	4.0	2.7	-.4	.8
MIL	35	10	43	1454.0	1513	9.4	133	491	3.0	689	4.3	4.02	92	.270	.326	6	-52	91	103	**.982**	**113**	162	**1.0**	-5.2	**10.5**	.0	-.3
BOS	29	7	42	1446.3	1572	9.8	158	493	3.1	767	4.8	4.34	95	.279	.335	-44	-33	102	104	.979	130	168	.0	-3.3	2.6	-.7	-1.7
CLE	34	8	25	1441.7	1531	9.6	120	529	3.3	794	5.0	4.43	97	.275	.336	-59	-20	106	97	.980	122	174	.5	-2.0	-5.9	-1.0	-2.6
WEST																											
CHI	35	12	48	1445.3	1355	8.4	128	**447**	**2.8**	877	5.5	3.67	112	.248	**.304**	63	73	102	94	.981	120	158	.6	7.3	.3	1.9	7.9
KC	19	8	**49**	1437.7	1535	9.6	133	471	2.9	593	3.7	4.25	98	.273	.327	-30	-16	102	99	.974	165	178	-1.9	-1.6	-3.9	**2.5**	2.9
TEX	43	11	32	1466.7	1392	8.5	**97**	471	2.9	826	5.1	**3.31**	**124**	.251	.310	**121**	**127**	101	104	**.982**	**113**	151	**1.0**	**12.7**	-11.5	-.0	-6.1
OAK	22	12	33	1454.3	1462	9.0	135	626	3.9	719	4.4	4.34	90	.262	.334	-45	-70	96	97	.974	157	157	-1.5	-7.0	-.0	1.1	.4
CAL	39	7	23	1474.0	1636	10.0	130	496	3.0	668	4.1	4.31	91	.284	.338	-40	-66	96	104	.977	154	**190**	-1.3	-6.6	.3	-1.1	-2.3
MIN	20	5	39	1437.3	1559	9.8	163	580	3.6	748	4.7	4.66	93	.279	.345	-96	-55	106	102	.980	121	170	.5	-5.5	-5.8	-.4	.1
SEA	25	9	39	1418.3	1455	9.2	145	544	3.5	**910**	**5.8**	4.12	100	.268	.334	-9	0	101	**105**	.978	136	159	-.3	.0	-13.0	-.5	-7.2
TOT	469	133	503	20281.0		9.2			3.1		4.9	4.06		.266	.330					.979	1831	2273					

Runs
Ripken-Bal 121
Murray-Bal 115
Cooper-Mil 106
Henderson-Oak 105
Moseby-Tor 104

Hits
Ripken-Bal 211
Boggs-Bos 210
Whitaker-Det 206
Cooper-Mil 203
Rice-Bos 191

Doubles
Ripken-Bal 47
Boggs-Bos 44
Yount-Mil 42
Parrish-Det 42

Triples
Yount-Mil 10
Herndon-Det 9
Griffin-Tor 9
Gibson-Det 9

Home Runs
Rice-Bos 39
Armas-Bos 36
Kittle-Chi 35
Murray-Bal 33

Total Bases
Rice-Bos 344
Ripken-Bal 343
Cooper-Mil 336
Murray-Bal 313
Winfield-NY 307

Runs Batted In
Rice-Bos 126
Cooper-Mil 126
Winfield-NY 116
Parrish-Det 114
Murray-Bal 111

Runs Produced
Cooper-Mil 202
Ripken-Bal 196
Murray-Bal 193
Winfield-NY 183
Rice-Bos 177

Bases On Balls
Henderson-Oak 103
Singleton-Bal 99
Boggs-Bos 92
Thornton-Cle 87
Murray-Bal 86

Batting Average
Boggs-Bos 361
Carew-Cal 339
Whitaker-Det 320
Trammell-Det 319
Ripken-Bal 318

On Base Percentage
Boggs-Bos 449
Henderson-Oak 415
Carew-Cal 411
Murray-Bal 398
Singleton-Bal 395

Slugging Average
Brett-KC 563
Rice-Bos 550
Murray-Bal 538
Fisk-Chi 518
Ripken-Bal 517

Production
Brett-KC 949
Murray-Bal 936
Boggs-Bos 935
Rice-Bos 914
Upshaw-Tor 891

Adjusted Production
Yount-Mil 156
Boggs-Bos 156
Brett-KC 155
Murray-Bal 154
Rice-Bos 146

Batter Runs
Boggs-Bos 50.6
Murray-Bal 44.9
Rice-Bos 38.7
Ripken-Bal 37.1
Brett-KC 36.3

Adjusted Batter Runs
Boggs-Bos 49.7
Murray-Bal 44.8
Yount-Mil 41.4
Rice-Bos 37.8
Ripken-Bal 36.9

Clutch Hitting Index
Simmons-Mil 145
Murphy-Oak 135
Franco-Cle 132
Hargrove-Cle 130
Parrish-Det 127

Runs Created
Murray-Bal 133
Boggs-Bos 130
Ripken-Bal 120
Yount-Mil 115
Whitaker-Det 114

Total Average
Murray-Bal 1.002
Boggs-Bos 972
Brett-KC 967
Moseby-Tor 910
Yount-Mil 909

Stolen Bases
Henderson-Oak 108
R.Law-Chi 77
Wilson-KC 59
Cruz-Sea-Chi 57
Sample-Tex 44

Stolen Base Average
Wilson-KC 88.1
R.Law-Chi 86.5
Washington-KC 85.1
Henderson-Oak 85.0

Stolen Base Runs
Henderson-Oak 21.0
R.Law-Chi 15.9
Wilson-KC 12.9
Cruz-Sea-Chi 9.9
Sample-Tex 8.4

Fielding Runs
Ward-Min 22.7
Grich-Cal 20.9
Boone-Cal 16.9
Bell-Tex 16.9
Ripken-Bal 16.0

Total Player Rating
Ripken-Bal 5.8
Boggs-Bos 5.8
Henderson-Oak 5.6
Grich-Cal 5.0
Rice-Bos 4.8

Wins
Hoyt-Chi 24
Dotson-Chi 22
Guidry-NY 21
Morris-Det 20
Petry-Det 19

Win Percentage
Dotson-Chi 759
McGregor-Bal 720
Hoyt-Chi 706
Guidry-NY 700
Boddicker-Bal 667

Games
Quisenberry-KC 69
VandeBerg-Sea 68
Davis-Min 66
T.Martinez-Bal 65
Stanley-Bos 64

Complete Games
Guidry-NY 21
Morris-Det 20
Stieb-Tor 14
Rawley-NY 13
McGregor-Bal 12

Shutouts
Boddicker-Bal 5
Stieb-Tor 4
Burns-Chi 4

Saves
Quisenberry-KC 45
Stanley-Bos 33
Davis-Min 30
Caudill-Sea 26
Ladd-Mil 25

Innings Pitched
Morris-Det 294
Stieb-Tor 278
Petry-Det 266
Hoyt-Chi 261
McGregor-Bal 260

Fewest Hits/Game
Boddicker-Bal 7.09
Stieb-Tor 7.22
Hough-Tex 7.82
Conroy-Oak 7.83
Dotson-Chi 7.84

Fewest BB/Game
Hoyt-Chi 1.07
McGregor-Bal 1.56
John-Cal 1.88
Honeycutt-Tex 1.90
Eckersley-Bos 1.99

Strikeouts
Morris-Det 232
Bannister-Chi 193
Stieb-Tor 187
Righetti-NY 169
Sutcliffe-Cle 160

Strikeouts/Game
Bannister-Chi 8.00
Morris-Det 7.10
Righetti-NY 7.01
Conroy-Oak 6.22
Gott-Tor 6.15

Wins Above Team
Dotson-Chi 6.2
Guidry-NY 5.4
Haas-Mil 5.0
Hoyt-Chi 4.9
Sutcliffe-Cle 4.9

Earned Run Average
Honeycutt-Tex 2.42
Boddicker-Bal 2.77
Stieb-Tor 3.04
Hough-Tex 3.18
McGregor-Bal 3.18

Adjusted ERA
Honeycutt-Tex 170
Boddicker-Bal 145
Stieb-Tor 144
Hough-Tex 129
Dotson-Chi 128

Opponents' Batting Avg.
Boddicker-Bal 216
Stieb-Tor 219
Conroy-Oak 232
Bannister-Chi 233
Morris-Det 233

Opponents' On Base Pct.
Hoyt-Chi 259
Boddicker-Bal 271
Morris-Det 285
Guidry-NY 287
Stieb-Tor 289

Starter Runs
Honeycutt-Tex 32.0
Stieb-Tor 31.4
Boddicker-Bal 25.8
McGregor-Bal 25.3
Hough-Tex 24.7

Adjusted Starter Runs
Stieb-Tor 41.1
Honeycutt-Tex 32.7
Hough-Tex 25.7
Boddicker-Bal 24.8
Dotson-Chi 24.0

Clutch Pitching Index
Honeycutt-Tex 140
Zahn-Cal 118
Hurst-Bos 113
Dotson-Chi 113
McGregor-Bal 113

Relief Runs
Quisenberry-KC 32.7
T.Martinez-Bal 19.5
Stanley-Bos 19.4
Gossage-NY 17.3
Lopez-Det 15.9

Adjusted Relief Runs
Quisenberry-KC 34.0
Stanley-Bos 20.5
T.Martinez-Bal 18.9
Gossage-NY 16.4
Barojas-Chi 15.9

Relief Ranking
Quisenberry-KC 42.4
Gossage-NY 39.9
Stanley-Bos 33.4
T.Martinez-Bal 28.5
Lopez-Det 21.9

Total Pitcher Index
Stieb-Tor 4.4
Honeycutt-Tex 3.9
Quisenberry-KC 3.7
Hough-Tex 3.1
Boddicker-Bal 3.0

Total Baseball Ranking
Ripken-Bal 5.8
Boggs-Bos 5.8
Henderson-Oak 5.6
Grich-Cal 5.0
Rice-Bos 4.8

TEAM	G	W	L	PCT	GB	R	OR	AB	H	2B	3B	HR	BB	SO	AVG	OBP	SLG	PRO	/A	BR	/A	PF	CHI	RC	TA	SB	CS	SBA	SBR
EAST																													
CHI	161	96	65	.596		**762**	658	5437	1415	240	47	136	**567**	967	.260	.333	.397	.730	111	78	11	110	103	729	.694	154	66	70	7
NY	162	90	72	.556	6.5	652	676	5438	1400	235	25	107	500	1001	.257	.322	.369	.691	100	1	1	100	100	645	.633	149	54	73	12
STL	162	84	78	.519	12.5	652	645	5433	1369	225	44	75	516	924	.252	.319	.351	.670	94	-34	-25	99	**105**	623	.627	**220**	71	76	**23**
PHI	162	81	81	.500	15.5	720	690	5614	1494	**248**	51	**147**	555	1084	**.266**	**.335**	**.407**	**.742**	**114**	**102**	**89**	102	92	**766**	**.707**	186	60	76	20
MON	161	78	83	.484	18	593	585	5439	1367	242	36	96	470	**782**	.251	.314	.362	.676	96	-31	24	91	96	630	.616	131	38	**78**	17
PIT	162	75	87	.463	21.5	615	**567**	5537	1412	237	33	98	438	841	.255	.312	.363	.675	95	-36	0	94	99	611	.593	96	62	61	-7
WEST																													
SD	162	92	70	.568		686	634	5504	1425	207	42	109	472	810	.259	.320	.371	.691	100	0	9	99	104	645	.629	152	68	69	5
HOU	162	80	82	.494	12	693	630	5548	1465	222	**67**	79	494	837	.264	.326	.371	.697	102	14	63	93	102	679	.632	105	61	63	-4
ATL	162	80	82	.494	12	632	655	5422	1338	234	27	111	555	896	.247	.319	.361	.680	97	-17	-79	110	99	623	.624	140	85	62	-8
LA	162	79	83	.488	13	580	600	5399	1316	213	23	102	488	829	.244	.308	.348	.656	90	-67	-90	104	99	573	.583	109	69	61	-8
CIN	162	70	92	.432	22	627	747	5498	1342	238	30	106	566	978	.244	.316	.356	.672	95	-34	-71	106	99	635	.624	160	63	72	10
SF	162	66	96	.407	26	682	807	5650	**1499**	229	26	112	528	980	.265	.330	.375	.705	104	31	57	96	96	686	.638	126	76	62	-7
TOT	971					7894		65919	16842	2770	451	1278	6149	10929	.255	.321	.369	.691								1728	773	69	55

TEAM	CG	SHO	SV	IP	H	H/G	HR	BB	BB/G	SO	SO/G	ERA	/A	OAVG	OOBA	PR	/A	PF	CPI	FA	E	DP	FW	PW	BW	SBW	DIF
EAST																											
CHI	19	8	50	1434.0	1458	9.2	99	**442**	**2.8**	879	5.5	3.75	104	.266	.317	-26	24	109	99	.981	121	137	1.1	2.5	1.2	.3	10.5
NY	12	15	50	1442.7	1371	8.6	104	573	3.6	1028	**6.4**	3.60	100	.252	.320	-1	0	100	101	.979	129	154	.6	.0	.1	.8	7.5
STL	19	12	**51**	1449.0	1427	8.9	94	494	3.1	808	5.0	3.58	99	.262	.320	0	-7	99	103	**.982**	**118**	**184**	**1.3**	-.7	-2.6	**1.9**	3.1
PHI	11	6	35	1458.3	1416	8.7	101	448	**2.8**	904	5.6	3.62	101	.252	**.304**	-4	3	101	92	.975	161	112	-1.3	.3	**9.3**	1.6	-10.0
MON	19	10	48	1431.0	1333	8.4	114	474	3.0	861	5.4	3.31	99	.248	.306	44	-5	91	103	.978	132	147	.4	-.5	2.5	1.3	-6.2
PIT	27	13	34	1470.0	1344	**8.2**	102	502	3.1	995	6.1	**3.11**	108	.245	**.304**	**78**	41	94	**105**	.980	128	142	.7	4.3	.0	-1.2	-9.8
WEST																											
SD	13	**17**	44	1460.3	**1327**	**8.2**	122	563	3.5	812	5.0	3.48	101	**.243**	.310	17	4	98	99	.978	138	144	.0	.4	.9	.0	9.5
HOU	24	13	29	1449.3	1350	8.4	91	502	3.1	950	5.9	3.32	99	.248	.308	43	-4	92	99	.979	133	160	.4	-.4	6.6	-.9	-6.7
ATL	17	7	49	1447.0	1401	8.7	122	525	3.3	859	5.3	3.57	110	.256	.317	2	58	110	**105**	.978	139	153	.0	6.1	-8.3	-1.3	2.5
LA	**39**	16	27	1460.7	1381	8.5	**76**	499	3.1	**1033**	**6.4**	3.17	**118**	.250	.309	68	**91**	104	102	.975	163	146	-1.4	**9.6**	-9.5	-1.3	.6
CIN	25	6	25	1461.3	1445	8.9	128	578	3.6	946	5.8	4.16	93	.258	.323	-92	-50	107	94	.977	139	116	.0	-5.3	-7.5	.6	1.1
SF	9	7	38	1461.0	1589	9.8	125	549	3.4	854	5.3	4.39	80	.278	.337	-130	-144	98	99	.973	173	134	-2.0	-15.1	6.0	-1.2	-2.7
TOT	234	130	480	17424.7		8.7			3.2		5.6	3.59		.255	.321					.978	1674	1729					

Runs
Sandberg-Chi 114
Wiggins-SD 106
Raines-Mon 106
Samuel-Phi 105
Matthews-Chi 101

Hits
Gwynn-SD 213
Sandberg-Chi 200
Raines-Mon 192
Samuel-Phi 191
Cruz-Hou 187

Doubles
Ray-Pit 38
Raines-Mon 38
Sandberg-Chi 36
Samuel-Phi 36

Triples
Sandberg-Chi 19
Samuel-Phi 19
Cruz-Hou 13

Home Runs
Schmidt-Phi 36
Murphy-Atl 36
Carter-Mon 27
Strawberry-NY 26
Cey-Chi 25

Total Bases
Murphy-Atl 332
Sandberg-Chi 331
Samuel-Phi 310
Carter-Mon 290
Schmidt-Phi 283

Runs Batted In
Schmidt-Phi 106
Carter-Mon 106
Murphy-Atl 100
Strawberry-NY 97
Cey-Chi 97

Runs Produced
Sandberg-Chi 179
Cruz-Hou 179
Matthews-Chi 169
Schmidt-Phi 163
Hernandez-NY 162

Bases On Balls
Matthews-Chi 103
Hernandez-NY 97
Schmidt-Phi 92
Thompson-Pit 87
Raines-Mon 87

Batting Average
Gwynn-SD .... .351
Lacy-Pit .... .321
C.Davis-SF .... .315
Sandberg-Chi .... .314
Ray-Pit .... .312

On Base Percentage
Matthews-Chi ...... .417
Hernandez-NY ..... .415
Gwynn-SD .... .411
Raines-Mon .... .395
Schmidt-Phi .... .388

Slugging Average
Murphy-Atl .... .547
Schmidt-Phi .... .536
Sandberg-Chi .... .520
C.Davis-SF .... .507
Durham-Chi .... .505

Production
Schmidt-Phi .... .924
Murphy-Atl .... .920
Sandberg-Chi ...... .889
Durham-Chi .... .877
C.Davis-SF .... .876

Adjusted Production
Schmidt-Phi 154
Carter-Mon 151
C.Davis-SF 150
Cruz-Hou 148
Raines-Mon 146

Batter Runs
Murphy-Atl 43.7
Schmidt-Phi 41.2
Sandberg-Chi 37.9
Hernandez-NY 35.4
Gwynn-SD 33.9

Adjusted Batter Runs
Schmidt-Phi 40.0
Raines-Mon 37.1
Murphy-Atl 36.7
Cruz-Hou 36.2
Carter-Mon 35.9

Clutch Hitting Index
Mumphrey-Hou 143
Davis-Chi 136
Garvey-SD 135
Matthews-Chi 135
Hernandez-NY 134

Runs Created
Sandberg-Chi 126
Raines-Mon 124
Murphy-Atl 123
Cruz-Hou 111
Carter-Mon 108

Total Average
Raines-Mon .... .975
Murphy-Atl .... .958
Schmidt-Phi .... .950
Sandberg-Chi ...... .929
Durham-Chi .... .910

Stolen Bases
Raines-Mon 75
Samuel-Phi 72
Wiggins-SD 70
L.Smith-StL 50

Stolen Base Average
Dilone-Mon 93.1
Raines-Mon 88.2
Cedeno-Cin 86.4
VanSlyke-StL 84.8
Stone-Phi 84.4

Stolen Base Runs
Raines-Mon 16.5
Samuel-Phi 12.6
Wilson-NY 8.4
Wiggins-SD 8.4
Redus-Cin 7.8

Fielding Runs
O.Smith-StL 30.9
Sandberg-Chi 23.0
Hubbard-Atl 22.1
Pena-Pit 18.5
Hernandez-NY 17.6

Total Player Rating
Sandberg-Chi 6.5
Carter-Mon 5.2
Raines-Mon 5.1
Schmidt-Phi 5.1
O.Smith-StL 5.1

Wins
Andujar-StL 20
Soto-Cin 18
Gooden-NY 17
Sutcliffe-Chi 16
Niekro-Hou 16

Win Percentage
Sutcliffe-Chi .... .941
Soto-Cin .... .720
Gooden-NY .... .654
Show-SD .... .625

Games
Power-Cin 78
Lavelle-SF 77
Minton-SF 74
Tekulve-Pit 72
Sutter-StL 71

Complete Games
Soto-Cin 13
Valenzuela-LA 12
Andujar-StL 12
Knepper-Hou 11
Mahler-Atl 9

Shutouts
Pena-LA 4
Hershiser-LA 4
Andujar-StL 4

Saves
Sutter-StL 45
Smith-Chi 33
Orosco-NY 31
Holland-Phi 29
Gossage-SD 25

Innings Pitched
Valenzuela-LA 261
Andujar-StL 261
Niekro-Hou 248
Rhoden-Pit 238
Soto-Cin 237

Fewest Hits/Game
Gooden-NY 6.65
Soto-Cin 6.87
DeLeon-Pit 6.89
Ryan-Hou 6.99

Fewest BB/Game
Gullickson-Mon 1.47
Candelaria-Pit 1.65
Whitson-SD 2.00
Pena-LA 2.08
Knepper-Hou 2.12

Strikeouts
Gooden-NY 276
Valenzuela-LA 240
Ryan-Hou 197
Soto-Cin 185
Carlton-Phi 163

Strikeouts/Game
Gooden-NY 11.39
Ryan-Hou 9.64
Valenzuela-LA 8.28
Berenyi-Cin-NY 7.27
DeLeon-Pit 7.17

Wins Above Team
Sutcliffe-Chi 7.4
Soto-Cin 6.9
Dawley-Hou 3.7
Rhoden-Pit 3.5
Perez-Atl 3.4

Earned Run Average
Pena-LA 2.49
Gooden-NY 2.60
Hershiser-LA 2.65
Rhoden-Pit 2.72
Candelaria-Pit 2.72

Adjusted ERA
Pena-LA 150
Hershiser-LA 141
Gooden-NY 138
Honeycutt-LA 132
Mahler-Atl 126

Opponents' Batting Avg.
Gooden-NY .... .202
Soto-Cin .... .209
Ryan-Hou .... .211
DeLeon-Pit .... .214
Hershiser-LA ..... .225

Opponents' On Base Pct.
Gooden-NY .... .268
Hershiser-LA ..... .278
Andujar-StL ...... .280
Soto-Cin .... .281
Ryan-Hou .... .284

Starter Runs
Pena-LA 24.3
Gooden-NY 23.9
Rhoden-Pit 22.9
Hershiser-LA 19.8
Denny-Phi 19.4

Adjusted Starter Runs
Pena-LA 27.5
Gooden-NY 24.1
Hershiser-LA 22.8
Denny-Phi 20.3
Valenzuela-LA 20.2

Clutch Pitching Index
McWilliams-Pit 129
Terrell-NY 124
Candelaria-Pit 122
Honeycutt-LA 117
Trout-Chi 117

Relief Runs
Sutter-StL 28.0
Dawley-Hou 18.1
Lefferts-SD 17.3
Sisk-NY 13.1
Andersen-Phi 12.3

Adjusted Relief Runs
Sutter-StL 27.4
Lefferts-SD 16.3
Dawley-Hou 14.8
Bedrosian-Atl 14.7
Sisk-NY 13.2

Relief Ranking
Sutter-StL 46.5
Bedrosian-Atl 28.0
Orosco-NY 24.0
Dawley-Hou 22.1
Power-Cin 19.5

Total Pitcher Index
Mahler-Atl 3.1
Rhoden-Pit 3.1
Valenzuela-LA 3.1
Sutter-StL 2.9
Sutcliffe-Chi 2.9

Total Baseball Ranking
Sandberg-Chi 6.5
Carter-Mon 5.2
Raines-Mon 5.1
Schmidt-Phi 5.1
O.Smith-StL 5.1

TEAM	G	W	L	PCT	GB	R	OR	AB	H	2B	3B	HR	BB	SO	AVG	OBP	SLG	PRO	/A	BR	/A	PF	CHI	RC	TA	SB	CS	SBA	SBR
EAST																													
DET	162	104	58	.642		**829**	**643**	5644	1529	254	46	**187**	602	941	.271	**.345**	.432	.777	113	103	**131**	96	98	**843**	**.742**	106	68	61	-8
TOR	163	89	73	.549	15	750	696	5687	1555	**275**	**68**	143	460	816	.273	.333	.421	.754	107	52	41	102	96	808	.723	**193**	67	**74**	**18**
NY	162	87	75	.537	17	758	679	5661	1560	**275**	32	130	534	**673**	.276	.342	.404	.746	106	47	91	94	97	773	.682	62	38	62	-3
BOS	162	86	76	.531	18	810	764	5648	**1598**	259	45	181	500	842	**.283**	.343	**.441**	**.784**	**115**	**112**	37	110	97	832	.722	38	25	60	-3
BAL	162	85	77	.525	19	681	667	5456	1374	234	23	160	**620**	884	.252	.331	.391	.722	99	-3	37	94	95	705	.665	51	36	59	-5
CLE	163	75	87	.463	29	761	766	5643	1498	222	39	123	600	815	.265	.339	.384	.723	100	4	-39	106	102	732	.670	126	77	62	-7
MIL	161	67	94	.416	36.5	641	734	5511	1446	232	36	96	432	**673**	.262	.319	.370	.689	90	-74	-15	92	102	621	.596	52	57	48	-18
WEST																													
KC	162	84	78	.519		673	686	5543	1487	269	52	117	400	832	.268	.320	.399	.719	98	-22	-16	99	99	694	.649	106	42	72	7
CAL	162	81	81	.500	3	696	697	5470	1363	211	30	150	556	928	.249	.322	.381	.703	94	-45	-54	101	**104**	663	.640	80	51	61	-6
MIN	162	81	81	.500	3	673	675	5562	1473	259	33	114	437	735	.265	.321	.385	.706	94	-44	-82	106	101	669	.620	39	30	57	-5
OAK	162	77	85	.475	7	738	796	5457	1415	257	29	158	568	871	.259	.332	.404	.736	102	18	78	92	101	736	.696	145	64	69	5
SEA	162	74	88	.457	10	682	774	5546	1429	244	34	129	519	871	.258	.326	.384	.710	96	-31	-46	102	99	700	.655	116	62	65	-1
CHI	162	74	88	.457	10	679	736	5513	1360	225	38	172	523	883	.247	.316	.395	.711	95	-36	-110	111	100	690	.660	109	49	69	3
TEX	161	69	92	.429	14.5	656	714	5569	1452	227	29	120	420	807	.261	.315	.377	.692	91	-74	-74	100	**104**	643	.609	81	50	62	-5
TOT	1134					10027		77910	20539	3443	534	1980	7171	11571	.264	.329	.398	.727								1304	716	65	-37

TEAM	CG	SHO	SV	IP	H	H/G	HR	BB	BB/G	SO	SO/G	ERA	/A	OAVG	OOBA	PR	/A	PF	CPI	FA	E	DP	FW	PW	BW	SBW	DIF
EAST																											
DET	19	8	**51**	1464.0	**1358**	**8.3**	130	489	3.0	914	5.6	**3.49**	108	**.245**	**.306**	**81**	43	94	98	.979	127	162	.3	4.3	**13.2**	-.5	5.7
TOR	34	10	33	1464.0	1433	8.8	140	528	3.2	875	5.4	3.86	104	.257	.319	21	27	101	99	.980	123	166	.5	2.7	4.1	**2.1**	-1.4
NY	15	12	43	1465.3	1485	9.1	**120**	518	3.2	**992**	**6.1**	3.78	98	.264	.323	34	-9	93	102	.977	142	**177**	-.5	-.9	9.2	-.0	-1.7
BOS	40	12	32	1442.0	1524	9.5	141	517	3.2	927	5.8	4.18	105	.269	.330	-29	33	110	99	.977	143	128	-.6	3.3	3.7	-.0	-1.4
BAL	**48**	**13**	32	1439.3	1393	8.7	137	512	3.2	714	4.5	3.71	101	.256	.317	44	6	94	102	**.981**	123	166	.5	.6	3.7	-.2	-.6
CLE	21	7	35	1467.7	1523	9.3	141	545	3.3	803	4.9	4.26	99	.269	.329	-43	-4	106	98	.977	146	163	-.8	-.4	-3.9	-.4	-.5
MIL	13	7	41	1433.0	1532	9.6	137	480	3.0	785	4.9	4.06	91	.274	.327	-10	-57	93	103	.978	136	156	-.2	-5.7	-1.5	-1.5	-4.5
WEST																											
KC	18	9	50	1444.0	1426	8.9	136	**433**	**2.7**	724	4.5	3.92	101	.258	.310	11	6	99	93	.979	131	157	.0	.6	-1.6	1.0	2.9
CAL	36	12	26	1458.0	1526	9.4	143	474	2.9	754	4.7	3.96	102	.270	.325	5	14	101	**104**	.980	128	170	.2	1.4	-5.4	-.3	4.1
MIN	32	9	38	1437.7	1429	8.9	159	463	2.9	713	4.5	3.85	**109**	.259	.317	22	**58**	106	101	.980	**120**	134	**.7**	**5.8**	-8.2	-.2	1.9
OAK	15	6	44	1430.0	1554	9.8	155	592	3.7	695	4.4	4.48	82	.277	.345	-77	-128	92	103	.975	146	159	-.8	-12.9	7.8	.8	1.0
SEA	26	4	35	1442.0	1497	9.3	138	619	3.9	972	**6.1**	4.31	96	.270	.342	-50	-30	103	102	.979	128	143	.2	-3.0	-4.6	.2	.2
CHI	43	9	32	1454.3	1416	8.8	155	483	3.0	840	5.2	4.13	107	.256	.314	-23	48	111	93	**.981**	122	160	.6	4.8	-11.1	.6	-1.9
TEX	38	6	21	1438.7	1443	9.0	148	518	3.2	863	5.4	3.91	103	.259	.322	13	17	101	101	.977	138	138	-.3	1.7	-7.4	-.2	-5.2
TOT	398	124	513	20280.0		9.1			3.2		5.1	3.99		.264	.329					.979	1853	2179					

Runs
Evans-Bos 121
Henderson-Oak 113
Boggs-Bos 109
Butler-Cle 108
Armas-Bos 107

Hits
Mattingly-NY 207
Boggs-Bos 203
Ripken-Bal 195
Winfield-NY 193

Doubles
Mattingly-NY 44
Parrish-Tex 42
Bell-Tor 39
Ripken-Bal 37
Evans-Bos 37

Triples
Moseby-Tor 15
Collins-Tor 15
Gibson-Det 10
Baines-Chi 10

Home Runs
Armas-Bos 43
Kingman-Oak 35
Thornton-Cle 33
Parrish-Det 33
Murphy-Oak 33

Total Bases
Armas-Bos 339
Evans-Bos 335
Ripken-Bal 327
Mattingly-NY 324
Easler-Bos 310

Runs Batted In
Armas-Bos 123
Rice-Bos 122
Kingman-Oak 118
Davis-Sea 116

Runs Produced
Evans-Bos 193
Rice-Bos 192
Winfield-NY 187
Armas-Bos 187

Bases On Balls
Murray-Bal 107
Davis-Sea 97
Evans-Bos 96
Thornton-Cle 91
Boggs-Bos 89

Batting Average
Mattingly-NY 343
Winfield-NY 340
Boggs-Bos 325
Bell-Tex 315
Trammell-Det 314

On Base Percentage
Murray-Bal 415
Boggs-Bos 409
Henderson-Oak 401
Winfield-NY 397
Davis-Sea 395

Slugging Average
Baines-Chi 541
Mattingly-NY 537
Evans-Bos 532
Armas-Bos 531
Hrbek-Min 522

Production
Evans-Bos 924
Mattingly-NY 923
Murray-Bal 923
Winfield-NY 912
Hrbek-Min 909

Adjusted Production
Murray-Bal 163
Mattingly-NY 162
Winfield-NY 160
Ripken-Bal 151
Henderson-Oak 150

Batter Runs
Murray-Bal 46.8
Evans-Bos 46.6
Mattingly-NY 41.3
Winfield-NY 38.4
Davis-Sea 37.5

Adjusted Batter Runs
Murray-Bal 51.5
Mattingly-NY 46.0
Winfield-NY 42.8
Ripken-Bal 41.4
Evans-Bos 37.8

Clutch Hitting Index
Simmons-Mil 131
Kingman-Oak 130
Franco-Cle 127
Bell-Tex 123
Davis-Sea 122

Runs Created
Evans-Bos 132
Murray-Bal 130
Ripken-Bal 122
Mattingly-NY 120
Easler-Bos 118

Total Average
Henderson-Oak . . . 1.018
Murray-Bal 998
Gibson-Det 949
Evans-Bos 944
Davis-Sea 938

Stolen Bases
Henderson-Oak 66
Collins-Tor 60
Butler-Cle 52
Pettis-Cal 48
Wilson-KC 47

Stolen Base Average
Wilson-KC 90.4
Tolleson-Tex 84.6
Perconte-Sea 82.9
Moseby-Tor 81.3
Collins-Tor 81.1

Stolen Base Runs
Wilson-KC 11.1
Collins-Tor 9.6
Henderson-Oak 9.0
Garcia-Tor 6.6
Moseby-Tor 6.3

Fielding Runs
Ripken-Bal 38.8
Boggs-Bos 23.1
Puckett-Min 22.2
Bell-Tex 21.1
Cruz-Chi 19.5

Total Player Rating
Ripken-Bal 9.0
Murray-Bal 5.0
Bell-Tex 4.8
Henderson-Oak 4.5
Boggs-Bos 4.4

Wins
Boddicker-Bal 20
Morris-Det 19
Blyleven-Cle 19
Viola-Min 18
Petry-Det 18

Win Percentage
Alexander-Tor 739
Blyleven-Cle 731
Petry-Det 692
Wilcox-Det 680

Games
Hernandez-Det 80
Quisenberry-KC 72
Lopez-Det 71
Camacho-Cle 69
Caudill-Oak 68

Complete Games
Hough-Tex 17
Boddicker-Bal 16
Dotson-Chi 14
Blyleven-Cle 12
Beattie-Sea 12

Shutouts
Zahn-Cal 5
Ojeda-Bos 5

Saves
Quisenberry-KC 44
Caudill-Oak 36
Hernandez-Det 32
Righetti-NY 31
Davis-Min 29

Innings Pitched
Stieb-Tor 267
Hough-Tex 266
Alexander-Tor 262
Boddicker-Bal 261
Viola-Min 258

Fewest Hits/Game
Stieb-Tor 7.25
Blyleven-Cle 7.49
Boddicker-Bal 7.52
Langston-Sea 7.52
Mason-Tex 7.78

Fewest BB/Game
Hoyt-Chi 1.64
Smithson-Min 1.93
Guidry-NY 2.02
Alexander-Tor 2.03
Haas-Mil 2.05

Strikeouts
Langston-Sea 204
Stieb-Tor 198
Witt-Cal 196
Blyleven-Cle 170
Hough-Tex 164

Strikeouts/Game
Langston-Sea 8.16
Witt-Cal 7.14
Moore-Sea 6.71
Stieb-Tor 6.67
Berenguer-Det 6.32

Wins Above Team
Blyleven-Cle 7.0
Alexander-Tor 5.3
Langston-Sea 4.8
Boddicker-Bal 4.6
Lopez-Det 4.2

Earned Run Average
Boddicker-Bal 2.79
Stieb-Tor 2.83
Blyleven-Cle 2.87
Niekro-NY 3.08
Black-KC 3.12

Adjusted ERA
Blyleven-Cle 148
Stieb-Tor 142
Boddicker-Bal 134
Viola-Min 131
Zahn-Cal 130

Opponents' Batting Avg.
Stieb-Tor 221
Blyleven-Cle 224
Boddicker-Bal 228
Langston-Sea 230
Berenguer-Det 232

Opponents' On Base Pct.
Black-KC 281
Mason-Tex 283
Alexander-Tor 283
Blyleven-Cle 283
Seaver-Chi 285

Starter Runs
Boddicker-Bal 34.8
Stieb-Tor 34.4
Blyleven-Cle 30.7
Alexander-Tor 25.2
Black-KC 25.0

Adjusted Starter Runs
Blyleven-Cle 37.2
Stieb-Tor 35.6
Viola-Min 28.8
Boddicker-Bal 27.9
Alexander-Tor 26.4

Clutch Pitching Index
Niekro-NY 125
Fontenot-NY 119
Cocanower-Mil 115
Hurst-Bos 113
Burris-Oak 113

Relief Runs
Hernandez-Det 32.1
Quisenberry-KC 19.2
Corbett-Cal 17.7
Righetti-NY 17.6
Camacho-Cle 17.3

Adjusted Relief Runs
Hernandez-Det 28.5
Camacho-Cle 20.0
Quisenberry-KC 18.8
Corbett-Cal 18.2
Righetti-NY 14.6

Relief Ranking
Hernandez-Det 36.6
Camacho-Cle 35.6
Quisenberry-KC 26.2
Righetti-NY 25.7
Caudill-Oak 23.8

Total Pitcher Index
Blyleven-Cle 4.0
Stieb-Tor 3.9
Boddicker-Bal 3.6
Black-KC 2.8
Hernandez-Det 2.8

Total Baseball Ranking
Ripken-Bal 9.0
Murray-Bal 5.0
Bell-Tex 4.8
Henderson-Oak 4.5
Boggs-Bos 4.4

TEAM	G	W	L	PCT	GB	R	OR	AB	H	2B	3B	HR	BB	SO	AVG	OBP	SLG	PRO	/A	BR	/A	PF	CHI	RC	TA	SB	CS	SBA	SBR
EAST																													
STL	162	101	61	.623		747	572	5467	1446	245	59	87	586	853	.264	.338	.379	.717	107	52	81	96	104	733	.710	314	96	77	37
NY	162	98	64	.605	3	695	635	5549	1425	239	35	134	546	872	.257	.326	.385	.711	105	31	50	97	99	691	.654	117	53	69	3
MON	161	84	77	.522	16.5	633	636	5429	1342	242	49	118	492	880	.247	.313	.375	.688	98	-18	23	94	100	633	.637	169	77	69	5
CHI	162	77	84	.478	23.5	686	729	5492	1397	239	28	150	562	937	.254	.326	.390	.716	106	40	-67	116	97	710	.681	182	49	79	25
PHI	162	75	87	.463	26	667	673	5477	1343	238	47	141	527	1095	.245	.314	.383	.697	100	0	-13	102	101	657	.643	122	51	71	6
PIT	161	57	104	.354	43.5	568	708	5436	1340	251	28	80	514	842	.247	.313	.347	.660	90	-63	-79	103	96	587	.589	110	60	65	-2
WEST																													
LA	162	95	67	.586		682	579	5502	1434	226	28	129	539	846	.261	.330	.382	.712	105	38	84	93	96	704	.663	136	58	70	6
CIN	162	89	72	.553	5.5	677	666	5431	1385	249	34	114	576	856	.255	.329	.376	.705	103	26	-8	105	99	672	.659	159	70	69	6
SD	162	83	79	.512	12	650	622	5507	1405	241	28	109	513	809	.255	.321	.368	.689	98	-8	-19	102	100	645	.615	60	39	61	-4
HOU	162	83	79	.512	12	706	691	5582	1457	261	42	121	477	873	.261	.322	.388	.710	104	25	51	96	102	684	.641	96	56	63	-4
ATL	162	66	96	.407	29	632	781	5526	1359	213	28	126	553	849	.246	.317	.363	.680	96	-27	-69	106	99	622	.607	72	52	58	-9
SF	162	62	100	.383	33	556	674	5420	1263	217	31	115	488	962	.233	.301	.348	.649	87	-92	-48	93	99	564	.580	99	55	64	-2
TOT	971					7899		65818	16596	2861	437	1424	6373	10674	.252	.321	.374	.695								1636	716	70	61

TEAM	CG	SHO	SV	IP	H	H/G	HR	BB	BB/G	SO	SO/G	ERA	/A	OAVG	OOBA	PR	/A	PF	CPI	FA	E	DP	FW	PW	BW	SBW	DIF
EAST																											
STL	37	20	44	1464.0	1343	8.3	98	453	2.8	798	4.9	3.10	108	.245	.301	79	39	93	102	.983	108	166	1.6	4.1	8.5	3.4	2.4
NY	32	19	37	1488.0	1306	7.9	111	515	3.1	1039	6.3	3.11	110	.236	.299	79	52	95	99	.982	115	138	1.2	5.5	5.3	-.2	5.3
MON	13	13	53	1457.0	1346	8.3	99	509	3.1	870	5.4	3.55	95	.246	.307	7	-29	94	93	.981	121	152	.8	-3.1	2.4	-.0	3.3
CHI	20	8	42	1442.3	1492	9.3	156	519	3.2	820	5.1	4.16	101	.270	.328	-90	5	117	103	.979	134	150	.0	.5	-7.0	2.1	.9
PHI	24	9	30	1447.0	1424	8.9	115	596	3.7	899	5.6	3.68	100	.258	.327	-14	-2	102	105	.978	139	142	-.2	-.2	-1.4	.0	-4.3
PIT	15	6	29	1445.3	1406	8.8	107	584	3.6	962	6.0	3.97	94	.255	.325	-61	-36	104	94	.979	133	127	.1	-3.8	-8.3	-.7	-10.8
WEST																											
LA	37	21	36	1465.0	1280	7.9	102	462	2.8	979	6.0	2.96	111	.234	.291	102	53	92	98	.974	166	131	-1.9	5.6	8.8	.0	1.4
CIN	24	11	45	1451.3	1347	8.4	131	535	3.3	910	5.6	3.71	102	.248	.310	-19	9	105	96	.980	122	142	.8	.9	-.8	.0	7.5
SD	26	19	44	1451.3	1399	8.7	127	443	2.7	727	4.5	3.40	107	.256	.308	29	38	101	106	.980	124	158	-.7	4.0	-2.0	-1.0	.3
HOU	17	9	42	1458.0	1393	8.6	119	543	3.4	909	5.6	3.66	94	.253	.317	-11	-35	96	100	.976	152	159	-1.0	-3.7	5.4	-1.0	2.3
ATL	9	9	29	1457.3	1512	9.3	134	642	4.0	776	4.8	4.19	93	.270	.342	-97	-49	108	104	.976	159	197	-1.4	-5.2	-7.3	-1.5	.3
SF	13	5	24	1448.0	1348	8.4	125	572	3.6	985	6.1	3.61	94	.247	.314	-3	-33	95	99	.976	148	134	-.8	-3.5	-5.0	-.7	-9.0
TOT	267	149	455	17474.7		8.5			3.3		5.5	3.59		.252	.321					.979	1621	1796					

Runs
Murphy-Atl 118
Raines-Mon 115
McGee-StL 114
Sandberg-Chi.......113
Coleman-StL 107

Hits
McGee-StL 216
Parker-Cin 198
Gwynn-SD 197
Sandberg-Chi.......186
Murphy-Atl 185

Doubles
Parker-Cin 42
Wilson-Phi 39
Herr-StL 38
Wallach-Mon 36

Triples
McGee-StL 18
Samuel-Phi 13
Raines-Mon 13
Garner-Hou 10
Coleman-StL 10

Home Runs
Murphy-Atl 37
Parker-Cin 34
Schmidt-Phi 33
Guerrero-LA 33
Carter-NY 32

Total Bases
Parker-Cin 350
Murphy-Atl 332
McGee-StL 308
Sandberg-Chi.......307
Schmidt-Phi 292

Runs Batted In
Parker-Cin 125
Murphy-Atl 111
Herr-StL 110
Moreland-Chi.......106
Wilson-Phi 102

Runs Produced
Herr-StL 199
Murphy-Atl 192
McGee-StL 186
Parker-Cin 179
Sandberg-Chi.......170

Bases On Balls
Murphy-Atl 90
Schmidt-Phi 87
Martinez-SD 87
Rose-Cin 86
Law-Mon 86

Batting Average
McGee-StL 353
Guerrero-LA 320
Raines-Mon 320
Gwynn-SD 317
Parker-Cin 312

On Base Percentage
Guerrero-LA 425
Scioscia-LA 409
Raines-Mon 407
Rose-Cin 398
Clark-StL 397

Slugging Average
Guerrero-LA 577
Parker-Cin 551
Murphy-Atl 539
Schmidt-Phi 532
Marshall-LA 515

Production
Guerrero-LA 1.002
Murphy-Atl 929
Parker-Cin 918
Schmidt-Phi 911
Clark-StL 899

Adjusted Production
Guerrero-LA 191
Clark-StL 157
Raines-Mon 156
McGee-StL 154
Schmidt-Phi 149

Batter Runs
Guerrero-LA 52.8
Murphy-Atl 47.6
Parker-Cin 42.5
Schmidt-Phi 38.5
Raines-Mon 37.5

Adjusted Batter Runs
Guerrero-LA 57.1
Murphy-Atl 42.7
Raines-Mon 42.0
McGee-StL 39.7
Parker-Cin 38.7

Clutch Hitting Index
Herr-StL 155
Pendleton-StL 151
Moreland-Chi 149
Brooks-Mon 146
Rose-Cin 144

Runs Created
Murphy-Atl 131
Raines-Mon 124
McGee-StL 123
Guerrero-LA 121
Sandberg-Chi.......117

Total Average
Guerrero-LA 1.098
Raines-Mon 1.044
Murphy-Atl 967
McGee-StL 959
Sandberg-Chi.......944

Stolen Bases
Coleman-StL 110
Raines-Mon 70
McGee-StL 56
Sandberg-Chi.......54
Samuel-Phi 53

Stolen Base Average
Lopes-Chi 92.2
Herr-StL 91.2
Raines-Mon 88.6
VanSlyke-StL 85.0
Davis-Cin 84.2

Stolen Base Runs
Coleman-StL 18.0
Raines-Mon 15.6
Lopes-Chi 11.7
Sandberg-Chi.......9.6
Herr-StL 7.5

Fielding Runs
Hubbard-Atl 56.8
Wallach-Mon 36.8
Pena-Pit 33.0
Pendleton-StL 26.4
Wilson-Phi 15.9

Total Player Rating
Guerrero-LA 6.4
Raines-Mon 5.7
McGee-StL 4.9
Wallach-Mon 4.6
Hubbard-Atl 4.4

Wins
Gooden-NY 24
Tudor-StL 21
Andujar-StL 21
Browning-Cin 20
Hershiser-LA 19

Win Percentage
Hershiser-LA 864
Gooden-NY 857
Smith-Mon 783
Darling-NY 727
Tudor-StL 724

Games
Burke-Mon 78
M.Davis-SF 77
Garrelts-SF 74
Carman-SF 71
Minton-SF 68

Complete Games
Gooden-NY 16
Valenzuela-LA 14
Tudor-StL 14
Cox-StL 10
Andujar-StL 10

Shutouts
Tudor-StL 10
Gooden-NY 8
Valenzuela-LA 5
Hershiser-LA 5

Saves
Reardon-Mon 41
Smith-Chi 33
Smith-Hou 27
Power-Cin 27
Gossage-SD 26

Innings Pitched
Gooden-NY 277
Tudor-StL 275
Valenzuela-LA 272
Andujar-StL 270
Mahler-Atl 267

Fewest Hits/Game
Fernandez-NY 5.72
Gooden-NY 6.43
Hershiser-LA 6.71
Tudor-StL 6.84
Soto-Cin 6.86

Fewest BB/Game
Hoyt-SD 86
Eckersley-Chi 1.01
Lynch-NY 1.27
Tudor-StL 1.60
Smith-Mon 1.66

Strikeouts
Gooden-NY 268
Soto-Cin 214
Ryan-Hou 209
Valenzuela-LA 208
Fernandez-NY 180

Strikeouts/Game
Fernandez-NY 9.53
Gooden-NY 8.71
DeLeon-Pit 8.23
Ryan-Hou 8.11
Soto-Cin 7.49

Wins Above Team
Gooden-NY 9.5
Hershiser-LA 7.7
Smith-Mon 6.7
Scott-Hou 5.3
Hawkins-SD 5.3

Earned Run Average
Gooden-NY 1.53
Tudor-StL 1.93
Hershiser-LA 2.03
Reuschel-Pit 2.27
Welch-LA 2.32

Adjusted ERA
Gooden-NY 224
Tudor-StL 173
Reuschel-Pit 165
Hershiser-LA 163
Welch-LA 142

Opponents' Batting Avg.
Fernandez-NY 181
Gooden-NY 201
Hershiser-LA 206
Tudor-StL 209
Soto-Cin 211

Opponents' On Base Pct.
Tudor-StL 248
Eckersley-Chi 252
Gooden-NY 253
Smith-Mon 264
Hershiser-LA 265

Starter Runs
Gooden-NY 63.5
Tudor-StL 50.7
Hershiser-LA 41.7
Valenzuela-LA 34.5
Reuschel-Pit 28.4

Adjusted Starter Runs
Gooden-NY 58.4
Tudor-StL 43.4
Hershiser-LA 33.8
Reuschel-Pit 31.8
Valenzuela-LA 25.5

Clutch Pitching Index
Darling-NY 120
Hawkins-SD 119
Show-SD 119
Reuss-LA 116
Gooden-NY 115

Relief Runs
Burke-Mon 15.9
Gossage-SD 15.5
Franco-Cin 15.5
Garrelts-SF 15.3
Carman-Phi 14.3

Adjusted Relief Runs
Franco-Cin 17.5
Gossage-SD 16.0
Carman-Phi 15.1
Garrelts-SF 13.1
Burke-Mon 12.9

Relief Ranking
Franco-Cin 28.6
Gossage-SD 26.4
Smith-Hou 24.2
Carman-Phi 23.2
Smith-Chi 22.3

Total Pitcher Index
Gooden-NY 7.9
Tudor-StL 5.1
Hershiser-LA 4.4
Reuschel-Pit 4.3
Valenzuela-LA 3.3

Total Baseball Ranking
Gooden-NY 7.9
Guerrero-LA 6.4
Raines-Mon 5.7
Tudor-StL 5.1
McGee-StL 4.9

TEAM	G	W	L	PCT	GB	R	OR	AB	H	2B	3B	HR	BB	SO	AVG	OBP	SLG	PRO	/A	BR	/A	PF	CHI	RC	TA	SB	CS	SBA	SBR
EAST																													
TOR	161	99	62	.615		759	**588**	5508	1482	281	**53**	158	503	807	.269	.334	.425	.759	106	43	36	101	98	767	.715	143	77	65	-2
NY	161	97	64	.602	2	**839**	660	5458	1458	272	31	176	620	771	.267	.347	.425	.772	110	82	**113**	96	101	821	**.754**	**155**	53	**75**	**15**
DET	161	84	77	.522	15	729	688	5575	1413	254	45	202	526	926	.253	.321	.424	.745	102	8	-38	106	97	765	.698	75	41	65	-1
BAL	161	83	78	.516	16	818	764	5517	1451	234	22	**214**	604	908	.263	.338	**.430**	.768	109	64	72	99	101	794	.722	69	43	62	-4
BOS	163	81	81	.500	18.5	800	720	5720	**1615**	**292**	31	162	562	816	**.282**	**.350**	.429	**.779**	**112**	**96**	78	102	92	**844**	.725	66	27	71	4
MIL	161	71	90	.441	28	690	802	5568	1467	250	44	101	462	**746**	.263	.322	.379	.701	91	-67	-100	105	103	666	.621	69	34	67	0
CLE	162	60	102	.370	39.5	729	861	5527	1465	254	31	116	492	817	.265	.327	.385	.712	94	-43	0	94	106	681	.648	132	72	65	-3
WEST																													
KC	162	91	71	.562		687	639	5500	1384	261	49	154	473	840	.252	.315	.401	.716	94	-46	-59	102	100	687	.663	128	**48**	73	10
CAL	162	90	72	.556	1	732	703	5442	1364	215	31	153	**648**	902	.251	.335	.386	.721	97	-16	-21	101	100	710	.678	106	51	68	1
CHI	163	85	77	.525	6	736	720	5470	1386	247	37	146	471	843	.253	.318	.392	.710	93	-54	-53	100	**109**	674	.650	108	56	66	0
MIN	162	77	85	.475	14	705	782	5509	1453	282	41	141	502	779	.264	.329	.407	.736	100	0	-23	103	96	729	.674	68	44	61	-5
OAK	162	77	85	.475	14	757	787	5581	1475	230	34	155	508	861	.264	.327	.401	.728	98	-14	39	93	104	725	.671	117	58	67	0
SEA	162	74	88	.457	17	719	818	5521	1410	277	38	171	564	942	.255	.328	.412	.740	101	7	47	95	96	739	.691	94	35	73	7
TEX	161	62	99	.385	28.5	617	785	5361	1359	213	41	129	530	819	.253	.324	.381	.705	92	-53	-112	108	93	652	.649	130	76	63	-6
TOT	1132					10317		77257	20182	3562	528	2178	7465	11777	.261	.330	.406	.735								1460	715	67	9

TEAM	CG	SHO	SV	IP	H	H/G	HR	BB	BB/G	SO	SO/G	ERA	/A	OAVG	OOBA	PR	/A	PF	CPI	FA	E	DP	FW	PW	BW	SBW	DIF
EAST																											
TOR	18	9	47	1448.0	**1312**	8.2	147	484	3.0	823	5.1	**3.31**	**124**	.242	**.303**	**135**	**129**	99	107	.980	125	164	.2	**12.8**	3.6	-.3	2.2
NY	25	9	**49**	1440.3	1373	8.6	157	518	3.2	907	5.7	3.69	106	.251	.313	73	33	94	104	.979	126	172	.2	3.3	**11.2**	**1.4**	.5
DET	31	**11**	40	1456.0	1313	**8.1**	141	556	3.4	943	5.8	3.78	116	**.240**	.308	58	98	106	94	.977	143	152	-.8	9.7	-3.8	-.2	-1.5
BAL	32	6	33	1427.3	1480	9.3	160	568	3.6	793	5.0	4.38	93	.269	.335	-36	-48	98	102	.979	129	168	-.0	-4.7	7.1	-.5	.6
BOS	35	8	29	1461.3	1487	9.2	130	540	3.3	913	5.6	4.06	104	.264	.328	14	24	102	101	.977	145	161	-.9	2.4	7.7	.3	-9.5
MIL	34	5	37	1437.0	1510	9.5	175	499	3.1	777	4.9	4.39	100	.270	.328	-38	-1	106	101	.977	142	153	-.7	-.0	-9.9	-.0	1.3
CLE	24	7	28	1421.0	1556	9.9	170	547	3.5	702	4.4	4.91	80	.280	.342	-121	-152	95	98	.977	141	161	-.7	-15.0	.0	-.4	-4.9
WEST																											
KC	27	**11**	41	1461.0	1433	8.8	**103**	463	**2.9**	846	5.2	3.49	120	.256	.312	107	115	101	103	.980	127	160	.0	11.4	-5.8	.9	3.4
CAL	22	8	41	1457.3	1453	9.0	171	514	3.2	767	4.7	3.91	107	.262	.323	38	41	101	**108**	**.982**	112	**202**	.9	4.1	-2.1	.0	6.1
CHI	20	8	39	1451.7	1411	8.7	161	569	3.5	**1023**	**6.3**	4.07	102	.255	.324	12	11	100	101	**.982**	**111**	152	**1.0**	1.1	-5.2	-.0	7.2
MIN	**41**	7	34	1426.3	1468	9.3	164	**462**	**2.9**	767	4.8	4.48	96	.268	.323	-52	-26	104	95	.980	120	139	.5	-2.6	-2.3	-.6	.9
OAK	10	6	41	1453.0	1451	9.0	172	607	3.8	785	4.9	4.41	88	.258	.329	-42	-88	93	97	.977	140	137	-.6	-8.7	3.9	-.0	1.5
SEA	23	8	30	1432.0	1456	9.2	154	637	4.0	868	5.5	4.68	85	.264	.340	-84	-114	95	96	.980	122	156	.4	-11.3	4.6	.6	-1.4
TEX	18	5	33	1411.7	1479	9.4	173	501	3.2	863	5.5	4.56	100	.268	.329	-64	0	110	97	.980	120	145	.5	.0	-11.1	-.7	-7.3
TOT	360	108	522	20184.0		9.0			3.3		5.3	4.15		.261	.330					.979	1803	2222					

Runs
Henderson-NY 146
Ripken-Bal 116
Murray-Bal 111
Evans-Bos 110
Brett-KC 108

Hits
Boggs-Bos 240
Mattingly-NY 211
Buckner-Bos 201
Puckett-Min 199
Baines-Chi 198

Doubles
Mattingly-NY 48
Buckner-Bos 46
Boggs-Bos 42
Cooper-Mil 39

Triples
Wilson-KC 21
Butler-Cle 14
Puckett-Min 13
Fernandez-Tor 10

Home Runs
Evans-Det 40
Fisk-Chi 37
Balboni-KC 36
Mattingly-NY 35
Thomas-Sea 32

Total Bases
Mattingly-NY 370
Brett-KC 322
Bradley-Sea 319
Boggs-Bos 312
Murray-Bal 305

Runs Batted In
Mattingly-NY 145
Murray-Bal 124
Winfield-NY 114
Baines-Chi 113
Brett-KC 112

Runs Produced
Mattingly-NY 217
Murray-Bal 204
Ripken-Bal 200
Henderson-NY 194
Winfield-NY 193

Bases On Balls
Evans-Bos 114
Harrah-Tex 113
Brett-KC 103
Henderson-NY 99
Boggs-Bos 96

Batting Average
Boggs-Bos .368
Brett-KC .335
Mattingly-NY .324
Henderson-NY .314
Butler-Cle .311

On Base Percentage
Boggs-Bos .452
Brett-KC .442
Harrah-Tex .437
Henderson-NY .422
Murray-Bal .387

Slugging Average
Brett-KC .585
Mattingly-NY .567
Barfield-Tor .536
Murray-Bal .523
Evans-Det .519

Production
Brett-KC 1.028
Mattingly-NY .946
Henderson-NY .938
Boggs-Bos .929
Murray-Bal .910

Adjusted Production
Brett-KC 175
Henderson-NY 162
Mattingly-NY 162
Boggs-Bos 151
Murray-Bal 148

Batter Runs
Brett-KC 63.4
Boggs-Bos 54.8
Mattingly-NY 47.5
Henderson-NY 45.5
Murray-Bal 38.3

Adjusted Batter Runs
Brett-KC 62.0
Boggs-Bos 52.7
Mattingly-NY 51.2
Henderson-NY 48.7
Murray-Bal 39.3

Clutch Hitting Index
Thornton-Cle 146
Meacham-NY 142
Boone-Cal 136
Baylor-NY 134
Buckner-Bos 132

Runs Created
Brett-KC 146
Boggs-Bos 143
Henderson-NY 138
Mattingly-NY 136
Murray-Bal 122

Total Average
Henderson-NY 1.181
Brett-KC 1.153
Gibson-Det .962
Boggs-Bos .954
Harrah-Tex .949

Stolen Bases
Henderson-NY 80
Pettis-Cal 56
Butler-Cle 47
Wilson-KC 43
Smith-KC 40

Stolen Base Average
Perconte-Sea 93.9
Henderson-NY 88.9
Gibson-Det 88.2
Pettis-Cal 86.2
Smith-KC 85.1

Stolen Base Runs
Henderson-NY 18.0
Pettis-Cal 11.4
Perconte-Sea 8.1
Smith-KC 7.8
Gibson-Det 6.6

Fielding Runs
Buckner-Bos 25.0
Grich-Cal 21.7
Gaetti-Min 21.0
Barfield-Tor 18.3
Schofield-Cal 16.1

Total Player Rating
Henderson-NY 7.4
Brett-KC 7.0
Boggs-Bos 5.5
Barfield-Tor 4.9
Murray-Bal 4.1

Wins
Guidry-NY 22
Saberhagen-KC 20
Viola-Min 18
Burns-Chi 18

Win Percentage
Guidry-NY .786
Saberhagen-KC .769
Leibrandt-KC .654
Higuera-Mil .652

Games
Quisenberry-KC 84
VandeBerg-Sea 76
Righetti-NY 74
Hernandez-Det 74
Nunez-Sea 70

Complete Games
Blyleven-Cle-Min 24
Moore-Sea 14
Hough-Tex 14
Morris-Det 13
Boyd-Bos 13

Shutouts
Blyleven-Cle-Min 5
Morris-Det 4
Burns-Chi 4

Saves
Quisenberry-KC 37
James-Chi 32
Moore-Cal 31
Hernandez-Det 31

Innings Pitched
Blyleven-Cle-Min 294
Boyd-Bos 272
Stieb-Tor 265
Alexander-Tor 261
Guidry-NY 259

Fewest Hits/Game
Stieb-Tor 7.00
Hough-Tex 7.13
Petry-Det 7.15
Morris-Det 7.42
Higuera-Mil 7.90

Fewest BB/Game
Haas-Mil 1.39
Saberhagen-KC 1.46
Guidry-NY 1.46
Butcher-Min 1.86
Key-Tor 2.11

Strikeouts
Blyleven-Cle-Min 206
Bannister-Chi 198
Morris-Det 191
Hurst-Bos 189
Witt-Cal 180

Strikeouts/Game
Bannister-Chi 8.45
Hurst-Bos 7.43
Burns-Chi 6.82
Morris-Det 6.69
Tanana-Tex-Det 6.66

Wins Above Team
Guidry-NY 7.1
Saberhagen-KC 6.7
Lamp-Tor 5.5
Moore-Sea 4.8
Higuera-Mil 4.8

Earned Run Average
Stieb-Tor 2.48
Leibrandt-KC 2.68
Saberhagen-KC 2.87
Key-Tor 3.00
Blyleven-Cle-Min 3.15

Adjusted ERA
Stieb-Tor 166
Leibrandt-KC 156
Saberhagen-KC 146
Hough-Tex 138
Key-Tor 137

Opponents' Batting Avg.
Stieb-Tor .213
Hough-Tex .215
Petry-Det .217
Morris-Det .225
Higuera-Mil .235

Opponents' On Base Pct.
Saberhagen-KC .269
Guidry-NY .276
Key-Tor .280
Hough-Tex .283
Petry-Det .285

Starter Runs
Stieb-Tor 49.1
Leibrandt-KC 38.7
Saberhagen-KC 33.3
Blyleven-Cle-Min 32.5
Key-Tor 27.1

Adjusted Starter Runs
Stieb-Tor 48.1
Leibrandt-KC 40.1
Hough-Tex 34.7
Saberhagen-KC 34.7
Morris-Det 30.4

Clutch Pitching Index
Leibrandt-KC 121
Romanick-Cal 117
Boddicker-Bal 115
Alexander-Tor 114
Stieb-Tor 112

Relief Runs
Moore-Cal 25.5
Quisenberry-KC 25.4
James-Chi 24.7
Cliburn-Cal 22.6
Harris-Tex 21.1

Adjusted Relief Runs
Harris-Tex 26.3
Quisenberry-KC 26.2
Moore-Cal 25.7
James-Chi 24.6
Cliburn-Cal 22.8

Relief Ranking
Moore-Cal 53.3
Quisenberry-KC 48.0
James-Chi 46.3
Hernandez-Det 43.8
Righetti-NY 29.5

Total Pitcher Index
Stieb-Tor 5.7
Leibrandt-KC 4.7
Saberhagen-KC 3.9
Hough-Tex 3.7
Key-Tor 3.2

Total Baseball Ranking
Henderson-NY 7.4
Brett-KC 7.0
Stieb-Tor 5.7
Boggs-Bos 5.5
Barfield-Tor 4.9

TEAM	G	W	L	PCT	GB	R	OR	AB	H	2B	3B	HR	BB	SO	AVG	OBP	SLG	PRO	/A	BR	/A	PF	CHI	RC	TA	SB	CS	SBA	SBR
EAST																													
NY	162	108	54	.667		783	578	5558	1462	261	31	148	631	968	.263	.341	.401	.742	111	84	114	96	100	773	.705	118	48	71	7
PHI	161	86	75	.534	21.5	739	713	5483	1386	266	39	154	589	1154	.253	.330	.400	.730	107	50	21	104	101	739	.699	153	59	72	11
STL	161	79	82	.491	28.5	601	611	5378	1270	216	48	58	568	905	.236	.311	.327	.638	82	-118	-138	103	108	584	.610	262	78	77	32
MON	161	78	83	.484	29.5	637	688	5508	1401	255	50	110	537	1016	.254	.324	.379	.703	100	0	16	98	94	676	.660	193	95	67	1
CHI	160	70	90	.438	37	680	781	5499	1409	258	27	155	508	966	.256	.321	.398	.719	104	21	-23	107	98	697	.666	132	62	68	2
PIT	162	64	98	.395	44	663	700	5456	1366	273	33	111	569	929	.250	.323	.374	.697	98	-11	-11	100	100	654	.645	152	84	64	-4
WEST																													
HOU	162	96	66	.593		654	569	5441	1388	244	32	125	536	916	.255	.325	.381	.706	101	3	-15	103	97	668	.657	163	75	68	4
CIN	162	86	76	.531	10	732	717	5536	1404	237	35	144	586	920	.254	.327	.387	.714	103	21	-8	104	103	712	.678	177	53	77	21
SF	162	83	79	.512	13	698	618	5501	1394	269	29	114	536	1087	.253	.324	.375	.699	99	-8	20	96	103	674	.650	148	93	61	-10
SD	162	74	88	.457	22	656	723	5515	1442	239	25	136	484	917	.261	.323	.388	.711	102	9	41	95	96	671	.641	96	68	59	-11
LA	162	73	89	.451	23	638	679	5471	1373	232	14	130	478	966	.251	.315	.370	.685	95	-41	-2	94	101	639	.629	155	67	70	6
ATL	161	72	89	.447	23.5	615	719	5384	1348	241	24	138	538	904	.250	.321	.381	.702	99	-4	-17	102	93	646	.639	93	76	55	-17
TOT	969					8096		65730	16643	2991	387	1523	6560	11648	.253	.324	.380	.704								1842	858	68	38

TEAM	CG	SHO	SV	IP	H	H/G	HR	BB	BB/G	SO	SO/G	ERA	/A	OAVG	OOBA	PR	/A	PF	CPI	FA	E	DP	FW	PW	BW	SBW	DIF
EAST																											
NY	27	11	46	1484.0	1304	7.9	103	509	3.1	1083	6.6	3.11	111	.236	.299	99	56	93	98	.978	138	145	.0	5.8	11.8	.4	8.9
PHI	22	11	39	1451.7	1473	9.1	130	553	3.4	874	5.4	3.85	100	.264	.327	-21	2	104	105	.978	137	157	.1	.2	2.2	.8	2.2
STL	17	4	46	1466.3	1364	8.4	135	485	3.0	761	4.7	3.37	114	.250	.308	56	75	103	106	.981	123	178	.9	7.8	-14.3	3.0	1.2
MON	15	9	50	1466.3	1350	8.3	119	566	3.5	1051	6.5	3.78	97	.245	.313	-10	-20	98	93	.979	133	132	.3	-2.1	1.7	-.2	-2.2
CHI	11	6	42	1445.0	1546	9.6	143	557	3.5	962	6.0	4.49	89	.278	.339	-124	-77	108	100	.980	124	147	.8	-8.0	-2.4	-.1	-.3
PIT	17	9	30	1450.7	1397	8.7	138	570	3.5	924	5.7	3.90	96	.254	.323	-30	-27	101	100	.978	143	134	-.2	-2.8	-1.1	-.7	-12.1
WEST																											
HOU	18	19	51	1456.3	1203	7.4	116	523	3.2	1160	7.2	3.15	120	.225	.291	92	101	102	93	.979	130	108	.5	10.5	-1.6	.0	5.5
CIN	14	8	45	1468.0	1465	9.0	136	524	3.2	924	5.7	3.91	99	.263	.321	-31	-6	104	101	.978	140	160	-.0	-.6	-.8	1.9	4.6
SF	18	10	35	1460.3	1264	7.8	121	591	3.6	992	6.1	3.33	106	.236	.309	61	30	95	101	.977	143	149	-.2	3.1	2.1	-1.4	-1.6
SD	13	7	32	1443.3	1406	8.8	150	607	3.8	934	5.8	3.99	89	.257	.328	-44	-68	96	102	.978	137	135	.1	-7.1	4.3	-1.5	-2.8
LA	35	14	25	1454.3	1428	8.8	115	499	3.1	1051	6.5	3.76	93	.256	.315	-7	-39	95	96	.971	181	118	-2.3	-4.1	-.2	.3	-1.7
ATL	17	5	39	1424.7	1443	9.1	117	576	3.6	932	5.9	3.97	97	.266	.333	-40	-21	103	103	.978	141	181	-.1	-2.2	-1.8	-2.1	-2.4
TOT	224	113	480	17471.0		8.6			3.4		6.0	3.72		.253	.324					.978	1670	1744					

Runs		Hits		Doubles		Triples		Home Runs		Total Bases	
Hayes-Phi	107	Gwynn-SD	211	Hayes-Phi	46	Webster-Mon	13	Schmidt-Phi	37	Parker-Cin	304
Gwynn-SD	107	Sax-LA	210	Sax-LA	43	Samuel-Phi	12	Parker-Cin	31	Schmidt-Phi	302
Schmidt-Phi	97	Raines-Mon	194	Dunston-Chi	37	Raines-Mon	10	Davis-Hou	31	Gwynn-SD	300
Davis-Cin	97	Hayes-Phi	186	Bream-Pit	37	Coleman-StL	8	Murphy-Atl	29	Murphy-Atl	293
		Bass-Hou	184	Samuel-Phi	36					Hayes-Phi	293

Runs Batted In		Runs Produced		Bases On Balls		Batting Average		On Base Percentage		Slugging Average	
Schmidt-Phi	119	Hayes-Phi	186	Hernandez-NY	94	Raines-Mon	.334	Raines-Mon	.415	Schmidt-Phi	.547
Parker-Cin	116	Schmidt-Phi	179	Schmidt-Phi	89	Sax-LA	.332	Hernandez-NY	.414	Strawberry-NY	.507
Carter-NY	105	Parker-Cin	174	C.Davis-SF	84	Gwynn-SD	.329	Schmidt-Phi	.395	McReynolds-SD	.504
Davis-Hou	101	Hernandez-NY	164	Oberkfell-Atl	83	Bass-Hou	.311	Sax-LA	.391	Davis-Hou	.493
Hayes-Phi	98	Carter-NY	162	Doran-Hou	81	Hernandez-NY	.310	Gwynn-SD	.382	Bass-Hou	.486

Production		Adjusted Production		Batter Runs		Adjusted Batter Runs		Clutch Hitting Index		Runs Created	
Schmidt-Phi	.942	Schmidt-Phi	151	Schmidt-Phi	44.0	Schmidt-Phi	41.0	Carter-NY	154	Raines-Mon	130
Raines-Mon	.891	Raines-Mon	149	Raines-Mon	38.0	Raines-Mon	39.8	Herr-StL	135	Schmidt-Phi	122
Strawberry-NY	.871	Strawberry-NY	144	Hernandez-NY	32.2	Hernandez-NY	35.4	Pendleton-StL	133	Gwynn-SD	113
McReynolds-SD	.867	Hernandez-NY	144	Hayes-Phi	30.3	Gwynn-SD	32.1	Ray-Pit	132	Hayes-Phi	111
Hayes-Phi	.861	McReynolds-SD	144	Gwynn-SD	28.4	Sax-LA	30.5	Cruz-Hou	131	Sax-LA	110

Total Average		Stolen Bases		Stolen Base Average		Stolen Base Runs		Fielding Runs		Total Player Rating	
Raines-Mon	1.062	Coleman-StL	107	Dernier-Chi	93.1	Coleman-StL	23.7	Hubbard-Atl	33.8	Raines-Mon	5.7
Schmidt-Phi	.993	Davis-Cin	80	Raines-Mon	88.6	Davis-Cin	17.4	Pendleton-StL	23.7	Gwynn-SD	5.2
Strawberry-NY	.943	Raines-Mon	70	Coleman-StL	88.4	Raines-Mon	15.6	Dunston-Chi	22.7	Hernandez-NY	4.6
Hernandez-NY	.876	Duncan-LA	48	Davis-Cin	87.9	Dernier-Chi	6.9	Ramirez-Atl	20.8	Davis-Cin	4.4
Hayes-Phi	.871			Leonard-SF	84.2			Thomas-Atl	20.2	Schmidt-Phi	3.4

Wins		Win Percentage		Games		Complete Games		Shutouts		Saves	
Valenzuela-LA	21	Ojeda-NY	.783	Lefferts-SD	83	Valenzuela-LA	20	Scott-Hou	5	Worrell-StL	36
Krukow-SF	20	Gooden-NY	.739	McDowell-NY	75	Rhoden-Pit	12	Knepper-Hou	5	Reardon-Mon	35
Scott-Hou	18	Fernandez-NY	.727	Worrell-StL	74	Gooden-NY	12	Welch-LA	3	Smith-Hou	33
Ojeda-NY	18	Darling-NY	.714	Franco-Cin	74	Krukow-SF	10	Valenzuela-LA	3	Smith-Chi	31
		Krukow-SF	.690	Tekulve-Phi	73						

Innings Pitched		Fewest Hits/Game		Fewest BB/Game		Strikeouts		Strikeouts/Game		Wins Above Team	
Scott-Hou	275	Scott-Hou	5.96	Eckersley-Chi	1.93	Scott-Hou	306	Scott-Hou	10.01	Valenzuela-LA	6.8
Valenzuela-LA	269	Youmans-Mon	5.96	Sanderson-Chi	1.96	Valenzuela-LA	242	Ryan-Hou	9.81	Krukow-SF	6.0
Knepper-Hou	258	Ryan-Hou	6.02	Krukow-SF	2.02	Youmans-Mon	202	Fernandez-NY	8.82	Ojeda-NY	4.4
Rhoden-Pit	254	Gooden-NY	7.09	Welch-LA	2.10	Gooden-NY	200	Youmans-Mon	8.30	Kerfeld-Hou	4.2
Gooden-NY	250	Fernandez-NY	7.10	Ojeda-NY	2.16	Fernandez-NY	200	Valenzuela-LA	8.10	Rhoden-Pit	4.1

Earned Run Average		Adjusted ERA		Opponents' Batting Avg.		Opponents' On Base Pct.		Starter Runs		Adjusted Starter Runs	
Scott-Hou	2.23	Scott-Hou	170	Scott-Hou	.186	Scott-Hou	.240	Scott-Hou	45.6	Scott-Hou	47.4
Ojeda-NY	2.57	Ojeda-NY	134	Ryan-Hou	.188	Krukow-SF	.266	Ojeda-NY	27.6	Rhoden-Pit	25.4
Darling-NY	2.81	Cox-StL	132	Youmans-Mon	.188	Ojeda-NY	.274	Rhoden-Pit	24.9	Cox-StL	22.7
Rhoden-Pit	2.83	Rhoden-Pit	132	Gooden-NY	.215	Gooden-NY	.275	Gooden-NY	24.2	Ruffin-Phi	22.7
Gooden-NY	2.84	Tudor-StL	131	Fernandez-NY	.216	Ryan-Hou	.281	Darling-NY	23.9	Tudor-StL	22.3

Clutch Pitching Index		Relief Runs		Adjusted Relief Runs		Relief Ranking		Total Pitcher Index		Total Baseball Ranking	
Dravecky-SD	115	Worrell-StL	18.9	Worrell-StL	20.3	Worrell-StL	49.2	Scott-Hou	5.4	Raines-Mon	5.7
Darling-NY	113	McGaffigan-Mon	17.0	Horton-StL	17.6	Smith-Chi	23.4	Rhoden-Pit	3.9	Scott-Hou	5.4
Garrelts-SF	110	Horton-StL	16.3	Tekulve-Phi	16.2	Tekulve-Phi	22.6	Tudor-StL	2.4	Gwynn-SD	5.2
Gullickson-Cin	110	Tekulve-Phi	14.4	McGaffigan-Mon	16.0	Orosco-NY	21.6	Ojeda-NY	2.1	Hernandez-NY	4.6
Tudor-StL	109	McCullers-SD	14.2	McCullers-SD	11.9	Garber-Atl	20.8	Horton-StL	2.1	Davis-Cin	4.4

TEAM	G	W	L	PCT	GB	R	OR	AB	H	2B	3B	HR	BB	SO	AVG	OBP	SLG	PRO	/A	BR	/A	PF	CHI	RC	TA	SB	CS	SBA	SBR
EAST																													
BOS	161	95	66	.590		794	696	5498	1488	**320**	21	144	595	**707**	.271	.349	.415	.764	107	59	62	100	97	792	.713	41	34	55	-7
NY	162	90	72	.556	5.5	797	738	5570	1512	275	23	188	645	911	.271	**.350**	**.430**	**.780**	**111**	**89**	65	103	93	**843**	**.755**	139	48	**74**	**13**
DET	162	87	75	.537	8.5	798	714	5512	1447	234	30	**198**	613	885	.263	.341	.424	.765	107	52	**86**	95	98	814	.741	138	58	70	7
TOR	163	86	76	.531	9.5	809	733	5716	1540	285	35	181	496	848	.269	.331	.427	.758	104	29	-9	105	102	796	.706	110	59	65	-1
CLE	163	84	78	.519	11.5	**831**	841	5702	**1620**	270	**45**	157	456	944	**.284**	.340	**.430**	.770	108	57	74	98	102	822	.720	**141**	54	72	10
MIL	161	77	84	.478	18	667	734	5461	1393	255	38	127	530	986	.255	.324	.385	.709	92	-58	-74	102	98	682	.651	100	50	67	0
BAL	162	73	89	.451	22.5	708	760	5524	1425	223	13	169	563	862	.258	.330	.395	.725	96	-27	-18	99	98	708	.661	64	34	65	0
WEST																													
CAL	162	92	70	.568		786	684	5433	1387	236	36	167	**671**	860	.255	.341	.404	.745	102	22	50	96	100	765	.714	109	42	72	8
TEX	162	87	75	.537	5	771	743	5529	1479	248	43	184	511	1088	.267	.333	.428	.761	105	37	70	96	99	761	.706	103	85	55	-19
KC	162	76	86	.469	16	654	**673**	5561	1403	264	**45**	137	474	919	.252	.315	.390	.705	90	-76	-76	100	98	683	.645	97	46	68	2
OAK	162	76	86	.469	16	731	760	5435	1370	213	25	163	553	983	.252	.325	.390	.715	93	-47	0	94	105	700	.673	139	61	70	5
CHI	162	72	90	.444	20	644	699	5406	1335	197	34	121	487	940	.247	.313	.363	.676	83	-124	-130	101	**107**	614	.612	115	54	68	2
MIN	162	71	91	.438	21	741	839	5531	1446	257	39	196	501	977	.261	.327	.428	.755	103	21	-40	108	97	756	.700	81	61	57	-11
SEA	162	67	95	.414	25	718	835	5498	1392	243	41	158	572	1148	.253	.327	.399	.726	96	-27	-64	105	100	706	.671	93	76	55	-17
TOT	1134					10449		77376	20237	3520	468	2290	7667	13058	.262	.332	.408	.740								1470	762	66	-15

TEAM	CG	SHO	SV	IP	H	H/G	HR	BB	BB/G	SO	SO/G	ERA	/A	OAVG	OOBA	PR	/A	PF	CPI	FA	E	DP	FW	PW	BW	SBW	DIF
EAST																											
BOS	36	6	41	1429.7	1469	9.2	167	**474**	**3.0**	1033	6.5	3.93	105	.266	.322	38	28	99	106	.979	129	146	-.1	2.8	6.1	-.6	6.3
NY	13	8	**58**	1443.3	1461	9.1	175	492	3.1	878	5.5	4.11	104	.262	.320	10	27	103	100	.979	127	153	.0	2.7	6.4	**1.4**	-1.4
DET	33	12	38	1443.7	1374	8.6	183	571	3.6	880	5.5	4.02	98	.250	.320	24	-11	95	100	.982	108	163	1.1	-1.1	**8.5**	.8	-3.3
TOR	16	12	44	1476.0	1467	8.9	164	487	**3.0**	1002	6.1	4.08	107	.260	.319	15	45	104	99	**.984**	**100**	150	**1.6**	4.4	-.9	.0	-.2
CLE	31	7	34	1447.7	1548	9.6	167	605	3.8	744	4.6	4.58	89	.273	.343	-64	-79	98	101	.975	157	148	-1.8	-7.8	7.3	1.1	4.2
MIL	29	12	32	1431.7	1478	9.3	158	494	3.1	952	6.0	4.01	107	.266	.325	26	46	103	104	.976	146	146	-1.1	4.5	-7.3	.1	.3
BAL	17	6	39	1436.7	1451	9.1	177	535	3.4	954	6.0	4.30	96	.262	.325	-20	-24	99	98	.978	135	163	-.5	-2.4	-1.8	.1	-3.5
WEST																											
CAL	29	12	40	1456.0	1356	**8.4**	153	478	**3.0**	955	5.9	3.84	104	.247	**.306**	54	22	95	94	.983	107	156	1.2	2.2	4.9	.9	1.8
TEX	15	8	41	1450.3	1356	**8.4**	145	836	5.2	**1059**	**6.6**	4.11	97	.253	.353	10	-21	95	**109**	.980	122	160	.3	-2.1	6.9	-1.8	2.6
KC	24	**13**	31	1440.7	1413	8.8	**121**	479	**3.0**	888	5.5	**3.82**	**109**	.257	.316	**56**	**57**	100	98	.980	123	153	.2	**5.6**	-7.5	.3	-3.7
OAK	22	8	37	1433.0	**1334**	**8.4**	166	667	4.2	937	5.9	4.31	91	**.246**	.327	-21	-62	94	94	.978	135	120	-.5	-6.1	.0	.6	1.0
CHI	18	8	38	1442.3	1361	8.5	143	561	3.5	895	5.6	3.93	108	.250	.319	39	48	101	97	.981	117	142	.6	4.7	-12.8	.3	-1.9
MIN	**39**	6	24	1432.7	1579	9.9	200	503	3.2	937	5.9	4.77	96	.280	.339	-94	-32	109	101	.980	118	168	.5	-3.1	-3.9	-1.0	-2.5
SEA	33	5	27	1439.7	1590	9.9	171	585	3.7	944	5.9	4.65	95	.282	.350	-76	-34	106	105	.975	156	**191**	-1.7	-3.3	-6.3	-1.6	-1.1
TOT	355	123	524	20203.3		9.0			3.5		5.8	4.18		.262	.332					.979	1780	2159					

Runs
Henderson-NY 130
Puckett-Min 119
Mattingly-NY 117
Carter-Cle 108

Hits
Mattingly-NY 238
Puckett-Min 223
Fernandez-Tor 213
Boggs-Bos 207

Doubles
Mattingly-NY 53
Boggs-Bos 47
Rice-Bos 39
Buckner-Bos 39
Barrett-Bos 39

Triples
Butler-Cle 14
Sierra-Tex 10
Fernandez-Tor 9
Carter-Cle 9

Home Runs
Barfield-Tor 40
Kingman-Oak 35
Gaetti-Min 34
Deer-Mil 33
Canseco-Oak 33

Total Bases
Mattingly-NY 388
Puckett-Min 365
Carter-Cle 341
Bell-Tor 341
Barfield-Tor 329

Runs Batted In
Carter-Cle 121
Canseco-Oak 117
Mattingly-NY 113
Rice-Bos 110

Runs Produced
Carter-Cle 200
Mattingly-NY 199
Rice-Bos 188
Puckett-Min 184
Bell-Tor 178

Bases On Balls
Boggs-Bos 105
Evans-Bos 97
Randolph-NY 94
Jackson-Cal 92
Evans-Det 91

Batting Average
Boggs-Bos 357
Mattingly-NY 352
Puckett-Min 328
Tabler-Cle 326
Rice-Bos 324

On Base Percentage
Boggs-Bos 455
Bradley-Sea 406
Brett-KC 404
Murray-Bal 400
Mattingly-NY 399

Slugging Average
Mattingly-NY 573
Barfield-Tor 559
Puckett-Min 537
Bell-Tor 532
Gaetti-Min 518

Production
Mattingly-NY 973
Boggs-Bos 942
Barfield-Tor 929
Puckett-Min 903
Brett-KC 885

Adjusted Production
Boggs-Bos 157
Mattingly-NY 156
Barfield-Tor 141
Gibson-Det 140
Brett-KC 139

Batter Runs
Mattingly-NY 55.6
Boggs-Bos 51.6
Barfield-Tor 39.0
Puckett-Min 37.1
Rice-Bos 32.6

Adjusted Batter Runs
Mattingly-NY 52.8
Boggs-Bos 51.9
Barfield-Tor 34.9
Rice-Bos 32.9
Puckett-Min 29.9

Clutch Hitting Index
Downing-Cal 132
Winfield-NY 132
Rice-Bos 128
Murray-Bal 127
Joyner-Cal 125

Runs Created
Mattingly-NY 150
Boggs-Bos 133
Puckett-Min 127
Barfield-Tor 122
Carter-Cle 116

Total Average
Boggs-Bos 997
Mattingly-NY 969
Henderson-NY 969
Gibson-Det 967
Barfield-Tor 950

Stolen Bases
Henderson-NY 87
Pettis-Cal 50
Cangelosi-Chi 50
Wilson-KC 34
Gibson-Det 34

Stolen Base Average
Felder-Mil 88.9
Davis-Oak 87.1
Gibson-Det 85.0
Henderson-NY 82.9

Stolen Base Runs
Henderson-NY 15.3
Pettis-Cal 7.2
Gibson-Det 6.6
Davis-Oak 5.7
Wilson-KC 5.4

Fielding Runs
Reynolds-Sea 29.0
Owen-Sea-Bos 23.8
Barfield-Tor 21.9
Gaetti-Min 21.4
Buckner-Bos 16.3

Total Player Rating
Barfield-Tor 4.9
Boggs-Bos 4.4
Ripken-Bal 3.8
Trammell-Det 3.5
Bernazard-Cle 3.5

Wins
Clemens-Bos 24
Morris-Det 21
Higuera-Mil 20
Witt-Cal 18
Rasmussen-NY 18

Win Percentage
Clemens-Bos 857
Rasmussen-NY 750
Morris-Det 724
Higuera-Mil 645
Witt-Cal 643

Games
Williams-Tex 80
Righetti-NY 74
Harris-Tex 73
Eichhorn-Tor 69

Complete Games
Candiotti-Cle 17
Blyleven-Min 16
Morris-Det 15
Higuera-Mil 15
Witt-Cal 14

Shutouts
Morris-Det 6
Hurst-Bos 4
Higuera-Mil 4

Saves
Righetti-NY 46
Aase-Bal 34
Henke-Tor 27
Hernandez-Det 24
Moore-Cal 21

Innings Pitched
Blyleven-Min 272
Witt-Cal 269
Morris-Det 267
Moore-Sea 266
Clemens-Bos 254

Fewest Hits/Game
Clemens-Bos 6.34
Rasmussen-NY 7.13
Witt-Cal 7.29
Hough-Tex 7.36
Cowley-Chi 7.39

Fewest BB/Game
Guidry-NY 1.78
Boyd-Bos 1.89
Blyleven-Min 1.92
Wegman-Mil 1.95
Sutton-Cal 2.13

Strikeouts
Langston-Sea 245
Clemens-Bos 238
Morris-Det 223
Blyleven-Min 215
Witt-Cal 208

Strikeouts/Game
Langston-Sea 9.23
Hurst-Bos 8.64
Clemens-Bos 8.43
Correa-Tex 8.42
Rijo-Oak 8.16

Wins Above Team
Clemens-Bos 9.7
Morris-Det 6.6
Rasmussen-NY 5.7
Higuera-Mil 5.7
Eichhorn-Tor 3.9

Earned Run Average
Clemens-Bos 2.48
Higuera-Mil 2.79
Witt-Cal 2.84
Hurst-Bos 3.00
Jackson-KC 3.19

Adjusted ERA
Clemens-Bos 166
Higuera-Mil 154
Witt-Cal 140
Hurst-Bos 137
Jackson-KC 131

Opponents' Batting Avg.
Clemens-Bos 195
Rasmussen-NY 217
Witt-Cal 221
Hough-Tex 221
Correa-Tex 223

Opponents' On Base Pct.
Clemens-Bos 251
Witt-Cal 275
Morris-Det 285
Sutton-Cal 286
Rasmussen-NY 288

Starter Runs
Clemens-Bos 47.8
Witt-Cal 39.8
Higuera-Mil 38.1
Morris-Det 26.9
Hurst-Bos 22.7

Adjusted Starter Runs
Clemens-Bos 46.2
Higuera-Mil 41.5
Witt-Cal 33.9
Hurst-Bos 21.6
Jackson-KC 20.5

Clutch Pitching Index
Hurst-Bos 123
Jackson-KC 121
Higuera-Mil 119
Stieb-Tor 119
Niekro-Cle 117

Relief Runs
Eichhorn-Tor 42.8
Righetti-NY 20.6
Harris-Tex 16.5
Clear-Mil 16.3
Mohorcic-Tex 14.7

Adjusted Relief Runs
Eichhorn-Tor 46.0
Righetti-NY 21.9
Clear-Mil 17.4
Harris-Tex 14.0
Plesac-Mil 13.5

Relief Ranking
Eichhorn-Tor 59.4
Righetti-NY 50.6
Clear-Mil 29.6
Plesac-Mil 27.3
Harris-Tex 26.2

Total Pitcher Index
Eichhorn-Tor 4.9
Clemens-Bos 4.8
Higuera-Mil 4.2
Witt-Cal 3.7
Key-Tor 2.4

Total Baseball Ranking
Barfield-Tor 4.9
Eichhorn-Tor 4.9
Clemens-Bos 4.8
Boggs-Bos 4.4
Higuera-Mil 4.2

TEAM	G	W	L	PCT	GB	R	OR	AB	H	2B	3B	HR	BB	SO	AVG	OBP	SLG	PRO	/A	BR	/A	PF	CHI	RC	TA	SB	CS	SBA	SBR
EAST																													
STL	162	95	67	.586		798	693	5500	1449	252	49	94	**644**	933	.263	**.343**	.378	.721	97	-8	3	99	**108**	740	.704	**248**	72	78	**31**
NY	162	92	70	.568	3	823	698	5601	**1499**	287	34	192	592	1012	.268	.341	**.434**	**.775**	111	81	92	99	99	848	.757	159	49	76	18
MON	162	91	71	.562	4	741	720	5527	1467	**310**	39	120	501	918	.265	.330	.401	.731	99	-5	-48	106	102	734	.689	166	74	69	5
PIT	162	80	82	.494	15	723	744	5536	1464	282	45	131	535	914	.264	.332	.403	.735	100	3	-27	104	98	741	.690	140	58	71	7
PHI	162	80	82	.494	15	702	749	5475	1390	248	51	169	547	1109	.254	.329	.410	.739	101	8	-21	104	95	736	.696	111	49	69	4
CHI	161	76	85	.472	18.5	720	801	5583	1475	244	33	**209**	504	1064	.264	.327	.432	.759	106	40	34	101	93	785	.714	109	48	69	4
WEST																													
SF	162	90	72	.556		783	**669**	5608	1458	274	32	205	511	1094	.260	.326	.430	.756	105	33	62	96	101	768	.710	126	59	57	-19
CIN	162	84	78	.519	6	783	752	5560	1478	262	29	192	514	928	.266	.331	.427	.758	106	42	16	104	101	786	.725	169	46	**79**	23
HOU	162	76	86	.469	14	648	678	5485	1386	238	28	122	526	936	.253	.321	.373	.694	90	-77	-24	93	100	669	.647	162	46	78	21
LA	162	73	89	.451	17	635	675	5517	1389	236	23	125	445	923	.252	.311	.371	.682	86	-107	-47	92	103	627	.614	128	59	68	3
ATL	161	69	92	.429	20.5	747	829	5428	1401	284	24	152	**641**	834	.258	.341	.403	.744	103	28	-32	108	98	747	.710	135	68	67	0
SD	162	65	97	.401	25	668	763	5456	1419	209	48	113	577	992	.260	.334	.378	.712	95	-33	-8	97	96	693	.674	198	91	69	5
TOT	971					8771		66276	17275	3126	435	1824	6577	11657	.261	.331	.404	.734								1851	757	71	101

TEAM	CG	SHO	SV	IP	H	H/G	HR	BB	BB/G	SO	SO/G	ERA	/A	OAVG	OOBA	PR	/A	PF	CPI	FA	E	DP	FW	PW	BW	SBW	DIF
EAST																											
STL	10	7	48	1466.0	1484	9.1	**129**	533	3.3	873	5.4	3.91	102	.265	.326	27	9	97	103	**.982**	116	172	.8	.9	.3	2.2	9.7
NY	16	7	**51**	1454.0	1407	8.7	135	510	3.2	1032	6.4	3.84	103	.254	.315	38	18	97	97	.978	137	137	-.4	1.8	**9.2**	1.0	-.5
MON	16	8	50	1450.3	1428	8.9	145	**446**	**2.8**	1012	6.3	3.92	**110**	.256	**.308**	26	64	106	95	.976	147	122	-.9	**6.4**	-4.8	-.3	9.7
PIT	25	**13**	39	1445.0	1377	8.6	164	562	3.5	914	5.7	4.20	102	.253	.319	-18	10	105	95	.980	123	147	.4	1.0	-2.7	-.1	.4
PHI	13	7	48	1448.3	1453	9.0	167	587	3.6	877	5.7	4.18	102	.263	.331	-16	13	105	103	.980	121	137	.5	1.3	-2.1	-.4	-.3
CHI	11	5	48	1434.7	1524	9.6	159	628	3.9	1024	6.4	4.55	91	.274	.345	-75	-65	102	103	.979	130	154	.0	-6.5	3.4	-.4	-1.0
WEST																											
SF	19	10	38	1471.0	1407	8.6	146	547	3.3	1038	6.4	**3.68**	105	.254	.319	65	30	95	**106**	.980	129	**183**	.0	3.0	6.2	-2.7	2.5
CIN	7	6	44	1452.3	1486	9.2	170	485	3.0	919	5.7	4.24	99	.267	.322	-26	-6	103	99	.979	130	137	.0	-.6	1.6	1.5	.5
HOU	13	**13**	33	1441.3	**1363**	**8.5**	141	525	3.3	**1137**	7.1	3.84	99	**.249**	.313	38	-7	93	96	.981	116	113	.8	-.7	-2.4	1.3	-4.0
LA	**29**	8	32	1455.0	1415	8.8	130	565	3.5	1097	6.8	3.72	101	.254	.321	58	6	92	103	.975	155	144	-1.4	.6	-4.7	-.5	-5.6
ATL	16	8	32	1427.7	1529	9.6	163	587	3.7	837	5.3	4.63	96	.276	.343	-86	-27	109	101	**.982**	116	170	.8	-2.7	-3.2	-.8	-5.6
SD	14	10	33	1433.3	1402	8.8	175	602	3.8	897	5.6	4.27	93	.255	.328	-30	-45	98	98	.976	147	135	-.9	-4.5	-.8	-.3	-9.5
TOT	189	98	496	17379.0		8.9			3.4		6.0	4.08		.261	.331					.979	1567	1751					

Runs
Raines-Mon 123
Coleman-StL 121
Davis-Cin 120
Gwynn-SD 119
Murphy-Atl 115

Hits
Gwynn-SD 218
Guerrero-LA 184
Smith-StL 182
Coleman-StL 180

Doubles
Wallach-Mon 42
Smith-StL 40
Galarraga-Mon 40

Triples
Samuel-Phi 15
Gwynn-SD 13
VanSlyke-Pit 11
McGee-StL 11
Coleman-StL 10

Home Runs
Dawson-Chi 49
Murphy-Atl 44
Strawberry-NY 39
Davis-Cin 37
Johnson-NY 36

Total Bases
Dawson-Chi 353
Samuel-Phi 329
Murphy-Atl 328
Strawberry-NY 310
Clark-SF 307

Runs Batted In
Dawson-Chi 137
Wallach-Mon 123
Schmidt-Phi 113
Clark-StL 106

Runs Produced
Wallach-Mon 186
Samuel-Phi 185
Davis-Cin 183
Smith-StL 179
Dawson-Chi 178

Bases On Balls
Clark-StL 136
Hayes-Phi 121
Murphy-Atl 115
Strawberry-NY 97
Raines-Mon 90

Batting Average
Gwynn-SD 370
Guerrero-LA 338
Raines-Mon 330
Kruk-SD 313
James-Atl 312

On Base Percentage
Clark-StL 461
Gwynn-SD 450
Raines-Mon 431
Guerrero-LA 421
Murphy-Atl 420

Slugging Average
Clark-StL 597
Davis-Cin 593
Strawberry-NY 583
Clark-SF 580
Murphy-Atl 580

Production
Clark-StL 1.058
Murphy-Atl 1.000
Davis-Cin 994
Strawberry-NY 984
Gwynn-SD 961

Adjusted Production
Clark-StL 180
Guerrero-LA 166
Gwynn-SD 159
Strawberry-NY 159
Clark-SF 154

Batter Runs
Clark-StL 54.3
Murphy-Atl 53.3
Gwynn-SD 49.6
Strawberry-NY 44.7
Raines-Mon 43.2

Adjusted Batter Runs
Clark-StL 55.2
Gwynn-SD 52.3
Guerrero-LA 48.8
Murphy-Atl 46.6
Strawberry-NY 45.8

Clutch Hitting Index
Herr-StL 200
McGee-StL 147
Pendleton-StL 142
Wallach-Mon 136
Kruk-SD 133

Runs Created
Murphy-Atl 143
Gwynn-SD 143
Strawberry-NY 132
Raines-Mon 132
Clark-StL 127

Total Average
Clark-StL 1.265
Davis-Cin 1.199
Raines-Mon 1.146
Strawberry-NY 1.134
Murphy-Atl 1.120

Stolen Bases
Coleman-StL 109
Gwynn-SD 56
Hatcher-Hou 53
Raines-Mon 50
Davis-Cin 50

Stolen Base Average
Sandberg-Chi 91.3
Raines-Mon 90.9
Davis-Cin 89.3
Hatcher-Hou 85.5
Coleman-StL 83.2

Stolen Base Runs
Coleman-StL 19.5
Raines-Mon 12.0
Davis-Cin 11.4
Hatcher-Hou 10.5
Gwynn-SD 9.6

Fielding Runs
Hubbard-Atl 22.6
Smith-StL 22.1
Davis-Cin 20.5
Virgil-Atl 19.2
Pendleton-StL 16.3

Total Player Rating
Davis-Cin 6.3
Gwynn-SD 5.9
Smith-StL 5.8
Murphy-Atl 4.9
Raines-Mon 4.2

Wins
Sutcliffe-Chi 18
Rawley-Phi 17
Scott-Hou 16
Hershiser-LA 16

Win Percentage
Gooden-NY 682
Sutcliffe-Chi 643
Welch-LA 625
Rawley-Phi 607
Smith-Atl 600

Games
Tekulve-Phi 90
Murphy-Cin 87
Williams-Cin 85
Robinson-SF -Pit .81
McCullers-SD 78

Complete Games
Reuschel-Pit-SF ..12
Valenzuela-LA 12
Hershiser-LA 10
Smith-Atl 9
Scott-Hou 8

Shutouts
Reuschel-Pit-SF ..4
Welch-LA 4

Saves
Bedrosian-Phi 40
Smith-Chi 36
Worrell-StL 33
Franco-Cin 32
McDowell-NY 25

Innings Pitched
Hershiser-LA 265
Welch-LA 252
Valenzuela-LA 251
Scott-Hou 248
Smith-Atl 242

Fewest Hits/Game
Ryan-Hou 6.54
Scott-Hou 7.22
Welch-LA 7.29
Dunne-Pit 7.90
Darling-NY 7.92

Fewest BB/Game
Reuschel-Pit-SF ..1.67
Heaton-Mon 1.73
Gullickson-Cin ...2.13
Forsch-StL 2.26
Drabek-Pit 2.35

Strikeouts
Ryan-Hou 270
Scott-Hou 233
Welch-LA 196
Valenzuela-LA 190
Hershiser-LA 190

Strikeouts/Game
Ryan-Hou 11.46
Scott-Hou 8.46
Sebra-Mon 7.93
Gooden-NY 7.40
Darling-NY 7.23

Wins Above Team
Sutcliffe-Chi 5.1
Leach-NY 4.9
Welch-LA 4.2
Smith-Atl 4.2
Dunne-Pit 3.9

Earned Run Average
Ryan-Hou 2.76
Dunne-Pit 3.04
Hershiser-LA 3.06
Reuschel-Pit-SF ..3.09
Gooden-NY 3.20

Adjusted ERA
Dunne-Pit 140
Ryan-Hou 137
Reuschel-Pit-SF ..135
Gooden-NY 124
Hershiser-LA 123

Opponents' Batting Avg.
Ryan-Hou 199
Scott-Hou 217
Welch-LA 221
Darling-NY 233
Dunne-Pit 240

Opponents' On Base Pct.
Scott-Hou 279
Reuschel-Pit-SF ..279
Ryan-Hou 281
Welch-LA 286
Drabek-Pit 293

Starter Runs
Ryan-Hou 31.1
Hershiser-LA 30.1
Reuschel-Pit-SF ..24.9
Welch-LA 24.2
Scott-Hou 23.4

Adjusted Starter Runs
Reuschel-Pit-SF ..27.1
Ryan-Hou 24.4
Dunne-Pit 22.2
Hershiser-LA 20.6
Martinez-Mon 16.5

Clutch Pitching Index
LaCoss-SF 124
Cox-StL 120
Dravecky-SD -SF ..112
Ruffin-Phi 112
Grant-SF -SD 111

Relief Runs
Burke-Mon 29.3
McGaffigan-Mon ...22.4
Williams-Cin 21.1
Robinson-SF -Pit .17.2
Smith-Hou 16.2

Adjusted Relief Runs
Burke-Mon 31.6
McGaffigan-Mon ...25.6
Williams-Cin 22.5
Robinson-SF -Pit .16.0
Franco-Cin 15.3

Relief Ranking
Burke-Mon 36.0
Franco-Cin 35.3
Worrell-StL 29.3
Bedrosian-Phi 25.8
Smith-Chi 23.9

Total Pitcher Index
Burke-Mon 3.2
Reuschel-Pit-SF ..3.1
Hershiser-LA 2.6
Dunne-Pit 2.5
McGaffigan-Mon ...2.4

Total Baseball Ranking
Davis-Cin 6.3
Gwynn-SD 5.9
Smith-StL 5.8
Murphy-Atl 4.9
Raines-Mon 4.2

TEAM	G	W	L	PCT	GB	R	OR	AB	H	2B	3B	HR	BB	SO	AVG	OBP	SLG	PRO	/A	BR	/A	PF	CHI	RC	TA	SB	CS	SBA	SBR
EAST																													
DET	162	98	64	.605		**896**	735	5649	1535	274	32	**225**	**653**	913	.272	.352	**.451**	**.803**	**111**	**91**	**114**	97	98	**910**	**.785**	106	50	68	2
TOR	162	96	66	.593	2	845	**655**	5635	1514	277	38	215	555	970	.269	.338	.446	.784	105	42	33	101	100	841	.750	126	50	72	8
MIL	162	91	71	.562	7	862	817	5625	1552	272	46	163	598	1040	.276	.349	.428	.777	104	40	20	102	101	852	.755	**176**	74	70	8
NY	162	89	73	.549	9	788	758	5511	1445	239	16	196	604	949	.262	.338	.418	.756	99	-5	13	98	100	773	.714	105	43	71	6
BOS	162	78	84	.481	20	842	825	5586	**1554**	273	26	174	606	**825**	**.278**	**.355**	.430	.785	107	61	68	99	96	855	.747	77	45	63	-3
BAL	162	67	95	.414	31	729	880	5576	1437	219	20	211	524	939	.258	.324	.418	.742	95	-46	-29	98	98	736	.681	69	45	61	-5
CLE	162	61	101	.377	37	742	957	5606	1476	267	30	187	489	977	.263	.326	.422	.748	96	-34	-55	103	98	772	.705	140	54	72	10
WEST																													
MIN	162	85	77	.525		786	806	5441	1422	258	35	196	523	898	.261	.330	.430	.760	99	-7	24	96	102	757	.715	113	65	63	-4
KC	162	83	79	.512	2	715	691	5499	1443	239	40	168	523	1034	.262	.330	.412	.742	95	-39	-70	104	96	747	.697	125	43	**74**	**12**
OAK	162	81	81	.500	4	806	789	5511	1432	263	33	199	593	1056	.260	.336	.428	.764	101	4	74	91	101	796	.735	140	63	69	4
SEA	162	78	84	.481	7	760	801	5508	1499	282	**48**	161	500	863	.272	.337	.428	.765	101	9	-11	103	96	788	.730	174	73	70	8
CHI	162	77	85	.475	8	748	746	5538	1427	**283**	36	173	487	971	.258	.321	.415	.736	93	-56	-123	109	102	737	.691	138	52	73	10
TEX	162	75	87	.463	10	823	849	5564	1478	264	35	194	567	1081	.266	.336	.430	.766	101	9	-18	104	102	798	.727	120	71	63	-6
CAL	162	75	87	.463	10	770	803	5570	1406	257	26	172	590	926	.252	.328	.401	.729	92	-64	-57	99	**104**	744	.690	125	44	**74**	11
TOT	1134					11112		77819	20620	3667	461	2634	7812	13442	.265	.336	.426	.761								1734	772	69	57

TEAM	CG	SHO	SV	IP	H	H/G	HR	BB	BB/G	SO	SO/G	ERA	/A	OAVG	OOBA	PR	/A	PF	CPI	FA	E	DP	FW	PW	BW	SBW	DIF
EAST																											
DET	33	10	31	1456.0	1430	8.8	180	563	3.5	976	6.0	4.02	106	.255	.323	69	38	96	103	.980	122	147	.1	3.6	**10.9**	-.2	2.6
TOR	18	8	43	1454.0	**1323**	**8.2**	158	567	3.5	1064	6.6	**3.74**	118	**.243**	**.313**	**114**	109	99	100	.982	111	148	.8	10.4	3.1	.4	.3
MIL	28	6	45	1464.0	1548	9.5	169	529	3.3	1039	6.4	4.62	98	.271	.331	-27	-12	102	96	.976	145	155	-1.3	-1.1	1.9	.4	10.2
NY	19	10	**47**	1446.3	1475	9.2	179	542	3.4	900	5.6	4.36	100	.265	.329	16	-3	97	101	.983	102	155	1.3	-.3	1.2	.2	5.5
BOS	**47**	**13**	16	1436.0	1584	9.9	190	517	3.2	1034	6.5	4.77	92	.282	.340	-50	-57	99	102	.982	110	158	.8	-5.4	6.5	-.7	-4.2
BAL	17	6	30	1439.7	1555	9.7	226	547	3.4	870	5.4	5.01	88	.276	.339	-88	-93	99	98	.982	111	**174**	.8	-8.9	-2.8	-.9	-2.3
CLE	24	8	25	1422.7	1566	9.9	219	606	3.8	849	5.4	5.28	88	.278	.347	-130	-98	105	97	.975	153	128	-1.8	-9.3	-5.2	.6	-4.2
WEST																											
MIN	16	4	39	1427.3	1465	9.2	210	564	3.6	990	6.2	4.63	92	.265	.335	-27	-55	96	100	**.984**	**98**	147	**1.6**	-5.2	2.3	-.8	6.2
KC	44	11	26	1424.0	1424	9.0	**128**	548	3.5	923	5.8	3.86	**120**	.261	.328	95	**121**	104	**105**	.979	131	151	-.5	**11.5**	-6.7	**.8**	-3.2
OAK	18	6	40	1445.7	1442	9.0	176	531	3.3	1042	6.5	4.32	94	.258	.322	21	-43	91	96	.977	142	122	-1.1	-4.1	7.1	.0	-1.8
SEA	39	10	33	1430.7	1503	9.5	199	**497**	**3.1**	919	5.8	4.49	102	.271	.328	-4	16	103	102	.980	122	150	.1	1.5	-1.0	.4	-4.0
CHI	29	12	37	1447.7	1436	8.9	189	537	3.3	792	4.9	4.30	113	.259	.324	25	86	109	99	.981	116	**174**	.5	8.2	-11.7	.6	-1.5
TEX	20	3	27	1444.3	1388	8.6	199	760	4.7	**1103**	**6.9**	4.63	100	.252	.344	-27	0	104	100	.976	151	148	-1.7	.0	-1.7	-1.0	-1.6
CAL	20	7	36	1457.3	1481	9.1	212	504	**3.1**	941	5.8	4.38	101	.264	.324	12	8	100	101	.981	117	162	.4	.8	-5.4	.7	-2.4
TOT	372	114	475	20195.7		9.2			3.5		6.0	4.46		.265	.336					.980	1731	2119					

Runs
Molitor-Mil 114
Bell-Tor 111
Whitaker-Det 110
Downing-Cal 110

Hits
Seitzer-KC 207
Puckett-Min 207
Trammell-Det 205
Boggs-Bos 200
Yount-Mil 198

Doubles
Molitor-Mil 41
Boggs-Bos 40

Triples
Wilson-KC 15
Polonia-Oak 10
P.Bradley-Sea 10
Yount-Mil 9

Home Runs
McGwire-Oak 49
Bell-Tor 47

Total Bases
Bell-Tor 369
McGwire-Oak 344
Puckett-Min 333
Trammell-Det 329
Boggs-Bos 324

Runs Batted In
Bell-Tor 134
Evans-Bos 123
McGwire-Oak 118
Joyner-Cal 117
Mattingly-NY 115

Runs Produced
Evans-Bos 198
Bell-Tor 198
Trammell-Det 186
Joyner-Cal 183
Yount-Mil 181

Bases On Balls
Evans-Bos 106
Downing-Cal 106
Boggs-Bos 105
Evans-Det 100
Butler-Cle 91

Batting Average
Boggs-Bos 363
Molitor-Mil 353
Trammell-Det 343
Puckett-Min 332
Mattingly-NY 327

On Base Percentage
Boggs-Bos 467
Molitor-Mil 438
Evans-Bos 422
Randolph-NY 415
Trammell-Det 406

Slugging Average
McGwire-Oak 618
Bell-Tor 605
Boggs-Bos 588
Evans-Bos 569
Molitor-Mil 566

Production
Boggs-Bos 1.055
Molitor-Mil 1.004
McGwire-Oak .... .992
Evans-Bos .... .991
Bell-Tor .... .962

Adjusted Production
Boggs-Bos 179
McGwire-Oak 172
Evans-Bos 161
Molitor-Mil 160
Trammell-Det 155

Batter Runs
Boggs-Bos 66.6
Evans-Bos 49.6
Molitor-Mil 44.8
McGwire-Oak 44.2
Trammell-Det 43.7

Adjusted Batter Runs
Boggs-Bos 67.3
McGwire-Oak 51.5
Evans-Bos 50.3
Trammell-Det 46.2
Molitor-Mil 43.2

Clutch Hitting Index
Griffin-Oak 132
Brock-Mil 132
Baines-Chi 130
Braggs-Mil 127
Tabler-Cle 127

Runs Created
Boggs-Bos 154
Trammell-Det 137
Evans-Bos 134
McGwire-Oak 131
Molitor-Mil 125

Total Average
Molitor-Mil 1.203
Boggs-Bos 1.177
Evans-Bos 1.074
McGwire-Oak 1.045
Trammell-Det 1.020

Stolen Bases
Reynolds-Sea 60
Wilson-KC 59
Redus-Chi 52
Molitor-Mil 45
Henderson-NY 41

Stolen Base Average
McDowell-Tex 92.3
Trammell-Det 91.3
Schofield-Cal 86.4
Moseby-Tor 84.8
Wilson-KC 84.3

Stolen Base Runs
Wilson-KC 11.1
Redus-Chi 9.0
Moseby-Tor 7.5
Molitor-Mil 7.5
Henderson-NY 7.5

Fielding Runs
Barrett-Bos 35.2
Reynolds-Sea 19.6
Surhoff-Mil 17.7
Guillen-Chi 17.4
Kennedy-Bal 16.6

Total Player Rating
Boggs-Bos 5.9
Trammell-Det 5.1
Molitor-Mil 4.5
Barrett-Bos 3.9
Fernandez-Tor 3.5

Wins
Stewart-Oak 20
Clemens-Bos 20
Langston-Sea 19

Win Percentage
Clemens-Bos .... .690
Key-Tor .... .680
Saberhagen-KC ..... .643
Higuera-Mil .... .643

Games
Eichhorn-Tor 89
Williams-Tex 85
Mohorcic-Tex 74
Henke-Tor 72
Musselman-Tor 68

Complete Games
Clemens-Bos 18
Saberhagen-KC 15
Hurst-Bos 15
Langston-Sea 14
Higuera-Mil 14

Shutouts
Clemens-Bos 7
Saberhagen-KC 4

Saves
Henke-Tor 34
Righetti-NY 31
Reardon-Min 31
Plesac-Mil 23
Buice-Cal 17

Innings Pitched
Hough-Tex 285
Clemens-Bos 282
Langston-Sea 272
Blyleven-Min 267
Morris-Det 266

Fewest Hits/Game
Key-Tor 7.24
Hough-Tex 7.52
Morris-Det 7.68
Stewart-Oak 7.72
DeLeon-Chi 7.73

Fewest BB/Game
Long-Chi 1.49
Saberhagen-KC 1.86
Sutton-Cal 1.92
Bannister-Chi 1.93
Young-Oak 1.95

Strikeouts
Langston-Sea 262
Clemens-Bos 256
Higuera-Mil 240
Hough-Tex 223
Morris-Det 208

Strikeouts/Game
Langston-Sea 8.67
Higuera-Mil 8.24
Clemens-Bos 8.17
Bosio-Mil 7.94
Nieves-Mil 7.48

Wins Above Team
Clemens-Bos 6.5
Alexander-Det 4.5
Saberhagen-KC 4.3
Stewart-Oak 4.2
Langston-Sea 4.1

Earned Run Average
Key-Tor 2.76
Viola-Min 2.89
Clemens-Bos 2.97
Saberhagen-KC 3.36
Morris-Det 3.38

Adjusted ERA
Key-Tor 160
Clemens-Bos 148
Viola-Min 148
Saberhagen-KC 138
Leibrandt-KC 136

Opponents' Batting Avg.
Key-Tor .... .221
Hough-Tex .... .223
Morris-Det .... .228
Stewart-Oak .... .229
DeLeon-Chi .... .230

Opponents' On Base Pct.
Key-Tor .... .269
Bannister-Chi ...... .282
Saberhagen-KC ..... .291
Young-Oak .... .291
Viola-Min .... .291

Starter Runs
Key-Tor 49.2
Clemens-Bos 46.6
Viola-Min 43.8
Morris-Det 31.7
Saberhagen-KC 31.2

Adjusted Starter Runs
Key-Tor 48.3
Clemens-Bos 45.1
Viola-Min 38.8
Saberhagen-KC 36.1
Leibrandt-KC 32.3

Clutch Pitching Index
Viola-Min 115
Rhoden-NY 113
Terrell-Det 110
Blyleven-Min 109
Gubicza-KC 107

Relief Runs
Henke-Tor 20.5
Eckersley-Oak 18.4
Eichhorn-Tor 18.4
Thigpen-Chi 17.1
Plesac-Mil 16.1

Adjusted Relief Runs
Thigpen-Chi 20.8
Henke-Tor 20.2
Eichhorn-Tor 17.9
Mohorcic-Tex 17.9
Williams-Tex 17.0

Relief Ranking
Thigpen-Chi 33.7
Plesac-Mil 32.2
Henke-Tor 28.1
Mohorcic-Tex 27.6
Williams-Tex 21.8

Total Pitcher Index
Key-Tor 5.1
Clemens-Bos 4.4
Viola-Min 3.8
Leibrandt-KC 3.7
Saberhagen-KC 3.7

Total Baseball Ranking
Boggs-Bos 5.9
Trammell-Det 5.1
Key-Tor 5.1
Molitor-Mil 4.5
Clemens-Bos 4.4

TEAM	G	W	L	PCT	GB	R	OR	AB	H	2B	3B	HR	BB	SO	AVG	OBP	SLG	PRO	/A	BR	/A	PF	CHI	RC	TA	SB	CS	SBA	SBR
EAST																													
NY	160	100	60	.625		703	532	5408	1387	251	24	152	544	842	.256	.328	.396	.724	114	95	156	90	97	717	.686	140	51	73	11
PIT	160	85	75	.531	15	651	616	5379	1327	240	45	110	553	947	.247	.321	.369	.690	104	33	47	98	98	648	.639	119	60	66	0
MON	163	81	81	.500	20	628	592	5573	1400	260	48	107	454	1053	.251	.311	.373	.684	102	12	-22	106	97	636	.628	189	89	68	3
CHI	163	77	85	.475	24	660	694	5675	1481	262	46	113	403	910	.261	.312	.383	.695	105	31	2	104	98	673	.625	120	46	72	8
STL	162	76	86	.469	25	578	633	5518	1373	207	33	71	484	827	.249	.312	.337	.649	93	-46	-71	104	98	601	.602	234	64	79	32
PHI	162	65	96	.404	35.5	597	734	5403	1294	246	31	106	489	981	.239	.308	.355	.663	96	-21	-28	101	99	599	.602	112	49	70	4
WEST																													
LA	162	94	67	.584		628	544	5431	1346	217	25	99	437	947	.248	.308	.352	.660	96	-31	-69	106	106	590	.591	131	46	74	12
CIN	161	87	74	.540	7	641	596	5426	1334	246	25	122	474	922	.246	.311	.368	.679	101	-5	-28	105	102	639	.640	207	56	79	29
SD	161	83	78	.516	11	594	583	5366	1325	205	35	94	494	892	.247	.313	.351	.664	97	-18	-1	97	98	594	.599	123	50	71	7
SF	162	83	79	.512	11.5	670	626	5450	1353	227	44	113	550	1023	.248	.321	.368	.689	104	31	69	94	100	650	.635	121	78	61	-10
HOU	162	82	80	.506	12.5	617	631	5494	1338	239	31	96	474	840	.244	.308	.351	.659	95	-31	11	93	103	604	.609	198	71	74	17
ATL	160	54	106	.338	39.5	555	741	5440	1319	228	28	96	432	848	.242	.301	.348	.649	92	-55	-82	104	98	549	.564	95	69	58	-12
TOT	969					7522		65563	16277	2828	415	1279	5793	11032	.248	.313	.363	.675								1789	729	71	99

TEAM	CG	SHO	SV	IP	H	H/G	HR	BB	BB/G	SO	SO/G	ERA	/A	OVAG	OOBA	PR	/A	PF	CPI	FA	E	DP	FW	PW	BW	SBW	DIF
EAST																											
NY	31	22	46	1439.0	1253	7.8	78	404	2.5	1100	6.9	2.91	104	.234	.287	86	19	88	97	.981	115	127	.9	2.0	16.8	.3	-.0
PIT	12	11	46	1440.7	1349	8.4	108	469	2.9	790	4.9	3.47	97	.250	.306	-3	-18	97	101	.980	125	126	.4	-1.9	5.1	-.9	2.4
MON	18	12	43	1482.7	1310	8.0	122	476	2.9	923	5.6	3.08	117	.237	.297	59	88	105	105	.978	142	145	-.6	9.5	-2.4	-.6	-6.0
CHI	30	10	29	1464.3	1494	9.2	115	490	3.0	897	5.5	3.84	94	.264	.321	-64	-37	105	102	.980	125	128	.4	-4.0	.2	-.0	-.6
STL	17	14	42	1470.7	1387	8.5	91	486	3.0	881	5.4	3.47	104	.251	.307	-3	23	105	99	.981	121	131	.6	2.5	-7.7	2.6	-1.2
PHI	16	6	36	1433.0	1447	9.1	118	628	3.9	859	5.4	4.14	86	.264	.336	-110	-93	103	102	.976	145	139	-.8	-10.0	-3.0	-.5	-1.2
WEST																											
LA	32	24	49	1463.3	1291	7.9	84	473	2.9	1029	6.3	2.96	122	.237	.295	78	106	105	102	.977	142	126	-.6	11.4	-7.4	.4	9.7
CIN	24	13	43	1455.0	1271	7.9	121	504	3.1	934	5.8	3.35	108	.236	.299	16	43	105	98	.980	125	131	.4	4.6	-3.0	2.2	2.3
SD	30	9	39	1449.0	1332	8.3	112	439	2.7	885	5.5	3.28	102	.246	.299	26	11	97	102	.981	120	147	.6	1.2	-.1	-.1	.9
SF	25	8	42	1462.3	1323	8.1	99	422	2.6	875	5.4	3.39	95	.242	.293	10	-27	93	93	.980	129	145	.1	-.3	7.4	-2.0	-.7
HOU	21	15	40	1474.7	1339	8.2	123	478	2.9	1049	6.4	3.41	95	.242	.299	6	-30	93	99	.978	138	124	-.4	-3.2	1.2	.9	2.5
ATL	14	4	25	1446.0	1481	9.2	108	524	3.3	810	5.0	4.09	90	.267	.327	-103	-64	107	100	.976	151	138	-1.1	-6.9	-8.8	-2.2	-7.0
TOT	270	153	480	17480.7		8.4			3.0		5.7	3.45		.248	.313					.979	1578	1607					

Runs
Butler-SF 109
Gibson-LA 106
Clark-SF 102
VanSlyke-Pit 101
Strawberry-NY 101

Hits
Galarraga-Mon 184
Dawson-Chi 179
Palmeiro-Chi 178
Sax-LA 175
Larkin-Cin 174

Doubles
Galarraga-Mon 42
Palmeiro-Chi 41
Sabo-Cin 40
Bream-Pit 37

Triples
VanSlyke-Pit 15
Coleman-StL 10
Young-Hou 9
Samuel-Phi 9
Butler-SF 9

Home Runs
Strawberry-NY 39
Davis-Hou 30
Galarraga-Mon 29
Clark-SF 29
McReynolds-NY 27

Total Bases
Galarraga-Mon 329
Dawson-Chi 298
VanSlyke-Pit 297
Strawberry-NY 296
Clark-SF 292

Runs Batted In
Clark-SF 109
Strawberry-NY 101
VanSlyke-Pit 100
Bonilla-Pit 100

Runs Produced
Clark-SF 182
VanSlyke-Pit 176
Strawberry-NY 163
Bonilla-Pit 163
Galarraga-Mon 162

Bases On Balls
Clark-SF 100
Butler-SF 97
Daniels-Cin 87
Johnson-NY 86

Batting Average
Gwynn-SD 313
Palmeiro-Chi 307
Dawson-Chi 303
Galarraga-Mon 302
Perry-Atl 300

On Base Percentage
Daniels-Cin 400
Butler-SF 395
Clark-SF 392
Gibson-LA 381
Gwynn-SD 374

Slugging Average
Strawberry-NY 545
Galarraga-Mon 540
Clark-SF 508
VanSlyke-Pit 506
Dawson-Chi 504

Production
Strawberry-NY 916
Clark-SF 900
Galarraga-Mon 894
Gibson-LA 864
Daniels-Cin 863

Adjusted Production
Strawberry-NY 177
Clark-SF 167
McReynolds-NY 152
Bonds-Pit 148
VanSlyke-Pit 147

Batter Runs
Clark-SF 44.3
Strawberry-NY 42.0
Galarraga-Mon 39.2
Gibson-LA 33.8
Daniels-Cin 33.2

Adjusted Batter Runs
Clark-SF 48.6
Strawberry-NY 48.5
Galarraga-Mon 35.4
Bonilla-Pit 33.8
VanSlyke-Pit 33.0

Clutch Hitting Index
Moreland-SD 142
Perry-Atl 129
Doran-Hou 124
Maldonado-SF 124
Davis-Cin 123

Runs Created
Clark-SF 120
Galarraga-Mon 114
Strawberry-NY 111
Gibson-LA 107
VanSlyke-Pit 107

Total Average
Strawberry-NY 990
Clark-SF 957
Daniels-Cin 940
Gibson-LA 940
Davis-Cin 936

Stolen Bases
Coleman-StL 81
Young-Hou 65
Smith-StL 57
Sabo-Cin 46
Nixon-Mon 46

Stolen Base Average
McReynolds-NY ...100.0
Davis-Cin 92.1
Gibson-LA 88.6
McGee-StL 87.2
Smith-StL 86.4

Stolen Base Runs
Smith-StL 11.7
McGee-StL 8.7
Davis-Cin 8.7
Coleman-StL 8.1
Larkin-Cin 7.8

Fielding Runs
Smith-StL 24.2
Sabo-Cin 15.8
Santiago-SD 15.2
Larkin-Cin 14.4
Bream-Pit 14.1

Total Player Rating
Strawberry-NY 4.9
Larkin-Cin 4.8
Smith-StL 4.8
VanSlyke-Pit 4.3
McReynolds-NY 4.2

Wins
Jackson-Cin 23
Hershiser-LA 23
Cone-NY 20
Reuschel-SF 19

Win Percentage
Cone-NY 870
Browning-Cin 783
Jackson-Cin 742
Hershiser-LA 742
Maddux-Chi 692

Games
Murphy-Cin 76
Robinson-Pit 75
Agosto-Hou 75
Tekulve-Phi 70
Franco-Cin 70

Complete Games
Jackson-Cin 15
Hershiser-LA 15
Show-SD 13
Sutcliffe-Chi 12
Gooden-NY 10

Shutouts
Hershiser-LA 8
Leary-LA 6
Jackson-Cin 6
Scott-Hou 5
Ojeda-NY 5

Saves
Franco-Cin 39
Gott-Pit 34
Worrell-StL 32
Davis-SD 28
Bedrosian-Phi 28

Innings Pitched
Hershiser-LA 267
Jackson-Cin 261
Browning-Cin 251
Mahler-Atl 249
Maddux-Chi 249

Fewest Hits/Game
Fernandez-NY 6.11
Perez-Mon 6.37
Scott-Hou 6.66
Rijo-Cin 6.67
Cone-NY 6.94

Fewest BB/Game
Smith-Mon 1.45
Mahler-Atl 1.52
Reuschel-SF 1.54
Ojeda-NY 1.56
Tudor-StL-LA 1.87

Strikeouts
Ryan-Hou 228
Cone-NY 213
DeLeon-StL 208
Scott-Hou 190
Fernandez-NY 189

Strikeouts/Game
Ryan-Hou 9.33
Fernandez-NY 9.10
Rijo-Cin 8.89
DeLeon-StL 8.32
Cone-NY 8.30

Wins Above Team
Cone-NY 7.9
Jackson-Cin 7.6
Hershiser-LA 6.7
Browning-Cin 6.5
Maddux-Chi 5.9

Earned Run Average
Magrane-StL 2.18
Cone-NY 2.22
Hershiser-LA 2.26
Tudor-StL-LA 2.33
Rijo-Cin 2.39

Adjusted ERA
Magrane-StL 166
Hershiser-LA 160
Tudor-StL-LA 154
Rijo-Cin 151
Perez-Mon 148

Opponents' Batting Avg.
Fernandez-NY 191
Perez-Mon 196
Scott-Hou 204
Rijo-Cin 209
Cone-NY 213

Opponents' On Base Pct.
Perez-Mon 248
Scott-Hou 255
Ojeda-NY 259
Hershiser-LA 267
Jackson-Cin 270

Starter Runs
Hershiser-LA 35.3
Cone-NY 31.5
Tudor-StL-LA 24.4
Magrane-StL 23.2
Perez-Mon 21.0

Adjusted Starter Runs
Hershiser-LA 40.4
Tudor-StL-LA 27.7
Magrane-StL 26.2
Jackson-Cin 25.8
Perez-Mon 24.6

Clutch Pitching Index
Tudor-StL-LA 134
Rawley-Phi 122
Moyer-Chi 118
Robinson-SF 113
Martinez-Mon 112

Relief Runs
Franco-Cin 17.9
Holton-LA 16.6
Pena-LA 16.0
Davis-SD 15.5
Myers-NY 13.0

Adjusted Relief Runs
Franco-Cin 19.5
Holton-LA 18.2
Pena-LA 17.8
Davis-SD 14.5
Harris-Phi 14.2

Relief Ranking
Franco-Cin 44.4
Davis-SD 29.3
Pena-LA 27.3
Myers-NY 21.6
Howell-LA 20.4

Total Pitcher Index
Hershiser-LA 5.4
Magrane-StL 3.5
Jackson-Cin 3.1
Tudor-StL-LA 3.1
Martinez-Mon 2.9

Total Baseball Ranking
Hershiser-LA 5.4
Strawberry-NY 4.9
Larkin-Cin 4.8
Smith-StL 4.8
VanSlyke-Pit 4.3

TEAM	G	W	L	PCT	GB	R	OR	AB	H	2B	3B	HR	BB	SO	AVG	OBP	SLG	PRO	/A	BR	/A	PF	CHI	RC	TA	SB	CS	SBA	SBR
EAST																													
BOS	162	89	73	.549		**813**	689	5545	**1569**	**310**	39	124	**623**	**728**	**.283**	**.360**	.420	**.780**	**118**	**140**	74	109	93	**842**	**.738**	65	36	64	-1
DET	162	88	74	.543	1	703	658	5433	1358	213	28	143	588	841	.250	.326	.378	.704	96	-19	21	94	102	673	.649	87	42	67	1
TOR	162	87	75	.537	2	763	680	5557	1491	271	**47**	**158**	521	935	.268	.334	.419	.753	109	68	70	100	98	771	.704	107	36	75	11
MIL	162	87	75	.537	2	682	**616**	5488	1409	258	26	113	439	911	.257	.316	.375	.691	93	-55	-78	103	**106**	648	.633	**159**	55	74	15
NY	161	85	76	.528	3.5	772	748	5592	1469	272	12	148	588	935	.263	.336	.395	.731	104	33	63	96	102	754	.693	146	39	**79**	**20**
CLE	162	78	84	.481	11	666	731	5505	1435	235	28	134	416	866	.261	.317	.387	.704	96	-34	-44	102	101	667	.633	97	50	66	0
BAL	161	54	107	.335	34.5	550	789	5358	1275	199	20	137	504	869	.238	.307	.359	.666	86	-100	-65	95	94	581	.593	69	44	61	-5
WEST																													
OAK	162	104	58	.642		800	620	5602	1474	251	22	156	580	926	.263	.339	.399	.738	106	49	**86**	95	103	763	.696	129	54	70	6
MIN	162	91	71	.562	13	759	672	5510	1508	294	31	151	528	832	.274	.343	**.421**	.764	113	93	49	106	94	785	.717	107	63	63	-5
KC	161	84	77	.522	19.5	704	648	5469	1419	275	40	121	486	944	.259	.324	.391	.715	99	-8	-29	103	102	696	.664	137	54	72	9
CAL	162	75	87	.463	29	714	771	5582	1458	258	31	124	469	819	.261	.324	.385	.709	98	-17	24	94	102	690	.641	86	52	62	-4
CHI	161	71	90	.441	32.5	631	757	5449	1327	224	35	132	446	908	.244	.305	.370	.675	88	-91	-72	97	105	609	.605	98	46	68	2
TEX	161	70	91	.435	33.5	637	735	5479	1378	228	39	112	542	1023	.252	.323	.369	.692	93	-46	-54	101	96	661	.639	130	57	70	5
SEA	161	68	93	.422	35.5	664	744	5436	1397	271	27	148	461	787	.257	.319	.398	.717	99	-6	-57	108	97	673	.652	95	61	61	-7
TOT	1131					9858		77005	19967	3559	425	1901	7191	12324	.259	.327	.391	.718								1512	689	69	40

TEAM	CG	SHO	SV	IP	H	H/G	HR	BB	BB/G	SO	SO/G	ERA	/A	OVAG	OOBA	PR	/A	PF	CPI	FA	E	DP	FW	PW	BW	SBW	DIF
EAST																											
BOS	26	14	37	1426.3	1415	8.9	143	493	3.1	**1085**	**6.8**	3.97	108	.258	.319	0	48	108	99	.984	93	123	1.5	4.9	7.5	-.4	-5.5
DET	34	8	36	1445.7	1361	8.5	150	497	3.1	890	5.5	3.71	100	.247	.309	40	1	94	99	.982	109	127	.6	.1	2.1	-.2	4.4
TOR	16	**17**	47	1449.0	1404	8.7	143	528	3.3	904	5.6	3.80	103	.256	.322	27	19	99	**105**	.982	110	170	.5	1.9	7.1	.8	-4.4
MIL	30	8	51	1449.3	1355	8.4	125	**437**	**2.7**	832	5.2	3.45	**118**	.247	**.300**	83	**100**	103	99	.981	120	146	-.0	**10.1**	-7.9	1.2	2.6
NY	16	5	43	1456.0	1512	9.3	157	487	3.0	861	5.3	4.24	89	.267	.325	-44	-73	96	100	.978	134	161	-.9	-7.4	6.4	**1.7**	4.7
CLE	35	10	46	1434.0	1501	9.4	120	442	2.8	812	5.1	4.16	97	.270	.322	-31	-17	102	97	.980	124	131	-.3	-1.7	-4.5	-.3	3.8
BAL	20	7	26	1416.0	1506	9.6	153	523	3.3	709	4.5	4.54	85	.274	.337	-90	-106	97	99	.980	119	172	.0	-10.7	-6.6	-.8	-8.4
WEST																											
OAK	22	9	**64**	1489.3	1376	8.3	116	553	3.3	984	5.9	**3.44**	107	.247	.312	**86**	41	93	104	.983	105	151	.8	4.1	**8.7**	.3	9.0
MIN	18	9	52	1431.7	1457	9.2	146	453	2.8	897	5.6	3.93	106	.266	.321	5	39	105	**105**	**.986**	**84**	155	**2.1**	3.9	5.0	-.8	-.2
KC	29	12	32	1428.3	1415	8.9	**102**	465	2.9	886	5.6	3.65	111	.258	.316	49	65	103	100	.980	124	147	-.3	6.6	-2.9	.6	-.5
CAL	26	9	33	1455.7	1503	9.3	135	568	3.5	817	5.1	4.32	87	.269	.335	-56	-90	95	101	.979	135	175	-.9	-9.1	2.4	-.7	2.3
CHI	11	9	43	1439.0	1467	9.2	138	533	3.3	754	4.7	4.12	95	.265	.327	-25	-34	99	101	.976	154	**177**	-2.1	-3.4	-7.3	-.0	3.4
TEX	**41**	11	31	1438.7	**1310**	**8.2**	129	654	4.1	912	5.7	4.05	100	**.243**	.326	-13	1	102	95	.979	131	145	-.7	.1	-5.5	.2	-4.6
SEA	28	11	28	1428.0	1385	8.7	144	558	3.5	981	6.2	4.15	103	.256	.324	-30	22	108	97	.980	123	168	-.2	2.2	-5.8	-1.0	-7.7
TOT	352	139	569	20187.0		8.9			3.2		5.5	3.96		.259	.327					.981	1665	2148					

Runs
Boggs-Bos 128
Canseco-Oak 120
Henderson-NY 118
Molitor-Mil 115
Puckett-Min 109

Hits
Puckett-Min 234
Boggs-Bos 214
Greenwell-Bos 192
Yount-Mil 190
Molitor-Mil 190

Doubles
Boggs-Bos 45
Ray-Cal 42
Puckett-Min 42
Brett-KC 42
Fernandez-Tor 41

Triples
Yount-Mil 11
Wilson-KC 11
Reynolds-Sea 11
Greenwell-Bos 8

Home Runs
Canseco-Oak 42
McGriff-Tor 34
McGwire-Oak 32
Murray-Bal 28
Gaetti-Min 28

Total Bases
Puckett-Min 358
Canseco-Oak 347
Greenwell-Bos 313
Brett-KC 300
Carter-Cle 297

Runs Batted In
Canseco-Oak 124
Puckett-Min 121
Greenwell-Bos 119
Evans-Bos 111
Winfield-NY 107

Runs Produced
Puckett-Min 206
Canseco-Oak 202
Evans-Bos 186
Greenwell-Bos 183
Boggs-Bos 181

Bases On Balls
Boggs-Bos 125
Clark-NY 113
Ripken-Bal 102
Davis-Sea 95
Greenwell-Bos 87

Batting Average
Boggs-Bos 366
Puckett-Min 356
Greenwell-Bos 325
Winfield-NY 322
Molitor-Mil 312

On Base Percentage
Boggs-Bos 480
Greenwell-Bos 420
Davis-Sea 416
Winfield-NY 398
Henderson-NY 397

Slugging Average
Canseco-Oak 569
McGriff-Tor 552
Gaetti-Min 551
Puckett-Min 545
Greenwell-Bos 531

Production
Boggs-Bos 970
Canseco-Oak 963
Greenwell-Bos 950
McGriff-Tor 930
Winfield-NY 928

Adjusted Production
Canseco-Oak 175
Winfield-NY 164
Boggs-Bos 158
McGriff-Tor 158
Henderson-Oak 155

Batter Runs
Boggs-Bos 65.8
Canseco-Oak 54.1
Greenwell-Bos 53.4
Puckett-Min 45.5
Winfield-NY 43.4

Adjusted Batter Runs
Boggs-Bos 58.3
Canseco-Oak 58.2
Winfield-NY 46.5
Greenwell-Bos 46.2
McGriff-Tor 41.2

Clutch Hitting Index
Evans-Bos 139
Greenwell-Bos 132
Larkin-Min 131
Hall-Cle 128
Clark-NY 127

Runs Created
Boggs-Bos 140
Canseco-Oak 136
Greenwell-Bos 134
Puckett-Min 126
Brett-KC 119

Total Average
Boggs-Bos 1.051
Canseco-Oak 1.046
Greenwell-Bos 1.019
Henderson-NY 988
McGriff-Tor 960

Stolen Bases
Henderson-NY 93
Pettis-Det 44
Molitor-Mil 41
Canseco-Oak 40

Stolen Base Average
Javier-Oak 95.2
Redus-Chi 92.9
Cotto-Sea 90.0
Henderson-NY 87.7
Yount-Mil 84.6

Stolen Base Runs
Henderson-NY 20.1
Pettis-Det 7.2
Redus-Chi 6.6

Fielding Runs
Guillen-Chi 42.8
Gruber-Tor 24.3
Schofield-Cal 21.2
White-KC 17.2
Allanson-Cle 15.0

Total Player Rating
Canseco-Oak 6.0
Boggs-Bos 5.5
Henderson-NY 4.9
Puckett-Min 4.8
Greenwell-Bos 4.7

Wins
Viola-Min 24
Stewart-Oak 21
Gubicza-KC 20

Win Percentage
Viola-Min 774
Hurst-Bos 750
Gubicza-KC 714
Davis-Oak 696
Stieb-Tor 667

Games
Crim-Mil 70
Thigpen-Chi 68
Williams-Tex 67
Henneman-Det 65

Complete Games
Stewart-Oak 14
Clemens-Bos 14
Witt-Tex 13
Witt-Cal 12
Swindell-Cle 12

Shutouts
Clemens-Bos 8
Swindell-Cle 4
Stieb-Tor 4
Gubicza-KC 4

Saves
Eckersley-Oak 45
Reardon-Min 42
Jones-Cle 37
Thigpen-Chi 34
Plesac-Mil 30

Innings Pitched
Stewart-Oak 276
Gubicza-KC 270
Clemens-Bos 264
Saberhagen-KC 261
Langston-Sea 261

Fewest Hits/Game
Robinson-Det 6.33
Higuera-Mil 6.66
Stieb-Tor 6.83
Witt-Tex 6.93
Hough-Tex 7.21

Fewest BB/Game
Anderson-Min 1.65
Swindell-Cle 1.67
Alexander-Det 1.81
Bosio-Mil 1.88
Viola-Min 1.91

Strikeouts
Clemens-Bos 291
Langston-Sea 235
Viola-Min 193
Stewart-Oak 192
Higuera-Mil 192

Strikeouts/Game
Clemens-Bos 9.92
Langston-Sea 8.10
Witt-Tex 7.66
Higuera-Mil 7.61
Moore-Sea 7.15

Wins Above Team
Viola-Min 8.3
Gubicza-KC 6.3
Hurst-Bos 5.8
Langston-Sea 3.9
Stieb-Tor 3.8

Earned Run Average
Anderson-Min 2.45
Higuera-Mil 2.46
Viola-Min 2.65
Gubicza-KC 2.70
Clemens-Bos 2.93

Adjusted ERA
Anderson-Min 170
Higuera-Mil 166
Viola-Min 158
Gubicza-KC 151
Clemens-Bos 146

Opponents' Batting Avg.
Robinson-Det 197
Higuera-Mil 207
Stieb-Tor 210
Witt-Tex 216
Clemens-Bos 220

Opponents' On Base Pct.
Higuera-Mil 260
Clemens-Bos 268
Robinson-Det 281
Swindell-Cle 283
Viola-Min 284

Starter Runs
Higuera-Mil 38.0
Gubicza-KC 37.9
Viola-Min 37.3
Anderson-Min 34.0
Clemens-Bos 30.3

Adjusted Starter Runs
Viola-Min 43.4
Gubicza-KC 41.0
Higuera-Mil 40.7
Clemens-Bos 39.5
Anderson-Min 38.8

Clutch Pitching Index
Anderson-Min 138
Davis-Oak 121
Candiotti-Cle 116
Leibrandt-KC 116
Viola-Min 115

Relief Runs
Henneman-Det 21.1
Jones-Cle 15.6
Harvey-Cal 15.5
Mirabella-Mil 15.4
Jackson-Sea 14.6

Adjusted Relief Runs
Henneman-Det 18.6
Jackson-Sea 18.2
Jones-Cle 16.4
Mirabella-Mil 16.1
Farr-KC 14.5

Relief Ranking
Henneman-Det 37.8
Jones-Cle 28.8
Reardon-Min 28.3
Harvey-Cal 26.4
Smith-Bos 24.2

Total Pitcher Index
Gubicza-KC 4.8
Higuera-Mil 4.6
Viola-Min 4.6
Anderson-Min 4.3
Clemens-Bos 4.1

Total Baseball Ranking
Canseco-Oak 6.0
Boggs-Bos 5.5
Henderson-NY 4.9
Puckett-Min 4.8
Gubicza-KC 4.8

The Player Register

The Player Register

The Player Register consists of the central batting, baserunning, and fielding statistics of every man who has batted in major league play since 1871, excepting those men who were primarily pitchers. A pitcher's complete batting record, however, is included for those pitchers who also, over the course of their careers, played in 100 or more games at another position—including pinch hitter—or played in more than half of their total major league games at a position other than pitcher. (Pitcher batting is also expressed in Batting Wins in the Pitcher Batting column of the Pitcher Register.)

The players are listed alphabetically by surname and, when more than one player bears the name, alphabetically by *given* name—not by "use name," by which we mean the name that may have been applied to him during his playing career. This is the standard method of alphabetizing used in other biographical reference works, and in the case of baseball it makes it easier to find a lesser-known player with a common surname like Smith or Johnson. This method also jibes with that employed in the Team Roster and Annual Record where, for example, Charles "Old Hoss" Radbourn is shown not as the puzzling O. Radbourn or H. Radbourn, as some reference books have it, but as C. Radbourn. On the whole, we have been conservative in ascribing nicknames, doing so only when the player was in fact known by that name during his playing days.

Each page of the Player Register is topped at the corner by a finding aid: in capital letters, the surname of, first, the player whose entry heads up the page and, second, the player whose entry concludes it. Another finding aid is the use of boldface numerals to indicate a league-leading total in those categories in which a player is truly attempting to excel (no boldface is given to the "leaders" in batter strikeouts, times caught stealing, at bats, or games played). Condensed type appears occasionally throughout this section; it has no special significance but is designed simply to accommodate unusually wide figures, such as the 4.000 slugging percentage of a man who, in his only at bat of the year, hit a home run.

The record for each man who played in more than one season is given in a line for each season, plus a career total line. If he played for more than one team in a given year, his totals for each team are stated on separate lines. And if the teams for which he played in his "traded year" are in the same league, then his full record is stated in both separate and combined fashion. (In the odd case of a man playing for three or more clubs in one year, with some of these clubs being in the same league, the combined total line will reflect only his play in that one league.) A man who played in only one year will have no additional career total line, since it would be identical to his seasonal listing.

Batting records for the National Association are included in The Player Register because the editors, like most baseball historians, regard it as a major league, inasmuch as it was the only professional league of its day and supplied the National League of 1876 with most of its players. We await completion of the SABR research project referred to in the Introduction to the Annual Record—which is expected to produce extra-base hits, earned runs, and a fairly full range of traditional statistics heretofore unavailable; until then, we must continue the recent practice of carrying separate totals for the National Association rather than integrating them into the career marks of those players whose major league tenures began before 1876 and concluded in that year or later.

Gaps remain elsewhere in the official record of baseball and in the ongoing process of sabermetric reconstruction. The reader will note occasional blank elements in biographical lines, or in single-season columns; these are not typographical lapses but are signs that the information does not exist or has not yet been found. In the totals lines of many players, an underlined figure indicates that the total reflects partial data, such as caught stealing for a man whose career covers the National League of 1918–1930 (during which this data was available only for 1920–1925), or batter strikeouts for a man whose career spanned both sides of the year 1909.

For a discussion of which data is missing for particular years, see the general introduction to Part 2. Here is a quick summation of the missing data:

Hit batters, 1900–1908 NL/AL, 1914–15 FL
Caught stealing, 1886–1914, 1916 for players with fewer than 20 stolen bases, 1917–1919, 1926–1950 NL; 1886–1891 AA; 1890 PL; 1901–1913, 1916 for players with fewer than 20 stolen bases, 1917–1919, 1927 AL; 1914–15 FL
Sacrifice hit, 1908–1930, 1939 (In these years fly balls scoring runners counted as sacrifice hits, and in 1927–1930 fly balls advancing runners to any base counted as sacrifices.)
Sacrifice fly, 1908–1930, 1939 (counted in these years but inseparable from sacrifice hits), 1940–1953 (not counted)
Runs batted in, 1882–1887, 1890 AA; 1884 UA
Strikeouts for batters, 1882–1888, 1890 AA; 1884 UA; 1897–1909 NL; 1901-1912 AL

For a key to the team and league abbreviations used in the Player Register, flip to the last page of this volume. For a guide to the other procedures and abbreviations employed in the Player Register, review the comments on the prodigiously extended playing record below.

Looking at the biographical line for any player, we see first his use name in full capitals, then his given name and nickname (and any other name he may have used or been born

YEAR	TM/L	G	AB	R	H	2B	3B	HR	RBI	BB	SO	AVG	OBP	SLG	PRO	/A	BR	/A	PF	CHI	RC	TA	SB	CS	SBR	FR	POS	TPR
■ KID DE LEON	Ponce de Leon, Juan "Castilian Kid" (also played in 1874 as Kid Madrid) b: 3/13/1460, Madrid, Spain d: 6/28/1963, St. Augustine, Fl. BR/TR, 5'11", 173 lbs. Deb: 5/21/1874 MUCH																											
1874	Bos-n	52	277	73	94							.339															*2	
1875	Wes-n	2	3	1	1							.333															/S	
1883	Bal-a	28	121	12	33	2	1	1			8	.273	.318	.331	.648	101	1	1	107	0	13	.545				0	CO/S	0.0
1884	Was-U	86	371	75	107	12	5	1			11	.288	.309	.356	.665	127	4	5	97	0	42	.542	0			0	1OC	0.9
	KC-U	1	4	1	0	0	0	0			0	.000	.000	.000	.000	-97	-0	0	87	0	0	.000	0			0	/1	0.0
	Yr	87	375	76	107	12	5	1			11	.287	.308	.355	.663	126	-0	-0	96	0	42	.540	0			0		0.0
1890	Cin-P	1	1	1	1	0	0	1	1	0		1.000	1.000	4.000	5.000	700	1	1	100	150	2	—	0			0	/2	0.0
1908	Pit-N	1	0	0	0	0	0	0	0	0		—	—	—	—	—	-0	0	90	0	0	—	0			0	/3	0.0
	Phi-A	9	31	5	9	3	0	0	2	0		.290	.290	.387	.677	113	1	0	108	110	3	.545				-1	/3	0.0
1909	Phi-A	148	541	73	165	27	19	4	85	26		.305	.343	.447	.790	146	27	26	102	126	88	.726	20			-5	*3	3.0
1910	Phi-A	146	561	83	159	25	15	2	74	34		.283	.329	.392	.721	123	14	13	102	115	77	.642	21			3	*3	2.4
1911	Phi-A	148	592	96	198	40	4	11	115	50		.334	.379	.505	.884	157	33	38	93	131	121	.865	38			-8	*3	3.3
1912	Phi-A	149	577	116	200	40	21	10	130	50		.347	.404	.541	.945	171	49	50	99	138	138	.976	40			9	*3	5.4
1913	Phi-A	149	564	116	190	34	9	12	117	63	31	.337	.413	.493	.906	171	46	48	97	138	130	.939	34			7	*3	6.1
1914	Phi-A	150	570	84	182	23	10	9	89	53	37	.319	.380	.442	.822	151	31	33	97	129	105	.794	19	20	-6	8	*3	4.1
1915	Nwk-F	2	8	5	4	2	1	1	4	0	2	.500	.500	1.38	1.88	304	3	3	101	156	3	2.250				-1	/3	0.1
1916	NY-A	100	360	46	97	23	2	10	52	36	30	.269	.344	.428	.772	130	13	12	101	118	59	.741	15			3	3	2.1
1917	NY-A	146	553	57	156	24	2	6	71	48	27	.282	.345	.365	.710	109	10	6	107	108	76	.642	18			11	*3	2.7
1918	NY-A	126	504	65	154	24	5	6	62	38	13	.306	.357	.409	.765	138	17	20	95	122	79	.703	8			11	*3	3.4
1919	NY-A	141	567	70	166	22	1	10	83	44	18	.293	.346	.388	.734	100	4	-0	106	103	82	.663	13			-2	*3	0.9
1921	NY-A	94	330	46	97	16	2	9	71	26	12	.294	.353	.436	.789	98	-0	-2	103	102	55	.747	8	5	-1	13	3	1.6
1922	NY-A	69	234	30	65	12	3	7	36	15	14	.278	.327	.444	.771	98	-1	-2	102	102	36	.716	1	3	-2	-8	3	-0.4
Total	2 n	54	280	74	95																							
Total	17	1694	6489	981	1983	329	100	100	992	502	184	.306	.354	.446	.800	130	247	246	100	120	1109	.822	235	28		41	*3C/SO12	35.6

with, such as the matronymic of a Latin American player). His date and place of birth follow "b" and his date and place of death follow "d". Years through 1900 are expressed fully, in four digits, and years after 1900 are expressed in their last two digits. Then come his manner of batting and throwing, abbreviated for a lefthanded batter who throws right as BL/TR (a switch-hitter would be shown as BB for "bats both" and a switch thrower as TB for "throws both"). Next, and for most players last, is the player's debut date in the major leagues, if known at this point. While we are able to report most of these thanks to SABR research, for some players we have had to list only the two digits representing their rookie years.

Some players continue in major league baseball after their playing days are through, as managers, coaches, or even umpires. A player whose biographical line concludes with an M can be located in the Manager Roster; one whose line bears a C will be listed in the Coach Roster; and one with a U occupies a place in the Umpire Roster. (In the last case we have placed a U on the biographical line only for those players who were employed as umpires by a league, for in the nineteenth century—and especially in the years of the National Association—literally hundreds of players were pressed into service as umpires for a game or two. It would be misleading to accord such players the same code we give to Bob Emslie or Babe Pinelli.) The select few who have been enshrined in the Baseball Hall of Fame are noted with an H. They are also listed in the Hall of Fame Roster found toward the end of Bill Deane's "Awards and Honors" essay in Part 1.

The explanations for the statistical column heads follow; for more technical information about formulas and calculations, see the Glossary. The vertical rules in the column-header line separate the stats into seven logical groupings: year, team, league; counting stats for batters; basic calculated averages; sabermetric figures of more complex calculation; baserunning stats; fielding stats; and Total Player Rating.

YEAR   Year of play (when a space in the column is blank, this indicates that the man has played for two or more clubs in the last year stated in the column; if those clubs were in the same league, then the man will also have a combined total line, beginning with the abbreviation "Yr" placed in the TEAM/L column)

Yr   Year's totals for play with two or more clubs in same league (see comments for YEAR)

TM/L   Team and League (see comments for YEAR)

G   Games

AB   At-bats

R   Runs

H   Hits (Bases on balls were counted as hits by scorers in 1887, but in *Total Baseball* they are not figured as times at bat nor hits nor outs.)

2B   Doubles

3B   Triples

HR   Home Runs

RBI   Runs Batted In

BB   Bases on Balls (Bases on balls were counted as outs by scorers in 1876, but in *Total Baseball* they are not figured as times at bat nor outs nor hits.)

SO   Strikeouts

AVG   Batting Average (Figured as hits over at-bats; mathematically meaningless averages created through a division by zero are rendered as dashes; see Kid De Leon's entry for 1908 with Pit-N.)

OBP   On Base Percentage (See comments for AVG)

SLG   Slugging Average (See comments for AVG, and note the use of condensed type to express Kid De Leon's maximum SLG in 1890.)

PRO   Production (On Base Percentage plus Slugging Average;

/A   Adjusted (This signifies that the stat to the immediate left is here normalized to league average and adjusted for home-park factor. A mark of 100 is a league-average performance. Pitcher batting is removed from all league batting statistics before normalization, for a variety of reasons expanded upon in the Glossary.)

BR   Batting Runs (Linear Weights measure of runs contributed *beyond* what a league-average batter or team might have contributed, defined as zero. Occasionally the curious figure of −0 will appear in this column, or in the columns of other Linear Weights measures of batting, baseruning, fielding, and the TPR. This "negative zero" figure signifies a run contribution that falls below the league average, but to so small a degree that it cannot be said to have cost the team a run.)

PF   Park Factor (A measure of run scoring at the batter's home park in a given year or, in the Totals line, of all his various home parks; above 100 signifies a park or aggregate of parks favorable to hitters, below 100 signifies a park or aggregate of parks unfavorable to hitters; see Home/Road section and Glossary for further data and technical information.)

CHI   Clutch Hitting Index (Actual RBIs over expected RBIs, adjusted for league average and position in batting order; see Glossary for precise formula.)

RC   Runs Created (Bill James's formulation for run contribution from a variety of batting and baserunning events; calculated variably to make maximum use of the data available in a given year; see Glossary.)

TA   Total Average (Tom Boswell's formulation for offensive contribution from a variety of batting and baserunning events; calculated variably to make maximum use of the data available in a given year; see Glossary.)

SB   Stolen Bases (for 1886 to the present)

CS   Caught Stealing (Available 1915, 1916 for players with 20 or more stolen bases, 1920–1925, 1951–date NL; 1914–1915, 1916 for players with 20 or more stolen bases, 1920–26, 1928–date AL.)

SBA   Stolen Base Average (Stolen bases divided by attempts; availability dependent upon CS as shown above.)

SBR   Stolen Base Runs (This is a Linear Weights measure of runs contributed *beyond* what a league-average base stealer might have gained, defined as zero and calculated on the basis of a 66.7 percent success rate, which computer simulations have shown to be the break-even point beyond which stolen bases have positive run value to the team; see the general introduction to Part 2 and the Glossary. The presence of SBR in the Player Register is dependent upon the availability of CS as shown above. Lifetime Stolen Base Runs are not totaled where data is incomplete, but seasonal SBRs are reflected in the seasonal Total Player Ratings, which in turn are added to form the lifetime Total Player Rating.)

FR   Fielding Runs (The Linear Weights measure of runs saved *beyond* what a league-average player at that position might have saved, defined as zero; this stat is calculated to take account of the particular demands of the different positions; see Glossary for formulas.)

POS   Positions played (This is a ranking from left to right by frequency of the positions played in the field or at designated hitter. An asterisk to the left of the position indicates, generally, that in a given year the man played about two-thirds of his team's scheduled games at that position; more precisely, it is figured at 20 games in 1871, 30 in 1872, 35 in 1873, 40 in 1874, and 50 in 1875; two-thirds of the scheduled games in 1876–1900, and 100 or more games since. When a slash separates positions, the man played those positions listed to the left of the slash in 10 or more games and the positions to the right of the slash in fewer than 10 games. If there is no slash, he played all positions listed in 10 or more games. For the POS [positions played] in the lifetime line, the asterisk signifies 1,000 games and the slash marks a dividing point of 100 games. A player's POS column will list him as a pinch runner or pinch hitter in only those years in which he appeared at no other position. The positions and their abbreviations are)

1: First base	P: Pitcher
2: Second base	D: Designated hitter
S: Shortstop	R: Runner (pinch)
3: Third base	H: Hitter (pinch)
O: Outfield	M: Manager (playing)
C: Catcher	

TPR   Total Player Rating (This is the sum of a player's Adjusted Batting Runs, Fielding Runs, and Base Stealing Runs, minus his positional adjustment, all divided by the Runs Per Win factor for that year— generally around 10, historically in the 9–11 range. For more information on the formula and the Runs Per Win concept, see the general introduction to Part 2 and the Glossary. In the lifetime line, the TPR is the sum of the seasonal TPRs. For men who were primarily pitchers but whose extent of play at other positions warrants a listing in the Player Register as well as the Pitcher Register, the TPR may be listed as 0.0; this signifies that their batting records are summed up in the Total Pitcher Index [TPI] column of the Pitcher Register.)

Total   For players whose careers include play in the National Association a well as other major leagues, two totals are given, as described above and as illustrated in Kid De Leon's record, where the record of his years in the National Association is shown alongside the notation "Total 2 n," where *2* stands for the number of years totaled and *n* stands for National Association. For players whose careers began in 1876 or later, the lifetime record is shown alongside the notation "Total x," where *x* stands for the number of post-1875 years totaled. Note the underlined entries in the record for Kid De Leon, reflecting the partial data for RBI, batter strikeouts, stolen bases, and times caught stealing.

YEAR	TM/L	G	AB	R	H	2B	3B	HR	RBI	BB	SO	AVG	OBP	SLG	PRO	/A	BR	/A	PF	CHI	RC	TA	SB	CS	SBR	FR	POS	TPR
■ **HANK AARON**	Aaron, Henry Louis "Hammerin' Hank" b: 2/5/34, Mobile, Ala. BR/TR, 6', 180 lbs. Deb: 4/13/54 H																											
1954	Mil-N	122	468	58	131	27	6	13	69	28	39	.280	.325	.447	.771	106	-2	2	93	116	64	.688	2	2	-1	-4	*O	-0.6
1955	Mil-N	153	602	105	189	**37**	9	27	106	49	61	.314	.369	.540	.908	148	31	36	93	112	114	.876	3	1	0	4	*O2	4.0
1956	Mil-N	153	609	106	**200**	**34**	14	26	92	37	54	**.328**	.369	.558	.927	146	36	37	99	99	115	.878	2	4	-2	9	*O	3.9
1957	Mil-N	151	615	**118**	198	27	6	**44**	**132**	57	58	.322	.379	.600	.979	**175**	48	56	90	105	136	.991	1	1	-0	9	*O	5.9
1958	Mil-N	153	601	109	196	34	4	30	95	59	49	.326	.387	.546	.933	161	37	45	89	90	121	.918	4	1	1	5	*O	4.6
1959	Mil-N	154	629	116	**223**	46	7	39	123	51	54	**.355**	.406	**.636**	**1.042**	**181**	**63**	**67**	95	85	**156**	**1.089**	8	0	2	-2	*O/3	**6.3**
1960	Mil-N	153	590	102	172	20	11	40	**126**	60	63	.292	.359	.566	.925	164	37	44	91	119	119	.952	16	7	1	9	*O/2	5.0
1961	Mil-N	155	603	115	197	**39**	10	34	120	56	64	.327	.386	.594	.979	**169**	46	**52**	92	112	132	1.014	21	9	1	-2	*O/3	4.2
1962	Mil-N	156	592	127	191	28	6	45	128	66	73	.323	.393	.618	1.012	168	54	55	99	107	140	1.066	15	7	0	14	*O/1	5.9
1963	Mil-N	161	631	**121**	201	29	4	**44**	**130**	78	94	.319	.394	**.586**	**.980**	177	**63**	**62**	101	105	**149**	**1.074**	31	5	**6**	-1	*O	**6.2**
1964	Mil-N	145	570	103	187	30	2	24	95	62	46	.328	.394	.514	.908	158	41	43	97	103	112	.922	22	4	4	12	*O2	5.8
1965	Mil-N	150	570	109	181	**40**	1	32	89	60	81	.318	.384	.560	.943	156	46	43	104	94	122	.990	24	4	5	-3	*O	4.1
1966	Atl-N	158	603	117	168	23	1	**44**	**127**	76	96	.279	.360	.539	.899	148	37	38	99	124	118	.936	21	3	5	12	*O/2	5.2
1967	Atl-N	155	600	**113**	184	37	3	**39**	109	63	97	.307	.373	**.573**	.946	160	50	47	104	94	126	.979	17	6	2	1	*O/2	4.5
1968	Atl-N	160	606	84	174	33	4	29	86	64	62	.287	.356	.498	.855	166	39	43	93	99	104	.862	28	5	5	14	*O1	**6.1**
1969	Atl-N	147	547	100	164	30	3	44	97	87	47	.300	.398	.607	1.005	172	56	54	104	81	128	1.057	9	10	-3	6	*O/1	5.0
1970	Atl-N	150	516	103	154	26	1	38	118	74	63	.298	.389	.574	.962	148	39	36	104	114	116	1.016	9	0	3	4	*O1	3.5
1971	Atl-N	139	495	95	162	22	3	47	118	71	58	.327	.414	**.669**	**1.082**	184	**65**	59	110	108	137	**1.181**	1	1	-0	-6	1O	4.8
1972	Atl-N	129	449	75	119	10	0	34	77	92	55	.265	.391	.514	.906	148	35	32	105	101	91	.945	4	0	1	0	*1O	2.7
1973	Atl-N	120	392	84	118	12	1	40	96	68	51	.301	.406	.643	1.048	165	45	39	113	104	104	1.142	1	1	-0	-2	*O	3.2
1974	Atl-N	112	340	47	91	16	0	20	69	39	29	.268	.343	.491	.834	125	13	11	105	117	58	.812	1	0	0	-8	O	0.0
1975	Mil-A	137	465	45	109	16	2	12	60	70	51	.234	.336	.355	.691	95	-2	-2	100	117	56	.634	0	1	-1	-1	*D/O	-0.2
1976	Mil-A	85	271	22	62	8	0	10	35	35	38	.229	.317	.369	.686	101	0	1	99	103	31	.619	0	1	-1	-0	D/O	0.0
Total	23	3298	12364	2174	3771	624	98	755	2297	1402	1383	.305	.377	.555	.932	156	878	901	99	104	2550	.983	240	73	28	70	*O1D/23	90.1
■ **TOMMIE AARON**	Aaron, Tommie Lee b: 8/5/39, Mobile, Ala. d: 8/4/84, Atlanta, Ga. BR/TR, 6'3", 190 lbs. Deb: 4/10/62 C																											
1962	Mil-N	141	334	54	77	20	2	8	38	41	58	.231	.315	.374	.689	85	-8	-7	99	100	40	.644	6	0	2	-5	*1O/23	-1.5
1963	Mil-N	72	135	6	27	6	1	1	15	11	27	.200	.260	.281	.542	55	-8	-8	101	154	8	.415	0	3	-2	-3	1O/23	-1.5
1965	Mil-N	8	16	1	3	0	0	0	1	1	2	.188	.235	.188	.423	20	-2	-2	104	138	1	.286	0	0	0	0	/1	-0.1
1968	Atl-N	98	283	21	69	10	3	1	25	21	37	.244	.296	.311	.607	89	-6	-4	93	116	24	.493	3	4	-2	-9	O1/3	-2.1
1969	Atl-N	49	60	13	15	2	0	1	5	6	6	.250	.318	.333	.652	80	-1	-2	104	87	6	.553	0	1	-1	0	1/O	-0.3
1970	Atl-N	44	63	3	13	2	0	2	7	3	10	.206	.242	.333	.576	50	-4	-5	104	101	4	.436	0	0	0	-2	1O	-0.8
1971	Atl-N	25	53	4	12	2	0	0	3	3	5	.226	.268	.264	.532	47	-3	-4	110	87	3	.386	0	0	0	0	1/3	-0.4
Total	7	437	944	102	216	42	6	13	94	86	145	.229	.293	.327	.621	75	-32	-31	99	112	86	.547	9	8	-2	-18	1O/32	-6.7
■ **JOHN ABADIE**	Abadie, John b: 11/4/1854, Philadelphia, Pa. d: 5/17/05, Pemberton, N.J. 6', 192 lbs. Deb: 6/10/1875																											
1875	Cen-n	11	46	4	10							.217															1	
	Atl-n	1	4	0	1							.250															/1	
	Yr	12	50	4	11							.220																
Total		12	50	4	11							.220																
■ **ED ABBATICCHIO**	Abbaticchio, Edward James "Batty" b: 4/15/1877, Latrobe, Pa. d: 1/6/57, Ft.Lauderdale, Fla. BR/TR, 5'11", 170 lbs. Deb: 9/04/1897																											
1897	Phi-N	3	10	0	3	0	0	0	0	1		.300	.364	.300	.664	82	-0	-0	96	0	1	.571	0			0	/2	0.0
1898	Phi-N	25	92	9	21	4	0	0	14	7		.228	.290	.272	.562	67	-4	-3	95	173	9	.521	4			0	3/2O	-0.2
1903	Bos-N	136	489	61	111	18	5	1	46	52		.227	.301	.290	.592	73	-18	-15	96	108	51	.574	23			10	*2S	0.3
1904	Bos-N	154	579	76	148	18	10	3	54	40		.256	.304	.337	.641	103	-1	2	97	93	68	.601	24			2	*S	0.4
1905	Bos-N	153	610	70	170	25	12	3	41	35		.279	.318	.374	.692	111	4	7	97	53	84	.666	30			-15	*S/O	-0.5
1907	Pit-N	147	496	63	130	14	7	2	82	65		.262	.348	.331	.678	109	10	8	105	**194**	71	.721	35			-27	*2	-1.9
1908	Pit-N	146	500	43	125	16	7	1	61	58		.250	.328	.316	.644	114	6	9	95	148	57	.635	22			-15	*2	-0.8
1909	Pit-N	36	87	13	20	0	0	1	16	19		.230	.368	.264	.632	93	1	0	105	224	9	.657	2			-1	S/2O	0.0
1910	Pit-N	3	3	0	0	0	0	0	0	0	0	.000	.000	.000	.000	-90	-1	-1	112	0	0	.000	0			0	/S	0.0
	Bos-N	52	178	20	44	4	2	0	10	12	16	.247	.295	.292	.587	63	-7	-10	114	68	16	.493	2			-3	S/2	-1.0
	Yr	55	181	20	44	4	2	0	10	12	16	.243	.290	.287	.577	60	-7	-11	114	65	16	.482	2			-3		-1.0
Total	9	855	3044	355	772	99	43	11	324	289	16	.254	.319	.325	.644	98	-8	-4	99	119	366	.626	142			-49	2S/3O	-3.7
■ **CHARLIE ABBEY**	Abbey, Charles S. b: 10/1868, Falls City, Neb. BL , 5'8.5", 169 lbs. Deb: 8/16/1893																											
1893	Was-N	31	116	11	30	1	4	0	12	12	6	.259	.333	.336	.670	89	-3	-1	90	86	16	.709	9			0	O	0.0
1894	Was-N	129	523	95	164	26	18	7	101	58	38	.314	.389	.472	.862	111	7	10	98	100	111	.955	31			6	*O	0.5
1895	Was-N	132	511	102	141	14	10	8	84	43	41	.276	.340	.389	.730	87	-8	-11	103	112	79	.749	28			2	*O	-1.6
1896	Was-N	79	301	47	79	12	6	1	49	27	20	.262	.331	.352	.683	86	-8	-5	95	132	41	.689	16			-10	O/P	-1.7
1897	Was-N	80	300	52	78	14	8	3	34	27		.260	.329	.390	.719	90	-4	-5	101	84	43	.707	9			3	O	-0.6
Total	5	451	1751	307	492	67	46	19	280	167	105	.281	.351	.404	.756	95	-16	-12	99	105	291	.787	93			1	O/P	-3.4
■ **FRED ABBOTT**	Abbott, Harry Frederick (born Harry Frederick Winbigler) b: 10/22/1874, Versailles, Ohio d: 6/11/35, Los Angeles, Cal. BR/TR, 5'10", 180 lbs. Deb: 4/25/03																											
1903	Cle-A	77	255	25	60	11	3	1	25	7		.235	.256	.314	.569	74	-9	-8	96	109	23	.487	8			1	C/1	0.2
1904	Cle-A	41	130	14	22	4	2	0	12	6		.169	.206	.231	.437	39	-9	-9	102	149	7	.352	2			-2	C/1	-0.7
1905	Phi-N	42	128	9	25	6	1	0	12	6		.195	.231	.258	.489	45	-8	-9	104	126	9	.417	4			1	C/1	-0.4
Total	3	160	513	48	107	21	6	1	49	19		.209	.237	.279	.516	58	-26	-26	100	123	39	.433	14			-0	C/1	-0.9
■ **ODY ABBOTT**	Abbott, Ody Cleon b: 9/5/1888, New Eagle, Pa. d: 4/13/33, Washington, D.C. BR/TR, 6'2", 180 lbs. Deb: 9/10/10																											
1910	StL-N	22	70	2	13	2	1	0	6	6	20	.186	.250	.243	.493	48	-5	-4	92	123	5	.456	3			2	O	-0.2
■ **DAVE ABERCROMBIE**	Abercrombie, David b: 5/1840, Falkirk, Scotland d: 9/2/16, Baltimore, Md. Deb: 10/21/1871																											
1871	Tro-n	1	4	0	0							.000															/S	
■ **CLIFF ABERSON**	Aberson, Clifford Alexander "Kif" b: 8/28/21, Chicago, Ill. d: 6/23/73, Vallejo, Cal. BR/TR, 6', 200 lbs. Deb: 7/18/47																											
1947	Chi-N	47	140	24	39	6	3	4	20	20	32	.279	.369	.450	.819	115	3	3	101	99	23	.783	0			-2	O	0.0
1948	Chi-N	12	32	1	6	1	0	1	6	5	10	.188	.297	.313	.610	70	-2	-1	93	173	3	.577	0			-0	/O	-0.1
1949	Chi-N	4	7	0	0	0	0	0	0	0	2	.000	.000	.000	.000	-99	-2	-2	94	0	0	.000	0			0	/O	-0.1
Total	3	63	179	25	45	7	3	5	26	25	44	.251	.343	.408	.751	100	-0	0	99	109	26	.726	0			-2	/O	-0.2
■ **SHAWN ABNER**	Abner, Shawn Wesley b: 6/17/66, Hamilton, Ohio BR/TR, 6'1", 190 lbs. Deb: 9/08/87																											
1987	SD-N	16	47	5	13	3	1	2	7	2	8	.277	.306	.511	.817	116	1	1	97	93	8	.794	1	0	0	1	O	0.1
1988	SD-N	37	83	6	15	3	0	2	5	4	19	.181	.227	.289	.516	49	-6	-6	97	67	5	.414	0	1	-1	-3	O	-1.0
Total	2	53	130	11	28	6	1	4	12	6	27	.215	.255	.369	.625	74	-5	-5	97	76	13	.538	1	1	-0	-2	/O	-0.9
■ **CAL ABRAMS**	Abrams, Calvin Ross b: 3/2/24, Philadelphia, Pa. BL/TL, 6', 185 lbs. Deb: 4/20/49																											
1949	Bro-N	8	24	6	2	1	0	0	0	7	6	.083	.290	.125	.415	15	-3	-3	102	0	1	.478	1			-1	/O	-0.3
1950	Bro-N	38	44	5	9	1	0	0	4	9	13	.205	.340	.227	.567	49	-3	-3	107	154	4	.543	0			-3	O	-0.6
1951	Bro-N	67	150	27	42	8	0	3	19	36	26	.280	.419	.393	.813	123	6	7	98	108	27	.852	3	2	-0	-2	O	0.4
1952	Bro-N	10	10	1	2	0	0	0	0	2	4	.200	.333	.200	.533	50	-1	-1	102	0	1	.500	0	0	0	-0	/O	0.0
	Cin-N	71	158	23	44	9	2	2	13	19	25	.278	.356	.399	.755	109	2	2	100	73	25	.722	1	0	0	-3	O	-0.1
	Yr	81	168	24	46	9	2	2	13	21	29	.274	.354	.387	.741	106	2	2	100	64	25	.707	1	0	0	-4		-0.1
1953	Pit-N	119	448	66	128	10	6	15	43	58	70	.286	.368	.435	.803	106	6	5	102	74	77	.788	4	4	-1	2	*O	0.1
1954	Pit-N	17	42	6	6	1	1	0	2	10	9	.143	.308	.214	.522	40	-4	-3	97	87	3	.500	0	0	0	0	O	-0.3
	Bal-A	115	423	67	124	22	7	6	25	72	67	.293	.401	.421	.822	131	17	20	95	47	76	.828	1	4	-2	1	*O	1.6
1955	Bal-A	118	309	56	75	12	3	6	32	89	69	.243	.416	.359	.776	123	10	15	90	93	52	.827	2	8	-4	0	O/1	0.5
1956	Chi-A	4	3	0	1	0	0	0	0	2	1	.333	.600	.333	.933	146	1	0	104	0	1	1.500	0	0	0	-0	/O	0.0

YEAR	TM/L	G	AB	R	H	2B	3B	HR	RBI	BB	SO	AVG	OBP	SLG	PRO	/A	BR	/A	PF	CHI	RC	TA	SB	CS	SBR	FR	POS	TPR
Total	8	567	1611	257	433	64	19	32	138	304	290	.269	.387	.392	.779	113	33	39	97	75	268	.798	12	18		-7	O/1	1.3
■ **JOE ABREU** Abreu, Joseph Lawrence b: 5/24/16, Oakland, Cal. BR/TR, 5'8", 160 lbs. Deb: 4/23/42																												
1942	Cin-N	9	28	4	6	1	0	1	3	4	4	.214	.313	.357	.670	95	-0	-0	101	86	3	.609	0			-0	/32	0.0
■ **BILL ABSTEIN** Abstein, William Henry "Big Bill" b: 2/2/1883, St.Louis, Mo. d: 4/8/40, St.Louis, Mo. BR/TR, 6', 185 lbs. Deb: 9/25/06																												
1906	Pit-N	8	20	2	4	0	0	0	3	0		.200	.200	.200	.400	25	-2	-2	104	274	1	.375	2			0	/2O	-0.1
1909	Pit-N	137	512	51	133	20	10	1	70	27		.260	.302	.344	.646	97	-1	-4	105	145	56	.588	16			-5	*1	-1.2
1910	StL-A	25	87	1	13	2	0	0	3	2		.149	.169	.172	.341	7	-9	-9	94	75	3	.270	3			-0	1	-0.9
Total	3	170	619	54	150	22	10	1	76	29		.242	.281	.315	.596	83	-12	-14	103	140	60	.531	21			-6	1/2O	-2.2
■ **MERITO ACOSTA** Acosta, Balmodero Pedro b: 5/19/1896, Havana, Cuba d: 11/17/63, Miami, Fla. BL/TL, 5'7", 140 lbs. Deb: 6/15/13																												
1913	Was-A	12	20	3	6	0	1	0	1	4	2	.300	.417	.400	.817	131	1	1	106	44	4	1.000	2			-3	/O	-0.2
1914	Was-A	38	74	10	19	2	2	0	4	11	18	.257	.353	.338	.691	107	1	1	101	60	8	.661	3	4	-2	-2	O	-0.3
1915	Was-A	72	163	20	34	4	1	0	18	28	15	.209	.338	.245	.584	74	-4	-4	101	153	17	.602	8	4	0	-6	O	-1.2
1916	Was-A	5	8	0	1	0	0	0	0	2	0	.125	.300	.125	.425	28	-1	-1	100	0	0	.429	0			1	/O	0.0
1918	Was-A	3	2	0	0	0	0	0	0	0	1	.000	.000	.000	.000	-96	-0	-0	104	0	0	.000	0			0	H	0.0
	Phi-A	49	169	23	51	3	3	0	14	18	10	.302	.369	.355	.724	114	4	3	104	90	24	.695	4			-2	O	-0.1
	Yr	52	171	23	51	3	3	0	14	18	11	.298	.365	.351	.716	111	4	3	104	85	24	.683	4			-2		-0.1
Total	5	179	436	56	111	9	7	0	37	63	46	.255	.354	.307	.661	96	2	0	102	105	53	.655	17	8		-12	O	-1.8
■ **JIMMY ADAIR** Adair, James Aubrey "Choppy" b: 1/25/07, Waxahachie, Tex. d: 12/9/82, Dallas, Tex. BR/TR, 5'10.5", 154 lbs. Deb: 8/24/31 C																												
1931	Chi-N	18	76	9	21	3	1	0	3	1	8	.276	.286	.342	.628	71	-4	-3	96	44	7	.509	1			-0	S	-0.1
■ **JERRY ADAIR** Adair, Kenneth Jerry b: 12/17/36, Sand Springs, Okla. d: 5/31/87, Tulsa, Okla. BR/TR, 6', 175 lbs. Deb: 9/02/58 C																												
1958	Bal-A	11	19	1	2	0	0	0	0	1	7	.105	.150	.105	.255	-30	-3	-3	94	0	0	.176	0	0	0	-1	S/2	-0.2
1959	Bal-A	12	35	3	11	0	1	0	2	1	5	.314	.333	.371	.705	96	-0	-0	97	61	4	.583	0	0	0	1	2/S	0.1
1960	Bal-A	3	5	1	1	0	0	1	1	0	0	.200	.200	.800	1.000	154	0	0	102	56	1	1.000	0	0	0	0	/2	0.1
1961	Bal-A	133	386	41	102	21	1	9	37	35	51	.264	.329	.394	.722	95	-5	-3	97	81	51	.664	5	2	0	5	*2S/3	1.7
1962	Bal-A	139	538	67	153	29	4	11	48	27	77	.284	.321	.414	.735	102	-4	-0	95	79	66	.636	7	7	-2	-2	*S2/3	0.5
1963	Bal-A	109	382	34	87	21	3	6	30	9	51	.228	.249	.346	.595	69	-19	-16	94	84	27	.463	3	3	-1	0	*2	-0.9
1964	Bal-A	155	569	56	141	20	3	9	47	28	72	.248	.284	.341	.625	69	-21	-25	105	92	50	.502	3	2	-0	5	*2	-0.3
1965	Bal-A	157	582	51	151	26	3	7	66	35	65	.259	.304	.351	.654	85	-12	-12	100	124	55	.536	6	4	-1	13	*2	1.0
1966	Bal-A	17	52	3	15	1	0	0	3	4	8	.288	.339	.308	.647	87	-1	-1	101	79	6	.526	0	0	0	0	2	0.0
	Chi-A	105	370	27	90	18	2	4	36	17	44	.243	.278	.335	.613	80	-12	-10	94	113	31	.490	3	2	-0	5	S2	0.4
	Yr	122	422	30	105	19	2	4	39	21	52	.249	.286	.332	.618	81	-13	-11	95	109	38	.495	3	2	-0	5		0.4
1967	Chi-A	28	98	6	20	4	0	0	9	4	17	.204	.243	.245	.488	47	-7	-6	94	159	5	.345	0	1	-1	0	2	-0.6
	Bos-A	89	316	41	92	13	1	3	26	13	35	.291	.323	.367	.690	90	1	-4	115	88	34	.555	1	4	-2	-4	3S2	-0.7
	Yr	117	414	47	112	17	1	3	35	17	52	.271	.304	.338	.642	82	-6	-10	110	107	40	.508	1	5	-3	-4		-1.3
1968	Bos-A	74	208	18	45	1	0	2	12	9	28	.216	.252	.250	.502	52	-12	-12	101	89	11	.358	0	0	0	0	S2/31	-0.8
1969	KC-A	126	432	29	108	9	1	5	48	20	36	.250	.288	.310	.598	65	-19	-21	103	129	32	.450	1	3	-2	-28	*2/S3	-4.8
1970	KC-A	7	27	0	4	0	0	0	1	5	3	.148	.281	.148	.429	22	-3	-3	98	87	1	.360	0	1	-1	-0	/2	-0.2
Total	13	1165	4019	378	1022	163	19	57	366	208	499	.254	.294	.347	.641	79	-117	-115	100	99	376	.544	29	29	-9	-5	2S/31	-4.7
■ **SPARKY ADAMS** Adams, Earl John b: 8/26/1894, Newtown, Pa. BR/TR, 5'5.5", 151 lbs. Deb: 9/18/22																												
1922	Chi-N	11	44	5	11	0	1	0	3	4	3	.250	.313	.295	.608	61	-3	-2	95	77	4	.514	1	2	-1	0	2	-0.2
1923	Chi-N	95	311	40	90	12	0	4	35	26	10	.289	.346	.367	.713	84	-5	-7	104	98	37	.671	20	19	-5	-8	S/O	-1.2
1924	Chi-N	117	418	66	117	11	5	1	27	40	20	.280	.344	.337	.682	82	-9	-9	101	70	48	.619	15	17	-6	-3	S2	-1.0
1925	Chi-N	149	627	95	180	29	8	2	48	44	15	.287	.341	.368	.709	83	-17	-15	97	64	80	.671	26	12	1	**25**	*2/S	0.9
1926	Chi-N	154	624	95	193	35	3	0	39	52	27	.309	.367	.375	.742	94	2	-4	106	51	86	.738	27			**24**	*23/S	2.7
1927	Chi-N	146	647	100	189	17	7	0	49	42	26	.292	.335	.340	.675	81	-17	-17	100	67	73	.629	26			7	23S	-0.3
1928	Pit-N	135	539	91	149	14	6	0	38	64	18	.276	.357	.325	.682	74	-14	-19	107	68	65	.644	8			-10	*2S/O	-2.3
1929	Pit-N	74	196	37	51	8	1	0	11	15	5	.260	.316	.311	.627	54	-13	-14	103	62	19	.552	3			-4	S23/O	-1.0
1930	StL-N	137	570	98	179	36	9	0	55	45	27	.314	.365	.409	.774	83	-11	-16	105	78	84	.731	7			-6	*32/S	-1.4
1931	StL-N	143	608	97	178	**46**	5	1	40	42	24	.293	.340	.390	.730	90	-4	-9	107	52	83	.691	16			-9	*3/S	-0.7
1932	StL-N	31	127	22	35	3	1	0	13	14	5	.276	.352	.315	.667	81	-3	-3	100	107	15	.598	0			-1	3	0.0
1933	StL-N	8	30	1	5	1	0	0	0	1	3	.167	.219	.200	.419	20	-3	-3	102	0	1	.296	0			0	/S3	-0.2
	Cin-N	137	538	59	141	21	1	1	22	44	30	.262	.320	.310	.631	82	-12	-11	99	43	56	.531	3			-3	*3/S	-1.0
	Yr	145	568	60	146	22	1	1	22	45	33	.257	.315	.305	.620	79	-15	-15	99	41	58	.519	3			-3		-1.2
1934	Cin-N	87	278	38	70	16	1	0	14	20	10	.252	.307	.317	.623	67	-13	-13	101	57	29	.533	2			-2	32	-0.8
Total	13	1424	5557	844	1588	249	48	9	394	453	223	.286	.343	.353	.695	82	-121	-142	103	64	679	.645	154	50		12	23S/O	-6.5
■ **BUSTER ADAMS** Adams, Elvin Clark b: 6/24/15, Trinidad, Col. BR/TR, 6', 180 lbs. Deb: 4/27/39																												
1939	StL-N	2	1	1	0	0	0	0	0	0	0	.000	.000	.000	.000	-95	-0	-0	105	0	0	.000	0			0	H	0.0
1943	StL-N	8	11	1	1	1	0	0	1	4	4	.091	.333	.182	.515	48	-1	-1	105	180	1	.600	0			-1	/O	-0.1
	Phi-N	111	418	48	107	14	7	4	38	39	67	.256	.319	.352	.671	100	-4	-1	94	91	48	.589	2			-1	*O	-0.5
	Yr	119	429	49	108	15	7	4	39	43	71	.252	.320	.347	.667	98	-4	-1	94	99	49	.590	2			-2		-0.6
1944	Phi-N	151	584	86	165	35	3	17	64	74	74	.283	.370	.440	.810	127	22	22	100	66	99	.791	2			5	*O	1.5
1945	Phi-N	14	56	6	13	3	1	2	8	5	5	.232	.295	.429	.724	103	-0	-0	96	89	7	.644	0			-2	O	-0.2
	StL-N	140	578	98	169	26	0	20	101	57	75	.292	.359	.441	.800	122	16	16	100	107	94	.763	3			-5	*O	0.4
	Yr	154	634	104	182	29	1	22	109	62	80	.287	.353	.440	.793	120	15	16	100	106	101	.754	3			-7		0.2
1946	StL-N	81	173	21	32	6	0	5	22	29	27	.185	.312	.306	.619	71	-5	-7	107	121	19	.611	3			-8	O	-1.6
1947	Phi-N	69	182	21	45	11	1	2	15	26	29	.247	.341	.352	.693	84	-4	-4	100	79	23	.657	2			-5	O	-0.9
Total	6	576	2003	282	532	96	12	50	249	234	281	.266	.346	.400	.747	110	24	26	99	90	290	.720	12			-16	O	-1.4
■ **GEORGE ADAMS** Adams, George b: Grafton, Mass. Deb: 6/14/1879																												
1879	Syr-N	4	13	0	3	0	0	0	0	1	1	.231	.286	.231	.516	82	-0	-0	89	0	1	.400				0	/O1	0.0
■ **GLENN ADAMS** Adams, Glenn Charles b: 10/4/47, Northbridge, Mass. BL/TR, 6'1", 180 lbs. Deb: 5/04/75																												
1975	SF-N	61	90	10	27	2	1	4	15	11	25	.300	.382	.478	.860	135	5	4	102	105	17	.875	1	0	0	-4	O	0.0
1976	SF-N	69	74	2	18	4	0	0	3	1	12	.243	.253	.297	.551	54	-4	-5	103	52	5	.400	1	0	0	-2	/O	-0.6
1977	Min-A	95	269	32	91	17	0	6	49	18	30	.338	.380	.468	.848	126	11	10	103	135	46	.778	0	2	-1	-5	DO	0.2
1978	Min-A	116	310	27	80	18	1	7	35	17	32	.258	.297	.390	.687	97	-4	-2	94	97	33	.573	0	1	-1	-1	*D/O	-0.3
1979	Min-A	119	326	34	98	13	1	8	49	25	27	.301	.356	.420	.776	100	4	0	109	117	50	.717	2	2	-1	-10	DO	-1.2
1980	Min-A	99	262	32	75	11	2	6	38	15	26	.286	.325	.412	.737	93	-0	-3	109	118	31	.619	2	4	-2	-2	DO	-0.6
1981	Min-A	72	220	13	46	10	0	2	24	20	26	.209	.275	.282	.557	58	-11	-12	105	138	15	.443	0	1	-1	0	D	-1.3
1982	Tor-A	30	66	2	17	4	0	1	11	4	5	.258	.300	.364	.664	75	-2	-2	109	163	7	.538	0	0	0	0	D	-0.1
Total	8	661	1617	152	452	79	5	34	224	111	183	.280	.327	.398	.725	96	-2	-11	104	118	204	.649	6	10	-4	-25	DO	-3.9
■ **DOUG ADAMS** Adams, Harold Douglas b: 1/27/43, Blue River, Wis. BL/TR, 6'3", 185 lbs. Deb: 9/08/69																												
1969	Chi-A	8	14	1	3	0	0	0	1	1	3	.214	.267	.214	.481	33	-1	-1	108	134	1	.333	0	0	0	0	/C	0.0
■ **HERB ADAMS** Adams, Herbert Loren b: 4/14/28, Hollywood, Cal. BL/TL, 5'9", 160 lbs. Deb: 9/17/48																												
1948	Chi-A	5	11	1	3	1	0	0	0	1	1	.273	.333	.364	.697	89	-0	-0	95	0	2	.625	0	0	0	2	/O	0.1
1949	Chi-A	56	208	26	61	5	3	0	16	9	16	.293	.323	.346	.669	79	-7	-7	98	78	23	.539	1	2	-1	1	O	-0.7
1950	Chi-A	34	118	12	24	2	3	0	2	12	7	.203	.288	.271	.559	45	-10	-10	97	22	10	.510	3	0	1	2	O	-0.6
Total	3	95	337	39	88	8	6	0	18	22	24	.261	.310	.320	.631	67	-18	-17	97	55	35	.538	4	2	0	4	/O	-1.2
■ **JIM ADAMS** Adams, James J. b: 1868, E.St.Louis, Ill. TR , Deb: 4/21/1890																												
1890	StL-a	1	4	0	1	0	0	0		0		.250	.250	.250	.500	42	-0	-0	116	0	0	.333	0			0	/C	0.0

YEAR	TM/L	G	AB	R	H	2B	3B	HR	RBI	BB	SO	AVG	OBP	SLG	PRO	/A	BR	/A	PF	CHI	RC	TA	SB	CS	SBR	FR	POS	TPR
■ BERT ADAMS	Adams, John Bertram b: 6/21/1891, Wharton, Tex. d: 6/24/40, Los Angeles, Cal. BB/TR, 6'1", 185 lbs. Deb: 8/30/10																											
1910	Cle-A	5	13	1	3	0	0	0	0	0		.231	.231	.231	.462	45	-1	-1	100	0	1	.300	0			-0	/C	0.0
1911	Cle-A	2	5	0	1	0	0	0	0	1		.200	.333	.200	.533	49	-0	-0	103	0	0	.500	0			0	/C	0.0
1912	Cle-A	20	54	5	11	2	1	0	6	4		.204	.259	.278	.536	53	-3	-3	101	133	4	.442	0			1	C	0.0
1915	Phi-N	24	27	1	3	0	0	0	2	2	3	.111	.172	.111	.284	-13	-4	-4	107	255	1	.208	0			-1	C/1	-0.3
1916	Phi-N	11	13	2	3	0	0	0	1	0	3	.231	.231	.231	.462	44	-1	-1	96	132	1	.300	0			-0	C	0.0
1917	Phi-N	43	107	4	22	4	1	1	7	0	20	.206	.206	.290	.495	47	-7	-7	108	79	6	.365	0			1	C/1	-0.4
1918	Phi-N	84	227	10	40	4	0	0	12	10	26	.176	.214	.194	.408	23	-20	-22	109	103	11	.321	5			-4	C	-2.2
1919	Phi-N	78	232	14	54	7	2	1	17	6	27	.233	.252	.293	.545	61	-11	-12	104	93	17	.438	4			3	C/1	-0.3
Total	8	267	678	37	137	17	4	2	45	23	79	.202	.229	.248	.477	42	-46	-51	106	103	40	.372	9			1	C/1	-3.2
■ DICK ADAMS	Adams, Richard Leroy b: 4/8/20, Tuolomne, Cal. BR/TL, 6', 185 lbs. Deb: 5/20/47																											
1947	Phi-A	37	89	9	18	2	3	2	11	2	18	.202	.220	.360	.579	59	-6	-6	100	106	7	.479	0	0	0	-1	1/O	-0.7
■ RICKY ADAMS	Adams, Ricky Lee b: 1/21/59, Upland, Cal. BR/TR, 6'2", 180 lbs. Deb: 9/15/82																											
1982	Cal-A	8	14	1	2	0	0	0	0	0	2	.143	.200	.143	.343	-4	-2	-2	100	0	0	.308	1	0	0	0	/S	0.0
1983	Cal-A	58	112	22	28	2	0	2	6	5	12	.250	.300	.321	.621	74	-4	-4	96	56	11	.517	1	1	-0	6	S3/2	0.5
1985	SF-N	54	121	12	23	3	1	2	10	5	23	.190	.228	.281	.509	45	-10	-9	93	100	7	.406	1	1	-0	-0	S3/2	-0.7
Total	3	120	247	35	53	5	1	4	16	10	37	.215	.260	.291	.551	55	-16	-14	95	74	19	.455	3	2	-0	7	/S32	-0.2
■ BOBBY ADAMS	Adams, Robert Henry b: 12/14/21, Tuolumne, Cal. BR/TR, 5'10.5", 160 lbs. Deb: 4/16/46 C																											
1946	Cin-N	94	311	35	76	13	3	4	24	18	32	.244	.292	.344	.636	77	-9	-10	104	75	31	.595	16			18	2/O3	1.1
1947	Cin-N	81	217	39	59	11	2	4	20	25	23	.272	.358	.396	.754	110	0	3	91	76	33	.775	9			-1	2	0.9
1948	Cin-N	87	262	33	78	20	3	1	21	25	23	.298	.361	.408	.770	104	3	2	103	72	39	.735	6			-3	2/3	0.3
1949	Cin-N	107	277	32	70	16	2	0	25	26	36	.253	.317	.325	.642	76	-11	-9	96	105	29	.563	4			-4	23	-0.9
1950	Cin-N	115	348	57	98	21	8	3	25	43	29	.282	.361	.414	.774	99	2	-0	105	63	55	.770	7			-1	23	0.0
1951	Cin-N	125	403	57	107	12	5	5	24	43	40	.266	.338	.357	.695	87	-7	-7	101	58	49	.615	4	10	-5	-1	32/O	-1.1
1952	Cin-N	154	637	85	180	25	4	6	48	49	67	.283	.334	.363	.696	93	-6	-6	100	66	77	.605	11	9	-2	8	*3	0.5
1953	Cin-N	150	607	99	167	14	6	8	49	58	67	.275	.338	.357	.696	82	-15	-15	99	70	78	.619	3	2	-0	8	*3	-1.0
1954	Cin-N	110	390	69	105	25	6	3	23	55	46	.269	.364	.387	.751	92	-1	-3	104	58	58	.718	2	5	-2	5	3/2	0.0
1955	Cin-N	64	150	23	41	11	2	2	20	20	21	.273	.370	.413	.783	102	2	1	106	119	24	.777	2	0	1	-0	3/2	0.1
	Chi-A	28	21	8	2	0	1	0	3	4	4	.095	.240	.190	.430	17	-3	-3	101	280	1	.421	0	0	0	-0	/32	-0.2
1956	Bal-A	41	111	19	25	6	1	0	7	25	15	.225	.368	.297	.665	82	-3	-2	94	79	15	.670	1	1	-0	-3	32	-0.2
1957	Chi-N	60	187	21	47	10	2	1	10	17	28	.251	.320	.342	.663	81	-6	-5	96	62	21	.572	0	3	-2	-4	3/2	-0.9
1958	Chi-N	62	96	14	27	4	4	0	4	6	15	.281	.324	.406	.730	91	-1	-1	101	42	13	.662	2	0	1	1	1/32	0.0
1959	Chi-N	3	2	0	0	0	0	0	0	0	1	.000	.000	.000	.000	-99	-1	-1	98	0	0	.000	0	0	0	0	/1	0.0
Total	14	1281	4019	591	1082	188	49	37	303	414	447	.269	.340	.368	.708	90	-54	-55	100	72	523	.666	67	30		22	32/1O	-1.4
■ BOB ADAMS	Adams, Robert Melvin b: 1/6/52, Pittsburgh, Pa. BR/TR, 6'2", 200 lbs. Deb: 7/10/77																											
1977	Det-A	15	24	2	6	1	0	2	2	0	5	.250	.250	.542	.792	104	0	-0	105	42	3	.722	0	0	0	0	/1C	0.0
■ MIKE ADAMS	Adams, Robert Michael b: 7/24/48, Cincinnati, Ohio BR/TR, 5'9", 180 lbs. Deb: 9/10/72																											
1972	Min-A	3	6	0	2	0	0	0	0	0	1	.333	.333	.333	.667	92	-0	-0	107	0	1	.500	0	0	0	-0	/O	0.0
1973	Min-A	55	66	21	14	2	0	3	6	17	18	.212	.381	.379	.760	110	2	2	104	69	11	.818	2	1	0	-2	O/D	0.0
1976	Chi-N	25	29	1	4	2	0	0	2	8	7	.138	.342	.207	.549	53	-1	-2	109	128	3	.600	0	0	0	-1	/O32	-0.2
1977	Chi-N	2	2	0	0	0	0	0	0	0	1	.000	.000	.000	.000	-88	-1	-1	114	0	0	.000	0	0	0	-1	/O	-0.1
1978	Oak-A	15	15	5	3	1	0	0	1	7	2	.200	.455	.267	.721	107	1	1	101	99	3	.917	0	0	0	-1	/23D	0.0
Total	5	100	118	27	23	5	0	3	9	32	29	.195	.375	.314	.689	92	1	0	105	85	17	.760	2	1	0	-4	/O23D	-0.3
■ SPENCER ADAMS	Adams, Spencer Dewey b: 6/21/1898, Layton, Utah d: 11/24/70, Salt Lake City, Ut BL/TR, 5'9", 158 lbs. Deb: 5/08/23																											
1923	Pit-N	25	56	11	14	0	1	0	4	6	6	.250	.323	.286	.608	64	-3	-3	97	88	5	.558	2	1	0	-0	2/S	-0.1
1925	Was-A	39	55	11	15	4	1	0	4	5	4	.273	.333	.382	.715	83	-2	-2	98	64	7	.659	1	1	-0	0	2/S3	0.0
1926	NY-A	28	25	7	3	1	0	0	1	3	7	.120	.214	.160	.374	-1	-4	-4	99	85	1	.364	1	0	0	-1	/23	-0.3
1927	StL-A	88	259	32	69	11	3	0	29	24	33	.266	.333	.332	.665	69	-10	-12	106	112	29	.595	1	0	0	2	23	-0.5
Total	4	180	395	61	101	16	5	0	38	38	50	.256	.324	.322	.646	66	-18	-20	103	100	43	.581	5	2	0	1	/23S	-0.9
■ JOE ADCOCK	Adcock, Joseph Wilbur b: 10/30/27, Coushatta, La. BR/TR, 6'4", 210 lbs. Deb: 4/23/50 M																											
1950	Cin-N	102	372	46	109	16	1	8	55	24	24	.293	.336	.406	.742	90	-4	-6	105	124	48	.644	2			4	O1	-0.4
1951	Cin-N	113	395	40	96	16	4	10	47	24	29	.243	.288	.380	.668	78	-13	-14	101	103	36	.540	1	2	-1	-0	*O	-1.8
1952	Cin-N	117	378	43	105	22	4	13	52	23	38	.278	.321	.460	.781	115	6	6	100	95	53	.693	1	4	-2	-9	O1	-0.8
1953	Mil-N	157	590	71	168	33	6	18	80	42	82	.285	.334	.453	.787	109	1	6	94	103	85	.704	3	2	-0	-4	*1	0.0
1954	Mil-N	133	500	73	154	27	5	23	87	44	58	.308	.367	.520	.887	137	19	24	93	110	95	.863	1	4	-2	-8	*1	0.8
1955	Mil-N	84	288	40	76	14	0	15	45	31	44	.264	.340	.469	.808	120	4	7	93	103	42	.740	0	2	-1	-2	1	0.0
1956	Mil-N	137	454	76	132	23	1	38	103	32	86	.291	.339	.597	.936	147	26	27	99	113	88	.916	1	0	-0	-0	*1	2.1
1957	Mil-N	65	209	31	60	13	2	12	38	20	51	.287	.352	.541	.893	150	10	12	90	106	38	.859	0	0	0	-0	1	0.7
1958	Mil-N	105	320	40	88	15	1	19	54	21	63	.275	.322	.506	.828	129	5	10	89	102	47	.748	0	0	0	1	1O	0.5
1959	Mil-N	115	404	53	118	19	2	25	76	32	77	.292	.344	.535	.879	137	16	18	95	108	73	.844	0	0	0	5	1O	1.6
1960	Mil-N	138	514	55	153	21	4	25	91	46	86	.298	.357	.500	.857	145	21	27	91	118	89	.814	2	2	-1	1	*1	2.1
1961	Mil-N	152	562	77	160	20	0	35	108	59	94	.285	.355	.507	.862	136	19	26	92	114	96	.819	2	1	0	-4	*1	1.3
1962	Mil-N	121	391	48	97	12	1	29	78	50	91	.248	.335	.506	.841	123	11	12	99	108	62	.804	2	0	1	-2	*1	0.7
1963	Cle-A	97	283	28	71	7	1	13	49	30	53	.251	.323	.420	.743	110	2	3	97	130	37	.679	1	2	-1	-3	1	-0.2
1964	LA-A	118	366	39	98	13	0	21	64	48	61	.268	.353	.475	.828	144	14	19	89	114	59	.784	0	2	-1	-0	*1	1.5
1965	Cal-A	122	349	30	84	14	0	14	47	37	74	.241	.315	.401	.716	104	1	2	98	107	43	.650	2	2	-1	0	1	-0.3
1966	Cal-A	83	231	33	63	10	3	18	48	31	48	.273	.359	.576	.935	165	19	19	99	108	43	.917	2	2	-1	0	1	1.7
Total	17	1959	6606	823	1832	295	35	336	1122	594	1059	.277	.339	.485	.824	125	158	198	95	110	1033	.798	20	25		-21	*1O	9.5
■ BOB ADDIS	Addis, Robert Gordon b: 11/6/25, Mineral, Ohio BL/TR, 6', 175 lbs. Deb: 9/01/50																											
1950	Bos-N	16	28	7	7	1	0	0	2	3	5	.250	.323	.286	.608	71	-1	-1	86	96	3	.571	1			-2	/O	-0.2
1951	Bos-N	85	199	23	55	7	0	1	24	9	10	.276	.308	.327	.634	72	-8	-8	98	136	20	.513	3	2	-0	-0	O	-0.9
1952	Chi-N	93	292	38	86	13	2	1	20	23	30	.295	.346	.363	.709	94	-1	-2	103	72	37	.619	4	4	-1	2	O	-0.3
1953	Chi-N	10	12	2	2	1	0	0	1	2	0	.167	.286	.250	.536	40	-1	-1	103	130	1	.500	0	0	0	1	/O	0.0
	Pit-N	4	3	0	0	0	0	0	0	0	2	.000	.000	.000	.000	-98	-1	-1	102	0	0	.000	0	0	0	0	H	0.0
	Yr	14	15	2	2	1	0	0	1	2	2	.133	.235	.200	.435	15	-2	-2	103	102	1	.385	0	0	0	1		0.0
Total	4	208	534	70	150	22	2	2	47	37	47	.281	.327	.341	.668	82	-13	-13	100	98	61	.582	8	6		1	O	-1.4
■ JIM ADDUCI	Adduci, James David b: 8/9/59, Chicago, Ill. BL/TR, 6'4", 200 lbs. Deb: 9/12/83																											
1983	StL-N	10	20	0	1	0	0	0	0	1	6	.050	.095	.050	.145	-60	-4	-4	98	0	0	.105	0	0	0	-0	/1O	-0.4
1986	Mil-A	3	11	2	1	1	0	0	0	1	2	.091	.167	.182	.348	-5	-2	-2	102	0	0	.300	0	0	0	-0	/1	-0.1
1988	Mil-A	44	94	8	25	6	1	1	15	0	15	.266	.266	.383	.649	77	-3	-3	103	153	9	.507	0	1	-1	-4	OD/1	-0.8
Total	3	57	125	10	27	7	1	1	15	2	23	.216	.228	.312	.540	48	-9	-9	102	113	9	.410	0	1	-1	-5	/O1D	-1.3
■ BOB ADDY	Addy, Robert Edward "Magnet" b: 1838, Rochester, N.Y. d: 4/10/10, Pocatello, Idaho BL/TL, 5'8", 160 lbs. Deb: 5/06/1871 M																											
1871	Rok-n	25	122	29	31							.254															*2/S	
1873	Phi-n	10	56	12	16							.286															2/M	
	Bos-n	31	162	37	55							.340															*O	
	Yr	41	218	49	71							.326																
1874	Har-n	50	208	26	55							.264															*2/3S	
1875	Phi-n	69	308	60	81							.263															*O/2	
1876	Chi-N	32	142	36	40	4	1	0	16	5	0	.282	.306	.324	.630	88	2	-4	125	120	14	.500				-0	O	-0.3

YEAR	TM/L	G	AB	R	H	2B	3B	HR	RBI	BB	SO	AVG	OBP	SLG	PRO	/A	BR	/A	PF	CHI	RC	TA	SB	CS	SBR	FR	POS	TPR
1877	Cin-N	57	245	27	68	2	3	0	31	6	5	.278	.295	.310	.605	111	-2	4	82	133	23	.463				4	*O/M	0.6
Total	4 n	185	856	164	238							.278															*O/M	
Total	2	89	387	63	108	6	4	0	47	11	5	.279	.299	.315	.614	100	-1	0	98	128	37	.477				4	O/23S	0.3
■ MORRIE ADERHOLT Aderholt, Morris Woodrow b: 9/13/15, Mt.Olive, N.C. d: 3/18/55, Sarasota, Fla. BL/TR, 6'1", 188 lbs. Deb: 9/13/39																												
1939	Was-A	7	25	5	5	0	0	1	4	2	6	.200	.259	.320	.579	52	-2	-2	90	123	2	.476	0	1	-1	1	/2	0.0
1940	Was-A	1	2	0	0	0	0	0	0	0	0	.000	.000	.000	.000	-99	-1	-1	93	0	0	.000	0	0	0	0	/2	0.0
1941	Was-A	11	14	3	2	0	0	0	1	1	3	.143	.200	.143	.343	-8	-2	-2	98	177	0	.250	0	0	0	0	/23	-0.1
1944	Bro-N	17	59	9	16	2	3	0	10	4	4	.271	.317	.407	.724	104	0	0	99	149	8	.651	0			-1	O	-0.1
1945	Bro-N	39	60	4	13	1	0	0	6	3	10	.217	.254	.233	.487	38	-5	-5	96	149	4	.362	0			-3	/O	-0.7
	Bos-N	31	102	15	34	4	0	2	11	9	6	.333	.387	.431	.819	113	4	2	112	76	18	.812	3			-1	O/2	0.0
	Yr	70	162	19	47	5	0	2	17	12	16	.290	.339	.358	.697	91	-1	-2	103	119	20	.629	3			-3		-0.7
Total	5	106	262	36	70	7	3	3	32	19	29	.267	.317	.351	.668	82	-6	-7	103	118	32	.588	3	1		-4	/O23	-0.9
■ DICK ADKINS Adkins, Richard Earl b: 3/3/20, Electra, Tex. d: 9/12/55, Electra, Tex. BR/TR, 5'10", 165 lbs. Deb: 9/19/42																												
1942	Phi-A	3	7	2	1	0	0	0	0	2	2	.143	.333	.143	.476	38	-0	-0	96	0	1	.500	0	0	0	0	/S	0.0
■ HENRY ADKINSON Adkinson, Henry Magee b: 9/1/1874, Chicago, Ill. d: 5/1/23, Salt Lake City, Ut. Deb: 9/25/1895																												
1895	StL-N	1	5	1	2	0	0	0	0	0	2	.400	.400	.400	.800	109	0	0	100	0	1	.667	0			0	/O	0.0
■ DAVE ADLESH Adlesh, David George b: 7/15/43, Long Beach, Cal. BR/TR, 6', 187 lbs. Deb: 5/12/63																												
1963	Hou-N	6	8	0	0	0	0	0	0	0	4	.000	.000	.000	.000	-99	-2	-2	92	0	0	.000	0	0	0	0	/C	-0.1
1964	Hou-N	3	10	0	2	0	0	0	0	0	5	.200	.200	.200	.400	14	-1	-1	96	0	0	.250	0	0	0	0	/C	0.0
1965	Hou-N	15	34	2	5	1	0	0	3	2	12	.147	.216	.176	.393	14	-4	-3	89	207	1	.300	0	0	0	1	C	-0.1
1966	Hou-N	3	6	0	0	0	0	0	0	0	4	.000	.000	.000	.000	-99	-2	-2	97	0	0	.000	0	0	0	0	/C	-0.1
1967	Hou-N	39	94	4	17	1	0	1	4	11	28	.181	.267	.223	.490	45	-7	-6	94	69	5	.386	0	0	0	1	C	-0.2
1968	Hou-N	40	104	3	19	1	1	0	4	5	27	.183	.227	.212	.439	33	-8	-8	99	77	5	.326	0	0	0	-2	C	-1.0
Total	6	106	256	9	43	3	1	1	11	18	80	.168	.228	.199	.427	27	-24	-23	95	85	12	.332	0	0	0	0	/C	-1.5
■ TROY AFENIR Afenir, Michael Troy b: 9/21/63, Escondido, Cal. BR/TR, 6'4", 185 lbs. Deb: 9/14/87																												
1987	Hou-N	10	20	1	6	1	0	0	1	0	12	.300	.300	.350	.650	77	-1	-1	93	57	2	.500	0	0	0	-1	C	0.0
■ TOMMIE AGEE Agee, Tommie Lee b: 8/9/42, Magnolia, Ala. BR/TR, 5'11", 195 lbs. Deb: 9/14/62																												
1962	Cle-A	5	14	0	3	0	0	0	2	0	4	.214	.214	.214	.429	16	-2	-2	98	265	1	.273	0	0	0	-0	/O	-0.1
1963	Cle-A	13	27	3	4	1	0	1	3	2	9	.148	.207	.296	.503	40	-2	-2	97	114	1	.417	0	0	0	-1	O	-0.3
1964	Cle-A	13	12	0	2	0	0	0	0	0	3	.167	.167	.167	.333	-7	-2	-2	103	0	0	.200	0	0	0	-3	O	-0.5
1965	Chi-A	10	19	2	3	1	0	0	3	2	6	.158	.238	.211	.449	31	-2	-2	92	311	1	.333	0	1	-1	-1	/O	-0.3
1966	Chi-A	160	629	98	172	27	8	22	86	41	127	.273	.328	.447	.775	127	15	19	94	100	88	.764	44	18	2	4	*O	2.1
1967	Chi-A	158	529	73	124	26	2	14	52	44	129	.234	.303	.371	.673	105	-2	2	94	93	58	.643	28	10	2	-4	*O	-0.4
1968	NY-N	132	368	30	80	12	3	5	17	15	103	.217	.256	.307	.563	67	-15	-15	102	56	27	.477	13	8	-1	-3	*O	-2.9
1969	NY-N	149	565	97	153	23	4	26	76	59	137	.271	.343	.464	.807	124	17	17	100	95	91	.789	12	9	-2	0	*O	0.7
1970	NY-N	153	636	107	182	30	7	24	75	55	156	.286	.345	.469	.813	111	12	9	104	69	101	.804	31	15	0	8	*O	1.1
1971	NY-N	113	425	58	121	19	0	14	50	50	84	.285	.363	.428	.791	128	13	15	96	96	68	.814	28	6	5	7	*O	2.5
1972	NY-N	114	422	52	96	23	0	13	47	53	92	.227	.319	.374	.694	101	-2	1	95	104	46	.632	8	9	-3	3	*O	-0.4
1973	Hou-N	83	204	30	48	5	2	8	15	16	55	.235	.294	.397	.691	95	-3	-2	95	57	22	.606	2	5	-2	-4	O	-1.1
	StL-N	26	62	8	11	3	1	3	7	5	13	.177	.239	.403	.642	83	-3	-2	91	83	3	.525	1	0	0	3	O	0.0
	Yr	109	266	38	59	8	3	11	22	21	68	.222	.281	.398	.680	92	-6	-4	94	64	27	.595	3	5	-2	-1		-1.1
Total	12	1129	3912	558	999	170	27	130	433	342	918	.255	.321	.412	.733	109	26	36	98	88	507	.718	167	81	2	9	*O	0.4
■ HARRY AGGANIS Agganis, Harry "The Golden Greek" b: 4/30/30, Lynn, Mass. d: 6/27/55, Cambridge, Mass. BL/TL, 6'2", 200 lbs. Deb: 4/13/54																												
1954	Bos-A	132	434	54	109	13	8	11	57	47	57	.251	.324	.394	.718	96	-3	-3	100	106	57	.671	6	3	0	3	*1	-0.3
1955	Bos-A	25	83	11	26	10	1	0	10	10	10	.313	.387	.458	.845	102	3	0	124	98	15	.833	2	0	1	0	1	0.0
Total	2	157	517	65	135	23	9	11	67	57	67	.261	.334	.404	.739	97	-0	-3	104	105	72	.706	8	3	1	3	1	-0.3
■ JOE AGLER Agler, Joseph Abram b: 6/12/1887, Coshocton, Ohio d: 4/26/71, Massillon, Ohio BL/TL, 5'11", 165 lbs. Deb: 10/01/12																												
1912	Was-A	2	1	0	0	0	0	0	0	0		.000	.000	.000	.000	-99	-0	-0	99	0	0	.000	0			0	H	0.0
1914	Buf-F	135	463	82	126	17	6	0	20	77	78	.272	.376	.335	.711	100	6	4	104	49	70	.751	21			3	1O	0.6
1915	Buf-F	25	73	11	13	1	2	0	2	20	0	.178	.355	.247	.601	80	-1	-1	100	41	7	.667	2			0	O/1	0.0
	Bal-F	72	214	28	46	4	2	0	14	34	0	.215	.323	.252	.575	66	-6	-8	107	93	23	.613	15			4	1/O2	-0.3
	Yr	97	287	39	59	5	4	0	16	54	0	.206	.331	.251	.582	70	-7	-9	105	80	30	.627	17			4		-0.3
Total	3	234	751	121	185	22	10	0	36	131	78	.246	.358	.302	.661	89	-1	-5	105	61	100	.700	38			7	1/O2	0.3
■ SAM AGNEW Agnew, Samuel Lester "Slam" b: 4/12/1887, Farmington, Mo. d: 7/19/51, Sonoma, Cal. BR/TR, 5'11", 185 lbs. Deb: 4/10/13																												
1913	StL-A	105	307	27	64	9	5	2	24	20	49	.208	.272	.290	.562	68	-14	-13	95	90	26	.523	11			3	*C	-0.1
1914	StL-A	113	311	22	66	5	4	0	16	24	63	.212	.279	.254	.533	62	-15	-14	98	76	23	.466	10	8	-2	-5	*C	-1.4
1915	StL-A	104	295	18	60	4	2	0	19	12	36	.203	.247	.231	.477	45	-21	-20	96	95	18	.380	5	2	0	-2	*C	-1.4
1916	Bos-A	40	67	4	14	2	1	0	7	6	4	.209	.293	.269	.562	74	-2	-2	94	139	6	.491	0			-5	C	-0.5
1917	Bos-A	85	260	17	54	6	2	0	16	19	30	.208	.267	.246	.513	52	-14	-16	108	90	17	.422	2			-4	C	-1.4
1918	Bos-A	72	199	11	33	8	0	0	6	11	26	.166	.221	.206	.427	30	-17	-16	95	53	9	.331	0			-6	C	-1.7
1919	Was-A	42	98	6	23	7	0	0	10	10	8	.235	.312	.306	.618	75	-3	-3	98	121	10	.560	1			2	C	0.1
Total	7	561	1537	105	314	41	14	2	98	102	216	.204	.265	.253	.518	56	-87	-84	98	87	111	.442	29	10		-17	C	-6.4
■ LUIS AGUAYO Aguayo, Luis (Muriel) b: 3/13/59, Vega Baja, P.R. BR/TR, 5'9", 173 lbs. Deb: 4/19/80																												
1980	Phi-N	20	47	7	13	1	2	1	8	2	3	.277	.306	.447	.753	100	0	-0	107	132	6	.686	1	1	-0	2	2/S	0.3
1981	Phi-N	45	84	11	18	4	0	1	7	6	15	.214	.283	.298	.580	58	-4	-5	112	98	8	.515	1	0	0	0	2S/3	0.0
1982	Phi-N	50	56	11	15	1	2	3	7	5	7	.268	.339	.518	.857	146	2	3	94	72	9	.837	1	1	-0	1	2S/3	0.5
1983	Phi-N	2	4	1	1	0	0	0	0	1	2	.250	.400	.250	.650	83	-0	-0	101	0	1	.667	0	0	0	-0	/S	0.0
1984	Phi-N	58	72	15	20	4	0	3	11	8	16	.278	.350	.458	.808	123	2	2	102	103	12	.774	0	0	0	-1	32S	0.3
1985	Phi-N	91	165	27	46	7	3	6	21	22	26	.279	.383	.467	.850	134	9	8	102	88	29	.841	1	0	0	-2	S2/3	1.1
1986	Phi-N	62	133	17	28	6	1	4	13	8	26	.211	.271	.361	.632	70	-5	-6	104	86	13	.550	1	1	-0	-1	2S/3	-0.5
1987	Phi-N	94	209	25	43	9	1	12	21	15	56	.206	.275	.431	.706	80	-6	-7	104	66	24	.643	0	0	0	-2	S/23	0.0
1988	Phi-N	49	97	9	24	3	0	3	5	13	17	.247	.336	.371	.707	102	1	0	101	44	13	.680	2	0	1	-1	S3/2	0.2
	NY-A	50	140	12	35	4	0	3	8	7	33	.250	.291	.343	.633	80	-5	-4	96	56	13	.505	0	2	-1	1	32/S	-0.2
Total	9	521	1007	135	243	39	9	36	101	87	201	.241	.313	.405	.718	95	-5	-8	102	77	127	.673	7	5	-1	-4	S2/3	1.7
■ CHARLIE AHEARN Ahearn, Charles b: Troy, N.Y. Deb: 6/19/1880																												
1880	Tro-N	1	4	1	1	0	0	0	0	0	0	.250	.250	.250	.500	63	-0	-0	110	0	0	.333				0	/C	0.0
■ WILLIE AIKENS Aikens, Willie Mays b: 10/14/54, Seneca, S.C. BL/TR, 6'3", 220 lbs. Deb: 5/17/77																												
1977	Cal-A	42	91	5	18	4	0	0	6	10	23	.198	.277	.242	.519	45	-7	-6	95	108	6	.434	1	2	-1	0	1D	-0.7
1979	Cal-A	116	379	59	106	18	0	21	81	61	79	.280	.381	.493	.874	145	19	23	93	125	71	.874	1	3	-2	-3	1D	1.5
1980	KC-A	151	543	70	151	24	0	20	98	64	88	.278	.362	.433	.794	119	13	14	98	132	82	.740	1	0	0	-5	*1D	0.0
1981	KC-A	101	349	45	93	16	0	17	53	62	47	.266	.382	.458	.840	143	20	21	99	104	62	.843	0	0	0	-5	1	1.3
1982	KC-A	134	466	50	131	29	1	17	74	45	70	.281	.348	.457	.805	119	12	12	100	114	69	.735	0	1	-1	-0	*1	0.8
1983	KC-A	125	410	49	124	26	1	23	72	45	75	.302	.374	.539	.913	146	26	26	101	97	78	.887	0	0	0	-2	*1/D	1.8
1984	Tor-A	93	234	21	48	7	0	11	26	29	56	.205	.298	.376	.674	84	-5	-5	102	86	26	.620	0	0	0	0	D/1	-0.5
1985	Tor-A	12	20	2	4	1	0	1	5	3	6	.200	.304	.400	.704	90	-0	-0	101	180	2	.647	0	0	0	0	D	0.0
Total	8	774	2492	301	675	125	2	110	415	319	444	.271	.358	.455	.813	124	78	84	99	113	398	.808	3	6	-3	-16	1D	4.2
■ DAN AINGE Ainge, Daniel Ray b: 3/17/59, Eugene, Ore. BR/TR, 6'4", 175 lbs. Deb: 5/21/79																												
1979	Tor-A	87	308	26	73	7	1	2	19	12	58	.237	.270	.286	.556	48	-22	-23	103	79	23	.424	1	0	0	2	2	-1.5

YEAR	TM/L	G	AB	R	H	2B	3B	HR	RBI	BB	SO	AVG	OBP	SLG	PRO	/A	BR	/A	PF	CHI	RC	TA	SB	CS	SBR	FR	POS	TPR
1980	Tor-A	38	111	11	27	6	1	0	4	2	29	.243	.263	.315	.578	58	-7	-7	100	45	9	.471	3	0	1	3	O/32D	-0.2
1981	Tor-A	86	246	20	46	6	2	0	14	23	41	.187	.259	.228	.487	37	-18	-21	111	98	15	.419	8	5	-1	-5	3/SO2D	-2.7
Total	3	211	665	57	146	19	4	2	37	37	128	.220	.265	.269	.534	46	-46	-51	106	81	47	.439	12	5	1	0	/23OSD	-4.4
■ EDDIE AINSMITH	Ainsmith, Edward Wilbur "Dorf" b: 2/4/1892, Cambridge, Mass. d: 9/6/81, Ft.Lauderdale, Fla BR/TR, 5'11", 180 lbs. Deb: 8/09/10																											
1910	Was-A	33	104	4	20	1	2	0	9	6		.192	.236	.240	.477	49	-6	-6	101	133	6	.369	0			2	C	-0.1
1911	Was-A	61	149	12	33	2	3	0	14	10		.221	.275	.275	.550	56	-9	-9	97	115	12	.491	5			6	C	0.3
1912	Was-A	60	186	22	42	7	2	0	22	14		.226	.280	.285	.565	62	-10	-9	99	139	17	.493	4			9	C	0.6
1913	Was-A	84	229	26	49	4	4	2	20	12	41	.214	.262	.293	.555	59	-12	-13	106	97	20	.550	17			-6	C/P	-1.3
1914	Was-A	58	151	11	34	7	0	0	13	9	28	.225	.273	.272	.545	63	-7	-7	101	119	12	.484	8	5	-1	-1	C	-0.5
1915	Was-A	47	120	13	24	4	2	0	6	10	18	.200	.267	.267	.534	59	-6	-6	101	64	9	.500	7	4	-0	2	C	-0.1
1916	Was-A	51	100	11	17	4	0	0	8	8	14	.170	.231	.210	.441	33	-8	-8	100	136	7	.386	3			-2	C	-0.8
1917	Was-A	125	350	38	67	17	4	0	42	40	48	.191	.280	.263	.543	71	-14	-11	92	164	30	.534	16			8	*C	0.7
1918	Was-A	96	292	22	62	10	9	0	20	29	44	.212	.283	.308	.592	75	-8	-10	104	81	27	.543	6			-1	C	-0.2
1919	Det-A	114	364	42	99	17	12	3	32	45	30	.272	.354	.409	.763	122	7	10	93	73	54	.770	9			-2	*C	1.3
1920	Det-A	69	186	19	43	5	3	1	19	14	19	.231	.285	.306	.591	55	-12	-13	103	111	17	.514	4	3	-1	-5	C/1	-1.2
1921	Det-A	35	98	6	27	5	2	0	12	13	7	.276	.360	.367	.728	90	-2	-1	96	114	14	.704	1	0	0	-1	C	0.0
	StL-N	27	62	5	18	0	1	0	5	3	4	.290	.323	.323	.646	75	-2	-2	95	92	7	.523	0	0	0	-2	C/1	-0.1
1922	StL-N	119	379	46	111	14	4	13	59	28	43	.293	.343	.454	.797	103	1	0	101	98	58	.749	2	3	-1	-2	*C	0.0
1923	StL-N	82	263	22	56	11	6	3	34	22	19	.213	.276	.335	.611	67	-16	-12	90	123	26	.556	4	0	1	-7	C	-1.2
	Bro-N	2	10	0	2	0	0	0	2	0	0	.200	.200	.200	.400	6	-1	-1	98	304	0	.222	0	1	-1	1	/C	0.0
	Yr	84	273	22	58	11	6	3	36	22	19	.212	.274	.330	.603	65	-17	-13	90	129	26	.542	4	1	1	-6		-1.2
1924	NY-N	10	5	0	3	0	0	0	0	0	0	.600	.600	.600	1.200	244	1	1	91	0	2	1.500	0	0	0	-0	/C	0.1
Total	15	1073	3048	299	707	108	54	22	317	263	315	.232	.296	.324	.620	76	-105	-98	98	110	317	.573	86	16		-1	C/1P	-2.5
■ GEORGE AITON	Aiton, George Wilson b: 12/29/1890, Kingman, Kan. d: 8/16/76, Van Nuys, Cal. BB/TR, 5'11.5", 175 lbs. Deb: 6/29/12																											
1912	StL-A	10	17	1	4	0	0	0	1	4		.235	.381	.235	.616	78	-0	-0	99	83	1	.615	0			-0	/O	0.0
■ JOHN AKE	Ake, John Leckie b: 8/29/1861, Altoona, Pa. d: 5/11/1887, La Crosse, Wis. 6'1", 180 lbs. Deb: 5/12/1884																											
1884	Bal-a	13	52	1	10	0	1	0		0		.192	.208	.231	.438	45	-3	-3	99	0	3	.310				0	/3OS	-0.2
■ BILL AKERS	Akers, William G. "Bump" b: 12/25/04, Chattanooga, Tenn. d: 4/13/62, Chattanooga, Tenn. BR/TR, 5'11", 178 lbs. Deb: 9/08/29																											
1929	Det-A	24	83	15	22	4	1	1	9	10	9	.265	.351	.373	.725	89	-2	-1	97	92	12	.721	2	0	1	-4	S	-0.1
1930	Det-A	85	233	36	65	8	5	9	40	36	34	.279	.375	.472	.848	108	5	3	105	97	42	.873	5	5	-2	0	S3	0.7
1931	Det-A	29	66	5	13	2	2	0	3	7	6	.197	.274	.288	.562	46	-5	-5	104	52	5	.481	0	1	-1	-1	S/2	-0.4
1932	Bos-N	36	93	8	24	3	1	1	17	10	15	.258	.330	.344	.674	87	-2	-1	93	181	11	.609	0			-1	3/2S	0.0
Total	4	174	475	64	124	17	9	11	69	63	64	.261	.349	.404	.753	93	-4	-5	101	106	70	.737	7	6		-6	/S32	0.2
■ GUS ALBERTS	Alberts, Augustus Peter b: 1861, Reading, Pa. d: 5/7/12, Idaho Springs, Colo BR/TR, 5'6.5", 180 lbs. Deb: 5/01/1884																											
1884	Pit-a	2	5	1	1	0	0	0		0		.200	.200	.200	.400	34	-0	-0	97	0	0	.250				0	/S	0.0
	Was-U	4	16	4	4	0	0	0		4		.250	.400	.250	.650	128	1	1	97	0	2	.667	0			0	/S	0.1
1888	Cle-a	102	364	51	75	10	6	1	48	41		.206	.299	.275	.573	90	-3	-2	97	148	39	.602	26			1	S3	0.1
1891	CM-a	12	41	6	4	0	0	0	2	7	5	.098	.260	.098	.358	4	-5	-6	112	147	1	.378	1			0	3	-0.4
Total	3	120	426	62	84	10	6	1	50	52	5	.197	.298	.256	.554	80	-8	-7	99	140	42	.576	27			1	/3S	-0.2
■ BUTCH ALBERTS	Alberts, Francis Burt b: 5/4/50, Williamsport, Pa. BR/TR, 6'2", 205 lbs. Deb: 9/07/78																											
1978	Tor-A	6	18	1	5	1	0	0	0	0	2	.278	.278	.333	.611	71	-1	-1	100	0	2	.462	0	0	0	0	/D	0.0
■ JACK ALBRIGHT	Albright, Harold John b: 6/30/21, St.Petersburg, Fl BR/TR, 5'9", 175 lbs. Deb: 5/19/47																											
1947	Phi-N	41	99	9	23	4	0	2	5	10	11	.232	.303	.333	.636	69	-5	-5	100	47	10	.564	1			-1	S	-0.2
■ LUIS ALCARAZ	Alcaraz, Angel Luis (Acosta) b: 6/20/41, Humacao, P.R. BR/TR, 5'9", 165 lbs. Deb: 9/13/67																											
1967	LA-N	17	60	1	14	1	0	0	3	1	13	.233	.246	.250	.496	48	-4	-4	88	83	3	.354	1	1	-0	0	2	-0.2
1968	LA-N	41	106	4	16	1	0	2	5	9	23	.151	.217	.217	.434	34	-9	-8	91	73	5	.355	1	1	-0	0	23/S	-0.7
1969	KC-A	22	79	15	20	2	1	1	7	7	9	.253	.314	.342	.656	81	-2	-2	103	95	8	.557	0	0	0	-5	2/3S	-0.6
1970	KC-A	35	120	10	20	5	1	1	14	4	13	.167	.194	.250	.444	22	-13	-13	98	172	6	.333	0	0	0	-1	2	-1.0
Total	4	115	365	30	70	9	2	4	29	21	58	.192	.236	.260	.496	43	-28	-26	95	111	22	.395	2	2	-1	-6	/23S	-2.5
■ SCOTTY ALCOCK	Alcock, John Forbes b: 11/29/1885, Wooster, Ohio d: 1/30/73, Wooster, Ohio BR/TR, 5'9.5", 160 lbs. Deb: 4/19/14																											
1914	Chi-A	54	156	12	27	4	2	0	7	7	14	.173	.213	.224	.438	31	-13	-14	103	75	8	.359	4	2	0	-2	3/2	-1.6
■ MIKE ALDRETE	Aldrete, Michael Peter b: 1/29/61, Carmel, Cal. BL/TL, 5'11", 180 lbs. Deb: 5/28/86																											
1986	SF-N	84	216	27	54	18	3	2	25	33	34	.250	.355	.389	.743	109	2	3	96	111	31	.714	1	3	-2	-2	1O	-0.2
1987	SF-N	126	357	50	116	18	2	9	51	43	50	.325	.398	.462	.860	132	15	17	96	106	68	.866	6	0	2	-1	O1	1.3
1988	SF-N	139	389	44	104	15	0	3	50	56	65	.267	.360	.329	.689	105	2	4	94	146	47	.633	6	5	-1	-4	*O1	-0.4
Total	3	349	962	121	274	51	5	14	126	132	149	.285	.372	.392	.764	117	19	25	95	123	146	.742	13	8	-1	-7	O/1	0.7
■ CHUCK ALENO	Aleno, Charles b: 2/19/17, St.Louis, Mo. BR/TR, 6'1.5", 215 lbs. Deb: 5/15/41																											
1941	Cin-N	54	169	23	41	7	3	1	18	11	16	.243	.289	.337	.626	77	-6	-6	99	108	16	.538	3			3	3/1	-0.2
1942	Cin-N	7	14	1	2	1	0	0	0	3	3	.143	.294	.214	.508	49	-1	-1	101	0	1	.500	0			0	/32	0.0
1943	Cin-N	7	10	0	3	0	0	0	1	2	1	.300	.417	.300	.717	109	0	0	99	120	1	.714	0			-1	/O	0.0
1944	Cin-N	50	127	10	21	3	0	1	15	15	15	.165	.259	.213	.471	35	-11	-10	95	179	8	.394	0			-2	3/1S	-1.0
Total	4	118	320	34	67	11	3	2	34	31	35	.209	.281	.281	.563	61	-17	-16	98	132	26	.488	3			-0	/31SO2	-1.2
■ DALE ALEXANDER	Alexander, David Dale "Moose" b: 4/26/03, Greenville, Tenn. d: 3/2/79, Greeneville, Tenn. BR/TR, 6'3", 210 lbs. Deb: 4/16/29																											
1929	Det-A	155	626	110	**215**	43	15	25	137	56	63	.343	.397	.580	.977	153	43	45	97	113	140	1.010	5	9	-4	-4	*1	1.4
1930	Det-A	154	602	86	196	33	8	20	135	42	56	.326	.372	.507	.878	115	17	13	105	130	112	.864	6	5	-1	-6	*1	-1.0
1931	Det-A	135	517	75	168	47	3	3	87	64	35	.325	.401	.445	.846	118	18	16	104	127	93	.843	5	8	-3	-6	*1/O	-0.5
1932	Det-A	23	16	0	4	0	0	0	4	6	2	.250	.455	.250	.705	86	0	0	102	335	2	.833	0	0	0	0	/1	0.0
	Bos-A	101	376	58	140	27	3	8	56	55	19	.372	.454	.524	.978	157	32	33	97	90	91	1.066	4	5	-2	3	*1	2.2
	Yr	124	392	58	144	27	3	8	60	61	21	.367	.454	.513	.966	153	32	33	98	138	93	1.055	4	5	-2	3		2.2
1933	Bos-A	94	313	40	88	14	1	5	40	25	22	.281	.336	.380	.716	89	-5	-5	101	100	40	.642	0	1	-1	0	1	-1.0
Total	5	662	2450	369	811	164	30	61	459	248	197	.331	.394	.497	.891	128	105	101	101	117	478	.895	20	28	-11	-13	1/O	1.1
■ GARY ALEXANDER	Alexander, Gary Wayne b: 3/27/53, Los Angeles, Cal. BR/TR, 6'2", 195 lbs. Deb: 9/12/75																											
1975	SF-N	3	3	1	0	0	0	0	0	1	2	.000	.250	.000	.250	-26	-0	-0	102	0	0	.333	0	0	0	0	/C	0.0
1976	SF-N	23	73	12	13	1	1	2	7	10	16	.178	.277	.301	.578	62	-3	-4	103	96	7	.541	1	0	0	-2	C	-0.4
1977	SF-N	51	119	17	36	4	2	5	20	20	33	.303	.411	.496	.907	136	8	7	104	108	24	.944	3	1	0	-3	C/O	0.4
1978	Oak-A	58	174	18	36	6	1	10	22	22	66	.207	.299	.425	.725	101	-0	-0	101	84	19	.647	0	3	-2	1	D/OC1	-0.1
	Cle-A	90	324	39	76	14	3	17	62	35	100	.235	.311	.454	.765	121	4	7	93	126	47	.726	0	2	-1	-4	CD	0.4
	Yr	148	498	57	112	20	4	27	84	57	166	.225	.307	.444	.751	113	4	7	96	110	70	.712	0	5	-3	-3		0.3
1979	Cle-A	110	358	54	82	9	2	15	54	46	100	.229	.319	.391	.710	85	-5	-8	106	112	46	.670	4	2	0	-5	CD/O	-0.8
1980	Cle-A	76	178	22	40	7	1	5	31	17	52	.225	.292	.360	.652	76	-6	-6	102	153	15	.536	0	4	-2	-1	DC/O	-0.8
1981	Pit-N	21	47	6	10	4	1	1	6	3	12	.213	.260	.404	.664	90	-1	-1	96	107	5	.579	0	0	0	1	/1O	0.0
Total	7	432	1276	169	293	45	11	55	202	154	381	.230	.315	.411	.726	98	-4	-5	101	115	163	.695	8	12	-5	-12	CD/O1	-1.3
■ HUGH ALEXANDER	Alexander, Hugh b: 7/10/17, Buffalo, Mo. BR/TR, 6', 190 lbs. Deb: 8/15/37																											
1937	Cle-A	7	11	0	1	0	0	0	0	0	5	.091	.091	.091	.182	-55	-3	-3	98	0	0	.200	1	0	0	-1	/O	-0.2
■ MATT ALEXANDER	Alexander, Matthew b: 1/30/47, Shreveport, La. BB/TR, 5'11", 168 lbs. Deb: 8/23/73																											
1973	Chi-N	12	5	4	1	0	0	0	1	1	1	.200	.333	.200	.533	47	-0	-0	108	402	1	1.000	2	0	1	-1	/O	0.0
1974	Chi-N	45	54	15	11	2	1	0	0	12	12	.204	.358	.278	.636	80	-1	-1	100	0	6	.735	8	4	0	-3	3/O2	-0.3

YEAR	TM/L	G	AB	R	H	2B	3B	HR	RBI	BB	SO	AVG	OBP	SLG	PRO	/A	BR	/A	PF	CHI	RC	TA	SB	CS	SBR	FR	POS	TPR
1975	Oak-A	63	10	16	1	0	0	0	0	1	1	.100	.182	.100	.282	-20	-2	-1	93	0	-7	1.000	17	10	-1	-4	DO/23	-0.5
1976	Oak-A	61	30	16	1	0	0	0	0	0	5	.033	.033	.033	.067	-81	-7	-7	100	0	-2	.583	20	7	2	-7	OD	-1.2
1977	Oak-A	90	42	24	10	1	0	0	2	4	6	.238	.304	.262	.566	59	-2	-2	95	72	0	.891	26	14	-1	-10	OS/23D	-1.1
1978	Pit-N	7	0	2	0	0	0	0	0	0	0	—	—	—	—	—	0	0	105	—	0	4.000	4	1	1	0	R	0.1
1979	Pit-N	44	13	16	7	0	1	0	1	0	0	.538	.538	.692	1.231	221	2	2	106	44	7	3.143	13	1	3	-2	O/S	0.3
1980	Pit-N	37	3	13	1	1	0	0	0	0	0	.333	.333	.667	1.000	167	0	0	103	0	-5	2.400	10	3	1	-0	/O2	0.1
1981	Pit-N	15	11	5	4	0	0	0	0	0	1	.364	.364	.364	.727	111	0	0	96	0	1	.778	3	2	-0	-1	/O	-0.1
Total	9	374	168	111	36	4	2	0	4	18	26	.214	.294	.262	.556	57	-9	-9	99	34	1	.954	103	42	6	-27	/OD3S2	-2.7
■ **WALT ALEXANDER** Alexander, Walter Ernest b: 3/5/1891, Atlanta, Ga. d: 12/29/78, Fort Worth, Tex. BR/TR, 5'10.5", 165 lbs. Deb: 6/21/12																												
1912	StL-A	37	97	5	17	4	0	0	5	8		.175	.245	.216	.462	33	-9	-8	99	79	6	.387	1			1	C	-0.3
1913	StL-A	43	110	5	15	2	1	0	7	4	36	.136	.174	.173	.347	2	-14	-13	95	131	3	.263	1			1	C	-0.9
1915	StL-A	1	1	0	0	0	0	0	0	0	0	.000	.000	.000	.000	-99	-0	-0	96	0	0	.000	0			0	/C	0.0
	NY-A	25	68	7	17	4	0	1	5	13	16	.250	.370	.353	.723	118	2	2	98	63	10	.750	2	1	0	2	C	0.6
	Yr	26	69	7	17	4	0	1	5	13	16	.246	.366	.348	.714	116	2	2	98	60	10	.736	2	1	0	2		0.6
1916	NY-A	36	78	8	20	6	1	0	3	13	20	.256	.376	.359	.735	119	3	2	101	38	11	.741	0			3	C	0.7
1917	NY-A	20	51	1	7	2	1	0	4	4	11	.137	.200	.216	.416	25	-5	-5	107	130	3	.364	1			1	C	-0.2
Total	5	162	405	26	76	18	3	1	24	42	83	.188	.271	.254	.525	55	-23	-22	99	87	32	.467	5	1		7	C	-0.1
■ **NIN ALEXANDER** Alexander, William Henry b: 11/24/1858, Pana, Ill. d: 12/22/33, Pana, Ill. 5'4.5", 163 lbs. Deb: 6/07/1884																												
1884	KC-U	19	65	2	9	0	0	0		1		.138	.152	.138	.290	-2	-7	-5	87	0	1	.179	0			0	C/SO	-0.4
	StL-a	1	4	0	0	0	0	0		0		.000	.000	.000	.000	-91	-1	-1	110	0	0	.000				0	/CO	0.0
Total	1	20	69	2	9	0	0	0		1		.130	.143	.130	.273	-8	-7	-6	88	0	1	.167				0	/COS	-0.4
■ **LUIS ALICEA** Alicea, Luis Rene (De Jesus) b: 7/29/65, Santurce, P.R. BB/TR, 5'9", 165 lbs. Deb: 4/23/88																												
1988	StL-N	93	297	20	63	10	4	1	24	25	32	.212	.278	.283	.561	59	-15	-16	104	110	22	.453	1	1	-0	3	2	-1.1
■ **ANDY ALLANSON** Allanson, Andrew Neal b: 12/22/61, Richmond, Va. BR/TR, 6'5", 220 lbs. Deb: 4/07/86																												
1986	Cle-A	101	293	30	66	7	3	1	29	14	36	.225	.263	.280	.543	50	-21	-20	98	136	22	.455	10	1	2	6	C	-0.5
1987	Cle-A	50	154	17	41	6	0	3	16	9	30	.266	.307	.364	.670	76	-5	-5	103	98	17	.569	1	1	-0	2	C	0.0
1988	Cle-A	133	434	44	114	11	0	5	50	25	63	.263	.307	.323	.630	75	-13	-14	102	128	42	.516	5	9	-4	15	*C	0.2
Total	3	284	881	91	221	24	3	9	95	48	129	.251	.293	.316	.608	67	-39	-39	100	125	81	.511	16	11	-2	22	C	-0.3
■ **NICK ALLEN** Allen, Artemus Ward b: 9/14/1888, Norton, Kan. d: 10/16/39, Hines, Ill. BR/TR, 6', 180 lbs. Deb: 5/01/14																												
1914	Buf-F	32	63	3	15	1	0	0	4	3	12	.238	.273	.254	.527	49	-4	-4	104	90	6	.479	4			0	C	-0.2
1915	Buf-F	84	215	14	44	7	1	0	17	18	34	.205	.266	.247	.513	52	-13	-13	100	116	16	.439	4			2	C	-0.8
1916	Chi-N	5	16	1	1	0	0	0	1	0	3	.063	.063	.063	.125	-53	-3	-3	117	397	0	.067	0			-0	/C	-0.3
1918	Cin-N	37	96	6	25	2	2	0	5	4	7	.260	.297	.323	.620	92	-1	-1	97	61	9	.507	0			2	C	0.4
1919	Cin-N	15	25	7	8	0	1	0	5	2	6	.320	.393	.400	.793	131	1	1	105	194	4	.765	0			0	C	0.2
1920	Cin-N	43	85	10	23	3	1	0	4	6	11	.271	.340	.329	.670	104	-1	1	90	55	10	.597	0	0	0	-1	C	0.2
Total	6	216	500	41	116	13	5	0	36	33	73	.232	.286	.278	.564	68	-20	-19	99	104	44	.482	8	0		3	C	-0.5
■ **BERNIE ALLEN** Allen, Bernard Keith b: 4/16/39, E. Liverpool, O. BL/TR, 6', 175 lbs. Deb: 4/10/62																												
1962	Min-A	159	573	79	154	27	7	12	64	62	82	.269	.340	.403	.743	95	-1	-4	105	97	80	.683	0	1	-1	-15	*2	-0.7
1963	Min-A	139	421	52	101	20	1	9	43	38	52	.240	.304	.356	.661	84	-9	-9	100	102	46	.580	0	0	0	-24	*2	-2.5
1964	Min-A	74	243	28	52	8	1	6	20	33	30	.214	.310	.329	.640	77	-7	-7	101	86	25	.581	1	2	-1	-5	2	-0.5
1965	Min-A	19	39	2	9	2	0	0	6	6	8	.231	.333	.282	.615	76	-1	-1	101	226	4	.567	0	0	0	-0	2/3	0.0
1966	Min-A	101	319	34	76	18	1	5	30	26	40	.238	.300	.348	.648	77	-6	-10	111	100	31	.551	2	3	-1	-7	2/3	-1.0
1967	Was-A	87	254	13	49	5	1	3	18	18	43	.193	.246	.256	.502	48	-16	-17	102	101	17	.402	1	2	-1	6	2	-1.0
1968	Was-A	120	373	31	90	12	4	6	40	28	35	.241	.301	.343	.644	104	-3	1	91	117	38	.557	2	0	1	4	*2/3	1.1
1969	Was-A	122	365	33	90	17	4	9	45	50	35	.247	.337	.389	.726	106	2	3	97	107	48	.684	5	4	-1	9	*2/3	1.6
1970	Was-A	104	261	31	61	7	1	8	29	43	21	.234	.342	.360	.702	97	-1	-0	96	99	34	.665	0	2	-1	11	23	1.8
1971	Was-A	97	229	18	61	11	1	4	22	33	27	.266	.359	.376	.734	117	3	5	92	92	33	.708	2	1	0	-1	23	0.5
1972	NY-A	84	220	26	50	9	0	9	21	23	42	.227	.300	.391	.691	113	1	3	92	78	26	.623	0	1	-1	2	32	0.8
1973	NY-A	17	57	5	13	3	0	0	4	5	5	.228	.290	.281	.571	61	-3	-3	101	98	5	.467	0	0	0	1	2/D	-0.1
	Mon-N	16	50	5	9	1	0	2	9	5	4	.180	.255	.320	.575	56	-3	-3	104	164	4	.512	0	0	0	-1	/23	-0.3
Total	12	1139	3404	357	815	140	21	73	351	370	424	.239	.315	.357	.673	90	-44	-43	100	102	391	.617	13	16	-6	-21	23/D	-0.3
■ **JACK ALLEN** Allen, Cyrus Alban b: 10/2/1855, Woodstock, Ill. d: 4/21/15, Girard, Pa. Deb: 5/01/1879																												
1879	Syr-N	11	48	7	9	2	1	0	3	1	5	.188	.204	.271	.475	62	-2	-1	89	71	3	.359				0	/3O	0.0
	Cle-N	16	60	7	7	1	1	0	4	1	9	.117	.131	.167	.298	-3	-6	-6	99	143	1	.208				0	3/O	-0.5
	Yr	27	108	14	16	3	2	0	7	2	14	.148	.164	.213	.377	24	-9	-8	95	117	4	.272				0		-0.5
Total	1	27	108	14	16	3	2	0	7	2	14	.148	.164	.213	.377	24	-9	-8	95	111	4	.272				0	/3O	-0.5
■ **ETHAN ALLEN** Allen, Ethan Nathan b: 1/1/04, Cincinnati, Ohio BR/TR, 6'1", 180 lbs. Deb: 6/21/26																												
1926	Cin-N	18	13	3	4	1	0	0	0	0	3	.308	.308	.385	.692	90	-0	-0	95	0	1	.556	0			-3	/O	-0.2
1927	Cin-N	111	359	54	106	26	4	2	20	14	23	.295	.325	.407	.732	95	-4	-3	100	46	46	.688	12			-8	O	-1.5
1928	Cin-N	129	485	55	148	30	7	1	62	27	29	.305	.343	.402	.745	98	-5	-2	96	114	65	.680	6			0	*O	-0.6
1929	Cin-N	143	538	69	157	27	11	6	64	20	21	.292	.317	.416	.734	81	-18	-18	99	92	68	.696	21			-1	*O	-2.8
1930	Cin-N	21	46	10	10	1	0	3	7	5	2	.217	.294	.435	.729	81	-2	-2	90	83	6	.722	1			-2	O	-0.3
	NY-N	76	238	48	73	9	2	7	31	12	23	.307	.340	.450	.790	91	-5	-4	98	83	35	.752	5			-2	O	-0.8
	Yr	97	284	58	83	10	2	10	38	17	25	.292	.332	.447	.779	90	-7	-5	96	84	41	.746	6			-3		-1.1
1931	NY-N	94	298	58	98	18	2	5	43	15	15	.329	.363	.453	.816	122	7	8	97	102	49	.785	6			-8	O	-0.2
1932	NY-N	54	103	13	18	6	2	1	7	1	12	.175	.198	.301	.499	32	-10	-10	99	77	6	.400	0			-3	O	-1.4
1933	StL-N	91	261	25	63	7	3	0	36	13	22	.241	.280	.291	.571	62	-12	-13	102	178	22	.460	3			9	O	-0.7
1934	Phi-N	145	581	87	192	**42**	4	10	85	33	47	.330	.370	.468	.838	113	18	11	108	107	99	.775	6			11	*O	1.5
1935	Phi-N	156	645	90	198	46	1	8	63	43	54	.307	.351	.419	.770	93	5	-7	114	68	100	.706	5			13	*O	0.0
1936	Phi-N	30	125	21	37	3	1	1	9	4	8	.296	.318	.360	.678	76	-3	-5	108	70	14	.576	4			2	O	-0.3
	Chi-N	91	373	47	110	18	6	3	39	13	30	.295	.322	.399	.722	89	-4	-7	105	93	47	.647	12			-2	O	-1.1
	Yr	121	498	68	147	21	7	4	48	17	38	.295	.321	.390	.711	86	-8	-11	106	88	62	.636	16			-0		-1.4
1937	StL-A	103	320	39	101	18	1	0	31	21	17	.316	.360	.378	.738	87	-6	-6	99	88	43	.655	3	4	-2	4	O	-0.5
1938	StL-A	19	33	4	10	3	1	0	4	2	4	.303	.343	.455	.797	98	-0	-0	100	90	5	.739	0	0	0	-1	/O	0.0
Total	13	1281	4418	623	1325	255	45	47	501	223	310	.300	.336	.410	.745	92	-40	-56	103	93	606	.688	84	4		10	*O	-8.9
■ **SLED ALLEN** Allen, Fletcher Manson b: 8/23/1886, West Plains, Mo. d: 10/16/59, Lubbock, Tex. TR, 6'1", 180 lbs. Deb: 5/04/10																												
1910	StL-A	14	23	3	3	1	0	0	1	1		.130	.231	.174	.405	29	-2	-2	94	92	1	.350	0			1	C/1	0.0
■ **HANK ALLEN** Allen, Harold Andrew b: 7/23/40, Wampum, Pa. BR/TR, 6', 190 lbs. Deb: 9/09/66																												
1966	Was-A	9	31	2	12	0	0	1	6	3	6	.387	.441	.484	.925	175	3	3	95	143	7	.947	0	0	0	0	/O	0.3
1967	Was-A	116	292	34	68	8	4	3	17	13	53	.233	.266	.318	.584	70	-11	-11	102	69	22	.462	3	4	-2	-10	O	-2.8
1968	Was-A	68	128	16	28	2	2	1	9	7	16	.219	.265	.289	.554	74	-5	-4	91	96	9	.433	0	0	0	-6	O32	-1.1
1969	Was-A	109	271	42	75	9	3	1	17	13	28	.277	.312	.343	.655	86	-6	-5	97	71	26	.561	12	3	2	-9	O/32	-1.5
1970	Was-A	22	38	3	8	2	0	0	4	5	9	.211	.302	.263	.565	60	-2	-2	96	162	3	.500	0	0	0	-3	O	-0.5
	Mil-A	28	61	4	14	4	0	0	4	7	5	.230	.309	.295	.604	69	-3	-2	98	90	5	.500	0	1	-1	-0	O/21	-0.3
	Yr	50	99	7	22	6	0	0	8	12	14	.222	.306	.283	.589	65	-5	-4	97	125	9	.500	0	1	-1	-3		-0.8
1972	Chi-A	9	21	1	3	0	0	0	0	0	2	.143	.143	.143	.286	-14	-3	-3	106	0	0	.158	0	0	0	1	/3	-0.2
1973	Chi-A	28	39	2	4	2	0	0	0	1	9	.103	.125	.154	.279	-21	-6	-6	102	0	0	.184	0	1	-1	-1	/31OC2	-0.8
Total	7	389	881	104	212	27	9	6	57	49	128	.241	.282	.312	.594	72	-34	-32	98	78	74	.501	15	9	-1	-28	O/321C	-6.9

YEAR TM/L	G	AB	R	H	2B	3B	HR	RBI	BB	SO	AVG	OBP	SLG	PRO	/A	BR	/A	PF	CHI	RC	TA	SB	CS	SBR	FR	POS	TPR
■ HEZEKIAH ALLEN	Allen, Hezekiah "Ki" b: 2/25/1863, Westport, Conn. d: 9/16/16, Saugatuck, Conn. 5'11", 160 lbs. Deb: 5/16/1884																										
1884 Phi-N	1	3	0	2	0	0	0	0	0	0	.667	.667	.667	1.333	348	1	1	92	0	1	2.000				0	/C	0.1
■ HAM ALLEN	Allen, Homer S. b: 8/1854, Hamden, Conn. d: 1/7/1892, Hamden, Conn. Deb: 4/27/1872																										
1872 Man-n	16	71	8	12							.169															O/S	
■ HORACE ALLEN	Allen, Horace Tanner "Pug" b: 6/11/1899, Deland, Fla. d: 7/5/81, Canton, N.C. BL/TR, 6', 187 lbs. Deb: 6/15/19																										
1919 Bro-N	4	7	0	0	0	0	0	0	0	2	.000	.000	.000	.000	-99	-2	-2	94	0	0	.000	0			0	/O	-0.1
■ JAMIE ALLEN	Allen, James Bradley b: 5/29/58, Yakima, Wash. BR/TR, 6', 205 lbs. Deb: 5/01/83																										
1983 Sea-A	86	273	23	61	10	0	4	21	33	52	.223	.309	.304	.613	70	-11	-11	100	88	26	.547	6	5	-1	-2	3/D	-1.3
■ PETE ALLEN	Allen, Jesse Hall b: 5/1/1868, Columbiana, Ohio d: 4/16/46, Philadelphia, Pa. BR/TR, 5'8.5", 185 lbs. Deb: 8/04/1893																										
1893 Cle-N	1	4	0	0	0	0	0	0	0	0	.000	.000	.000	.000	-96	-1	-1	104	0	0	.000	0			0	/C	0.0
■ KIM ALLEN	Allen, Kim Bryant b: 4/5/53, Fontana, Cal. BR/TR, 5'11", 175 lbs. Deb: 9/02/80																										
1980 Sea-A	23	51	9	12	3	0	0	3	8	3	.235	.350	.294	.644	76	-1	-1	103	78	6	.791	10	3	1	-1	2/OS	0.0
1981 Sea-A	19	3	1	0	0	0	0	0	0	2	.000	.000	.000	.000	-99	-1	-1	100	0	-0	.500	2	1	0	-1	/2OD	-0.1
Total 2	42	54	10	12	3	0	0	3	8	5	.222	.333	.278	.611	68	-2	-2	103	74	6	.783	12	4	1	-1	/2ODS	-0.1
■ MYRON ALLEN	Allen, Myron Smith "Zeke" b: 3/22/1854, Kingston, N.Y. d: 3/8/24, Kingston, N.Y. 5'8", 150 lbs. Deb: 7/19/1883																										
1883 NY-N	1	4	0	0	0	0	0	1	0	2	.000	.000	.000	.000	-99	-1	-1	100	0	0	.000				0	/P	0.0
1886 Bos-N	1	3	0	0	0	0	0	0	0	1	.000	.000	.000	.000	-99	-1	-1	97	0	0	.000	0			0	/2	0.0
1887 Cle-a	117	463	66	128	22	10	4		36		.276	.335	.393	.728	107	3	5	98	0	71	.743	26			5	*O/3SP	0.4
1888 KC-a	37	136	23	29	6	4	0	10	9		.213	.267	.316	.583	84	-2	-3	106	71	13	.533	4			6	O/P	0.1
Total 4	156	606	89	157	28	14	4	11	45	3	.259	.317	.371	.688	100	-1	0	99	16	84	.682	30			10	O/P3S2	0.5
■ DICK ALLEN	Allen, Richard Anthony b: 3/8/42, Wampum, Pa. BR/TR, 5'11", 187 lbs. Deb: 9/03/63																										
1963 Phi-N	10	24	6	7	2	1	0	2	0	5	.292	.292	.458	.750	109	0	0	103	76	2	.579	0	0	0	-1	/O3	0.0
1964 Phi-N	162	632	**125**	201	38	**13**	29	91	67	138	.318	.383	.557	.940	163	50	51	99	82	135	.953	3	4	-2	8	*3	5.0
1965 Phi-N	161	619	93	187	31	14	20	85	74	150	.302	.378	.494	.873	152	36	41	95	93	119	.888	15	2	3	-2	*3/S	3.6
1966 Phi-N	141	524	112	166	25	10	40	110	68	136	.317	.398	**.632**	**1.030**	**179**	**57**	**56**	101	109	**131**	**1.105**	10	6	-1	-5	3O	4.9
1967 Phi-N	122	463	89	142	31	10	23	77	75	117	.307	**.404**	.566	**.970**	167	46	44	104	85	109	**1.069**	20	5	3	-4	*3/2S	3.8
1968 Phi-N	152	521	87	137	17	9	33	90	74	161	.263	.356	.520	.876	165	38	39	97	105	97	.887	7	7	-2	-10	*O3	2.3
1969 Phi-N	118	438	79	126	23	3	32	89	64	144	.288	.378	.573	.952	166	36	37	98	99	95	.997	9	3	1	-10	*1	1.9
1970 StL-N	122	459	88	128	17	5	34	101	71	118	.279	.378	.560	.938	139	30	26	106	116	97	.974	5	4	-1	-8	13/O	0.9
1971 LA-N	155	549	82	162	24	1	23	90	93	113	.295	.398	.468	.866	146	35	36	99	119	102	.873	8	1	2	3	3O1	3.8
1972 Chi-A	148	506	90	156	28	5	**37**	**113**	**99**	126	.308	**.422**	**.603**	**1.025**	**191**	**66**	**63**	106	120	**131**	**1.143**	19	8	1	-4	*1/3	5.1
1973 Chi-A	72	250	39	79	20	3	16	41	33	51	.316	.398	.612	1.010	177	26	25	102	82	59	1.066	7	2	1	0	1/2D	2.2
1974 Chi-A	128	462	84	139	23	1	**32**	88	57	89	.301	.379	**.563**	**.942**	165	39	38	102	99	96	.956	7	1	2	-10	*1/2D	2.5
1975 Phi-N	119	416	54	97	21	3	12	62	58	109	.233	.330	.385	.714	96	-1	-2	101	125	52	.679	11	2	2	3	*1	-0.3
1976 Phi-N	85	298	52	80	16	1	15	49	37	63	.268	.349	.480	.829	124	12	10	107	102	47	.813	11	4	1	-3	1	0.4
1977 Oak-A	54	171	19	41	4	0	5	31	24	36	.240	.337	.351	.688	92	-2	-1	95	164	20	.628	1	3	-2	0	1/D	-0.5
Total 15	1749	6332	1099	1848	320	79	351	1119	894	1556	.292	.381	.534	.914	155	469	463	101	105	1290	.974	133	52	9	-45	13O/2DS	35.6
■ BOB ALLEN	Allen, Robert b: 1896, BR/TR, 5'10", 180 lbs. Deb: 8/20/19																										
1919 Phi-A	9	22	3	3	1	0	0	0	3	7	.136	.269	.182	.451	26	-2	-2	106	0	1	.421	0			-2	/O	-0.4
■ BOB ALLEN	Allen, Robert Gilman b: 7/10/1867, Marion, Ohio d: 5/14/43, Little Rock, Ark. BR/TR, 5'11", 175 lbs. Deb: 4/19/1890 M																										
1890 Phi-N	133	456	69	103	15	11	2	57	87	54	.226	.356	.320	.676	92	3	-3	108	116	58	.711	13			**33**	*S/M	2.5
1891 Phi-N	118	438	46	97	7	4	1	51	43	44	.221	.291	.263	.554	67	-19	-16	95	129	38	.499	12			10	*S	0.0
1892 Phi-N	152	563	77	128	20	14	2	64	61	60	.227	.304	.323	.627	88	-6	-9	104	107	61	.595	15			12	*S	0.9
1893 Phi-N	124	471	86	126	19	12	8	90	71	40	.268	.369	.410	.779	109	7	7	100	116	76	.803	8			17	*S	2.2
1894 Phi-N	40	149	26	38	10	3	0	19	17	11	.255	.335	.362	.698	73	-7	-6	95	97	20	.685	4			-4	S	-0.5
1897 Bos-N	34	119	33	38	5	0	1	24	18		.319	.409	.387	.795	106	3	2	107	146	20	.802	1			0	S/O2	0.1
1900 Cin-N	5	15	0	2	1	0	0	1	0		.133	.133	.200	.333	-8	-2	-2	92	104	0	.231	0			0	/SM	-0.1
Total 7	606	2211	337	532	77	44	14	306	297	209	.241	.334	.334	.668	89	-21	-28	102	116	273	.656	53			69	S/2O	5.1
■ ROD ALLEN	Allen, Roderick Bernet b: 10/5/59, Los Angeles, Cal. BR/TR, 6'1", 185 lbs. Deb: 4/07/83																										
1983 Sea-A	11	12	1	2	0	0	0	0	0	1	.167	.167	.167	.333	-8	-2	-2	100	0	0	.200	0	0	0	0	/OD	-0.1
1984 Det-A	15	27	6	8	1	0	0	3	2	8	.296	.367	.333	.700	99	-0	0	96	133	4	.684	1	0	0	-0	D/O	0.0
1988 Cle-A	5	11	1	1	1	0	0	0	0	2	.091	.091	.182	.273	-25	-2	-2	102	0	0	.200	0	0	0	0	/D	-0.1
Total 3	31	50	8	11	2	0	0	3	2	11	.220	.264	.260	.524	47	-4	-3	98	75	4	.436	1	0	0	-0	/DO	-0.2
■ RON ALLEN	Allen, Ronald Fredrick b: 12/23/43, Wampum, Pa. BB/TR, 6'3", 205 lbs. Deb: 8/11/72																										
1972 StL-N	7	11	2	1	0	0	1	1	3	5	.091	.286	.364	.649	79	-0	-0	105	59	1	.636	0	0	0	0	/1	0.0
■ GARY ALLENSON	Allenson, Gary Martin b: 2/4/55, Culver City, Cal. BR/TR, 5'11", 185 lbs. Deb: 4/08/79																										
1979 Bos-A	108	241	27	49	10	2	3	22	20	42	.203	.267	.299	.566	49	-16	-19	107	104	19	.468	1	1	-0	-24	*C/3	-3.7
1980 Bos-A	36	70	9	25	6	0	0	10	13	11	.357	.458	.443	.901	145	6	5	102	126	15	.958	2	2	-1	2	C/3D	0.8
1981 Bos-A	47	139	23	31	8	0	5	25	23	33	.223	.337	.388	.726	102	2	1	106	142	18	.684	0	0	0	-2	C	0.1
1982 Bos-A	92	264	25	54	11	0	6	33	38	39	.205	.307	.314	.621	64	-10	-14	110	131	26	.557	0	3	-2	-2	C	-1.2
1983 Bos-A	84	230	19	53	11	0	3	30	27	43	.230	.317	.317	.634	74	-7	-8	101	143	23	.548	0	1	-1	-3	C	-0.6
1984 Bos-A	35	83	9	19	2	0	2	8	9	14	.229	.304	.325	.630	67	-3	-4	110	97	7	.522	0	0	0	-0	C	-0.1
1985 Tor-A	14	34	2	4	1	0	0	3	0	10	.118	.118	.147	.265	-28	-6	-6	101	238	0	.161	0	0	0	-0	C	-0.5
Total 7	416	1061	114	235	49	2	19	131	130	192	.221	.309	.325	.635	71	-35	-44	106	129	109	.579	3	7	-3	-29	C/3D	-5.2
■ GENE ALLEY	Alley, Leonard Eugene b: 7/10/40, Richmond, Va. BR/TR, 5'10", 160 lbs. Deb: 9/04/63																										
1963 Pit-N	17	51	3	11	1	0	0	0	2	12	.216	.245	.235	.481	40	-4	-4	99	0	3	.333	0	1	-1	1	/32S	-0.2
1964 Pit-N	81	209	30	44	3	1	6	13	21	56	.211	.289	.321	.609	71	-8	-8	101	63	20	.533	0	1	-1	9	S/32	0.5
1965 Pit-N	153	500	47	126	21	6	5	47	32	82	.252	.302	.348	.650	83	-12	-12	100	103	52	.561	7	2	1	20	*S2/3	2.5
1966 Pit-N	147	579	88	173	28	10	7	43	27	83	.299	.336	.418	.753	107	6	5	101	73	79	.668	8	8	-2	16	*S	3.1
1967 Pit-N	152	550	59	158	25	7	6	55	36	70	.287	.339	.391	.730	108	6	6	100	100	70	.649	10	5	0	10	*S	3.5
1968 Pit-N	133	474	48	116	20	2	4	39	39	78	.245	.309	.321	.630	88	-6	-6	101	102	45	.546	13	5	1	18	*S2	3.0
1969 Pit-N	82	285	28	70	3	2	8	32	19	48	.246	.295	.354	.649	86	-8	-6	95	103	29	.556	4	0	1	11	2S/3	1.4
1970 Pit-N	121	426	46	104	16	5	8	41	31	70	.244	.300	.362	.662	79	-15	-13	97	91	46	.589	7	3	0	27	*S/23	2.8
1971 Pit-N	114	348	38	79	8	7	6	28	35	43	.227	.298	.342	.640	81	-9	-9	99	83	36	.588	9	2	2	-5	*S/3	0.3
1972 Pit-N	119	347	30	86	12	2	3	36	38	52	.248	.322	.320	.642	81	-7	-8	103	123	36	.567	4	3	-1	6	*S/3	1.1
1973 Pit-N	76	158	25	32	3	2	2	8	20	28	.203	.292	.285	.577	66	-8	-7	92	63	12	.493	1	0	0	3	S/3	0.3
Total 11	1195	3927	442	999	140	44	55	342	300	622	.254	.312	.354	.666	88	-65	-61	99	92	428	.601	63	30	1	115	S2/3	18.3
■ GAIR ALLIE	Allie, Gair Roosevelt b: 10/28/31, Statesville, N.C. BR/TR, 6'1", 190 lbs. Deb: 4/13/54																										
1954 Pit-N	121	418	38	83	8	6	3	30	56	84	.199	.296	.268	.564	50	-31	-29	97	100	37	.504	1	1	-0	-17	S3	-4.0
■ BOB ALLIETTA	Allietta, Robert George b: 5/1/52, New Bedford, Mass. BR/TR, 6', 190 lbs. Deb: 5/06/75																										
1975 Cal-A	21	45	4	8	1	0	1	2	1	6	.178	.196	.267	.462	31	-4	-4	95	51	2	.342	0	0	0	-2	C	-0.5
■ ANDY ALLISON	Allison, Andrew K. b: 1848, New York, N.Y. 5'10", 150 lbs. Deb: 5/07/1872																										
1872 Eck-n	25	107	11	15							.140															1/O	
■ ART ALLISON	Allison, Arthur Algernon b: 1/29/1849, Philadelphia, Pa. d: 2/25/16, Washington, D.C. 5'8", 150 lbs. Deb: 5/04/1871																										
1871 Cle-n	29	140	27	36							.257															*O	
1872 Cle-n	18	88	12	23							.261															O	

YEAR	TM/L	G	AB	R	H	2B	3B	HR	RBI	BB	SO	AVG	OBP	SLG	PRO	/A	BR	/A	PF	CHI	RC	TA	SB	CS	SBR	FR	POS	TPR
1873	Res-n	23	102	12	31							.304															O/1C	
1875	Nat-n	27	118	16	20							.169															1/OC	
	Har-n	35	161	26	39							.242															O/2	
	Yr	62	279	42	59							.211																
1876	Lou-N	31	130	9	27	2	1	0	10	2	6	.208	.220	.238	.458	51	-6	-7	104	115	7	.320				5	O/1	-0.1
Total	4 n	132	609	93	149							.245															O/1	
■ **DOUG ALLISON** Allison, Douglas b: 1846, Philadelphia, Pa. d: 12/19/16, Washington, D.C. BR/TR, 5'10.5", 160 lbs. Deb: 5/05/1871																												
1871	Oly-n	27	132	28	44							.333															*C	
1872	Tro-n	23	119	21	38							.319															C/S	
	Eck-n	18	87	20	26							.299															C	
	Yr	41	206	41	64							.311																
1873	Res-n	18	91	11	25							.275															C/O	
	Mut-n	11	53	6	13							.245															C	
	Yr	29	144	17	38							.264																
1874	Mut-n	65	326	65	88							.270															*OC	
1875	Har-n	61	293	38	68							.232															*C/1	
1876	Har-N	44	163	19	43	4	0	0	15	3	9	.264	.277	.288	.565	82	-2	-4	108	108	13	.417				6	C/O	0.4
1877	Har-N	29	115	14	17	2	0	0	6	3	7	.148	.169	.165	.335	7	-12	-10	89	109	3	.224				3	C	-0.5
1878	Pro-N	19	76	9	22	2	0	0	7	1	8	.289	.299	.316	.614	104	0	0	98	101	7	.463				0	C/P	0.1
1879	Pro-N	1	5	0	0	0	0	0	0	0	1	.000	.000	.000	.000	-99	-1	-1	102	0	0	.000				0	/C	0.0
1883	Bal-a	1	3	2	2	0	0	0		0		.667	.667	.667	1.333	309	1	1	107	0	1	2.000				0	/OC	0.1
Total	5 n	223	1101	189	302							.274															/OC	
Total	5	94	362	44	84	8	0	0	28	7	25	.232	.247	.254	.501	64	-14	-14	100	104	25	.356				9	C/O1PS	0.1
■ **MILO ALLISON** Allison, Milo Henry b: 10/16/1890, Elk Rapids, Mich. d: 6/18/57, Kenosha, Wis. BL/TR, 6', 163 lbs. Deb: 9/26/13																												
1913	Chi-N	2	6	1	2	0	0	0	0	0	1	.333	.333	.333	.667	92	-0	-0	99	0	1	.750	1			0	/O	0.0
1914	Chi-N	1	1	0	1	0	0	0	0	0	0	1.000	1.000	1.000	2.000	504	0	0	98	0	1	—	0			0	H	0.0
1916	Cle-A	14	18	10	5	0	0	0	0	6	1	.278	.458	.278	.736	122	1	1	100	0	3	.846	0			-1	/O	0.0
1917	Cle-A	32	35	4	5	0	0	0	0	9	7	.143	.318	.143	.461	36	-2	-3	114	0	3	.567	3			-2	O	-0.6
Total	4	49	60	15	13	0	0	0	0	15	9	.217	.373	.217	.590	72	-0	-1	108	0	7	.681	4			-4	/O	-0.6
■ **BILL ALLISON** Allison, William Andrew b: 9/18/1848, Philadelphia, Pa. d: 6/12/23, Deb: 5/21/1872																												
1872	Eck-n	3	11	3	2							.182															/O2	
■ **BOB ALLISON** Allison, William Robert b: 7/11/34, Raytown, Mo. BR/TR, 6'3", 205 lbs. Deb: 9/16/58																												
1958	Was-A	11	35	1	7	1	0	0	0	2	5	.200	.243	.229	.472	32	-3	-3	97	0	1	.323	0	2	-1	0	O	-0.4
1959	Was-A	150	570	83	149	18	**9**	30	85	60	92	.261	.334	.482	.816	121	15	15	100	88	85	.776	13	8	-1	-10	*O	-0.3
1960	Was-A	144	501	79	126	30	3	15	69	92	94	.251	.370	.413	.783	109	10	9	102	109	79	.784	11	9	-2	6	*O/1	0.7
1961	Min-A	159	556	83	136	21	3	29	105	103	100	.245	.367	.450	.817	110	15	10	106	129	93	.811	2	7	-4	6	*O1	0.5
1962	Min-A	149	519	102	138	24	8	29	102	84	115	.266	.372	.511	.883	129	26	23	105	117	102	.914	8	5	-1	5	*O	2.2
1963	Min-A	148	527	**99**	143	25	4	35	91	90	109	.271	.381	.533	**.914**	**152**	39	**38**	100	105	113	**.969**	6	1	1	-1	*O	3.4
1964	Min-A	149	492	90	141	27	4	32	86	92	99	.287	.406	.553	.959	162	45	44	101	101	119	1.061	10	1	2	2	1O	4.5
1965	Min-A	135	438	71	102	14	5	23	78	73	114	.233	.345	.445	.790	121	14	13	101	125	73	.816	10	2	2	8	*O/1	1.9
1966	Min-A	70	168	34	37	6	1	8	19	30	34	.220	.348	.411	.759	105	5	2	111	86	27	.812	6	0	2	-2	O	0.0
1967	Min-A	153	496	73	128	21	6	24	75	74	114	.258	.357	.470	.826	133	27	23	107	105	87	.836	6	4	-1	-6	*O	1.3
1968	Min-A	145	469	63	116	16	8	22	52	52	98	.247	.325	.456	.781	127	19	16	106	80	65	.737	9	7	-2	-8	*O1	0.1
1969	Min-A	81	189	18	43	8	2	8	27	29	39	.228	.333	.418	.751	107	2	2	102	105	24	.703	2	4	-2	-4	O/1	-0.5
1970	Min-A	47	72	15	15	5	0	1	7	14	20	.208	.345	.319	.664	86	-1	-1	98	109	9	.661	1	0	0	-3	O/1	-0.4
Total	13	1541	5032	811	1281	216	53	256	796	795	1033	.255	.360	.471	.831	126	211	191	103	105	877	.864	84	50	-5	-7	*O1	13.0
■ **MEL ALMADA** Almada, Baldomero Melo b: 2/7/13, Hwatabampo, Sonora, Mexico d: 8/13/88, Hermosillo, Mexico BL/TL, 6', 170 lbs. Deb: 9/08/33																												
1933	Bos-A	14	44	11	15	0	0	1	3	11	3	.341	.473	.409	.882	134	3	3	101	49	10	1.067	3	1	0	0	O	0.3
1934	Bos-A	23	90	7	21	2	1	0	10	6	8	.233	.281	.278	.559	42	-7	-8	106	136	7	.479	3	2	-0	4	O	-0.3
1935	Bos-A	151	607	85	176	27	9	3	59	55	34	.290	.350	.379	.729	82	-10	-17	108	89	83	.695	20	9	1	-7	*O/1	-2.3
1936	Bos-A	96	320	40	81	16	4	1	21	24	15	.253	.305	.338	.643	55	-22	-24	106	61	33	.551	2	4	-2	-2	O	-2.6
1937	Bos-A	32	110	17	26	6	2	1	9	15	6	.236	.328	.355	.683	70	-5	-5	103	75	13	.635	0	1	-1	-5	O/1	-1.1
	Was-A	100	433	74	134	21	4	4	33	38	21	.309	.365	.404	.769	99	-4	-0	94	52	66	.743	12	4	1	10	*O	0.7
	Yr	132	543	91	160	27	6	5	42	53	27	.295	.357	.394	.751	92	-9	-6	96	58	79	.719	12	5	1	5		-0.4
1938	Was-A	47	197	24	48	7	4	1	15	8	16	.244	.277	.335	.612	55	-15	-14	95	78	19	.527	4	1	1	9	O	-0.3
	StL-A	102	436	77	149	22	2	3	37	38	22	.342	.398	.422	.820	106	5	5	100	56	74	.801	9	5	-0	-3	*O	0.1
	Yr	149	633	101	197	29	6	4	52	46	38	.311	.362	.395	.757	91	-10	-9	98	63	92	.708	13	6	0	6		-0.2
1939	StL-A	42	134	17	32	2	1	1	7	10	8	.239	.292	.291	.583	49	-10	-10	100	56	12	.481	1	0	0	-0	O	-1.0
	Bro-N	39	112	11	24	4	0	0	3	9	17	.214	.273	.250	.523	38	-9	-10	107	39	8	.433	2			3	O	-0.7
Total	7	646	2483	363	706	107	27	15	197	214	150	.284	.342	.367	.710	79	-74	-82	102	68	324	.657	56	27		9	O/1	-7.2
■ **RAFAEL ALMEIDA** Almeida, Rafael D. "Mike" b: 7/30/1887, Havana, Cuba d: 3/68, Havana, Cuba BR/TR, 5'9", 164 lbs. Deb: 7/04/11																												
1911	Cin-N	36	96	9	30	5	1	0	15	9	16	.313	.383	.385	.769	126	2	3	92	137	16	.773	3			-0	3/2S	0.4
1912	Cin-N	16	59	9	13	4	3	0	10	5	8	.220	.281	.390	.671	89	-2	-1	92	155	6	.609	0			0	3	0.0
1913	Cin-N	50	130	14	34	4	2	3	21	11	16	.262	.324	.392	.716	102	0	0	102	127	17	.698	4			-2	3/OS2	-0.2
Total	3	102	285	32	77	13	6	3	46	25	40	.270	.335	.389	.725	107	1	2	96	136	39	.702	7			-3	/3OS2	0.2
■ **BILL ALMON** Almon, William Francis b: 11/21/52, Providence, R.I. BR/TR, 6'3", 180 lbs. Deb: 9/02/74																												
1974	SD-N	16	38	4	12	1	0	0	3	2	9	.316	.350	.342	.692	101	-0	0	93	89	5	.615	1	0	0	-0	S	0.2
1975	SD-N	6	10	0	4	0	0	0	0	0	1	.400	.400	.400	.800	123	0	0	100	0	2	.667	0	0	0	1	/S	0.1
1976	SD-N	14	57	6	14	3	0	1	6	2	9	.246	.271	.351	.622	85	-2	-1	89	96	6	.568	3	1	0	-1	S	0.0
1977	SD-N	155	613	75	160	18	11	2	43	37	114	.261	.303	.336	.639	81	-25	-15	88	86	61	.553	20	9	1	16	*S	2.3
1978	SD-N	138	405	39	102	19	2	0	21	33	74	.252	.308	.309	.617	79	-14	-11	93	67	40	.557	17	5	2	1	*3S/2	-0.7
1979	SD-N	100	198	20	45	3	0	1	8	21	48	.227	.301	.258	.559	56	-12	-11	96	59	16	.491	6	5	-1	-0	2S/O	-0.5
1980	Mon-N	18	38	2	10	1	1	0	3	1	5	.263	.282	.342	.624	74	-1	-1	99	91	3	.467	0	0	0	-0	S/2	0.0
	NY-N	48	112	13	19	3	2	0	4	8	27	.170	.225	.232	.457	29	-11	-10	96	61	6	.387	2	0	1	-4	S2/3	-1.0
	Yr	66	150	15	29	4	3	0	7	9	32	.193	.239	.260	.499	40	-12	-12	97	71	10	.413	2	0	1	-4		-1.0
1981	Chi-A	103	349	46	105	10	2	4	41	21	60	.301	.344	.375	.719	108	3	3	100	112	46	.669	16	6	1	14	*S	2.6
1982	Chi-A	111	308	40	79	10	4	4	26	25	49	.256	.314	.354	.668	85	-7	-6	97	86	34	.602	10	8	-2	12	*S/D	1.4
1983	Oak-A	143	451	45	120	29	1	4	63	26	67	.266	.309	.361	.670	88	-10	-8	96	141	51	.625	26	8	3	-13	S31O/2D	-1.6
1984	Oak-A	106	211	24	47	11	0	7	16	10	42	.223	.258	.374	.632	79	-8	-6	92	64	18	.540	5	7	-3	-10	O1D/3CS	-2.2
1985	Pit-N	88	244	33	66	17	0	6	29	22	61	.270	.333	.414	.747	105	2	2	103	97	32	.702	10	7	-1	-2	SO/13	0.0
1986	Pit-N	102	196	29	43	7	2	7	27	30	38	.219	.323	.383	.706	94	-2	-2	100	112	25	.716	11	4	1	-8	O3S/1	-0.8
1987	Pit-N	19	20	5	4	1	0	0	1	1	5	.200	.238	.250	.488	28	-2	-2	104	80	1	.375	0	0	0	-1	/SO3	-0.2
	NY-N	49	54	8	13	3	0	0	4	8	16	.241	.339	.296	.635	71	-2	-2	99	100	6	.610	1	0	0	-0	S2/1O	0.1
	Yr	68	74	13	17	4	0	0	5	9	21	.230	.313	.284	.597	60	-4	-4	100	95	7	.544	1	0	0	-1		-0.1
1988	Phi-N	20	26	1	3	2	0	0	1	3	11	.115	.207	.192	.399	15	-3	-3	101	80	1	.348	0	0	0	-0	/3S1	-0.2
Total	15	1236	3330	390	846	138	25	36	296	250	636	.254	.307	.343	.650	83	-95	-74	95	92	354	.600	128	60	2	3	S3O2/1DC	-0.5
■ **ROBERTO ALOMAR** Alomar, Roberto (Velazquez) b: 2/5/68, Salinas, P.R. BB/TR, 6', 155 lbs. Deb: 4/22/88																												
1988	SD-N	143	545	84	145	24	6	9	41	47	83	.266	.328	.382	.709	106	2	4	97	74	68	.670	24	6	4	13	*2	2.6
■ **SANDY ALOMAR** Alomar, Santos (Velazquez) Jr. b: 6/18/66, Salinas, P.R. BR/TR, 6'5", 200 lbs. Deb: 9/30/88																												
1988	SD-N	1	1	0	0	0	0	0	0	0	1	.000	.000	.000	.000	-99	-0	-0	97	0	0	.000	0	0	0	0	H	0.0

■ **SANDY ALOMAR** Alomar, Santos Sr. (Conde) b: 10/19/43, Salinas, P.R. BB/TR, 5'9", 140 lbs. Deb: 9/15/64 C

YEAR	TM/L	G	AB	R	H	2B	3B	HR	RBI	BB	SO	AVG	OBP	SLG	PRO	/A	BR	/A	PF	CHI	RC	TA	SB	CS	SBR	FR	POS	TPR
1964	Mil-N	19	53	3	13	1	0	0	6	0	11	.245	.245	.264	.509	45	-4	-4	97	176	3	.366	1	0	0	2	S	0.0
1965	Mil-N	67	108	16	26	1	1	0	8	4	12	.241	.268	.269	.536	50	-7	-7	104	114	7	.489	12	5	1	-1	S2	-0.1
1966	Atl-N	31	44	4	4	1	0	0	2	1	10	.091	.111	.114	.225	-38	-8	-8	99	168	1	.150	0	0	0	-1	2/S	-0.7
1967	NY-N	15	22	1	0	0	0	0	0	0	6	.000	.000	.000	.000	-99	-6	-6	99	0	0	.000	0	0	0	0	S/32	-0.4
	Chi-A	12	15	4	3	0	0	0	0	2	0	.200	.294	.200	.494	52	-1	-1	94	0	1	.538	2	0	1	0	/S2	0.1
1968	Chi-A	133	363	41	92	8	2	0	12	20	42	.253	.294	.287	.581	76	-10	-11	101	49	32	.512	21	8	2	-13	23/SO	-1.9
1969	Chi-A	22	58	8	13	2	0	0	4	4	6	.224	.274	.259	.533	46	-4	-4	108	107	5	.467	2	0	1	4	2	0.1
	Cal-A	134	559	60	140	10	2	1	30	36	48	.250	.296	.281	.577	62	-28	-28	99	65	50	.494	18	3	4	-7	*2	-2.6
	Yr	156	617	68	153	12	2	1	34	40	54	.248	.294	.279	.573	60	-32	-32	101	72	54	.492	20	3	4	-3		-2.5
1970	Cal-A	162	672	82	169	18	2	2	36	49	65	.251	.303	.293	.596	71	-31	-24	92	62	64	.540	35	12	3	12	*2S/3	0.7
1971	Cal-A	162	689	77	179	24	3	4	42	41	60	.260	.301	.321	.622	77	-22	-21	99	64	70	.571	39	10	6	18	*2S	1.2
1972	Cal-A	155	610	65	146	20	3	1	25	47	55	.239	.294	.287	.581	83	-20	-12	88	52	52	.500	20	12	-1	6	*2/S	0.2
1973	Cal-A	136	470	45	112	7	1	0	28	34	44	.238	.290	.257	.547	57	-27	-25	96	93	39	.486	25	10	2	-6	*2S	-2.0
1974	Cal-A	46	54	12	12	0	1	0	1	2	8	.222	.250	.259	.509	50	-4	-3	92	28	4	.419	2	0	1	-0	S2/3OD	0.0
	NY-A	76	279	35	75	8	0	1	27	14	25	.269	.304	.308	.612	80	-9	-7	96	122	25	.495	6	4	-1	-3	2	-0.7
	Yr	122	333	47	87	8	1	1	28	16	33	.261	.295	.300	.595	76	-12	-10	94	86	29	.484	8	4	0	-3		-0.7
1975	NY-A	151	489	61	117	18	4	2	39	26	58	.239	.278	.305	.582	65	-23	-23	99	97	44	.529	28	6	5	-8	*2/S	-2.1
1976	NY-A	67	163	20	39	4	0	1	10	13	12	.239	.295	.282	.578	70	-6	-6	99	78	14	.534	12	7	-1	2	2/S31O	-0.1
1977	Tex-A	69	83	21	22	3	0	1	11	8	13	.265	.337	.337	.674	81	-2	-2	105	141	10	.641	4	3	-1	0	D2/SO13	0.0
1978	Tex-A	24	29	3	6	1	0	0	1	1	7	.207	.233	.241	.475	35	-3	-2	96	56	2	.348	0	0	0	0	/123SD	-0.1
Total	15	1481	4760	558	1168	126	19	13	282	302	482	.245	.291	.288	.579	68	-214	-194	96	75	421	.518	227	80	20	5	*2S/3D1O	-8.4

■ **FELIPE ALOU** Alou, Felipe Rojas (born Felipe Rojas (Alou)) b: 5/12/35, Haina, D.R. BR/TR, 6', 195 lbs. Deb: 6/08/58 C

YEAR	TM/L	G	AB	R	H	2B	3B	HR	RBI	BB	SO	AVG	OBP	SLG	PRO	/A	BR	/A	PF	CHI	RC	TA	SB	CS	SBR	FR	POS	TPR
1958	SF-N	75	182	21	46	9	2	4	16	19	34	.253	.327	.390	.717	89	-3	-3	100	80	24	.683	4	2	0	-3	O	-0.7
1959	SF-N	95	247	38	68	13	2	10	33	17	38	.275	.322	.466	.788	112	2	3	95	92	36	.733	5	3	-0	-5	O	-0.2
1960	SF-N	106	322	48	85	17	3	8	44	16	42	.264	.303	.410	.713	104	-4	0	90	114	39	.645	10	2	2	-6	O	-0.6
1961	SF-N	132	415	59	120	19	0	18	52	26	41	.289	.334	.465	.799	111	5	5	98	85	62	.748	11	4	1	-1	*O	-0.1
1962	SF-N	154	561	96	177	30	3	25	98	33	66	.316	.359	.513	.872	130	23	22	101	109	103	.851	10	7	-1	-2	*O	1.1
1963	SF-N	157	565	75	159	31	9	20	82	27	87	.281	.321	.474	.795	132	17	19	96	107	83	.741	11	2	2	5	*O	1.9
1964	Mil-N	121	415	60	105	26	3	9	51	30	41	.253	.310	.395	.705	100	-2	-0	97	110	51	.640	5	2	0	-6	O1	-0.9
1965	Mil-N	143	555	80	165	29	2	23	78	31	63	.297	.340	.481	.821	123	19	17	104	102	90	.777	8	4	0	-2	O1/3S	0.9
1966	Atl-N	154	666	**122**	**218**	32	6	31	74	24	51	.327	.362	.533	.895	147	38	39	99	61	123	.850	5	7	-3	7	1O/3S	3.8
1967	Atl-N	140	574	76	157	26	3	15	43	32	50	.274	.320	.408	.727	102	4	1	104	56	73	.646	6	5	-1	-5	1O	-1.1
1968	Atl-N	160	662	72	**210**	37	5	11	57	48	56	.317	.367	.438	.805	151	32	37	93	66	103	.748	12	11	-3	2	*O	3.2
1969	Atl-N	123	476	54	134	13	1	5	32	23	23	.282	.320	.345	.665	83	-9	-11	104	76	51	.549	4	6	-2	-2	*O	-2.3
1970	Oak-A	154	575	70	156	25	3	8	55	32	31	.271	.311	.367	.678	89	-12	-9	97	97	63	.581	10	5	0	9	*O/1	-0.6
1971	Oak-A	2	8	0	2	1	0	0	0	0	1	.250	.250	.375	.625	75	-0	-0	101	0	1	.500	0	0	0	1	/O	0.0
	NY-A	131	461	52	133	20	6	8	69	32	24	.289	.337	.410	.747	114	6	7	97	135	59	.655	5	5	-2	-6	O1	-0.5
	Yr	133	469	52	135	21	6	8	69	32	25	.288	.336	.409	.745	114	5	7	97	133	60	.653	5	5	-2	-6		-0.5
1972	NY-A	120	324	33	90	18	1	6	37	22	27	.278	.328	.395	.723	124	5	8	92	106	41	.632	1	0	0	-5	1O	-0.7
1973	NY-A	93	280	25	66	12	0	4	27	9	25	.236	.260	.321	.581	62	-14	-15	101	104	22	.452	0	1	-1	-1	1O	-2.1
	Mon-N	19	48	4	10	1	0	1	4	2	4	.208	.240	.292	.532	45	-4	-4	104	95	2	.381	0	1	-1	1	O/1	-0.4
1974	Mil-A	3	3	0	0	0	0	0	0	0	2	.000	.000	.000	.000	-98	-1	-1	102	0	0	.000	0	0	0	-1	/O	-0.1
Total	17	2082	7339	985	2101	359	49	206	852	423	706	.286	.330	.433	.763	114	101	116	98	91	1028	.709	107	67	-8	-20	*O1/3S	0.6

■ **JESUS ALOU** Alou, Jesus Maria Rojas (born Jesus Maria Rojas (Alou)) b: 3/24/42, Haina, D.R. BR/TR, 6'2", 190 lbs. Deb: 9/10/63 C

YEAR	TM/L	G	AB	R	H	2B	3B	HR	RBI	BB	SO	AVG	OBP	SLG	PRO	/A	BR	/A	PF	CHI	RC	TA	SB	CS	SBR	FR	POS	TPR
1963	SF-N	16	24	3	6	1	0	0	5	0	3	.250	.280	.292	.572	68	-1	-1	96	300	1	.400	0	1	-1	-3	O	-0.5
1964	SF-N	115	376	42	103	11	0	3	28	13	35	.274	.305	.327	.632	78	-11	-11	100	87	35	.507	6	6	-2	-1	*O	-1.6
1965	SF-N	143	543	76	162	19	4	9	52	13	40	.298	.318	.398	.716	91	-1	-7	111	91	61	.590	8	5	-1	2	*O	-1.0
1966	SF-N	110	370	41	96	13	1	1	20	9	22	.259	.281	.308	.589	65	-18	-17	97	72	28	.444	5	5	-2	-8	*O	-3.0
1967	SF-N	129	510	55	149	15	4	5	30	14	39	.292	.316	.367	.683	94	-4	-5	101	63	55	.545	1	7	-4	-6	*O	-2.1
1968	SF-N	120	419	26	110	15	4	0	39	9	23	.263	.280	.317	.597	81	-11	-11	98	124	31	.432	1	4	-2	1	*O	-1.8
1969	Hou-N	115	452	49	112	19	4	5	34	15	30	.248	.278	.341	.619	71	-18	-18	102	85	38	.493	4	6	-2	-1	*O	-2.9
1970	Hou-N	117	458	59	140	27	3	1	44	21	15	.306	.338	.384	.722	99	-5	-1	94	97	55	.600	3	2	-0	-6	*O	-1.2
1971	Hou-N	122	433	41	121	21	4	2	40	13	17	.279	.307	.360	.667	95	-8	-4	93	100	43	.533	3	7	-3	5	*O	-0.6
1972	Hou-N	52	93	8	29	4	1	0	11	7	5	.312	.366	.376	.743	105	2	1	106	129	11	.623	0	2	-1	-3	O	-0.4
1973	Hou-N	28	55	7	13	2	0	1	8	1	6	.236	.276	.327	.603	70	-3	-2	95	153	4	.467	0	0	0	-3	O	-0.5
	Oak-A	36	108	10	33	3	0	1	11	2	6	.306	.318	.361	.679	104	-2	0	87	103	12	.532	0	0	0	0	O/D	0.0
1974	Oak-A	96	220	13	59	8	0	2	15	5	9	.268	.291	.332	.623	78	-6	-7	100	75	19	.471	0	0	0	-2	DO	-0.8
1975	NY-N	62	102	8	27	3	0	0	11	4	5	.265	.299	.294	.593	68	-5	-4	95	142	8	.438	0	1	-1	-2	O	-0.7
1978	Hou-N	77	139	7	45	5	1	2	19	6	5	.324	.352	.417	.769	121	2	3	95	118	19	.653	0	0	0	-3	O	0.0
1979	Hou-N	42	43	3	11	4	0	0	10	6	7	.256	.347	.349	.696	100	-0	0	90	264	4	.583	0	0	0	-1	/O1	-0.1
Total	15	1380	4345	448	1216	170	26	32	377	138	267	.280	.307	.353	.660	86	-89	-84	99	96	426	.545	31	46	-18	-29	*O/D1	-17.2

■ **MATTY ALOU** Alou, Mateo Rojas (born Mateo Rojas (Alou)) b: 12/22/38, Haina, D.R. BL/TL, 5'9", 160 lbs. Deb: 9/26/60

YEAR	TM/L	G	AB	R	H	2B	3B	HR	RBI	BB	SO	AVG	OBP	SLG	PRO	/A	BR	/A	PF	CHI	RC	TA	SB	CS	SBR	FR	POS	TPR
1960	SF-N	4	3	1	1	0	0	0	0	0	0	.333	.333	.333	.667	93	-0	-0	90	0	0	.500	0	0	0	-0	/O	0.0
1961	SF-N	81	200	38	62	7	2	6	24	15	18	.310	.358	.455	.813	116	4	4	98	89	32	.757	3	2	-0	-5	O	-0.4
1962	SF-N	78	195	28	57	8	1	3	14	14	17	.292	.349	.390	.739	97	-0	-1	101	65	27	.676	3	1	0	-4	O	-0.7
1963	SF-N	63	76	4	11	1	0	0	2	2	13	.145	.177	.158	.335	-3	-10	-10	96	70	2	.224	0	1	-1	-3	O	-1.5
1964	SF-N	110	250	28	66	4	2	1	14	11	25	.264	.303	.308	.611	72	-9	-9	100	72	23	.505	5	3	-0	-5	O	-1.7
1965	SF-N	117	324	37	75	12	2	2	18	17	28	.231	.274	.299	.573	56	-17	-21	111	72	24	.474	10	2	2	-5	*O/P	-2.8
1966	Pit-N	141	535	86	183	18	9	2	27	24	44	**.342**	.375	.421	.795	120	15	15	101	50	84	.746	23	15	-2	9	*O	1.8
1967	Pit-N	139	550	87	186	21	7	2	28	24	42	.338	.372	.413	.785	125	17	17	100	53	85	.724	16	10	-1	4	*O/1	1.5
1968	Pit-N	146	558	59	185	28	4	0	52	27	26	.332	.365	.396	.761	127	19	18	101	105	79	.682	18	10	-1	5	*O	1.8
1969	Pit-N	162	698	105	**231**	**41**	6	1	48	42	35	.331	.371	.411	.782	125	17	21	95	59	109	.735	22	8	2	-1	*O	1.3
1970	Pit-N	155	677	97	201	21	8	1	47	30	18	.297	.331	.356	.687	87	-15	-13	97	65	79	.593	19	11	-1	-1	*O	-2.0
1971	StL-N	149	609	85	192	28	6	7	74	34	27	.315	.355	.415	.771	117	13	13	101	106	89	.711	19	10	-0	4	O1	1.0
1972	StL-N	108	404	46	127	17	2	3	31	24	23	.314	.354	.389	.743	106	6	3	105	78	54	.659	11	4	1	-1	1O	-0.2
	Oak-A	32	121	11	34	5	0	1	16	11	12	.281	.346	.347	.693	110	1	2	97	157	15	.629	2	1	0	-2	O/1	-0.1
1973	NY-A	123	497	59	147	22	1	2	28	30	43	.296	.340	.356	.696	96	-2	-3	101	58	57	.581	5	2	0	-3	O1/D	-1.0
	StL-N	11	11	1	3	0	0	0	1	1	0	.273	.333	.273	.606	77	-0	-0	91	134	1	.400	0	0	0	0	/1O	0.0
1974	SD-N	48	81	8	16	3	0	0	3	5	6	.198	.244	.235	.479	37	-7	-6	93	61	4	.353	0	0	0	-2	O/1	-0.9
Total	15	1667	5789	780	1777	236	50	31	427	311	377	.307	.346	.381	.727	104	30	31	100	74	764	.662	156	80	-1	-10	*O1/DP	-3.9

■ **WHITEY ALPERMAN** Alperman, Charles Augustus b: 11/11/1879, Etna, Pa. d: 12/25/42, Pittsburgh, Pa. BR/TR, 5'10", 180 lbs. Deb: 4/13/06

YEAR	TM/L	G	AB	R	H	2B	3B	HR	RBI	BB	SO	AVG	OBP	SLG	PRO	/A	BR	/A	PF	CHI	RC	TA	SB	CS	SBR	FR	POS	TPR
1906	Bro-N	128	441	38	111	15	7	3	46	6		.252	.262	.338	.600	102	-8	-2	87	108	43	.509	13			-3	*2S/3	-0.4
1907	Bro-N	141	558	44	130	23	**16**	2	39	13		.233	.250	.342	.593	92	-11	-8	94	66	50	.488	5			18	*23S	1.3
1908	Bro-N	70	213	17	42	3	1	1	15	9		.197	.230	.235	.464	52	-12	-11	95	109	11	.357	2			1	2/3OS	-1.0
1909	Bro-N	111	420	35	104	19	12	1	41	2		.248	.262	.357	.619	94	-6	-6	99	103	39	.522	7			11	*2	0.4
Total	4	450	1632	134	387	60	36	7	141	30		.237	.254	.331	.584	90	-38	-27	94	93	144	.484	27			27	2/S3O	0.3

■ **TOM ALSTON** Alston, Thomas Edison b: 1/31/31, Greensboro, N.C. BL/TR, 6'5", 210 lbs. Deb: 4/13/54

YEAR	TM/L	G	AB	R	H	2B	3B	HR	RBI	BB	SO	AVG	OBP	SLG	PRO	/A	BR	/A	PF	CHI	RC	TA	SB	CS	SBR	FR	POS	TPR
1954	StL-N	66	244	28	60	14	2	4	34	24	41	.246	.319	.369	.687	78	-8	-8	100	134	27	.610	3	5	-2	5	1	-0.7
1955	StL-N	13	8	0	1	0	0	0	0	0	0	.125	.125	.125	.250	-33	-2	-2	101	0	0	.143	0	0	0	0	/1	-0.1
1956	StL-N	3	2	0	0	0	0	0	0	0	0	.000	.000	.000	.000	-99	-1	-1	99	0	0	.000	0	0	0	0	/1	0.0
1957	StL-N	9	17	2	5	1	0	0	2	1	5	.294	.333	.353	.686	84	-0	-0	101	138	2	.583	0	0	0	0	/1	0.0

YEAR	TM/L	G	AB	R	H	2B	3B	HR	RBI	BB	SO	AVG	OBP	SLG	PRO	/A	BR	/A	PF	CHI	RC	TA	SB	CS	SBR	FR	POS	TPR
Total	4	91	271	30	66	15	2	4	36	25	46	.244	.312	.358	.670	74	-10	-10	100	129	30	.605	3	5	-2	5	/1	-0.8

■ **WALTER ALSTON** Alston, Walter Emmons "Smokey" b: 12/1/11, Venice, Ohio d: 10/1/84, Oxford, Ohio BR/TR, 6'2", 195 lbs. Deb: 9/27/36 MH

1936	StL-N	1	1	0	0	0	0	0	0	0	1	.000	.000	.000	.000	-99	-0	-0	94	0	0	.000	0			0	/1	0.0

■ **DELL ALSTON** Alston, Wendell b: 9/22/52, Valhalla, N.Y. BL/TR, 6', 180 lbs. Deb: 5/17/77

1977	NY-A	22	40	10	13	4	0	1	4	3	4	.325	.372	.500	.872	137	2	2	99	69	6	.813	3	3	-1	0	D/O	0.1
1978	NY-A	3	3	0	0	0	0	0	0	0	2	.000	.000	.000	.000	-99	-1	-1	99	0	0	.000	0	0	0	0	H	0.0
	Oak-A	58	173	17	36	2	0	1	10	10	21	.208	.251	.237	.488	38	-14	-14	101	90	10	.419	11	10	-3	-6	O/1D	-2.5
	Yr	61	176	17	36	2	0	1	10	10	23	.205	.247	.233	.480	35	-15	-15	101	85	10	.411	11	10	-3	-6		-2.5
1979	Cle-A	54	62	10	18	0	2	1	12	10	10	.290	.389	.403	.792	108	2	1	106	165	10	.813	4	4	-1	-6	O	-0.7
1980	Cle-A	52	54	11	12	1	2	0	9	5	7	.222	.311	.315	.626	70	-2	-2	102	206	5	.553	2	4	-2	-4	O/D	-0.8
Total	4	189	332	48	79	7	4	3	35	28	44	.238	.301	.310	.611	68	-13	-14	102	121	30	.556	20	21	-7	-16	O/D1	-3.9

■ **JESSE ALTENBURG** Altenburg, Jesse Howard b: 1/2/1893, Ashley, Mich. d: 3/12/73, Lansing, Mich. BL/TR, 5'9", 158 lbs. Deb: 9/19/16

1916	Pit-N	8	14	2	6	1	1	0	0	1	1	.429	.467	.643	1.110	228	2	2	105	0	4	1.250	0			-3	/O	0.0
1917	Pit-N	11	17	1	3	0	0	0	3	0	4	.176	.176	.176	.353	8	-2	-2	100	386	1	.214	0			-1	/O	-0.3
Total	2	19	31	3	9	1	1	0	3	1	5	.290	.313	.387	.700	112	0	0	102	205	5	.591	0			-4	/O	-0.3

■ **DAVE ALTIZER** Altizer, David Tilden "Filipino" b: 11/6/1876, Pearl, Ill. d: 5/14/64, Pleasant Hill, Ill BL/TR, 5'10.5", 160 lbs. Deb: 5/29/06

1906	Was-A	115	433	56	111	9	5	1	27	35		.256	.312	.307	.619	105	-1	3	91	69	54	.637	37			-18	*S/O	-1.4
1907	Was-A	147	540	60	145	15	5	2	42	34		.269	.312	.326	.638	117	3	9	90	87	68	.628	38			-15	S1O	-0.6
1908	Was-A	67	205	19	46	1	1	0	18	13		.224	.271	.239	.510	71	-7	-6	95	138	15	.440	8			-1	23/1S	-0.7
	Cle-A	29	89	11	19	1	2	0	5	7		.213	.271	.270	.540	73	-2	-3	106	78	8	.543	7			-1	O/S	-0.4
	Yr	96	294	30	65	2	3	0	23	20		.221	.271	.248	.519	72	-9	-8	99	121	23	.472	15			-1		-1.1
1909	Chi-A	116	382	47	89	6	7	1	20	39		.233	.330	.293	.623	100	1	2	97	71	44	.662	27			8	O1	0.8
1910	Cin-N	3	10	3	6	0	0	0	0	3	0	.600	.692	.600	1.292	275	3	3	101	0	4	2.250	0			0	/S	0.3
1911	Cin-N	37	75	8	17	4	1	0	4	9	5	.227	.318	.307	.624	82	-2	-2	92	59	8	.603	2			-2	S/12O	-0.1
Total	6	514	1734	204	433	36	21	4	116	140	5	.250	.312	.302	.614	102	-6	6	94	83	202	.614	119			-27	SO1/23	-2.1

■ **GEORGE ALTMAN** Altman, George Lee b: 3/20/33, Goldsboro, N.C. BL/TR, 6'4", 200 lbs. Deb: 4/11/59

1959	Chi-N	135	420	54	103	14	4	12	47	34	80	.245	.312	.383	.696	85	-10	-9	98	96	51	.625	1	0	0	-2	*O	-1.2
1960	Chi-N	119	334	50	89	16	4	13	51	32	67	.266	.332	.455	.788	115	5	6	98	108	51	.750	4	3	-1	-4	O1	-0.1
1961	Chi-N	138	518	77	157	28	**12**	27	96	40	92	.303	.358	.560	.917	139	27	27	100	107	105	.926	6	2	1	6	*O/1	2.5
1962	Chi-N	147	534	74	170	27	5	22	74	62	89	.318	.394	.511	.906	133	31	27	106	88	110	.947	19	7	2	1	*O1	2.1
1963	StL-N	135	464	62	127	18	7	9	47	47	93	.274	.343	.401	.744	106	8	5	107	93	66	.713	13	4	2	3	*O	0.3
1964	NY-N	124	422	48	97	14	1	9	47	18	70	.230	.263	.332	.595	70	-19	-17	95	115	35	.487	4	2	0	6	*O	-1.4
1965	Chi-N	90	196	24	46	7	1	4	23	19	36	.235	.302	.342	.644	80	-5	-5	102	121	21	.582	3	2	-0	-5	O/1	-1.2
1966	Chi-N	88	185	19	41	6	0	5	17	14	37	.222	.276	.335	.612	69	-8	-8	100	93	17	.523	2	2	-1	-5	O/1	-1.5
1967	Chi-N	15	18	1	2	2	0	0	1	2	8	.111	.200	.222	.422	20	-2	-2	102	104	1	.375	0	0	0	-1	/O1	-0.3
Total	9	991	3091	409	832	132	34	101	403	268	572	.269	.331	.432	.763	106	29	24	101	101	456	.734	52	22	2	-2	O/1	-0.8

■ **JOE ALTOBELLI** Altobelli, Joseph Salvatore b: 5/26/32, Detroit, Mich. BL/TL, 6', 185 lbs. Deb: 4/14/55 MC

1955	Cle-A	42	75	8	15	3	0	2	5	5	14	.200	.259	.320	.579	53	-5	-5	104	62	6	.492	0	1	-1	0	1	-0.7
1957	Cle-A	83	87	9	18	3	2	0	9	5	14	.207	.258	.287	.545	48	-6	-6	102	142	7	.472	3	2	-0	-0	1/O	-0.7
1961	Min-A	41	95	10	21	2	1	3	14	13	14	.221	.315	.358	.673	75	-3	-4	106	127	11	.618	0	0	0	-3	O/1	-0.7
Total	3	166	257	27	54	8	3	5	28	23	42	.210	.280	.323	.603	60	-14	-15	104	114	24	.534	3	3	-1	-3	/1O	-2.1

■ **GEORGE ALUSIK** Alusik, George Joseph b: 2/11/35, Ashley, Pa. BR/TR, 6'3.5", 175 lbs. Deb: 9/11/58

1958	Det-A	2	2	0	0	0	0	0	0	0	1	.000	.000	.000	.000	-96	-1	-1	104	0	0	.000	0	0	0	-0	/O	0.0
1961	Det-A	15	14	0	2	0	0	0	2	1	4	.143	.200	.143	.343	-7	-2	-2	96	392	1	.250	0	0	0	-0	/O	-0.2
1962	Det-A	2	2	0	0	0	0	0	0	0	0	.000	.000	.000	.000	-90	-1	-1	111	0	0	.000	0	0	0	0	H	0.0
	KC-A	90	209	29	57	10	1	11	35	16	29	.273	.327	.488	.815	116	4	4	100	103	33	.764	1	1	-0	-1	O/1	0.1
	Yr	92	211	29	57	10	1	11	35	16	29	.270	.325	.483	.808	114	3	3	**100**	101	32	.755	1	1	-0	-1		0.1
1963	KC-A	87	221	28	59	11	0	9	37	26	33	.267	.347	.439	.786	110	6	4	**108**	125	33	.734	0	1	-1	-2	O	-0.1
1964	KC-A	102	204	18	49	10	1	3	19	30	36	.240	.343	.343	.686	88	-1	-3	105	102	25	.634	0	0	0	-3	O1	-0.7
Total	5	298	652	75	167	31	2	23	93	73	103	.256	.335	.416	.750	101	5	2	104	115	91	.708	1	2	-1	-7	O/1	-0.9

■ **LUIS ALVARADO** Alvarado, Luis Cesar (Martinez) b: 1/15/49, La Jas, P.R. BR/TR, 5'9", 162 lbs. Deb: 9/13/68

1968	Bos-A	11	46	3	6	2	0	0	1	1	11	.130	.167	.174	.341	3	-5	-5	101	47	1	.244	0	0	0	0	S	-0.4
1969	Bos-A	6	5	0	0	0	0	0	0	0	2	.000	.000	.000	.000	-95	-1	-1	105	0	0	.000	0	1	-1	0	/S	-0.1
1970	Bos-A	59	183	19	41	11	0	1	10	9	30	.224	.260	.301	.561	49	-12	-14	111	70	13	.436	1	2	-1	-2	3S	-1.4
1971	Chi-A	99	264	22	57	14	1	0	8	11	34	.216	.247	.277	.524	49	-18	-18	98	45	18	.403	1	2	-1	3	S2	-0.7
1972	Chi-A	103	254	30	54	4	1	4	29	13	36	.213	.254	.283	.537	56	-13	-15	106	144	15	.411	2	2	-1	-2	S2/3	-0.8
1973	Chi-A	80	203	21	47	7	2	0	20	4	20	.232	.250	.286	.536	49	-14	-14	102	135	14	.429	6	2	1	-5	2S3/D	-1.4
1974	Chi-A	8	10	1	1	0	0	0	0	0	1	.100	.100	.100	.200	-42	-2	-2	102	0	0	.111	0	0	0	0	/S23	0.0
	StL-N	17	36	3	5	2	0	0	1	2	6	.139	.184	.194	.379	6	-5	-5	104	55	1	.281	0	0	0	0	S	-0.2
	Cle-A	61	114	12	25	2	0	0	12	6	14	.219	.258	.237	.495	43	-8	-8	101	175	7	.366	1	1	-0	2	2/SD	-0.3
1976	StL-N	16	42	5	12	1	0	0	3	3	6	.286	.333	.310	.643	80	-1	-1	104	89	5	.533	0	0	0	-0	2	0.0
1977	NY-N	1	2	0	0	0	0	0	0	0	0	.000	.000	.000	.000	-99	-1	-1	96	0	0	.000	0	0	0	0	/2	0.0
	Det-A	2	1	0	0	0	0	0	0	0	0	.000	.000	.000	.000	-96	-0	-0	105	0	0	.000	0	0	0	0	/3	0.0
Total	9	463	1160	116	248	43	4	5	84	49	160	.214	.248	.271	.518	46	-79	-84	103	100	74	.409	11	10	-3	-4	S2/3D	-5.3

■ **ORLANDO ALVAREZ** Alvarez, Jesus Manuel Orlando (Monge) b: 2/28/52, Rio Grande, P.R. BR/TR, 6', 165 lbs. Deb: 9/01/73

1973	LA-N	4	4	0	1	1	0	0	0	0	1	.250	.250	.500	.750	103	-0	-0	100	0	1	.667	0	0	0	0	H	0.0
1974	LA-N	2	1	0	0	0	0	0	0	0	0	.000	.000	.000	.000	-99	-0	-0	93	0	0	.000	0	0	0	-0	/O	0.0
1975	LA-N	4	4	0	0	0	0	0	0	0	1	.000	.000	.000	.000	-99	-1	-1	95	0	0	.000	0	0	0	0	H	0.0
1976	Cal-A	15	42	4	7	1	0	2	8	0	3	.167	.167	.333	.500	48	-3	-3	92	154	2	.400	0	0	0	-1	O/D	-0.4
Total	4	25	51	4	8	2	0	2	8	0	5	.157	.157	.314	.471	37	-5	-4	93	126	3	.372	0	0	0	-1	/OD	-0.4

■ **OSSIE ALVAREZ** Alvarez, Oswaldo (Gonzalez) b: 10/19/33, Matanzas, Cuba BR/TR, 5'10", 165 lbs. Deb: 4/19/58

1958	Was-A	87	196	20	41	3	0	0	5	16	26	.209	.269	.224	.493	39	-16	-16	97	46	13	.389	1	1	-0	4	S2/3	-0.1
1959	Det-A	8	2	0	1	0	0	0	0	0	1	.500	.500	.500	1.000	158	0	0	111	0	1	1.000	0	0	0	0	H	0.0
Total	2	95	198	20	42	3	0	0	5	16	27	.212	.271	.227	.498	40	-16	-15	97	45	13	.395	1	1	-0	4	/S23	-0.1

■ **ROGELIO ALVAREZ** Alvarez, Rogelio (Hernandez) b: 4/18/38, Pinar Del Rio, Cuba BR/TR, 5'11", 183 lbs. Deb: 9/18/60

1960	Cin-N	3	9	1	1	0	0	0	0	0	3	.111	.111	.111	.222	-40	-2	-2	98	0	0	.125	0	0	0	0	/1	-0.1
1962	Cin-N	14	28	1	6	0	0	0	2	1	10	.214	.241	.214	.456	23	-3	-3	102	131	2	.318	0	0	0	0	1	-0.2
Total	2	17	37	2	7	0	0	0	2	1	13	.189	.211	.189	.400	9	-5	-5	101	100	2	.267	0	0	0	0	/1	-0.3

■ **MAX ALVIS** Alvis, Roy Maxwell b: 2/2/38, Jasper, Tex. BR/TR, 5'11", 185 lbs. Deb: 9/11/62

1962	Cle-A	12	51	1	11	2	0	0	3	2	13	.216	.245	.255	.500	36	-5	-5	98	88	3	.439	3	1	0	-1	3	-0.5
1963	Cle-A	158	602	81	165	32	7	22	67	36	109	.274	.326	.460	.786	121	12	15	97	87	90	.738	9	7	-2	-6	*3	0.9
1964	Cle-A	107	381	51	96	14	3	18	53	29	77	.252	.315	.446	.761	106	4	2	103	102	53	.712	5	5	-2	-3	*3	0.0
1965	Cle-A	159	604	88	149	24	2	21	61	47	121	.247	.311	.397	.708	101	-1	0	98	89	74	.653	12	8	-1	-20	*3	-2.1
1966	Cle-A	157	596	67	146	22	3	17	55	50	98	.245	.306	.378	.683	94	-4	-5	101	89	66	.599	4	7	-3	-6	*3	-1.8
1967	Cle-A	161	637	66	163	23	4	21	70	38	107	.256	.302	.403	.705	106	3	5	100	88	73	.608	3	10	-5	-7	*3	-0.5
1968	Cle-A	131	452	38	101	17	3	8	37	41	91	.223	.294	.327	.621	87	-7	-7	101	94	42	.540	5	5	-2	-19	*3	-2.7
1969	Cle-A	66	191	13	43	6	0	1	15	14	26	.225	.278	.272	.550	58	-12	-10	94	109	13	.424	1	1	-0	-4	3/S	-1.4
1970	Mil-A	62	115	16	21	2	0	3	12	5	20	.183	.217	.278	.495	36	-10	-10	98	118	5	.376	1	2	-1	1	3	-0.9

YEAR	TM/L	G	AB	R	H	2B	3B	HR	RBI	BB	SO	AVG	OBP	SLG	PRO	/A	BR	/A	PF	CHI	RC	TA	SB	CS	SBR	FR	POS	TPR
Total	9	1013	3629	421	895	142	22	111	373	262	662	.247	.304	.390	.693	98	-19	-17	99	92	420	.630	43	46	-15	-65	3/S	-9.0
■ BILLY ALVORD	Alvord, William Charles "Uncle Bill" b: 8/1863, St.Louis, Mo. d: 08, Buffalo, N.Y. 5'10", 187 lbs. Deb: 1885																											
1885	StL-N	2	5	0	0	0	0	0	0	1	2	.000	.167	.000	.167	-46	-1	-1	92	0	0	.200				0	/3	0.0
1889	KC-a	50	186	23	43	8	9	0	18	10	35	.231	.270	.370	.641	79	-5	-7	106	76	20	.573	3			0	3/S2	-0.5
1890	Tol-a	116	495	69	135	13	16	2		22		.273	.304	.376	.679	100	-1	-3	103	0	64	.636	21			1	*3	-0.3
1891	Cle-N	13	59	7	17	2	2	1	7	0	7	.288	.300	.441	.741	111	1	0	105	68	8	.643	0			0	3	0.0
	Was-a	81	312	28	73	8	3	0	30	11	38	.234	.260	.279	.539	59	-18	-16	95	102	24	.423	3			15	3	0.2
1893	Cle-N	3	12	2	2	0	0	0	2	0	1	.167	.167	.167	.333	-10	-2	-2	104	274	0	.200	0			0	/3	-0.1
Total	5	265	1069	129	270	31	30	3	57	44	83	.253	.283	.346	.629	83	-26	-28	101	49	117	.553	27			16	3/2S	-0.7
■ BRANT ALYEA	Alyea, Garrabrant Ryerson b: 12/8/40, Passaic, N.J. BR/TR, 6'3", 215 lbs. Deb: 9/11/65																											
1965	Was-A	8	13	3	3	0	0	2	6	1	4	.231	.286	.692	.978	169	1	1	100	166	2	.909	0	0	0	-0	/1O	0.0
1968	Was-A	53	150	18	40	11	1	6	23	10	39	.267	.317	.473	.790	150	6	7	91	111	21	.707	0	0	0	-1	O	0.6
1969	Was-A	104	237	29	59	4	0	11	40	34	67	.249	.346	.405	.751	113	3	4	97	124	32	.695	1	3	-2	-8	O/1	-0.7
1970	Min-A	94	258	34	75	12	1	16	61	28	51	.291	.367	.531	.898	147	15	16	98	133	46	.864	3	3	-1	-8	O	0.3
1971	Min-A	79	158	13	28	4	0	2	15	24	38	.177	.290	.241	.530	49	-10	-10	104	139	11	.464	1	1	-0	-8	O	-2.2
1972	Oak-A	20	31	3	6	1	0	1	2	3	5	.194	.265	.323	.587	77	-1	-1	97	64	3	.500	0	0	0	3	/O	0.2
	StL-N	13	19	0	3	1	0	0	1	0	6	.158	.158	.211	.368	4	-2	-2	105	103	1	.250	0	0	0	1	/O	-0.1
Total	6	371	866	100	214	33	2	38	148	100	210	.247	.329	.421	.751	114	12	14	98	126	115	.722	5	7	-3	-21	O/1	-1.9
■ JOEY AMALFITANO	Amalfitano, John Joseph b: 1/23/34, San Pedro, Cal. BR/TR, 5'11", 175 lbs. Deb: 5/03/54 MC																											
1954	NY-N	9	5	2	0	0	0	0	0	0	4	.000	.000	.000	.000	-95	-1	-1	105	0	0	.000	0	0	0	0	/32	0.0
1955	NY-N	36	22	8	5	1	1	0	1	2	2	.227	.292	.364	.655	74	-1	-1	99	51	2	.588	0	0	0	0	/S3	0.0
1960	SF-N	106	328	47	91	15	3	1	27	26	31	.277	.336	.351	.687	98	-5	-1	90	93	39	.596	2	3	-1	-1	32/SO	0.0
1961	SF-N	109	384	64	98	11	4	2	23	44	59	.255	.332	.320	.652	75	-13	-12	98	73	44	.596	7	4	-0	-21	2/3	-2.1
1962	Hou-N	117	380	44	90	12	5	1	27	45	43	.237	.319	.303	.622	73	-16	-13	93	90	36	.537	4	4	-1	-4	*2/3	-0.7
1963	SF-N	54	137	11	24	3	0	1	7	12	18	.175	.247	.219	.466	37	-11	-11	96	89	6	.363	2	6	-3	-3	2/3	-1.5
1964	Chi-N	100	324	51	78	19	6	4	27	40	42	.241	.333	.373	.707	94	0	-2	105	83	38	.639	2	7	-4	8	2/1S	1.0
1965	Chi-N	67	96	13	26	4	0	0	8	12	14	.271	.364	.313	.676	91	-0	-1	102	111	12	.630	2	2	-1	1	2/S	0.2
1966	Chi-N	41	38	8	6	2	0	0	3	4	10	.158	.238	.211	.449	26	-4	-4	100	158	2	.364	0	0	0	-1	2/3S	-0.3
1967	Chi-N	4	1	0	0	0	0	0	0	0	1	.000	.000	.000	.000	-99	-0	-0	102	0	0	.000	0	0	0	0	H	0.0
Total	10	643	1715	248	418	67	19	9	123	185	224	.244	.322	.321	.642	79	-52	-45	97	87	180	.579	19	26	-10	-21	2/3S10	-3.4
■ RUBEN AMARO	Amaro, Ruben (Mora) b: 1/6/36, Vera Cruz, Mexico BR/TR, 5'11", 170 lbs. Deb: 6/29/58 C																											
1958	StL-N	40	76	8	17	2	1	0	0	5	8	.224	.272	.276	.548	43	-6	-7	106	0	5	.413	0	1	-1	-4	S/2	-0.8
1960	Phi-N	92	264	25	61	9	1	0	16	21	32	.231	.293	.273	.565	52	-16	-18	107	90	21	.455	0	1	-1	-10	S	-2.6
1961	Phi-N	135	381	34	98	14	9	1	32	53	59	.257	.351	.349	.700	92	-6	-2	94	95	49	.647	1	0	0	9	*S/12	1.9
1962	Phi-N	79	226	24	55	10	0	0	19	30	28	.243	.335	.288	.622	79	-9	-7	95	115	23	.564	5	2	0	4	S/1	0.4
1963	Phi-N	115	217	25	47	9	2	2	19	19	31	.217	.280	.304	.584	66	-9	-10	103	111	18	.486	0	1	-1	4	S3/1	0.0
1964	Phi-N	129	299	31	79	11	0	4	34	16	37	.264	.308	.341	.649	84	-7	-6	99	122	30	.528	1	6	-3	-2	S1/230	-0.8
1965	Phi-N	118	184	26	39	7	0	0	15	27	22	.212	.316	.250	.566	65	-8	-7	95	135	15	.493	1	1	-0	5	1S/2	0.1
1966	NY-A	14	23	0	5	0	0	0	3	0	2	.217	.217	.217	.435	27	-2	-2	94	252	1	.250	0	0	0	-1	S	-0.1
1967	NY-A	130	417	31	93	12	0	1	17	43	49	.223	.297	.259	.556	70	-17	-14	94	64	32	.457	3	2	-0	5	*S/31	0.0
1968	NY-A	47	41	3	5	1	0	0	0	9	6	.122	.280	.146	.426	32	-3	-3	101	0	2	.417	0	0	0	0	S1	-0.2
1969	Cal-A	41	27	4	6	0	0	0	1	4	6	.222	.323	.222	.545	55	-1	-1	99	67	3	.476	0	0	0	-0	1/2S3	-0.1
Total	11	940	2155	211	505	75	13	8	156	227	280	.234	.310	.292	.603	71	-84	-78	98	95	200	.528	11	14	-5	9	S1/320	-2.2
■ WAYNE AMBLER	Ambler, Wayne Harper b: 11/8/15, Abington, Pa. BR/TR, 5'8.5", 165 lbs. Deb: 6/04/37																											
1937	Phi-A	56	162	3	35	5	0	0	11	13	8	.216	.274	.247	.521	34	-17	-15	94	94	12	.425	1	0	0	-2	2	-1.0
1938	Phi-A	120	393	42	92	21	2	0	38	48	31	.234	.317	.298	.615	54	-27	-28	101	110	40	.553	2	1	0	-21	*S/2	-3.7
1939	Phi-A	95	227	15	48	13	0	0	24	22	25	.211	.281	.269	.550	42	-20	-19	97	133	17	.444	1	0	0	-4	S2	-1.3
Total	3	271	782	60	175	39	2	0	73	83	64	.224	.298	.279	.577	47	-64	-62	98	113	69	.494	4	1	1	-27	S/2	-6.0
■ ED AMELUNG	Amelung, Edward Allen b: 4/13/59, Fullerton, Cal. BL/TL, 6', 185 lbs. Deb: 7/28/84																											
1984	LA-N	34	46	7	10	0	0	0	4	2	4	.217	.250	.217	.467	31	-4	-4	104	157	2	.385	3	2	-0	-3	O	-0.8
1986	LA-N	8	11	0	1	0	0	0	0	0	4	.091	.091	.091	.182	-53	-2	-2	94	0	0	.091	0	0	0	-0	/O	-0.2
Total	2	42	57	7	11	0	0	0	4	2	8	.193	.220	.193	.413	16	-6	-6	102	127	2	.327	3	2	-0	-3	/O	-1.0
■ SANDY AMOROS	Amoros, Edmundo (Isasi) b: 1/30/30, Havana, Cuba BL/TL, 5'7.5", 170 lbs. Deb: 8/22/52																											
1952	Bro-N	20	44	10	11	3	1	0	3	5	14	.250	.327	.364	.690	90	-1	-1	102	73	6	.667	1	0	0	-1	O	-0.1
1954	Bro-N	79	263	44	72	18	6	9	34	31	24	.274	.353	.490	.843	116	6	6	101	86	45	.814	1	4	-2	4	O	0.5
1955	Bro-N	119	388	59	96	16	7	10	51	55	45	.247	.350	.402	.752	95	0	-2	104	111	57	.744	10	5	0	0	*O	-0.3
1956	Bro-N	114	292	53	76	11	8	16	58	59	51	.260	.386	.517	.903	136	18	17	103	123	61	.955	3	4	-2	-10	O	0.2
1957	Bro-N	106	238	40	66	7	1	7	26	46	42	.277	.401	.403	.804	100	8	2	116	92	41	.822	3	2	-0	-3	O	-0.2
1959	LA-N	5	5	1	1	0	0	0	1	0	1	.200	.200	.200	.400	7	-1	-1	102	404	0	.250	0	0	0	0	H	0.0
1960	LA-N	9	14	1	2	0	0	0	0	3	2	.143	.294	.143	.437	21	-1	-2	115	0	1	.417	0	0	0	1	/O	0.0
	Det-A	65	67	7	10	0	0	1	7	12	10	.149	.278	.194	.473	30	-6	-6	102	171	4	.431	0	0	0	-1	O	-0.7
Total	7	517	1311	215	334	55	23	43	180	211	189	.255	.363	.430	.793	105	23	13	106	107	215	.810	18	15	-4	-10	O	-0.6
■ ALF ANDERSON	Anderson, Alfred Walton b: 1/28/14, Gainesville, Ga. d: 6/23/85, Albany, Ga. BR/TR, 5'11", 165 lbs. Deb: 4/20/41																											
1941	Pit-N	70	223	32	48	7	2	1	10	14	30	.215	.265	.278	.543	52	-14	-15	103	56	17	.444	2			-6	S	-1.5
1942	Pit-N	54	166	24	45	4	1	0	7	18	19	.271	.342	.307	.650	90	-1	-2	101	51	18	.589	4			-7	S	-0.5
1946	Pit-N	2	1	0	0	0	0	0	0	1	0	.000	.500	.000	.500	47	0	0	103	0	0	.500	0				H	0.0
Total	3	126	390	56	93	11	3	1	17	33	49	.238	.300	.290	.589	68	-15	-16	102	53	35	.513	6			-12	S	-2.0
■ ANDY ANDERSON	Anderson, Andy Holm b: 11/13/22, Bremerton, Wash. d: 7/18/82, Seattle, Wash. BR/TR, 5'11", 172 lbs. Deb: 5/10/48																											
1948	StL-A	51	87	13	24	5	1	1	12	8	15	.276	.337	.391	.728	88	-1	-2	106	110	10	.600	0	0	0	2	2S/1	0.1
1949	StL-A	71	136	10	17	3	0	1	5	14	21	.125	.207	.169	.376	-0	-20	-20	100	66	5	.298	0	1	-1	-3	S/23	-2.2
Total	2	122	223	23	41	8	1	2	17	22	36	.184	.257	.256	.513	35	-21	-22	102	83	15	.422	0	1	-1	-1	/S231	-2.1
■ BRADY ANDERSON	Anderson, Brady Kevin b: 1/8/64, Silver Spring, Md. BL/TL, 6'1", 170 lbs. Deb: 4/04/88																											
1988	Bos-A	41	148	14	34	5	3	0	12	15	35	.230	.317	.304	.621	69	-5	-6	109	108	16	.576	4	2	0	3	O	-0.3
	Bal-A	53	177	17	35	8	1	1	9	8	40	.198	.232	.271	.504	43	-14	-13	95	70	11	.422	6	4	-1	9	O	-0.5
	Yr	94	325	31	69	13	4	1	21	23	75	.212	.273	.286	.559	56	-19	-19	101	88	27	.494	10	6	-1	11		-0.8
Total	1	94	325	31	69	13	4	1	21	23	75	.212	.273	.286	.559	56	-19	-19	102	88	27	.494	10	6	-1	11	/O	-0.8
■ DAVE ANDERSON	Anderson, David Carter b: 8/1/60, Louisville, Ky. BR/TR, 6'2", 185 lbs. Deb: 5/08/83																											
1983	LA-N	61	115	12	19	4	2	1	2	12	15	.165	.244	.261	.505	40	-9	-9	100	24	8	.480	6	3	0	2	S/3	-0.3
1984	LA-N	121	374	51	94	16	2	3	34	45	55	.251	.335	.329	.664	84	-5	-7	104	101	44	.631	15	5	2	15	*S3	2.2
1985	LA-N	77	221	24	44	6	0	4	18	35	42	.199	.311	.281	.592	72	-9	-7	93	97	21	.557	5	4	-1	8	3S/2	0.2
1986	LA-N	92	216	31	53	9	0	1	15	22	39	.245	.315	.301	.616	75	-8	-7	94	88	20	.526	5	1	1	1	3S/2	-0.1
1987	LA-N	108	265	32	62	12	3	1	13	24	43	.234	.300	.313	.613	68	-14	-11	92	60	26	.557	9	5	-0	2	S3/2	-0.1
1988	LA-N	116	285	31	71	10	2	2	20	32	45	.249	.327	.319	.646	81	-4	-6	106	82	30	.569	4	2	0	6	S23	0.6
Total	6	575	1476	181	343	57	9	12	102	170	239	.232	.314	.308	.621	74	-50	-48	99	82	148	.579	44	20	1	34	S3/2	2.5
■ DWAIN ANDERSON	Anderson, Dwain Cleaven b: 11/23/47, Oakland, Cal. BR/TR, 5'11", 165 lbs. Deb: 9/03/71																											
1971	Oak-A	16	37	3	10	2	1	0	3	5	9	.270	.372	.378	.750	112	1	1	101	87	5	.714	0	1	-1	0	S/23	0.2
1972	Oak-A	3	7	2	0	0	0	0	0	1	4	.000	.125	.000	.125	-63	-1	-1	97	0	0	.143	0	0	0	0	/S3	0.0
	StL-N	57	135	12	36	4	1	1	8	8	23	.267	.313	.333	.646	80	-3	-4	105	68	13	.519	0	1	-1	-1	S3/2	0.0

YEAR	TM/L	G	AB	R	H	2B	3B	HR	RBI	BB	SO	AVG	OBP	SLG	PRO	/A	BR	/A	PF	CHI	RC	TA	SB	CS	SBR	FR	POS	TPR
1973	StL-N	18	17	5	2	0	0	0	0	4	4	.118	.286	.118	.403	17	-2	-2	91	0	1	.400	0	0	0	-1	/SO	-0.1
	SD-N	53	107	11	13	0	0	0	3	14	29	.121	.223	.121	.345	-2	-15	-14	94	93	4	.302	2	0	1	0	S/3	-0.7
	Yr	71	124	16	15	0	0	0	3	18	33	.121	.232	.121	.353	1	-16	-15	93	69	5	.315	2	0	1	-0		-0.8
1974	Cle-A	2	3	0	1	0	0	0	0	0	1	.333	.333	.333	.667	92	-0	-0	101	0	0	.500	0	0	0	0	/2	0.0
Total	4	149	306	33	62	6	2	1	14	32	70	.203	.282	.245	.527	50	-20	-20	99	73	23	.451	2	2	-1	-1	/S32O	-0.6
■ GOAT ANDERSON Anderson, Edward John b: 1/13/1880, Cleveland, Ohio d: 3/15/23, South Bend, Ind. TR, Deb: 4/11/07																												
1907	Pit-N	127	413	73	85	3	1	1	12	80		.206	.335	.225	.560	74	-6	-8	105	50	41	.610	27			12	*O/2	0.0
■ FERRELL ANDERSON Anderson, Ferrell Jack "Andy" b: 1/9/18, Maple City, Kan. d: 3/12/78, Joplin, Mo. BR/TR, 6'1", 200 lbs. Deb: 4/16/46																												
1946	Bro-N	79	199	19	51	10	0	2	14	18	21	.256	.330	.337	.667	87	-3	-3	103	72	22	.584	1			-1	C	-0.1
1953	StL-N	18	35	1	10	2	0	0	1	0	4	.286	.286	.343	.629	62	-2	-2	102	32	4	.480	0	0	0	-0	C	-0.1
Total	2	97	234	20	61	12	0	2	15	18	25	.261	.324	.338	.662	83	-5	-5	102	66	26	.590	1	0		-1	/C	-0.2
■ GEORGE ANDERSON Anderson, George Jendrus "Andy" (Born George Andrew Jendrus) b: 9/26/1889, Cleveland, Ohio d: 5/28/62, Cleveland, Ohio BL/TR, 5'8.5", 160 lbs. Deb: 5/26/14																												
1914	Bro-F	98	364	58	115	13	3	3	24	31	50	.316	.370	.393	.762	118	9	9	101	60	61	.763	16			5	O	0.9
1915	Bro-F	136	511	70	135	23	9	2	39	52	54	.264	.332	.356	.688	106	3	4	98	79	70	.676	20			-10	*O	-1.3
1918	StL-N	35	132	20	39	4	5	0	6	15	7	.295	.380	.402	.782	148	7	8	93	38	20	.763	0			-3	O	0.3
Total	3	269	1007	148	289	40	17	5	69	98	111	.287	.352	.375	.727	116	18	20	98	67	151	.717	36			-9	O	-0.1
■ SPARKY ANDERSON Anderson, George Lee b: 2/22/34, Bridgewater, S.Dak BR/TR, 5'9", 170 lbs. Deb: 4/10/59 MC																												
1959	Phi-N	152	477	42	104	9	3	0	34	42	53	.218	.283	.249	.532	43	-38	-37	99	116	32	.423	6	9	-4	-2	*2	-3.1
■ HAL ANDERSON Anderson, Harold b: 2/10/04, St.Louis, Mo. d: 5/1/74, St.Louis, Mo. BR/TR, 5'11", 160 lbs. Deb: 4/12/32																												
1932	Chi-A	9	32	4	8	0	0	0	2	0	1	.250	.250	.250	.500	34	-3	-3	87	84	2	.320	0	1	-1	1	/O	-0.2
■ HARRY ANDERSON Anderson, Harry Walter b: 9/10/31, North East, Md. BL/TR, 6'3", 205 lbs. Deb: 4/18/57																												
1957	Phi-N	118	400	53	107	15	4	17	61	36	61	.268	.337	.452	.790	112	5	6	98	111	61	.745	2	3	-1	1	*O	0.3
1958	Phi-N	140	515	80	155	34	6	23	97	59	95	.301	.376	.524	.900	138	26	27	98	**121**	100	.888	0	2	-1	-4	O1	1.6
1959	Phi-N	142	508	50	122	28	6	14	63	43	95	.240	.306	.402	.707	87	-11	-10	99	106	62	.639	1	1	-0	14	*O	0.1
1960	Phi-N	38	93	10	23	2	0	5	12	10	19	.247	.333	.430	.763	100	1	0	107	89	13	.722	0	0	0	-1	O1	-0.1
	Cin-N	42	66	6	11	3	0	1	9	11	20	.167	.286	.258	.543	51	-4	-4	98	183	6	.509	0	0	0	-1	1/O	-0.5
	Yr	80	159	16	34	5	0	6	21	21	39	.214	.313	.358	.672	81	-4	-4	103	139	20	.640	0	0	0	-1	O/1	-0.6
1961	Cin-N	4	4	0	1	0	0	0	0	0	1	.250	.250	.250	.500	32	-0	-0	104	0	0	.333	0	0	0	0	H	0.0
Total	5	484	1586	199	419	82	16	60	242	159	291	.264	.337	.450	.787	109	16	18	99	114	242	.760	3	6	-3	10	O/1	1.4
■ JIM ANDERSON Anderson, James Lea b: 2/23/57, Los Angeles, Cal. BR/TR, 6', 170 lbs. Deb: 7/02/78																												
1978	Cal-A	48	108	6	21	7	0	0	7	11	16	.194	.269	.259	.528	48	-7	-7	102	99	7	.424	0	0	0	-4	S/2	-0.7
1979	Cal-A	96	234	33	58	13	1	3	23	17	31	.248	.302	.350	.652	81	-8	-6	93	97	24	.560	3	2	-0	-1	S3/2C	0.3
1980	Sea-A	116	317	46	72	7	0	8	30	27	39	.227	.294	.325	.619	67	-13	-15	103	92	30	.531	2	4	-2	4	S3/2CD	-0.6
1981	Sea-A	70	162	12	33	7	0	2	19	17	29	.204	.283	.284	.567	64	-7	-7	100	143	12	.486	3	5	-2	-0	S/3	-0.4
1983	Tex-A	50	102	8	22	1	1	0	6	5	8	.216	.252	.245	.497	37	-9	-9	101	94	6	.365	1	2	-1	-2	S2/3OCD	-0.8
1984	Tex-A	39	47	2	5	0	0	0	1	4	7	.106	.176	.106	.283	-20	-8	-8	100	80	1	.214	0	0	0	-1	S/32	-0.6
Total	6	419	970	107	211	35	2	13	86	81	130	.218	.281	.298	.579	60	-52	-51	99	102	81	.497	9	13	-5	-4	S/32DCO	-2.8
■ JOHN ANDERSON Anderson, John Joseph "Honest John" b: 12/14/1873, Sasbourg, Norway d: 7/23/49, Worcester, Mass. BB/TR, 6'2", 180 lbs. Deb: 9/08/1894																												
1894	Bro-N	17	63	14	19	1	3	1	19	3	3	.302	.333	.460	.794	97	-1	-1	94	164	12	.886	7			0	O/3	0.0
1895	Bro-N	102	419	76	120	11	14	9	87	12	29	.286	.314	.444	.758	102	-5	-1	94	121	68	.759	24			-7	*O	-1.3
1896	Bro-N	108	430	70	135	23	17	1	55	18	23	.314	.344	.453	.798	127	5	14	87	85	82	.854	37			-4	O1	0.5
1897	Bro-N	117	492	93	160	28	12	4	85	17		.325	.355	.455	.811	114	9	8	102	101	92	.831	29			-1	*O/1	-0.1
1898	Bro-N	6	21	1	3	2	0	0	2	1		.143	.217	.238	.455	34	-2	-2	95	123	1	.389	0			0	/1	-0.1
	Was-N	110	430	70	131	28	18	9	71	23		.305	.356	.516	.872	149	26	24	102	83	87	.916	18			7	O1	2.3
	Bro-N	19	69	11	19	3	4	0	8	5		.275	.333	.435	.768	129	2	2	95	82	11	.760	2			-1	O/1	0.0
	Yr	135	520	82	153	33	**22**	9	81	29		.294	.347	.494	.841	142	25	25	101	86	99	.869	20			6		2.2
1899	Bro-N	117	439	65	118	18	7	3	92	27		.269	.317	.362	.679	84	-7	-11	105	178	60	.670	25			-5	O1	-1.7
1901	Mil-A	138	576	90	190	46	7	8	99	24		.330	.357	.476	.832	138	22	26	95	93	113	.863	35			1	*1O	1.9
1902	StL-A	126	524	60	149	29	6	4	85	21		.284	.312	.385	.697	92	-5	-7	102	116	69	.635	15			-7	*1/O	-1.1
1903	StL-A	138	550	65	156	34	8	2	78	23		.284	.312	.385	.698	116	6	9	95	114	73	.637	16			6	*1/O	1.6
1904	NY-A	143	558	62	155	27	12	3	82	23		.278	.306	.385	.692	107	11	4	112	**145**	74	.640	20			10	*O1	0.8
1905	NY-A	32	99	12	23	3	1	0	14	8		.232	.290	.283	.573	82	-2	-2	102	178	11	.592	9			-1	O/1	-0.4
	Was-A	101	400	50	116	21	6	1	38	22		.290	.327	.380	.707	121	11	9	104	75	58	.690	22			7	O/1	1.2
	Yr	133	499	62	139	24	7	1	52	30		.279	.319	.361	.680	114	9	7	104	102	69	.669	31			6		0.8
1906	Was-A	151	583	62	158	25	4	3	70	19		.271	.294	.343	.637	111	-1	5	91	129	72	.607	**39**			11	*O	1.1
1907	Was-A	87	333	33	96	12	4	0	44	34		.288	.354	.348	.703	140	11	14	90	120	49	.713	19			-11	1O	0.1
1908	Chi-A	123	355	36	93	17	1	0	47	30		.262	.319	.315	.635	115	4	6	94	158	41	.622	21			0	O/1	0.2
Total	14	1635	6341	870	1841	328	124	48	976	310	55	.290	.326	.404	.730	115	82	100	98	118	974	.720	338			5	*O1/3	5.0
■ MIKE ANDERSON Anderson, Michael Allen b: 6/22/51, Florence, S.C. BR/TR, 6'2", 200 lbs. Deb: 9/02/71																												
1971	Phi-N	26	89	11	22	5	1	2	5	13	28	.247	.343	.393	.736	105	1	1	103	51	13	.716	0	0	0	3	O	0.3
1972	Phi-N	36	103	8	20	5	1	2	5	19	36	.194	.320	.320	.640	85	-2	-2	97	53	12	.639	1	0	0	4	O	0.1
1973	Phi-N	87	193	32	49	9	1	9	28	19	53	.254	.324	.451	.775	104	3	1	108	99	27	.718	0	3	-2	-5	O	-0.8
1974	Phi-N	145	395	35	99	22	2	5	34	37	75	.251	.315	.354	.669	84	-7	-9	103	85	41	.576	2	1	0	4	*O/1	-1.0
1975	Phi-N	115	247	24	64	10	3	4	28	17	66	.259	.312	.372	.684	88	-4	-5	101	104	27	.586	1	2	-1	-7	*O/1	-1.7
1976	StL-N	86	199	17	58	8	1	1	12	26	30	.291	.376	.357	.733	105	3	2	104	62	27	.673	1	1	-0	-0	O/1	0.0
1977	StL-N	94	154	18	34	4	1	4	17	14	31	.221	.286	.338	.623	69	-7	-7	96	106	14	.540	2	3	-1	-11	O	-2.1
1978	Bal-A	53	32	2	3	0	1	0	3	3	10	.094	.171	.156	.328	-8	-5	-4	91	237	1	.276	0	0	0	-16	O	-2.2
1979	Phi-N	79	78	12	18	4	0	1	2	13	14	.231	.341	.321	.661	84	-2	-1	97	28	9	.609	1	2	-1	-15	O/P	-1.9
Total	9	721	1490	159	367	67	11	28	134	161	343	.246	.321	.362	.684	89	-20	-23	102	84	173	.627	8	12	-5	-44	O/1P	-9.3
■ ERNIE ANDRES Andres, Ernest Henry "Junie" b: 1/11/18, Jeffersonville, Ind. BR/TR, 6'1", 200 lbs. Deb: 4/16/46																												
1946	Bos-A	15	41	0	4	2	0	0	1	3	5	.098	.159	.146	.305	-13	-6	-7	114	63	1	.237	0	0	0	-0	3	-0.5
■ KIM ANDREW Andrew, Kim Darrell b: 11/14/53, Glendale, Cal. BR/TR, 5'10", 160 lbs. Deb: 4/16/75																												
1975	Bos-A	2	2	0	1	0	0	0	0	0	0	.500	.500	.500	1.000	169	0	0	109	0	1	1.000	0	0	0	0	/2	0.0
■ FRED ANDREWS Andrews, Fred b: 5/4/52, Lafayette, La. BR/TR, 5'8", 163 lbs. Deb: 9/26/76																												
1976	Phi-N	4	6	1	4	0	0	0	0	2	0	.667	.778	.667	1.444	291	2	2	107	0	4	2.667	1	1	-0	0	/2	0.2
1977	Phi-N	12	23	3	4	0	1	0	2	1	5	.174	.208	.261	.469	25	-2	-2	100	133	1	.400	1	0	0	1	/2	0.0
Total	2	16	29	4	8	0	1	0	2	3	5	.276	.364	.345	.708	91	-0	-0	102	97	5	.696	2	1	0	1	/2	0.2
■ ED ANDREWS Andrews, George Edward b: 4/5/1859, Painesville, Ohio d: 8/12/34, W.Palm Beach, Fla. BR/TR, 5'8", 160 lbs. Deb: 5/01/1884																												
1884	Phi-N	109	420	74	93	21	2	0	23	9	42	.221	.238	.281	.519	68	-18	-13	92	68	29	.388				-29	*2	-3.5
1885	Phi-N	103	421	77	112	15	3	0	23	32	25	.266	.318	.316	.634	102	3	1	104	52	43	.534				1	*O/2	0.0
1886	Phi-N	107	437	93	109	15	4	2	28	31	35	.249	.299	.316	.615	89	-6	-5	98	56	59	.686	**56**			4	*O/2	0.0
1887	Phi-N	104	464	110	151	19	7	4	67	21	21	.325	.359	.422	.781	122	11	13	97	88	93	.885	57			-2	*O/21	1.0
1888	Phi-N	124	528	75	126	14	4	3	44	21	41	.239	.272	.297	.569	73	-10	-19	114	82	53	.537	35			-6	*O	-2.6
1889	Phi-N	10	39	10	11	1	0	0	7	2	4	.282	.317	.308	.625	73	-1	-1	104	177	6	.750	7			-2	/O2	-0.2
	Ind-N	40	173	32	53	11	0	0	22	5	10	.306	.330	.370	.700	89	-1	-3	109	99	24	.642	7			-4	O/2	-0.7
	Yr	50	212	42	64	12	0	0	29	7	14	.302	.327	.358	.686	86	-2	-5	108	118	30	.662	14			-5		-0.9
1890	Bro-P	94	395	84	100	14	2	3	38	40	32	.253	.323	.322	.645	70	-14	-18	106	81	49	.641	21			-2	*O	-1.9
1891	CM-a	83	356	47	75	7	4	0	26	33	35	.211	.279	.253	.532	49	-20	-27	112	74	32	.520	22			15	O	-1.3

YEAR	TM/L	G	AB	R	H	2B	3B	HR	RBI	BB	SO	AVG	OBP	SLG	PRO	/A	BR	/A	PF	CHI	RC	TA	SB	CS	SBR	FR	POS	TPR
Total	8	774	3233	602	830	117	26	12	278	194	245	.257	.301	.320	.621	83	-57	-73	104	74	389	.600	205			-25	O2/1	-9.2
■ **JIM ANDREWS**	Andrews, James Pratt b: 6/5/1865, Shelburne Falls, Mass. d: 12/27/07, Chicago, Ill. Deb: 4/19/1890																											
1890	Chi-N	53	202	32	38	4	2	3	17	23	41	.188	.278	.272	.550	57	-9	-12	109	85	19	.555	11			-1	O	-1.2
■ **MIKE ANDREWS**	Andrews, Michael Jay b: 7/9/43, Los Angeles, Cal. BR/TR, 6'3", 195 lbs. Deb: 9/18/66																											
1966	Bos-A	5	18	1	3	0	0	0	0	0	2	.167	.167	.167	.333	-4	-2	-3	109	0	1	.200	0	0	0	0	/2	-0.1
1967	Bos-A	142	494	79	130	20	0	8	40	62	72	.263	.348	.352	.700	94	6	-2	115	86	63	.645	7	7	-2	-4	*2/S	-0.3
1968	Bos-A	147	536	77	145	22	1	7	45	81	57	.271	.369	.354	.724	120	16	16	101	88	75	.684	3	8	-4	2	*2/S3	2.1
1969	Bos-A	121	464	79	136	26	2	15	59	71	53	.293	.393	.455	.847	130	24	21	105	82	88	.857	1	1	-0	10	*2	3.7
1970	Bos-A	151	589	91	149	28	1	17	65	81	63	.253	.346	.390	.737	93	3	-5	111	83	84	.701	2	1	0	-29	*2	-1.9
1971	Chi-A	109	330	45	93	16	0	12	47	67	36	.282	.405	.439	.844	142	20	21	98	106	62	.871	3	5	-2	-4	21	1.8
1972	Chi-A	148	505	58	111	18	0	7	50	70	78	.220	.317	.297	.614	79	-8	-12	106	129	54	.560	2	2	-1	-9	*2/1	-1.5
1973	Chi-A	52	159	10	32	9	0	0	10	23	28	.201	.302	.258	.560	58	-8	-9	102	96	12	.474	0	1	-1	0	D/123	-0.9
	Oak-A	18	21	1	4	1	0	0	0	3	1	.190	.292	.238	.530	58	-1	-1	87	0	1	.444	0	0	0	-0	/2D	0.0
	Yr	70	180	11	36	10	0	0	10	26	29	.200	.301	.256	.557	59	-9	-9	98	73	16	.493	0	1	-1	-0		-0.9
Total	8	893	3116	441	803	140	4	66	316	458	390	.258	.356	.369	.724	103	49	27	106	94	439	.702	18	25	-10	-33	2/1DS3	2.9
■ **ROB ANDREWS**	Andrews, Robert Patrick b: 12/11/52, Santa Monica, Cal. BR/TR, 6', 185 lbs. Deb: 4/07/75																											
1975	Hou-N	103	277	29	66	5	4	0	19	31	34	.238	.315	.285	.600	71	-12	-10	94	93	27	.550	12	5	1	5	2/S	0.1
1976	Hou-N	109	410	42	105	8	5	0	23	33	27	.256	.312	.300	.612	86	-13	-7	86	76	37	.503	7	3	0	11	*2/S	1.0
1977	SF-N	127	436	60	115	11	3	0	25	56	33	.264	.348	.303	.650	73	-13	-15	104	77	49	.580	5	6	-2	-12	*2	-2.2
1978	SF-N	79	177	21	39	3	3	1	11	20	18	.220	.299	.288	.588	71	-8	-6	92	81	17	.539	5	1	1	-5	2/S	-0.5
1979	SF-N	75	154	22	40	3	0	2	13	8	9	.260	.296	.318	.614	73	-7	-5	92	94	14	.508	4	1	1	-2	2/3	-0.3
Total	5	493	1454	174	365	30	15	3	91	148	121	.251	.320	.298	.619	76	-53	-43	95	82	143	.554	33	16	0	-3	2/S3	-1.9
■ **STAN ANDREWS**	Andrews, Stanley Joseph "Polo" (born Stanley Joseph Andruskewicz) b: 4/17/17, Lynn, Mass. BR/TR, 5'11", 178 lbs. Deb: 6/11/39																											
1939	Bos-N	13	26	1	6	0	0	0	1	1	2	.231	.259	.231	.490	36	-2	-2	92	61	1	.333	0			0	C	-0.1
1940	Bos-N	19	33	1	6	0	0	0	2	0	3	.182	.182	.182	.364	1	-4	-4	99	124	1	.259	1			1	C	-0.2
1944	Bro-N	4	8	1	1	0	0	0	1	1	2	.125	.222	.125	.347	-0	-1	-1	99	359	0	.286	0			0	/C	0.0
1945	Bro-N	21	49	5	8	0	1	0	2	5	4	.163	.255	.204	.459	30	-5	-4	96	69	3	.372	0			-1	C	-0.4
	Phi-N	13	33	3	11	2	0	1	6	1	5	.333	.353	.485	.838	136	1	1	96	110	6	.818	1			-0	C	0.1
	Yr	34	82	8	19	2	1	1	8	6	9	.232	.292	.317	.609	72	-4	-3	96	87	8	.540	1			-1		-0.3
Total	4	70	149	11	32	2	1	1	12	8	16	.215	.259	.262	.521	46	-11	-11	96	104	11	.427	2			-0	/C	-0.6
■ **WALLY ANDREWS**	Andrews, William Walter b: 9/18/1859, Philadelphia, Pa. d: 1/20/40, Indianapolis, Ind. 6'3", 170 lbs. Deb: 5/22/1884																											
1884	Lou-a	14	49	10	10	5	1	0		4		.204	.264	.347	.611	113	0	1	89	0	5	.538				0	/13OS	0.1
1888	Lou-a	26	93	12	18	6	3	0	6	13		.194	.292	.323	.615	110	0	2	91	61	10	.640	5			0	1	0.2
Total	2	40	142	22	28	11	4	0	6	17		.197	.283	.331	.614	111	0	3	90	41	15	.605	5			0	/13SO	0.3
■ **FRED ANDRUS**	Andrus, Frederick Hotham b: 8/23/1850, Washington, Mich. d: 11/10/37, Detroit, Mich. BR/TR, 6'2", 185 lbs. Deb: 7/25/1876																											
1876	Chi-N	8	36	6	11	3	0	0	2	0	5	.306	.306	.389	.694	104	1	-0	125	49	4	.560				0	/O	0.0
1884	Chi-N	1	5	3	1	0	0	0	0	1	0	.200	.333	.200	.533	67	-0	-0	108	0	0	.500				0	/P	0.0
Total	2	9	41	9	12	3	0	0	2	1	5	.293	.310	.366	.675	100	1	-0	123	42	5	.552				0	/OP	0.0
■ **BILL ANDRUS**	Andrus, William Morgan "Andy" b: 7/25/07, Beaumont, Tex. d: 3/12/82, Washington, D.C. BR/TR, 6', 185 lbs. Deb: 9/19/31																											
1931	Was-A	3	7	0	0	0	0	0	1	0	1	.000	.000	.000	.000	-99	-2	-2	101	0	0	.000	0	0	0	0	/3	-0.1
1937	Phi-N	3	2	0	0	0	0	0	0	0	2	.000	.000	.000	.000	-93	-1	-1	108	0	0	.000	0			0	/3	0.0
Total	2	6	9	0	0	0	0	0	1	0	3	.000	.000	.000	.000	-98	-3	-3	102	0	0	.000	0	0		0	/3	-0.1
■ **WYMAN ANDRUS**	Andrus, Wyman W. b: 1858, Orono, Ontario, Can. d: 6/17/35, Miles City, Mon. Deb: 9/15/1885																											
1885	Pro-N	1	4	0	0	0	0	0	0	0	1	.000	.000	.000	.000	-99	-1	-1	91	0	0	.000				0	/3	0.0
■ **TOM ANGLEY**	Angley, Thomas Samuel b: 10/2/04, Baltimore, Md. d: 10/26/52, Wichita, Kan. BL/TR, 5'8", 190 lbs. Deb: 4/23/29																											
1929	Chi-N	5	16	1	4	1	0	0	6	2	2	.250	.333	.313	.646	60	-1	-1	101	419	2	.583	0			0	/C	0.0
■ **PAT ANKENMAN**	Ankenman, Frederick Norman b: 12/23/12, Houston, Tex. BR/TR, 5'4", 125 lbs. Deb: 4/16/36																											
1936	StL-N	1	3	0	0	0	0	0	0	0	3	.000	.000	.000	.000	-99	-1	-1	94	0	0	.000	0			0	/S	0.0
1943	Bro-N	1	2	1	1	0	0	0	0	0	0	.500	.500	.500	1.000	190	0	0	100	0	1	1.000	0			0	/S	0.0
1944	Bro-N	13	24	1	6	1	0	0	3	0	2	.250	.250	.292	.542	53	-2	-2	99	154	2	.368	0			-1	2/S	0.0
Total	3	15	29	2	7	1	0	0	3	0	5	.241	.241	.276	.517	45	-2	-2	99	127	2	.348	0			-1	/2S	0.0
■ **BILL ANNIS**	Annis, William Perley b: 3/8/1857, Stoneham, Mass. d: 6/10/23, Kennebunkport, Me BR, 5'7", 150 lbs. Deb: 5/01/1884																											
1884	Bos-N	27	96	17	17	2	0	0	3	0	8	.177	.177	.198	.375	18	-9	-9	98	54	3	.241				0	O	-0.7
■ **CAP ANSON**	Anson, Adrian Constantine b: 4/11/1852, Marshalltown, Iowa d: 4/14/22, Chicago, Ill. BR/TR, 6', 227 lbs. Deb: 5/06/1871 MH																											
1871	Rok-n	25	122	30	43							.352															*3/C2O	
1872	Ath-n	45	231	60	88							.381															*3	
1873	Ath-n	51	272	52	96							.353															*13/2C0	
1874	Ath-n	55	267	51	98							.367															13/OS	
1875	Ath-n	69	330	84	105							.318															10C/3M	
1876	Chi-N	66	309	63	110	9	7	2	59	12	8	.356	.380	.450	.830	140	24	12	125	132	54	.759				12	*3/C	2.0
1877	Chi-N	59	255	52	86	**19**	1	0	32	9	3	.337	.360	.420	.779	147	13	13	98	97	39	.686				1	*3C	1.6
1878	Chi-N	60	261	55	89	12	2	0	40	13	1	.341	.372	.402	.775	143	15	12	108	124	40	.686				-5	*O/23C	0.3
1879	Chi-N	51	227	40	72	20	1	0	34	2	2	.317	.323	.414	.737	134	9	8	105	122	31	.619				0	1/M	0.4
1880	Chi-N	86	356	54	120	24	1	1	**74**	14	12	.337	.362	.419	.781	156	23	21	105	**171**	55	.691				0	*1/3S2M	1.6
1881	Chi-N	84	343	67	**137**	21	7	1	**82**	26	4	**.399**	**.442**	.510	**.952**	**183**	**39**	**35**	108	**169**	**79**	**.976**				8	*1/CSM	2.8
1882	Chi-N	82	348	69	126	29	8	1	**83**	20	7	.362	.397	.500	.897	183	33	32	101	**167**	71	.874				-0	*1/CM	1.6
1883	Chi-N	98	413	70	127	36	5	0	68	18	9	.308	.336	.419	.755	117	14	8	109	144	60	.668				4	*1/POCM	0.0
1884	Chi-N	112	475	108	159	30	3	21	**102**	29	13	.335	.373	.543	.916	171	45	39	108	116	99	.908				-1	*1/CSPM	2.3
1885	Chi-N	112	464	100	144	**35**	7	7	**108**	34	13	.310	.357	.461	.819	144	32	23	114	169	78	.775				-4	*1/CM	0.0
1886	Chi-N	125	504	117	187	35	11	10	**147**	55	19	.371	.433	.544	.977	168	58	45	116	152	134	1.129	29			6	*1CM	2.6
1887	Chi-N	122	472	107	164	33	13	7	102	60	18	.347	.422	.517	.939	139	41	27	116	114	117	1.078	27			10	*1/CM	1.4
1888	Chi-N	134	515	101	177	20	12	12	**84**	47	24	**.344**	**.400**	.499	**.899**	176	51	46	107	99	117	.985	28			9	*1M	4.0
1889	Chi-N	134	518	100	161	32	7	7	117	86	19	.311	.414	.440	.854	142	31	32	99	135	108	.969	27			9	*1M	2.6
1890	Chi-N	139	504	95	157	14	5	7	107	**113**	23	.312	**.443**	.401	.844	137	39	31	109	139	105	1.009	29			2	*1/C2M	2.1
1891	Chi-N	136	540	81	157	24	8	8	**120**	75	29	.291	.378	.409	.788	124	23	17	106	**151**	92	.820	17			8	*1/CM	1.8
1892	Chi-N	146	559	62	152	25	9	1	74	67	30	.272	.354	.354	.708	126	12	19	92	109	77	.693	13			-6	*1/M	0.1
1893	Chi-N	103	398	70	125	24	2	0	91	68	12	.314	.415	.384	.800	111	12	9	104	**172**	71	.861	13			-4	*1/M	0.4
1894	Chi-N	83	340	82	132	28	4	5	99	40	15	.388	.457	.538	.995	131	24	19	108	146	94	1.168	17			4	1/2M	1.8
1895	Chi-N	122	474	87	159	23	6	2	91	55	23	.335	.408	.422	.830	113	14	11	103	131	89	.857	12			-1	*1/M	1.0
1896	Chi-N	108	402	72	133	18	2	2	90	49	10	.331	.407	.400	.808	107	11	5	108	165	77	.881	24			2	*1C/M	0.8
1897	Chi-N	114	424	67	121	17	3	3	75	60		.285	.379	.361	.740	98	1	1	100	143	64	.752	11			1	*1C/M	0.1
Total	5 n	245	1222	277	430							.352															*1C/M	
Total	22	2276	9101	1719	2995	528	124	97	1879	952	294	.329	.395	.446	.841	139	564	466	107	139	1751	.867	247			54	*13C/O2SP	31.3
■ **JOE ANTOLICK**	Antolick, Joseph b: 4/11/16, Hokendauqua, Pa. BR/TR, 6', 185 lbs. Deb: 9/20/44																											
1944	Phi-N	4	6	1	2	0	0	0	0	1	0	.333	.429	.333	.762	116	0	0	100	0	1	.750	0			0	/C	0.0
■ **JOHN ANTONELLI**	Antonelli, John Lawrence b: 7/15/15, Memphis, Tenn. BR/TR, 5'10.5", 165 lbs. Deb: 9/16/44																											
1944	StL-N	8	21	0	4	1	0	0	1	0	4	.190	.190	.238	.429	20	-2	-2	101	72	1	.294	0			-0	/132	-0.1

YEAR	TM/L	G	AB	R	H	2B	3B	HR	RBI	BB	SO	AVG	OBP	SLG	PRO	/A	BR	/A	PF	CHI	RC	TA	SB	CS	SBR	FR	POS	TPR
1945	StL-N	2	3	0	0	0	0	0	0	0	1	.000	.000	.000	.000	-99	-1	-1	100	0	0	.000	0			0	/3	0.0
	Phi-N	125	504	50	129	27	2	1	28	24	24	.256	.292	.323	.616	74	-21	-18	96	56	45	.488	1			-6	*32/1S	-2.3
	Yr	127	507	50	129	27	2	1	28	24	25	.254	.291	.321	.612	73	-21	-19	96	55	45	.485	1			-6		-2.3
Total	2	135	528	50	133	28	2	1	29	24	29	.252	.287	.318	.605	71	-24	-21	97	57	46	.477	1			-6	3/21S	-2.4
■ **BILL ANTONELLO**	Antonello, William James b: 5/19/27, Brooklyn, N.Y. BR/TR, 5'11", 185 lbs. Deb: 4/30/53																											
1953	Bro-N	40	43	9	7	1	1	1	4	2	11	.163	.200	.302	.502	28	-5	-5	104	97	2	.405	0	0	0	-6	O	-1.1
■ **LUIS APARICIO**	Aparicio, Luis Ernesto (Montiel) b: 4/29/34, Maracaibo, Venez. BR/TR, 5'9", 160 lbs. Deb: 4/17/56 H																											
1956	Chi-A	152	533	69	142	19	6	3	56	34	63	.266	.312	.341	.653	69	-22	-25	104	110	59	.589	**21**	4	**4**	0	*S	-0.6
1957	Chi-A	143	575	82	148	22	6	3	41	52	55	.257	.319	.332	.651	79	-17	-16	99	78	65	.613	**28**	8	4	-3	*S	-0.4
1958	Chi-A	145	557	76	148	20	9	2	40	35	38	.266	.310	.345	.655	82	-15	-14	98	86	62	.608	**29**	6	**5**	14	*S	2.6
1959	Chi-A	152	612	98	157	18	5	6	51	52	40	.257	.318	.332	.650	81	-17	-15	97	87	70	.656	**56**	13	**9**	2	*S	0.8
1960	Chi-A	153	600	86	166	20	7	2	61	43	39	.277	.326	.343	.669	80	-15	-16	101	119	73	.663	**51**	8	**11**	**31**	*S	**3.7**
1961	Chi-A	156	625	90	170	24	4	6	45	38	33	.272	.315	.352	.667	79	-20	-19	99	78	72	.650	**53**	13	**8**	11	*S	1.0
1962	Chi-A	153	581	72	140	23	5	7	40	32	36	.241	.282	.334	.616	68	-29	-26	95	75	54	.556	**31**	12	2	13	*S	-0.1
1963	Bal-A	146	601	73	150	18	8	5	45	36	35	.250	.294	.331	.625	80	-20	-16	94	78	62	.593	**40**	6	**8**	2	*S	0.2
1964	Bal-A	146	578	93	154	20	3	10	37	49	51	.266	.327	.363	.690	87	-6	-10	105	63	71	.703	**57**	17	**7**	-0	*S	-0.2
1965	Bal-A	144	564	67	127	20	10	8	40	46	56	.225	.287	.339	.626	77	-17	-17	100	74	57	.585	26	7	4	0	*S	-0.7
1966	Bal-A	151	659	97	182	25	8	6	41	33	42	.276	.312	.366	.677	93	-6	-7	101	57	74	.602	25	11	1	13	*S	1.7
1967	Bal-A	134	546	55	127	22	5	4	31	29	44	.233	.273	.313	.586	77	-19	-16	95	68	47	.507	18	5	2	-12	*S	-1.8
1968	Chi-A	155	622	55	164	24	4	4	36	33	43	.264	.303	.334	.637	92	-6	-7	101	67	61	.543	17	11	-2	28	*S	3.5
1969	Chi-A	156	599	77	168	24	5	5	51	66	29	.280	.354	.362	.716	93	2	-4	108	85	81	.688	24	4	5	30	*S	3.9
1970	Chi-A	146	552	86	173	29	3	5	43	53	34	.313	.375	.404	.779	109	12	8	106	77	85	.725	8	3	1	22	*S	4.4
1971	Bos-A	125	491	56	114	23	0	4	45	35	43	.232	.286	.303	.589	64	-22	-25	106	110	44	.495	6	4	-1	-27	*S	-4.2
1972	Bos-A	110	436	47	112	26	3	3	39	26	28	.257	.302	.351	.653	89	-4	-6	105	107	45	.549	3	3	-1	-10	*S	-0.6
1973	Bos-A	132	499	56	135	17	1	0	49	43	33	.271	.328	.309	.637	76	-12	-16	106	132	53	.557	13	1	3	-8	*S	-0.2
Total	18	2599	10230	1335	2677	394	92	83	791	735	742	.262	.313	.343	.655	82	-236	-247	101	85	1137	.620	506	136	70	105	*S	13.0
■ **LUKE APPLING**	Appling, Lucius Benjamin b: 4/2/09, High Point, N.C. BR/TR, 5'10", 183 lbs. Deb: 9/10/30 MCH																											
1930	Chi-A	6	26	2	8	2	0	0	2	0	0	.308	.308	.385	.692	72	-1	-1	103	70	3	.667	2	0	1	-1	/S	0.0
1931	Chi-A	96	297	36	69	13	4	1	28	29	27	.232	.303	.313	.616	67	-16	-13	92	96	30	.574	9	2	2	-5	S/2	-0.8
1932	Chi-A	139	489	66	134	20	10	3	63	40	36	.274	.329	.374	.703	94	-14	-4	87	110	60	.639	9	8	-2	9	S23	1.0
1933	Chi-A	151	612	90	197	36	10	6	85	56	29	.322	.379	.443	.822	116	15	14	101	104	100	.782	6	11	-5	11	*S	3.0
1934	Chi-A	118	452	75	137	28	6	2	61	59	27	.303	.384	.405	.788	104	4	4	99	114	73	.775	3	1	0	-6	*S/2	0.6
1935	Chi-A	153	525	94	161	28	6	1	71	122	40	.307	.437	.389	.826	106	20	12	109	123	100	.914	12	6	0	**21**	*S	3.8
1936	Chi-A	138	526	111	204	31	7	6	128	85	25	**.388**	.474	.508	.981	143	40	41	99	**154**	131	1.107	10	6	-1	16	*S	5.7
1937	Chi-A	154	574	98	182	42	8	4	77	86	28	.317	.407	.439	.846	110	14	12	103	106	107	.888	18	10	-1	14	*S	3.0
1938	Chi-A	81	294	41	89	14	0	0	44	42	17	.303	.392	.350	.742	89	-4	-3	98	147	42	.707	1	3	-2	4	S	0.3
1939	Chi-A	148	516	82	162	16	6	0	56	105	37	.314	.430	.368	.798	99	11	6	107	105	90	.832	16	9	-1	1	*S	1.9
1940	Chi-A	150	566	96	197	27	13	0	79	69	35	.348	.420	.442	.862	119	23	20	104	121	109	.839	3	5	-2	-2	*S	2.7
1941	Chi-A	154	592	93	186	26	8	1	57	82	32	.314	.399	.390	.789	117	11	17	94	83	98	.769	12	8	-1	1	*S	1.9
1942	Chi-A	142	543	78	142	26	4	3	53	63	23	.262	.342	.341	.682	93	-5	-4	99	93	70	.649	17	5	2	1	*S	0.7
1943	Chi-A	155	585	63	192	33	2	3	80	90	29	**.328**	**.419**	.407	.825	141	35	34	101	114	109	.860	27	8	3	8	*S	4.9
1945	Chi-A	18	57	12	21	2	2	1	10	12	7	.368	.478	.526	1.005	201	7	8	95	112	16	1.194	1	0	0	1	S	1.0
1946	Chi-A	149	582	59	180	27	5	1	55	71	41	.309	.384	.378	.762	117	13	15	97	90	88	.705	6	4	-1	12	*S	2.9
1947	Chi-A	139	503	67	154	29	0	8	49	64	28	.306	.386	.412	.797	126	16	18	97	83	81	.757	8	6	-1	2	*S/3	1.9
1948	Chi-A	139	497	63	156	16	2	0	47	94	35	.314	.423	.354	.777	113	12	15	95	96	82	.773	10	4	1	13	3S	2.6
1949	Chi-A	142	492	82	148	21	5	5	58	121	24	.301	.439	.394	.833	124	22	24	98	101	90	.850	7	12	-5	-1	*S	1.8
1950	Chi-A	50	128	11	30	3	4	0	13	12	8	.234	.300	.320	.620	61	-8	-8	97	109	12	.524	2	0	1	1	S1/2	-0.4
Total	20	2422	8856	1319	2749	440	102	45	1116	1302	528	.310	.399	.398	.798	112	196	207	99	107	1493	.807	179	108	-11	98	*S/321	38.5
■ **JACK ARAGON**	Aragon, Angel Valdes (Reyes) b: 11/20/15, Havana, Cuba d: 4/4/88, Clearwater, Fla. BR/TR, 5'10", 176 lbs. Deb: 8/13/41																											
1941	NY-N	1	0	0	0	0	0	0	0	0	0	—	—	—	—	—	0	0	103	—	—	—	0			0	R	0.0
■ **ANGEL ARAGON**	Aragon, Angel (Valdes) "Pete" b: 8/2/1890, Havana, Cuba d: 1/24/52, New York, N.Y. BR/TR, 5'5", 150 lbs. Deb: 8/20/14																											
1914	NY-A	6	7	1	1	0	0	0	0	1	2	.143	.333	.143	.476	44	-0	-0	100	0	0	.500	0			-0	/O	0.0
1916	NY-A	12	24	1	5	0	0	0	3	2	2	.208	.269	.208	.478	43	-2	-2	101	214	2	.474	2			0	/3O	0.0
1917	NY-A	14	45	2	3	1	0	0	2	2	2	.067	.106	.089	.195	-38	-8	-8	107	179	1	.143	0			0	/O3S	-0.8
Total	3	32	76	4	9	1	0	0	5	5	6	.118	.183	.132	.315	-4	-10	-10	104	171	3	.269	2			-0	/3OS	-0.8
■ **MAURICE ARCHDEACON**	Archdeacon, Maurice John "Flash" b: 12/14/1898, St.Louis, Mo. d: 9/5/54, St.Louis, Mo. BL/TL, 5'8", 153 lbs. Deb: 9/17/23																											
1923	Chi-A	22	87	23	35	5	1	0	4	6	8	.402	.441	.483	.924	145	6	6	98	34	17	.909	2	3	-1	-2	O	0.1
1924	Chi-A	95	288	59	92	9	3	0	25	40	30	.319	.410	.372	.781	106	3	5	97	77	47	.798	11	7	-1	-0	O	-0.1
1925	Chi-A	10	9	2	1	0	0	0	0	2	1	.111	.273	.111	.384	0	-1	-1	96	0	0	.375	0	0	0	0	/O	0.0
Total	3	127	384	84	128	14	4	0	29	48	39	.333	.413	.391	.803	112	7	9	97	66	65	.808	13	10	-2	-2	/O	0.0
■ **JIMMY ARCHER**	Archer, James Patrick b: 5/13/1883, Dublin, Ireland d: 3/29/58, Milwaukee, Wis. BR/TR, 5'10", 168 lbs. Deb: 9/06/04																											
1904	Pit-N	7	20	1	3	0	0	0	1	0		.150	.150	.150	.300	-6	-2	-2	99	122	0	.176	0			-0	/CO	-0.1
1907	Det-A	18	42	6	5	0	0	0	0	4		.119	.196	.119	.315	2	-4	-4	102	0	1	.243	0			0	C/2	-0.2
1909	Chi-N	80	261	31	60	9	2	1	30	12		.230	.266	.291	.558	74	-9	-9	101	138	21	.468	5			-5	C	-0.9
1910	Chi-N	98	313	36	81	17	6	2	41	14	49	.259	.293	.371	.663	93	-5	-5	101	117	36	.591	6			0	C1	-0.2
1911	Chi-N	116	387	41	98	18	5	4	41	18	43	.253	.288	.357	.645	83	-12	-10	97	92	41	.561	5			2	*C1/2	-0.1
1912	Chi-N	120	385	35	109	20	2	5	58	22	36	.283	.330	.384	.715	92	-4	-6	104	120	51	.659	7			-3	*C	-0.1
1913	Chi-N	111	368	38	98	14	7	2	44	19	27	.266	.311	.359	.670	92	-5	-4	99	116	41	.593	4			9	*C	1.0
1914	Chi-N	79	248	17	64	9	2	0	19	9	9	.258	.284	.310	.595	78	-8	-7	98	89	21	.473	1			-0	C	-0.4
1915	Chi-N	97	309	21	75	11	5	1	27	11	38	.243	.273	.320	.594	78	-9	-9	102	101	27	.488	5	6	-2	9	C	0.3
1916	Chi-N	77	205	11	45	6	2	1	30	12	24	.220	.269	.283	.552	60	-7	-11	117	195	18	.469	3			-3	C/3	-1.1
1917	Chi-N	2	2	0	0	0	0	0	0	0	1	.000	.000	.000	.000	-96	-0	-0	105	0	0	.000	0			0	H	0.0
1918	Pit-N	24	58	4	9	1	2	0	3	1	6	.155	.197	.241	.438	31	-5	-5	106	81	3	.347	0			1	C/1	-0.1
	Bro-N	9	22	3	6	0	1	0	0	1	5	.273	.304	.364	.668	102	0	-0	101	0	2	.563	0			1	/C	0.1
	Cin-N	9	26	2	7	1	0	0	2	1	3	.269	.296	.308	.604	87	-1	-0	97	95	2	.474	0			0	/C1	0.1
	Yr	42	106	9	22	2	3	0	5	3	14	.208	.243	.283	.526	58	-5	-6	103	68	7	.417	0			2		0.1
Total	12	847	2646	246	660	106	34	16	296	124	241	.249	.288	.333	.621	80	-70	-75	101	114	264	.533	36	6		10	C/1230	-1.7
■ **GEORGE ARCHIE**	Archie, George Albert b: 4/27/14, Nashville, Tenn. BR/TR, 6', 170 lbs. Deb: 9/14/38																											
1938	Det-A	3	2	1	0	0	0	0	0	0	1	.000	.000	.000	.000	-99	-1	-1	100	0	0	.000	0	0	0	0	H	0.0
1941	Was-A	105	379	45	102	20	4	3	48	30	42	.269	.324	.367	.691	84	-10	-9	98	117	45	.612	8	4	0	-7	31	-1.1
	StL-A	9	29	3	11	3	0	0	5	7	3	.379	.500	.483	.983	161	3	3	100	126	8	1.150	2	0	1	0	/1	0.4
	Yr	114	408	48	113	23	4	3	53	37	45	.277	.339	.375	.714	90	-7	-6	98	119	56	.668	10	4	1	-6		-0.7
1946	StL-A	4	11	1	2	1	0	0	0	0	1	.182	.182	.273	.455	26	-1	-1	98	0	1	.333	0	0	0	0	/1	0.0
Total	3	121	421	50	115	24	4	3	53	37	47	.273	.333	.371	.704	88	-9	-7	98	115	53	.658	10	4	1	-6	/31	-0.7
■ **JOSE ARCIA**	Arcia, Jose Raimundo (Orta) b: 8/22/43, Havana, Cuba BR/TR, 6'3", 170 lbs. Deb: 4/10/68																											
1968	Chi-N	59	84	15	16	4	0	1	8	3	24	.190	.218	.274	.492	42	-6	-7	112	130	5	.382	0	0	0	-2	O2/S3	-0.8
1969	SD-N	120	302	35	65	11	3	0	10	14	47	.215	.255	.272	.526	49	-21	-20	97	49	20	.446	14	7	0	-5	2S/3O1	-1.6
1970	SD-N	114	229	28	51	9	3	0	17	12	36	.223	.282	.288	.570	56	-15	-14	95	100	18	.471	3	6	-3	3	S2/3O	-0.2
Total	3	293	615	78	132	24	6	1	35	29	107	.215	.260	.278	.538	51	-42	-40	98	79	43	.453	17	13	-3	-4	S/2O31	-2.6

YEAR	TM/L	G	AB	R	H	2B	3B	HR	RBI	BB	SO	AVG	OBP	SLG	PRO	/A	BR	/A	PF	CHI	RC	TA	SB	CS	SBR	FR	POS	TPR
■ DAN ARDELL Ardell, Daniel Miers b: 5/27/41, Seattle, Wash. BL/TL, 6'2", 190 lbs. Deb: 9/14/61																												
1961	LA-A	7	4	1	1	0	0	0	0	1	2	.250	.400	.250	.650	70	-0	-0	111	0	1	.667	0	0	0	0	/1	0.0
■ JOE ARDNER Ardner, Joseph A. "Old Hoss" b: 2/27/1858, Mt.Vernon, Ohio d: 9/15/35, Cleveland, Ohio BR/TR, Deb: 5/01/1884																												
1884	Cle-N	26	92	6	16	1	1	0	4	1	24	.174	.183	.207	.389	22	-8	-8	102	72	4	.263				0	2/3	-0.7
1890	Cle-N	84	323	28	72	13	1	0	35	17	40	.223	.266	.269	.535	62	-17	-14	94	124	26	.458	9			-7	2	-1.6
Total	2	110	415	34	88	14	2	0	39	18	64	.212	.248	.255	.504	53	-25	-23	96	113	30	.413	9			-7	2/3	-2.3
■ HANK ARFT Arft, Henry Irven "Bow Wow" b: 1/28/22, Manchester, Mo. BL/TL, 5'10.5", 190 lbs. Deb: 7/27/48																												
1948	StL-A	69	248	25	59	10	3	5	38	45	43	.238	.355	.363	.718	86	-3	-5	106	129	34	.687	1	2	-1	-0	1	-0.1
1949	StL-A	6	5	1	1	1	0	0	2	0	1	.200	.200	.400	.600	57	-0	-0	100	343	0	.500	0	0	0	0	H	0.0
1950	StL-A	98	280	45	75	16	4	1	32	46	48	.268	.375	.364	.739	84	-3	-6	107	105	43	.729	3	2	-0	-3	1	-1.2
1951	StL-A	112	345	44	90	16	5	7	42	41	34	.261	.339	.397	.736	94	-1	-3	105	95	48	.684	4	6	-2	3	1	-0.3
1952	StL-A	15	28	1	4	3	1	0	4	5	7	.143	.273	.321	.594	67	-1	-1	97	166	3	.560	0	0	0	-0	1	-0.1
Total	5	300	906	116	229	46	13	13	118	137	133	.253	.352	.375	.727	88	-8	-16	105	111	128	.708	8	10	-4	-1	1	-1.7
■ BUZZ ARLETT Arlett, Russell Loris b: 1/3/1899, Elmhurst, Cal. d: 5/16/64, Minneapolis, Minn. BB/TR, 6'3.5", 225 lbs. Deb: 4/14/31																												
1931	Phi-N	121	418	65	131	26	7	18	72	45	39	.313	.387	.538	.925	138	27	23	106	94	90	.969	3			6	O1	2.3
■ TONY ARMAS Armas, Antonio Rafael (Machado) b: 7/2/53, Anzoatequi, Venez. BR/TR, 5'11", 182 lbs. Deb: 9/06/76																												
1976	Pit-N	4	6	0	2	0	0	0	1	0	2	.333	.333	.333	.667	89	-0	-0	100	193	1	.500	0	0	0	-0	/O	0.0
1977	Oak-A	118	363	26	87	8	2	13	53	20	99	.240	.279	.380	.660	82	-12	-10	95	119	37	.556	1	2	-1	2	*O/S	-1.1
1978	Oak-A	91	239	17	51	6	1	2	13	10	62	.213	.251	.272	.523	47	-17	-17	101	72	16	.400	1	2	-1	-4	O/D	-2.5
1979	Oak-A	80	278	29	69	9	3	11	34	16	67	.248	.292	.421	.712	101	-5	-1	89	89	33	.628	1	0	0	8	O	0.4
1980	Oak-A	158	628	87	175	18	8	35	109	29	128	.279	.313	.500	.813	126	13	17	95	108	89	.732	5	3	-0	12	*O	2.6
1981	Oak-A	109	440	51	115	24	3	**22**	76	19	115	.261	.295	.480	.775	125	9	11	96	114	61	.714	5	1	1	6	*O	1.6
1982	Oak-A	138	536	58	125	19	2	28	89	33	128	.233	.279	.433	.712	97	-8	-5	95	119	61	.628	2	2	-1	9	*O/D	0.0
1983	Bos-A	145	574	77	125	23	2	36	107	29	131	.218	.258	.453	.711	90	-10	-11	101	120	55	.605	0	1	-1	1	*OD	-1.1
1984	Bos-A	157	639	107	171	29	5	**43**	**123**	32	156	.268	.304	.531	.834	114	18	10	110	111	97	.771	1	3	-2	-6	*OD	0.0
1985	Bos-A	103	385	50	102	17	5	23	64	18	90	.265	.301	.514	.816	116	8	6	102	97	54	.734	0	0	0	1	OD	0.7
1986	Bos-A	121	425	40	112	21	4	11	58	24	77	.264	.306	.409	.715	94	-4	-4	100	112	49	.610	0	3	-2	1	*O/D	-0.8
1987	Cal-A	28	81	8	16	3	1	3	9	1	11	.198	.207	.370	.578	50	-6	-6	99	92	5	.471	1	0	0	-5	O	-1.0
1988	Cal-A	120	368	42	100	20	2	13	49	22	87	.272	.313	.443	.756	116	3	6	94	96	46	.655	1	3	-2	-6	*O/D	-0.3
Total	13	1372	4962	592	1250	197	38	240	785	253	1153	.252	.290	.452	.742	103	-12	-3	99	108	603	.675	18	20	-7	20	*O/DS	-1.5
■ ED ARMBRISTER Armbrister, Edison Rosanda b: 7/4/48, Nassau, Bahamas BR/TR, 5'11", 160 lbs. Deb: 8/31/73																												
1973	Cin-N	18	37	5	8	3	1	1	5	2	8	.216	.256	.432	.689	94	-1	-1	93	106	4	.621	0	0	0	-2	O	-0.2
1974	Cin-N	9	7	0	2	0	0	0	0	1	1	.286	.375	.286	.661	88	-0	-0	98	0	1	.600	0	0	0	-1	/O	-0.1
1975	Cin-N	59	65	9	12	1	0	0	2	5	19	.185	.254	.200	.454	26	-6	-7	104	59	4	.400	3	1	0	-6	O	-1.3
1976	Cin-N	73	78	20	23	3	2	2	7	6	22	.295	.345	.462	.807	124	3	2	103	64	13	.845	7	3	0	-5	O	-0.3
1977	Cin-N	65	78	12	20	4	3	1	5	10	21	.256	.341	.423	.764	104	0	0	100	56	9	.716	5	6	-2	-4	O	-0.6
Total	5	224	265	46	65	11	6	4	19	24	71	.245	.310	.377	.688	88	-4	-5	101	64	31	.657	15	10	-2	-18	/O	-2.5
■ CHARLIE ARMBRUSTER Armbruster, Charles A. b: 8/30/1880, Cincinnati, Ohio d: 10/7/64, Grants Pass, Ore. TR , 5'9", 180 lbs. Deb: 7/17/05																												
1905	Bos-A	35	91	13	18	4	0	0	6	18		.198	.330	.242	.572	84	-1	-1	100	97	8	.589	3			-0	C	0.3
1906	Bos-A	72	201	9	29	6	1	0	6	25		.144	.239	.184	.423	35	-14	-14	98	59	10	.372	2			7	C/1	-0.1
1907	Bos-A	23	60	2	6	1	0	0	0	8		.100	.206	.117	.323	4	-6	-6	101	0	2	.296	1			2	C	-0.1
	Chi-A	1	3	0	0	0	0	0	0	1		.000	.250	.000	.250	-17	-0	-0	104	0	0	.333	0			0	/C	0.0
	Yr	24	63	2	6	1	0	0	0	9		.095	.208	.111	.319	4	-6	-6	101	0	2	.298	1			2		-0.1
Total	3	131	355	24	53	11	1	0	12	52		.149	.258	.186	.444	42	-21	-21	99	59	20	.411	6			9	C/1	0.1
■ HARRY ARMBRUSTER Armbruster, Henry "Army" b: 3/20/1882, Cincinnati, Ohio d: 12/10/53, Cincinnati, Ohio BL/TL, 5'10", 190 lbs. Deb: 4/30/06																												
1906	Phi-A	91	265	40	63	6	3	2	24	43		.238	.344	.306	.650	113	4	6	94	100	33	.678	13			-0	O	0.3
■ GEORGE ARMSTRONG Armstrong, George Noble "Dodo" b: 6/3/24, Orange, N.J. BR/TR, 5'10", 190 lbs. Deb: 4/26/46																												
1946	Phi-A	8	6	0	1	1	0	0	0	1	1	.167	.286	.333	.619	69	-0	-0	104	0	1	.600	0	0	0	0	/C	0.0
■ SAM ARMSTRONG Armstrong, Samuel b: 1850, Baltimore, Md. 6'2", 160 lbs. Deb: 6/26/1871																												
1871	Kek-n	12	48	9	11							.229															O	
■ HARRY ARNDT Arndt, Harry J. b: 2/12/1879, South Bend, Ind. d: 3/24/21, South Bend, Ind. TR , Deb: 7/02/02																												
1902	Det-A	10	34	4	5	0	1	0	7	6		.147	.275	.206	.481	36	-3	-3	99	349	2	.448	0			0	O/1	-0.2
	Bal-A	68	248	41	63	7	4	2	28	35		.254	.346	.339	.685	90	-2	-2	102	109	33	.692	9			1	O/23S	-0.4
	Yr	78	282	45	68	7	5	2	35	41		.241	.337	.323	.660	84	-4	-5	102	144	35	.659	9			1		-0.6
1905	StL-N	113	415	40	101	11	6	2	36	24		.243	.285	.313	.598	88	-11	-6	91	97	42	.532	13			-14	2/O3S	-1.5
1906	StL-N	69	256	30	69	7	9	2	26	19		.270	.320	.391	.711	123	6	6	101	95	34	.663	5			11	3/1O	1.5
1907	StL-N	11	32	3	6	1	0	0	2	1		.188	.212	.219	.431	38	-2	-2	96	108	2	.308	0			0	/13	-0.1
Total	4	271	985	118	244	26	20	6	99	85		.248	.307	.333	.640	94	-11	-7	97	109	113	.594	27			-2	/2O3S1	-0.7
■ CHRIS ARNOLD Arnold, Christopher Paul b: 11/6/47, Long Beach, Cal. BR/TR, 5'10", 160 lbs. Deb: 9/07/71																												
1971	SF-N	6	13	2	3	0	0	1	3	1	2	.231	.286	.462	.747	109	0	0	100	136	2	.700	0	0	0	0	/2	0.0
1972	SF-N	51	84	8	19	3	1	1	4	8	12	.226	.293	.321	.615	75	-3	-3	100	55	7	.507	0	1	-1	-1	3/2S	-0.3
1973	SF-N	49	54	7	16	2	0	1	13	8	11	.296	.387	.389	.776	110	1	1	105	218	8	.725	0	0	0	-0	/C23	0.1
1974	SF-N	78	174	22	42	7	3	1	26	15	27	.241	.305	.333	.639	73	-5	-7	108	165	19	.560	1	1	-0	-1	2/3S	-0.6
1975	SF-N	29	41	4	8	0	0	0	0	4	8	.195	.267	.195	.462	29	-4	-4	102	0	2	.333	0	0	0	1	/2O	-0.2
1976	SF-N	60	69	4	15	0	1	0	5	6	16	.217	.280	.246	.526	49	-4	-5	103	113	4	.397	0	0	0	0	/231S	-0.3
Total	6	273	435	47	103	12	5	4	51	42	76	.237	.305	.315	.620	71	-15	-17	104	126	42	.536	1	2	-1	-1	/23CSO1	-1.3
■ BILLY ARNOLD Arnold, Willis S. b: 3/2/1851, Middletown, Conn. d: 1/18/1899, Albany, N.Y. Deb: 4/26/1872																												
1872	Man-n	2	8	2	1							.125															/O	
■ MORRIE ARNOVICH Arnovich, Morris "Snooker" b: 11/16/10, Superior, Wis. d: 7/20/59, Superior, Wis. BR/TR, 5'10", 168 lbs. Deb: 9/14/36																												
1936	Phi-N	13	48	4	15	3	0	1	7	1	3	.313	.353	.438	.790	103	1	0	108	105	7	.686	0			2	O	0.1
1937	Phi-N	117	410	60	119	27	4	10	60	34	32	.290	.349	.449	.798	107	8	4	108	101	63	.741	5			7	*O	0.5
1938	Phi-N	139	502	47	138	29	0	4	72	42	37	.275	.333	.357	.690	89	-7	-7	100	139	60	.595	2			19	*O	0.9
1939	Phi-N	134	491	68	159	25	2	5	67	58	28	.324	.397	.413	.811	126	15	19	94	119	83	.789	7			12	*O	2.8
1940	Phi-N	39	141	13	28	2	1	0	12	14	15	.199	.276	.227	.503	41	-11	-11	97	147	9	.398	0			2	O	-0.9
	Cin-N	62	211	17	60	10	2	0	21	13	10	.284	.326	.351	.677	86	-4	-4	101	105	23	.553	1			1	O	-0.4
	Yr	101	352	30	88	12	3	0	33	27	25	.250	.305	.301	.606	68	-15	-15	99	123	32	.496	1			3		-1.3
1941	NY-N	85	207	25	58	8	3	2	22	23	14	.280	.352	.377	.729	102	2	1	103	95	27	.656	2			-4	O	-0.5
1946	NY-N	1	3	0	0	0	0	0	0	0	0	.000	.000	.000	.000	-99	-1	-1	102	0	0	.000	0			-0	/O	0.0
Total	7	590	2013	234	577	104	12	22	261	185	139	.287	.350	.383	.733	100	3	1	101	118	272	.685	17			38	O	2.5
■ TUG ARUNDEL Arundel, John Thomas b: 6/30/1862, Auburn, N.Y. d: 9/5/12, Auburn, N.Y. Deb: 5/23/1882																												
1882	Phi-a	1	5	0	0	0	0	0		0		.000	.000	.000	.000	-90	-1	-1	112	0	0	.000				0	/C	0.0
1884	Tol-a	15	47	6	4	0	0	0		3		.085	.140	.085	.225	-23	-6	-6	104	0	1	.163				0	C	-0.5
1887	Ind-N	43	157	13	31	4	0	0	13	8	12	.197	.241	.223	.464	32	-14	-13	96	117	11	.413	8			-3	C/O1	-0.9
1888	Was-N	17	51	2	10	0	1	0	3	5	10	.196	.268	.235	.503	66	-2	-2	96	90	4	.439	1			0	C	-0.1
Total	4	76	260	21	45	4	1	0	16	16	22	.173	.224	.196	.420	27	-23	-22	98	88	15	.358	9			-3	/CO1	-1.5
■ RANDY ASADOOR Asadoor, Randall Carl b: 10/20/62, Fresno, Cal. BR/TR, 6'1", 185 lbs. Deb: 9/14/86																												
1986	SD-N	15	55	9	20	5	0	0	7	3	13	.364	.397	.455	.851	141	3	3	95	114	9	.784	1	2	-1	-0	3/2	0.1

YEAR	TM/L	G	AB	R	H	2B	3B	HR	RBI	BB	SO	AVG	OBP	SLG	PRO	/A	BR	/A	PF	CHI	RC	TA	SB	CS	SBR	FR	POS	TPR
■ **JIM ASBELL**	Asbell, James Marion "Big Train" b: 6/22/14, Dallas Tex. d: 7/6/67, San Mateo, Cal. BR/TR, 6', 195 lbs. Deb: 5/08/38																											
1938	Chi-N	17	33	6	6	2	0	0	3	3	9	.182	.250	.242	.492	34	-3	-3	105	136	2	.407	0			-1	O	-0.3
■ **CASPER ASBJORNSON**	Asbjornson, Robert Anthony (Name Changed To Asby) b: 6/19/09, Concord, Mass. d: 1/21/70, Williamsport, Pa. BR/TR, 6'1", 196 lbs. Deb: 9/17/28																											
1928	Bos-A	6	16	0	3	1	0	0	1	1	1	.188	.235	.250	.485	28	-2	-2	98	86	1	.385	0	0	0	-0	/C	0.0
1929	Bos-A	17	29	1	3	0	0	0	0	1	6	.103	.133	.103	.237	-38	-6	-6	102	0	0	.154	0	0	0	0	C	-0.4
1931	Cin-N	45	118	13	36	7	1	0	22	7	23	.305	.349	.381	.731	101	-1	0	95	174	16	.646	0			0	C	0.2
1932	Cin-N	29	58	5	10	2	0	1	4	0	15	.172	.186	.259	.445	19	-7	-6	96	83	3	.333	0			0	C	-0.5
Total	4	97	221	19	52	10	1	1	27	9	45	.235	.272	.303	.575	55	-15	-14	97	122	20	.462	0	0		0	/C	-0.7
■ **RICHIE ASHBURN**	Ashburn, Rich "Whitey" b: 3/19/27, Tilden, Neb. BL/TR, 5'10", 170 lbs. Deb: 4/20/48																											
1948	Phi-N	117	463	78	154	17	4	2	40	60	22	.333	.410	.400	.810	127	16	19	94	68	82	.897	**32**			**13**	*O	2.3
1949	Phi-N	154	662	84	188	18	11	1	37	58	38	.284	.343	.349	.692	85	-12	-13	101	51	82	.622	9			18	*O	-0.3
1950	Phi-N	151	594	84	180	25	**14**	2	41	63	32	.303	.372	.402	.774	106	4	7	97	62	91	.748	14			3	*O	0.4
1951	Phi-N	154	643	92	**221**	31	5	4	63	50	37	.344	.393	.426	.819	124	19	22	97	75	118	.822	29	6	5	**26**	*O	4.7
1952	Phi-N	154	613	93	173	31	6	1	42	75	30	.282	.362	.357	.720	99	2	2	101	65	86	.681	16	11	-2	13	*O	1.0
1953	Phi-N	156	622	110	**205**	25	9	2	57	61	35	.330	.394	.408	.802	111	11	12	99	76	109	.784	14	6	1	22	*O	2.6
1954	Phi-N	153	559	111	175	16	8	1	41	**125**	46	.313	**.442**	.376	.818	117	22	23	99	67	107	.886	11	8	-2	13	*O	2.8
1955	Phi-N	140	533	91	180	32	9	3	42	105	36	**.338**	**.449**	.448	.898	137	37	35	102	59	117	.981	12	10	-2	7	*O	3.6
1956	Phi-N	154	628	94	190	26	8	3	50	79	45	.303	.385	.384	.769	114	10	15	94	73	101	.756	10	1	2	21	*O	3.3
1957	Phi-N	156	626	93	186	26	8	0	33	**94**	44	.297	.392	.364	.756	107	9	10	98	52	95	.737	13	10	-2	**27**	*O	3.1
1958	Phi-N	152	615	98	**215**	24	**13**	2	33	**97**	48	**.350**	**.441**	.441	.882	137	36	38	98	43	129	.957	30	12	2	14	*O	4.9
1959	Phi-N	153	564	86	150	16	2	1	20	79	42	.266	.362	.307	.669	81	-12	-12	99	44	66	.614	9	11	-4	-3	*O	-2.0
1960	Chi-N	151	547	99	159	16	5	0	40	**116**	50	.291	**.416**	.338	.754	111	14	16	98	84	91	.803	16	4	2	-7	*O	0.6
1961	Chi-N	109	307	49	79	7	4	0	19	55	27	.257	.375	.306	.682	84	-5	-5	100	82	39	.668	7	6	-2	-3	O	-1.3
1962	NY-N	135	389	60	119	7	3	7	28	81	39	.306	.426	.393	.819	117	17	14	104	63	72	.875	12	7	-1	5	O/2	1.3
Total	15	2189	8365	1322	2574	317	109	29	586	1198	571	.308	.397	.382	.779	111	169	185	99	64	1386	.793	234	92		167	*O/2	27.0
■ **ALAN ASHBY**	Ashby, Alan Dean b: 7/8/51, Long Beach, Cal. BB/TR, 6'2", 185 lbs. Deb: 7/03/73																											
1973	Cle-A	11	29	4	5	1	0	1	3	2	11	.172	.226	.310	.536	51	-2	-2	97	98	2	.458	0	0	0	0	C	0.0
1974	Cle-A	10	7	1	1	0	0	0	0	1	2	.143	.250	.143	.393	15	-1	-1	101	0	0	.333	0	0	0	0	/C	0.0
1975	Cle-A	90	254	32	57	10	1	5	32	30	42	.224	.309	.331	.639	81	-6	-6	100	124	26	.565	3	2	-0	0	C/13D	-0.3
1976	Cle-A	89	247	26	59	5	1	4	32	27	49	.239	.314	.316	.630	85	-4	-4	100	137	24	.536	0	2	-1	2	C/13	0.0
1977	Tor-A	124	396	25	83	16	3	2	29	50	51	.210	.301	.280	.582	58	-21	-23	103	98	34	.495	0	2	-1	14	*C	-0.6
1978	Tor-A	81	264	27	69	15	0	9	29	28	32	.261	.334	.420	.755	111	4	4	100	83	35	.684	1	1	-0	6	C	1.1
1979	Hou-N	108	336	25	68	15	2	2	35	26	70	.202	.264	.277	.541	53	-24	-20	90	140	24	.438	0	0	0	-9	*C	-2.7
1980	Hou-N	116	352	30	90	19	2	3	48	35	40	.256	.323	.347	.670	89	-6	-5	98	145	38	.575	0	0	0	-12	*C	-1.5
1981	Hou-N	83	255	20	69	13	0	4	33	35	33	.271	.359	.369	.727	121	3	7	88	122	34	.665	0	2	-1	2	C	1.0
1982	Hou-N	100	339	40	87	14	2	12	49	27	53	.257	.313	.416	.729	103	0	1	99	111	44	.660	2	0	1	-1	C	0.1
1983	Hou-N	87	275	31	63	18	1	8	34	31	38	.229	.307	.389	.696	102	-4	-0	90	103	31	.616	0	0	0	-5	C	-0.2
1984	Hou-N	66	191	16	50	7	0	4	27	20	22	.262	.335	.361	.696	103	-1	1	93	131	24	.621	0	0	0	-1	C	0.2
1985	Hou-N	65	189	20	53	8	0	8	25	24	27	.280	.364	.450	.814	132	7	8	96	91	29	.759	0	0	0	0	C	1.0
1986	Hou-N	120	315	24	81	15	0	7	38	39	56	.257	.339	.371	.710	93	-1	-2	103	110	40	.651	1	0	0	-18	*C	-1.8
1987	Hou-N	125	386	53	111	16	0	14	63	50	52	.288	.371	.438	.809	122	8	12	93	119	61	.759	0	1	-1	-14	*C	0.6
1988	Hou-N	73	227	19	54	10	0	7	33	29	36	.238	.324	.374	.699	107	0	2	93	124	28	.640	0	0	0	-6	C	0.0
Total	16	1348	4062	393	1000	182	12	90	510	454	614	.246	.323	.363	.687	94	-48	-30	96	117	475	.633	7	10	-4	-42	*C/13D	-3.1
■ **TUCKER ASHFORD**	Ashford, Thomas Steven b: 12/4/54, Memphis, Tenn. BR/TR, 6'1", 195 lbs. Deb: 9/21/76																											
1976	SD-N	4	5	0	3	1	0	0	0	1	0	.600	.667	.800	1.467	356	2	2	89	0	4	3.500	2	0	1	0	/3	0.2
1977	SD-N	81	249	25	54	18	0	3	24	21	35	.217	.280	.325	.606	71	-14	-10	88	107	22	.517	2	3	-1	0	3S/2	-0.9
1978	SD-N	75	155	11	38	11	0	3	26	14	31	.245	.308	.374	.682	97	-2	-1	93	154	18	.608	1	0	0	1	321	0.0
1980	Tex-A	15	32	2	4	0	0	0	3	3	3	.125	.200	.125	.325	-9	-5	-5	100	293	1	.241	0	0	0	1	3/S	-0.3
1981	NY-A	3	0	0	0	0	0	0	0	0	0	—	—	—	—	—	0	0	100	—	—	—	0	0	0	0	/2	0.0
1983	NY-N	35	56	3	10	0	1	0	2	7	4	.179	.270	.214	.484	36	-5	-5	99	66	3	.404	0	0	0	0	32/C	-0.4
1984	KC-A	9	13	1	2	1	0	0	0	1	2	.154	.214	.231	.445	23	-1	-1	99	0	0	.333	0	0	0	0	/3	0.0
Total	7	222	510	42	111	31	1	6	55	47	75	.218	.285	.318	.603	70	-25	-20	91	124	49	.533	5	3	-0	3	3/21SC	-1.4
■ **TOM ASMUSSEN**	Asmussen, Thomas William b: 9/26/1876, Chicago, Ill. d: 8/21/63, Arlington Heights Ill. TR, Deb: 8/10/07																											
1907	Bos-N	2	5	0	0	0	0	0	0	0		.000	.000	.000	.000	-99	-1	-1	95	0	0	.000	0			0	/C	0.0
■ **KEN ASPROMONTE**	Aspromonte, Kenneth Joseph b: 9/22/31, Brooklyn, N.Y. BR/TR, 6', 180 lbs. Deb: 9/02/57 M																											
1957	Bos-A	24	78	9	21	5	0	0	4	17	10	.269	.400	.333	.733	93	1	0	110	62	11	.705	0	1	-1	-0	2	0.0
1958	Bos-A	6	16	0	2	0	0	0	0	3	1	.125	.263	.125	.388	10	-2	-2	105	0	1	.333	0	0	0	0	/2	0.0
	Was-A	92	253	15	57	9	1	5	27	25	28	.225	.297	.328	.626	75	-10	-9	97	110	23	.531	1	1	-0	-2	23/S	-0.4
	Yr	98	269	15	59	9	1	5	27	28	29	.219	.295	.316	.611	70	-12	-11	97	104	24	.520	1	1	-0	-1		-0.4
1959	Was-A	70	225	31	55	12	0	2	14	26	39	.244	.323	.324	.647	78	-6	-6	100	70	23	.561	2	1	0	-2	2S/1O	-0.4
1960	Was-A	4	3	0	0	0	0	0	0	0	1	.000	.000	.000	.000	-98	-1	-1	102	0	0	.000	0	0	0	0	H	0.0
	Cle-A	117	459	65	133	20	1	10	48	53	32	.290	.366	.403	.769	110	6	7	98	84	69	.722	4	1	1	-21	23	-0.6
	Yr	121	462	65	133	20	1	10	48	53	33	.288	.364	.400	.764	109	5	6	98	81	69	.716	4	1	1	-21		-0.6
1961	LA-A	66	238	29	53	10	0	2	14	33	21	.223	.322	.290	.612	58	-11	-15	111	77	24	.547	0	0	0	8	2	0.1
	Cle-A	22	70	5	16	6	1	0	5	6	3	.229	.289	.343	.632	71	-3	-3	96	82	6	.526	0	0	0	-3	2	-0.2
	Yr	88	308	34	69	16	1	2	19	39	24	.224	.315	.302	.617	61	-14	-18	108	79	32	.554	0	0	0	5		-0.1
1962	Cle-A	20	28	4	4	2	0	0	1	6	5	.143	.294	.214	.508	40	-2	-2	98	66	2	.500	0	0	0	0	/23	0.0
	Mil-N	34	79	11	23	2	0	0	7	6	5	.291	.349	.316	.665	81	-2	-2	99	110	7	.508	0	1	-1	-0	2/3	-0.1
1963	Chi-N	20	34	2	5	3	0	0	4	4	4	.147	.237	.235	.472	35	-3	-3	105	210	2	.400	0	0	0	1	/21	-0.1
Total	7	475	1483	171	369	69	3	19	124	179	149	.249	.332	.338	.670	82	-33	-35	101	87	169	.619	7	5	-1	-17	2/3S1O	-1.7
■ **BOB ASPROMONTE**	Aspromonte, Robert Thomas b: 6/19/38, Brooklyn, N.Y. BR/TR, 6'2", 170 lbs. Deb: 9/19/56																											
1956	Bro-N	1	1	0	0	0	0	0	0	0	1	.000	.000	.000	.000	-97	-0	-0	103	0	0	.000	0	0	0	0	H	0.0
1960	LA-N	21	55	1	10	1	0	1	6	0	6	.182	.196	.255	.451	19	-6	-7	115	143	3	.348	1	0	0	2	S/3	-0.3
1961	LA-N	47	58	7	14	3	0	0	2	4	12	.241	.290	.293	.583	54	-4	-4	102	47	5	.457	0	0	0	0	/3S2	-0.2
1962	Hou-N	149	534	59	142	18	4	11	59	46	54	.266	.333	.376	.710	97	-7	-2	93	101	67	.636	4	5	-2	-0	*3S/2	0.0
1963	Hou-N	136	468	42	100	9	5	8	49	40	57	.214	.277	.306	.583	73	-19	-15	92	126	38	.487	3	1	0	-17	*3/1	-3.4
1964	Hou-N	157	553	51	155	20	3	12	69	35	54	.280	.332	.392	.725	107	2	5	96	114	69	.635	6	7	-2	-16	*3	-2.3
1965	Hou-N	152	578	53	152	15	2	5	52	38	54	.263	.312	.322	.634	89	-16	-8	89	114	57	.518	2	2	-1	-0	*3/1S	-1.5
1966	Hou-N	152	560	55	141	16	3	8	52	35	63	.252	.298	.334	.632	77	-18	-17	97	106	50	.503	0	4	-2	-9	*3/1S	-3.1
1967	Hou-N	137	486	51	143	24	5	6	58	45	44	.294	.356	.401	.758	125	11	15	94	115	67	.678	2	2	-1	-6	*3	0.1
1968	Hou-N	124	409	25	92	9	2	1	46	35	57	.225	.289	.264	.553	68	-16	-15	99	178	30	.440	1	0	0	-1	3O/1S	-2.0
1969	Atl-N	82	198	16	50	8	1	3	24	13	19	.253	.305	.348	.654	80	-5	-6	104	123	21	.549	0	1	-1	-2	O3S/2	-0.7
1970	Atl-N	62	127	5	27	3	0	0	7	13	13	.213	.286	.236	.522	40	-10	-11	104	91	9	.413	0	0	0	2	3/S1O	-0.8
1971	NY-N	104	342	21	77	9	1	5	33	29	25	.225	.286	.301	.587	69	-15	-14	96	114	27	.468	0	2	-1	-1	3	-1.6
Total	13	1324	4369	386	1103	135	26	60	457	333	459	.252	.310	.336	.646	86	-103	-79	95	118	441	.560	19	24	-9	-47	*3/OS12	-15.8
■ **BRIAN ASSELSTINE**	Asselstine, Brian Hanly b: 9/23/53, Santa Barbara, Cal BL/TR, 6'1", 175 lbs. Deb: 9/14/76																											
1976	Atl-N	11	33	2	7	0	0	1	3	1	2	.212	.235	.303	.538	47	-2	-3	111	89	3	.423	0	0	0	0	/O	-0.2
1977	Atl-N	83	124	12	26	6	0	4	17	9	10	.210	.263	.355	.618	57	-7	-9	113	121	12	.540	1	0	0	-2	O	-1.1
1978	Atl-N	39	103	11	28	3	3	2	13	11	16	.272	.353	.417	.771	103	2	1	112	105	16	.753	2	1	0	-2	O	-0.2
1979	Atl-N	8	10	1	1	0	0	0	0	1	2	.100	.182	.100	.282	-19	-2	-2	109	0	0	.200	0	0	0	-0	/O	-0.1

YEAR	TM/L	G	AB	R	H	2B	3B	HR	RBI	BB	SO	AVG	OBP	SLG	PRO	/A	BR	/A	PF	CHI	RC	TA	SB	CS	SBR	FR	POS	TPR
1980	Atl-N	87	218	18	62	13	1	3	25	11	37	.284	.322	.394	.716	98	-1	-1	101	104	24	.589	1	3	-2	-7	O	-1.2
1981	Atl-N	56	86	8	22	5	0	2	10	5	7	.256	.297	.384	.680	92	-1	-1	100	101	9	.574	1	0	0	-2	O	-0.2
Total	6	284	574	52	146	27	4	12	68	38	74	.254	.304	.378	.682	83	-10	-15	106	105	63	.603	5	4	-1	-14	O	-3.0

■ **JOE ASTROTH** Astroth, Joseph Henry b: 9/1/22, East Alton, Ill. BR/TR, 5'9", 187 lbs. Deb: 8/13/45

YEAR	TM/L	G	AB	R	H	2B	3B	HR	RBI	BB	SO	AVG	OBP	SLG	PRO	/A	BR	/A	PF	CHI	RC	TA	SB	CS	SBR	FR	POS	TPR
1945	Phi-A	10	17	1	1	0	0	0	1	0	1	.059	.111	.059	.170	-54	-3	-3	94	362	0	.125	0	0	0	0	/C	-0.2
1946	Phi-A	4	7	0	1	0	0	0	0	0	2	.143	.143	.143	.286	-19	-1	-1	104	0	0	.143	0	0	0	0	/C	0.0
1949	Phi-A	55	148	18	36	4	1	0	12	21	13	.243	.337	.284	.621	66	-7	-7	99	98	15	.542	1	0	0	2	C	-0.1
1950	Phi-A	39	110	11	36	3	1	1	18	18	3	.327	.422	.400	.822	124	3	4	90	132	18	.765	0	0	0	1	C	0.6
1951	Phi-A	64	187	30	46	10	2	2	19	18	13	.246	.312	.353	.665	75	-6	-7	106	94	21	.575	0	1	-1	6	C	0.2
1952	Phi-A	104	337	24	84	7	2	1	36	25	27	.249	.305	.291	.596	60	-15	-19	111	133	27	.465	2	2	-1	10	*C	-0.4
1953	Phi-A	82	260	28	77	15	2	3	24	27	12	.296	.367	.404	.771	106	3	2	102	78	38	.696	1	0	0	15	C	2.0
1954	Phi-A	77	226	22	50	8	1	1	23	21	19	.221	.296	.279	.575	59	-13	-12	98	132	20	.489	0	0	0	4	C	-0.5
1955	KC-A	101	274	29	69	4	1	5	23	47	33	.252	.373	.328	.702	89	-2	-2	101	82	35	.662	2	3	-1	4	*C	0.4
1956	KC-A	8	13	0	1	0	0	0	0	0	1	.077	.077	.077	.154	-59	-3	-3	101	0	0	.083	0	0	0	1	/C	-0.1
Total	10	544	1579	163	401	51	10	13	156	177	124	.254	.334	.324	.658	77	-44	-48	102	107	175	.598	6	6	-2	41	C	1.9

■ **CHARLIE ATHERTON** Atherton, Charles Morgan Herbert "Prexy" b: 10/19/1873, New Brunswick, N.J d: 12/19/34, Vienna, Austria 5'10", 160 lbs. Deb: 5/30/1899

YEAR	TM/L	G	AB	R	H	2B	3B	HR	RBI	BB	SO	AVG	OBP	SLG	PRO	/A	BR	/A	PF	CHI	RC	TA	SB	CS	SBR	FR	POS	TPR
1899	Was-N	65	242	28	60	5	6	0	23	21		.248	.313	.318	.631	79	-8	-6	96	97	25	.560	2			-7	3/O	-1.1

■ **ED ATKINSON** Atkinson, Edward b: Baltimore, Md. Deb: 10/22/1873

YEAR	TM/L	G	AB	R	H	2B	3B	HR	RBI	BB	SO	AVG	OBP	SLG	PRO	/A	BR	/A	PF	CHI	RC	TA	SB	CS	SBR	FR	POS	TPR
1873	Nat-n	2	9	2	0							.000															/O	

■ **LEFTY ATKINSON** Atkinson, Hubert Berley b: 6/4/04, Chicago, Ill. d: 2/12/61, Chicago, Ill. BL/TL, 5'6.5", 149 lbs. Deb: 8/05/27

YEAR	TM/L	G	AB	R	H	2B	3B	HR	RBI	BB	SO	AVG	OBP	SLG	PRO	/A	BR	/A	PF	CHI	RC	TA	SB	CS	SBR	FR	POS	TPR
1927	Was-A	1	1	1	0	0	0	0	0	0	0	.000	.000	.000	.000	-99	-0	-0	97	0	0	.000	0	0	0	0	H	0.0

■ **DICK ATTREAU** Attreau, Richard Gilbert b: 4/8/1897, Chicago, Ill. d: 7/5/64, Chicago, Ill. BL/TL, 6', 160 lbs. Deb: 9/14/26

YEAR	TM/L	G	AB	R	H	2B	3B	HR	RBI	BB	SO	AVG	OBP	SLG	PRO	/A	BR	/A	PF	CHI	RC	TA	SB	CS	SBR	FR	POS	TPR
1926	Phi-N	17	61	9	14	1	1	0	5	6	5	.230	.299	.279	.577	54	-4	-4	103	104	5	.489	0			-0	1	-0.4
1927	Phi-N	44	83	17	17	1	1	1	11	14	18	.205	.320	.277	.597	63	-4	-4	96	148	8	.576	1			0	1	-0.5
Total	2	61	144	26	31	2	2	1	16	20	23	.215	.311	.278	.589	59	-8	-8	99	130	13	.540	1			-0	/1	-0.9

■ **TOBY ATWELL** Atwell, Maurice Dailey b: 3/8/24, Leesburg, Va. BL/TR, 5'9.5", 185 lbs. Deb: 4/15/52

YEAR	TM/L	G	AB	R	H	2B	3B	HR	RBI	BB	SO	AVG	OBP	SLG	PRO	/A	BR	/A	PF	CHI	RC	TA	SB	CS	SBR	FR	POS	TPR
1952	Chi-N	107	362	36	105	16	3	2	31	40	22	.290	.362	.367	.730	99	2	1	103	89	49	.654	2	1	0	-2	*C	0.1
1953	Chi-N	24	74	10	17	2	0	1	8	13	7	.230	.345	.297	.642	67	-3	-3	103	125	9	.614	0	0	0	1	C	0.0
	Pit-N	53	139	11	34	6	0	0	17	20	12	.245	.352	.288	.640	68	-5	-6	102	166	14	.558	0	0	0	1	C	-0.1
	Yr	77	213	21	51	8	0	1	25	33	19	.239	.349	.291	.640	68	-8	-9	102	155	23	.576	0	0	0	1		-0.1
1954	Pit-N	96	287	36	83	8	4	3	26	43	21	.289	.387	.376	.764	103	2	3	97	87	42	.716	2	3	-1	12	C	1.5
1955	Pit-N	71	207	21	44	8	0	1	18	40	16	.213	.343	.266	.608	66	-9	-8	97	126	21	.571	0	1	-1	3	C	-0.3
1956	Pit-N	12	18	0	2	0	0	0	3	1	5	.111	.158	.111	.269	-25	-3	-3	102	634	0	.167	0	0	0	-0	/C	-0.2
	Mil-N	15	30	2	5	1	0	2	7	4	1	.167	.265	.400	.665	76	-1	-1	99	164	3	.640	0	0	0	0	C	0.0
	Yr	27	48	2	7	1	0	2	10	5	6	.146	.226	.292	.518	38	-4	-4	100	396	3	.463	0	0	0	-0		-0.2
Total	5	378	1117	116	290	41	7	9	110	161	84	.260	.357	.333	.690	85	-18	-18	100	118	139	.655	4	5	-2	14	C	1.0

■ **BILL ATWOOD** Atwood, William Franklin b: 9/25/11, Rome, Ga. BR/TR, 5'11.5", 190 lbs. Deb: 4/15/36

YEAR	TM/L	G	AB	R	H	2B	3B	HR	RBI	BB	SO	AVG	OBP	SLG	PRO	/A	BR	/A	PF	CHI	RC	TA	SB	CS	SBR	FR	POS	TPR
1936	Phi-N	71	192	21	58	9	2	2	29	11	15	.302	.346	.401	.747	93	0	-2	108	124	27	.647	0			-2	C	-0.1
1937	Phi-N	87	279	27	68	15	1	2	32	30	27	.244	.317	.326	.643	69	-9	-12	108	119	32	.585	3			-1	C	-0.9
1938	Phi-N	102	281	27	55	8	1	3	28	25	26	.196	.261	.263	.525	44	-21	-21	100	122	19	.421	0			-5	C	-2.2
1939	Phi-N	4	6	0	0	0	0	0	1	2	3	.000	.250	.000	.250	-29	-1	-1	94	0	0	.500	1			0	/C	0.0
1940	Phi-N	78	203	7	39	9	0	0	22	25	18	.192	.284	.236	.520	46	-15	-14	97	170	14	.438	0			3	C	-0.7
Total	5	342	961	82	220	41	4	7	112	93	89	.229	.299	.302	.601	62	-46	-51	103	131	92	.523	4			-4	C	-3.9

■ **JAKE ATZ** Atz, Jacob Henry b: 7/1/1879, Washington, D.C. d: 5/22/45, New Orleans, La. BR/TR, 5'9.5", 160 lbs. Deb: 9/24/02

YEAR	TM/L	G	AB	R	H	2B	3B	HR	RBI	BB	SO	AVG	OBP	SLG	PRO	/A	BR	/A	PF	CHI	RC	TA	SB	CS	SBR	FR	POS	TPR
1902	Was-A	3	10	1	1	0	0	0	0	0		.100	.100	.100	.200	-45	-2	-2	99	0	0	.111	0			0	/2	-0.1
1907	Chi-A	4	8	0	1	0	0	0	0	0		.125	.125	.125	.250	-19	-1	-1	104	0	0	.143	0			0	/3O	0.0
1908	Chi-A	83	206	24	40	3	0	0	27	31		.194	.300	.209	.508	72	-6	-4	94	236	15	.500	9			1	2S/3	-0.4
1909	Chi-A	119	381	39	90	18	3	0	22	38		.236	.309	.299	.608	95	-3	-2	97	76	38	.577	14			-2	*2/OS	-0.7
Total	4	209	605	64	132	21	3	0	49	69		.218	.300	.263	.563	83	-11	-9	96	130	53	.535	23			-1	2/SO3	-1.2

■ **CHUB AUBREY** Aubrey, Harry Herbert "Harry" or "Chub" b: 7/5/1880, St.Joseph, Mo. d: 9/18/53, Baltimore, Md. TR , Deb: 4/22/03

YEAR	TM/L	G	AB	R	H	2B	3B	HR	RBI	BB	SO	AVG	OBP	SLG	PRO	/A	BR	/A	PF	CHI	RC	TA	SB	CS	SBR	FR	POS	TPR
1903	Bos-N	96	325	26	69	8	2	0	27	18		.212	.254	.249	.503	47	-23	-21	96	107	23	.414	7			-13	S/2O	-2.8

■ **RICK AUERBACH** Auerbach, Frederick Steven b: 2/15/50, Woodland Hills, Cal BR/TR, 6', 165 lbs. Deb: 4/13/71

YEAR	TM/L	G	AB	R	H	2B	3B	HR	RBI	BB	SO	AVG	OBP	SLG	PRO	/A	BR	/A	PF	CHI	RC	TA	SB	CS	SBR	FR	POS	TPR
1971	Mil-A	79	236	22	48	10	0	1	9	20	40	.203	.271	.258	.530	49	-15	-16	103	57	17	.446	3	2	-0	-4	S	-1.2
1972	Mil-A	153	554	50	121	16	3	2	30	43	62	.218	.277	.269	.546	66	-25	-22	95	83	42	.479	24	8	2	-21	*S	-2.7
1973	Mil-A	6	10	2	1	1	0	0	0	0	1	.100	.100	.200	.300	-18	-2	-2	96	0	0	.200	0	1	-1	-0	/S	-0.1
1974	LA-N	45	73	12	25	0	0	1	4	8	9	.342	.407	.384	.791	132	3	3	93	50	11	.741	4	2	0	-2	S2/3	0.4
1975	LA-N	85	170	18	38	9	0	0	12	18	22	.224	.298	.276	.574	63	-9	-8	95	99	13	.479	3	2	-0	-12	S/23	-1.1
1976	LA-N	36	47	7	6	0	0	0	1	6	6	.128	.226	.128	.354	2	-6	-6	100	64	1	.267	0	1	-1	-1	S/32	-0.5
1977	Cin-N	33	45	5	7	2	0	0	3	4	7	.156	.224	.200	.424	15	-5	-5	100	133	2	.333	0	0	0	0	2S	-0.1
1978	Cin-N	63	55	17	18	6	0	2	5	7	12	.327	.413	.545	.958	161	5	5	103	55	13	1.026	1	0	0	0	S2/3	0.8
1979	Cin-N	62	100	17	21	8	1	1	12	14	19	.210	.307	.340	.647	78	-3	-3	97	128	11	.593	0	1	-1	2	3S/2	0.0
1980	Cin-N	24	33	5	11	1	1	1	4	3	5	.333	.389	.515	.904	148	2	2	102	79	5	.800	0	3	-2	-0	/S32	0.1
1981	Sea-A	38	84	12	13	3	0	1	6	4	15	.155	.202	.226	.428	23	-8	-8	100	107	4	.342	1	1	-0	-0	S	-0.5
Total	11	624	1407	167	309	56	5	9	86	127	198	.220	.287	.286	.573	66	-64	-60	98	83	119	.510	36	21	-2	-38	S/23	-4.9

■ **DAVE AUGUSTINE** Augustine, David Ralph b: 11/28/49, Follansbee, W.Va. BR/TR, 6'2", 174 lbs. Deb: 9/03/73

YEAR	TM/L	G	AB	R	H	2B	3B	HR	RBI	BB	SO	AVG	OBP	SLG	PRO	/A	BR	/A	PF	CHI	RC	TA	SB	CS	SBR	FR	POS	TPR
1973	Pit-N	11	7	1	2	1	0	0	0	0	1	.286	.286	.429	.714	104	-0	-0	92	0	0	.500	0	0	0	-2	/O	-0.2
1974	Pit-N	18	22	3	4	0	0	0	0	0	5	.182	.182	.182	.364	2	-3	-3	98	0	0	.200	0	1	-1	1	O	-0.2
Total	2	29	29	4	6	1	0	0	0	0	6	.207	.207	.241	.448	26	-3	-3	96	0	1	.280	0	1	-1	-1	/O	-0.4

■ **TEX AULDS** Aulds, Leycester Doyle b: 12/28/20, Farmerville, La. BR/TR, 6'2", 185 lbs. Deb: 5/25/47

YEAR	TM/L	G	AB	R	H	2B	3B	HR	RBI	BB	SO	AVG	OBP	SLG	PRO	/A	BR	/A	PF	CHI	RC	TA	SB	CS	SBR	FR	POS	TPR
1947	Bos-A	3	4	0	1	0	0	0	0	0	1	.250	.250	.250	.500	36	-0	-0	108	0	0	.333	0	0	0	0	/C	0.0

■ **DOUG AULT** Ault, Douglas Reagan b: 3/9/50, Beaumont, Tex. BR/TL, 6'3", 200 lbs. Deb: 9/09/76

YEAR	TM/L	G	AB	R	H	2B	3B	HR	RBI	BB	SO	AVG	OBP	SLG	PRO	/A	BR	/A	PF	CHI	RC	TA	SB	CS	SBR	FR	POS	TPR
1976	Tex-A	9	20	0	6	1	0	0	0	1	3	.300	.333	.350	.683	98	-0	-0	102	0	2	.571	0	0	0	0	/1D	0.0
1977	Tor-A	129	445	44	109	22	3	11	64	39	68	.245	.311	.382	.693	86	-8	-9	103	127	48	.603	4	4	-1	5	*1/D	-1.1
1978	Tor-A	54	104	10	25	1	1	3	7	17	14	.240	.352	.356	.708	100	0	0	100	60	13	.647	0	0	0	-3	1/OD	-0.3
1980	Tor-A	64	144	12	28	5	1	3	15	14	23	.194	.275	.306	.581	59	-8	-8	100	110	12	.500	0	1	-1	0	1D/O	-1.0
Total	4	256	713	66	168	29	5	17	86	71	108	.236	.311	.362	.673	83	-15	-17	102	110	75	.615	4	5	-2	2	1/DO	-2.4

■ **HENRY AUSTIN** Austin, Henry C. b: 1844, Brooklyn, N.Y. d: 9/3/1895, Amityville, N.Y. Deb: 4/28/1873

YEAR	TM/L	G	AB	R	H	2B	3B	HR	RBI	BB	SO	AVG	OBP	SLG	PRO	/A	BR	/A	PF	CHI	RC	TA	SB	CS	SBR	FR	POS	TPR
1873	Res-n	23	106	11	24							.226															O	

■ **JIMMY AUSTIN** Austin, James Philip "Pepper" b: 12/8/1879, Swansea, Wales d: 3/6/65, Laguna Beach, Cal. BB/TR, 5'7.5", 155 lbs. Deb: 4/19/09 MC

YEAR	TM/L	G	AB	R	H	2B	3B	HR	RBI	BB	SO	AVG	OBP	SLG	PRO	/A	BR	/A	PF	CHI	RC	TA	SB	CS	SBR	FR	POS	TPR
1909	NY-A	136	437	37	101	11	5	1	39	32		.231	.285	.286	.571	81	-10	-10	99	117	42	.560	30			9	*3S/2	0.5
1910	NY-A	133	432	46	94	11	4	2	36	47		.218	.305	.275	.580	76	-8	-12	107	109	45	.577	22			2	*3	-0.4
1911	StL-A	148	541	84	141	25	11	2	45	69		.261	.351	.359	.709	103	-0	4	95	67	79	.738	26			18	*3	2.2
1912	StL-A	149	536	57	135	14	8	2	44	38		.252	.306	.319	.625	80	-15	-15	99	88	62	.601	28			2	*3	-1.4
1913	StL-A	142	489	56	130	18	6	2	42	45	51	.266	.338	.339	.677	103	-1	2	95	89	66	.713	37			9	*3M	1.5
1914	StL-A	130	466	55	111	16	4	0	30	40	59	.238	.300	.290	.590	79	-13	-12	98	88	41	.519	20	23	-8	-2	*3	-2.0
1915	StL-A	141	477	61	127	6	6	1	30	64	60	.266	.355	.310	.666	104	2	4	96	72	59	.636	18	15	-4	11	*3	1.9
1916	StL-A	129	411	55	85	15	6	1	28	74	59	.207	.333	.280	.613	89	-5	-3	95	86	47	.650	19			-5	*3	-0.1

YEAR	TM/L	G	AB	R	H	2B	3B	HR	RBI	BB	SO	AVG	OBP	SLG	PRO	/A	BR	/A	PF	CHI	RC	TA	SB	CS	SBR	FR	POS	TPR
1917	StL-A	127	455	61	109	18	8	0	19	50	46	.240	.319	.314	.633	99	-3	-0	95	46	50	.604	13			11	*3/S	1.8
1918	StL-A	110	367	42	97	14	4	0	20	53	32	.264	.359	.324	.683	107	4	5	99	63	49	.707	18			-16	S3M	-0.7
1919	StL-A	106	396	54	94	9	9	1	21	42	31	.237	.314	.313	.627	79	-12	-11	97	64	40	.583	8			8	3	0.4
1920	StL-A	83	280	38	76	11	3	1	32	31	15	.271	.352	.343	.695	76	-5	-10	111	116	35	.639	2	4	-2	-5	3	-1.0
1921	StL-A	27	66	8	18	2	1	0	2	4	7	.273	.324	.333	.657	67	-3	-3	101	31	7	.592	2	1	0	-1	S/23	-0.1
1922	StL-A	15	31	6	9	3	1	0	1	3	2	.290	.353	.452	.805	103	0	0	106	26	5	.773	0	0	0	1	/32	0.2
1923	StL-A	1	0	0	0	0	0	0	0	0	0	—	—	—	—	—	0	0	104	—	—	—	0	0	0	0	/M	0.0
1925	StL-A	1	1	0	0	0	0	0	0	0	0	.000	.000	.000	.000	-93	-0	-0	108	0	0	.000	0	0	0	0	/3	0.0
1926	StL-A	1	2	1	1	1	0	0	1	0	0	.500	.500	1.000	1.500	283	0	0	101	170	1	3.000	1	0	0	0	/3	0.1
1929	StL-A	1	1	0	0	0	0	0	0	0	1	.000	.000	.000	.000	-99	-0	-0	100	0	0	.000	0	0	0	0	/3	0.0
Total	18	1580	5388	661	1328	174	76	13	390	592	363	.246	.326	.314	.640	90	-70	-60	98	82	635	.627	244	43		43	*3S/2	2.9
■ **CHICK AUTRY**	Autry, Martin Gordon b: 3/5/03, Martindale, Tex. d: 1/26/50, Savannah, Ga. BR/TR, 6', 180 lbs. Deb: 4/20/24																											
1924	NY-A	2	0	1	0	0	0	0	0	0	0	—	1.000	—	1.314	251	0	0	99	0	0	—	0	0	0	0	/C	0.0
1926	Cle-A	3	7	1	1	0	0	0	0	1	0	.143	.250	.143	.393	4	-1	-1	100	0	0	.333	0	0	0	0	/C	0.0
1927	Cle-A	16	43	5	11	4	1	0	7	0	6	.256	.256	.395	.651	69	-2	-2	97	137	4	.531	0	0	0	1	C	0.0
1928	Cle-A	22	60	6	18	6	1	1	9	1	7	.300	.311	.483	.795	100	0	-0	106	97	9	.714	0	0	0	2	C	0.3
1929	Chi-A	43	96	7	20	6	0	1	12	1	8	.208	.224	.302	.527	36	-10	-9	95	128	6	.397	0	2	-1	1	C	-0.5
1930	Chi-A	34	71	1	18	1	1	0	5	4	8	.254	.293	.296	.589	49	-5	-6	103	79	6	.472	0	0	0	0	C	-0.2
Total	6	120	277	21	68	17	3	2	33	7	29	.245	.269	.350	.619	59	-18	-18	100	106	26	.502	0	2	-1	4	/C	-0.4
■ **CHICK AUTRY**	Autry, William Askew b: 1/2/1885, Humboldt, Tenn. d: 1/16/76, Santa Rosa, Cal. BL/TL, 5'11", 168 lbs. Deb: 9/18/07																											
1907	Cin-N	7	25	3	5	0	0	0	0	1		.200	.231	.200	.431	38	-2	-2	95	0	1	.300	0			0	/O	-0.1
1909	Cin-N	9	33	3	6	2	0	0	4	2		.182	.229	.242	.471	50	-2	-2	94	193	2	.407	1			0	/1	-0.1
	Bos-N	65	199	16	39	4	0	0	13	21		.196	.279	.216	.495	57	-10	-9	96	110	13	.444	5			6	1/O	-0.4
	Yr	74	232	19	45	6	0	0	17	23		.194	.272	.220	.492	56	-12	-11	96	123	15	.439	6			6		-0.5
Total	2	81	257	22	50	6	0	0	17	24		.195	.269	.218	.486	54	-14	-12	96	110	16	.425	6			6	/1O	-0.6
■ **EARL AVERILL**	Averill, Earl Douglas b: 9/9/31, Cleveland, O. BR/TR, 5'10", 185 lbs. Deb: 4/19/56																											
1956	Cle-A	42	93	12	22	6	0	3	14	14	25	.237	.343	.398	.740	94	-1	-1	101	114	13	.703	0	1	-1	-5	C	-0.5
1958	Cle-A	17	55	2	10	1	0	2	7	4	7	.182	.250	.309	.559	56	-4	-3	94	122	4	.489	1	0	0	0	3	-0.1
1959	Chi-N	74	186	22	44	10	0	10	34	15	39	.237	.300	.452	.752	98	-1	-1	98	121	25	.697	0	1	-1	-2	C3/O2	-0.1
1960	Chi-N	52	102	14	24	4	0	1	13	11	16	.235	.316	.304	.620	72	-4	-4	98	155	10	.537	1	1	-0	-5	C/3O	-0.7
	Chi-A	10	14	2	3	0	0	0	2	4	2	.214	.389	.214	.603	67	-0	-0	101	261	2	.636	0	0	0	0	/C	0.0
1961	LA-A	115	323	56	86	9	0	21	59	62	70	.266	.388	.489	.877	119	16	11	111	105	64	.907	1	0	0	-7	C/O2	0.3
1962	LA-A	92	187	21	41	9	0	4	22	43	47	.219	.368	.332	.700	88	-1	-2	102	118	26	.716	0	0	0	-4	O/C	-0.7
1963	Phi-N	47	71	8	19	2	0	3	8	9	14	.268	.350	.423	.773	118	2	2	103	86	11	.722	0	0	0	-2	C/O13	0.0
Total	7	449	1031	137	249	41	0	44	159	162	220	.242	.349	.409	.758	100	7	2	104	117	154	.756	3	3	-1	-25	C/O321	-1.8
■ **EARL AVERILL**	Averill, Howard Earl "Rock" b: 5/21/02, Snohomish, Wash. d: 8/16/83, Everett, Wash. BL/TR, 5'9.5", 172 lbs. Deb: 4/16/29 H																											
1929	Cle-A	151	597	110	198	43	13	18	96	63	53	.332	.398	.538	.936	138	34	33	100	84	125	.971	13	13	-4	-8	*O	1.4
1930	Cle-A	139	534	102	181	33	8	19	119	56	48	.339	.404	.537	.941	130	29	25	105	122	116	.986	10	7	-1	-5	*O	1.2
1931	Cle-A	155	627	140	209	36	10	32	143	68	38	.333	.404	.576	.979	146	48	42	106	99	144	1.040	9	9	-3	-7	*O	2.1
1932	Cle-A	153	631	116	198	37	14	32	124	75	40	.314	.392	.569	.961	135	41	33	108	88	140	1.009	5	8	-3	16	*O	3.6
1933	Cle-A	151	599	83	180	39	16	11	92	54	29	.301	.363	.474	.837	115	16	12	105	103	104	.824	3	1	0	-2	*O	0.5
1934	Cle-A	154	598	128	187	48	6	31	113	99	44	.313	.414	.569	.982	151	46	45	101	84	145	1.080	4	3	-1	6	*O	4.4
1935	Cle-A	140	563	109	162	34	13	19	79	70	58	.288	.368	.496	.863	122	16	17	99	77	105	.884	8	4	0	-6	*O	0.9
1936	Cle-A	152	614	136	**232**	39	**15**	28	126	65	35	.378	.438	.627	1.065	152	56	51	106	92	168	1.179	3	3	-1	-9	*O	3.3
1937	Cle-A	156	609	121	182	33	11	21	92	88	65	.299	.387	.493	.880	123	19	21	98	84	119	.912	5	4	-1	-13	*O	0.1
1938	Cle-A	134	482	101	159	27	15	14	93	81	48	.330	.429	.535	.965	142	32	33	99	107	115	1.068	5	2	0	1	*O	3.0
1939	Cle-A	24	55	8	15	8	0	1	7	6	12	.273	.344	.473	.817	109	0	1	98	81	9	.780	0	1	-1	-3	O	-0.2
	Det-A	87	309	58	81	20	6	10	58	43	30	.262	.354	.463	.817	97	3	-3	111	115	53	.816	4	2	0	-4	O	-0.8
	Yr	111	364	66	96	28	6	11	65	49	42	.264	.353	.464	.817	99	3	-2	108	109	62	.811	4	3	-1	-7		-1.0
1940	Det-A	64	118	10	33	4	1	2	20	5	14	.280	.309	.381	.690	70	-4	-6	111	142	14	.568	0	0	0	-5	O	-1.0
1941	Bos-N	8	17	2	2	0	0	0	2	1	4	.118	.211	.118	.328	-6	-2	-2	93	361	1	.267	0			1	/O	-0.1
Total	13	1668	6353	1224	2019	401	128	238	1164	774	518	.318	.395	.534	.928	132	334	303	103	96	1358	.972	69	57		-38	*O	18.4
■ **BOBBY AVILA**	Avila, Roberto Francisco (Gonzalez) b: 4/2/24, Vera Cruz, Mexico BR/TR, 5'10", 175 lbs. Deb: 4/30/49																											
1949	Cle-A	31	14	3	3	0	0	0	3	1	3	.214	.267	.214	.481	29	-1	-1	98	343	1	.333	0	0	0	0	/2	0.0
1950	Cle-A	80	201	39	60	10	2	1	21	29	17	.299	.390	.383	.773	101	0	1	98	91	32	.752	5	0	2	-9	2/S	-0.1
1951	Cle-A	141	542	76	165	21	3	10	58	60	31	.304	.374	.410	.783	118	9	13	95	87	84	.738	14	8	-1	5	*2	2.3
1952	Cle-A	150	597	102	179	26	**11**	7	45	67	36	.300	.371	.415	.787	131	15	22	91	60	93	.739	12	10	-2	-15	*2	1.2
1953	Cle-A	141	559	85	160	22	3	8	55	58	27	.286	.355	.379	.735	103	-1	3	95	83	75	.664	10	8	-2	15	*2	2.4
1954	Cle-A	143	555	112	189	27	2	15	67	59	31	.341	.405	.477	.882	133	32	27	106	79	109	.874	9	7	-2	14	*2/S	4.7
1955	Cle-A	141	537	83	146	22	4	13	61	82	47	.272	.370	.400	.771	103	7	4	104	86	81	.728	1	4	-2	4	*2	1.4
1956	Cle-A	138	513	74	115	14	2	10	54	70	68	.224	.323	.318	.641	69	-22	-23	101	111	57	.616	17	4	3	2	*2	-0.7
1957	Cle-A	129	463	60	124	19	3	5	48	46	47	.268	.335	.354	.690	87	-7	-8	102	108	55	.603	2	4	-2	-6	*23	-0.9
1958	Cle-A	113	375	54	95	21	3	5	30	55	45	.253	.350	.365	.716	103	-0	3	94	81	50	.678	5	7	-3	-0	23	0.6
1959	Bal-A	20	47	1	8	0	0	0	0	4	5	.170	.235	.170	.406	14	-6	-5	97	0	1	.273	0	0	0	-1	O/23	-0.6
	Bos-A	22	45	7	11	0	0	3	6	6	11	.244	.333	.444	.778	106	1	0	106	81	6	.703	0	0	0	0	2	0.1
	Yr	42	92	8	19	0	0	3	6	10	16	.207	.284	.304	.589	61	-5	-5	102	43	8	.500	0	0	0	-1		-0.5
	Mil-N	51	172	29	41	3	2	3	19	24	31	.238	.332	.331	.663	81	-5	-4	95	119	22	.636	3	0	1	-5	2	-0.4
Total	11	1300	4620	725	1296	185	35	80	467	561	399	.281	.360	.388	.748	104	23	33	98	87	666	.724	78	52	-8	4	*2/3OS	10.0
■ **RAMON AVILES**	Aviles, Ramon Antonio (Miranda) b: 1/22/52, Manati, P.R. BR/TR, 5'9", 155 lbs. Deb: 7/10/77																											
1977	Bos-A	1	0	0	0	0	0	0	0	0	0	—	—	—	—	—	0	-0	117	—	0	—	0	0	0	0	/2	0.0
1979	Phi-N	27	61	7	17	2	0	0	12	8	8	.279	.371	.311	.683	91	-1	-0	97	250	8	.622	0	0	0	1	2	0.2
1980	Phi-N	51	101	12	28	6	0	2	9	10	9	.277	.342	.396	.738	98	1	-0	107	77	13	.658	0	0	0	-0	S2	0.4
1981	Phi-N	38	28	2	6	1	0	0	3	3	5	.214	.290	.250	.540	48	-2	-2	112	168	2	.455	0	0	0	1	23/S	0.1
Total	4	117	190	21	51	9	0	2	24	21	22	.268	.344	.347	.692	88	-1	-3	105	148	24	.633	0	0	0	1	/2S3	0.7
■ **BENNY AYALA**	Ayala, Benigno (Felix) b: 2/7/51, Yauco, P.R. BR/TR, 6'1", 185 lbs. Deb: 8/27/74																											
1974	NY-N	23	68	9	16	1	0	2	8	7	17	.235	.316	.338	.654	83	-2	-1	99	106	7	.564	0	0	0	-0	O	-0.2
1976	NY-N	22	26	2	3	0	0	1	2	2	6	.115	.179	.231	.409	17	-3	-3	92	86	1	.333	0	1	-1	-1	/O	-0.4
1977	StL-N	1	3	0	1	0	0	0	0	0	1	.333	.333	.333	.667	83	-0	-0	96	0	0	.500	0	0	0	2	/O	0.2
1979	Bal-A	42	86	15	22	5	0	6	13	6	9	.256	.304	.523	.828	122	2	2	97	79	13	.773	0	0	0	-4	OD	-0.2
1980	Bal-A	76	170	28	45	8	1	10	33	19	21	.265	.339	.500	.839	126	6	6	101	112	28	.806	0	0	0	-3	DO	0.2
1981	Bal-A	44	86	12	24	2	0	3	13	11	9	.279	.367	.407	.774	124	3	3	99	116	13	.723	0	1	-1	0	D/O	0.3
1982	Bal-A	64	128	17	39	6	0	6	24	5	14	.305	.331	.492	.823	123	3	3	100	118	19	.742	1	1	-0	-5	OD/1	-0.2
1983	Bal-A	47	104	12	23	7	0	4	13	9	18	.221	.283	.404	.687	86	-2	-2	100	94	12	.614	0	0	0	-3	OD	-0.5
1984	Bal-A	60	118	9	25	6	0	4	24	8	24	.212	.262	.364	.626	76	-5	-4	94	174	10	.531	1	1	-0	-4	DO	-0.8
1985	Cle-A	46	76	10	19	7	0	2	15	4	17	.250	.287	.421	.709	97	-1	-1	94	157	9	.610	0	0	0	-5	O/D	-0.5
Total	10	425	865	114	217	42	1	38	145	71	136	.251	.309	.434	.743	105	1	3	98	118	113	.688	2	4	-2	-22	OD/1	-2.1
■ **DICK AYLWARD**	Aylward, Richard John "Dandy" b: 6/4/25, Baltimore, Md. d: 6/11/83, Spring Valley, Cal. BR/TR, 6', 190 lbs. Deb: 5/01/53																											
1953	Cle-A	4	3	0	0	0	0	0	0	0	1	.000	.000	.000	.000	-99	-1	-1	95	0	0	.000	0	0	0	-0	/C	0.0
■ **JOE AZCUE**	Azcue, Jose Joaquin (Lopez) b: 8/18/39, Cienfuegos, Cuba BR/TR, 6', 190 lbs. Deb: 8/03/60																											
1960	Cin-N	14	31	1	3	0	0	0	3	2	6	.097	.152	.097	.248	-31	-6	-5	98	406	0	.172	0	1	-1	1	C	-0.4

YEAR	TM/L	G	AB	R	H	2B	3B	HR	RBI	BB	SO	AVG	OBP	SLG	PRO	/A	BR	/A	PF	CHI	RC	TA	SB	CS	SBR	FR	POS	TPR
1962	KC-A	72	223	18	51	9	1	2	25	17	27	.229	.292	.305	.597	61	-12	-12	100	134	20	.509	1	0	0	-1	C	-0.8
1963	KC-A	2	4	0	0	0	0	0	0	0	1	.000	.000	.000	.000	-93	-1	-1	108	0	0	.000	0	0	0	0	/C	0.0
	Cle-A	94	320	26	91	16	0	14	46	15	46	.284	.316	.466	.782	120	6	7	97	101	42	.679	1	1	-0	0	C	0.9
	Yr	96	324	26	91	16	0	14	46	15	47	.281	.313	.460	.773	117	5	6	97	99	42	.668	1	1	-0	1		0.9
1964	Cle-A	83	271	20	74	9	1	4	34	16	38	.273	.318	.358	.676	85	-4	-5	103	132	30	.567	0	2	-1	7	C	0.3
1965	Cle-A	111	335	16	77	7	0	2	35	27	54	.230	.293	.269	.562	62	-17	-16	98	151	24	.445	2	1	0	-10	*C	-1.9
1966	Cle-A	98	302	22	83	10	1	9	37	20	22	.275	.324	.404	.728	106	3	2	101	104	38	.634	0	2	-1	-17	C	-1.2
1967	Cle-A	86	295	33	74	12	5	11	34	22	35	.251	.309	.437	.747	118	6	6	100	89	37	.664	0	3	-2	8	C	1.9
1968	Cle-A	115	357	23	100	10	0	4	42	28	33	.280	.332	.342	.674	104	2	2	101	134	40	.566	1	1	-0	-6	C	0.0
1969	Cle-A	7	24	1	7	0	0	1	1	4	3	.292	.393	.417	.810	134	1	1	94	31	4	.824	0	0	0	1	/C	0.2
	Bos-A	19	51	7	11	2	0	0	3	4	5	.216	.273	.255	.528	46	-4	-4	105	93	3	.395	0	0	0	0	C	-0.2
	Cal-A	80	248	15	54	6	0	1	19	27	28	.218	.300	.254	.554	56	-14	-14	99	116	17	.440	0	1	-1	7	C	-0.1
	Yr	106	323	23	72	8	0	2	23	35	36	.223	.303	.266	.569	60	-16	-16	100	107	25	.462	0	1	-1	8		-0.1
1970	Cal-A	114	351	19	85	13	1	2	25	24	40	.242	.294	.302	.596	71	-17	-13	92	90	30	.475	0	0	0	-14	*C	-2.6
1972	Cal-A	3	2	0	0	0	0	0	0	0	1	.000	.000	.000	.000	-99	-0	-0	88	0	0	.000	0	0	0	0	/C	0.0
	Mil-A	11	14	0	2	0	0	0	0	1	5	.143	.200	.143	.343	3	-2	-2	95	0	0	.250	0	0	0	0	/C	-0.1
	Yr	14	16	0	2	0	0	0	0	1	6	.125	.176	.125	.301	-10	-2	-2	94	0	0	.214	0	0	0	0		-0.1
Total	11	909	2828	201	712	94	9	50	304	207	344	.252	.307	.344	.651	85	-59	-55	99	118	287	.565	5	12	-6	-24	C	-4.0
■ **CHARLIE BABB** Babb, Charles Amos b: 2/20/1873, Milwaukie, Ore. d: 3/20/54, Portland, Ore. BB/TR, 5'10", 165 lbs. Deb: 4/17/03																												
1903	NY-N	121	424	68	105	15	8	0	46	45		.248	.320	.321	.641	79	-8	-12	106	111	52	.636	22			-7	*S/3	-1.1
1904	Bro-N	151	521	49	138	18	3	0	53	53		.265	.333	.311	.644	106	2	5	95	127	67	.650	34			-6	*S	0.0
1905	Bro-N	75	235	27	44	8	2	0	17	27		.187	.271	.238	.509	56	-12	-11	96	108	18	.487	10			-1	S1/32	-1.2
Total	3	347	1180	144	287	41	13	0	116	125		.243	.316	.300	.616	86	-18	-18	99	117	137	.610	66			-14	S/132	-2.3
■ **LOREN BABE** Babe, Loren Rolland "Bee Bee" b: 1/11/28, Pisgah, Iowa d: 2/14/84, Omaha, Neb. BL/TR, 5'10", 180 lbs. Deb: 8/19/52 C																												
1952	NY-A	12	21	1	2	1	0	0	0	4	4	.095	.240	.143	.383	8	-3	-3	98	0	1	.421	1	0	0	0	/3	-0.1
1953	NY-A	5	18	2	6	1	0	2	6	0	2	.333	.333	.722	1.056	192	2	2	93	117	4	1.083	0	0	0	1	/3	0.2
	Phi-A	103	343	34	77	16	2	0	20	35	20	.224	.300	.283	.583	57	-20	-21	102	76	30	.486	0	1	-1	6	3/S	-1.9
	Yr	108	361	36	83	17	2	2	26	35	22	.230	.302	.305	.606	63	-18	-19	102	79	34	.510	0	1	-1	6		-1.7
Total	2	120	382	37	85	18	2	2	26	39	26	.223	.298	.296	.594	60	-21	-21	102	74	36	.505	1	1	-0	7	3/S	-1.8
■ **CHARLIE BABINGTON** Babington, Charles Percy b: 5/4/1895, Cranston, R.I. d: 3/22/57, Providence, R.I. BR/TR, 6', 170 lbs. Deb: 7/20/15																												
1915	NY-N	28	33	5	8	3	1	0	2	0	4	.242	.265	.394	.659	107	-0	0	91	59	4	.600	1			-4	O/1	-0.3
■ **SHOOTY BABITT** Babitt, Mack Neal b: 3/9/59, Oakland, Cal. BR/TR, 5'8", 174 lbs. Deb: 4/09/81																												
1981	Oak-A	54	156	10	40	1	3	0	14	13	13	.256	.314	.301	.615	81	-4	-3	96	117	14	.516	5	4	-1	-8	2	-1.1
■ **WALLY BACKMAN** Backman, Walter Wayne b: 9/22/59, Hillsboro, Ore. BB/TR, 5'9", 160 lbs. Deb: 9/02/80																												
1980	NY-N	27	93	12	30	1	1	0	9	11	14	.323	.400	.355	.755	117	2	3	96	110	13	.681	2	3	-1	-2	2/S	0.2
1981	NY-N	26	36	5	10	2	0	0	0	4	7	.278	.350	.333	.683	94	-0	-0	101	0	5	.654	1	0	0	1	2/3	0.1
1982	NY-N	96	261	37	71	13	2	3	22	49	47	.272	.387	.372	.759	115	7	7	99	81	39	.759	8	7	-2	-1	2/3OS	0.9
1983	NY-N	26	42	6	7	0	1	0	3	2	8	.167	.205	.214	.419	16	-5	-5	99	132	2	.297	0	0	0	1	2/3	-0.3
1984	NY-N	128	436	68	122	19	2	1	26	56	63	.280	.362	.339	.701	98	1	1	100	69	57	.702	32	9	4	-3	*2/S	0.6
1985	NY-N	145	520	77	142	24	5	1	38	36	72	.273	.321	.344	.666	89	-10	-8	97	85	61	.626	30	12	2	-10	*2/S	-1.6
1986	NY-N	124	387	67	124	18	2	1	27	36	32	.320	.378	.385	.763	116	7	9	96	71	59	.725	13	7	-0	-13	*2	-0.2
1987	NY-N	94	300	43	75	6	1	1	23	25	43	.250	.308	.287	.594	60	-17	-17	99	103	28	.524	11	3	2	-8	2	-2.0
1988	NY-N	99	294	44	89	12	0	0	17	41	49	.303	.390	.344	.733	124	7	10	90	67	42	.704	9	5	-0	-0	2	1.3
Total	9	765	2369	359	670	95	14	7	165	260	335	.283	.354	.344	.698	98	-8	1	97	80	306	.676	106	46	4	-36	2/S3O	-1.0
■ **EDDIE BACON** Bacon, Edgar Suter b: 4/8/1895, Franklin Co., Ky. d: 10/2/63, Frankfurt, Ky. Deb: 8/13/17																												
1917	Phi-A	4	6	1	3	1	0	0	2	0	0	.500	.500	.667	1.167	273	1	1	94	179	2	1.333	0			1	/P	0.2
■ **ART BADER** Bader, Arthur Herman b: 9/21/1886, St.Louis, Mo. d: 4/5/57, St.Louis, Mo. BR/TR, 5'10", 170 lbs. Deb: 8/02/04																												
1904	StL-A	2	3	0	0	0	0	0	0	1		.000	.250	.000	.250	-16	-0	-0	95	0	0	.333	0			0	/O	0.0
■ **RED BADGRO** Badgro, Morris Hiram b: 12/1/02, Orilla, Wash. BL/TR, 6', 190 lbs. Deb: 6/20/29																												
1929	StL-A	54	148	27	42	12	0	1	18	11	15	.284	.342	.385	.727	87	-3	-3	100	103	20	.670	1	0	0	-6	O	-0.9
1930	StL-A	89	234	30	56	18	3	1	27	13	27	.239	.285	.355	.640	57	-14	-17	108	104	23	.552	3	5	-2	-0	O	-1.9
Total	2	143	382	57	98	30	3	2	45	24	42	.257	.307	.366	.674	68	-17	-20	105	104	43	.595	4	5	-2	-7	/O	-2.8
■ **JOSE BAEZ** Baez, Jose Antonio (born Jose Antonio Mota (Baez)) b: 12/31/53, San Cristobal, D.R. BR/TR, 5'8", 160 lbs. Deb: 4/06/77																												
1977	Sea-A	91	305	39	79	14	1	1	17	19	20	.259	.305	.321	.626	74	-12	-11	96	67	30	.532	6	1	1	8	2/3D	0.5
1978	Sea-A	23	50	8	8	0	1	0	2	6	7	.160	.250	.200	.450	27	-5	-5	102	79	3	.405	1	0	0	3	2/3D	0.0
Total	2	114	355	47	87	14	2	1	19	25	27	.245	.297	.304	.601	67	-17	-15	97	68	34	.524	7	1	2	11	/2D3	0.5
■ **BILL BAGWELL** Bagwell, William Mallory "Big Bill" b: 2/24/1896, Choudrant, La. d: 10/5/76, Choudrant, La. BL/TL, 6'1", 175 lbs. Deb: 4/17/23																												
1923	Bos-N	56	93	8	27	4	2	2	10	6	12	.290	.333	.441	.774	103	0	0	100	75	14	.712	0	0	0	-4	O	-0.3
1925	Phi-A	36	50	4	15	2	1	0	10	2	2	.300	.327	.380	.707	77	-2	-2	103	176	6	.600	0	0	0	-2	/O	-0.3
Total	2	92	143	12	42	6	3	2	20	8	14	.294	.331	.420	.751	93	-2	-2	101	110	20	.673	0	0	0	-5	/O	-0.6
■ **FRANK BAHRET** Bahret, Frank J. b: Baltimore, Md. Deb: 4/17/1884																												
1884	Bal-U	2	8	0	0	0	0	0		0		.000	.000	.000	.000	-91	-2	-2	110	0	0	.000	0			0	/O	-0.1
■ **GENE BAILEY** Bailey, Arthur Eugene b: 11/25/1893, Pearsall, Tex. d: 11/14/73, Houston, Tex. BR/TR, 5'8", 160 lbs. Deb: 9/10/17																												
1917	Phi-A	5	12	1	1	0	0	0	0	1	1	.083	.154	.083	.237	-29	-2	-2	94	0	0	.182	0			-1	/O	-0.3
1919	Bos-N	4	6	0	2	0	0	0	1	0	2	.333	.333	.333	.667	103	-0	0	98	194	1	.750	1			-1	/O	0.0
1920	Bos-N	13	24	2	2	0	0	0	0	3	3	.083	.185	.083	.269	-22	-4	-4	96	0	1	.217	0	1	-1	-1	/O	-0.5
	Bos-A	46	135	14	31	2	0	0	5	9	15	.230	.283	.244	.527	42	-11	-11	96	53	9	.405	2	7	-4	-5	O	-2.1
1923	Bro-N	127	411	71	109	11	7	1	42	43	34	.265	.343	.333	.677	81	-11	-10	98	106	49	.631	9	7	-2	-5	*O/1	-1.8
1924	Bro-N	18	46	7	11	3	0	1	4	7	6	.239	.340	.370	.709	91	-1	-0	99	73	6	.714	1	0	0	2	O	0.1
Total	5	213	634	95	156	16	7	2	52	63	61	.246	.321	.303	.624	69	-28	-26	97	87	66	.558	13	15		-10	O/1	-4.6
■ **FRED BAILEY** Bailey, Frederick Middleton "Penny" b: 8/16/1895, Mt.Hope, W.Va. d: 8/16/72, Huntington, W.Va. BL/TL, 5'11", 150 lbs. Deb: 8/19/16																												
1916	Bos-N	6	10	0	1	0	0	0	1	0	3	.100	.100	.100	.200	-42	-2	-2	93	397	0	.111	0			-1	/O	-0.2
1917	Bos-N	50	110	9	21	2	1	1	5	9	25	.191	.270	.255	.525	64	-5	-4	96	62	8	.483	3			-0	O	-0.5
1918	Bos-N	4	4	1	1	0	0	0	0	0	1	.250	.250	.250	.500	56	-0	-0	94	0	0	.333	0			0	H	0.0
Total	3	60	124	10	23	2	1	1	6	9	29	.185	.257	.242	.499	56	-7	-6	96	85	8	.446	3			-1	/O	-0.7
■ **BILL BAILEY** Bailey, Harry Lewis b: 11/19/1881, Shawnee, Ohio d: 10/27/67, Seattle, Wash. BL/TR, 5'10.5", 170 lbs. Deb: 4/21/11																												
1911	NY-A	5	9	1	1	0	0	0	0	0		.111	.111	.111	.222	-34	-2	-2	111	0	0	.125	0			-1	/O3	-0.2
■ **ED BAILEY** Bailey, Lonas Edgar b: 4/15/31, Strawberry Plains, Tenn. BL/TR, 6'2", 205 lbs. Deb: 9/26/53																												
1953	Cin-N	2	8	1	3	1	0	0	1	1	3	.375	.444	.500	.944	147	1	1	99	86	2	1.000	0	0	0	0	/C	0.1
1954	Cin-N	73	183	21	36	2	3	9	20	35	34	.197	.326	.388	.714	82	-4	-5	104	80	26	.718	1	0	0	0	C	-0.2
1955	Cin-N	21	39	3	8	1	1	1	4	4	10	.205	.326	.359	.685	77	-1	-1	106	95	4	.636	0	0	0	0	C	0.0
1956	Cin-N	118	383	59	115	8	2	28	75	52	50	.300	.388	.551	.939	137	27	23	108	107	83	.975	2	0	1	10	*C	3.6
1957	Cin-N	122	391	54	102	15	2	20	48	73	69	.261	.380	.463	.843	119	16	13	105	83	72	.870	5	3	-0	8	*C	2.6
1958	Cin-N	112	360	39	90	23	1	11	59	47	61	.250	.338	.411	.749	90	-1	-5	107	135	51	.715	2	2	-1	7	C	0.7
1959	Cin-N	121	379	43	100	13	0	12	40	62	53	.264	.370	.393	.763	100	4	2	103	87	58	.744	2	0	1	18	*C	2.8
1960	Cin-N	133	441	52	115	19	3	13	67	59	70	.261	.351	.406	.756	108	5	6	98	125	65	.719	1	0	0	7	*C	1.9
1961	Cin-N	12	43	4	13	4	0	0	2	3	5	.302	.348	.395	.743	93	-0	-0	104	48	6	.667	0	0	0	-0	C	0.0

YEAR	TM/L	G	AB	R	H	2B	3B	HR	RBI	BB	SO	AVG	OBP	SLG	PRO	/A	BR	/A	PF	CHI	RC	TA	SB	CS	SBR	FR	POS	TPR
	SF-N	107	340	39	81	9	1	13	51	42	41	.238	.329	.385	.714	90	-5	-4	98	121	42	.654	1	5	-3	1	*C/O	0.2
	Yr	119	383	43	94	13	1	13	53	45	46	.245	.331	.386	.717	91	-5	-5	99	114	48	.656	1	5	-3	1		0.2
1962	SF-N	96	254	32	59	9	1	17	45	42	42	.232	.354	.476	.831	119	8	7	101	103	44	.842	1	1	-0	2	C	0.9
1963	SF-N	105	308	41	81	8	0	21	68	50	64	.263	.368	.494	.861	152	19	20	96	133	54	.849	0	6	-4	8	C	2.9
1964	Mil-N	95	271	30	71	10	1	5	34	34	39	.262	.346	.362	.708	103	1	2	97	123	35	.652	2	0	1	-3	C	0.2
1965	SF-N	24	28	1	3	0	0	0	3	6	7	.107	.265	.107	.372	8	-3	-4	111	415	1	.321	0	0	0	-0	C/1	-0.3
	Chi-N	66	150	13	38	6	0	5	23	34	28	.253	.391	.393	.785	120	6	6	102	129	23	.769	0	1	-1	-2	C/1	0.5
	Yr	90	178	14	41	6	0	5	26	40	35	.230	.372	.348	.720	100	3	2	104	210	24	.699	0	1	-1	-2		0.2
1966	Cal-A	5	3	0	0	0	0	0	0	1	1	.000	.250	.000	.250	-21	-0	-0	99	0	0	.333	0	0	0	0	H	0.0
Total	14	1212	3581	432	915	128	15	155	540	545	577	.256	.358	.429	.787	110	69	59	102	113	566	.792	17	18	-6	55	*C/1O	15.9

■ MARK BAILEY Bailey, John Mark b: 11/4/61, Springfield, Mo. BB/TR, 6'5", 195 lbs. Deb: 4/27/84

YEAR	TM/L	G	AB	R	H	2B	3B	HR	RBI	BB	SO	AVG	OBP	SLG	PRO	/A	BR	/A	PF	CHI	RC	TA	SB	CS	SBR	FR	POS	TPR
1984	Hou-N	108	344	38	73	16	1	9	34	53	71	.212	.321	.343	.664	94	-5	-2	93	92	40	.620	0	1	-1	-2	*C	-0.1
1985	Hou-N	114	332	47	88	14	0	10	45	67	70	.265	.390	.398	.788	126	12	14	96	111	51	.763	0	2	-1	-0	*C/1	1.7
1986	Hou-N	57	153	9	27	5	0	4	15	28	45	.176	.304	.288	.591	62	-7	-8	103	107	13	.545	1	1	-0	-9	C/1	-1.6
1987	Hou-N	35	64	5	13	1	0	0	3	10	21	.203	.311	.219	.530	47	-5	-4	93	85	5	.463	1	0	0	-2	C	-0.3
1988	Hou-N	8	23	1	3	0	0	0	0	5	6	.130	.286	.130	.416	25	-2	-2	93	0	1	.364	0	1	-1	-1	/C	-0.2
Total	5	322	916	100	204	36	1	23	97	163	213	.223	.342	.340	.681	95	-7	-2	96	98	109	.667	2	5	-2	-14	C/1	-0.5

■ BOB BAILEY Bailey, Robert Sherwood b: 10/13/42, Long Beach, Cal. BR/TR, 6'1", 180 lbs. Deb: 9/14/62

YEAR	TM/L	G	AB	R	H	2B	3B	HR	RBI	BB	SO	AVG	OBP	SLG	PRO	/A	BR	/A	PF	CHI	RC	TA	SB	CS	SBR	FR	POS	TPR
1962	Pit-N	14	42	6	7	2	1	0	6	6	10	.167	.271	.262	.533	43	-3	-3	102	215	3	.500	1	1	-0	-0	3	-0.3
1963	Pit-N	154	570	60	130	15	3	12	45	58	98	.228	.305	.328	.633	83	-12	-11	99	90	58	.568	10	9	-2	6	*3/S	-0.7
1964	Pit-N	143	530	73	149	26	3	11	51	44	78	.281	.337	.404	.741	107	5	5	101	86	68	.664	10	8	-2	0	*3O/S	-0.3
1965	Pit-N	159	626	87	160	28	3	11	49	70	93	.256	.330	.363	.693	95	-3	-3	100	75	72	.619	10	14	-5	-14	*3O	-3.0
1966	Pit-N	126	380	51	106	19	3	13	46	47	65	.279	.361	.447	.809	122	13	12	101	92	60	.775	5	3	-0	-1	3O	0.9
1967	LA-N	116	322	21	73	8	2	4	28	40	50	.227	.314	.301	.615	87	-9	-4	88	106	29	.534	5	5	-2	-3	3O/1S	-1.4
1968	LA-N	105	322	24	73	9	3	8	39	38	69	.227	.310	.348	.658	107	-1	3	91	121	35	.587	1	2	-1	0	3/SO	0.2
1969	Mon-N	111	358	46	95	16	6	9	53	40	76	.265	.341	.419	.760	111	5	5	100	120	49	.698	3	3	-1	3	1O/3	0.0
1970	Mon-N	131	352	77	101	19	3	28	84	72	70	.287	.409	.597	1.006	166	34	34	100	111	86	1.083	5	3	-0	-8	3O1	2.0
1971	Mon-N	157	545	65	137	21	4	14	83	97	105	.251	.364	.382	.746	113	11	12	99	**143**	78	.733	13	7	-0	-10	*3O/1	0.0
1972	Mon-N	143	489	55	114	10	4	16	57	59	112	.233	.317	.368	.685	92	-4	-5	102	105	56	.623	6	7	-2	-3	*3/O1	-1.2
1973	Mon-N	151	513	77	140	25	4	26	86	88	99	.273	.380	.489	.870	134	29	26	104	107	90	.854	5	8	-3	-3	*3/O	1.6
1974	Mon-N	152	507	69	142	20	2	20	73	100	107	.280	.400	.446	.845	130	28	25	104	101	89	.840	4	7	-3	-9	O3	0.9
1975	Mon-N	106	227	23	62	5	0	5	30	46	38	.273	.398	.361	.759	103	6	3	108	120	34	.751	4	4	-1	-6	O/3	-0.5
1976	Cin-N	69	124	17	37	6	1	6	23	16	26	.298	.379	.508	.887	146	8	8	103	109	22	.840	0	0	0	-5	O3	0.1
1977	Cin-N	49	79	9	20	2	1	2	11	12	10	.253	.352	.380	.731	96	-0	-0	100	122	11	.694	1	1	-0	-1	1/O	-0.2
	Bos-A	2	2	0	0	0	0	0	0	0	1	.000	.000	.000	.000	-85	-1	-1	117	0	0	.000	0	0	0	0	H	0.0
1978	Bos-A	43	94	12	18	3	0	4	9	19	19	.191	.333	.351	.684	86	-0	-1	107	79	12	.696	2	1	0	0	D/3O	-0.1
Total	17	1931	6082	772	1564	234	43	189	773	852	1126	.257	.350	.403	.753	111	106	104	100	105	852	.740	85	83	-24	-56	*3O1/DS	-2.0

■ BOB BAILOR Bailor, Robert Michael b: 3/10/51, Connellsville, Pa. BR/TR, 5'11", 170 lbs. Deb: 9/06/75

YEAR	TM/L	G	AB	R	H	2B	3B	HR	RBI	BB	SO	AVG	OBP	SLG	PRO	/A	BR	/A	PF	CHI	RC	TA	SB	CS	SBR	FR	POS	TPR
1975	Bal-A	5	7	0	1	0	0	0	0	1	0	.143	.250	.143	.393	15	-1	-1	91	0	0	.333	0	0	0	1	/S2	0.0
1976	Bal-A	9	6	2	2	0	1	0	0	0	0	.333	.333	.667	1.000	193	1	1	98	0	1	.800	0	1	-1	0	/SD	0.0
1977	Tor-A	122	496	62	154	21	5	5	32	17	26	.310	.336	.403	.739	98	-0	-2	103	63	66	.659	15	6	1	8	OS/D	1.1
1978	Tor-A	154	621	74	164	29	7	1	52	38	21	.264	.312	.338	.650	83	-14	-14	100	85	66	.548	5	6	-2	20	*O3/S	0.0
1979	Tor-A	130	414	50	95	11	5	1	38	36	27	.229	.300	.287	.588	58	-23	-25	103	120	37	.526	14	8	-1	1	*O/3	-2.8
1980	Tor-A	117	347	44	82	14	2	1	16	36	33	.236	.312	.297	.609	68	-15	-15	100	59	33	.550	12	8	-1	9	OS3/P2D	-0.7
1981	NY-N	51	81	11	23	3	1	0	8	8	11	.284	.356	.346	.701	99	0	0	101	112	10	.639	2	0	1	-4	S2O/3	0.0
1982	NY-N	110	376	44	104	14	1	0	31	20	17	.277	.317	.319	.636	79	-11	-10	99	101	41	.579	20	3	4	-2	S23	0.0
1983	NY-N	118	340	33	85	8	0	1	30	20	23	.250	.294	.282	.576	61	-18	-17	99	120	28	.502	18	3	4	2	S23/O	-0.3
1984	LA-N	65	131	11	36	4	0	0	8	8	1	.275	.317	.305	.622	73	-4	-5	104	78	13	.515	3	1	0	4	23S	0.1
1985	LA-N	74	118	8	29	3	1	0	7	3	5	.246	.270	.288	.559	61	-7	-6	93	82	9	.424	1	0	0	3	32/SO	-0.1
Total	11	955	2937	339	775	107	23	9	222	187	164	.264	.312	.325	.638	76	-92	-94	100	89	305	.569	90	36	5	40	OS23/DP	-2.7

■ HAROLD BAINES Baines, Harold Douglass b: 3/15/59, Easton, Md. BL/TL, 6'2", 175 lbs. Deb: 4/10/80

YEAR	TM/L	G	AB	R	H	2B	3B	HR	RBI	BB	SO	AVG	OBP	SLG	PRO	/A	BR	/A	PF	CHI	RC	TA	SB	CS	SBR	FR	POS	TPR
1980	Chi-A	141	491	55	125	23	6	13	49	19	65	.255	.284	.405	.689	90	-11	-9	97	82	50	.574	2	4	-2	-14	*O/D	-2.7
1981	Chi-A	82	280	42	80	11	7	10	41	12	41	.286	.320	.482	.802	129	9	9	100	97	41	.745	6	2	1	-5	O/D	0.3
1982	Chi-A	161	608	89	165	29	8	25	105	49	95	.271	.326	.469	.794	118	11	13	97	119	91	.751	10	3	1	-2	*O	0.7
1983	Chi-A	156	596	76	167	33	2	20	99	49	85	.280	.336	.443	.779	109	9	7	103	127	85	.715	7	5	-1	-1	*O	0.3
1984	Chi-A	147	569	72	173	28	10	29	94	54	75	.304	.364	**.541**	.906	133	35	27	111	101	109	.885	1	2	-1	-1	*O	2.1
1985	Chi-A	160	640	86	198	29	3	22	113	42	89	.309	.353	.467	.820	122	19	19	100	118	98	.736	1	1	-0	-18	*O/D	-0.1
1986	Chi-A	145	570	72	169	29	2	21	88	38	89	.296	.343	.465	.808	117	14	13	101	103	87	.738	2	1	0	8	*O/D	1.7
1987	Chi-A	132	505	59	148	26	4	20	93	46	82	.293	.353	.479	.832	110	13	7	109	130	84	.783	0	0	0	-1	*D/O	0.5
1988	Chi-A	158	599	55	166	39	1	13	81	67	109	.277	.351	.411	.762	116	11	13	97	120	83	.692	0	0	0	-1	*D/O	1.2
Total	9	1282	4858	606	1391	247	43	173	763	376	730	.286	.339	.462	.800	116	109	99	102	112	730	.758	29	18	-2	-34	OD	4.0

■ AL BAIRD Baird, Albert Wells b: 6/2/1895, Cleburne, Tex. d: 11/27/76, Shreveport, La. BR/TR, 5'9", 160 lbs. Deb: 9/10/17

YEAR	TM/L	G	AB	R	H	2B	3B	HR	RBI	BB	SO	AVG	OBP	SLG	PRO	/A	BR	/A	PF	CHI	RC	TA	SB	CS	SBR	FR	POS	TPR
1917	NY-N	10	24	1	7	0	0	0	4	2	2	.292	.346	.292	.638	99	-0	0	97	220	3	.647	2			-0	/2S	0.0
1919	NY-N	38	83	8	20	1	0	0	5	5	9	.241	.284	.253	.537	62	-4	-4	100	93	6	.460	3			2	2/S3	0.0
Total	2	48	107	9	27	1	0	0	9	7	11	.252	.298	.262	.560	70	-4	-4	99	122	9	.500	5			1	/2S3	0.0

■ DOUG BAIRD Baird, Howard Douglas b: 9/27/1891, St.Charles, Mo. d: 6/13/67, Thomasville, Ga. BR/TR, 5'9.5", 148 lbs. Deb: 4/18/15

YEAR	TM/L	G	AB	R	H	2B	3B	HR	RBI	BB	SO	AVG	OBP	SLG	PRO	/A	BR	/A	PF	CHI	RC	TA	SB	CS	SBR	FR	POS	TPR
1915	Pit-N	145	512	49	112	26	12	1	53	37	88	.219	.277	.322	.599	82	-13	-12	99	123	51	.570	29	12	2	-1	*3O/2	-0.7
1916	Pit-N	128	430	41	93	10	7	1	28	24	49	.216	.263	.279	.542	63	-17	-19	105	90	32	.473	20	16	-4	-18	32O	-4.1
1917	Pit-N	43	135	17	35	6	1	0	18	20	19	.259	.355	.319	.673	108	2	2	100	165	18	.710	8			-2	3/2	0.0
	StL-N	104	364	38	92	19	12	0	24	23	52	.253	.301	.371	.672	104	1	1	102	70	45	.654	18			11	*3/O	1.1
	Yr	147	499	55	127	25	13	0	42	43	71	.255	.316	.357	.673	105	3	3	101	99	63	.669	26			9		1.1
1918	StL-N	82	316	41	78	12	8	2	25	25	42	.247	.304	.354	.659	108	-0	2	93	77	40	.685	25			8	3/SO	1.3
1919	Phi-N	66	242	33	61	13	3	2	30	22	28	.252	.317	.355	.672	98	1	-0	104	134	30	.674	13			10	3	1.1
	StL-N	16	33	4	7	0	1	0	4	2	3	.212	.257	.273	.530	63	-2	-1	94	173	3	.500	2			-0	/32O	-0.1
	Bro-N	20	60	6	11	0	1	0	8	1	10	.183	.197	.217	.413	26	-6	-5	94	239	3	.347	3			-2	3	-0.7
	Yr	102	335	43	79	13	5	2	42	25	41	.236	.291	.322	.613	84	-7	-7	100	164	36	.594	18			8		0.3
1920	Bro-N	6	6	1	2	0	0	0	1	2	1	.333	.556	.333	.889	143	1	1	111	193	2	1.250	0	0	0	0	/3	0.1
	NY-N	7	8	0	1	0	0	0	0	1	3	.125	.222	.125	.347	1	-1	-1	100	0	0	.286	0	0	0	0	/3	0.0
	Yr	13	14	1	3	0	0	0	1	3	4	.214	.389	.214	.603	73	-0	-0	105	104	2	.636	0	0	0	0		0.1
Total	6	617	2106	230	492	86	45	6	191	157	295	.234	.291	.326	.616	87	-33	-33	100	108	223	.593	118	28		7	3/O2S	-2.0

■ CHARLIE BAKER Baker, Charles A. b: 1856, Westboro, Mass. Deb: 8/01/1884

YEAR	TM/L	G	AB	R	H	2B	3B	HR	RBI	BB	SO	AVG	OBP	SLG	PRO	/A	BR	/A	PF	CHI	RC	TA	SB	CS	SBR	FR	POS	TPR
1884	CP-U	15	57	5	8	2	0	1		0		.140	.140	.228	.368	23	-4	-4	99	0	2	.265	0			0	O/S2	-0.3

■ CHUCK BAKER Baker, Charles Joseph b: 12/6/52, Seattle, Wash. BR/TR, 5'11", 180 lbs. Deb: 4/07/78

YEAR	TM/L	G	AB	R	H	2B	3B	HR	RBI	BB	SO	AVG	OBP	SLG	PRO	/A	BR	/A	PF	CHI	RC	TA	SB	CS	SBR	FR	POS	TPR
1978	SD-N	44	58	8	12	1	0	0	3	2	15	.207	.233	.224	.457	31	-6	-5	93	91	3	.319	0	0	0	2	2S	0.0
1980	SD-N	9	22	0	3	1	0	0	0	0	4	.136	.136	.182	.318	-13	-3	-3	93	0	1	.211	0	0	0	0	/S	-0.1
1981	Min-A	40	66	6	12	0	3	0	6	1	8	.182	.194	.273	.467	32	-6	-6	105	130	3	.333	0	0	0	-2	S/23D	-0.5
Total	3	93	146	14	27	2	3	0	9	3	27	.185	.201	.240	.441	25	-15	-14	98	95	7	.311	0	0	0	-0	/S2D3	-0.6

■ DAVE BAKER Baker, David Glenn b: 11/25/57, Lacona, Iowa BL/TR, 6', 185 lbs. Deb: 9/12/82

YEAR	TM/L	G	AB	R	H	2B	3B	HR	RBI	BB	SO	AVG	OBP	SLG	PRO	/A	BR	/A	PF	CHI	RC	TA	SB	CS	SBR	FR	POS	TPR
1982	Tor-A	9	20	3	5	1	0	0	2	3	3	.250	.400	.300	.700	88	0	-0	109	133	3	.733	0	0	0	-1	/3	0.0

YEAR	TM/L	G	AB	R	H	2B	3B	HR	RBI	BB	SO	AVG	OBP	SLG	PRO	/A	BR	/A	PF	CHI	RC	TA	SB	CS	SBR	FR	POS	TPR
■ **DEL BAKER**	Baker, Delmer David b: 5/3/1892, Sherwood, Ore. d: 9/11/73, San Antonio, Tex. BR/TR, 5'11.5", 176 lbs. Deb: 4/16/14 MC																											
1914	Det-A	43	70	4	15	2	1	0	1	6	9	.214	.276	.271	.548	64	-3	-3	102	20	5	.439	0	2	-1	-2	C	-0.3
1915	Det-A	68	134	16	33	3	3	0	15	15	15	.246	.327	.313	.640	85	-1	-3	108	121	16	.598	3	1	0	-7	C	-0.4
1916	Det-A	61	98	7	15	4	0	0	6	11	8	.153	.245	.194	.439	31	-8	-9	105	113	6	.398	2			-6	C	-1.2
Total	3	172	302	27	63	9	4	0	22	32	32	.209	.289	.265	.554	63	-12	-15	106	96	27	.492	5	<u>3</u>		-15	C	-1.9
■ **DOUG BAKER**	Baker, Douglas Lee b: 4/3/61, Fullerton, Cal. BB/TR, 5'9", 165 lbs. Deb: 7/02/84																											
1984	Det-A	43	108	15	20	4	1	0	12	7	22	.185	.241	.241	.482	35	-10	-9	96	184	7	.416	3	0	1	-1	S/2D	-0.5
1985	Det-A	15	27	4	5	1	0	0	1	0	9	.185	.185	.222	.407	10	-3	-3	106	66	1	.273	0	0	0	-1	S/2	-0.2
1986	Det-A	13	24	1	3	1	0	0	0	2	7	.125	.192	.167	.359	-1	-3	-3	95	0	1	.286	0	0	0	0	S/2D	-0.1
1987	Det-A	8	1	0	0	0	0	0	0	0	1	.000	.000	.000	.000	-99	-0	-0	97	0	0	.000	0	0	0	0	/S23	0.0
1988	Min-A	11	7	1	0	0	0	0	0	0	5	.000	.000	.000	.000	-94	-2	-2	106	0	0	.000	0	0	0	-0	/S23	-0.1
Total	5	90	167	21	28	6	1	0	13	9	44	.168	.215	.216	.430	20	-18	-18	98	131	9	.353	3	0	1	-1	/S23D	-0.9
■ **GENE BAKER**	Baker, Eugene Walter b: 6/15/25, Davenport, Iowa BR/TR, 6'1", 170 lbs. Deb: 9/20/53 C																											
1953	Chi-N	7	22	1	5	1	0	0	0	1	4	.227	.261	.273	.534	38	-2	-2	103	0	2	.444	1	0	0	-1	/2	-0.1
1954	Chi-N	135	541	68	149	32	5	13	61	47	55	.275	.336	.425	.761	96	-3	-4	101	86	76	.692	4	5	-2	1	*2	0.3
1955	Chi-N	154	609	82	163	29	7	11	52	49	57	.268	.324	.392	.717	89	-10	-10	100	68	76	.640	9	7	-2	7	*2	0.8
1956	Chi-N	140	546	65	141	23	3	12	57	39	54	.258	.311	.377	.689	85	-13	-12	99	96	62	.596	4	3	-1	15	*2	1.5
1957	Chi-N	12	44	4	11	3	1	1	10	6	3	.250	.353	.432	.785	114	1	1	96	200	7	.743	0	0	0	-1	3	0.0
	Pit-N	111	365	36	97	19	4	2	36	29	29	.266	.322	.356	.678	87	-9	-6	94	110	41	.586	3	2	-0	-3	3S2	-0.5
	Yr	123	409	40	108	22	5	3	46	35	32	.264	.325	.364	.689	90	-8	-5	94	120	49	.608	3	2	-0	-4		-0.5
1958	Pit-N	29	56	3	14	2	1	0	7	8	6	.250	.344	.321	.665	81	-2	-1	95	161	6	.591	0	0	0	-2	3/2	-0.2
1960	Pit-N	33	37	5	9	0	0	0	4	2	9	.243	.282	.243	.525	46	-3	-3	99	180	3	.379	0	0	0	0	/32	-0.1
1961	Pit-N	9	10	1	1	0	0	0	0	3	2	.100	.308	.100	.408	15	-1	-1	99	0	0	.444	0	0	0	0	/3	0.0
Total	8	630	2230	265	590	109	21	39	227	184	219	.265	.323	.385	.708	88	-42	-37	99	92	272	.647	21	17	-4	17	2/3S	1.7
■ **FLOYD BAKER**	Baker, Floyd Wilson b: 10/10/16, Luray, Va. BL/TR, 5'9", 160 lbs. Deb: 5/04/43 C																											
1943	StL-A	22	46	5	8	2	0	0	4	6	4	.174	.269	.217	.487	43	-3	-3	100	146	3	.400	0	1	-1	-2	S/3	-0.5
1944	StL-A	44	97	10	17	3	0	0	5	11	5	.175	.259	.206	.465	33	-8	-8	102	90	6	.407	2	0	1	-1	2S	-0.7
1945	Chi-A	82	208	22	52	8	0	0	19	23	12	.250	.325	.288	.613	82	-5	-4	95	115	22	.541	3	2	-0	-0	32	-0.3
1946	Chi-A	9	24	2	6	1	0	0	3	2	3	.250	.308	.292	.599	70	-1	-1	97	163	2	.500	0	0	0	1	/3	0.0
1947	Chi-A	105	371	61	98	12	3	0	22	66	28	.264	.375	.313	.688	96	-1	1	97	74	49	.670	9	7	-2	12	*3/2S	1.4
1948	Chi-A	104	335	47	72	8	3	0	18	73	26	.215	.359	.257	.615	68	-13	-11	95	72	35	.594	4	10	-5	12	32/S	-0.5
1949	Chi-A	125	388	38	101	15	4	1	40	84	32	.260	.392	.327	.719	93	-1	0	98	105	59	.735	3	1	0	11	*3/S2	1.1
1950	Chi-A	83	186	26	59	7	0	0	11	32	10	.317	.417	.355	.772	102	2	3	97	58	30	.744	1	1	-0	3	3/2O	0.3
1951	Chi-A	82	133	24	35	6	1	0	14	25	12	.263	.380	.323	.703	94	-0	0	97	116	18	.660	0	1	-1	-1	3/2S	-0.2
1952	Was-A	79	263	27	69	8	0	0	33	30	17	.262	.342	.293	.635	78	-7	-7	100	160	30	.564	1	0	0	-4	2/S3	-0.7
1953	Was-A	9	7	0	0	0	0	0	0	1	0	.000	.222	.000	.222	-38	-1	-1	94	0	0	.286	0	0	0	0	/3	0.0
	Bos-A	81	172	22	47	4	2	0	24	24	10	.273	.365	.320	.685	79	-2	-4	109	162	21	.606	0	2	-1	-0	32	-0.6
	Yr	90	179	22	47	4	2	0	24	25	10	.263	.359	.307	.666	76	-4	-5	107	145	21	.590	0	2	-1	-0		-0.6
1954	Bos-A	21	20	1	4	2	0	0	3	0	1	.200	.200	.300	.500	35	-2	-2	100	190	1	.375	0	0	0	0	/32	-0.1
	Phi-N	23	22	0	5	0	0	0	0	5	4	.227	.370	.227	.598	61	-1	-1	99	0	2	.588	0	0	0	0	/32	0.0
1955	Phi-N	5	8	0	0	0	0	0	0	0	1	.000	.000	.000	.000	-98	-2	-2	102	0	0	.000	0	0	0	-0	/3	-0.2
Total	13	874	2280	285	573	76	13	1	196	382	165	.251	.360	.297	.658	82	-47	-41	98	102	279	.628	23	25	-8	30	32/SO	-1.0
■ **FRANK BAKER**	Baker, Frank b: 1/11/44, Bartow, Fla. BL/TR, 5'10", 180 lbs. Deb: 7/27/69																											
1969	Cle-A	52	172	21	44	5	3	3	15	14	34	.256	.316	.372	.688	97	-2	-1	94	82	20	.609	2	1	0	-0	O	-0.2
1971	Cle-A	73	181	18	38	12	1	1	23	12	34	.210	.263	.304	.567	57	-10	-11	106	162	13	.460	1	3	-2	-6	O	-2.1
Total	2	125	353	39	82	17	4	4	38	26	68	.232	.289	.337	.626	76	-12	-12	100	123	33	.538	3	4	-2	-7	/O	-2.3
■ **FRANK BAKER**	Baker, Frank Watts b: 10/29/46, Meridian, Miss. BL/TR, 6'2", 178 lbs. Deb: 8/09/70																											
1970	NY-A	35	117	6	27	4	1	0	11	14	26	.231	.323	.282	.605	74	-5	-3	92	138	11	.538	1	2	-1	1	S	0.0
1971	NY-A	43	79	9	11	2	0	0	2	16	22	.139	.284	.165	.449	31	-7	-7	97	63	5	.457	3	0	1	5	S	0.3
1973	Bal-A	44	63	10	12	1	2	1	11	7	7	.190	.271	.317	.589	61	-3	-4	107	188	6	.529	0	0	0	1	S/213	0.2
1974	Bal-A	24	29	3	5	1	0	0	0	3	5	.172	.250	.207	.457	35	-2	-2	93	0	1	.360	0	0	0	1	S/23	0.0
Total	4	146	288	28	55	8	3	1	24	40	60	.191	.294	.250	.544	55	-17	-16	97	113	24	.500	4	2	0	7	S/231	0.5
■ **GEORGE BAKER**	Baker, George F. b: 1859, St.Louis, Mo. Deb: 5/24/1883																											
1883	Bal-a	7	22	0	5	0	0	0		0		.227	.227	.227	.455	44	-1	-1	107	0	1	.294				0	/SCO	0.0
1884	StL-U	80	317	39	52	6	0	0		5		.164	.177	.183	.360	21	-25	-27	104	0	11	.238	0			7	C/O23S	-1.3
1885	StL-N	38	131	5	16	0	0	0	5	9	28	.122	.179	.122	.301	-1	-14	-13	92	111	3	.217				-6	C/3O2	-1.4
1886	KC-N	1	4	1	1	0	0	0	0	0	1	.250	.250	.250	.500	49	-0	-0	107	0	0	.333	0			0	/C	0.0
Total	4	126	474	45	74	6	0	0	<u>5</u>	14	<u>29</u>	.156	.180	.169	.349	17	-41	-41	100	32	15	.235	0			1	C/O3S2	-2.7
■ **HOWARD BAKER**	Baker, Howard Francis b: 3/1/1888, Bridgeport, Conn. d: 1/16/64, Bridgeport, Conn. BR/TR, 5'11", 175 lbs. Deb: 8/11/12																											
1912	Cle-A	11	30	1	5	0	0	0	2	5		.167	.286	.167	.452	30	-3	-3	101	133	1	.400	0			0	3	-0.1
1914	Chi-A	15	47	4	13	1	1	0	5	3	8	.277	.320	.340	.660	95	-0	-0	103	117	5	.600	2	1	0	-0	3	0.0
1915	Chi-A	2	2	0	0	0	0	0	0	0	2	.000	.000	.000	.000	-99	-0	-0	98	0	0	.000	0			0	H	0.0
	NY-N	1	3	0	0	0	0	0	0	0	0	.000	.000	.000	.000	-99	-1	-1	91	0	0	.000	0			0	/3	0.0
Total	3	29	82	5	18	1	1	0	7	8	<u>10</u>	.220	.289	.256	.545	60	-4	-4	102	117	7	.477	2	<u>1</u>		0	/3	-0.1
■ **JACK BAKER**	Baker, Jack Edward b: 5/4/50, Birmingham, Ala. BR/TR, 6'5", 225 lbs. Deb: 9/11/76																											
1976	Bos-A	12	23	1	3	0	0	1	2	1	5	.130	.167	.261	.428	22	-2	-3	110	85	1	.333	0	0	0	-0	/1D	-0.2
1977	Bos-A	2	3	0	0	0	0	0	0	0	1	.000	.000	.000	.000	-85	-1	-1	117	0	0	.000	0	0	0	0	/1	0.0
Total	2	14	26	1	3	0	0	1	2	1	6	.115	.148	.231	.379	8	-3	-3	111	76	1	.304	0	0	0	-0	/1D	-0.2
■ **JESSE BAKER**	Baker, Jesse Eugene b: 2/9/1897, New York d: 7/25/60, Pomona, Cal. 5'4", 140 lbs. Deb: 9/14/19																											
1919	Was-A	1	0	0	0	0	0	0	1	0	0	—	—	—	—	—	0	0	98	—	—	—	0			0	/S	0.0
■ **FRANK BAKER**	Baker, John Franklin "Home Run" b: 3/13/1886, Trappe, Md. d: 6/28/63, Trappe, Md. BL/TR, 5'11", 173 lbs. Deb: 9/21/08 H																											
1908	Phi-A	9	31	5	9	3	0	0	2	0		.290	.290	.387	.677	113	1	0	108	64	3	.545	0			-1	/3	0.0
1909	Phi-A	148	541	73	165	27	**19**	4	85	26		.305	.343	.447	.790	146	27	26	102	137	87	.779	20			-5	*3	3.0
1910	Phi-A	146	561	83	159	25	15	2	74	34		.283	.329	.392	.721	123	14	13	102	128	79	.694	21			3	*3	2.4
1911	Phi-A	148	592	96	198	40	4	**11**	115	50		.334	.388	.505	.893	160	36	42	93	113	130	.987	38			-8	*3	3.3
1912	Phi-A	149	577	116	200	40	21	**10**	**130**	50		.347	.404	.541	.945	171	49	50	99	134	140	1.082	40			9	*3	5.4
1913	Phi-A	149	564	116	190	34	9	**12**	**117**	63	31	.337	.413	.493	.906	171	46	48	97	140	122	1.029	34			7	*3	6.1
1914	Phi-A	150	570	84	182	23	10	**9**	89	53	37	.319	.380	.442	.822	151	31	33	97	127	95	.801	19	20	-6	8	*3	4.1
1916	NY-A	100	360	46	97	23	2	10	52	36	30	.269	.344	.428	.772	130	13	12	101	103	58	.798	15			3	3	2.1
1917	NY-A	146	553	57	156	24	2	6	71	48	27	.282	.345	.365	.710	109	10	6	107	123	72	.688	18			11	*3	2.7
1918	NY-A	126	504	65	154	24	5	6	62	38	13	.306	.357	.409	.765	138	17	20	95	97	74	.726	8			11	*3	3.4
1919	NY-A	141	567	70	166	22	1	10	83	44	18	.293	.346	.388	.734	100	4	-0	106	116	77	.696	13			-2	*3	0.9
1921	NY-A	94	330	46	97	16	2	9	71	26	12	.294	.353	.436	.789	98	-0	-2	103	142	51	.765	8	5	-1	13	3	1.6
1922	NY-A	69	234	30	65	12	3	7	36	15	14	.278	.327	.444	.771	98	-1	-2	102	103	33	.709	1	3	-2	-8	3	-0.4
Total	13	1575	5984	887	1838	313	93	96	987	483	<u>182</u>	.307	.364	.442	.806	135	246	247	100	123	1020	.818	235	<u>28</u>		41	*3	34.6
■ **DUSTY BAKER**	Baker, Johnnie B b: 6/15/49, Riverside, Cal. BR/TR, 6'2", 183 lbs. Deb: 9/07/68 C																											
1968	Atl-N	6	5	0	2	0	0	0	0	0	1	.400	.400	.400	.800	151	0	0	93	0	1	.667	0	0	0	-1	/O	0.0
1969	Atl-N	3	7	0	0	0	0	0	0	0	3	.000	.000	.000	.000	-97	-2	-2	104	0	0	.000	0	0	0	-1	/O	-0.2
1970	Atl-N	13	24	3	7	0	0	0	4	2	4	.292	.346	.292	.638	70	-1	-1	104	222	2	.500	0	0	0	-2	O	-0.2

YEAR	TM/L	G	AB	R	H	2B	3B	HR	RBI	BB	SO	AVG	OBP	SLG	PRO	/A	BR	/A	PF	CHI	RC	TA	SB	CS	SBR	FR	POS	TPR
1971	Atl-N	29	62	2	14	2	0	0	4	1	14	.226	.238	.258	.496	37	-5	-6	110	102	3	.340	0	1	-1	-1	O	-0.7
1972	Atl-N	127	446	62	143	27	2	17	76	45	68	.321	.388	.504	.892	145	30	28	105	115	85	.871	4	7	-3	8	*O	2.9
1973	Atl-N	159	604	101	174	29	4	21	99	67	72	.288	.364	.454	.818	111	21	11	113	125	103	.828	24	3	5	4	*O	1.4
1974	Atl-N	149	574	80	147	35	0	20	69	71	87	.256	.339	.422	.761	107	8	5	105	85	83	.744	18	7	1	-4	*O	-0.3
1975	Atl-N	142	494	63	129	18	2	19	72	67	57	.261	.349	.421	.770	119	9	12	95	107	74	.751	12	7	-1	6	*O	1.2
1976	LA-N	112	384	36	93	13	0	4	39	31	54	.242	.300	.307	.608	73	-14	-13	100	118	33	.490	2	4	-2	-7	*O	-2.7
1977	LA-N	153	533	86	155	26	1	30	86	58	89	.291	.367	.512	.879	133	24	24	100	97	99	.863	2	6	-3	-13	*O	0.2
1978	LA-N	149	522	62	137	24	1	11	66	47	66	.262	.327	.375	.702	97	-3	-2	99	117	66	.648	12	3	2	-4	*O	-1.0
1979	LA-N	151	554	86	152	29	1	23	88	56	70	.274	.342	.455	.797	116	11	11	100	111	84	.758	11	4	1	6	*O	1.4
1980	LA-N	153	579	80	170	26	4	29	97	43	66	.294	.346	.503	.848	139	24	26	97	108	96	.812	12	10	-2	-2	*O	1.7
1981	LA-N	103	400	48	128	17	3	9	49	29	43	.320	.367	.445	.812	132	15	16	98	99	63	.757	10	7	-1	-2	*O	1.0
1982	LA-N	147	570	80	171	19	1	23	88	56	62	.300	.366	.458	.824	137	22	26	95	111	96	.810	17	10	-1	-11	*O	1.2
1983	LA-N	149	531	71	138	25	1	15	73	72	59	.260	.350	.395	.746	106	6	6	100	120	78	.722	7	1	2	-6	*O	0.0
1984	SF-N	100	243	31	71	7	2	3	32	40	27	.292	.392	.374	.767	121	7	8	96	125	39	.758	4	1	1	-4	O	0.3
1985	Oak-A	111	343	48	92	15	1	14	52	50	47	.268	.361	.440	.802	127	9	13	93	107	54	.769	2	1	0	-5	1OD	0.3
1986	Oak-A	83	242	25	58	8	0	4	19	27	37	.240	.316	.322	.638	80	-8	-6	94	84	24	.544	0	1	-1	-5	OD/1	-1.2
Total	19	2039	7117	964	1981	320	23	242	1013	762	926	.278	.351	.432	.782	116	154	155	100	109	1084	.767	137	73	-3	-42	*O/1D	5.3

■ **PHIL BAKER** Baker, Philip b: 9/19/1856, Philadelphia, Pa. d: 6/4/40, Washington, D.C. 5'8", 152 lbs. Deb: 5/01/1883

YEAR	TM/L	G	AB	R	H	2B	3B	HR	RBI	BB	SO	AVG	OBP	SLG	PRO	/A	BR	/A	PF	CHI	RC	TA	SB	CS	SBR	FR	POS	TPR
1883	Bal-a	28	121	22	33	2	1	1		8		.273	.318	.331	.648	102	1	0	107	0	13	.545				0	CO/S	0.0
1884	Was-U	86	371	75	107	12	5	1		11		.288	.309	.356	.665	128	9	11	97	0	42	.542	0			0	1OC	0.9
1886	Was-N	81	325	37	72	6	5	1	34	20	32	.222	.267	.280	.547	71	-13	-10	94	104	29	.502	16			-4	1OC	-2.1
Total	3	195	817	134	212	20	11	3	34	39	32	.259	.293	.322	.615	101	-3	1	97	42	84	.526	16			-3	/1OCS	-1.2

■ **TRACY BAKER** Baker, Tracy Lee b: 11/7/1891, Pendleton, Ore. d: 3/14/75, Placerville, Cal. BR/TR, 6'1", 180 lbs. Deb: 6/19/11

YEAR	TM/L	G	AB	R	H	2B	3B	HR	RBI	BB	SO	AVG	OBP	SLG	PRO	/A	BR	/A	PF	CHI	RC	TA	SB	CS	SBR	FR	POS	TPR
1911	Bos-A	1	0	0	0	0	0	0	0	0		—	—	—	—	—	0	0	99	—	—	—	0			0	/1	0.0

■ **BILL BAKER** Baker, William Presley b: 2/22/11, Paw Creek, N.C. BR/TR, 6', 200 lbs. Deb: 5/04/40 C

YEAR	TM/L	G	AB	R	H	2B	3B	HR	RBI	BB	SO	AVG	OBP	SLG	PRO	/A	BR	/A	PF	CHI	RC	TA	SB	CS	SBR	FR	POS	TPR
1940	Cin-N	27	69	5	15	1	1	0	7	4	8	.217	.260	.261	.521	44	-5	-5	101	144	4	.414	2			-1	C	-0.5
1941	Cin-N	2	1	0	0	0	0	0	0	1	1	.000	.500	.000	.500	49	0	0	99	0	0	1.000	0			0	/C	0.0
	Pit-N	35	67	5	15	3	0	0	6	11	0	.224	.333	.269	.602	69	-2	-2	103	120	7	.537	0			-1	C	0.0
	Yr	37	68	5	15	3	0	0	6	12	1	.221	.338	.265	.602	69	-2	-2	102	114	7	.545	0			-1		0.0
1942	Pit-N	18	17	1	2	0	0	0	2	1	0	.118	.167	.118	.284	-16	-2	-2	101	371	0	.200	0			0	C	-0.1
1943	Pit-N	63	172	12	47	6	3	1	26	22	6	.273	.365	.360	.726	105	3	2	104	144	23	.687	3			3	C	0.8
1946	Pit-N	53	113	7	27	4	0	1	8	12	6	.239	.312	.301	.613	72	-4	-4	103	81	11	.517	0			-0	C/1	-0.3
1948	StL-N	45	119	13	35	10	1	0	15	15	7	.294	.373	.395	.768	107	2	2	101	120	17	.716	1			-0	C	0.4
1949	StL-N	20	30	2	4	1	0	0	4	2	2	.133	.188	.167	.354	-4	-4	-5	110	302	1	.269	0			-0	C	-0.4
Total	7	263	588	45	145	25	5	2	68	68	30	.247	.328	.316	.644	79	-13	-16	103	138	63	.594	6			1	C/1	-0.1

■ **JOHN BALAZ** Balaz, John Lawrence b: 11/24/50, Toronto, Ont., Can. BR/TR, 6'3", 180 lbs. Deb: 9/10/74

YEAR	TM/L	G	AB	R	H	2B	3B	HR	RBI	BB	SO	AVG	OBP	SLG	PRO	/A	BR	/A	PF	CHI	RC	TA	SB	CS	SBR	FR	POS	TPR
1974	Cal-A	14	42	4	10	0	0	1	5	2	10	.238	.289	.310	.598	78	-2	-1	92	123	4	.500	0	0	0	-2	O	-0.2
1975	Cal-A	45	120	10	29	8	1	1	10	5	25	.242	.272	.350	.622	79	-4	-4	95	85	12	.511	0	0	0	-1	OD	-0.4
Total	2	59	162	14	39	8	1	2	15	7	35	.241	.276	.340	.616	79	-6	-5	94	95	16	.508	0	0	0	-3	/OD	-0.6

■ **STEVE BALBONI** Balboni, Stephen Charles b: 1/16/57, Brockton, Mass. BR/TR, 6'3", 225 lbs. Deb: 4/22/81

YEAR	TM/L	G	AB	R	H	2B	3B	HR	RBI	BB	SO	AVG	OBP	SLG	PRO	/A	BR	/A	PF	CHI	RC	TA	SB	CS	SBR	FR	POS	TPR
1981	NY-A	4	7	2	2	1	1	0	2	1	4	.286	.375	.714	1.089	207	1	1	100	157	2	1.200	0	0	0	0	/1D	0.1
1982	NY-A	33	107	8	20	2	1	2	4	6	34	.187	.230	.280	.510	41	-9	-9	96	44	7	.409	0	0	0	-2	1/D	-1.0
1983	NY-A	32	86	8	20	2	0	5	17	8	23	.233	.298	.430	.728	99	-1	-0	99	128	11	.662	0	0	0	-1	1/D	-0.1
1984	KC-A	126	438	58	107	23	2	28	77	45	139	.244	.320	.498	.818	123	12	12	99	104	69	.785	0	0	0	-4	*1/D	0.0
1985	KC-A	160	600	74	146	28	2	36	88	52	166	.243	.309	.477	.786	109	7	6	102	94	86	.733	1	1	-0	-8	*1	-1.2
1986	KC-A	138	512	54	117	25	1	29	88	43	146	.229	.290	.451	.741	99	-2	-2	100	112	67	.682	0	0	0	-4	*1	-1.5
1987	KC-A	121	386	44	80	11	1	24	60	34	97	.207	.275	.427	.702	80	-10	-13	104	101	43	.634	0	0	0	-0	1D	-1.7
1988	KC-A	21	63	2	9	2	0	2	5	1	20	.143	.156	.270	.426	16	-7	-7	103	86	3	.333	0	0	0	-1	1/D	-0.8
	Sea-A	97	350	44	88	15	1	21	61	23	67	.251	.299	.480	.779	106	5	2	108	107	48	.708	0	1	-1	-1	D1	-0.1
	Yr	118	413	46	97	17	1	23	66	24	87	.235	.279	.448	.726	94	-2	-5	107	104	49	.646	0	1	-1	-2		-0.9
Total	8	732	2549	294	589	109	9	147	402	213	696	.231	.294	.454	.748	100	-4	-10	102	101	336	.703	1	2	-1	-21	1D	-6.3

■ **BOBBY BALCENA** Balcena, Robert Rudolph b: 8/1/28, San Pedro, Cal. BR/TL, 5'7", 160 lbs. Deb: 9/16/56

YEAR	TM/L	G	AB	R	H	2B	3B	HR	RBI	BB	SO	AVG	OBP	SLG	PRO	/A	BR	/A	PF	CHI	RC	TA	SB	CS	SBR	FR	POS	TPR
1956	Cin-N	7	2	2	0	0	0	0	0	0	1	.000	.000	.000	.000	-92	-1	-1	108	0	0	.000	0	0	0	-1	/O	0.0

■ **KID BALDWIN** Baldwin, Clarence Geoghan b: 11/1/1864, Newport, Ky. d: 7/12/1897, Cincinnati, Ohio BR/TR, 5'6", 147 lbs. Deb: 7/27/1884

YEAR	TM/L	G	AB	R	H	2B	3B	HR	RBI	BB	SO	AVG	OBP	SLG	PRO	/A	BR	/A	PF	CHI	RC	TA	SB	CS	SBR	FR	POS	TPR
1884	KC-U	50	191	19	37	5	3	1		4		.194	.210	.267	.477	69	-8	-4	87	0	11	.357	0			-1	CO/23	-0.1
	CP-U	1	1	0	1	0	0	0		0		1.000	1.000	1.000	2.000	582	0	0	99	0	1	—	0			0	/C	0.0
	Yr	51	192	19	38	5	3	1		4		.198	.214	.271	.485	72	-7	-3	87	0	11	.364	0			-1		-0.1
1885	Cin-a	34	126	9	17	1	0	1		3		.135	.155	.167	.322	3	-13	-14	104	0	3	.220				0	C/O2P3	-1.2
1886	Cin-a	87	315	41	72	8	7	3		8		.229	.252	.327	.579	86	-7	-5	96	0	30	.514	12			-4	C3/O	-0.3
1887	Cin-a	96	388	46	98	15	10	1		6		.253	.271	.351	.622	69	-14	-20	108	0	41	.548	13			-9	*C/O	-0.9
1888	Cin-a	67	271	27	59	11	3	1	25	3		.218	.235	.292	.526	70	-9	-9	101	97	20	.420	4			-1	C/O1	-0.2
1889	Cin-a	60	223	34	55	14	2	1	34	5	32	.247	.273	.341	.614	72	-8	-9	105	125	23	.542	7			-1	C/O31	-0.3
1890	Cin-N	22	72	5	11	0	0	0	10	3	6	.153	.187	.153	.339	0	-9	-10	108	275	2	.262	2			0	C/O	-0.8
	Phi-a	24	90	5	21	1	2	0		4		.233	.274	.289	.563	70	-4	-3	97	0	8	.478	2			0	C/3	-0.2
Total	7	441	1677	186	371	55	27	8	69	36	38	.221	.243	.301	.544	65	-72	-75	101	44	140	.454	40			-15	C/O321P	-4.0

■ **FRANK BALDWIN** Baldwin, Frank De Witt b: 12/25/28, High Bridge, N.J. BR/TR, 5'11", 195 lbs. Deb: 4/22/53

YEAR	TM/L	G	AB	R	H	2B	3B	HR	RBI	BB	SO	AVG	OBP	SLG	PRO	/A	BR	/A	PF	CHI	RC	TA	SB	CS	SBR	FR	POS	TPR
1953	Cin-N	16	20	0	2	0	0	0	0	1	9	.100	.143	.100	.243	-36	-4	-4	99	0	0	.158	0	0	0	0	/C	-0.2

■ **HENRY BALDWIN** Baldwin, Henry Clay "Ted" b: 6/13/1894, Chadds Ford, Pa. d: 2/24/64, West Chester, Pa. BR/TR, 5'11", 180 lbs. Deb: 5/22/27

YEAR	TM/L	G	AB	R	H	2B	3B	HR	RBI	BB	SO	AVG	OBP	SLG	PRO	/A	BR	/A	PF	CHI	RC	TA	SB	CS	SBR	FR	POS	TPR
1927	Phi-N	6	16	1	5	0	0	0	1	1	2	.313	.353	.313	.665	82	-0	-0	96	70	2	.545	0			0	/S3	0.0

■ **REGGIE BALDWIN** Baldwin, Reginald Conrad b: 8/19/54, River Rouge, Mich. BR/TR, 6'1", 195 lbs. Deb: 5/25/78

YEAR	TM/L	G	AB	R	H	2B	3B	HR	RBI	BB	SO	AVG	OBP	SLG	PRO	/A	BR	/A	PF	CHI	RC	TA	SB	CS	SBR	FR	POS	TPR
1978	Hou-N	38	67	5	17	5	0	1	11	3	3	.254	.286	.373	.659	87	-2	-1	95	156	6	.528	0	0	0	-0	C	0.0
1979	Hou-N	14	20	0	4	1	0	0	1	0	1	.200	.200	.250	.450	24	-2	-2	90	79	1	.278	0	0	0	0	/C1	-0.1
Total	2	52	87	5	21	6	0	1	12	3	4	.241	.267	.345	.611	73	-4	-3	94	139	7	.485	0	0	0	-0	/C1	-0.1

■ **BILLY BALDWIN** Baldwin, Robert Harvey b: 6/9/51, Tazewell, Va. BL/TL, 6', 175 lbs. Deb: 7/29/75

YEAR	TM/L	G	AB	R	H	2B	3B	HR	RBI	BB	SO	AVG	OBP	SLG	PRO	/A	BR	/A	PF	CHI	RC	TA	SB	CS	SBR	FR	POS	TPR
1975	Det-A	30	95	8	21	3	0	4	8	5	14	.221	.260	.379	.639	76	-3	-4	104	64	10	.573	2	1	0	3	O/D	0.0
1976	NY-N	9	22	4	6	1	1	1	5	1	2	.273	.304	.545	.850	150	1	1	92	128	4	.813	0	0	0	1	/O	0.2
Total	2	39	117	12	27	4	1	5	13	6	16	.231	.268	.410	.679	88	-2	-2	101	76	13	.615	2	1	0	4	/OD	0.2

■ **MIKE BALENTI** Balenti, Michael Richard b: 7/3/1886, Calumet, Okla. d: 8/4/55, Altus, Okla. BR/TR, 5'11", 175 lbs. Deb: 7/19/11

YEAR	TM/L	G	AB	R	H	2B	3B	HR	RBI	BB	SO	AVG	OBP	SLG	PRO	/A	BR	/A	PF	CHI	RC	TA	SB	CS	SBR	FR	POS	TPR
1911	Cin-N	8	8	2	2	0	0	0	0	0	1	.250	.250	.250	.500	44	-1	-1	92	0	1	.833	3			-1	/SO	0.0
1913	StL-A	70	211	17	38	2	4	0	11	6	32	.180	.206	.227	.434	28	-20	-19	95	81	10	.335	3			-5	S/O	-2.0
Total	2	78	219	19	40	2	4	0	11	6	33	.183	.208	.228	.436	29	-21	-19	95	79	12	.352	6			-5	/SO	-2.0

■ **LEE BALES** Bales, Wesley Owen b: 12/4/44, Los Angeles, Cal. BB/TR, 5'10.5", 165 lbs. Deb: 8/07/66

YEAR	TM/L	G	AB	R	H	2B	3B	HR	RBI	BB	SO	AVG	OBP	SLG	PRO	/A	BR	/A	PF	CHI	RC	TA	SB	CS	SBR	FR	POS	TPR
1966	Atl-N	12	16	4	1	0	0	0	0	0	5	.063	.063	.063	.125	-66	-3	-3	99	0	0	.067	0	0	0	-0	/23	-0.3
1967	Hou-N	19	27	4	3	0	0	0	2	8	7	.111	.314	.111	.425	29	-2	-2	94	276	2	.462	1	1	-0	-0	/2S	-0.1
Total	2	31	43	8	4	0	0	0	2	8	12	.093	.235	.093	.328	-3	-6	-5	95	190	2	.317	1	1	-0	-1	/23S	-0.4

■ **ART BALL** Ball, Arthur Clark b: 1873, Indiana d: 12/26/15, Chicago, Ill. TR , Deb: 8/01/1894

YEAR	TM/L	G	AB	R	H	2B	3B	HR	RBI	BB	SO	AVG	OBP	SLG	PRO	/A	BR	/A	PF	CHI	RC	TA	SB	CS	SBR	FR	POS	TPR
1894	StL-N	1	3	0	1	0	0	0	0	0	1	.333	.333	.333	.667	62	-0	-0	101	0	0	.500	0			0	/2	0.0

YEAR	TM/L	G	AB	R	H	2B	3B	HR	RBI	BB	SO	AVG	OBP	SLG	PRO	/A	BR	/A	PF	CHI	RC	TA	SB	CS	SBR	FR	POS	TPR
1898	Bal-N	32	81	7	15	2	0	0	8	7		.185	.258	.210	.468	36	-6	-7	103	142	5	.409	2			0	3S/2O	-0.5
Total	2	33	84	7	16	2	0	0	8	7	1	.190	.261	.214	.475	37	-7	-7	103	138	5	.412	2			0	/3S2O	-0.5
■ NEAL BALL Ball, Cornelius b: 4/22/1881, Grand Haven, Mich. d: 10/15/57, Bridgeport, Conn. BR/TR, 5'7", 145 lbs. Deb: 9/12/07																												
1907	NY-A	15	44	5	9	1	1	0	4	1		.205	.222	.273	.495	54	-2	-2	109	119	3	.400	1			1	S/2	-0.1
1908	NY-A	132	446	34	110	16	2	0	38	21		.247	.281	.291	.572	92	-6	-4	95	112	43	.545	32			-5	*S/2	-0.5
1909	NY-A	8	29	5	6	1	1	0	3	3		.207	.281	.310	.592	87	-0	-0	99	136	3	.609	2			-2	/2	-0.2
	Cle-A	96	324	29	83	13	2	1	25	17		.256	.295	.318	.613	92	-3	-4	102	93	34	.573	17			-14	S	-1.6
	Yr	104	353	34	89	14	3	1	28	20		.252	.294	.317	.611	91	-4	-4	102	97	37	.576	19			-16		-1.8
1910	Cle-A	53	119	12	25	3	1	0	12	9		.210	.266	.252	.518	62	-5	-5	100	148	9	.457	4			-1	S/2O3	-0.7
1911	Cle-A	116	412	45	122	14	9	3	45	27		.296	.339	.396	.735	102	1	-0	103	90	62	.728	21			1	23/S	0.1
1912	Cle-A	37	132	12	30	4	1	0	14	9		.227	.277	.273	.549	57	-7	-8	101	132	11	.510	7			2	2	-0.5
	Bos-A	18	45	10	9	2	0	0	6	3		.200	.250	.244	.494	39	-3	-4	107	182	4	.528	5			-1	2	-0.4
	Yr	55	177	22	39	6	1	0	20	12		.220	.270	.266	.535	52	-11	-12	103	151	15	.514	12			1		-0.9
1913	Bos-A	23	58	9	10	2	0	0	4	9	13	.172	.294	.207	.501	46	-4	-4	103	118	4	.521	3			-1	2/S3	-0.4
Total	7	498	1609	161	404	56	17	4	151	99	13	.251	.295	.314	.610	85	-30	-31	101	110	174	.580	92			-20	S2/3O	-4.3
■ JIM BALL Ball, James Chandler b: 2/22/1884, Hartford, Md. d: 4/7/63, Glendale, Cal. BR/TR, 5'11", 175 lbs. Deb: 9/21/07																												
1907	Bos-N	10	36	3	6	2	0	0	3	2		.167	.211	.222	.433	39	-3	-2	95	145	2	.333	0			0	C	-0.1
1908	Bos-N	6	15	1	1	0	0	0	0	1		.067	.125	.067	.192	-36	-2	-2	104	0	0	.143	0			0	/C	-0.1
Total	2	16	51	4	7	2	0	0	3	3		.137	.185	.176	.362	16	-5	-5	98	102	2	.273	0			0	/C	-0.2
■ PELHAM BALLENGER Ballenger, Pelham Ashby b: 2/6/1894, Gilreath Mill, S.C. d: 12/8/48, W.Gantt Township, S.C. BR/TR, 5'11", 160 lbs. Deb: 5/07/28																												
1928	Was-A	3	9	0	1	0	0	0	0	0	1	.111	.111	.111	.222	-41	-2	-2	102	0	0	.125	0	0	0	0	/3	-0.1
■ HAL BAMBERGER Bamberger, Harold Earl "Dutch" b: 10/29/24, Lebanon, Pa. BL/TR, 6', 173 lbs. Deb: 9/15/48																												
1948	NY-N	7	12	0	1	0	0	0	0	1	2	.083	.154	.083	.237	-34	-2	-2	100	0	0	.182	0			-0	/O	-0.2
■ STUD BANCKER Bancker, John b: Philadelphia, Pa. Deb: 4/21/1875																												
1875	NH-n	19	77	3	11							.143															C/2S3	
■ DAVE BANCROFT Bancroft, David James "Beauty" b: 4/20/1891, Sioux City, Iowa d: 10/9/72, Superior, Wis. BB/TR, 5'9.5", 160 lbs. Deb: 4/14/15 MCH																												
1915	Phi-N	153	563	85	143	18	2	7	30	77	62	.254	.346	.330	.676	98	6	1	107	49	64	.626	15	27	-12	5	*S	-0.1
1916	Phi-N	142	477	53	101	10	0	3	33	74	57	.212	.323	.252	.574	81	-9	-7	96	108	46	.566	15			22	*S	2.6
1917	Phi-N	127	478	56	116	22	5	4	43	44	42	.243	.307	.335	.641	90	-2	-6	108	93	52	.602	14			**27**	*S/2O	2.6
1918	Phi-N	125	499	69	132	19	4	0	26	54	36	.265	.338	.319	.656	92	2	-3	109	55	55	.613	11			18	*S	1.9
1919	Phi-N	92	335	45	91	13	7	0	25	31	30	.272	.333	.352	.686	102	3	1	104	84	41	.643	8			9	S	1.5
1920	Phi-N	42	171	23	51	7	2	0	5	9	12	.298	.337	.363	.700	93	0	-2	109	27	19	.575	1	7	-4	6	S	0.3
	NY-N	108	442	79	132	29	7	0	31	33	32	.299	.349	.396	.745	114	8	8	100	61	61	.686	7	5	-1	23	*S	3.7
	Yr	150	613	102	183	36	9	0	36	42	44	.299	.346	.387	.732	108	8	6	102	51	80	.654	8	12	-5	**29**		4.0
1921	NY-N	153	606	121	193	26	15	6	67	66	23	.318	.389	.441	.830	122	18	21	98	76	106	.837	17	10	-1	18	*S	5.0
1922	NY-N	156	651	117	209	41	5	4	60	79	27	.321	.397	.418	.815	107	13	9	104	64	111	.817	16	11	-2	22	*S	3.7
1923	NY-N	107	444	80	135	33	3	1	31	62	23	.304	.391	.399	.789	107	8	7	101	52	72	.785	8	7	-2	11	S2	2.4
1924	Bos-N	79	319	49	89	11	1	2	21	37	24	.279	.356	.339	.694	93	-5	-2	94	58	40	.641	4	4	-1	1	SM	0.4
1925	Bos-N	128	479	75	153	29	8	2	49	64	22	.319	.400	.426	.826	119	10	15	94	88	85	.833	7	4	-0	12	*SM	3.5
1926	Bos-N	127	453	70	141	18	6	1	44	64	29	.311	.399	.384	.783	129	10	20	86	91	72	.779	3			-2	*S/3M	2.5
1927	Bos-N	111	375	44	91	13	4	1	31	43	36	.243	.322	.307	.629	74	-15	-12	93	94	38	.577	5			5	*S/3M	0.3
1928	Bro-N	149	515	47	127	19	5	0	51	59	20	.247	.326	.303	.629	66	-25	-24	99	119	53	.577	7			3	*S	0.0
1929	Bro-N	104	358	35	99	11	3	1	44	29	11	.277	.331	.332	.663	69	-19	-16	94	123	40	.598	7			-5	*S	-0.5
1930	NY-N	10	17	0	1	1	0	0	0	2	1	.059	.158	.118	.276	-33	-4	-4	98	0	0	.250	0			0	/S	-0.1
Total	16	1913	7182	1048	2004	320	77	32	591	827	487	.279	.355	.358	.714	98	-1	6	100	78	954	.679	145	75		176	*S/23O	29.7
■ CHRIS BANDO Bando, Christopher Michael b: 2/4/56, Cleveland, Ohio BB/TR, 6', 195 lbs. Deb: 8/13/81																												
1981	Cle-A	21	47	3	10	3	0	0	6	2	2	.213	.245	.277	.521	54	-3	-3	93	181	3	.395	0	0	0	-0	C/D	-0.1
1982	Cle-A	66	184	13	39	6	1	3	16	24	30	.212	.303	.304	.607	67	-8	-8	100	98	17	.530	0	0	0	-6	C/3	-1.0
1983	Cle-A	48	121	15	31	3	0	4	15	15	19	.256	.338	.380	.718	92	-0	-1	105	101	15	.635	0	1	-1	-2	C	0.0
1984	Cle-A	75	220	38	64	11	0	12	41	33	35	.291	.383	.505	.888	135	13	12	106	111	41	.873	1	2	-1	2	C/13D	1.6
1985	Cle-A	73	173	11	24	4	1	0	13	22	21	.139	.236	.173	.409	15	-20	-19	94	172	7	.333	0	1	-1	5	C	-1.0
1986	Cle-A	92	254	28	68	9	0	2	26	22	49	.268	.329	.327	.655	82	-6	-6	98	116	27	.544	0	1	-1	5	C	0.3
1987	Cle-A	89	211	20	46	9	0	5	16	12	28	.218	.260	.332	.592	55	-13	-14	103	75	17	.480	0	0	0	2	C	-0.4
1988	Cle-A	32	72	6	9	1	0	1	8	8	12	.125	.222	.181	.403	14	-8	-8	102	199	3	.328	0	0	0	3	C	-0.4
	Det-A	1	0	0	0	0	0	0	0	0	0	—	—	—	—	—	0	0	94	—	—	—	0	0	0	0	/C	0.0
	Yr	33	72	6	9	1	0	1	8	8	12	.125	.222	.181	.403	14	-8	-8	101	199	4	.349	0	0	0	3		-0.4
Total	8	497	1282	134	291	46	2	27	141	138	196	.227	.303	.329	.632	73	-46	-47	101	119	134	.565	1	5	-3	9	C/3D1	-1.0
■ SAL BANDO Bando, Salvatore Leonard b: 2/13/44, Cleveland, O. BR/TR, 6', 195 lbs. Deb: 9/03/66 C																												
1966	KC-A	11	24	1	7	1	1	0	1	1	3	.292	.320	.417	.737	117	0	0	94	42	3	.647	0	0	0	-0	/3	0.0
1967	KC-A	47	130	11	25	3	2	0	6	16	24	.192	.295	.246	.541	62	-6	-6	100	78	11	.495	1	0	0	-4	3	-0.8
1968	Oak-A	162	605	67	152	25	5	9	67	51	78	.251	.317	.354	.670	105	2	3	98	126	69	.608	13	4	2	-11	*3/O	-0.1
1969	Oak-A	162	609	106	171	25	3	31	113	111	82	.281	.401	.484	.885	159	41	48	92	112	124	.921	1	4	-2	-13	*3	3.6
1970	Oak-A	155	502	93	132	20	2	20	75	118	88	.263	.409	.430	.839	136	27	30	97	117	94	.883	6	10	-4	-20	*3	0.5
1971	Oak-A	153	538	75	146	23	1	24	94	86	55	.271	.380	.452	.831	134	27	26	101	129	93	.823	3	7	-3	-16	*3	0.1
1972	Oak-A	152	535	64	126	20	3	15	77	78	55	.236	.342	.368	.711	115	10	11	97	141	70	.678	3	1	0	5	*3/2	2.5
1973	Oak-A	162	592	97	170	**32**	3	29	98	82	84	.287	.378	.498	.876	166	36	46	87	107	**113**	.881	4	2	0	-21	*3/D	2.2
1974	Oak-A	146	498	84	121	21	2	22	103	86	79	.243	.360	.426	.786	125	18	18	100	**154**	80	.782	2	3	-1	-8	*3/D	1.0
1975	Oak-A	160	562	64	129	24	1	15	78	87	80	.230	.338	.356	.694	103	-1	4	93	125	73	.673	7	1	2	-13	*3	-0.4
1976	Oak-A	158	550	75	132	18	2	27	84	76	74	.240	.337	.427	.764	123	16	16	100	104	84	.777	20	6	2	-4	*3/SD	1.6
1977	Mil-A	159	580	65	145	27	3	17	82	75	89	.250	.339	.395	.734	104	0	4	95	123	81	.696	4	2	0	0	*3D/2S	0.1
1978	Mil-A	152	540	85	154	20	6	17	78	72	52	.285	.375	.439	.814	121	22	18	106	109	92	.797	3	2	-0	13	*3D/1	3.0
1979	Mil-A	130	476	57	117	14	3	9	43	57	42	.246	.330	.345	.675	82	-11	-11	100	88	54	.601	2	0	1	-4	*3D/1P2	-1.2
1980	Mil-A	78	254	28	50	12	1	5	31	29	35	.197	.282	.311	.593	66	-13	-11	95	129	22	.533	5	3	-0	-0	3D/1	-1.2
1981	Mil-A	32	65	10	13	4	0	2	9	6	3	.200	.268	.354	.621	81	-2	-2	96	121	6	.556	1	1	-0	-1	3/1D	-0.2
Total	16	2019	7060	982	1790	289	38	242	1039	1031	923	.254	.355	.408	.763	120	165	194	97	119	1069	.764	75	46	-5	-98	*3/D1S2PO	10.7
■ ERNIE BANKS Banks, Ernest b: 1/31/31, Dallas, Tex. BR/TR, 6'1", 180 lbs. Deb: 9/17/53 CH																												
1953	Chi-N	10	35	3	11	1	1	2	6	4	5	.314	.385	.571	.956	141	2	2	103	92	8	1.000	0	0	0	-1	S	0.2
1954	Chi-N	154	593	70	163	19	7	19	79	40	50	.275	.328	.427	.755	94	-6	-6	101	106	80	.678	6	10	-4	-1	*S	0.0
1955	Chi-N	154	596	98	176	29	9	44	117	45	72	.295	.347	.596	.942	144	34	34	100	103	117	.936	9	3	1	5	*S	4.4
1956	Chi-N	139	538	82	160	25	8	28	85	52	62	.297	.359	.530	.889	137	25	26	99	94	99	.871	6	9	-4	-13	*S	1.9
1957	Chi-N	156	594	113	169	34	6	43	102	70	85	.285	.363	.579	.942	154	39	42	96	95	123	.964	8	4	0	-19	*S3	2.8
1958	Chi-N	154	617	119	193	23	11	**47**	**129**	52	87	.313	.370	**.614**	.984	154	46	45	101	99	135	.993	4	4	-1	-2	*S	5.2
1959	Chi-N	155	589	97	179	25	6	45	**143**	64	72	.304	.379	.596	.975	157	44	46	98	126	126	.981	2	4	-2	5	*S	5.3
1960	Chi-N	156	597	94	162	32	7	**41**	117	71	69	.271	.353	.554	.907	147	34	36	98	111	113	.900	1	3	-2	13	*S	5.3
1961	Chi-N	138	511	75	142	22	4	29	80	54	75	.278	.349	.507	.856	124	16	16	100	95	88	.827	1	2	-1	11	*SO/1	3.4
1962	Chi-N	154	610	87	164	20	6	37	104	30	71	.269	.311	.503	.814	108	9	4	106	104	89	.749	5	1	1	0	*1/3	0.1
1963	Chi-N	130	432	41	98	20	1	18	64	39	73	.227	.297	.403	.700	95	-1	-4	105	120	50	.631	0	3	-2	-2	*1	-0.9
1964	Chi-N	157	591	67	156	29	6	23	95	36	84	.264	.310	.450	.760	105	7	3	105	119	77	.675	1	2	-1	11	*1	0.9
1965	Chi-N	163	612	79	162	25	3	28	106	55	64	.265	.331	.453	.784	116	14	13	102	129	87	.724	3	5	-2	-8	*1	-0.5
1966	Chi-N	141	511	52	139	23	7	15	75	29	59	.272	.317	.432	.750	106	3	3	100	121	66	.657	0	1	-1	2	*1/3	-0.1

YEAR	TM/L	G	AB	R	H	2B	3B	HR	RBI	BB	SO	AVG	OBP	SLG	PRO	/A	BR	/A	PF	CHI	RC	TA	SB	CS	SBR	FR	POS	TPR
1967	Chi-N	151	573	68	158	26	4	23	95	27	93	.276	.312	.455	.767	115	10	9	102	122	74	.670	2	2	-1	0	*1	0.2
1968	Chi-N	150	552	71	136	27	0	32	83	27	67	.246	.288	.469	.757	111	13	6	112	100	72	.685	2	0	1	-2	*1	0.0
1969	Chi-N	155	565	60	143	19	2	23	106	42	101	.253	.313	.416	.729	96	0	-4	107	143	71	.650	0	0	0	-1	*1	-1.7
1970	Chi-N	72	222	25	56	6	2	12	44	20	33	.252	.317	.459	.776	88	1	-5	120	124	32	.719	0	0	0	-1	1	-1.0
1971	Chi-N	39	83	4	16	2	0	3	6	6	14	.193	.247	.325	.572	56	-4	-5	110	68	7	.485	0	0	0	1	1	-0.6
Total	19	2528	9421	1305	2583	407	90	512	1636	763	1236	.274	.333	.500	.833	122	288	263	102	111	1513	.811	50	53	-17	-1	*1S/3O	24.9

■ GEORGE BANKS Banks, George Edward b: 9/24/38, Pacolet Mills, S.C. d: 3/1/85, Spartanburg, S.C. BR/TR, 5'11", 185 lbs. Deb: 4/15/62

YEAR	TM/L	G	AB	R	H	2B	3B	HR	RBI	BB	SO	AVG	OBP	SLG	PRO	/A	BR	/A	PF	CHI	RC	TA	SB	CS	SBR	FR	POS	TPR
1962	Min-A	63	103	22	26	0	2	4	15	21	27	.252	.384	.408	.792	108	3	2	105	110	16	.771	0	0	0	-2	O/3	0.0
1963	Min-A	25	71	5	11	4	0	3	8	9	21	.155	.259	.338	.597	66	-3	-3	100	101	6	.548	0	0	0	-1	3	-0.3
1964	Min-A	1	1	0	0	0	0	0	0	0	1	.000	.000	.000	.000	-99	-0	-0	101	0	0	.000	0	0	0	0	H	0.0
	Cle-A	9	17	6	5	1	0	2	3	6	6	.294	.478	.706	1.184	218	3	3	103	71	6	1.500	0	0	0	-0	/O23	0.3
	Yr	10	18	6	5	1	0	2	3	6	7	.278	.458	.667	1.125	203	3	3	103	63	6	1.385	0	0	0	-0		0.3
1965	Cle-A	4	5	0	1	1	0	0	0	1	3	.200	.333	.400	.733	109	0	0	98	0	0	.600	0	1	-1	0	/3	0.0
1966	Cle-A	4	4	0	1	0	0	0	1	0	1	.250	.250	.250	.500	44	-0	-0	101	420	0	.333	0	0	0	0	H	0.0
Total	5	106	201	33	44	6	2	9	27	37	59	.219	.346	.403	.749	102	2	1	103	105	30	.759	0	1	-1	-3	/3O2	0.0

■ BILL BANKSTON Bankston, Wilborn Everett b: 5/25/1893, Barnesville, Ga. d: 2/26/70, Griffin, Ga. BL/TR, 5'11", 180 lbs. Deb: 8/15/15

YEAR	TM/L	G	AB	R	H	2B	3B	HR	RBI	BB	SO	AVG	OBP	SLG	PRO	/A	BR	/A	PF	CHI	RC	TA	SB	CS	SBR	FR	POS	TPR
1915	Phi-A	11	36	6	5	1	1	1	2	2	5	.139	.205	.306	.511	55	-2	-2	96	49	2	.484	1			-0	/O	-0.2

■ JIM BANNING Banning, James M. b: 1866, New York, N.Y. BL/TR, Deb: 1888

YEAR	TM/L	G	AB	R	H	2B	3B	HR	RBI	BB	SO	AVG	OBP	SLG	PRO	/A	BR	/A	PF	CHI	RC	TA	SB	CS	SBR	FR	POS	TPR
1888	Was-N	1	0	0	0	0	0	0	0	0	0	—	—	—	—	—	0	0	96	—	—	—	0			0	/C	0.0
1889	Was-N	2	1	0	0	0	0	0	0	0	0	.000	.000	.000	.000	-99	-0	-0	92	0	0	.000	0			0	/C	0.0
Total	2	3	1	0	0	0	0	0	0	0	0	.000	.000	.000	.000	-99	-0	-0	92	0	2	.000	0			0	/C	0.0

■ ALAN BANNISTER Bannister, Alan b: 9/3/51, Montebello, Cal. BR/TR, 5'11", 170 lbs. Deb: 7/13/74

YEAR	TM/L	G	AB	R	H	2B	3B	HR	RBI	BB	SO	AVG	OBP	SLG	PRO	/A	BR	/A	PF	CHI	RC	TA	SB	CS	SBR	FR	POS	TPR
1974	Phi-N	26	25	4	3	0	0	0	1	3	7	.120	.241	.120	.361	3	-3	-3	103	129	1	.318	0	0	0	-1	/OS	-0.4
1975	Phi-N	24	61	10	16	3	1	0	0	1	9	.262	.274	.344	.618	70	-3	-3	101	0	5	.500	2	2	-1	2	O/2S	0.0
1976	Chi-A	73	145	19	36	6	2	0	8	14	21	.248	.319	.317	.636	87	-2	-2	99	67	17	.646	12	4	1	-4	OS/23D	-0.4
1977	Chi-A	139	560	87	154	20	3	3	57	54	49	.275	.341	.338	.678	86	-10	-9	99	110	66	.593	4	3	-1	-31	*S/2O	-2.4
1978	Chi-A	49	107	16	24	3	2	0	8	11	12	.224	.303	.290	.592	67	-4	-5	101	102	9	.523	3	3	-1	-3	DO/S2	-0.8
1979	Chi-A	136	506	71	144	28	8	2	55	43	40	.285	.344	.383	.728	94	-2	-4	102	112	69	.695	22	6	3	-13	2O3/1D	-1.2
1980	Chi-A	45	130	16	25	6	0	0	9	12	16	.192	.261	.238	.499	39	-11	-10	97	113	8	.436	5	2	0	-3	O3	-1.3
	Cle-A	81	262	41	86	17	4	1	32	28	25	.328	.393	.435	.828	124	10	9	102	107	46	.821	9	2	2	-7	2O/3S	0.5
	Yr	126	392	57	111	23	4	1	41	40	41	.283	.350	.370	.719	97	-1	-1	100	110	54	.684	14	4	2	-10		-0.8
1981	Cle-A	68	232	36	61	11	1	1	17	16	19	.263	.310	.332	.642	91	-4	-3	93	83	27	.630	16	2	4	-3	O2/1S	-0.1
1982	Cle-A	101	348	40	93	16	1	4	41	42	41	.267	.348	.353	.701	93	-2	-2	100	124	47	.697	18	5	2	-2	O2/S3D	0.0
1983	Cle-A	117	377	51	100	25	4	5	45	31	43	.265	.326	.393	.719	92	-2	-4	105	108	48	.648	6	6	-2	-5	O2/1D	-1.0
1984	Hou-N	9	20	2	4	2	0	0	0	2	2	.200	.273	.300	.573	66	-1	-1	93	0	2	.500	0	0	0	1	/SO	0.0
	Tex-A	47	112	20	33	2	1	2	9	21	17	.295	.410	.384	.794	121	4	4	100	73	20	.850	3	0	1	-3	2/O13D	0.3
1985	Tex-A	57	122	17	32	4	1	1	6	14	17	.262	.338	.336	.674	79	-2	-3	108	54	15	.677	8	2	1	-3	DO2/31	-0.4
Total	12	972	3007	430	811	143	28	19	288	292	318	.270	.337	.355	.692	90	-32	-36	101	101	381	.662	108	37	10	-75	O2S/D31	-7.2

■ JIMMY BANNON Bannon, James Henry "Foxy Grandpa" b: 5/5/1871, Amesbury, Mass. d: 3/24/48, Glen Rock, N.J. BR , 5'5", 160 lbs. Deb: 6/15/1893

YEAR	TM/L	G	AB	R	H	2B	3B	HR	RBI	BB	SO	AVG	OBP	SLG	PRO	/A	BR	/A	PF	CHI	RC	TA	SB	CS	SBR	FR	POS	TPR
1893	StL-N	26	107	9	36	3	4	0	15	4	5	.336	.366	.439	.805	117	2	2	99	89	21	.845	8			0	O/SP	0.2
1894	Bos-N	128	494	130	166	29	10	13	114	62	42	.336	.414	.514	.928	110	20	6	113	109	128	1.119	47			19	*O/P	1.3
1895	Bos-N	123	489	101	171	35	5	6	74	54	31	.350	.420	.479	.898	130	25	23	103	87	113	1.009	28			8	*O/P	1.7
1896	Bos-N	89	343	52	86	9	5	0	50	32	23	.251	.316	.306	.623	61	-16	-21	108	140	39	.599	16			-1	O/2S3	-2.2
Total	4	366	1433	292	459	76	24	19	253	152	101	.320	.390	.447	.836	106	31	11	107	107	300	.926	99			26	O/S23P	1.0

■ TOM BANNON Bannon, Thomas Edward "Ward Six" b: 5/8/1869, S.Groveland, Mass. d: 1/26/50, Lynn, Mass. 5'8", 175 lbs. Deb: 5/10/1895

YEAR	TM/L	G	AB	R	H	2B	3B	HR	RBI	BB	SO	AVG	OBP	SLG	PRO	/A	BR	/A	PF	CHI	RC	TA	SB	CS	SBR	FR	POS	TPR
1895	NY-N	37	159	33	43	6	2	0	8	7	8	.270	.301	.333	.635	69	-8	-7	95	40	23	.690	20			0	O1	-0.5
1896	NY-N	2	7	1	1	1	0	0	0	1	1	.143	.250	.286	.536	43	-1	-1	99	0	1	.500	0			0	/O	0.0
Total	2	39	166	34	44	7	2	0	8	8	9	.265	.299	.331	.630	68	-9	-7	95	39	23	.680	20			0	/O1	-0.5

■ WALTER BARBARE Barbare, Walter Lawrence "Dinty" b: 8/11/1891, Greenville, S.C. d: 10/28/65, Greenville, S.C. BR/TR, 6', 162 lbs. Deb: 9/17/14

YEAR	TM/L	G	AB	R	H	2B	3B	HR	RBI	BB	SO	AVG	OBP	SLG	PRO	/A	BR	/A	PF	CHI	RC	TA	SB	CS	SBR	FR	POS	TPR
1914	Cle-A	15	52	6	16	2	2	0	5	2	5	.308	.345	.423	.769	128	2	2	102	87	7	.650	1	4	-2	1	3/S	0.1
1915	Cle-A	77	246	15	47	3	1	0	11	10	27	.191	.235	.211	.446	32	-20	-21	104	72	14	.353	6	5	-1	7	3/1	-1.3
1916	Cle-A	13	48	3	11	1	0	0	3	4	9	.229	.288	.250	.538	62	-2	-2	100	95	4	.432	0			1	3	0.0
1918	Bos-A	13	29	2	5	3	0	0	2	0	1	.172	.172	.276	.448	37	-2	-2	95	91	2	.375	1			0	3/S	-0.2
1919	Pit-N	85	293	34	80	11	5	1	34	18	18	.273	.317	.355	.672	97	0	-1	105	126	36	.629	11			-19	3/2	-2.2
1920	Pit-N	57	186	9	51	5	2	0	12	9	11	.274	.308	.323	.630	80	-5	-5	101	77	18	.536	5	3	-0	-7	S2/3	-0.9
1921	Bos-N	134	550	66	166	22	7	0	49	24	28	.302	.331	.367	.698	91	-12	-7	93	86	68	.611	11	4	1	-10	*S/23	-0.3
1922	Bos-N	106	373	38	86	5	4	0	40	21	22	.231	.272	.265	.537	41	-34	-30	94	144	28	.425	2	0	1	-6	231	-3.1
Total	8	500	1777	173	462	52	21	1	156	88	121	.260	.297	.315	.612	71	-73	-68	98	102	177	.518	37	16		-33	3S/21	-7.9

■ RED BARBARY Barbary, Donald Odell b: 6/20/20, Simpsonville, S.C BR/TR, 6'3", 190 lbs. Deb: 5/22/43

YEAR	TM/L	G	AB	R	H	2B	3B	HR	RBI	BB	SO	AVG	OBP	SLG	PRO	/A	BR	/A	PF	CHI	RC	TA	SB	CS	SBR	FR	POS	TPR
1943	Was-A	1	1	0	0	0	0	0	0	0	0	.000	.000	.000	.000	-96	-0	-0	104	0	0	.000	0	0	0	0	H	0.0

■ JAP BARBEAU Barbeau, William Joseph b: 6/10/1882, New York, N.Y. d: 9/10/69, Milwaukee, Wis. BR/TR, 5'5", 140 lbs. Deb: 9/27/05

YEAR	TM/L	G	AB	R	H	2B	3B	HR	RBI	BB	SO	AVG	OBP	SLG	PRO	/A	BR	/A	PF	CHI	RC	TA	SB	CS	SBR	FR	POS	TPR
1905	Cle-A	11	37	1	10	1	1	0	2	1		.270	.289	.351	.641	105	0	0	100	56	4	.556	1			0	2	0.0
1906	Cle-A	42	129	8	25	5	3	0	12	9		.194	.246	.279	.525	64	-5	-5	103	121	10	.481	5			1	3/S	-0.2
1909	Pit-N	91	350	60	77	16	3	0	25	37		.220	.302	.283	.585	79	-6	-8	105	88	34	.582	19			-7	3	-1.4
	StL-N	48	175	23	44	3	0	0	5	28		.251	.370	.269	.639	103	2	3	96	37	22	.718	14			2	3	0.6
	Yr	139	525	83	121	19	3	0	30	65		.230	.326	.278	.604	87	-5	-6	102	71	57	.626	33			-4		-0.8
1910	StL-N	7	21	4	4	0	1	0	2	3	3	.190	.292	.286	.577	75	-1	-1	92	116	2	.529	0			0	/32	0.0
Total	4	199	712	96	160	25	8	0	46	78	3	.225	.309	.282	.591	84	-10	-12	102	80	73	.592	39			-3	3/2S	-1.0

■ DAVE BARBEE Barbee, David Monroe b: 5/7/05, Greensboro, N.C. d: 7/1/68, Albermarle, N.C. BR/TR, 5'11.5", 178 lbs. Deb: 7/29/26

YEAR	TM/L	G	AB	R	H	2B	3B	HR	RBI	BB	SO	AVG	OBP	SLG	PRO	/A	BR	/A	PF	CHI	RC	TA	SB	CS	SBR	FR	POS	TPR
1926	Phi-A	19	47	7	8	1	1	1	5	2	4	.170	.220	.298	.518	29	-5	-6	118	100	3	.436	0	0	0	-0	O	-0.6
1932	Pit-N	97	327	37	84	22	6	5	55	18	38	.257	.300	.407	.706	88	-6	-6	99	138	40	.634	1			-0	O	-1.1
Total	2	116	374	44	92	23	7	6	60	20	42	.246	.290	.393	.683	80	-11	-12	102	133	44	.606	1	0		-1	/O	-1.7

■ CHARLIE BARBER Barber, Charles D. b: 1854, Philadelphia, Pa. d: 11/23/10, Philadelphia, Pa. BR/TR, Deb: 4/17/1884

YEAR	TM/L	G	AB	R	H	2B	3B	HR	RBI	BB	SO	AVG	OBP	SLG	PRO	/A	BR	/A	PF	CHI	RC	TA	SB	CS	SBR	FR	POS	TPR
1884	Cin-U	55	204	38	41	1	4	0		11		.201	.242	.245	.487	60	-7	-10	108	0	12	.374	0			3	3	-0.4

■ TURNER BARBER Barber, Tyrus Turner b: 7/9/1893, Lavinia, Tenn. d: 10/20/68, Milan, Tenn. BL/TR, 5'11", 170 lbs. Deb: 8/19/15

YEAR	TM/L	G	AB	R	H	2B	3B	HR	RBI	BB	SO	AVG	OBP	SLG	PRO	/A	BR	/A	PF	CHI	RC	TA	SB	CS	SBR	FR	POS	TPR
1915	Was-A	20	53	9	16	1	1	0	6	6	7	.302	.383	.358	.742	121	2	2	101	107	7	.650	0	3	-2	-3	O	-0.3
1916	Was-A	15	33	3	7	0	1	1	5	2	3	.212	.257	.364	.621	86	-1	-1	100	119	3	.538	0			-3	O	-0.4
1917	Chi-N	7	28	2	6	1	0	0	2	2	8	.214	.267	.250	.517	56	-1	-1	105	106	2	.455	1			1	/O	0.0
1918	Chi-N	55	123	11	29	3	2	0	10	9	16	.236	.293	.293	.586	77	-3	-3	102	105	11	.521	3			-3	O/1	-0.8
1919	Chi-N	76	230	26	72	9	4	0	21	14	17	.313	.355	.387	.742	122	6	6	100	92	33	.703	7			-5	O	0.0
1920	Chi-N	94	340	27	90	10	5	0	50	9	26	.265	.290	.324	.613	77	-11	-11	99	179	31	.496	5	6	-2	-4	1O/2	-1.9
1921	Chi-N	127	452	73	142	14	4	1	54	41	24	.314	.379	.369	.748	93	1	-3	107	119	64	.687	5	9	-4	3	*O	-0.9
1922	Chi-N	84	226	35	70	7	4	0	29	30	9	.310	.391	.376	.767	104	1	3	95	119	35	.762	7	4	-0	-6	O1	-0.5
1923	Bro-N	13	46	3	10	2	0	0	8	2	2	.217	.250	.261	.511	36	-4	-4	98	235	3	.378	0	1	-1	-1	O	-0.5
Total	9	491	1531	189	442	47	21	2	185	115	112	.289	.343	.351	.694	92	-11	-13	101	129	189	.622	28	23		-21	O/12	-5.3

■ JIM BARBIERI Barbieri, James Patrick b: 9/15/41, Schenectady, N.Y. BL/TR, 5'7", 155 lbs. Deb: 7/05/66

YEAR	TM/L	G	AB	R	H	2B	3B	HR	RBI	BB	SO	AVG	OBP	SLG	PRO	/A	BR	/A	PF	CHI	RC	TA	SB	CS	SBR	FR	POS	TPR
1966	LA-N	39	82	9	23	5	0	0	3	9	7	.280	.352	.341	.693	97	-0	-0	97	45	11	.661	2	0	1	0	O	0.0

YEAR	TM/L	G	AB	R	H	2B	3B	HR	RBI	BB	SO	AVG	OBP	SLG	PRO	/A	BR	/A	PF	CHI	RC	TA	SB	CS	SBR	FR	POS	TPR
■ **GEORGE BARCLAY** Barclay, George Oliver "Deerfoot" b: 5/16/1876, Millville, Pa. d: 4/3/09, Philadelphia, Pa. TR , 5'10", 162 lbs. Deb: 4/17/02																												
1902	StL-N	137	543	79	163	14	2	3	53	31		.300	.338	.350	.688	120	9	12	95	89	76	.661	30			-9	*O	-0.7
1903	StL-N	108	419	37	104	10	8	0	42	15		.248	.274	.310	.584	71	-18	-16	96	110	40	.498	12			-12	*O	-3.2
1904	StL-N	103	375	41	75	7	4	1	28	12		.200	.225	.248	.473	48	-23	-23	99	109	25	.397	14			-14	*O	-4.3
	Bos-N	24	93	5	21	3	1	0	10	2		.226	.242	.280	.522	65	-4	-4	97	149	7	.431	3			0	O	-0.4
	Yr	127	468	46	96	10	5	1	38	14		.205	.228	.254	.482	51	-27	-27	98	117	32	.403	17			-14		-4.7
1905	Bos-N	29	108	5	19	1	0	0	7	2		.176	.191	.185	.376	14	-11	-11	97	124	4	.270	2			-1	O	-1.4
Total	4	401	1538	167	382	35	15	4	140	62		.248	.278	.298	.576	78	-48	-42	97	105	152	.503	61			-36	O	-10.0
■ **JESSE BARFIELD** Barfield, Jesse Lee b: 10/29/59, Joliet, Ill. BR/TR, 6'4", 215 lbs. Deb: 9/03/81																												
1981	Tor-A	25	95	7	22	3	2	2	9	4	19	.232	.270	.368	.638	74	-2	-4	111	91	8	.550	4	3	-1	4	O	0.0
1982	Tor-A	139	394	54	97	13	2	18	58	42	79	.246	.323	.426	.750	96	2	-3	109	104	54	.695	1	4	-2	-9	*O/D	-1.7
1983	Tor-A	128	388	58	98	13	3	27	68	22	110	.253	.300	.510	.810	109	7	3	108	95	55	.746	2	5	-2	-0	*O/D	0.0
1984	Tor-A	110	320	51	91	14	1	14	49	35	81	.284	.359	.466	.824	124	11	11	102	102	55	.822	8	2	1	4	*O/D	1.4
1985	Tor-A	155	539	94	156	34	9	27	84	66	143	.289	.371	.536	.907	143	33	32	101	92	106	.941	22	8	2	18	*O	4.9
1986	Tor-A	158	589	107	170	35	2	**40**	108	69	146	.289	.371	.559	.929	143	40	36	105	102	122	.950	8	8	-2	22	*O	**4.9**
1987	Tor-A	159	590	89	155	25	3	28	84	58	141	.263	.332	.458	.789	106	6	5	101	97	87	.737	3	5	-2	1	*O	0.0
1988	Tor-A	136	468	62	114	21	5	18	56	41	108	.244	.306	.425	.731	103	0	1	100	90	60	.676	7	3	0	15	*O/D	1.3
Total	8	1010	3383	522	903	158	27	174	516	337	827	.267	.338	.484	.822	118	97	82	104	97	546	.813	55	38	-6	56	O/D	10.8
■ **AL BARKER** Barker, Alfred L b: 1/18/1839, Rockford, Ill. d: 9/15/12, Rockford, Ill. Deb: 6/01/1871																												
1871	Rok-n	1	5	0	1							.200															/O	
■ **RAY BARKER** Barker, Raymond Herrell "Buddy" b: 3/12/36, Martinsburg.W.Va. BL/TR, 6', 192 lbs. Deb: 9/13/60																												
1960	Bal-A	5	6	0	0	0	0	0	0	0	3	.000	.000	.000	.000	-98	-2	-2	102	0	0	.000	0	0	0	-0	/O	-0.1
1965	Cle-A	11	6	0	0	0	0	0	0	2	2	.000	.250	.000	.250	-23	-1	-1	98	0	0	.333	0	0	0	0	/1	0.0
	NY-A	98	205	21	52	11	0	7	31	20	46	.254	.329	.410	.739	107	2	2	101	122	28	.688	1	0	0	2	1/3	0.1
	Yr	109	211	21	52	11	0	7	31	22	48	.246	.326	.398	.724	104	1	1	101	110	28	.675	1	0	0	2		0.1
1966	NY-A	61	75	11	14	5	0	3	13	4	20	.187	.228	.373	.601	74	-3	-3	94	147	7	.525	0	0	0	1	1	-0.2
1967	NY-A	17	26	2	2	0	0	0	0	3	5	.077	.172	.077	.249	-26	-4	-4	94	0	0	.208	0	0	0	0	1	-0.4
Total	4	192	318	34	68	16	0	10	44	29	76	.214	.286	.358	.644	84	-8	-7	99	113	35	.588	1	0	0	3	1/3O	-0.6
■ **RED BARKLEY** Barkley, John Duncan b: 9/19/13, Childress, Tex. BR/TR, 5'11", 160 lbs. Deb: 9/02/37																												
1937	StL-A	31	101	9	27	6	0	0	14	14	17	.267	.357	.327	.683	74	-4	-4	99	145	13	.649	1	0	0	-2	2	-0.1
1939	Bos-N	12	11	1	0	0	0	0	0	1	2	.000	.083	.000	.083	-83	-3	-3	92	0	0	.091	0			0	/S3	-0.1
1943	Bro-N	20	51	6	16	3	0	0	7	4	7	.314	.364	.373	.736	113	1	1	100	133	7	.686	1			-1	S	0.2
Total	3	63	163	16	43	9	0	0	21	19	26	.264	.341	.319	.660	76	-6	-5	99	132	20	.608	2	0		-2	/2S3	0.0
■ **SAM BARKLEY** Barkley, Samuel E. b: 5/24/1858, Wheeling, W.Va. d: 4/20/12, Wheeling, W.Va. TR , 5'11.5", Deb: 5/01/1884 M																												
1884	Tol-a	104	435	71	133	**39**	9	1		22		.306	.342	.444	.786	152	26	24	104	0	68	.719				25	*2/C	**4.6**
1885	StL-a	106	418	67	112	18	10	2		25		.268	.312	.373	.686	127	9	13	93	0	50	.598				7	*21	2.2
1886	Pit-a	122	478	77	127	32	8	0		58		.266	.345	.366	.711	135	15	21	93	0	70	.726	22			-3	*2/O1	1.5
1887	Pit-N	89	340	44	76	10	4	1	35	30	24	.224	.294	.285	.579	68	-16	-12	93	114	31	.519	6			-5	12	-1.9
1888	KC-a	116	482	67	104	21	6	3	51	26		.216	.262	.303	.565	78	-9	-13	106	87	43	.505	15			-9	*2/M	-1.7
1889	KC-a	45	176	36	50	6	2	0	23	15	20	.284	.340	.341	.681	91	-1	-2	106	116	24	.659	8			-12	2/1	-1.0
Total	6	582	2329	362	602	126	39	7	109	176	44	.258	.314	.355	.669	111	24	30	99	43	285	.617	51			4	2/1OC	3.7
■ **TOM BARLOW** Barlow, Thomas H. Deb: 5/02/1872																												
1872	Atl-n	35	174	31	48							.276															*C/S	
1873	Atl-n	55	283	48	71							.251															*C	
1874	Har-n	32	157	37	49							.312															S	
1875	NH-n	1	5	0	1							.200															/S	
	Atl-n	1	4	1	0							.000															/2	
	Yr	2	9	1	1							.111																
Total	4 n	124	623	117	169							.271															/2	
■ **BRUCE BARMES** Barmes, Bruce Raymond "Squeaky" b: 10/23/29, Vincennes, Ind. BL/TR, 5'8", 165 lbs. Deb: 9/13/53																												
1953	Was-A	5	5	1	1	0	0	0	0	0	0	.200	.200	.200	.400	9	-1	-1	94	0	0	.250	0	0	0	0	/O	0.0
■ **BABE BARNA** Barna, Herbert Paul b: 3/2/15, Clarksburg, W.Va. d: 5/18/72, Charleston, W.Va. BL/TR, 6'2", 210 lbs. Deb: 9/16/37																												
1937	Phi-A	14	36	10	14	2	0	2	9	2	6	.389	.421	.611	1.032	167	3	3	94	110	9	1.136	1	0	0	-3	/O1	0.0
1938	Phi-A	9	30	4	4	0	0	0	2	3	5	.133	.212	.133	.345	-12	-5	-5	101	169	1	.269	0	0	0	-1	/O	-0.5
1941	NY-N	10	42	5	9	3	0	1	5	2	6	.214	.250	.357	.607	68	-2	-2	103	96	4	.515	0			1	O	-0.1
1942	NY-N	104	331	39	85	8	7	6	58	38	48	.257	.333	.378	.711	105	3	2	103	150	44	.664	3			-4	O	-0.3
1943	NY-N	40	113	11	23	5	1	1	12	16	9	.204	.302	.292	.594	75	-4	-3	96	120	11	.571	3			-2	O	-0.6
	Bos-A	30	112	19	19	4	1	2	10	15	24	.170	.268	.277	.545	57	-6	-6	104	104	9	.505	2	1	0	-4	O	-1.2
Total	5	207	664	88	154	22	9	12	96	76	98	.232	.311	.346	.657	87	-11	-12	101	133	78	.615	9	1		-14	O/1	-2.7
■ **RED BARNES** Barnes, Emile Deering b: 12/25/03, Suggsville, Ala. d: 7/3/59, Mobile, Ala. BL/TR, 5'10.5", 158 lbs. Deb: 9/29/27																												
1927	Was-A	3	11	5	4	1	0	0	0	1	3	.364	.417	.455	.871	130	0	0	97	0	2	.857	0	0	0	0	/O	0.1
1928	Was-A	114	417	82	127	22	15	6	51	55	38	.305	.391	.472	.863	124	16	15	102	86	80	.898	7	3	0	-2	*O	0.8
1929	Was-A	72	130	16	26	5	2	1	15	13	12	.200	.273	.292	.565	46	-11	-11	100	125	11	.500	1	0	0	-5	O	-1.5
1930	Was-A	12	12	1	2	1	0	0	0	0	3	.167	.167	.250	.417	4	-2	-2	101	0	0	.300	0	0	0	0	H	-0.1
	Chi-A	85	266	48	66	12	7	1	31	26	20	.248	.317	.357	.675	69	-12	-13	103	105	31	.624	4	2	0	7	O	-0.7
	Yr	97	278	49	68	13	7	1	31	26	23	.245	.311	.353	.664	66	-14	-15	103	92	32	.608	4	2	0	7		-0.8
Total	4	286	836	152	225	41	24	8	97	95	76	.269	.347	.404	.752	92	-8	-10	102	96	125	.731	12	5	1	1	O	-1.4
■ **EPPIE BARNES** Barnes, Everett Duane b: 12/1/1900, Ossining, N.Y. d: 11/17/80, Mineola, N.Y. BL/TL, 5'9", 175 lbs. Deb: 9/25/23																												
1923	Pit-N	2	2	0	1	0	0	0	0	0	1	.500	.500	.500	1.000	170	0	0	97	0	0	1.000	0	0	0	0	/1	0.0
1924	Pit-N	2	5	0	0	0	0	0	0	0	1	.000	.000	.000	.000	-94	-1	-1	106	0	0	.000	0	0	0	0	/1	-0.1
Total	2	4	7	0	1	0	0	0	0	0	2	.143	.143	.143	.286	-23	-1	-1	104	0	0	.167	0	0	0	0	/1	-0.1
■ **HONEY BARNES** Barnes, John Francis b: 1/29/1900, Fulton, N.Y. d: 6/18/81, Lockport, N.Y. BL/TR, 5'10", 175 lbs. Deb: 4/20/26																												
1926	NY-A	1	0	0	0	0	0	0	0	1	0	—	1.000	—	1.143	213	0	0	99	0	0	—	0	0	0	0	/C	0.0
■ **LUTE BARNES** Barnes, Luther Owens b: 4/28/47, Forest City, Iowa BR/TR, 5'10", 160 lbs. Deb: 8/06/72																												
1972	NY-N	24	72	5	17	2	2	0	6	6	4	.236	.295	.319	.614	78	-2	-2	95	107	6	.500	0	1	-1	-4	2/S	-0.5
1973	NY-N	3	2	2	1	0	0	0	0	1	0	.500	.500	.500	1.000	177	0	0	101	402	1	1.000	0	0	0	0	H	0.0
Total	2	27	74	7	18	2	2	0	7	6	5	.243	.300	.324	.624	81	-2	-2	95	114	7	.526	0	1	-1	-4	/2S	-0.5
■ **ROSS BARNES** Barnes, Roscoe Charles b: 5/8/1850, Mt.Morris, N.Y. d: 2/5/15, Chicago, Ill. BR/TR, 5'8.5", 145 lbs. Deb: 5/05/1871																												
1871	Bos-n	31	172	66	65							.378															2S/3	
1872	Bos-n	45	240	81	97							.404															*2	
1873	Bos-n	60	338	126	136							.402															*23	
1874	Bos-n	52	277	73	94							.339															*2	
1875	Bos-n	78	398	116	148							.372															*2	
1876	Chi-N	66	322	**126**	**138**	**21**	**14**	1	59	**20**	8	**.429**	**.462**	**.590**	**1.052**	198	**50**	**37**	125	89	**90**	**1.141**				2	*2/P	**3.3**
1877	Chi-N	22	92	16	25	1	0	0	5	7	4	.272	.323	.283	.606	94	-0	-0	98	63	9	.493				-7	2	-0.5
1879	Cin-N	77	323	55	86	9	2	1	30	16	25	.266	.301	.316	.617	109	2	4	95	106	31	.498				6	*S2	1.3
1881	Bos-N	69	295	42	80	14	1	0	17	16	16	.271	.309	.325	.634	109	0	4	91	53	30	.521				0	*S/2	0.8
Total	5 n	266	1425	462	540							.379															*S/2	

YEAR	TM/L	G	AB	R	H	2B	3B	HR	RBI	BB	SO	AVG	OBP	SLG	PRO	/A	BR	/A	PF	CHI	RC	TA	SB	CS	SBR	FR	POS	TPR
Total	4	234	1032	239	329	45	17	2	111	59	53	.319	.356	.401	.757	140	51	45	104	82	160	.673				0	2S/3P	4.9
■ SAM BARNES	Barnes, Samuel Thomas b: 12/18/1899, Suggsville, Ala. d: 2/19/81, Montgomery, Ala. BL/TR, 5'8", 150 lbs. Deb: 9/14/21																											
1921	Det-A	7	11	2	2	1	0	0	0	2	1	.182	.357	.273	.630	65	-1	-0	96	0	1	.667	0	0	0	-0	/2	0.0
■ BILL BARNES	Barnes, William H. b: Indianapolis, Ind. Deb: 9/27/1884																											
1884	StP-U	8	30	2	6	1	0	0		0		.200	.200	.233	.433	46	-2	-2	100	0	1	.292	0			0	/O	0.0
■ SKEETER BARNES	Barnes, William Henry b: 3/3/57, Cincinnati, Ohio BR/TR, 5'11", 175 lbs. Deb: 9/06/83																											
1983	Cin-N	15	34	5	7	0	0	1	4	7	3	.206	.372	.294	.666	84	-0	-0	103	122	4	.724	2	2	-1	-1	/13	-0.1
1984	Cin-N	32	42	5	5	0	0	1	3	4	6	.119	.196	.190	.386	8	-5	-5	106	107	2	.316	0	0	0	-1	3/O	-0.6
1985	Mon-N	19	26	0	4	1	0	0	0	0	2	.154	.154	.192	.346	-4	-4	-3	94	0	0	.208	0	1	-1	1	/3O1	-0.3
1987	StL-N	4	4	1	1	0	0	1	3	0	0	.250	.250	1.000	1.250	215	1	1	99	171	1	1.333	0	0	0	0	/3	0.1
Total	4	70	106	11	17	1	0	3	10	11	11	.160	.252	.255	.507	41	-8	-9	102	91	7	.457	2	3	-1	-1	/31O	-0.9
■ ED BARNEY	Barney, Edmund J. b: 1/23/1890, Amery, Wis. d: 10/4/67, Rice Lake, Wis. BL/TR, 5'10.5", 178 lbs. Deb: 7/22/15																											
1915	NY-A	11	36	1	7	0	0	0	8	3	6	.194	.256	.194	.451	36	-3	-3	98	389	2	.400	2	1	0	1	O	-0.2
	Pit-N	32	99	16	27	1	2	0	5	11	12	.273	.363	.323	.686	110	2	2	99	61	13	.707	7	3	0	3	O	0.5
1916	Pit-N	45	137	16	27	4	0	0	9	23	15	.197	.313	.226	.539	64	-4	-5	105	118	13	.564	8			7	O	0.0
Total	2	88	272	33	61	5	2	0	22	37	33	.224	.324	.257	.581	76	-6	-6	102	131	29	.591	17	4		10	/O	0.3
■ CLYDE BARNHART	Barnhart, Clyde Lee "Pooch" b: 12/29/1895, Buck Valley, Pa. d: 1/21/80, Hagerstown, Md. BR/TR, 5'10", 155 lbs. Deb: 9/22/20																											
1920	Pit-N	12	46	5	15	4	2	0	5	1	2	.326	.340	.500	.840	138	2	2	101	86	8	.806	1	0	0	-0	3	0.3
1921	Pit-N	124	449	66	116	15	13	3	62	32	36	.258	.312	.370	.682	77	-13	-16	103	133	53	.607	3	3	-1	-15	*3	-3.0
1922	Pit-N	75	209	30	69	7	5	1	38	25	7	.330	.402	.426	.828	110	5	4	104	144	37	.824	3	2	-0	-6	3O	0.0
1923	Pit-N	114	327	60	106	25	13	9	72	47	21	.324	.409	.563	.972	159	26	27	97	120	74	1.035	5	7	-3	1	O	2.1
1924	Pit-N	102	344	49	95	6	11	3	51	30	17	.276	.338	.384	.721	87	-3	-6	106	134	46	.680	8	4	0	0	O	-0.7
1925	Pit-N	142	539	85	175	32	11	4	114	59	25	.325	.391	.447	.838	112	12	11	102	**170**	96	.837	9	5	-0	-8	*O	0.0
1926	Pit-N	76	203	26	39	3	0	0	10	23	13	.192	.278	.207	.484	28	-19	-22	112	82	13	.409	1			-7	O	-3.1
1927	Pit-N	108	360	66	115	25	5	3	54	37	19	.319	.384	.442	.826	118	11	10	102	112	61	.812	2			1	O	0.7
1928	Pit-N	61	196	18	58	6	2	4	30	11	9	.296	.333	.408	.741	87	-2	-4	107	116	26	.681	3			-3	O/3	-0.8
Total	9	814	2673	405	788	123	62	27	436	265	149	.295	.360	.418	.777	101	18	6	103	131	413	.747	35	21		-37	O3	-4.5
■ VIC BARNHART	Barnhart, Victor Dee b: 9/1/22, Hagerstown, Md. BR/TR, 6', 188 lbs. Deb: 10/01/44																											
1944	Pit-N	1	2	0	1	0	0	0	0	1	1	.500	.667	.500	1.167	220	1	1	105	0	1	2.000	0			-0	/S	0.0
1945	Pit-N	71	201	21	54	7	0	0	19	9	11	.269	.300	.303	.603	66	-9	-10	103	108	17	.462	2			-3	S/3	-0.6
1946	Pit-N	2	1	0	0	0	0	0	0	0	0	.000	.000	.000	.000	-97	-0	-0	103	0	0	.000	0			0	H	0.0
Total	3	74	204	21	55	7	0	0	19	10	12	.270	.304	.304	.608	67	-9	-9	103	106	17	.497	2			-4	/S3	-0.6
■ BILLY BARNIE	Barnie, William Harrison "Bald Billy" b: 1/26/1853, New York, N.Y. d: 7/15/1900, Hartford, Conn. 5'7", 157 lbs. Deb: 5/07/1874 M																											
1874	Har-n	45	184	19	36							.196															CO/S	
1875	Wes-n	10	37	3	4							.108															/CO	
	Mut-n	10	40	1	6							.150															/CO	
	Yr	20	77	4	10							.130																
1883	Bal-a	17	55	7	11	0	0	0		2		.200	.228	.200	.428	37	-4	-4	107	0	3	.295				0	C/OSM	-0.3
1886	Bal-a	2	6	0	0	0	0	0		1		.000	.143	.000	.143	-59	-1	-1	91	0	0	.167	0			0	/OC	0.0
Total	2 n	65	261	23	46							.176															/OC	
Total	2	19	61	7	11	0	0	0		3		.180	.219	.180	.399	28	-5	-5	105	0	3	.280	0			0	/COS	-0.3
■ DICK BARONE	Barone, Richard Anthony b: 10/13/32, San Jose, Cal. BR/TR, 5'9", 165 lbs. Deb: 9/22/60																											
1960	Pit-N	3	6	0	0	0	0	0	0	0	1	.000	.000	.000	.000	-99	-2	-2	99	0	0	.000	0	0	0	0	/S	0.0
■ SCOTTY BARR	Barr, Hyder Edward b: 10/6/1886, Bristol, Tenn. d: 12/2/34, Ft.Worth, Tex. BR/TR, 6', 175 lbs. Deb: 8/22/08																											
1908	Phi-A	19	56	4	8	2	0	0	1	3		.143	.186	.179	.365	19	-5	-5	108	38	2	.271	0			-1	2/31O	-0.6
1909	Phi-A	22	51	5	4	1	0	0	1	11		.078	.254	.098	.352	12	-5	-5	102	77	2	.404	2			-4	O/1	-1.0
Total	2	41	107	9	12	3	0	0	2	14		.112	.221	.140	.361	16	-9	-10	105	58	3	.337	2			-4	/O213	-1.6
■ CUNO BARRAGAN	Barragan, Facundo b: 6/20/32, Sacramento, Cal. BR/TR, 5'11", 180 lbs. Deb: 9/01/61																											
1961	Chi-N	10	28	3	6	0	0	1	2	2	7	.214	.267	.321	.588	55	-2	-2	100	67	2	.478	0	0	0	-0	C	0.0
1962	Chi-N	58	134	11	27	6	1	0	12	21	28	.201	.310	.261	.571	52	-8	-9	106	135	11	.487	0	2	-1	-5	C	-1.4
1963	Chi-N	1	1	0	0	0	0	0	0	0	1	.000	.000	.000	.000	-95	-0	-0	105	0	0	.000	0	0	0	0	/C	0.0
Total	3	69	163	14	33	6	1	1	14	23	36	.202	.301	.270	.571	52	-10	-11	105	123	13	.508	0	2	-1	-6	/C	-1.4
■ GERMAN BARRANCA	Barranca, German (Costales) b: 10/19/56, Verzcruz, Mex. BL/TR, 6', 160 lbs. Deb: 9/02/79																											
1979	KC-A	5	5	3	3	1	0	0	0	0	0	.600	.600	.800	1.400	260	1	1	105	0	2	2.333	3	1	0	0	/23	0.1
1980	KC-A	7	0	3	0	0	0	0	0	0	0	—	—	—	—	—	0	0	98	—	—	—	0	0	0	0	/R	0.0
1981	Cin-N	9	6	2	2	0	0	0	1	0	0	.333	.333	.333	.667	89	-0	-0	101	196	1	.500	0	0	0	0	/H	0.0
1982	Cin-N	46	51	11	13	1	3	0	2	2	9	.255	.283	.392	.675	85	-1	-1	102	39	6	.615	2	0	1	0	/2	0.0
Total	4	67	62	19	18	2	3	0	3	2	9	.290	.313	.419	.732	100	0	-0	102	51	11	.717	5	1	1	0	/23	0.1
■ JIMMY BARRETT	Barrett, James Erigena b: 3/28/1875, Athol, Mass. d: 10/24/21, Detroit, Mich. BL/TR, 5'9", 170 lbs. Deb: 9/13/1899																											
1899	Cin-N	26	92	30	34	2	4	0	10	18		.370	.477	.478	.956	157	10	9	106	67	23	1.155	4			0	O	0.8
1900	Cin-N	137	545	114	172	11	7	5	42	72		.316	.395	.389	.784	130	17	24	92	50	104	.879	44			0	*O	1.2
1901	Det-A	135	542	110	159	16	9	4	65	76		.293	.380	.378	.758	110	13	4	110	82	90	.802	26			13	*O	1.3
1902	Det-A	136	509	93	154	19	6	4	44	74		.303	.391	.387	.778	120	16	17	99	61	89	.831	24			8	*O	1.5
1903	Det-A	136	517	95	163	13	10	2	31	**74**		.315	**.401**	.391	.792	145	29	31	97	46	94	.856	27			4	*O	2.7
1904	Det-A	162	624	83	167	10	5	0	31	**79**		.268	.350	.300	.650	114	10	13	96	53	72	.615	15			11	*O	1.6
1905	Det-A	20	67	2	17	1	0	0	3	6		.254	.315	.269	.584	89	-1	-1	98	61	6	.480	0			1	O	0.0
1906	Cin-N	5	12	1	0	0	0	0	0	2		.000	.143	.000	.143	-47	-2	-2	115	0	0	.167	0			0	/O	-0.2
1907	Bos-A	106	390	52	95	11	6	1	28	38		.244	.311	.310	.621	99	1	0	101	85	39	.549	3			6	O	0.1
1908	Bos-A	3	8	0	1	0	0	0	1	1		.125	.222	.125	.347	15	-1	-1	98	376	0	.286	0			0	/O	0.0
Total	10	866	3306	580	962	83	47	16	255	440		.291	.374	.359	.733	119	92	95	99	62	518	.756	143			43	O	9.0
■ JOHNNY BARRETT	Barrett, John Joseph "Jack" b: 12/18/15, Lowell, Mass. d: 8/17/74, Seabrook Beach, N.H. BL/TL, 5'10.5", 170 lbs. Deb: 4/14/42																											
1942	Pit-N	111	332	56	82	11	6	0	26	48	42	.247	.347	.316	.664	94	-1	-1	101	92	40	.654	10			5	O	0.2
1943	Pit-N	130	290	41	67	12	3	1	32	32	23	.231	.316	.303	.619	76	-7	-9	104	127	30	.571	5			-13	O	-2.6
1944	Pit-N	149	568	99	153	24	**19**	7	83	86	56	.269	.366	.415	.782	114	16	13	105	111	93	.834	**28**			-8	*O	-0.7
1945	Pit-N	142	507	97	130	29	4	15	67	79	68	.256	.357	.418	.775	111	11	8	103	92	81	.827	25			-13	*O	-1.0
1946	Pit-N	32	71	7	12	3	0	0	6	8	11	.169	.253	.211	.464	31	-6	-7	103	149	4	.407	1			-3	O	-1.0
	Bos-N	24	43	3	10	3	0	0	6	12	1	.233	.400	.302	.702	107	1	1	95	172	6	.735	0			-3	O	-0.1
	Yr	56	114	10	22	6	0	0	12	20	12	.193	.313	.246	.559	60	-5	-5	99	162	10	.527	1			-6		-1.1
Total	5	588	1811	303	454	82	32	23	220	265	201	.251	.349	.369	.718	100	14	6	103	108	255	.744	69			-34	O	-5.2
■ MARTY BARRETT	Barrett, Martin F. b: 11/1860, Port Huron, N.Y. d: 1/29/10, Holyoke, Mass. BR/TR, 5'9", 170 lbs. Deb: 6/24/1884																											
1884	Bos-N	3	6	0	0	0	0	0	0	0	4	.000	.000	.000	.000	-99	-1	-1	98	0	0	.000				0	/C	0.0
	Ind-a	5	13	1	1	1	0	0		1		.077	.143	.154	.297	-2	-1	-1	96	0	0	.250				0	/C	0.0
Total	1	8	19	1	1	1	0	0	0	1	4	.053	.100	.105	.205	-34	-3	-3	97	0	0	.167				0	/C	0.0
■ MARTY BARRETT	Barrett, Martin Glenn b: 6/23/58, Arcadia, Cal. BR/TR, 5'10", 175 lbs. Deb: 9/06/82																											
1982	Bos-A	8	18	0	1	0	0	0	0	0	1	.056	.056	.056	.111	-63	-4	-4	110	0	0	.056	0	0	0	-0	/2	-0.3
1983	Bos-A	33	44	7	10	1	1	0	2	3	1	.227	.277	.295	.572	57	-3	-3	101	60	4	.457	0	0	0	-3	2/D	-0.4
1984	Bos-A	139	475	56	144	23	3	3	45	42	25	.303	.361	.383	.744	96	5	-1	110	94	66	.671	5	3	-0	-2	*2	0.2

YEAR	TM/L	G	AB	R	H	2B	3B	HR	RBI	BB	SO	AVG	OBP	SLG	PRO	/A	BR	/A	PF	CHI	RC	TA	SB	CS	SBR	FR	POS	TPR
1985	Bos-A	156	534	59	142	26	0	5	56	56	50	.266	.338	.343	.681	85	-8	-10	102	112	62	.603	7	5	-1	15	*2	1.0
1986	Bos-A	158	625	94	179	39	4	4	60	65	31	.286	.355	.381	.735	102	3	3	100	92	87	.685	15	7	0	-1	*2	1.0
1987	Bos-A	137	559	72	164	23	0	3	43	51	38	.293	.354	.351	.704	90	-7	-7	99	74	74	.645	15	2	3	**35**	*2	3.9
1988	Bos-A	150	612	83	173	28	1	1	65	40	35	.283	.334	.337	.670	81	-9	-16	109	109	69	.568	7	3	0	5	*2	0.0
Total	7	781	2867	371	813	140	9	16	271	257	181	.284	.345	.355	.700	89	-23	-38	104	95	362	.640	49	20	3	50	2/D	5.4

■ **BOB BARRETT** Barrett, Robert Schley "Jumbo" b: 1/27/1899, Atlanta, Ga. d: 1/18/82, Atlanta, Ga. BR/TR, 5'11", 175 lbs. Deb: 4/30/23

YEAR	TM/L	G	AB	R	H	2B	3B	HR	RBI	BB	SO	AVG	OBP	SLG	PRO	/A	BR	/A	PF	CHI	RC	TA	SB	CS	SBR	FR	POS	TPR
1923	Chi-N	3	3	0	1	0	0	0	0	0	0	.333	.333	.333	.667	73	-0	-0	104	0	0	.500	0	0	0	0	H	0.0
1924	Chi-N	54	133	12	32	2	3	5	21	7	29	.241	.279	.414	.692	82	-4	-4	101	109	15	.624	1	0	0	0	21/3	-0.4
1925	Chi-N	14	32	1	10	1	0	0	7	1	4	.313	.333	.344	.677	75	-1	-1	97	226	3	.542	1	2	-1	1	/32	0.0
	Bro-N	1	1	0	0	0	0	0	1	0	0	.000	.000	.000	.000	-99	-0	-0	94	0	0	.000	0	0	0	0	H	0.0
	Yr	15	33	1	10	1	0	0	8	1	4	.303	.324	.333	.657	70	-2	-1	97	226	3	.520	1	2	-1	1		0.0
1927	Bro-N	99	355	29	92	10	2	5	38	14	22	.259	.289	.341	.630	66	-17	-18	103	100	34	.521	1			-3	3	-1.5
1929	Bos-A	68	126	15	34	10	0	0	19	10	6	.270	.324	.349	.673	72	-5	-5	102	148	15	.613	3	1	0	1	3/12O	-0.1
Total	5	239	650	57	169	23	5	10	86	32	61	.260	.296	.357	.653	71	-27	-29	102	117	68	.560	6	3		-1	3/21O	-2.0

■ **TOM BARRETT** Barrett, Thomas Loren b: 4/2/60, San Fernando, Cal. BB/TR, 5'9", 157 lbs. Deb: 7/02/88

YEAR	TM/L	G	AB	R	H	2B	3B	HR	RBI	BB	SO	AVG	OBP	SLG	PRO	/A	BR	/A	PF	CHI	RC	TA	SB	CS	SBR	FR	POS	TPR
1988	Phi-N	36	54	5	11	1	0	0	3	7	8	.204	.306	.222	.529	53	-3	-3	101	100	4	.455	0	0	0	-1	2	-0.3

■ **BILL BARRETT** Barrett, William b: Washington, D.C. Deb: 7/08/1871

YEAR	TM/L	G	AB	R	H	2B	3B	HR	RBI	BB	SO	AVG	OBP	SLG	PRO	/A	BR	/A	PF	CHI	RC	TA	SB	CS	SBR	FR	POS	TPR
1871	Kek-n	1	5	1	1							.200															/C3	
1872	Oly-n	1	5	0	0							.000															/C	
	Atl-n	7	30	4	8							.267															/O	
	Yr	8	35	4	8							.229																
1873	Bal-n	1	4	0	1							.250															/SO	
Total	3 n	10	44	5	10							.227															/SO	

■ **BILL BARRETT** Barrett, William Joseph "Whispering Bill" b: 5/28/1900, Cambridge, Mass. d: 1/26/51, Cambridge, Mass. BR/TR, 6', 175 lbs. Deb: 5/13/21

YEAR	TM/L	G	AB	R	H	2B	3B	HR	RBI	BB	SO	AVG	OBP	SLG	PRO	/A	BR	/A	PF	CHI	RC	TA	SB	CS	SBR	FR	POS	TPR
1921	Phi-A	14	30	3	7	2	1	0	3	0	5	.233	.233	.367	.600	49	-2	-3	103	93	2	.478	0	0	0	-1	/SP31	-0.1
1923	Chi-A	44	162	17	44	7	2	2	23	9	24	.272	.310	.377	.686	81	-5	-5	98	120	20	.678	12	3	2	0	O/3	-0.5
1924	Chi-A	119	406	52	110	18	5	2	56	30	38	.271	.326	.355	.680	78	-15	-14	97	123	47	.627	15	10	-2	-16	SO/3	-2.2
1925	Chi-A	81	245	44	89	23	3	3	40	24	27	.363	.420	.518	.938	143	14	15	96	98	52	.963	5	6	-2	-8	2O/S3	0.5
1926	Chi-A	111	368	46	113	31	4	6	61	25	26	.307	.353	.462	.815	121	4	9	92	110	59	.782	9	7	-2	-8	*O/1	-0.8
1927	Chi-A	147	556	62	159	35	9	4	83	52	46	.286	.347	.403	.750	92	-5	-7	102	124	77	.746	20	0	6	2	*O	-1.3
1928	Chi-A	76	235	34	65	11	2	3	26	14	30	.277	.320	.379	.699	84	-6	-6	99	91	29	.647	8	3	1	-1	O2	-0.6
1929	Chi-A	3	1	0	0	0	0	0	0	2	0	.000	.667	.000	.667	91	0	0	95	0	0	2.000	0	0	0	0	H	0.0
	Bos-A	111	370	57	100	23	4	3	35	51	38	.270	.363	.378	.742	90	-4	-5	102	82	53	.737	11	8	-2	1	*O/3	-0.8
	Yr	114	371	57	100	23	4	3	35	53	38	.270	.365	.377	.743	90	-3	-4	102	80	54	.742	11	8	-2	1		-0.8
1930	Bos-A	6	18	3	3	1	0	0	1	1	3	.167	.211	.222	.433	11	-2	-2	93	83	1	.333	0	0	0	-1	/O	-0.3
	Was-A	6	4	0	0	0	0	0	0	1	2	.000	.200	.000	.200	-44	-1	-1	101	0	0	.250	0	0	0	-0	/O	0.0
	Yr	12	22	3	3	1	0	0	1	2	5	.136	.208	.182	.390	-0	-3	-3	97	48	1	.316	0	0	0	-2		-0.3
Total	9	718	2395	318	690	151	30	23	328	209	239	.288	.347	.405	.752	96	-23	-17	98	108	340	.727	80	37	2	-31	O/S23P1	-6.1

■ **JOSE BARRIOS** Barrios, Jose Manuel b: 6/26/57, New York, N.Y. BR/TR, 6'4", 195 lbs. Deb: 4/23/82

YEAR	TM/L	G	AB	R	H	2B	3B	HR	RBI	BB	SO	AVG	OBP	SLG	PRO	/A	BR	/A	PF	CHI	RC	TA	SB	CS	SBR	FR	POS	TPR
1982	SF-N	10	19	2	3	0	0	0	0	1	4	.158	.200	.158	.358	1	-2	-2	94	0	0	.235	0	0	0	0	/1	-0.2

■ **JIM BARRON** Barron, James b: St.Louis.Mo. Deb: 6/19/1874

YEAR	TM/L	G	AB	R	H	2B	3B	HR	RBI	BB	SO	AVG	OBP	SLG	PRO	/A	BR	/A	PF	CHI	RC	TA	SB	CS	SBR	FR	POS	TPR
1874	Bal-n	16	76	6	22							.289															O	

■ **RED BARRON** Barron, David Irenus b: 6/21/1900, Clarksville, Ga. d: 10/4/82, Atlanta, Ga. BR/TR, 5'11.5", 185 lbs. Deb: 6/10/29

YEAR	TM/L	G	AB	R	H	2B	3B	HR	RBI	BB	SO	AVG	OBP	SLG	PRO	/A	BR	/A	PF	CHI	RC	TA	SB	CS	SBR	FR	POS	TPR
1929	Bos-N	10	21	3	4	1	0	0	1	1	4	.190	.227	.238	.465	16	-3	-3	94	68	1	.471	2			0	/O	-0.2

■ **FRANK BARROWS** Barrows, Frank Lewis b: Boston, Mass. Deb: 5/20/1871

YEAR	TM/L	G	AB	R	H	2B	3B	HR	RBI	BB	SO	AVG	OBP	SLG	PRO	/A	BR	/A	PF	CHI	RC	TA	SB	CS	SBR	FR	POS	TPR
1871	Bos-n	18	87	13	14							.161															O/2	

■ **CUKE BARROWS** Barrows, Roland b: 10/20/1883, Gray, Maine d: 2/10/55, Gorham, Maine BL/TR, 5'8", 158 lbs. Deb: 9/18/09

YEAR	TM/L	G	AB	R	H	2B	3B	HR	RBI	BB	SO	AVG	OBP	SLG	PRO	/A	BR	/A	PF	CHI	RC	TA	SB	CS	SBR	FR	POS	TPR
1909	Chi-A	5	20	1	3	0	0	0	2	0		.150	.190	.150	.340	8	-2	-2	97	222	1	.235	0			-1	/O	-0.3
1910	Chi-A	6	20	0	4	0	0	0	1	3		.200	.304	.200	.504	61	-1	-1	95	94	1	.438	0			-1	/O	-0.2
1911	Chi-A	13	46	5	9	2	0	0	4	7		.196	.315	.239	.554	57	-2	-2	97	130	4	.568	2			-3	O	-0.5
1912	Chi-A	8	13	0	3	0	0	0	2	2		.231	.333	.231	.564	63	-1	-1	99	223	1	.600	1			-0	/O	0.0
Total	4	32	99	6	19	2	0	0	9	12		.192	.292	.212	.504	50	-6	-6	97	152	7	.475	3			-5	/O	-1.0

■ **SHAD BARRY** Barry, John C. b: 9/28/1876, Newburgh, N.Y. d: 11/27/36, Los Angeles, Cal. BR/TR, Deb: 5/30/1899

YEAR	TM/L	G	AB	R	H	2B	3B	HR	RBI	BB	SO	AVG	OBP	SLG	PRO	/A	BR	/A	PF	CHI	RC	TA	SB	CS	SBR	FR	POS	TPR
1899	Was-N	78	247	31	71	7	5	1	33	12		.287	.328	.368	.697	97	-3	-1	96	108	34	.665	11			0	O1S3/2	0.0
1900	Bos-N	81	254	40	66	10	7	1	37	13		.260	.296	.366	.662	70	-6	-14	120	120	31	.612	9			0	OS2/13	-1.2
1901	Bos-N	11	40	3	7	2	0	0	6	2		.175	.214	.225	.439	26	-4	-4	112	227	2	.364	1			1	O	-0.3
	Phi-N	67	252	35	62	10	0	1	22	15		.246	.288	.298	.586	70	-9	-10	103	96	26	.542	13			-1	23O/S	-0.8
	Yr	78	292	38	69	12	0	1	28	17		.236	.278	.288	.566	64	-12	-14	104	118	28	.516	14			0		-1.1
1902	Phi-N	138	543	65	156	20	6	3	58	44		.287	.341	.363	.704	113	12	9	105	86	74	.659	14			-4	*O/1	-0.4
1903	Phi-N	138	550	75	152	24	5	1	60	30		.276	.314	.344	.657	97	-8	-3	92	106	69	.616	26			4	*O1/3	-.8
1904	Phi-N	35	122	15	25	2	0	0	3	11		.205	.271	.221	.492	58	-6	-5	93	41	8	.412	2			4	O/3	-0.1
	Chi-N	73	263	29	69	7	2	1	26	17		.262	.307	.316	.623	94	-2	-2	101	117	30	.577	12			-1	O13/S2	-0.4
	Yr	108	385	44	94	9	2	1	29	28		.244	.295	.286	.581	83	-8	-7	98	93	38	.522	14			3		-0.5
1905	Chi-N	27	104	10	22	2	0	0	10	5		.212	.248	.231	.478	42	-7	-7	105	153	7	.415	5			0	1	-0.8
	Cin-N	125	494	90	160	11	12	1	56	33		.324	.366	.401	.767	127	18	16	103	93	80	.740	16			-9	*1/O	0.2
	Yr	152	598	100	182	13	12	1	66	38		.304	.346	.371	.717	112	11	9	103	105	86	.675	21			-8		-0.6
1906	Cin-N	73	279	38	80	10	5	1	33	26		.287	.348	.369	.717	109	8	4	115	100	41	.704	11			5	1O	0.7
	StL-N	62	237	26	59	9	1	0	12	15		.249	.294	.295	.589	85	-4	-4	101	60	23	.511	6			2	O1/3	-0.4
	Yr	135	516	64	139	19	6	1	45	41		.269	.323	.335	.658	99	4	-1	108	82	63	.613	17			7		0.3
1907	StL-N	81	294	30	73	5	2	0	19	28		.248	.314	.279	.593	92	-3	-2	96	84	28	.516	4			-10	O	-1.7
1908	StL-N	74	268	24	61	8	1	0	11	19		.228	.279	.265	.544	81	-7	-5	94	63	21	.478	9			8	O/S	0.2
	NY-N	37	67	5	10	1	1	0	5	9		.149	.250	.194	.444	42	-4	-4	104	148	3	.404	1			-3	O	-0.8
	Yr	111	335	29	71	9	2	0	16	28		.212	.273	.251	.523	71	-11	-10	97	92	24	.462	10			5		-0.6
Total	10	1100	4014	516	1073	128	47	10	391	279		.267	.315	.330	.646	94	-24	-33	102	96	478	.594	140			-4	O1/23S	-6.4

■ **JACK BARRY** Barry, John Joseph b: 4/26/1887, Meriden, Conn. d: 4/23/61, Shrewsbury, Mass. BR/TR, 5'9", 158 lbs. Deb: 7/13/08 M

YEAR	TM/L	G	AB	R	H	2B	3B	HR	RBI	BB	SO	AVG	OBP	SLG	PRO	/A	BR	/A	PF	CHI	RC	TA	SB	CS	SBR	FR	POS	TPR
1908	Phi-A	40	135	13	30	4	3	0	8	10		.222	.276	.296	.572	82	-2	-3	108	77	12	.524	5			-3	2S/3	-0.6
1909	Phi-A	124	409	56	88	11	2	1	23	44		.215	.307	.259	.566	77	-8	-9	102	83	36	.551	17			-20	*S	-2.9
1910	Phi-A	145	487	64	126	19	5	3	60	52		.259	.336	.337	.673	109	7	6	102	131	61	.651	14			-27	*S	-2.0
1911	Phi-A	127	442	73	117	18	7	1	63	38		.265	.333	.344	.677	96	-7	-2	93	140	62	.698	30			-24	*S	-1.3
1912	Phi-A	139	483	76	126	19	9	0	55	47		.261	.335	.337	.673	93	-4	-4	99	115	63	.669	22			-5	*S	0.3
1913	Phi-A	134	455	62	125	20	6	3	85	44	32	.275	.349	.365	.714	113	5	7	97	**176**	64	.706	15			-9	*S	1.0
1914	Phi-A	140	467	57	113	12	0	0	42	53	34	.242	.324	.268	.592	80	-11	-9	97	129	48	.556	22	13	-1	3	*S	0.6
1915	Phi-A	54	194	16	43	6	2	0	15	15	9	.222	.284	.273	.558	70	-8	-7	96	102	16	.487	6	5	-1	-6	S	-0.9
	Bos-A	78	248	30	65	13	2	0	26	24	11	.262	.342	.331	.672	102	1	1	99	110	32	.612	0			-8	2	-0.8
	Yr	132	442	46	108	19	4	0	41	39	20	.244	.317	.305	.622	88	-7	-6	98	107	48	.555	6	5	-1	-14		-1.7
1916	Bos-A	94	330	28	67	6	1	0	20	17	24	.203	.277	.227	.505	55	-19	-16	94	101	27	.445	8			0	2	-1.4
1917	Bos-A	116	388	45	83	9	0	2	30	47	27	.214	.305	.253	.558	65	-12	-16	108	110	39	.528	12			-2	*2M	-1.1
1919	Bos-A	31	108	13	26	5	1	0	2	5	5	.241	.293	.306	.599	75	-5	-3	91	22	11	.524	2			-1	2	-0.1
Total	11	1222	4146	533	1009	142	38	10	429	396	142	.243	.320	.303	.623	87	-63	-56	99	118	471	.596	153	18		-101	S2/3	-9.2

YEAR	TM/L	G	AB	R	H	2B	3B	HR	RBI	BB	SO	AVG	OBP	SLG	PRO	/A	BR	/A	PF	CHI	RC	TA	SB	CS	SBR	FR	POS	TPR
■ RICH BARRY	Barry, Richard Donovan b: 9/12/40, Berkeley, Cal. BR/TR, 6'4", 205 lbs. Deb: 7/04/69																											
1969	Phi-N	20	32	4	6	1	0	0	0	5	6	.188	.316	.219	.535	53	-2	-2	98	0	2	.464	0	0	0	-1	/O	-0.2
■ DICK BARTELL	Bartell, Richard William "Rowdy Richard" b: 11/22/07, Chicago, Ill. BR/TR, 5'9", 160 lbs. Deb: 10/02/27 C																											
1927	Pit-N	1	2	0	0	0	0	0	0	2	0	.000	.500	.000	.500	43	0	0	102	0	0	1.000	0			-0	/S	0.0
1928	Pit-N	72	233	27	71	8	4	1	36	21	18	.305	.377	.386	.763	93	1	-2	107	138	34	.747	4			-6	2S/3	-0.3
1929	Pit-N	143	610	101	184	40	13	2	57	40	29	.302	.347	.420	.766	86	-11	-15	103	66	86	.725	11			-16	S2	-1.6
1930	Pit-N	129	475	69	152	32	13	4	75	39	34	.320	.378	.467	.845	106	2	5	97	113	82	.848	8			2	*S	1.6
1931	Phi-N	135	554	88	160	43	7	0	34	27	38	.289	.325	.392	.717	87	-7	-12	106	49	72	.642	6			-1	*S/2	-0.1
1932	Phi-N	154	614	118	189	48	7	1	53	64	47	.308	.379	.414	.792	101	13	3	112	68	102	.781	8			10	*S	2.5
1933	Phi-N	152	587	78	159	25	5	1	37	56	46	.271	.340	.336	.675	79	-3	-16	118	61	73	.606	6			8	*S	0.2
1934	Phi-N	146	604	102	187	30	4	0	37	64	59	.310	.384	.373	.757	95	6	-1	108	51	92	.727	13			13	*S	1.5
1935	NY-N	137	539	60	141	28	4	14	53	37	52	.262	.316	.406	.722	96	-6	-4	96	78	72	.656	5			11	*S	1.3
1936	NY-N	145	510	71	152	31	3	8	42	40	36	.298	.355	.418	.773	107	5	5	100	64	79	.719	6			**43**	*S	5.4
1937	NY-N	128	516	91	158	38	2	14	62	40	38	.306	.367	.469	.836	126	18	18	100	69	92	.809	5			**37**	*S	**6.2**
1938	NY-N	127	481	67	126	26	1	9	49	55	60	.262	.347	.376	.724	96	0	-2	103	90	67	.679	4			23	*S	3.0
1939	Chi-N	105	336	37	80	24	2	3	34	42	25	.238	.335	.348	.683	83	-7	-7	101	99	41	.647	6			2	*S/3	0.1
1940	Det-A	139	528	76	123	24	3	7	53	76	53	.233	.335	.330	.665	66	-20	-29	111	104	65	.639	12	2	2	14	*S	0.0
1941	Det-A	5	12	0	2	1	0	0	1	2	2	.167	.333	.250	.583	53	-1	-1	106	118	1	.545	0	1	-1	0	/S	0.0
	NY-N	104	373	44	113	20	0	5	35	52	29	.303	.394	.397	.791	119	13	12	103	82	60	.775	6			4	3S	1.8
1942	NY-N	90	316	53	77	10	3	5	24	44	34	.244	.351	.342	.692	100	3	2	103	77	41	.669	4			10	3S	1.5
1943	NY-N	99	337	48	91	14	0	5	28	47	27	.270	.371	.356	.727	115	6	8	96	76	47	.705	5			9	3S	2.1
1946	NY-N	5	2	0	0	0	0	0	0	0	0	.000	.000	.000	.000	-99	-1	-1	102	0	0	.000	0			0	/32	0.0
Total	18	2016	7629	1130	2165	442	71	79	710	748	627	.284	.355	.391	.747	96	13	-35	105	77	1107	.721	109	3		163	*S32	25.2
■ TONY BARTIROME	Bartirome, Anthony Joseph b: 5/9/32, Pittsburgh, Pa. BL/TL, 5'10", 155 lbs. Deb: 4/19/52 C																											
1952	Pit-N	124	355	32	78	10	3	0	16	26	37	.220	.273	.265	.538	50	-24	-24	100	66	28	.439	3	3	-1	-2	*1	-3.1
■ BOYD BARTLEY	Bartley, Boyd Owen b: 2/11/20, Chicago, Ill. BR/TR, 5'8.5", 165 lbs. Deb: 5/30/43																											
1943	Bro-N	9	21	0	1	0	0	0	1	1	3	.048	.091	.048	.139	-60	-4	-4	100	361	0	.100	0			-0	/S	-0.3
■ IRV BARTLING	Bartling, Irving Henry b: 6/27/14, Bay City, Mich. d: 6/12/73, Westland, Mich. BR/TR, 6', 175 lbs. Deb: 9/08/38																											
1938	Phi-A	14	46	5	8	1	1	0	5	3	7	.174	.224	.239	.464	16	-6	-6	101	154	3	.368	0	0	0	-3	S/3	-0.7
■ HARRY BARTON	Barton, Harry Lamb b: 1/20/1875, Chester, Pa. d: 1/25/55, Upland, Pa. BB/TR, 5'6.5", 155 lbs. Deb: 4/15/05																											
1905	Phi-A	29	60	5	10	2	1	0	3	3		.167	.206	.233	.440	37	-4	-5	109	76	3	.380	2			-1	C/13O	-0.4
■ BOB BARTON	Barton, Robert Wilbur b: 7/30/41, Norwood, O. BR/TR, 6', 175 lbs. Deb: 9/17/65																											
1965	SF-N	4	7	1	4	0	0	0	1	0	0	.571	.571	.571	1.143	202	1	1	111	104	2	1.333	0	0	0	0	/C	0.1
1966	SF-N	43	91	1	16	2	1	0	3	5	5	.176	.219	.220	.439	23	-9	-9	97	63	4	.325	0	0	0	-2	C	-1.0
1967	SF-N	7	19	0	4	0	0	0	1	0	2	.211	.250	.211	.461	33	-2	-2	101	104	1	.313	0	0	0	0	/C	0.0
1968	SF-N	46	92	4	24	2	0	0	5	7	18	.261	.313	.283	.596	82	-2	-2	98	81	9	.478	0	0	0	-2	C	-0.2
1969	SF-N	49	106	5	18	2	0	0	1	9	19	.170	.241	.189	.430	22	-11	-11	101	20	5	.326	0	0	0	-4	C	-1.2
1970	SD-N	61	188	15	41	6	0	4	16	15	37	.218	.279	.314	.593	62	-11	-10	95	87	16	.500	1	1	-0	-1	C	-0.8
1971	SD-N	121	376	23	94	17	2	5	23	35	49	.250	.317	.346	.663	91	-6	-4	96	65	36	.551	0	5	-3	5	*C	0.0
1972	SD-N	29	88	1	17	1	0	0	9	2	19	.193	.211	.205	.416	21	-9	-8	88	205	4	.297	2	0	1	-1	C	-0.6
1973	Cin-N	3	1	0	0	0	0	0	0	1	0	.000	.500	.000	.500	53	0	0	93	0	0	1.000	0	0	0	0	/C	0.0
1974	SD-N	30	81	4	19	1	0	0	7	13	19	.235	.340	.247	.587	71	-3	-2	93	135	8	.516	0	0	0	1	C	0.0
Total	10	393	1049	54	237	31	3	9	66	87	168	.226	.288	.287	.575	65	-52	-48	96	83	85	.483	3	6	-3	-5	C	-3.7
■ VINCE BARTON	Barton, Vincent David b: 2/1/08, Edmonton, Alberta, Canada d: 9/13/73, Toronto, Ont., Can BL/TR, 6', 180 lbs. Deb: 7/17/31																											
1931	Chi-N	66	239	45	57	10	1	13	50	21	40	.238	.323	.452	.775	111	1	3	96	124	36	.764	1			-4	O	-0.4
1932	Chi-N	36	134	19	30	2	3	3	15	8	22	.224	.273	.351	.623	64	-7	-7	104	102	13	.538	0			-2	O	-1.1
Total	2	102	373	64	87	12	4	16	65	29	62	.233	.306	.416	.721	93	-5	-5	99	116	50	.682	1			-6	/O	-1.5
■ DAVE BARTOSCH	Bartosch, David Robert b: 3/24/17, St.Louis, Mo. BR/TR, 6'1", 190 lbs. Deb: 4/28/45																											
1945	StL-N	24	47	9	12	1	0	0	1	6	3	.255	.340	.277	.616	72	-2	-2	100	27	5	.543	0			0	O	-0.1
■ MONTY BASGALL	Basgall, Romanus b: 2/8/22, Pfeifer, Kan. BR/TR, 5'10.5", 175 lbs. Deb: 4/19/48 C																											
1948	Pit-N	38	51	12	11	1	0	2	6	3	5	.216	.259	.353	.612	61	-3	-3	104	94	5	.512	0			1	2	0.0
1949	Pit-N	107	308	25	67	9	1	2	26	31	32	.218	.291	.273	.564	52	-21	-21	101	109	25	.472	1			-2	2/3	-1.9
1951	Pit-N	55	153	15	32	5	2	0	9	12	14	.209	.271	.268	.539	43	-12	-13	107	85	10	.415	0	0	0	2	2	-0.9
Total	3	200	512	52	110	15	3	4	41	46	51	.215	.282	.279	.561	50	-35	-37	103	100	40	.467	1	0		-0	2/3	-2.8
■ AL BASHANG	Bashang, Albert C. b: 8/22/1888, Cincinnati, Ohio d: 6/23/67, Cincinnati, Ohio BB/TR, 5'8", 150 lbs. Deb: 7/30/12																											
1912	Det-A	6	12	3	1	0	0	0	0	3		.083	.267	.083	.350	2	-1	-1	95	0	0	.364	0			-2	/O	-0.3
1918	Bro-N	2	5	0	1	0	0	0	0	0	0	.200	.200	.200	.400	22	-0	-0	101	0	0	.250	0			0	/O	0.0
Total	2	8	17	3	2	0	0	0	0	3	0	.118	.250	.118	.368	8	-2	-2	96	0	0	.333	0			-1	/O	-0.3
■ WALT BASHORE	Bashore, Walter Franklin (born Walter Franklin Beshore) b: 10/6/09, Harrisburg, Pa. d: 9/26/84, Sebring, Fla. BR/TR, 6', 170 lbs. Deb: 7/14/36																											
1936	Phi-N	10	10	1	2	0	0	0	0	1	3	.200	.273	.200	.473	27	-1	-1	108	0	1	.375	0			-3	/O3	-0.3
■ EDDIE BASINSKI	Basinski, Edwin Frank "Bazooka" or "Fiddler" b: 11/4/22, Buffalo, N.Y. BR/TR, 6'1", 172 lbs. Deb: 5/20/44																											
1944	Bro-N	39	105	13	27	4	1	0	9	6	10	.257	.310	.314	.624	77	-3	-3	99	98	11	.532	1			-6	2/S	-0.4
1945	Bro-N	108	336	30	88	9	4	0	33	11	33	.262	.293	.313	.606	71	-15	-13	96	109	29	.463	0			-9	*S/2	-1.0
1947	Pit-N	56	161	15	32	6	2	4	17	18	27	.199	.279	.335	.615	62	-9	-9	101	95	15	.537	0			-10	2	-1.2
Total	3	203	602	58	147	19	7	4	59	35	70	.244	.292	.319	.611	70	-27	-25	98	103	55	.509	1			-24	S/2	-2.6
■ JOHN BASS	Bass, John E. b: 1850, Baltimore, Md. 5'6", 150 lbs. Deb: 5/04/1871																											
1871	Cle-n	22	91	18	25							.275															*3	
1872	Atl-n	1	4	0	1							.250															/O	
1877	Har-N	1	4	1	1	0	0	0	0	0	0	.250	.250	.250	.500	65	-0	-0	89	0	0	.333				0	/O	0.0
Total	2 n	23	95	18	26							.274															/O	
■ KEVIN BASS	Bass, Kevin Charles b: 5/12/59, Menlo Park, Cal. BB/TR, 6', 183 lbs. Deb: 4/09/82																											
1982	Mil-A	18	9	4	0	0	0	0	0	1	1	.000	.100	.000	.100	-74	-2	-2	94	0	0	.111	0	0	0	-5	O/D	-0.7
	Hou-N	12	24	2	1	0	0	0	1	0	8	.042	.042	.042	.083	-77	-6	-6	99	392	0	.042	0	0	0	-1	/O	-0.6
1983	Hou-N	88	195	25	46	7	3	2	18	6	27	.236	.259	.333	.592	70	-10	-8	90	100	16	.477	2	2	-1	-8	O	-1.7
1984	Hou-N	121	331	33	86	17	5	2	29	6	57	.260	.279	.360	.639	85	-10	-8	93	91	32	.528	5	5	-2	0	O	-1.2
1985	Hou-N	150	539	72	145	27	5	16	68	31	63	.269	.316	.427	.743	110	3	5	96	99	71	.694	19	8	1	1	*O	0.3
1986	Hou-N	157	591	83	184	33	5	20	79	38	72	.311	.359	.486	.845	127	23	21	103	96	97	.811	22	13	-1	0	*O	1.8
1987	Hou-N	157	592	83	168	31	5	19	85	53	77	.284	.347	.449	.796	117	7	13	93	111	90	.770	21	8	2	7	*O	1.4
1988	Hou-N	157	541	57	138	27	2	14	72	42	65	.255	.316	.390	.706	109	0	5	93	116	66	.682	31	6	6	-3	*O	0.4
Total	7	860	2822	359	768	142	25	73	352	177	370	.272	.321	.418	.739	108	5	20	95	106	372	.701	100	42	5	-8	O/D	-0.3
■ RANDY BASS	Bass, Randy William b: 3/13/54, Lawton, Okla. BL/TR, 6'1", 210 lbs. Deb: 9/03/77																											
1977	Min-A	9	19	0	2	0	0	0	0	0	5	.105	.105	.105	.211	-41	-4	-4	103	0	0	.118	0	0	0	0	/D	-0.3
1978	KC-A	2	2	0	0	0	0	0	0	0	0	.000	.000	.000	.000	-98	-1	-1	102	0	0	.000	0	0	0	0	H	0.0
1979	Mon-N	2	1	0	0	0	0	0	0	0	0	.000	.000	.000	.000	-98	-0	-0	102	0	0	.000	0	0	0	0	/1	0.0
1980	SD-N	19	49	5	14	0	1	3	8	7	7	.286	.386	.510	.896	159	3	4	93	93	10	.943	0	0	0	0	1	0.3
1981	SD-N	69	176	13	37	4	1	4	20	20	28	.210	.294	.313	.607	77	-6	-5	93	117	15	.517	0	1	-1	-1	1	-0.8
1982	SD-N	13	30	1	6	0	0	1	8	2	4	.200	.273	.300	.573	65	-2	-1	92	261	3	.500	0	0	0	-0	/1	-0.1

YEAR	TM/L	G	AB	R	H	2B	3B	HR	RBI	BB	SO	AVG	OBP	SLG	PRO	/A	BR	/A	PF	CHI	RC	TA	SB	CS	SBR	FR	POS	TPR
	Tex-A	16	48	5	10	2	0	1	6	1	7	.208	.240	.313	.553	54	-3	-3	93	133	4	.436	0	0	0	-0	/1D	-0.2
Total	6	130	325	24	69	6	2	9	42	30	51	.212	.287	.326	.613	76	-12	-10	94	122	32	.543	0	1	-1	-1	/1D	-1.1

■ DOC BASS Bass, Williams Capers (Also Played One Game In 1918 Under Name Of Johnson) b: 12/4/1899, Macon, Ga. d: 1/12/70, Macon, Ga. BL/TL, 5'10", 165 lbs. Deb: 7/29/18

YEAR	TM/L	G	AB	R	H	2B	3B	HR	RBI	BB	SO	AVG	OBP	SLG	PRO	/A	BR	/A	PF	CHI	RC	TA	SB	CS	SBR	FR	POS	TPR
1918	Bos-N	2	1	1	1	0	0	0	0	0	0	1.000	1.000	1.000	2.000	545	0	0	94	0	2	—	1			0	/H	0.1

■ CHARLEY BASSETT Bassett, Charles Edwin b: 2/9/1863, Central Falls, R.I. d: 5/28/42, Pawtucket, R.I. BR/TR, 5'10", 150 lbs. Deb: 7/22/1884

YEAR	TM/L	G	AB	R	H	2B	3B	HR	RBI	BB	SO	AVG	OBP	SLG	PRO	/A	BR	/A	PF	CHI	RC	TA	SB	CS	SBR	FR	POS	TPR
1884	Pro-N	27	79	10	11	2	1	0	6	4	15	.139	.181	.190	.371	16	-7	-8	102	138	3	.279				0	3/SO2	-0.6
1885	Pro-N	82	285	21	41	8	2	0	16	19	60	.144	.197	.186	.383	27	-23	-20	91	107	11	.295				-5	2S3/C	-1.9
1886	KC-N	90	342	41	89	19	8	2	32	36	43	.260	.331	.380	.711	109	7	3	107	74	46	.680	6			7	S/3	0.9
1887	Ind-N	119	452	41	104	14	6	1	47	25	31	.230	.278	.294	.572	63	-23	-20	96	113	45	.540	25			13	*2	0.0
1888	Ind-N	128	481	58	116	20	3	2	60	32	41	.241	.297	.308	.604	100	-2	1	95	148	52	.575	24			-17	*2	-1.0
1889	Ind-N	127	477	64	117	12	5	4	68	37	38	.245	.304	.317	.620	69	-16	-23	109	127	52	.572	15			4	*2	-0.6
1890	NY-N	100	410	52	98	13	8	0	54	29	25	.239	.300	.310	.610	84	-11	-7	95	123	43	.567	14			13	*2	0.8
1891	NY-N	130	524	60	136	19	8	4	68	36	29	.260	.312	.349	.661	101	-5	0	94	108	64	.616	16			4	*3/2	0.7
1892	NY-N	35	130	9	27	2	3	0	16	6	10	.208	.254	.269	.523	61	-6	-6	98	143	9	.417	0			-0	2/3	-0.5
	Lou-N	79	313	36	67	5	5	2	35	15	19	.214	.250	.281	.531	67	-15	-11	92	121	27	.484	16			-1	3/2	-0.6
	Yr	114	443	45	94	7	8	2	51	21	29	.212	.251	.278	.529	65	-21	-18	94	129	36	.464	16			-1		-1.1
Total	9	917	3493	392	806	114	49	15	402	239	311	.231	.285	.304	.590	78	-101	-90	98	118	351	.538	116			17	23S/OC	-2.8

■ JOHNNY BASSLER Bassler, John Landis b: 6/3/1885, Mechanics Grove, Pa. d: 6/29/79, Santa Monica, Cal BL/TR, 5'9", 170 lbs. Deb: 7/11/13 C

YEAR	TM/L	G	AB	R	H	2B	3B	HR	RBI	BB	SO	AVG	OBP	SLG	PRO	/A	BR	/A	PF	CHI	RC	TA	SB	CS	SBR	FR	POS	TPR
1913	Cle-A	1	2	0	0	0	0	0	0	0	0	.000	.000	.000	.000	-95	-0	-1	106	0	0	.000	0			0	/C	0.0
1914	Cle-A	43	77	5	14	1	1	0	6	15	8	.182	.323	.221	.543	62	-3	-3	102	132	6	.554	3	2	-0	1	C/3O	0.0
1921	Det-A	119	388	37	119	18	5	0	56	58	16	.307	.401	.379	.780	104	3	5	96	131	63	.778	2	1	0	-5	*C	0.3
1922	Det-A	121	372	41	120	14	0	0	41	62	12	.323	.422	.360	.782	108	7	8	98	109	62	.791	2	1	0	-8	*C	0.4
1923	Det-A	135	383	45	114	12	3	0	49	76	13	.298	.414	.345	.759	105	5	7	97	127	61	.775	2	2	-1	1	*C	1.6
1924	Det-A	124	379	43	131	20	3	1	68	62	11	.346	.441	.422	.864	124	17	17	100	138	76	.912	2	1	0	-6	*C	1.8
1925	Det-A	121	344	40	96	19	3	0	52	74	6	.279	.408	.352	.760	95	1	1	99	144	56	.791	1	1	-0	-11	*C	-0.2
1926	Det-A	66	174	20	53	8	1	0	22	45	6	.305	.447	.362	.810	116	7	8	97	119	33	.893	0	0	0	-4	C	0.8
1927	Det-A	81	200	19	57	7	0	0	24	45	9	.285	.416	.320	.736	86	1	-2	108	125	30	.769	1	0	0	1	C	0.1
Total	9	811	2319	250	704	99	16	1	318	437	81	.304	.416	.361	.777	104	37	42	99	128	387	.800	13	8		-30	C/O3	4.8

■ CHARLIE BASTIAN Bastian, Charles J. b: 7/4/1860, Philadelphia, Pa. d: 1/18/32, Pennsauken, N.J. BR/TR, 5'6.5", 145 lbs. Deb: 8/18/1884

YEAR	TM/L	G	AB	R	H	2B	3B	HR	RBI	BB	SO	AVG	OBP	SLG	PRO	/A	BR	/A	PF	CHI	RC	TA	SB	CS	SBR	FR	POS	TPR
1884	WiL-U	17	60	6	12	1	3	2		3		.200	.238	.417	.655	114	1	1	103	0	6	.583	0			0	2/PS	0.1
	KC-U	11	46	6	9	3	0	1		4		.196	.260	.326	.586	112	-0	1	87	0	4	.514	0			0	2	0.1
	Yr	28	106	12	21	4	3	3		7		.198	.248	.377	.625	112	1	2	97	0	10	.553	0			0		0.2
1885	Phi-N	103	389	63	65	11	5	4	29	35	82	.167	.236	.252	.488	56	-17	-19	104	88	24	.410				-1	*S	-1.3
1886	Phi-N	105	373	46	81	9	11	2	38	33	73	.217	.281	.316	.597	83	-8	-7	98	102	42	.616	29			-8	*2S/3	-0.9
1887	Phi-N	60	221	33	47	11	1	1	21	19	29	.213	.284	.285	.569	62	-11	-10	97	100	22	.552	11			-7	2S/3	-1.2
1888	Phi-N	80	275	30	53	4	1	1	17	27	41	.193	.282	.225	.507	57	-9	-14	114	95	21	.486	12			13	23/S	0.0
1889	Chi-N	46	155	19	21	0	0	0	10	25	46	.135	.256	.135	.391	12	-17	-17	99	142	6	.351	1			-2	S/2	-1.5
1890	Chi-P	80	283	38	54	10	5	0	29	33	37	.191	.287	.261	.548	46	-20	-23	104	109	23	.507	4			-11	S2/3	-2.3
1891	CM-a	1	4	0	0	0	0	0	0	0	0	.000	.000	.000	.000	-90	-1	-1	112	0	0	.000	0			0	/2	0.0
	Phi-N	1	0	0	0	0	0	0	0	0	0	—	—	—	—	—	0	0	95	—	—	—	0			0	/S	0.0
Total	8	504	1806	241	342	49	26	11	144	179	308	.189	.268	.264	.532	59	-84	-90	102	97	148	.497	57			-16	S2/3P	-7.0

■ EMIL BATCH Batch, Emil "Heinie" or "Ace" b: 1/21/1880, Brooklyn, N.Y. d: 8/23/26, Brooklyn, N.Y. BR/TR, 5'7", 170 lbs. Deb: 9/13/04

YEAR	TM/L	G	AB	R	H	2B	3B	HR	RBI	BB	SO	AVG	OBP	SLG	PRO	/A	BR	/A	PF	CHI	RC	TA	SB	CS	SBR	FR	POS	TPR
1904	Bro-N	28	94	9	24	1	2	2	7	1		.255	.263	.372	.635	102	-1	-0	95	62	11	.600	6			-1	3	0.0
1905	Bro-N	145	568	64	143	20	11	5	49	26		.252	.285	.352	.637	95	-8	-5	96	76	64	.581	21			-8	*3	-0.2
1906	Bro-N	59	203	23	52	7	6	0	11	15		.256	.307	.350	.657	123	1	4	87	58	23	.589	3			0	O/3	0.4
1907	Bro-N	116	388	38	96	10	3	0	31	23		.247	.290	.289	.578	88	-8	-5	94	107	35	.486	7			9	*O/23S	0.0
Total	4	348	1253	134	315	38	22	7	98	65		.251	.288	.334	.622	98	-15	-7	94	82	134	.554	37			-0	3O/2S	0.2

■ JOHN BATEMAN Bateman, John Alvin b: 7/21/42, Killeen, Tex. BR/TR, 6'3", 210 lbs. Deb: 4/19/63

YEAR	TM/L	G	AB	R	H	2B	3B	HR	RBI	BB	SO	AVG	OBP	SLG	PRO	/A	BR	/A	PF	CHI	RC	TA	SB	CS	SBR	FR	POS	TPR
1963	Hou-N	128	404	23	85	8	6	10	59	13	103	.210	.251	.334	.585	73	-18	-14	92	150	33	.479	0	0	0	10	*C	0.0
1964	Hou-N	74	221	18	42	8	0	5	19	17	48	.190	.251	.294	.545	55	-14	-13	96	97	14	.439	0	1	-1	6	C	-0.4
1965	Hou-N	45	142	15	28	3	1	7	14	12	37	.197	.260	.380	.640	88	-5	-3	89	77	11	.532	0	1	-1	5	C	0.3
1966	Hou-N	131	433	39	121	24	3	17	70	20	74	.279	.319	.467	.785	118	8	9	97	116	58	.690	0	0	0	10	*C	2.2
1967	Hou-N	76	252	16	48	9	0	2	17	17	53	.190	.247	.250	.497	46	-19	-17	94	102	14	.385	0	0	0	4	C	-0.9
1968	Hou-N	111	350	28	87	19	0	4	33	23	46	.249	.301	.337	.638	92	-4	-4	99	107	31	.518	1	1	-0	-9	*C	-0.9
1969	Mon-N	74	235	16	49	4	0	8	19	12	44	.209	.250	.328	.578	60	-13	-13	100	75	17	.462	0	2	-1	1	C	-0.9
1970	Mon-N	139	520	51	123	21	5	15	68	28	75	.237	.277	.383	.660	75	-20	-21	100	110	51	.567	8	4	0	8	*C	-0.6
1971	Mon-N	139	492	34	119	17	3	10	56	19	87	.242	.276	.350	.625	77	-17	-16	99	115	40	.490	1	0	0	-1	*C	-1.4
1972	Mon-N	18	29	0	7	1	0	0	3	3	4	.241	.313	.276	.588	67	-1	-1	102	154	2	.478	0	0	0	-0	/C	0.0
	Phi-N	82	252	10	56	9	0	3	17	8	39	.222	.249	.294	.543	55	-16	-15	97	84	17	.413	0	1	-1	-6	C	-1.7
	Yr	100	281	10	63	10	0	3	20	11	43	.224	.256	.292	.548	56	-17	-16	98	98	20	.422	0	1	-1	-6		-1.7
Total	10	1017	3330	250	765	123	18	81	375	172	610	.230	.273	.350	.624	77	-118	-107	97	109	289	.534	10	10	-3	28	C	-4.3

■ CHARLIE BATES Bates, Charles William b: 9/17/07, Philadelphia, Pa. d: 1/29/80, Topeka, Kan. BR/TR, 5'10", 165 lbs. Deb: 9/22/27

YEAR	TM/L	G	AB	R	H	2B	3B	HR	RBI	BB	SO	AVG	OBP	SLG	PRO	/A	BR	/A	PF	CHI	RC	TA	SB	CS	SBR	FR	POS	TPR
1927	Phi-A	9	38	5	9	2	2	0	2	3	5	.237	.293	.395	.687	80	-1	-1	97	43	4	.724	3	0	1	-1	/O	-0.2

■ DEL BATES Bates, Delbert Oakley b: 6/12/40, Seattle, Wash. BL/TR, 6'2", 195 lbs. Deb: 5/06/70

YEAR	TM/L	G	AB	R	H	2B	3B	HR	RBI	BB	SO	AVG	OBP	SLG	PRO	/A	BR	/A	PF	CHI	RC	TA	SB	CS	SBR	FR	POS	TPR
1970	Phi-N	22	60	1	8	2	0	0	1	6	15	.133	.257	.167	.424	17	-7	-7	96	39	3	.364	0	1	-1	-1	C	-0.7

■ BUD BATES Bates, Hubert Edgar b: 3/16/12, Los Angeles, Cal. d: 4/19/87, Long Beach, Cal. BR/TR, 6', 165 lbs. Deb: 9/16/39

YEAR	TM/L	G	AB	R	H	2B	3B	HR	RBI	BB	SO	AVG	OBP	SLG	PRO	/A	BR	/A	PF	CHI	RC	TA	SB	CS	SBR	FR	POS	TPR
1939	Phi-N	15	58	8	15	2	0	1	2	2	8	.259	.283	.345	.628	72	-3	-2	94	34	5	.500	1			3	O	0.1

■ JOHNNY BATES Bates, John William b: 8/21/1882, Steubenville, Ohio d: 2/10/49, Steubenville, Ohio BL/TL, 5'7", 168 lbs. Deb: 4/12/06

YEAR	TM/L	G	AB	R	H	2B	3B	HR	RBI	BB	SO	AVG	OBP	SLG	PRO	/A	BR	/A	PF	CHI	RC	TA	SB	CS	SBR	FR	POS	TPR
1906	Bos-N	140	504	52	127	21	5	6	54	36		.252	.302	.349	.651	105	2	1	100	108	57	.586	9			-9	*O	-1.1
1907	Bos-N	126	447	52	116	18	12	2	49	39		.260	.319	.367	.686	123	8	10	95	111	57	.647	11			-11	*O	-0.6
1908	Bos-N	127	445	48	115	14	6	1	29	35		.258	.313	.324	.636	102	3	1	104	77	51	.618	25			-1	*O	-0.1
1909	Bos-N	63	236	27	68	15	3	1	23	20		.288	.354	.390	.744	138	9	10	96	78	37	.780	15			3	O	1.1
	Phi-N	77	266	43	78	11	1	1	15	28		.293	.365	.353	.718	117	8	6	106	60	41	.777	22			2	O	0.6
	Yr	140	502	70	146	26	4	2	38	48		.291	.360	.371	.730	126	17	16	102	68	78	.778	37			4		1.7
1910	Phi-N	135	498	91	152	26	11	3	61	61	49	.305	.385	.420	.805	141	22	25	96	94	93	.882	31			6	*O	2.8
1911	Cin-N	148	518	89	151	24	13	1	61	103	59	.292	.415	.394	.808	138	24	30	92	106	99	.943	33			-0	*O	2.5
1912	Cin-N	81	239	45	69	12	7	1	29	47	16	.289	.406	.410	.816	134	10	12	92	97	45	.912	10			10	O	1.9
1913	Cin-N	131	407	63	113	13	7	6	51	67	30	.278	.387	.388	.776	120	14	14	102	107	67	.857	21			2	*O	1.4
1914	Cin-N	58	155	29	39	7	5	2	15	28	17	.252	.380	.400	.780	126	7	6	105	80	25	.845	4			-5	O	0.0
	Chi-N	9	8	2	1	0	0	0	1	1	1	.125	.300	.125	.425	28	-1	-1	98	363	0	.429	0			-0	/O	0.0
	Yr	67	163	31	40	7	5	2	16	29	18	.245	.376	.387	.762	122	7	6	104	119	25	.821	4			-5		0.0
	Bal-F	59	190	24	58	6	3	1	29	38	18	.305	.421	.384	.805	133	10	10	99	146	35	.886	6			-3	O	0.4
Total	9	1154	3913	565	1087	167	73	25	417	503	190	.278	.364	.377	.741	124	116	126	98	98	608	.776	187			-9	*O	8.9

■ RAY BATES Bates, Raymond b: 2/8/1890, Paterson, N.J. d: 8/15/70, Tucson, Ariz. BR/TR, 6', 165 lbs. Deb: 5/31/13

YEAR	TM/L	G	AB	R	H	2B	3B	HR	RBI	BB	SO	AVG	OBP	SLG	PRO	/A	BR	/A	PF	CHI	RC	TA	SB	CS	SBR	FR	POS	TPR
1913	Cle-A	27	30	4	5	0	2	0	4	3	9	.167	.265	.300	.565	62	-1	-2	106	158	3	.640	3			-1	3/O	-0.1
1917	Phi-A	127	485	47	115	20	7	2	66	21	39	.237	.277	.320	.597	88	-12	-9	94	**156**	45	.524	12			6	*3	0.2
Total	2	154	515	51	120	20	9	2	70	24	48	.233	.277	.318	.595	86	-14	-11	94	156	47	.532	15			5	3/O	0.1

YEAR	TM/L	G	AB	R	H	2B	3B	HR	RBI	BB	SO	AVG	OBP	SLG	PRO	/A	BR	/A	PF	CHI	RC	TA	SB	CS	SBR	FR	POS	TPR
■ BILL BATHE	Bathe, William David b: 10/14/60, Downey, Cal. BR/TR, 6'2", 200 lbs. Deb: 4/12/86																											
1986	Oak-A	39	103	9	19	3	0	5	11	2	20	.184	.208	.359	.567	55	-7	-6	94	84	7	.465	0	0	0	-4	C	-0.7
■ RAFAEL BATISTA	Batista, Rafael (Sanchez) b: 10/20/47, San Pedro De Macoris, D.R. BL/TL, 6'1", 195 lbs. Deb: 6/17/73																											
1973	Hou-N	12	15	2	4	0	0	0	2	1	6	.267	.313	.267	.579	65	-1	-1	95	201	1	.455	0	0	0	0	/1	0.0
1975	Hou-N	10	10	0	3	1	0	0	0	0	4	.300	.300	.400	.700	99	-0	-0	94	0	1	.500	0	0	0	0	H	0.0
Total	2	22	25	2	7	1	0	0	2	1	10	.280	.308	.320	.628	78	-1	-1	95	124	2	.474	0	0	0	0	/1	0.0
■ BILL BATSCH	Batsch, William Mc Kinley b: 5/18/1892, Mingo Junction, O. d: 12/31/63, Canton, Ohio BR/TR, 5'10.5", 168 lbs. Deb: 9/09/16																											
1916	Pit-N	1	0	0	0	0	0	0	0	1	0	—	1.000	—	1.320	301	0	0	105	0	0	—	0			0	H	0.0
■ LARRY BATTAM	Battam, Lawrence J. b: 5/1/1878, Brooklyn, N.Y. d: 1/27/38, Brooklyn, N.Y. 5'11", Deb: 9/28/1895																											
1895	NY-N	2	4	0	1	0	0	0	0	2	1	.250	.500	.250	.750	105	0	0	95	0	1	1.000	0			0	/3	0.0
■ GEORGE BATTEN	Batten, George Burnett b: 10/7/1891, Haddonfield, N.J. d: 8/4/72, New Port Richey, Fla. BR/TR, 5'11", 165 lbs. Deb: 9/28/12																											
1912	NY-A	1	3	0	0	0	0	0	0	0		.000	.000	.000	.000	-99	-1	-1	101	0	0	.000	0			0	/2	0.0
■ EARL BATTEY	Battey, Earl Jesse b: 1/5/35, Los Angeles, Cal. BR/TR, 6'1", 205 lbs. Deb: 9/10/55																											
1955	Chi-A	5	7	1	2	0	0	0	0	1	1	.286	.444	.286	.730	99	0	0	101	0	1	.667	0	0	0	-0	/C	0.0
1956	Chi-A	4	4	1	1	0	0	0	0	1	1	.250	.400	.250	.650	72	-0	-0	104	0	0	.400	0	0	0	0	/C	0.0
1957	Chi-A	48	115	12	20	2	3	3	6	11	38	.174	.246	.322	.568	54	-8	-8	99	51	8	.480	0	2	-1	-1	C	-0.7
1958	Chi-A	68	168	24	38	8	0	8	26	24	34	.226	.330	.417	.747	106	1	1	98	111	24	.729	1	0	0	2	C	0.5
1959	Chi-A	26	64	9	14	1	2	2	7	8	13	.219	.306	.391	.696	93	-1	-1	97	89	8	.660	0	0	0	0	C	0.1
1960	Was-A	137	466	49	126	24	2	15	60	48	68	.270	.349	.427	.776	107	6	4	102	96	67	.719	4	5	-2	12	*C	2.2
1961	Min-A	133	460	70	139	24	1	17	55	53	66	.302	.378	.470	.847	118	17	13	106	82	78	.804	3	3	-1	9	*C	1.9
1962	Min-A	148	522	58	146	20	3	11	57	57	48	.280	.351	.393	.743	95	0	-3	105	97	70	.662	0	0	0	-4	*C	0.1
1963	Min-A	147	508	64	145	17	1	26	84	61	75	.285	.371	.476	.847	135	25	25	100	112	89	.821	0	0	0	-5	*C	2.2
1964	Min-A	131	405	33	110	17	1	12	52	51	49	.272	.354	.407	.762	110	7	7	101	110	54	.683	1	1	-0	-25	*C	-1.3
1965	Min-A	131	394	36	117	22	2	6	60	50	23	.297	.379	.409	.788	122	14	13	101	139	63	.750	0	0	0	-16	*C	0.7
1966	Min-A	115	364	30	93	12	1	4	34	43	30	.255	.339	.327	.666	83	-2	-7	111	109	39	.589	4	1	1	-13	*C	-1.4
1967	Min-A	48	109	6	18	3	1	0	8	13	24	.165	.254	.211	.465	36	-8	-9	107	145	6	.379	0	0	0	-10	C	-1.7
Total	13	1141	3586	393	969	150	17	104	449	421	470	.270	.351	.409	.760	106	50	36	103	105	508	.732	13	12	-3	-50	*C	2.6
■ JOE BATTIN	Battin, Joseph V. b: 11/11/1851, Philadelphia, Pa. d: 12/10/37, Akron, Ohio BR/TR, Deb: 8/11/1871 M																											
1871	Cle-n	1	4	0	0							.000															/O	
1873	Ath-n	1	6	4	3							.500															/O	
1874	Ath-n	51	228	41	62							.272															*2/OS	
1875	StL-n	66	278	32	73							.263															*2/3	
1876	StL-N	64	283	34	85	11	4	0	46	6	6	.300	.315	.367	.682	145	8	13	88	144	34	.556				14	*3/2	2.2
1877	StL-N	57	226	28	45	3	7	1	22	6	17	.199	.220	.288	.507	58	-10	-11	102	116	15	.392				-2	32/OP	-0.8
1882	Pit-a	34	133	13	28	5	1	1		3		.211	.228	.286	.514	74	-4	-3	97	0	9	.390				18	3	1.2
1883	Pit-a	98	388	42	83	9	6	1		11		.214	.236	.276	.511	69	-15	-11	94	0	26	.387				28	*3/PM	1.6
1884	Pit-a	43	158	10	28	1	2	0		3		.177	.198	.209	.406	36	-11	-10	97	0	7	.285				7	3M	-0.2
	CP-U	18	69	8	13	2	0	0		0		.188	.188	.217	.406	37	-4	-4	99	0	3	.268	0			0	3M	-0.3
	Bal-U	17	59	3	6	1	0	0		0		.102	.102	.119	.220	-23	-7	-8	110	0	1	.132	0			0	3	-0.6
	Yr	35	128	11	19	3	0	0		0		.148	.148	.172	.320	8	-12	-13	105	0	3	.202	0			0		-0.9
1890	Syr-a	29	119	15	25	2	1	0		8		.210	.260	.244	.504	56	-7	-6	90	0	10	.479	8			0	3	-0.4
Total	4 n	119	516	77	138							.267															3	
Total	6	360	1435	153	313	34	21	3	68	37	23	.218	.238	.277	.516	70	-52	-41	95	46	103	.396	8			65	32/OSP	2.7
■ JIM BATTLE	Battle, James Milton b: 3/26/01, Bailey, Tex. d: 9/30/65, Chico, Cal. BR/TR, 6'1", 170 lbs. Deb: 9/09/27																											
1927	Chi-A	6	8	1	3	0	1	0	0	0	1	.375	.375	.625	1.000	153	1	1	102	0	2	1.000	0	0	0	0	/3S	0.1
■ MATT BATTS	Batts, Matthew Daniel b: 10/16/21, San Antonio, Tex. BR/TR, 5'11", 200 lbs. Deb: 9/10/47																											
1947	Bos-A	7	16	3	8	1	0	1	5	1	1	.500	.529	.750	1.279	235	3	3	108	123	7	1.625	0	0	0	0	/C	0.3
1948	Bos-A	46	118	13	37	12	0	1	24	15	9	.314	.391	.441	.832	121	4	4	100	147	21	.788	0	0	0	-1	C	0.6
1949	Bos-A	60	157	23	38	9	1	3	31	25	22	.242	.350	.369	.719	84	-2	-4	107	159	22	.691	1	0	0	-1	C	-0.1
1950	Bos-A	75	238	27	65	15	3	4	34	18	19	.273	.327	.412	.739	77	-5	-10	114	107	31	.646	0	0	0	-1	C	-0.7
1951	Bos-A	11	29	1	4	1	0	0	2	1	2	.138	.167	.172	.339	-8	-4	-5	108	143	1	.231	0	0	0	-1	C	-0.4
	StL-A	79	248	26	75	17	1	5	31	21	21	.302	.357	.440	.796	109	4	3	105	89	38	.725	2	0	1	5	C	1.2
	Yr	90	277	27	79	18	1	5	33	22	23	.285	.338	.412	.749	97	-0	-2	105	97	38	.667	2	0	1	4		0.8
1952	Det-A	56	173	11	41	4	1	3	13	14	22	.237	.298	.324	.622	74	-7	-6	99	75	17	.526	1	0	0	-1	C	-0.3
1953	Det-A	116	374	38	104	24	3	6	43	24	36	.278	.322	.406	.728	98	-4	-2	98	94	48	.631	2	3	-1	4	*C	0.4
1954	Det-A	12	21	1	6	1	0	0	5	2	4	.286	.348	.333	.681	87	-0	-0	100	271	3	.600	0	0	0	0	/C	0.0
	Chi-A	55	158	16	36	7	1	3	19	17	15	.228	.303	.342	.645	74	-5	-6	104	114	15	.538	0	1	-1	-1	C	-0.5
	Yr	67	179	17	42	8	1	3	24	19	19	.235	.308	.341	.649	75	-6	-6	103	146	17	.544	0	1	-1	-1		-0.5
1955	Cin-N	26	71	4	18	4	1	0	13	4	11	.254	.293	.338	.631	63	-3	-4	106	219	6	.500	0	0	0	0	C	-0.2
1956	Cin-N	3	2	0	0	0	0	0	0	0	1	.000	.333	.000	.333	0	-0	-0	108	0	0	.500	0	0	0	0	H	0.0
Total	10	546	1605	163	432	95	11	26	220	143	163	.269	.330	.391	.721	89	-20	-28	104	114	208	.662	6	4	-1	5	C	0.3
■ HANK BAUER	Bauer, Henry Albert b: 7/31/22, E.St.Louis, Ill. BR/TR, 6', 192 lbs. Deb: 9/06/48 MC																											
1948	NY-A	19	50	6	9	1	1	1	9	6	13	.180	.268	.300	.568	51	-4	-4	100	169	5	.537	1	0	0	-1	O	-0.4
1949	NY-A	103	301	56	82	6	6	10	45	37	42	.272	.354	.432	.786	107	2	2	100	96	47	.739	2	2	-1	-5	O	-0.5
1950	NY-A	113	415	72	133	16	2	13	70	35	41	.320	.380	.463	.843	116	9	9	99	107	75	.801	2	3	-1	1	*O	0.6
1951	NY-A	118	348	53	103	19	3	10	54	42	39	.296	.373	.454	.827	134	11	15	92	103	60	.802	5	2	0	-4	*O	0.6
1952	NY-A	141	553	86	162	31	6	17	74	50	61	.293	.355	.463	.818	129	18	19	98	95	91	.772	6	7	-2	-2	*O	1.1
1953	NY-A	133	437	77	133	20	6	10	57	59	45	.304	.394	.446	.841	136	18	22	93	94	81	.832	2	3	-1	-0	*O	1.7
1954	NY-A	114	377	73	111	16	5	12	54	40	42	.294	.362	.459	.821	125	11	12	99	98	63	.789	4	4	-1	-9	*O	0.0
1955	NY-A	139	492	97	137	20	5	20	53	56	65	.278	.362	.461	.823	123	13	14	98	70	86	.824	8	4	0	2	*O/C	1.0
1956	NY-A	147	539	96	130	18	7	26	84	59	72	.241	.318	.445	.764	101	-3	-2	99	101	77	.723	4	2	0	-9	*O	-1.7
1957	NY-A	137	479	70	124	22	9	18	65	42	64	.259	.324	.455	.779	118	5	9	94	96	71	.742	7	2	1	-11	*O	-0.9
1958	NY-A	128	452	62	121	22	6	12	50	32	56	.268	.318	.423	.740	99	-0	-2	103	88	60	.668	3	2	-0	-10	*O	-1.9
1959	NY-A	114	341	44	81	20	0	9	39	33	54	.238	.309	.375	.684	94	-7	-3	93	99	41	.628	4	2	0	-17	*O	-2.6
1960	KC-A	95	255	30	70	15	0	3	31	21	36	.275	.332	.369	.701	90	-4	-3	99	118	30	.597	1	0	0	-8	O	-1.3
1961	KC-A	43	106	11	28	3	1	3	18	9	8	.264	.322	.396	.718	89	-2	-2	102	138	14	.658	1	0	0	-5	OM	-0.7
Total	14	1544	5145	833	1424	229	57	164	703	521	638	.277	.347	.439	.786	114	68	87	97	97	801	.763	50	33	-5	-79	*O/C	-5.0
■ PADDY BAUMANN	Baumann, Charles John b: 12/20/1885, Indianapolis, Ind. d: 11/20/69, Indianapolis, Ind. BR/TR, 5'9", 160 lbs. Deb: 8/10/11																											
1911	Det-A	26	94	8	24	2	4	0	11	6		.255	.307	.362	.669	80	-2	-3	108	111	11	.600	1			2	2/O	0.0
1912	Det-A	13	42	3	11	1	0	0	7	6		.262	.354	.286	.640	88	-1	-0	95	195	6	.710	4			1	/32O	0.0
1913	Det-A	50	191	31	57	7	4	1	22	16	18	.298	.353	.393	.745	119	4	4	99	96	28	.709	4			-3	2	0.0
1914	Det-A	3	11	1	0	0	0	0	0	2	1	.000	.154	.000	.154	-52	-2	-2	102	0	0	.182	0			0	/2	-0.2
1915	NY-A	76	219	30	64	13	1	2	28	28	32	.292	.380	.388	.768	132	9	9	98	105	33	.758	9	10	-3	7	23/O	1.4
1916	NY-A	79	237	35	68	5	3	1	25	19	16	.287	.352	.346	.698	108	3	3	101	105	33	.686	10			-3	O3/2	0.0
1917	NY-A	49	110	10	24	2	1	0	8	4	9	.218	.246	.255	.500	49	-7	-7	107	103	7	.395	2			-3	2/O3	-1.0
Total	7	296	904	118	248	30	13	4	101	81	76	.274	.340	.350	.690	103	4	3	101	106	117	.655	30	10		0	2/3O	0.2
■ JIM BAUMER	Baumer, James Sloan b: 1/29/31, Tulsa, Okla. BR/TR, 6'2", 185 lbs. Deb: 9/14/49																											
1949	Chi-A	8	10	2	4	1	1	0	2	2	1	.400	.571	.700	1.271	241	2	2	98	98	5	1.833	0	0	0	0	/S	0.2
1961	Cin-N	10	24	0	3	0	0	0	0	0	9	.125	.125	.125	.250	-32	-5	-5	104	0	0	.143	0	0	0	-1	/2	-0.3

YEAR	TM/L	G	AB	R	H	2B	3B	HR	RBI	BB	SO	AVG	OBP	SLG	PRO	/A	BR	/A	PF	CHI	RC	TA	SB	CS	SBR	FR	POS	TPR
Total	2	18	34	2	7	1	1	0	2	2	10	.206	.289	.294	.584	54	-2	-2	102	36	5	.519	0	0	0	-1	/2S	-0.1
■ **JOHN BAUMGARTNER**	Baumgartner, John Edward b: 5/29/31, Birmingham, Ala. BR/TR, 6'1", 190 lbs. Deb: 4/14/53																											
1953	Det-A	7	27	3	5	0	0	0	2	0	5	.185	.185	.185	.370	0	-4	-4	98	148	1	.227	0	0	0	1	/3	-0.3
■ **FRANK BAUMHOLTZ**	Baumholtz, Frank Conrad b: 10/7/18, Midvale, Ohio BL/TL, 5'10.5", 175 lbs. Deb: 4/15/47																											
1947	Cin-N	151	643	96	182	32	9	5	45	56	53	.283	.341	.384	.726	102	-7	1	91	55	88	.664	6			-1	*O	-0.5
1948	Cin-N	128	415	57	123	19	5	4	30	27	32	.296	.344	.395	.739	96	-1	-2	103	64	57	.678	8			1	*O	-0.8
1949	Cin-N	27	81	12	19	5	3	1	8	6	8	.235	.295	.407	.703	90	-2	-1	96	84	10	.625	0			1	O	-0.1
	Chi-N	58	164	15	37	4	2	1	15	9	21	.226	.270	.293	.563	54	-12	-10	94	111	14	.472	2			-4	O	-1.6
	Yr	85	245	27	56	9	5	2	23	15	29	.229	.279	.331	.609	66	-13	-12	95	103	24	.529	2			-3		-1.7
1951	Chi-N	146	560	62	159	28	10	2	50	49	36	.284	.346	.380	.726	98	-3	-1	97	94	74	.644	5	4	-1	-21	*O	-2.7
1952	Chi-N	103	409	59	133	17	4	4	35	27	27	.325	.371	.416	.787	114	10	8	103	72	64	.712	5	7	-3	-1	*O	0.2
1953	Chi-N	133	520	75	159	36	7	3	25	42	36	.306	.359	.419	.778	99	2	-0	103	46	82	.715	3	3	-1	-16	*O	-2.1
1954	Chi-N	90	303	38	90	12	6	4	28	20	15	.297	.343	.416	.758	96	-2	-2	101	80	42	.670	1	3	-2	1	O	-0.4
1955	Chi-N	105	280	23	81	12	5	1	27	16	24	.289	.330	.379	.709	88	-5	-5	100	100	33	.589	0	1	-1	1	O	-0.5
1956	Phi-N	76	100	13	27	0	0	0	9	6	6	.270	.318	.270	.588	64	-5	-5	94	141	8	.436	0	2	-1	-1	O	-0.6
1957	Phi-N	2	2	0	0	0	0	0	0	0	0	.000	.000	.000	.000	-99	-1	-1	98	0	0	.000	0	0	0	0	H	0.0
Total	10	1019	3477	450	1010	165	51	25	272	258	258	.290	.342	.389	.731	96	-26	-19	99	74	470	.666	30	20		-40	O	-9.1
■ **JIM BAXES**	Baxes, Dimitrios Speros b: 7/5/28, San Francisco, Cal BR/TR, 6'1", 190 lbs. Deb: 4/11/59																											
1959	LA-N	11	33	4	10	1	0	2	5	4	7	.303	.395	.515	.910	138	2	2	102	88	6	.885	1	0	0	1	3	0.3
	Cle-A	77	247	35	59	11	0	15	34	21	47	.239	.299	.466	.764	110	1	2	97	84	30	.677	0	1	-1	-9	23	-0.5
Total	1	88	280	39	69	12	0	17	39	25	54	.246	.310	.471	.782	114	3	4	97	84	36	.710	1	1	-0	-8	/23	-0.2
■ **MIKE BAXES**	Baxes, Michael b: 12/18/30, San Francisco, Cal BR/TR, 5'10", 175 lbs. Deb: 4/17/56																											
1956	KC-A	73	106	9	24	3	1	1	5	18	15	.226	.339	.302	.641	70	-4	-4	101	53	12	.588	0	1	-1	2	S/2	0.3
1958	KC-A	73	231	31	49	10	1	0	8	21	24	.212	.286	.264	.550	50	-15	-16	106	53	17	.448	1	6	-3	4	2/S	-1.1
Total	2	146	337	40	73	13	2	1	13	39	39	.217	.303	.276	.579	56	-19	-20	104	53	29	.495	1	7	-4	6	/S2	-0.8
■ **JOHN BAXTER**	Baxter, John b: Spokane, Wash. Deb: 4/19/07																											
1907	StL-N	6	21	1	4	0	0	0	0	0		.190	.190	.190	.381	21	-2	-2	96	0	1	.235	0			0	/1	-0.1
■ **HARRY BAY**	Bay, Harry Elbert "Deerfoot" b: 1/17/1878, Pontiac, Ill. d: 3/20/52, Peoria, Ill. BL/TL, 5'8", 138 lbs. Deb: 7/23/01																											
1901	Cin-N	41	157	25	33	1	2	1	3	13		.210	.271	.261	.532	59	-8	-7	95	24	12	.468	4			2	O	-0.9
1902	Cin-N	6	16	3	6	0	0	0	1	2		.375	.444	.375	.819	142	1	1	110	58	3	.800	0			-0	/O	0.1
	Cle-A	108	455	71	132	10	5	0	23	36		.290	.342	.334	.676	93	-5	-3	97	43	61	.650	22			11	*O	0.1
1903	Cle-A	140	579	94	169	15	12	1	35	29		.292	.326	.364	.690	113	6	8	96	51	85	.695	**45**			4	*O	0.4
1904	Cle-A	132	506	69	122	12	9	3	36	43		.241	.301	.318	.619	97	-0	-1	102	76	61	.630	**38**			-4	*O	-1.5
1905	Cle-A	144	552	90	166	18	10	0	22	36		.301	.344	.370	.713	129	17	17	100	37	85	.715	36			-1	*O	1.0
1906	Cle-A	68	280	47	77	8	3	0	14	26		.275	.337	.325	.662	106	4	3	103	48	37	.660	17			-1	O	0.0
1907	Cle-A	34	95	14	17	1	1	0	7	10		.179	.257	.211	.468	55	-5	-4	93	125	7	.474	7			3	O	-0.2
1908	Cle-A	2	0	0	0	0	0	0	0	0		—	—	—	—	—	0	0	106	—	—	—	0			0	R	0.0
Total	8	675	2640	413	722	65	42	5	141	195		.273	.323	.336	.659	103	9	14	99	52	359	.652	169			13	O	-1.0
■ **DICK BAYLESS**	Bayless, Harry Owen b: 9/6/1883, Joplin, Mo. d: 12/16/20, Santa Rita, N.M. 5'9", 178 lbs. Deb: 9/09/08																											
1908	Cin-N	19	71	7	16	1	0	1	3	6		.225	.286	.282	.567	81	-1	-1	103	44	5	.473	0			0	O	-0.1
■ **DON BAYLOR**	Baylor, Don Edward b: 6/28/49, Austin, Tex. BR/TR, 6'1", 190 lbs. Deb: 9/18/70																											
1970	Bal-A	8	17	4	4	0	0	0	4	2	3	.235	.316	.235	.551	56	-1	-1	97	405	1	.500	1	1	-0	1	/O	0.0
1971	Bal-A	1	2	0	0	0	0	0	1	2	1	.000	.600	.000	.600	80	0	0	103	0	0	1.500	0	0	0	0	/O	0.1
1972	Bal-A	102	320	33	81	13	3	11	38	29	50	.253	.332	.416	.748	125	8	9	98	96	47	.780	24	2	6	-4	O/1	0.8
1973	Bal-A	118	405	64	116	20	4	11	51	35	48	.286	.362	.437	.799	116	13	9	107	95	65	.832	32	9	4	-4	*O/1D	0.6
1974	Bal-A	137	489	66	133	22	1	10	59	43	56	.272	.343	.382	.726	117	6	10	93	109	65	.712	29	12	2	-17	*O/1D	-0.8
1975	Bal-A	145	524	79	148	21	6	25	76	53	64	.282	.363	.489	.851	153	26	32	91	90	90	.874	32	17	-1	-4	*O/1D	2.4
1976	Oak-A	157	595	85	147	25	1	15	68	58	72	.247	.334	.368	.702	106	5	5	100	95	80	.741	52	12	8	-10	O1D	-0.1
1977	Cal-A	154	561	87	141	27	0	25	75	62	76	.251	.339	.433	.772	115	7	11	95	99	81	.766	26	12	1	-2	OD1	0.5
1978	Cal-A	158	591	103	151	26	0	34	99	56	71	.255	.338	.472	.810	124	19	18	102	109	93	.808	22	9	1	-2	*DO1	1.5
1979	Cal-A	162	628	**120**	186	33	3	36	**139**	71	51	.296	.377	.530	.908	153	37	43	93	116	126	.942	22	12	-1	-2	OD/1	3.5
1980	Cal-A	90	340	39	85	12	2	5	51	24	32	.250	.320	.341	.661	85	-8	-6	96	161	36	.581	6	6	-2	1	OD	-0.7
1981	Cal-A	103	377	52	90	18	1	17	66	42	51	.239	.326	.427	.753	111	7	5	104	129	51	.703	3	3	-1	1	D/1O	0.5
1982	Cal-A	157	608	80	160	24	1	24	93	57	69	.263	.333	.424	.758	106	5	5	100	119	84	.706	10	4	1	0	*D	0.6
1983	NY-A	144	534	82	162	33	3	21	85	40	53	.303	.366	.494	.861	136	25	26	99	104	96	.859	17	7	1	-0	*D/O1	2.6
1984	NY-A	134	493	84	129	29	1	27	89	38	68	.262	.343	.489	.832	135	18	21	94	112	83	.808	1	1	-0	-1	*D/O	2.0
1985	NY-A	142	477	70	110	24	1	23	91	52	90	.231	.336	.430	.766	113	6	9	96	134	70	.738	0	4	-2	0	*D	0.6
1986	Bos-A	160	585	93	139	23	1	31	94	62	111	.238	.346	.439	.785	114	12	12	100	113	91	.771	3	5	-2	1	*D1/O	0.9
1987	Bos-A	108	339	64	81	8	0	16	57	40	47	.239	.360	.404	.764	104	3	4	99	123	52	.763	5	2	0	0	D	0.3
	Min-A	20	49	3	14	1	0	0	6	5	12	.286	.397	.306	.703	95	-0	0	96	160	6	.615	0	1	-1	0	D	0.0
	Yr	128	388	67	95	9	0	16	63	45	59	.245	.364	.392	.756	103	3	4	99	130	61	.769	5	3	-0	0		0.3
1988	Oak-A	92	264	28	58	7	0	7	34	34	44	.220	.335	.326	.661	91	-4	-2	95	126	30	.617	0	1	-1	0	D	-0.1
Total	19	2292	8198	1236	2135	366	28	338	1276	805	1069	.260	.346	.436	.782	119	183	212	97	113	1247	.796	285	120	14	-43	*DO1	15.2
■ **JACK BEACH**	Beach, Stonewall Jackson b: 1862, Alexandria, Va. d: 7/23/1896, Alexandria, Va. Deb: 5/01/1884																											
1884	Was-a	8	31	3	3	2	0	0		0		.097	.097	.161	.258	-18	-4	-3	88	0	0	.179				0	/O	-0.2
■ **JOHNNY BEALL**	Beall, John Woolf b: 3/12/1882, Beltsville, Md. d: 6/14/26, Beltsville, Md. BL/TR, 6', 180 lbs. Deb: 4/17/13																											
1913	Cle-A	6	6	0	1	0	0	0	1	0	2	.167	.167	.167	.333	-2	-1	-1	106	355	0	.200	0			0	H	0.0
	Chi-A	17	60	10	16	0	1	2	3	0	0	.267	.279	.400	.679	103	-1	-0	95	36	6	.591	1			2	O	0.0
	Yr	23	66	10	17	0	1	2	4	0	2	.258	.269	.379	.647	91	-1	-1	98	135	6	.551	1			2		0.0
1915	Cin-N	10	34	3	8	1	0	0	3	5	10	.235	.350	.265	.615	85	-0	-0	103	135	3	.556	0	1	-1	2	O	0.0
1916	Cin-N	6	21	3	7	2	0	1	4	3	7	.333	.417	.571	.988	206	3	3	98	112	5	1.143	1			1	/O	0.3
1918	StL-N	19	49	2	11	1	0	0	6	3	6	.224	.269	.245	.514	61	-2	-2	93	189	4	.395	0			-2	O	-0.5
Total	4	58	170	18	43	4	1	3	17	11	25	.253	.306	.341	.647	97	-2	-1	97	122	19	.570	2	1		2	/O	-0.2
■ **BOB BEALL**	Beall, Robert Brooks b: 4/24/48, Portland, Ore. BB/TL, 5'11", 180 lbs. Deb: 5/12/75																											
1975	Atl-N	20	31	2	7	2	0	0	1	6	9	.226	.351	.290	.642	84	-1	-0	95	43	4	.625	0	0	0	-0	/1	0.0
1978	Atl-N	108	185	29	45	8	0	1	16	36	27	.243	.369	.303	.672	80	-1	-4	112	108	22	.651	4	5	-2	-1	1/O	-0.8
1979	Atl-N	17	15	1	2	2	0	0	1	3	4	.133	.278	.267	.544	45	-1	-1	109	99	1	.538	0	0	0	0	/1	0.0
1980	Pit-N	3	3	0	0	0	0	0	0	0	1	.000	.000	.000	.000	-97	-1	-1	103	0	0	.000	0	0	0	0	/H	0.0
Total	4	148	234	32	54	12	0	1	18	45	41	.231	.357	.295	.652	76	-3	-6	109	97	28	.643	4	5	-2	-1	/1O	-0.8
■ **TOMMY BEALS**	Beals, Thomas L. (played under name of W.Thomas In 1871 And 1873) b: Hartford, Conn. d: 10/2/15, San Francisco, Cal. BR, 5'5", 144 lbs. Deb: 7/27/1871																											
1871	Oly-n	10	38	7	7							.184															/O2	
1872	Oly-n	9	39	8	11							.282															/2SO	
1873	Nat-n	37	170	35	46							.271															2C/O	
1874	Bos-n	18	98	20	20							.204															2/O	
1875	Bos-n	35	157	38	46							.293															2O	
1880	Chi-N	13	46	4	7	0	0	0	3	1	6	.152	.170	.152	.322	10	-4	-4	105	156	1	.205				0	O/2	-0.3
Total	5 n	109	502	108	130							.259															O/2	

YEAR	TM/L	G	AB	R	H	2B	3B	HR	RBI	BB	SO	AVG	OBP	SLG	PRO	/A	BR	/A	PF	CHI	RC	TA	SB	CS	SBR	FR	POS	TPR
■ **CHARLIE BEAMON**	Beamon, Charles Alfonzo Jr. b: 12/4/53, Oakland, Cal. BL/TL, 6'1", 183 lbs. Deb: 9/11/78																											
1978	Sea-A	10	11	2	2	0	0	0	0	1	1	.182	.250	.182	.432	23	-1	-1	102	0	1	.333	0	0	0	0	/1D	0.0
1979	Sea-A	27	25	5	5	1	0	0	0	0	5	.200	.200	.240	.440	18	-3	-3	100	0	1	.333	1	0	0	-1	/1O	-0.3
1981	Tor-A	8	15	1	3	1	0	0	0	2	2	.200	.294	.267	.561	56	-1	-1	111	0	1	.500	0	0	0	0	/D1	0.0
Total	3	45	51	8	10	2	0	0	0	3	8	.196	.241	.235	.476	31	-5	-5	104	0	3	.390	1	0	0	-1	/D1O	-0.3
■ **JOE BEAN**	Bean, Joseph William b: 3/18/1874, Boston, Mass. d: 2/15/61, Atlanta, Ga. TR, 5'8", 138 lbs. Deb: 4/28/02																											
1902	NY-N	48	176	13	39	2	1	0	5	5		.222	.243	.244	.487	52	-10	-10	100	43	13	.416	9			-5	S	-1.3
■ **BILL BEAN**	Bean, William Daro b: 5/11/64, Santa Ana, Cal. BL/TL, 6' ", 185 lbs. Deb: 4/25/87																											
1987	Det-A	26	66	6	17	2	0	0	4	5	11	.258	.310	.288	.598	63	-4	-3	97	84	6	.490	1	1	-0	1	O	-0.2
1988	Det-A	10	11	2	2	0	1	0	0	0	2	.182	.182	.364	.545	52	-1	-1	94	0	1	.444	0	0	0	-1	/O1D	-0.1
Total	2	36	77	8	19	2	1	0	4	5	13	.247	.293	.299	.591	61	-4	-4	97	73	7	.492	1	1	-0	0	/O1D	-0.3
■ **BILLY BEANE**	Beane, William Lamar b: 3/29/62, Orlando, Fla. BR/TR, 6'4", 195 lbs. Deb: 9/13/84																											
1984	NY-N	5	10	0	1	0	0	0	0	0	2	.100	.100	.100	.200	-44	-2	-2	100	0	0	.100	0	1	-1	-2	/O	-0.4
1985	NY-N	8	8	0	2	1	0	0	1	0	3	.250	.250	.375	.625	75	-0	-0	97	133	1	.500	0	0	0	-1	/O	0.0
1986	Min-A	80	183	20	39	6	0	3	15	11	54	.213	.258	.295	.553	47	-12	-14	108	95	12	.438	2	3	-1	-6	O/D	-2.2
1987	Min-A	12	15	1	4	2	0	0	1	0	6	.267	.267	.400	.667	78	-1	-0	96	66	2	.545	0	0	0	-1	/O	-0.1
1988	Det-A	6	6	1	1	0	0	0	1	0	2	.167	.167	.167	.333	-7	-1	-1	94	398	0	.200	0	0	0	-2	/O	-0.2
Total	5	111	222	22	47	9	0	3	18	11	67	.212	.249	.293	.542	45	-16	-18	106	98	15	.436	2	4	-2	-11	/OD	-2.9
■ **TED BEARD**	Beard, Cramer Theodore b: 1/7/21, Woodsboro, Md. BL/TL, 5'8", 165 lbs. Deb: 9/05/48																											
1948	Pit-N	25	81	15	16	1	3	0	7	12	18	.198	.316	.284	.600	61	-4	-4	104	116	8	.646	5			3	O	-0.2
1949	Pit-N	14	24	1	2	0	0	0	1	2	2	.083	.154	.083	.237	-34	-5	-5	101	188	0	.182	0			-3	O	-0.8
1950	Pit-N	61	177	32	41	6	2	4	12	27	45	.232	.333	.356	.689	79	-4	-5	103	62	22	.664	3			2	O	-0.4
1951	Pit-N	22	48	7	9	1	0	1	3	6	14	.188	.291	.271	.562	49	-3	-4	107	72	4	.513	0	0	0	-1	O	-0.4
1952	Pit-N	15	44	5	8	2	1	0	3	7	9	.182	.294	.273	.567	58	-2	-2	100	98	4	.568	2	0	1	0	O	-0.1
1957	Chi-A	38	78	15	16	1	0	0	7	18	14	.205	.354	.218	.572	60	-3	-3	99	163	7	.585	3	2	-0	-2	O	-0.6
1958	Chi-A	19	22	5	2	0	0	1	2	6	5	.091	.286	.227	.513	44	-2	-2	98	100	2	.700	3	0	1	-3	O	-0.4
Total	7	194	474	80	94	11	6	6	35	78	107	.198	.315	.285	.600	61	-24	-25	102	101	49	.607	16	2		-5	O	-2.9
■ **OLLIE BEARD**	Beard, Oliver Perry b: 5/2/1862, Lexington, Ky. d: 5/28/29, Cincinnati, Ohio BR/TR, 5'11", 180 lbs. Deb: 4/17/1889																											
1889	Cin-a	141	558	96	159	13	14	1	77	35	39	.285	.328	.364	.692	94	-2	-6	105	113	80	.689	36			34	*S	3.2
1890	Cin-N	122	492	64	132	17	15	3	72	44	13	.268	.331	.382	.713	102	5	-1	108	106	74	.733	30			-6	*S/3	-0.7
1891	Lou-a	68	257	35	62	4	5	0	24	33	9	.241	.330	.296	.626	91	-5	-1	90	97	28	.600	7			3	3/S	0.4
Total	3	331	1307	195	353	34	34	4	173	112	61	.270	.330	.357	.687	97	-2	-8	103	107	182	.688	73			32	S/3	2.9
■ **LEW BEASLEY**	Beasley, Lewis Paige b: 8/27/48, Sparta, Va. BL/TR, 5'10", 172 lbs. Deb: 5/21/77																											
1977	Tex-A	25	32	5	7	1	0	0	3	2	2	.219	.265	.250	.515	39	-3	-3	105	149	2	.423	1	1	-0	-6	O/SD	-0.9
■ **DAVE BEATLE**	Beatle, David b: 1861, New York, N.Y. 6'2", 200 lbs. Deb: 6/17/1884																											
1884	Det-N	1	3	0	0	0	0	0	0	0	2	.000	.000	.000	.000	-99	-1	-1	94	0	0	.000				0	/OC	0.0
■ **DESMOND BEATTY**	Beatty, Aloysius Desmond "Desperate" b: 4/7/1893, Baltimore, Md. d: 10/6/69, Norway, Maine BR/TR, 5'8.5", 158 lbs. Deb: 9/28/14																											
1914	NY-N	2	3	0	0	0	0	0	1	0	0	.000	.000	.000	.000	-99	-1	-1	96	0	-0	.000	0			0	/S3	0.0
■ **JIM BEAUCHAMP**	Beauchamp, James Edward b: 8/21/39, Vinita, Okla. BR/TR, 6'2", 190 lbs. Deb: 9/22/63																											
1963	StL-N	4	3	0	0	0	0	0	0	0	2	.000	.000	.000	.000	-93	-1	-1	107	0	0	.000	0	0	0	0	H	0.0
1964	Hou-N	23	55	6	9	2	0	2	4	5	16	.164	.246	.309	.555	57	-3	-3	96	71	4	.489	0	0	0	-2	O/1	-0.5
1965	Hou-N	24	53	5	10	1	0	0	4	5	11	.189	.259	.208	.466	37	-5	-4	89	151	3	.348	0	2	-1	-0	/O1	-0.5
	Mil-N	4	3	0	0	0	0	0	0	1	1	.000	.250	.000	.250	-22	-0	-0	104	0	0	.250	0	1	-1	0	/1	0.0
	Yr	28	56	5	10	1	0	0	4	6	12	.179	.258	.196	.454	33	-5	-4	91	135	3	.347	0	3	-2	-0		-0.5
1967	Atl-N	4	3	0	0	0	0	0	1	0	0	.000	.000	.000	.000	-96	-1	-1	104	0	0	.000	0	0	0	0	H	0.0
1968	Cin-N	31	57	10	15	2	0	2	14	4	19	.263	.311	.404	.715	102	1	0	111	203	7	.628	0	0	0	0	O/1	0.0
1969	Cin-N	43	60	8	15	1	0	1	8	5	13	.250	.308	.317	.624	76	-2	-2	99	146	6	.533	0	0	0	-2	/O1	-0.3
1970	Hou-N	31	26	3	5	0	0	1	4	3	7	.192	.276	.308	.584	60	-2	-1	94	141	2	.478	0	1	-1	-5	O	-0.7
	StL-N	44	58	8	15	2	0	1	6	8	11	.259	.348	.345	.693	81	-1	-1	106	101	8	.698	2	0	1	0	O/1	-0.1
	Yr	75	84	11	20	2	0	2	10	11	18	.238	.326	.333	.660	76	-3	-3	101	120	10	.631	2	1	0	-5		-0.8
1971	StL-N	77	162	24	38	8	3	2	16	9	26	.235	.279	.358	.637	79	-5	-5	101	102	16	.550	3	1	0	-1	1/O	-0.9
1972	NY-N	58	120	10	29	1	0	5	19	7	33	.242	.289	.375	.664	92	-2	-2	95	130	13	.570	0	0	0	-1	1/O	-0.5
1973	NY-N	50	61	5	17	1	1	0	14	7	11	.279	.353	.328	.681	89	-1	-1	101	281	8	.622	1	0	0	-0	1	0.0
Total	10	393	661	79	153	18	4	14	90	54	150	.231	.292	.334	.627	77	-21	-21	99	138	66	.553	6	5	-1	-11	1/O	-3.5
■ **GINGER BEAUMONT**	Beaumont, Clarence Howeth b: 7/23/1876, Rochester, Wis. d: 4/10/56, Burlington, Wis. BL/TR, 5'8", 190 lbs. Deb: 4/21/1899																											
1899	Pit-N	111	437	90	154	15	8	3	38	41		.352	.416	.444	.860	141	24	25	99	55	96	.965	31			6	*O/1	2.3
1900	Pit-N	138	567	105	158	14	9	4	50	40		.279	.326	.356	.682	88	-7	-10	103	64	77	.658	27			-13	*O	-3.1
1901	Pit-N	133	558	120	185	14	5	8	72	44		.332	.380	.418	.798	133	24	24	101	83	105	.839	36			-8	*O	0.2
1902	Pit-N	130	541	100	**193**	21	6	0	67	39		**.357**	.400	.418	.818	147	34	31	105	91	106	.856	33			0	*O	2.2
1903	Pit-N	141	613	**137**	**209**	30	6	7	68	44		.341	.385	.444	.829	132	29	25	105	64	116	.839	23			3	*O	1.9
1904	Pit-N	153	615	97	**185**	12	12	3	54	34		.301	.337	.374	.711	123	14	15	99	73	89	.679	28			-4	*O	0.5
1905	Pit-N	103	384	60	126	12	8	3	40	22		.328	.365	.424	.789	132	16	15	104	86	69	.798	21			5	O	1.3
1906	Pit-N	80	310	48	82	9	3	2	32	19		.265	.307	.332	.639	97	-0	-2	104	103	33	.539	1			-4	O	-0.7
1907	Bos-N	150	580	67	**187**	19	14	4	62	37		.322	.363	.424	.787	156	30	33	95	88	101	.784	25			8	*O	3.9
1908	Bos-N	125	476	66	127	20	6	2	52	42		.267	.326	.347	.673	113	9	7	104	112	56	.630	13			-12	*O	-0.5
1909	Bos-N	123	407	35	107	11	4	0	60	35		.263	.321	.310	.631	101	-1	0	96	177	43	.577	12			0	*O	-0.3
1910	Chi-N	76	172	30	46	5	1	2	22	28	14	.267	.373	.343	.716	108	3	3	101	118	24	.730	4			-3	O	-0.1
Total	12	1463	5660	955	1759	182	82	38	617	425	14	.311	.360	.392	.752	125	177	167	101	89	915	.745	254			-21	*O/1	7.6
■ **GEORGE BECHTEL**	Bechtel, George A. b: 1848, Philadelphia, Pa. 5'11", 165 lbs. Deb: 5/20/1871																											
1871	Ath-n	20	94	23	30							.319															O/P3	
1872	Mut-n	52	262	64	79							.302															*O/1	
1873	Phi-n	53	266	54	62							.233															*O/P	
1874	Phi-n	31	153	29	43							.281															O/P	
1875	Cen-n	14	64	12	17							.266															P	
	Ath-n	34	154	32	45							.292															O/P	
	Yr	48	218	44	62							.284																
1876	Lou-N	14	55	2	10	1	0	0	2	0	1	.182	.182	.200	.382	26	-4	-4	104	63	2	.244				0	O	-0.3
	NY-N	2	10	2	3	0	0	0	0	0	0	.300	.300	.300	.600	115	-0	0	87	0	1	.429				0	/O	0.0
	Yr	16	65	4	13	1	0	0	2	0	1	.200	.200	.215	.415	38	-4	-4	102	59	3	.269				0		-0.3
Total	5 n	204	993	214	276							.278															/O	
■ **CLYDE BECK**	Beck, Clyde Eugene "Jersey" b: 1/6/02, Bassett, Cal. BR/TR, 5'10", 176 lbs. Deb: 5/19/26																											
1926	Chi-N	30	81	10	16	0	0	1	4	7	15	.198	.261	.235	.496	32	-7	-8	106	63	5	.400	0			5	2	-0.1
1927	Chi-N	117	391	44	101	20	5	2	44	43	37	.258	.332	.350	.682	83	-9	-9	100	108	46	.621	0			8	23/S	-0.1
1928	Chi-N	131	483	72	124	18	4	3	52	58	58	.257	.341	.329	.670	80	-16	-12	95	112	56	.624	3			4	3S/2	0.0
1929	Chi-N	54	190	28	40	7	0	0	9	19	24	.211	.282	.247	.530	32	-20	-20	101	66	14	.460	3			2	3S	-1.2
1930	Chi-N	83	244	32	52	7	0	6	34	36	32	.213	.314	.316	.630	50	-19	-21	105	123	26	.599	2			-1	S2/3	-1.1
1931	Cin-N	53	136	17	21	4	2	0	19	21	14	.154	.272	.213	.485	34	-13	-12	95	234	10	.452	1			0	3/S	-0.8
Total	6	468	1525	203	354	56	11	12	162	184	180	.232	.317	.307	.624	63	-83	-82	99	116	156	.569	9			18	32S	-3.3

YEAR	TM/L	G	AB	R	H	2B	3B	HR	RBI	BB	SO	AVG	OBP	SLG	PRO	/A	BR	/A	PF	CHI	RC	TA	SB	CS	SBR	FR	POS	TPR
■ **ERVE BECK** Beck, Ervin Thomas "Dutch" b: 7/19/1878, Toledo, Ohio d: 12/23/16, Toledo, Ohio BR/TR, 5'10", 168 lbs. Deb: 9/19/1899																												
1899	Bro-N	8	24	2	4	2	0	0	2	0		.167	.167	.250	.417	14	-3	-3	105	102	1	.300	0			0	/2S	-0.2
1901	Cle-A	135	539	78	156	26	8	6	79	23		.289	.319	.401	.719	106	-1	3	95	113	73	.642	7			-11	*2	-1.1
1902	Cin-N	48	187	19	57	10	3	1	20	3		.305	.316	.406	.722	113	4	2	110	89	25	.623	2			-1	2/1O	0.2
	Det-A	41	162	23	48	4	0	2	22	4		.296	.313	.358	.671	88	-3	-3	99	120	20	.570	3			1	1/O	0.0
Total	3	232	912	122	265	42	11	9	123	30		.291	.313	.390	.704	101	-3	-0	99	109	119	.615	12			-11	2/1OS	-1.1
■ **FRED BECK** Beck, Frederick Thomas b: 11/17/1886, Havana, Ill. d: 3/12/62, Havana, Ill. BL/TL, 6'1", 180 lbs. Deb: 09																												
1909	Bos-N	96	334	20	66	4	6	3	27	17		.198	.245	.272	.518	64	-16	-14	96	100	22	.437	5			3	O1	-1.5
1910	Bos-N	154	571	52	157	32	9	**10**	64	19	55	.275	.307	.415	.722	97	3	-7	114	89	73	.655	8			13	*O1	0.1
1911	Cin-N	41	87	7	16	1	2	2	20	1	13	.184	.193	.310	.504	44	-8	-7	92	205	5	.423	2			-1	O/1	-0.8
	Phi-N	66	210	26	59	8	3	3	25	17	21	.281	.346	.390	.737	99	1	-1	108	93	29	.702	3			-7	O	-0.9
	Yr	107	297	33	75	9	5	5	45	18	34	.253	.304	.367	.671	86	-6	-7	101	138	34	.613	5			-8		-1.7
1914	Chi-F	157	555	51	155	23	4	11	77	44	66	.279	.332	.395	.727	118	5	11	91	113	79	.680	9			-12	*1	0.2
1915	Chi-F	121	373	35	83	9	3	5	38	24	38	.223	.270	.303	.572	71	-15	-14	97	107	33	.486	4			-4	*1	-1.6
Total	5	635	2130	191	536	77	27	34	251	122	193	.252	.297	.361	.658	91	-29	-31	101	105	243	.588	31			-9	1O	-4.5
■ **ZINN BECK** Beck, Zinn Bertram b: 9/30/1885, Steubenville, O. d: 3/19/81, W.Palm Beach, Fla. BR/TR, 5'10.5", 160 lbs. Deb: 9/14/13																												
1913	StL-N	10	30	4	5	1	0	0	2	-4	10	.167	.265	.200	.465	36	-2	-2	93	121	2	.440	1			1	/S3	0.0
1914	StL-N	137	457	42	106	15	11	3	45	28	32	.232	.282	.333	.615	79	-11	-13	104	103	45	.564	14			-4	*3S	-1.2
1915	StL-N	70	223	21	52	9	4	0	15	12	31	.233	.282	.309	.591	79	-6	-6	100	83	18	.481	3	10	-5	2	3/S2	-0.6
1916	StL-N	62	184	8	41	7	1	0	10	14	21	.223	.281	.272	.553	73	-6	-6	97	79	15	.476	3			0	3/12	-0.4
1918	NY-A	11	8	0	0	0	0	0	1	0	1	.000	.000	.000	.000	-99	-2	-2	95	0	-0	.000	0			0	/13	-0.1
Total	5	290	902	75	204	32	16	3	73	58	95	.226	.279	.307	.586	75	-28	-29	101	93	80	.514	21	10		-0	3/S12	-2.3
■ **HEINE BECKENDORF** Beckendorf, Henry Ward b: 6/15/1884, New York, N.Y. d: 9/15/49, Jackson Heights, N.Y. BR/TR, 5'9", 174 lbs. Deb: 4/16/09																												
1909	Det-A	15	27	1	7	1	0	0	1	2		.259	.310	.296	.607	83	-0	-1	110	48	2	.500	0			-1	C	0.0
1910	Det-A	3	7	0	3	0	0	0	2	1		.429	.500	.429	.929	188	1	1	102	246	1	1.000	0			0	/C	0.1
	Was-A	37	103	8	15	1	0	0	10	5		.146	.207	.155	.363	14	-10	-10	101	231	3	.273	0			2	C	-0.4
	Yr	40	110	8	18	1	0	0	12	6		.164	.227	.173	.400	25	-9	-9	101	238	4	.304	0			2		-0.3
Total	2	55	137	9	25	2	0	0	13	8		.182	.243	.197	.440	37	-10	-10	103	196	7	.339	0			2	/C	-0.3
■ **BEALS BECKER** Becker, David Beals b: 7/5/1886, El Dorado, Kan. d: 8/16/43, Huntington Park, Cal. BL/TL, 5'9", 170 lbs. Deb: 4/19/08																												
1908	Pit-N	20	65	4	10	0	1	0	0	2		.154	.179	.185	.364	18	-6	-6	95	0	2	.291	2			0	O	-0.5
	Bos-N	43	171	13	47	3	1	0	7	7		.275	.303	.304	.607	93	-1	-2	104	50	17	.532	7			1	O	0.0
	Yr	63	236	17	57	3	2	0	7	9		.242	.269	.271	.541	74	-7	-7	101	34	19	.458	9			1		-0.5
1909	Bos-N	152	562	60	138	15	6	6	24	47		.246	.305	.326	.631	101	-3	-1	96	46	60	.594	21			1	*O	-0.5
1910	NY-N	80	126	18	36	2	4	3	24	14	25	.286	.357	.437	.794	138	5	5	95	131	23	.889	11			-4	O/1	0.0
1911	NY-N	88	172	28	45	11	1	1	20	26	22	.262	.359	.355	.713	97	1	-0	102	106	28	.835	19			-6	O	-0.7
1912	NY-N	125	402	66	106	18	8	6	58	54	35	.264	.354	.393	.747	100	2	0	104	113	66	.824	30			4	*O	0.1
1913	Cin-N	30	108	11	32	5	3	0	14	6	12	.296	.333	.398	.731	107	1	1	102	121	14	.645	0			2	O	0.2
	Phi-N	88	306	53	99	19	10	9	44	22	30	.324	.369	.539	.908	141	21	16	112	85	62	.957	11			2	O/1	1.7
	Yr	118	414	64	131	24	13	9	58	28	42	.316	.360	.502	.862	132	22	17	109	95	75	.873	11			4		1.9
1914	Phi-N	138	514	76	167	25	5	9	66	37	59	.325	.370	.446	.816	142	25	25	100	99	87	.813	16			7	*O	3.0
1915	Phi-N	112	338	38	83	16	4	11	35	26	48	.246	.301	.414	.716	108	5	2	107	77	40	.663	12	15	-5	-7	O	-1.4
Total	8	876	2764	367	763	114	43	45	292	241	231	.276	.335	.397	.732	114	49	42	102	84	399	.730	129	15		-0	O/1	1.9
■ **HEINZ BECKER** Becker, Heinz Reinhard "Dutch" b: 8/26/15, Berlin, Germany BB/TR, 6'2", 200 lbs. Deb: 4/21/43																												
1943	Chi-N	24	69	5	10	0	0	0	2	9	6	.145	.244	.145	.389	14	-7	-7	99	72	3	.306	0			-1	1	-0.9
1945	Chi-N	67	133	25	38	8	2	2	27	17	16	.286	.375	.421	.796	122	4	4	99	151	22	.765	0			-1	1	0.3
1946	Chi-N	9	7	0	2	0	0	0	1	1	1	.286	.375	.286	.661	94	-0	0	94	187	1	.600	0			0	H	0.0
	Cle-A	50	147	15	44	10	1	0	17	23	18	.299	.401	.381	.782	135	5	7	89	115	25	.781	1	0	0	2	1	0.7
1947	Cle-A	2	2	0	0	0	0	0	0	0	1	.000	.000	.000	.000	-99	-1	-1	96	0	0	.000	0	0	0	0	H	0.0
Total	4	152	358	45	94	18	3	2	47	50	42	.263	.359	.346	.706	104	1	3	94	121	50	.678	1	0		0	/1	0.1
■ **JOE BECKER** Becker, Joseph Edward b: 6/25/08, St.Louis, Mo. BR/TR, 6'1", 180 lbs. Deb: 5/10/36 C																												
1936	Cle-A	22	50	5	9	3	1	1	11	5	4	.180	.255	.340	.595	43	-5	-5	106	178	4	.537	0	0	0	0	C	-0.2
1937	Cle-A	18	33	3	11	2	1	0	2	3	4	.333	.405	.455	.860	119	1	1	98	46	6	.864	0	0	0	0	C	0.2
Total	2	40	83	8	20	5	2	1	13	8	8	.241	.315	.386	.701	72	-4	-4	102	125	11	.651	0	0	0	0	/C	0.0
■ **MARTY BECKER** Becker, Martin Henry b: 12/22/1893, Tiffin, Ohio d: 9/25/57, Cincinnati, Ohio BB/TL, 5'8.5", 155 lbs. Deb: 9/08/15																												
1915	NY-N	17	52	5	13	2	0	0	3	2	9	.250	.278	.288	.566	78	-2	-1	91	76	6	.513	3			2	O	0.1
■ **GLENN BECKERT** Beckert, Glenn Alfred b: 10/12/40, Pittsburgh, Pa. BR/TR, 6'1", 190 lbs. Deb: 4/12/65																												
1965	Chi-N	154	614	73	147	21	3	3	30	28	52	.239	.276	.298	.574	61	-31	-32	102	69	47	.450	6	8	-3	13	*2	-1.4
1966	Chi-N	153	656	73	188	23	7	1	59	26	36	.287	.318	.348	.665	85	-13	-13	100	95	73	.558	10	4	1	-19	*2/S	-2.3
1967	Chi-N	146	597	91	167	32	3	5	40	30	25	.280	.314	.369	.683	93	-5	-6	102	68	68	.586	10	3	1	3	*2	0.8
1968	Chi-N	155	643	**98**	189	28	4	4	37	31	20	.294	.328	.369	.697	97	6	-2	112	55	79	.599	8	4	0	5	*2	1.4
1969	Chi-N	131	543	69	158	22	1	1	37	24	24	.291	.328	.341	.669	82	-9	-13	107	76	60	.554	6	0	2	7	*2	0.6
1970	Chi-N	143	591	99	170	15	6	3	36	32	22	.288	.324	.349	.673	67	-17	-32	120	62	66	.556	4	1	1	10	*2/O	-0.5
1971	Chi-N	131	530	80	181	18	5	2	42	24	24	.342	.370	.406	.776	109	13	7	110	74	76	.659	3	2	-0	1	*2	1.5
1972	Chi-N	120	474	51	128	22	2	3	43	23	17	.270	.307	.344	.650	74	-10	-18	114	109	47	.523	2	1	0	21	*2	1.2
1973	Chi-N	114	372	38	95	13	0	0	29	30	15	.255	.314	.290	.605	63	-15	-19	108	108	32	.476	0	2	-1	6	2	-1.0
1974	SD-N	64	172	11	44	1	0	0	7	11	8	.256	.301	.262	.562	62	-9	-8	93	60	14	.434	0	0	0	-2	2/3	-0.8
1975	SD-N	9	16	2	6	1	0	0	0	1	0	.375	.412	.438	.849	136	1	1	100	0	3	.800	0	0	0	0	/3	0.1
Total	11	1320	5208	685	1473	196	31	22	360	260	243	.283	.319	.345	.664	81	-90	-135	107	77	565	.565	49	25	-0	44	*2/3OS	-0.4
■ **JAKE BECKLEY** Beckley, Jacob Peter "Eagle Eye" b: 8/4/1867, Hannibal, Mo. d: 6/25/18, Kansas City, Mo. BL/TL, 5'10", 200 lbs. Deb: 1888																												
1888	Pit-N	71	283	35	97	15	3	0	27	7	22	.343	.363	.417	.780	159	15	17	95	79	51	.790	20			-3	1	0.7
1889	Pit-N	123	522	91	157	24	10	9	97	29	29	.301	.345	.437	.781	134	11	21	89	109	84	.751	11			2	*1/O	1.1
1890	Pit-P	121	516	109	167	38	**22**	10	120	42	32	.324	.381	.541	.922	160	31	39	92	102	116	.989	18			-0	*1	2.1
1891	Pit-N	133	554	94	162	20	19	4	73	44	46	.292	.353	.419	.772	125	18	16	101	77	89	.758	13			12	*1	2.2
1892	Pit-N	151	614	102	145	21	19	10	96	31	44	.236	.288	.381	.669	111	-0	6	94	118	78	.659	30			20	*1	1.3
1893	Pit-N	131	542	108	164	32	19	5	106	54	26	.303	.386	.459	.846	119	20	14	106	116	105	.894	15			11	*1	1.9
1894	Pit-N	131	533	121	183	36	18	7	120	43	16	.343	.412	.518	.930	132	21	27	94	107	125	1.026	21			6	*1	2.6
1895	Pit-N	129	530	104	174	31	19	5	110	24	20	.328	.381	.487	.868	129	18	21	97	99	109	.907	20			-7	*1	1.4
1896	Pit-N	59	217	44	55	7	5	3	32	22	28	.253	.349	.373	.723	99	-2	1	93	105	32	.747	8			1	1/O2	0.3
	NY-N	46	182	37	55	8	4	5	38	9	7	.302	.352	.473	.825	120	4	4	99	115	35	.874	11			-0	1/O	0.5
	Yr	105	399	81	110	15	9	8	70	31	35	.276	.351	.419	.769	109	2	5	96	110	67	.803	19			0		0.8
1897	NY-N	17	68	8	17	2	3	1	11	2		.250	.301	.412	.713	91	-1	-1	98	110	9	.686	2			2	1	0.0
	Cin-N	97	365	76	126	17	9	7	76	18		.345	.395	.499	.894	128	19	14	107	116	83	.983	23			-4	*1	0.8
	Yr	114	433	84	143	19	12	8	87	20		.330	.380	.485	.865	123	17	13	106	116	92	.931	25			-2		0.8
1898	Cin-N	118	459	86	135	20	12	4	72	28		.294	.337	.416	.754	110	9	4	108	114	68	.701	6			-1	*1	0.3
1899	Cin-N	134	513	87	171	27	16	3	99	40		.333	.386	.466	.852	129	24	20	106	130	102	.886	20			4	*1	2.3
1900	Cin-N	141	558	98	190	26	10	2	94	40		.341	.385	.434	.818	140	21	28	92	125	104	.829	23			5	*1	3.1
1901	Cin-N	140	580	78	178	36	13	3	79	28		.307	.339	.429	.768	131	16	20	95	90	88	.699	4			-3	*1	1.7
1902	Cin-N	129	531	82	175	23	7	5	69	34		.330	.370	.427	.797	135	28	22	110	87	92	.775	15			-3	*1/P	1.5
1903	Cin-N	120	459	85	150	29	10	2	81	42		.327	.383	.447	.830	127	22	17	109	131	90	.874	23			5	*1	1.7
1904	StL-N	142	551	72	179	22	9	1	67	35		.325	.365	.403	.768	141	24	25	99	105	89	.737	17			-11	*1	0.8

YEAR	TM/L	G	AB	R	H	2B	3B	HR	RBI	BB	SO	AVG	OBP	SLG	PRO	/A	BR	/A	PF	CHI	RC	TA	SB	CS	SBR	FR	POS	TPR
1905	StL-N	134	514	48	147	20	10	1	57	30		.286	.325	.370	.695	119	5	10	91	99	67	.632	12			-7	*1	-0.2
1906	StL-N	87	320	29	79	16	6	0	44	13		.247	.276	.334	.611	91	-4	-4	101	159	31	.510	3			-3	1	-1.1
1907	StL-N	32	115	6	24	3	0	0	7	1		.209	.216	.235	.450	44	-8	-7	96	100	6	.308	0			1	1	-0.8
Total	20	2386	9526	1600	2930	473	243	87	1575	616	270	.308	.358	.436	.794	127	292	313	99	108	1654	.790	315			24	*1/OP2	24.2
■ JULIO BECQUER	Becquer, Julio (Villegas) b: 12/20/31, Havana, Cuba BL/TL, 5'11.5", 178 lbs. Deb: 9/13/55																											
1955	Was-A	10	14	1	3	0	0	0	1	0	1	.214	.214	.214	.429	17	-2	-2	91	124	1	.273	0	0	0	0	/1	-0.1
1957	Was-A	105	186	14	42	6	2	2	22	10	29	.226	.269	.312	.581	59	-11	-11	98	136	13	.462	3	3	-1	-1	1	-1.2
1958	Was-A	86	164	10	39	3	0	0	12	8	21	.238	.273	.256	.529	48	-12	-11	97	115	10	.383	1	2	-1	1	1/O	-1.2
1959	Was-A	108	220	20	59	12	5	1	26	8	17	.268	.297	.382	.679	85	-5	-5	100	118	22	.558	3	2	-0	2	1	-0.3
1960	Was-A	110	298	41	75	15	7	4	35	12	35	.252	.283	.389	.672	78	-9	-10	102	107	27	.539	1	3	-2	-5	1/P	-2.1
1961	LA-A	11	8	0	0	0	0	0	0	1	5	.000	.111	.000	.111	-61	-2	-2	111	0	0	.125	0	0	0	0	/1	-0.2
	Min-A	57	84	13	20	1	2	5	18	2	12	.238	.256	.476	.732	86	-2	-2	106	128	9	.636	0	1	-1	-0	1/OP	-0.4
	Yr	68	92	13	20	1	2	5	18	3	17	.217	.242	.435	.677	72	-4	-4	107	107	9	.581	0	1	-1	-0		-0.6
1963	Min-A	1	0	1	0	0	0	0	0	0	0	—	—	—	—	—	0	0	100	—	—	—	0	0	0	0	H	0.0
Total	7	488	974	100	238	37	16	12	114	41	120	.244	.277	.352	.629	70	-43	-43	100	117	91	.529	8	11	-4	-3	1/OP	-5.5
■ HOWIE BEDELL	Bedell, Howard William b: 9/29/35, Clearfield, Pa. BL/TR, 6'1", 185 lbs. Deb: 4/10/62 C																											
1962	Mil-N	58	138	15	27	1	2	0	2	11	22	.196	.255	.232	.487	32	-13	-13	99	25	9	.393	1	0	0	-6	O	-2.1
1968	Phi-N	9	7	0	1	0	0	0	1	1	0	.143	.250	.143	.393	21	-1	-1	97	421	0	.333	0	0	0	0	H	0.0
Total	2	67	145	15	28	1	2	0	3	12	22	.193	.255	.228	.482	32	-14	-14	99	45	9	.393	1	0	0	-6	/O	-2.1
■ GENE BEDFORD	Bedford, William Eugene b: 12/2/1896, Dallas, Tex. d: 10/6/77, San Antonio, Tex. BB/TR, 5'8", 170 lbs. Deb: 6/25/25																											
1925	Cle-A	2	3	1	0	0	0	0	0	0	1	.000	.000	.000	.000	-94	-1	-1	106	0	0	.000	0	0	0	0	/2	0.0
■ ED BEECHER	Beecher, Edward "Scrap Iron" b: 5/1876 Indiana Deb: 9/26/1897																											
1897	StL-N	3	12	1	4	0	0	0	1	0		.333	.333	.333	.667	84	-0	-0	93	75	2	.625	1			0	/O	0.0
1898	Cle-N	8	25	1	5	2	0	0	0	0		.200	.200	.280	.480	40	-2	-2	96	0	1	.350	0			0	/O	-0.1
Total	2	11	37	2	9	2	0	0	1	0		.243	.243	.297	.541	55	-2	-2	95	24	3	.429	1			0	/O	-0.1
■ ED BEECHER	Beecher, Edward H. b: 7/2/1860, Guilford, Conn. d: 9/12/35, Hartford, Conn. BL, 5'10", 185 lbs. Deb: 6/28/1887																											
1887	Pit-N	41	169	15	41	8	0	2	22	7	8	.243	.281	.325	.606	74	-7	-5	93	118	18	.563	8			7	O	0.2
1889	Was-N	42	179	20	53	9	0	0	30	5	4	.296	.319	.346	.665	95	-3	-1	92	139	21	.563	3			-1	O/1	-0.2
1890	Buf-P	126	536	69	159	22	10	3	90	29	23	.297	.341	.392	.733	106	-3	5	92	119	78	.690	14			-5	*O/P	-0.3
1891	Was-a	58	235	35	57	11	3	2	28	27	9	.243	.333	.340	.674	100	-1	1	95	81	33	.725	17			2	O	0.0
	Phi-a	16	71	9	15	2	4	0	7	3	4	.211	.243	.352	.595	70	-3	-3	103	71	8	.625	7			-1	O	-0.4
	Yr	74	306	44	72	13	7	2		30	13	.235	.314	.343	.657	93	-4	-3	97	80	41	.701	24			1		-0.4
Total	4	283	1190	148	325	52	17	7	177	71	48	.273	.322	.363	.685	97	-17	-4	93	111	159	.655	49			2	O/1P	-0.7
■ JODIE BEELER	Beeler, Joseph Sam b: 11/26/21, Dallas, Tex. BR/TR, 6', 170 lbs. Deb: 9/21/44																											
1944	Cin-N	3	3	0	0	0	0	0	0	0	2	.000	.000	.000	.000	-99	-1	-1	95	0	0	.000	0			0	/23	0.0
■ GENE BEGLEY	Begley, Eugene T. b: 6/1861, Brooklyn, N.Y. Deb: 9/11/1886																											
1886	NY-N	5	16	1	2	0	0	0	1	1	3	.125	.176	.125	.301	-8	-2	-2	89	163	1	.286	1			0	/CO	-0.1
■ JIM BEGLEY	Begley, James Lawrence "Imp" b: 9/19/02, San Francisco, Cal. d: 2/20/57, San Francisco, Cal BR/TR, 5'6", 145 lbs. Deb: 5/28/24																											
1924	Cin-N	2	5	1	1	0	0	0	0	2	0	.200	.429	.200	.629	73	-0	-0	101	0	1	.750	0	0	0	0	/2	0.0
■ STEVE BEHEL	Behel, Stephen Arnold Douglas b: 11/6/1860, Earlville, Ill. d: 2/15/45, Los Angeles, Cal. Deb: 9/27/1884																											
1884	Mil-U	9	33	5	8	1	0	0		3		.242	.306	.273	.578	97	0	0	100	0	3	.480	0			0	/O	0.0
1886	NY-a	59	224	32	46	5	2	0		22		.205	.279	.246	.525	64	-8	-9	104	0	20	.528	16			-6	O	-1.4
Total	2	68	257	37	54	6	2	0		25		.210	.283	.249	.532	68	-8	-9	103	0	23	.522	16			-6	/O	-1.4
■ OLLIE BEJMA	Bejma, Alojzy Frank b: 9/12/07, South Bend, Ind. BR/TR, 5'10", 165 lbs. Deb: 4/24/34																											
1934	StL-A	95	262	39	71	16	3	2	29	40	36	.271	.376	.378	.754	91	-1	-2	104	92	40	.756	3	2	-0	-1	S23/O	0.0
1935	StL-A	64	198	18	38	8	2	2	26	27	21	.192	.289	.283	.572	45	-15	-17	107	142	18	.525	1	0	0	-1	2/S3	-1.4
1936	StL-A	67	139	19	36	2	3	2	18	27	21	.259	.380	.360	.739	81	-3	-4	103	104	21	.748	0	0	0	-2	2/3S	-0.2
1939	Chi-A	90	307	52	77	9	3	8	44	36	27	.251	.331	.378	.709	76	-9	-12	107	108	39	.647	1	3	-2	-1	2/S3	-1.0
Total	4	316	906	128	222	35	11	14	117	130	105	.245	.343	.354	.697	75	-28	-36	105	110	118	.664	5	5	-2	-4	2/S3O	-2.6
■ MARK BELANGER	Belanger, Mark Henry b: 6/8/44, Pittsfield, Mass. BR/TR, 6'1", 170 lbs. Deb: 8/07/65																											
1965	Bal-A	11	3	1	1	0	0	0	0	0	0	.333	.333	.333	.667	90	-0	-0	100	0	0	.333	0	1	-1	0	/S	0.0
1966	Bal-A	8	19	2	3	1	0	0	0	0	3	.158	.158	.211	.368	5	-2	-2	101	0	1	.250	0	0	0	0	/S	-0.1
1967	Bal-A	69	184	19	32	5	0	1	10	12	46	.174	.224	.217	.442	33	-16	-15	95	97	10	.372	6	1	1	-3	S2/3	-1.4
1968	Bal-A	145	472	40	98	13	0	2	21	40	114	.208	.275	.248	.523	58	-22	-23	102	73	35	.445	10	1	2	11	*S	0.0
1969	Bal-A	150	530	76	152	17	4	2	50	53	54	.287	.354	.345	.699	93	-1	-4	104	108	66	.635	14	6	1	-6	*S	-0.2
1970	Bal-A	145	459	53	100	6	5	1	36	52	65	.218	.304	.259	.564	59	-26	-24	97	119	42	.518	13	2	3	-4	*S	-1.3
1971	Bal-A	150	500	67	133	19	4	0	35	73	48	.266	.367	.320	.687	93	1	-1	103	91	63	.651	10	8	-2	1	*S	1.6
1972	Bal-A	113	285	36	53	9	1	2	16	18	53	.186	.239	.246	.485	46	-20	-19	98	88	18	.403	6	3	0	1	*S	-0.6
1973	Bal-A	154	470	60	106	15	1	0	27	49	54	.226	.305	.262	.567	57	-23	-27	107	86	41	.501	13	6	0	5	*S	-0.1
1974	Bal-A	155	493	54	111	14	4	5	36	51	69	.225	.300	.300	.601	79	-16	-12	93	87	49	.555	17	7	1	10	*S	1.2
1975	Bal-A	152	442	44	100	11	1	3	27	36	53	.226	.286	.276	.562	66	-23	-18	91	79	40	.503	16	4	2	**29**	*S	2.9
1976	Bal-A	153	522	66	141	22	2	1	40	51	64	.270	.337	.326	.663	97	-2	-1	98	91	60	.619	27	17	-2	17	*S	2.4
1977	Bal-A	144	402	39	83	13	4	2	30	43	68	.206	.288	.274	.562	58	-25	-21	93	102	34	.512	15	8	-0	**31**	*S	2.6
1978	Bal-A	135	348	39	74	13	0	0	16	40	55	.213	.305	.250	.555	63	-18	-14	91	73	29	.489	6	6	-2	**26**	*S	2.1
1979	Bal-A	101	198	28	33	6	2	0	9	29	33	.167	.276	.217	.493	36	-18	-17	97	80	15	.462	5	1	1	-5	S	-0.8
1980	Bal-A	113	268	37	61	7	3	0	22	12	25	.228	.261	.276	.537	47	-19	-20	101	116	20	.436	6	3	0	-1	*S	-1.1
1981	Bal-A	64	139	9	23	3	2	1	10	12	25	.165	.242	.237	.479	39	-11	-11	99	109	8	.405	2	1	0	2	S	-0.3
1982	LA-N	54	50	6	12	1	0	0	4	5	10	.240	.309	.260	.569	64	-2	-2	95	121	4	.475	1	0	0	0	S/2	0.2
Total	18	2016	5784	676	1316	175	33	20	389	576	839	.228	.302	.280	.582	67	-245	-230	98	93	533	.528	167	75	5	116	*S/23	7.1
■ WAYNE BELARDI	Belardi, Carroll Wayne b: 9/5/30, Calistoga, Cal. BL/TL, 6'1", 185 lbs. Deb: 4/18/50																											
1950	Bro-N	10	10	0	0	0	0	0	0	0	4	.000	.000	.000	.000	-94	-3	-3	107	0	0	.000				0	/1	-0.2
1951	Bro-N	3	3	1	1	0	1	0	0	0	2	.333	.333	1.000	1.333	250	1	1	98	0	1	1.500	0	0	0	0	H	0.1
1953	Bro-N	69	163	19	39	3	2	11	34	16	40	.239	.311	.485	.796	100	0	-1	104	118	26	.762	0	0	0	2	1	0.0
1954	Bro-N	11	9	0	2	0	0	0	1	2	3	.222	.364	.222	.586	56	-0	-0	101	197	1	.571	0	0	0	0	H	0.0
	Det-A	88	250	27	58	7	1	11	24	33	34	.232	.333	.400	.733	100	-0	-0	100	68	35	.702	1	0	0	1	1	0.0
1955	Det-A	3	3	0	0	0	0	0	0	0	1	.000	.000	.000	.000	-99	-1	-1	97	0	0	.000	0	0	0	0	H	0.0
1956	Det-A	79	154	24	43	3	1	6	15	15	13	.279	.373	.429	.801	115	3	3	97	67	25	.774	0	0	0	-2	1/O	0.0
Total	6	263	592	71	143	13	5	28	74	66	97	.242	.332	.422	.754	100	-1	-1	100	82	88	.731	1	0		1	1/O	-0.1
■ IRA BELDEN	Belden, Ira Allison b: 4/16/1874, Cleveland, Ohio d: 7/15/16, Lakewood, Ohio 5'11", 175 lbs. Deb: 9/17/1897																											
1897	Cle-N	8	30	5	8	0	2	0	4	2		.267	.333	.400	.733	86	-0	-1	111	99	4	.682	0			0	/O	0.0
■ BUDDY BELL	Bell, David Gus b: 8/27/51, Pittsburgh, Pa. BR/TR, 6'1", 180 lbs. Deb: 4/15/72																											
1972	Cle-A	132	466	49	119	21	1	9	36	34	29	.255	.310	.363	.673	93	-1	-4	107	78	52	.589	5	6	-2	0	*O/3	-1.0
1973	Cle-A	156	631	86	169	23	7	14	59	49	47	.268	.327	.393	.720	105	1	3	97	77	76	.633	7	15	-7	24	*3/O	1.8
1974	Cle-A	116	423	51	111	15	1	7	46	35	29	.262	.323	.352	.675	94	-3	-3	101	113	46	.571	1	3	-2	-0	*3/D	-0.3
1975	Cle-A	153	553	66	150	20	4	10	59	51	72	.271	.334	.376	.710	101	0	0	100	97	69	.635	6	5	-1	-5	*3	-0.2
1976	Cle-A	159	604	75	170	26	2	7	60	44	49	.281	.332	.366	.698	105	3	3	100	101	71	.595	3	8	-4	6	*3/1	0.6
1977	Cle-A	129	479	64	140	23	4	11	64	45	63	.292	.354	.426	.780	114	8	9	98	113	68	.695	1	8	-5	7	*3O	0.9

YEAR	TM/L	G	AB	R	H	2B	3B	HR	RBI	BB	SO	AVG	OBP	SLG	PRO	/A	BR	/A	PF	CHI	RC	TA	SB	CS	SBR	FR	POS	TPR
1978	Cle-A	142	556	71	157	27	8	6	62	39	43	.282	.329	.392	.721	109	1	6	93	110	65	.606	1	3	-2	25	*3/D	2.8
1979	Tex-A	162	670	89	200	42	3	18	101	30	45	.299	.331	.451	.782	109	6	6	100	105	95	.694	5	4	-1	17	*3S	2.8
1980	Tex-A	129	490	76	161	24	4	17	83	40	39	.329	.379	.498	.877	138	25	25	100	112	88	.829	3	1	0	15	*3/S	3.9
1981	Tex-A	97	360	44	106	16	1	10	64	42	30	.294	.373	.428	.801	143	15	19	91	144	58	.768	3	3	-1	**27**	3/S	4.6
1982	Tex-A	148	537	62	159	27	2	13	67	70	50	.296	.379	.426	.806	130	17	22	93	106	87	.775	5	4	-1	**37**	*3/S	5.5
1983	Tex-A	156	618	75	171	35	3	14	66	50	48	.277	.335	.411	.746	103	3	2	101	84	78	.653	3	5	-2	17	*3	1.7
1984	Tex-A	148	553	88	174	36	5	11	83	63	54	.315	.388	.458	.845	133	26	26	100	123	95	.800	2	1	0	21	*3	4.8
1985	Tex-A	84	313	33	74	13	3	4	32	33	21	.236	.311	.335	.647	71	-10	-13	108	115	31	.557	3	2	-0	10	3	-0.5
	Cin-N	67	247	28	54	15	2	6	36	34	27	.219	.313	.368	.682	86	-3	-5	105	139	27	.613	0	1	-1	-6	3	-1.1
1986	Cin-N	155	568	89	158	29	3	20	75	73	49	.278	.365	.445	.811	117	18	15	104	101	91	.771	2	8	-4	0	*3/2	0.8
1987	Cin-N	143	522	74	148	19	2	17	70	71	39	.284	.370	.425	.796	106	9	7	104	108	84	.766	4	1	1	-17	*3	-1.0
1988	Cin-N	21	54	3	10	0	0	0	3	7	3	.185	.279	.185	.464	34	-4	-5	105	120	3	.370	0	0	0	1	3/1	-0.3
	Hou-N	74	269	24	68	10	1	7	37	19	29	.253	.302	.375	.678	100	-3	-1	93	124	29	.576	1	1	-0	-1	3/1	-0.2
	Yr	95	323	27	78	10	1	7	40	26	32	.241	.298	.344	.642	87	-7	-6	96	124	32	.543	1	1	-0	1		-0.5
Total	17	2371	8913	1147	2499	421	56	201	1103	829	766	.280	.344	.408	.752	109	108	113	100	106	1213	.701	55	79	-31	179	*3O/S1D2	25.6

■ **GUS BELL** Bell, David Russell b: 11/15/28, Louisville, Ky. BL/TR, 6'1.5", 190 lbs. Deb: 5/30/50

YEAR	TM/L	G	AB	R	H	2B	3B	HR	RBI	BB	SO	AVG	OBP	SLG	PRO	/A	BR	/A	PF	CHI	RC	TA	SB	CS	SBR	FR	POS	TPR
1950	Pit-N	111	422	62	119	22	11	8	53	28	46	.282	.333	.443	.776	100	0	-1	103	99	63	.726	4			2	*O	-0.2
1951	Pit-N	149	600	80	167	27	**12**	16	89	42	41	.278	.330	.443	.773	99	3	-2	107	116	88	.702	1	4	-2	0	*O	-0.7
1952	Pit-N	131	468	53	117	21	5	16	59	36	72	.250	.306	.419	.725	100	-2	-2	100	96	61	.651	1	4	-2	-9	*O	-1.6
1953	Cin-N	151	610	102	183	37	5	30	105	48	72	.300	.354	.525	.879	127	21	22	99	96	113	.837	0	2	-1	9	*O	2.1
1954	Cin-N	153	619	104	185	38	7	17	101	48	58	.299	.353	.465	.818	107	9	6	104	113	100	.767	5	3	-0	-3	*O	-0.2
1955	Cin-N	154	610	88	188	30	6	27	104	54	57	.308	.364	.510	.874	122	24	20	106	114	114	.854	4	4	-1	-14	*O	0.2
1956	Cin-N	150	603	82	176	31	4	29	84	50	66	.292	.349	.501	.850	115	20	14	108	88	105	.822	6	2	1	-11	*O	-0.2
1957	Cin-N	121	510	65	149	20	3	13	61	30	54	.292	.335	.420	.755	96	0	-3	105	96	70	.664	0	1	-1	-5	*O	-1.2
1958	Cin-N	112	385	42	97	16	2	10	46	36	40	.252	.318	.382	.699	78	-9	-13	107	107	46	.624	2	3	-1	7	*O	-0.9
1959	Cin-N	148	580	59	170	27	2	19	115	29	44	.293	.329	.445	.774	101	2	-1	103	**156**	81	.683	2	3	-1	4	*O	0.0
1960	Cin-N	143	515	65	135	19	5	12	62	29	40	.262	.303	.388	.691	89	-10	-9	98	109	60	.600	4	3	-1	-0	*O	-1.3
1961	Cin-N	103	235	27	60	10	1	3	33	18	21	.255	.308	.345	.653	70	-9	-10	104	148	25	.556	1	1	-0	-8	O	-2.2
1962	NY-N	30	101	8	15	2	0	1	6	10	7	.149	.225	.198	.423	14	-12	-13	104	103	5	.337	0	1	-1	4	O	-1.0
	Mil-N	79	214	28	61	11	3	5	24	12	17	.285	.323	.435	.758	102	-0	0	99	88	30	.673	0	0	0	-6	O	-0.8
	Yr	109	315	36	76	13	3	6	30	22	24	.241	.291	.359	.650	73	-12	-13	100	93	33	.556	0	1	-1	-2		-1.8
1963	Mil-N	3	3	0	1	0	0	0	0	0	0	.333	.333	.333	.667	92	-0	-0	101	0	0	.500	0	0	0	0	H	0.0
1964	Mil-N	3	3	0	0	0	0	0	0	0	1	.000	.000	.000	.000	-99	-1	-1	97	0	0	.000	0	0	0	0	H	0.0
Total	15	1741	6478	865	1823	311	66	206	942	470	636	.281	.333	.445	.778	102	37	8	103	109	962	.728	30	31		-30	*O	-8.0

■ **FERN BELL** Bell, Fern Lee "Danny" b: 1/21/13, Ada, Okla. BR/TR, 6', 180 lbs. Deb: 4/17/39

YEAR	TM/L	G	AB	R	H	2B	3B	HR	RBI	BB	SO	AVG	OBP	SLG	PRO	/A	BR	/A	PF	CHI	RC	TA	SB	CS	SBR	FR	POS	TPR
1939	Pit-N	83	262	44	75	5	8	2	34	42	18	.286	.385	.389	.774	109	5	5	100	115	42	.764	2			3	O/3	0.6
1940	Pit-N	6	3	0	0	0	0	0	1	1	1	.000	.250	.000	.250	-27	-0	-0	95	0	0	.333	0			0	H	0.0
Total	2	89	265	44	75	5	8	2	35	43	19	.283	.383	.385	.768	107	4	4	100	114	42	.774	2			3	/O3	0.6

■ **FRANK BELL** Bell, Frank Gustav b: 1863, Cincinnati, Ohio d: 4/14/1891, Cincinnati, Ohio Deb: 1885

YEAR	TM/L	G	AB	R	H	2B	3B	HR	RBI	BB	SO	AVG	OBP	SLG	PRO	/A	BR	/A	PF	CHI	RC	TA	SB	CS	SBR	FR	POS	TPR
1885	Bro-a	10	29	5	5	0	1	0		0		.172	.200	.241	.441	39	-2	-2	104	0	1	.333				0	/CO3	-0.1

■ **JAY BELL** Bell, Jay Stuart b: 12/11/65, Eglin A.F.B., Fla. BR/TR, 6'1", 180 lbs. Deb: 9/29/86

YEAR	TM/L	G	AB	R	H	2B	3B	HR	RBI	BB	SO	AVG	OBP	SLG	PRO	/A	BR	/A	PF	CHI	RC	TA	SB	CS	SBR	FR	POS	TPR
1986	Cle-A	5	14	3	5	2	0	1	4	2	3	.357	.438	.714	1.152	213	2	2	98	123	5	1.333	0	0	0	0	/2D	0.2
1987	Cle-A	38	125	14	27	9	1	2	13	8	31	.216	.269	.352	.621	62	-7	-7	103	104	13	.561	2	0	1	-7	S	-1.0
1988	Cle-A	73	211	23	46	5	1	2	21	21	53	.218	.292	.280	.571	60	-11	-11	102	128	18	.500	4	2	0	-11	S/D	-1.9
Total	3	116	350	40	78	16	2	5	38	31	87	.223	.290	.323	.613	67	-15	-16	102	120	36	.549	6	2	1	-18	S/D2	-2.7

■ **RUDY BELL** Bell, John (born Rudolph Fred Baerwald) b: 1/1/1881, Wausau, Wis. d: 7/28/55, Albuquerque, N.M. BR/TR, 5'8.5", 158 lbs. Deb: 9/16/07

YEAR	TM/L	G	AB	R	H	2B	3B	HR	RBI	BB	SO	AVG	OBP	SLG	PRO	/A	BR	/A	PF	CHI	RC	TA	SB	CS	SBR	FR	POS	TPR
1907	NY-A	17	52	4	11	2	1	0	3	3		.212	.255	.288	.543	69	-2	-2	109	71	5	.537	4			2	O	0.0

■ **GEORGE BELL** Bell, Jorge (Mathey) b: 10/21/59, San Pedro De Macoris, D.R. BR/TR, 6'1", 190 lbs. Deb: 4/09/81

YEAR	TM/L	G	AB	R	H	2B	3B	HR	RBI	BB	SO	AVG	OBP	SLG	PRO	/A	BR	/A	PF	CHI	RC	TA	SB	CS	SBR	FR	POS	TPR
1981	Tor-A	60	163	19	38	2	1	5	12	5	27	.233	.256	.350	.606	66	-6	-8	111	65	14	.508	3	2	-0	0	O/D	-0.9
1983	Tor-A	39	112	5	30	5	4	2	17	4	17	.268	.305	.438	.743	94	-0	-1	108	121	13	.644	1	1	-0	-3	O/D	-0.4
1984	Tor-A	159	606	85	177	39	4	26	87	24	86	.292	.328	.498	.826	123	18	17	102	93	95	.775	11	2	2	-2	*O/3D	1.2
1985	Tor-A	157	607	87	167	28	6	28	95	43	90	.275	.331	.479	.811	118	14	13	101	106	97	.800	21	6	3	1	*O/3	1.4
1986	Tor-A	159	641	101	198	38	6	31	108	41	62	.309	.352	.532	.884	131	31	27	105	105	113	.839	7	8	-3	0	*OD/3	1.9
1987	Tor-A	156	610	111	188	32	4	47	**134**	39	75	.308	.357	.605	.962	148	41	40	101	111	125	.955	5	1	1	-4	*O/23D	3.1
1988	Tor-A	156	614	78	165	27	5	24	97	34	66	.269	.308	.446	.754	109	5	5	100	118	78	.663	4	2	0	-12	*O/D	-0.9
Total	7	886	3353	486	963	171	30	163	550	190	423	.287	.331	.502	.833	122	103	93	102	105	536	.803	52	22	2	-20	O/D32	5.4

■ **KEVIN BELL** Bell, Kevin Robert b: 7/13/55, Los Angeles, Cal. BR/TR, 6', 195 lbs. Deb: 6/16/76

YEAR	TM/L	G	AB	R	H	2B	3B	HR	RBI	BB	SO	AVG	OBP	SLG	PRO	/A	BR	/A	PF	CHI	RC	TA	SB	CS	SBR	FR	POS	TPR
1976	Chi-A	68	230	24	57	7	6	5	20	18	56	.248	.305	.396	.701	105	1	1	99	72	28	.633	2	1	0	-1	3/D	0.0
1977	Chi-A	9	28	4	5	1	0	1	6	3	8	.179	.258	.321	.579	57	-2	-2	99	198	3	.522	0	0	0	-1	/S3O	-0.1
1978	Chi-A	54	68	9	13	0	0	2	5	5	19	.191	.257	.279	.536	50	-4	-5	101	79	5	.448	1	0	0	2	3/D	-0.1
1979	Chi-A	70	200	20	49	8	1	4	22	15	43	.245	.298	.355	.653	73	-7	-8	102	102	20	.557	2	4	-2	12	3/S	0.3
1980	Chi-A	92	191	16	34	5	2	1	11	29	37	.178	.286	.241	.527	48	-14	-13	97	88	15	.469	0	0	0	2	3/SD	-0.9
1982	Oak-A	4	9	1	3	1	0	0	0	0	2	.333	.333	.444	.778	117	0	0	95	0	1	.667	0	0	0	0	/3D	0.0
Total	6	297	726	74	161	22	9	13	64	70	165	.222	.292	.331	.623	74	-26	-26	99	89	72	.556	5	5	-2	15	3/SDO	-0.8

■ **LES BELL** Bell, Lester Rowland b: 12/14/01, Harrisburg, Pa. d: 12/26/85, Hershey, Pa. BR/TR, 5'11", 165 lbs. Deb: 9/18/23

YEAR	TM/L	G	AB	R	H	2B	3B	HR	RBI	BB	SO	AVG	OBP	SLG	PRO	/A	BR	/A	PF	CHI	RC	TA	SB	CS	SBR	FR	POS	TPR
1923	StL-N	15	51	5	19	2	1	0	9	9	7	.373	.467	.451	.918	159	4	5	90	140	12	1.031	1	0	0	-1	S	0.5
1924	StL-N	17	57	5	14	3	2	1	5	3	7	.246	.295	.421	.716	88	-1	-1	103	68	7	.651	0	0	0	0	S	0.0
1925	StL-N	153	586	80	167	29	9	11	88	43	47	.285	.334	.422	.755	90	-8	-10	102	114	82	.693	4	5	-2	-1	*3/S	-0.2
1926	StL-N	155	581	85	189	33	14	17	100	54	62	.325	.383	.518	.901	137	32	30	102	104	112	.929	9			-22	*3	0.9
1927	StL-N	115	390	48	101	26	6	9	65	34	63	.259	.320	.426	.746	92	-2	-6	107	118	52	.713	5			-12	*3S	-1.1
1928	Bos-N	153	591	58	164	36	7	10	91	40	45	.277	.323	.413	.736	94	-9	-7	97	125	77	.667	1			5	*3	0.0
1929	Bos-N	139	483	58	144	23	5	9	72	50	42	.298	.364	.422	.786	100	-4	1	94	109	74	.761	4			-23	*3/2S	-1.0
1930	Chi-N	74	248	35	69	15	4	5	47	24	27	.278	.342	.431	.773	81	-6	-8	105	133	36	.737	1			-2	3/1	-0.8
1931	Chi-N	75	252	30	71	17	1	4	32	19	22	.282	.332	.405	.737	101	-1	0	96	100	35	.669	0			7	3	1.1
Total	9	896	3239	404	938	184	49	66	509	276	322	.290	.346	.438	.784	102	3	2	100	114	486	.746	25	5		-49	3/S12	-0.6

■ **BEAU BELL** Bell, Roy Chester b: 8/20/07, Bellville, Tex. d: 9/14/77, College Station, Tex. BR/TR, 6'2", 185 lbs. Deb: 4/16/35

YEAR	TM/L	G	AB	R	H	2B	3B	HR	RBI	BB	SO	AVG	OBP	SLG	PRO	/A	BR	/A	PF	CHI	RC	TA	SB	CS	SBR	FR	POS	TPR
1935	StL-A	76	220	20	55	8	2	3	17	16	16	.250	.304	.345	.649	63	-11	-13	107	68	23	.566	1	1	-0	-6	O1/3	-1.9
1936	StL-A	155	616	100	212	40	12	11	123	60	55	.344	.403	.502	.905	118	21	18	103	123	126	.923	4	1	1	-3	*O1	0.8
1937	StL-A	156	642	82	**218**	**51**	8	14	117	53	54	.340	.391	.509	.900	127	23	25	99	104	127	.899	2	2	-1	0	*O1/3	1.5
1938	StL-A	147	526	91	138	35	3	13	84	71	46	.262	.350	.414	.765	91	-8	-8	100	113	79	.742	1	3	-2	4	*O/1	-0.4
1939	StL-A	11	32	4	7	1	0	1	5	4	3	.219	.324	.344	.668	71	-1	-1	100	121	4	.615	0	0	0	-1	/O	-0.1
	Det-A	54	134	14	32	4	2	0	24	24	16	.239	.358	.299	.657	63	-5	-8	111	203	15	.596	0	1	-1	0	O	-0.8
	Yr	65	166	18	39	5	2	1	29	28	19	.235	.352	.307	.659	64	-7	-9	109	190	19	.604	0	1	-1	-1		-0.9
1940	Cle-A	120	444	55	124	22	2	4	58	34	41	.279	.332	.365	.697	86	-13	-8	93	123	55	.603	2	2	-1	-6	O1	-2.1
1941	Cle-A	48	104	12	20	4	3	0	9	10	8	.192	.270	.288	.558	47	-8	-8	101	106	8	.472	1	2	-1	-3	O1	-1.2
Total	7	767	2718	378	806	165	32	46	437	272	239	.297	.362	.432	.794	99	-2	-4	100	116	437	.759	11	12	-4	-14	O/13	-4.2

■ **TERRY BELL** Bell, Terence William b: 10/27/62, Dayton, Ohio BR/TR, 6', 195 lbs. Deb: 9/03/86

YEAR	TM/L	G	AB	R	H	2B	3B	HR	RBI	BB	SO	AVG	OBP	SLG	PRO	/A	BR	/A	PF	CHI	RC	TA	SB	CS	SBR	FR	POS	TPR
1986	KC-A	8	3	0	0	0	0	0	0	2	1	.000	.400	.000	.400	22	-0	-0	100	0	0	.667	0	0	0	0	/C	0.0
1987	Atl-N	1	1	0	0	0	0	0	0	0	1	.000	.000	.000	.000	-92	-0	-0	108	0	0	.000	0	0	0	0	/H	0.0

YEAR	TM/L	G	AB	R	H	2B	3B	HR	RBI	BB	SO	AVG	OBP	SLG	PRO	/A	BR	/A	PF	CHI	RC	TA	SB	CS	SBR	FR	POS	TPR
Total	2	9	4	0	0	0	0	0	0	2	2	.000	.333	.000	.333	1	-0	-0	101	0	0	.500	0	0	0	0	/C	0.0
■ **ZEKE BELLA**	Bella, John b: 8/23/30, Greenwich, Conn. BR/TL, 5'11", 185 lbs. Deb: 9/11/57																											
1957	NY-A	5	10	0	1	0	0	0	0	1	2	.100	.182	.100	.282	-22	-2	-2	94	0	0	.222	0	0	0	1	/O	0.0
1959	KC-A	47	82	10	17	2	1	1	9	9	14	.207	.293	.293	.586	61	-4	-4	101	131	6	.486	0	0	0	-4	O/1	-0.9
Total	2	52	92	10	18	2	1	1	9	10	16	.196	.282	.272	.553	52	-6	-6	100	117	7	.456	0	0	0	-4	/O1	-0.9
■ **STEVE BELLAN**	Bellan, Esteban Enrique b: 1850, Cuba d: 8/8/32, Havana, Cuba 5'6", 154 lbs. Deb: 5/09/1871																											
1871	Tro-n	29	136	25	29							.213															*3/S	
1872	Tro-n	23	115	22	32							.278															/S3O	
1873	Mut-n	7	37	4	7							.189															/3	
Total	3 n	59	288	51	68							.236															/3	
■ **RAFAEL BELLIARD**	Belliard, Rafael Leonidas b: 10/24/61, Pueblo Nuevo, D.R. BR/TR, 5'9", 139 lbs. Deb: 9/06/82																											
1982	Pit-N	9	2	3	1	0	0	0	0	0	0	.500	.500	.500	1.000	164	0	0	110	0	1	2.000	1	0	0	0	/S	0.1
1983	Pit-N	4	1	1	0	0	0	0	0	0	1	.000	.000	.000	.000	-97	-0	-0	103	0	0	.000	0	0	0	0	/S	0.0
1984	Pit-N	20	22	3	5	0	0	0	0	0	1	.227	.227	.227	.455	30	-2	-2	94	0	1	.500	4	1	1	0	S/2	0.0
1985	Pit-N	17	20	1	4	0	0	0	1	0	5	.200	.200	.200	.400	12	-2	-2	103	100	1	.250	0	0	0	1	S	0.0
1986	Pit-N	117	309	33	72	5	2	0	31	26	54	.233	.299	.262	.561	56	-18	-18	100	153	26	.494	12	2	2	5	S2	0.0
1987	Pit-N	81	203	26	42	4	3	1	15	20	25	.207	.288	.271	.559	47	-15	-16	104	103	17	.500	5	1	1	-3	S/2	-0.9
1988	Pit-N	122	286	28	61	0	4	0	11	26	47	.213	.288	.241	.529	55	-16	-16	98	64	21	.449	7	1	2	-9	*S/2	-1.5
Total	7	370	843	95	185	9	9	1	58	72	133	.219	.289	.255	.544	52	-53	-54	100	105	66	.484	29	5	6	-5	S/2	-2.3
■ **JACK BELLMAN**	Bellman, John Hutchins "Happy Jack" b: 3/4/1864, Taylorsville, Ky. d: 12/8/31, Louisville, Ky. Deb: 4/23/1889																											
1889	StL-a	1	2	1	1	0	0	0	0	1	0	.500	.667	.500	1.167	212	1	0	112	0	1	2.000	0			0	/C	0.0
■ **ROB BELLOIR**	Belloir, Robert Edward b: 7/13/48, Heidelberg, Ger. BR/TR, 5'10", 155 lbs. Deb: 8/02/75																											
1975	Atl-N	43	105	11	23	2	1	0	9	7	8	.219	.268	.257	.525	49	-8	-7	95	129	7	.391	0	0	0	-2	S/2	-0.4
1976	Atl-N	30	60	5	12	2	0	0	4	5	7	.200	.262	.233	.495	37	-5	-5	111	110	4	.396	0	0	0	0	S3/2	-0.3
1977	Atl-N	6	1	2	0	0	0	0	0	0	0	.000	.000	.000	.000	-89	-0	-0	113	0	0	.000	0	0	0	0	/S	0.0
1978	Atl-N	2	1	0	1	1	0	0	0	0	0	1.000	1.000	2.000	3.000	644	1	1	112	0	2	—	0	0	0	0	/S3	0.1
Total	4	81	167	18	36	5	1	0	13	12	15	.216	.268	.257	.526	47	-12	-12	101	121	13	.420	0	0	0	-2	/S32	-0.6
■ **HARRY BEMIS**	Bemis, Harry Parker b: 2/1/1874, Farmington, N.H. d: 5/23/47, Cleveland, Ohio BR/TR, 5'6.5", 155 lbs. Deb: 4/23/02																											
1902	Cle-A	93	317	42	99	12	7	1	29	19		.312	.351	.404	.755	114	4	6	97	73	47	.688	3			-2	C/O2	1.0
1903	Cle-A	92	314	31	82	20	3	1	41	8		.261	.280	.354	.633	94	-4	-3	96	130	33	.534	5			0	C1/2	0.7
1904	Cle-A	97	336	35	76	11	6	0	25	8		.226	.244	.295	.539	71	-11	-11	102	96	26	.435	6			-5	C1/2	-0.8
1905	Cle-A	70	226	27	66	13	3	0	28	13		.292	.331	.376	.707	127	6	6	100	118	30	.631	3			-4	C/231	0.9
1906	Cle-A	93	297	28	82	13	5	2	30	12		.276	.304	.374	.678	110	4	3	103	93	37	.609	8			-8	C	0.2
1907	Cle-A	65	172	12	43	7	0	0	19	7		.250	.279	.291	.570	90	-3	-2	93	136	16	.481	5			-5	C/1	-0.2
1908	Cle-A	91	277	23	62	9	1	0	33	7		.224	.243	.264	.506	63	-10	-12	106	170	20	.437	14			-8	C/1	-1.3
1909	Cle-A	42	123	4	23	2	3	0	13	0		.187	.194	.252	.446	40	-9	-9	102	162	6	.340	2			1	C	-0.5
1910	Cle-A	61	167	11	36	5	1	1	16	5		.216	.238	.275	.514	61	-8	-8	100	121	12	.412	3			-2	C	-0.5
Total	9	704	2229	213	569	92	29	5	234	79		.255	.281	.329	.610	89	-32	-31	100	117	227	.520	49			-32	C/123O	-0.5
■ **JOHNNY BENCH**	Bench, Johnny Lee b: 12/7/47, Oklahoma City, Okla. BR/TR, 6'1", 197 lbs. Deb: 8/28/67																											
1967	Cin-N	26	86	7	14	3	1	1	6	5	19	.163	.209	.256	.465	30	-8	-9	109	99	4	.351	0	1	-1	-2	C	-0.9
1968	Cin-N	154	564	67	155	40	2	15	82	31	96	.275	.315	.433	.748	110	14	7	111	122	71	.650	1	5	-3	14	*C	2.7
1969	Cin-N	148	532	83	156	23	1	26	90	49	86	.293	.357	.487	.844	136	23	24	99	109	92	.817	6	6	-2	13	*C	4.6
1970	Cin-N	158	605	97	177	35	4	**45**	**148**	54	102	.293	.351	.587	.937	140	36	32	104	124	121	.937	5	2	0	3	*CO1/3	3.9
1971	Cin-N	149	562	80	134	19	2	27	61	49	83	.238	.300	.423	.723	107	-0	2	96	82	66	.644	2	1	0	-1	*C1O/3	0.3
1972	Cin-N	147	538	87	145	22	2	**40**	**125**	100	84	.270	.386	.541	.927	**172**	44	49	93	132	110	.957	6	6	-2	4	*CO/13	**6.0**
1973	Cin-N	152	557	83	141	17	3	25	104	83	83	.253	.350	.429	.779	123	12	17	93	**141**	82	.743	4	1	1	-2	*CO/13	2.2
1974	Cin-N	160	621	108	174	38	2	33	**129**	80	90	.280	.365	.507	.872	145	33	35	98	127	114	.869	5	4	-1	-7	*C3/1	3.3
1975	Cin-N	142	530	83	150	39	1	28	110	65	108	.283	.363	.519	.882	137	29	26	104	121	101	.901	11	0	3	-1	*CO/1	3.2
1976	Cin-N	135	465	62	109	24	1	16	74	81	95	.234	.350	.394	.744	108	8	6	103	126	69	.760	13	2	3	2	*C/O1	1.9
1977	Cin-N	142	494	67	136	34	2	31	109	58	95	.275	.353	.540	.893	136	23	23	100	124	92	.882	2	4	-2	-11	*C/O13	0.8
1978	Cin-N	120	393	52	102	17	1	23	73	50	83	.260	.345	.483	.828	126	14	13	103	112	65	.811	4	2	0	-12	*C1/O	0.4
1979	Cin-N	130	464	73	128	19	0	22	80	67	73	.276	.367	.459	.826	127	16	18	97	116	79	.814	4	2	0	9	*C/1	3.0
1980	Cin-N	114	360	52	90	12	0	24	68	41	64	.250	.330	.483	.813	122	11	10	102	109	57	.786	4	2	0	-7	*C	0.5
1981	Cin-N	52	178	14	55	8	0	8	25	17	21	.309	.369	.489	.858	140	9	9	101	88	31	.806	0	2	-1	-4	1/C	0.3
1982	Cin-N	119	399	44	103	16	0	13	38	37	58	.258	.321	.396	.717	97	-1	-2	102	76	48	.628	1	2	-1	-5	*3/1C	-1.0
1983	Cin-N	110	310	32	79	15	2	12	54	24	38	.255	.308	.432	.741	100	0	-1	103	126	37	.645	0	1	-1	-6	31/CO	-1.0
Total	17	2158	7658	1091	2048	381	24	389	1376	891	1278	.267	.345	.476	.821	127	264	260	100	117	1240	.816	68	43	-5	-11	*C31O	30.2
■ **ART BENEDICT**	Benedict, Arthur M. b: 3/31/1862, Cornwall, Ill. d: 1/20/48, Denver, Colo. BR/TR, Deb: 5/14/1883																											
1883	Phi-N	3	15	3	4	1	0	0	4	0	4	.267	.267	.333	.600	90	-0	-0	90	239	1	.455				0	/2	0.0
■ **BRUCE BENEDICT**	Benedict, Bruce Edwin b: 8/18/55, Birmingham, Ala. BR/TR, 6'1", 175 lbs. Deb: 8/18/78																											
1978	Atl-N	22	52	3	13	2	0	0	1	6	6	.250	.328	.288	.616	66	-2	-2	112	26	5	.538	0	0	0	1	C	0.0
1979	Atl-N	76	204	14	46	11	0	0	15	33	18	.225	.333	.279	.613	63	-8	-10	109	104	20	.552	1	3	-2	-3	C	-1.3
1980	Atl-N	120	359	18	91	14	1	2	34	28	36	.253	.309	.315	.624	74	-12	-12	101	113	34	.514	3	3	-1	0	*C	-1.1
1981	Atl-N	90	295	26	78	12	1	5	35	33	21	.264	.344	.363	.707	101	1	1	100	115	37	.637	1	1	-0	11	C	1.4
1982	Atl-N	118	386	34	95	11	1	3	44	37	40	.246	.317	.303	.620	69	-12	-16	107	137	37	.528	4	4	-1	-1	*C	-1.7
1983	Atl-N	134	423	43	126	13	1	2	43	61	24	.298	.388	.348	.735	100	6	3	106	111	57	.673	1	3	-2	4	*C	1.0
1984	Atl-N	95	300	26	67	8	1	4	25	34	25	.223	.304	.297	.601	63	-12	-15	110	97	27	.512	1	2	-1	8	C	-0.4
1985	Atl-N	70	208	12	42	6	0	0	20	22	12	.202	.281	.231	.512	42	-15	-16	106	166	13	.406	0	1	-1	3	C	-1.1
1986	Atl-N	64	160	11	36	10	1	0	13	15	10	.225	.299	.300	.599	64	-7	-8	102	108	13	.496	1	0	0	6	C	0.0
1987	Atl-N	37	95	4	14	1	0	1	5	17	15	.147	.277	.189	.466	24	-10	-11	108	95	6	.417	0	1	-1	5	C	-0.3
1988	Atl-N	90	236	11	57	7	0	0	19	19	26	.242	.298	.271	.569	62	-10	-12	104	119	20	.454	0	2	-1	-1	C	-0.9
Total	11	916	2718	202	665	95	6	17	254	305	233	.245	.324	.303	.626	72	-81	-99	105	116	270	.555	12	20	-8	34	C	-4.4
■ **JOE BENES**	Benes, Joseph Anthony "Bananas" b: 1/8/01, Long Island City, N.Y. d: 3/7/75, Elmhurst, N.J. BR/TR, 5'8.5", 158 lbs. Deb: 5/09/31																											
1931	StL-N	10	12	1	2	0	0	0	0	2	1	.167	.333	.167	.500	36	-1	-1	107	0	1	.500	0			0	/S23	0.0
■ **BENNY BENGOUGH**	Bengough, Bernard Oliver b: 7/27/1898, Niagara Falls, N.Y. d: 12/22/68, Philadelphia, Pa. BR/TR, 5'7.5", 168 lbs. Deb: 5/18/23 C																											
1923	NY-A	19	53	1	7	2	0	0	3	4	2	.132	.193	.170	.363	-4	-8	-8	104	114	2	.283	0	0	0	-1	C	-0.7
1924	NY-A	11	16	4	5	1	1	0	3	2	0	.313	.389	.500	.889	129	1	1	99	124	3	.909	0	0	0	-0	C	0.1
1925	NY-A	95	283	17	73	14	2	0	23	19	9	.258	.305	.322	.626	61	-18	-16	96	85	28	.519	0	2	-1	4	C	-0.7
1926	NY-A	36	84	9	32	6	0	0	14	7	4	.381	.435	.452	.887	132	4	4	99	125	17	.904	1	0	0	1	C	0.7
1927	NY-A	31	85	6	21	3	3	0	10	4	4	.247	.281	.353	.634	64	-5	-5	100	111	8	.531	0	0	0	-1	C	-0.4
1928	NY-A	58	161	12	43	3	1	0	9	7	8	.267	.302	.298	.600	63	-10	-8	92	64	15	.475	0	0	0	-5	C	-0.8
1929	NY-A	23	62	5	12	2	1	0	7	0	2	.194	.194	.258	.452	15	-8	-8	99	150	3	.320	0	0	0	-0	C	-0.5
1930	NY-A	44	102	10	24	4	2	0	12	3	8	.235	.257	.314	.571	49	-9	-7	90	124	8	.462	1	0	0	-3	C	-0.5
1931	StL-A	40	140	6	35	4	1	0	12	4	4	.250	.271	.293	.564	47	-11	-11	102	97	10	.417	0	3	-2	3	C	-0.6
1932	StL-A	54	139	13	35	7	1	0	15	12	4	.252	.311	.317	.628	63	-8	-8	100	114	14	.533	0	1	-1	2	C	-0.2
Total	10	411	1125	83	287	46	12	0	108	62	45	.255	.295	.317	.613	60	-71	-66	97	101	108	.501	2	6	-3	-1	C	-3.6
■ **JUAN BENIQUEZ**	Beniquez, Juan Jose (Torres) b: 5/13/50, San Sebastian, P.R. BR/TR, 5'11", 150 lbs. Deb: 9/04/71																											
1971	Bos-A	16	57	8	17	2	0	0	4	3	4	.298	.333	.333	.667	85	-1	-1	106	88	6	.568	3	1	0	-3	S	-0.2

YEAR	TM/L	G	AB	R	H	2B	3B	HR	RBI	BB	SO	AVG	OBP	SLG	PRO	/A	BR	/A	PF	CHI	RC	TA	SB	CS	SBR	FR	POS	TPR
1972	Bos-A	33	99	10	24	4	1	1	8	7	11	.242	.292	.333	.626	82	-2	-2	105	93	10	.545	2	0	1	-2	S	0.0
1974	Bos-A	106	389	60	104	14	3	5	33	25	61	.267	.313	.357	.671	87	-4	-7	107	86	41	.603	19	11	-1	-4	O/D	-1.4
1975	Bos-A	78	254	43	74	14	4	2	17	25	26	.291	.359	.402	.761	106	5	2	109	60	34	.690	7	10	-4	3	OD3	0.0
1976	Tex-A	145	478	49	122	14	4	0	33	39	56	.255	.315	.301	.617	79	-11	-12	102	88	47	.546	17	6	2	13	*O/2	0.0
1977	Tex-A	123	424	56	114	19	6	10	50	43	43	.269	.338	.413	.750	99	2	-1	105	97	55	.718	26	18	-3	-1	*O	-0.7
1978	Tex-A	127	473	61	123	17	3	11	50	20	59	.260	.294	.378	.673	91	-9	-7	96	95	48	.570	10	12	-4	-7	*O	-2.1
1979	NY-A	62	142	19	36	6	1	4	17	9	17	.254	.307	.394	.702	92	-3	-2	96	96	16	.614	3	3	-1	-5	O/3	-0.9
1980	Sea-A	70	237	26	54	10	0	6	21	17	25	.228	.280	.346	.626	68	-10	-11	103	82	20	.515	2	3	-1	6	O/D	-0.7
1981	Cal-A	58	166	18	30	5	0	3	13	15	16	.181	.253	.265	.518	47	-11	-12	104	96	11	.434	2	1	0	-4	O/D	-1.7
1982	Cal-A	112	196	25	52	11	2	3	24	15	21	.265	.321	.388	.709	93	-2	-2	100	113	25	.642	3	0	1	-25	*O	-2.9
1983	Cal-A	92	315	44	96	15	0	3	34	15	29	.305	.344	.381	.725	104	-0	2	96	103	39	.619	4	2	0	-1	O/D	0.0
1984	Cal-A	110	354	60	119	17	0	8	39	18	43	.336	.373	.452	.825	125	13	12	101	84	55	.724	0	3	-2	-4	O	0.3
1985	Cal-A	132	411	54	125	13	5	8	42	34	46	.304	.364	.418	.783	113	8	8	101	85	59	.705	4	3	-1	-11	O1D/3S	-0.7
1986	Bal-A	113	343	48	103	15	0	6	36	40	49	.300	.378	.397	.775	114	7	8	99	93	51	.710	2	3	-1	-3	O3D1	0.0
1987	KC-A	57	174	14	41	7	0	3	26	11	26	.236	.285	.328	.613	60	-9	-10	104	157	14	.486	0	0	0	-3	OD/13	-1.3
	Tor-A	39	81	6	23	5	1	5	21	5	13	.284	.333	.556	.889	130	3	3	101	140	14	.836	0	0	0	-2	D/O1	0.1
	Yr	96	255	20	64	12	1	8	47	16	39	.251	.300	.400	.700	82	-6	-7	103	152	31	.619	0	0	0	-4		-1.2
1988	Tor-A	27	58	9	17	2	0	1	8	8	6	.293	.379	.379	.758	113	1	1	100	127	8	.667	0	0	0	-0	D/O	0.1
Total	17	1500	4651	610	1274	190	30	79	476	349	551	.274	.329	.379	.707	95	-21	-30	102	94	553	.649	104	76	-14	-54	*OD/13S2	-12.1

■ STAN BENJAMIN Benjamin, Alfred Stanley b: 5/20/14, Framingham, Mass. BR/TR, 6'2", 194 lbs. Deb: 9/16/39

YEAR	TM/L	G	AB	R	H	2B	3B	HR	RBI	BB	SO	AVG	OBP	SLG	PRO	/A	BR	/A	PF	CHI	RC	TA	SB	CS	SBR	FR	POS	TPR
1939	Phi-N	12	50	4	7	2	1	0	2	1	6	.140	.157	.220	.377	0	-7	-7	94	64	1	.271	1			-0	/O3	-0.6
1940	Phi-N	8	9	1	2	0	0	0	1	1	1	.222	.300	.222	.522	47	-1	-1	97	185	1	.429	0			0	/O	0.0
1941	Phi-N	129	480	47	113	20	7	3	27	20	81	.235	.266	.325	.591	68	-23	-21	97	60	39	.507	17			-5	*O/123	-3.2
1942	Phi-N	78	210	24	47	8	3	2	8	10	27	.224	.262	.319	.581	74	-9	-7	94	41	18	.503	5			-1	O1	-1.1
1945	Cle-A	14	21	1	7	2	0	0	3	0	0	.333	.333	.429	.762	122	0	0	99	121	3	.600	0	1	-1	1	/O	0.1
Total	5	241	770	77	176	32	11	5	41	32	115	.229	.260	.318	.578	66	-39	-36	96	58	61	.506	23	1		-4	O/132	-4.8

■ IKE BENNERS Benners, Isaac B. b: Philadelphia, Pa. BL, 175 lbs. Deb: 5/01/1884

YEAR	TM/L	G	AB	R	H	2B	3B	HR	RBI	BB	SO	AVG	OBP	SLG	PRO	/A	BR	/A	PF	CHI	RC	TA	SB	CS	SBR	FR	POS	TPR
1884	Bro-a	49	189	25	38	11	5	1		7		.201	.237	.328	.565	87	-3	-2	98	0	15	.470				-6	O	-0.8
	WiL-U	6	22	0	1	0	0	0		1		.045	.087	.045	.132	-53	-3	-4	103	0	0	.095	0			0	/O	-0.2
Total	1	55	211	25	39	11	5	1		8		.185	.222	.299	.520	72	-6	-6	98	0	15	.424	0			-6	/O	-1.0

■ CHARLIE BENNETT Bennett, Charles Wesley b: 11/21/1854, New Castle, Pa. d: 2/24/27, Detroit, Mich. BR/TR, 5'11", 180 lbs. Deb: 5/01/1878

YEAR	TM/L	G	AB	R	H	2B	3B	HR	RBI	BB	SO	AVG	OBP	SLG	PRO	/A	BR	/A	PF	CHI	RC	TA	SB	CS	SBR	FR	POS	TPR
1878	Mil-N	49	184	16	45	9	0	1	12	10	26	.245	.284	.310	.593	89	-1	-2	107	69	17	.482				-13	CO	-1.5
1880	Wor-N	51	193	20	44	9	3	0	18	10	30	.228	.266	.306	.572	83	-1	-4	113	118	16	.463				-4	C/O	-0.3
1881	Det-N	76	299	44	90	18	7	7	64	18	37	.301	.341	.478	.819	145	18	15	106	144	50	.770				14	*C/3O	2.7
1882	Det-N	84	342	43	103	16	10	5	51	20	33	.301	.340	.450	.790	148	19	18	102	108	54	.728				6	*C3/2S1	2.6
1883	Det-N	92	371	56	113	34	7	5	55	26	59	.305	.350	.474	.825	162	21	26	91	106	63	.783				12	*C2O	**3.6**
1884	Det-N	90	341	37	90	18	6	3	40	36	40	.264	.334	.378	.713	132	10	14	94	96	44	.657				3	*C/OS321	2.1
1885	Det-N	91	349	49	94	24	13	5	60	47	37	.269	.356	.456	.812	165	25	26	97	106	58	.808				5	CO3	3.3
1886	Det-N	72	235	37	57	13	5	4	34	48	29	.243	.371	.391	.763	121	11	8	109	109	37	.809	4			8	C/OS	1.8
1887	Det-N	46	160	26	39	6	5	3	20	30	22	.244	.363	.400	.763	112	4	3	102	86	26	.835	7			2	C/O1	0.9
1888	Det-N	74	258	32	68	12	4	5	29	31	40	.264	.347	.399	.746	142	12	13	98	90	38	.737	4			8	C/1	2.3
1889	Bos-N	82	247	42	57	8	2	4	28	21	43	.231	.296	.328	.624	74	-8	-9	102	90	27	.584	7			-4	C	-0.9
1890	Bos-N	85	281	59	60	17	2	3	40	72	56	.214	.377	.320	.698	96	6	1	111	124	37	.769	6			3	C	0.8
1891	Bos-N	75	256	35	55	9	3	5	39	42	61	.215	.332	.332	.664	86	-0	-5	112	116	30	.662	3			2	C	0.2
1892	Bos-N	35	114	19	23	4	0	1	16	27	23	.202	.355	.263	.618	79	0	-2	113	152	13	.692	6			0	C	-0.1
1893	Bos-N	60	191	34	40	6	0	4	27	40	36	.209	.352	.304	.656	75	-5	-6	103	106	23	.695	5			-9	C	-0.7
Total	15	1062	3821	549	978	203	67	55	533	478	572	.256	.340	.387	.728	119	111	95	103	108	532	.707	42			32	C/O32S1	16.8

■ HERSCHEL BENNETT Bennett, Herschel Emmett b: 9/21/1896, Elwood, Mo. d: 9/9/64, Springfield, Mo. BL/TR, 5'9.5", 160 lbs. Deb: 4/19/23

YEAR	TM/L	G	AB	R	H	2B	3B	HR	RBI	BB	SO	AVG	OBP	SLG	PRO	/A	BR	/A	PF	CHI	RC	TA	SB	CS	SBR	FR	POS	TPR
1923	StL-A	5	4	0	0	0	0	0	0	1	1	.000	.200	.000	.200	-43	-1	-1	104	0	0	.250	0	0	0	-0	/O	0.0
1924	StL-A	41	94	16	31	4	3	1	11	3	6	.330	.364	.468	.832	106	1	0	107	77	16	.794	1	0	0	-4	O	-0.4
1925	StL-A	93	298	46	83	11	6	2	37	18	16	.279	.324	.376	.700	72	-11	-14	108	105	34	.610	4	8	-4	-2	O	-2.4
1926	StL-A	80	225	33	60	14	2	1	26	22	21	.267	.337	.360	.697	81	-6	-6	101	105	28	.645	2	1	0	3	O	-0.6
1927	StL-A	93	256	40	68	12	2	3	30	14	21	.266	.311	.363	.675	70	-10	-12	106	98	28	.617	6	0	2	-0	O	-1.5
Total	5	312	877	135	242	41	13	7	104	58	65	.276	.327	.376	.704	77	-27	-33	105	99	108	.637	13	9	-2	-4	O	-4.9

■ FRED BENNETT Bennett, James Fred "Red" b: 3/15/02, Atkins, Ark. d: 5/12/57, Atkins, Ark. BR/TR, 5'9", 185 lbs. Deb: 4/13/28

YEAR	TM/L	G	AB	R	H	2B	3B	HR	RBI	BB	SO	AVG	OBP	SLG	PRO	/A	BR	/A	PF	CHI	RC	TA	SB	CS	SBR	FR	POS	TPR
1928	StL-A	7	8	0	2	1	0	0	0	0	2	.250	.250	.375	.625	60	-0	-1	104	0	1	.500	0	0	0	0	/O	0.0
1931	Pit-N	32	89	6	25	5	0	1	7	7	4	.281	.333	.371	.704	89	-1	-1	101	69	11	.625	0			-2	O	-0.4
Total	2	39	97	6	27	6	0	1	7	7	6	.278	.327	.371	.698	86	-2	-2	101	64	12	.614	0	0		-2	/O	-0.4

■ JOE BENNETT Bennett, Joseph Rosenblum b: 7/2/1900, New York, N.Y. d: 7/11/87, Morro Bay, Cal. BR/TR, 5'9", 168 lbs. Deb: 7/05/23

YEAR	TM/L	G	AB	R	H	2B	3B	HR	RBI	BB	SO	AVG	OBP	SLG	PRO	/A	BR	/A	PF	CHI	RC	TA	SB	CS	SBR	FR	POS	TPR
1923	Phi-N	1	0	0	0	0	0	0	0	0	0	—	—	—	—	—	0	0	114	—	—	—	0	0	0	0	/3	0.0

■ PUG BENNETT Bennett, Justin Titus b: 2/20/1874, Ponca, Neb. d: 9/12/35, Kirkland, Wash. TR, 5'11", 165 lbs. Deb: 4/12/06

YEAR	TM/L	G	AB	R	H	2B	3B	HR	RBI	BB	SO	AVG	OBP	SLG	PRO	/A	BR	/A	PF	CHI	RC	TA	SB	CS	SBR	FR	POS	TPR
1906	StL-N	153	595	66	156	16	7	1	34	56		.262	.326	.318	.643	102	2	2	101	57	70	.604	20			-2	*2	0.0
1907	StL-N	87	324	20	72	8	2	0	21	21		.222	.270	.259	.529	70	-12	-11	96	91	25	.444	7			-3	2/3	-1.3
Total	2	240	919	86	228	24	9	1	55	77		.248	.306	.297	.603	91	-10	-9	99	69	95	.546	27			-5	2/3	-1.3

■ VERN BENSON Benson, Vernon Adair b: 9/19/24, Granite Quarry, N.C. BL/TR, 5'10", 160 lbs. Deb: 7/31/43 MC

YEAR	TM/L	G	AB	R	H	2B	3B	HR	RBI	BB	SO	AVG	OBP	SLG	PRO	/A	BR	/A	PF	CHI	RC	TA	SB	CS	SBR	FR	POS	TPR
1943	Phi-A	2	2	0	0	0	0	0	0	0	0	.000	.000	.000	.000	-99	-0	-0	101	0	0	.000	0	0	0	0	H	0.0
1946	Phi-A	7	5	1	0	0	0	0	0	1	3	.000	.167	.000	.167	-49	-1	-1	104	0	0	.200	0	0	0	-0	/O	0.0
1951	StL-N	13	46	8	12	3	1	1	7	6	8	.261	.346	.435	.781	108	1	0	101	120	8	.765	0	0	0	1	/3O	0.1
1952	StL-N	20	47	6	9	2	0	2	5	5	9	.191	.269	.362	.631	75	-2	-2	98	85	5	.579	0	0	0	0	3	0.0
1953	StL-N	13	4	2	0	0	0	0	0	1	2	.000	.200	.000	.200	-41	-1	-1	102	0	0	.250	0	0	0	0	H	0.0
Total	5	55	104	17	21	5	1	3	12	13	22	.202	.291	.356	.646	76	-4	-4	100	91	13	.602	0	0	0	1	/3O	0.1

■ JACK BENTLEY Bentley, John Needles b: 3/8/1895, Sandy Spring, Md. d: 10/24/69, Olney, Md. BL/TL, 5'11.5", 200 lbs. Deb: 9/06/13

YEAR	TM/L	G	AB	R	H	2B	3B	HR	RBI	BB	SO	AVG	OBP	SLG	PRO	/A	BR	/A	PF	CHI	RC	TA	SB	CS	SBR	FR	POS	TPR
1913	Was-A	3	3	0	0	0	0	0	0	0	0	.000	.000	.000	.000	-95	-1	-1	106	0	0	.000	0			0	/P	0.0
1914	Was-A	30	40	7	11	2	0	0	4	0	5	.275	.275	.325	.600	79	-1	-1	101	115	4	.448	0			-1	P	0.0
1915	Was-A	4	2	0	0	0	0	0	0	0	1	.000	.000	.000	.000	-99	-0	-0	101	0	0	.000	0			-0	/P	0.0
1916	Was-A	2	0	0	0	0	0	0	0	0	0	—	—	—	—	—	0	0	100	—	—	—	0			0	/P	0.0
1923	NY-N	52	89	9	38	6	2	1	14	3	4	.427	.446	.573	1.019	165	8	8	101	91	22	1.059	0	0	0	-1	P	0.0
1924	NY-N	46	98	12	26	5	1	0	6	3	13	.265	.287	.337	.624	73	-5	-4	91	66	9	.500	0	0	0	-1	P	0.0
1925	NY-N	64	99	10	30	5	2	3	18	9	11	.303	.361	.485	.846	115	2	2	99	112	17	.826	0	0	0	-2	P/O1	0.5
1926	Phi-N	75	240	19	62	12	3	2	27	5	4	.258	.273	.358	.632	67	-11	-12	103	102	22	.511	0			-2	1/P	-1.4
	NY-N	3	4	0	1	0	0	0	0	0	0	.250	.250	.250	.500	36	-0	-0	98	0	0	.333	0			0	/P	0.0
	Yr	78	244	19	63	12	3	2	27	5	4	.258	.273	.357	.630	66	-12	-13	103	99	23	.508	0			-2		-1.4
1927	NY-N	8	9	1	2	0	0	1	2	1	1	.222	.300	.556	.856	125	0	0	100	87	1	.857	0			0	/P1	0.1
Total	9	287	584	58	170	30	8	7	71	21	39	.291	.316	.406	.722	92	-8	-8	100	95	77	.623	0	0		-5	P/1O	-0.8

■ BUTCH BENTON Benton, Alfred Lee b: 8/24/57, Tampa, Fla. BR/TR, 6'1", 190 lbs. Deb: 9/14/78

YEAR	TM/L	G	AB	R	H	2B	3B	HR	RBI	BB	SO	AVG	OBP	SLG	PRO	/A	BR	/A	PF	CHI	RC	TA	SB	CS	SBR	FR	POS	TPR
1978	NY-N	4	4	1	2	0	0	0	2	0	0	.500	.600	.500	1.100	214	1	1	98	397	1	1.500	0	0	0	0	/C	0.1
1980	NY-N	12	21	0	1	0	0	0	0	2	4	.048	.167	.048	.214	-39	-4	-4	96	0	0	.190	0	0	0	0	/C	-0.2
1982	Chi-N	4	7	0	1	0	0	0	1	0	1	.143	.143	.143	.286	-19	-1	-1	103	392	0	.167	0	0	0	0	/C	0.0
1985	Cle-A	31	67	5	12	4	0	0	7	3	9	.179	.214	.239	.453	25	-7	-7	94	174	3	.339	0	0	0	2	C	-0.3

YEAR	TM/L	G	AB	R	H	2B	3B	HR	RBI	BB	SO	AVG	OBP	SLG	PRO	/A	BR	/A	PF	CHI	RC	TA	SB	CS	SBR	FR	POS	TPR
Total	4	51	99	6	16	4	0	0	10	5	14	.162	.217	.202	.419	17	-11	-11	95	159	5	.321	0	0	0	3	/C	-0.4
■ **RABBIT BENTON**	Benton, Stanley W. "Stan" b: 9/29/01, Canal City, Ky. d: 6/7/84, Mesquite, Tex. BR/TR, 5'7", 150 lbs. Deb: 9/13/22																											
1922	Phi-N	6	19	1	4	1	0	0	3	2	1	.211	.286	.263	.549	37	-2	-2	113	210	2	.467	0	0	0	1	/2	0.0
■ **TODD BENZINGER**	Benzinger, Todd Eric b: 2/11/63, Dayton, Ky. BB/TR, 6'1", 185 lbs. Deb: 6/21/87																											
1987	Bos-A	73	223	36	62	11	1	8	43	22	41	.278	.348	.444	.792	110	3	3	99	139	34	.753	5	4	-1	9	O/1	0.9
1988	Bos-A	120	405	47	103	28	1	13	70	22	80	.254	.294	.425	.719	91	-2	-7	109	132	48	.629	2	3	-1	-10	1O/D	-2.3
Total	2	193	628	83	165	39	2	21	113	44	121	.263	.314	.432	.746	97	1	-3	105	135	82	.680	7	7	-2	-1	O/1D	-1.4
■ **DENNIS BERAN**	Beran, Dennis Martin b: 10/8/1887, Merrimac, Mass. d: 4/28/43, Boston, Mass. BR/TL, Deb: 8/11/12																											
1912	Chi-A	2	4	1	1	0	0	0	0	0		.250	.250	.250	.500	44	-0	-0	99	0	0	.333	0			-1	/O	0.0
■ **JOHNNY BERARDINO**	Berardino, John "Bernie" b: 5/1/17, Los Angeles, Cal. BR/TR, 5'11.5", 175 lbs. Deb: 4/22/39																											
1939	StL-A	126	468	42	120	24	5	5	58	37	36	.256	.314	.361	.675	72	-20	-21	100	109	53	.594	6	2	1	0	*2/3S	-1.4
1940	StL-A	142	523	71	135	31	4	16	85	32	46	.258	.301	.424	.725	81	-13	-17	106	116	64	.639	6	8	-3	10	*S2/3	0.1
1941	StL-A	128	469	48	127	30	4	5	89	41	27	.271	.332	.384	.716	89	-8	-8	100	**165**	57	.621	3	5	-2	-15	*S/3	-2.1
1942	StL-A	29	74	11	21	6	0	1	10	4	2	.284	.329	.405	.735	102	0	-0	104	107	11	.704	3	1	0	0	/S312	0.1
1946	StL-A	144	582	70	154	29	5	5	68	34	58	.265	.306	.357	.664	87	-13	-12	98	123	61	.547	2	4	-2	-4	*2	-0.5
1947	StL-A	90	306	29	80	22	1	1	20	44	26	.261	.358	.350	.708	95	-0	-1	102	68	40	.663	6	5	-1	2	2	0.5
1948	Cle-A	66	147	19	28	5	1	2	10	27	16	.190	.328	.279	.607	63	-7	-7	99	72	14	.563	0	1	-1	0	21S/3	-0.5
1949	Cle-A	50	116	11	23	6	1	0	13	14	14	.198	.295	.267	.563	51	-9	-8	98	144	10	.495	0	1	-1	-1	3/2S	-0.9
1950	Cle-A	4	5	1	2	0	0	0	3	1	0	.400	.500	.400	.900	135	0	0	98	518	1	1.000	0	0	0	-0	/23	0.0
	Pit-N	40	131	12	27	3	1	1	12	19	11	.206	.307	.267	.574	51	-9	-9	103	122	11	.491	0			0	2/3	-0.7
1951	StL-A	39	119	13	27	7	1	0	13	17	18	.227	.324	.303	.626	67	-5	-6	105	129	12	.563	1	1	-0	-1	3/21O	-0.7
1952	Cle-A	35	32	5	3	0	0	0	2	10	8	.094	.310	.094	.403	17	-3	-3	91	249	2	.433	0	1	-1	-0	/2S31	-0.2
	Pit-N	19	56	2	8	4	0	0	4	4	6	.143	.200	.214	.414	15	-7	-7	100	130	2	.327	0	0	0	1	2	-0.4
Total	11	912	3028	334	755	167	23	36	387	284	268	.249	.316	.355	.672	78	-93	-98	101	121	339	.608	27	29		-8	2S/31O	-6.7
■ **LOU BERBERET**	Berberet, Louis Joseph b: 11/20/29, Long Beach, Cal. BL/TR, 5'11", 200 lbs. Deb: 9/17/54																											
1954	NY-A	5	5	1	2	0	0	0	3	1	1	.400	.500	.400	.900	150	0	0	99	569	1	1.000	0	0	0	0	/C	0.1
1955	NY-A	2	5	1	2	0	0	0	2	1	0	.400	.500	.400	.900	148	0	0	98	373	1	1.000	0	0	0	0	/C	0.1
1956	Was-A	95	207	25	54	6	3	4	27	46	33	.261	.402	.377	.779	105	4	4	102	112	33	.794	0	0	0	0	C	0.5
1957	Was-A	99	264	24	69	11	2	7	36	41	38	.261	.365	.398	.763	111	4	5	98	113	37	.712	0	1	-1	5	C	1.2
1958	Was-A	5	6	0	1	0	0	0	0	4	1	.167	.500	.167	.667	95	0	0	97	0	1	1.000	0	0	0	0	/C	0.0
	Bos-A	57	167	11	35	5	3	2	18	31	32	.210	.337	.311	.648	76	-4	-5	105	124	18	.604	0	2	-1	-3	C	-0.8
	Yr	62	173	11	36	5	3	2	18	35	33	.208	.344	.306	.651	77	-3	-4	104	114	19	.618	0	2	-1	-3		-0.8
1959	Det-A	100	338	38	73	8	2	13	44	35	59	.216	.290	.367	.656	71	-10	-15	111	106	36	.580	0	0	0	1	C	-0.8
1960	Det-A	85	232	18	45	4	0	5	23	41	31	.194	.318	.276	.593	61	-11	-12	102	114	22	.560	2	0	1	-5	C	-1.0
Total	7	448	1224	118	281	34	10	31	153	200	195	.230	.341	.350	.691	85	-16	-22	104	115	150	.669	2	3	-1	-1	C	-0.7
■ **MOE BERG**	Berg, Morris b: 3/2/02, New York, N.Y. d: 5/29/72, Belleville, N.J. BR/TR, 6'1", 185 lbs. Deb: 7/04/23 C																											
1923	Bro-N	49	129	9	24	3	2	0	6	2	5	.186	.198	.240	.439	16	-16	-15	98	68	6	.324	1	0	0	1	S/2	-0.9
1926	Chi-A	41	113	4	25	6	0	0	7	6	9	.221	.261	.274	.535	43	-10	-9	92	77	8	.411	0	2	-1	0	S/23	-0.6
1927	Chi-A	35	69	4	17	4	0	0	4	4	10	.246	.288	.304	.592	53	-5	-5	102	63	6	.481	0	0	0	-1	2C/S3	-0.3
1928	Chi-A	76	224	25	55	16	0	0	29	14	25	.246	.302	.317	.619	63	-12	-12	99	140	23	.535	2	1	0	0	C	-0.6
1929	Chi-A	107	352	32	101	7	0	0	47	17	16	.287	.323	.307	.630	67	-19	-16	95	149	36	.524	5	1	1	3	*C	-0.1
1930	Chi-A	20	61	4	7	3	0	0	7	1	5	.115	.129	.164	.293	-26	-12	-12	103	232	1	.204	0	0	0	0	C	-0.8
1931	Cle-A	10	13	1	1	1	0	0	0	1	1	.077	.143	.154	.297	-21	-2	-2	106	0	0	.250	0	0	0	0	/C	-0.1
1932	Was-A	75	195	16	46	8	1	1	26	8	13	.236	.266	.303	.569	47	-16	-15	100	140	16	.453	1	1	-0	-10	C	-2.0
1933	Was-A	40	65	8	12	3	0	2	9	4	5	.185	.232	.323	.555	48	-5	-5	96	111	5	.472	0	0	0	-2	C	-0.4
1934	Was-A	33	86	5	21	4	0	0	6	6	4	.244	.301	.291	.592	53	-6	-6	101	80	8	.523	2	0	1	-2	C	-0.3
	Cle-A	29	97	4	25	3	1	0	9	1	7	.258	.265	.309	.575	48	-8	-8	101	100	8	.431	0	0	0	-1	C	-0.5
	Yr	62	183	9	46	7	1	0	15	7	11	.251	.283	.301	.583	50	-14	-14	101	91	16	.474	2	0	1	-3		-0.8
1935	Bos-A	38	98	13	28	5	0	2	12	5	3	.286	.320	.398	.718	78	-2	-4	108	91	12	.629	0	0	0	1	C	-0.1
1936	Bos-A	39	125	9	30	4	1	0	19	2	6	.240	.264	.288	.552	34	-13	-14	106	171	10	.421	0	0	0	2	C	-0.7
1937	Bos-A	47	141	13	36	3	1	0	20	5	4	.255	.281	.291	.572	43	-12	-13	103	167	12	.438	0	0	0	-0	C	-0.8
1938	Bos-A	10	12	0	4	0	0	0	0	0	1	.333	.333	.333	.667	66	-1	-1	102	0	1	.500	0	0	0	-0	/C1	0.0
1939	Bos-A	14	33	3	9	1	0	1	5	2	3	.273	.314	.394	.708	74	-1	-1	108	105	4	.600	0	0	0	0	C	0.0
Total	15	663	1813	150	441	71	6	6	206	78	117	.243	.278	.299	.577	49	-140	-138	100	126	156	.464	11	5	0	-9	C/S231	-8.2
■ **AUGIE BERGAMO**	Bergamo, August Samuel b: 2/14/17, Detroit, Mich. d: 8/19/74, Grosse Pointe City, Mich. BL/TL, 5'9", 165 lbs. Deb: 4/25/44																											
1944	StL-N	80	192	35	55	6	3	2	19	35	23	.286	.399	.380	.779	119	7	7	101	86	32	.784	0			-9	O/1	-0.5
1945	StL-N	94	304	51	96	17	2	3	44	43	21	.316	.401	.414	.815	127	12	12	100	113	55	.813	0			-3	O/1	0.5
Total	2	174	496	86	151	23	5	5	63	78	44	.304	.400	.401	.801	124	19	19	100	102	88	.806	0			-12	O/1	0.0
■ **MARTY BERGEN**	Bergen, Martin b: 10/25/1871, N.Brookfield, Mass d: 1/19/1900, N.Brookfield, Mass TR , 5'10", 170 lbs. Deb: 4/17/1896																											
1896	Bos-N	65	245	39	66	6	4	4	37	11	22	.269	.309	.376	.684	76	-7	-10	108	105	31	.626	6			0	C/1	-0.3
1897	Bos-N	87	327	47	81	11	3	2	45	18		.248	.295	.318	.613	59	-17	-21	107	122	33	.533	5			-3	C/O	-1.0
1898	Bos-N	120	446	62	125	16	5	3	60	13		.280	.302	.359	.661	88	-6	-9	104	109	52	.570	9			-7	*C/1	-0.6
1899	Bos-N	72	260	32	67	11	3	1	34	10		.258	.290	.335	.625	70	-10	-12	105	118	27	.534	4			-2	C	-0.8
Total	4	344	1278	180	339	44	15	10	176	52	22	.265	.299	.347	.646	74	-40	-52	106	114	143	.563	24			-12	C/1O	-2.7
■ **BILL BERGEN**	Bergen, William Aloysius b: 6/13/1878, N.Brookfield, Mass. d: 12/19/43, Worcester, Mass. BR/TR, 6', 184 lbs. Deb: 5/06/01																											
1901	Cin-N	87	308	15	55	6	4	1	17	8		.179	.199	.234	.433	28	-28	-26	95	76	15	.324	2			5	C	-1.0
1902	Cin-N	89	322	19	58	8	3	0	36	14		.180	.214	.224	.438	33	-24	-27	110	176	16	.333	2			10	C	-0.8
1903	Cin-N	58	207	21	47	4	2	0	19	7		.227	.252	.266	.518	45	-14	-16	109	111	15	.400	2			-3	C	-1.3
1904	Bro-N	96	329	17	60	4	2	0	12	9		.182	.204	.207	.411	30	-27	-25	95	66	15	.297	3			15	C/1	-0.2
1905	Bro-N	79	247	12	47	3	2	0	22	7		.190	.213	.219	.431	31	-21	-20	96	142	13	.325	4			6	C	-0.5
1906	Bro-N	103	353	9	56	3	3	0	19	7		.159	.175	.184	.359	15	-35	-30	87	109	12	.249	2			10	*C	-1.3
1907	Bro-N	51	138	2	22	3	0	0	14	1		.159	.165	.181	.347	10	-14	-13	94	212	4	.233	1			-2	C	-1.2
1908	Bro-N	99	302	8	53	8	2	0	15	5		.175	.189	.215	.404	32	-24	-22	95	89	11	.285	1			12	C	-0.5
1909	Bro-N	112	346	16	48	1	1	1	15	10		.139	.163	.156	.319	-0	-40	-40	99	96	9	.228	4			16	*C	-1.8
1910	Bro-N	89	249	11	40	2	1	0	14	6	39	.161	.180	.177	.357	4	-31	-29	95	111	9	.239	0			10	C	-1.5
1911	Bro-N	84	227	8	30	3	1	0	10	14	42	.132	.183	.154	.337	-6	-32	-31	97	97	7	.259	2			4	C	-2.0
Total	11	947	3028	138	516	45	21	2	193	88	81	.170	.194	.201	.395	21	-290	-281	97	111	126	.287	23			83	C/1	-12.1
■ **CLARENCE BERGER**	Berger, Clarence Edward b: 11/1/1894, E.Cleveland, Ohio d: 6/30/59, Washington, D.C. BL/TR, 6', 185 lbs. Deb: 9/23/14																											
1914	Pit-N	6	13	2	1	0	0	0	0	1	4	.077	.143	.077	.220	-37	-2	-2	92	0	0	.167	0			-2	/O	-0.4
■ **JOHNNY BERGER**	Berger, John Henne b: 8/27/01, Philadelphia, Pa. d: 5/7/79, Lake Charles, La. BR/TR, 5'9", 165 lbs. Deb: 4/20/22																											
1922	Phi-A	2	1	0	1	0	0	0	0	0	0	1.000	1.000	1.000	2.000	405	0	0	104	0	1	—	1	0	0	0	/C	0.1
1927	Was-A	9	15	1	4	0	0	0	1	2	3	.267	.353	.267	.620	65	-1	-1	97	83	1	.545	0	0	0	0	/C	0.0
Total	2	11	16	1	5	0	0	0	1	2	3	.313	.389	.313	.701	86	-0	-0	97	78	3	.727	1	0	0	0	/C	0.1
■ **TUN BERGER**	Berger, John Henry b: 12/6/1867, Pittsburgh, Pa. d: 6/10/07, Pittsburgh, Pa. TR , 204 lbs. Deb: 5/09/1890																											
1890	Pit-N	104	391	64	104	18	4	0	40	35	23	.266	.337	.332	.670	111	-1	7	88	98	49	.638	11			1	OSC/23	0.6
1891	Pit-N	43	134	15	32	2	1	1	14	12	10	.239	.315	.291	.606	78	-3	-4	101	97	14	.569	4			0	C2/SO	-0.2
1892	Was-N	26	97	9	14	2	1	0	3	7	9	.144	.210	.186	.395	20	-9	-10	105	52	5	.349	3			0	S/C	-0.8
Total	3	173	622	88	150	22	6	1	57	54	42	.241	.313	.301	.614	88	-13	-6	93	91	67	.572	18			1	/SCO23	-0.4

YEAR	TM/L	G	AB	R	H	2B	3B	HR	RBI	BB	SO	AVG	OBP	SLG	PRO	/A	BR	/A	PF	CHI	RC	TA	SB	CS	SBR	FR	POS	TPR
■ **JOE BERGER**		Berger, Joseph August "Fats" b: 12/20/1886, St.Louis, Mo. d: 3/6/56, Rock Island, Ill. BR/TR, 5'10.5", 170 lbs. Deb: 4/11/13																										
1913	Chi-A	79	223	27	48	6	2	2	20	36	28	.215	.330	.287	.616	85	-4	-3	95	102	23	.617	6			0	2/S3	-0.3
1914	Chi-A	47	148	11	23	3	1	0	3	13	9	.155	.224	.189	.413	23	-14	-14	103	40	6	.323	2	8	-4	1	S2/3	-1.6
Total	2	126	371	38	71	9	3	2	23	49	37	.191	.289	.248	.537	60	-18	-17	98	78	29	.490	8	8		1	/2S3	-1.9
■ **BOZE BERGER**		Berger, Louis William b: 5/13/10, Baltimore, Md. BR/TR, 6'2", 180 lbs. Deb: 8/17/32																										
1932	Cle-A	1	1	0	0	0	0	0	0	0	1	.000	.000	.000	.000	-92	-0	-0	108	0	0	.000	0	0	0	-0	/S	0.0
1935	Cle-A	124	461	62	119	27	5	5	43	34	97	.258	.310	.371	.681	76	-18	-17	99	80	53	.614	7	5	-1	12	*2/S13	-0.1
1936	Cle-A	28	52	1	9	2	0	0	3	1	14	.173	.189	.212	.400	-1	-8	-9	106	88	2	.279	0	0	0	1	/123S	-0.7
1937	Chi-A	52	130	19	31	5	0	5	13	15	24	.238	.322	.392	.714	77	-5	-5	103	67	17	.680	1	1	-0	-1	3/2S	-0.4
1938	Chi-A	118	470	60	102	15	3	3	36	43	80	.217	.284	.281	.565	43	-43	-41	98	91	40	.488	4	1	1	1	S2/3	-3.0
1939	Bos-A	20	30	4	9	2	0	0	2	1	10	.300	.323	.367	.689	70	-1	-1	108	61	4	.571	0	0	0	0	S/32	0.0
Total	6	343	1144	146	270	51	8	13	97	94	226	.236	.296	.329	.624	59	-75	-74	100	83	116	.551	12	7	-1	12	2/S31	-4.2
■ **WALLY BERGER**		Berger, Walter Antone b: 10/10/05, Chicago, Ill. d: 11/30/88, Redondo Beach, Cal. BR/TR, 6'2", 198 lbs. Deb: 4/15/30																										
1930	Bos-N	151	555	98	172	27	14	38	119	54	69	.310	.375	.614	.990	138	27	30	97	96	124	1.050	3			-1	*O	1.6
1931	Bos-N	156	617	94	199	44	8	19	84	55	70	.323	.380	.512	.892	139	32	32	99	77	122	.923	13			4	*O/1	2.8
1932	Bos-N	145	602	90	185	34	6	17	73	33	66	.307	.346	.468	.815	125	13	18	93	78	98	.775	5			0	*O1	0.8
1933	Bos-N	137	528	84	165	37	8	27	106	41	77	.313	.365	.566	.932	**169**	40	43	96	111	113	.935	2			1	*O	3.7
1934	Bos-N	150	615	92	183	35	8	34	121	49	65	.298	.352	.546	.899	160	29	41	86	96	119	.874	2			-3	*O	2.9
1935	Bos-N	150	589	91	174	39	4	**34**	**130**	50	80	.295	.355	.548	.903	145	30	33	96	117	115	.886	3			7	*O	3.2
1936	Bos-N	138	534	88	154	23	3	25	91	53	84	.288	.361	.483	.844	132	18	22	95	103	95	.814	1			1	*O	1.7
1937	Bos-N	30	113	14	31	9	1	5	22	11	33	.274	.344	.504	.848	141	4	5	90	117	21	.831	0			-3	O	0.1
	NY-N	59	199	40	58	11	2	12	43	18	30	.291	.359	.548	.907	143	11	11	100	107	39	.911	3			-0	O	0.8
	Yr	89	312	54	89	20	3	17	65	29	63	.285	.354	.532	.886	142	15	16	97	111	61	.886	3			-3		0.9
1938	NY-N	16	32	5	6	0	0	0	4	2	4	.188	.235	.188	.423	17	-4	-4	103	241	2	.308	0			1	/O	-0.1
	Cin-N	99	407	74	125	23	4	16	56	29	44	.307	.356	.501	.857	137	17	18	98	85	73	.814	2			-1	O	1.5
	Yr	115	439	79	131	23	4	16	60	31	48	.298	.347	.478	.826	127	13	14	98	109	74	.773	2			0		1.4
1939	Cin-N	97	329	36	85	15	1	14	44	36	63	.258	.341	.438	.778	105	3	2	103	87	50	.744	1			-8	O	-0.7
1940	Cin-N	2	2	0	0	0	0	0	0	0	1	.000	.000	.000	.000	-99	-1	-1	101	0	0	.000	0			0	H	0.0
	Phi-N	20	41	3	13	2	0	1	5	4	8	.317	.378	.439	.817	128	1	2	97	88	7	.793	1			-2	O/1	0.0
	Yr	22	43	3	13	2	0	1	5	4	9	.302	.362	.419	.780	118	1	1	97	80	6	.742	1			-2		0.0
Total	11	1350	5163	809	1550	299	59	242	898	435	694	.300	.359	.522	.881	139	222	254	95	96	977	.886	36			-2	*O/1	18.3
■ **JOHN BERGH**		Bergh, John Baptist b: 10/8/1857, Boston, Mass. d: 4/16/1883, Boston, Mass. Deb: 8/05/1876																										
1876	Phi-N	1	4	0	0	0	0	0	0	0	2	.000	.000	.000	.000	-99	-1	-1	99	0	0	.000				0	/OC	0.0
1880	Bos-N	11	40	2	8	3	0	0	0	2	5	.200	.238	.275	.513	80	-1	-1	92	0	3	.406				0	C	0.0
Total	2	12	44	2	8	3	0	0	0	2	7	.182	.217	.250	.467	62	-2	-1	92	0	3	.361				0	/CO	0.0
■ **MARTY BERGHAMMER**		Berghammer, Martin Andrew "Pepper" b: 6/18/1888, Elliott, Pa. d: 12/21/57, Pittsburgh, Pa. BL/TR, 5'9", 172 lbs. Deb: 9/08/11																										
1911	Chi-A	2	5	0	0	0	0	0	0	0		.000	.167	.000	.167	-54	-1	-1	97	0	0	.200	0			0	/2	0.0
1913	Cin-N	74	188	25	41	4	1	1	13	10	29	.218	.269	.266	.535	52	-12	-12	102	89	17	.537	16			6	S2	-0.2
1914	Cin-N	77	112	15	25	2	0	0	6	10	18	.223	.287	.241	.528	55	-6	-6	105	81	8	.471	4			3	S2	-0.2
1915	Pit-F	132	469	96	114	10	6	0	33	83	44	.243	.357	.290	.647	89	-0	-3	104	77	62	.690	26			-43	*S	-3.9
Total	4	285	774	136	180	16	7	1	52	103	91	.233	.326	.275	.601	75	-19	-22	103	80	87	.616	46			-35	S/2	-4.3
■ **AL BERGMAN**		Bergman, Alfred Henry "Dutch" b: 9/27/1890, Peru, Ind. d: 6/20/61, Fort Wayne, Ind. BR/TR, 5'7", 155 lbs. Deb: 8/29/16																										
1916	Cle-A	8	14	2	3	0	1	0	0	2	4	.214	.313	.357	.670	101	-0	0	100	0	2	.636	0			0	/2	0.0
■ **DAVE BERGMAN**		Bergman, David Bruce b: 6/6/53, Evanston, Ill. BL/TL, 6'1.5", 185 lbs. Deb: 8/26/75																										
1975	NY-A	7	17	0	0	0	0	0	0	2	4	.000	.105	.000	.105	-69	-4	-4	99	0	0	.118	0	0	0	0	/O	-0.3
1977	NY-A	5	4	1	1	0	0	0	1	0	0	.250	.250	.250	.500	37	-0	-0	99	396	0	.333	0	0	0	-1	/O1	0.0
1978	Hou-N	104	186	15	43	5	1	0	12	39	32	.231	.364	.269	.633	84	-3	-2	95	95	20	.615	2	0	1	-1	1O	-0.5
1979	Hou-N	13	15	4	6	0	0	1	2	0	3	.400	.400	.600	1.000	187	1	1	90	66	4	1.000	0	0	0	0	/1	0.1
1980	Hou-N	90	78	12	20	6	1	0	3	10	10	.256	.341	.359	.700	98	-0	-0	98	42	10	.661	1	0	0	-1	1/O	-0.3
1981	Hou-N	6	6	1	1	0	0	1	1	0	0	.167	.167	.667	.833	145	0	0	88	56	1	.800	0	0	0	0	/1	0.0
	SF-N	63	145	16	37	9	0	3	13	19	18	.255	.341	.379	.721	99	1	0	105	80	19	.679	2	0	1	-1	1O	-0.1
	Yr	69	151	17	38	9	0	4	14	19	18	.252	.335	.391	.726	102	1	0	104	78	20	.684	2	0	1	-1		-0.1
1982	SF-N	100	121	22	33	3	1	4	14	18	11	.273	.367	.413	.780	126	3	4	94	89	20	.798	3	0	1	1	1/O	0.3
1983	SF-N	90	140	16	40	4	1	6	24	24	21	.286	.394	.457	.851	134	7	7	101	116	25	.858	2	1	0	-0	1/O	0.5
1984	Det-A	120	271	42	74	8	5	7	44	33	40	.273	.358	.417	.775	118	6	7	96	131	41	.741	3	4	-2	7	*1/O	0.5
1985	Det-A	69	140	8	25	2	0	3	7	14	15	.179	.253	.257	.510	38	-12	-13	106	62	9	.413	0	0	0	3	1/OD	-1.1
1986	Det-A	65	130	14	30	6	1	1	9	21	16	.231	.338	.315	.653	84	-3	-2	95	81	15	.602	0	0	0	2	1/OD	-0.2
1987	Det-A	91	172	25	47	7	3	6	22	30	23	.273	.384	.453	.838	126	6	7	97	91	32	.858	0	1	-1	1	1/OD	0.0
1988	Det-A	116	289	37	85	14	0	5	35	38	34	.294	.376	.394	.771	123	7	10	94	108	43	.714	0	2	-1	-1	1DO/3	0.4
Total	13	939	1714	213	442	64	13	37	187	248	227	.258	.353	.375	.728	104	10	16	97	96	240	.706	13	8	-1	9	1/OD3	-0.7
■ **FRANK BERKELBACH**		Berkelbach, Francis P. b: Philadelphia, Pa. 6', 182 lbs. Deb: 7/04/1884																										
1884	Cin-a	6	25	3	6	0	1	0		0		.240	.296	.320	.616	98	0	-0	106	0	2	.526				0	/O	0.0
■ **NATE BERKENSTOCK**		Berkenstock, Nathan b: 1831, Pennsylvania d: 2/23/1900, Philadelphia, Pa. Deb: 10/30/1871																										
1871	Ath-n	1	4	0	0							.000															/O	
■ **BOB BERMAN**		Berman, Robert Leon b: 1/24/1899, New York, N.Y. d: 8/2/88, Bridgeport, Conn. BR/TR, 5'8", 147 lbs. Deb: 6/04/18																										
1918	Was-A	2	0	0	0	0	0	0	0	0	0	—	—	—	—	—	0	0	104	—	—	—	0			0	/C	0.0
■ **CURT BERNARD**		Bernard, Curtis Henry b: 2/18/1878, Parkersburg, W.Va. d: 4/10/55, Culver City, Cal. BL/TR, 5'10", 150 lbs. Deb: 9/17/00																										
1900	NY-N	20	71	9	18	2	0	0	8	6		.254	.312	.282	.593	68	-3	-3	97	127	7	.509	1			0	O/S	-0.2
1901	NY-N	23	76	11	17	0	2	0	6	7		.224	.289	.276	.565	73	-3	-2	91	97	7	.508	2			-2	O/2S3	-0.4
Total	2	43	147	20	35	2	2	0	14	13		.238	.300	.279	.579	70	-6	-5	94	112	14	.509	3			-2	/O2S3	-0.6
■ **TONY BERNAZARD**		Bernazard, Antonio (Garcia) b: 8/24/56, Caguas, P.R. BB/TR, 5'9", 150 lbs. Deb: 7/13/79																										
1979	Mon-N	22	40	11	12	2	0	1	8	15	12	.300	.500	.425	.925	151	5	4	102	158	9	1.063	1	2	-1	-0	2	0.4
1980	Mon-N	82	183	26	41	7	1	5	18	17	41	.224	.290	.355	.645	80	-5	-5	99	89	19	.619	9	2	2	-2	2S	0.0
1981	Chi-A	106	384	53	106	14	4	6	34	54	66	.276	.368	.380	.748	116	10	10	100	86	56	.713	4	4	-1	1	*2/S	1.4
1982	Chi-A	137	540	90	138	25	9	11	56	67	88	.256	.340	.396	.736	104	2	4	97	80	78	.715	11	0	3	28	*2	4.1
1983	Chi-A	59	233	30	61	16	2	2	26	17	45	.262	.312	.373	.685	85	-4	-5	103	105	27	.596	2	1	0	4	2	0.1
	Sea-A	80	300	35	80	18	1	6	30	38	52	.267	.353	.393	.746	106	3	3	100	76	44	.772	21	8	2	4	2	1.1
	Yr	139	533	65	141	34	3	8	56	55	97	.265	.336	.385	.720	97	-1	-2	101	89	73	.704	23	9	2	8		1.2
1984	Cle-A	140	439	44	97	15	4	2	38	43	70	.221	.293	.287	.580	58	-22	-26	106	115	37	.523	20	13	-2	5	*2/D	-1.5
1985	Cle-A	153	500	73	137	26	3	11	59	69	72	.274	.363	.404	.767	117	8	12	94	102	75	.755	17	9	-0	-11	*2/S	0.7
1986	Cle-A	146	562	88	169	28	4	17	73	53	77	.301	.367	.456	.823	126	19	21	98	100	96	.816	17	8	0	8	*2	3.5
1987	Cle-A	79	293	39	70	12	1	11	30	25	49	.239	.301	.399	.700	82	-7	-8	103	81	35	.649	7	4	-0	-9	2	-1.0
	Oak-A	61	214	34	57	14	1	3	19	30	30	.266	.357	.383	.740	107	-0	3	91	85	29	.695	4	4	-1	-1	2/D	0.4
	Yr	140	507	73	127	26	2	14	49	55	79	.250	.325	.393	.718	92	-7	-5	98	83	66	.675	11	8	-2	-10		-0.6
Total	9	1065	3688	523	968	177	30	75	391	428	602	.262	.342	.388	.730	101	7	13	99	94	507	.715	113	55	1	28	2/SD	9.2
■ **JUAN BERNHARDT**		Bernhardt, Juan Ramon (Coradin) b: 8/31/53, San Pedro De Macoris, D.R. BR/TR, 5'11", 160 lbs. Deb: 7/10/76																										
1976	NY-A	10	21	1	4	1	0	0	1	0	4	.190	.190	.238	.429	25	-2	-2	99	77	1	.294	0	0	0	-1	/O3D	-0.3
1977	Sea-A	89	305	32	74	9	2	7	30	5	26	.243	.260	.354	.614	68	-15	-14	96	92	25	.481	2	3	-1	-1	D3/1	-1.6

YEAR	TM/L	G	AB	R	H	2B	3B	HR	RBI	BB	SO	AVG	OBP	SLG	PRO	/A	BR	/A	PF	CHI	RC	TA	SB	CS	SBR	FR	POS	TPR
1978	Sea-A	54	165	13	38	9	0	2	12	9	10	.230	.274	.321	.595	66	-7	-8	102	80	14	.489	1	1	-0	-1	13/D	-1.0
1979	Sea-A	1	1	0	1	0	0	0	0	0	0	1.000	1.000	1.000	2.000	441	0	0	100	0	1	—	0	0	0	0	/H	0.0
Total	4	154	492	46	117	19	2	9	43	14	40	.238	.263	.339	.603	66	-24	-23	98	87	41	.493	3	4	-2	-3	/D31O	-2.9
■ CARLOS BERNIER Bernier, Carlos (Rodriguez) b: 1/28/29, Juana Diaz, P.R. BR/TR, 5'9", 180 lbs. Deb: 4/22/53																												
1953	Pit-N	105	310	48	66	7	8	3	31	51	53	.213	.332	.316	.648	69	-13	-13	102	113	32	.625	15	14	-4	11	O	-0.8
■ JOHNNY BERO Bero, John George b: 12/22/22, Gary, W.Va. d: 5/11/85, Gardena, Cal. BL/TR, 6', 170 lbs. Deb: 9/26/48																												
1948	Det-A	4	9	2	0	0	0	0	0	1	1	.000	.100	.000	.100	-75	-2	-2	96	0	0	.111	0	0	0	0	/2	-0.1
1951	StL-A	61	160	24	34	5	0	5	17	26	30	.213	.323	.338	.660	75	-5	-6	105	88	19	.623	1	1	-0	-5	S/2	-0.6
Total	2	65	169	26	34	5	0	5	17	27	31	.201	.311	.320	.631	68	-7	-8	104	84	19	.590	1	1	-0	-5	/S2	-0.7
■ DALE BERRA Berra, Dale Anthony b: 12/13/56, Ridgewood, N.J. BR/TR, 6', 180 lbs. Deb: 8/22/77																												
1977	Pit-N	17	40	0	7	1	0	0	3	1	8	.175	.195	.200	.395	6	-5	-5	103	150	2	.273	0	0	0	1	3	-0.4
1978	Pit-N	56	135	16	28	2	0	6	14	13	20	.207	.287	.356	.642	75	-4	-5	105	84	14	.600	3	1	0	-1	3/S	-0.5
1979	Pit-N	44	123	11	26	5	0	3	15	11	17	.211	.276	.325	.601	60	-6	-7	106	121	10	.500	0	0	0	-1	S3	-0.6
1980	Pit-N	93	245	21	54	8	2	6	31	16	52	.220	.271	.343	.614	68	-10	-11	103	120	22	.523	2	0	1	-3	3S/2	-0.8
1981	Pit-N	81	232	21	56	12	0	2	27	17	34	.241	.302	.319	.621	79	-7	-6	96	132	24	.583	11	1	3	-3	3S2	-0.3
1982	Pit-N	156	529	64	139	25	5	10	61	33	83	.263	.311	.386	.697	85	-5	-12	110	102	59	.601	6	6	-2	6	*S/3	0.4
1983	Pit-N	161	537	51	135	25	1	10	52	61	84	.251	.328	.358	.685	87	-7	-9	103	93	63	.626	8	5	-1	17	*S	2.3
1984	Pit-N	136	450	31	100	16	0	9	52	34	78	.222	.278	.318	.596	71	-20	-17	94	120	38	.492	1	3	-2	5	*S/3	0.0
1985	NY-A	48	109	8	25	5	1	1	8	7	20	.229	.276	.321	.597	66	-6	-5	96	83	9	.494	1	1	-0	-4	3/S	-0.9
1986	NY-A	42	108	10	25	7	0	2	13	9	14	.231	.297	.352	.648	74	-3	-4	103	118	12	.578	0	0	0	2	S3/D	-0.1
1987	Hou-N	19	45	3	8	3	0	0	2	8	12	.178	.302	.244	.546	51	-3	-3	93	73	4	.514	0	0	0	-1	S/2	-0.1
Total	11	853	2553	236	603	109	9	49	278	210	422	.236	.297	.344	.641	76	-78	-85	102	108	258	.575	32	17	-1	18	S3/2D	-1.0
■ YOGI BERRA Berra, Lawrence Peter b: 5/12/25, St.Louis, Mo. BL/TR, 5'7.5", 185 lbs. Deb: 9/22/46 MCH																												
1946	NY-A	7	22	3	8	1	0	2	4	1	1	.364	.391	.682	1.073	195	3	3	100	72	6	1.143	0	0	0	0	/C	0.3
1947	NY-A	83	293	41	82	15	3	11	54	13	12	.280	.310	.464	.775	118	3	4	97	118	41	.680	0	1	-1	-6	CO	0.1
1948	NY-A	125	469	70	143	24	10	14	98	25	24	.305	.341	.488	.830	119	9	9	100	125	77	.763	3	3	-1	-4	CO	0.7
1949	NY-A	116	415	59	115	20	2	20	91	22	25	.277	.323	.480	.802	110	2	2	100	120	65	.746	2	1	0	-2	*C	0.5
1950	NY-A	151	597	116	192	30	6	28	124	55	12	.322	.383	.533	.915	133	26	27	99	113	125	.911	4	2	0	3	*C	3.3
1951	NY-A	141	547	92	161	19	4	27	88	44	20	.294	.350	.492	.842	137	17	23	92	95	92	.791	5	4	-1	11	*C	4.1
1952	NY-A	142	534	97	146	17	1	30	98	66	24	.273	.358	.478	.835	134	21	22	98	112	95	.820	2	3	-1	4	*C	3.3
1953	NY-A	137	503	80	149	23	5	27	108	50	32	.296	.363	.523	.886	148	24	29	93	119	98	.868	0	3	-2	-5	*C	2.6
1954	NY-A	151	584	88	179	28	6	22	125	56	29	.307	.371	.488	.859	135	26	26	99	**143**	107	.831	0	1	-1	6	*C/3	3.9
1955	NY-A	147	541	84	147	20	3	27	108	60	20	.272	.352	.470	.821	122	13	15	98	127	90	.791	1	0	0	5	*C	2.5
1956	NY-A	140	521	93	155	29	2	30	105	65	29	.298	.381	.534	.914	141	28	29	99	109	108	.934	3	2	-0	13	*C/O	4.2
1957	NY-A	134	482	74	121	14	2	24	82	57	24	.251	.331	.438	.769	116	5	9	94	117	69	.722	1	2	-1	7	*C/O	2.0
1958	NY-A	122	433	60	115	17	3	22	90	35	35	.266	.323	.471	.795	113	8	6	103	136	67	.753	3	0	1	10	CO/1	1.7
1959	NY-A	131	472	64	134	25	1	19	69	43	38	.284	.349	.462	.811	130	13	17	93	101	77	.769	1	2	-1	7	*C/O	3.0
1960	NY-A	120	359	46	99	14	1	15	62	38	23	.276	.350	.446	.796	120	7	9	94	118	55	.746	2	1	0	-3	CO	0.8
1961	NY-A	119	395	62	107	11	0	22	61	35	28	.271	.333	.466	.799	115	5	7	96	96	62	.756	2	0	1	2	OC	0.6
1962	NY-A	86	232	25	52	8	0	10	35	24	18	.224	.302	.388	.690	90	-6	-4	94	116	26	.617	0	1	-1	3	CO	0.0
1963	NY-A	64	147	20	43	6	0	8	28	15	17	.293	.362	.497	.859	137	7	7	101	121	26	.833	1	0	0	4	C	1.2
1965	NY-N	4	9	1	2	0	0	0	0	0	3	.222	.222	.222	.444	26	-1	-1	100	0	0	.286	0	0	0	-0	/C	0.0
Total	19	2120	7555	1175	2150	321	49	358	1430	704	414	.285	.350	.482	.832	126	208	239	97	117	1284	.816	30	26	-7	54	*CO/13	34.8
■ RAY BERRES Berres, Raymond Frederick b: 8/31/07, Kenosha, Wis. BR/TR, 5'9", 170 lbs. Deb: 4/24/34 C																												
1934	Bro-N	39	79	7	17	4	0	0	3	1	16	.215	.225	.266	.491	33	-8	-7	95	51	5	.349	0			-1	C	-0.6
1936	Bro-N	105	267	16	64	10	1	1	13	14	35	.240	.280	.296	.576	53	-17	-19	105	56	21	.450	1			-16	*C	-3.0
1937	Pit-N	2	6	0	1	0	0	0	0	0	0	.167	.167	.167	.333	-9	-1	-1	102	0	0	.200	0			0	/C	0.0
1938	Pit-N	40	100	7	23	2	0	0	6	8	10	.230	.287	.250	.537	49	-7	-7	100	87	7	.402	0			2	C	-0.3
1939	Pit-N	81	231	22	53	6	1	0	16	11	25	.229	.267	.264	.532	43	-18	-18	100	96	15	.396	1			0	C	-1.5
1940	Pit-N	21	32	2	6	0	0	0	2	1	1	.188	.212	.188	.400	12	-4	-4	95	124	1	.259	0			-0	C	-0.2
	Bos-N	85	229	12	44	4	1	0	14	18	19	.192	.251	.218	.469	31	-21	-21	99	104	13	.356	0			5	C	-1.2
	Yr	106	261	14	50	4	1	0	16	19	20	.192	.246	.215	.461	29	-25	-25	98	109	14	.346	0			4		-1.4
1941	Bos-N	120	279	21	56	10	0	1	19	17	20	.201	.247	.247	.494	42	-23	-20	93	95	15	.374	2			-10	*C	-1.8
1942	NY-N	12	32	0	6	0	0	0	1	2	3	.188	.235	.188	.423	24	-3	-3	103	62	1	.296	0			0	C	-0.2
1943	NY-N	20	28	1	4	1	0	0	0	1	2	.143	.172	.179	.351	1	-4	-3	96	0	1	.240	0			0	C	-0.2
1944	NY-N	16	17	4	8	0	0	1	2	1	0	.471	.526	.647	1.173	221	3	3	104	51	5	1.300	0			0	C	0.3
1945	NY-N	20	30	4	5	0	0	0	2	2	3	.167	.219	.167	.385	8	-4	-4	100	139	1	.269	0			0	C	-0.2
Total	11	561	1330	96	287	37	3	3	78	76	134	.216	.260	.255	.515	42	-106	-104	99	84	87	.404	4			-20	C	-8.9
■ KEN BERRY Berry, Allen Kent b: 5/10/41, Kansas City, Mo. BR/TR, 6', 175 lbs. Deb: 9/09/62																												
1962	Chi-A	3	6	2	2	0	0	0	0	0	0	.333	.333	.333	.667	84	-0	-0	95	0	1	.500	0	0	0	1	/O	0.1
1963	Chi-A	4	5	2	1	0	0	0	0	1	1	.200	.333	.200	.533	51	-0	-0	104	0	0	.500	0	0	0	0	/O2	0.0
1964	Chi-A	12	32	4	12	1	0	1	4	5	3	.375	.459	.500	.959	175	3	3	96	89	7	.955	0	1	-1	-2	O	0.1
1965	Chi-A	157	472	51	103	17	4	12	42	28	96	.218	.269	.347	.617	80	-17	-13	92	87	45	.533	4	2	0	-3	*O	-2.2
1966	Chi-A	147	443	50	120	20	2	8	34	28	63	.271	.317	.379	.696	105	-1	2	94	74	51	.605	7	10	-4	-6	*O	-1.4
1967	Chi-A	147	485	49	117	14	4	7	41	46	68	.241	.311	.330	.641	95	-6	-3	94	95	49	.563	9	8	-2	-4	*O	-1.4
1968	Chi-A	153	504	49	127	21	2	7	32	25	64	.252	.289	.343	.632	90	-7	-7	101	71	46	.515	6	6	-2	-3	*O	-2.0
1969	Chi-A	130	297	25	69	12	2	4	18	24	50	.232	.296	.327	.623	68	-11	-14	108	66	27	.523	1	2	-1	-12	*O	-3.0
1970	Chi-A	141	463	45	128	12	2	7	50	43	61	.276	.346	.356	.702	89	-3	-6	106	109	54	.615	6	4	-1	-2	*O	-1.4
1971	Cal-A	111	298	29	66	17	0	3	22	18	33	.221	.273	.309	.581	65	-14	-14	99	89	23	.472	3	2	-0	-3	*O	-2.1
1972	Cal-A	119	409	41	118	15	3	5	39	35	47	.289	.348	.377	.724	130	8	13	88	98	56	.658	5	3	-0	10	*O	2.2
1973	Cal-A	136	415	48	118	11	2	3	36	26	50	.284	.328	.342	.670	93	-6	-4	96	94	41	.528	1	6	-3	-4	*O	-1.5
1974	Mil-A	98	267	21	64	9	2	1	24	18	26	.240	.295	.300	.595	70	-10	-10	102	114	24	.498	3	1	0	4	OD	-0.8
1975	Cle-A	25	40	6	8	1	0	0	1	1	7	.200	.238	.225	.463	32	-4	-4	100	43	2	.324	0	1	-1	-3	O/D	-0.7
Total	14	1383	4136	422	1053	150	23	58	343	298	569	.255	.309	.344	.653	90	-67	-56	98	89	425	.574	45	46	-14	-25	*O/D2	-14.1
■ CHARLIE BERRY Berry, Charles Francis b: 10/18/02, Philipsburg, N.J. d: 9/6/72, Evanston, Ill. BR/TR, 6', 185 lbs. Deb: 6/15/25 UC																												
1925	Phi-A	10	14	1	3	1	0	0	3	0	2	.214	.214	.286	.500	25	-2	-2	103	251	1	.364	0	0	0	-0	/C	-0.1
1928	Bos-A	80	177	18	46	7	3	1	19	21	19	.260	.342	.350	.692	84	-4	-4	98	100	22	.644	1	1	-0	-5	C	-0.4
1929	Bos-A	77	207	19	50	11	4	1	21	15	29	.242	.302	.348	.650	66	-11	-11	102	96	21	.571	2	4	-2	-0	C	-0.5
1930	Bos-A	88	256	31	74	9	6	6	35	16	22	.289	.331	.441	.772	101	-3	-0	93	89	38	.720	2	0	1	4	C	1.1
1931	Bos-A	111	357	41	101	16	2	6	49	29	38	.283	.337	.389	.726	96	-5	-2	94	103	48	.672	4	0	1	1	*C	0.8
1932	Bos-A	10	32	0	6	3	0	0	6	3	2	.188	.257	.281	.538	41	-3	-3	97	223	2	.462	0	0	0	1	C	-0.1
	Chi-A	72	226	33	69	15	6	4	31	21	23	.305	.364	.478	.842	133	5	9	87	86	40	.841	3	0	1	4	C	1.6
	Yr	82	258	33	75	18	6	4	37	24	25	.291	.351	.453	.805	121	2	6	88	106	42	.787	3	0	1	4		1.5
1933	Chi-A	86	271	25	69	8	3	2	28	17	16	.255	.301	.328	.629	66	-13	-14	101	98	27	.530	0	0	0	-7	C	-1.5
1934	Phi-A	99	269	14	72	10	2	0	34	22	23	.268	.323	.320	.643	68	-13	-12	97	132	29	.553	1	0	0	-7	C	-0.9
1935	Phi-A	62	190	14	48	7	3	3	29	10	20	.253	.290	.368	.658	69	-9	-9	100	125	20	.563	0	0	0	2	C	-0.4
1936	Phi-A	13	17	0	1	1	0	0	1	6	2	.059	.304	.118	.422	8	-2	-2	101	162	1	.500	0	0	0	-0	C	-0.1
1938	Phi-A	1	2	0	0	0	0	0	0	0	0	.000	.000	.000	.000	-99	-1	-1	101	0	0	.000	0	0	0	0	/C	0.0
Total	11	709	2018	196	539	88	29	23	256	160	196	.267	.322	.374	.696	83	-62	-50	96	107	251	.628	13	5	1	-8	C	-0.5

YEAR	TM/L	G	AB	R	H	2B	3B	HR	RBI	BB	SO	AVG	OBP	SLG	PRO	/A	BR	/A	PF	CHI	RC	TA	SB	CS	SBR	FR	POS	TPR
■ **CHARLIE BERRY**	Berry, Charles Joseph b: 9/6/1860, Elizabeth, N.J. d: 1/22/40, Phillipsburg, N.J. BR/TR, 5'11", 175 lbs. Deb: 4/30/1884																											
1884	Alt-U	7	25	2	6	0	0	0		0		.240	.240	.240	.480	62	-1	-1	101	0	1	.316	0			0	/2	0.0
	KC-U	29	118	15	29	6	1	1		1		.246	.252	.339	.591	113	-0	2	87	0	10	.461	0			-4	2/O3	-0.1
	CP-U	7	27	4	3	2	0	0		0		.111	.111	.185	.296	-1	-3	-3	99	0	1	.208	0			0	/2	-0.1
	Yr	43	170	21	38	8	1	1		1		.224	.228	.300	.528	84	-4	-2	91	0	12	.394	0			-4		-0.2
Total	1	43	170	21	38	8	1	1		1		.224	.228	.300	.528	85	-4	-2	91	0	12	.394	0			-4	/2O3	-0.2
■ **CLAUDE BERRY**	Berry, Claude Elzy "Admiral" b: 2/14/1880, Losantville, Ind. d: 2/1/74, Richmond, Ind. BR/TR, 5'7", 165 lbs. Deb: 4/22/04																											
1904	Chi-A	3	1	1	0	0	0	0	0	1		.000	.500	.000	.500	70	0	0	99	0	0	1.000	0			0	/C	0.0
1906	Phi-A	10	30	2	7	0	0	0	2	2		.233	.281	.233	.515	68	-1	-1	94	104	2	.435	1			1	C	0.1
1907	Phi-A	8	19	2	4	2	0	0	1	2		.211	.286	.316	.602	88	-0	-0	106	60	2	.533	0			1	/C	0.1
1914	Pit-F	124	411	35	98	18	9	2	36	26	50	.238	.284	.341	.624	83	-12	-9	94	89	44	.550	6			-7	*C	-1.0
1915	Pit-F	100	292	32	56	11	1	1	26	29	42	.192	.265	.247	.511	50	-17	-19	104	125	23	.458	7			6	C	-1.0
Total	5	245	753	72	165	31	10	3	65	60	92	.219	.277	.299	.576	69	-31	-29	98	103	72	.509	14			1	C	-1.8
■ **NEIL BERRY**	Berry, Cornelius John b: 1/11/22, Kalamazoo, Mich. BR/TR, 5'10", 168 lbs. Deb: 4/20/48																											
1948	Det-A	87	256	46	68	8	1	0	16	37	23	.266	.358	.305	.663	80	-7	-6	96	69	31	.595	1	3	-2	-4	S2	-0.9
1949	Det-A	109	329	38	78	9	1	0	18	27	24	.237	.299	.271	.569	48	-23	-27	108	69	27	.462	4	2	0	-13	2/S	-3.7
1950	Det-A	39	40	9	10	1	0	0	7	6	11	.250	.348	.275	.623	63	-2	-2	97	220	5	.567	0	0	0	1	S/23	0.0
1951	Det-A	67	157	17	36	5	2	0	9	10	15	.229	.275	.287	.562	49	-11	-12	106	71	13	.476	4	2	0	-1	S2/3	-0.9
1952	Det-A	73	189	22	43	4	3	0	13	22	19	.228	.311	.280	.592	66	-8	-8	99	92	17	.507	1	3	-2	0	S/3	-0.5
1953	StL-A	57	99	14	28	1	2	0	11	9	10	.283	.343	.333	.676	78	-2	-3	107	123	11	.558	1	2	-1	-2	32/S	-0.4
	Chi-A	5	8	1	1	0	0	0	0	1	1	.125	.222	.125	.347	-4	-1	-1	106	0	0	.250	0	0	0	0	/2	0.0
	Yr	62	107	15	29	1	2	0	11	10	11	.271	.333	.318	.651	72	-3	-4	107	115	12	.556	1	2	-1	-1		-0.4
1954	Bal-A	5	9	1	1	0	0	0	0	1	2	.111	.200	.111	.311	-14	-1	-1	95	0	0	.250	0	0	0	0	/S	0.0
Total	7	442	1087	148	265	28	9	0	74	113	105	.244	.317	.286	.603	61	-56	-60	102	83	104	.525	11	12	-4	-18	S2/3	-6.4
■ **JOE BERRY**	Berry, Joseph Howard Jr. "Nig" b: 12/31/1894, Philadelphia, Pa. d: 4/29/76, Philadelphia, Pa. BB/TR, 5'10.5", 159 lbs. Deb: 7/18/21																											
1921	NY-N	9	6	0	2	0	1	0	2	1	1	.333	.429	.667	1.095	190	1	1	98	183	2	1.250	0	0	0	0	/2	0.1
1922	NY-N	6	0	0	0	0	0	0	0	0	0	—	—	—	—	—	0	0	104	—	—	—	0	0	0	0	R	0.0
Total	2	15	6	0	2	0	1	0	2	1	1	.333	.429	.667	1.095	190	1	1	98	183	4	1.250	0	0	0	0	/2	0.1
■ **JOE BERRY**	Berry, Joseph Howard Sr. "Hodge" b: 9/10/1872, Wheeling, W.Va. d: 3/13/61, Allenwood, N.J. BB/TR, 5'9", 172 lbs. Deb: 9/04/02																											
1902	Phi-N	1	4	0	1	0	0	0	1	1		.250	.400	.250	.650	98	0	0	105	299	1	1.000	1			0	/C	0.0
■ **TOM BERRY**	Berry, Thomas Haney b: 12/31/1842, Chester, Pa. d: 6/6/15, Chester, Pa. 5'6", 140 lbs. Deb: 9/02/1871																											
1871	Ath-n	1	4	0	1							.250															/O	
■ **DAMON BERRYHILL**	Berryhill, Damon Scott b: 12/3/63, South Laguna, Cal. BB/TR, 6' ", 210 lbs. Deb: 9/05/87																											
1987	Chi-N	12	28	2	5	1	0	0	1	3	5	.179	.258	.214	.472	27	-3	-3	101	66	1	.360	0	1	-1	0	C	-0.2
1988	Chi-N	95	309	19	80	19	1	7	38	17	56	.259	.298	.395	.692	93	-2	-4	104	106	33	.583	1	0	0	2	C	0.4
Total	2	107	337	21	85	20	1	7	39	20	61	.252	.294	.380	.674	87	-5	-6	104	103	35	.564	1	1	-0	2	C	0.2
■ **HARRY BERTE**	Berte, Harry Thomas b: 5/10/1872, Covington, Ky. d: 5/6/52, Los Angeles, Cal. TR , Deb: 03																											
1903	StL-N	4	15	1	5	0	0	0	1	1		.333	.375	.333	.708	109	0	0	96	68	2	.600	0			0	/2S	0.1
■ **DICK BERTELL**	Bertell, Richard George b: 11/21/35, Oak Park, Ill. BR/TR, 6'0.5", 200 lbs. Deb: 9/22/60																											
1960	Chi-N	5	15	0	2	0	0	0	2	3	1	.133	.278	.133	.411	17	-2	-2	98	406	1	.385	0	0	0	-1	/C	-0.1
1961	Chi-N	92	267	20	73	7	1	2	33	15	33	.273	.312	.330	.642	70	-11	-11	100	142	26	.512	0	0	0	-3	C	-0.6
1962	Chi-N	77	215	19	65	6	2	2	18	13	30	.302	.345	.377	.722	88	-2	-3	106	82	27	.613	0	1	-1	-8	C	-1.0
1963	Chi-N	100	322	15	75	7	2	2	14	24	41	.233	.286	.286	.572	62	-14	-16	105	60	25	.451	0	2	-1	4	C	-1.0
1964	Chi-N	112	353	29	84	11	3	4	35	33	67	.238	.307	.320	.627	73	-10	-13	105	115	34	.534	2	1	0	-4	*C	-1.3
1965	Chi-N	34	84	6	18	2	0	0	7	11	10	.214	.305	.238	.543	54	-5	-5	102	145	7	.463	0	0	0	-1	C	-0.4
	SF-N	22	48	1	9	1	0	0	3	7	5	.188	.291	.208	.499	39	-3	-4	111	124	3	.425	0	0	0	-1	C	-0.3
	Yr	56	132	7	27	3	0	0	10	18	15	.205	.300	.227	.527	48	-8	-9	105	139	10	.453	0	0	0	-2		-0.7
1967	Chi-N	2	6	1	1	0	1	0	0	0	1	.167	.167	.500	.667	82	-0	-0	102	0	1	.600	0	0	0	0	/C	0.0
Total	7	444	1310	91	327	34	9	10	112	106	188	.250	.307	.312	.619	69	-47	-54	104	107	124	.527	2	4	-2	-13	C	-4.7
■ **HARRY BERTHRONG**	Berthrong, Henry W. b: 1/1/1844, Mumford, N.Y. d: 4/28/28, Chelsea, Mass. TR , 5'6.5", 140 lbs. Deb: 5/05/1871																											
1871	Oly-n	17	78	17	17							.218															O/23	
■ **RENO BERTOIA**	Bertoia, Reno Peter b: 1/8/35, St.Vito Udine, Italy BR/TR, 5'11.5", 185 lbs. Deb: 9/22/53																											
1953	Det-A	1	1	0	0	0	0	0	0	0	1	.000	.000	.000	.000	-99	-0	-0	98	0	0	.000	0	0	0	0	/2	0.0
1954	Det-A	54	37	13	6	2	0	1	2	5	9	.162	.262	.297	.559	53	-3	-2	100	54	3	.548	1	0	0	-1	2/3S	-0.2
1955	Det-A	38	68	13	14	2	1	1	10	5	11	.206	.260	.309	.569	54	-5	-4	97	155	6	.473	0	0	0	-0	3/2S	-0.3
1956	Det-A	22	66	7	12	2	0	1	5	6	12	.182	.260	.258	.518	38	-6	-6	97	93	4	.414	0	0	0	-1	2/3	-0.4
1957	Det-A	97	295	28	81	16	2	4	28	19	43	.275	.327	.383	.710	87	-3	-6	107	88	36	.616	2	3	-1	-6	3/S2	-1.0
1958	Det-A	86	240	28	56	6	0	6	27	20	35	.233	.298	.333	.631	71	-9	-10	104	110	25	.563	5	2	0	0	3/SO	-0.5
1959	Was-A	90	308	33	73	10	0	8	29	29	48	.237	.305	.347	.652	79	-9	-9	100	89	30	.556	2	5	-2	-3	2/3S	-1.2
1960	Was-A	121	460	44	122	17	7	4	45	26	58	.265	.316	.359	.674	81	-12	-13	102	105	50	.571	3	5	-2	-2	*32	-1.3
1961	Min-A	35	104	17	22	2	0	1	8	20	12	.212	.339	.260	.598	59	-5	-6	106	104	10	.553	0	0	0	-2	3	-0.4
	KC-A	39	120	12	29	2	0	0	13	9	15	.242	.295	.258	.553	48	-8	-9	102	164	9	.423	1	0	0	3	3/2	-0.2
	Det-A	24	46	6	10	1	0	1	4	3	8	.217	.265	.304	.570	54	-3	-3	96	92	4	.528	2	0	1	-2	3/2S	-0.2
	Yr	98	270	35	61	5	0	2	25	32	35	.226	.308	.267	.575	54	-17	-17	102	128	26	.512	3	0	1	-0		-0.8
1962	Det-A	5	0	3	0	0	0	0	0	0	0	—	—	—	—	—	0	0	111	—	—	—	0	0	0	0	/2S3	0.0
Total	10	612	1745	204	425	60	10	27	171	142	252	.244	.306	.336	.642	72	-63	-68	102	104	203	.569	16	15	-4	-14	32/SO	-5.7
■ **BOB BESCHER**	Bescher, Robert Henry b: 2/25/1884, London, Ohio d: 11/29/42, London, Ohio BB/TL, 6'1", 200 lbs. Deb: 9/05/08																											
1908	Cin-N	32	114	16	31	5	5	0	17	9		.272	.325	.404	.729	131	4	4	103	150	18	.783	10			3	O	0.8
1909	Cin-N	124	446	73	107	17	6	1	34	56		.240	.335	.312	.647	109	3	6	94	84	63	.758	**54**			-2	*O	0.0
1910	Cin-N	150	589	95	147	20	10	4	48	81	75	.250	.344	.338	.682	98	1	-0	101	68	91	.801	**70**			8	*O	0.2
1911	Cin-N	153	599	106	165	32	10	1	45	102	78	.275	.385	.367	.753	121	13	20	92	59	115	.940	**81**			-6	*O	0.8
1912	Cin-N	145	548	**120**	154	29	11	4	38	83	61	.281	.381	.396	.777	122	12	18	92	49	107	.947	**67**			-2	*O	1.2
1913	Cin-N	141	511	86	132	22	11	1	37	**94**	68	.258	.377	.350	.727	106	10	9	102	65	77	.828	38			-7	*O	0.0
1914	NY-N	135	512	82	138	23	4	6	35	45	48	.270	.336	.365	.701	113	5	8	96	66	70	.733	36			1	*O	0.5
1915	StL-N	130	486	71	128	15	7	4	34	52	53	.263	.342	.348	.690	109	6	6	100	69	61	.674	27	19	-3	2	*O	0.1
1916	StL-N	151	561	78	132	24	8	6	43	60	50	.235	.316	.339	.654	105	1	4	97	79	67	.669	39	12	5	-16	*O	-2.0
1917	StL-N	42	110	10	17	1	1	1	8	20	13	.155	.290	.209	.499	53	-5	-5	102	119	8	.505	3			-4	O	-1.1
1918	Cle-A	25	60	12	20	2	1	0	6	17	5	.333	.487	.400	.887	155	7	6	108	91	13	1.125	3			-1	O	0.5
Total	11	1228	4536	749	1171	190	74	28	345	619	451	.258	.353	.351	.704	110	56	75	97	70	689	.791	428	31		-24	*O	1.0
■ **BESTICK**	Bestick Deb:6/10/1872																											
1872	Eck-n	4	14	0	3							.214															/C	
■ **JIM BESWICK**	Beswick, James William b: 2/12/58, Wilkinsburg, Pa. BB/TR, 6'1", 180 lbs. Deb: 8/09/78																											
1978	SD-N	17	20	2	1	0	0	0	0	1	7	.050	.095	.050	.145	-63	-4	-4	93	0	0	.095	0	0	0	-1	/O	-0.5
■ **FRANK BETCHER**	Betcher, Franklin Lyle (born Franklin Lyle Bettger) b: 2/15/1888, Philadelphia, Pa. d: 11/27/81, Wynnewood, Pa. BB/TR, 5'11", 173 lbs. Deb: 5/21/10																											
1910	StL-N	35	89	7	18	2	0	0	6	7	14	.202	.276	.225	.500	50	-6	-5	92	105	6	.423	1			-2	S/32O	-0.6
■ **BILL BETHEA**	Bethea, William Lamar "Spot" b: 1/1/42, Houston, Tex. BR/TR, 6', 175 lbs. Deb: 9/13/64																											
1964	Min-A	10	30	4	5	1	0	0	2	4	4	.167	.265	.200	.465	31	-3	-3	101	141	2	.400	0	0	0	-0	/2S	-0.2

YEAR	TM/L	G	AB	R	H	2B	3B	HR	RBI	BB	SO	AVG	OBP	SLG	PRO	/A	BR	/A	PF	CHI	RC	TA	SB	CS	SBR	FR	POS	TPR
■ **LARRY BETTENCOURT**	Bettencourt, Lawrence Joseph b: 9/22/05, Newark, Cal. d: 9/15/78, New Orleans, La. BR/TR, 5'11", 195 lbs. Deb: 6/02/28																											
1928	StL-A	67	159	30	45	9	4	4	24	22	19	.283	.377	.465	.842	116	5	4	104	96	29	.870	2	1	0	-4	3/OC	0.1
1931	StL-A	74	206	27	53	9	2	3	26	31	35	.257	.357	.364	.721	88	-2	-3	102	102	28	.712	4	3	-1	-3	O	-0.9
1932	StL-A	27	30	4	4	1	0	1	3	7	6	.133	.297	.267	.564	47	-2	-2	100	91	3	.615	1	0	0	-0	/O3	-0.1
Total	3	168	395	61	102	19	6	8	53	60	60	.258	.360	.397	.758	96	0	-1	103	99	60	.764	7	4	-0	-7	/O3C	-0.9
■ **BRUNO BETZEL**	Betzel, Christian Frederick Albert John Henry David b: 12/6/1894, Chattanooga, Ohio d: 2/7/65, W.Hollywood, Fla. BR/TR, 5'9", 158 lbs. Deb: 9/03/14																											
1914	StL-N	7	9	2	0	0	0	0	0	1	1	.000	.100	.000	.100	-67	-2	-2	104	0	0	.111	0			0	/23	-0.1
1915	StL-N	117	367	42	92	12	4	0	27	18	48	.251	.291	.305	.596	80	-9	-9	100	92	33	.497	10	13	-5	5	*3/2S	-0.4
1916	StL-N	142	510	49	119	15	11	1	37	39	77	.233	.288	.312	.600	87	-10	-8	97	96	47	.541	22	16	-3	19	*23/O	1.6
1917	StL-N	106	328	24	71	4	3	1	17	20	47	.216	.266	.256	.522	59	-15	-16	102	75	24	.447	9			11	2O/3	0.0
1918	StL-N	76	230	18	51	6	7	0	13	12	16	.222	.260	.309	.569	78	-8	-6	93	69	20	.508	8			4	3O2	-0.1
Total	5	448	1444	135	333	37	25	2	94	90	189	.231	.278	.295	.573	76	-44	-41	98	85	124	.500	49	29		39	23/OS	1.0
■ **KURT BEVACQUA**	Bevacqua, Kurt Anthony b: 1/23/47, Miami Beach, Fla. BR/TR, 6', 180 lbs. Deb: 6/22/71																											
1971	Cle-A	55	137	9	28	3	1	3	13	4	28	.204	.227	.307	.534	47	-9	-10	106	104	9	.407	0	0	0	-1	2/O3S	-1.0
1972	Cle-A	19	35	2	4	0	0	1	1	3	10	.114	.184	.200	.384	13	-4	-4	107	42	1	.313	0	0	0	-3	O/3	-0.7
1973	KC-A	99	276	39	71	8	3	2	40	25	42	.257	.321	.330	.651	77	-6	-9	109	162	29	.553	2	3	-1	-5	32DO/1	-1.5
1974	Pit-N	18	35	1	4	1	0	0	0	2	10	.114	.162	.143	.305	-15	-5	-5	98	0	0	.206	0	0	0	-1	/3O	-0.5
	KC-A	39	90	10	19	0	0	0	3	9	20	.211	.290	.211	.501	43	-6	-7	106	62	6	.400	1	1	-0	-1	13/2SD	-0.7
1975	Mil-A	104	258	30	59	14	0	2	24	26	45	.229	.302	.306	.608	72	-9	-9	100	108	24	.522	3	4	-2	-5	32/S1D	-1.3
1976	Mil-A	12	7	3	1	0	0	0	0	0	0	.143	.143	.143	.286	-16	-1	-1	99	0	0	.167	0	0	0	0	/2D	0.0
1977	Tex-A	39	96	13	32	7	2	5	28	6	13	.333	.373	.604	.977	154	8	7	105	152	18	.901	0	1	-1	-5	O3/12D	0.1
1978	Tex-A	90	248	21	55	12	0	6	30	18	31	.222	.274	.343	.617	75	-10	-8	96	115	22	.512	1	2	-1	-2	3D2/1	-1.0
1979	SD-N	114	297	23	75	12	4	1	34	38	25	.253	.337	.330	.667	86	-6	-5	96	133	31	.575	2	5	-2	4	32/1O	-0.4
1980	SD-N	62	71	4	19	6	1	0	12	6	1	.268	.325	.380	.705	103	-0	0	93	176	9	.630	1	1	-0	-1	3/O21	0.0
	Pit-N	22	43	1	7	1	0	0	4	6	7	.163	.280	.186	.466	31	-4	-4	103	198	2	.395	0	0	0	-1	/31	-0.4
	Yr	84	114	5	26	7	1	0	16	12	8	.228	.307	.307	.614	75	-4	-4	96	184	11	.538	1	1	-0	-1		-0.4
1981	Pit-N	29	27	2	7	1	0	1	4	4	6	.259	.355	.407	.762	121	1	1	96	112	4	.714	0	0	0	0	/23	0.1
1982	SD-N	64	123	15	31	9	0	0	24	17	22	.252	.343	.325	.668	96	-2	-0	92	235	14	.608	2	0	1	-2	1/O3	-0.2
1983	SD-N	74	156	17	38	7	0	2	24	18	33	.244	.322	.327	.649	81	-4	-4	99	167	16	.556	0	3	-2	-0	13O	-0.7
1984	SD-N	59	80	7	16	3	0	1	9	14	19	.200	.326	.275	.601	71	-3	-3	99	141	7	.529	0	0	0	-1	13/O	-0.4
1985	SD-N	71	138	17	33	6	0	3	25	25	17	.239	.356	.348	.704	96	0	0	102	175	18	.676	0	0	0	-2	3/1O	-0.2
Total	15	970	2117	214	499	90	11	27	275	221	329	.236	.309	.327	.636	78	-60	-61	100	138	210	.567	12	20	-8	-24	321/ODS	-8.8
■ **HAL BEVAN**	Bevan, Joseph Harold b: 11/15/30, New Orleans, La. d: 10/5/68, New Orleans, La. BR/TR, 6'2", 198 lbs. Deb: 4/24/52																											
1952	Bos-A	1	1	0	0	0	0	0	0	0	0	.000	.000	.000	.000	-94	-0	-0	107	0	0	.000	0	0	0	0	/3	0.0
	Phi-A	8	17	1	6	0	0	0	4	0	1	.353	.353	.353	.706	87	-0	-0	111	249	2	.667	2	0	1	0	/3	0.0
	Yr	9	18	1	6	0	0	0	4	0	1	.333	.333	.333	.667	78	-0	-1	110	221	2	.615	2	0	1	0		0.0
1955	KC-A	3	3	0	0	0	0	0	0	0	0	.000	.000	.000	.000	-99	-1	-1	101	0	0	.000	0	0	0	0	/3	0.0
1961	Cin-N	3	3	1	1	0	0	1	1	0	2	.333	.333	1.333	1.667	304	1	1	104	58	1	2.000	0	0	0	0	H	0.1
Total	3	15	24	2	7	0	0	1	5	0	3	.292	.292	.417	.708	86	-0	-1	109	184	3	.706	2	0	1	0	/3	0.1
■ **E. P. BEVANS**	Bevans, E. P. b: 1848, New York TR, 5'8", 138 lbs. Deb: 5/09/1871																											
1871	Tro-n	3	15	7	5							.333															/2	
1872	Atl-n	10	44	7	9							.205															/2SO	
Total	2 n	13	59	14	14							.237															/2SO	
■ **MONTE BEVILLE**	Beville, Henry Monte b: 2/24/1875, Dublin, Ind. d: 1/24/55, Grand Rapids, Mich BL/TR, 5'11", 180 lbs. Deb: 4/24/03																											
1903	NY-A	82	258	23	50	14	1	0	29	16		.194	.241	.256	.497	50	-15	-15	100	158	17	.413	4			-9	C/1	-1.4
1904	NY-A	9	22	2	6	2	0	0	2	2		.273	.333	.364	.697	109	1	0	112	93	3	.625	0			0	/1C	0.1
	Det-A	54	174	14	36	5	1	0	13	8		.207	.242	.247	.489	59	-8	-7	96	113	11	.384	2			3	C1	0.0
	Yr	63	196	16	42	7	1	0	15	10		.214	.252	.260	.513	66	-8	-7	98	111	14	.409	2			3		0.1
Total	2	145	454	39	92	21	2	0	44	26		.203	.246	.258	.504	57	-23	-22	99	138	31	.412	6			-6	C/1	-1.3
■ **BUDDY BIANCALANA**	Biancalana, Roland Americo b: 2/2/60, Larkspur, Cal. BB/TR, 5'11", 160 lbs. Deb: 9/12/82																											
1982	KC-A	3	2	0	1	0	1	0	0	1	0	.500	.667	1.500	2.167	474	1	1	100	0	1	2.000	0	0	0	0	/S	0.1
1983	KC-A	6	15	2	3	0	0	0	0	0	7	.200	.200	.200	.400	10	-2	-2	101	0	1	.333	1	0	0	-0	/S	-0.1
1984	KC-A	66	134	18	26	6	1	2	9	6	44	.194	.229	.299	.527	45	-10	-10	99	78	9	.420	1	2	-1	2	S2/D	-0.4
1985	KC-A	81	138	21	26	5	1	1	6	17	34	.188	.277	.261	.538	48	-10	-10	102	61	10	.462	1	4	-2	6	S/2D	0.0
1986	KC-A	100	190	24	46	4	4	2	8	15	50	.242	.298	.337	.634	73	-7	-7	100	45	20	.568	5	1	1	-3	S2	-0.2
1987	KC-A	37	47	4	10	1	0	1	7	1	10	.213	.229	.298	.527	38	-4	-4	104	164	3	.395	0	0	0	2	S2/D	0.0
	Hou-N	18	24	1	1	0	0	0	0	1	12	.042	.080	.042	.122	-72	-6	-6	93	0	0	.087	0	0	0	-1	S/2	-0.4
Total	6	311	550	70	113	16	7	6	30	41	157	.205	.261	.293	.553	51	-37	-38	100	64	44	.473	8	7	-2	6	S/2D	-1.0
■ **TOMMY BIANCO**	Bianco, Thomas Anthony b: 12/16/52, Rockville Cntr, N.Y BB/TR, 5'11", 190 lbs. Deb: 5/28/75																											
1975	Mil-A	18	34	6	6	1	0	0	0	3	7	.176	.263	.206	.469	34	-3	-3	100	0	2	.379	0	0	0	-0	/31D	-0.3
■ **HANK BIASATTI**	Biasatti, Henry Arcado b: 1/14/22, Beano, Italy BL/TL, 5'11", 175 lbs. Deb: 4/23/49																											
1949	Phi-A	21	24	6	2	2	0	0	2	8	5	.083	.313	.167	.479	29	-2	-2	99	171	2	.545	0	0	0	0	/1	-0.1
■ **DANTE BICHETTE**	Bichette, Alphonse Dante b: 11/18/63, W.Palm Beach, Fla. BR/TR, 6'3", 215 lbs. Deb: 9/05/88																											
1988	Cal-A	21	46	1	12	2	0	0	8	0	7	.261	.261	.304	.565	61	-3	-2	94	227	4	.412	0	0	0	0	O	-0.1
■ **OSCAR BIELASKI**	Bielaski, Oscar b: 3/21/1847, Washington, D.C. d: 11/8/11, Washington, D.C. BR/TR, Deb: 4/24/1872																											
1872	Nat-n	10	47	12	8							.170															O	
1873	Nat-n	38	187	35	49							.262															*O	
1874	Bal-n	28	126	18	26							.206															O/12	
1875	Chi-n	52	211	21	49							.232															*O	
1876	Chi-N	32	139	24	29	3	0	0	10	2	3	.209	.220	.230	.450	40	-7	-12	125	108	7	.309				-3	O	-1.3
Total	4 n	128	571	86	132							.231															O	
■ **LOU BIERBAUER**	Bierbauer, Louis W. b: 9/23/1865, Erie, Pa. d: 1/31/26, Erie, Pa. BL/TR, 5'8", 140 lbs. Deb: 4/17/1886																											
1886	Phi-a	137	522	56	118	17	5	2		21		.226	.256	.289	.545	72	-17	-17	100	0	45	.473	19			-5	*2/CSP	-1.9
1887	Phi-a	126	530	74	144	19	7	1		13		.272	.289	.340	.629	77	-17	-17	99	0	65	.604	40			-11	*2/P	-2.1
1888	Phi-a	134	535	83	143	20	9	0	80	25		.267	.301	.338	.640	107	4	3	101	140	66	.615	34			21	*23/P	2.5
1889	Phi-a	130	549	80	167	27	7	7	105	29	30	.304	.344	.417	.761	121	11	13	98	127	87	.730	17			36	*2/C	4.3
1890	Bro-P	133	589	128	180	31	11	7	99	40	15	.306	.350	.431	.781	104	6	-0	106	95	97	.758	16			21	*2	2.2
1891	Pit-N	121	500	60	103	13	6	1	47	28	19	.206	.252	.262	.514	51	-31	-32	101	98	37	.438	12			-3	*2	-2.8
1892	Pit-N	152	649	81	153	20	9	8	65	25	29	.236	.264	.331	.595	87	-17	-12	94	80	61	.506	11			16	*2	0.5
1893	Pit-N	128	528	84	150	19	11	4	94	36	12	.284	.335	.384	.719	87	-7	-13	106	122	73	.672	11			14	*2	0.1
1894	Pit-N	130	525	86	159	19	13	3	107	26	9	.303	.337	.406	.743	85	-18	-12	94	136	80	.708	19			7	*2	0.2
1895	Pit-N	117	466	53	120	13	11	0	69	19	8	.258	.290	.333	.622	64	-27	-24	97	132	51	.561	18			14	*2	-0.2
1896	Pit-N	59	258	33	74	10	6	0	39	5	7	.287	.300	.372	.672	84	-9	-6	93	124	32	.587	7			12	2	0.6
1897	StL-N	12	46	1	10	0	0	0	1	0		.217	.217	.217	.435	17	-5	-5	93	30	3	.333	2			0	2	-0.3
1898	StL-N	4	9	0	0	0	0	0	0	1		.000	.100	.000	.100	-66	-2	-2	106	0	0	.111	0			0	/2S3	-0.1
Total	13	1383	5706	819	1521	208	95	33	706	268	129	.267	.301	.354	.655	85	-130	-124	99	94	697	.599	206			122	*2/3CPS	3.0
■ **CHARLIE BIERMAN**	Bierman, Charles S. b: 1845, Hoboken, N.J. d: 8/4/1879, Hoboken, N.J. 6', 180 lbs. Deb: 6/21/1871																											
1871	Kek-n	1	3	0	0							.000															/1	

YEAR	TM/L	G	AB	R	H	2B	3B	HR	RBI	BB	SO	AVG	OBP	SLG	PRO	/A	BR	/A	PF	CH!	RC	TA	SB	CS	SBR	FR	POS	TPR
■ **CARSON BIGBEE** Bigbee, Carson Lee "Skeeter" b: 3/31/1895, Waterloo, Ore. d: 10/17/64, Portland, Ore. BL/TR, 5'9", 157 lbs. Deb: 8/25/16																												
1916	Pit-N	43	164	17	41	3	6	0	3	7	14	.250	.285	.341	.626	88	-2	-3	105	22	19	.585	8			-4	2O/3	-0.7
1917	Pit-N	133	469	46	112	11	6	0	21	37	16	.239	.301	.288	.589	81	-10	-9	100	61	46	.549	19			-0	*O2/S	-1.3
1918	Pit-N	92	310	47	79	11	3	1	19	42	10	.255	.344	.319	.663	97	2	0	106	75	40	.693	19			-1	O	-0.5
1919	Pit-N	125	478	61	132	11	4	2	27	37	26	.276	.332	.328	.660	94	0	-3	105	62	59	.659	31			11	*O	0.4
1920	Pit-N	137	550	78	154	19	15	4	32	45	28	.280	.341	.391	.732	109	7	6	101	48	74	.723	31	15	0	6	*O	0.5
1921	Pit-N	147	632	100	204	23	17	3	42	41	19	.323	.364	.427	.791	105	8	5	103	48	94	.741	21	20	-6	17	*O	0.9
1922	Pit-N	150	614	113	215	29	15	5	99	56	13	.350	.405	.471	.876	121	24	21	104	109	116	.894	24	15	-2	14	*O	2.6
1923	Pit-N	123	499	79	149	18	7	0	54	43	15	.299	.355	.363	.718	93	-6	-4	97	93	65	.655	10	9	-2	6	*O	-0.3
1924	Pit-N	89	282	42	74	4	1	0	15	26	12	.262	.331	.284	.615	62	-12	-15	106	68	29	.577	15	7	0	-2	O	-1.7
1925	Pit-N	66	126	31	30	7	0	0	8	7	8	.238	.278	.294	.572	45	-10	-11	102	77	10	.469	2	2	-1	-8	O	-1.8
1926	Pit-N	42	68	15	15	3	1	2	4	3	0	.221	.264	.382	.646	64	-3	-4	112	43	7	.604	2			-4	O	-0.8
Total	11	1147	4192	629	1205	139	75	17	324	344	161	.287	.345	.369	.713	96	-2	-16	103	69	558	.685	182	68		35	*O/2S3	-2.7
■ **LYLE BIGBEE** Bigbee, Lyle Randolph "Al" b: 8/22/1893, Sweet Home, Ore. d: 8/5/42, Portland, Ore. BL/TR, 6', 180 lbs. Deb: 4/15/20																												
1920	Phi-A	38	75	5	14	2	0	1	8	9	12	.187	.282	.253	.536	45	-6	-5	94	128	6	.492	1	0	0	-2	OP	-0.6
1921	Pit-N	5	2	0	0	0	0	0	0	0	1	.000	.000	.000	.000	-97	-1	-1	103	0	0	.000	0	0	0	0	/P	0.0
Total	2	43	77	5	14	2	0	1	8	9	13	.182	.276	.247	.523	42	-7	-6	94	125	6	.476	1	0	0	-2	/PO	-0.6
■ **ELLIOT BIGELOW** Bigelow, Elliot Allardice "Babe" or "Gilly" b: 10/13/1897, Tarpon Springs, Fla. d: 8/10/33, Tampa, Fla. BL/TL, 5'11", 185 lbs. Deb: 4/18/29																												
1929	Bos-A	100	211	23	60	16	0	1	26	23	18	.284	.357	.374	.732	87	-3	-4	102	108	28	.671	1	4	-2	-14	O	-2.0
■ **CRAIG BIGGIO** Biggio, Craig Alan b: 12/14/65, Smithtown, N.Y. BR/TR, 5'11", 185 lbs. Deb: 6/26/88																												
1988	Hou-N	50	123	14	26	6	1	3	5	7	29	.211	.254	.350	.603	77	-5	-4	93	38	11	.566	6	1	1	-4	C	-0.4
■ **GEORGE BIGNELL** Bignell, George William b: 7/18/1858, Taunton, Mass. d: 1/16/25, Providence, R.I. Deb: 9/27/1884																												
1884	Mil-U	4	9	4	2	0	0	0		1		.222	.300	.222	.522	79	-0	-0	100	0	1	.429	0			0	/C	0.0
■ **LARRY BIITTNER** Biittner, Lawrence David b: 7/27/45, Pocahontas, Ia. BL/TL, 6'2", 205 lbs. Deb: 7/17/70																												
1970	Was-A	2	2	0	0	0	0	0	0	0	0	.000	.000	.000	.000	-99	-1	-1	96	0	0	.000	0	0	0	0	H	0.0
1971	Was-A	66	171	12	44	4	1	0	16	16	20	.257	.324	.292	.617	82	-5	-4	92	131	16	.507	1	0	0	1	O/1	-0.4
1972	Tex-A	137	382	34	99	18	1	3	31	29	37	.259	.315	.335	.650	99	-3	-1	94	95	40	.546	1	3	-2	-3	1O	-1.5
1973	Tex-A	83	258	19	65	8	2	1	12	20	21	.252	.308	.310	.618	77	-9	-8	97	57	24	.507	1	0	0	-1	O1/D	-1.0
1974	Mon-N	18	26	2	7	1	0	0	3	0	2	.269	.269	.308	.577	58	-1	-2	104	145	2	.421	0	0	0	1	/O	0.0
1975	Mon-N	121	346	34	109	13	5	3	28	34	33	.315	.376	.408	.784	109	9	5	108	72	51	.708	2	1	0	-2	O	0.0
1976	Mon-N	11	32	2	6	1	0	0	1	0	3	.188	.188	.219	.406	15	-4	-4	100	55	1	.250	0	0	0	1	/O	-0.2
	Chi-N	78	192	21	47	13	1	0	17	10	6	.245	.286	.323	.609	66	-7	-9	109	106	17	.483	0	2	-1	-2	1O	-1.5
	Yr	89	224	23	53	14	1	0	18	10	9	.237	.272	.308	.580	60	-11	-13	108	100	18	.452	0	2	-1	-1		-1.7
1977	Chi-N	138	493	74	147	28	1	12	62	35	36	.298	.346	.432	.778	94	5	-4	114	100	70	.690	2	1	0	-1	1O/P	-1.1
1978	Chi-N	120	343	32	88	15	1	4	50	23	37	.257	.305	.341	.646	73	-9	-13	110	154	35	.534	0	1	-1	2	1O	-1.6
1979	Chi-N	111	272	35	79	13	3	3	50	21	23	.290	.341	.393	.735	89	-0	-4	112	171	34	.632	1	1	-0	-5	O1	-1.1
1980	Chi-N	127	273	21	68	12	2	1	34	18	33	.249	.300	.319	.619	69	-10	-12	106	150	25	.505	1	3	-2	-1	1O	-1.8
1981	Cin-N	42	61	1	13	4	0	0	8	4	4	.213	.262	.279	.540	53	-4	-4	101	185	4	.412	0	0	0	1	/1O	-0.2
1982	Cin-N	97	184	18	57	9	2	2	24	17	16	.310	.374	.413	.787	117	5	5	102	115	27	.706	1	0	0	-3	O1	0.1
1983	Tex-A	66	116	5	32	5	1	0	18	9	16	.276	.328	.336	.664	82	-2	-3	101	180	13	.571	0	0	0	1	1/OD	-0.1
Total	14	1217	3151	310	861	144	20	29	354	236	287	.273	.326	.359	.685	87	-37	-57	105	116	358	.603	10	12	-4	-12	O1/DP	-10.4
■ **DANN BILARDELLO** Bilardello, Dann James b: 5/26/59, Santa Cruz, Cal. BR/TR, 6', 185 lbs. Deb: 4/11/83																												
1983	Cin-N	109	298	27	71	18	0	9	38	15	49	.238	.277	.389	.666	81	-8	-9	103	105	30	.565	2	1	0	-8	*C	-1.4
1984	Cin-N	68	182	16	38	7	0	2	10	19	34	.209	.287	.280	.567	57	-9	-11	106	69	14	.470	0	1	-1	-7	C	-1.7
1985	Cin-N	42	102	6	17	0	0	1	9	4	15	.167	.206	.196	.402	12	-12	-12	105	156	3	.278	0	0	0	-5	C	-1.6
1986	Mon-N	79	191	12	37	5	0	4	17	14	32	.194	.249	.283	.532	47	-14	-14	98	103	13	.434	1	0	0	-10	C	-2.2
Total	4	298	773	61	163	30	0	16	74	52	130	.211	.263	.312	.575	58	-44	-46	102	102	61	.485	3	2	-0	-30	C	-6.9
■ **STEVE BILKO** Bilko, Stephen Thomas b: 11/13/28, Nanticoke, Pa. d: 3/7/78, Wilkes-Barre, Pa. BR/TR, 6'1", 230 lbs. Deb: 9/22/49																												
1949	StL-N	6	17	3	5	2	0	0	2	5	6	.294	.455	.412	.866	121	1	1	110	108	4	1.000	0			-0	/1	0.1
1950	StL-N	10	33	1	6	1	0	0	2	4	10	.182	.270	.212	.482	28	-3	-3	103	110	2	.393	0			0	/1	-0.3
1951	StL-N	21	72	5	16	4	0	2	12	9	10	.222	.309	.361	.670	79	-2	-2	101	148	9	.614	0	0	0	-1	1	-0.2
1952	StL-N	20	72	7	19	6	1	1	6	4	15	.264	.303	.417	.719	100	-1	-0	98	72	9	.618	0	0	0	1	1	0.0
1953	StL-N	154	570	72	143	23	3	21	84	70	125	.251	.334	.412	.746	92	-6	-7	102	112	79	.688	0	1	-1	8	*1	-0.1
1954	StL-N	8	14	1	2	0	0	0	1	3	1	.143	.294	.143	.437	18	-2	-2	100	197	0	.357	0	0	0	0	/1	-0.1
	Chi-N	47	92	11	22	8	1	4	12	11	24	.239	.320	.478	.799	104	0	0	101	84	12	.724	0	0	0	2	1	0.1
	Yr	55	106	12	24	8	1	4	13	14	25	.226	.317	.434	.751	93	-1	-1	100	104	13	.682	0	0	0	2		0.0
1958	Cin-N	31	87	12	23	4	2	4	17	10	20	.264	.340	.494	.834	109	2	1	107	128	13	.768	0	0	0	0	1	0.0
	LA-N	47	101	13	21	1	2	7	18	8	37	.208	.266	.465	.731	85	-2	-3	105	109	11	.655	0	0	0	0	1	-0.4
	Yr	78	188	25	44	5	4	11	35	18	57	.234	.301	.479	.780	97	-0	-2	106	118	27	.730	0	0	0	0		-0.4
1960	Det-A	78	222	20	46	11	2	9	25	27	31	.207	.293	.396	.690	83	-5	-6	102	85	25	.628	0	1	-1	-1	1	-1.0
1961	LA-A	114	294	49	82	16	1	20	59	58	81	.279	.398	.544	.942	134	21	17	111	105	65	.986	1	1	-0	-3	1/O	0.5
1962	LA-A	64	164	26	47	9	1	8	38	25	35	.287	.387	.500	.887	134	9	8	102	142	32	.894	1	1	-0	-3	1	0.1
Total	10	600	1738	220	432	85	13	76	276	234	395	.249	.339	.444	.782	102	13	4	104	110	262	.768	2	4		3	1/O	-1.3
■ **JOSH BILLINGS** Billings, John Augustus b: 11/30/1891, Grantville, Kan. d: 12/30/81, Santa Monica, Cal. BR/TR, 5'11", 165 lbs. Deb: 9/09/13																												
1913	Cle-A	1	3	0	0	0	0	0	0	0	3	.000	.000	.000	.000	-95	-1	-1	106	0	0	.000	0			0	/C	0.0
1914	Cle-A	11	8	2	2	1	0	0	0	1	1	.250	.333	.375	.708	110	0	0	102	0	1	.833	1			0	/C	0.1
1915	Cle-A	8	21	2	4	1	0	0	0	0	6	.190	.190	.238	.429	27	-2	-2	104	0	1	.353	1			1	/CO	0.0
1916	Cle-A	22	31	2	5	0	0	0	1	2	11	.161	.212	.161	.373	12	-3	-3	100	71	1	.269	0			0	C	-0.2
1917	Cle-A	66	129	8	23	3	2	0	9	8	21	.178	.243	.233	.475	39	-9	-11	114	108	8	.406	2			-0	C	-0.7
1918	Cle-A	2	3	0	1	0	0	0	0	0	0	.333	.333	.333	.667	94	-0	-0	108	0	0	.500	0			0	/C	0.0
1919	StL-A	38	76	9	15	1	1	0	3	1	12	.197	.218	.237	.455	28	-7	-7	97	60	4	.328	0			0	C/1	-0.5
1920	StL-A	66	155	19	43	5	2	0	11	11	10	.277	.353	.335	.688	74	-3	-6	111	74	20	.634	1	0	0	1	C	-0.1
1921	StL-A	20	46	2	10	0	0	0	4	0	7	.217	.217	.217	.435	11	-6	-6	101	137	2	.278	0	0	0	0	C	-0.4
1922	StL-A	5	7	0	3	1	0	0	1	0	0	.429	.429	.571	1.000	150	1	1	106	89	2	1.000	0	0	0	0	/C	0.1
1923	StL-A	4	9	0	0	0	0	0	0	0	2	.000	.000	.000	.000	-96	-3	-3	104	0	0	.000	0	0	0	0	/C	-0.1
Total	11	243	488	44	106	12	5	0	29	23	73	.217	.268	.262	.530	45	-33	-38	108	80	40	.437	5	0		2	C/1O	-1.8
■ **DICK BILLINGS** Billings, Richard Arlin b: 12/4/42, Detroit, Mich. BR/TR, 6'1", 195 lbs. Deb: 9/11/68																												
1968	Was-A	12	33	3	6	1	0	1	3	5	13	.182	.289	.303	.593	87	-1	-0	91	99	3	.536	0	0	0	-0	/O3	0.0
1969	Was-A	27	37	3	5	0	0	0	0	6	8	.135	.256	.135	.391	12	-4	-4	97	0	1	.306	0	1	-1	-1	/O3	-0.5
1970	Was-A	11	24	3	6	2	0	1	1	2	3	.250	.308	.458	.766	113	0	0	96	29	3	.684	0	0	0	-1	/C	0.0
1971	Was-A	116	349	32	86	14	0	6	48	21	54	.246	.299	.338	.637	87	-10	-7	92	144	34	.535	2	5	-2	2	CO/3	-0.4
1972	Tex-A	133	469	41	119	15	1	5	58	29	77	.254	.300	.322	.622	90	-9	-6	94	**149**	42	.497	1	5	-3	-4	CO/31	-1.4
1973	Tex-A	81	280	17	50	11	0	3	32	20	43	.179	.238	.250	.488	39	-23	-22	97	162	15	.383	1	1	-0	1	C/O1D	-2.0
1974	Tex-A	16	31	2	7	1	0	0	0	4	6	.226	.314	.258	.572	69	-1	-1	96	0	3	.560	2	0	1	0	C/OD	0.0
	StL-N	1	5	0	1	0	0	0	0	0	1	.200	.200	.200	.400	12	-1	-1	104	0	0	.250	0	0	0	0	/C	0.0
1975	StL-N	3	3	0	0	0	0	0	0	0	2	.000	.000	.000	.000	-97	-1	-1	103	0	0	.000	0	0	0	0	H	0.0
Total	8	400	1231	101	280	44	1	16	142	87	207	.227	.283	.304	.587	73	-49	-42	95	137	102	.494	6	12	-5	-1	C/O31D	-4.3
■ **GEORGE BINKS** Binks, George Alvin "Bingo" (born George Alvin Binkowski) b: 7/11/16, Chicago, Ill. BL/TL, 6', 175 lbs. Deb: 9/23/44																												
1944	Was-A	5	12	0	3	0	0	0	0	0	1	.250	.250	.250	.500	48	-1	-1	90	0	1	.333	0	0	0	-1	/O	-0.1

YEAR	TM/L	G	AB	R	H	2B	3B	HR	RBI	BB	SO	AVG	OBP	SLG	PRO	/A	BR	/A	PF	CHI	RC	TA	SB	CS	SBR	FR	POS	TPR
1945	Was-A	145	550	62	153	32	6	6	81	34	52	.278	.324	.391	.715	115	3	7	93	128	69	.634	11	7	-1	10	*O1	1.0
1946	Was-A	65	134	13	26	3	0	0	12	6	16	.194	.229	.216	.445	27	-14	-12	92	157	7	.324	1	0	0	0	O	-1.3
1947	Phi-A	104	333	33	86	19	4	2	34	23	36	.258	.308	.357	.665	84	-8	-8	100	100	38	.592	8	2	1	-2	O1	-1.2
1948	Phi-A	17	41	2	4	1	0	0	2	2	2	.098	.140	.122	.261	-30	-8	-8	102	135	1	.211	1	0	0	-3	O	-1.0
	StL-A	15	23	2	5	0	0	0	1	2	1	.217	.280	.217	.497	31	-2	-2	106	68	2	.389	0	0	0	-1	/O1	-0.2
	Yr	32	64	4	9	1	0	0	3	4	3	.141	.191	.156	.347	-7	-10	-10	104	108	2	.273	1	0	0	-4		-1.2
Total	5	351	1093	112	277	55	10	8	130	67	108	.253	.299	.344	.643	86	-29	-24	96	121	117	.567	21	9	1	3	O/1	-2.8
■ **STEVE BIRAS**	Biras, Stephen Alexander b: 2/26/22, E.St.Louis, Ill. d: 4/21/65, St.Louis, Mo. BR/TR, 5'11", 185 lbs. Deb: 9/15/44																											
1944	Cle-A	2	2	0	2	0	0	0	2	0	0	1.000	1.000	1.000	2.000	472	1	1	100	361	2	—	0	0	0	0	/2	0.1
■ **JUD BIRCHALL**	Birchall, Adoniram Judson b: 1858, Germantown, Pa. d: 12/22/1887, Philadelphia, Pa. Deb: 5/02/1882																											
1882	Phi-a	75	338	65	89	12	1	0		8		.263	.280	.305	.585	87	-1	-7	112	0	30	.446				-1	*O/2	-0.7
1883	Phi-a	96	449	95	108	10	1	1		19		.241	.271	.274	.545	74	-11	-13	103	0	34	.416				5	*O	-0.6
1884	Phi-a	54	221	36	57	2	2	0		4		.258	.287	.285	.572	79	-2	-7	114	0	19	.439				1	O/3	-0.5
Total	3	225	1008	196	254	24	4	1		31		.252	.278	.287	.564	79	-15	-27	108	0	82	.431				5	O/32	-1.8
■ **FRANK BIRD**	Bird, Frank Zepherin "Dodo" b: 3/10/1869, Spencer, Mass. d: 5/20/58, Worcester, Mass. BR/TR, 5'10", 195 lbs. Deb: 4/16/1892																											
1892	StL-N	17	50	9	10	3	1	1	1	6	11	.200	.286	.360	.646	102	-0	0	95	15	6	.650	2			0	C	0.0
■ **GEORGE BIRD**	Bird, George Raymond b: 6/23/1850, Stillman Valley, Ill. d: 11/9/40, Rockford, Ill. 5'9", 150 lbs. Deb: 5/06/1871																											
1871	Rok-n	25	112	18	24							.214															*O	
■ **DAVE BIRDSALL**	Birdsall, David Solomon b: 7/16/1838, New York, N.Y. d: 12/30/1896, Boston, Mass. BR/TR, 5'9", 126 lbs. Deb: 5/05/1871																											
1871	Bos-n	29	155	51	43							.277															*O/C	
1872	Bos-n	14	78	10	14							.179															C/O	
1873	Bos-n	3	12	4	1							.083															/O	
Total	3 n	46	245	65	58							.237															/O	
■ **JOE BIRMINGHAM**	Birmingham, Joseph Leo "Dode" b: 8/6/1884, Elmira, N.Y. d: 4/24/46, Tampico, Mexico BR/TR, 5'10", 185 lbs. Deb: 9/12/06 M																											
1906	Cle-A	10	41	5	13	2	1	0	6	1		.317	.333	.415	.748	132	1	1	103	123	6	.714	2			-0	/O3	0.1
1907	Cle-A	136	476	55	112	10	9	1	33	16		.235	.260	.300	.561	86	-11	-8	93	82	44	.500	23			13	*O/S	-0.2
1908	Cle-A	122	413	32	88	10	1	2	38	19		.213	.248	.257	.504	62	-15	-18	106	130	28	.431	15			1	*O/S	-2.6
1909	Cle-A	100	343	29	99	10	5	1	38	19		.289	.333	.356	.689	115	6	6	102	119	43	.643	12			-23	O	-2.4
1910	Cle-A	104	367	41	84	11	2	0	35	23		.229	.284	.270	.553	74	-11	-11	100	133	33	.512	18			9	*O/3	-0.7
1911	Cle-A	125	447	55	136	18	5	2	51	15		.304	.334	.380	.714	96	-2	-4	103	100	61	.662	16			5	*O3	-0.6
1912	Cle-A	107	369	49	94	19	3	0	45	26		.255	.311	.322	.633	80	-9	-10	101	129	42	.596	15			1	O/1M	-1.4
1913	Cle-A	47	131	16	37	9	1	0	15	8	22	.282	.324	.366	.690	96	-0	-1	106	111	18	.670	7			-1	OM	-0.3
1914	Cle-A	19	47	2	6	0	0	0	4	2	5	.128	.163	.128	.291	-12	-6	-7	102	250	1	.190	0	1	-1	-3	OM	-1.1
Total	9	770	2634	284	669	89	27	6	265	129	27	.254	.293	.315	.609	85	-48	-52	101	116	277	.552	108	1		1	O/31S	-9.2
■ **JOHN BISCHOFF**	Bischoff, John George "Smiley" b: 10/28/1894, Granite City, Ill. d: 12/28/81, Granite City, Ill. BR/TR, 5'7", 165 lbs. Deb: 4/18/25																											
1925	Chi-A	7	11	1	1	0	0	0	0	1	5	.091	.167	.091	.258	-35	-2	-2	96	0	0	.200	0	0	0	0	/C	-0.1
	Bos-A	41	133	13	37	9	1	1	16	6	11	.278	.309	.383	.693	79	-6	-5	95	99	15	.592	1	2	-1	3	C	0.0
	Yr	48	144	14	38	9	1	1	16	7	16	.264	.298	.361	.659	70	-8	-7	95	85	15	.556	1	2	-1	3		-0.1
1926	Bos-A	59	127	6	33	11	2	0	19	15	16	.260	.343	.378	.721	87	-2	-2	101	134	16	.670	1	3	-2	0	C	0.0
Total	2	107	271	20	71	20	3	1	35	22	32	.262	.320	.369	.689	78	-10	-9	98	112	32	.610	2	5	-2	3	/C	-0.1
■ **FRANK BISHOP**	Bishop, Frank H. b: 9/21/1860, Belvidere, Ill. d: 6/18/29, Chicago, Ill. Deb: 5/27/1884																											
1884	CP-U	4	16	1	3	1	0	0		0		.188	.188	.250	.438	47	-1	-1	99	0	1	.308	0			0	/3S	0.0
■ **MAX BISHOP**	Bishop, Max Frederick "Tilly" or "Camera Eye" b: 9/5/1899, Waynesboro, Pa. d: 2/24/62, Waynesboro, Pa. BL/TR, 5'8.5", 165 lbs. Deb: 4/15/24																											
1924	Phi-A	91	294	52	75	13	2	2	21	54	30	.255	.380	.333	.713	85	-4	-4	99	68	41	.725	4	3	-1	10	2	0.7
1925	Phi-A	105	368	66	103	18	4	4	27	87	37	.280	.420	.383	.803	102	7	5	103	63	65	.858	5	9	-4	10	*2	1.5
1926	Phi-A	122	400	77	106	20	2	0	33	116	41	.265	.431	.325	.756	84	8	-4	118	91	67	.839	4	5	-2	10	*2	0.9
1927	Phi-A	117	372	80	103	15	1	0	22	105	28	.277	.442	.323	.764	104	9	11	97	62	62	.885	8	0	2	-3	*2	1.2
1928	Phi-A	126	472	104	149	27	5	6	50	97	36	.316	.435	.432	.868	125	25	23	103	68	95	.943	9	9	-3	-6	*2	2.0
1929	Phi-A	129	475	102	110	19	6	3	36	**128**	44	.232	.398	.316	.713	79	-3	-10	109	67	70	.764	1	4	-2	-12	*2	-2.0
1930	Phi-A	130	441	117	111	27	6	10	38	128	60	.252	.426	.408	.834	113	16	16	99	64	88	.955	3	2	-0	-1	*2	1.4
1931	Phi-A	130	497	115	146	30	4	5	37	112	51	.294	.426	.400	.826	113	20	16	105	49	94	.898	3	1	0	-2	*2	2.0
1932	Phi-A	114	409	89	104	24	2	5	37	110	43	.254	.412	.359	.772	89	7	-3	114	81	69	.844	2	2	-1	-1	*2	0.0
1933	Phi-A	117	391	80	115	27	1	4	42	106	46	.294	.446	.399	.845	136	21	27	92	88	78	.940	1	5	-3	-11	*2	1.1
1934	Bos-A	97	253	65	66	13	1	1	22	82	22	.261	.445	.332	.777	97	7	5	106	84	46	.905	3	2	-0	0	21	0.4
1935	Bos-A	60	122	19	28	3	1	1	14	28	14	.230	.377	.295	.673	70	-3	-5	108	122	16	.677	0	2	-1	2	21/S	-0.3
Total	12	1338	4494	966	1216	236	35	41	379	1153	452	.271	.423	.366	.789	102	109	77	104	72	790	.865	43	44	-14	-5	*2/1S	8.9
■ **MIKE BISHOP**	Bishop, Michael b: 11/5/58, Santa Maria, Cal. BR/TR, 6'2", 188 lbs. Deb: 4/16/83																											
1983	NY-N	3	8	2	1	1	0	0	0	3	4	.125	.364	.250	.614	74	-0	-0	99	0	1	.714	0	0	0	0	/C	0.0
■ **RIVINGTON BISLAND**	Bisland, Rivington Martin b: 2/17/1890, New York, N.Y. d: 1/11/73, Salzburg, Austria BR/TR, 5'9", 155 lbs. Deb: 9/13/12																											
1912	Pit-N	1	1	0	0	0	0	0	0	0	0	.000	.000	.000	.000	-99	-0	-0	99	0	0	.000	0			0	H	0.0
1913	StL-A	12	44	3	6	0	0	0	3	2	5	.136	.191	.136	.328	-4	-6	-5	95	181	1	.237	0			-1	S	-0.5
1914	Cle-A	18	57	9	6	1	0	0	2	6	2	.105	.190	.123	.313	-5	-7	-7	102	107	1	.268	2	5	-2	-1	S/3	-1.0
Total	3	31	102	12	12	1	0	0	5	8	7	.118	.189	.127	.317	-6	-13	-13	99	137	2	.253	2	5		-2	/S3	-1.5
■ **DEL BISSONETTE**	Bissonette, Adelphia Louis b: 9/6/1899, Winthrop, Me. d: 6/9/72, Augusta, Maine BL/TL, 5'11", 180 lbs. Deb: 4/11/28 MC																											
1928	Bro-N	155	587	90	188	30	13	25	106	70	75	.320	.396	.543	.940	145	36	37	99	102	125	.997	5			-3	*1	1.6
1929	Bro-N	116	431	68	121	28	10	12	75	46	58	.281	.351	.476	.827	109	1	4	94	109	71	.819	2			-5	*1	-0.5
1930	Bro-N	146	572	102	192	33	13	16	113	56	66	.336	.396	.523	.919	119	18	18	101	119	115	.947	4			-7	*1	0.3
1931	Bro-N	152	587	90	170	19	14	12	87	59	53	.290	.354	.431	.785	109	8	7	101	114	93	.758	4			-6	*1	-1.0
1933	Bro-N	35	114	9	28	7	0	1	10	2	17	.246	.259	.333	.592	70	-5	-5	97	92	9	.462	2			-1	1	-0.6
Total	5	604	2291	359	699	117	50	66	391	233	269	.305	.371	.486	.857	119	59	62	99	110	412	.858	17			-23	1	-0.2
■ **RED BITTMAN**	Bittman, Henry P. b: 7/22/1862, Cincinnati, Ohio d: 11/8/29, Cincinnati, Ohio Deb: 10/10/1889																											
1889	KC-a	4	14	2	4	0	0	0	2	1	1	.286	.333	.286	.619	75	-0	-0	106	143	2	.600	1			0	/2	0.0
■ **GEORGE BJORKMAN**	Bjorkman, George Anton b: 8/26/56, Ontario, Cal. BR/TR, 6'2", 190 lbs. Deb: 7/10/83																											
1983	Hou-N	29	75	8	17	4	0	2	14	16	29	.227	.370	.360	.730	114	1	2	90	168	11	.746	0	0	0	-2	C	0.1
■ **JOHN BLACK**	Black, John Falcnor "Jack" (born John Falcnor Haddow) b: 2/23/1890, Covington, Ky. d: 3/20/62, Rutherford, N.J. BR/TR, 6'1", 185 lbs. Deb: 6/20/11																											
1911	StL-A	54	186	13	28	4	0	0	7	10		.151	.202	.172	.374	5	-24	-23	95	75	7	.304	4			-2	1	-2.3
■ **BILL BLACK**	Black, John William "Jigger" b: 8/12/1899, Philadelphia, Pa. d: 1/14/68, Philadelphia, Pa. BL/TR, 5'11", 168 lbs. Deb: 5/04/24																											
1924	Chi-A	6	5	0	1	0	0	0	0	0	0	.200	.200	.200	.400	3	-1	-1	97	0	0	.250	0	0	0	0	/2	0.0
■ **BOB BLACK**	Black, Robert Benjamin b: 12/10/1862, Cincinnati, Ohio d: 3/21/33, Sioux City, Iowa Deb: 8/17/1884																											
1884	KC-U	38	146	25	36	14	2	1		10		.247	.295	.390	.685	149	5	8	87	0	17	.609	0			0	OP/2S	0.7
■ **ETHAN BLACKABY**	Blackaby, Ethan Allen b: 7/24/40, Cincinnati, O. BL/TL, 5'11", 190 lbs. Deb: 9/06/62																											
1962	Mil-N	6	13	0	2	1	0	0	0	1	8	.154	.214	.231	.445	20	-1	-1	99	0	1	.364	0	0	0	-1	/O	-0.1
1964	Mil-N	9	12	0	1	0	0	0	1	1	2	.083	.154	.083	.237	-32	-2	-2	97	410	0	.182	0	0	0	-2	/O	-0.3
Total	2	15	25	0	3	1	0	0	1	2	10	.120	.185	.160	.345	-4	-4	-4	98	198	1	.273	0	0	0	-2	/O	-0.4

■ **EARL BLACKBURN** Blackburn, Earl Stuart b: 11/1/1892, Leesville, Ohio d: 8/3/66, Mansfield, Ohio BR/TR, 5'11", 180 lbs. Deb: 9/17/12

YEAR	TM/L	G	AB	R	H	2B	3B	HR	RBI	BB	SO	AVG	OBP	SLG	PRO	/A	BR	/A	PF	CHI	RC	TA	SB	CS	SBR	FR	POS	TPR
1912	Pit-N	1	0	0	0	0	0	0	0	0	0	—	—	—	—	—	0	0	99	—	—	—	0			0	/C	0.0
	Cin-N	1	0	0	0	0	0	0	0	1	0	—	1.000	—	1.160	246	0	0	92	0	0	—	0			0	/C	0.0
	Yr	2	0	0	0	0	0	0	0	1	0	—	1.000	—	1.160	238	0	0	95	0	0	—	0			0		0.0
1913	Cin-N	17	27	1	7	0	0	0	3	2	5	.259	.310	.259	.570	63	-1	-1	102	156	3	.550	2			1	C	0.0
1915	Bos-N	3	6	0	1	0	0	0	0	2	1	.167	.375	.167	.542	68	-0	-0	98	0	0	.600	0			0	/C	0.0
1916	Bos-N	47	110	12	30	4	4	0	7	9	21	.273	.328	.382	.710	127	2	3	93	66	15	.663	2			-2	C	0.4
1917	Chi-N	2	2	0	0	0	0	0	0	0	0	.000	.000	.000	.000	-96	-0	-0	105	0	0	.000	0			0	H	0.0
Total	5	71	145	13	38	4	4	0	10	14	27	.262	.327	.345	.672	109	1	2	95	78	19	.636	4			-1	/C	0.4

■ **LENA BLACKBURNE** Blackburne, Russell Aubrey "Slats" b: 10/23/1886, Clifton Heights, Pa. d: 2/29/68, Riverside, N.J. BR/TR, 5'11", 160 lbs. Deb: 4/14/10 MC

YEAR	TM/L	G	AB	R	H	2B	3B	HR	RBI	BB	SO	AVG	OBP	SLG	PRO	/A	BR	/A	PF	CHI	RC	TA	SB	CS	SBR	FR	POS	TPR
1910	Chi-A	75	242	16	42	3	1	0	10	19		.174	.245	.194	.439	40	-17	-15	95	80	13	.370	4			5	S	-0.9
1912	Chi-A	5	1	0	0	0	0	0	0	1		.000	.500	.000	.500	47	0	0	99	0	1	2.000	1			0	/S3	0.0
1914	Chi-A	144	474	52	105	10	5	1	35	66	58	.222	.324	.270	.594	76	-10	-12	103	106	49	.586	25	15	-1	4	*2	-1.0
1915	Chi-A	96	283	33	61	5	1	0	25	35	34	.216	.304	.240	.544	64	-12	-11	98	125	25	.502	13	11	-3	-11	3/S	-2.1
1918	Cin-N	125	435	34	99	8	10	1	45	25	30	.228	.271	.299	.570	76	-14	-13	97	131	36	.482	6			5	*S	-0.4
1919	Bos-N	31	80	5	21	3	1	0	4	6	7	.262	.322	.325	.647	97	-0	-0	98	60	9	.610	3			2	3/12S	0.2
	Phi-N	72	291	32	58	10	5	2	19	10	22	.199	.228	.289	.517	53	-17	-18	104	72	20	.416	2			9	3/1	-0.9
	Yr	103	371	37	79	13	6	2	23	16	29	.213	.249	.296	.546	63	-17	-18	102	69	30	.455	5			10		-0.7
1927	Chi-A	1	1	1	1	0	0	0	1	0	0	1.000	1.000	1.000	2.000	412	0	0	102	333	1	—	0	0	0	0	H	0.0
1929	Chi-A	1	0	0	0	0	0	0	0	0	0	—	—	—	—	—	0	0	95	—	—	—	0	0	0	0	/PM	0.0
Total	8	550	1807	173	387	39	23	4	139	162	151	.214	.284	.268	.552	68	-70	-69	100	104	155	.494	54	26		14	S32/1P	-5.1

■ **GEORGE BLACKERBY** Blackerby, George Franklin b: 11/10/03, Gluther, Okla. BR/TR, 6'1", 176 lbs. Deb: 8/10/28

YEAR	TM/L	G	AB	R	H	2B	3B	HR	RBI	BB	SO	AVG	OBP	SLG	PRO	/A	BR	/A	PF	CHI	RC	TA	SB	CS	SBR	FR	POS	TPR
1928	Chi-A	30	83	8	21	0	0	0	12	4	10	.253	.287	.253	.540	43	-7	-7	99	196	6	.429	2	1	0	-2	O	-0.8

■ **FRED BLACKWELL** Blackwell, Fredrick William " b: 9/7/1891, Bowling Green, Ky. d: 12/8/75, Morgantown, Ky. BL/TR, 5'1.5 ", 160 lbs. Deb: 9/25/17

YEAR	TM/L	G	AB	R	H	2B	3B	HR	RBI	BB	SO	AVG	OBP	SLG	PRO	/A	BR	/A	PF	CHI	RC	TA	SB	CS	SBR	FR	POS	TPR
1917	Pit-N	3	10	1	2	0	0	0	2	0	3	.200	.200	.200	.400	23	-1	-1	100	386	0	.250	0			0	/C	0.0
1918	Pit-N	8	13	1	2	0	0	0	4	3	4	.154	.313	.154	.466	41	-1	-1	106	757	1	.455	0			0	/C	0.0
1919	Pit-N	24	65	3	14	3	0	0	4	3	9	.215	.261	.262	.522	55	-3	-4	105	91	5	.412	0			-1	C	-0.3
Total	3	35	88	5	18	3	0	0	10	6	16	.205	.263	.239	.502	50	-5	-5	105	234	6	.400	0			-1	/C	-0.3

■ **TIM BLACKWELL** Blackwell, Timothy P b: 8/19/52, San Diego, Cal. BB/TR, 5'11", 170 lbs. Deb: 7/03/74

YEAR	TM/L	G	AB	R	H	2B	3B	HR	RBI	BB	SO	AVG	OBP	SLG	PRO	/A	BR	/A	PF	CHI	RC	TA	SB	CS	SBR	FR	POS	TPR
1974	Bos-A	44	122	9	30	1	1	0	8	10	21	.246	.308	.270	.579	63	-5	-6	107	95	10	.469	1	1	-0	1	C	-0.3
1975	Bos-A	59	132	15	26	3	2	0	6	19	13	.197	.303	.250	.553	53	-7	-8	109	70	11	.486	0	0	0	0	C/D	-0.6
1976	Phi-N	4	8	0	2	0	0	0	1	0	1	.250	.250	.250	.500	39	-1	-1	107	193	1	.333	0	0	0	-0	/C	0.0
1977	Phi-N	1	0	1	0	0	0	0	0	0	0	—	—	—	—	—	0	0	100	—	—	—	0	0	0	0	/C	0.0
	Mon-N	16	22	3	2	1	0	0	0	2	7	.091	.167	.136	.303	-18	-4	-4	98	0	0	.238	0	0	0	1	C	-0.2
	Yr	17	22	4	2	1	0	0	0	2	7	.091	.167	.136	.303	-18	-4	-4	98	0	0	.238	0	0	0	1		-0.2
1978	Chi-N	49	103	8	23	3	0	0	7	23	17	.223	.370	.252	.623	70	-2	-3	110	107	11	.595	0	0	0	-8	C	-1.0
1979	Chi-N	63	122	8	20	3	1	0	12	32	25	.164	.342	.205	.547	47	-7	-9	112	190	11	.552	0	0	0	-6	C	-1.2
1980	Chi-N	103	320	24	87	16	4	5	30	41	62	.272	.355	.394	.748	102	4	2	106	84	46	.699	0	1	-1	15	*C	2.0
1981	Chi-N	58	158	21	37	10	2	1	11	23	23	.234	.331	.342	.673	88	-1	-2	104	76	19	.637	2	1	0	3	C	0.2
1982	Mon-N	23	42	2	8	2	1	0	3	3	11	.190	.244	.286	.530	45	-3	-3	105	98	3	.429	0	0	0	1	C	-0.1
1983	Mon-N	6	15	0	3	1	0	0	2	1	3	.200	.250	.267	.517	43	-1	-1	102	198	1	.385	0	0	0	1	/C	0.0
Total	10	426	1044	91	238	40	11	6	80	154	183	.228	.329	.305	.634	73	-26	-35	107	99	114	.591	3	3	-1	8	C/D	-1.2

■ **RAY BLADES** Blades, Francis Raymond b: 8/6/1896, Mt.Vernon, Ill. d: 5/18/79, Lincoln, Ill. BR/TR, 5'7.5", 163 lbs. Deb: 8/19/22 MC

YEAR	TM/L	G	AB	R	H	2B	3B	HR	RBI	BB	SO	AVG	OBP	SLG	PRO	/A	BR	/A	PF	CHI	RC	TA	SB	CS	SBR	FR	POS	TPR
1922	StL-N	37	130	27	39	2	4	3	21	25	21	.300	.428	.446	.874	124	6	6	101	116	26	.957	3	3	-1	1	O/S3	0.5
1923	StL-N	98	317	48	78	21	5	5	44	37	46	.246	.342	.391	.733	103	-3	2	90	111	45	.722	4	2	0	4	O/3	0.2
1924	StL-N	131	456	86	142	21	13	11	68	35	38	.311	.373	.487	.860	126	18	17	103	99	81	.848	7	9	-3	1	*O/23	1.2
1925	StL-N	122	462	112	158	37	8	12	57	59	47	.342	.423	.535	.958	140	31	30	102	76	105	1.019	6	8	-3	-3	*O/3	1.9
1926	StL-N	107	416	81	127	17	12	8	43	62	57	.305	.409	.462	.871	131	22	21	102	61	80	.938	6			-2	*O	1.5
1927	StL-N	61	180	33	57	8	5	2	29	28	22	.317	.414	.450	.864	123	9	7	107	117	34	.927	3			-15	O	-0.9
1928	StL-N	51	85	9	20	7	1	1	19	20	26	.235	.393	.376	.769	102	1	1	100	193	14	.831	0			-2	O	-0.1
1930	StL-N	45	101	26	40	6	2	4	25	21	15	.396	.504	.614	1.118	161	13	12	105	116	32	1.393	1			-2	O	0.6
1931	StL-N	35	67	10	19	4	0	1	5	10	7	.284	.392	.388	.780	104	2	1	107	61	11	.813	1			-5	O	-0.4
1932	StL-N	80	201	35	46	10	1	3	29	34	31	.229	.340	.333	.674	82	-4	-4	100	142	25	.665	2			-6	O/3	-1.4
Total	10	767	2415	467	726	133	51	50	340	331	310	.301	.395	.460	.855	123	95	92	101	99	453	.890	33	22		-30	O/32S	3.1

■ **RICK BLADT** Bladt, Richard Alan b: 12/9/46, Santa Cruz, Cal. BR/TR, 6'1", 160 lbs. Deb: 6/15/69

YEAR	TM/L	G	AB	R	H	2B	3B	HR	RBI	BB	SO	AVG	OBP	SLG	PRO	/A	BR	/A	PF	CHI	RC	TA	SB	CS	SBR	FR	POS	TPR
1969	Chi-N	10	13	1	2	0	0	0	1	0	5	.154	.154	.154	.308	-13	-2	-2	107	200	0	.182	0	0	0	1	/O	-0.1
1975	NY-A	52	117	13	26	3	1	1	11	11	8	.222	.295	.291	.585	67	-5	-5	99	114	11	.553	6	2	1	1	O	-0.4
Total	2	62	130	14	28	3	1	1	12	11	13	.215	.282	.277	.559	59	-7	-7	99	122	11	.514	6	2	1	1	/O	-0.5

■ **RAE BLAEMIRE** Blaemire, Rae Bertrum b: 2/8/11, Gary, Ind. d: 12/23/75, Champaign, Ill. BR/TR, 6', 178 lbs. Deb: 9/13/41

YEAR	TM/L	G	AB	R	H	2B	3B	HR	RBI	BB	SO	AVG	OBP	SLG	PRO	/A	BR	/A	PF	CHI	RC	TA	SB	CS	SBR	FR	POS	TPR
1941	NY-N	2	5	0	2	0	0	0	0	0	0	.400	.400	.400	.800	122	0	0	103	0	1	.667	0			0	/C	0.1

■ **FOOTSIE BLAIR** Blair, Clarence Vick b: 7/13/1900, Interprise, Okla. d: 7/1/82, Texarkana, Tex. BL/TR, 6'1", 180 lbs. Deb: 4/28/29

YEAR	TM/L	G	AB	R	H	2B	3B	HR	RBI	BB	SO	AVG	OBP	SLG	PRO	/A	BR	/A	PF	CHI	RC	TA	SB	CS	SBR	FR	POS	TPR
1929	Chi-N	26	72	10	23	5	0	1	8	3	4	.319	.347	.431	.777	90	-1	-1	101	81	10	.714	1			1	/312	0.0
1930	Chi-N	134	578	97	158	24	12	6	59	20	58	.273	.306	.388	.693	63	-33	-37	105	89	66	.619	9			7	*23	-1.4
1931	Chi-N	86	240	31	62	19	5	3	29	14	26	.258	.302	.417	.719	95	-4	-3	96	95	31	.652	1			-4	21/3	-0.5
Total	3	246	890	138	243	48	17	10	96	37	88	.273	.308	.399	.707	73	-38	-41	102	90	107	.635	11			3	2/13	-1.9

■ **BUDDY BLAIR** Blair, Louis Nathan b: 9/10/10, Columbia, Miss. BL/TR, 6', 186 lbs. Deb: 4/14/42

YEAR	TM/L	G	AB	R	H	2B	3B	HR	RBI	BB	SO	AVG	OBP	SLG	PRO	/A	BR	/A	PF	CHI	RC	TA	SB	CS	SBR	FR	POS	TPR
1942	Phi-A	137	484	48	135	26	8	5	66	30	30	.279	.325	.397	.722	106	-0	2	96	115	59	.612	1	6	-3	-4	*3	-0.3

■ **PAUL BLAIR** Blair, Paul L b: 2/1/44, Cushing, Okla. BR/TR, 6', 168 lbs. Deb: 9/09/64

YEAR	TM/L	G	AB	R	H	2B	3B	HR	RBI	BB	SO	AVG	OBP	SLG	PRO	/A	BR	/A	PF	CHI	RC	TA	SB	CS	SBR	FR	POS	TPR
1964	Bal-A	8	1	0	0	0	0	0	0	0	1	.000	.000	.000	.000	-95	-0	-0	105	0	0	.000	0	1	-1	-2	/O	-0.2
1965	Bal-A	119	364	49	85	19	2	5	25	32	52	.234	.303	.338	.640	82	-9	-9	100	75	38	.576	8	5	-1	-2	*O	-1.6
1966	Bal-A	133	303	35	84	20	2	6	33	15	36	.277	.311	.416	.727	106	2	2	101	96	37	.638	5	6	-2	-4	*O	-0.9
1967	Bal-A	151	552	72	162	27	**12**	11	64	50	68	.293	.357	.446	.803	144	24	28	95	98	87	.759	8	6	-1	16	*O	4.1
1968	Bal-A	141	421	48	89	22	1	7	38	37	60	.211	.278	.318	.597	79	-10	-11	102	105	39	.524	4	2	0	-4	*O/3	-2.2
1969	Bal-A	150	625	102	178	32	5	26	76	40	72	.285	.330	.477	.807	119	16	13	104	72	97	.776	20	6	2	17	*O	3.0
1970	Bal-A	133	480	79	128	24	2	18	65	56	93	.267	.347	.438	.784	119	9	11	97	102	74	.788	24	11	1	13	*O/3	2.0
1971	Bal-A	141	516	75	135	24	8	10	44	32	94	.262	.306	.397	.703	95	-3	-5	103	78	60	.630	14	11	-2	-4	*O	-1.6
1972	Bal-A	142	477	47	111	20	8	8	49	25	78	.233	.271	.358	.629	88	-10	-9	98	105	41	.521	7	8	-3	3	*O	-1.3
1973	Bal-A	146	500	73	140	25	3	10	64	43	72	.280	.337	.402	.739	100	4	-0	107	109	67	.693	18	8	1	1	*O/D	-0.2
1974	Bal-A	151	552	77	144	27	4	17	62	43	59	.261	.317	.417	.733	118	5	10	93	89	73	.706	27	9	3	-0	*O	0.9
1975	Bal-A	140	440	51	96	13	4	5	31	25	82	.218	.260	.300	.560	64	-25	-20	91	81	34	.481	17	11	-2	-10	*O/1D	-3.6
1976	Bal-A	145	375	29	74	16	0	3	16	22	49	.197	.246	.264	.510	50	-24	-23	98	57	23	.430	15	6	1	-15	*O/D	-4.2
1977	NY-A	83	164	20	43	4	3	4	25	9	16	.262	.309	.396	.705	92	-2	-2	99	129	18	.608	3	2	-0	-10	O/D	-1.4
1978	NY-A	75	125	10	22	5	0	2	13	9	17	.176	.231	.264	.495	39	-10	-10	99	132	7	.398	1	1	-0	-10	O/2S3	-2.1
1979	NY-A	2	5	0	1	0	0	0	0	0	1	.200	.200	.200	.400	9	-1	-1	96	0	0	.250	0	0	0	0	/O	0.0
	Cin-N	75	140	7	21	4	1	2	15	11	27	.150	.212	.236	.448	23	-15	-15	97	152	7	.358	0	0	0	-4	O	-2.1
1980	NY-A	12	2	2	0	0	0	0	0	0	0	.000	.000	.000	.000	-99	-1	-1	99	0	0	.000	0	0	0	-4	O	-0.4
Total	17	1947	6042	776	1513	282	55	134	620	449	877	.250	.305	.382	.687	96	-49	-40	99	92	702	.638	171	93	-5	-19	*O/23SD1	-11.8

■ **WALTER BLAIR** Blair, Walter Allen "Heavy" b: 10/13/1883, Landrus, Pa. d: 8/20/48, Lewisburg, Pa. BR/TR, 6', 185 lbs. Deb: 9/17/07 M

YEAR	TM/L	G	AB	R	H	2B	3B	HR	RBI	BB	SO	AVG	OBP	SLG	PRO	/A	BR	/A	PF	CHI	RC	TA	SB	CS	SBR	FR	POS	TPR
1907	NY-A	7	22	1	4	0	0	0	1	2		.182	.250	.182	.432	36	-1	-2	109	89	1	.333	0			0	/C	0.0

YEAR	TM/L	G	AB	R	H	2B	3B	HR	RBI	BB	SO	AVG	OBP	SLG	PRO	/A	BR	/A	PF	CHI	RC	TA	SB	CS	SBR	FR	POS	TPR
1908	NY-A	76	211	9	40	5	1	1	13	11		.190	.230	.237	.467	56	-11	-10	95	92	12	.380	4			-7	C/O1	-1.1
1909	NY-A	42	110	5	23	2	2	0	11	7		.209	.269	.264	.533	69	-4	-4	99	146	8	.460	2			-2	C	-0.3
1910	NY-A	6	22	2	5	0	1	0	2	0		.227	.227	.318	.545	66	-1	-1	107	108	1	.412	0			-0	/C	0.0
1911	NY-A	85	222	18	43	9	2	0	26	16		.194	.257	.252	.510	38	-17	-21	111	157	16	.430	2			-7	C/1	-1.7
1914	Buf-F	128	378	22	92	11	2	0	33	32	64	.243	.302	.283	.586	65	-15	-17	104	111	36	.507	6			0	*C	-1.0
1915	Buf-F	98	290	23	65	15	3	2	20	18	32	.224	.269	.317	.587	73	-10	-10	100	74	27	.507	4			3	CM	-0.5
Total	7	442	1255	80	272	42	11	3	106	86	96	.217	.270	.275	.545	60	-59	-64	103	110	100	.462	18			-13	C/O1	-4.6
■ HARRY BLAKE	Blake, Harry Cooper b: 6/16/1874, Portsmouth, Ohio d: 10/14/19, Chicago, Ill. 5'7", 165 lbs. Deb: 7/07/1894																											
1894	Cle-N	73	296	51	78	15	4	1	51	30	22	.264	.335	.351	.687	61	-16	-22	111	139	36	.628	1			2	O	-1.8
1895	Cle-N	84	315	50	87	10	1	3	45	30	33	.276	.341	.343	.684	81	-9	-8	97	110	42	.658	11			-3	O	-1.3
1896	Cle-N	104	383	66	92	12	5	1	43	46	30	.240	.322	.305	.627	62	-17	-23	110	105	42	.595	10			3	*O/S	-2.3
1897	Cle-N	32	117	17	30	3	1	1	15	12		.256	.331	.325	.656	68	-4	-6	111	109	15	.644	5			0	O	-0.4
1898	Cle-N	136	474	65	116	18	7	0	58	69		.245	.341	.312	.653	94	-4	-0	96	121	56	.640	12			9	*O/1	0.0
1899	StL-N	97	292	50	70	9	4	2	41	43		.240	.341	.318	.660	78	-5	-9	108	127	38	.694	16			-3	O/2S1C	-1.5
Total	6	526	1877	299	473	67	22	8	253	230	85	.252	.336	.324	.659	75	-55	-68	104	119	228	.640	55			8	O/21SC	-7.3
■ LINC BLAKELY	Blakely, Lincoln Howard b: 2/12/12, Oakland, Cal. d: 9/28/76, Oakland, Cal. BR/TR, 6', 180 lbs. Deb: 4/29/34																											
1934	Cin-N	34	102	11	23	1	1	0	10	5	14	.225	.269	.255	.523	41	-8	-9	101	139	6	.388	1			4	O	-0.5
■ BOB BLAKISTON	Blakiston, Robert J. (born Robert J. Blackstone) b: 10/2/1855, San Francisco, Cal. d: 12/25/18, San Francisco, Cal Deb: 5/02/1882																											
1882	Phi-a	72	281	40	64	4	1	0		9		.228	.252	.249	.501	62	-9	-13	112	0	18	.364				1	O3/2	-1.2
1883	Phi-a	44	167	26	41	3	3	0		9		.246	.284	.299	.583	86	-2	-3	103	0	15	.468				-3	O/13	-0.4
1884	Phi-a	32	128	21	33	6	0	0		11		.258	.336	.305	.640	99	2	-0	114	0	13	.568				4	O/312S	0.3
	Ind-a	6	18	0	4	1	0	0		1		.222	.263	.278	.541	82	-0	-0	96	0	1	.429				0	/1O	0.0
	Yr	38	146	21	37	7	0	0		12		.253	.327	.301	.629	98	2	-1	112	0	15	.550				4		0.3
Total	3	154	594	87	142	14	4	0		30		.239	.280	.276	.556	78	-9	-17	109	0	47	.438				2	O/312S	-1.3
■ JOHNNY BLANCHARD	Blanchard, John Edwin b: 2/26/33, Minneapolis, Minn. BL/TR, 6'1", 193 lbs. Deb: 9/25/55																											
1955	NY-A	1	3	0	0	0	0	0	0	1	0	.000	.250	.000	.250	-29	-1	-1	98	0	0	.333	0	0	0	0	/C	0.0
1959	NY-A	49	59	6	10	1	0	2	4	7	12	.169	.258	.288	.546	54	-4	-4	93	68	4	.471	0	0	0	-2	C/O1	-0.4
1960	NY-A	53	99	8	24	3	1	4	14	6	17	.242	.292	.414	.707	94	-2	-1	94	103	12	.623	0	0	0	0	C	0.0
1961	NY-A	93	243	38	74	10	1	21	54	27	28	.305	.383	.613	.996	168	20	22	96	100	56	1.034	1	0	0	2	CO	2.2
1962	NY-A	93	246	33	57	7	0	13	39	28	32	.232	.313	.419	.731	101	-2	-0	94	109	33	.688	0	0	0	-2	OC/1	-0.3
1963	NY-A	76	218	22	49	4	0	16	45	26	30	.225	.307	.463	.771	112	3	3	101	126	31	.730	0	0	0	-10	O	-0.8
1964	NY-A	77	161	18	41	8	0	7	28	24	24	.255	.351	.435	.786	114	4	3	103	130	24	.754	1	0	0	2	CO/1	0.6
1965	NY-A	12	34	1	5	1	0	1	3	7	3	.147	.293	.265	.557	59	-2	-2	101	104	3	.533	0	0	0	0	C	0.0
	KC-A	52	120	10	24	2	0	2	11	8	16	.200	.256	.267	.522	50	-8	-8	97	120	8	.414	0	0	0	-2	OC	-1.0
	Yr	64	154	11	29	3	0	3	14	15	19	.188	.265	.266	.531	52	-10	-9	98	119	11	.445	0	0	0	-2		-1.0
	Mil-N	10	10	1	1	0	0	1	2	2	1	.100	.250	.400	.650	77	-0	-0	104	118	1	.667	0	0	0	-0	/O	0.0
Total	8	516	1193	137	285	36	2	67	200	136	163	.239	.320	.441	.761	109	8	13	97	111	173	.739	2	0	1	-12	OC/1	0.3
■ DAMASO BLANCO	Blanco, Damaso (Caripe) b: 12/11/41, Curiepe, Venez. BR/TR, 5'10", 165 lbs. Deb: 5/26/72																											
1972	SF-N	39	20	5	7	1	0	0	2	4	3	.350	.458	.400	.858	146	2	2	100	103	4	.933	2	1	0	-0	3/S2	0.2
1973	SF-N	28	12	4	0	0	0	0	0	1	2	.000	.077	.000	.077	-73	-3	-3	105	0	0	.083	0	0	0	-0	/3S2	-0.2
1974	SF-N	5	1	0	0	0	0	0	0	0	1	.000	.000	.000	.000	-93	-0	-0	108	0	0	1.000	1	0	0	0	H	0.0
Total	3	72	33	9	7	1	0	0	2	5	6	.212	.316	.242	.558	58	-2	-2	102	65	4	.593	3	1	0	-0	/3S2	0.0
■ OSSIE BLANCO	Blanco, Oswaldo Carlos (Diaz) b: 9/8/45, Caracas, Venez. BR/TR, 6', 185 lbs. Deb: 5/26/70																											
1970	Chi-A	34	66	4	13	0	0	0	8	3	14	.197	.232	.197	.429	18	-7	-8	106	249	3	.291	0	1	-1	-0	1/O	-0.9
1974	Cle-A	18	36	1	7	0	0	0	2	7	4	.194	.326	.194	.520	52	-2	-2	101	112	2	.424	0	3	-2	-0	1/D	-0.4
Total	2	52	102	5	20	0	0	0	10	10	18	.196	.268	.196	.464	31	-9	-10	104	197	5	.345	0	4	-2	-0	/1DO	-1.3
■ COONIE BLANK	Blank, Frank Ignatz b: 10/18/1892, St.Louis, Mo. d: 12/8/61, St.Louis, Mo. BR/TR, 5'11", 165 lbs. Deb: 09																											
1909	StL-N	1	2	0	0	0	0	0	0	0		.000	.000	.000	.000	-99	-0	-0	96	0	0	.000	0			0	/C	0.0
■ CLIFF BLANKENSHIP	Blankenship, Clifford Douglas b: 4/10/1880, Columbus, Ga. d: 4/26/56, Oakland, Cal. BR/TR, 5'10.5", 165 lbs. Deb: 4/17/05																											
1905	Cin-N	19	56	8	11	1	1	0	7	4		.196	.250	.250	.500	49	-3	-4	103	174	4	.422	1			-1	1	-0.5
1907	Was-A	37	102	4	23	2	0	0	6	3		.225	.248	.245	.493	65	-5	-4	90	86	7	.392	3			-2	C/1	-0.4
1909	Was-A	39	60	4	15	1	0	0	9	0		.250	.250	.267	.517	70	-3	-2	90	217	4	.400	2			0	C/O	0.0
Total	3	95	218	16	49	4	1	0	22	7		.225	.249	.252	.501	62	-11	-9	93	144	15	.402	6			-3	/C1O	-0.9
■ LANCE BLANKENSHIP	Blankenship, Lance Robert b: 12/6/63, Portland, Ore. BR/TR, 6', 185 lbs. Deb: 9/04/88																											
1988	Oak-A	10	3	1	0	0	0	0	0	0	1	.000	.000	.000	.000	-99	-1	-1	95	0	0	.000	0	1	-1	0	/2D	0.0
■ LARVELL BLANKS	Blanks, Larvell b: 1/28/50, Del Rio, Tex. BR/TR, 5'8", 167 lbs. Deb: 7/19/72																											
1972	Atl-N	33	85	10	28	5	0	1	7	7	12	.329	.380	.424	.804	122	3	3	105	74	13	.717	0	0	0	-2	2/S3	0.3
1973	Atl-N	17	18	1	4	0	0	0	0	1	3	.222	.263	.222	.485	32	-2	-2	113	0	1	.333	0	0	0	0	/32S	-0.1
1974	Atl-N	3	8	0	2	0	0	0	1	0	0	.250	.250	.250	.500	38	-1	-1	105	193	1	.333	0	0	0	0	/S	0.0
1975	Atl-N	141	471	49	110	13	3	3	38	38	43	.234	.294	.293	.587	66	-23	-21	95	100	40	.485	4	3	-1	-12	*S2	-1.8
1976	Cle-A	104	328	45	92	8	7	5	41	30	31	.280	.341	.393	.734	115	6	6	100	109	41	.632	1	2	-1	3	S2/3D	1.5
1977	Cle-A	105	322	43	92	10	4	6	38	19	37	.286	.327	.398	.725	99	-2	-1	98	103	42	.637	3	0	1	-7	S32/D	0.2
1978	Cle-A	70	193	19	49	10	0	2	20	10	16	.254	.291	.337	.627	81	-6	-5	93	111	18	.497	0	0	0	-3	S2/3D	-0.3
1979	Tex-A	68	120	13	24	5	0	1	15	11	9	.200	.267	.267	.534	45	-9	-9	100	165	9	.443	0	0	0	-4	S2	-0.6
1980	Atl-N	88	221	23	45	6	0	2	12	16	27	.204	.257	.258	.515	44	-16	-17	101	75	14	.402	1	2	-1	3	S3/2	-0.8
Total	9	629	1766	203	446	57	14	20	172	132	178	.253	.306	.335	.640	81	-51	-46	98	103	179	.551	9	7	-2	-22	S2/3D	-1.6
■ DON BLASINGAME	Blasingame, Don Lee b: 3/16/32, Corinth, Miss. BL/TR, 5'10", 160 lbs. Deb: 9/20/55																											
1955	StL-N	5	16	4	6	1	0	0	0	6	0	.375	.545	.438	.983	164	2	2	101	0	4	1.273	1	1	-0	-0	/2S	0.2
1956	StL-N	150	587	94	153	22	7	0	27	72	52	.261	.344	.322	.666	81	-14	-13	99	58	70	.611	8	8	-2	11	2S/3	0.7
1957	StL-N	154	650	108	176	25	7	8	58	71	49	.271	.343	.368	.711	91	-7	-7	101	79	87	.682	21	9	1	26	*2	3.2
1958	StL-N	143	547	71	150	19	10	2	36	57	47	.274	.344	.356	.700	81	-10	-15	106	78	69	.656	20	5	3	-1	*2	-0.5
1959	StL-N	150	615	90	178	26	7	1	24	67	42	.289	.361	.359	.720	89	-4	-8	105	37	83	.670	15	15	-5	18	*2	1.7
1960	SF-N	136	523	72	123	12	8	2	31	49	53	.235	.303	.300	.603	73	-24	-17	90	82	52	.547	14	2	3	-11	*2	-1.3
1961	SF-N	3	1	1	0	0	0	0	0	2	1	.000	.667	.000	.667	98	0	0	98	0	0	2.000	0	0	0	0	H	0.0
	Cin-N	123	450	59	100	18	4	1	21	39	38	.222	.287	.287	.574	51	-30	-32	104	68	38	.483	4	3	-1	-12	*2	-3.0
	Yr	126	451	60	100	18	4	1	21	41	39	.222	.289	.286	.576	51	-30	-32	104	66	39	.488	4	3	-1	-12		-3.0
1962	Cin-N	141	494	77	139	9	7	2	35	63	44	.281	.365	.340	.705	89	-4	-5	102	81	66	.655	4	3	-1	-9	*2	-0.2
1963	Cin-N	18	31	4	5	2	0	0	0	7	5	.161	.316	.226	.542	57	-1	-2	104	0	3	.519	0	1	-1	-1	2/3	-0.2
	Was-A	69	254	29	65	10	2	2	12	24	18	.256	.320	.335	.655	86	-5	-4	98	56	29	.583	3	2	-0	3	2	0.3
1964	Was-A	143	506	56	135	17	2	1	34	40	44	.267	.321	.314	.635	77	-15	-15	101	91	54	.549	8	5	-1	-11	*2	-1.3
1965	Was-A	129	403	47	90	8	8	1	18	35	45	.223	.289	.290	.579	65	-18	-18	100	62	36	.498	5	4	-1	-9	*2	-2.3
1966	Was-A	68	200	18	43	9	0	1	11	18	21	.215	.280	.275	.555	63	-10	-9	95	80	17	.475	2	1	0	-3	2/S	-0.6
	KC-A	12	19	1	3	0	0	0	1	2	3	.158	.238	.158	.396	17	-2	-2	94	140	1	.294	0	1	-1	0	/2	-0.1
	Yr	80	219	19	46	9	0	1	12	20	24	.210	.276	.265	.541	60	-12	-11	95	90	17	.457	2	2	-1	-3		-0.7
Total	12	1444	5296	731	1366	178	62	21	308	552	462	.258	.330	.327	.657	79	-142	-145	100	69	610	.602	105	60	-4	0	*2/S3	-3.4
■ JOHNNY BLATNIK	Blatnik, John Louis b: 3/10/21, Bridgeport, Ohio BR/TR, 6', 195 lbs. Deb: 4/21/48																											
1948	Phi-N	121	415	56	108	27	8	6	45	31	77	.260	.315	.407	.722	100	-5	-2	94	92	51	.643	3			-1	*O	-0.9
1949	Phi-N	6	8	3	1	0	0	0	0	4	1	.125	.417	.125	.542	52	-0	-0	101	0	1	.714	0			-0	/O	0.0

YEAR	TM/L	G	AB	R	H	2B	3B	HR	RBI	BB	SO	AVG	OBP	SLG	PRO	/A	BR	/A	PF	CHI	RC	TA	SB	CS	SBR	FR	POS	TPR
1950	Phi-N	4	4	0	1	0	0	0	0	2	3	.250	.500	.250	.750	107	0	0	97	0	1	1.000	0			0	/O	0.0
	StL-N	7	20	0	3	0	0	0	1	3	2	.150	.261	.150	.411	11	-3	-3	103	129	1	.333	0			-1	/O	-0.3
	Yr	11	24	0	4	0	0	0	1	5	5	.167	.310	.167	.477	29	-2	-2	101	82	1	.429	0			-1		-0.3
Total	3	138	447	59	113	27	8	6	46	40	83	.253	.317	.389	.706	95	-7	-4	95	90	54	.654	3			-3	O	-1.2

■ **BUDDY BLATTNER** Blattner, Robert Garnett b: 2/8/20, St.Louis, Mo. BR/TR, 6'0.5", 180 lbs. Deb: 4/18/42

YEAR	TM/L	G	AB	R	H	2B	3B	HR	RBI	BB	SO	AVG	OBP	SLG	PRO	/A	BR	/A	PF	CHI	RC	TA	SB	CS	SBR	FR	POS	TPR
1942	StL-N	19	23	3	1	0	0	0	1	3	6	.043	.185	.043	.229	-29	-4	-4	108	371	0	.217	0			0	S/2	-0.2
1946	NY-N	126	420	63	107	18	6	11	49	56	52	.255	.351	.405	.755	112	8	7	102	92	63	.765	12			-1	*2/1	1.0
1947	NY-N	55	153	28	40	9	2	0	13	21	19	.261	.351	.346	.697	85	-3	-3	101	91	20	.684	4			3	23	0.3
1948	NY-N	8	20	3	4	1	0	0	0	3	2	.200	.304	.250	.554	52	-1	-1	100	0	2	.625	2			0	/2	0.0
1949	Phi-N	64	97	15	24	6	0	5	21	19	17	.247	.371	.464	.835	122	3	3	101	132	18	.853	0			-1	23/S	0.3
Total	5	272	713	112	176	34	8	16	84	102	96	.247	.347	.384	.731	101	4	2	101	104	103	.744	18			1	2/3S1	1.4

■ **JEFF BLAUSER** Blauser, Jeffrey Michael b: 11/8/65, Los Gatos, Cal. BR/TR, 6' ", 170 lbs. Deb: 7/05/87

YEAR	TM/L	G	AB	R	H	2B	3B	HR	RBI	BB	SO	AVG	OBP	SLG	PRO	/A	BR	/A	PF	CHI	RC	TA	SB	CS	SBR	FR	POS	TPR
1987	Atl-N	51	165	11	40	6	3	2	15	18	34	.242	.328	.352	.679	74	-4	-6	108	93	19	.652	7	3	0	4	S	0.4
1988	Atl-N	18	67	7	16	3	1	2	7	2	11	.239	.271	.403	.674	87	-1	-1	104	90	7	.566	0	1	-1	-0	/2S	-0.1
Total	2	69	232	18	56	9	4	4	22	20	45	.241	.313	.366	.679	77	-6	-8	107	92	26	.641	7	4	-0	4	/S2	0.3

■ **MARV BLAYLOCK** Blaylock, Marvin Edward b: 9/30/29, Ft.Smith, Ark. BL/TL, 6'1.5", 175 lbs. Deb: 9/26/50

YEAR	TM/L	G	AB	R	H	2B	3B	HR	RBI	BB	SO	AVG	OBP	SLG	PRO	/A	BR	/A	PF	CHI	RC	TA	SB	CS	SBR	FR	POS	TPR
1950	NY-N	1	1	0	0	0	0	0	0	0	0	.000	.000	.000	.000	-99	-0	-0	98	0	0	.000	0			0	H	0.0
1955	Phi-N	113	259	30	54	7	7	3	24	31	43	.208	.296	.324	.620	63	-13	-14	102	104	27	.581	6	1	1	2	1/O	-1.5
1956	Phi-N	136	460	61	117	14	8	10	50	50	86	.254	.330	.385	.715	97	-5	-2	94	104	60	.661	5	1	1	-7	*1/O	-1.3
1957	Phi-N	37	26	5	4	0	0	2	4	3	8	.154	.313	.385	.697	88	-0	-0	98	104	4	.727	0	0	0	0	1/O	0.0
Total	4	287	746	96	175	21	15	15	78	84	137	.235	.317	.363	.680	84	-19	-16	97	104	90	.649	11	2		-5	1/O	-2.8

■ **CURT BLEFARY** Blefary, Curtis Le Roy b: 7/5/43, Brooklyn, N.Y. BL/TR, 6'2", 195 lbs. Deb: 4/14/65

YEAR	TM/L	G	AB	R	H	2B	3B	HR	RBI	BB	SO	AVG	OBP	SLG	PRO	/A	BR	/A	PF	CHI	RC	TA	SB	CS	SBR	FR	POS	TPR
1965	Bal-A	144	462	72	120	23	4	22	70	88	73	.260	.382	.470	.851	141	27	27	100	105	87	.881	4	2	0	0	*O	2.3
1966	Bal-A	131	419	73	107	14	3	23	64	73	56	.255	.373	.468	.841	139	24	23	101	103	77	.857	1	4	-2	-8	*O1	0.9
1967	Bal-A	155	554	69	134	19	5	22	81	73	94	.242	.339	.413	.752	128	15	19	95	121	81	.732	4	4	-1	6	*O1	1.8
1968	Bal-A	137	451	50	90	8	1	15	39	65	66	.200	.306	.322	.627	88	-4	-5	102	90	49	.598	6	3	0	-3	OC1	-1.2
1969	Hou-N	155	542	66	137	26	7	12	67	77	79	.253	.350	.393	.743	106	7	6	102	110	77	.719	8	7	-2	7	*1/O	-0.1
1970	NY-A	99	269	34	57	6	0	9	37	43	37	.212	.327	.335	.662	90	-6	-3	92	128	31	.620	1	3	-2	-13	O/1	-2.1
1971	NY-A	21	36	4	7	1	0	1	2	3	5	.194	.256	.306	.562	60	-2	-2	97	58	3	.467	0	0	0	-1	/O1	-0.2
	Oak-A	50	101	15	22	2	0	5	12	15	15	.218	.325	.386	.711	100	0	0	101	91	13	.679	0	1	-1	-2	CO/32	-0.2
	Yr	71	137	19	29	3	0	6	14	18	20	.212	.308	.365	.673	90	-2	-2	99	82	16	.627	0	1	-1	-3		-0.4
1972	Oak-A	8	11	1	5	2	0	0	1	0	1	.455	.455	.636	1.091	229	2	2	97	60	3	1.167	0	0	0	0	/12O	0.2
	SD-N	74	102	10	20	3	0	3	9	19	18	.196	.322	.314	.636	92	-2	-1	88	90	11	.614	0	0	0	-1	C/13O	-0.1
Total	8	974	2947	394	699	104	20	112	382	456	444	.237	.345	.400	.745	115	61	66	99	107	432	.743	24	24	-7	-14	O1/C32	1.3

■ **IKE BLESSITT** Blessitt, Isaiah b: 9/30/49, Detroit, Mich. BR/TR, 5'11", 185 lbs. Deb: 9/07/72

YEAR	TM/L	G	AB	R	H	2B	3B	HR	RBI	BB	SO	AVG	OBP	SLG	PRO	/A	BR	/A	PF	CHI	RC	TA	SB	CS	SBR	FR	POS	TPR
1972	Det-A	4	5	0	0	0	0	0	0	0	2	.000	.000	.000	.000	-88	-1	-1	113	0	0	.000	0	0	0	0	/O	-0.1

■ **NED BLIGH** Bligh, Edwin Forrest b: 6/30/1864, Brooklyn, N.Y. d: 4/18/1892, Brooklyn, N.Y. BR/TR, 5'11", 172 lbs. Deb: 6/26/1886

YEAR	TM/L	G	AB	R	H	2B	3B	HR	RBI	BB	SO	AVG	OBP	SLG	PRO	/A	BR	/A	PF	CHI	RC	TA	SB	CS	SBR	FR	POS	TPR
1886	Bal-a	3	9	0	0	0	0	0		1		.000	.100	.000	.100	-74	-2	-2	91	0	0	.111	0			0	/C	0.0
1888	Cin-a	3	5	0	0	0	0	0	0	0		.000	.000	.000	.000	-99	-1	-1	101	0	0	.000	0			0	/CO	0.0
1889	Col-a	28	93	6	13	1	1	0	5	4	14	.140	.200	.172	.372	8	-11	-10	91	89	4	.313	2			0	C	-0.7
1890	Col-a	8	29	2	6	2	0	0		2		.207	.258	.276	.534	60	-2	-1	99	0	2	.435	0			0	/C	0.0
	Lou-a	24	73	9	15	0	0	1		9		.205	.293	.247	.539	57	-3	-4	107	0	6	.483	1			0	C	-0.3
	Yr	32	102	11	21	2	0	1	0	11		.206	.283	.255	.538	58	-5	-6	105	0	8	.469	1			0		-0.3
Total	4	66	209	17	34	3	1	1	5	16	14	.163	.232	.201	.433	29	-19	-18	98	39	12	.366	3			0	/CO	-1.0

■ **ELMER BLISS** Bliss, Elmer Ward b: 3/9/1875, Penfield, Pa. d: 3/18/62, Bradford, Pa. BL/TR, 6', 180 lbs. Deb: 03

YEAR	TM/L	G	AB	R	H	2B	3B	HR	RBI	BB	SO	AVG	OBP	SLG	PRO	/A	BR	/A	PF	CHI	RC	TA	SB	CS	SBR	FR	POS	TPR
1903	NY-A	1	3	0	0	0	0	0	0	0		.000	.000	.000	.000	-99	-1	-1	100	0	0	.000	0			-0	/P	0.0
1904	NY-A	1	1	0	0	0	0	0	0	0		.000	.000	.000	.000	-89	-0	-0	112	0	0	.000	0			0	/O	0.0
Total	2	2	4	0	0	0	0	0	0	0		.000	.000	.000	.000	-97	-1	-1	103	0	0	.000	0			-0	/OP	0.0

■ **FRANK BLISS** Bliss, Howard Frank b: 2/15/1844, Mount Carmel, Ill. d: 7/25/19, Janesville, Wis. Deb: 6/20/1878

YEAR	TM/L	G	AB	R	H	2B	3B	HR	RBI	BB	SO	AVG	OBP	SLG	PRO	/A	BR	/A	PF	CHI	RC	TA	SB	CS	SBR	FR	POS	TPR
1878	Mil-N	2	8	1	1	0	0	0	0	0	0	.125	.125	.125	.250	-17	-1	-1	107	0	0	.143				0	/3C	0.0

■ **JACK BLISS** Bliss, John Joseph Albert b: 1/9/1882, Vancouver, Wash. d: 10/23/68, Temple City, Cal. BR/TR, 5'9", 185 lbs. Deb: 5/10/08

YEAR	TM/L	G	AB	R	H	2B	3B	HR	RBI	BB	SO	AVG	OBP	SLG	PRO	/A	BR	/A	PF	CHI	RC	TA	SB	CS	SBR	FR	POS	TPR
1908	StL-N	44	136	9	29	4	0	1	5	8		.213	.257	.265	.522	73	-5	-4	94	49	10	.439	3			1	C	0.0
1909	StL-N	35	113	12	25	2	1	1	8	12		.221	.307	.283	.590	88	-2	-1	96	83	10	.545	2			-0	C	0.0
1910	StL-N	16	33	2	2	0	0	0	3	4	8	.061	.162	.061	.223	-38	-6	-5	92	523	0	.194	0			-1	C	-0.5
1911	StL-N	97	258	36	59	6	4	1	27	42	25	.229	.341	.295	.636	78	-6	-6	101	116	28	.628	5			0	C/S	0.0
1912	StL-N	49	114	11	28	3	1	0	18	19	14	.246	.372	.289	.662	83	-2	-2	100	184	14	.686	3			4	C	0.5
Total	5	241	654	70	143	15	6	3	61	85	47	.219	.316	.274	.590	74	-20	-19	98	130	62	.558	13			5	C/S	0.0

■ **BRUNO BLOCK** Block, James John (born James John Blochowicz) b: 3/13/1885, Wisconsin Rapids, Wis. d: 8/6/37, S.Milwaukee, Wis. BR/TR, 5'9", 185 lbs. Deb: 8/05/07

YEAR	TM/L	G	AB	R	H	2B	3B	HR	RBI	BB	SO	AVG	OBP	SLG	PRO	/A	BR	/A	PF	CHI	RC	TA	SB	CS	SBR	FR	POS	TPR
1907	Was-A	24	57	3	8	2	1	0	2	2		.140	.169	.211	.380	25	-5	-4	90	60	2	.286	0			-1	C	-0.3
1910	Chi-A	55	152	12	32	1	1	0	9	13		.211	.273	.230	.503	61	-7	-6	95	95	11	.425	3			2	C	0.0
1911	Chi-A	39	115	11	35	6	1	1	18	6		.304	.339	.400	.739	109	0	1	97	124	15	.650	0			-6	C	0.0
1912	Chi-A	46	136	8	35	5	6	0	26	7		.257	.294	.382	.676	94	-2	-2	99	167	16	.594	1			-2	C	0.1
1914	Chi-F	44	105	8	21	4	1	0	14	11	17	.200	.276	.257	.533	58	-6	-5	91	187	8	.464	1			1	C	-0.2
Total	5	208	565	42	131	18	10	1	69	39	17	.232	.281	.304	.586	76	-20	-17	95	132	52	.498	5			-7	C	-0.4

■ **CY BLOCK** Block, Seymour b: 5/4/19, Brooklyn, N.Y. BR/TR, 6', 180 lbs. Deb: 9/07/42

YEAR	TM/L	G	AB	R	H	2B	3B	HR	RBI	BB	SO	AVG	OBP	SLG	PRO	/A	BR	/A	PF	CHI	RC	TA	SB	CS	SBR	FR	POS	TPR
1942	Chi-N	9	33	6	12	1	1	0	4	3	3	.364	.417	.455	.871	161	2	2	96	101	6	.909	2			-1	/32	0.2
1945	Chi-N	2	7	1	1	0	0	0	1	0	0	.143	.143	.143	.286	-21	-1	-1	99	347	0	.167	0			0	/23	0.0
1946	Chi-N	6	13	2	3	0	0	0	0	4	0	.231	.412	.231	.643	90	0	0	94	0	2	.700	0			0	/3	0.0
Total	3	17	53	9	16	1	1	0	5	7	3	.302	.383	.358	.742	119	1	1	96	101	8	.757	2			-1	/32	0.2

■ **TERRY BLOCKER** Blocker, Terry Fennell b: 8/18/59, Columbia, S.C. BL/TL, 6'2", 195 lbs. Deb: 4/11/85

YEAR	TM/L	G	AB	R	H	2B	3B	HR	RBI	BB	SO	AVG	OBP	SLG	PRO	/A	BR	/A	PF	CHI	RC	TA	SB	CS	SBR	FR	POS	TPR
1985	NY-N	18	15	1	1	0	0	0	0	1	2	.067	.125	.067	.192	-46	-3	-3	97	0	0	.143	0	0	0	-1	/O	-0.3
1988	Atl-N	66	198	13	42	4	2	2	10	10	20	.212	.250	.283	.533	50	-12	-13	104	64	13	.411	1	1	-0	0	O	-1.5
Total	2	84	213	14	43	4	2	2	10	11	22	.202	.241	.268	.509	44	-15	-16	104	60	13	.390	1	1	-0	-1	/O	-1.8

■ **WES BLOGG** Blogg, Wesley C. b: 1855, Norfolk, Va. d: 3/1897, Deb: 1883

YEAR	TM/L	G	AB	R	H	2B	3B	HR	RBI	BB	SO	AVG	OBP	SLG	PRO	/A	BR	/A	PF	CHI	RC	TA	SB	CS	SBR	FR	POS	TPR
1883	Pit-a	9	34	0	5	0	0	0		0		.147	.147	.147	.294	-5	-4	-4	94	0	1	.172				0	/CO	-0.2

■ **RON BLOMBERG** Blomberg, Ronald Mark "Boomer" b: 8/23/48, Atlanta, Ga. BL/TR, 6'1.5", 195 lbs. Deb: 9/10/69

YEAR	TM/L	G	AB	R	H	2B	3B	HR	RBI	BB	SO	AVG	OBP	SLG	PRO	/A	BR	/A	PF	CHI	RC	TA	SB	CS	SBR	FR	POS	TPR
1969	NY-A	4	6	0	3	0	0	0	0	1	0	.500	.571	.500	1.071	212	1	1	95	0	2	1.333	0	0	0	-0	/O	0.1
1971	NY-A	64	199	30	64	6	2	7	31	14	23	.322	.366	.477	.844	142	9	10	97	109	33	.787	2	4	-2	-5	O	0.1
1972	NY-A	107	299	36	80	22	1	14	49	38	26	.268	.356	.488	.844	162	18	20	92	109	53	.831	0	2	-1	-3	1	0.7
1973	NY-A	100	301	45	99	13	1	12	57	34	25	.329	.397	.498	.895	150	20	20	101	120	60	.890	2	0	1	-1	D1	1.8
1974	NY-A	90	264	39	82	11	2	10	48	29	33	.311	.383	.481	.864	154	16	18	96	120	49	.851	2	1	0	-1	DO	1.7
1975	NY-A	34	106	18	27	8	2	4	17	13	10	.255	.336	.481	.817	130	4	4	99	104	17	.780	0	0	0	0	D/O	0.4
1976	NY-A	1	2	0	0	0	0	0	0	0	0	.000	.000	.000	.000	-99	-0	-0	99	0	0	.000	0	0	0	0	/D	0.0
1978	Chi-A	61	156	16	36	7	0	5	22	11	17	.231	.281	.372	.653	81	-4	-4	101	119	17	.570	0	0	0	-0	D/1	-0.4
Total	8	461	1333	184	391	67	8	52	224	140	134	.293	.363	.473	.835	142	64	68	97	114	231	.822	6	7	-2	-10	D1/O	4.4

■ **JOE BLONG** Blong, Joseph Myles b: 9/17/1853, St.Louis, Mo. d: 9/22/1892, St.Louis, Mo. BR/TR, Deb: 5/04/1875

YEAR	TM/L	G	AB	R	H	2B	3B	HR	RBI	BB	SO	AVG	OBP	SLG	PRO	/A	BR	/A	PF	CHI	RC	TA	SB	CS	SBR	FR	POS	TPR
1875	RS-n	16	70	3	10							.143															P/O	

YEAR	TM/L	G	AB	R	H	2B	3B	HR	RBI	BB	SO	AVG	OBP	SLG	PRO	/A	BR	/A	PF	CHI	RC	TA	SB	CS	SBR	FR	POS	TPR
1876	StL-N	62	264	30	62	7	4	0	30	2	9	.235	.241	.292	.532	87	-6	-1	88	134	19	.391				0	*O/P	-0.1
1877	StL-N	58	218	17	47	8	3	0	13	4	22	.216	.230	.280	.510	59	-10	-10	102	74	14	.380				-2	*OP	-0.8
Total	2	120	482	47	109	15	7	0	43	6	31	.226	.236	.286	.522	73	-16	-12	94	107	33	.386				-2	O/P	-0.9
■ **JIMMY BLOODWORTH** Bloodworth, James Henry b: 7/26/17, Tallahassee, Fla. BR/TR, 5'11", 180 lbs. Deb: 9/14/37																												
1937	Was-A	15	50	3	11	2	1	0	8	5	8	.220	.291	.300	.591	52	-4	-4	94	183	4	.500	0	1	-1	-1	2	-0.2
1939	Was-A	83	318	34	92	24	1	4	40	10	26	.289	.313	.409	.722	92	-9	-5	90	97	37	.600	3	1	0	6	2/O	0.4
1940	Was-A	119	469	47	115	17	8	11	70	16	71	.245	.272	.386	.658	74	-24	-19	93	125	46	.543	3	1	0	8	21/3	-0.5
1941	Was-A	142	506	59	124	24	3	7	66	41	58	.245	.303	.346	.649	73	-22	-20	98	119	54	.553	1	1	-0	22	*2/3S	1.3
1942	Det-A	137	533	62	129	23	1	13	57	35	63	.242	.295	.362	.657	75	-13	-21	113	92	54	.553	2	8	-4	14	*2/S	-0.6
1943	Det-A	129	474	41	114	23	4	6	52	29	59	.241	.289	.344	.632	80	-11	-14	106	107	39	.503	4	7	-3	3	*2	-0.8
1946	Det-A	76	249	26	61	8	1	5	36	12	26	.245	.285	.345	.631	70	-9	-11	108	136	22	.512	3	3	-1	1	2	-0.5
1947	Pit-N	88	316	27	79	9	0	7	48	16	39	.250	.290	.345	.635	67	-15	-15	101	137	30	.520	1			-18	2	-2.3
1949	Cin-N	134	452	40	118	27	1	9	59	27	36	.261	.304	.385	.689	87	-12	-9	96	111	51	.587	1			-6	21/3	-1.1
1950	Cin-N	4	14	1	3	1	0	0	1	2	0	.214	.313	.286	.598	56	-1	-1	105	98	1	.545	0			0	/2	0.0
	Phi-N	54	96	6	22	2	0	0	13	6	12	.229	.275	.250	.525	40	-8	-8	97	209	7	.395	0			-1	2/13	-0.8
	Yr	58	110	7	25	3	0	0	14	8	12	.227	.280	.255	.534	43	-9	-9	98	203	8	.414	0			-1		-0.8
1951	Phi-N	21	42	2	6	0	0	0	1	3	9	.143	.200	.143	.343	-6	-6	-6	97	64	1	.263	1	0	0	-1	/21	-0.6
Total	11	1002	3519	348	874	160	20	62	451	202	407	.248	.292	.358	.650	75	-134	-134	100	116	346	.561	19	22		27	2/13OS	-5.7
■ **BUD BLOOMFIELD** Bloomfield, Clyde Stalcup b: 1/5/36, Oklahoma City, Okla. BR/TR, 5'11.5", 175 lbs. Deb: 9/25/63																												
1963	StL-N	1	0	0	0	0	0	0	0	0	0	—	—	—	—	—	0	0	107	—	—	—	0	0	0	0	/3	0.0
1964	Min-A	7	7	1	1	0	0	0	0	0	0	.143	.143	.143	.286	-20	-1	-1	101	0	0	.167	0	0	0	-0	/2S	0.0
Total	2	8	7	1	1	0	0	0	0	0	0	.143	.143	.143	.286	-20	-1	-1	101	0	346	.167	0	0	0	-0	/2S3	0.0
■ **JACK BLOTT** Blott, John Leonard b: 8/24/02, Girard, Ohio d: 6/11/64, Ann Arbor, Mich. BR/TR, 6', 210 lbs. Deb: 7/30/24																												
1924	Cin-N	2	1	0	0	0	0	0	0	0	0	.000	.000	.000	.000	-99	-0	-0	101	0	0	.000	0	0	0	0	/C	0.0
■ **BERT BLUE** Blue, Bird Wayne b: 12/14/1876, Bettsville, Ohio d: 12/14/28, Detroit, Mich. TR, 6'3", 200 lbs. Deb: 6/15/08																												
1908	StL-A	11	24	2	9	1	2	0	1	3		.375	.444	.583	1.028	229	4	3	103	27	6	1.133	0			1	/C	0.6
	Phi-A	6	18	2	3	0	0	0	1	0		.167	.167	.167	.333	9	-2	-2	108	125	0	.200	0			1	/C	0.0
	Yr	17	42	4	12	1	2	0	2	3		.286	.333	.405	.738	136	2	2	105	63	5	.667	0			1		0.6
Total	1	17	42	4	12	1	2	0	2	3		.286	.333	.405	.738	135	2	2	105	66	7	.667	0			1	/C	0.6
■ **LU BLUE** Blue, Luzerne Atwell b: 3/5/1897, Washington, D.C. d: 7/28/58, Alexandria, Va. BB/TL, 5'10", 165 lbs. Deb: 4/14/21																												
1921	Det-A	153	585	103	180	33	11	5	75	103	47	.308	.416	.427	.843	120	18	22	96	103	107	.879	13	17	-6	-6	*1	0.7
1922	Det-A	145	584	131	175	31	9	6	45	82	48	.300	.392	.414	.807	113	12	13	98	55	100	.819	8	5	-1	1	*1	0.2
1923	Det-A	129	504	100	143	27	7	1	46	96	40	.284	.402	.371	.773	108	8	11	97	71	81	.796	9	11	-4	5	*1	0.5
1924	Det-A	108	395	81	123	26	7	2	50	64	26	.311	.413	.428	.840	117	12	13	100	100	75	.891	9	4	0	0	*1	0.7
1925	Det-A	150	532	91	163	18	9	3	94	83	29	.306	.403	.391	.794	103	5	6	99	148	92	.837	19	5	3	-0	*1	0.4
1926	Det-A	128	429	92	123	24	14	1	52	90	18	.287	.413	.415	.828	120	14	16	97	100	81	.904	13	7	-0	-6	*1/O	0.5
1927	Det-A	112	365	71	95	17	9	1	42	71	28	.260	.384	.364	.748	88	-0	-5	108	105	55	.811	13	0	4	-2	*1	-1.0
1928	StL-A	154	549	116	154	32	11	14	80	105	43	.281	.400	.455	.855	120	22	19	104	100	107	.923	12	7	-1	2	*1	1.2
1929	StL-A	151	573	111	168	40	10	6	61	126	32	.293	.422	.429	.852	120	23	23	100	68	114	.939	12	6	0	-3	*1	0.0
1930	StL-A	117	425	85	100	27	5	4	42	81	44	.235	.363	.351	.713	76	-10	-15	108	83	60	.741	12	7	-1	2	*1	-2.4
1931	Chi-A	155	589	119	179	23	15	1	62	127	60	.304	.430	.399	.829	129	24	31	92	74	113	.915	13	3	2	-3	*1	1.5
1932	Chi-A	112	373	51	93	21	2	0	43	64	21	.249	.364	.316	.680	89	-10	-2	87	124	49	.706	17	6	2	7	*1	-0.4
1933	Bro-N	1	1	0	0	0	0	0	0	0	0	.000	.000	.000	.000	-99	-0	-0	97	0	0	.000	0			0	/1	0.0
Total	13	1615	5904	1151	1696	319	109	44	692	1092	436	.287	.402	.401	.803	110	119	131	99	92	1033	.852	150	78		-2	*1/O	1.9
■ **OSSIE BLUEGE** Bluege, Oswald Louis b: 10/24/1900, Chicago, Ill. d: 10/15/85, Edina, Minn. BR/TR, 5'11", 162 lbs. Deb: 4/24/22 MC																												
1922	Was-A	19	61	5	12	1	0	0	2	7	7	.197	.300	.213	.513	39	-6	-5	92	55	5	.469	1	0	0	1	3/S	0.0
1923	Was-A	109	379	48	93	15	7	2	42	48	53	.245	.343	.338	.680	84	-10	-7	95	109	48	.654	5	3	-0	4	*3/2	0.9
1924	Was-A	117	402	59	113	15	4	2	49	39	36	.281	.358	.353	.711	85	-9	-8	98	112	53	.670	7	5	-1	-15	*32/S	-1.3
1925	Was-A	145	522	77	150	27	4	4	79	59	56	.287	.362	.377	.739	90	-9	-7	98	129	73	.712	16	13	-3	3	*3/S	0.1
1926	Was-A	139	487	69	132	19	8	3	65	70	46	.271	.368	.361	.730	93	-5	-3	98	122	69	.723	12	9	-2	-16	*3/S	-0.8
1927	Was-A	146	503	71	138	21	10	1	66	57	47	.274	.354	.362	.716	89	-9	-7	97	121	66	.710	15	0	5	14	*3	1.6
1928	Was-A	146	518	78	154	33	7	2	75	46	27	.297	.364	.400	.763	99	1	-0	102	123	79	.754	18	6	2	12	*3/2	1.5
1929	Was-A	64	220	35	65	6	0	5	31	19	15	.295	.354	.391	.745	92	-3	-2	100	105	31	.704	6	4	-1	1	32S	0.1
1930	Was-A	134	476	64	138	27	7	3	69	51	40	.290	.368	.395	.763	92	-3	-4	101	119	73	.757	15	8	-0	-1	*3	0.0
1931	Was-A	152	570	82	155	25	7	8	98	50	39	.272	.336	.382	.718	88	-10	-10	101	136	74	.680	16	10	-1	-5	*3/S	-0.6
1932	Was-A	149	507	64	131	22	4	5	64	84	41	.258	.367	.347	.714	86	-8	-7	100	115	71	.710	9	7	-2	5	*3	0.5
1933	Was-A	140	501	63	131	14	0	6	71	55	34	.261	.338	.325	.663	80	-16	-13	96	133	58	.602	6	7	-2	-6	*3	-0.9
1934	Was-A	99	285	39	70	9	2	0	11	23	15	.246	.306	.291	.598	54	-19	-19	101	44	27	.509	2	1	0	7	3S/2O	-0.9
1935	Was-A	100	320	44	84	14	3	0	34	37	21	.262	.341	.325	.666	80	-12	-8	92	111	37	.605	2	2	-1	8	S3/2	0.2
1936	Was-A	90	319	43	92	12	1	1	55	38	16	.288	.375	.342	.716	80	-9	-8	98	162	44	.687	5	3	-0	1	2S3	-0.1
1937	Was-A	42	127	12	36	4	2	1	13	13	9	.283	.355	.370	.725	88	-3	-2	94	89	17	.674	1	1	-0	-2	S/13	-0.2
1938	Was-A	58	184	25	48	12	1	0	21	21	11	.261	.340	.337	.677	74	-8	-7	95	114	22	.635	3	1	0	1	2S/13	-0.3
1939	Was-A	18	59	5	9	0	0	0	3	7	2	.153	.242	.153	.395	3	-9	-8	90	113	2	.327	1	0	0	0	1/2S3	-0.7
Total	18	1867	6440	883	1751	276	67	43	848	724	515	.272	.352	.356	.707	85	-147	-127	98	118	848	.676	140	80	-6	11	*3S2/1O	-0.9
■ **OTTO BLUEGE** Bluege, Otto Adam "Squeaky" b: 7/20/09, Chicago, Ill. d: 6/28/77, Chicago, Ill. BR/TR, 5'10", 154 lbs. Deb: 4/12/32																												
1932	Cin-N	1	0	1	0	0	0	0	0	0	0	—	—	—	—	—	0	0	96	—	—	—	0			0	R	0.0
1933	Cin-N	108	291	17	62	6	2	0	18	26	29	.213	.278	.247	.525	52	-18	-17	99	94	19	.405	0			-10	S2/3	-2.1
Total	2	109	291	18	62	6	2	0	18	26	29	.213	.278	.247	.525	52	-18	-17	99	94	868	.405	0			-10	/S23	-2.1
■ **RED BLUHM** Bluhm, Harvey Fred b: 6/27/1894, Cleveland, Ohio d: 5/7/52, Flint, Mich. BR/TR, 5'11", 165 lbs. Deb: 7/03/18																												
1918	Bos-A	1	1	0	0	0	0	0	0	0	0	.000	.000	.000	.000	-99	-0	-0	95	0	0	.000	0			0	H	0.0
■ **CHET BOAK** Boak, Chester Robert b: 6/19/35, New Castle, Pa. d: 11/28/83, Emporium, Pa. BR/TR, 6', 180 lbs. Deb: 9/18/60																												
1960	KC-A	5	13	1	2	0	0	0	1	0	2	.154	.214	.154	.368	1	-2	-2	99	196	1	.273	0	0	0	0	/2	0.0
1961	Was-A	5	7	0	0	0	0	0	0	1	1	.000	.125	.000	.125	-67	-2	-2	95	0	0	.250	1	0	0	0	/2	0.0
Total	2	10	20	1	2	0	0	0	1	1	3	.100	.182	.100	.282	-22	-3	-3	97	125	1	.263	1	0	0	0	/2	0.0
■ **RANDY BOBB** Bobb, Mark Randall b: 1/1/48, Los Angeles, Cal. d: 6/13/82, Carnelian Bay, Cal BR/TR, 6'1", 185 lbs. Deb: 8/15/68																												
1968	Chi-N	7	8	0	1	0	0	0	0	1	2	.125	.222	.125	.347	6	-1	-1	112	0	0	.286	0	0	0	0	/C	0.0
1969	Chi-N	3	2	0	0	0	0	0	0	0	1	.000	.000	.000	.000	-94	-1	-1	107	0	0	.000	0	0	0	0	/C	0.0
Total	2	10	10	0	1	0	0	0	0	1	3	.100	.182	.100	.282	-13	-1	-2	111	0	0	.222	0	0	0	0	/C	0.0
■ **JOHN BOCCABELLA** Boccabella, John Dominic b: 6/29/41, San Francisco, Cal BR/TR, 6'1", 195 lbs. Deb: 9/02/63																												
1963	Chi-N	24	74	7	14	4	1	1	5	6	21	.189	.250	.311	.561	58	-4	-4	105	81	5	.460	0	1	-1	-0	1	-0.5
1964	Chi-N	9	23	4	9	2	1	0	6	0	3	.391	.391	.565	.957	157	2	2	105	189	5	.867	0	0	0	-0	/1O	0.1
1965	Chi-N	6	12	2	4	0	0	2	4	1	2	.333	.385	.833	1.218	228	2	2	102	104	4	1.375	0	0	0	-0	/1O	0.1
1966	Chi-N	75	206	22	47	9	0	6	25	14	39	.228	.277	.359	.636	75	-7	-7	100	114	19	.527	0	1	-1	0	O1/C	-1.0
1967	Chi-N	25	35	0	6	1	1	0	8	3	7	.171	.256	.257	.514	47	-2	-2	102	368	2	.433	0	0	0	-1	/O1C	-0.4
1968	Chi-N	7	14	0	1	0	0	0	1	2	2	.071	.188	.071	.259	-18	-2	-2	112	421	0	.231	0	0	0	-0	/CO	-0.2
1969	Mon-N	40	86	4	9	2	0	1	6	6	30	.105	.172	.163	.335	-6	-12	-12	100	141	2	.278	1	0	0	0	C	-0.9
1970	Mon-N	61	145	18	39	3	1	5	17	11	24	.269	.321	.407	.727	93	-2	-2	100	89	18	.636	0	1	-1	3	1C/3	0.0
1971	Mon-N	74	177	15	39	11	0	3	15	14	26	.220	.281	.333	.615	74	-6	-6	99	90	15	.510	0	1	-1	1	C1/3	-0.7
1972	Mon-N	83	207	14	47	8	1	1	10	9	29	.227	.263	.290	.553	55	-12	-12	102	65	15	.428	1	2	-1	-4	C/13	-1.4

YEAR	TM/L	G	AB	R	H	2B	3B	HR	RBI	BB	SO	AVG	OBP	SLG	PRO	/A	BR	/A	PF	CHI	RC	TA	SB	CS	SBR	FR	POS	TPR
1973	Mon-N	118	403	25	94	13	0	7	46	26	57	.233	.281	.318	.599	63	-19	-21	104	124	33	.480	1	1	-0	-1	*C/1	-1.5
1974	SF-N	29	80	6	11	3	0	0	5	4	6	.138	.179	.175	.354	-1	-11	-12	108	138	2	.254	0	0	0	-2	C	-1.2
Total	12	551	1462	117	320	56	5	26	148	96	246	.219	.269	.317	.587	62	-74	-78	102	116	122	.493	3	7	-3	-4	C1/O3	-7.6
■ MILT BOCEK Bocek, Milton Frank b: 7/16/12, Chicago, Ill. BR/TR, 6'1", 185 lbs. Deb: 9/03/33																												
1933	Chi-A	11	22	3	8	1	0	1	3	4	6	.364	.462	.545	1.007	164	2	2	101	67	6	1.143	0	0	0	-2	/O	0.0
1934	Chi-A	19	38	3	8	1	0	0	3	5	5	.211	.302	.237	.539	41	-3	-3	99	111	3	.467	0	0	0	2	O	0.0
Total	2	30	60	6	16	2	0	1	6	9	11	.267	.362	.350	.712	86	-1	-1	100	94	9	.682	0	0	0	1	/O	0.0
■ BRUCE BOCHTE Bochte, Bruce Anton b: 11/12/50, Pasadena, Cal. BL/TL, 6'3", 195 lbs. Deb: 7/19/74																												
1974	Cal-A	57	196	24	53	4	1	5	26	18	23	.270	.335	.378	.712	113	1	3	92	117	24	.651	6	3	0	-3	O1	-0.1
1975	Cal-A	107	375	41	107	19	3	3	48	45	43	.285	.365	.376	.741	116	6	9	95	125	53	.687	3	4	-2	-6	*1/D	-0.5
1976	Cal-A	146	466	53	120	17	1	2	49	64	53	.258	.350	.311	.661	103	-1	4	92	125	52	.592	4	5	-2	-1	O1/D	-0.3
1977	Cal-A	25	100	12	29	4	0	2	8	7	4	.290	.336	.390	.726	103	-0	0	95	68	12	.645	3	2	-0	4	O/D	0.3
	Cle-A	112	392	52	119	19	1	5	43	40	38	.304	.368	.395	.763	111	5	7	98	102	54	.678	3	2	-0	3	O1/D	0.5
	Yr	137	492	64	148	23	1	7	51	47	42	.301	.362	.394	.756	109	5	7	97	96	68	.677	6	4	-1	7		0.8
1978	Sea-A	140	486	58	128	25	3	11	51	60	47	.263	.346	.395	.741	106	6	5	102	91	67	.684	3	4	-2	-2	OD/1	0.0
1979	Sea-A	150	554	81	175	38	6	16	100	67	64	.316	.392	.493	.884	137	29	29	100	127	100	.843	2	2	-1	5	*1	2.5
1980	Sea-A	148	520	62	156	34	4	13	78	72	81	.300	.385	.456	.841	126	23	20	103	112	90	.812	2	3	-1	4	*1D	1.4
1981	Sea-A	99	335	39	87	16	0	6	30	47	53	.260	.354	.361	.715	107	4	4	100	86	44	.668	1	3	-2	-5	1O/D	-0.5
1982	Sea-A	144	509	58	151	21	0	12	70	67	71	.297	.382	.409	.790	107	14	8	109	117	79	.753	8	5	-1	-8	O1D	-0.4
1984	Oak-A	148	469	58	124	23	0	5	52	52	59	.264	.338	.345	.683	98	-6	-0	92	117	54	.597	2	5	-2	-13	*1/D	-2.4
1985	Oak-A	137	424	48	125	17	1	14	60	49	58	.295	.368	.439	.807	129	12	16	93	104	67	.758	3	1	0	-9	*1	0.0
1986	Oak-A	125	407	57	104	13	1	6	43	65	68	.256	.358	.337	.695	98	-2	1	94	113	52	.653	3	2	-0	-4	*1/D	-1.0
Total	12	1538	5233	643	1478	250	21	100	658	653	662	.282	.363	.396	.759	113	92	106	98	111	749	.730	43	41	-12	-36	*1O/D	-0.5
■ BRUCE BOCHY Bochy, Bruce Douglas b: 4/16/55, Landes De Bussac, France BR/TR, 6'3", 205 lbs. Deb: 7/19/78																												
1978	Hou-N	54	154	8	41	8	0	3	15	11	35	.266	.315	.377	.692	98	-2	-1	95	89	16	.570	0	0	0	-1	C	0.0
1979	Hou-N	56	129	11	28	4	0	1	6	13	25	.217	.294	.271	.565	61	-8	-6	90	63	10	.462	0	0	0	-3	C	-0.7
1980	Hou-N	22	22	0	4	1	0	0	0	5	7	.182	.357	.227	.584	68	-1	-1	98	0	2	.611	0	0	0	-0	C/1	0.0
1982	NY-N	17	49	4	15	4	0	2	8	4	6	.306	.358	.510	.869	143	2	3	99	101	9	.829	0	0	0	2	C/1	0.5
1983	SD-N	23	42	2	9	1	1	0	3	0	9	.214	.214	.286	.500	38	-4	-4	99	99	2	.343	0	0	0	0	C	-0.2
1984	SD-N	37	92	10	21	5	1	4	15	3	21	.228	.253	.435	.687	91	-2	-2	99	113	9	.581	0	1	-1	-1	C	-0.2
1985	SD-N	48	112	16	30	2	0	6	13	6	30	.268	.305	.446	.752	106	1	0	102	76	15	.675	0	0	0	2	C	0.4
1986	SD-N	63	127	16	32	9	0	8	22	14	23	.252	.326	.512	.838	134	4	5	95	99	21	.816	1	0	0	1	C	0.7
1987	SD-N	38	75	8	12	3	0	2	11	11	21	.160	.267	.280	.547	47	-6	-6	97	163	5	.478	0	1	-1	1	C	-0.3
Total	9	358	802	75	192	37	2	26	93	67	177	.239	.300	.388	.687	92	-14	-11	96	93	89	.620	1	2	-1	0	C/1	0.2
■ EDDIE BOCKMAN Bockman, Joseph Edward b: 7/26/20, Santa Ana, Cal. BR/TR, 5'9", 175 lbs. Deb: 9/11/46																												
1946	NY-A	4	12	2	1	1	0	0	0	1	4	.083	.154	.167	.321	-10	-2	-2	100	0	0	.273	0	0	0	0	/3	0.0
1947	Cle-A	46	66	8	17	2	2	1	14	5	17	.258	.310	.394	.704	99	-1	-0	96	178	9	.633	0	0	0	3	3/2SO	0.3
1948	Pit-N	70	176	23	42	7	1	4	23	17	35	.239	.309	.358	.667	77	-5	-6	104	115	19	.589	2			5	3/2	-0.1
1949	Pit-N	79	220	21	49	6	1	6	19	23	31	.223	.296	.341	.637	70	-9	-10	101	77	23	.580	3			4	3/2	-0.4
Total	4	199	474	54	109	16	4	11	56	46	87	.230	.299	.350	.650	74	-17	-18	101	103	51	.592	5	<u>0</u>		12	3/2OS	-0.2
■ PING BODIE Bodie, Frank Stephan (born Francesco Stephano Pezzolo) b: 10/8/1887, San Francisco, Cal. d: 12/17/61, San Francisco, Cal BR/TR, 5'8", 195 lbs. Deb: 4/22/11																												
1911	Chi-A	145	551	75	159	27	13	4	97	49		.289	.348	.407	.754	114	6	9	97	147	82	.735	14			0	*O2	-0.1
1912	Chi-A	137	472	58	139	24	7	5	72	43		.294	.358	.407	.765	120	11	12	99	118	73	.754	12			-7	*O	-0.3
1913	Chi-A	127	406	39	107	14	8	8	48	35	57	.264	.325	.397	.722	117	4	6	95	94	54	.679	5			-10	*O	-1.0
1914	Chi-A	107	327	21	75	9	5	3	29	21	35	.229	.278	.315	.593	76	-10	-11	103	97	32	.521	12	11	-3	-6	O	-2.8
1917	Phi-A	148	557	51	162	28	11	7	74	53	40	.291	.356	.418	.774	145	22	27	94	101	86	.765	13			8	*O/1	2.8
1918	NY-A	91	324	36	83	12	6	3	46	27	24	.256	.319	.358	.677	110	1	3	95	137	39	.631	6			2	O	0.0
1919	NY-A	134	475	45	132	27	8	6	59	36	46	.278	.334	.406	.740	102	3	-0	106	103	67	.723	15			-13	*O	-2.2
1920	NY-A	129	471	63	139	26	12	7	79	40	30	.295	.350	.446	.796	107	5	4	102	123	70	.740	6	14	-7	-15	*O	-2.7
1921	NY-A	31	87	5	15	2	2	0	12	8	8	.172	.242	.241	.483	23	-10	-11	103	196	5	.397	0	1	-1	-5	O	-1.7
Total	9	1049	3670	393	1011	169	72	43	516	312	<u>240</u>	.275	.335	.396	.731	111	32	38	99	117	508	.695	83	<u>26</u>		-46	O/21	-8.0
■ TONY BOECKEL Boeckel, Norman Doxie b: 8/25/1892, Los Angeles, Cal. d: 2/16/24, Torrey Pines, Cal. BR/TR, 5'10.5", 175 lbs. Deb: 7/23/17																												
1917	Pit-N	64	219	16	58	11	1	0	23	8	31	.265	.297	.324	.621	91	-3	-3	100	127	22	.540	6			-3	3	-0.6
1919	Pit-N	45	152	18	38	9	2	0	16	18	20	.250	.333	.336	.669	96	1	-0	105	129	20	.711	11			-7	3	-0.7
	Bos-N	95	365	42	91	11	5	1	26	35	13	.249	.317	.315	.632	92	-4	-3	98	91	38	.588	10			4	3	0.1
	Yr	140	517	60	129	20	7	1	42	53	33	.250	.322	.321	.643	93	-3	-3	100	104	58	.624	21			-4		-0.6
1920	Bos-N	153	582	70	156	28	5	3	62	38	50	.268	.314	.349	.663	93	-8	-5	96	120	62	.590	18	15	-4	-7	*3/S2	-0.9
1921	Bos-N	153	592	93	185	20	13	10	84	52	41	.313	.370	.441	.811	122	12	18	93	112	95	.794	20	15	-3	-12	*3	0.3
1922	Bos-N	119	402	61	116	19	6	6	47	35	32	.289	.349	.410	.759	101	-3	0	94	92	58	.735	14	8	-1	-8	*3	0.0
1923	Bos-N	148	568	72	169	32	4	7	79	51	31	.298	.357	.405	.762	101	1	1	100	117	83	.722	11	8	-2	-12	*3/S	-0.7
Total	6	777	2880	372	813	130	36	27	337	237	218	.282	.339	.381	.720	102	-4	8	97	111	378	.679	90	<u>46</u>		-44	3/S2	-2.5
■ LEN BOEHMER Boehmer, Leonard Joseph Stephen b: 6/28/41, Flint Hill, Mo. BR/TR, 6'1", 192 lbs. Deb: 6/18/67																												
1967	Cin-N	2	3	0	0	0	0	0	0	0	0	.000	.000	.000	.000	-92	-1	-1	109	0	0	.000	0	0	0	0	/2	0.0
1969	NY-A	45	108	5	19	4	0	0	7	8	10	.176	.233	.213	.446	27	-11	-10	95	122	5	.333	0	1	-1	0	1/32S	-1.2
1971	NY-A	3	5	0	0	0	0	0	0	0	0	.000	.000	.000	.000	-99	-1	-1	97	0	0	.000	0	0	0	0	/3	0.0
Total	3	50	116	5	19	4	0	0	7	8	10	.164	.218	.198	.416	18	-13	-12	96	114	5	.316	0	1	-1	0	/132S	-1.2
■ TERRY BOGENER Bogener, Terry Wayne b: 9/28/55, Hannibal, Mo. BL/TL, 6', 193 lbs. Deb: 6/14/82																												
1982	Tex-A	24	60	6	13	2	1	1	4	4	8	.217	.288	.333	.621	75	-2	-2	93	69	6	.560	2	0	1	-3	O/D	-0.4
■ WADE BOGGS Boggs, Wade Anthony b: 6/15/58, Omaha, Neb. BL/TR, 6'2", 190 lbs. Deb: 4/10/82																												
1982	Bos-A	104	338	51	118	14	1	5	44	35	21	.349	.410	.441	.851	121	17	12	110	107	61	.808	1	0	0	3	13/OD	1.4
1983	Bos-A	153	582	100	210	44	7	5	74	92	36	**.361**	**.449**	.486	.935	156	**51**	**50**	101	93	130	.972	3	3	-1	10	*3	5.8
1984	Bos-A	158	625	109	203	31	4	6	55	89	44	.325	.409	.416	.825	117	29	20	110	70	110	.805	3	2	-0	23	*3/D	4.4
1985	Bos-A	161	653	107	**240**	42	3	8	78	96	61	**.368**	**.452**	.478	.929	151	55	53	102	81	143	.954	2	1	0	9	*3	5.5
1986	Bos-A	149	580	107	207	47	2	8	71	**105**	44	**.357**	**.455**	.486	.942	**159**	53	53	100	80	133	**.997**	0	4	-2	-0	*3	4.4
1987	Bos-A	147	551	108	200	40	6	24	89	105	48	**.363**	**.467**	.588	**1.055**	**180**	**68**	**68**	99	86	**154**	**1.177**	1	3	-2	-0	*3/1D	**5.9**
1988	Bos-A	155	584	**128**	214	**45**	6	5	58	**125**	34	**.366**	**.480**	.490	**.970**	158	**66**	**58**	109	68	**140**	**1.051**	2	3	-1	-2	*3/D	5.5
Total	7	1027	3913	710	1392	263	29	61	469	647	288	.356	.448	.485	.933	150	337	314	104	82	872	1.002	12	16	-6	43	3/1DO	32.9
■ CHARLIE BOHN Bohn, Charles b: 1857, Cleveland, Ohio d: 8/1/03, Cleveland, Ohio Deb: 6/20/1882																												
1882	Lou-a	4	13	0	2	0	0	0		0		.154	.154	.154	.308	4	-1	-1	94	0	0	.182				0	/OP	0.0
■ SAM BOHNE Bohne, Samuel Arthur (born Samuel Arthur Cohen) b: 10/22/1896, San Francisco, Cal d: 5/23/77, Palo Alto, Cal. BR/TR, 5'8.5", 175 lbs. Deb: 9/09/16																												
1916	StL-N	14	38	3	9	0	0	0	0	4	6	.237	.310	.237	.546	71	-1	-1	97	0	4	.552	3			-1	S	0.0
1921	Cin-N	153	613	98	175	28	16	3	44	54	38	.285	.347	.398	.745	96	-2	-3	101	55	83	.713	26	22	-5	3	*23	-0.4
1922	Cin-N	112	383	53	105	14	5	3	51	39	18	.274	.344	.360	.705	86	-10	-7	96	124	49	.671	13	8	-1	9	2S	0.1
1923	Cin-N	139	539	77	136	18	10	3	47	48	37	.252	.316	.340	.655	75	-21	-19	98	91	56	.590	16	19	-7	14	23/S1	-0.9
1924	Cin-N	100	349	42	89	15	9	4	46	18	24	.255	.293	.384	.677	80	-11	-11	101	115	39	.609	9	6	-1	-2	2S3	-1.1
1925	Cin-N	73	214	24	55	9	1	2	24	14	14	.257	.303	.336	.639	65	-12	-11	97	109	22	.564	6	4	-1	1	S2/O13	-0.5
1926	Cin-N	25	54	8	11	0	2	0	5	4	8	.204	.259	.278	.536	47	-4	-4	95	115	4	.465	1			-1	S	-0.3
	Bro-N	47	125	4	25	3	2	1	11	12	9	.200	.270	.280	.550	49	-9	-9	99	100	10	.480	1			-3	23	-1.0
	Yr	72	179	12	36	3	4	1	16	16	17	.201	.267	.279	.546	48	-13	-13	98	107	14	.476	2			-4		-1.3

YEAR	TM/L	G	AB	R	H	2B	3B	HR	RBI	BB	SO	AVG	OBP	SLG	PRO	/A	BR	/A	PF	CHI	RC	TA	SB	CS	SBR	FR	POS	TPR
Total	7	663	2315	309	605	87	45	16	228	193	154	.261	.321	.359	.679	80	-71	-66	99	92	266	.626	75	59		21	2S3/O1	-4.1
■ **BRUCE BOISCLAIR** Boisclair, Bruce Armand b: 12/9/52, Putnam, Conn. BL/TL, 6'2", 185 lbs. Deb: 9/11/74																												
1974	NY-N	7	12	0	3	1	0	0	1	1	4	.250	.308	.333	.641	80	-0	-0	99	96	1	.500	0	0	0	1	/O	0.1
1976	NY-N	110	286	42	82	13	3	2	13	28	55	.287	.350	.374	.724	115	2	5	92	44	38	.679	9	5	-0	-2	O	0.0
1977	NY-N	127	307	41	90	21	1	4	44	31	57	.293	.360	.407	.767	110	3	4	96	128	46	.721	6	4	-1	-9	O/1	-0.8
1978	NY-N	107	214	24	48	7	1	4	15	23	43	.224	.300	.322	.622	75	-7	-7	98	73	21	.549	3	3	-1	-5	O/1	-1.6
1979	NY-N	59	98	7	18	5	1	0	4	3	24	.184	.216	.255	.471	29	-10	-9	95	63	5	.345	0	2	-1	-2	O/1	-1.3
Total	5	410	917	114	241	47	6	10	77	86	183	.263	.327	.360	.687	94	-13	-7	95	82	111	.630	18	14	-3	-18	O/1	-3.6
■ **BOB BOKEN** Boken, Robert Anthony b: 2/23/08, Maryville, Ill. BR/TR, 6'2", 165 lbs. Deb: 4/25/33																												
1933	Was-A	55	133	19	37	5	2	3	26	9	16	.278	.324	.414	.737	98	-2	-1	96	135	18	.667	0	0	0	0	23S	0.1
1934	Was-A	11	27	5	6	1	1	0	6	3	1	.222	.300	.333	.633	63	-2	-2	101	223	3	.667	2	0	1	1	/32	0.0
	Chi-A	81	297	30	70	9	1	3	40	15	32	.236	.275	.303	.578	49	-23	-23	99	138	25	.474	2	1	0	-12	2S	-2.8
	Yr	92	324	35	76	10	2	3	46	18	33	.235	.277	.306	.583	50	-25	-24	100	150	28	.490	4	1	1	-12		-2.8
Total	2	147	457	54	113	15	4	6	72	27	49	.247	.291	.337	.628	64	-26	-25	98	142	46	.539	4	1	1	-12	/2S3	-2.7
■ **BOLAND** Boland Deb: 9/04/1875																												
1875	Atl-n	1	4	0	0							.000															/O	
■ **ED BOLAND** Boland, Edward John b: 4/18/08, Long Island City, N.Y. BL/TL, 5'10", 165 lbs. Deb: 9/18/34																												
1934	Phi-N	8	30	2	9	1	1	0	5	0	2	.300	.300	.400	.700	79	-1	-1	108	150	4	.619	1			-2	/O	-0.2
1935	Phi-N	30	47	5	10	0	0	0	4	4	6	.213	.275	.213	.487	29	-4	-5	114	144	3	.405	1			-3	O	-0.7
1944	Was-A	19	59	4	16	4	0	0	14	0	6	.271	.271	.339	.610	82	-2	-2	90	253	5	.455	0	0	0	-2	O	-0.3
Total	3	57	136	11	35	5	1	0	23	4	14	.257	.279	.309	.587	60	-7	-8	102	191	12	.471	2	0		-6	/O	-1.2
■ **CHARLIE BOLD** Bold, Charles Dickens "Dutch" b: 10/27/1894, Karlskrona, Sweden d: 7/29/78, Chelsea, Mass. BR/TR, 6'2", 185 lbs. Deb: 8/24/14																												
1914	StL-A	2	1	0	0	0	0	0	0	0	1	.000	.000	.000	.000	-99	-0	-0	98	0	0	.000	0			0	/1	0.0
■ **CARL BOLES** Boles, Carl Theodore b: 10/31/34, Center Point, Ark. BR/TR, 5'11", 185 lbs. Deb: 8/02/62																												
1962	SF-N	19	24	4	9	0	0	0	1	0	6	.375	.375	.375	.750	101	0	0	101	44	3	.529	0	0	0	-2	/O	-0.1
■ **JOE BOLEY** Boley, John Peter (born John Peter Bolinsky) b: 7/19/1896, Mahanoy City, Pa. d: 12/30/62, Mahanoy City, Pa. BR/TR, 5'11", 170 lbs. Deb: 4/12/27																												
1927	Phi-A	118	370	49	115	18	8	1	52	26	14	.311	.361	.411	.772	103	-0	2	97	112	54	.741	8	0	2	-5	*S	0.6
1928	Phi-A	132	425	49	112	20	3	0	49	32	11	.264	.317	.325	.641	67	-19	-21	103	122	46	.561	5	1	1	-19	*S	-2.5
1929	Phi-A	91	303	36	76	17	6	2	47	24	16	.251	.310	.366	.676	68	-13	-16	109	137	36	.608	1	0	0	-14	S/3	-1.9
1930	Phi-A	121	420	41	116	22	2	4	55	32	26	.276	.335	.367	.701	78	-14	-14	99	110	53	.628	0	0	0	-9	*S	-0.8
1931	Phi-A	67	224	26	51	9	3	0	20	15	13	.228	.282	.295	.577	49	-16	-17	105	100	19	.483	1	1	-0	-5	S/2	-1.5
1932	Phi-A	10	34	2	7	2	0	0	4	1	4	.206	.229	.265	.493	24	-4	-4	114	149	2	.357	0	1	-1	-0	S	-0.3
	Cle-A	1	4	0	1	0	0	0	0	0	0	.250	.250	.250	.500	28	-0	-0	108	0	0	.333	0	0	0	0	/S	0.0
	Yr	11	38	2	8	2	0	0	4	1	4	.211	.231	.263	.494	24	-4	-5	113	149	2	.355	0	1	-1	-0		-0.3
Total	6	540	1780	203	478	88	22	7	227	130	84	.269	.323	.354	.677	74	-66	-71	102	117	210	.605	15	3	3	-51	S/23	-6.4
■ **JIM BOLGER** Bolger, James Cyril "Dutch" b: 2/23/32, Cincinnati, Ohio BR/TR, 6'2", 180 lbs. Deb: 6/24/50																												
1950	Cin-N	2	1	0	0	0	0	0	0	0	0	.000	.000	.000	.000	-96	-0	-0	105	0	0	.000	0			-1	/O	0.0
1951	Cin-N	2	0	1	0	0	0	0	0	0	0	—	—	—	—	—	0	0	101	—	0	—	1	0	0	0	R	0.0
1954	Cin-N	5	3	1	1	0	0	0	0	0	1	.333	.333	.333	.667	72	-0	-0	104	0	0	.500	0	0	0	-1	/O	0.0
1955	Chi-N	64	160	19	33	5	4	0	7	9	17	.206	.257	.287	.545	44	-13	-13	100	62	11	.447	2	2	-1	1	O	-1.2
1957	Chi-N	112	273	28	75	4	1	5	29	10	36	.275	.308	.352	.659	80	-9	-8	96	108	27	.519	0	1	-1	6	O/3	-0.3
1958	Chi-N	84	120	15	27	4	1	1	11	9	20	.225	.285	.300	.585	55	-8	-8	101	117	10	.479	0	1	-1	-6	O	-1.5
1959	Cle-A	8	7	0	0	0	0	0	0	1	1	.000	.125	.000	.125	-65	-2	-2	97	0	0	.143	0	0	0	0	H	-0.1
	Phi-N	35	48	1	4	1	0	0	1	3	8	.083	.137	.104	.241	-35	-9	-9	99	81	0	.167	0	0	0	-1	/O	-0.9
Total	7	312	612	65	140	14	6	6	48	32	83	.229	.274	.301	.574	54	-41	-40	98	93	49	.469	3	4		-1	O/3	-4.0
■ **FRANK BOLLING** Bolling, Frank Elmore b: 11/16/31, Mobile, Ala. BR/TR, 6'1", 175 lbs. Deb: 4/13/54																												
1954	Det-A	117	368	46	87	15	2	6	38	36	51	.236	.304	.337	.641	76	-13	-13	100	101	38	.560	3	5	-2	-13	*2	-2.4
1956	Det-A	102	366	53	103	21	7	7	45	42	51	.281	.359	.434	.793	112	4	6	97	95	60	.777	6	2	1	-3	*2	1.1
1957	Det-A	146	576	72	149	27	6	15	40	57	64	.259	.328	.405	.732	92	-2	-7	107	60	73	.656	4	9	-4	1	*2	-0.1
1958	Det-A	154	610	91	164	25	4	14	75	54	54	.269	.332	.392	.724	95	-1	-4	104	94	81	.660	6	4	-1	9	*2	1.5
1959	Det-A	127	459	56	122	18	3	13	55	45	37	.266	.341	.403	.744	93	2	-4	111	99	65	.693	2	2	-1	-1	*2	-0.1
1960	Det-A	139	536	64	136	20	4	9	59	40	48	.254	.308	.356	.664	78	-16	-17	102	108	58	.580	7	4	-0	-1	*2	-0.8
1961	Mil-N	148	585	86	153	16	4	15	56	57	62	.262	.330	.379	.710	95	-10	-4	92	81	70	.628	7	3	0	-1	*2	1.4
1962	Mil-N	122	406	45	110	17	4	9	43	35	45	.271	.335	.399	.734	97	-2	-2	99	90	55	.666	2	2	-1	-8	*2	0.0
1963	Mil-N	142	542	73	132	18	2	5	43	41	47	.244	.300	.312	.612	76	-16	-16	101	104	52	.509	2	1	0	-3	*2	-1.1
1964	Mil-N	120	352	35	70	11	1	5	34	21	44	.199	.248	.278	.526	50	-24	-23	97	123	24	.416	0	1	-1	-10	*2	-2.5
1965	Mil-N	148	535	55	141	26	3	7	50	24	41	.264	.295	.363	.658	81	-12	-15	104	98	54	.533	0	4	-2	-9	*2	-1.8
1966	Atl-N	75	227	16	48	7	0	1	18	10	14	.211	.248	.256	.503	41	-18	-18	99	124	14	.383	1	1	-0	-5	2	-1.9
Total	12	1540	5562	692	1415	221	40	106	556	462	558	.254	.315	.366	.681	85	-108	-117	101	95	643	.613	40	38	-11	-43	*2	-6.7
■ **JACK BOLLING** Bolling, John Edward b: 2/20/17, Mobile, Ala. BL/TL, 5'11", 168 lbs. Deb: 6/10/39																												
1939	Phi-N	69	211	27	61	11	0	3	13	11	10	.289	.324	.384	.708	95	-3	-2	94	53	25	.632	6			0	1	-0.6
1944	Bro-N	56	131	21	46	14	1	1	25	14	4	.351	.418	.496	.914	158	10	10	99	132	27	.899	0			0	1	0.8
Total	2	125	342	48	107	25	1	4	38	25	14	.313	.361	.427	.788	120	7	8	96	84	52	.745	6			0	/1	0.2
■ **MILT BOLLING** Bolling, Milton Joseph b: 8/9/30, Mississippi City, Miss. BR/TR, 6'1", 177 lbs. Deb: 9/10/52																												
1952	Bos-A	11	36	4	8	1	0	1	3	3	5	.222	.282	.333	.615	66	-2	-2	107	75	3	.517	0	1	-1	1	S	0.0
1953	Bos-A	109	323	30	85	12	1	5	28	23	41	.263	.318	.353	.671	74	-9	-13	109	80	37	.573	1	4	-2	8	*S	0.2
1954	Bos-A	113	370	42	92	20	3	6	36	47	55	.249	.340	.368	.707	93	-3	-3	100	89	49	.663	2	4	-2	8	*S/3	1.2
1955	Bos-A	6	5	0	1	0	0	0	0	0	1	.200	.200	.200	.400	6	-1	-1	124	0	0	.250	0	0	0	0	/S	0.0
1956	Bos-A	45	118	19	25	3	2	3	8	18	20	.212	.321	.347	.669	75	-4	-4	103	60	14	.619	0	1	-1	0	S3/2	-0.1
1957	Bos-A	1	1	0	0	0	0	0	0	0	0	.000	.000	.000	.000	-91	-0	-0	110	0	0	.000	0	0	0	0	H	0.0
	Was-A	91	277	29	63	12	1	4	19	18	59	.227	.279	.321	.601	65	-14	-14	98	74	22	.487	2	2	-1	3	2S/3	-0.5
	Yr	92	278	29	63	12	1	4	19	18	59	.227	.279	.320	.599	64	-15	-14	98	73	22	.485	2	2	-1	3		-0.5
1958	Det-A	24	31	3	6	2	0	0	0	5	7	.194	.306	.258	.564	55	-2	-2	104	0	3	.520	0	0	0	-1	S/23	0.0
Total	7	400	1161	127	280	50	7	19	94	114	188	.241	.314	.345	.660	77	-34	-38	103	77	129	.594	5	12	-6	18	S/23	0.8
■ **DON BOLLWEG** Bollweg, Donald Raymond b: 2/12/21, Wheaton, Ill. BL/TL, 6'1", 190 lbs. Deb: 9/28/50																												
1950	StL-N	4	11	1	2	0	0	0	1	1	1	.182	.250	.182	.432	15	-1	-1	103	193	0	.300	0			0	/1	-0.1
1951	StL-N	6	9	1	1	0	0	0	2	0	1	.111	.111	.222	.333	-12	-1	-1	101	387	0	.250	0	0	0	0	/1	-0.1
1953	NY-A	70	155	24	46	6	4	6	24	21	31	.297	.384	.503	.887	149	8	10	93	93	33	.927	1	0	0	-1	1	0.8
1954	Phi-A	103	268	35	60	15	3	5	24	35	33	.224	.320	.358	.678	87	-5	-5	98	82	33	.637	1	0	0	2	1	-0.4
1955	KC-A	12	9	1	1	0	0	0	2	3	2	.111	.333	.111	.444	23	-1	-1	101	746	0	.500	0	0	0	0	/1	0.0
Total	5	195	452	62	110	22	7	11	53	60	68	.243	.337	.396	.733	102	-1	1	97	109	67	.716	2	0		1	1	0.2
■ **CECIL BOLTON** Bolton, Cecil Glenford "Glenn" b: 2/13/04, Booneville, Miss. BL/TR, 6'4", 195 lbs. Deb: 9/21/28																												
1928	Cle-A	4	13	1	2	0	2	0	0	2	2	.154	.267	.462	.728	83	-0	-0	106	0	2	.727	0	0	0	0	/1	0.0
■ **CLIFF BOLTON** Bolton, William Clifton b: 4/10/07, High Point, N.C. d: 4/21/79, Lexington, N.C. BL/TR, 5'9", 160 lbs. Deb: 4/20/31																												
1931	Was-A	23	43	3	11	1	1	0	6	1	5	.256	.273	.326	.598	56	-3	-3	101	141	4	.469	0	0	0	-0	C	-0.1
1933	Was-A	33	39	4	16	1	1	0	6	6	3	.410	.500	.487	.987	169	4	4	96	105	10	1.130	0	0	0	-0	/CO	0.4
1934	Was-A	42	148	12	40	9	1	1	17	11	9	.270	.321	.365	.686	76	-5	-6	101	100	18	.620	2	0	1	-3	C	-0.3

YEAR	TM/L	G	AB	R	H	2B	3B	HR	RBI	BB	SO	AVG	OBP	SLG	PRO	/A	BR	/A	PF	CHI	RC	TA	SB	CS	SBR	FR	POS	TPR
1935	Was-A	110	375	47	114	18	11	2	55	57	13	.304	.397	.427	.824	124	9	14	92	112	66	.832	0	1	-1	-11	*C	0.5
1936	Was-A	86	289	41	84	18	4	2	51	25	12	.291	.349	.401	.751	87	-7	-6	98	135	41	.691	1	2	-1	-2	C	-0.1
1937	Det-A	27	57	6	15	2	0	1	7	8	6	.263	.354	.351	.705	72	-2	-3	109	104	8	.667	0	0	0	-0	C	-0.1
1941	Was-A	14	11	0	0	0	0	0	1	1	2	.000	.083	.000	.083	-78	-3	-3	98	0	0	.091	0	0	0	0	/C	-0.2
Total	7	335	962	113	280	49	18	6	143	109	50	.291	.365	.398	.763	98	-7	-2	96	116	146	.727	3	3	-1	-17	C/O	0.1
■ WALT BOND	Bond, Walter Franklin b: 10/19/37, Denmark, Tenn. d: 9/14/67, Houston, Tex. BL/TR, 6'7", 228 lbs. Deb: 4/19/60																											
1960	Cle-A	40	131	19	29	2	1	5	18	13	14	.221	.306	.366	.673	83	-4	-3	98	112	15	.648	4	1	1	2	O	-0.1
1961	Cle-A	38	52	7	9	1	1	2	7	6	10	.173	.271	.346	.617	66	-3	-3	96	114	5	.591	1	0	0	-1	O	-0.3
1962	Cle-A	12	50	10	19	3	0	6	17	4	9	.380	.426	.800	1.226	227	8	8	98	103	17	1.406	1	0	0	0	O	0.8
1964	Hou-N	148	543	63	138	16	7	20	85	38	90	.254	.312	.420	.732	108	2	5	96	128	70	.660	2	2	-1	-7	1O	-0.7
1965	Hou-N	117	407	46	107	17	2	7	47	42	51	.263	.339	.366	.705	111	0	6	89	117	52	.645	2	1	0	-3	1O	-0.2
1967	Min-A	10	16	4	5	1	0	1	5	3	1	.313	.421	.563	.984	176	2	2	107	174	4	1.091	0	0	0	0	/O	0.2
Total	6	365	1199	149	307	40	11	41	179	106	175	.256	.325	.410	.736	110	6	14	94	121	163	.698	10	4	1	-9	O1	-0.3
■ BARRY BONDS	Bonds, Barry Lamar b: 7/24/64, Riverside, Cal. BL/TL, 6'1", 185 lbs. Deb: 5/30/86																											
1986	Pit-N	113	413	72	92	26	3	16	48	65	102	.223	.331	.416	.748	105	3	3	100	92	64	.828	36	7	7	10	*O	1.7
1987	Pit-N	150	551	99	144	34	9	25	59	54	88	.261	.331	.492	.822	110	10	7	104	69	93	.855	32	10	4	6	*O	1.0
1988	Pit-N	144	538	97	152	30	5	24	58	72	82	.283	.369	.491	.860	148	32	33	98	73	100	.887	17	11	-2	1	*O	3.1
Total	3	407	1502	268	388	90	17	65	165	191	272	.258	.345	.471	.815	121	44	42	101	77	257	.865	85	28	9	16	O	5.8
■ BOBBY BONDS	Bonds, Bobby Lee b: 3/15/46, Riverside, Cal. BR/TR, 6'1", 190 lbs. Deb: 6/25/68 C																											
1968	SF-N	81	307	55	78	10	5	9	35	38	84	.254	.338	.407	.745	126	9	10	98	93	46	.763	16	7	1	6	O	1.4
1969	SF-N	158	622	**120**	161	25	6	32	90	81	187	.259	.353	.473	.826	128	24	23	101	89	114	.907	45	4	**11**	-4	*O	2.3
1970	SF-N	157	663	134	200	36	10	26	78	77	189	.302	.376	.504	.880	139	31	35	96	65	134	.962	48	10	**8**	13	*O	4.7
1971	SF-N	155	619	110	178	32	4	33	102	62	137	.288	.357	.512	.869	144	34	34	100	96	115	.893	26	8	3	6	*O	4.0
1972	SF-N	153	626	118	162	29	5	26	80	60	137	.259	.329	.446	.774	118	13	14	100	79	96	.803	44	6	**10**	10	*O	2.8
1973	SF-N	160	643	**131**	182	34	4	39	96	87	148	.283	.372	.530	.902	140	40	36	105	74	130	.977	43	17	3	9	*O	4.2
1974	SF-N	150	567	97	145	22	8	21	71	95	134	.256	.366	.434	.800	114	19	13	108	78	100	.883	41	11	6	7	*O	2.1
1975	NY-A	145	529	93	143	26	3	32	85	89	137	.270	.378	.512	.891	152	35	36	99	86	103	.952	30	17	-1	12	*OD	4.4
1976	Cal-A	99	378	48	100	10	3	10	54	41	90	.265	.341	.386	.727	123	6	10	92	113	50	.733	30	15	0	-8	O/D	0.0
1977	Cal-A	158	592	103	156	23	9	37	115	74	141	.264	.347	.520	.868	140	26	30	95	115	107	.918	41	18	2	-1	*OD	2.5
1978	Chi-A	26	90	8	25	4	0	2	8	10	10	.278	.350	.389	.739	107	1	1	101	79	13	.739	6	2	1	1	O/D	0.2
	Tex-A	130	475	85	126	15	4	29	82	69	110	.265	.361	.497	.858	144	24	27	96	106	82	.903	37	20	-1	3	*OD	2.7
	Yr	156	565	93	151	19	4	31	90	79	120	.267	.359	.480	.839	138	25	28	97	102	96	.882	43	22	-0	4		2.9
1979	Cle-A	146	538	93	148	24	1	25	85	74	135	.275	.371	.463	.834	117	19	14	106	107	92	.865	34	23	-4	8	*OD	1.4
1980	StL-N	86	231	37	47	5	3	5	24	33	74	.203	.308	.316	.624	73	-7	-8	103	108	25	.637	15	5	2	-5	O	-1.4
1981	Chi-N	45	163	26	35	7	1	6	19	24	44	.215	.323	.380	.703	95	-0	-1	104	99	19	.674	5	6	-2	3	O	0.0
Total	14	1849	7043	1258	1886	302	66	332	1024	914	1757	.268	.356	.471	.827	129	274	274	100	91	1224	.890	461	169	37	61	*O/D	31.3
■ GEORGE BONE	Bone, George Drummond b: 8/28/1876, New Haven, Conn. d: 5/26/18, West Haven, Conn. BB/TR, 5'7", 152 lbs. Deb: 9/18/01																											
1901	Mil-A	12	43	6	13	2	0	0	6	4		.302	.362	.349	.711	105	0	0	95	129	6	.633	0			1	S	0.2
■ NINO BONGIOVANNI	Bongiovanni, Anthony Thomas b: 12/12/11, Pike's Peak, La. BL/TL, 5'10", 175 lbs. Deb: 4/23/38																											
1938	Cin-N	2	7	0	2	1	0	0	0	0	0	.286	.286	.429	.714	96	-0	-0	98	0	1	.600	0			0	/O	0.0
1939	Cin-N	66	159	17	41	6	0	0	16	9	8	.258	.298	.296	.593	58	-9	-9	103	125	15	.471	0			1	O	-0.9
Total	2	68	166	17	43	7	0	0	16	9	8	.259	.297	.301	.598	60	-9	-10	103	120	15	.476	0			1	/O	-0.9
■ JUAN BONILLA	Bonilla, Juan Guillermo b: 2/12/55, Santurce, P.R. BR/TR, 5'9", 170 lbs. Deb: 4/09/81																											
1981	SD-N	99	369	30	107	13	2	1	25	25	23	.290	.338	.344	.683	101	-3	0	93	77	41	.568	4	9	-4	-8	2	-0.5
1982	SD-N	45	182	21	51	6	2	0	8	11	15	.280	.325	.335	.660	92	-4	-2	92	49	20	.545	0	1	-1	-10	2	-1.0
1983	SD-N	152	556	55	132	17	4	4	45	50	40	.237	.304	.304	.608	69	-23	-22	99	100	50	.508	3	0	1	-14	*2	-3.0
1985	NY-A	8	16	0	2	1	0	0	2	0	3	.125	.125	.188	.313	-17	-3	-2	96	264	0	.214	0	0	0	0	/2	-0.1
1986	Bal-A	102	284	33	69	10	1	1	18	25	21	.243	.311	.296	.607	68	-12	-12	99	82	25	.489	0	0	0	-5	23/D	-1.3
1987	NY-A	23	55	6	14	3	0	1	3	5	6	.255	.317	.364	.680	83	-1	-1	98	52	6	.581	0	0	0	0	2/3D	0.1
Total	6	429	1462	145	375	50	9	7	101	116	108	.256	.315	.317	.632	79	-45	-39	97	85	142	.542	7	10	-4	-36	2/3D	-5.8
■ BOBBY BONILLA	Bonilla, Roberto Martin Antonio b: 2/23/63, New York, N.Y. BB/TR, 6'3", 210 lbs. Deb: 4/09/86																											
1986	Chi-A	75	234	27	63	10	2	2	26	33	49	.269	.362	.355	.717	96	0	-0	101	116	32	.688	4	1	1	-0	O1	-0.2
	Pit-N	63	192	28	46	6	2	1	17	29	39	.240	.342	.307	.650	80	-4	-4	100	109	21	.600	4	4	-1	-4	O/13	-1.0
1987	Pit-N	141	466	58	140	33	3	15	77	39	64	.300	.357	.481	.838	115	12	10	104	114	78	.791	3	5	-2	-12	3O/1	-0.7
1988	Pit-N	159	584	87	160	32	7	24	100	85	82	.274	.370	.476	.846	145	32	34	98	121	106	.855	3	5	-2	-1	*3	3.2
Total	3	438	1476	200	409	81	14	42	220	186	234	.277	.361	.436	.797	119	41	39	100	117	238	.785	14	15	-5	-18	3O/1	1.3
■ LUTHER BONIN	Bonin, Ernest Luther "Bonnie" b: 1/13/1888, Green Hill, Ind. d: 1/3/65, Sycamore, Ohio BL/TR, 5'9.5", 178 lbs. Deb: 4/13/13																											
1913	StL-A	1	1	0	0	0	0	0	0	0	0	.000	.000	.000	.000	-99	-0	-0	95	0	0	.000	0			0	H	0.0
1914	Buf-F	20	76	6	14	4	1	0	4	7	11	.184	.253	.263	.516	46	-5	-6	104	69	6	.484	3			0	O	-0.6
Total	2	21	77	6	14	4	1	0	4	7	11	.182	.250	.260	.510	44	-5	-6	104	68	6	.476	3			0	/O	-0.6
■ BARRY BONNELL	Bonnell, Robert Barry b: 10/27/53, Clermont County, O. BR/TR, 6'3", 190 lbs. Deb: 5/04/77																											
1977	Atl-N	100	360	41	108	11	0	1	45	37	32	.300	.368	.339	.707	81	-3	-9	113	147	45	.636	7	5	-1	8	O3	-0.4
1978	Atl-N	117	304	36	73	11	3	1	16	20	30	.240	.287	.306	.593	59	-14	-18	112	66	23	.496	12	6	0	-4	*O3	-2.7
1979	Atl-N	127	375	47	97	20	3	12	45	26	55	.259	.312	.424	.736	90	-2	-6	109	91	46	.664	8	7	-2	-2	*O/3	-1.3
1980	Tor-A	130	463	55	124	22	4	13	56	37	59	.268	.325	.417	.742	102	0	0	100	96	59	.658	3	4	-2	7	*O/D	0.4
1981	Tor-A	66	227	21	50	7	4	4	28	12	25	.220	.262	.339	.602	65	-9	-12	111	126	18	.500	4	3	-1	2	O	-1.2
1982	Tor-A	140	437	59	128	26	3	6	49	32	51	.293	.345	.407	.753	98	4	-1	109	100	63	.712	14	2	3	-11	*O/3D	-1.2
1983	Tor-A	121	377	49	120	21	3	10	54	33	52	.318	.373	.469	.843	120	16	11	108	102	64	.809	10	7	-1	-7	*O/3D	0.2
1984	Sea-A	110	363	42	96	15	4	8	48	25	51	.264	.315	.394	.709	93	-3	-4	102	115	43	.627	5	2	0	-5	O3/1D	-1.1
1985	Sea-A	48	111	9	27	8	0	1	10	6	19	.243	.282	.342	.624	74	-5	-4	95	97	10	.517	1	2	-1	-1	O/1D	-0.5
1986	Sea-A	17	51	4	10	2	0	0	4	1	13	.196	.212	.235	.447	21	-5	-6	105	133	2	.295	0	1	-1	-1	/O1D	-0.7
Total	10	976	3068	363	833	143	24	56	355	229	387	.272	.325	.389	.713	89	-21	-48	107	105	374	.658	64	39	-4	-14	O/3D1	-8.5
■ FRANK BONNER	Bonner, Frank J. b: 8/20/1869, Lowell, Mass. d: 12/31/05, Kansas City, Mo. TR, 5'7.5", 169 lbs. Deb: 4/26/1894																											
1894	Bal-N	33	118	27	38	10	2	0	24	17	5	.322	.412	.441	.852	108	2	2	99	127	27	1.025	12			0	2/O3S	0.2
1895	Bal-N	11	42	9	14	1	1	0	7	5	1	.333	.404	.405	.809	104	1	0	107	122	9	.929	4			0	3/C	0.0
	StL-N	15	59	3	8	0	1	1	8	1	8	.136	.164	.220	.384	-1	-9	-9	100	142	3	.333	2			0	3/O	-0.6
	Yr	26	101	12	22	1	2	1	15	6	9	.218	.269	.297	.566	46	-8	-9	103	138	10	.544	6			0		-0.6
1896	Bro-N	9	34	8	6	2	0	0	5	2	8	.176	.263	.235	.498	38	-3	-2	87	191	2	.464	1			0	/2	-0.1
1899	Was-N	85	347	41	95	20	4	2	44	18		.274	.313	.372	.685	94	-6	-3	96	88	43	.615	6			-0	2	0.1
1902	Cle-A	34	132	14	37	6	0	0	14	5		.280	.307	.326	.632	79	-4	-4	97	109	14	.516	1			3	2	0.1
	Phi-A	11	44	2	8	0	0	0	3	0		.182	.182	.182	.364	2	-6	-6	108	126	1	.222	0			-3	2	-0.8
	Yr	45	176	16	45	6	0	0	17	5		.256	.276	.290	.566	59	-10	-10	100	116	15	.435	1			-0		-0.7
1903	Bos-N	48	173	11	38	5	0	1	10	7		.220	.250	.266	.516	50	-12	-11	96	67	12	.407	2			0	2S	-0.7
Total	6	246	949	115	244	44	8	4	115	55	22	.257	.302	.333	.635	75	-36	-33	97	103	112	.574	28			-1	2/S3OC	-1.8
■ BOBBY BONNER	Bonner, Robert Averill b: 8/12/56, Uvalde, Tex. BR/TR, 6', 185 lbs. Deb: 9/12/80																											
1980	Bal-A	4	4	1	0	0	0	0	1	0	0	.000	.000	.000	.000	-99	-1	-1	101	0	0	.000	0	0	0	0	/S	0.0
1981	Bal-A	10	27	6	8	2	0	0	2	1	4	.296	.321	.370	.692	100	-0	-0	99	78	4	.632	1	0	0	0	/S	0.1
1982	Bal-A	41	77	8	13	3	1	0	5	3	12	.169	.200	.234	.434	19	-9	-9	100	111	3	.313	0	0	0	-2	S/2	-0.6
1983	Bal-A	6	0	0	0	0	0	0	0	0	0	—	—	—	—	—	0	0	100	—	—	—	0	0	0	0	/2D	0.0

YEAR	TM/L	G	AB	R	H	2B	3B	HR	RBI	BB	SO	AVG	OBP	SLG	PRO	/A	BR	/A	PF	CHI	RC	TA	SB	CS	SBR	FR	POS	TPR
Total	4	61	108	15	21	5	1	0	8	4	16	.194	.223	.259	.482	34	-10	-10	100	99	10	.379	1	0	0	-2	/S2D	-0.5
■ **ZEKE BONURA** Bonura, Henry John b: 9/20/08, New Orleans, La. d: 3/9/87, New Orleans, La. BR/TR, 6', 210 lbs. Deb: 4/17/34																												
1934	Chi-A	127	510	86	154	35	4	27	110	64	31	.302	.380	.545	.925	137	25	26	99	98	106	.955	0	2	-1	3	*1	0.5
1935	Chi-A	138	550	107	162	34	4	21	92	57	28	.295	.364	.485	.849	108	13	6	109	100	99	.853	4	0	1	2	*1	-0.4
1936	Chi-A	148	587	120	194	39	7	12	138	94	29	.330	.426	.482	.908	125	25	26	99	148	126	.975	4	2	0	11	*1	1.4
1937	Chi-A	116	447	79	154	41	2	19	100	49	24	.345	.412	.573	.984	142	30	29	103	116	107	1.061	5	1	1	-1	*1	1.3
1938	Was-A	137	540	72	156	27	3	22	114	44	29	.289	.346	.472	.818	109	0	4	95	122	88	.788	2	2	-1	2	*1	-1.1
1939	NY-N	123	455	75	146	26	6	11	85	46	22	.321	.388	.477	.865	133	20	21	99	132	80	.810	1			1	*1	0.8
1940	Was-A	79	311	41	85	16	3	3	45	40	13	.273	.358	.373	.731	97	-4	-1	93	125	45	.685	2	0	1	-2	1	-0.5
	Chi-N	49	182	20	48	14	0	4	20	10	4	.264	.302	.407	.709	94	-2	-2	100	88	18	.582	1			0	1	-0.5
Total	7	917	3582	600	1099	232	29	119	704	404	180	.307	.380	.487	.867	121	108	109	100	119	670	.874	19	7		15	1	1.5
■ **EVERETT BOOE** Booe, Everett Little b: 9/28/1891, Mocksville, N.C. d: 5/21/69, Kenedy, Tex. BL/TR, 5'8.5", 165 lbs. Deb: 4/13/13																												
1913	Pit-N	29	80	9	16	0	2	0	2	6	9	.200	.256	.250	.506	47	-6	-5	96	36	5	.438	2			0	O	-0.5
1914	Ind-F	20	31	5	7	1	0	0	6	7	0	.226	.368	.258	.626	73	-0	-1	111	271	5	.792	4			0	/OS	0.0
	Buf-F	76	241	29	54	9	2	0	14	21	0	.224	.286	.278	.564	59	-12	-13	104	75	22	.513	8			-3	O/S32	-1.9
	Yr	96	272	34	61	10	2	0	20	28	0	.224	.297	.276	.572	61	-12	-14	106	119	26	.545	12			-3		-1.9
Total	2	125	352	43	77	10	4	0	22	34	9	.219	.288	.270	.557	58	-18	-19	103	86	32	.520	14			-2	/OS32	-2.4
■ **BUDDY BOOKER** Booker, Richard Lee b: 5/28/42, Lynchburg, Va. BL/TR, 5'10", 170 lbs. Deb: 6/04/66																												
1966	Cle-A	18	28	6	6	1	0	2	5	2	6	.214	.267	.464	.731	104	0	0	101	110	3	.625	0	0	0	-1	C	0.0
1968	Chi-A	5	5	0	0	0	0	0	0	1	2	.000	.167	.000	.167	-46	-1	-1	101	0	0	.200	0	0	0	0	/C	0.0
Total	2	23	33	6	6	1	0	2	5	3	8	.182	.250	.394	.644	82	-1	-1	101	92	3	.593	0	0	0	-1	/C	0.0
■ **ROD BOOKER** Booker, Roderick Stewart b: 9/4/58, Los Angeles, Cal. BL/TR, 6' ", 175 lbs. Deb: 4/29/87																												
1987	StL-N	44	47	9	13	1	1	0	8	7	7	.277	.370	.340	.711	91	-0	-0	99	200	7	.735	2	0	1	-1	2/3S	0.0
1988	StL-N	18	35	6	12	3	0	0	3	4	3	.343	.410	.429	.839	136	2	2	104	80	6	.840	2	2	-1	0	3/2	0.2
Total	2	62	82	15	25	4	1	0	11	11	10	.305	.387	.378	.765	110	2	2	101	149	13	.780	4	2	0	-0	/23S	0.2
■ **AL BOOL** Bool, Albert J. b: 8/24/1897, Lincoln, Neb. d: 9/27/81, Lincoln, Neb. BR/TR, 5'11", 180 lbs. Deb: 9/29/28																												
1928	Was-A	2	7	0	1	0	0	0	1	0	0	.143	.143	.143	.286	-24	-1	-1	102	350	0	.167	0	0	0	0	/C	0.0
1930	Pit-N	78	216	30	56	12	4	7	46	25	29	.259	.336	.449	.785	90	-5	-4	97	134	32	.762	0			5	C	0.4
1931	Bos-N	49	85	5	16	1	0	0	6	9	13	.188	.266	.200	.466	27	-9	-8	99	126	5	.377	0			-1	C	-0.7
Total	3	129	308	35	73	13	4	7	53	34	42	.237	.313	.373	.686	72	-15	-14	98	136	38	.634	0	0		4	C	-0.3
■ **IKE BOONE** Boone, Isaac Morgan b: 2/17/1897, Samantha, Ala. d: 8/1/58, Northport, Ala. BL/TR, 6', 195 lbs. Deb: 4/22/22																												
1922	NY-N	2	2	0	1	0	0	0	0	0	1	.500	.500	.500	1.000	153	0	0	104	0	0	1.000	0	0	0	0	H	0.0
1923	Bos-A	5	15	1	4	0	1	0	2	1	0	.267	.313	.400	.712	85	-0	-0	102	114	2	.583	0	1	-1	0	/O	0.0
1924	Bos-A	128	487	72	164	31	4	13	98	54	32	.337	.404	.497	.901	127	22	20	104	122	99	.920	2	2	-1	-11	*O	0.0
1925	Bos-A	133	476	79	157	34	5	9	68	60	19	.330	.406	.479	.885	130	18	22	95	91	94	.898	1	4	-2	-14	*O	-0.4
1927	Chi-A	29	53	10	12	4	0	1	11	3	4	.226	.268	.358	.626	60	-3	-3	102	166	5	.537	0	0	0	-3	O	-0.5
1930	Bro-N	40	101	13	30	9	1	3	13	14	8	.297	.383	.495	.878	110	2	2	101	76	19	.901	0			-4	O	-0.3
1931	Bro-N	6	5	0	1	0	0	0	0	1	1	.200	.333	.200	.533	46	-0	-0	101	0	0	.500	0			0	H	0.0
1932	Bro-N	13	21	2	3	1	0	0	2	5	2	.143	.308	.190	.498	39	-2	-2	96	186	2	.500	0			-1	/O	-0.3
Total	8	356	1160	177	372	79	11	26	194	138	67	.321	.394	.475	.869	121	36	37	100	107	221	.873	3	7		-31	O	-1.5
■ **LUKE BOONE** Boone, Lute Joseph "Danny" b: 5/6/1890, Pittsburgh, Pa. d: 7/29/82, Pittsburgh, Pa. BR/TR, 5'9", 160 lbs. Deb: 9/09/13																												
1913	NY-A	6	12	3	4	0	0	0	1	3	1	.333	.467	.333	.800	134	1	1	101	89	2	.875	0			-0	/S	0.1
1914	NY-A	106	370	34	82	8	2	0	21	31	41	.222	.285	.254	.539	62	-17	-17	100	85	26	.448	10	18	-8	12	2/3O	-1.3
1915	NY-A	130	431	44	88	12	2	5	43	41	53	.204	.285	.276	.562	69	-17	-16	98	111	35	.506	14	17	-6	**20**	*2S/3	-0.2
1916	NY-A	46	124	14	23	4	0	1	8	8	10	.185	.252	.242	.494	48	-8	-8	101	87	10	.475	7			0	3S/2	-0.6
1918	Pit-N	27	91	7	18	3	0	0	3	8	6	.198	.263	.231	.493	48	-5	-6	106	55	6	.411	1			-4	S/2	-0.9
Total	5	315	1028	102	215	27	4	6	76	91	111	.209	.282	.261	.543	63	-46	-46	100	94	79	.476	32	35		27	2/S3O	-2.9
■ **RAY BOONE** Boone, Raymond Otis "Ike" b: 7/27/23, San Diego, Cal. BR/TR, 6', 172 lbs. Deb: 9/03/48																												
1948	Cle-A	6	5	0	2	1	0	0	1	0	1	.400	.400	.600	1.000	166	0	0	99	113	1	1.000	0	0	0	0	/S	0.1
1949	Cle-A	86	258	39	65	4	4	4	26	38	17	.252	.352	.345	.697	87	-5	-4	98	88	32	.626	0	2	-1	5	S	0.0
1950	Cle-A	109	365	53	110	14	6	7	58	56	27	.301	.397	.430	.827	114	8	9	98	113	65	.817	4	3	-1	-6	*S	0.7
1951	Cle-A	151	544	65	127	14	1	12	51	48	36	.233	.302	.329	.631	74	-23	-19	95	87	55	.547	5	3	-0	-2	*S	-1.1
1952	Cle-A	103	316	57	83	8	2	7	45	53	33	.263	.372	.367	.739	117	4	8	91	123	45	.698	0	1	-1	5	S/32	1.8
1953	Cle-A	34	112	21	27	1	2	4	21	24	21	.241	.375	.393	.768	113	2	3	95	142	18	.767	1	2	-1	3	S	0.7
	Det-A	101	385	73	120	16	6	22	93	48	47	.312	.395	.556	.951	158	29	30	98	130	89	.989	2	1	0	5	3/S	3.0
	Yr	135	497	94	147	17	8	26	114	72	68	.296	.390	.519	.909	148	30	32	97	134	107	.942	3	3	-1	9		3.7
1954	Det-A	148	543	76	160	19	7	20	85	71	53	.295	.378	.466	.844	130	23	23	100	109	95	.819	4	2	0	3	*3/S	1.8
1955	Det-A	135	500	61	142	22	7	20	**116**	50	49	.284	.350	.476	.826	124	12	14	97	148	80	.773	1	1	-0	-2	*3	1.4
1956	Det-A	131	481	77	148	14	6	25	81	77	46	.308	.406	.518	.924	147	30	33	97	99	103	.951	0	0	0	-6	*3	2.8
1957	Det-A	129	462	48	126	25	3	12	65	57	47	.273	.356	.418	.774	103	7	3	107	114	68	.720	1	1	-0	-6	*1/3	-0.3
1958	Det-A	39	114	16	27	4	1	6	20	14	13	.237	.326	.447	.773	106	1	1	104	116	16	.717	0	2	-1	0	1	0.0
	Chi-A	77	246	25	60	12	1	7	41	18	33	.244	.298	.386	.684	88	-5	-4	98	142	27	.596	1	1	-0	-2	1	-0.8
	Yr	116	360	41	87	16	2	13	61	32	46	.242	.307	.406	.713	94	-4	-4	100	134	44	.642	1	3	-2	-2		-0.8
1959	Chi-A	9	21	3	5	0	0	1	5	7	5	.238	.429	.381	.810	128	1	1	97	179	5	1.000	1	0	0	-0	/1	0.1
	KC-A	61	132	19	36	6	0	2	12	27	17	.273	.396	.364	.760	109	3	3	101	87	21	.760	1	0	0	-1	1/3	0.2
	Yr	70	153	22	41	6	0	3	17	34	22	.268	.401	.366	.767	111	4	4	101	102	25	.793	2	0	1	-1		0.3
	Mil-N	13	15	3	3	0	0	1	2	4	2	.200	.368	.400	.768	110	0	0	95	90	2	.769	0	0	0	0	/1	0.0
1960	Mil-N	7	12	3	3	1	0	0	4	5	1	.250	.471	.333	.804	137	1	1	91	406	2	1.000	0	0	0	0	/1	0.1
	Bos-A	34	78	6	16	1	0	1	11	11	15	.205	.303	.256	.560	51	-5	-5	103	187	6	.484	0	0	0	0	1	-0.6
Total	13	1373	4589	645	1260	162	46	151	737	608	463	.275	.363	.429	.791	115	84	96	98	116	731	.783	21	19	-5	-3	3S1/2	9.9
■ **BOB BOONE** Boone, Robert Raymond b: 11/19/47, San Diego, Cal. BR/TR, 6'2.5", 195 lbs. Deb: 9/10/72																												
1972	Phi-N	16	51	4	14	1	0	1	4	5	7	.275	.339	.353	.692	100	-0	0	97	78	6	.615	1	0	0	-1	C	0.0
1973	Phi-N	145	521	42	136	20	2	10	61	41	36	.261	.315	.365	.680	81	-9	-14	108	114	60	.591	3	4	-2	17	*C	1.0
1974	Phi-N	146	488	41	118	24	3	3	52	35	29	.242	.298	.322	.620	71	-18	-20	103	121	45	.514	3	1	0	-11	*C	-2.5
1975	Phi-N	97	289	28	71	14	2	2	20	32	14	.246	.323	.329	.652	80	-7	-8	101	77	30	.563	1	3	-2	-4	C/3	-0.9
1976	Phi-N	121	361	40	98	18	2	4	54	45	44	.271	.354	.366	.719	97	3	-0	107	144	45	.647	2	5	-2	-8	*C/1	-0.5
1977	Phi-N	132	440	55	125	26	4	11	66	42	54	.284	.349	.436	.786	109	6	5	100	117	66	.735	5	5	-2	-1	*C/3	0.1
1978	Phi-N	132	435	48	123	18	4	12	62	46	37	.283	.353	.425	.778	110	10	7	105	111	62	.709	2	5	-2	-6	*C/1O	0.1
1979	Phi-N	119	398	38	114	21	3	9	58	49	33	.286	.367	.422	.790	118	9	11	97	120	61	.741	1	4	-2	-2	*C/3	1.0
1980	Phi-N	141	480	34	110	23	1	9	55	48	41	.229	.301	.338	.638	72	-14	-19	107	115	48	.559	3	4	-2	4	*C	-1.3
1981	Phi-N	76	227	19	48	7	0	4	24	22	16	.211	.281	.295	.576	57	-11	-14	112	119	18	.487	2	2	-1	-6	C	-2.0
1982	Cal-A	143	472	42	121	17	0	7	58	39	34	.256	.313	.337	.650	78	-14	-14	100	129	51	.547	0	2	-1	18	*C	1.1
1983	Cal-A	142	468	46	120	18	0	9	52	24	42	.256	.293	.353	.645	80	-15	-13	96	106	44	.522	4	3	-1	17	*C	1.0
1984	Cal-A	139	450	33	91	16	1	3	32	25	45	.202	.244	.262	.506	40	-37	-37	101	100	28	.391	3	3	-1	8	*C	-2.1
1985	Cal-A	150	460	37	114	17	0	5	55	37	35	.248	.308	.317	.625	71	-17	-18	101	136	45	.519	1	2	-1	7	*C	-0.5
1986	Cal-A	144	442	48	98	12	2	7	49	43	30	.222	.291	.305	.596	66	-22	-20	96	125	39	.499	1	0	0	-4	*C	-1.5
1987	Cal-A	128	389	42	94	18	0	3	33	35	36	.242	.306	.311	.617	66	-19	-18	99	101	37	.511	0	2	-1	-1	*C/D	-0.9
1988	Cal-A	122	352	38	104	17	0	5	39	29	26	.295	.352	.386	.739	113	4	6	94	103	47	.653	2	2	-1	-8	*C	0.3
Total	17	2093	6723	635	1699	287	24	104	774	597	559	.253	.315	.349	.664	82	-152	-165	102	115	732	.590	34	47	-18	19	*C/13DO	-7.6

YEAR	TM/L	G	AB	R	H	2B	3B	HR	RBI	BB	SO	AVG	OBP	SLG	PRO	/A	BR	/A	PF	CHI	RC	TA	SB	CS	SBR	FR	POS	TPR
■ **AMOS BOOTH**	Booth, Amos Smith "Darling" b: 9/14/1853, Cincinnati, O. d: 7/1/21, Miamisburg, Ohio BR/TR, Deb: 4/25/1876																											
1876	Cin-N	63	272	31	71	3	0	0	14	9	11	.261	.285	.272	.557	96	-4	1	90	55	22	.413				-21	3CS/OP	-1.7
1877	Cin-N	44	157	16	27	2	1	0	13	12	10	.172	.231	.197	.428	44	-11	-6	82	145	7	.331				0	SCP2/3O	-0.5
1880	Cin-N	1	2	0	0	0	0	0	0	0	0	.000	.000	.000	.000	-99	-0	-0	99	0	0	.000				0	/3	0.0
1882	Bal-a	1	3	0	0	0	0	0		0		.000	.000	.000	.000	-99	-1	-1	92	0	0	.000				0	/3	0.0
	Lou-a	1	4	0	0	0	0	0		0		.000	.000	.000	.000	-99	-1	-1	94	0	0	.000				0	/2	0.0
	Yr	2	7	0	0	0	0	0		0		.000	.000	.000	.000	-99	-1	-1	93	0	0	.000				0		0.0
Total	4	110	438	47	98	5	1	0	27	21	21	.224	.259	.240	.499	74	-16	-7	87	87	29	.371				-21	/CS3P2O	-2.2
■ **EDDIE BOOTH**	Booth, Edward H. b: Brooklyn, N.Y. Deb: 4/26/1872																											
1872	Man-n	24	116	26	39							.336															2/O	
	Atl-n	14	64	10	16							.250															O/2	
	Yr	38	180	36	55							.306																
1873	Res-n	18	77	9	23							.299															O/2	
	Atl-n	15	70	8	12							.171															O	
	Yr	33	147	17	35							.238																
1874	Atl-n	44	194	24	46							.237															*O	
1875	Mut-n	68	286	33	57							.199															*O/2	
1876	NY-N	57	228	17	49	2	1	0	7	2	4	.215	.222	.232	.454	59	-11	-7	87	46	12	.307				-2	*O/2P	-0.7
Total	4 n	183	807	110	193							.239															*O/2P	
■ **FRENCHY BORDAGARAY**	Bordagaray, Stanley George b: 1/3/10, Coalinga, Cal. BR/TR, 5'7.5", 175 lbs. Deb: 4/17/34																											
1934	Chi-A	29	87	12	28	3	1	0	2	3	8	.322	.344	.379	.724	87	-2	-2	99	20	11	.607	1	2	-1	-1	O	-0.3
1935	Bro-N	120	422	69	119	19	6	1	39	17	29	.282	.319	.363	.682	88	-10	-7	94	90	51	.632	18			5	*O	-0.6
1936	Bro-N	125	372	63	117	21	3	4	31	17	42	.315	.346	.419	.766	100	2	-0	105	65	54	.707	12			3	O2/3	0.0
1937	StL-N	96	300	43	88	11	4	1	37	15	25	.293	.331	.367	.698	89	-5	-5	101	118	37	.636	11			-4	3O	-0.7
1938	StL-N	81	156	19	44	5	1	0	21	8	9	.282	.325	.327	.652	72	-4	-6	111	149	17	.548	2			1	O/3	-0.5
1939	Cin-N	63	122	19	24	5	1	0	12	9	10	.197	.252	.254	.506	35	-11	-11	103	142	8	.434	3			-7	O/2	-1.8
1941	NY-A	36	73	10	19	1	0	0	4	6	8	.260	.325	.274	.599	61	-4	-4	98	71	7	.519	1	0	0	-3	O	-0.7
1942	Bro-N	48	58	11	14	2	0	0	5	3	3	.241	.279	.276	.555	61	-3	-3	102	116	4	.467	2			-4	O	-0.6
1943	Bro-N	89	268	47	81	18	2	0	19	30	15	.302	.379	.384	.763	121	8	8	100	67	42	.751	6			-7	O3	0.0
1944	Bro-N	130	501	85	141	26	4	6	51	36	22	.281	.331	.385	.716	102	-0	1	99	92	64	.627	2			-14	3O	-1.0
1945	Bro-N	113	273	32	70	9	6	2	49	29	15	.256	.328	.355	.683	94	-4	-2	96	165	33	.646	7			-12	3O	-1.5
Total	11	930	2632	410	745	120	28	14	270	173	186	.283	.331	.366	.697	91	-32	-32	100	99	329	.643	65	2		-42	O3/2	-7.7
■ **PAT BORDERS**	Borders, Patrick Lance b: 5/14/63, Columbus, Ohio BR/TR, 6'2", 190 lbs. Deb: 4/06/88																											
1988	Tor-A	56	154	15	42	6	3	5	21	3	24	.273	.287	.448	.735	103	-0	-0	100	99	18	.615	0	0	0	-1	C/23D	0.1
■ **GLENN BORGMANN**	Borgmann, Glenn Dennis b: 5/25/50, Paterson, N.J. BR/TR, 6'4", 210 lbs. Deb: 7/01/72																											
1972	Min-A	56	175	11	41	4	0	3	14	25	25	.234	.330	.309	.639	85	-1	-3	107	93	18	.572	0	0	0	-11	C	-1.4
1973	Min-A	12	34	7	9	2	0	0	9	6	10	.265	.375	.324	.699	95	0	0	104	322	5	.680	0	0	0	0	C	0.0
1974	Min-A	128	345	33	87	8	1	3	45	39	44	.252	.330	.307	.637	83	-6	-6	101	154	36	.552	2	1	0	-7	*C	-0.9
1975	Min-A	125	352	34	73	15	2	2	33	47	59	.207	.304	.278	.583	61	-15	-18	107	122	31	.507	0	1	-1	-7	*C	-2.2
1976	Min-A	24	65	10	16	3	0	1	6	19	7	.246	.417	.338	.755	125	3	3	98	92	11	.808	1	1	-0	2	C	0.6
1977	Min-A	17	43	12	11	1	0	2	7	11	9	.256	.407	.419	.826	122	2	2	103	116	8	.879	0	0	0	2	C	0.4
1978	Min-A	49	123	16	26	4	1	3	15	18	17	.211	.312	.333	.645	86	-3	-2	94	118	15	.608	0	0	0	1	C/D	0.1
1979	Min-A	31	70	4	14	3	0	0	8	12	11	.200	.317	.243	.560	49	-4	-5	109	181	6	.508	1	0	0	1	C	-0.1
1980	Chi-A	32	87	10	19	2	0	2	14	14	9	.218	.327	.310	.637	78	-3	-2	97	165	10	.594	0	0	0	-5	C	-0.5
Total	9	474	1294	137	296	42	4	16	151	191	191	.229	.329	.304	.634	79	-26	-31	103	136	140	.591	4	3	-1	-23	C/D	-4.0
■ **BOB BORKOWSKI**	Borkowski, Robert Vilarian b: 1/27/26, Dayton, Ohio BR/TR, 6', 182 lbs. Deb: 4/22/50																											
1950	Chi-N	85	256	27	70	7	4	4	29	16	30	.273	.319	.379	.698	79	-7	-8	105	103	29	.590	1			3	O/1	-0.7
1951	Chi-N	58	89	9	14	1	0	0	10	3	16	.157	.185	.169	.353	-4	-13	-13	97	258	2	.225	0	0	0	-4	O	-1.7
1952	Cin-N	126	377	42	95	11	4	4	24	26	53	.252	.300	.334	.634	76	-13	-12	100	68	39	.531	1	3	-2	1	*O/1	-1.5
1953	Cin-N	94	249	32	67	11	1	7	29	21	41	.269	.328	.406	.734	91	-4	-3	99	93	34	.654	0	1	-1	-10	O/1	-1.5
1954	Cin-N	73	162	13	43	12	1	1	19	8	18	.265	.304	.370	.674	72	-6	-7	104	119	15	.531	0	2	-1	-1	O/1	-1.0
1955	Cin-N	25	18	1	3	1	0	0	1	1	2	.167	.211	.222	.433	14	-2	-2	106	101	1	.313	0	0	0	-4	O/1	-0.6
	Bro-N	9	19	2	2	0	0	0	0	1	6	.105	.150	.105	.255	-29	-4	-4	104	0	0	.176	0	0	0	-3	/O	-0.6
	Yr	34	37	3	5	1	0	0	1	2	8	.135	.179	.162	.342	-8	-6	-6	105	77	1	.250	0	0	0	-7		-1.2
Total	6	470	1170	126	294	43	10	16	112	76	166	.251	.299	.346	.645	71	-48	-50	101	101	120	.551	2	6		-18	O/1	-7.6
■ **RED BOROM**	Borom, Edward Jones b: 10/30/15, Spartanburg, S.C. BL/TR, 5'11", 180 lbs. Deb: 4/23/44																											
1944	Det-A	7	14	1	1	0	0	0	1	2	2	.071	.188	.071	.259	-23	-2	-2	105	361	0	.214	0	0	0	0	/2S	-0.1
1945	Det-A	55	130	19	35	4	0	0	9	7	8	.269	.307	.300	.607	72	-4	-5	106	83	13	.505	4	2	0	4	2/3S	0.0
Total	2	62	144	20	36	4	0	0	10	9	10	.250	.294	.278	.572	62	-6	-7	106	112	13	.473	4	2	0	4	/23S	-0.1
■ **STEVE BOROS**	Boros, Stephen b: 9/3/36, Flint, Mich. BR/TR, 6', 185 lbs. Deb: 6/19/57 MC																											
1957	Det-A	24	41	4	6	1	0	0	2	1	8	.146	.167	.171	.337	-7	-6	-6	107	113	1	.216	0	0	0	-1	/3S	-0.6
1958	Det-A	6	2	0	0	0	0	0	0	0	0	.000	.000	.000	.000	-96	-1	-1	104	0	0	.000	0	0	0	0	/2	0.0
1961	Det-A	116	396	51	107	18	2	5	62	68	42	.270	.388	.364	.751	106	4	7	96	156	61	.749	4	2	0	-21	*3	-0.6
1962	Det-A	116	356	46	81	14	1	16	47	53	62	.228	.333	.407	.740	88	-1	-6	111	97	50	.721	3	1	0	-13	*3/2	-1.6
1963	Chi-N	41	90	9	19	5	1	3	7	12	19	.211	.304	.389	.693	93	-0	-1	105	67	11	.635	0	2	-1	-2	1O	-0.4
1964	Cin-N	117	370	31	95	12	3	2	31	47	43	.257	.344	.322	.665	86	-4	-5	103	102	41	.597	4	1	1	-4	*3	-1.5
1965	Cin-N	2	0	0	0	0	0	0	0	0	0	—	—	—	—	—	0	0	104	—	—	—	0	0	0	0	/3	0.0
Total	7	422	1255	141	308	50	7	26	149	181	174	.245	.346	.359	.705	90	-7	-13	103	116	205	.687	11	6	-0	-39	3/1O2S	-4.7
■ **BABE BORTON**	Borton, William Baker b: 8/14/1888, Marion, Ill. d: 7/29/54, Berkeley, Cal. BL/TL, 6', 178 lbs. Deb: 9/02/12																											
1912	Chi-A	31	105	15	39	3	1	0	17	8		.371	.416	.419	.835	141	5	6	99	131	19	.803	1			2	1	0.8
1913	Chi-A	28	80	9	22	5	0	0	13	23	5	.275	.442	.338	.780	135	5	5	95	174	12	.897	1			0	1	0.6
	NY-A	33	108	8	14	1	0	1	11	18	19	.130	.260	.167	.427	25	-10	-10	101	190	5	.404	1			1	1	-0.8
	Yr	61	188	17	36	6	0	1	24	41	24	.191	.342	.239	.581	72	-5	-4	98	186	15	.592	2			1		-0.2
1915	StL-F	159	549	**97**	157	20	14	3	83	**92**	64	.286	.388	.390	.778	125	25	21	105	142	95	.824	17			-7	*1	1.7
1916	StL-A	66	98	10	22	1	2	1	12	19	13	.224	.350	.306	.657	102	0	1	95	130	11	.658	1			-0	1	0.0
Total	4	317	940	139	254	30	17	5	136	160	101	.270	.377	.354	.732	114	25	23	102	148	142	.752	21			-4	1	2.3
■ **DON BOSCH**	Bosch, Donald John b: 7/15/42, San Francisco, Cal BB/TR, 5'10", 160 lbs. Deb: 9/19/66																											
1966	Pit-N	3	2	0	0	0	0	0	0	0	0	.000	.000	.000	.000	-99	-1	-1	101	0	0	.000	0	0	0	-0	/O	0.0
1967	NY-N	44	93	7	13	0	1	0	2	5	24	.140	.184	.161	.345	-0	-12	-12	99	55	3	.274	3	1	0	-3	O	-1.7
1968	NY-N	50	111	14	19	1	0	3	7	9	33	.171	.233	.261	.495	47	-7	-7	102	78	6	.396	0	2	-1	4	O	-0.6
1969	Mon-N	49	112	13	20	5	0	1	4	8	20	.179	.233	.250	.483	35	-10	-10	100	52	7	.398	1	0	0	-1	O	-1.2
Total	4	146	318	34	52	6	1	4	13	22	77	.164	.218	.226	.444	28	-29	-30	101	61	16	.363	4	3	-1	0	O	-3.5
■ **RICK BOSETTI**	Bosetti, Richard Alan b: 8/5/53, Redding, Cal. BR/TR, 5'11", 185 lbs. Deb: 9/09/76																											
1976	Phi-N	13	18	6	5	1	0	0	0	1	3	.278	.316	.333	.649	79	-0	-1	107	0	2	.714	3	0	1	0	/O	0.0
1977	StL-N	41	69	12	16	0	0	0	3	6	11	.232	.303	.232	.535	48	-5	-5	96	75	5	.474	4	4	-1	-4	O	-1.1
1978	Tor-A	136	568	61	147	25	5	5	42	30	65	.259	.300	.347	.646	81	-15	-15	100	69	58	.541	6	10	-4	18	*O	-0.4
1979	Tor-A	162	619	59	161	35	2	8	65	22	70	.260	.289	.362	.651	72	-23	-26	103	107	58	.538	13	12	-3	11	*O	-2.3
1980	Tor-A	53	188	24	40	7	1	4	18	15	29	.213	.278	.324	.603	65	-9	-9	100	98	16	.526	4	6	-2	3	O	-0.8
1981	Tor-A	25	47	5	11	2	0	0	4	2	6	.234	.265	.277	.542	51	-3	-3	111	120	3	.375	0	2	-1	-1	O/D	-0.5

YEAR	TM/L	G	AB	R	H	2B	3B	HR	RBI	BB	SO	AVG	OBP	SLG	PRO	/A	BR	/A	PF	CHI	RC	TA	SB	CS	SBR	FR	POS	TPR
	Oak-A	9	19	4	2	0	0	0	1	3	3	.105	.227	.105	.333	-2	-2	-2	96	196	1	.294	0	0	0	0	/OD	-0.2
	Yr	34	66	9	13	2	0	0	5	5	9	.197	.254	.227	.481	37	-5	-6	107	144	4	.364	0	2	-1	-1		-0.7
1982	Oak-A	6	15	1	3	0	0	0	0	0	1	.200	.200	.200	.400	11	-2	-2	95	0	0	.231	0	0	0	2	/O	0.0
Total	7	445	1543	172	385	70	8	17	133	79	188	.250	.290	.338	.628	71	-60	-63	101	90	143	.536	30	34	-11	29	O/D	-5.3
■ **THAD BOSLEY**	Bosley, Thaddis b: 9/17/56, Oceanside, Cal. BL/TL, 6'3", 175 lbs. Deb: 6/29/77																											
1977	Cal-A	58	212	19	63	10	2	0	19	16	32	.297	.349	.363	.713	100	-1	0	95	100	27	.631	5	4	-1	3	O	0.0
1978	Chi-A	66	219	25	59	5	1	2	13	13	32	.269	.310	.329	.639	79	-6	-6	101	66	20	.554	12	11	-3	4	O	-0.6
1979	Chi-A	36	77	13	24	1	1	1	8	9	14	.312	.384	.390	.773	107	1	1	102	93	12	.782	4	1	1	0	O	0.1
1980	Chi-A	70	147	12	33	2	0	2	14	10	27	.224	.274	.279	.553	54	-10	-9	97	116	10	.446	3	2	-0	-6	O	-1.5
1981	Mil-A	42	105	11	24	2	0	0	3	6	13	.229	.270	.248	.518	52	-7	-6	96	45	7	.395	2	1	0	-6	O/D	-1.3
1982	Sea-A	22	46	3	8	1	0	0	2	4	8	.174	.240	.196	.436	19	-5	-5	109	89	2	.400	3	1	0	-5	O	-1.0
1983	Chi-N	43	72	12	21	4	1	2	12	10	12	.292	.378	.458	.836	129	3	3	101	122	13	.846	1	1	-0	-2	O	0.1
1984	Chi-N	55	98	17	29	2	2	2	14	13	22	.296	.378	.418	.797	112	3	2	110	117	17	.831	5	1	1	-4	O	-0.2
1985	Chi-N	108	180	25	59	6	3	7	27	20	29	.328	.395	.511	.906	130	12	9	116	95	37	.936	5	1	1	-6	O	0.3
1986	Chi-N	87	120	15	33	4	1	1	9	18	24	.275	.370	.350	.720	93	1	-0	107	80	17	.700	3	0	1	-10	O	-1.0
1987	KC-A	80	140	13	39	6	1	1	16	9	26	.279	.322	.357	.679	78	-4	-4	104	120	16	.573	0	0	0	-6	OD	-1.0
1988	KC-A	15	21	1	4	0	0	0	2	2	6	.190	.261	.190	.451	28	-2	-2	103	199	1	.353	0	0	0	-2	/OD	-0.3
	Cal-A	35	75	9	21	5	0	0	7	6	12	.280	.333	.347	.680	96	-1	-0	94	107	9	.579	1	1	-0	-1	O/D	-0.2
	Yr	50	96	10	25	5	0	0	9	8	18	.260	.317	.313	.630	80	-3	-2	97	138	10	.527	1	1	-0	-3		-0.5
Total	12	717	1512	175	417	48	12	18	146	136	257	.276	.336	.359	.695	90	-14	-18	103	96	188	.646	44	24	-1	-42	O/D	-6.6
■ **HARLEY BOSS**	Boss, Elmer Harley "Lefty" b: 11/19/08, Hodge, La. d: 5/15/64, Nashville, Tenn. BL/TL, 5'11.5", 185 lbs. Deb: 7/19/28																											
1928	Was-A	12	12	1	3	0	0	0	2	3	1	.250	.400	.250	.650	73	-0	-0	102	229	1	.667	0	0	0	0	/1	0.0
1929	Was-A	28	66	9	18	2	1	0	6	2	6	.273	.294	.333	.627	61	-4	-4	100	93	6	.500	0	0	0	1	1	-0.5
1930	Was-A	3	3	0	0	0	0	0	0	0	0	.000	.000	.000	.000	-99	-1	-1	101	0	0	.000	0	0	0	0	/1	0.0
1933	Cle-A	112	438	54	118	17	7	1	53	25	27	.269	.310	.347	.657	71	-17	-20	105	121	46	.554	2	5	-2	6	*1	-2.2
Total	4	155	519	64	139	19	8	1	61	30	34	.268	.309	.341	.650	69	-22	-25	104	120	54	.545	2	5	-2	6	1	-2.7
■ **HENRY BOSTICK**	Bostick, Henry Landers (born Henry Lipschitz) b: 1/11/1895, Boston, Mass. d: 9/16/68, Denver, Colo. BR/TR, Deb: 5/18/15																											
1915	Phi-A	2	7	0	0	0	0	0	2	1	1	.000	.125	.000	.125	-65	-1	-1	96	0	0	.143	0			0	/3	0.0
■ **LYMAN BOSTOCK**	Bostock, Lyman Wesley b: 11/22/50, Birmingham, Ala. d: 9/23/78, Gary, Ind. BL/TR, 6'1", 180 lbs. Deb: 4/08/75																											
1975	Min-A	98	369	52	104	21	5	0	29	28	42	.282	.332	.366	.698	91	-2	-5	107	84	44	.600	2	3	-1	-1	O/D	-0.9
1976	Min-A	128	474	75	153	21	9	4	60	33	37	.323	.368	.430	.798	136	19	20	98	109	71	.731	12	6	0	-1	*O	1.7
1977	Min-A	153	593	104	199	36	12	14	90	51	59	.336	.394	.508	.901	140	36	34	103	110	116	.897	16	7	1	-10	*O	1.9
1978	Cal-A	147	568	74	168	24	4	5	71	59	36	.296	.364	.379	.743	107	8	7	102	129	72	.664	15	12	-3	15	*O/D	1.6
Total	4	526	2004	305	624	102	30	23	250	171	174	.311	.368	.427	.795	120	62	56	102	111	303	.753	45	28	-3	3	O/D	4.3
■ **DARYL BOSTON**	Boston, Daryl Lamont b: 1/4/63, Cincinnati, Ohio BL/TL, 6'3", 185 lbs. Deb: 5/13/84																											
1984	Chi-A	35	83	8	14	3	1	0	3	4	20	.169	.207	.229	.436	18	-9	-10	111	63	5	.420	6	0	2	-3	O/D	-1.2
1985	Chi-A	95	232	20	53	13	1	3	15	14	44	.228	.272	.332	.604	65	-12	-12	100	69	20	.527	8	6	-1	1	O/D	-1.2
1986	Chi-A	56	199	29	53	11	3	5	22	21	33	.266	.336	.427	.763	106	2	2	101	89	28	.742	9	5	-0	2	O/D	0.2
1987	Chi-A	103	337	51	87	21	2	10	29	25	68	.258	.309	.421	.731	85	-4	-8	109	67	43	.686	12	6	0	3	O/D	-0.7
1988	Chi-A	105	281	37	61	12	2	15	31	21	44	.217	.272	.434	.706	97	-3	-3	97	74	32	.667	9	3	1	0	O/D	-0.2
Total	5	394	1132	145	268	60	9	33	100	85	209	.237	.290	.393	.683	82	-26	-31	103	73	128	.646	44	20	1	3	O/D	-3.1
■ **KEN BOSWELL**	Boswell, Kenneth George b: 2/23/46, Austin, Tex. BL/TR, 6', 170 lbs. Deb: 9/18/67																											
1967	NY-N	11	40	2	9	3	0	1	4	1	5	.225	.244	.375	.619	75	-1	-1	99	94	3	.471	0	0	0	0	/23	0.0
1968	NY-N	75	284	37	74	7	2	4	11	16	27	.261	.302	.342	.644	91	-3	-3	102	45	29	.555	7	2	1	-5	2	-0.3
1969	NY-N	102	362	48	101	14	7	3	32	36	47	.279	.348	.381	.729	104	2	2	100	89	47	.661	7	3	0	-5	2	0.5
1970	NY-N	105	351	32	89	13	2	5	44	41	32	.254	.335	.345	.680	79	-8	-10	104	126	39	.606	5	4	-1	-14	*2	-1.3
1971	NY-N	116	392	46	107	20	1	5	40	36	31	.273	.337	.367	.705	103	0	2	96	102	48	.628	5	2	0	-17	*2	-1.0
1972	NY-N	100	355	35	75	9	1	9	33	32	35	.211	.276	.318	.595	72	-15	-13	95	99	29	.495	2	2	-1	-24	2	-3.4
1973	NY-N	76	110	12	25	2	1	2	14	12	11	.227	.303	.318	.621	72	-4	-4	101	137	11	.547	0	0	0	1	3/2	-0.3
1974	NY-N	96	222	19	48	6	1	2	15	18	19	.216	.278	.279	.557	57	-13	-13	99	85	16	.443	0	1	-1	1	23/O	-1.2
1975	Hou-N	86	178	16	43	8	2	0	21	30	12	.242	.354	.309	.663	90	-2	-1	94	148	19	.593	0	3	-2	1	23	0.0
1976	Hou-N	91	126	12	33	8	1	0	18	8	8	.262	.306	.341	.647	97	-3	-1	86	161	11	.515	1	0	0	-1	3/2O	-0.1
1977	Hou-N	72	97	7	21	1	1	0	12	10	12	.216	.290	.247	.537	49	-7	-6	93	200	6	.420	0	0	0	0	2/3	-0.3
Total	11	930	2517	266	625	91	19	31	244	240	239	.248	.316	.337	.652	85	-55	-49	98	107	259	.587	27	17	-2	-63	2/3O	-7.4
■ **JOHN BOTTARINI**	Bottarini, John Charles b: 9/14/08, Crockett, Cal. d: 10/8/76, Jemez Springs, N.M. BR/TR, 6', 190 lbs. Deb: 4/22/37																											
1937	Chi-N	26	40	3	11	3	0	1	7	5	10	.275	.370	.425	.795	112	1	1	103	126	7	.793	0			-1	C/O	0.0
■ **JIM BOTTOMLEY**	Bottomley, James Leroy "Sunny Jim" b: 4/23/1900, Oglesby, Ill. d: 12/11/59, St.Louis, Mo. BL/TL, 6', 180 lbs. Deb: 8/18/22 MCH																											
1922	StL-N	37	151	29	49	8	5	5	35	6	13	.325	.358	.543	.902	128	6	5	101	134	29	.903	3	1	0	-0	1	0.5
1923	StL-N	134	523	79	194	34	14	8	94	45	44	.371	.425	.535	.960	168	39	47	90	115	117	.994	4	6	-2	-5	*1	2.8
1924	StL-N	137	528	87	167	31	12	14	111	35	35	.316	.362	.500	.862	126	20	18	103	140	94	.841	5	4	-1	-11	*1/2	0.1
1925	StL-N	153	619	92	**227**	**44**	12	21	128	47	36	.367	.413	.578	.992	147	46	44	102	104	145	1.035	3	4	-2	-4	*1	2.1
1926	StL-N	154	603	98	180	**40**	14	19	**120**	58	52	.299	.364	.506	.870	129	25	23	102	122	109	.877	4			-15	*1	0.3
1927	StL-N	152	574	95	174	31	15	19	124	74	49	.303	.387	.509	.896	129	31	25	107	119	112	.947	8			-11	*1	0.4
1928	StL-N	149	576	123	187	42	**20**	**31**	**136**	71	54	.325	.402	.628	1.030	166	53	53	100	113	142	1.147	10			-13	*1	2.3
1929	StL-N	146	560	108	176	31	12	29	137	70	54	.314	.391	.568	.959	137	29	30	98	123	122	1.021	3			-7	*1	1.5
1930	StL-N	131	487	92	148	33	7	15	97	44	36	.304	.368	.493	.860	101	4	-0	105	120	86	.867	5			-10	*1	-1.3
1931	StL-N	108	382	73	133	34	5	9	75	34	24	.348	.403	.534	.937	140	26	23	107	118	84	.972	3			1	1	1.6
1932	StL-N	91	311	45	92	16	3	11	48	25	32	.296	.350	.473	.823	119	8	8	100	99	52	.799	2			-2	1	0.2
1933	Cin-N	145	549	57	137	23	9	13	83	42	28	.250	.311	.395	.706	102	-0	1	99	129	68	.633	3			-8	*1	-1.0
1934	Cin-N	142	556	72	158	31	11	11	78	33	40	.284	.324	.439	.763	101	0	-0	101	108	80	.683	1			-3	*1	-1.4
1935	Cin-N	107	399	44	103	21	1	1	49	18	24	.258	.294	.323	.617	70	-19	-16	93	137	37	.495	3			1	1	-1.6
1936	StL-A	140	544	72	162	39	11	12	95	44	55	.298	.354	.476	.830	100	0	-2	103	106	92	.801	0	0	0	-10	*1	-2.7
1937	StL-A	65	109	11	26	7	0	1	12	18	15	.239	.346	.330	.677	72	-4	-4	99	105	14	.663	1	0	0	-0	1M	-0.6
Total	16	1991	7471	1177	2313	465	151	219	1422	664	591	.310	.369	.500	.869	125	262	253	101	118	1384	.870	58	15		-97	*1/2	3.2
■ **ED BOUCHEE**	Bouchee, Edward Francis b: 3/7/33, Livingston, Mont. BL/TL, 6', 200 lbs. Deb: 9/19/56																											
1956	Phi-N	9	22	0	6	2	0	0	1	5	6	.273	.407	.364	.771	116	1	1	94	53	4	.813	0	0	0	-0	/1	0.0
1957	Phi-N	154	574	78	168	35	8	17	76	84	91	.293	.396	.470	.866	134	29	30	98	94	110	.876	1	0	0	4	*1	2.0
1958	Phi-N	89	334	55	86	19	5	9	39	51	74	.257	.356	.425	.781	108	3	4	98	101	51	.752	1	0	0	-1	1	-0.2
1959	Phi-N	136	499	75	142	29	4	15	74	70	74	.285	.378	.449	.827	120	15	16	99	107	85	.799	0	4	-2	-2	*1	0.1
1960	Phi-N	22	65	1	17	4	0	0	8	9	11	.262	.360	.323	.683	83	-1	-1	107	155	8	.633	0	0	0	1	1	-0.1
	Chi-N	98	299	33	71	11	1	5	44	45	51	.237	.341	.331	.672	87	-5	-4	98	157	37	.641	2	0	1	1	1	-0.6
	Yr	120	364	34	88	15	1	5	52	54	62	.242	.344	.330	.674	86	-6	-5	100	158	46	.642	2	0	1	1		-0.7
1961	Chi-N	112	319	49	79	12	3	12	38	58	77	.248	.372	.417	.789	109	6	6	100	91	53	.801	1	4	-2	-2	*1	-0.4
1962	NY-N	50	87	7	14	2	0	3	10	18	17	.161	.305	.287	.592	58	-5	-5	104	116	8	.573	0	0	0	1	1	-0.4
Total	7	670	2199	298	583	114	21	61	290	340	401	.265	.370	.419	.790	112	43	46	99	108	357	.796	5	8	-3	1	1	0.4
■ **AL BOUCHER**	Boucher, Alexander Francis "Bo" b: 11/13/1881, Franklin, Mass. d: 6/23/74, Torrance, Cal. BR/TR, 5'8.5", 156 lbs. Deb: 4/16/14																											
1914	StL-F	147	516	62	119	26	4	2	49	52	88	.231	.301	.308	.609	71	-17	-20	106	109	56	.564	13			-3	*3	-2.1
■ **MEDRIC BOUCHER**	Boucher, Medric Charles Francis b: 3/12/1886, St.Louis, Mo. d: 3/12/74, Martinez, Cal. BR/TR, 5'10", 165 lbs. Deb: 6/03/14																											
1914	Bal-F	16	16	2	5	1	1	0	2	1	0	.313	.353	.500	.853	144	1	1	99	90	3	.818	0			0	/C1O	0.1

YEAR	TM/L	G	AB	R	H	2B	3B	HR	RBI	BB	SO	AVG	OBP	SLG	PRO	/A	BR	/A	PF	CHI	RC	TA	SB	CS	SBR	FR	POS	TPR
	Pit-F	1	1	0	0	0	0	0	0	0	0	.000	.000	.000	.000	-99	-0	-0	94	0	0	.000	0			0	H	0.0
	Yr	17	17	2	5	1	1	0	2	1	0	.294	.333	.471	.804	130	1	1	99	90	3	.750	0			0		0.1
Total	1	17	17	2	5	1	1	0	2	1	0	.294	.333	.471	.804	130	1	1	99	85	3	.750	0			0	/CO1	0.1
■ **LOU BOUDREAU** Boudreau, Louis b: 7/17/17, Harvey, Ill. BR/TR, 5'11", 185 lbs. Deb: 9/09/38 MH																												
1938	Cle-A	1	1	0	0	0	0	0	0	1	0	.000	.500	.000	.500	36	0	0	99	0	0	1.000	0	0	0	0	/3	0.0
1939	Cle-A	53	225	42	58	15	4	0	19	28	24	.258	.340	.360	.700	81	-7	-6	98	68	28	.642	2	1	0	-2	S	-0.2
1940	Cle-A	155	627	97	185	46	10	9	101	73	39	.295	.370	.443	.814	118	10	16	93	106	103	.767	6	3	0	12	*S	3.9
1941	Cle-A	148	579	95	149	**45**	8	10	56	85	57	.257	.355	.415	.770	102	3	2	101	63	92	.757	9	4	0	15	*S	2.1
1942	Cle-A	147	506	57	143	18	10	2	58	75	39	.283	.379	.370	.749	121	10	16	92	108	73	.698	7	16	-8	1	*SM	1.7
1943	Cle-A	152	539	69	154	32	7	3	67	90	31	.286	.388	.388	.776	141	22	28	90	119	87	.750	4	7	-3	**28**	*S/CM	**5.7**
1944	Cle-A	150	584	91	191	**45**	5	3	67	73	39	**.327**	.406	.437	.843	141	33	33	100	88	112	.847	11	3	2	23	*S/CM	**6.8**
1945	Cle-A	97	345	50	106	24	1	3	48	35	20	.307	.374	.409	.783	129	12	13	99	123	53	.706	0	4	-2	-2	SM	1.2
1946	Cle-A	140	515	51	151	30	6	6	62	40	14	.293	.345	.410	.755	125	6	13	89	109	72	.675	6	7	-2	15	*SM	2.8
1947	Cle-A	150	538	79	165	**45**	3	4	67	67	10	.307	.388	.424	.811	131	20	22	96	109	95	.785	1	0	0	15	*SM	3.8
1948	Cle-A	152	560	116	199	34	6	18	106	98	9	.355	.453	.534	.987	164	53	54	99	107	143	1.063	3	2	-0	10	*S/CM	6.1
1949	Cle-A	134	475	53	135	20	3	4	60	70	10	.284	.381	.364	.745	100	0	2	98	113	68	.686	0	1	-1	4	S3/12M	0.6
1950	Cle-A	81	260	23	70	13	2	1	29	31	5	.269	.349	.346	.695	80	-8	-7	98	108	32	.612	1	2	-1	-4	S/123M	-0.8
1951	Bos-A	82	273	37	73	18	1	5	47	30	12	.267	.353	.396	.748	95	1	-2	108	137	39	.690	1	0	0	5	S3/1	0.6
1952	Bos-A	4	2	1	0	0	0	0	2	0	0	.000	.000	.000	.000	-94	-1	-1	107	0	0	.000	0	0	0	0	/S3M	0.0
Total	15	1646	6029	861	1779	385	66	68	789	796	309	.295	.380	.415	.795	121	154	184	96	104	996	.786	51	50	-15	121	*S/312C	34.3
■ **CHRIS BOURJOS** Bourjos, Christopher b: 10/16/55, Chicago, Ill. BR/TR, 6', 185 lbs. Deb: 8/31/80																												
1980	SF-N	13	22	4	5	1	0	1	2	2	7	.227	.292	.409	.701	98	-0	-0	96	66	2	.611	0	0	0	-2	/O	-0.1
■ **PAT BOURQUE** Bourque, Patrick Daniel b: 3/23/47, Worcester, Mass. BL/TL, 6', 210 lbs. Deb: 9/06/71																												
1971	Chi-N	14	37	3	7	0	1	1	3	3	9	.189	.250	.324	.574	56	-2	-2	110	81	3	.484	0	0	0	0	1	-0.2
1972	Chi-N	11	27	3	7	1	0	0	5	2	2	.259	.310	.296	.607	64	-1	-1	114	257	3	.500	0	0	0	0	/1	-0.1
1973	Chi-N	57	139	11	29	6	0	7	20	16	21	.209	.299	.403	.702	86	-2	-3	108	104	18	.676	1	1	-0	3	1	-0.1
	Oak-A	23	42	8	8	4	1	2	9	15	10	.190	.404	.476	.880	169	3	4	87	136	9	1.000	0	0	0	-0	D/1	0.4
1974	Oak-A	73	96	6	22	4	0	1	16	15	20	.229	.333	.302	.635	83	-2	-2	100	197	10	.571	0	2	-1	-1	1/D	-0.5
	Min-A	23	64	5	14	2	0	1	8	7	11	.219	.296	.297	.593	70	-2	-2	101	143	6	.500	0	0	0	1	1	-0.1
	Yr	96	160	11	36	6	0	2	24	22	31	.225	.319	.300	.619	78	-4	-4	101	186	16	.547	0	2	-1	1		-0.6
Total	4	201	405	36	87	17	2	12	61	58	73	.215	.316	.356	.672	87	-5	-7	103	144	48	.635	1	3	-2	4	1/D	-0.6
■ **LARRY BOWA** Bowa, Lawrence Robert b: 12/6/45, Sacramento, Cal. BB/TR, 5'10", 155 lbs. Deb: 4/07/70 MC																												
1970	Phi-N	145	547	50	137	17	6	0	34	21	48	.250	.278	.303	.582	58	-35	-32	96	81	45	.490	24	13	-1	-20	*S/2	-3.4
1971	Phi-N	159	650	74	162	18	5	0	25	36	61	.249	.294	.292	.586	65	-28	-30	103	52	59	.515	28	11	2	10	*S	0.2
1972	Phi-N	152	579	67	145	11	**13**	1	31	32	51	.250	.292	.320	.612	76	-20	-18	97	72	54	.523	17	9	-0	5	*S	0.4
1973	Phi-N	122	446	42	94	11	3	0	23	24	31	.211	.253	.249	.502	37	-36	-41	108	85	28	.402	10	6	-1	0	*S	-2.5
1974	Phi-N	162	669	97	184	19	10	1	36	23	52	.275	.300	.338	.638	76	-21	-23	103	54	69	.570	39	11	5	-14	*S	-1.5
1975	Phi-N	136	583	79	178	18	9	2	38	24	32	.305	.335	.377	.712	96	-3	-4	101	57	75	.643	24	6	4	-13	*S	0.2
1976	Phi-N	156	624	71	155	15	9	0	49	32	31	.248	.285	.301	.586	62	-28	-33	107	106	55	.512	30	8	4	-12	*S	-2.7
1977	Phi-N	154	624	93	175	19	3	4	41	32	32	.280	.316	.340	.655	75	-21	-21	100	78	70	.596	32	3	8	6	*S	1.4
1978	Phi-N	156	654	78	192	31	5	3	43	24	40	.294	.320	.370	.690	87	-8	-12	105	65	80	.622	27	5	5	8	*S	1.4
1979	Phi-N	147	539	74	130	17	11	0	31	61	32	.241	.319	.314	.633	76	-19	-17	97	77	57	.585	20	9	1	-10	*S	-1.0
1980	Phi-N	147	540	57	144	16	4	2	39	24	28	.267	.302	.322	.624	69	-19	-23	107	88	53	.540	21	6	3	-13	*S	-1.7
1981	Phi-N	103	360	34	102	14	3	0	31	26	17	.283	.332	.339	.670	81	-4	-9	112	100	40	.601	16	7	1	-8	*S	-0.5
1982	Chi-N	142	499	50	123	15	7	0	29	39	38	.246	.302	.305	.607	68	-19	-21	103	76	47	.514	8	3	1	-28	*S	-4.1
1983	Chi-N	147	499	73	133	20	5	2	43	35	30	.267	.315	.339	.653	80	-13	-13	101	97	56	.567	7	3	0	21	*S	2.2
1984	Chi-N	133	391	33	87	14	2	0	17	28	24	.223	.274	.269	.543	48	-24	-29	110	63	30	.458	10	4	1	5	*S	-0.9
1985	Chi-N	72	195	13	48	6	4	0	13	11	20	.246	.286	.318	.604	59	-8	-12	116	83	18	.517	5	1	1	9	S	0.3
	NY-N	14	19	2	2	1	0	0	2	2	2	.105	.190	.158	.348	-2	-3	-3	97	266	1	.294	0	0	0	-1	/S2	-0.2
	Yr	86	214	15	50	7	4	0	15	13	22	.234	.278	.304	.581	55	-11	-14	113	114	20	.503	5	1	1	8		0.1
Total	16	2247	8418	987	2191	262	99	15	525	474	569	.260	.301	.320	.621	70	-310	-343	103	76	836	.554	318	105	32	-55	*S/2	-12.4
■ **BENNY BOWCOCK** Bowcock, Benjamin James b: 10/28/1879, Fall River, Mass. d: 6/16/61, New Bedford, Mass BR/TR, 5'7", 150 lbs. Deb: 03																												
1903	StL-A	14	50	7	16	3	1	1	10	3		.320	.358	.480	.838	160	3	3	95	136	9	.824	1			-2	2	0.1
■ **TIM BOWDEN** Bowden, David Timon b: 8/15/1891, Mcdonough, Ga. d: 10/25/49, Emory, Ga. BL/TR, 5'10", 175 lbs. Deb: 9/17/14																												
1914	StL-A	7	9	0	2	0	0	0	0	1	6	.222	.300	.222	.522	59	-0	-0	98	0	1	.429	0			-1	/O	-0.1
■ **CHICK BOWEN** Bowen, Emmons Joseph b: 7/26/1897, New Haven, Conn. d: 8/9/48, New Haven, Conn. BR/TR, 5'7", 165 lbs. Deb: 9/15/19																												
1919	NY-N	3	5	0	1	0	0	0	1	1	2	.200	.333	.200	.533	62	-0	-0	100	389	0	.500	0			-0	/O	0.0
■ **SAM BOWEN** Bowen, Samuel Thomas b: 9/18/52, Brunswick, Ga. BR/TR, 5'9", 170 lbs. Deb: 8/25/77																												
1977	Bos-A	3	2	0	0	0	0	0	0	0	2	.000	.000	.000	.000	-85	-1	-1	117	0	0	.000	0	0	0	-1	/O	0.0
1978	Bos-A	6	7	3	1	0	0	1	1	1	2	.143	.250	.571	.821	116	0	0	107	56	1	.833	0	0	0	-1	/O	-0.1
1980	Bos-A	7	13	0	2	0	0	0	0	2	3	.154	.267	.154	.421	18	-1	-1	102	0	1	.455	1	0	0	1	/O	0.0
Total	3	16	22	3	3	0	0	1	1	3	7	.136	.240	.273	.513	39	-2	-2	105	18	2	.526	1	0	0	-1	/O	-0.1
■ **SAM BOWENS** Bowens, Samuel Edward b: 3/23/39, Wilmington, N.C. BR/TR, 6'1.5", 188 lbs. Deb: 9/07/63																												
1963	Bal-A	15	48	8	16	3	1	1	9	4	5	.333	.385	.500	.885	155	3	3	94	139	9	.879	1	1	-0	-2	O	0.1
1964	Bal-A	139	501	58	132	25	2	22	71	42	99	.263	.325	.453	.779	108	8	5	105	105	71	.718	4	3	-1	4	*O	0.4
1965	Bal-A	84	203	16	33	4	1	7	20	10	41	.163	.202	.296	.497	39	-17	-17	100	102	10	.425	7	1	2	-3	O	-2.1
1966	Bal-A	89	243	26	51	9	1	6	20	17	52	.210	.275	.329	.605	72	-9	-9	101	86	21	.547	9	3	1	2	O	-0.9
1967	Bal-A	62	120	13	22	2	1	5	12	11	43	.183	.258	.342	.599	80	-4	-3	95	89	10	.549	3	4	-2	-3	O	-0.8
1968	Was-A	57	115	14	22	4	0	4	7	11	39	.191	.262	.330	.592	86	-3	-2	91	60	11	.527	0	0	0	-1	O	-0.4
1969	Was-A	33	57	6	11	1	0	0	4	5	14	.193	.258	.211	.469	33	-5	-5	97	134	3	.375	1	1	-0	-5	O	-1.1
Total	7	479	1287	141	287	48	6	45	143	100	293	.223	.284	.375	.659	85	-26	-27	101	98	136	.608	25	13	-0	-7	O	-4.8
■ **FRANK BOWERMAN** Bowerman, Frank Eugene "Mike" b: 12/5/1868, Romeo, Mich. d: 11/30/48, Romeo, Mich. BR/TR, 6'2", 190 lbs. Deb: 8/24/1895 M																												
1895	Bal-N	1	1	0	0	0	0	0	0	0	0	.000	.000	.000	.000	-93	-0	-0	107	0	0	.000	0			0	/C	0.0
1896	Bal-N	4	16	0	2	0	0	0	4	1	0	.125	.176	.125	.301	-18	-3	-3	102	588	0	.214	0			0	/C1	-0.1
1897	Bal-N	38	130	16	41	5	0	1	21	1		.315	.331	.377	.708	93	-2	-1	95	118	18	.618	3			-3	C	0.1
1898	Bal-N	5	16	5	7	1	0	0	1	2		.438	.526	.500	1.026	193	2	2	103	38	5	1.333	1			0	/C	0.2
	Pit-N	69	241	17	66	6	3	0	29	7		.274	.297	.324	.621	82	-7	-6	98	115	25	.514	4			4	C/1	0.2
	Yr	74	257	22	73	7	3	0	30	9		.284	.313	.335	.648	90	-4	-3	98	110	29	.554	5			4		0.4
1899	Pit-N	109	424	49	110	16	10	3	53	11		.259	.286	.366	.652	81	-13	-12	99	101	48	.576	10			12	C1	0.5
1900	NY-N	80	270	25	65	5	3	1	42	6		.241	.257	.293	.550	55	-17	-16	97	160	23	.463	10			15	C/S	0.5
1901	NY-N	59	191	20	38	5	3	0	14	7		.199	.227	.257	.484	46	-14	-12	91	96	12	.386	3			-0	C/2S31	-0.5
1902	NY-N	107	367	38	93	14	6	0	26	13		.253	.279	.324	.603	88	-6	-6	100	77	37	.526	12			2	C/1	0.6
1903	NY-N	64	210	22	58	6	2	1	31	6		.276	.296	.338	.634	77	-5	-7	106	135	23	.539	5			0	C/1O	-0.1
1904	NY-N	93	289	38	67	11	4	2	27	16		.232	.272	.318	.590	80	-6	-8	105	101	28	.518	7			-6	C/12P	-0.6
1905	NY-N	98	297	37	80	8	1	3	41	12		.269	.298	.333	.631	89	-4	-5	101	132	32	.539	6			-10	C1/2	-0.7
1906	NY-N	103	285	23	65	7	3	1	42	15		.228	.267	.284	.551	73	-9	-9	100	182	24	.459	5			-1	C1	-0.5
1907	NY-N	96	311	31	81	8	2	0	32	17		.260	.299	.299	.598	85	-4	-6	105	130	32	.526	11			-7	C1	-0.8
1908	Bos-N	86	254	16	58	8	1	1	25	13		.228	.266	.280	.545	73	-7	-8	104	130	19	.449	4			2	C1	-0.3
1909	Bos-N	33	99	6	21	2	0	0	4	2		.212	.228	.232	.460	45	-7	-6	96	63	5	.321	0			2	CM	-0.2

YEAR	TM/L	G	AB	R	H	2B	3B	HR	RBI	BB	SO	AVG	OBP	SLG	PRO	/A	BR	/A	PF	CHI	RC	TA	SB	CS	SBR	FR	POS	TPR
Total	15	1045	3401	343	852	102	38	13	392	129	0	.251	.280	.314	.594	77	-102	-102	100	122	331	.505	81			13	C1/2S3PO	-1.7
■ BILLY BOWERS	Bowers, Grover Bill b: 3/25/23, Parkin, Ark. BL/TR, 5'9.5", 176 lbs. Deb: 4/24/49																											
1949	Chi-A	26	78	5	15	2	1	0	6	4	5	.192	.232	.244	.475	26	-9	-8	98	108	4	.353	1	1	-0	1	O	-0.8
■ FRANK BOWES	Bowes, Frank M. b: 1865, Bath, N.Y. d: 1/21/1895, New York, N.Y. TR, 5'9", 160 lbs. Deb: 4/17/1890																											
1890	BB-a	61	232	28	51	5	2	0		7		.220	.246	.259	.504	50	-15	-15	100	0	18	.436	11			0	CO3/1S	-1.2
■ WELDON BOWLIN	Bowlin, Lois Weldon "Hoss" b: 12/10/40, Paragould, Ark. BR/TR, 5'9", 155 lbs. Deb: 9/27/67																											
1967	KC-A	2	5	0	1	0	0	0	0	0	0	.200	.200	.200	.400	19	-1	-1	100	0	0	.250	0	0	0	0	/3	0.0
■ STEVE BOWLING	Bowling, Stephen Shaddon b: 6/26/52, Tulsa, Okla. BR/TR, 6', 185 lbs. Deb: 9/07/76																											
1976	Mil-A	14	42	4	7	2	0	0	2	2	5	.167	.205	.214	.419	23	-4	-4	99	85	2	.314	0	0	0	2	O/D	-0.1
1977	Tor-A	89	194	19	40	8	1	1	13	37	42	.206	.333	.273	.607	66	-8	-8	103	92	18	.558	2	3	-1	0	O	-1.1
Total	2	103	236	23	47	10	1	1	15	39	47	.199	.313	.263	.575	59	-12	-12	102	91	20	.515	2	3	-1	3	O/D	-1.2
■ ELMER BOWMAN	Bowman, Elmari Wilhelm "Big Bow" b: 3/19/1897, Proctor, Vt. BR/TR, 6'0.5", 193 lbs. Deb: 8/03/20																											
1920	Was-A	2	1	1	0	0	0	0	0	1	0	.000	.500	.000	.500	43	0	0	95	0	0	1.000	0	0	0	0	H	0.0
■ ERNIE BOWMAN	Bowman, Ernest Ferrell b: 7/28/35, Johnson City, Tenn. BR/TR, 5'10", 160 lbs. Deb: 4/12/61																											
1961	SF-N	38	38	10	8	0	2	0	2	1	8	.211	.231	.316	.547	44	-3	-3	98	67	3	.484	2	0	1	-2	2S/3	-0.1
1962	SF-N	46	42	9	8	1	0	1	4	1	10	.190	.227	.286	.513	36	-4	-4	101	105	2	.389	0	1	-1	-1	23S	-0.2
1963	SF-N	81	125	10	23	3	0	0	4	0	15	.184	.184	.208	.392	13	-14	-13	96	65	4	.255	1	2	-1	-4	S23	-1.3
Total	3	165	205	29	39	4	2	1	10	2	33	.190	.202	.244	.446	25	-21	-20	97	74	9	.327	3	3	-1	-6	/S23	-1.6
■ JOE BOWMAN	Bowman, Joseph Emil b: 6/17/10, Argentine, Kan. BL/TR, 6'2", 190 lbs. Deb: 4/18/32																											
1932	Phi-A	7	1	0	1	0	0	0	0	0	0	1.000	1.000	1.000	2.000	368	0	0	114	0	1	—	0	0	0	1	/P	0.0
1934	NY-N	31	29	4	5	0	1	0	4	2	3	.172	.226	.241	.467	26	-3	-3	98	206	2	.375	0			-0	P	0.0
1935	Phi-N	49	67	6	13	1	1	1	7	4	7	.194	.239	.284	.523	35	-6	-7	114	115	5	.436	1			-1	P/O	0.0
1936	Phi-N	44	77	9	15	1	0	0	6	6	14	.195	.253	.208	.461	23	-8	-9	108	133	4	.349	0			-3	P	0.0
1937	Pit-N	35	47	3	10	1	0	0	4	5	9	.213	.288	.234	.523	42	-4	-4	102	131	3	.410	0			0	P	0.0
1938	Pit-N	18	21	5	7	0	1	0	1	1	3	.333	.364	.429	.792	117	0	0	100	40	4	.714	0			-1	P	0.0
1939	Pit-N	70	96	9	33	8	1	0	18	5	9	.344	.382	.448	.830	123	3	3	100	153	17	.766	0			0	P	0.0
1940	Pit-N	57	90	11	22	5	1	1	14	14	14	.244	.352	.356	.708	100	-0	0	95	148	12	.662	0			0	P	0.0
1941	Pit-N	22	31	4	8	1	0	0	1	1	2	.258	.281	.290	.572	60	-2	-2	103	40	2	.417	0			-0	P	0.0
1944	Bos-A	59	100	7	20	5	2	0	16	5	19	.200	.238	.290	.528	52	-7	-6	98	199	7	.432	1	0	0	-2	P	-0.4
1945	Bos-A	9	9	0	2	0	0	0	1	1	1	.222	.300	.222	.522	55	-1	-0	95	181	1	.429	0	0	0	-0	/P	0.0
	Cin-N	29	71	4	5	2	1	0	3	2	9	.070	.096	.127	.223	-41	-13	-13	94	116	1	.176	1			-2	P	0.0
Total	11	430	639	62	141	24	8	2	75	46	90	.221	.275	.293	.568	55	-39	-40	101	141	58	.476	3	0		-8	P/O	-0.4
■ BOB BOWMAN	Bowman, Robert Leroy b: 5/10/31, Laytonville, Cal. BR/TR, 6'1", 195 lbs. Deb: 4/16/55																											
1955	Phi-N	3	3	0	0	0	0	0	0	0	0	.000	.000	.000	.000	-98	-1	-1	102	0	0	.000	0	0	0	-0	/O	0.0
1956	Phi-N	6	16	2	3	0	1	1	2	0	6	.188	.188	.500	.688	81	-1	-1	94	77	2	.615	0	0	0	-1	/O	-0.1
1957	Phi-N	99	237	31	63	8	2	6	23	27	50	.266	.356	.392	.748	103	1	2	98	86	35	.708	0	0	0	-5	O	-0.5
1958	Phi-N	91	184	31	53	11	2	8	24	16	30	.288	.345	.500	.845	122	5	5	98	85	31	.794	0	1	-1	-8	O	-0.4
1959	Phi-N	57	79	7	10	0	0	2	5	5	23	.127	.179	.203	.381	1	-11	-11	99	92	3	.292	0	0	0	-1	O/P	-1.1
Total	5	256	519	71	129	19	5	17	54	48	109	.249	.319	.403	.722	93	-7	-6	98	86	70	.668	0	1	-1	-16	O/P	-2.1
■ BILL BOWMAN	Bowman, William G. b: 1869, Chicago, Ill. 5'11", 180 lbs. Deb: 6/18/1891																											
1891	Chi-N	15	45	2	4	1	0	0	5	5	9	.089	.196	.111	.307	-8	-6	-6	106	292	1	.268	0			0	C	-0.5
■ RED BOWSER	Bowser, James H. b: Greensburg, Pa. Deb: 9/13/10																											
1910	Chi-A	1	2	0	0	0	0	0	0	0		.000	.000	.000	.000	-99	-0	-0	95	0	0	.000	0			-0	/O	0.0
■ FRANK BOYD	Boyd, Frank Jay b: 4/2/1868, West Middletown, Pa d: 12/16/37, Oil City, Pa. BR/TR, Deb: 5/18/1893																											
1893	Cle-N	2	5	3	1	1	0	0	3	1	0	.200	.333	.400	.733	93	-0	-0	104	411	1	.750	0			0	/C	0.0
■ JAKE BOYD	Boyd, Jacob Henry b: 1/19/1874, Martinsburg, W.Va. d: 8/12/32, Gettysburg, Pa. TL, 160 lbs. Deb: 9/20/1894																											
1894	Was-N	6	21	1	3	0	0	0	1	1	4	.143	.182	.143	.325	-21	-4	-4	98	92	1	.333	2			0	/OP	-0.2
1895	Was-N	51	157	29	42	5	1	1	16	20	28	.268	.375	.331	.706	82	-2	-3	103	81	21	.704	2			0	OP2/S3	-0.2
1896	Was-N	4	13	1	1	0	0	0	1	1	1	.077	.200	.077	.277	-26	-2	-2	95	288	0	.250	0			0	/P	0.0
Total	3	61	191	31	46	5	1	1	18	22	33	.241	.344	.293	.637	65	-9	-9	102	96	22	.621	4			0	/OP2S3	-0.4
■ BOB BOYD	Boyd, Robert Richard "The Rope" b: 10/1/26, Potts Camp, Miss. BL/TL, 5'10", 170 lbs. Deb: 9/08/51																											
1951	Chi-A	12	18	3	3	0	1	0	4	3	3	.167	.286	.278	.563	55	-1	-1	97	286	2	.533	0	0	0	0	/1	0.0
1953	Chi-A	55	165	20	49	6	2	3	23	13	11	.297	.352	.412	.764	100	1	-0	106	111	23	.675	1	4	-2	-1	1O	-0.3
1954	Chi-A	29	56	10	10	3	0	0	5	4	3	.179	.233	.232	.465	27	-6	-6	104	146	3	.388	2	0	1	-2	O1	-0.7
1956	Bal-A	70	225	28	70	8	3	2	11	30	14	.311	.395	.400	.795	117	4	6	94	44	35	.729	0	5	-3	-2	1/O	-0.1
1957	Bal-A	141	485	73	154	16	8	4	34	55	31	.318	.389	.408	.798	127	14	18	93	65	80	.758	2	4	-2	-3	*1/O	1.2
1958	Bal-A	125	401	58	124	21	5	7	36	25	24	.309	.353	.439	.792	124	8	11	94	73	62	.721	1	1	-0	-3	1	0.5
1959	Bal-A	128	415	42	110	20	2	3	41	29	14	.265	.315	.345	.659	83	-11	-9	97	106	44	.553	3	1	0	-9	*1	-1.7
1960	Bal-A	71	82	9	26	5	2	0	9	6	5	.317	.364	.427	.790	111	1	1	102	101	12	.683	0	0	0	-0	1	0.0
1961	KC-A	26	48	7	11	2	0	0	9	1	2	.229	.245	.271	.516	37	-4	-4	102	271	2	.350	0	2	-1	0	/1	-0.5
	Mil-N	36	41	3	10	0	0	0	3	1	7	.244	.262	.244	.506	38	-4	-3	92	121	3	.344	0	0	0	0	/1	-0.3
Total	9	693	1936	253	567	81	23	19	175	167	114	.293	.351	.388	.739	105	3	13	96	89	266	.673	9	17	-8	-20	1/O	-1.9
■ BILL BOYD	Boyd, William J. b: 12/22/1852, New York d: 10/1/12, Queens, N.Y. Deb: 4/22/1872 M																											
1872	Mut-n	35	169	25	43							.254															*3/SO	
1873	Atl-n	48	233	31	63							.270															*O/3	
1874	Har-n	26	123	22	47							.382															3O	
1875	Atl-n	36	154	14	45							.292															2O/31M	
Total	4 n	145	679	92	198							.292															2O/31M	
■ CLETE BOYER	Boyer, Cletis Leroy b: 2/9/37, Cassville, Mo. BR/TR, 6', 165 lbs. Deb: 6/05/55 C																											
1955	KC-A	47	79	3	19	1	0	0	6	3	17	.241	.268	.253	.521	40	-7	-7	101	112	5	.365	0	0	0	-0	S32	-0.4
1956	KC-A	67	129	15	28	3	1	1	4	11	24	.217	.284	.279	.563	49	-10	-10	101	38	10	.471	1	1	-0	2	2/3	-0.3
1957	KC-A	10	0	0	0	0	0	0	0	0	0	—	—	—	—	—	0	0	99	—	—	—	0	0	0	0	/23	0.0
1959	NY-A	47	114	4	20	2	0	0	3	6	23	.175	.217	.193	.410	14	-13	-12	93	54	5	.302	1	0	0	2	S3	-0.8
1960	NY-A	124	393	54	95	20	1	14	46	23	85	.242	.289	.405	.693	90	-10	-7	94	90	44	.607	2	3	-1	15	3S	1.1
1961	NY-A	148	504	61	113	19	5	11	55	63	83	.224	.313	.347	.660	79	-17	-14	96	106	55	.592	1	3	-2	**32**	*3S/O	2.4
1962	NY-A	158	566	85	154	24	1	18	68	51	106	.272	.335	.413	.749	107	-0	5	94	96	76	.675	3	2	-0	**36**	*3	4.1
1963	NY-A	152	557	59	140	20	3	12	54	33	91	.251	.296	.363	.658	83	-13	-13	101	97	60	.568	4	2	0	18	*3/S2	0.7
1964	NY-A	147	510	43	111	10	5	8	52	36	93	.218	.271	.304	.574	58	-28	-30	103	123	41	.481	6	1	1	18	*3S	-0.8
1965	NY-A	148	514	69	129	23	6	18	58	39	79	.251	.306	.424	.730	104	2	1	101	90	63	.654	4	1	1	**28**	*3/S	3.3
1966	NY-A	144	500	59	120	22	4	14	57	46	48	.240	.307	.384	.691	104	-2	2	94	104	60	.632	6	0	2	19	3S	2.4
1967	Atl-N	154	572	63	140	18	3	26	96	39	81	.245	.295	.423	.718	99	1	-2	104	127	68	.644	6	3	0	3	*3/S	-0.6
1968	Atl-N	71	273	19	62	7	2	4	17	16	32	.227	.275	.311	.586	81	-8	-6	93	78	22	.479	2	0	1	-1	3	-0.7
1969	Atl-N	144	496	57	124	16	1	14	57	55	87	.250	.330	.371	.701	93	-2	-5	104	103	58	.623	3	7	-3	-3	*3	-1.0
1970	Atl-N	134	475	44	117	14	1	16	62	41	71	.246	.308	.381	.689	80	-12	-15	104	107	53	.602	2	5	-2	9	*3/S	-1.0
1971	Atl-N	30	98	10	24	1	0	6	19	8	11	.245	.302	.439	.741	98	1	-1	110	127	13	.680	0	0	0	1	3/S	0.1
Total	16	1725	5780	645	1396	200	33	162	654	470	931	.242	.301	.372	.673	86	-119	-114	99	101	645	.608	41	28	-5	178	*3S/2O	8.5

YEAR	TM/L	G	AB	R	H	2B	3B	HR	RBI	BB	SO	AVG	OBP	SLG	PRO	/A	BR	/A	PF	CHI	RC	TA	SB	CS	SBR	FR	POS	TPR
■ **KEN BOYER**	Boyer, Kenton Lloyd b: 5/20/31, Liberty, Mo. d: 9/7/82, St.Louis, Mo. BR/TR, 6'1.5", 190 lbs. Deb: 4/12/55 MC																											
1955	StL-N	147	530	78	140	27	2	18	62	37	67	.264	.313	.425	.738	93	-6	-6	101	92	67	.690	22	17	-4	5	*3S	-0.5
1956	StL-N	150	595	91	182	30	2	26	98	38	65	.306	.349	.494	.843	124	18	19	99	118	97	.786	8	3	1	8	*3	2.7
1957	StL-N	142	544	79	144	18	3	19	62	44	77	.265	.321	.414	.734	95	-4	-5	101	93	70	.673	12	8	-1	-6	*O3	-1.3
1958	StL-N	150	570	101	175	21	9	23	90	49	53	.307	.365	.496	.861	118	20	15	106	112	100	.832	11	6	-0	22	*3/OS	3.7
1959	StL-N	149	563	86	174	18	5	28	94	67	77	.309	.384	.508	.892	129	29	25	105	109	112	.913	12	6	0	11	*3S	3.2
1960	StL-N	151	552	95	168	26	10	32	97	56	77	.304	.373	.562	.934	140	38	32	108	103	111	.936	8	7	-2	16	*3	4.5
1961	StL-N	153	589	109	194	26	11	24	95	68	91	.329	.400	.533	.933	128	38	28	113	105	126	.951	6	3	0	13	*3	3.3
1962	StL-N	160	611	92	178	27	5	24	98	75	104	.291	.370	.470	.839	114	21	14	109	114	105	.824	12	7	-1	3	*3	2.0
1963	StL-N	159	617	86	176	28	2	24	111	70	90	.285	.360	.454	.814	124	26	21	107	140	98	.766	1	0	0	-14	*3	0.9
1964	StL-N	162	628	100	185	30	10	24	**119**	70	85	.295	.367	.489	.856	124	32	23	112	136	107	.813	3	5	-2	3	*3	1.6
1965	StL-N	144	535	71	139	18	2	13	75	57	73	.260	.332	.374	.706	92	-0	-5	107	138	64	.621	2	7	-4	-9	*3	-2.4
1966	NY-N	136	496	62	132	28	2	14	61	30	64	.266	.308	.415	.723	105	-2	2	94	105	59	.628	4	3	-1	13	*3/1	1.2
1967	NY-N	56	166	17	39	7	2	3	13	26	22	.235	.339	.355	.694	100	0	1	99	79	20	.649	2	1	0	2	3/1	0.0
	Chi-A	57	180	17	47	5	1	4	21	7	25	.261	.289	.367	.655	99	-2	-1	94	112	18	.525	0	2	-1	2	31	0.0
1968	Chi-A	10	24	0	3	0	0	0	0	1	6	.125	.160	.125	.285	-13	-3	-3	101	0	0	.174	0	0	0	0	/31	-0.3
	LA-N	83	221	20	60	7	2	6	41	16	34	.271	.324	.403	.726	129	4	6	91	161	29	.655	2	2	-1	0	31	0.5
1969	LA-N	25	34	0	7	2	0	0	4	2	7	.206	.250	.265	.515	45	-3	-2	99	178	2	.379	0	0	0	0	/1	-0.2
Total	15	2034	7455	1104	2143	318	68	282	1141	713	1017	.287	.351	.462	.813	115	207	164	105	115	1184	.794	105	77	-15	69	*3O/1S	18.9
■ **DOE BOYLAND**	Boyland, Dorian Scott b: 1/6/55, Chicago, Ill. BL/TL, 6'4", 200 lbs. Deb: 9/04/78																											
1978	Pit-N	6	8	1	2	0	0	0	1	0	1	.250	.250	.250	.500	38	-1	-1	105	198	1	.333	0	0	0	0	/1	0.0
1979	Pit-N	4	3	0	0	0	0	0	0	0	2	.000	.000	.000	.000	-95	-1	-1	106	0	0	.000	0	0	0	0	/H	0.0
1981	Pit-N	11	8	0	0	0	0	0	0	1	3	.000	.111	.000	.111	-69	-2	-2	96	0	0	.125	0	0	0	0	/H	-0.1
Total	3	21	19	1	2	0	0	0	1	1	6	.105	.150	.105	.255	-27	-3	-3	101	79	1	.176	0	0	0	0	/1	-0.1
■ **EDDIE BOYLE**	Boyle, Edward J. b: 5/8/1874, Cincinnati, Ohio d: 2/9/41, Cincinnati, Ohio 6'3", 200 lbs. Deb: 4/17/1896																											
1896	Lou-N	3	9	0	0	0	0	0	0	2	2	.000	.182	.000	.182	-50	-2	-2	98	0	0	.222	0			0	/C	-0.1
	Pit-N	2	5	0	0	0	0	0	0	0	1	.000	.000	.000	.000	-99	-1	-1	93	0	0	.000	0			0	/C	0.0
	Yr	5	14	0	0	0	0	0	0	2	3	.000	.125	.000	.125	-67	-3	-3	96	0	0	.143	0			0		-0.1
Total	1	5	14	0	0	0	0	0	0	2	3	.000	.125	.000	.125	-67	-3	-3	97	0	0	.143	0			0	/C	-0.1
■ **JIM BOYLE**	Boyle, James John b: 1/19/04, Cincinnati, Ohio d: 12/24/58, Cincinnati, Ohio BR/TR, 6', 180 lbs. Deb: 6/20/26																											
1926	NY-N	1	0	0	0	0	0	0	0	0	0	—	—	—	—	—	0	0	98	—	—	—	0			0	/C	0.0
■ **JACK BOYLE**	Boyle, John Anthony "Honest Jack" b: 3/22/1866, Cincinnati, Ohio d: 1/7/13, Cincinnati, Ohio BL/TR, 6'4", 190 lbs. Deb: 10/08/1886																											
1886	Cin-a	1	5	0	1	0	0	0		0		.200	.200	.200	.400	28	-0	-0	96	0	0	.250	0			0	/C	0.0
1887	StL-a	88	350	48	66	3	1	2		20		.189	.237	.220	.457	27	-33	-38	110	0	20	.373	7			-17	C/O13	-3.3
1888	StL-a	71	257	33	62	8	1	1	23	13		.241	.286	.292	.578	80	-3	-7	111	90	25	.523	11			8	C/O	0.8
1889	StL-a	99	347	54	85	11	4	4	42	21	42	.245	.301	.334	.636	74	-8	-15	112	94	37	.569	5			-11	C3/O12	-1.4
1890	Chi-P	100	369	56	96	9	5	1	49	44	29	.260	.347	.320	.667	77	-9	-12	104	113	46	.652	11			-3	C3S/1O	-0.9
1891	StL-a	123	439	78	123	18	8	5	79	47	36	.280	.365	.392	.757	105	12	1	114	122	72	.791	19			-16	CS/3O21	-0.9
1892	NY-N	120	436	52	80	8	8	0	32	36	40	.183	.252	.239	.491	51	-26	-25	98	96	29	.433	10			7	C1/OS	-1.4
1893	Phi-N	116	504	105	144	29	9	4	81	41	30	.286	.351	.403	.754	102	1	1	100	109	81	.767	22			7	*1/C2	0.6
1894	Phi-N	114	495	98	149	21	10	4	88	45	26	.301	.363	.408	.771	92	-10	-5	95	120	83	.783	21			2	*1/32	-0.1
1895	Phi-N	133	565	90	143	17	4	0	67	35	23	.253	.302	.297	.600	57	-36	-35	99	118	56	.524	13			-6	*1	-3.0
1896	Phi-N	40	145	17	43	4	1	1	28	6	7	.297	.346	.359	.705	86	-2	-3	102	147	20	.647	3			0	C1	-0.1
1897	Phi-N	75	288	37	73	9	1	2	36	19		.253	.306	.313	.619	68	-14	-12	96	112	29	.535	3			-3	C1	-0.6
1898	Phi-N	6	22	0	2	0	1	0	3	1		.091	.130	.182	.312	-10	-3	-3	95	231	1	.250	0			0	/1C	-0.2
Total	13	1086	4222	668	1067	137	53	24	528	328	233	.253	.315	.327	.643	75	-132	-154	103	103	499	.600	125			-31	C1/3SO2	-10.5
■ **JACK BOYLE**	Boyle, John Bellew b: 7/9/1889, Morris, Ill. d: 4/3/71, Ft.Lauderdale, Fla. BL/TR, 5'11.5", 165 lbs. Deb: 6/28/12																											
1912	Phi-N	15	25	4	7	1	0	0	2	1	5	.280	.308	.320	.628	72	-1	-1	100	84	2	.500	0			0	/3S	0.0
■ **BUZZ BOYLE**	Boyle, Ralph Francis b: 2/9/08, Cincinnati, Ohio d: 11/12/78, Cincinnati, Ohio BL/TL, 5'11.5", 170 lbs. Deb: 9/11/29																											
1929	Bos-N	17	57	8	15	2	1	1	2	6	11	.263	.333	.386	.719	83	-2	-1	94	28	7	.714	2			-2	O	-0.3
1930	Bos-N	1	1	0	0	0	0	0	0	0	1	.000	.000	.000	.000	-99	-0	-0	97	0	0	.000	0			-0	/O	0.0
1933	Bro-N	93	338	38	101	13	4	0	31	16	24	.299	.331	.361	.691	101	-1	-0	97	97	42	.607	7			-5	O	-1.1
1934	Bro-N	128	472	88	144	26	10	7	48	51	44	.305	.376	.447	.823	126	14	17	95	76	84	.815	8			11	*O	2.2
1935	Bro-N	127	475	51	129	17	9	4	44	43	45	.272	.332	.371	.703	94	-7	-3	94	86	62	.646	7			2	*O	-0.6
Total	5	366	1343	185	389	58	24	12	125	116	125	.290	.347	.395	.743	107	3	12	95	83	196	.704	24			6	O	0.2
■ **GIBBY BRACK**	Brack, Gilbert Herman b: 3/29/08, Chicago, Ill. d: 1/20/60, Greenville, Tex. BR/TR, 5'9", 170 lbs. Deb: 4/23/37																											
1937	Bro-N	112	372	60	102	27	9	5	38	44	93	.274	.351	.435	.786	108	6	4	104	77	60	.779	9			2	*O	0.2
1938	Bro-N	40	56	10	12	2	1	1	6	4	14	.214	.267	.339	.606	69	-3	-2	96	99	5	.545	1			2	O	0.0
	Phi-N	72	282	40	81	20	4	4	28	18	30	.287	.332	.429	.761	108	2	2	100	81	41	.689	2			2	O	0.3
	Yr	112	338	50	93	22	5	5	34	22	44	.275	.321	.414	.736	102	-0	0	99	88	46	.664	3			4		0.3
1939	Phi-N	91	270	40	78	21	4	6	41	26	49	.289	.351	.463	.814	125	6	8	94	105	45	.776	1			-2	O1	0.3
Total	3	315	980	150	273	70	18	16	113	92	186	.279	.341	.436	.777	110	12	12	100	87	151	.750	13			4	O/1	0.8
■ **BUDDY BRADFORD**	Bradford, Charles William b: 7/25/44, Mobile, Ala. BR/TR, 5'11", 170 lbs. Deb: 9/09/66																											
1966	Chi-A	14	28	3	4	0	0	0	0	2	6	.143	.200	.143	.343	0	-4	-3	94	0	1	.250	0	0	0	-3	/O	-0.6
1967	Chi-A	24	20	6	2	1	0	0	1	1	7	.100	.143	.150	.293	-14	-3	-3	94	139	1	.278	1	0	0	-4	O	-0.7
1968	Chi-A	103	281	32	61	11	0	5	24	23	67	.217	.281	.310	.591	78	-7	-7	101	101	24	.517	8	4	0	-5	O	-1.8
1969	Chi-A	93	273	36	70	8	2	11	27	34	75	.256	.347	.421	.769	105	5	2	108	73	42	.756	5	2	0	-4	O	-0.3
1970	Chi-A	32	91	8	17	3	0	2	8	10	30	.187	.267	.286	.553	50	-6	-7	106	101	6	.457	1	2	-1	-1	O	-1.0
	Cle-A	75	163	25	32	6	1	7	23	21	43	.196	.292	.374	.666	72	-4	-7	115	113	16	.593	0	1	-1	-0	O/3	-1.0
	Yr	107	254	33	49	9	1	9	31	31	73	.193	.283	.343	.626	64	-10	-14	112	111	24	.556	1	3	-2	-1		-2.0
1971	Cle-A	20	38	4	6	2	1	0	3	6	10	.158	.273	.263	.536	50	-2	-3	106	122	3	.471	0	0	0	1	O	-0.2
	Cin-N	79	100	17	20	3	0	2	12	14	23	.200	.316	.290	.606	75	-3	-3	96	140	10	.595	4	2	0	-13	O	-1.9
1972	Chi-A	35	48	13	13	2	0	2	8	4	13	.271	.340	.438	.777	123	2	1	106	124	6	.725	3	2	-0	-4	O	-0.4
1973	Chi-A	53	168	24	40	3	1	8	15	17	43	.238	.316	.411	.726	101	0	-0	102	63	20	.672	4	5	-2	8	O	0.5
1974	Chi-A	39	96	16	32	2	0	5	10	13	11	.333	.418	.510	.929	163	8	8	102	61	20	.928	1	2	-1	-4	O/D	0.3
1975	Chi-A	25	58	8	9	3	1	2	15	8	22	.155	.290	.345	.635	76	-2	-2	103	222	6	.654	3	2	-0	-2	O/D	-0.4
	StL-N	50	81	12	22	1	0	4	15	12	24	.272	.366	.432	.798	117	2	2	103	123	12	.734	0	2	-1	-2	O	-0.1
1976	Chi-A	55	160	20	35	5	2	4	14	19	37	.219	.309	.350	.659	94	-1	-1	99	79	20	.664	6	0	2	-5	O/D	-0.5
Total	11	697	1605	224	363	50	8	52	175	184	411	.226	.313	.364	.678	90	-14	-22	104	97	185	.651	36	24	-4	-38	O/D3	-8.1
■ **VIC BRADFORD**	Bradford, Henry Victor b: 3/5/15, Brownsville, Tenn. BR/TR, 6'2", 190 lbs. Deb: 5/01/43																											
1943	NY-N	6	5	1	1	0	0	0	1	1	1	.200	.333	.200	.533	58	-0	-0	96	361	0	.500	0			0	/O	0.0
■ **BRADLEY**	Bradley 5'10", 185 lbs. Deb: 5/21/1884																											
1884	Was-U	1	3	0	0	0	0	0		2		.000	.400	.000	.400	47	0	0	97	0	0	.667	0			0	/O	0.0
■ **GEORGE BRADLEY**	Bradley, George Washington "Grin" b: 7/13/1852, Reading, Pa. d: 10/2/31, Philadelphia, Pa. BR/TR, 5'10.5", 175 lbs. Deb: 5/04/1875																											
1875	StL-n	61	250	28	67							.268															*P/3O	
1876	StL-N	64	265	29	66	7	6	0	28	3	12	.249	.257	.321	.578	105	-2	3	88	114	22	.442				3	*P	0.0
1877	Chi-N	55	214	31	52	7	3	0	12	6	19	.243	.264	.304	.567	80	-5	-5	98	64	18	.438				-8	*P3/1O	0.0
1879	Tro-N	63	251	36	62	9	5	0	23	1	20	.247	.250	.323	.573	93	-3	-1	93	102	21	.434				5	P/31OS	0.0
1880	Pro-N	82	309	32	70	7	6	0	23	5	38	.227	.239	.288	.527	81	-7	-5	96	96	22	.393				16	*3P/O1	1.0

YEAR	TM/L	G	AB	R	H	2B	3B	HR	RBI	BB	SO	AVG	OBP	SLG	PRO	/A	BR	/A	PF	CHI	RC	TA	SB	CS	SBR	FR	POS	TPR
1881	Det-N	1	4	0	0	0	0	0	0	0	0	.000	.000	.000	.000	-94	-1	-1	106	0	0	.000				0	/S	0.0
	Cle-N	60	241	21	60	10	1	2	18	4	25	.249	.261	.324	.585	86	-5	-4	96	76	21	.453				-8	3/PSO	-0.6
	Yr	61	245	21	60	10	1	2	18	4	25	.245	.257	.318	.575	83	-6	-5	96	75	21	.443				-8		-0.6
1882	Cle-N	30	115	16	21	5	0	0	6	4	16	.183	.210	.226	.436	45	-7	-6	90	79	6	.319				0	P/O1	0.0
1883	Cle-N	4	16	0	5	0	1	0	1	0	1	.313	.313	.438	.750	119	0	0	105	52	2	.636				0	/S	0.0
	Phi-a	76	312	47	73	8	5	1		8		.234	.253	.301	.554	76	-8	-9	103	0	24	.427				1	3PO/1	-0.5
1884	Cin-U	58	226	31	43	4	7	0		7		.190	.215	.270	.485	58	-8	-11	108	0	13	.372	0			3	PO/S1	0.0
1886	Phi-a	13	48	1	4	0	1	0		1		.083	.102	.125	.227	-28	-7	-7	100	0	1	.205	2			0	S	-0.5
1888	Bal-a	1	3	0	0	0	0	0	0	0		.000	.000	.000	.000	-99	-1	-1	96	0	0	.000	0			0	/S	0.0
Total	10	507	2004	244	456	57	35	3	111	39	131	.228	.242	.295	.538	77	-55	-46	97	63	150	.409	2			11	P3/OS1	-0.6
■ **GEORGE BRADLEY** Bradley, George Washington b: 4/1/14, Greenwood, Ark. d: 10/19/82, Lawrenceburg, Tenn BR/TR, 6'1.5", 185 lbs. Deb: 4/28/46																												
1946	StL-A	4	12	2	2	1	0	0	3	0	1	.167	.167	.250	.417	16	-1	-1	98	380	0	.250	0	0	0	-0	/O	-0.1
■ **HUGH BRADLEY** Bradley, Hugh Frederick "Corns" b: 5/23/1885, Grafton, Mass. d: 1/26/49, Worcester, Mass. BR/TR, 5'10", 175 lbs. Deb: 4/25/10																												
1910	Bos-A	32	83	8	14	6	2	0	7	5		.169	.216	.289	.505	59	-4	-4	99	108	6	.449	2			-1	1/CO	-0.4
1911	Bos-A	12	41	9	13	2	0	1	4	2		.317	.364	.439	.803	125	1	1	99	64	7	.786	1			-0	1	0.1
1912	Bos-A	40	137	16	26	11	1	1	19	15		.190	.275	.307	.581	62	-6	-8	107	144	13	.550	3			-1	1	-0.7
1914	Pit-F	118	427	41	131	20	6	0	61	27	27	.307	.348	.382	.730	115	5	8	94	138	63	.666	7			-2	*1	0.8
1915	Pit-F	26	66	3	18	4	1	0	6	4	0	.273	.314	.364	.678	97	-0	-0	104	90	8	.625	2			0	O	0.0
	Bro-F	37	126	7	31	3	2	0	18	4	0	.246	.269	.302	.571	70	-5	-5	98	171	12	.505	6			0	1/OC	-0.4
	New-F	12	33	0	5	0	0	0	2	2	0	.152	.200	.152	.352	5	-4	-4	94	144	1	.321	2			0	/1	-0.3
	Yr	75	225	10	54	7	3	0	26	10	0	.240	.272	.298	.570	69	-9	-9	99	142	21	.509	10			0		-0.7
Total	5	277	913	84	238	46	12	2	117	59	27	.261	.307	.344	.651	91	-14	-12	98	134	110	.590	23			-5	1/OC	-0.9
■ **JACK BRADLEY** Bradley, John Thomas b: 9/20/1893, Denver, Colo. d: 3/18/69, Tulsa, Okla. BR/TR, 5'11", 175 lbs. Deb: 6/18/16																												
1916	Cle-A	2	3	0	0	0	0	0	0	0	1	.000	.000	.000	.000	-99	-1	-1	100	0	0	.000	0			0	/C	0.0
■ **MARK BRADLEY** Bradley, Mark Allen b: 12/3/56, Elizabethtown, Ky. BR/TR, 6'1", 180 lbs. Deb: 9/03/81																												
1981	LA-N	9	6	2	1	1	0	0	0	0	1	.167	.167	.333	.500	40	-1	-0	98	0	0	.400	0	0	0	-1	/O	-0.1
1982	LA-N	8	3	1	1	0	0	0	0	0	0	.333	.333	.333	.667	92	-0	-0	95	0	0	.500	0	0	0	-1	/O	0.0
1983	NY-N	73	104	10	21	4	0	3	5	11	35	.202	.278	.327	.605	68	-5	-5	99	46	9	.563	4	2	0	-5	O	-1.0
Total	3	90	113	13	23	5	0	3	5	11	36	.204	.274	.327	.602	67	-5	-5	98	43	10	.553	4	2	0	-7	/O	-1.1
■ **PHIL BRADLEY** Bradley, Philip Poole b: 3/11/59, Bloomington, Ind. BR/TR, 6', 185 lbs. Deb: 9/02/83																												
1983	Sea-A	23	67	8	18	2	0	0	5	8	5	.269	.347	.299	.645	80	-2	-2	100	98	8	.620	3	1	0	-1	O/D	-0.2
1984	Sea-A	124	322	49	97	12	4	0	24	34	61	.301	.373	.363	.737	103	3	3	102	82	46	.732	21	8	2	-2	*O/D	0.0
1985	Sea-A	159	641	100	192	33	8	26	88	55	129	.300	.366	.498	.863	141	29	34	95	78	116	.864	22	9	1	4	*O	3.6
1986	Sea-A	143	526	88	163	27	4	12	50	77	134	.310	.406	.445	.851	126	27	23	105	78	99	.885	21	12	-1	-3	*O	1.4
1987	Sea-A	158	603	101	179	38	10	14	67	84	119	.297	.390	.463	.853	123	25	23	103	74	113	.909	40	10	6	-4	*O	1.9
1988	Phi-N	154	569	77	150	30	5	11	56	54	106	.264	.344	.392	.736	110	9	8	101	93	78	.692	11	9	-2	6	*O	0.9
Total	6	761	2728	423	799	142	31	63	290	312	554	.293	.375	.437	.812	122	92	89	101	81	460	.839	118	49	6	-0	O/D	7.6
■ **SCOTT BRADLEY** Bradley, Scott William b: 3/22/60, Glen Ridge, N.J. BL/TR, 5'11", 185 lbs. Deb: 9/09/84																												
1984	NY-A	9	21	3	6	1	0	0	2	1	1	.286	.318	.333	.652	86	-1	-0	94	114	2	.533	0	0	0	-1	/OC	0.0
1985	NY-A	19	49	4	8	2	1	0	1	1	5	.163	.196	.245	.441	21	-5	-5	96	33	2	.326	0	0	0	0	/CD	-0.4
1986	Chi-A	9	21	3	6	0	0	0	0	1	0	.286	.375	.286	.661	84	-0	-0	101	0	2	.500	0	2	-1	-0	/OD	-0.1
	Sea-A	68	199	17	60	8	3	5	28	12	7	.302	.347	.447	.795	110	4	3	105	107	27	.689	1	0	0	-0	C/D	0.6
	Yr	77	220	20	66	8	3	5	28	13	7	.300	.350	.432	.782	108	4	2	105	95	29	.673	1	2	-1	-0		0.5
1987	Sea-A	102	342	34	95	15	1	5	43	15	18	.278	.314	.371	.685	80	-9	-10	103	121	36	.556	0	1	-1	6	C/3OD	0.1
1988	Sea-A	103	335	45	86	17	1	4	33	17	16	.257	.297	.349	.646	75	-9	-12	108	102	32	.525	1	1	-0	9	C/O31	0.0
Total	5	310	967	106	261	43	6	14	107	47	47	.270	.311	.370	.681	82	-20	-26	104	104	102	.578	2	4	-2	14	C/DO31	0.2
■ **BILL BRADLEY** Bradley, William Joseph b: 2/13/1878, Cleveland, Ohio d: 3/11/54, Cleveland, Ohio BR/TR, 6', 185 lbs. Deb: 8/26/1899 M																												
1899	Chi-N	35	129	26	40	6	1	2	18	12		.310	.373	.419	.792	124	4	4	96	97	22	.798	4			0	3/S	0.4
1900	Chi-N	122	444	63	125	21	8	5	49	27		.282	.323	.399	.721	109	-1	4	93	81	63	.683	14			14	*31	1.7
1901	Cle-A	133	516	95	151	28	13	1	55	26		.293	.327	.403	.730	109	1	6	95	87	75	.682	15			10	*3/P	1.2
1902	Cle-A	137	550	104	187	39	12	11	77	27		.340	.371	.515	.885	150	31	33	97	85	112	.884	11			12	*3	3.9
1903	Cle-A	136	536	101	168	36	22	6	68	25		.313	.344	.496	.840	157	31	34	96	83	101	.848	21			12	*3	4.5
1904	Cle-A	154	609	94	183	32	8	5	83	26		.300	.329	.404	.733	132	21	20	102	114	91	.692	23			8	*3	3.7
1905	Cle-A	146	541	63	145	34	6	0	51	27		.268	.303	.353	.656	110	5	5	100	101	66	.606	22			14	*3	2.6
1906	Cle-A	82	302	32	83	15	2	2	25	18		.275	.316	.358	.673	109	4	3	103	81	39	.635	13			-1	3	0.8
1907	Cle-A	139	498	48	111	20	1	0	34	35		.223	.274	.267	.541	80	-14	-10	93	97	43	.486	20			5	*3	0.4
1908	Cle-A	148	548	70	133	24	7	1	46	29		.243	.281	.318	.598	91	-3	-6	106	103	52	.533	18			-18	*3S	-1.8
1909	Cle-A	95	334	30	62	6	3	0	22	19		.186	.236	.222	.458	44	-21	-22	102	121	18	.382	8			-2	3/12	-2.3
1910	Cle-A	61	214	12	42	3	0	0	12	10		.196	.236	.210	.446	40	-15	-15	100	100	12	.360	6			1	3	-1.2
1914	Bro-F	7	6	1	3	1	0	0	3	0	0	.500	.500	.667	1.167	231	1	1	101	271	2	1.333	0			0	HM	0.1
1915	KC-F	66	203	15	38	9	1	0	9	9	18	.187	.222	.241	.463	38	-16	-15	97	66	13	.388	6			4	3	-1.0
Total	14	1461	5430	754	1471	274	84	33	552	290	18	.271	.308	.371	.679	108	29	42	98	95	709	.628	181			58	*3/S12P	13.0
■ **DALLAS BRADSHAW** Bradshaw, Dallas Carl "Windy" b: 11/23/1895, Wolf Creek, Ill. d: 12/11/39, Herrin, Ill. BL/TR, 5'7", 145 lbs. Deb: 6/05/17																												
1917	Phi-A	2	4	0	0	0	0	0	0	0	1	.000	.000	.000	.000	-99	-1	-1	94	0	0	.000	0			0	/2	0.0
■ **GEORGE BRADSHAW** Bradshaw, George Thomas b: 9/12/24, Salisbury, N.C. BR/TR, 6'2", 185 lbs. Deb: 8/10/52																												
1952	Was-A	10	23	3	5	2	0	0	6	1	2	.217	.280	.304	.584	62	-1	-1	100	320	2	.450	0	0	0	0	/C	0.0
■ **BRADY** Brady Deb:9/25/1875																												
1875	Chi-n	1	4	1	1							.250															/O	
■ **CLIFF BRADY** Brady, Clifford Francis b: 3/6/1897, St.Louis, Mo. d: 9/25/74, Belleville, Ill. BR/TR, 5'5.5", 140 lbs. Deb: 8/08/20																												
1920	Bos-A	53	180	16	41	5	1	0	12	13	12	.228	.284	.267	.550	48	-14	-13	96	88	14	.443	0	1	-1	3	2	-0.8
■ **BOB BRADY** Brady, Robert Jay b: 11/8/22, Lewistown, Pa. BL/TR, 6'1", 175 lbs. Deb: 8/24/46																												
1946	Bos-N	3	5	0	1	0	0	0	0	1	1	.200	.333	.200	.533	56	-0	-0	95	0	0	.500	0			0	/C	0.0
1947	Bos-N	1	1	0	0	0	0	0	0	0	0	.000	.000	.000	.000	-99	-0	-0	97	0	0	.000	0			0	H	0.0
Total	2	4	6	0	1	0	0	0	0	1	1	.167	.286	.167	.452	30	-1	-1	95	0	0	.400	0			0	/C	0.0
■ **STEVE BRADY** Brady, Stephen A. b: 7/14/1851, Worcester, Mass. d: 11/1/17, Hartford, Conn. 175 lbs. Deb: 7/23/1874																												
1874	Har-n	25	110	18	37							.336															3/O	
1875	Nat-n	19	83	4	11							.133															2/O1	
1883	NY-a	97	432	69	117	12	6	0		11		.271	.289	.326	.615	91	-1	-6	108	0	42	.483				4	*1O	-0.8
1884	NY-a	112	485	102	122	11	3	0		21		.252	.283	.287	.569	89	-6	-6	100	0	40	.441				-2	*O/12	-0.8
1885	NY-a	108	434	60	128	14	5	3		25		.295	.342	.371	.713	153	14	25	84	0	56	.627				-10	*O/123	0.9
1886	NY-a	124	466	56	112	8	5	0		35		.240	.298	.279	.577	80	-8	-11	104	0	45	.520	16			-8	*O/1	-2.0
Total	2 n	44	193	22	48							.249															*O/1	
Total	4	441	1817	287	479	45	19	3		92		.264	.302	.314	.617	100	-1	2	99	0	183	.514	16			-16	O/123	-2.7
■ **TOM BRADY** Brady, Thomas A. b: Hartford, Conn. d: 8/27/22, Hartford, Conn. Deb: 9/25/1875																												
1875	Har-n	1	4	0	0							.000															/O	
■ **BOBBY BRAGAN** Bragan, Robert Randall "Nig" b: 10/30/17, Birmingham, Ala. BR/TR, 5'10.5", 175 lbs. Deb: 4/16/40 MC																												
1940	Phi-N	132	474	36	105	14	1	7	44	28	34	.222	.265	.300	.565	57	-29	-28	97	102	37	.454	2			-2	*S/3	-1.6

YEAR	TM/L	G	AB	R	H	2B	3B	HR	RBI	BB	SO	AVG	OBP	SLG	PRO	/A	BR	/A	PF	CHI	RC	TA	SB	CS	SBR	FR	POS	TPR
1941	Phi-N	154	557	37	140	19	3	4	69	26	29	.251	.285	.318	.603	72	-23	-22	97	134	48	.484	7			-8	*S/23	-1.6
1942	Phi-N	109	335	17	73	12	2	2	15	20	21	.218	.264	.284	.548	64	-17	-15	94	55	24	.426	0			3	SC/23	-0.6
1943	Bro-N	74	220	17	58	7	2	2	24	15	16	.264	.311	.341	.652	88	-4	-4	100	107	23	.533	0			-1	C3	-0.2
1944	Bro-N	94	266	26	71	8	4	0	17	13	14	.267	.304	.327	.631	78	-8	-8	99	70	25	.502	2			-7	SC/32	-0.5
1947	Bro-N	25	36	3	7	2	0	0	3	7	3	.194	.326	.250	.576	52	-2	-2	105	123	4	.586	1			0	C	-0.1
1948	Bro-N	9	12	0	2	0	0	0	0	1	0	.167	.231	.167	.397	9	-2	-2	104	0	1	.300	0			0	/C	0.0
Total	7	597	1900	136	456	62	12	15	172	110	117	.240	.282	.309	.591	69	-86	-80	97	99	160	.492	12			-15	SC/32	-4.6
■ **GLENN BRAGGS** Braggs, Glenn Erick b: 10/17/62, San Bernardino, Cal BR/TR, 6'3", 210 lbs. Deb: 7/18/86																												
1986	Mil-A	58	215	19	51	8	2	4	18	11	47	.237	.278	.349	.626	69	-9	-10	102	84	20	.515	1	1	-0	0	O/D	-1.0
1987	Mil-A	132	505	67	136	28	7	13	77	47	96	.269	.336	.430	.766	100	2	-0	102	127	69	.711	12	5	1	11	*O/D	0.7
1988	Mil-A	72	272	30	71	14	0	10	42	14	60	.261	.309	.423	.732	99	0	-1	103	122	34	.664	6	4	-1	2	OD	0.0
Total	3	262	992	116	258	50	9	27	137	72	203	.260	.317	.410	.727	93	-7	-11	103	117	122	.677	19	10	-0	13	O/D	-0.3
■ **DAVE BRAIN** Brain, David Leonard b: 1/24/1879, Hereford, England d: 5/25/59, Los Angeles, Cal. BR/TR, 5'10", 170 lbs. Deb: 4/24/01																												
1901	Chi-A	5	20	2	7	1	0	0	5	1		.350	.381	.400	.781	120	1	1	99	209	3	.692	0			-0	/2	0.0
1903	StL-N	119	464	44	107	8	15	1	60	25		.231	.270	.319	.589	72	-19	-17	96	123	47	.543	21			1	S3	-1.0
1904	StL-N	127	488	57	130	24	12	7	72	17		.266	.291	.408	.699	118	7	8	99	127	65	.654	18			-4	S3O2/1	0.5
1905	StL-N	44	158	11	36	4	5	1	17	8		.228	.265	.335	.601	88	-4	-3	91	108	15	.533	4			-5	S/3O	-0.7
	Pit-N	85	307	31	79	17	6	3	46	15		.257	.292	.381	.673	98	-0	-2	104	129	37	.614	8			5	3/S	0.9
	Yr	129	465	42	115	21	11	4	63	23		.247	.283	.366	.648	95	-5	-5	100	123	53	.586	12			-0		0.2
1906	Bos-N	139	525	43	131	19	5	5	45	29		.250	.289	.333	.622	96	-4	-4	100	83	55	.546	11			21	*3	1.3
1907	Bos-N	133	509	60	142	24	9	**10**	56	29		.279	.318	.420	.738	140	16	19	95	92	73	.689	10			21	*3/O	4.4
1908	Cin-N	16	55	4	6	0	0	0	1	8		.109	.222	.109	.331	8	-5	-5	103	61	1	.286	0			0	O	-0.6
	NY-N	11	17	2	3	0	0	0	1	2		.176	.263	.176	.440	41	-1	-1	104	128	1	.429	1			0	/2O3S	0.0
	Yr	27	72	6	9	0	0	0	2	10		.125	.232	.125	.357	16	-6	-7	103	91	2	.317	1			0		-0.6
Total	7	679	2543	254	641	97	52	27	303	134		.252	.290	.363	.652	101	-11	-5	98	108	298	.594	73			38	3S/O21	4.8
■ **FRED BRAINERD** Brainerd, Frederick F. b: 2/17/1892, Champaign, Ill. d: 4/17/59, Galveston, Tex. BR/TR, 6', 176 lbs. Deb: 10/06/14																												
1914	NY-N	2	5	1	1	0	0	0	0	1	0	.200	.333	.200	.533	63	-0	-0	96	0	1	.500	0			-0	/2	0.0
1915	NY-N	91	249	31	50	7	2	1	21	21	44	.201	.266	.257	.523	64	-12	-10	91	120	17	.447	6	7	-2	2	13/S2O	-1.2
1916	NY-N	2	7	0	0	0	0	0	0	0	0	.000	.000	.000	.000	-99	-2	-2	96	0	0	.000	0			0	/3	-0.1
Total	3	95	261	32	51	7	2	1	21	22	44	.195	.261	.249	.510	60	-14	-12	92	114	17	.433	6	7		2	/13S2O	-1.3
■ **ART BRAMHALL** Bramhall, Arthur Washington b: 2/22/09, Oak Park, Ill. d: 9/4/85, Madison, Wis. BR/TR, 5'11", 170 lbs. Deb: 4/18/35																												
1935	Phi-N	2	1	0	0	0	0	0	0	0	0	.000	.000	.000	.000	-88	-0	-0	114	0	0	.000	0			0	/S3	0.0
■ **AL BRANCATO** Brancato, Albert "Bronk" b: 5/29/19, Philadelphia, Pa. BR/TR, 5'9.5", 188 lbs. Deb: 9/07/39																												
1939	Phi-A	21	68	12	14	5	0	1	8	8	4	.206	.299	.324	.622	61	-4	-4	97	108	7	.561	1	0	0	-1	3/S	-0.3
1940	Phi-A	107	298	42	57	11	2	1	23	28	36	.191	.265	.252	.517	36	-29	-27	96	107	20	.429	3	1	0	-13	S3	-2.9
1941	Phi-A	144	530	60	124	20	9	2	49	59	49	.234	.311	.317	.628	66	-26	-26	101	102	54	.540	1	5	-3	-18	*S/3	-4.1
1945	Phi-A	10	34	3	4	1	0	0	0	1	3	.118	.143	.147	.290	-17	-5	-5	94	0	1	.200	0	0	0	0	S	-0.4
Total	4	282	930	117	199	37	11	4	80	96	92	.214	.290	.290	.580	54	-64	-62	99	100	81	.507	5	6	-2	-31	S/3	-7.7
■ **RON BRAND** Brand, Ronald George b: 1/13/40, Los Angeles, Cal. BR/TR, 5'7.5", 167 lbs. Deb: 5/26/63																												
1963	Pit-N	46	66	8	19	2	0	1	7	10	11	.288	.390	.364	.753	120	2	2	99	109	10	.729	0	0	0	-1	C/23	0.3
1965	Hou-N	117	391	27	92	6	3	2	37	19	34	.235	.281	.281	.563	66	-21	-16	89	132	28	.452	10	5	0	13	*C/3O	0.0
1966	Hou-N	56	123	12	30	2	0	0	10	9	13	.244	.306	.260	.566	61	-6	-6	97	131	9	.426	0	2	-1	-0	C/2O3	-0.6
1967	Hou-N	84	215	22	52	8	1	0	18	23	17	.242	.321	.288	.609	81	-6	-4	94	120	21	.538	4	0	1	3	C/2O	0.4
1968	Hou-N	43	81	7	13	2	0	0	4	9	11	.160	.261	.185	.446	36	-6	-6	99	112	5	.386	1	1	-0	-2	C/3O	-0.8
1969	Mon-N	103	287	19	74	12	0	0	20	30	19	.258	.330	.300	.630	77	-8	-8	100	93	27	.524	2	3	-1	0	C/O	-0.3
1970	Mon-N	72	126	10	30	2	3	0	9	9	16	.238	.289	.302	.590	58	-7	-7	100	92	12	.505	2	1	0	-1	S3/CO2	-0.5
1971	Mon-N	47	56	3	12	0	0	0	1	3	5	.214	.254	.214	.469	34	-5	-5	99	34	3	.356	1	1	-0	-1	S/3OC2	-0.3
Total	8	568	1345	108	322	34	7	3	106	112	126	.239	.305	.282	.586	69	-57	-50	95	112	114	.507	20	13	-2	11	C/S3O2	-1.8
■ **JACKIE BRANDT** Brandt, John George b: 4/28/34, Omaha, Neb. BR/TR, 5'11", 165 lbs. Deb: 4/21/56																												
1956	StL-N	27	42	9	12	3	0	1	3	4	5	.286	.362	.429	.790	113	1	1	99	60	6	.719	0	1	-1	-4	O	-0.4
	NY-N	98	351	45	105	16	8	11	47	17	31	.299	.332	.484	.816	119	7	8	97	100	55	.751	3	4	-2	-2	O	0.1
	Yr	125	393	54	117	19	8	12	50	21	36	.298	.335	.478	.813	118	7	9	98	92	62	.750	3	5	-2	-5		-0.3
1958	SF-N	18	52	7	13	1	0	0	3	6	5	.250	.328	.269	.597	60	-3	-3	100	89	5	.538	1	0	0	-0	O	-0.2
1959	SF-N	137	429	63	116	16	5	12	57	35	69	.270	.325	.415	.740	100	-3	-1	95	108	58	.689	11	4	1	-4	*O3/12	-0.6
1960	Bal-A	145	511	73	130	24	6	15	65	47	69	.254	.321	.413	.734	95	-3	-5	102	101	69	.680	5	3	-0	-9	*O/31	-1.9
1961	Bal-A	139	516	93	153	18	5	16	72	62	51	.297	.373	.444	.817	121	13	15	97	108	85	.791	10	2	2	-8	*O/3	0.4
1962	Bal-A	143	505	76	129	29	5	19	75	55	64	.255	.333	.446	.779	114	5	8	95	108	76	.751	9	3	1	0	*O/3	0.4
1963	Bal-A	142	451	49	112	15	5	15	61	34	85	.248	.301	.404	.705	102	-4	-0	94	112	51	.618	4	5	-2	-8	*O/3	-1.4
1964	Bal-A	137	523	66	127	25	1	13	47	45	104	.243	.306	.369	.676	83	-9	-13	105	91	59	.595	1	4	-2	10	*O	-1.0
1965	Bal-A	96	243	35	59	17	0	8	24	21	40	.243	.303	.412	.715	101	-0	-0	100	80	30	.642	1	2	-1	-1	O	-0.5
1966	Phi-N	82	164	16	41	6	1	1	15	17	36	.250	.320	.317	.638	77	-4	-5	101	115	16	.535	0	2	-1	-10	O	-1.8
1967	Phi-N	16	19	1	2	1	0	0	1	0	6	.105	.105	.158	.263	-25	-3	-3	104	138	0	.176	0	0	0	-1	/O	-0.4
	Hou-N	41	89	7	21	4	1	1	15	8	9	.236	.299	.337	.636	87	-2	-1	94	188	9	.551	0	0	0	-2	1/O3	-0.4
	Yr	57	108	8	23	5	1	1	16	8	15	.213	.267	.306	.573	66	-5	-5	97	177	9	.477	0	0	0	-3		-0.8
Total	11	1221	3895	540	1020	175	37	112	485	351	574	.262	.325	.412	.737	101	-7	2	98	104	520	.693	45	30	-4	-37	*O/312	-7.7
■ **OTIS BRANNAN** Brannan, Otis Owen b: 3/13/1899, Greenbrier, Ark. d: 6/6/67, Little Rock, Ark. BR/TR, 5'9", 160 lbs. Deb: 4/11/28																												
1928	StL-A	135	483	68	118	18	3	10	66	60	19	.244	.333	.356	.689	78	-13	-15	104	114	59	.639	3	9	-5	-4	*2	-1.5
1929	StL-A	23	51	4	15	1	0	1	8	4	4	.294	.345	.373	.718	85	-1	-1	100	124	7	.639	0	0	0	2	2	0.1
Total	2	158	534	72	133	19	3	11	74	64	23	.249	.334	.358	.692	79	-14	-17	103	115	66	.639	3	9	-5	-2	2	-1.4
■ **MIKE BRANNOCK** Brannock, Michael J. b: Chicago, Ill. Deb: 10/21/1871																												
1871	Chi-n	3	13	2	1							.077															/3	
1875	Chi-n	2	9	2	1							.111															/3	
Total	2 n	5	22	4	2							.091															/3	
■ **DUD BRANOM** Branom, Edgar Dudley b: 11/30/1897, Sulphur Springs, Tex. d: 2/4/80, Sun City, Ariz. BL/TL, 6'1", 190 lbs. Deb: 4/12/27																												
1927	Phi-A	30	94	8	22	1	0	0	13	2	5	.234	.250	.245	.495	30	-10	-9	97	188	6	.375	2	0	1	-0	1	-1.0
■ **KITTY BRANSFIELD** Bransfield, William Edward b: 1/7/1875, Worcester, Mass. d: 5/1/47, Worcester, Mass. BR/TR, 5'11", 207 lbs. Deb: 8/22/1898																												
1898	Bos-N	5	9	2	2	0	1	0	1	0		.222	.222	.444	.667	88	-0	-0	104	76	1	.571	0			0	/C1	0.0
1901	Pit-N	139	566	92	167	26	16	0	91	29		.295	.329	.398	.727	112	8	7	101	143	84	.694	23			-11	*1	-0.2
1902	Pit-N	102	413	49	126	21	7	1	69	17		.305	.333	.397	.730	121	11	9	105	151	64	.711	23			-5	*1	0.0
1903	Pit-N	127	505	69	134	23	7	2	57	33		.265	.310	.350	.661	86	-7	-11	105	106	60	.601	13			4	*1	-0.9
1904	Pit-N	139	520	47	116	17	9	0	60	22		.223	.255	.290	.545	70	-19	-19	99	154	42	.455	11			-2	*1	-2.8
1905	Phi-N	151	580	55	150	23	9	3	76	27		.259	.292	.345	.636	87	-8	-11	104	134	68	.591	27			-3	*1	-2.0
1906	Phi-N	140	524	47	144	28	5	1	60	16		.275	.296	.353	.649	113	0	5	92	123	60	.561	12			-1	*1	-0.1
1907	Phi-N	94	348	25	81	15	2	0	38	14		.233	.262	.287	.550	71	-11	-12	104	152	29	.457	8			-3	1	-1.9
1908	Phi-N	144	527	53	160	25	7	3	71	23		.304	.333	.395	.727	135	18	18	100	133	76	.711	30			-1	*1	1.5
1909	Phi-N	140	527	47	154	27	6	1	59	18		.292	.319	.372	.691	109	7	3	106	114	66	.627	17			4	*1	0.5
1910	Phi-N	123	427	39	102	17	4	3	52	20	34	.239	.275	.319	.593	76	-17	-14	96	125	40	.514	10			-1	*1	-1.7
1911	Phi-N	23	43	4	11	1	1	0	3	0	5	.256	.256	.326	.581	58	-2	-3	108	72	4	.469	1			0	/1	-0.2
	Chi-N	3	10	0	4	2	0	0	0	2	2	.400	.500	.600	1.100	215	2	2	97	0	3	1.333	0			0	/1	0.1

YEAR	TM/L	G	AB	R	H	2B	3B	HR	RBI	BB	SO	AVG	OBP	SLG	PRO	/A	BR	/A	PF	CHI	RC	TA	SB	CS	SBR	FR	POS	TPR
	Yr	26	53	4	15	3	1	0	3	2	7	.283	.309	.377	.686	86	-1	-1	106	67	6	.605	1			0		-0.1
Total	12	1330	4999	529	1351	225	74	14	637	221	41	.270	.302	.353	.655	98	-18	-26	101	132	596	.594	175			-18	*1/C	-7.7
■ **MARSHALL BRANT** Brant, Marshall Lee b: 9/17/55, Garberville, Cal. BR/TR, 6'5", 185 lbs. Deb: 10/01/80																												
1980	NY-A	3	6	0	0	0	0	0	0	0	3	.000	.000	.000	.000	-99	-2	-2	99	0	0	.000	0	0	0	0	/1D	-0.1
1983	Oak-A	5	14	2	2	0	0	0	2	0	3	.143	.143	.143	.286	-22	-2	-2	96	391	0	.167	0	0	0	-0	/1D	-0.2
Total	2	8	20	2	2	0	0	0	2	0	6	.100	.100	.100	.200	-46	-4	-4	97	274	0	.111	0	0	0	-0	/1D	-0.3
■ **MICKEY BRANTLEY** Brantley, Michael Charles b: 6/17/61, Catskill, N.Y. BR/TR, 5'10", 180 lbs. Deb: 8/09/86																												
1986	Sea-A	27	102	12	20	3	2	3	7	10	21	.196	.268	.353	.621	65	-5	-5	105	66	9	.547	1	1	-0	2	O	-0.3
1987	Sea-A	92	351	52	106	23	2	14	54	24	44	.302	.347	.499	.845	119	10	9	103	105	62	.845	13	4	2	-0	O/D	0.7
1988	Sea-A	149	577	76	152	25	4	15	56	26	64	.263	.298	.399	.696	87	-7	-12	108	86	66	.622	18	7	1	-11	*O	-2.4
Total	3	268	1030	140	278	51	8	32	117	60	129	.270	.311	.428	.740	95	-1	-9	106	90	137	.689	32	12	2	-9	O/D	-2.0
■ **KITTY BRASHEAR** Brashear, Norman C. b: 8/27/1877, Mansfield, Ohio d: 12/22/34, Los Angeles, Cal. 5'11", 205 lbs. Deb: 4/25/02																												
1902	StL-N	110	388	36	107	8	2	1	40	32		.276	.331	.314	.645	106	1	4	95	113	44	.580	9			3	12O/S	0.4
■ **ROY BRASHEAR** Brashear, Roy Parks b: 1/3/1874, Ashtabula, Ohio d: 4/20/51, Los Angeles, Cal. TR , Deb: 6/25/1899																												
1899	Lou-N	3	2	0	1	0	0	0	0	0		.500	.500	.500	1.000	172	0	0	103	0	1	1.000	0			0	/P	0.0
1903	Phi-N	20	75	9	17	3	0	0	4	6		.227	.284	.267	.551	64	-4	-3	92	68	6	.483	2			-1	2/1	-0.2
Total	2	23	77	9	18	3	0	0	4	6		.234	.289	.273	.562	67	-4	-3	92	66	7	.492	2			-1	/2P1	-0.2
■ **JOE BRATCHER** Bratcher, Joseph Warlick "Goobers" b: 7/22/1898, Grand Saline, Tex d: 10/13/77, Fort Worth, Tex. BL/TR, 5'8.5", 140 lbs. Deb: 8/26/24																												
1924	StL-N	4	1	1	0	0	0	0	0	0	0	.000	.000	.000	.000	-98	-0	-0	103	0	0	.000	0	0	0	-0	/O	0.0
■ **FRED BRATSCHI** Bratschi, Frederick Oscar "Fritz" b: 1/16/1892, Alliance, Ohio d: 1/10/62, Massillon, Ohio BR/TR, 5'10", 170 lbs. Deb: 7/24/21																												
1921	Chi-A	16	28	0	8	1	0	0	3	0	2	.286	.286	.321	.607	55	-2	-2	99	114	2	.450	0	0	0	0	/O	-0.1
1926	Bos-A	72	167	12	46	10	1	0	19	14	15	.275	.335	.347	.682	77	-5	-6	101	111	20	.598	0	1	-1	-8	O	-1.5
1927	Bos-A	1	1	0	0	0	0	0	0	0	0	.000	.000	.000	.000	-99	-0	-0	95	0	0	.000	0	0	0	0	H	0.0
Total	3	89	196	12	54	11	1	0	22	14	17	.276	.327	.342	.669	73	-8	-8	101	111	22	.573	0	1	-1	-7	/O	-1.6
■ **STEVE BRAUN** Braun, Stephen Russell b: 5/8/48, Trenton, N.J. BL/TR, 5'10", 180 lbs. Deb: 4/06/71																												
1971	Min-A	128	343	51	87	12	2	5	35	48	50	.254	.354	.344	.698	94	1	-1	104	107	44	.670	8	3	1	-15	32S/O	-1.6
1972	Min-A	121	402	40	116	21	0	2	50	45	38	.289	.363	.356	.719	107	8	5	107	140	51	.636	4	5	-2	-1	32S/O	0.8
1973	Min-A	115	361	46	102	28	5	6	42	74	48	.283	.409	.438	.846	133	22	20	104	94	68	.882	4	3	-1	-5	*3/O	1.2
1974	Min-A	129	453	53	127	12	1	8	40	56	51	.280	.362	.364	.726	108	7	7	101	85	62	.676	4	4	-1	-4	*O3	0.0
1975	Min-A	136	453	70	137	18	3	11	45	66	55	.302	.392	.428	.821	123	21	17	107	76	79	.801	0	2	-1	-3	*O/132D	0.9
1976	Min-A	122	417	73	120	12	3	3	61	67	43	.288	.388	.353	.740	120	13	13	98	153	63	.742	12	4	1	0	DO3	1.5
1977	Sea-A	139	451	51	106	19	1	5	31	80	59	.235	.353	.315	.668	87	-7	-5	96	80	54	.641	8	3	1	2	*OD/3	-0.4
1978	Sea-A	32	74	11	17	4	0	3	15	9	5	.230	.313	.405	.719	99	-0	-0	102	152	9	.656	1	0	0	-1	D/O	0.0
	KC-A	64	137	16	36	10	1	0	14	28	16	.263	.388	.350	.738	107	3	3	102	115	21	.760	3	2	-0	-4	O3	-0.2
	Yr	96	211	27	53	14	1	3	29	37	21	.251	.363	.370	.733	104	3	2	102	129	32	.739	4	2	0	-5		-0.2
1979	KC-A	58	116	15	31	2	0	4	10	22	11	.267	.384	.388	.772	103	2	1	105	67	19	.770	0	0	0	0	OD/3	0.1
1980	KC-A	14	23	0	1	0	0	0	1	2	2	.043	.120	.043	.163	-54	-5	-5	98	390	0	.136	0	0	0	-2	/OD	-0.6
	Tor-A	37	55	4	15	2	0	1	9	8	5	.273	.365	.364	.729	101	0	0	100	153	7	.667	0	0	0	0	D/3	0.0
	Yr	51	78	4	16	2	0	1	10	10	7	.205	.295	.269	.565	56	-5	-4	99	225	6	.484	0	0	0	-2		-0.6
1981	StL-N	44	46	9	9	2	1	0	2	15	7	.196	.393	.283	.676	93	1	0	102	60	7	.763	1	0	0	-1	O/3	0.0
1982	StL-N	58	62	6	17	4	0	0	4	11	10	.274	.384	.339	.722	100	1	1	103	75	8	.681	0	0	0	-2	/O3	-0.1
1983	StL-N	78	92	8	25	2	1	3	7	21	7	.272	.407	.413	.820	130	4	5	98	59	17	.855	0	1	-1	-5	O/3	0.0
1984	StL-N	86	98	6	27	3	1	0	16	17	17	.276	.383	.327	.709	102	1	1	99	196	14	.690	0	0	0	-5	O/3	-0.4
1985	StL-N	64	67	7	16	4	0	1	6	10	9	.239	.346	.343	.689	98	-0	0	96	92	9	.667	0	0	0	-2	O	-0.2
Total	15	1425	3650	466	989	155	19	52	388	579	433	.271	.373	.367	.740	108	72	63	102	106	532	.736	45	27	-3	-47	O3D/2S1	1.0
■ **ANGEL BRAVO** Bravo, Angel Alfonso (Urdaneta) b: 8/4/42, Maracaibo, Venez. BL/TL, 5'8", 150 lbs. Deb: 6/06/69																												
1969	Chi-A	27	90	10	26	4	2	1	3	3	5	.289	.319	.411	.730	95	0	-1	108	30	12	.662	2	0	1	-2	O	-0.2
1970	Cin-N	65	65	10	18	1	1	0	3	9	13	.277	.365	.323	.688	82	-1	-1	104	55	8	.625	0	1	-1	-5	O	-0.7
1971	Cin-N	5	5	0	1	0	0	0	0	0	1	.200	.200	.200	.400	14	-1	-1	96	0	0	.250	0	0	0	0	H	0.0
	SD-N	52	58	6	9	2	0	0	6	8	12	.155	.269	.190	.458	33	-5	-5	96	222	3	.400	0	1	-1	-3	/O	-0.8
	Yr	57	63	6	10	2	0	0	6	8	13	.159	.264	.190	.454	32	-6	-5	96	203	4	.389	0	1	-1	-3		-0.8
Total	3	149	218	26	54	7	3	1	12	20	31	.248	.317	.321	.638	74	-6	-7	103	91	24	.566	2	2	-1	-9	/O	-1.7
■ **BUSTER BRAY** Bray, Clarence Wilbur b: 4/1/13, Birmingham, Ala. d: 9/4/82, Evansville, Ind. BL/TL, 6', 170 lbs. Deb: 4/18/41																												
1941	Bos-N	4	11	2	1	1	0	0	1	1	2	.091	.167	.182	.348	-2	-2	-1	93	181	0	.300	0			-0	/O	-0.1
■ **FRANK BRAZILL** Brazill, Frank Leo b: 8/11/1899, Spangler, Pa. d: 11/3/76, Oakland, Cal. BL/TR, 5'11.5", 175 lbs. Deb: 4/13/21																												
1921	Phi-A	66	177	17	48	3	1	0	19	23	21	.271	.361	.299	.661	68	-7	-8	103	123	20	.602	2	4	-2	-4	1/3	-1.1
1922	Phi-A	6	13	0	1	0	0	0	1	0	1	.077	.077	.077	.154	-57	-3	-3	104	358	0	.083	0	0	0	0	/3	-0.2
Total	2	72	190	17	49	3	1	0	20	23	22	.258	.344	.284	.628	60	-10	-11	103	137	20	.559	2	4	-2	-4	/13	-1.3
■ **SID BREAM** Bream, Sid b: 8/3/60, Carlisle, Pa. BL/TL, 6'4", 215 lbs. Deb: 9/01/83																												
1983	LA-N	15	11	0	2	0	0	0	2	2	2	.182	.308	.182	.490	39	-1	-1	100	396	1	.400	0	0	0	0	/1	0.0
1984	LA-N	27	49	2	9	3	0	0	6	6	9	.184	.273	.245	.518	45	-3	-4	104	196	4	.463	1	0	0	1	1	-0.2
1985	LA-N	24	53	4	7	0	0	3	6	7	10	.132	.233	.302	.535	52	-4	-3	93	96	4	.500	0	0	0	0	1	-0.3
	Pit-N	26	95	14	27	7	0	3	15	11	14	.284	.358	.453	.811	122	3	3	103	122	14	.730	0	2	-1	0	1	0.1
	Yr	50	148	18	34	7	0	6	21	18	24	.230	.313	.399	.712	100	-1	-0	98	111	18	.642	0	2	-1	0		-0.2
1986	Pit-N	154	522	73	140	37	5	16	77	60	73	.268	.345	.450	.795	117	12	12	100	111	79	.767	13	7	-0	17	*1/O	2.3
1987	Pit-N	149	516	64	142	25	3	13	65	49	69	.275	.338	.411	.749	93	-2	-5	104	105	66	.673	9	8	-2	8	*1	-0.7
1988	Pit-N	148	462	50	122	37	0	10	65	47	64	.264	.333	.409	.742	115	7	8	98	119	61	.683	9	9	-3	14	*1	1.4
Total	6	543	1708	207	449	109	8	45	236	182	241	.263	.335	.415	.750	105	12	10	101	116	228	.714	32	26	-6	40	1/O	2.6
■ **JIM BREAZEALE** Breazeale, James Leo b: 10/3/49, Houston, Tex. BL/TR, 6'2", 210 lbs. Deb: 9/13/69																												
1969	Atl-N	2	1	1	0	0	0	0	0	2	0	.000	.667	.000	.667	97	0	0	104	0	0	2.000	0	0	0	0	/1	0.0
1971	Atl-N	10	21	1	4	0	0	1	3	0	3	.190	.190	.333	.524	42	-2	-2	110	122	1	.412	0	0	0	0	/1	-0.1
1972	Atl-N	52	85	10	21	2	0	5	17	6	12	.247	.297	.447	.744	104	1	0	105	132	10	.657	0	1	-1	0	1/3	-0.1
1978	Chi-A	25	72	8	15	3	0	3	13	8	10	.208	.287	.375	.663	84	-2	-2	101	143	8	.593	0	0	0	-0	1/D	-0.2
Total	4	89	179	20	40	5	0	9	33	16	25	.223	.287	.402	.689	90	-2	-3	104	133	20	.620	0	1	-1	-0	/1D3	-0.4
■ **DANNY BREEDEN** Breeden, Danny Richard b: 6/27/42, Albany, Ga. BR/TR, 5'11.5", 185 lbs. Deb: 7/24/69																												
1969	Cin-N	3	8	0	1	0	0	0	1	0	3	.125	.125	.125	.250	-30	-1	-1	99	401	0	.143	0	0	0	0	/C	0.0
1971	Chi-N	25	65	3	10	1	0	0	4	9	18	.154	.267	.169	.436	24	-6	-7	110	148	4	.368	0	0	0	-1	C	-0.7
Total	2	28	73	3	11	1	0	0	5	9	21	.151	.253	.164	.417	19	-7	-8	109	172	4	.344	0	0	0	-1	/C	-0.7
■ **HAL BREEDEN** Breeden, Harold Noel b: 6/28/44, Albany, Ga. BR/TL, 6'2", 200 lbs. Deb: 4/07/71																												
1971	Chi-N	23	36	1	5	1	0	1	2	2	7	.139	.184	.250	.434	20	-4	-4	110	68	2	.355	0	0	0	0	/1	-0.4
1972	Mon-N	42	87	6	20	2	0	3	10	7	15	.230	.287	.356	.644	80	-2	-2	102	103	9	.559	0	0	0	0	1/O	-0.3
1973	Mon-N	105	258	36	71	10	6	15	43	29	45	.275	.353	.535	.888	137	14	13	104	94	47	.867	0	1	-1	3	1	1.3
1974	Mon-N	79	190	14	47	13	0	2	20	24	35	.247	.332	.347	.679	86	-2	-3	104	107	21	.596	0	1	-1	2	1	-0.3
1975	Mon-N	24	37	4	5	2	0	0	1	7	5	.135	.273	.189	.462	28	-3	-4	108	55	2	.424	0	0	0	1	1	-0.3
Total	5	273	608	61	148	28	6	21	76	69	107	.243	.323	.413	.735	100	2	-1	104	95	81	.695	0	2	-1	6	1/O	-0.0
■ **MARV BREEDING** Breeding, Marvin Eugene b: 3/8/34, Decatur, Ala. BR/TR, 6', 175 lbs. Deb: 4/19/60																												
1960	Bal-A	152	551	69	147	25	2	3	43	35	80	.267	.314	.336	.650	74	-19	-20	102	89	59	.560	10	4	1	9	*2	0.0

YEAR	TM/L	G	AB	R	H	2B	3B	HR	RBI	BB	SO	AVG	OBP	SLG	PRO	/A	BR	/A	PF	CHI	RC	TA	SB	CS	SBR	FR	POS	TPR
1961	Bal-A	90	244	32	51	8	0	1	16	14	33	.209	.252	.254	.506	37	-22	-21	97	96	16	.411	5	2	0	3	2	-0.7
1962	Bal-A	95	240	27	59	10	1	2	18	8	41	.246	.273	.321	.594	63	-14	-12	95	86	21	.478	2	2	-1	0	2/S3	-0.7
1963	Was-A	58	197	20	54	7	2	1	14	7	21	.274	.299	.345	.644	82	-5	-5	98	82	20	.524	1	1	-0	1	32/S	-0.2
	LA-N	20	36	6	6	0	0	0	1	2	5	.167	.211	.167	.377	11	-4	-4	95	70	2	.300	1	0	0	-0	2/S3	-0.2
Total	4	415	1268	154	317	50	5	7	92	66	180	.250	.289	.314	.603	64	-64	-63	99	88	118	.507	19	9	0	13	2/3S	-1.8
■ **HERB BREMER** Bremer, Herbert Frederick b: 10/26/13, Chicago, Ill. d: 11/28/79, Columbus, Ga. BR/TR, 6', 195 lbs. Deb: 9/16/37																												
1937	StL-N	11	33	2	7	1	0	0	3	2	4	.212	.257	.242	.500	36	-3	-3	101	135	2	.370	0			0	C	-0.2
1938	StL-N	50	151	14	33	5	1	2	14	9	36	.219	.262	.305	.567	50	-9	-12	111	97	13	.471	1			1	C	-0.8
1939	StL-N	9	9	0	1	0	0	0	1	0	2	.111	.111	.111	.222	-38	-2	-2	105	367	0	.125	0			-0	/C	-0.1
Total	3	70	193	16	41	6	1	2	18	11	42	.212	.255	.285	.540	44	-14	-16	109	116	15	.441	1			1	/C	-1.1
■ **SAM BRENEGAN** Brenegan, Olaf Selmar b: 9/1/1890, Galesville, Wis. d: 4/20/56, Galesville, Wis. BL/TR, 6'2", 185 lbs. Deb: 4/24/14																												
1914	Pit-N	1	0	0	0	0	0	0	0	0	0	—	—	—	—	—	0	0	92	—	—	—	0			0	/C	0.0
■ **BOB BRENLY** Brenly, Robert Earl b: 2/25/54, Coshocton, Ohio BR/TR, 6'2", 210 lbs. Deb: 8/14/81																												
1981	SF-N	19	45	5	15	2	1	1	4	6	4	.333	.423	.489	.912	150	4	3	105	63	9	.906	0	1	-1	-0	C/3O	0.3
1982	SF-N	65	180	26	51	4	1	4	15	18	26	.283	.352	.383	.735	113	2	3	94	73	25	.707	6	2	1	1	C/3	0.5
1983	SF-N	104	281	36	63	12	2	7	34	37	48	.224	.319	.356	.675	86	-5	-5	101	111	30	.629	10	7	-1	3	C1/O	0.0
1984	SF-N	145	506	74	147	28	0	20	80	48	52	.291	.355	.464	.820	134	19	21	96	108	79	.764	6	9	-4	-3	*C1/O	1.8
1985	SF-N	133	440	41	97	16	1	19	56	57	62	.220	.313	.391	.704	102	-3	1	93	99	55	.657	1	4	-2	5	*C31	0.8
1986	SF-N	149	472	60	116	26	0	16	62	74	97	.246	.352	.403	.754	112	6	9	96	104	71	.757	10	6	-1	-14	*C31	-0.4
1987	SF-N	123	375	55	100	19	1	18	51	47	85	.267	.353	.467	.820	120	8	10	96	89	63	.819	10	7	-1	1	*C/13	1.8
1988	SF-N	73	206	13	39	7	0	5	22	20	40	.189	.268	.296	.564	66	-10	-9	94	116	17	.488	1	2	-1	-7	C	-1.3
Total	8	811	2505	310	628	114	6	90	324	307	414	.251	.337	.409	.745	110	20	33	96	101	348	.726	44	38	-10	-14	C/31O	3.5
■ **JACK BRENNAN** Brennan, John Gottlieb (born John Gottlieb Dorn) b: 1862, St.Louis, Mo. d: 10/18/04, Philadelphia, Pa. Deb: 7/14/1884																												
1884	StL-U	56	231	38	50	6	1	0		12		.216	.255	.251	.506	69	-6	-8	104	0	15	.387	0			-3	CO/3S	-0.6
1885	StL-N	3	10	0	1	0	0	0	1	1	1	.100	.182	.100	.282	-8	-1	-1	92	355	0	.222				0	/O3	0.0
1888	KC-a	34	118	5	20	2	0	0	6	3		.169	.203	.186	.390	26	-9	-10	106	82	5	.306	3			0	C/O3	-0.9
1889	Phi-a	31	113	12	25	4	0	0	15	10	15	.221	.285	.257	.541	58	-6	-6	98	151	9	.455	1			0	C/O23	-0.4
1890	Cle-P	59	233	32	59	3	7	0	26	13	29	.253	.304	.326	.630	76	-10	-7	92	95	26	.580	8			-6	C3/O	-0.8
Total	5	183	705	87	155	15	8	0	48	39	45	.220	.267	.264	.530	61	-33	-31	99	75	55	.442	12			-9	C/O32S	-2.7
■ **BILL BRENZEL** Brenzel, William Richard b: 3/3/10, Oakland, Cal. BR/TR, 5'10", 173 lbs. Deb: 4/13/32																												
1932	Pit-N	9	24	0	1	1	0	0	2	0	4	.042	.042	.083	.125	-68	-6	-6	99	372	0	.087	0			0	/C	-0.4
1934	Cle-A	15	51	4	11	3	0	0	3	2	1	.216	.245	.275	.520	34	-5	-5	101	71	4	.400	0	0	0	-1	C	-0.3
1935	Cle-A	52	142	12	31	5	1	0	14	6	10	.218	.250	.268	.518	34	-14	-14	99	125	10	.407	2	2	-1	-5	C	-1.7
Total	3	76	217	16	43	9	1	0	19	8	15	.198	.227	.249	.476	23	-25	-25	100	139	13	.364	2	2		-6	/C	-2.4
■ **ROGER BRESNAHAN** Bresnahan, Roger Philip "The Duke Of Tralee" b: 6/11/1879, Toledo, Ohio d: 12/4/44, Toledo, Ohio BR/TR, 5'9", 200 lbs. Deb: 8/27/1897 MCH																												
1897	Was-N	6	16	1	6	0	0	0	3	1		.375	.412	.375	.787	109	0	0	101	146	3	.700	0			0	/PO	0.0
1900	Chi-N	2	2	0	0	0	0	0	0	0		.000	.000	.000	.000	-99	-1	-1	93	0	0	.000	0			0	/C	0.0
1901	Bal-A	86	295	40	79	9	9	1	32	23		.268	.321	.369	.690	87	-3	-6	107	92	39	.657	10			-8	C/O3P2	-0.6
1902	Bal-A	65	235	30	64	8	6	4	34	21		.272	.332	.409	.741	104	2	1	102	106	37	.754	12			-7	3CO	-0.4
	NY-N	51	178	16	51	9	3	1	22	16		.287	.345	.388	.733	128	6	6	100	112	27	.717	6			6	OC/1S3	1.2
1903	NY-N	113	406	87	142	30	8	4	55	61		.350	.435	.493	.927	157	37	33	106	80	104	1.117	34			8	O1C/3	3.4
1904	NY-N	109	402	81	114	22	7	5	33	58		.284	.374	.410	.784	137	22	20	105	59	68	.819	13			-3	O1/S23	1.4
1905	NY-N	104	331	58	100	18	3	0	46	50		.302	.394	.375	.768	130	15	15	101	132	54	.801	11			-13	C/O	1.0
1906	NY-N	124	405	69	114	22	4	0	43	81		.281	.401	.356	.757	139	23	23	100	115	70	.859	25			-1	CO	3.1
1907	NY-N	110	328	57	83	9	7	4	38	61		.253	.370	.360	.730	124	14	12	105	113	50	.792	15			-10	C/1O3	1.1
1908	NY-N	140	449	70	127	25	3	1	54	**83**		.283	.395	.359	.753	138	26	24	104	134	68	.801	14			-25	*C	0.7
1909	StL-N	72	234	27	57	4	1	0	23	46		.244	.370	.269	.639	104	3	4	96	135	27	.684	11			-1	C/23M	0.7
1910	StL-N	88	234	35	65	15	3	0	27	55	17	.278	.419	.368	.787	142	12	15	92	109	42	.923	13			-5	C/OPM	1.4
1911	StL-N	81	227	22	63	17	8	3	41	45	19	.278	.404	.463	.866	141	14	14	101	122	44	.957	4			0	C/2M	1.9
1912	StL-N	48	108	8	36	7	2	1	15	14	9	.333	.419	.463	.882	142	7	7	100	95	22	.972	4			4	CM	1.2
1913	Chi-N	69	162	20	37	5	2	1	21	21	11	.228	.324	.302	.627	81	-4	-3	99	147	18	.632	7			4	C	0.4
1914	Chi-N	101	248	42	69	10	4	0	24	49	20	.278	.401	.351	.752	127	10	11	98	100	40	.849	14			-0	C2/O	1.5
1915	Chi-N	77	221	19	45	8	1	1	19	29	23	.204	.296	.262	.558	68	-7	-8	102	119	22	.592	19	3	**4**	7	CM	0.8
Total	17	1446	4481	682	1252	218	71	26	530	714	99	.279	.380	.377	.757	125	177	167	102	109	734	.813	212	3		-44	CO/312PS	18.8
■ **RUBE BRESSLER** Bressler, Raymond Bloom b: 10/23/1894, Coder, Pa. d: 11/7/66, Cincinnati, Ohio BR/TL, 6', 187 lbs. Deb: 4/24/14																												
1914	Phi-A	29	51	6	11	1	1	0	4	6	7	.216	.310	.275	.585	78	-1	-1	97	107	5	.525	0			-2	P	0.0
1915	Phi-A	33	55	9	8	0	1	1	4	9	13	.145	.277	.236	.513	56	-3	-3	96	85	4	.489	0			0	P	0.0
1916	Phi-A	4	5	1	1	0	1	0	1	0	0	.200	.200	.600	.800	142	0	0	98	119	1	.750	0			-0	/P	0.0
1917	Cin-N	3	5	0	1	0	0	0	0	0	2	.200	.200	.200	.400	25	-0	-0	92	0	0	.250	0			-0	/P	0.0
1918	Cin-N	23	62	10	17	5	0	0	6	5	4	.274	.328	.355	.683	112	1	1	97	103	7	.600	0			3	P/O	0.0
1919	Cin-N	61	165	22	34	3	4	2	17	23	15	.206	.311	.309	.620	82	-2	-3	105	116	17	.595	2			0	OP	-0.2
1920	Cin-N	21	30	4	8	1	0	0	3	1	4	.267	.290	.300	.590	78	-1	-1	90	129	3	.500	1	0	0	-0	P/O1	0.0
1921	Cin-N	109	323	41	99	18	6	1	54	39	20	.307	.385	.409	.793	109	6	6	101	147	52	.777	5	5	-2	-8	O/1	-0.8
1922	Cin-N	52	53	7	14	0	2	0	8	4	4	.264	.316	.340	.655	72	-2	-2	96	155	6	.590	1	0	0	-1	/1O	-0.2
1923	Cin-N	54	119	25	33	3	1	0	18	20	4	.277	.399	.319	.718	94	-0	0	98	167	17	.747	3	1	0	-1	1/O	-0.1
1924	Cin-N	115	383	41	133	14	13	4	49	22	20	.347	.389	.483	.872	132	17	17	101	91	69	.846	9	10	-3	3	1O	1.3
1925	Cin-N	97	319	43	111	17	6	4	61	40	16	.348	.424	.476	.900	133	16	17	97	132	66	.953	9	5	-0	-2	1O	0.8
1926	Cin-N	86	297	58	106	15	9	1	51	37	20	.357	.433	.478	.911	153	20	23	95	124	61	.969	3			-8	O/1	1.1
1927	Cin-N	124	467	43	136	14	8	3	77	32	22	.291	.338	.375	.713	91	-6	-6	100	155	58	.640	4			3	*O	-0.7
1928	Bro-N	145	501	78	148	29	13	4	70	80	33	.295	.398	.429	.827	117	15	15	99	116	88	.856	2			-8	*O	0.1
1929	Bro-N	136	456	72	145	22	8	9	77	67	27	.318	.406	.461	.867	121	12	16	94	113	86	.907	4			-3	*O	0.2
1930	Bro-N	109	335	53	100	12	8	3	52	51	19	.299	.394	.409	.803	94	-1	-1	101	123	56	.826	4			2	O/1	-0.5
1931	Bro-N	67	153	22	43	4	5	0	26	11	10	.281	.329	.373	.702	87	-3	-3	101	163	19	.618	0			-7	O/1	-1.0
1932	Phi-N	27	83	9	19	6	1	0	6	2	5	.229	.247	.325	.572	47	-6	-7	112	83	7	.453	0			3	O	-0.4
	StL-N	10	19	0	3	0	0	0	2	0	1	.158	.158	.158	.316	-15	-3	-3	100	248	1	.188	0			-0	/O	-0.3
	Yr	37	102	9	22	6	1	0	8	2	6	.216	.231	.294	.525	37	-9	-10	109	130	7	.400	0			2		-0.7
Total	19	1305	3881	544	1170	164	87	32	586	449	246	.301	.378	.413	.791	109	58	65	99	126	623	.779	47	21		-27	O1P	-0.7
■ **EDDIE BRESSOUD** Bressoud, Edward Francis b: 5/2/32, Los Angeles, Cal. BR/TR, 6'1", 175 lbs. Deb: 6/14/56																												
1956	NY-N	49	163	15	37	4	2	0	9	12	20	.227	.284	.276	.560	53	-11	-10	97	84	13	.454	1	0	0	-4	S	-1.0
1957	NY-N	49	127	11	34	2	2	5	10	4	19	.268	.301	.433	.734	92	-1	-2	102	59	16	.635	0	1	-1	4	S3	0.3
1958	SF-N	66	137	19	36	5	3	0	8	14	22	.263	.331	.343	.674	79	-4	-4	100	70	16	.587	0	1	-1	-1	2/3S	-0.2
1959	SF-N	104	315	36	79	17	2	9	26	28	55	.251	.312	.403	.715	93	-6	-4	95	68	40	.646	0	0	0	-8	S/123	-0.8
1960	SF-N	116	386	37	87	19	6	9	43	35	72	.225	.293	.376	.669	91	-10	-5	90	101	41	.588	1	2	-1	-5	*S	-0.6
1961	SF-N	59	14	14	24	6	0	3	11	11	23	.211	.280	.342	.622	65	-6	-6	98	92	9	.526	1	1	-0	-4	S/32	-0.6
1962	Bos-A	153	599	79	166	40	9	14	68	46	118	.277	.331	.444	.775	104	4	2	102	93	85	.702	2	3	-1	21	*S	3.1
1963	Bos-A	140	497	61	129	23	6	20	60	52	93	.260	.332	.451	.783	111	11	7	106	90	75	.738	1	1	-0	-12	*S	0.2
1964	Bos-A	158	566	86	166	41	3	15	55	72	99	.293	.374	.456	.830	127	24	22	102	78	99	.810	1	1	-0	-13	*S	1.0
1965	Bos-A	107	296	29	67	11	1	8	25	29	77	.226	.298	.351	.649	78	-7	-9	107	81	32	.575	0	1	-1	2	S/3O	-0.3
1966	NY-N	133	405	48	91	15	5	10	49	47	107	.225	.307	.360	.667	90	-8	-5	94	117	45	.599	2	2	-1	9	S3/12	1.1
1967	StL-N	52	67	8	9	1	1	1	1	9	18	.134	.237	.224	.461	32	-6	-6	101	23	4	.414	0	0	0	-0	S/3	0.0

YEAR	TM/L	G	AB	R	H	2B	3B	HR	RBI	BB	SO	AVG	OBP	SLG	PRO	/A	BR	/A	PF	CHI	RC	TA	SB	CS	SBR	FR	POS	TPR
Total	12	1186	3672	443	925	184	40	94	365	359	723	.252	.321	.401	.721	97	-20	-19	100	87	474	.671	9	13	-5	-12	*S/2310	2.2
■ **JIM BRETON** Breton, John Frederick b: 7/15/1891, Chicago, Ill. d: 5/30/73, Beloit, Wis. BR/TR, 5'10.5", 178 lbs. Deb: 8/25/13																												
1913	Chi-A	12	30	1	5	1	1	0	2	1	5	.167	.194	.267	.460	36	-3	-2	95	89	1	.360	0			1	/S3	0.0
1914	Chi-A	81	231	21	49	7	2	0	24	24	42	.212	.292	.260	.552	64	-9	-10	103	150	20	.505	9	6	-1	-3	3	-1.3
1915	Chi-A	16	36	3	5	1	0	0	1	5	9	.139	.262	.167	.429	29	-3	-3	98	57	3	.438	2	1	0	-2	3/2S	-0.3
Total	3	109	297	25	59	9	3	0	27	30	56	.199	.279	.249	.528	57	-15	-16	102	132	24	.482	11	7		-4	/3S2	-1.6
■ **GEORGE BRETT** Brett, George Howard b: 5/15/53, Glen Dale, W.Va. BL/TR, 6', 185 lbs. Deb: 8/02/73																												
1973	KC-A	13	40	2	5	2	0	0	0	0	5	.125	.125	.175	.300	-15	-6	-7	109	0	1	.200	0	0	0	-1	3	-0.8
1974	KC-A	133	457	49	129	21	5	2	47	21	38	.282	.314	.363	.677	89	-4	-8	106	107	50	.570	8	5	-1	-6	*3/S	-1.2
1975	KC-A	159	634	84	**195**	35	**13**	11	89	46	49	.308	.356	.456	.812	126	22	20	102	112	102	.766	13	10	-2	-5	*3/S	1.6
1976	KC-A	159	645	94	**215**	34	**14**	7	67	49	36	**.333**	.381	.462	.843	146	36	36	100	78	**114**	.822	21	11	-0	2	*3/S	4.0
1977	KC-A	139	564	105	176	32	13	22	88	55	24	.312	.375	.532	.907	143	33	33	100	92	108	.900	14	12	-3	20	*3/SD	4.6
1978	KC-A	128	510	79	150	**45**	8	9	62	39	35	.294	.345	.467	.812	124	16	15	102	89	83	.807	23	7	3	5	*3/S	2.2
1979	KC-A	154	645	119	**212**	42	**20**	23	107	51	36	.329	.378	.563	.941	142	43	38	105	92	134	.956	17	10	-1	16	*3/1	5.3
1980	KC-A	117	449	87	175	33	9	24	118	58	22	**.390**	**.461**	**.664**	**1.124**	**207**	**65**	**66**	98	132	**135**	**1.278**	15	6	1	3	*3/1	**6.7**
1981	KC-A	89	347	42	109	27	7	6	43	27	23	.314	.365	.484	.849	145	18	19	99	96	60	.837	14	6	1	-9	3	1.1
1982	KC-A	144	552	101	166	32	9	21	82	71	51	.301	.381	.505	.887	141	32	32	100	92	107	.895	6	1	1	-2	*3O	2.8
1983	KC-A	123	464	90	144	38	2	25	93	57	39	.310	.387	**.563**	**.949**	155	36	35	101	104	100	.967	0	1	-1	-10	*31O/D	2.3
1984	KC-A	104	377	42	107	21	3	13	69	38	37	.284	.349	.459	.808	123	11	11	99	137	58	.746	0	2	-1	4	*3	1.6
1985	KC-A	155	550	108	184	38	5	30	112	103	49	.335	.442	**.585**	**1.028**	**175**	**63**	**62**	102	114	**146**	1.153	9	1	2	14	*3/D	7.0
1986	KC-A	124	441	70	128	28	4	16	73	80	45	.290	.404	.481	.885	141	28	28	100	118	89	.925	1	2	-1	7	*3/SD	2.9
1987	KC-A	115	427	71	124	18	2	22	78	72	47	.290	.394	.496	.890	130	24	21	104	108	85	.921	6	3	0	0	1D3	1.1
1988	KC-A	157	589	90	180	42	3	24	103	82	51	.306	.393	.509	.903	146	41	39	103	106	119	.934	14	3	2	-8	*1D/S	2.6
Total	16	2013	7691	1233	2399	488	117	255	1231	849	587	.312	.382	.505	.887	142	458	441	102	103	1492	.913	161	80	0	29	*31/DOS	43.8
■ **TONY BREWER** Brewer, Anthony Bruce b: 11/25/57, Shreveport, La. BR/TR, 5'11", 190 lbs. Deb: 8/01/84																												
1984	LA-N	24	37	3	4	1	0	1	4	4	9	.108	.195	.216	.411	15	-4	-4	104	142	2	.382	1	0	0	-2	O	-0.6
■ **MIKE BREWER** Brewer, Michael Quinn b: 10/24/59, Shreveport, La. BR/TR, 6'5", 190 lbs. Deb: 6/11/86																												
1986	KC-A	12	18	0	3	1	0	0	0	2	6	.167	.250	.222	.472	31	-2	-2	100	0	1	.375	0	1	-1	-2	/OD	-0.4
■ **CHARLIE BREWSTER** Brewster, Charles Lawrence b: 12/27/16, Marthaville, La. BR/TR, 5'8.5", 175 lbs. Deb: 5/02/43																												
1943	Cin-N	7	8	0	1	0	0	0	0	0	1	.125	.125	.125	.250	-28	-1	-1	99	0	0	.143	0			0	/2	0.0
	Phi-N	49	159	13	35	2	0	0	12	10	19	.220	.275	.233	.508	50	-11	-9	94	117	11	.397	1			-12	S	-1.8
	Yr	56	167	13	36	2	0	0	12	10	20	.216	.268	.228	.496	46	-12	-11	94	102	11	.383	1			-12		-1.8
1944	Chi-N	10	44	4	11	2	0	0	2	5	7	.250	.327	.295	.622	75	-1	-1	101	48	4	.529	0			0	S	0.0
1946	Cle-A	3	2	0	0	0	0	0	0	1	1	.000	.333	.000	.333	-2	-0	-0	89	0	0	.500	0	0	0	0	/S	0.0
Total	3	69	213	17	47	4	0	0	14	16	28	.221	.281	.239	.521	53	-13	-12	95	97	15	.422	1	0		-12	/S2	-1.8
■ **FRITZ BRICKELL** Brickell, Fritz Darrell b: 3/19/35, Wichita, Kan. d: 10/15/65, Wichita, Kan. BR/TR, 5'5.5", 157 lbs. Deb: 4/30/58																												
1958	NY-A	2	0	0	0	0	0	0	0	0	0	—	—	—	—	—	0	0	103	—	—	—	0	0	0	0	/2	0.0
1959	NY-A	18	39	4	10	1	0	1	4	1	10	.256	.275	.359	.634	78	-2	-1	93	93	4	.500	0	0	0	1	S/2	0.1
1961	LA-A	21	49	3	6	0	0	0	3	6	9	.122	.218	.122	.341	-6	-7	-8	111	196	1	.255	0	0	0	1	S	-0.5
Total	3	41	88	7	16	1	0	1	7	7	19	.182	.242	.227	.469	27	-9	-9	103	152	20	.355	0	0	0	2	/S2	-0.4
■ **FRED BRICKELL** Brickell, George Frederick b: 11/9/06, Saffordville, Kan. d: 4/8/61, Wichita, Kan. BL/TR, 5'7", 160 lbs. Deb: 8/19/26																												
1926	Pit-N	24	55	11	19	3	1	0	4	3	6	.345	.379	.436	.816	106	1	1	112	58	9	.750	0			-1	O	0.0
1927	Pit-N	32	21	6	6	1	0	1	4	1	0	.286	.318	.476	.794	108	0	0	102	108	3	.733	0			-1	/O	0.0
1928	Pit-N	81	202	34	65	4	4	3	41	20	18	.322	.383	.426	.809	104	4	2	107	154	33	.810	5			0	O	0.0
1929	Pit-N	60	118	13	37	4	2	0	17	7	12	.314	.352	.381	.733	79	-3	-4	103	129	15	.679	3			-1	O	-0.6
1930	Pit-N	68	219	36	65	9	3	1	14	15	20	.297	.342	.379	.721	76	-9	-8	97	56	28	.656	3			-3	O	-1.3
	Phi-N	53	240	33	59	12	6	0	17	13	21	.246	.290	.346	.636	50	-19	-21	106	61	24	.547	1			7	O	-1.5
	Yr	121	459	69	124	21	9	1	31	28	41	.270	.315	.362	.677	62	-28	-28	101	59	51	.597	4			3		-2.8
1931	Phi-N	130	514	77	130	14	5	1	31	42	39	.253	.316	.305	.621	64	-22	-27	106	73	52	.544	5			-2	*O	-3.4
1932	Phi-N	45	66	9	22	6	1	0	2	4	5	.333	.389	.455	.843	113	3	1	112	25	12	.864	2			1	O	0.1
1933	Phi-N	8	13	2	4	1	1	0	1	1	0	.308	.357	.538	.896	130	1	1	118	54	3	.889	0			1	/O	0.1
Total	8	501	1448	221	407	54	23	6	131	106	121	.281	.334	.363	.697	75	-45	-55	105	82	178	.633	19			1	O	-6.6
■ **GEORGE BRICKLEY** Brickley, George Vincent b: 7/19/1894, Everett, Mass. d: 2/23/47, Everett, Mass. BR/TR, 5'9", 180 lbs. Deb: 9/26/13																												
1913	Phi-A	5	12	0	2	0	1	0	0	0	4	.167	.231	.333	.564	67	-1	-1	97	0	1	.500	0			-1	/O	-0.1
■ **JIM BRIDEWESER** Brideweser, James Ehrenfeld b: 2/13/27, Lancaster, Ohio BR/TR, 6', 165 lbs. Deb: 9/29/51																												
1951	NY-A	2	8	1	3	0	0	0	0	0	1	.375	.375	.375	.750	113	0	0	92	0	1	.600	0	0	0	0	/S	0.0
1952	NY-A	42	38	12	10	0	0	0	2	3	5	.263	.317	.263	.580	64	-2	-2	98	75	3	.433	0	0	0	1	S/23	0.0
1953	NY-A	7	3	3	3	0	1	0	3	1	0	1.000	1.000	1.667	2.667	657	2	2	93	222	5	—	0	0	0	0	/S	0.3
1954	Bal-A	73	204	18	54	7	2	0	12	15	27	.265	.318	.319	.637	78	-7	-6	95	70	20	.526	1	1	-0	-2	S2	-0.3
1955	Chi-A	34	58	6	12	3	2	0	4	3	7	.207	.246	.328	.573	53	-4	-4	101	79	4	.449	0	0	0	1	S/32	0.0
1956	Chi-A	10	11	0	2	1	0	0	1	0	3	.182	.250	.273	.523	36	-1	-1	104	124	1	.444	0	0	0	0	S	0.0
	Det-A	70	156	23	34	4	0	0	10	20	19	.218	.307	.244	.550	49	-11	-11	97	98	13	.480	3	1	0	-2	S2/3	-0.6
	Yr	80	167	23	36	5	0	0	11	20	22	.216	.303	.246	.549	48	-13	-12	98	103	13	.478	3	1	0	-2		-0.6
1957	Bal-A	91	142	16	38	7	1	1	18	21	15	.268	.362	.352	.714	103	-0	1	93	134	19	.670	2	0	1	-1	S/32	0.7
Total	7	329	620	79	156	22	6	1	50	63	77	.252	.323	.311	.634	75	-23	-20	96	95	66	.561	6	2	1	-3	S/23	0.1
■ **ROCKY BRIDGES** Bridges, Everett Lamar b: 8/7/27, Refugio, Tex. BR/TR, 5'8", 170 lbs. Deb: 4/17/51 C																												
1951	Bro-N	63	134	13	34	7	0	1	15	10	10	.254	.306	.328	.634	72	-6	-5	98	123	12	.495	0	0	0	-0	32/S	-0.4
1952	Bro-N	51	56	9	11	3	0	0	2	7	9	.196	.286	.250	.536	49	-4	-4	102	56	4	.438	0	1	-1	1	2S/3	-0.1
1953	Cin-N	122	432	52	98	13	2	1	21	37	42	.227	.288	.273	.561	48	-33	-32	99	69	35	.464	6	3	0	9	*2/S3	-1.7
1954	Cin-N	53	52	4	12	1	0	0	2	7	7	.231	.322	.250	.572	50	-3	-4	104	61	4	.476	0	1	-1	0	S23	-0.1
1955	Cin-N	95	168	20	48	4	0	1	18	15	19	.286	.344	.327	.672	75	-4	-6	106	126	19	.568	1	1	-0	0	3S/2	-0.4
1956	Cin-N	71	19	9	4	0	0	0	1	4	3	.211	.348	.211	.558	51	-1	-1	108	106	1	.529	1	2	-1	-2	3/2SO	-0.2
1957	Cin-N	5	1	1	0	0	0	0	0	1	1	.000	.500	.000	.500	47	-0	0	105	0	0	1.000	0	0	0	0	/2S3	0.0
	Was-A	120	391	40	89	17	2	3	47	40	32	.228	.303	.304	.607	68	-18	-17	98	145	34	.502	0	2	-1	14	*S2/3	0.5
1958	Was-A	116	377	38	99	14	3	5	28	27	32	.263	.317	.355	.672	88	-8	-6	97	75	38	.552	0	3	-2	8	*S/23	1.6
1959	Det-A	116	381	38	102	16	3	3	35	30	35	.268	.323	.349	.672	76	-8	-13	111	97	40	.559	1	2	-1	-1	*S/2	-0.5
1960	Det-A	10	5	0	1	0	0	0	0	0	0	.200	.200	.200	.400	8	-1	-1	102	0	0	.200	0	0	0	-0	/3S	0.0
	Cle-A	10	27	1	9	0	0	0	3	1	2	.333	.357	.333	.690	90	-0	-0	98	131	3	.526	0	0	0	-0	/S3	0.0
	Yr	20	32	1	10	0	0	0	3	1	2	.313	.333	.313	.646	76	-1	-1	100	65	3	.478	0	0	0	-0		0.0
	StL-N	3	0	0	0	0	0	0	0	0	0	—	—	—	—	—	0	0	108	—	—	—	0	0	0	0	/2	0.0
1961	LA-A	84	229	20	55	5	1	2	15	26	37	.240	.320	.297	.617	59	-10	-14	111	79	23	.539	1	0	0	7	2S/3	0.2
Total	11	919	2272	245	562	80	11	16	187	205	229	.247	.312	.313	.625	67	-96	-103	102	97	218	.540	10	15	-6	35	S23/O	-1.1
■ **AL BRIDWELL** Bridwell, Albert Henry b: 1/4/1884, Friendship, Ohio d: 1/23/69, Portsmouth, Ohio BL/TR, 5'9", 170 lbs. Deb: 4/16/05																												
1905	Cin-N	82	254	17	64	3	1	0	17	19		.252	.304	.272	.576	72	-8	-8	103	86	24	.505	8			7	3O/2S1	0.1
1906	Bos-N	120	459	41	104	9	1	0	22	44		.227	.294	.251	.545	72	-14	-14	100	62	36	.465	6			10	*S/O	0.3
1907	Bos-N	140	509	49	111	8	2	0	26	61		.218	.302	.242	.543	76	-14	-11	95	85	43	.505	17			7	*S	0.2
1908	NY-N	147	467	53	133	14	1	0	46	52		.285	.356	.319	.676	114	12	9	104	121	59	.662	20			9	*S	1.8
1909	NY-N	145	476	59	140	11	5	0	55	67		.294	.386	.338	.724	120	18	15	105	127	73	.786	32			1	*S	1.9
1910	NY-N	142	492	74	136	15	7	0	48	73	23	.276	.374	.335	.710	113	7	11	95	107	68	.719	14			2	*S	1.8

YEAR	TM/L	G	AB	R	H	2B	3B	HR	RBI	BB	SO	AVG	OBP	SLG	PRO	/A	BR	/A	PF	CHI	RC	TA	SB	CS	SBR	FR	POS	TPR
1911	NY-N	76	263	28	71	10	1	0	31	33	10	.270	.358	.316	.673	87	-3	-4	102	134	33	.661	8			2	S	0.1
	Bos-N	51	182	29	53	5	0	0	10	33	8	.291	.403	.319	.721	99	3	2	103	62	25	.729	2			-2	S	0.2
	Yr	127	445	57	124	15	1	0	41	66	18	.279	.377	.317	.694	92	0	-2	103	106	59	.688	10			0		0.3
1912	Bos-N	31	106	6	25	5	1	0	14	5	5	.236	.270	.302	.572	53	-7	-8	107	147	9	.481	2			-6	S	-0.9
1913	Chi-N	136	405	35	97	6	6	1	37	74	28	.240	.358	.291	.650	88	-3	-3	99	111	47	.666	12			1	*S	0.7
1914	StL-F	117	381	46	90	6	5	1	33	71	18	.236	.356	.286	.642	81	-4	-7	106	113	47	.649	9			0	*S2	0.0
1915	StL-F	65	175	20	40	3	2	0	9	25	6	.229	.325	.269	.594	73	-4	-5	105	69	19	.578	6			3	23/1	-0.1
Total	11	1252	4169	457	1064	95	32	2	348	557	98	.255	.345	.295	.640	91	-16	-22	101	102	484	.623	136			33	*S/2301	6.1
■ **BUNNY BRIEF**	Brief, Anthony Vincent (born Antonio Bordetzki) b: 7/3/1892, Remus, Mich. d: 2/10/63, Milwaukee, Wis. BR/TR, 6', 185 lbs. Deb: 9/22/12																											
1912	StL-A	15	42	9	13	3	0	0	5	6		.310	.408	.381	.789	128	2	2	99	104	8	.862	2			-1	/O1	0.0
1913	StL-A	85	258	24	56	11	6	1	26	21	46	.217	.284	.318	.602	80	-9	-7	95	109	24	.540	3			4	1/O	-0.3
1915	Chi-A	48	154	13	33	6	2	2	17	16	28	.214	.305	.318	.623	88	-3	-2	98	107	16	.606	8	6	-1	-1	1	-0.6
1917	Pit-N	36	115	15	25	5	1	2	11	15	21	.217	.318	.330	.649	99	0	0	100	98	14	.656	4			-1	1	0.0
Total	4	184	569	61	127	25	9	5	59	58	95	.223	.306	.325	.631	90	-9	-7	97	106	62	.603	17	6		2	1/O	-0.9
■ **CHARLIE BRIGGS**	Briggs, Charles R. b: 1861, Batavia, Ill. 5'7", 170 lbs. Deb: 5/02/1884																											
1884	CP-U	49	182	29	31	8	2	1		11		.170	.218	.253	.470	59	-7	-7	99	0	10	.377	0			-2	O2/S	-0.8
■ **DAN BRIGGS**	Briggs, Dan Lee b: 11/18/52, Scotia, Cal. BL/TL, 6', 180 lbs. Deb: 9/10/75																											
1975	Cal-A	13	31	3	7	1	0	1	3	2	6	.226	.273	.355	.628	80	-1	-1	95	82	2	.500	0	2	-1	-1	/1OD	-0.2
1976	Cal-A	77	248	19	53	13	2	1	14	13	47	.214	.256	.294	.550	66	-13	-10	92	71	17	.424	0	3	-2	2	1O/D	-1.3
1977	Cal-A	59	74	6	12	2	0	1	4	8	14	.162	.244	.230	.474	32	-7	-7	95	79	4	.385	0	0	0	0	1O	-0.9
1978	Cle-A	15	49	4	8	0	1	1	1	4	9	.163	.226	.265	.492	41	-4	-4	93	25	3	.395	0	0	0	2	O	-0.1
1979	SD-N	104	227	34	47	4	3	8	30	18	45	.207	.280	.357	.637	75	-9	-8	96	113	23	.576	2	1	0	-4	1O	-1.5
1981	Mon-N	9	11	0	1	0	0	0	0	0	3	.091	.091	.091	.182	-49	-2	-2	99	0	0	.091	0	1	-1	-1	/1O	-0.3
1982	Chi-N	48	48	1	6	0	0	0	1	0	9	.125	.143	.125	.268	-24	-8	-8	103	65	1	.163	0	0	0	-2	O/1	-1.0
Total	7	325	688	67	134	20	6	12	53	45	133	.195	.251	.294	.545	56	-44	-40	95	82	50	.456	2	7	-4	-2	1O/D	-5.3
■ **GRANT BRIGGS**	Briggs, Grant b: 3/16/1865, Pittsburgh, Pa. d: 5/31/28, Pittsburgh, Pa. Deb: 4/17/1890																											
1890	Syr-a	86	316	44	57	6	5	0		16		.180	.222	.231	.453	39	-26	-21	90	0	18	.375	7			-0	CO/3S	-1.4
1891	Lou-a	1	4	0	1	0	0	0	0	0	0	.250	.250	.250	.500	50	-0	-0	90	0	0	.333	0			0	/C	0.0
1892	StL-N	23	57	2	4	1	0	0	1	6	16	.070	.172	.088	.260	-21	-8	-8	95	61	1	.283	3			0	C/O	-0.6
1895	Lou-N	1	3	0	0	0	0	0	0	0	1	.000	.000	.000	.000	-99	-1	-1	95	0	0	.000	0			0	/C	0.0
Total	4	111	380	46	62	7	5	0	1	22	17	.163	.213	.208	.421	28	-35	-30	91	10	20	.355	10			-0	/CO3S	-2.0
■ **JOHN BRIGGS**	Briggs, John Edward b: 3/10/44, Paterson, N.J. BL/TL, 6'1", 190 lbs. Deb: 4/17/64																											
1964	Phi-N	61	66	16	17	2	0	1	6	9	12	.258	.347	.333	.680	94	-0	-0	99	98	8	.615	1	1	-0	-2	O/1	-0.3
1965	Phi-N	93	229	47	54	9	4	4	23	42	44	.236	.354	.362	.717	108	2	4	95	100	33	.723	3	2	-0	-1	O	0.0
1966	Phi-N	81	255	43	72	13	5	10	23	41	55	.282	.382	.490	.872	139	15	14	101	62	50	.904	3	2	-0	-8	O	0.5
1967	Phi-N	106	332	47	77	12	4	9	30	41	72	.232	.316	.373	.690	93	-1	-3	104	82	40	.639	3	5	-2	1	O	-0.8
1968	Phi-N	110	338	36	86	13	1	7	31	58	72	.254	.365	.361	.726	122	10	11	97	91	49	.727	8	5	-1	-1	O1	0.5
1969	Phi-N	124	361	51	86	20	3	12	46	64	78	.238	.353	.410	.763	115	7	8	98	100	56	.781	9	6	-1	1	*O/1	0.3
1970	Phi-N	110	341	43	92	15	7	9	47	39	65	.270	.345	.434	.779	111	3	5	96	104	48	.719	5	4	-1	5	O	0.4
1971	Phi-N	10	22	3	4	1	0	0	3	6	2	.182	.357	.227	.584	67	-1	-1	103	244	2	.611	0	0	0	-1	/O	-0.1
	Mil-A	125	375	51	99	11	1	21	59	71	79	.264	.383	.467	.849	135	21	20	103	103	71	.879	1	2	-1	-0	O1	1.4
1972	Mil-A	135	418	58	111	14	1	21	65	54	67	.266	.351	.455	.805	145	20	22	95	107	67	.776	1	2	-1	-3	*O1	1.4
1973	Mil-A	142	488	78	120	20	7	18	57	87	83	.246	.362	.426	.788	127	16	18	96	87	80	.815	15	9	-1	4	*O/D	1.7
1974	Mil-A	154	554	72	140	30	8	17	73	71	102	.253	.338	.428	.765	116	13	12	102	106	82	.739	9	7	-2	-1	*O/D	0.5
1975	Mil-A	28	74	12	22	1	0	3	5	20	13	.297	.447	.432	.879	149	6	6	100	47	15	.945	0	2	-1	2	O/D	0.6
	Min-A	87	264	44	61	9	2	7	39	60	41	.231	.373	.360	.733	101	5	3	107	129	41	.782	6	2	1	0	1O/D	0.0
	Yr	115	338	56	83	10	2	10	44	80	54	.246	.390	.376	.766	111	11	9	105	109	56	.819	6	4	-1	2		0.6
Total	12	1366	4117	601	1041	170	43	139	507	663	785	.253	.357	.416	.773	120	116	118	100	98	643	.782	64	49	-10	-3	*O1/D	6.1
■ **HARRY BRIGHT**	Bright, Harry James b: 9/22/29, Kansas City, Mo. BR/TR, 6', 190 lbs. Deb: 8/07/58																											
1958	Pit-N	15	24	4	6	1	0	1	3	1	6	.250	.280	.417	.697	86	-1	-1	95	95	3	.611	0	0	0	-1	/3	-0.1
1959	Pit-N	40	48	4	12	1	0	3	8	5	10	.250	.321	.458	.779	101	0	-0	103	104	7	.750	0	0	0	-1	/O32	0.0
1960	Pit-N	4	4	0	0	0	0	0	0	0	2	.000	.000	.000	.000	-99	-1	-1	99	0	0	.000	0	0	0	0	H	0.0
1961	Was-A	72	183	20	44	6	0	4	21	19	23	.240	.312	.339	.651	78	-7	-6	95	111	18	.551	0	2	-1	2	3/C2	-0.1
1962	Was-A	113	392	55	107	15	4	17	67	26	51	.273	.321	.462	.783	107	3	3	101	117	54	.703	2	1	0	-1	1/C3	-0.4
1963	Cin-N	1	1	0	0	0	0	0	0	0	1	.000	.000	.000	.000	-96	-0	-0	104	0	0	.000	0	0	0	0	/1	0.0
	NY-A	60	157	15	37	7	0	7	23	13	31	.236	.298	.414	.712	97	-1	-1	101	112	19	.637	0	0	0	2	13	0.0
1964	NY-A	4	5	0	1	0	0	0	0	1	1	.200	.333	.200	.533	51	-0	-0	103	0	0	.500	0	0	0	0	/1	0.0
1965	Chi-N	27	25	1	7	1	0	0	4	0	8	.280	.280	.320	.600	67	-1	-1	102	207	2	.444	0	0	0	0	H	0.0
Total	8	336	839	99	214	31	4	32	126	65	133	.255	.311	.416	.727	95	-8	-7	99	114	104	.667	2	3	-1	2	1/3CO2	-0.6
■ **GREG BRILEY**	Briley, Gregory "Peewee" b: 5/24/65, Bethel, N.C. BL/TR, 5'9", 165 lbs. Deb: 6/27/88																											
1988	Sea-A	13	36	6	9	2	0	1	4	5	6	.250	.341	.389	.730	97	0	-0	108	94	5	.679	0	1	-1	-2	O	-0.2
■ **BILL BRINKER**	Brinker, William Hutchinson "Dode" b: 8/30/1883, Warrensburg, Mo. d: 2/5/65, Arcadia, Cal. BB/TR, 6'1", 190 lbs. Deb: 4/24/12																											
1912	Phi-N	9	18	1	4	1	0	0	2	2	3	.222	.300	.278	.578	58	-1	-1	100	135	1	.500	0			-0	/3O	0.0
■ **CHUCK BRINKMAN**	Brinkman, Charles Ernest b: 9/16/44, Cincinnati, O. BR/TR, 6'1", 185 lbs. Deb: 7/10/69																											
1969	Chi-A	14	15	2	1	0	0	0	0	1	5	.067	.125	.067	.192	-42	-3	-3	108	0	0	.143	0	0	0	-0	C	-0.2
1970	Chi-A	9	20	4	5	1	0	0	0	3	3	.250	.348	.300	.648	76	-0	-1	106	0	2	.600	0	0	0	0	/C	0.0
1971	Chi-A	15	20	0	4	0	0	0	1	3	5	.200	.304	.200	.504	46	-1	-1	98	102	1	.438	0	0	0	0	C	0.0
1972	Chi-A	35	52	1	7	0	0	0	0	4	7	.135	.196	.135	.331	-0	-6	-7	106	0	1	.229	0	0	0	-1	C	-0.8
1973	Chi-A	63	139	13	26	6	0	1	10	11	37	.187	.252	.252	.503	41	-11	-11	102	103	9	.405	0	0	0	1	C	-0.8
1974	Chi-A	8	14	1	2	0	0	0	0	1	3	.143	.200	.143	.343	-0	-2	-2	102	0	0	.231	0	0	0	0	/C	-0.1
	Pit-N	4	7	1	1	0	0	0	1	0	0	.143	.143	.143	.286	-20	-1	-1	98	386	0	.167	0	0	0	0	/C	0.0
Total	6	148	267	22	46	7	0	1	12	23	60	.172	.241	.210	.450	28	-25	-26	103	71	15	.362	0	0	0	-0	C	-1.9
■ **ED BRINKMAN**	Brinkman, Edwin Albert b: 12/8/41, Cincinnati, O. BR/TR, 6', 170 lbs. Deb: 9/06/61 C																											
1961	Was-A	4	11	0	1	0	0	0	0	1	1	.091	.167	.091	.258	-31	-2	-2	95	0	0	.200	0	0	0	0	/3	-0.1
1962	Was-A	54	133	8	22	7	1	0	4	11	28	.165	.229	.233	.462	25	-14	-14	101	51	6	.368	1	0	0	-4	S3	-1.5
1963	Was-A	145	514	44	117	20	3	7	45	31	86	.228	.277	.319	.596	68	-23	-22	98	104	46	.502	5	3	-0	7	*S	-0.8
1964	Was-A	132	447	54	100	20	3	8	34	26	99	.224	.273	.336	.608	67	-20	-20	101	83	41	.513	2	2	-1	-1	*S	-2.2
1965	Was-A	154	444	35	82	13	2	5	35	38	82	.185	.252	.257	.509	45	-32	-32	100	113	28	.413	1	2	-1	-8	*S	-3.6
1966	Was-A	158	582	42	133	18	9	7	48	29	105	.229	.265	.326	.592	73	-24	-21	95	97	45	.476	7	9	-3	10	*S	-0.4
1967	Was-A	109	320	21	60	9	2	1	18	24	58	.188	.253	.237	.490	45	-21	-22	102	95	20	.393	1	3	-2	10	*S	-0.5
1968	Was-A	77	193	12	36	3	0	0	6	19	31	.187	.259	.202	.462	45	-13	-11	91	66	10	.356	0	0	0	-0	S/2O	-0.7
1969	Was-A	151	576	71	153	18	5	2	43	50	42	.266	.330	.325	.654	86	-12	-10	97	95	59	.545	2	2	-1	14	*S	1.1
1970	Was-A	158	625	63	164	17	2	1	40	60	41	.262	.332	.301	.633	79	-19	-16	96	82	62	.538	8	9	-3	**32**	*S	2.6
1971	Det-A	159	527	40	120	18	2	1	37	44	54	.228	.296	.275	.571	65	-25	-23	96	102	42	.464	1	4	-2	14	*S	0.6
1972	Det-A	156	516	42	105	19	1	6	49	38	51	.203	.262	.279	.541	54	-25	-32	113	129	37	.435	0	0	0	4	*S	-1.3
1973	Det-A	162	515	55	122	16	4	7	40	34	79	.237	.285	.324	.610	71	-20	-21	101	84	44	.486	0	1	-1	-17	*S	-1.7
1974	Det-A	153	502	55	111	15	3	14	54	29	71	.221	.268	.347	.614	71	-17	-21	106	98	45	.516	2	0	1	2	*S/3	-0.5
1975	StL-N	28	75	6	18	4	0	1	6	7	10	.240	.313	.333	.647	77	-2	-2	103	83	7	.550	0	0	0	-0	S	0.0
	Tex-A	1	2	0	0	0	0	0	0	0	1	.000	.000	.000	.000	-99	-1	-1	100	0	0	.000	0	0	0	0	/3	0.0

YEAR	TM/L	G	AB	R	H	2B	3B	HR	RBI	BB	SO	AVG	OBP	SLG	PRO	/A	BR	/A	PF	CHI	RC	TA	SB	CS	SBR	FR	POS	TPR
	NY-A	44	63	2	11	4	1	0	2	3	6	.175	.224	.270	.494	39	-5	-5	99	45	3	.382	0	0	0	-1	S/23	-0.2
	Yr	45	65	2	11	4	1	0	2	3	7	.169	.217	.262	.479	35	-6	-6	99	44	3	.368	0	0	0	-1		-0.2
Total	15	1845	6045	550	1355	201	38	60	461	444	845	.224	.282	.300	.581	65	-276	-274	100	95	497	.492	30	35	-12	60	*S/32O	-9.2
■ **LEON BRINKOPF**	Brinkopf, Leon Clarence b: 10/20/26, Cape Girardeau, Mo BR/TR, 5'11.5", 185 lbs. Deb: 4/18/52																											
1952	Chi-N	9	22	1	4	0	0	0	2	4	5	.182	.308	.182	.490	38	-2	-2	103	195	2	.444	0	0	0	-0	/S	-0.1
■ **FATTY BRIODY**	Briody, Charles F. "Alderman" b: 8/13/1858, Lansinsburg, N.Y. d: 6/22/03, Chicago, Ill. TR, 5'8.5", 190 lbs. Deb: 6/16/1880																											
1880	Tro-N	1	4	0	0	0	0	0	0	0	0	.000	.000	.000	.000	-91	-1	-1	110	0	0	.000				0	/C	0.0
1882	Cle-N	53	194	30	50	13	0	0	13	9	13	.258	.291	.325	.615	108	-1	2	90	71	19	.500				2	C	0.8
1883	Cle-N	40	145	23	34	5	1	0	10	3	13	.234	.250	.283	.533	59	-7	-8	105	86	11	.396				3	C/213	-0.2
1884	Cle-N	43	148	17	25	6	0	1	12	6	19	.169	.201	.230	.431	34	-11	-11	102	111	7	.325				12	C/O	0.3
	Cin-U	22	89	11	30	2	2	0		1		.337	.344	.404	.749	141	5	3	108	0	13	.627	0			0	C	0.3
1885	StL-N	62	215	14	42	9	0	1	17	12	23	.195	.238	.251	.489	63	-10	-7	92	106	13	.382				-4	C/O32	-0.5
1886	KC-N	56	215	14	51	10	3	0	29	3	35	.237	.248	.312	.559	65	-8	-10	107	144	17	.427	0			9	C/O1	0.2
1887	Det-N	33	128	24	29	6	1	1	26	9	10	.227	.283	.313	.595	66	-6	-6	102	190	13	.566	6			6	C	0.3
1888	KC-a	13	48	1	10	1	0	0	8	1		.208	.224	.229	.454	45	-3	-3	106	222	3	.316	0			0	C	-0.2
Total	8	323	1186	134	271	52	7	3	115	44	113	.228	.257	.292	.548	71	-40	-41	100	111	95	.434	6			27	C/2013	1.0
■ **GEORGE BRISTOW**	Bristow, George T. b: 5/1870, Paw Paw, Ill. Deb: 4/15/1899																											
1899	Cle-N	3	8	0	1	1	0	0	0	0		.125	.222	.250	.472	35	-1	-1	89	0	0	.429	0			0	/O	0.0
■ **GUS BRITTAIN**	Brittain, August Schuster b: 11/29/09, Wilmington, N.C. d: 2/16/74, Wilmington, N.C. BR/TR, 5'10", 192 lbs. Deb: 7/22/37																											
1937	Cin-N	3	6	0	1	0	0	0	0	0	3	.167	.167	.167	.333	-10	-1	-1	91	0	0	.200	0			0	/C	0.0
■ **GIL BRITTON**	Britton, Stephen Gilbert b: 9/21/1891, Parsons, Kan. d: 6/20/83, Parsons, Kan. BR/TR, 5'10", 160 lbs. Deb: 9/20/13																											
1913	Pit-N	3	12	0	0	0	0	0	0	0	2	.000	.000	.000	.000	-99	-3	-3	96	0	0	.000	0			0	/S	-0.2
■ **GREG BROCK**	Brock, Gregory Allen b: 6/14/57, Mc Minnville, Ore. BL/TR, 6'3", 200 lbs. Deb: 9/01/82																											
1982	LA-N	18	17	1	2	1	0	0	1	1	5	.118	.167	.176	.343	-4	-2	-2	95	131	1	.267	0	0	0	0	/1	-0.2
1983	LA-N	146	455	64	102	14	2	20	66	83	81	.224	.345	.396	.741	105	4	4	100	109	64	.733	5	1	1	2	*1	0.1
1984	LA-N	88	271	33	61	6	0	14	34	39	37	.225	.323	.402	.725	99	1	-0	104	88	37	.722	8	0	2	4	1	0.4
1985	LA-N	129	438	64	110	19	0	21	66	54	72	.251	.333	.438	.772	123	8	12	93	105	65	.737	4	2	0	-0	*1	0.8
1986	LA-N	115	325	33	76	13	0	16	52	37	60	.234	.312	.422	.734	107	-1	2	94	112	42	.680	2	5	-2	6	1	0.2
1987	Mil-A	141	532	81	159	29	3	13	85	57	63	.299	.373	.438	.811	113	13	11	102	132	88	.780	5	4	-1	3	*1	0.0
1988	Mil-A	115	364	53	77	16	1	6	50	63	48	.212	.333	.310	.643	79	-7	-9	103	155	39	.617	6	2	1	10	*1/D	-0.5
Total	7	752	2402	329	587	98	6	90	354	334	366	.244	.339	.403	.742	104	16	17	99	119	336	.729	30	14	1	25	1/D	0.8
■ **JOHN BROCK**	Brock, John Roy b: 10/16/1896, Hamilton, Ill. d: 10/27/51, Clayton, Mo. BR/TR, 5'6.5", 165 lbs. Deb: 8/10/17																											
1917	StL-N	7	15	4	6	1	0	0	2	0	2	.400	.400	.467	.867	163	1	1	102	110	3	1.000	2			0	/C	0.2
1918	StL-N	27	52	9	11	2	0	0	4	3	10	.212	.255	.250	.505	58	-3	-2	93	116	4	.512	5			0	C/O	0.0
Total	2	34	67	13	17	3	0	0	6	3	12	.254	.286	.299	.584	82	-2	-1	95	115	8	.600	7			0	/CO	0.2
■ **LOU BROCK**	Brock, Louis Clark b: 6/18/39, El Dorado, Ark. BL/TL, 5'11.5", 170 lbs. Deb: 9/10/61 H																											
1961	Chi-N	4	11	1	1	0	0	0	0	1	3	.091	.167	.091	.258	-29	-2	-2	100	0	0	.200	0	0	0	-0	/O	-0.2
1962	Chi-N	123	434	73	114	24	7	9	35	35	96	.263	.322	.412	.734	90	-3	-7	106	68	58	.702	16	7	1	-3	*O	-1.4
1963	Chi-N	148	547	79	141	19	11	9	37	31	122	.258	.302	.382	.684	91	-4	-7	105	67	64	.638	24	12	0	-4	*O	-1.9
1964	Chi-N	52	215	30	54	9	2	2	14	13	40	.251	.300	.340	.640	76	-6	-7	105	70	23	.587	10	3	1	3	O	-0.4
	StL-N	103	419	81	146	21	9	12	44	27	87	.348	.391	.527	.918	139	30	24	112	62	86	.976	33	15	1	0	*O	2.3
	Yr	155	634	111	200	30	11	14	58	40	127	.315	.360	.464	.824	118	24	17	110	65	108	.839	43	18	2	3		1.9
1965	StL-N	155	631	107	182	35	8	16	69	45	116	.288	.345	.445	.791	114	17	12	107	77	99	.835	63	27	3	3	*O	1.3
1966	StL-N	156	643	94	183	24	12	15	46	31	134	.285	.321	.429	.750	106	4	4	100	53	91	.792	**74**	18	**11**	-2	*O	1.0
1967	StL-N	159	689	**113**	206	32	12	21	76	24	109	.299	.328	.472	.800	125	20	20	101	72	106	.803	**52**	18	5	1	*O	2.0
1968	StL-N	159	660	92	184	**46**	**14**	6	51	46	124	.279	.329	.418	.747	129	17	20	95	65	98	.787	**62**	12	**11**	-4	*O	2.2
1969	StL-N	157	655	97	195	33	10	12	47	50	115	.298	.349	.434	.783	119	15	15	100	52	105	.817	**53**	14	8	-6	*O	0.8
1970	StL-N	155	664	114	202	29	5	13	57	60	99	.304	.363	.422	.784	103	9	4	106	61	105	.805	51	15	6	-7	*O	-0.3
1971	StL-N	157	640	**126**	200	37	7	7	61	76	107	.313	.386	.425	.811	129	27	26	101	75	114	.890	**64**	19	**8**	-11	*O	1.8
1972	StL-N	153	621	81	193	26	8	3	42	47	93	.311	.360	.393	.753	108	11	8	105	66	93	.785	**63**	18	8	-7	*O	0.2
1973	StL-N	160	650	110	193	29	8	7	63	71	112	.297	.366	.398	.765	123	12	19	91	80	101	.823	**70**	20	9	-7	*O	1.4
1974	StL-N	153	635	105	194	25	7	3	48	61	88	.306	.368	.381	.749	106	9	7	104	71	98	.878	**118**	33	**16**	-3	*O	1.4
1975	StL-N	136	528	78	163	27	6	3	47	38	64	.309	.359	.400	.758	107	7	5	103	88	79	.794	56	16	7	-2	*O	0.5
1976	StL-N	133	498	73	150	24	5	4	67	35	75	.301	.348	.394	.742	106	6	4	104	127	65	.746	56	19	5	-7	*O	-0.1
1977	StL-N	141	489	69	133	22	6	2	46	30	74	.272	.317	.354	.670	83	-14	-12	96	103	52	.622	35	24	-4	-20	*O	-4.0
1978	StL-N	92	298	31	66	9	0	0	12	17	29	.221	.263	.252	.515	47	-22	-20	95	63	21	.452	17	5	2	-9	O	-3.2
1979	StL-N	120	405	56	123	15	4	5	38	23	43	.304	.346	.398	.743	98	1	-1	105	85	54	.691	21	12	-1	-9	O	-1.4
Total	19	2616	10332	1610	3023	486	141	149	900	761	1730	.293	.344	.410	.754	108	135	112	102	73	1512	.785	938	307	97	-95	*O	2.0
■ **MATT BRODERICK**	Broderick, Matthew Thomas b: 12/1/1877, Lattimer Mines, Pa. d: 2/26/40, Freeland, Pa. TR, 5'6.5", 135 lbs. Deb: 03																											
1903	Bro-N	2	2	0	0	0	0	0	0	0		.000	.000	.000	.000	-99	-1	-1	101	0	0	.000	0			0	/2	0.0
■ **STEVE BRODIE**	Brodie, Walter Scott b: 9/11/1868, Warronton, Va. d: 10/30/35, Baltimore, Md. BL, 5'11", 180 lbs. Deb: 4/21/1890																											
1890	Bos-N	132	514	77	152	19	9	0	67	66	20	.296	.387	.368	.755	111	18	9	111	113	87	.815	29			4	*O	0.9
1891	Bos-N	133	523	84	136	13	6	2	78	63	39	.260	.351	.319	.670	87	1	-9	112	139	69	.685	25			4	*O	-1.0
1892	StL-N	154	602	85	152	10	9	4	60	52	31	.252	.316	.319	.635	99	-4	0	95	96	71	.613	28			4	*O2/3	0.0
1893	StL-N	107	469	71	149	16	8	2	79	33	16	.318	.376	.399	.775	109	6	6	99	99	88	.850	41			8	*O	0.8
	Bal-N	25	97	18	35	7	2	0	19	12	2	.361	.446	.474	.921	138	7	6	107	120	25	1.113	8			-3	O	0.1
	Yr	132	566	89	184	23	10	2	98	45	18	.325	.389	.412	.800	114	13	12	101	104	112	.893	49			4		0.9
1894	Bal-N	129	573	134	210	25	11	3	113	18	8	.366	.399	.464	.863	110	9	9	99	120	126	.934	42			-8	*O	-0.5
1895	Bal-N	131	528	85	184	27	10	2	134	26	15	.348	.394	.449	.843	111	15	8	107	**163**	110	.907	35			1	*O	-0.1
1896	Bal-N	132	516	98	153	19	11	2	87	36	17	.297	.363	.388	.751	98	1	-1	102	129	84	.769	25			9	*O	0.0
1897	Pit-N	100	370	47	108	7	12	2	53	25		.292	.348	.392	.740	99	-1	-0	98	109	56	.718	11			-2	*O	-0.7
1898	Pit-N	42	156	15	41	5	0	0	21	6		.263	.303	.295	.598	76	-5	-5	98	146	15	.504	3			2	O	-0.4
	Bal-N	23	98	12	30	3	2	0	19	5		.306	.346	.378	.724	107	1	1	103	137	14	.676	3			2	O	0.1
	Yr	65	254	27	71	8	2	0	40	11		.280	.320	.327	.646	88	-4	-4	99	145	29	.568	6			4		-0.3
1899	Bal-N	137	531	82	164	26	1	3	87	31		.309	.372	.379	.750	101	8	1	108	122	84	.744	19			1	*O	-0.5
1901	Bal-A	83	306	41	95	6	6	2	41	25		.310	.363	.389	.751	103	5	2	107	110	48	.725	9			7	O	0.7
1902	NY-N	109	416	37	117	8	2	3	42	22		.281	.317	.332	.649	102	1	1	100	95	48	.572	11			8	*O	0.1
Total	12	1437	5699	886	1726	191	89	25	900	420	148	.303	.363	.381	.744	103	59	28	103	120	924	.754	289			37	*O/23	-0.5
■ **JACK BROHAMER**	Brohamer, John Anthony b: 2/26/50, Maywood, Cal. BL/TR, 5'10", 165 lbs. Deb: 4/18/72																											
1972	Cle-A	136	527	49	123	13	2	5	35	27	46	.233	.272	.294	.566	64	-21	-25	107	91	42	.449	3	2	-0	9	*2/3	-0.9
1973	Cle-A	102	300	29	66	12	1	4	29	32	23	.220	.295	.307	.602	72	-12	-11	97	110	28	.515	0	2	-1	13	2	0.5
1974	Cle-A	101	315	33	85	11	1	2	30	26	22	.270	.331	.330	.662	90	-3	-4	101	107	36	.574	2	1	0	6	2	0.7
1975	Cle-A	69	217	15	53	5	0	6	16	14	14	.244	.290	.350	.640	81	-6	-6	100	65	21	.538	2	2	-1	-4	2	-0.8
1976	Chi-A	119	354	33	89	12	2	7	40	44	28	.251	.339	.356	.695	104	2	3	99	105	43	.628	1	3	-2	7	*2/3	1.6
1977	Chi-A	59	152	26	39	10	3	2	20	21	8	.257	.351	.401	.752	105	1	1	99	118	23	.728	0	0	0	-3	32/D	0.0
1978	Bos-A	81	244	34	57	14	1	1	25	25	13	.234	.305	.311	.616	69	-8	-11	107	125	23	.520	1	3	-2	-2	3D2	-1.2
1979	Bos-A	64	192	25	51	7	1	1	11	15	15	.266	.319	.328	.647	70	-7	-8	107	64	18	.513	0	3	-2	-2	23	-0.9
1980	Bos-A	21	57	5	18	2	0	1	6	4	3	.316	.361	.404	.764	107	1	1	102	90	8	.659	0	0	0	-1	3/2D	0.0
	Cle-A	53	142	13	32	5	1	1	15	14	6	.225	.295	.296	.591	61	-7	-8	102	130	12	.483	0	1	-1	-4	2/D	-0.9

YEAR	TM/L	G	AB	R	H	2B	3B	HR	RBI	BB	SO	AVG	OBP	SLG	PRO	/A	BR	/A	PF	CHI	RC	TA	SB	CS	SBR	FR	POS	TPR
	Yr	74	199	18	50	7	1	2	21	18	9	.251	.313	.327	.640	74	-6	-7	102	120	20	.535	0	1	-1	-5		-0.9
Total	9	805	2500	262	613	91	12	30	227	222	178	.245	.309	.327	.636	79	-60	-67	102	100	253	.554	9	17	-8	19	23/D	-1.9

■ HERMAN BRONKIE Bronkie, Herman Charles "Dutch" b: 3/31/1885, S.Manchester, Conn d: 5/27/68, Somers, Conn. BR/TR, 5'9", 165 lbs. Deb: 9/20/10

YEAR	TM/L	G	AB	R	H	2B	3B	HR	RBI	BB	SO	AVG	OBP	SLG	PRO	/A	BR	/A	PF	CHI	RC	TA	SB	CS	SBR	FR	POS	TPR
1910	Cle-A	5	9	1	2	0	0	0	0	1		.222	.300	.222	.522	64	-0	-0	100	0	1	.571	1			0	/3S	0.0
1911	Cle-A	2	6	0	1	0	0	0	0	0		.167	.167	.167	.333	-7	-1	-1	103	0	0	.200	0			0	/3	0.0
1912	Cle-A	6	16	1	0	0	0	0	0	1		.000	.059	.000	.059	-82	-4	-4	101	0	0	.063	0			0	/3	-0.3
1914	Chi-N	1	1	1	1	1	0	0	1	0	0	1.000	1.000	2.000	3.000	799	1	1	98	181	2	—	0			0	/3	0.1
1918	StL-N	18	68	7	15	3	0	1	7	2	4	.221	.243	.309	.552	73	-3	-2	93	117	5	.434	0			2	3	0.0
1919	StL-A	67	196	23	50	6	4	0	14	23	23	.255	.336	.327	.663	89	-3	-2	97	79	22	.616	2			2	32/1	0.3
1922	StL-A	23	64	7	18	4	1	0	2	6	7	.281	.343	.375	.718	82	-1	-2	106	30	8	.625	0	2	-1	1	3	0.0
Total	7	122	360	40	87	14	5	1	24	33	34	.242	.307	.317	.624	77	-11	-11	98	71	38	.549	3	2		5	/321S	0.1

■ TOM BROOKENS Brookens, Thomas Dale b: 8/10/53, Chambersburg, Pa. BR/TR, 5'10", 165 lbs. Deb: 7/10/79

YEAR	TM/L	G	AB	R	H	2B	3B	HR	RBI	BB	SO	AVG	OBP	SLG	PRO	/A	BR	/A	PF	CHI	RC	TA	SB	CS	SBR	FR	POS	TPR
1979	Det-A	60	190	23	50	5	2	4	21	11	40	.263	.310	.374	.684	87	-5	-4	96	97	23	.644	10	3	1	4	32	0.3
1980	Det-A	151	509	64	140	25	9	10	66	32	71	.275	.319	.418	.738	95	-1	-4	105	106	64	.664	13	11	-3	-2	*3/2SD	-0.8
1981	Det-A	71	239	19	58	10	1	4	25	14	43	.243	.290	.343	.633	78	-6	-7	105	104	23	.545	5	3	-0	-2	3	-0.9
1982	Det-A	140	398	40	92	15	3	9	58	27	63	.231	.280	.352	.632	72	-16	-16	100	139	36	.531	5	9	-4	-4	*32/SO	-2.3
1983	Det-A	138	332	50	71	13	3	6	32	29	46	.214	.281	.325	.606	69	-15	-13	96	99	32	.556	10	4	1	-9	*3S2/D	-1.9
1984	Det-A	113	224	32	55	11	4	5	26	19	33	.246	.307	.397	.705	97	-2	-1	96	100	27	.650	6	6	-2	-6	3S2/D	-0.4
1985	Det-A	156	485	54	115	34	6	7	47	27	78	.237	.277	.375	.653	72	-17	-20	106	92	50	.582	14	5	1	-1	*3/S2CD	-2.3
1986	Det-A	98	281	42	76	11	2	3	25	20	42	.270	.321	.356	.677	89	-6	-4	95	91	32	.608	11	8	-2	-2	32SD/O	-0.5
1987	Det-A	143	444	59	107	15	3	13	59	33	63	.241	.296	.376	.673	80	-14	-13	97	114	49	.599	7	4	-0	1	*3S2	-1.1
1988	Det-A	136	441	62	107	23	5	5	38	44	74	.243	.316	.351	.667	92	-8	-4	94	89	49	.594	4	4	-1	-3	*3/2S	-0.7
Total	10	1206	3543	445	871	162	38	66	397	256	553	.246	.299	.369	.668	83	-89	-87	100	104	385	.607	85	57	-9	-22	32S/DOC	-10.6

■ HUBIE BROOKS Brooks, Hubert b: 9/24/56, Los Angeles, Cal. BR/TR, 6', 178 lbs. Deb: 9/04/80

YEAR	TM/L	G	AB	R	H	2B	3B	HR	RBI	BB	SO	AVG	OBP	SLG	PRO	/A	BR	/A	PF	CHI	RC	TA	SB	CS	SBR	FR	POS	TPR
1980	NY-N	24	81	8	25	2	1	1	10	5	9	.309	.364	.395	.759	116	1	2	96	113	12	.690	1	1	-0	-1	3	0.1
1981	NY-N	98	358	34	110	21	2	4	38	23	65	.307	.351	.411	.761	115	7	6	101	96	50	.687	9	5	-0	-2	3/OS	0.0
1982	NY-N	126	457	40	114	21	2	2	40	28	76	.249	.300	.317	.617	74	-17	-16	99	106	43	.515	6	3	0	-15	*3	-3.4
1983	NY-N	150	586	53	147	18	4	5	58	24	96	.251	.285	.321	.606	69	-26	-25	99	120	51	.486	6	4	-1	3	*3/2	-2.8
1984	NY-N	153	561	61	159	23	2	16	73	48	79	.283	.342	.417	.759	112	9	9	100	104	75	.684	6	5	-1	-20	*3S	-1.0
1985	Mon-N	156	605	67	163	34	7	13	100	34	79	.269	.314	.413	.727	109	-0	4	94	146	71	.626	6	9	-4	-33	*S	-2.1
1986	Mon-N	80	306	50	104	18	5	14	58	25	60	.340	.393	.569	.962	166	25	26	98	113	65	.953	4	2	0	-15	S	1.9
1987	Mon-N	112	430	57	113	22	3	14	72	24	72	.263	.303	.426	.729	85	-7	-10	106	130	54	.648	4	3	-1	-16	*S	-1.3
1988	Mon-N	151	588	61	164	35	2	20	90	35	108	.279	.321	.447	.768	112	12	8	106	118	78	.683	7	3	0	-7	*O	-0.2
Total	9	1050	3972	431	1099	194	28	89	539	246	644	.277	.323	.407	.729	102	3	3	100	118	497	.660	49	35	-6	-105	3SO/2	-8.8

■ MANDY BROOKS Brooks, Jonathan Joseph (born Jonathan Joseph Brozek) b: 8/18/1897, Milwaukee, Wis. d: 6/17/62, Kirkwood, Mo. BR/TR, 5'9", 165 lbs. Deb: 5/30/25

YEAR	TM/L	G	AB	R	H	2B	3B	HR	RBI	BB	SO	AVG	OBP	SLG	PRO	/A	BR	/A	PF	CHI	RC	TA	SB	CS	SBR	FR	POS	TPR
1925	Chi-N	90	349	55	98	25	7	14	72	19	28	.281	.322	.513	.835	112	3	4	97	123	57	.827	10	3	1	3	O	0.5
1926	Chi-N	26	48	7	9	1	0	1	6	5	5	.188	.278	.271	.549	45	-3	-4	106	130	4	.487	0			-2	O	-0.6
Total	2	116	397	62	107	26	7	15	78	24	33	.270	.316	.484	.800	104	-1	0	98	124	61	.782	10	3		1	O	-0.1

■ BOBBY BROOKS Brooks, Robert b: 11/1/45, Los Angeles, Cal. BR/TR, 5'8.5", 165 lbs. Deb: 9/01/69

YEAR	TM/L	G	AB	R	H	2B	3B	HR	RBI	BB	SO	AVG	OBP	SLG	PRO	/A	BR	/A	PF	CHI	RC	TA	SB	CS	SBR	FR	POS	TPR
1969	Oak-A	29	79	13	19	5	0	3	10	20	24	.241	.400	.418	.818	140	4	5	92	96	15	.871	0	2	-1	0	O	0.3
1970	Oak-A	7	18	2	6	1	0	2	5	1	7	.333	.368	.722	1.091	200	2	2	97	106	4	1.077	0	1	-1	-1	/O	0.0
1972	Oak-A	15	39	4	7	0	0	0	5	8	8	.179	.319	.179	.499	53	-2	-2	97	299	2	.429	0	1	-1	3	O	0.0
1973	Cal-A	4	7	0	1	0	0	0	0	0	3	.143	.143	.143	.286	-20	-1	-1	96	0	0	.167	0	0	0	-0	/O	-0.1
Total	4	55	143	19	33	6	0	5	20	29	42	.231	.364	.378	.742	118	3	4	94	148	21	.737	0	4	-2	1	/O	0.2

■ SIG BROSKIE Broskie, Sigmund Theodore "Chops" b: 3/23/11, Iselin, Pa. d: 5/17/75, Canton, Ohio BR/TR, 5'11.5", 200 lbs. Deb: 9/11/40

YEAR	TM/L	G	AB	R	H	2B	3B	HR	RBI	BB	SO	AVG	OBP	SLG	PRO	/A	BR	/A	PF	CHI	RC	TA	SB	CS	SBR	FR	POS	TPR
1940	Bos-N	11	22	1	6	1	0	0	4	1	2	.273	.304	.318	.623	73	-1	-1	99	212	2	.500	0			0	C	0.0

■ TONY BROTTEM Brottem, Anton Christian b: 4/30/1892, Halstead, Minn. d: 8/5/29, Chicago, Ill. BR/TR, 6'0.5", 176 lbs. Deb: 4/17/16

YEAR	TM/L	G	AB	R	H	2B	3B	HR	RBI	BB	SO	AVG	OBP	SLG	PRO	/A	BR	/A	PF	CHI	RC	TA	SB	CS	SBR	FR	POS	TPR
1916	StL-N	26	33	3	6	1	0	0	4	3	10	.182	.250	.212	.462	44	-2	-2	97	227	2	.407	1			0	C/O	-0.1
1918	StL-N	2	4	0	0	0	0	0	0	1	0	.000	.200	.000	.200	-40	-1	-1	93	0	0	.250	0			0	/1	0.0
1921	Was-A	4	7	1	1	0	0	0	0	2	1	.143	.333	.143	.476	26	-1	-1	99	0	0	.500	0	0	0	0	/C	0.0
	Pit-N	30	91	6	22	2	0	0	9	3	11	.242	.266	.264	.530	39	-8	-8	103	138	6	.386	0	1	-1	0	C	-0.6
Total	3	62	135	10	29	3	0	0	13	9	22	.215	.264	.237	.501	38	-11	-11	101	146	9	.393	1	1		0	/C1O	-0.7

■ CAL BROUGHTON Broughton, Cecil Calvert b: 12/28/1860, Magnolia, Wis. d: 3/15/39, Evansville, Wis. BR/TR, Deb: 5/02/1883

YEAR	TM/L	G	AB	R	H	2B	3B	HR	RBI	BB	SO	AVG	OBP	SLG	PRO	/A	BR	/A	PF	CHI	RC	TA	SB	CS	SBR	FR	POS	TPR
1883	Cle-N	4	10	2	2	0	0	0	1	2	2	.200	.333	.200	.533	64	-0	-0	105	173	1	.500				0	/C	0.0
	Bal-a	9	32	1	6	0	0	0		1		.188	.212	.188	.400	28	-2	-3	107	0	1	.269				0	/CO	-0.1
1884	Mil-U	11	39	5	12	5	0	0		0		.308	.308	.436	.744	149	2	2	100	0	5	.630	0			0	/CO	0.2
1885	StL-a	4	17	1	1	0	0	0		0		.059	.059	.059	.118	-67	-3	-3	93	0	0	.063				0	/C	-0.2
	NY-a	11	41	1	6	1	0	0		1		.146	.167	.171	.337	10	-4	-3	84	0	1	.229				0	C	-0.2
	Yr	15	58	2	7	1	0	0		1		.121	.136	.138	.274	-14	-7	-6	86	0	1	.176				0		-0.4
1888	Det-N	1	4	0	0	0	0	0	0	0	0	.000	.000	.000	.000	-99	-1	-1	98	0	0	.000	0			0	/C	0.0
Total	4	40	143	10	27	6	0	0	1	4	2	.189	.211	.231	.442	45	-9	-8	96	14	9	.319	0			0	/CO	-0.3

■ MARK BROUHARD Brouhard, Mark Steven b: 5/22/56, Burbank.Cal. BR/TR, 6'1", 210 lbs. Deb: 4/12/80

YEAR	TM/L	G	AB	R	H	2B	3B	HR	RBI	BB	SO	AVG	OBP	SLG	PRO	/A	BR	/A	PF	CHI	RC	TA	SB	CS	SBR	FR	POS	TPR
1980	Mil-A	45	125	17	29	6	0	5	16	7	24	.232	.278	.400	.678	88	-3	-2	95	96	13	.596	1	0	0	-0	DO1	-0.3
1981	Mil-A	60	186	19	51	6	3	2	20	7	41	.274	.308	.371	.679	99	-2	-1	96	104	19	.552	1	1	-0	0	O/D	-0.1
1982	Mil-A	40	108	16	29	4	1	4	10	9	17	.269	.336	.435	.771	117	1	2	94	68	14	.682	0	3	-2	1	O/D	0.0
1983	Mil-A	56	185	25	51	10	1	7	23	9	39	.276	.316	.454	.770	119	2	4	92	86	23	.655	0	4	-2	3	OD	0.3
1984	Mil-A	66	197	20	47	7	0	6	22	16	36	.239	.302	.365	.668	91	-4	-2	92	97	21	.577	0	3	-2	2	O/D	-0.3
1985	Mil-A	37	108	11	28	7	2	1	13	5	26	.259	.298	.389	.687	83	-2	-3	105	115	12	.585	0	0	0	-3	O/D	-0.5
Total	6	304	909	108	235	40	7	25	104	53	183	.259	.307	.400	.707	100	-8	-2	95	95	103	.624	2	11	-6	2	O/D1	-0.9

■ ART BROUTHERS Brouthers, Arthur H. b: 11/25/1882, Montgomery, Ala. d: 9/28/59, Charleston, S.C. TR , 6'1", Deb: 4/14/06

YEAR	TM/L	G	AB	R	H	2B	3B	HR	RBI	BB	SO	AVG	OBP	SLG	PRO	/A	BR	/A	PF	CHI	RC	TA	SB	CS	SBR	FR	POS	TPR
1906	Phi-A	37	144	18	30	5	1	0	14	5		.208	.235	.257	.492	59	-7	-6	94	146	10	.404	4			1	3/2	-0.2

■ DAN BROUTHERS Brouthers, Dennis Joseph "Big Dan" b: 5/8/1858, Sylvan Lake, N.Y. d: 8/3/32, E.Orange, N.J. BL/TL, 6'2", 207 lbs. Deb: 6/23/1879 H

YEAR	TM/L	G	AB	R	H	2B	3B	HR	RBI	BB	SO	AVG	OBP	SLG	PRO	/A	BR	/A	PF	CHI	RC	TA	SB	CS	SBR	FR	POS	TPR
1879	Tro-N	39	168	17	46	12	1	4	17	1	18	.274	.278	.429	.707	138	5	6	93	68	21	.598				-4	1/P	0.0
1880	Tro-N	3	12	0	2	0	0	0	1	1	0	.167	.231	.167	.397	34	-1	-1	110	175	0	.300				0	/1	0.0
1881	Buf-N	65	270	60	86	18	9	**8**	45	18	22	.319	.361	**.541**	.902	178	24	24	101	81	54	.891				-5	O1	1.3
1882	Buf-N	84	351	71	**129**	23	11	6	63	21	7	**.368**	**.403**	**.547**	**.950**	**193**	**39**	**37**	104	97	**79**	**.959**				1	*1	2.1
1883	Buf-N	98	425	85	**159**	41	**17**	3	**97**	16	17	**.374**	**.397**	**.572**	**.969**	**190**	**44**	**44**	100	141	**99**	**.974**				1	*1/3P	2.8
1884	Buf-N	94	398	82	130	22	15	14	79	33	20	.327	.378	**.563**	**.941**	**180**	41	37	107	90	87	.959				1	*1/3	2.4
1885	Buf-N	98	407	87	146	32	11	7	59	34	10	.359	.408	**.543**	**.951**	**207**	47	**47**	99	73	92	**.977**				-2	*1	2.6
1886	Det-N	121	489	139	181	**40**	15	**11**	72	66	16	.370	.445	**.581**	**1.026**	193	**66**	**59**	109	65	139	1.205	21			-8	*1	2.6
1887	Det-N	123	500	**153**	169	**36**	20	12	101	71	9	.338	**.426**	.562	**.988**	**172**	52	50	102	87	138	**1.184**	34			-5	*1	2.1
1888	Det-N	129	522	**118**	160	**33**	11	9	66	68	13	.307	.399	.464	.862	180	48	49	98	76	113	.983	34			-3	*1	3.3
1889	Bos-N	126	485	105	181	26	9	7	118	66	6	**.373**	.462	.507	.969	170	**51**	**49**	102	127	127	1.145	22			1	*1	3.4
1890	Bos-P	123	460	117	152	36	9	1	97	99	17	.330	**.466**	.454	.921	139	40	33	107	120	113	1.149	28			2	*1	1.8
1891	Bos-a	130	486	117	170	26	19	5	108	87	20	**.350**	**.471**	**.512**	**.983**	**188**	**59**	**61**	99	125	135	**1.237**	31			-8	*1	3.9
1892	Bro-N	152	588	121	**197**	30	20	5	**124**	84	30	**.335**	.432	.480	**.911**	**175**	**58**	**57**	101	123	**138**	**1.056**	31			11	*1	5.1
1893	Bro-N	77	282	57	95	21	11	2	59	52	10	.337	.450	.511	.961	174	25	31	91	103	71	1.128	9			3	1	2.7
1894	Bal-N	123	525	137	182	39	23	9	128	67	9	.347	.425	.560	.985	139	32	33	99	106	145	1.178	38			-0	*1	2.6
1895	Bal-N	5	23	2	6	2	0	0	5	1	1	.261	.292	.348	.639	62	-1	-1	107	151	2	.529	0			0	/1	0.0

YEAR	TM/L	G	AB	R	H	2B	3B	HR	RBI	BB	SO	AVG	OBP	SLG	PRO	/A	BR	/A	PF	CHI	RC	TA	SB	CS	SBR	FR	POS	TPR
	Lou-N	24	97	13	30	10	1	2	15	11	2	.309	.380	.495	.874	133	4	4	95	75	19	.896	1			0	1	0.4
	Yr	29	120	15	36	12	1	2	20	12	3	.300	.364	.467	.830	118	2	3	97	93	21	.821	1			0		0.4
1896	Phi-N	57	218	42	75	13	3	1	41	44	11	.344	.462	.445	.907	140	17	16	102	104	49	1.063	7			-3	1	1.3
1904	NY-N	2	5	0	0	0	0	0	0	0		.000	.000	.000	.000	-95	-1	-1	105	0	0	.000	0			0	/1	0.0
Total	19	1673	6711	1523	2296	460	205	106	1295	840	238	.342	.423	.519	.942	171	648	634	101	101	1622	1.061	256			-18	*1/OP3	40.4
■ **JOE BROVIA** Brovia, Joseph John "Ox" b: 2/18/22, Davenport, Cal. BL/TR, 6'3", 195 lbs. Deb: 7/03/55																												
1955	Cin-N	21	18	0	2	0	0	0	4	1	6	.111	.158	.111	.269	-26	-3	-3	106	810	0	.188	0	0	0	0	H	-0.2
■ **FRANK BROWER** Brower, Frank Willard "Turkeyfoot" b: 3/26/1893, Gainesville, Va. d: 11/20/60, Baltimore, Md. BL/TR, 6'2", 180 lbs. Deb: 8/14/20																												
1920	Was-A	36	119	21	37	7	2	1	13	9	11	.311	.374	.429	.803	118	2	3	95	85	19	.771	1	1	-0	-1	O/13	0.0
1921	Was-A	83	203	31	53	12	3	1	35	18	7	.261	.330	.365	.695	78	-7	-7	99	156	25	.636	1	1	-0	1	O/1	-0.8
1922	Was-A	139	471	61	138	20	6	9	71	52	25	.293	.375	.418	.793	116	5	11	92	116	76	.788	8	6	-1	-9	*O/1	-0.8
1923	Cle-A	126	397	77	113	25	8	16	66	62	32	.285	.392	.509	.901	134	21	20	101	90	82	.962	6	5	-1	-1	*1/O	1.2
1924	Cle-A	66	107	16	30	10	1	3	20	27	9	.280	.434	.477	.910	140	7	7	97	110	24	1.038	1	1	-0	-1	1/PO	0.5
Total	5	450	1297	206	371	74	20	30	205	168	84	.286	.379	.443	.822	118	28	35	96	110	227	.836	17	14	-3	-11	O1/P3	0.1
■ **LOUIS BROWER** Brower, Louis Lester b: 7/1/1900, Cleveland, Ohio BR/TR, 5'10", 155 lbs. Deb: 6/13/31																												
1931	Det-A	21	62	3	10	1	0	0	6	8	5	.161	.278	.177	.455	21	-7	-7	104	180	4	.423	1	0	0	-1	S/2	-0.5
■ **BOB BROWER** Brower, Robert Richard b: 1/10/60, Jamaica, N.Y. BR/TR, 5'11", 185 lbs. Deb: 9/03/86																												
1986	Tex-A	21	9	3	1	1	0	0	0	0	3	.111	.111	.222	.333	-12	-1	-1	96	0	-0	.300	1	2	-1	-5	O/D	-0.7
1987	Tex-A	127	303	63	79	10	3	14	46	36	66	.261	.339	.452	.791	105	4	2	104	103	47	.800	15	9	-1	-7	*O/D	-0.7
1988	Tex-A	82	201	29	45	7	0	1	11	27	38	.224	.316	.274	.589	66	-8	-9	101	75	18	.551	10	5	0	-4	OD	-1.3
Total	3	230	513	95	125	18	3	15	57	63	107	.244	.326	.378	.705	89	-6	-8	102	90	66	.690	26	16	-2	-16	O/D	-2.7
■ **BROWN** Brown Deb:8/31/1874																												
1874	Bal-n	1	5	0	0							.000															/S	
■ **CURTIS BROWN** Brown, Curtis b: 9/14/45, Sacramento, Cal. BR/TR, 5'11", 180 lbs. Deb: 5/27/73																												
1973	Mon-N	1	4	0	0	0	0	0	0	0	0	.000	.000	.000	.000	-96	-1	-1	104	0	0	.000	0	0	0	0	/O	0.0
■ **DARRELL BROWN** Brown, Darrell Wayne b: 10/29/55, Oklahoma City, Okla BB/TR, 6', 184 lbs. Deb: 4/11/31																												
1981	Det-A	16	4	4	1	0	0	0	0	0	1	.250	.250	.250	.500	42	-0	-0	105	0	0	.667	1	0	0	-2	/OD	-0.2
1982	Oak-A	8	18	2	6	0	1	0	3	1	2	.333	.368	.444	.813	128	1	1	95	150	3	.833	1	0	0	-1	/OD	0.0
1983	Min-A	91	309	40	84	6	2	0	22	10	28	.272	.297	.304	.601	63	-14	-16	105	91	26	.456	3	3	-1	1	O/D	-1.6
1984	Min-A	95	260	36	71	9	3	1	19	14	16	.273	.310	.342	.653	76	-7	-9	106	82	27	.549	4	1	1	6	OD	-0.3
Total	4	210	591	82	162	15	6	1	44	25	47	.274	.305	.325	.630	70	-21	-25	105	89	57	.518	9	4	0	3	O/D	-2.1
■ **DELOS BROWN** Brown, Delos Hight b: 10/4/1892, Anna, Ill. d: 12/21/64, Carbondale, Ill. BR/TR, 5'9", 160 lbs. Deb: 6/12/14																												
1914	Chi-A	1	1	0	0	0	0	0	0	0	1	.000	.000	.000	.000	-97	-0	-0	103	0	0	.000	0			0	H	0.0
■ **DRUMMOND BROWN** Brown, Drummond Nicol b: 1/31/1885, Los Angeles, Cal. d: 1/27/27, Parkville, Mo. BR/TR, 6', 180 lbs. Deb: 4/25/13																												
1913	Bos-N	15	34	3	11	1	0	1	2	2	9	.324	.361	.441	.802	136	1	1	95	40	5	.739	0			0	C	0.2
1914	KC-F	31	58	4	11	3	0	0	5	7	6	.190	.277	.241	.518	52	-4	-3	95	129	5	.468	1			-1	C/1	-0.3
1915	KC-F	77	227	13	55	10	1	1	26	12	23	.242	.280	.308	.589	77	-8	-7	97	128	22	.494	3			-6	C/1	-1.1
Total	3	123	319	20	77	14	1	2	33	21	38	.241	.288	.310	.599	78	-10	-9	96	119	32	.512	4			-7	C/1	-1.2
■ **EARL BROWN** Brown, Earl James "Snitz" b: 3/5/11, Louisville, Ky. BL/TL, 6', 175 lbs. Deb: 9/12/35																												
1935	Pit-N	9	32	6	8	2	0	0	6	2	8	.250	.294	.313	.607	59	-2	-2	107	221	3	.462	0			-0	/1	-0.1
1936	Pit-N	8	23	7	7	1	2	0	3	1	4	.304	.333	.522	.855	130	1	1	98	89	3	.722	0			0	/O1	0.1
1937	Phi-N	105	332	42	97	19	3	6	52	21	41	.292	.342	.422	.763	98	2	-1	108	119	48	.693	4			-0	O1	-0.4
1938	Phi-N	21	74	4	19	4	0	0	8	5	11	.257	.304	.311	.615	69	-3	-3	100	128	7	.491	0			0	1/O	-0.3
Total	4	143	461	59	131	26	5	6	69	29	64	.284	.332	.401	.733	93	-2	-5	106	126	60	.669	4			-0	/O1	-0.7
■ **ED BROWN** Brown, Edward P. b: Chicago, Ill. TR , Deb: 8/19/1882																												
1882	StL-a	17	60	4	11	0	0	0		4		.183	.234	.183	.418	43	-3	-3	100	0	3	.306				0	O/2P	-0.2
1884	Tol-a	42	153	13	27	3	0	0		2		.176	.187	.196	.383	26	-12	-12	104	0	6	.254				-8	3/O2CP	-1.8
Total	2	59	213	17	38	3	0	0		6		.178	.201	.192	.393	31	-15	-16	102	0	8	.269				-8	/3O2PC	-2.0
■ **EDDIE BROWN** Brown, Edward William "Glass Arm Eddie" b: 7/17/1891, Milligan, Neb. d: 9/10/56, Vallejo, Cal. BR/TR, 6'3", 190 lbs. Deb: 9/26/20																												
1920	NY-N	3	8	1	1	1	0	0	0	0	3	.125	.125	.250	.375	6	-1	-1	100	0	0	.286	0	0	0	0	/O	0.0
1921	NY-N	70	128	16	36	6	2	0	12	4	11	.281	.324	.359	.683	83	-4	-3	98	96	15	.598	1	0	0	-2	O	-0.5
1924	Bro-N	114	455	56	140	30	4	5	78	26	15	.308	.345	.424	.769	106	3	3	99	145	65	.694	3	5	-2	-0	*O	-0.1
1925	Bro-N	153	618	88	189	39	11	5	99	22	18	.306	.332	.429	.761	99	-8	-3	94	133	86	.674	3	4	-2	5	*O	-0.3
1926	Bos-N	153	612	71	**201**	31	8	2	84	23	20	.328	.355	.415	.770	123	5	16	86	118	86	.691	5			-3	*O	0.6
1927	Bos-N	155	558	64	171	35	6	2	75	28	20	.306	.340	.401	.741	105	-3	2	93	116	73	.680	11			-4	*O/1	-0.7
1928	Bos-N	142	523	45	140	28	2	2	59	24	22	.268	.305	.340	.645	70	-25	-23	97	116	53	.554	6			1	*O/1	-2.5
Total	7	790	2902	341	878	170	33	16	407	127	109	.303	.334	.400	.735	100	-33	-8	94	124	379	.654	29	9		-3	O/1	-3.5
■ **RANDY BROWN** Brown, Edwin Randolph b: 8/29/44, Leesburg, Fla. BL/TR, 5'7", 170 lbs. Deb: 9/11/69																												
1969	Cal-A	13	25	3	4	1	0	0	0	6	1	.160	.323	.200	.523	49	-1	-1	99	0	2	.524	0	0	0	0	C/O	0.0
1970	Cal-A	5	4	0	0	0	0	0	0	0	0	.000	.000	.000	.000	-99	-1	-1	92	0	0	.000	0	0	0	0	/C	0.0
Total	2	18	29	3	4	1	0	0	0	6	1	.138	.286	.172	.458	31	-3	-2	98	0	2	.440	0	0	0	0	/CO	0.0
■ **FRED BROWN** Brown, Fred Herbert b: 4/12/1879, Ossipee, N.H. d: 2/3/55, Somersworth, N.H. BR/TR, 5'10.5", 190 lbs. Deb: 5/04/01																												
1901	Bos-N	7	14	1	2	0	0	0	2	0		.143	.143	.143	.286	-14	-2	-2	112	335	0	.167	0			1	/O	-0.1
1902	Bos-N	2	6	1	2	1	0	0	0	0		.333	.333	.500	.833	166	0	0	95	0	1	.750	0			0	/O	0.0
Total	2	9	20	2	4	1	0	0	2	0		.200	.200	.250	.450	32	-2	-2	107	234	1	.313	0			1	/O	-0.1
■ **IKE BROWN** Brown, Isaac b: 4/13/42, Memphis, Tenn. BR/TR, 6', 190 lbs. Deb: 6/17/69																												
1969	Det-A	70	170	24	39	4	3	5	12	26	43	.229	.338	.376	.715	96	0	-0	103	61	21	.667	2	3	-1	-1	23/OS	0.0
1970	Det-A	56	94	17	27	5	0	4	15	13	26	.287	.380	.468	.848	128	4	4	103	108	17	.841	0	0	0	-1	2/O3	0.5
1971	Det-A	59	110	20	28	1	0	8	19	19	25	.255	.364	.482	.846	144	6	6	96	101	19	.828	0	1	-1	-1	1/O23S	0.4
1972	Det-A	51	84	12	21	3	0	2	10	17	23	.250	.376	.357	.733	105	3	1	113	116	11	.686	1	2	-1	1	O1/2S3	0.0
1973	Det-A	42	76	12	22	2	1	1	9	15	13	.289	.407	.382	.788	122	3	3	101	110	12	.772	0	1	-1	-2	1O/3D	0.0
1974	Det-A	2	2	0	0	0	0	0	0	0	0	.000	.000	.000	.000	-94	-1	-1	106	0	0	.000	0	0	0	0	/3	0.0
Total	6	280	536	85	137	15	4	20	65	90	130	.256	.366	.410	.776	116	16	14	103	93	80	.778	3	7	-3	-4	/21O3SD	0.9
■ **JIM BROWN** Brown, James Donaldson "Don" or "Moose" b: 3/31/1897, Laurel, Ind. BR/TR, 6', 178 lbs. Deb: 9/13/15																												
1915	StL-N	1	2	0	1	0	0	0	0	2	1	.500	.750	.500	1.250	281	1	1	100	0	1	3.000	0			-0	/O	0.1
1916	Phi-A	14	42	6	10	2	1	1	5	4	9	.238	.304	.405	.709	115	0	0	98	89	6	.656	0			-1	O	-0.1
Total	2	15	44	6	11	2	1	1	5	6	10	.250	.340	.409	.749	127	1	1	98	82	6	.727	0			-1	/O	0.0
■ **JIMMY BROWN** Brown, James Roberson b: 4/25/10, Jamesville, N.C. d: 12/29/77, Bath, N.C. BB/TR, 5'8.5", 165 lbs. Deb: 4/23/37 C																												
1937	StL-N	138	525	86	145	20	9	2	53	27	29	.276	.313	.360	.673	82	-13	-14	101	104	58	.573	10			-11	*2S/3	-1.7
1938	StL-N	108	382	50	115	12	6	0	38	27	9	.301	.350	.364	.714	87	-1	-7	111	99	50	.641	7			-5	2S3	-0.6
1939	StL-N	147	645	88	192	31	8	3	51	32	18	.298	.335	.384	.719	88	-7	-11	105	63	83	.622	4			-5	*S2	-0.7
1940	StL-N	107	454	56	127	17	4	0	30	24	15	.280	.317	.335	.652	78	-12	-13	102	70	48	.557	9			-13	23S	-2.0
1941	StL-N	132	549	81	168	28	9	3	56	45	22	.306	.363	.406	.769	106	12	5	110	84	83	.704	2			10	*32	1.7
1942	StL-N	145	606	75	155	28	4	1	71	52	11	.256	.315	.320	.635	79	-11	-16	108	118	63	.543	4			-2	23S	-1.2
1943	StL-N	34	110	6	20	4	2	0	8	6	1	.182	.224	.255	.479	36	-9	-10	105	103	7	.378	0			1	2/3S	-0.7
1946	Pit-N	79	241	23	58	6	0	0	12	18	5	.241	.293	.266	.559	57	-13	-14	103	70	18	.445	3			-0	S2/3	-1.1

YEAR	TM/L	G	AB	R	H	2B	3B	HR	RBI	BB	SO	AVG	OBP	SLG	PRO	/A	BR	/A	PF	CHI	RC	TA	SB	CS	SBR	FR	POS	TPR
Total	8	890	3512	465	980	146	42	9	319	231	110	.279	.326	.352	.678	84	-55	-80	106	88	411	.598	39			-24	23S	-6.3
■ JAKE BROWN	Brown, Jerald Ray b: 3/22/48, Sumrall, Miss. d: 12/18/81, Houston, Tex. BR/TR, 6'2", 200 lbs. Deb: 5/17/75																											
1975	SF-N	41	43	6	9	3	0	0	4	5	13	.209	.292	.279	.571	58	-2	-2	102	129	4	.500	0	0	0	-3	O	-0.6
■ CHRIS BROWN	Brown, John Christopher b: 8/15/61, Jackson, Miss. BR/TR, 6', 185 lbs. Deb: 9/03/84																											
1984	SF-N	23	84	6	24	7	0	1	11	9	19	.286	.362	.405	.766	120	2	2	96	119	12	.708	2	1	0	-4	3	-0.1
1985	SF-N	131	432	50	117	20	3	16	61	38	78	.271	.345	.442	.787	127	10	14	93	102	61	.718	2	3	-1	5	*3	1.9
1986	SF-N	116	416	57	132	16	3	7	49	33	43	.317	.380	.421	.801	126	12	14	96	102	65	.762	13	9	-2	-15	*3/S	-0.4
1987	SF-N	38	132	17	32	6	0	6	17	9	16	.242	.306	.424	.730	95	-2	-1	96	92	14	.627	1	3	-2	1	3/S	-0.1
	SD-N	44	155	17	36	3	0	6	23	11	30	.232	.296	.368	.664	77	-6	-5	97	125	16	.583	3	1	0	-0	3	-0.5
	Yr	82	287	34	68	9	0	12	40	20	46	.237	.300	.394	.694	85	-8	-7	96	110	32	.622	4	4	-1	1		-0.6
1988	SD-N	80	247	14	58	6	0	2	19	19	49	.235	.297	.283	.581	69	-10	-9	97	100	20	.465	0	0	0	-2	3	-1.1
Total	5	432	1466	161	399	58	6	38	180	119	235	.272	.339	.398	.737	108	7	15	95	104	188	.689	21	17	-4	-16	3/S	-0.3
■ LINDSAY BROWN	Brown, John Lindsay "Red" b: 7/22/11, Mason, Tex. d: 1/1/67, San Antonio, Tex. BR/TR, 5'10", 160 lbs. Deb: 7/13/37																											
1937	Bro-N	48	115	16	31	3	1	0	6	3	17	.270	.288	.313	.601	61	-6	-7	104	60	10	.455	1			-5	S	-0.7
■ LARRY BROWN	Brown, Larry Leslie b: 3/1/40, Shinnston, W.Va. BR/TR, 5'10", 160 lbs. Deb: 7/06/63																											
1963	Cle-A	74	247	28	63	6	0	5	18	22	27	.255	.319	.340	.659	88	-5	-4	97	78	27	.581	4	3	-1	-8	S2	-0.7
1964	Cle-A	115	335	33	77	12	1	12	40	24	55	.230	.285	.379	.664	81	-8	-9	103	104	34	.570	1	2	-1	9	*2/S	0.9
1965	Cle-A	124	438	52	111	22	2	8	40	38	62	.253	.316	.368	.683	95	-4	-3	98	91	51	.606	5	7	-3	1	S2	0.1
1966	Cle-A	105	340	29	78	12	0	3	17	36	58	.229	.309	.291	.600	72	-11	-11	101	66	30	.504	0	1	-1	-8	S2	-1.4
1967	Cle-A	152	485	38	110	16	2	7	37	53	62	.227	.311	.311	.622	84	-9	-9	100	92	48	.547	4	4	-1	1	*S	0.1
1968	Cle-A	154	495	43	116	18	3	6	35	43	46	.234	.302	.319	.621	88	-7	-7	101	85	47	.528	1	1	-0	-13	*S	-1.0
1969	Cle-A	132	469	48	112	10	2	4	24	44	43	.239	.305	.294	.600	72	-19	-16	94	66	43	.508	5	3	-0	-4	*S3/2	-1.5
1970	Cle-A	72	155	17	40	5	2	0	15	20	14	.258	.343	.316	.659	72	-3	-6	115	124	17	.579	1	0	0	2	S32	0.0
1971	Cle-A	13	50	4	11	1	0	0	5	3	3	.220	.278	.240	.518	45	-3	-4	106	180	3	.390	0	0	0	-2	S	-0.3
	Oak-A	70	189	14	37	2	1	1	9	7	19	.196	.228	.233	.461	31	-17	-17	101	78	9	.329	1	2	-1	1	S23	-1.4
	Yr	83	239	18	48	3	1	1	14	10	22	.201	.239	.234	.473	34	-21	-21	101	96	12	.345	1	2	-1	-1		-1.7
1972	Oak-A	47	142	11	26	2	0	0	4	13	8	.183	.252	.197	.449	36	-11	-11	97	60	6	.328	0	0	0	-2	2/3	-1.1
1973	Bal-A	17	28	4	7	0	0	1	5	5	4	.250	.364	.357	.721	97	0	0	107	151	4	.682	0	0	0	1	3/2	0.0
1974	Tex-A	54	76	10	15	2	0	0	5	9	13	.197	.282	.224	.506	49	-5	-5	96	116	4	.394	0	0	0	0	3/2S	-0.2
Total	12	1129	3449	331	803	108	13	47	254	317	414	.233	.301	.313	.614	77	-102	-102	100	87	324	.538	22	23	-7	-21	S23	-6.5
■ LEON BROWN	Brown, Leon b: 11/16/49, Sacramento, Cal. BR/TR, 6', 185 lbs. Deb: 5/19/76																											
1976	NY-N	64	70	11	15	3	0	0	2	4	4	.214	.257	.257	.514	50	-5	-4	92	43	3	.387	2	4	-2	-6	O	-1.3
■ LEW BROWN	Brown, Lewis J. "Blower" b: 2/1/1858, Leominster, Mass. d: 1/16/1889, Boston, Mass. BR/TR, 5'10.5", 185 lbs. Deb: 6/17/1876 M																											
1876	Bos-N	45	195	23	41	6	6	2	21	3	22	.210	.222	.333	.556	87	-3	-2	95	106	15	.442				1	C/O	0.1
1877	Bos-N	58	221	27	56	12	8	1	31	6	33	.253	.273	.394	.667	99	2	-1	108	117	24	.564				13	*C/1	1.2
1878	Pro-N	58	243	44	74	21	6	1	43	7	37	.305	.324	.453	.777	157	13	14	98	137	37	.692				6	*C1/OP	2.0
1879	Pro-N	53	229	23	59	13	4	2	38	4	24	.258	.270	.376	.646	109	2	2	102	148	24	.529				-4	C/O	-0.1
	Chi-N	6	21	2	6	1	0	0	3	1	4	.286	.318	.333	.652	110	0	0	105	150	2	.533				0	/1M	0.0
	Yr	59	250	25	65	14	4	2	41	5	28	.260	.275	.372	.647	109	3	2	102	150	26	.530				-4		-0.1
1881	Det-N	27	108	16	26	3	1	3	14	3	16	.241	.261	.370	.632	90	-1	-2	106	105	11	.524				-0	1	-0.4
	Pro-N	18	75	9	18	3	1	0	10	4	13	.240	.278	.307	.585	90	-1	-1	93	145	7	.474				-0	O/1	0.0
	Yr	45	183	25	44	6	2	3	24	7	29	.240	.268	.344	.613	90	-2	-2	101	123	17	.504				-1		-0.4
1883	Bos-N	14	54	5	13	4	1	0	9	3	6	.241	.281	.352	.633	85	-1	-1	106	168	5	.537				0	1	0.0
	Lou-a	14	60	6	11	2	1	0		1		.183	.197	.250	.447	46	-4	-3	94	0	3	.327				0	1/C	-0.2
1884	Bos-U	85	325	50	75	18	3	1		13		.231	.260	.314	.574	95	-2	-1	98	0	27	.460	0			10	C1/OP	1.0
Total	7	378	1531	205	379	83	31	10	169	45	155	.248	.269	.362	.631	104	6	5	100	96	155	.520	0			25	C1/OP	3.6
■ MARTY BROWN	Brown, Marty Leo b: 1/23/63, Lawton, Okla. BR/TR, 6'1", 190 lbs. Deb: 9/04/88																											
1988	Cin-N	10	16	0	3	1	0	0	2	1	2	.188	.235	.250	.485	37	-1	-1	105	200	1	.357	0	1	-1	0	/3	-0.1
■ MIKE BROWN	Brown, Michael Charles b: 12/29/59, San Francisco, Cal. BR/TR, 6'2", 195 lbs. Deb: 7/21/83																											
1983	Cal-A	31	104	12	24	5	1	3	9	7	20	.231	.279	.385	.664	84	-3	-2	96	72	11	.578	1	0	0	-2	O	-0.3
1984	Cal-A	62	148	19	42	8	3	7	22	13	23	.284	.342	.520	.862	133	6	6	101	89	22	.776	0	2	-1	-7	O/D	-0.2
1985	Cal-A	60	153	23	41	9	1	4	20	7	21	.268	.304	.418	.723	95	-1	-1	101	104	16	.590	0	1	-1	-4	O/D	-0.6
	Pit-N	57	205	29	68	18	2	5	33	22	27	.332	.396	.512	.909	148	14	14	103	112	40	.884	2	2	-1	-3	O	0.9
1986	Pit-N	87	243	18	53	7	0	4	26	27	32	.218	.296	.296	.593	64	-12	-12	100	123	20	.500	2	3	-1	-4	O	-1.9
1988	Cal-A	18	50	4	11	2	0	0	3	1	12	.220	.235	.260	.495	41	-4	-4	94	92	3	.341	0	0	0	-1	O	-0.4
Total	5	315	903	105	239	49	7	23	113	77	135	.265	.323	.411	.734	101	1	0	100	104	112	.674	5	8	-3	-20	O/D	-2.5
■ OLIVER BROWN	Brown, Oliver E. b: 1849, Brooklyn, N.Y. d: 9/23/32, Brooklyn, N.Y. Deb: 8/01/1872																											
1872	Atl-n	4	17	0	1							.059															/O	
1875	Atl-n	3	14	0	1							.071															/1	
Total	2 n	7	31	0	2							.065															/1	
■ OLLIE BROWN	Brown, Ollie Lee "Downtown" b: 2/11/44, Tuscaloosa, Ala. BR/TR, 6'2", 178 lbs. Deb: 9/10/65																											
1965	SF-N	6	10	0	2	1	0	0	0	0	2	.200	.200	.300	.500	35	-1	-1	111	0	1	.375	0	0	0	-1	/O	-0.1
1966	SF-N	115	348	32	81	7	1	7	33	33	66	.233	.303	.319	.622	75	-12	-11	97	105	30	.517	2	5	-2	-2	*O	-1.9
1967	SF-N	120	412	44	110	12	1	13	53	25	65	.267	.315	.396	.711	101	1	0	101	109	47	.602	0	2	-1	-3	*O	-0.9
1968	SF-N	40	95	7	22	4	0	0	11	3	23	.232	.270	.274	.544	65	-4	-4	98	178	7	.432	1	0	0	-7	O	-1.3
1969	SD-N	151	568	76	150	18	3	20	61	44	97	.264	.320	.412	.732	107	2	4	97	88	73	.667	10	6	-1	6	*O	0.1
1970	SD-N	139	534	79	156	34	1	23	89	34	78	.292	.335	.489	.823	124	11	14	95	111	82	.759	5	3	-0	5	*O	1.2
1971	SD-N	145	484	36	132	16	0	9	55	52	74	.273	.347	.362	.709	105	2	4	96	113	61	.638	3	3	-1	3	*O	0.1
1972	SD-N	23	70	3	12	2	0	0	3	5	9	.171	.227	.200	.427	25	-7	-6	88	88	3	.322	0	0	0	0	O	-0.6
	Oak-A	20	54	5	13	1	0	1	4	6	14	.241	.317	.315	.631	91	-1	-1	97	84	6	.571	1	1	-0	-1	O	-0.1
	Mil-A	66	179	21	50	8	0	3	25	17	24	.279	.345	.374	.719	120	3	4	95	137	20	.603	0	2	-1	6	O/3	0.9
	Yr	86	233	26	63	9	0	4	29	23	38	.270	.339	.361	.699	113	3	4	96	126	26	.596	1	3	-2	6		0.8
1973	Mil-A	97	296	28	83	10	1	7	32	33	53	.280	.356	.392	.748	115	5	6	96	92	42	.698	4	1	1	-2	D/O	0.5
1974	Hou-N	27	69	8	15	1	0	3	6	4	15	.217	.260	.362	.623	74	-3	-3	98	68	6	.518	0	0	0	-1	O	-0.4
	Phi-N	43	99	11	24	5	2	4	13	6	20	.242	.286	.455	.740	101	-0	-0	103	88	11	.630	0	1	-1	-7	O	-0.9
	Yr	70	168	19	39	6	2	7	19	10	35	.232	.275	.417	.692	91	-3	-3	101	81	17	.593	0	1	-1	-7		-1.3
1975	Phi-N	84	145	19	44	12	0	6	26	15	29	.303	.369	.510	.879	140	8	7	101	109	28	.874	1	1	-0	-13	O	-0.8
1976	Phi-N	92	209	30	53	10	1	5	30	33	33	.254	.355	.383	.738	102	3	1	107	122	31	.728	2	1	0	-6	O	-0.7
1977	Phi-N	53	70	5	17	3	1	1	13	4	14	.243	.284	.357	.641	70	-3	-3	100	186	6	.526	1	1	-0	-5	O	-0.8
Total	13	1221	3642	404	964	144	11	102	454	314	616	.265	.326	.394	.720	104	3	12	98	108	455	.664	30	27	-7	-25	O/D3	-5.7
■ OSCAR BROWN	Brown, Oscar Lee b: 2/8/46, Long Beach, Cal. BR/TR, 6', 175 lbs. Deb: 9/03/69																											
1969	Atl-N	7	4	2	1	0	0	0	0	0	1	.250	.250	.250	.500	39	-0	-0	104	0	0	.333	0	0	0	-1	/O	0.0
1970	Atl-N	28	47	6	18	2	1	1	7	7	7	.383	.473	.532	1.005	162	5	5	104	97	11	1.031	0	2	-1	-5	O	-0.1
1971	Atl-N	27	43	4	9	4	0	0	5	3	8	.209	.261	.302	.563	54	-2	-3	110	157	4	.471	0	0	0	-2	O	-0.4
1972	Atl-N	76	164	19	37	5	1	3	16	4	29	.226	.244	.323	.567	57	-9	-10	105	106	11	.429	0	2	-1	-5	O	-1.9
1973	Atl-N	22	58	3	12	3	0	0	0	3	10	.207	.246	.259	.505	35	-5	-6	113	0	4	.383	0	0	0	2	O	-0.4
Total	5	160	316	34	77	14	2	4	28	17	55	.244	.284	.339	.623	69	-11	-14	107	91	30	.512	0	4	-2	-10	O	-2.8

YEAR	TM/L	G	AB	R	H	2B	3B	HR	RBI	BB	SO	AVG	OBP	SLG	PRO	/A	BR	/A	PF	CHI	RC	TA	SB	CS	SBR	FR	POS	TPR
■ DICK BROWN	Brown, Richard Ernest b: 1/17/35, Shinnston, W.Va. d: 4/17/70, Baltimore, Md. BR/TR, 6'2", 176 lbs. Deb: 6/20/57																											
1957	Cle-A	34	114	10	30	4	0	4	22	4	23	.263	.288	.404	.692	86	-3	-3	102	150	13	.593	1	1	-0	-2	C	-0.3
1958	Cle-A	68	173	20	41	5	0	7	20	14	27	.237	.305	.387	.693	94	-3	-2	94	91	21	.630	1	0	0	-6	C	-0.6
1959	Cle-A	48	141	15	31	7	0	5	16	11	39	.220	.290	.376	.666	84	-4	-3	97	93	16	.604	0	0	0	-2	C	-0.2
1960	Chi-A	16	43	4	7	0	0	3	5	3	11	.163	.217	.372	.589	56	-3	-3	101	78	3	.514	0	0	0	1	C	0.0
1961	Det-A	93	308	32	82	12	2	16	45	22	57	.266	.315	.474	.789	112	2	4	96	91	42	.706	0	2	-1	-11	C	-0.8
1962	Det-A	134	431	40	104	12	0	12	40	21	66	.241	.280	.353	.632	62	-20	-26	111	84	40	.516	0	1	-1	-1	*C	-2.0
1963	Bal-A	59	171	13	42	7	0	2	13	15	35	.246	.310	.322	.632	83	-5	-4	94	89	18	.550	1	0	0	4	C	0.1
1964	Bal-A	88	230	24	59	6	0	8	32	12	45	.257	.296	.387	.683	84	-4	-5	105	120	24	.578	2	0	1	-4	C	-0.5
1965	Bal-A	96	255	17	59	9	1	5	30	17	53	.231	.282	.333	.615	74	-9	-9	100	124	22	.510	2	2	-1	-0	C	-0.3
Total	9	636	1866	175	455	62	3	62	223	119	356	.244	.293	.380	.673	82	-48	-51	101	101	199	.594	7	6	-2	-22	C	-4.6
■ BOBBY BROWN	Brown, Robert William "Doc" b: 10/25/24, Seattle, Wash. BL/TR, 6'1", 180 lbs. Deb: 9/22/46																											
1946	NY-A	7	24	1	8	1	0	0	1	4	0	.333	.429	.375	.804	125	1	1	100	45	4	.722	0	0	0	0	/S3	0.2
1947	NY-A	69	150	21	45	6	1	1	18	21	9	.300	.390	.373	.763	117	3	4	97	112	23	.703	0	2	-1	-4	3S/O	0.0
1948	NY-A	113	363	62	109	19	5	3	48	48	16	.300	.383	.405	.788	110	6	6	100	104	60	.748	0	1	-1	-5	3S2/O	0.0
1949	NY-A	104	343	61	97	14	4	6	61	38	18	.283	.359	.399	.759	100	-0	-0	100	135	50	.705	4	3	-1	-3	3/O	-0.3
1950	NY-A	95	277	33	74	4	2	4	37	39	18	.267	.360	.339	.699	80	-8	-7	99	121	35	.634	3	1	0	-2	3	-1.0
1951	NY-A	103	313	44	84	15	2	6	51	47	18	.268	.369	.387	.756	114	3	7	92	131	49	.735	1	1	-0	-6	3	-0.2
1952	NY-A	29	89	6	22	2	0	1	14	9	6	.247	.323	.303	.627	77	-3	-3	98	174	9	.543	1	1	-0	3	3	0.0
1954	NY-A	28	60	5	13	1	0	1	7	8	3	.217	.309	.283	.592	64	-3	-3	99	133	5	.490	0	1	-1	1	3	-0.2
Total	8	548	1619	233	452	62	14	22	237	214	88	.279	.367	.376	.742	101	-0	5	98	123	234	.713	9	10	-3	-15	3/S2O	-1.5
■ BOBBY BROWN	Brown, Rogers Lee b: 5/24/54, Norfolk, Va. BB/TR, 6'2", 190 lbs. Deb: 4/05/79																											
1979	Tor-A	4	10	1	0	0	0	0	0	2	1	.000	.167	.000	.167	-49	-2	-2	103	0	0	.200	0	0	0	-0	/O	-0.2
	NY-A	30	68	7	17	3	1	0	3	2	17	.250	.271	.324	.595	63	-4	-4	96	52	6	.500	2	1	0	-2	O	-0.5
	Yr	34	78	8	17	3	1	0	3	4	18	.218	.256	.282	.538	47	-6	-6	96	46	6	.452	2	1	0	-2		-0.7
1980	NY-A	137	412	65	107	12	5	14	47	29	82	.260	.308	.415	.723	97	-3	-3	99	86	52	.707	27	8	3	4	*O/D	0.2
1981	NY-A	31	62	5	14	1	0	0	6	5	15	.226	.284	.242	.526	52	-4	-4	100	157	5	.471	4	2	0	-1	O/D	-0.4
1982	Sea-A	79	245	29	59	7	1	4	17	17	32	.241	.290	.327	.617	63	-10	-13	109	74	25	.641	28	6	5	3	O/D	-0.7
1983	SD-N	57	225	40	60	5	3	5	22	23	38	.267	.335	.382	.717	99	-1	-0	99	83	31	.777	27	9	3	-2	O	0.0
1984	SD-N	85	171	28	43	7	2	3	29	11	33	.251	.297	.368	.665	87	-4	-3	99	158	18	.652	16	4	2	-2	O	-0.4
1985	SD-N	79	84	8	13	3	0	0	6	5	20	.155	.202	.190	.393	10	-10	-10	102	149	3	.351	6	4	-1	-5	O	-1.7
Total	7	502	1277	183	313	38	12	26	130	94	238	.245	.297	.355	.652	78	-37	-39	101	98	140	.657	110	34	13	-5	O/D	-3.7
■ SAM BROWN	Brown, Samuel Wakefield b: 5/21/1878, Webster, Pa. d: 11/8/31, Mount Pleasant, Pa. BR/TR, Deb: 4/21/06																											
1906	Bos-N	71	231	12	48	6	1	0	20	13		.208	.250	.242	.492	55	-12	-12	100	133	15	.399	4			7	CO3/12	-0.2
1907	Bos-N	70	208	17	40	6	0	0	14	12		.192	.236	.221	.458	47	-13	-12	95	115	11	.345	0			2	C/1	-0.5
Total	2	141	439	29	88	12	1	0	34	25		.200	.244	.232	.476	51	-25	-24	98	124	27	.373	4			9	/CO312	-0.7
■ TOMMY BROWN	Brown, Thomas Michael "Buckshot" b: 12/6/27, Brooklyn, N.Y. BR/TR, 6'1", 170 lbs. Deb: 8/03/44																											
1944	Bro-N	46	146	17	24	4	0	0	8	8	17	.164	.208	.192	.400	13	-17	-17	99	102	6	.288	0			-10	S	-2.1
1945	Bro-N	57	196	13	48	3	4	2	19	6	16	.245	.267	.332	.599	69	-10	-9	96	93	17	.490	3			-6	S/O	-0.8
1947	Bro-N	15	34	3	8	1	0	0	2	1	6	.235	.257	.265	.522	37	-3	-3	105	82	2	.370	0			-1	/3OS	-0.3
1948	Bro-N	54	145	18	35	4	0	2	20	7	17	.241	.281	.310	.591	57	-8	-9	104	147	12	.470	1			-3	3/1	-1.3
1949	Bro-N	41	89	14	27	2	0	3	18	6	8	.303	.347	.427	.774	105	1	0	102	144	13	.698	0			-2	O	-0.2
1950	Bro-N	48	86	15	25	2	1	8	20	11	9	.291	.378	.616	.994	147	7	6	107	100	19	1.000	0			0	O	0.5
1951	Bro-N	11	25	2	4	2	0	0	1	2	4	.160	.222	.240	.462	25	-3	-3	98	64	1	.381	0	0	0	0	/O	-0.2
	Phi-N	78	196	24	43	2	1	10	32	15	21	.219	.278	.393	.671	81	-7	-6	97	116	19	.577	1	2	-1	-8	O21/3	-1.5
	Yr	89	221	26	47	4	1	10	33	17	25	.213	.272	.376	.648	75	-9	-9	97	110	21	.554	1	2	-1	-8		-1.7
1952	Phi-N	18	25	2	4	1	0	1	2	4	3	.160	.276	.320	.596	64	-1	-1	101	71	3	.571	0	0	0	-1	/1O	-0.2
	Chi-N	61	200	24	64	11	0	3	24	12	24	.320	.358	.420	.778	111	4	3	103	101	29	.678	1	2	-1	-7	S2/1	-0.3
	Yr	79	225	26	68	12	0	4	26	16	27	.302	.349	.409	.757	106	3	2	103	95	32	.665	1	2	-1	-8		-0.5
1953	Chi-N	65	138	19	27	7	1	2	13	13	17	.196	.279	.304	.584	51	-10	-10	103	106	11	.492	1	0	0	-3	S/O	-1.0
Total	9	494	1280	151	309	39	7	31	159	85	142	.241	.292	.355	.647	74	-47	-48	101	109	132	.562	7	4		-41	S/O321	-7.4
■ TOM BROWN	Brown, Thomas T. b: 9/21/1860, Liverpool, England d: 10/27/27, Washington, D.C. BL/TR, 5'10", 168 lbs. Deb: 1882 M																											
1882	Bal-a	45	181	30	55	5	2	1		6		.304	.326	.370	.696	145	6	8	92	0	22	.579				0	O/P	0.7
1883	Col-a	97	420	69	115	12	7	5		20		.274	.307	.371	.678	135	8	16	87	0	49	.577				-4	*O/P	1.1
1884	Col-a	107	451	93	123	9	11	5		24		.273	.315	.375	.690	131	13	15	97	0	55	.601				-8	*O/P	0.5
1885	Pit-a	108	437	81	134	16	12	4		34		.307	.366	.426	.792	144	27	22	106	0	70	.749				-7	*O/P	0.8
1886	Pit-a	115	460	106	131	11	11	1		56		.285	.365	.363	.728	141	18	24	93	0	74	.775	30			6	*O/P	2.3
1887	Pit-N	47	192	30	47	3	4	0	6	11	40	.245	.289	.302	.591	71	-9	-6	93	34	21	.566	12			3	O	-0.1
	Ind-N	36	140	20	25	3	0	2	9	8	25	.179	.228	.243	.471	34	-13	-12	96	73	11	.487	13			-2	O	-1.0
	Yr	83	332	50	72	6	4	2	15	19	65	.217	.263	.277	.541	55	-21	-18	94	51	32	.531	25			2		-1.1
1888	Bos-N	107	420	62	104	10	7	9	49	30	68	.248	.299	.369	.668	108	7	3	106	102	62	.734	46			-6	*O	-0.2
1889	Bos-N	90	362	93	84	10	5	2	24	59	56	.232	.341	.304	.645	81	-6	-7	102	53	61	.838	63			2	O	-0.7
1890	Bos-P	128	543	146	150	23	14	4	61	86	84	.276	.378	.392	.770	101	8	1	107	64	113	.969	79			2	*O	-0.1
1891	Bos-a	137	589	**177**	**189**	30	**21**	5	71	70	96	.321	.397	.469	.865	153	38	39	99	61	**155**	1.140	**106**			-12	*O	1.8
1892	Lou-N	153	660	105	150	16	8	2	45	47	94	.227	.284	.285	.569	80	-21	-13	92	62	77	.624	78			16	*O	-0.1
1893	Lou-N	122	529	104	127	15	7	5	54	56	63	.240	.319	.323	.642	75	-21	-17	96	69	77	.741	**66**			27	*O	0.4
1894	Lou-N	129	536	122	136	22	14	9	57	60	73	.254	.332	.397	.730	87	-22	-9	88	57	95	.855	66			2	*O	-1.1
1895	StL-N	83	350	72	76	11	4	1	31	48	44	.217	.315	.280	.595	56	-22	-22	100	74	43	.664	34			7	O	-1.7
	Was-N	34	134	25	32	8	3	2	16	18	16	.239	.329	.388	.717	84	-3	-4	103	74	20	.765	8			-8	O	-1.1
	Yr	117	484	97	108	19	7	3	47	66	60	.223	.319	.310	.629	64	-25	-25	101	75	63	.691	42			-1		-2.8
1896	Was-N	116	435	87	128	17	6	2	59	58	49	.294	.385	.375	.759	108	4	8	95	107	75	.831	28			-7	*O	-0.5
1897	Was-N	116	469	91	137	17	2	5	45	52		.292	.364	.369	.733	95	-1	-2	101	62	74	.756	25			1	*O/M	-0.8
1898	Was-N	16	55	8	9	1	0	0	2	5		.164	.233	.182	.415	21	-5	-6	102	62	3	.391	3			0	O/M	-0.4
Total	17	1786	7363	1521	1952	239	138	64	529	748	708	.265	.337	.361	.698	103	6	39	97	51	1157	.760	657			12	*O/P	-0.2
■ TOM BROWN	Brown, Thomas William b: 12/12/40, Laureldale, Pa. BB/TL, 6'1", 190 lbs. Deb: 4/08/63																											
1963	Was-A	61	116	8	17	4	0	1	4	11	45	.147	.227	.207	.433	23	-12	-12	98	62	6	.380	2	1	0	-2	O1	-1.5
■ WILLARD BROWN	Brown, Willard "Big Bill" or "California" b: 1866, San Francisco, Cal. d: 12/20/1897, San Francisco, Cal BR/TR, 6'2", 190 lbs. Deb: 5/10/1887																											
1887	NY-N	49	170	17	37	3	2	0	25	10	15	.218	.273	.259	.532	47	-11	-13	107	175	15	.504	10			1	C/3O	-0.5
1888	NY-N	20	59	4	16	1	0	0	6	1	8	.271	.283	.288	.571	91	-1	-1	93	126	5	.442	1			0	C	0.0
1889	NY-N	40	139	16	36	10	0	1	29	9	9	.259	.318	.353	.670	84	-2	-3	105	166	18	.650	6			-18	C/O	-1.7
1890	NY-P	60	230	47	64	8	4	4	43	13	13	.278	.320	.400	.720	86	-3	-7	109	113	32	.669	5			0	CO/132	-0.4
1891	Phi-N	115	441	62	107	20	4	0	50	34	35	.243	.303	.306	.609	83	-11	-8	95	110	44	.539	7			3	*1C/O	-0.6
1893	Bal-N	7	32	5	4	3	0	0	5	1	3	.125	.152	.219	.370	-1	-5	-5	107	188	1	.286	0			-0	/1	-0.4
	Lou-N	111	461	80	140	23	7	1	85	50	32	.304	.373	.390	.764	109	4	7	96	135	72	.748	9			-1	*1/C	0.4
	Yr	118	493	85	144	26	7	1	90	51	35	.292	.360	.379	.739	101	-1	2	97	139	72	.711	9			-1		0.0
1894	Lou-N	13	48	5	10	2	0	0	9	5	7	.208	.283	.250	.533	35	-5	-4	88	219	4	.474	1			0	1	-0.2
	StL-N	3	9	0	1	0	0	0	0	0	2	.111	.111	.111	.222	-45	-2	-2	101	0	0	.125	0			0	/1	-0.1
	Yr	16	57	5	11	2	0	0	9	5	9	.193	.258	.228	.486	21	-7	-6	91	192	4	.413	1			0		-0.3
Total	7	418	1589	236	415	70	17	6	252	123	124	.261	.319	.338	.657	83	-37	-36	99	134	191	.606	39			-15	1C/O32	-3.5

YEAR	TM/L	G	AB	R	H	2B	3B	HR	RBI	BB	SO	AVG	OBP	SLG	PRO	/A	BR	/A	PF	CHI	RC	TA	SB	CS	SBR	FR	POS	TPR
■ WILLARD BROWN	Brown, Willard Jessie b: 6/26/15, Shreveport, La. BR/TR, 5'11.5", 200 lbs. Deb: 7/19/47																											
1947	StL-A	21	67	4	12	3	0	1	6	0	7	.179	.179	.269	.448	23	-7	-7	102	105	2	.339	2	2	-1	-1	O	-0.9
■ GATES BROWN	Brown, William James b: 5/2/39, Crestline, O. BL/TR, 5'11", 220 lbs. Deb: 6/19/63 C																											
1963	Det-A	55	82	16	22	3	1	2	14	8	13	.268	.341	.402	.743	104	1	1	104	150	11	.688	2	1	0	3	O	0.3
1964	Det-A	123	426	65	116	22	6	15	54	31	53	.272	.328	.458	.785	121	8	10	96	97	64	.753	11	4	1	4	*O	1.1
1965	Det-A	96	227	33	58	14	2	10	43	17	33	.256	.307	.467	.774	111	4	3	105	131	34	.750	6	0	2	1	O	0.4
1966	Det-A	88	169	27	45	5	1	7	27	18	19	.266	.344	.432	.776	119	5	4	102	121	26	.756	3	0	1	-4	O	0.0
1967	Det-A	51	91	17	17	1	1	2	9	13	15	.187	.288	.286	.574	71	-3	-3	99	117	8	.506	0	0	0	-2	O	-0.6
1968	Det-A	67	92	15	34	7	2	6	15	12	4	.370	.442	.685	1.127	223	15	14	106	79	28	1.250	0	0	0	-2	O/1	1.3
1969	Det-A	60	93	13	19	1	2	1	6	5	17	.204	.253	.290	.543	50	-6	-7	103	80	7	.434	0	0	0	0	O	-0.6
1970	Det-A	81	124	18	28	3	0	3	24	20	14	.226	.338	.323	.661	80	-2	-3	103	198	15	.616	0	0	0	-2	O	-0.5
1971	Det-A	82	195	37	66	2	3	11	29	21	17	.338	.408	.549	.957	177	18	19	96	85	44	.993	4	2	0	-8	O	0.9
1972	Det-A	103	252	33	58	5	0	10	31	26	28	.230	.307	.369	.676	89	-0	-4	113	105	29	.617	3	0	1	-1	O	-0.5
1973	Det-A	125	377	48	89	11	1	12	50	52	41	.236	.330	.366	.696	95	-1	-2	101	113	44	.632	1	1	-0	-1	*D/O	-0.2
1974	Det-A	73	99	7	24	2	0	4	17	10	15	.242	.312	.384	.696	94	-0	-1	106	134	12	.632	0	0	0	0	D	0.0
1975	Det-A	47	35	1	6	2	0	1	3	9	6	.171	.356	.314	.670	87	-0	-0	104	82	4	.677	0	0	0	0	H	0.0
Total	13	1051	2262	330	582	78	19	84	322	242	275	.257	.333	.420	.753	111	37	31	102	113	324	.732	30	8	4	-11	OD/1	1.6
■ BILL BROWN	Brown, William Verna "Verna" b: 7/8/1893, Coleman, Tex. d: 5/13/65, Lubbock, Tex. BL/TL, 5'8", 185 lbs. Deb: 8/15/12																											
1912	StL-A	9	20	0	4	0	0	0	1	0		.200	.200	.200	.400	15	-2	-2	99	83	1	.250	0			-1	/O	-0.3
■ BYRON BROWNE	Browne, Byron Ellis b: 12/27/42, St.Joseph, Mo. BR/TR, 6'2", 190 lbs. Deb: 9/09/65																											
1965	Chi-N	4	6	0	0	0	0	0	0	0	2	.000	.000	.000	.000	-98	-2	-2	102	0	0	.000	0	0	0	-1	/O	-0.2
1966	Chi-N	120	419	46	102	15	7	16	51	40	143	.243	.317	.427	.744	104	2	2	100	96	57	.694	3	3	-1	-3	*O	-0.4
1967	Chi-N	10	19	3	3	2	0	0	2	4	5	.158	.304	.263	.568	63	-1	-1	102	166	2	.588	1	1	-0	-1	/O	-0.2
1968	Hou-N	10	13	0	3	0	0	0	1	4	6	.231	.412	.231	.643	98	0	0	99	140	1	.636	0	0	0	2	/O	0.2
1969	StL-N	22	53	9	12	0	1	1	7	11	14	.226	.359	.321	.680	92	-0	-0	100	140	6	.651	0	0	0	4	O	0.3
1970	Phi-N	104	270	29	67	17	2	10	36	33	72	.248	.330	.437	.767	108	1	2	96	94	36	.700	1	2	-1	-2	O	-0.4
1971	Phi-N	58	68	5	14	3	0	3	5	8	23	.206	.289	.382	.672	86	-1	-1	103	58	8	.630	0	0	0	-9	O	-1.1
1972	Phi-N	21	21	2	4	0	0	0	0	1	8	.190	.227	.190	.418	20	-2	-2	97	0	1	.278	0	0	0	-3	/O	-0.5
Total	8	349	869	94	205	37	10	30	102	101	273	.236	.319	.405	.724	99	-2	-1	99	95	111	.690	5	6	-2	-13	O	-2.3
■ GEORGE BROWNE	Browne, George Edward b: 1/12/1876, Richmond, Va. d: 12/9/20, Hyde Park, N.Y. BL/TR, 5'10.5", 160 lbs. Deb: 9/27/01																											
1901	Phi-N	8	26	2	5	1	0	0	4	1		.192	.222	.231	.453	32	-2	-2	103	223	2	.429	2			1	/O	-0.1
1902	Phi-N	70	281	41	73	7	1	0	26	16		.260	.300	.292	.591	80	-5	-7	105	97	29	.524	11			-2	O	-1.4
	NY-N	53	216	30	69	9	5	0	14	9		.319	.347	.407	.754	135	8	8	100	47	36	.748	13			3	O	0.7
	Yr	123	497	71	142	16	6	0	40	25		.286	.320	.342	.662	103	3	1	103	76	64	.617	24			0		-0.7
1903	NY-N	141	591	105	185	20	3	3	45	43		.313	.360	.372	.732	104	8	3	106	55	91	.714	27			5	*O	0.0
1904	NY-N	150	596	**99**	169	16	5	4	39	39		.284	.328	.347	.675	105	7	3	105	58	78	.632	24			-13	*O	-1.6
1905	NY-N	127	536	95	157	16	14	4	43	20		.293	.318	.397	.716	114	8	7	101	57	78	.683	26			-7	*O	-0.9
1906	NY-N	122	477	61	126	10	4	0	37	27		.264	.304	.302	.605	91	-6	-6	100	83	55	.578	32			-11	*O	-2.0
1907	NY-N	127	458	54	119	11	10	5	37	31		.260	.307	.360	.667	105	2	2	105	83	57	.622	15			4	*O	0.1
1908	Bos-N	138	536	61	122	10	6	1	34	36		.228	.276	.274	.550	75	-13	-15	104	84	43	.483	17			5	*O	-1.3
1909	Chi-N	12	39	7	8	0	1	0	1	5		.205	.295	.256	.552	72	-1	-1	101	37	4	.581	3			0	O	-0.1
	Was-A	103	393	40	107	15	5	1	16	17		.272	.308	.344	.651	117	1	5	90	43	44	.587	13			4	*O	0.6
1910	Was-A	7	22	1	4	0	0	0	0	1		.182	.217	.182	.399	25	-2	-2	101	0	1	.278	0			-2	/O	-0.3
	Chi-A	30	112	17	27	4	1	0	4	12		.241	.315	.295	.609	96	-1	-0	95	43	12	.588	5			-3	O	-0.4
	Yr	37	134	18	31	4	1	0	4	13		.231	.299	.276	.575	84	-3	-2	96	35	12	.534	5			-5		-0.7
1911	Bro-N	8	12	1	4	0	0	0	2	1	1	.333	.385	.333	.718	105	0	0	97	169	2	.875	2			-0	/O	0.0
1912	Phi-N	6	5	0	1	0	0	0	0	1	0	.200	.333	.200	.533	47	-0	-0	100	0	0	.500	0			0	H	0.0
Total	12	1102	4300	614	1176	119	55	18	302	259	1	.273	.315	.339	.655	100	6	-5	102	67	530	.612	190			-17	*O	-6.7
■ JERRY BROWNE	Browne, Jerome Austin b: 2/13/66, Christiansted, V.I. BB/TR, 5'10", 140 lbs. Deb: 9/06/86																											
1986	Tex-A	12	24	6	10	2	0	0	3	1	4	.417	.440	.500	.940	164	2	2	96	100	4	.813	0	2	-1	-0	/2	0.1
1987	Tex-A	132	454	63	123	16	6	1	38	61	50	.271	.360	.339	.699	85	-6	-8	104	99	59	.689	27	17	-2	-2	*2/D	-0.2
1988	Tex-A	73	214	26	49	9	2	1	17	25	33	.229	.310	.304	.613	72	-7	-8	101	99	20	.554	7	5	-1	-6	2/D	-1.0
Total	3	217	692	95	182	27	8	2	58	87	87	.263	.347	.334	.681	84	-11	-14	103	99	83	.657	34	24	-4	-9	2/D	-1.1
■ PIDGE BROWNE	Browne, Prentice Almont b: 3/21/29, Peekskill, N.Y. BL/TL, 6'1", 190 lbs. Deb: 4/13/62																											
1962	Hou-N	65	100	8	21	4	2	1	10	13	9	.210	.301	.320	.621	72	-5	-4	93	113	8	.517	0	0	0	1	1	-0.3
■ PETE BROWNING	Browning, Louis Rogers "The Gladiator" b: 7/17/1861, Louisville, Ky. d: 9/10/05, Louisville, Ky. BR/TR, 6', 180 lbs. Deb: 5/02/1882																											
1882	Lou-a	69	288	67	109	17	3	5		26		**.378**	**.430**	**.510**	**.940**	**231**	**35**	**38**	94	0	**65**	**.966**				10	2S3	**4.5**
1883	Lou-a	84	358	95	121	15	11	2		23		.338	.378	.458	.836	178	27	30	94	0	64	.789				-8	OS3/21	1.9
1884	Lou-a	103	447	101	150	33	8	4		13		.336	.357	.472	.829	193	33	40	89	0	77	.761				-12	3O1/2P	2.5
1885	Lou-a	112	481	98	**174**	34	10	9		25		**.362**	**.393**	.530	**.923**	189	**48**	47	102	0	**103**	**.912**				4	*O	**3.9**
1886	Lou-a	112	467	86	159	29	6	2		30		**.340**	.389	.441	.830	150	33	27	108	0	92	.873	26			-12	*O	0.9
1887	Lou-a	134	547	137	220	35	16	4		55		.402	.464	.547	1.011	172	62	55	107	0	191	1.422	103			-6	*O	3.6
1888	Lou-a	99	383	58	120	22	8	3	72	37		.313	.380	.436	.816	**182**	28	33	91	130	79	.928	36			-5	*O	2.3
1889	Lou-a	83	324	39	83	19	5	2	32	34	30	.256	.327	.364	.691	103	-1	2	96	78	47	.718	21			-4	O	-0.4
1890	Cle-P	118	493	112	184	**40**	8	5	93	75	36	**.373**	.459	.517	.976	**177**	47	**55**	92	83	136	1.191	35			4	*O	**4.2**
1891	Pit-N	50	203	35	59	14	1	5	28	27	31	.291	.377	.443	.820	139	11	10	101	67	36	.847	4			4	O	1.0
	Cin-N	55	216	29	74	10	3	0	33	24	23	.343	.413	.417	.830	158	13	16	91	103	43	.901	12			-1	O	1.1
	Yr	105	419	64	133	24	4	5	61	51	54	.317	.395	.430	.825	148	23	26	96	86	79	.874	16			3		2.1
1892	Lou-N	21	77	10	19	4	0	0	4	12	7	.247	.348	.299	.647	107	0	1	92	57	10	.690	5			-1	O	0.0
	Cin-N	83	307	47	93	12	5	3	52	40	25	.303	.383	.404	.787	136	16	14	103	127	52	.804	8			-5	O/1	0.5
	Yr	104	384	57	112	16	5	3	56	52	32	.292	.376	.383	.759	130	16	15	101	113	62	.779	13			-6		0.5
1893	Lou-N	57	220	38	78	11	3	1	37	44	15	.355	.466	.445	.912	151	17	19	96	96	51	1.070	8			-5	O	0.9
1894	StL-N	2	7	1	1	0	0	0	0	0	0	.143	.143	.143	.286	-30	-1	-1	101	0	0	.167	0			0	/O	0.0
	Bro-N	1	2	1	2	0	0	0	2	1	0	1.000	1.000	1.000	2.000	411	1	1	94	276	2	—	0			0	/O	0.1
	Yr	3	9	2	3	0	0	0	2	1	0	.333	.400	.333	.733	81	-0	-0	99	92	1	.667	0			0		0.1
Total	13	1183	4820	954	1646	295	87	45	353	466	167	.341	.403	.467	.870	166	369	387	98	46	1048	.946	258			-37	O/32S1P	27.0
■ BILL BRUBAKER	Brubaker, Wilbur Lee b: 11/7/10, Cleveland, Ohio d: 4/2/78, Laguna Hills, Cal. BR/TR, 6'2", 185 lbs. Deb: 9/08/32																											
1932	Pit-N	7	24	3	10	3	0	0	4	3	4	.417	.481	.542	1.023	176	3	3	99	117	6	1.214	1			0	/3	0.3
1933	Pit-N	2	2	0	0	0	0	0	0	0	0	.000	.000	.000	.000	-99	-1	-0	95	0	0	.000	0			0	/3	0.0
1934	Pit-N	3	6	0	2	1	0	0	1	1	0	.333	.429	.500	.929	141	0	0	105	120	1	1.000	0			0	/3	0.1
1935	Pit-N	6	11	1	0	0	0	0	0	2	5	.000	.154	.000	.154	-51	-2	-3	107	0	0	.182	0			0	/3	-0.1
1936	Pit-N	145	554	77	160	27	4	6	102	50	96	.289	.352	.384	.736	101	-1	1	98	**160**	76	.662	5			-13	*3	-0.1
1937	Pit-N	120	413	57	105	20	4	6	48	47	51	.254	.335	.366	.700	88	-5	-6	102	104	52	.632	2			4	*3/S1	0.3
1938	Pit-N	45	112	18	33	5	0	3	19	9	14	.295	.347	.420	.767	110	1	1	100	123	16	.707	2			2	3/1SO	0.2
1939	Pit-N	100	345	41	80	23	1	7	43	29	51	.232	.297	.365	.662	77	-12	-12	100	107	36	.585	3			1	23/S	-0.7
1940	Pit-N	38	78	8	15	3	1	0	7	8	16	.192	.267	.256	.524	47	-6	-5	95	130	6	.444	0			1	3/S1	-0.3
1943	Bos-N	13	19	3	8	3	0	0	1	2	2	.421	.476	.579	1.055	193	3	2	106	33	5	1.182	0			0	/31	0.3
Total	10	479	1564	208	413	85	10	22	225	151	239	.264	.333	.373	.706	91	-19	-19	100	125	200	.659	13			-6	3/21SO	0.0
■ LOU BRUCE	Bruce, Louis R. b: 1/16/1877, St.Regis, N.Y. d: 2/9/68, Ilion, N.Y. BL/TR, 5'5", 145 lbs. Deb: 6/22/04																											
1904	Phi-A	30	101	9	27	3	0	0	8	5		.267	.302	.297	.599	90	-1	-1	102	101	10	.500	2			1	O/P23	-0.1

YEAR	TM/L	G	AB	R	H	2B	3B	HR	RBI	BB	SO	AVG	OBP	SLG	PRO	/A	BR	/A	PF	CHI	RC	TA	SB	CS	SBR	FR	POS	TPR
■ **EARLE BRUCKER** Brucker, Earle Francis Jr. b: 8/29/25, Los Angeles, Cal. BL/TR, 6'2", 210 lbs. Deb: 10/02/48																												
1948	Phi-A	2	6	0	1	1	0	0	0	1	1	.167	.286	.333	.619	63	-0	-0	102	0	1	.600	0	0	0	0	/C	0.0
■ **EARLE BRUCKER** Brucker, Earle Francis Sr. b: 5/6/01, Albany, N.Y. d: 5/8/81, San Diego, Cal. BR/TR, 5'11", 175 lbs. Deb: 4/19/37 MC																												
1937	Phi-A	102	317	40	82	16	5	6	37	48	30	.259	.356	.397	.754	96	-5	-2	94	88	47	.738	1	2	-1	-4	C	0.0
1938	Phi-A	53	171	26	64	21	1	3	35	19	16	.374	.437	.561	.998	147	13	13	101	113	42	1.074	1	1	-0	-1	C/1	1.1
1939	Phi-A	62	172	18	50	15	1	3	31	24	16	.291	.381	.442	.823	113	3	4	97	123	28	.777	0	1	-1	2	C	0.7
1940	Phi-A	23	46	3	9	1	1	0	2	6	3	.196	.288	.261	.549	46	-4	-4	96	60	3	.439	0	0	0	0	C	-0.1
1943	Phi-A	1	1	0	0	0	0	0	0	0	0	.000	.000	.000	.000	-99	-0	-0	101	0	0	.000	0	0	0	0	H	0.0
Total	5	241	707	87	205	53	8	12	105	97	65	.290	.376	.438	.815	109	7	11	96	100	120	.810	2	4	-2	-3	C/1	1.7
■ **FRANK BRUGGY** Bruggy, Frank Leo b: 5/4/1891, Elizabeth, N.J. d: 4/5/59, Elizabeth, N.J. BR/TR, 5'11", 195 lbs. Deb: 4/13/21																												
1921	Phi-N	96	277	28	86	11	2	5	28	23	37	.310	.370	.419	.788	106	4	3	102	78	44	.767	6	2	1	1	C/1	1.0
1922	Phi-A	53	111	10	31	7	0	0	9	6	11	.279	.322	.342	.664	70	-4	-5	104	85	12	.561	1	2	-1	0	C	-0.4
1923	Phi-A	54	105	4	22	3	0	1	6	4	9	.210	.245	.267	.512	35	-10	-10	100	66	7	.405	1	1	-0	-1	C/1	-0.8
1924	Phi-A	50	113	9	30	6	0	0	8	8	15	.265	.314	.319	.633	64	-6	-6	99	73	12	.578	4	0	1	-2	C	-0.3
1925	Cin-N	6	14	2	3	0	0	0	1	2	0	.214	.313	.214	.527	38	-1	-1	97	119	1	.455	0	0	0	-1	/C	-0.1
Total	5	259	620	53	172	27	2	6	52	43	72	.277	.329	.356	.686	79	-18	-20	101	77	76	.620	12	5	1	-2	C/1	-0.6
■ **MIKE BRUMLEY** Brumley, Anthony Michael b: 4/9/63, Oklahoma City, Okla. BB/TR, 5'10", 165 lbs. Deb: 6/16/87																												
1987	Chi-N	39	104	8	21	2	2	1	9	10	30	.202	.278	.288	.567	50	-7	-8	101	109	9	.558	7	1	2	1	S/2	0.0
■ **MIKE BRUMLEY** Brumley, Tony Mike b: 7/10/38, Granite, Okla. BL/TR, 5'10", 195 lbs. Deb: 4/18/64																												
1964	Was-A	136	426	36	104	19	2	2	35	40	54	.244	.310	.312	.623	73	-14	-15	101	107	40	.519	1	1	-0	1	*C	-0.9
1965	Was-A	79	216	15	45	4	0	3	15	20	33	.208	.282	.269	.550	57	-12	-12	100	93	16	.458	1	1	-0	6	C	0.0
1966	Was-A	9	18	1	2	1	0	0	0	0	2	.111	.111	.167	.278	-23	-3	-3	95	0	0	.188	0	0	0	0	/C	-0.1
Total	3	224	660	52	151	24	2	5	50	60	89	.229	.296	.294	.590	66	-29	-29	100	99	57	.507	2	2	-1	8	C	-1.0
■ **GLENN BRUMMER** Brummer, Glenn Edward b: 11/23/54, Olney, Ill. BR/TR, 6', 185 lbs. Deb: 5/25/81																												
1981	StL-N	21	30	2	6	1	0	0	2	1	2	.200	.226	.233	.459	30	-3	-3	102	112	2	.320	0	0	0	-1	C	-0.3
1982	StL-N	35	64	4	15	4	0	0	8	0	12	.234	.234	.297	.531	46	-5	-5	103	165	5	.429	2	0	1	-1	C	-0.4
1983	StL-N	45	87	7	24	7	0	0	9	10	11	.276	.351	.356	.707	98	-0	0	98	115	10	.600	1	3	-2	-1	C	0.0
1984	StL-N	28	58	3	12	0	0	1	3	3	7	.207	.246	.259	.505	42	-4	-4	99	65	3	.353	0	0	0	0	C	-0.2
1985	Tex-A	49	108	7	30	4	0	0	5	11	22	.278	.355	.315	.670	79	-2	-3	108	58	11	.565	1	5	-3	-2	C/OD	-0.5
Total	5	178	347	23	87	16	0	1	27	25	54	.251	.305	.305	.610	68	-14	-15	103	97	30	.507	4	8	-4	-4	C/DO	-1.4
■ **TOM BRUNANSKY** Brunansky, Thomas Andrew b: 8/20/60, Covina, Cal. BR/TR, 6'4", 205 lbs. Deb: 4/09/81																												
1981	Cal-A	11	33	7	5	0	0	3	6	8	10	.152	.317	.424	.741	108	1	0	104	102	5	.821	1	0	0	3	O	0.3
1982	Min-A	127	463	77	126	30	1	20	46	71	101	.272	.378	.471	.849	131	22	22	100	70	84	.849	1	2	-1	16	*O	3.2
1983	Min-A	151	542	70	123	24	5	28	82	61	95	.227	.310	.445	.754	100	2	-1	105	101	72	.705	2	5	-2	5	*O/D	0.0
1984	Min-A	155	567	75	144	21	0	32	85	57	94	.254	.322	.460	.782	108	9	5	106	97	81	.727	4	5	-2	1	*O/D	0.0
1985	Min-A	157	567	71	137	28	4	27	90	71	86	.242	.326	.448	.774	106	7	4	103	113	83	.742	5	3	-0	-0	*O	0.1
1986	Min-A	157	593	69	152	28	1	23	75	53	98	.256	.318	.423	.742	93	0	-7	108	99	78	.689	12	4	1	3	*O/D	-0.6
1987	Min-A	155	532	83	138	22	2	32	85	74	104	.259	.354	.489	.843	127	17	20	96	97	90	.837	11	11	-3	4	*OD	1.6
1988	Min-A	14	49	5	9	1	0	1	6	7	11	.184	.286	.265	.551	52	-3	-3	106	152	4	.500	1	2	-1	-3	O/D	-0.6
	StL-N	143	523	69	128	22	4	22	79	79	82	.245	.348	.428	.776	117	16	13	104	115	79	.773	16	6	1	-1	*O	1.0
Total	8	1070	3869	526	962	176	17	188	554	481	681	.249	.335	.449	.784	110	70	54	103	100	576	.773	53	38	-7	28	*O/D	5.0
■ **ARLO BRUNSBERG** Brunsberg, Arlo Adolph b: 8/15/40, Fertile, Minn. BL/TR, 6', 195 lbs. Deb: 9/23/66																												
1966	Det-A	2	3	1	1	1	0	0	0	0	0	.333	.500	.667	1.167	227	1	1	102	0	1	1.500	0	0	0	0	/C	0.1
■ **BOB BRUSH** Brush, Robert b: 3/8/1875, Osage, Iowa d: 4/2/44, San Bernadino, Cal. Deb: 4/20/07																												
1907	Bos-N	2	2	0	0	0	0	0	0	0	0	.000	.000	.000	.000	-99	-0	-0	95	0	0	.000	0			0	/1	0.0
■ **BILL BRUTON** Bruton, William Haron b: 12/22/25, Panola, Ala. BL/TR, 6'0.5", 169 lbs. Deb: 4/13/53																												
1953	Mil-N	151	613	82	153	18	14	1	41	44	100	.250	.306	.330	.636	70	-31	-26	94	69	65	.579	**26**	11	1	4	*O	-2.5
1954	Mil-N	142	567	89	161	20	7	4	30	40	78	.284	.336	.365	.701	88	-14	-9	93	57	73	.675	**34**	13	2	-3	*O	-1.4
1955	Mil-N	149	636	106	175	30	12	9	47	43	72	.275	.325	.403	.728	99	-8	-2	93	59	86	.692	**25**	11	1	10	*O	0.5
1956	Mil-N	147	525	73	143	23	**15**	8	56	26	63	.272	.308	.419	.727	94	-6	-5	99	99	66	.646	8	6	-1	-2	*O	-1.4
1957	Mil-N	79	306	41	85	16	9	5	30	19	35	.278	.322	.438	.760	113	0	4	90	85	44	.727	11	4	1	-3	O	0.0
1958	Mil-N	100	325	47	91	11	3	3	28	27	37	.280	.339	.360	.699	95	-6	-2	89	92	41	.625	4	1	1	-12	O	-1.5
1959	Mil-N	133	478	72	138	22	6	6	41	35	54	.289	.339	.397	.736	100	-3	-0	95	81	64	.675	13	5	1	-3	*O	-0.3
1960	Mil-N	151	629	**112**	180	27	**13**	12	54	41	97	.286	.332	.428	.760	117	4	11	91	63	89	.717	22	13	-1	-2	*O	0.3
1961	Det-A	160	596	99	153	15	5	17	63	61	66	.257	.329	.384	.713	94	-9	-5	96	90	79	.688	22	6	3	3	*O	-0.4
1962	Det-A	147	561	90	156	27	5	16	74	55	67	.278	.348	.430	.777	97	6	-2	111	108	84	.745	14	7	0	10	*O	0.3
1963	Det-A	145	524	84	134	21	8	8	48	59	70	.256	.331	.372	.703	93	-2	-4	104	94	67	.665	14	7	0	3	*O	-0.5
1964	Det-A	106	296	42	82	11	5	5	33	32	54	.277	.348	.399	.746	112	3	5	96	105	42	.729	14	5	1	4	O	0.7
Total	12	1610	6056	937	1651	241	102	94	545	482	793	.273	.329	.393	.722	96	-65	-36	96	82	801	.688	207	89	9	10	*O	-6.2
■ **ED BRUYETTE** Bruyette, Edward T. b: 8/31/1874, Wanawa, Wis. d: 8/5/40, Peshastin, Wash. BL , 5'10", 170 lbs. Deb: 8/06/01																												
1901	Mil-A	26	82	7	15	3	0	0	4	12		.183	.287	.220	.507	46	-6	-5	95	70	6	.463	1			-3	O/2S3	-0.7
■ **BILLY BRYAN** Bryan, William Ronald b: 12/4/38, Morgan, Ga. BL/TR, 6'4", 200 lbs. Deb: 9/12/61																												
1961	KC-A	9	19	2	3	0	0	1	2	2	7	.158	.238	.316	.554	46	-2	-2	102	87	1	.471	0	0	0	0	/C	-0.1
1962	KC-A	25	74	5	11	2	1	2	7	5	32	.149	.203	.284	.486	29	-8	-8	100	103	5	.413	0	0	0	-0	C	-0.6
1963	KC-A	24	65	11	11	1	1	3	7	9	22	.169	.270	.354	.624	68	-2	-3	108	92	6	.582	0	0	0	2	C	0.0
1964	KC-A	93	220	19	53	9	2	13	36	16	69	.241	.292	.477	.770	105	2	1	105	106	29	.699	0	0	0	-3	C	0.0
1965	KC-A	108	325	36	82	11	5	14	51	29	87	.252	.317	.446	.764	118	5	7	97	113	47	.718	0	0	0	7	C	2.1
1966	KC-A	32	76	0	10	4	0	0	7	6	17	.132	.195	.184	.379	10	-9	-8	94	210	3	.294	0	0	0	0	C/1	-0.7
	NY-A	27	69	5	15	2	0	4	5	5	19	.217	.270	.420	.691	102	-1	-0	94	51	8	.618	0	0	0	2	C/1	0.3
	Yr	59	145	5	25	6	0	4	12	11	36	.172	.231	.297	.527	54	-10	-9	94	141	10	.446	0	0	0	2		-0.4
1967	NY-A	16	12	1	2	0	0	1	2	5	3	.167	.412	.417	.828	154	1	1	94	104	3	1.000	0	0	0	0	/C	0.1
1968	Was-A	40	108	7	22	3	0	3	8	14	27	.204	.301	.315	.616	95	-2	-1	91	80	11	.557	0	1	-1	3	C	0.4
Total	8	374	968	86	209	32	9	41	125	91	283	.216	.285	.395	.680	92	-14	-13	99	108	112	.625	0	1	-1	12	C/1	1.5
■ **DEREK BRYANT** Bryant, Derek Roszell b: 10/9/51, Lexington, Ky. BR/TR, 5'11", 185 lbs. Deb: 4/24/79																												
1979	Oak-A	39	106	8	19	2	1	0	13	10	10	.179	.250	.217	.467	31	-11	-9	89	217	6	.363	0	0	0	-2	O/D	-1.2
■ **DON BRYANT** Bryant, Donald Ray b: 7/13/41, Jasper, Fla. BR/TR, 6'5", 200 lbs. Deb: 7/17/66 C																												
1966	Chi-N	13	26	2	8	2	0	0	4	1	4	.308	.357	.385	.742	106	0	0	100	168	4	.684	1	0	0	1	C	0.2
1969	Hou-N	31	59	2	11	1	0	1	6	4	13	.186	.250	.254	.504	41	-5	-5	102	134	4	.408	0	0	0	-1	C	-0.3
1970	Hou-N	15	24	2	5	0	0	0	3	1	8	.208	.240	.208	.448	23	-3	-2	94	233	1	.316	0	0	0	0	C	-0.1
Total	3	59	109	6	24	3	0	1	13	6	25	.220	.274	.275	.549	53	-7	-7	99	163	9	.459	1	0	0	0	/C	-0.2
■ **G. BRYANT** Bryant, G. Deb: 1885																												
1885	Det-N	1	4	0	0	0	0	0	1	0	2	.000	.000	.000	.000	-99	-1	-1	97	0	0	.000				0	/2	0.0
■ **RALPH BRYANT** Bryant, Ralph Wendell b: 5/20/61, Fort Gaines, Ga. BL/TR, 6'2", 200 lbs. Deb: 9/08/85																												
1985	LA-N	6	6	0	2	0	0	0	0	0	2	.333	.333	.333	.667	94	-0	-0	93	199	1	.500	0	0	0	-1	/O	0.0
1986	LA-N	27	75	15	19	4	2	6	13	5	25	.253	.309	.600	.909	154	4	4	94	82	13	.879	0	1	-1	-1	O	0.2
1987	LA-N	46	69	7	17	2	1	2	10	10	24	.246	.350	.391	.741	105	-0	1	92	121	10	.755	2	1	0	-3	O	-0.2
Total	3	79	150	22	38	6	3	8	24	15	51	.253	.329	.493	.823	128	4	5	93	105	24	.816	2	2	-1	-5	/O	0.0

YEAR	TM/L	G	AB	R	H	2B	3B	HR	RBI	BB	SO	AVG	OBP	SLG	PRO	/A	BR	/A	PF	CHI	RC	TA	SB	CS	SBR	FR	POS	TPR
■ **STEVE BRYE**	Brye, Stephen Robert b: 2/4/49, Alameda, Cal. BR/TR, 6', 190 lbs. Deb: 9/03/70																											
1970	Min-A	9	11	1	2	1	0	0	2	2	4	.182	.308	.273	.580	62	-1	-1	98	270	1	.556	0	0	0	-2	/O	-0.1
1971	Min-A	28	107	10	24	1	0	3	11	7	15	.224	.272	.318	.590	64	-5	-5	104	111	9	.500	3	1	0	2	O	-0.4
1972	Min-A	100	253	18	61	9	3	0	12	17	38	.241	.292	.300	.592	71	-7	-9	107	66	22	.490	3	1	0	2	O	-1.0
1973	Min-A	92	278	39	73	9	5	6	33	35	43	.263	.345	.396	.741	104	3	2	104	101	38	.692	3	5	-2	-4	O/D	-0.5
1974	Min-A	135	488	52	138	32	1	2	41	22	59	.283	.320	.365	.685	96	-3	-3	101	89	54	.564	1	3	-2	-5	*O	-1.3
1975	Min-A	86	246	41	62	13	1	9	34	21	37	.252	.316	.423	.739	100	2	-1	107	100	32	.675	2	1	0	-5	O/D	-0.6
1976	Min-A	87	258	33	68	11	0	2	23	13	31	.264	.299	.329	.628	85	-6	-5	98	97	24	.497	1	2	-1	-7	O/D	-1.5
1977	Mil-A	94	241	27	60	14	3	7	28	16	39	.249	.298	.419	.718	98	-3	-1	95	91	30	.640	1	0	0	3	O/D	0.0
1978	Pit-N	66	115	16	27	7	0	1	9	11	10	.235	.307	.322	.629	72	-4	-4	105	89	12	.560	2	1	0	-7	O	-1.3
Total	9	697	1997	237	515	97	13	30	193	144	276	.258	.311	.365	.676	90	-23	-28	102	93	222	.599	16	14	-4	-23	O/D	-6.7
■ **HAL BUBSER**	Bubser, Harold Fred b: 9/28/1895, Chicago, Ill. d: 6/22/59, Melrose Park, Ill BR/TR, 5'11", 170 lbs. Deb: 4/15/22																											
1922	Chi-A	3	3	0	0	0	0	0	0	0	2	.000	.000	.000	.000	-99	-1	-1	101	0	0	.000	0	0	0	0	H	0.0
■ **JOHNNY BUCHA**	Bucha, John George b: 1/22/25, Allentown, Pa. BR/TR, 5'11", 190 lbs. Deb: 5/02/48																											
1948	StL-N	2	1	0	0	0	0	0	0	1	0	.000	.500	.000	.500	45	0	0	101	0	0	1.000	0			0	/C	0.0
1950	StL-N	22	36	1	5	1	0	0	1	4	7	.139	.225	.167	.392	5	-5	-5	103	64	1	.303	0			0	C	-0.4
1953	Det-A	60	158	17	35	9	0	1	14	20	14	.222	.309	.297	.606	66	-8	-7	98	104	16	.535	1	1	-0	2	C	-0.2
Total	3	84	195	18	40	10	0	1	15	25	21	.205	.295	.272	.567	54	-13	-12	99	95	17	.497	1	1		2	/C	-0.6
■ **JERRY BUCHEK**	Buchek, Gerald Peter b: 5/9/42, St.Louis, Mo. BR/TR, 5'11", 185 lbs. Deb: 6/30/61																											
1961	StL-N	31	90	6	12	2	0	0	9	0	28	.133	.152	.156	.308	-16	-15	-17	113	259	1	.190	0	0	0	-1	S	-1.4
1963	StL-N	3	4	0	1	0	0	0	0	0	2	.250	.250	.250	.500	41	-0	-0	107	0	0	.333	0	0	0	0	/S	0.0
1964	StL-N	35	30	7	6	0	2	0	1	3	11	.200	.273	.333	.606	62	-1	-2	112	41	3	.542	0	0	0	0	S/23	0.0
1965	StL-N	55	166	17	41	8	3	3	21	13	46	.247	.302	.386	.687	86	-2	-3	107	119	19	.605	1	0	0	-0	2S/3	0.0
1966	StL-N	100	284	23	67	10	4	4	25	23	71	.236	.293	.342	.635	76	-9	-9	100	96	26	.519	0	5	-3	3	2S/3	-0.2
1967	NY-N	124	411	35	97	11	2	14	41	26	101	.236	.285	.375	.659	88	-8	-7	99	87	41	.562	3	5	-2	2	23/S	0.0
1968	NY-N	73	192	8	35	4	0	1	11	10	53	.182	.234	.219	.453	36	-15	-15	102	103	9	.337	1	1	-0	-3	32/O	-2.0
Total	7	421	1177	96	259	35	11	22	108	75	312	.220	.271	.325	.595	67	-50	-53	102	107	98	.501	5	11	-5	1	2S/3O	-3.6
■ **JIM BUCHER**	Bucher, James Quinter b: 3/11/11, Manassas, Va. BL/TR, 5'11", 170 lbs. Deb: 4/18/34																											
1934	Bro-N	47	84	12	19	5	2	0	8	4	7	.226	.261	.333	.595	61	-5	-5	95	103	7	.500	1			1	2/3	0.0
1935	Bro-N	123	473	72	143	22	1	7	58	10	33	.302	.317	.397	.714	97	-7	-3	94	102	58	.596	4			2	23O	0.1
1936	Bro-N	110	370	49	93	12	8	2	41	29	27	.251	.306	.343	.649	71	-13	-16	105	109	40	.569	5			-4	32O	-1.5
1937	Bro-N	125	380	44	96	11	2	4	37	20	18	.253	.295	.324	.619	65	-17	-19	104	99	37	.521	5			-8	23/O	-2.3
1938	StL-N	17	57	7	13	3	1	0	7	2	2	.228	.254	.316	.570	50	-4	-4	111	141	4	.435	0			-1	2/3	-0.3
1944	Bos-A	80	277	39	76	9	2	4	31	19	13	.274	.326	.365	.690	99	-1	-1	98	99	33	.595	3	3	-1	0	32	0.0
1945	Bos-A	52	151	19	34	4	3	0	11	7	13	.225	.264	.291	.556	64	-8	-7	95	90	11	.434	1	3	-2	2	3/2	-0.5
Total	7	554	1792	242	474	66	19	17	193	91	113	.265	.302	.351	.653	79	-56	-55	100	103	192	.562	19	6		-8	32/O	-4.5
■ **KEVIN BUCKLEY**	Buckley, Kevin John b: 1/16/59, Quincy, Mass. BR/TR, 6'1", 200 lbs. Deb: 9/04/84																											
1984	Tex-A	5	7	1	2	1	0	0	0	2	4	.286	.444	.429	.873	143	1	1	100	0	2	1.000	0	0	0	0	/D	0.1
■ **DICK BUCKLEY**	Buckley, Richard D. b: 9/21/1858, Troy, N.Y. d: 12/12/29, Pittsburgh, Pa. TR, 5'10", Deb: 1888																											
1888	Ind-N	71	260	28	71	9	3	5	22	6	24	.273	.289	.388	.678	122	4	6	95	69	31	.587	4			-9	C3/O1	-0.1
1889	Ind-N	68	260	35	67	11	0	8	41	15	32	.258	.301	.392	.693	87	-3	-7	109	99	33	.637	5			-18	C3/O1	-2.0
1890	NY-N	70	266	39	68	11	0	2	26	23	35	.256	.324	.320	.644	95	-3	-1	95	88	29	.581	3			6	C/3	0.9
1891	NY-N	75	253	23	55	9	1	4	31	11	30	.217	.258	.308	.567	71	-11	-9	94	100	21	.480	3			4	C/3	0.1
1892	StL-N	121	410	43	93	17	4	5	52	22	34	.227	.275	.324	.599	87	-10	-7	95	108	39	.527	7			-4	*C/1	-0.3
1893	StL-N	9	23	2	4	1	0	0	1	0	0	.174	.174	.217	.391	5	-3	-3	99	55	1	.263	0			0	/C	-0.2
1894	StL-N	29	89	5	16	1	2	1	3	6	3	.180	.240	.270	.509	23	-11	-12	101	31	6	.438	1			-1	C/1	-0.7
	Phi-N	43	160	18	47	7	3	1	26	6	13	.294	.327	.394	.721	78	-7	-5	95	109	21	.628	0			4	C/1	0.2
	Yr	72	249	23	63	8	5	2	29	12	16	.253	.295	.349	.645	58	-18	-17	98	78	27	.554	1			3		-0.5
1895	Phi-N	38	112	20	28	6	1	0	14	9	17	.250	.333	.321	.655	72	-5	-4	99	109	13	.619	2			-0	C	0.0
Total	8	524	1833	213	449	72	14	26	216	98	188	.245	.291	.342	.633	84	-49	-42	97	93	195	.557	25			-18	C/31O	-2.1
■ **BILL BUCKNER**	Buckner, William Joseph b: 12/14/49, Vallejo, Cal. BL/TL, 6', 185 lbs. Deb: 9/21/69																											
1969	LA-N	1	1	0	0	0	0	0	0	0	0	.000	.000	.000	.000	-99	-0	-0	99	0	0	.000	0	0	0	0	H	0.0
1970	LA-N	28	68	6	13	3	1	0	4	3	7	.191	.225	.265	.490	34	-7	-6	90	86	4	.375	0	1	-1	0	O/1	-0.6
1971	LA-N	108	358	37	99	15	1	5	41	11	18	.277	.307	.366	.673	91	-5	-5	99	114	40	.568	4	1	1	-0	O1	-0.8
1972	LA-N	105	383	47	122	14	3	5	37	17	13	.319	.349	.410	.759	123	7	9	94	90	52	.668	10	3	1	-1	O1	0.5
1973	LA-N	140	575	68	158	20	0	8	46	17	34	.275	.299	.351	.650	79	-17	-17	100	87	58	.539	12	2	2	-8	1O	-3.0
1974	LA-N	145	580	83	182	30	3	7	58	30	24	.314	.352	.412	.764	122	9	14	93	91	81	.717	31	13	2	-7	*O/1	0.3
1975	LA-N	92	288	30	70	11	2	6	31	17	15	.243	.290	.358	.648	83	-9	-7	95	99	27	.560	8	3	1	0	O	-0.9
1976	LA-N	154	642	76	193	28	4	7	60	26	26	.301	.329	.389	.718	104	1	1	100	82	82	.655	28	9	3	-2	*O/1	-0.2
1977	Chi-N	122	426	40	121	27	0	11	60	21	23	.284	.319	.425	.744	86	-3	-10	114	112	52	.644	7	5	-1	4	1	-1.1
1978	Chi-N	117	446	47	144	26	1	5	74	18	17	.323	.349	.419	.768	103	7	2	110	148	59	.656	7	5	-1	8	*1	0.6
1979	Chi-N	149	591	72	168	34	7	14	66	30	28	.284	.321	.437	.758	93	2	-7	112	92	78	.675	9	4	0	16	*1	0.3
1980	Chi-N	145	578	69	187	41	3	10	68	30	18	**.324**	.357	.457	.814	118	18	14	106	97	90	.727	1	2	-1	2	1O	0.9
1981	Chi-N	106	421	45	131	**35**	3	10	75	26	16	.311	.353	.480	.832	129	17	15	104	134	65	.757	5	2	0	0	*1	1.3
1982	Chi-N	161	657	93	201	34	5	15	105	36	26	.306	.347	.441	.788	115	15	13	103	118	98	.728	15	5	2	16	*1	2.2
1983	Chi-N	153	626	79	175	**38**	6	16	66	25	30	.280	.313	.436	.749	104	2	1	101	78	83	.677	12	4	1	17	*1O	1.3
1984	Chi-N	21	43	3	9	0	0	0	2	1	1	.209	.244	.209	.454	26	-4	-5	110	87	2	.314	0	0	0	1	/1O	-0.3
	Bos-A	114	439	51	122	21	2	11	67	24	38	.278	.323	.410	.733	92	0	-6	110	128	55	.639	2	2	-1	7	*1	-0.6
1985	Bos-A	162	673	89	201	46	3	16	110	30	36	.299	.330	.447	.778	108	8	6	102	132	96	.713	18	4	3	**25**	*1	2.3
1986	Bos-A	153	629	73	168	39	2	18	102	40	25	.267	.315	.421	.736	100	-2	-1	100	122	76	.643	6	4	-1	16	*1D	0.4
1987	Bos-A	75	286	23	78	6	1	2	42	13	19	.273	.304	.322	.626	68	-13	-13	99	174	25	.480	1	3	-2	-2	1	-2.2
	Cal-A	57	183	16	56	12	1	3	32	9	7	.306	.339	.432	.770	104	1	1	99	145	26	.685	1	0	0	-0	D/1	0.0
	Yr	132	469	39	134	18	2	5	74	22	26	.286	.318	.365	.682	82	-12	-12	99	163	55	.572	2	3	-1	-2		-2.2
1988	Cal-A	19	43	1	9	0	0	0	9	4	0	.209	.277	.209	.486	41	-3	-3	94	398	3	.417	2	0	1	0	D/1	-0.2
	KC-A	89	242	18	62	14	0	3	34	13	19	.256	.294	.351	.645	77	-7	-8	103	144	24	.540	3	1	0	-1	D1	-0.9
	Yr	108	285	19	71	14	0	3	43	17	19	.249	.291	.330	.621	72	-10	-11	102	192	27	.525	5	1	1	-1		-1.1
Total	20	2416	9178	1066	2669	494	48	172	1189	441	440	.291	.326	.411	.738	101	17	-10	102	112	1177	.674	182	73	11	92	*1OD	-0.7
■ **MARK BUDASKA**	Budaska, Mark David b: 12/27/52, Sharon, Pa. BB/TL, 6', 180 lbs. Deb: 6/06/78																											
1978	Oak-A	4	4	0	1	1	0	0	0	1	2	.250	.400	.500	.900	150	0	0	101	0	1	1.000	0	0	0	-1	/O	0.0
1981	Oak-A	9	32	3	5	1	0	0	2	4	10	.156	.250	.188	.438	29	-3	-3	96	133	2	.357	0	1	-1	0	/D	-0.3
Total	2	13	36	3	6	2	0	0	2	5	12	.167	.268	.222	.491	44	-3	-2	96	117	2	.419	0	1	-1	-1	/DO	-0.3
■ **BUDD**	Budd Deb:9/10/1890																											
1890	Cle-P	1	4	0	0	0	0	0	0	0	3	.000	.000	.000	.000	-99	-1	-1	92	0	0	.000	0			0	/O	0.0
■ **DON BUDDIN**	Buddin, Donald Thomas b: 5/5/34, Turbeville, S.C. BR/TR, 5'11", 178 lbs. Deb: 4/17/56																											
1956	Bos-A	114	377	49	90	24	0	5	37	65	62	.239	.357	.342	.699	83	-6	-8	103	96	49	.664	2	0	1	-1	*S	0.1
1958	Bos-A	136	497	74	118	25	2	12	43	82	106	.237	.350	.368	.718	93	1	-3	105	83	66	.679	0	4	-2	14	*S	2.8
1959	Bos-A	151	485	75	117	24	1	10	53	92	99	.241	.368	.357	.724	94	3	-1	106	105	72	.734	6	1	1	-7	*S	0.5
1960	Bos-A	124	428	62	105	21	5	6	36	62	59	.245	.342	.360	.702	87	-5	-7	103	84	53	.652	4	2	0	-11	*S	-0.8
1961	Bos-A	115	339	58	89	22	3	6	42	72	45	.263	.395	.398	.793	111	9	8	102	107	58	.818	2	1	0	-3	*S	1.2

YEAR	TM/L	G	AB	R	H	2B	3B	HR	RBI	BB	SO	AVG	OBP	SLG	PRO	/A	BR	/A	PF	CHI	RC	TA	SB	CS	SBR	FR	POS	TPR
1962	Hou-N	40	80	10	13	4	1	2	10	17	17	.162	.316	.313	.629	75	-3	-2	93	127	8	.606	0	0	0	1	S/3	0.2
	Det-A	31	83	14	19	3	0	0	4	20	16	.229	.385	.265	.650	71	-1	-3	111	72	11	.688	1	0	0	-5	S/23	-0.5
Total	6	711	2289	342	551	123	12	41	225	410	404	.241	.360	.359	.719	92	-3	-15	104	95	317	.724	15	8	-0	-13	S/32	3.5
■ **STEVE BUECHELE** Buechele, Steven Bernard b: 9/26/61, Lancaster, Cal. BR/TR, 6'2", 190 lbs. Deb: 7/19/85																												
1985	Tex-A	69	219	22	48	6	3	6	21	14	38	.219	.272	.356	.629	65	-9	-12	108	87	18	.527	3	2	-0	7	3/2	-0.6
1986	Tex-A	153	461	54	112	19	2	18	54	35	98	.243	.303	.410	.713	97	-5	-2	96	89	54	.638	5	8	-3	4	*32/O	-0.3
1987	Tex-A	136	363	45	86	20	0	13	50	28	66	.237	.293	.399	.693	79	-10	-12	104	108	42	.615	2	2	-1	-8	*32/O	-2.0
1988	Tex-A	155	503	68	126	21	4	16	58	65	79	.250	.342	.404	.746	107	6	5	101	92	71	.707	2	4	-2	8	*3/2	1.2
Total	4	513	1546	189	372	66	9	53	183	142	281	.241	.310	.398	.708	91	-18	-20	101	94	185	.653	12	16	-6	11	3/2O	-1.7
■ **CHARLIE BUELOW** Buelow, Charles John b: 1/12/1877, Dubuque, Iowa d: 5/4/51, Dubuque, Iowa BR/TR, Deb: 6/01/01																												
1901	NY-N	22	72	3	8	4	0	0	4	2		.111	.135	.167	.302	-13	-10	-9	91	112	2	.219	0			2	3/2	-0.5
■ **FRITZ BUELOW** Buelow, Frederick William b: 2/13/1876, Berlin, Germany d: 12/27/33, Detroit, Mich. BR/TR, 5'10.5", 170 lbs. Deb: 9/28/1899																												
1899	StL-N	7	15	4	7	0	2	0	2	2		.467	.556	.733	1.289	238	3	3	108	56	6	1.750	0			0	/CO	0.3
1900	StL-N	6	17	2	4	0	0	0	3	0		.235	.235	.235	.471	34	-2	-1	93	234	1	.308	0			0	/CO	0.0
1901	Det-A	70	231	28	52	5	5	2	29	11		.225	.260	.316	.576	55	-12	-16	110	116	20	.480	2			-5	C	-1.3
1902	Det-A	66	224	23	50	5	2	2	29	9		.223	.253	.290	.543	52	-15	-14	99	135	18	.443	3			-1	C/1	-0.9
1903	Det-A	63	192	24	41	3	6	1	13	6		.214	.237	.307	.545	66	-8	-8	97	76	15	.457	4			-2	C/1	-0.1
1904	Det-A	42	136	6	15	1	1	0	5	8		.110	.160	.132	.292	-6	-16	-15	96	104	3	.231	2			2	C	-1.0
	Cle-A	42	119	11	21	4	1	0	5	11		.176	.246	.227	.473	51	-6	-6	102	69	7	.408	2			-2	C	-0.4
	Yr	84	255	17	36	5	2	0	10	19		.141	.201	.176	.377	22	-22	-21	99	88	10	.311	4			-1		-1.4
1905	Cle-A	75	239	11	41	4	1	1	18	6		.172	.192	.209	.401	29	-19	-19	100	121	11	.318	7			-5	C/O13	-1.9
1906	Cle-A	34	86	7	14	2	0	0	7	9		.163	.242	.186	.428	35	-6	-6	103	159	4	.347	0			-2	C	-0.6
1907	StL-A	26	75	9	11	1	0	0	1	7		.147	.220	.160	.380	23	-6	-6	98	30	3	.297	0			0	C	-0.3
Total	9	431	1334	125	256	25	18	6	112	69		.192	.232	.251	.483	45	-87	-89	101	107	89	.394	20			-16	C/O13	-6.2
■ **ART BUES** Bues, Arthur Frederick b: 3/3/1888, Milwaukee, Wis. d: 11/7/54, Whitefish Bay, Wis. BR/TR, 5'11", 184 lbs. Deb: 4/17/13																												
1913	Bos-N	2	1	0	0	0	0	0	0	0	1	.000	.000	.000	.000	-99	-0	-0	95	0	0	.000	0			0	/23	0.0
1914	Chi-N	14	45	3	10	1	1	0	4	5	6	.222	.300	.289	.589	77	-1	-1	98	112	4	.543	1			-1	3	-0.1
Total	2	16	46	3	10	1	1	0	4	5	7	.217	.294	.283	.577	73	-2	-1	98	109	4	.528	1			-1	/32	-0.1
■ **CHARLIE BUFFINTON** Buffinton, Charles G. b: 6/14/1861, Fall River, Mass. d: 9/23/07, Fall River, Mass. BR/TR, 6'1", 180 lbs. Deb: 5/17/1882 M																												
1882	Bos-N	15	50	5	13	1	0	0	4	2	3	.260	.288	.280	.568	81	-1	-1	103	96	4	.432				0	/OP1	0.0
1883	Bos-N	86	341	28	81	8	3	1	26	6	24	.238	.251	.287	.538	59	-15	-18	106	91	25	.400				-7	OP/1	-1.4
1884	Bos-N	87	352	48	94	18	3	1	39	16	12	.267	.299	.344	.643	104	0	2	98	115	37	.531				4	PO1	0.0
1885	Bos-N	82	338	26	81	12	3	1	33	3	26	.240	.246	.302	.548	82	-9	-6	94	116	26	.409				5	PO1	0.0
1886	Bos-N	44	176	27	51	4	1	1	30	6	12	.290	.313	.341	.654	102	-0	0	97	164	20	.552	3			0	1P	0.0
1887	Phi-N	66	269	34	72	12	1	1	46	11	3	.268	.299	.331	.630	79	-8	-7	97	157	30	.553	8			7	PO1	0.0
1888	Phi-N	46	160	14	29	4	1	0	12	7	5	.181	.216	.219	.434	35	-10	-13	114	123	8	.328	1			9	P/O	0.0
1889	Phi-N	47	154	16	32	2	0	0	21	9	5	.208	.256	.221	.477	34	-13	-14	104	184	9	.361	0			2	P/O	0.0
1890	Phi-P	42	150	24	41	3	2	1	24	9	3	.273	.319	.340	.659	76	-5	-5	102	122	17	.569	1			2	P/O1M	0.0
1891	Bos-a	58	181	16	34	2	1	1	16	19	15	.188	.269	.227	.495	45	-13	-12	99	105	11	.415	0			6	PO/1	0.0
1892	Bal-N	13	43	7	15	1	1	0	4	3	6	.349	.391	.419	.810	147	2	2	100	68	8	.786	1			0	P	0.0
Total	11	586	2214	245	543	67	16	7	255	91	114	.245	.276	.299	.576	73	-72	-73	100	124	195	.462	14			28	PO/1	-1.4
■ **DON BUFORD** Buford, Donald Alvin b: 2/2/37, Linden, Tex. BB/TR, 5'7", 160 lbs. Deb: 9/14/63 C																												
1963	Chi-A	12	42	9	12	1	2	0	5	5	7	.286	.362	.405	.766	110	1	1	104	125	6	.742	1	0	0	-0	/32	0.1
1964	Chi-A	135	442	62	116	14	6	4	30	46	62	.262	.339	.348	.687	96	-4	-1	96	77	54	.638	12	7	-1	2	23	1.0
1965	Chi-A	155	586	93	166	22	5	10	47	67	76	.283	.361	.389	.750	123	11	17	92	80	87	.730	17	7	1	18	*23	**4.6**
1966	Chi-A	163	607	85	148	26	7	8	52	69	71	.244	.324	.349	.673	99	-4	0	94	89	74	.692	51	22	2	11	*32O	1.4
1967	Chi-A	156	535	61	129	10	9	4	32	65	51	.241	.324	.316	.640	96	-5	-1	94	75	58	.626	34	21	-2	4	*32/O	0.4
1968	Bal-A	130	426	65	120	13	4	15	46	57	46	.282	.372	.437	.808	141	24	23	102	87	74	.859	27	12	1	5	O2/3	3.1
1969	Bal-A	144	554	99	161	31	3	11	64	96	62	.291	.400	.417	.817	124	25	23	104	86	97	.844	19	18	-5	-2	*O2/3	1.3
1970	Bal-A	144	504	99	137	15	2	17	66	109	55	.272	.409	.411	.820	131	24	26	97	110	97	.904	16	8	0	4	*O/23	2.5
1971	Bal-A	122	449	**99**	130	19	4	19	54	89	62	.290	.415	.477	.891	147	34	33	103	78	97	.991	15	7	0	-1	*O	3.0
1972	Bal-A	125	408	46	84	6	2	5	22	69	83	.206	.326	.267	.594	80	-8	-7	98	76	40	.572	8	3	1	-4	*O	-1.5
Total	10	1286	4553	718	1203	157	44	93	418	672	575	.264	.364	.379	.743	116	98	112	98	85	686	.763	200	105	-3	36	O23	15.9
■ **JAY BUHNER** Buhner, Jay Campbell b: 8/13/64, Louisville, Ky. BR/TR, 6'3", 205 lbs. Deb: 9/11/87																												
1987	NY-A	7	22	0	5	2	0	0	1	1	6	.227	.261	.318	.579	55	-1	-1	98	57	2	.444	0	0	0	0	/O	0.0
1988	NY-A	25	69	8	13	0	0	3	13	3	25	.188	.253	.319	.572	62	-4	-4	96	167	6	.491	0	0	0	1	O	-0.2
	Sea-A	60	192	28	43	13	1	10	25	25	68	.224	.323	.458	.781	108	4	2	108	86	29	.760	1	1	-0	8	O	0.8
	Yr	85	261	36	56	13	1	13	38	28	93	.215	.305	.421	.727	97	-0	-1	104	112	34	.690	1	1	-0	9		0.6
Total	2	92	283	36	61	15	1	13	39	29	99	.216	.302	.413	.715	94	-1	-3	104	103	36	.674	1	1	-0	9	/O	0.6
■ **HARRY BUKER** Buker, Henry L. "Happy" Deb: 6/11/1884																												
1884	Det-N	30	111	5	15	1	0	0	3	4	15	.135	.165	.144	.309	-2	-13	-12	94	66	3	.208				0	SO	-0.9
■ **GEORGE BULLARD** Bullard, George Donald "Curly" b: 10/24/28, Lynn, Mass. BR/TR, 5'9.5", 165 lbs. Deb: 9/17/54																												
1954	Det-A	4	1	0	0	0	0	0	0	0	0	.000	.000	.000	.000	-99	-0	-0	100	0	0	.000	0	0	0	0	/S	0.0
■ **SIM BULLAS** Bullas, Simeon Edward b: 4/10/1861, Cleveland, Ohio d: 1/14/08, Cleveland, Ohio 5'7.5", 150 lbs. Deb: 5/02/1884																												
1884	Tol-a	13	45	4	4	0	1	0		1		.089	.109	.133	.242	-20	-6	-6	104	0	1	.171				0	C/O	-0.4
■ **BUD BULLING** Bulling, Terry Charles "Terry" b: 12/15/52, Lynwood, Cal. BR/TR, 6'1", 200 lbs. Deb: 7/03/77																												
1977	Min-A	15	32	2	5	1	0	0	5	5	5	.156	.270	.188	.458	27	-3	-3	103	330	2	.393	0	0	0	1	C/D	-0.1
1981	Sea-A	62	154	15	38	3	0	2	15	21	20	.247	.341	.305	.646	88	-2	-2	100	111	18	.585	0	0	0	-11	C	-1.0
1982	Sea-A	56	154	17	34	7	0	1	8	19	16	.221	.306	.286	.592	58	-7	-9	109	68	13	.512	2	1	0	-6	C	-1.1
1983	Sea-A	5	5	0	0	0	0	0	0	0	0	.000	.000	.000	.000	-99	-1	-1	100	0	0	.000	0	0	0	0	/C	0.0
Total	4	138	345	34	77	11	0	3	28	45	41	.223	.315	.281	.596	66	-13	-15	104	111	33	.539	2	1	0	-16	C/D	-2.2
■ **ERIC BULLOCK** Bullock, Eric Gerald b: 2/16/60, Los Angeles, Cal. BL/TL, 5'11", 185 lbs. Deb: 8/26/85																												
1985	Hou-N	18	25	3	7	2	0	0	2	1	3	.280	.308	.360	.668	90	-1	-0	96	88	2	.526	0	1	-1	-2	/O	-0.2
1986	Hou-N	6	21	0	1	0	0	0	1	0	3	.048	.048	.048	.095	-72	-5	-5	103	399	0	.150	2	0	1	-1	/O	-0.5
1988	Min-A	16	17	3	5	0	0	0	3	3	1	.294	.400	.294	.694	92	0	-0	106	239	3	.750	1	0	0	-1	/OD	0.0
Total	3	40	63	6	13	2	0	0	6	4	7	.206	.254	.238	.492	37	-5	-5	101	230	5	.431	3	1	0	-3	/OD	-0.7
■ **AL BUMBRY** Bumbry, Alonza Benjamin (born Alonza Benjamin Bumbrey) b: 4/21/47, Fredericksburg, Va. BL/TR, 5'8", 170 lbs. Deb: 9/05/72 C																												
1972	Bal-A	9	11	5	4	0	1	0	0	0	0	.364	.364	.545	.909	172	1	1	98	0	2	.875	1	1	-0	0	/O	0.0
1973	Bal-A	110	356	73	120	15	**11**	7	34	34	49	.337	.399	.500	.899	142	24	21	107	67	72	.948	23	10	1	-11	O/D	0.8
1974	Bal-A	94	270	35	63	10	3	1	19	21	46	.233	.291	.304	.595	77	-10	-8	93	88	25	.542	12	4	1	-5	O/D	-1.3
1975	Bal-A	114	349	47	94	19	4	2	32	32	81	.269	.338	.364	.702	108	-1	4	91	92	47	.688	16	3	3	-3	DO/3	0.3
1976	Bal-A	133	450	71	113	15	7	9	36	43	76	.251	.318	.376	.693	105	1	2	98	72	57	.720	42	10	7	0	*OD	0.7
1977	Bal-A	133	518	74	164	31	3	4	41	45	88	.317	.373	.411	.785	122	11	15	93	77	83	.762	19	8	1	-5	*O	0.6
1978	Bal-A	33	114	21	27	5	2	2	6	17	15	.237	.346	.368	.714	111	1	2	91	50	15	.702	5	3	-0	1	O	0.2
1979	Bal-A	148	569	80	162	29	1	7	49	43	74	.285	.338	.376	.714	95	-6	-4	97	85	76	.699	37	12	4	-7	*O	-1.1
1980	Bal-A	160	645	118	205	29	9	9	53	78	75	.318	.394	.433	.826	125	26	25	101	60	118	.878	44	11	7	9	*O	3.7
1981	Bal-A	101	392	61	107	18	2	1	27	51	51	.273	.360	.337	.696	103	3	3	99	69	49	.676	22	15	-2	-1	*O	-0.1
1982	Bal-A	150	562	77	147	20	4	5	40	44	77	.262	.315	.338	.653	80	-15	-15	100	80	60	.565	10	5	0	1	*O/D	-1.8

YEAR	TM/L	G	AB	R	H	2B	3B	HR	RBI	BB	SO	AVG	OBP	SLG	PRO	/A	BR	/A	PF	CHI	RC	TA	SB	CS	SBR	FR	POS	TPR
1983	Bal-A	124	378	63	104	14	4	3	31	31	33	.275	.330	.357	.687	89	-5	-5	100	84	47	.636	12	5	1	-11	*OD	-1.7
1984	Bal-A	119	344	47	93	12	1	3	24	25	35	.270	.320	.337	.657	87	-8	-6	94	77	35	.562	9	5	-0	-10	O/D	-1.8
1985	SD-N	68	95	6	19	3	0	1	10	7	9	.200	.255	.263	.518	44	-7	-7	102	142	6	.425	2	0	1	-1	O	-0.8
Total	14	1496	5053	778	1422	220	52	54	402	471	709	.281	.345	.378	.723	103	14	29	98	77	692	.712	254	92	21	-42	*O/D3	-2.3
■ **JOSH BUNCE** Bunce, Joshua b: 5/10/1847, Brooklyn, N.Y. d: 4/28/12, Brooklyn, N.Y. Deb: 8/27/1877																												
1877	Har-N	1	4	0	0	0	0	0	0	0	0	.000	.000	.000	.000	-99	-1	-1	89	0	0	.000				0	/O	0.0
■ **NELSON BURBRINK** Burbrink, Nelson Edward b: 12/28/21, Cincinnati, Ohio BR/TR, 5'10", 195 lbs. Deb: 6/05/55																												
1955	StL-N	58	170	11	47	8	1	0	15	14	13	.276	.335	.335	.670	78	-5	-5	101	107	19	.566	1	1	-0	-1	C	-0.4
■ **AL BURCH** Burch, Albert William b: 10/7/1883, Albany, N.Y. d: 10/5/26, Brooklyn, N.Y. BL/TR, 5'8.5", 160 lbs. Deb: 6/19/06																												
1906	StL-N	91	335	40	89	5	1	0	11	37		.266	.339	.287	.625	96	0	0	101	40	39	.602	15			9	O	0.8
1907	StL-N	48	154	18	35	3	1	0	5	17		.227	.304	.260	.564	82	-3	-3	96	48	15	.538	7			-3	O	-0.8
	Bro-N	40	120	12	35	2	2	0	12	11		.292	.351	.342	.693	126	3	4	94	111	17	.671	5			3	O/2	0.6
	Yr	88	274	30	70	5	3	0	17	28		.255	.325	.296	.620	101	-0	1	95	77	31	.593	12			-0		-0.2
1908	Bro-N	123	456	45	111	8	4	2	18	33		.243	.294	.292	.586	94	-5	-3	95	48	42	.525	15			28	*O	2.7
1909	Bro-N	152	601	80	163	20	6	1	30	51		.271	.329	.329	.659	107	4	5	99	47	75	.658	38			3	*O/1	0.2
1910	Bro-N	103	352	41	83	8	3	1	20	22	30	.236	.281	.284	.565	68	-16	-14	95	69	31	.502	13			-1	O1	-1.8
1911	Bro-N	54	167	18	38	2	3	0	7	15	22	.228	.291	.275	.567	61	-9	-9	97	51	14	.496	3			3	O/2	-0.6
Total	6	611	2185	254	554	48	20	4	103	186	52	.254	.312	.299	.612	92	-27	-20	97	53	232	.574	96			43	O/12	1.1
■ **ERNIE BURCH** Burch, Earnest W. b: 1856, Dekalb Co., Ill. BL , Deb: 8/15/1884																												
1884	Cle-N	32	124	9	26	4	0	0	7	5	24	.210	.240	.242	.482	51	-7	-7	102	85	7	.357				5	O	-0.1
1886	Bro-a	113	456	78	119	22	6	2		39		.261	.321	.349	.669	111	6	6	100	0	58	.638	16			-14	*O	-0.9
1887	Bro-a	49	188	47	55	4	4	2		29		.293	.395	.388	.784	123	7	7	99	0	36	.902	15			-1	O	0.4
Total	3	194	768	134	200	30	10	4	7	73	24	.260	.328	.341	.669	105	6	6	100	13	101	.651	31			-10	O	-0.6
■ **BOB BURDA** Burda, Edward Robert b: 7/16/38, St.Louis, Mo. BL/TL, 5'11", 174 lbs. Deb: 8/25/62																												
1962	StL-N	7	14	0	1	0	0	0	0	3	1	.071	.235	.071	.307	-12	-2	-2	109	0	1	.385	1	0	0	-0	/O	-0.2
1965	SF-N	31	27	0	3	0	0	0	5	5	6	.111	.250	.111	.361	5	-3	-4	111	691	1	.308	0	0	0	0	1/O	-0.3
1966	SF-N	37	43	3	7	3	0	0	2	2	5	.163	.200	.233	.433	20	-5	-5	97	84	2	.324	0	0	0	-1	/1O	-0.6
1969	SF-N	97	161	20	37	8	0	6	27	21	12	.230	.319	.391	.710	97	-1	-1	101	134	21	.661	0	1	-1	-1	1O	-0.7
1970	SF-N	28	23	1	6	0	0	0	3	5	2	.261	.414	.261	.675	89	-0	0	96	194	3	.706	0	0	0	0	/1O	0.0
	Mil-A	78	222	19	55	9	0	4	20	16	17	.248	.307	.342	.649	80	-7	-6	98	92	24	.558	1	0	0	-9	O/1	-1.7
1971	StL-N	65	71	6	21	0	0	1	12	10	11	.296	.390	.338	.728	107	1	1	101	181	10	.673	0	0	0	-1	1/O	0.0
1972	Bos-A	45	73	4	12	1	0	2	9	8	11	.164	.247	.260	.507	48	-4	-5	105	150	4	.422	0	0	0	1	1/O	-0.5
Total	7	388	634	53	142	21	0	13	78	70	65	.224	.306	.319	.625	75	-20	-21	101	148	64	.563	2	1	0	-11	1/O	-4.0
■ **JACK BURDOCK** Burdock, John Joseph "Black Jack" b: 1851, Brooklyn, N.Y. d: 11/28/31, Brooklyn, N.Y. BR/TR, 5'9.5", 158 lbs. Deb: 5/02/1872 M																												
1872	Atl-n	35	176	27	44							.250															*S/C2	
1873	Atl-n	55	261	56	62							.238															*2	
1874	Mut-n	61	284	46	78							.275															*3	
1875	Har-n	73	360	72	102							.283															*2/3	
1876	Har-N	69	309	66	80	9	1	0	23	13	16	.259	.289	.294	.583	87	-1	-5	108	75	27	.454				-4	*2/3	-0.7
1877	Har-N	58	277	35	72	6	0	0	9	2	16	.260	.265	.282	.547	81	-9	-4	89	34	21	.390				4	*2/3	0.2
1878	Bos-N	60	246	37	64	12	6	0	25	3	17	.260	.269	.358	.627	97	1	-2	108	102	24	.500				**20**	*2	2.1
1879	Bos-N	84	359	64	86	10	3	0	36	9	28	.240	.258	.284	.542	73	-8	-12	107	131	27	.407				23	*2	1.3
1880	Bos-N	86	356	58	90	17	4	2	35	8	26	.253	.269	.340	.609	114	2	5	92	97	33	.485				11	*2	1.8
1881	Bos-N	73	282	36	67	12	4	1	24	7	18	.238	.256	.319	.575	87	-7	-3	91	95	24	.451				-12	*2/S	-1.1
1882	Bos-N	83	319	36	76	6	7	0	27	9	24	.238	.259	.301	.560	77	-7	-9	103	97	25	.432				4	*2	-0.2
1883	Bos-N	96	400	80	132	27	8	5	88	14	35	.330	.353	.475	.828	140	23	19	106	**158**	69	.761				-2	*2/M	1.0
1884	Bos-N	87	361	65	97	14	4	6	49	15	52	.269	.298	.380	.677	114	4	5	98	115	42	.576				-1	*2/3	0.5
1885	Bos-N	45	169	18	24	5	0	0	7	8	18	.142	.181	.172	.352	15	-16	-14	94	86	5	.255				-5	2	-1.3
1886	Bos-N	59	221	26	48	6	1	0	25	11	27	.217	.254	.253	.508	56	-12	-11	97	148	15	.405	3			-10	2	-1.6
1887	Bos-N	65	237	36	61	6	0	0	29	18	22	.257	.320	.283	.603	72	-8	-8	98	136	28	.614	19			-25	2	-2.4
1888	Bos-N	22	79	5	16	0	0	0	4	2	5	.203	.232	.203	.434	39	-5	-6	106	90	4	.317	1			0	2	-0.5
	Bro-a	70	246	15	30	1	2	1	8	8		.122	.166	.154	.320	4	-25	-27	105	59	8	.278	9			-0	2	-2.3
1891	Bro-N	3	12	1	1	0	0	0	1	1	1	.083	.154	.083	.237	-30	-2	-2	97	309	0	.182	0			0	/2	-0.1
Total	4 n	224	1081	201	286							.265															/2	
Total	14	960	3873	578	944	131	40	15	390	128	305	.244	.270	.310	.580	83	-70	-72	100	105	354	.468	32			2	*2/3SC	-3.3
■ **PETE BURG** Burg, Joseph Peter b: 6/4/1882, Chicago, Ill. d: 4/28/69, Joliet, Ill. TR , 5'1", 150 lbs. Deb: 9/26/10																												
1910	Bos-N	13	46	7	15	0	1	0	10	7	12	.326	.415	.370	.785	113	2	1	114	197	9	.935	5			1	3/S	0.2
■ **SMOKY BURGESS** Burgess, Forrest Harrill b: 2/6/27, Caroleen, N.C. BL/TR, 5'8.5", 185 lbs. Deb: 4/19/49																												
1949	Chi-N	46	56	4	15	0	0	1	12	4	4	.268	.317	.321	.638	76	-2	-2	94	215	6	.524	0			0	/C	0.0
1951	Chi-N	94	219	21	55	4	2	2	20	21	12	.251	.317	.315	.632	72	-9	-8	97	103	21	.529	2	0	1	-1	C	-0.7
1952	Phi-N	110	371	49	110	27	2	6	56	49	21	.296	.380	.429	.809	123	13	12	101	126	65	.797	3	1	0	3	*C	1.9
1953	Phi-N	102	312	31	91	17	5	4	36	37	17	.292	.370	.417	.787	106	3	4	99	99	48	.735	3	2	-0	-2	C	0.7
1954	Phi-N	108	345	41	127	27	5	4	46	42	11	.368	.437	.510	.947	148	25	25	99	96	75	.940	1	5	-3	3	C	2.6
1955	Phi-N	7	21	4	4	2	0	1	1	3	1	.190	.292	.429	.720	86	-0	-0	102	34	2	.600	0	0	0	1	/C	0.1
	Cin-N	116	421	67	129	15	3	20	77	47	35	.306	.377	.499	.876	123	18	15	106	118	78	.852	1	1	-0	2	*C	2.0
	Yr	123	442	71	133	17	3	21	78	50	36	.301	.373	.495	.869	121	18	15	105	113	81	.844	1	1	-0	3		2.1
1956	Cin-N	90	229	28	63	10	0	12	39	26	18	.275	.349	.476	.825	110	6	4	108	114	37	.785	0	1	-1	5	C	1.0
1957	Cin-N	90	205	29	58	14	1	14	39	24	16	.283	.358	.566	.924	136	12	11	105	102	41	.927	0	0	0	3	C	1.6
1958	Cin-N	99	251	28	71	12	1	6	31	22	20	.283	.343	.410	.753	92	-1	-3	107	106	34	.670	0	0	0	5	C	0.5
1959	Pit-N	114	377	41	112	28	5	11	59	31	16	.297	.354	.485	.839	117	11	9	103	110	62	.785	0	0	0	-9	*C	0.6
1960	Pit-N	110	337	33	99	15	2	7	39	35	13	.294	.360	.412	.773	112	6	6	99	99	50	.710	0	1	-1	1	C	1.1
1961	Pit-N	100	323	37	98	17	3	12	52	30	16	.303	.366	.486	.852	125	11	11	99	109	57	.819	1	0	0	-2	C	1.7
1962	Pit-N	103	360	38	118	19	2	13	61	31	19	.328	.381	.500	.881	131	17	16	102	112	68	.847	0	1	-1	4	*C	2.1
1963	Pit-N	91	264	20	74	10	1	6	37	24	14	.280	.343	.394	.736	113	4	5	99	127	32	.635	0	1	-1	-3	C	0.4
1964	Pit-N	68	171	9	42	3	1	2	17	13	14	.246	.303	.310	.613	72	-6	-6	101	118	14	.496	2	1	0	-3	C	-0.7
	Chi-A	7	5	1	1	0	0	1	1	2	0	.200	.429	.800	1.229	244	1	1	96	61	2	1.500	0	0	0	0	H	0.1
1965	Chi-A	80	77	2	22	4	0	2	24	11	7	.286	.375	.416	.791	135	3	4	92	262	12	.754	0	0	0	-1	/C	0.3
1966	Chi-A	79	67	0	21	5	0	0	15	11	8	.313	.418	.388	.806	141	4	4	94	242	12	.826	0	0	0	0	/C	0.4
1967	Chi-A	77	60	2	8	1	0	2	11	14	8	.133	.307	.250	.557	71	-2	-2	94	218	5	.556	0	0	0	0	H	-0.1
Total	18	1691	4471	485	1318	230	33	126	673	477	270	.295	.364	.446	.810	116	112	105	101	117	722	.787	13	14		9	*C	15.6
■ **TOM BURGESS** Burgess, Thomas Roland "Tim" b: 9/1/27, London, Ont., Can. BL/TL, 6', 180 lbs. Deb: 4/17/54 C																												
1954	StL-N	17	21	2	1	1	0	0	1	3	9	.048	.167	.095	.262	-30	-4	-4	100	197	0	.250	0	0	0	-1	/O	-0.5
1962	LA-A	87	143	17	28	7	1	2	13	36	20	.196	.358	.301	.658	78	-3	-3	102	105	18	.698	2	0	1	-3	1/O	-0.7
Total	2	104	164	19	29	8	1	2	14	39	29	.177	.335	.274	.609	64	-7	-7	102	116	19	.632	2	0	1	-4	/1O	-1.2
■ **BILL BURGO** Burgo, William Ross b: 11/5/19, Johnstown, Pa. BR/TR, 5'8", 185 lbs. Deb: 9/22/43																												
1943	Phi-A	17	70	12	26	4	2	1	9	4	1	.371	.421	.529	.950	175	7	6	101	72	16	.935	0	2	-1	2	O	0.7
1944	Phi-A	27	88	6	21	2	0	1	3	7	3	.239	.316	.295	.612	75	-3	-3	101	37	8	.514	1	3	-2	1	O	-0.3
Total	2	44	158	18	47	6	2	2	12	11	4	.297	.362	.399	.761	118	4	4	101	53	23	.678	1	5	-3	3	/O	0.4

YEAR	TM/L	G	AB	R	H	2B	3B	HR	RBI	BB	SO	AVG	OBP	SLG	PRO	/A	BR	/A	PF	CHI	RC	TA	SB	CS	SBR	FR	POS	TPR
■ BILL BURICH	Burich, William Max b: 5/29/18, Calumet, Mich. BR/TR, 6', 180 lbs. Deb: 4/15/42																											
1942	Phi-N	25	80	3	23	1	0	0	7	6	13	.287	.337	.300	.637	92	-1	-1	94	108	8	.552	2			1	S/3	0.2
1946	Phi-N	2	1	1	0	0	0	0	0	0	0	.000	.000	.000	.000	-99	-0	-0	95	0	0	.000	0			0	/3	0.0
Total	2	27	81	4	23	1	0	0	7	6	13	.284	.333	.296	.630	90	-1	-1	94	107	8	.552	2			1	/S3	0.2
■ MACK BURK	Burk, Mack Edwin b: 4/21/35, Nacogdoches, Tex. BR/TR, 6'4", 180 lbs. Deb: 5/25/56																											
1956	Phi-N	15	1	3	1	0	0	0	0	0	0	1.000	1.000	1.000	2.000	467	0	0	94	0	1	—	0	0	0	0	/C	0.1
1958	Phi-N	1	1	0	0	0	0	0	0	0	1	.000	.000	.000	.000	-99	-0	-0	98	0	0	.000	0	0	0	0	H	0.0
Total	2	16	2	3	1	0	0	0	0	0	1	.500	.500	.500	1.000	174	0	0	96	0	1	1.000	0	0	0	0	/C	0.1
■ CHRIS BURKAM	Burkam, Chauncey De Pew b: 10/13/1892, Benton Harbor, Mich. d: 5/9/64, Kalamazoo, Mich. BL/TR, 5'11", 175 lbs. Deb: 6/24/15																											
1915	StL-A	1	1	0	0	0	0	0	0	0	1	.000	.000	.000	.000	-99	-0	-0	96	0	0	.000	0			0	H	0.0
■ DAN BURKE	Burke, Daniel L. b: 10/25/1868, Abington, Mass. d: 3/20/33, Taunton, Mass. BR/TR, 5'10", 190 lbs. Deb: 4/18/1890																											
1890	Roc-a	32	102	14	22	1	0	0		17		.216	.333	.225	.559	73	-3	-2	93	0	9	.538	2			0	O/C1	-0.1
	Syr-a	9	20	1	0	0	0	0		5		.000	.231	.000	.231	-33	-3	-3	90	0	0	.300	0			0	/C	-0.1
	Yr	41	122	15	22	1	0	0	0	22		.180	.315	.189	.504	55	-6	-4	92	0	8	.490	2			0		-0.2
1892	Bos-N	1	4	0	0	0	0	0	0	0	2	.000	.000	.000	.000	-88	-1	-1	113	0	0	.000	0			0	/C	0.0
Total	2	42	126	15	22	1	0	0	0	22	2	.175	.307	.183	.489	50	-7	-5	93	0	9	.471	2			0	/OC1	-0.2
■ EDDIE BURKE	Burke, Edward D. b: 10/6/1866, Northumberland, Pa. d: 11/26/07, Utica, N.Y. BR/TR, 5'6", 161 lbs. Deb: 4/19/1890																											
1890	Phi-N	100	430	85	113	16	11	4	50	49	40	.263	.349	.379	.728	106	8	3	108	75	72	.814	38			5	*O/2	0.5
	Pit-N	31	124	17	26	5	2	1	7	14	9	.210	.295	.306	.601	88	-4	-1	88	45	13	.602	6			0	O	0.0
	Yr	131	554	102	139	21	13	5	57	63	49	.251	.337	.363	.700	103	5	2	103	68	85	.764	44			5		0.5
1891	CM-a	35	144	31	34	9	0	1	21	12	19	.236	.337	.319	.657	81	-1	-4	112	107	18	.682	7			2	O	-0.3
1892	Cin-N	15	41	6	6	1	0	0	4	9	4	.146	.300	.171	.471	43	-2	-2	103	175	3	.514	2			0	O/3	-0.1
	NY-N	89	363	81	94	10	5	6	41	46	37	.259	.350	.364	.714	120	9	10	98	72	62	.836	42			-2	2O	0.7
	Yr	104	404	87	100	11	5	6	45	55	41	.248	.345	.344	.689	112	7	7	99	89	65	.799	44			-2		0.6
1893	NY-N	135	537	122	150	23	10	9	80	51	32	.279	.369	.410	.778	105	7	4	104	85	104	.904	54			0	*O	0.0
1894	NY-N	136	566	121	172	23	11	4	77	37	35	.304	.357	.405	.762	85	-14	-14	100	85	96	.787	34			-7	*O	-2.2
1895	NY-N	39	167	38	43	6	2	1	12	7	9	.257	.299	.335	.635	69	-9	-7	95	50	21	.645	14			2	O	-0.6
	Cin-N	56	228	52	61	8	6	1	25	22	14	.268	.343	.368	.711	79	-5	-8	108	77	36	.772	19			2	O	-0.8
	Yr	95	395	90	104	14	8	2	37	29	23	.263	.325	.354	.679	75	-14	-15	102	67	58	.718	33			3		-1.4
1896	Cin-N	122	521	120	177	24	9	1	52	41	29	.340	.392	.426	.818	112	14	10	105	58	111	.930	53			3	*O	0.4
1897	Cin-N	95	387	71	103	17	1	1	41	29		.266	.327	.323	.650	69	-14	-18	107	83	49	.641	22			6	*O	-1.6
Total	8	853	3508	744	979	142	57	29	410	317	228	.279	.352	.377	.729	94	-10	-29	103	77	586	.793	291			11	O/23	-4.0
■ FRANK BURKE	Burke, Frank Aloysius b: 2/16/1880, Carbon, Co., Pa. d: 9/17/46, Los Angeles, Cal. TR , Deb: 9/14/06																											
1906	NY-N	8	9	2	3	1	1	0	1	1		.333	.400	.667	1.067	235	1	1	100	61	3	1.333	1			0	/O	0.1
1907	Bos-N	43	129	6	23	0	1	0	8	11		.178	.243	.194	.437	40	-9	-8	95	121	7	.368	3			-2	O	-1.3
Total	2	51	138	8	26	1	2	0	9	12		.188	.253	.225	.478	54	-7	-7	96	117	10	.420	4			-2	/O	-1.2
■ GLENN BURKE	Burke, Glenn Lawrence b: 11/16/52, Oakland, Cal. BR/TR, 6', 195 lbs. Deb: 4/09/76																											
1976	LA-N	25	46	9	11	2	0	0	5	3	8	.239	.300	.283	.583	66	-2	-2	100	148	4	.526	3	2	-0	-3	O	-0.5
1977	LA-N	83	169	16	43	8	0	1	13	5	22	.254	.280	.320	.600	60	-10	-10	100	91	15	.545	13	5	1	-11	O	-2.2
1978	LA-N	16	19	2	4	0	0	0	2	0	4	.211	.211	.211	.421	18	-2	-2	99	198	1	.333	1	0	0	-4	O	-0.6
	Oak-A	78	200	19	47	6	1	1	14	10	26	.235	.271	.290	.561	57	-11	-11	101	91	14	.494	15	8	-0	1	O/1D	-1.2
1979	Oak-A	23	89	4	19	2	1	0	4	4	10	.213	.247	.258	.506	41	-8	-7	89	71	5	.405	3	1	0	0	O	-0.6
Total	4	225	523	50	124	18	2	2	38	22	70	.237	.271	.291	.561	55	-33	-32	98	96	38	.505	35	16	1	-17	O/D1	-5.1
■ JIMMY BURKE	Burke, James Timothy "Sunset Jimmy" b: 10/12/1874, St.Louis, Mo. d: 3/26/42, St.Louis, Mo. BR/TR, 5'7", 160 lbs. Deb: 10/06/1898 MC																											
1898	Cle-N	13	38	1	4	1	0	0	1	2		.105	.150	.132	.282	-19	-6	-5	96	60	1	.235	1			0	3	-0.4
1899	StL-N	2	6	1	2	0	0	0	0	1		.333	.429	.333	.762	105	0	0	108	0	1	.750	0			0	/2	0.0
1901	Mil-A	64	233	24	48	8	0	0	26	17		.206	.260	.240	.500	43	-18	-16	95	149	17	.427	6			-5	3	-2.0
	Chi-A	42	148	20	39	5	0	0	21	12		.264	.319	.297	.616	74	-5	-5	99	154	18	.615	11			-3	S3	-0.4
	Yr	106	381	44	87	13	0	0	47	29		.228	.283	.262	.545	55	-23	-21	97	152	34	.497	17			-8		-2.4
	Pit-N	14	51	4	10	0	0	0	4	4		.196	.255	.196	.451	33	-4	-4	101	136	3	.341	0			1	3	-0.1
1902	Pit-N	60	203	24	60	12	2	0	26	17		.296	.350	.374	.724	119	6	5	105	118	30	.713	9			1	2O/3S	0.7
1903	StL-N	115	431	55	123	13	3	0	42	23		.285	.322	.329	.651	91	-7	-5	96	101	56	.627	28			8	32/O	0.4
1904	StL-N	118	406	37	92	10	3	0	37	15		.227	.254	.266	.520	63	-18	-17	99	128	33	.446	17			-4	*3	-1.7
1905	StL-N	122	431	34	97	9	5	1	30	21		.225	.261	.276	.537	68	-20	-16	91	87	36	.464	15			5	*3M	-0.1
Total	7	550	1947	200	475	58	13	1	187	112		.244	.285	.289	.574	72	-72	-64	97	115	194	.517	87			4	3/2SO	-3.6
■ JOHN BURKE	Burke, John Patrick b: 1/27/1877, Hazelton, Pa. d: 8/4/50, Jersey City, N.J. BR/TR, Deb: 6/27/02																											
1902	NY-N	4	13	0	2	0	0	0	0	0		.154	.154	.154	.308	-4	-2	-2	100	0	0	.182	0			1	/PO	0.0
■ JOE BURKE	Burke, Joseph A. b: Cincinnati, Ohio 5'7", 160 lbs. Deb: 9/26/1890																											
1890	StL-a	2	6	3	4	0	0	0		1		.667	.750	.667	1.417	279	2	2	116	0	3	3.000	0			0	/3	0.2
1891	CM-a	1	4	0	1	0	0	0	1	0	2	.250	.250	.250	.500	40	-0	-0	112	295	0	.333	0			0	/2	0.0
Total	2	3	10	3	5	0	0	0	1	1	2	.500	.583	.500	1.083	193	2	1	115	98	3	1.400	0			0	/32	0.2
■ LEO BURKE	Burke, Leo Patrick b: 5/6/34, Hagerstown, Md. BR/TR, 5'11", 185 lbs. Deb: 9/07/58																											
1958	Bal-A	7	11	4	5	1	0	1	4	1	2	.455	.500	.818	1.318	272	2	2	94	134	5	1.667	0	0	0	-1	/O3	0.1
1959	Bal-A	5	10	0	2	0	0	0	1	0	5	.200	.273	.200	.473	33	-1	-1	97	197	0	.333	0	0	0	0	/23	0.0
1961	LA-A	6	5	0	0	0	0	0	0	0	1	.000	.000	.000	.000	-90	-1	-1	111	0	0	.000	0	0	0	0	H	0.0
1962	LA-A	19	64	8	17	1	0	4	14	5	11	.266	.329	.469	.797	109	1	1	102	132	10	.750	0	0	0	-1	O/3S	0.0
1963	StL-N	30	49	6	10	2	1	1	5	4	12	.204	.264	.347	.611	69	-2	-2	107	105	4	.525	0	0	0	-2	O/3	-0.4
	Chi-N	27	49	4	9	0	0	2	7	4	13	.184	.245	.306	.551	55	-3	-3	105	140	3	.452	0	1	-1	2	2/1	-0.1
	Yr	57	98	10	19	2	1	3	12	8	25	.194	.255	.327	.581	62	-4	-5	106	123	8	.494	0	1	-1	-1		-0.5
1964	Chi-N	59	103	11	27	3	1	1	14	7	31	.262	.315	.340	.655	80	-2	-3	105	151	11	.551	0	0	0	-0	O/231C	-0.3
1965	Chi-N	12	10	0	2	0	0	0	0	0	4	.200	.200	.200	.400	13	-1	-1	102	0	0	.222	0	0	0	-0	/CO	-0.1
Total	7	165	301	33	72	7	2	9	45	21	79	.239	.295	.365	.661	81	-7	-8	104	132	34	.580	0	1	-1	-3	/O231CS	-0.8
■ LES BURKE	Burke, Leslie Kingston "Buck" b: 12/18/02, Lynn, Mass. d: 5/6/75, Danvers, Mass. BL/TR, 5'9", 168 lbs. Deb: 5/02/23																											
1923	Det-A	7	10	2	1	0	0	0	2	0	1	.100	.100	.100	.200	-49	-2	-2	97	684	0	.111	0	0	0	0	/32	-0.1
1924	Det-A	72	241	30	61	10	4	0	17	22	20	.253	.321	.328	.649	68	-12	-12	100	71	26	.571	2	4	-2	3	2/S	-0.7
1925	Det-A	77	180	32	52	6	3	0	24	17	8	.289	.357	.356	.712	82	-5	-5	99	125	25	.674	4	1	1	5	2	0.3
1926	Det-A	38	75	9	17	1	0	0	4	7	3	.227	.301	.240	.541	44	-6	-6	97	75	6	.450	1	2	-1	0	2/3S	-0.4
Total	4	194	506	73	131	17	7	0	47	46	32	.259	.327	.320	.647	67	-25	-24	99	102	56	.576	7	7	-2	8	2/3S	-0.9
■ MIKE BURKE	Burke, Michael E. b: Cincinnati, Ohio d: 6/9/1889, Albany, N.Y. BR/TR, 6', 190 lbs. Deb: 5/01/1879																											
1879	Cin-N	28	117	13	26	3	0	0	8	2	5	.222	.235	.248	.483	63	-5	-4	95	102	7	.341				0	S/O3	-0.3
■ PAT BURKE	Burke, Patrick Edward b: 5/13/01, St.Louis, Mo. d: 7/7/65, St.Louis, Mo. BR/TR, 5'10.5", 170 lbs. Deb: 9/23/24																											
1924	StL-A	1	3	0	0	0	0	0	1	0	0	.000	.000	.000	.000	-93	-1	-1	107	0	0	.000	0	0	0	0	/3	0.0
■ JESSE BURKETT	Burkett, Jesse Cail "Crab" b: 12/4/1868, Wheeling, W.Va. d: 5/27/53, Worcester, Mass. BL/TL, 5'8", 155 lbs. Deb: 4/22/1890 H																											
1890	NY-N	101	401	67	124	23	13	4	60	33	52	.309	.366	.461	.827	151	20	23	95	97	75	.848	14			-1	OP	1.9
1891	Cle-N	40	167	29	45	7	4	0	13	23	19	.269	.358	.359	.717	106	3	2	105	56	22	.689	1			-2	O	-0.1
1892	Cle-N	145	608	119	167	15	14	6	66	67	59	.275	.348	.375	.723	117	15	12	103	73	94	.753	36			1	*O	0.8
1893	Cle-N	125	511	145	178	25	15	6	82	98	23	.348	.459	.491	.951	149	45	41	104	72	137	1.186	39			-9	*O	2.2

YEAR	TM/L	G	AB	R	H	2B	3B	HR	RBI	BB	SO	AVG	OBP	SLG	PRO	/A	BR	/A	PF	CHI	RC	TA	SB	CS	SBR	FR	POS	TPR
1894	Cle-N	125	523	138	187	27	14	8	94	84	27	.358	.447	.509	.956	119	30	18	111	77	135	1.128	28			-6	*O/P	0.3
1895	Cle-N	131	550	153	**225**	22	13	5	83	74	31	**.409**	.486	.524	1.009	168	56	59	97	66	164	1.265	41			-5	*O	3.5
1896	Cle-N	133	586	**160**	**240**	27	16	6	72	49	19	**.410**	.461	.541	1.002	151	56	47	110	54	166	1.176	34			-2	*O	3.0
1897	Cle-N	127	517	129	198	28	7	2	60	76		.383	.468	.476	.944	138	44	34	111	60	132	1.119	28			-2	*O	1.9
1898	Cle-N	150	624	114	213	18	9	0	42	69		.341	.415	.399	.814	143	33	37	96	44	114	.842	19			-11	*O	1.5
1899	StL-N	141	558	116	221	21	8	7	71	67		.396	.463	.500	.963	155	54	47	108	64	144	1.107	25			-5	*O/2	2.9
1900	StL-N	141	559	88	203	11	15	7	68	62		.363	.427	.474	.901	162	40	46	93	66	130	1.008	32			1	*O	3.2
1901	StL-N	142	601	**142**	**226**	20	15	10	75	59		**.376**	**.432**	.509	.941	**181**	**57**	**60**	97	65	**147**	1.045	27			1	*O	4.5
1902	StL-A	138	553	97	169	29	9	5	52	71		.306	.385	.418	.802	122	20	18	102	60	100	.846	23			8	*O/PS3	1.7
1903	StL-A	132	515	73	151	20	7	3	40	52		.293	.358	.377	.735	129	16	19	95	61	77	.723	17			-4	*O	0.6
1904	StL-A	147	575	72	156	15	10	2	27	78		.271	.358	.343	.701	132	19	23	95	43	77	.685	12			4	*O	2.0
1905	Bos-A	148	573	78	147	12	13	4	47	67		.257	.334	.344	.678	117	13	13	100	71	72	.650	13			-3	*O	0.3
Total	16	2066	8421	1720	2850	320	182	75	952	1029	230	.338	.413	.446	.860	142	522	500	101	64	1785	.937	389			-33	*O/P3S2	30.2
■ ELLIS BURKS	Burks, Ellis Rena b: 9/11/64, Vicksburg, Miss. BR/TR, 6'2", 175 lbs. Deb: 4/30/87																											
1987	Bos-A	133	558	94	152	30	2	20	59	41	98	.272	.324	.441	.765	102	0	1	99	74	85	.765	27	6	5	9	*O/D	1.0
1988	Bos-A	144	540	93	159	37	5	18	92	62	89	.294	.370	.481	.852	125	27	20	109	123	99	.879	25	9	2	6	*O/D	2.5
Total	2	277	1098	187	311	67	7	38	151	103	187	.283	.347	.461	.808	114	27	21	104	99	184	.822	52	15	7	14	O/D	3.5
■ RICK BURLESON	Burleson, Richard Paul "Rooster" b: 4/29/51, Lynwood, Cal. BR/TR, 5'10", 165 lbs. Deb: 5/04/74																											
1974	Bos-A	114	384	36	109	22	0	4	44	21	34	.284	.324	.372	.697	94	-1	-4	107	112	43	.581	3	3	-1	-7	S2/3	-0.2
1975	Bos-A	158	580	66	146	25	1	6	62	45	44	.252	.309	.329	.638	74	-15	-22	109	116	58	.540	8	5	-1	-0	*S	-0.6
1976	Bos-A	152	540	75	157	27	1	7	42	60	37	.291	.367	.383	.750	109	15	8	110	72	76	.703	14	9	-1	-5	*S	1.2
1977	Bos-A	154	663	80	194	36	7	3	52	47	69	.293	.341	.382	.723	82	-3	-18	117	68	83	.635	13	12	-3	12	*S	0.9
1978	Bos-A	145	626	75	155	32	5	5	49	40	71	.248	.297	.339	.636	73	-18	-24	107	74	60	.533	8	8	-2	16	*S	0.1
1979	Bos-A	153	627	93	174	32	5	5	60	35	54	.278	.319	.368	.687	79	-14	-20	107	90	72	.590	9	5	-0	26	*S	2.4
1980	Bos-A	155	644	89	179	29	2	8	51	62	51	.278	.343	.366	.710	93	-4	-5	102	68	76	.622	12	13	-4	**31**	*S	3.3
1981	Cal-A	109	430	53	126	17	1	5	33	42	38	.293	.360	.372	.732	107	7	5	104	65	58	.657	4	6	-2	23	*S	3.4
1982	Cal-A	11	45	4	7	1	0	0	2	6	3	.156	.255	.178	.433	21	-5	-5	100	86	2	.350	0	0	0	1	S	-0.2
1983	Cal-A	33	119	22	34	7	0	0	11	12	12	.286	.351	.345	.696	96	-1	-0	96	107	13	.576	0	2	-1	6	S	0.6
1984	Cal-A	7	4	2	0	0	0	0	0	0	2	.000	.000	.000	.000	-99	-1	-1	101	0	0	.000	0	0	0	0	/H	0.0
1986	Cal-A	93	271	35	77	14	0	5	29	33	32	.284	.364	.391	.755	111	3	5	96	95	40	.709	1	3	-2	1	DS/23	0.6
1987	Bal-A	62	206	26	43	14	1	2	14	17	30	.209	.279	.316	.594	59	-12	-12	98	79	17	.494	0	2	-1	-3	2/D	-1.0
Total	13	1346	5139	656	1401	256	23	50	449	420	477	.273	.331	.361	.692	87	-48	-92	107	83	599	.622	72	68	-19	102	*S/2D3	10.5
■ HERCULES BURNETT	Burnett, Hercules H. b: 8/13/1865, Louisville, Ky. d: 10/4/36, Louisville, Ky. BR , Deb: 1888																											
1888	Lou-a	1	4	1	0	0	0	0	0	1		.000	.200	.000	.200	-35	-1	-0	91	0	0	.500	1			0	/O	0.0
1895	Lou-N	5	17	6	7	0	1	2	3	2	2	.412	.474	.882	1.356	260	3	4	95	40	8	1.900	2			0	/O1	0.3
Total	2	6	21	7	7	0	1	2	3	3	2	.333	.417	.714	1.131	215	3	3	94	32	8	1.500	3			0	/O1	0.3
■ JOHNNY BURNETT	Burnett, John Henderson b: 11/1/04, Bartow, Fla. d: 8/13/59, Tampa, Fla. BL/TR, 5'11", 175 lbs. Deb: 5/07/27																											
1927	Cle-A	17	8	5	0	0	0	0	0	0	3	.000	.000	.000	.000	-99	-2	-2	97	0	0	.125	1	0	0	0	/2	-0.1
1928	Cle-A	3	10	3	5	0	0	0	1	0	1	.500	.500	.500	1.000	155	1	1	106	69	2	1.000	0	0	0	0	/S	0.1
1929	Cle-A	19	33	2	5	1	0	0	2	1	2	.152	.200	.182	.382	-1	-5	-5	100	114	1	.286	0	0	0	2	S/2	0.0
1930	Cle-A	54	170	28	53	13	0	0	20	17	8	.312	.378	.388	.766	90	-1	-2	105	101	26	.723	2	2	-1	1	3S	0.1
1931	Cle-A	111	427	85	128	25	5	1	52	39	25	.300	.360	.389	.749	91	-2	-5	106	104	61	.701	5	2	0	7	S23/O	1.0
1932	Cle-A	129	512	81	152	23	5	4	53	46	27	.297	.359	.385	.744	86	-5	-11	108	90	72	.682	2	5	-2	-19	*S2	-2.1
1933	Cle-A	83	261	39	71	11	2	1	29	23	14	.272	.333	.341	.674	76	-8	-9	105	105	31	.604	3	2	-0	0	S23	-0.4
1934	Cle-A	72	208	28	61	11	2	3	30	18	11	.293	.352	.409	.761	95	-1	-2	101	107	30	.709	1	1	-0	1	3/S2O	0.0
1935	StL-A	70	206	17	46	10	1	0	26	19	16	.223	.289	.282	.570	45	-16	-18	107	152	18	.488	1	0	0	-1	3S2	-1.5
Total	9	558	1835	288	521	94	15	9	213	163	107	.284	.345	.366	.712	80	-38	-54	106	105	241	.648	15	12	-3	-8	S32/O	-2.9
■ JACK BURNETT	Burnett, John P. b: 12/2/1889, Missouri d: 9/8/29, Taft, Cal. Deb: 7/02/07																											
1907	StL-N	59	206	18	49	8	4	0	12	15		.238	.290	.316	.605	95	-2	-1	96	74	21	.541	5			-4	O	-0.8
■ C.B. BURNS	Burns, Charles Birmingham b: 5/15/1879, Bay View, Md. d: 6/6/68, Havre De Grace, Md BR/TR, 6', 175 lbs. Deb: 8/19/02																											
1902	Bal-A	1	1	0	1	0	0	0	0	0		1.000	1.000	1.000	2.000	451	0	0	102	0	1	—	0			0	H	0.0
■ ED BURNS	Burns, Edward James b: 10/31/1888, San Francisco, Cal d: 6/1/42, Monterey, Cal. BR/TR, 5'6", 165 lbs. Deb: 6/25/12																											
1912	StL-N	1	1	0	0	0	0	0	1	0	0	.000	.000	.000	.000	-99	-0	-0	100	0	0	.000	0			0	/C	0.0
1913	Phi-N	17	30	3	6	3	0	0	3	6	3	.200	.351	.300	.651	78	-0	-1	112	121	4	.750	2			0	C	0.0
1914	Phi-N	70	139	8	36	3	4	0	16	20	12	.259	.352	.338	.690	105	2	2	100	123	18	.699	5			4	C	0.8
1915	Phi-N	67	174	11	42	5	0	0	16	20	12	.241	.327	.270	.597	76	-3	-4	107	130	16	.530	1			-4	C	-0.4
1916	Phi-N	78	219	14	51	8	1	0	14	16	18	.233	.294	.279	.573	80	-6	-5	96	91	20	.494	3			-5	C/SO	-0.6
1917	Phi-N	20	49	2	10	1	0	0	6	1	5	.204	.220	.224	.444	34	-4	-4	108	210	3	.359	2			0	C	-0.2
1918	Phi-N	68	184	10	38	1	1	0	9	20	9	.207	.288	.223	.511	52	-9	-11	109	83	12	.432	1			-3	C	-0.8
Total	7	321	796	48	183	21	6	0	65	83	59	.230	.308	.271	.579	73	-20	-24	104	111	72	.522	14			-8	C/OS	-1.2
■ GEORGE BURNS	Burns, George Henry "Tioga George" b: 1/31/1893, Niles, Ohio d: 1/7/78, Kirkland, Wash. BR/TR, 6'1.5", 180 lbs. Deb: 4/14/14																											
1914	Det-A	137	478	55	139	22	5	5	57	32	56	.291	.351	.389	.740	120	12	11	102	109	70	.719	23	13	-1	-5	*1	0.6
1915	Det-A	105	392	49	99	18	3	5	50	22	51	.253	.301	.352	.653	88	-4	-8	108	113	45	.588	9	3	1	-4	*1	-1.6
1916	Det-A	135	479	60	137	22	6	4	73	22	30	.286	.327	.382	.709	108	5	3	105	136	66	.655	12			-9	*1	-0.8
1917	Det-A	119	407	42	92	14	10	1	40	15	33	.226	.264	.317	.581	79	-13	-12	98	109	34	.486	3			-5	*1	-2.2
1918	Phi-A	130	505	61	**178**	22	9	6	70	23	25	.352	.390	.467	.857	152	33	31	104	106	91	.841	8			5	*1/O	3.1
1919	Phi-A	126	470	63	139	29	9	8	57	19	18	.296	.339	.447	.786	113	10	7	106	90	72	.773	15			1	1O	-0.1
1920	Phi-A	22	60	1	14	3	0	1	7	6	7	.233	.313	.333	.647	76	-2	-2	94	107	7	.674	4	0	1	-0	O	-0.1
	Cle-A	44	56	7	15	4	1	0	13	4	3	.268	.339	.375	.714	86	-1	-1	104	217	8	.683	1	0	0	-0	1/O	0.0
	Yr	66	116	8	29	7	1	1	20	10	10	.250	.326	.353	.679	80	-3	-3	100	182	15	.678	5	0	2	-1		-0.1
1921	Cle-A	84	244	52	88	21	4	0	49	13	19	.361	.398	.480	.877	124	8	8	99	143	46	.854	2	1	0	1	1	0.8
1922	Bos-A	147	558	71	171	32	5	12	73	20	28	.306	.341	.446	.787	108	1	4	96	93	85	.735	8	2	1	1	*1	-0.5
1923	Bos-A	146	551	91	181	47	5	7	82	45	33	.328	.386	.470	.856	123	19	18	102	106	100	.849	9	7	-2	-1	*1	0.8
1924	Cle-A	129	462	64	143	37	5	4	66	29	27	.310	.370	.437	.807	111	4	7	97	104	77	.802	14	5	1	8	*1	0.9
1925	Cle-A	127	488	69	164	41	4	6	79	24	24	.336	.371	.473	.844	106	8	3	106	108	83	.818	16	11	-2	-0	*1	-0.1
1926	Cle-A	151	603	97	**216**	**64**	3	4	114	28	33	.358	.394	.494	.889	131	25	26	100	132	116	.881	13	7	-0	1	*1	1.9
1927	Cle-A	140	549	84	175	51	2	3	78	42	27	.319	.375	.435	.810	113	8	10	97	111	88	.805	13	0	4	-0	*1	0.4
1928	Cle-A	82	209	29	52	12	1	5	30	17	11	.249	.323	.388	.711	81	-5	-6	106	107	26	.663	2	3	-1	1	1	-0.8
	NY-A	4	4	1	2	0	0	0	0	0	1	.500	.500	.500	1.000	178	0	0	92	0	1	1.000	0	0	0	0	/1	0.0
	Yr	86	213	30	54	12	1	5	30	17	12	.254	.326	.390	.716	83	-4	-6	105	103	27	.667	2	3	-1	1		-0.8
1929	NY-A	9	9	0	0	0	0	0	0	0	4	.000	.000	.000	.000	-99	-3	-3	99	0	0	.000	0	0	0	0	H	-0.2
	Phi-A	29	49	5	13	5	0	1	11	2	3	.265	.294	.429	.723	77	-1	-2	109	157	6	.667	1	0	0	-0	1	-0.4
	Yr	38	58	5	13	5	0	1	11	2	7	.224	.250	.362	.612	52	-4	-5	106	120	5	.533	1	0	0	-0		-0.6
Total	16	1866	6573	901	2018	444	72	72	949	363	433	.307	.354	.429	.783	112	104	93	101	112	1021	.748	153	52		-7	*1/O	1.7
■ GEORGE BURNS	Burns, George Joseph b: 11/24/1889, Utica, N.Y. d: 8/15/66, Gloversville, N.Y. BR/TR, 5'7", 160 lbs. Deb: 10/03/11 C																											
1911	NY-N	6	17	2	1	0	0	0	0	1	0	.059	.111	.059	.170	-51	-3	-4	102	0	0	.125	0			-1	/O	-0.4
1912	NY-N	29	51	11	15	4	0	0	3	8	8	.294	.400	.373	.773	108	1	1	104	53	10	.972	7			-4	O	-0.3
1913	NY-N	150	605	81	173	37	4	2	54	58	74	.286	.352	.370	.723	103	6	4	103	74	88	.755	40			10	*O	1.1
1914	NY-N	154	561	**100**	170	35	10	3	60	89	53	.303	.403	.417	.820	151	34	37	96	86	**113**	**.997**	**62**			5	*O	4.0
1915	NY-N	155	622	83	169	27	14	3	51	56	57	.272	.333	.375	.707	125	10	16	91	69	79	.670	27	20	-4	-3	*O	0.5

YEAR	TM/L	G	AB	R	H	2B	3B	HR	RBI	BB	SO	AVG	OBP	SLG	PRO	/A	BR	/A	PF	CHI	RC	TA	SB	CS	SBR	FR	POS	TPR
1916	NY-N	155	623	**105**	174	24	8	5	41	63	47	.279	.346	.368	.714	125	15	18	96	58	82	.695	37	26	-5	2	*O	1.7
1917	NY-N	152	597	**103**	180	25	13	5	45	**75**	55	.302	.380	.412	.792	147	32	34	97	57	**102**	.868	40			5	*O	3.8
1918	NY-N	119	465	80	135	22	6	4	51	43	37	.290	.354	.389	.743	130	15	16	98	88	74	.809	40			-8	*O	0.2
1919	NY-N	139	534	**86**	162	30	9	2	46	**82**	37	.303	**.396**	.404	.801	141	30	30	100	70	**96**	**.909**	**40**			1	*O	2.8
1920	NY-N	154	631	**115**	181	35	9	6	46	**76**	48	.287	.365	.399	.765	120	18	18	100	57	91	.746	22	22	-7	-18	*O	-1.6
1921	NY-N	149	605	111	181	28	9	4	61	**80**	24	.299	.386	.395	.781	110	10	12	98	77	93	.775	19	20	-6	-9	*O/3	-0.9
1922	Cin-N	156	631	104	180	20	10	1	53	78	38	.285	.366	.353	.719	90	-10	-6	96	71	83	.703	30	23	-5	-4	*O	-1.9
1923	Cin-N	154	614	99	168	27	13	3	45	**101**	46	.274	.376	.375	.751	101	2	4	98	57	90	.746	12	14	-5	-4	*O	-0.8
1924	Cin-N	93	336	43	86	19	2	2	33	29	21	.256	.315	.342	.657	76	-11	-11	101	101	36	.574	3	6	-3	1	O	-1.4
1925	Phi-N	88	349	65	102	29	1	1	22	33	20	.292	.353	.390	.743	78	-5	-13	116	60	47	.678	4	8	-4	-2	O	-1.9
Total	15	1853	7241	1188	2077	362	108	41	611	872	565	.287	.366	.384	.749	115	143	156	98	70	1085	.765	383	139		-27	*O/3	4.9

■ JIM BURNS Burns, James M. b: Quincy, Ill. 5'7", 168 lbs. Deb: 1888

YEAR	TM/L	G	AB	R	H	2B	3B	HR	RBI	BB	SO	AVG	OBP	SLG	PRO	/A	BR	/A	PF	CHI	RC	TA	SB	CS	SBR	FR	POS	TPR
1888	KC-a	15	66	13	20	0	0	0	4	1		.303	.343	.303	.646	105	1	0	106	52	9	.652	6			0	O	0.0
1889	KC-a	134	579	103	176	23	11	5	97	20	68	.304	.335	.408	.743	107	8	2	106	106	100	.792	56			-10	*O/3	-1.0
1891	Was-a	20	82	15	26	6	0	0	10	6	10	.317	.378	.390	.768	129	2	3	95	80	13	.750	2			0	O/S	0.3
Total	3	169	727	131	222	29	11	5	111	27	78	.305	.341	.396	.737	109	11	5	105	98	123	.774	64			-10	O/S3	-0.7

■ JACK BURNS Burns, John Irving "Slug" b: 8/31/07, Cambridge, Mass. d: 4/18/75, Brighton, Mass. BL/TL, 5'10.5", 175 lbs. Deb: 9/17/30 C

YEAR	TM/L	G	AB	R	H	2B	3B	HR	RBI	BB	SO	AVG	OBP	SLG	PRO	/A	BR	/A	PF	CHI	RC	TA	SB	CS	SBR	FR	POS	TPR
1930	StL-A	8	30	5	9	3	0	0	2	5	5	.300	.400	.400	.800	96	0	-0	108	53	5	.810	0	0	0	0	/1	0.0
1931	StL-A	144	570	75	148	27	7	4	70	42	58	.260	.312	.353	.664	72	-22	-24	102	115	63	.606	19	12	-2	18	*1	-1.9
1932	StL-A	150	617	111	188	33	8	11	70	61	43	.305	.368	.438	.806	108	7	7	100	68	100	.793	17	11	-2	4	*1	-0.5
1933	StL-A	144	556	89	160	43	4	7	71	56	51	.288	.353	.417	.770	90	2	-9	115	99	81	.735	11	11	-3	3	*1	-1.8
1934	StL-A	154	612	86	157	28	8	13	73	62	47	.257	.327	.392	.719	82	-15	-19	104	84	81	.683	9	3	1	0	*1	-4.1
1935	StL-A	143	549	77	157	28	1	5	67	68	49	.286	.366	.368	.734	85	-6	-12	107	111	78	.695	3	2	-0	-8	*1	-3.2
1936	StL-A	9	14	2	3	1	0	0	1	3	1	.214	.353	.286	.639	58	-1	-1	103	81	2	.636	0	0	0	-0	/1	0.0
	Det-A	138	558	96	158	36	3	4	63	79	45	.283	.375	.380	.755	91	-10	-5	95	88	82	.730	4	8	-4	2	*1	-2.2
	Yr	147	572	98	161	37	3	4	64	82	46	.281	.374	.378	.752	90	-11	-7	96	88	84	.728	4	8	-4	2		-2.2
Total	7	890	3506	541	980	199	31	44	417	376	299	.280	.351	.392	.742	88	-44	-63	104	93	493	.707	63	47	-9	19	1	-13.7

■ JACK BURNS Burns, John Joseph b: 5/13/1880, Avoca, Pa. d: 6/24/57, Waterford, Conn. BR/TR, 5'10", 160 lbs. Deb: 03

YEAR	TM/L	G	AB	R	H	2B	3B	HR	RBI	BB	SO	AVG	OBP	SLG	PRO	/A	BR	/A	PF	CHI	RC	TA	SB	CS	SBR	FR	POS	TPR
1903	Det-A	11	37	2	10	0	0	0	3	1		.270	.289	.270	.560	73	-1	-1	97	108	3	.407	0			0	2	0.0
1904	Det-A	4	16	3	2	0	0	0	1	1		.125	.176	.125	.301	-3	-2	-2	96	161	1	.286	1			0	/2	-0.1
Total	2	15	53	5	12	0	0	0	4	2		.226	.255	.226	.481	51	-3	-3	96	124	4	.366	1			0	/2	-0.1

■ JOE BURNS Burns, Joseph Francis b: 3/26/1889, Ipswich, Mass. d: 7/12/87, Beverly, Ma. BL/TL, 5'11", 170 lbs. Deb: 6/08/10

YEAR	TM/L	G	AB	R	H	2B	3B	HR	RBI	BB	SO	AVG	OBP	SLG	PRO	/A	BR	/A	PF	CHI	RC	TA	SB	CS	SBR	FR	POS	TPR
1910	Cin-N	1	1	0	1	0	0	0	0	0	0	1.000	1.000	1.000	2.000	478	0	0	101	0	2	—	1			0	H	0.0
1913	Det-A	4	13	0	5	0	0	0	1	2	4	.385	.500	.385	.885	161	1	1	99	72	2	1.000	0			-1	/O	0.1
Total	2	5	14	0	6	0	0	0	1	2	4	.429	.529	.429	.958	183	2	2	99	68	4	1.250	1			-1	/O	0.1

■ JOE BURNS Burns, Joseph Francis b: 2/25/1900, Trenton, N.J. d: 1/7/86, Trenton, N.J. BR/TR, 6', 175 lbs. Deb: 4/18/24

YEAR	TM/L	G	AB	R	H	2B	3B	HR	RBI	BB	SO	AVG	OBP	SLG	PRO	/A	BR	/A	PF	CHI	RC	TA	SB	CS	SBR	FR	POS	TPR
1924	Chi-A	8	19	1	2	0	0	0	0	0	2	.105	.105	.105	.211	-47	-4	-4	97	0	0	.118	0	0	0	0	/C	-0.2

■ JOE BURNS Burns, Joseph James b: 6/17/16, Bryn Mawr, Pa. d: 6/24/74, Bryn Mawr, Pa. BR/TR, 5'10.5", 175 lbs. Deb: 4/24/43

YEAR	TM/L	G	AB	R	H	2B	3B	HR	RBI	BB	SO	AVG	OBP	SLG	PRO	/A	BR	/A	PF	CHI	RC	TA	SB	CS	SBR	FR	POS	TPR
1943	Bos-N	52	135	12	28	3	0	1	5	8	25	.207	.262	.252	.514	46	-9	-10	106	49	8	.407	2			3	3/O	-0.7
1944	Phi-A	28	75	5	18	2	0	1	8	4	8	.240	.278	.307	.585	66	-3	-3	101	111	7	.466	0	1	-1	-1	3/2	-0.4
1945	Phi-A	31	90	7	23	1	1	0	3	4	17	.256	.287	.289	.576	72	-4	-3	94	42	7	.429	0	1	-1	-3	O/31	-0.7
Total	3	111	300	24	69	6	1	2	16	16	50	.230	.274	.277	.550	58	-16	-16	101	62	22	.438	2	2		-1	/3O21	-1.8

■ PAT BURNS Burns, Patrick Deb: 8/11/1884

YEAR	TM/L	G	AB	R	H	2B	3B	HR	RBI	BB	SO	AVG	OBP	SLG	PRO	/A	BR	/A	PF	CHI	RC	TA	SB	CS	SBR	FR	POS	TPR
1884	Bal-a	6	25	3	5	2	1	0		3		.200	.286	.360	.646	113	0	0	99	0	3	.600				0	/1	0.0
	Bal-U	1	4	0	2	0	0	0		0		.500	.500	.500	1.000	217	1	0	110	0	1	1.000	0			0	/1	0.0
Total	1	7	29	3	7	2	1	0		3		.241	.313	.379	.692	128	1	1	100	0	4	.636	0			0	/1	0.0

■ DICK BURNS Burns, Richard Simon b: 12/26/1863, Holyoke, Mass. d: 11/11/37, Holyoke, Mass. BL , 140 lbs. Deb: 5/03/1883

YEAR	TM/L	G	AB	R	H	2B	3B	HR	RBI	BB	SO	AVG	OBP	SLG	PRO	/A	BR	/A	PF	CHI	RC	TA	SB	CS	SBR	FR	POS	TPR
1883	Det-N	37	140	11	26	7	1	0	5	2	22	.186	.197	.250	.447	38	-11	-9	91	50	7	.325				-6	OP	-1.1
1884	Cin-U	79	350	84	107	17	**12**	4		5		.306	.315	.457	.773	147	20	16	108	0	52	.679	0			-2	OP/S	0.0
1885	StL-N	14	54	2	12	2	1	0	4	3	8	.222	.263	.296	.559	87	-1	-1	92	92	4	.452				0	O/P	0.0
Total	3	130	544	97	145	26	14	4	9	10	30	.267	.280	.388	.668	114	8	6	102	22	63	.554				-7	/OPS	-1.1

■ TOM BURNS Burns, Thomas Everett b: 3/30/1857, Honesdale, Pa. d: 3/19/02, Jersey City, N.J. BR/TR, 5'7", 152 lbs. Deb: 5/01/1880 M

YEAR	TM/L	G	AB	R	H	2B	3B	HR	RBI	BB	SO	AVG	OBP	SLG	PRO	/A	BR	/A	PF	CHI	RC	TA	SB	CS	SBR	FR	POS	TPR
1880	Chi-N	85	333	47	103	17	3	0	43	12	23	.309	.333	.378	.712	134	14	11	105	127	43	.600				-30	*S/3CP	-1.3
1881	Chi-N	84	342	41	95	20	3	4	42	14	22	.278	.306	.389	.695	108	6	2	108	107	42	.595				-4	*S/32	0.3
1882	Chi-N	84	355	55	88	23	6	0	48	15	28	.248	.278	.346	.625	98	-0	-1	101	139	35	.517				-7	2S	-0.1
1883	Chi-N	97	405	69	119	37	7	2	67	13	31	.294	.316	.435	.750	115	12	6	109	135	57	.661				3	*S2/O	1.1
1884	Chi-N	83	343	54	84	14	2	7	94	13	50	.245	.272	.359	.631	90	-2	-6	108	**229**	34	.525				-2	*S/3	0.0
1885	Chi-N	111	445	82	121	23	9	7	71	16	48	.272	.297	.411	.708	112	12	4	114	123	56	.614				-9	*S/2	0.0
1886	Chi-N	112	445	64	123	18	10	3	65	14	40	.276	.298	.382	.680	91	2	-9	116	121	57	.618	15			13	*3	0.8
1887	Chi-N	115	424	57	112	20	10	3	60	34	32	.264	.320	.380	.700	82	-3	-14	116	111	63	.731	32			16	*3/O	0.2
1888	Chi-N	134	483	60	115	12	6	3	70	26	49	.238	.281	.306	.588	83	-5	-10	107	**163**	52	.573	34			9	*3	0.5
1889	Chi-N	136	525	64	127	27	6	4	66	32	57	.242	.288	.339	.627	77	-18	-17	99	106	58	.578	18			3	*3	-0.3
1890	Chi-N	139	538	86	149	17	6	5	86	57	45	.277	.348	.359	.707	99	6	-2	109	132	85	.761	44			-1	*3	0.2
1891	Chi-N	59	243	36	55	8	1	1	17	21	21	.226	.288	.280	.568	63	-10	-12	106	74	25	.569	18			-1	3/SO	-1.0
1892	Pit-N	12	39	7	8	0	0	0	4	3	8	.205	.262	.205	.467	46	-3	-2	94	154	2	.387	1			0	/3OM	-0.1
Total	13	1251	4920	722	1299	236	69	39	733	270	454	.264	.303	.364	.667	95	11	-49	108	131	610	.616	162			-11	3S/2OCP	0.3

■ OYSTER BURNS Burns, Thomas P. b: 9/6/1864, Philadelphia, Pa. d: 11/11/28, Brooklyn, N.Y. BR/TR, 5'8", 183 lbs. Deb: 8/18/1884

YEAR	TM/L	G	AB	R	H	2B	3B	HR	RBI	BB	SO	AVG	OBP	SLG	PRO	/A	BR	/A	PF	CHI	RC	TA	SB	CS	SBR	FR	POS	TPR
1884	WiL-U	2	7	0	1	0	1	0		1		.143	.250	.429	.679	122	0	0	103	0	1	.667	0			0	/S	0.0
	Bal-a	35	131	34	39	2	6	6		7		.298	.348	.542	.890	191	12	13	99	0	25	.880				0	O2/P3	1.1
1885	Bal-a	78	321	47	74	11	6	5		16		.231	.280	.349	.629	95	0	-3	106	0	32	.543				5	OPS/321D	0.0
1887	Bal-a	140	551	122	188	33	19	9		63		.341	.414	.519	.933	168	46	50	96	0	146	1.135	58			-22	*S3/P2	2.0
1888	Bal-a	79	325	54	97	18	9	4	42	24		.298	.349	.446	.795	164	20	22	96	69	60	.846	23			-7	OS/P32	1.2
	Bro-a	52	204	40	58	9	6	2	25	14		.284	.339	.417	.756	139	10	9	105	79	37	.842	21			-13	SO/2	-0.3
	Yr	131	529	94	155	27	15	6	67	38		.293	.345	.435	.780	154	30	30	100	73	97	.845	44			-21		0.9
1889	Bro-a	131	504	105	153	19	13	5	100	68	26	.304	.391	.423	.813	139	24	28	96	133	98	.903	32			-3	*OS	1.7
1890	Bro-N	119	472	102	134	22	12	**13**	**128**	51	42	.284	.359	.464	.823	141	23	23	100	144	88	.873	21			-6	*O/3	1.3
1891	Bro-N	123	470	75	134	24	13	4	83	53	30	.285	.358	.417	.775	131	16	18	97	123	80	.804	21			4	*O/S3	1.4
1892	Bro-N	141	542	88	171	27	18	4	96	65	42	.315	.395	.454	.849	156	39	38	101	121	113	.943	33			-8	*O/3S	2.3
1893	Bro-N	109	415	68	112	22	8	7	60	36	16	.270	.334	.412	.746	110	-2	5	91	87	63	.743	14			-1	*O/S	0.0
1894	Bro-N	124	505	106	179	32	14	5	107	44	18	.354	.409	.503	.912	128	17	23	94	116	119	1.015	30			-5	*O	0.7
1895	Bro-N	20	76	7	14	0	1	0	7	8	2	.184	.271	.211	.481	28	-8	-7	94	129	4	.403	0			0	O	-0.5
	NY-N	33	114	21	35	5	3	1	25	14	6	.307	.388	.430	.817	119	2	4	95	137	23	.937	10			0	O/1	0.3
	Yr	53	190	28	49	5	4	1	32	22	8	.258	.341	.342	.683	83	-6	-4	94	137	26	.702	10			0		-0.2
Total	11	1186	4637	869	1389	224	129	65	673	464	182	.300	.368	.446	.814	137	199	220	98	90	890	.873	263			-58	OS/3P21D	11.2

■ ALEX BURR Burr, Alexander Thomson b: 11/1/1893, Chicago, Ill. d: 11/1/18, France BR/TR, 6'3.5", 190 lbs. Deb: 4/21/14

YEAR	TM/L	G	AB	R	H	2B	3B	HR	RBI	BB	SO	AVG	OBP	SLG	PRO	/A	BR	/A	PF	CHI	RC	TA	SB	CS	SBR	FR	POS	TPR
1914	NY-A	1	0	0	0	0	0	0	0	0	0	—	—	—	—	—	0	0	100	—	—	—	0			-0	/O	0.0

■ BUSTER BURRELL Burrell, Frank Andrew b: 12/22/1866, E.Weymouth, Mass. d: 5/8/62, S.Weymouth, Mass. BR/TR, 5'10", 165 lbs. Deb: 8/01/1891

YEAR	TM/L	G	AB	R	H	2B	3B	HR	RBI	BB	SO	AVG	OBP	SLG	PRO	/A	BR	/A	PF	CHI	RC	TA	SB	CS	SBR	FR	POS	TPR
1891	NY-N	15	53	1	5	0	0	0	1	3	12	.094	.158	.094	.252	-27	-8	-8	94	58	1	.229	2			0	C/O	-0.6

YEAR	TM/L	G	AB	R	H	2B	3B	HR	RBI	BB	SO	AVG	OBP	SLG	PRO	/A	BR	/A	PF	CHI	RC	TA	SB	CS	SBR	FR	POS	TPR
1895	Bro-N	12	28	7	4	0	0	1	5	4	3	.143	.250	.250	.500	32	-3	-3	94	140	2	.458	0			0	C	-0.1
1896	Bro-N	62	206	19	62	11	3	0	23	15	13	.301	.348	.383	.732	108	-2	3	87	84	29	.660	1			-9	C	0.0
1897	Bro-N	33	103	15	25	2	0	2	18	10		.243	.310	.320	.630	67	-5	-5	102	135	11	.564	1			0	C/1	-0.3
Total	4	122	390	42	96	13	3	3	47	32	28	.246	.305	.318	.623	73	-17	-12	93	98	42	.548	4			-9	C/1O	-1.0
■ LARRY BURRIGHT Burright, Larry Allen "Possum" b: 7/10/37, Roseville, Ill. BR/TR, 5'11", 170 lbs. Deb: 4/12/62																												
1962	LA-N	115	249	35	51	6	5	4	30	21	67	.205	.267	.317	.584	60	-16	-13	93	130	20	.505	4	3	-1	1	*2/S	-0.2
1963	NY-N	41	100	9	22	2	1	0	3	8	25	.220	.291	.260	.551	60	-5	-5	99	48	8	.474	1	0	0	0	S2/3	-0.1
1964	NY-N	3	7	0	0	0	0	0	0	0	0	.000	.000	.000	.000	-99	-2	-2	95	0	0	.000	0	0	0	0	/2	0.0
Total	3	159	356	44	73	8	6	4	33	29	92	.205	.269	.295	.564	57	-23	-20	95	104	29	.493	5	3	-0	2	2/S3	-0.3
■ PAUL BURRIS Burris, Paul Robert b: 7/21/23, Hickory, N.C. BR/TR, 6', 190 lbs. Deb: 10/02/48																												
1948	Bos-N	2	4	0	2	0	0	0	0	0	0	.500	.500	.500	1.000	169	0	0	102	0	1	1.000	0			0	/C	0.1
1950	Bos-N	10	23	1	4	1	0	0	3	1	2	.174	.208	.217	.426	14	-3	-3	86	231	1	.286	0			1	/C	-0.1
1952	Bos-N	55	168	14	37	4	0	2	21	7	19	.220	.256	.280	.535	51	-12	-11	95	155	10	.393	0	0	0	0	C	-0.9
1953	Mil-N	2	1	0	0	0	0	0	0	0	0	.000	.000	.000	.000	-99	-0	-0	94	0	0	.000	0	0	0	0	/C	0.0
Total	4	69	196	15	43	5	0	2	24	8	21	.219	.254	.276	.529	49	-15	-13	94	160	12	.412	0	0		1	/C	-0.9
■ HENRY BURROUGHS Burroughs, Henry F. b: 1845, Detroit, Mich. 5'8", 147 lbs. Deb: 5/05/1871																												
1871	Oly-n	12	63	11	14							.222															/O3	
1872	Oly-n	2	8	1	1							.125															/O	
Total	2 n	14	71	12	15							.211															/O	
■ JEFF BURROUGHS Burroughs, Jeffrey Alan b: 3/7/51, Long Beach, Cal. BR/TR, 6'1", 200 lbs. Deb: 7/20/70																												
1970	Was-A	6	12	1	2	0	0	0	1	2	5	.167	.286	.167	.452	29	-1	-1	96	202	1	.400	0	0	0	-0	/O	-0.1
1971	Was-A	59	181	20	42	9	0	5	25	22	55	.232	.319	.365	.683	101	-2	0	92	126	22	.629	1	0	0	-3	O	-0.4
1972	Tex-A	22	65	4	12	1	0	1	3	5	22	.185	.243	.246	.489	48	-4	-4	94	66	3	.368	0	2	-1	-1	O/1	-0.7
1973	Tex-A	151	526	71	147	17	1	30	85	67	88	.279	.362	.487	.849	141	25	27	97	99	95	.837	0	0	0	9	*O/1D	3.2
1974	Tex-A	152	554	84	167	33	2	25	**118**	91	104	.301	.405	.504	.908	**167**	**45**	**48**	96	126	113	.926	2	3	-1	-10	*O/1D	3.4
1975	Tex-A	152	585	81	132	20	0	29	94	79	155	.226	.319	.409	.727	105	3	3	100	117	76	.687	4	4	-1	-10	*O/D	-1.2
1976	Tex-A	158	604	71	143	22	2	18	86	69	93	.237	.317	.369	.686	98	0	-1	102	126	69	.609	0	0	0	-6	*O/D	-1.0
1977	Atl-N	154	579	91	157	19	1	41	114	86	126	.271	.365	.520	.885	119	28	18	113	114	114	.907	4	1	1	-8	*O	0.5
1978	Atl-N	153	488	72	147	30	6	23	77	**117**	92	.301	**.436**	.529	.965	151	50	42	112	95	116	**1.047**	1	2	-1	-8	*O	2.9
1979	Atl-N	116	397	49	89	14	1	11	47	73	75	.224	.349	.348	.696	83	-3	-8	109	115	50	.667	2	2	-1	-6	*O	-1.8
1980	Atl-N	99	278	35	73	14	0	13	51	35	57	.263	.349	.453	.802	121	8	8	101	122	45	.781	1	1	-0	-8	O	-0.3
1981	Sea-A	89	319	32	81	13	1	10	41	41	64	.254	.339	.395	.734	111	5	5	100	105	43	.679	0	1	-1	-13	O/D	-1.1
1982	Oak-A	113	285	42	79	13	2	16	48	45	61	.277	.376	.505	.881	146	16	18	95	100	54	.876	1	3	-2	-6	DO	0.9
1983	Oak-A	121	401	43	108	15	1	10	56	47	79	.269	.346	.387	.733	106	1	4	96	118	51	.650	0	2	-1	0	*D	0.3
1984	Oak-A	58	71	5	15	1	0	2	8	18	23	.211	.371	.310	.681	99	-0	1	92	114	9	.690	0	0	0	-2	D/O	0.0
1985	Tor-A	86	191	19	49	9	3	6	28	34	36	.257	.369	.429	.798	117	6	5	101	111	30	.773	0	1	-1	0	D	0.5
Total	16	1689	5536	720	1443	230	20	240	882	831	1135	.261	.359	.439	.798	121	177	165	102	113	892	.799	16	22	-8	-73	*OD/1	5.1
■ DICK BURRUS Burrus, Maurice Lennon b: 1/29/1898, Hatteras, N.C. d: 2/2/72, Elizabeth City, N.C BL/TL, 5'11", 175 lbs. Deb: 6/23/19																												
1919	Phi-A	70	194	17	50	3	4	0	8	9	25	.258	.294	.314	.609	67	-8	-9	106	48	18	.507	2			-1	1O	-1.4
1920	Phi-A	71	135	11	25	8	0	0	10	5	7	.185	.225	.244	.470	26	-15	-14	94	106	7	.354	0	3	-2	-0	1/O	-1.5
1925	Bos-N	152	588	82	200	41	4	5	87	51	29	.340	.396	.449	.845	123	15	20	94	117	104	.821	8	9	-3	1	*1	0.2
1926	Bos-N	131	486	59	131	21	1	3	61	37	16	.270	.324	.335	.659	90	-15	-6	86	125	53	.580	4			13	*1	0.2
1927	Bos-N	72	220	22	70	8	3	0	32	17	10	.318	.370	.382	.752	109	1	3	93	133	31	.700	3			0	1	0.0
1928	Bos-N	64	137	15	37	6	0	3	13	19	8	.270	.367	.380	.747	98	-0	0	97	76	20	.740	1			1	1	-0.1
Total	6	560	1760	206	513	87	12	11	211	138	95	.291	.347	.373	.720	97	-22	-5	93	110	231	.654	18	12		14	1/O	-2.6
■ FRANK BURT Burt, Frank J. b: Camden, N.J. Deb: 5/02/1882																												
1882	Bal-a	10	36	2	4	2	1	0		1		.111	.135	.222	.357	20	-3	-3	92	0	1	.281				0	O	-0.1
■ ELLIS BURTON Burton, Ellis Narrington b: 8/12/36, Los Angeles, Cal. BB/TR, 5'11", 160 lbs. Deb: 9/18/58																												
1958	StL-N	8	30	5	7	0	1	2	4	3	8	.233	.324	.500	.824	107	0	0	106	83	4	.760	0	1	-1	-1	/O	0.0
1960	StL-N	29	28	5	6	1	0	0	2	4	14	.214	.313	.250	.563	52	-2	-2	108	116	2	.458	0	2	-1	-8	O	-1.1
1963	Cle-A	26	31	6	6	3	0	1	1	4	4	.194	.286	.387	.673	89	-1	-0	97	28	3	.615	0	0	0	-4	O	-0.4
	Chi-N	93	322	45	74	16	1	12	41	36	59	.230	.315	.398	.712	99	2	-0	105	111	41	.677	6	3	0	-0	O	-0.5
1964	Chi-N	42	105	12	20	3	2	2	7	17	22	.190	.303	.314	.618	71	-3	-4	105	74	11	.614	4	0	1	-1	O	-0.4
1965	Chi-N	17	40	6	7	1	0	0	4	1	10	.175	.195	.200	.395	11	-5	-5	102	207	2	.303	1	0	0	0	O	-0.4
Total	5	215	556	79	120	24	4	17	59	65	117	.216	.304	.365	.669	85	-8	-11	105	104	64	.643	11	6	-0	-14	O	-2.8
■ JIM BUSBY Busby, James Franklin b: 1/8/27, Kenedy, Tex. BR/TR, 6'1", 175 lbs. Deb: 4/23/50 C																												
1950	Chi-A	18	48	5	10	0	0	0	4	1	5	.208	.224	.208	.433	12	-6	-6	97	138	2	.268	0	2	-1	1	O	-0.6
1951	Chi-A	143	477	59	135	15	2	5	68	40	46	.283	.344	.354	.698	92	-7	-5	97	132	58	.649	26	11	1	-3	*O	-1.1
1952	Chi-A	16	39	5	5	0	0	0	0	2	7	.128	.171	.128	.299	-16	-6	-6	100	0	1	.189	0	2	-1	1	O	-0.6
	Was-A	129	512	58	125	24	4	2	47	22	48	.244	.281	.318	.599	66	-24	-24	100	110	44	.480	5	6	-2	6	*O	-2.4
	Yr	145	551	63	130	24	4	2	47	24	55	.236	.273	.305	.578	61	-30	-30	100	98	44	.457	5	8	-3	7		-3.0
1953	Was-A	150	586	68	183	28	7	6	82	38	45	.312	.358	.415	.773	115	6	10	94	123	90	.715	13	6	0	14	*O	2.0
1954	Was-A	155	628	83	187	22	7	7	80	43	56	.298	.346	.389	.734	102	-0	1	98	110	88	.681	17	2	**4**	7	*O	0.9
1955	Was-A	47	191	23	44	6	2	6	14	13	22	.230	.279	.377	.656	83	-8	-5	91	56	20	.596	5	0	2	6	O	0.0
	Chi-A	99	337	38	82	13	4	1	27	25	37	.243	.296	.315	.610	64	-17	-18	101	92	32	.523	7	3	0	-1	O	-2.3
	Yr	146	528	61	126	19	6	7	41	38	59	.239	.290	.337	.627	70	-25	-23	98	81	54	.555	12	3	2	4		-2.3
1956	Cle-A	135	494	72	116	17	3	12	50	43	47	.235	.301	.354	.656	72	-21	-22	101	90	52	.584	8	3	1	-2	*O	-2.9
1957	Cle-A	30	74	9	14	2	1	2	4	1	8	.189	.200	.324	.524	40	-6	-6	102	53	4	.391	0	1	-1	-1	O	-0.9
	Bal-A	86	288	31	72	10	1	3	19	23	36	.250	.305	.323	.628	77	-11	-9	93	74	30	.550	6	3	0	5	O	-0.8
	Yr	116	362	40	86	12	2	5	23	24	44	.238	.285	.323	.608	69	-17	-15	95	69	34	.519	6	4	-1	4		-1.7
1958	Bal-A	113	215	32	51	7	2	3	19	24	37	.237	.322	.330	.653	85	-5	-4	94	95	24	.612	6	4	-1	-12	*O/3	-2.3
1959	Bos-A	61	102	16	23	8	0	1	5	5	18	.225	.269	.333	.602	61	-5	-6	106	53	8	.482	0	1	-1	-4	O	-1.1
1960	Bos-A	1	0	0	0	0	0	0	0	0	0	—	—	—	—	—	0	0	103	—	—	—	0	0	0	-0	/O	0.0
	Bal-A	79	159	25	41	7	1	0	12	20	14	.258	.341	.314	.655	77	-4	-5	102	94	17	.576	2	3	-1	-1	O	-0.9
	Yr	80	159	25	41	7	1	0	12	20	14	.258	.341	.314	.655	77	-4	-5	102	93	17	.576	2	3	-1	-1		-0.9
1961	Bal-A	75	89	15	23	3	1	0	6	8	10	.258	.320	.315	.634	72	-4	-3	97	84	10	.567	2	0	1	-14	O	-1.8
1962	Hou-N	15	11	2	2	0	0	0	1	2	3	.182	.308	.182	.490	38	-1	-1	93	197	1	.400	0	1	-1	-3	O/C	-0.4
Total	13	1352	4250	541	1113	162	35	48	438	310	439	.262	.316	.350	.666	82	-121	-109	98	101	489	.603	97	48	0	-1	*O/C3	-15.2
■ PAUL BUSBY Busby, Paul Miller "Red" b: 8/25/18, Waynesboro, Miss. BL/TR, 6'1", 175 lbs. Deb: 9/14/41																												
1941	Phi-N	10	16	3	5	0	0	0	2	0	1	.313	.313	.313	.625	79	-1	-0	97	144	2	.455	0			-1	/O	0.0
1943	Phi-N	26	40	13	10	1	0	0	5	2	1	.250	.286	.275	.561	67	-2	-2	94	164	3	.469	2			0	O	-0.1
Total	2	36	56	16	15	1	0	0	7	2	2	.268	.293	.286	.579	70	-2	-2	94	159	5	.465	2			-1	/O	-0.1
■ ED BUSCH Busch, Edgar John b: 11/16/17, Lebanon, Ill. d: 1/17/87, St.Clair Co., Ill. BR/TR, 5'10", 175 lbs. Deb: 9/30/43																												
1943	Phi-A	4	17	2	5	0	0	0	0	1	2	.294	.368	.294	.663	94	-0	-0	101	0	2	.538	0	1	-1	-0	/S	0.0
1944	Phi-A	140	484	41	131	11	3	0	40	29	17	.271	.313	.306	.619	76	-14	-15	101	98	44	.487	5	3	-0	-14	*S2/3	-2.2
1945	Phi-A	126	416	37	104	10	3	0	35	32	9	.250	.305	.288	.594	78	-14	-11	94	105	37	.474	2	3	-1	2	*S/231	-0.5
Total	3	270	917	80	240	21	6	0	75	62	28	.262	.311	.298	.608	77	-29	-26	98	99	82	.496	7	7	-2	-13	S/231	-2.7
■ DONIE BUSH Bush, Owen Joseph b: 10/8/1887, Indianapolis, Ind. d: 3/28/72, Indianapolis, Ind. BB/TR, 5'6", 140 lbs. Deb: 9/18/08 M																												
1908	Det-A	20	68	13	20	1	1	0	4	7		.294	.360	.338	.698	128	2	2	101	67	9	.667	2			-1	S	0.2

YEAR	TM/L	G	AB	R	H	2B	3B	HR	RBI	BB	SO	AVG	OBP	SLG	PRO	/A	BR	/A	PF	CHI	RC	TA	SB	CS	SBR	FR	POS	TPR
1909	Det-A	157	532	114	145	18	2	0	33	**88**		.273	.380	.314	.694	108	17	11	110	81	82	.806	53			4	*S	2.1
1910	Det-A	142	496	90	130	13	4	3	34	**78**		.262	.365	.323	.687	113	12	11	102	72	78	.790	49			10	*S/3	2.5
1911	Det-A	150	561	126	130	18	5	1	36	**98**		.232	.349	.287	.636	72	-12	-19	108	66	73	.705	42			15	*S	1.0
1912	Det-A	144	511	107	118	14	8	2	38	**117**		.231	.377	.301	.679	100	3	7	95	70	72	.786	35			28	*S	4.7
1913	Det-A	152	593	98	149	19	10	1	40	80	32	.251	.344	.322	.666	96	-2	-1	99	63	77	.718	44			4	*S	1.7
1914	Det-A	157	596	97	150	18	4	0	32	**112**	54	.252	.373	.295	.668	99	7	5	102	59	71	.691	35	26	-5	**33**	*S	5.2
1915	Det-A	155	561	99	128	12	8	1	44	118	44	.228	.364	.283	.648	87	2	-5	108	82	65	.683	35	27	-6	8	*S	1.2
1916	Det-A	145	550	73	124	5	9	0	34	75	42	.225	.319	.267	.587	73	-14	-17	105	73	57	.568	19			-14	*S	-2.1
1917	Det-A	147	581	**112**	163	18	3	0	24	80	40	.281	.370	.322	.691	114	11	13	98	40	78	.725	34			-16	*S	0.2
1918	Det-A	128	500	74	117	10	3	0	22	79	31	.234	.340	.266	.606	86	-7	-5	97	52	48	.580	9			-21	*S	-1.9
1919	Det-A	129	509	82	124	11	6	0	26	75	36	.244	.343	.289	.632	84	-12	-7	93	55	57	.639	22			-6	*S	-0.2
1920	Det-A	141	506	85	133	18	5	1	33	73	32	.263	.357	.324	.681	79	-11	-14	103	67	66	.666	15	7	0	-16	*S	-1.5
1921	Det-A	104	402	72	113	6	5	0	27	45	23	.281	.355	.321	.676	76	-14	-12	96	69	48	.603	6	11	-5	-11	S2	-1.4
	Was-A	23	84	15	18	1	0	0	2	12	4	.214	.313	.226	.539	40	-7	-7	99	37	7	.515	4	2	0	-1	S	-0.4
	Yr	127	486	87	131	7	5	0	29	57	27	.270	.347	.305	.652	70	-22	-19	97	64	55	.587	10	13	-5	-11		-1.8
1922	Was-A	41	134	17	32	4	1	0	7	21	7	.239	.342	.284	.626	70	-6	-5	92	67	14	.583	1	1	-0	2	3/2	0.1
1923	Was-A	10	22	6	9	0	0	0	0	0	1	.409	.409	.409	.818	122	0	1	95	0	3	.643	0	1	-1	0	/32M	0.1
Total	16	1945	7206	1280	1803	186	74	9	436	1158	346	.250	.356	.300	.657	90	-31	-41	101	65	905	.686	405	75		19	*S/32	11.5
■ RANDY BUSH	Bush, Robert Randall b: 10/5/58, Dover, Del. BL/TL, 6'1", 186 lbs. Deb: 5/01/82																											
1982	Min-A	55	119	13	29	6	1	4	13	8	28	.244	.308	.412	.719	95	-1	-1	100	85	16	.659	0	0	0	-1	D/O	-0.1
1983	Min-A	124	373	43	93	24	3	11	56	34	51	.249	.324	.418	.742	97	1	-2	105	116	50	.684	0	1	-1	0	*D/1	-0.1
1984	Min-A	113	311	46	69	17	1	11	43	31	60	.222	.301	.389	.690	85	-5	-7	106	111	38	.641	1	2	-1	0	D/1	-0.7
1985	Min-A	97	234	26	56	13	3	10	35	24	30	.239	.323	.449	.772	105	3	1	103	103	36	.757	3	0	1	-6	OD/1	-0.4
1986	Min-A	130	357	50	96	19	7	7	45	39	63	.269	.348	.420	.768	101	5	1	108	105	53	.731	5	3	-0	-11	*O/1D	-1.2
1987	Min-A	122	293	46	74	10	2	11	46	43	49	.253	.354	.413	.767	108	2	4	96	119	45	.776	10	3	1	-10	O/1D	-0.6
1988	Min-A	136	394	51	103	20	3	14	51	58	49	.261	.369	.434	.803	117	14	11	106	95	64	.807	8	6	-1	-9	*O/1D	-0.1
Total	7	777	2081	275	520	109	20	68	289	237	330	.250	.337	.420	.756	102	19	8	104	107	301	.740	27	15	-1	-38	OD/1	-3.2
■ DOC BUSHONG	Bushong, Albert John b: 9/15/1856, Philadelphia, Pa. d: 8/19/08, Brooklyn, N.Y. BR/TR, 5'11", 165 lbs. Deb: 7/19/1875																											
1875	Atl-n	1	5	0	3							.600															/C	
1876	Phi-N	5	21	4	1	0	0	0	1	0	0	.048	.048	.048	.095	-69	-4	-4	99	345	0	.050				0	/C	-0.2
1880	Wor-N	41	146	13	25	3	0	0	19	1	16	.171	.177	.192	.369	22	-11	-13	113	248	5	.240				15	C/O3	0.4
1881	Wor-N	76	275	35	64	7	4	0	21	21	23	.233	.287	.287	.574	77	-5	-7	105	94	23	.474				16	*C	0.7
1882	Wor-N	69	253	20	40	4	1	1	15	5	17	.158	.174	.194	.368	18	-22	-22	100	99	9	.254				3	*C	-1.2
1883	Cle-N	63	215	15	37	5	0	0	9	7	19	.172	.198	.195	.394	19	-20	-21	105	74	9	.275				15	C	-0.2
1884	Cle-N	62	203	24	48	6	1	0	10	17	11	.236	.295	.276	.571	79	-4	-5	102	61	17	.471				3	C/O	0.3
1885	StL-a	85	300	42	80	13	5	0		11		.267	.297	.343	.640	112	1	4	93	0	31	.527				4	*C/3	1.8
1886	StL-a	107	386	56	86	8	0	1		31		.223	.281	.251	.532	62	-13	-20	111	0	31	.467	12			9	*C/1	-0.3
1887	StL-a	53	201	35	51	4	0	0		11		.254	.299	.274	.573	57	-10	-13	110	0	21	.547	14			-0	C/O3	-0.3
1888	Bro-a	69	253	23	53	5	1	0	16	5		.209	.231	.237	.468	50	-13	-15	105	81	16	.380	9			-9	C	-1.5
1889	Bro-a	25	84	15	13	1	0	0	8	9	7	.155	.237	.167	.403	18	-9	-8	96	163	4	.352	2			0	C	-0.6
1890	Bro-N	16	55	5	13	2	0	0	7	6	4	.236	.311	.273	.584	72	-2	-2	100	141	5	.548	2			0	C/O	-0.1
Total	12	671	2392	287	511	58	12	2	106	124	97	.214	.254	.250	.505	56	-111	-126	104	68	172	.408	39			55	C/O31	-1.2
■ JOE BUSKEY	Buskey, Joseph Henry "Jazzbow" b: 12/18/02, Cumberland, Md. d: 4/11/49, Cumberland, Md. BR/TR, 5'10", 175 lbs. Deb: 4/19/26																											
1926	Phi-N	5	8	1	0	0	0	0	0	1	1	.000	.111	.000	.111	-66	-2	-2	103	0	0	.125	0			0	/S	-0.1
■ MIKE BUSKEY	Buskey, Michael Thomas b: 1/13/49, San Francisco, Cal. BR/TR, 5'11", 160 lbs. Deb: 9/02/77																											
1977	Phi-N	6	7	1	2	0	1	0	1	0	1	.286	.375	.571	.946	149	0	0	100	100	2	1.000	0	0	0	0	/S	0.2
■ RAY BUSSE	Busse, Raymond Edward b: 9/25/48, Daytona Beach, Fla. BR/TR, 6'4", 175 lbs. Deb: 7/24/71																											
1971	Hou-N	10	34	2	5	3	0	0	4	2	9	.147	.194	.235	.430	23	-4	-3	93	204	2	.345	0	0	0	0	/S3	-0.2
1973	StL-N	24	70	6	10	4	2	2	5	5	21	.143	.200	.343	.543	53	-5	-5	91	67	3	.446	0	1	-1	-3	S	-0.4
	Hou-N	15	17	1	1	0	0	0	0	1	12	.059	.111	.059	.170	-54	-3	-3	95	0	0	.125	0	0	0	0	/S3	-0.2
	Yr	39	87	7	11	4	2	2	5	6	33	.126	.183	.287	.470	31	-9	-8	92	43	5	.403	0	1	-1	-3		-0.6
1974	Hou-N	19	34	3	7	1	0	0	0	3	12	.206	.270	.235	.506	43	-3	-2	98	0	2	.379	0	0	0	0	/3	-0.2
Total	3	68	155	12	23	8	2	2	9	11	54	.148	.205	.265	.469	32	-15	-14	93	74	7	.385	0	1	-1	-2	/S3	-1.0
■ HANK BUTCHER	Butcher, Henry Joseph b: 7/12/1886, Chicago, Ill. d: 12/28/79, Hazel Crest, Ill. BR/TR, 5'10", 180 lbs. Deb: 7/08/11																											
1911	Cle-A	38	133	21	32	7	3	1	11	11		.241	.303	.361	.664	83	-3	-4	103	74	17	.683	9			0	O	-0.5
1912	Cle-A	24	82	9	16	4	1	1	10	6		.195	.250	.305	.555	58	-5	-5	101	122	6	.485	1			1	O	-0.4
Total	2	62	215	30	48	11	4	2	21	17		.223	.283	.340	.623	73	-8	-9	102	92	23	.605	10			1	/O	-0.9
■ SAL BUTERA	Butera, Salvatore Philip b: 9/25/52, Richmond Hill, N.Y BR/TR, 6', 190 lbs. Deb: 4/10/80																											
1980	Min-A	34	85	4	23	1	0	0	2	3	6	.271	.303	.282	.586	57	-4	-5	109	32	7	.424	0	0	0	1	C/D	-0.2
1981	Min-A	62	167	13	40	7	1	0	18	22	14	.240	.328	.293	.621	77	-4	-5	105	144	16	.526	0	0	0	4	C/1D	0.2
1982	Min-A	54	126	9	32	2	0	0	8	17	12	.254	.347	.270	.617	72	-4	-4	100	94	12	.520	0	0	0	1	C	0.0
1983	Det-A	4	5	1	1	0	0	0	0	0	0	.200	.200	.200	.400	11	-1	-1	96	0	0	.250	0	0	0	0	/C	0.0
1984	Mon-N	3	3	0	0	0	0	0	0	1	0	.000	.250	.000	.250	-27	-0	-0	91	0	0	.333	0	0	0	0	/C	0.0
1985	Mon-N	67	120	11	24	1	0	3	12	13	12	.200	.284	.283	.567	63	-6	-6	94	111	11	.495	0	0	0	-9	C/P	-1.2
1986	Cin-N	56	113	14	27	6	1	2	16	21	10	.239	.358	.363	.721	95	1	-0	104	136	15	.681	0	0	0	-1	C/P	0.0
1987	Cin-N	5	11	1	2	0	0	1	2	1	6	.182	.250	.455	.705	79	-0	-0	104	100	1	.667	0	0	0	0	/C	0.0
	Min-A	51	111	7	19	5	0	1	12	7	16	.171	.220	.243	.464	25	-12	-11	96	160	5	.343	0	0	0	-4	C	-1.0
1988	Tor-A	23	60	3	14	2	1	1	6	1	9	.233	.246	.350	.596	65	-3	-3	100	99	5	.468	0	0	0	-0	C	-0.1
Total	9	359	801	63	182	24	3	8	76	86	85	.227	.304	.295	.599	66	-34	-35	101	115	71	.524	0	0	0	-8	C/DP1	-2.3
■ ED BUTKA	Butka, Edward Luke "Babe" b: 1/7/16, Canonsburg, Pa. BR/TR, 6'3", 193 lbs. Deb: 9/26/43																											
1943	Was-A	3	9	0	3	1	0	0	1	0	3	.333	.333	.444	.778	122	0	0	104	91	1	.667	0	0	0	0	/1	0.0
1944	Was-A	15	41	1	8	1	0	0	1	2	11	.195	.233	.220	.452	33	-4	-3	90	40	2	.333	0	0	0	-0	1	-0.4
Total	2	18	50	1	11	2	0	0	2	2	14	.220	.250	.260	.510	50	-4	-3	92	49	4	.385	0	0	0	-0	/1	-0.4
■ ART BUTLER	Butler, Arthur Edward (born Arthur Edward Bouthillier) b: 12/19/1887, Fall River, Mass. d: 10/7/84, Fall River, Mass. BR/TR, 5'9", 160 lbs. Deb: 4/14/11																											
1911	Bos-N	27	68	11	12	2	0	0	2	6	6	.176	.263	.206	.469	31	-6	-6	103	48	4	.393	0			0	3/2S	-0.5
1912	Pit-N	43	154	19	42	4	2	1	17	15	13	.273	.337	.344	.681	88	-3	-2	99	104	19	.625	2			-4	2	-0.7
1913	Pit-N	82	214	40	60	9	3	0	20	32	14	.280	.379	.350	.729	114	4	5	96	97	31	.766	9			-11	2S/3O	-0.4
1914	StL-N	86	274	29	55	12	3	1	24	39	23	.201	.311	.277	.589	73	-7	-9	104	112	28	.612	14			-10	S/O	-1.6
1915	StL-N	130	469	73	119	12	5	1	31	47	34	.254	.323	.307	.630	91	-4	-4	100	85	52	.599	26	14	-1	-30	*S	-3.5
1916	StL-N	86	110	9	23	5	0	0	7	7	12	.209	.256	.255	.511	59	-6	-5	97	99	8	.437	3			-4	O/2S3	-1.0
Total	6	454	1289	181	311	44	13	3	101	146	102	.241	.323	.303	.626	84	-22	-22	100	95	141	.605	54	14		-59	S/2O3	-7.7
■ BRETT BUTLER	Butler, Brett Morgan b: 6/15/57, Los Angeles, Cal. BL/TL, 5'10", 160 lbs. Deb: 8/20/81																											
1981	Atl-N	40	126	17	32	2	3	0	4	19	17	.254	.352	.317	.669	91	-1	-1	100	39	17	.716	9	1	2	-0	O	0.0
1982	Atl-N	89	240	35	52	2	0	0	7	25	35	.217	.291	.225	.516	43	-17	-19	107	51	19	.508	21	8	2	-6	O	-2.4
1983	Atl-N	151	549	84	154	21	**13**	5	37	54	56	.281	.347	.393	.741	99	4	0	106	65	76	.737	39	22	-2	8	*O	0.5
1984	Cle-A	159	602	108	162	25	9	3	49	86	62	.269	.364	.355	.720	94	3	-2	106	84	87	.762	52	22	2	5	*O	0.0
1985	Cle-A	152	591	106	184	28	14	5	50	63	42	.311	.379	.431	.810	129	19	23	94	71	100	.841	47	20	2	15	*O/D	3.7
1986	Cle-A	161	587	92	163	17	**14**	4	51	70	65	.278	.359	.375	.733	104	3	5	98	93	84	.729	32	15	1	0	*O	0.1
1987	Cle-A	137	522	91	154	25	8	9	41	91	55	.295	.401	.425	.826	117	19	17	103	58	97	.897	33	16	0	9	*O	2.1

YEAR	TM/L	G	AB	R	H	2B	3B	HR	RBI	BB	SO	AVG	OBP	SLG	PRO	/A	BR	/A	PF	CHI	RC	TA	SB	CS	SBR	FR	POS	TPR
1988	SF-N	157	568	**109**	163	27	9	6	43	97	64	.287	.395	.398	.793	136	25	29	94	75	99	.867	43	20	1	-2	*O	2.6
Total	8	1046	3785	642	1064	147	70	32	282	505	396	.281	.368	.382	.750	107	55	54	100	72	578	.788	276	124	8	29	*O/D	6.6
■ **FRANK BUTLER** Butler, Frank Dean "Stuffy" or "Goldbrick" b: 7/18/1860, Savannah, Ga. d: 7/10/45, Jacksonville, Fla BL/TL, Deb: 7/30/1895																												
1895	NY-N	5	22	5	6	1	0	0	2	1	1	.273	.304	.318	.623	66	-1	-1	95	70	2	.500	0			0	/O	0.0
■ **KID BUTLER** Butler, Frank E. b: 1862, Boston, Mass. d: 4/9/21, S.Boston, Mass. Deb: 5/20/1884																												
1884	Bos-U	71	255	36	43	15	0	0		12		.169	.206	.227	.433	47	-14	-13	98	0	12	.330	0			-5	O2/S3	-1.5
■ **JOHN BUTLER** Butler, John Albert (played under name of Frederick King In 1901) b: 7/26/1879, Boston, Mass. d: 2/2/50, Boston, Mass. BR/TR, 5'7", 170 lbs. Deb: 9/28/01																												
1901	Mil-A	1	3	0	0	0	0	0	0	1		.000	.250	.000	.250	-26	-0	-0	95	0	0	.333	0			0	/C	0.0
1904	StL-N	12	37	0	6	1	0	0	1	4		.162	.244	.189	.433	36	-3	-3	99	52	2	.355	0			-2	C	-0.2
1906	Bro-N	1	0	0	0	0	0	0	0	0		—	—	—	—	—	0	0	87	—	—	—	0			0	/C	0.0
1907	Bro-N	30	79	6	10	1	0	0	2	9		.127	.216	.139	.355	14	-8	-7	94	69	2	.290	0			-1	C/O	-0.6
Total	4	44	119	6	16	2	0	0	3	14		.134	.226	.151	.377	20	-11	-10	96	62	6	.311	0			-3	/CO	-0.8
■ **JOHNNY BUTLER** Butler, John Stephen "Trolley Line" b: 3/20/1893, Fall River, Kan. d: 4/29/67, Seal Beach, Cal. BR/TR, 6', 175 lbs. Deb: 4/18/26 C																												
1926	Bro-N	147	501	54	135	27	5	1	68	54	44	.269	.346	.349	.696	88	-7	-7	99	135	62	.656	6			-2	*S3/2	0.0
1927	Bro-N	149	521	39	124	13	6	2	57	34	33	.238	.292	.298	.590	57	-31	-32	103	126	46	.514	9			-10	S3	-3.0
1928	Chi-N	62	174	17	47	7	0	0	16	19	7	.270	.352	.310	.662	79	-6	-4	95	105	20	.614	2			0	3/S	-0.2
1929	StL-N	17	55	5	9	1	1	0	5	4	5	.164	.220	.218	.439	9	-8	-8	98	143	3	.348	0			-1	/3S	-0.5
Total	4	375	1251	115	315	48	12	3	146	111	89	.252	.320	.317	.636	70	-52	-52	100	127	130	.575	17			-13	S3/2	-3.7
■ **DICK BUTLER** Butler, Richard H. b: Brooklyn, N.Y. Deb: 6/16/1897																												
1897	Lou-N	10	38	3	7	0	0	0	2	0		.184	.184	.184	.368	-2	-5	-5	95	85	2	.258	1			0	C	-0.4
1899	Was-N	12	36	4	10	0	1	0	1	2		.278	.316	.333	.649	84	-1	-1	96	26	4	.577	1			0	C	0.0
Total	2	22	74	7	17	0	1	0	3	2		.230	.250	.257	.507	40	-6	-6	96	55	6	.404	2			0	/C	-0.4
■ **BILL BUTLER** Butler, W. J. b: 1861, New Orleans, La. Deb: 6/29/1884																												
1884	Ind-a	9	31	7	7	3	2	0		1		.226	.250	.452	.702	131	1	1	96	0	4	.625				0	/O	0.1
■ **KID BUTLER** Butler, Willis Everett b: 8/9/1887, Franklin, Pa. d: 2/22/64, Richmond, Cal. BR/TR, 5'11", 155 lbs. Deb: 4/30/07																												
1907	StL-A	20	59	4	13	2	0	0	6	2		.220	.246	.254	.500	62	-3	-2	98	143	4	.391	1			0	2/3S	-0.2
■ **FRANK BUTTERY** Buttery, Frank b: 5/13/1851, Silver Mine, Conn. d: 12/16/02, Silver Mine, Conn. Deb: 4/26/1872																												
1872	Man-n	17	88	18	26							.295															/P3O	
■ **JOE BUZAS** Buzas, Joseph John b: 10/2/19, Alpha, N.J. BR/TR, 6'1", 180 lbs. Deb: 4/17/45																												
1945	NY-A	30	65	8	17	2	1	0	6	2	5	.262	.284	.323	.607	71	-2	-3	107	103	6	.500	2	0	1	-1	S	-0.1
■ **BURLEY BYERS** Byers, Burley (born Christopher A. Bayer) b: 12/19/1875, Louisville, Ky. d: 5/30/33, Louisville, Ky. 175 lbs. Deb: 6/17/1899																												
1899	Lou-N	1	3	0	0	0	0	0	0	0		.000	.000	.000	.000	-97	-1	-1	103	0	0	.000	0			0	/S	0.0
■ **BILL BYERS** Byers, James William b: 10/3/1877, Bridgeton, Ind. d: 9/8/48, Baltimore, Md. TR , 5'7", Deb: 4/15/04																												
1904	StL-N	19	60	3	13	0	0	0	4	1		.217	.230	.217	.446	40	-4	-4	99	113	3	.298	0			-3	C/1	-0.5
■ **RANDY BYERS** Byers, Randell Parker b: 10/2/64, Bridgeton, N.J. BL/TR, 6'2", 180 lbs. Deb: 9/07/87																												
1987	SD-N	10	16	1	5	1	0	0	1	1	5	.313	.353	.375	.728	96	-0	-0	97	66	2	.727	1	0	0	0	/O	0.0
1988	SD-N	11	10	0	2	1	0	0	0	0	5	.200	.200	.300	.500	43	-1	-1	97	0	1	.375	0	0	0	-1	/O	-0.1
Total	2	21	26	1	7	2	0	0	1	1	10	.269	.296	.346	.642	77	-1	-1	97	42	3	.579	1	0	0	-1	/O	-0.1
■ **SAMMY BYRD** Byrd, Samuel Dewey "Babe Ruth's Legs" b: 10/15/07, Bremen, Ga. d: 5/11/81, Mesa, Ariz. BR/TR, 5'10.5", 175 lbs. Deb: 5/12/29																												
1929	NY-A	62	170	32	53	12	0	5	28	28	18	.312	.409	.471	.880	128	7	8	99	101	33	.901	1	4	-2	-1	O	0.2
1930	NY-A	92	218	46	62	12	2	6	31	30	18	.284	.371	.440	.811	117	2	6	90	90	38	.834	5	1	1	-14	O	-0.9
1931	NY-A	115	248	51	67	18	2	3	32	29	26	.270	.349	.395	.744	97	-2	-1	98	99	36	.735	5	0	2	-10	O	-1.3
1932	NY-A	105	209	49	62	12	1	8	30	30	20	.297	.385	.478	.863	128	7	9	95	81	39	.879	1	2	-1	-14	O	-0.8
1933	NY-A	85	107	26	30	6	1	2	11	15	12	.280	.369	.411	.780	117	1	3	91	73	17	.756	0	1	-1	-17	O	-1.5
1934	NY-A	106	191	32	47	8	0	3	23	18	22	.246	.318	.335	.653	72	-9	-8	96	105	21	.582	1	2	-1	-13	*O	-2.1
1935	Cin-N	121	416	51	109	25	4	9	52	37	51	.262	.322	.406	.729	101	-4	0	93	98	56	.669	4			-3	*O	-0.7
1936	Cin-N	59	141	17	35	8	0	2	13	11	11	.248	.303	.348	.650	77	-5	-4	97	84	15	.545	0			-0	O	-0.5
Total	8	745	1700	304	465	101	10	38	220	198	178	.274	.350	.412	.762	104	-2	11	95	93	255	.735	17	10		-71	O	-7.6
■ **BOBBY BYRNE** Byrne, Robert Matthew b: 12/31/1884, St.Louis, Mo. d: 12/31/64, Wayne, Pa. BR/TR, 5'7.5", 145 lbs. Deb: 4/11/07																												
1907	StL-N	149	559	55	143	11	5	0	29	35		.256	.300	.293	.593	92	-8	-6	96	64	57	.529	21			22	*3/S	1.8
1908	StL-N	127	439	27	84	7	1	0	14	23		.191	.232	.212	.443	46	-27	-24	94	59	24	.372	16			8	*3/S	-1.4
1909	StL-N	105	421	61	90	13	6	1	33	46		.214	.302	.280	.582	85	-8	-6	96	86	40	.580	21			6	*3	0.2
	Pit-N	46	168	31	43	6	2	0	7	32		.256	.387	.315	.703	114	6	5	105	41	23	.776	8			-3	3	0.3
	Yr	151	589	92	133	19	8	1	40	78		.226	.327	.290	.618	94	-2	-1	99	73	64	.634	29			3		0.5
1910	Pit-N	148	602	101	**178**	**43**	12	2	52	66	27	.296	.366	.417	.783	115	21	12	112	61	104	.835	36			-8	*3	0.5
1911	Pit-N	153	598	96	155	24	17	2	52	67	41	.259	.342	.366	.708	97	-1	-2	101	69	82	.716	23			-3	*3	0.0
1912	Pit-N	130	528	99	152	31	11	3	35	54	40	.288	.358	.405	.764	110	6	7	99	47	83	.777	20			-16	*3	-0.8
1913	Pit-N	113	448	54	121	22	0	1	47	29	28	.270	.322	.326	.647	89	-9	-6	96	110	49	.581	10			-9	*3	-1.6
	Phi-N	19	58	9	13	1	0	1	4	5	3	.224	.308	.293	.601	64	-2	-3	112	73	6	.578	2			-1	3	-0.4
	Yr	132	506	63	134	23	0	2	51	34	31	.265	.320	.322	.642	85	-11	-9	98	106	54	.581	12			-10		-2.0
1914	Phi-N	126	467	61	127	12	1	0	26	45	44	.272	.339	.302	.640	91	-4	-4	100	71	49	.579	9			1	*23	-0.2
1915	Phi-N	105	387	50	81	6	4	0	21	39	28	.209	.290	.245	.536	58	-16	-19	107	81	28	.450	4	12	-6	-3	*3	-2.6
1916	Phi-N	48	141	22	33	10	1	0	9	14	7	.234	.308	.319	.627	97	-1	-0	96	79	17	.611	6			-1	3	-0.1
1917	Phi-N	13	14	1	5	0	0	0	0	1	2	.357	.400	.357	.757	124	1	0	108	0	2	.667	0			0	/3	0.0
	Chi-A	1	1	0	0	0	0	0	0	0	0	.000	.000	.000	.000	-99	-0	-0	98	0	0	.000	0			0	/2	0.0
Total	11	1283	4831	667	1225	186	60	10	329	456	220	.254	.323	.323	.646	91	-43	-47	101	70	564	.617	176	12		-7	*32/S	-4.3
■ **JIM BYRNES** Byrnes, James Joseph b: 1/5/1880, San Francisco, Cal. d: 7/31/41, San Francisco, Cal BR/TR, 5'9", 150 lbs. Deb: 4/19/06																												
1906	Phi-A	10	23	2	4	0	1	0	0	0		.174	.174	.261	.435	39	-2	-2	94	0	1	.316	0			1	/C	0.0
■ **MILT BYRNES** Byrnes, Milton John "Skippy" b: 11/15/16, St.Louis, Mo. d: 2/1/79, St.Louis, Mo. BL/TL, 5'10.5", 170 lbs. Deb: 4/21/43																												
1943	StL-A	129	429	58	120	28	7	4	50	54	49	.280	.362	.406	.767	124	13	13	100	98	65	.714	1	4	-2	3	*O	1.1
1944	StL-A	128	407	63	120	20	4	4	45	68	50	.295	.396	.393	.789	123	16	15	102	94	67	.758	1	7	-4	4	*O	1.2
1945	StL-A	133	442	53	110	29	4	8	59	78	84	.249	.363	.387	.750	102	12	3	115	112	69	.736	1	3	-2	11	*O/1	0.8
Total	3	390	1278	174	350	77	15	16	154	200	183	.274	.373	.395	.768	115	41	32	106	102	201	.749	3	14	-8	18	O/1	3.1
■ **PUTSY CABALLERO** Caballero, Ralph Joseph b: 11/5/27, New Orleans, La. BR/TR, 5'10", 170 lbs. Deb: 9/14/44																												
1944	Phi-N	4	4	0	0	0	0	0	0	0	1	.000	.000	.000	.000	-99	-1	-1	100	0	0	.000	0			-0	/3	0.0
1945	Phi-N	9	1	1	0	0	0	0	1	0	0	.000	.000	.000	.000	-99	-0	-0	96	0	0	.000	0			-0	/3	0.0
1947	Phi-N	2	7	2	1	0	0	0	0	1	0	.143	.250	.143	.393	7	-1	-1	100	0	0	.333	0			0	/23	0.0
1948	Phi-N	113	351	33	86	12	1	0	19	24	18	.245	.293	.285	.578	61	-21	-18	94	71	29	.478	7			-2	32	-1.9
1949	Phi-N	29	68	8	19	3	0	0	3	0	3	.279	.279	.324	.603	61	-4	-4	101	51	6	.431	0			-2	2/S	-0.4
1950	Phi-N	46	24	12	4	0	0	0	0	2	2	.167	.231	.167	.397	7	-3	-3	97	0	1	.350	1			-0	/23S	-0.2
1951	Phi-N	84	161	15	30	3	2	1	11	12	7	.186	.243	.248	.491	33	-15	-15	97	99	9	.381	1	2	-1	-11	2/3S	-2.4
1952	Phi-N	35	42	10	10	3	0	0	6	2	3	.238	.273	.310	.582	61	-2	-2	101	180	2	.432	1	0	0	0	/S23	0.0
Total	8	322	658	81	150	21	3	1	40	41	34	.228	.273	.274	.547	50	-48	-45	96	79	47	.449	10	2		-14	23/S	-4.9
■ **ENOS CABELL** Cabell, Enos Milton b: 10/8/49, Fort Riley, Kan. BR/TR, 6'4", 170 lbs. Deb: 9/17/72																												
1972	Bal-A	3	5	0	0	0	0	0	1	0	0	.000	.000	.000	.000	-99	-1	-1	98	0	0	.000	0	0	0	0	/1	-0.1

YEAR	TM/L	G	AB	R	H	2B	3B	HR	RBI	BB	SO	AVG	OBP	SLG	PRO	/A	BR	/A	PF	CHI	RC	TA	SB	CS	SBR	FR	POS	TPR
1973	Bal-A	32	47	12	10	2	0	1	3	3	7	.213	.260	.319	.579	58	-2	-3	107	65	3	.463	1	3	-2	0	1/3	-0.5
1974	Bal-A	80	174	24	42	4	2	3	17	7	20	.241	.271	.339	.610	80	-6	-5	93	98	14	.504	5	3	-0	-1	103/2D	-0.7
1975	Hou-N	117	348	43	92	17	6	2	43	18	53	.264	.306	.365	.671	91	-8	-5	94	125	38	.597	12	3	2	-1	O13	-0.8
1976	Hou-N	144	586	85	160	13	7	2	43	29	79	.273	.310	.329	.639	94	-15	-6	86	80	61	.579	35	8	6	-11	*3/1	-1.3
1977	Hou-N	150	625	101	176	36	7	16	68	27	55	.282	.315	.438	.753	108	-2	3	93	81	82	.722	42	22	-1	-3	*3/1S	-0.1
1978	Hou-N	162	660	92	195	31	8	7	71	22	80	.295	.323	.398	.722	106	-1	3	95	95	81	.654	33	15	1	-14	*31/S	-1.1
1979	Hou-N	155	603	60	164	30	5	6	67	21	68	.272	.300	.368	.668	90	-17	-10	90	117	60	.596	37	18	0	-19	*31	-3.8
1980	Hou-N	152	604	69	167	23	8	2	55	26	84	.276	.307	.351	.658	85	-14	-13	98	106	61	.562	21	13	-2	-17	*3/1	-3.3
1981	SF-N	96	396	41	101	20	1	2	36	10	47	.255	.275	.326	.601	67	-16	-19	105	111	33	.474	6	7	-2	6	13	-1.9
1982	Det-A	125	464	45	121	17	3	2	37	15	48	.261	.285	.323	.609	67	-21	-22	100	97	41	.504	15	6	1	-4	13/O	-2.8
1983	Det-A	121	392	62	122	23	5	5	46	16	41	.311	.340	.434	.774	116	5	7	96	97	51	.654	4	8	-4	8	*1/3SD	0.7
1984	Hou-N	127	436	52	135	17	3	8	44	21	47	.310	.343	.417	.760	122	6	10	93	84	56	.654	8	11	-4	-3	*1	0.0
1985	Hou-N	60	143	20	35	8	1	2	14	16	15	.245	.321	.357	.677	93	-2	-1	96	98	16	.614	3	1	0	-1	1	-0.2
	LA-N	57	192	20	56	11	0	0	22	14	21	.292	.340	.349	.689	100	-2	-0	93	131	24	.630	6	2	1	5	31/O	0.5
	Yr	117	335	40	91	19	1	2	36	30	36	.272	.332	.352	.684	97	-4	-1	95	115	42	.636	9	3	1	5		0.3
1986	LA-N	107	277	27	71	11	0	2	29	14	26	.256	.297	.318	.615	74	-12	-10	94	123	26	.530	10	4	1	3	1O/3	-0.8
Total	15	1688	5952	753	1647	263	56	60	596	259	691	.277	.309	.370	.679	93	-108	-70	94	100	646	.614	238	124	-3	-52	31O/DS2	-16.2
■ **AL CABRERA**	Cabrera, Alfredo A. b: 1883, Canary Islands d: Havana, Cuba TR , Deb: 5/16/13																											
1913	StL-N	1	2	0	0	0	0	0	0	0	0	.000	.000	.000	.000	-99	-1	-0	93	0	0	.000	0			0	/S	0.0
■ **CRAIG CACEK**	Cacek, Craig Thomas b: 9/10/54, Hollywood, Cal. BR/TR, 6'1", 200 lbs. Deb: 6/18/77																											
1977	Hou-N	7	20	0	1	0	0	0	1	1	3	.050	.095	.050	.145	-65	-5	-4	93	400	0	.095	0	0	0	0	/1	-0.3
■ **CHARLIE CADY**	Cady, Charles B. b: 12/1865, Chicago, Ill. d: 6/7/09, Kankakee, Ill. 5'11", 180 lbs. Deb: 9/05/1883																											
1883	Cle-N	3	11	0	0	0	0	0	0	1	5	.000	.083	.000	.083	-69	-2	-2	105	0	0	.091				0	/OP	-0.1
1884	CP-U	6	20	4	2	1	1	0		1		.100	.143	.250	.393	31	-1	-1	99	0	1	.333	0			0	/PO	0.0
	KC-U	2	3	0	0	0	0	0		0		.000	.000	.000	.000	-99	-1	-1	87	0	0	.000	0			0	/C2	0.0
	Yr	8	23	4	2	1	1	0		1		.087	.125	.217	.342	14	-2	-2	96	0	1	.286	0			0		0.0
Total	2	11	34	4	2	1	1	0	0	2	5	.059	.111	.147	.258	-17	-4	-4	100	0	1	.219	0			0	/PO2C	-0.1
■ **HICK CADY**	Cady, Forrest Leroy b: 1/26/1886, Bishop Hill, Ill. d: 3/3/46, Cedar Rapids, Iowa BR/TR, 6'2", 179 lbs. Deb: 4/26/12																											
1912	Bos-A	47	135	19	35	13	2	0	9	10		.259	.324	.385	.710	96	0	-1	107	58	17	.650	0			-5	C/1	0.0
1913	Bos-A	40	96	10	24	5	2	0	6	5	14	.250	.294	.344	.638	84	-2	-2	103	65	10	.556	1			-0	C	0.0
1914	Bos-A	61	159	14	41	6	1	0	8	12	22	.258	.310	.308	.618	88	-3	-3	98	61	16	.529	2	1	0	-5	C	-0.3
1915	Bos-A	78	205	25	57	10	2	0	17	19	25	.278	.342	.346	.689	107	1	2	99	81	25	.607	0	2	-1	-5	C	0.1
1916	Bos-A	78	162	5	31	6	3	0	13	15	16	.191	.264	.265	.529	63	-8	-7	94	108	12	.450	0			-8	C/1	-1.3
1917	Bos-A	17	46	4	7	1	1	0	2	1	6	.152	.170	.217	.388	17	-5	-5	108	72	2	.282	0			-1	C	-0.4
1919	Phi-N	34	98	6	21	6	0	1	19	4	8	.214	.252	.306	.559	65	-4	-4	104	224	8	.468	1			1	C	-0.1
Total	7	355	901	83	216	47	11	1	74	66	91	.240	.297	.320	.616	83	-21	-21	100	92	89	.531	4	3		-23	C/1	-2.0
■ **TOM CAFEGO**	Cafego, Thomas b: 8/21/11, Whipple, W.Va. d: 10/29/61, Detroit, Mich. BL/TR, 5'10", 160 lbs. Deb: 9/03/37																											
1937	StL-A	4	4	1	0	0	0	0	0	0	1	.000	.000	.000	.000	-99	-1	-1	99	0	0	.000	0	0	0	-0	/O	-0.1
■ **JOE CAFFIE**	Caffie, Joseph Clifford "Rabbit" b: 2/14/31, Ramer, Ala. BL/TR, 5'10.5", 180 lbs. Deb: 9/13/56																											
1956	Cle-A	12	38	7	13	0	0	0	1	4	8	.342	.432	.342	.774	105	1	1	101	29	6	.815	3	2	-0	1	O	0.1
1957	Cle-A	32	89	14	24	2	1	3	10	4	11	.270	.301	.416	.717	92	-1	-1	102	86	11	.612	0	1	-1	0	O	-0.2
Total	2	44	127	21	37	2	1	3	11	8	19	.291	.343	.394	.737	97	-0	-1	101	67	17	.670	3	3	-1	1	/O	-0.1
■ **BEN CAFFYN**	Caffyn, Benjamin Thomas b: 2/10/1880, Peoria, Ill. d: 11/22/42, Peoria, Ill. BL/TL, Deb: 8/21/06																											
1906	Cle-A	30	103	16	20	4	0	0	3	12		.194	.278	.233	.511	60	-4	-4	103	46	7	.458	2			-1	O	-0.6
■ **WAYNE CAGE**	Cage, Wayne Levell b: 11/23/51, Monroe, La. BL/TL, 6'4", 205 lbs. Deb: 4/22/78																											
1978	Cle-A	36	98	11	24	6	1	4	13	9	28	.245	.308	.449	.757	119	1	2	93	92	13	.692	1	2	-1	0	D1	0.1
1979	Cle-A	29	56	6	13	2	0	1	6	5	16	.232	.295	.321	.617	63	-3	-3	106	110	5	.500	0	2	-1	0	/1D	-0.4
Total	2	65	154	17	37	8	1	5	19	14	44	.240	.304	.403	.706	96	-2	-1	98	98	17	.631	1	4	-2	0	/D1	-0.3
■ **JOHN CAHILL**	Cahill, John Patrick Francis "Patsy" b: 1864, San Francisco, Cal. d: 11/1/01, Pleasanton, Cal. BR/TR, 5'7.5", 168 lbs. Deb: 5/31/1884																											
1884	Col-a	59	210	28	46	3	3	0		6		.219	.248	.262	.510	71	-7	-6	97	0	14	.384				-3	O/SP	-0.8
1886	StL-N	125	463	43	92	17	6	1	32	9	79	.199	.214	.268	.482	48	-30	-27	95	84	31	.402	16			1	*O/PS3	-2.1
1887	Ind-N	68	263	22	54	4	3	0	26	9	5	.205	.234	.243	.478	36	-23	-21	96	133	24	.517	34			-4	O/3PS	-2.0
Total	3	252	936	93	192	24	12	1	58	24	84	.205	.227	.260	.487	49	-60	-54	96	79	68	.430	50			-6	O/3PS	-4.9
■ **TOM CAHILL**	Cahill, Thomas H. b: 10/1868, Fall River, Mass. d: 12/25/1894, Scranton, Pa. Deb: 4/09/1891																											
1891	Lou-a	120	433	70	111	18	7	3	47	41	51	.256	.329	.351	.680	108	-2	5	90	86	64	.739	39			-0	CSO/23	0.7
■ **GEORGE CAITHAMER**	Caithamer, George Theodore "Sidel" b: 7/22/10, Chicago, Ill. d: 6/1/54, Chicago, Ill. BR/TR, 5'7.5", 160 lbs. Deb: 9/17/34																											
1934	Chi-A	5	19	1	6	1	0	0	3	1	5	.316	.350	.368	.718	86	-0	-0	99	146	2	.615	0	0	0	1	/C	0.0
■ **IVAN CALDERON**	Calderon, Ivan (Perez) b: 3/19/62, Fajardo, P.R. BR/TR, 5'11", 160 lbs. Deb: 8/10/84																											
1984	Sea-A	11	24	2	5	1	0	1	1	2	5	.208	.269	.375	.644	74	-1	-1	102	33	2	.545	1	0	0	-0	O	0.0
1985	Sea-A	67	210	37	60	16	4	8	28	19	45	.286	.351	.514	.865	141	9	11	95	84	34	.821	4	2	0	1	O/1D	1.0
1986	Sea-A	37	131	13	31	5	0	2	13	6	33	.237	.275	.321	.596	59	-7	-8	105	108	12	.510	3	1	0	-0	O	-0.8
	Chi-A	13	33	3	10	2	1	0	2	3	6	.303	.361	.424	.785	113	1	1	101	57	5	.739	0	0	0	-1	/OD	0.0
	Yr	50	164	16	41	7	1	2	15	9	39	.250	.293	.341	.635	70	-6	-7	104	97	17	.556	3	1	0	-1		-0.8
1987	Chi-A	144	542	93	159	38	2	28	83	60	109	.293	.365	.526	.891	123	26	19	109	95	102	.888	10	5	0	2	*O/D	1.6
1988	Chi-A	73	264	40	56	14	0	14	35	34	66	.212	.302	.424	.726	104	-0	1	97	96	33	.688	4	4	-1	-0	O/D	-0.1
Total	5	345	1204	188	321	76	7	53	162	124	264	.267	.337	.473	.811	114	28	23	103	92	188	.799	22	12	-1	2	O/D1	1.7
■ **SAM CALDERONE**	Calderone, Samuel Francis b: 2/6/26, Beverly, N.J. BR/TR, 5'10.5", 185 lbs. Deb: 4/19/50																											
1950	NY-N	34	67	9	20	1	0	1	12	2	5	.299	.319	.358	.677	79	-2	-2	98	171	7	.531	0			0	C	0.0
1953	NY-N	35	45	4	10	2	0	0	8	1	4	.222	.239	.267	.506	32	-4	-4	98	260	3	.371	0	0	0	-1	C	-0.3
1954	Mil-N	22	29	3	11	2	0	0	5	4	4	.379	.455	.448	.903	146	2	2	93	151	6	.895	0	0	0	0	C	0.3
Total	3	91	141	16	41	5	0	1	25	7	13	.291	.324	.348	.672	78	-5	-4	97	194	16	.554	0	0		-1	/C	0.0
■ **BRUCE CALDWELL**	Caldwell, Bruce b: 2/8/06, Ashton, R.I. d: 2/15/59, West Haven, Conn. BR/TR, 6', 195 lbs. Deb: 6/30/28																											
1928	Cle-A	18	27	2	6	1	1	0	3	2	2	.222	.300	.333	.633	63	-1	-2	106	114	3	.619	1	0	0	-2	O/1	-0.3
1932	Bro-N	7	11	2	1	0	0	0	2	2	2	.091	.231	.091	.322	-10	-2	-2	96	744	0	.300	0			0	/1	-0.1
Total	2	25	38	4	7	1	1	0	5	4	4	.184	.279	.263	.542	43	-3	-3	103	305	3	.516	1	0		-2	/O1	-0.4
■ **RAY CALDWELL**	Caldwell, Raymond Benjamin "Rube" or "Sum" b: 4/26/1888, Corydon, Pa. d: 8/17/67, Salamanca, N.Y. BL/TR, 6'2", 190 lbs. Deb: 9/09/10																											
1910	NY-A	6	6	0	0	0	0	0	0	0		.000	.000	.000	.000	-93	-1	-1	107	0	0	.000	0			-0	/P	0.0
1911	NY-A	59	147	14	40	4	1	0	17	11		.272	.323	.313	.636	70	-4	-6	111	125	16	.579	5			-2	PO	0.0
1912	NY-A	41	76	18	18	1	2	0	6	5		.237	.284	.303	.587	67	-3	-3	101	87	7	.552	4			1	P	0.0
1913	NY-A	59	97	10	28	3	2	0	11	3	15	.289	.310	.361	.671	95	-1	-1	101	112	11	.594	3			-1	P/O	0.2
1914	NY-A	59	113	9	22	4	0	0	10	7	24	.195	.248	.230	.478	44	-8	-8	100	144	7	.391	2	1	0	-3	P/1	0.0
1915	NY-A	72	144	27	35	4	1	4	20	9	32	.243	.288	.368	.656	98	-2	-1	98	105	15	.589	4	3	-1	-3	P	0.0
1916	NY-A	45	93	6	19	2	0	0	4	2	17	.204	.221	.226	.447	34	-8	-8	101	68	5	.324	1			-1	P/O	-0.6
1917	NY-A	63	124	12	32	6	1	2	12	16	16	.258	.343	.371	.714	110	3	2	107	83	16	.696	2			-3	P/O	0.0
1918	NY-A	65	151	14	44	10	0	1	18	13	23	.291	.352	.377	.729	127	3	4	95	109	20	.682	2			-1	PO	0.6
1919	Bos-A	33	48	5	13	1	1	0	4	0	9	.271	.271	.333	.604	76	-2	-2	91	91	4	.457	0			-2	P/O	0.0
	Cle-A	6	23	4	8	4	0	0	2	0	4	.348	.348	.522	.870	134	1	1	107	62	4	.800	0			-1	/P	0.0

YEAR	TM/L	G	AB	R	H	2B	3B	HR	RBI	BB	SO	AVG	OBP	SLG	PRO	/A	BR	/A	PF	CHI	RC	TA	SB	CS	SBR	FR	POS	TPR
	Yr	39	71	9	21	5	1	0	6	0	13	.296	.296	.394	.690	99	-1	-1	94	88	8	.560	0			-3		0.0
1920	Cle-A	41	89	17	19	3	0	0	7	10	13	.213	.300	.247	.547	44	-7	-7	104	112	7	.458	0	2	-1	-3	P	0.0
1921	Cle-A	38	53	2	11	4	0	1	3	2	5	.208	.236	.340	.576	46	-5	-5	99	49	4	.476	0	0	0	-0	P	0.0
Total	12	587	1164	138	289	46	8	8	114	78	158	.248	.297	.322	.619	78	-34	-36	101	102	117	.544	23	6		-19	P/O1	0.2
■ **JACK CALHOUN** Calhoun, John Charles "Red" b: 12/14/1879, Pittsburgh, Pa. d: 2/27/47, Cincinnati, Ohio BR/TR, 6', 185 lbs. Deb: 6/27/02																												
1902	StL-N	20	64	3	10	2	1	0	8	8		.156	.250	.219	.469	49	-4	-3	95	202	4	.426	1			-1	3/1O	-0.4
■ **BILL CALHOUN** Calhoun, William Davitte "Mary" b: 6/23/1890, Rockmart, Ga. d: 2/11/55, Sandersville, Ga. BL/TL, 6', 180 lbs. Deb: 4/24/13																												
1913	Bos-N	6	13	0	1	0	0	0	0	0	3	.077	.077	.077	.154	-59	-3	-3	95	0	0	.083	0			0	/1	-0.2
■ **MARTY CALLAGHAN** Callaghan, Martin Francis b: 6/9/1900, Norwood, Mass. d: 6/23/75, Norfolk, Mass. BL/TL, 5'10", 157 lbs. Deb: 4/13/22																												
1922	Chi-N	74	175	31	45	7	4	0	20	17	17	.257	.326	.343	.669	77	-7	-6	95	116	20	.602	2	3	-1	-10	O	-1.7
1923	Chi-N	61	129	18	29	1	3	0	14	8	18	.225	.275	.279	.554	45	-10	-11	104	137	9	.448	2	5	-2	-5	O	-1.8
1928	Cin-N	81	238	29	69	11	4	0	24	27	10	.290	.362	.370	.732	96	-2	-1	96	97	33	.710	5			-3	O	-0.6
1930	Cin-N	79	225	28	62	9	2	0	16	19	25	.276	.335	.333	.668	69	-13	-10	90	74	25	.589	1			3	O	-0.8
Total	4	295	767	106	205	28	13	0	74	71	70	.267	.332	.338	.669	74	-32	-27	95	101	87	.602	10	8		-15	O	-4.9
■ **DAVE CALLAHAN** Callahan, David Joseph b: 7/20/1888, Ottawa, Ill. d: 10/28/69, Ottawa, Ill. BL/TR, 5'10", 165 lbs. Deb: 9/14/10																												
1910	Cle-A	13	44	6	8	1	0	0	2	4		.182	.265	.205	.470	48	-3	-3	100	84	4	.528	5			0	O	-0.2
1911	Cle-A	6	16	1	4	0	1	0	0	1		.250	.294	.375	.669	84	-0	-0	103	0	2	.583	0			1	/O	0.0
Total	2	19	60	7	12	1	1	0	2	5		.200	.273	.250	.523	59	-3	-3	100	62	5	.542	5			1	/O	-0.2
■ **ED CALLAHAN** Callahan, Edward J. b: Boston, Mass. Deb: 7/19/1884																												
1884	StL-U	1	3	0	0	0	0	0		0		.000	.000	.000	.000	-97	-1	-1	104	0	0	.000	0			0	/O	0.0
	KC-U	3	11	0	4	0	0	0		0		.364	.364	.364	.727	168	0	1	87	0	1	.571	0			0	/S	0.1
	Bos-U	4	13	2	5	0	0	0		1		.385	.429	.385	.813	180	1	1	98	0	2	.750	0			0	/O	0.1
	Yr	8	27	2	9	0	0	0		1		.333	.357	.333	.690	142	1	1	95	0	3	.556	0			0		0.2
Total	1	8	27	2	9	0	0	0		1		.333	.357	.333	.690	143	1	1	94	0	4	.556	0			0	/OS	0.2
■ **NIXEY CALLAHAN** Callahan, James Joseph b: 3/18/1874, Fitchburg, Mass. d: 10/4/34, Boston, Mass. BR/TR, 5'10.5", 180 lbs. Deb: 5/12/1894 M																												
1894	Phi-N	9	21	4	5	0	0	0	0	0	7	.238	.238	.238	.476	17	-3	-3	95	0	1	.313	0			0	/P	0.0
1897	Chi-N	94	360	60	105	18	6	3	47	10		.292	.318	.400	.718	91	-6	-6	100	92	51	.667	12			0	2POS/3	-0.4
1898	Chi-N	43	164	27	43	7	5	0	22	4		.262	.280	.366	.646	84	-4	-4	103	113	18	.554	3			2	P/OS21	0.0
1899	Chi-N	47	150	21	39	4	3	0	18	8		.260	.306	.327	.633	79	-5	-4	96	113	18	.613	9			5	P/OS2	0.0
1900	Chi-N	32	115	16	27	3	2	0	9	6		.235	.273	.296	.568	63	-6	-5	93	84	11	.511	5			7	P	0.0
1901	Chi-A	45	118	15	39	7	3	1	19	10		.331	.383	.466	.849	138	6	6	99	103	26	.949	10			5	P/32	0.0
1902	Chi-A	70	218	27	51	7	2	0	13	6		.234	.254	.284	.539	53	-15	-13	95	69	17	.431	4			5	PO/S	0.0
1903	Chi-A	118	439	47	128	26	5	2	56	20		.292	.322	.387	.710	124	7	11	92	117	64	.688	24			-2	*3/OPM	0.9
1904	Chi-A	132	482	66	126	23	2	0	54	39		.261	.317	.317	.634	104	3	3	99	140	59	.621	29			-3	*O2M	-0.7
1905	Chi-A	96	345	50	94	18	6	1	43	29		.272	.329	.368	.697	127	9	10	97	125	52	.725	26			-1	O	0.5
1911	Chi-A	120	466	64	131	13	5	3	60	15		.281	.306	.350	.656	86	-12	-10	97	125	63	.672	45			-7	*O	-2.6
1912	Chi-A	111	408	45	111	9	7	1	52	12		.272	.298	.336	.634	82	-11	-11	99	126	47	.576	19			-14	*OM	-3.1
1913	Chi-A	6	9	0	2	0	0	0	0	0	2	.222	.222	.222	.444	32	-1	-1	95	0	0	.286	0			0	/OM	0.0
Total	13	923	3295	442	901	135	46	11	393	159	9	.273	.309	.352	.661	95	-38	-27	97	115	427	.634	186			-3	OP3/2S1	-5.4
■ **JIM CALLAHAN** Callahan, James Timothy "Red" (born James Timothy Callaghan) b: 1/4/1880, Mansfield, Pa. d: 3/25/68, Carnegie, Pa. 5'9", 145 lbs. Deb: 5/25/02																												
1902	NY-N	1	4	0	0	0	0	0	0	1		.000	.200	.000	.200	-36	-1	-1	100	0	0	.250	0			0	/O	0.0
■ **LEO CALLAHAN** Callahan, Leo David b: 8/9/1890, Jamaica Plain, Mass d: 5/2/82, Erie, Pa. BL/TL, 5'8", 142 lbs. Deb: 4/09/13																												
1913	Bro-N	33	41	6	7	3	1	0	3	4	5	.171	.244	.293	.537	51	-3	-3	104	91	3	.471	0			-2	/O	-0.4
1919	Phi-N	81	235	26	54	14	4	1	9	29	19	.230	.317	.336	.653	93	-1	-2	104	43	26	.630	5			1	O	-0.2
Total	2	114	276	32	61	17	5	1	12	33	24	.221	.306	.330	.636	86	-3	-4	104	50	29	.605	5			-1	/O	-0.6
■ **PAT CALLAHAN** Callahan, Patrick Henry b: 10/15/1866, Cleveland, Ohio d: 2/4/40, Louisville, Ky. Deb: 5/01/1884																												
1884	Ind-a	61	258	38	67	8	5	2		8		.260	.282	.353	.635	113	2	3	96	0	26	.518				-9	3	-0.3
■ **WESLEY CALLAHAN** Callahan, Wesley Leroy b: 7/3/1888, Lyons, Ind. d: 9/13/53, Dayton, Ohio TR, 5'7.5", 155 lbs. Deb: 9/07/13																												
1913	StL-N	7	14	0	4	0	0	0	1	2	2	.286	.375	.286	.661	97	-0	0	93	91	2	.700	1			-0	/S	0.0
■ **FRANK CALLAWAY** Callaway, Frank Burnett b: 2/26/1898, Knoxville, Tenn. d: 8/21/87, Knoxville, Tenn. BR/TR, 6', 170 lbs. Deb: 9/17/21																												
1921	Phi-A	14	50	7	12	1	1	0	4	2	11	.240	.283	.300	.583	47	-4	-4	103	93	5	.500	1	0	0	-2	S	-0.3
1922	Phi-A	29	48	5	13	0	2	0	4	0	13	.271	.271	.354	.625	59	-3	-3	104	84	4	.486	0	0	0	-0	2/3S	-0.1
Total	2	43	98	12	25	1	3	0	8	2	24	.255	.277	.327	.604	53	-7	-7	104	89	9	.493	1	0	0	-2	/S23	-0.4
■ **JOHNNY CALLISON** Callison, John Wesley b: 3/12/39, Qualls, Okla. BL/TR, 5'10", 175 lbs. Deb: 9/09/58																												
1958	Chi-A	18	64	10	19	4	2	1	12	6	14	.297	.357	.469	.826	128	2	2	98	149	11	.804	1	0	0	2	O	0.3
1959	Chi-A	49	104	12	18	3	0	3	12	13	20	.173	.271	.288	.560	56	-7	-6	97	121	7	.478	0	1	-1	-5	O	-1.3
1960	Phi-N	99	288	36	75	11	5	9	30	45	70	.260	.360	.427	.787	107	7	4	107	81	46	.771	0	4	-2	4	O	0.3
1961	Phi-N	138	455	74	121	20	11	9	47	69	76	.266	.366	.418	.784	115	6	10	94	89	74	.788	10	4	1	1	*O	0.5
1962	Phi-N	157	603	107	181	26	**10**	23	83	54	96	.300	.363	.491	.854	134	22	26	95	95	110	.845	10	3	1	26	*O	4.4
1963	Phi-N	157	626	96	178	36	11	26	78	50	111	.284	.339	.502	.841	135	29	27	103	74	107	.815	8	3	1	5	*O	2.6
1964	Phi-N	162	654	101	179	30	10	31	104	36	95	.274	.318	.492	.810	126	19	19	99	99	103	.766	6	3	0	18	*O	3.4
1965	Phi-N	160	619	93	162	25	**16**	32	101	57	117	.262	.330	.509	.839	140	25	29	95	108	105	.822	6	5	-1	5	*O	2.8
1966	Phi-N	155	612	93	169	**40**	7	11	55	56	83	.276	.340	.418	.758	108	8	7	101	85	86	.699	8	8	-2	6	*O	0.6
1967	Phi-N	149	556	62	145	30	5	14	64	55	63	.261	.331	.408	.739	106	7	4	104	104	72	.677	6	12	-5	-2	*O	-1.0
1968	Phi-N	121	398	46	97	18	4	14	40	42	70	.244	.321	.415	.735	123	9	10	97	83	54	.690	4	3	-1	2	*O	0.7
1969	Phi-N	134	495	66	131	29	5	16	64	49	73	.265	.335	.440	.775	118	9	10	98	102	74	.733	2	1	0	15	*O	1.9
1970	Chi-N	147	477	65	126	23	2	19	68	60	63	.264	.350	.440	.790	92	7	-6	120	99	75	.771	7	2	1	-2	*O	-1.2
1971	Chi-N	103	290	27	61	12	1	8	38	36	55	.210	.302	.341	.643	75	-7	-10	110	126	31	.589	2	1	0	-4	O	-1.8
1972	NY-A	92	275	28	71	10	0	9	34	18	34	.258	.304	.393	.696	115	1	3	92	105	33	.614	3	0	1	-3	O	0.0
1973	NY-A	45	136	10	24	4	0	1	10	4	24	.176	.200	.228	.428	20	-14	-15	101	116	5	.303	1	1	-0	-4	OD	-2.0
Total	16	1886	6652	926	1757	321	89	226	840	650	1064	.264	.333	.441	.774	114	123	117	101	97	992	.747	74	51	-8	64	*O/D	10.2
■ **JACK CALVO** Calvo, Jacinto (Gonzalez) (Born Jacinto Del Calvo) b: 6/11/1894, Havana, Cuba d: 6/15/65, Miami, Fla. BL/TL, 5'10", 156 lbs. Deb: 5/09/13																												
1913	Was-A	17	33	5	8	0	0	1	2	1	4	.242	.265	.333	.598	71	-1	-1	106	51	3	.480	0			-3	O	-0.5
1920	Was-A	17	23	5	1	0	1	0	2	2	2	.043	.120	.130	.250	-35	-5	-4	95	234	0	.227	0	0	0	-4	O	-0.8
Total	2	34	56	10	9	0	1	1	4	3	6	.161	.203	.250	.453	26	-6	-6	101	128	4	.362	0	0		-7	/O	-1.3
■ **HANK CAMELLI** Camelli, Henry Richard b: 12/12/14, Gloucester, Mass. BR/TR, 5'11", 190 lbs. Deb: 10/03/43																												
1943	Pit-N	1	3	1	0	0	0	0	0	1	0	.000	.250	.000	.250	-24	-0	-0	104	0	0	.333	0			0	/C	0.0
1944	Pit-N	63	125	14	37	5	1	1	10	18	12	.296	.385	.376	.761	109	3	2	105	72	18	.691	0			-3	C	0.2
1945	Pit-N	1	2	0	0	0	0	0	0	1	0	.000	.333	.000	.333	-3	-0	-0	103	0	0	.500	0			0	/C	0.0
1946	Pit-N	42	96	8	20	2	2	0	5	8	9	.208	.269	.271	.540	52	-6	-6	103	72	7	.442	0			-0	C	-0.5
1947	Bos-N	52	150	10	29	8	1	1	11	18	18	.193	.280	.280	.560	51	-11	-10	97	91	11	.465	0			-0	C	-0.8
Total	5	159	376	33	86	15	4	2	26	46	39	.229	.313	.306	.619	70	-15	-15	101	78	36	.540	0			-4	C	-1.1
■ **JACK CAMERON** Cameron, John William "Happy Jack" b: 1885, Canada d: 8/17/51, Boston, Mass. Deb: 9/13/06																												
1906	Bos-N	18	61	3	11	0	0	0	4	2		.180	.206	.180	.387	22	-5	-5	100	135	2	.260	0			-1	O/P	-0.6
■ **DOLPH CAMILLI** Camilli, Adolph Louis b: 4/23/07, San Francisco, Cal BL/TL, 5'10", 185 lbs. Deb: 9/09/33																												
1933	Chi-N	16	58	8	13	2	1	2	7	4	11	.224	.274	.397	.671	92	-1	-1	97	92	6	.638	3			1	1	0.0

YEAR	TM/L	G	AB	R	H	2B	3B	HR	RBI	BB	SO	AVG	OBP	SLG	PRO	/A	BR	/A	PF	CHI	RC	TA	SB	CS	SBR	FR	POS	TPR
1934	Chi-N	32	120	17	33	8	0	4	19	5	25	.275	.315	.442	.757	103	-0	0	98	107	18	.701	1			0	1	-0.1
	Phi-N	102	378	52	100	20	3	12	68	48	69	.265	.350	.429	.779	99	4	-0	108	131	59	.749	3			-4	*1	-1.2
	Yr	134	498	69	133	28	3	16	87	53	94	.267	.342	.432	.774	100	4	-0	106	126	77	.738	4			-4		-1.3
1935	Phi-N	156	602	88	157	23	5	25	83	65	113	.261	.336	.440	.776	94	5	-6	114	93	93	.753	9			-1	*1	-0.9
1936	Phi-N	151	530	106	167	29	13	28	102	116	84	.315	.441	.577	1.018	159	58	52	108	98	148	1.162	5			-10	*1	2.8
1937	Phi-N	131	475	101	161	23	7	27	80	90	82	.339	**.446**	.587	1.034	165	55	49	108	85	137	**1.189**	6			6	*1	4.6
1938	Bro-N	146	509	106	128	25	11	24	100	**119**	101	.251	.393	.485	.879	147	31	35	96	120	110	.964	6			2	*1	2.4
1939	Bro-N	157	565	105	164	30	12	26	104	**110**	107	.290	.409	.524	.933	139	42	36	107	108	128	.995	1			10	*1	2.7
1940	Bro-N	142	512	92	147	29	13	23	96	89	83	.287	.397	.529	.926	142	39	33	108	111	114	1.005	9			-6	*1	1.5
1941	Bro-N	149	529	92	151	29	6	**34**	**120**	104	115	.285	.407	.556	.962	164	**50**	**48**	103	116	**128**	**1.057**	3			2	*1	2.9
1942	Bro-N	150	524	89	132	23	7	26	109	97	85	.252	.372	.471	.843	143	31	30	102	127	97	.888	10			0	*1	2.0
1943	Bro-N	95	353	56	87	15	6	6	43	65	48	.246	.365	.374	.739	114	8	8	100	110	52	.733	2			3	1	0.7
1945	Bos-A	63	198	24	42	5	2	2	19	35	38	.212	.330	.288	.618	84	-4	-3	95	109	21	.584	2	0	1	1	1	-0.2
Total	12	1490	5353	936	1482	261	86	239	950	947	961	.277	.388	.492	.880	135	319	281	105	109	1111	.946	60	0		2	*1	17.2

■ DOUG CAMILLI Camilli, Douglas Joseph b: 9/22/36, Philadelphia, Pa. BR/TR, 5′11″, 195 lbs. Deb: 9/25/60 C

YEAR	TM/L	G	AB	R	H	2B	3B	HR	RBI	BB	SO	AVG	OBP	SLG	PRO	/A	BR	/A	PF	CHI	RC	TA	SB	CS	SBR	FR	POS	TPR
1960	LA-N	6	24	4	8	2	0	1	3	1	4	.333	.385	.542	.926	130	2	1	115	81	5	.938	0	0	0	0	/C	0.2
1961	LA-N	13	30	3	4	0	0	3	4	1	9	.133	.161	.433	.595	50	-2	-2	102	73	2	.519	0	0	0	0	C	0.0
1962	LA-N	45	88	16	25	5	2	4	22	12	21	.284	.370	.523	.893	147	4	5	93	149	16	.866	0	0	0	-1	C	0.5
1963	LA-N	49	117	9	19	1	1	3	10	11	22	.162	.234	.265	.499	46	-9	-8	95	105	7	.412	0	0	0	1	C	-0.5
1964	LA-N	50	123	1	22	3	0	0	10	8	19	.179	.229	.203	.432	25	-12	-11	92	164	6	.314	0	0	0	-5	C	-1.5
1965	Was-A	75	193	13	37	6	1	3	18	16	34	.192	.257	.280	.537	52	-12	-12	100	119	14	.447	0	0	0	5	C	-0.2
1966	Was-A	44	107	5	22	4	0	2	8	3	19	.206	.234	.299	.533	55	-7	-6	95	88	7	.404	0	0	0	2	C	-0.2
1967	Was-A	30	82	5	15	1	0	2	5	4	16	.183	.221	.268	.489	43	-6	-6	102	74	5	.382	0	0	0	4	C	0.0
1969	Was-A	1	3	0	1	0	0	0	0	0	2	.333	.333	.333	.667	90	-0	-0	97	0	0	.500	0	0	0	0	/C	0.0
Total	9	313	767	56	153	22	4	18	80	56	146	.199	.257	.309	.566	61	-42	-39	97	115	61	.482	0	0	0	6	C	-1.7

■ LOU CAMILLI Camilli, Louis Steven b: 9/24/46, El Paso, Tex. BB/TR, 5′10″, 170 lbs. Deb: 8/09/69

YEAR	TM/L	G	AB	R	H	2B	3B	HR	RBI	BB	SO	AVG	OBP	SLG	PRO	/A	BR	/A	PF	CHI	RC	TA	SB	CS	SBR	FR	POS	TPR
1969	Cle-A	13	14	0	0	0	0	0	0	0	3	.000	.000	.000	.000	-99	-4	-4	94	0	-0	.000	0	0	0	-1	3	-0.4
1970	Cle-A	16	15	0	0	0	0	0	0	2	2	.000	.118	.000	.118	-57	-3	-4	115	0	0	.125	0	0	0	0	/S23	-0.2
1971	Cle-A	39	81	5	16	2	0	0	0	8	10	.198	.270	.222	.492	38	-6	-7	106	0	5	.382	0	0	0	-1	S2	-0.4
1972	Cle-A	39	41	2	6	2	0	0	3	3	8	.146	.205	.195	.400	18	-4	-4	107	157	2	.314	0	0	0	0	/S2	-0.3
Total	4	107	151	7	22	4	0	0	3	13	23	.146	.213	.172	.386	11	-17	-18	106	42	7	.302	0	0	0	-2	/S23	-1.3

■ KEN CAMINITI Caminiti, Kenneth Gene b: 4/21/63, Hanford, Cal. BB/TR, 6′3″, 200 lbs. Deb: 7/16/87

YEAR	TM/L	G	AB	R	H	2B	3B	HR	RBI	BB	SO	AVG	OBP	SLG	PRO	/A	BR	/A	PF	CHI	RC	TA	SB	CS	SBR	FR	POS	TPR
1987	Hou-N	63	203	10	50	7	1	3	23	12	44	.246	.288	.335	.623	70	-10	-9	93	119	19	.503	0	0	0	2	3	-0.7
1988	Hou-N	30	83	5	15	2	0	1	7	5	18	.181	.227	.241	.468	37	-7	-6	93	122	4	.352	0	0	0	-0	3	-0.6
Total	2	93	286	15	65	9	1	4	30	17	62	.227	.271	.308	.578	61	-18	-15	93	120	23	.469	0	0	0	1	/3	-1.3

■ HOWIE CAMP Camp, Howard Lee "Red" b: 7/1/1893, Mumford, Ala. d: 5/8/60, Eastaboga, Ala. BL/TR, 5′9″, 169 lbs. Deb: 9/19/17

YEAR	TM/L	G	AB	R	H	2B	3B	HR	RBI	BB	SO	AVG	OBP	SLG	PRO	/A	BR	/A	PF	CHI	RC	TA	SB	CS	SBR	FR	POS	TPR
1917	NY-A	5	21	3	6	1	0	0	0	1	2	.286	.318	.333	.652	93	-0	-0	107	0	2	.533	0			1	/O	0.0

■ LEW CAMP Camp, Llewellyn Robert b: 2/22/1868, Columbus, Ohio d: 10/1/48, Omaha, Neb. BL/TR, 6′, 175 lbs. Deb: 8/26/1892

YEAR	TM/L	G	AB	R	H	2B	3B	HR	RBI	BB	SO	AVG	OBP	SLG	PRO	/A	BR	/A	PF	CHI	RC	TA	SB	CS	SBR	FR	POS	TPR
1892	StL-N	42	145	19	30	3	1	2	13	17	27	.207	.294	.283	.577	80	-4	-3	95	87	16	.617	12			-16	3/O	-1.4
1893	Chi-N	38	156	37	41	7	7	2	17	19	19	.263	.347	.436	.782	105	2	1	104	60	35	1.026	30			0	3O/2S	0.0
1894	Chi-N	8	33	1	6	2	0	0	1	1	6	.182	.206	.242	.448	8	-5	-5	108	35	2	.333	0			0	/2	-0.3
Total	3	88	334	57	77	12	8	4	31	37	52	.231	.311	.350	.661	85	-7	-8	100	69	53	.770	42			-16	/32OS	-1.7

■ ROY CAMPANELLA Campanella, Roy b: 11/19/21, Philadelphia, Pa. BR/TR, 5′9.5″, 190 lbs. Deb: 4/20/48 H

YEAR	TM/L	G	AB	R	H	2B	3B	HR	RBI	BB	SO	AVG	OBP	SLG	PRO	/A	BR	/A	PF	CHI	RC	TA	SB	CS	SBR	FR	POS	TPR
1948	Bro-N	83	279	32	72	11	3	9	45	36	45	.258	.345	.416	.761	101	2	0	104	118	42	.743	3			6	C	1.2
1949	Bro-N	130	436	65	125	22	2	22	82	67	36	.287	.385	.498	.883	133	22	21	102	109	86	.901	3			1	*C	2.6
1950	Bro-N	126	437	70	123	19	3	31	89	55	51	.281	.364	.551	.916	129	22	18	107	105	84	.903	1			7	*C	2.8
1951	Bro-N	143	505	90	164	33	1	33	108	53	51	.325	.393	.590	.983	164	42	43	98	107	114	.983	1	2	-1	8	*C	5.0
1952	Bro-N	128	468	73	126	18	1	22	97	57	59	.269	.352	.453	.805	120	14	13	102	139	72	.761	8	4	0	4	*C	1.9
1953	Bro-N	144	519	103	162	26	3	41	**142**	67	58	.312	.395	.611	1.006	152	43	40	104	128	128	1.054	4	2	0	8	*C	5.3
1954	Bro-N	111	397	43	82	14	3	19	51	42	49	.207	.286	.401	.686	76	-15	-16	101	95	42	.614	1	4	-2	12	*C	-0.3
1955	Bro-N	123	446	81	142	20	1	32	107	56	41	.318	.402	.583	.985	151	37	34	104	124	101	1.009	2	3	-1	2	*C	3.7
1956	Bro-N	124	388	39	85	6	1	20	73	66	61	.219	.334	.394	.728	92	-2	-3	103	145	49	.684	1	0	0	0	*C	0.0
1957	Bro-N	103	330	31	80	9	0	13	62	34	50	.242	.321	.388	.709	77	-5	-12	116	154	40	.640	1	0	0	6	*C	0.0
Total	10	1215	4205	627	1161	178	18	242	856	533	501	.276	.362	.500	.861	123	159	138	104	122	759	.876	25	15		52	*C	22.2

■ BERT CAMPANERIS Campaneris, Dagoberto (Blanco) "Campy" (born Dagoberto Campaneria (Blanco)) b: 3/9/42, Pueblo Nuevo, Cuba BR/TR, 5′10″, 160 lbs. Deb: 7/23/64

YEAR	TM/L	G	AB	R	H	2B	3B	HR	RBI	BB	SO	AVG	OBP	SLG	PRO	/A	BR	/A	PF	CHI	RC	TA	SB	CS	SBR	FR	POS	TPR
1964	KC-A	67	269	27	69	14	3	4	22	15	41	.257	.306	.375	.681	84	-5	-6	105	87	32	.634	10	2	2	-4	SO/3	-0.9
1965	KC-A	144	578	67	156	23	**12**	6	42	41	71	.270	.328	.382	.710	104	1	3	97	64	76	.722	**51**	19	4	-10	*SO/PC123	0.0
1966	KC-A	142	573	82	153	29	10	5	42	25	72	.267	.303	.379	.682	101	-5	-1	94	73	70	.686	**52**	10	**10**	-15	*S	0.1
1967	KC-A	147	601	85	149	29	6	3	32	36	82	.248	.298	.331	.629	86	-11	-11	100	57	64	.631	**55**	16	**7**	-16	*S	-1.0
1968	Oak-A	159	642	87	**177**	25	9	4	38	50	69	.276	.332	.361	.693	112	8	9	98	58	82	.707	**62**	22	**5**	2	*S/O	3.0
1969	Oak-A	135	547	71	142	15	2	2	25	30	62	.260	.303	.305	.608	77	-22	-17	92	61	59	.629	62	8	**14**	-2	*S	0.0
1970	Oak-A	147	603	97	168	28	4	22	64	36	73	.279	.323	.448	.771	114	6	9	97	68	91	.782	**42**	10	7	-10	*S	1.8
1971	Oak-A	134	569	80	143	18	4	5	47	29	64	.251	.290	.323	.613	73	-21	-21	101	85	56	.566	34	7	6	3	*S	0.2
1972	Oak-A	149	625	85	150	25	2	8	32	32	88	.240	.279	.325	.604	82	-17	-15	97	51	59	.580	**52**	14	**7**	12	*S	2.2
1973	Oak-A	151	601	89	150	17	6	4	46	50	79	.250	.311	.318	.629	89	-17	-8	87	86	63	.592	34	10	4	3	*S	2.0
1974	Oak-A	134	527	77	153	18	8	2	41	47	81	.290	.348	.366	.715	105	4	4	100	72	70	.694	34	15	1	-4	*S/D	1.2
1975	Oak-A	137	509	69	135	15	3	4	46	50	71	.265	.339	.330	.669	96	-6	-1	93	104	60	.630	24	12	0	-20	*S	-0.7
1976	Oak-A	149	536	67	137	14	1	1	52	63	80	.256	.337	.291	.628	85	-8	-7	100	133	64	.665	54	12	**9**	-3	*S	0.8
1977	Tex-A	150	552	77	140	19	7	5	46	47	86	.254	.317	.341	.657	76	-15	-19	105	95	60	.606	27	20	-4	24	*S	1.9
1978	Tex-A	98	269	30	50	5	3	1	17	20	36	.186	.247	.238	.485	39	-22	-21	96	100	19	.472	22	4	4	10	S/D	0.0
1979	Tex-A	8	9	2	1	0	0	0	0	1	3	.111	.200	.111	.311	-14	-1	-1	100	0	0	.375	1	0	0	-1	/S	-0.1
	Cal-A	85	239	27	56	4	4	0	15	19	32	.234	.296	.285	.581	62	-14	-11	93	85	21	.518	12	4	1	-0	S	0.0
	Yr	93	248	29	57	4	4	0	15	20	35	.230	.293	.278	.571	59	-15	-13	93	77	21	.512	13	4	2	-2		-0.1
1980	Cal-A	77	210	32	53	8	1	2	18	14	33	.252	.302	.329	.631	76	-8	-7	96	94	21	.566	10	5	0	-13	S/2D	-1.4
1981	Cal-A	55	82	11	21	2	1	1	10	5	10	.256	.299	.341	.640	81	-2	-2	104	126	9	.603	5	2	0	-1	3/S2	-0.2
1983	NY-A	60	143	19	46	5	0	0	11	8	9	.322	.358	.357	.714	99	-0	-0	99	84	16	.602	6	7	-2	1	23	0.0
Total	19	2328	8684	1181	2249	313	86	79	646	618	1142	.259	.313	.342	.655	89	-154	-123	97	79	992	.648	649	199	75	-45	*S/3O2D1C	8.9

■ AL CAMPANIS Campanis, Alexander Sebastian (born Alessandro Campani) b: 11/2/16, Cos, Greece BB/TR, 6′, 185 lbs. Deb: 9/23/43

YEAR	TM/L	G	AB	R	H	2B	3B	HR	RBI	BB	SO	AVG	OBP	SLG	PRO	/A	BR	/A	PF	CHI	RC	TA	SB	CS	SBR	FR	POS	TPR
1943	Bro-N	7	20	3	2	0	0	0	0	4	5	.100	.250	.100	.350	3	-2	-2	100	0	1	.333	0			-1	/2	-0.3

■ JIM CAMPANIS Campanis, James Alexander b: 2/9/44, New York, N.Y. BR/TR, 6′, 195 lbs. Deb: 9/20/66

YEAR	TM/L	G	AB	R	H	2B	3B	HR	RBI	BB	SO	AVG	OBP	SLG	PRO	/A	BR	/A	PF	CHI	RC	TA	SB	CS	SBR	FR	POS	TPR
1966	LA-N	1	1	0	0	0	0	0	0	0	0	.000	.000	.000	.000	-99	-0	-0	97	0	0	.000	0	0	0	0	/C	0.0
1967	LA-N	41	62	3	10	1	0	2	2	9	14	.161	.268	.274	.542	63	-4	-3	88	36	5	.481	0	0	0	-1	C	-0.2
1968	LA-N	4	11	0	1	0	0	0	0	1	2	.091	.167	.091	.258	-23	-2	-1	91	0	0	.182	0	0	0	0	/C	0.0
1969	KC-A	30	83	4	13	5	0	0	5	5	19	.157	.205	.217	.421	17	-9	-9	103	111	3	.311	0	0	0	-1	C	-0.9
1970	KC-A	31	54	6	7	0	0	2	2	4	14	.130	.203	.241	.444	22	-6	-6	98	43	2	.353	0	0	0	0	C/O	-0.5
1973	Pit-N	6	6	0	1	0	0	0	0	0	0	.167	.167	.167	.333	-8	-1	-1	92	0	0	.200	0	0	0	0	H	0.0
Total	6	113	217	13	32	6	0	4	9	19	49	.147	.219	.230	.450	28	-21	-20	96	63	10	.378	0	0	0	-2	/CO	-1.6

■ COUNT CAMPAU Campau, Charles Columbus b: 10/17/1863, Detroit, Mich. d: 4/3/38, New Orleans, La. BL/TR, 5′11″, 160 lbs. Deb: 1888 M

YEAR	TM/L	G	AB	R	H	2B	3B	HR	RBI	BB	SO	AVG	OBP	SLG	PRO	/A	BR	/A	PF	CHI	RC	TA	SB	CS	SBR	FR	POS	TPR
1888	Det-N	70	251	28	51	5	3	1	18	19	36	.203	.259	.259	.518	69	-9	-8	98	95	24	.555	27			-5	O	-1.3

YEAR	TM/L	G	AB	R	H	2B	3B	HR	RBI	BB	SO	AVG	OBP	SLG	PRO	/A	BR	/A	PF	CHI	RC	TA	SB	CS	SBR	FR	POS	TPR
1890	StL-a	75	314	68	101	9	11	**10**		26		.322	.374	.516	.889	142	23	15	116	0	76	1.052	36			3	O/31M	1.2
1894	Was-N	2	7	1	1	0	0	0	0	1	4	.143	.250	.143	.393	-2	-1	-1	98	0	0	.333	0			0	/O	0.0
Total	3	147	572	97	153	14	14	11	18	46	40	.267	.322	.399	.721	112	13	6	108	41	101	.804	63			-2	O/13	-0.1
■ VIN CAMPBELL	Campbell, Arthur Vincent b: 1/30/1888, St.Louis, Mo. d: 11/16/69, Towson, Md. BL/TR, 6', 185 lbs. Deb: 6/06/08																											
1908	Chi-N	1	1	0	0	0	0	0	0	0		.000	.000	.000	.000	-94	-0	-0	106	0	0	.000	0			0	H	0.0
1910	Pit-N	97	282	42	92	9	5	4	21	26	23	.326	.391	.436	.827	126	14	10	112	54	55	.895	17			-5	O	0.3
1911	Pit-N	42	93	12	29	3	1	0	10	8	7	.312	.366	.366	.732	104	1	1	101	99	14	.750	6			-3	O	-0.2
1912	Bos-N	145	624	102	185	32	9	3	48	32	44	.296	.334	.391	.725	91	-4	-10	107	55	87	.679	19			-2	*O	-1.5
1914	Ind-F	134	544	92	173	23	11	7	44	37	47	.318	.361	.439	.801	116	19	12	111	54	99	.814	26			-2	*O	0.2
1915	New-F	127	525	78	163	18	10	1	44	29	35	.310	.347	.389	.735	125	10	14	94	68	82	.710	24			-8	*O	0.0
Total	6	546	2069	326	642	85	36	15	167	132	156	.310	.354	.408	.762	111	40	26	105	60	337	.753	92			-20	O	-1.2
■ BRUCE CAMPBELL	Campbell, Bruce Douglas b: 10/20/09, Chicago, Ill. BL/TR, 6'1", 185 lbs. Deb: 9/12/30																											
1930	Chi-A	5	10	4	5	1	1	0	5	1	2	.500	.545	.800	1.345	230	2	2	103	207	4	1.800	0	0	0	-0	/O	0.1
1931	Chi-A	4	17	4	7	2	0	2	5	0	4	.412	.444	.882	1.327	261	3	3	92	75	7	1.600	0	0	0	-0	/O	0.2
1932	Chi-A	7	18	3	4	1	0	0	2	0	2	.222	.222	.278	.500	33	-2	-2	87	134	1	.333	0	1	-1	-1	/O	-0.2
	StL-A	139	593	83	169	35	11	14	85	40	102	.285	.336	.452	.788	102	0	0	100	81	90	.748	7	5	-1	2	*O	-0.3
	Yr	146	611	86	173	36	11	14	87	40	104	.283	.333	.447	.780	101	-2	-1	99	85	90	.734	7	6	-2	1		-0.5
1933	StL-A	148	567	87	157	38	8	16	106	69	77	.277	.357	.457	.814	100	11	-1	115	122	95	.821	10	4	1	-6	*O	-1.0
1934	StL-A	138	481	62	134	25	6	9	74	51	64	.279	.350	.412	.762	92	-3	-6	104	112	71	.729	5	4	-1	-0	*O	-0.8
1935	Cle-A	80	308	56	100	26	3	7	54	31	33	.325	.390	.497	.887	129	12	13	99	112	60	.900	2	1	0	-10	O	0.2
1936	Cle-A	76	172	35	64	15	2	6	30	19	17	.372	.440	.587	1.028	144	14	12	106	82	45	1.138	2	1	0	-6	O	0.5
1937	Cle-A	134	448	82	135	42	11	4	61	67	49	.301	.392	.471	.863	119	12	14	98	96	85	.887	4	5	-2	-4	*O	0.3
1938	Cle-A	133	511	90	148	27	12	12	72	53	57	.290	.360	.460	.820	105	2	3	99	95	85	.816	11	7	-1	0	*O	0.2
1939	Cle-A	130	450	84	129	23	13	8	72	67	48	.287	.383	.449	.832	114	9	11	98	110	81	.838	7	6	-2	-6	*O	0.0
1940	Det-A	103	297	56	84	15	5	8	44	45	28	.283	.381	.448	.829	102	7	2	111	101	51	.798	2	7	-4	-5	O	-1.1
1941	Det-A	141	512	72	141	28	10	15	93	68	67	.275	.364	.457	.821	109	11	7	106	120	90	.808	3	3	-1	-11	*O	-1.2
1942	Was-A	122	378	41	105	17	5	5	63	37	34	.278	.344	.389	.733	111	3	5	96	137	51	.654	0	6	-4	-1	O	-0.6
Total	13	1360	4762	759	1382	295	87	106	766	548	584	.290	.367	.455	.822	109	81	62	103	107	815	.815	53	50	-14	-49	*O	-3.7
■ SOUP CAMPBELL	Campbell, Clarence b: 3/7/15, Sparta, Va. BL/TR, 6'1", 188 lbs. Deb: 4/21/40																											
1940	Cle-A	35	62	8	14	1	0	0	2	7	12	.226	.304	.242	.546	47	-5	-4	93	48	5	.449	0	0	0	-1	O	-0.6
1941	Cle-A	104	328	36	82	10	4	3	35	31	21	.250	.317	.332	.649	71	-13	-14	101	105	32	.538	1	9	-5	5	O	-1.7
Total	2	139	390	44	96	11	4	3	37	38	33	.246	.315	.318	.633	68	-18	-18	99	96	37	.526	1	9	-5	4	/O	-2.3
■ DAVE CAMPBELL	Campbell, David Wilson b: 1/14/42, Manistee, Mich. BR/TR, 6'1", 180 lbs. Deb: 9/17/67																											
1967	Det-A	2	2	0	0	0	0	0	0	0	1	.000	.000	.000	.000	-99	-0	-0	99	0	0	.000	0	0	0	0	/1	0.0
1968	Det-A	9	8	1	1	0	0	1	2	1	3	.125	.222	.500	.722	107	0	0	106	122	1	.714	0	0	0	-0	/2	0.0
1969	Det-A	32	39	4	4	1	0	0	2	4	15	.103	.205	.128	.333	-5	-5	-6	103	161	1	.278	0	1	-1	0	1/23	-0.6
1970	SD-N	154	581	71	127	28	2	12	40	40	115	.219	.270	.336	.606	64	-33	-30	95	71	54	.544	18	6	2	21	*2	1.0
1971	SD-N	108	365	38	83	14	2	7	29	37	75	.227	.299	.334	.633	82	-10	-9	96	84	38	.573	9	6	-1	-1	23/S1O	-0.7
1972	SD-N	33	100	6	24	5	0	0	3	11	12	.240	.315	.290	.605	83	-3	-2	88	42	8	.488	0	4	-2	-1	3/2	-0.5
1973	SD-N	33	98	2	22	3	0	0	8	7	15	.224	.276	.255	.531	51	-7	-6	94	129	6	.407	1	1	-0	1	2/13	-0.4
	StL-N	13	21	1	0	0	0	0	1	1	6	.000	.045	.000	.045	-95	-5	-5	91	0	0	.048	0	0	0	0	/2	-0.4
	Hou-N	9	15	1	4	2	0	0	2	0	4	.267	.267	.400	.667	87	-0	-0	95	134	2	.545	0	0	0	-0	/31O	0.0
	Yr	55	134	4	26	5	0	0	11	8	25	.194	.239	.231	.471	33	-12	-11	93	101	8	.367	1	1	-0	0		-0.8
1974	Hou-N	35	23	4	2	1	0	0	2	1	8	.087	.125	.130	.255	-29	-4	-4	98	257	1	.238	1	0	0	-0	/213O	-0.3
Total	8	428	1252	128	267	54	4	20	89	102	254	.213	.274	.311	.584	64	-69	-62	95	83	110	.520	29	18	-2	18	2/31OS	-1.9
■ JIM CAMPBELL	Campbell, James Robert b: 6/24/37, Palo Alto, Cal. BR/TR, 6', 190 lbs. Deb: 7/17/62																											
1962	Hou-N	27	86	6	19	4	0	3	6	6	23	.221	.272	.372	.644	76	-4	-3	93	58	8	.543	0	0	0	4	C	0.1
1963	Hou-N	55	158	9	35	3	0	4	19	10	40	.222	.268	.316	.584	73	-7	-5	92	129	12	.462	0	0	0	4	C	0.0
Total	2	82	244	15	54	7	0	7	25	16	63	.221	.269	.336	.605	74	-11	-8	92	104	20	.497	0	0	0	7	/C	0.1
■ JIM CAMPBELL	Campbell, James Robert b: 1/10/43, Hartsville, S.C. BL/TR, 6', 205 lbs. Deb: 4/11/70																											
1970	StL-N	13	13	0	3	0	0	0	1	0	3	.231	.231	.231	.462	23	-1	-1	106	129	1	.300	0	0	0	0	H	0.0
■ JOE CAMPBELL	Campbell, Joseph Earl b: 3/10/44, Louisville, Ky. BR/TR, 6'1", 175 lbs. Deb: 5/03/67																											
1967	Chi-N	1	3	0	0	0	0	0	0	0	3	.000	.000	.000	.000	-99	-1	-1	102	0	0	.000	0	0	0	-0	/O	0.0
■ MARC CAMPBELL	Campbell, Marc Thaddeus b: 11/29/1884, Punxsutawney, Pa. d: 2/13/46, New Bethlehem, Pa. BL/TR, 5'10", 155 lbs. Deb: 9/30/07																											
1907	Pit-N	2	4	0	1	0	0	0	1	1		.250	.400	.250	.650	101	0	0	105	379	0	.667	0			0	/S	0.0
■ MIKE CAMPBELL	Campbell, Michael b: New Jersey Deb: 4/28/1873																											
1873	Res-n	21	89	9	13							.146															1/SO	
■ PAUL CAMPBELL	Campbell, Paul Mc Laughlin b: 9/1/17, Paw Creek, N.C. BL/TL, 5'10", 185 lbs. Deb: 4/15/41																											
1941	Bos-A	1	0	0	0	0	0	0	0	0	0	—	—	—	—	—	0	0	103	—	—	—	0	0	0	0	R	0.0
1942	Bos-A	26	15	4	1	0	0	0	0	1	5	.067	.125	.067	.192	-44	-3	-3	104	0	0	.214	1	0	0	-2	/O	-0.4
1946	Bos-A	28	26	3	3	1	0	0	0	2	7	.115	.179	.154	.332	-6	-4	-4	114	0	1	.261	0	0	0	0	/1	-0.4
1948	Det-A	59	83	15	22	1	1	1	11	1	10	.265	.274	.337	.611	64	-5	-4	96	120	8	.475	0	0	0	0	1	-0.2
1949	Det-A	87	255	38	71	15	4	3	30	24	32	.278	.343	.404	.747	90	-2	-5	108	92	38	.697	3	3	-1	-1	1	-0.5
1950	Det-A	3	1	1	0	0	0	0	0	0	0	.000	.000	.000	.000	-99	-0	-0	97	0	0	.000	0	0	0	0	H	0.0
Total	6	204	380	61	97	17	5	4	41	28	54	.255	.308	.358	.666	73	-14	-17	106	87	47	.589	4	3	-1	-3	1/O	-1.5
■ RON CAMPBELL	Campbell, Ronald Thomas b: 4/5/40, Chattanooga, Tenn. BR/TR, 6'1", 180 lbs. Deb: 9/01/64																											
1964	Chi-N	26	92	7	25	6	1	1	10	1	21	.272	.280	.391	.671	82	-2	-2	105	105	10	.544	0	1	-1	3	2	0.2
1965	Chi-N	2	2	0	0	0	0	0	0	0	0	.000	.000	.000	.000	-98	-1	-1	102	0	0	.000	0	0	0	0	H	0.0
1966	Chi-N	24	60	4	13	1	0	0	4	6	5	.217	.288	.233	.521	47	-4	-4	100	120	4	.412	1	1	-0	1	S/3	-0.2
Total	3	52	154	11	38	7	1	1	14	7	26	.247	.280	.325	.604	67	-6	-7	103	110	13	.479	1	2	-1	4	/2S3	0.0
■ SAM CAMPBELL	Campbell, Samuel b: Philadelphia, Pa. Deb: 10/11/1890																											
1890	Phi-a	2	5	0	0	0	0	0		1		.000	.167	.000	.167	-51	-1	-1	97	0	0	.200	0			0	/2	0.0
■ GILLY CAMPBELL	Campbell, William Gilthorpe b: 2/13/08, Kansas City, Kan. d: 2/21/73, Los Angeles, Cal. BL/TR, 5'7.5", 182 lbs. Deb: 4/25/33																											
1933	Chi-N	46	89	11	25	3	1	1	10	7	4	.281	.347	.371	.718	108	1	1	97	104	12	.646	0			0	C	0.2
1935	Cin-N	88	218	26	56	7	0	3	30	42	7	.257	.379	.330	.710	99	-0	2	93	134	30	.702	3			2	C/1O	0.3
1936	Cin-N	89	235	28	63	13	1	1	40	43	14	.268	.384	.345	.728	101	1	2	97	169	35	.718	2			1	C/1	0.5
1937	Cin-N	18	40	3	11	2	0	0	2	5	1	.275	.356	.325	.681	94	-1	-0	91	55	5	.621	0			0	C	0.0
1938	Bro-N	54	126	10	31	5	0	0	11	19	9	.246	.354	.286	.639	81	-3	-2	96	110	13	.564	0			-2	C	-0.1
Total	5	295	708	78	186	30	2	5	93	116	35	.263	.371	.332	.703	97	-2	3	95	134	95	.686	5			1	C/1O	0.9
■ FRANK CAMPOS	Campos, Francisco Jose (Lopez) b: 5/11/24, Havana, Cuba BL/TL, 5'11", 180 lbs. Deb: 9/11/51																											
1951	Was-A	8	26	4	11	3	1	0	3	0	1	.423	.423	.615	1.038	187	3	3	95	67	7	1.067	0	0	0	-2	/O	0.0
1952	Was-A	53	112	9	29	6	1	0	8	1	13	.259	.278	.330	.609	69	-5	-5	100	81	11	.476	0	0	0	-2	O	-0.8
1953	Was-A	10	9	0	1	0	0	0	2	1	0	.111	.200	.111	.311	-15	-1	-1	94	741	0	.222	0	0	0	0	H	0.0
Total	3	71	147	13	41	9	2	0	13	2	14	.279	.298	.367	.665	84	-4	-4	99	122	18	.542	0	0	0	-5	/O	-0.8
■ SIL CAMPUSANO	Campusano, Silvestre (Diaz) b: 12/31/65, Santo Domingo, D.R. BR/TR, 6', 160 lbs. Deb: 4/04/88																											
1988	Tor-A	73	142	14	31	10	2	2	12	9	33	.218	.284	.359	.643	79	-4	-4	100	84	16	.577	0	0	0	-9	O/D	-1.4

YEAR	TM/L	G	AB	R	H	2B	3B	HR	RBI	BB	SO	AVG	OBP	SLG	PRO	/A	BR	/A	PF	CHI	RC	TA	SB	CS	SBR	FR	POS	TPR
■ JIM CANAVAN Canavan, James Edward b: 11/26/1866, New Bedford, Mass. d: 5/27/49, New Bedford, Mass. BR/TR, 5'8", 160 lbs. Deb: 4/08/1891																												
1891	CM-a	136	568	107	135	15	18	10	87	43	54	.238	.297	.380	.677	86	-6	-17	112	98	74	.674	28			-12	*S2	-2.0
1892	Chi-N	118	439	48	73	10	11	0	32	48	48	.166	.248	.239	.488	53	-27	-22	92	99	35	.508	33			-2	*2/OS	-2.0
1893	Cin-N	121	461	65	104	13	7	5	64	51	20	.226	.305	.317	.622	66	-22	-23	101	111	55	.644	31			-5	*O/23	-2.6
1894	Cin-N	101	356	77	97	16	9	13	70	62	25	.272	.380	.478	.858	107	4	4	100	94	71	.946	13			1	*O/S321	0.0
1897	Bro-N	63	240	25	52	9	3	2	34	26		.217	.296	.304	.600	59	-14	-14	102	133	25	.580	9			-23	2	-2.7
Total	5	539	2064	322	461	63	48	30	287	230	147	.223	.304	.344	.648	77	-64	-71	102	105	261	.663	114			-40	O2S/31	-9.3
■ CASEY CANDAELE Candaele, Casey Todd b: 1/12/61, Lompoc, Cal. BB/TR, 5'9", 160 lbs. Deb: 6/05/86																												
1986	Mon-N	30	104	9	24	4	1	0	6	5	15	.231	.266	.288	.555	54	-7	-6	98	80	6	.432	3	5	-2	4	2/3	-0.4
1987	Mon-N	138	449	62	122	23	4	1	23	38	28	.272	.331	.347	.679	76	-12	-16	106	58	51	.594	7	10	-4	-3	2OS/1	-2.1
1988	Mon-N	36	116	9	20	5	1	0	4	10	11	.172	.238	.233	.471	34	-10	-10	106	59	6	.369	1	0	0	3	2	-0.6
	Hou-N	21	31	2	5	3	0	0	1	1	6	.161	.188	.258	.446	29	-3	-3	93	50	1	.333	0	1	-1	-2	2/O3	-0.5
	Yr	57	147	11	25	8	1	0	5	11	17	.170	.228	.238	.466	34	-13	-13	101	57	9	.382	1	1	-0	1		-1.1
Total	3	225	700	82	171	35	6	1	34	54	60	.244	.300	.316	.616	64	-32	-35	104	61	64	.528	11	16	-6	1	2/OS31	-3.6
■ JOHN CANGELOSI Cangelosi, John Anthony b: 3/10/63, Brooklyn, N.Y. BB/TL, 5'8", 150 lbs. Deb: 6/30/85																												
1985	Chi-A	5	2	2	0	0	0	0	0	0	1	.000	.333	.000	.333	1	-0	-0	100	0	0	.500	0	0	0	-1	/OD	0.0
1986	Chi-A	137	438	65	103	16	3	2	32	71	61	.235	.351	.299	.650	80	-9	-10	101	95	55	.725	50	17	5	1	*O/D	-0.6
1987	Pit-N	104	182	44	50	8	3	4	18	46	33	.275	.429	.418	.846	120	9	8	104	82	39	1.035	21	6	3	-2	O	0.7
1988	Pit-N	75	118	18	30	4	1	0	8	17	16	.254	.353	.305	.658	93	-1	-0	98	89	15	.685	9	4	0	-0	O/P	0.0
Total	4	321	740	129	183	28	7	6	58	134	111	.247	.371	.328	.700	92	-1	-2	101	90	109	.803	80	27	8	-2	O/DP	0.1
■ RIP CANNELL Cannell, Virgin Wirt b: 1/23/1880, S.Bridgton, Maine d: 8/26/48, Bridgton, Maine BL/TR, 5'10.5", 180 lbs. Deb: 4/14/04																												
1904	Bos-N	100	346	32	81	5	1	0	18	23		.234	.282	.254	.536	70	-12	-11	97	76	28	.457	10			0	O	-1.4
1905	Bos-N	154	567	52	140	14	4	0	36	51		.247	.309	.286	.595	82	-13	-11	97	82	57	.539	17			-13	*O	-3.5
Total	2	254	913	84	221	19	5	0	54	74		.242	.299	.274	.573	78	-25	-22	97	80	85	.507	27			-12	O	-4.9
■ CHRIS CANNIZZARO Cannizzaro, Christopher John b: 5/3/38, Oakland, Cal. BR/TR, 6', 190 lbs. Deb: 4/17/60 C																												
1960	StL-N	7	9	0	2	0	0	0	1	1	3	.222	.300	.222	.522	42	-1	-1	108	203	1	.429	0	0	0	-0	/C	0.0
1961	StL-N	6	2	0	1	0	0	0	0	0	0	.500	.500	.500	1.000	147	0	0	113	0	1	1.000	0	0	0	0	/C	0.0
1962	NY-N	59	133	9	32	2	1	0	9	19	26	.241	.340	.271	.611	64	-6	-6	104	99	13	.533	1	1	-0	-2	C/O	-0.7
1963	NY-N	16	33	4	8	1	0	0	4	1	8	.242	.265	.273	.537	55	-2	-2	99	187	3	.400	0	0	0	-1	C	-0.1
1964	NY-N	60	164	11	51	10	0	0	10	14	28	.311	.369	.372	.741	115	2	3	95	67	21	.628	0	5	-3	3	C	0.6
1965	NY-N	114	251	17	46	8	2	0	7	28	60	.183	.270	.231	.502	43	-18	-18	100	50	16	.415	0	2	-1	-12	*C	-2.9
1968	Pit-N	25	58	5	14	2	2	1	7	9	13	.241	.343	.397	.740	120	2	2	101	113	8	.696	0	0	0	-2	C	0.0
1969	SD-N	134	418	23	92	14	3	4	33	42	81	.220	.291	.297	.588	67	-19	-18	97	97	34	.484	0	1	-1	3	*C	-0.6
1970	SD-N	111	341	27	95	13	3	5	42	48	49	.279	.369	.378	.748	106	2	4	95	113	47	.687	2	7	-4	-2	*C	0.3
1971	SD-N	21	63	2	12	1	0	1	8	11	10	.190	.320	.254	.574	67	-3	-2	96	171	4	.483	0	0	0	1	C	0.0
	Chi-N	71	197	18	42	8	1	5	23	28	24	.213	.314	.340	.654	78	-4	-6	110	114	19	.571	0	0	0	-2	C	-0.6
	Yr	92	260	20	54	9	1	6	31	39	34	.208	.316	.319	.635	75	-6	-8	107	129	26	.566	0	0	0	-1		-0.6
1972	LA-N	73	200	14	48	6	0	2	18	31	38	.240	.342	.300	.642	89	-3	-2	94	112	22	.580	0	1	-1	-4	C	-0.2
1973	LA-N	17	21	0	4	0	0	0	3	3	3	.190	.292	.190	.482	36	-2	-2	100	301	1	.412	0	0	0	0	C	0.0
1974	SD-N	26	60	2	11	1	0	0	4	6	11	.183	.258	.200	.458	31	-6	-5	93	129	3	.346	0	0	0	0	C	-0.3
Total	13	740	1950	132	458	66	12	18	169	241	354	.235	.321	.309	.630	78	-56	-52	98	103	192	.564	3	17	-9	-18	C/O	-4.5
■ JOE CANNON Cannon, Joseph Jerome b: 7/13/53, Camp Lejune, N.C. BL/TR, 6'3", 193 lbs. Deb: 9/22/77																												
1977	Hou-N	9	17	3	2	2	0	0	1	0	5	.118	.118	.235	.353	-9	-3	-2	93	100	0	.313	1	1	-0	0	/O	-0.2
1978	Hou-N	8	18	1	4	0	0	0	1	0	1	.222	.222	.222	.444	26	-2	-2	95	99	1	.267	0	1	-1	-1	/O	-0.3
1979	Tor-A	61	142	14	30	1	1	1	5	1	34	.211	.217	.254	.470	26	-15	-15	103	49	8	.422	12	2	2	-3	O	-1.6
1980	Tor-A	70	50	16	4	0	0	0	4	0	14	.080	.098	.080	.178	-51	-10	-10	100	390	0	.146	2	2	-1	-9	O/D	-2.0
Total	4	148	227	34	40	3	1	1	11	1	54	.176	.183	.211	.395	7	-29	-30	101	133	9	.337	15	6	1	-13	/OD	-4.1
■ JOSE CANSECO Canseco, Jose (Capas) b: 7/2/64, Havana, Cuba BR/TR, 6'3", 195 lbs. Deb: 9/02/85																												
1985	Oak-A	29	96	16	29	3	0	5	13	4	31	.302	.330	.490	.820	130	2	3	93	83	15	.754	1	1	-0	1	O	0.3
1986	Oak-A	157	600	85	144	29	1	33	117	65	175	.240	.322	.457	.779	118	8	13	94	120	89	.762	15	7	0	-4	*O/D	0.5
1987	Oak-A	159	630	81	162	35	3	31	113	50	157	.257	.314	.470	.784	115	3	11	91	123	91	.745	15	3	3	7	*OD	1.6
1988	Oak-A	158	610	120	187	34	0	**42**	**124**	78	128	.307	.394	**.569**	.963	**175**	54	58	95	110	136	1.046	40	16	2	0	*O/D	**6.0**
Total	4	503	1936	302	522	101	4	111	367	197	491	.270	.343	.498	.841	136	67	85	93	116	330	.860	71	27	5	4	O/D	8.4
■ BART CANTZ Cantz, Bartholomew L. b: 1/29/1860, Philadelphia, Pa. d: 2/12/43, Philadelphia, Pa. Deb: 1888																												
1888	Bal-a	37	126	7	21	2	1	0	9	2		.167	.180	.198	.378	24	-11	-10	96	108	5	.257	0			0	C/O	-0.8
1889	Bal-a	20	69	6	12	2	0	0	8	4	14	.174	.219	.203	.422	22	-7	-7	100	163	4	.351	2			0	C/O	-0.5
1890	Phi-a	5	22	1	1	0	0	0		0		.045	.045	.045	.091	-75	-5	-5	97	0	0	.048	0			0	/C	-0.3
Total	3	62	217	14	34	4	1	0	17	6	14	.157	.179	.184	.364	13	-22	-21	97	115	8	.262	2			0	/CO	-1.6
■ NICK CAPRA Capra, Nick Lee b: 3/8/58, Denver, Colo. BR/TR, 5'8", 165 lbs. Deb: 9/06/82																												
1982	Tex-A	13	15	2	4	0	0	1	1	3	4	.267	.421	.467	.888	155	1	1	93	40	3	1.000	2	1	0	1	/O	0.2
1983	Tex-A	8	2	2	0	0	0	0	0	0	0	.000	.000	.000	.000	-99	-1	-1	101	0	0	.000	0	0	0	-2	/O	-0.1
1985	Tex-A	8	8	1	1	0	0	0	0	0	0	.125	.125	.125	.250	-29	-1	-1	108	0	0	.143	0	0	0	-1	/O	-0.2
1988	KC-A	14	29	3	4	1	0	0	0	2	3	.138	.194	.172	.366	3	-4	-4	103	0	1	.286	1	0	0	-2	O/2D	-0.5
Total	4	43	54	8	9	1	0	1	1	5	7	.167	.250	.241	.491	37	-5	-5	100	13	4	.449	3	1	0	-4	/OD2	-0.6
■ PAT CAPRI Capri, Patrick Nicholas b: 11/27/18, New York, N.Y. BR/TR, 6'0.5", 170 lbs. Deb: 7/16/44																												
1944	Bos-N	7	1	1	0	0	0	0	0	0	1	.000	.000	.000	.000	-99	-0	-0	95	0	0	.000	0			0	/2	0.0
■ RALPH CAPRON Capron, Ralph Earl b: 6/16/1889, Minneapolis, Minn d: 9/19/80, Los Angeles, Cal. BL/TR, 5'11.5", 165 lbs. Deb: 4/25/12																												
1912	Pit-N	1	0	0	0	0	0	0	0	0	0	—	—	—	—	—	0	0	99	—	—	—	0			0	R	0.0
1913	Phi-N	2	1	1	0	0	0	0	0	0	0	.000	.000	.000	.000	-89	-0	-0	112	0	0	.000	0			-0	/O	0.0
Total	2	3	1	1	0	0	0	0	0	0	0	.000	.000	.000	.000	-89	-0	-0	112	0	0	.000	0			-0	/O	0.0
■ JOHN CARBINE Carbine, John C. b: 10/12/1855, Syracuse, N.Y. d: 9/11/15, Chicago, Ill. 6', 187 lbs. Deb: 5/08/1875																												
1875	Wes-n	10	39	1	2							.051															1	
1876	Lou-N	7	25	3	4	0	0	0	1	0	0	.160	.160	.160	.320	7	-2	-3	104	84	1	.190				0	/1O	-0.1
Total		7	25	3	4	0	0	0	1	0	0	.160	.160	.160	.320	7	-2	-3	104	84	1	.190				0	/1O	-0.1
■ BERNIE CARBO Carbo, Bernardo b: 8/5/47, Detroit, Mich. BL/TR, 5'11", 173 lbs. Deb: 9/02/69																												
1969	Cin-N	4	3	0	0	0	0	0	0	0	2	.000	.000	.000	.000	-99	-1	-1	99	0	0	.000	0	0	0	0	H	0.0
1970	Cin-N	125	365	54	113	19	3	21	63	94	77	.310	.456	.551	1.006	161	40	38	104	93	100	1.179	10	4	1	-8	*O	2.5
1971	Cin-N	106	310	33	68	20	1	5	20	54	56	.219	.339	.339	.678	96	-2	-0	96	68	38	.655	2	1	0	-2	O	-0.5
1972	Cin-N	19	21	2	3	0	0	0	0	6	3	.143	.357	.143	.500	50	-1	-1	93	0	2	.556	0	0	0	0	/O	0.0
	StL-N	99	302	42	78	13	1	7	34	57	56	.258	.385	.377	.762	112	9	8	105	103	47	.759	0	1	-1	6	O/3	0.9
	Yr	118	323	44	81	13	1	7	34	63	59	.251	.383	.362	.745	109	8	7	103	87	48	.744	0	1	-1	6		0.9
1973	StL-N	111	308	42	88	18	0	8	40	58	52	.286	.401	.422	.823	141	14	18	91	104	56	.845	2	0	1	3	O	1.8
1974	Bos-A	117	338	40	84	20	0	12	61	58	90	.249	.365	.414	.779	116	12	9	107	136	52	.774	4	3	-1	-4	OD	0.3
1975	Bos-A	107	319	64	82	21	3	15	50	83	69	.257	.412	.483	.895	140	25	21	109	96	68	.972	2	4	-2	-3	OD	1.5
1976	Bos-A	17	55	5	13	4	0	2	6	8	17	.236	.333	.418	.752	108	1	1	110	79	8	.762	1	0	0	-0	D/O	0.1
	Mil-A	69	183	20	43	7	0	3	15	33	55	.235	.352	.322	.674	99	1	1	99	85	22	.633	1	2	-1	3	OD	0.2
	Yr	86	238	25	56	11	0	5	21	41	72	.235	.348	.345	.692	102	2	2	101	85	30	.661	2	2	-1	3		0.3
1977	Bos-A	86	228	36	66	6	1	15	34	47	72	.289	.411	.522	.933	130	18	12	117	82	51	.994	1	2	-1	-0	O/D	0.9

YEAR	TM/L	G	AB	R	H	2B	3B	HR	RBI	BB	SO	AVG	OBP	SLG	PRO	/A	BR	/A	PF	CHI	RC	TA	SB	CS	SBR	FR	POS	TPR
1978	Bos-A	17	46	7	12	3	0	1	6	8	8	.261	.370	.391	.762	106	1	1	107	113	6	.711	1	1	-0	1	/OD	0.1
	Cle-A	60	174	21	50	8	0	4	16	20	31	.287	.364	.402	.766	124	4	5	93	77	25	.708	1	0	0	-2	D/O	0.4
	Yr	77	220	28	62	11	0	5	22	28	39	.282	.365	.400	.765	119	5	6	96	86	33	.721	2	1	0	-1		0.5
1979	StL-N	52	64	6	18	1	0	3	12	10	22	.281	.378	.438	.816	116	2	2	105	128	12	.848	1	0	0	-6	O	-0.3
1980	StL-N	14	11	0	2	0	0	0	0	1	0	.182	.250	.182	.432	22	-1	-1	103	0	1	.333	0	0	0	0	H	0.0
	Pit-N	7	6	0	2	0	0	0	1	1	1	.333	.429	.333	.762	112	0	0	103	198	1	.750	0	0	0	0	/H	0.0
	Yr	21	17	0	4	0	0	0	1	2	1	.235	.316	.235	.551	54	-1	-1	103	66	2	.462	0	0	0	0		0.0
Total	12	1010	2733	372	722	140	9	96	358	538	611	.264	.389	.427	.816	125	124	113	103	96	489	.863	26	18	-3	-12	OD/3	7.9
■ JOSE CARDENAL	Cardenal, Jose Rosario Domec (born Jose Rosario Domec (Cardenal)) b: 10/7/43, Matanzas, Cuba BR/TR, 5'10", 150 lbs. Deb: 4/14/63																											
1963	SF-N	9	5	1	1	0	0	0	2	1	1	.200	.333	.200	.533	60	-0	-0	96	841	0	.400	0	1	-1	-1	/O	-0.1
1964	SF-N	20	15	3	0	0	0	0	0	2	3	.000	.118	.000	.118	-64	-3	-3	100	0	0	.267	2	0	1	-3	O	-0.6
1965	Cal-A	134	512	58	128	23	2	11	57	27	72	.250	.290	.367	.657	87	-11	-9	98	113	54	.626	37	17	1	6	*O/32	-0.7
1966	Cal-A	154	561	67	155	15	3	16	48	34	69	.276	.322	.399	.721	107	4	4	99	76	72	.676	24	11	1	4	*O	0.3
1967	Cal-A	108	381	40	90	13	5	6	27	15	63	.236	.269	.344	.613	84	-10	-9	96	77	35	.527	10	5	0	-2	*O	-1.4
1968	Cle-A	157	583	78	150	21	7	7	44	39	74	.257	.306	.353	.659	98	-1	-2	101	88	65	.632	40	18	1	8	*O	0.2
1969	Cle-A	146	557	75	143	26	3	11	45	49	58	.257	.317	.373	.690	98	-6	-3	94	79	67	.669	36	6	7	4	*O/3	0.5
1970	StL-N	148	552	73	162	32	6	10	74	45	70	.293	.348	.428	.775	100	4	0	106	110	81	.746	26	9	2	-5	*O	-0.8
1971	StL-N	89	301	37	73	12	4	7	48	29	35	.243	.309	.379	.688	93	-3	-3	101	145	35	.649	12	3	2	8	O	0.4
	Mil-A	53	198	20	51	10	0	3	32	13	20	.258	.307	.354	.660	84	-4	-4	103	175	21	.596	9	5	-0	9	O	0.2
1972	Chi-N	143	533	96	155	24	6	17	70	55	58	.291	.358	.454	.812	114	20	11	114	104	83	.794	25	14	-1	-5	*O	0.0
1973	Chi-N	145	522	80	158	33	2	11	68	58	62	.303	.378	.437	.815	115	19	13	108	111	86	.801	19	7	2	-3	*O	0.5
1974	Chi-N	143	542	75	159	35	3	13	72	56	67	.293	.361	.441	.802	123	16	16	100	102	84	.778	23	9	2	8	*O	2.1
1975	Chi-N	154	574	85	182	30	2	9	68	77	50	.317	.402	.423	.825	124	25	22	104	103	103	.863	34	12	3	11	*O	3.1
1976	Chi-N	136	521	64	156	25	2	8	47	32	39	.299	.341	.401	.742	101	6	0	109	82	71	.690	23	14	-2	0	*O	-0.5
1977	Chi-N	100	226	33	54	12	1	3	18	28	30	.239	.325	.341	.666	69	-6	-10	114	84	24	.600	5	4	-1	-8	O/2S	-2.1
1978	Phi-N	87	201	27	50	12	0	4	33	23	16	.249	.326	.368	.694	89	-2	-3	105	152	23	.623	2	3	-1	-7	1O	-1.3
1979	Phi-N	29	48	4	10	3	0	0	9	8	8	.208	.321	.271	.592	65	-2	-2	97	274	4	.537	1	0	0	-2	O/1	-0.4
	NY-N	11	37	8	11	4	0	2	4	6	3	.297	.409	.568	.977	172	3	4	95	60	10	1.115	1	0	0	-1	/O1	0.3
	Yr	40	85	12	21	7	0	2	13	14	11	.247	.360	.400	.760	111	1	2	96	222	14	.797	2	0	1	-3		-0.1
1980	NY-N	26	42	4	7	1	0	0	4	6	4	.167	.271	.190	.461	32	-4	-4	96	198	2	.359	0	1	-1	1	/O1	-0.3
	KC-A	25	53	8	18	2	0	0	5	5	5	.340	.397	.377	.774	115	1	1	98	97	9	.714	0	0	0	-4	O	-0.2
Total	18	2017	6964	936	1913	333	46	138	775	608	807	.275	.335	.395	.730	102	46	20	103	103	928	.716	329	139	15	17	*O/132S	-0.8
■ LEO CARDENAS	Cardenas, Leonardo Lazaro (Alfonso) "Chico" b: 12/17/38, Matanzas, Cuba BR/TR, 5'11", 150 lbs. Deb: 7/25/60																											
1960	Cin-N	48	142	13	33	2	4	1	12	6	32	.232	.264	.324	.587	61	-8	-8	98	99	12	.473	0	0	0	-2	S	-0.8
1961	Cin-N	74	198	23	61	18	1	5	24	15	39	.308	.357	.485	.842	116	6	5	104	87	33	.789	1	0	0	-6	S	0.5
1962	Cin-N	153	589	77	173	31	4	10	60	39	99	.294	.343	.411	.754	99	1	-1	102	92	79	.658	2	5	-2	-7	*S	0.3
1963	Cin-N	158	565	42	133	22	4	7	48	23	101	.235	.270	.326	.596	68	-22	-24	104	100	46	.476	3	5	-2	-3	*S	-1.5
1964	Cin-N	163	597	61	150	32	2	9	69	41	110	.251	.302	.357	.658	82	-12	-15	103	120	63	.564	4	4	-1	-10	*S	-1.4
1965	Cin-N	156	557	65	160	25	11	11	57	60	100	.287	.358	.431	.788	117	16	13	104	88	81	.722	1	4	-2	-2	*S	2.8
1966	Cin-N	160	568	59	145	25	4	20	81	45	87	.255	.311	.419	.730	89	-0	-10	114	117	69	.657	9	4	0	-14	*S	-1.0
1967	Cin-N	108	379	30	97	14	3	2	21	34	77	.256	.320	.325	.645	78	-7	-11	109	69	38	.553	4	5	-2	-14	*S	-1.5
1968	Cin-N	137	452	45	106	13	2	7	41	36	83	.235	.294	.319	.612	75	-9	-14	111	105	39	.507	2	1	0	-22	*S	-2.2
1969	Min-A	160	578	67	162	24	4	10	70	66	96	.280	.358	.388	.746	106	8	6	102	113	78	.678	5	6	-2	**31**	*S	4.4
1970	Min-A	160	588	67	145	34	4	11	65	42	101	.247	.301	.374	.675	87	-13	-12	98	106	65	.584	2	5	-2	2	*S	0.1
1971	Min-A	153	554	59	146	25	4	18	75	51	69	.264	.327	.421	.747	106	6	4	104	109	73	.674	3	3	-1	-1	*S	1.9
1972	Cal-A	150	551	25	123	11	2	6	42	35	73	.223	.272	.283	.555	74	-24	-17	88	107	41	.436	1	2	-1	3	*S	0.0
1973	Cle-A	72	195	9	42	4	0	0	12	13	42	.215	.264	.236	.500	43	-15	-14	97	102	11	.370	1	4	-2	1	S/3	-0.6
1974	Tex-A	34	92	5	25	3	0	0	7	2	14	.272	.287	.304	.592	73	-4	-3	96	98	8	.449	1	0	0	-0	3S/D	-0.1
1975	Tex-A	55	102	15	24	2	0	1	5	14	12	.235	.328	.284	.612	75	-3	-3	100	60	11	.551	0	0	0	1	3/S2	0.0
Total	16	1941	6707	662	1725	285	49	118	689	522	1135	.257	.313	.367	.681	89	-80	-103	103	102	748	.607	39	48	-17	-45	*S/3D2	0.9
■ ROD CAREW	Carew, Rodney Cline b: 10/1/45, Gatun, C.Z. BL/TR, 6', 170 lbs. Deb: 4/11/67																											
1967	Min-A	137	514	66	150	22	7	8	51	37	91	.292	.342	.409	.750	113	13	9	107	96	68	.660	5	9	-4	-9	*2	0.0
1968	Min-A	127	461	46	126	27	2	1	42	26	71	.273	.314	.347	.661	94	-1	-3	106	113	49	.569	12	4	1	-3	*2/S	0.0
1969	Min-A	123	458	79	152	30	4	8	56	37	72	**.332**	.386	.467	.853	135	22	21	102	96	83	.850	19	8	1	4	*2	3.2
1970	Min-A	51	191	27	70	12	3	4	28	11	28	.366	.407	.524	.930	157	14	14	98	103	39	.914	4	6	-2	-3	2/1	1.4
1971	Min-A	147	577	88	177	16	10	2	48	45	81	.307	.358	.380	.737	105	7	4	104	92	73	.630	6	7	-2	-21	*2/3	-1.3
1972	Min-A	142	535	61	170	21	6	0	51	43	60	**.318**	.371	.379	.750	115	16	12	107	111	75	.681	12	6	0	5	*2	2.8
1973	Min-A	149	580	98	**203**	30	**11**	6	62	62	55	**.350**	.415	.471	.885	144	39	36	104	89	113	.924	41	16	3	14	*2	**5.9**
1974	Min-A	153	599	86	**218**	30	5	3	55	74	49	**.364**	**.435**	.446	.880	152	45	44	101	75	**118**	.918	38	16	2	17	*2	**7.1**
1975	Min-A	143	535	89	192	24	4	14	80	64	40	**.359**	**.428**	.497	.926	150	44	39	107	106	118	1.011	35	9	5	11	*21/D	5.8
1976	Min-A	156	605	97	200	29	12	9	90	67	52	.331	.398	.463	.861	154	**40**	**41**	98	119	111	**.904**	49	22	2	2	*1/2	3.9
1977	Min-A	155	616	**128**	**239**	38	**16**	14	100	69	55	**.388**	**.452**	.570	**1.022**	**171**	**67**	**65**	103	107	**160**	**1.126**	23	13	-1	5	*1/2D	**5.9**
1978	Min-A	152	564	85	188	26	10	5	70	78	62	**.333**	**.415**	.441	.857	149	34	38	94	111	105	.885	27	7	4	4	*1/2O	4.0
1979	Cal-A	110	409	78	130	15	3	3	44	73	46	.318	.421	.391	.812	130	16	21	93	96	73	.848	18	8	1	-5	*1/D	1.0
1980	Cal-A	144	540	74	179	34	7	3	59	59	38	.331	.398	.437	.835	134	23	26	96	100	92	.816	23	15	-2	-6	*1D	1.1
1981	Cal-A	93	364	57	111	17	1	2	21	45	45	.305	.381	.374	.755	114	10	8	104	51	53	.730	16	9	-1	-1	1/D	0.5
1982	Cal-A	138	523	88	167	25	5	3	44	67	49	.319	.399	.403	.802	121	18	18	100	85	83	.759	10	17	-7	1	*1	0.8
1983	Cal-A	129	472	66	160	24	2	2	44	57	48	.339	.411	.411	.822	133	20	23	96	88	78	.772	6	7	-2	-7	1D/2	1.0
1984	Cal-A	93	329	42	97	8	1	3	31	40	39	.295	.371	.353	.724	100	2	2	101	101	44	.658	4	3	-1	-3	1/D	-0.6
1985	Cal-A	127	443	69	124	17	3	2	39	64	47	.280	.372	.345	.717	97	1	1	101	99	60	.672	5	5	-2	-8	*1	-1.5
Total	19	2469	9315	1424	3053	445	112	92	1015	1018	1028	.328	.395	.429	.825	131	431	419	101	97	1595	.835	353	187	-6	-2	*12/DS3O	41.0
■ ANDY CAREY	Carey, Andrew Arthur (born Andrew Arthur Nordstrom) b: 10/18/31, Oakland, Cal. BR/TR, 6'1.5", 190 lbs. Deb: 5/02/52																											
1952	NY-A	16	40	6	6	0	0	0	1	3	10	.150	.209	.150	.359	1	-5	-5	98	62	1	.250	0	0	0	1	3/S	-0.3
1953	NY-A	51	81	14	26	5	0	4	8	9	12	.321	.389	.531	.920	158	5	6	93	54	17	.947	2	1	0	3	3/S2	0.7
1954	NY-A	122	411	60	124	14	6	8	65	43	38	.302	.377	.423	.801	120	11	12	99	124	64	.746	5	5	-2	14	*3	1.8
1955	NY-A	135	510	73	131	19	**11**	7	47	44	51	.257	.317	.378	.696	88	-11	-10	98	87	60	.613	3	3	-1	11	*3	0.3
1956	NY-A	132	422	54	100	18	2	7	50	45	53	.237	.313	.339	.652	73	-17	-16	99	114	45	.591	9	6	-1	1	*3	-1.3
1957	NY-A	85	247	30	63	6	5	6	33	15	42	.255	.311	.393	.704	97	-4	-2	94	113	29	.617	2	2	-1	-0	3	0.0
1958	NY-A	102	315	39	90	19	4	12	45	34	43	.286	.366	.486	.852	129	14	13	103	95	57	.836	1	2	-1	9	3	2.5
1959	NY-A	41	101	11	26	1	0	3	9	7	17	.257	.306	.356	.662	88	-3	-2	93	79	10	.550	1	1	-0	1	3	0.0
1960	NY-A	4	3	1	1	0	0	0	1	0	1	.333	.333	.333	.667	86	-0	-0	94	392	0	.500	0	0	0	-0	/3O	0.0
	KC-A	102	343	30	80	14	4	12	53	26	52	.233	.289	.402	.692	86	-8	-8	99	119	36	.591	0	0	0	1	3	-0.5
	Yr	106	346	31	81	14	4	12	54	26	53	.234	.290	.402	.691	86	-9	-8	99	133	36	.591	0	0	0	0		-0.5
1961	KC-A	39	123	20	30	6	2	3	11	15	23	.244	.336	.398	.734	94	-1	-1	102	74	17	.688	0	0	0	3	3	0.4
	Chi-A	56	143	21	38	12	3	0	14	11	24	.266	.327	.392	.719	92	-2	-2	99	98	19	.645	0	1	-1	0	3	0.1
	Yr	95	266	41	68	18	5	3	25	26	47	.256	.331	.395	.726	93	-3	-3	100	89	37	.675	0	1	-1	3		0.5
1962	LA-N	53	111	12	26	5	1	2	13	16	23	.234	.336	.351	.687	91	-2	-1	93	114	14	.651	0	0	0	0	3	0.0
Total	11	938	2850	371	741	119	38	64	350	268	389	.260	.329	.396	.725	97	-23	-16	98	103	369	.679	23	21	-6	44	3/SO2	3.7
■ SCOOPS CAREY	Carey, George C. b: 12/4/1870, E.Liverpool, Ohio d: 12/17/16, E.Liverpool, Ohio BR/TR, 175 lbs. Deb: 4/26/1895																											
1895	Bal-N	123	490	59	128	21	6	1	75	27	32	.261	.305	.335	.640	62	-25	-31	107	128	52	.544	2			-8	*1/OS3	-2.8
1898	Lou-N	8	32	1	6	1	1	0	1	1		.188	.212	.281	.493	44	-2	-2	96	36	2	.385	0			0	/1	-0.1
1902	Was-A	120	452	46	142	35	11	0	60	20		.314	.343	.440	.783	119	9	10	99	101	71	.716	3			3	*1	1.3

YEAR	TM/L	G	AB	R	H	2B	3B	HR	RBI	BB	SO	AVG	OBP	SLG	PRO	/A	BR	/A	PF	CHI	RC	TA	SB	CS	SBR	FR	POS	TPR
1903	Was-A	48	183	8	37	3	2	0	23	4		.202	.219	.240	.460	37	-13	-14	105	199	10	.329	0			-2	1	-1.6
Total	4	299	1157	114	313	60	20	1	159	52	32	.271	.304	.360	.664	79	-31	-37	103	126	135	.565	5			-7	1/3SO	-3.2
■ MAX CAREY Carey, Max George "Scoops" (born Maximilian Carnarius) b: 1/11/1890, Terre Haute, Ind. d: 5/30/76, Miami, Fla. BB/TR, 5'11.5", 170 lbs. Deb: 10/03/10 MCH																												
1910	Pit-N	2	6	2	3	0	1	0	2	2	1	.500	.625	.833	1.458	291	2	2	112	142	3	2.333	0			2	/O	0.3
1911	Pit-N	129	427	77	110	15	10	5	43	44	75	.258	.337	.375	.712	98	-1	-2	101	85	64	.751	27			0	*O	-0.4
1912	Pit-N	150	587	114	177	23	8	5	66	61	79	.302	.372	.394	.766	111	8	10	99	80	104	.834	45			5	*O	0.9
1913	Pit-N	154	620	**99**	172	23	10	5	49	55	67	.277	.339	.371	.710	107	2	5	96	64	92	.779	**61**			22	*O	2.5
1914	Pit-N	156	593	76	144	25	**17**	1	31	59	56	.243	.313	.347	.661	104	-3	2	92	52	72	.679	38			6	*O	0.4
1915	Pit-N	140	564	76	143	26	5	3	27	57	58	.254	.326	.333	.660	101	1	2	99	45	66	.651	**36**	17	1	17	*O	1.7
1916	Pit-N	154	599	90	158	23	11	7	42	59	58	.264	.337	.374	.711	113	13	10	105	60	87	.767	**63**	19	8	**24**	*O	3.3
1917	Pit-N	155	588	82	174	21	12	1	51	58	38	.296	.369	.378	.746	130	22	22	100	84	94	.812	**46**			22	*O	4.3
1918	Pit-N	126	468	70	128	14	6	3	48	**62**	25	.274	.363	.348	.712	111	12	9	106	93	76	.844	**58**			15	*O	1.9
1919	Pit-N	66	244	41	75	10	2	0	9	25	24	.307	.376	.365	.741	117	8	6	105	38	38	.793	18			5	O	1.0
1920	Pit-N	130	485	74	140	18	4	1	35	59	31	.289	.369	.348	.718	106	7	6	101	76	72	.797	**52**	10	**10**	-3	*O	0.5
1921	Pit-N	140	521	85	161	34	4	7	56	70	30	.309	.395	.430	.825	114	16	14	103	81	95	.901	37	12	4	12	*O	2.2
1922	Pit-N	155	629	140	207	28	12	10	70	**80**	26	.329	.408	.459	.868	119	24	21	104	68	131	1.000	**51**	2	**14**	13	*O	3.9
1923	Pit-N	153	610	120	188	32	**19**	6	63	73	28	.308	.388	.452	.841	125	20	23	97	67	117	.947	**51**	8	**11**	**16**	*O	**4.2**
1924	Pit-N	149	599	113	178	30	9	7	55	58	17	.297	.366	.412	.778	102	8	3	106	65	97	.832	**49**	13	**7**	6	*O	1.2
1925	Pit-N	133	542	109	186	39	13	5	44	66	19	.343	.418	.491	.909	129	28	26	102	49	118	1.041	**46**	11	**7**	6	*O	3.3
1926	Pit-N	86	324	46	72	14	5	0	28	30	14	.222	.288	.296	.584	51	-19	-25	112	107	28	.540	10			2	O	-2.5
	Bro-N	27	100	18	26	3	1	0	7	8	5	.260	.315	.310	.625	69	-4	-4	99	83	10	.527	0			-0	O	-0.4
	Yr	113	424	64	98	17	6	0	35	38	19	.231	.294	.300	.594	55	-24	-29	109	102	38	.537	10			2		-2.9
1927	Bro-N	144	538	70	143	30	10	1	54	64	18	.266	.345	.364	.709	88	-7	-9	103	91	69	.742	32			13	*O	-0.1
1928	Bro-N	108	296	41	73	11	0	2	19	47	24	.247	.354	.304	.658	74	-10	-9	99	70	34	.704	18			-9	O	-2.1
1929	Bro-N	19	23	2	7	0	0	0	1	3	2	.304	.407	.304	.712	84	-0	-0	94	49	3	.688	0			-1	/O	0.0
Total	20	2476	9363	1545	2665	419	159	69	800	1040	695	.285	.361	.385	.746	107	127	112	101	70	1471	.805	738	92		170	*O	26.1
■ ROGER CAREY Carey, Roger J. Deb: 7/09/1887																												
1887	NY-N	1	4	0	0	0	0	0	2	0	1	.000	.000	.000	.000	-93	-1	-1	107	0	0	.000	0			0	/2	0.0
■ TOM CAREY Carey, Thomas Francis Aloysius "Scoops" b: 10/11/06, Hoboken, N.J. d: 2/21/70, Rochester, N.Y. BR/TR, 5'8.5", 170 lbs. Deb: 7/19/35 C																												
1935	StL-A	76	296	29	86	18	4	0	42	13	11	.291	.320	.378	.699	75	-9	-12	107	130	35	.590	0	2	-1	-3	2	-1.1
1936	StL-A	134	488	58	133	27	6	1	57	27	25	.273	.315	.359	.673	64	-27	-30	103	104	55	.581	2	1	0	-10	*2/S	-2.6
1937	StL-A	130	487	54	134	24	1	1	40	21	26	.275	.306	.335	.641	62	-29	-28	99	84	49	.524	1	2	-1	-7	2S/3	-2.3
1939	Bos-A	54	161	17	39	6	2	0	20	3	9	.242	.265	.304	.569	42	-14	-15	108	138	12	.429	0	0	0	6	2S	-0.5
1940	Bos-A	43	62	4	20	4	0	0	7	2	1	.323	.344	.387	.731	88	-1	-1	101	105	8	.591	0	0	0	1	S/23	0.2
1941	Bos-A	25	21	7	4	0	0	0	0	0	0	.190	.190	.190	.381	1	-3	-3	103	0	1	.235	0	0	0	0	/2S3	-0.1
1942	Bos-A	1	1	0	1	0	0	0	1	0	0	1.000	1.000	1.000	2.000	447	0	0	104	352	1	—	0	0	0	0	/2	0.1
1946	Bos-A	3	5	0	1	0	0	0	0	0	1	.200	.200	.200	.400	10	-1	-1	114	0	0	.200	0	0	0	0	/2	0.0
Total	8	466	1521	169	418	79	13	2	167	66	73	.275	.308	.348	.655	63	-83	-89	103	105	162	.545	3	5	-2	-13	2/S3	-6.3
■ TOM CAREY Carey, Thomas John (born J. J. Norton) b: 1849, Brooklyn, N.J. d: 2/13/1899, Los Angeles, Cal. TR , 5'8", 145 lbs. Deb: 5/04/1871 M																												
1871	Kek-n	19	85	15	20							.235															2/S	
1872	Bal-n	41	196	39	58							.296															2/S3O1	
1873	Bal-n	55	292	72	95							.325															*2/S3M	
1874	Mut-n	64	292	55	83							.284															*S2M	
1875	Har-n	85	390	63	99							.254															*S	
1876	Har-N	68	289	51	78	7	0	0	26	3	4	.270	.277	.294	.572	84	-3	-6	108	109	24	.417				-0	*S	-0.6
1877	Har-N	60	274	38	70	3	2	1	20	0	9	.255	.255	.292	.547	81	-9	-4	89	79	21	.392				-4	*S	-0.6
1878	Pro-N	61	253	33	60	10	3	0	24	0	14	.237	.237	.300	.538	77	-7	-6	98	113	18	.394				1	*S	0.0
1879	Cle-N	80	335	30	80	14	1	0	32	5	20	.239	.250	.287	.537	77	-8	-8	99	112	25	.396				-4	*S	-0.6
Total	5 n	264	1255	244	355							.283															*S	
Total	4	269	1151	152	288	34	6	1	102	8	47	.250	.255	.293	.548	79	-26	-25	99	104	88	.400				-7	S2/3O1	-1.8
■ BOBBY CARGO Cargo, Robert J. "Chic" b: 1871, Pittsburgh, Pa. BR/TR, Deb: 10/06/1892																												
1892	Pit-N	2	4	0	1	0	0	0	0	0	0	.250	.250	.250	.500	56	-0	-0	94	0	0	.333	0			0	/S	0.0
■ FRED CARISCH Carisch, Frederick Behlmer b: 11/14/1881, Fountain City, Wis d: 4/19/77, San Gabriel, Cal. BR/TR, 5'10.5", 174 lbs. Deb: 03 C																												
1903	Pit-N	5	18	4	6	4	0	1	5	0		.333	.333	.722	1.056	191	2	2	105	100	4	1.083	0			-1	/C	0.2
1904	Pit-N	37	125	9	31	3	1	0	8	9		.248	.299	.288	.587	84	-2	-2	99	83	12	.511	3			-1	C1	-0.1
1905	Pit-N	32	107	7	22	0	3	0	8	2		.206	.220	.262	.482	43	-7	-8	104	99	7	.365	1			-2	C	-0.6
1906	Pit-N	4	12	0	1	0	0	0	0	1		.083	.154	.083	.237	-24	-2	-2	104	0	0	.273	1			-0	/C	-0.1
1912	Cle-A	25	70	4	19	3	1	0	5	1		.271	.282	.343	.625	77	-2	-2	101	69	7	.549	3			2	C	0.1
1913	Cle-A	82	222	11	48	4	2	0	26	21	19	.216	.287	.252	.539	55	-12	-13	106	165	17	.483	6			2	C	-0.4
1914	Cle-A	40	102	8	22	3	2	0	5	12	18	.216	.298	.284	.583	74	-3	-3	102	65	9	.524	2	2	-1	4	C	0.2
1923	Det-A	2	0	0	0	0	0	0	0	0	0	—	—	—	—	—	0	0	97	—	—	—	0	0	0	0	/C	0.0
Total	8	227	656	43	149	17	9	1	57	46	37	.227	.279	.285	.564	66	-26	-29	103	109	66	.491	16	2		3	C/1	-0.7
■ FRED CARL Carl, Frederick E. b: 1856, Washington, D.C. d: 5/4/19, Washington, D.C. TL , 5'6", 158 lbs. Deb: 7/25/1889																												
1889	Lou-a	25	99	13	20	2	2	0	13	16	22	.202	.313	.263	.576	69	-4	-3	96	123	8	.532	0			0	O/23	-0.2
■ LEW CARL Carl, Lewis b: Baltimore, Md. Deb: 9/09/1874																												
1874	Bal-n	1	4	0	0							.000															/C	
■ JIM CARLETON Carleton, James b: 1849, New York 5'8", 155 lbs. Deb: 5/04/1871																												
1871	Cle-n	29	136	31	32							.235															*1	
1872	Cle-n	7	38	8	12							.316															1	
Total	2 n	36	174	39	44							.253															1	
■ JIM CARLIN Carlin, James Arthur b: 2/23/18, Wylam, Ala. BR/TR, 5'11", 165 lbs. Deb: 7/26/41																												
1941	Phi-N	16	21	2	3	1	0	1	2	3	4	.143	.250	.333	.583	65	-1	-1	97	72	2	.526	0			-4	/O3	-0.4
■ WALTER CARLISLE Carlisle, Walter G. "Rosy" b: 7/6/1883, Yorkshire, England d: 5/27/45, Los Angeles, Cal. BB/TR, Deb: 5/08/08																												
1908	Bos-A	3	10	0	1	0	0	0	0	1		.100	.182	.100	.282	-7	-1	-1	98	0	0	.333	1			0	/O	0.0
■ SWEDE CARLSTROM Carlstrom, Albin Oscar b: 10/26/1886, Elizabeth, N.J. d: 4/28/35, Elizabeth, N.J. BR/TR, 6', 167 lbs. Deb: 9/13/11																												
1911	Bos-A	2	6	0	1	0	0	0	0	0		.167	.167	.167	.333	-7	-1	-1	99	0	0	.200	0			-0	/S	0.0
■ CLEO CARLYLE Carlyle, Hiram Cleo b: 9/7/02, Fairburn, Ga. d: 11/12/67, Los Angeles, Cal. BL/TR, 6', 170 lbs. Deb: 5/16/27																												
1927	Bos-A	95	278	31	65	12	8	1	28	36	40	.234	.324	.345	.669	78	-11	-9	95	94	32	.643	4	0	1	-9	O	-2.1
■ ROY CARLYLE Carlyle, Roy Edward "Dizzy" b: 12/10/1900, Buford, Ga. d: 11/22/56, Norcross, Ga. BL/TR, 6'2.5", 195 lbs. Deb: 4/16/25																												
1925	Was-A	1	1	0	0	0	0	0	0	0	1	.000	.000	.000	.000	-99	-0	-0	98	0	0	.000	0	0	0	0	H	0.0
	Bos-A	93	276	36	90	20	3	7	49	16	28	.326	.365	.496	.862	123	6	8	95	104	49	.829	1	1	-0	-7	O	-0.4
	Yr	94	277	36	90	20	3	7	49	16	29	.325	.364	.495	.859	122	5	7	95	103	49	.824	1	1	-0	-7		-0.4
1926	Bos-A	45	165	22	47	6	2	2	16	4	18	.285	.310	.382	.692	79	-6	-6	101	80	19	.585	0	0	0	-5	O	-1.3
	NY-A	35	52	3	20	5	1	0	11	4	9	.385	.439	.519	.958	150	4	4	99	138	12	1.000	0	0	0	-4	O	0.0
	Yr	80	217	25	67	11	3	2	27	8	27	.309	.342	.415	.757	96	-2	-2	100	107	30	.673	0	0	0	-9		-1.3
Total	2	174	494	61	157	31	6	9	76	24	56	.318	.354	.460	.814	111	4	6	97	100	80	.757	1	1	-0	-15	O	-1.7

YEAR	TM/L	G	AB	R	H	2B	3B	HR	RBI	BB	SO	AVG	OBP	SLG	PRO	/A	BR	/A	PF	CHI	RC	TA	SB	CS	SBR	FR	POS	TPR
■ GEORGE CARMAN Carman, George Wartman b: Doylestown, Pa. d: 6/16/29, Lancaster, Pa. Deb: 9/04/1890																												
1890	Phi-a	28	97	9	17	2	0	0		8		.175	.245	.196	.441	33	-8	-8	97	0	6	.412	5			0	SO/23	-0.6
■ DUKE CARMEL Carmel, Leon James b: 4/23/37, New York, N.Y. BL/TL, 6'3", 202 lbs. Deb: 9/10/59																												
1959	StL-N	10	23	2	3	1	0	0	3	1	6	.130	.167	.174	.341	-9	-4	-4	105	303	1	.238	0	1	-1	-1	O	-0.5
1960	StL-N	4	3	0	0	0	0	0	0	1	1	.000	.250	.000	.250	-23	-1	-1	108	0	0	.500	1	1	-0	-0	/1O	0.0
1963	StL-N	57	44	9	10	1	0	1	2	9	11	.227	.358	.318	.677	90	0	-0	107	49	6	.676	0	0	0	-7	O/1	-0.9
	NY-N	47	149	11	35	5	3	3	18	16	37	.235	.309	.369	.678	95	-1	-1	99	118	18	.629	2	2	-1	4	O1	0.1
	Yr	104	193	20	45	6	3	4	20	25	48	.233	.321	.358	.679	92	-1	-2	104	81	24	.640	2	2	-1	-3		-0.8
1965	NY-A	6	8	0	0	0	0	0	0	0	5	.000	.000	.000	.000	-99	-2	-2	101	0	0	.000	0	0	0	0	/1	-0.1
Total	4	124	227	22	48	7	3	4	23	27	60	.211	.295	.322	.617	75	-7	-7	102	116	24	.563	3	4	-2	-5	/O1	-1.4
■ EDDIE CARNETT Carnett, Edwin Elliott "Lefty" b: 10/21/16, Springfield, Mo. BL/TL, 6', 185 lbs. Deb: 4/19/41																												
1941	Bos-N	2	0	0	0	0	0	0	0	0	0	—	—	—	—	—	0	0	93	—	—	—	0			0	/P	0.0
1944	Chi-A	126	457	51	126	18	8	1	60	26	35	.276	.322	.357	.678	94	-4	-4	100	133	55	.589	5	2	0	-1	O1/P	-0.8
1945	Cle-A	30	73	5	16	7	0	0	7	2	9	.219	.250	.315	.565	64	-4	-4	99	110	5	.441	0	1	-1	-0	O/P	-0.5
Total	3	158	530	56	142	25	8	1	67	28	44	.268	.312	.351	.663	90	-8	-8	100	130	84	.574	5	3		-1	O/1P	-1.3
■ JOHN CARNEY Carney, John Joseph "Handsome Jack" b: 11/10/1866, Salem, Mass. d: 10/19/25, Litchfield, N.H. BR/TR, 5'10.5", 175 lbs. Deb: 4/24/1889																												
1889	Was-N	69	273	25	63	7	0	1	29	14	14	.231	.271	.267	.538	57	-17	-14	92	116	24	.476	12			-5	1O	-1.9
1890	Buf-P	28	107	11	29	3	0	0	13	7	14	.271	.333	.299	.632	78	-4	-2	92	113	12	.564	2			0	1/O	-0.1
	Cle-P	25	89	15	31	5	3	0	21	14	5	.348	.442	.472	.914	160	6	8	92	139	22	1.086	6			0	O/1	0.6
	Yr	53	196	26	60	8	3	0	34	21	19	.306	.385	.378	.762	116	2	6	92	128	32	.787	8			0		0.5
1891	CM-a	130	477	69	135	15	10	6	66	48	26	.283	.356	.394	.750	105	10	1	112	95	76	.766	20			3	*1	-0.1
Total	3	252	946	120	258	30	13	7	129	83	59	.273	.338	.354	.693	94	-5	-7	102	107	133	.682	40			-2	1/O	-1.5
■ PAT CARNEY Carney, Patrick Joseph "Doc" b: 8/7/1876, Holyoke, Mass. d: 1/9/53, Worcester, Mass. BL/TL, 6', 200 lbs. Deb: 9/20/01																												
1901	Bos-N	13	55	6	16	2	1	0	6	3		.291	.328	.364	.691	92	0	-1	112	87	7	.590	0			-1	O	-0.2
1902	Bos-N	137	522	75	141	17	4	2	65	42		.270	.324	.330	.654	109	3	6	95	134	66	.633	27			-8	*O/P	-1.2
1903	Bos-N	110	392	37	94	12	4	1	49	28		.240	.290	.298	.589	72	-15	-13	96	134	38	.520	10			12	OP/1	-0.3
1904	Bos-N	78	279	24	57	5	2	0	11	12		.204	.237	.237	.474	50	-17	-16	97	62	17	.378	6			-0	O/P1	-1.8
Total	4	338	1248	142	308	36	11	3	131	85		.247	.295	.300	.595	83	-29	-24	97	116	128	.535	43			3	O/P1	-3.5
■ BILL CARNEY Carney, William John b: 3/25/1874, St.Paul, Minn. d: 7/31/38, Hopkins, Minn. BB/TR, 5'10", Deb: 8/22/04																												
1904	Chi-N	2	7	0	0	0	0	0	0	1		.000	.125	.000	.125	-59	-1	-1	101	0	0	.143	0			0	/O	0.0
■ HICK CARPENTER Carpenter, Warren William b: 8/16/1855, Grafton, Mass. d: 4/18/37, San Diego, Cal. BR/TL, 5'11", 186 lbs. Deb: 5/01/1879																												
1879	Syr-N	65	261	30	53	6	0	0	20	2	15	.203	.209	.226	.435	49	-15	-11	89	126	13	.293				1	13O/2	-1.1
1880	Cin-N	77	300	32	72	6	4	0	23	2	15	.240	.245	.287	.532	80	-6	-6	99	103	22	.386				5	*3/1S	0.0
1881	Wor-N	83	347	40	75	12	2	2	31	3	19	.216	.223	.280	.502	54	-17	-19	105	111	22	.368				0	*3	-1.1
1882	Cin-a	80	351	78	**120**	15	5	1		10		.342	.360	.422	.782	150	22	18	109	0	55	.684				-1	*3	1.2
1883	Cin-a	95	436	99	129	18	4	3		18		.296	.324	.376	.700	121	12	9	103	0	54	.593				-6	*3	0.4
1884	Cin-a	108	474	80	121	16	2	4		6		.255	.271	.323	.593	90	-3	-7	106	0	42	.462				-12	*3/O	-1.5
1885	Cin-a	112	473	89	131	12	8	2		9		.277	.295	.349	.644	102	2	-1	104	0	50	.518				-7	*3	0.0
1886	Cin-a	111	458	67	101	8	5	2		18		.221	.262	.273	.535	72	-16	-13	96	0	36	.445	8			-6	*3	-1.2
1887	Cin-a	127	498	70	124	12	6	1		19		.249	.282	.303	.585	60	-23	-31	108	0	56	.583	44			-16	*3	-4.0
1888	Cin-a	136	551	68	147	14	5	3	67	5		.267	.280	.327	.607	96	-3	-4	101	112	69	.616	59			-12	*3	-1.4
1889	Cin-a	123	486	67	127	23	6	0	63	18	41	.261	.293	.333	.627	76	-14	-17	105	118	63	.643	47			-28	*3/1	-3.7
1892	StL-N	1	3	0	1	0	0	0	0	1	1	.333	.500	.333	.833	164	0	0	95	0	1	1.000	0			0	/3	0.0
Total	12	1118	4638	720	1201	142	47	18	204	111	91	.259	.281	.321	.602	87	-62	-82	103	47	482	.520	158			-81	*3/1O2S	-12.4
■ CHARLIE CARR Carr, Charles Carbitt b: 12/27/1876, Coatesville, Pa. d: 11/25/32, Memphis, Tenn. BR/TR, 6'2", 195 lbs. Deb: 9/15/1898																												
1898	Was-N	20	73	6	14	2	0	0	4	2		.192	.213	.219	.433	25	-7	-7	102	77	4	.339	2			0	1	-0.6
1901	Phi-A	2	8	0	1	0	0	0	0	0		.125	.125	.125	.250	-30	-1	-1	100	0	0	.143	0			0	/1	0.0
1903	Det-A	135	548	59	154	23	11	2	79	10		.281	.294	.374	.668	104	-1	1	97	130	65	.571	10			12	*1	1.5
1904	Det-A	92	360	29	77	13	3	0	40	14		.214	.243	.267	.510	66	-15	-13	96	149	25	.410	6			6	1	-0.5
	Cle-A	32	120	9	27	5	1	0	7	4		.225	.250	.283	.533	69	-4	-4	102	81	9	.409	0			-2	1	-0.5
	Yr	124	480	38	104	18	4	0	47	18		.217	.245	.271	.516	67	-19	-17	97	133	34	.410	6			4		-1.0
1905	Cle-A	89	306	29	72	12	4	1	31	13		.235	.266	.310	.577	85	-6	-6	100	115	29	.513	12			1	1	-0.6
1906	Cin-N	22	94	9	18	2	3	0	10	2		.191	.208	.277	.485	46	-5	-7	115	121	6	.368	0			1	1	-0.7
1914	Ind-F	115	441	44	129	11	10	3	69	26	47	.293	.332	.383	.715	94	2	-4	111	148	66	.686	19			-0	*1	-0.1
Total	7	507	1950	185	492	68	32	6	240	71	47	.252	.279	.329	.608	84	-37	-41	102	129	203	.523	49			18	1	-1.5
■ LEW CARR Carr, Lewis Smith b: 8/15/1872, Union Springs, N.Y d: 6/15/54, Moravia, N.Y. TR , 6'2", 200 lbs. Deb: 7/04/01																												
1901	Pit-N	9	28	2	7	1	1	0	4	2		.250	.300	.357	.657	92	-0	-0	101	134	3	.571	0			0	/S3	0.0
■ CHICO CARRASQUEL Carrasquel, Alfonso (Colon) b: 1/23/28, Caracas, Venez. BR/TR, 6', 170 lbs. Deb: 4/18/50																												
1950	Chi-A	141	524	72	148	21	5	4	46	66	46	.282	.368	.365	.733	91	-8	-6	97	83	73	.665	0	2	-1	9	*S	0.8
1951	Chi-A	147	538	41	142	22	4	2	58	46	39	.264	.325	.331	.656	80	-17	-14	97	115	60	.584	14	4	2	16	*S	1.3
1952	Chi-A	100	359	36	89	7	4	1	42	33	27	.248	.315	.298	.613	71	-14	-13	100	145	36	.520	2	2	-1	-4	S	-1.2
1953	Chi-A	149	552	72	154	30	4	2	47	38	47	.279	.330	.359	.689	81	-11	-15	106	87	65	.589	5	3	-0	6	*S	0.2
1954	Chi-A	155	620	106	158	28	3	12	62	85	67	.255	.349	.368	.717	93	-2	-5	104	77	84	.681	7	6	-2	12	*S	1.9
1955	Chi-A	145	523	83	134	11	2	11	52	61	59	.256	.338	.348	.686	84	-11	-11	101	92	64	.620	1	1	-0	4	*S	0.8
1956	Cle-A	141	474	60	115	15	1	7	48	52	61	.243	.325	.323	.648	71	-19	-20	101	105	51	.567	0	4	-2	-18	*S/3	-2.6
1957	Cle-A	125	392	37	108	14	1	8	57	41	53	.276	.356	.378	.734	99	1	0	102	131	51	.654	0	2	-1	-9	*S	0.0
1958	Cle-A	49	156	14	40	6	0	2	21	14	12	.256	.318	.333	.651	84	-4	-3	94	145	16	.550	0	0	0	-4	S3	-0.1
	KC-A	59	160	19	34	5	1	2	13	21	15	.213	.304	.294	.598	62	-7	-8	106	98	15	.523	0	1	-1	-3	3S	-0.7
	Yr	108	316	33	74	11	1	4	34	35	27	.234	.311	.313	.624	72	-12	-12	100	121	33	.545	0	1	-1	-6		-0.8
1959	Bal-A	114	346	28	77	13	0	4	28	34	41	.223	.294	.295	.589	64	-18	-16	97	97	30	.493	2	3	-1	1	S2/31	-0.8
Total	10	1325	4644	568	1199	172	25	55	474	491	467	.258	.334	.342	.676	82	-109	-111	101	102	546	.616	31	28	-8	12	*S/321	-0.4
■ CAM CARREON Carreon, Camilo b: 8/6/37, Colton, Cal. d: 9/2/87, Tucson, Ariz. BR/TR, 6'1.5", 190 lbs. Deb: 9/27/59																												
1959	Chi-A	1	1	0	0	0	0	0	0	0	0	.000	.000	.000	.000	-99	-0	-0	97	0	0	.000	0	0	0	0	/C	0.0
1960	Chi-A	8	17	2	4	0	0	0	2	1	3	.235	.278	.235	.513	40	-1	-1	101	196	1	.385	0	0	0	0	/C	0.0
1961	Chi-A	78	229	32	62	5	1	4	27	21	24	.271	.332	.354	.686	84	-5	-5	99	114	26	.583	0	1	-1	-2	C	-0.7
1962	Chi-A	106	313	31	80	19	1	4	37	33	37	.256	.329	.361	.690	90	-6	-4	95	117	36	.607	1	1	-0	-4	C	-0.2
1963	Chi-A	101	270	28	74	10	1	2	35	23	32	.274	.333	.341	.674	86	-3	-5	104	149	30	.568	1	1	-0	-12	C	-1.6
1964	Chi-A	37	95	12	26	5	0	0	4	7	13	.274	.330	.326	.656	87	-2	-1	96	55	9	.527	0	0	0	-5	C	-0.5
1965	Cle-A	19	52	6	12	2	1	1	7	9	6	.231	.344	.365	.710	104	0	0	98	132	6	.674	1	1	-0	-2	C	0.0
1966	Bal-A	4	9	2	2	2	0	0	2	3	2	.222	.417	.444	.861	146	1	1	101	210	2	1.000	0	0	0	0	/C	0.1
Total	8	354	986	113	260	43	4	11	114	97	117	.264	.331	.349	.680	87	-17	-16	99	122	111	.612	3	4	-2	-23	C	-2.9
■ MARK CARREON Carreon, Mark Steven b: 7/19/63, Chicago, Ill. BR/TL, 6' ", 170 lbs. Deb: 9/08/87																												
1987	NY-N	9	12	0	3	0	0	0	1	1	1	.250	.308	.250	.558	51	-1	-1	99	133	1	.400	0	1	-1	-1	/O	-0.2
1988	NY-N	7	9	5	5	2	0	1	1	2	1	.556	.636	1.111	1.747	435	4	4	90	31	7	3.000	0	0	0	-1	/O	0.2
Total	2	16	21	5	8	2	0	1	2	3	2	.381	.458	.619	1.077	203	3	3	95	86	7	1.143	0	1	-1	-3	/O	0.0
■ BILL CARRIGAN Carrigan, William Francis "Rough" b: 10/22/1883, Lewiston, Me. d: 7/8/69, Lewiston, Me. BR/TR, 5'9", 175 lbs. Deb: 7/07/06 M																												
1906	Bos-A	37	109	5	23	0	0	0	10	5		.211	.246	.211	.457	46	-7	-6	98	158	7	.360	3			4	C	0.0
1908	Bos-A	57	149	13	35	5	2	0	14	3		.235	.250	.295	.545	80	-4	-4	98	119	11	.421	1			5	C/1	0.7

YEAR	TM/L	G	AB	R	H	2B	3B	HR	RBI	BB	SO	AVG	OBP	SLG	PRO	/A	BR	/A	PF	CHI	RC	TA	SB	CS	SBR	FR	POS	TPR
1909	Bos-A	94	280	25	83	13	2	1	36	17		.296	.341	.368	.709	113	7	4	109	131	35	.629	2			-1	C/1	1.0
1910	Bos-A	114	342	36	85	11	1	3	53	23		.249	.307	.313	.620	95	-2	-2	99	169	37	.568	10			-11	*C	-0.1
1911	Bos-A	72	232	29	67	6	1	1	30	26		.289	.373	.336	.709	99	1	1	99	125	31	.691	5			-0	C/1	0.8
1912	Bos-A	87	266	24	70	7	1	0	24	38		.263	.359	.297	.656	83	-2	-5	107	101	31	.643	7			-7	C	-0.2
1913	Bos-A	87	256	17	62	15	5	0	28	27	26	.242	.319	.340	.659	90	-3	-3	103	114	29	.629	6			-0	CM	0.3
1914	Bos-A	81	178	18	45	5	1	1	22	40	18	.253	.395	.309	.704	115	5	6	98	142	24	.726	1	2	-1	-8	CM	0.3
1915	Bos-A	46	95	10	19	3	0	0	7	16	12	.200	.321	.232	.553	66	-3	-3	99	108	8	.513	0			-3	CM	-0.2
1916	Bos-A	33	63	7	17	2	1	0	11	11	3	.270	.378	.333	.712	122	2	2	94	187	9	.739	2			-5	CM	-0.1
Total	10	708	1970	184	506	67	14	6	235	206	59	.257	.333	.314	.648	94	-6	-10	102	133	221	.602	37	2		-27	C/1	2.5
■ **DIXIE CARROLL**	Carroll, Dorsey Lee b: 5/9/1891, Paducah, Ky. d: 10/13/84, Jacksonville, Fla BL/TR, 5'11", 165 lbs. Deb: 9/12/19																											
1919	Bos-N	15	49	10	13	3	1	0	7	7	1	.265	.379	.367	.747	128	2	2	98	154	8	.889	5			3	O	0.5
■ **CHICK CARROLL**	Carroll, Edward b: 10/20/1897, Chicago, Ill. d: 2/18/41, Hines, Ill. Deb: 4/17/1884																											
1884	Was-U	4	16	1	4	0	0	0		0		.250	.250	.250	.500	72	-1	-0	97	0	1	.333	0			0	/O	0.0
■ **FRED CARROLL**	Carroll, Frederick Herbert b: 7/2/1864, Sacramento, Cal. d: 11/7/04, San Rafael, Cal. BR/TR, 5'11", 185 lbs. Deb: 5/01/1884																											
1884	Col-a	69	252	46	70	13	5	6		13		.278	.326	.440	.766	155	14	15	97	0	37	.709				11	CO	2.7
1885	Pit-a	71	280	45	75	13	8	0		7		.268	.298	.371	.669	106	4	1	106	0	32	.566				-0	CO	0.8
1886	Pit-a	122	486	92	140	28	11	5		52		.288	.362	.422	.783	159	27	33	93	0	83	.812	20			13	CO1/S	4.3
1887	Pit-N	102	421	71	138	24	15	6	54	36	21	.328	.383	.499	.882	156	25	30	93	64	92	.958	23			-12	OC1/S	2.0
1888	Pit-N	97	366	62	91	14	5	2	48	32	31	.249	.326	.331	.657	119	6	9	95	130	46	.658	18			-9	CO/13	0.1
1889	Pit-N	91	318	80	105	21	11	2	51	85	26	.330	**.486**	.484	**.970**	**195**	39	46	89	84	86	**1.263**	19			-4	CO/13	3.4
1890	Pit-P	111	416	95	124	20	7	2	71	75	22	.298	.418	.394	.813	130	16	23	92	121	85	.976	35			-13	CO/1	0.8
1891	Pit-N	91	353	55	77	13	4	4	48	48	36	.218	.315	.312	.627	83	-6	-7	101	110	43	.659	22			6	O	-0.4
Total	8	754	2892	546	820	146	66	27	272	348	136	.284	.370	.408	.778	138	125	150	95	68	504	.827	137			-8	CO/13S	13.7
■ **SCRAPPY CARROLL**	Carroll, John E. b: 8/27/1860, Buffalo, N.Y. d: 11/14/42, Buffalo, N.Y. 5'7.5", Deb: 9/27/1884																											
1884	StP-U	9	31	3	3	1	0	0		2		.097	.152	.129	.281	-4	-3	-3	100	0	1	.214	0			0	/O3	-0.2
1885	Buf-N	13	40	1	3	0	0	0	1	2	8	.075	.119	.075	.194	-37	-6	-6	99	116	0	.135				0	O	-0.5
1887	Cle-a	57	216	30	43	5	1	0		15		.199	.264	.231	.495	41	-17	-16	98	0	19	.509	19			-5	O/32	-1.7
Total	3	79	287	34	49	6	1	0	1	19	8	.171	.232	.199	.431	27	-26	-25	98	16	20	.416	19			-5	/O32	-2.4
■ **PAT CARROLL**	Carroll, Patrick b: Philadelphia, Pa. d: 2/14/16, Philadelphia, Pa. Deb: 5/10/1884																											
1884	Alt-U	11	49	4	13	1	0	0		1		.265	.280	.286	.566	90	-0	-1	101	0	4	.417	0			0	/CO	0.0
	Phi-U	5	19	1	3	1	0	0		0		.158	.158	.211	.368	25	-1	-1	93	0	1	.250	0			0	/C	0.0
	Yr	16	68	5	16	2	0	0		1		.235	.246	.265	.511	74	-2	-2	99	0	5	.365	0			0		0.0
Total	1	16	68	5	16	2	0	0		1		.235	.246	.265	.511	74	-2	-2	99	0	5	.365	0			0	/CO	0.0
■ **DOC CARROLL**	Carroll, Ralph Arthur "Red" b: 12/28/1891, Worcester, Mass. d: 6/27/83, Worcester, Mass. BR/TR, 6', 170 lbs. Deb: 6/27/16																											
1916	Phi-A	10	22	1	2	0	0	0	0	1	8	.091	.167	.091	.258	-23	-3	-3	98	0	1	.200	0			2	C	0.0
■ **CLIFF CARROLL**	Carroll, Samuel Clifford b: 10/18/1859, Clay Grove, Iowa d: 6/12/23, Portland, Ore. BB, 5'8", 163 lbs. Deb: 8/03/1882																											
1882	Pro-N	10	41	4	5	0	0	0	2	0	4	.122	.122	.122	.244	-20	-5	-6	106	137	1	.139				0	O	-0.4
1883	Pro-N	58	238	37	63	12	3	1	20	4	28	.265	.277	.353	.630	89	-3	-3	101	81	24	.503				5	O	0.2
1884	Pro-N	113	452	90	118	16	4	3	54	29	39	.261	.306	.334	.640	100	1	-0	102	123	47	.539				3	*O	0.1
1885	Pro-N	104	426	62	99	12	3	1	40	29	29	.232	.281	.282	.563	90	-8	-2	91	98	35	.456				3	*O	-0.2
1886	Was-N	111	433	73	99	11	6	2	22	44	26	.229	.300	.296	.595	87	-8	-4	94	46	49	.608	31			-2	*O	-0.3
1887	Was-N	103	420	79	104	17	4	4	37	17	30	.248	.291	.336	.627	79	-14	-11	95	72	54	.655	40			1	*O	-0.7
1888	Pit-N	5	20	1	0	0	0	0	0	0	8	.000	.000	.000	.000	-99	-4	-4	95	0	0	.100	2			0	/O	-0.3
1890	Chi-N	136	582	134	166	16	6	7	65	53	34	.285	.352	.369	.721	103	10	1	109	72	90	.743	34			12	*O	0.9
1891	Chi-N	130	515	87	132	20	8	7	80	50	42	.256	.340	.367	.707	101	6	0	106	118	77	.744	31			-4	*O	-0.9
1892	StL-N	101	407	82	111	14	8	4	49	47	22	.273	.363	.376	.739	132	14	17	95	79	68	.814	30			2	*O	1.4
1893	Bos-N	120	438	80	98	7	5	2	54	88	28	.224	.360	.276	.636	70	-14	-16	103	123	55	.715	29			4	*O	-1.3
Total	11	991	3972	729	995	125	47	31	423	361	290	.251	.320	.329	.649	93	-26	-28	100	91	499	.642	197			22	O	-1.5
■ **TOM CARROLL**	Carroll, Thomas Edward b: 9/17/36, Jamaica, N.Y. BR/TR, 6'3", 186 lbs. Deb: 5/07/55																											
1955	NY-A	14	6	3	2	0	0	0	0	0	2	.333	.333	.333	.667	81	-0	-0	98	0	1	.500	0	0	0	0	/S	0.0
1956	NY-A	36	17	11	6	0	0	0	0	1	3	.353	.389	.353	.742	98	-0	0	99	0	3	.727	1	0	0	0	3/S	0.1
1959	KC-A	14	7	1	1	0	0	0	1	0	1	.143	.143	.143	.286	-21	-1	-1	101	394	0	.167	0	0	0	0	/S3	0.0
Total	3	64	30	15	9	0	0	0	1	1	6	.300	.323	.300	.623	68	-1	-1	99	89	3	.524	1	0	0	0	/3S	0.1
■ **KIT CARSON**	Carson, Walter Lloyd b: 11/15/12, Colton, Cal. d: 6/21/83, BL/TL, 6', 180 lbs. Deb: 7/21/34																											
1934	Cle-A	5	18	4	5	2	1	0	1	2	3	.278	.350	.500	.850	117	0	0	101	38	3	.846	0	0	0	-1	/O	0.0
1935	Cle-A	16	22	1	5	2	0	0	1	2	6	.227	.292	.318	.610	58	-1	-1	99	48	2	.500	0	1	-1	-1	/O	-0.1
Total	2	21	40	5	10	4	1	0	2	4	9	.250	.318	.400	.718	85	-1	-1	100	44	5	.645	0	1	-1	-2	/O	-0.1
■ **FRANK CARSWELL**	Carswell, Frank Willis "Tex" or "Wheels" b: 11/6/19, Palestine, Tex. BR/TR, 6', 195 lbs. Deb: 4/17/53																											
1953	Det-A	16	15	2	4	0	0	0	2	3	1	.267	.389	.267	.656	82	-0	-0	98	185	2	.636	0	0	0	-1	/O	-0.1
■ **GARY CARTER**	Carter, Gary Edmund b: 4/8/54, Culver City, Cal. BR/TR, 6'2", 205 lbs. Deb: 9/16/74																											
1974	Mon-N	9	27	5	11	0	1	1	6	1	2	.407	.429	.593	1.021	176	3	3	104	122	7	1.188	2	0	1	0	/CO	0.4
1975	Mon-N	144	503	58	136	20	1	17	68	72	83	.270	.363	.416	.778	107	11	6	108	103	80	.763	5	2	0	-9	OC/3	-0.3
1976	Mon-N	91	311	31	68	8	1	6	38	30	43	.219	.289	.309	.598	70	-12	-12	100	131	28	.504	0	2	-1	5	CO	-0.6
1977	Mon-N	154	522	86	148	29	2	31	84	58	103	.284	.361	.525	.886	137	24	25	98	92	98	.881	5	5	-2	14	*C/O	3.5
1978	Mon-N	157	533	76	136	27	1	20	72	62	70	.255	.338	.422	.760	116	8	11	96	102	77	.731	10	6	-1	25	*C/1	4.0
1979	Mon-N	141	505	74	143	26	5	22	75	40	62	.283	.342	.485	.827	120	14	13	102	97	82	.781	3	2	-0	22	*C	3.8
1980	Mon-N	154	549	76	145	25	5	29	101	58	78	.264	.336	.486	.822	128	18	19	99	115	89	.793	3	2	-0	24	*C	4.7
1981	Mon-N	100	374	48	94	20	2	16	68	35	35	.251	.317	.444	.761	115	6	6	99	132	51	.698	1	5	-3	7	*C/1	1.2
1982	Mon-N	154	557	91	163	32	1	29	97	78	64	.293	.385	.510	.895	141	37	33	105	109	107	.892	2	5	-2	21	*C	5.5
1983	Mon-N	145	541	63	146	37	3	17	79	51	57	.270	.341	.444	.784	114	11	10	102	114	80	.729	1	1	-0	29	*C/1	4.4
1984	Mon-N	159	596	75	175	32	1	27	**106**	64	57	.294	.368	.487	.854	151	30	36	91	119	108	.840	2	2	-1	11	*C1	5.2
1985	NY-N	149	555	83	156	17	1	32	100	69	46	.281	.367	.488	.855	141	28	29	97	115	97	.830	1	1	-0	5	*C/1O	4.1
1986	NY-N	132	490	81	125	14	2	24	105	62	63	.255	.346	.439	.785	120	10	13	96	**155**	72	.736	1	0	0	6	*C/1O3	2.2
1987	NY-N	139	523	55	123	18	2	20	83	42	73	.235	.293	.392	.685	81	-17	-16	99	128	58	.599	0	0	0	5	*C/1O	0.0
1988	NY-N	129	455	39	110	16	2	11	46	34	52	.242	.304	.358	.663	89	-6	-1	90	96	50	.575	0	2	-1	-11	*C/13	-0.7
Total	15	1957	7041	941	1879	321	30	302	1128	756	888	.267	.343	.450	.792	120	164	174	99	114	1084	.772	36	35	-10	153	*CO/13	37.4
■ **HOWIE CARTER**	Carter, John Howard b: 10/13/04, New York, N.Y. BR/TR, 5'10", 154 lbs. Deb: 6/21/26																											
1926	Cin-N	5	1	0	0	0	0	0	0	0	0	.000	.000	.000	.000	-99	-0	-0	95	0	0	.000	0			0	/2S	0.0
■ **JOE CARTER**	Carter, Joseph b: 3/7/60, Oklahoma City, Okla. BR/TR, 6'3", 215 lbs. Deb: 7/30/83																											
1983	Chi-N	23	51	6	9	1	1	0	1	0	21	.176	.176	.235	.412	13	-6	-6	101	33	2	.302	1	0	0	-1	O	-0.7
1984	Cle-A	66	244	32	67	6	1	13	41	11	48	.275	.309	.467	.776	105	3	1	106	107	34	.699	2	4	-2	3	O/1	0.0
1985	Cle-A	143	489	64	128	27	0	15	59	25	74	.262	.300	.409	.709	98	-6	-3	94	96	60	.668	24	6	4	1	*O1/23D	0.0
1986	Cle-A	162	663	108	200	36	9	29	**121**	32	95	.302	.339	.514	.853	132	24	26	98	119	116	.851	29	7	5	5	*O1	2.7
1987	Cle-A	149	588	83	155	27	2	32	106	27	105	.264	.306	.480	.786	102	2	0	103	119	87	.781	31	6	6	0	1O/D	-0.3
1988	Cle-A	157	621	85	168	36	6	27	98	35	82	.271	.317	.478	.795	118	13	12	102	99	96	.789	27	5	5	7	*O	2.1
Total	6	700	2656	378	727	133	19	116	426	130	425	.274	.314	.469	.783	111	30	31	100	107	394	.771	114	28	17	14	O1/D32	3.8

■ BLACKIE CARTER Carter, Otis Leonard b: 9/30/02, Langley, S.C. d: 9/10/76, Greenville, S.C. BR/TR, 5'10", 175 lbs. Deb: 10/03/25

YEAR	TM/L	G	AB	R	H	2B	3B	HR	RBI	BB	SO	AVG	OBP	SLG	PRO	/A	BR	/A	PF	CHI	RC	TA	SB	CS	SBR	FR	POS	TPR
1925	NY-N	1	4	0	0	0	0	0	0	0	1	.000	.000	.000	.000	-99	-1	-1	99	0	0	.000	0	0	0	1	/O	0.0
1926	NY-N	5	17	4	4	1	0	1	1	1	0	.235	.278	.471	.748	101	-0	-0	98	31	2	.692	0			0	/O	0.0
Total	2	6	21	4	4	1	0	1	1	1	1	.190	.227	.381	.608	61	-1	-1	98	26	2	.529	0	0		1	/O	0.0

■ ED CARTWRIGHT Cartwright, Edward Charles "Jumbo" b: 10/6/1859, Johnstown, Pa. d: 24, Florida BR/TR, 5'10", 220 lbs. Deb: 7/10/1890

YEAR	TM/L	G	AB	R	H	2B	3B	HR	RBI	BB	SO	AVG	OBP	SLG	PRO	/A	BR	/A	PF	CHI	RC	TA	SB	CS	SBR	FR	POS	TPR
1890	StL-a	75	300	70	90	12	4	8		29		.300	.367	.447	.814	123	15	7	116	0	60	.914	26			-2	1	0.2
1894	Was-N	132	507	88	149	35	13	12	106	57	43	.294	.374	.485	.859	110	5	7	98	110	106	.955	31			-0	*1	0.6
1895	Was-N	122	472	95	156	34	17	3	90	54	41	.331	.400	.494	.894	128	22	19	103	110	116	1.070	50			13	*1	2.8
1896	Was-N	133	499	76	138	15	10	1	62	54	44	.277	.350	.353	.702	92	-8	-4	95	102	73	.720	28			-0	*1	0.0
1897	Was-N	33	124	19	29	4	0	0	15	8		.234	.286	.266	.552	47	-9	-9	101	136	12	.537	9			2	1	-0.6
Total	5	495	1902	348	562	100	44	24	273	202	128	.295	.368	.432	.800	108	25	21	101	92	368	.883	144			12	1	3.0

■ RICO CARTY Carty, Ricardo Adolfo Jacobo (born Ricardo Adolfo Jacobo (Carty)) b: 9/1/39, San Pedro De Macoris, D.R. BR/TR, 6'3", 200 lbs. Deb: 9/15/63

YEAR	TM/L	G	AB	R	H	2B	3B	HR	RBI	BB	SO	AVG	OBP	SLG	PRO	/A	BR	/A	PF	CHI	RC	TA	SB	CS	SBR	FR	POS	TPR
1963	Mil-N	2	2	0	0	0	0	0	0	0	2	.000	.000	.000	.000	-99	-1	-1	101	0	0	.000	0	0	0	0	H	0.0
1964	Mil-N	133	455	72	150	28	4	22	88	43	78	.330	.391	.554	.945	168	37	39	97	114	94	.926	1	2	-1	-6	*O	3.0
1965	Mil-N	83	271	37	84	18	1	10	35	17	44	.310	.357	.494	.852	132	13	11	104	88	44	.779	1	4	-2	-3	O	0.4
1966	Atl-N	151	521	73	170	25	2	15	76	60	74	.326	.396	.468	.864	141	29	30	99	113	94	.828	4	6	-2	3	*OC/13	2.8
1967	Atl-N	134	444	41	113	16	2	15	64	49	70	.255	.330	.401	.731	104	5	3	104	119	55	.661	4	3	-1	1	*O/1	-0.2
1969	Atl-N	104	304	47	104	15	0	16	58	32	28	.342	.405	.549	.954	159	26	25	104	108	61	.909	0	2	-1	-8	O	1.1
1970	Atl-N	136	478	84	175	23	3	25	101	77	46	**.366**	**.456**	.584	1.040	169	54	52	104	113	125	1.108	1	2	-1	-6	*O	3.8
1972	Atl-N	86	271	31	75	12	2	6	29	44	33	.277	.378	.402	.780	116	9	8	105	94	42	.750	0	0	0	-4	O	0.0
1973	Tex-A	86	306	24	71	12	0	3	33	36	39	.232	.315	.301	.616	76	-10	-9	97	131	30	.537	2	0	1	-4	OD	-1.3
	Chi-N	22	70	4	15	0	0	1	8	6	10	.214	.276	.257	.533	45	-5	-6	108	153	4	.393	0	0	0	-1	O	-0.7
	Oak-A	7	8	1	2	1	0	1	1	2	1	.250	.400	.750	1.150	250	1	1	87	44	3	1.333	0	0	0	0	/D	0.1
1974	Cle-A	33	91	6	33	5	0	1	16	5	9	.363	.396	.451	.846	142	5	5	101	143	15	.742	0	0	0	-0	D/1	0.4
1975	Cle-A	118	383	57	118	19	1	18	64	45	31	.308	.384	.504	.888	150	25	25	100	100	70	.855	2	2	-1	-2	D1O	2.0
1976	Cle-A	152	552	67	171	34	0	13	83	67	45	.310	.384	.442	.827	142	30	30	100	119	92	.780	1	1	-0	0	*D1/O	3.0
1977	Cle-A	127	461	50	129	23	1	15	80	56	51	.280	.358	.432	.790	117	10	11	98	133	68	.729	1	2	-1	0	*D/1	1.0
1978	Tor-A	104	387	51	110	16	0	20	68	36	41	.284	.345	.481	.826	130	14	14	100	116	64	.782	1	1	-0	0	*D	1.4
	Oak-A	41	141	19	39	5	1	11	31	21	16	.277	.370	.560	.931	157	11	11	101	116	27	.909	0	0	0	0	D	1.1
	Yr	145	528	70	149	21	1	31	99	57	57	.282	.352	.502	.854	137	25	25	100	116	94	.832	1	1	-0	0		2.5
1979	Tor-A	132	461	48	118	26	0	12	55	46	45	.256	.325	.390	.715	89	-5	-7	103	100	54	.630	3	1	0	0	*D	-0.6
Total	15	1651	5606	712	1677	278	17	204	890	642	663	.299	.372	.464	.836	131	248	241	101	113	941	.824	21	26	-9	-30	OD/1C3	17.3

■ BOB CARUTHERS Caruthers, Robert Lee "Parisian Bob" b: 1/5/1864, Memphis, Tenn. d: 8/5/11, Peoria, Ill. BL/TR, 5'7", 138 lbs. Deb: 9/07/1884 MU

YEAR	TM/L	G	AB	R	H	2B	3B	HR	RBI	BB	SO	AVG	OBP	SLG	PRO	/A	BR	/A	PF	CHI	RC	TA	SB	CS	SBR	FR	POS	TPR
1884	StL-a	23	82	15	21	2	0	2		4		.256	.291	.354	.644	102	1	-0	110	0	9	.541				0	OP	0.0
1885	StL-a	60	222	37	50	10	2	1		20		.225	.289	.302	.591	96	-2	0	93	0	20	.506				0	P/O	0.0
1886	StL-a	87	317	91	106	21	14	4		64		.334	.448	.527	.974	186	42	**36**	111	0	89	1.223	26			-5	PO/2	0.0
1887	StL-a	98	364	102	130	23	11	8		66		.357	.463	.547	1.010	168	44	37	110	0	118	1.368	49			8	OP/1	4.0
1888	Bro-a	94	335	58	77	10	5	5	53	45		.230	.328	.334	.662	111	8	5	105	132	45	.713	23			3	OP	1.1
1889	Bro-a	59	172	45	43	8	3	2	31	44	17	.250	.408	.366	.775	129	8	9	96	128	30	.915	9			2	P/O1	0.0
1890	Bro-N	71	238	46	63	7	4	1	29	47	18	.265	.397	.340	.737	117	8	8	100	106	38	.834	13			-5	OP	0.0
1891	Bro-N	56	171	24	48	5	3	2	23	25	13	.281	.372	.380	.753	125	5	6	97	94	26	.764	4			0	PO/2	0.0
1892	StL-N	143	513	76	142	16	8	3	69	86	29	.277	.386	.357	.742	134	21	25	95	117	82	.803	24			-10	*OP/21M	1.0
1893	Chi-N	1	3	0	0	0	0	0	0	0	1	.000	.000	.000	.000	-97	-1	-1	104	0	0	.000	0			0	/O	0.0
	Cin-N	13	48	14	14	2	0	1	8	16	1	.292	.477	.396	.873	133	4	4	101	86	11	1.176	4			0	O	0.3
	Yr	14	51	14	14	2	0	1	8	16	2	.275	.456	.373	.828	122	3	3	102	80	11	1.081	4			0		0.3
Total	10	705	2465	508	694	104	50	29	213	417	79	.282	.391	.400	.790	137	138	129	102	70	468	.891	152			-7	OP/12	6.4

■ PAUL CASANOVA Casanova, Paulino (Ortiz) b: 12/21/41, Colon, Matanzas, Cuba BR/TR, 6'4", 180 lbs. Deb: 9/18/65

YEAR	TM/L	G	AB	R	H	2B	3B	HR	RBI	BB	SO	AVG	OBP	SLG	PRO	/A	BR	/A	PF	CHI	RC	TA	SB	CS	SBR	FR	POS	TPR
1965	Was-A	5	13	2	4	1	0	0	1	1	3	.308	.357	.385	.742	111	0	0	100	83	2	.667	0	0	0	0	/C	0.1
1966	Was-A	122	429	45	109	16	5	13	44	14	78	.254	.279	.406	.685	99	-5	-2	95	87	46	.576	1	2	-1	6	*C	0.9
1967	Was-A	141	528	47	131	19	1	9	53	17	65	.248	.274	.339	.613	79	-14	-15	102	109	44	.477	1	1	-0	23	*C	1.8
1968	Was-A	96	322	19	63	6	0	4	25	7	52	.196	.213	.252	.464	44	-24	-21	91	115	16	.328	0	1	-1	10	*C	-0.8
1969	Was-A	124	379	26	82	9	2	4	37	18	52	.216	.257	.282	.540	52	-25	-24	97	125	26	.414	0	0	0	9	*C	-0.7
1970	Was-A	104	328	25	75	17	3	6	30	10	47	.229	.254	.354	.607	68	-16	-15	96	91	28	.492	0	0	0	-10	*C	-2.4
1971	Was-A	94	311	19	63	9	1	5	26	14	52	.203	.239	.286	.525	52	-22	-19	92	102	19	.402	0	3	-2	8	C	-0.9
1972	Atl-N	49	136	8	28	3	0	2	10	4	28	.206	.229	.272	.501	40	-11	-11	105	96	6	.353	0	1	-1	-0	C	-1.0
1973	Atl-N	82	236	18	51	7	0	7	18	11	36	.216	.254	.335	.589	55	-13	-16	113	72	18	.474	0	2	-1	-2	C	-1.5
1974	Atl-N	42	104	5	21	0	0	0	8	5	17	.202	.239	.202	.440	23	-10	-11	105	147	5	.306	0	0	0	1	C	-0.8
Total	10	859	2786	214	627	87	12	50	252	101	430	.225	.254	.319	.573	64	-140	-135	98	103	210	.461	2	10	-5	44	C	-5.3

■ GEORGE CASE Case, George Washington b: 11/11/15, Trenton, N.J. BR/TR, 6', 183 lbs. Deb: 9/08/37 C

YEAR	TM/L	G	AB	R	H	2B	3B	HR	RBI	BB	SO	AVG	OBP	SLG	PRO	/A	BR	/A	PF	CHI	RC	TA	SB	CS	SBR	FR	POS	TPR
1937	Was-A	22	90	14	26	6	2	0	11	3	5	.289	.312	.400	.712	83	-3	-3	94	107	11	.631	2	1	0	-1	O	-0.3
1938	Was-A	107	433	69	132	27	3	2	40	39	28	.305	.362	.395	.757	94	-7	-3	95	81	63	.720	11	6	-0	-2	*O	-0.4
1939	Was-A	128	530	103	160	20	7	2	35	56	36	.302	.369	.377	.746	101	-6	2	90	51	80	.781	**51**	17	**5**	-6	*O	-0.2
1940	Was-A	154	656	109	192	29	5	5	56	52	39	.293	.349	.375	.724	94	-11	-4	93	67	94	.706	**35**	10	**5**	-7	*O	-1.6
1941	Was-A	153	649	95	176	32	8	2	53	51	37	.271	.325	.354	.680	82	-19	-17	98	70	82	.647	**33**	9	**5**	14	*O	-0.7
1942	Was-A	125	513	101	164	26	2	5	43	44	30	.320	.377	.407	.784	126	14	17	96	65	88	.826	**44**	6	**10**	-2	*O	1.7
1943	Was-A	141	613	**102**	180	36	5	1	52	41	27	.294	.341	.374	.715	105	6	3	104	71	88	.742	**61**	14	**10**	-2	*O	0.7
1944	Was-A	119	464	63	116	14	2	2	32	49	22	.250	.326	.302	.627	89	-11	-5	90	84	50	.644	49	18	4	9	*O	0.4
1945	Was-A	123	504	72	148	19	5	1	31	49	27	.294	.360	.357	.717	116	6	10	93	54	68	.691	30	16	-1	4	*O	0.9
1946	Cle-A	118	484	46	109	23	4	1	22	34	38	.225	.280	.295	.576	69	-26	-19	89	51	43	.531	**28**	11	**2**	-4	*O	-2.9
1947	Was-A	36	80	11	12	1	0	0	2	8	8	.150	.227	.162	.390	10	-10	-9	97	57	5	.377	5	1	1	0	O	-0.9
Total	11	1226	5016	785	1415	233	43	21	377	426	297	.282	.341	.358	.699	96	-67	-29	94	66	670	.699	349	109	39	4	*O	-3.3

■ DENNIS CASEY Casey, Dennis Patrick b: 3/30/1858, Binghamton, N.Y. d: 1/19/09, Binghamton, N.Y. BL/TR, 5'9", 164 lbs. Deb: 8/18/1884

YEAR	TM/L	G	AB	R	H	2B	3B	HR	RBI	BB	SO	AVG	OBP	SLG	PRO	/A	BR	/A	PF	CHI	RC	TA	SB	CS	SBR	FR	POS	TPR
1884	WiL-U	2	8	1	2	1	0	0		0		.250	.250	.375	.625	106	0	0	103	0	1	.500	0			0	/O	0.0
	Bal-a	37	149	20	37	7	4	3		5		.248	.273	.409	.682	123	3	4	99	0	17	.589				-0	O	0.3
1885	Bal-a	63	264	50	76	10	5	3		21		.288	.347	.398	.745	130	12	9	106	0	37	.686				-6	O	0.0
Total	2	102	421	71	115	18	9	6		26		.273	.320	.401	.721	128	15	13	103	0	55	.647				-6	O	0.3

■ DOC CASEY Casey, James Patrick b: 3/15/1870, Lawrence, Mass. d: 12/31/36, Detroit, Mich. BL/TR, 5'6", Deb: 9/14/1898

YEAR	TM/L	G	AB	R	H	2B	3B	HR	RBI	BB	SO	AVG	OBP	SLG	PRO	/A	BR	/A	PF	CHI	RC	TA	SB	CS	SBR	FR	POS	TPR
1898	Was-N	28	112	13	31	2	0	0	15	3		.277	.302	.295	.596	72	-4	-4	102	146	15	.642	15			0	3/SC	-0.3
1899	Was-N	9	34	3	4	2	0	0	2	2		.118	.167	.176	.343	-5	-5	-5	96	108	1	.300	1			-1	/3	-0.4
	Bro-N	134	525	75	141	14	8	1	43	25		.269	.308	.331	.640	74	-16	-20	105	79	63	.602	27			-18	*3	-3.4
	Yr	143	559	78	145	16	8	1	45	27		.259	.299	.322	.621	70	-21	-24	104	82	64	.580	28			-19		-3.8
1900	Bro-N	1	3	0	1	0	0	0	1	0		.333	.333	.333	.667	80	-0	-0	108	313	0	.500	0			0	/3	0.0
1901	Det-A	128	540	105	153	16	9	2	46	32		.283	.323	.357	.681	82	-7	-15	110	63	75	.669	34			1	*3	-1.4
1902	Det-A	132	520	69	142	18	7	3	55	44		.273	.330	.352	.682	92	-6	-5	99	91	69	.659	22			2	*3	-0.6
1903	Chi-N	112	435	56	126	8	3	1	40	19		.290	.319	.329	.648	91	-8	-5	95	93	50	.560	11			-19	*3	-2.2
1904	Chi-N	136	548	71	147	20	4	1	43	18		.268	.292	.325	.616	92	-6	-6	101	77	59	.541	21			-8	*3/C	-0.8
1905	Chi-N	144	526	66	122	21	10	1	56	41		.232	.287	.316	.603	78	-12	-15	105	122	55	.567	22			-7	*3/S	-1.1
1906	Bro-N	149	571	71	133	17	8	0	34	52		.233	.297	.291	.588	98	-9	-1	87	65	57	.548	22			-17	*3	-2.5
1907	Bro-N	141	527	55	122	19	3	0	19	34		.231	.278	.279	.557	81	-14	-11	94	47	46	.486	16			-5	*3	-1.8
Total	10	1114	4341	584	1122	137	52	9	354	270		.258	.303	.320	.623	85	-88	-88	99	81	493	.577	191			-71	*3/CS	-14.5

YEAR	TM/L	G	AB	R	H	2B	3B	HR	RBI	BB	SO	AVG	OBP	SLG	PRO	/A	BR	/A	PF	CHI	RC	TA	SB	CS	SBR	FR	POS	TPR
■ **JOE CASEY**	Casey, Joseph Felix b: 8/15/1887, Boston, Mass. d: 6/2/66, Melrose, Mass. BR/TR, 5'9", 180 lbs. Deb: 10/01/09																											
1909	Det-A	3	5	1	0	0	0	0	0	1		.000	.167	.000	.167	-42	-1	-1	110	0	0	.200	0			-0	/C	0.0
1910	Det-A	23	62	3	12	3	0	0	2	2		.194	.231	.242	.473	47	-4	-4	102	49	4	.380	1			0	C	-0.1
1911	Det-A	15	33	2	5	0	0	0	3	3		.152	.222	.152	.374	5	-4	-5	108	203	1	.286	0			-1	C/O	-0.4
1918	Was-A	9	17	3	4	0	0	0	2	2	2	.235	.316	.235	.551	64	-1	-1	104	182	1	.462	0			0	/C	0.0
Total	4	50	117	9	21	3	0	0	7	8	2	.179	.238	.205	.443	32	-9	-10	104	111	6	.354	1			-1	/CO	-0.5
■ **BOB CASEY**	Casey, Orrin Robinson b: 1859, Canada 5'11", 190 lbs. Deb: 7/17/1882																											
1882	Det-N	9	39	5	9	2	1	1	7	0	15	.231	.231	.410	.641	99	-0	-0	102	119	4	.533				0	/32	0.0
■ **DAVE CASH**	Cash, David b: 6/11/48, Utica, N.Y. BR/TR, 5'11", 170 lbs. Deb: 9/13/69																											
1969	Pit-N	18	61	8	17	3	1	0	4	9	9	.279	.371	.361	.732	112	1	1	95	74	9	.717	2	0	1	4	2	0.7
1970	Pit-N	64	210	30	66	7	6	1	28	17	25	.314	.368	.419	.787	114	3	4	97	119	30	.716	5	2	0	13	2	2.3
1971	Pit-N	123	478	79	138	17	4	2	34	46	33	.289	.351	.354	.705	101	1	2	99	84	61	.642	13	5	1	5	*23/S	1.4
1972	Pit-N	99	425	58	120	22	4	3	30	22	31	.282	.318	.374	.692	93	-3	-4	103	65	48	.592	9	9	-3	**27**	2	2.8
1973	Pit-N	116	436	59	118	21	2	2	31	38	36	.271	.329	.342	.671	94	-8	-3	92	85	49	.571	2	5	-2	7	23	0.5
1974	Phi-N	162	687	89	206	26	11	2	58	46	33	.300	.352	.378	.730	101	4	1	103	73	93	.670	20	8	1	**30**	*2	4.2
1975	Phi-N	162	699	111	**213**	40	3	4	57	56	34	.305	.360	.388	.747	106	7	6	101	67	100	.688	13	6	0	10	*2	2.4
1976	Phi-N	160	666	92	189	14	**12**	1	56	54	13	.284	.339	.345	.685	88	-4	-10	107	82	75	.586	10	12	-4	-1	*2	-0.7
1977	Mon-N	153	650	91	188	42	7	0	43	52	33	.289	.344	.375	.719	94	-6	-5	98	62	82	.652	21	12	-1	-4	*2	0.0
1978	Mon-N	159	658	66	166	26	3	3	43	37	29	.252	.292	.315	.607	73	-27	-24	96	70	58	.498	12	6	0	-17	*2	-3.3
1979	Mon-N	76	187	24	60	11	1	2	19	12	12	.321	.362	.422	.784	111	3	3	102	89	27	.715	7	4	-0	-1	2	0.4
1980	SD-N	130	397	25	90	14	2	1	23	35	21	.227	.289	.280	.569	64	-21	-18	93	80	30	.463	6	5	-1	1	*2	-0.9
Total	12	1422	5554	732	1571	243	56	21	426	424	309	.283	.336	.358	.694	93	-50	-47	100	76	661	.626	120	74	-8	73	*2/3S	9.8
■ **NORM CASH**	Cash, Norman Dalton b: 11/10/34, Justiceburg, Tex. d: 10/12/86, Beaver Island, Mich. BL/TL, 6', 185 lbs. Deb: 6/18/58																											
1958	Chi-A	13	8	2	2	0	0	0	0	0	1	.250	.250	.250	.500	39	-1	-1	98	0	1	.333	0	0	0	-1	/O	-0.1
1959	Chi-A	58	104	16	25	0	1	4	16	18	9	.240	.378	.375	.753	111	2	2	97	124	17	.788	1	1	-0	-1	1	0.1
1960	Det-A	121	353	64	101	16	3	18	63	65	58	.286	.406	.501	.907	142	24	23	102	107	79	.992	4	2	0	-2	1/O	1.5
1961	Det-A	159	535	119	**193**	22	8	41	132	124	85	**.361**	**.488**	.662	**1.150**	**213**	**86**	**89**	96	111	**178**	**1.372**	11	5	0	5	*1	**7.6**
1962	Det-A	148	507	94	123	16	2	39	89	104	82	.243	.385	.513	.897	125	30	22	111	99	104	.957	6	3	0	5	*1/O	1.7
1963	Det-A	147	493	67	133	19	1	26	79	89	76	.270	.388	.471	.858	134	29	26	104	109	94	.884	2	3	-1	3	*1	2.5
1964	Det-A	144	479	63	123	15	5	23	83	70	66	.257	.355	.453	.808	129	16	18	96	125	78	.791	2	1	0	2	*1	1.7
1965	Det-A	142	467	79	124	23	1	30	82	77	62	.266	.374	.512	.886	141	31	28	105	106	91	.911	6	6	-2	2	*1	2.3
1966	Det-A	160	603	98	168	18	3	32	93	66	91	.279	.354	.478	.831	133	28	27	102	108	101	.798	2	1	0	5	*1	2.8
1967	Det-A	152	488	64	118	16	5	22	72	81	100	.242	.354	.430	.785	132	20	21	99	111	78	.786	3	2	-0	9	*1	1.9
1968	Det-A	127	411	50	108	15	1	25	63	39	70	.263	.331	.487	.818	137	21	18	106	98	63	.769	1	1	-0	6	*1	2.1
1969	Det-A	142	483	81	135	15	4	22	74	63	80	.280	.370	.464	.833	128	21	19	103	105	85	.824	2	1	0	1	*1	1.1
1970	Det-A	130	370	58	96	18	2	15	53	72	58	.259	.387	.441	.828	124	16	15	103	103	64	.825	0	1	-1	2	*1	1.0
1971	Det-A	135	452	72	128	10	3	32	91	59	86	.283	.375	.531	.905	161	32	34	96	113	93	.933	1	0	0	-1	*1	2.8
1972	Det-A	137	440	51	114	16	0	22	61	50	64	.259	.340	.445	.786	117	17	11	113	99	66	.742	0	2	-1	0	*1	-0.3
1973	Det-A	121	363	51	95	19	0	19	40	47	73	.262	.359	.471	.830	131	16	15	101	69	63	.828	1	0	0	0	*1/D	0.9
1974	Det-A	53	149	17	34	3	2	7	12	19	30	.228	.327	.416	.744	106	2	1	106	57	21	.726	1	1	-0	0	1	0.0
Total	17	2089	6705	1046	1820	241	41	377	1103	1043	1091	.271	.377	.488	.865	138	390	369	103	104	1278	.905	43	30	-5	33	*1/OD	29.6
■ **RON CASH**	Cash, Ronald Forrest b: 11/20/49, Atlanta, Ga. BR/TR, 6', 180 lbs. Deb: 9/04/73																											
1973	Det-A	14	39	8	16	1	1	0	6	5	5	.410	.477	.487	.964	171	4	4	101	124	9	1.000	0	0	0	-0	/O3	0.3
1974	Det-A	20	62	6	14	2	0	0	5	0	11	.226	.226	.258	.484	37	-5	-5	106	123	3	.314	0	1	-1	1	1/3	-0.5
Total	2	34	101	14	30	3	1	0	11	5	16	.297	.330	.347	.677	90	-1	-1	104	123	12	.541	0	1	-1	0	/13O	-0.2
■ **ED CASKIN**	Caskin, Edward James b: 12/30/1851, Danvers, Mass. d: 10/9/24, Danvers, Mass. BR/TR, 5'9.5", 165 lbs. Deb: 5/01/1879																											
1879	Tro-N	70	304	32	78	13	2	0	21	2	14	.257	.261	.313	.574	95	-4	-1	93	75	25	.429				9	SC/2	0.9
1880	Tro-N	82	333	36	75	5	4	0	28	7	24	.225	.241	.264	.505	65	-10	-14	110	123	22	.368				7	*S/C	-0.2
1881	Tro-N	63	234	33	53	7	1	0	21	13	29	.226	.267	.265	.532	68	-8	-8	100	120	17	.414				-3	*S	-0.5
1883	NY-N	95	383	47	91	11	2	1	40	14	25	.238	.264	.285	.549	67	-15	-15	100	131	30	.421				-2	*S2/C	-1.1
1884	NY-N	100	351	49	81	11	1	1	40	34	55	.231	.299	.276	.575	84	-6	-5	98	140	30	.485				0	*S/C	0.4
1885	StL-N	71	262	31	47	3	0	0	12	12	22	.179	.215	.191	.406	35	-19	-16	92	85	11	.288				-2	3/CS	-1.5
1886	NY-N	1	4	1	2	0	0	0	1	0	1	.500	.500	.500	1.000	231	0	1	89	173	1	1.000	0			0	/S	0.0
Total	7	482	1871	229	427	50	10	2	163	82	170	.228	.261	.269	.529	70	-61	-59	99	115	136	.405	0			9	S/3C2	-2.0
■ **HARRY CASSADY**	Cassady, Harry Delbert (born Harry Delbert Cassaday) b: 7/20/1880, Belleflower, Ill. d: 4/19/69, Fresno, Cal. BL, 5'8", 145 lbs. Deb: 8/08/04																											
1904	Pit-N	12	44	8	9	0	0	0	3	2		.205	.239	.205	.444	39	-3	-3	99	124	3	.371	2			0	O	-0.3
1905	Was-A	10	30	1	4	0	0	0	1	0		.133	.133	.133	.267	-14	-4	-4	104	89	1	.154	0			1	/O	-0.3
Total	2	22	74	9	13	0	0	0	4	2		.176	.197	.176	.373	18	-7	-7	101	110	3	.279	2			1	/O	-0.6
■ **JOHN CASSIDY**	Cassidy, John P. b: 1857, Brooklyn, N.Y. d: 7/2/1891, Brooklyn, N.Y. TL, 5'8", 168 lbs. Deb: 4/24/1875																											
1875	Atl-n	40	167	13	28							.168															PO/1	
	NH-n	6	24	3	3							.125															/1	
	Yr	46	191	16	31							.162																
1876	Har-N	12	47	6	13	2	0	0	8	1	0	.277	.292	.319	.611	95	0	-0	108	184	4	.471				0	/O1	0.0
1877	Har-N	60	251	43	95	10	5	0	27	3	3	.378	.386	.458	.844	**184**	18	22	89	81	45	.756				-5	*O/P	1.3
1878	Chi-N	60	256	33	68	7	1	0	29	9	11	.266	.291	.301	.591	87	-1	-4	108	135	23	.457				7	*O/C	-0.1
1879	Tro-N	9	37	4	7	1	0	0	1	2	4	.189	.231	.216	.447	52	-2	-2	93	42	2	.333				0	/O1	0.0
1880	Tro-N	83	352	40	89	14	8	0	29	12	34	.253	.277	.338	.616	97	3	-2	110	86	34	.498				-4	*O/2	-0.8
1881	Tro-N	85	370	57	82	13	3	1	11	18	21	.222	.258	.281	.539	69	-13	-13	100	31	27	.424				-10	*O/S	-2.2
1882	Tro-N	29	121	14	21	3	1	0	9	3	16	.174	.194	.215	.408	32	-9	-8	95	112	5	.290				0	O3	-0.7
1883	Pro-N	89	366	46	87	16	5	0	42	9	38	.238	.256	.309	.565	70	-13	-13	101	132	30	.437				-1	*O/21	-0.9
1884	Bro-a	106	433	57	109	11	6	2		19		.252	.286	.319	.605	102	0	2	98	0	41	.491				-9	*O/3S	-0.7
1885	Bro-a	54	221	36	47	6	2	1		8		.213	.250	.271	.521	64	-8	-9	104	0	15	.408				-9	O	-1.8
Total	10	587	2454	336	618	83	31	4	156	84	127	.252	.278	.316	.594	90	-25	-28	101	68	227	.471				-31	O/P13S2C	-5.9
■ **JOE CASSIDY**	Cassidy, Joseph Phillip b: 2/8/1883, Chester, Pa. d: 3/25/06, Chester, Pa. BR/TR, Deb: 4/18/04																											
1904	Was-A	152	581	63	140	12	**19**	1	33	15		.241	.260	.332	.592	96	-9	-4	93	67	56	.510	17			-5	SO3	-1.0
1905	Was-A	151	576	67	124	16	4	1	43	25		.215	.248	.262	.510	61	-24	-26	104	96	44	.440	23			**36**	*S	1.5
Total	2	303	1157	130	264	28	23	2	76	40		.228	.254	.297	.551	77	-32	-31	98	81	100	.475	40			30	S/O3	0.5
■ **PETE CASSIDY**	Cassidy, Peter Francis b: 4/8/1873, Wilmington, Del. d: 7/9/29, Wilmington, Del. BR/TR, 5'10", 165 lbs. Deb: 4/18/1896																											
1896	Lou-N	49	184	16	39	1	1	0	12	7	7	.212	.256	.228	.485	30	-18	-18	98	84	12	.400	5			-2	1S	-1.5
1899	Bro-N	6	20	2	3	1	0	0	4	1		.150	.261	.200	.461	28	-2	-2	105	313	1	.471	1			0	/3S	-0.1
	Was-N	46	178	21	56	13	0	3	32	9		.315	.358	.438	.796	126	4	6	96	119	30	.779	5			0	1/3S	0.5
	Yr	52	198	23	59	14	0	3	36	10		.298	.347	.414	.762	115	3	4	97	148	31	.741	6			0		0.4
Total	2	101	382	39	98	15	1	3	48	17	7	.257	.304	.325	.629	73	-16	-14	97	113	44	.567	11			-2	/1S3	-1.1
■ **JACK CASSINI**	Cassini, Jack Dempsey "Gabby" or "Scat" b: 10/26/19, Dearborn, Mich. BR/TR, 5'10", 175 lbs. Deb: 4/19/49																											
1949	Pit-N	8	0	3	0	0	0	0	0	0	0	—	—	—	—	—	0	0	101	—	—	—	0			0	R	0.0
■ **JIM CASTIGLIA**	Castiglia, James Vincent b: 9/30/18, Passaic, N.J. BL/TR, 5'11", 200 lbs. Deb: 4/14/42																											
1942	Phi-A	16	18	2	7	0	0	0	2	1	3	.389	.421	.389	.810	133	1	1	96	101	3	.727	0	0	0	0	/C	0.1

YEAR	TM/L	G	AB	R	H	2B	3B	HR	RBI	BB	SO	AVG	OBP	SLG	PRO	/A	BR	/A	PF	CHI	RC	TA	SB	CS	SBR	FR	POS	TPR
■ PETE CASTIGLIONE Castiglione, Peter Paul b: 2/13/21, Greenwich, Conn. BR/TR, 5'11", 175 lbs. Deb: 9/10/47																												
1947	Pit-N	13	50	6	14	0	0	0	1	2	5	.280	.308	.280	.588	56	-3	-3	101	27	4	.444	0			-2	S	-0.3
1948	Pit-N	4	2	0	0	0	0	0	0	0	0	.000	.000	.000	.000	-96	-1	-1	104	0	0	.500	1			0	/S	0.0
1949	Pit-N	118	448	57	120	20	2	6	43	20	43	.268	.299	.362	.661	76	-16	-16	101	92	49	.554	2			6	3S/O	-0.7
1950	Pit-N	94	263	29	67	10	3	3	22	23	23	.255	.317	.350	.667	73	-9	-10	103	84	29	.576	1			-1	3S/21	-0.7
1951	Pit-N	132	482	62	126	19	4	7	42	34	28	.261	.311	.361	.672	75	-14	-18	107	85	55	.575	2	2	-1	11	3S	-0.5
1952	Pit-N	67	214	27	57	9	1	4	18	17	8	.266	.323	.374	.697	93	-2	-2	100	76	27	.623	3	3	-1	-2	3/1O	-0.3
1953	Pit-N	45	159	14	33	2	1	4	21	5	14	.208	.236	.308	.545	40	-14	-15	102	137	11	.427	1	1	-0	3	3	-1.2
	StL-N	67	52	9	9	2	0	0	3	2	5	.173	.204	.212	.415	8	-7	-7	102	106	2	.283	0	0	0	0	3/2S	-0.6
	Yr	112	211	23	42	4	1	4	24	7	19	.199	.228	.284	.513	32	-21	-22	102	120	14	.399	1	1	-0	3		-1.8
1954	StL-N	5	0	1	0	0	0	0	0	0	0	—	—	—	—	—	0	0	100	—	—	—	0	0	0	0	/3	0.0
Total	8	545	1670	205	426	62	11	24	150	103	126	.255	.300	.349	.648	71	-66	-72	103	89	191	.559	10	6		15	3/S21O	-4.3
■ TONY CASTILLO Castillo, Anthony b: 6/14/57, San Jose, Cal. BR/TR, 6'4", 190 lbs. Deb: 9/22/78																												
1978	SD-N	5	8	0	1	0	0	0	1	0	2	.125	.125	.125	.250	-32	-1	-1	93	397	0	.143	0	0	0	-0	/C	-0.1
■ MANNY CASTILLO Castillo, Esteban Manuel Antonio (Cabrera) b: 4/1/57, Santo Domingo, D.R. BB/TR, 5'9", 160 lbs. Deb: 9/01/80																												
1980	KC-A	7	10	1	2	0	0	0	0	0	0	.200	.200	.200	.400	10	-1	-1	98	0	0	.250	0	0	0	0	/32D	0.0
1982	Sea-A	138	506	49	130	29	1	3	49	22	35	.257	.291	.336	.627	65	-20	-26	109	112	46	.496	2	8	-4	-11	*3/2	-4.4
1983	Sea-A	91	203	13	42	6	3	0	24	7	20	.207	.237	.266	.503	38	-17	-17	100	174	12	.380	1	1	-0	-1	31/2PD	-1.8
Total	3	236	719	63	174	35	4	3	73	29	55	.242	.274	.314	.589	58	-38	-44	106	128	58	.468	3	9	-5	-12	3/21DP	-6.2
■ JUAN CASTILLO Castillo, Juan (Bryas) b: 1/25/62, San Pedro De Macoris, D.R. BB/TR, 5'11", 162 lbs. Deb: 4/12/86																												
1986	Mil-A	26	54	6	9	0	1	0	5	5	12	.167	.250	.204	.454	26	-5	-6	102	181	3	.375	1	1	-0	-2	2/S3OD	-0.6
1987	Mil-A	116	321	44	72	11	4	3	28	33	76	.224	.303	.312	.614	63	-16	-17	102	102	33	.565	15	7	0	-3	2S/3	-1.0
1988	Mil-A	54	90	10	20	0	0	0	2	3	14	.222	.247	.222	.470	31	-8	-8	103	40	5	.352	2	0	1	-1	23S/OD	-0.6
Total	3	196	465	60	101	11	5	3	35	41	102	.217	.286	.282	.568	53	-29	-31	103	100	41	.520	18	8	1	-6	2/S3DO	-2.2
■ MARTY CASTILLO Castillo, Martin Horace b: 1/16/57, Long Beach, Cal. BR/TR, 6'1", 190 lbs. Deb: 8/19/81																												
1981	Det-A	6	8	1	1	0	0	0	0	0	2	.125	.125	.125	.250	-26	-1	-1	105	0	0	.143	0	0	0	-0	/3CO	-0.1
1982	Det-A	1	0	0	0	0	0	0	0	0	0	—	—	—	—	—	0	0	100	—	—	—	0	0	0	0	/C	0.0
1983	Det-A	67	119	10	23	4	0	2	10	7	22	.193	.238	.277	.515	43	-10	-9	96	100	8	.420	2	0	1	-4	3C	-1.1
1984	Det-A	70	141	16	33	5	2	4	17	10	33	.234	.285	.383	.668	86	-4	-3	96	103	15	.580	1	0	0	-3	C3/D	-0.2
1985	Det-A	57	84	4	10	2	0	2	5	2	19	.119	.140	.214	.354	-5	-12	-13	106	83	2	.260	0	2	-1	-1	C3	-1.3
Total	5	201	352	31	67	11	2	8	32	19	76	.190	.232	.301	.533	46	-27	-26	98	95	25	.444	3	2	-0	-8	3/CDO	-2.7
■ CARMELO CASTILLO Castillo, Monte Carmelo b: 6/8/58, San Pedro De Macoris, D.R. BR/TR, 6'1", 185 lbs. Deb: 7/17/82																												
1982	Cle-A	47	120	11	25	4	0	2	11	6	17	.208	.258	.292	.549	50	-8	-8	100	107	9	.443	0	0	0	-2	O/D	-1.1
1983	Cle-A	23	36	9	10	2	1	1	3	4	6	.278	.366	.472	.838	122	1	1	105	59	6	.852	1	1	-0	-2	O/D	0.0
1984	Cle-A	87	211	36	55	9	2	10	36	21	32	.261	.333	.464	.798	111	5	3	106	112	30	.735	1	3	-2	-9	O/D	-0.8
1985	Cle-A	67	184	27	45	5	1	11	25	11	40	.245	.298	.462	.760	111	0	2	94	84	24	.703	3	0	1	-4	O/D	-0.1
1986	Cle-A	85	205	34	57	9	0	8	32	9	48	.278	.312	.439	.751	105	0	1	98	112	25	.646	2	1	0	-3	OD	-0.2
1987	Cle-A	89	220	27	55	17	0	11	31	16	52	.250	.301	.477	.778	100	0	-1	103	90	33	.735	1	1	-0	-2	DO	-0.3
1988	Cle-A	66	176	12	48	8	0	4	14	5	31	.273	.297	.386	.683	88	-3	-3	102	70	19	.597	6	2	1	-7	O/D	-1.0
Total	7	464	1152	156	295	54	4	47	152	72	226	.256	.306	.432	.738	99	-4	-5	101	95	146	.684	14	8	-1	-28	OD	-3.5
■ JOHN CASTINO Castino, John Anthony b: 10/23/54, Evanston, Ill. BR/TR, 5'11", 175 lbs. Deb: 4/06/79																												
1979	Min-A	148	393	49	112	13	8	5	52	27	72	.285	.333	.397	.729	88	-3	-7	109	117	52	.647	5	2	0	5	*3/S	0.1
1980	Min-A	150	546	67	165	17	7	13	64	29	67	.302	.337	.430	.768	100	5	-1	109	93	75	.676	7	5	-1	23	*3S	2.2
1981	Min-A	101	381	41	102	13	9	6	36	18	52	.268	.303	.396	.699	95	-1	-3	105	88	45	.606	4	5	-2	10	3/2	0.6
1982	Min-A	117	410	48	99	12	6	6	37	36	51	.241	.306	.344	.650	78	-12	-12	100	95	41	.554	2	5	-2	-11	23/OD	-2.1
1983	Min-A	142	563	83	156	30	4	11	57	62	54	.277	.350	.403	.753	101	6	2	105	76	81	.700	4	2	0	4	*2/3D	1.0
1984	Min-A	8	27	5	12	1	0	0	3	5	2	.444	.531	.481	1.013	173	4	3	106	94	6	1.059	0	0	0	1	/3	0.4
Total	6	666	2320	293	646	86	34	41	249	177	298	.278	.331	.398	.729	95	-1	-18	106	92	300	.665	22	19	-5	31	32/SOD	2.2
■ VINCE CASTINO Castino, Vincent Charles b: 10/11/17, Willisville, Ill. d: 3/6/67, Sacramento, Cal. BR/TR, 5'9", 175 lbs. Deb: 6/24/43																												
1943	Chi-A	33	101	14	23	1	0	2	16	12	11	.228	.310	.297	.607	77	-3	-3	101	162	10	.519	0	0	0	0	C	0.0
1944	Chi-A	29	78	8	18	5	0	0	3	10	13	.231	.326	.295	.621	78	-2	-2	100	47	8	.548	0	1	-1	0	C	0.0
1945	Chi-A	26	36	2	8	1	0	0	4	3	7	.222	.282	.250	.532	58	-2	-2	95	161	2	.400	0	0	0	0	C	0.0
Total	3	88	215	24	49	7	0	2	23	25	31	.228	.311	.288	.600	74	-7	-7	100	119	20	.521	0	1	-1	1	/C	0.0
■ DON CASTLE Castle, Donald Hardy b: 2/1/50, Kokomo, Ind. BL/TL, 6'1", 205 lbs. Deb: 9/11/73																												
1973	Tex-A	4	13	0	4	1	0	0	2	1	3	.308	.357	.385	.742	112	0	0	97	157	1	.545	0	0	0	0	/D	0.0
■ JOHN CASTLE Castle, John Francis b: 6/1/1883, Honey Brook, Pa. d: 4/13/29, Philadelphia, Pa. 5'10.5", Deb: 4/30/10																												
1910	Phi-N	3	4	1	1	0	0	0	0	0	0	.250	.250	.250	.500	48	-0	-0	96	0	0	.667	1			-1	/O	0.0
■ FOSTER CASTLEMAN Castleman, Foster Ephraim b: 1/1/31, Nashville, Tenn. BR/TR, 6', 175 lbs. Deb: 8/04/54																												
1954	NY-N	13	12	0	3	0	0	0	1	0	3	.250	.308	.250	.558	45	-1	-1	105	131	1	.400	0	0	0	0	/3	0.0
1955	NY-N	15	28	3	6	1	0	2	4	2	4	.214	.267	.464	.731	91	-1	-1	99	85	4	.682	0	0	0	1	/23	0.0
1956	NY-N	124	385	33	87	16	3	14	45	15	50	.226	.259	.392	.651	74	-16	-15	97	98	37	.552	2	1	0	8	*3/S2	-0.7
1957	NY-N	18	37	7	6	2	0	1	1	2	8	.162	.205	.297	.502	32	-4	-4	102	30	2	.419	0	0	0	0	/32S	-0.2
1958	Bal-A	98	200	15	34	5	0	3	14	16	34	.170	.242	.240	.482	35	-18	-17	94	98	12	.401	2	0	1	-9	S/23O	-1.2
Total	5	268	662	58	136	24	3	20	65	35	99	.205	.252	.341	.593	60	-40	-37	97	95	55	.508	4	1	1	-0	3/S2O	-2.1
■ LOUIS CASTRO Castro, Louis M. "Jud" b: 1877, Columbia, South America d: Venezuela TR , 5'7", Deb: 4/23/02																												
1902	Phi-A	42	143	18	35	8	1	1	15	4		.245	.265	.336	.601	62	-7	-8	108	97	14	.500	2			-7	2/OS	-1.3
■ DANNY CATER Cater, Danny Anderson b: 2/25/40, Austin, Tex. BR/TR, 6', 170 lbs. Deb: 4/14/64																												
1964	Phi-N	60	152	13	45	9	1	1	13	7	15	.296	.327	.388	.715	102	-0	0	99	86	18	.593	1	0	0	-1	O/13	-0.1
1965	Chi-A	142	514	74	139	18	4	14	55	33	65	.270	.318	.403	.721	112	1	6	92	94	61	.621	3	3	-1	-10	*O3/1	-1.0
1966	Chi-A	21	60	3	11	1	1	0	4	0	10	.183	.197	.233	.430	24	-6	-6	94	120	3	.353	3	1	0	-4	O	-1.0
	KC-A	116	425	47	124	16	3	7	52	28	37	.292	.337	.393	.730	116	5	8	94	118	53	.623	1	4	-2	-3	13O	-0.1
	Yr	137	485	50	135	17	4	7	56	28	47	.278	.320	.373	.694	105	-1	2	94	119	55	.587	4	5	-2	-7		-1.1
1967	KC-A	142	529	55	143	17	4	4	46	34	56	.270	.319	.340	.659	95	-3	-3	100	106	54	.548	4	5	-2	-7	3O1	-1.7
1968	Oak-A	147	504	53	146	28	3	6	62	35	43	.290	.338	.393	.731	123	12	13	98	125	61	.630	8	7	-2	-5	*1O/2	0.0
1969	Oak-A	152	584	64	153	24	2	10	76	28	40	.262	.298	.361	.659	91	-14	-9	92	129	55	.526	1	4	-2	3	*1O/2	-1.8
1970	NY-A	155	582	64	175	26	5	6	76	34	44	.301	.341	.393	.735	111	1	6	92	127	74	.629	4	2	0	0	*13/O	0.0
1971	NY-A	121	428	39	118	16	5	4	50	19	25	.276	.310	.364	.674	93	-6	-5	97	121	42	.535	0	3	-2	4	13	-0.8
1972	Bos-A	92	317	32	75	17	1	8	39	15	33	.237	.275	.372	.648	87	-5	-6	105	115	28	.521	0	1	-1	4	1	-1.3
1973	Bos-A	63	195	30	61	12	0	1	24	10	22	.313	.350	.390	.739	102	2	0	106	119	25	.621	0	0	0	0	13/D	-0.1
1974	Bos-A	56	126	14	31	5	0	5	20	10	13	.246	.312	.405	.716	98	1	-0	107	119	15	.640	1	0	0	-0	1D	-0.1
1975	StL-N	22	35	3	8	2	0	0	2	1	3	.229	.250	.286	.536	47	-3	-3	103	77	3	.407	0	0	0	0	1	-0.2
Total	12	1289	4451	491	1229	191	29	66	519	254	406	.276	.318	.377	.695	102	-16	2	97	116	492	.608	26	30	-10	-20	1O3/D2	-8.2
■ ELI CATES Cates, Eli Eldo b: 1/26/1877, Greensfork, Ind. d: 5/29/64, Richmond, Ind. BR/TR, 5'9.5", 175 lbs. Deb: 4/20/08																												
1908	Was-A	40	59	5	11	1	1	0	3	6		.186	.262	.237	.499	67	-2	-2	95	80	3	.417	0			1	P/2	0.1
■ TED CATHER Cather, Theodore P b: 5/20/1889, Chester, Pa. d: 4/9/45, Elkton, Md. BR/TR, 5'10.5", 178 lbs. Deb: 9/23/12																												
1912	StL-N	5	19	4	8	1	1	0	2	0	4	.421	.421	.579	1.000	173	2	2	100	62	5	1.091	1			2	/O	0.3
1913	StL-N	67	183	16	39	8	4	0	12	9	24	.213	.250	.301	.551	61	-11	-9	93	79	15	.493	7			-10	O/P1	-2.0

YEAR	TM/L	G	AB	R	H	2B	3B	HR	RBI	BB	SO	AVG	OBP	SLG	PRO	/A	BR	/A	PF	CHI	RC	TA	SB	CS	SBR	FR	POS	TPR
1914	StL-N	39	99	11	27	7	0	0	13	3	15	.273	.294	.343	.638	86	-2	-2	104	139	11	.569	4			-0	O	-0.3
	Bos-N	50	145	19	43	11	2	0	27	7	28	.297	.338	.400	.738	114	3	2	104	169	21	.725	7			-8	O	-0.7
	Yr	89	244	30	70	18	2	0	40	10	43	.287	.320	.377	.697	103	1	0	104	157	32	.661	11			-8		-1.0
1915	Bos-N	40	102	10	21	3	1	2	18	15	19	.206	.319	.314	.633	94	-1	-0	98	181	11	.600	2	4	-2	-7	O	-1.0
Total	4	201	548	60	138	30	8	2	72	34	90	.252	.300	.347	.647	91	-8	-8	99	133	62	.601	21	4		-23	O/1P	-3.7
■ HOWDY CATON	Caton, James Howard "Buster" b: 7/16/1896, Zanesville, Ohio d: 1/8/48, Zanesville, Ohio BR/TR, 5'6", 165 lbs. Deb: 9/17/17																											
1917	Pit-N	14	57	6	12	1	2	0	4	6	7	.211	.286	.298	.584	80	-1	-1	100	78	5	.511	0			-2	S	-0.3
1918	Pit-N	80	303	37	71	5	7	0	17	32	16	.234	.312	.297	.609	81	-4	-6	106	69	31	.586	12			-10	S	-1.5
1919	Pit-N	39	102	13	18	1	2	0	5	12	10	.176	.263	.225	.489	45	-6	-7	105	84	7	.440	2			-4	S3/O	-1.1
1920	Pit-N	98	352	29	83	11	5	0	27	33	19	.236	.305	.295	.600	72	-12	-12	101	102	32	.514	4	9	-4	-24	S	-3.8
Total	4	231	814	85	184	18	16	0	53	83	52	.226	.301	.287	.588	72	-24	-27	103	86	74	.531	18	9		-40	S/3O	-6.7
■ TOM CATTERSON	Catterson, Thomas Henry b: 8/25/1884, Warwick, R.I. d: 2/5/20, Portland, Maine BL , 5'10", 170 lbs. Deb: 9/19/08																											
1908	Bro-N	19	68	5	13	1	1	1	2	5		.191	.247	.279	.526	73	-2	-2	95	37	4	.436	0			5	O	0.3
1909	Bro-N	9	18	0	4	0	0	0	1	3		.222	.333	.222	.556	74	-0	-0	99	91	1	.500	0			0	/O	0.0
Total	2	28	86	5	17	1	1	1	3	8		.198	.266	.267	.533	74	-3	-2	96	49	6	.449	0			5	/O	0.3
■ JAKE CAULFIELD	Caulfield, John Joseph b: 11/23/17, Los Angeles, Cal. BR/TR, 5'11", 170 lbs. Deb: 4/24/46																											
1946	Phi-A	44	94	13	26	8	0	0	10	4	11	.277	.306	.362	.668	82	-2	-2	104	112	10	.543	0	0	0	-3	S/3	-0.4
■ WAYNE CAUSEY	Causey, James Wayne b: 12/26/36, Ruston, La. BL/TR, 5'10.5", 175 lbs. Deb: 6/05/55																											
1955	Bal-A	68	175	14	34	2	1	1	9	17	25	.194	.269	.234	.504	41	-16	-13	90	76	12	.413	0	1	-1	-3	3/2S	-1.5
1956	Bal-A	53	88	7	15	0	1	1	4	8	23	.170	.240	.227	.467	25	-10	-9	94	65	5	.373	0	0	0	-1	3/2	-0.8
1957	Bal-A	14	10	2	2	0	0	0	1	5	2	.200	.500	.200	.700	106	1	1	93	198	2	1.000	0	0	0	0	/23	0.1
1961	KC-A	104	312	37	86	14	1	8	49	37	28	.276	.352	.404	.756	100	1	0	102	128	46	.706	0	0	0	11	3S/2	1.8
1962	KC-A	117	305	40	77	14	1	4	38	41	30	.252	.345	.344	.689	86	-5	-5	100	129	38	.636	2	0	1	-3	S3/2	-0.2
1963	KC-A	139	554	72	155	32	4	8	44	56	54	.280	.346	.395	.741	100	6	1	108	73	77	.680	4	2	0	3	*S/3	1.1
1964	KC-A	157	604	82	170	31	4	8	49	88	65	.281	.379	.386	.765	109	14	11	105	71	90	.722	0	1	-1	-8	*S2/3	0.4
1965	KC-A	144	513	48	134	17	8	3	34	61	48	.261	.342	.343	.685	98	-2	0	97	81	63	.617	1	3	-2	-12	S23	-0.8
1966	KC-A	28	79	1	18	0	0	0	5	7	6	.228	.291	.228	.519	54	-5	-4	94	117	5	.406	1	0	0	-2	3S	-0.5
	Chi-A	78	164	23	40	8	2	0	13	24	13	.244	.340	.317	.657	96	-1	-0	94	105	20	.619	2	0	1	1	2/S3	0.7
	Yr	106	243	24	58	8	2	0	18	31	19	.239	.325	.288	.613	82	-6	-4	94	109	26	.556	3	0	1	-1		0.2
1967	Chi-A	124	292	21	66	10	3	1	28	32	35	.226	.305	.291	.596	82	-8	-6	94	133	27	.515	2	5	-2	-0	2/S	-0.5
1968	Chi-A	59	100	8	18	2	0	0	7	14	7	.180	.287	.200	.487	49	-6	-6	101	150	7	.427	0	0	0	-4	2	-0.8
	Cal-A	4	11	0	0	0	0	0	0	0	1	.000	.000	.000	.000	-99	-3	-3	94	0	0	.000	0	0	0	0	/2	-0.2
	Yr	63	111	8	18	2	0	0	7	14	8	.162	.262	.180	.442	36	-8	-8	100	143	6	.372	0	0	0	-3		-1.0
	Atl-N	16	37	2	4	0	1	1	4	0	4	.108	.108	.243	.351	3	-4	-4	93	140	1	.273	0	0	0	0	/2S3	-0.3
Total	11	1105	3244	357	819	130	26	35	285	390	341	.252	.335	.341	.676	90	-37	-37	100	96	394	.625	12	12	-4	-18	S23	-1.5
■ JOHN CAVANAUGH	Cavanaugh, John J. b: 6/5/1900, Scranton, Pa. d: 1/14/61, New Brunswick, N.J 5'9", 158 lbs. Deb: 7/07/19																											
1919	Phi-N	1	1	0	0	0	0	0	0	0	1	.000	.000	.000	.000	-96	-0	-0	104	0	0	.000	0			0	/3	0.0
■ PHIL CAVARRETTA	Cavarretta, Philip Joseph b: 7/19/16, Chicago, Ill. BL/TL, 5'11.5", 175 lbs. Deb: 9/16/34 MC																											
1934	Chi-N	7	21	5	8	0	1	1	6	2	3	.381	.435	.619	1.054	183	2	2	98	135	6	1.231	1			0	/1	0.2
1935	Chi-N	146	589	85	162	28	12	8	82	39	61	.275	.322	.404	.726	95	-6	-5	99	120	79	.649	4			3	*1	-0.4
1936	Chi-N	124	458	55	125	18	1	9	56	17	36	.273	.306	.376	.682	79	-12	-15	105	100	53	.592	8			3	*1	-2.1
1937	Chi-N	106	329	43	94	18	7	5	56	32	35	.286	.349	.429	.778	107	4	3	103	129	50	.741	7			0	O1	-0.1
1938	Chi-N	92	268	29	64	11	4	1	28	14	27	.239	.287	.321	.608	64	-12	-14	105	114	25	.514	4			-6	O1	-2.3
1939	Chi-N	22	55	4	15	3	1	0	0	4	3	.273	.322	.364	.686	83	-1	-1	101	0	6	.634	2			-1	1/O	-0.3
1940	Chi-N	65	193	34	54	11	4	2	22	31	18	.280	.388	.409	.797	121	6	7	100	96	33	.823	3			0	1	0.2
1941	Chi-N	107	346	46	99	18	4	6	40	53	28	.286	.384	.413	.797	133	13	16	94	91	58	.791	2			-5	O1	0.3
1942	Chi-N	136	482	59	130	28	4	3	54	71	42	.270	.365	.363	.728	118	10	12	96	111	71	.718	7			-1	O1	0.5
1943	Chi-N	143	530	93	154	27	9	8	73	75	42	.291	.382	.421	.802	133	23	24	99	113	89	.788	3			-8	*1/O	1.0
1944	Chi-N	152	614	106	**197**	35	15	5	82	67	42	.321	.390	.451	.841	135	30	30	101	89	111	.822	4			-7	*1O	1.1
1945	Chi-N	132	498	94	177	34	10	6	97	81	34	**.355**	**.449**	.500	.949	**166**	46	47	99	121	119	1.037	5			-3	*1O	3.8
1946	Chi-N	139	510	89	150	28	10	8	78	88	54	.294	.401	.435	.836	146	28	31	94	125	92	.838	2			5	O1	3.1
1947	Chi-N	127	459	56	144	22	5	2	63	58	35	.314	.391	.397	.787	108	8	8	101	132	76	.759	2			3	*O1	0.5
1948	Chi-N	111	334	41	93	16	5	3	40	35	29	.278	.349	.383	.732	105	-1	2	93	109	48	.694	4			1	1O	0.0
1949	Chi-N	105	360	46	106	22	4	8	49	45	31	.294	.374	.444	.819	126	10	13	94	102	62	.800	2			9	1O	2.0
1950	Chi-N	82	256	49	70	11	1	10	31	40	31	.273	.376	.441	.817	109	6	4	105	84	45	.817	1			4	1/O	0.5
1951	Chi-N	89	206	24	64	7	1	6	28	27	28	.311	.393	.442	.835	128	8	8	97	99	39	.826	0	0	0	0	1M	0.8
1952	Chi-N	41	63	7	15	1	1	1	8	9	3	.238	.333	.333	.667	83	-1	-1	103	130	8	.625	0	0	0	0	1M	-0.1
1953	Chi-N	27	21	3	6	3	0	0	3	6	3	.286	.444	.429	.873	125	1	1	103	130	5	1.000	0	0	0	0	HM	0.1
1954	Chi-A	71	158	21	50	6	0	3	24	26	12	.316	.419	.411	.831	124	7	7	104	123	31	.890	4	0	1	-5	1/O	0.1
1955	Chi-A	6	4	1	0	0	0	0	0	0	1	.000	.000	.000	.000	-99	-1	-1	101	0	0	.000	0	0	0	0	/1	0.0
Total	22	2030	6754	990	1977	347	99	95	920	820	598	.293	.372	.416	.788	118	170	178	99	110	1106	.781	65	0		-10	*1O	8.9
■ IKE CAVENEY	Caveney, James Christopher b: 12/10/1894, San Francisco, Cal d: 7/6/49, San Francisco, Cal BR/TR, 5'9", 168 lbs. Deb: 4/12/22																											
1922	Cin-N	118	394	41	94	12	9	3	54	29	33	.239	.301	.338	.638	67	-21	-19	96	136	41	.569	6	6	-2	-5	*S	-1.6
1923	Cin-N	138	488	58	135	21	9	4	63	26	41	.277	.315	.381	.696	85	-13	-12	98	114	58	.611	5	4	-1	-2	*S	-0.2
1924	Cin-N	95	337	36	92	19	1	4	32	14	21	.273	.310	.371	.681	81	-9	-9	101	87	38	.585	2	3	-1	-4	S/2	-0.7
1925	Cin-N	115	358	38	89	9	5	2	47	28	31	.249	.303	.318	.622	61	-22	-21	97	139	36	.535	2	0	1	2	*S	-0.7
Total	4	466	1577	173	410	61	24	13	196	97	126	.260	.307	.354	.661	74	-66	-60	98	120	174	.577	15	13	-3	-10	S/2	-3.2
■ CESAR CEDENO	Cedeno, Cesar (Encarnacion) b: 2/25/51, Santo Domingo, D.R. BR/TR, 6'2", 175 lbs. Deb: 6/20/70																											
1970	Hou-N	90	355	46	110	21	4	7	42	15	57	.310	.341	.451	.792	118	4	7	94	92	53	.755	17	4	3	-1	O	0.5
1971	Hou-N	161	611	85	161	**40**	6	10	81	25	102	.264	.296	.398	.693	102	-6	-1	93	123	70	.622	20	9	1	-7	*O/1	-1.3
1972	Hou-N	139	559	103	179	**39**	8	22	82	56	62	.320	.387	.537	.924	151	43	39	106	88	115	1.010	55	21	4	5	*O	4.4
1973	Hou-N	139	525	86	168	35	2	25	70	41	79	.320	.377	.537	.914	159	34	37	95	83	102	.987	56	15	8	11	*O	5.0
1974	Hou-N	160	610	95	164	29	5	26	102	64	103	.269	.342	.461	.803	126	17	18	98	116	99	.860	57	17	7	11	*O	3.1
1975	Hou-N	131	500	93	144	31	3	13	63	62	52	.288	.374	.440	.814	133	18	21	94	90	85	.881	50	17	5	-0	*O	2.2
1976	Hou-N	150	575	89	171	26	5	18	83	55	51	.297	.360	.454	.814	150	22	31	86	108	94	.862	58	15	8	4	*O	3.9
1977	Hou-N	141	530	92	148	36	8	14	71	47	50	.279	.350	.457	.807	124	10	16	93	106	89	.889	61	14	10	4	*O	2.5
1978	Hou-N	50	192	31	54	8	2	7	23	15	24	.281	.333	.453	.786	125	4	5	95	89	31	.868	23	2	6	6	O	1.6
1979	Hou-N	132	470	57	123	27	4	6	54	64	52	.262	.354	.374	.728	109	1	7	90	117	63	.728	30	13	1	4	1O	0.7
1980	Hou-N	137	499	71	154	32	8	10	73	66	72	.309	.390	.465	.855	141	27	28	98	117	93	.930	48	15	5	-0	*O	2.9
1981	Hou-N	82	306	42	83	19	0	5	34	24	31	.271	.326	.382	.709	114	-0	4	88	107	37	.653	12	7	-1	1	1O	0.1
1982	Cin-N	138	492	52	142	35	1	8	57	41	41	.289	.348	.413	.761	110	8	6	102	100	67	.702	16	11	-2	-3	*O/1	0.0
1983	Cin-N	98	332	40	77	16	0	9	39	33	53	.232	.307	.361	.669	82	-7	-8	103	107	38	.635	13	9	-2	2	O1	-1.0
1984	Cin-N	110	380	59	105	24	2	10	47	25	54	.276	.323	.429	.752	104	4	1	106	95	52	.720	19	3	4	-1	O1	0.0
1985	Cin-N	83	220	24	53	12	0	3	30	19	35	.241	.310	.336	.646	77	-6	-7	105	144	23	.593	9	5	-0	-2	O1	-1.1
	StL-N	28	76	14	33	4	1	6	19	5	7	.434	.469	.750	1.219	247	13	14	96	101	26	1.457	5	1	1	-2	1/O	1.2
	Yr	111	296	38	86	16	1	9	49	24	42	.291	.350	.443	.792	117	8	7	103	134	47	.789	14	6	1	-4		0.1
1986	LA-N	37	78	5	18	2	1	0	6	7	13	.231	.294	.282	.576	63	-4	-4	94	109	7	.492	1	1	-0	-5	O	-0.9
Total	17	2006	7310	1084	2087	436	60	199	976	664	938	.285	.350	.443	.793	124	180	215	96	105	1144	.835	550	179	58	27	*O1	23.8
■ ORLANDO CEPEDA	Cepeda, Orlando Manuel (Penne) "Baby Bull" or "Cha Cha" b: 9/17/37, Ponce, P.R. BR/TR, 6'2", 210 lbs. Deb: 4/15/58 C																											
1958	SF-N	148	603	88	188	**38**	4	25	96	29	84	.312	.346	.512	.859	123	18	18	100	109	97	.802	15	11	-2	-3	*1	0.3

YEAR	TM/L	G	AB	R	H	2B	3B	HR	RBI	BB	SO	AVG	OBP	SLG	PRO	/A	BR	/A	PF	CHI	RC	TA	SB	CS	SBR	FR	POS	TPR
1959	SF-N	151	605	92	192	35	4	27	105	33	100	.317	.358	.522	.880	137	25	28	95	113	110	.873	23	9	2	-8	*1O/3	1.1
1960	SF-N	151	569	81	169	36	3	24	96	34	91	.297	.345	.497	.843	142	20	27	90	112	95	.815	15	6	1	-2	O1	2.0
1961	SF-N	152	585	105	182	28	4	**46**	**142**	39	91	.311	.363	.609	.972	155	41	42	98	123	118	.963	12	8	-1	-6	1O	2.5
1962	SF-N	162	625	105	191	26	1	35	114	37	97	.306	.350	.518	.869	128	24	23	101	111	108	.830	10	4	1	-8	*1/O	1.0
1963	SF-N	156	579	100	183	33	4	34	97	37	70	.316	.367	.563	.930	171	45	48	96	97	113	.914	8	3	1	-7	*1/O	4.1
1964	SF-N	142	529	75	161	27	2	31	97	43	83	.304	.366	.539	.904	151	35	35	100	107	101	.896	9	4	0	-4	*1/O	2.7
1965	SF-N	33	34	1	6	1	0	1	5	3	9	.176	.243	.294	.537	46	-2	-3	111	159	2	.448	0	0	1	-1	/1O	-0.3
1966	SF-N	19	49	5	14	2	0	3	15	4	11	.286	.352	.510	.862	140	2	2	97	185	9	.833	0	1	-1	-2	/O1	0.0
	StL-N	123	452	65	137	24	0	17	58	34	69	.303	.369	.469	.838	131	19	19	100	98	75	.800	9	8	-2	-2	*1	0.9
	Yr	142	501	70	151	26	0	20	73	38	80	.301	.367	.473	.840	132	22	22	99	111	83	.803	9	9	-3	-5		0.9
1967	StL-N	151	563	91	183	37	0	25	**111**	62	75	.325	.403	.524	.927	162	47	46	101	132	118	.955	11	2	2	-1	*1	4.3
1968	StL-N	157	600	71	149	26	2	16	73	43	96	.248	.308	.378	.687	111	3	6	95	118	68	.611	8	6	-1	-4	*1	-0.5
1969	Atl-N	154	573	74	147	28	2	22	88	55	76	.257	.327	.428	.755	106	6	4	104	120	79	.716	12	5	1	1	*1	-0.6
1970	Atl-N	148	567	87	173	33	0	34	111	47	75	.305	.368	.543	.911	135	31	27	104	111	108	.894	6	5	-1	1	*1	1.5
1971	Atl-N	71	250	31	69	10	1	14	44	22	29	.276	.335	.492	.827	120	9	6	110	111	35	.744	3	6	-3	-2	1	-0.2
1972	Atl-N	28	84	6	25	3	0	4	9	7	17	.298	.352	.476	.828	127	3	3	105	71	14	.783	0	0	0	-0	1	0.1
	Oak-A	3	3	0	0	0	0	0	0	0	0	.000	.000	.000	.000	-99	-1	-1	97	0	0	.000	0	0	0	0	H	0.0
1973	Bos-A	142	550	51	159	25	0	20	86	50	81	.289	.352	.444	.795	116	16	12	106	118	79	.712	0	2	-1	0	*D	1.1
1974	KC-A	33	107	3	23	5	0	1	18	9	16	.215	.282	.290	.572	61	-5	-6	106	208	8	.472	1	0	0	0	D	-0.5
Total	17	2124	7927	1131	2351	417	27	379	1365	588	1170	.297	.353	.499	.852	134	337	339	100	115	1338	.846	142	80	-5	-48	*1OD/3	19.5

■ ED CERMAK Cermak, Edward Hugo b: 3/10/1882, Cleveland, Ohio d: 11/22/11, Cleveland, Ohio BR/TR, 5'11", 170 lbs. Deb: 9/09/01

YEAR	TM/L	G	AB	R	H	2B	3B	HR	RBI	BB	SO	AVG	OBP	SLG	PRO	/A	BR	/A	PF	CHI	RC	TA	SB	CS	SBR	FR	POS	TPR
1901	Cle-A	1	4	0	0	0	0	0	0	0		.000	.000	.000	.000	-99	-1	-1	95	0	0	.000	0			0	/O	0.0

■ RICK CERONE Cerone, Richard Aldo b: 5/19/54, Newark, N.J. BR/TR, 5'11", 192 lbs. Deb: 8/17/75

YEAR	TM/L	G	AB	R	H	2B	3B	HR	RBI	BB	SO	AVG	OBP	SLG	PRO	/A	BR	/A	PF	CHI	RC	TA	SB	CS	SBR	FR	POS	TPR
1975	Cle-A	7	12	1	3	1	0	0	0	1	0	.250	.308	.333	.641	81	-0	-0	100	0	1	.556	0	0	0	0	/C	0.0
1976	Cle-A	7	16	1	2	0	0	0	1	0	2	.125	.125	.125	.250	-27	-3	-3	100	192	0	.143	0	0	0	0	/CD	-0.1
1977	Tor-A	31	100	7	20	4	0	1	10	6	12	.200	.245	.270	.515	39	-8	-9	103	132	6	.398	0	0	0	3	C	-0.4
1978	Tor-A	88	282	25	63	8	2	3	20	23	32	.223	.284	.298	.582	64	-13	-14	100	85	23	.472	0	3	-2	6	C/D	-0.6
1979	Tor-A	136	469	47	112	27	4	7	61	37	40	.239	.296	.358	.654	73	-17	-19	103	127	50	.566	1	4	-2	13	*C	-0.1
1980	NY-A	147	519	70	144	30	4	14	85	32	56	.277	.327	.432	.758	107	3	4	99	127	70	.671	1	3	-2	-1	*C	0.7
1981	NY-A	71	234	23	57	13	2	2	21	12	24	.244	.280	.342	.622	78	-7	-7	100	96	20	.487	0	2	-1	1	C	-0.4
1982	NY-A	89	300	29	68	10	0	5	28	19	27	.227	.275	.310	.585	63	-16	-15	96	104	23	.459	0	2	-1	-1	C	-1.2
1983	NY-A	80	246	18	54	7	0	2	22	15	29	.220	.267	.272	.540	50	-17	-17	99	118	18	.421	0	0	0	-3	C/3	-1.5
1984	NY-A	38	120	8	25	3	0	2	13	9	15	.208	.269	.283	.553	57	-8	-7	94	130	9	.450	1	0	0	2	C	-0.2
1985	Atl-N	96	282	15	61	9	0	3	25	29	25	.216	.292	.280	.572	57	-14	-17	106	113	20	.456	0	3	-2	4	C	-1.1
1986	Mil-A	68	216	22	56	14	0	4	18	15	28	.259	.310	.380	.690	86	-4	-4	102	76	25	.596	1	1	-0	13	C	1.1
1987	NY-A	113	284	28	69	12	1	4	23	30	46	.243	.324	.335	.658	78	-9	-8	98	86	31	.576	0	1	-1	-13	*C/P1	-1.2
1988	Bos-A	84	264	31	71	13	1	3	27	20	32	.269	.328	.360	.687	85	-3	-6	109	103	31	.593	0	0	0	-2	C/D	-0.3
Total	14	1055	3344	325	805	151	14	50	354	248	368	.241	.297	.339	.636	74	-116	-120	101	109	327	.548	4	19	-10	21	*C/D1P3	-5.3

■ BOB CERV Cerv, Robert Henry b: 5/5/26, Weston, Neb. BR/TR, 6', 200 lbs. Deb: 8/01/51

YEAR	TM/L	G	AB	R	H	2B	3B	HR	RBI	BB	SO	AVG	OBP	SLG	PRO	/A	BR	/A	PF	CHI	RC	TA	SB	CS	SBR	FR	POS	TPR
1951	NY-A	12	28	4	6	1	0	0	2	4	6	.214	.313	.250	.563	58	-2	-1	92	102	2	.478	0	0	0	-2	/O	-0.3
1952	NY-A	36	87	11	21	3	2	1	8	9	22	.241	.313	.356	.669	88	-2	-2	98	88	10	.597	0	1	-1	-1	O	-0.4
1953	NY-A	8	6	0	0	0	0	0	0	1	1	.000	.143	.000	.143	-63	-1	-1	93	0	0	.167	0	0	0	0	H	0.0
1954	NY-A	56	100	14	26	6	0	5	13	11	17	.260	.333	.470	.803	119	2	2	99	79	14	.734	0	2	-1	-6	O	-0.5
1955	NY-A	55	85	17	29	4	2	3	22	7	16	.341	.411	.541	.952	158	6	7	98	149	20	1.053	4	0	1	-3	O	0.4
1956	NY-A	54	115	16	35	5	6	3	25	18	13	.304	.398	.530	.929	145	7	7	99	133	24	.940	0	1	-1	-4	O	0.1
1957	KC-A	124	345	35	94	14	2	11	44	20	57	.272	.314	.420	.734	100	-2	-1	99	98	42	.630	1	1	-0	-3	O	-0.9
1958	KC-A	141	515	93	157	20	7	38	104	50	82	.305	.372	.592	.964	152	41	37	106	105	106	.955	3	3	-1	3	*O	3.1
1959	KC-A	125	463	61	132	22	4	20	87	35	87	.285	.339	.479	.819	121	13	12	101	124	72	.760	3	2	-0	2	*O	0.8
1960	KC-A	23	78	14	20	1	1	6	12	10	17	.256	.341	.526	.867	132	3	3	99	81	14	.850	0	0	0	2	O	0.5
	NY-A	87	216	32	54	11	1	8	28	30	36	.250	.349	.421	.771	114	2	4	94	95	32	.738	0	0	0	3	O/1	0.5
	Yr	110	294	46	74	12	2	14	40	40	53	.252	.347	.449	.796	119	6	7	95	93	47	.774	0	0	0	5		1.0
1961	LA-A	18	57	3	9	3	0	2	6	1	8	.158	.172	.316	.488	25	-6	-7	111	98	2	.365	0	0	0	-3	O	-1.0
	NY-A	57	118	17	32	5	1	6	20	12	17	.271	.344	.483	.827	123	3	3	96	104	18	.772	1	0	0	-0	O/1	0.2
	Yr	75	175	20	41	8	1	8	26	13	25	.234	.291	.429	.720	90	-3	-3	100	104	21	.643	1	0	0	-3		-0.8
1962	NY-A	14	17	1	2	1	0	0	0	2	3	.118	.250	.176	.426	18	-2	-2	94	0	1	.400	0	0	0	-0	/O	-0.1
	Hou-N	19	31	2	7	0	0	2	3	2	10	.226	.273	.419	.692	89	-1	-1	93	62	3	.577	0	0	0	-1	/O	-0.1
Total	12	829	2261	320	624	96	26	105	374	212	392	.276	.343	.481	.823	122	62	61	100	105	361	.805	12	10	-2	-13	O/1	2.3

■ RON CEY Cey, Ronald Charles b: 2/15/48, Tacoma, Wash. BR/TR, 5'10", 185 lbs. Deb: 9/03/71

YEAR	TM/L	G	AB	R	H	2B	3B	HR	RBI	BB	SO	AVG	OBP	SLG	PRO	/A	BR	/A	PF	CHI	RC	TA	SB	CS	SBR	FR	POS	TPR
1971	LA-N	2	2	0	0	0	0	0	0	0	2	.000	.000	.000	.000	-99	-1	-1	99	0	0	.000	0	0	0	0	H	0.0
1972	LA-N	11	37	3	10	1	0	1	3	7	10	.270	.400	.378	.778	130	1	2	94	74	6	.815	0	0	0	1	3	0.2
1973	LA-N	152	507	60	124	18	4	15	80	74	77	.245	.343	.385	.728	101	2	2	100	137	66	.675	1	1	-0	**22**	*3	2.0
1974	LA-N	159	577	88	151	20	2	18	97	76	68	.262	.355	.397	.751	119	9	14	93	**140**	82	.705	1	1	-0	17	*3	2.9
1975	LA-N	158	566	72	160	29	2	25	101	78	74	.283	.376	.473	.850	142	27	31	95	121	101	.846	5	2	0	-4	*3	2.6
1976	LA-N	145	502	69	139	18	3	23	80	89	74	.277	.389	.462	.851	141	29	29	100	108	92	.857	0	4	-2	8	*3	3.5
1977	LA-N	153	564	77	136	22	3	30	110	93	106	.241	.351	.450	.801	113	11	11	100	**136**	92	.795	3	4	-2	16	*3	2.4
1978	LA-N	159	555	84	150	32	0	23	84	96	96	.270	.384	.452	.837	134	27	28	99	110	99	.842	2	5	-2	8	*3	3.4
1979	LA-N	150	487	77	137	20	1	28	81	86	85	.281	.391	.499	.890	142	29	30	100	100	97	.918	3	3	-1	-1	*3	2.2
1980	LA-N	157	551	81	140	25	0	28	77	69	92	.254	.342	.452	.794	124	14	17	97	93	84	.758	2	2	-1	8	*3	2.4
1981	LA-N	85	312	42	90	15	2	13	50	40	55	.288	.375	.474	.849	143	16	17	98	111	55	.827	0	2	-1	7	3	2.1
1982	LA-N	150	556	62	141	23	1	24	79	57	99	.254	.327	.428	.755	116	6	10	95	102	76	.697	3	2	-0	12	*3	1.9
1983	Chi-N	159	581	73	160	33	1	24	90	62	85	.275	.350	.460	.810	122	17	16	101	111	90	.757	0	0	0	-19	*3	-0.7
1984	Chi-N	146	505	71	121	27	0	25	97	61	108	.240	.329	.442	.770	104	9	3	110	130	74	.740	3	2	-0	-21	*3	-2.0
1985	Chi-N	145	500	64	116	18	2	22	63	58	106	.232	.317	.408	.725	87	0	-10	116	95	65	.676	1	1	-0	-10	*3	-2.0
1986	Chi-N	97	256	42	70	21	0	13	36	44	66	.273	.386	.508	.894	136	16	14	107	85	53	.927	0	0	0	-3	3	0.9
1987	Oak-A	45	104	12	23	6	0	4	11	22	32	.221	.362	.394	.756	112	1	2	91	83	16	.753	0	0	0	0	D/13	0.1
Total	17	2073	7162	977	1868	328	21	316	1139	1012	1235	.261	.357	.445	.802	121	216	216	100	113	1149	.804	24	29	-10	40	*3/D1	21.9

■ ELIO CHACON Chacon, Elio (Rodirguez) b: 10/26/36, Caracas, Venez. BR/TR, 5'9", 160 lbs. Deb: 4/20/60

YEAR	TM/L	G	AB	R	H	2B	3B	HR	RBI	BB	SO	AVG	OBP	SLG	PRO	/A	BR	/A	PF	CHI	RC	TA	SB	CS	SBR	FR	POS	TPR
1960	Cin-N	49	116	14	21	1	0	0	7	14	23	.181	.275	.190	.464	30	-11	-11	98	129	8	.458	7	1	2	-4	2/O	-0.9
1961	Cin-N	61	132	26	35	4	2	2	5	21	22	.265	.374	.371	.745	95	1	-0	104	37	20	.723	1	4	-2	-6	2/O	-0.3
1962	NY-N	118	368	49	87	10	3	2	27	76	64	.236	.369	.296	.665	78	-6	-9	104	93	44	.658	12	7	-1	-8	*S/23	-0.6
Total	3	228	616	89	143	15	5	4	39	111	109	.232	.353	.292	.645	73	-17	-19	103	87	71	.633	20	12	-1	-18	S/2O3	-1.8

■ CHET CHADBOURNE Chadbourne, Chester James "Pop" b: 10/28/1884, Parkman, Me. d: 6/21/43, Los Angeles, Cal. BL/TR, 5'9", 170 lbs. Deb: 9/17/06

YEAR	TM/L	G	AB	R	H	2B	3B	HR	RBI	BB	SO	AVG	OBP	SLG	PRO	/A	BR	/A	PF	CHI	RC	TA	SB	CS	SBR	FR	POS	TPR
1906	Bos-A	11	43	7	13	1	0	0	3	3		.302	.348	.326	.673	115	1	1	98	69	5	.600	1			0	2/S	0.1
1907	Bos-A	10	38	0	11	0	0	0	1	7		.289	.400	.289	.689	122	2	1	101	28	5	.704	1			-0	O	0.1
1914	KC-F	147	581	92	161	22	8	1	37	69	49	.277	.354	.348	.702	107	3	7	95	56	90	.745	42			9	*O	0.9
1915	KC-F	152	587	75	133	16	9	1	35	62	29	.227	.300	.290	.590	78	-17	-15	97	63	64	.575	29			-1	*O	-2.4
1918	Bos-N	27	104	9	27	2	1	0	6	5	5	.260	.300	.298	.598	88	-2	-1	94	70	11	.545	5			-0	O	-0.3
Total	5	347	1353	183	345	41	18	2	82	146	83	.255	.328	.316	.644	93	-14	-7	96	60	175	.648	78			9	O/2S	-1.6

■ DAVE CHALK Chalk, David Lee b: 8/30/50, Del Rio, Tex. BR/TR, 5'10", 175 lbs. Deb: 9/04/73

YEAR	TM/L	G	AB	R	H	2B	3B	HR	RBI	BB	SO	AVG	OBP	SLG	PRO	/A	BR	/A	PF	CHI	RC	TA	SB	CS	SBR	FR	POS	TPR
1973	Cal-A	24	69	14	16	2	0	0	6	9	13	.232	.329	.261	.590	71	-3	-2	96	131	6	.509	0	0	0	-1	S	0.0
1974	Cal-A	133	465	44	117	9	3	5	31	30	57	.252	.307	.316	.623	86	-12	-8	92	77	41	.516	10	10	-3	-4	S3	-0.7

YEAR	TM/L	G	AB	R	H	2B	3B	HR	RBI	BB	SO	AVG	OBP	SLG	PRO	/A	BR	/A	PF	CHI	RC	TA	SB	CS	SBR	FR	POS	TPR
1975	Cal-A	149	513	59	140	24	2	3	56	66	49	.273	.358	.345	.703	105	2	5	95	118	64	.635	6	9	-4	3	*3	0.7
1976	Cal-A	142	438	39	95	14	1	0	33	49	62	.217	.310	.253	.563	72	-17	-12	92	114	36	.474	0	0	0	-4	*S3	-1.0
1977	Cal-A	149	519	58	144	27	2	3	45	52	69	.277	.349	.355	.703	98	-4	-0	95	94	65	.639	12	8	-1	-1	*3/2S	-0.4
1978	Cal-A	135	470	42	119	12	0	1	34	38	34	.253	.318	.285	.604	70	-17	-18	102	100	43	.500	5	8	-3	-11	S23/D	-2.3
1979	Tex-A	9	8	0	2	0	0	0	0	0	0	.250	.250	.250	.500	35	-1	-1	100	0	0	.286	0	0	0	0	/S2	0.0
	Oak-A	66	212	15	47	6	0	2	13	29	14	.222	.318	.278	.596	71	-10	-7	89	78	20	.529	2	1	0	-8	2S3	-1.0
	Yr	75	220	15	49	6	0	2	13	29	14	.223	.316	.277	.593	68	-11	-8	90	69	21	.522	2	1	0	-8		-1.0
1980	KC-A	69	167	19	42	10	1	1	20	18	27	.251	.332	.341	.673	86	-3	-3	98	130	19	.595	1	1	-0	0	32/SD	-0.1
1981	KC-A	27	49	2	11	3	0	0	5	4	2	.224	.283	.286	.569	65	-2	-2	99	140	4	.450	0	1	-1	-2	32/S	-0.3
Total	9	903	2910	292	733	107	9	15	243	295	327	.252	.328	.310	.638	85	-67	-47	95	102	299	.573	36	38	-12	-28	3S2/D	-5.1

■ **JOE CHAMBERLAIN** Chamberlain, Joseph Jeremiah b: 5/10/10, San Francisco, Cal d: 1/28/83, San Francisco, Cal. BR/TR, 6'1", 175 lbs. Deb: 4/17/34

YEAR	TM/L	G	AB	R	H	2B	3B	HR	RBI	BB	SO	AVG	OBP	SLG	PRO	/A	BR	/A	PF	CHI	RC	TA	SB	CS	SBR	FR	POS	TPR
1934	Chi-A	43	141	13	34	5	1	2	17	6	38	.241	.272	.333	.605	56	-10	-10	99	107	13	.500	1	1	-0	-0	S3/2	-0.7

■ **AL CHAMBERS** Chambers, Albert Eugene b: 3/24/61, Harrisburg, Pa. BL/TL, 6'4", 217 lbs. Deb: 7/23/83

YEAR	TM/L	G	AB	R	H	2B	3B	HR	RBI	BB	SO	AVG	OBP	SLG	PRO	/A	BR	/A	PF	CHI	RC	TA	SB	CS	SBR	FR	POS	TPR
1983	Sea-A	31	67	11	14	3	0	1	7	18	20	.209	.376	.299	.675	89	-0	-0	100	119	9	.691	0	1	-1	-1	D/O	0.0
1984	Sea-A	22	49	4	11	1	0	1	4	3	12	.224	.269	.306	.575	58	-3	-3	102	89	4	.513	2	1	0	-2	O/D	-0.5
1985	Sea-A	4	4	0	0	0	0	0	0	0	2	.000	.000	.000	.000	-99	-1	-1	95	0	0	.000	0	0	0	0	/H	0.0
Total	3	57	120	15	25	4	0	2	11	21	34	.208	.326	.292	.618	72	-4	-4	100	104	13	.598	2	2	-1	-3	/DO	-0.5

■ **CHRIS CHAMBLISS** Chambliss, Carroll Christopher b: 12/26/48, Dayton, O. BL/TR, 6'1", 195 lbs. Deb: 5/28/71 C

YEAR	TM/L	G	AB	R	H	2B	3B	HR	RBI	BB	SO	AVG	OBP	SLG	PRO	/A	BR	/A	PF	CHI	RC	TA	SB	CS	SBR	FR	POS	TPR
1971	Cle-A	111	415	49	114	20	4	9	48	40	83	.275	.341	.407	.749	105	6	3	106	106	58	.687	2	0	1	-5	*1	-0.6
1972	Cle-A	121	466	51	136	27	2	6	44	26	63	.292	.329	.397	.726	108	8	4	107	96	59	.626	3	4	-2	-3	*1	-1.3
1973	Cle-A	155	572	70	156	30	2	11	53	58	76	.273	.343	.390	.733	109	5	7	97	83	74	.658	4	8	-4	5	*1	0.0
1974	Cle-A	17	67	8	22	4	0	0	7	5	5	.328	.375	.388	.763	119	2	2	101	112	9	.660	0	1	-1	-0	1	0.0
	NY-A	110	400	38	97	16	3	6	43	23	43	.243	.284	.343	.626	83	-11	-9	96	111	38	.513	0	0	0	4	*1	-1.0
	Yr	127	467	46	119	20	3	6	50	28	48	.255	.297	.349	.646	88	-10	-8	96	112	47	.534	0	1	-1	3		-1.0
1975	NY-A	150	562	66	171	38	4	9	72	29	50	.304	.340	.434	.774	119	11	12	99	104	77	.667	0	1	-1	0	*1	0.3
1976	NY-A	156	641	79	188	32	6	17	96	27	80	.293	.325	.441	.766	124	15	16	99	117	90	.677	1	0	0	-2	*1/D	0.6
1977	NY-A	157	600	90	172	32	6	17	90	45	73	.287	.338	.445	.783	113	9	10	99	114	85	.707	4	0	1	-4	*1	-0.1
1978	NY-A	162	625	81	171	26	3	12	90	41	60	.274	.323	.382	.706	99	-3	-2	99	137	79	.623	2	1	0	5	*1/D	-0.3
1979	NY-A	149	554	61	155	27	3	18	63	34	53	.280	.327	.437	.764	109	2	5	96	83	78	.693	3	2	-0	-0	*1D	-0.2
1980	Atl-N	158	602	83	170	37	2	18	72	49	73	.282	.340	.440	.781	115	12	11	101	95	90	.729	7	3	0	0	*1	0.4
1981	Atl-N	107	404	44	110	25	2	8	51	44	41	.272	.345	.403	.749	112	6	7	100	113	56	.693	4	1	1	7	*1	1.1
1982	Atl-N	157	534	57	144	25	2	20	86	57	57	.270	.340	.436	.776	108	11	6	107	115	79	.735	7	3	0	9	*1	0.8
1983	Atl-N	131	447	59	125	24	3	20	78	63	68	.280	.369	.481	.850	127	20	17	106	115	78	.831	2	7	-4	-1	*1	0.7
1984	Atl-N	135	389	47	100	14	0	9	44	58	54	.257	.355	.362	.717	93	3	-2	110	103	51	.668	1	2	-1	-1	*1	-0.7
1985	Atl-N	101	170	16	40	7	0	3	21	18	22	.235	.309	.329	.638	74	-5	-6	106	129	17	.548	0	0	0	0	1	-0.6
1986	Atl-N	97	122	13	38	8	0	2	14	15	24	.311	.387	.426	.813	122	4	4	102	96	20	.761	0	2	-1	0	1	0.2
1988	NY-A	1	1	0	0	0	0	0	0	0	1	.000	.000	.000	.000	-99	-0	-0	96	0	0	.000	0	0	0	0	/H	0.0
Total	17	2175	7571	912	2109	392	42	185	972	632	926	.279	.336	.415	.751	109	94	85	101	107	1036	.698	40	35	-9	14	*1/D	-0.7

■ **MIKE CHAMPION** Champion, Robert Michael b: 2/10/55, Montgomery, Ala. BR/TR, 6', 185 lbs. Deb: 9/14/76

YEAR	TM/L	G	AB	R	H	2B	3B	HR	RBI	BB	SO	AVG	OBP	SLG	PRO	/A	BR	/A	PF	CHI	RC	TA	SB	CS	SBR	FR	POS	TPR
1976	SD-N	11	38	4	9	2	0	1	2	1	3	.237	.256	.368	.625	86	-1	-1	89	45	3	.500	0	0	0	-0	2	0.0
1977	SD-N	150	507	35	116	14	6	1	43	27	85	.229	.271	.286	.557	56	-36	-28	88	116	39	.440	3	3	-1	-31	*2	-5.2
1978	SD-N	32	53	3	12	0	2	0	4	5	13	.226	.293	.302	.595	72	-2	-2	93	99	5	.500	0	0	0	1	2/3	0.0
Total	3	193	598	42	137	16	8	2	49	33	101	.229	.272	.293	.564	59	-40	-31	88	110	47	.458	3	3	-1	-31	2/3	-5.2

■ **FRANK CHANCE** Chance, Frank Leroy "Husk" or "The Peerless Leader" b: 9/9/1877, Fresno, Cal. d: 9/15/24, Los Angeles, Cal. BR/TR, 6', 190 lbs. Deb: 4/29/1898 MH

YEAR	TM/L	G	AB	R	H	2B	3B	HR	RBI	BB	SO	AVG	OBP	SLG	PRO	/A	BR	/A	PF	CHI	RC	TA	SB	CS	SBR	FR	POS	TPR
1898	Chi-N	53	147	32	41	4	3	1	14	7		.279	.338	.367	.705	101	1	0	103	74	21	.698	7			0	CO/1	0.0
1899	Chi-N	64	192	37	55	6	2	1	22	15		.286	.344	.354	.699	98	-1	-0	96	95	28	.693	10			-6	C/O1	-0.1
1900	Chi-N	56	149	26	44	9	3	0	13	15		.295	.360	.396	.756	120	2	4	93	69	25	.781	8			-7	C/1	0.2
1901	Chi-N	69	241	38	67	12	4	0	36	29		.278	.356	.361	.717	110	4	4	100	141	42	.822	27			1	OC/1	0.1
1902	Chi-N	75	240	39	69	9	4	1	31	35		.287	.378	.371	.749	139	11	12	96	119	45	.883	27			-1	1C/O	1.2
1903	Chi-N	125	441	83	144	24	10	2	81	78		.327	.428	.440	.868	157	32	35	95	138	114	**1.141**	**67**			-3	*1/C	2.7
1904	Chi-N	124	451	89	140	16	10	6	49	36		.310	.361	.430	.792	146	24	23	101	90	87	.875	42			6	*1/C	2.5
1905	Chi-N	118	392	92	124	16	12	2	70	78		.316	.430	.434	.863	153	33	31	105	146	92	1.067	38			1	*1M	2.7
1906	Chi-N	136	474	**103**	151	24	10	3	71	70		.319	**.406**	.430	.837	153	37	33	107	129	109	**1.025**	**57**			-1	*1M	2.9
1907	Chi-N	111	382	58	112	19	2	1	50	51		.293	.376	.361	.738	126	16	14	106	142	67	.830	35			3	*1M	1.5
1908	Chi-N	129	452	65	123	27	4	2	55	37		.272	.327	.363	.690	115	11	8	106	132	60	.693	27			3	*1M	0.9
1909	Chi-N	93	324	53	88	16	4	0	46	30		.272	.341	.346	.686	114	6	5	101	158	47	.742	29			-2	1M	0.2
1910	Chi-N	88	295	54	88	12	8	0	36	37	15	.298	.395	.393	.788	129	13	12	101	110	52	.865	16			-3	1M	0.9
1911	Chi-N	31	88	23	21	6	3	1	17	25	13	.239	.432	.409	.841	141	6	7	97	150	20	1.119	9			-1	1M	0.4
1912	Chi-N	2	5	2	1	0	0	0	0	3	0	.200	.500	.200	.700	92	0	0	104	0	1	1.250	1			0	/1M	0.0
1913	NY-A	12	24	3	5	0	0	0	6	8	1	.208	.406	.208	.615	80	0	0	101	427	2	.737	1			0	/1M	0.0
1914	NY-A	1	0	0	0	0	0	0	0	0	0	—	—	—	—	—	0	0	100	—	—	—	0			0	/1M	0.0
Total	17	1287	4297	797	1273	200	79	20	597	554	29	.296	.380	.394	.774	133	195	189	101	127	814	.884	401			-10	1C/O	16.1

■ **BOB CHANCE** Chance, Robert b: 9/10/40, Statesboro, Ga. BL/TR, 6'2", 196 lbs. Deb: 9/04/63

YEAR	TM/L	G	AB	R	H	2B	3B	HR	RBI	BB	SO	AVG	OBP	SLG	PRO	/A	BR	/A	PF	CHI	RC	TA	SB	CS	SBR	FR	POS	TPR
1963	Cle-A	16	52	5	15	4	0	2	7	1	10	.288	.302	.481	.783	119	1	1	97	94	7	.667	0	1	-1	-2	O	-0.1
1964	Cle-A	120	390	45	109	16	1	14	75	40	101	.279	.351	.433	.784	114	9	8	103	151	58	.734	3	3	-1	-8	1O	-0.4
1965	Was-A	72	199	20	51	9	0	4	14	18	44	.256	.318	.362	.680	93	-2	-2	100	69	23	.588	0	1	-1	0	1/O	-0.4
1966	Was-A	37	57	1	10	3	0	1	8	2	23	.175	.203	.281	.484	40	-5	-4	95	177	3	.367	0	0	0	-0	1	-0.5
1967	Was-A	27	42	5	9	2	0	3	7	7	13	.214	.340	.476	.816	136	2	2	102	101	8	.848	0	0	0	0	1	0.1
1969	Cal-A	5	7	0	1	0	0	0	1	0	4	.143	.143	.143	.286	-20	-1	-1	99	401	0	.167	0	0	0	0	/1	0.0
Total	6	277	747	76	195	34	1	24	112	68	195	.261	.326	.406	.732	104	4	3	101	126	98	.679	3	5	-2	-10	1/O	-1.3

■ **DARREL CHANEY** Chaney, Darrel Lee b: 3/9/48, Hammond, Ind. BB/TR, 6'2", 188 lbs. Deb: 4/11/69

YEAR	TM/L	G	AB	R	H	2B	3B	HR	RBI	BB	SO	AVG	OBP	SLG	PRO	/A	BR	/A	PF	CHI	RC	TA	SB	CS	SBR	FR	POS	TPR
1969	Cin-N	93	209	21	40	5	2	0	15	24	75	.191	.278	.234	.512	45	-15	-15	99	123	15	.441	1	0	0	-7	S	-1.1
1970	Cin-N	57	95	7	22	3	0	1	4	3	26	.232	.263	.295	.557	47	-7	-7	104	50	8	.446	1	1	-0	-0	S2/3	-0.1
1971	Cin-N	10	24	2	3	0	0	0	1	1	3	.125	.160	.125	.285	-19	-4	-4	96	136	0	.182	0	1	-1	-0	/S23	-0.3
1972	Cin-N	83	196	29	49	7	2	2	19	29	28	.250	.347	.337	.683	102	-0	1	93	108	24	.636	1	3	-2	-2	S23	0.6
1973	Cin-N	105	227	27	41	7	1	0	14	26	50	.181	.268	.220	.488	39	-19	-17	93	112	15	.424	4	3	-1	5	S23	-0.1
1974	Cin-N	117	135	27	27	6	1	2	16	26	33	.200	.329	.304	.633	79	-3	-3	98	131	14	.607	1	2	-1	-4	32S	-0.5
1975	Cin-N	71	160	18	35	6	0	2	26	14	38	.219	.282	.294	.575	57	-9	-10	104	190	14	.500	3	0	1	2	S23	-0.1
1976	Atl-N	153	496	42	125	20	8	1	50	54	92	.252	.327	.331	.657	78	-8	-14	111	115	54	.579	5	7	-3	-6	*S/23	-0.9
1977	Atl-N	74	209	22	42	7	2	3	15	17	44	.201	.261	.297	.558	44	-15	-19	113	85	15	.449	0	0	0	-5	S2	-1.6
1978	Atl-N	89	245	27	55	9	1	3	20	25	48	.224	.296	.306	.602	61	-10	-14	112	94	24	.529	1	0	0	-8	S/32	-1.5
1979	Atl-N	63	117	15	19	5	0	0	10	19	34	.162	.279	.205	.485	31	-10	-12	109	165	8	.446	2	1	0	-0	S/23C	-0.7
Total	11	915	2113	237	458	75	17	14	190	238	471	.217	.297	.288	.585	61	-101	-113	105	117	191	.519	19	18	-5	-24	S23/C	-6.3

■ **LES CHANNELL** Channell, Lester Clark "Goat" or "Gint" b: 3/3/1886, Crestline, Ohio d: 5/8/54, Denver, Colo. BL/TL, 6', 180 lbs. Deb: 5/11/10

YEAR	TM/L	G	AB	R	H	2B	3B	HR	RBI	BB	SO	AVG	OBP	SLG	PRO	/A	BR	/A	PF	CHI	RC	TA	SB	CS	SBR	FR	POS	TPR
1910	NY-A	6	19	3	6	0	0	0	3	2		.316	.381	.316	.697	110	0	0	107	185	3	.769	2			-1	/O	0.0
1914	NY-A	1	1	0	1	1	0	0	0	0	0	1.000	1.000	2.000	3.000	800	1	1	100	0	2	—	0			0	H	0.1
Total	2	7	20	3	7	1	0	0	3	2	0	.350	.409	.400	.809	143	1	1	107	176	5	.923	2			-1	/O	0.1

■ **CHARLIE CHANT** Chant, Charles Joseph b: 8/7/51, Bell, Cal. BR/TR, 6', 190 lbs. Deb: 9/12/75

YEAR	TM/L	G	AB	R	H	2B	3B	HR	RBI	BB	SO	AVG	OBP	SLG	PRO	/A	BR	/A	PF	CHI	RC	TA	SB	CS	SBR	FR	POS	TPR
1975	Oak-A	5	5	1	0	0	0	0	0	0	0	.000	.000	.000	.000	-99	-1	-1	93	0	0	.000	0	0	0	-2	/OD	-0.3
1976	StL-N	15	14	0	2	0	0	0	0	0	4	.143	.143	.143	.286	-18	-2	-2	104	0	0	.167	0	0	0	-2	O	-0.5

YEAR	TM/L	G	AB	R	H	2B	3B	HR	RBI	BB	SO	AVG	OBP	SLG	PRO	/A	BR	/A	PF	CHI	RC	TA	SB	CS	SBR	FR	POS	TPR
Total	2	20	19	1	2	0	0	0	0	0	4	.105	.105	.105	.211	-40	-3	-3	101	0	0	.118	0	0	0	-4	/OD	-0.8
■ ED CHAPLIN	Chaplin, Bert Edgar (born Bert Edgar Chapman) b: 9/25/1893, Pelzer, S.C. d: 8/15/78, Sanford, Fla. BL/TR, 5'7", 158 lbs. Deb: 9/04/20																											
1920	Bos-A	4	5	2	1	1	0	0	1	4	1	.200	.556	.400	.956	163	1	1	96	176	2	1.500	0	0	0	0	/C	0.1
1921	Bos-A	3	2	0	0	0	0	0	0	0	1	.000	.000	.000	.000	-99	-1	-1	100	0	0	.000	0	0	0	0	/C	0.0
1922	Bos-A	28	69	8	13	1	1	0	6	9	9	.188	.282	.232	.514	37	-6	-6	96	134	5	.474	2	1	0	1	C	-0.4
Total	3	35	76	10	14	2	1	0	7	13	11	.184	.303	.237	.540	44	-6	-6	96	135	7	.524	2	1	0	1	/C	-0.3
■ CALVIN CHAPMAN	Chapman, Calvin Louis b: 12/20/10, Courtland, Miss. BL/TR, 5'9", 160 lbs. Deb: 9/10/35																											
1935	Cin-N	15	53	6	18	1	0	0	3	4	5	.340	.386	.358	.744	109	0	1	93	58	8	.714	2			-0	S/2	0.1
1936	Cin-N	96	219	35	54	7	3	1	22	16	19	.247	.301	.320	.620	70	-10	-9	97	107	22	.548	5			-3	O2/3	-1.0
Total	2	111	272	41	72	8	3	1	25	20	24	.265	.317	.327	.645	77	-10	-8	96	97	30	.576	7			-3	/O2S3	-0.9
■ GLENN CHAPMAN	Chapman, Glenn Justice "Pete" b: 1/21/06, Cambridge City, Ind. BR/TR, 5'11.5", 170 lbs. Deb: 4/18/34																											
1934	Bro-N	67	93	19	26	5	1	1	10	7	19	.280	.330	.387	.717	96	-1	-0	95	92	12	.647	1			-10	O2	-1.0
■ HARRY CHAPMAN	Chapman, Harry E. b: 10/26/1887, Severance, Kan. d: 10/21/18, Nevada, Mo. BR/TR, 5'11", 160 lbs. Deb: 10/06/12																											
1912	Chi-N	1	4	1	1	0	1	0	1	0	0	.250	.250	.750	1.000	162	0	0	104	114	1	1.333	1			0	/C	0.0
1913	Cin-N	2	2	0	1	0	0	0	0	0	1	.500	.500	.500	1.000	183	0	0	102	0	0	1.000	0			0	H	0.0
1914	StL-F	64	181	16	38	2	1	0	14	13	27	.210	.263	.232	.495	40	-13	-15	106	120	12	.399	2			6	C/12O	-0.6
1915	StL-F	62	186	19	37	6	3	1	29	22	24	.199	.284	.280	.563	64	-7	-9	105	190	17	.523	4			1	C	-0.5
1916	StL-A	18	31	2	3	0	0	0	0	2	5	.097	.152	.097	.248	-27	-5	-5	95	0	1	.179	0			-1	C	-0.4
Total	5	147	404	38	80	8	5	1	44	37	57	.198	.265	.250	.515	49	-25	-27	104	144	32	.448	7			6	C/O21	-1.5
■ JACK CHAPMAN	Chapman, John Curtis b: 5/8/1843, Brooklyn, N.Y. d: 6/10/16, Brooklyn, N.Y. TR, 5'11", 170 lbs. Deb: 5/05/1874 M																											
1874	Atl-n	53	248	32	64							.258															*O/1	
1875	StL-n	43	187	27	46							.246															O	
1876	Lou-N	17	67	4	16	1	0	0	5	1	3	.239	.250	.254	.504	66	-2	-3	104	101	4	.353				-3	O/3	-0.4
Total	2 n	96	435	59	110							.253															O/3	
■ JOHN CHAPMAN	Chapman, John Joseph b: 10/15/1899, Centralia, Pa. d: 11/3/53, Philadelphia, Pa. BR/TR, 5'10.5", 175 lbs. Deb: 6/28/24																											
1924	Phi-A	19	71	7	20	4	1	0	7	4	8	.282	.329	.366	.695	80	-2	-2	99	94	9	.608	0	0	0	-1	S	0.0
■ KELVIN CHAPMAN	Chapman, Kelvin Keith b: 6/2/56, Willits, Cal. BR/TR, 5'11", 173 lbs. Deb: 4/05/79																											
1979	NY-N	35	80	7	12	1	2	0	4	5	15	.150	.200	.213	.413	13	-10	-9	95	93	4	.319	0	0	0	-1	2/3	-0.8
1984	NY-N	75	197	27	57	13	0	3	23	19	30	.289	.358	.401	.759	113	4	4	100	102	26	.701	8	7	-2	-2	2/3	0.2
1985	NY-N	62	144	16	25	3	0	0	7	9	15	.174	.232	.194	.427	21	-15	-15	97	100	7	.352	5	4	-1	-3	2/3	-1.8
Total	3	172	421	50	94	17	2	3	34	33	60	.223	.286	.295	.581	63	-21	-20	98	100	36	.512	13	11	-3	-5	2/3	-2.4
■ RAY CHAPMAN	Chapman, Raymond Johnson b: 1/15/1891, Beaver Dam, Ky. d: 8/17/20, New York, N.Y. BR/TR, 5'10", 170 lbs. Deb: 8/30/12																											
1912	Cle-A	31	109	29	34	6	3	0	19	10		.312	.375	.422	.797	126	4	4	101	146	22	.893	10			-3	S	0.3
1913	Cle-A	141	508	78	131	19	7	3	39	46	51	.258	.322	.341	.662	89	-5	-8	106	73	67	.663	29			-7	*S/O	-0.3
1914	Cle-A	106	375	59	103	16	10	2	42	48	48	.275	.358	.387	.745	121	11	10	102	110	58	.776	24	9	2	-5	S2	1.5
1915	Cle-A	154	570	101	154	14	17	3	67	70	82	.270	.353	.370	.723	112	12	9	104	100	84	.742	36	15	2	9	*S	3.5
1916	Cle-A	109	346	50	80	10	5	0	27	50	46	.231	.330	.289	.619	86	-5	-4	100	98	41	.614	21	14	-2	4	S32	0.6
1917	Cle-A	156	563	98	170	28	13	2	36	61	65	.302	.370	.409	.779	120	25	15	114	48	105	.873	52			**24**	*S	4.9
1918	Cle-A	128	446	**84**	119	19	8	1	32	**84**	46	.267	.390	.352	.742	115	17	13	108	64	74	.847	30			5	*S/O	2.9
1919	Cle-A	115	433	75	130	23	10	3	53	31	38	.300	.351	.420	.772	109	8	4	107	89	72	.772	18			1	*S	1.5
1920	Cle-A	111	435	97	132	27	8	3	49	52	38	.303	.380	.423	.803	109	9	6	104	77	72	.804	13	9	-2	12	*S	2.6
Total	9	1051	3785	671	1053	162	81	17	364	452	414	.278	.358	.377	.735	109	76	48	106	83	595	.767	233	47		40	S/23O	17.5
■ SAM CHAPMAN	Chapman, Samuel Blake b: 4/11/16, Tiburon, Cal. BR/TR, 6', 180 lbs. Deb: 5/16/38																											
1938	Phi-A	114	406	60	105	17	7	17	63	55	94	.259	.353	.461	.813	101	0	-1	101	91	67	.816	3	4	-2	-1	*O	-0.2
1939	Phi-A	140	498	74	134	24	6	15	64	51	62	.269	.338	.432	.770	98	-5	-3	97	85	73	.735	11	4	1	3	*O1	-0.4
1940	Phi-A	134	508	88	140	26	3	23	75	46	96	.276	.337	.474	.811	113	4	7	96	93	78	.747	2	6	-3	1	*O	-0.3
1941	Phi-A	143	552	97	178	29	9	25	106	47	49	.322	.378	.543	.921	140	30	29	101	102	110	.896	6	9	-4	11	*O	2.6
1945	Phi-A	9	30	3	6	2	0	0	1	2	4	.200	.250	.267	.517	53	-2	-2	94	45	2	.417	0	0	0	-0	/O	-0.2
1946	Phi-A	146	545	77	142	22	5	20	67	54	66	.261	.327	.429	.757	106	6	3	104	92	73	.675	1	3	-2	0	*O	-0.5
1947	Phi-A	149	551	84	139	18	5	14	83	65	70	.252	.331	.379	.710	97	-3	-3	100	129	71	.644	3	4	-2	5	*O	-0.5
1948	Phi-A	123	445	58	115	18	6	13	70	55	50	.258	.341	.413	.755	99	-1	-2	102	108	63	.705	6	1	1	3	*O	-0.2
1949	Phi-A	154	589	89	164	24	4	24	108	80	68	.278	.367	.455	.822	118	12	13	99	115	97	.781	3	4	-2	8	*O	1.5
1950	Phi-A	144	553	93	139	20	6	23	95	68	79	.251	.338	.434	.772	107	-5	3	90	112	83	.731	3	3	-1	7	*O	0.6
1951	Phi-A	18	65	7	11	1	0	0	5	12	12	.169	.299	.185	.483	31	-6	-6	106	158	4	.429	0	0	0	1	O	-0.5
	Cle-A	94	246	24	56	9	1	6	36	27	32	.228	.304	.346	.650	80	-9	-7	95	125	27	.587	3	0	1	-12	O/1	-2.1
	Yr	112	311	31	67	10	1	6	41	39	44	.215	.303	.312	.615	69	-15	-13	96	132	32	.556	3	0	1	-12		-2.6
Total	11	1368	4988	754	1329	210	52	180	773	562	682	.266	.342	.438	.780	107	21	32	99	105	749	.756	41	38	-11	24	*O/1	-0.2
■ BEN CHAPMAN	Chapman, William Benjamin b: 12/25/08, Nashville, Tenn. BR/TR, 6', 190 lbs. Deb: 4/15/30 MC																											
1930	NY-A	138	513	74	162	31	10	10	81	43	58	.316	.371	.474	.845	125	9	18	90	100	91	.846	14	6	1	-5	32	1.5
1931	NY-A	149	600	120	189	28	11	17	122	75	77	.315	.396	.483	.879	132	27	29	98	125	119	.993	**61**	23	**5**	8	*O2	3.0
1932	NY-A	151	581	101	174	41	15	10	107	71	55	.299	.381	.473	.854	126	17	21	95	120	107	.915	**38**	18	1	2	*O	1.6
1933	NY-A	147	565	112	176	36	4	9	98	72	45	.312	.393	.437	.830	132	18	25	91	126	99	.860	**27**	18	-3	12	*O	2.7
1934	NY-A	149	588	82	181	21	**13**	5	86	67	68	.308	.381	.413	.795	110	6	9	96	118	94	.801	26	16	-2	1	*O	0.6
1935	NY-A	140	553	118	160	38	8	8	74	61	39	.289	.361	.430	.791	112	3	9	93	102	87	.787	17	10	-1	14	*O	1.8
1936	NY-A	36	139	19	37	14	3	1	21	15	20	.266	.338	.432	.769	94	-3	-2	95	110	20	.731	1	2	-1	5	O	0.1
	Was-A	97	401	91	133	36	7	4	60	69	18	.332	.431	.486	.917	129	19	21	98	81	89	1.033	19	7	2	2	O	1.8
	Yr	133	540	110	170	50	10	5	81	84	38	.315	.408	.472	.880	121	16	19	97	90	109	.950	20	9	1	6		1.9
1937	Was-A	35	130	23	34	7	1	0	12	26	7	.262	.385	.331	.715	87	-3	-1	94	101	20	.802	8	0	2	1	O	0.1
	Bos-A	113	423	76	130	23	11	7	57	57	35	.307	.391	.463	.854	111	10	8	103	95	79	.921	27	12	1	7	*O/S	1.1
	Yr	148	553	99	164	30	12	7	69	83	42	.297	.389	.432	.822	106	7	7	101	97	99	.893	**35**	12	**3**	8		1.2
1938	Bos-A	127	480	92	163	40	8	6	80	65	33	.340	.418	.494	.912	125	22	20	102	112	102	.975	13	6	0	6	*O/3	2.4
1939	Cle-A	149	545	101	158	31	9	6	82	87	30	.290	.390	.413	.802	108	7	9	98	121	91	.806	18	6	2	-9	*O	-0.2
1940	Cle-A	143	548	82	157	40	6	4	50	78	45	.286	.377	.403	.781	110	4	10	93	75	85	.753	13	7	-0	3	*O	0.2
1941	Was-A	28	110	9	28	6	0	1	10	10	6	.255	.317	.336	.653	75	-4	-4	98	94	10	.538	2	2	-1	0	O	-0.5
	Chi-A	57	190	26	43	9	1	2	19	19	14	.226	.297	.316	.612	66	-11	-9	94	102	19	.536	2	2	-1	2	O	-0.9
	Yr	85	300	35	71	15	1	3	29	29	20	.237	.304	.323	.627	70	-15	-13	95	100	31	.553	4	4	-1	2		-1.4
1944	Bro-N	20	38	11	14	4	0	0	11	5	4	.368	.442	.474	.916	159	3	3	99	219	9	1.000	1			-2	P	0.0
1945	Bro-N	13	22	2	3	0	0	0	3	2	1	.136	.208	.136	.345	-3	-3	-3	96	347	1	.250	0			1	P	0.0
	Phi-N	24	51	4	16	2	0	0	4	2	1	.314	.340	.353	.693	96	-1	-0	96	77	5	.513	0			-2	O/3PM	-0.1
	Yr	37	73	6	19	2	0	0	7	4	2	.260	.299	.288	.586	66	-4	-3	96	181	5	.431	0			-1		-0.1
1946	Phi-N	1	1	1	0	0	0	0	0	0	0	.000	.000	.000	.000	-99	-0	-0	95	0	0	.000	0			0	/PM	0.0
Total	15	1717	6478	1144	1958	407	107	90	977	824	556	.302	.383	.440	.823	116	120	162	96	109	1127	.856	287	135		46	*O/32PS	15.2
■ FRED CHAPMAN	Chapman, William Fred "Chappie" b: 7/17/16, Liberty, S.C. BR/TR, 6'1", 185 lbs. Deb: 9/15/39																											
1939	Phi-A	15	49	5	14	1	1	0	1	1	3	.286	.300	.347	.647	67	-3	-2	97	20	5	.543	1	0	0	-0	S	0.0
1940	Phi-A	26	69	6	11	1	0	0	4	6	10	.159	.227	.174	.401	6	-10	-9	96	120	3	.311	1	1	-0	-3	S	-0.9
1941	Phi-A	35	69	1	11	1	0	0	4	4	15	.159	.205	.174	.379	1	-10	-10	101	118	2	.279	1	2	-1	-1	S/32	-1.0
Total	3	76	187	12	36	3	1	0	9	11	28	.193	.237	.219	.457	20	-22	-22	98	94	11	.355	3	3	-1	-5	/S32	-1.9

YEAR	TM/L	G	AB	R	H	2B	3B	HR	RBI	BB	SO	AVG	OBP	SLG	PRO	/A	BR	/A	PF	CHI	RC	TA	SB	CS	SBR	FR	POS	TPR
■ **HARRY CHAPPAS** Chappas, Harry Perry b: 10/26/57, Mt.Ranier, Md. BB/TR, 5'3", 150 lbs. Deb: 9/07/78																												
1978	Chi-A	20	75	11	20	1	0	0	6	6	11	.267	.329	.280	.609	72	-2	-3	101	100	8	.509	1	2	-1	-1	S	-0.2
1979	Chi-A	26	59	9	17	1	0	1	4	5	5	.288	.354	.356	.710	90	-0	-1	102	64	7	.622	1	1	-0	-1	S	0.1
1980	Chi-A	26	50	6	8	2	0	0	2	4	10	.160	.236	.200	.436	22	-5	-5	97	78	2	.341	0	2	-1	1	S/2D	-0.2
Total	3	72	184	26	45	4	0	1	12	15	26	.245	.312	.283	.594	65	-8	-8	100	82	17	.500	2	5	-2	-1	/SD2	-0.3
■ **LARRY CHAPPELL** Chappell, La Verne Ashford b: 2/19/1890, Mc Clusky, Ill. d: 11/8/18, San Francisco, Cal. BL/TR, 6', 186 lbs. Deb: 7/18/13																												
1913	Chi-A	60	208	20	48	8	1	0	15	18	22	.231	.295	.279	.574	72	-8	-7	95	97	18	.525	7			-2	O	-1.2
1914	Chi-A	21	39	3	9	0	0	0	1	4	11	.231	.302	.231	.533	59	-2	-2	103	42	3	.433	0			-2	/O	-0.4
1915	Chi-A	1	1	0	0	0	0	0	0	0	0	.000	.000	.000	.000	-99	-0	-0	98	0	0	.000	0			0	H	0.0
1916	Cle-A	3	2	0	0	0	0	0	0	1	0	.000	.333	.000	.333	1	-0	-0	100	0	0	1.000	1			0	H	0.0
	Bos-N	20	53	4	12	1	1	0	9	2	8	.226	.268	.283	.551	75	-2	-2	93	238	4	.463	1			-2	O	-0.4
1917	Bos-N	4	2	0	0	0	0	0	1	0	1	.000	.000	.000	.000	-99	-0	-0	96	0	0	.000	0			-0	/O	0.0
Total	5	109	305	27	69	9	2	0	26	25	42	.226	.289	.269	.558	68	-13	-11	96	112	26	.500	9			-6	/O	-2.0
■ **JOE CHARBONEAU** Charboneau, Joseph b: 6/17/55, Belvidere, Ill. BR/TR, 6'2", 205 lbs. Deb: 4/11/80																												
1980	Cle-A	131	453	76	131	17	2	23	87	49	70	.289	.362	.488	.850	128	19	17	102	119	72	.786	2	4	-2	-1	OD	1.3
1981	Cle-A	48	138	14	29	7	1	4	18	7	22	.210	.248	.362	.611	79	-5	-4	93	114	11	.509	1	0	0	-2	OD	-0.5
1982	Cle-A	22	56	7	12	2	1	2	9	5	7	.214	.290	.393	.683	85	-1	-1	100	128	6	.609	0	0	0	-4	O/D	-0.5
Total	3	201	647	97	172	26	4	29	114	61	99	.266	.333	.453	.786	115	12	12	100	119	90	.751	3	4	-2	-6	O/D	0.3
■ **ED CHARLES** Charles, Edwin Douglas b: 4/29/33, Daytona Beach, Fla. BR/TR, 5'10", 170 lbs. Deb: 4/11/62																												
1962	KC-A	147	535	81	154	24	7	17	74	54	70	.288	.358	.454	.812	117	12	12	100	102	89	.811	20	4	4	7	*3/2	2.5
1963	KC-A	158	603	82	161	28	2	15	79	58	79	.267	.336	.395	.731	97	4	-2	108	124	77	.671	15	8	-0	-9	*3	-0.9
1964	KC-A	150	557	69	134	25	2	16	63	64	92	.241	.323	.379	.702	90	-4	-7	105	109	66	.647	12	7	-1	-16	*3	-2.1
1965	KC-A	134	480	55	129	19	7	8	56	44	72	.269	.335	.387	.723	108	3	5	97	113	64	.677	13	4	2	-4	*3/2S	0.4
1966	KC-A	118	385	52	110	18	8	9	42	30	53	.286	.337	.444	.782	130	11	13	94	89	56	.737	12	5	1	-7	*3/1O	0.4
1967	KC-A	19	61	5	15	1	0	0	5	12	13	.246	.378	.262	.641	93	0	0	100	133	7	.625	1	0	0	-1	3	0.0
	NY-N	101	323	32	77	13	2	3	31	24	58	.238	.305	.319	.624	80	-9	-8	99	115	33	.548	4	1	1	6	3	-0.6
1968	NY-N	117	369	41	102	11	1	15	53	28	57	.276	.331	.434	.764	125	12	11	102	109	52	.701	5	4	-1	-2	*3/1	0.8
1969	NY-N	61	169	21	35	8	1	3	18	18	31	.207	.287	.320	.607	69	-7	-7	100	115	15	.542	4	2	0	-3	3	-0.9
Total	8	1005	3482	438	917	147	30	86	421	332	525	.263	.332	.397	.729	104	23	18	101	110	458	.701	86	35	5	-29	3/12OS	-0.4
■ **CHAPPY CHARLES** Charles, Raymond (born Charles Shuh Achenbach) b: 3/25/1881, Phillipsburg, N.J. d: 8/4/59, Bethlehem, Pa. BR/TR, 5'11", 175 lbs. Deb: 4/15/08																												
1908	StL-N	121	454	39	93	14	3	1	17	19		.205	.237	.256	.492	63	-21	-18	94	53	29	.416	15			-5	2S3	-2.7
1909	StL-N	99	339	33	80	7	3	0	29	31		.236	.309	.274	.584	86	-6	-5	96	116	30	.525	7			-11	2S/3	-1.8
	Cin-N	13	43	3	11	2	0	0	5	4		.256	.319	.302	.621	100	-0	0	94	143	5	.594	2			1	2/S	0.1
	Yr	112	382	36	91	9	3	0	34	35		.238	.310	.277	.588	87	-6	-5	96	120	34	.533	9			-10		-1.7
1910	Cin-N	4	15	1	2	0	1	0	0	0	1	.133	.133	.267	.400	16	-2	-2	101	0	0	.308	0			-0	/S	-0.1
Total	3	237	851	76	186	23	7	1	51	54	1	.219	.269	.266	.535	74	-29	-25	95	82	64	.465	24			-15	2/S3	-4.5
■ **MIKE CHARTAK** Chartak, Michael George "Shotgun" b: 4/28/16, Brooklyn, N.Y. d: 7/25/67, Cedar Rapids, Ia. BL/TL, 6'2", 180 lbs. Deb: 9/13/40																												
1940	NY-A	11	15	2	2	1	0	0	3	5	5	.133	.350	.200	.550	47	-1	-1	99	361	2	.615	0	0	0	-1	/O	-0.1
1942	NY-A	5	5	0	0	0	0	0	0	0	0	.000	.000	.000	.000	-99	-1	-1	99	0	0	.000	0	0	0	0	H	0.0
	Was-A	24	92	11	20	4	2	1	8	14	16	.217	.321	.337	.658	89	-2	-1	96	88	10	.600	0	1	-1	-1	O	-0.4
	StL-A	73	237	37	59	11	2	9	43	40	27	.249	.362	.426	.788	116	7	6	104	118	39	.785	3	3	-1	4	O	0.5
	Yr	102	334	48	79	15	4	10	51	54	43	.237	.346	.395	.741	106	4	3	102	106	49	.723	3	4	-2	3		0.1
1943	StL-A	108	344	38	88	16	2	10	37	39	55	.256	.333	.401	.734	114	6	5	100	80	47	.670	1	3	-2	-3	O1	-0.2
1944	StL-A	35	72	8	17	2	1	1	7	6	9	.236	.304	.333	.637	80	-2	-2	102	94	8	.554	0	0	0	-1	1/O	-0.3
Total	4	256	765	96	186	34	7	21	98	104	112	.243	.337	.388	.725	106	7	6	101	101	105	.697	4	7	-3	-2	O/1	-0.5
■ **HAL CHASE** Chase, Harold Homer "Prince Hal" b: 2/13/1883, Los Gatos, Cal. d: 5/18/47, Colusa, Cal. BR/TL, 6', 175 lbs. Deb: 4/14/05 M																												
1905	NY-A	128	465	60	116	16	6	3	49	15		.249	.273	.329	.602	91	-5	-6	102	110	49	.544	22			-8	*1/S2	-1.7
1906	NY-A	151	597	84	193	23	10	0	76	13		.323	.338	.395	.733	109	19	6	120	113	91	.686	28			-3	*1/2	-0.1
1907	NY-A	125	498	72	143	23	3	2	69	19		.287	.313	.357	.671	107	7	3	109	118	67	.645	32			-2	*1/O	-0.1
1908	NY-A	106	405	50	104	11	3	1	36	15		.257	.283	.306	.590	98	-4	-2	95	102	41	.551	27			-3	1/2O3	-0.7
1909	NY-A	118	474	60	134	17	3	4	63	20		.283	.317	.357	.674	113	5	6	99	118	59	.641	25			1	*1/S	0.7
1910	NY-A	130	524	67	152	20	5	3	73	16		.290	.312	.365	.677	104	5	0	107	130	71	.667	40			-5	*1M	0.0
1911	NY-A	133	527	82	166	32	7	3	62	21		.315	.342	.419	.762	101	6	-2	111	97	87	.773	36			2	*1/O2M	0.3
1912	NY-A	131	522	61	143	21	9	4	58	17		.274	.299	.372	.671	90	-8	-9	101	90	67	.649	33			-3	*1/2	-1.0
1913	NY-A	39	146	15	31	2	4	0	9	11	13	.212	.268	.281	.548	60	-8	-8	101	83	11	.496	5			1	1/2O	-0.7
	Chi-A	102	384	49	110	11	10	2	39	16	41	.286	.320	.383	.703	111	1	3	95	96	47	.639	9			0	*1	0.3
	Yr	141	530	64	141	13	14	2	48	27	54	.266	.305	.355	.660	96	-7	-5	97	93	57	.596	14			1		-0.4
1914	Chi-A	58	206	27	55	10	5	0	20	23	19	.267	.343	.364	.708	109	3	2	103	106	28	.697	9	4	0	2	1	0.6
	Buf-F	75	291	43	101	19	9	3	48	6	31	.347	.360	.505	.865	140	15	14	104	118	58	.858	10			1	1	1.7
1915	Buf-F	145	567	85	165	31	10	**17**	89	20	50	.291	.315	.471	.786	131	17	18	100	107	94	.771	23			1	*1/O	2.2
1916	Cin-N	142	542	66	**184**	29	12	4	82	19	48	**.339**	.363	.459	.822	155	30	31	98	127	93	.789	22	11	0	-2	1O2	2.8
1917	Cin-N	152	602	71	167	28	15	4	86	15	49	.277	.296	.394	.690	120	5	9	92	141	72	.630	21			-2	*1	0.6
1918	Cin-N	74	259	30	78	12	6	2	38	13	15	.301	.339	.417	.756	134	8	9	97	129	37	.707	5			-2	1/O	0.6
1919	NY-N	110	408	58	116	17	7	5	45	17	40	.284	.318	.397	.715	115	6	6	100	105	54	.678	16			-3	*1	0.2
Total	15	1919	7417	980	2158	322	124	57	942	276	306	.291	.318	.391	.709	112	103	81	102	113	1028	.674	363	15		-24	*1/O2S3	5.7
■ **BUSTER CHATHAM** Chatham, Charles L b: 12/25/01, West, Tex. d: 12/15/75, Waco, Tex. BR/TR, 5'5", 150 lbs. Deb: 6/01/30																												
1930	Bos-N	112	404	48	108	20	11	5	56	37	41	.267	.332	.408	.740	80	-15	-13	97	114	54	.716	8			-9	3S	-1.6
1931	Bos-N	17	44	4	10	1	0	1	3	6	6	.227	.320	.318	.638	73	-2	-2	99	63	5	.588	0			-1	/S3	0.0
Total	2	129	448	52	118	21	11	6	59	43	47	.263	.331	.400	.730	79	-17	-15	97	108	59	.703	8			-9	/3S	-1.6
■ **JIM CHATTERTON** Chatterton, James M. b: 10/14/1864, Brooklyn, N.Y. d: 12/15/44, Tewksbury, Mass. Deb: 6/07/1884																												
1884	KC-U	4	15	4	2	1	0	0		2		.133	.235	.200	.435	56	-1	-0	87	0	1	.385	0			0	/O1P	0.0
■ **OSSIE CHAVARRIA** Chavarria, Osvaldo (Quijano) b: 8/5/40, Colon, Panama BR/TR, 5'11", 155 lbs. Deb: 4/14/66																												
1966	KC-A	86	191	26	46	10	0	2	10	18	43	.241	.306	.325	.631	87	-4	-3	94	62	19	.546	3	2	-0	-5	OS2/13	-0.8
1967	KC-A	38	59	2	6	2	0	0	4	7	16	.102	.209	.136	.345	4	-7	-7	100	209	2	.321	1	0	0	-2	2/3OS	-0.8
Total	2	124	250	28	52	12	0	2	14	25	59	.208	.283	.280	.563	66	-11	-10	95	97	21	.500	4	2	0	-7	/2OS31	-1.6
■ **HARRY CHEEK** Cheek, Harry G. b: 1879, Sedalia, Mo. d: 6/25/56, Paramas, N.J. TR , Deb: 5/12/10																												
1910	Phi-N	2	4	1	2	1	0	0	0	0	0	.500	.500	.750	1.250	275	1	1	96	0	1	1.500	0			0	/C	0.1
■ **PAUL CHERVINKO** Chervinko, Paul b: 7/28/10, Trauger, Pa. d: 6/3/76, Danville, Ill. BR/TR, 5'8", 185 lbs. Deb: 5/30/37																												
1937	Bro-N	30	48	1	7	0	1	0	2	3	16	.146	.196	.188	.384	4	-6	-7	104	80	2	.286	0			-1	C	-0.6
1938	Bro-N	12	27	0	4	0	0	0	3	2	0	.148	.207	.148	.355	-1	-4	-4	96	271	1	.240	0			-0	C	-0.3
Total	2	42	75	1	11	0	1	0	5	5	16	.147	.200	.173	.373	3	-10	-10	101	149	2	.273	0			-1	/C	-0.9
■ **CUPID CHILDS** Childs, Clarence Algernon b: 8/8/1867, Calvert Co., Md. d: 11/8/12, Baltimore, Md. BL/TR, 5'8", 185 lbs. Deb: 1888																												
1888	Phi-N	2	4	0	0	0	0	0	0	0	0	.000	.000	.000	.000	-88	-1	-1	114	0	0	.000	0			0	/2	0.0
1890	Syr-a	126	493	109	170	**33**	14	2		72		.345	.434	**.481**	**.915**	**191**	47	**55**	90	0	130	1.149	56			12	*2/S	**6.1**
1891	Cle-N	141	551	120	155	21	12	2	83	97	32	.281	.395	.374	.769	121	23	19	105	110	99	.881	39			-14	*2	0.8
1892	Cle-N	145	558	**136**	177	14	11	3	53	117	20	.317	**.443**	.398	.841	152	47	44	103	61	113	.982	26			-7	*2	3.5
1893	Cle-N	124	485	145	158	19	10	3	65	120	12	.326	.463	.425	.888	134	36	32	104	71	109	1.080	23			7	*2	3.1
1894	Cle-N	118	479	143	169	21	12	2	52	107	11	.353	.475	.459	.935	116	30	18	111	55	116	1.126	17			-5	*2	1.6

YEAR	TM/L	G	AB	R	H	2B	3B	HR	RBI	BB	SO	AVG	OBP	SLG	PRO	/A	BR	/A	PF	CHI	RC	TA	SB	CS	SBR	FR	POS	TPR
1895	Cle-N	119	462	96	133	15	3	4	90	74	24	.288	.393	.359	.752	100	2	5	97	136	75	.809	20			9	*2	1.7
1896	Cle-N	132	498	106	177	24	9	1	106	100	18	.355	.467	.446	.913	131	39	30	110	131	118	1.093	25			**42**	*2	**6.2**
1897	Cle-N	114	444	105	150	15	9	1	61	74		.338	.435	.419	.854	116	23	14	111	83	94	.976	25			17	*2	3.4
1898	Cle-N	110	413	90	119	9	4	1	31	69		.288	.395	.337	.732	118	11	14	96	58	60	.752	9			7	*2	2.4
1899	StL-N	125	464	73	123	11	11	1	48	74		.265	.369	.343	.711	91	2	-4	108	87	64	.721	11			-15	*2	-0.9
1900	Chi-N	137	531	67	128	14	5	0	44	57		.241	.315	.286	.601	74	-21	-15	93	80	54	.556	15			12	*2	0.4
1901	Chi-N	63	236	24	61	9	0	0	21	29		.258	.340	.297	.636	87	-2	-2	100	96	25	.583	3			12	2	1.3
Total	13	1456	5618	1214	1720	205	100	20	654	990	117	.306	.414	.389	.803	120	235	208	102	80	1057	.896	269			78	*2/S	29.6

■ **PETE CHILDS** Childs, Peter Pierre b: 11/15/1871, Philadelphia, Pa. d: 2/15/22, Philadelphia, Pa. TR , Deb: 4/24/01

YEAR	TM/L	G	AB	R	H	2B	3B	HR	RBI	BB	SO	AVG	OBP	SLG	PRO	/A	BR	/A	PF	CHI	RC	TA	SB	CS	SBR	FR	POS	TPR
1901	StL-N	29	79	12	21	1	0	0	8	14		.266	.376	.278	.655	97	0	1	97	122	8	.621	0			-2	2/OS	0.0
	Chi-N	60	210	23	48	5	1	0	14	26		.229	.314	.262	.575	70	-7	-7	100	87	19	.525	4			10	2	0.7
	Yr	89	289	35	69	6	1	0	22	40		.239	.331	.266	.598	77	-7	-6	99	100	28	.550	4			8		0.7
1902	Phi-N	123	403	25	78	5	0	0	25	34		.194	.256	.206	.462	42	-25	-27	105	104	23	.378	6			-11	*2	-3.1
Total	2	212	692	60	147	11	1	0	47	74		.212	.289	.231	.520	57	-31	-34	103	101	51	.448	10			-2	2/OS	-2.4

■ **PEARCE CHILES** Chiles, Pearce Nuget "What's the Use" b: 5/28/1867, Deepwater, Mo. Deb: 4/18/1899

YEAR	TM/L	G	AB	R	H	2B	3B	HR	RBI	BB	SO	AVG	OBP	SLG	PRO	/A	BR	/A	PF	CHI	RC	TA	SB	CS	SBR	FR	POS	TPR
1899	Phi-N	97	338	57	108	28	7	2	76	16		.320	.352	.462	.814	129	10	11	97	144	58	.778	6			-0	O12	0.7
1900	Phi-N	33	111	13	24	6	2	1	23	6		.216	.256	.333	.590	65	-6	-5	98	180	11	.540	4			0	12/O	-0.4
Total	2	130	449	70	132	34	9	3	99	22		.294	.328	.430	.758	113	4	6	97	153	69	.713	10			-0	/O12	0.3

■ **RICH CHILES** Chiles, Richard Francis b: 11/22/49, Sacramento, Cal. BL/TL, 5'11", 170 lbs. Deb: 9/20/71

YEAR	TM/L	G	AB	R	H	2B	3B	HR	RBI	BB	SO	AVG	OBP	SLG	PRO	/A	BR	/A	PF	CHI	RC	TA	SB	CS	SBR	FR	POS	TPR
1971	Hou-N	67	119	12	27	5	1	2	15	6	20	.227	.270	.336	.606	76	-5	-4	93	133	10	.495	0	1	-1	-4	O	-0.9
1972	Hou-N	9	11	0	3	1	0	0	2	1	1	.273	.333	.364	.697	92	-0	-0	106	205	1	.625	0	0	0	0	/O	0.0
1973	NY-N	8	25	2	3	2	0	0	1	0	2	.120	.120	.200	.320	-13	-4	-4	101	80	0	.208	0	0	0	2	/O	-0.1
1976	Hou-N	5	4	1	2	1	0	0	0	0	0	.500	.500	.750	1.250	291	1	1	86	0	2	1.500	0	0	0	-0	/O	0.1
1977	Min-A	108	261	31	69	16	1	3	36	23	17	.264	.329	.368	.696	87	-4	-5	103	136	32	.611	0	1	-1	-3	DO	-0.8
1978	Min-A	87	198	22	53	12	0	1	22	20	25	.268	.341	.343	.684	99	-1	0	94	122	22	.583	1	2	-1	-5	O/D	-0.7
Total	6	284	618	68	157	37	2	6	76	50	65	.254	.315	.350	.665	86	-13	-12	98	129	67	.574	1	4	-2	-10	O/D	-2.4

■ **DINO CHIOZZA** Chiozza, Dino Joseph "Dynamo" b: 6/30/12, Memphis, Tenn. d: 4/23/72, Memphis, Tenn. BL/TR, 6', 170 lbs. Deb: 7/14/35

YEAR	TM/L	G	AB	R	H	2B	3B	HR	RBI	BB	SO	AVG	OBP	SLG	PRO	/A	BR	/A	PF	CHI	RC	TA	SB	CS	SBR	FR	POS	TPR
1935	Phi-N	2	0	1	0	0	0	0	0	0	0	—	—	—	—	—	0	0	114	—	—	—	0			0	/S	0.0

■ **LOU CHIOZZA** Chiozza, Louis Peo b: 5/17/10, Tallulah, La. d: 2/28/71, Memphis, Tenn. BL/TR, 6', 172 lbs. Deb: 4/17/34

YEAR	TM/L	G	AB	R	H	2B	3B	HR	RBI	BB	SO	AVG	OBP	SLG	PRO	/A	BR	/A	PF	CHI	RC	TA	SB	CS	SBR	FR	POS	TPR
1934	Phi-N	134	484	66	147	28	5	0	44	34	35	.304	.357	.382	.739	90	-1	-6	108	87	68	.674	9			-12	23O	-0.7
1935	Phi-N	124	472	71	134	26	6	3	47	33	44	.284	.333	.383	.717	81	-5	-14	114	95	64	.646	5			11	*2/3	0.6
1936	Phi-N	144	572	83	170	32	6	1	48	37	39	.297	.346	.379	.726	88	-4	-10	108	82	80	.684	17			-0	O23	-0.9
1937	NY-N	117	439	49	102	11	2	4	29	20	30	.232	.266	.294	.560	52	-30	-30	100	76	36	.457	6			1	3O/2	-2.4
1938	NY-N	57	179	15	42	7	2	3	17	12	7	.235	.283	.346	.629	70	-7	-8	103	87	18	.568	5			0	2O/3	-0.5
1939	NY-N	40	142	19	38	3	1	3	12	9	10	.268	.311	.366	.677	82	-4	-4	99	73	17	.610	3			0	3/S	-0.1
Total	6	616	2288	303	633	107	22	14	197	145	165	.277	.324	.361	.685	79	-50	-71	107	84	283	.622	45			-0	23O/S	-4.0

■ **WALT CHIPPLE** Chipple, Walter John (born Walter John Chlipala) b: 9/26/18, Utica, N.Y. d: 6/8/88, Tonawanda, N.Y. BR/TR, 6'0.5", 168 lbs. Deb: 4/17/45

YEAR	TM/L	G	AB	R	H	2B	3B	HR	RBI	BB	SO	AVG	OBP	SLG	PRO	/A	BR	/A	PF	CHI	RC	TA	SB	CS	SBR	FR	POS	TPR
1945	Was-A	18	44	4	6	0	0	0	5	5	6	.136	.224	.136	.361	6	-5	-5	93	301	1	.275	0	1	-1	4	O	-0.2

■ **TOM CHISM** Chism, Thomas Raymond b: 5/9/55, Chester, Pa. BL/TL, 6'1", 195 lbs. Deb: 9/13/79

YEAR	TM/L	G	AB	R	H	2B	3B	HR	RBI	BB	SO	AVG	OBP	SLG	PRO	/A	BR	/A	PF	CHI	RC	TA	SB	CS	SBR	FR	POS	TPR
1979	Bal-A	6	3	0	0	0	0	0	0	0	0	.000	.000	.000	.000	-99	-1	-1	97	0	0	.000	0	0	0	0	/1	0.0

■ **HARRY CHITI** Chiti, Harry b: 11/16/32, Kincaid, Ill. BR/TR, 6'2.5", 221 lbs. Deb: 9/27/50

YEAR	TM/L	G	AB	R	H	2B	3B	HR	RBI	BB	SO	AVG	OBP	SLG	PRO	/A	BR	/A	PF	CHI	RC	TA	SB	CS	SBR	FR	POS	TPR
1950	Chi-N	3	6	0	2	0	0	0	0	0	0	.333	.333	.333	.667	72	-0	-0	105	0	1	.500	0			0	/C	0.0
1951	Chi-N	9	31	1	11	2	0	0	5	2	2	.355	.394	.419	.813	122	1	1	97	152	4	.652	0	0	0	0	/C	0.1
1952	Chi-N	32	113	14	31	5	0	5	13	5	8	.274	.305	.451	.756	104	1	0	103	77	15	.651	0	1	-1	-1	C	0.0
1955	Chi-N	113	338	24	78	6	1	11	41	25	68	.231	.286	.352	.638	68	-16	-16	100	109	33	.541	0	0	0	-4	*C	-1.6
1956	Chi-N	72	203	17	43	6	4	4	18	19	35	.212	.283	.340	.622	67	-10	-9	99	94	18	.527	0	0	0	3	C	-0.4
1958	KC-A	103	295	32	79	11	3	9	44	18	48	.268	.316	.417	.733	95	-1	-3	106	118	37	.653	3	2	-0	3	C	0.1
1959	KC-A	55	162	20	44	11	1	5	25	17	26	.272	.344	.444	.789	113	3	3	101	113	22	.703	0	1	-1	3	C	0.8
1960	KC-A	58	190	16	42	7	0	5	28	17	33	.221	.288	.337	.625	69	-9	-8	99	139	18	.532	1	0	0	5	C	0.0
	Det-A	37	104	9	17	0	0	2	5	10	12	.163	.237	.221	.458	24	-11	-11	102	67	4	.344	0	3	-2	-2	C	-1.2
	Yr	95	294	25	59	7	0	7	33	27	45	.201	.270	.296	.566	53	-20	-20	100	112	23	.475	1	3	-2	3		-1.2
1961	Det-A	5	12	0	1	0	0	0	0	1	2	.083	.154	.083	.237	-36	-2	-2	96	0	0	.167	0	0	0	-0	/C	-0.2
1962	NY-N	15	41	2	8	1	0	0	0	1	8	.195	.233	.220	.452	21	-4	-5	104	0	2	.314	0	0	0	-1	C	-0.4
Total	10	502	1495	135	356	49	9	41	179	115	242	.238	.296	.365	.661	77	-48	-51	101	104	153	.586	4	7		7	C	-2.8

■ **FELIX CHOUINARD** Chouinard, Felix George b: 10/5/1887, Hines, Ill. d: 4/28/55, Hines, Ill. BL/TR, 5'7", 150 lbs. Deb: 9/11/10

YEAR	TM/L	G	AB	R	H	2B	3B	HR	RBI	BB	SO	AVG	OBP	SLG	PRO	/A	BR	/A	PF	CHI	RC	TA	SB	CS	SBR	FR	POS	TPR
1910	Chi-A	24	82	6	16	3	2	0	9	8		.195	.275	.280	.555	78	-2	-2	95	153	7	.545	4			5	O/2	0.2
1911	Chi-A	14	17	3	3	0	0	0	0	0		.176	.176	.176	.353	-1	-2	-2	97	0	0	.214	0			0	/2O	-0.1
1914	Pit-F	9	30	2	9	1	0	1	3	0	0	.300	.300	.433	.733	115	0	0	94	68	4	.667	1			0	/2OS	0.0
	Bro-F	32	79	7	20	1	2	0	8	4	0	.253	.289	.316	.606	73	-3	-3	101	115	8	.542	3			0	O	-0.2
	Bal-F	5	9	3	4	0	0	0	1	0	0	.444	.444	.444	.889	156	1	1	99	90	2	.800	0			0	/O	0.1
	Yr	46	118	12	33	2	2	1	12	4	0	.280	.303	.356	.659	89	-2	-2	99	107	14	.588	4			0		-0.1
1915	Bro-F	4	4	1	2	0	0	0	2	0	0	.500	.500	.500	1.000	201	0	0	98	361	1	1.000	0			0	/O	0.0
Total	4	88	221	22	54	5	4	1	23	12	0	.244	.286	.317	.603	80	-6	-6	97	119	23	.545	8			6	/O2S	0.0

■ **HARRY CHOZEN** Chozen, Harry b: 9/27/15, Winnebago, Minn. BR/TR, 5'9.5", 190 lbs. Deb: 9/21/37

YEAR	TM/L	G	AB	R	H	2B	3B	HR	RBI	BB	SO	AVG	OBP	SLG	PRO	/A	BR	/A	PF	CHI	RC	TA	SB	CS	SBR	FR	POS	TPR
1937	Cin-N	1	4	0	1	0	0	0	0	0	0	.250	.250	.250	.500	40	-0	-0	91	0	0	.333	0			0	/C	0.0

■ **NEIL CHRISLEY** Chrisley, Barbra O'Neil b: 12/16/31, Calhoun Falls, S.C BL/TR, 6'3", 187 lbs. Deb: 4/15/57

YEAR	TM/L	G	AB	R	H	2B	3B	HR	RBI	BB	SO	AVG	OBP	SLG	PRO	/A	BR	/A	PF	CHI	RC	TA	SB	CS	SBR	FR	POS	TPR
1957	Was-A	26	51	6	8	2	1	0	3	7	7	.157	.259	.235	.494	37	-5	-4	98	99	4	.442	0	0	0	-1	O	-0.6
1958	Was-A	105	233	19	50	7	4	5	26	16	18	.215	.265	.343	.608	68	-11	-10	97	110	19	.505	1	3	-2	0	O/3	-1.6
1959	Det-A	65	106	7	14	3	0	6	11	12	10	.132	.227	.330	.557	46	-8	-9	111	82	8	.516	0	0	0	-3	O	-1.2
1960	Det-A	96	220	27	56	10	3	5	24	19	26	.255	.317	.395	.712	90	-3	-3	102	92	28	.645	2	0	1	2	O/1	-0.2
1961	Mil-N	10	9	1	2	0	0	0	0	1	1	.222	.300	.222	.522	45	-1	-1	92	0	1	.429	0	0	0	0	H	0.0
Total	5	302	619	60	130	22	8	16	64	55	62	.210	.277	.349	.626	69	-27	-28	101	96	60	.561	3	3	-1	-3	O/13	-3.6

■ **LLOYD CHRISTENBURY** Christenbury, Lloyd Reid "Low" b: 10/19/1893, Mecklenburg Co., N.C. d: 12/13/44, Birmingham, Ala. BL/TR, 5'7", 165 lbs. Deb: 9/20/19

YEAR	TM/L	G	AB	R	H	2B	3B	HR	RBI	BB	SO	AVG	OBP	SLG	PRO	/A	BR	/A	PF	CHI	RC	TA	SB	CS	SBR	FR	POS	TPR
1919	Bos-N	7	31	5	9	1	0	0	4	2	2	.290	.333	.323	.656	100	-0	0	98	134	3	.545	0			1	/O	0.1
1920	Bos-N	65	106	17	22	2	2	0	14	13	12	.208	.300	.264	.564	65	-5	-4	96	193	9	.494	0	1	-1	-3	O/S23	-0.7
1921	Bos-N	62	125	34	44	6	2	3	16	21	7	.352	.449	.504	.953	163	10	12	93	82	28	1.035	3	4	-2	-0	2/S3	1.0
1922	Bos-N	71	152	22	38	5	2	1	13	18	11	.250	.337	.329	.666	77	-6	-4	94	86	17	.610	2	4	-2	-0	O/23	-0.6
Total	4	205	414	78	113	14	6	4	47	54	32	.273	.362	.365	.727	102	-0	3	95	115	58	.690	5	9		-2	/O2S3	-0.2

■ **BRUCE CHRISTENSEN** Christensen, Bruce Ray b: 2/22/48, Madison, Wis. BL/TR, 5'11", 160 lbs. Deb: 7/17/71

YEAR	TM/L	G	AB	R	H	2B	3B	HR	RBI	BB	SO	AVG	OBP	SLG	PRO	/A	BR	/A	PF	CHI	RC	TA	SB	CS	SBR	FR	POS	TPR
1971	Cal-A	29	63	4	17	1	0	0	3	6	5	.270	.333	.286	.619	78	-2	-2	99	68	6	.490	0	1	-1	-1	S	0.0

■ **JOHN CHRISTENSEN** Christensen, John Lawrence b: 9/5/60, Downey, Cal. BR/TR, 6'3", 205 lbs. Deb: 9/13/84

YEAR	TM/L	G	AB	R	H	2B	3B	HR	RBI	BB	SO	AVG	OBP	SLG	PRO	/A	BR	/A	PF	CHI	RC	TA	SB	CS	SBR	FR	POS	TPR
1984	NY-N	5	11	2	3	2	0	0	3	1	2	.273	.333	.455	.788	120	0	0	100	235	1	.667	0	1	-1	-2	/O	-0.2
1985	NY-N	51	113	10	21	4	1	3	13	19	23	.186	.303	.319	.622	76	-4	-3	97	115	11	.577	1	2	-1	-6	O	-1.1
1987	Sea-A	53	132	19	32	6	1	2	12	12	28	.242	.306	.348	.654	72	-5	-5	103	92	14	.583	2	0	1	-4	O/D	-0.8
1988	Min-A	23	38	5	10	4	0	0	5	3	5	.263	.349	.368	.717	95	0	-0	106	142	5	.655	0	0	0	-3	O	-0.3
Total	4	132	294	36	66	16	2	5	33	35	58	.224	.311	.344	.655	78	-8	-9	101	113	32	.608	3	3	-1	-15	O/D	-2.4

YEAR	TM/L	G	AB	R	H	2B	3B	HR	RBI	BB	SO	AVG	OBP	SLG	PRO	/A	BR	/A	PF	CHI	RC	TA	SB	CS	SBR	FR	POS	TPR
■ CUCKOO CHRISTENSEN	Christensen, Walter Niels "Seacap" b: 10/24/1899, San Francisco, Cal d: 12/20/84, Menlo Park, Cal. BL/TL, 5'6.5", 156 lbs. Deb: 4/13/26																											
1926	Cin-N	114	329	41	115	15	7	0	41	40	18	.350	.426	.438	.864	140	17	20	95	98	62	.916	8			-9	O	0.7
1927	Cin-N	57	185	25	47	6	0	0	16	20	16	.254	.330	.286	.617	66	-8	-8	100	106	18	.565	4			-1	O	-1.0
Total	2	171	514	66	162	21	7	0	57	60	34	.315	.392	.383	.775	113	9	12	97	101	80	.778	12			-10	O	-0.3
■ BOB CHRISTIAN	Christian, Robert Charles b: 10/17/45, Chicago, Ill. d: 2/20/74, San Diego, Cal. BR/TR, 5'10", 180 lbs. Deb: 9/02/68																											
1968	Det-A	3	3	0	1	1	0	0	0	0	0	.333	.333	.667	1.000	185	0	0	106	0	1	1.000	0	0	0	-0	/1O	0.0
1969	Chi-A	39	129	11	28	4	0	3	16	10	19	.217	.279	.318	.596	61	-6	-7	108	128	12	.529	3	0	1	-0	O	-0.7
1970	Chi-A	12	15	3	4	0	0	1	3	1	4	.267	.313	.467	.779	106	0	0	106	121	2	.727	0	0	0	-1	/O	0.0
Total	3	54	147	14	33	5	0	4	19	11	23	.224	.283	.340	.623	68	-6	-7	108	125	15	.570	3	0	1	-2	/O1	-0.7
■ MARK CHRISTMAN	Christman, Marquette Joseph b: 10/21/13, Maplewood, Mo. d: 10/9/76, St.Louis, Mo. BR/TR, 5'11", 175 lbs. Deb: 4/20/38																											
1938	Det-A	95	318	35	79	6	4	1	44	27	21	.248	.307	.302	.609	53	-23	-23	100	150	31	.531	5	2	0	7	3S	-1.1
1939	Det-A	6	16	0	4	2	0	0	0	0	2	.250	.250	.375	.625	52	-1	-1	111	0	1	.429	0	0	0	-0	/3	-0.1
	StL-A	79	222	27	48	6	3	0	20	20	10	.216	.281	.270	.551	41	-20	-20	100	113	16	.446	2	1	0	4	S/2	-0.7
	Yr	85	238	27	52	8	3	0	20	20	12	.218	.279	.277	.556	42	-21	-21	101	105	18	.449	2	1	0	4		-0.8
1943	StL-A	98	336	31	91	11	5	2	35	19	19	.271	.318	.351	.669	95	-3	-3	100	103	38	.557	0	3	-2	-2	3S12	-0.6
1944	StL-A	148	547	56	148	25	1	6	83	47	37	.271	.332	.353	.684	94	-3	-4	102	**145**	64	.592	5	2	0	3	*3/1	-0.1
1945	StL-A	78	289	32	80	7	4	4	34	19	19	.277	.328	.370	.698	89	0	-5	115	105	36	.605	1	0	0	1	3	-0.1
1946	StL-A	128	458	40	118	22	2	1	41	22	29	.258	.295	.321	.616	73	-18	-17	98	106	41	.479	0	2	-1	1	3S	-1.0
1947	Was-A	110	374	27	83	15	2	1	33	33	16	.222	.287	.281	.568	60	-21	-20	97	115	30	.469	4	4	-1	-3	*S/2	-2.4
1948	Was-A	120	409	38	106	17	2	1	40	25	19	.259	.303	.318	.621	63	-21	-23	103	102	37	.488	0	3	-2	-18	*S/32	-4.1
1949	Was-A	49	112	8	24	2	0	3	18	8	7	.214	.273	.313	.585	60	-8	-7	91	140	9	.473	0	0	0	-0	3/1S2	-0.6
Total	9	911	3081	294	781	113	23	19	348	220	179	.253	.306	.324	.630	72	-117	-122	101	119	302	.538	17	17	-5	-7	3S/12	-10.8
■ STEVE CHRISTMAS	Christmas, Stephen Randall b: 12/9/57, Orlando, Fla. BL/TR, 6', 190 lbs. Deb: 9/01/83																											
1983	Cin-N	9	17	0	1	0	0	0	1	1	3	.059	.111	.059	.170	-50	-3	-4	103	396	0	.118	0	0	0	-0	/C	-0.3
1984	Chi-A	12	11	1	4	1	0	1	4	0	2	.364	.364	.727	1.091	175	1	1	111	145	3	1.143	0	0	0	0	/C	0.1
1986	Chi-N	3	9	0	1	1	0	0	2	0	1	.111	.111	.222	.333	-10	-1	-1	107	399	0	.250	0	0	0	0	/C1	0.0
Total	3	24	37	1	6	2	0	1	7	1	6	.162	.184	.297	.482	29	-4	-4	106	324	3	.387	0	0	0	-0	/C1	-0.2
■ JOE CHRISTOPHER	Christopher, Joseph O'Neal b: 12/13/35, Frederiksted, V.I. BR/TR, 5'10", 175 lbs. Deb: 5/26/59																											
1959	Pit-N	15	12	6	0	0	0	0	0	1	4	.000	.077	.000	.077	-75	-3	-3	103	0	0	.083	0	0	0	-3	/O	-0.5
1960	Pit-N	50	56	21	13	2	0	1	3	5	8	.232	.295	.321	.617	69	-2	-2	99	58	6	.558	1	0	0	-3	O	-0.4
1961	Pit-N	76	186	25	49	7	3	0	14	18	24	.263	.328	.333	.662	77	-6	-6	99	91	19	.581	6	4	-1	-4	O	-1.3
1962	NY-N	119	271	36	66	10	2	6	32	35	42	.244	.339	.362	.700	85	-4	-5	104	109	36	.698	11	3	2	-7	O	-1.5
1963	NY-N	64	149	19	33	5	1	1	8	13	21	.221	.297	.289	.586	70	-6	-5	99	73	13	.496	1	3	-2	-5	O	-1.5
1964	NY-N	154	543	78	163	26	8	16	76	48	92	.300	.363	.466	.829	138	23	26	95	106	88	.777	6	5	-1	-0	*O	2.1
1965	NY-N	148	437	38	109	18	3	5	40	35	82	.249	.314	.339	.652	84	-9	-9	100	102	46	.564	4	4	-1	-6	*O	-2.0
1966	Bos-A	12	13	1	1	0	0	0	0	2	4	.077	.200	.077	.277	-15	-2	-2	109	0	0	.250	0	0	0	-1	/O	-0.2
Total	8	638	1667	224	434	68	17	29	173	157	277	.260	.331	.374	.705	96	-9	-7	99	97	208	.661	29	19	-3	-27	O	-5.3
■ LOYD CHRISTOPHER	Christopher, Loyd Eugene b: 12/31/19, Richmond, Cal. BR/TR, 6'2", 190 lbs. Deb: 4/20/45																											
1945	Bos-A	8	14	4	4	0	0	0	4	3	2	.286	.412	.286	.697	109	0	0	95	362	2	.700	0	0	0	-0	/O	0.0
	Chi-N	1	0	0	0	0	0	0	0	0	0	—	—	—	—	—	0	0	99	—	—	—	0			-0	/O	0.0
1947	Chi-A	7	23	1	5	0	1	0	0	2	4	.217	.280	.304	.584	65	-1	-1	97	0	1	.429	0	1	-1	1	/O	0.0
Total	2	16	37	5	9	0	1	0	4	5	6	.243	.333	.297	.631	82	-1	-1	96	146	5	.516	0	1		1	/O	0.0
■ HI CHURCH	Church, Hiram Lincoln b: Central Square, N.Y. Deb: 8/28/1890																											
1890	BB-a	3	9	1	1	0	0	0		0		.111	.111	.111	.222	-34	-1	-1	100	0	0	.125	0			0	/O	0.0
■ JOHN CHURRY	Churry, John b: 11/26/1900, Johnstown, Pa. d: 2/8/70, Zanesville, Ohio BR/TR, 5'9", 172 lbs. Deb: 5/24/24																											
1924	Chi-N	6	7	0	1	1	0	0	0	2	0	.143	.333	.286	.619	67	-0	-0	101	0	1	.667	0	0	0	0	/C	0.0
1925	Chi-N	3	6	1	3	0	0	0	1	0	0	.500	.500	.500	1.000	160	1	1	97	119	1	1.000	0	0	0	0	/C	0.1
1926	Chi-N	2	4	0	0	0	0	0	0	1	2	.000	.200	.000	.200	-40	-1	-1	106	0	0	.250	0			0	/C	0.0
1927	Chi-N	1	1	0	1	0	0	0	0	0	0	1.000	1.000	1.000	2.000	436	0	0	100	0	1	—	0			0	/C	0.1
Total	4	12	18	1	5	1	0	0	1	3	2	.278	.381	.333	.714	89	-0	-0	101	34	3	.692	0	0		0	/C	0.2
■ LARRY CIAFFONE	Ciaffone, Lawrence Thomas "Symphony Larry" b: 8/17/24, Brooklyn, N.Y. BR/TR, 5'9.5", 185 lbs. Deb: 4/17/51																											
1951	StL-N	5	5	0	0	0	0	0	0	1	2	.000	.167	.000	.167	-51	-1	-1	101	0	0	.200	0	0	0	-0	/O	0.0
■ DARRYL CIAS	Cias, Darryl Richard b: 4/23/57, New York, N.Y. BR/TR, 5'11", 190 lbs. Deb: 4/27/83																											
1983	Oak-A	19	18	1	6	1	0	0	1	2	4	.333	.400	.389	.789	124	1	1	96	56	3	.833	1	0	0	0	C	0.2
■ JOE CICERO	Cicero, Joseph Francis "Dode" b: 11/18/10, Atlantic City, N.J d: 3/30/83, Clearwater, Fla. BR/TR, 5'8", 167 lbs. Deb: 9/20/29																											
1929	Bos-A	10	32	6	10	2	2	0	4	0	2	.313	.313	.500	.813	104	0	-0	102	86	5	.727	0	0	0	-0	/O	0.0
1930	Bos-A	18	30	5	5	1	2	0	4	1	5	.167	.194	.333	.527	33	-3	-3	93	133	2	.440	0	0	0	-2	/O3	-0.4
1945	Phi-A	12	19	3	3	0	0	0	0	1	6	.158	.238	.158	.396	17	-2	-2	94	0	1	.313	0	0	0	-2	/O	-0.4
Total	3	40	81	14	18	3	4	0	8	2	13	.222	.250	.358	.608	60	-5	-5	96	82	8	.508	0	0	0	-5	/O3	-0.8
■ TED CIESLAK	Cieslak, Thaddeus Walter b: 11/22/16, Milwaukee, Wis. BR/TR, 5'10", 175 lbs. Deb: 4/18/44																											
1944	Phi-N	85	220	18	54	10	0	2	11	21	17	.245	.314	.318	.632	78	-6	-6	100	52	22	.541	1			-1	3/O	-0.5
■ AL CIHOCKI	Cihocki, Albert Joseph b: 5/7/24, Nanticoke, Pa. d: 11/9/87, Newark, Del. BR/TR, 5'11", 185 lbs. Deb: 4/17/45																											
1945	Cle-A	92	283	21	60	9	3	0	24	11	48	.212	.241	.265	.507	48	-20	-19	99	116	19	.384	2	1	0	-9	S32	-2.7
■ ED CIHOCKI	Cihocki, Edward Joseph "Cy" b: 5/9/07, Wilmington, Del. BR/TR, 5'8", 163 lbs. Deb: 5/29/32																											
1932	Phi-A	1	1	0	0	0	0	0	0	0	0	.000	.000	.000	.000	-88	-0	-0	114	0	0	.000	0	0	0	0	H	0.0
1933	Phi-A	33	97	6	14	2	3	0	9	7	16	.144	.202	.227	.429	15	-12	-11	92	136	5	.349	0	0	0	-2	S/23	-0.9
Total	2	34	98	6	14	2	3	0	9	7	16	.143	.200	.224	.424	13	-13	-12	92	135	5	.345	0	0	0	-2	/S32	-0.9
■ GINO CIMOLI	Cimoli, Gino Nicholas b: 12/18/29, San Francisco, Cal. BR/TR, 6'1", 180 lbs. Deb: 4/19/56																											
1956	Bro-N	73	36	3	4	1	0	0	4	1	8	.111	.135	.139	.274	-25	-6	-6	103	338	1	.212	1	0	0	-20	O	-2.9
1957	Bro-N	142	532	88	156	22	5	10	57	39	86	.293	.346	.410	.756	88	2	-9	116	97	76	.680	3	1	0	4	*O	-0.8
1958	LA-N	109	325	35	80	6	3	9	27	18	49	.246	.292	.366	.658	70	-13	-15	105	76	30	.542	3	3	-1	-15	*O	-3.4
1959	StL-N	143	519	61	145	40	7	8	72	37	83	.279	.330	.430	.759	96	-1	-4	105	120	70	.684	7	0	2	5	*O	0.1
1960	Pit-N	101	307	36	82	14	4	0	28	32	43	.267	.338	.339	.677	87	-5	-5	99	109	35	.590	1	0	0	-0	O	-0.7
1961	Pit-N	21	67	4	20	3	1	0	6	2	13	.299	.319	.373	.692	83	-2	-2	99	97	7	.529	0	0	0	-1	O	-0.2
	Mil-N	37	117	12	23	5	0	3	4	11	15	.197	.266	.316	.582	58	-8	-7	92	35	10	.505	1	0	0	-1	O	-0.8
	Yr	58	184	16	43	8	1	3	10	13	28	.234	.284	.337	.621	68	-10	-8	95	59	18	.528	1	0	0	-1		-1.0
1962	KC-A	152	550	67	151	20	**15**	10	71	40	89	.275	.326	.420	.746	99	-2	-2	100	110	74	.667	2	1	0	-8	*O	-1.5
1963	KC-A	145	529	56	139	19	11	4	48	39	72	.263	.316	.363	.679	83	-7	-12	108	100	60	.586	3	1	0	5	*O	-1.1
1964	KC-A	4	9	1	0	0	0	0	0	0	1	.000	.000	.000	.000	-96	-2	-2	105	0	0	.000	0	0	0	-0	/O	-0.2
	Bal-A	38	58	6	8	3	2	0	3	2	13	.138	.167	.259	.425	15	-7	-7	105	85	2	.333	0	0	0	-9	O	-1.8
	Yr	42	67	7	8	3	2	0	3	2	14	.119	.145	.224	.369	1	-9	-9	105	77	2	.283	0	0	0	-10		-2.0
1965	Cal-A	4	5	1	0	0	0	0	1	0	2	.000	.000	.000	.000	-99	-1	-1	98	0	0	.000	0	0	0	0	/O	0.0
Total	10	969	3054	370	808	133	48	44	321	221	474	.265	.317	.383	.700	84	-52	-72	105	103	365	.633	21	6	3	-41	O	-13.3
■ FRANK CIPRIANI	Cipriani, Frank Dominick b: 4/14/41, Buffalo, N.Y. BR/TR, 6', 180 lbs. Deb: 9/08/61																											
1961	KC-A	13	36	2	9	0	0	0	2	2	4	.250	.289	.250	.539	45	-3	-3	102	87	3	.393	0	0	0	-1	O	-0.3

YEAR	TM/L	G	AB	R	H	2B	3B	HR	RBI	BB	SO	AVG	OBP	SLG	PRO	/A	BR	/A	PF	CHI	RC	TA	SB	CS	SBR	FR	POS	TPR
■ **GEORGE CISAR**	Cisar, George Joseph b: 8/25/12, Chicago, Ill. BR/TR, 6', 175 lbs. Deb: 9/09/37																											
1937	Bro-N	20	29	8	6	0	0	0	4	2	6	.207	.258	.207	.465	27	-3	-3	104	240	1	.440	3			-3	O	-0.6
■ **BILL CISSELL**	Cissell, Chalmer William b: 1/3/04, Perryville, Mo. d: 3/15/49, Chicago, Ill. BR/TR, 5'11", 170 lbs. Deb: 4/11/28																											
1928	Chi-A	125	443	66	115	22	3	1	60	29	41	.260	.307	.330	.636	68	-21	-21	99	141	46	.581	18	6	2	-1	*S	-0.7
1929	Chi-A	152	618	83	173	27	12	5	62	28	53	.280	.312	.387	.699	83	-21	-16	95	89	72	.636	26	17	-2	-3	*S	-0.7
1930	Chi-A	141	562	82	152	28	9	2	48	28	32	.270	.307	.363	.670	67	-27	-29	103	80	62	.597	16	9	-1	-8	*23S	-3.1
1931	Chi-A	109	409	42	90	13	5	1	46	16	26	.220	.256	.284	.540	45	-35	-31	92	130	31	.474	18	6	2	-7	S2/3	-2.4
1932	Chi-A	12	43	7	11	1	1	1	5	1	0	.256	.273	.395	.668	81	-2	-1	87	84	5	.563	0	0	0	2	S	0.1
	Cle-A	131	541	78	173	35	6	6	93	28	25	.320	.354	.440	.794	96	3	-4	108	129	80	.744	18	15	-4	3	*2/S	0.2
	Yr	143	584	85	184	36	7	7	98	29	25	.315	.349	.437	.785	96	1	-5	107	126	85	.730	18	15	-4	5		0.3
1933	Cle-A	112	409	53	94	21	3	6	33	31	29	.230	.284	.340	.624	62	-22	-24	105	71	39	.548	6	6	-2	-1	2S/3	-2.3
1934	Bos-A	102	416	71	111	13	4	4	44	28	23	.267	.315	.346	.661	66	-19	-22	106	100	46	.595	11	4	1	1	2/S3	-1.3
1937	Phi-A	34	117	15	31	7	0	1	14	17	10	.265	.358	.350	.709	85	-3	-2	94	111	16	.674	0	0	0	-2	2	0.0
1938	NY-N	38	149	19	40	6	0	2	18	6	11	.268	.297	.349	.646	74	-5	-6	103	114	14	.513	1			3	2/3	0.0
Total	9	956	3707	516	990	173	43	29	423	212	250	.267	.308	.360	.669	73	-153	-157	101	105	412	.600	114	63		-12	2S/3	-10.2
■ **MOOSE CLABAUGH**	Clabaugh, John William b: 11/13/01, Albany, Mo. d: 7/11/84, Tucson, Arizona BL/TR, 6', 185 lbs. Deb: 8/30/26																											
1926	Bro-N	11	14	2	1	1	0	0	1	0	1	.071	.133	.143	.276	-26	-3	-3	99	173	0	.231	0			-1	/O	-0.2
■ **BOBBY CLACK**	Clack, Robert S. "Gentlemanly Bob" (born Robert S. Clark) b: 1851, Brooklyn, N.Y. d: 10/22/33, Danvers, Mass. BR/TR, 5'9", 153 lbs. Deb: 5/15/1874																											
1874	Atl-n	32	134	22	21							.157															O/1	
1875	Atl-n	17	60	1	6							.100															O	
1876	Cin-N	32	118	10	19	0	1	0	5	5	12	.161	.195	.178	.373	28	-9	-7	90	82	4	.263				1	O/213P	-0.5
Total	2 n	49	194	23	27							.139															O/213P	
■ **DANNY CLAIRE**	Claire, David Matthew b: 11/17/1897, Ludington, Mich. d: 1/7/56, Las Vegas, Nev. BR/TR, 5'8", 164 lbs. Deb: 9/17/20																											
1920	Det-A	3	7	1	1	0	0	0	0	0	0	.143	.143	.143	.286	-23	-1	-1	103	0	0	.167	0	0	0	0	/S	0.0
■ **BILL CLANCEY**	Clancey, William Edward b: 4/12/1878, Redfield, N.Y. d: 2/10/48, Oriskany, N.Y. TR , Deb: 4/14/05																											
1905	Pit-N	56	227	23	52	11	3	2	24	4		.229	.242	.330	.573	69	-9	-10	104	99	19	.469	3			-3	1/O	-1.5
■ **AL CLANCY**	Clancy, Albert Harrison b: 8/14/1888, Santa Fe, N.Mex. d: 10/17/51, Las Cruces, N.Mex. BR/TR, 5'10.5", 175 lbs. Deb: 6/20/11																											
1911	StL-A	3	5	0	0	0	0	0	0	0		.000	.167	.000	.167	-55	-1	-1	95	0	0	.200	0			0	/3	0.0
■ **BUD CLANCY**	Clancy, John William b: 9/15/1900, Odell, Ill. d: 9/26/68, Ottumwa, Iowa BL/TL, 6', 170 lbs. Deb: 8/29/24																											
1924	Chi-A	13	35	5	9	1	0	0	6	3	2	.257	.316	.286	.602	58	-2	-2	97	198	3	.571	3	2	-0	-1	/1	-0.2
1925	Chi-A	4	3	0	0	0	0	0	0	1	0	.000	.250	.000	.250	-34	-1	-1	96	0	0	.333	0	0	0	0	H	0.0
1926	Chi-A	12	38	3	13	2	2	0	7	1	1	.342	.375	.500	.875	138	1	2	92	125	7	.840	0	0	0	0	1	0.1
1927	Chi-A	130	464	46	139	21	2	3	53	24	24	.300	.337	.373	.710	82	-11	-13	102	99	57	.625	4	0	1	-3	*1	-1.9
1928	Chi-A	130	487	64	132	19	11	2	37	42	25	.271	.331	.368	.699	84	-12	-11	99	73	60	.629	6	9	-4	6	*1	-1.4
1929	Chi-A	92	290	36	82	14	6	3	45	16	19	.283	.320	.403	.724	90	-7	-5	95	122	38	.651	3	1	0	1	1	-1.2
1930	Chi-A	68	234	28	57	8	3	3	27	12	18	.244	.286	.342	.628	57	-15	-16	103	101	23	.545	3	1	0	-1	1	-2.1
1932	Bro-N	53	196	14	60	4	2	0	16	6	13	.306	.327	.347	.674	85	-5	-4	96	89	22	.544	0			1	1	-0.5
1934	Phi-N	20	49	8	12	0	0	1	7	6	4	.245	.339	.306	.645	68	-2	-2	108	140	6	.595	0			-0	1	-0.2
Total	9	522	1796	204	504	69	26	12	198	111	106	.281	.325	.368	.693	81	-54	-52	99	98	216	.612	19	13		4	1	-7.4
■ **UKE CLANTON**	Clanton, Eucal "Cat" b: 2/19/1898, Powell, Mo. d: 2/24/60, Antlers, Okla. BL/TL, 5'8", 165 lbs. Deb: 9/21/22																											
1922	Cle-A	1	1	0	0	0	0	0	0	0	1	.000	.000	.000	.000	-98	-0	-0	102	0	0	.000	0	0	0	0	/1	0.0
■ **AARON CLAPP**	Clapp, Aaron Bronson b: 7/1856 Ithaca, N.Y. d: 1/13/14, Sayre, Pa. TR , 5'8", 175 lbs. Deb: 5/01/1879																											
1879	Tro-N	36	146	24	39	9	3	0	18	6	10	.267	.296	.370	.666	126	3	4	93	124	16	.561				-2	1O	0.0
■ **JOHN CLAPP**	Clapp, John Edgar b: 7/17/1851, Ithaca, N.Y. d: 12/18/04, Ithaca, N.Y. BR/TR, 5'7", 175 lbs. Deb: 4/26/1872 M																											
1872	Man-n	19	98	30	30							.306															CM	
1873	Ath-n	45	219	35	63							.288															*C/S2	
1874	Ath-n	39	169	46	56							.331															CO/S	
1875	Ath-n	60	298	65	74							.248															C	
1876	StL-N	64	298	60	91	4	2	0	29	8	2	.305	.324	.332	.656	136	6	12	88	85	33	.517				7	*C/O2	1.9
1877	StL-N	60	255	47	81	6	6	0	34	8	6	.318	.338	.388	.727	126	8	7	102	103	34	.615				-5	*CO/1	0.4
1878	Ind-N	63	263	42	80	10	2	0	29	13	8	.304	.337	.357	.694	148	8	13	87	100	32	.585				-3	*O1/CS2M	0.6
1879	Buf-N	70	292	47	77	12	5	1	36	11	11	.264	.290	.349	.640	96	3	-3	114	116	30	.526				-8	*C/OM	-1.0
1880	Cin-N	80	323	33	91	16	4	1	20	21	10	.282	.326	.365	.691	135	12	12	99	53	39	.599				21	*COM	**3.6**
1881	Cle-N	68	261	47	66	12	2	0	25	**35**	6	.253	.341	.314	.655	112	4	5	96	112	29	.600				-3	CO	0.1
1883	NY-N	20	73	6	13	0	0	0	5	5	4	.178	.231	.178	.409	27	-6	-6	100	136	3	.300				0	C/OM	-0.4
Total	4 n	163	784	176	223							.284															C/OM	
Total	7	425	1765	282	499	60	21	2	178	101	47	.283	.322	.344	.665	120	34	41	98	95	201	.559				9	CO/1S2	5.2
■ **DENNY CLARE**	Clare, Dennis J. b: 1852, Brooklyn, N.Y. d: 11/26/28, Brooklyn, N.Y. Deb: 9/14/1872																											
1872	Atl-n	2	7	1	1							.143															/2	
■ **DOUG CLAREY**	Clarey, Douglas William b: 4/20/54, Los Angeles, Cal. BR/TR, 6', 180 lbs. Deb: 4/20/76																											
1976	StL-N	9	4	2	1	0	0	1	2	0	1	.250	.250	1.000	1.250	233	1	1	104	110	1	1.333	0	0	0	0	/2	0.1
■ **ALLIE CLARK**	Clark, Alfred Aloysius b: 6/16/23, S.Amboy, N.J. BR/TR, 6', 185 lbs. Deb: 8/05/47																											
1947	NY-A	24	67	9	25	5	0	1	14	5	2	.373	.417	.493	.909	158	5	5	97	143	12	.809	0	0	0	-1	O	0.4
1948	Cle-A	81	271	43	84	5	2	9	38	23	13	.310	.364	.443	.807	116	4	5	99	87	41	.711	0	2	-1	-9	O/31	-0.6
1949	Cle-A	35	74	8	13	4	0	1	9	4	7	.176	.218	.270	.488	29	-8	-8	98	134	4	.381	0	0	0	-5	O/1	-1.2
1950	Cle-A	59	163	19	35	6	1	6	21	11	10	.215	.264	.374	.639	63	-10	-10	98	92	12	.511	0	1	-1	-4	O	-1.4
1951	Cle-A	3	10	3	3	2	0	1	3	1	2	.300	.364	.800	1.164	220	1	1	95	97	3	1.286	0	0	0	-1	/O	0.0
	Phi-A	56	161	20	40	10	1	4	22	15	7	.248	.320	.398	.718	88	-2	-3	106	103	20	.654	2	0	1	-1	O3	-0.4
	Yr	59	171	23	43	12	1	5	25	16	9	.251	.323	.421	.744	95	-1	-2	105	105	23	.687	2	0	1	-2		-0.4
1952	Phi-A	71	186	23	51	12	0	7	29	10	19	.274	.315	.452	.766	101	2	-1	111	103	24	.660	0	2	-1	-6	O/1	-0.9
1953	Phi-A	20	74	6	15	4	0	3	13	3	5	.203	.234	.378	.612	62	-4	-5	102	133	6	.508	0	0	0	-1	O	-0.5
	Chi-A	9	15	0	1	0	0	0	0	0	5	.067	.067	.067	.133	-60	-3	-4	106	0	-0	.059	0	0	0	-0	/1O	-0.3
	Yr	29	89	6	16	4	0	3	13	3	10	.180	.207	.326	.532	40	-8	-8	103	96	5	.421	0	0	0	-1		-0.8
Total	7	358	1021	131	267	48	4	32	149	72	70	.262	.312	.410	.722	91	-16	-19	102	103	123	.651	2	5	-2	-26	O/31	-4.9
■ **DAD CLARK**	Clark, Alfred Robert "Fred" b: 7/16/1873, San Francisco, Cal d: 7/26/56, Ogden, Utah BL/TL, 5'11", 170 lbs. Deb: 7/03/02																											
1902	Chi-N	12	43	1	8	1	0	0	2	4		.186	.255	.209	.465	47	-3	-2	96	78	3	.400	1			-0	1	-0.2
■ **EARL CLARK**	Clark, Bailey Earl b: 11/6/07, Washington, D.C. d: 1/16/38, Washington, D.C. BR/TR, 5'10", 160 lbs. Deb: 8/17/27																											
1927	Bos-N	13	44	6	12	1	0	0	3	2	4	.273	.304	.295	.600	66	-2	-2	93	81	4	.469	0			-1	O	-0.3
1928	Bos-N	28	112	18	34	9	1	0	10	4	8	.304	.339	.402	.741	96	-1	-1	97	84	15	.654	0			1	O	0.0
1929	Bos-N	84	279	43	88	13	3	1	30	12	30	.315	.346	.394	.740	88	-7	-5	94	91	37	.675	6			2	O	-0.8
1930	Bos-N	82	233	29	69	11	3	3	28	7	22	.296	.320	.408	.727	76	-10	-9	97	93	29	.646	3			3	O	-0.9
1931	Bos-N	16	50	8	11	2	0	0	4	7	4	.220	.316	.260	.576	57	-3	-3	99	110	5	.538	1			0	O	-0.3
1932	Bos-N	50	44	11	11	2	0	0	4	2	7	.250	.283	.295	.578	60	-3	-3	93	114	4	.485	1			-3	O	-0.5
1933	Bos-N	7	23	3	8	1	0	0	1	2	1	.348	.400	.391	.791	131	1	1	96	43	4	.688	0			-1	/O	0.0
1934	StL-A	13	41	4	7	2	0	0	1	1	3	.171	.190	.220	.410	5	-6	-6	104	37	2	.294	0	0	0	0	/O	-0.5
Total	8	293	826	122	240	41	7	4	81	37	79	.291	.324	.372	.696	78	-32	-27	96	88	98	.613	11	0		1	O	-3.3

YEAR	TM/L	G	AB	R	H	2B	3B	HR	RBI	BB	SO	AVG	OBP	SLG	PRO	/A	BR	/A	PF	CHI	RC	TA	SB	CS	SBR	FR	POS	TPR
■ **DANNY CLARK** Clark, Daniel Curran b: 1/18/1894, Meridian, Miss. d: 5/23/37, Meridian, Miss. BL/TR, 5'9", 167 lbs. Deb: 4/12/22																												
1922	Det-A	83	185	31	54	11	3	3	26	15	11	.292	.345	.432	.777	104	-0	1	98	104	28	.733	1	0	0	-1	2/O3	0.2
1924	Bos-A	104	325	36	90	23	3	2	54	51	19	.277	.378	.385	.763	94	-0	-2	104	136	49	.752	4	7	-3	8	3	0.9
1927	StL-N	58	72	8	17	2	2	0	13	8	7	.236	.313	.319	.632	65	-3	-4	107	198	7	.564	0			1	/O	-0.2
Total	3	245	582	75	161	36	8	5	93	74	37	.277	.360	.392	.752	93	-3	-5	102	134	85	.722	5	7		8	/32O	0.9
■ **DAVE CLARK** Clark, David Earl b: 9/3/62, Tupelo, Miss. BL/TR, 6'2", 200 lbs. Deb: 9/03/86																												
1986	Cle-A	18	58	10	16	1	0	3	9	7	11	.276	.354	.448	.802	121	1	2	98	102	10	.791	1	0	0	1	O/D	0.2
1987	Cle-A	29	87	11	18	5	0	3	12	2	24	.207	.225	.368	.593	53	-6	-6	103	117	6	.479	1	0	0	0	OD	-0.5
1988	Cle-A	63	156	11	41	4	1	3	18	17	28	.263	.335	.359	.694	93	-1	-1	102	110	17	.584	0	2	-1	-4	DO	-0.6
Total	3	110	301	32	75	10	1	9	39	26	63	.249	.309	.379	.688	87	-5	-6	101	110	32	.602	2	2	-1	-3	/DO	-0.9
■ **GLEN CLARK** Clark, Glen Ester b: 3/7/41, Austin, Tex. BB/TR, 6'1", 190 lbs. Deb: 6/03/67																												
1967	Atl-N	4	4	0	0	0	0	0	0	0	1	.000	.000	.000	.000	-96	-1	-1	104	0	0	.000	0	0	0	0	H	0.0
■ **PEP CLARK** Clark, Harry b: 3/20/1883, Union City, Ohio d: 6/8/65, Milwaukee, Wis. BR/TR, 5'7.5", 175 lbs. Deb: 03																												
1903	Chi-A	15	65	7	20	4	2	0	9	2		.308	.328	.431	.759	139	2	3	92	100	11	.778	5			-0	3	0.2
■ **JACK CLARK** Clark, Jack Anthony b: 11/10/55, New Brighton, Pa. BR/TR, 6'2", 175 lbs. Deb: 9/12/75																												
1975	SF-N	8	17	3	4	0	0	0	2	1	2	.235	.278	.235	.513	43	-1	-1	102	193	1	.462	1	0	0	0	/O3	0.0
1976	SF-N	26	102	14	23	6	2	2	10	8	18	.225	.282	.382	.664	85	-2	-2	103	75	12	.654	6	2	1	5	O	0.2
1977	SF-N	136	413	64	104	17	4	13	51	49	73	.252	.334	.407	.741	94	-1	-4	104	99	58	.722	12	4	1	4	*O	-0.1
1978	SF-N	156	592	90	181	46	8	25	98	50	72	.306	.363	.537	.900	162	36	42	92	105	109	.883	15	11	-2	11	*O	4.6
1979	SF-N	143	527	84	144	25	2	26	86	63	95	.273	.352	.476	.828	134	17	22	92	110	88	.815	11	8	-2	6	*O/3	2.2
1980	SF-N	127	437	77	124	20	8	22	82	74	52	.284	.390	.517	.907	158	31	34	96	118	87	.921	2	5	-2	-4	*O	2.4
1981	SF-N	99	385	60	103	19	2	17	53	45	45	.268	.346	.460	.805	121	13	11	105	88	59	.759	1	1	-0	6	O	1.4
1982	SF-N	157	563	90	154	30	3	27	103	90	91	.274	.375	.481	.856	147	30	34	94	122	98	.840	6	9	-4	-3	*O	2.7
1983	SF-N	135	492	82	132	25	0	20	66	74	79	.268	.365	.441	.806	121	16	15	101	100	80	.788	5	3	-0	7	*O/1	2.0
1984	SF-N	57	203	33	65	9	1	11	44	43	29	.320	.439	.537	.976	180	22	23	96	129	47	1.034	1	1	-0	-2	O/1	1.9
1985	StL-N	126	442	71	124	26	3	22	87	83	88	.281	.397	.502	.899	157	32	34	96	127	89	.928	1	4	-2	-12	*1O	1.7
1986	StL-N	65	232	34	55	12	2	9	23	45	61	.237	.363	.422	.786	112	6	5	103	78	38	.797	1	1	-0	-1	1	0.1
1987	StL-N	131	419	93	120	23	1	35	106	**136**	139	.286	**.461**	**.597**	**1.058**	**180**	**54**	**55**	99	126	127	**1.265**	1	2	-1	-7	*1/O	3.9
1988	NY-A	150	496	81	120	14	0	27	93	113	141	.242	.385	.433	.818	134	23	26	96	127	88	.849	3	2	-0	-1	*DO1	2.4
Total	14	1516	5320	876	1453	272	36	256	904	874	985	.273	.377	.482	.859	140	274	293	97	111	982	.895	66	53	-12	11	*O1D/3	25.4
■ **JIM CLARK** Clark, James (born James Petrosky) b: 9/21/27, Bagley, Pa. BR/TR, 5'9", 150 lbs. Deb: 8/17/48																												
1948	Was-A	9	12	1	3	0	0	0	0	0	2	.250	.250	.250	.500	32	-1	-1	103	0	1	.333	0	0	0	-0	/S3	0.0
■ **JIM CLARK** Clark, James Edward b: 4/30/47, Kansas City, Kan. BR/TR, 6'1", 190 lbs. Deb: 7/16/71																												
1971	Cle-A	13	18	2	3	0	1	0	0	2	7	.167	.250	.278	.528	47	-1	-1	106	0	1	.438	0	0	0	0	/O1	-0.1
■ **JIM CLARK** Clark, James Francis b: 12/26/1887, Brooklyn, N.Y. d: 3/20/69, Beaumont, Tex. BR/TR, 5'11", 175 lbs. Deb: 9/02/11																												
1911	StL-N	14	18	2	3	0	1	0	3	3	4	.167	.286	.278	.563	57	-1	-1	101	203	2	.667	2			-3	/O	-0.3
1912	StL-N	2	1	0	0	0	0	0	0	0	1	.000	.000	.000	.000	-99	-0	-0	100	0	0	.000	0			0	H	0.0
Total	2	16	19	2	3	0	1	0	3	3	5	.158	.273	.263	.536	50	-1	-1	101	194	2	.625	2			-3	/O	-0.3
■ **JERALD CLARK** Clark, Jerald Dwayne b: 8/10/63, Crockett, Tex. BR/TR, 6'4", 189 lbs. Deb: 9/19/88																												
1988	SD-N	6	15	0	3	1	0	0	3	0	4	.200	.200	.267	.467	34	-1	-1	97	300	1	.333	0	0	0	1	/O	0.0
■ **CAP CLARK** Clark, John Carrol b: 9/19/06, Snow Camp, N.C. d: 2/16/57, Fayetteville, N.C. BL/TR, 5'11", 180 lbs. Deb: 4/23/38																												
1938	Phi-N	52	74	11	19	1	1	0	4	9	10	.257	.337	.297	.635	75	-2	-2	100	66	8	.564	0			-1	C	-0.1
■ **MEL CLARK** Clark, Melvin Earl b: 7/7/26, Letart, W.Va. BR/TR, 6', 180 lbs. Deb: 9/11/51																												
1951	Phi-N	10	31	2	10	1	0	1	3	0	3	.323	.323	.452	.774	109	0	0	97	68	4	.636	0	1	-1	-1	/O	-0.1
1952	Phi-N	47	155	20	52	6	4	1	15	6	13	.335	.364	.445	.809	122	4	4	101	81	25	.722	2	1	0	2	O/3	0.6
1953	Phi-N	60	198	31	59	10	4	0	19	11	17	.298	.338	.389	.727	90	-3	-3	99	96	24	.604	1	0	0	-2	O	-0.5
1954	Phi-N	83	233	26	56	9	7	1	24	17	21	.240	.292	.352	.644	68	-12	-11	99	111	21	.518	0	1	-1	-0	O	-1.3
1955	Phi-N	10	32	3	5	3	0	0	1	3	4	.156	.229	.250	.479	26	-3	-3	102	51	2	.379	0	0	0	3	/O	0.0
1957	Det-A	5	7	0	0	0	0	0	1	0	3	.000	.000	.000	.000	-93	-2	-2	107	0	0	.000	0	0	0	0	/O	-0.1
Total	6	215	656	82	182	29	15	3	63	37	61	.277	.318	.381	.699	85	-16	-15	99	94	75	.611	3	3	-1	3	O/3	-1.4
■ **SPIDER CLARK** Clark, Owen F. b: 9/16/1867, Brooklyn, N.Y. d: 2/8/1892, Brooklyn, N.Y. TR, 5'10", 150 lbs. Deb: 5/02/1889																												
1889	Was-N	38	145	19	37	7	2	3	22	6	18	.255	.285	.393	.678	98	-3	-1	92	101	19	.657	8			0	CS/O32	0.0
1890	Buf-P	69	260	45	69	11	1	1	25	20	16	.265	.325	.327	.652	83	-9	-5	92	79	31	.607	8			0	OC2/13SP	-0.3
Total	2	107	405	64	106	18	3	4	47	26	34	.262	.311	.351	.662	88	-11	-6	92	87	50	.625	16			0	/OC2S13P	-0.3
■ **BOB CLARK** Clark, Robert Cale b: 6/13/55, Sacramento, Cal. BR/TR, 6', 190 lbs. Deb: 8/21/79																												
1979	Cal-A	19	54	8	16	2	2	1	5	5	11	.296	.356	.463	.819	129	1	2	93	69	8	.738	1	1	-0	3	O	0.3
1980	Cal-A	78	261	26	60	10	1	5	23	11	42	.230	.266	.333	.600	66	-14	-12	96	88	21	.478	0	1	-1	12	O	-0.2
1981	Cal-A	34	88	12	22	2	1	4	19	7	18	.250	.305	.432	.737	106	1	0	104	149	11	.662	0	0	0	1	O	0.1
1982	Cal-A	102	90	11	19	1	0	2	8	0	29	.211	.211	.289	.500	36	-8	-8	100	100	5	.375	1	0	0	-29	*O	-4.0
1983	Cal-A	76	212	17	49	9	1	5	21	9	45	.231	.262	.354	.616	71	-10	-9	96	91	18	.494	0	0	0	-11	O/3D	-2.0
1984	Mil-A	58	169	17	44	7	2	2	16	16	35	.260	.328	.361	.689	99	-2	-0	92	95	17	.568	1	5	-3	-5	O	-0.9
1985	Mil-A	29	93	6	21	3	0	0	8	7	19	.226	.280	.258	.538	46	-6	-7	105	132	6	.421	1	1	-0	3	O	-0.4
Total	7	396	967	97	231	34	7	19	100	55	199	.239	.282	.347	.629	75	-38	-34	97	100	87	.533	4	8	-4	-27	O/D3	-7.1
■ **BOB CLARK** Clark, Robert H. b: 3/18/1863, Covington, Ky. d: 8/21/19, Covington, Ky. BR/TR, 5'10", 175 lbs. Deb: 4/17/1886																												
1886	Bro-a	71	269	37	58	8	2	0		17		.216	.262	.260	.522	65	-10	-11	100	0	23	.479	14			-6	COS	-1.1
1887	Bro-a	48	177	24	47	3	1	0		7		.266	.297	.294	.591	68	-8	-7	99	0	20	.577	15			-4	C/O	-0.2
1888	Bro-a	45	150	23	36	5	3	1	20	9		.240	.292	.333	.625	99	1	-1	105	113	18	.632	11			-2	C/O1	0.1
1889	Bro-a	53	182	32	50	5	2	0	22	26	7	.275	.368	.324	.693	104	1	3	96	109	29	.788	18			6	C	1.2
1890	Bro-N	43	151	24	33	3	3	0	15	15	8	.219	.306	.278	.584	72	-5	-5	100	110	16	.602	10			-15	C/O	-1.4
1891	Cin-N	16	54	2	6	0	0	0	3	6	9	.111	.213	.111	.324	-4	-7	-6	91	149	2	.333	3			0	C	-0.4
1893	Lou-N	12	28	3	3	1	0	0	3	5	5	.107	.242	.143	.385	5	-4	-4	96	205	1	.360	0			0	C/OS	-0.2
Total	7	288	1011	145	233	25	11	1	63	85	29	.230	.296	.280	.576	74	-32	-30	99	68	110	.576	71			-21	C/OS1	-2.0
■ **RON CLARK** Clark, Ronald Bruce b: 1/14/43, Ft.Worth, Tex. BR/TR, 5'10", 175 lbs. Deb: 9/11/66 C																												
1966	Min-A	5	1	1	1	0	0	0	1	0	0	1.000	1.000	1.000	2.000	428	0	0	111	420	1	—	0	0	0	0	/3	0.0
1967	Min-A	20	60	7	10	3	1	2	11	4	9	.167	.219	.350	.569	61	-3	-3	107	170	4	.472	0	0	0	-1	3	-0.3
1968	Min-A	104	227	14	42	5	1	1	13	16	44	.185	.245	.229	.474	42	-15	-17	106	101	14	.386	3	2	-0	-0	3S2	-1.3
1969	Min-A	5	8	0	1	0	0	0	0	0	0	.125	.125	.125	.250	-29	-1	-1	102	0	0	.125	0	0	0	0	/3	0.0
	Sea-A	57	163	9	32	5	0	0	12	13	29	.196	.260	.227	.487	38	-14	-13	98	130	11	.394	1	0	0	-3	S3/21	-1.4
	Yr	62	171	9	33	5	0	0	12	13	29	.193	.254	.222	.476	35	-15	-15	99	120	11	.381	1	0	0	-3		-1.4
1971	Oak-A	2	1	0	0	0	0	0	0	1	0	.000	.500	.000	.500	52	0	0	101	0	0	1.000	0	0	0	0	H	0.0
1972	Oak-A	14	15	1	4	2	0	0	1	2	4	.267	.353	.400	.753	128	0	1	97	70	2	.667	0	0	0	-0	2/3	0.1
	Mil-A	22	54	8	10	1	1	2	5	5	11	.185	.254	.352	.606	83	-2	-1	95	84	5	.522	0	0	0	-2	23	-0.1
	Yr	36	69	9	14	3	1	2	6	7	15	.203	.276	.362	.639	93	-1	-1	96	80	7	.561	0	0	0	-2		0.0
1975	Phi-N	1	1	0	0	0	0	0	0	0	1	.000	.000	.000	.000	-99	-0	-0	101	0	0	.000	0	0	0	0	H	0.0
Total	7	230	530	40	100	16	3	5	43	41	98	.189	.251	.258	.509	49	-34	-35	102	114	35	.428	4	2	0	-6	/3S21	-3.0
■ **ROY CLARK** Clark, Roy Elliott "Pepper" b: 5/11/1874, New Haven, Conn. d: 11/1/25, Bridgeport, Conn. BL/TR, 5'8", 170 lbs. Deb: 4/19/02																												
1902	NY-N	21	76	4	11	1	0	0	3	1		.145	.156	.158	.314	-2	-9	-9	100	88	3	.277	5			1	O	-1.0

■ WILL CLARK Clark, William Nuschler b: 3/17/64, New Orleans, La. BL/TL, 6'2", 190 lbs. Deb: 4/08/86

YEAR	TM/L	G	AB	R	H	2B	3B	HR	RBI	BB	SO	AVG	OBP	SLG	PRO	/A	BR	/A	PF	CHI	RC	TA	SB	CS	SBR	FR	POS	TPR
1986	SF-N	111	408	66	117	27	2	11	41	34	76	.287	.346	.444	.790	121	8	10	96	78	62	.738	4	7	-3	2	*1	0.6
1987	SF-N	150	529	89	163	29	5	35	91	49	98	.308	.372	.580	.953	154	34	37	96	90	109	.951	5	17	-9	1	*1	2.1
1988	SF-N	162	575	102	162	31	6	29	**109**	**100**	129	.282	.392	.508	.900	167	**44**	**49**	94	122	**120**	.957	9	1	2	-4	*1	4.1
Total	3	423	1512	257	442	87	13	75	241	183	303	.292	.373	.516	.889	150	87	96	95	99	290	.899	18	25	-10	-1	1	6.8

■ WILLIE CLARK Clark, William Otis "Wee Willie" b: 8/16/1872, Pittsburgh, Pa. d: 11/13/32, Pittsburgh, Pa. Deb: 6/20/1895

YEAR	TM/L	G	AB	R	H	2B	3B	HR	RBI	BB	SO	AVG	OBP	SLG	PRO	/A	BR	/A	PF	CHI	RC	TA	SB	CS	SBR	FR	POS	TPR
1895	NY-N	23	88	9	23	3	2	0	16	5	6	.261	.301	.341	.642	71	-4	-4	95	152	10	.554	1			0	1	-0.2
1896	NY-N	72	247	38	72	12	4	0	33	15	12	.291	.352	.372	.724	94	-2	-2	99	103	36	.703	8			-4	1	-0.2
1897	NY-N	116	431	63	122	17	12	1	75	37		.283	.352	.385	.737	98	-2	-0	98	132	66	.744	18			3	*1/O3	0.1
1898	Pit-N	57	209	29	64	9	7	1	31	22		.306	.378	.431	.808	138	9	10	98	107	35	.786	0			0	1	1.0
1899	Pit-N	80	298	49	85	13	10	0	44	35		.285	.375	.396	.771	116	7	8	99	121	50	.808	11			-0	1	0.8
Total	5	348	1273	188	366	54	35	2	199	114	18	.288	.359	.390	.748	106	8	12	98	121	197	.744	38			-2	1/O3	1.5

■ BILL CLARK Clark, William Winfield b: 4/11/1875, Circleville, Ohio d: 4/15/59, Los Angeles, Cal. BR/TR, 5'10", 175 lbs. Deb: 7/12/1897

YEAR	TM/L	G	AB	R	H	2B	3B	HR	RBI	BB	SO	AVG	OBP	SLG	PRO	/A	BR	/A	PF	CHI	RC	TA	SB	CS	SBR	FR	POS	TPR
1897	Lou-N	7	26	2	6	0	0	0	2	1		.231	.259	.231	.490	33	-2	-2	95	99	2	.400	1			0	/2P3	-0.1

■ ARTIE CLARKE Clarke, Arthur Franklin b: 5/6/1865, Providence, R.I. d: 11/14/49, Brookline, Mass. BR/TR, 5'8", 155 lbs. Deb: 4/19/1890

YEAR	TM/L	G	AB	R	H	2B	3B	HR	RBI	BB	SO	AVG	OBP	SLG	PRO	/A	BR	/A	PF	CHI	RC	TA	SB	CS	SBR	FR	POS	TPR
1890	NY-N	101	395	55	89	12	8	0	49	32	38	.225	.290	.296	.586	77	-14	-10	95	134	48	.644	44			1	CO32/S	-0.6
1891	NY-N	48	174	17	33	2	2	0	21	15	16	.190	.254	.224	.478	44	-13	-11	94	160	11	.418	5			-13	C/3O	-1.8
Total	2	149	569	72	122	14	10	0	70	47	54	.214	.279	.274	.553	67	-26	-21	95	142	59	.573	49			-12	/CO32S	-2.4

■ FRED CLARKE Clarke, Fred Clifford "Cap" b: 10/3/1872, Winterset, Iowa d: 8/14/60, Winfield, Kan. BL/TR, 5'10.5", 165 lbs. Deb: 6/30/1894 MH

YEAR	TM/L	G	AB	R	H	2B	3B	HR	RBI	BB	SO	AVG	OBP	SLG	PRO	/A	BR	/A	PF	CHI	RC	TA	SB	CS	SBR	FR	POS	TPR
1894	Lou-N	75	310	54	83	11	7	7	48	25	27	.268	.330	.416	.747	91	-11	-4	88	76	52	.806	25			3	O	-0.4
1895	Lou-N	132	550	96	191	21	5	4	82	34	24	.347	.396	.425	.821	120	12	17	95	90	111	.886	40			10	*O	1.3
1896	Lou-N	131	517	96	168	15	18	9	79	43	34	.325	.392	.476	.868	133	22	24	98	80	113	.966	34			-1	*O	1.2
1897	Lou-N	128	518	120	202	30	13	6	67	45		.390	.461	.533	.994	173	50	54	95	58	157	1.269	57			5	*OM	4.2
1898	Lou-N	149	599	116	184	23	12	3	47	48		.307	.373	.401	.774	129	20	23	96	49	107	.827	40			3	*OM	1.6
1899	Lou-N	148	602	122	206	23	9	5	70	49		.342	.405	.435	.840	129	29	25	103	68	129	.944	49			-2	*O/SM	1.3
1900	Pit-N	106	399	84	110	15	12	3	32	51		.276	.358	.396	.754	107	6	5	103	58	66	.796	21			-0	*OM	-0.3
1901	Pit-N	129	527	118	171	24	15	6	60	51		.324	.384	.461	.845	146	31	31	101	68	105	.890	23			-2	*O/S3M	1.5
1902	Pit-N	113	459	103	145	27	14	2	53	51		.316	.384	.449	.833	151	32	29	105	75	93	.911	29			-9	*OM	1.2
1903	Pit-N	104	427	88	150	**32**	15	5	70	41		.351	.408	**.532**	**.940**	**162**	37	34	105	82	104	1.043	21			-3	*O/SM	2.4
1904	Pit-N	72	278	51	85	7	11	0	25	22		.306	.357	.410	.767	140	12	12	99	77	46	.762	11			-5	OM	0.5
1905	Pit-N	141	525	95	157	18	15	2	51	55		.299	.366	.402	.767	126	20	18	104	87	88	.788	24			4	*OM	1.2
1906	Pit-N	118	417	69	129	14	**13**	1	39	40		.309	.370	.412	.782	140	22	20	104	86	72	.799	18			5	*OM	2.5
1907	Pit-N	148	501	97	145	18	13	2	59	68		.289	.374	.389	.764	135	26	23	105	118	89	.843	37			-2	*OM	1.8
1908	Pit-N	151	551	83	146	18	15	2	53	65		.265	.343	.363	.706	134	18	21	95	95	75	.714	24			1	*OM	2.3
1909	Pit-N	152	550	97	158	16	11	3	68	**80**		.287	.384	.373	.756	130	26	23	105	122	89	.821	31			11	*OM	3.1
1910	Pit-N	123	429	57	113	23	9	2	63	53	23	.263	.350	.373	.723	99	6	-1	112	140	62	.725	12			9	*OM	0.4
1911	Pit-N	110	392	73	127	25	13	5	49	53	27	.324	.407	.492	.900	150	27	27	101	84	82	.974	10			1	*OM	2.4
1913	Pit-N	9	13	0	1	1	0	0	0	0	0	.077	.077	.154	.231	-37	-2	-2	96	0	0	.167	0			-1	/OM	-0.2
1914	Pit-N	2	2	0	0	0	0	0	0	0	0	.000	.000	.000	.000	-99	-0	-0	92	0	0	.000	0			0	HM	0.0
1915	Pit-N	1	2	0	1	0	0	0	0	0	0	.500	.500	.500	1.000	206	0	0	99	0	1	1.000	0			-0	/OM	0.0
Total	21	2242	8568	1619	2672	361	220	67	1015	874	135	.312	.382	.429	.810	133	383	379	101	84	1639	.873	506			27	*O/S3	28.0

■ HARRY CLARKE Clarke, Harry Corson b: 1861, d: 3/3/23, Long Beach, Cal. Deb: 8/28/1889

YEAR	TM/L	G	AB	R	H	2B	3B	HR	RBI	BB	SO	AVG	OBP	SLG	PRO	/A	BR	/A	PF	CHI	RC	TA	SB	CS	SBR	FR	POS	TPR
1889	Was-N	1	3	0	0	0	0	0	0	0	1	.000	.000	.000	.000	-99	-1	-1	92	0	0	.000	0			0	/O	0.0

■ HORACE CLARKE Clarke, Horace Meredith b: 6/2/40, Frederiksted, St.Croix, V.I. BB/TR, 5'9", 170 lbs. Deb: 5/13/65

YEAR	TM/L	G	AB	R	H	2B	3B	HR	RBI	BB	SO	AVG	OBP	SLG	PRO	/A	BR	/A	PF	CHI	RC	TA	SB	CS	SBR	FR	POS	TPR
1965	NY-A	51	108	13	28	1	0	1	9	6	6	.259	.298	.296	.595	69	-4	-4	101	107	10	.482	2	1	0	3	3/2S	0.0
1966	NY-A	96	312	37	83	10	4	6	28	27	24	.266	.326	.381	.708	110	1	3	94	86	40	.650	5	3	-0	-3	S2/3	0.5
1967	NY-A	143	588	74	160	17	0	3	29	42	64	.272	.321	.316	.637	94	-8	-4	94	55	64	.570	21	4	4	9	*2	1.4
1968	NY-A	148	579	52	133	6	1	2	26	23	46	.230	.259	.254	.513	55	-31	-32	101	77	39	.412	20	7	2	**30**	*2	0.6
1969	NY-A	156	641	82	183	26	7	4	48	53	41	.285	.340	.367	.707	102	-2	1	95	67	83	.670	33	13	2	-2	*2	0.8
1970	NY-A	158	686	81	172	24	2	4	46	35	35	.251	.289	.309	.598	70	-33	-27	92	72	62	.510	23	7	3	-7	*2	-1.6
1971	NY-A	159	625	76	156	23	7	2	41	64	43	.250	.321	.318	.640	84	-14	-12	97	79	66	.576	17	7	1	-4	*2	-0.8
1972	NY-A	147	547	65	132	20	2	3	37	56	44	.241	.316	.302	.618	91	-9	-5	92	94	56	.568	18	6	2	8	*2	1.5
1973	NY-A	148	590	60	155	21	0	2	35	47	48	.263	.319	.308	.628	77	-17	-17	101	65	56	.523	11	10	-3	10	*2	-0.3
1974	NY-A	24	47	3	11	1	0	0	1	4	5	.234	.294	.255	.549	62	-2	-2	96	33	4	.459	1	0	0	-0	2/D	0.0
	SD-N	42	90	5	17	1	0	0	4	8	6	.189	.255	.200	.455	31	-8	-8	93	86	5	.356	0	0	0	-1	2	-0.7
Total	10	1272	4813	548	1230	150	23	27	304	365	362	.256	.310	.313	.623	82	-128	-106	96	74	482	.559	151	58	11	43	*2/S3D	1.4

■ NIG CLARKE Clarke, Jay Justin b: 12/15/1882, Amherstburg, Ont., Canada d: 6/15/49, River Rouge, Mich BB/TR, 5'8", 165 lbs. Deb: 4/26/05

YEAR	TM/L	G	AB	R	H	2B	3B	HR	RBI	BB	SO	AVG	OBP	SLG	PRO	/A	BR	/A	PF	CHI	RC	TA	SB	CS	SBR	FR	POS	TPR
1905	Cle-A	5	9	2	1	1	0	0	1	1		.111	.200	.222	.422	35	-1	-1	100	178	0	.375	0			0	/C	0.0
	Det-A	3	7	1	3	0	0	1	1	0		.429	.429	.857	1.286	313	1	1	98	40	3	1.500	0			0	/C	0.2
	Cle-A	37	114	9	23	5	1	0	8	10		.202	.266	.263	.529	70	-4	-4	100	95	8	.440	0			-3	C	-0.2
	Yr	45	130	12	27	6	1	1	10	11		.208	.270	.292	.562	80	-3	-3	100	106	10	.476	0			-3		0.0
1906	Cle-A	57	179	22	64	12	4	1	21	13		.358	.401	.486	.887	174	16	15	103	85	37	.896	3			-5	C	1.6
1907	Cle-A	120	390	44	105	19	6	3	33	35		.269	.329	.372	.701	135	11	14	93	78	50	.642	3			-13	*C	1.2
1908	Cle-A	97	290	34	70	8	6	1	27	30		.241	.313	.321	.633	102	3	1	106	106	30	.586	6			-8	C	0.3
1909	Cle-A	55	164	15	45	4	2	0	14	9		.274	.316	.323	.639	100	0	-0	102	102	16	.538	1			1	C	0.5
1910	Cle-A	21	58	4	9	2	0	0	2	8		.155	.258	.190	.447	40	-4	-4	100	67	3	.388	0			-1	C	-0.2
1911	StL-A	82	256	22	55	10	1	0	18	26		.215	.287	.262	.549	56	-16	-14	95	91	20	.473	2			5	C/1	0.0
1919	Phi-N	26	62	4	15	3	0	0	2	4	5	.242	.299	.290	.589	75	-2	-2	104	43	5	.511	1			1	C	0.0
1920	Pit-N	3	7	0	0	0	0	0	0	2	4	.000	.222	.000	.222	-32	-1	-1	101	0	0	.286	0	0	0	0	/C	0.0
Total	9	506	1536	157	390	64	20	6	127	138	9	.254	.316	.333	.650	104	5	7	99	88	173	.583	16	0		-23	C/1	3.4

■ JOSH CLARKE Clarke, Joshua Baldwin "Pepper" b: 3/8/1879, Winfield, Kan. d: 7/2/62, Ventura, Cal. BL/TR, 5'10", 180 lbs. Deb: 6/15/1898

YEAR	TM/L	G	AB	R	H	2B	3B	HR	RBI	BB	SO	AVG	OBP	SLG	PRO	/A	BR	/A	PF	CHI	RC	TA	SB	CS	SBR	FR	POS	TPR
1898	Lou-N	6	18	0	3	0	0	0	0	1		.167	.211	.167	.377	10	-2	-2	96	0	1	.267	0			0	/O	-0.1
1905	StL-N	50	167	31	43	3	2	3	18	27		.257	.361	.353	.714	126	4	6	91	97	25	.758	8			-2	O2/S	0.4
1908	Cle-A	131	492	70	119	8	4	1	21	76		.242	.343	.280	.624	100	7	4	106	48	58	.673	37			-16	*O	-2.0
1909	Cle-A	4	12	1	0	0	0	0	0	2		.000	.143	.000	.143	-53	-2	-2	102	0	0	.167	0			0	/O	-0.2
1911	Bos-N	32	120	16	28	7	3	1	4	29	22	.233	.387	.367	.753	108	3	2	103	25	19	.870	6			4	O	0.5
Total	5	223	809	118	193	18	9	5	43	135	22	.239	.348	.302	.650	102	10	8	102	53	103	.700	51			-14	O/2S	-1.4

■ GREY CLARKE Clarke, Richard Grey "Noisy" b: 9/26/12, Fulton, Ala. BR/TR, 5'9", 183 lbs. Deb: 4/19/44

YEAR	TM/L	G	AB	R	H	2B	3B	HR	RBI	BB	SO	AVG	OBP	SLG	PRO	/A	BR	/A	PF	CHI	RC	TA	SB	CS	SBR	FR	POS	TPR
1944	Chi-A	63	169	14	44	10	1	0	27	22	6	.260	.352	.331	.684	96	-0	-0	100	174	19	.588	0	4	-2	2	3	0.0

■ SUMPTER CLARKE Clarke, Sumpter Mills b: 10/18/1897, Savannah, Ga. d: 3/16/62, Knoxville, Tenn. BR/TR, 5'11", 170 lbs. Deb: 9/27/20

YEAR	TM/L	G	AB	R	H	2B	3B	HR	RBI	BB	SO	AVG	OBP	SLG	PRO	/A	BR	/A	PF	CHI	RC	TA	SB	CS	SBR	FR	POS	TPR
1920	Chi-N	1	3	0	1	0	0	0	0	0	1	.333	.333	.333	.667	93	-0	-0	99	0	0	.500	0	0	0	0	/3	0.0
1923	Cle-A	1	3	0	0	0	0	0	0	0	0	.000	.000	.000	.000	-99	-1	-1	101	0	0	.000	0	0	0	-0	/O	0.0
1924	Cle-A	35	104	17	24	6	1	0	11	6	12	.231	.273	.308	.580	51	-8	-8	97	114	9	.475	0	0	0	-6	O	-1.4
Total	3	37	110	17	25	6	1	0	11	6	13	.227	.267	.300	.567	48	-9	-9	97	108	9	.459	0	0	0	-6	/O3	-1.4

■ TOMMY CLARKE Clarke, Thomas Aloysius b: 5/9/1888, New York, N.Y. d: 8/14/45, Corona, N.Y. BR/TR, 5'11", 175 lbs. Deb: 09 C

YEAR	TM/L	G	AB	R	H	2B	3B	HR	RBI	BB	SO	AVG	OBP	SLG	PRO	/A	BR	/A	PF	CHI	RC	TA	SB	CS	SBR	FR	POS	TPR
1909	Cin-N	18	52	5	13	3	2	0	10	6		.250	.328	.385	.712	130	1	2	94	182	7	.744	3			-2	C	0.1
1910	Cin-N	64	151	19	42	6	5	1	20	19	17	.278	.370	.404	.774	124	5	5	101	109	23	.771	1			-1	C	0.7
1911	Cin-N	86	203	20	49	6	7	1	25	25	22	.241	.328	.355	.682	99	-3	-0	92	113	26	.662	4			-1	C/1	0.4
1912	Cin-N	72	146	19	41	7	2	0	22	28	14	.281	.400	.356	.756	117	3	5	92	142	25	.857	9			-0	C	0.8

YEAR	TM/L	G	AB	R	H	2B	3B	HR	RBI	BB	SO	AVG	OBP	SLG	PRO	/A	BR	/A	PF	CHI	RC	TA	SB	CS	SBR	FR	POS	TPR
1913	Cin-N	114	330	29	87	11	8	1	38	39	40	.264	.345	.355	.700	98	1	0	102	115	39	.658	2			9	*C	1.5
1914	Cin-N	113	313	30	82	13	7	2	25	31	30	.262	.332	.367	.700	103	3	1	105	75	39	.667	6			-5	*C	0.0
1915	Cin-N	96	226	23	65	7	2	0	21	33	22	.288	.381	.336	.717	115	7	6	103	105	32	.713	7	3	0	1	C	1.2
1916	Cin-N	78	177	10	42	10	1	0	17	24	20	.237	.328	.305	.633	97	-0	0	98	125	20	.637	8			3	C	0.6
1917	Cin-N	58	110	11	32	3	3	1	13	11	12	.291	.361	.400	.761	144	4	5	92	107	16	.744	2			0	C	0.8
1918	Chi-N	1	0	0	0	0	0	0	0	0	0	—	—	—	—	—	0	0	102	—	—	—	0			0	/C	0.0
Total	10	700	1708	166	453	66	37	6	191	216	177	.265	.351	.358	.709	109	21	24	99	111	243	.700	42	3		4	C/1	6.1
■ BOILERYARD CLARKE	Clarke, William Jones b: 10/18/1868, New York, N.Y. d: 7/29/59, Princeton, N.J. BR/TR, 5'11.5", 170 lbs. Deb: 5/01/1893																											
1893	Bal-N	49	183	23	32	1	3	1	24	19	14	.175	.274	.230	.504	33	-17	-19	107	149	12	.457	2			0	C1	-1.2
1894	Bal-N	28	100	18	24	8	0	1	19	16	14	.240	.361	.350	.711	74	-4	-4	99	141	14	.737	2			0	C/1	-0.2
1895	Bal-N	67	241	38	70	15	3	0	35	13	18	.290	.350	.378	.727	83	-4	-7	107	110	35	.708	8			4	C/1	0.2
1896	Bal-N	80	300	48	89	14	7	2	71	14	12	.297	.345	.410	.755	98	-0	-1	102	162	46	.720	7			-11	C1	-0.5
1897	Bal-N	64	241	32	65	7	1	1	38	9		.270	.320	.320	.640	75	-10	-8	95	142	27	.568	5			-18	C/1	-1.4
1898	Bal-N	82	285	26	69	5	2	0	27	4		.242	.289	.274	.563	62	-13	-14	103	105	24	.458	2			-1	C1	-0.8
1899	Bos-N	60	223	25	50	3	2	2	32	10		.224	.270	.283	.553	51	-14	-16	105	145	18	.457	2			-4	C	-1.4
1900	Bos-N	81	270	35	85	5	2	1	30	9		.315	.337	.359	.696	79	-2	-10	120	94	33	.573	0			7	C/1	0.2
1901	Was-A	110	422	58	118	15	5	3	54	23		.280	.317	.360	.677	90	-6	-6	99	108	52	.599	7			-4	*C/1	0.0
1902	Was-A	87	291	31	78	16	0	6	40	23		.268	.322	.385	.707	98	-1	-1	99	101	37	.638	1			-5	C	0.1
1903	Was-A	126	465	35	111	14	6	2	38	15		.239	.262	.308	.570	68	-16	-19	105	97	42	.480	12			-5	1C	-1.9
1904	Was-A	85	275	23	58	8	1	0	17	17		.211	.257	.247	.504	67	-11	-9	93	95	19	.415	5			6	C1	0.3
1905	NY-N	31	50	2	9	0	0	1	4	4		.180	.241	.240	.481	44	-3	-3	101	93	3	.415	1			-1	1C	-0.3
Total	13	950	3346	394	858	111	32	20	429	176	58	.256	.304	.327	.631	75	-102	-116	103	117	363	.553	54			-32	C1	-6.9
■ STU CLARKE	Clarke, William Stuart b: 1/24/06, San Francisco, Cal d: 8/26/85, Hayward, Cal. BR/TR, 5'8.5", 160 lbs. Deb: 7/17/29																											
1929	Pit-N	57	178	20	47	5	7	2	21	19	21	.264	.338	.404	.743	80	-5	-6	103	92	24	.725	3			-7	S3/2	-0.5
1930	Pit-N	4	9	2	4	0	1	0	2	1	0	.444	.500	.667	1.167	184	1	1	97	115	3	1.400	0			-0	/2	0.1
Total	2	61	187	22	51	5	8	2	23	20	21	.273	.346	.417	.763	85	-4	-5	103	93	27	.750	3			-7	/S32	-0.4
■ BUZZ CLARKSON	Clarkson, James Buster b: 3/13/18, Hopkins, S.C. BR/TR, 5'11", 210 lbs. Deb: 4/30/52																											
1952	Bos-N	14	25	3	5	0	0	0	1	3	3	.200	.286	.200	.486	39	-2	-2	95	78	2	.400	0	0	0	0	/S3	-0.1
■ ELLIS CLARY	Clary, Ellis "Cat" b: 9/11/16, Valdosta, Ga. BR/TR, 5'8", 160 lbs. Deb: 6/07/42 C																											
1942	Was-A	76	240	34	66	9	0	0	16	45	25	.275	.394	.313	.706	105	3	4	96	75	35	.701	2	0	1	-8	2/3	0.0
1943	Was-A	73	254	36	65	19	1	0	19	44	31	.256	.370	.339	.709	104	4	3	104	82	35	.697	8	4	0	-5	3/S	0.0
	StL-A	23	69	15	19	2	0	0	5	11	6	.275	.375	.304	.679	99	1	0	100	87	9	.635	1	2	-1	1	3/2	0.0
	Yr	96	323	51	84	21	1	0	24	55	37	.260	.371	.331	.702	103	5	4	103	84	46	.706	9	6	-1	-4		0.0
1944	StL-A	25	49	6	13	1	1	0	4	12	9	.265	.410	.327	.736	110	2	1	102	90	8	.806	1	0	0	0	3/2	0.2
1945	StL-A	26	38	6	8	1	0	1	2	2	3	.211	.250	.316	.566	55	-2	-3	115	48	3	.438	0	2	-1	0	3/2	-0.2
Total	4	223	650	97	171	32	2	1	46	114	74	.263	.376	.323	.699	101	7	7	101	79	89	.698	12	8	-1	-12	3/2S	0.0
■ DAIN CLAY	Clay, Dain Elmer "Sniffy" or "Ding-A-Ling" b: 7/10/19, Hicksville, Ohio BR/TR, 5'1.5", 160 lbs. Deb: 6/12/43																											
1943	Cin-N	49	93	19	25	2	4	0	9	8	14	.269	.333	.376	.710	105	0	1	99	93	12	.652	1			-8	O	-0.8
1944	Cin-N	110	356	51	89	15	0	0	17	17	18	.250	.290	.292	.582	67	-17	-15	95	59	31	.484	8			-6	O	-2.9
1945	Cin-N	153	656	81	184	29	2	1	50	37	58	.280	.321	.335	.656	88	-16	-11	94	67	71	.577	19			1	*O	-1.7
1946	Cin-N	121	435	52	99	17	0	2	22	53	40	.228	.318	.280	.599	68	-15	-18	104	68	43	.560	11			1	*O	-1.9
Total	4	433	1540	203	397	63	6	3	98	115	130	.258	.314	.312	.626	78	-48	-43	98	67	157	.563	39			-12	O	-7.3
■ BILL CLAY	Clay, Frederick C. b: 11/23/1874, Baltimore, Md. d: 10/12/17, York, Pa. TR , Deb: 8/08/02																											
1902	Phi-N	3	8	1	2	0	0	0	1	0		.250	.250	.250	.500	53	-0	-0	105	173	1	.333	0			-0	/O	0.0
■ CHET CLEMENS	Clemens, Chester Spurgeon b: 5/10/17, San Fernando, Cal. BR/TR, 6', 175 lbs. Deb: 9/13/39																											
1939	Bos-N	9	23	2	5	0	0	0	1	1	3	.217	.250	.217	.467	29	-2	-2	92	73	1	.389	1			-1	/O	-0.3
1944	Bos-N	19	17	7	3	1	1	0	2	2	2	.176	.263	.353	.616	76	-1	-1	95	120	2	.571	0			-2	/O	-0.3
Total	2	28	40	9	8	1	1	0	3	3	5	.200	.256	.275	.531	49	-3	-3	93	94	3	.469	1			-3	/O	-0.6
■ CLEM CLEMENS	Clemens, Clement Lambert "Count" (born Clement Lambert Ulatowski) b: 11/21/1886, Chicago, Ill. d: 11/2/67, St.Petersburg, Fla. BR/TR, 5'11", 176 lbs. Deb: 5/15/14																											
1914	Chi-F	13	27	4	4	0	0	0	2	3	0	.148	.233	.148	.381	12	-3	-3	91	180	1	.304	0			0	/C	-0.2
1915	Chi-F	11	22	3	3	1	0	0	3	1	0	.136	.174	.182	.356	5	-3	-3	97	270	1	.263	0			0	/C2	-0.2
1916	Chi-N	10	15	0	0	0	0	0	0	1	6	.000	.063	.000	.063	-68	-3	-3	117	0	0	.067	0			-0	/C	-0.3
Total	3	34	64	7	7	1	0	0	5	5	6	.109	.174	.125	.299	-11	-9	-9	99	169	2	.228	0			-0	/C2	-0.7
■ DOUG CLEMENS	Clemens, Douglas Horace b: 6/9/39, Leesport, Pa. BL/TR, 6', 180 lbs. Deb: 10/02/60																											
1960	StL-N	1	0	0	0	0	0	0	0	0	0	—	—	—	—	—	0	0	108	—	—	—	0	0	0	0	/O	0.0
1961	StL-N	6	12	1	2	1	0	0	0	3	1	.167	.333	.250	.583	51	-1	-1	113	0	1	.600	0	0	0	-1	/O	-0.1
1962	StL-N	48	93	12	22	1	1	1	12	17	19	.237	.355	.301	.656	72	-2	-3	109	153	11	.608	0	0	0	-6	O	-1.0
1963	StL-N	5	6	1	1	0	0	1	2	1	2	.167	.286	.667	.952	154	0	0	107	120	1	1.000	0	0	0	0	/O	0.1
1964	StL-N	33	78	8	16	4	3	1	9	6	16	.205	.271	.372	.642	70	-2	-4	112	115	8	.571	0	0	0	-1	O	-0.4
	Chi-N	54	140	23	39	10	2	2	12	18	22	.279	.365	.421	.786	115	4	3	105	76	22	.757	0	0	0	1	O	0.3
	Yr	87	218	31	55	14	5	3	21	24	38	.252	.332	.404	.736	98	2	-0	108	92	31	.691	0	0	0	0		-0.1
1965	Chi-N	128	340	36	75	11	0	4	26	38	53	.221	.303	.288	.591	66	-14	-15	102	98	29	.511	5	8	-3	-7	*O	-2.9
1966	Phi-N	79	121	10	31	1	0	1	15	16	25	.256	.353	.289	.642	80	-2	-3	101	166	14	.587	1	0	0	-1	O/1	-0.4
1967	Phi-N	69	73	2	13	5	0	0	4	8	15	.178	.268	.247	.515	46	-5	-5	104	92	5	.435	0	0	0	-3	O	-0.8
1968	Phi-N	29	57	6	12	1	1	2	8	7	13	.211	.297	.368	.665	101	-0	0	97	125	6	.609	0	0	0	-1	O	-0.1
Total	9	452	920	99	211	34	7	12	88	114	166	.229	.319	.321	.640	77	-22	-26	104	111	100	.588	6	8	-3	-18	O/1	-5.3
■ BOB CLEMENS	Clemens, Robert Baxter b: 8/9/1886, Mt.Hebron, Mo. d: 4/5/64, Marshall, Mo. BR/TR, 5'9", 163 lbs. Deb: 9/17/14																											
1914	StL-A	7	13	1	3	0	1	0	3	2	1	.231	.375	.385	.760	132	1	1	98	225	1	.667	0	2	-1	-1	/O	-0.1
■ WALLY CLEMENT	Clement, Wallace Oakes b: 7/21/1881, Auburn, Me. d: 11/1/53, Coral Gables, Fla. BL/TR, 5'11", 175 lbs. Deb: 8/17/08																											
1908	Phi-N	16	36	0	8	3	0	0	1	0		.222	.222	.306	.528	70	-1	-1	100	35	3	.464	2			0	/O	-0.1
1909	Phi-N	3	3	0	0	0	0	0	0	0		.000	.000	.000	.000	-94	-1	-1	106	0	0	.000	0			0	H	0.0
	Bro-N	92	340	35	88	8	4	0	17	18		.259	.296	.306	.602	89	-6	-5	99	63	33	.528	11			-7	O	-1.7
	Yr	95	343	35	88	8	4	0	17	18		.257	.294	.303	.597	87	-6	-6	99	61	32	.522	11			-7		-1.7
Total	2	111	379	35	96	11	4	0	18	18		.253	.287	.303	.591	86	-8	-7	99	60	35	.516	13			-7	/O	-1.8
■ ROBERTO CLEMENTE	Clemente, Roberto (Walker) "Bob" b: 8/18/34, Carolina, P.R. d: 12/31/72, San Juan, P.R. BR/TR, 5'11", 175 lbs. Deb: 4/17/55 H																											
1955	Pit-N	124	474	48	121	23	11	5	47	18	60	.255	.285	.382	.667	77	-18	-16	97	99	46	.546	2	5	-2	13	*O	-0.7
1956	Pit-N	147	543	66	169	30	7	7	60	13	58	.311	.332	.431	.763	101	1	-0	102	101	72	.652	6	6	-2	7	*O/23	0.0
1957	Pit-N	111	451	42	114	17	7	4	30	23	45	.253	.289	.348	.637	75	-19	-16	94	78	41	.508	0	4	-2	13	*O	-0.8
1958	Pit-N	140	519	69	150	24	10	6	50	31	41	.289	.329	.408	.738	99	-5	-2	95	92	67	.650	8	2	1	**22**	*O	1.7
1959	Pit-N	105	432	60	128	17	7	4	50	15	51	.296	.324	.396	.720	88	-6	-8	103	117	52	.603	2	3	-1	7	*O	-0.3
1960	Pit-N	144	570	89	179	22	6	16	94	39	72	.314	.360	.458	.818	123	17	17	99	131	87	.734	4	5	-2	2	*O	1.3
1961	Pit-N	146	572	100	201	30	10	23	89	35	59	**.351**	.392	.559	.951	150	39	39	99	98	119	.928	4	1	1	14	*O	4.4
1962	Pit-N	144	538	95	168	28	9	10	74	35	73	.312	.355	.454	.809	113	11	9	102	109	81	.730	6	4	-1	12	*O	1.3
1963	Pit-N	152	600	77	192	23	8	17	76	31	64	.320	.357	.470	.827	138	26	27	99	102	94	.758	12	2	2	-2	*O	2.1
1964	Pit-N	155	622	95	**211**	40	7	12	87	51	87	**.339**	.391	.484	.875	143	37	36	101	102	118	.851	5	2	0	-7	*O	2.7
1965	Pit-N	152	589	91	194	21	14	10	65	43	78	**.329**	.380	.463	.843	137	28	28	100	94	101	.799	8	0	2	12	*O	4.0
1966	Pit-N	154	638	105	202	31	11	29	119	46	109	.317	.363	.536	.899	145	38	37	101	112	119	.868	7	5	-1	-2	*O	3.1
1967	Pit-N	147	585	103	**209**	26	10	23	110	41	103	**.357**	.402	.554	.956	**171**	**52**	**52**	100	123	**126**	.962	9	1	2	-2	*O	4.8

YEAR	TM/L	G	AB	R	H	2B	3B	HR	RBI	BB	SO	AVG	OBP	SLG	PRO	/A	BR	/A	PF	CHI	RC	TA	SB	CS	SBR	FR	POS	TPR
1968	Pit-N	132	502	74	146	18	12	18	57	51	77	.291	.357	.482	.839	149	30	29	101	86	82	.796	2	3	-1	0	*O	2.5
1969	Pit-N	138	507	87	175	20	**12**	19	91	56	73	.345	.413	.544	.958	176	45	48	95	112	109	.963	4	1	1	6	*O	4.9
1970	Pit-N	108	412	65	145	22	10	14	60	38	66	.352	.409	.556	.965	161	32	34	97	91	93	.993	3	0	1	5	*O	3.4
1971	Pit-N	132	522	82	178	29	8	13	86	26	65	.341	.372	.502	.874	147	29	30	99	119	90	.792	1	2	-1	9	*O	3.5
1972	Pit-N	102	378	68	118	19	7	10	60	29	49	.312	.361	.479	.840	133	17	16	103	119	61	.764	0	0	0	5	O	1.7
Total	18	2433	9454	1416	3000	440	166	240	1305	621	1230	.317	.362	.475	.837	130	353	362	99	105	1557	.803	83	46	-3	113	*O/23	39.6
■ **ED CLEMENTS**	Clements, Edward b: Philadelphia, Pa. Deb: 6/24/1890																											
1890	Pit-N	1	1	0	0	0	0	0	0	0	0	.000	.000	.000	.000	-99	-0	-0	88	0	0	.000	0			0	/S	0.0
■ **JACK CLEMENTS**	Clements, John J. b: 7/24/1864, Philadelphia, Pa. d: 5/23/41, Norristown, Pa. BL/TL, 5'8.5", 204 lbs. Deb: 4/22/1884 M																											
1884	Phi-U	41	177	37	50	13	2	3		9		.282	.317	.429	.747	162	9	11	93	0	25	.669	0			0	OC/S	1.0
	Phi-N	9	30	3	7	0	0	0	0	4	8	.233	.324	.233	.557	85	-1	-0	92	0	2	.478				0	/C	0.0
1885	Phi-N	52	188	14	36	11	3	1	14	2	30	.191	.200	.298	.498	57	-9	-10	104	84	11	.382				-8	CO	-1.2
1886	Phi-N	54	185	15	38	5	1	0	11	7	34	.205	.234	.243	.478	46	-12	-11	98	80	12	.381	4			5	C/O	-0.2
1887	Phi-N	66	246	48	69	13	7	1	47	9	24	.280	.317	.402	.719	104	-0	1	97	142	34	.672	7			5	C/3S	1.1
1888	Phi-N	86	326	26	80	8	4	1	32	10	36	.245	.276	.304	.580	76	-5	-11	114	115	29	.472	3			-2	C/O	-0.9
1889	Phi-N	78	310	51	88	17	1	4	35	29	21	.284	.347	.384	.731	101	2	0	104	84	43	.685	3			-7	C	-0.4
1890	Phi-N	97	381	64	120	23	8	7	74	45	30	.315	.392	.472	.864	143	26	21	108	118	76	.912	10			0	C/1M	2.4
1891	Phi-N	107	423	58	131	29	4	4	75	43	19	.310	.380	.426	.806	144	20	23	95	121	71	.791	3			-5	*C/1	2.4
1892	Phi-N	109	402	50	106	25	6	8	76	43	40	.264	.339	.415	.755	124	14	11	104	125	61	.743	7			6	*C	2.2
1893	Phi-N	94	376	64	107	20	3	17	80	39	29	.285	.360	.489	.849	127	12	12	100	95	69	.859	3			-9	*C/1	0.9
1894	Phi-N	45	159	26	55	6	5	3	36	24	7	.346	.455	.503	.959	140	10	12	95	114	40	1.135	6			2	C	1.3
1895	Phi-N	88	322	64	127	27	2	13	75	22	7	.394	.446	.612	1.058	175	34	34	99	89	91	1.179	3			-10	*C	2.5
1896	Phi-N	57	184	35	66	5	7	5	45	17	14	.359	.427	.543	.971	154	15	14	102	113	45	1.051	2			-1	C	1.5
1897	Phi-N	55	185	18	44	4	2	6	36	12		.238	.305	.378	.684	85	-5	-4	96	120	23	.645	3			-2	C	0.0
1898	StL-N	99	335	39	86	19	5	3	41	21		.257	.314	.370	.684	93	-1	-4	106	95	40	.614	1			-1	C	0.1
1899	Cle-N	4	12	1	3	0	0	0	0	0		.250	.308	.250	.558	63	-1	-0	89	0	1	.444	0			0	/C	0.0
1900	Bos-N	16	42	6	13	1	0	1	10	3		.310	.356	.405	.760	93	1	-1	120	156	6	.690	0			0	C	0.0
Total	17	1157	4283	619	1226	226	60	77	687	339	299	.286	.347	.421	.768	118	109	99	102	103	680	.738	55			-27	*C/O13S	12.7
■ **VERNE CLEMONS**	Clemons, Verne James "Stinger" or "Tubby" b: 9/8/1891, Clemons, Iowa d: 5/5/59, Bay Pines, Fla. BR/TR, 5'9.5", 190 lbs. Deb: 4/22/16																											
1916	StL-A	4	7	0	1	1	0	0	0	0	1	.143	.143	.286	.429	30	-1	-1	95	0	0	.333	0			0	/C	0.0
1919	StL-N	88	239	14	63	13	2	2	22	26	13	.264	.336	.360	.696	116	3	5	94	93	29	.659	4			2	C	1.3
1920	StL-N	112	338	17	95	10	6	1	36	30	12	.281	.340	.355	.695	102	0	1	98	113	42	.619	1	1	-0	-4	*C	0.4
1921	StL-N	117	341	29	109	16	2	2	48	33	17	.320	.380	.396	.776	111	4	6	95	125	53	.724	0	0	0	-9	*C	0.4
1922	StL-N	71	160	9	41	4	0	0	15	18	5	.256	.331	.281	.613	59	-9	-9	101	116	16	.538	1	0	0	-1	C	-0.8
1923	StL-N	57	130	6	37	9	1	0	13	10	11	.285	.345	.369	.714	98	-2	-0	90	95	17	.645	0	0	0	-3	C	-0.1
1924	StL-N	25	56	3	18	3	0	0	6	2	3	.321	.345	.375	.720	91	-1	-1	103	104	7	.605	0	0	0	-1	C	0.0
Total	7	474	1271	78	364	56	11	5	140	119	62	.286	.348	.360	.708	99	-5	1	96	110	164	.643	6	1		-15	C	1.2
■ **DONN CLENDENON**	Clendenon, Donn Alvin b: 7/15/35, Neosho, Mo. BR/TR, 6'4", 209 lbs. Deb: 9/22/61																											
1961	Pit-N	9	35	7	11	1	1	0	2	5	10	.314	.400	.400	.800	114	1	1	99	55	6	.792	0	0	0	1	/O	0.1
1962	Pit-N	80	222	39	67	8	5	7	28	26	58	.302	.378	.477	.855	125	9	8	102	87	42	.920	16	4	2	-0	1O	0.7
1963	Pit-N	154	563	65	155	28	7	15	57	39	136	.275	.328	.430	.758	118	11	12	99	85	75	.708	22	13	-1	5	*1	1.4
1964	Pit-N	133	457	53	129	23	8	12	64	26	96	.282	.324	.446	.770	113	8	7	101	109	62	.705	12	8	-1	-3	*1	0.0
1965	Pit-N	162	612	89	184	32	14	14	96	48	128	.301	.356	.467	.824	130	24	24	100	129	99	.779	9	9	-3	1	*1/3	1.5
1966	Pit-N	155	571	80	171	22	10	28	98	52	142	.299	.360	.520	.880	140	31	30	101	110	102	.853	8	7	-2	-2	*1	1.9
1967	Pit-N	131	478	46	119	15	2	13	56	34	107	.249	.300	.370	.670	91	-6	-6	100	110	49	.571	4	4	-1	2	*1	-1.1
1968	Pit-N	158	584	63	150	20	6	17	87	47	163	.257	.313	.399	.712	111	8	7	101	132	72	.645	10	3	1	8	*1	1.2
1969	Mon-N	38	129	14	31	6	1	4	14	6	32	.240	.274	.395	.669	85	-3	-3	100	89	11	.538	0	2	-1	3	1O	-0.3
	NY-N	72	202	31	51	5	0	12	37	19	62	.252	.323	.455	.778	115	4	3	100	116	30	.744	3	2	-0	-1	1/O	-0.2
	Yr	110	331	45	82	11	1	16	51	25	94	.248	.304	.432	.736	104	1	0	100	107	43	.676	3	4	-2	1		-0.5
1970	NY-N	121	396	65	114	18	3	22	97	39	91	.288	.353	.515	.868	125	15	13	104	139	68	.832	4	1	1	0	*1	0.5
1971	NY-N	88	263	29	65	10	0	11	37	21	78	.247	.305	.411	.716	105	-0	1	96	107	29	.618	1	2	-1	-1	1	-0.6
1972	StL-N	61	136	13	26	4	0	4	9	17	37	.191	.281	.309	.590	64	-6	-7	105	68	10	.504	1	2	-1	1	1	-0.9
Total	12	1362	4648	594	1273	192	57	159	682	379	1140	.274	.331	.442	.774	116	94	91	101	111	657	.740	90	57	-7	12	*1/O3	4.2
■ **ELMER CLEVELAND**	Cleveland, Elmer Ellsworth b: 9/15/1862, Washington, D.C. d: 10/8/13, Zimmerman, Pa. BR/TR, Deb: 8/29/1884																											
1884	Cin-U	29	115	24	37	9	1	1		4		.322	.345	.443	.788	153	7	6	108	0	18	.705	0			1	3	0.7
1888	NY-N	9	34	6	8	0	2	2	5	3	1	.235	.297	.529	.827	174	2	3	93	79	6	.846	1			0	/3	0.2
	Pit-N	30	108	10	24	2	1	2	11	5	23	.222	.270	.315	.584	93	-1	-1	95	100	10	.524	3			0	3	0.0
	Yr	39	142	16	32	2	3	4	16	8	24	.225	.276	.366	.643	112	1	2	94	97	16	.600	4			0		0.2
1891	Col-a	12	41	12	7	0	0	0	4	12	9	.171	.370	.171	.541	66	-1	-0	89	146	4	.706	4			0	3	0.0
Total	3	80	298	52	76	11	4	5	20	24	33	.255	.317	.369	.686	122	7	8	98	69	38	.653	8			1	/3	0.9
■ **STAN CLIBURN**	Cliburn, Stanley Gene b: 12/19/56, Jackson, Miss. BR/TR, 6', 195 lbs. Deb: 5/06/80																											
1980	Cal-A	54	56	7	10	2	0	2	6	3	9	.179	.220	.321	.542	49	-4	-4	96	97	4	.447	0	0	0	-6	C	-0.6
■ **HARLOND CLIFT**	Clift, Harlond Benton "Darkie" b: 8/12/12, El Reno, Okla. BR/TR, 5'11", 180 lbs. Deb: 4/17/34																											
1934	StL-A	147	572	104	149	30	10	14	56	84	100	.260	.357	.421	.778	96	0	-3	104	58	91	.786	7	2	1	-17	*3	-1.7
1935	StL-A	137	475	101	140	26	4	11	69	83	39	.295	.406	.436	.842	111	16	11	107	100	89	.876	0	3	-2	-7	*3/2	0.3
1936	StL-A	152	576	145	174	40	11	20	73	115	68	.302	.424	.514	.938	126	31	27	103	59	134	1.059	12	4	1	2	*3	2.8
1937	StL-A	155	571	103	175	36	7	29	118	98	80	.306	.413	.546	.960	142	36	37	99	107	134	1.057	8	5	-1	**40**	*3	**7.1**
1938	StL-A	149	534	119	155	25	7	34	118	118	67	.290	.423	.554	.977	143	38	38	100	106	133	1.117	10	5	0	14	*3	5.0
1939	StL-A	151	526	90	142	25	2	15	84	**111**	55	.270	.402	.411	.813	108	11	10	100	115	97	.855	4	3	-1	12	*3	1.7
1940	StL-A	150	523	92	143	29	5	20	87	104	62	.273	.396	.463	.859	115	20	15	106	110	103	.899	9	8	-2	7	*3	2.6
1941	StL-A	154	584	108	149	33	9	17	84	113	93	.255	.376	.430	.806	113	13	13	100	95	102	.820	6	4	-1	0	*3	1.9
1942	StL-A	143	541	108	148	39	4	7	55	106	48	.274	.394	.399	.794	119	21	18	104	79	95	.813	6	4	-1	4	*3/S	2.4
1943	StL-A	105	379	43	88	11	3	3	25	54	37	.232	.329	.301	.630	85	-6	-6	100	79	40	.570	5	4	-1	14	*3	0.9
	Was-A	8	30	4	9	0	0	0	4	5	3	.300	.417	.300	.717	107	1	1	104	156	4	.682	0	0	0	-1	/3	0.0
	Yr	113	409	47	97	11	3	3	29	59	40	.237	.336	.301	.637	86	-5	-5	101	85	48	.596	5	4	-1	13		0.9
1944	Was-A	12	44	4	7	3	0	0	3	3	3	.159	.213	.227	.440	29	-4	-4	90	110	2	.342	0	0	0	0	3	-0.3
1945	Was-A	119	375	49	79	12	0	8	53	76	58	.211	.349	.307	.656	98	-1	2	93	138	48	.657	2	1	0	-4	*3	0.0
Total	12	1582	5730	1070	1558	309	62	178	829	1070	713	.272	.390	.441	.831	116	173	158	102	94	1072	.878	69	43	-5	66	*3/2S	22.7
■ **FLEA CLIFTON**	Clifton, Herman Earl b: 12/12/09, Cincinnati, Ohio BR/TR, 5'10", 160 lbs. Deb: 4/29/34																											
1934	Det-A	16	16	3	1	0	0	0	1	1	2	.063	.118	.063	.180	-54	-4	-4	98	334	0	.133	0	0	0	0	/32	-0.2
1935	Det-A	43	110	15	28	5	0	0	9	5	13	.255	.293	.300	.593	56	-8	-7	97	93	10	.494	2	1	0	-1	3/2S	-0.6
1936	Det-A	13	26	5	5	1	0	0	1	4	3	.192	.300	.231	.531	34	-3	-3	95	54	2	.455	0	1	-1	0	/S32	-0.1
1937	Det-A	15	43	4	5	1	0	0	2	7	10	.116	.240	.140	.380	-2	-7	-7	109	114	2	.421	3	0	1	-1	/3S2	-0.5
Total	4	87	195	27	39	7	0	0	13	17	28	.200	.268	.236	.504	30	-21	-21	99	111	14	.437	5	2	0	-2	/3S2	-1.4
■ **MONK CLINE**	Cline, John P. b: 3/3/1858, Ohio d: 9/23/16, Louisville, Ky. BL/TL, 5'4", 150 lbs. Deb: 7/04/1882																											
1882	Bal-a	44	172	18	38	6	2	0		3		.221	.234	.279	.513	78	-5	-3	92	0	12	.381				6	O/S23	0.2
1884	Lou-a	94	396	91	115	16	7	2		27		.290	.342	.381	.723	156	17	24	89	0	53	.648				8	*O/S	2.8
1885	Lou-a	2	9	0	2	1	0	0		0		.222	.222	.333	.556	74	-0	-0	102	0	1	.429				0	/O3	0.0
1888	KC-a	73	293	45	69	13	2	0	19	20		.235	.289	.294	.582	84	-3	-6	106	63	34	.612	29			5	O/23	-0.2
1891	Lou-a	21	76	13	23	3	1	0	12	19	3	.303	.442	.368	.811	150	5	6	90	109	14	.925	2			0	O	0.5

YEAR	TM/L	G	AB	R	H	2B	3B	HR	RBI	BB	SO	AVG	OBP	SLG	PRO	/A	BR	/A	PF	CHI	RC	TA	SB	CS	SBR	FR	POS	TPR
Total	5	234	946	167	247	39	12	2	31	69	3	.261	.315	.334	.649	117	14	21	95	30	113	.604	31			20	O/S23	3.3
■ **TY CLINE**	Cline, Tyrone Alexander b: 6/15/39, Hampton, S.C. BL/TL, 6'0.5", 170 lbs. Deb: 9/14/60																											
1960	Cle-A	7	26	2	8	1	1	0	2	0	4	.308	.308	.423	.731	98	-0	-0	98	73	3	.579	0	0	0	2	/O	0.1
1961	Cle-A	12	43	9	9	2	1	0	1	6	1	.209	.333	.302	.636	74	-2	-1	96	32	5	.647	1	0	0	-1	O	-0.2
1962	Cle-A	118	375	53	93	15	5	2	28	28	50	.248	.309	.331	.639	74	-15	-13	98	85	39	.557	5	4	-1	-4	*O	-2.2
1963	Mil-N	72	174	17	41	2	1	0	10	10	31	.236	.285	.259	.544	57	-9	-9	101	93	14	.437	2	1	0	4	O	-0.8
1964	Mil-N	101	116	22	35	4	2	1	13	8	22	.302	.362	.397	.759	117	2	3	97	109	18	.695	0	1	-1	-7	O/1	-0.6
1965	Mil-N	123	220	27	42	5	3	0	10	16	50	.191	.246	.241	.487	36	-18	-19	104	78	14	.392	2	2	-1	-5	O/1	-2.8
1966	Chi-N	7	17	3	6	0	0	0	2	0	2	.353	.353	.353	.706	97	-0	-0	100	140	2	.583	1	0	0	-1	/O	0.0
	Atl-N	42	71	12	18	0	0	0	6	3	11	.254	.303	.254	.556	57	-4	-4	99	140	5	.446	2	1	0	-2	O/1	-0.7
	Yr	49	88	15	24	0	0	0	8	3	13	.273	.312	.273	.585	65	-4	-4	99	143	8	.478	3	1	0	-3		-0.7
1967	Atl-N	10	8	0	0	0	0	0	0	0	3	.000	.111	.000	.111	-63	-2	-2	104	0	0	.125	0	0	0	-0	/O	-0.1
	SF-N	64	122	18	33	5	5	0	4	9	13	.270	.326	.393	.719	104	1	1	101	34	16	.659	2	1	0	-4	O	-0.5
	Yr	74	130	18	33	5	5	0	4	9	16	.254	.312	.369	.681	93	-1	-1	101	30	16	.616	2	1	0	-4		-0.6
1968	SF-N	116	291	37	65	6	3	1	28	11	26	.223	.254	.275	.529	60	-15	-14	98	142	20	.397	0	2	-1	-5	O1	-2.8
1969	Mon-N	101	209	26	50	5	3	2	12	32	22	.239	.346	.321	.666	87	-2	-2	100	66	25	.636	4	3	-1	3	O1	-0.3
1970	Mon-N	2	2	0	1	0	0	0	0	0	0	.500	.500	.500	1.000	169	0	0	100	0	1	1.000	0	0	0	0	H	0.0
	Cin-N	48	63	13	17	7	1	0	8	12	11	.270	.387	.413	.799	110	2	1	104	119	11	.813	1	2	-1	-1	O/1	-0.1
	Yr	50	65	13	18	7	1	0	8	12	11	.277	.390	.415	.805	111	2	1	104	115	11	.816	1	2	-1	-1		-0.1
1971	Cin-N	69	97	12	19	1	0	0	1	18	16	.196	.333	.206	.540	58	-5	-4	96	20	8	.525	2	2	-1	-4	O/1	-1.0
Total	12	892	1834	251	437	53	25	6	125	153	262	.238	.304	.304	.609	72	-66	-65	99	88	180	.532	22	19	-5	-25	O/1	-12.0
■ **GENE CLINES**	Clines, Eugene Anthony b: 10/6/46, San Pablo, Cal. BR/TR, 5'9", 170 lbs. Deb: 6/28/70 C																											
1970	Pit-N	31	37	4	15	2	0	0	3	2	5	.405	.436	.459	.895	145	2	2	97	68	7	.840	2	1	0	-2	/O	0.0
1971	Pit-N	97	273	52	84	12	4	1	24	22	36	.308	.366	.392	.758	116	6	6	99	89	42	.750	15	6	1	4	O	0.9
1972	Pit-N	107	311	52	104	15	6	0	17	16	47	.334	.371	.421	.792	121	10	9	103	53	47	.732	12	6	0	-6	O	0.0
1973	Pit-N	110	304	42	80	11	3	1	23	26	36	.263	.327	.329	.656	90	-7	-4	92	90	30	.564	8	7	-2	-1	O	-0.9
1974	Pit-N	107	276	29	62	5	1	0	14	30	40	.225	.310	.250	.560	59	-15	-14	98	78	23	.515	14	2	3	6	O	-0.7
1975	NY-N	82	203	25	46	6	3	0	10	11	21	.227	.270	.286	.555	57	-13	-12	95	67	15	.448	4	4	-1	2	O	-1.3
1976	Tex-A	116	446	52	123	12	3	0	38	16	52	.276	.307	.316	.623	81	-10	-11	102	106	39	.493	11	9	-2	1	*OD	-1.5
1977	Chi-N	101	239	27	70	12	2	3	41	25	25	.293	.362	.397	.760	91	2	-3	114	158	34	.685	1	2	-1	-10	O	-1.5
1978	Chi-N	109	229	31	59	10	2	0	17	21	28	.258	.323	.319	.641	72	-6	-9	110	92	24	.556	4	3	-1	-8	O	-2.0
1979	Chi-N	10	10	0	2	0	0	0	0	0	1	.200	.200	.200	.400	8	-1	-1	112	0	0	.250	0	0	0	0	/H	0.0
Total	10	870	2328	314	645	85	24	5	187	169	291	.277	.331	.341	.672	88	-32	-36	101	91	260	.611	71	40	-3	-12	O/D	-7.0
■ **BILLY CLINGMAN**	Clingman, William Frederick b: 11/21/1869, Cincinnati, Ohio d: 5/14/58, Cincinnati, Ohio BB/TR, 5'11", 150 lbs. Deb: 9/09/1890																											
1890	Cin-N	7	27	2	7	1	0	0	5	1	0	.259	.286	.296	.582	66	-1	-1	108	193	2	.450	0			0	/S2	0.0
1891	CM-a	1	5	0	1	1	0	0		0	0	.200	.200	.400	.600	65	-0	-0	112	0	0	.500	0			0	/2	0.0
1895	Pit-N	106	382	69	99	16	4	0	45	41	43	.259	.334	.322	.656	74	-15	-13	97	104	49	.654	19			13	*3	0.2
1896	Lou-N	121	423	57	99	10	2	2	37	57	51	.234	.329	.281	.611	65	-20	-19	98	87	47	.611	19			19	*3	0.5
1897	Lou-N	113	395	59	90	14	7	2	47	37		.228	.302	.314	.616	68	-20	-17	95	108	43	.590	14			27	*3	0.9
1898	Lou-N	154	538	65	138	12	6	0	50	51		.257	.327	.301	.628	86	-10	-7	96	95	59	.582	15			11	3S/O2	0.8
1899	Lou-N	109	366	67	96	15	4	2	44	46		.262	.348	.342	.689	89	-3	-5	103	105	49	.689	13			-13	*S	-0.9
1900	Chi-N	47	159	15	33	6	0	0	11	17		.208	.284	.245	.529	53	-11	-9	93	90	13	.492	6			-16	S	-1.8
1901	Was-A	137	480	66	116	10	7	2	56	42		.242	.303	.304	.607	71	-18	-17	99	119	48	.544	10			18	*S	0.8
1903	Cle-A	21	64	10	18	1	1	0	7	11		.281	.387	.328	.715	123	2	2	96	122	9	.739	2			1	2/S3	0.4
Total	10	816	2839	410	697	86	31	8	302	303	94	.246	.322	.306	.628	75	-96	-86	98	103	320	.601	98			61	3S/2O	0.9
■ **JIM CLINTON**	Clinton, James Lawrence "Big Jim" b: 8/10/1850, New York, N.Y. d: 9/3/21, Brooklyn, N.Y. BR/TR, 5'8.5", 174 lbs. Deb: 5/21/1872 M																											
1872	Eck-n	24	101	11	19							.188															/3/OS2M	
1873	Res-n	9	40	5	9							.225															/3O	
1874	Atl-n	2	11	3	2							.182															/2O	
1875	Atl-n	22	83	3	10							.120															P/O12	
1876	Lou-N	16	65	8	22	2	0	0	0	0	0	.338	.338	.369	.708	130	2	2	104	0	8	.558				0	O/1P	0.2
1882	Wor-N	26	98	9	16	2	0	0	3	7	13	.163	.219	.184	.403	31	-7	-7	100	59	4	.305				-4	O	-1.0
1883	Bal-a	94	399	69	125	16	8	0		27		.313	.357	.393	.750	132	19	14	107	0	57	.672				4	*O/2	1.7
1884	Bal-a	104	437	82	118	12	6	3		29		.270	.334	.346	.680	127	13	14	99	0	52	.605				-2	*O/2	0.9
1885	Cin-a	105	408	48	97	5	5	0		15		.238	.277	.275	.551	74	-10	-12	104	0	32	.431				-1	*O	-1.7
1886	Bal-a	23	83	8	15	1	0	0		4		.181	.227	.193	.420	37	-6	-5	91	0	4	.353	3			0	O	-0.3
Total	4 n	57	235	22	40							.170															O	
Total	6	368	1490	224	393	38	19	3	3	82	13	.264	.311	.321	.632	103	11	5	102	4	158	.532	3			-3	O/3P21S	-0.2
■ **LOU CLINTON**	Clinton, Luciean Louis b: 10/13/37, Ponca City, Okla. BR/TR, 6'1", 185 lbs. Deb: 4/22/60																											
1960	Bos-A	96	298	37	68	17	5	6	37	20	66	.228	.283	.379	.663	75	-10	-12	103	111	29	.569	4	3	-1	0	O	-1.5
1961	Bos-A	17	51	4	13	2	1	0	3	2	10	.255	.283	.333	.616	63	-3	-3	102	69	5	.500	0	0	0	3	O	0.0
1962	Bos-A	114	398	63	117	24	10	18	75	34	79	.294	.351	.540	.891	133	18	17	102	111	75	.875	2	1	0	0	*O	1.4
1963	Bos-A	148	560	71	130	23	7	22	77	49	118	.232	.295	.416	.711	91	-4	-8	106	114	65	.633	0	0	0	8	*O	-0.4
1964	Bos-A	37	120	15	31	4	3	3	6	9	33	.258	.310	.417	.727	98	-0	-0	102	43	15	.645	1	0	0	4	O	0.3
	LA-A	91	306	30	76	18	0	9	38	31	40	.248	.320	.395	.715	110	-1	3	89	111	40	.664	3	0	1	3	O	0.3
	Yr	128	426	45	107	22	3	12	44	40	73	.251	.317	.401	.718	106	-1	3	92	92	57	.667	4	0	1	7		0.6
1965	Cal-A	89	222	29	54	12	3	1	8	23	37	.243	.317	.338	.655	88	-4	-3	98	43	23	.571	2	3	-1	-2	O	-0.9
	KC-A	1	1	0	0	0	0	0	0	0	0	.000	.000	.000	.000	-99	-0	-0	97	0	0	.000	0	0	0	-0	/O	0.0
	Cle-A	12	34	2	6	1	0	1	2	3	7	.176	.243	.294	.537	53	-2	-2	98	64	3	.464	0	0	0	0	/O	-0.1
	Yr	102	257	31	60	13	3	2	10	26	44	.233	.306	.331	.637	83	-6	-6	98	45	28	.570	2	3	-1	-2		-1.0
1966	NY-A	80	159	18	35	10	2	5	21	16	27	.220	.291	.403	.694	104	-1	0	94	112	19	.630	0	0	0	-8	O	-1.0
1967	NY-A	6	4	1	2	1	0	0	2	1	1	.500	.600	.750	1.350	315	1	1	94	278	2	2.000	0	0	0	-0	/O	0.1
Total	8	691	2153	270	532	112	31	65	269	188	418	.247	.310	.418	.728	99	-6	-6	100	99	275	.681	12	7	-1	8	O	-1.8
■ **ED CLOUGH**	Clough, Edgar George "Big Ed" or "Spec" b: 10/28/06, Wiconisco, Pa. d: 1/30/44, Harrisburg, Pa. BL/TL, 6', 188 lbs. Deb: 8/28/24																											
1924	StL-N	7	14	0	1	0	0	0	1	0	3	.071	.071	.071	.143	-60	-3	-3	103	365	0	.077	0	0	0	0	/O	-0.2
1925	StL-N	3	4	0	1	0	0	0	0	0	0	.250	.250	.250	.500	28	-0	-0	102	0	0	.333	0	0	0	-0	/P	0.0
1926	StL-N	1	1	0	0	0	0	0	0	0	0	.000	.000	.000	.000	-98	-0	-0	102	0	0	.000	0			0	/P	0.0
Total	3	11	19	0	2	0	0	0	1	0	3	.105	.105	.105	.211	-43	-4	-4	102	269	0	.118	0	0		0	/OP	-0.2
■ **OTIS CLYMER**	Clymer, Otis Edgar b: 1/27/1876, Pine Grove, Pa. d: 2/27/26, St.Paul, Minn. BB/TR, 5'11", 180 lbs. Deb: 4/14/05																											
1905	Pit-N	96	365	74	108	11	5	0	23	19		.296	.331	.353	.684	102	2	0	104	66	52	.665	23			-3	O/1	-0.8
1906	Pit-N	11	45	7	11	0	1	0	1	3		.244	.292	.289	.581	80	-1	-1	104	24	4	.500	1			-0	O	-0.1
1907	Pit-N	22	66	8	15	2	0	0	4	4		.227	.271	.258	.529	64	-2	-3	105	89	6	.510	5			1	O/1	-0.1
	Was-A	57	206	30	65	5	5	1	16	18		.316	.371	.403	.773	165	11	14	90	70	38	.844	18			-13	O	-0.1
1908	Was-A	110	368	32	93	11	4	1	35	20		.253	.291	.313	.604	103	-1	1	95	114	37	.560	19			5	O2/3	0.1
1909	Was-A	45	138	11	27	5	2	0	6	17		.196	.284	.261	.545	80	-4	-2	90	65	12	.541	7			-5	O	-1.0
1913	Chi-N	30	105	16	24	5	1	0	7	14	18	.229	.319	.295	.615	77	-3	-3	99	84	12	.667	9			-1	O	-0.3
	Bos-N	14	37	4	12	3	1	0	6	3	3	.324	.375	.459	.834	145	2	2	95	128	7	.880	2			-1	O	0.0
	Yr	44	142	20	36	8	2	0	13	17	21	.254	.333	.338	.671	94	-1	-1	97	100	18	.717	11			-2		-0.3
Total	6	385	1330	182	355	42	19	2	98	98	21	.267	.317	.332	.649	105	4	8	97	82	168	.639	84			-17	O/231	-2.3

YEAR	TM/L	G	AB	R	H	2B	3B	HR	RBI	BB	SO	AVG	OBP	SLG	PRO	/A	BR	/A	PF	CHI	RC	TA	SB	CS	SBR	FR	POS	TPR
■ **BILL CLYMER**	Clymer, William Johnston "Derby Day Bill" b: 12/18/1873, Philadelphia, Pa. d: 12/26/36, Philadelphia, Pa. Deb: 6/26/1891 C																											
1891	Phi-a	3	11	0	0	0	0	0	0	1	2	.000	.154	.000	.154	-53	-2	-2	103	0	0	.273	1			0	/S	-0.1
■ **GIL COAN**	Coan, Gilbert Fitzgerald b: 5/18/22, Monroe, N.C. BL/TR, 6', 180 lbs. Deb: 4/27/46																											
1946	Was-A	59	134	17	28	3	2	3	9	7	37	.209	.269	.328	.597	72	-6	-5	92	65	12	.523	2	2	-1	-3	O	-1.0
1947	Was-A	11	42	5	21	3	2	0	3	5	6	.500	.553	.667	1.220	246	8	8	97	38	17	1.591	2	1	0	0	O	0.8
1948	Was-A	138	513	56	119	13	9	7	60	41	78	.232	.298	.333	.631	66	-25	-27	103	112	55	.593	23	9	2	11	*O	-1.9
1949	Was-A	111	358	36	78	7	8	3	25	29	58	.218	.278	.307	.586	60	-25	-21	91	72	32	.514	9	6	-1	3	O	-2.0
1950	Was-A	104	366	58	111	17	4	7	50	28	46	.303	.359	.429	.788	102	-0	0	99	97	60	.762	10	5	0	-3	O	-0.3
1951	Was-A	135	538	85	163	25	7	9	62	39	62	.303	.357	.426	.782	116	7	10	95	92	85	.731	8	5	-1	**24**	*O	2.8
1952	Was-A	107	332	50	68	11	6	5	20	32	35	.205	.277	.319	.596	65	-16	-16	100	62	32	.548	9	4	0	0	O	-1.8
1953	Was-A	68	168	28	33	1	4	2	17	22	23	.196	.301	.286	.586	62	-9	-8	94	117	17	.580	7	0	**2**	1	O	-0.6
1954	Bal-A	94	265	29	74	11	1	2	20	16	17	.279	.323	.351	.674	89	-6	-4	95	77	31	.607	9	4	0	-1	O	-0.6
1955	Bal-A	61	130	18	31	7	1	1	11	13	15	.238	.313	.331	.643	81	-5	-3	90	89	14	.592	4	2	0	-6	O	-1.0
	Chi-A	17	17	0	3	0	0	0	1	0	5	.176	.176	.176	.353	-5	-2	-3	101	124	1	.214	0	0	0	-1	/O	-0.3
	Yr	78	147	18	34	7	1	1	12	13	20	.231	.298	.313	.611	70	-7	-6	92	98	15	.557	4	2	0	-6		-1.3
	NY-N	9	13	0	2	0	0	0	0	0	1	.154	.154	.154	.308	-18	-2	-2	99	0	0	.182	0	0	0	-2	/O	-0.3
1956	NY-N	4	1	2	0	0	0	0	0	0	1	.000	.000	.000	.000	-99	-0	-0	97	0	0	.000	0	0	0	0	H	0.0
Total	11	918	2877	384	731	98	44	39	278	232	384	.254	.316	.359	.675	84	-83	-72	97	88	355	.630	83	38	2	24	O	-6.2
■ **JOE COBB**	Cobb, Joseph Stanley (born Joseph Stanley Serafin) b: 1/24/1895, Hudson, Pa. d: 12/24/47, Allentown, Pa. BR/TR, 5'9", 170 lbs. Deb: 4/25/18																											
1918	Det-A	1	0	0	0	0	0	0	0	1	0	—	1.000	—	1.359	321	0	0	97	0	0	—	0			0	H	0.0
■ **TY COBB**	Cobb, Tyrus Raymond "The Georgia Peach" b: 12/18/1886, Narrows, Ga. d: 7/17/61, Atlanta, Ga. BL/TR, 6'1", 175 lbs. Deb: 8/30/05 MH																											
1905	Det-A	41	150	19	36	6	0	1	15	10		.240	.287	.300	.587	90	-2	-2	98	118	14	.500	2			2	O	-0.1
1906	Det-A	98	358	45	113	15	5	1	34	19		.316	.350	.394	.744	125	13	10	108	91	59	.747	23			9	O	1.7
1907	Det-A	150	605	97	**212**	28	14	5	**119**	24		**.350**	.375	**.468**	**.843**	**168**	**44**	**43**	102	137	**128**	**.906**	**49**			14	*O	5.2
1908	Det-A	150	581	88	**188**	**36**	**20**	4	**108**	34		**.324**	.361	**.475**	**.836**	**172**	**44**	**43**	101	135	**110**	**.888**	39			5	*O	4.5
1909	Det-A	156	573	**116**	**216**	33	10	**9**	**107**	48		**.377**	**.431**	**.517**	**.947**	**181**	**63**	**57**	110	123	**157**	**1.193**	**76**			12	*O	**6.9**
1910	Det-A	140	506	**106**	194	35	13	8	91	64		.383	**.456**	**.551**	**1.008**	**211**	68	67	102	118	**156**	**1.321**	65			-2	*O	6.3
1911	Det-A	146	591	**147**	**248**	**47**	**24**	8	**127**	44		**.420**	.467	**.621**	**1.088**	187	**78**	**72**	108	106	**207**	**1.464**	**83**			7	*O	6.5
1912	Det-A	140	553	119	**227**	30	23	7	83	43		**.410**	.458	**.586**	**1.043**	**209**	68	**72**	95	85	174	**1.328**	61			-5	*O	5.7
1913	Det-A	122	428	70	167	18	16	4	67	58	31	**.390**	**.467**	.535	1.002	**195**	52	52	99	105	124	**1.314**	52			2	*O	5.0
1914	Det-A	97	345	69	127	22	11	2	57	57	22	.368	.466	.513	.979	191	42	41	102	124	89	1.170	35	17	0	-3	O	3.6
1915	Det-A	156	563	**144**	**208**	31	13	3	99	118	43	**.369**	**.486**	.487	**.973**	177	**72**	**65**	108	114	**155**	**1.267**	**96**	38	6	-6	*O	5.9
1916	Det-A	145	542	**113**	201	31	10	5	68	78	39	.371	.452	.493	.944	176	58	55	105	91	**136**	**1.137**	**68**	24	6	9	*O/1	6.0
1917	Det-A	152	588	107	**225**	**44**	**23**	7	102	61	34	**.383**	**.444**	**.571**	**1.016**	**215**	**75**	**76**	98	99	**165**	**1.256**	**55**			6	*O	**7.9**
1918	Det-A	111	421	83	161	19	**14**	3	64	41	21	**.382**	**.440**	**.515**	**.955**	**195**	**44**	**46**	97	109	**105**	**1.131**	34			-4	01/P23	3.9
1919	Det-A	124	497	92	**191**	36	13	1	70	38	22	**.384**	.429	.515	.944	176	42	46	93	94	116	1.056	28			9	*O	4.7
1920	Det-A	112	428	86	143	28	8	2	63	58	28	.334	.416	.451	.867	126	20	18	103	107	82	.905	14	10	-2	2	*O	0.8
1921	Det-A	128	507	124	197	37	16	12	101	56	19	.389	.452	.596	1.048	172	50	53	96	108	134	1.178	22	15	-2	20	*OM	5.5
1922	Det-A	137	526	99	211	42	16	4	99	55	24	.401	.462	.565	1.026	170	52	54	98	121	133	1.113	9	13	-5	-1	*OM	3.6
1923	Det-A	145	556	103	189	40	7	6	88	66	14	.340	.413	.469	.882	136	27	30	97	114	108	.899	9	10	-3	-1	*OM	1.2
1924	Det-A	155	625	115	211	38	10	4	74	85	18	.338	.418	.450	.867	124	25	25	100	80	121	.911	23	14	-2	2	*OM	1.3
1925	Det-A	121	415	97	157	31	12	12	102	65	12	.378	.468	.598	**1.066**	**170**	45	46	99	123	118	**1.240**	13	9	-2	-8	*O/PM	2.5
1926	Det-A	79	233	48	79	18	5	4	62	26	2	.339	.408	.511	.918	143	13	14	97	161	49	.981	9	4	0	-3	OM	0.7
1927	Phi-A	134	490	104	175	32	7	5	93	67	12	.357	.440	.482	.921	144	31	34	97	131	104	1.048	22	0	7	-5	*O	1.9
1928	Phi-A	95	353	54	114	27	4	1	40	34	16	.323	.389	.431	.819	112	8	7	103	90	58	.789	5	8	-3	-6	O	-0.6
Total	24	3034	11434	2245	4190	724	294	118	1933	1249	357	.366	.432	.512	.945	168	1033	1025	101	111	2801	1.091	892	162		54	*O/1P32	90.6
■ **DAVE COBLE**	Coble, David Lamar b: 12/24/12, Monroe, N.C. d: 10/15/71, Orlando, Fla. BR/TR, 6'1", 183 lbs. Deb: 5/01/39																											
1939	Phi-N	15	25	2	7	1	0	0	0	0	3	.280	.280	.320	.600	65	-1	-1	94	0	2	.421	0			-0	C	0.0
■ **DAVE COCHRANE**	Cochrane, David Carter b: 1/31/63, Riverside, Cal. BB/TR, 6'2", 180 lbs. Deb: 9/02/86																											
1986	Chi-A	19	62	4	12	2	0	1	2	5	22	.194	.254	.274	.528	44	-5	-5	101	40	4	.423	0	0	0	-1	3/S	-0.5
■ **GEORGE COCHRAN**	Cochran, George Leslie b: 2/12/1889, Rusk, Tex. d: 5/21/60, Harbor City, Cal. TR , Deb: 7/29/18																											
1918	Bos-A	24	60	7	7	0	0	0	3	10	6	.117	.264	.117	.381	16	-6	-5	95	156	2	.415	3			0	3/S	-0.5
■ **MICKEY COCHRANE**	Cochrane, Gordon Stanley b: 4/6/03, Bridgewater, Mass. d: 6/28/62, Lake Forest, Ill. BL/TR, 5'10.5", 180 lbs. Deb: 4/14/25 MCH																											
1925	Phi-A	134	420	69	139	21	5	6	55	44	19	.331	.397	.448	.845	111	9	8	103	89	76	.846	7	4	-0	-14	*C	0.1
1926	Phi-A	120	370	50	101	8	9	8	47	56	15	.273	.369	.408	.777	87	2	-8	118	91	60	.782	5	2	0	-3	*C	-0.2
1927	Phi-A	126	432	80	146	20	6	12	80	50	7	.338	.409	.495	.904	138	22	24	97	109	86	.962	9	0	3	-4	*C	2.4
1928	Phi-A	131	468	92	137	26	12	10	57	76	25	.293	.395	.464	.859	122	19	17	103	84	89	.896	7	7	-2	2	*C	2.4
1929	Phi-A	135	514	113	170	37	8	7	95	69	8	.331	.412	.475	.887	117	23	16	109	130	103	.920	7	6	-2	-6	*C	1.9
1930	Phi-A	130	487	110	174	42	5	10	85	55	18	.357	.424	.526	.949	140	30	31	99	101	111	1.013	5	0	2	-6	*C	3.3
1931	Phi-A	122	459	87	160	31	6	17	89	56	21	.349	.423	.553	.976	147	37	33	105	102	108	1.043	2	3	-1	-5	*C	3.3
1932	Phi-A	139	518	118	152	35	4	23	112	100	22	.293	.412	.510	.921	120	31	19	114	119	115	1.003	0	1	-1	10	*C/O	3.3
1933	Phi-A	130	429	104	138	30	4	15	60	106	22	.322	**.459**	.515	.974	172	42	47	92	77	109	1.138	8	6	-1	0	*C	4.8
1934	Det-A	129	437	74	140	32	1	2	76	78	26	.320	.428	.412	.840	120	16	17	98	139	83	.897	8	4	0	-7	*CM	2.1
1935	Det-A	115	411	93	131	33	3	5	47	96	15	.319	.452	.450	.902	139	27	29	97	85	91	1.018	5	5	-2	3	*CM	3.1
1936	Det-A	44	126	24	34	8	0	2	17	46	15	.270	.465	.381	.846	116	6	7	95	102	27	1.022	1	1	-0	-4	CM	0.5
1937	Det-A	27	98	27	30	10	1	2	12	25	4	.306	.452	.490	.941	126	7	5	109	73	23	1.072	0	1	-1	-1	CM	0.5
Total	13	1482	5169	1041	1652	333	64	119	832	857	217	.320	.419	.478	.897	128	269	246	103	102	1082	.961	64	40	-5	-36	*C/O	27.5
■ **JIM COCKMAN**	Cockman, James b: 4/26/1873, Guelph, Ont., Can. d: 9/28/47, Guelph, Ont., Can. BR/TR, 5'6", 145 lbs. Deb: 9/28/05																											
1905	NY-A	13	38	5	4	0	0	0	2	4		.105	.190	.105	.296	-4	-4	-4	102	178	1	.294	2			-0	3	-0.4
■ **JACK COFFEY**	Coffey, John Francis b: 1/28/1887, New York, N.Y. d: 2/14/66, Bronx, N.Y. BR/TR, 5'11", 178 lbs. Deb: 09																											
1909	Bos-N	73	257	21	48	4	4	0	20	11		.187	.229	.233	.462	46	-17	-16	96	124	13	.364	2			-1	S	-1.7
1918	Det-A	22	67	7	14	0	2	0	4	8	6	.209	.303	.269	.571	75	-2	-2	97	81	6	.547	2			-3	2	-0.3
	Bos-A	15	44	5	7	1	0	1	2	3	2	.159	.213	.250	.463	42	-3	-3	95	52	3	.432	2			0	3/2	-0.3
	Yr	37	111	12	21	1	2	1	6	11	8	.189	.268	.261	.530	62	-6	-5	96	71	9	.500	4			-3		-0.6
Total	2	110	368	33	69	5	6	1	26	22	8	.188	.241	.242	.483	51	-23	-21	96	107	22	.405	6			-4	/S23	-2.3
■ **FRANK COGGINS**	Coggins, Franklin b: 5/22/44, Griffin, Ga. BB/TR, 6'2", 187 lbs. Deb: 9/10/67																											
1967	Was-A	19	75	9	23	3	0	1	8	2	17	.307	.325	.387	.711	107	1	0	102	110	9	.582	1	0	0	2	2	0.3
1968	Was-A	62	171	15	30	6	1	0	7	9	33	.175	.217	.222	.439	36	-14	-12	91	79	8	.331	1	1	-0	2	2	-0.9
1972	Chi-N	6	1	1	0	0	0	0	0	1	0	.000	.500	.000	.500	46	0	0	114	0	0	1.000	0	0	0	0	H	0.0
Total	3	87	247	25	53	9	1	1	15	12	50	.215	.251	.271	.522	60	-13	-12	95	88	17	.415	2	1	0	4	/2	-0.6
■ **RICH COGGINS**	Coggins, Richard Allen b: 12/7/50, Indianapolis, Ind. BL/TL, 5'8", 170 lbs. Deb: 8/29/72																											
1972	Bal-A	16	39	5	13	4	0	0	1	1	6	.333	.350	.436	.786	136	1	1	98	25	5	.643	0	2	-1	4	O	0.4
1973	Bal-A	110	389	54	124	19	9	7	41	28	24	.319	.365	.468	.832	124	16	12	107	79	65	.808	17	9	-0	5	*O/D	1.4
1974	Bal-A	113	411	53	100	13	3	4	32	29	31	.243	.301	.319	.620	85	-11	-8	93	90	42	.591	26	6	4	1	*O	-0.5
1975	Mon-N	13	37	1	10	3	1	0	4	1	7	.270	.289	.405	.695	84	-1	-1	108	103	4	.593	0	0	0	-1	O	-0.2
	NY-A	51	107	7	24	1	0	1	6	7	16	.224	.272	.262	.534	52	-7	-7	99	74	8	.437	3	3	-1	-2	O/D	-1.0
1976	NY-A	7	4	1	1	0	0	0	1	0	1	.250	.250	.250	.500	47	-0	-0	99	384	0	.667	1	0	0	-0	/O	0.0
	Chi-A	32	96	4	15	2	0	0	5	6	15	.156	.206	.177	.383	13	-10	-10	99	113	4	.313	3	1	0	-2	O/D	-1.3
	Yr	39	100	5	16	2	0	0	6	6	16	.160	.208	.180	.388	14	-11	-11	99	171	4	.326	4	1	1	-3		-1.3

YEAR	TM/L	G	AB	R	H	2B	3B	HR	RBI	BB	SO	AVG	OBP	SLG	PRO	/A	BR	/A	PF	CHI	RC	TA	SB	CS	SBR	FR	POS	TPR
Total	5	342	1083	125	287	42	13	12	90	72	100	.265	.314	.361	.675	92	-12	-12	100	86	129	.633	50	21	2	4	O/D	-1.2

■ **ED COGSWELL** Cogswell, Edward b: 2/25/1854, England d: 7/27/1888, Fitchburg, Mass. BR/TR, 5'8", 150 lbs. Deb: 7/11/1879

YEAR	TM/L	G	AB	R	H	2B	3B	HR	RBI	BB	SO	AVG	OBP	SLG	PRO	/A	BR	/A	PF	CHI	RC	TA	SB	CS	SBR	FR	POS	TPR
1879	Bos-N	49	236	51	76	8	1	1	18	8	5	.322	.344	.377	.721	128	9	7	107	59	31	.606				1	1	0.3
1880	Tro-N	47	209	41	63	7	3	0	13	11	10	.301	.336	.364	.700	124	8	5	110	54	26	.596				1	1	0.4
1882	Wor-N	13	51	10	7	1	0	0	1	6	6	.137	.228	.157	.385	26	-4	-4	100	37	2	.318				0	1	-0.3
Total	3	109	496	102	146	16	4	1	32	25	21	.294	.328	.349	.677	116	13	8	108	54	59	.566				1	1	0.4

■ **ALTA COHEN** Cohen, Alta Albert "Schoolboy" b: 12/25/08, New York, N.Y. BL/TL, 5'10.5", 170 lbs. Deb: 4/15/31

YEAR	TM/L	G	AB	R	H	2B	3B	HR	RBI	BB	SO	AVG	OBP	SLG	PRO	/A	BR	/A	PF	CHI	RC	TA	SB	CS	SBR	FR	POS	TPR
1931	Bro-N	1	3	1	2	0	0	0	0	0	0	.667	.667	.667	1.333	256	1	1	101	0	1	2.000	0			1	/O	0.2
1932	Bro-N	9	32	1	5	1	0	0	1	3	7	.156	.229	.188	.416	14	-4	-4	96	63	2	.333	0			1	/O	-0.3
1933	Phi-N	19	32	6	6	1	0	0	1	6	4	.188	.316	.219	.535	47	-2	-2	118	54	2	.464	0			-0	/O	-0.2
Total	3	29	67	8	13	2	0	0	2	9	11	.194	.289	.224	.513	41	-5	-5	107	56	5	.429	0			2	/O	-0.3

■ **ANDY COHEN** Cohen, Andrew Howard b: 10/25/04, Baltimore, Md. d: 10/29/88, El Paso, Tex. BR/TR, 5'8", 155 lbs. Deb: 6/06/26 MC

YEAR	TM/L	G	AB	R	H	2B	3B	HR	RBI	BB	SO	AVG	OBP	SLG	PRO	/A	BR	/A	PF	CHI	RC	TA	SB	CS	SBR	FR	POS	TPR
1926	NY-N	32	35	4	9	0	1	0	8	1	2	.257	.278	.314	.592	60	-2	-2	98	252	3	.462	0			0	2S/3	0.0
1928	NY-N	129	504	64	138	24	7	9	59	31	17	.274	.318	.403	.721	86	-11	-12	102	93	63	.653	3			-0	*2/S3	-0.9
1929	NY-N	101	347	40	102	12	2	5	47	11	15	.294	.319	.383	.703	74	-15	-15	100	109	41	.608	3			8	2/S3	-0.3
Total	3	262	886	108	249	36	10	14	114	43	34	.281	.317	.392	.709	80	-28	-29	101	105	106	.628	6			8	2/S3	-1.2

■ **JIMMIE COKER** Coker, James Goodwin b: 3/28/36, Holly Hill, S.C. BR/TR, 5'11", 195 lbs. Deb: 9/11/58

YEAR	TM/L	G	AB	R	H	2B	3B	HR	RBI	BB	SO	AVG	OBP	SLG	PRO	/A	BR	/A	PF	CHI	RC	TA	SB	CS	SBR	FR	POS	TPR
1958	Phi-N	2	6	0	1	0	0	0	0	0	0	.167	.167	.167	.333	-12	-1	-1	98	0	0	.167	0	0	0	0	/C	0.0
1960	Phi-N	81	252	18	54	5	3	6	34	23	45	.214	.290	.329	.620	64	-11	-13	107	137	24	.534	0	3	-2	10	C	-0.1
1961	Phi-N	11	25	3	10	1	0	1	4	7	4	.400	.531	.560	1.091	203	4	4	94	95	9	1.467	1	0	0	0	C	0.5
1962	Phi-N	5	3	0	0	0	0	0	1	1	2	.000	.250	.000	.250	-28	-1	-0	95	0	0	.333	0	0	0	0	H	0.0
1963	SF-N	4	5	0	1	0	0	0	0	1	2	.200	.333	.200	.533	60	-0	-0	96	0	0	.500	0	0	0	0	/C	0.0
1964	Cin-N	11	32	3	10	2	0	1	4	3	5	.313	.371	.469	.840	131	1	1	103	91	5	.783	0	0	0	1	C	0.3
1965	Cin-N	24	61	3	15	2	0	2	9	8	16	.246	.333	.377	.710	96	0	-0	104	129	8	.660	0	0	0	2	C	0.3
1966	Cin-N	50	111	9	28	3	0	4	14	8	5	.252	.303	.387	.690	79	-2	-3	114	107	13	.600	0	1	-1	-1	C/O	-0.4
1967	Cin-N	45	97	8	18	2	1	2	4	4	20	.186	.218	.289	.506	40	-7	-8	109	49	5	.390	0	1	-1	-1	C	-0.8
Total	9	233	592	44	137	15	4	16	70	55	99	.231	.301	.351	.652	75	-16	-21	107	109	64	.580	1	5	-3	11	C/O	-0.2

■ **ROCKY COLAVITO** Colavito, Rocco Domenico b: 8/10/33, New York, N.Y. BR/TR, 6'3", 190 lbs. Deb: 9/10/55 C

YEAR	TM/L	G	AB	R	H	2B	3B	HR	RBI	BB	SO	AVG	OBP	SLG	PRO	/A	BR	/A	PF	CHI	RC	TA	SB	CS	SBR	FR	POS	TPR
1955	Cle-A	5	9	3	4	2	0	0	0	0	2	.444	.444	.667	1.111	188	1	1	104	0	3	1.200	0	0	0	2	/O	0.3
1956	Cle-A	101	322	55	89	11	4	21	65	49	46	.276	.375	.531	.906	135	16	16	101	104	67	.933	0	1	-1	-3	O	0.8
1957	Cle-A	134	461	66	116	26	0	25	84	71	80	.252	.353	.471	.823	121	14	14	102	116	76	.799	1	6	-3	7	*O	1.0
1958	Cle-A	143	489	80	148	26	3	41	113	84	89	.303	.407	**.620**	1.027	**189**	53	56	94	108	122	1.084	0	2	-1	6	*O1/P	**5.3**
1959	Cle-A	154	588	90	151	24	0	**42**	111	71	86	.257	.339	.512	.851	135	22	25	97	108	101	.832	3	3	-1	5	*O	2.1
1960	Det-A	145	555	67	138	18	1	35	87	53	80	.249	.319	.474	.793	110	6	5	102	98	78	.734	3	6	-3	4	*O	0.1
1961	Det-A	163	583	129	169	30	2	45	140	113	75	.290	.407	.580	.987	167	52	55	96	123	141	1.056	1	2	-1	8	*O	5.4
1962	Det-A	161	601	90	164	30	2	37	112	96	68	.273	.375	.514	.889	123	31	22	111	112	117	.899	2	0	1	14	*O	3.0
1963	Det-A	160	597	91	162	29	2	22	91	84	78	.271	.362	.437	.799	119	20	17	104	123	95	.764	0	0	0	4	*O	1.6
1964	KC-A	160	588	89	161	31	2	34	102	83	56	.274	.368	.507	.875	135	33	29	105	114	110	.876	3	1	0	2	*O	2.6
1965	Cle-A	162	592	92	170	25	2	26	**108**	**93**	63	.287	.387	.468	.855	144	35	36	98	134	**110**	.856	1	1	-0	2	*O	3.3
1966	Cle-A	151	533	68	127	13	0	30	72	76	81	.238	.337	.432	.768	117	14	13	101	100	74	.720	2	1	0	5	*O	1.3
1967	Cle-A	63	191	10	46	9	0	5	21	24	31	.241	.329	.366	.695	105	2	1	100	103	23	.634	2	2	-1	-2	O	-0.2
	Chi-A	60	190	20	42	4	1	3	29	25	10	.221	.312	.300	.612	87	-4	-2	94	183	19	.550	1	1	-0	-5	O	-0.9
	Yr	123	381	30	88	13	1	8	50	49	41	.231	.320	.333	.654	96	-2	-1	97	143	44	.604	3	3	-1	-7		-1.1
1968	LA-N	40	113	8	23	3	0	3	11	15	18	.204	.297	.310	.607	91	-2	-1	91	105	9	.515	0	1	-1	-2	O	-0.5
	NY-A	39	91	13	20	2	2	5	13	14	17	.220	.330	.451	.781	133	4	4	101	99	14	.778	0	0	0	-6	O/P	-0.2
Total	14	1841	6503	971	1730	283	21	374	1159	951	880	.266	.362	.489	.851	133	296	291	101	115	1157	.870	19	27	-11	42	*O/1P	25.0

■ **MIKE COLBERN** Colbern, Michael Malloy b: 4/19/55, Santa Monica, Cal. BR/TR, 6'3", 205 lbs. Deb: 7/18/78

YEAR	TM/L	G	AB	R	H	2B	3B	HR	RBI	BB	SO	AVG	OBP	SLG	PRO	/A	BR	/A	PF	CHI	RC	TA	SB	CS	SBR	FR	POS	TPR
1978	Chi-A	48	141	11	38	5	1	2	20	1	36	.270	.285	.362	.646	80	-4	-4	101	139	14	.514	0	1	-1	0	C/D	-0.2
1979	Chi-A	32	83	5	20	5	1	0	8	4	25	.241	.276	.325	.601	60	-5	-5	102	114	8	.484	0	0	0	-1	C	-0.4
Total	2	80	224	16	58	10	2	2	28	5	61	.259	.281	.348	.630	72	-9	-9	101	129	22	.506	0	1	-1	-1	/CD	-0.6

■ **NATE COLBERT** Colbert, Nathan b: 4/9/46, St.Louis, Mo. BR/TR, 6'2", 190 lbs. Deb: 4/14/66

YEAR	TM/L	G	AB	R	H	2B	3B	HR	RBI	BB	SO	AVG	OBP	SLG	PRO	/A	BR	/A	PF	CHI	RC	TA	SB	CS	SBR	FR	POS	TPR
1966	Hou-N	19	7	3	0	0	0	0	0	0	4	.000	.000	.000	.000	-99	-2	-2	97	0	0	.000	0	0	0	0	H	-0.1
1968	Hou-N	20	53	5	8	1	0	0	4	1	23	.151	.167	.170	.336	1	-6	-6	99	187	1	.229	1	1	-0	0	O/1	-0.8
1969	SD-N	139	483	64	123	20	9	24	66	45	123	.255	.322	.482	.804	127	12	14	97	89	72	.761	6	4	-1	3	*1	0.6
1970	SD-N	156	572	84	148	17	6	38	86	56	150	.259	.329	.509	.838	127	14	18	95	84	93	.805	3	5	-2	-8	*1/3	-0.5
1971	SD-N	156	565	81	149	25	3	27	84	63	119	.264	.342	.462	.804	131	18	21	96	106	87	.766	5	2	0	0	*1	1.0
1972	SD-N	151	563	87	141	27	2	38	111	70	127	.250	.335	.508	.843	155	25	33	88	121	95	.848	15	6	1	7	*1	3.2
1973	SD-N	145	529	73	143	25	2	22	80	54	146	.270	.347	.450	.797	127	13	17	94	112	80	.761	9	8	-2	3	*1	1.1
1974	SD-N	119	368	53	76	16	0	14	54	62	108	.207	.323	.364	.687	98	-4	-0	93	118	46	.681	10	2	2	0	1O	-0.3
1975	Det-A	45	156	16	23	4	2	4	18	17	52	.147	.231	.276	.507	41	-12	-13	104	128	9	.432	0	2	-1	-2	1/D	-1.8
	Mon-N	38	81	10	14	4	1	4	11	5	31	.173	.230	.395	.625	66	-4	-5	108	97	7	.559	0	0	0	1	1	-0.4
1976	Mon-N	14	40	5	8	2	0	2	6	9	16	.200	.347	.400	.747	111	1	1	100	105	6	.848	3	1	0	1	/O1	0.2
	Oak-A	2	5	0	0	0	0	0	0	1	3	.000	.167	.000	.167	-49	-1	-1	100	0	0	.200	0	0	0	0	/D	0.0
Total	10	1004	3422	481	833	141	25	173	520	383	902	.243	.324	.451	.775	120	55	77	95	106	497	.764	52	31	-3	5	1/OD3	2.2

■ **DICK COLE** Cole, Richard Roy b: 5/6/26, Long Beach, Cal. BR/TR, 6'2", 175 lbs. Deb: 4/27/51 C

YEAR	TM/L	G	AB	R	H	2B	3B	HR	RBI	BB	SO	AVG	OBP	SLG	PRO	/A	BR	/A	PF	CHI	RC	TA	SB	CS	SBR	FR	POS	TPR
1951	StL-N	15	36	4	7	1	0	0	3	6	5	.194	.310	.222	.532	45	-3	-3	101	145	3	.483	0	0	0	1	2	0.0
	Pit-N	42	106	9	25	4	0	1	11	15	9	.236	.331	.302	.632	67	-4	-5	107	122	11	.547	0	1	-1	1	2/S	-0.2
	Yr	57	142	13	32	5	0	1	14	21	14	.225	.325	.282	.607	62	-6	-8	105	130	14	.530	0	1	-1	2		-0.2
1953	Pit-N	97	235	29	64	13	1	0	23	38	26	.272	.374	.336	.710	85	-3	-4	102	114	32	.665	2	2	-1	-6	S/21	-0.3
1954	Pit-N	138	486	40	131	22	5	1	40	41	48	.270	.326	.342	.668	77	-18	-16	97	95	52	.552	0	0	0	-10	S32	-1.9
1955	Pit-N	77	239	16	54	8	3	0	21	18	22	.226	.286	.285	.570	54	-16	-15	97	125	19	.463	0	0	0	-0	32S	-1.3
1956	Pit-N	72	99	7	21	2	1	0	9	11	9	.212	.291	.253	.543	47	-7	-7	102	152	7	.434	0	0	0	-0	32/S	-0.5
1957	Mil-N	15	14	1	1	0	0	0	0	3	5	.071	.235	.071	.307	-14	-2	-2	90	0	0	.286	0	0	0	1	2/13	0.0
Total	6	456	1215	106	303	50	10	2	107	132	124	.249	.324	.312	.636	69	-53	-51	99	112	125	.562	2	3	-1	-14	S23/1	-4.2

■ **WILLIS COLE** Cole, Willis Russell b: 1/6/1882, Milton Junction, Wis. d: 10/11/65, Madison, Wis. BR/TR, 5'8", 170 lbs. Deb: 8/22/09

YEAR	TM/L	G	AB	R	H	2B	3B	HR	RBI	BB	SO	AVG	OBP	SLG	PRO	/A	BR	/A	PF	CHI	RC	TA	SB	CS	SBR	FR	POS	TPR
1909	Chi-A	46	165	17	39	7	3	0	16	16		.236	.308	.315	.623	99	-1	-0	97	126	16	.571	3			-5	O	-0.7
1910	Chi-A	22	80	6	14	2	1	0	2	4		.175	.224	.225	.449	43	-6	-5	95	43	4	.348	0			2	O	-0.4
Total	2	68	245	23	53	9	4	0	18	20		.216	.281	.286	.567	81	-6	-5	96	99	21	.495	3			-3	/O	-1.1

■ **CHOO CHOO COLEMAN** Coleman, Clarence b: 8/25/37, Orlando, Fla. BL/TR, 5'9", 165 lbs. Deb: 4/16/61

YEAR	TM/L	G	AB	R	H	2B	3B	HR	RBI	BB	SO	AVG	OBP	SLG	PRO	/A	BR	/A	PF	CHI	RC	TA	SB	CS	SBR	FR	POS	TPR
1961	Phi-N	34	47	3	6	1	0	0	4	2	8	.128	.180	.149	.329	-12	-8	-7	94	231	1	.238	0	0	0	0	C	-0.5
1962	NY-N	55	152	24	38	7	2	6	17	11	24	.250	.305	.441	.746	94	-1	-2	104	79	19	.681	2	4	-2	-2	C	-0.4
1963	NY-N	106	247	22	44	0	0	3	9	24	49	.178	.264	.215	.479	40	-19	-18	99	61	15	.410	5	5	-2	-6	C/O	-2.5
1966	NY-N	6	16	2	3	0	0	0	0	0	4	.188	.188	.188	.375	5	-2	-2	94	0	1	.231	0	0	0	-0	/C	-0.1
Total	4	201	462	51	91	8	2	9	30	37	85	.197	.267	.281	.548	53	-29	-29	100	82	36	.476	7	9	-3	-8	C/O	-3.5

■ **CURT COLEMAN** Coleman, Curtis Hancock b: 2/18/1887, Salem, Ore. d: 7/1/80, Newport, Ore. BL/TR, 5'11", 180 lbs. Deb: 4/13/12

YEAR	TM/L	G	AB	R	H	2B	3B	HR	RBI	BB	SO	AVG	OBP	SLG	PRO	/A	BR	/A	PF	CHI	RC	TA	SB	CS	SBR	FR	POS	TPR
1912	NY-A	12	37	8	9	4	0	0	4	7		.243	.364	.351	.715	103	0	0	101	103	5	.714	0			-0	3	0.0

■ **DAVE COLEMAN** Coleman, David Lee b: 10/26/50, Dayton, Ohio BR/TR, 6'3", 195 lbs. Deb: 4/13/77

YEAR	TM/L	G	AB	R	H	2B	3B	HR	RBI	BB	SO	AVG	OBP	SLG	PRO	/A	BR	/A	PF	CHI	RC	TA	SB	CS	SBR	FR	POS	TPR
1977	Bos-A	11	12	1	0	0	0	0	0	1	3	.000	.077	.000	.077	-66	-3	-3	117	0	0	.083	0	0	0	-3	/O	-0.6

YEAR	TM/L	G	AB	R	H	2B	3B	HR	RBI	BB	SO	AVG	OBP	SLG	PRO	/A	BR	/A	PF	CHI	RC	TA	SB	CS	SBR	FR	POS	TPR
■ JERRY COLEMAN	Coleman, Gerald Francis b: 9/14/24, San Jose, Cal. BR/TR, 6', 165 lbs. Deb: 4/20/49 M																											
1949	NY-A	128	447	54	123	21	5	2	42	63	44	.275	.367	.358	.725	92	-4	-4	100	89	62	.681	8	6	-1	3	*2/S	0.0
1950	NY-A	153	522	69	150	19	6	6	69	67	38	.287	.372	.381	.753	94	-4	-4	99	110	79	.708	3	2	-0	-14	*2/S	-0.6
1951	NY-A	121	362	48	90	11	2	3	43	31	36	.249	.315	.315	.630	77	-15	-11	92	125	37	.546	6	1	1	2	*2S	-0.1
1952	NY-A	11	42	6	17	2	1	0	4	5	4	.405	.468	.500	.968	173	4	4	98	75	10	1.000	0	1	-1	2	2	0.6
1953	NY-A	8	10	1	2	0	0	0	0	0	2	.200	.200	.200	.400	9	-1	-1	93	0	0	.250	0	0	0	0	/2S	0.0
1954	NY-A	107	300	39	65	7	1	3	21	26	29	.217	.279	.277	.556	53	-20	-19	99	87	24	.461	3	0	1	10	2S/3	-0.2
1955	NY-A	43	96	12	22	5	0	0	8	11	11	.229	.321	.281	.602	64	-5	-4	98	111	9	.506	0	2	-1	0	S2/3	-0.1
1956	NY-A	80	183	15	47	5	1	0	18	12	33	.257	.306	.295	.601	60	-11	-10	99	124	16	.476	1	2	-1	4	2S3	0.0
1957	NY-A	72	157	23	42	7	2	2	12	20	21	.268	.354	.376	.730	106	0	2	94	73	20	.659	1	1	-0	1	23/S	0.5
Total	9	723	2119	267	558	77	18	16	217	235	218	.263	.341	.339	.680	83	-55	-48	98	102	257	.625	22	15	-2	8	2S/3	0.1
■ GORDY COLEMAN	Coleman, Gordon Calvin b: 7/5/34, Rockville, Md. BL/TR, 6'3", 208 lbs. Deb: 9/19/59																											
1959	Cle-A	6	15	5	8	0	1	0	2	1	2	.533	.563	.667	1.229	245	3	3	97	79	6	1.571	0	0	0	0	/1	0.3
1960	Cin-N	66	251	26	68	10	1	6	32	12	32	.271	.309	.390	.700	92	-4	-3	98	114	31	.608	1	1	-0	2	1	-0.4
1961	Cin-N	150	520	63	149	27	4	26	87	45	67	.287	.346	.504	.850	117	15	12	104	105	88	.809	1	3	-2	9	*1	1.0
1962	Cin-N	136	476	73	132	13	1	28	86	36	68	.277	.332	.485	.817	114	9	8	102	108	73	.758	2	3	-1	1	*1	0.4
1963	Cin-N	123	365	38	90	20	2	14	59	29	51	.247	.306	.427	.733	104	3	2	104	125	47	.667	1	0	0	-0	*1	0.0
1964	Cin-N	89	198	18	48	6	2	5	27	13	30	.242	.292	.369	.661	82	-4	-5	103	126	20	.563	2	0	1	1	1	-0.4
1965	Cin-N	108	325	39	98	19	0	14	57	24	38	.302	.351	.489	.841	129	14	12	104	118	55	.790	0	0	0	-2	1	0.7
1966	Cin-N	91	227	20	57	7	0	5	37	16	45	.251	.300	.348	.648	70	-6	-10	114	165	24	.557	2	1	0	-3	1	-1.7
1967	Cin-N	4	7	0	0	0	0	0	0	1	0	.000	.125	.000	.125	-56	-1	-2	109	0	0	.143	0	0	0	0	/1	-0.1
Total	9	773	2384	282	650	102	11	98	387	177	333	.273	.326	.448	.774	106	29	18	104	118	344	.726	9	8	-2	9	1	-0.2
■ JOHN COLEMAN	Coleman, John Francis b: 3/6/1863, Saratoga Spgs., N.Y d: 5/31/22, Detroit, Mich. BL/TR, 5'9.5", 170 lbs. Deb: 5/01/1883																											
1883	Phi-N	90	354	33	83	12	8	0	32	15	39	.234	.266	.314	.579	83	-10	-5	90	106	30	.465				12	PO/2	0.0
1884	Phi-N	43	171	16	42	7	2	0	22	8	20	.246	.279	.310	.589	92	-3	-1	92	151	15	.473				0	OP/1	0.0
	Phi-a	28	107	16	22	2	3	2		5		.206	.241	.336	.578	78	-1	-4	114	0	9	.482				0	O/P1	-0.2
1885	Phi-a	96	398	71	119	15	12	2		25		.299	.345	.412	.757	137	18	16	103	0	58	.688				-3	*O/P	0.7
1886	Phi-a	121	492	67	121	18	16	0		33		.246	.296	.348	.644	103	1	1	100	0	60	.631	28			3	*O/1P2	0.0
	Pit-a	11	43	3	15	2	1	0		2		.349	.378	.442	.820	172	3	3	93	0	8	.786	1			-2	O	0.0
	Yr	132	535	70	136	20	17	0		35		.254	.302	.355	.658	108	4	4	99	0	68	.642	29			1		0.0
1887	Pit-N	115	475	75	139	21	11	2	54	31	40	.293	.337	.396	.733	112	3	8	93	83	74	.729	25			-3	*O/1	0.6
1888	Pit-N	116	438	49	101	11	4	0	26	29	52	.231	.285	.274	.558	85	-9	-5	95	82	39	.499	15			2	O1	-0.3
1889	Phi-a	6	19	1	1	0	0	0	1	1	3	.053	.100	.053	.153	-57	-4	-4	98	286	0	.167	1			0	/PO	0.0
1890	Pit-N	3	11	1	2	0	0	0	0	3	0	.182	.357	.182	.539	69	-0	-0	88	0	1	.667	1			0	/OP	0.0
Total	8	629	2508	332	645	88	57	6	135	152	154	.257	.302	.345	.647	102	-2	11	97	57	295	.589	71			9	OP/12	0.8
■ ED COLEMAN	Coleman, Parke Edward b: 12/1/01, Canby, Ore. d: 8/5/64, Oregon City, Ore. BL/TR, 6'2", 200 lbs. Deb: 4/15/32																											
1932	Phi-A	26	73	13	25	7	1	1	13	1	6	.342	.351	.507	.858	105	2	0	114	109	13	.813	1	0	0	0	O	0.0
1933	Phi-A	102	388	48	109	26	3	6	68	19	51	.281	.318	.410	.728	100	-6	-2	92	131	50	.645	0	0	0	-4	O	-0.7
1934	Phi-A	101	329	53	92	14	6	14	60	29	34	.280	.342	.486	.828	115	4	5	97	99	55	.803	0	1	-1	-4	O	0.0
1935	Phi-A	10	13	0	1	0	0	0	0	0	3	.077	.077	.077	.154	-60	-3	-3	100	0	0	.083	0	0	0	-0	/O	-0.2
	StL-A	108	397	66	114	15	9	17	71	53	41	.287	.373	.499	.871	116	13	9	107	99	75	.884	0	2	-1	-6	*O	0.1
	Yr	118	410	66	115	15	9	17	71	53	44	.280	.364	.485	.850	111	10	6	106	90	74	.852	0	2	-1	-6		-0.1
1936	StL-A	92	137	13	40	5	4	2	34	15	17	.292	.366	.431	.797	93	-1	-2	103	169	22	.773	0	0	0	-3	O	-0.4
Total	5	439	1337	193	381	67	23	40	246	117	152	.285	.345	.459	.804	107	8	8	100	115	215	.770	1	3	-2	-18	O	-1.2
■ RAY COLEMAN	Coleman, Raymond Leroy b: 6/4/22, Dunsmuir, Cal. BL/TR, 5'11", 170 lbs. Deb: 4/22/47																											
1947	StL-A	110	343	34	89	9	7	2	30	26	32	.259	.314	.344	.658	81	-9	-9	102	89	33	.536	2	5	-2	-6	O	-2.2
1948	StL-A	17	29	2	5	0	1	0	2	2	5	.172	.226	.241	.467	23	-3	-3	106	96	1	.385	1	0	0	-1	/O	-0.3
	Phi-A	68	210	32	51	6	6	0	21	31	17	.243	.340	.329	.669	77	-6	-7	102	103	23	.601	4	3	-1	4	O	-0.4
	Yr	85	239	34	56	6	7	0	23	33	22	.234	.327	.318	.645	70	-9	-10	102	103	25	.579	5	3	-0	3		-0.7
1950	StL-A	117	384	54	104	25	6	8	55	32	37	.271	.330	.430	.760	87	-6	-10	107	100	52	.691	7	5	-1	6	O	-0.5
1951	StL-A	91	341	41	96	16	5	5	55	24	32	.282	.329	.402	.731	92	-3	-5	105	132	43	.633	3	4	-2	4	O	-0.5
	Chi-A	51	181	21	50	8	7	3	21	15	14	.276	.332	.448	.779	113	1	2	97	83	26	.705	2	3	-1	5	O	0.4
	Yr	142	522	62	146	24	12	8	76	39	46	.280	.330	.418	.747	99	-1	-2	102	115	73	.675	5	7	-3	8		-0.1
1952	Chi-A	85	195	19	42	7	1	2	14	13	17	.215	.264	.292	.557	55	-12	-12	100	83	15	.440	0	0	0	-4	O	-1.9
	StL-A	20	46	5	9	3	0	0	1	5	4	.196	.288	.261	.549	55	-3	-3	97	31	4	.486	0	0	0	-2	O	-0.5
	Yr	105	241	24	51	10	1	2	15	18	21	.212	.269	.286	.556	55	-15	-15	99	74	21	.463	0	0	0	-7		-2.4
Total	5	559	1729	208	446	74	33	20	199	148	158	.258	.318	.374	.692	83	-40	-46	103	99	198	.627	19	20	-6	5	O	-5.9
■ BOB COLEMAN	Coleman, Robert Hunter b: 9/26/1890, Huntingburg, Ind. d: 7/16/59, Boston, Mass. BR/TR, 6'2", 190 lbs. Deb: 6/13/13 MC																											
1913	Pit-N	24	50	5	9	2	0	0	9	7	8	.180	.281	.220	.501	46	-3	-3	96	297	3	.439	0			0	C	-0.1
1914	Pit-N	73	150	11	40	4	1	1	14	15	32	.267	.333	.327	.660	104	-0	1	92	98	17	.609	3			-4	C	0.0
1916	Cle-A	19	28	3	6	2	0	0	4	7	6	.214	.371	.286	.657	98	0	0	100	179	3	.682	0			0	C	0.1
Total	3	116	228	19	55	8	1	1	27	29	46	.241	.327	.298	.625	90	-4	-2	94	153	23	.578	3			-4	C	0.0
■ VINCE COLEMAN	Coleman, Vincent Maurice b: 9/22/60, Jacksonville, Fla. BB/TR, 6', 170 lbs. Deb: 4/18/85																											
1985	StL-N	151	636	107	170	20	10	1	40	50	115	.267	.321	.335	.656	87	-14	-10	96	64	79	.755	**110**	25	**18**	7	*O	1.1
1986	StL-N	154	600	94	139	13	8	0	29	60	98	.232	.304	.280	.584	60	-30	-32	103	66	67	.704	**107**	14	**24**	2	*O	-0.9
1987	StL-N	151	623	121	180	14	10	3	43	70	126	.289	.364	.358	.721	93	-5	-4	99	65	96	.858	**109**	22	**20**	3	*O	1.3
1988	StL-N	153	616	77	160	20	10	3	38	49	111	.260	.315	.339	.655	85	-9	-12	104	67	71	.698	**81**	27	8	3	*O	-0.5
Total	4	609	2475	399	649	67	38	7	150	229	450	.262	.326	.328	.655	81	-58	-58	100	66	313	.759	407	88	69	15	O	1.0
■ CAD COLES	Coles, Cadwallader R. b: 1/17/1889, Rockhill, S.C. d: 6/30/42, Miami, Fla. BL/TR, 6'0.5", 174 lbs. Deb: 4/16/14																											
1914	KC-F	78	194	17	49	7	3	1	25	5	30	.253	.271	.335	.606	77	-7	-6	95	133	20	.524	6			-6	O/1	-1.4
■ CHUCK COLES	Coles, Charles Edward b: 6/27/31, Fredericktown, Pa BL/TL, 5'9", 180 lbs. Deb: 9/19/58																											
1958	Cin-N	5	11	0	2	1	0	0	2	2	6	.182	.308	.273	.580	51	-1	-1	107	275	1	.556	0	0	0	1	/O	0.0
■ DARNELL COLES	Coles, Darnell b: 6/2/62, San Bernardino, Cal BR/TR, 6'1", 170 lbs. Deb: 9/04/83																											
1983	Sea-A	27	92	9	26	7	0	1	6	7	12	.283	.333	.391	.725	99	-0	-0	100	61	8	.558	0	3	-2	-1	3	-0.2
1984	Sea-A	48	143	15	23	3	1	0	6	17	26	.161	.259	.196	.455	27	-14	-14	102	85	8	.389	2	1	0	-4	3/OD	-1.7
1985	Sea-A	27	59	8	14	4	0	1	5	9	17	.237	.348	.356	.704	99	-0	0	95	83	8	.674	0	1	-1	2	S/3OD	0.2
1986	Det-A	142	521	67	142	30	2	20	86	45	84	.273	.337	.453	.790	119	10	13	95	118	81	.753	6	2	1	-4	*3/SOD	0.5
1987	Det-A	53	149	14	27	5	1	4	15	15	23	.181	.265	.309	.574	54	-10	-10	97	103	13	.508	0	1	-1	-2	3/1OSD	-1.2
	Pit-N	40	119	20	27	8	0	6	24	19	20	.227	.338	.445	.784	101	1	0	104	135	17	.755	1	3	-2	-5	O3/1	-0.7
1988	Pit-N	68	211	20	49	13	1	5	36	20	41	.232	.308	.374	.682	97	-1	-1	98	153	25	.620	1	1	-0	-4	O/13	-0.7
	Sea-A	55	195	32	57	10	1	10	34	17	26	.292	.361	.508	.869	131	10	8	108	107	35	.848	3	2	-0	-5	O/1D	0.2
Total	6	460	1489	185	365	80	6	47	212	149	249	.245	.322	.402	.723	99	-5	-3	99	113	195	.682	13	14	-5	-23	3O/DS1	-3.6
■ CHRIS COLETTA	Coletta, Christopher Michael b: 8/2/44, Brooklyn, N.Y. BL/TL, 5'11", 190 lbs. Deb: 8/15/72																											
1972	Cal-A	14	30	5	9	1	0	1	7	1	4	.300	.323	.433	.756	140	1	1	88	183	4	.636	0	0	0	-2	/O	-0.1
■ ED COLGAN	Colgan, William H. b: E.St.Louis, Ill. d: 8/13/1895, Great Falls, Mont. Deb: 5/03/1884																											
1884	Pit-a	48	161	10	25	4	1	0		3		.155	.171	.193	.363	21	-13	-13	97	0	5	.250				4	C/O	-0.4
■ BILL COLIVER	Coliver, William J. b: 1867, Detroit, Mich. d: 3/24/1888, Detroit, Mich. Deb: 1885																											
1885	Bos-N	1	4	0	0	0	0	0	0	0	1	.000	.000	.000	.000	-99	-1	-1	94	0	0	.000				0	/O	0.0

YEAR	TM/L	G	AB	R	H	2B	3B	HR	RBI	BB	SO	AVG	OBP	SLG	PRO	/A	BR	/A	PF	CHI	RC	TA	SB	CS	SBR	FR	POS	TPR
■ CHUB COLLINS Collins, Charles b: 1862, Dundas, Ont., Canada d: 5/20/14, Dundas, Ont., Can. Deb: 5/01/1884																												
1884	Buf-N	45	169	24	30	6	0	0	20	14	36	.178	.240	.213	.453	41	-10	-12	107	195	9	.360				0	2/S	-0.9
	Ind-a	38	138	18	31	3	1	0		9		.225	.272	.261	.533	80	-3	-2	96	0	10	.421				-8	2	-0.8
1885	Det-N	14	55	8	10	0	2	0	6	0	11	.182	.182	.255	.436	41	-4	-3	97	152	3	.311				0	S	-0.2
Total	2	97	362	50	71	9	3	0	26	23	47	.196	.244	.238	.482	55	-17	-18	101	114	22	.375				-8	/2S	-1.9
■ WILSON COLLINS Collins, Cyril Wilson b: 5/7/1889, Pulaski, Tenn. d: 2/28/41, Knoxville, Tenn. BR/TR, 5'9.5", 165 lbs. Deb: 5/12/13																												
1913	Bos-N	16	3	3	1	0	0	0	0	0	1	.333	.333	.333	.667	96	-0	-0	95	0	0	.500	0			-4	/O	-0.3
1914	Bos-N	27	35	5	9	0	0	0	1	2	8	.257	.297	.257	.554	63	-1	-2	104	40	3	.423	0			-4	O	-0.6
Total	2	43	38	8	10	0	0	0	1	2	9	.263	.300	.263	.563	65	-2	-2	103	37	3	.429	0			-8	/O	-0.9
■ DAN COLLINS Collins, Daniel Thomas b: 7/12/1854, St.Louis, Mo. d: 9/21/1883, New Orleans, La. Deb: 6/08/1874																												
1874	Chi-n	3	12	1	1							.083															/POS	
1876	Lou-N	7	28	3	4	1	0	0	9	0	2	.143	.143	.179	.321	6	-3	-3	104	620	1	.208				0	/O	-0.2
Total	1	7	28	3	4	1	0	0	9	0	2	.143	.143	.179	.321	6	-3	-3	104	620	1	.208				0	/OPS	-0.2
■ DAVE COLLINS Collins, David S b: 10/20/52, Rapid City, S.D. BB/TL, 5'11", 175 lbs. Deb: 6/07/75																												
1975	Cal-A	93	319	41	85	13	4	3	29	36	55	.266	.343	.361	.703	104	0	2	95	92	42	.710	24	10	1	2	OD	0.3
1976	Cal-A	99	365	45	96	12	1	4	28	40	55	.263	.336	.334	.670	105	-1	3	92	85	43	.669	32	19	-2	2	OD	0.1
1977	Sea-A	120	402	46	96	9	3	5	28	33	66	.239	.301	.313	.615	71	-17	-15	96	80	41	.588	25	10	2	-2	OD	-1.7
1978	Cin-N	102	102	13	22	1	0	0	7	15	18	.216	.316	.225	.542	52	-6	-6	103	121	7	.506	7	7	-2	-2	O	-1.1
1979	Cin-N	122	396	59	126	16	4	3	35	27	48	.318	.365	.402	.766	112	5	6	97	82	58	.716	16	9	-1	-7	O1	-0.4
1980	Cin-N	144	551	94	167	20	4	3	35	53	68	.303	.367	.370	.738	105	6	5	102	69	84	.827	79	21	11	-7	*O	0.4
1981	Cin-N	95	360	63	98	18	6	3	23	41	41	.272	.356	.381	.737	108	5	5	101	66	52	.755	26	10	2	-4	O	0.0
1982	NY-A	111	348	41	88	12	3	3	25	28	49	.253	.318	.330	.648	81	-10	-8	96	81	37	.588	13	8	-1	-4	O1/D	-1.5
1983	Tor-A	118	402	55	109	12	4	1	34	43	67	.271	.345	.328	.673	80	-6	-11	108	100	51	.680	31	7	5	4	*O/1D	-0.2
1984	Tor-A	128	441	59	136	24	**15**	2	44	33	41	.308	.369	.444	.813	122	14	14	102	89	81	.934	60	14	10	-1	*O/1D	1.8
1985	Oak-A	112	379	52	95	16	4	4	29	29	37	.251	.306	.346	.651	84	-11	-8	93	80	42	.638	29	8	4	1	O	-0.3
1986	Det-A	124	419	44	113	18	2	1	27	44	49	.270	.342	.329	.671	89	-7	-5	95	76	49	.645	27	12	1	1	OD	-0.4
1987	Cin-N	57	85	19	25	5	0	0	5	11	12	.294	.388	.353	.741	95	0	-0	104	66	14	.852	9	0	3	-1	O	0.0
1988	Cin-N	99	174	12	41	6	2	0	14	11	27	.236	.289	.293	.582	64	-7	-8	105	110	16	.526	7	2	1	-3	O/1	-1.1
Total	14	1524	4743	643	1297	182	52	32	363	444	633	.273	.340	.354	.694	94	-35	-26	99	83	617	.711	385	137	33	-21	*OD/1	-4.1
■ EDDIE COLLINS Collins, Edward Trowbridge Jr. b: 11/23/16, Lansdowne, Pa. BL/TR, 5'10", 175 lbs. Deb: 7/04/39																												
1939	Phi-A	32	21	6	5	1	0	0	0	0	3	.238	.238	.286	.524	34	-2	-2	97	0	2	.438	1	0	0	-1	/O2	-0.2
1941	Phi-A	80	219	29	53	6	3	0	12	20	24	.242	.305	.297	.602	59	-13	-13	101	65	21	.509	2	1	0	-1	O	-1.5
1942	Phi-A	20	34	6	8	2	0	0	4	4	2	.235	.316	.294	.610	75	-1	-1	96	141	4	.577	1	0	0	-3	/O	-0.4
Total	3	132	274	41	66	9	3	0	16	24	29	.241	.302	.296	.598	59	-16	-16	100	70	26	.522	4	1	1	-5	/O2	-2.1
■ EDDIE COLLINS Collins, Edward Trowbridge Sr. "Cocky" (a.k.a. Edward T. Sullivan In 1906) b: 5/2/1887, Millerton, N.Y. d: 3/25/51, Boston, Mass. BL/TR, 5'9", 175 lbs. Deb: 9/17/06 MCH																												
1906	Phi-A	6	15	2	3	0	0	0	0	0		.200	.200	.200	.400	28	-1	-1	94	0	1	.250	0			0	/S23	0.0
1907	Phi-A	14	20	0	5	0	0	0	2	0		.250	.250	.250	.500	58	-1	-1	106	143	1	.333	0			0	/S	0.0
1908	Phi-A	102	330	39	90	18	7	1	40	16		.273	.306	.379	.685	116	8	5	108	117	39	.621	8			-9	2SO	-0.4
1909	Phi-A	153	572	104	198	30	10	3	56	62		.346	.416	.449	.865	170	49	48	102	72	132	1.048	67			7	*2/S	5.6
1910	Phi-A	153	583	81	188	16	15	3	81	49		.322	.381	.417	.798	147	33	32	102	114	122	.959	**81**			**33**	*2	5.9
1911	Phi-A	132	493	92	180	22	13	3	73	62		.365	.451	.481	.932	172	43	48	93	96	124	1.125	38			-3	*2	4.2
1912	Phi-A	153	543	**137**	189	25	11	0	64	101		.348	.450	.435	.885	154	44	44	99	87	136	1.130	63			15	*2	5.6
1913	Phi-A	148	534	**125**	184	23	13	3	73	85	37	.345	.441	.453	.894	167	46	48	97	99	126	1.109	54			13	*2	5.9
1914	Phi-A	152	526	**122**	181	23	14	2	85	97	31	**.344**	**.452**	.452	.904	177	52	53	97	126	120	**1.064**	58	30	-1	2	*2	5.8
1915	Chi-A	155	521	118	173	22	10	4	77	**119**	27	.332	.460	.436	.896	172	52	54	98	105	116	1.050	46	30	-4	13	*2	**6.3**
1916	Chi-A	155	545	87	168	14	17	0	52	86	36	.308	.405	.396	.802	130	31	25	108	83	99	.867	40	21	-1	-5	*2	2.6
1917	Chi-A	156	564	91	163	18	12	0	67	89	16	.289	.389	.363	.752	133	24	25	98	104	98	.873	53			-25	*2	1.1
1918	Chi-A	97	330	51	91	8	2	2	30	73	13	.276	.407	.330	.737	122	14	13	101	91	54	.854	22			-6	2	1.4
1919	Chi-A	140	518	87	165	19	7	4	80	68	27	.319	.400	.405	.805	120	20	17	105	115	97	.887	**33**			3	*2	3.3
1920	Chi-A	153	601	115	222	37	13	3	75	69	19	.369	.436	.489	.925	151	41	44	96	77	132	.992	19	8	1	10	*2	5.5
1921	Chi-A	139	526	79	177	20	10	2	58	66	11	.337	.412	.424	.836	115	14	14	99	92	94	.844	12	10	-2	30	*2	4.2
1922	Chi-A	154	598	92	194	20	12	1	69	73	16	.324	.401	.403	.804	109	12	11	101	89	101	.810	20	12	-1	-10	*2	1.0
1923	Chi-A	145	505	89	182	22	5	5	67	84	8	.360	.455	.453	.909	142	34	36	98	99	109	1.040	**49**	29	-3	-2	*2	3.4
1924	Chi-A	152	556	108	194	27	7	6	86	89	16	.349	.441	.455	.896	136	30	33	97	111	119	1.021	**42**	17	**2**	-7	*2	3.0
1925	Chi-A	118	425	80	147	26	3	3	80	87	8	.346	.461	.442	.904	136	26	29	96	144	96	1.049	19	6	2	-9	*2M	2.5
1926	Chi-A	106	375	66	129	32	4	1	62	62	8	.344	.441	.459	.900	147	22	27	92	127	80	.984	13	8	-1	-9	*2M	2.1
1927	Phi-A	95	226	50	76	12	1	1	15	56	9	.336	.468	.412	.880	134	14	16	97	52	47	1.033	6	0	2	-2	2/S	1.5
1928	Phi-A	36	33	3	10	3	0	0	7	4	4	.303	.378	.394	.772	100	0	0	103	185	5	.739	0	0	0	0	/2S	0.0
1929	Phi-A	9	7	0	0	0	0	0	0	2	0	.000	.222	.000	.222	-35	-1	-2	109	0	0	.286	0	0	0	0	H	0.0
1930	Phi-A	3	2	1	1	0	0	0	0	0	0	.500	.500	.500	1.000	155	0	0	99	0	0	1.000	0	0	0	0	H	0.0
Total	25	2826	9948	1819	3310	437	186	47	1299	1499	286	.333	.424	.428	.852	142	604	620	99	100	2050	.966	743	171		40	*2/SO3	70.5
■ HUB COLLINS Collins, Hubert B. b: 4/15/1864, Louisville, Ky. d: 5/21/1892, Brooklyn, N.Y. BR/TR, Deb: 9/04/1886																												
1886	Lou-a	27	101	12	29	3	2	0		5		.287	.321	.356	.677	106	1	0	108	0	14	.667	7			0	O/3S21	0.0
1887	Lou-a	130	559	122	162	22	8	1		39		.290	.338	.363	.701	91	-2	-9	107	0	95	.793	71			-0	*O2/1S3	-0.9
1888	Lou-a	116	485	117	149	26	11	2	50	41		.307	.366	.419	.785	171	29	36	91	62	99	.923	62			15	O2S	4.4
	Bro-a	12	42	16	13	5	1	0	3	9		.310	.442	.476	.918	190	5	5	105	40	13	1.345	9			0	2	0.4
	Yr	128	527	133	162	**31**	12	2	53	50		.307	.373	.423	.796	172	35	41	92	60	112	.956	71			15		**4.8**
1889	Bro-a	138	560	139	149	18	3	2	73	80	41	.266	.365	.320	.684	102	2	6	96	97	91	.805	65			0	*2	0.8
1890	Bro-N	129	510	**148**	142	32	7	3	69	85	47	.278	.385	.386	.771	127	21	20	100	87	111	1.005	85			1	*2	2.3
1891	Bro-N	107	435	82	120	16	5	3	31	59	63	.276	.365	.356	.721	116	9	11	97	48	70	.787	32			-21	2O	-0.8
1892	Bro-N	21	87	17	26	5	1	0	17	14	13	.299	.396	.379	.775	135	4	4	101	136	15	.836	4			0	O	0.4
Total	7	680	2779	653	790	127	38	11	243	332	164	.284	.365	.369	.734	119	70	74	99	60	509	.861	335			-4	2O/S13	6.6
■ HUGH COLLINS Collins, Hugh Deb: 8/01/1887																												
1887	NY-a	1	4	0	1	0	0	0		0		.250	.250	.250	.500	47	-0	-0	88	0	0	.333	0			0	/C	0.0
■ RIPPER COLLINS Collins, James Anthony b: 3/30/04, Altoona, Pa. d: 4/15/70, New Haven, Conn. BB/TL, 5'9", 165 lbs. Deb: 4/18/31 C																												
1931	StL-N	89	279	34	84	20	10	4	59	18	24	.301	.350	.487	.837	115	8	6	107	142	48	.810	1			1	1/O	0.1
1932	StL-N	149	549	82	153	28	8	21	91	38	67	.279	.329	.474	.802	113	8	8	100	107	87	.770	4			-7	1O	-0.7
1933	StL-N	132	493	66	153	26	7	10	68	38	49	.310	.363	.452	.816	129	20	19	102	103	81	.768	7			3	*1	1.9
1934	StL-N	154	600	116	200	40	12	**35**	128	57	50	.333	.393	**.615**	**1.008**	146	53	42	114	103	148	1.046	2			8	*1	3.6
1935	StL-N	150	578	109	181	36	10	23	122	65	45	.313	.385	.529	.915	138	35	32	104	124	125	.930	0			-0	*1	2.7
1936	StL-N	103	277	48	81	15	3	13	48	48	30	.292	.399	.509	.908	151	18	20	94	94	61	.955	1			-1	1/O	1.2
1937	Chi-N	115	456	77	125	16	5	16	71	32	46	.274	.329	.436	.765	104	3	1	103	110	64	.690	2			3	*1	-0.2
1938	Chi-N	143	490	78	131	22	8	13	61	54	48	.267	.344	.424	.768	105	7	3	105	91	73	.715	1			8	*1	0.0
1941	Pit-N	49	62	5	13	2	2	0	11	6	14	.210	.279	.306	.586	63	-3	-3	103	209	6	.510	0			-1	1/O	-0.5
Total	9	1084	3784	615	1121	205	65	135	659	356	373	.296	.360	.492	.852	125	149	128	104	110	694	.848	18			12	1/O	8.1
■ JIMMY COLLINS Collins, James Joseph b: 1/16/1870, Buffalo, N.Y. d: 3/6/43, Buffalo, N.Y. BR/TR, 5'9", 178 lbs. Deb: 4/19/1895 MH																												
1895	Bos-N	11	38	10	8	3	0	1	8	4	4	.211	.302	.368	.671	72	-2	-2	103	132	4	.633	0			0	O	0.0
	Lou-N	96	373	65	104	17	5	6	49	33	16	.279	.352	.399	.751	100	-3	1	95	87	58	.755	12			16	3O/2S	1.4
	Yr	107	411	75	112	20	5	7	57	37	20	.273	.347	.397	.744	97	-4	-1	96	93	62	.742	12			16		1.4
1896	Bos-N	84	304	48	90	10	9	1	46	30	12	.296	.374	.398	.772	98	3	-1	108	109	50	.790	10			20	3/S	1.9

YEAR	TM/L	G	AB	R	H	2B	3B	HR	RBI	BB	SO	AVG	OBP	SLG	PRO	/A	BR	/A	PF	CHI	RC	TA	SB	CS	SBR	FR	POS	TPR
1897	Bos-N	134	529	103	183	28	13	6	132	41		.346	.400	.482	.882	126	26	20	107	144	110	.916	14			20	*3	3.4
1898	Bos-N	152	597	107	196	35	5	**15**	111	40		.328	.377	.479	.856	143	34	31	104	107	115	.860	12			12	*3	4.3
1899	Bos-N	151	599	98	166	28	11	5	92	40		.277	.334	.386	.719	95	-1	-6	105	110	83	.679	12			20	*3	1.2
1900	Bos-N	142	586	104	178	25	5	6	95	34		.304	.342	.394	.736	87	3	-14	120	115	89	.706	23			11	*3/S	-0.1
1901	Bos-A	138	564	108	187	42	16	6	94	34		.332	.370	.495	.864	145	28	31	97	96	113	.881	19			14	*3M	3.7
1902	Bos-A	108	429	71	138	21	10	6	61	24		.322	.358	.459	.817	128	14	15	99	99	79	.821	18			9	*3M	1.9
1903	Bos-A	130	540	88	160	33	17	5	72	24		.296	.326	.448	.774	118	19	12	112	89	89	.761	23			10	*3M	2.1
1904	Bos-A	156	631	85	171	33	13	3	67	27		.271	.301	.379	.680	111	10	7	105	89	80	.620	19			7	*3M	2.1
1905	Bos-A	131	508	66	140	26	5	4	65	37		.276	.325	.370	.695	122	12	12	100	112	69	.660	18			8	*3M	2.7
1906	Bos-A	37	142	17	39	8	4	1	16	4		.275	.295	.408	.703	123	3	3	98	101	18	.612	1			-2	3M	0.4
1907	Bos-A	41	158	12	46	8	0	0	10	10		.291	.333	.342	.675	116	3	3	101	64	20	.607	4			0	3	0.6
	Phi-A	100	365	39	100	21	1	0	35	24		.274	.319	.337	.656	105	4	2	106	108	41	.570	4			-4	3	0.4
	Yr	141	523	51	146	29	1	0	45	34		.279	.323	.338	.662	108	7	5	105	95	61	.581	8			-4		1.0
1908	Phi-A	115	433	34	94	14	3	0	30	20		.217	.252	.263	.515	64	-15	-18	108	105	28	.410	5			-9	*3	-2.2
Total	14	1726	6796	1055	2000	352	117	65	983	426	32	.294	.340	.409	.749	112	142	95	105	105	1046	.718	194			131	*3/OS2	23.8

■ **ZIP COLLINS** Collins, John Edgar b: 5/2/1892, Brooklyn, N.Y. d: 12/19/83, Manassas, Va. BL/TL, 5'11", 152 lbs. Deb: 7/31/14

YEAR	TM/L	G	AB	R	H	2B	3B	HR	RBI	BB	SO	AVG	OBP	SLG	PRO	/A	BR	/A	PF	CHI	RC	TA	SB	CS	SBR	FR	POS	TPR
1914	Pit-N	49	182	14	44	2	0	0	15	8	10	.242	.277	.253	.530	63	-9	-8	92	125	13	.420	3			1	O	-0.8
1915	Pit-N	101	354	51	104	8	5	1	23	24	38	.294	.340	.353	.693	111	4	5	99	70	44	.607	6	7	-2	1	O	0.1
	Bos-N	5	14	3	4	1	1	0	0	2	1	.286	.375	.500	.875	167	1	1	98	0	3	1.000	1			0	/O	0.2
	Yr	106	368	54	108	9	6	1	23	26	39	.293	.342	.359	.700	114	5	6	99	67	47	.622	7	7	-2	1		0.3
1916	Bos-N	93	268	39	56	1	6	1	18	18	42	.209	.261	.269	.530	68	-12	-10	93	95	21	.448	4			-5	O	-1.9
1917	Bos-N	9	27	3	4	0	1	0	2	0	4	.148	.148	.222	.370	13	-3	-3	96	129	1	.261	0			0	/O	-0.2
1921	Phi-A	24	71	14	20	5	1	0	5	6	5	.282	.354	.380	.735	85	-1	-2	103	63	9	.679	1	2	-1	1	O	-0.2
Total	5	281	916	124	232	17	14	2	63	58	100	.253	.301	.309	.610	86	-20	-16	96	88	92	.521	15	9		-1	O	-2.8

■ **SHANO COLLINS** Collins, John Francis b: 12/4/1885, Charlestown, Mass. d: 9/10/55, Newton, Mass. BR/TR, 6', 185 lbs. Deb: 4/21/10 M

YEAR	TM/L	G	AB	R	H	2B	3B	HR	RBI	BB	SO	AVG	OBP	SLG	PRO	/A	BR	/A	PF	CHI	RC	TA	SB	CS	SBR	FR	POS	TPR
1910	Chi-A	97	315	29	62	10	8	1	24	25		.197	.258	.289	.547	75	-11	-9	95	96	26	.502	10			-3	O1	-1.5
1911	Chi-A	106	370	48	97	16	12	4	48	20		.262	.309	.403	.712	101	-3	-1	97	103	50	.689	14			6	1/2O	0.6
1912	Chi-A	153	579	75	168	34	10	2	81	29		.290	.330	.394	.723	108	3	3	99	122	83	.701	26			-14	*O1	-1.5
1913	Chi-A	148	535	53	128	26	9	1	47	32	60	.239	.286	.327	.613	83	-16	-13	95	99	55	.570	22			-5	*O	-2.7
1914	Chi-A	154	598	61	164	34	9	3	65	27	49	.274	.312	.376	.688	104	2	-0	103	100	71	.629	30	24	-5	4	*O	-1.1
1915	Chi-A	153	576	73	148	24	17	2	85	28	50	.257	.298	.368	.666	102	-4	-2	98	141	70	.635	38	19	0	2	*O1	-0.8
1916	Chi-A	143	527	74	128	28	12	0	42	59	51	.243	.323	.342	.664	92	-1	-6	108	88	65	.647	16			-2	*O/1	-1.7
1917	Chi-A	82	252	38	59	13	3	1	14	10	27	.234	.269	.321	.590	82	-7	-7	98	60	24	.554	14			-6	O	-1.9
1918	Chi-A	103	365	30	100	18	11	1	56	17	19	.274	.310	.392	.702	111	3	2	101	143	45	.638	7			12	O/1	1.0
1919	Chi-A	63	179	21	50	6	3	1	16	7	11	.279	.317	.363	.681	87	-3	-4	105	85	21	.605	3			-0	O/1	-0.7
1920	Chi-A	133	495	70	150	21	10	1	63	23	24	.303	.339	.392	.731	97	-6	-3	96	115	65	.658	12	9	-2	-11	*1O	-1.5
1921	Bos-A	141	542	63	155	29	12	4	69	18	38	.286	.314	.406	.720	83	-16	-16	100	108	68	.651	15	8	-0	3	*O/1	-2.3
1922	Bos-A	135	472	33	128	24	7	1	52	7	30	.271	.289	.358	.647	70	-24	-21	96	108	46	.533	7	9	-3	-6	*O/1	-3.8
1923	Bos-A	97	342	41	79	10	5	0	18	11	29	.231	.265	.289	.555	45	-27	-28	102	63	25	.450	7	8	-3	-1	O	-3.9
1924	Bos-A	89	240	37	70	17	5	0	28	18	17	.292	.349	.404	.753	90	-3	-4	104	95	33	.693	4	6	-2	-9	O1	-1.8
1925	Bos-A	2	3	1	1	0	0	0	1	0	0	.333	.333	.333	.667	73	-0	-0	95	335	0	.500	0	0	0	-0	/O	0.0
Total	16	1799	6390	747	1687	310	133	22	709	331	405	.264	.306	.364	.671	90	-114	-109	100	105	748	.615	225	83		-30	*O1/2	-23.6

■ **JOE COLLINS** Collins, Joseph Edward (born Joseph Edward Kollonige) b: 12/3/22, Scranton, Pa. BL/TL, 6', 185 lbs. Deb: 9/25/48

YEAR	TM/L	G	AB	R	H	2B	3B	HR	RBI	BB	SO	AVG	OBP	SLG	PRO	/A	BR	/A	PF	CHI	RC	TA	SB	CS	SBR	FR	POS	TPR
1948	NY-A	5	5	0	1	1	0	0	2	0	1	.200	.200	.400	.600	57	-0	-0	100	338	0	.500	0	0	0	0	H	0.0
1949	NY-A	7	10	2	1	0	0	0	4	6	2	.100	.438	.100	.538	46	-0	-0	100	0	1	.778	0	0	0	0	/1	0.0
1950	NY-A	108	205	47	48	8	3	8	28	31	34	.234	.335	.420	.754	93	-3	-3	99	88	31	.758	5	0	2	-4	1/O	-0.9
1951	NY-A	125	262	52	75	8	5	9	48	34	23	.286	.368	.458	.826	134	8	11	92	117	44	.815	9	7	-2	-3	*1O	0.4
1952	NY-A	122	428	69	120	16	8	18	59	55	47	.280	.364	.481	.845	137	18	20	98	86	77	.829	4	2	0	-2	*1	1.1
1953	NY-A	127	387	72	104	11	2	17	44	59	36	.269	.365	.439	.805	126	9	13	93	74	65	.783	2	6	-3	-2	*1/O	0.5
1954	NY-A	130	343	67	93	20	2	12	46	51	37	.271	.365	.446	.812	123	10	11	99	92	58	.802	2	2	-1	1	*1	0.8
1955	NY-A	105	278	40	65	9	1	13	45	44	32	.234	.343	.414	.756	105	1	2	98	109	40	.725	0	2	-1	0	1O	-0.3
1956	NY-A	100	262	38	59	5	3	7	43	34	33	.225	.316	.347	.664	76	-10	-9	99	143	30	.617	3	1	0	-1	O1	-1.3
1957	NY-A	79	149	17	30	1	0	2	10	24	18	.201	.312	.248	.560	59	-9	-7	94	92	12	.508	2	1	0	-1	1O	-0.9
Total	10	908	2329	404	596	79	24	86	329	338	263	.256	.351	.421	.772	112	25	36	96	98	360	.768	27	21	-5	-11	1O	-0.6

■ **KEVIN COLLINS** Collins, Kevin Michael "Casey" b: 8/4/46, Springfield, Mass. BL/TR, 6'1", 180 lbs. Deb: 9/01/65

YEAR	TM/L	G	AB	R	H	2B	3B	HR	RBI	BB	SO	AVG	OBP	SLG	PRO	/A	BR	/A	PF	CHI	RC	TA	SB	CS	SBR	FR	POS	TPR
1965	NY-N	11	23	3	4	1	0	0	0	1	9	.174	.208	.217	.426	20	-2	-2	100	0	1	.300	0	1	-1	0	/3S	-0.2
1967	NY-N	4	10	1	1	0	0	0	0	0	3	.100	.100	.100	.200	-43	-2	-2	99	0	0	.200	1	0	0	0	/2	-0.1
1968	NY-N	58	154	12	31	5	2	1	13	7	37	.201	.236	.279	.515	53	-9	-9	102	119	10	.397	0	1	-1	-1	3/2S	-1.1
1969	NY-N	16	40	1	6	3	0	1	2	3	10	.150	.209	.300	.509	41	-3	-3	100	53	3	.441	0	0	0	-1	3	-0.3
	Mon-N	52	96	5	23	5	1	2	12	8	16	.240	.298	.375	.673	87	-2	-2	100	115	11	.587	0	0	0	0	23	0.0
	Yr	68	136	6	29	8	1	3	14	11	26	.213	.272	.353	.625	74	-5	-5	100	101	13	.541	0	0	0	-0		-0.3
1970	Det-A	25	24	2	5	1	0	1	3	1	10	.208	.240	.375	.615	65	-1	-1	103	101	2	.526	0	0	0	0	/1	0.0
1971	Det-A	35	41	6	11	2	1	1	4	0	12	.268	.268	.439	.707	102	-0	-0	96	78	4	.581	0	0	0	0	/3O2	0.0
Total	6	201	388	30	81	17	4	6	34	20	97	.209	.248	.320	.567	62	-20	-20	101	96	31	.468	1	2	-1	-2	/32SO1	-1.7

■ **ORTH COLLINS** Collins, Orth Stein "Buck" b: 4/27/1880, Lafayette, Ind. d: 12/13/49, Ft.Lauderdale, Fla BL/TR, 6', 150 lbs. Deb: 6/01/04

YEAR	TM/L	G	AB	R	H	2B	3B	HR	RBI	BB	SO	AVG	OBP	SLG	PRO	/A	BR	/A	PF	CHI	RC	TA	SB	CS	SBR	FR	POS	TPR
1904	NY-A	5	17	3	6	1	1	0	1	1		.353	.389	.529	.918	171	2	1	112	42	4	.909	0			0	/O	0.2
1909	Was-A	8	7	0	0	0	0	0	0	0		.000	.000	.000	.000	-99	-2	-1	90	0	0	.000	0			0	/OP	-0.1
Total	2	13	24	3	6	1	1	0	1	1		.250	.280	.375	.655	102	0	-0	106	30	4	.556	0			0	/OP	0.1

■ **RIP COLLINS** Collins, Robert Joseph b: 9/18/09, Pittsburgh, Pa. d: 4/19/69, Pittsburgh, Pa. BR/TR, 5'11", 176 lbs. Deb: 4/28/40

YEAR	TM/L	G	AB	R	H	2B	3B	HR	RBI	BB	SO	AVG	OBP	SLG	PRO	/A	BR	/A	PF	CHI	RC	TA	SB	CS	SBR	FR	POS	TPR
1940	Chi-N	47	120	11	25	3	0	1	14	14	18	.208	.296	.258	.555	54	-7	-7	100	153	9	.500	4			0	C	-0.4
1944	NY-A	3	3	0	1	0	0	0	0	1	0	.333	.500	.333	.833	132	0	0	106	0	1	1.000	0	0	0	0	/C	0.1
Total	2	50	123	11	26	3	0	1	14	15	18	.211	.302	.260	.562	57	-7	-7	100	148	10	.536	4	0		0	/C	-0.3

■ **PAT COLLINS** Collins, Tharon Leslie b: 9/13/1896, Sweet Sprgs., Mo. d: 5/20/60, Kansas City, Kan. BR/TR, 5'9", 178 lbs. Deb: 9/05/19

YEAR	TM/L	G	AB	R	H	2B	3B	HR	RBI	BB	SO	AVG	OBP	SLG	PRO	/A	BR	/A	PF	CHI	RC	TA	SB	CS	SBR	FR	POS	TPR
1919	StL-A	11	21	2	3	1	0	0	1	4	2	.143	.280	.190	.470	34	-2	-2	97	91	1	.444	0			0	/C	0.0
1920	StL-A	23	28	5	6	1	0	0	6	3	5	.214	.290	.250	.540	40	-2	-3	111	301	2	.455	0	0	0	0	/C	-0.1
1921	StL-A	58	111	9	27	3	0	1	10	16	17	.243	.339	.297	.636	63	-6	-6	101	95	12	.595	1	0	0	0	C	-0.3
1922	StL-A	63	127	14	39	6	0	8	23	21	21	.307	.405	.543	.949	138	9	7	106	88	28	1.011	0	1	-1	2	C/1	0.9
1923	StL-A	85	181	9	32	8	0	3	30	15	45	.177	.240	.271	.511	33	-18	-19	104	177	13	.430	0	0	0	2	C	-1.2
1924	StL-A	32	54	9	17	2	0	1	11	11	14	.315	.431	.407	.838	109	2	1	107	145	10	.868	0	1	-1	0	C	0.2
1926	NY-A	102	290	41	83	11	3	7	35	73	55	.286	.433	.417	.850	123	14	14	99	84	59	.952	3	2	-0	3	*C	2.2
1927	NY-A	92	251	38	69	9	3	7	36	54	24	.275	.407	.418	.825	115	8	8	100	95	45	.885	0	0	0	-3	C	0.7
1928	NY-A	70	136	18	30	5	0	6	14	35	16	.221	.380	.390	.770	111	2	3	92	68	23	.830	0	0	0	-5	C	0.3
1929	Bos-N	7	5	1	0	0	0	0	2	3	1	.000	.375	.000	.375	2	-1	-1	94	0	1	.600	0			0	/C	0.0
Total	10	543	1204	146	306	46	6	33	168	235	200	.254	.378	.385	.762	99	5	4	100	105	194	.783	4	4		-0	C/1	2.7

■ **BILL COLLINS** Collins, William J. b: 1863, Dublin, Ireland d: 6/8/1893, New York, N.Y. BR , Deb: 1889

YEAR	TM/L	G	AB	R	H	2B	3B	HR	RBI	BB	SO	AVG	OBP	SLG	PRO	/A	BR	/A	PF	CHI	RC	TA	SB	CS	SBR	FR	POS	TPR
1889	Phi-a	1	4	0	1	0	0	0	1	1	0	.250	.400	.250	.650	91	0	0	98	247	1	1.000	1			0	/C	0.0
1890	Phi-a	1	1	0	0	0	0	0		0		.000	.000	.000	.000	-99	-0	-0	97	0	0	.000	0			0	/S	0.0
1891	Cle-N	2	3	0	0	0	0	0	0	0	0	.000	.000	.000	.000	-95	-1	-1	105	0	0	.000	0			0	/OC	0.0
Total	3	4	8	0	1	0	0	0	1	1	0	.125	.222	.125	.347	2	-1	-1	100	137	1	.429	1			0	/COS	0.0

YEAR	TM/L	G	AB	R	H	2B	3B	HR	RBI	BB	SO	AVG	OBP	SLG	PRO	/A	BR	/A	PF	CHI	RC	TA	SB	CS	SBR	FR	POS	TPR
■ BILL COLLINS	Collins, William Shirley b: 3/27/1882, Chesterton, Ind. d: 6/26/61, San Bernadino, Cal. BB/TR, 6', 170 lbs. Deb: 4/14/10																											
1910	Bos-N	151	584	67	141	6	7	3	40	43	48	.241	.308	.291	.599	66	-18	-29	114	69	63	.591	36			1	*O	-3.4
1911	Bos-N	17	44	8	6	1	1	0	8	1	8	.136	.156	.205	.360	0	-6	-6	103	301	2	.368	4			0	O/3	-0.5
	Chi-N	7	5	2	1	1	0	0	0	1	3	.200	.333	.400	.733	109	0	0	97	0	1	.750	0			-2	/O	-0.1
	Yr	24	49	10	7	2	1	0	8	2	11	.143	.176	.224	.401	12	-6	-6	101	225	3	.405	4			-1		-0.6
1913	Bro-N	32	95	8	18	1	0	0	4	8	11	.189	.267	.200	.467	33	-8	-8	104	76	5	.403	2			-2	O	-1.1
1914	Buf-F	21	47	6	7	2	2	0	2	1	8	.149	.167	.277	.443	25	-5	-5	104	55	2	.350	0			-3	O	-0.8
Total	4	228	775	91	173	11	10	3	54	54	78	.223	.287	.275	.562	56	-37	-48	111	81	74	.538	42			-5	O/3	-5.9
■ FRANK COLMAN	Colman, Frank Lloyd b: 3/2/18, London, Ont., Canada d: 2/21/83, London, Ont., Can. BL/TL, 5'11", 186 lbs. Deb: 9/12/42																											
1942	Pit-N	10	37	2	5	0	0	1	2	2	2	.135	.179	.216	.396	15	-4	-4	101	69	2	.313	0			1	/O	-0.3
1943	Pit-N	32	59	9	16	2	2	0	4	8	7	.271	.358	.373	.731	107	1	1	104	66	9	.698	0			-0	O	0.0
1944	Pit-N	99	226	30	61	9	5	6	53	25	27	.270	.345	.434	.779	112	5	4	105	164	34	.729	0			-5	O/1	-0.5
1945	Pit-N	77	153	18	32	11	1	4	30	9	16	.209	.253	.373	.626	70	-7	-7	103	151	14	.528	0			-3	1O	-1.0
1946	Pit-N	26	53	3	9	3	0	1	6	2	7	.170	.214	.283	.497	39	-4	-5	103	124	3	.409	0			0	/O1	-0.4
	NY-A	5	15	2	4	0	0	1	5	1	1	.267	.313	.467	.779	115	0	0	100	190	2	.727	0	0	0	-1	/O	0.0
1947	NY-A	22	28	2	3	0	0	2	6	2	6	.107	.167	.321	.488	35	-3	-3	97	147	2	.440	0	0	0	-1	/O	-0.3
Total	6	271	571	66	130	25	8	15	106	49	66	.228	.291	.378	.669	85	-11	-14	104	140	65	.605	0	0		-8	O/1	-2.5
■ BOB COLUCCIO	Coluccio, Robert Pasquali b: 10/2/51, Centralia, Wash. BR/TR, 5'11", 183 lbs. Deb: 4/15/73																											
1973	Mil-A	124	438	65	98	21	8	15	58	54	92	.224	.313	.411	.724	107	1	3	96	103	58	.710	13	6	0	10	*OD	1.0
1974	Mil-A	138	394	42	88	13	4	6	31	43	61	.223	.305	.322	.627	79	-10	-11	102	84	40	.584	15	9	-1	-6	*O/D	-2.1
1975	Mil-A	22	62	8	12	0	1	1	5	11	11	.194	.324	.274	.599	70	-2	-2	100	96	5	.536	1	4	-2	2	O	-0.2
	Chi-A	61	161	22	33	4	2	4	13	13	34	.205	.269	.329	.598	66	-7	-8	103	77	15	.542	4	0	1	-6	O/D	-1.4
	Yr	83	223	30	45	4	3	5	18	24	45	.202	.285	.314	.599	67	-9	-10	102	83	21	.546	5	4	-1	-4		-1.6
1977	Chi-A	20	37	4	10	0	0	0	7	6	2	.270	.372	.270	.642	79	-1	-1	99	277	4	.533	0	2	-1	-1	O	-0.3
1978	StL-N	5	3	0	0	0	0	0	0	1	2	.000	.250	.000	.250	-26	-0	-0	95	0	0	.333	0	0	0	-1	/O	0.0
Total	5	370	1095	141	241	38	15	26	114	128	202	.220	.306	.353	.660	87	-19	-19	100	98	122	.635	33	21	-3	-2	O/D	-3.0
■ EARLE COMBS	Combs, Earle Bryan "The Kentucky Colonel" b: 5/14/1899, Pebworth, Ky. d: 7/21/76, Richmond, Ky. BL/TR, 6', 185 lbs. Deb: 4/16/24 CH																											
1924	NY-A	24	35	10	14	5	0	0	2	4	2	.400	.462	.543	1.004	160	3	3	99	35	8	1.045	0	1	-1	-3	O	0.0
1925	NY-A	150	593	117	203	36	13	3	61	65	43	.342	.411	.462	.873	126	20	24	96	69	112	.881	12	13	-4	-4	*O	0.2
1926	NY-A	145	606	113	181	31	12	8	56	47	23	.299	.352	.429	.781	104	1	2	99	59	92	.738	8	6	-1	-5	*O	-1.4
1927	NY-A	152	648	137	**231**	36	**23**	6	64	62	31	.356	.414	.511	.925	139	37	37	100	54	134	.983	15	0	5	-2	*O	2.3
1928	NY-A	149	626	118	194	33	**21**	7	56	77	33	.310	.387	.463	.850	133	21	28	92	53	114	.861	10	8	-2	2	*O	1.9
1929	NY-A	142	586	119	202	33	15	3	65	69	32	.345	.414	.468	.881	128	25	26	99	69	115	.905	11	7	-1	-7	*O	1.1
1930	NY-A	137	532	129	183	30	**22**	7	82	74	26	.344	.424	.523	.947	155	33	42	90	96	120	1.025	16	10	-1	-1	*O	3.0
1931	NY-A	138	563	120	179	31	13	5	58	68	34	.318	.394	.446	.840	123	18	20	98	76	103	.860	11	3	2	-6	*O	0.6
1932	NY-A	144	591	143	190	32	10	9	65	81	16	.321	.405	.455	.860	128	22	26	95	71	110	.866	3	9	-5	-7	*O	0.8
1933	NY-A	122	417	86	125	22	16	5	64	47	19	.300	.372	.465	.837	133	12	17	91	102	73	.838	6	4	-1	-8	*O	0.5
1934	NY-A	63	251	47	80	13	5	2	25	40	9	.319	.412	.434	.847	124	8	10	96	64	48	.884	3	1	0	1	O	1.0
1935	NY-A	89	298	47	84	7	4	3	35	36	10	.282	.359	.362	.722	94	-5	-2	93	102	40	.668	1	3	-2	-4	O	-0.7
Total	12	1455	5746	1186	1866	309	154	58	633	670	278	.325	.397	.462	.859	128	197	234	96	72	1068	.872	96	65	-10	-44	*O	9.3
■ MERL COMBS	Combs, Merrill Russell b: 12/11/19, Los Angeles, Cal. d: 7/8/81, Riverside, Cal. BL/TR, 6', 172 lbs. Deb: 9/12/47 C																											
1947	Bos-A	17	68	8	15	1	0	1	6	9	9	.221	.329	.279	.609	65	-2	-3	108	89	7	.536	0	0	0	-0	3	-0.2
1949	Bos-A	14	24	5	5	1	0	0	1	9	0	.208	.424	.250	.674	75	-0	-0	107	57	4	.789	0	0	0	1	/3S	0.1
1950	Bos-A	1	0	0	0	0	0	0	0	1	0	—	1.000	—	1.250	204	0	0	114	0	0	—	0	0	0	0	H	0.0
	Was-A	37	102	19	25	1	0	0	6	22	16	.245	.379	.255	.634	65	-4	-4	99	80	12	.600	0	0	0	-1	S	-0.2
	Yr	38	102	19	25	1	0	0	6	23	16	.245	.384	.255	.639	66	-4	-4	100	78	12	.613	0	0	0	-1		-0.2
1951	Cle-A	19	28	2	5	2	0	0	2	2	3	.179	.233	.250	.483	32	-3	-3	95	102	2	.391	0	0	0	0	S	-0.1
1952	Cle-A	52	139	11	23	1	1	1	10	14	15	.165	.242	.209	.450	29	-14	-12	91	117	8	.361	0	1	-1	2	S/2	-0.7
Total	5	140	361	45	73	6	1	2	25	57	43	.202	.314	.241	.555	52	-23	-22	98	94	32	.502	0	1	-1	3	/S32	-1.1
■ WAYNE COMER	Comer, Harry Wayne b: 2/3/44, Shenandoah, Va. BR/TR, 5'1", 175 lbs. Deb: 9/17/67																											
1967	Det-A	4	3	0	1	0	0	0	0	0	0	.333	.333	.333	.667	98	-0	-0	99	0	0	.500	0	0	0	-0	/O	0.0
1968	Det-A	48	48	8	6	0	1	1	3	2	7	.125	.160	.229	.389	16	-5	-5	106	92	1	.283	0	0	0	-6	O/C	-1.4
1969	Sea-A	147	481	88	118	18	1	15	54	82	79	.245	.356	.380	.737	108	6	7	98	97	70	.747	18	7	1	14	*O/C3	1.9
1970	Mil-A	13	17	1	1	0	0	0	1	0	3	.059	.059	.059	.118	-69	-4	-4	98	405	0	.059	0	0	0	-1	/O	-0.4
	Was-A	77	129	21	30	4	0	0	8	22	16	.233	.349	.264	.612	74	-4	-3	96	95	14	.598	4	1	1	-9	O/3	-1.4
	Yr	90	146	22	31	4	0	0	9	22	19	.212	.320	.240	.559	58	-8	-7	96	144	13	.525	4	1	1	-10		-1.8
1972	Det-A	27	9	1	1	0	0	0	1	0	1	.111	.111	.111	.222	-30	-1	-2	113	418	0	.111	0	1	-1	-6	O	-0.9
Total	5	316	687	119	157	22	2	16	67	106	106	.229	.333	.336	.670	90	-8	-7	99	106	85	.670	22	9	1	-8	O/3C	-2.2
■ CHARLIE COMISKEY	Comiskey, Charles Albert "Commy" or "The Old Roman" b: 8/15/1859, Chicago, Ill. d: 10/26/31, Eagle River, Wis. BR/TR, 6', 180 lbs. Deb: 5/02/1882 MH																											
1882	StL-a	78	329	58	80	9	5	1		4		.243	.252	.310	.562	89	-4	-4	100	0	26	.426				-1	*1/P	-0.4
1883	StL-a	96	401	87	118	17	9	2		11		.294	.313	.397	.710	118	11	6	108	0	51	.601				-2	*1/OM	-0.3
1884	StL-a	108	460	76	110	17	6	2		5		.239	.255	.315	.571	80	-6	-13	110	0	38	.443				2	*1/2PM	-1.4
1885	StL-a	83	340	68	87	15	7	2		14		.256	.293	.359	.652	116	3	6	93	0	37	.553				1	*1M	0.0
1886	StL-a	131	578	95	147	15	9	3		10		.254	.267	.327	.594	78	-10	-20	111	0	63	.557	41			6	*1/2OM	-1.7
1887	StL-a	125	538	139	180	22	5	4		27		.335	.374	.416	.790	112	16	7	110	0	131	1.047	117			5	*1/2OM	0.8
1888	StL-a	137	576	102	157	22	5	6	83	12		.273	.292	.359	.652	100	5	-4	111	117	84	.704	72			-3	*1/O2M	-1.3
1889	StL-a	137	587	105	168	28	10	3	102	19	19	.286	.312	.383	.695	89	-3	-14	112	120	93	.745	65			-1	*1/O2PM	-2.2
1890	Chi-P	88	377	53	92	11	3	0	59	14	17	.244	.277	.289	.566	51	-26	-28	104	157	41	.561	34			-2	1M	-3.1
1891	StL-a	141	580	86	152	16	2	3	93	33	25	.262	.310	.312	.622	71	-15	-28	114	**144**	70	.612	41			2	*1/OM	-2.8
1892	Cin-N	141	551	61	125	14	6	3	71	32	16	.227	.274	.290	.565	70	-19	-22	103	137	53	.531	30			-0	*1M	-3.0
1893	Cin-N	64	259	38	57	12	1	0	26	11	2	.220	.257	.274	.531	42	-22	-22	101	102	21	.460	9			-6	1M	-2.3
1894	Cin-N	61	220	26	58	8	0	0	33	5	5	.264	.289	.300	.589	44	-20	-20	100	138	23	.519	10			-4	1/OM	-1.7
Total	13	1390	5796	994	1531	206	68	29	467	197	84	.264	.293	.338	.631	83	-89	-156	107	72	730	.614	419			-1	*1/2OP	-19.4
■ JIM COMMAND	Command, James Dalton "Igor" b: 10/15/28, Grand Rapids, Mich BL/TR, 6'2", 200 lbs. Deb: 6/20/54																											
1954	Phi-N	9	18	1	4	1	0	1	6	2	4	.222	.300	.444	.744	92	-0	-0	99	215	3	.714	0	0	0	0	/3	0.0
1955	Phi-N	5	5	0	0	0	0	0	0	0	0	.000	.000	.000	.000	-98	-1	-1	102	0	0	.000	0	0	0	0	H	0.0
Total	2	14	23	1	4	1	0	1	6	2	4	.174	.240	.348	.588	52	-2	-2	99	172	3	.526	0	0	0	0	/3	0.0
■ ADAM COMOROSKY	Comorosky, Adam b: 12/9/05, Swoyersville, Pa. d: 3/2/51, Swoyersville, Pa. BR/TR, 5'10", 167 lbs. Deb: 9/13/26																											
1926	Pit-N	8	15	2	4	1	1	0	0	1	2	.267	.313	.467	.779	96	0	-0	112	0	2	.818	1			-2	/O	-0.1
1927	Pit-N	18	61	5	14	1	0	0	4	3	1	.230	.266	.246	.512	37	-5	-5	102	93	4	.383	0			1	O	-0.4
1928	Pit-N	51	176	22	52	6	3	2	34	15	6	.295	.354	.398	.752	90	-1	-3	107	159	25	.702	1			1	O	-0.2
1929	Pit-N	127	473	86	152	26	11	6	97	40	22	.321	.377	.461	.838	103	5	2	103	144	80	.869	19			-6	*O	-1.2
1930	Pit-N	152	597	112	187	47	**23**	12	119	51	33	.313	.371	.529	.900	118	12	15	97	112	114	.939	14			2	*O	0.6
1931	Pit-N	99	350	37	85	12	1	1	48	34	28	.243	.310	.291	.601	62	-18	-18	101	166	34	.555	11			-1	O	-2.3
1932	Pit-N	108	370	54	106	18	4	4	46	25	20	.286	.337	.389	.726	95	-3	-2	99	110	50	.678	7			6	O	-0.2
1933	Pit-N	64	162	18	46	8	1	1	15	4	9	.284	.301	.364	.665	84	-3	-2	95	91	16	.524	2			-2	O	-0.4
1934	Cin-N	127	446	46	115	12	6	0	40	34	23	.258	.315	.312	.626	68	-19	-20	101	106	44	.513	1			-1	*O	-2.5
1935	Cin-N	59	137	22	34	3	1	2	14	7	14	.248	.290	.328	.618	70	-7	-5	93	99	13	.514	1			-3	O	-0.9
Total	10	813	2787	404	795	134	51	28	417	214	158	.285	.339	.400	.739	91	-38	-38	100	123	382	.702	57			-3	O	-7.6

■ PETE COMPTON Compton, Anna Sebastian "Bash" b: 9/28/1889, San Marcos, Tex. d: 2/3/78, Kansas City, Mo. BL/TL, 5'11", 170 lbs. Deb: 9/06/11

YEAR	TM/L	G	AB	R	H	2B	3B	HR	RBI	BB	SO	AVG	OBP	SLG	PRO	/A	BR	/A	PF	CHI	RC	TA	SB	CS	SBR	FR	POS	TPR
1911	StL-A	28	107	9	29	4	0	0	5	8		.271	.322	.308	.630	80	-3	-3	95	54	11	.551	2			-0	O	-0.4
1912	StL-A	100	268	26	75	6	4	2	30	21		.280	.337	.354	.691	99	-1	-1	99	99	35	.668	11			1	O	-0.3
1913	StL-A	63	100	14	18	5	2	2	17	13	13	.180	.274	.330	.604	80	-3	-3	95	155	9	.585	2			-4	O	-0.8
1915	StL-F	2	8	0	2	0	0	0	3	0	0	.250	.250	.250	.500	46	-1	-1	105	551	1	.333	0			0	/O	0.0
	Bos-N	35	116	10	28	7	1	1	12	8	11	.241	.290	.345	.635	94	-1	-1	98	107	13	.584	4	1	1	1	O	0.0
1916	Bos-N	34	98	13	20	2	0	0	8	7	7	.204	.264	.224	.489	55	-6	-5	93	144	7	.449	5			-0	O	-0.6
	Pit-N	5	16	1	1	0	0	0	0	2	5	.063	.211	.063	.273	-14	-2	-2	105	0	0	.267	0			-0	/O	-0.2
	Yr	39	114	14	21	2	0	0	8	9	12	.184	.256	.202	.458	44	-8	-7	94	130	8	.419	5			-1		-0.8
1918	NY-N	21	60	5	13	0	1	0	5	5	4	.217	.277	.250	.527	63	-3	-3	98	126	4	.468	2			-1	O	-0.4
Total	6	288	773	78	186	24	8	5	80	64	40	.241	.302	.312	.614	82	-20	-17	97	111	81	.570	26	1		-5	O	-2.7

■ MIKE COMPTON Compton, Michael Lynn b: 8/15/44, Stamford, Tex. BR/TR, 5'10", 180 lbs. Deb: 4/17/70

YEAR	TM/L	G	AB	R	H	2B	3B	HR	RBI	BB	SO	AVG	OBP	SLG	PRO	/A	BR	/A	PF	CHI	RC	TA	SB	CS	SBR	FR	POS	TPR
1970	Phi-N	47	110	8	18	0	1	1	7	9	22	.164	.240	.209	.449	22	-12	-12	96	104	6	.366	0	0	0	-2	C	-1.1

■ CLINT CONATSER Conatser, Clinton Astor "Connie" b: 7/24/21, Los Angeles, Cal. BR/TR, 5'11", 182 lbs. Deb: 4/21/48

YEAR	TM/L	G	AB	R	H	2B	3B	HR	RBI	BB	SO	AVG	OBP	SLG	PRO	/A	BR	/A	PF	CHI	RC	TA	SB	CS	SBR	FR	POS	TPR
1948	Bos-N	90	224	30	62	9	3	3	23	32	27	.277	.370	.384	.754	103	2	2	102	91	34	.717	0			-6	O	-0.9
1949	Bos-N	53	152	10	40	6	0	3	16	14	19	.263	.325	.362	.687	87	-3	-3	97	94	17	.585	0			0	O	-0.4
Total	2	143	376	40	102	15	3	6	39	46	46	.271	.352	.375	.727	97	-1	-1	100	92	51	.671	0			-6	O	-1.3

■ DAVE CONCEPCION Concepcion, David Ismael (Benitez) b: 6/17/48, Aragua, Venez. BR/TR, 6'2", 155 lbs. Deb: 4/06/70

YEAR	TM/L	G	AB	R	H	2B	3B	HR	RBI	BB	SO	AVG	OBP	SLG	PRO	/A	BR	/A	PF	CHI	RC	TA	SB	CS	SBR	FR	POS	TPR
1970	Cin-N	101	265	38	69	6	3	1	19	23	45	.260	.326	.317	.643	70	-10	-11	104	85	27	.577	10	2	2	-3	S/2	0.0
1971	Cin-N	130	327	24	67	4	4	1	20	18	51	.205	.246	.251	.497	43	-25	-24	96	96	19	.399	9	3	1	-5	*S2/3O	-1.4
1972	Cin-N	119	378	40	79	13	2	2	29	32	65	.209	.274	.270	.544	59	-22	-19	93	110	27	.472	13	6	0	-4	*S/32	-1.0
1973	Cin-N	89	328	39	94	18	3	8	46	21	55	.287	.331	.433	.764	118	4	6	93	113	47	.756	22	5	4	8	S/O	3.1
1974	Cin-N	160	594	70	167	25	1	14	82	44	79	.281	.337	.397	.734	107	3	4	98	116	80	.722	41	6	9	13	*S/O	4.4
1975	Cin-N	140	507	62	139	23	1	5	49	39	51	.274	.328	.353	.682	85	-8	-10	104	100	59	.647	33	6	6	17	*S/3	2.9
1976	Cin-N	152	576	74	162	28	7	9	69	49	68	.281	.339	.401	.740	106	6	4	103	105	77	.694	21	10	0	15	*S	3.5
1977	Cin-N	156	572	59	155	26	3	8	64	46	77	.271	.325	.369	.694	86	-11	-11	100	111	69	.651	29	7	5	12	*S	2.6
1978	Cin-N	153	565	75	170	33	4	6	67	51	83	.301	.360	.405	.765	110	10	9	103	110	82	.726	23	10	1	4	*S	2.7
1979	Cin-N	149	590	91	166	25	3	16	84	64	73	.281	.352	.415	.767	111	7	9	97	109	85	.731	19	7	2	20	*S	4.6
1980	Cin-N	156	622	72	162	31	8	5	77	37	107	.260	.303	.360	.663	83	-14	-15	102	**135**	65	.568	12	2	2	-13	*S/2	-0.8
1981	Cin-N	106	421	57	129	28	0	5	67	37	61	.306	.364	.409	.772	118	10	10	101	135	60	.690	4	5	-2	5	*S	2.6
1982	Cin-N	147	572	48	164	25	4	5	53	45	61	.287	.339	.371	.709	96	-1	-3	102	97	68	.622	13	6	0	12	*S/13	2.2
1983	Cin-N	143	528	54	123	22	0	1	47	56	81	.233	.307	.280	.587	62	-25	-27	103	130	43	.501	14	9	-1	-11	*S/31	-2.8
1984	Cin-N	154	531	46	130	26	1	4	58	52	72	.245	.312	.320	.632	74	-15	-19	106	127	56	.587	22	6	3	-21	*S3/1	-2.6
1985	Cin-N	155	560	59	141	19	2	7	48	50	67	.252	.316	.330	.647	77	-14	-17	105	95	54	.559	16	12	-2	-24	*S/3	-3.3
1986	Cin-N	90	311	42	81	13	2	3	30	26	43	.260	.318	.344	.662	79	-7	-9	104	105	33	.596	13	2	3	-1	S123	-0.2
1987	Cin-N	104	279	32	89	15	0	1	33	28	24	.319	.381	.384	.765	100	2	1	104	120	39	.685	4	3	-1	-3	213/S	-0.2
1988	Cin-N	84	197	11	39	9	0	0	8	18	23	.198	.265	.244	.509	45	-13	-14	105	67	13	.421	3	2	-0	2	21S/3P	-1.2
Total	19	2488	8723	993	2326	389	48	101	950	736	1186	.267	.325	.357	.682	88	-122	-135	101	111	1005	.644	321	109	31	22	*S23/1OP	15.1

■ ONIX CONCEPCION Concepcion, Onix Cardona (Cardona) b: 10/5/57, Dorado, P.R. BR/TR, 5'6", 160 lbs. Deb: 8/30/80

YEAR	TM/L	G	AB	R	H	2B	3B	HR	RBI	BB	SO	AVG	OBP	SLG	PRO	/A	BR	/A	PF	CHI	RC	TA	SB	CS	SBR	FR	POS	TPR
1980	KC-A	12	15	1	2	0	0	0	2	0	1	.133	.133	.133	.267	-27	-3	-3	98	390	0	.143	0	0	0	-0	/S	-0.2
1981	KC-A	2	0	0	0	0	0	0	0	0	0	—	—	—	—	—	0	0	99	—	—	—	0	0	0	0	/S	0.0
1982	KC-A	74	205	17	48	9	1	0	15	5	18	.234	.256	.288	.544	49	-14	-14	100	102	14	.409	2	1	0	-3	S2/D	-1.1
1983	KC-A	80	219	22	53	11	3	0	20	12	12	.242	.284	.320	.604	65	-10	-11	101	112	20	.538	10	3	1	-2	32S/D	-0.9
1984	KC-A	90	287	36	81	9	2	1	23	14	33	.282	.322	.338	.660	84	-6	-6	99	92	31	.572	9	6	-1	3	S/23	0.3
1985	KC-A	131	314	32	64	5	1	2	20	16	29	.204	.256	.245	.501	37	-26	-27	102	96	19	.393	4	4	-1	9	*S/2	-0.9
1987	Pit-N	1	1	0	1	0	0	0	0	0	0	1.000	1.000	1.000	2.000	414	0	0	104	0	1	—	0	0	0	0	/H	0.0
Total	7	390	1041	108	249	34	7	3	80	47	93	.239	.279	.294	.573	58	-60	-60	101	103	86	.483	25	14	-1	7	S/23D	-2.8

■ RAMON CONDE Conde, Ramon Luis b: 12/29/34, Juana Diaz, P.R. BR/TR, 5'8", 172 lbs. Deb: 7/17/62

YEAR	TM/L	G	AB	R	H	2B	3B	HR	RBI	BB	SO	AVG	OBP	SLG	PRO	/A	BR	/A	PF	CHI	RC	TA	SB	CS	SBR	FR	POS	TPR
1962	Chi-A	14	16	0	0	0	0	0	1	3	3	.000	.158	.000	.158	-56	-4	-3	95	0	0	.167	0	0	0	-1	/3	-0.3

■ FRED CONE Cone, Joseph Frederick b: 5/1848, Rockford, Ill. d: 4/13/09, Chicago, Ill. 5'9.5", 171 lbs. Deb: 5/05/1871

YEAR	TM/L	G	AB	R	H	2B	3B	HR	RBI	BB	SO	AVG	OBP	SLG	PRO	/A	BR	/A	PF	CHI	RC	TA	SB	CS	SBR	FR	POS	TPR
1871	Bos-n	18	85	17	20							.235															O	

■ BUNK CONGALTON Congalton, William Millar b: 1/24/1875, Guelph, Ont., Can. d: 8/16/37, Cleveland, Ohio BL/TL, 5'11", 190 lbs. Deb: 4/18/02

YEAR	TM/L	G	AB	R	H	2B	3B	HR	RBI	BB	SO	AVG	OBP	SLG	PRO	/A	BR	/A	PF	CHI	RC	TA	SB	CS	SBR	FR	POS	TPR
1902	Chi-N	45	179	14	40	3	0	1	24	7		.223	.253	.257	.510	61	-9	-8	96	179	13	.403	3			-5	O	-1.6
1905	Cle-A	12	47	4	17	0	0	0	5	2		.362	.388	.362	.749	141	2	2	100	101	8	.733	3			-0	O	0.1
1906	Cle-A	117	419	51	134	13	5	3	50	24		.320	.357	.396	.753	134	17	16	103	106	65	.709	12			-20	*O	-0.9
1907	Cle-A	9	22	2	4	0	0	0	2	4		.182	.308	.182	.490	63	-1	-1	93	179	1	.444	0			0	/O	0.0
	Bos-A	124	496	44	142	11	8	2	47	20		.286	.314	.353	.667	113	7	6	101	89	60	.588	13			-5	*O	-0.5
	Yr	133	518	46	146	11	8	2	49	24		.282	.314	.346	.659	112	6	6	100	97	62	.581	13			-5		-0.5
Total	4	307	1163	115	337	27	13	6	128	57		.290	.323	.351	.674	113	17	16	101	111	147	.600	31			-30	O	-2.9

■ TONY CONIGLIARO Conigliaro, Anthony Richard b: 1/7/45, Revere, Mass. BR/TR, 6'3", 185 lbs. Deb: 4/16/64

YEAR	TM/L	G	AB	R	H	2B	3B	HR	RBI	BB	SO	AVG	OBP	SLG	PRO	/A	BR	/A	PF	CHI	RC	TA	SB	CS	SBR	FR	POS	TPR
1964	Bos-A	111	404	69	117	21	2	24	52	35	78	.290	.354	.530	.883	139	22	21	102	79	72	.848	2	4	-2	2	*O	1.8
1965	Bos-A	138	521	82	140	21	5	**32**	82	51	116	.269	.340	.512	.852	129	25	20	107	99	91	.834	4	2	0	12	*O	2.9
1966	Bos-A	150	558	77	148	26	7	28	93	52	112	.265	.333	.487	.821	121	22	16	109	116	91	.787	0	2	-1	-2	*O	0.8
1967	Bos-A	95	349	59	100	11	5	20	67	27	58	.287	.346	.519	.865	133	21	16	115	118	62	.841	4	6	-2	2	O	1.3
1969	Bos-A	141	506	57	129	21	3	20	82	48	111	.255	.324	.427	.751	104	4	1	105	122	68	.689	2	4	-2	-11	*O	-1.5
1970	Bos-A	146	560	89	149	20	1	36	116	43	93	.266	.327	.498	.826	113	16	9	111	129	90	.788	4	2	0	0	*O	0.3
1971	Cal-A	74	266	23	59	18	0	4	15	23	52	.222	.286	.335	.621	76	-9	-9	99	62	23	.527	3	3	-1	5	O	-0.6
1975	Bos-A	21	57	8	7	1	0	2	9	8	9	.123	.231	.246	.476	32	-5	-6	109	173	4	.442	1	0	0	0	D	-0.5
Total	8	876	3221	464	849	139	23	166	516	287	629	.264	.330	.476	.806	117	97	69	107	108	501	.781	20	23	-8	8	O/D	4.5

■ BILLY CONIGLIARO Conigliaro, William Michael b: 8/15/47, Revere, Mass. BR/TR, 6', 180 lbs. Deb: 4/11/69

YEAR	TM/L	G	AB	R	H	2B	3B	HR	RBI	BB	SO	AVG	OBP	SLG	PRO	/A	BR	/A	PF	CHI	RC	TA	SB	CS	SBR	FR	POS	TPR
1969	Bos-A	32	80	14	23	6	2	4	7	9	23	.287	.367	.563	.929	149	6	5	105	49	17	.949	1	1	-0	-5	O	0.0
1970	Bos-A	114	398	59	108	16	3	18	58	35	73	.271	.341	.462	.803	108	10	4	111	101	59	.741	3	7	-3	4	*O	0.1
1971	Bos-A	101	351	42	92	26	1	11	33	25	68	.262	.311	.436	.747	104	3	1	106	74	45	.670	3	2	-0	9	*O	0.7
1972	Mil-A	52	191	22	44	6	2	7	16	8	54	.230	.261	.393	.654	97	-3	-2	95	71	18	.553	1	0	0	7	O	0.5
1973	Oak-A	48	110	5	22	2	2	0	14	9	26	.200	.261	.255	.515	52	-8	-6	87	196	8	.422	1	0	0	0	O/2	-0.6
Total	5	347	1130	142	289	56	10	40	128	86	244	.256	.313	.429	.742	104	8	3	104	93	147	.689	9	10	-3	16	O/2	0.7

■ JOCKO CONLAN Conlan, John Bertrand b: 12/6/1899, Chicago, Ill. BL/TL, 5'7.5", 165 lbs. Deb: 7/06/34 UH

YEAR	TM/L	G	AB	R	H	2B	3B	HR	RBI	BB	SO	AVG	OBP	SLG	PRO	/A	BR	/A	PF	CHI	RC	TA	SB	CS	SBR	FR	POS	TPR
1934	Chi-A	63	225	35	56	11	3	0	16	19	7	.249	.310	.324	.635	64	-12	-12	99	75	24	.556	2	2	-1	2	O	-1.0
1935	Chi-A	65	140	20	40	7	1	0	15	14	6	.286	.355	.350	.705	76	-3	-5	109	104	18	.650	3	3	-1	-2	O	-0.7
Total	2	128	365	55	96	18	4	0	31	33	13	.263	.327	.334	.662	69	-15	-17	103	86	41	.591	5	5	-2	-0	/O	-1.7

■ JOCKO CONLON Conlon, Arthur Joseph b: 12/10/1897, Woburn, Mass. BR/TR, 5'7", 145 lbs. Deb: 4/17/23

YEAR	TM/L	G	AB	R	H	2B	3B	HR	RBI	BB	SO	AVG	OBP	SLG	PRO	/A	BR	/A	PF	CHI	RC	TA	SB	CS	SBR	FR	POS	TPR
1923	Bos-N	59	147	23	32	3	0	0	17	11	11	.218	.299	.238	.537	43	-12	-12	100	171	11	.441	0	3	-2	-2	2/S3	-1.3

■ BERT CONN Conn, Albert Thomas b: 9/22/1879, Philadelphia, Pa. d: 11/2/44, Philadelphia, Pa. TR, Deb: 9/16/1898

YEAR	TM/L	G	AB	R	H	2B	3B	HR	RBI	BB	SO	AVG	OBP	SLG	PRO	/A	BR	/A	PF	CHI	RC	TA	SB	CS	SBR	FR	POS	TPR
1898	Phi-N	1	3	1	1	0	1	0	1	0		.333	.333	1.000	1.333	297	1	1	95	101	1	1.500	0			0	/P	0.0
1900	Phi-N	6	9	4	3	1	0	0	1	0		.333	.333	.444	.778	118	0	0	98	78	1	.667	0			0	/P	0.0
1901	Phi-N	5	18	2	4	1	0	0	0	0		.222	.222	.278	.500	45	-1	-1	103	0	1	.357	0			-0	/2	0.0
Total	3	12	30	7	8	2	1	0	2	0		.267	.267	.400	.667	90	-1	-1	100	33	4	.545	0			-0	/2P	0.0

YEAR	TM/L	G	AB	R	H	2B	3B	HR	RBI	BB	SO	AVG	OBP	SLG	PRO	/A	BR	/A	PF	CHI	RC	TA	SB	CS	SBR	FR	POS	TPR
■ **FRITZIE CONNALLY** Connally, Fritzie Lee b: 5/19/58, Bryan, Tex. BR/TR, 6'3", 210 lbs. Deb: 9/09/83																												
1983	Chi-N	8	10	0	1	0	0	0	0	0	5	.100	.100	.100	.200	-44	-2	-2	101	0	0	.111	0	0	0	-0	/3	-0.1
1985	Bal-A	50	112	16	26	4	0	3	15	19	21	.232	.348	.348	.697	93	-1	-1	99	124	15	.678	0	0	0	0	3/1D	-0.1
Total	2	58	122	16	27	4	0	3	15	19	26	.221	.331	.328	.659	82	-3	-2	99	115	15	.625	0	0	0	0	/31D	-0.2
■ **BRUCE CONNATSER** Connatser, Broadus Milburn b: 9/19/02, Sevierville, Tenn d: 1/27/71, Terre Haute, Ind. BR/TR, 5'11.5", 170 lbs. Deb: 9/15/31																												
1931	Cle-A	12	49	5	14	3	0	0	4	2	3	.286	.327	.347	.674	73	-2	-2	106	82	6	.571	0	0	0	0	1	-0.2
1932	Cle-A	23	60	8	14	3	1	0	4	4	8	.233	.281	.317	.598	50	-4	-5	108	70	6	.522	1	0	0	-0	1	-0.5
Total	2	35	109	13	28	6	1	0	8	6	11	.257	.302	.330	.632	60	-6	-7	107	76	11	.543	1	0	0	-0	/1	-0.7
■ **FRANK CONNAUGHTON** Connaughton, Frank H. b: 1/1/1869, Clinton, Mass. d: 12/1/42, Boston, Mass. BR/TR, 5'9", 165 lbs. Deb: 5/28/1894																												
1894	Bos-N	46	171	42	59	9	2	2	33	16	8	.345	.407	.456	.864	97	3	-1	113	108	34	.884	3			-6	S/CO	-0.3
1896	NY-N	88	315	53	82	3	2	2	43	25	7	.260	.319	.302	.620	67	-15	-14	99	125	38	.618	22			0	SO	-1.1
1906	Bos-N	12	44	3	9	0	0	0	1	3		.205	.255	.205	.460	45	-3	-3	100	43	3	.371	1			1	S/2	0.0
Total	3	146	530	98	150	12	4	4	77	44	15	.283	.343	.343	.686	77	-15	-18	103	113	75	.674	26			-5	/SOC2	-1.4
■ **GENE CONNELL** Connell, Eugene Joseph b: 5/10/06, Hazelton, Pa. d: 8/31/37, Waverly, N.Y. BR/TR, 6'0.5", 180 lbs. Deb: 7/04/31																												
1931	Phi-N	6	12	1	3	0	0	0	0	0	3	.250	.250	.250	.500	33	-1	-1	106	0	1	.333	0			0	/C	0.0
■ **JOE CONNELL** Connell, Joseph Bernard b: 1/16/02, Bethlehem, Pa. d: 9/21/77, Trexlertown, Pa. BL/TL, 5'8", 165 lbs. Deb: 6/15/26																												
1926	NY-N	2	1	0	0	0	0	0	0	0	0	.000	.000	.000	.000	-99	-0	-0	98	0	0	.000	0			0	H	0.0
■ **PETE CONNELL** Connell, Peter J. b: Brooklyn, N.Y. Deb: 9/03/1886																												
1886	NY-a	1	5	0	0	0	0	0		0		.000	.000	.000	.000	-97	-1	-1	104	0	0	.000	0			0	/3	0.0
■ **TERRY CONNELL** Connell, Terence G. b: 6/17/1855, Philadelphia, Pa. d: 3/25/24, Philadelphia, Pa. Deb: 6/20/1874																												
1874	Chi-n	1	4	0	0							.000															/C	
■ **TOM CONNELLY** Connelly, Thomas Martin b: 10/20/1897, Chicago, Ill. d: 2/18/41, Hines, Ill. BL/TR, 5'11.5", 165 lbs. Deb: 9/24/20																												
1920	NY-A	1	1	0	0	0	0	0	0	0	0	.000	.000	.000	.000	-98	-0	-0	102	0	0	.000	0	0	0	0	H	0.0
1921	NY-A	4	5	0	1	0	0	0	0	1	0	.200	.333	.200	.533	38	-0	-0	103	0	0	.500	0	0	0	0	/O	0.0
Total	2	5	6	0	1	0	0	0	0	1	0	.167	.286	.167	.452	18	-1	-1	103	0	0	.400	0	0	0	0	/O	0.0
■ **ED CONNOLLY** Connolly, Edward Joseph Sr b: 7/17/08, Brooklyn, N.Y. d: 11/12/63, Pittsfield, Mass. BR/TR, 5'8.5", 180 lbs. Deb: 9/20/29																												
1929	Bos-A	5	8	0	0	0	0	0	0	0	2	.000	.000	.000	.000	-98	-2	-2	102	0	0	.000	0	0	0	0	/C	-0.1
1930	Bos-A	27	48	1	9	2	0	0	7	4	3	.188	.250	.229	.479	24	-6	-5	93	211	3	.385	0	0	0	1	C	-0.1
1931	Bos-A	42	93	3	7	1	0	0	3	5	18	.075	.131	.086	.217	-45	-19	-18	94	124	1	.163	0	0	0	-1	C	-1.3
1932	Bos-A	75	222	9	50	8	4	0	21	20	27	.225	.289	.297	.587	54	-16	-15	97	107	20	.497	0	1	-1	6	C	-0.4
Total	4	149	371	13	66	11	4	0	31	29	50	.178	.239	.229	.469	23	-43	-41	96	122	24	.376	0	1	-1	7	C	-1.9
■ **RED CONNOLLY** Connolly, John M. b: 1863, New York, N.Y. d: 3/2/1896, New York, N.Y. Deb: 7/01/1886																												
1886	StL-N	2	7	0	0	0	0	0	0	0	3	.000	.000	.000	.000	-99	-2	-2	95	0	0	.000	0			0	/O	0.0
■ **JOE CONNOLLY** Connolly, Joseph Aloysius b: 2/12/1888, N.Smithfield, R.I. d: 9/1/43, Springfield, R.I. BL/TR, 5'7.5", 165 lbs. Deb: 4/10/13																												
1913	Bos-N	126	427	79	120	18	11	5	57	66	47	.281	.379	.410	.788	132	16	19	95	111	72	.847	18			-3	*O	1.4
1914	Bos-N	120	399	64	122	28	10	9	65	49	36	.306	.393	.494	.886	156	31	29	104	107	80	.960	12			-8	*O	1.9
1915	Bos-N	104	305	48	91	14	8	0	23	39	35	.298	.387	.397	.784	140	15	16	98	73	48	.788	13	12	-3	-1	O	0.9
1916	Bos-N	62	110	11	25	5	2	0	12	14	13	.227	.320	.309	.629	101	-0	0	93	140	13	.635	5			-1	O	-0.1
Total	4	412	1241	202	358	65	31	14	157	168	131	.288	.380	.425	.805	140	61	64	98	103	212	.847	48	12		-14	O	4.1
■ **JOE CONNOLLY** Connolly, Joseph George "Coaster Joe" b: 6/4/1896, San Francisco, Cal d: 3/30/60, San Francisco, Cal BR/TR, 6', 170 lbs. Deb: 10/01/21																												
1921	NY-N	2	4	0	0	0	0	0	0	1	1	.000	.200	.000	.200	-44	-1	-1	98	0	0	.250	0	0	0	0	/O	0.0
1922	Cle-A	12	45	6	11	2	1	0	6	5	8	.244	.320	.333	.653	69	-2	-2	102	146	5	.618	1	0	0	2	O	0.0
1923	Cle-A	52	109	25	33	10	1	3	25	13	7	.303	.377	.495	.872	127	4	4	101	136	20	.872	1	2	-1	-11	O	-1.0
1924	Bos-A	14	10	1	1	0	0	0	1	2	2	.100	.250	.100	.350	-7	-2	-2	104	331	0	.333	0	0	0	-1	/O	-0.2
Total	4	80	168	32	45	12	2	3	32	21	18	.268	.349	.417	.766	99	-0	-1	101	147	26	.744	2	2	-1	-10	/O	-1.2
■ **BUD CONNOLLY** Connolly, Mervin Thomas "Mike" b: 5/25/01, San Francisco, Cal d: 6/12/64, Berkeley, Cal. BR/TR, 5'8", 154 lbs. Deb: 5/03/25																												
1925	Bos-A	43	107	12	28	7	1	0	21	23	9	.262	.392	.346	.738	93	-1	-0	95	190	15	.732	0	3	-2	1	S/3	0.4
■ **TOM CONNOLLY** Connolly, Thomas Francis "Blackie" or "Ham" b: 12/30/1892, Boston, Mass. d: 5/14/66, Boston, Mass. BL/TR, 5'11", 175 lbs. Deb: 5/12/15																												
1915	Was-A	50	141	14	26	3	2	0	7	14	19	.184	.268	.234	.502	50	-9	-9	101	72	9	.454	5	4	-1	-3	3O/S	-1.3
■ **NED CONNOR** Connor, Edward b: 1850, New York 5'9", 156 lbs. Deb: 5/18/1871																												
1871	Tro-n	7	33	7	6							.182															/1O2	
■ **JIM CONNOR** Connor, James Matthew (born James Matthew O'Connor) b: 5/11/1863, Port Jervis, N.Y. d: 9/3/50, Providence, R.I. BR/TR, Deb: 7/11/1892																												
1892	Chi-N	9	34	0	2	0	0	0	0	1	7	.059	.111	.059	.170	-52	-6	-6	92	0	0	.125	0			0	/2	-0.4
1897	Chi-N	77	285	40	83	10	5	3	38	24		.291	.355	.393	.748	99	-0	-0	100	94	44	.743	10			20	2	2.2
1898	Chi-N	138	505	51	114	9	9	0	67	42		.226	.289	.279	.568	63	-22	-24	103	147	45	.504	11			-5	*2	-2.1
1899	Chi-N	69	234	26	48	7	1	0	24	18		.205	.265	.244	.508	43	-18	-17	96	132	17	.441	6			-3	23	-1.4
Total	4	293	1058	117	247	26	15	3	129	85	7	.233	.296	.295	.591	66	-46	-47	100	124	107	.534	27			13	2/3	-1.7
■ **JOE CONNOR** Connor, Joseph Francis b: 12/8/1874, Waterbury, Conn. d: 11/8/57, Waterbury, Conn. BR/TR, 6'2", 185 lbs. Deb: 9/09/1895																												
1895	StL-N	2	7	0	0	0	0	0	1	0	2	.000	.000	.000	.000	-99	-2	-2	100	0	0	.000	0			0	/3	-0.1
1900	Bos-N	7	19	2	4	0	0	0	4	2		.211	.286	.211	.496	33	-1	-2	120	313	1	.467	1			0	/C	-0.1
1901	Mil-A	38	102	10	28	3	1	1	9	6		.275	.315	.353	.668	91	-2	-1	95	73	13	.622	4			1	C/23O	0.3
	Cle-A	37	121	13	17	3	1	0	6	7		.140	.188	.182	.369	4	-15	-14	95	86	5	.298	2			2	C/OS	-0.7
	Yr	75	223	23	45	6	2	1	15	13		.202	.246	.260	.506	44	-17	-16	95	80	16	.433	6			4		-0.4
1905	NY-A	8	22	4	5	1	0	0	2	3		.227	.320	.273	.593	89	-0	-0	102	119	2	.588	1			-1	/C1	0.0
Total	4	92	271	29	54	7	2	1	22	18	2	.199	.249	.251	.500	43	-21	-20	97	98	21	.433	8			3	/CO31S2	-0.6
■ **ROGER CONNOR** Connor, Roger b: 7/1/1857, Waterbury, Conn. d: 1/4/31, Waterbury, Conn. BL/TL, 6'3", 220 lbs. Deb: 5/01/1880 MH																												
1880	Tro-N	83	340	53	113	18	8	3	47	13	21	.332	.357	.459	.816	158	25	21	110	110	57	.744				-9	*3	1.1
1881	Tro-N	85	367	55	107	17	6	2	31	15	20	.292	.319	.387	.706	121	8	8	100	64	46	.604				2	*1	0.0
1882	Tro-N	81	349	65	115	22	**18**	4	42	13	20	.330	.354	.530	.884	188	30	32	95	63	67	.846				0	1O3	2.2
1883	NY-N	98	409	80	146	28	15	1	50	25	16	.357	.394	.506	.900	171	35	35	100	73	84	.882				2	*1	2.1
1884	NY-N	116	477	98	151	28	4	4	82	38	32	.317	.367	.417	.784	149	26	27	98	118	75	.727				-1	2O3	2.4
1885	NY-N	110	455	102	**169**	23	15	1	65	51	8	**.371**	**.435**	.495	.929	183	**52**	45	109	86	**100**	.965				3	*1	2.7
1886	NY-N	118	485	105	172	29	**20**	7	71	41	15	.355	.405	.540	.945	**209**	49	57	89	71	116	1.022	17			9	*1	4.0
1887	NY-N	127	471	113	134	26	22	17	104	75	50	.285	.392	.541	.933	148	38	32	107	101	120	1.131	43			4	*1	1.3
1888	NY-N	134	481	98	140	15	17	14	71	**73**	44	.291	.389	.480	.869	**193**	45	**50**	93	99	103	.982	27			-1	*1/2	3.5
1889	NY-N	131	496	117	157	32	17	13	**130**	93	46	.317	.426	**.528**	.955	160	47	43	105	137	124	1.115	21			-9	*1/3	2.0
1890	NY-P	123	484	133	169	24	15	**13**	103	88	32	.349	.450	**.541**	**.992**	153	**48**	40	109	99	131	1.184	22			11	*1	3.0
1891	NY-N	129	479	112	139	29	13	7	94	83	39	.290	.399	.449	.848	159	32	37	94	123	99	.968	27			1	*1	3.0
1892	Phi-N	155	564	123	166	**37**	11	12	73	116	39	.294	.420	.463	.883	162	52	48	104	73	122	1.018	22			-8	*1	2.6
1893	NY-N	135	511	111	156	25	8	11	105	91	26	.305	.413	.450	.863	127	26	22	104	116	108	.980	24			2	*1/3	1.9
1894	NY-N	22	82	10	24	7	0	1	14	8	0	.293	.356	.415	.770	87	-2	-2	100	106	13	.759	2			1	1/O	0.0
	StL-N	99	380	83	122	28	25	7	79	51	17	.321	.410	.582	.991	137	22	22	101	87	100	1.143	17			6	*1	2.2
	Yr	121	462	93	146	35	25	8	93	59	17	.316	.400	.552	.952	128	21	20	101	91	112	1.073	19			7		2.2
1895	StL-N	103	398	78	131	29	9	8	77	63	10	.329	.423	.508	.931	142	26	26	100	92	92	1.034	9			4	*1	2.6
1896	StL-N	126	483	71	137	21	9	11	72	52	14	.284	.356	.433	.788	115	6	10	95	83	80	.789	10			13	*1M	2.2
1897	StL-N	22	83	13	19	3	1	1	12	13		.229	.333	.325	.659	82	-3	-2	93	124	10	.672	3			0	1	0.0

YEAR	TM/L	G	AB	R	H	2B	3B	HR	RBI	BB	SO	AVG	OBP	SLG	PRO	/A	BR	/A	PF	CHI	RC	TA	SB	CS	SBR	FR	POS	TPR
Total	18	1997	7794	1620	2467	441	233	137	1322	1002	449	.317	.397	.486	.883	154	563	552	101	95	1645	.952	244			32	*13/2O	38.8
■ **JERRY CONNORS** Connors, Jeremiah b: Philadelphia, Pa. Deb: 7/11/1892																												
1892	Phi-N	1	3	0	0	0	0	0	0	0	1	.000	.000	.000	.000	-96	-1	-1	104	0	0	.000	0			0	/O	0.0
■ **JOE CONNORS** Connors, Joseph P. b: Paterson, N.J. Deb: 5/03/1884																												
1884	Alt-U	3	11	0	1	0	0	0		0		.091	.091	.091	.182	-38	-2	-2	101	0	0	.100	0			0	/P3O	0.0
	KC-U	3	11	2	1	0	0	0		1		.091	.167	.091	.258	-12	-1	-1	87	0	0	.200	0			0	/OP	0.0
	Yr	6	22	2	2	0	0	0		1		.091	.130	.091	.221	-25	-3	-3	94	0	0	.150	0			0		0.0
Total	1	6	22	2	2	0	0	0		1		.091	.130	.091	.221	-26	-3	-3	94	0	0	.150	0			0	/OP3	0.0
■ **CHUCK CONNORS** Connors, Kevin Joseph Aloysius b: 4/10/21, Brooklyn, N.Y. BL/TL, 6'5", 190 lbs. Deb: 5/01/49																												
1949	Bro-N	1	1	0	0	0	0	0	0	0	0	.000	.000	.000	.000	-99	-0	-0	102	0	0	.000	0			0	H	0.0
1951	Chi-N	66	201	16	48	5	1	2	18	12	25	.239	.282	.303	.585	59	-12	-11	97	104	19	.503	4	0	1	0	1	-1.0
Total	2	67	202	16	48	5	1	2	18	12	25	.238	.280	.302	.582	58	-12	-12	97	103	19	.500	4	0		0	/1	-1.0
■ **MERV CONNORS** Connors, Mervyn James b: 1/23/14, Berkeley, Cal. BR/TR, 6'2", 192 lbs. Deb: 9/04/37																												
1937	Chi-A	28	103	12	24	4	1	2	12	14	19	.233	.325	.350	.674	68	-5	-5	103	104	12	.650	2	1	0	-1	3	-0.4
1938	Chi-A	24	62	14	22	4	0	6	13	9	17	.355	.437	.710	1.146	187	8	8	98	71	19	1.325	0	0	0	-1	1	0.4
Total	2	52	165	26	46	8	1	8	25	23	36	.279	.367	.485	.852	112	3	3	101	91	32	.875	2	1	0	-2	/31	0.0
■ **BEN CONROY** Conroy, Bernard Patrick b: 3/14/1871, Philadelphia, Pa. d: 11/25/37, Philadelphia, Pa. 160 lbs. Deb: 4/21/1890																												
1890	Phi-a	117	404	45	69	13	1	0		45		.171	.262	.208	.470	42	-29	-27	97	0	27	.451	17			-4	S2/O	-2.1
■ **WID CONROY** Conroy, William Edward b: 4/5/1877, Camden, N.J. d: 12/6/59, Mt.Holly, N.J. BR/TR, 5'9", 158 lbs. Deb: 4/25/01 C																												
1901	Mil-A	131	503	74	129	20	6	5	64	36		.256	.306	.350	.656	88	-11	-8	95	112	62	.623	21			13	*S3	1.1
1902	Pit-N	99	365	55	89	10	6	1	47	24		.244	.290	.312	.603	83	-5	-8	105	142	37	.536	10			5	S/O	0.1
1903	NY-A	126	503	74	137	23	12	1	45	32		.272	.316	.372	.688	107	4	4	100	75	71	.689	33			2	*3/S	0.5
1904	NY-A	140	489	58	119	18	12	1	52	43		.243	.305	.335	.640	93	3	-4	112	119	61	.641	30			8	*3S/O	0.9
1905	NY-A	101	385	55	105	19	11	2	25	32		.273	.329	.395	.723	129	13	12	102	50	60	.746	25			0	3OS1/2	1.4
1906	NY-A	148	567	67	139	17	10	4	54	47		.245	.303	.332	.635	84	0	-12	120	87	68	.624	32			-3	OS/3	-1.9
1907	NY-A	140	530	58	124	12	11	3	51	30		.234	.275	.315	.590	83	-7	-12	109	110	59	.586	41			17	*OS	0.0
1908	NY-A	141	531	44	126	22	3	1	39	14		.237	.257	.296	.553	85	-12	-9	95	97	44	.479	23			18	*32O	1.7
1909	Was-A	139	488	44	119	13	4	1	20	37		.244	.298	.293	.592	97	-7	-2	90	56	48	.556	24			3	*32/OS	0.6
1910	Was-A	103	351	36	89	11	3	1	27	30		.254	.314	.311	.625	95	-2	-2	101	91	38	.576	11			-1	3O/2	-0.3
1911	Was-A	106	349	40	81	11	4	2	28	20		.232	.282	.304	.585	65	-18	-16	97	84	33	.530	12			5	3O/2	-1.1
Total	11	1374	5061	605	1257	176	82	22	452	345		.248	.297	.329	.626	91	-41	-56	103	93	580	.598	262			67	3SO/21	3.0
■ **BILL CONROY** Conroy, William Frederick "Pep" b: 1/9/1899, Chicago, Ill. d: 1/23/70, Chicago, Ill. BR/TR, 5'8.5", 160 lbs. Deb: 4/18/23																												
1923	Was-A	18	60	6	8	2	2	0	2	4	9	.133	.188	.233	.421	11	-8	-8	95	49	3	.346	0	0	0	0	3/1O	-0.6
■ **BILL CONROY** Conroy, William Gordon b: 2/26/15, Bloomington, Ill. BR/TR, 6', 185 lbs. Deb: 9/21/35																												
1935	Phi-A	1	4	0	1	1	0	0	0	1	0	.250	.400	.500	.900	132	0	0	100	0	1	1.000	0	0	0	0	/C	0.0
1936	Phi-A	1	2	0	1	0	0	0	0	0	1	.500	.500	.500	1.000	147	0	0	101	0	0	1.000	0	0	0	0	/C	0.0
1937	Phi-A	26	60	4	12	1	1	0	3	7	9	.200	.284	.250	.534	38	-6	-5	94	69	5	.479	1	0	0	-1	C/1	-0.3
1942	Bos-A	83	250	22	50	4	2	4	20	40	47	.200	.315	.280	.595	66	-10	-11	104	86	26	.559	2	0	1	-1	C	-0.1
1943	Bos-A	39	89	13	16	5	0	1	6	18	19	.180	.336	.270	.606	75	-2	-2	104	81	9	.592	0	0	0	-0	C	0.0
1944	Bos-A	19	47	6	10	2	0	0	4	11	9	.213	.362	.255	.617	80	-1	-1	98	120	5	.605	0	0	0	0	C	0.1
Total	6	169	452	45	90	13	3	5	33	77	85	.199	.322	.274	.596	66	-18	-19	102	85	46	.576	3	0	1	-2	C/1	-0.3
■ **BILLY CONSOLO** Consolo, William Angelo b: 8/18/34, Cleveland, Ohio BR/TR, 5'11", 180 lbs. Deb: 4/20/53 C																												
1953	Bos-A	47	65	9	14	2	1	1	6	2	23	.215	.239	.323	.562	46	-5	-5	109	93	5	.453	1	2	-1	0	32	-0.5
1954	Bos-A	91	242	23	55	7	1	1	11	33	69	.227	.325	.277	.602	66	-10	-10	100	60	24	.542	2	1	0	5	S32	-0.1
1955	Bos-A	8	18	4	4	0	0	0	0	5	4	.222	.391	.222	.614	55	-0	-1	124	0	2	.600	0	0	0	-1	/2	-0.1
1956	Bos-A	48	11	13	2	0	0	0	1	3	5	.182	.357	.182	.539	45	-1	-1	103	187	1	.556	0	0	0	0	2	0.1
1957	Bos-A	68	196	26	53	6	1	4	19	23	48	.270	.347	.372	.719	88	-1	-3	110	88	25	.647	1	3	-2	5	S2/3	0.5
1958	Bos-A	46	72	13	9	2	1	0	5	6	14	.125	.192	.181	.373	3	-10	-10	105	154	2	.288	0	0	0	1	2S/3	-0.6
1959	Bos-A	10	14	3	3	1	0	0	0	2	5	.214	.313	.286	.598	62	-1	-1	106	0	1	.545	0	0	0	-0	/S	0.0
	Was-A	79	202	25	43	5	3	0	10	36	54	.213	.332	.267	.599	67	-8	-8	100	73	21	.562	1	0	0	5	S/2	0.3
	Yr	89	216	28	46	6	3	0	10	38	59	.213	.331	.269	.599	66	-9	-9	101	65	22	.561	1	0	0	5		0.3
1960	Was-A	100	174	23	36	4	2	3	15	25	29	.207	.310	.305	.615	66	-8	-8	102	95	17	.556	1	1	-0	1	S2/3	0.0
1961	Min-A	11	5	1	0	0	0	0	0	0	1	.000	.000	.000	.000	-94	-1	-1	106	0	0	.000	0	0	0	-0	/2S3	0.0
1962	Phi-N	13	5	3	2	0	0	0	0	0	1	.400	.400	.400	.800	122	0	0	95	0	1	.667	0	0	0	0	/3	0.0
	LA-A	28	20	4	2	0	0	0	0	3	11	.100	.217	.100	.317	-11	-3	-3	102	0	1	.368	2	0	1	0	3/S2	-0.1
	KC-A	54	154	11	37	4	2	0	16	23	33	.240	.339	.292	.631	72	-5	-5	100	141	16	.566	1	3	-2	-2	S	-0.6
	Yr	82	174	15	39	4	2	0	16	26	44	.224	.325	.270	.595	62	-9	-9	101	93	17	.543	3	3	-1	-2		-0.7
Total	10	603	1178	158	260	31	11	9	83	161	297	.221	.316	.289	.605	64	-53	-58	103	88	116	.552	9	10	-3	14	S2/3	-1.1
■ **JACK CONWAY** Conway, Jack Clements b: 7/30/19, Bryan, Tex. BR/TR, 5'11", 175 lbs. Deb: 9/09/41																												
1941	Cle-A	2	2	0	1	0	0	0	1	0	0	.500	.500	.500	1.000	164	0	0	101	354	1	1.000	0	0	0	0	/S	0.0
1946	Cle-A	68	258	24	58	6	2	0	18	20	36	.225	.281	.264	.544	59	-16	-13	89	107	20	.435	2	2	-1	-6	2S/3	-1.5
1947	Cle-A	34	50	3	9	2	0	0	5	3	8	.180	.226	.220	.446	25	-5	-5	96	167	2	.311	0	0	0	1	S/23	-0.3
1948	NY-N	24	49	8	12	2	1	1	3	5	10	.245	.315	.388	.703	89	-1	-1	100	51	6	.632	0			0	2/S3	0.1
Total	4	128	359	35	80	10	3	1	27	28	54	.223	.279	.276	.555	60	-22	-18	91	108	28	.457	2	2		-5	/2S3	-1.7
■ **OWEN CONWAY** Conway, Owen Sylvester b: 10/23/1890, New York, N.Y. d: 3/12/42, Philadelphia, Pa. TR , Deb: 6/21/15																												
1915	Phi-A	4	15	2	1	0	0	0	0	0	3	.067	.067	.067	.133	-63	-3	-3	96	0	0	.071	0			0	/3	-0.2
■ **RIP CONWAY** Conway, Richard Daniel b: 4/18/1896, White Bear, Minn. d: 12/3/71, St.Paul, Minn. 5'6", 160 lbs. Deb: 4/16/18																												
1918	Bos-N	14	24	4	4	0	0	0	2	2	4	.167	.231	.167	.397	23	-2	-2	94	189	1	.350	1			0	/23	-0.1
■ **BILL CONWAY** Conway, William F. b: 11/28/1861, Lowell, Mass. d: 12/28/43, Somerville, Mass. 5'8", 170 lbs. Deb: 7/28/1884																												
1884	Phi-N	1	4	0	0	0	0	0	0	0	1	.000	.000	.000	.000	-99	-1	-1	92	0	0	.000				0	/C	0.0
1886	Bal-a	7	14	4	2	0	0	0		7		.143	.429	.143	.571	93	0	1	91	0	1	.750	0			0	/C	0.1
Total	2	8	18	4	2	0	0	0	0	7	1	.111	.360	.111	.471	58	-0	-0	91	0	1	.563	0			0	/C	0.1
■ **ED CONWELL** Conwell, Edward James "Irish" b: 1/29/1890, Chicago, Ill. d: 5/1/26, Norwood Park, Ill. BR/TR, 5'11", 155 lbs. Deb: 9/22/11																												
1911	StL-N	1	1	0	0	0	0	0	0	0	1	.000	.000	.000	.000	-99	-0	-0	101	0	0	.000	0			0	/3	0.0
■ **HERB CONYERS** Conyers, Herbert Leroy b: 1/8/21, Cowgill, Mo. d: 9/16/64, Cleveland, Ohio BL/TR, 6'5", 210 lbs. Deb: 4/18/50																												
1950	Cle-A	7	9	2	3	0	0	1	1	1	2	.333	.400	.667	1.067	173	1	1	98	38	3	1.333	1	0	0	0	/1	0.1
■ **DALE COOGAN** Coogan, Dale Roger b: 8/14/30, Los Angeles, Cal. BL/TL, 6'1", 190 lbs. Deb: 4/22/50																												
1950	Pit-N	53	129	19	31	6	1	1	13	17	24	.240	.338	.326	.663	74	-4	-5	103	111	15	.598	0			-0	1	-0.5
■ **DAN COOGAN** Coogan, Daniel George b: 2/16/1875, Philadelphia, Pa. d: 10/28/42, Philadelphia, Pa. 128 lbs. Deb: 4/25/1895																												
1895	Was-N	26	77	9	17	2	1	0	7	13	6	.221	.333	.273	.606	57	-4	-5	103	93	8	.583	1			0	S/CO3	-0.3
■ **JIM COOK** Cook, James Fitchie b: 11/10/1879, Dundee, Ill. d: 6/17/49, St.Louis, Mo. BR/TR, 5'9", 163 lbs. Deb: 03																												
1903	Chi-N	8	26	3	4	1	0	0	2	2		.154	.214	.192	.407	18	-3	-3	95	129	1	.364	1			1	/O21	-0.1
■ **DOC COOK** Cook, Luther Almus b: 6/24/1886, Witt, Tex. d: 6/30/73, Lawrenceburg, Tenn. BL/TR, 6', 170 lbs. Deb: 8/07/13																												
1913	NY-A	20	72	9	19	2	1	0	1	10	4	.264	.369	.319	.688	101	1	1	101	14	9	.679	1			1	O	0.1
1914	NY-A	131	470	59	133	11	3	1	40	44	60	.283	.356	.326	.681	105	4	4	100	102	53	.629	26	32	-11	-11	*O	-2.8

YEAR	TM/L	G	AB	R	H	2B	3B	HR	RBI	BB	SO	AVG	OBP	SLG	PRO	/A	BR	/A	PF	CHI	RC	TA	SB	CS	SBR	FR	POS	TPR
1915	NY-A	132	476	70	129	16	5	2	33	62	43	.271	.364	.338	.703	112	8	9	98	71	63	.712	29	18	-2	-6	*O	-0.6
1916	NY-A	4	10	0	1	0	0	0	1	0	2	.100	.100	.100	.200	-39	-2	-2	101	357	0	.111	0			-1	/O	-0.2
Total	4	287	1028	138	282	29	9	3	75	116	109	.274	.359	.329	.687	107	11	12	99	83	125	.665	56	50		-16	O	-3.5
■ PAUL COOK	Cook, Paul b: 5/5/1863, Caledonia, N.Y. d: 5/26/05, Rochester, N.Y. BR/TR, Deb: 9/13/1884																											
1884	Phi-N	3	12	0	1	0	0	0	0	0	2	.083	.083	.083	.167	-51	-2	-2	92	0	0	.091				0	/C	-0.1
1886	Lou-a	66	262	28	54	5	2	0		10		.206	.235	.240	.476	47	-15	-18	108	0	17	.380	6			-2	1C/O	-1.9
1887	Lou-a	61	223	34	55	4	2	0		11		.247	.294	.283	.577	59	-11	-13	107	0	24	.554	15			-15	C/1	-1.4
1888	Lou-a	57	185	20	34	2	0	0	13	5		.184	.222	.195	.416	40	-13	-10	91	108	10	.358	9			-18	C/OS	-2.0
1889	Lou-a	81	286	34	65	10	1	0	15	15	48	.227	.287	.269	.556	63	-14	-12	96	57	26	.507	11			3	C/OS1	-0.1
1890	Bro-P	58	218	32	55	3	3	0	31	14	18	.252	.303	.294	.597	58	-12	-14	106	132	22	.534	7			-1	C1/O	-1.0
1891	Lou-a	45	153	21	35	3	1	0	23	11	17	.229	.285	.261	.546	65	-8	-6	90	166	13	.475	4			-9	C1	-1.1
	StL-a	7	25	3	5	0	0	0	1	1	2	.200	.259	.200	.459	30	-2	-3	114	58	1	.350	0			2	/C	0.0
	Yr	52	178	24	40	3	1	0		12	19	.225	.281	.253	.534	59	-10	-8	94	155	14	.457	4			-7		-1.1
Total	7	378	1364	172	304	27	9	0	83	67	87	.223	.270	.256	.526	55	-76	-78	101	68	113	.461	52			-40	C/1OS	-7.6
■ CLIFF COOK	Cook, Raymond Clifford b: 8/20/36, Dallas, Tex. BR/TR, 6', 185 lbs. Deb: 9/09/59																											
1959	Cin-N	9	21	3	8	2	1	0	5	2	8	.381	.435	.571	1.006	160	2	2	103	168	6	1.154	1	0	0	-0	/3	0.2
1960	Cin-N	54	149	9	31	7	0	3	13	8	51	.208	.248	.315	.564	54	-10	-10	98	94	12	.462	0	0	0	2	3/O	-0.8
1961	Cin-N	4	5	0	0	0	0	0	0	0	4	.000	.000	.000	.000	-96	-1	-1	104	0	0	.000	0	0	0	0	/3	0.0
1962	Cin-N	6	5	0	0	0	0	0	0	0	2	.000	.000	.000	.000	-98	-1	-1	102	0	0	.000	0	0	0	0	/3	0.0
	NY-N	40	112	12	26	6	1	2	9	4	34	.232	.277	.357	.634	66	-5	-6	104	77	12	.558	1	0	0	-2	3O	-0.7
	Yr	46	117	12	26	6	1	2	9	4	36	.222	.266	.342	.608	60	-7	-7	104	67	11	.527	1	0	0	-2		-0.7
1963	NY-N	50	106	9	15	2	1	2	8	12	37	.142	.229	.236	.465	34	-9	-9	99	108	6	.398	0	1	-1	-1	O/31	-1.2
Total	5	163	398	33	80	17	3	7	35	26	136	.201	.255	.312	.567	55	-25	-25	100	95	35	.484	2	1	0	-1	/3O1	-2.5
■ DUSTY COOKE	Cooke, Allen Lindsey b: 6/23/07, Swepsonville, N.C d: 11/21/87, Raleigh, N.C. BL/TR, 6'1", 205 lbs. Deb: 4/15/30 MC																											
1930	NY-A	92	216	43	55	12	3	6	29	32	61	.255	.353	.421	.775	107	-1	2	90	88	32	.766	4	6	-2	-6	O	-0.7
1931	NY-A	27	39	10	13	1	0	1	6	8	11	.333	.447	.436	.883	135	2	2	98	99	9	1.074	4	1	1	-1	O	0.2
1932	NY-A	3	0	1	0	0	0	0	0	1	0	—	1.000	—	1.436	299	0	0	95	0	0	—	0	0	0	0	H	0.0
1933	Bos-A	119	454	86	133	35	10	5	54	67	71	.293	.386	.447	.833	119	14	14	101	88	81	.856	7	5	-1	0	*O	0.8
1934	Bos-A	74	168	34	41	8	5	1	26	36	25	.244	.377	.369	.746	88	-1	-2	106	134	26	.814	7	2	1	-4	O	-0.5
1935	Bos-A	100	294	51	90	18	6	3	34	46	24	.306	.400	.439	.839	108	9	5	108	84	52	.854	6	8	-3	-2	O	0.0
1936	Bos-A	111	341	58	93	20	3	6	47	72	48	.273	.401	.402	.803	93	2	-2	106	98	60	.853	4	3	-1	0	O	-0.3
1938	Cin-N	82	233	41	64	15	1	2	33	28	36	.275	.355	.373	.728	103	1	1	98	128	33	.667	0			3	O	0.3
Total	8	608	1745	324	489	109	28	24	229	290	276	.280	.384	.416	.800	105	26	21	102	99	294	.819	32	25		-9	O	-0.2
■ FRED COOKE	Cooke, Frederick B. b: Paulding, Ohio Deb: 7/30/1897																											
1897	Cle-N	5	17	2	5	2	0	0	3	3		.294	.400	.412	.812	106	1	0	111	128	3	.833	0			0	/O	0.0
■ DUFF COOLEY	Cooley, Duff Gordan "Dick" b: 3/14/1873, Dallas, Tex. d: 8/9/37, Dallas, Tex. BL/TR, Deb: 7/27/1893																											
1893	StL-N	29	107	20	37	2	3	0	21	8	9	.346	.391	.421	.812	119	3	3	99	128	21	.871	8			0	OC/S	0.2
1894	StL-N	54	206	35	61	3	1	1	21	12	16	.296	.335	.335	.670	63	-12	-12	101	82	26	.607	7			-5	O3/S1	-1.5
1895	StL-N	132	563	106	191	9	20	7	75	36	29	.339	.382	.464	.846	120	15	15	100	66	113	.879	27			10	*O/3SC	1.2
1896	StL-N	40	166	29	51	5	3	0	13	7	3	.307	.335	.373	.709	93	-3	-2	95	58	25	.704	12			-1	O	-0.4
	Phi-N	64	287	63	88	6	4	2	22	18	16	.307	.348	.376	.724	91	-3	-4	102	48	45	.724	18			-6	O	-1.1
	Yr	104	453	92	139	11	7	2	35	25	19	.307	.343	.375	.718	92	-6	-5	99	52	70	.717	30			-7		-1.5
1897	Phi-N	133	566	124	186	14	13	4	40	51		.329	.384	.420	.805	120	13	17	96	41	106	.842	31			4	*O/1	0.9
1898	Phi-N	149	629	123	196	24	12	4	55	48		.312	.360	.407	.767	130	17	22	95	54	101	.741	17			-1	*O	1.2
1899	Phi-N	94	406	75	112	15	8	1	31	29		.276	.329	.360	.688	94	-5	-3	97	55	54	.656	15			-4	1O/2	-0.4
1900	Pit-N	66	249	30	50	8	1	0	22	14		.201	.243	.241	.484	35	-21	-22	103	121	17	.417	9			-6	1	-2.5
1901	Bos-N	63	240	27	62	13	3	0	27	14		.258	.299	.338	.637	77	-4	-8	112	118	26	.562	5			6	O1	-0.6
1902	Bos-N	135	548	73	162	26	8	0	58	34		.296	.337	.372	.709	127	12	15	95	87	80	.687	27			4	*O/1	1.0
1903	Bos-N	138	553	76	160	26	10	1	70	44		.289	.342	.378	.720	111	5	8	96	94	83	.712	27			-1	*O1	0.0
1904	Bos-N	122	467	41	127	18	7	5	70	24		.272	.308	.373	.680	116	5	7	97	130	59	.624	14			-14	*O/1	-1.2
1905	Det-A	97	377	25	93	11	9	1	32	26		.247	.295	.332	.627	103	0	1	98	79	40	.556	7			6	O	0.2
Total	13	1316	5364	847	1576	180	102	26	557	365	73	.294	.339	.380	.719	106	21	36	98	78	797	.695	224			-6	*O1/3CS2	-3.0
■ CECIL COOMBS	Coombs, Cecil Lysander b: 3/18/1888, Moweaqua, Ill. d: 11/25/75, Fort Worth, Tex. BR/TR, 5'9", 160 lbs. Deb: 8/07/14																											
1914	Chi-A	7	23	1	4	1	0	0	1	1	7	.174	.208	.217	.426	27	-2	-2	103	75	1	.300	0	1	-1	1	/O	-0.1
■ JACK COOMBS	Coombs, John Wesley "Colby Jack" b: 11/18/1882, Le Grand, Iowa d: 4/15/57, Palestine, Tex. BB/TR, 6', 185 lbs. Deb: 7/05/06 M																											
1906	Phi-A	24	67	9	16	2	0	0	3	1		.239	.250	.269	.519	68	-3	-2	94	61	5	.412	2			-0	P	0.0
1907	Phi-A	24	48	4	8	0	0	1	4	0		.167	.167	.229	.396	25	-4	-4	106	102	2	.300	1			0	P	0.0
1908	Phi-A	78	220	24	56	9	5	1	23	9		.255	.284	.355	.638	102	1	-0	108	107	23	.567	6			7	OP/1	0.9
1909	Phi-A	37	83	4	14	4	0	0	10	4		.169	.216	.217	.433	36	-6	-6	102	214	4	.348	1			0	P	0.0
1910	Phi-A	46	132	20	29	3	0	0	9	7		.220	.270	.242	.512	59	-6	-6	102	104	9	.427	3			-5	P	0.0
1911	Phi-A	52	141	31	45	6	1	2	23	8		.319	.356	.418	.774	125	2	4	93	120	22	.750	5			-3	P	0.0
1912	Phi-A	55	110	10	28	2	0	0	13	14		.255	.344	.273	.617	77	-3	-3	99	145	11	.561	1			-1	P	0.0
1913	Phi-A	2	3	1	1	1	0	0	0	0	2	.333	.333	.667	1.000	198	0	0	97	0	1	1.000	0			-0	/P	0.0
1914	Phi-A	5	11	0	3	1	0	0	2	1	1	.273	.333	.364	.697	113	0	0	97	188	1	.625	0			-0	/PO	0.0
1915	Bro-N	29	75	8	21	1	1	0	5	2	17	.280	.299	.320	.619	86	-1	-1	101	80	7	.473	0	1	-1	-4	P	0.0
1916	Bro-N	27	61	2	11	2	0	0	3	2	10	.180	.206	.213	.419	28	-5	-5	103	92	3	.300	0			-5	P	0.0
1917	Bro-N	32	44	4	10	0	1	0	2	4	9	.227	.292	.273	.564	71	-1	-1	104	64	4	.500	1			-3	P	0.0
1918	Bro-N	46	113	6	19	3	2	0	3	7	5	.168	.223	.230	.453	38	-8	-9	101	44	6	.372	1			-7	PO	0.0
1920	Det-A	2	2	0	0	0	0	0	0	0	0	.000	.000	.000	.000	-97	-1	-1	103	0	0	.000	0	0	0	-0	/P	0.0
Total	14	459	1110	123	261	34	10	4	100	59	44	.235	.277	.295	.571	74	-34	-35	101	107	97	.485	21	1		-21	P/O1	0.9
■ WILLIAM COON	Coon, William K. b: 3/21/1855, Pennsylvania d: 8/30/15, Burlington, N.J. Deb: 9/04/1875																											
1875	Ath-n	4	14	1	2							.143															/C	
1876	Phi-N	54	220	30	50	5	1	0	22	2	4	.227	.234	.259	.493	65	-8	-8	99	133	14	.347				-8	OC/32P	-1.3
Total		54	220	30	50	5	1	0	22	2	4	.227	.234	.259	.493	65	-8	-8	99	133	14	.347				-8	/OC23P	-1.3
■ JIMMY COONEY	Cooney, James Edward "Scoops" b: 8/24/1894, Cranston, R.I. BR/TR, 5'11", 160 lbs. Deb: 9/22/17																											
1917	Bos-A	11	36	4	8	1	0	0	3	6	2	.222	.333	.250	.583	72	-1	-1	108	115	4	.536	0			0	2/S	0.0
1919	NY-N	5	14	3	3	0	0	0	1	0	0	.214	.214	.214	.429	29	-1	-1	100	130	1	.273	0			1	/S2	0.0
1924	StL-N	110	383	44	113	20	8	1	57	20	20	.295	.330	.397	.727	92	-4	-5	103	134	48	.657	12	10	-2	-0	S/32	0.1
1925	StL-N	54	187	27	51	11	2	0	18	4	5	.273	.292	.353	.645	63	-10	-11	102	97	18	.518	1	3	-2	-3	S2/O	-1.1
1926	Chi-N	141	513	52	129	18	5	1	47	23	10	.251	.288	.312	.599	58	-28	-32	106	102	45	.513	11			16	*S	-0.5
1927	Chi-N	33	132	16	32	2	0	0	6	8	7	.242	.286	.258	.543	46	-10	-10	100	59	10	.430	1			2	S	-0.4
	Phi-N	76	259	33	70	12	1	0	15	13	9	.270	.305	.324	.629	71	-12	-10	96	62	25	.534	4			1	S	-0.2
	Yr	109	391	49	102	14	1	0	21	21	16	.261	.299	.302	.600	63	-21	-20	98	62	35	.498	5			2		-0.6
1928	Bos-N	18	51	2	7	0	0	0	3	2	5	.137	.170	.137	.307	-19	-9	-9	97	153	1	.227	1			-2	S/2	-0.8
Total	7	448	1575	181	413	64	16	2	150	76	58	.262	.298	.327	.625	65	-74	-79	102	101	153	.532	30	13		14	S/23O	-2.9
■ JIMMY COONEY	Cooney, James Joseph b: 7/9/1865, Cranston, R.I. d: 7/1/03, Cranston, R.I. BB/TR, 5'9", 155 lbs. Deb: 4/19/1890																											
1890	Chi-N	135	574	114	156	19	10	4	52	73	23	.272	.360	.361	.721	103	11	2	109	62	93	.792	45			-8	*S/C	-0.6
1891	Chi-N	118	465	84	114	15	3	0	42	48	17	.245	.318	.290	.609	75	-11	-15	106	96	51	.587	21			2	*S	-0.6
1892	Chi-N	65	238	18	41	1	0	0	20	23	5	.172	.248	.176	.425	33	-19	-16	92	149	13	.386	10			-10	S	-2.1

YEAR	TM/L	G	AB	R	H	2B	3B	HR	RBI	BB	SO	AVG	OBP	SLG	PRO	/A	BR	/A	PF	CHI	RC	TA	SB	CS	SBR	FR	POS	TPR
	Was-N	6	25	5	4	0	1	0	4	4	3	.160	.276	.240	.516	55	-1	-1	105	177	2	.524	1			-3	/S	-0.3
	Yr	71	263	23	45	1	1	0	24	27	8	.171	.251	.183	.433	35	-20	-18	93	153	15	.399	11			-13		-2.4
Total	3	324	1302	221	315	35	14	4	118	148	48	.242	.324	.300	.623	81	-20	-31	105	92	159	.632	77			-20	S/C	-3.6

■ JOHNNY COONEY Cooney, John Walter b: 3/18/01, Cranston, R.I. d: 7/8/86, Sarasota, Fla. BR/TL, 5'10", 165 lbs. Deb: 4/19/21 MC

YEAR	TM/L	G	AB	R	H	2B	3B	HR	RBI	BB	SO	AVG	OBP	SLG	PRO	/A	BR	/A	PF	CHI	RC	TA	SB	CS	SBR	FR	POS	TPR
1921	Bos-N	8	5	0	1	0	0	0	0	0	1	.200	.200	.200	.400	7	-1	-1	93	0	0	.250	0	0	0	0	/P	0.0
1922	Bos-N	4	8	0	0	0	0	0	0	0	1	.000	.000	.000	.000	-99	-2	-2	94	0	0	.000	0	0	0	0	/P	0.0
1923	Bos-N	42	66	7	25	1	0	0	3	4	2	.379	.414	.394	.808	115	2	2	100	41	11	.714	0	1	-1	0	PO/1	0.0
1924	Bos-N	55	130	10	33	2	1	0	4	9	5	.254	.302	.285	.587	62	-7	-6	94	39	11	.455	0	4	-2	1	PO/1	0.0
1925	Bos-N	54	103	17	33	7	0	0	13	3	6	.320	.346	.388	.734	93	-2	-1	94	116	14	.643	1	0	0	0	P/1O	0.0
1926	Bos-N	64	126	17	38	3	2	0	18	13	7	.302	.367	.357	.724	111	-0	2	86	138	17	.727	6			3	1P/O	0.7
1927	Bos-N	10	1	3	0	0	0	0	0	0	0	.000	.000	.000	.000	-99	-0	-0	93	0	0	.000	0			0	H	0.0
1928	Bos-N	33	41	2	7	0	0	0	2	4	3	.171	.244	.171	.415	11	-5	-5	97	102	2	.324	0			3	P/1O	0.0
1929	Bos-N	41	72	10	23	4	1	0	6	3	3	.319	.355	.403	.758	93	-1	-1	94	71	10	.694	1			2	OP	0.2
1930	Bos-N	4	3	0	0	0	0	0	0	0	0	.000	.000	.000	.000	-99	-1	-1	97	0	0	.000	0			1	/P	0.0
1935	Bro-N	10	29	3	9	0	1	0	1	3	2	.310	.375	.379	.754	110	0	0	94	33	5	.700	0			-0	O	0.0
1936	Bro-N	130	507	71	143	17	5	0	30	24	15	.282	.315	.335	.650	71	-18	-21	105	64	54	.525	3			3	*O	-2.3
1937	Bro-N	120	430	61	126	18	5	0	37	22	10	.293	.327	.358	.686	83	-8	-11	104	88	49	.573	5			2	*O/1	-1.3
1938	Bos-N	120	432	45	117	25	5	0	17	22	12	.271	.308	.352	.660	92	-12	-5	88	41	47	.546	2			-5	*O1	-1.3
1939	Bos-N	118	368	39	101	8	1	2	27	21	8	.274	.317	.318	.635	78	-15	-11	92	80	37	.514	2			-0	*O/1	-1.2
1940	Bos-N	108	365	40	116	14	3	0	21	25	9	.318	.363	.373	.736	105	2	3	99	57	50	.648	4			-3	O/1	-0.3
1941	Bos-N	123	442	52	141	25	2	0	29	27	15	.319	.358	.385	.743	117	5	9	93	63	59	.637	3			0	*O/1	0.4
1942	Bos-N	74	198	23	41	6	0	0	7	23	5	.207	.290	.237	.527	58	-11	-10	95	55	15	.444	2			-13	O1	-2.7
1943	Bro-N	37	34	7	7	0	0	0	2	4	3	.206	.289	.206	.495	44	-2	-2	100	103	2	.429	1			0	/1O	-0.2
1944	Bro-N	7	4	0	3	0	0	0	1	0	0	.750	.750	.750	1.500	326	1	1	99	120	2	3.000	0			-0	/O	0.1
	NY-A	10	8	1	1	0	0	0	1	1	0	.125	.222	.125	.347	1	-1	-1	106	361	0	.286	0	0	0	-0	/O	-0.1
Total	20	1172	3372	408	965	130	26	2	219	208	107	.286	.329	.342	.671	86	-77	-61	96	69	383	.579	30	5		-7	OP/1	-8.0

■ PHIL COONEY Cooney, Philip Clarence (born Philip Clarence Cohen) b: 9/14/1882, New York, N.Y. d: 10/6/57, New York, N, Y. BR/TR, 5'8", 155 lbs. Deb: 9/27/05

YEAR	TM/L	G	AB	R	H	2B	3B	HR	RBI	BB	SO	AVG	OBP	SLG	PRO	/A	BR	/A	PF	CHI	RC	TA	SB	CS	SBR	FR	POS	TPR
1905	NY-A	1	3	0	0	0	0	0	0	0		.000	.000	.000	.000	-98	-1	-1	102	0	0	.000	0			0	/3	0.0

■ BILL COONEY Cooney, William A. "Cush" b: 4/4/1887, Boston, Mass. d: 11/6/28, Roxbury, Mass. TR , Deb: 09

YEAR	TM/L	G	AB	R	H	2B	3B	HR	RBI	BB	SO	AVG	OBP	SLG	PRO	/A	BR	/A	PF	CHI	RC	TA	SB	CS	SBR	FR	POS	TPR
1909	Bos-N	5	10	0	3	0	0	0	0	0		.300	.300	.300	.600	91	-0	-0	96	0	1	.429	0			-0	/P2S	0.0
1910	Bos-N	8	12	2	3	0	0	0	1	2	0	.250	.357	.250	.607	68	-0	-0	114	116	1	.556	0			-1	/O	-0.1
Total	2	13	22	2	6	0	0	0	1	2	0	.273	.333	.273	.606	77	-0	-1	107	68	2	.500	0			-1	/POS2	-0.1

■ CECIL COOPER Cooper, Cecil Celester b: 12/20/49, Brenham, Tex. BL/TL, 6'2", 165 lbs. Deb: 9/08/71

YEAR	TM/L	G	AB	R	H	2B	3B	HR	RBI	BB	SO	AVG	OBP	SLG	PRO	/A	BR	/A	PF	CHI	RC	TA	SB	CS	SBR	FR	POS	TPR
1971	Bos-A	14	42	9	13	4	1	0	3	5	4	.310	.396	.452	.848	132	2	2	106	64	8	.897	1	0	0	-0	1	0.1
1972	Bos-A	12	17	0	4	1	0	0	2	2	5	.235	.316	.294	.610	78	-0	-0	105	167	2	.538	0	0	0	0	/1	0.0
1973	Bos-A	30	101	12	24	2	0	3	11	7	12	.238	.287	.347	.634	73	-3	-4	106	98	10	.538	1	2	-1	-1	1	-0.7
1974	Bos-A	121	414	55	114	24	1	8	43	32	74	.275	.329	.396	.725	101	4	0	107	90	54	.646	2	5	-2	-1	1D	-0.6
1975	Bos-A	106	305	49	95	17	6	14	44	19	33	.311	.358	.544	.902	140	19	16	109	81	57	.871	1	4	-2	0	D1	1.2
1976	Bos-A	123	451	66	127	22	6	15	78	16	62	.282	.308	.457	.764	110	10	4	110	122	64	.701	7	1	2	-3	1D	0.0
1977	Mil-A	160	643	86	193	31	7	20	78	28	110	.300	.329	.463	.793	119	10	14	95	91	93	.720	13	8	-1	6	*1D	1.0
1978	Mil-A	107	407	60	127	23	2	13	54	32	72	.312	.362	.474	.836	126	17	14	106	97	69	.789	3	4	-2	-1	1D	0.9
1979	Mil-A	150	590	83	182	**44**	1	24	106	56	77	.308	.368	.508	.877	134	27	27	100	116	110	.873	15	3	3	-8	*1D	1.3
1980	Mil-A	153	622	96	219	33	4	25	**122**	39	42	.352	.392	.539	.931	161	43	47	95	112	126	.925	17	6	2	3	*1D	4.2
1981	Mil-A	106	416	70	133	**35**	1	12	60	28	30	.320	.367	.495	.862	153	24	26	96	103	70	.799	5	4	-1	0	*1/D	2.3
1982	Mil-A	155	654	104	205	38	3	32	121	32	53	.313	.345	.528	.873	144	29	34	94	105	118	.831	2	3	-1	1	*1/D	3.0
1983	Mil-A	160	661	106	203	37	3	30	**126**	37	63	.307	.345	.508	.853	143	26	33	92	111	110	.790	2	1	0	-9	*1/D	1.7
1984	Mil-A	148	603	63	166	28	3	11	67	27	59	.275	.309	.386	.695	99	-8	-2	92	106	70	.599	8	2	1	3	*1D	-0.5
1985	Mil-A	154	631	82	185	39	8	16	99	30	77	.293	.327	.456	.784	107	9	5	105	112	86	.698	10	3	1	-2	*1D	-0.3
1986	Mil-A	134	542	46	140	24	1	12	75	41	87	.258	.312	.373	.684	84	-10	-12	102	121	60	.585	1	2	-1	-5	1D	-2.3
1987	Mil-A	63	250	25	62	13	0	6	36	17	51	.248	.296	.372	.668	75	-9	-9	102	137	27	.575	1	1	-0	0	D	-0.9
Total	17	1896	7349	1012	2192	415	47	241	1125	448	911	.298	.340	.466	.806	122	188	194	99	107	1134	.764	89	49	-3	-16	*1D	10.4

■ CLAUDE COOPER Cooper, Claude William b: 4/1/1892, Troupe, Tex. d: 1/21/74, Plainview, Tex. BL/TL, 5'9", 158 lbs. Deb: 4/14/13

YEAR	TM/L	G	AB	R	H	2B	3B	HR	RBI	BB	SO	AVG	OBP	SLG	PRO	/A	BR	/A	PF	CHI	RC	TA	SB	CS	SBR	FR	POS	TPR
1913	NY-N	27	30	11	9	4	0	0	4	4	6	.300	.382	.433	.816	129	1	1	103	112	6	.952	3			-4	O	-0.2
1914	Bro-F	113	399	56	96	14	11	2	25	26	60	.241	.287	.346	.633	80	-11	-11	101	64	49	.624	25			1	*O	-1.6
1915	Bro-F	153	527	75	155	26	12	2	63	77	78	.294	.384	.400	.784	135	23	25	98	111	97	.858	31			17	*O1	3.9
1916	Phi-N	56	104	9	20	2	0	0	11	7	15	.192	.250	.212	.462	44	-7	-6	96	199	6	.369	1			-3	O/1	-1.1
1917	Phi-N	24	29	5	3	1	0	0	1	5	4	.103	.235	.138	.373	15	-3	-3	108	96	1	.346	0			-3	O	-0.7
Total	5	373	1089	156	283	47	23	4	104	119	163	.260	.333	.356	.690	103	4	6	99	102	159	.705	60			7	O/1	0.3

■ GARY COOPER Cooper, Gary Nathaniel b: 12/22/56, Savannah, Ga. BB/TR, 6'3", 175 lbs. Deb: 8/25/80

YEAR	TM/L	G	AB	R	H	2B	3B	HR	RBI	BB	SO	AVG	OBP	SLG	PRO	/A	BR	/A	PF	CHI	RC	TA	SB	CS	SBR	FR	POS	TPR
1980	Atl-N	21	2	3	0	0	0	0	0	0	1	.000	.000	.000	.000	-99	-1	-1	101	0	-1	.667	2	1	0	-4	O	-0.4

■ PAT COOPER Cooper, Orge Patterson b: 11/26/17, Albemarle, N.C. BR/TR, 6'3", 180 lbs. Deb: 5/11/46

YEAR	TM/L	G	AB	R	H	2B	3B	HR	RBI	BB	SO	AVG	OBP	SLG	PRO	/A	BR	/A	PF	CHI	RC	TA	SB	CS	SBR	FR	POS	TPR
1946	Phi-A	1	0	0	0	0	0	0	0	0	0	—	—	—	—	—	0	0	104	—	—	—	0	0	0	0	/P	0.0
1947	Phi-A	13	16	0	4	2	0	0	3	0	5	.250	.250	.375	.625	72	-1	-1	100	184	2	.500	0	0	0	0	/1	0.0
Total	2	14	16	0	4	2	0	0	3	0	5	.250	.250	.375	.625	72	-1	-1	100	184	1	.500	0	0	0	0	/1P	0.0

■ WALKER COOPER Cooper, William Walker "Walk" b: 1/8/15, Atherton, Mo. BR/TR, 6'3", 210 lbs. Deb: 9/25/40 C

YEAR	TM/L	G	AB	R	H	2B	3B	HR	RBI	BB	SO	AVG	OBP	SLG	PRO	/A	BR	/A	PF	CHI	RC	TA	SB	CS	SBR	FR	POS	TPR
1940	StL-N	6	19	3	6	1	0	0	2	2	2	.316	.381	.368	.749	105	0	0	102	106	3	.769	1			-0	/C	0.0
1941	StL-N	68	200	19	49	9	1	1	20	13	14	.245	.291	.315	.606	64	-8	-10	110	109	17	.487	1			0	C	-0.3
1942	StL-N	125	438	58	123	32	7	7	65	29	29	.281	.327	.434	.761	112	10	6	108	114	57	.673	4			3	*C	1.1
1943	StL-N	122	449	52	143	30	4	9	81	19	19	.318	.349	.463	.812	128	17	14	105	127	69	.721	1			-4	*C	1.6
1944	StL-N	112	397	56	126	25	5	13	72	20	19	.317	.352	.504	.855	138	18	18	101	108	65	.787	4			3	C	2.5
1945	StL-N	4	18	3	7	0	0	0	1	0	1	.389	.389	.389	.778	116	0	0	100	52	3	.636	0			0	/C	0.1
1946	NY-N	87	280	29	75	10	1	8	46	17	12	.268	.310	.396	.706	98	-1	-2	102	127	32	.595	0			1	C	0.1
1947	NY-N	140	515	79	157	24	8	35	122	24	43	.305	.339	.586	.926	141	26	25	101	113	97	.892	2			2	*C	2.9
1948	NY-N	91	290	40	77	12	0	16	54	28	29	.266	.332	.472	.805	116	5	5	100	109	42	.736	1			-6	C	0.5
1949	NY-N	42	147	14	31	4	2	4	21	7	8	.211	.261	.347	.608	61	-8	-9	102	126	11	.484	0			-1	C	-0.8
	Cin-N	82	307	34	86	9	2	16	62	21	24	.280	.330	.479	.809	120	5	7	96	122	46	.739	0			1	C	1.0
	Yr	124	454	48	117	13	4	20	83	28	32	.258	.308	.436	.744	100	-4	-2	98	124	60	.668	0			0		0.2
1950	Cin-N	15	47	3	9	3	0	0	4	0	5	.191	.191	.255	.447	16	-6	-6	105	129	2	.308	0			-1	C	-0.5
	Bos-N	102	337	52	111	19	3	14	60	30	26	.329	.389	.528	.917	161	18	25	86	105	69	.906	1			6	C	3.2
	Yr	117	384	55	120	22	3	14	64	30	31	.313	.367	.495	.862	140	13	19	88	109	69	.824	1			5		2.7
1951	Bos-N	109	342	42	107	14	1	18	59	28	18	.313	.367	.518	.884	138	16	17	98	99	64	.841	1	1	-0	5	C	2.1
1952	Bos-N	102	349	33	82	12	1	10	55	22	32	.235	.282	.361	.643	81	-12	-10	95	138	36	.547	1	0	0	0	C	-0.7
1953	Mil-N	53	137	12	30	6	0	3	16	12	15	.219	.287	.328	.615	64	-8	-7	94	116	12	.522	1	0	0	2	C	-0.2
1954	Pit-N	14	15	0	3	2	0	0	1	2	1	.200	.294	.333	.627	65	-1	-1	97	79	1	.538	0	0	0	0	/C	0.0
	Chi-N	57	158	21	49	10	2	7	32	21	23	.310	.398	.532	.929	139	9	9	101	120	32	.922	0	0	0	-2	C	0.8
	Yr	71	173	21	52	12	2	7	33	23	24	.301	.389	.514	.903	133	9	9	100	113	34	.891	0	0	0	-2		0.8
1955	Chi-N	54	111	11	31	8	1	7	15	6	19	.279	.322	.559	.881	128	4	4	100	73	19	.831	0	0	0	-1	C	0.4
1956	StL-N	40	68	5	18	5	1	2	14	3	8	.265	.296	.456	.752	99	-0	-0	99	160	8	.654	0	0	0	1	C	0.1
1957	StL-N	48	78	7	21	5	1	3	10	5	10	.269	.313	.474	.788	107	1	1	101	90	9	.667	0	0	0	1	C	0.2
Total	18	1473	4702	573	1341	240	40	173	812	309	357	.285	.332	.464	.796	116	84	86	100	115	695	.751	18	1		9	*C	14.1

YEAR	TM/L	G	AB	R	H	2B	3B	HR	RBI	BB	SO	AVG	OBP	SLG	PRO	/A	BR	/A	PF	CHI	RC	TA	SB	CS	SBR	FR	POS	TPR
■ JOEY CORA	Cora, Jose Manuel (Amaro) b: 5/14/65, Caguas, P.R. BB/TR, 5'8", 150 lbs. Deb: 4/06/87																											
1987	SD-N	77	241	23	57	7	2	0	13	28	26	.237	.319	.282	.601	63	-13	-12	97	76	22	.563	15	11	-2	2	2/S	-0.9
■ GENE CORBETT	Corbett, Eugene Louis b: 10/25/13, Winona, Minn. BL/TR, 6'1.5", 190 lbs. Deb: 9/19/36																											
1936	Phi-N	6	21	1	3	0	0	0	2	2	3	.143	.217	.143	.360	-1	-3	-3	108	236	1	.263	0			-0	/1	-0.3
1937	Phi-N	7	12	4	4	2	0	0	1	0	0	.333	.333	.500	.833	114	0	0	108	60	2	.750	0			0	/32	0.0
1938	Phi-N	24	75	7	6	1	0	2	7	6	11	.080	.148	.173	.321	-12	-12	-12	100	133	2	.271	0			0	1	-1.3
Total	3	37	108	12	13	3	0	2	10	8	14	.120	.181	.204	.385	5	-14	-15	103	146	5	.313	0			-0	/132	-1.6
■ CLAUDE CORBITT	Corbitt, Claude Elliott b: 7/21/15, Sunbury, N.C. d: 5/1/78, Cincinnati, Ohio BR/TR, 5'10", 170 lbs. Deb: 9/23/45																											
1945	Bro-N	2	4	1	2	0	0	0	0	1	0	.500	.600	.500	1.100	217	1	1	96	0	1	1.500	0			0	/3	0.1
1946	Cin-N	82	274	25	68	10	1	1	16	23	13	.248	.309	.303	.612	71	-9	-11	104	69	27	.524	3			4	S	0.0
1948	Cin-N	87	258	24	66	11	0	0	18	14	16	.256	.297	.298	.595	60	-14	-15	103	88	24	.497	4			-1	23S	-1.1
1949	Cin-N	44	94	10	17	1	0	0	3	9	1	.181	.252	.191	.444	22	-10	-10	96	63	5	.350	1			-2	S2/3	-0.8
Total	4	215	630	60	153	22	1	1	37	47	30	.243	.297	.286	.583	60	-33	-35	102	75	57	.494	8			1	S/23	-1.8
■ ART CORCORAN	Corcoran, Arthur Andrew "Bunny" b: 11/23/1894, Roxbury, Mass. d: 7/27/58, Chelsea, Mass. TR , Deb: 9/09/15																											
1915	Phi-A	1	4	0	0	0	0	0	0	0	2	.000	.000	.000	.000	-99	-1	-1	96	0	0	.000	0			0	/3	0.0
■ JOHN CORCORAN	Corcoran, John A. b: 1873, Cincinnati, Ohio d: 11/1/01, Cincinnati, Ohio TL , Deb: 9/17/1895																											
1895	Pit-N	6	20	0	3	0	0	0	1	0	2	.150	.150	.150	.300	-22	-4	-3	97	93	0	.176	0			0	/S3	-0.2
■ JACK CORCORAN	Corcoran, John H. b: 1860, Lowell, Mass. Deb: 5/01/1884																											
1884	Bro-a	52	185	17	39	4	3	0		8		.211	.251	.265	.516	73	-6	-5	98	0	13	.404				-6	C/O2SP	-0.6
■ MICKEY CORCORAN	Corcoran, Michael Joseph b: 8/26/1882, Buffalo, N.Y. d: 12/9/50, Buffalo, N.Y. BR/TR, 5'8", 165 lbs. Deb: 9/15/10																											
1910	Cin-N	14	46	3	10	3	0	0	7	5	9	.217	.308	.283	.590	72	-2	-2	101	191	4	.528	0			-1	2	-0.2
■ TOMMY CORCORAN	Corcoran, Thomas William "Corky" b: 1/4/1869, New Haven, Conn. d: 6/25/60, Plainfield, Conn. BR/TR, 5'9", 164 lbs. Deb: 4/19/1890																											
1890	Pit-P	123	503	80	117	14	13	1	61	38	45	.233	.289	.318	.607	69	-27	-19	92	108	60	.630	43			-3	*S	-1.1
1891	Phi-a	133	511	84	130	11	15	7	71	29	56	.254	.307	.376	.683	95	-4	-6	103	98	70	.685	30			12	*S	0.9
1892	Bro-N	151	613	77	145	11	6	1	74	34	51	.237	.281	.279	.560	70	-22	-23	101	138	61	.530	39			-6	*S	-1.9
1893	Bro-N	115	459	61	126	11	10	2	58	27	12	.275	.318	.355	.673	89	-14	-6	91	100	58	.619	14			14	*S	0.9
1894	Bro-N	129	576	123	173	21	20	5	92	25	17	.300	.329	.432	.762	89	-17	-11	94	85	95	.762	33			-8	*S	-0.8
1895	Bro-N	127	535	81	142	17	10	2	69	23	11	.265	.299	.346	.645	72	-26	-21	94	107	62	.580	17			14	*S	0.2
1896	Bro-N	132	532	63	154	15	7	3	73	15	13	.289	.310	.361	.671	89	-18	-7	87	111	66	.593	16			20	*S	1.2
1897	Cin-N	109	445	76	128	30	5	3	57	13		.288	.311	.398	.709	82	-9	-14	107	95	61	.653	15			3	S2	-0.4
1898	Cin-N	153	619	80	155	28	15	2	87	26		.250	.281	.354	.634	78	-15	-22	108	124	68	.569	19			9	*S	-0.4
1899	Cin-N	137	537	91	149	11	8	0	81	28		.277	.314	.328	.642	74	-16	-20	106	**150**	67	.611	32			-2	*S2	-1.2
1900	Cin-N	127	523	64	128	21	9	1	54	22		.245	.275	.325	.600	73	-24	-18	92	94	56	.554	27			-10	*S/2	-1.3
1901	Cin-N	31	115	14	24	3	3	0	15	11		.209	.278	.287	.565	69	-5	-4	95	161	11	.549	6			-3	S	-0.4
1902	Cin-N	138	538	54	136	18	4	0	54	11		.253	.268	.301	.569	70	-16	-21	110	118	50	.480	20			-14	*S/2	-3.0
1903	Cin-N	115	459	61	113	18	7	2	73	12		.246	.265	.329	.594	65	-19	-24	109	**158**	44	.506	12			1	*S	-1.5
1904	Cin-N	150	578	55	133	17	9	2	74	19		.230	.255	.301	.556	64	-19	-29	114	159	50	.476	19			0	*S	-2.9
1905	Cin-N	151	605	70	150	21	11	2	85	23		.248	.275	.329	.604	79	-15	-17	103	139	64	.549	28			19	*S	0.5
1906	Cin-N	117	430	29	89	13	1	1	33	19		.207	.241	.249	.489	47	-23	-30	115	116	28	.393	8			-8	*S	-3.5
1907	NY-N	62	226	21	60	9	2	0	24	7		.265	.288	.323	.611	88	-3	-4	105	132	24	.536	9			-13	2	-1.7
Total	18	2200	8804	1184	2252	289	155	34	1135	382	205	.256	.289	.335	.624	75	-290	-297	102	120	996	.572	387			26	*S2	-16.4
■ TIM CORCORAN	Corcoran, Timothy Michael b: 3/19/53, Glendale, Cal. BL/TL, 5'11", 175 lbs. Deb: 5/18/77																											
1977	Det-A	55	103	13	29	3	0	3	15	6	9	.282	.321	.398	.719	91	-1	-1	105	119	12	.603	0	1	-1	-0	O/D	-0.2
1978	Det-A	116	324	37	86	13	1	1	27	24	27	.265	.326	.321	.647	77	-7	-10	108	100	33	.544	3	2	-0	-8	*O/D	-2.1
1979	Det-A	18	22	4	5	1	0	0	6	4	2	.227	.346	.273	.619	72	-1	-1	96	384	2	.579	1	1	-0	-1	/O1	-0.2
1980	Det-A	84	153	20	44	7	1	3	18	22	10	.288	.381	.405	.786	110	4	3	105	99	23	.739	0	2	-1	-2	1O/D	-0.3
1981	Min-A	22	51	4	9	3	0	0	4	6	7	.176	.263	.235	.498	43	-4	-4	105	130	3	.400	0	0	0	-0	1/D	-0.4
1983	Phi-N	3	0	0	0	0	0	0	0	0	0	—	—	—	—	—	0	-0	101	—	0	—	0	0	0	0	/1	0.0
1984	Phi-N	102	208	30	71	13	1	5	36	37	27	.341	.443	.486	.929	158	19	18	102	122	45	.965	0	1	-1	-3	1O	1.3
1985	Phi-N	103	182	11	39	6	1	0	22	29	20	.214	.322	.258	.581	63	-8	-8	102	186	16	.510	0	0	0	-0	1/O	-1.0
1986	NY-N	6	7	1	0	0	0	0	0	2	0	.000	.222	.000	.222	-35	-1	-1	96	0	0	.286	0	0	0	0	/1	0.0
Total	9	509	1050	120	283	46	4	12	128	130	102	.270	.354	.355	.709	94	2	-4	104	128	136	.664	4	7	-3	-15	1O/D	-2.9
■ FRED COREY	Corey, Frederick Harrison b: 1857, S.Kingston, R.I. d: 11/27/12, Providence, R.I. BR/TR, Deb: 5/01/1878																											
1878	Pro-N	7	21	3	3	0	0	0	1	0	2	.143	.143	.143	.286	-6	-2	-2	98	113	0	.167				0	/P21	0.0
1880	Wor-N	41	138	11	24	8	1	0	6	4	27	.174	.197	.246	.444	44	-7	-9	113	64	7	.333				-8	OP/S31	0.0
1881	Wor-N	51	203	22	45	8	4	0	10	5	10	.222	.240	.300	.541	66	-7	-9	105	58	15	.418				-2	OP/S	-0.9
1882	Wor-N	64	255	33	63	7	12	0	29	5	31	.247	.262	.369	.630	100	-0	-0	100	110	25	.516				-6	SPO/31	-0.2
1883	Phi-a	71	298	45	77	16	2	1		12		.258	.287	.336	.623	97	-0	-1	103	0	29	.507				2	3PO/2SCD	0.1
1884	Phi-a	104	439	64	121	17	16	5		17		.276	.306	.421	.727	120	17	8	114	0	58	.642				10	*3	1.7
1885	Phi-a	94	384	61	94	14	8	1		17		.245	.282	.331	.613	93	-2	-4	103	0	37	.507				7	*3/SP	0.7
Total	7	432	1738	239	427	70	43	7	46	60	70	.246	.273	.348	.620	94	-2	-18	106	29	172	.510				4	3/POS21D	1.4
■ MARK COREY	Corey, Mark Mundell b: 11/3/55, Tucumcari, N.Mex. BR/TR, 6'2", 200 lbs. Deb: 9/01/79																											
1979	Bal-A	13	13	1	2	0	0	0	1	0	4	.154	.154	.154	.308	-17	-2	-2	97	192	0	.250	1	0	0	-3	O	-0.4
1980	Bal-A	36	36	7	10	2	0	1	2	5	7	.278	.366	.417	.783	113	1	1	101	43	6	.741	0	1	-1	-12	O	-1.1
1981	Bal-A	10	8	2	0	0	0	0	0	2	2	.000	.200	.000	.200	-39	-1	-1	99	0	0	.250	0	0	0	-2	/O	-0.3
Total	3	59	57	10	12	2	0	1	3	7	13	.211	.297	.298	.595	64	-3	-3	100	67	6	.543	1	1	-0	-17	/O	-1.8
■ CHUCK CORGAN	Corgan, Charles Howard b: 12/4/02, Wagoner, Okla. d: 6/13/28, Wagoner, Okla. BB/TR, 5'11", 180 lbs. Deb: 9/19/25																											
1925	Bro-N	14	47	4	8	1	1	0	0	3	9	.170	.220	.234	.454	17	-6	-6	94	0	3	.359	0	0	0	0	S	-0.3
1927	Bro-N	19	57	3	15	1	0	0	1	4	4	.263	.311	.281	.592	58	-3	-3	103	22	5	.476	0			-1	2/S	-0.3
Total	2	33	104	7	23	2	1	0	1	7	13	.221	.270	.260	.530	40	-9	-9	99	12	8	.420	0	0		-1	/S2	-0.6
■ ROY CORHAN	Corhan, Roy George "Irish" b: 10/21/1887, Indianapolis, Ind. d: 11/24/58, San Francisco, Cal BR/TR, 5'9.5", 165 lbs. Deb: 4/20/11																											
1911	Chi-A	43	131	14	28	6	2	0	8	15		.214	.304	.290	.594	68	-6	-5	97	71	12	.553	2			11	S	0.9
1916	StL-N	92	295	30	62	6	3	0	18	20	31	.210	.265	.251	.516	61	-14	-13	97	97	24	.476	15			-6	S	-1.6
Total	2	135	426	44	90	12	5	0	26	35	31	.211	.277	.263	.540	63	-20	-18	97	88	36	.500	17			5	S	-0.7
■ POP CORKHILL	Corkhill, John Stewart b: 4/11/1858, Parkesburg, Pa. d: 4/4/21, Pennsauken, N.J. BL/TR, 5'10", 180 lbs. Deb: 5/01/1883																											
1883	Cin-a	88	375	53	81	10	8	2		3		.216	.222	.301	.524	65	-14	-16	103	0	26	.395				-3	*O/S21	-1.5
1884	Cin-a	110	452	85	124	13	11	4		6		.274	.290	.378	.668	113	8	5	106	0	51	.552				8	*OS/13P	1.0
1885	Cin-a	112	440	64	111	10	8	1		7		.252	.275	.318	.594	86	-5	-8	104	0	40	.468				16	*O/P1	0.1
1886	Cin-a	129	540	81	143	9	8	4		23		.265	.302	.333	.636	105	-0	3	96	0	63	.587	24			-0	*O3/1SP	0.0
1887	Cin-a	128	541	79	168	19	11	5		14		.311	.333	.414	.747	101	5	-3	108	0	87	.729	30			11	*O/P	0.2
1888	Cin-a	118	490	68	133	11	9	1	74	15		.271	.299	.337	.635	106	3	2	101	140	59	.591	27			3	*O/P12	0.0
	Bro-a	19	71	17	27	4	3	1	19	4		.380	.429	.563	.992	211	9	9	105	140	19	1.114	3			1	O	0.8
	Yr	137	561	85	160	15	12	2	93	19		.285	.316	.365	.681	120	12	11	101	141	76	.648	30			4		0.8
1889	Bro-a	138	537	91	134	21	9	8	78	42	24	.250	.308	.367	.674	97	-6	-2	96	107	69	.655	22			10	*O/S1	0.2
1890	Bro-N	51	204	23	46	4	2	1	21	15	11	.225	.279	.279	.558	64	-9	-9	100	112	18	.494	6			7	O/1	-0.2
1891	Phi-a	83	349	50	73	7	7	0	31	26	15	.209	.268	.269	.537	54	-20	-22	103	92	29	.486	12			4	O	-1.7
	Cin-N	1	4	0	0	0	0	0	0	0	1	.000	.000	.000	.000	-99	-1	-1	91	0	0	.000	0			1	/O	0.0
	Pit-N	41	145	16	33	1	1	3	20	7	10	.228	.268	.310	.578	69	-6	-6	101	108	14	.536	7			1	O	-0.6

YEAR	TM/L	G	AB	R	H	2B	3B	HR	RBI	BB	SO	AVG	OBP	SLG	PRO	/A	BR	/A	PF	CHI	RC	TA	SB	CS	SBR	FR	POS	TPR
	Yr	42	149	16	33	1	1	3	20	7	11	.221	.261	.302	.563	65	-7	-7	101	105	14	.517	7			2		-0.6
1892	Pit-N	68	256	23	47	1	4	0	25	12	19	.184	.229	.219	.448	39	-19	-17	94	140	15	.368	6			5	O	-1.3
Total	10	1086	4404	650	1120	110	81	30	268	174	80	.254	.288	.337	.625	90	-55	-65	101	56	489	.557	137			62	*O/1PS32	-3.0
■ **PAT CORRALES** Corrales, Patrick b: 3/20/41, Los Angeles, Cal. BR/TR, 6', 180 lbs. Deb: 8/02/64 MC																												
1964	Phi-N	2	1	1	0	0	0	0	0	1	0	.000	.500	.000	.500	55	0	0	99	0	0	1.000	0	0	0	0	H	0.0
1965	Phi-N	63	174	16	39	8	1	2	15	25	42	.224	.325	.316	.641	86	-4	-2	95	102	19	.583	0	0	0	2	C	0.2
1966	StL-N	28	72	5	13	2	0	0	3	2	17	.181	.224	.208	.432	21	-8	-8	100	84	3	.323	1	0	0	2	C	-0.4
1968	Cin-N	20	56	3	15	4	0	0	6	6	16	.268	.349	.339	.688	96	1	0	111	133	7	.619	0	0	0	2	C	0.3
1969	Cin-N	29	72	10	19	5	0	1	5	8	17	.264	.346	.375	.721	103	0	0	99	67	9	.643	0	1	-1	2	C	0.4
1970	Cin-N	43	106	9	25	5	1	1	10	8	22	.236	.289	.330	.620	63	-5	-6	104	102	9	.506	0	0	0	2	C	-0.1
1971	Cin-N	40	94	6	17	2	0	0	6	6	17	.181	.230	.202	.432	24	-9	-9	96	129	5	.321	0	0	0	0	C	-0.8
1972	Cin-N	2	1	0	0	0	0	0	0	2	0	.000	.667	.000	.667	111	0	0	93	0	0	2.000	0	0	0	0	/C	0.1
	SD-N	44	119	6	23	0	0	0	6	11	26	.193	.267	.193	.460	37	-10	-9	88	107	7	.361	0	0	0	-1	C	-0.7
	Yr	46	120	6	23	0	0	0	6	13	26	.192	.276	.192	.468	40	-10	-8	89	102	7	.378	0	0	0	-1		-0.6
1973	SD-N	29	72	7	15	2	1	0	3	6	10	.208	.278	.264	.542	54	-5	-4	94	63	6	.448	0	0	0	1	C	0.0
Total	9	300	767	63	166	28	3	4	54	75	167	.216	.292	.276	.569	62	-39	-37	97	99	64	.489	1	1	-0	10	C	-1.0
■ **VIC CORRELL** Correll, Victor Crosby b: 2/5/46, Washington, D.C. BR/TR, 5'10", 185 lbs. Deb: 10/04/72																												
1972	Bos-A	1	4	1	2	0	0	0	1	0	1	.500	.500	.500	1.000	188	0	0	105	213	1	1.000	0	0	0	0	/C	0.1
1974	Atl-N	73	202	20	48	15	1	4	29	21	38	.238	.322	.381	.703	92	-1	-2	105	126	25	.642	0	0	0	3	C	0.3
1975	Atl-N	103	325	37	70	12	1	11	39	42	66	.215	.307	.360	.667	89	-7	-5	95	101	34	.593	0	2	-1	4	C	0.1
1976	Atl-N	69	200	26	45	6	2	5	16	21	37	.225	.302	.350	.652	76	-4	-7	111	72	20	.564	0	1	-1	1	C	-0.2
1977	Atl-N	54	144	16	30	7	0	7	16	22	33	.208	.317	.403	.720	81	-2	-4	113	81	18	.692	2	3	-1	3	C	-0.3
1978	Cin-N	52	105	9	25	7	0	1	6	8	17	.238	.292	.333	.625	72	-4	-4	103	63	8	.489	0	2	-1	-3	C	-0.7
1979	Cin-N	48	133	14	31	12	0	1	15	14	26	.233	.311	.346	.657	81	-4	-3	97	121	14	.581	0	0	0	3	C	0.1
1980	Cin-N	10	19	1	8	1	0	0	3	0	2	.421	.421	.474	.895	147	1	1	102	132	4	.818	0	0	0	-0	C	0.1
Total	8	410	1132	124	259	60	4	29	125	128	220	.229	.312	.366	.677	85	-20	-25	103	97	125	.627	2	8	-4	11	C	-0.5
■ **PHIL CORRIDAN** Corridan, Philip Deb: 7/16/1884																												
1884	CP-U	2	7	1	1	0	0	0		0		.143	.143	.143	.286	-3	-1	-1	99	0	0	.167	0			0	/2O	0.0
■ **JOHN CORRIDEN** Corriden, John Michael Jr. b: 10/6/18, Logansport, Ind. BB/TR, 5'6", 160 lbs. Deb: 4/20/46																												
1946	Bro-N	1	0	1	0	0	0	0	0	0	0	—	—	—	—	—	0	0	103	—	—	—	0			0	R	0.0
■ **RED CORRIDEN** Corriden, John Michael Sr. b: 9/4/1887, Logansport, Ind. d: 9/28/59, Indianapolis, Ind BR/TR, 5'9", 165 lbs. Deb: 9/08/10 MC																												
1910	StL-A	26	84	19	13	3	0	1	4	13		.155	.268	.226	.494	58	-4	-3	94	71	7	.521	5			2	S3	0.0
1912	Det-A	38	138	22	28	6	0	0	5	15		.203	.286	.246	.532	55	-8	-7	95	52	11	.491	4			2	3/2S	-0.4
1913	Chi-N	46	97	13	17	3	0	2	9	10	14	.175	.252	.268	.520	49	-7	-6	99	102	7	.500	4			1	S/23	-0.3
1914	Chi-N	107	318	42	73	9	5	3	29	35	33	.230	.323	.318	.641	92	-3	-2	98	96	37	.645	13			-21	S/32	-2.1
1915	Chi-N	6	3	1	0	0	0	0	0	2	1	.000	.571	.000	.571	78	1	1	102	0	0	1.333	0			-0	/3O	0.0
Total	5	223	640	97	131	21	5	6	47	75	48	.205	.300	.281	.581	74	-21	-19	97	83	62	.576	26			-17	S/32O	-2.8
■ **JESS CORTAZZO** Cortazzo, John Francis b: 9/26/04, Wilmerding, Pa. d: 3/4/63, Pittsburgh, Pa. BR/TR, 5'3.5", 142 lbs. Deb: 9/01/23																												
1923	Chi-A	1	1	0	0	0	0	0	0	0	0	.000	.000	.000	.000	-99	-0	-0	98	0	0	.000	0	0	0	0	H	0.0
■ **JOE COSCARART** Coscarart, Joseph Marvin b: 11/18/09, Escondido, Cal. BR/TR, 6', 185 lbs. Deb: 4/26/35																												
1935	Bos-N	86	284	30	67	11	2	1	29	16	28	.236	.277	.299	.576	57	-18	-16	96	119	23	.458	2			-7	3S2	-1.8
1936	Bos-N	104	367	28	90	11	2	2	44	19	37	.245	.292	.302	.594	63	-20	-18	95	136	31	.466	0			-0	3/S2	-0.9
Total	2	190	651	58	157	22	4	3	73	35	65	.241	.285	.301	.586	61	-39	-34	95	128	55	.469	2			-7	3/S2	-2.7
■ **PETE COSCARART** Coscarart, Peter Joseph b: 6/16/13, Escondido, Cal. BR/TR, 5'11.5", 175 lbs. Deb: 4/26/38																												
1938	Bro-N	32	79	10	12	3	0	0	6	9	18	.152	.256	.190	.445	25	-8	-8	96	145	5	.388	0			0	2	-0.5
1939	Bro-N	115	419	59	116	22	2	4	43	46	56	.277	.354	.368	.721	88	-2	-6	107	97	58	.695	10			-10	*2/3S	-1.1
1940	Bro-N	143	506	55	120	24	4	9	58	53	59	.237	.311	.354	.664	77	-12	-17	108	107	56	.596	5			-27	*2	-3.5
1941	Bro-N	43	62	13	8	1	0	0	5	7	12	.129	.217	.145	.363	3	-8	-8	103	201	2	.304	1			-2	2/S	-0.8
1942	Pit-N	133	487	57	111	12	4	3	29	38	56	.228	.288	.287	.575	68	-19	-20	101	74	42	.477	2			-22	*S2	-3.4
1943	Pit-N	133	491	57	119	19	6	0	48	46	48	.242	.307	.305	.613	74	-14	-17	104	118	47	.524	4			-7	2S/3	-1.7
1944	Pit-N	139	554	89	146	30	4	4	42	41	57	.264	.315	.354	.669	84	-9	-13	105	77	62	.590	10			-6	*2/SO	-0.4
1945	Pit-N	123	392	59	95	17	2	8	38	55	55	.242	.341	.357	.699	91	-2	-4	103	80	50	.655	2			11	*2/S	1.7
1946	Pit-N	3	2	0	1	1	0	0	0	0	0	.500	.500	1.000	1.500	310	1	1	103	0	1	2.000	0			0	/S	0.1
Total	9	864	2992	399	728	129	22	28	269	295	361	.243	.314	.329	.644	77	-75	-92	105	96	322	.587	34			-61	2S/3O	-9.6
■ **RAY COSEY** Cosey, Donald Ray b: 2/15/56, San Raphael, Cal. BL/TL, 5'10", 185 lbs. Deb: 4/14/80																												
1980	Oak-A	9	9	0	1	0	0	0	0	0	0	.111	.111	.111	.222	-41	-2	-2	95	0	0	.125	0	0	0	0	/H	-0.1
■ **DAN COSTELLO** Costello, Daniel Francis "Dashing Dan" b: 9/9/1891, Jessup, Pa. d: 3/26/36, Pittsburgh, Pa. BL/TR, 6'0.5", 185 lbs. Deb: 7/02/13																												
1913	NY-A	2	2	1	1	0	0	0	0	0	0	.500	.500	.500	1.000	191	0	0	101	0	0	1.000	0			0	H	0.0
1914	Pit-N	21	64	7	19	1	0	0	5	8	16	.297	.375	.313	.688	114	1	1	92	91	8	.667	2			-1	O	0.0
1915	Pit-N	71	125	16	27	4	1	0	11	7	23	.216	.258	.264	.522	59	-6	-6	99	127	10	.475	7	1	2	-5	O	-1.1
1916	Pit-N	60	159	11	38	1	3	0	8	6	23	.239	.267	.283	.550	66	-6	-7	105	71	13	.446	3			-3	O	-1.2
Total	4	154	350	35	85	6	4	0	24	21	62	.243	.286	.283	.569	73	-11	-11	100	94	32	.496	12	1		-9	/O	-2.3
■ **HENRY COTE** Cote, Henry Joseph b: 2/19/1864, Troy, N.Y. d: 4/28/40, Troy, N.Y. Deb: 9/16/1894																												
1894	Lou-N	10	31	7	9	2	2	0	3	5	6	.290	.389	.484	.873	126	1	1	88	55	7	1.000	2			0	C	0.1
1895	Lou-N	10	33	10	10	0	0	0	5	3	3	.303	.361	.303	.664	78	-1	-1	95	140	4	.652	2			0	C	0.0
Total	2	20	64	17	19	2	2	0	8	8	9	.297	.375	.391	.766	101	-1	1	92	97	11	.822	4			0	/C	0.1
■ **PETE COTE** Cote, Warren Peter b: 8/30/02, Cambridge, Mass. d: 10/17/87, Middleton, Mass. BR/TR, 5'6", 148 lbs. Deb: 6/18/26																												
1926	NY-N	2	1	0	0	0	0	0	0	0	0	.000	.000	.000	.000	-99	-0	-0	98	0	0	.000	0			0	H	0.0
■ **ED COTTER** Cotter, Edward Chrsitopher b: 7/4/04, Hartford, Conn. d: 6/14/59, Hartford, Conn. BR/TR, 6', 185 lbs. Deb: 6/12/26																												
1926	Phi-N	17	26	3	8	0	1	0	1	1	4	.308	.333	.385	.718	90	-0	-0	103	35	3	.667	1			0	/3S	0.0
■ **HOOKS COTTER** Cotter, Harvey Louis b: 5/22/1900, Holden, Mo. d: 8/6/55, Los Angeles, Cal. BL/TL, 5'10", 160 lbs. Deb: 4/15/22																												
1922	Chi-N	1	1	0	1	1	0	0	0	0	0	1.000	1.000	2.000	3.000	691	1	1	95	0	2	—	0	0	0	0	H	0.1
1924	Chi-N	98	310	39	81	16	4	4	33	36	31	.261	.338	.377	.716	91	-3	-4	101	93	40	.667	3	5	-2	-2	1	-1.1
Total	2	99	311	39	82	17	4	4	33	36	31	.264	.340	.383	.723	92	-3	-3	101	93	42	.675	3	5	-2	-2	/1	-1.0
■ **DICK COTTER** Cotter, Richard Raphael b: 10/12/1889, Manchester, N.H. d: 4/4/45, Brooklyn, N.Y. TR , 5'11", 172 lbs. Deb: 8/17/11																												
1911	Phi-N	20	46	2	13	0	0	0	5	5	7	.283	.353	.283	.636	73	-1	-2	108	130	5	.576	1			0	C	0.0
1912	Chi-N	26	54	6	15	0	2	0	10	6	13	.278	.361	.352	.713	92	-0	-0	104	177	7	.692	1			-0	C	0.0
Total	2	46	100	8	28	0	2	0	15	11	20	.280	.357	.320	.677	83	-1	-2	105	156	12	.639	2			-0	/C	0.0
■ **TOM COTTER** Cotter, Thomas B. b: 9/30/1866, Waltham, Mass. d: 11/22/06, Brookline, Mass. BR/TR, 5'10.5", 149 lbs. Deb: 9/03/1891																												
1891	Bos-a	6	12	1	3	0	0	0	4	1	2	.250	.308	.250	.558	63	-1	-1	99	386	1	.444	0			0	/CO	0.0
■ **CHUCK COTTIER** Cottier, Charles Keith b: 1/8/36, Delta, Colo. BR/TR, 5'10.5", 175 lbs. Deb: 4/17/59 MC																												
1959	Mil-N	10	24	1	3	1	0	0	1	3	7	.125	.222	.167	.389	6	-3	-3	95	101	1	.333	0	0	0	-1	2	-0.2
1960	Mil-N	95	229	29	52	8	0	3	19	14	21	.227	.278	.301	.579	64	-13	-10	91	99	20	.478	1	0	0	-7	2	-0.8
1961	Det-A	10	7	2	2	0	0	0	1	1	1	.286	.375	.286	.661	83	-0	-0	96	196	1	.600	0	0	0	-1	/S2	0.0
	Was-A	101	337	37	79	14	4	2	34	30	51	.234	.299	.318	.616	68	-17	-15	95	120	34	.557	9	1	2	8	*2	0.8
	Yr	111	344	39	81	14	4	2	35	31	52	.235	.301	.317	.617	68	-17	-15	95	129	35	.558	9	1	2	8		0.8

YEAR	TM/L	G	AB	R	H	2B	3B	HR	RBI	BB	SO	AVG	OBP	SLG	PRO	/A	BR	/A	PF	CHI	RC	TA	SB	CS	SBR	FR	POS	TPR
1962	Was-A	136	443	50	107	14	6	6	40	44	57	.242	.313	.341	.654	75	-15	-15	101	94	49	.603	14	8	-1	12	*2	0.6
1963	Was-A	113	337	30	69	16	4	5	21	24	63	.205	.258	.320	.578	62	-18	-17	98	71	28	.489	2	1	0	5	2S/3	-0.4
1964	Was-A	73	137	16	23	6	2	3	10	19	33	.168	.269	.307	.576	59	-7	-8	101	83	12	.543	2	0	1	-5	2/3S	-0.6
1965	Was-A	7	1	1	0	0	0	0	0	0	0	.000	.000	.000	.000	-99	-0	-0	100	0	0	.000	0	0	0	0	H	0.0
1968	Cal-A	33	67	2	13	4	1	0	1	2	15	.194	.217	.284	.501	54	-4	-4	94	23	4	.389	0	0	0	0	3/2	-0.2
1969	Cal-A	2	2	0	0	0	0	0	0	0	0	.000	.000	.000	.000	-99	-1	-1	99	0	0	.000	0	0	0	0	/2	0.0
Total	9	580	1584	168	348	63	17	19	127	137	248	.220	.284	.317	.601	66	-79	-73	97	92	150	.539	28	10	2	13	2/S3	-0.8

■ **HENRY COTTO** Cotto, Henry b: 1/5/61, New York, N.Y. BR/TR, 6'2", 178 lbs. Deb: 4/05/84

YEAR	TM/L	G	AB	R	H	2B	3B	HR	RBI	BB	SO	AVG	OBP	SLG	PRO	/A	BR	/A	PF	CHI	RC	TA	SB	CS	SBR	FR	POS	TPR
1984	Chi-N	105	146	24	40	5	0	0	8	10	23	.274	.325	.308	.633	71	-4	-6	110	70	16	.591	9	3	1	-11	O	-1.9
1985	NY-A	34	56	4	17	1	0	1	6	3	12	.304	.339	.375	.714	99	-0	-0	96	99	7	.610	1	1	-0	-4	O	-0.4
1986	NY-A	35	80	11	17	3	0	1	6	2	17	.213	.232	.287	.519	40	-7	-7	103	92	5	.424	3	0	1	-0	O/D	-0.6
1987	NY-A	68	149	21	35	10	0	5	20	6	35	.235	.269	.403	.672	78	-5	-5	98	106	14	.577	4	2	0	-6	O	-1.1
1988	Sea-A	133	386	50	100	18	1	8	33	23	53	.259	.304	.373	.677	82	-6	-10	108	78	46	.660	27	3	6	3	*O/D	-0.2
Total	5	375	817	110	209	37	1	15	73	44	140	.256	.297	.359	.656	77	-23	-28	105	84	87	.616	44	9	8	-17	O/D	-4.2

■ **DENNIS COUGHLIN** Coughlin, Dennis F. Deb: 4/27/1872

YEAR	TM/L	G	AB	R	H	2B	3B	HR	RBI	BB	SO	AVG	OBP	SLG	PRO	/A	BR	/A	PF	CHI	RC	TA	SB	CS	SBR	FR	POS	TPR
1872	Nat-n	8	37	5	12							.324															/OS2	

■ **BILL COUGHLIN** Coughlin, William Paul "Scranton Bill" b: 7/12/1878, Scranton, Pa. d: 5/7/43, Scranton, Pa. BR/TR, 5'9", 140 lbs. Deb: 8/09/1899

YEAR	TM/L	G	AB	R	H	2B	3B	HR	RBI	BB	SO	AVG	OBP	SLG	PRO	/A	BR	/A	PF	CHI	RC	TA	SB	CS	SBR	FR	POS	TPR
1899	Was-N	6	24	2	3	0	1	0	3	1		.125	.160	.208	.368	2	-3	-3	96	195	1	.333	1			0	/3	-0.2
1901	Was-A	137	506	76	139	17	13	6	70	25		.275	.309	.395	.704	97	-4	-3	99	103	68	.657	16			0	*3	-0.5
1902	Was-A	123	469	84	141	27	4	6	71	26		.301	.337	.414	.751	111	5	6	99	117	77	.759	29			-3	3S2	0.4
1903	Was-A	125	473	56	116	18	3	1	31	9		.245	.259	.302	.562	66	-18	-21	105	81	46	.510	30			-0	*3/SO	-2.2
1904	Was-A	65	265	28	73	15	4	0	17	9		.275	.299	.362	.662	120	3	5	93	57	33	.599	10			1	3	0.9
	Det-A	56	206	22	47	6	0	0	17	5		.228	.246	.257	.504	64	-9	-8	96	122	14	.371	1			-6	3	-1.3
	Yr	121	471	50	120	21	4	0	34	14		.255	.276	.316	.593	95	-6	-3	94	87	45	.496	11			-5		-0.4
1905	Det-A	137	489	48	123	20	6	0	44	34		.252	.300	.317	.617	100	-1	-0	98	107	53	.560	16			-7	*3	-0.2
1906	Det-A	147	498	54	117	15	5	2	60	36		.235	.287	.297	.584	78	-9	-13	108	145	53	.564	31			-11	*3	-1.4
1907	Det-A	134	519	80	126	10	2	0	46	35		.243	.291	.270	.560	79	-11	-11	102	113	46	.483	15			-8	*3	-1.2
1908	Det-A	119	405	32	87	5	1	0	23	23		.215	.257	.232	.489	60	-17	-17	101	94	25	.399	10			-13	*3	-2.4
Total	9	1049	3854	482	972	133	39	15	382	203		.252	.290	.319	.608	86	-63	-66	101	107	415	.552	159			-47	3/S2O	-8.1

■ **MARLAN COUGHTRY** Coughtry, James Marlan b: 9/11/34, Hollywood, Cal. BL/TR, 6'1", 170 lbs. Deb: 9/02/60

YEAR	TM/L	G	AB	R	H	2B	3B	HR	RBI	BB	SO	AVG	OBP	SLG	PRO	/A	BR	/A	PF	CHI	RC	TA	SB	CS	SBR	FR	POS	TPR
1960	Bos-A	15	19	3	3	0	0	0	0	5	8	.158	.333	.158	.491	36	-1	-2	103	0	1	.500	0	0	0	0	2/3	0.0
1962	LA-A	11	22	0	4	0	0	0	2	0	6	.182	.182	.182	.364	-2	-3	-3	102	198	1	.222	0	0	0	0	/32	-0.2
	KC-A	6	11	1	2	0	0	0	1	4	3	.182	.400	.182	.582	63	-0	-0	100	198	1	.667	0	0	0	0	/3	0.0
	Cle-A	3	2	1	1	0	0	0	1	1	1	.500	.667	.500	1.167	225	1	1	98	397	1	2.000	0	0	0	0	H	0.1
	Yr	20	35	2	7	0	0	0	4	5	10	.200	.300	.200	.500	37	-3	-3	101	248	3	.429	0	0	0	0		-0.1
Total	2	35	54	5	10	0	0	0	4	10	18	.185	.313	.185	.498	37	-4	-4	102	133	4	.455	0	0	0	1	/23	-0.1

■ **BOB COULSON** Coulson, Robert Jackson b: 6/17/1887, Courtney, Pa. d: 9/11/53, Washington, Pa. BR/TR, 5'10.5", 175 lbs. Deb: 8/04/08

YEAR	TM/L	G	AB	R	H	2B	3B	HR	RBI	BB	SO	AVG	OBP	SLG	PRO	/A	BR	/A	PF	CHI	RC	TA	SB	CS	SBR	FR	POS	TPR
1908	Cin-N	8	18	3	6	1	1	0	1	3		.333	.429	.500	.929	194	2	2	103	43	4	1.000	0			1	/O	0.3
1910	Bro-N	25	89	14	22	3	4	1	13	6	14	.247	.302	.404	.707	111	0	1	95	118	13	.776	9			-1	O	0.0
1911	Bro-N	146	521	52	122	23	7	0	50	42	78	.234	.301	.305	.606	72	-21	-19	97	113	57	.604	32			-3	*O	-2.6
1914	Pit-F	18	64	7	13	1	0	0	3	7	10	.203	.282	.219	.500	47	-4	-4	94	82	5	.451	2			-3	O	-0.7
Total	4	197	692	76	163	28	12	1	67	58	102	.236	.303	.315	.618	78	-24	-21	97	109	79	.620	43			-5	O	-3.0

■ **CHIP COULTER** Coulter, Thomas Lee b: 6/5/45, Steubenville, O. BB/TR, 5'10", 172 lbs. Deb: 9/18/69

YEAR	TM/L	G	AB	R	H	2B	3B	HR	RBI	BB	SO	AVG	OBP	SLG	PRO	/A	BR	/A	PF	CHI	RC	TA	SB	CS	SBR	FR	POS	TPR
1969	StL-N	6	19	3	6	1	1	0	4	2	6	.316	.381	.474	.855	139	1	1	100	178	3	.786	0	1	-1	-0	/2	0.0

■ **CLINT COURTNEY** Courtney, Clinton Dawson "Scrap Iron" b: 3/16/27, Hall Summit, La. d: 6/16/75, Rochester, N.Y. BL/TR, 5'8", 180 lbs. Deb: 9/29/51 C

YEAR	TM/L	G	AB	R	H	2B	3B	HR	RBI	BB	SO	AVG	OBP	SLG	PRO	/A	BR	/A	PF	CHI	RC	TA	SB	CS	SBR	FR	POS	TPR
1951	NY-A	1	2	0	0	0	0	0	0	1	1	.000	.333	.000	.333	-5	-0	-0	92	0	0	.500	0	0	0	0	/C	0.0
1952	StL-A	119	413	38	118	24	3	5	50	39	26	.286	.349	.395	.743	110	3	5	97	105	58	.663	0	2	-1	7	*C	1.7
1953	StL-A	106	355	28	89	12	2	4	19	25	20	.251	.302	.330	.631	66	-15	-18	107	54	33	.509	0	1	-1	-3	*C	-1.7
1954	Bal-A	122	397	25	107	18	3	4	37	30	7	.270	.326	.360	.686	92	-7	-5	95	91	46	.591	2	1	0	2	*C	0.2
1955	Chi-A	19	37	7	14	3	0	1	10	7	0	.378	.477	.541	1.018	172	4	4	101	162	9	1.080	0	0	0	-0	C	0.4
	Was-A	75	238	26	71	8	4	2	30	19	9	.298	.353	.391	.743	110	-0	3	91	113	33	.661	0	0	0	1	C	0.6
	Yr	94	275	33	85	11	4	3	40	26	9	.309	.371	.411	.782	118	4	7	93	125	43	.722	0	0	0	0		1.0
1956	Was-A	101	283	31	85	20	3	5	44	20	10	.300	.365	.445	.811	111	5	4	102	117	43	.731	0	5	-3	0	C	0.3
1957	Was-A	91	232	23	62	14	1	6	27	16	11	.267	.346	.414	.760	109	2	3	98	94	33	.705	0	0	0	4	C	0.9
1958	Was-A	134	450	46	113	18	0	8	62	48	23	.251	.335	.344	.680	91	-7	-5	97	**142**	52	.603	1	5	-3	5	*C	-0.1
1959	Was-A	72	189	19	44	4	1	2	18	20	19	.233	.310	.296	.606	67	-8	-8	100	114	18	.517	0	1	-1	-3	C	-0.8
1960	Bal-A	83	154	14	35	3	0	1	12	30	14	.227	.380	.266	.646	76	-3	-3	102	107	18	.632	0	1	-1	-5	C	-0.4
1961	KC-A	1	1	0	0	0	0	0	0	0	0	.000	.000	.000	.000	-98	-0	-0	102	0	0	.000	0	0	0	0	H	0.0
	Bal-A	22	45	3	12	2	0	0	4	10	3	.267	.400	.311	.711	95	0	0	97	112	6	.706	0	0	0	-0	C	0.0
	Yr	23	46	3	12	2	0	0	4	10	3	.261	.393	.304	.697	91	-0	0	97	107	6	.686	0	0	0	-0		0.0
Total	11	946	2796	260	750	126	17	38	313	265	143	.268	.341	.366	.708	94	-26	-20	99	105	349	.648	3	16	-9	8	C	1.1

■ **ERNIE COURTNEY** Courtney, Edward Ernest b: 1/20/1875, Des Moines, Iowa d: 2/29/20, Buffalo, N.Y. BL/TR, 5'10", Deb: 4/17/02

YEAR	TM/L	G	AB	R	H	2B	3B	HR	RBI	BB	SO	AVG	OBP	SLG	PRO	/A	BR	/A	PF	CHI	RC	TA	SB	CS	SBR	FR	POS	TPR
1902	Bos-N	48	165	23	36	3	0	0	17	13		.218	.275	.236	.512	63	-7	-6	95	154	12	.426	3			1	O/S	-0.7
	Bal-A	1	4	3	2	0	1	0	1	1		.500	.600	1.000	1.600	334	1	1	102	71	2	2.500	0			-0	/3	0.1
1903	NY-A	25	79	7	21	3	3	1	8	7		.266	.326	.418	.743	124	2	2	100	80	11	.707	1			0	S/21	0.4
	Det-A	23	74	7	17	0	0	0	6	5		.230	.278	.230	.508	57	-4	-3	97	127	5	.404	1			-2	3/S	-0.5
	Yr	48	153	14	38	3	3	1	14	12		.248	.303	.327	.630	92	-2	-1	99	104	16	.557	2			-2		-0.1
1905	Phi-N	155	601	77	165	14	7	2	77	47		.275	.327	.331	.658	94	-1	-4	104	126	72	.603	17			-18	*3	-1.0
1906	Phi-N	116	398	53	94	12	2	0	42	45		.236	.314	.276	.590	94	-5	-1	92	147	37	.530	6			-11	31/OS	-1.8
1907	Phi-N	130	440	42	107	17	4	2	43	55		.243	.327	.314	.641	99	3	1	104	120	48	.598	6			-6	31/2SO	-0.6
1908	Phi-N	60	160	14	29	3	0	0	6	15		.181	.251	.200	.451	46	-9	-9	100	72	8	.366	1			0	31/2S	-0.9
Total	6	558	1921	226	471	52	17	5	200	188		.245	.312	.298	.610	89	-19	-20	100	125	197	.548	35			-35	3/1OS2	-5.0

■ **DEE COUSINEAU** Cousineau, Edward Thomas b: 12/16/1898, Watertown, Mass. d: 7/14/51, Watertown, Mass. BR/TR, 6', 170 lbs. Deb: 10/06/23

YEAR	TM/L	G	AB	R	H	2B	3B	HR	RBI	BB	SO	AVG	OBP	SLG	PRO	/A	BR	/A	PF	CHI	RC	TA	SB	CS	SBR	FR	POS	TPR
1923	Bos-N	1	2	1	2	0	0	0	2	0	0	1.000	1.000	1.000	2.000	430	1	1	100	352	2	—	0	0	0	0	/C	0.1
1924	Bos-N	3	2	0	0	0	0	0	0	0	0	.000	.000	.000	.000	-99	-1	-1	94	0	0	.000	0	0	0	0	/C	0.0
1925	Bos-N	1	0	0	0	0	0	0	0	0	0	—	—	—	—	—	0	0	94	—	—	—	0	0	0	0	/C	0.0
Total	3	5	4	1	2	0	0	0	2	0	0	.500	.500	.500	1.000	172	0	0	97	176	2	1.000	0	0	0	0	/C	0.1

■ **JACK COVENEY** Coveney, John Patrick b: 6/10/1880, S.Natick, Mass. d: 3/28/61, Waverly, Mass. TR , 5'9", 175 lbs. Deb: 03

YEAR	TM/L	G	AB	R	H	2B	3B	HR	RBI	BB	SO	AVG	OBP	SLG	PRO	/A	BR	/A	PF	CHI	RC	TA	SB	CS	SBR	FR	POS	TPR
1903	StL-N	4	14	0	2	0	0	0	0	0		.143	.143	.143	.286	-18	-2	-2	96	0	0	.167	0			0	/C	0.0

■ **SAM COVINGTON** Covington, Clarence Otto b: 12/17/1892, Henryville, Tenn. d: 1/4/63, Denison, Tex. BL/TR, 6'1", 190 lbs. Deb: 8/25/13

YEAR	TM/L	G	AB	R	H	2B	3B	HR	RBI	BB	SO	AVG	OBP	SLG	PRO	/A	BR	/A	PF	CHI	RC	TA	SB	CS	SBR	FR	POS	TPR
1913	StL-A	20	60	3	9	0	1	0	4	4	6	.150	.203	.183	.386	14	-7	-6	95	129	2	.353	3			1	1	-0.5
1917	Bos-N	17	66	8	13	2	0	1	10	5	5	.197	.264	.273	.537	67	-3	-2	96	162	5	.472	1			0	1	-0.2
1918	Bos-N	3	3	0	1	0	0	0	0	0	0	.333	.333	.333	.667	110	0	0	94	0	0	.500	0			0	H	0.0
Total	3	40	129	11	23	2	1	1	14	9	11	.178	.237	.233	.470	43	-9	-9	96	143	8	.415	4			1	/1	-0.7

■ **WES COVINGTON** Covington, John Wesley b: 3/27/32, Laurinburg, N.C. BL/TR, 6'1", 205 lbs. Deb: 4/19/56

YEAR	TM/L	G	AB	R	H	2B	3B	HR	RBI	BB	SO	AVG	OBP	SLG	PRO	/A	BR	/A	PF	CHI	RC	TA	SB	CS	SBR	FR	POS	TPR
1956	Mil-N	75	138	17	39	4	0	2	16	16	20	.283	.361	.355	.716	95	-1	-0	99	123	19	.663	1	0	0	-5	O	-0.6
1957	Mil-N	96	328	51	93	4	8	21	65	29	44	.284	.345	.537	.882	147	14	18	90	113	61	.876	4	1	1	-2	O	1.4
1958	Mil-N	90	294	43	97	12	1	24	74	20	35	.330	.382	.622	1.005	179	24	28	89	120	68	1.020	0	0	0	-9	O	1.7

YEAR	TM/L	G	AB	R	H	2B	3B	HR	RBI	BB	SO	AVG	OBP	SLG	PRO	/A	BR	/A	PF	CHI	RC	TA	SB	CS	SBR	FR	POS	TPR
1959	Mil-N	103	373	38	104	17	3	7	45	26	41	.279	.331	.397	.728	98	-4	-2	95	110	46	.625	0	1	-1	-6	O	-0.9
1960	Mil-N	95	281	25	70	16	1	10	35	15	37	.249	.290	.420	.709	101	-4	-1	91	96	31	.608	1	2	-1	-9	O	-1.3
1961	Mil-N	9	21	3	4	1	0	0	0	2	4	.190	.261	.238	.499	37	-2	-2	92	0	1	.412	0	0	0	-2	/O	-0.3
	Chi-A	22	59	5	17	1	0	4	15	4	5	.288	.333	.508	.842	123	2	2	99	140	9	.773	0	0	0	-2	O	0.0
	KC-A	17	44	3	7	0	0	1	6	4	7	.159	.260	.227	.487	31	-4	-4	102	181	3	.410	0	0	0	-2	O	-0.6
	Yr	39	103	8	24	1	0	5	21	8	12	.233	.301	.388	.689	82	-3	-3	100	161	12	.617	0	0	0	-4		-0.6
	Phi-N	57	165	23	50	9	0	7	26	15	17	.303	.361	.485	.846	130	5	6	94	104	28	.798	0	0	0	-5	O	-0.1
1962	Phi-N	116	304	36	86	12	1	9	44	19	44	.283	.329	.418	.747	104	-1	1	95	113	40	.652	0	0	0	-13	O	-1.6
1963	Phi-N	119	353	46	107	24	1	17	64	26	56	.303	.354	.521	.876	145	21	20	103	114	63	.839	1	0	0	-13	*O	0.2
1964	Phi-N	129	339	37	95	18	0	13	58	38	50	.280	.358	.448	.806	127	12	12	99	125	55	.772	0	0	0	-17	*O	-0.8
1965	Phi-N	101	235	27	58	10	1	15	45	26	47	.247	.324	.489	.814	133	7	9	95	117	37	.780	0	0	0	-5	O	0.2
1966	Chi-N	9	11	0	1	0	0	0	0	1	2	.091	.167	.091	.258	-26	-2	-2	100	0	0	.200	0	0	0	0	/O	-0.1
	LA-N	37	33	1	4	0	1	1	6	6	5	.121	.293	.273	.565	60	-2	-2	97	210	3	.567	0	0	0	-0	/O	-0.1
	Yr	46	44	1	5	0	1	1	6	7	7	.114	.264	.227	.491	39	-4	-3	98	169	3	.475	0	0	0	-0		-0.2
Total	11	1075	2978	355	832	128	17	131	499	247	414	.279	.339	.466	.805	123	65	84	95	115	463	.774	7	4	-0	-90	O	-2.9
■ BILLY COWAN	Cowan, Billy Roland b: 8/28/38, Calhoun City, Miss. BR/TR, 6', 170 lbs. Deb: 9/09/63																											
1963	Chi-N	14	36	1	9	1	1	1	2	0	11	.250	.250	.417	.667	84	-1	-1	105	47	3	.536	0	1	-1	-1	O	-0.2
1964	Chi-N	139	497	52	120	16	4	19	50	18	128	.241	.269	.404	.674	82	-10	-13	105	80	53	.601	12	3	2	-9	*O	-2.5
1965	NY-N	82	156	16	28	8	2	3	9	4	45	.179	.205	.314	.519	44	-12	-12	100	64	9	.432	3	2	-0	-5	O/2S	-2.0
	Mil-N	19	27	4	5	1	0	0	0	0	9	.185	.185	.222	.407	14	-3	-3	104	0	1	.273	0	0	0	-2	O	-0.5
	Yr	101	183	20	33	9	2	3	9	4	54	.180	.202	.301	.503	39	-15	-15	101	53	11	.414	3	2	-0	-7		-2.5
1967	Phi-N	34	59	11	9	0	0	3	6	4	14	.153	.206	.305	.511	43	-4	-5	104	92	4	.451	1	0	0	-4	O/23	-0.9
1969	NY-A	32	48	5	8	0	0	1	3	3	9	.167	.216	.229	.445	26	-5	-5	95	86	2	.326	0	0	0	-2	O	-0.6
	Cal-A	28	56	10	17	1	0	4	10	3	9	.304	.350	.536	.886	146	3	3	99	96	10	.850	0	0	0	0	O/1	0.3
	Yr	60	104	15	25	1	0	5	13	6	18	.240	.288	.394	.683	92	-2	-2	97	92	12	.600	0	0	0	-2		-0.3
1970	Cal-A	68	134	20	37	9	1	5	25	11	29	.276	.336	.470	.806	131	3	5	92	130	21	.750	0	1	-1	-6	O1/3	-0.3
1971	Cal-A	74	174	12	48	8	0	4	20	7	41	.276	.304	.391	.695	97	-2	-1	99	102	20	.589	1	1	-0	-3	O/1	-0.5
1972	Cal-A	3	3	0	0	0	0	0	0	0	2	.000	.000	.000	.000	-99	-1	-1	88	0	0	.000	0	0	0	0	H	0.0
Total	8	493	1190	131	281	44	8	40	125	50	297	.236	.269	.387	.657	82	-31	-33	101	85	124	.580	17	8	0	-31	O/132S	-7.2
■ AL COWENS	Cowens, Alfred Edward b: 10/25/51, Los Angeles, Cal. BR/TR, 6'1", 197 lbs. Deb: 4/06/74																											
1974	KC-A	110	269	28	65	7	1	1	25	23	38	.242	.304	.286	.590	66	-10	-12	106	123	23	.495	5	0	2	-8	*O/3D	-2.1
1975	KC-A	120	328	44	91	13	8	4	42	28	36	.277	.342	.402	.744	108	4	3	102	112	44	.696	12	7	-1	-5	*O/D	-0.4
1976	KC-A	152	581	71	154	23	6	3	59	26	50	.265	.300	.341	.641	87	-10	-10	100	112	57	.553	23	16	-3	5	*O/D	-1.1
1977	KC-A	162	606	98	189	32	14	23	112	41	64	.312	.363	.525	.888	138	31	30	100	117	109	.865	16	12	-2	2	*O/D	2.4
1978	KC-A	132	485	63	133	24	8	5	63	31	54	.274	.326	.388	.713	98	-1	-2	102	125	62	.655	14	6	1	6	*O/3D	0.2
1979	KC-A	136	516	69	152	18	7	9	73	40	44	.295	.349	.409	.758	98	3	-1	105	120	71	.688	10	8	-2	-3	*O	-1.0
1980	Cal-A	34	119	11	27	5	0	1	17	12	21	.227	.303	.294	.597	67	-6	-5	96	178	11	.510	1	2	-1	1	O/D	-0.4
	Det-A	108	403	58	113	15	3	5	42	37	40	.280	.342	.370	.712	90	-2	-5	105	102	51	.636	5	6	-2	-4	*O/D	-1.2
	Yr	142	522	69	140	20	3	6	59	49	61	.268	.333	.352	.686	85	-8	-10	103	121	62	.609	6	8	-3	-3		-1.6
1981	Det-A	85	253	27	66	11	4	1	18	22	36	.261	.322	.348	.670	89	-2	-4	105	77	29	.591	3	3	-1	-4	O	-1.0
1982	Sea-A	146	560	72	151	39	8	20	78	46	81	.270	.326	.475	.801	107	11	5	109	101	84	.757	11	7	-1	2	*O/D	0.1
1983	Sea-A	110	356	39	73	19	2	7	35	23	38	.205	.257	.329	.586	60	-20	-20	100	99	28	.510	10	2	2	-0	OD	-1.8
1984	Sea-A	139	524	60	145	34	2	15	78	27	83	.277	.315	.435	.750	103	2	1	102	116	66	.662	9	5	-0	-5	*O/D	-0.8
1985	Sea-A	122	452	59	120	32	5	14	69	30	56	.265	.313	.451	.764	112	3	6	95	113	56	.662	0	0	0	-2	*O/D	0.2
1986	Sea-A	28	82	5	15	4	0	0	6	3	18	.183	.212	.232	.443	20	-9	-9	105	126	4	.329	1	0	0	-1	O/D	-0.9
Total	13	1584	5534	704	1494	276	68	108	717	389	659	.270	.322	.403	.725	98	-6	-23	102	113	694	.674	120	74	-8	-17	*O/D3	-7.8
■ DICK COX	Cox, Elmer Joseph b: 9/30/1897, Pasadena, Cal. d: 6/1/66, Morro Bay, Cal. BR/TR, 5'7.5", 158 lbs. Deb: 4/16/25																											
1925	Bro-N	122	434	68	143	23	10	7	64	37	29	.329	.382	.477	.859	126	12	16	94	100	79	.844	4	3	-1	-6	*O	0.5
1926	Bro-N	124	398	53	118	17	4	1	45	46	20	.296	.375	.367	.742	101	2	2	99	104	56	.721	6			-8	*O	-1.0
Total	2	246	832	121	261	40	14	8	109	83	49	.314	.379	.424	.803	114	14	18	96	102	135	.784	10	3		-15	O	-0.5
■ FRANK COX	Cox, Francis Bernhardt "Runt" b: 8/29/1857, Waltham, Mass. d: 6/24/28, Hartford, Conn. 5'6", Deb: 8/13/1884																											
1884	Det-N	27	102	6	13	3	1	0	4	2	36	.127	.144	.176	.321	0	-11	-10	94	78	3	.225				0	S	-0.8
■ JIM COX	Cox, James Charles b: 5/28/50, Bloomington, Ill. BR/TR, 5'11", 175 lbs. Deb: 7/19/73																											
1973	Mon-N	9	15	1	2	1	0	0	0	1	4	.133	.188	.200	.387	7	-2	-2	104	0	1	.308	0	0	0	-0	/2	-0.1
1974	Mon-N	77	236	29	52	9	1	2	26	23	36	.220	.292	.292	.585	61	-11	-13	104	134	20	.490	2	3	-1	3	2	-0.6
1975	Mon-N	11	27	1	7	1	0	1	5	1	2	.259	.286	.407	.693	84	-0	-1	108	138	2	.591	1	0	0	0	/2	0.0
1976	Mon-N	13	29	2	5	0	1	0	2	2	2	.172	.226	.241	.467	32	-3	-3	100	110	1	.360	0	0	0	0	2	-0.1
Total	4	110	307	33	66	11	2	3	33	27	44	.215	.281	.293	.574	58	-16	-18	104	125	24	.494	3	3	-1	4	/2	-0.8
■ JEFF COX	Cox, Jeffrey Lindon b: 11/9/55, Los Angeles, Cal. BR/TR, 5'11", 170 lbs. Deb: 7/01/80																											
1980	Oak-A	59	169	20	36	3	0	0	9	14	23	.213	.273	.231	.504	42	-14	-12	95	90	12	.436	8	5	-1	-12	2	-2.1
1981	Oak-A	2	0	0	0	0	0	0	0	0	0	—	—	—	—	—	0	0	96	—	—	—	0	0	0	0	/2	0.0
Total	2	61	169	20	36	3	0	0	9	14	23	.213	.273	.231	.504	42	-14	-12	95	90	23	.442	8	5	-1	-12	/2	-2.1
■ LARRY COX	Cox, Larry Eugene b: 9/11/47, Bluffton, Ohio BR/TR, 5'10", 178 lbs. Deb: 4/18/73 C																											
1973	Phi-N	1	0	0	0	0	0	0	0	0	0	—	—	—	—	—	0	0	108	—	—	—	0	0	0	0	/C	0.0
1974	Phi-N	30	53	5	9	2	0	0	4	4	9	.170	.241	.208	.449	26	-5	-5	103	140	3	.356	0	0	0	-1	C	-0.5
1975	Phi-N	11	5	0	1	0	0	0	1	1	0	.200	.333	.200	.533	50	-0	-0	101	387	0	.600	1	0	0	0	C	0.0
1977	Sea-A	35	93	6	23	6	0	2	6	10	12	.247	.320	.376	.697	93	-1	-1	96	58	11	.630	1	1	-0	0	C	0.0
1978	Chi-N	59	121	10	34	5	0	2	18	12	16	.281	.346	.372	.718	91	0	-1	110	140	15	.626	0	0	0	-7	C	-0.6
1979	Sea-A	100	293	32	63	11	3	4	36	22	39	.215	.270	.314	.584	57	-18	-18	100	133	24	.483	2	1	0	-6	C	-1.8
1980	Sea-A	105	243	18	49	6	2	4	20	19	36	.202	.260	.292	.552	49	-17	-18	103	94	17	.444	1	2	-1	-12	*C	-2.5
1981	Tex-A	5	13	0	3	1	0	0	0	0	4	.231	.231	.308	.538	59	-1	-1	91	0	1	.400	0	0	0	1	/C	0.0
1982	Chi-N	2	4	1	0	0	0	0	0	2	1	.000	.333	.000	.333	1	-0	-0	103	0	0	.500	0	0	0	0	/C	0.0
Total	9	348	825	72	182	31	5	12	85	70	117	.221	.282	.314	.596	62	-42	-45	102	113	95	.518	5	4	-1	-24	C	-5.4
■ BOBBY COX	Cox, Robert Joe b: 5/21/41, Tulsa, Okla. BR/TR, 5'11", 180 lbs. Deb: 4/14/68 MC																											
1968	NY-A	135	437	33	100	15	1	7	41	41	85	.229	.302	.316	.618	86	-6	-7	101	113	42	.537	3	2	-0	2	*3	-0.1
1969	NY-A	85	191	17	41	7	1	2	17	34	41	.215	.336	.293	.629	81	-5	-4	95	110	19	.572	0	1	-1	6	3/2	0.3
Total	2	220	628	50	141	22	2	9	58	75	126	.225	.313	.309	.622	85	-11	-10	99	112	61	.558	3	3	-1	8	3/2	0.2
■ BILLY COX	Cox, William Richard b: 8/29/19, Newport, Pa. d: 3/30/78, Harrisburg, Pa. BR/TR, 5'10", 150 lbs. Deb: 9/20/41																											
1941	Pit-N	10	37	4	10	3	1	0	2	3	2	.270	.325	.405	.730	102	0	0	103	49	5	.679	1			-1	S	0.0
1946	Pit-N	121	411	32	119	22	6	2	36	26	15	.290	.333	.387	.720	101	1	-0	103	81	54	.642	4			-8	*S	0.0
1947	Pit-N	132	529	75	145	30	7	15	54	29	28	.274	.313	.442	.755	98	-4	-4	101	76	74	.692	5			-15	*S	-0.8
1948	Bro-N	88	237	36	59	13	2	3	15	38	19	.249	.353	.359	.711	89	-2	-3	104	60	31	.677	3			-4	3/S2	-0.7
1949	Bro-N	100	390	48	91	18	2	8	40	30	18	.233	.290	.351	.641	70	-17	-18	102	95	39	.562	5			5	*3	-1.0
1950	Bro-N	119	451	62	116	17	2	8	44	35	24	.257	.311	.357	.668	70	-17	-21	107	94	48	.577	6			16	*32/S	-0.3
1951	Bro-N	142	455	62	127	25	4	9	51	37	30	.279	.336	.411	.747	102	-1	1	98	92	64	.677	5	5	-2	-5	*3/S	-0.6
1952	Bro-N	116	455	56	118	12	3	6	34	25	32	.259	.301	.338	.639	76	-15	-15	102	79	43	.528	10	12	-4	-2	*3S/2	-1.9
1953	Bro-N	100	327	44	95	18	1	10	44	37	21	.291	.363	.443	.806	105	4	3	104	98	54	.763	2	2	-1	-2	3/S2	-0.1
1954	Bro-N	77	226	26	53	9	2	2	17	21	13	.235	.300	.319	.618	60	-13	-13	101	86	21	.514	0	0	0	1	32/S	-1.0
1955	Bal-A	53	194	25	41	7	2	3	14	17	16	.211	.275	.314	.589	65	-12	-9	90	76	16	.494	1	2	-1	-5	32/S	-1.2
Total	11	1058	3712	470	974	174	32	66	351	298	218	.262	.318	.380	.698	86	-73	-81	102	84	448	.636	42	21		-19	3S/2	-7.6

YEAR	TM/L	G	AB	R	H	2B	3B	HR	RBI	BB	SO	AVG	OBP	SLG	PRO	/A	BR	/A	PF	CHI	RC	TA	SB	CS	SBR	FR	POS	TPR
■ TED COX	Cox, William Ted b: 1/24/55, Oklahoma City, Okla BR/TR, 6'3", 195 lbs. Deb: 9/18/77																											
1977	Bos-A	13	58	11	21	3	1	1	6	3	6	.362	.393	.500	.893	121	3	2	117	64	12	.865	0	0	0	0	D	0.2
1978	Cle-A	82	227	14	53	7	0	1	19	16	30	.233	.287	.278	.564	64	-12	-10	93	114	18	.447	0	1	-1	-2	O3D/1S	-1.4
1979	Cle-A	78	189	17	40	6	0	4	22	14	27	.212	.273	.307	.580	53	-12	-13	106	121	14	.481	3	4	-2	-10	3O/2	-2.4
1980	Sea-A	83	247	17	60	9	0	2	23	19	25	.243	.297	.304	.601	63	-12	-13	103	111	21	.482	0	0	0	1	3	-1.1
1981	Tor-A	16	50	6	15	4	0	2	9	5	10	.300	.364	.500	.864	132	3	2	111	114	9	.833	0	1	-1	-0	3/1D	0.1
Total	5	272	771	65	189	29	1	10	79	57	98	.245	.300	.324	.624	70	-29	-32	102	111	75	.532	3	6	-3	-12	3/OD12S	-4.6
■ TOOTS COYNE	Coyne, TR, Deb: 9/28/14																											
1914	Phi-A	1	2	0	0	0	0	0	0	0	2	.000	.000	.000	.000	-99	-0	-0	97	0	0	.000	0			0	/3	0.0
■ ESTEL CRABTREE	Crabtree, Estel Crayton "Crabby" b: 8/19/03, Crabtree, Ohio d: 1/4/67, Logan, Ohio BL/TR, 6', 168 lbs. Deb: 4/18/29 C																											
1929	Cin-N	1	1	0	0	0	0	0	0	0	0	.000	.000	.000	.000	-99	-0	-0	99	0	0	.000	0			0	H	0.0
1931	Cin-N	117	443	70	119	12	12	4	37	23	33	.269	.309	.377	.686	88	-11	-8	95	75	53	.605	3			13	*O/31	0.0
1932	Cin-N	108	402	38	110	14	9	2	35	23	26	.274	.316	.368	.684	87	-9	-7	96	86	48	.599	2			3	O	-1.0
1933	StL-N	23	34	6	9	3	0	0	3	2	3	.265	.306	.353	.658	86	-1	-1	102	94	4	.600	1			0	/O	0.0
1941	StL-N	77	167	27	57	6	3	5	28	26	24	.341	.439	.503	.942	150	15	13	110	102	39	1.009	1			-8	O/3	0.4
1942	StL-N	10	9	1	3	2	0	0	2	1	3	.333	.400	.556	.956	165	1	1	108	148	2	1.000	0			0	H	0.1
1943	Cin-N	95	254	25	70	12	0	2	26	25	17	.276	.345	.346	.692	101	0	1	99	100	29	.592	1			-4	O	-0.5
1944	Cin-N	58	98	7	28	4	1	0	11	13	3	.286	.369	.347	.716	107	1	1	95	116	12	.627	0			-4	O/1	-0.4
Total	8	489	1408	174	396	53	25	13	142	113	109	.281	.339	.382	.721	100	-4	-1	98	90	186	.658	8			0	O/31	-1.4
■ HARRY CRAFT	Craft, Harry Francis "Wildfire" b: 4/19/15, Ellisville, Miss. BR/TR, 6'1", 185 lbs. Deb: 9/19/37 MC																											
1937	Cin-N	10	42	7	13	2	1	0	4	1	3	.310	.326	.405	.730	107	-0	0	91	81	5	.600	0			1	O	0.0
1938	Cin-N	151	612	70	165	28	9	15	83	29	46	.270	.305	.418	.723	99	-5	-3	98	106	77	.632	3			9	*O	0.2
1939	Cin-N	134	502	58	129	20	7	13	67	27	54	.257	.299	.402	.701	84	-11	-13	103	104	61	.625	5			-1	*O	-1.5
1940	Cin-N	115	422	47	103	18	5	6	48	17	46	.244	.277	.353	.630	72	-17	-17	101	109	41	.525	2			4	*O/1	-1.7
1941	Cin-N	119	413	48	103	15	2	10	59	33	43	.249	.308	.368	.676	91	-6	-6	99	119	46	.599	4			-3	*O	-1.3
1942	Cin-N	37	113	7	20	2	1	0	6	3	11	.177	.205	.212	.418	22	-11	-11	101	93	5	.295	0			3	O	-0.9
Total	6	566	2104	237	533	85	25	44	267	110	203	.253	.294	.380	.674	85	-51	-50	100	107	236	.594	14			12	O/1	-5.2
■ ROD CRAIG	Craig, Rodney Paul b: 1/12/58, Los Angeles, Cal. BB/TR, 6'1", 195 lbs. Deb: 9/11/79																											
1979	Sea-A	16	52	9	20	8	1	0	6	1	5	.385	.396	.577	.973	159	4	4	100	77	12	.970	1	1	-0	-2	O	0.1
1980	Sea-A	70	240	30	57	15	1	3	20	17	35	.237	.293	.346	.639	72	-9	-10	103	86	22	.541	3	6	-3	3	O	-1.0
1982	Cle-A	49	65	7	15	2	0	0	1	4	6	.231	.275	.262	.537	48	-5	-5	100	23	4	.429	3	1	0	-5	O/D	-0.9
1986	Chi-A	10	10	3	2	0	0	0	0	2	2	.200	.333	.200	.533	50	-1	-1	101	0	1	.500	0	0	0	-1	/O	-0.1
Total	4	145	367	49	94	25	2	3	27	24	48	.256	.305	.360	.665	79	-10	-11	102	71	39	.587	7	8	-3	-5	O/D	-1.9
■ DOC CRAMER	Cramer, Roger Maxwell "Flit" b: 7/22/05, Beach Haven, N.J. BL/TR, 6'2", 185 lbs. Deb: 9/18/29 C																											
1929	Phi-A	2	6	0	0	0	0	0	0	0	2	.000	.000	.000	.000	-92	-2	-2	109	0	0	.000	0	0	0	1	/O	0.0
1930	Phi-A	30	82	12	19	1	1	0	6	2	8	.232	.250	.268	.518	32	-9	-8	99	90	5	.381	0	0	0	-2	O/S	-0.9
1931	Phi-A	65	223	37	58	8	2	2	20	11	15	.260	.301	.341	.642	65	-11	-12	105	80	23	.548	2	1	0	4	O	-1.0
1932	Phi-A	92	384	73	129	27	6	3	46	17	27	.336	.367	.461	.828	99	7	-1	114	84	64	.777	3	1	0	12	O	0.7
1933	Phi-A	152	661	109	195	27	8	8	75	36	24	.295	.331	.396	.728	100	-9	-1	92	77	86	.645	5	4	-1	0	*O	-0.6
1934	Phi-A	153	649	99	202	29	9	6	46	40	35	.311	.353	.411	.765	99	-4	-2	97	48	93	.686	1	5	-3	2	*O	-0.4
1935	Phi-A	149	644	96	214	37	4	3	70	37	34	.332	.373	.416	.789	104	4	4	100	74	99	.723	6	7	-2	-1	*O	0.0
1936	Bos-A	154	643	99	188	31	7	0	41	49	20	.292	.347	.362	.710	71	-25	-31	106	50	82	.631	4	6	-2	12	*O	-2.2
1937	Bos-A	133	560	90	171	22	11	0	51	35	14	.305	.351	.384	.735	82	-13	-15	103	72	76	.663	8	6	-1	2	*O	-1.7
1938	Bos-A	148	658	116	198	36	8	0	71	51	19	.301	.354	.380	.734	82	-16	-19	102	83	87	.657	4	9	-4	5	*O/P	-1.5
1939	Bos-A	137	589	110	183	30	6	0	56	36	17	.311	.352	.382	.734	81	-11	-18	108	74	77	.626	3	3	-1	-3	*O	-2.3
1940	Bos-A	150	661	94	**200**	27	12	1	51	36	29	.303	.340	.384	.724	87	-13	-13	101	63	86	.614	3	5	-2	3	*O	-2.1
1941	Was-A	154	660	93	180	25	6	2	66	37	15	.273	.317	.338	.655	75	-26	-24	98	90	71	.543	4	1	1	-12	*O	-4.3
1942	Det-A	151	630	71	166	26	4	0	43	43	18	.263	.314	.317	.631	69	-19	-29	113	67	63	.518	4	4	-1	-2	*O	-4.3
1943	Det-A	140	606	79	182	18	4	1	43	31	13	.300	.335	.348	.684	95	-1	-5	106	63	73	.568	4	3	-1	-2	*O	-1.1
1944	Det-A	143	578	69	169	20	9	2	42	37	21	.292	.337	.369	.706	96	0	-3	105	73	74	.613	6	5	-1	-12	*O	-2.1
1945	Det-A	141	541	62	149	22	8	6	58	36	21	.275	.324	.379	.703	98	1	-3	106	100	65	.600	2	9	-5	-12	*O	-2.6
1946	Det-A	68	204	26	60	8	2	1	26	15	8	.294	.342	.368	.710	91	-1	-3	108	127	26	.620	3	0	1	-4	O	-0.7
1947	Det-A	73	157	21	42	2	2	2	30	20	5	.268	.350	.344	.694	90	-1	-2	104	184	17	.578	0	4	-2	0	O	-0.5
1948	Det-A	4	4	1	0	0	0	0	1	3	0	.000	.429	.000	.429	20	-0	-0	96	0	0	.750	0	0	0	0	/O	0.0
Total	20	2239	9140	1357	2705	396	109	37	842	572	345	.296	.340	.375	.715	87	-146	-185	103	76	1168	.631	62	73	-25	-9	*O/PS	-27.6
■ DICK CRAMER	Cramer, William B. b: Brooklyn, N.Y. d: 8/12/1885, Camden, N.J. Deb: 5/12/1883																											
1883	NY-N	2	6	0	0	0	0	0	0	1	5	.000	.143	.000	.143	-52	-1	-1	100	0	0	.167				0	/O	0.0
■ DEL CRANDALL	Crandall, Delmar Wesley b: 3/5/30, Ontario, Cal. BR/TR, 6'1.5", 180 lbs. Deb: 6/17/49 MC																											
1949	Bos-N	67	228	21	60	10	1	4	34	9	18	.263	.291	.368	.660	78	-8	-7	97	133	22	.540	2			-0	C	-0.5
1950	Bos-N	79	255	21	56	11	0	4	37	13	24	.220	.257	.310	.567	56	-20	-15	86	157	20	.449	0			5	C/1	-0.7
1953	Mil-N	116	382	55	104	13	1	15	51	33	47	.272	.330	.429	.759	102	-3	0	94	95	53	.682	2	1	0	7	*C	1.3
1954	Mil-N	138	463	60	112	18	2	21	64	40	56	.242	.306	.425	.732	95	-10	-5	93	97	57	.652	0	3	-2	3	*C	0.0
1955	Mil-N	133	440	61	104	15	2	26	62	40	56	.236	.303	.457	.760	106	-3	1	93	90	58	.702	2	1	0	9	*C	1.4
1956	Mil-N	112	311	37	74	14	2	16	48	35	30	.238	.317	.450	.767	104	1	1	99	108	44	.725	1	2	-1	-2	*C	0.1
1957	Mil-N	118	383	45	97	11	2	15	46	30	38	.253	.309	.410	.719	101	-5	-1	90	94	45	.628	1	2	-1	7	*C/O1	1.1
1958	Mil-N	131	427	50	116	23	1	18	63	48	38	.272	.351	.457	.807	125	7	13	89	105	66	.770	4	1	1	12	*C	3.2
1959	Mil-N	150	518	65	133	19	2	21	72	46	48	.257	.321	.423	.744	101	-4	-0	95	105	65	.666	5	1	1	**25**	*C	3.4
1960	Mil-N	142	537	81	158	14	1	19	77	34	36	.294	.341	.430	.771	121	6	13	91	115	74	.683	4	6	-2	23	*C	4.0
1961	Mil-N	15	30	3	6	3	0	0	1	1	0	.200	.226	.300	.526	41	-3	-2	92	45	2	.400	0	0	0	1	/C	0.0
1962	Mil-N	107	350	35	104	12	3	8	45	27	24	.297	.351	.417	.768	106	3	3	99	104	46	.669	3	4	-2	15	C/1	1.7
1963	Mil-N	86	259	18	52	4	0	3	28	18	22	.201	.253	.251	.504	45	-18	-18	101	159	14	.380	1	4	-2	0	C/1	-1.9
1964	SF-N	69	195	12	45	8	1	3	11	22	21	.231	.309	.328	.637	79	-5	-5	100	62	18	.544	0	3	-2	4	C	0.0
1965	Pit-N	60	140	11	30	2	0	2	10	14	10	.214	.290	.271	.562	59	-7	-7	100	94	11	.478	1	0	0	-6	C	-1.0
1966	Cle-A	50	108	10	25	2	0	4	8	14	9	.231	.320	.361	.681	94	-1	-1	101	66	12	.616	0	0	0	-9	C	-0.7
Total	16	1573	5026	585	1276	179	18	179	657	424	477	.254	.315	.404	.718	97	-69	-30	94	106	607	.661	26	28		94	*C/1O	11.4
■ DOC CRANDALL	Crandall, James Otis b: 10/8/1887, Wadena, Ind. d: 8/17/51, Bell, Cal. BR/TR, 5'10.5", 180 lbs. Deb: 4/24/08																											
1908	NY-N	34	72	8	16	4	0	2	6	4		.222	.263	.361	.624	97	-0	-1	104	72	7	.536	0			-1	P/2	0.0
1909	NY-N	30	41	4	10	0	1	1	1	1		.244	.262	.366	.628	92	-1	-1	105	20	4	.516	0			2	P	0.0
1910	NY-N	45	73	10	25	2	4	1	13	5	7	.342	.385	.521	.905	172	5	6	95	111	15	.896	0			-1	P/S	0.0
1911	NY-N	61	113	12	27	1	4	2	21	8	16	.239	.295	.372	.667	84	-3	-3	102	148	13	.616	2			1	P/S2	0.0
1912	NY-N	50	80	9	25	6	2	0	19	6	7	.313	.360	.438	.798	113	2	1	104	183	13	.745	0			-0	P/21	0.0
1913	NY-N	31	25	4	7	2	1	0	2	1	5	.280	.308	.440	.748	109	0	0	103	66	3	.667	0			0	P/2	0.0
	StL-N	2	2	0	0	0	0	0	0	0	2	.000	.000	.000	.000	-99	-1	-0	93	0	0	.000	0			0	H	0.0
	NY-N	15	22	3	8	2	0	0	2	2	3	.364	.417	.455	.871	145	1	1	103	73	4	.857	0			1	P	0.0
	Yr	48	49	7	15	4	1	0	4	3	10	.306	.346	.429	.775	118	1	1	102	67	7	.706	0			1		0.0
1914	StL-F	118	278	40	86	16	5	2	41	58	32	.309	.429	.424	.853	137	19	17	106	119	54	.932	3			-15	2P/SO	0.8
1915	StL-F	84	141	18	40	2	2	1	19	27	15	.284	.399	.348	.746	116	5	5	105	132	22	.792	4			3	P	0.0
1916	StL-A	16	12	0	1	0	0	0	0	2	4	.083	.214	.083	.298	-11	-2	-1	95	0	0	.273	0			-0	/P	-0.1
1918	Bos-N	14	28	1	8	0	0	0	2	4	3	.286	.375	.286	.661	109	0	1	94	95	3	.600	0			-0	/PO	0.1
Total	10	500	887	109	253	35	19	9	126	118	94	.285	.370	.398	.768	119	28	25	103	117	136	.759	9			-10	P/2SO1	0.8

■ **ED CRANE** Crane, Edward Nicholas "Cannon-Ball" b: 5/1862, Boston, Mass. d: 9/19/1896, Rochester, N.Y. BR/TR, 5'10.5", 204 lbs. Deb: 4/17/1884

YEAR	TM/L	G	AB	R	H	2B	3B	HR	RBI	BB	SO	AVG	OBP	SLG	PRO	/A	BR	/A	PF	CHI	RC	TA	SB	CS	SBR	FR	POS	TPR
1884	Bos-U	101	428	83	122	23	6	12		14		.285	.308	.451	.759	156	23	24	98	0	61	.676	0			-12	OC/1P	1.1
1885	Pro-N	1	2	0	0	0	0	0	0	1	1	.000	.333	.000	.333	16	-0	-0	91	0	0	.500				0	/O	0.0
	Buf-N	13	51	5	14	0	1	2	9	3	8	.275	.315	.431	.746	141	2	2	99	118	7	.676				0	O	0.2
	Yr	14	53	5	14	0	1	2	9	4	9	.264	.316	.415	.731	137	2	2	99	110	7	.667				0		0.2
1886	Was-N	80	292	20	50	11	3	0	20	13	54	.171	.207	.229	.436	35	-23	-21	94	99	16	.364	8			0	OP/C	-1.7
1888	NY-N	12	37	3	6	2	0	1	2	3	11	.162	.225	.297	.522	72	-1	-1	93	51	3	.484	1			0	P	0.0
1889	NY-N	29	103	16	21	1	0	2	11	13	21	.204	.293	.272	.565	57	-5	-6	105	98	10	.573	6			0	P/1	0.0
1890	NY-P	43	146	27	46	5	4	0	16	10	26	.315	.363	.404	.767	98	1	-1	109	74	24	.750	5			-1	P	0.0
1891	CM-a	34	110	13	17	0	0	1	7	8	28	.155	.212	.182	.394	13	-12	-14	112	88	5	.344	4			0	P/O	0.0
	Cin-N	15	46	3	5	0	0	0	2	3	12	.109	.163	.109	.272	-21	-7	-6	91	117	1	.268	3			0	P	0.0
1892	NY-N	48	163	20	40	1	1	0	14	11	30	.245	.297	.264	.561	73	-5	-5	98	100	14	.463	2			-0	P/O	0.0
1893	NY-N	12	26	8	12	1	0	0	3	7	0	.462	.576	.500	1.076	183	4	4	104	63	8	1.429	0			0	P/1O	0.0
	Bro-N	3	5	1	2	1	0	0	0	0	0	.400	.400	.600	1.000	184	0	0	91	0	1	1.000	0			0	/PO	0.0
	Yr	15	31	9	14	2	0	0	3	7	0	.452	.553	.516	1.069	186	5	5	101	55	9	1.353	0			0		0.0
Total	9	391	1409	199	335	45	15	18	84	86	191	.238	.283	.329	.612	87	-24	-24	100	65	150	.541	29			-13	PO/C1	-0.4

■ **FRED CRANE** Crane, Frederick William Hotchkiss b: 11/4/1840, Saybrook, Conn. d: 4/27/25, Brooklyn, N.Y. Deb: 5/26/1873

YEAR	TM/L	G	AB	R	H	2B	3B	HR	RBI	BB	SO	AVG	OBP	SLG	PRO	/A	BR	/A	PF	CHI	RC	TA	SB	CS	SBR	FR	POS	TPR
1873	Res-n	1	4	0	1							.250															/2	
1875	Atl-n	21	81	7	17							.210															1/O	
Total	2 n	22	85	7	18							.212															1/O	

■ **SAM CRANE** Crane, Samuel Byren "Lucky" or "Red" b: 9/13/1894, Harrisburg, Pa. d: 11/12/55, Philadelphia, Pa. BR/TR, 5'11.5", 154 lbs. Deb: 10/02/14

YEAR	TM/L	G	AB	R	H	2B	3B	HR	RBI	BB	SO	AVG	OBP	SLG	PRO	/A	BR	/A	PF	CHI	RC	TA	SB	CS	SBR	FR	POS	TPR
1914	Phi-A	2	6	0	0	0	0	0	0	2	3	.000	.250	.000	.250	-25	-1	-1	97	0	0	.333	0			0	/S	0.0
1915	Phi-A	8	23	3	2	2	0	0	1	0	4	.087	.087	.174	.261	-23	-4	-3	96	85	0	.190	0			-1	/S2	-0.3
1916	Phi-A	2	4	1	1	0	0	0	0	2	1	.250	.500	.250	.750	128	0	0	98	0	1	1.000	0			0	/S	0.1
1917	Was-A	32	95	6	17	2	0	0	4	4	14	.179	.212	.200	.412	28	-9	-8	92	76	4	.295	0			-1	S	-0.7
1920	Cin-N	54	144	20	31	4	0	0	9	7	9	.215	.261	.243	.504	51	-10	-8	90	99	9	.419	5	4	-1	-8	S3/2O	-1.6
1921	Cin-N	73	215	20	50	10	2	0	16	14	14	.233	.292	.298	.590	56	-13	-14	101	92	19	.494	2	5	-2	-12	S/3O	-2.1
1922	Bro-N	3	8	1	2	1	0	0	0	0	1	.250	.333	.375	.708	87	-0	-0	95	0	1	.667	0	0	0	-0	/S	0.0
Total	7	174	495	51	103	19	2	0	30	29	46	.208	.262	.255	.516	47	-36	-34	96	87	34	.421	7	9		-22	S/32O	-4.6

■ **SAM CRANE** Crane, Samuel Newhall b: 1/2/1854, Springfield, Mass. d: 6/26/25, New York, N.Y. BR/TR, Deb: 1880 M

YEAR	TM/L	G	AB	R	H	2B	3B	HR	RBI	BB	SO	AVG	OBP	SLG	PRO	/A	BR	/A	PF	CHI	RC	TA	SB	CS	SBR	FR	POS	TPR
1880	Buf-N	10	31	4	4	0	0	0	2	1	8	.129	.156	.129	.285	-2	-3	-3	91	183	1	.185				0	2/OM	-0.2
1883	NY-a	96	349	57	82	8	5	0		13		.235	.262	.287	.549	71	-9	-13	108	0	27	.423				-14	*2/O	-2.1
1884	Cin-U	80	309	56	72	9	3	1		11		.233	.259	.291	.551	80	-4	-8	108	0	24	.426	0			-9	*2M	-1.7
1885	Det-N	68	245	23	47	4	6	1	20	13	45	.192	.233	.269	.502	64	-10	-9	97	103	16	.399				-7	2	-0.8
1886	Det-N	47	185	24	26	2	2	1	12	8	34	.141	.176	.189	.365	10	-19	-22	109	105	8	.321	8			-1	2/SO	-1.9
	StL-N	39	116	10	20	3	1	0	7	13	27	.172	.256	.216	.471	47	-7	-6	95	91	8	.458	6			-5	2	-0.8
	Yr	86	301	34	46	5	3	1	19	21	61	.153	.208	.199	.407	24	-27	-28	102	100	16	.373	14			-6		-2.7
1887	Was-N	7	30	6	9	1	1	0	1	1	6	.300	.323	.400	.723	106	0	0	95	23	6	.857	5			0	/S	0.0
1890	NY-N	2	6	0	0	0	0	0	0	0	0	.000	.000	.000	.000	-99	-1	-1	95	0	0	.167	1			0	/1O	0.0
	Pit-N	22	82	3	16	3	0	0	3	0	5	.195	.205	.232	.437	32	-7	-6	88	49	5	.379	5			0	2/SO	-0.4
	NY-N	2	6	0	0	0	0	0	0	0	0	.000	.000	.000	.000	-99	-1	-1	95	0	0	.167	1			0	/2	0.0
	Yr	26	94	3	16	3	0	0	3	0	5	.170	.179	.202	.381	14	-10	-9	89	43	5	.346	7			0		-0.4
Total	7	373	1359	183	276	30	18	3	45	60	125	.203	.237	.258	.496	56	-64	-70	103	49	94	.404	26			-37	2/SO1	-7.9

■ **GAVVY CRAVATH** Cravath, Clifford Carlton "Cactus" b: 3/23/1881, Escondido, Cal. d: 5/23/63, Laguna Beach, Cal. BR/TR, 5'10.5", 186 lbs. Deb: 4/18/08 MC

YEAR	TM/L	G	AB	R	H	2B	3B	HR	RBI	BB	SO	AVG	OBP	SLG	PRO	/A	BR	/A	PF	CHI	RC	TA	SB	CS	SBR	FR	POS	TPR
1908	Bos-A	94	277	43	71	10	11	1	34	38		.256	.346	.383	.729	142	13	13	98	117	38	.728	6			6	O/1	1.7
1909	Chi-A	19	50	7	9	0	0	1	8	19		.180	.406	.240	.646	108	2	2	97	210	6	.829	3			-2	O	0.0
	Was-A	4	6	0	0	0	0	0	1	1		.000	.143	.000	.143	-61	-1	-1	90	0	0	.167	0			0	/O	0.0
	Yr	23	56	7	9	0	0	1	9	20		.161	.382	.214	.596	93	1	1	96	182	6	.745	3			-2		0.0
1912	Phi-N	130	436	63	124	30	9	11	70	47	77	.284	.358	.470	.828	125	14	14	100	101	78	.865	15			6	*O	1.5
1913	Phi-N	147	525	78	**179**	34	14	**19**	**128**	55	63	.341	.407	**.568**	**.974**	**157**	**50**	**42**	112	134	**120**	**1.058**	10			-10	*O	3.1
1914	Phi-N	149	499	76	149	27	8	**19**	100	83	72	.299	.402	.499	**.901**	**167**	**43**	**43**	100	126	103	.997	14			1	*O	4.2
1915	Phi-N	150	522	**89**	149	31	7	**24**	**115**	**86**	77	.285	**.393**	**.510**	**.902**	**160**	**47**	**42**	107	138	**105**	**.966**	11	9	-2	2	*O	**4.1**
1916	Phi-N	137	448	70	127	21	8	11	70	64	89	.283	**.379**	.440	.819	**158**	29	31	96	123	80	.857	9			-9	*O	1.9
1917	Phi-N	140	503	70	141	29	16	**12**	83	70	57	.280	.369	.473	.842	146	35	30	108	124	88	.870	6			-10	*O	1.7
1918	Phi-N	121	426	43	99	27	5	**8**	54	54	46	.232	.320	.376	.696	103	6	2	109	113	51	.679	7			-9	*O	-1.4
1919	Phi-N	83	214	34	73	18	5	**12**	45	35	21	.341	.438	.640	1.078	214	**32**	31	104	101	61	1.291	8			-6	OM	2.5
1920	Phi-N	46	45	2	13	5	0	1	11	9	12	.289	.407	.467	.874	139	3	3	109	177	9	.938	0	0	0	-2	/OM	0.0
Total	11	1220	3951	575	1134	232	83	119	719	561	514	.287	.379	.478	.857	149	272	252	104	124	740	.907	89	9		-35	*O/1	19.3

■ **BILL CRAVER** Craver, William H. b: 1844, Troy, N.Y. d: 6/17/01, Troy, N.Y. BR/TR, 5'9", 160 lbs. Deb: 5/09/1871 M

YEAR	TM/L	G	AB	R	H	2B	3B	HR	RBI	BB	SO	AVG	OBP	SLG	PRO	/A	BR	/A	PF	CHI	RC	TA	SB	CS	SBR	FR	POS	TPR
1871	Tro-n	27	122	26	37							.303															2/SC1M	
1872	Bal-n	33	180	52	50							.278															C/O32M	
1873	Bal-n	36	185	38	52							.281															CS/O1	
1874	Phi-n	55	275	71	95							.345															*2/CM	
1875	Cen-n	14	68	8	18							.265															/S31M	
	Ath-n	54	264	71	83							.314															2/C	
	Yr	68	332	79	101							.304																
1876	NY-N	56	246	24	55	4	0	0	22	2	7	.224	.230	.240	.470	65	-11	-6	87	121	14	.319				-26	2C/S	-2.8
1877	Lou-N	57	238	33	63	5	2	0	29	5	11	.265	.280	.303	.582	63	-4	-16	132	139	21	.440				1	*S	-1.1
Total	5 n	219	1094	266	335							.306															*S	
Total	2	113	484	57	118	9	2	0	51	7	18	.244	.255	.271	.525	64	-15	-22	109	130	35	.377				-25	2S/C031	-3.9

■ **PAT CRAWFORD** Crawford, Clifford Rankin b: 1/28/02, Society Hill, S.C. BL/TR, 5'11", 170 lbs. Deb: 4/18/29

YEAR	TM/L	G	AB	R	H	2B	3B	HR	RBI	BB	SO	AVG	OBP	SLG	PRO	/A	BR	/A	PF	CHI	RC	TA	SB	CS	SBR	FR	POS	TPR
1929	NY-N	65	57	13	17	3	0	3	24	11	5	.298	.412	.509	.921	127	3	3	100	216	12	1.025	1			0	/13	0.2
1930	NY-N	25	76	11	21	3	2	3	17	7	2	.276	.345	.487	.832	101	-0	-0	98	127	13	.818	0			0	2/1	0.2
	Cin-N	76	224	24	65	7	1	3	26	23	10	.290	.359	.371	.729	85	-8	-4	90	97	30	.686	2			-3	21	0.0
	Yr	101	300	35	86	10	3	6	43	30	12	.287	.355	.400	.755	89	-8	-4	92	106	43	.720	2			-2		0.2
1933	StL-N	91	224	24	60	8	2	0	21	14	9	.268	.317	.321	.638	81	-5	-5	102	110	23	.527	1			0	12/3	-0.4
1934	StL-N	61	70	3	19	2	0	0	16	5	3	.271	.320	.300	.620	59	-3	-4	114	275	7	.491	0			0	/32	-0.2
Total	4	318	651	75	182	23	5	9	104	60	29	.280	.344	.372	.716	86	-14	-11	98	135	85	.658	4			-2	/213	-0.2

■ **FORREST CRAWFORD** Crawford, Forrest A. b: 5/10/1881, Rockdale, Tex. d: 3/29/08, Austin, Tex. TR , Deb: 7/30/06

YEAR	TM/L	G	AB	R	H	2B	3B	HR	RBI	BB	SO	AVG	OBP	SLG	PRO	/A	BR	/A	PF	CHI	RC	TA	SB	CS	SBR	FR	POS	TPR
1906	StL-N	45	145	8	30	3	1	0	11	7		.207	.243	.241	.485	52	-8	-8	101	115	9	.374	1			0	S/3	-0.6
1907	StL-N	7	22	0	5	0	0	0	3	2		.227	.292	.227	.519	67	-1	-1	96	232	1	.412	0			1	/S	0.0
Total	2	52	167	8	35	3	1	0	14	9		.210	.250	.240	.490	54	-9	-9	100	131	10	.379	1			1	/S3	-0.6

■ **GEORGE CRAWFORD** Crawford, George Deb: 10/09/1890

YEAR	TM/L	G	AB	R	H	2B	3B	HR	RBI	BB	SO	AVG	OBP	SLG	PRO	/A	BR	/A	PF	CHI	RC	TA	SB	CS	SBR	FR	POS	TPR
1890	Phi-a	5	17	1	2	0	0	0		0		.118	.118	.118	.235	-31	-3	-3	97	0	0	.200	1			0	/OS	-0.1

■ **GLENN CRAWFORD** Crawford, Glenn Martin "Shorty" b: 12/2/13, North Branch, Mich. d: 1/2/72, Saginaw, Mich. BL/TR, 5'9", 165 lbs. Deb: 4/22/45

YEAR	TM/L	G	AB	R	H	2B	3B	HR	RBI	BB	SO	AVG	OBP	SLG	PRO	/A	BR	/A	PF	CHI	RC	TA	SB	CS	SBR	FR	POS	TPR
1945	StL-N	4	3	0	0	0	0	0	0	1	0	.000	.250	.000	.250	-27	-0	-0	100	0	0	.333	0			-0	/O	0.0
	Phi-N	82	302	41	89	13	2	2	24	36	15	.295	.372	.371	.743	111	4	5	96	75	45	.716	5			2	OS2	1.0
	Yr	86	305	41	89	13	2	2	24	37	15	.292	.370	.367	.737	109	3	5	97	71	45	.711	5			1		1.0
1946	Phi-N	1	1	1	0	0	0	0	0	0	0	.000	.000	.000	.000	-99	-0	-0	95	0	0	.000	0			0	H	0.0
Total	2	87	306	42	89	13	2	2	24	37	15	.291	.369	.366	.735	109	3	4	96	74	45	.714	5			1	/OS2	1.0

YEAR	TM/L	G	AB	R	H	2B	3B	HR	RBI	BB	SO	AVG	OBP	SLG	PRO	/A	BR	/A	PF	CHI	RC	TA	SB	CS	SBR	FR	POS	TPR
■ KEN CRAWFORD	Crawford, Kenneth Daniel b: 10/31/1894, South Bend, Ind. d: 11/11/76, Pittsburgh, Pa. BL/TR, 5'9", 145 lbs. Deb: 9/06/15																											
1915	Bal-F	23	82	4	20	2	1	0	7	1	18	.244	.253	.293	.546	57	-4	-5	107	105	6	.403	0			0	1/O	-0.4
■ JAKE CRAWFORD	Crawford, Rufus b: 3/20/28, Campbell, Mo. BR/TR, 6'1.5", 185 lbs. Deb: 9/07/52																											
1952	StL-A	7	11	1	2	1	0	0	0	1	5	.182	.250	.273	.523	47	-1	-1	97	0	1	.556	1	0	0	-0	/O	0.0
■ SAM CRAWFORD	Crawford, Samuel Earl "Wahoo Sam" b: 4/18/1880, Wahoo, Neb. d: 6/15/68, Hollywood, Cal. BL/TL, 6', 190 lbs. Deb: 9/10/1899 H																											
1899	Cin-N	31	127	25	39	3	7	1	20	2		.307	.318	.465	.782	110	2	1	106	105	21	.761	6			2	O	0.1
1900	Cin-N	101	389	68	101	15	15	7	59	28		.260	.309	.429	.739	114	1	6	92	104	57	.726	14			7	*O	0.4
1901	Cin-N	131	515	91	170	20	16	**16**	104	37		.330	.375	.524	.899	170	38	41	95	105	109	.928	13			-1	*O	2.6
1902	Cin-N	140	555	92	185	18	**22**	3	78	47		.333	.385	.461	**.847**	149	**40**	33	110	98	107	.862	16			5	*O	2.9
1903	Det-A	137	550	88	184	23	**25**	4	89	25		.335	.363	.489	.853	161	35	37	97	101	**107**	.852	18			13	*O	4.2
1904	Det-A	150	562	49	143	22	16	2	73	44		.254	.309	.361	.670	119	9	11	96	125	71	.637	20			2	*O	0.5
1905	Det-A	154	575	73	171	38	10	6	75	50		.297	.354	.430	.783	153	32	33	98	97	97	.790	22			9	*O1	3.9
1906	Det-A	145	563	65	166	25	16	2	72	38		.295	.339	.407	.746	125	22	16	108	98	88	.733	24			-4	*O1	0.7
1907	Det-A	144	582	**102**	188	34	17	4	81	37		.323	.363	.460	.824	162	39	39	102	91	107	.820	18			-0	*O/1	3.3
1908	Det-A	152	591	102	184	33	16	**7**	80	37		.311	.352	.457	.809	163	39	38	101	99	97	.791	15			-5	*O1	3.0
1909	Det-A	156	589	83	185	**35**	14	6	97	47		.314	.366	.452	.817	143	37	30	110	127	105	.851	30			-16	*O1	1.0
1910	Det-A	154	588	83	170	26	**19**	5	**120**	37		.289	.332	.423	.756	134	21	20	102	**178**	89	.734	20			-13	*O/1	0.0
1911	Det-A	146	574	109	217	36	14	7	115	61		.378	.438	.526	.964	156	52	46	108	116	147	1.120	37			-18	*O	1.6
1912	Det-A	149	581	81	189	30	21	4	109	42		.325	.373	.470	.843	148	28	32	95	135	116	.913	41			-21	*O	0.1
1913	Det-A	153	609	78	193	32	**23**	9	83	52	28	.317	.371	.489	.860	153	36	37	99	87	110	.873	13			-15	*O1	1.4
1914	Det-A	157	582	74	183	22	**26**	8	**104**	69	31	.314	.388	.483	.871	159	42	41	102	123	113	.906	25	16	-2	-16	*O	1.4
1915	Det-A	156	612	81	183	31	**19**	5	**112**	66	29	.299	.367	.436	.804	130	28	22	108	130	102	.806	24	14	-1	-22	*O	-1.0
1916	Det-A	100	322	41	92	11	13	0	42	37	10	.286	.359	.401	.760	123	11	9	105	116	51	.765	10			-17	O/1	-1.3
1917	Det-A	61	104	6	18	4	0	2	12	4	6	.173	.204	.269	.473	45	-7	-7	98	127	6	.372	0			-1	1/O	-0.9
Total	19	2517	9570	1391	2961	458	309	98	1525	760	104	.309	.361	.453	.813	144	504	485	102	114	1700	.823	366	30		-111	*O1	23.9
■ WILLIE CRAWFORD	Crawford, Willie Murphy b: 9/7/46, Los Angeles, Cal. BL/TL, 6'1", 197 lbs. Deb: 9/16/64																											
1964	LA-N	10	16	3	5	1	0	0	0	1	7	.313	.353	.375	.728	114	0	0	92	0	2	.667	1	1	-0	0	/O	0.0
1965	LA-N	52	27	10	4	0	0	0	0	2	8	.148	.207	.148	.355	2	-3	-3	91	0	1	.348	2	0	1	-2	/O	-0.4
1966	LA-N	6	0	1	0	0	0	0	0	0	0	—	—	—	—	—	0	0	97	—	—	—	0	0	0	0	R	0.0
1967	LA-N	4	4	0	1	0	0	0	0	1	3	.250	.400	.250	.650	102	0	0	88	0	1	.667	0	0	0	-1	/O	0.0
1968	LA-N	61	175	25	44	12	1	4	14	20	64	.251	.335	.400	.735	132	4	6	91	72	24	.694	1	3	-2	2	O	0.4
1969	LA-N	129	389	64	96	17	5	11	41	49	85	.247	.331	.401	.732	106	2	3	99	87	52	.690	4	5	-2	-5	*O	-1.0
1970	LA-N	109	299	48	70	8	6	8	40	33	88	.234	.314	.381	.696	95	-7	-2	90	112	36	.643	4	4	-1	1	O	-0.6
1971	LA-N	114	342	64	96	16	6	9	40	28	49	.281	.337	.442	.778	120	8	8	99	91	51	.728	5	2	0	-9	O	-0.3
1972	LA-N	96	243	28	61	7	3	8	27	35	55	.251	.350	.403	.753	121	5	7	94	91	34	.724	4	2	0	-8	O	-0.5
1973	LA-N	145	457	75	135	26	2	14	66	78	91	.295	.399	.453	.852	135	25	24	100	107	88	.895	12	5	1	1	*O	2.0
1974	LA-N	139	468	73	138	23	4	11	61	64	88	.295	.380	.432	.811	136	18	22	93	100	77	.787	7	8	-3	-8	*O	0.6
1975	LA-N	124	373	46	98	15	2	9	46	49	43	.263	.348	.386	.734	109	2	5	95	104	52	.702	5	5	-2	-6	*O	-0.6
1976	StL-N	120	392	49	119	17	5	9	50	37	53	.304	.365	.441	.806	123	14	12	104	96	62	.750	2	1	0	-2	*O	0.7
1977	Hou-N	42	114	14	29	3	0	2	18	16	10	.254	.346	.333	.679	90	-2	-1	93	164	14	.628	0	0	0	-4	O	-0.5
	Oak-A	59	136	7	25	7	1	1	16	18	20	.184	.279	.272	.551	54	-9	-8	95	159	10	.474	0	0	0	2	OD	-0.6
Total	14	1210	3435	507	921	152	35	86	419	431	664	.268	.351	.408	.759	116	56	73	96	101	506	.739	47	36	-8	-39	O/D	-0.8
■ GEORGE CREAMER	Creamer, George W. (born George W. Triebel) b: 1855, Philadelphia, Pa. d: 6/27/1886, Philadelphia, Pa. BR/TR, 6'2", Deb: 5/01/1878 M																											
1878	Mil-N	50	193	30	41	7	3	0	15	5	15	.212	.232	.280	.512	63	-7	-8	107	96	13	.388				-8	2O/3	-1.4
1879	Syr-N	15	60	3	13	2	0	0	3	1	2	.217	.230	.250	.480	65	-3	-2	89	74	4	.340				0	2/SO	-0.1
1880	Wor-N	85	306	40	61	6	3	0	27	4	21	.199	.210	.239	.448	46	-15	-20	113	138	16	.314				-8	*2	-2.4
1881	Wor-N	80	309	42	64	9	2	0	25	11	27	.207	.234	.249	.484	49	-17	-19	105	115	18	.359				-8	*2	-2.2
1882	Wor-N	81	286	27	65	16	6	1	29	14	24	.227	.263	.336	.599	91	-3	-3	100	101	26	.498				11	*2	0.9
1883	Pit-a	91	369	54	94	7	9	0		20		.255	.293	.322	.616	105	-0	3	94	0	36	.505				5	*2	0.9
1884	Pit-a	98	339	38	62	8	5	0		16		.183	.224	.236	.460	54	-17	-15	97	0	18	.354				14	*2M	0.1
Total	7	500	1862	234	400	55	28	1	99	71	89	.215	.244	.276	.520	68	-61	-63	101	69	131	.402				7	2/O3S	-4.2
■ BIRDIE CREE	Cree, William Franklin b: 10/23/1882, Khedive, Pa. d: 11/8/42, Sunbury, Pa. BR/TR, 5'6", 150 lbs. Deb: 9/17/08																											
1908	NY-A	21	78	5	21	0	2	0	4	7		.269	.329	.321	.650	119	1	2	95	53	8	.579	1			-0	O	0.0
1909	NY-A	104	343	48	90	6	3	2	27	30		.262	.338	.315	.653	107	3	4	99	93	39	.621	10			9	O/S23	1.1
1910	NY-A	134	467	58	134	19	16	4	73	40		.287	.353	.422	.775	133	22	18	107	132	79	.820	28			-5	*O	0.7
1911	NY-A	137	520	90	181	30	22	4	88	56		.348	.415	.513	.928	143	40	32	111	113	129	1.103	48			5	*O/S2	2.6
1912	NY-A	50	190	25	63	11	6	0	22	20		.332	.409	.453	.862	144	12	11	101	82	39	.969	12			-1	O	0.8
1913	NY-A	145	534	51	145	25	6	1	63	50	51	.272	.338	.346	.685	100	0	-0	101	126	68	.671	22			-4	*O	-1.2
1914	NY-A	77	275	45	85	18	5	0	40	30	24	.309	.389	.411	.800	141	14	14	100	141	43	.769	4	9	-4	4	O	1.0
1915	NY-A	74	196	23	42	8	2	0	15	36	22	.214	.353	.276	.628	90	-1	-1	98	94	20	.636	7	8	-3	-2	O	-0.7
Total	8	742	2603	345	761	117	62	11	332	269	97	.292	.368	.398	.765	124	92	80	103	114	425	.795	132	17		7	O/S23	4.3
■ CONNIE CREEDEN	Creeden, Cornelius Stephen b: 7/21/15, Danvers, Mass. d: 11/30/69, Santa Ana, Cal. BL/TL, 6'1", 200 lbs. Deb: 4/28/43																											
1943	Bos-N	5	4	0	1	0	0	0	1	1	0	.250	.400	.250	.650	85	0	-0	106	361	1	.667	0			0	H	0.0
■ PAT CREEDEN	Creeden, Patrick Francis "Whoops" b: 5/23/06, Newburyport, Mass. BL/TR, 5'8", 175 lbs. Deb: 4/14/31																											
1931	Bos-A	5	8	0	0	0	0	0	0	1	3	.000	.111	.000	.111	-73	-2	-2	94	0	0	.125	0	0	0	-0	/2	-0.1
■ MARTY CREEGAN	Creegan, Martin b: San Francisco, Cal. Deb: 4/17/1884																											
1884	Was-U	9	33	4	5	0	0	0		1		.152	.176	.152	.328	12	-3	-3	97	0	1	.214	0			0	/OC31	-0.1
■ GUS CREELY	Creely, August L. b: 6/6/1870, Florissant, Mo. d: 4/22/34, St.Louis, Mo. 5'6", 150 lbs. Deb: 10/09/1890																											
1890	StL-a	4	15	0	0	0	0	0		0		.000	.000	.000	.000	-86	-4	-4	116	0	0	.067	1			0	/S	-0.3
■ PETE CREGAN	Cregan, Peter James "Peekskill Pete" b: 4/13/1875, Kingston, N.Y. d: 5/18/45, New York, N.Y. BR/TR, 5'7.5", 150 lbs. Deb: 9/08/1899																											
1899	NY-N	1	2	0	0	0	0	0	0	0		.000	.000	.000	.000	-99	-1	-1	97	0	0	.000	0			0	/O	0.0
1903	Cin-N	6	19	0	2	0	0	0	0	1		.105	.150	.105	.255	-24	-3	-3	109	0	0	.176	0			1	/O	-0.2
Total	2	7	21	0	2	0	0	0	0	1		.095	.136	.095	.232	-31	-4	-4	108	0	0	.158	0			1	/O	-0.2
■ BERNIE CREGER	Creger, Bernard Odell b: 3/21/27, Wytheville, Va. BR/TR, 6', 175 lbs. Deb: 4/29/47																											
1947	StL-N	15	16	3	3	1	0	0	0	1	3	.188	.235	.250	.485	27	-2	-2	106	0	1	.429	1			0	S	0.0
■ CREEPY CRESPI	Crespi, Frank Angelo Joseph b: 2/16/18, St.Louis, Mo. BR/TR, 5'8.5", 175 lbs. Deb: 9/14/38																											
1938	StL-N	7	19	2	5	2	0	0	1	2	7	.263	.333	.368	.702	83	-0	-0	111	52	2	.600	0			-1	/S	0.0
1939	StL-N	15	29	3	5	1	0	0	6	3	6	.172	.250	.207	.457	23	-3	-3	105	367	2	.375	0			-0	/2S	-0.2
1940	StL-N	3	11	2	3	1	0	0	0	1	2	.273	.333	.364	.697	90	-0	-0	102	0	1	.750	1			-1	/3S	0.0
1941	StL-N	146	560	85	156	24	2	4	46	57	58	.279	.355	.350	.705	90	1	-6	110	85	72	.639	3			-0	*2	0.3
1942	StL-N	93	292	33	71	4	2	0	35	27	29	.243	.309	.271	.580	65	-10	-13	108	164	26	.489	4			-5	2/S	-1.2
Total	5	264	911	125	240	32	4	4	88	90	102	.263	.336	.321	.657	80	-13	-23	109	117	104	.591	8			-7	2/S3	-1.1
■ LOU CRIGER	Criger, Louis b: 2/3/1872, Elkhart, Ind. d: 5/14/34, Tucson, Ariz. BR/TR, 5'10", 165 lbs. Deb: 9/21/1896																											
1896	Cle-N	2	5	0	0	0	0	0	0	1	0	.000	.167	.000	.167	-48	-1	-1	110	0	0	.400	1			0	/C	0.0
1897	Cle-N	39	138	15	31	4	1	0	22	23		.225	.340	.268	.608	58	-6	-9	111	177	15	.617	5			-0	C/1	-0.3
1898	Cle-N	84	287	43	80	13	4	1	32	40		.279	.373	.362	.735	119	7	9	96	92	40	.720	2			15	C	2.7
1899	StL-N	77	258	39	66	4	5	2	44	28		.256	.333	.333	.667	79	-4	-8	108	150	34	.677	14			-4	C	-0.6
1900	StL-N	80	288	31	78	8	6	2	38	4		.271	.281	.361	.642	84	-9	-6	93	108	31	.538	5			10	C/3	0.9

YEAR	TM/L	G	AB	R	H	2B	3B	HR	RBI	BB	SO	AVG	OBP	SLG	PRO	/A	BR	/A	PF	CHI	RC	TA	SB	CS	SBR	FR	POS	TPR
1901	Bos-A	76	268	26	62	6	3	0	24	11		.231	.262	.276	.538	52	-18	-16	97	102	22	.447	7			10	C/1	0.0
1902	Bos-A	83	266	32	68	16	6	0	28	27		.256	.324	.361	.685	92	-3	-3	99	96	34	.657	7			5	C/O	0.9
1903	Bos-A	96	317	41	61	7	10	3	31	26		.192	.254	.306	.560	61	-12	-16	112	105	27	.500	5			8	C	0.4
1904	Bos-A	98	299	34	63	10	5	2	34	27		.211	.276	.298	.574	80	-5	-7	105	134	25	.496	1			0	C	0.4
1905	Bos-A	109	313	33	62	6	7	1	36	54		.198	.316	.272	.588	89	-2	-2	100	146	29	.574	5			-1	*C	0.9
1906	Bos-A	7	17	0	3	1	0	0	1	1		.176	.222	.235	.458	45	-1	-1	98	91	1	.429	1			1	/C	0.1
1907	Bos-A	75	226	12	41	4	0	0	14	19		.181	.245	.199	.444	43	-14	-14	101	111	12	.357	2			8	C	0.1
1908	Bos-A	84	237	12	45	4	2	0	25	13		.190	.232	.224	.456	51	-13	-12	98	177	12	.349	1			10	C	0.7
1909	StL-A	74	212	15	36	1	1	0	9	25		.170	.261	.184	.444	44	-13	-11	92	89	10	.381	2			7	C	0.1
1910	NY-A	27	69	3	13	2	0	0	4	10		.188	.291	.217	.509	55	-3	-3	107	99	4	.446	0			-2	C	-0.2
1912	StL-A	1	2	1	0	0	0	0	0	0		.000	.000	.000	.000	-99	-1	-1	99	0	0	.000	0			0	/C	0.0
Total	16	1012	3202	337	709	86	50	11	342	309	0	.221	.291	.290	.581	73	-97	-102	101	121	297	.522	58			67	C/1O3	6.1

■ **DAVE CRIPE** Cripe, David Gordon b: 4/7/51, Ramona, Cal. BR/TR, 6', 180 lbs. Deb: 9/10/78

YEAR	TM/L	G	AB	R	H	2B	3B	HR	RBI	BB	SO	AVG	OBP	SLG	PRO	/A	BR	/A	PF	CHI	RC	TA	SB	CS	SBR	FR	POS	TPR
1978	KC-A	7	13	1	2	0	0	0	1	0	2	.154	.154	.154	.308	-13	-2	-2	102	198	0	.182	0	0	0	0	/3	-0.1

■ **DAVE CRISCIONE** Criscione, David Gerald b: 9/2/51, Dunkirk, N.Y. BR/TR, 5'8", 185 lbs. Deb: 7/17/77

YEAR	TM/L	G	AB	R	H	2B	3B	HR	RBI	BB	SO	AVG	OBP	SLG	PRO	/A	BR	/A	PF	CHI	RC	TA	SB	CS	SBR	FR	POS	TPR
1977	Bal-A	7	9	1	3	0	0	1	1	0	1	.333	.333	.667	1.000	177	1	1	93	44	2	1.000	0	0	0	0	/C	0.1

■ **TONY CRISCOLA** Criscola, Anthony Paul b: 7/9/15, Walla Walla, Wash. BL/TR, 5'11.5", 180 lbs. Deb: 4/15/42

YEAR	TM/L	G	AB	R	H	2B	3B	HR	RBI	BB	SO	AVG	OBP	SLG	PRO	/A	BR	/A	PF	CHI	RC	TA	SB	CS	SBR	FR	POS	TPR
1942	StL-A	91	158	17	47	9	2	1	13	8	13	.297	.331	.399	.730	101	0	-0	104	69	22	.646	2	2	-1	-14	O	-1.9
1943	StL-A	29	52	4	8	0	0	0	1	8	7	.154	.267	.154	.421	24	-5	-5	100	46	3	.364	0	0	0	-2	O	-0.7
1944	Cin-N	64	157	14	36	3	2	0	14	14	12	.229	.297	.274	.570	64	-8	-7	95	117	13	.468	0			0	O	-0.9
Total	3	184	367	35	91	12	4	1	28	30	32	.248	.307	.311	.617	75	-12	-12	100	86	38	.523	2	2		-16	O	-3.5

■ **PAT CRISHAM** Crisham, Patrick J. b: 6/4/1877, Amesbury, Mass. d: 6/12/15, Syracuse, N.Y. 6', 168 lbs. Deb: 5/05/1899

YEAR	TM/L	G	AB	R	H	2B	3B	HR	RBI	BB	SO	AVG	OBP	SLG	PRO	/A	BR	/A	PF	CHI	RC	TA	SB	CS	SBR	FR	POS	TPR
1899	Bal-N	53	172	23	50	5	3	0	20	4		.291	.311	.355	.665	78	-4	-6	108	101	21	.574	4			0	1C	-0.4

■ **JOE CRISP** Crisp, Joseph Shelby b: 7/8/1889, Higginsville, Mo. d: 2/5/39, Kansas City, Mo. BR/TR, 6'4", 200 lbs. Deb: 9/02/10

YEAR	TM/L	G	AB	R	H	2B	3B	HR	RBI	BB	SO	AVG	OBP	SLG	PRO	/A	BR	/A	PF	CHI	RC	TA	SB	CS	SBR	FR	POS	TPR
1910	StL-A	1	1	0	0	0	0	0	0	0		.000	.000	.000	.000	-99	-0	-0	94	0	0	.000	0			0	/C	0.0
1911	StL-A	1	1	0	1	0	0	0	0	0		1.000	1.000	1.000	2.000	482	0	0	95	0	1	—	0			0	/H	0.0
Total	2	2	2	0	1	0	0	0	0	0		.500	.500	.500	1.000	206	0	0	95	0	1	1.000	0			0	/C	0.0

■ **DODE CRISS** Criss, Dode b: 3/12/1885, Sherman, Miss. d: 9/8/55, Sherman, Miss. BL/TR, 6'2", 200 lbs. Deb: 4/20/08

YEAR	TM/L	G	AB	R	H	2B	3B	HR	RBI	BB	SO	AVG	OBP	SLG	PRO	/A	BR	/A	PF	CHI	RC	TA	SB	CS	SBR	FR	POS	TPR
1908	StL-A	64	82	15	28	6	0	0	14	9		.341	.407	.415	.821	165	6	6	103	155	14	.815	1			-2	O/P1	0.5
1909	StL-A	35	48	2	14	6	1	0	7	0		.292	.306	.458	.764	154	2	2	92	123	6	.676	0			-1	P	0.4
1910	StL-A	70	91	11	21	4	2	1	11	11		.231	.320	.352	.672	117	1	2	94	116	11	.657	2			-0	1/P	0.3
1911	StL-A	58	83	10	21	3	1	2	15	11		.253	.347	.386	.733	110	1	1	95	133	11	.710	0			-0	1/P	0.2
Total	4	227	304	38	84	19	4	3	47	31		.276	.349	.395	.744	133	10	11	97	132	42	.714	3			-3	/P1O	1.4

■ **CHES CRIST** Crist, Chester Arthur "Squak" b: 2/10/1882, Cozaddale, Ohio d: 1/7/57, Cincinnati, Ohio TR , 5'11", 165 lbs. Deb: 5/18/06

YEAR	TM/L	G	AB	R	H	2B	3B	HR	RBI	BB	SO	AVG	OBP	SLG	PRO	/A	BR	/A	PF	CHI	RC	TA	SB	CS	SBR	FR	POS	TPR
1906	Phi-N	6	11	1	0	0	0	0	0	0		.000	.000	.000	.000	-99	-2	-2	92	0	0	.000	0			-0	/C	-0.1

■ **HUGHIE CRITZ** Critz, Hugh Melville b: 9/17/1900, Starkville, Miss. d: 1/10/80, Greenwood, Miss. BR/TR, 5'8", 147 lbs. Deb: 5/31/24

YEAR	TM/L	G	AB	R	H	2B	3B	HR	RBI	BB	SO	AVG	OBP	SLG	PRO	/A	BR	/A	PF	CHI	RC	TA	SB	CS	SBR	FR	POS	TPR
1924	Cin-N	102	413	67	133	15	14	3	35	19	18	.322	.352	.448	.800	112	7	6	101	70	63	.766	19	11	-1	-3	2/S	-0.2
1925	Cin-N	144	541	74	150	14	8	2	51	34	17	.277	.321	.344	.665	72	-24	-22	97	100	59	.579	13	13	-4	18	*2	-0.8
1926	Cin-N	155	607	96	164	24	14	3	79	39	25	.270	.316	.371	.687	89	-14	-10	95	124	70	.616	7			23	*2	2.0
1927	Cin-N	113	396	50	110	10	8	4	49	16	18	.278	.306	.374	.680	81	-11	-11	100	109	44	.598	7			-3	*2	-1.5
1928	Cin-N	153	641	95	190	21	11	5	52	37	24	.296	.335	.387	.722	92	-12	-8	96	61	81	.672	18			-15	*2	-2.1
1929	Cin-N	107	425	55	105	17	9	1	50	27	21	.247	.292	.336	.629	56	-31	-30	99	113	41	.559	9			8	*2/S	-1.6
1930	Cin-N	28	104	15	24	3	2	0	11	6	6	.231	.273	.298	.571	42	-11	-9	90	125	8	.475	1			-2	2	-0.6
	NY-N	124	558	93	148	17	11	4	50	24	26	.265	.296	.357	.652	58	-40	-38	98	72	57	.561	7			3	*2	-1.7
	Yr	152	662	108	172	20	13	4	61	30	32	.260	.292	.347	.639	56	-50	-46	96	83	65	.547	8			2		-2.3
1931	NY-N	66	238	33	69	7	2	4	17	8	17	.290	.313	.387	.700	90	-5	-4	97	58	29	.615	4			-2	2	-0.2
1932	NY-N	151	659	90	182	32	7	2	50	34	27	.276	.313	.355	.668	80	-19	-18	99	67	74	.570	3			3	*2	-0.3
1933	NY-N	133	558	68	137	18	5	2	33	23	24	.246	.279	.306	.586	68	-24	-23	99	62	48	.465	4			**40**	*2	2.8
1934	NY-N	137	571	77	138	17	1	6	40	19	24	.242	.269	.306	.575	55	-38	-36	98	72	47	.447	3			**27**	*2	0.4
1935	NY-N	65	219	19	41	0	3	2	14	3	10	.187	.198	.242	.440	18	-25	-24	96	86	10	.319	2			-1	2	-1.9
Total	12	1478	5930	832	1591	195	95	38	531	289	257	.268	.303	.352	.656	74	-247	-228	98	83	631	.569	97	24		97	*2/S	-5.7

■ **DAVEY CROCKETT** Crockett, Daniel Solomon b: 10/5/1875, Roanoke, Va. d: 2/23/61, Charlottesville, Va. BL/TR, 6'1", 175 lbs. Deb: 7/11/01

YEAR	TM/L	G	AB	R	H	2B	3B	HR	RBI	BB	SO	AVG	OBP	SLG	PRO	/A	BR	/A	PF	CHI	RC	TA	SB	CS	SBR	FR	POS	TPR
1901	Det-A	28	102	10	29	2	2	0	14	6		.284	.324	.343	.667	79	-2	-3	110	129	12	.575	1			-0	1	-0.4

■ **ART CROFT** Croft, Arthur F. b: 1/23/1855, St.Louis, Mo. d: 3/16/1884, St.Louis, Mo. Deb: 5/04/1875

YEAR	TM/L	G	AB	R	H	2B	3B	HR	RBI	BB	SO	AVG	OBP	SLG	PRO	/A	BR	/A	PF	CHI	RC	TA	SB	CS	SBR	FR	POS	TPR
1875	RS-n	18	72	4	11							.153															O	
1877	StL-N	54	220	23	51	5	2	0	27	1	15	.232	.235	.273	.508	59	-10	-10	102	162	14	.361				-2	1O/2	-1.2
1878	Ind-N	60	222	22	35	6	0	0	16	5	23	.158	.176	.185	.361	22	-19	-15	87	135	7	.246				-1	*1/O	-1.3
Total	2	114	442	45	86	11	2	0	43	6	38	.195	.205	.229	.434	42	-29	-25	94	148	22	.301				-3	/1O2	-2.5

■ **HARRY CROFT** Croft, Henry T. b: 8/1/1875, Chicago, Ill. d: 12/11/33, Oak Park, Ill. Deb: 5/19/1899

YEAR	TM/L	G	AB	R	H	2B	3B	HR	RBI	BB	SO	AVG	OBP	SLG	PRO	/A	BR	/A	PF	CHI	RC	TA	SB	CS	SBR	FR	POS	TPR
1899	Lou-N	2	2	0	0	0	0	0	0	0		.000	.000	.000	.000	-97	-1	-1	103	0	0	.000	0			0		0.0
	Phi-N	2	7	0	1	0	0	0	0	1		.143	.250	.143	.393	11	-1	-1	97	0	0	.333	0			0	/2	0.0
	Yr	4	9	0	1	0	0	0	0	1		.111	.200	.111	.311	-12	-1	-1	100	0	0	.250	0			0		0.0
1901	Chi-N	3	12	1	4	0	0	0	4	0		.333	.333	.333	.667	96	-0	-0	100	354	1	.500	0			-2	/O	-0.2
Total	2	7	21	1	5	0	0	0	4	1		.238	.273	.238	.511	47	-1	-1	99	193	2	.375	0			-2	/O2	-0.2

■ **FRED CROLIUS** Crolius, Fred Joseph b: 12/16/1876, Jersey City, N.J. d: 8/25/60, Ormond Beach, Fla. Deb: 4/19/01

YEAR	TM/L	G	AB	R	H	2B	3B	HR	RBI	BB	SO	AVG	OBP	SLG	PRO	/A	BR	/A	PF	CHI	RC	TA	SB	CS	SBR	FR	POS	TPR
1901	Bos-N	49	200	22	48	4	1	1	13	9		.240	.273	.285	.558	57	-9	-12	112	64	18	.474	6			-6	O	-2.2
1902	Pit-N	9	38	4	10	2	1	0	7	0		.263	.263	.368	.632	91	-0	-1	105	183	4	.500	0			-2	/O	-0.3
Total	2	58	238	26	58	6	2	1	20	9		.244	.271	.298	.570	62	-10	-13	111	82	21	.478	6			-8	/O	-2.5

■ **WARREN CROMARTIE** Cromartie, Warren Livingston b: 9/29/53, Miami Beach, Fla. BL/TL, 6', 180 lbs. Deb: 9/06/74

YEAR	TM/L	G	AB	R	H	2B	3B	HR	RBI	BB	SO	AVG	OBP	SLG	PRO	/A	BR	/A	PF	CHI	RC	TA	SB	CS	SBR	FR	POS	TPR
1974	Mon-N	8	17	2	3	0	0	0	0	3	3	.176	.300	.176	.476	34	-1	-1	104	0	1	.500	1	0	0	-1	/O	-0.1
1976	Mon-N	33	81	8	17	1	0	0	2	1	5	.210	.220	.222	.442	25	-8	-8	100	43	3	.294	1	2	-1	-2	O	-1.1
1977	Mon-N	155	620	64	175	41	7	5	50	33	40	.282	.323	.395	.718	93	-8	-7	98	82	77	.631	10	3	1	2	*O	-0.8
1978	Mon-N	159	607	77	180	32	6	10	56	33	60	.297	.340	.418	.758	116	8	11	96	83	82	.671	8	8	-2	17	*O/1	2.0
1979	Mon-N	158	659	84	181	46	5	8	46	38	78	.275	.315	.396	.711	91	-8	-10	102	56	79	.621	8	7	-2	12	*O	-0.3
1980	Mon-N	162	597	74	172	33	5	14	70	51	64	.288	.346	.430	.777	116	12	12	99	95	80	.696	8	8	-2	-5	*1/O	-0.2
1981	Mon-N	99	358	41	109	19	2	6	42	39	27	.304	.373	.419	.792	126	12	12	99	100	55	.735	2	3	-1	-2	1O	0.6
1982	Mon-N	144	497	59	126	24	3	14	62	69	60	.254	.348	.398	.746	103	7	3	105	103	71	.717	3	0	1	6	*O/1	0.8
1983	Mon-N	120	360	37	100	26	2	3	43	43	48	.278	.356	.386	.743	104	4	3	102	115	49	.697	8	3	1	8	*O/1	1.0
Total	9	1038	3796	446	1063	222	30	60	371	310	385	.280	.337	.402	.739	103	16	15	100	86	497	.685	49	34	-6	36	O1	1.9

■ **NED CROMPTON** Crompton, Edward b: 2/12/1889, Liverpool, England d: 9/28/50, Aspinwall, Pa. BL/TL, 5'10.5", 175 lbs. Deb: 9/13/09

YEAR	TM/L	G	AB	R	H	2B	3B	HR	RBI	BB	SO	AVG	OBP	SLG	PRO	/A	BR	/A	PF	CHI	RC	TA	SB	CS	SBR	FR	POS	TPR
1909	StL-A	17	63	7	10	2	1	0	2	7		.159	.254	.222	.476	55	-3	-3	92	49	4	.434	1			-2	O	-0.5
1910	Cin-N	1	2	0	0	0	0	0	0	0	2	.000	.000	.000	.000	-99	-1	-1	101	0	0	.000	0			-0	/O	0.0
Total	2	18	65	7	10	2	1	0	2	7	2	.154	.247	.215	.462	50	-4	-3	92	47	4	.418	1			-2	/O	-0.5

■ **HERB CROMPTON** Crompton, Herbert Bryan "Workhorse" b: 11/7/11, Taylor Ridge, Ill. d: 8/5/63, Moline, Ill. BR/TR, 6', 185 lbs. Deb: 4/26/37

YEAR	TM/L	G	AB	R	H	2B	3B	HR	RBI	BB	SO	AVG	OBP	SLG	PRO	/A	BR	/A	PF	CHI	RC	TA	SB	CS	SBR	FR	POS	TPR
1937	Was-A	2	3	0	1	0	0	0	0	0	0	.333	.333	.333	.667	73	-0	-0	94	0	0	.500	0	0	0	0	/C	0.0
1945	NY-A	36	99	6	19	3	0	0	12	2	7	.192	.208	.222	.430	23	-10	-10	107	197	4	.289	0	0	0	-0	C	-0.8
Total	2	38	102	6	20	3	0	0	12	2	7	.196	.212	.225	.437	25	-10	-11	107	192	5	.294	0	0	0	-0	/C	-0.8

YEAR	TM/L	G	AB	R	H	2B	3B	HR	RBI	BB	SO	AVG	OBP	SLG	PRO	/A	BR	/A	PF	CHI	RC	TA	SB	CS	SBR	FR	POS	TPR
■ **DAN CRONIN**	Cronin, Daniel T. b: 4/1857, S.Boston, Mass. d: 11/30/1885, Boston, Mass. 5′8″, 170 lbs. Deb: 7/08/1884																											
1884	CP-U	1	4	1	1	0	0	0		0		.250	.250	.250	.500	70	-0	-0	99	0	0	.333	0			0	/2	0.0
	StL-U	1	5	0	0	0	0	0		0		.000	.000	.000	.000	-97	-1	-1	104	0	0	.000	0			0	/O	0.0
	Yr	2	9	1	1	0	0	0		0		.111	.111	.111	.222	-24	-1	-1	101	0	0	.125	0			0		0.0
Total	1	2	9	1	1	0	0	0		0		.111	.111	.111	.222	-24	-1	-1	102	0	0	.125	0			0	/O2	0.0
■ **JIM CRONIN**	Cronin, James John b: 8/7/05, Richmond, Cal. d: 6/10/83, Concord, Cal. BB/TR, 5′10.5″, 150 lbs. Deb: 7/04/29																											
1929	Phi-A	25	56	7	13	2	1	0	4	5	7	.232	.295	.304	.599	50	-4	-5	109	80	5	.512	0	0	0	-2	2/S3	-0.4
■ **JOE CRONIN**	Cronin, Joseph Edward b: 10/12/06, San Francisco, Cal d: 9/7/84, Osterville, Mass. BR/TR, 5′11.5″, 180 lbs. Deb: 4/29/26 MH																											
1926	Pit-N	38	83	9	22	2	2	0	11	6	15	.265	.315	.337	.652	67	-3	-4	112	136	9	.557	0			-0	2/S	-0.2
1927	Pit-N	12	22	2	5	1	0	0	3	2	3	.227	.292	.273	.564	51	-1	-2	102	175	2	.471	0			-0	/2S1	-0.1
1928	Was-A	63	227	23	55	10	4	0	25	22	27	.242	.309	.322	.631	65	-11	-12	102	120	25	.576	4	0	1	2	S	-0.2
1929	Was-A	145	494	72	139	29	8	8	61	85	37	.281	.388	.421	.809	109	8	9	100	92	84	.821	5	9	-4	6	*S/2	2.2
1930	Was-A	154	587	127	203	41	9	13	126	72	36	.346	.422	.513	.934	134	34	33	101	130	129	1.003	17	10	-1	26	*S	6.5
1931	Was-A	156	611	103	187	44	13	12	126	81	52	.306	.391	.480	.870	127	25	25	101	134	116	.896	10	9	-2	13	*S	4.5
1932	Was-A	143	557	95	177	43	**18**	6	116	66	45	.318	.393	.492	.885	128	23	24	100	**141**	109	.909	7	5	-1	7	*S	3.7
1933	Was-A	152	602	89	186	**45**	11	5	118	87	49	.309	.398	.445	.843	128	22	26	96	**147**	111	.862	5	4	-1	9	*SM	4.2
1934	Was-A	127	504	68	143	30	9	7	101	53	28	.284	.353	.421	.774	98	-1	-2	101	**153**	78	.759	8	0	2	16	*SM	2.4
1935	Bos-A	144	556	70	164	37	14	9	95	63	40	.295	.370	.460	.830	105	11	4	108	121	96	.823	3	3	-1	-17	*S/1M	-0.5
1936	Bos-A	81	295	36	83	22	4	2	43	32	21	.281	.354	.403	.757	82	-6	-9	106	114	43	.712	1	3	-2	-4	S3M	-0.9
1937	Bos-A	148	570	102	175	40	4	18	110	84	73	.307	.402	.486	.887	119	21	18	103	110	116	.935	5	3	-0	-14	*SM	1.1
1938	Bos-A	143	530	98	172	**51**	5	17	94	91	60	.325	.428	.536	.964	137	35	33	102	101	126	1.066	7	5	-1	7	*SM	4.2
1939	Bos-A	143	520	97	160	33	3	19	107	87	48	.308	.407	.492	.899	119	24	17	108	122	104	.909	6	6	-2	6	*SM	3.2
1940	Bos-A	149	548	104	156	35	6	24	111	83	65	.285	.380	.502	.882	125	22	21	101	118	112	.908	7	5	-1	7	*S/3M	3.7
1941	Bos-A	143	518	98	161	38	8	16	95	82	55	.311	.406	.508	.914	136	31	29	103	110	107	.911	1	4	-2	5	*S3/OM	3.5
1942	Bos-A	45	79	7	24	3	0	4	24	15	21	.304	.415	.494	.909	149	6	6	104	166	16	.915	0	1	-1	-0	3/1SM	0.5
1943	Bos-A	59	77	8	24	4	0	5	29	11	4	.312	.398	.558	.956	172	7	7	104	183	17	.964	0	0	0	-0	3M	0.7
1944	Bos-A	76	191	24	46	7	0	5	28	34	19	.241	.358	.356	.714	107	2	3	98	122	25	.667	1	4	-2	-2	1M	-0.4
1945	Bos-A	3	8	1	3	0	0	0	1	3	2	.375	.545	.375	.920	178	1	1	95	121	2	1.200	0	0	0	0	/3M	0.1
Total	20	2124	7579	1233	2285	515	118	170	1424	1059	700	.301	.390	.468	.857	119	250	225	102	124	1426	.881	87	71		66	*S/312O	38.2
■ **BILL CRONIN**	Cronin, William Patrick "Crungy" b: 12/26/02, W.Newton, Mass. d: 10/26/66, Newton, Mass. BR/TR, 5′9″, 167 lbs. Deb: 7/04/28																											
1928	Bos-N	3	2	1	0	0	0	0	0	1	0	.000	.333	.000	.333	-6	-0	-0	97	0	0	.500	0			0	/C	0.0
1929	Bos-N	6	9	0	1	0	0	0	0	0	0	.111	.111	.111	.222	-48	-2	-2	94	0	0	.125	0			0	/C	0.0
1930	Bos-N	66	178	19	45	9	1	0	17	4	8	.253	.277	.315	.592	44	-17	-16	97	105	15	.466	0			-6	C	-1.5
1931	Bos-N	51	107	8	22	6	1	0	10	7	5	.206	.267	.280	.548	48	-8	-8	99	119	8	.459	0			-1	C	-0.6
Total	4	126	296	28	68	15	2	0	27	12	13	.230	.269	.294	.563	42	-27	-26	98	106	24	.452	0			-7	C	-2.1
■ **TOM CROOKE**	Crooke, Thomas Aloysius b: 7/26/1884, Washington, D.C. d: 4/5/29, Quantico, Va. BR/TR, 6′, 180 lbs. Deb: 9/29/09																											
1909	Was-A	3	7	2	2	1	0	0	2	2		.286	.444	.429	.873	196	1	1	90	257	2	1.200	1			0	/1	0.1
1910	Was-A	8	21	1	4	1	0	0	1	1		.190	.227	.238	.465	45	-1	-1	101	74	1	.353	0			0	/1	0.0
Total	2	11	28	3	6	2	0	0	3	3		.214	.290	.286	.576	83	-1	-1	98	127	3	.545	1			0	/1	0.1
■ **JACK CROOKS**	Crooks, John Charles b: 11/9/1865, St.Paul, Minn. d: 2/2/18, St.Louis, Mo. BR/TR, 170 lbs. Deb: 9/26/1889 M																											
1889	Col-a	12	43	13	14	2	3	0	7	10	4	.326	.463	.512	.975	198	5	6	91	80	15	1.483	10			0	2	0.5
1890	Col-a	135	485	86	107	5	4	1		96		.221	.357	.254	.611	84	-4	-4	99	0	66	.749	57			-9	*2/3O	-0.6
1891	Col-a	138	519	110	127	19	13	0	46	103	47	.245	.379	.331	.710	119	10	20	89	67	86	.852	50			22	*2	**4.3**
1892	StL-N	128	445	82	95	7	4	7	38	**136**	52	.213	.400	.294	.694	119	17	20	95	68	63	.834	23			-1	*23/OM	1.8
1893	StL-N	128	448	93	106	10	9	1	48	**121**	37	.237	.408	.306	.714	94	4	4	99	99	70	.871	31			5	*3/SC	0.9
1895	Was-N	117	409	80	114	19	8	6	57	68	39	.279	.392	.408	.800	105	8	5	103	88	82	.946	36			10	*2	1.8
1896	Was-N	25	84	20	24	3	0	3	20	16	8	.286	.406	.429	.835	129	3	4	95	131	16	.917	2			-6	2/3	0.0
	Lou-N	39	122	19	29	5	1	2	15	20	8	.238	.354	.344	.698	88	-2	-1	98	90	18	.774	8			0	2	0.0
	Yr	64	206	39	53	8	1	5	35	36	16	.257	.376	.379	.754	104	2	3	97	108	34	.830	10			-5		0.0
1898	StL-N	72	225	33	52	4	2	1	20	40		.231	.359	.280	.639	82	-1	-3	106	93	24	.642	3			5	2/3SO	0.4
Total	8	794	2780	536	668	74	44	21	251	610	195	.240	.385	.321	.706	104	38	51	97	69	440	.837	220			26	23/SOC	9.1
■ **ED CROSBY**	Crosby, Edward Carlton b: 5/26/49, Long Beach, Cal. BL/TR, 6′2″, 175 lbs. Deb: 7/12/70																											
1970	StL-N	38	95	9	24	4	1	0	6	7	5	.253	.311	.316	.626	64	-4	-5	106	78	10	.528	0	0	0	4	S/32	0.4
1972	StL-N	101	276	27	60	9	1	0	19	18	27	.217	.270	.257	.528	48	-18	-19	105	110	18	.405	1	1	-0	0	S23	-1.2
1973	StL-N	22	39	4	5	2	1	0	1	4	4	.128	.209	.231	.440	24	-4	-4	91	45	2	.382	0	0	0	-0	/S23	-0.2
	Cin-N	36	51	4	11	1	1	0	5	7	12	.216	.333	.275	.608	75	-2	-1	93	143	5	.548	0	1	-1	1	S/2	0.3
	Yr	58	90	8	16	3	2	0	6	11	16	.178	.282	.256	.537	54	-6	-5	92	107	7	.474	0	1	-1	1		0.1
1974	Cle-A	37	86	11	18	3	0	0	6	6	12	.209	.261	.244	.505	46	-6	-6	101	112	6	.386	0	1	-1	-0	3S/2	-0.5
1975	Cle-A	61	128	12	30	3	0	0	7	13	14	.234	.305	.258	.563	61	-6	-6	100	81	9	.434	0	4	-2	2	S23	-0.2
1976	Cle-A	2	2	0	1	0	0	0	0	0	0	.500	.500	.500	1.000	194	0	0	100	0	1	1.000	0	0	0	0	/3D	0.0
Total	6	297	677	67	149	22	4	0	44	55	74	.220	.284	.264	.548	54	-40	-41	102	99	50	.449	1	7	-4	7	S/23D	-1.4
■ **FRANKIE CROSETTI**	Crosetti, Frank Peter Joseph "Crow" b: 10/4/10, San Francisco, Cal. BR/TR, 5′10″, 165 lbs. Deb: 4/12/32 C																											
1932	NY-A	116	398	47	96	20	9	5	57	51	51	.241	.335	.374	.709	87	-10	-7	95	116	53	.684	3	2	-0	-1	S3/2	0.1
1933	NY-A	136	451	71	114	20	5	9	60	55	40	.253	.337	.379	.716	98	-7	-1	91	101	61	.686	4	1	1	-8	*S	0.2
1934	NY-A	138	554	85	147	22	10	11	67	61	58	.265	.344	.401	.744	96	-8	-4	96	84	78	.709	5	6	-2	-7	*S3/2	-0.4
1935	NY-A	87	305	49	78	17	6	8	50	41	27	.256	.351	.430	.781	109	0	3	93	112	48	.785	3	1	0	-15	S	-0.5
1936	NY-A	151	632	137	182	35	7	15	78	90	83	.288	.387	.437	.824	109	4	10	95	69	113	.867	18	7	1	-9	*S	1.0
1937	NY-A	149	611	127	143	29	5	11	49	86	105	.234	.340	.352	.692	73	-23	-25	102	58	79	.686	13	7	-0	1	*S	-1.4
1938	NY-A	157	631	113	166	35	3	9	55	106	97	.263	.382	.371	.752	85	-7	-13	105	62	98	.801	**27**	12	1	**18**	*S	1.4
1939	NY-A	152	656	109	153	25	5	10	56	65	81	.233	.315	.332	.647	72	-34	-26	91	66	71	.589	11	7	-1	9	*S	-0.2
1940	NY-A	145	546	84	106	23	4	4	31	72	77	.194	.299	.273	.572	50	-40	-39	99	74	47	.527	14	8	-1	-13	*S	-3.8
1941	NY-A	50	148	13	33	2	2	1	22	18	14	.223	.320	.284	.603	62	-8	-8	98	173	13	.512	0	2	-1	5	S3	-0.1
1942	NY-A	74	285	50	69	5	5	4	23	31	31	.242	.335	.337	.672	90	-3	-3	99	79	35	.617	1	1	-0	1	3/S2	0.0
1943	NY-A	95	348	36	81	8	1	2	20	36	47	.233	.317	.279	.596	78	-10	-9	96	72	33	.518	4	4	-1	-2	S	-1.1
1944	NY-A	55	197	20	47	4	2	5	30	11	21	.239	.299	.355	.654	81	-4	-5	106	130	20	.563	3	0	1	-1	S	-0.1
1945	NY-A	130	441	57	105	12	0	4	48	59	65	.238	.341	.293	.634	79	-6	-10	107	126	52	.603	7	1	2	-9	*S	-1.2
1946	NY-A	28	59	4	17	3	0	0	3	8	2	.288	.382	.339	.721	102	1	1	100	57	8	.644	0	3	-2	2	S	0.1
1947	NY-A	3	1	0	0	0	0	0	0	0	0	.000	.000	.000	.000	-99	-0	-0	97	0	0	.000	0	0	0	0	/2S	0.0
1948	NY-A	17	14	4	4	0	1	0	0	2	0	.286	.375	.429	.804	113	0	0	100	0	3	.800	0	0	0	-0	/2S	0.0
Total	17	1683	6277	1006	1541	260	65	98	649	792	799	.245	.341	.354	.695	84	-155	-135	98	85	812	.676	113	62	-3	-30	*S3/2	-6.0
■ **AMOS CROSS**	Cross, Amos C. b: 1861, Czechoslovakia d: 7/16/1888, Cleveland, Ohio Deb: 1885																											
1885	Lou-a	35	130	11	37	2	1	0		0		.285	.290	.315	.605	92	-1	-2	102	0	12	.452				-7	C	-0.2
1886	Lou-a	74	283	51	78	14	6	1		44		.276	.375	.378	.753	128	14	10	108	0	46	.805	13			-23	C1/SO	-0.7
1887	Lou-a	8	28	0	3	0	0	0		1		.107	.138	.107	.245	-28	-5	-5	107	0	0	.160	0			0	/C1O	-0.3
Total	3	117	441	62	118	16	7	1		45		.268	.338	.342	.681	108	8	4	106	0	59	.653	13			-30	/C1OS	-1.2
■ **CLARENCE CROSS**	Cross, Clarence (born Clarence Crause) b: 3/4/1856, St.Louis, Mo. d: 6/23/31, Seattle, Wash. Deb: 5/05/1884																											
1884	Alt-U	2	7	1	4	1	0	0		2		.571	.667	.714	1.381	362	2	2	101	0	3	2.333	0			0	/3	0.2
	Phi-U	2	9	0	2	0	0	0		0		.222	.222	.222	.444	55	-0	-0	93	0	0	.286	0			0	/S	0.0
	KC-U	25	93	13	20	1	0	0		6		.215	.263	.226	.488	76	-3	-1	87	0	6	.370	0			4	S/3	0.3
	Yr	29	109	14	26	2	0	0		8		.239	.291	.257	.547	98	-1	1	88	0	8	.434	0			4		0.5

YEAR	TM/L	G	AB	R	H	2B	3B	HR	RBI	BB	SO	AVG	OBP	SLG	PRO	/A	BR	/A	PF	CHI	RC	TA	SB	CS	SBR	FR	POS	TPR
1887	NY-a	16	55	9	11	2	1	0		2		.200	.267	.273	.539	60	-3	-2	88	0	4	.455	0			0	S/3	-0.1
Total	2	45	164	23	37	4	1	0		10		.226	.282	.262	.545	83	-5	-1	88	0	14	.441	0			4	/S3	0.4
■ **FRANK CROSS**	Cross, Frank Atwell "Mickey" b: 1/20/1873, Cleveland, Ohio d: 11/2/32, Geauga Lake, Ohio TR, Deb: 5/20/01																											
1901	Cle-A	1	5	0	3	0	0	0	0	0		.600	.600	.600	1.200	250	1	1	95	0	2	1.500	0			0	/O	0.1
■ **JEFF CROSS**	Cross, Joffre James b: 8/28/18, Tulsa, Okla. BR/TR, 5'11", 160 lbs. Deb: 9/27/42																											
1942	StL-N	1	4	0	1	0	0	0	1	0	0	.250	.250	.250	.500	43	-0	-0	108	378	0	.333	0			0	/S	0.0
1946	StL-N	49	69	17	15	3	0	0	6	10	8	.217	.316	.261	.577	61	-3	-3	107	124	6	.582	4			2	S/23	0.0
1947	StL-N	51	49	4	5	1	0	0	3	10	6	.102	.254	.122	.377	3	-7	-7	106	185	2	.348	0			1	3S/2	-0.5
1948	StL-N	2	0	0	0	0	0	0	0	0	0	—	—	—	—	—	0	0	101	—	—	—	0			0	R	0.0
	Chi-N	16	20	1	2	0	0	0	0	0	4	.100	.100	.100	.200	-49	-4	-4	93	0	0	.111	0			0	/S2	-0.2
	Yr	18	20	1	2	0	0	0	0	0	4	.100	.100	.100	.200	-49	-4	-4	94	0	0	.111	0			0		-0.2
Total	4	119	142	22	23	4	0	0	10	20	18	.162	.265	.190	.456	26	-14	-15	105	137	11	.429	4			3	/S32	-0.7
■ **LAVE CROSS**	Cross, Lafayette Napoleon b: 5/12/1866, Milwaukee, Wis. d: 9/6/27, Toledo, Ohio BR/TR, 5'8.5", 155 lbs. Deb: 4/23/1887 M																											
1887	Lou-a	54	203	32	54	8	3	0		15		.266	.320	.335	.655	79	-4	-7	107	0	27	.664	15			-3	CO	-0.1
1888	Lou-a	47	181	20	41	3	0	0	15	2		.227	.239	.243	.482	63	-9	-6	91	104	13	.407	10			-1	CO/S	-0.2
1889	Phi-a	55	199	22	44	8	2	0	23	14	9	.221	.272	.281	.554	61	-11	-10	98	117	19	.523	11			15	C	0.9
1890	Phi-P	63	245	42	73	7	8	3	47	12	6	.298	.331	.429	.759	101	0	-1	102	115	37	.709	5			4	CO	0.4
1891	Phi-a	110	402	66	121	20	14	5	52	38	23	.301	.366	.458	.823	134	18	16	103	77	74	.851	14			1	OC3/S2	1.5
1892	Phi-N	140	541	84	149	15	10	4	69	39	16	.275	.328	.362	.690	106	6	2	104	104	72	.653	18			-5	3CO2/S	0.3
1893	Phi-N	96	415	81	124	17	6	4	78	26	7	.299	.342	.398	.739	98	-2	-2	100	123	64	.722	18			3	C3OS/1	0.4
1894	Phi-N	119	529	123	204	34	9	7	125	29	7	.386	.421	.524	.944	135	24	29	95	123	128	1.015	21			24	*3C/S2	3.8
1895	Phi-N	125	535	95	145	26	9	2	101	35	8	.271	.319	.364	.684	79	-18	-17	99	149	71	.651	21			28	*3	1.0
1896	Phi-N	106	406	63	104	23	5	1	73	32	14	.256	.312	.345	.657	73	-15	-16	102	150	47	.599	8			10	3S/2OC	-0.1
1897	Phi-N	88	344	37	89	17	5	3	51	10		.259	.282	.363	.645	75	-15	-13	96	114	39	.573	10			-5	32/OS	-1.2
1898	StL-N	151	602	71	191	28	8	3	79	28		.317	.348	.405	.753	112	12	7	106	100	92	.696	14			17	*3/S	2.6
1899	Cle-N	38	154	15	44	5	0	1	20	8		.286	.325	.338	.663	94	-3	-1	89	98	18	.573	2			3	3M	0.2
	StL-N	103	403	61	122	14	5	4	64	17		.303	.333	.392	.725	94	-1	-5	108	122	58	.665	11			27	*3	1.9
	Yr	141	557	76	166	19	5	5	84	25		.298	.330	.377	.707	94	-4	-6	103	116	76	.639	13			30		2.1
1900	StL-N	16	61	6	18	1	0	0	6	1		.295	.306	.311	.618	78	-2	-2	93	101	6	.488	1			-1	3	-0.1
	Bro-N	117	461	73	135	14	6	4	67	25		.293	.329	.375	.704	90	-3	-8	108	120	65	.669	20			3	*3	-0.2
	Yr	133	522	79	153	15	6	4	73	26		.293	.327	.368	.694	89	-5	-9	106	118	71	.648	21			2		-0.3
1901	Phi-A	100	424	82	139	28	12	2	73	19		.328	.357	.465	.821	128	15	15	100	100	80	.839	23			11	*3	2.1
1902	Phi-A	137	559	90	191	39	8	0	108	27		.342	.372	.440	.812	116	19	12	108	139	103	.810	25			7	*3	1.4
1903	Phi-A	137	559	60	163	22	4	2	90	10		.292	.304	.356	.660	96	-1	-4	104	152	66	.563	14			-3	*3/1	-0.8
1904	Phi-A	155	607	73	176	31	10	1	71	13		.290	.305	.379	.684	116	10	9	102	109	75	.587	10			-10	*3	0.5
1905	Phi-A	146	583	68	155	29	5	0	77	26		.266	.297	.333	.630	93	0	-6	109	136	62	.533	8			-20	*3	-2.2
1906	Was-A	130	494	55	130	14	6	1	46	28		.263	.303	.322	.625	107	-2	3	91	99	55	.566	19			-7	*3	0.6
1907	Was-A	41	161	13	32	8	0	0	10	10		.199	.246	.248	.494	66	-7	-5	90	86	11	.411	3			2	3	0.0
Total	21	2274	9068	1332	2644	411	135	47	1345	464	90	.292	.327	.382	.710	101	10	-9	102	116	1284	.662	301			101	*3CO/S21	12.7
■ **MONTE CROSS**	Cross, Montford Montgomery b: 8/31/1869, Philadelphia, Pa. d: 6/21/34, Philadelphia, Pa. BR/TR, 6'2", 180 lbs. Deb: 9/27/1892																											
1892	Bal-N	15	50	5	8	0	0	0	2	4	10	.160	.222	.160	.382	17	-5	-5	100	77	2	.333	2			0	S	-0.4
1894	Pit-N	13	43	14	19	1	5	2	13	5	4	.442	.520	.837	1.357	239	9	9	94	85	22	2.042	6			0	S	0.7
1895	Pit-N	108	393	67	101	14	13	3	54	38	38	.257	.327	.382	.709	87	-10	-7	97	97	63	.788	39			-17	*S/2	-1.2
1896	StL-N	125	427	66	104	10	6	6	52	58	48	.244	.342	.337	.679	86	-10	-6	95	94	65	.768	40			-16	*S	-1.8
1897	StL-N	131	462	59	132	17	11	4	55	62		.286	.379	.396	.775	114	6	12	93	84	86	.879	38			25	*S	3.4
1898	Phi-N	149	525	68	135	25	5	1	50	55		.257	.334	.330	.664	98	-3	1	95	88	66	.651	20			9	*S	1.6
1899	Phi-N	154	557	85	143	25	6	3	65	56		.257	.333	.339	.673	90	-9	-6	97	103	73	.674	26			-6	*S	-0.1
1900	Phi-N	131	466	59	94	11	3	3	62	51		.202	.280	.258	.538	52	-30	-28	98	**153**	40	.511	19			-7	*S	-2.0
1901	Phi-N	139	483	49	95	14	1	1	44	52		.197	.275	.236	.511	49	-28	-30	103	128	39	.490	24			-17	*S	-4.0
1902	Phi-A	137	497	72	115	22	2	3	59	32		.231	.278	.302	.580	57	-25	-31	108	125	48	.521	17			12	*S	-0.6
1903	Phi-A	137	470	44	116	21	2	3	45	49		.247	.318	.319	.637	90	-2	-4	104	104	59	.650	31			8	*S/2	1.0
1904	Phi-A	153	503	33	95	23	4	1	38	46		.189	.257	.256	.513	63	-19	-20	102	110	39	.475	19			-18	*S	-4.1
1905	Phi-A	78	248	28	67	17	2	0	24	19		.270	.322	.355	.677	107	5	2	109	97	32	.635	8			-21	S/2	-1.7
1906	Phi-A	134	445	32	89	23	3	1	40	50		.200	.281	.272	.553	80	-11	-8	94	120	41	.542	22			2	*S	-0.4
1907	Phi-A	77	248	37	51	9	5	0	18	39		.206	.314	.282	.596	87	-1	-2	106	94	28	.640	17			5	S	0.5
Total	15	1681	5817	718	1364	232	68	31	621	616	100	.234	.311	.314	.625	81	-134	-125	99	108	703	.629	328			-41	*S/2	-9.1
■ **FRANK CROSSIN**	Crossin, Frank Patrick b: 6/15/1891, Avondale, Pa. d: 12/6/65, Kingston, Pa. BR/TR, 5'10", 160 lbs. Deb: 9/24/12																											
1912	StL-A	8	22	2	5	0	0	0	2	1		.227	.261	.227	.488	40	-2	-2	99	133	1	.412	1			0	/C	0.0
1913	StL-A	4	4	1	1	0	0	0	0	1	1	.250	.500	.250	.750	127	0	0	95	0	0	1.000	0			0	/C	0.1
1914	StL-A	43	90	5	11	1	1	0	5	10	10	.122	.225	.156	.381	15	-9	-9	98	134	4	.367	3			-2	C	-0.7
Total	3	55	116	8	17	1	1	0	7	12	11	.147	.244	.172	.417	25	-11	-10	98	128	6	.394	4			-2	/C	-0.6
■ **JOE CROTTY**	Crotty, Joseph P. b: 12/24/1860, Cincinnati, O. d: 6/22/26, Minneapolis, Minn BR, Deb: 5/04/1882																											
1882	Lou-a	5	20	1	2	0	0	0		0		.100	.100	.100	.200	-35	-3	-2	94	0	0	.111				0	/C	-0.1
	StL-a	8	28	2	4	1	0	0		3		.143	.226	.179	.404	38	-2	-2	100	0	1	.333				0	/CO	-0.1
	Yr	13	48	3	6	1	0	0		3		.125	.176	.146	.322	10	-4	-4	97	0	1	.238				0		-0.2
1884	Cin-U	21	84	11	22	4	2	1		1		.262	.271	.393	.663	113	2	1	108	0	9	.548	0			0	C	0.1
1885	Lou-a	39	129	14	20	2	0	0		3		.155	.193	.171	.363	17	-12	-12	102	0	4	.257				-7	C/1	-1.2
1886	NY-a	14	47	6	8	0	1	0		4		.170	.250	.213	.463	45	-3	-3	104	0	3	.462	3			0	C	-0.2
Total	4	87	308	34	56	7	3	1		11		.182	.220	.234	.454	47	-17	-19	103	0	18	.357	3			-7	/C1O	-1.5
■ **JACK CROUCH**	Crouch, Jack Albert "Roxy" b: 6/12/03, Salisbury, N.C. d: 8/25/72, Leesburg, Fla. BR/TR, 5'9", 165 lbs. Deb: 9/18/30																											
1930	StL-A	6	14	1	2	1	0	0	1	1	3	.143	.200	.214	.414	5	-2	-2	108	111	1	.333	0	0	0	0	/C	0.0
1931	StL-A	8	12	0	0	0	0	0	1	0	4	.000	.000	.000	.000	-98	-3	-3	102	0	0	.000	0	0	0	0	/C	-0.1
1933	StL-A	19	30	1	5	0	0	1	5	2	6	.167	.219	.267	.485	24	-3	-4	115	152	2	.400	0	0	0	0	/C	-0.2
	Cin-N	10	16	5	2	0	0	0	1	0	0	.125	.222	.125	.347	1	-2	-2	99	188	1	.357	1			0	/C	-0.1
Total	3	43	72	7	9	1	0	1	8	3	13	.125	.182	.181	.362	-3	-11	-12	108	128	3	.302	1	0		1	/C	-0.4
■ **FRANK CROUCHER**	Croucher, Frank Donald "Dingle" b: 7/23/14, San Antonio, Tex. d: 5/21/80, Houston, Tex. BR/TR, 5'11", 165 lbs. Deb: 4/18/39																											
1939	Det-A	97	324	38	87	15	0	5	40	16	42	.269	.303	.361	.664	62	-16	-21	111	102	33	.542	2	2	-1	-6	S/2	-1.6
1940	Det-A	37	57	3	6	0	0	0	2	4	5	.105	.164	.105	.269	-26	-11	-12	111	120	1	.196	0	0	0	1	S/23	-0.7
1941	Det-A	136	489	51	124	21	4	2	39	33	72	.254	.305	.325	.630	63	-24	-28	106	85	50	.527	2	0	1	-3	*S	-2.5
1942	Was-A	26	65	2	18	1	1	0	5	3	9	.277	.309	.323	.632	81	-2	-2	96	84	6	.471	0	0	0	-2	2	-0.2
Total	4	296	935	94	235	37	5	7	86	56	128	.251	.296	.324	.620	58	-52	-62	107	93	90	.518	4	2	0	-10	S/23	-5.0
■ **BUCK CROUSE**	Crouse, Clyde Elsworth b: 1/6/1897, Anderson, Ind. d: 10/23/83, Muncie, Ind. BL/TR, 5'8", 158 lbs. Deb: 8/01/23																											
1923	Chi-A	23	70	6	18	2	1	1	7	3	4	.257	.297	.357	.654	73	-3	-3	98	85	7	.558	0	0	0	-0	C	0.0
1924	Chi-A	94	305	30	79	10	1	1	44	23	12	.259	.319	.308	.627	64	-17	-16	97	150	32	.544	3	2	-0	10	C	0.0
1925	Chi-A	54	131	18	46	7	0	2	25	12	4	.351	.410	.450	.860	124	4	5	96	129	24	.839	1	2	-1	-0	C	0.6
1926	Chi-A	49	135	10	32	4	1	0	17	14	7	.237	.309	.281	.590	60	-9	-7	92	152	13	.505	0	0	0	-4	C	-0.7
1927	Chi-A	85	222	22	53	11	0	0	20	21	10	.239	.307	.288	.596	54	-14	-15	102	104	20	.533	4	0	1	1	C	-1.0
1928	Chi-A	78	218	17	55	5	2	2	20	19	14	.252	.315	.321	.636	68	-10	-10	99	90	22	.557	3	4	-2	0	C	-0.5
1929	Chi-A	45	107	11	29	7	0	2	12	5	7	.271	.316	.393	.708	86	-3	-2	95	86	14	.654	3	0	1	1	C	0.3
1930	Chi-A	42	118	14	30	8	1	0	15	17	10	.254	.348	.339	.687	73	-4	-5	103	124	15	.652	1	1	-0	0	C	0.0

YEAR	TM/L	G	AB	R	H	2B	3B	HR	RBI	BB	SO	AVG	OBP	SLG	PRO	/A	BR	/A	PF	CHI	RC	TA	SB	CS	SBR	FR	POS	TPR
Total	8	470	1306	128	342	54	6	8	160	114	68	.262	.326	.331	.657	72	-57	-53	98	119	147	.586	14	9	-1	8	C	-1.3
■ DON CROW	Crow, Donald Le Roy b: 8/18/58, Yakima, Wash. BR/TR, 6'4", 200 lbs. Deb: 7/25/82																											
1982	LA-N	4	4	0	0	0	0	0	0	0	3	.000	.000	.000	.000	-99	-1	-1	95	0	0	.000	0	0	0	-0	/C	0.0
■ GEORGE CROWE	Crowe, George Daniel b: 3/22/23, Whiteland, Ind. BL/TL, 6'2", 210 lbs. Deb: 4/16/52																											
1952	Bos-N	73	217	25	56	13	1	4	20	18	25	.258	.329	.382	.712	102	-1	0	95	82	28	.635	0	1	-1	1	1	-0.1
1953	Mil-N	47	42	6	12	2	0	2	6	2	7	.286	.333	.476	.810	115	0	1	94	90	7	.742	0	0	0	0	/1	0.0
1955	Mil-N	104	303	41	85	12	4	15	55	45	44	.281	.375	.495	.870	138	13	16	93	114	59	.895	1	0	0	-1	1	0.9
1956	Cin-N	77	144	22	36	2	1	10	23	11	28	.250	.312	.486	.798	102	2	0	108	97	22	.761	0	0	0	-0	1	-0.1
1957	Cin-N	133	494	71	134	20	1	31	92	32	62	.271	.317	.504	.821	110	9	6	105	114	77	.765	1	1	-0	2	*1	-0.2
1958	Cin-N	111	345	31	95	12	5	7	61	41	51	.275	.352	.400	.752	92	-0	-3	107	159	50	.700	1	0	0	0	1/2	-0.8
1959	StL-N	77	103	14	31	6	0	8	29	5	12	.301	.333	.592	.926	134	5	5	105	138	18	.868	0	0	0	0	1	0.4
1960	StL-N	73	72	5	17	3	0	4	13	5	16	.236	.286	.444	.730	89	-1	-1	108	120	8	.627	0	0	0	0	/1	-0.1
1961	StL-N	7	7	0	1	0	0	0	0	0	1	.143	.143	.143	.286	-21	-1	-1	113	0	0	.167	0	0	0	0	H	0.0
Total	9	702	1727	215	467	70	12	81	299	159	246	.270	.335	.466	.801	110	26	21	102	118	269	.773	3	2	-0	1	1/2	-0.0
■ ED CROWLEY	Crowley, Edgar Jewel b: 8/20/06, Watkinsville, Ga. d: 4/14/70, Birmingham, Ala. BR/TR, 6'1", 180 lbs. Deb: 6/21/28																											
1928	Was-A	2	1	0	0	0	0	0	0	0	0	.000	.000	.000	.000	-99	-0	-0	102	0	0	.000	0	0	0	0	/3	0.0
■ JOHN CROWLEY	Crowley, John A. b: 1/12/1862, Lawrence, Mass. d: 9/23/1896, Lawrence, Mass. 5'10", 164 lbs. Deb: 5/01/1884																											
1884	Phi-N	48	168	26	41	7	3	0	19	15	21	.244	.306	.321	.627	106	-0	2	92	123	17	.543				-20	C	-1.1
■ TERRY CROWLEY	Crowley, Terrence Michael b: 2/16/47, Staten Island, N.Y. BL/TL, 6', 180 lbs. Deb: 9/04/69 C																											
1969	Bal-A	7	18	2	6	0	0	0	3	1	4	.333	.368	.333	.702	94	-0	-0	104	201	2	.583	0	0	0	-0	/1O	0.0
1970	Bal-A	83	152	25	39	5	0	5	20	35	26	.257	.396	.388	.784	121	5	6	97	109	25	.814	2	0	1	-4	O1	0.0
1971	Bal-A	18	23	2	4	0	0	0	1	3	4	.174	.269	.174	.443	27	-2	-2	103	102	1	.333	0	0	0	-2	/O1	-0.4
1972	Bal-A	97	247	30	57	10	0	11	29	32	26	.231	.321	.405	.726	118	5	5	98	91	32	.672	0	0	0	-8	O1	-0.6
1973	Bal-A	54	131	16	27	4	0	3	15	16	14	.206	.297	.305	.603	65	-5	-6	107	120	12	.528	0	0	0	-2	DO/1	-0.8
1974	Cin-N	84	125	11	30	12	0	1	20	10	16	.240	.301	.360	.661	86	-3	-3	98	161	13	.576	1	0	0	-3	O/1	-0.5
1975	Cin-N	66	71	8	19	6	0	1	11	7	6	.268	.333	.394	.728	97	0	-0	104	137	8	.603	0	0	0	0	/1O	0.0
1976	Atl-N	7	6	0	0	0	0	0	1	0	0	.000	.000	.000	.000	-90	-2	-2	111	0	-0	.000	0	0	0	0	H	-0.1
	Bal-A	33	61	5	15	1	0	0	5	7	11	.246	.333	.262	.596	78	-2	-1	98	120	6	.511	0	0	0	0	D/1	0.0
1977	Bal-A	18	22	3	8	1	0	1	9	1	3	.364	.391	.545	.937	163	2	2	93	238	5	.929	0	0	0	0	/1D	0.2
1978	Bal-A	62	95	9	24	2	0	0	12	8	12	.253	.317	.274	.591	74	-4	-3	91	182	8	.467	0	0	0	0	D/O1	-0.2
1979	Bal-A	61	63	8	20	5	1	1	8	14	13	.317	.449	.476	.925	154	5	6	97	93	14	1.000	0	0	0	0	D/1	0.5
1980	Bal-A	92	233	33	67	8	0	12	50	29	21	.288	.366	.476	.843	128	9	9	101	133	40	.805	0	0	0	0	D/1	0.9
1981	Bal-A	68	134	12	33	6	0	4	25	29	12	.246	.380	.381	.761	121	5	5	99	155	21	.769	0	0	0	0	D/1	0.5
1982	Bal-A	65	93	8	22	2	0	3	17	21	9	.237	.377	.355	.732	103	1	1	100	162	13	.711	0	0	0	0	D1	0.1
1983	Mon-N	50	44	2	8	0	0	0	3	9	4	.182	.333	.182	.515	46	-3	-3	102	148	3	.474	0	0	0	0	/1	-0.2
Total	15	865	1518	174	379	62	1	42	229	222	181	.250	.348	.375	.723	104	12	13	99	131	202	.702	3	0	1	-18	DO/1	-0.6
■ BILL CROWLEY	Crowley, William Michael b: 4/8/1857, Philadelphia, Pa. d: 7/14/1891, Gloucester, Mass. BR/TR, 5'7.5", 159 lbs. Deb: 4/26/1875																											
1875	Phi-n	9	37	4	4							.108															/O312	
1877	Lou-N	61	238	30	67	9	3	1	23	4	13	.282	.293	.357	.651	79	1	-10	132	90	26	.520				7	*O/SC32	-0.4
1879	Buf-N	60	261	41	75	9	5	0	30	6	14	.287	.303	.360	.664	103	5	-0	114	99	29	.538				1	OC/12	0.0
1880	Buf-N	85	354	57	95	16	4	0	20	19	23	.268	.306	.336	.642	129	7	11	91	53	37	.533				-7	*OC	0.3
1881	Bos-N	72	279	33	71	12	0	0	31	14	15	.254	.290	.297	.588	93	-5	-1	91	137	25	.466				-4	*O	-0.5
1883	Phi-a	23	96	16	24	4	3	0		3		.250	.273	.354	.627	98	-0	-0	103	0	10	.514				0	O/1	0.0
	Cle-N	11	41	3	12	5	0	0	5	1	7	.293	.310	.415	.724	113	1	1	105	104	5	.621				0	O	0.0
1884	Bos-N	108	407	50	110	14	6	6	61	33	74	.270	.325	.378	.703	123	10	11	98	124	51	.630				-8	*O	0.2
1885	Buf-N	92	344	29	83	14	1	1	36	21	32	.241	.285	.297	.581	89	-4	-4	99	126	30	.471				-5	*O	-0.9
Total	7	512	2020	259	537	83	22	8	206	101	178	.266	.301	.341	.641	104	14	7	102	101	213	.532				-16	O/C123S	-1.3
■ WALTON CRUISE	Cruise, Walton Edwin b: 5/6/1890, Childersburg, Ala. d: 1/9/75, Sylacauga, Ala. BL/TR, 6', 175 lbs. Deb: 4/14/14																											
1914	StL-N	95	256	20	58	9	3	4	28	25	42	.227	.303	.332	.635	85	-4	-5	104	105	26	.586	3			-3	O	-1.0
1916	StL-N	3	3	0	2	0	0	0	0	1	0	.667	.750	.667	1.417	349	1	1	97	0	2	3.000	0			-0	/O	0.1
1917	StL-N	153	529	70	156	20	10	5	59	38	73	.295	.343	.399	.742	125	16	15	102	103	76	.713	16			-20	*O	-1.0
1918	StL-N	70	240	34	65	5	4	6	39	30	26	.271	.359	.400	.759	141	10	11	93	132	35	.749	2			-9	O	0.0
1919	StL-N	9	21	0	2	1	0	0	0	1	6	.095	.136	.143	.279	-17	-3	-3	94	0	0	.211	0			-2	/O1	-0.4
	Bos-N	73	241	23	52	7	0	1	21	17	29	.216	.267	.257	.525	59	-12	-11	98	126	18	.460	8			-3	O	-1.8
	Yr	82	262	23	54	8	0	1	21	18	35	.206	.257	.248	.505	54	-15	-14	97	112	18	.438	8			-4		-2.2
1920	Bos-N	91	288	40	80	7	5	1	21	31	26	.278	.352	.347	.699	105	1	3	96	79	37	.654	5	3	-0	-8	O	-1.1
1921	Bos-N	108	344	47	119	16	7	8	55	48	24	.346	.429	.503	.932	157	24	28	93	102	75	1.000	10	8	-2	-6	*O/1	1.5
1922	Bos-N	104	352	51	98	15	10	4	46	44	20	.278	.360	.412	.772	105	-0	3	94	104	54	.752	4	4	-1	-2	*O/1	-0.3
1923	Bos-N	21	38	4	8	2	0	0	0	3	2	.211	.268	.263	.531	41	-3	-3	100	0	3	.467	1	0	0	-1	/O	-0.3
1924	Bos-N	9	9	4	4	1	0	1	3	0	2	.444	.444	.889	1.333	265	2	2	94	99	3	1.600	0	0	0	0	H	0.2
Total	10	736	2321	293	644	83	39	30	272	238	250	.277	.348	.386	.733	113	32	41	97	103	329	.706	49	15		-54	O/1	-4.1
■ GENE CRUMLING	Crumling, Eugene Leon b: 4/5/22, Wrightsville, Pa. BR/TR, 6', 180 lbs. Deb: 9/11/45																											
1945	StL-N	6	12	0	1	0	0	0	1	0	1	.083	.083	.083	.167	-54	-2	-2	100	347	0	.091	0			0	/C	-0.1
■ BUDDY CRUMP	Crump, Arthur Elliott b: 11/29/01, Norfolk, Va. d: 9/7/76, Raleigh, N.C. BL/TL, 5'10", 156 lbs. Deb: 9/28/24																											
1924	NY-N	1	4	0	0	0	0	0	1	0	1	.000	.000	.000	.000	-99	-1	-1	91	0	0	.000	0	0	0	-0	/O	-0.1
■ PRESS CRUTHERS	Cruthers, Charles Preston b: 9/8/1890, Marshallton, Del. d: 12/27/76, Kenosha, Wis. BR/TR, 5'9", 152 lbs. Deb: 9/29/13																											
1913	Phi-A	3	12	0	3	0	0	0	0	0	0	.250	.250	.333	.583	73	-1	-0	97	0	1	.444	0			0	/2	0.0
1914	Phi-A	4	15	1	3	0	1	0	0	0	4	.200	.200	.333	.533	62	-1	-1	97	0	1	.385	0	1	-1	0	/2	-0.1
Total	2	7	27	1	6	0	1	0	0	0	4	.222	.222	.333	.556	67	-1	-1	97	0	2	.409	0	1		0	/2	-0.1
■ TOMMY CRUZ	Cruz, Cirilo (Dilan) b: 2/15/51, Arroyo, P.R. BL/TL, 5'9", 165 lbs. Deb: 9/04/73																											
1973	StL-N	3	0	1	0	0	0	0	0	0	0	—	—	—	—	—	0	0	91	—	—	—	0	0	0	-0	/O	0.0
1977	Chi-A	4	2	1	0	0	0	0	0	0	0	.000	.000	.000	.000	-99	-1	-1	99	0	0	.000	0	0	0	-1	/O	0.0
Total	2	7	2	2	0	0	0	0	0	0	0	.000	.000	.000	.000	-99	-1	-1	99	0	2	.000	0	0	0	-1	/O	0.0
■ HEITY CRUZ	Cruz, Hector Louis (Dilan) b: 4/2/53, Arroyo, P.R. BR/TR, 5'11", 170 lbs. Deb: 8/11/73																											
1973	StL-N	11	11	1	0	0	0	0	0	1	3	.000	.083	.000	.083	-83	-3	-2	91	0	0	.091	0	0	0	-1	/O	-0.3
1975	StL-N	23	48	7	7	2	2	0	6	2	4	.146	.180	.271	.451	23	-5	-5	103	178	2	.357	0	0	0	-0	3/O	-0.5
1976	StL-N	151	526	54	120	17	1	13	71	42	119	.228	.288	.338	.626	74	-17	-19	104	129	50	.532	1	0	0	-18	*3	-4.1
1977	StL-N	118	339	50	80	19	2	6	42	46	56	.236	.329	.357	.686	88	-7	-5	96	121	41	.637	4	3	-1	-8	*O/3	-1.7
1978	Chi-N	30	76	8	18	5	0	2	9	3	6	.237	.266	.382	.647	72	-2	-3	110	102	6	.516	0	0	0	0	O/3	-0.3
	SF-N	79	197	19	44	8	1	6	24	21	39	.223	.301	.365	.667	93	-4	-2	92	106	20	.584	0	2	-1	-1	O3	-0.6
	Yr	109	273	27	62	13	1	8	33	24	45	.227	.292	.370	.662	87	-7	-5	97	106	28	.575	0	2	-1	-1		-0.9
1979	SF-N	16	25	2	3	0	0	0	1	3	7	.120	.214	.120	.334	-7	-4	-3	92	132	1	.250	0	0	0	-1	/O3	-0.4
	Cin-N	74	182	24	44	10	2	4	27	31	39	.242	.352	.385	.737	104	1	1	97	130	24	.687	0	1	-1	1	O	0.0
	Yr	90	207	26	47	10	2	4	28	34	46	.227	.336	.353	.689	91	-3	-2	97	132	24	.633	0	1	-1	-0		-0.4
1980	Cin-N	52	75	5	16	4	1	1	5	8	16	.213	.289	.333	.622	72	-3	-3	102	71	7	.550	0	0	0	-4	O	-0.8
1981	Chi-N	53	109	15	25	5	0	7	15	17	24	.229	.333	.468	.801	121	3	3	104	82	17	.787	2	2	-1	-2	3O	0.0
1982	Chi-N	17	19	1	4	1	0	0	0	2	4	.211	.286	.263	.549	53	-1	-1	103	0	1	.438	0	0	0	-1	/O	-0.2
Total	9	624	1607	186	361	71	9	39	200	176	317	.225	.303	.353	.656	82	-41	-40	100	116	170	.601	7	8	-3	-36	O3	-8.9

YEAR	TM/L	G	AB	R	H	2B	3B	HR	RBI	BB	SO	AVG	OBP	SLG	PRO	/A	BR	/A	PF	CHI	RC	TA	SB	CS	SBR	FR	POS	TPR
■ **HENRY CRUZ** Cruz, Henry (Acosta) b: 2/27/52, Christiansted, V.I. BL/TL, 6′, 175 lbs. Deb: 4/18/75																												
1975	LA-N	53	94	8	25	3	1	0	5	7	6	.266	.317	.319	.636	81	-3	-2	95	64	10	.543	1	1	-0	-8	O	-1.2
1976	LA-N	49	88	8	16	2	1	4	14	9	11	.182	.258	.364	.621	75	-3	-3	100	123	8	.547	0	2	-1	-2	O	-0.6
1977	Chi-A	16	21	3	6	0	0	2	5	1	3	.286	.318	.571	.890	137	1	1	99	110	4	.867	0	0	0	-3	/O	-0.1
1978	Chi-A	53	77	13	17	2	1	2	10	8	11	.221	.302	.351	.653	82	-2	-2	101	120	8	.571	0	1	-1	-3	O/D	-0.6
Total	4	171	280	32	64	7	3	8	34	25	31	.229	.294	.361	.655	84	-7	-6	98	102	29	.577	1	4	-2	-16	O/D	-2.5
■ **JOSE CRUZ** Cruz, Jose (Dilan) b: 8/8/47, Arroyo, P.R. BL/TL, 6′, 170 lbs. Deb: 9/19/70																												
1970	StL-N	6	17	2	6	1	0	0	1	4	0	.353	.500	.412	.912	139	2	1	106	55	4	1.000	0	0	0	2	/O	0.3
1971	StL-N	83	292	46	80	13	2	9	27	49	35	.274	.380	.425	.805	127	12	12	101	74	49	.814	6	3	0	-1	O	0.8
1972	StL-N	117	332	33	78	14	4	2	23	36	54	.235	.312	.319	.631	76	-8	-10	105	84	35	.582	9	3	1	-1	*O	-1.5
1973	StL-N	132	406	51	92	22	5	10	57	51	66	.227	.314	.379	.694	101	-5	-0	91	124	50	.663	10	4	1	-4	*O	-0.8
1974	StL-N	107	161	24	42	4	3	5	20	20	27	.261	.343	.416	.759	108	2	2	104	94	23	.734	4	2	0	-6	O/1	-0.6
1975	Hou-N	120	315	44	81	15	2	9	49	52	44	.257	.364	.403	.767	120	6	9	94	123	49	.765	6	3	0	1	O	0.6
1976	Hou-N	133	439	49	133	21	5	4	61	53	46	.303	.378	.401	.779	140	13	21	86	125	70	.796	28	11	2	6	*O	2.5
1977	Hou-N	157	579	87	173	31	10	17	87	69	67	.299	.373	.475	.848	136	21	27	93	113	104	.896	44	23	-1	2	*O	2.3
1978	Hou-N	153	565	79	178	34	9	10	83	57	57	.315	.378	.460	.838	141	25	29	95	120	102	.874	37	9	6	-0	*O/1	2.9
1979	Hou-N	157	558	73	161	33	7	9	72	72	66	.289	.370	.421	.791	128	13	20	90	115	91	.825	36	14	2	0	*O	1.8
1980	Hou-N	160	612	79	185	29	7	11	91	60	66	.302	.365	.426	.791	123	17	18	98	130	97	.795	36	11	4	6	*O	2.3
1981	Hou-N	107	409	53	109	16	5	13	55	35	49	.267	.324	.425	.750	126	5	10	88	107	54	.682	5	7	-3	5	*O	1.1
1982	Hou-N	155	570	62	157	27	2	9	68	60	67	.275	.345	.377	.723	103	2	3	99	117	75	.683	21	11	-0	-6	*O	-0.5
1983	Hou-N	160	594	85	**189**	28	8	14	92	65	86	.318	.386	.463	.849	149	28	36	90	122	109	.873	30	16	-1	3	*O	3.6
1984	Hou-N	160	600	96	187	28	13	12	95	73	68	.312	.386	.462	.848	148	31	36	93	126	111	.867	22	8	2	4	*O	3.7
1985	Hou-N	141	544	69	163	34	4	9	79	43	74	.300	.351	.426	.777	121	11	14	96	129	81	.733	16	5	2	3	*O	1.6
1986	Hou-N	141	479	48	133	22	4	10	72	55	86	.278	.352	.403	.755	105	6	4	103	131	68	.699	3	4	-2	-2	*O	-0.1
1987	Hou-N	126	365	47	88	17	4	11	38	36	65	.241	.309	.400	.709	93	-8	-4	93	85	47	.660	4	1	1	3	O	-0.4
1988	NY-A	38	80	9	16	2	0	1	7	8	8	.200	.273	.262	.535	53	-5	-5	96	116	5	.433	0	1	-1	-2	D/O	-0.7
Total	19	2353	7917	1036	2251	391	94	165	1077	898	1031	.284	.358	.420	.778	122	169	222	95	116	1223	.783	317	136	14	12	*O/D1	18.9
■ **JULIO CRUZ** Cruz, Julio Luis b: 12/2/54, Brooklyn, N.Y. BB/TR, 5′9″, 165 lbs. Deb: 7/04/77																												
1977	Sea-A	60	199	25	51	3	1	1	7	24	29	.256	.336	.296	.633	77	-6	-5	96	46	22	.628	15	6	1	6	2/D	0.6
1978	Sea-A	147	550	77	129	14	1	1	25	69	66	.235	.321	.269	.590	66	-21	-23	102	63	58	.631	59	10	**12**	23	*2/SD	2.0
1979	Sea-A	107	414	70	112	16	2	1	29	62	61	.271	.366	.326	.692	88	-4	-4	100	71	59	.774	49	9	9	14	*2	2.3
1980	Sea-A	119	422	66	88	9	3	2	16	59	49	.209	.307	.258	.565	55	-24	-25	103	57	42	.617	45	7	9	6	*2/D	-0.3
1981	Sea-A	94	352	57	90	12	3	2	24	39	40	.256	.335	.324	.659	91	-3	-3	100	83	45	.726	43	8	**8**	13	2/S	2.1
1982	Sea-A	154	549	83	133	22	5	8	49	57	71	.242	.317	.344	.661	75	-13	-20	109	94	66	.678	46	13	6	6	*2/S3D	0.0
1983	Sea-A	61	181	24	46	10	1	2	12	20	22	.254	.335	.354	.689	90	-2	-2	100	67	25	.826	33	6	6	4	2/D	1.0
	Chi-A	99	334	47	84	9	4	1	40	29	44	.251	.315	.311	.626	71	-12	-13	103	146	35	.600	24	6	4	9	2	0.2
	Yr	160	515	71	130	19	5	3	52	49	66	.252	.322	.326	.648	78	-14	-15	102	116	61	.685	57	12	10	12		1.2
1984	Chi-A	143	415	42	92	14	4	5	43	45	58	.222	.298	.311	.609	62	-17	-23	111	119	40	.556	14	6	1	20	*2	0.4
1985	Chi-A	91	234	28	46	2	3	0	15	32	40	.197	.299	.231	.529	48	-16	-16	100	110	17	.482	8	5	-1	4	2/D	-0.8
1986	Chi-A	81	209	38	45	2	0	0	19	42	28	.215	.347	.225	.571	60	-9	-10	101	161	20	.565	7	2	1	-2	2/D	-0.6
Total	10	1156	3859	557	916	113	27	23	279	478	508	.237	.324	.299	.622	71	-128	-144	103	90	430	.657	343	78	56	101	*2/DS3	6.9
■ **TODD CRUZ** Cruz, Todd Ruben b: 11/23/55, Highland Park, Mich BR/TR, 6′, 175 lbs. Deb: 9/04/78																												
1978	Phi-N	3	4	0	2	0	0	0	2	0	0	.500	.500	.500	1.000	171	0	0	105	397	1	.667	0	1	-1	0	/S	0.0
1979	KC-A	55	118	9	24	7	0	2	15	3	19	.203	.230	.314	.543	43	-9	-10	105	134	8	.423	0	1	-1	-4	S/3	-0.8
1980	Cal-A	18	40	5	11	3	0	1	5	5	8	.275	.356	.425	.781	118	1	1	96	97	6	.759	0	0	0	-2	S/32O	0.0
	Chi-A	90	293	23	68	11	1	2	18	9	54	.232	.260	.297	.557	54	-19	-18	97	75	22	.433	2	1	0	11	S	0.0
	Yr	108	333	28	79	14	1	3	23	14	62	.237	.272	.312	.585	62	-19	-17	96	80	28	.469	2	1	0	9		0.0
1982	Sea-A	136	492	44	113	20	2	16	57	12	95	.230	.248	.376	.624	63	-23	-28	109	100	37	.489	2	10	-5	11	*S	-1.0
1983	Sea-A	65	216	21	41	4	2	7	21	7	56	.190	.222	.324	.546	48	-16	-16	100	90	15	.444	1	3	-2	10	S	-0.2
	Bal-A	81	221	16	46	9	1	3	27	15	52	.208	.262	.299	.560	54	-14	-14	100	141	14	.445	3	4	-2	-2	3/2	-1.7
	Yr	146	437	37	87	13	3	10	48	22	108	.199	.242	.311	.554	51	-30	-30	100	119	30	.447	4	7	-3	8		-1.9
1984	Bal-A	96	142	15	31	4	0	3	9	8	33	.218	.265	.310	.575	62	-8	-7	94	68	11	.462	1	4	-2	2	3/PD	-0.5
Total	6	544	1526	133	336	58	6	34	154	59	317	.220	.253	.333	.585	58	-88	-92	102	100	113	.479	9	24	-12	26	S3/2DPO	-4.2
■ **MIKE CUBBAGE** Cubbage, Michael Lee b: 7/21/50, Charlottesville, Va BL/TR, 6′, 180 lbs. Deb: 4/07/74																												
1974	Tex-A	9	15	0	0	0	0	0	0	0	4	.000	.000	.000	.000	-99	-4	-4	96	0	0	.000	0	0	0	0	/32	-0.3
1975	Tex-A	58	143	12	32	6	0	4	21	18	14	.224	.311	.350	.660	87	-3	-2	100	130	17	.602	0	0	0	2	2/3D	0.1
1976	Tex-A	14	32	2	7	0	0	0	0	7	7	.219	.359	.219	.578	70	-1	-1	102	0	3	.538	0	0	0	-0	/23D	0.0
	Min-A	104	342	40	89	19	5	3	49	42	37	.260	.346	.371	.718	112	5	6	98	138	44	.655	1	1	-0	1	3/2D	0.7
	Yr	118	374	42	96	19	5	3	49	49	44	.257	.347	.358	.706	108	4	5	99	122	48	.647	1	1	-0	1		0.7
1977	Min-A	129	417	60	110	16	5	9	55	37	49	.264	.324	.391	.715	91	-4	-5	103	115	53	.638	1	4	-2	7	*3/D	-0.2
1978	Min-A	125	394	40	111	12	7	7	57	40	44	.282	.349	.401	.750	117	6	9	94	126	56	.694	3	1	0	4	*3/2	1.2
1979	Min-A	94	243	26	67	10	1	2	23	39	26	.276	.376	.350	.726	89	1	-2	109	97	33	.672	1	8	-5	2	3D/12	-0.3
1980	Min-A	103	285	29	70	9	0	8	42	23	37	.246	.304	.361	.666	75	-7	-11	109	129	32	.577	0	1	-1	8	13/2D	-0.7
1981	NY-N	67	80	9	17	2	2	1	4	9	15	.213	.292	.325	.617	74	-3	-3	101	54	8	.538	0	0	0	0	3	-0.3
Total	8	703	1951	218	503	74	20	34	251	215	233	.258	.333	.369	.702	94	-9	-14	101	117	245	.645	6	15	-7	24	3/12D	0.2
■ **AL CUCCINELLO** Cuccinello, Alfred Edward b: 11/26/14, Long Island City, N.Y. BR/TR, 5′10″, 165 lbs. Deb: 5/17/35																												
1935	NY-N	54	165	27	41	7	1	4	20	1	20	.248	.262	.376	.638	72	-8	-7	96	97	15	.500	0			-1	2/3	-0.3
■ **TONY CUCCINELLO** Cuccinello, Anthony Francis "Cooch" or "Chick" b: 11/8/07, Long Island City, N.Y. BR/TR, 5′7″, 160 lbs. Deb: 4/15/30 C																												
1930	Cin-N	125	443	64	138	22	5	10	78	47	44	.312	.380	.451	.832	111	1	8	90	119	75	.833	5			-6	*32/S	0.4
1931	Cin-N	154	575	67	181	39	11	2	93	54	28	.315	.374	.431	.805	122	13	17	95	138	96	.769	1			6	*2	2.9
1932	Bro-N	154	597	76	168	32	6	12	77	46	47	.281	.337	.415	.752	105	1	4	96	107	86	.706	5			19	*2	3.3
1933	Bro-N	134	485	58	122	31	4	9	65	44	40	.252	.316	.388	.704	104	-0	2	97	116	57	.621	4			-19	*23	-0.8
1934	Bro-N	140	528	59	138	32	2	14	94	49	45	.261	.325	.409	.734	101	-4	-0	95	134	73	.668	0			4	*23	1.6
1935	Bro-N	102	360	49	105	20	3	8	53	40	35	.292	.366	.431	.796	120	7	10	94	109	57	.746	3			9	23	2.5
1936	Bos-N	150	565	68	174	26	3	7	86	58	49	.308	.374	.402	.776	115	9	13	95	130	89	.715	1			22	*2	4.2
1937	Bos-N	152	575	77	156	36	4	11	80	61	40	.271	.341	.405	.746	113	2	9	90	115	83	.688	2			-10	*2	0.6
1938	Bos-N	147	555	62	147	25	2	9	76	52	32	.265	.331	.366	.697	104	-6	2	88	127	67	.614	4			-28	*2	-1.5
1939	Bos-N	81	310	42	95	17	1	2	40	26	26	.306	.360	.387	.747	110	1	4	92	123	43	.674	5			-1	2	0.6
1940	Bos-N	34	126	14	34	9	0	0	19	8	9	.270	.319	.341	.660	83	-3	-3	99	167	13	.552	1			1	3	-0.2
	NY-N	88	307	26	64	9	2	5	36	16	42	.208	.248	.300	.547	50	-21	-21	100	125	21	.433	1			7	23	-1.1
	Yr	122	433	40	98	18	2	5	55	24	51	.226	.269	.312	.580	60	-24	-24	100	138	35	.471	2			7		-1.3
1942	Bos-N	40	104	8	21	3	0	1	8	9	11	.202	.265	.260	.525	57	-6	-6	95	99	7	.430	1			-0	32	-0.4
1943	Bos-N	13	19	0	0	0	0	0	2	3	1	.000	.136	.000	.136	-56	-4	-4	106	0	0	.158	0			0	/32S	-0.3
	Chi-A	34	103	5	28	5	0	2	11	13	13	.272	.353	.379	.732	113	2	2	101	89	15	.705	3	1	0	-1	3	0.2
1944	Chi-A	38	130	5	34	3	0	0	17	8	16	.262	.304	.285	.589	69	-5	-5	100	166	12	.459	0	0	0	2	3/2	-0.3
1945	Chi-A	118	402	50	124	25	3	2	49	45	19	.308	.379	.400	.780	133	14	16	95	108	64	.737	6	2	1	-2	*3	1.9
Total	15	1704	6184	730	1729	334	46	94	884	579	497	.280	.343	.394	.737	106	-1	48	94	122	857	.689	42	3		2	*23/S	13.6
■ **JIM CUDWORTH** Cudworth, James Alaric "Cuddy" b: 8/22/1858, Fairhaven, Mass. d: 12/21/43, Middleboro, Mass. BR/TR, 6′, 165 lbs. Deb: 7/27/1884																												
1884	KC-U	32	116	7	17	3	1	0		2		.147	.161	.190	.351	21	-10	-7	87	0	4	.242	0			0	1O/P	-0.5

YEAR	TM/L	G	AB	R	H	2B	3B	HR	RBI	BB	SO	AVG	OBP	SLG	PRO	/A	BR	/A	PF	CHI	RC	TA	SB	CS	SBR	FR	POS	TPR
■ **MANUEL CUETO** Cueto, Manuel "Potato" b: 2/8/1892, Guanajay, Cuba d: 6/29/42, Regla, Havana, Cuba BR/TR, 5'5", 157 lbs. Deb: 6/25/14																												
1914	StL-F	19	43	2	4	0	0	0	2	5	0	.093	.188	.093	.281	-17	-6	-7	106	180	1	.231	0			0	3/S2	-0.6
1917	Cin-N	56	140	10	28	3	0	1	11	16	17	.200	.287	.243	.529	68	-6	-4	92	115	11	.491	4			-1	O/2C	-0.6
1918	Cin-N	47	108	14	32	5	1	0	14	19	5	.296	.406	.361	.767	139	6	6	97	136	18	.829	4			-4	O2/SC	0.3
1919	Cin-N	29	88	10	22	2	0	0	4	10	4	.250	.340	.273	.613	81	-1	-2	105	65	10	.621	5			4	O/3	0.1
Total	4	151	379	36	86	10	1	1	31	50	26	.227	.323	.266	.590	81	-7	-7	98	117	39	.573	13			-1	/O2SC3	-0.8
■ **JOHN CULLEN** Cullen, John J. b: Marysville, Cal. Deb: 8/18/1884																												
1884	Bal-U	3	11	1	1	1	0	0		1		.091	.167	.182	.348	16	-1	-1	110	0	0	.300	0			0	/C	0.0
■ **LEON CULBERSON** Culberson, Delbert Leon "Lee" b: 8/6/19, Hall's Station, Ga. BR/TR, 5'11", 180 lbs. Deb: 5/16/43																												
1943	Bos-A	81	312	36	85	16	6	3	34	31	35	.272	.338	.391	.729	109	5	3	104	100	46	.720	14	0	4	2	O	0.8
1944	Bos-A	75	282	41	67	11	5	2	21	20	20	.238	.288	.333	.621	79	-9	-8	98	77	27	.536	6	4	-1	4	O	-0.6
1945	Bos-A	97	331	26	91	21	6	6	45	20	37	.275	.316	.429	.745	122	4	6	95	102	41	.646	4	3	-1	2	O	0.5
1946	Bos-A	59	179	34	56	10	1	3	18	16	19	.313	.369	.430	.799	107	5	2	114	80	29	.744	3	2	-0	-6	O/3	-0.6
1947	Bos-A	47	84	10	20	1	0	0	11	12	10	.238	.354	.250	.604	64	-3	-4	108	193	9	.552	1	1	-0	-4	O/3	-0.9
1948	Was-A	12	29	1	5	0	0	0	2	8	5	.172	.351	.172	.524	41	-2	-2	103	135	2	.500	0	0	0	-2	O	-0.3
Total	6	371	1217	148	324	59	18	14	131	107	126	.266	.327	.379	.706	100	1	-2	102	100	153	.662	28	10	2	-3	O/3	-1.1
■ **JOHN CULLEN** Cullen, John J. Deb: 8/18/1884																												
1884	WiL-U	9	31	2	6	0	0	0		1		.194	.219	.194	.412	39	-2	-2	103	0	1	.280	0			0	/OS	-0.1
■ **TIM CULLEN** Cullen, Timothy Leo b: 2/16/42, San Francisco, Cal. BR/TR, 6'1", 185 lbs. Deb: 8/08/66																												
1966	Was-A	18	34	8	8	1	0	0	0	2	8	.235	.278	.265	.542	60	-2	-2	95	0	3	.423	0	0	0	-0	/32	-0.1
1967	Was-A	124	402	35	95	7	0	2	31	40	47	.236	.307	.269	.576	70	-13	-14	102	113	35	.483	4	5	-2	11	S23/O	0.1
1968	Chi-A	72	155	16	31	7	0	2	13	15	23	.200	.275	.284	.559	69	-6	-6	101	111	12	.472	0	0	0	-8	2	-1.2
	Was-A	47	114	8	31	4	2	1	16	7	12	.272	.325	.368	.694	120	1	2	91	152	14	.600	0	0	0	1	S2/3	0.7
	Yr	119	269	24	62	11	2	3	29	22	35	.230	.296	.320	.616	89	-4	-4	97	128	27	.531	0	0	0	-7		-0.5
1969	Was-A	119	249	22	52	7	0	1	15	14	27	.209	.257	.249	.506	43	-19	-18	97	93	14	.374	1	1	-0	6	*2/S3	-0.8
1970	Was-A	123	262	22	56	10	2	1	18	31	38	.214	.304	.279	.583	64	-13	-12	96	96	22	.505	3	2	-0	12	*2/S	1.2
1971	Was-A	125	403	34	77	13	4	2	26	33	47	.191	.252	.258	.510	48	-29	-26	92	96	26	.412	2	0	1	5	2S	-1.1
1972	Oak-A	72	142	10	37	8	1	0	15	5	17	.261	.286	.331	.617	86	-3	-3	97	133	13	.477	0	1	-1	-2	2/3S	0.0
Total	7	700	1761	155	387	57	9	9	134	147	219	.220	.283	.278	.561	64	-85	-78	97	106	138	.473	10	9	-2	24	2S/3O	-1.2
■ **ROY CULLENBINE** Cullenbine, Roy Joseph b: 10/18/15, Nashville, Tenn. BB/TR, 6'1", 190 lbs. Deb: 4/19/38																												
1938	Det-A	25	67	12	19	1	3	0	9	12	9	.284	.392	.388	.780	96	-0	-0	100	117	11	.833	2	0	1	-1	O	0.0
1939	Det-A	75	179	31	43	9	2	6	23	34	29	.240	.362	.413	.775	88	-0	-4	111	84	29	.777	0	1	-1	-6	O/1	-1.0
1940	Bro-N	22	61	8	11	1	0	1	9	23	11	.180	.405	.246	.651	77	0	-1	108	185	8	.784	2			0	O	0.0
	StL-A	86	257	41	59	11	2	7	31	50	34	.230	.359	.370	.729	84	-3	-5	106	97	38	.728	0	1	-1	-2	O/1	-1.1
1941	StL-A	149	501	82	159	29	9	9	98	121	43	.317	.452	.465	.917	143	38	38	100	136	120	1.034	6	4	-1	1	*O1	2.9
1942	StL-A	38	109	15	21	7	1	2	14	30	20	.193	.367	.330	.697	93	1	0	104	117	16	.725	0	1	-1	-0	O/1	-0.2
	Was-A	64	241	30	69	19	0	2	35	44	18	.286	.396	.390	.787	127	9	10	96	131	41	.785	1	2	-1	3	O3	1.0
	NY-A	21	77	16	28	7	0	2	17	18	2	.364	.484	.532	1.017	187	10	10	99	112	22	1.157	0	1	-1	1	O/1	0.9
	Yr	123	427	61	118	33	1	6	66	92	40	.276	.405	.400	.805	128	19	20	99	125	79	.841	1	4	-2	4		1.7
1943	Cle-A	138	488	66	141	24	4	8	56	96	58	.289	.407	.404	.811	152	27	34	90	98	89	.827	3	4	-2	-1	*O1	2.9
1944	Cle-A	154	571	98	162	34	5	16	80	87	49	.284	.380	.445	.825	135	28	28	100	101	102	.818	4	4	-1	-5	*O	1.7
1945	Cle-A	8	13	3	1	1	0	0	0	11	0	.077	.500	.154	.654	95	1	1	99	0	2	1.083	0	0	0	-1	/O3	0.0
	Det-A	146	523	80	145	27	5	18	93	102	36	.277	.398	.451	.849	138	34	30	106	112	103	.882	2	0	1	11	*O	3.7
	Yr	154	536	83	146	28	5	18	93	**113**	36	.272	.402	.444	.846	138	35	31	106	106	106	**.888**	2	0	1	9		3.7
1946	Det-A	113	328	63	110	21	0	15	56	88	39	.335	.477	.537	1.014	169	42	38	108	96	95	1.202	3	0	1	-1	O1	3.4
1947	Det-A	142	464	82	104	18	1	24	78	137	51	.224	.401	.422	.823	124	24	21	104	113	91	.903	3	2	-0	13	*1	3.1
Total	10	1181	3879	627	1072	209	32	110	599	853	399	.276	.408	.432	.840	131	211	201	102	111	769	.904	26	20		12	O1/3	17.3
■ **DICK CULLER** Culler, Richard Broadus b: 1/15/15, High Point, N.C. d: 6/16/64, Chapel Hill, N.C. BR/TR, 5'9.5", 155 lbs. Deb: 9/19/36																												
1936	Phi-A	9	38	3	9	0	0	0	1	1	3	.237	.256	.237	.493	22	-5	-5	101	35	2	.345	0	0	0	1	/2S	-0.2
1943	Chi-A	53	148	9	32	5	1	0	11	16	11	.216	.297	.264	.560	64	-6	-7	101	103	11	.480	4	5	-2	-0	32/S	-0.7
1944	Bos-N	8	28	2	2	0	0	0	0	4	2	.071	.188	.071	.259	-27	-5	-4	95	0	0	.222	0			0	/S	-0.3
1945	Bos-N	136	527	87	138	12	1	2	30	50	35	.262	.328	.300	.628	67	-16	-25	112	67	54	.547	7			-5	*S/3	-1.6
1946	Bos-N	134	482	70	123	15	3	0	33	62	18	.255	.342	.299	.641	88	-9	-6	95	87	51	.575	7			-8	*S	-0.4
1947	Bos-N	77	214	20	53	5	1	0	19	19	15	.248	.309	.280	.589	59	-13	-12	97	117	19	.482	1			-6	S	-1.1
1948	Chi-N	48	89	4	15	2	0	0	5	13	3	.169	.275	.191	.466	30	-9	-8	93	110	5	.385	0			4	S/2	0.1
1949	NY-N	7	1	0	0	0	0	0	0	1	0	.000	.500	.000	.500	45	0	0	102	0	0	1.000	0			0	/S	0.1
Total	8	472	1527	195	372	39	6	2	99	166	87	.244	.320	.281	.601	67	-62	-66	102	84	144	.534	19	5		-15	S/32	-4.1
■ **NICK CULLOP** Cullop, Henry Nicholas "Tomato Face" b: 10/16/1900, St.Louis, Mo. d: 12/8/78, Westerville, Ohio BR/TR, 6', 200 lbs. Deb: 4/14/26																												
1926	NY-A	2	2	0	1	0	0	0	0	0	1	.500	.500	.500	1.000	162	0	0	99	0	0	1.000	0	0	0	0	H	0.0
1927	Was-A	15	23	2	5	2	0	0	1	1	6	.217	.250	.304	.554	45	-2	-2	97	47	2	.444	0	0	0	-1	/O1	-0.2
	Cle-A	32	68	9	16	2	3	1	8	9	19	.235	.333	.397	.730	92	-1	-1	97	89	9	.712	0	0	0	3	O/P	0.1
	Yr	47	91	11	21	4	3	1	9	10	25	.231	.314	.374	.687	80	-3	-3	97	77	11	.643	0	0	0	2		-0.1
1929	Bro-N	13	41	7	8	2	2	1	5	8	7	.195	.327	.415	.741	87	-1	-1	94	86	6	.758	0			1	O/1	0.0
1930	Cin-N	7	22	2	4	0	0	1	5	1	9	.182	.217	.318	.536	30	-3	-2	90	172	1	.444	0			1	/O	-0.1
1931	Cin-N	104	334	29	88	23	7	8	48	21	86	.263	.309	.446	.755	106	-1	1	95	99	47	.699	1			-5	O	-0.8
Total	5	173	490	49	122	29	12	11	67	40	128	.249	.308	.424	.733	96	-8	-5	95	97	65	.682	1	0		-2	O/1P	-1.0
■ **WIL CULMER** Culmer, Wilfred Hillard b: 11/11/58, Nassau, Bahamas BR/TR, 6'4", 210 lbs. Deb: 4/12/83																												
1983	Cle-A	7	19	0	2	0	0	0	1	0	4	.105	.105	.105	.211	-40	-4	-4	105	195	0	.105	0	1	-1	-1	/OD	-0.5
■ **BENNY CULP** Culp, Benjamin Baldy b: 1/19/14, Philadelphia, Pa. BR/TR, 5'9", 175 lbs. Deb: 9/17/42 C																												
1942	Phi-N	1	0	0	0	0	0	0	0	0	0	—	—	—	—	—	0	0	94	—	—	—	0			0	/C	0.0
1943	Phi-N	10	24	4	5	1	0	0	2	3	3	.208	.296	.250	.546	62	-1	-1	94	120	2	.450	0			0	C	0.0
1944	Phi-N	4	2	1	0	0	0	0	0	0	0	.000	.000	.000	.000	-99	-1	-1	100	0	0	.000	0			0	/C	0.0
Total	3	15	26	5	5	1	0	0	2	3	3	.192	.276	.231	.507	50	-2	-2	94	112	2	.429	0			0	/C	0.0
■ **JACK CUMMINGS** Cummings, John William b: 4/1/04, Pittsburgh, Pa. d: 10/5/62, W.Mifflin, Pa. BR/TR, 6', 195 lbs. Deb: 9/11/26																												
1926	NY-N	7	16	3	5	3	0	0	4	4	2	.313	.450	.500	.950	159	1	2	98	173	4	1.091	0			-1	/C	0.1
1927	NY-N	43	80	8	29	6	1	2	14	5	10	.363	.407	.538	.944	152	6	6	100	100	17	.961	0			-3	C	0.5
1928	NY-N	33	27	4	9	2	0	2	9	3	4	.333	.400	.630	1.030	162	2	2	102	139	7	1.111	0			-0	/C	0.2
1929	NY-N	3	3	0	1	0	0	0	0	0	0	.333	.333	.333	.667	66	-0	-0	100	0	0	.500	0			0	/C	0.0
	Bos-N	3	6	0	1	0	0	0	1	0	2	.167	.167	.167	.333	-18	-1	-1	94	342	0	.200	0			0	/C	0.0
	Yr	6	9	0	2	0	0	0	1	0	2	.222	.222	.222	.444	11	-1	-1	97	171	0	.286	0			0		0.0
Total	4	89	132	15	45	11	1	4	28	12	18	.341	.400	.530	.930	145	8	8	100	126	28	.954	0			-4	/C	0.8
■ **JOE CUNNINGHAM** Cunningham, Joseph Robert b: 8/27/31, Paterson, N.J. BL/TL, 6', 180 lbs. Deb: 6/30/54 C																												
1954	StL-N	85	310	40	88	11	3	11	50	43	40	.284	.375	.445	.820	112	6	6	100	117	55	.814	1	1	-0	7	1	1.0
1956	StL-N	4	3	1	0	0	0	0	0	1	1	.000	.250	.000	.250	-25	-1	-1	99	0	0	.333	0	0	0	0	/1	0.0
1957	StL-N	122	261	50	83	15	0	9	52	56	29	.318	.447	.479	.926	148	22	21	101	142	61	1.027	3	3	-1	-5	1O	0.9
1958	StL-N	131	337	61	105	20	3	12	57	82	23	.312	.450	.496	.946	141	29	26	106	116	80	1.045	4	4	-1	-5	1O	1.3
1959	StL-N	144	458	65	158	28	6	7	60	88	47	.345	**.456**	.478	.934	142	38	35	105	103	104	.997	2	6	-3	-6	*O1	2.2
1960	StL-N	139	492	68	138	28	3	6	39	59	59	.280	.364	.386	.751	98	6	0	108	78	70	.694	1	7	-4	-8	*O1	-1.6
1961	StL-N	113	322	60	92	11	2	7	40	53	32	.286	.404	.398	.802	101	9	3	113	108	58	.835	1	0	0	-8	O1	-0.9

YEAR	TM/L	G	AB	R	H	2B	3B	HR	RBI	BB	SO	AVG	OBP	SLG	PRO	/A	BR	/A	PF	CHI	RC	TA	SB	CS	SBR	FR	POS	TPR
1962	Chi-A	149	526	91	155	32	7	8	70	101	59	.295	.415	.428	.843	134	25	29	95	118	102	.880	3	3	-1	-7	*1/O	1.1
1963	Chi-A	67	210	32	60	12	1	1	31	33	23	.286	.393	.367	.759	110	6	5	104	162	33	.747	1	0	0	-4	1	0.0
1964	Chi-A	40	108	13	27	7	0	0	10	14	15	.250	.352	.315	.667	91	-1	-1	96	125	13	.622	0	1	-1	-1	1	-0.2
	Was-A	49	126	15	27	4	0	0	7	23	13	.214	.344	.246	.590	67	-4	-5	101	96	12	.538	0	1	-1	-1	1	-0.7
	Yr	89	234	28	54	11	0	0	17	37	28	.231	.348	.278	.626	78	-6	-5	98	110	25	.575	0	2	-1	-1		-0.9
1965	Was-A	95	201	29	46	9	1	3	20	46	27	.229	.375	.328	.703	102	3	3	100	111	27	.693	0	1	-1	0	1	0.0
1966	Was-A	3	8	0	1	0	0	0	0	0	1	.125	.125	.125	.250	-29	-1	-1	95	0	0	.143	0	0	0	0	/1	-0.1
Total	12	1141	3362	525	980	177	26	64	436	599	369	.291	.406	.417	.823	119	136	122	103	112	614	.857	16	27	-11	-37	1O	3.0

■ **RAY CUNNINGHAM** Cunningham, Raymond Lee b: 1/17/08, Mesquite, Tex. BR/TR, 5'7.5", 150 lbs. Deb: 9/16/31

YEAR	TM/L	G	AB	R	H	2B	3B	HR	RBI	BB	SO	AVG	OBP	SLG	PRO	/A	BR	/A	PF	CHI	RC	TA	SB	CS	SBR	FR	POS	TPR
1931	StL-N	3	4	0	0	0	0	0	1	0	0	.000	.000	.000	.000	-94	-1	-1	107	0	0	.000	0			0	/3	0.0
1932	StL-N	11	22	4	4	1	0	0	0	3	4	.182	.280	.227	.507	38	-2	-2	100	0	2	.444	0			-0	/32	0.0
Total	2	14	26	4	4	1	0	0	1	3	4	.154	.241	.192	.434	18	-3	-3	101	0	2	.364	0			-0	/32	0.0

■ **BILL CUNNINGHAM** Cunningham, William Aloysius b: 7/30/1895, San Francisco, Cal d: 9/26/53, Colusa, Cal. BR/TR, 5'8", 155 lbs. Deb: 7/14/21 C

YEAR	TM/L	G	AB	R	H	2B	3B	HR	RBI	BB	SO	AVG	OBP	SLG	PRO	/A	BR	/A	PF	CHI	RC	TA	SB	CS	SBR	FR	POS	TPR
1921	NY-N	40	76	10	21	2	1	1	12	3	3	.276	.313	.368	.681	82	-2	-2	98	142	8	.571	0	1	-1	-3	O	-0.5
1922	NY-N	85	229	37	75	15	2	2	33	7	9	.328	.350	.437	.787	98	0	-1	104	109	33	.704	4	5	-2	0	O/3	-0.4
1923	NY-N	79	203	22	55	7	1	5	27	10	9	.271	.305	.389	.694	81	-6	-6	101	101	24	.627	5	2	0	-3	O/2	-1.0
1924	Bos-N	114	437	44	119	15	8	1	40	32	27	.272	.326	.350	.676	87	-11	-8	94	99	51	.607	8	5	-1	8	*O	-0.2
Total	4	318	945	113	270	39	12	9	112	52	48	.286	.326	.381	.707	88	-19	-17	98	105	116	.631	17	13	-3	2	O/23	-2.1

■ **BILL CUNNINGHAM** Cunningham, William James b: 6/9/1888, Schenectady, N.Y. d: 2/21/46, Schenectady, N.Y. BR/TR, 5'9", 170 lbs. Deb: 9/12/10

YEAR	TM/L	G	AB	R	H	2B	3B	HR	RBI	BB	SO	AVG	OBP	SLG	PRO	/A	BR	/A	PF	CHI	RC	TA	SB	CS	SBR	FR	POS	TPR
1910	Was-A	21	74	3	22	5	1	0	14	12		.297	.402	.392	.794	148	5	5	101	157	14	.885	4			-1	2	0.2
1911	Was-A	94	331	34	63	10	5	3	37	19		.190	.239	.278	.517	45	-26	-25	97	126	25	.459	10			-6	2	-3.0
1912	Was-A	8	27	5	5	1	0	1	8	3		.185	.267	.333	.600	72	-1	-1	99	227	3	.636	2			-0	/2	-0.1
Total	3	123	432	42	90	16	6	4	59	34		.208	.271	.301	.572	64	-22	-21	98	138	41	.535	16			-7	2	-2.9

■ **DOC CURLEY** Curley, Walter James b: 3/12/1874, Upton, Mass. d: 9/23/20, Framingham, Mass. BR/TR, Deb: 9/12/1899

YEAR	TM/L	G	AB	R	H	2B	3B	HR	RBI	BB	SO	AVG	OBP	SLG	PRO	/A	BR	/A	PF	CHI	RC	TA	SB	CS	SBR	FR	POS	TPR
1899	Chi-N	10	37	7	4	0	1	0	2	3		.108	.195	.162	.357	-0	-5	-5	96	108	1	.303	0			0	2	-0.3

■ **PETE CURREN** Curren, Peter b: Baltimore, Md. Deb: 9/12/1876

YEAR	TM/L	G	AB	R	H	2B	3B	HR	RBI	BB	SO	AVG	OBP	SLG	PRO	/A	BR	/A	PF	CHI	RC	TA	SB	CS	SBR	FR	POS	TPR
1876	Phi-N	3	12	5	4	1	0	0	2	0	0	.333	.333	.417	.750	150	1	1	99	135	2	.625				0	/CO	0.1

■ **PERRY CURRIN** Currin, Perry Gilmore b: 9/27/28, Washington, D.C. BL/TR, 6', 175 lbs. Deb: 6/29/47

YEAR	TM/L	G	AB	R	H	2B	3B	HR	RBI	BB	SO	AVG	OBP	SLG	PRO	/A	BR	/A	PF	CHI	RC	TA	SB	CS	SBR	FR	POS	TPR
1947	StL-A	3	2	0	0	0	0	0	0	1	0	.000	.333	.000	.333	-3	-0	-0	102	0	0	.500	0	0	0	0	/S	0.0

■ **TONY CURRY** Curry, George Anthony b: 12/22/38, Nassau, Bahamas BL/TL, 5'11", 185 lbs. Deb: 4/12/60

YEAR	TM/L	G	AB	R	H	2B	3B	HR	RBI	BB	SO	AVG	OBP	SLG	PRO	/A	BR	/A	PF	CHI	RC	TA	SB	CS	SBR	FR	POS	TPR
1960	Phi-N	95	245	26	64	14	2	6	34	16	53	.261	.309	.408	.717	88	-2	-5	107	117	31	.636	0	2	-1	-9	O	-1.6
1961	Phi-N	15	36	3	7	2	0	0	3	1	8	.194	.216	.250	.466	25	-4	-4	94	134	2	.345	0	0	0	-1	/O	-0.4
1966	Cle-A	19	16	4	2	0	0	0	3	3	8	.125	.263	.125	.388	15	-2	-2	101	630	1	.357	0	0	0	0	H	-0.1
Total	3	129	297	33	73	16	2	6	40	20	69	.246	.296	.374	.669	77	-8	-10	105	150	34	.584	0	2	-1	-9	/O	-2.1

■ **JIM CURRY** Curry, James E. b: 3/10/1893, Camden, N.J. d: 8/2/38, Lakeland, N.J. BR/TR, 5'11", 160 lbs. Deb: 10/02/09

YEAR	TM/L	G	AB	R	H	2B	3B	HR	RBI	BB	SO	AVG	OBP	SLG	PRO	/A	BR	/A	PF	CHI	RC	TA	SB	CS	SBR	FR	POS	TPR
1909	Phi-A	1	4	1	1	0	0	0	0	0		.250	.250	.250	.500	57	-0	-0	102	0	0	.333	0			0	/2	0.0
1911	NY-A	4	11	3	2	0	0	0	0	1		.182	.250	.182	.432	19	-1	-1	111	0	0	.333	0			0	/2	0.0
1918	Det-A	5	20	1	5	1	0	0	0	0	0	.250	.286	.300	.586	79	-1	-1	97	0	2	.467	0			-0	/2	0.0
Total	3	10	35	5	8	1	0	0	0	1	0	.229	.270	.257	.527	55	-2	-2	102	0	2	.407	0			-0	/2	0.0

■ **GENE CURTIS** Curtis, Eugene Holmes "Euge" b: 5/5/1883, Bethany, W.Va. d: 1/1/19, Steubenville, Ohio BR/TR, 6'3", 220 lbs. Deb: 03

YEAR	TM/L	G	AB	R	H	2B	3B	HR	RBI	BB	SO	AVG	OBP	SLG	PRO	/A	BR	/A	PF	CHI	RC	TA	SB	CS	SBR	FR	POS	TPR
1903	Pit-N	5	19	2	8	1	0	0	3	1		.421	.450	.474	.924	158	2	1	105	109	4	.909	0			-0	/O	0.1

■ **FRED CURTIS** Curtis, Frederick Marion b: 10/30/1880, Beaver Lake, Mich. d: 4/5/39, Minneapolis, Minn. BR/TR, 6'1", Deb: 7/24/05

YEAR	TM/L	G	AB	R	H	2B	3B	HR	RBI	BB	SO	AVG	OBP	SLG	PRO	/A	BR	/A	PF	CHI	RC	TA	SB	CS	SBR	FR	POS	TPR
1905	NY-A	2	9	0	2	1	0	0	2	1		.222	.300	.333	.633	101	0	0	102	205	1	.714	1			0	/1	0.0

■ **HARRY CURTIS** Curtis, Harry Albert b: 2/19/1883, Portland, Maine d: 8/1/51, Evanston, Ill. TR , Deb: 8/28/07

YEAR	TM/L	G	AB	R	H	2B	3B	HR	RBI	BB	SO	AVG	OBP	SLG	PRO	/A	BR	/A	PF	CHI	RC	TA	SB	CS	SBR	FR	POS	TPR
1907	NY-N	6	9	2	2	0	0	0	1	2		.222	.364	.222	.586	82	0	-0	105	189	1	.857	2			-0	/C	0.0

■ **JIM CURTIS** Curtis, James D. BL , 5'8.5", 157 lbs. Deb: 7/15/1891

YEAR	TM/L	G	AB	R	H	2B	3B	HR	RBI	BB	SO	AVG	OBP	SLG	PRO	/A	BR	/A	PF	CHI	RC	TA	SB	CS	SBR	FR	POS	TPR
1891	Cin-N	27	108	11	29	3	3	1	13	9	19	.269	.331	.380	.710	119	1	3	91	83	15	.684	3			0	O	0.2
	Was-a	29	103	17	26	3	2	0	12	13	16	.252	.347	.320	.668	99	-0	0	95	107	12	.649	2			0	O	0.0
Total	1	56	211	28	55	6	5	1	25	22	35	.261	.339	.351	.690	109	1	3	93	95	27	.667	5			0	/O	0.2

■ **GUY CURTWRIGHT** Curtwright, Guy Paxton b: 10/18/12, Holliday, Mo. BR/TR, 5'11", 200 lbs. Deb: 4/21/43

YEAR	TM/L	G	AB	R	H	2B	3B	HR	RBI	BB	SO	AVG	OBP	SLG	PRO	/A	BR	/A	PF	CHI	RC	TA	SB	CS	SBR	FR	POS	TPR
1943	Chi-A	138	488	67	142	20	7	3	48	69	60	.291	.382	.379	.761	122	16	16	101	96	74	.732	13	12	-3	-2	*O	0.8
1944	Chi-A	72	198	22	50	8	2	2	23	23	21	.253	.330	.343	.674	93	-2	-2	100	112	23	.609	4	3	-1	0	O	-0.3
1945	Chi-A	98	324	51	91	15	7	4	32	39	29	.281	.358	.407	.766	128	9	11	95	80	49	.716	3	4	-2	3	O	0.9
1946	Chi-A	23	55	7	11	2	0	0	5	11	14	.200	.333	.236	.570	63	-2	-2	97	146	4	.500	0	1	-1	0	O	-0.2
Total	4	331	1065	147	294	45	16	9	108	142	124	.276	.363	.374	.737	115	21	23	99	97	150	.709	20	20	-6	1	O	1.2

■ **TONY CUSICK** Cusick, Andrew Daniel "And b: 1860, Fall River, Mass. d: 8/6/29, Chicago, Ill. BR/TR, 5'9.5", 190 lbs. Deb: 8/21/1884

YEAR	TM/L	G	AB	R	H	2B	3B	HR	RBI	BB	SO	AVG	OBP	SLG	PRO	/A	BR	/A	PF	CHI	RC	TA	SB	CS	SBR	FR	POS	TPR
1884	WiL-U	11	34	0	5	0	0	0		1		.147	.171	.147	.318	8	-3	-3	103	0	1	.207	0			0	/CSO23	-0.2
	Phi-N	9	29	2	4	0	0	0	1	0	3	.138	.138	.138	.276	-14	-4	-3	92	86	1	.160				0	/C	-0.2
1885	Phi-N	39	141	12	25	1	0	0	5	1	24	.177	.183	.184	.367	18	-12	-13	104	68	5	.233				-4	C/O	-1.2
1886	Phi-N	29	104	10	23	5	1	0	4	3	14	.221	.243	.288	.531	62	-5	-5	98	44	8	.420	1			0	C/O1	-0.3
1887	Phi-N	7	24	3	7	1	0	0	5	3	1	.292	.393	.333	.726	109	0	1	97	196	3	.706	0			0	/C12	0.0
Total	4	95	332	27	64	7	1	0	15	8	42	.193	.214	.220	.434	36	-24	-24	100	66	17	.310	1			-4	/CO1S23	-1.9

■ **JACK CUSICK** Cusick, John Peter b: 6/12/28, Weehawken, N.J. BR/TR, 6', 170 lbs. Deb: 4/24/51

YEAR	TM/L	G	AB	R	H	2B	3B	HR	RBI	BB	SO	AVG	OBP	SLG	PRO	/A	BR	/A	PF	CHI	RC	TA	SB	CS	SBR	FR	POS	TPR
1951	Chi-N	65	164	16	29	3	2	2	16	17	29	.177	.254	.256	.510	39	-15	-14	97	129	11	.436	2	1	0	-1	S	-1.0
1952	Bos-N	49	78	5	13	1	0	0	6	6	9	.167	.226	.179	.406	15	-9	-9	95	167	2	.278	0	1	-1	1	S/3	-0.7
Total	2	114	242	21	42	4	2	2	22	23	38	.174	.245	.231	.477	31	-24	-22	97	141	13	.389	2	2	-1	-0	/S3	-1.7

■ **NED CUTHBERT** Cuthbert, Edgar Edward b: 6/20/1845, Philadelphia, Pa. d: 2/6/05, St.Louis, Mo. BR/TR, 5'6", 140 lbs. Deb: 5/20/1871 M

YEAR	TM/L	G	AB	R	H	2B	3B	HR	RBI	BB	SO	AVG	OBP	SLG	PRO	/A	BR	/A	PF	CHI	RC	TA	SB	CS	SBR	FR	POS	TPR
1871	Ath-n	28	162	47	39							.241															*O/C	
1872	Ath-n	46	265	80	87							.328															*O	
1873	Phi-n	51	284	79	75							.264															*O	
1874	Chi-n	58	306	64	79							.258															*O/C	
1875	StL-n	68	308	69	82							.266															*O/C	
1876	StL-N	63	283	46	70	10	1	0	25	7	4	.247	.266	.290	.555	97	-4	1	88	99	22	.418				-7	*O	-0.5
1877	Cin-N	12	56	6	10	5	0	0	2	1	2	.179	.193	.268	.461	53	-4	-2	82	39	3	.348				0	O	-0.1
1882	StL-a	60	233	28	52	16	5	0		17		.223	.276	.335	.611	105	2	2	100	0	22	.525				-4	*OM	-0.2
1883	StL-a	21	71	3	12	1	0	0		4		.169	.213	.183	.396	27	-5	-6	108	0	3	.288				0	O/1	-0.5
1884	Bal-U	44	168	29	34	5	0	0		10		.202	.247	.232	.479	57	-6	-9	110	0	10	.366	0			-5	O	-1.2
Total	5 n	251	1325	339	362							.273															O	
Total	5	200	811	112	178	37	6	0	27	39	6	.219	.255	.280	.535	80	-18	-14	97	36	60	.420	0			-16	O/C1	-2.5

■ **GEORGE CUTSHAW** Cutshaw, George William "Clancy" b: 7/27/1887, Wilmington, Ill. d: 8/22/73, San Diego, Cal. BR/TR, 5'9", 160 lbs. Deb: 4/25/12

YEAR	TM/L	G	AB	R	H	2B	3B	HR	RBI	BB	SO	AVG	OBP	SLG	PRO	/A	BR	/A	PF	CHI	RC	TA	SB	CS	SBR	FR	POS	TPR
1912	Bro-N	102	357	41	100	14	4	0	28	31	16	.280	.341	.342	.683	91	-6	-4	95	79	47	.665	16			-1	2/3S	-0.7
1913	Bro-N	147	592	72	158	23	13	7	80	39	22	.267	.315	.385	.701	95	-2	-5	104	103	80	.712	39			18	*2	0.9
1914	Bro-N	153	583	69	150	22	12	2	78	30	32	.257	.297	.346	.644	90	-8	-9	101	144	67	.621	34			26	*2	1.7
1915	Bro-N	154	566	68	139	18	9	0	62	34	35	.246	.293	.309	.602	81	-13	-13	101	143	53	.536	28	23	-5	17	*2	0.0
1916	Bro-N	154	581	58	151	21	4	2	63	25	32	.260	.292	.320	.612	85	-9	-11	103	138	58	.531	27	20	-4	8	*2	0.1
1917	Bro-N	135	487	42	126	17	7	4	49	21	26	.259	.292	.347	.639	92	-4	-6	104	107	54	.593	22			-10	*2	-0.8

YEAR	TM/L	G	AB	R	H	2B	3B	HR	RBI	BB	SO	AVG	OBP	SLG	PRO	/A	BR	/A	PF	CHI	RC	TA	SB	CS	SBR	FR	POS	TPR
1918	Pit-N	126	463	56	132	16	10	5	68	27	18	.285	.326	.395	.721	113	9	6	106	138	66	.713	25			-2	*2	1.2
1919	Pit-N	139	512	49	124	15	8	3	51	30	22	.242	.287	.320	.607	78	-11	-14	105	121	54	.598	36			-10	*2	-2.2
1920	Pit-N	131	488	56	123	16	8	0	47	23	10	.252	.287	.318	.605	73	-17	-18	101	124	44	.517	17	14	-3	2	*2	-1.6
1921	Pit-N	98	350	46	119	18	4	0	53	11	11	.340	.362	.414	.776	101	2	1	103	134	52	.725	14	5	1	-22	2	-1.8
1922	Det-A	132	499	57	133	14	8	2	61	20	13	.267	.300	.339	.639	68	-25	-24	98	127	52	.550	11	5	0	3	*2	-1.0
1923	Det-A	45	143	15	32	1	2	0	13	9	5	.224	.279	.259	.538	44	-12	-11	97	120	12	.446	2	1	0	-3	2/3	-1.1
Total	12	1516	5621	629	1487	195	89	25	653	300	242	.265	.305	.344	.649	86	-97	-108	102	124	639	.603	271	68		27	*2/3S	-5.3
■ **KIKI CUYLER**	Cuyler, Hazen Shirley b: 8/30/1899, Harrisville, Mich. d: 2/11/50, Ann Arbor, Mich. BR/TR, 5'10.5", 180 lbs. Deb: 9/29/21 CH																											
1921	Pit-N	1	3	0	0	0	0	0	0	0	1	.000	.000	.000	.000	-97	-1	-1	103	0	0	.000	0	0	0	-0	/O	0.0
1922	Pit-N	1	0	0	0	0	0	0	0	0	0	—	—	—	—	—	0	0	104	—	—	—	0	0	0	0	R	0.0
1923	Pit-N	11	40	4	10	1	1	0	2	5	3	.250	.348	.325	.673	81	-1	-1	97	57	4	.636	2	3	-1	0	O	-0.1
1924	Pit-N	117	466	94	165	27	16	9	85	30	62	.354	.402	.539	.940	141	32	28	106	107	101	1.026	32	11	3	6	*O	3.4
1925	Pit-N	153	617	**144**	220	43	**26**	18	102	58	56	.357	.423	.598	1.021	155	53	51	102	82	158	1.173	41	13	5	6	*O	5.3
1926	Pit-N	157	614	**113**	197	31	15	8	92	50	66	.321	.380	.459	.840	111	22	11	112	100	105	.902	**35**			15	*O	2.0
1927	Pit-N	85	285	60	88	13	7	3	31	37	36	.309	.394	.435	.829	119	10	9	102	82	49	.934	20			4	O	1.0
1928	Chi-N	133	499	92	142	25	9	17	79	51	61	.285	.359	.473	.832	123	11	15	95	104	84	.927	**37**			7	*O	1.6
1929	Chi-N	139	509	111	183	29	7	15	102	66	56	.360	.438	.532	.970	137	33	32	101	113	118	1.181	**43**			8	*O	2.6
1930	Chi-N	156	642	155	228	50	17	13	134	72	49	.355	.428	.547	.975	127	37	31	105	105	148	1.135	**37**			-0	*O	1.7
1931	Chi-N	154	613	100	202	37	12	9	88	72	54	.330	.404	.473	.877	141	32	36	96	95	122	.925	13			3	*O	3.0
1932	Chi-N	110	446	58	130	19	9	10	77	29	43	.291	.340	.442	.782	104	5	2	104	121	68	.756	9			-4	*O	-0.8
1933	Chi-N	70	262	37	83	13	3	5	35	21	29	.317	.376	.447	.823	138	12	13	97	106	43	.772	4			-8	O	0.1
1934	Chi-N	142	559	80	189	**42**	8	6	69	31	62	.338	.377	.474	.851	129	20	22	98	93	101	.829	15			-3	*O	1.2
1935	Chi-N	45	157	22	42	5	1	4	18	10	16	.268	.331	.389	.720	93	-2	-1	99	89	21	.669	3			2	O	0.0
	Cin-N	62	223	36	56	8	3	2	22	27	18	.251	.337	.341	.678	89	-5	-3	93	102	28	.651	5			0	O	-0.4
	Yr	107	380	58	98	13	4	6	40	37	34	.258	.335	.361	.695	91	-6	-4	96	98	50	.665	8			3		-0.4
1936	Cin-N	144	567	96	185	29	11	7	74	47	67	.326	.380	.453	.833	128	19	21	97	100	102	.828	16			-12	*O	0.3
1937	Cin-N	117	406	48	110	12	4	0	32	36	50	.271	.333	.320	.654	86	-11	-7	91	90	43	.572	10			-7	*O	-1.8
1938	Bro-N	82	253	45	69	10	8	2	23	34	23	.273	.363	.399	.763	114	4	6	96	78	39	.753	6			-1	O	0.3
Total	18	1879	7161	1295	2299	394	157	128	1065	676	752	.321	.386	.474	.860	125	270	265	100	99	1336	.915	328	27		17	*O	19.4
■ **AL CYPERT**	Cypert, Alfred Boyd "Cy" b: 8/8/1889, Little Rock, Ark. d: 1/9/73, Washington, D.C. BR/TR, 5'10.5", 150 lbs. Deb: 6/27/14																											
1914	Cle-A	1	1	0	0	0	0	0	0	0	0	.000	.000	.000	.000	-98	-0	-0	102	0	0	.000	0			0	/3	0.0
■ **PAUL DADE**	Dade, Lonnie Paul b: 12/7/51, Seattle, Wash. BR/TR, 6'1", 185 lbs. Deb: 9/12/75																											
1975	Cal-A	11	30	5	6	4	0	0	1	6	7	.200	.333	.333	.667	94	-0	-0	95	38	4	.667	0	0	0	0	/O3D	0.0
1976	Cal-A	13	9	2	1	0	0	0	1	3	3	.111	.333	.111	.444	37	-1	-0	92	384	0	.444	0	0	0	-1	/O23D	0.0
1977	Cle-A	134	461	65	134	15	3	3	45	32	58	.291	.339	.356	.695	92	-6	-4	98	103	54	.617	16	8	0	0	O3/2D	-0.7
1978	Cle-A	93	307	37	78	12	1	3	20	34	45	.254	.332	.329	.661	93	-5	-2	93	72	35	.618	12	9	-2	2	O/D	-0.3
1979	Cle-A	44	170	22	48	4	1	3	18	12	22	.282	.330	.371	.700	84	-3	-4	106	102	21	.674	12	6	0	1	O/3D	-0.4
	SD-N	76	283	38	78	19	2	1	19	14	48	.276	.314	.367	.682	89	-6	-5	96	72	32	.616	13	5	1	7	3/O	0.0
1980	SD-N	68	53	17	10	0	0	0	3	12	10	.189	.338	.189	.527	54	-3	-2	93	119	4	.520	4	5	-2	-1	3/O2	-0.5
Total	6	439	1313	186	355	54	7	10	107	113	193	.270	.331	.345	.676	89	-23	-18	97	90	151	.633	57	33	-3	9	O3/D2	-1.9
■ **ANGELO DAGRES**	Dagres, Angelo George "Junior" b: 8/22/34, Newburyport, Mass. BL/TL, 5'11", 175 lbs. Deb: 9/11/55																											
1955	Bal-A	8	15	5	4	0	0	0	3	1	2	.267	.313	.267	.579	63	-1	-1	90	280	2	.455	0	0	0	-1	/O	-0.1
■ **BILL DAHLEN**	Dahlen, William Frederick "Bad Bill" b: 1/5/1870, Helliston, N.Y. d: 12/5/50, Brooklyn, N.Y. BR/TR, 5'9", 180 lbs. Deb: 4/22/1891 M																											
1891	Chi-N	135	549	114	143	18	13	9	76	67	60	.260	.348	.390	.738	110	12	7	106	88	84	.761	21			11	3OS	1.6
1892	Chi-N	143	581	114	169	23	19	5	58	45	56	.291	.347	.422	.769	145	22	28	92	61	109	.862	60			24	S3/O2	**5.5**
1893	Chi-N	116	485	113	146	28	15	5	64	58	30	.301	.381	.452	.833	119	16	12	104	66	98	.923	31			8	*SO2/3	1.9
1894	Chi-N	121	502	149	179	32	14	15	107	76	33	.357	.444	.566	1.010	134	37	29	108	79	148	1.254	42			**32**	S3	**4.8**
1895	Chi-N	129	516	106	131	19	10	7	62	61	51	.254	.344	.370	.714	83	-10	-13	103	72	81	.779	38			29	*S/O	2.1
1896	Chi-N	125	474	137	167	30	19	9	74	64	36	.352	.438	.553	.990	150	44	36	108	71	140	1.254	51			21	*S	4.8
1897	Chi-N	75	276	67	80	18	8	6	40	43		.290	.399	.478	.877	133	14	14	100	83	60	1.005	15			**28**	S	3.6
1898	Chi-N	142	521	96	151	35	8	1	79	58		.290	.380	.393	.774	121	19	16	103	122	90	.832	27			14	*S	3.4
1899	Bro-N	121	428	87	121	22	7	4	76	67		.283	.392	.395	.787	114	14	11	105	136	80	.896	29			9	*S3	2.3
1900	Bro-N	133	483	87	125	16	11	1	69	73		.259	.356	.344	.700	89	-0	-6	108	135	72	.754	31			18	*S	2.3
1901	Bro-N	131	511	69	136	17	9	4	82	30		.266	.307	.358	.665	89	-4	-8	106	149	65	.629	23			12	*S/2	1.0
1902	Bro-N	138	527	67	139	25	8	2	74	43		.264	.319	.353	.672	115	5	9	95	141	67	.642	20			-7	*S	0.8
1903	Bro-N	138	474	71	124	17	9	1	64	82		.262	.371	.342	.712	104	7	6	101	132	74	.794	34			17	*S	2.9
1904	NY-N	145	523	70	140	26	2	2	**80**	44		.268	.325	.337	.661	101	4	1	105	**170**	74	.697	47			24	*S	2.7
1905	NY-N	148	520	67	126	20	4	7	81	62		.242	.323	.337	.660	98	0	-0	101	152	70	.695	37			16	*S/O	1.9
1906	NY-N	143	471	60	113	18	3	1	49	76		.240	.346	.297	.643	103	5	5	100	132	55	.648	16			-2	*S	1.1
1907	NY-N	143	464	40	96	20	1	0	34	51		.207	.285	.254	.540	67	-14	-17	105	111	38	.489	11			5	*S	-0.6
1908	Bos-N	144	524	50	125	23	2	3	48	35		.239	.286	.307	.593	88	-5	-7	104	115	47	.516	10			19	*S	1.1
1909	Bos-N	69	197	22	46	6	1	2	16	29		.234	.332	.305	.636	103	1	1	96	88	21	.616	4			-0	S/23	0.1
1910	Bro-N	3	2	0	0	0	0	0	0	0	0	.000	.000	.000	.000	-99	-1	-0	95	0	-0	.000	0			0	HM	0.0
1911	Bro-N	1	3	0	0	0	0	0	0	0	3	.000	.000	.000	.000	-99	-1	-1	97	0	0	.000	0			0	/SM	0.0
Total	21	2443	9031	1586	2457	413	163	84	1233	1064	269	.272	.353	.382	.735	109	165	123	103	111	1473	.781	547			278	*S3/O2	43.3
■ **BABE DAHLGREN**	Dahlgren, Ellsworth Tenney b: 6/15/12, San Francisco, Cal BR/TR, 6', 190 lbs. Deb: 4/16/35 C																											
1935	Bos-A	149	525	77	138	27	7	9	63	56	67	.263	.337	.392	.730	82	-10	-16	108	94	71	.691	6	5	-1	-6	*1	-3.6
1936	Bos-A	16	57	6	16	3	1	1	7	7	1	.281	.359	.421	.780	87	-1	-1	106	86	9	.786	2	1	0	0	1	-0.2
1937	NY-A	1	1	0	0	0	0	0	0	0	0	.000	.000	.000	.000	-98	-0	-0	102	0	0	.000	0	0	0	0	H	0.0
1938	NY-A	27	43	8	8	1	0	0	1	1	7	.186	.205	.209	.414	4	-6	-7	105	38	2	.286	0	0	0	-1	/31	-0.6
1939	NY-A	144	531	71	125	18	6	15	89	57	54	.235	.312	.377	.689	82	-21	-14	91	125	61	.616	2	3	-1	-7	*1	-3.3
1940	NY-A	155	568	51	150	24	4	12	73	46	54	.264	.325	.384	.709	84	-15	-14	99	106	69	.615	1	1	-0	-10	*1	-2.9
1941	Bos-N	44	166	20	39	8	1	7	30	16	13	.235	.306	.422	.728	111	0	1	93	126	20	.649	0			1	1/3	-0.2
	Chi-N	99	359	50	101	20	1	16	59	43	39	.281	.360	.476	.836	143	15	18	94	99	62	.816	2			-9	1	-0.4
	Yr	143	525	70	140	28	2	23	89	59	52	.267	.343	.459	.802	133	16	20	93	108	85	.774	2			-8		-0.6
1942	Chi-N	17	56	4	12	1	0	0	6	4	2	.214	.267	.232	.499	48	-4	-3	96	171	3	.362	0			-0	1	-0.4
	StL-A	2	2	0	0	0	0	0	0	0	0	.000	.000	.000	.000	-96	-1	-1	104	0	0	.000	0	0	0	0	H	0.0
	Bro-N	17	19	2	1	0	0	0	0	4	5	.053	.217	.053	.270	-19	-3	-3	102	0	0	.263	0			0	1	-0.3
1943	Phi-N	136	508	55	146	19	2	5	56	50	39	.287	.354	.362	.716	114	5	9	94	108	62	.620	2			-9	13S/C	-0.1
1944	Pit-N	158	599	67	173	28	7	12	101	47	56	.289	.347	.419	.766	109	11	7	105	129	84	.686	2			8	*1	0.2
1945	Pit-N	144	531	57	133	24	8	5	75	51	51	.250	.318	.354	.673	84	-10	-12	103	131	57	.575	1			1	*1	-1.6
1946	StL-A	28	80	2	14	1	0	0	9	8	13	.175	.250	.188	.438	24	-8	-8	98	228	4	.333	0	1	-1	1	1	-0.9
Total	12	1137	4045	470	1056	174	37	82	569	390	401	.261	.329	.383	.713	93	-47	-44	99	116	505	.660	18	11		-31	*1/3SC	-14.3
■ **JOHN DAILEY**	Dailey, John J. b: Brooklyn, N.Y. Deb: 7/12/1875																											
1875	Nat-n	26	106	15	22							.208															S/32	
	Atl-n	2	8	3	1							.125															/1O	
	Yr	28	114	18	23							.202																
■ **VINCE DAILEY**	Dailey, Vincent Perry b: 12/25/1864, Osceola, Pa. d: 11/14/19, Hornell, N.Y. 6', 200 lbs. Deb: 4/21/1890																											
1890	Cle-N	64	246	41	71	5	7	0	32	33	23	.289	.373	.366	.739	126	6	9	94	103	41	.800	17			-1	O/P	0.6

YEAR	TM/L	G	AB	R	H	2B	3B	HR	RBI	BB	SO	AVG	OBP	SLG	PRO	/A	BR	/A	PF	CHI	RC	TA	SB	CS	SBR	FR	POS	TPR
■ **CON DAILY**	Daily, Cornelius F. b: 9/11/1864, Blackstone, Mass. d: 6/14/28, Brooklyn, N.Y. BL , 6', 192 lbs. Deb: 6/09/1884																											
1884	Phi-U	2	8	0	0	0	0	0		0		.000	.000	.000	.000	-99	-2	-2	93	0	0	.000	0			0	/C	0.0
1885	Pro-N	60	223	20	58	6	1	0	19	12	20	.260	.298	.296	.594	101	-2	1	91	102	20	.473				-1	C/1O	0.4
1886	Bos-N	50	180	25	43	4	2	0	21	19	29	.239	.312	.283	.595	84	-3	-2	97	137	17	.526	2			-7	C	-0.4
1887	Bos-N	36	120	12	19	5	0	0	13	9	8	.158	.229	.200	.429	22	-12	-12	98	167	7	.416	7			-6	C	-1.1
1888	Ind-N	57	202	14	44	6	1	0	14	10	28	.218	.255	.257	.512	69	-8	-6	95	98	17	.487	15			5	C/O312	0.0
1889	Ind-N	62	219	35	55	6	2	0	26	28	21	.251	.347	.297	.643	76	-4	-7	109	122	28	.677	14			-8	C/O13	-1.2
1890	Bro-P	46	168	20	42	6	3	0	35	15	14	.250	.315	.321	.637	68	-7	-9	106	177	19	.603	6			-10	C/1O	-1.2
1891	Bro-N	60	206	25	66	10	1	0	30	15	13	.320	.378	.379	.756	126	6	7	97	112	33	.743	7			-0	C/OS1	1.0
1892	Bro-N	80	278	38	65	10	1	0	28	38	21	.234	.328	.277	.605	84	-4	-4	101	114	32	.629	18			2	CO	0.2
1893	Bro-N	61	215	33	57	4	2	1	32	20	12	.265	.342	.316	.658	85	-6	-3	91	126	28	.671	13			0	C/O	0.1
1894	Bro-N	67	234	40	60	14	7	0	32	31	22	.256	.351	.376	.727	81	-9	-6	94	102	35	.747	8			4	C/1	0.3
1895	Bro-N	40	142	17	30	3	2	1	11	10	18	.211	.268	.282	.550	46	-12	-10	94	71	12	.482	3			0	C/O	-0.5
1896	Chi-N	9	27	1	2	0	0	0	1	1	2	.074	.107	.074	.181	-47	-6	-6	108	144	0	.160	1			0	/C	-0.4
Total	13	630	2222	280	541	74	22	2	262	208	208	.243	.314	.299	.613	77	-67	-59	98	119	249	.588	94			-20	C/O13S2	-2.8
■ **ED DAILY**	Daily, Edward M. b: 9/7/1862, Providence, R.I. d: 10/21/1891, Washington, D.C. BR/TR, Deb: 1885																											
1885	Phi-N	50	184	22	38	8	2	1	13	0	25	.207	.207	.288	.495	57	-9	-9	104	82	11	.363				-4	P	0.0
1886	Phi-N	79	309	40	70	17	1	4	50	7	34	.227	.244	.327	.571	73	-11	-10	98	153	31	.548	23			1	OP	-0.6
1887	Phi-N	26	106	18	30	11	1	1	17	3	9	.283	.303	.434	.737	107	0	1	97	109	17	.750	8			0	O/P	0.1
	Was-N	78	311	39	78	6	10	2	36	14	27	.251	.285	.354	.639	82	-9	-7	95	101	40	.648	26			-8	O/P	-1.2
	Yr	104	417	57	108	17	11	3	53	17	36	.259	.290	.374	.664	88	-9	-6	96	104	56	.673	34			-8		-1.1
1888	Was-N	110	453	56	102	8	4	8	39	7	42	.225	.239	.313	.552	80	-12	-10	96	74	45	.553	44			2	*O/P1	-0.9
1889	Col-a	136	578	105	148	22	8	3	70	38	65	.256	.303	.337	.640	93	-13	-4	91	87	79	.684	60			-6	*O/P	-1.1
1890	BB-a	91	394	68	94	15	7	1		24		.239	.284	.320	.604	80	-11	-11	100	0	51	.667	49			3	OP	-0.9
	NY-N	4	15	1	2	1	0	0	1	0	4	.133	.133	.200	.333	-2	-2	-2	95	101	0	.231	0			0	/OP	-0.1
	Lou-a	23	80	24	20	0	2	0		13		.250	.355	.300	.655	89	0	-1	107	0	13	.833	13			-1	PO	0.0
1891	Lou-a	22	64	10	16	2	0	0	8	8	6	.250	.342	.281	.624	90	-1	-0	90	128	8	.646	4			0	P/O	0.0
	Was-a	21	79	13	18	2	0	0	6	11	10	.228	.322	.253	.575	71	-3	-2	95	92	9	.639	8			0	O	-0.1
	Yr	43	143	23	34	4	0	0	14	19	16	.238	.331	.266	.597	80	-4	-2	93	114	17	.642	12			0		-0.1
Total	7	640	2573	396	616	92	35	20	240	125	222	.239	.276	.326	.602	82	-70	-56	96	80	305	.615	235			-14	OP/1	-4.8
■ **GEORGE DAISEY**	Daisey, George K. b: Altoona, Pa. 5'11", 190 lbs. Deb: 5/31/1884																											
1884	Alt-U	1	4	0	0	0	0	0		0		.000	.000	.000	.000	-99	-1	-1	101	0	0	.000	0			0	/O	0.0
■ **JOHN DALEY**	Daley, John Francis b: 5/25/1887, Pittsburgh, Pa. d: 8/31/88, Mansfield, Ohio BR/TR, 5'7.5", 155 lbs. Deb: 7/19/12																											
1912	StL-A	17	52	7	9	0	0	1	3	9		.173	.317	.231	.548	58	-2	-2	99	68	5	.628	4			-0	S	0.0
■ **JUD DALEY**	Daley, Judson Lawrence b: 3/14/1884, S.Coventry, Conn. d: 1/26/67, Gasden, Ala. BL/TR, 5'8", 172 lbs. Deb: 9/19/11																											
1911	Bro-N	19	65	8	15	2	1	0	7	2	8	.231	.286	.292	.578	64	-3	-3	97	127	6	.520	2			1	O	-0.1
1912	Bro-N	61	199	22	51	9	1	1	13	24	17	.256	.342	.327	.669	87	-4	-3	95	66	24	.628	2			3	O	-0.1
Total	2	80	264	30	66	11	2	1	20	26	25	.250	.329	.318	.647	82	-7	-6	96	80	30	.601	4			4	/O	-0.2
■ **PETE DALEY**	Daley, Peter Harvey b: 1/14/30, Grass Valley, Cal. BR/TR, 6', 195 lbs. Deb: 5/03/55																											
1955	Bos-A	17	50	4	11	2	1	0	5	3	6	.220	.264	.300	.564	41	-4	-5	124	124	4	.462	0	0	0	1	C	-0.2
1956	Bos-A	59	187	22	50	11	3	5	29	18	30	.267	.338	.439	.777	101	0	-0	103	112	25	.696	1	0	0	0	C	0.1
1957	Bos-A	78	191	17	43	10	0	3	25	16	31	.225	.288	.325	.613	61	-9	-11	110	139	16	.503	0	0	0	-6	C	-1.3
1958	Bos-A	27	56	10	18	2	1	2	8	7	11	.321	.397	.500	.897	138	4	3	105	94	10	.854	0	0	0	-1	C	0.2
1959	Bos-A	65	169	9	38	7	0	1	11	13	31	.225	.280	.284	.564	52	-10	-12	106	85	14	.470	1	1	-0	-0	C	-0.8
1960	KC-A	73	228	19	60	10	2	5	25	16	41	.263	.311	.390	.702	90	-4	-4	99	94	26	.597	0	0	0	5	C/O	0.4
1961	Was-A	72	203	12	39	7	1	2	17	14	37	.192	.244	.266	.510	38	-19	-17	95	111	11	.386	0	1	-1	-0	C	-1.8
Total	7	391	1084	93	259	49	8	18	120	87	187	.239	.297	.349	.646	71	-41	-46	103	108	106	.561	2	2	-1	-1	C/O	-3.4
■ **TOM DALEY**	Daley, Thomas Francis "Pete" b: 11/13/1884, Dubois, Pa. d: 12/2/34, Los Angeles, Cal. BL/TR, 5'5", 168 lbs. Deb: 8/29/08																											
1908	Cin-N	14	46	5	5	0	0	0	1	3		.109	.163	.109	.272	-11	-6	-6	103	78	1	.220	1			0	O	-0.6
1913	Phi-A	62	141	13	36	2	1	0	11	13	28	.255	.327	.284	.611	82	-3	-3	97	98	14	.562	4			1	O	-0.3
1914	Phi-A	28	86	17	22	1	3	0	7	12	14	.256	.347	.337	.684	109	1	1	97	91	9	.634	4	7	-3	2	O	0.0
	NY-A	68	191	36	48	6	4	0	9	38	13	.251	.378	.325	.703	112	5	5	100	54	24	.722	8	8	-2	8	O	0.7
	Yr	96	277	53	70	7	7	0	16	50	27	.253	.369	.329	.697	111	5	6	99	66	33	.694	12	15	-5	10		0.7
1915	NY-A	10	8	2	2	0	0	0	1	2	2	.250	.400	.250	.650	96	0	0	98	170	1	.833	1			0	/O	0.0
Total	4	182	472	73	113	9	8	0	29	68	57	.239	.339	.292	.631	91	-3	-3	99	78	49	.607	18	15		11	O	-0.2
■ **DOM DALLESSANDRO**	Dallessandro, Nicholas Dominic "Dim Dom" b: 10/3/13, Reading, Pa. d: 4/29/88, Indianapolis, Ind. BL/TL, 5'6", 168 lbs. Deb: 4/24/37																											
1937	Bos-A	68	147	18	34	7	1	0	11	27	16	.231	.351	.293	.643	62	-7	-8	103	88	17	.632	2	1	0	-6	O	-1.3
1940	Chi-N	107	287	33	77	19	6	1	36	34	13	.268	.348	.387	.735	103	1	2	100	117	40	.694	4			-4	O	-0.4
1941	Chi-N	140	486	73	132	36	2	6	85	68	37	.272	.362	.391	.753	120	9	13	94	151	72	.720	3			-11	*O	-0.2
1942	Chi-N	96	264	30	69	12	4	4	43	36	18	.261	.350	.383	.733	119	5	6	96	141	35	.684	4			-0	O	0.5
1943	Chi-N	87	176	13	39	8	3	1	31	40	14	.222	.369	.318	.687	100	2	2	99	190	24	.705	1			-4	O	-0.3
1944	Chi-N	117	381	53	116	19	4	8	74	61	29	.304	.400	.438	.839	135	20	20	101	139	70	.839	1			-2	*O	1.0
1946	Chi-N	65	89	4	20	2	2	1	9	23	12	.225	.384	.326	.710	109	1	2	94	105	12	.707	1			-3	O	-0.1
1947	Chi-N	66	115	18	33	7	1	1	14	21	11	.287	.397	.391	.788	109	3	2	101	108	18	.759	0			-2	O	0.0
Total	8	746	1945	242	520	110	23	22	303	310	150	.267	.369	.381	.750	112	34	39	98	136	287	.748	16	1		-32	O	-0.8
■ **ABNER DALRYMPLE**	Dalrymple, Abner Frank b: 9/9/1857, Warren, Ill. d: 1/25/39, Warren, Ill. BL/TR, 5'10.5", 175 lbs. Deb: 5/01/1878																											
1878	Mil-N	61	271	52	96	10	4	0	15	6	29	.354	.368	.421	.789	149	16	14	107	39	43	.686				6	*O	1.4
1879	Chi-N	71	333	47	97	25	1	0	23	4	29	.291	.300	.372	.672	114	7	4	105	56	38	.542				-13	*O	-0.9
1880	Chi-N	86	382	**91**	**126**	25	12	0	36	3	18	.330	.335	.458	.793	158	25	22	105	66	60	.695				3	*O	2.1
1881	Chi-N	82	362	72	117	22	4	1	37	15	22	.323	.350	.414	.764	129	16	12	108	74	54	.673				-8	*O	0.2
1882	Chi-N	84	397	96	117	25	11	1	36	14	18	.295	.319	.421	.739	133	15	14	101	62	55	.646				-2	*O	1.0
1883	Chi-N	80	363	78	108	24	4	2	37	11	29	.298	.318	.402	.720	107	7	2	109	73	48	.616				-2	*O	0.2
1884	Chi-N	111	521	111	161	18	9	22	69	14	39	.309	.327	.505	.832	146	32	26	108	62	88	.769				3	*O	2.4
1885	Chi-N	113	492	109	135	27	12	**11**	61	46	42	.274	.336	.445	.782	133	28	18	114	73	76	.742				-2	*O	1.2
1886	Chi-N	82	331	62	77	7	12	3	26	33	44	.233	.302	.353	.656	85	-0	-9	116	65	41	.654	16			3	O	-0.3
1887	Pit-N	92	358	45	76	18	5	2	31	45	43	.212	.311	.307	.618	79	-11	-7	93	79	44	.674	29			3	*O	-0.2
1888	Pit-N	57	227	19	50	9	2	0	14	6	28	.220	.247	.278	.524	73	-8	-6	95	76	18	.441	7			-2	O	-0.8
1891	CM-a	32	135	31	42	7	5	1	22	7	18	.311	.345	.459	.804	119	5	2	112	104	24	.806	6			0	O	0.2
Total	12	951	4172	813	1202	217	81	43	407	204	359	.288	.323	.410	.732	121	130	92	106	68	588	.667	58			-10	O	6.5
■ **CLAY DALRYMPLE**	Dalrymple, Clayton Errol b: 12/3/36, Chico, Cal. BL/TR, 6', 190 lbs. Deb: 4/24/60																											
1960	Phi-N	82	158	11	43	6	2	4	21	15	21	.272	.347	.411	.758	99	2	0	107	111	22	.697	0	0	0	4	C	0.7
1961	Phi-N	129	378	23	83	11	1	5	42	30	30	.220	.284	.294	.578	57	-25	-22	94	134	30	.471	0	2	-1	3	*C	-0.9
1962	Phi-N	123	370	40	102	13	3	11	54	70	32	.276	.396	.416	.813	125	13	15	95	114	65	.824	1	3	-2	5	*C	2.1
1963	Phi-N	142	452	40	114	15	3	10	40	45	55	.252	.327	.365	.692	96	-0	-1	103	86	54	.618	0	2	-1	-15	*C	-1.4
1964	Phi-N	127	382	36	91	16	3	6	46	39	40	.238	.309	.343	.652	84	-8	-8	99	127	41	.569	0	1	-1	-3	*C	-0.7
1965	Phi-N	103	301	14	64	5	5	4	23	34	37	.213	.293	.302	.595	72	-12	-10	95	93	27	.510	0	1	-1	4	*C	-0.3
1966	Phi-N	114	331	30	81	13	3	4	39	60	57	.245	.365	.338	.704	96	1	1	101	132	46	.692	0	0	0	-3	*C	0.0
1967	Phi-N	101	268	12	46	7	1	3	21	36	49	.172	.272	.239	.511	45	-18	-19	104	119	18	.438	1	2	-1	-2	C	-1.7
1968	Phi-N	85	241	19	50	9	1	3	26	22	57	.207	.277	.290	.567	72	-9	-8	97	139	19	.477	1	2	-1	-2	C	-0.8
1969	Bal-A	37	80	8	19	1	1	3	6	13	8	.237	.344	.387	.732	101	1	0	104	60	10	.657	0	0	0	0	C	0.2

YEAR	TM/L	G	AB	R	H	2B	3B	HR	RBI	BB	SO	AVG	OBP	SLG	PRO	/A	BR	/A	PF	CHI	RC	TA	SB	CS	SBR	FR	POS	TPR
1970	Bal-A	13	32	4	7	1	0	1	3	7	4	.219	.359	.344	.703	98	-0	0	97	87	4	.720	0	0	0	-1	C	0.0
1971	Bal-A	23	49	6	10	1	0	1	6	16	13	.204	.409	.286	.695	97	1	1	103	144	8	.795	0	0	0	-1	C	0.1
Total	12	1079	3042	243	710	98	23	55	327	387	403	.233	.324	.335	.659	85	-55	-51	99	115	343	.610	3	13	-7	-11	*C	-2.7
■ BILL DALRYMPLE	Dalrymple, William Dunn b: 2/7/1891, Baltimore, Md. d: 7/14/67, San Diego, Cal. TR , Deb: 7/06/15																											
1915	StL-A	3	2	0	0	0	0	0	0	0	0	.000	.000	.000	.000	-99	-0	-0	96	0	0	.000	0			0	/3	0.0
■ JACK DALTON	Dalton, Talbot Percy b: 7/3/1885, Henderson, Tenn. BR/TR, 5'10.5", 187 lbs. Deb: 6/20/10																											
1910	Bro-N	77	273	33	62	9	4	1	21	26	30	.227	.304	.300	.604	80	-8	-7	95	91	27	.555	5			2	O	-0.7
1914	Bro-N	128	442	65	141	13	8	1	45	53	39	.319	.396	.391	.787	133	20	20	101	95	74	.824	19			-2	*O	1.6
1915	Buf-F	132	437	68	128	17	3	2	46	50	38	.293	.366	.359	.725	115	9	10	100	104	71	.761	28			-2	*O	0.2
1916	Det-A	8	11	1	2	0	0	0	0	0	5	.182	.182	.182	.364	9	-1	-1	105	0	0	.222	0			-1	/O	-0.2
Total	4	345	1163	167	333	39	15	4	112	129	112	.286	.361	.356	.717	113	20	22	99	96	173	.725	52			-4	O	0.9
■ BERT DALY	Daly, Albert Joseph b: 4/8/1881, Bayonne, N.J. d: 9/3/52, Bayonne, N.J. BR/TR, 5'9", 170 lbs. Deb: 03																											
1903	Phi-A	10	21	2	4	0	2	0	4	1		.190	.227	.381	.608	78	-1	-1	104	180	2	.529	0			0	/23S	0.0
■ SUN DALY	Daly, James J. b: 1/6/1865, Rutland, Vt. d: 4/30/38, Albany, N.Y. Deb: N/A.																											
1892	Bal-N	13	48	5	12	0	2	0	7	1	4	.250	.265	.333	.599	82	-1	-1	100	134	4	.472	0			0	O	0.0
■ JOE DALY	Daly, Joseph John b: 9/21/1868, Conshohocken, Pa. d: 3/21/43, Philadelphia, Pa. TR , 5'8", 157 lbs. Deb: 9/19/1890																											
1890	Phi-a	21	75	8	21	4	1	0		3		.280	.308	.360	.668	102	-0	-0	97	0	9	.574	1			0	O/C	0.0
1891	Cle-N	1	3	0	0	0	0	0	0	0	2	.000	.000	.000	.000	-95	-1	-1	105	0	0	.000	0			0	/O	0.0
1892	Bos-N	1	0	0	0	0	0	0	0	0	0	—	—	—	—	—	0	0	113	—	—	—	0			0	/C	0.0
Total	3	23	78	8	21	4	1	0	0	3	2	.269	.296	.346	.642	94	-1	-1	97	0	9	.544	1			0	/OC	0.0
■ TOM DALY	Daly, Thomas Daniel b: 12/12/1891, St.John, N.B., Can. d: 11/7/46, Medford, Mass. BR/TR, 5'11.5", 171 lbs. Deb: 9/23/13 C																											
1913	Chi-A	1	3	0	0	0	0	0	0	0	0	.000	.000	.000	.000	-99	-1	-1	95	0	0	.000	0			0	/C	0.0
1914	Chi-A	61	133	13	31	2	0	0	8	7	13	.233	.271	.248	.520	55	-7	-8	103	91	9	.406	3	4	-2	-6	O/3C1	-1.7
1915	Chi-A	29	47	5	9	1	0	0	3	5	9	.191	.269	.213	.482	45	-3	-3	98	102	3	.395	0			-1	C/1	-0.1
1916	Cle-A	31	73	3	16	1	1	0	8	1	2	.219	.230	.260	.490	47	-5	-5	100	150	4	.351	0			-0	C/O	-0.4
1918	Chi-N	1	1	0	0	0	0	0	0	0	0	.000	.000	.000	.000	-98	-0	-0	102	0	0	.000	0			0	/C	0.0
1919	Chi-N	25	50	4	11	0	1	0	1	2	5	.220	.250	.260	.510	53	-3	-3	100	30	3	.385	0			0	C	-0.1
1920	Chi-N	44	90	12	28	6	0	0	13	2	6	.311	.333	.378	.711	105	0	0	99	148	11	.603	1	1	-0	1	C	0.3
1921	Chi-N	51	143	12	34	7	1	0	22	8	8	.238	.278	.301	.579	50	-10	-11	107	188	12	.468	1	2	-1	1	C	-0.6
Total	8	243	540	49	129	17	3	0	55	25	43	.239	.274	.281	.555	59	-28	-30	102	129	42	.438	5	7		-4	C/O31	-2.6
■ TOM DALY	Daly, Thomas Peter "Tido" b: 2/7/1866, Philadelphia, Pa. d: 10/29/39, Brooklyn, N.Y. BB/TR, 5'7", 170 lbs. Deb: 4/30/1887																											
1887	Chi-N	74	256	45	53	10	4	2	17	22	25	.207	.270	.301	.571	51	-14	-21	116	64	29	.631	29			22	C/OS21	0.7
1888	Chi-N	65	219	34	42	2	6	0	29	10	26	.192	.230	.256	.486	53	-10	-12	107	186	16	.435	10			16	C/O	0.6
1889	Was-N	71	250	39	75	13	5	1	40	38	28	.300	.394	.404	.798	136	10	13	92	117	48	.903	18			10	C/12OS	2.0
1890	Bro-N	82	292	55	71	9	4	5	43	32	43	.243	.326	.353	.679	100	0	-0	100	112	41	.719	20			2	C1/O	0.6
1891	Bro-N	58	200	29	50	11	5	2	27	21	34	.250	.327	.385	.712	112	2	3	97	97	28	.713	7			0	C1S/O	0.3
1892	Bro-N	124	446	76	114	15	6	4	51	64	61	.256	.355	.343	.698	112	9	8	101	97	68	.771	34			-8	3OC2	0.4
1893	Bro-N	126	470	94	136	21	14	8	70	76	65	.289	.388	.445	.833	136	16	25	91	87	96	.949	32			-18	23	0.5
1894	Bro-N	123	492	135	168	22	10	8	82	77	42	.341	.436	.476	.911	129	20	26	94	77	127	1.133	51			-21	*2	1.0
1895	Bro-N	120	455	89	128	17	8	2	68	52	52	.281	.359	.367	.726	95	-6	-1	94	116	72	.765	28			-19	*2	-0.9
1896	Bro-N	67	224	43	63	13	6	3	29	33	25	.281	.385	.433	.819	135	6	12	87	80	46	.957	19			-6	2/C	0.6
1898	Bro-N	23	73	11	24	3	1	0	11	14		.329	.443	.397	.840	153	5	6	95	117	16	1.020	6			0	2	0.5
1899	Bro-N	141	498	95	156	24	9	5	88	69		.313	.403	.428	.831	125	23	20	105	125	106	.968	43			15	*2	3.9
1900	Bro-N	97	343	72	107	17	3	4	55	46		.312	.393	.414	.807	117	13	9	108	114	68	.911	27			-14	2/1O	0.0
1901	Bro-N	133	520	88	164	**38**	10	3	90	42		.315	.367	.444	.811	129	24	19	106	133	98	.854	31			14	*2	4.1
1902	Chi-A	137	489	57	110	22	3	1	54	55		.225	.303	.288	.592	69	-21	-18	95	131	50	.567	19			-13	*2	-2.4
1903	Chi-A	43	150	20	31	11	0	0	19	20		.207	.300	.280	.580	83	-4	-2	92	173	15	.571	6			-11	2	-1.2
	Cin-N	80	307	42	90	14	9	1	38	16		.293	.328	.407	.735	102	3	-1	109	101	44	.673	5			-8	2	-0.3
Total	16	1564	5684	1024	1582	262	103	49	811	687	401	.278	.359	.387	.746	109	78	87	99	111	968	.805	385			-38	*2C3/O1S	10.4
■ BILL DAM	Dam, Elbridge Rust b: 4/4/1885, Cambridge, Mass. d: 6/22/30, Quincy, Mass. Deb: 09																											
1909	Bos-N	1	2	1	1	1	0	0	0	1		.500	.667	1.000	1.667	437	1	1	96	0	1	3.000	0			0	/O	0.1
■ JACK DAMASKA	Damaska, Jack Lloyd b: 8/21/37, Beaver Falls, Pa. BR/TR, 5'11", 168 lbs. Deb: 7/03/63																											
1963	StL-N	5	5	1	1	0	0	0	1	0	4	.200	.200	.200	.400	14	-1	-1	107	420	0	.250	0	0	0	-0	/2O	0.0
■ HARRY DAMRAU	Damrau, Harry Robert (Also Known As Arthur Lee Whitehorn) b: 9/11/1890, Newburgh, N.Y. d: 8/21/57, Staten Island, N.Y BR/TR, 5'10", 178 lbs. Deb: 9/17/15																											
1915	Phi-A	16	56	4	11	1	0	0	3	5	17	.196	.262	.214	.477	44	-4	-4	96	87	3	.391	1	1	-0	0	3	-0.2
■ JAKE DANIEL	Daniel, Handley Jacob b: 4/22/11, Roanoke, Ala. BL/TL, 5'11", 175 lbs. Deb: 7/24/37																											
1937	Bro-N	12	27	3	5	1	0	0	3	3	4	.185	.267	.222	.489	33	-2	-3	104	180	2	.409	0			0	/1	-0.2
■ BERT DANIELS	Daniels, Bernard Elmer b: 10/13/1882, Danville, Ill. d: 6/6/58, Cedar Grove, N.J. BR/TR, 5'9.5", 180 lbs. Deb: 6/25/10																											
1910	NY-A	95	356	68	90	13	8	1	17	41		.253	.356	.343	.699	111	10	6	107	44	58	.827	41			-5	O/31	-0.1
1911	NY-A	131	462	74	132	16	9	2	31	48		.286	.375	.372	.747	98	7	-0	111	62	80	.842	40			-7	*O	-1.5
1912	NY-A	133	496	72	136	25	11	2	41	51		.274	.363	.381	.744	111	9	8	101	67	82	.819	37			5	*O	0.6
1913	NY-A	94	320	52	69	13	5	0	22	44	36	.216	.343	.287	.630	84	-4	-4	101	90	38	.721	27			-2	O	-1.1
1914	Cin-N	71	269	29	59	9	7	0	19	19	40	.219	.276	.305	.581	69	-10	-11	105	81	25	.557	14			-4	O	-1.8
Total	5	524	1903	295	486	76	40	5	130	203	76	.255	.349	.345	.695	98	13	-1	105	67	283	.770	159			-13	O/31	-3.9
■ TONY DANIELS	Daniels, Frederick Clinton b: 12/28/24, Gastonia, N.C. BR/TR, 5'9.5", 185 lbs. Deb: 6/12/45																											
1945	Phi-N	76	230	15	46	3	2	0	10	12	22	.200	.249	.230	.479	35	-21	-19	96	65	13	.359	1			-3	2/3	-1.6
■ JACK DANIELS	Daniels, Harold Jack "Sour Mash Jack" b: 12/21/27, Chester, Pa. BL/TL, 5'10", 165 lbs. Deb: 4/18/52																											
1952	Bos-N	106	219	31	41	5	1	2	14	28	30	.187	.288	.247	.535	52	-14	-13	95	91	18	.484	3	3	-1	-12	O	-2.9
■ KAL DANIELS	Daniels, Kalvoski b: 8/20/63, Vienna, Ga. BL/TR, 5'11", 185 lbs. Deb: 4/09/86																											
1986	Cin-N	74	181	34	58	10	4	6	23	22	30	.320	.400	.519	.919	145	13	12	104	82	40	1.031	15	2	3	-2	O	1.3
1987	Cin-N	108	368	73	123	24	1	26	64	60	62	.334	.429	.617	1.046	167	40	38	104	85	100	1.212	26	8	3	1	O	3.7
1988	Cin-N	140	495	95	144	29	1	18	64	87	94	.291	**.400**	.463	.863	139	33	30	105	96	98	.940	27	6	5	1	*O	3.3
Total	3	322	1044	202	325	63	6	50	151	169	186	.311	.410	.527	.937	151	86	80	105	90	238	1.063	68	16	11	-1	O	8.3
■ LAW DANIELS	Daniels, Lawrence Long b: 7/14/1862, Newton, Mass. d: 1/7/29, Waltham, Mass. 5'10", 170 lbs. Deb: 4/25/1887																											
1887	Bal-a	48	165	23	41	5	1	0		8		.248	.287	.291	.578	66	-8	-7	96	0	16	.516	7			0	CO/12S3	-0.5
1888	KC-a	61	218	32	44	2	0	1	28	14		.202	.260	.225	.484	55	-9	-11	106	164	18	.494	20			0	OC/3S	-1.0
Total	2	109	383	55	85	7	1	1	28	22		.222	.271	.253	.525	60	-17	-18	102	94	35	.503	27			0	/CO13S2	-1.5
■ BUCK DANNER	Danner, Henry Frederick b: 6/8/1891, Dedham, Mass. d: 9/21/49, Boston, Mass. BR/TR, 5'6", 135 lbs. Deb: 9/17/15																											
1915	Phi-A	3	12	1	3	0	0	0	0	0	1	.250	.250	.250	.500	52	-1	-1	96	0	1	.444	1			-0	/S	0.0
■ HARRY DANNING	Danning, Harry "Harry The Horse" b: 9/6/11, Los Angeles, Cal. BR/TR, 6'1", 190 lbs. Deb: 7/30/33																											
1933	NY-N	3	2	0	0	0	0	0	0	1	0	.000	.333	.000	.333	2	-0	-0	99	0	0	.333	0			0	/C	0.0
1934	NY-N	53	97	8	32	7	0	1	7	1	9	.330	.337	.433	.770	107	0	1	98	56	12	.629	1			-1	C	0.0
1935	NY-N	65	152	16	37	11	1	2	20	9	16	.243	.286	.368	.654	77	-6	-5	96	116	16	.546	0			-1	C	-0.5
1936	NY-N	32	69	3	11	2	2	0	4	1	5	.159	.183	.246	.429	15	-8	-8	100	83	2	.302	0			1	C	-0.6
1937	NY-N	93	292	30	84	12	4	8	51	18	20	.288	.331	.438	.770	107	2	2	100	121	42	.681	0			0	C	0.5

YEAR	TM/L	G	AB	R	H	2B	3B	HR	RBI	BB	SO	AVG	OBP	SLG	PRO	/A	BR	/A	PF	CHI	RC	TA	SB	CS	SBR	FR	POS	TPR
1938	NY-N	120	448	59	137	26	3	9	60	23	40	.306	.345	.438	.783	110	7	6	103	99	66	.689	1			3	*C	1.3
1939	NY-N	135	520	79	163	28	5	16	74	35	42	.313	.359	.479	.838	125	15	16	99	97	87	.786	4			**18**	*C	3.8
1940	NY-N	140	524	65	157	34	4	13	91	35	31	.300	.349	.454	.803	120	13	13	100	124	79	.730	3			**21**	*C	3.9
1941	NY-N	130	459	58	112	22	4	7	56	30	25	.244	.292	.355	.647	79	-12	-14	103	110	46	.543	1			21	*C/1	1.8
1942	NY-N	119	408	45	114	20	3	1	34	34	29	.279	.335	.350	.685	98	0	-1	103	86	46	.583	3			1	*C	0.3
Total	10	890	2971	363	847	162	26	57	397	187	217	.285	.330	.415	.745	104	12	9	101	104	395	.676	13			63	C/1	10.5
■ **IKE DANNING**	Danning, Ike b: 1/20/05, Los Angeles, Cal. d: 3/30/83, Santa Monica, Cal BR/TR, 5'10", 160 lbs. Deb: 9/21/28																											
1928	StL-A	2	6	0	3	0	0	0	1	1	2	.500	.571	.500	1.071	177	1	1	104	114	2	1.333	0	0	0	0	/C	0.1
■ **FATS DANTONIO**	Dantonio, John James b: 12/31/19, New Orleans, La. BR/TR, 5'8", 165 lbs. Deb: 9/18/44																											
1944	Bro-N	3	7	0	1	0	0	0	0	0	1	.143	.143	.143	.286	-20	-1	-1	99	0	0	.143	0			0	/C	0.0
1945	Bro-N	47	128	12	32	6	1	0	12	11	6	.250	.309	.313	.622	76	-5	-4	96	104	13	.545	3			-3	C	-0.5
Total	2	50	135	12	33	6	1	0	12	11	7	.244	.301	.304	.605	71	-6	-5	96	99	13	.524	3			-2	/C	-0.5
■ **BABE DANZIG**	Danzig, Harold P. b: 4/30/1887, Binghamton, N.Y. d: 7/14/31, San Francisco, Cal BR/TR, 6'2", 205 lbs. Deb: 4/12/09																											
1909	Bos-A	6	13	0	2	0	0	0	0	2		.154	.313	.154	.466	44	-1	-1	109	0	1	.455	0			0	/1	0.0
■ **CLIFF DAPPER**	Dapper, Clifford Roland b: 1/2/20, Los Angeles, Cal. BR/TR, 6'2", 190 lbs. Deb: 4/19/42																											
1942	Bro-N	8	17	2	8	1	0	1	9	2	2	.471	.526	.706	1.232	254	3	3	102	222	7	1.556	0			-0	/C	0.3
■ **CLIFF DARINGER**	Daringer, Clifford Clarence "Shanty" b: 4/10/1885, Hayden, Ind. d: 12/26/71, Sacramento, Cal. BL/TR, 5'7.5", 155 lbs. Deb: 4/20/14																											
1914	KC-F	64	160	12	42	2	1	0	16	11	7	.262	.310	.287	.597	75	-6	-5	95	125	19	.559	9			-2	S32	-0.4
■ **ROLLA DARINGER**	Daringer, Rolla Harrison b: 11/15/1888, N.Vernon, Ind. d: 5/23/74, Seymour, Ind. BL/TR, 5'10", 155 lbs. Deb: 9/19/14																											
1914	StL-N	2	4	1	2	1	0	0	0	1	2	.500	.600	.750	1.350	289	1	1	104	0	2	2.000	0			0	/S	0.1
1915	StL-N	10	23	3	2	0	0	0	0	9	5	.087	.344	.087	.431	33	-1	-1	100	0	1	.500	0	1	-1	-2	S	-0.3
Total	2	12	27	4	4	1	0	0	0	10	7	.148	.378	.185	.564	72	-0	-0	101	0	3	.625	0	1		-2	/S	-0.2
■ **AL DARK**	Dark, Alvin Ralph "Blackie" b: 1/7/22, Comanche, Okla. BR/TR, 5'11", 185 lbs. Deb: 7/14/46 MC																											
1946	Bos-N	15	13	0	3	3	0	0	1	0	3	.231	.231	.462	.692	99	-0	-0	95	62	1	.600	0			-0	S/O	0.0
1948	Bos-N	137	543	85	175	39	6	3	48	24	36	.322	.353	.433	.786	110	7	6	102	75	84	.712	4			-12	*S	0.9
1949	Bos-N	130	529	74	146	23	5	3	53	31	43	.276	.317	.355	.673	83	-15	-13	97	107	59	.573	5			-6	*S/3	-0.5
1950	NY-N	154	587	79	164	36	5	16	67	39	60	.279	.331	.440	.770	102	-1	0	98	86	85	.721	9			-13	*S	0.3
1951	NY-N	156	646	114	196	**41**	7	14	69	42	39	.303	.352	.454	.805	113	12	11	102	77	104	.754	12	7	-1	2	*S	2.5
1952	NY-N	151	589	92	177	29	3	14	73	47	39	.301	.357	.431	.788	115	14	12	102	102	92	.729	6	6	-2	4	*S	1.8
1953	NY-N	155	647	126	194	41	6	23	88	28	34	.300	.335	.488	.823	113	8	10	98	86	102	.753	7	2	1	1	*S2O/3P	2.0
1954	NY-N	154	644	98	189	26	6	20	70	27	40	.293	.327	.446	.773	94	-3	-7	105	76	89	.684	5	3	-0	5	*S	0.7
1955	NY-N	115	475	77	134	20	3	9	45	22	32	.282	.321	.394	.714	90	-8	-7	99	82	60	.622	2	1	0	-4	*S	-0.7
1956	NY-N	48	206	19	52	12	0	2	17	8	13	.252	.284	.340	.624	69	-10	-9	97	82	19	.497	0	0	0	-5	S	-1.1
	StL-N	100	413	54	118	14	7	4	37	21	33	.286	.323	.383	.706	90	-7	-6	99	88	50	.603	3	1	0	-3	S	-0.1
	Yr	148	619	73	170	26	7	6	54	29	46	.275	.310	.368	.679	83	-16	-15	98	87	71	.573	3	1	0	-8		-1.2
1957	StL-N	140	583	80	169	25	8	4	64	29	56	.290	.328	.381	.709	89	-9	-9	101	120	72	.607	3	4	-2	12	*S/3	0.6
1958	StL-N	18	64	7	19	0	0	1	5	2	6	.297	.318	.344	.662	71	-2	-3	106	83	6	.500	0	0	0	-0	/S3	-0.2
	Chi-N	114	464	54	137	16	4	3	43	29	23	.295	.343	.366	.710	88	-7	-8	101	95	57	.601	1	1	-0	2	*3	-0.5
	Yr	132	528	61	156	16	4	4	48	31	29	.295	.340	.364	.704	85	-10	-11	101	94	64	.593	1	1	-0	1		-0.7
1959	Chi-N	136	477	60	126	22	9	6	45	55	50	.264	.344	.386	.730	95	-3	-2	98	92	66	.683	1	1	-0	1	*3/1S	-0.5
1960	Phi-N	55	198	29	48	5	1	3	14	19	14	.242	.315	.323	.638	70	-6	-8	107	79	20	.551	1	1	-0	-5	3/1	-1.4
	Mil-N	50	141	16	42	6	2	1	18	7	13	.298	.336	.390	.726	108	-0	1	91	126	18	.618	0	0	0	-1	O1/32	0.0
	Yr	105	339	45	90	11	3	4	32	26	27	.265	.323	.351	.674	85	-7	-7	99	102	40	.589	1	1	-0	-6		-1.4
Total	14	1828	7219	1064	2089	358	72	126	757	430	534	.289	.334	.411	.745	98	-31	-32	100	90	987	.681	59	27		-23	*S3/O21P	3.8
■ **DELL DARLING**	Darling, Conrad b: 12/21/1861, Erie, Pa. d: 11/20/04, Erie, Pa. BR/TR, 5'8", 170 lbs. Deb: 7/03/1883																											
1883	Buf-N	6	18	1	3	0	0	0	1	2	5	.167	.250	.167	.417	30	-1	-1	100	116	1	.333				0	/C	0.0
1887	Chi-N	38	141	28	45	7	4	3	20	22	18	.319	.411	.489	.900	130	10	6	116	84	37	1.146	19			0	OC	0.5
1888	Chi-N	20	75	12	16	3	1	2	7	3	12	.213	.253	.360	.613	89	-0	-1	107	80	7	.525	0			0	C	0.0
1889	Chi-N	36	120	14	23	1	1	0	7	25	22	.192	.331	.217	.548	57	-6	-6	99	82	11	.577	5			2	C	-0.2
1890	Chi-P	58	221	45	57	12	4	2	39	29	28	.258	.352	.376	.727	92	-1	-3	104	127	32	.732	5			0	1S/CO23	-0.1
1891	StL-a	17	53	9	7	1	3	0	9	10	11	.132	.270	.264	.534	48	-3	-4	114	186	4	.522	0			0	C/2S	-0.3
Total	6	175	628	109	151	24	13	7	83	91	96	.240	.340	.354	.694	90	-1	-9	107	108	91	.725	29			2	C/1OS23	-0.1
■ **JACK DARRAGH**	Darragh, James S. b: 7/17/1866, Ebensburg, Pa. d: 8/12/39, Rochester, Pa. Deb: 5/13/1891																											
1891	Lou-a	1	2	0	1	0	0	0	0	0	0	.500	.500	.500	1.000	211	0	0	90	0	1	1.000	0			0	/1	0.0
■ **BOBBY DARWIN**	Darwin, Arthur Bobby Lee b: 2/16/43, Los Angeles, Cal. BR/TR, 6'2", 190 lbs. Deb: 9/30/62																											
1962	LA-A	1	1	0	0	0	0	0	0	0	1	.000	.000	.000	.000	-98	-0	-0	102	0	0	.000	0	0	0	0	/P	0.0
1969	LA-N	6	0	1	0	0	0	0	0	0	0	—	—	—	—	—	0	0	99	—	—	—	0	0	0	-0	/P	0.0
1971	LA-N	11	20	2	5	1	0	1	4	2	9	.250	.318	.450	.768	117	0	0	99	136	3	.733	0	0	0	0	/O	0.0
1972	Min-A	145	513	48	137	20	2	22	80	38	145	.267	.327	.442	.770	119	16	12	107	116	67	.682	2	3	-1	3	*O	1.2
1973	Min-A	145	560	69	141	20	2	18	90	46	137	.252	.312	.391	.703	93	-3	-6	104	137	64	.616	5	2	0	-2	*O/D	-1.1
1974	Min-A	152	575	67	152	13	7	25	94	37	127	.264	.324	.442	.766	118	12	11	101	115	80	.699	1	3	-2	-4	*O	0.2
1975	Min-A	48	169	26	37	6	0	5	18	18	44	.219	.309	.343	.652	78	-3	-5	107	97	17	.586	2	0	1	-4	OD	-0.9
	Mil-A	55	186	19	46	6	2	8	23	11	54	.247	.300	.430	.730	104	0	0	100	85	24	.676	4	1	1	0	O/D	0.0
	Yr	103	355	45	83	12	2	13	41	29	98	.234	.304	.389	.693	92	-3	-5	103	91	44	.650	6	1	1	-4		-0.9
1976	Mil-A	25	73	6	18	3	1	1	5	6	16	.247	.321	.356	.677	99	-0	-0	99	66	8	.596	0	0	0	-1	O/D	-0.1
	Bos-A	43	106	9	19	5	2	3	13	2	35	.179	.216	.349	.565	58	-5	-7	110	109	8	.483	1	0	0	-2	OD	-0.9
	Yr	68	179	15	37	8	3	4	18	8	51	.207	.260	.352	.612	74	-6	-7	106	94	17	.535	1	0	0	-3		-1.0
1977	Bos-A	4	9	1	2	1	0	0	1	0	4	.222	.222	.333	.556	42	-1	-1	117	132	0	.375	0	0	0	-0	/OD	0.0
	Chi-N	11	12	2	2	1	0	0	0	0	5	.167	.167	.250	.417	9	-2	-2	114	0	1	.300	0	0	0	-0	/O	-0.1
Total	9	646	2224	250	559	76	16	83	328	160	577	.251	.312	.412	.724	103	14	3	104	115	272	.674	15	9	-1	-11	O/DP	-1.7
■ **DOUG DASCENZO**	Dascenzo, Douglas Craig b: 6/30/64, Cleveland, Ohio BB/TL, 5'7", 150 lbs. Deb: 9/02/88																											
1988	Chi-N	26	75	9	16	3	0	0	4	9	4	.213	.298	.253	.551	57	-4	-4	104	84	6	.548	6	1	1	3	O	0.0
■ **WALLY DASHIELL**	Dashiell, John Wallace b: 5/9/02, Jewett, Tex. d: 5/20/72, Pensacola, Fla. BR/TR, 5'9.5", 170 lbs. Deb: 4/20/24																											
1924	Chi-A	1	2	0	0	0	0	0	0	0	0	.000	.000	.000	.000	-99	-1	-1	97	0	0	.000	0	0	0	0	/S	0.0
■ **HARRY DAUBERT**	Daubert, Harry "Jake" b: 6/19/1892, Columbus, Ohio d: 1/8/44, Detroit, Mich. BR/TR, 6', 160 lbs. Deb: 9/04/15																											
1915	Pit-N	1	1	0	0	0	0	0	0	0	1	.000	.000	.000	.000	-99	-0	-0	99	0	0	.000	0			0	H	0.0
■ **JAKE DAUBERT**	Daubert, Jacob Ellsworth b: 4/7/1884, Shamokin, Pa. d: 10/9/24, Cincinnati, Ohio BL/TL, 5'10.5", 160 lbs. Deb: 4/14/10																											
1910	Bro-N	144	552	67	146	15	15	8	50	47	53	.264	.328	.389	.717	115	4	8	95	64	79	.714	23			-3	*1	0.3
1911	Bro-N	149	573	89	176	17	8	5	45	51	56	.307	.366	.391	.757	115	9	11	97	56	94	.778	32			3	*1	0.8
1912	Bro-N	145	559	81	172	19	16	3	66	48	45	.308	.369	.415	.784	120	11	14	95	98	95	.814	29			1	*1	0.9
1913	Bro-N	139	508	76	178	17	7	2	52	44	40	**.350**	.405	.423	.829	131	25	22	104	91	94	.870	25			3	*1	1.9
1914	Bro-N	126	474	89	156	17	7	6	45	30	34	**.329**	.375	.432	.808	139	22	22	101	70	85	.833	25			-6	*1	1.5
1915	Bro-N	150	544	62	164	21	8	2	47	57	48	.301	.369	.381	.749	125	19	18	101	81	81	.702	11	13	-5	8	*1	1.5
1916	Bro-N	127	478	75	151	16	7	3	33	38	39	.316	.371	.397	.769	132	21	19	103	63	80	.757	21	7	2	2	*1	1.8
1917	Bro-N	125	468	59	122	4	4	2	30	51	30	.261	.341	.299	.640	94	1	-1	104	70	53	.601	11			7	*1	0.5
1918	Bro-N	108	396	50	122	12	**15**	2	47	27	18	.308	.360	.429	.789	138	18	18	101	107	63	.774	10			1	*1	1.7
1919	Cin-N	140	537	79	148	10	12	2	44	35	23	.276	.322	.350	.672	97	1	-2	105	78	66	.607	11			-1	*1	-0.5

YEAR	TM/L	G	AB	R	H	2B	3B	HR	RBI	BB	SO	AVG	OBP	SLG	PRO	/A	BR	/A	PF	CHI	RC	TA	SB	CS	SBR	FR	POS	TPR
1920	Cin-N	142	553	97	168	28	13	4	48	47	29	.304	.362	.423	.785	139	18	25	90	67	83	.741	11	13	-5	-9	*1	1.1
1921	Cin-N	136	516	69	158	18	12	2	64	24	16	.306	.341	.399	.740	94	-4	-4	101	117	70	.673	12	6	0	1	*1	-0.6
1922	Cin-N	156	610	114	205	15	**22**	12	66	56	21	.336	.395	.492	.886	133	25	29	96	61	115	.884	14	17	-6	-1	*1	1.9
1923	Cin-N	125	500	63	146	27	10	2	54	40	20	.292	.349	.398	.747	99	-2	-1	98	89	68	.694	11	12	-4	-1	*1	-0.8
1924	Cin-N	102	405	47	114	14	9	1	31	28	17	.281	.331	.368	.699	87	-7	-8	101	71	48	.611	5	10	-5	6	*1	-1.0
Total	15	2014	7673	1117	2326	250	165	56	722	623	489	.303	.360	.401	.760	117	159	168	99	78	1174	.738	251	78		15	*1	11.0
■ **RICH DAUER**	Dauer, Richard Fremont b: 7/27/52, San Bernardino, Cal. BR/TR, 6', 180 lbs. Deb: 9/11/76																											
1976	Bal-A	11	39	0	4	0	0	0	3	1	3	.103	.146	.103	.249	-27	-6	-6	98	294	1	.171	0	0	0	0	2	-0.5
1977	Bal-A	96	304	38	74	15	1	5	25	20	28	.243	.294	.349	.643	80	-11	-8	93	82	30	.538	1	0	0	3	2/3D	0.2
1978	Bal-A	133	459	57	121	23	0	6	46	26	22	.264	.303	.353	.656	92	-10	-5	91	101	44	.525	0	4	-2	1	23/D	-0.2
1979	Bal-A	142	479	63	123	20	0	9	61	36	36	.257	.310	.355	.665	81	-14	-13	97	119	51	.556	0	1	-1	-10	*23	-1.6
1980	Bal-A	152	557	71	158	32	0	2	63	46	19	.284	.342	.352	.693	90	-6	-7	101	124	64	.586	3	2	-0	7	*23	0.7
1981	Bal-A	96	369	41	97	27	0	4	38	27	18	.263	.318	.369	.687	98	-1	-1	99	106	44	.597	0	0	0	-8	2/3	-0.6
1982	Bal-A	158	558	75	156	24	2	8	57	50	34	.280	.340	.373	.713	96	-3	-3	100	100	70	.620	0	1	-1	-28	*23	-2.5
1983	Bal-A	140	459	49	108	19	0	5	41	47	29	.235	.309	.309	.618	71	-17	-18	100	102	42	.516	1	1	-0	-19	*23	-3.2
1984	Bal-A	127	397	29	101	26	0	2	24	24	23	.254	.297	.335	.632	79	-14	-11	94	69	36	.503	1	3	-2	-8	*2/3	-1.4
1985	Bal-A	85	208	25	42	7	0	2	14	20	7	.202	.275	.264	.540	49	-14	-14	99	91	14	.432	0	1	-1	-8	23/1	-2.0
Total	10	1140	3829	448	984	193	3	43	372	297	219	.257	.313	.343	.655	83	-98	-85	97	104	396	.568	6	13	-6	-70	23/D1	-11.1
■ **DOC DAUGHERTY**	Daugherty, Harold Ray b: 10/12/27, Paris, Pa. BR/TR, 6', 180 lbs. Deb: 4/22/51																											
1951	Det-A	1	1	0	0	0	0	0	0	0	1	.000	.000	.000	.000	-95	-0	-0	106	0	0	.000	0	0	0	0	H	0.0
■ **JACK DAUGHERTY**	Daugherty, John Michael b: 7/3/60, Hialeah, Fla. BB/TL, 6' ", 188 lbs. Deb: 9/01/87																											
1987	Mon-N	11	10	1	1	1	0	0	1	0	3	.100	.100	.200	.300	-22	-2	-2	106	200	0	.222	0	0	0	0	/1	-0.1
■ **BOB DAUGHTERS**	Daughters, Robert Francis "Red" b: 8/5/14, Cincinnati, Ohio d: 8/23/88, Southbury, Conn. BR/TR, 6'2", 185 lbs. Deb: 4/24/37																											
1937	Bos-A	1	0	1	0	0	0	0	0	0	0	—	—	—	—	—	0	0	103	—	—	—	0	0	0	0	R	0.0
■ **DARREN DAULTON**	Daulton, Darren Arthur b: 1/3/62, Arkansas City, Kan. BL/TR, 6', 185 lbs. Deb: 9/25/83																											
1983	Phi-N	2	3	1	1	0	0	0	0	1	1	.333	.500	.333	.833	134	0	0	101	0	1	1.000	0	0	0	0	/C	0.0
1985	Phi-N	36	103	14	21	3	1	4	11	16	37	.204	.311	.369	.680	88	-1	-2	102	88	13	.687	3	0	1	3	C	0.3
1986	Phi-N	49	138	18	31	4	0	8	21	38	41	.225	.395	.428	.823	122	7	6	104	101	26	.901	2	3	-1	2	C	0.8
1987	Phi-N	53	129	10	25	6	0	3	13	16	37	.194	.283	.310	.593	55	-8	-9	104	106	13	.538	0	0	0	3	C/1	-0.1
1988	Phi-N	58	144	13	30	6	0	1	12	17	26	.208	.292	.271	.563	62	-7	-7	101	114	12	.496	2	1	0	4	C/1	0.0
Total	5	198	517	56	108	19	1	16	57	88	142	.209	.325	.342	.667	82	-9	-11	103	102	65	.658	7	4	-0	12	C/1	1.0
■ **YO-YO DAVALILLO**	Davalillo, Pompeyo Antonio (Romero) b: 6/30/31, Caracas, Venez. BR/TR, 5'3", 140 lbs. Deb: 8/01/53																											
1953	Was-A	19	58	10	17	1	0	0	2	1	7	.293	.305	.310	.615	70	-3	-2	94	41	6	.476	1	0	0	-3	S	-0.3
■ **VIC DAVALILLO**	Davalillo, Victor Jose (Romero) b: 7/31/36, Cabimas, Venez. BL/TL, 5'7", 150 lbs. Deb: 4/09/63																											
1963	Cle-A	90	370	44	108	18	5	7	36	16	41	.292	.323	.424	.747	111	3	4	97	81	50	.658	3	3	-1	12	O	1.3
1964	Cle-A	150	577	64	156	26	2	6	51	34	77	.270	.312	.354	.666	82	-12	-14	103	103	65	.596	21	11	-0	8	*O	-1.2
1965	Cle-A	142	505	67	152	19	1	5	40	35	50	.301	.346	.372	.719	106	3	4	98	83	68	.684	26	7	4	10	*O	1.3
1966	Cle-A	121	344	42	86	6	4	3	19	24	37	.250	.299	.317	.616	76	-10	-11	101	68	32	.522	8	6	-1	-6	*O	-2.3
1967	Cle-A	139	359	47	103	17	5	2	22	10	30	.287	.308	.379	.687	102	-0	-0	100	65	39	.571	6	7	-2	-2	*O	-0.9
1968	Cle-A	51	180	15	43	2	3	2	13	3	19	.239	.255	.317	.572	72	-6	-7	101	88	13	.476	8	6	-1	2	O	-0.9
	Cal-A	93	339	34	101	15	4	1	18	15	34	.298	.328	.375	.702	120	4	6	94	60	41	.636	17	10	-1	1	O	0.3
	Yr	144	519	49	144	17	7	3	31	18	53	.277	.303	.355	.658	102	-2	-0	96	71	55	.580	25	16	-2	3		-0.6
1969	Cal-A	33	71	10	11	1	1	0	1	6	5	.155	.231	.197	.428	21	-8	-7	99	29	4	.400	3	0	1	-3	O/1	-1.0
	StL-N	63	98	15	26	3	0	2	10	7	8	.265	.314	.357	.671	88	-2	-2	100	98	10	.566	1	1	-0	-1	O/P	-0.4
1970	StL-N	111	183	29	57	14	3	1	33	13	19	.311	.357	.437	.794	105	3	1	106	154	28	.740	4	1	1	-5	O	-0.5
1971	Pit-N	99	295	48	84	14	6	1	33	11	31	.285	.315	.383	.698	98	-2	-2	99	116	36	.627	10	2	2	1	O1	-0.1
1972	Pit-N	117	368	59	117	19	2	4	28	26	44	.318	.368	.413	.781	118	10	9	103	70	59	.765	14	1	4	-3	O/1	0.5
1973	Pit-N	59	83	9	15	1	0	1	3	2	7	.181	.200	.229	.429	20	-9	-8	92	55	3	.296	0	2	-1	-2	1O	-1.2
	Oak-A	38	64	5	12	1	0	0	4	3	4	.188	.224	.203	.427	24	-7	-6	87	121	3	.308	0	0	0	-2	O/1D	-0.8
1974	Oak-A	17	23	0	4	0	0	0	1	2	2	.174	.240	.174	.414	21	-2	-2	100	98	1	.316	0	0	0	-2	/OD	-0.4
1977	LA-N	24	48	3	15	2	0	0	4	0	6	.313	.313	.354	.667	78	-2	-2	100	94	5	.515	0	0	0	-2	O	-0.3
1978	LA-N	75	77	15	24	1	1	1	11	3	7	.312	.338	.390	.727	104	0	0	99	132	10	.636	2	1	0	-7	O/1	-0.8
1979	LA-N	29	27	2	7	1	0	0	2	2	0	.259	.310	.296	.607	67	-1	-1	100	99	3	.600	2	0	1	-1	/O	-0.1
1980	LA-N	7	6	1	1	0	0	0	0	0	1	.167	.167	.167	.333	-7	-1	-1	97	0	0	.200	0	0	0	0	/1	0.0
Total	16	1458	4017	509	1122	160	37	36	329	212	422	.279	.317	.364	.682	94	-38	-37	100	86	472	.613	125	58	3	-2	*O/1DP	-7.5
■ **JERRY DaVANON**	DaVanon, Frank Gerald b: 8/21/45, Oceanside, Cal. BR/TR, 5'11", 175 lbs. Deb: 4/11/69																											
1969	SD-N	24	59	4	8	1	0	0	3	3	12	.136	.177	.153	.330	-7	-8	-8	97	134	1	.214	0	3	-2	-1	2/S	-0.8
	StL-N	16	40	7	12	3	0	1	7	6	8	.300	.391	.450	.841	136	2	2	100	134	7	.800	0	0	0	2	S	0.6
	Yr	40	99	11	20	4	0	1	10	9	20	.202	.269	.273	.541	53	-6	-6	98	137	6	.429	0	3	-2	1		-0.2
1970	StL-N	11	18	2	2	1	0	0	0	2	5	.111	.200	.167	.367	-1	-3	-3	106	0	1	.294	0	0	0	-1	/32	-0.3
1971	Bal-A	38	81	14	19	5	0	0	4	12	20	.235	.340	.296	.637	79	-2	-2	103	68	8	.552	0	0	0	-0	2S/31	0.0
1973	Cal-A	41	49	6	12	3	0	0	2	3	9	.245	.288	.306	.595	70	-2	-2	96	52	4	.487	1	2	-1	-1	S2/3	0.0
1974	StL-N	30	40	4	6	1	0	0	4	4	5	.150	.261	.175	.436	23	-4	-4	104	221	2	.361	0	1	-1	-0	S/32O	-0.3
1975	Hou-N	32	97	15	27	4	2	1	10	16	7	.278	.386	.392	.778	123	3	3	94	94	16	.781	2	0	1	2	S/23	0.9
1976	Hou-N	61	107	19	31	3	3	1	20	21	12	.290	.411	.402	.813	152	6	7	86	167	18	.813	0	2	-1	1	2S/3	1.0
1977	StL-N	9	8	2	0	0	0	0	0	1	2	.000	.111	.000	.111	-70	-2	-2	96	0	0	.125	0	0	0	0	/2	0.0
Total	8	262	499	73	117	21	5	3	50	68	80	.234	.332	.315	.647	86	-10	-8	96	115	56	.597	3	8	-4	2	S/23O1	1.1
■ **JIM DAVENPORT**	Davenport, James Houston b: 8/17/33, Siluria, Ala. BR/TR, 5'11", 170 lbs. Deb: 4/15/58 MC																											
1958	SF-N	134	434	70	111	22	3	12	41	33	64	.256	.319	.403	.722	89	-7	-7	100	80	57	.655	1	3	-2	-7	*3/S	-1.4
1959	SF-N	123	469	65	121	16	3	6	38	28	65	.258	.303	.343	.646	75	-19	-16	95	91	50	.541	0	1	-1	0	*3/S	-2.0
1960	SF-N	112	363	43	91	15	3	6	38	26	58	.251	.308	.358	.666	91	-9	-5	90	104	39	.567	0	2	-1	2	*3/S	-0.5
1961	SF-N	137	436	64	121	28	4	12	65	45	65	.278	.348	.443	.790	110	5	6	98	115	67	.744	4	3	-1	-1	*3	-0.1
1962	SF-N	144	485	83	144	25	5	14	58	45	76	.297	.359	.456	.815	116	11	11	101	87	76	.752	2	5	-2	-1	*3	1.0
1963	SF-N	147	460	40	116	19	3	4	36	32	87	.252	.301	.333	.633	86	-11	-8	96	92	46	.532	5	2	0	-18	*32/S	-2.5
1964	SF-N	116	297	24	70	10	6	2	26	29	46	.236	.304	.330	.634	78	-8	-8	100	103	29	.542	2	0	1	-4	S32	-0.6
1965	SF-N	106	271	29	68	14	3	4	31	21	47	.251	.307	.369	.676	81	-4	-7	111	115	30	.578	0	0	0	-9	3S2	-1.2
1966	SF-N	111	305	42	76	6	2	9	30	22	40	.249	.302	.370	.672	88	-6	-5	97	90	33	.576	1	1	-0	-3	S32/1	-0.2
1967	SF-N	124	295	42	81	10	3	5	30	39	50	.275	.367	.380	.747	113	7	6	101	98	41	.693	1	4	-2	1	3S2	0.6
1968	SF-N	113	272	27	61	1	1	1	17	26	32	.224	.292	.246	.538	64	-12	-11	98	102	19	.419	0	3	-2	-4	3S/2	-1.6
1969	SF-N	112	303	20	73	10	1	2	42	29	37	.241	.307	.300	.608	70	-11	-12	101	174	27	.494	0	1	-1	-3	*3/1SO	-1.4
1970	SF-N	22	37	3	9	1	0	0	4	7	6	.243	.364	.270	.634	76	-1	-1	96	155	4	.607	0	0	0	-1	3	-0.1
Total	13	1501	4427	552	1142	177	37	77	456	382	673	.258	.320	.367	.687	90	-65	-57	99	103	519	.618	16	25	-10	-48	*3S2/1O	-10.0
■ **ANDRE DAVID**	David, Andre Anter b: 5/18/58, Hollywood, Cal. BL/TL, 6', 170 lbs. Deb: 6/29/84																											
1984	Min-A	33	48	5	12	2	0	1	5	7	11	.250	.357	.354	.711	92	0	-0	106	100	6	.658	0	0	0	-4	O/D	-0.4
1986	Min-A	5	5	0	1	0	0	0	0	0	2	.200	.333	.200	.533	47	-0	-0	108	0	0	.500	0	0	0	0	/D	0.0
Total	2	38	53	5	13	2	0	1	5	7	13	.245	.355	.340	.694	88	-0	-1	106	90	6	.675	0	0	0	-4	/OD	-0.4
■ **CLAUDE DAVIDSON**	Davidson, Claude Boucher "Davey" b: 10/13/1896, Boston, Mass. d: 4/18/56, Weymouth, Mass. BL/TR, 5'11", 155 lbs. Deb: 4/25/18																											
1918	Phi-A	31	81	4	15	1	0	0	4	5	9	.185	.233	.198	.430	29	-7	-7	104	91	4	.318	0			-0	2/O3	-0.7
1919	Was-A	2	7	1	3	0	0	0	0	1	1	.429	.500	.429	.929	165	1	1	98	0	2	1.000	0			0	/3	0.1

YEAR	TM/L	G	AB	R	H	2B	3B	HR	RBI	BB	SO	AVG	OBP	SLG	PRO	/A	BR	/A	PF	CHI	RC	TA	SB	CS	SBR	FR	POS	TPR
Total	2	33	88	5	18	1	0	0	4	6	10	.205	.255	.216	.471	40	-6	-7	104	83	6	.357	0			0	/2O3	-0.6
■ **HOMER DAVIDSON** Davidson, Homer Hurd "Divvy" b: 10/14/1884, Cleveland, Ohio d: 7/26/48, Detroit, Mich. TR, 5'10.5", 155 lbs. Deb: 4/25/08																												
1908	Cle-A	9	4	2	0	0	0	0	0	0		.000	.000	.000	.000	-94	-1	-1	106	0	-0	.250	1			0	/CO	0.0
■ **MARK DAVIDSON** Davidson, John Mark b: 2/15/61, Knoxville, Tenn. BR/TR, 6'2", 180 lbs. Deb: 6/20/86																												
1986	Min-A	36	68	5	8	3	0	0	2	6	22	.118	.189	.162	.351	-2	-10	-10	108	72	2	.297	2	3	-1	-4	O/D	-1.6
1987	Min-A	102	150	32	40	4	1	1	14	13	26	.267	.325	.327	.652	78	-5	-4	96	107	17	.612	9	2	2	-13	O/D	-1.7
1988	Min-A	100	106	22	23	7	0	1	10	10	20	.217	.291	.311	.602	65	-4	-5	106	110	9	.528	3	3	-1	-18	O/3D	-2.6
Total	3	238	324	59	71	14	1	2	26	29	68	.219	.285	.287	.572	55	-19	-20	102	101	28	.519	14	8	-1	-35	O/D3	-5.9
■ **BILL DAVIDSON** Davidson, William Simpson b: 5/10/1884, Lafayette, Ind. d: 5/23/54, Lincoln, Neb. BR/TR, 5'10", 170 lbs. Deb: 09																												
1909	Chi-N	2	7	2	1	0	0	0	0	1		.143	.250	.143	.393	23	-1	-1	101	0	0	.500	1			0	/O	0.0
1910	Bro-N	136	509	48	121	13	7	0	34	24	54	.238	.277	.291	.568	69	-23	-20	95	85	48	.523	27			2	*O	-2.4
1911	Bro-N	87	292	33	68	3	4	1	26	16	21	.233	.275	.281	.556	57	-18	-17	97	103	27	.522	18			-8	O	-2.6
Total	3	225	808	83	190	16	11	1	60	41	75	.235	.276	.286	.562	64	-42	-38	96	91	75	.523	46			-5	O	-5.0
■ **CHICK DAVIES** Davies, Lloyd Garrison b: 3/6/1892, Peabody, Mass. d: 9/5/73, Middletown, Conn. BL/TL, 5'8", 145 lbs. Deb: 7/11/14																												
1914	Phi-A	19	46	6	11	3	1	0	5	5	13	.239	.314	.348	.662	102	-0	-0	97	117	6	.629	1			1	O/P	0.1
1915	Phi-A	56	132	13	24	5	3	0	11	14	31	.182	.270	.265	.535	63	-7	-6	96	107	10	.473	2	4	-2	5	O/P	-0.3
1925	NY-N	4	6	1	0	0	0	0	0	0	1	.000	.000	.000	.000	-99	-2	-2	99	0	0	.000	0	0	0	0	/PO	0.0
1926	NY-N	38	18	4	4	0	0	0	1	3	5	.222	.333	.222	.556	53	-1	-1	98	86	1	.500	0			1	P	0.0
Total	4	117	202	24	39	8	4	0	17	22	50	.193	.279	.272	.551	65	-10	-9	97	104	17	.491	3	4		7	/PO	-0.2
■ **LEFTY DAVIS** Davis, Alphonzo De Ford b: 2/4/1875, Nashville, Tenn. d: 2/4/19, Collins, N.Y. BL/TL, 5'10", 170 lbs. Deb: 4/18/01																												
1901	Bro-N	25	91	11	19	2	0	0	7	10		.209	.287	.231	.518	50	-5	-6	106	114	7	.486	4			-1	O/2	-0.8
	Pit-N	87	335	87	105	8	11	2	33	56		.313	.412	.421	.833	144	21	21	101	66	69	.952	22			3	O	1.5
	Yr	112	426	98	124	10	11	2	40	66		.291	.386	.380	.766	123	16	15	102	78	74	.841	26			2		0.7
1902	Pit-N	59	232	52	65	7	3	0	20	35		.280	.375	.336	.711	116	8	6	105	77	37	.790	19			5	O	0.7
1903	NY-A	104	372	54	88	10	0	0	25	43		.237	.316	.263	.579	77	-8	-8	100	97	35	.535	11			-19	*O/S	-3.6
1907	Cin-N	73	266	28	61	5	5	1	25	23		.229	.291	.297	.588	90	-4	-3	95	111	26	.541	9			9	O	0.3
Total	4	348	1296	232	338	32	19	3	110	167		.261	.345	.322	.667	102	12	10	101	89	175	.677	65			-4	O/S2	-1.9
■ **ALVIN DAVIS** Davis, Alvin Glenn b: 9/9/60, Riverside, Cal. BL/TR, 6'1", 195 lbs. Deb: 4/11/84																												
1984	Sea-A	152	567	80	161	34	3	27	116	97	78	.284	.395	.497	.892	142	38	36	102	122	117	.938	5	4	-1	-3	*1/D	2.2
1985	Sea-A	155	578	78	166	33	1	18	78	90	71	.287	.385	.441	.826	133	23	27	95	96	101	.813	1	2	-1	-6	*1	1.0
1986	Sea-A	135	479	66	130	18	1	18	72	76	68	.271	.375	.426	.800	113	14	11	105	118	78	.780	0	3	-2	-2	*1D	0.0
1987	Sea-A	157	580	86	171	37	2	29	100	72	84	.295	.375	.516	.890	131	29	26	103	110	111	.876	0	0	0	-7	*1	0.3
1988	Sea-A	140	478	67	141	24	1	18	69	95	53	.295	.416	.462	.878	135	34	29	108	106	95	.912	1	1	-0	-4	*1D	1.8
Total	5	739	2682	377	769	146	8	110	435	430	354	.287	.389	.470	.859	131	137	129	102	110	501	.886	7	10	-4	-22	1/D	5.3
■ **BILL DAVIS** Davis, Arthur Willard b: 6/6/42, Graceville, Minn. BL/TL, 6'7", 215 lbs. Deb: 9/16/65																												
1965	Cle-A	10	10	0	3	1	0	0	0	0	1	.300	.300	.400	.700	99	-0	-0	98	0	1	.571	0	0	0	0	H	0.0
1966	Cle-A	23	38	2	6	1	0	1	4	6	9	.158	.273	.263	.536	54	-2	-2	101	129	3	.485	0	0	0	-0	/1	-0.2
1969	SD-N	31	57	1	10	1	0	0	1	8	18	.175	.288	.193	.481	38	-5	-4	97	36	3	.408	0	0	0	0	1	-0.4
Total	3	64	105	3	19	3	0	1	5	14	28	.181	.283	.238	.521	50	-7	-7	99	67	8	.455	0	0	0	0	/1	-0.6
■ **BROCK DAVIS** Davis, Bryshear Barnett b: 10/19/43, Oakland, Cal. BL/TL, 5'10", 160 lbs. Deb: 4/09/63																												
1963	Hou-N	34	55	7	11	2	0	1	2	4	10	.200	.254	.291	.545	61	-3	-3	92	44	4	.444	0	0	0	-2	O	-0.4
1964	Hou-N	1	3	0	0	0	0	0	0	1	1	.000	.250	.000	.250	-23	-0	-0	96	0	0	.333	0	0	0	0	/O	0.0
1966	Hou-N	10	27	2	4	1	0	0	1	5	4	.148	.281	.185	.466	34	-2	-2	97	84	2	.478	1	0	0	0	/O	-0.1
1970	Chi-N	6	3	0	0	0	0	0	0	0	1	.000	.000	.000	.000	-83	-1	-1	120	0	0	.000	0	0	0	-0	/O	0.0
1971	Chi-N	106	301	22	77	7	5	0	28	35	34	.256	.337	.312	.650	77	-5	-8	110	121	33	.567	0	6	-4	-0	O	-1.6
1972	Mil-A	85	154	17	49	2	0	0	12	12	23	.318	.367	.331	.699	114	2	3	95	98	18	.611	6	4	-1	-5	O	-0.3
Total	6	242	543	48	141	12	5	1	43	57	73	.260	.332	.306	.638	82	-10	-12	103	104	58	.558	7	10	-4	-6	O	-2.4
■ **CHILI DAVIS** Davis, Charles Theodore b: 1/17/60, Kingston, Jamaica BB/TR, 6'3", 195 lbs. Deb: 4/10/81																												
1981	SF-N	8	15	1	2	0	0	0	0	1	2	.133	.188	.133	.321	-7	-2	-2	105	0	0	.357	2	0	1	-1	/O	-0.2
1982	SF-N	154	641	86	167	27	6	19	76	45	115	.261	.311	.410	.721	107	-2	3	94	82	79	.668	24	13	-1	10	*O	1.2
1983	SF-N	137	486	54	113	21	2	11	59	55	108	.233	.311	.352	.662	82	-11	-12	101	117	52	.599	10	12	-4	5	*O	-1.3
1984	SF-N	137	499	87	157	21	6	21	81	42	74	.315	.369	.507	.876	150	28	30	96	103	89	.848	12	8	-1	12	*O	3.8
1985	SF-N	136	481	53	130	25	2	13	56	62	74	.270	.354	.412	.765	121	9	13	93	100	68	.735	15	7	0	0	*O	1.1
1986	SF-N	153	526	71	146	28	3	13	70	84	96	.278	.378	.416	.794	124	16	19	96	110	83	.792	16	13	-3	6	*O	1.9
1987	SF-N	149	500	80	125	22	1	24	76	72	109	.250	.347	.442	.789	112	5	8	96	106	78	.793	16	9	-1	-9	*O	-0.7
1988	Cal-A	158	600	81	161	29	3	21	93	56	118	.268	.331	.432	.762	119	9	13	94	122	82	.701	9	10	-3	-5	*O/D	0.2
Total	8	1032	3748	513	1001	173	23	122	511	417	696	.267	.341	.423	.765	116	52	73	96	105	530	.746	104	72	-12	17	O/D	6.0
■ **DOUG DAVIS** Davis, Douglas Raymond b: 9/24/62, Bloomsburg, Pa. BR/TR, 6', 180 lbs. Deb: 7/08/88																												
1988	Cal-A	6	12	1	0	0	0	0	0	0	3	.000	.077	.000	.077	-81	-3	-3	94	0	0	.083	0	0	0	0	/C3	-0.2
■ **ERIC DAVIS** Davis, Eric Keith b: 5/29/62, Los Angeles, Cal. BR/TR, 6'2", 165 lbs. Deb: 5/19/84																												
1984	Cin-N	57	174	33	39	10	1	10	30	24	48	.224	.322	.466	.787	112	4	3	106	106	28	.841	10	2	2	8	O	1.1
1985	Cin-N	56	122	26	30	3	3	8	18	7	39	.246	.287	.516	.803	114	2	2	105	82	19	.896	16	3	3	-1	O	0.2
1986	Cin-N	132	415	97	115	15	3	27	71	68	100	.277	.380	.523	.903	140	27	24	104	95	95	1.155	80	11	17	4	*O	4.4
1987	Cin-N	129	474	120	139	23	4	37	100	84	134	.293	.401	.593	.994	154	41	39	104	108	124	1.199	50	6	11	21	*O	**6.3**
1988	Cin-N	135	472	81	129	18	3	26	93	65	124	.273	.365	.489	.854	136	27	24	105	123	90	.936	35	3	9	-8	*O	2.2
Total	5	509	1657	357	452	69	14	108	312	248	445	.273	.369	.527	.896	138	101	91	105	107	356	1.062	191	25	42	23	O	14.2
■ **GEORGE DAVIS** Davis, George Stacey b: 8/23/1870, Cohoes, N.Y. d: 10/17/40, Philadelphia, Pa. BB/TR, 5'9", 180 lbs. Deb: 4/19/1890 M																												
1890	Cle-N	136	526	98	139	22	9	6	73	53	34	.264	.336	.375	.711	116	6	11	94	109	75	.713	22			13	*O/2S	1.9
1891	Cle-N	136	570	115	165	35	12	3	89	53	29	.289	.354	.409	.763	118	17	12	105	103	100	.820	42			6	*O3/P	1.1
1892	Cle-N	144	597	95	144	27	12	5	82	58	51	.241	.312	.352	.663	99	1	-2	103	108	79	.678	36			-4	3OS/2	-0.1
1893	NY-N	133	549	112	195	22	27	11	119	42	20	.355	.410	.554	.964	152	42	38	104	102	143	1.107	37			-1	*3/S	3.1
1894	NY-N	122	477	120	168	26	19	8	91	66	10	.352	.435	.537	.972	136	28	29	100	86	132	1.184	40			-0	*3	2.0
1895	NY-N	110	430	108	146	36	9	5	101	55	12	.340	.417	.500	.917	146	25	29	95	118	112	1.127	48			9	312/OM	3.1
1896	NY-N	124	494	98	158	25	12	6	99	50	24	.320	.387	.455	.842	125	17	18	99	113	108	.973	48			9	3S/O1	2.6
1897	NY-N	130	519	112	183	31	10	10	**134**	41		.353	.406	.509	.915	146	31	33	98	141	137	1.119	65			19	*S	4.6
1898	NY-N	121	486	80	149	20	5	2	86	32		.307	.351	.381	.731	118	7	11	95	131	76	.724	26			**33**	*S	**4.5**
1899	NY-N	108	416	68	140	21	5	1	57	37		.337	.393	.418	.812	129	15	17	97	95	84	.895	34			**43**	*S	**5.9**
1900	NY-N	114	426	69	136	20	4	3	61	35		.319	.371	.406	.777	120	10	12	97	111	77	.817	29			21	*SM	4.0
1901	NY-N	130	491	69	148	26	7	7	65	40		.301	.354	.426	.780	140	17	23	91	100	86	.805	27			12	*S3M	4.0
1902	Chi-A	132	485	76	145	27	7	3	93	65		.299	.382	.402	.784	125	15	18	95	**159**	88	.856	31			-2	*S/1	2.5
1903	NY-N	4	15	2	4	0	0	0	1	1		.267	.313	.267	.579	63	-1	-1	106	85	1	.455	0			-0	/S	0.0
1904	Chi-A	152	563	75	142	27	15	1	69	43		.252	.305	.359	.664	113	8	8	99	121	73	.658	32			17	*S	2.9
1905	Chi-A	151	550	74	153	28	3	1	55	60		.278	.349	.345	.695	127	16	18	97	98	79	.708	31			13	*S	3.8
1906	Chi-A	133	484	63	134	26	6	0	80	41		.277	.333	.355	.689	128	10	15	92	**179**	68	.686	27			12	*S/2	3.1
1907	Chi-A	132	466	59	111	16	2	1	52	47		.238	.308	.288	.596	89	-3	-5	104	104	47	.552	15			6	*S	0.4
1908	Chi-A	128	419	41	91	14	1	0	26	41		.217	.287	.255	.542	83	-8	-6	94	93	36	.518	22			2	2S/1	-0.6
1909	Chi-A	28	68	5	9	1	0	0	2	10		.132	.253	.147	.400	28	-5	-5	97	77	3	.424	4			1	1/2	-0.4
Total	20	2368	9031	1539	2660	450	165	73	1435	870	180	.295	.359	.405	.764	123	246	272	98	117	1605	.814	616			208	*S3O2/1P	48.4

YEAR	TM/L	G	AB	R	H	2B	3B	HR	RBI	BB	SO	AVG	OBP	SLG	PRO	/A	BR	/A	PF	CHI	RC	TA	SB	CS	SBR	FR	POS	TPR
■ **KIDDO DAVIS**	Davis, George Willis b: 2/12/02, Bridgeport, Conn. d: 3/4/83, Bridgeport, Conn. BR/TR, 5'11", 178 lbs. Deb: 6/15/26																											
1926	NY-A	1	0	0	0	0	0	0	0	0	0	—	—	—	—	—	0	0	99	—	—	—	0	0	0	-0	/O	0.0
1932	Phi-N	137	576	100	178	39	6	5	57	44	56	.309	.359	.424	.783	98	8	-1	112	79	90	.766	16			10	*O	0.0
1933	NY-N	126	434	61	112	20	4	7	37	25	30	.258	.298	.371	.669	91	-6	-6	99	76	47	.587	10			-12	*O	-2.6
1934	StL-N	16	33	6	10	3	0	1	4	3	1	.303	.361	.485	.846	109	1	0	114	76	6	.833	1			1	/O	0.1
	Phi-N	100	393	50	115	25	5	3	48	27	28	.293	.338	.405	.743	90	-1	-6	108	109	55	.656	1			15	*O	0.5
	Yr	116	426	56	125	28	5	4	52	30	29	.293	.340	.411	.751	92	-0	-5	109	105	61	.672	2			16		0.6
1935	NY-N	47	91	16	24	7	1	2	6	10	4	.264	.343	.429	.772	110	1	1	96	48	14	.754	2			-2	O	0.0
1936	NY-N	47	67	6	16	1	0	0	5	6	5	.239	.301	.254	.555	51	-4	-4	100	104	6	.442	0			-1	O	-0.5
1937	NY-N	56	76	20	20	10	0	0	9	10	7	.263	.356	.395	.751	104	1	1	100	108	11	.724	1			-9	O	-1.0
	Cin-N	40	136	19	35	6	0	1	5	16	6	.257	.340	.324	.663	89	-3	-1	91	39	16	.590	1			3	O	0.0
	Yr	96	212	39	55	16	0	1	14	26	13	.259	.346	.349	.695	93	-3	-1	96	80	28	.646	2			-7		-1.0
1938	Cin-N	5	18	3	5	1	0	0	0	1	4	.278	.316	.333	.649	80	-1	-0	98	0	2	.538	0			0	/O	0.0
Total	8	575	1824	281	515	112	16	19	171	142	141	.282	.336	.393	.728	94	-5	-16	105	81	1850	.683	32	0		5	O	-3.5
■ **GERRY DAVIS**	Davis, Gerald Edward b: 12/25/58, Trenton, N.J. BR/TR, 6', 185 lbs. Deb: 9/20/83																											
1983	SD-N	5	15	3	5	2	0	0	1	3	4	.333	.444	.467	.911	154	1	1	99	56	3	1.000	1	0	0	0	/O	0.2
1985	SD-N	44	58	10	17	3	1	0	2	5	7	.293	.349	.379	.729	102	0	0	102	36	7	.628	0	0	0	-5	O	-0.4
Total	2	49	73	13	22	5	1	0	3	8	11	.301	.370	.397	.768	113	2	1	101	41	11	.717	1	0	0	-4	/O	-0.2
■ **GLENN DAVIS**	Davis, Glenn Earle b: 3/28/61, Jacksonville, Fla. BR/TR, 6'3", 210 lbs. Deb: 9/02/84																											
1984	Hou-N	18	61	6	13	5	0	2	8	4	12	.213	.262	.393	.655	88	-2	-1	93	104	7	.583	0	0	0	-0	1	-0.1
1985	Hou-N	100	350	51	95	11	0	20	64	27	68	.271	.336	.474	.810	129	10	12	96	115	53	.749	0	0	0	-2	1/O	0.7
1986	Hou-N	158	574	91	152	32	3	31	101	64	72	.265	.348	.493	.841	126	22	20	103	113	100	.827	3	1	0	2	*1	1.6
1987	Hou-N	151	578	70	145	35	2	27	93	47	84	.251	.313	.458	.771	109	-1	4	93	114	80	.713	4	1	1	3	*1	0.0
1988	Hou-N	152	561	78	152	26	0	30	99	53	77	.271	.346	.478	.823	144	24	28	93	117	91	.794	4	3	-1	-1	*1	2.0
Total	5	579	2124	296	557	109	5	110	365	195	313	.262	.333	.474	.807	125	53	63	96	114	330	.786	11	5	0	1	1/O	4.2
■ **HARRY DAVIS**	Davis, Harry Albert "Stinky" b: 5/7/08, Shreveport, La. BL/TL, 5'10.5", 160 lbs. Deb: 4/13/32																											
1932	Det-A	141	590	92	159	32	13	4	74	60	53	.269	.339	.388	.727	86	-11	-12	102	89	80	.692	12	7	-1	-3	*1	-2.8
1933	Det-A	66	173	24	37	8	2	0	14	22	8	.214	.303	.283	.586	53	-11	-12	107	95	16	.525	2	3	-1	-1	1	-1.6
1937	StL-A	120	450	89	124	25	3	3	35	71	26	.276	.374	.364	.739	88	-7	-6	99	73	65	.729	7	6	-2	-3	*1/O	-2.1
Total	3	327	1213	205	320	65	18	7	123	153	87	.264	.347	.364	.712	82	-28	-31	101	84	161	.680	21	16	-3	-7	1/O	-6.5
■ **HARRY DAVIS**	Davis, Harry H "Jasper" b: 7/19/1873, Philadelphia, Pa. d: 8/11/47, Philadelphia, Pa. BR/TR, 5'10", 180 lbs. Deb: 9/21/1895 M																											
1895	NY-N	7	24	1	7	0	1	0	6	2	0	.292	.346	.375	.721	93	-0	-0	95	186	4	.706	1			0	/1	0.0
1896	NY-N	64	233	43	64	11	10	2	50	31	20	.275	.372	.433	.805	115	5	6	99	143	45	.905	16			-4	O1	0.0
	Pit-N	44	168	24	32	5	6	0	23	13	21	.190	.257	.292	.548	49	-13	-12	93	138	15	.537	9			-1	1O/S	-0.9
	Yr	108	401	67	96	16	16	2	73	44	41	.239	.325	.374	.699	89	-8	-6	96	142	58	.741	25			-5		-0.9
1897	Pit-N	111	429	70	131	10	**28**	2	63	26		.305	.355	.473	.828	122	10	12	98	93	82	.862	21			-5	13O/S	0.5
1898	Pit-N	58	222	31	65	9	13	1	24	12		.293	.332	.464	.796	133	7	8	98	72	37	.783	7			-1	1/O	0.6
	Lou-N	37	138	18	30	5	2	1	16	7		.217	.255	.304	.560	64	-7	-6	96	110	13	.509	6			0	1/2O	-0.5
	Was-N	1	3	0	0	0	0	0	0	0		.000	.000	.000	.000	-98	-1	-1	102	0	0	.000	0			0	/1	0.0
	Yr	96	363	49	95	14	15	2	40	19		.262	.300	.399	.700	105	-1	1	97	88	49	.664	13			-1		0.1
1899	Was-N	18	64	3	12	2	3	0	8	8		.188	.288	.313	.600	70	-3	-2	96	130	6	.596	2			0	1	-0.1
1901	Phi-A	117	496	92	152	28	10	8	76	23		.306	.337	.452	.789	119	11	11	100	85	85	.779	21			6	*1	1.1
1902	Phi-A	133	561	89	172	**43**	8	6	92	30		.307	.342	.444	.786	109	12	5	108	100	97	.789	28			7	*1/O	1.3
1903	Phi-A	106	420	77	125	29	7	5	55	24		.298	.336	.436	.771	127	15	14	104	96	71	.783	24			-3	*1/O	1.2
1904	Phi-A	102	404	54	125	21	11	**10**	62	23		.309	.347	.490	.837	163	28	27	102	90	75	.835	12			-3	*1	2.9
1905	Phi-A	149	602	**92**	171	**47**	6	**8**	**83**	43		.284	.332	.422	.754	129	26	20	109	94	99	.773	36			-1	*1	1.6
1906	Phi-A	145	551	94	161	40	8	**12**	**96**	49		.292	.350	.459	.809	165	33	37	94	116	99	.833	23			-0	*1	3.5
1907	Phi-A	149	582	84	155	**37**	8	**8**	87	42		.266	.316	.399	.714	122	17	14	106	117	82	.689	20			4	*1	1.7
1908	Phi-A	147	513	65	127	23	9	5	62	61		.248	.328	.357	.684	116	15	11	108	125	64	.684	20			2	*1	1.0
1909	Phi-A	149	530	73	142	22	11	4	75	51		.268	.338	.374	.711	122	15	14	102	146	71	.706	20			-6	*1	0.8
1910	Phi-A	139	492	61	122	19	4	1	41	53		.248	.332	.309	.641	99	2	1	102	104	57	.624	17			-4	*1	0.2
1911	Phi-A	57	183	27	36	9	1	1	22	24		.197	.297	.273	.570	64	-10	-8	93	140	16	.531	2			-0	1	-0.6
1912	Cle-A	2	5	0	0	0	0	0	0	0		.000	.000	.000	.000	-99	-1	-1	101	0	0	.000	0			0	/1M	0.0
1913	Phi-A	7	17	2	6	2	0	0	4	1	4	.353	.389	.471	.859	157	1	1	97	178	3	.818	0			0	/1	0.1
1914	Phi-A	5	7	0	3	0	0	0	2	1	0	.429	.556	.429	.984	202	1	1	97	250	1	.833	0	2	-1	0	/1	0.0
1915	Phi-A	5	3	0	1	0	0	0	4	0	0	.333	.333	.333	.667	104	-0	0	96	0	0	.500	0			0	/1	0.0
1916	Phi-A	4	6	0	1	0	0	0	1	1	2	.167	.286	.167	.452	37	-0	-0	98	357	0	.400	0			1	/O	0.0
1917	Phi-A	1	1	0	0	0	0	0	0	0	0	.000	.000	.000	.000	-99	-0	-0	94	0	0	.000	0			0	H	0.0
Total	22	1757	6654	1000	1840	362	146	74	952	525	47	.277	.333	.408	.741	119	163	149	102	110	1021	.739	285	2		-10	*1/O32S	14.4
■ **TOMMY DAVIS**	Davis, Herman Thomas b: 3/21/39, Brooklyn, N.Y. BR/TR, 6'2", 195 lbs. Deb: 9/22/59 C																											
1959	LA-N	1	1	0	0	0	0	0	0	0	1	.000	.000	.000	.000	-98	-0	-0	102	0	0	.000	0	0	0	0	H	0.0
1960	LA-N	110	352	43	97	18	1	11	44	13	35	.276	.305	.426	.731	85	-2	-9	115	98	45	.650	6	2	1	-7	O/3	-1.7
1961	LA-N	132	460	60	128	13	2	15	58	32	53	.278	.328	.413	.741	93	-4	-5	102	102	59	.665	10	4	1	0	O3	-1.1
1962	LA-N	163	665	120	**230**	27	9	27	**153**	33	65	**.346**	.379	.535	.914	153	37	43	93	**146**	129	.893	18	6	2	-2	*O3	3.5
1963	LA-N	146	556	69	181	19	3	16	88	29	59	**.326**	.363	.457	.820	142	24	27	95	130	86	.751	15	10	-2	-4	*O3	1.6
1964	LA-N	152	592	70	163	20	5	14	86	29	68	.275	.314	.397	.711	107	-2	4	92	135	69	.619	11	8	-2	4	*O	0.2
1965	LA-N	17	60	3	15	1	1	0	9	2	4	.250	.274	.300	.574	67	-3	-2	91	211	3	.431	2	1	0	-0	O	-0.3
1966	LA-N	100	313	27	98	11	1	3	27	16	36	.313	.347	.383	.730	106	1	2	97	88	38	.607	3	3	-1	-6	O/3	-0.6
1967	NY-N	154	577	72	174	32	0	16	73	31	71	.302	.345	.440	.785	124	16	17	99	106	84	.713	9	3	1	-8	*O/1	0.3
1968	Chi-A	132	456	30	122	5	3	8	50	16	48	.268	.292	.344	.637	92	-5	-6	101	121	42	.503	4	2	0	-6	*O/1	-1.9
1969	Sea-A	123	454	52	123	29	1	6	80	30	46	.271	.322	.379	.701	97	-4	-3	98	172	53	.639	19	4	3	-9	*O/1	-1.1
	Hou-N	24	79	2	19	3	0	1	9	8	9	.241	.318	.316	.635	77	-2	-2	102	129	8	.556	1	1	-0	-1	O	-0.4
1970	Hou-N	57	213	24	60	12	2	3	30	7	25	.282	.305	.399	.704	93	-5	-3	94	124	25	.629	8	3	1	-4	O	-0.7
	Chi-N	11	42	4	11	2	0	2	8	1	1	.262	.279	.452	.731	77	-1	-2	120	127	5	.645	0	0	0	-1	O	-0.2
	Yr	68	255	28	71	14	2	5	38	8	26	.278	.300	.408	.708	90	-5	-5	98	126	32	.642	8	3	1	-4		-0.9
	Oak-A	66	200	17	58	9	1	1	27	8	18	.290	.321	.360	.681	90	-4	-3	97	146	21	.553	2	4	-2	-8	O/1	-1.4
1971	Oak-A	79	219	26	71	8	1	3	42	15	19	.324	.368	.411	.778	120	6	6	101	173	31	.704	7	1	2	-0	1O/23	0.5
1972	Chi-N	15	26	3	7	1	0	0	6	2	3	.269	.321	.308	.629	70	-1	-1	114	308	2	.500	0	1	-1	0	/1O	-0.1
	Bal-A	26	82	9	21	3	0	0	6	6	18	.256	.307	.293	.600	81	-2	-2	98	104	7	.500	2	0	1	-1	O/1	-0.3
1973	Bal-A	137	552	53	169	20	3	7	89	30	56	.306	.343	.391	.734	99	4	-1	107	**156**	72	.643	11	3	2	0	*D/1	0.0
1974	Bal-A	158	626	67	181	20	1	11	84	34	49	.289	.329	.377	.706	111	1	7	93	130	73	.597	6	2	1	0	*D	0.7
1975	Bal-A	116	460	43	130	14	1	6	57	23	52	.283	.317	.357	.673	99	-7	-2	91	123	49	.549	2	0	1	0	*D	0.0
1976	Cal-A	72	219	16	58	5	0	3	26	15	18	.265	.315	.329	.644	96	-3	-1	92	123	20	.506	0	1	-1	0	D/1	-0.1
	KC-A	8	19	1	5	0	0	0	0	1	0	.263	.300	.263	.563	66	-1	-1	100	0	1	.400	0	0	0	0	/D	0.0
	Yr	80	238	17	63	5	0	3	26	16	18	.265	.314	.324	.637	94	-4	-2	93	113	25	.531	0	1	-1	0		-0.1
Total	18	1999	7223	811	2121	272	35	153	1052	381	754	.294	.332	.405	.736	108	44	63	98	130	923	.672	136	59	5	-52	*OD3/12	-3.1
■ **IKE DAVIS**	Davis, Isaac Marion b: 6/14/1895, Pueblo, Col. d: 4/2/84, Tucson, Ariz. BR/TR, 5'7", 140 lbs. Deb: 4/23/19																											
1919	Was-A	8	14	0	0	0	0	0	0	0	6	.000	.000	.000	.000	-99	-4	-4	98	0	0	.000	0			-0	/S	-0.3
1924	Chi-A	10	33	5	8	1	1	0	4	2	5	.242	.286	.333	.619	61	-2	-2	97	120	3	.520	0	0	0	-1	*S	-0.1
1925	Chi-A	146	562	105	135	31	9	0	61	71	58	.240	.333	.327	.660	71	-27	-23	96	107	66	.637	19	14	-3	8	*S	0.4
Total	3	164	609	110	143	32	10	0	65	73	69	.235	.324	.320	.644	67	-33	-28	96	105	69	.613	19	14		7	S	0.0

YEAR	TM/L	G	AB	R	H	2B	3B	HR	RBI	BB	SO	AVG	OBP	SLG	PRO	/A	BR	/A	PF	CHI	RC	TA	SB	CS	SBR	FR	POS	TPR
■ IRA DAVIS	Davis, J. Ira "Slats" b: 7/8/1870, Philadelphia, Pa. d: 12/21/42, Brooklyn, N.Y. Deb: 4/22/1899																											
1899	NY-N	6	17	3	4	1	1	0	2	0		.235	.235	.412	.647	80	-1	-1	97	88	2	.615	1			0	/S1	0.0
■ JACKE DAVIS	Davis, Jacke Sylvesta b: 3/5/36, Carthage, Tex. BR/TR, 5'11", 160 lbs. Deb: 4/19/62																											
1962	Phi-N	48	75	9	16	0	1	1	6	4	20	.213	.253	.280	.533	45	-6	-6	95	99	5	.426	1	0	0	-6	O	-1.1
■ JUMBO DAVIS	Davis, James J. b: 9/5/1861, New York, N, Y. d: 2/14/21, St.Louis, Mo. BL/TR, 5'11", 195 lbs. Deb: 7/27/1884																											
1884	KC-U	7	29	3	6	0	0	0		0		.207	.207	.207	.414	46	-2	-1	87	0	1	.261	0			0	/3	0.0
1886	Bal-a	60	216	23	42	5	2	1		11		.194	.240	.250	.490	61	-11	-8	91	0	16	.454	12			3	3	-0.1
1887	Bal-a	130	485	81	150	23	19	8		28		.309	.353	.485	.838	140	20	24	96	0	103	.946	49			-1	3S	1.6
1888	KC-a	121	491	70	131	22	8	3	61	20		.267	.304	.363	.666	109	8	3	106	94	68	.683	42			30	*3/S	3.0
1889	KC-a	62	241	40	64	4	3	0	30	17	35	.266	.319	.307	.626	76	-6	-8	106	118	32	.667	25			-1	3	-0.6
	StL-a	2	4	1	0	0	0	0	0	1	1	.000	.200	.000	.200	-36	-1	-1	112	0	0	.250	0			0	/SO	0.0
	Yr	64	245	41	64	4	3	0	30	18	36	.261	.317	.302	.619	74	-6	-9	106	116	32	.657	25			-1		-0.6
1890	StL-a	21	71	8	18	3	1	0		9		.254	.338	.324	.661	84	-0	-2	116	0	10	.698	5			-1	3	-0.2
	BB-a	38	142	33	43	9	2	2		15		.303	.385	.437	.822	145	8	8	100	0	28	.919	10			-5	3	0.2
	Yr	59	213	41	61	12	3	2		24		.286	.369	.399	.768	122	8	6	106	0	38	.842	15			-6		0.0
1891	Was-a	12	44	7	14	3	2	0	9	7	5	.318	.412	.477	.889	165	3	4	95	131	12	1.200	8			0	3	0.3
Total	7	453	1723	266	468	69	37	14	100	108	41	.272	.322	.379	.701	110	20	19	101	46	272	.742	151			26	3/SO	4.2
■ JODY DAVIS	Davis, Jody Richard b: 11/12/56, Gainesville, Ga. BR/TR, 6'4", 192 lbs. Deb: 4/21/81																											
1981	Chi-N	56	180	14	46	5	1	4	21	21	28	.256	.337	.361	.698	94	-0	-1	104	107	21	.617	0	1	-1	3	C	0.2
1982	Chi-N	130	418	41	109	20	2	12	52	36	92	.261	.321	.404	.725	98	0	-1	103	99	55	.652	0	1	-1	13	*C	1.2
1983	Chi-N	151	510	56	138	31	2	24	84	33	93	.271	.317	.480	.798	117	10	9	101	105	72	.718	0	2	-1	0	*C	1.4
1984	Chi-N	150	523	55	134	25	2	19	94	47	99	.256	.319	.421	.739	96	3	-3	110	136	63	.658	5	6	-2	8	*C	0.7
1985	Chi-N	142	482	47	112	30	0	17	58	48	83	.232	.302	.400	.702	82	-4	-14	116	95	57	.630	1	0	0	5	*C	-0.3
1986	Chi-N	148	528	61	132	27	2	21	74	41	110	.250	.304	.428	.732	93	-2	-6	107	104	66	.650	0	1	-1	19	*C/1	1.5
1987	Chi-N	125	428	57	106	12	2	19	51	52	91	.248	.332	.418	.750	96	-2	-2	101	88	58	.692	1	2	-1	0	*C	0.7
1988	Chi-N	88	249	19	57	9	0	6	33	29	51	.229	.312	.337	.649	83	-4	-5	104	129	25	.564	0	3	-2	2	C	-0.1
	Atl-N	2	8	2	2	0	0	1	3	0	1	.250	.250	.625	.875	138	0	0	104	153	1	.833	0	0	0	0	/C	0.0
	Yr	90	257	21	59	9	0	7	36	29	52	.230	.310	.346	.656	84	-4	-5	104	131	29	.592	0	3	-2	2		-0.1
Total	8	992	3326	352	836	159	11	123	470	307	648	.251	.316	.417	.733	96	1	-24	106	107	418	.682	7	16	-8	50	C/1	5.3
■ JOHN DAVIS	Davis, John Humphrey "Red" b: 7/15/15, Laurel Run, Pa. BR/TR, 5'11", 172 lbs. Deb: 9/09/41																											
1941	NY-N	21	70	8	15	3	0	0	5	8	12	.214	.295	.257	.552	55	-4	-4	103	100	6	.473	0			1	3	-0.3
■ CRASH DAVIS	Davis, Lawrence Columbus b: 7/14/19, Canon, Ga. BR/TR, 6', 173 lbs. Deb: 6/15/40																											
1940	Phi-A	23	67	4	18	1	1	0	9	3	10	.269	.310	.313	.623	65	-4	-3	96	155	7	.510	1	0	0	-2	2/S	-0.3
1941	Phi-A	39	105	8	23	3	0	0	8	11	16	.219	.293	.248	.541	44	-8	-8	101	109	9	.446	0	0	0	-1	21	-0.7
1942	Phi-A	86	272	31	61	8	1	2	26	21	30	.224	.282	.283	.565	61	-15	-14	96	110	22	.457	1	0	0	-7	2S/1	-1.7
Total	3	148	444	43	102	12	2	2	43	35	56	.230	.289	.279	.568	57	-27	-25	97	117	37	.466	2	0	1	-10	/2S1	-2.7
■ MIKE DAVIS	Davis, Michael Dwayne b: 6/11/59, San Diego, Cal. BL/TL, 6'2", 175 lbs. Deb: 4/10/80																											
1980	Oak-A	51	95	11	20	2	1	1	8	7	14	.211	.265	.284	.549	53	-6	-6	95	104	7	.462	2	1	0	-1	O/1D	-0.6
1981	Oak-A	17	20	0	1	1	0	0	0	2	4	.050	.136	.100	.236	-32	-3	-3	96	0	0	.200	0	0	0	-0	/O1D	-0.3
1982	Oak-A	23	75	12	30	4	0	1	10	2	8	.400	.416	.493	.909	156	5	5	95	100	15	.894	3	2	-0	0	O/1	0.5
1983	Oak-A	128	443	61	122	24	4	8	62	27	74	.275	.324	.402	.726	103	-1	1	96	120	56	.701	32	15	1	10	*O/D	1.0
1984	Oak-A	134	382	47	88	18	3	9	46	31	66	.230	.290	.364	.654	87	-11	-7	92	110	40	.601	14	9	-1	2	*O/D	-0.9
1985	Oak-A	154	547	92	157	34	1	24	82	50	99	.287	.349	.484	.833	135	18	23	93	98	91	.832	24	10	1	7	*O	2.9
1986	Oak-A	142	489	77	131	28	3	19	55	34	91	.268	.317	.454	.771	115	4	8	94	79	72	.770	27	4	6	7	*O	1.6
1987	Oak-A	139	494	69	131	32	1	22	72	42	94	.265	.324	.468	.792	118	4	11	91	99	72	.765	19	7	2	-10	*OD	-0.1
1988	LA-N	108	281	29	55	11	2	2	17	25	59	.196	.261	.270	.532	50	-17	-19	106	83	20	.460	7	3	0	-5	O	-2.7
Total	9	896	2826	398	735	154	15	86	352	220	509	.260	.316	.416	.732	105	-8	14	94	98	374	.715	128	51	8	10	O/D1	1.4
■ ODIE DAVIS	Davis, Odie Ernest b: 8/13/55, San Antonio, Tex. BR/TR, 6'1", 178 lbs. Deb: 9/03/80																											
1980	Tex-A	17	8	0	1	0	0	0	0	0	2	.125	.125	.125	.250	-31	-1	-1	100	0	0	.143	0	0	0	0	S/3	0.0
■ OTIS DAVIS	Davis, Otis Allen "Scat" b: 9/24/20, Charleston, Ark. BL/TL, 6', 160 lbs. Deb: 4/22/46																											
1946	Bro-N	1	0	1	0	0	0	0	0	0	0	—	—	—	—	—	0	0	103	—	—	—	0			0	R	0.0
■ DICK DAVIS	Davis, Richard Earl b: 9/25/53, Long Beach, Cal. BR/TR, 6'3", 190 lbs. Deb: 7/12/77																											
1977	Mil-A	22	51	7	14	2	0	0	6	1	8	.275	.288	.314	.602	67	-3	-2	95	149	4	.447	0	0	0	-3	O/D	-0.4
1978	Mil-A	69	218	28	54	10	1	5	26	7	23	.248	.278	.372	.649	77	-6	-8	106	107	20	.529	2	5	-2	-1	DO	-1.1
1979	Mil-A	91	335	51	89	13	1	12	41	16	46	.266	.299	.418	.717	91	-5	-5	100	91	38	.614	3	3	-1	-2	DO	-0.9
1980	Mil-A	106	365	50	99	26	2	4	30	11	43	.271	.298	.386	.684	91	-8	-5	95	76	40	.578	5	3	-0	-3	DO	-0.9
1981	Phi-N	45	96	12	32	6	1	2	19	8	13	.333	.390	.479	.870	130	6	4	112	143	18	.836	1	2	-1	-6	O	-0.3
1982	Phi-N	28	68	5	19	3	1	2	7	2	9	.279	.300	.441	.741	112	0	1	94	76	8	.623	1	0	0	-1	O	0.0
	Tor-A	3	7	0	2	0	0	0	2	0	1	.286	.286	.286	.571	53	-0	-0	109	400	0	.333	0	0	0	0	/OD	0.0
	Pit-N	39	77	7	14	2	1	2	10	5	9	.182	.232	.312	.543	46	-5	-6	110	131	6	.469	1	0	0	-5	O	-1.1
Total	6	403	1217	160	323	62	7	27	141	50	152	.265	.298	.394	.692	88	-22	-22	101	100	134	.605	13	13	-4	-20	OD	-4.7
■ BRANDY DAVIS	Davis, Robert Brandon b: 9/10/28, Newark, Del. BR/TR, 6', 170 lbs. Deb: 4/15/52 C																											
1952	Pit-N	55	95	14	17	1	1	0	1	11	28	.179	.264	.211	.475	33	-8	-8	100	19	7	.500	9	2	2	-2	O	-0.9
1953	Pit-N	12	39	5	8	2	0	0	2	0	3	.205	.205	.256	.462	19	-5	-5	102	78	2	.303	0	2	-1	-0	/O	-0.5
Total	2	67	134	19	25	3	1	0	3	11	31	.187	.248	.224	.472	29	-13	-13	100	35	9	.442	9	4	0	-2	/O	-1.4
■ BOB DAVIS	Davis, Robert John Eugene b: 3/1/52, Pryor, Okla. BR/TR, 6', 180 lbs. Deb: 4/06/73																											
1973	SD-N	5	11	1	1	0	0	0	0	0	5	.091	.091	.091	.182	-53	-2	-2	94	0	0	.100	0	0	0	0	/C	-0.1
1975	SD-N	43	128	6	30	3	2	0	7	11	31	.234	.310	.289	.599	67	-5	-5	100	73	12	.505	0	0	0	0	C	-0.3
1976	SD-N	51	83	7	17	0	1	0	5	5	13	.205	.250	.229	.479	41	-7	-6	89	101	5	.364	0	0	0	-2	C	-0.5
1977	SD-N	48	94	9	17	2	0	1	10	5	24	.181	.238	.234	.472	31	-10	-8	88	160	5	.367	0	0	0	-3	C	-1.1
1978	SD-N	19	40	3	8	1	0	0	2	1	5	.200	.220	.225	.445	26	-4	-4	93	88	1	.278	0	1	-1	-1	C	-0.4
1979	Tor-A	32	89	6	11	2	0	1	8	6	15	.124	.188	.180	.367	-0	-13	-13	103	162	2	.271	0	0	0	3	C	-0.8
1980	Tor-A	91	218	18	47	11	0	4	19	12	25	.216	.260	.321	.581	58	-13	-13	100	90	17	.461	0	0	0	0	C	-0.8
1981	Cal-A	1	2	0	0	0	0	0	0	0	0	.000	.000	.000	.000	-96	-1	-1	104	0	0	.000	0	0	0	0	/C	0.0
Total	8	290	665	50	131	19	3	6	51	40	118	.197	.250	.262	.512	42	-54	-52	97	106	42	.413	0	1	-1	-2	C	-4.0
■ RON DAVIS	Davis, Ronald Everette b: 10/21/41, Roanoke Rapids, N.C BR/TR, 6', 175 lbs. Deb: 8/01/62																											
1962	Hou-N	6	14	1	3	0	0	0	1	1	7	.214	.267	.214	.481	33	-1	-1	93	131	1	.417	1	0	0	0	/O	0.0
1966	Hou-N	48	194	21	48	10	1	2	19	13	26	.247	.308	.340	.648	82	-5	-4	97	98	20	.559	2	2	-1	9	O	0.2
1967	Hou-N	94	285	31	73	19	1	7	38	17	48	.256	.303	.404	.706	107	-1	1	94	116	34	.635	5	3	-0	-1	O	-0.3
1968	Hou-N	52	217	22	46	10	1	1	12	13	48	.212	.269	.281	.550	66	-9	-9	99	68	16	.443	0	4	-2	4	O	-1.0
	StL-N	33	79	11	14	4	2	0	5	5	17	.177	.226	.278	.505	53	-5	-4	95	96	5	.418	1	0	0	1	O	-0.4
	Yr	85	296	33	60	14	3	1	17	18	65	.203	.258	.280	.538	63	-14	-13	98	80	22	.438	1	4	-2	5		-1.4
1969	Pit-N	62	64	10	15	1	1	0	4	7	14	.234	.310	.281	.591	70	-3	-2	95	89	6	.510	0	0	0	-13	O	-1.8
Total	5	295	853	96	199	44	6	10	79	56	160	.233	.288	.334	.622	82	-24	-20	96	96	83	.543	9	9	-3	0	O	-3.3
■ STEVE DAVIS	Davis, Steven Michael b: 12/30/53, Oakland, Cal. BR/TR, 6'1", 200 lbs. Deb: 9/23/79																											
1979	Chi-N	3	4	0	0	0	0	0	1	0	0	.000	.000	.000	.000	-89	-1	-1	112	0	0	.000	0	0	0	0	/23	0.0

YEAR	TM/L	G	AB	R	H	2B	3B	HR	RBI	BB	SO	AVG	OBP	SLG	PRO	/A	BR	/A	PF	CHI	RC	TA	SB	CS	SBR	FR	POS	TPR
■ TOD DAVIS	Davis, Thomas Oscar b: 7/24/24, Los Angeles, Cal. d: 2/79, W.Covina, Cal. BR/TR, 6'2", 190 lbs. Deb: 4/27/49																											
1949	Phi-A	31	75	7	20	0	1	1	6	9	16	.267	.345	.333	.679	81	-2	-2	99	73	10	.607	0	0	0	1	S3/2	0.0
1951	Phi-A	11	15	0	1	0	0	0	0	1	3	.067	.125	.067	.192	-45	-3	-3	106	0	0	.133	0	0	0	0	/23	-0.2
Total	2	42	90	7	21	0	1	1	6	10	19	.233	.310	.289	.599	60	-5	-5	100	62	10	.514	0	0	0	1	/S32	-0.2
■ TRENCH DAVIS	Davis, Trench Neal b: 9/12/60, Baltimore, Md. BL/TL, 6'3", 171 lbs. Deb: 6/04/85																											
1985	Pit-N	2	7	1	1	0	0	0	0	0	0	.143	.143	.143	.286	-19	-1	-1	103	0	0	.286	1	0	0	-1	/O	-0.1
1986	Pit-N	15	23	2	3	0	0	0	1	0	4	.130	.130	.130	.261	-28	-4	-4	100	133	0	.143	0	0	0	-0	/O	-0.4
1987	Atl-N	6	3	0	0	0	0	0	0	0	1	.000	.000	.000	.000	-92	-1	-1	108	0	0	.000	0	0	0	0	/H	0.0
Total	3	23	33	3	4	0	0	0	1	0	5	.121	.121	.121	.242	-33	-6	-6	101	93	0	.172	1	0	0	-1	/O	-0.5
■ SPUD DAVIS	Davis, Virgil Lawrence b: 12/20/04, Birmingham, Ala. d: 8/14/84, Birmingham, Ala. BR/TR, 6'1", 197 lbs. Deb: 4/30/28 MC																											
1928	StL-N	2	5	1	1	0	0	0	1	1	0	.200	.333	.200	.533	42	-0	-0	100	356	0	.500	0			0	/C	0.0
	Phi-N	67	163	16	46	2	0	3	18	15	11	.282	.343	.350	.692	78	-4	-5	104	97	19	.615	0			5	C	0.3
	Yr	69	168	17	47	2	0	3	19	16	11	.280	.342	.345	.688	77	-5	-5	104	110	20	.612	0			5		0.3
1929	Phi-N	98	263	31	90	18	0	7	48	19	17	.342	.391	.490	.881	107	7	3	110	110	49	.873	1			-1	C	0.8
1930	Phi-N	106	329	41	103	16	1	14	65	17	20	.313	.349	.495	.844	95	-0	-4	106	109	54	.805	1			-2	C	0.0
1931	Phi-N	120	393	30	128	32	1	4	51	36	28	.326	.382	.443	.825	114	12	9	106	98	68	.792	0			3	*C	1.7
1932	Phi-N	125	402	44	135	23	5	14	70	40	39	.336	.399	.522	.921	130	26	20	112	103	86	.948	1			-7	*C	1.7
1933	Phi-N	141	495	51	173	28	3	9	65	32	24	.349	.395	.473	.867	125	30	20	118	96	89	.796	2			7	*C	3.2
1934	StL-N	107	347	45	104	22	4	9	65	34	27	.300	.366	.464	.830	106	10	4	114	125	58	.773	0			0	C	0.7
1935	StL-N	102	315	28	100	24	2	1	60	33	30	.317	.386	.416	.802	111	8	6	104	162	54	.758	0			-6	C/1	0.0
1936	StL-N	112	363	24	99	26	2	4	59	35	34	.273	.342	.388	.730	102	-2	1	94	137	48	.649	0			-4	*C/3	0.0
1937	Cin-N	76	209	19	56	10	1	3	33	23	15	.268	.341	.368	.709	101	-2	1	91	138	26	.625	0			-0	C	0.2
1938	Cin-N	12	36	3	6	1	0	0	1	5	6	.167	.286	.194	.480	35	-3	-3	98	52	2	.406	0			-0	C	-0.2
	Phi-N	70	215	11	53	7	0	2	23	14	14	.247	.293	.307	.600	65	-10	-10	100	115	17	.466	1			-3	C	-1.0
	Yr	82	251	14	59	8	0	2	24	19	20	.235	.292	.291	.582	61	-13	-13	100	107	20	.461	1			-3		-1.2
1939	Phi-N	87	202	10	62	8	1	0	23	24	20	.307	.383	.356	.740	106	1	3	94	117	29	.669	0			-2	C	0.3
1940	Pit-N	99	285	23	93	14	1	5	39	35	20	.326	.404	.435	.839	138	13	15	95	104	48	.778	0			-1	C	1.8
1941	Pit-N	57	107	3	27	4	1	0	6	11	11	.252	.322	.308	.630	76	-3	-3	103	66	10	.512	0			-1	C	0.1
1944	Pit-N	54	93	6	28	7	0	2	14	10	8	.301	.369	.441	.810	121	3	3	105	107	15	.761	0			-2	C	0.3
1945	Pit-N	23	33	2	8	2	0	0	6	2	2	.242	.306	.303	.609	67	-1	-1	103	208	3	.481	0			-0	C	-0.1
Total	16	1458	4255	388	1312	244	22	77	647	386	326	.308	.369	.430	.799	108	84	56	105	114	676	.762	6			-14	*C/13	9.8
■ WILLIE DAVIS	Davis, William Henry b: 4/15/40, Mineral Springs, Ark. BL/TL, 5'11", 180 lbs. Deb: 9/08/60																											
1960	LA-N	22	88	12	28	6	1	2	10	4	12	.318	.348	.477	.825	107	3	1	115	89	12	.742	3	5	-2	2	O	0.0
1961	LA-N	128	339	56	86	19	6	12	45	27	46	.254	.318	.451	.769	99	-0	-1	102	96	49	.749	12	5	1	-8	*O	-1.4
1962	LA-N	157	600	103	171	18	**10**	21	85	42	72	.285	.338	.453	.791	119	7	13	93	106	92	.782	32	7	5	6	*O	1.5
1963	LA-N	156	515	60	126	19	8	9	60	25	61	.245	.284	.365	.649	90	-11	-8	95	117	51	.589	25	11	1	6	*O	-0.9
1964	LA-N	157	613	91	180	23	7	12	77	22	59	.294	.319	.413	.732	113	2	8	92	116	82	.707	42	13	5	19	*O	2.8
1965	LA-N	142	558	52	133	24	3	10	57	14	81	.238	.266	.346	.612	77	-23	-17	91	112	51	.542	25	9	2	0	*O	-2.0
1966	LA-N	153	624	74	177	31	6	11	61	15	68	.284	.305	.405	.710	98	-5	-3	97	95	76	.636	21	10	0	2	*O	-0.5
1967	LA-N	143	569	65	146	27	9	6	41	29	65	.257	.296	.367	.663	101	-9	-2	88	79	62	.597	20	6	2	-1	*O	-0.7
1968	LA-N	160	643	86	161	24	10	7	31	31	88	.250	.286	.351	.637	100	-9	-3	91	51	68	.594	36	10	5	0	*O	-0.6
1969	LA-N	129	498	66	155	23	8	11	59	33	39	.311	.359	.456	.815	129	17	18	99	96	79	.791	24	10	1	-1	*O	1.1
1970	LA-N	146	593	92	181	23	**16**	8	93	29	54	.305	.339	.438	.777	119	4	12	90	135	88	.759	38	14	3	10	*O	1.8
1971	LA-N	158	641	84	198	33	10	10	74	23	47	.309	.333	.438	.771	118	12	13	99	103	88	.692	20	8	1	5	*O	1.4
1972	LA-N	149	615	81	178	22	7	19	79	27	61	.289	.320	.441	.761	122	9	13	94	95	87	.710	20	3	4	4	*O	1.6
1973	LA-N	152	599	82	171	29	9	16	77	29	62	.285	.324	.444	.768	110	6	6	100	104	86	.720	17	5	2	-2	*O	0.0
1974	Mon-N	153	611	86	180	27	9	12	89	27	69	.295	.328	.427	.755	105	5	2	104	123	85	.709	25	7	3	-3	*O	-0.3
1975	Tex-A	42	169	16	42	8	2	5	17	4	25	.249	.270	.408	.678	90	-3	-3	100	79	18	.649	13	5	1	2	O	-0.1
	StL-N	98	350	41	102	19	6	6	50	14	27	.291	.326	.431	.758	106	3	1	103	117	50	.705	10	1	2	4	O	0.4
1976	SD-N	141	493	61	132	18	10	5	46	19	34	.268	.298	.375	.673	102	-8	-2	89	89	56	.596	14	2	3	2	*O	-0.1
1979	Cal-A	43	56	9	14	2	1	0	2	4	7	.250	.300	.321	.621	73	-3	-2	93	43	5	.523	1	0	0	-1	/OD	-0.2
Total	18	2429	9174	1217	2561	395	138	182	1053	418	977	.279	.314	.412	.726	107	-3	47	95	101	1186	.689	398	131	41	43	*O/D	3.8
■ BUTCH DAVIS	Davis, Wallace Mc Arthur b: 6/19/58, Martin Co., N.C. BR/TR, 6', 185 lbs. Deb: 8/23/83																											
1983	KC-A	33	122	13	42	2	6	2	18	4	19	.344	.365	.508	.873	135	6	6	101	106	21	.814	4	3	-1	1	O	0.5
1984	KC-A	41	116	11	17	3	0	2	12	10	19	.147	.214	.224	.438	22	-12	-12	99	150	5	.385	4	3	-1	-1	O/D	-1.5
1987	Pit-N	7	7	3	1	1	0	0	0	1	3	.143	.250	.286	.536	40	-1	-1	104	0	1	.500	0	0	0	0	/O	0.0
1988	Bal-A	13	25	2	6	1	0	0	0	0	8	.240	.240	.280	.520	47	-2	-2	95	0	1	.381	1	0	0	-0	O/D	-0.1
Total	4	94	270	29	66	7	6	4	30	15	49	.244	.284	.359	.643	76	-9	-9	100	113	28	.571	9	6	-1	-1	/OD	-1.1
■ ANDRE DAWSON	Dawson, Andre Fernando b: 7/10/54, Miami, Fla. BR/TR, 6'3", 180 lbs. Deb: 9/11/76																											
1976	Mon-N	24	85	9	20	4	1	0	7	5	13	.235	.278	.306	.584	65	-4	-4	100	106	7	.478	1	2	-1	3	O	-0.2
1977	Mon-N	139	525	64	148	26	9	19	65	34	93	.282	.328	.474	.802	114	7	8	98	87	82	.785	21	7	2	2	*O	0.7
1978	Mon-N	157	609	84	154	24	8	25	72	30	128	.253	.301	.442	.743	110	1	4	96	88	80	.717	28	11	2	14	*O	1.4
1979	Mon-N	155	639	90	176	24	12	25	92	27	115	.275	.311	.468	.779	107	5	4	102	86	91	.760	35	10	5	-2	*O	0.2
1980	Mon-N	151	577	96	178	41	7	17	87	44	69	.308	.364	.492	.856	138	27	28	99	109	105	.882	34	9	5	11	*O	3.9
1981	Mon-N	103	394	71	119	21	3	24	64	35	50	.302	.369	.553	.923	161	29	29	99	92	83	1.004	26	4	5	12	*O	4.6
1982	Mon-N	148	608	107	183	37	7	23	83	34	96	.301	.346	.498	.845	127	25	21	105	84	106	.867	39	10	6	13	*O	3.9
1983	Mon-N	159	633	104	**189**	36	10	32	113	38	81	.299	.347	.539	.886	140	32	31	102	108	113	.881	25	11	1	6	*O	3.6
1984	Mon-N	138	533	73	132	23	6	17	86	41	80	.248	.304	.409	.713	108	-3	3	91	133	65	.656	13	5	1	12	*O	1.1
1985	Mon-N	139	529	65	135	27	2	23	91	29	92	.255	.299	.444	.743	112	1	5	94	126	67	.685	13	4	2	-0	*O	0.3
1986	Mon-N	130	496	65	141	32	2	20	78	37	79	.284	.341	.478	.819	126	14	16	98	111	75	.784	18	12	-2	-3	*O	0.9
1987	Chi-N	153	621	90	178	24	2	**49**	**137**	32	103	.287	.329	.568	.897	131	25	24	101	116	111	.874	11	3	2	3	*O	2.1
1988	Chi-N	157	591	78	179	31	8	24	79	37	73	.303	.348	.504	.852	136	30	27	104	87	100	.818	12	4	1	-4	*O	2.1
Total	13	1753	6840	996	1932	350	77	298	1054	423	1072	.282	.331	.487	.818	125	190	196	99	102	1085	.818	276	92	28	65	*O	24.6
■ BOOTS DAY	Day, Charles Frederick b: 8/31/47, Ilion, N.Y. BL/TL, 5'9", 160 lbs. Deb: 6/15/69																											
1969	StL-N	11	6	1	0	0	0	0	0	1	1	.000	.143	.000	.143	-57	-1	-1	100	0	0	.143	0	0	0	-0	/O	-0.1
1970	Chi-N	11	8	2	2	0	0	0	0	0	3	.250	.250	.250	.500	29	-1	-1	120	0	0	.286	0	0	0	-1	/O	-0.1
	Mon-N	41	108	14	29	4	0	0	5	6	18	.269	.307	.306	.613	65	-5	-5	100	59	10	.506	3	2	-0	2	O	-0.4
	Yr	52	116	16	31	4	0	0	5	6	21	.267	.303	.302	.605	60	-6	-7	104	46	10	.494	3	2	-0	1		-0.5
1971	Mon-N	127	371	53	105	10	2	4	33	33	39	.283	.343	.353	.696	99	-1	-0	99	94	47	.635	9	4	0	-1	*O	-0.4
1972	Mon-N	128	386	32	90	7	4	0	30	29	44	.233	.288	.272	.560	59	-20	-21	102	117	31	.450	3	6	-3	-10	*O	-4.2
1973	Mon-N	101	207	36	57	7	0	4	28	21	28	.275	.342	.367	.709	93	-1	-2	104	128	26	.622	0	3	-2	-3	O	-0.8
1974	Mon-N	52	65	8	12	0	0	0	2	5	8	.185	.243	.185	.427	20	-7	-7	104	64	3	.309	0	0	0	-3	O	-1.0
Total	6	471	1151	146	295	28	6	8	98	95	141	.256	.314	.312	.626	75	-35	-37	102	102	117	.540	15	15	-5	-16	O	-7.0
■ BRIAN DAYETT	Dayett, Brian Kelly b: 1/22/57, New London, Conn. BR/TR, 5'10", 180 lbs. Deb: 9/11/83																											
1983	NY-A	11	29	3	6	0	1	0	5	2	4	.207	.258	.276	.534	48	-2	-2	99	244	2	.435	0	0	0	1	/O	0.0
1984	NY-A	64	127	14	31	8	0	4	23	9	14	.244	.299	.402	.701	98	-2	-1	94	146	15	.616	0	0	0	-10	O/D	-1.2
1985	Chi-N	22	26	1	6	0	0	1	4	0	6	.231	.259	.346	.605	58	-1	-2	116	133	2	.476	0	0	0	-2	O	-0.4
1986	Chi-N	24	67	7	18	4	0	4	11	6	10	.269	.329	.507	.836	119	2	2	107	95	10	.769	0	1	-1	-2	O	-0.1
1987	Chi-N	97	177	20	49	14	1	5	25	20	37	.277	.350	.452	.802	110	3	2	101	105	29	.763	0	0	0	-14	O	-1.4
Total	5	218	426	45	110	26	2	14	68	37	71	.258	.320	.427	.748	101	-0	-0	100	126	58	.691	0	1	-1	-28	O/D	-3.1

YEAR	TM/L	G	AB	R	H	2B	3B	HR	RBI	BB	SO	AVG	OBP	SLG	PRO	/A	BR	/A	PF	CHI	RC	TA	SB	CS	SBR	FR	POS	TPR
■ CHARLIE DEAL Deal, Charles Albert b: 10/30/1891, Wilkinsburg, Pa. d: 9/6/79, Covina, Cal. BR/TR, 5'11", 160 lbs. Deb: 7/19/12																												
1912	Det-A	41	142	13	32	4	2	0	11	9		.225	.272	.282	.553	61	-8	-7	95	94	12	.482	4			2	3	-0.5
1913	Det-A	16	50	3	11	0	2	0	3	1	7	.220	.235	.300	.535	57	-3	-3	99	71	4	.462	2			0	3	-0.1
	Bos-N	10	36	6	11	1	0	0	3	2	1	.306	.359	.333	.692	104	0	0	95	93	5	.640	1			0	2	0.0
1914	Bos-N	79	257	17	54	13	2	0	23	20	23	.210	.270	.276	.546	60	-12	-13	104	117	21	.473	4			2	3/S	-0.9
1915	StL-F	65	223	21	72	12	4	1	27	12	16	.323	.357	.426	.783	125	8	7	105	101	40	.775	10			5	3	1.4
1916	StL-A	23	74	7	10	1	0	0	10	6	8	.135	.200	.149	.349	5	-9	-8	95	325	3	.328	4			-1	3/2	-0.8
	Chi-N	2	8	2	2	1	0	0	3	0	0	.250	.250	.375	.625	77	-0	-0	117	405	1	.500	0			0	/3	0.0
1917	Chi-N	135	449	46	114	11	3	0	47	19	18	.254	.284	.292	.576	73	-13	-15	105	141	41	.478	10			4	*3	-1.3
1918	Chi-N	119	414	43	99	9	3	2	34	21	13	.239	.279	.290	.569	72	-13	-14	102	104	37	.489	11			-3	*3	-1.7
1919	Chi-N	116	405	37	117	23	5	2	52	12	12	.289	.316	.385	.701	110	4	4	100	127	52	.635	11			6	*3	1.1
1920	Chi-N	129	450	48	108	10	5	3	39	20	14	.240	.285	.304	.589	70	-18	-17	99	105	39	.486	5	8	-3	10	*3	-0.4
1921	Chi-N	115	422	52	122	19	8	3	66	13	9	.289	.310	.393	.704	80	-10	-14	107	141	50	.597	3	5	-2	11	*3	-0.3
Total	10	850	2930	295	752	104	34	11	318	135	121	.257	.293	.327	.620	79	-74	-82	102	125	304	.535	65	13		36	3/2S	-3.5
■ LINDSAY DEAL Deal, Fred Lindsay b: 9/3/11, Lenoir, N.C. d: 4/18/79, Little Rock, Ark. BL/TR, 6', 175 lbs. Deb: 9/13/39																												
1939	Bro-N	4	7	0	0	0	0	0	0	0	2	.000	.000	.000	.000	-93	-2	-2	107	0	0	.000	0			0	/O	-0.1
■ SNAKE DEAL Deal, John Wesley b: 1/21/1879, Lancaster, Pa. d: 5/9/44, Harrisburg, Pa. BR/TR, 6', 164 lbs. Deb: 7/09/06																												
1906	Cin-N	65	231	13	48	4	3	0	21	6		.208	.228	.251	.479	44	-14	-17	115	135	17	.432	15			1	1	-2.0
■ PAT DEALY Dealy, Patrick E. b: Moosup, Conn. d: 12/16/24, Buffalo, N.Y. BR/TR, Deb: 9/30/1884																												
1884	StP-U	5	15	2	2	0	0	0		0		.133	.133	.133	.267	-10	-2	-2	100	0	0	.154	0			0	/CO	0.0
1885	Bos-N	35	130	18	29	4	1	1	9	2	14	.223	.235	.292	.527	75	-4	-3	94	78	9	.396				2	C/3OS1	0.1
1886	Bos-N	15	46	9	15	1	1	0	3	4	4	.326	.380	.391	.771	139	2	2	97	54	9	.871	5			0	C/O	0.2
1887	Was-N	58	312	33	85	8	2	1	18	8	8	.272	.295	.321	.616	76	-11	-9	95	46	41	.643	36			0	CS/O3	-0.7
1890	Syr-a	18	66	9	12	1	0	0		5		.182	.250	.197	.447	37	-5	-4	90	0	4	.426	4			0	C/3O	-0.3
Total	5	131	569	71	143	14	4	2	30	19	26	.251	.279	.301	.580	75	-21	-16	95	47	64	.559	45			2	/CS3O1	-0.7
■ CHUBBY DEAN Dean, Alfred Lovill b: 8/24/16, Mt.Airy, N.C. d: 12/21/70, Riverside, Cal. BL/TL, 5'11", 181 lbs. Deb: 4/14/36																												
1936	Phi-A	111	342	41	98	21	3	1	48	24	24	.287	.337	.374	.711	75	-14	-14	101	119	44	.638	3	2	-0	-2	1	-2.3
1937	Phi-A	104	309	36	81	14	4	2	31	42	10	.262	.350	.353	.703	83	-10	-7	94	92	41	.668	2	1	0	-2	1/P	-1.6
1938	Phi-A	16	20	3	6	2	0	0	1	1	4	.300	.333	.400	.733	82	-1	-1	101	42	3	.643	0	0	0	1	/P	0.1
1939	Phi-A	80	77	12	27	4	0	0	19	8	4	.351	.412	.403	.814	112	1	2	97	207	12	.709	0	0	0	1	P	0.0
1940	Phi-A	67	90	6	26	2	0	0	6	16	9	.289	.396	.311	.707	90	-1	-0	96	77	13	.677	0	0	0	1	P/1	0.5
1941	Phi-A	27	37	0	9	2	0	0	9	4	3	.243	.317	.297	.614	63	-2	-2	101	290	4	.536	0	0	0	0	P/1	0.0
	Cle-A	17	25	2	4	1	0	0	2	3	2	.160	.250	.200	.450	20	-3	-3	101	142	1	.348	0	0	0	1	/P	0.0
	Yr	44	62	2	13	3	0	0	11	7	5	.210	.290	.258	.548	46	-5	-5	101	239	5	.451	0	0	0	1		0.0
1942	Cle-A	70	101	4	27	1	0	0	7	11	7	.267	.339	.277	.617	81	-3	-2	92	88	10	.506	0	0	0	-3	P	0.0
1943	Cle-A	41	46	2	9	0	0	0	5	6	2	.196	.288	.196	.484	47	-3	-3	90	203	3	.375	0	0	0	-1	P	0.0
Total	8	533	1047	106	287	47	7	3	128	115	65	.274	.347	.341	.688	79	-34	-29	96	119	129	.625	5	3	-0	-5	P1	-3.3
■ DORY DEAN Dean, Charles Wilson b: 11/6/1852, Cincinnati, Ohio d: 5/4/35, Nashville, Tenn. BR/TR, Deb: N/A.																												
1874	Bal-n	45	212	29	49							.231															*O/2	
1876	Cin-N	34	138	9	36	3	1	0	4	2	13	.261	.271	.297	.569	100	-2	1	90	35	11	.422				-0	P/OS	0.0
Total	2	34	138	9	36	3	1	0	4	2	13	.261	.271	.297	.569	100	-2	1	90	35	11	.422				-0	/OPS2	0.0
■ TOMMY DEAN Dean, Tommy Douglas b: 8/30/45, Iuka, Miss. BR/TR, 6', 165 lbs. Deb: 9/17/67																												
1967	LA-N	12	28	1	4	1	0	0	2	0	9	.143	.143	.179	.321	-10	-4	-4	88	166	1	.208	0	0	0	0	S	-0.1
1969	SD-N	101	273	14	48	9	2	2	9	27	54	.176	.252	.245	.498	41	-22	-21	97	49	17	.409	0	3	-2	-7	S/2	-1.8
1970	SD-N	61	158	18	35	5	1	2	13	11	29	.222	.272	.304	.576	57	-10	-9	95	93	13	.480	2	0	1	3	S	0.1
1971	SD-N	41	70	2	8	0	0	0	1	4	13	.114	.162	.114	.276	-21	-11	-11	96	51	2	.203	1	0	0	-0	S3/2	-0.7
Total	4	215	529	35	95	15	3	4	25	42	105	.180	.241	.242	.483	36	-47	-44	96	68	33	.396	3	3	-1	-4	S/32	-2.5
■ HARRY DEANE Deane, John Henry b: 5/6/1846, Trenton, N.J. d: 5/31/25, Indianapolis, Ind. 5'7", 150 lbs. Deb: 7/20/1871 M																												
1871	Kek-n	5	24	3	4							.167															/OM	
■ BUDDY DEAR Dear, Paul Stanford b: 12/1/05, Norfolk, Va. BR/TR, 5'8", 143 lbs. Deb: 9/09/27																												
1927	Was-A	2	1	1	0	0	0	0	0	0	0	.000	.000	.000	.000	-99	-0	-0	97	0	0	.000	0	0	0	0	/2	0.0
■ CHARLIE DeARMOND DeArmond, Charles Hommer "Hummer" b: 2/13/1877, Okeana, Ohio d: 12/17/33, Morning Sun, Ohio BR/TR, 5'10", 165 lbs. Deb: 03																												
1903	Cin-N	11	39	10	11	2	1	0	7	3		.282	.333	.385	.718	97	0	-0	109	153	5	.679	1			1	3	0.0
■ JOHN DEASLEY Deasley, John b: 1/1861, Philadelphia, Pa. d: 12/25/10, Philadelphia, Pa. Deb: 6/17/1884																												
1884	Was-U	31	134	20	29	1	1	0		3		.216	.234	.239	.472	62	-5	-5	97	0	8	.333	0			-1	S	-0.3
	KC-U	13	40	3	7	2	0	0		2		.175	.214	.225	.439	56	-2	-1	87	0	2	.333	0			0	S	0.0
	Yr	44	174	23	36	3	1	0		5		.207	.229	.236	.465	61	-7	-6	94	0	10	.333	0			-1		-0.3
Total	1	44	174	23	36	3	1	0		5		.207	.229	.236	.465	61	-7	-6	94	0	10	.333	0			-1	/S	-0.3
■ PAT DEASLEY Deasley, Thomas H. b: 11/17/1857, Ireland d: 4/1/43, Philadelphia, Pa. BR/TR, 5'8.5", 154 lbs. Deb: 5/18/1881																												
1881	Bos-N	43	147	13	35	5	2	0	8	5	10	.238	.263	.299	.562	83	-4	-2	91	63	12	.438				-3	C/OS1	-0.5
1882	Bos-N	67	264	36	70	8	0	0	29	7	22	.265	.284	.295	.580	84	-4	-5	103	128	23	.438				-1	*CO/S	-0.1
1883	StL-a	58	206	27	53	2	1	0		6		.257	.278	.277	.555	73	-5	-7	108	0	16	.412				2	C/O	0.0
1884	StL-a	75	254	27	52	5	4	0		7		.205	.235	.256	.491	57	-10	-14	110	0	16	.371				-1	*C/O1	-0.7
1885	NY-N	54	207	22	53	5	1	0	24	9	20	.256	.287	.290	.577	79	-3	-6	109	142	18	.448				-3	C/OS	-0.3
1886	NY-N	41	143	18	38	6	1	0	17	4	12	.266	.286	.322	.607	95	-3	-0	89	120	14	.495	2			0	CO	0.0
1887	NY-N	30	118	12	37	5	0	0	23	9	7	.314	.367	.356	.723	97	1	-1	107	179	17	.679	3			0	C/3S	0.0
1888	Was-N	34	127	6	20	1	0	0	4	2	18	.157	.171	.165	.336	9	-13	-12	96	70	4	.234	2			0	C/OS2	-1.1
Total	8	402	1466	161	358	37	9	0	105	49	89	.244	.271	.282	.552	73	-40	-47	103	82	119	.427	7			-7	C/OS312	-2.7
■ HANK DeBERRY DeBerry, John Herman b: 12/29/1894, Savannah, Tenn. d: 9/10/51, Savannah, Tenn. BR/TR, 5'11", 195 lbs. Deb: 9/12/16																												
1916	Cle-A	15	33	7	9	4	0	0	4	6	9	.273	.385	.394	.779	134	2	2	100	110	5	.792	0			0	C	0.2
1917	Cle-A	25	33	3	9	2	0	0	1	2	7	.273	.333	.333	.667	90	0	-0	114	33	3	.583	0			0	/C	0.0
1922	Bro-N	85	259	29	78	10	1	3	35	20	9	.301	.354	.382	.736	94	-4	-2	95	113	36	.681	4	1	1	-1	C	-0.1
1923	Bro-N	78	235	21	67	11	6	1	48	20	12	.285	.346	.396	.742	98	-2	-1	98	176	33	.692	2	1	0	9	C	1.1
1924	Bro-N	77	218	20	53	10	3	3	26	20	21	.243	.307	.358	.665	78	-7	-7	99	109	24	.590	0	1	-1	8	C	0.1
1925	Bro-N	67	193	26	50	8	1	2	24	16	8	.259	.322	.342	.664	75	-9	-7	94	119	22	.593	2	2	-1	10	C	0.5
1926	Bro-N	48	115	6	33	11	0	0	13	8	5	.287	.333	.383	.716	93	-1	-1	99	102	14	.634	0			2	C	0.2
1927	Bro-N	68	201	15	47	3	2	1	21	17	8	.234	.294	.284	.577	54	-13	-13	103	122	17	.487	1			7	C	-0.1
1928	Bro-N	82	258	19	65	8	2	0	23	18	15	.252	.301	.298	.599	58	-16	-16	99	106	23	.508	3			-3	C	-1.2
1929	Bro-N	68	210	13	55	11	1	1	25	17	15	.262	.317	.338	.655	66	-12	-11	94	116	23	.574	1			5	C	0.0
1930	Bro-N	35	95	11	28	3	0	0	14	4	10	.295	.323	.326	.650	57	-6	-6	101	156	10	.522	0			-1	C	-0.4
Total	11	648	1850	170	494	81	16	11	234	148	119	.267	.323	.346	.669	76	-68	-62	98	122	210	.593	13	5		35	C	0.3
■ ADAM DEBUS Debus, Adam Joseph b: 10/7/1892, Chicago, Ill. d: 5/13/77, Chicago, Ill. BR/TR, 5'10.5", 150 lbs. Deb: 7/14/17																												
1917	Pit-N	38	131	9	30	5	4	0	7	7	14	.229	.279	.328	.607	86	-2	-2	100	64	12	.535	2			-5	S3	-0.7
■ DOUG DeCINCES DeCinces, Douglas Vernon b: 8/29/50, Burbank, Cal. BR/TR, 6'2", 190 lbs. Deb: 9/09/73																												
1973	Bal-A	10	18	2	2	0	0	0	3	1	5	.111	.158	.111	.269	-22	-3	-3	107	590	0	.188	0	0	0	0	/32S	-0.2
1974	Bal-A	1	1	0	0	0	0	0	0	1	0	.000	.500	.000	.500	58	0	0	93	0	0	1.000	0	0	0	0	/3	0.0
1975	Bal-A	61	167	20	42	6	3	4	23	13	32	.251	.309	.395	.705	108	-1	1	91	113	20	.620	0	1	-1	5	3S2/1	0.7

YEAR	TM/L	G	AB	R	H	2B	3B	HR	RBI	BB	SO	AVG	OBP	SLG	PRO	/A	BR	/A	PF	CHI	RC	TA	SB	CS	SBR	FR	POS	TPR
1976	Bal-A	129	440	36	103	17	2	11	42	29	68	.234	.285	.357	.641	89	-8	-7	98	85	43	.557	8	4	0	-3	*321/SD	-0.9
1977	Bal-A	150	522	63	135	28	3	19	69	64	86	.259	.342	.433	.775	118	7	12	93	99	75	.733	8	8	-2	13	*3/12D	1.9
1978	Bal-A	142	511	72	146	37	1	28	80	46	81	.286	.347	.526	.873	157	27	32	91	91	89	.844	7	7	-2	12	*32	4.2
1979	Bal-A	120	422	67	97	27	1	16	61	54	68	.230	.322	.412	.734	99	-3	-1	97	108	56	.696	5	3	-0	-1	*3	0.0
1980	Bal-A	145	489	64	122	23	2	16	64	49	83	.249	.322	.403	.724	97	-2	-3	101	102	59	.662	11	6	-0	23	*3/1	2.0
1981	Bal-A	100	346	49	91	23	2	13	55	41	32	.263	.343	.454	.797	129	12	13	99	112	51	.737	0	3	-2	-2	*3/1O	1.0
1982	Cal-A	153	575	94	173	42	5	30	97	66	80	.301	.374	.548	.922	149	38	38	100	101	113	.915	7	5	-1	24	*3/S	5.7
1983	Cal-A	95	370	49	104	19	3	18	65	32	56	.281	.338	.495	.833	132	12	14	96	114	59	.778	2	0	1	14	3D	2.8
1984	Cal-A	146	547	77	147	23	3	20	82	53	79	.269	.333	.431	.765	108	7	6	101	117	77	.703	4	1	1	-5	*3/D	0.3
1985	Cal-A	120	427	50	104	22	1	20	78	47	71	.244	.321	.440	.762	105	3	3	101	127	55	.692	1	4	-2	-8	*3/D	-1.0
1986	Cal-A	140	512	69	131	20	3	26	96	52	74	.256	.327	.459	.786	116	8	10	96	125	72	.724	2	2	-1	-7	*3/SD	0.0
1987	Cal-A	133	453	65	106	23	0	16	63	70	87	.234	.339	.391	.730	95	-3	-2	99	114	61	.698	3	4	-2	-3	*3/1SD	-0.8
	StL-N	4	9	1	2	2	0	0	1	0	2	.222	.222	.444	.667	72	-0	-0	99	100	1	.571	0	0	0	0	/3	0.0
Total	15	1649	5809	778	1505	312	29	237	879	618	904	.259	.333	.445	.778	116	93	112	98	109	832	.754	58	48	-11	63	*3/2D1SO	15.7
■ **HARRY DECKER**	Decker, Earl Harry b: 9/3/1854, Lockport, Ill. BR/TR, 180 lbs. Deb: 8/23/1884																											
1884	Ind-a	4	15	1	4	1	0	0		1		.267	.313	.333	.646	118	0	0	96	0	2	.545				0	/C	0.0
	KC-U	23	75	8	10	2	0	0		5		.133	.188	.160	.348	21	-6	-4	87	0	2	.262	0			0	OC	-0.3
1886	Det-N	14	54	2	12	1	0	0	5	2	9	.222	.250	.241	.491	46	-3	-4	109	128	3	.357	0			0	C/O	-0.3
	Was-N	7	23	0	5	1	1	0	2	1	5	.217	.250	.348	.598	86	-1	-0	94	81	2	.500	0			0	/C3S	0.0
	Yr	21	77	2	17	2	1	0	7	3	14	.221	.250	.273	.523	57	-4	-4	104	118	5	.400	0			0		-0.3
1889	Phi-N	11	30	4	3	0	0	0	2	2	5	.100	.156	.100	.256	-26	-5	-5	104	199	1	.222	1			0	/2CO	-0.4
1890	Phi-N	5	19	5	7	1	0	0	2	4	1	.368	.478	.421	.899	153	2	2	108	73	6	1.333	4			-1	/1OC	0.0
	Pit-N	92	354	52	97	14	3	5	38	26	36	.274	.324	.373	.697	120	1	8	88	83	46	.646	8			-11	C1/O2S	0.2
	Yr	97	373	57	104	15	3	5	40	30	37	.279	.333	.375	.708	122	3	10	89	83	52	.677	12			-12		0.2
Total	4	156	570	72	138	20	4	5	49	41	56	.242	.293	.318	.611	91	-11	-4	92	79	62	.544	13			-12	C/O12S3	-0.8
■ **FRANK DECKER**	Decker, Frank b: 2/26/1856, St.Louis, Mo. d: 2/5/40, St.Louis, Mo. BR/TR, Deb: 6/25/1879																											
1879	Syr-N	3	10	0	1	0	0	0	0	0	3	.100	.100	.100	.200	-38	-1	-1	89	0	0	.111				0	/CO1	0.0
1882	StL-a	2	8	0	2	0	0	0		0		.250	.250	.250	.500	69	-0	-0	100	0	1	.333				0	/2	0.0
Total	2	5	18	0	3	0	0	0	0	0	3	.167	.167	.167	.333	12	-2	-1	94	0	1	.200				0	/2C1O	0.0
■ **GEORGE DECKER**	Decker, George A "Gentleman George" b: 6/1/1869, York, Pa. d: 6/9/09, Compton, Cal. BL/TL, 6'1", 180 lbs. Deb: 7/11/1892																											
1892	Chi-N	78	291	32	66	6	7	1	28	20	49	.227	.277	.306	.582	84	-8	-5	92	95	28	.524	9			-2	O2	-0.8
1893	Chi-N	81	328	57	89	9	8	2	48	24	22	.271	.325	.366	.691	82	-8	-10	104	106	47	.703	22			1	O12/S	-0.7
1894	Chi-N	91	384	74	120	17	6	8	92	24	17	.313	.361	.451	.811	89	-3	-9	108	136	72	.852	23			-4	1O/32S	-0.9
1895	Chi-N	73	297	51	82	9	7	2	41	17	22	.276	.324	.374	.698	79	-9	-10	103	104	41	.665	11			-9	O1/3S2	-1.9
1896	Chi-N	107	421	68	118	23	11	5	61	23	14	.280	.318	.423	.740	89	-4	-10	108	97	64	.729	20			-3	O1	-1.4
1897	Chi-N	111	428	72	124	12	7	5	63	24		.290	.333	.386	.719	91	-6	-6	100	104	60	.671	11			-4	O1/2	-1.3
1898	StL-N	76	286	26	74	10	0	1	45	20		.259	.314	.304	.618	75	-7	-9	106	160	29	.538	4			-8	1	-1.5
	Lou-N	42	148	27	44	4	3	0	19	9		.297	.342	.365	.707	109	1	2	96	108	22	.702	9			0	1/O	0.2
	Yr	118	434	53	118	14	3	1	64	29		.272	.323	.325	.648	86	-6	-8	102	143	51	.592	13			-8		-1.3
1899	Lou-N	38	135	13	36	8	0	1	18	12		.267	.336	.348	.684	87	-2	-2	103	113	17	.646	3			-2	1	-0.2
	Was-N	4	9	0	0	0	0	0	0	0		.000	.000	.000	.000	-99	-2	-2	96	0	0	.000	0			0	/1O	-0.1
	Yr	42	144	13	36	8	0	1	18	12		.250	.316	.326	.643	77	-4	-5	103	104	16	.593	3			-2		-0.3
Total	8	701	2727	420	753	98	49	25	415	173	124	.276	.324	.376	.700	86	-48	-63	103	113	381	.674	112			-31	O1/23S	-8.6
■ **ARTIE DEDE**	Dede, Arthur Richard b: 7/12/1895, Brooklyn, N.Y. d: 9/6/71, Keene, N.H. BR/TR, 5'9", 155 lbs. Deb: 10/04/16																											
1916	Bro-N	1	1	0	0	0	0	0	0	0	0	.000	.000	.000	.000	-97	-0	-0	103	0	0	.000	0			0	/C	0.0
■ **ROD DEDEAUX**	Dedeaux, Raoul Martial b: 2/17/15, New Orleans, La. BR/TR, 5'11", 160 lbs. Deb: 9/28/35																											
1935	Bro-N	2	4	0	1	0	0	0	1	0	0	.250	.250	.250	.500	37	-0	-0	94	361	0	.333	0			0	/S	0.0
■ **JIM DEE**	Dee, James D. b: Buffalo, N.Y. Deb: 7/30/1884																											
1884	Pit-a	12	40	0	5	0	0	0		1		.125	.146	.125	.271	-10	-5	-4	97	0	1	.171				0	S	-0.3
■ **SHORTY DEE**	Dee, Maurice Leo b: 10/4/1889, Halifax, N.S., Can. d: 8/12/71, Jamaica Plain, Mass. BR/TR, 5'6", 155 lbs. Deb: 9/14/15																											
1915	StL-A	1	3	1	0	0	0	0	0	1	0	.000	.250	.000	.250	-26	-0	-0	96	0	0	.250	0	1	-1	0	/S	0.0
■ **ROB DEER**	Deer, Robert George b: 9/29/60, Orange, Cal. BR/TR, 6'3", 210 lbs. Deb: 9/04/84																											
1984	SF-N	13	24	5	4	0	0	3	3	7	10	.167	.375	.542	.917	161	2	2	96	53	5	1.048	1	1	-0	-0	/O	0.1
1985	SF-N	78	162	22	30	5	1	8	20	23	71	.185	.286	.377	.663	90	-4	-2	93	94	19	.632	0	1	-1	-3	O1	-0.7
1986	Mil-A	134	466	75	108	17	3	33	86	72	179	.232	.338	.494	.832	121	15	14	102	106	82	.852	5	2	0	4	*O/1	1.4
1987	Mil-A	134	474	71	113	15	2	28	80	86	186	.238	.361	.456	.817	113	12	11	102	109	85	.864	12	4	1	5	*O1/D	1.2
1988	Mil-A	135	492	71	124	24	0	23	85	51	153	.252	.331	.441	.772	110	9	7	103	125	74	.753	9	5	-0	5	*O/D	0.9
Total	5	494	1618	244	379	61	6	95	274	239	599	.234	.338	.456	.794	113	35	31	102	110	266	.811	27	13	0	11	O/1D	2.9
■ **CHARLIE DEES**	Dees, Charles Henry b: 6/24/35, Birmingham, Ala. BL/TL, 6'1", 173 lbs. Deb: 5/26/63																											
1963	LA-A	60	202	23	62	11	1	3	27	11	31	.307	.367	.416	.782	130	5	7	91	121	30	.711	3	3	-1	1	1	0.6
1964	LA-A	26	26	3	2	1	0	0	1	1	4	.077	.143	.115	.258	-31	-4	-4	89	141	0	.231	1	2	-1	0	1	-0.5
1965	Cal-A	12	32	1	5	0	0	0	1	1	8	.156	.182	.156	.338	-3	-4	-4	98	83	1	.241	1	2	-1	0	/1	-0.5
Total	3	98	260	27	69	12	1	3	29	13	43	.265	.323	.354	.677	98	-3	-1	92	119	31	.601	5	7	-3	1	/1	-0.4
■ **TONY DeFATE**	DeFate, Clyde Herbert b: 2/22/1895, Kansas City, Mo. d: 9/3/63, New Orleans, La. BR/TR, 5'8.5", 158 lbs. Deb: 4/18/17																											
1917	StL-N	14	14	0	2	0	0	0	1	4	5	.143	.333	.143	.476	48	-1	-1	102	193	1	.500	0			0	/32	0.0
	Det-A	3	2	1	0	0	0	0	0	0	1	.000	.000	.000	.000	-99	-0	-0	98	0	0	.000	0			0	/2	0.0
Total	1	17	16	1	2	0	0	0	1	4	6	.125	.300	.125	.425	32	-1	-1	101	174	1	.429	0			0	/32	0.0
■ **ARTURO DeFREITAS**	DeFreitas, Arturo Marcelino (Simon) b: 4/26/53, San Pedro De Macoris, D.R. BR/TR, 6'2", 195 lbs. Deb: 9/07/78																											
1978	Cin-N	9	19	1	4	1	0	1	2	1	4	.211	.250	.421	.671	82	-1	-1	103	72	2	.600	0	0	0	0	/1	0.0
1979	Cin-N	23	34	2	7	2	0	0	4	0	16	.206	.206	.265	.471	28	-3	-3	97	176	2	.321	0	0	0	-0	/1O	-0.3
Total	2	32	53	3	11	3	0	1	6	1	20	.208	.222	.321	.543	48	-4	-4	99	137	4	.419	0	0	0	-0	/1O	-0.3
■ **RUBE DeGROFF**	DeGroff, Edward Arthur b: 9/2/1879, Hyde Park, N.Y. d: 12/17/55, Poughkeepsie, N.Y. BL , 5'11", Deb: 9/22/05																											
1905	StL-N	15	56	3	14	2	1	0	5	5		.250	.311	.321	.633	99	-1	0	91	93	6	.571	1			0	O	0.0
1906	StL-N	1	4	1	0	0	0	0	0	0		.000	.000	.000	.000	-99	-1	-1	101	0	0	.000	0			0	/O	0.0
Total	2	16	60	4	14	2	1	0	5	5		.233	.292	.300	.592	86	-1	-1	92	87	6	.522	1			0	/O	0.0
■ **HERMAN DEHLMAN**	Dehlman, Herman J. b: 1850, Catasaqua, Pa. d: 3/13/1885, Wilkes-Barre, Pa. Deb: 5/02/1872																											
1872	Atl-n	35	164	26	33							.201															*1	
1873	Atl-n	54	236	50	50							.212															*1	
1874	Atl-n	53	232	40	51							.220															*1	
1875	StL-n	67	284	43	61							.215															*1	
1876	StL-N	64	245	40	45	6	0	0	9	9	10	.184	.213	.208	.421	46	-15	-10	88	61	11	.300				0	*1	-0.7
1877	StL-N	32	119	24	22	4	0	0	11	7	21	.185	.230	.218	.449	41	-7	-8	102	146	6	.340				-4	1/O	-1.1
Total	4 n	209	916	159	195							.213															1/O	
Total	2	96	364	64	67	10	0	0	20	16	31	.184	.218	.212	.430	45	-22	-18	92	89	17	.313				-3	1/O	-1.8
■ **JIM DEIDEL**	Deidel, James Lawrence b: 6/6/49, Denver, Col. BR/TR, 6'2", 195 lbs. Deb: 5/31/74																											
1974	NY-A	2	2	0	0	0	0	0	0	0	0	.000	.000	.000	.000	-99	-1	-0	96	0	0	.000	0	0	0	0	/C	0.0

YEAR	TM/L	G	AB	R	H	2B	3B	HR	RBI	BB	SO	AVG	OBP	SLG	PRO	/A	BR	/A	PF	CHI	RC	TA	SB	CS	SBR	FR	POS	TPR
■ **PEP DEININGER** Deininger, Otto Charles b: 10/10/1877, Wasseralfingen, Germany d: 9/25/50, Boston, Mass. BL/TL, 5'8.5", 180 lbs. Deb: 4/26/02																												
1902	Bos-A	2	6	0	2	1	1	0	0	0		.333	.333	.833	1.167	219	1	1	99	0	2	1.250	0			-0	/P	0.0
1908	Phi-N	1	0	0	0	0	0	0	0	0		—	—	—	—	—	0	0	100	—	—	—	0			0	/O	0.0
1909	Phi-N	55	169	22	44	9	0	0	16	11		.260	.309	.314	.623	89	-1	-2	106	110	17	.560	5			1	O/2	-0.2
Total	3	58	175	22	46	10	1	0	16	11		.263	.310	.331	.642	94	-0	-2	106	106	21	.581	5			1	/OP2	-0.2
■ **PAT DEISEL** Deisel, Edward b: 4/29/1876, Ripley, Ohio d: 4/17/48, Cincinnati, Ohio BR/TR, 5'5", 145 lbs. Deb: 8/21/02																												
1902	Bro-N	1	3	0	2	0	0	0	1	1		.667	.750	.667	1.417	361	1	1	95	183	2	3.000	0			0	/C	0.1
1903	Cin-N	2	0	0	0	0	0	0	0	1		—	1.000	—	1.667	352	0	0	109	0	0	—	0			0	/C	0.0
Total	2	3	3	0	2	0	0	0	1	2		.667	.800	.667	1.467	363	1	1	98	147	2	4.000	0			0	/C	0.1
■ **BILL DEITRICK** Deitrick, William Alexander b: 4/20/02, Hanover Co., Va. d: 5/6/46, Bethesda, Md. BR/TR, 5'10", 160 lbs. Deb: 9/19/27																												
1927	Phi-N	5	6	1	1	0	0	0	0	0	0	.167	.167	.167	.333	-11	-1	-1	96	0	0	.200	0			0	/S	0.0
1928	Phi-N	52	100	13	20	6	0	0	7	17	10	.200	.322	.260	.582	52	-6	-7	104	96	9	.563	1			-0	O/S	-0.6
Total	2	57	106	14	21	6	0	0	7	17	10	.198	.315	.255	.569	49	-7	-8	104	91	9	.541	1			-0	/OS	-0.6
■ **MIKE DEJAN** Dejan, Michael Dan b: 1/13/15, Cleveland, Ohio d: 2/2/53, W.Los Angeles, Cal. BL/TL, 6'1", 185 lbs. Deb: 7/13/40																												
1940	Cin-N	12	16	1	3	0	1	0	2	3	3	.188	.316	.313	.628	73	-1	-1	101	148	2	.571	0			-0	/O	0.0
■ **IVAN DeJESUS** DeJesus, Ivan (Alvarez) b: 1/9/53, Santurce, P.R. BR/TR, 5'11", 175 lbs. Deb: 9/13/74																												
1974	LA-N	3	3	1	1	0	0	0	0	0	2	.333	.333	.333	.667	94	-0	-0	93	0	0	.500	0	0	0	0	/S	0.0
1975	LA-N	63	87	10	16	2	1	0	2	11	15	.184	.276	.230	.505	44	-7	-6	95	39	6	.438	1	2	-1	-7	S	-0.6
1976	LA-N	22	41	4	7	2	1	0	2	4	9	.171	.244	.268	.513	46	-3	-3	100	70	2	.405	0	1	-1	0	S/3	-0.2
1977	Chi-N	155	624	91	166	31	7	3	40	56	90	.266	.330	.353	.683	73	-14	-25	114	67	75	.636	24	12	0	**36**	*S	3.3
1978	Chi-N	160	619	**104**	172	24	7	3	35	74	78	.278	.357	.354	.711	90	1	-6	110	59	84	.713	41	12	5	14	*S	2.7
1979	Chi-N	160	636	92	180	26	10	5	52	59	82	.283	.346	.379	.725	87	-1	-11	112	71	83	.672	24	20	-5	4	*S	0.4
1980	Chi-N	157	618	78	160	26	3	3	33	60	81	.259	.328	.325	.654	78	-13	-17	106	60	72	.646	44	16	4	15	*S	2.0
1981	Chi-N	106	403	49	78	8	4	0	13	46	61	.194	.276	.233	.509	44	-28	-30	104	52	30	.479	21	9	1	9	*S	-0.8
1982	Phi-N	161	536	53	128	21	5	3	59	54	70	.239	.311	.313	.624	80	-17	-13	94	133	55	.567	14	4	2	-9	*S/3	-0.8
1983	Phi-N	158	497	60	126	15	7	4	45	53	77	.254	.325	.336	.661	83	-10	-11	101	100	56	.605	11	4	1	-13	*S	-0.9
1984	Phi-N	144	435	40	112	15	3	0	35	43	76	.257	.327	.306	.633	77	-11	-12	102	103	43	.557	12	5	1	-7	*S	-0.3
1985	StL-N	59	72	11	16	5	0	0	7	4	16	.222	.263	.292	.555	58	-4	-4	96	133	6	.466	2	2	-1	2	3S	-0.1
1986	NY-A	7	4	1	0	0	0	0	0	1	1	.000	.200	.000	.200	-38	-1	-1	103	0	0	.250	0	0	0	0	/S	0.0
1987	SF-N	9	10	0	2	0	0	0	1	0	2	.200	.200	.200	.400	7	-1	-1	96	200	0	.222	0	1	-1	1	/S	0.0
1988	Det-A	7	17	1	3	0	0	0	0	1	4	.176	.222	.176	.399	14	-2	-2	94	0	1	.286	0	0	0	-0	/S	-0.1
Total	15	1371	4602	595	1167	175	48	21	324	466	664	.254	.324	.326	.651	77	-112	-143	105	79	514	.618	194	88	5	44	*S/3	4.6
■ **MARK DeJOHN** DeJohn, Mark Stephen b: 9/18/53, Middletown, Conn. BB/TR, 5'11", 170 lbs. Deb: 4/28/82																												
1982	Det-A	24	21	1	4	2	0	0	1	4	4	.190	.320	.286	.606	68	-1	-1	100	67	3	.647	1	0	0	-0	S/32	0.1
■ **WILLIAM DeKONING** DeKoning, William Callahan b: 12/19/18, Brooklyn, N.Y. d: 7/26/79, Palm Harbor, Fla. BR/TR, 5'11", 185 lbs. Deb: 5/27/45																												
1945	NY-N	3	1	0	0	0	0	0	0	0	1	.000	.000	.000	.000	-99	-0	-0	100	0	0	.000	0			0	/C	0.0
■ **ED DELAHANTY** Delahanty, Edward James "Big Ed" b: 10/30/1867, Cleveland, Ohio d: 7/2/03, Niagara Falls, N.Y BR/TR, 6'1", 170 lbs. Deb: 1888																												
1888	Phi-N	74	290	40	66	12	2	1	31	12	26	.228	.261	.293	.554	69	-7	-12	114	134	33	.607	38			-11	2O	-2.0
1889	Phi-N	56	246	37	72	13	3	0	27	14	17	.293	.333	.370	.703	94	-1	-3	104	78	38	.718	19			0	O2/S	-0.1
1890	Cle-P	115	517	107	154	26	13	3	64	24	30	.298	.339	.416	.755	112	0	8	92	69	83	.749	25			-11	S2O/31	0.1
1891	Phi-N	128	543	92	132	19	9	5	86	33	50	.243	.296	.339	.635	91	-10	-6	95	121	63	.608	25			-1	*O1/2	-1.0
1892	Phi-N	123	477	79	146	30	**21**	6	91	31	32	.306	.360	**.495**	.855	153	31	28	104	117	98	.921	29			8	*O/3	3.0
1893	Phi-N	132	595	145	219	35	18	**19**	**146**	47	20	.368	.423	**.583**	1.007	169	**55**	**55**	100	95	**167**	1.173	37			27	*O2/1	**6.2**
1894	Phi-N	114	489	147	199	39	18	4	131	60	16	.407	.478	.585	1.063	165	48	53	95	117	151	1.290	21			16	*O1/3S2	4.7
1895	Phi-N	116	480	149	194	**49**	10	11	106	86	31	.404	**.500**	.617	**1.117**	**192**	**68**	**69**	99	80	175	**1.517**	46			9	*O/S23	5.5
1896	Phi-N	123	499	131	198	**44**	17	13	**126**	62	22	.397	.472	**.631**	**1.103**	**188**	**66**	**65**	102	91	170	1.405	37			16	*O1/2	6.1
1897	Phi-N	129	530	109	200	40	15	5	96	60		.377	.444	.538	.982	169	47	51	96	83	142	1.136	26			7	*O/1	4.1
1898	Phi-N	144	548	115	183	36	9	4	92	77		.334	.422	.454	.877	163	41	**46**	95	103	**133**	1.071	**58**			3	*O	3.7
1899	Phi-N	146	581	135	**238**	**55**	9	9	**137**	55		**.410**	.463	**.582**	**1.045**	**195**	**70**	**72**	97	111	**175**	1.242	30			-3	*O	5.3
1900	Phi-N	131	539	82	174	32	10	2	109	41		.323	.371	.430	.801	126	16	18	98	138	94	.792	16			-4	*1	1.4
1901	Phi-N	139	542	106	192	**38**	16	8	108	65		.354	.423	.528	**.951**	173	54	52	103	112	137	**1.086**	29			1	O1	4.2
1902	Was-A	123	473	103	178	**43**	14	10	93	62		**.376**	**.449**	**.590**	**1.038**	**191**	**57**	**58**	99	88	**136**	**1.210**	16			-8	*O1	4.0
1903	Was-A	42	156	22	52	11	1	1	21	12		.333	.381	.436	.817	139	9	8	105	102	28	.798	3			4	O/1	0.9
Total	16	1835	7505	1599	2597	522	185	101	1464	741	244	.346	.410	.505	.915	155	544	562	99	102	1821	1.031	455			54	*O12/S3	46.1
■ **FRANK DELAHANTY** Delahanty, Frank George "Pudgie" b: 1/29/1883, Cleveland, Ohio d: 7/22/66, Cleveland, Ohio BR/TR, 5'9", 160 lbs. Deb: 8/23/05																												
1905	NY-A	9	27	0	6	1	0	0	2	1		.222	.250	.259	.509	62	-1	-1	102	102	2	.381	0			0	/1O	-0.1
1906	NY-A	92	307	37	73	11	8	2	41	16		.238	.276	.345	.621	80	-2	-9	120	136	33	.568	11			-2	O	-1.5
1907	Cle-A	15	52	3	9	0	1	0	4	4		.173	.232	.212	.444	46	-3	-3	93	138	3	.395	2			-0	O	-0.3
1908	NY-A	37	125	12	32	1	2	0	10	10		.256	.311	.296	.607	105	0	1	95	103	14	.602	9			0	O	0.0
1914	Buf-F	79	274	29	55	4	7	2	27	23	0	.201	.263	.288	.551	55	-15	-17	104	117	27	.562	21			-6	O	-2.7
	Pit-F	41	159	25	38	4	4	1	7	11	0	.239	.288	.333	.622	82	-5	-4	94	48	18	.587	7			-2	O/2	-0.7
	Yr	120	433	54	93	8	11	3	34	34	0	.215	.272	.305	.577	64	-20	-21	101	94	45	.571	28			-7		-3.4
1915	Pit-F	14	42	3	10	1	0	0	3	1	0	.238	.256	.262	.518	51	-2	-3	104	98	3	.375	0			0	O	-0.2
Total	6	287	986	109	223	22	22	5	94	66	0	.226	.275	.308	.583	72	-29	-35	106	110	99	.550	50			-9	O/12	-5.5
■ **JIM DELAHANTY** Delahanty, James Christopher b: 6/20/1879, Cleveland, Ohio d: 10/17/53, Cleveland, Ohio BR/TR, 5'10.5", 170 lbs. Deb: 4/19/01																												
1901	Chi-N	17	63	4	12	2	0	0	4	3		.190	.227	.222	.449	32	-5	-5	100	97	4	.431	5			-1	3/2	-0.5
1902	NY-N	7	26	3	6	1	0	0	3	1		.231	.259	.269	.528	65	-1	-1	100	157	2	.400	0			2	/O	0.1
1904	Bos-N	142	499	56	142	27	8	3	60	27		.285	.321	.389	.710	125	11	13	97	110	69	.664	16			3	*32/OP	2.1
1905	Bos-N	125	461	50	119	11	8	5	55	28		.258	.301	.349	.650	98	-3	-2	97	115	53	.588	12			-6	*O/P	-1.6
1906	Cin-N	115	379	63	106	21	4	1	39	45		.280	.356	.364	.720	110	12	6	115	103	58	.747	21			-7	*3/SO	-0.4
1907	StL-A	33	95	8	21	3	0	0	6	5		.221	.260	.253	.513	67	-4	-3	98	89	8	.473	6			0	3/O2	-0.1
	Was-A	108	404	44	118	18	7	2	54	36		.292	.350	.386	.736	152	17	21	90	126	62	.734	18			-12	23/O1	1.1
	Yr	141	499	52	139	21	7	2	60	41		.279	.333	.361	.694	134	13	17	92	118	70	.681	24			-12		1.0
1908	Was-A	83	287	33	91	11	4	1	30	24		.317	.370	.394	.764	158	16	17	95	99	46	.781	16			-1	2	1.6
1909	Was-A	90	302	18	67	13	5	1	21	23		.222	.290	.308	.598	99	-4	-1	90	86	27	.536	4			0	2	-0.2
	Det-A	46	150	29	38	10	1	0	20	17		.253	.364	.333	.697	109	5	3	110	163	21	.759	9			1	2	0.3
	Yr	136	452	47	105	23	6	1	41	40		.232	.316	.316	.632	103	1	2	97	113	48	.608	13			1		0.1
1910	Det-A	106	378	67	111	16	3	2	45	43		.294	.379	.368	.747	131	16	16	102	121	59	.772	15			-14	*2	-0.5
1911	Det-A	144	542	83	184	30	14	3	94	56		.339	.411	.463	.874	133	33	26	108	129	110	.927	15			-3	123	2.4
1912	Det-A	78	266	34	76	14	1	0	41	42		.286	.397	.346	.743	119	7	9	95	157	41	.789	9			1	2O	0.7
1914	Bro-F	74	214	28	62	13	5	0	15	25	21	.290	.364	.397	.761	117	5	5	101	64	35	.750	4			-1	2/1	0.5
1915	Bro-F	17	25	0	6	1	0	0	2	3	3	.240	.321	.280	.601	81	-1	-0	98	103	3	.579	1			0	/2	0.0
Total	13	1185	4091	520	1159	191	60	18	489	378	24	.283	.350	.373	.722	121	104	104	100	115	598	.714	151			-37	23O/1SP	5.5
■ **JOE DELAHANTY** Delahanty, Joseph Nicholas b: 10/18/1875, Cleveland, Ohio d: 1/9/36, Cleveland, Ohio BR/TR, 5'9", 168 lbs. Deb: 9/30/07																												
1907	StL-N	7	22	3	7	0	0	1	2	0		.318	.318	.455	.773	150	1	1	96	58	4	.867	3			1	/O	0.1
1908	StL-N	140	499	37	127	14	11	1	44	32		.255	.299	.333	.632	111	1	5	94	106	51	.562	11			-14	*O	-1.1
1909	StL-N	123	411	28	88	16	4	2	54	42		.214	.292	.287	.579	84	-9	-7	96	162	36	.536	10			-6	O2	-1.7
Total	3	270	932	68	222	30	15	4	100	74		.238	.296	.315	.612	100	-7	-2	95	130	91	.556	24			-19	O/2	-2.7

YEAR	TM/L	G	AB	R	H	2B	3B	HR	RBI	BB	SO	AVG	OBP	SLG	PRO	/A	BR	/A	PF	CHI	RC	TA	SB	CS	SBR	FR	POS	TPR
■ **TOM DELAHANTY**	Delahanty, Thomas James b: 3/9/1872, Cleveland, Ohio d: 1/10/51, Sanford, Fla. TR , 5'8", 175 lbs. Deb: 9/29/1894																											
1894	Phi-N	1	4	0	1	0	0	0	0	0	1	.250	.250	.250	.500	23	-0	-0	95	0	0	.333	0			0	/2	0.0
1896	Cle-N	16	56	11	13	4	0	0	4	8	4	.232	.338	.304	.642	65	-2	-3	110	69	7	.698	4			0	3	-0.2
	Pit-N	1	3	1	1	0	0	0	0	0	0	.333	.333	.333	.667	83	-0	-0	93	0	0	.500	0			0	/S	0.0
	Yr	17	59	12	14	4	0	0	4	8	4	.237	.338	.305	.643	66	-2	-3	109	69	8	.689	4			0		-0.2
1897	Lou-N	1	4	1	1	1	0	0	2	0		.250	.250	.500	.750	102	-0	-0	95	310	1	.667	0			0	/2	0.0
Total	3	19	67	13	16	5	0	0	6	8	5	.239	.329	.313	.642	66	-3	-4	108	75	8	.667	4			0	/32S	-0.2
■ **MIKE de la HOZ**	De la Hoz, Miguel Angel (Piloto) b: 10/2/38, Havana, Cuba BR/TR, 5'11", 175 lbs. Deb: 7/22/60																											
1960	Cle-A	49	160	20	41	6	2	6	23	9	12	.256	.300	.431	.731	97	-2	-1	98	103	19	.627	0	0	0	-1	S/3	0.1
1961	Cle-A	61	173	20	45	10	0	3	23	7	10	.260	.297	.370	.667	80	-6	-5	96	123	18	.553	0	0	0	-5	2S3	-0.5
1962	Cle-A	12	12	0	1	0	0	0	0	0	3	.083	.083	.083	.167	-56	-3	-3	98	0	0	.091	0	0	0	0	/2	-0.1
1963	Cle-A	67	150	15	40	10	0	5	25	9	29	.267	.313	.433	.746	110	1	2	97	131	20	.664	0	0	0	1	2/3SO	0.5
1964	Mil-N	78	189	25	55	7	1	4	12	14	22	.291	.346	.402	.748	114	3	3	97	56	25	.664	1	1	-0	-1	23/S	0.3
1965	Mil-N	81	176	15	45	3	2	2	11	8	21	.256	.296	.330	.625	73	-6	-7	104	71	16	.493	0	1	-1	1	S32/1	-0.2
1966	Atl-N	71	110	11	24	3	0	2	7	5	18	.218	.252	.300	.552	54	-7	-7	99	75	8	.432	0	1	-1	1	3/2S	-0.7
1967	Atl-N	74	143	10	29	3	0	3	14	4	14	.203	.224	.287	.511	43	-10	-11	104	116	8	.390	1	0	0	1	23/S	-0.9
1969	Cin-N	1	1	0	0	0	0	0	0	0	1	.000	.000	.000	.000	-99	-0	-0	99	0	0	.000	0	0	0	0	H	0.0
Total	9	494	1114	116	280	42	5	25	115	56	130	.251	.292	.365	.657	82	-30	-29	99	95	114	.565	2	3	-1	-4	32S/01	-1.5
■ **BILL DeLANCEY**	DeLancey, William Pinkney b: 11/28/11, Greensboro, N.C. d: 11/28/46, Phoenix, Ariz. BL/TR, 5'11.5", 185 lbs. Deb: 9/11/32																											
1932	StL-N	8	26	1	5	0	2	0	2	2	1	.192	.250	.346	.596	58	-2	-2	100	83	2	.524	0			1	/C	0.0
1934	StL-N	93	253	41	80	18	3	13	40	41	37	.316	.414	.565	.979	140	22	17	114	79	62	1.045	1			0	C	1.9
1935	StL-N	103	301	37	84	14	5	6	41	42	34	.279	.369	.419	.788	107	6	4	104	103	50	.761	0			-6	C	-0.2
1940	StL-N	15	18	0	4	0	0	0	2	0	2	.222	.222	.222	.444	22	-2	-2	102	185	1	.267	0			-0	C	-0.1
Total	4	219	598	79	173	32	10	19	85	85	74	.289	.380	.472	.851	118	24	18	108	94	115	.869	1			-6	C	1.6
■ **BILL DELANEY**	Delaney, William L. b: 3/4/1863, Cincinnati, O. d: 3/1/42, Canton, Ohio BR/TR, Deb: 8/21/1890																											
1890	Cle-N	36	116	16	22	1	1	1	7	21	19	.190	.314	.241	.555	69	-4	-3	94	70	11	.574	5			-11	2	-1.0
■ **JESUS De La ROSA**	De La Rosa, Jesus b: 7/28/53, Santo Domingo, D.R BR/TR, 6'1", 153 lbs. Deb: 8/02/75																											
1975	Hou-N	3	3	1	1	1	0	0	0	0	0	.333	.333	.667	1.000	183	0	0	94	0	1	1.000	0	0	0	0	H	0.0
■ **PUCHY DELGADO**	Delgado, Luis Felipe (Robles) b: 2/2/54, Hatillo, P.R. BB/TL, 5'11", 170 lbs. Deb: 9/06/77																											
1977	Sea-A	13	22	4	4	0	0	0	2	1	8	.182	.217	.182	.399	11	-3	-3	96	198	1	.278	0	0	0	-2	O	-0.4
■ **BOBBY Del GRECO**	Del Greco, Robert George b: 4/7/33, Pittsburgh, Pa. BR/TR, 5'10.5", 185 lbs. Deb: 4/16/52																											
1952	Pit-N	99	341	34	74	14	2	1	20	38	70	.217	.301	.279	.580	62	-17	-17	100	81	30	.505	6	5	-1	4	O	-1.6
1956	Pit-N	14	20	4	4	0	0	2	3	3	3	.200	.304	.500	.804	109	0	0	102	79	3	.765	0	0	0	-1	/O3	-0.1
	StL-N	102	270	29	58	16	2	5	18	32	50	.215	.312	.344	.656	77	-9	-8	99	70	31	.614	1	1	-0	-12	O	-2.4
	Yr	116	290	33	62	16	2	7	21	35	53	.214	.311	.355	.666	79	-9	-8	99	72	35	.628	1	1	-0	-13		-2.5
1957	Chi-N	20	40	2	8	2	0	0	3	10	17	.200	.360	.250	.610	70	-1	-1	96	124	5	.636	1	0	0	-0	O	-0.1
	NY-A	8	7	3	3	0	0	0	0	2	2	.429	.556	.429	.984	184	1	1	94	0	2	1.500	1	0	0	-1	/O	0.0
1958	NY-A	12	5	1	1	0	0	0	0	1	1	.200	.333	.200	.533	49	-0	-0	103	0	0	.400	0	1	-1	-4	O	-0.5
1960	Phi-N	100	300	48	71	16	4	10	26	54	64	.237	.355	.417	.772	103	5	2	107	68	46	.761	1	5	-3	8	O	0.5
1961	Phi-N	41	112	14	29	5	0	2	11	12	17	.259	.346	.357	.704	93	-2	-1	94	96	14	.640	0	0	0	3	O/23	0.1
	KC-A	74	239	34	55	14	1	5	21	30	31	.230	.319	.360	.678	79	-6	-7	102	81	29	.628	1	0	0	2	O	-0.7
1962	KC-A	132	338	61	86	21	1	9	38	49	62	.254	.370	.402	.772	108	5	5	100	93	55	.783	4	1	1	5	*O	0.6
1963	KC-A	121	306	40	65	7	1	8	29	40	52	.212	.313	.320	.634	73	-8	-11	108	99	32	.578	1	2	-1	-3	*O/3	-1.8
1965	Phi-N	8	4	1	0	0	0	0	0	0	3	.000	.000	.000	.000	-99	-1	-1	95	0	0	.000	0	0	0	-1	/O	-0.2
Total	9	731	1982	271	454	95	11	42	169	271	372	.229	.331	.352	.683	85	-33	-38	102	84	247	.658	16	15	-4	-1	O/32	-6.2
■ **JUAN DELIS**	Delis, Juan Francisco b: 2/27/28, Santiago, Cuba BR/TR, 5'11", 170 lbs. Deb: 4/16/55																											
1955	Was-A	54	132	12	25	3	1	0	11	3	15	.189	.219	.227	.446	22	-15	-14	91	137	6	.324	1	2	-1	-1	3/O2	-1.5
■ **EDDIE DELKER**	Delker, Edward Alberts b: 4/17/07, De Alto, Pa. BR/TR, 5'10.5", 170 lbs. Deb: 4/28/29																											
1929	StL-N	22	40	5	6	0	1	0	3	2	12	.150	.209	.200	.409	2	-6	-6	98	128	2	.324	0			-1	/S23	-0.4
1931	StL-N	1	2	0	1	1	0	0	2	0	0	.500	.500	1.000	1.500	275	1	0	107	356	1	2.000	0			0	/3	0.0
1932	StL-N	20	42	1	5	4	0	0	2	8	7	.119	.260	.214	.474	29	-4	-4	100	83	3	.459	0			1	2/3S	-0.1
	Phi-N	30	62	7	10	1	1	1	7	6	14	.161	.235	.258	.493	29	-6	-7	112	137	4	.423	0			-4	2	-0.8
	Yr	50	104	8	15	5	1	1	9	14	21	.144	.246	.240	.486	29	-10	-11	107	117	7	.438	0			-3		-0.9
1933	Phi-N	25	41	6	7	3	1	0	1	0	12	.171	.171	.293	.463	26	-4	-5	118	31	2	.353	0			0	2/3	-0.3
Total	4	98	187	19	29	9	3	1	15	16	45	.155	.225	.251	.477	25	-20	-21	107	103	12	.405	0			-3	/23S	-1.6
■ **BERT DELMAS**	Delmas, Albert Charles b: 5/20/11, San Francisco, Cal d: 12/4/79, Huntington Beach, Cal. BL/TR, 5'11", 165 lbs. Deb: 9/10/33																											
1933	Bro-N	12	28	4	7	0	0	0	0	1	7	.250	.276	.250	.526	53	-2	-2	97	0	2	.381	0			-1	2	-0.1
■ **LUIS De Los SANTOS**	De Los Santos, Luis Manuel b: 12/29/66, San Cristobal, D.R. BR/TR, 6'5", 190 lbs. Deb: 9/07/88																											
1988	KC-A	11	22	1	2	1	1	0	1	4	4	.091	.231	.227	.458	28	-2	-2	103	79	1	.391	0	0	0	-0	/1D	-0.2
■ **GARTON Del SAVIO**	DelSavio, Garton Orville b: 11/26/13, New York, N.Y. BR/TR, 5'9.5", 165 lbs. Deb: 4/24/43																											
1943	Phi-N	4	11	0	1	0	0	0	0	1	0	.091	.167	.091	.258	-26	-2	-2	94	0	0	.200	0			-1	/S	-0.2
■ **JIM DELSING**	Delsing, James Henry b: 11/13/25, Rudolph, Wis. BL/TR, 5'10", 175 lbs. Deb: 4/21/48																											
1948	Chi-A	20	63	5	12	0	0	0	5	5	12	.190	.261	.190	.451	22	-7	-7	95	141	3	.340	0	0	0	0	O	-0.6
1949	NY-A	9	20	5	7	1	0	1	3	1	2	.350	.381	.550	.931	144	1	1	100	73	4	.923	0	0	0	-1	/O	0.0
1950	NY-A	12	10	2	4	0	0	0	2	2	0	.400	.500	.400	.900	133	1	1	99	173	2	1.000	0	0	0	0	H	0.1
	StL-A	69	209	25	55	5	2	0	15	20	23	.263	.328	.306	.634	59	-11	-13	107	81	21	.525	1	4	-2	6	O	-0.9
	Yr	81	219	27	59	5	2	0	17	22	23	.269	.336	.311	.647	63	-11	-13	106	97	23	.542	1	4	-2	6		-0.8
1951	StL-A	131	449	59	112	20	2	8	45	56	39	.249	.338	.356	.694	84	-7	-10	105	89	52	.613	2	9	-5	5	*O	-1.4
1952	StL-A	93	298	34	76	13	6	1	34	26	29	.255	.323	.349	.672	90	-5	-4	97	119	33	.583	3	3	-1	6	O	-0.1
	Det-A	33	113	14	31	2	1	3	15	11	8	.274	.344	.389	.733	105	1	1	99	108	16	.687	1	0	0	-1	O	0.0
	Yr	126	411	48	107	15	7	4	49	37	37	.260	.329	.360	.689	94	-5	-4	98	117	53	.630	4	3	-1	4		-0.1
1953	Det-A	138	479	77	138	26	6	11	62	66	39	.288	.380	.436	.816	123	14	16	98	97	84	.798	1	3	-2	-6	*O	0.4
1954	Det-A	122	371	39	92	24	2	6	38	49	38	.248	.337	.372	.709	94	-3	-3	100	92	48	.664	4	4	-1	-2	*O	-0.8
1955	Det-A	114	356	49	85	15	2	10	60	48	40	.239	.331	.376	.707	93	-5	-4	97	136	47	.668	2	0	1	-7	*O	-1.5
1956	Det-A	10	12	0	0	0	0	0	0	3	3	.000	.250	.000	.250	-30	-2	-2	97	0	0	.333	0	0	0	-1	/O	-0.2
	Chi-A	55	41	11	5	3	0	0	2	10	13	.122	.294	.195	.489	30	-4	-4	104	93	3	.528	1	0	0	-8	O	-1.2
	Yr	65	53	11	5	3	0	0	2	13	16	.094	.284	.151	.435	17	-6	-6	103	79	4	.479	1	0	0	-9		-1.4
1960	KC-A	16	40	2	10	3	0	0	5	3	5	.250	.302	.325	.627	71	-2	-2	99	151	4	.533	0	0	0	1	O	-0.1
Total	10	822	2461	322	627	112	21	40	286	300	251	.255	.340	.366	.706	91	-30	-31	100	104	320	.665	15	23	-9	-10	O	-6.3
■ **JOE DeMAESTRI**	DeMaestri, Joseph Paul "Oats" b: 12/9/28, San Francisco, Cal. BR/TR, 6', 170 lbs. Deb: 4/19/51																											
1951	Chi-A	56	74	8	15	0	2	1	3	5	11	.203	.253	.297	.550	50	-6	-5	97	43	5	.422	0	4	-2	1	S2/3	-0.3
1952	StL-A	81	186	13	42	9	1	1	18	8	25	.226	.258	.301	.559	57	-12	-11	97	114	14	.430	0	1	-1	-6	S/23	-1.4
1953	Phi-A	111	420	53	107	17	3	6	35	24	39	.255	.297	.352	.649	73	-16	-17	102	80	42	.526	0	1	-1	-15	*S	-2.4
1954	Phi-A	146	539	49	124	16	3	8	40	20	63	.230	.262	.315	.577	58	-33	-32	98	80	42	.452	1	4	-2	-10	*S/23	-3.3
1955	KC-A	123	457	42	114	14	1	6	37	20	47	.249	.285	.324	.609	63	-24	-25	101	85	39	.483	3	5	-2	-11	*S	-2.4
1956	KC-A	133	434	41	101	16	1	6	39	25	73	.233	.279	.316	.595	56	-28	-29	101	94	37	.488	3	3	-1	8	*S/2	-0.8
1957	KC-A	135	461	44	113	14	6	9	33	22	82	.245	.282	.360	.643	75	-18	-17	99	69	44	.540	6	1	1	-8	*S	-1.2
1958	KC-A	139	442	32	97	11	1	6	38	16	84	.219	.248	.290	.538	45	-32	-35	106	104	29	.407	1	0	0	1	*S	-1.4

YEAR	TM/L	G	AB	R	H	2B	3B	HR	RBI	BB	SO	AVG	OBP	SLG	PRO	/A	BR	/A	PF	CHI	RC	TA	SB	CS	SBR	FR	POS	TPR
1959	KC-A	118	352	31	86	16	5	6	34	28	65	.244	.307	.369	.677	84	-8	-8	101	90	38	.586	1	0	0	0	*S	0.1
1960	NY-A	49	35	8	8	1	0	0	2	0	9	.229	.229	.257	.486	33	-3	-3	94	87	2	.333	0	0	0	0	2S	0.0
1961	NY-A	30	41	1	6	0	0	0	2	0	13	.146	.146	.146	.293	-22	-7	-7	96	131	1	.167	0	0	0	1	S/23	-0.3
Total	11	1121	3441	322	813	114	23	49	281	168	511	.236	.275	.325	.601	62	-187	-189	101	87	293	.498	15	19	-7	-37	*S/23	-13.4
■ **FRANK DEMAREE**	Demaree, Joseph Franklin (born Joseph Franklin Dimaria) b: 6/10/10, Winters, Cal. d: 8/30/58, Los Angeles, Cal. BR/TR, 5'11.5", 185 lbs. Deb: 7/22/32																											
1932	Chi-N	23	56	4	14	3	0	0	6	2	7	.250	.288	.304	.592	57	-3	-3	104	131	5	.476	0			-1	O	-0.4
1933	Chi-N	134	515	68	140	24	6	6	51	22	42	.272	.304	.377	.681	96	-5	-4	97	96	59	.575	4			-3	*O	-1.5
1935	Chi-N	107	385	60	125	19	4	2	66	26	23	.325	.369	.410	.779	110	5	6	99	145	58	.705	6			3	O	0.4
1936	Chi-N	154	605	93	212	34	3	16	96	49	30	.350	.400	.496	.896	133	34	30	105	104	119	.857	4			-4	*O	1.8
1937	Chi-N	154	615	104	199	36	6	17	115	57	31	.324	.382	.485	.866	131	28	26	103	114	112	.825	6			0	*O	1.9
1938	Chi-N	129	476	63	130	15	7	8	62	45	34	.273	.341	.384	.725	94	-0	-3	105	110	62	.642	1			-8	*O	-1.3
1939	NY-N	150	560	68	170	27	2	11	79	66	40	.304	.381	.418	.799	116	13	14	99	115	89	.746	2			-6	*O	0.5
1940	NY-N	121	460	68	139	18	6	7	61	45	39	.302	.364	.413	.777	114	9	9	100	114	71	.727	5			-10	*O	-0.4
1941	NY-N	16	35	3	6	0	0	0	1	4	1	.171	.256	.171	.428	21	-4	-4	103	60	1	.313	0			0	O	-0.3
	Bos-N	48	113	20	26	5	2	2	15	12	5	.230	.304	.363	.667	94	-2	-1	93	115	12	.604	2			-4	O	-0.6
	Yr	64	148	23	32	5	2	2	16	16	6	.216	.293	.318	.610	75	-6	-5	96	102	14	.542	2			-4		-0.9
1942	Bos-N	64	187	18	42	5	0	3	24	17	10	.225	.289	.299	.589	76	-7	-6	95	137	15	.490	2			3	O	-0.3
1943	StL-N	39	86	5	25	2	0	0	9	8	4	.291	.351	.314	.665	89	-1	-1	105	120	9	.537	1			-4	O	-0.5
1944	StL-A	16	51	4	13	2	0	0	6	6	3	.255	.333	.294	.627	79	-1	-1	102	144	6	.553	0	0	0	-2	O	-0.3
Total	12	1155	4144	578	1241	190	36	72	591	359	269	.299	.357	.415	.772	111	67	62	101	114	616	.732	33	0		-35	*O	-1.0
■ **BILLY DeMARS**	DeMars, William Lester "Kid" b: 8/26/25, Brooklyn, N.Y. BR/TR, 5'10", 160 lbs. Deb: 5/18/48 C																											
1948	Phi-A	18	29	3	5	0	0	0	1	5	3	.172	.294	.172	.467	25	-3	-3	102	68	2	.417	0	0	0	0	/S23	-0.1
1950	StL-A	61	178	25	44	5	1	0	13	22	13	.247	.330	.287	.617	55	-11	-12	107	88	17	.518	0	1	-1	-7	S/3	-1.6
1951	StL-A	1	4	1	1	0	0	0	0	1	0	.250	.400	.250	.650	75	-0	-0	105	0	1	.667	0	0	0	0	/S	0.0
Total	3	80	211	29	50	5	1	0	14	28	16	.237	.326	.270	.597	52	-14	-15	106	83	20	.525	0	1	-1	-7	/S32	-1.7
■ **JOHN DeMERIT**	DeMerit, John Stephen "Thumper" b: 1/8/36, West Bend, Wis. BR/TR, 6'1.5", 195 lbs. Deb: 6/18/57																											
1957	Mil-N	33	34	8	5	0	0	0	1	0	8	.147	.147	.147	.294	-23	-6	-5	90	83	1	.207	1	0	0	-2	O	-0.6
1958	Mil-N	3	3	1	2	0	0	0	0	0	0	.667	.667	.667	1.333	285	1	1	89	0	1	2.000	0	0	0	-0	/O	0.0
1959	Mil-N	11	5	4	1	0	0	0	0	1	2	.200	.333	.200	.533	49	-0	-0	95	0	0	.500	0	0	0	-0	/O	0.0
1961	Mil-N	32	74	5	12	3	0	2	5	5	19	.162	.225	.284	.509	37	-7	-6	92	75	5	.422	0	0	0	0	O	-0.6
1962	NY-N	14	16	3	3	0	0	1	1	2	4	.188	.278	.375	.653	71	-1	-1	104	44	2	.615	0	0	0	-3	/O	-0.3
Total	5	93	132	21	23	3	0	3	7	8	33	.174	.227	.265	.492	33	-13	-12	93	68	9	.413	1	0	0	-5	/O	-1.5
■ **DON DEMETER**	Demeter, Donald Lee b: 6/25/35, Oklahoma City, Okla BR/TR, 6'4", 190 lbs. Deb: 9/18/56																											
1956	Bro-N	3	3	1	1	0	0	1	1	0	1	.333	.333	1.333	1.667	311	1	1	103	60	1	2.000	0	0	0	-0	/O	0.1
1958	LA-N	43	106	11	20	2	0	5	8	5	32	.189	.225	.349	.574	47	-8	-9	105	64	8	.494	2	3	-1	-2	O	-1.3
1959	LA-N	139	371	55	95	11	1	18	70	16	87	.256	.298	.437	.734	91	-5	-6	102	131	45	.654	5	6	-2	-12	*O	-2.1
1960	LA-N	64	168	23	46	7	1	9	29	8	34	.274	.311	.488	.799	99	3	-0	115	108	25	.734	0	1	-1	-4	O	-0.7
1961	LA-N	15	29	3	5	0	0	1	2	3	6	.172	.250	.276	.526	39	-3	-3	102	73	2	.423	0	0	0	-1	O	-0.3
	Phi-N	106	382	54	98	18	4	20	68	19	74	.257	.300	.482	.782	110	0	3	94	115	54	.719	2	1	0	1	O1	-0.1
	Yr	121	411	57	103	18	4	21	70	22	80	.251	.297	.467	.764	104	-2	0	95	110	56	.699	2	1	0	0		-0.4
1962	Phi-N	153	550	85	169	24	3	29	107	41	93	.307	.366	.520	.886	142	26	30	95	115	101	.850	2	7	-4	-7	*3O/1	1.8
1963	Phi-N	154	515	63	133	20	2	22	83	31	93	.258	.308	.433	.741	108	6	4	103	121	66	.662	1	4	-2	-2	*O31	-0.6
1964	Det-A	134	441	57	113	22	1	22	80	17	85	.256	.292	.460	.752	110	1	4	96	126	58	.684	4	1	1	2	O1	0.2
1965	Det-A	122	389	50	108	16	4	16	58	23	65	.278	.328	.463	.790	116	10	8	105	106	56	.724	4	2	0	-3	O1	0.0
1966	Det-A	32	99	12	21	5	0	5	12	3	19	.212	.235	.414	.649	81	-3	-3	102	90	8	.542	1	0	0	5	O/1	0.1
	Bos-A	73	226	31	66	13	1	9	29	5	42	.292	.310	.478	.788	113	6	3	109	90	33	.706	1	0	0	2	O/1	0.3
	Yr	105	325	43	87	18	1	14	41	8	61	.268	.287	.458	.746	103	3	0	107	91	42	.664	2	0	1	7		0.4
1967	Bos-A	20	43	7	12	5	0	1	4	3	11	.279	.326	.465	.791	115	2	1	115	73	7	.742	0	0	0	-0	O/3	0.0
	Cle-A	51	121	15	25	4	0	5	12	6	16	.207	.256	.364	.619	81	-3	-3	100	85	10	.520	0	0	0	1	O/3	-0.3
	Yr	71	164	22	37	9	0	6	16	9	27	.226	.274	.390	.665	90	-2	-2	104	82	17	.573	0	0	0	1		-0.3
Total	11	1109	3443	467	912	147	17	163	563	180	658	.265	.309	.459	.769	109	32	29	101	112	474	.713	22	25	-8	-20	O31	-2.9
■ **STEVE DEMETER**	Demeter, Stephen b: 1/27/35, Homer City, Pa. BR/TR, 5'9.5", 185 lbs. Deb: 7/29/59 C																											
1959	Det-A	11	18	1	2	1	0	0	1	0	1	.111	.111	.167	.278	-22	-3	-3	111	131	0	.176	0	0	0	-0	/3	-0.3
1960	Cle-A	4	5	0	0	0	0	0	0	0	1	.000	.000	.000	.000	-99	-1	-1	98	0	0	.000	0	0	0	-0	/3	-0.1
Total	2	15	23	1	2	1	0	0	1	0	2	.087	.087	.130	.217	-38	-4	-5	108	103	0	.143	0	0	0	-0	/3	-0.4
■ **RAY DEMMITT**	Demmitt, Charles Raymond b: 2/2/1884, Illiopolis, Ill. d: 2/19/56, Glen Ellyn, Ill. BL/TR, 5'8", 170 lbs. Deb: 4/12/09																											
1909	NY-A	123	427	68	105	12	12	4	30	55		.246	.340	.358	.698	121	11	12	99	74	56	.714	16			15	*O	2.5
1910	StL-A	10	23	4	4	1	0	0	2	3		.174	.296	.217	.514	65	-1	-1	94	148	1	.474	0			0	/O	0.0
1914	Det-A	1	0	0	0	0	0	0	0	0	0	—	—	—	—	—	0	0	102	—	—	—	0			0	R	0.0
	Chi-A	146	515	63	133	13	12	2	46	61	48	.258	.344	.342	.685	103	5	3	103	100	60	.634	12	20	-8	0	*O	-1.4
	Yr	147	515	63	133	13	12	2	46	61	48	.258	.344	.342	.685	103	5	3	103	100	60	.634	12	20	-8	0		-1.4
1915	Chi-A	9	6	0	0	0	0	0	0	1	2	.000	.143	.000	.143	-58	-1	-1	98	0	0	.167	0			-1	/O	-0.2
1917	StL-A	14	53	6	15	1	2	0	7	0	8	.283	.296	.377	.674	111	-0	0	95	128	6	.579	1			-4	O	-0.4
1918	StL-A	116	405	45	114	23	5	1	61	38	35	.281	.346	.370	.716	117	7	8	99	148	55	.687	10			2	*O	0.4
1919	StL-A	79	202	19	48	11	2	1	19	14	27	.238	.290	.327	.617	75	-8	-7	97	100	19	.545	3			-10	O	-2.1
Total	7	498	1631	205	419	61	33	8	165	172	120	.257	.334	.349	.684	107	13	13	100	106	199	.650	42	20		3	O	-1.2
■ **GENE DeMONTREVILLE**	DeMontreville, Eugene Napoleon b: 3/26/1874, St.Paul, Minn. d: 2/18/35, Memphis, Tenn. BR/TR, 5'8", 165 lbs. Deb: 8/20/1894																											
1894	Pit-N	2	8	0	2	0	0	0	0	1	4	.250	.333	.250	.583	47	-1	-1	94	0	1	.500	0			0	/S	0.0
1895	Was-N	12	46	7	10	1	3	0	9	3	4	.217	.265	.370	.635	62	-3	-3	103	151	6	.694	5			0	S	-0.1
1896	Was-N	133	533	94	183	24	5	8	77	29	27	.343	.381	.452	.833	127	15	19	95	89	105	.860	28			10	*S	2.5
1897	Was-N	133	566	92	193	27	8	3	93	21		.341	.366	.433	.799	111	9	8	101	95	103	.796	30			13	*S2	2.1
1898	Bal-N	151	567	93	186	19	2	0	86	52		.328	.394	.369	.763	118	19	16	103	132	104	.840	49			2	*2S	2.1
1899	Chi-N	82	310	43	87	6	3	0	40	17		.281	.328	.319	.648	83	-8	-6	96	131	42	.659	26			6	S	0.4
	Bal-N	60	240	40	67	13	4	1	36	10		.279	.313	.379	.693	85	-3	-6	108	124	36	.717	21			8	2	0.5
	Yr	142	550	83	154	19	7	1	76	27		.280	.322	.345	.667	84	-11	-12	101	129	78	.684	47			14		0.9
1900	Bro-N	69	234	34	57	8	1	0	28	10		.244	.275	.286	.561	53	-14	-16	108	131	25	.554	21			-1	2S/3O1	-1.3
1901	Bos-N	140	577	83	173	14	4	5	72	17		.300	.320	.364	.684	90	-1	-10	112	95	77	.624	25			3	*23	0.3
1902	Bos-N	124	481	51	125	16	5	0	53	12		.260	.278	.314	.592	88	-10	-8	95	129	50	.522	23			-15	*2S	-1.5
1903	Was-A	12	44	0	12	2	0	0	3	0		.273	.273	.318	.591	74	-1	-1	105	79	4	.438	0			0	2/S	0.0
1904	StL-A	4	9	0	1	0	0	0	0	2		.111	.273	.111	.384	27	-1	-1	95	0	0	.375	0			-0	/2	0.0
Total	11	922	3615	537	1096	130	35	17	497	174	35	.303	.339	.373	.711	99	1	-8	102	112	553	.703	228			25	2S/3O1O	5.0
■ **LEE DeMONTREVILLE**	DeMontreville, Leon b: 9/23/1879, St.Paul, Minn. d: 3/22/62, Pelham Manor, N.Y. TR , 5'7", 140 lbs. Deb: 03																											
1903	StL-N	26	70	8	17	3	1	0	7	8		.243	.321	.314	.635	86	-1	-1	96	102	8	.623	3			0	S/2O	0.0
■ **RICK DEMPSEY**	Dempsey, John Rikard b: 9/13/49, Fayetteville, Tenn. BR/TR, 6', 190 lbs. Deb: 9/23/69																											
1969	Min-A	5	6	1	3	1	0	0	0	1	0	.500	.571	.667	1.238	240	1	1	102	0	2	1.667	0	0	0	0	/C	0.1
1970	Min-A	5	7	1	0	0	0	0	0	1	1	.000	.125	.000	.125	-64	-2	-2	98	0	0	.125	0	0	0	0	/C	-0.1
1971	Min-A	6	13	2	4	1	0	0	0	1	1	.308	.357	.385	.742	106	0	0	104	0	2	.600	0	0	0	-0	/C	0.0
1972	Min-A	25	40	0	8	1	0	0	0	6	8	.200	.304	.225	.529	55	-2	-2	107	0	3	.441	0	0	0	-2	C	-0.4
1973	NY-A	6	11	0	2	0	0	0	0	0	1	3	.182	.250	.182	.432	23	-1	-1	101	0	0	.300	0	0	0	0	/C	0.0
1974	NY-A	43	109	12	26	3	0	2	12	8	7	.239	.291	.321	.612	79	-3	-3	96	115	9	.500	1	0	0	3	C/OD	0.1

YEAR	TM/L	G	AB	R	H	2B	3B	HR	RBI	BB	SO	AVG	OBP	SLG	PRO	/A	BR	/A	PF	CHI	RC	TA	SB	CS	SBR	FR	POS	TPR
1975	NY-A	71	145	18	38	8	0	1	11	21	15	.262	.355	.338	.693	98	0	0	99	81	18	.625	0	0	0	3	CD/O3	0.4
1976	NY-A	21	42	1	5	0	0	0	2	5	4	.119	.213	.119	.332	-1	-5	-5	99	154	1	.270	0	0	0	1	/CO	-0.4
	Bal-A	59	174	11	37	2	0	0	10	13	17	.213	.275	.224	.499	48	-11	-11	98	98	11	.393	1	1	-0	0	C/O	-0.8
	Yr	80	216	12	42	2	0	0	12	18	21	.194	.263	.204	.466	39	-16	-16	98	115	13	.367	1	1	-0	1		-1.2
1977	Bal-A	91	270	27	61	7	4	3	34	34	34	.226	.317	.315	.632	78	-9	-7	93	143	27	.557	2	3	-1	2	C	-0.3
1978	Bal-A	136	441	41	114	25	0	6	32	48	54	.259	.331	.356	.687	103	-3	2	91	72	53	.622	7	3	0	4	*C	1.0
1979	Bal-A	124	368	48	88	23	0	6	41	38	37	.239	.310	.351	.661	80	-11	-10	97	107	39	.570	0	1	-1	1	*C	-0.3
1980	Bal-A	119	362	51	95	26	3	9	40	36	45	.262	.334	.425	.760	106	3	3	101	86	50	.703	3	1	0	4	*C/O1D	1.2
1981	Bal-A	92	251	24	54	10	1	6	15	32	36	.215	.306	.335	.641	86	-5	-4	99	58	26	.576	0	1	-1	-8	C/D	-0.9
1982	Bal-A	125	344	35	88	15	1	5	36	46	37	.256	.344	.349	.692	91	-3	-3	100	107	42	.617	0	3	-2	-6	*C/D	-0.3
1983	Bal-A	128	347	33	80	16	2	4	32	40	54	.231	.315	.323	.638	76	-11	-11	100	101	36	.563	1	1	-0	-4	*C	-0.8
1984	Bal-A	109	330	37	76	11	0	11	34	40	58	.230	.315	.364	.679	93	-5	-3	94	89	37	.607	1	2	-1	7	*C	0.9
1985	Bal-A	132	362	54	92	19	0	12	52	50	87	.254	.346	.406	.752	106	3	4	99	113	55	.725	0	1	-1	-4	*C	0.5
1986	Bal-A	122	327	42	68	15	1	13	29	45	78	.208	.309	.379	.689	88	-6	-5	99	71	41	.655	1	0	0	-8	*C	-0.5
1987	Cle-A	60	141	16	25	10	0	1	9	23	29	.177	.297	.270	.566	51	-9	-10	103	88	12	.517	0	0	0	2	C	-0.2
1988	LA-N	77	167	25	42	13	0	7	30	25	44	.251	.349	.455	.804	122	6	5	106	124	27	.791	1	0	0	-3	C	0.6
Total	20	1556	4257	479	1006	206	12	86	419	514	649	.236	.321	.351	.672	88	-73	-61	98	94	493	.624	18	17	-5	-8	*C/OD13	-0.2

■ **TOD DENNEHEY** Dennehey, Thomas Francis b: 5/12/1899, Philadelphia, Pa. d: 8/8/77, Philadelphia, Pa. BL/TL, 5'10", 180 lbs. Deb: 4/21/23

YEAR	TM/L	G	AB	R	H	2B	3B	HR	RBI	BB	SO	AVG	OBP	SLG	PRO	/A	BR	/A	PF	CHI	RC	TA	SB	CS	SBR	FR	POS	TPR
1923	Phi-N	9	24	4	7	2	0	0	2	1	3	.292	.320	.375	.695	73	-1	-1	114	78	3	.588	0	0	0	-1	/O	-0.2

■ **OTTO DENNING** Denning, Otto George "Dutch" b: 12/28/12, Hays, Kan. BR/TR, 6', 180 lbs. Deb: 4/15/42

YEAR	TM/L	G	AB	R	H	2B	3B	HR	RBI	BB	SO	AVG	OBP	SLG	PRO	/A	BR	/A	PF	CHI	RC	TA	SB	CS	SBR	FR	POS	TPR
1942	Cle-A	92	214	15	45	14	0	1	19	18	14	.210	.275	.290	.564	64	-12	-10	92	103	18	.468	0	0	0	-5	C/O	-0.4
1943	Cle-A	37	129	8	31	6	0	0	13	5	1	.240	.269	.287	.555	69	-6	-5	90	128	9	.433	3	1	0	-2	1	-0.7
Total	2	129	343	23	76	20	0	1	32	23	15	.222	.272	.289	.561	66	-18	-15	91	112	27	.462	3	1	0	-7	/C1O	-1.1

■ **JERRY DENNY** Denny, Jeremiah Dennis (born Jeremiah Dennis Eldridge) b: 3/16/1859, New York, N.Y. d: 8/16/27, Houston, Tex. BR/TR, 5'11.5", 180 lbs. Deb: 5/02/1881

YEAR	TM/L	G	AB	R	H	2B	3B	HR	RBI	BB	SO	AVG	OBP	SLG	PRO	/A	BR	/A	PF	CHI	RC	TA	SB	CS	SBR	FR	POS	TPR
1881	Pro-N	85	320	38	77	16	2	1	24	5	44	.241	.252	.313	.565	82	-9	-6	93	83	26	.432				3	*3	0.4
1882	Pro-N	84	329	54	81	10	9	2	42	4	46	.246	.255	.350	.605	87	-3	-6	106	119	30	.480				9	*3	0.4
1883	Pro-N	98	393	73	108	26	8	8	55	9	48	.275	.291	.443	.734	118	8	8	101	98	52	.642				11	*3	1.7
1884	Pro-N	110	439	57	109	22	9	6	59	14	58	.248	.272	.380	.652	101	1	-0	102	112	46	.548				-4	*3/12C	-0.7
1885	Pro-N	83	318	40	71	14	4	3	24	12	53	.223	.252	.321	.572	92	-6	-2	91	80	26	.462				-0	*3	0.0
1886	StL-N	119	475	58	122	24	6	9	62	14	68	.257	.278	.389	.668	107	-1	3	95	92	57	.609	16			**27**	*3/S	3.1
1887	Ind-N	122	510	86	165	34	12	11	97	13	22	.324	.344	.502	.846	140	21	24	96	99	101	.872	29			14	*3/SO2	3.3
1888	Ind-N	126	524	92	137	27	7	12	63	9	79	.261	.277	.408	.685	124	9	12	95	80	70	.664	32			12	*3S/2OP	2.7
1889	Ind-N	133	578	96	163	24	0	18	112	27	63	.282	.314	.417	.731	97	1	-7	109	109	85	.699	22			10	*3/2S	1.0
1890	NY-N	114	437	50	93	18	7	3	42	28	62	.213	.270	.307	.576	73	-18	-14	95	91	40	.520	11			4	*3/S2	-0.4
1891	NY-N	4	16	0	4	1	0	0	1	0	3	.250	.250	.313	.563	69	-1	-1	94	59	2	.583	2			0	/3	0.0
	Cle-N	36	138	17	31	5	0	0	21	12	23	.225	.291	.261	.552	60	-6	-7	105	173	12	.486	3			0	3/O	-0.6
	Phi-N	19	73	5	21	1	1	0	11	4	6	.288	.325	.329	.653	97	-1	-0	95	136	8	.558	1			0	1/3	0.0
	Yr	59	227	22	56	7	1	0	33	16	32	.247	.299	.286	.586	72	-8	-8	101	158	22	.515	6			0		-0.6
1893	Lou-N	44	175	22	43	5	4	1	22	9	15	.246	.283	.337	.620	68	-9	-8	96	99	18	.545	4			-1	S/3	-0.5
1894	Lou-N	60	221	26	61	11	7	0	32	13	12	.276	.325	.389	.714	83	-10	-5	88	105	32	.700	10			3	3	-0.2
Total	13	1237	4946	714	1286	238	76	74	667	173	602	.260	.287	.384	.671	100	-24	-9	98	100	605	.605	130			88	*3/S12OPC	10.2

■ **BUCKY DENT** Dent, Russell Earl (born Russell Earl O'Dey) b: 11/25/51, Savannah, Ga. BR/TR, 5'9", 170 lbs. Deb: 6/01/73

YEAR	TM/L	G	AB	R	H	2B	3B	HR	RBI	BB	SO	AVG	OBP	SLG	PRO	/A	BR	/A	PF	CHI	RC	TA	SB	CS	SBR	FR	POS	TPR
1973	Chi-A	40	117	17	29	2	0	0	10	10	18	.248	.313	.265	.577	63	-5	-6	102	127	10	.478	2	3	-1	0	S/23	-0.1
1974	Chi-A	154	496	55	136	15	3	5	45	28	48	.274	.317	.347	.664	89	-6	-7	102	95	54	.552	3	4	-2	12	*S	1.5
1975	Chi-A	157	602	52	159	29	4	3	58	36	48	.264	.306	.341	.646	80	-15	-17	103	110	60	.525	2	4	-2	29	*S	2.6
1976	Chi-A	158	562	44	138	18	4	2	52	43	45	.246	.301	.302	.604	78	-16	-15	99	116	52	.497	3	5	-2	-4	*S	-1.3
1977	NY-A	158	477	54	118	18	4	8	49	39	28	.247	.306	.352	.658	80	-14	-13	99	101	52	.566	1	1	-0	-9	*S	-0.3
1978	NY-A	123	379	40	92	11	1	5	40	23	24	.243	.290	.317	.606	71	-15	-14	99	117	34	.497	3	1	0	-10	*S	-1.3
1979	NY-A	141	431	47	99	14	2	2	32	37	30	.230	.292	.285	.577	59	-26	-23	96	95	39	.478	0	0	0	31	*S	2.4
1980	NY-A	141	489	57	128	26	2	5	52	48	37	.262	.330	.354	.684	88	-8	-7	99	110	59	.603	0	3	-2	17	*S	1.9
1981	NY-A	73	227	20	54	11	0	7	27	19	17	.238	.302	.379	.681	95	-2	-2	100	99	27	.611	0	1	-1	-4	S	0.0
1982	NY-A	59	160	11	27	1	1	0	9	8	11	.169	.208	.188	.396	10	-20	-19	96	120	6	.271	0	0	0	1	S	-1.2
	Tex-A	46	146	16	32	9	0	1	14	13	10	.219	.283	.301	.584	65	-8	-6	93	119	13	.491	0	0	0	0	S	-0.1
	Yr	105	306	27	59	10	1	1	23	21	21	.193	.245	.242	.486	36	-27	-25	95	121	20	.382	0	0	0	2		-1.3
1983	Tex-A	131	417	36	99	15	2	2	34	23	31	.237	.279	.297	.576	58	-23	-24	101	102	34	.460	3	7	-3	-5	*S/D	-2.4
1984	KC-A	11	9	2	3	0	0	0	1	1	2	.333	.400	.333	.733	106	0	0	99	133	1	.667	0	0	0	0	/S3	0.1
Total	12	1392	4512	451	1114	169	23	40	423	328	349	.247	.300	.321	.621	74	-157	-154	100	107	442	.528	17	29	-12	59	*S/32D	1.8

■ **SAM DENTE** Dente, Samuel Joseph "Blackie" b: 4/26/22, Harrison, N.J. BR/TR, 5'11", 175 lbs. Deb: 7/10/47

YEAR	TM/L	G	AB	R	H	2B	3B	HR	RBI	BB	SO	AVG	OBP	SLG	PRO	/A	BR	/A	PF	CHI	RC	TA	SB	CS	SBR	FR	POS	TPR
1947	Bos-A	46	168	14	39	4	2	0	11	19	15	.232	.310	.280	.590	60	-8	-9	108	88	15	.485	0	1	-1	-1	3	-0.9
1948	StL-A	98	267	26	72	11	2	0	22	22	8	.270	.328	.326	.653	70	-10	-12	106	85	29	.547	1	3	-2	7	S/3	-0.5
1949	Was-A	153	590	48	161	24	4	1	53	31	24	.273	.309	.332	.641	76	-27	-21	91	93	58	.513	4	4	-1	-10	*S	-3.0
1950	Was-A	155	603	56	144	20	5	2	59	39	19	.239	.286	.299	.585	50	-47	-46	99	116	49	.456	1	1	-0	-2	*S2	-3.7
1951	Was-A	88	273	21	65	8	1	0	29	25	10	.238	.302	.275	.577	59	-16	-15	95	138	22	.468	3	0	1	-10	S2/3	-1.8
1952	Chi-A	62	145	12	32	0	1	0	11	5	8	.221	.257	.234	.491	37	-12	-12	100	121	8	.345	0	0	0	-2	S3/2O1	-1.2
1953	Chi-A	2	0	0	0	0	0	0	0	0	0	—	—	—	—	—	0	0	106	—	—	—	0	0	0	0	/S	0.0
1954	Cle-A	68	169	18	45	7	1	1	19	14	4	.266	.322	.337	.660	76	-4	-6	106	120	18	.550	0	0	0	-4	S/2	-0.4
1955	Cle-A	73	105	10	27	4	0	0	10	12	8	.257	.333	.295	.629	67	-4	-5	104	120	11	.538	0	0	0	1	S3/2	0.3
Total	9	745	2320	205	585	78	16	4	214	167	96	.252	.303	.305	.608	63	-129	-125	99	108	219	.508	9	9	-3	-19	S/32O1	-11.2

■ **MIKE DEPANGHER** Depangher, Michael Anthony b: 9/11/1858, Marysville, Cal. d: 7/7/15, San Francisco, Cal 5'8", 190 lbs. Deb: 8/08/1884

YEAR	TM/L	G	AB	R	H	2B	3B	HR	RBI	BB	SO	AVG	OBP	SLG	PRO	/A	BR	/A	PF	CHI	RC	TA	SB	CS	SBR	FR	POS	TPR
1884	Phi-N	4	10	0	2	0	0	0	0	1	3	.200	.273	.200	.473	56	-1	-0	92	0	1	.375				0	/C	0.0

■ **TONY DePHILLIPS** DePhillips, Anthony Andrew b: 9/20/12, New York, N.Y. BR/TR, 6'2", 185 lbs. Deb: 4/25/43

YEAR	TM/L	G	AB	R	H	2B	3B	HR	RBI	BB	SO	AVG	OBP	SLG	PRO	/A	BR	/A	PF	CHI	RC	TA	SB	CS	SBR	FR	POS	TPR
1943	Cin-N	35	20	0	2	1	0	0	2	1	5	.100	.143	.150	.293	-16	-3	-3	99	241	1	.222	0			1	C	0.0

■ **GENE DERBY** Derby, Eugene A. b: 2/1860 New Hampshire d: 10/12/28, Buffalo, N.Y. Deb: 1885

YEAR	TM/L	G	AB	R	H	2B	3B	HR	RBI	BB	SO	AVG	OBP	SLG	PRO	/A	BR	/A	PF	CHI	RC	TA	SB	CS	SBR	FR	POS	TPR
1885	Bal-a	10	31	4	4	0	0	0		1		.129	.182	.129	.311	1	-3	-4	106	0	1	.222				0	/CO	-0.2

■ **BOB DERNIER** Dernier, Robert Eugene b: 1/5/57, Kansas City, Mo. BR/TR, 6', 160 lbs. Deb: 9/07/80

YEAR	TM/L	G	AB	R	H	2B	3B	HR	RBI	BB	SO	AVG	OBP	SLG	PRO	/A	BR	/A	PF	CHI	RC	TA	SB	CS	SBR	FR	POS	TPR
1980	Phi-N	10	7	5	4	0	0	0	1	1	0	.571	.625	.571	1.196	220	1	1	107	99	4	2.667	3	0	1	1	/O	0.3
1981	Phi-N	10	4	0	3	0	0	0	0	0	0	.750	.750	.750	1.500	291	1	1	112	0	2	2.500	2	1	0	-2	/O	0.0
1982	Phi-N	122	370	56	92	10	2	4	21	36	69	.249	.317	.319	.636	84	-10	-7	94	63	41	.666	42	12	5	6	*O	0.3
1983	Phi-N	122	221	41	51	10	0	1	15	18	21	.231	.289	.290	.578	60	-12	-12	101	89	22	.654	35	7	6	-7	*O	-1.4
1984	Chi-N	143	536	94	149	26	5	3	32	63	60	.278	.356	.362	.718	93	3	-3	110	65	75	.743	45	17	3	-2	*O	-0.7
1985	Chi-N	121	469	63	119	20	3	1	21	40	44	.254	.316	.316	.632	67	-14	-23	116	59	51	.608	31	8	5	3	*O	-1.8
1986	Chi-N	108	324	32	73	14	1	4	18	22	41	.225	.275	.312	.586	58	-17	-20	107	63	30	.577	27	2	7	-4	*O	-1.9
1987	Chi-N	93	199	38	63	4	4	8	21	19	19	.317	.379	.497	.876	129	8	8	101	68	37	.918	16	7	1	-8	O	-0.2
1988	Phi-N	68	166	19	48	3	1	1	10	9	19	.289	.330	.337	.667	91	-2	-2	101	68	19	.627	13	6	0	-2	O	-0.4
Total	9	797	2296	348	602	87	16	22	139	208	273	.262	.326	.343	.668	81	-40	-56	106	66	281	.693	214	60	28	-15	O	-5.8

■ **CLAUD DERRICK** Derrick, Claud Lester "Deek" b: 6/11/1886, Burton, Ga. d: 7/15/74, Clayton, Ga. BR/TR, 6', 175 lbs. Deb: 9/08/10

YEAR	TM/L	G	AB	R	H	2B	3B	HR	RBI	BB	SO	AVG	OBP	SLG	PRO	/A	BR	/A	PF	CHI	RC	TA	SB	CS	SBR	FR	POS	TPR
1910	Phi-A	2	1	0	0	0	0	0	0	0		.000	.000	.000	.000	-98	-0	-0	102	0	0	.000	0			0	/S	0.0
1911	Phi-A	36	100	14	23	1	2	0	5	7		.230	.294	.280	.574	65	-5	-4	93	60	11	.571	7			-2	2/S13	-0.4
1912	Phi-A	21	58	7	14	0	1	0	7	5		.241	.313	.276	.588	69	-2	-2	99	146	6	.523	1			-1	S	0.0

YEAR	TM/L	G	AB	R	H	2B	3B	HR	RBI	BB	SO	AVG	OBP	SLG	PRO	/A	BR	/A	PF	CHI	RC	TA	SB	CS	SBR	FR	POS	TPR
1913	NY-A	23	65	7	19	1	0	1	7	5	8	.292	.352	.354	.706	106	1	1	101	96	8	.674	2			-2	S/32	0.0
1914	Cin-N	3	6	2	2	1	0	0	1	0	0	.333	.333	.500	.833	140	0	0	105	121	1	1.000	1			0	/S	0.1
	Chi-N	28	96	5	21	3	1	0	13	5	13	.219	.257	.271	.528	58	-5	-5	98	185	7	.440	2			-8	/S	-1.2
	Yr	31	102	7	23	4	1	0	14	5	13	.225	.262	.284	.546	63	-5	-5	99	183	8	.468	3			-7		-1.1
Total	5	113	326	35	79	6	4	1	33	22	21	.242	.298	.294	.593	73	-12	-11	97	120	33	.547	13			-11	/S231	-1.5
■ MIKE DERRICK Derrick, James Michael b: 9/19/43, Columbia, S.C. BL/TR, 6', 190 lbs. Deb: 4/09/70																												
1970	Bos-A	24	33	3	7	1	0	0	5	0	11	.212	.212	.242	.455	23	-3	-4	111	253	1	.286	0	1	-1	0	/O1	-0.3
■ RUSS DERRY Derry, Alva Russell b: 10/7/16, Princeton, Mo. BL/TR, 6'1", 180 lbs. Deb: 7/04/44																												
1944	NY-A	38	114	14	29	3	0	4	14	20	19	.254	.366	.386	.752	108	3	2	106	90	19	.765	1	0	0	-3	O	0.0
1945	NY-A	78	253	37	57	6	2	13	45	31	49	.225	.312	.419	.731	104	3	1	107	112	34	.685	1	0	0	3	O	0.1
1946	Phi-A	69	184	17	38	8	5	0	14	27	54	.207	.311	.304	.616	69	-6	-7	104	95	20	.568	0	0	0	4	O	-0.5
1949	StL-N	2	2	0	0	0	0	0	0	0	2	.000	.000	.000	.000	-91	-1	-1	110	0	0	.000	0			0	H	0.0
Total	4	187	553	68	124	17	7	17	73	78	124	.224	.322	.373	.695	92	-2	-6	106	101	72	.671	2	0		4	O	-0.4
■ JOE DeSA DeSa, Joseph b: 7/27/59, Honolulu, Hawaii d: 12/20/86, San Juan, P.R. BL/TL, 5'11", 170 lbs. Deb: 9/06/80																												
1980	StL-N	7	11	0	3	0	0	0	0	0	2	.273	.273	.273	.545	51	-1	-1	103	0	1	.333	0	0	0	-0	/1O	0.0
1985	Chi-A	28	44	5	8	2	0	2	7	3	6	.182	.234	.364	.598	61	-3	-3	100	126	4	.528	0	0	0	-0	/1OD	-0.3
Total	2	35	55	5	11	2	0	2	7	3	8	.200	.241	.345	.587	59	-3	-3	100	102	4	.500	0	0	0	-1	/1DO	-0.3
■ GENE DESAUTELS Desautels, Eugene Abraham "Red" b: 6/13/07, Worcester, Mass. BR/TR, 5'11", 170 lbs. Deb: 6/22/30																												
1930	Det-A	42	126	13	24	4	2	0	9	7	9	.190	.239	.254	.493	24	-15	-15	105	93	8	.412	2	0	1	-3	C	-1.2
1931	Det-A	3	11	1	1	0	0	0	1	0	1	.091	.091	.091	.182	-50	-2	-2	104	330	0	.100	0	0	0	0	/C	-0.1
1932	Det-A	28	72	8	17	2	0	0	2	13	11	.236	.360	.264	.624	63	-3	-3	102	35	8	.600	0	0	0	-1	C	-0.2
1933	Det-A	30	42	5	6	1	0	0	4	4	6	.143	.234	.167	.401	7	-6	-6	107	191	2	.333	0	0	0	-2	C	-0.6
1937	Bos-A	96	305	33	74	10	3	0	27	36	26	.243	.325	.295	.620	56	-19	-21	103	103	31	.549	1	2	-1	-1	C	-1.3
1938	Bos-A	108	333	47	97	16	2	2	48	57	31	.291	.396	.369	.766	91	-1	-3	102	126	53	.768	1	1	-0	-8	*C	-0.7
1939	Bos-A	76	226	26	55	14	0	0	21	33	13	.243	.340	.305	.645	61	-11	-14	108	103	27	.603	3	1	0	1	C	-0.6
1940	Bos-A	71	222	19	50	7	1	0	17	32	13	.225	.328	.266	.594	56	-13	-14	101	104	21	.517	0	1	-1	-8	C	-1.6
1941	Cle-A	66	189	20	38	5	1	1	17	14	12	.201	.260	.254	.514	36	-17	-18	101	118	14	.418	1	0	0	-2	C	-1.4
1942	Cle-A	62	162	14	40	5	0	0	9	12	13	.247	.303	.278	.581	70	-8	-6	92	70	15	.472	1	0	0	-4	C	-0.1
1943	Cle-A	68	185	14	38	6	1	0	19	11	16	.205	.250	.249	.499	51	-13	-11	90	151	12	.393	2	0	1	0	C	-0.7
1945	Cle-A	10	9	1	1	0	0	0	0	1	1	.111	.200	.111	.311	-9	-1	-1	99	0	0	.250	0	0	0	0	C	0.0
1946	Phi-A	52	130	10	28	3	1	0	13	12	16	.215	.282	.254	.536	48	-9	-9	104	150	10	.434	1	1	-0	4	C	-0.2
Total	13	712	2012	211	469	73	11	3	187	232	168	.233	.315	.285	.600	57	-118	-123	101	112	201	.532	12	6	0	-23	C	-8.7
■ ORESTES DESTRADE Destrade, Orestes (Cucuas) b: 5/8/62, Santiago, Cuba BB/TR, 6'4", 210 lbs. Deb: 9/11/87																												
1987	NY-A	9	19	5	5	0	0	0	1	5	5	.263	.417	.263	.680	89	-0	0	98	80	2	.667	0	0	0	0	/1D	0.0
1988	Pit-N	36	47	2	7	1	0	1	3	5	17	.149	.231	.234	.465	35	-4	-4	98	86	3	.400	0	0	0	1	/1	-0.3
Total	2	45	66	7	12	1	0	1	4	10	22	.182	.289	.242	.532	52	-4	-4	98	84	5	.481	0	0	0	1	/1D	-0.3
■ BOB DETHERAGE Detherage, Robert Wayne b: 9/20/54, Springfield, Mo. BR/TR, 6', 180 lbs. Deb: 4/11/80																												
1980	KC-A	20	26	2	8	2	0	1	7	1	4	.308	.333	.500	.833	127	1	1	98	171	4	.789	1	1	-0	-6	O	-0.5
■ GEORGE DETORE Detore, George Francis b: 11/11/06, Utica, N.Y. BR/TR, 5'8", 170 lbs. Deb: 9/14/30																												
1930	Cle-A	3	12	0	2	1	0	0	2	0	2	.167	.167	.250	.417	4	-2	-2	105	234	1	.300	0	0	0	0	/3	-0.1
1931	Cle-A	30	56	3	15	6	0	0	7	8	2	.268	.359	.375	.734	88	-0	-1	106	110	7	.674	0	2	-1	1	3S/2	0.1
Total	2	33	68	3	17	7	0	0	9	8	4	.250	.329	.353	.682	74	-2	-3	106	130	8	.604	0	2	-1	1	/3S2	0.0
■ DUCKY DETWEILER Detweiler, Robert Sterling b: 2/15/19, Trumbauersville, Pa. BR/TR, 5'11", 178 lbs. Deb: 9/12/42																												
1942	Bos-N	12	44	3	14	2	1	0	5	2	7	.318	.348	.409	.757	127	1	1	95	105	6	.645	0			0	3	0.1
1946	Bos-N	1	1	0	0	0	0	0	0	0	0	.000	.000	.000	.000	-99	-0	-0	95	0	0	.000	0			0	H	0.0
Total	2	13	45	3	14	2	1	0	5	2	7	.311	.340	.400	.740	122	1	1	95	103	6	.645	0			0	/3	0.1
■ MIKE DEVEREAUX Devereaux, Michael b: 4/10/63, Casper, Wyo. BR/TR, 6' ", 195 lbs. Deb: 9/02/87																												
1987	LA-N	19	54	7	12	3	0	0	4	3	10	.222	.263	.278	.541	47	-4	-4	92	106	4	.488	3	1	0	-2	O	-0.5
1988	LA-N	30	43	4	5	1	0	0	2	2	10	.116	.156	.140	.295	-14	-6	-7	106	133	1	.205	0	1	-1	-5	O	-1.3
Total	2	49	97	11	17	4	0	0	6	5	20	.175	.216	.216	.432	19	-11	-10	98	118	5	.354	3	2	-0	-7	/O	-1.8
■ MICKEY DEVINE Devine, William Patrick b: 5/9/1892, Albany, N.Y. d: 10/1/37, Albany, N.Y. BR/TR, 5'10", 165 lbs. Deb: 8/02/18																												
1918	Phi-N	4	8	0	1	1	0	0	0	0	1	.125	.125	.250	.375	12	-1	-1	109	0	0	.286	0			0	/C	0.0
1920	Bos-A	8	12	1	2	0	0	0	0	1	2	.167	.231	.167	.397	7	-2	-2	96	0	1	.400	1	0	0	0	/C	0.0
1925	NY-N	21	33	6	9	3	0	0	4	2	3	.273	.314	.364	.678	73	-1	-1	99	119	4	.583	0	0	0	-0	C/3	0.0
Total	3	33	53	7	12	4	0	0	4	3	6	.226	.268	.302	.570	50	-4	-4	100	74	5	.488	1	0		0	/C3	0.0
■ BERNIE DeVIVEIROS DeViveiros, Bernard John b: 4/19/01, Oakland, Cal. BR/TR, 5'7", 160 lbs. Deb: 9/13/24																												
1924	Chi-A	1	1	0	0	0	0	0	0	0	0	.000	.000	.000	.000	-99	-0	-0	97	0	0	.000	0	0	0	0	/S	0.0
1927	Det-A	24	22	4	5	1	0	0	2	2	8	.227	.292	.273	.564	44	-2	-2	108	111	2	.529	1	0	0	0	S/3	0.0
Total	2	25	23	4	5	1	0	0	2	2	8	.217	.280	.261	.541	38	-2	-2	108	106	2	.500	1	0	0	0	/S3	0.0
■ ART DEVLIN Devlin, Arthur Mc Arthur b: 10/16/1879, Washington, D.C. d: 9/18/48, Jersey City, N.J. BR/TR, 6', 175 lbs. Deb: 4/14/04 C																												
1904	NY-N	130	474	81	133	16	8	1	66	62		.281	.364	.354	.718	118	16	13	105	136	75	.771	33			5	*3	2.4
1905	NY-N	153	525	74	129	14	7	2	61	66		.246	.330	.310	.640	92	-2	-3	101	128	75	.727	**59**			5	*3	1.3
1906	NY-N	148	498	76	149	23	8	2	65	74		.299	.390	.390	.779	145	29	29	100	126	99	.923	54			**28**	*3	5.5
1907	NY-N	143	491	61	136	16	2	1	54	63		.277	.359	.324	.683	110	12	9	105	134	73	.732	38			-1	*3/S	0.9
1908	NY-N	157	534	59	135	18	4	2	45	62		.253	.331	.313	.643	103	6	4	104	106	60	.622	19			13	*3	2.4
1909	NY-N	143	491	61	130	19	8	0	56	65		.265	.362	.336	.698	113	13	10	105	126	68	.737	26			15	*3	3.0
1910	NY-N	147	493	71	128	17	5	2	67	62	32	.260	.353	.327	.679	103	1	4	95	143	69	.712	28			8	*3	1.3
1911	NY-N	95	260	42	71	16	2	0	25	42	19	.273	.386	.350	.736	104	4	3	102	93	40	.783	9			7	3/12S	1.3
1912	Bos-N	124	436	59	126	18	8	0	54	51	37	.289	.367	.367	.734	94	2	-3	107	116	62	.726	11			-5	1S3/O	-0.6
1913	Bos-N	73	210	19	48	7	5	0	12	29	17	.229	.328	.310	.637	87	-4	-3	95	67	23	.642	8			-3	3	-0.6
Total	10	1313	4412	603	1185	164	57	10	505	576	105	.269	.357	.338	.695	108	76	64	102	122	642	.739	285			70	*3/1S20	16.9
■ JIM DEVLIN Devlin, James Alexander b: 1849, Philadelphia, Pa. d: 10/10/1883, Philadelphia, Pa. BR/TR, 5'11", 175 lbs. Deb: 4/21/1873																												
1873	Phi-n	22	104	18	26							.250															1/3SO	
1874	Chi-n	44	215	28	59							.274															1O/3	
1875	Chi-n	70	336	60	95							.283															1P/O	
1876	Lou-N	68	298	38	94	14	1	0	28	1	11	.315	.318	.369	.687	123	8	6	104	83	36	.544				3	*P/1	0.0
1877	Lou-N	61	268	38	72	6	3	1	27	7	27	.269	.287	.325	.612	70	-2	-15	132	98	26	.480				3	*P	0.0
Total	3 n	136	655	106	180							.275															*P	
Total	2	129	566	76	166	20	4	1	55	8	38	.293	.303	.348	.651	94	6	-9	117	90	61	.512				6	P/1O3S	0.0
■ JIM DEVLIN Devlin, James Raymond b: 8/25/22, Plains, Pa. BL/TR, 5'11.5", 165 lbs. Deb: 4/27/44																												
1944	Cle-A	1	1	0	0	0	0	0	0	0	0	.000	.000	.000	.000	-99	-0	-0	100	0	0	.000	0	0	0	0	/C	0.0
■ REX DeVOGT DeVogt, Rex Eugene b: 1/4/1888, Clare, Mich. d: 11/9/35, Alma, Mich. BR/TR, 5'9", 170 lbs. Deb: 4/17/13																												
1913	Bos-N	3	6	0	0	0	0	0	0	0	3	.000	.000	.000	.000	-99	-2	-1	95	0	0	.000	0			0	/C	0.0
■ JOSH DEVORE Devore, Joshua D. b: 11/13/1887, Murray City, Ohio d: 10/6/54, Chillicothe, Ohio BL/TL, 5'6", 160 lbs. Deb: 9/25/08																												
1908	NY-N	5	6	1	1	0	0	0	2	1		.167	.286	.167	.452	45	-0	-0	104	768	1	.600	1			0	/O	0.0
1909	NY-N	22	28	6	4	1	0	0	1	2		.143	.250	.179	.429	32	-2	-2	105	73	2	.500	3			0	O	-0.2

YEAR	TM/L	G	AB	R	H	2B	3B	HR	RBI	BB	SO	AVG	OBP	SLG	PRO	/A	BR	/A	PF	CHI	RC	TA	SB	CS	SBR	FR	POS	TPR
1910	NY-N	133	490	92	149	11	10	2	27	46	67	.304	.371	.380	.750	125	12	15	95	52	84	.824	43			-8	*O	0.3
1911	NY-N	149	565	96	158	19	10	3	50	81	69	.280	.376	.365	.740	105	8	6	102	69	99	.870	61			2	*O	0.4
1912	NY-N	106	327	66	90	14	6	2	37	51	43	.275	.381	.373	.754	103	5	3	104	97	56	.865	27			-8	O	-0.7
1913	NY-N	16	21	4	4	0	1	0	1	3	4	.190	.320	.286	.606	72	-1	-1	103	61	3	.941	6			-2	/O	-0.2
	Cin-N	66	217	30	58	6	4	3	14	12	21	.267	.309	.373	.682	93	-2	-3	102	56	29	.698	17			0	O	-0.3
	Phi-N	23	39	9	11	1	0	0	5	4	7	.282	.364	.308	.671	83	-0	-1	112	151	4	.607	0			-3	O	-0.3
	Yr	105	277	43	73	7	5	3	20	19	32	.264	.318	.357	.675	89	-3	-4	104	79	37	.706	23			-5		-0.8
1914	Phi-N	30	53	5	16	2	0	0	7	4	5	.302	.351	.340	.690	105	0	0	100	141	6	.595	0			3	/O	0.3
	Bos-N	51	128	22	29	4	0	1	5	18	14	.227	.327	.281	.608	78	-2	-3	104	46	12	.576	2			-8	O	-1.2
	Yr	81	181	27	45	6	0	1	12	22	19	.249	.333	.298	.632	86	-2	-3	103	83	19	.581	2			-5		-0.9
Total	7	601	1874	331	520	58	31	11	149	222	230	.277	.361	.359	.720	104	18	15	101	73	297	.796	160			-23	O	-1.9

■ AL DeVORMER DeVormer, Albert E. b: 8/19/1891, Grand Rapids, Mich d: 8/29/66, Grand Rapids, Mich BR/TR, 6'0.5", 175 lbs. Deb: 8/04/18

YEAR	TM/L	G	AB	R	H	2B	3B	HR	RBI	BB	SO	AVG	OBP	SLG	PRO	/A	BR	/A	PF	CHI	RC	TA	SB	CS	SBR	FR	POS	TPR
1918	Chi-A	8	19	2	5	2	0	0	0	0	4	.263	.263	.368	.632	90	-0	-0	101	0	2	.571	1			-0	/CO	0.0
1921	NY-A	22	49	6	17	4	0	0	7	2	4	.347	.373	.429	.801	101	0	0	103	114	8	.781	2	0	1	-1	C	0.0
1922	NY-A	24	59	8	12	4	1	0	11	1	6	.203	.217	.305	.522	34	-6	-6	102	219	4	.404	0	0	0	-1	C/1	-0.5
1923	Bos-A	74	209	20	54	7	3	0	18	6	21	.258	.282	.321	.603	58	-13	-14	102	92	19	.497	3	0	1	4	C/1	-0.4
1927	NY-N	68	141	14	35	3	1	2	21	11	11	.248	.312	.326	.638	71	-6	-6	100	141	14	.566	1			-5	C/1	-0.6
Total	5	196	477	50	123	20	5	2	57	20	46	.258	.292	.333	.625	64	-25	-26	101	121	48	.534	7	0		-3	C/1O	-1.5

■ WALT DEVOY Devoy, Walter Joseph b: 3/14/1886, St.Louis, Mo. d: 12/17/53, St.Louis, Mo. Deb: 9/13/09

YEAR	TM/L	G	AB	R	H	2B	3B	HR	RBI	BB	SO	AVG	OBP	SLG	PRO	/A	BR	/A	PF	CHI	RC	TA	SB	CS	SBR	FR	POS	TPR
1909	StL-A	19	69	7	17	3	1	0	8	3		.246	.278	.319	.597	96	-1	-1	92	148	7	.558	4			1	O/1	0.0

■ JEFF DeWILLIS DeWillis, Jeffrey Allen b: 4/13/65, Houston, Tex. BR/TR, 6'2", 170 lbs. Deb: 4/19/87

YEAR	TM/L	G	AB	R	H	2B	3B	HR	RBI	BB	SO	AVG	OBP	SLG	PRO	/A	BR	/A	PF	CHI	RC	TA	SB	CS	SBR	FR	POS	TPR
1987	Tor-A	13	25	2	3	1	0	1	2	2	12	.120	.185	.280	.465	21	-3	-3	101	80	1	.409	0	0	0	-0	C	-0.1

■ CHARLIE DEXTER Dexter, Charles Dana b: 6/15/1876, Evansville, Ind. d: 6/9/34, Cedar Rapids, Iowa TR , 5'7", 155 lbs. Deb: 4/17/1896

YEAR	TM/L	G	AB	R	H	2B	3B	HR	RBI	BB	SO	AVG	OBP	SLG	PRO	/A	BR	/A	PF	CHI	RC	TA	SB	CS	SBR	FR	POS	TPR
1896	Lou-N	107	402	65	112	18	7	3	37	17	34	.279	.318	.381	.698	87	-9	-8	98	67	57	.679	21			-2	CO	-0.6
1897	Lou-N	76	257	43	72	12	5	2	46	21		.280	.342	.389	.731	99	-2	-0	95	129	39	.735	12			0	OC3/S	0.0
1898	Lou-N	112	421	76	132	13	5	1	66	26		.314	.361	.375	.736	118	7	10	96	131	75	.806	44			-1	O/2C	0.2
1899	Lou-N	80	295	47	76	7	1	1	33	21		.258	.316	.298	.614	69	-11	-12	103	113	35	.612	21			5	O/S	-1.0
1900	Chi-N	40	125	7	25	5	0	2	20	1		.200	.206	.288	.494	40	-11	-10	93	149	8	.390	2			0	CO/2	-0.8
1901	Chi-N	116	460	46	123	9	5	1	66	16		.267	.292	.315	.607	78	-13	-13	100	158	50	.543	22			4	1302/C	-0.7
1902	Chi-N	69	266	30	60	12	0	2	26	19		.226	.277	.293	.570	81	-7	-6	96	113	26	.534	13			-6	31O	-1.2
	Bos-N	48	183	33	47	3	0	1	18	16		.257	.317	.290	.606	93	-2	-1	95	107	22	.625	16			-3	S2/O3	-0.1
	Yr	117	449	63	107	15	0	3	44	35		.238	.293	.292	.585	86	-9	-6	96	112	48	.570	29			-10		-1.3
1903	Bos-N	123	457	82	102	15	1	3	34	61		.223	.315	.280	.595	75	-15	-12	96	77	52	.623	32			2	*O/SC	-1.4
Total	8	771	2866	429	749	94	24	16	346	198	34	.261	.313	.328	.641	85	-62	-52	97	113	364	.632	183			-2	OC/312S	-5.6

■ BO DIAZ Diaz, Baudilio Jose (Seijas) b: 3/23/53, Cua, Venezuela BR/TR, 5'11", 185 lbs. Deb: 9/06/77

YEAR	TM/L	G	AB	R	H	2B	3B	HR	RBI	BB	SO	AVG	OBP	SLG	PRO	/A	BR	/A	PF	CHI	RC	TA	SB	CS	SBR	FR	POS	TPR
1977	Bos-A	2	1	0	0	0	0	0	0	0	1	.000	.000	.000	.000	-85	-0	-0	117	0	0	.000	0	0	0	0	/C	0.0
1978	Cle-A	44	127	12	30	4	0	2	11	4	17	.236	.260	.315	.575	65	-7	-6	93	94	10	.444	0	0	0	-2	C	-0.6
1979	Cle-A	15	32	0	5	2	0	0	1	2	6	.156	.206	.219	.425	14	-4	-4	106	55	1	.321	0	0	0	-1	C	-0.3
1980	Cle-A	76	207	15	47	11	2	3	32	7	27	.227	.252	.343	.595	60	-11	-12	102	156	14	.459	1	0	0	-4	C	-1.1
1981	Cle-A	63	182	25	57	19	0	7	38	13	23	.313	.362	.533	.895	166	12	14	93	126	32	.843	2	2	-1	-1	C/D	1.4
1982	Phi-N	144	525	69	151	29	1	18	85	36	87	.288	.337	.450	.786	126	11	15	94	117	72	.695	3	6	-3	-13	*C	0.0
1983	Phi-N	136	471	49	111	17	0	15	64	38	57	.236	.295	.367	.663	82	-12	-13	101	116	49	.572	1	4	-2	0	*C	-1.0
1984	Phi-N	27	75	5	16	4	0	1	9	5	13	.213	.262	.307	.569	58	-4	-4	102	136	5	.444	0	0	0	-1	C	-0.4
1985	Phi-N	26	76	9	16	5	1	2	16	6	7	.211	.268	.382	.650	78	-2	-3	102	182	6	.538	0	0	0	2	C	0.0
	Cin-N	51	161	12	42	8	0	3	15	15	18	.261	.328	.366	.694	89	-1	-2	105	88	19	.600	0	0	0	-7	C	-0.7
	Yr	77	237	21	58	13	1	5	31	21	25	.245	.309	.371	.680	86	-4	-5	104	122	27	.595	0	0	0	-5		-0.7
1986	Cin-N	134	474	50	129	21	0	10	56	40	52	.272	.329	.380	.709	91	-4	-6	104	108	59	.619	1	1	-0	-3	*C	-0.6
1987	Cin-N	140	496	49	134	28	1	15	82	19	73	.270	.304	.421	.725	87	-9	-11	104	129	59	.619	1	0	0	3	*C	0.3
1988	Cin-N	92	315	26	69	9	0	10	35	7	41	.219	.238	.343	.581	62	-15	-17	105	101	20	.439	0	2	-1	-1	C	-1.5
Total	12	950	3142	321	807	157	5	86	444	192	422	.257	.302	.392	.694	90	-46	-49	101	118	347	.611	9	15	-6	-28	C/D	-4.5

■ EDGAR DIAZ Diaz, Edgar (Serrano) b: 2/8/64, Santurce, P.R. BR/TR, 6', 155 lbs. Deb: 9/16/86

YEAR	TM/L	G	AB	R	H	2B	3B	HR	RBI	BB	SO	AVG	OBP	SLG	PRO	/A	BR	/A	PF	CHI	RC	TA	SB	CS	SBR	FR	POS	TPR
1986	Mil-A	5	13	0	3	0	0	0	0	1	3	.231	.286	.231	.516	43	-1	-1	102	0	1	.400	0	0	0	-1	/S	0.0

■ MARIO DIAZ Diaz, Mario Rafael (Torres) b: 1/10/62, Humacao, P.R. BR/TR, 5'10", 145 lbs. Deb: 9/12/87

YEAR	TM/L	G	AB	R	H	2B	3B	HR	RBI	BB	SO	AVG	OBP	SLG	PRO	/A	BR	/A	PF	CHI	RC	TA	SB	CS	SBR	FR	POS	TPR
1987	Sea-A	11	23	4	7	0	1	0	3	0	4	.304	.304	.391	.696	82	-1	-1	103	133	3	.563	0	0	0	0	S	0.0
1988	Sea-A	28	72	6	22	5	0	0	9	3	5	.306	.333	.375	.708	91	-0	-1	108	132	8	.566	0	0	0	-0	S/213	0.0
Total	2	39	95	10	29	5	1	0	12	3	9	.305	.327	.379	.705	89	-1	-2	106	133	11	.565	0	0	0	-0	/S231	0.0

■ MIKE DIAZ Diaz, Michael Anthony b: 4/15/60, San Francisco, Cal. BR/TR, 6'2", 195 lbs. Deb: 9/15/83

YEAR	TM/L	G	AB	R	H	2B	3B	HR	RBI	BB	SO	AVG	OBP	SLG	PRO	/A	BR	/A	PF	CHI	RC	TA	SB	CS	SBR	FR	POS	TPR
1983	Chi-N	6	7	2	2	1	0	0	1	0	0	.286	.286	.429	.714	95	-0	-0	101	132	1	.600	0	0	0	0	/C	0.0
1986	Pit-N	97	209	22	56	9	0	12	36	19	43	.268	.335	.483	.818	123	6	6	100	105	33	.767	0	1	-1	-2	O1/3C	0.2
1987	Pit-N	103	241	28	58	8	2	16	48	31	42	.241	.335	.490	.824	110	5	3	104	115	40	.810	1	0	0	-3	O1/C	-0.1
1988	Pit-N	47	74	6	17	3	0	0	5	16	13	.230	.367	.270	.637	87	-1	-0	98	100	8	.610	0	0	0	-5	O/1C	-0.5
	Chi-A	40	152	12	36	6	0	3	12	5	30	.237	.266	.336	.601	69	-7	-6	97	81	12	.467	0	1	-1	-4	1/D	-1.2
Total	4	293	683	70	169	27	2	31	102	71	128	.247	.324	.429	.753	103	3	2	101	103	94	.712	1	2	-1	-13	/1OC3D	-1.6

■ PAUL DICKEN Dicken, Paul Franklin b: 10/2/43, Deland, Fla. BR/TR, 6'5", 195 lbs. Deb: 6/07/64

YEAR	TM/L	G	AB	R	H	2B	3B	HR	RBI	BB	SO	AVG	OBP	SLG	PRO	/A	BR	/A	PF	CHI	RC	TA	SB	CS	SBR	FR	POS	TPR
1964	Cle-A	11	11	0	0	0	0	0	0	0	5	.000	.000	.000	.000	-97	-3	-3	103	0	0	.000	0	0	0	0	H	-0.2
1966	Cle-A	2	2	0	0	0	0	0	0	0	1	.000	.000	.000	.000	-99	-1	-1	101	0	0	.000	0	0	0	0	H	0.0
Total	2	13	13	0	0	0	0	0	0	0	6	.000	.000	.000	.000	-97	-3	-3	103	0	0	.000	0	0	0	0		-0.2

■ BUTTERCUP DICKERSON Dickerson, Lewis Pessano b: 10/11/1858, Tyaskin, Md. d: 7/23/20, Baltimore, Md. BL/TR, 5'6", 140 lbs. Deb: 7/15/1878

YEAR	TM/L	G	AB	R	H	2B	3B	HR	RBI	BB	SO	AVG	OBP	SLG	PRO	/A	BR	/A	PF	CHI	RC	TA	SB	CS	SBR	FR	POS	TPR
1878	Cin-N	29	123	17	38	5	1	0	9	0	7	.309	.309	.366	.675	127	2	3	95	72	14	.529				-3	O	-0.1
1879	Cin-N	81	350	73	102	18	**14**	2	57	3	27	.291	.297	.440	.737	147	14	17	95	132	47	.633				-4	*O	0.9
1880	Tro-N	30	119	15	23	2	2	0	10	2	3	.193	.207	.244	.450	47	-6	-7	110	128	6	.323				6	O/S	-0.2
	Wor-N	31	133	22	39	8	6	0	20	1	2	.293	.299	.444	.742	131	6	4	113	109	18	.638				-3	O	0.0
	Yr	61	252	37	62	10	8	0	30	3	5	.246	.255	.349	.604	92	0	-3	111	121	23	.479				3		-0.2
1881	Wor-N	80	367	48	116	18	6	1	31	8	8	.316	.331	.406	.737	124	12	9	105	61	51	.625				9	*O	1.6
1883	Pit-a	85	355	62	88	15	1	0		17		.248	.282	.296	.578	92	-5	-1	94	0	30	.457				1	*O/S2	0.0
1884	StL-U	46	211	49	77	15	1	0		8		.365	.388	.445	.834	175	17	16	104	0	37	.761	0			4	O/3	1.7
	Bal-a	13	56	9	12	2	1	0		4		.214	.290	.286	.576	92	-0	-0	99	0	5	.500				0	O/3	0.0
	Lou-a	8	28	6	4	0	2	1		3		.143	.226	.393	.619	113	0	1	89	0	3	.583				0	/O	0.0
	Yr	21	84	15	16	2	3	1		7		.190	.269	.321	.590	99	-0	0	95	0	7	.529				0		0.0
1885	Buf-N	5	21	1	1	1	0	0	0	1	4	.048	.091	.095	.186	-40	-3	-3	99	0	0	.150				0	/O	-0.2
Total	7	408	1763	302	500	84	34	4	127	47	51	.284	.303	.377	.680	121	38	38	100	60	211	.565				10	O/S32	3.7

■ GEORGE DICKEY Dickey, George Willard "Skeets" b: 7/10/15, Kensett, Ark. d: 6/16/76, Dewitt, Ark. BB/TR, 6'2", 180 lbs. Deb: 9/21/35

YEAR	TM/L	G	AB	R	H	2B	3B	HR	RBI	BB	SO	AVG	OBP	SLG	PRO	/A	BR	/A	PF	CHI	RC	TA	SB	CS	SBR	FR	POS	TPR
1935	Bos-A	5	11	1	0	0	0	0	1	1	3	.000	.083	.000	.083	-71	-3	-3	108	0	0	.091	0	0	0	0	/C	-0.2
1936	Bos-A	10	23	0	1	1	0	0	0	2	3	.043	.120	.087	.207	-45	-6	-6	106	0	0	.182	0	0	0	0	C	-0.3
1941	Chi-A	32	55	6	11	1	0	2	8	5	7	.200	.267	.327	.594	60	-4	-3	94	118	5	.511	0	0	0	1	C	0.0
1942	Chi-A	59	116	6	27	3	0	1	17	9	11	.233	.288	.284	.572	62	-6	-6	99	166	10	.457	0	0	0	0	C	-0.1
1946	Chi-A	37	78	8	15	1	0	0	1	12	13	.192	.300	.205	.505	44	-6	-5	97	24	5	.418	0	2	-1	2	C	-0.2
1947	Chi-A	83	211	15	47	6	0	1	27	34	25	.223	.331	.265	.596	69	-8	-7	97	168	22	.560	4	2	0	-1	C	-0.1
Total	6	226	494	36	101	12	0	4	54	63	62	.204	.294	.253	.547	53	-32	-30	97	128	41	.481	4	4	-1	2	C	-0.9

YEAR	TM/L	G	AB	R	H	2B	3B	HR	RBI	BB	SO	AVG	OBP	SLG	PRO	/A	BR	/A	PF	CHI	RC	TA	SB	CS	SBR	FR	POS	TPR
■ **BILL DICKEY**	Dickey, William Malcolm b: 6/6/07, Bastrop, La. BL/TR, 6'1.5", 185 lbs. Deb: 8/15/28 MCH																											
1928	NY-A	10	15	1	3	1	1	0	2	0	2	.200	.200	.400	.600	59	-1	-1	92	114	1	.500	0	0	0	-0	/C	0.0
1929	NY-A	130	447	60	145	30	6	10	65	14	16	.324	.346	.485	.832	113	6	7	99	90	73	.774	4	3	-1	-4	*C	1.3
1930	NY-A	109	366	55	124	25	7	5	65	21	14	.339	.375	.486	.861	130	8	14	90	112	67	.848	7	1	2	-7	*C	1.5
1931	NY-A	130	477	65	156	17	10	6	78	39	20	.327	.378	.442	.820	117	10	12	98	112	80	.783	2	1	0	-7	*C	1.3
1932	NY-A	108	423	66	131	20	4	15	84	34	13	.310	.361	.482	.843	122	9	12	95	115	72	.811	2	4	-2	-8	*C	0.8
1933	NY-A	130	478	58	152	24	8	14	97	47	14	.318	.381	.490	.871	142	19	26	91	120	89	.867	3	4	-2	11	*C	3.8
1934	NY-A	104	395	56	127	24	4	12	72	38	18	.322	.384	.494	.878	131	14	16	96	106	74	.867	0	3	-2	5	*C	2.7
1935	NY-A	120	448	54	125	26	6	14	81	35	11	.279	.339	.458	.797	112	1	6	93	114	70	.762	1	1	-0	-3	*C	0.5
1936	NY-A	112	423	99	153	26	8	22	107	46	16	.362	.428	.617	1.045	164	35	39	95	108	111	1.140	0	2	-1	-6	*C	3.5
1937	NY-A	140	530	87	176	35	2	29	133	73	22	.332	.417	.570	.987	144	37	36	102	124	128	1.073	3	2	-0	1	*C	4.2
1938	NY-A	132	454	84	142	27	4	27	115	75	22	.313	.412	.568	.981	136	30	26	105	117	111	1.083	3	0	1	-4	*C	2.3
1939	NY-A	128	480	98	145	23	3	24	105	77	37	.302	.403	.512	.915	145	24	31	91	118	104	.965	5	0	2	0	*C	3.7
1940	NY-A	106	372	45	92	11	1	9	54	48	32	.247	.336	.355	.691	81	-11	-10	99	125	46	.628	0	3	-2	4	*C	0.0
1941	NY-A	109	348	35	99	15	5	7	71	45	17	.284	.371	.417	.788	110	5	6	98	151	56	.750	2	1	0	-6	*C	0.6
1942	NY-A	82	268	28	79	13	1	2	38	26	11	.295	.359	.373	.732	107	2	3	99	126	34	.635	2	2	-1	1	C	1.3
1943	NY-A	85	242	29	85	18	2	4	33	41	12	.351	.445	.492	.937	180	24	25	96	92	57	.994	2	1	0	-1	C	2.9
1946	NY-A	54	134	10	35	8	0	2	10	19	12	.261	.357	.366	.723	102	1	1	100	69	17	.651	0	1	-1	-0	CM	0.2
Total	17	1789	6300	930	1969	343	72	202	1210	678	289	.313	.382	.486	.868	128	216	248	97	115	1193	.872	36	29	-7	-23	*C	30.6
■ **JOHNNY DICKSHOT**	Dickshot, John Oscar "Ugly" (born John Oscar Dicksus) b: 1/24/10, Waukegan, Ill. BR/TR, 6', 195 lbs. Deb: 4/16/36																											
1936	Pit-N	9	9	2	2	0	0	0	1	1	2	.222	.300	.222	.522	44	-1	-1	98	177	1	.429	0			-0	/O	0.0
1937	Pit-N	82	264	42	67	8	4	3	33	26	36	.254	.323	.348	.672	80	-6	-7	102	118	29	.572	0			-4	O	-1.3
1938	Pit-N	29	35	3	8	0	0	0	4	8	5	.229	.372	.229	.601	68	-1	-1	100	181	4	.704	3			-2	O	-0.2
1939	NY-N	10	34	3	8	0	0	0	5	5	3	.235	.333	.235	.569	56	-2	-2	99	234	3	.464	0			-1	O	-0.2
1944	Chi-A	62	162	18	41	8	5	0	15	13	10	.253	.313	.364	.677	93	-2	-2	100	92	20	.615	2	0	1	-4	O	-0.6
1945	Chi-A	130	486	74	147	19	10	4	58	48	41	.302	.366	.407	.774	130	15	18	95	106	75	.740	18	3	**4**	-1	*O	1.6
Total	6	322	990	142	273	35	19	7	116	101	97	.276	.345	.371	.715	104	3	5	98	115	131	.671	23	3		-12	O	-0.7
■ **BOB DIDIER**	Didier, Robert Daniel b: 2/16/49, Hattiesburg, Miss. BB/TR, 6', 190 lbs. Deb: 4/07/69 C																											
1969	Atl-N	114	352	30	90	16	1	0	32	34	39	.256	.321	.307	.628	74	-10	-12	104	119	36	.530	1	3	-2	-13	*C	-1.9
1970	Atl-N	57	168	9	25	2	1	0	7	12	11	.149	.210	.173	.383	4	-23	-24	104	94	6	.295	1	0	0	-5	C	-2.5
1971	Atl-N	51	155	9	34	4	1	0	5	6	17	.219	.248	.258	.507	40	-12	-13	110	51	10	.371	0	0	0	-0	C	-1.3
1972	Atl-N	13	40	5	12	2	1	0	5	2	4	.300	.349	.400	.749	107	1	0	105	128	6	.655	0	0	0	-0	C	0.1
1973	Det-A	7	22	3	10	1	0	0	1	3	0	.455	.520	.500	1.020	187	3	3	101	36	6	1.167	0	0	0	1	/C	0.4
1974	Bos-A	5	14	0	1	0	0	0	1	2	1	.071	.188	.071	.259	-22	-2	-2	107	393	0	.231	0	0	0	0	/C	-0.1
Total	6	247	751	56	172	25	4	0	51	59	72	.229	.287	.273	.560	54	-43	-48	105	103	64	.460	2	3	-1	-17	C	-5.3
■ **ERNIE DIEHL**	Diehl, Ernest Guy b: 10/2/1877, Cincinnati, Ohio d: 11/6/58, Miami, Fla. BR/TR, 6'1", 190 lbs. Deb: 5/31/03																											
1903	Pit-N	1	3	0	1	0	0	0	0	0		.333	.333	.333	.667	88	-0	-0	105	0	0	.500	0			0	/O	0.0
1904	Pit-N	12	37	6	6	0	0	0	4	6		.162	.279	.162	.441	39	-2	-2	99	249	3	.484	3			0	/O	-0.2
1906	Bos-N	3	11	1	5	0	1	0	0	0		.455	.455	.636	1.091	243	2	2	100	0	3	1.167	0			-0	/OS	0.2
1909	Bos-N	1	4	1	2	1	0	0	0	0		.500	.500	.750	1.250	302	1	1	96	0	1	1.500	0			0	/O	0.1
Total	4	17	55	8	14	1	1	0	4	6		.255	.328	.309	.637	99	0	0	100	175	8	.634	3			0	/OS	0.1
■ **CHUCK DIERING**	Diering, Charles Edward Allen b: 2/5/23, St.Louis, Mo. BR/TR, 5'10", 165 lbs. Deb: 4/15/47																											
1947	StL-N	105	74	22	16	3	1	2	11	19	22	.216	.383	.365	.748	94	1	-0	106	123	12	.847	3			-22	O	-2.4
1948	StL-N	7	7	2	0	0	0	0	0	2	2	.000	.222	.000	.222	-35	-1	-1	101	0	0	.375	1			-1	/O	-0.1
1949	StL-N	131	369	60	97	21	8	3	38	35	49	.263	.328	.388	.716	83	-5	-10	110	94	49	.652	1			-9	*O	-2.5
1950	StL-N	89	204	34	51	12	0	3	18	35	38	.250	.360	.353	.713	86	-2	-3	103	86	28	.692	1			-3	O	-0.8
1951	StL-N	64	85	9	22	5	1	0	8	6	15	.259	.308	.341	.649	74	-3	-3	101	107	9	.538	0	1	-1	-6	O	-1.1
1952	NY-N	41	23	2	4	1	1	0	2	4	3	.174	.296	.304	.601	65	-1	-1	102	111	2	.524	0	2	-1	-11	O	-1.4
1954	Bal-A	128	418	35	108	14	1	2	29	56	57	.258	.351	.311	.662	87	-8	-6	95	83	46	.585	3	7	-3	10	*O	-0.1
1955	Bal-A	137	371	38	95	16	2	3	31	57	45	.256	.355	.334	.689	96	-6	-1	90	87	45	.637	5	8	-3	-12	*O3S	-1.9
1956	Bal-A	50	97	15	18	4	0	1	4	23	19	.186	.342	.258	.599	64	-5	-4	94	53	10	.588	2	5	-2	0	O/3	-0.7
Total	9	752	1648	217	411	76	14	14	141	237	250	.249	.346	.338	.684	85	-31	-29	99	88	201	.647	16	23		-53	O/3S	-11.0
■ **DICK DIETZ**	Dietz, Richard Allen b: 9/18/41, Crawfordsville, Ind. BR/TR, 6'1", 195 lbs. Deb: 6/18/66																											
1966	SF-N	13	23	1	1	0	0	0	0	0	9	.043	.083	.043	.127	-65	-5	-5	97	0	0	.087	0	0	0	-0	/C	-0.4
1967	SF-N	56	120	10	27	3	0	4	19	25	44	.225	.363	.350	.713	104	2	2	101	146	16	.701	0	1	-1	-1	C	0.3
1968	SF-N	98	301	21	82	14	2	6	38	34	68	.272	.348	.392	.740	125	9	9	98	118	42	.684	1	1	-0	-6	C	0.7
1969	SF-N	79	244	28	56	8	1	11	35	53	53	.230	.373	.406	.779	117	8	7	101	106	38	.779	0	0	0	-9	C	0.3
1970	SF-N	148	493	82	148	36	2	22	107	109	106	.300	.430	.515	.945	159	41	44	96	132	113	1.011	0	1	-1	10	*C	5.8
1971	SF-N	142	453	58	114	19	0	19	72	97	86	.252	.388	.419	.808	129	21	21	100	121	79	.834	1	3	-2	-9	*C	1.4
1972	LA-N	27	56	4	9	1	0	1	6	14	11	.161	.329	.232	.561	66	-2	-2	94	154	5	.604	2	0	1	-1	C	-0.1
1973	Atl-N	83	139	22	41	8	1	3	24	49	25	.295	.479	.432	.910	136	14	12	113	140	32	1.048	0	0	0	-0	1C	1.1
Total	8	646	1829	226	478	89	6	66	301	381	402	.261	.392	.425	.817	130	87	88	99	125	326	.862	4	6	-2	-17	C/1	9.1
■ **ROY DIETZEL**	Dietzel, Leroy Louis b: 1/9/31, Baltimore, Md. BR/TR, 6', 190 lbs. Deb: 9/02/54																											
1954	Was-A	9	21	1	5	0	0	0	1	5	4	.238	.385	.238	.623	75	-0	-0	98	76	2	.588	0	0	0	0	/23	0.0
■ **JAY DIFANI**	Difani, Clarence Joseph b: 12/21/23, Crystal City, Mo. BR/TR, 6', 170 lbs. Deb: 4/23/48																											
1948	Was-A	2	2	0	0	0	0	0	0	0	2	.000	.000	.000	.000	-97	-1	-1	103	0	0	.000	0	0	0	0	H	0.0
1949	Was-A	2	1	0	1	1	0	0	0	0	0	1.000	1.000	2.000	3.000	749	1	1	91	0	2	—	0	0	0	0	/2	0.1
Total	2	4	3	0	1	1	0	0	0	0	2	.333	.333	.667	1.000	163	0	0	99	0	2	1.000	0	0	0	0	/2	0.1
■ **STEVE DIGNAN**	Dignan, Stephen E. b: 5/16/1859, Boston, Mass. d: 7/11/1881, Boston, Mass. Deb: 6/01/1880																											
1880	Bos-N	8	34	4	11	1	0	0	4	0	3	.324	.324	.353	.676	141	1	1	92	117	4	.522				0	/O	0.1
	Wor-N	3	10	1	3	0	1	0	2	0	1	.300	.300	.500	.800	147	1	0	113	146	2	.714				0	/O	0.0
	Yr	11	44	5	14	1	1	0	6	0	4	.318	.318	.386	.705	141	2	2	97	135	6	.567				0		0.1
Total	1	11	44	5	14	1	1	0	6	0	4	.318	.318	.386	.705	142	2	2	97	123	6	.567				0	/O	0.1
■ **DON DILLARD**	Dillard, David Donald b: 1/8/37, Greenville, S.C. BL/TR, 6'1", 200 lbs. Deb: 4/24/59																											
1959	Cle-A	10	10	0	4	0	0	0	1	0	2	.400	.400	.400	.800	125	0	0	97	98	2	.667	0	0	0	0	H	0.0
1960	Cle-A	6	7	0	1	0	0	0	0	1	3	.143	.250	.143	.393	9	-1	-1	98	0	0	.286	0	0	0	-0	/O	0.0
1961	Cle-A	74	147	27	40	5	0	7	17	15	28	.272	.340	.449	.788	113	2	2	96	76	23	.750	0	0	0	-3	O	-0.2
1962	Cle-A	95	174	22	40	5	1	5	14	11	25	.230	.276	.356	.632	70	-8	-8	98	72	16	.529	0	1	-1	-9	O	-1.9
1963	Mil-N	67	119	9	28	6	4	1	12	5	21	.235	.272	.378	.650	84	-3	-3	101	105	11	.531	0	2	-1	-1	O	-0.6
1965	Mil-N	20	19	1	3	0	0	1	3	0	6	.158	.158	.316	.474	29	-2	-2	104	138	0	.333	0	0	0	-0	/O	-0.1
Total	6	272	476	59	116	16	5	14	47	32	85	.244	.293	.387	.679	86	-12	-10	98	83	53	.595	0	3	-2	-14	O	-2.8
■ **PAT DILLARD**	Dillard, Robert Lee b: 6/12/1874, Chattanooga, Tenn d: 7/22/07, Denver, Colo. Deb: 4/21/00																											
1900	StL-N	57	183	24	42	5	2	0	12	13		.230	.281	.279	.559	61	-11	-9	93	73	17	.504	7			0	O3/S	-0.7
■ **STEVE DILLARD**	Dillard, Stephen Bradley b: 2/8/51, Memphis, Tenn. BR/TR, 6'1", 180 lbs. Deb: 9/28/75																											
1975	Bos-A	1	5	2	2	0	0	0	0	0	0	.400	.400	.400	.800	116	0	0	109	0	1	1.000	1	0	0	-0	/2	0.0
1976	Bos-A	57	167	22	46	14	0	1	15	17	20	.275	.342	.377	.720	100	2	0	110	87	20	.652	6	4	-1	-4	32S/D	-0.2
1977	Bos-A	66	141	22	34	7	0	1	13	7	13	.241	.277	.312	.589	51	-8	-11	117	110	12	.495	4	3	-1	0	2/SD	-0.6
1978	Det-A	56	130	21	29	5	2	0	7	6	11	.223	.257	.292	.550	50	-8	-9	108	73	9	.417	1	2	-1	6	2/D	-0.1
1979	Chi-N	89	166	31	47	6	1	5	24	17	24	.283	.353	.422	.775	98	2	-0	112	112	25	.724	1	0	0	11	2/3	1.5

YEAR	TM/L	G	AB	R	H	2B	3B	HR	RBI	BB	SO	AVG	OBP	SLG	PRO	/A	BR	/A	PF	CHI	RC	TA	SB	CS	SBR	FR	POS	TPR
1980	Chi-N	100	244	31	55	8	1	4	27	20	54	.225	.287	.316	.602	64	-11	-12	106	120	22	.515	2	2	-1	4	32/S	-0.6
1981	Chi-N	53	119	18	26	7	1	2	11	8	20	.218	.268	.345	.612	70	-5	-5	104	92	11	.521	0	0	0	4	2/3S	0.1
1982	Chi-A	16	41	1	7	3	1	0	5	1	5	.171	.190	.293	.483	31	-4	-4	97	167	2	.361	0	1	-1	2	2	0.0
Total	8	438	1013	148	246	50	6	13	102	76	147	.243	.297	.343	.640	72	-30	-41	109	104	102	.564	15	12	-3	24	2/3SD	0.1
■ **PICKLES DILLHOEFER** Dillhoefer, William Martin b: 10/13/1894, Cleveland, Ohio d: 2/23/22, St.Louis, Mo. BR/TR, 5'7", 154 lbs. Deb: 4/16/17																												
1917	Chi-N	42	95	3	12	1	1	0	8	2	9	.126	.144	.158	.302	-7	-12	-12	105	206	3	.217	1			1	C	-1.0
1918	Phi-N	8	11	0	1	0	0	0	0	1	1	.091	.167	.091	.258	-19	-2	-2	109	0	0	.400	2			0	/C	0.0
1919	StL-N	45	108	11	23	3	2	0	12	8	6	.213	.267	.278	.545	68	-5	-4	94	155	9	.506	5			1	C	0.0
1920	StL-N	76	224	26	59	8	3	0	13	13	7	.263	.304	.326	.630	83	-6	-5	98	69	22	.530	2	1	0	-3	C	-0.2
1921	StL-N	76	162	19	39	4	4	0	15	11	7	.241	.289	.315	.604	63	-9	-8	95	108	15	.516	2	1	0	-4	C	-0.7
Total	5	247	600	59	134	16	10	0	48	35	30	.223	.266	.283	.549	59	-33	-31	98	115	49	.464	12	2		-5	C	-1.9
■ **BOB DILLINGER** Dillinger, Robert Bernard "Duke" "Duke" b: 9/17/18, Glendale, Cal. BR/TR, 5'11.5", 170 lbs. Deb: 4/16/46																												
1946	StL-A	83	225	33	63	6	3	0	11	19	30	.280	.341	.333	.675	91	-3	-2	98	56	27	.608	8	1	**2**	1	3/S	0.5
1947	StL-A	137	571	70	168	23	6	3	37	56	38	.294	.361	.371	.733	102	4	2	102	53	80	.713	**34**	13	**2**	6	*3	1.4
1948	StL-A	153	644	110	**207**	34	10	2	44	65	34	.321	.385	.415	.799	106	12	7	106	47	105	.775	**28**	11	2	-15	*3	-1.1
1949	StL-A	137	544	68	176	22	13	1	51	51	40	.324	.385	.417	.802	112	9	9	100	67	87	.760	**20**	14	-2	-21	*3	-1.3
1950	Phi-A	84	356	55	110	21	9	3	41	31	20	.309	.366	.444	.810	119	3	8	90	75	57	.750	5	3	-0	2	3	0.6
	Pit-N	58	222	23	64	8	2	1	9	13	22	.288	.328	.356	.684	78	-6	-7	103	43	24	.575	4			1	3	-0.6
1951	Pit-N	12	43	3	10	3	0	0	0	1	0	.233	.250	.302	.552	45	-3	-4	107	0	2	.432	2	0	1	1	3	-0.1
	Chi-A	89	299	39	90	6	4	0	20	15	17	.301	.337	.348	.684	88	-6	-5	97	69	34	.568	5	5	-2	-4	3	-1.2
Total	6	753	2904	401	888	123	47	10	213	251	201	.306	.363	.391	.754	102	9	8	100	57	417	.727	106	47		-28	3/S	-1.8
■ **POP DILLON** Dillon, Frank Edward b: 10/17/1873, Normal, Ill. d: 9/12/31, Pasadena, Cal. BL , Deb: 9/08/1899																												
1899	Pit-N	30	121	21	31	5	0	0	20	5		.256	.286	.298	.583	63	-6	-6	99	180	12	.511	5			0	1	-0.4
1900	Pit-N	5	18	3	2	1	0	0	1	0		.111	.111	.167	.278	-22	-3	-3	103	104	0	.188	0			0	/1	-0.2
1901	Det-A	74	281	40	81	14	6	1	42	15		.288	.324	.391	.716	91	-1	-5	110	120	41	.695	14			-1	1	-0.8
1902	Det-A	66	243	21	50	6	3	0	22	16		.206	.255	.255	.510	43	-18	-18	99	119	17	.415	2			4	1	-1.1
	Bal-A	2	7	1	2	0	1	0	0	2		.286	.444	.571	1.016	179	1	1	102	0	2	1.200	0			0	/1	0.1
	Yr	68	250	22	52	6	4	0	22	18		.208	.261	.264	.525	48	-18	-17	99	117	18	.434	2			4		-1.0
1904	Bro-N	135	511	60	132	18	6	0	31	40		.258	.312	.317	.629	101	-2	1	95	62	56	.567	13			3	*1	-0.1
Total	5	312	1181	146	298	44	16	1	116	78		.252	.299	.319	.618	81	-29	-30	100	99	128	.554	34			6	1	-2.5
■ **PACKY DILLON** Dillon, Packard Andrew b: St.Louis, Mo. d: 1/8/1890, Guelph, Ont., Canada Deb: 5/04/1875																												
1875	RS-n	3	16	1	3							.188															/C	
■ **MIGUEL DILONE** Dilone, Miguel Angel (Reyes) b: 11/1/54, Santiago, D.R. BB/TR, 6', 160 lbs. Deb: 9/02/74																												
1974	Pit-N	12	2	3	0	0	0	0	0	1	0	.000	.333	.000	.333	-1	-0	-0	98	0	0	1.500	2	0	1	-1	/O	0.0
1975	Pit-N	18	6	8	0	0	0	0	0	0	1	.000	.000	.000	.000	-99	-2	-2	99	0	-0	.250	2	2	-1	-0	/O	-0.2
1976	Pit-N	16	17	7	4	0	0	0	0	0	0	.235	.235	.235	.471	34	-1	-1	100	0	1	.643	5	1	1	1	/O	0.0
1977	Pit-N	29	44	5	6	0	0	0	0	2	3	.136	.174	.136	.310	-15	-7	-7	103	0	2	.526	12	0	4	-2	O	-0.6
1978	Oak-A	135	258	34	59	8	0	1	14	23	30	.229	.294	.271	.566	60	-13	-14	101	76	21	.643	50	23	1	-3	OD/3	-1.8
1979	Oak-A	30	91	15	17	1	2	1	6	6	7	.187	.237	.275	.512	42	-8	-7	89	82	5	.457	6	5	-1	-2	O	-1.0
	Chi-N	43	36	14	11	0	0	0	1	2	5	.306	.342	.306	.648	70	-1	-2	112	36	4	.933	15	5	2	-4	O	-0.4
1980	Cle-A	132	528	82	180	30	9	0	40	28	45	.341	.376	.432	.808	118	15	13	102	73	89	.855	61	18	8	1	*OD	2.0
1981	Cle-A	72	269	33	78	5	5	0	19	18	28	.290	.334	.346	.680	103	-1	1	93	81	31	.676	29	10	3	5	OD	0.8
1982	Cle-A	104	379	50	89	12	3	3	25	25	36	.235	.286	.306	.592	62	-19	-19	100	81	35	.575	33	5	7	-6	O/D	-2.1
1983	Cle-A	32	68	15	13	3	1	0	7	10	5	.191	.295	.265	.560	53	-4	-4	105	152	6	.579	5	1	1	0	O	-0.2
	Chi-A	4	3	1	0	0	0	0	0	0	0	.000	.000	.000	.000	-97	-1	-1	103	0	0	.333	1	0	0	-1	/OD	0.0
	Yr	36	71	16	13	3	1	0	7	10	5	.183	.284	.254	.537	47	-5	-5	105	139	6	.576	6	1	1	-0		-0.2
	Pit-N	7	0	1	0	0	0	0	0	0	0	—	—	—	—	—	0	0	103	—	6	—	2	0	1	0	/R	0.1
1984	Mon-N	88	169	28	47	8	2	1	10	17	18	.278	.348	.367	.714	110	1	2	91	60	26	.836	27	2	7	-1	O	0.7
1985	Mon-N	51	84	10	16	0	2	0	6	6	11	.190	.244	.238	.483	38	-7	-7	94	119	4	.440	7	3	0	-1	O	-0.8
	SD-N	27	46	8	10	0	1	0	1	4	8	.217	.280	.261	.541	51	-3	-3	102	33	4	.667	10	3	1	-1	O	-0.3
	Yr	78	130	18	26	0	3	0	7	10	19	.200	.257	.246	.503	43	-10	-10	96	91	9	.536	17	6	2	-2		-1.1
Total	12	800	2000	314	530	67	25	6	129	142	197	.265	.316	.333	.648	81	-53	-50	99	76	235	.698	267	78	33	-15	O/D3	-3.8
■ **DOM DiMAGGIO** DiMaggio, Dominic Paul "The Little Professor" b: 2/12/17, San Francisco, Cal BR/TR, 5'9", 168 lbs. Deb: 4/16/40																												
1940	Bos-A	108	418	81	126	32	6	8	46	41	46	.301	.367	.464	.831	113	8	8	101	78	73	.805	7	6	-2	6	O	0.5
1941	Bos-A	144	584	117	165	37	6	8	58	90	57	.283	.385	.408	.792	106	11	8	103	68	101	.806	13	6	0	2	*O	0.2
1942	Bos-A	151	622	110	178	36	8	14	48	70	52	.286	.364	.437	.801	120	20	17	104	48	103	.786	16	10	-1	15	*O	2.1
1946	Bos-A	142	534	85	169	24	7	7	73	66	58	.316	.393	.427	.820	113	22	13	114	118	92	.788	10	6	-1	3	*O	0.8
1947	Bos-A	136	513	75	145	21	5	8	71	74	62	.283	.376	.390	.766	105	11	6	108	124	80	.744	10	6	-1	15	*O	1.4
1948	Bos-A	155	648	127	185	40	4	9	87	101	58	.285	.383	.401	.785	109	10	10	100	88	110	.784	10	2	2	10	*O	1.6
1949	Bos-A	145	605	126	186	34	5	8	60	96	55	.307	.404	.420	.824	110	18	12	107	64	110	.828	9	7	-2	10	*O	1.7
1950	Bos-A	141	588	**131**	193	30	**11**	7	70	82	68	.328	.414	.452	.866	106	21	9	114	74	117	.889	**15**	4	**2**	6	*O	1.3
1951	Bos-A	146	639	**113**	189	34	4	12	72	73	53	.296	.370	.418	.788	104	12	5	108	73	101	.736	4	7	-3	-4	*O	-0.6
1952	Bos-A	128	486	81	143	20	1	6	33	57	61	.294	.371	.377	.747	101	7	2	107	65	70	.687	6	8	-3	-6	*O	-0.9
1953	Bos-A	3	3	0	1	0	0	0	0	0	1	.333	.333	.333	.667	74	-0	-0	109	0	0	.500	0	0	0	0	H	0.0
Total	11	1399	5640	1046	1680	308	57	87	618	750	571	.298	.383	.419	.802	109	140	90	107	79	958	.807	100	62	-7	57	*O	8.1
■ **JOE DiMAGGIO** DiMaggio, Joseph Paul "Joltin' Joe" or "The Yankee Clipper" b: 11/25/14, Martinez, Cal. BR/TR, 6'2", 193 lbs. Deb: 5/13/36 CH																												
1936	NY-A	138	637	132	206	44	**15**	29	125	24	39	.323	.352	.576	.928	132	19	25	95	79	127	.926	4	0	1	0	*O	1.9
1937	NY-A	151	621	**151**	215	35	15	**46**	167	64	37	.346	.412	**.673**	1.085	166	61	60	102	99	173	1.207	3	0	1	6	*O	5.5
1938	NY-A	145	599	129	194	32	13	32	140	59	21	.324	.386	.581	.967	132	33	28	105	102	136	1.022	6	1	1	0	*O	2.6
1939	NY-A	120	462	108	176	32	6	30	126	52	20	**.381**	.448	.671	1.119	**199**	56	**62**	91	109	139	1.242	3	0	1	5	*O	**5.7**
1940	NY-A	132	508	93	179	28	9	31	133	61	30	**.352**	.425	.626	1.051	**171**	51	52	99	124	135	1.104	1	2	-1	-2	*O	3.7
1941	NY-A	139	541	122	193	43	11	30	**125**	76	13	.357	.440	.643	1.083	187	64	66	98	107	162	1.213	4	2	0	7	*O	6.0
1942	NY-A	154	610	123	186	29	13	21	114	68	36	.305	.376	.498	.875	146	34	35	99	116	120	.869	4	2	0	-0	*O	2.4
1946	NY-A	132	503	81	146	20	8	25	95	59	24	.290	.367	.511	.878	143	28	27	100	115	96	.862	1	0	0	0	*O	2.2
1947	NY-A	141	534	97	168	31	10	20	97	64	32	.315	.391	.522	.913	158	37	39	97	112	112	.918	3	0	1	1	*O	3.5
1948	NY-A	153	594	110	190	26	11	**39**	**155**	67	30	.320	.396	.598	.994	162	49	49	100	118	140	1.014	1	1	-0	-2	*O	3.9
1949	NY-A	76	272	58	94	14	6	14	67	55	18	.346	.459	.596	1.055	177	32	32	100	119	76	1.153	0	1	-1	-3	O	2.5
1950	NY-A	139	525	114	158	33	10	32	122	80	33	.301	.394	**.585**	.979	149	35	36	99	111	125	1.018	0	0	0	-2	*O/1	2.9
1951	NY-A	116	415	72	109	22	4	12	71	61	36	.263	.365	.422	.787	123	8	13	92	123	65	.752	0	0	0	0	*O	0.8
Total	13	1736	6821	1390	2214	389	131	361	1537	790	369	.325	.398	.579	.977	156	507	522	98	109	1606	1.039	30	9	4	10	*O/1	43.6
■ **VINCE DiMAGGIO** DiMaggio, Vincent Paul b: 9/6/12, Martinez, Cal. d: 10/3/86, N.Hollywood, Cal. BR/TR, 5'11", 183 lbs. Deb: 4/19/37																												
1937	Bos-N	132	493	56	126	18	4	13	69	39	111	.256	.311	.387	.699	98	-9	-2	90	110	61	.636	8			10	*O	0.1
1938	Bos-N	150	540	71	123	28	3	14	61	65	134	.228	.313	.369	.682	99	-10	-1	88	93	68	.658	11			7	*O/2	0.3
1939	Cin-N	8	14	1	1	1	0	0	2	2	10	.071	.188	.143	.330	-10	-2	-2	103	367	0	.308	0			0	/O	-0.1
1940	Cin-N	2	4	2	1	0	0	0	0	1	0	.250	.400	.250	.650	82	-0	-0	101	0	0	.500	0			0	/O	0.0
	Pit-N	110	356	59	103	26	0	19	54	37	83	.289	.364	.522	.887	149	19	22	95	82	68	.919	11			4	*O	2.2
	Yr	112	360	61	104	26	0	19	54	38	83	.289	.365	.519	.884	148	19	22	95	81	69	.916	11			4		2.2
1941	Pit-N	151	528	73	141	27	5	21	100	68	100	.267	.354	.456	.810	124	18	17	103	121	88	.813	10			0	*O	1.1
1942	Pit-N	143	496	57	118	22	3	15	75	52	87	.238	.311	.385	.697	102	1	0	101	120	59	.650	10			14	*O	1.1
1943	Pit-N	157	580	64	144	41	2	15	88	70	126	.248	.329	.403	.733	107	7	4	104	116	80	.709	11			8	*O/S	0.7

YEAR	TM/L	G	AB	R	H	2B	3B	HR	RBI	BB	SO	AVG	OBP	SLG	PRO	/A	BR	/A	PF	CHI	RC	TA	SB	CS	SBR	FR	POS	TPR
1944	Pit-N	109	342	41	82	20	4	9	50	33	83	.240	.307	.401	.707	93	-2	-4	105	109	42	.662	6			4	*O/3	-0.8
1945	Phi-N	127	452	64	116	25	3	19	84	43	91	.257	.321	.451	.773	118	6	8	96	114	67	.757	12			7	*O	0.9
1946	Phi-N	6	19	1	4	1	0	0	1	0	7	.211	.211	.263	.474	36	-2	-2	95	75	1	.313	0			-1	/O	-0.2
	NY-N	15	25	2	0	0	0	0	0	2	5	.000	.074	.000	.074	-77	-6	-6	102	0	0	.074	0			-0	O	-0.6
	Yr	21	44	3	4	1	0	0	1	2	12	.091	.130	.114	.244	-31	-8	-8	100	25	1	.167	0			-1		-0.8
Total	10	1110	3849	491	959	209	24	125	584	412	837	.249	.324	.413	.737	108	21	33	98	109	535	.724	79			52	*O/3S2	4.7
■ MIKE DIMMEL	Dimmel, Michael Wayne b: 10/16/54, Albert Lea, Minn. BR/TR, 6', 180 lbs. Deb: 9/02/77																											
1977	Bal-A	25	5	8	0	0	0	0	0	0	1	.000	.000	.000	.000	-99	-1	-1	93	0	0	.200	1	0	0	-7	O	-0.8
1978	Bal-A	8	0	2	0	0	0	0	0	0	0	—	—	—	—	—	0	0	91	—	0	.000	0	1	-1	-3	/O	-0.3
1979	StL-N	6	3	1	1	0	0	0	0	0	0	.333	.333	.333	.667	79	-0	-0	105	0	0	.333	0	1	-1	-2	/O	-0.2
Total	3	39	8	11	1	0	0	0	0	0	1	.125	.125	.125	.250	-32	-1	-1	97	0	0	.222	1	2	-1	-11	/O	-1.3
■ KERRY DINEEN	Dineen, Kerry Michael b: 7/1/52, Englewood, N.J. BL/TL, 5'11", 165 lbs. Deb: 6/14/75																											
1975	NY-A	7	22	3	8	1	0	0	1	2	1	.364	.417	.409	.826	136	1	1	99	43	4	.786	0	0	0	1	/O	0.2
1976	NY-A	4	7	0	2	0	0	0	1	1	2	.286	.375	.286	.661	96	0	0	99	192	1	.667	1	1	-0	-0	/O	0.0
1978	Phi-N	5	8	0	2	1	0	0	0	1	0	.250	.333	.375	.708	93	-0	-0	105	0	1	.571	0	0	0	-0	/O	0.0
Total	3	16	37	3	12	2	0	0	2	4	3	.324	.390	.378	.769	118	1	1	100	62	5	.704	1	1	-0	0	/O	0.2
■ VANCE DINGES	Dinges, Vance George b: 5/29/15, Elizabeth, N.J. BL/TL, 6'2", 175 lbs. Deb: 4/17/45																											
1945	Phi-N	109	397	46	114	15	4	1	36	35	17	.287	.346	.353	.699	98	-3	-1	96	93	49	.622	5			3	O1	-0.1
1946	Phi-N	50	104	7	32	5	1	1	10	9	12	.308	.363	.404	.767	124	2	3	95	83	15	.697	2			0	1/O	0.1
Total	2	159	501	53	146	20	5	2	46	44	29	.291	.350	.363	.713	103	-0	2	96	90	64	.652	7			3	/1O	0.0
■ BOB DiPIETRO	DiPietro, Robert Louis Paul b: 9/1/27, San Francisco, Cal BR/TR, 5'11", 185 lbs. Deb: 9/23/51																											
1951	Bos-A	4	11	0	1	0	0	0	0	1	1	.091	.167	.091	.258	-27	-2	-2	108	0	0	.182	0	0	0	0	/O	-0.1
■ BENNY DISTEFANO	Distefano, Benito James b: 1/23/62, Brooklyn, N.Y. BL/TL, 6'1", 195 lbs. Deb: 5/18/84																											
1984	Pit-N	45	78	10	13	1	2	3	9	5	13	.167	.226	.346	.572	62	-5	-4	94	98	5	.478	0	1	-1	-0	O1	-0.6
1986	Pit-N	31	39	3	7	1	0	1	5	1	5	.179	.200	.282	.482	31	-4	-4	100	142	2	.375	0	0	0	-1	/O1	-0.4
1988	Pit-N	16	29	6	10	3	1	1	6	3	4	.345	.406	.621	1.027	195	3	3	98	114	7	1.050	0	0	0	0	/1O	0.3
Total	3	92	146	19	30	5	3	5	20	9	22	.205	.256	.384	.640	80	-5	-4	97	113	14	.559	0	1	-1	-1	/O1	-0.7
■ DUTCH DISTEL	Distel, George Adam b: 4/15/1896, Madison, Ind. d: 2/12/67, Madison, Ind. BR/TR, 5'9", 165 lbs. Deb: 6/21/18																											
1918	StL-N	8	17	3	3	1	1	0	1	2	3	.176	.263	.353	.616	93	-0	-0	93	63	2	.571	0			0	/2SO	0.0
■ JACK DITTMER	Dittmer, John Douglas b: 1/10/28, Elkader, Iowa BL/TR, 6'1", 175 lbs. Deb: 6/17/52																											
1952	Bos-N	93	326	26	63	7	2	7	41	26	26	.193	.255	.291	.546	54	-22	-20	95	141	24	.452	1	0	0	-6	2	-2.2
1953	Mil-N	138	504	54	134	22	1	9	63	18	35	.266	.293	.367	.660	75	-22	-19	94	118	53	.538	1	0	0	-20	*2	-3.1
1954	Mil-N	66	192	22	47	8	0	6	20	19	17	.245	.322	.380	.703	88	-5	-3	93	86	24	.633	0	1	-1	2	2	0.1
1955	Mil-N	38	72	4	9	1	1	1	4	4	15	.125	.171	.208	.379	0	-10	-10	93	90	3	.297	0	0	0	2	2	-0.4
1956	Mil-N	44	102	8	25	4	0	1	6	8	8	.245	.300	.314	.614	66	-5	-5	99	72	10	.519	0	0	0	-0	2	-0.1
1957	Det-A	16	22	3	5	1	0	0	2	2	1	.227	.292	.273	.564	51	-1	-2	107	132	2	.471	0	0	0	-0	/32	-0.1
Total	6	395	1218	117	283	43	4	24	136	77	102	.232	.281	.333	.614	66	-66	-58	95	114	116	.524	2	1	0	-22	2/3	-5.8
■ LEO DIXON	Dixon, Leo Moses b: 9/1894, Chicago, Ill. d: 4/11/84, Chicago, Ill. BR/TR, 5'11", 170 lbs. Deb: 4/14/25																											
1925	StL-A	76	205	27	46	11	1	1	19	24	42	.224	.318	.302	.620	54	-13	-16	108	98	21	.578	3	2	-0	3	C	-0.7
1926	StL-A	33	89	7	17	3	1	0	8	11	14	.191	.294	.247	.541	42	-7	-8	101	124	7	.474	1	4	-2	3	C	-0.3
1927	StL-A	36	103	6	20	3	1	0	12	7	6	.194	.245	.243	.488	25	-11	-12	106	160	6	.386	0	0	0	3	C	-0.7
1929	Cin-N	14	30	0	5	2	0	0	2	3	7	.167	.242	.233	.476	19	-4	-4	99	98	2	.400	0			1	C	-0.1
Total	4	159	427	40	88	19	3	1	41	45	69	.206	.291	.272	.562	42	-36	-39	105	118	36	.496	4	6		9	C	-1.8
■ DAN DOBBEK	Dobbek, Daniel John b: 12/6/34, Ontonagon, Mich. BL/TR, 6', 195 lbs. Deb: 9/09/59																											
1959	Was-A	16	60	8	15	1	2	1	5	5	13	.250	.308	.383	.691	88	-1	-1	100	80	7	.622	0	0	0	-0	O	-0.1
1960	Was-A	110	248	32	54	8	2	10	30	35	41	.218	.317	.387	.704	88	-4	-4	102	93	31	.673	4	3	-1	-1	O	-0.9
1961	Min-A	72	125	12	21	3	1	4	14	13	18	.168	.257	.304	.561	46	-9	-10	106	110	10	.500	1	2	-1	-7	O	-1.9
Total	3	198	433	52	90	12	5	15	49	53	72	.208	.299	.363	.661	75	-14	-16	103	96	48	.623	5	5	-2	-8	O	-2.9
■ JOHN DOBBS	Dobbs, John Gordon b: 6/3/1876, Chattanooga, Tenn. d: 9/9/34, Charlotte, N.C. BL/TR, 5'9.5", 170 lbs. Deb: 4/20/01																											
1901	Cin-N	109	435	71	119	17	4	2	27	36		.274	.329	.345	.674	103	-1	2	95	51	57	.649	19			4	*O/3	-0.2
1902	Cin-N	63	256	39	76	7	3	1	16	19		.297	.345	.359	.705	109	6	3	110	51	35	.656	7			0	O	-0.1
	Chi-N	59	235	31	71	8	2	0	35	18		.302	.352	.353	.705	125	6	7	96	129	31	.634	3			-8	O	-0.6
	Yr	122	491	70	147	15	5	1	51	37		.299	.348	.356	.705	116	11	10	103	89	66	.645	10			-8		-0.7
1903	Chi-N	16	61	8	14	1	1	0	4	7		.230	.309	.279	.588	73	-2	-2	95	73	5	.511	0			2	O	0.0
	Bro-N	111	414	61	98	15	7	2	59	48		.237	.316	.321	.637	82	-8	-9	101	131	51	.646	23			11	*O	-0.3
	Yr	127	475	69	112	16	8	2	63	55		.236	.315	.316	.631	81	-10	-11	101	124	56	.628	23			12		-0.3
1904	Bro-N	101	363	36	90	16	2	0	30	28		.248	.302	.303	.605	93	-4	-2	95	106	37	.546	11			6	O/2S	0.0
1905	Bro-N	123	460	59	117	21	4	2	36	31		.254	.301	.330	.632	94	-6	-3	96	84	52	.577	15			-14	*O	-2.7
Total	5	582	2224	305	585	85	23	7	207	187		.263	.320	.331	.652	98	-10	-5	98	91	268	.611	78			1	O/3S2	-3.9
■ LARRY DOBY	Doby, Lawrence Eugene b: 12/13/24, Camden, S.C. BL/TR, 6'1", 180 lbs. Deb: 7/05/47 MC																											
1947	Cle-A	29	32	3	5	1	0	0	2	1	11	.156	.182	.188	.369	3	-4	-4	96	123	1	.241	0	0	0	0	/21S	-0.3
1948	Cle-A	121	439	83	132	23	9	14	66	54	77	.301	.384	.490	.873	133	19	20	99	89	84	.873	9	9	-3	9	*O	2.1
1949	Cle-A	147	547	106	153	25	3	24	85	91	90	.280	.389	.468	.857	129	21	23	98	85	104	.873	10	9	-2	-9	*O	0.7
1950	Cle-A	142	503	110	164	25	5	25	102	98	71	.326	**.442**	.545	**.986**	**155**	**42**	**43**	98	107	**130**	**1.090**	8	6	-1	-9	*O	2.8
1951	Cle-A	134	447	84	132	27	5	20	69	101	81	.295	.428	.512	.941	**162**	37	41	95	87	108	1.034	4	1	1	-6	*O	2.9
1952	Cle-A	140	519	**104**	143	26	8	**32**	104	90	111	.276	.383	**.541**	.924	**171**	38	44	91	109	116	**.979**	5	2	0	3	*O	**4.5**
1953	Cle-A	149	513	92	135	18	5	29	102	96	121	.263	.385	.487	.873	141	26	29	95	114	105	.917	3	2	-0	-12	*O	1.2
1954	Cle-A	153	577	94	157	18	4	**32**	**126**	85	94	.272	.368	.484	.852	124	25	20	106	135	108	.864	3	1	0	2	*O	2.0
1955	Cle-A	131	491	91	143	17	5	26	75	61	100	.291	.372	.505	.877	129	22	20	104	91	95	.884	2	0	1	-2	*O	1.2
1956	Chi-A	140	504	89	135	22	3	24	102	102	105	.268	.395	.466	.861	121	22	19	104	**131**	100	.905	0	1	-1	-1	*O	1.0
1957	Chi-A	119	416	57	120	27	2	14	79	56	79	.288	.376	.464	.839	129	17	17	99	136	71	.811	2	3	-1	-10	*O	0.0
1958	Cle-A	89	247	41	70	10	1	13	45	26	49	.283	.352	.490	.842	137	9	11	94	113	41	.790	0	2	-1	-2	O	0.3
1959	Det-A	18	55	5	12	3	1	0	4	8	9	.218	.317	.309	.627	66	-2	-3	111	93	6	.581	0	0	0	-1	O	-0.4
	Chi-A	21	58	1	14	1	1	0	9	2	13	.241	.267	.293	.560	55	-4	-3	97	208	5	.444	1	0	0	-0	O/1	-0.3
	Yr	39	113	6	26	4	2	0	13	10	22	.230	.293	.301	.594	61	-6	-6	103	157	11	.511	1	0	0	-1		-0.7
Total	13	1533	5348	960	1515	243	52	253	970	871	1011	.283	.387	.490	.877	136	267	276	99	110	1074	.924	47	36	-8	-37	*O/21S	17.7
■ ORAN DODD	Dodd, Oran A. b: 9/14/1889, Bagwell, Tex. d: 3/31/29, Newport, Ark. BR/TR, 5'8", 150 lbs. Deb: 7/26/12																											
1912	Pit-N	5	9	0	0	0	0	0	1	1	3	.000	.100	.000	.100	-72	-2	-2	99	0	0	.111	0			0	/32	-0.1
■ TOM DODD	Dodd, Thomas Marion b: 8/15/58, Portland, Ore. BR/TR, 6', 190 lbs. Deb: 7/25/86																											
1986	Bal-A	8	13	1	3	0	0	1	2	2	2	.231	.375	.462	.837	129	1	1	99	88	2	.818	0	0	0	0	/3D	0.1
■ JOHN DODGE	Dodge, John Lewis b: 4/27/1889, Bolivar, Tenn. d: 6/19/16, Mobile, Ala. BR/TR, 5'11.5", 165 lbs. Deb: 8/29/12																											
1912	Phi-N	30	92	3	11	1	0	0	3	4	11	.120	.156	.130	.287	-21	-15	-15	100	84	2	.222	2			-1	3/2S	-1.5
1913	Phi-N	3	3	0	1	0	0	0	0	2	0	.333	.600	.333	.933	152	1	1	112	0	1	1.500	0			0	/S	0.1
	Cin-N	94	323	35	78	8	8	4	45	10	34	.241	.269	.353	.622	75	-11	-12	102	130	32	.559	11			-4	3	-1.7
	Yr	97	326	35	79	8	8	4	45	12	34	.242	.274	.353	.626	77	-11	-11	102	126	33	.567	11			-4		-1.6
Total	2	127	418	38	90	9	8	4	48	16	45	.215	.248	.304	.552	55	-26	-27	101	118	35	.482	13			-5	3/2S	-3.1

YEAR	TM/L	G	AB	R	H	2B	3B	HR	RBI	BB	SO	AVG	OBP	SLG	PRO	/A	BR	/A	PF	CHI	RC	TA	SB	CS	SBR	FR	POS	TPR
■ **PAT DODSON** Dodson, Patrick Neal b: 10/11/59, Santa Monica, Cal. BL/TL, 6'4", 210 lbs. Deb: 9/05/86																												
1986	Bos-A	9	12	3	5	2	0	1	3	3	3	.417	.533	.833	1.367	268	3	3	100	92	6	1.857	0	0	0	0	/1	0.3
1987	Bos-A	26	42	4	7	3	0	2	6	8	13	.167	.300	.381	.681	81	-1	-1	99	109	5	.686	0	0	0	-0	1/D	-0.2
1988	Bos-A	17	45	5	8	3	1	1	1	6	17	.178	.275	.356	.630	69	-2	-2	109	21	5	.595	0	0	0	-1	1	-0.3
Total	3	52	99	12	20	8	1	4	10	17	33	.202	.319	.424	.743	97	0	-0	104	68	16	.747	0	0	0	-1	/1D	-0.2
■ **JOHN DOE** Doe, John (Name Unknown) Deb: 5/18/1872																												
1872	Eck-n	1	3	1	1							.333															/C	
■ **BOBBY DOERR** Doerr, Robert Pershing b: 4/7/18, Los Angeles, Cal. BR/TR, 5'11", 175 lbs. Deb: 4/20/37 CH																												
1937	Bos-A	55	147	22	33	5	1	2	14	18	25	.224	.313	.313	.626	57	-9	-10	103	92	15	.568	2	4	-2	-1	2	-0.7
1938	Bos-A	145	509	70	147	26	7	5	80	59	39	.289	.363	.397	.760	88	-7	-9	102	127	74	.715	5	10	-5	8	*2	0.0
1939	Bos-A	127	525	75	167	28	2	12	73	38	32	.318	.365	.448	.813	99	5	-2	108	96	78	.714	1	10	-6	**27**	*2	2.2
1940	Bos-A	151	595	87	173	37	10	22	105	57	53	.291	.353	.497	.850	117	14	13	101	111	104	.819	10	5	0	17	*2	3.5
1941	Bos-A	132	500	74	141	28	4	16	93	43	43	.282	.339	.450	.789	104	3	1	103	123	78	.731	1	3	-2	-2	*2	0.9
1942	Bos-A	144	545	71	158	35	5	15	102	67	55	.290	.369	.455	.824	126	22	19	104	130	95	.796	4	4	-1	10	*2	3.2
1943	Bos-A	155	604	78	163	32	3	16	75	62	59	.270	.339	.412	.751	115	13	11	104	98	86	.696	8	8	-2	15	*2	3.1
1944	Bos-A	125	468	95	152	30	10	15	81	58	31	.325	.399	**.528**	.927	167	38	39	98	106	103	.951	5	2	0	0	*2	4.5
1946	Bos-A	151	583	95	158	34	9	18	116	66	67	.271	.346	.453	.799	107	16	5	114	147	90	.748	5	6	-2	**29**	*2	4.5
1947	Bos-A	146	561	79	145	23	10	17	95	59	47	.258	.329	.426	.755	101	5	-1	108	128	74	.678	3	3	-1	**22**	*2	2.8
1948	Bos-A	140	527	94	150	23	6	27	111	83	49	.285	.386	.505	.891	135	26	26	100	114	107	.908	3	2	-0	9	*2	3.6
1949	Bos-A	139	541	91	167	30	9	18	109	75	33	.309	.393	.497	.890	126	26	20	107	123	101	.850	2	2	-1	**22**	*2	4.2
1950	Bos-A	149	586	103	172	29	**11**	27	120	67	42	.294	.367	.519	.886	109	19	6	114	110	109	.854	3	4	-2	9	*2	2.2
1951	Bos-A	106	402	60	116	21	2	13	73	57	33	.289	.378	.448	.826	114	13	9	108	121	71	.808	2	1	0	4	*2	1.6
Total	14	1865	7093	1094	2042	381	89	223	1247	809	608	.288	.362	.461	.823	114	181	128	106	117	1185	.809	54	64	-22	168	*2	35.6
■ **JOHN DOHERTY** Doherty, John Michael b: 8/22/51, Woburn, Mass. BL/TL, 5'11", 185 lbs. Deb: 6/01/74																												
1974	Cal-A	74	223	20	57	14	1	3	15	8	13	.256	.281	.368	.649	93	-5	-3	92	65	23	.541	2	1	0	-2	1/D	-0.8
1975	Cal-A	30	94	7	19	3	0	1	12	8	12	.202	.265	.266	.531	53	-6	-6	95	165	7	.436	1	1	-0	-2	1/D	-0.8
Total	2	104	317	27	76	17	1	4	27	16	25	.240	.276	.338	.614	80	-11	-8	93	95	29	.514	3	2	-0	-4	/1D	-1.6
■ **COZY DOLAN** Dolan, Albert J. (born James Alberts) b: 12/23/1889, Chicago, Ill. d: 12/10/58, Chicago, Ill. BR/TR, 5'10", 160 lbs. Deb: 09 C																												
1909	Cin-N	3	6	2	1	0	0	0	0	2		.167	.375	.167	.542	74	-0	0	94	0	0	.600	0			0	/3	0.0
1911	NY-A	19	69	19	21	1	2	0	6	8		.304	.385	.377	.761	102	1	0	111	83	14	.979	12			-1	3	0.0
1912	NY-A	17	60	15	12	1	3	0	11	5		.200	.273	.317	.589	67	-3	-3	101	205	7	.625	5			-1	3	-0.3
	Phi-N	11	50	8	14	2	2	0	7	1	10	.280	.294	.400	.694	89	-1	-1	100	102	6	.667	3			-0	3	0.0
1913	Phi-N	55	126	15	33	4	0	0	8	1	21	.262	.273	.294	.567	55	-6	-8	112	79	12	.516	9			-2	OS/231	-0.9
	Pit-N	35	133	22	27	5	2	0	9	15	14	.203	.289	.271	.559	63	-7	-6	96	87	13	.623	14			-2	3	-0.8
	Yr	90	259	37	60	9	2	0	17	16	35	.232	.282	.282	.563	58	-13	-15	106	83	25	.573	23			-4		-1.7
1914	StL-N	126	421	76	101	16	3	4	32	55	74	.240	.335	.321	.655	92	-1	-3	104	84	57	.741	42			-4	O3	-0.9
1915	StL-N	111	322	53	90	14	9	2	38	34	37	.280	.356	.398	.753	127	11	11	100	108	49	.753	17	11	-2	-9	O	-0.2
1922	NY-N	1	0	0	0	0	0	0	0	0	0	—	—	—	—	—	0	0	104	—	—	—	0	0	0	0	R	0.0
Total	7	378	1187	210	299	43	21	6	111	121	156	.252	.328	.339	.666	93	-5	-10	103	96	208	.710	102	11		-19	O3/S21	-3.1
■ **JOE DOLAN** Dolan, Joseph b: 2/24/1873, Baltimore, Md. d: 3/24/38, Omaha, Neb. TR , 5'10", 155 lbs. Deb: 8/11/1896																												
1896	Lou-N	44	165	14	35	2	1	3	18	9	12	.212	.253	.291	.544	45	-13	-13	98	93	14	.485	6			6	S	-0.5
1897	Lou-N	36	133	10	28	2	2	0	7	8		.211	.271	.256	.526	43	-11	-10	95	64	11	.486	6			0	S2	-0.8
1899	Phi-N	61	222	27	57	6	3	1	30	11		.257	.295	.324	.619	74	-9	-8	97	125	23	.527	3			-14	2	-1.6
1900	Phi-N	74	257	39	51	7	3	1	27	16		.198	.245	.261	.506	42	-20	-20	98	121	19	.451	10			0	32S	-1.7
1901	Phi-N	10	37	0	3	0	0	0	2	2		.081	.128	.081	.209	-37	-6	-6	103	227	0	.147	0			-1	2	-0.6
	Phi-A	98	338	50	73	21	2	1	38	26		.216	.272	.299	.571	60	-18	-18	100	115	29	.491	3			4	S3/2O	-0.9
Total	5	323	1152	140	247	38	11	6	122	72	12	.214	.263	.282	.545	51	-78	-75	98	113	97	.474	28			-5	S2/3O	-6.1
■ **BIDDY DOLAN** Dolan, Leon BR , 6', Deb: 4/16/14																												
1914	Ind-F	32	103	13	23	4	2	1	15	12	13	.223	.304	.330	.634	74	-2	-4	111	149	13	.637	5			0	1	-0.3
■ **COZY DOLAN** Dolan, Patrick Henry b: 12/3/1872, Cambridge, Mass. d: 3/29/07, Louisville, Ky. BL/TL, Deb: N/A.																												
1895	Bos-N	26	83	12	20	4	1	0	7	6	7	.241	.300	.313	.613	58	-5	-5	103	75	9	.571	3			0	P/O	0.0
1896	Bos-N	6	14	4	2	0	0	0	0	0	1	.143	.143	.143	.286	-22	-2	-3	108	0	0	.167	0			0	/P	0.0
1900	Chi-N	13	48	5	13	1	0	0	2	2		.271	.300	.292	.592	71	-2	-2	93	45	5	.514	2			0	O	-0.1
1901	Chi-N	43	171	29	45	1	2	0	16	7		.263	.292	.292	.585	72	-6	-6	100	113	16	.476	3			1	O	-0.9
	Bro-N	66	253	33	66	11	1	0	29	17		.261	.307	.312	.620	77	-6	-8	106	125	27	.551	7			3	O	-1.1
	Yr	109	424	62	111	12	3	0	45	24		.262	.301	.304	.606	75	-12	-14	104	122	43	.521	10			3		-2.0
1902	Bro-N	141	592	72	166	16	7	1	54	33		.280	.318	.336	.655	110	2	6	95	80	73	.601	24			-4	*O	-0.9
1903	Chi-A	27	104	16	27	5	1	0	7	6		.260	.300	.327	.627	97	-1	-0	92	79	12	.584	5			3	1/O	0.3
	Cin-N	93	385	64	111	20	3	0	58	28		.288	.337	.356	.692	91	-0	-5	109	120	51	.642	11			-16	O	-2.5
1904	Cin-N	129	465	88	132	8	10	6	51	39		.284	.339	.383	.722	109	13	5	114	101	69	.709	19			-3	*O1	-0.2
1905	Cin-N	22	77	7	18	2	1	0	4	7		.234	.298	.286	.583	74	-2	-2	103	64	7	.525	2			-0	1/O	-0.3
	Bos-N	112	433	44	119	11	7	3	48	27		.275	.317	.353	.671	105	0	2	97	99	57	.640	21			-0	*O/P1	-0.5
	Yr	134	510	51	137	13	8	3	52	34		.269	.314	.343	.657	100	-2	-0	98	94	64	.622	23			-1		-0.8
1906	Bos-N	152	549	54	136	20	4	0	39	55		.248	.316	.299	.615	94	-3	-3	100	83	59	.571	17			2	*O/2P1	-0.4
Total	9	830	3174	428	855	99	37	10	315	227	8	.269	.318	.333	.652	95	-12	-21	102	95	384	.604	114			-17	O/1P2	-6.6
■ **TOM DOLAN** Dolan, Thomas J. b: 1/10/1859, New York, N.Y. d: 1/16/13, St.Louis, Mo. BR/TR, Deb: 9/30/1879																												
1879	Chi-N	1	4	0	0	0	0	0	0	0	2	.000	.000	.000	.000	-95	-1	-1	105	0	0	.000				0	/C	0.0
1882	Buf-N	22	89	12	14	0	1	0	8	2	11	.157	.176	.180	.356	14	-8	-9	104	172	3	.240				-5	C/O3	-1.0
1883	StL-a	81	295	32	63	9	2	1		9		.214	.237	.268	.505	58	-12	-16	108	0	19	.379				4	CO/P	-0.6
1884	StL-a	35	137	19	36	6	2	0		6		.263	.299	.336	.634	100	1	-1	110	0	14	.525				-8	C/O	-0.5
	StL-U	19	69	9	13	3	0	0		4		.188	.233	.232	.465	56	-3	-3	104	0	4	.357	0			0	C/3O	-0.2
1885	StL-N	3	9	1	2	0	0	0	0	2	1	.222	.364	.222	.586	100	0	0	92	0	1	.571				0	/C	0.0
1886	StL-N	15	44	8	11	3	0	0	1	7	9	.250	.353	.318	.671	111	1	1	95	23	6	.697	2			0	C	0.1
	Bal-a	38	125	13	19	3	2	0		8		.152	.203	.208	.411	33	-10	-8	91	0	7	.396	8			-6	C/O	-0.9
1888	StL-a	11	36	1	7	1	0	0	1	1		.194	.216	.222	.438	39	-2	-3	111	37	2	.345	1			0	C	-0.2
Total	7	225	808	95	165	25	7	1	10	39	23	.204	.242	.256	.498	58	-34	-39	104	21	56	.401	11			-14	C/O3P	-3.3
■ **LESTER DOLE** Dole, Lester Carrington b: 7/8/1855, Meriden, Conn. d: 12/10/18, Concord, N.H. 5'11", Deb: 5/27/1875																												
1875	NH-n	1	4	1	2							.500															/O	
■ **FRANK DOLJACK** Doljack, Frank Joseph "Dolie" b: 10/5/07, Cleveland, Ohio d: 1/23/48, Cleveland, Ohio BR/TR, 5'11", 175 lbs. Deb: 9/04/30																												
1930	Det-A	20	74	10	19	5	1	3	17	2	11	.257	.286	.473	.759	84	-2	-2	105	131	9	.679	0	1	-1	0	O	-0.2
1931	Det-A	63	187	20	52	13	3	4	20	15	17	.278	.335	.444	.779	99	0	-1	104	69	28	.745	3	2	-0	6	O	0.1
1932	Det-A	8	26	5	10	1	0	1	7	2	2	.385	.429	.538	.967	146	2	2	102	138	6	1.063	1	0	0	-2	/O	0.0
1933	Det-A	42	147	18	42	5	2	0	22	14	13	.286	.348	.347	.695	79	-3	-4	107	147	17	.604	2	6	-3	2	O	-0.5
1934	Det-A	56	120	15	28	7	1	1	19	13	15	.233	.313	.333	.647	69	-6	-6	98	147	13	.602	2	1	0	-2	O/1	-0.8
1943	Cle-A	3	7	0	0	0	0	0	0	1	2	.000	.125	.000	.125	-69	-1	-1	90	0	0	.143	0	0	0	-1	/O	-0.1
Total	6	192	561	68	151	31	7	9	85	47	60	.269	.329	.398	.726	86	-10	-13	103	117	73	.669	8	10	-4	3	O/1	-1.5
■ **SHE DONAHUE** Donahue, Charles Michael b: 6/29/1877, Oswego, N.Y. d: 8/28/47, New York, N.Y. BR/TR, 5'9", Deb: 4/29/04																												
1904	StL-N	4	15	1	4	0	0	0	2	0		.267	.267	.267	.533	67	-1	-1	99	187	2	.636	3			0	/2S	0.0
	Phi-N	58	200	21	43	4	0	0	14	3		.215	.227	.235	.462	47	-13	-11	93	111	13	.363	7			-6	S3/12	-1.7

YEAR	TM/L	G	AB	R	H	2B	3B	HR	RBI	BB	SO	AVG	OBP	SLG	PRO	/A	BR	/A	PF	CHI	RC	TA	SB	CS	SBR	FR	POS	TPR
	Yr	62	215	22	47	4	0	0	16	3		.219	.229	.237	.467	49	-14	-12	93	119	14	.381	10			-6		-1.7
Total	1	62	215	22	47	4	0	0	16	3		.219	.229	.237	.467	49	-14	-12	93	116	14	.381	10			-6	/S321	-1.7

■ **JIM DONAHUE** Donahue, James Augustus b: 1/8/1862, Lockport, Ill. d: 4/19/35, Lockport, Ill. TR , 6', 175 lbs. Deb: 4/19/1886

YEAR	TM/L	G	AB	R	H	2B	3B	HR	RBI	BB	SO	AVG	OBP	SLG	PRO	/A	BR	/A	PF	CHI	RC	TA	SB	CS	SBR	FR	POS	TPR
1886	NY-a	49	186	14	37	0	0	0		10		.199	.251	.199	.450	42	-12	-13	104	0	10	.342	1			0	OC	-1.0
1887	NY-a	60	220	33	62	4	1	1		21		.282	.350	.323	.673	103	-2	3	88	0	28	.633	6			-1	C/O132	0.8
1888	KC-a	88	337	29	79	11	3	1	28	21		.234	.281	.294	.575	82	-5	-8	106	87	32	.516	12			-4	CO/32	-0.3
1889	KC-a	67	252	30	59	5	4	0	32	21	20	.234	.293	.286	.579	63	-11	-13	106	130	25	.544	12			-6	CO3	-1.1
1891	Col-a	77	280	27	61	4	3	0	35	31	18	.218	.298	.254	.552	68	-13	-9	89	145	22	.479	2			10	C/O1	0.4
Total	5	341	1275	133	298	24	11	2	95	104	38	.234	.295	.275	.570	72	-42	-39	99	81	117	.506	33			-1	C/O312	-1.2

■ **JIGGS DONAHUE** Donahue, John Augustus b: 7/13/1879, Springfield, Ohio d: 7/19/13, Columbus, Ohio BL/TL, 6'1", 178 lbs. Deb: 9/10/00

YEAR	TM/L	G	AB	R	H	2B	3B	HR	RBI	BB	SO	AVG	OBP	SLG	PRO	/A	BR	/A	PF	CHI	RC	TA	SB	CS	SBR	FR	POS	TPR
1900	Pit-N	3	10	1	2	0	1	0	3	0		.200	.200	.400	.600	63	-1	-1	103	234	1	.625	1			0	/CO	0.0
1901	Pit-N	2	0	1	0	0	0	0	0	0		—	—	—	—	—	0	0	101	—	—	—	0			0	/CO	0.0
	Mil-A	37	107	10	34	5	4	0	16	10		.318	.376	.439	.815	134	4	5	95	107	20	.836	4			1	C1	0.6
1902	StL-A	30	89	11	21	1	1	1	7	12		.236	.327	.303	.630	75	-2	-3	102	77	10	.603	2			-1	C/1	-0.1
1904	Chi-A	102	367	47	91	9	7	1	48	25		.248	.296	.319	.615	97	-1	-1	99	158	42	.591	21			8	*1	1.0
1905	Chi-A	149	533	71	153	22	4	1	76	44		.287	.341	.349	.690	126	13	15	97	**152**	76	.689	32			11	*1	2.5
1906	Chi-A	154	556	70	143	17	7	1	57	48		.257	.316	.318	.635	110	1	6	92	122	69	.632	36			9	*1	1.2
1907	Chi-A	157	609	75	158	16	4	0	68	28		.259	.292	.299	.591	87	-7	-9	104	128	63	.525	27			21	*1	1.0
1908	Chi-A	93	304	22	62	8	2	0	22	25		.204	.264	.243	.508	71	-10	-8	94	114	22	.467	14			4	1	-0.6
1909	Chi-A	2	4	0	0	0	0	0	2	1		.000	.200	.000	.200	-37	-1	-1	97	0	0	.250	0			0	/1	0.0
	Was-A	84	283	13	67	12	1	0	28	22		.237	.294	.286	.580	93	-5	-2	90	136	25	.523	9			-2	1	-0.4
	Yr	86	287	13	67	12	1	0	30	23		.233	.293	.282	.575	91	-6	-3	90	133	25	.518	9			-2		-0.4
Total	9	813	2862	321	731	90	31	4	327	215		.255	.308	.313	.620	100	-9	2	97	132	329	.590	146			51	1/CO	5.2

■ **JOHN DONAHUE** Donahue, John Frederick "Jiggs" b: 4/19/1894, Roxbury, Mass. d: 10/3/49, Boston, Mass. BB/TR, 5'8", 170 lbs. Deb: 9/25/23

YEAR	TM/L	G	AB	R	H	2B	3B	HR	RBI	BB	SO	AVG	OBP	SLG	PRO	/A	BR	/A	PF	CHI	RC	TA	SB	CS	SBR	FR	POS	TPR
1923	Bos-A	10	36	5	10	4	0	0	1	4	5	.278	.350	.389	.739	93	-0	-0	102	26	5	.667	0	1	-1	3	/O	0.1

■ **PAT DONAHUE** Donahue, Patrick William b: 11/8/1884, Springfield, Ohio d: 1/31/66, Springfield, Ohio BR/TR, 6', 175 lbs. Deb: 5/29/08

YEAR	TM/L	G	AB	R	H	2B	3B	HR	RBI	BB	SO	AVG	OBP	SLG	PRO	/A	BR	/A	PF	CHI	RC	TA	SB	CS	SBR	FR	POS	TPR
1908	Bos-A	35	86	8	17	2	0	1	6	9		.198	.274	.256	.529	76	-2	-2	98	90	6	.449	0			3	C/1	0.5
1909	Bos-A	64	176	14	42	4	1	2	25	17		.239	.309	.307	.616	87	-1	-3	109	161	17	.552	2			-1	C	0.1
1910	Bos-A	2	4	0	0	0	0	0	0	0		.000	.000	.000	.000	-99	-1	-1	99	0	0	.000	0			-0	/C	0.0
	Phi-A	14	34	2	5	0	0	0	4	3		.147	.237	.147	.384	20	-3	-3	102	296	1	.345	1			1	C	0.0
	Cle-A	2	6	0	1	0	0	0	0	0		.167	.167	.167	.333	4	-1	-1	100	0	0	.200	0			0	/C1	0.0
	Phi-A	1	1	0	0	0	0	0	0	0		.000	.000	.000	.000	-98	-0	-0	102	0	0	.000	0			0	/C	0.0
	Yr	19	45	2	6	0	0	0	4	3		.133	.204	.133	.337	6	-5	-5	102	233	1	.282	1			1		0.0
Total	3	118	307	24	65	6	1	3	35	29		.212	.284	.267	.551	72	-8	-10	105	151	24	.479	3			3	C/1	0.6

■ **TIM DONAHUE** Donahue, Timothy Cornelius "Bridget" b: 6/8/1870, Raynham, Mass. d: 6/12/02, Taunton, Mass. BL/TR, 5'11", 180 lbs. Deb: 7/28/1891

YEAR	TM/L	G	AB	R	H	2B	3B	HR	RBI	BB	SO	AVG	OBP	SLG	PRO	/A	BR	/A	PF	CHI	RC	TA	SB	CS	SBR	FR	POS	TPR
1891	Bos-a	4	7	0	0	0	0	0	0	0	5	.000	.000	.000	.000	-99	-2	-2	99	0	0	.000	0			0	/C	-0.1
1895	Chi-N	63	219	29	59	9	1	2	36	20	25	.269	.339	.347	.686	76	-7	-8	103	123	28	.650	5			-3	C	-0.4
1896	Chi-N	57	188	27	41	10	1	0	20	11	15	.218	.276	.282	.558	45	-14	-17	108	109	18	.537	11			4	C	-0.5
1897	Chi-N	58	188	28	45	7	3	0	21	9		.239	.281	.309	.590	57	-12	-12	100	106	18	.503	3			4	C/S1	0.0
1898	Chi-N	122	396	52	87	12	3	0	39	49		.220	.318	.265	.583	68	-13	-15	103	112	40	.579	17			-3	*C	-0.8
1899	Chi-N	92	278	39	69	9	3	0	29	34		.248	.345	.302	.647	84	-6	-4	96	106	33	.646	10			-2	C/1	0.0
1900	Chi-N	67	216	21	51	10	1	0	17	19		.236	.298	.292	.590	70	-10	-7	93	84	22	.545	8			-10	C/2	-1.0
1902	Was-A	3	8	0	2	0	0	0	1	0		.250	.250	.250	.500	41	-1	-1	99	165	1	.333	0			0	/C	0.0
Total	8	466	1500	196	354	57	12	2	163	142	45	.236	.312	.294	.606	67	-63	-65	101	107	159	.577	54			-10	C/1S2	-2.8

■ **JOHN DONALDSON** Donaldson, John David b: 5/5/43, Charlotte, N.C. BL/TR, 5'11", 160 lbs. Deb: 8/26/66

YEAR	TM/L	G	AB	R	H	2B	3B	HR	RBI	BB	SO	AVG	OBP	SLG	PRO	/A	BR	/A	PF	CHI	RC	TA	SB	CS	SBR	FR	POS	TPR
1966	KC-A	15	30	4	4	0	0	0	1	3	4	.133	.212	.133	.345	2	-4	-4	94	105	1	.308	1	0	0	-0	/2	-0.2
1967	KC-A	105	377	27	104	16	5	0	28	37	39	.276	.344	.345	.689	105	3	3	100	95	47	.625	6	3	0	-9	*2/S	-0.2
1968	Oak-A	127	363	37	80	9	2	2	27	45	44	.220	.310	.273	.582	79	-9	-8	98	110	32	.510	5	5	-2	3	2/3S	-0.3
1969	Oak-A	12	13	1	1	0	0	0	0	2	4	.077	.200	.077	.277	-22	-2	-2	92	0	0	.250	0	0	0	0	/2	-0.1
	Sea-A	95	338	22	79	8	3	1	19	36	36	.234	.307	.284	.592	67	-15	-14	98	79	32	.521	6	1	1	-9	2/3S	-1.8
	Yr	107	351	23	80	8	3	1	19	38	40	.228	.303	.276	.580	65	-17	-16	98	70	32	.509	6	1	1	-9		-1.9
1970	Oak-A	41	89	4	22	2	1	1	11	9	6	.247	.316	.326	.642	80	-3	-2	97	139	9	.557	1	0	0	-0	2/S3	0.0
1974	Oak-A	10	15	1	2	0	0	0	0	0	0	.133	.133	.133	.267	-23	-2	-2	100	0	0	.154	0	0	0	-0	/23	-0.1
Total	6	405	1225	96	292	35	11	4	86	132	133	.238	.314	.295	.609	79	-31	-29	98	96	121	.548	19	9	0	-15	2/3S	-2.7

■ **LEN DONDERO** Dondero, Leonard Peter "Mike" b: 9/12/03, Newark, Cal. BR/TR, 5'11", 178 lbs. Deb: 4/21/29

YEAR	TM/L	G	AB	R	H	2B	3B	HR	RBI	BB	SO	AVG	OBP	SLG	PRO	/A	BR	/A	PF	CHI	RC	TA	SB	CS	SBR	FR	POS	TPR
1929	StL-A	19	31	2	6	0	0	1	8	0	4	.194	.194	.290	.484	23	-4	-4	100	228	2	.360	0	0	0	-1	3/2	-0.2

■ **MIKE DONLIN** Donlin, Michael Joseph "Turkey Mike" b: 5/30/1878, Peoria, Ill. d: 9/24/33, Hollywood, Cal. BL/TL, 5'9", 170 lbs. Deb: 7/19/1899

YEAR	TM/L	G	AB	R	H	2B	3B	HR	RBI	BB	SO	AVG	OBP	SLG	PRO	/A	BR	/A	PF	CHI	RC	TA	SB	CS	SBR	FR	POS	TPR
1899	StL-N	66	266	49	86	9	6	6	27	17		.323	.366	.470	.836	122	10	7	108	56	54	.906	20			-5	O1/SP	0.0
1900	StL-N	78	276	40	90	8	6	10	48	14		.326	.359	.507	.866	150	13	16	93	90	57	.903	14			0	O1	1.1
1901	Bal-A	121	476	107	162	23	13	5	67	53		.340	.406	.475	.881	137	30	25	107	77	108	.994	33			-19	O1	0.3
1902	Cin-N	34	143	30	41	5	4	0	9	9		.287	.329	.378	.707	109	3	1	110	50	21	.706	9			0	O/PS	0.0
1903	Cin-N	126	496	110	174	25	18	7	67	56		.351	.417	.516	.933	154	**43**	37	109	69	120	1.050	26			13	*O/1	4.0
1904	Cin-N	60	236	42	84	11	7	1	38	18		.356	.402	.475	.876	151	19	15	114	107	55	.993	21			6	O/1	2.0
	NY-N	42	132	17	37	7	3	2	14	10		.280	.331	.424	.755	128	5	4	105	83	19	.705	1			1	O	0.4
	Yr	102	368	59	121	18	10	3	52	28		.329	.376	.457	.833	144	24	20	111	98	73	.883	22			7		2.4
1905	NY-N	150	606	**124**	216	31	16	7	80	56		.356	.411	.495	.906	170	52	52	101	75	140	.997	33			-18	*O	2.4
1906	NY-N	37	121	15	38	5	1	1	14	11		.314	.371	.397	.768	142	6	6	100	102	22	.819	9			1	O/1	0.6
1908	NY-N	155	593	71	198	26	13	6	106	23		.334	.359	.452	.811	154	37	34	104	151	104	.813	30			-6	*O	3.0
1911	NY-N	12	12	3	4	0	0	1	1	0	1	.333	.333	.583	.917	151	1	1	102	34	3	1.125	2			-1	/O	0.0
	Bos-N	56	222	33	70	16	1	2	34	22	17	.315	.377	.423	.800	120	7	6	103	110	38	.809	7			1	O	0.5
	Yr	68	234	36	74	16	1	3	35	22	18	.316	.375	.432	.807	121	8	7	103	97	41	.825	9			-0		0.5
1912	Pit-N	77	244	27	77	9	8	2	35	20	16	.316	.370	.443	.812	123	7	7	99	103	43	.820	8			-4	O	0.1
1914	NY-N	35	31	1	5	1	1	1	3	3	5	.161	.235	.355	.590	78	-1	-1	96	78	2	.538	0			0	H	0.0
Total	12	1049	3854	669	1282	176	97	51	543	312	39	.333	.383	.468	.851	144	232	210	104	91	786	.907	213			-32	O/1PS	14.4

■ **JIM DONNELLY** Donnelly, James B. b: 7/19/1865, New Haven, Conn. d: 3/5/15, Meriden, Conn. BR , Deb: 7/11/1884

YEAR	TM/L	G	AB	R	H	2B	3B	HR	RBI	BB	SO	AVG	OBP	SLG	PRO	/A	BR	/A	PF	CHI	RC	TA	SB	CS	SBR	FR	POS	TPR
1884	KC-U	6	23	2	3	1	0	0		1		.130	.167	.174	.341	18	-2	-1	87	0	1	.250	0			0	/3C	0.0
	Ind-a	40	134	22	34	2	2	0		5		.254	.301	.299	.599	103	0	1	96	0	12	.490				0	3/SO2	0.1
1885	Det-N	56	211	24	49	4	3	1	22	10	29	.232	.267	.294	.561	83	-4	-4	97	120	17	.444				-3	3/1	-0.4
1886	KC-N	113	438	51	88	11	3	0	38	36	57	.201	.262	.240	.501	50	-24	-28	107	113	32	.449	16			-0	*3	-2.0
1887	Was-N	117	425	51	85	9	6	1	46	16	26	.200	.234	.256	.491	39	-35	-32	95	129	36	.500	42			11	*3/S	-1.6
1888	Was-N	122	428	43	86	9	4	0	23	20	16	.201	.242	.241	.482	58	-20	-18	96	82	36	.497	44			-11	*3/S	-2.3
1889	Was-N	4	13	3	2	0	0	0	0	2	0	.154	.267	.154	.421	22	-1	-1	92	0	1	.455	1			0	/3	0.0
1890	StL-a	11	42	11	14	0	0	0		8		.333	.451	.333	.784	116	3	1	116	0	9	1.000	5			0	3	0.1
1891	Col-a	17	54	6	13	0	0	0	9	13	5	.241	.388	.241	.629	94	-0	1	89	204	8	.805	7			0	3	0.1
1896	Bal-N	106	396	70	130	14	10	0	71	34	11	.328	.387	.414	.801	111	8	7	102	127	80	.902	38			-6	*3	0.5
1897	Pit-N	44	161	22	31	4	0	0	14	16		.193	.270	.217	.487	32	-15	-15	98	124	14	.508	14			-1	3	-1.3
	NY-N	23	85	19	16	3	0	0	11	9		.188	.266	.224	.489	32	-8	-8	98	173	7	.493	6			-6	3	-1.1
	Yr	67	246	41	47	7	0	0	25	25		.191	.268	.220	.488	32	-24	-23	98	142	20	.503	20			-6		-2.4
1898	StL-N	1	1	0	1	0	0	0	0	0		1.000	1.000	1.000	2.000	455	0	0	106	0	1	—	0			0	/3	0.0
Total	11	660	2411	324	552	57	28	2	234	170	144	.229	.284	.278	.562	66	-99	-97	99	108	254	.554	173			-15	3/SO21C	-7.9

YEAR	TM/L	G	AB	R	H	2B	3B	HR	RBI	BB	SO	AVG	OBP	SLG	PRO	/A	BR	/A	PF	CHI	RC	TA	SB	CS	SBR	FR	POS	TPR
■ **T. J.DONNELLY**	Donnelly, T. J. Deb: 5/13/1871																											
1871	Kek-n	9	35	8	7							.200															/O3	
1873	Nat-n	30	141	15	35							.248															S2/O	
1874	Phi-n	5	21	2	5							.238															/SO2	
Total	3 n	44	197	25	47							.239															/SO2	
■ **JOE DONOHUE**	Donohue, Joseph F. b: 1869, Syracuse, N.Y. Deb: 8/24/1891																											
1891	Phi-N	6	22	2	7	1	0	0	2	1	3	.318	.375	.364	.739	124	1	1	95	74	3	.667	0			0	/OS	0.1
■ **TOM DONOHUE**	Donohue, Thomas James b: 11/15/52, Mineola, N.Y. BR/TR, 6', 185 lbs. Deb: 4/06/79																											
1979	Cal-A	38	107	13	24	3	1	3	14	3	29	.224	.259	.355	.614	69	-6	-5	93	114	10	.536	2	0	1	-2	C	-0.3
1980	Cal-A	84	218	18	41	4	1	2	14	7	63	.188	.217	.243	.460	27	-22	-21	96	93	12	.371	5	1	1	-15	C	-3.1
Total	2	122	325	31	65	7	2	5	28	10	92	.200	.231	.280	.511	41	-28	-26	95	100	23	.425	7	1	2	-16	C	-3.4
■ **FRED DONOVAN**	Donovan, Frederick Maurice b: 7/4/1864, New Hampshire d: 3/7/16, Bloomington, Ill. Deb: 6/23/1895																											
1895	Cle-N	3	12	1	1	0	0	0	1	1	2	.083	.154	.083	.237	-38	-2	-2	97	296	0	.182	0			0	/C	-0.1
■ **JERRY DONOVAN**	Donovan, Jeremiah Francis b: 9/3/1876, Lock Haven, Pa. d: 6/27/38, St.Petersburg, Fla. BR/TR, Deb: 4/12/06																											
1906	Phi-N	61	166	11	33	4	0	0	15	6		.199	.227	.223	.450	45	-11	-10	92	148	9	.338	2			-5	C/SO	-1.1
■ **MIKE DONOVAN**	Donovan, Michael Berchman b: 10/18/1881, Brooklyn, N.Y. d: 2/3/38, New York, N.Y. BR/TR, 5'8", 155 lbs. Deb: 5/29/04																											
1904	Cle-A	2	2	0	0	0	0	0	0	0		.000	.000	.000	.000	-99	-0	-0	102	0	0	.000	0			0	/S	0.0
1908	NY-A	5	19	2	5	1	0	0	2	0		.263	.263	.316	.579	94	-0	-0	95	133	1	.429	0			1	/3	0.2
Total	2	7	21	2	5	1	0	0	2	0		.238	.238	.286	.524	74	-1	-1	96	120	1	.375	0			1	/3S	0.2
■ **PATSY DONOVAN**	Donovan, Patrick Joseph b: 3/16/1865, County Cork, Ireland d: 12/25/53, Lawrence, Mass. BL/TL, 5'11.5", 175 lbs. Deb: 4/19/1890 M																											
1890	Bos-N	32	140	17	36	0	0	0	9	8	17	.257	.307	.257	.564	60	-6	-8	111	67	14	.538	10			0	O	-0.6
	Bro-N	28	105	17	23	5	1	0	8	5	5	.219	.268	.286	.554	63	-5	-5	100	82	9	.488	3			0	O	-0.4
	Yr	60	245	34	59	5	1	0	17	13	22	.241	.290	.269	.559	62	-11	-13	106	75	23	.516	13			0		-1.0
1891	Lou-a	105	439	73	141	10	3	2	53	30	18	.321	.375	.371	.747	129	10	17	90	80	73	.765	27			0	*O	1.0
	Was-a	17	70	9	14	1	0	0	3	4	5	.200	.243	.214	.458	35	-6	-5	95	56	4	.357	1			-3	O	-0.7
	Yr	122	509	82	155	11	3	2	56	34	23	.305	.358	.350	.707	116	4	11	91	77	75	.701	28			-3		0.3
1892	Was-N	40	163	29	39	3	3	0	12	11	13	.239	.295	.294	.590	77	-4	-5	105	74	19	.621	16			1	O	-0.4
	Pit-N	90	388	77	114	15	3	2	26	20	16	.294	.333	.363	.697	120	5	8	94	48	62	.745	40			-2	O	0.3
	Yr	130	551	106	153	18	6	2	38	31	29	.278	.322	.343	.665	106	1	3	97	56	81	.706	56			-1		-0.1
1893	Pit-N	113	499	114	158	5	8	2	56	42	8	.317	.373	.371	.744	94	1	-5	106	77	88	.809	46			-2	*O	-0.8
1894	Pit-N	132	576	145	174	21	10	4	76	33	12	.302	.345	.394	.739	84	-20	-13	94	77	95	.761	41			6	*O	-1.1
1895	Pit-N	125	519	114	160	17	6	1	58	47	19	.308	.375	.370	.745	98	-2	1	97	72	88	.788	36			-7	*O	-1.3
1896	Pit-N	131	573	113	183	20	5	3	59	35	18	.319	.370	.387	.757	109	2	9	93	64	102	.810	48			5	*O	0.4
1897	Pit-N	120	479	82	154	16	7	0	57	25		.322	.360	.384	.744	100	-1	1	98	96	80	.760	34			1	*OM	-0.5
1898	Pit-N	147	610	112	184	16	9	0	37	34		.302	.346	.357	.703	107	3	5	98	44	92	.704	41			-20	*O	-2.2
1899	Pit-N	121	531	82	156	11	7	1	55	17		.294	.322	.347	.668	87	-11	-10	99	80	69	.619	26			-14	*OM	-2.8
1900	StL-N	126	503	78	159	11	1	0	61	38		.316	.364	.342	.706	105	0	5	93	107	81	.741	**45**			-1	*O	-0.6
1901	StL-N	130	531	92	161	23	5	1	73	27		.303	.337	.371	.708	111	5	7	97	129	78	.681	28			1	*OM	-0.4
1902	StL-N	126	502	70	158	12	4	0	35	28		.315	.351	.355	.706	126	11	14	95	65	76	.698	34			10	*OM	1.6
1903	StL-N	105	410	63	134	15	3	0	40	25		.327	.366	.378	.744	118	7	10	96	80	67	.743	25			13	*OM	1.5
1904	Was-A	125	436	30	100	6	0	0	19	24		.229	.270	.243	.513	70	-16	-13	93	68	34	.438	17			6	*OM	-1.5
1906	Bro-N	7	21	1	5	0	0	0	0	0		.238	.238	.238	.476	58	-1	-1	87	0	1	.313	0			-0	/OM	0.0
1907	Bro-N	1	1	0	0	0	0	0	0	0		.000	.000	.000	.000	-99	-0	-0	94	0	0	.000	0			-0	/OM	0.0
Total	17	1821	7496	1318	2253	207	75	16	737	453	131	.301	.345	.355	.700	100	-28	11	96	77	1134	.704	518			-7	*O	-8.5
■ **TOM DONOVAN**	Donovan, Thomas Joseph BR/TR, 6'2", 168 lbs. Deb: 9/10/01																											
1901	Cle-A	18	71	9	18	3	1	0	5	0		.254	.254	.324	.577	64	-4	-3	95	70	6	.453	1			-2	O/P	-0.4
■ **RED DOOIN**	Dooin, Charles Sebastian b: 6/12/1879, Cincinnati, Ohio d: 5/14/52, Rochester, N.Y. BR/TR, 5'9.5", 165 lbs. Deb: 4/18/02 M																											
1902	Phi-N	94	333	20	77	7	3	0	35	10		.231	.254	.270	.524	60	-15	-17	105	137	25	.422	8			-3	C/O	-1.1
1903	Phi-N	62	188	18	41	5	1	0	14	8		.218	.250	.255	.505	49	-13	-11	92	94	15	.442	9			2	C/1O	-0.4
1904	Phi-N	108	355	41	86	11	4	6	36	8		.242	.259	.346	.605	95	-6	-3	93	93	37	.543	15			4	C/1O3	0.9
1905	Phi-N	113	380	45	95	13	5	0	36	10		.250	.269	.311	.580	71	-13	-15	104	106	36	.491	12			4	*C/3	0.1
1906	Phi-N	113	351	25	86	19	1	0	32	13		.245	.272	.305	.577	89	-8	-5	92	109	34	.509	15			-11	*C	-0.7
1907	Phi-N	101	313	18	66	8	4	0	14	15		.211	.247	.262	.509	59	-14	-16	104	65	23	.433	10			11	C/2O	0.3
1908	Phi-N	133	435	28	108	17	4	0	41	17		.248	.277	.306	.582	88	-7	-7	100	121	40	.520	20			12	*C	1.4
1909	Phi-N	141	468	42	105	14	1	2	38	21		.224	.264	.271	.535	63	-19	-22	106	106	35	.457	14			5	*C	-0.7
1910	Phi-N	103	331	30	80	13	4	0	30	22	17	.242	.289	.305	.594	76	-12	-10	96	104	31	.530	10			2	C/OM	-0.4
1911	Phi-N	74	247	18	81	15	1	1	16	14	12	.328	.366	.409	.775	109	5	2	108	52	39	.735	6			2	CM	0.9
1912	Phi-N	69	184	20	43	9	0	0	22	5	12	.234	.262	.283	.544	49	-13	-13	100	142	15	.475	8			2	CM	-0.7
1913	Phi-N	55	129	6	33	4	1	0	13	3	9	.256	.273	.302	.575	57	-6	-8	112	121	10	.448	1			1	CM	-0.3
1914	Phi-N	53	118	10	21	2	0	1	8	4	14	.178	.205	.220	.425	26	-11	-11	100	100	6	.351	4			3	CM	-0.6
1915	Cin-N	10	31	2	10	0	0	0	0	2	5	.323	.364	.323	.686	106	0	0	103	0	4	.619	1			0	C	0.1
	NY-N	46	124	9	27	2	2	0	9	3	15	.218	.236	.266	.502	57	-7	-6	91	104	8	.364	0	2	-1	-4	C	-0.9
	Yr	56	155	11	37	2	2	0	9	5	20	.239	.262	.277	.540	68	-7	-6	93	86	11	.408	1	2	-1	-4		-0.8
1916	NY-N	15	17	1	2	0	0	0	0	0	3	.118	.118	.118	.235	-29	-3	-2	96	0	0	.133	0			-1	C	-0.2
Total	15	1290	4004	333	961	139	31	10	344	155	87	.240	.270	.298	.567	72	-142	-144	100	103	359	.488	133	2		29	*C/O132	-2.3
■ **MICKEY DOOLAN**	Doolan, Michael Joseph "Doc" (born Michael Joseph Doolittle) b: 5/7/1880, Ashland, Pa. d: 11/1/51, Orlando, Fla. BR/TR, 5'10.5", 170 lbs. Deb: 4/14/05 C																											
1905	Phi-N	136	492	53	125	27	11	1	48	24		.254	.289	.360	.649	91	-5	-7	104	95	57	.594	17			-15	*S	-1.9
1906	Phi-N	154	535	41	123	19	7	1	55	27		.230	.267	.297	.564	84	-15	-10	92	126	48	.490	16			3	*S	0.0
1907	Phi-N	145	509	33	104	19	7	1	47	25		.204	.242	.275	.517	61	-22	-24	104	127	39	.452	18			12	*S	-0.6
1908	Phi-N	129	445	29	104	25	4	2	49	17		.234	.262	.321	.583	88	-7	-7	100	129	37	.484	5			-4	*S	-1.5
1909	Phi-N	147	493	39	108	12	10	1	35	37		.219	.276	.290	.566	72	-14	-18	106	89	40	.499	10			19	*S	0.3
1910	Phi-N	148	536	58	141	31	6	2	57	35	56	.263	.315	.354	.670	99	-5	-2	96	103	64	.625	16			16	*S	2.1
1911	Phi-N	146	512	51	122	23	6	1	49	44	65	.238	.301	.313	.614	67	-20	-25	108	104	52	.564	14			19	*S	0.0
1912	Phi-N	146	532	47	137	26	6	1	62	34	59	.258	.305	.335	.639	74	-20	-20	100	118	56	.557	6			10	*S	0.4
1913	Phi-N	151	518	32	113	12	6	1	43	29	68	.218	.262	.270	.533	47	-33	-40	112	111	40	.464	17			12	*S/2	-1.9
1914	Bal-F	145	486	58	119	23	6	1	53	40	47	.245	.302	.323	.625	80	-13	-13	99	122	61	.619	30			23	*S	2.1
1915	Bal-F	119	404	41	75	13	7	2	21	24	0	.186	.231	.267	.499	44	-27	-30	107	66	28	.432	10			25	*S	0.3
	Chi-F	24	86	9	23	1	1	0	9	2	0	.267	.284	.302	.586	76	-3	-3	97	125	9	.524	5			-2	S	-0.2
	Yr	143	490	50	98	14	8	2	30	26	0	.200	.240	.273	.514	49	-30	-33	105	77	37	.446	15			23		0.1
1916	Chi-N	28	70	4	15	2	1	0	5	8	7	.214	.295	.271	.566	64	-2	-3	117	104	6	.491	0			-3	S	-0.5
	NY-N	18	51	4	12	3	1	1	3	2	4	.235	.264	.392	.656	105	-0	-0	96	52	6	.590	1			3	S/2	0.4
	Yr	46	121	8	27	5	2	1	8	10	11	.223	.282	.322	.605	79	-2	-3	109	86	12	.532	1			0		-0.1
1918	Bro-N	92	308	14	55	8	2	0	18	22	24	.179	.233	.218	.451	37	-23	-23	101	104	18	.383	8			4	2	-1.6
Total	13	1728	5977	513	1376	244	81	15	554	370	330	.230	.277	.306	.582	71	-209	-226	102	108	562	.518	173			122	*S/2	-2.6
■ **HARRY DOOMS**	Dooms, Henry E. "Jack" b: 1/30/1867, St.Louis, Mo. d: 12/1899, St.Louis, Mo. Deb: 8/07/1892																											
1892	Lou-N	1	4	0	0	0	0	0	0	1	3	.000	.200	.000	.200	-41	-1	-1	92	0	0	.250	0			0	/O	0.0
■ **TOM DORAN**	Doran, Thomas J. "Long Tom" b: 12/2/1880, Westchester Co., N.Y. d: 6/22/10, New York, N.Y. TR, 5'11", 152 lbs. Deb: 4/19/04																											
1904	Bos-A	12	32	1	4	0	1	0	0	0	4	.125	.222	.188	.410	31	-2	-2	105	0	2	.393	1			0	C	-0.1
1905	Bos-A	3	3	0	0	0	0	0	0	0	0	.000	.000	.000	.000	-99	-1	-1	100	0	0	.000	0			0	/C	0.0

YEAR	TM/L	G	AB	R	H	2B	3B	HR	RBI	BB	SO	AVG	OBP	SLG	PRO	/A	BR	/A	PF	CHI	RC	TA	SB	CS	SBR	FR	POS	TPR
	Det-A	34	94	8	15	3	0	0	4	8		.160	.225	.191	.417	35	-7	-7	98	79	5	.354	2			1	C	-0.2
	Yr	37	97	8	15	3	0	0	4	8		.155	.219	.186	.405	31	-7	-7	98	73	4	.341	2			1		-0.2
1906	Bos-A	2	3	1	0	0	0	0	0	0		.000	.000	.000	.000	-99	-1	-1	98	0	0	.000	0			0	/C	0.0
Total	3	51	132	10	19	3	1	0	4	12		.144	.215	.182	.397	28	-10	-10	100	56	6	.345	3			1	/C	-0.3

■ **BILL DORAN** Doran, William Donald b: 5/28/58, Cincinnati, Ohio BR/TR, 6', 175 lbs. Deb: 9/06/82

YEAR	TM/L	G	AB	R	H	2B	3B	HR	RBI	BB	SO	AVG	OBP	SLG	PRO	/A	BR	/A	PF	CHI	RC	TA	SB	CS	SBR	FR	POS	TPR
1982	Hou-N	26	97	11	27	3	0	0	6	4	11	.278	.307	.309	.616	74	-4	-3	99	80	10	.557	5	0	2	-0	2	0.0
1983	Hou-N	154	535	70	145	12	7	8	39	86	67	.271	.372	.364	.736	116	7	13	90	72	76	.718	12	12	-4	2	*2	1.8
1984	Hou-N	147	548	92	143	18	11	4	41	66	69	.261	.343	.356	.698	104	-1	4	93	82	70	.671	21	12	-1	9	*2S	1.8
1985	Hou-N	148	578	84	166	31	6	14	59	71	69	.287	.365	.434	.799	128	18	21	96	77	92	.789	23	15	-2	8	*2	2.9
1986	Hou-N	145	550	92	152	29	3	6	37	81	57	.276	.371	.373	.744	103	7	5	103	58	81	.773	42	19	1	-32	*2	-2.4
1987	Hou-N	162	625	82	177	23	3	16	79	82	64	.283	.369	.406	.775	113	7	13	93	92	99	.787	31	11	3	-13	*2/S	0.6
1988	Hou-N	132	480	66	119	18	1	7	53	65	60	.248	.339	.333	.672	100	-2	2	93	124	59	.653	17	4	3	-0	*2	0.9
Total	7	914	3413	497	929	134	31	55	314	455	397	.272	.359	.378	.737	110	32	55	95	83	487	.743	151	73	2	-26	2/S	5.6

■ **BILL DORAN** Doran, William James b: 6/14/1898, San Francisco, Cal. d: 3/9/78, Santa Monica, Cal. BL/TR, 5'11.5", 175 lbs. Deb: 6/23/22

YEAR	TM/L	G	AB	R	H	2B	3B	HR	RBI	BB	SO	AVG	OBP	SLG	PRO	/A	BR	/A	PF	CHI	RC	TA	SB	CS	SBR	FR	POS	TPR
1922	Cle-A	3	2	0	1	0	0	0	0	1	0	.500	.667	.500	1.167	204	0	0	102	0	1	2.000	0	0	0	0	/3	0.1

■ **JERRY DORGAN** Dorgan, Jeremiah F. b: 1856, Meriden, Conn. d: 6/10/1891, New Haven, Conn. BL/TR, Deb: 7/08/1880

YEAR	TM/L	G	AB	R	H	2B	3B	HR	RBI	BB	SO	AVG	OBP	SLG	PRO	/A	BR	/A	PF	CHI	RC	TA	SB	CS	SBR	FR	POS	TPR
1880	Wor-N	10	35	2	7	1	0	0	1	0	1	.200	.200	.229	.429	40	-2	-3	113	46	2	.286				0	/OC	-0.1
1882	Phi-a	44	181	25	51	9	1	0		4		.282	.297	.343	.640	103	3	-0	112	0	19	.508				-2	CO/3	-0.2
1884	Ind-a	34	141	22	42	6	1	0		2		.298	.317	.355	.672	126	3	4	96	0	16	.545				-1	O/C	0.2
	Bro-a	4	13	2	4	0	0	0		0		.308	.308	.308	.615	107	0	0	98	0	1	.444				0	/C	0.0
	Yr	38	154	24	46	6	1	0		2		.299	.316	.351	.667	125	3	4	97	0	18	.537				-1		0.2
1885	Det-N	39	161	23	46	6	2	0	24	8	10	.286	.320	.348	.667	119	3	3	97	131	18	.557				-3	O	0.0
Total	4	131	531	74	150	22	4	0	25	14	11	.282	.303	.339	.642	109	6	4	103	44	56	.514				-7	/OC3	-0.1

■ **MIKE DORGAN** Dorgan, Michael Cornelius b: 10/2/1853, Middletown, Conn. d: 4/26/09, Syracuse, N.Y. BR/TR, 5'9", 180 lbs. Deb: 5/08/1877 M

YEAR	TM/L	G	AB	R	H	2B	3B	HR	RBI	BB	SO	AVG	OBP	SLG	PRO	/A	BR	/A	PF	CHI	RC	TA	SB	CS	SBR	FR	POS	TPR
1877	StL-N	60	266	45	82	9	7	0	23	9	13	.308	.331	.395	.726	125	8	8	102	64	36	.620				-7	*OC/3S2	0.0
1879	Syr-N	59	270	38	72	11	5	1	17	4	13	.267	.277	.356	.633	120	2	6	89	52	27	.505				1	1O3/SCP2	0.5
1880	Pro-N	79	321	45	79	10	1	0	31	10	18	.246	.269	.283	.552	91	-4	-2	96	132	25	.417				1	*O/3PM	-0.3
1881	Wor-N	51	220	36	61	5	0	0	18	8	4	.277	.303	.300	.603	86	-2	-4	105	91	20	.465				-0	1O/SM	-0.7
	Det-N	8	34	5	8	1	0	0	5	1	0	.235	.257	.265	.522	60	-1	-2	106	170	2	.385				1	/O31	0.0
	Yr	59	254	41	69	6	0	0	23	9	4	.272	.297	.295	.592	82	-4	-6	105	103	23	.454				1		-0.7
1883	NY-N	64	261	32	61	11	3	0	27	2	23	.234	.240	.299	.538	63	-12	-12	100	127	19	.400				-6	O/CP	-1.3
1884	NY-N	83	341	61	94	11	6	1	48	13	27	.276	.302	.352	.654	107	2	3	98	142	37	.538				-2	OP/C2	0.0
1885	NY-N	89	347	60	113	17	8	0	46	11	24	.326	.346	.421	.767	134	17	12	109	112	52	.671				-3	*O/1	0.6
1886	NY-N	118	442	61	129	19	4	2	79	29	37	.292	.335	.367	.702	128	7	15	89	162	59	.639	9			-15	*O/1	0.2
1887	NY-N	71	283	41	73	10	0	0	34	15	20	.258	.302	.293	.596	63	-12	-15	107	134	33	.586	22			-4	O/1	-1.5
1890	Syr-a	33	139	19	30	8	0	0		16		.216	.301	.273	.575	79	-5	-2	90	0	14	.578	8			0	O	-0.1
Total	10	715	2924	443	802	112	34	4	328	118	179	.274	.303	.340	.643	102	0	7	98	112	325	.544	39			-33	O/1CP3S2	-2.6

■ **CHARLIE DORMAN** Dorman, Charles William "Slats" b: 4/23/1898, San Francisco, Cal d: 11/15/28, San Francisco, Cal BR/TR, 6'2", 185 lbs. Deb: 5/14/23

YEAR	TM/L	G	AB	R	H	2B	3B	HR	RBI	BB	SO	AVG	OBP	SLG	PRO	/A	BR	/A	PF	CHI	RC	TA	SB	CS	SBR	FR	POS	TPR
1923	Chi-A	1	2	0	1	0	0	0	0	0	0	.500	.500	.500	1.000	167	0	0	98	0	0	1.000	0	0	0	0	/C	0.0

■ **RED DORMAN** Dorman, Dwight Dexter "Curlie" b: 10/3/05, Jacksonville, Ill. d: 12/7/74, Anaheim, Cal. BR/TR, 5'10.5", 180 lbs. Deb: 8/21/28

YEAR	TM/L	G	AB	R	H	2B	3B	HR	RBI	BB	SO	AVG	OBP	SLG	PRO	/A	BR	/A	PF	CHI	RC	TA	SB	CS	SBR	FR	POS	TPR
1928	Cle-A	25	77	12	28	6	0	0	11	9	6	.364	.430	.442	.872	122	4	3	106	111	15	.898	1	0	0	-1	O	0.1

■ **BRIAN DORSETT** Dorsett, Brian Richard b: 4/9/61, Terre Haute, Ind. BR/TR, 6'3", 215 lbs. Deb: 9/08/87

YEAR	TM/L	G	AB	R	H	2B	3B	HR	RBI	BB	SO	AVG	OBP	SLG	PRO	/A	BR	/A	PF	CHI	RC	TA	SB	CS	SBR	FR	POS	TPR
1987	Cle-A	5	11	2	3	0	0	1	3	0	3	.273	.333	.545	.879	125	0	0	103	133	2	.875	0	0	0	0	/C	0.1
1988	Cal-A	7	11	0	1	0	0	0	2	1	5	.091	.167	.091	.258	-27	-2	-2	94	795	0	.200	0	0	0	-0	/C	-0.1
Total	2	12	22	2	4	0	0	1	5	1	8	.182	.250	.318	.568	55	-1	-1	98	464	2	.500	0	0	0	-0	/C	0.0

■ **JERRY DORSEY** Dorsey, Jeremiah b: 1885, Oakland, Cal. BL/TL, 5'11", 175 lbs. Deb: 9/23/11

YEAR	TM/L	G	AB	R	H	2B	3B	HR	RBI	BB	SO	AVG	OBP	SLG	PRO	/A	BR	/A	PF	CHI	RC	TA	SB	CS	SBR	FR	POS	TPR
1911	Pit-N	2	6	0	0	0	0	0	0	0	1	.000	.000	.000	.000	-99	-2	-2	101	0	0	.000	0			0	/O	0.0

■ **HERM DOSCHER** Doscher, John Henry Sr. b: 12/20/1852, New York, N.Y. d: 3/20/34, Buffalo, N.Y. BR/TR, 5'10", 182 lbs. Deb: 9/05/1872

YEAR	TM/L	G	AB	R	H	2B	3B	HR	RBI	BB	SO	AVG	OBP	SLG	PRO	/A	BR	/A	PF	CHI	RC	TA	SB	CS	SBR	FR	POS	TPR
1872	Atl-n	6	26	4	9							.346															/O	
1873	Atl-n	1	6	1	1							.167															/O	
1875	Nat-n	21	75	3	12							.160															3/S	
1879	Tro-N	47	191	16	42	8	0	0	18	2	10	.220	.228	.262	.490	65	-8	-6	93	134	12	.349				-4	3	-0.7
	Chi-N	3	11	1	2	0	0	0	1	0	3	.182	.182	.182	.364	19	-1	-1	105	175	0	.222				-1	/3	-0.1
	Yr	50	202	17	44	8	0	0	19	2	13	.218	.225	.257	.483	62	-9	-7	94	139	12	.342				-5		-0.8
1881	Cle-N	5	19	2	4	0	0	0	0	0	2	.211	.211	.211	.421	34	-1	-1	96	0	1	.267				0	/3	0.0
1882	Cle-N	25	104	7	25	2	0	0	10	0	11	.240	.240	.260	.500	67	-5	-3	90	132	7	.342				-2	3/OS	-0.3
Total	3 n	28	107	8	22							.206															3/OS	
Total	3	80	325	26	73	10	0	0	29	2	26	.225	.229	.255	.485	62	-15	-11	93	127	20	.337				-6	3/OS	-1.1

■ **DUTCH DOTTERER** Dotterer, Henry John b: 11/11/31, Syracuse, N.Y. BR/TR, 6', 209 lbs. Deb: 9/25/57

YEAR	TM/L	G	AB	R	H	2B	3B	HR	RBI	BB	SO	AVG	OBP	SLG	PRO	/A	BR	/A	PF	CHI	RC	TA	SB	CS	SBR	FR	POS	TPR
1957	Cin-N	4	12	0	1	0	0	0	2	1	2	.083	.154	.083	.237	-32	-2	-2	105	829	0	.182	0	0	0	0	/C	-0.1
1958	Cin-N	11	28	1	7	1	0	1	2	2	4	.250	.300	.393	.693	76	-1	-1	107	59	3	.619	0	0	0	1	/C	0.0
1959	Cin-N	52	161	21	43	7	0	2	17	16	23	.267	.333	.348	.681	79	-4	-5	103	111	19	.595	0	0	0	8	C	0.6
1960	Cin-N	33	79	4	18	5	0	2	11	13	10	.228	.337	.367	.704	94	-1	-0	98	128	10	.656	0	1	-1	1	C	0.2
1961	Was-A	7	19	1	5	2	0	0	1	3	5	.263	.364	.368	.732	101	-0	0	95	56	3	.714	0	0	0	0	/C	0.0
Total	5	107	299	27	74	15	0	5	33	35	44	.247	.326	.348	.674	80	-8	-8	102	135	36	.615	0	1	-1	10	C	0.7

■ **CHARLIE DOUGHERTY** Dougherty, Charles William b: 2/7/1862, Darlington, Wis. d: 2/18/25, Milwaukee, Wis. Deb: 4/17/1884

YEAR	TM/L	G	AB	R	H	2B	3B	HR	RBI	BB	SO	AVG	OBP	SLG	PRO	/A	BR	/A	PF	CHI	RC	TA	SB	CS	SBR	FR	POS	TPR
1884	Alt-U	23	85	6	22	5	0	0		2		.259	.276	.318	.594	99	-0	-0	101	0	8	.460	0			0	2/OS	0.0

■ **PATSY DOUGHERTY** Dougherty, Patrick Henry b: 10/27/1876, Andover, N.Y. d: 4/30/40, Bolivar, N.Y. BL/TR, 6'2", 190 lbs. Deb: 4/19/02

YEAR	TM/L	G	AB	R	H	2B	3B	HR	RBI	BB	SO	AVG	OBP	SLG	PRO	/A	BR	/A	PF	CHI	RC	TA	SB	CS	SBR	FR	POS	TPR
1902	Bos-A	108	438	77	150	12	6	0	34	42		.342	.400	.397	.797	124	15	16	99	57	80	.819	20			-8	*O/3	0.2
1903	Bos-A	139	590	**106**	**195**	19	12	4	59	33		.331	.366	.424	.790	124	27	18	112	70	107	.805	35			5	*O	1.5
1904	Bos-A	49	195	33	53	5	4	0	4	25		.272	.355	.338	.693	117	6	5	105	19	28	.711	10			0	O	0.2
	NY-A	106	452	80	128	13	10	6	22	19		.283	.312	.396	.708	112	12	6	112	36	61	.645	11			-27	*O	-3.0
	Yr	155	647	**113**	181	18	14	6	26	44		.280	.326	.379	.704	114	18	11	110	31	89	.665	21			-27		-2.8
1905	NY-A	116	418	56	110	9	6	3	29	17		.263	.292	.335	.627	99	-1	-1	102	71	50	.601	28			5	*O/3	-0.1
1906	NY-A	12	52	3	10	2	0	0	4	0		.192	.192	.231	.423	28	-4	-5	120	105	2	.286	0			-0	O	-0.6
	Chi-A	75	253	30	59	9	4	1	27	19		.233	.287	.312	.599	97	-3	-1	92	122	26	.562	11			-17	O	-2.3
	Yr	87	305	33	69	11	4	1	31	19		.226	.272	.298	.570	84	-7	-6	96	121	28	.513	11			-17		-2.9
1907	Chi-A	148	533	69	144	17	2	1	59	36		.270	.316	.315	.632	100	-2	0	104	131	65	.609	33			-8	*O	-1.7
1908	Chi-A	138	482	68	134	11	6	0	45	58		.278	.356	.326	.681	132	15	18	94	114	71	.753	**47**			-0	*O	1.3
1909	Chi-A	139	491	71	140	23	13	1	55	51		.285	.359	.391	.751	141	21	23	97	115	80	.812	36			-22	*O	-0.4
1910	Chi-A	127	443	45	110	8	6	1	43	41		.248	.318	.300	.618	99	-3	-0	95	119	48	.601	22			-11	*O	-1.8
1911	Chi-A	76	211	39	61	10	9	0	32	26		.289	.380	.422	.802	128	7	8	97	122	41	.927	19			-6	O	-0.2
Total	10	1233	4558	677	1294	138	78	17	413	367		.284	.339	.360	.699	115	95	87	102	91	659	.703	272			-89	*O/3	-6.9

■ **JOHN DOUGLAS** Douglas, John Franklin b: 9/14/17, Thayer, W.Va. d: 2/11/84, Miami, Fla. BL/TL, 6'2.5", 195 lbs. Deb: 4/21/45

YEAR	TM/L	G	AB	R	H	2B	3B	HR	RBI	BB	SO	AVG	OBP	SLG	PRO	/A	BR	/A	PF	CHI	RC	TA	SB	CS	SBR	FR	POS	TPR
1945	Bro-N	5	9	0	0	0	0	0	0	2	4	.000	.182	.000	.182	-49	-2	-2	96	0	0	.222	0			0	/1	-0.1

■ **ASTYANAX DOUGLASS** Douglass, Astyanax Saunders b: 9/19/1899, Covington, Tex. d: 1/26/75, El Paso, Tex. BL/TR, 6'1", 190 lbs. Deb: 7/30/21

YEAR	TM/L	G	AB	R	H	2B	3B	HR	RBI	BB	SO	AVG	OBP	SLG	PRO	/A	BR	/A	PF	CHI	RC	TA	SB	CS	SBR	FR	POS	TPR
1921	Cin-N	4	7	1	1	0	0	0	0	0	1	.143	.143	.143	.286	-24	-1	-1	101	0	0	.167	0	0	0	0	/C	0.0

YEAR	TM/L	G	AB	R	H	2B	3B	HR	RBI	BB	SO	AVG	OBP	SLG	PRO	/A	BR	/A	PF	CHI	RC	TA	SB	CS	SBR	FR	POS	TPR
1925	Cin-N	7	17	1	3	0	0	0	1	1	3	.176	.222	.176	.399	3	-2	-2	97	119	1	.286	0	0	0	-0	/C	-0.1
Total	2	11	24	2	4	0	0	0	1	1	4	.167	.200	.167	.367	-4	-4	-4	98	85	1	.250	0	0	0	-0	/C	-0.1
■ KLONDIKE DOUGLASS	Douglass, William Bingham b: 5/10/1872, Boston, Pa. d: 12/13/53, Bend, Ore. BL/TR, 6', 200 lbs. Deb: 4/23/1896																											
1896	StL-N	81	296	42	78	6	4	1	28	35	15	.264	.351	.321	.672	84	-7	-5	95	87	41	.702	18			-7	O/CS	-1.3
1897	StL-N	125	516	77	170	15	3	6	50	52		.329	.403	.405	.808	124	15	20	93	56	91	.824	12			3	CO1/3S	2.4
1898	Phi-N	146	582	105	150	26	4	2	48	55		.258	.328	.326	.655	95	-6	-1	95	65	70	.623	18			1	*1	0.0
1899	Phi-N	77	275	26	70	6	6	0	27	10		.255	.293	.320	.613	72	-11	-10	97	94	29	.537	7			-5	C/31O	-0.9
1900	Phi-N	50	160	23	48	9	4	0	25	13		.300	.353	.406	.759	114	2	3	98	120	26	.759	7			-6	C/3	0.1
1901	Phi-N	51	173	14	56	6	1	0	23	11		.324	.364	.370	.734	112	4	3	103	120	28	.726	10			-1	C/1O	0.7
1902	Phi-N	109	408	37	95	12	3	0	37	23		.233	.274	.277	.551	68	-13	-16	105	120	33	.454	6			1	1CO	-1.6
1903	Phi-N	105	377	43	96	5	4	1	36	28		.255	.306	.297	.603	80	-12	-8	92	103	37	.520	6			-2	1	-1.2
1904	Phi-N	3	10	1	3	0	0	0	1	0		.300	.300	.300	.600	94	-0	-0	93	122	1	.429	0			-0	/1	0.0
Total	9	747	2797	368	766	85	29	10	275	227	15	.274	.335	.336	.670	94	-30	-14	96	88	356	.629	84			-16	1CO/3S	-1.8
■ TAYLOR DOUTHIT	Douthit, Taylor Lee b: 4/22/01, Little Rock, Ark. d: 5/28/86, Fremont, Cal. BR/TR, 5'11.5", 175 lbs. Deb: 9/14/23																											
1923	StL-N	9	27	3	5	0	2	0	0	0	4	.185	.185	.333	.519	38	-3	-2	90	0	2	.455	1	0	0	-0	/O	-0.2
1924	StL-N	53	173	24	48	13	1	0	13	16	19	.277	.349	.364	.713	89	-2	-2	103	75	23	.672	4	3	-1	3	O	0.0
1925	StL-N	30	73	13	20	3	1	1	8	2	6	.274	.312	.384	.695	75	-3	-3	102	92	9	.604	0	0	0	-0	O	-0.2
1926	StL-N	139	530	96	163	20	4	3	52	55	46	.308	.375	.377	.752	101	4	2	102	83	76	.763	23			14	*O	1.1
1927	StL-N	130	488	81	128	29	6	5	50	52	45	.262	.336	.377	.713	85	-6	-11	107	93	62	.678	6			3	*O	-1.3
1928	StL-N	154	648	111	191	35	3	3	43	84	36	.295	.384	.372	.756	98	2	2	100	53	95	.757	11			21	*O	1.7
1929	StL-N	150	613	128	206	42	7	9	62	79	49	.336	.416	.471	.888	121	21	23	98	58	120	.936	8			-1	*O	0.7
1930	StL-N	154	664	109	201	41	10	7	93	60	38	.303	.364	.426	.790	86	-10	-15	105	91	102	.758	4			-1	*O	-2.4
1931	StL-N	36	133	21	44	11	2	1	21	11	9	.331	.386	.466	.852	120	5	4	107	117	25	.843	1			2	O	0.4
	Cin-N	95	374	42	98	9	1	0	24	42	24	.262	.340	.291	.631	75	-13	-11	95	69	40	.569	4			1	O	-1.4
	Yr	131	507	63	142	20	3	1	45	53	33	.280	.352	.337	.689	87	-8	-7	98	83	64	.636	5			3		-1.0
1932	Cin-N	96	333	28	81	12	1	0	25	31	29	.243	.311	.285	.597	64	-17	-15	96	100	32	.520	3			8	O	-1.3
1933	Cin-N	1	0	1	0	0	0	0	0	0	0	—	—	—	—	—	0	0	99	—	—	—	0			0	R	0.0
	Chi-N	27	71	8	16	5	0	0	5	11	7	.225	.329	.296	.625	82	-2	-1	97	89	6	.557	2			0	O	-0.1
	Yr	28	71	9	16	5	0	0	5	11	7	.225	.329	.296	.625	82	-2	-1	97	86	6	.557	2			0		-0.1
Total	11	1074	4127	665	1201	220	38	29	396	443	312	.291	.364	.384	.748	93	-22	-30	101	77	624	.725	67	3		48	*O	-3.0
■ CLARENCE DOW	Dow, Clarence G. b: 10/11/1854, Charlestown, Mass. d: 3/11/1893, Somerville, Mass. Deb: 9/22/1884																											
1884	Bos-U	1	6	1	2	0	0	0				.333	.333	.333	.667	128	0	0	98	0	1	.500	0			0	/O	0.0
■ JOHN DOWD	Dowd, John Leo b: 1/3/1891, S.Weymouth, Mass. d: 1/31/81, Ft.Lauderdale, Fla BR/TR, 5'8", 170 lbs. Deb: 7/03/12																											
1912	NY-A	10	31	1	6	1	0	0	0	6		.194	.342	.226	.568	62	-1	-1	101	0	2	.560	0			-1	S	0.0
■ SNOOKS DOWD	Dowd, Raymond Bernard b: 12/20/1897, Springfield, Mass. d: 4/4/62, Northampton, Mass. BR/TR, 5'8", 163 lbs. Deb: 4/27/19																											
1919	Det-A	1	0	0	0	0	0	0	0	0	0	—	—	—	—	—	0	0	93	—	—	—	0			0	R	0.0
	Phi-A	13	18	4	3	0	0	0	6	0	5	.167	.167	.167	.333	-6	-3	-3	106	725	1	.333	2			-0	/2S3O	-0.2
	Yr	14	18	4	3	0	0	0	6	0	5	.167	.167	.167	.333	-6	-3	-3	105	674	1	.333	2			-0		-0.2
1926	Bro-N	2	8	0	0	0	0	0	0	0	0	.000	.000	.000	.000	-99	-2	-2	99	0	0	.000	0			-0	/2	-0.1
Total	2	16	26	4	3	0	0	0	6	0	5	.115	.115	.115	.231	-35	-5	-5	104	502	3	.217	2			-0	/2SO3	-0.3
■ TOMMY DOWD	Dowd, Thomas Jefferson "Buttermilk Tommy" b: 4/20/1869, Holyoke, Mass. d: 7/2/33, Holyoke, Mass. BR/TR, 5'8", 173 lbs. Deb: 4/08/1891 M																											
1891	Bos-a	4	11	1	1	0	0	0	0	0	1	.091	.091	.091	.182	-48	-2	-2	99	0	0	.100	0			0	/O	-0.1
	Was-a	112	464	66	120	9	10	1	44	19	44	.259	.291	.328	.618	83	-14	-11	95	79	57	.616	39			-15	*2/O	-1.5
	Yr	116	475	67	121	9	10	1	44	19	45	.255	.286	.322	.608	80	-16	-13	96	76	56	.602	39			-15		-1.6
1892	Was-N	144	584	94	142	9	10	1	50	34	49	.243	.286	.298	.584	75	-16	-20	105	92	65	.584	49			-28	2O3/S	-4.4
1893	StL-N	132	581	114	164	18	7	1	54	49	23	.282	.340	.343	.683	84	-13	-13	99	65	90	.741	59			8	*O/2	-0.7
1894	StL-N	123	524	92	142	16	8	4	62	54	33	.271	.341	.355	.696	69	-25	-27	101	75	76	.715	31			-5	*O/23	-3.0
1895	StL-N	129	505	95	163	19	16	7	74	30	31	.323	.364	.465	.830	115	9	10	100	86	99	.871	30			2	*O3/2	0.1
1896	StL-N	126	521	93	138	17	11	5	46	42	19	.265	.322	.369	.691	88	-13	-9	95	55	77	.721	40			-15	2OM	-2.0
1897	StL-N	35	145	25	38	9	1	0	9	6		.262	.291	.338	.629	72	-7	-5	93	57	18	.617	11			-5	O/2M	-1.0
	Phi-N	91	391	68	114	14	4	0	43	19		.292	.324	.348	.672	83	-12	-9	96	89	55	.668	30			-2	O2	-1.3
	Yr	126	536	93	152	23	5	0	52	25		.284	.316	.345	.661	80	-19	-14	95	80	73	.654	41			-7		-2.3
1898	StL-N	139	586	70	143	17	7	0	32	30		.244	.288	.297	.585	66	-23	-27	106	48	56	.510	16			-7	*O2	-4.0
1899	Cle-N	147	605	81	168	17	6	2	35	48		.278	.334	.336	.669	96	-10	-1	89	44	79	.645	28			-3	*O	-1.1
1901	Bos-A	138	594	104	159	18	7	3	52	38		.268	.312	.337	.648	84	-14	-12	97	68	74	.623	33			5	*O/13	-0.7
Total	10	1320	5511	903	1492	163	87	24	501	369	200	.271	.319	.345	.664	83	-140	-124	98	68	746	.661	366			-65	O2/3S1	-19.7
■ KEN DOWELL	Dowell, Kenneth Allen b: 1/19/61, Sacramento, Cal. BR/TR, 5'9", 160 lbs. Deb: 6/24/87																											
1987	Phi-N	15	39	4	5	0	0	0	1	2	5	.128	.171	.128	.299	-19	-7	-7	104	80	1	.200	0	0	0	-0	S	-0.5
■ JOE DOWIE	Dowie, Joseph E. b: 1866, New Orleans, La. 5'8", 150 lbs. Deb: 7/10/1889																											
1889	Bal-a	20	75	12	17	5	0	0	8	2	10	.227	.266	.293	.559	61	-4	-4	100	106	7	.534	5			0	O	-0.2
■ RED DOWNEY	Downey, Alexander Cummings b: 2/6/1889, Aurora, Ind. d: 7/10/49, Detroit, Mich. BL/TL, 5'11", 174 lbs. Deb: 09																											
1909	Bro-N	19	78	7	20	1	0	0	8	2		.256	.275	.269	.544	71	-3	-3	99	120	7	.466	4			0	O	-0.3
■ TOM DOWNEY	Downey, Thomas Edward b: 1/1/1884, Lewiston, Me. d: 8/3/61, Passaic, N.J. BR/TR, 5'10", 178 lbs. Deb: 09																											
1909	Cin-N	119	416	39	96	9	6	1	32	32		.231	.287	.288	.576	85	-10	-7	94	96	37	.528	16			-7	*S/C	-1.4
1910	Cin-N	111	378	43	102	9	3	2	32	34	28	.270	.335	.325	.660	92	-3	-4	101	88	46	.623	12			-2	S3	-0.2
1911	Cin-N	111	360	50	94	16	7	0	36	44	38	.261	.345	.344	.689	102	-3	1	92	98	46	.677	10			-8	S/231O	-0.3
1912	Phi-N	54	171	27	50	6	3	1	23	21	20	.292	.370	.380	.750	105	2	2	100	116	26	.736	3			-2	3/S	0.0
	Chi-N	13	22	4	4	0	2	0	4	1	5	.182	.217	.364	.581	55	-1	-2	104	168	2	.500	0			1	/S32	0.0
	Yr	67	193	31	54	6	5	1	27	22	25	.280	.353	.378	.732	99	0	-0	101	128	28	.705	3			-1		0.0
1914	Buf-F	151	541	69	118	20	3	2	42	40	55	.218	.272	.277	.549	55	-30	-33	104	103	54	.532	35			13	*2S/3	-1.7
1915	Buf-F	92	282	24	56	9	1	1	19	26	26	.199	.266	.248	.514	53	-16	-16	100	94	23	.473	11			2	23/S1	-1.3
Total	6	651	2170	256	520	69	25	7	188	198	172	.240	.305	.304	.609	78	-62	-59	99	99	235	.576	87			-1	S23/1OC	-4.9
■ BRIAN DOWNING	Downing, Brian Jay b: 10/9/50, Los Angeles, Cal. BR/TR, 5'10", 170 lbs. Deb: 5/31/73																											
1973	Chi-A	34	73	5	13	1	0	2	4	10	17	.178	.277	.274	.551	54	-4	-4	102	60	6	.476	0	0	0	0	OC/3D	-0.4
1974	Chi-A	108	293	41	66	12	1	10	39	51	72	.225	.344	.375	.719	105	4	3	102	110	38	.682	0	1	-1	-2	CO/D	0.2
1975	Chi-A	138	420	58	101	12	1	7	41	76	75	.240	.361	.324	.685	92	0	-2	103	100	54	.681	13	4	2	18	*C/D	2.2
1976	Chi-A	104	317	38	81	14	0	3	30	40	55	.256	.341	.328	.669	97	-0	0	99	102	39	.631	7	3	0	-2	CD	0.2
1977	Chi-A	69	169	28	48	4	2	4	25	34	21	.284	.410	.402	.812	123	7	7	99	124	30	.833	1	2	-1	6	C/OD	1.3
1978	Cal-A	133	412	42	105	15	0	7	46	52	47	.255	.347	.342	.689	93	-1	-2	102	112	49	.625	3	2	-0	-8	*C/D	-0.6
1979	Cal-A	148	509	87	166	27	3	12	75	77	57	.326	.420	.462	.881	149	30	36	93	109	99	.882	3	3	-1	-8	*CD	3.1
1980	Cal-A	30	93	5	27	6	0	2	25	12	12	.290	.371	.419	.791	121	2	3	96	217	13	.699	0	2	-1	-3	CD	0.0
1981	Cal-A	93	317	47	79	14	0	9	41	46	35	.249	.351	.379	.730	106	5	4	104	111	43	.684	1	1	-0	-4	OC/D	0.0
1982	Cal-A	158	623	109	175	37	2	28	84	86	58	.281	.373	.482	.854	132	29	29	100	77	114	.849	2	1	0	-4	*O	1.9
1983	Cal-A	113	403	68	99	15	1	19	53	62	59	.246	.353	.429	.782	119	9	11	96	92	63	.768	1	2	-1	-3	OD	0.6
1984	Cal-A	156	539	65	148	28	2	23	91	70	66	.275	.365	.462	.827	125	21	20	101	116	89	.789	0	4	-2	-3	*OD	1.0
1985	Cal-A	150	520	80	137	23	1	20	85	78	61	.263	.373	.427	.800	118	16	15	101	122	86	.797	5	3	-0	-5	*OD	0.8
1986	Cal-A	152	513	90	137	27	4	20	95	90	84	.267	.394	.452	.846	136	26	28	96	**132**	96	.871	4	4	-1	-5	*OD	1.8
1987	Cal-A	155	567	110	154	29	3	29	77	**106**	85	.272	.401	.487	.888	136	33	34	99	81	117	.944	5	5	-2	-4	*DO	2.5
1988	Cal-A	135	484	80	117	18	2	25	64	81	63	.242	.366	.442	.808	133	19	22	94	93	81	.815	3	4	-2	0	*D	2.1

YEAR	TM/L	G	AB	R	H	2B	3B	HR	RBI	BB	SO	AVG	OBP	SLG	PRO	/A	BR	/A	PF	CHI	RC	TA	SB	CS	SBR	FR	POS	TPR
Total	16	1876	6252	953	1653	282	22	220	875	971	867	.264	.372	.422	.794	121	194	204	99	105	1019	.808	48	41	-10	-26	OCD/3	16.7
■ **RED DOWNS** Downs, Jerome Willis b: 8/22/1883, Neola, Iowa d: 10/19/39, Council Bluffs, Ia BR/TR, 5'11", 155 lbs. Deb: 5/02/07																												
1907	Det-A	105	374	28	82	13	5	1	42	13		.219	.245	.289	.534	71	-12	-13	102	138	28	.425	3			-11	2O/S3	-2.7
1908	Det-A	84	289	29	64	10	3	1	35	5		.221	.235	.287	.522	70	-10	-10	101	156	19	.400	2			-5	2/3	-1.9
1912	Bro-N	9	32	2	8	3	0	0	3	1	5	.250	.273	.344	.616	71	-2	-1	95	92	4	.625	3			0	/2	-0.1
	Chi-N	43	95	9	25	4	3	1	14	9	17	.263	.327	.400	.727	95	-1	-1	104	115	14	.743	5			1	2/S3	0.1
	Yr	52	127	11	33	7	3	1	17	10	22	.260	.314	.386	.700	89	-2	-2	102	113	18	.713	8			1		0.0
Total	3	241	790	68	179	30	11	3	94	28	22	.227	.253	.304	.557	74	-24	-26	101	140	64	.460	13			-15	2/OS3	-4.6
■ **TOM DOWSE** Dowse, Thomas Joseph b: 8/12/1866, Ireland d: 12/14/46, Riverside, Cal. BR/TR, 5'11", 175 lbs. Deb: 4/21/1890																												
1890	Cle-N	40	159	20	33	2	1	0	9	12	22	.208	.267	.233	.500	51	-10	-9	94	78	11	.421	3			0	O1/CP	-0.7
1891	Col-a	55	201	24	45	7	0	0	22	13	22	.224	.278	.259	.536	63	-11	-8	89	125	15	.442	2			-0	C/O	-0.4
1892	Lou-N	41	145	10	21	2	0	0	7	2	15	.145	.173	.159	.332	2	-17	-15	92	93	4	.234	1			0	C1/O2	-1.4
	Cin-N	1	4	0	0	0	0	0	0	0	0	.000	.000	.000	.000	-97	-1	-1	103	0	0	.000	0			0	/C	0.0
	Phi-N	16	54	3	10	0	0	0	6	2	4	.185	.228	.185	.413	25	-5	-5	104	184	3	.318	1			0	C	-0.4
	Was-N	7	27	5	7	1	0	0	2	0	3	.259	.259	.296	.556	66	-1	-1	105	78	2	.400	0			0	/OC	0.0
	Yr	65	230	18	38	3	0	0	15	4	22	.165	.193	.178	.372	14	-24	-23	97	117	9	.266	2			0		-1.8
Total	3	160	590	62	116	12	1	0	46	29	66	.197	.243	.220	.463	41	-45	-39	93	107	35	.365	7			-0	C/O12P	-2.9
■ **BRIAN DOYLE** Doyle, Brian Reed b: 1/26/55, Glasgow, Ky. BL/TR, 5'10", 160 lbs. Deb: 4/30/78																												
1978	NY-A	39	52	6	10	0	0	0	0	0	3	.192	.192	.192	.385	9	-6	-6	99	0	1	.213	0	3	-2	0	2/S3	-0.5
1979	NY-A	20	32	2	4	2	0	0	5	3	1	.125	.200	.188	.387	5	-4	-4	96	320	1	.310	0	0	0	1	2/3	-0.2
1980	NY-A	34	75	8	13	1	0	1	5	6	7	.173	.235	.227	.461	27	-8	-7	99	97	4	.375	1	1	-0	1	2S/3	-0.4
1981	Oak-A	17	40	2	5	0	0	0	3	1	2	.125	.146	.125	.271	-22	-6	-6	96	235	1	.162	0	1	-1	-3	2	-0.9
Total	4	110	199	18	32	3	0	1	13	10	13	.161	.201	.191	.392	10	-24	-24	98	137	7	.283	1	5	-3	-1	/2S3	-2.0
■ **CONNY DOYLE** Doyle, Cornelius J. b: 1858, Holyoke, Mass. d: 1/18/27, E.Orange, N.J. 5'10", 185 lbs. Deb: 6/23/1883																												
1883	Phi-N	16	68	3	15	3	2	0	3	0	15	.221	.221	.324	.544	70	-3	-2	90	50	5	.415				0	O	-0.1
■ **ED DOYLE** Doyle, Edward H. b: 1853, Illinois d: 2/6/29, Havre, Mont. Deb: 8/22/1884																												
1884	Pit-a	15	58	8	17	3	2	0		2		.293	.317	.414	.730	144	2	3	97	0	8	.634				0	O/S	0.2
■ **DANNY DOYLE** Doyle, Howard James b: 1/24/17, Mcloud, Okla. BB/TR, 6'1", 195 lbs. Deb: 9/14/43																												
1943	Bos-A	13	43	2	9	1	0	0	6	7	9	.209	.320	.233	.553	61	-2	-2	104	219	3	.459	0	1	-1	0	C	-0.1
■ **JIM DOYLE** Doyle, James Francis b: 12/25/1881, Detroit, Mich. d: 2/1/12, Syracuse, N.Y. BR/TR, 5'10", 168 lbs. Deb: 5/04/10																												
1910	Cin-N	7	13	1	2	2	0	0	1	0	2	.154	.154	.308	.462	34	-1	-1	101	87	1	.364	0			-0	/3O	-0.1
1911	Chi-N	130	472	69	133	23	12	5	62	40	54	.282	.340	.413	.754	114	5	7	97	102	73	.755	19			4	*3	1.6
Total	2	137	485	70	135	25	12	5	63	40	56	.278	.336	.410	.746	112	4	6	97	101	73	.743	19			4	3/O	1.5
■ **JEFF DOYLE** Doyle, Jeffrey Donald b: 10/2/56, Havre, Mont. BL/TR, 5'9", 160 lbs. Deb: 9/13/83																												
1983	StL-N	13	37	4	11	1	2	0	2	1	3	.297	.316	.432	.748	108	0	0	98	49	4	.607	0	0	0	-1	2	0.0
■ **JACK DOYLE** Doyle, John Joseph "Dirty Jack" b: 10/25/1869, Killorgin, Ireland d: 12/31/58, Holyoke, Mass. BR/TR, 5'9", 155 lbs. Deb: 8/27/1889 M																												
1889	Col-a	11	36	6	10	1	1	0	3	6	6	.278	.381	.361	.742	126	1	2	91	67	9	1.077	9			0	/CO2	0.1
1890	Col-a	77	298	47	80	17	7	2		13		.268	.299	.393	.692	107	0	1	99	0	44	.720	27			-9	CS/O23	-0.2
1891	Cle-N	69	250	43	69	14	4	0	43	26	44	.276	.351	.364	.715	105	4	2	105	140	41	.796	24			0	CO3/S	0.2
1892	Cle-N	24	88	17	26	4	1	1	14	6	10	.295	.340	.398	.738	121	2	2	103	115	14	.742	5			0	O/C1S	0.2
	NY-N	90	366	61	109	22	1	5	55	18	30	.298	.336	.404	.740	128	10	11	98	110	65	.821	42			0	2CO3/S	1.0
	Yr	114	454	78	135	26	2	6	69	24	40	.297	.337	.403	.740	127	12	13	99	112	79	.806	47			0		1.2
1893	NY-N	82	318	56	102	17	5	1	51	27	12	.321	.383	.415	.798	110	6	4	104	105	67	.944	40			-1	CO/S31	0.6
1894	NY-N	105	422	90	155	30	8	3	100	35	3	.367	.420	.498	.917	123	16	16	100	133	108	1.086	42			-0	*1/C	1.3
1895	NY-N	82	319	52	100	21	3	1	66	24	12	.313	.365	.408	.773	107	1	4	95	147	62	.872	35			-0	12/3CM	0.4
1896	Bal-N	118	487	116	165	29	4	1	101	42	15	.339	.400	.421	.821	116	14	13	102	135	114	1.019	73			-10	*1/2	0.5
1897	Bal-N	114	460	91	163	29	4	1	87	29		.354	.394	.441	.835	129	15	19	95	126	107	.993	62			3	*1	1.7
1898	Was-N	43	177	26	54	2	2	2	26	7		.305	.335	.373	.708	103	1	0	102	105	26	.675	9			-1	1/2M	0.0
	NY-N	82	297	42	84	15	3	1	43	12		.283	.317	.364	.681	103	-2	1	95	119	40	.643	14			0	O1S/3C	0.0
	Yr	125	474	68	138	17	5	3	69	19		.291	.324	.367	.691	103	-1	1	97	115	65	.655	23			-1		0.0
1899	NY-N	118	448	55	134	15	7	3	76	33		.299	.351	.384	.735	107	3	4	97	136	75	.774	35			5	*1/C	1.0
1900	NY-N	133	505	69	135	24	1	1	66	34		.267	.314	.325	.638	80	-14	-12	97	131	64	.627	34			5	*1	-0.4
1901	Chi-N	75	285	21	66	9	2	0	39	7		.232	.250	.277	.527	54	-16	-16	100	168	22	.429	8			5	1	-1.0
1902	NY-N	49	186	21	56	13	0	1	19	10		.301	.337	.387	.724	126	5	5	100	84	28	.708	10			2	1	0.5
	Was-A	78	312	52	77	15	2	1	20	29		.247	.311	.317	.628	77	-10	-9	99	57	34	.574	7			-6	2/1OC	-1.1
1903	Bro-N	139	524	84	164	27	6	0	91	54		.313	.377	.387	.765	119	15	14	101	139	92	.808	34			2	*1	1.1
1904	Bro-N	8	22	2	5	1	0	0	2	6		.227	.393	.273	.666	114	1	1	95	124	3	.765	1			0	/1	0.1
	Phi-N	66	236	20	52	10	3	1	22	19		.220	.278	.301	.579	87	-5	-3	93	115	21	.511	4			-4	1/2	-0.9
	Yr	74	258	22	57	11	3	1	24	25		.221	.290	.298	.588	90	-5	-2	93	118	24	.532	5			-3		-0.8
1905	NY-A	1	3	0	0	0	0	0	0	0		.000	.000	.000	.000	-98	-1	-1	102	0	0	.000	0			0	/1	0.0
Total	17	1564	6039	971	1806	315	64	25	924	437	132	.299	.350	.385	.734	107	45	55	99	118	1036	.781	515			-9	*1CO2/S3	5.1
■ **JOE DOYLE** Doyle, Joseph K. b: Cincinnati, Ohio Deb: 4/20/1872																												
1872	Nat-n	8	36	4	8							.222															/S23	
■ **LARRY DOYLE** Doyle, Lawrence Joseph "Laughing Larry" b: 7/31/1886, Caseyville, Ill. d: 3/1/74, Saranac Lake, N.Y. BL/TR, 5'10", 165 lbs. Deb: 7/22/07																												
1907	NY-N	69	227	16	59	3	0	0	16	20		.260	.320	.273	.593	83	-3	-4	105	100	21	.506	3			-15	2	-2.0
1908	NY-N	104	377	65	116	16	9	0	33	22		.308	.346	.398	.744	134	16	14	104	89	56	.724	17			-6	*2	0.8
1909	NY-N	147	570	86	**172**	27	11	6	49	45		.302	.360	.419	.779	137	27	24	105	67	95	.809	31			-16	*2	0.7
1910	NY-N	151	575	97	164	21	14	8	69	71	26	.285	.369	.412	.781	134	20	24	95	81	101	.856	39			-17	*2	1.0
1911	NY-N	143	526	102	163	25	**25**	13	77	71	39	.310	.397	.527	.924	154	39	37	102	79	124	**1.077**	38			-19	*2	1.5
1912	NY-N	143	558	98	184	33	8	10	90	56	20	.330	.393	.471	.864	131	27	24	104	99	116	.955	36			-4	*2	1.5
1913	NY-N	132	482	67	135	25	6	5	73	59	29	.280	.364	.388	.752	112	11	9	103	139	78	.833	38			-13	*2	-0.7
1914	NY-N	145	539	87	140	19	8	5	63	58	25	.260	.343	.353	.695	112	6	9	96	107	69	.689	17			-19	*2	-1.2
1915	NY-N	150	591	86	**189**	**40**	10	4	70	32	28	**.320**	.358	.442	.799	155	27	33	91	94	94	.757	22	18	-4	-9	*2	2.2
1916	NY-N	113	441	55	118	24	10	2	47	27	23	.268	.316	.381	.697	118	6	8	96	95	60	.669	17			15	*2	2.9
	Chi-N	9	38	6	15	5	1	1	7	1	1	.395	.410	.658	1.068	193	5	5	117	95	11	1.217	2			0	/2	0.6
	Yr	122	479	61	133	29	11	3	54	28	24	.278	.323	.403	.726	126	11	13	97	96	70	.705	19			15		3.5
1917	Chi-N	135	476	48	121	19	5	6	61	48	28	.254	.323	.353	.675	102	4	2	105	134	56	.623	5			6	*2	1.7
1918	NY-N	75	257	38	67	7	4	3	36	37	10	.261	.354	.354	.708	119	6	7	98	139	34	.726	10			-8	2	0.3
1919	NY-N	113	381	61	110	14	10	7	52	31	17	.289	.350	.433	.783	135	16	16	100	111	59	.786	12			7	*2	2.8
1920	NY-N	137	471	48	134	21	2	4	50	47	28	.285	.352	.363	.715	106	4	5	100	108	61	.668	11	9	-2	-22	*2	-1.6
Total	14	1766	6509	960	1887	299	123	74	793	625	274	.290	.356	.408	.764	127	211	211	100	101	1035	.780	298	27		-120	*2	10.5
■ **DENNY DOYLE** Doyle, Robert Dennis b: 1/17/44, Glasgow, Ky. BL/TR, 5'9", 175 lbs. Deb: 4/07/70																												
1970	Phi-N	112	413	43	86	10	7	2	16	33	64	.208	.267	.281	.548	49	-31	-29	96	52	31	.459	6	5	-1	-12	*2	-3.0
1971	Phi-N	95	342	34	79	12	1	3	24	19	31	.231	.281	.298	.580	62	-16	-17	103	90	29	.480	4	2	0	8	2	-0.4
1972	Phi-N	123	442	33	110	14	2	1	26	31	33	.249	.298	.296	.594	72	-17	-16	97	81	38	.483	6	7	-2	-6	*2	-1.7
1973	Phi-N	116	370	45	101	9	3	3	26	31	32	.273	.329	.338	.667	79	-7	-11	108	78	41	.569	1	3	-2	4	*2	-0.3
1974	Cal-A	147	511	47	133	19	2	1	34	25	49	.260	.296	.311	.607	81	-17	-12	92	84	46	.487	6	7	-2	16	*2/S	0.8
1975	Cal-A	8	15	0	1	0	0	0	0	1	1	.067	.125	.067	.192	-47	-3	-3	95	0	0	.143	0	0	0	1	/23	-0.1

YEAR	TM/L	G	AB	R	H	2B	3B	HR	RBI	BB	SO	AVG	OBP	SLG	PRO	/A	BR	/A	PF	CHI	RC	TA	SB	CS	SBR	FR	POS	TPR
	Bos-A	89	310	50	96	21	2	4	36	14	11	.310	.342	.429	.771	107	6	2	109	95	43	.677	5	7	-3	-15	2/3S	-1.2
	Yr	97	325	50	97	21	2	4	36	15	12	.298	.331	.412	.744	101	3	-0	108	87	42	.646	5	7	-3	-15		-1.3
1976	Bos-A	117	432	51	108	15	5	0	26	22	39	.250	.286	.308	.594	67	-15	-20	110	77	37	.482	8	5	-1	-18	*2	-3.3
1977	Bos-A	137	455	54	109	13	6	2	49	29	50	.240	.291	.308	.599	54	-23	-33	117	133	40	.489	2	4	-2	-2	*2	-2.5
Total	8	944	3290	357	823	113	28	16	237	205	310	.250	.296	.316	.612	69	-123	-139	104	86	305	.515	38	40	-13	-24	2/3S	-11.7
DRAKE Drake Deb:6/29/1884																												
1884	Was-a	2	7	0	2	1	0	0		0		.286	.286	.429	.714	150	0	0	88	0	1	.600				0	/O	0.0
DELOS DRAKE Drake, Delos Daniel b: 12/3/1886, Girard, Ohio d: 10/3/65, Findlay, Ohio BR/TR, 5'11.5", 170 lbs. Deb: 4/30/11																												
1911	Det-A	95	315	37	88	9	9	1	36	17		.279	.324	.375	.699	88	-3	-7	108	101	44	.700	20			-11	O/1	-2.3
1914	StL-F	138	514	51	129	18	8	3	42	31	57	.251	.294	.335	.628	75	-14	-18	106	89	59	.571	17			3	*O1	-2.1
1915	StL-F	102	343	32	91	23	4	1	41	23	27	.265	.311	.364	.676	95	-1	-3	105	115	43	.611	6			0	O/1	-0.7
Total	3	335	1172	120	308	50	21	5	119	71	84	.263	.307	.354	.661	84	-18	-27	106	100	146	.617	43			-8	O/1	-5.1
LARRY DRAKE Drake, Larry Francis b: 5/4/21, Mc Kinney, Tex. d: 7/14/85, Houston, Tex. BL/TR, 6'1.5", 195 lbs. Deb: 7/20/45																												
1945	Phi-A	1	2	0	0	0	0	0	0	0	2	.000	.000	.000	.000	-99	-1	-0	94	0	0	.000	0	0	0	0	/O	0.0
1948	Was-A	4	7	0	2	0	0	0	1	1	3	.286	.375	.286	.661	75	-0	-0	103	169	1	.600	0	0	0	-0	/O	0.0
Total	2	5	9	0	2	0	0	0	1	1	5	.222	.300	.222	.522	42	-1	-1	101	135	1	.429	0	0	0	-0	/O	0.0
SAMMY DRAKE Drake, Samuel Harrison b: 10/7/34, Little Rock, Ark. BB/TR, 5'11", 175 lbs. Deb: 4/17/60																												
1960	Chi-N	15	15	5	1	0	0	0	0	1	4	.067	.125	.067	.192	-47	-3	-3	98	0	0	.143	0	0	0	0	/32	-0.2
1961	Chi-N	13	5	1	0	0	0	0	0	1	1	.000	.167	.000	.167	-51	-1	-1	100	0	0	.200	0	0	0	-0	/O	0.0
1962	NY-N	25	52	2	10	0	0	0	7	6	12	.192	.276	.192	.468	27	-5	-5	104	276	3	.381	0	0	0	0	2/3	-0.3
Total	3	53	72	8	11	0	0	0	7	8	17	.153	.237	.153	.390	7	-9	-9	102	200	3	.311	0	0	0	0	/23O	-0.5
SOLLY DRAKE Drake, Solomon Louis b: 10/23/30, Little Rock, Ark. BB/TR, 6', 170 lbs. Deb: 4/17/56																												
1956	Chi-N	65	215	29	55	9	1	2	15	23	35	.256	.331	.335	.665	81	-6	-5	99	83	26	.636	9	5	-0	8	O	0.0
1959	LA-N	9	8	2	2	0	0	0	0	1	3	.250	.333	.250	.583	57	-0	-0	102	0	1	.667	1	0	0	-1	/O	-0.1
	Phi-N	67	62	10	9	1	0	0	3	8	15	.145	.243	.161	.404	10	-8	-8	99	121	3	.397	5	5	-2	-8	O	-1.7
	Yr	76	70	12	11	1	0	0	3	9	18	.157	.253	.171	.425	16	-8	-8	100	107	3	.422	6	5	-1	-9		-1.8
Total	2	141	285	41	66	10	1	2	18	32	53	.232	.311	.295	.606	64	-14	-14	99	89	29	.576	15	10	-2	-2	/O	-1.8
JAKE DRAUBY Drauby, Jacob C. b: 1865, Harrisburg, Pa. 5'10", 163 lbs. Deb: 10/03/1892																												
1892	Was-N	10	34	3	7	0	1	0	3	2	12	.206	.250	.265	.515	55	-2	-2	105	102	2	.407	0			0	3	-0.1
BILL DREESEN Dreesen, William Richard b: 7/26/04, New York, N.Y. d: 11/9/71, Mt.Vernon, N.Y. BL/TR, 5'7.5", 160 lbs. Deb: 5/01/31																												
1931	Bos-N	48	180	38	40	10	4	1	10	23	23	.222	.310	.339	.649	75	-6	-6	99	53	20	.607	1			1	3	-0.1
BILL DRESCHER Drescher, William Clayton "Dutch" b: 5/23/21, Congers, N.Y. d: 5/15/68, Hammerstraw, N.Y. BL/TR, 6'2", 190 lbs. Deb: 4/19/44																												
1944	NY-A	4	7	0	1	0	0	0	0	0	0	.143	.143	.143	.286	-17	-1	-1	106	0	0	.143	0	0	0	0	/C	0.0
1945	NY-A	48	126	10	34	3	1	0	15	8	5	.270	.313	.310	.623	76	-3	-4	107	139	12	.485	0	2	-1	-0	C	-0.2
1946	NY-A	5	6	0	2	1	0	0	1	0	0	.333	.333	.500	.833	130	0	0	100	127	1	.750	0	0	0	0	/C	0.0
Total	3	57	139	10	37	4	1	0	16	8	5	.266	.306	.309	.615	73	-4	-5	107	132	13	.490	0	2	-1	-0	/C	-0.2
CHUCK DRESSEN Dressen, Charles Walter b: 9/20/1898, Decatur, Ill. d: 8/10/66, Detroit, Mich. BR/TR, 5'5.5", 146 lbs. Deb: 4/17/25 MC																												
1925	Cin-N	76	215	35	59	8	2	3	19	12	4	.274	.319	.372	.691	78	-8	-7	97	76	26	.623	5	3	-0	6	3/2O	0.1
1926	Cin-N	127	474	76	126	27	11	4	48	49	31	.266	.338	.395	.733	102	-2	1	95	88	63	.687	0			19	*3/SO	2.1
1927	Cin-N	144	548	78	160	36	10	2	55	71	32	.292	.376	.405	.781	109	9	9	100	75	85	.781	7			14	*3/S	3.0
1928	Cin-N	135	498	72	145	26	3	1	59	43	22	.291	.355	.361	.716	91	-8	-5	96	122	64	.677	10			-2	*3	-0.4
1929	Cin-N	110	401	49	98	22	3	1	36	41	21	.244	.321	.322	.642	60	-25	-25	99	99	42	.601	8			-5	3/2	-2.0
1930	Cin-N	33	19	0	4	0	0	0	1	1	3	.211	.250	.211	.461	14	-3	-2	90	86	1	.333	0			-0	3/2	-0.1
1931	Cin-N	5	15	0	1	0	0	0	0	1	1	.067	.125	.067	.192	-49	-3	-3	95	0	0	.143	0			0	/3	-0.2
1933	NY-N	16	45	3	10	4	0	0	3	1	4	.222	.239	.311	.550	57	-3	-3	99	81	3	.405	0			-1	3	-0.2
Total	8	646	2215	313	603	123	29	11	221	219	118	.272	.343	.369	.711	88	-43	-35	97	92	285	.670	30	3		30	3/2OS	2.3
LEE DRESSEN Dressen, Lee August b: 7/23/1889, Ellinwodd, Kan. d: 6/30/31, Diller, Neb. BL/TL, 6', 165 lbs. Deb: 4/21/14																												
1914	StL-N	46	103	16	24	2	1	0	7	11	20	.233	.307	.272	.579	70	-3	-4	104	91	9	.519	2			1	1	-0.3
1918	Det-A	31	107	10	19	1	2	0	3	21	10	.178	.323	.224	.547	67	-3	-3	97	48	9	.557	2			-3	1	-0.8
Total	2	77	210	26	43	3	3	0	10	32	30	.205	.316	.248	.563	69	-7	-7	100	68	18	.539	4			-2	/1	-1.1
CAMERON DREW Drew, Cameron Steward b: 2/12/64, Boston, Mass. BR/TL, 6'5", 215 lbs. Deb: 9/09/88																												
1988	Hou-N	7	16	1	3	0	1	0	1	0	1	.188	.188	.313	.500	44	-1	-1	93	80	1	.385	0	0	0	0	/O	0.0
DAVE DREW Drew, David Deb: 5/14/1884																												
1884	Phi-U	2	9	1	4	0	0	0		0		.444	.444	.444	.889	217	1	1	93	0	2	.800	0			0	/P2S	0.1
	Was-U	13	53	8	16	1	2	0		1		.302	.315	.396	.711	144	2	2	97	0	7	.595	0			0	/S1O	0.2
	Yr	15	62	9	20	1	2	0		1		.323	.333	.403	.737	154	3	3	96	0	9	.619	0			0		0.3
Total	1	15	62	9	20	1	2	0		1		.323	.333	.403	.737	154	3	3	96	0	9	.619	0			0	/S1O2P	0.3
FRANK DREWS Drews, Frank John b: 5/25/16, Buffalo, N.Y. d: 4/22/72, Buffalo, N.Y. BR/TR, 5'10", 175 lbs. Deb: 8/13/44																												
1944	Bos-N	46	141	14	29	9	1	0	10	25	14	.206	.329	.284	.613	78	-4	-3	95	90	15	.574	0			6	2	0.8
1945	Bos-N	49	147	13	30	4	1	0	19	16	18	.204	.282	.245	.527	42	-10	-13	112	183	12	.444	0			-3	2	-1.1
Total	2	95	288	27	59	13	2	0	29	41	32	.205	.306	.264	.570	58	-14	-16	103	136	26	.515	0			4	/2	-0.3
DAN DRIESSEN Driessen, Daniel b: 7/29/51, Hilton Head, S.C. BL/TR, 5'11", 187 lbs. Deb: 6/09/73																												
1973	Cin-N	102	366	49	110	15	2	4	47	24	37	.301	.347	.385	.732	110	1	4	93	123	48	.655	8	3	1	1	31/O	0.3
1974	Cin-N	150	470	63	132	23	6	7	56	48	62	.281	.349	.400	.749	111	6	7	98	103	66	.702	10	5	0	-15	*31/O	-1.3
1975	Cin-N	88	210	38	59	8	1	7	38	35	30	.281	.389	.429	.817	121	9	7	104	132	36	.846	10	3	1	-6	1O	0.0
1976	Cin-N	98	219	32	54	11	1	7	44	43	32	.247	.370	.402	.772	116	7	6	103	155	35	.819	14	1	4	-4	1O	0.3
1977	Cin-N	151	536	75	161	31	4	17	91	64	85	.300	.378	.468	.846	126	20	20	100	123	95	.873	31	13	2	-3	*1	1.1
1978	Cin-N	153	524	68	131	23	3	16	70	75	79	.250	.348	.397	.745	105	7	5	103	111	76	.759	28	9	3	2	*1	0.5
1979	Cin-N	150	515	72	129	24	3	18	75	62	77	.250	.334	.414	.748	106	2	4	97	114	74	.728	11	5	0	-5	*1	-0.7
1980	Cin-N	154	524	81	139	36	1	14	74	**93**	68	.265	.382	.418	.800	121	20	18	102	115	88	.832	19	6	2	-3	*1	1.1
1981	Cin-N	82	233	35	55	14	0	7	33	40	31	.236	.353	.386	.739	108	4	4	101	117	33	.717	2	4	-2	-4	1	-0.5
1982	Cin-N	149	516	64	139	25	1	17	57	82	62	.269	.372	.421	.792	118	17	15	102	85	85	.798	11	6	-0	-6	*1	0.2
1983	Cin-N	122	386	57	107	17	1	12	57	75	51	.277	.395	.420	.814	122	16	15	103	116	66	.824	6	4	-1	-6	*1	0.3
1984	Cin-N	81	218	27	61	13	0	7	28	37	25	.280	.384	.436	.820	123	10	8	106	95	38	.822	2	1	0	-5	1	0.1
	Mon-N	51	169	20	43	11	0	9	32	17	15	.254	.323	.479	.802	134	4	6	91	116	24	.742	0	1	-1	2	1	0.7
	Yr	132	387	47	104	24	0	16	60	54	40	.269	.358	.455	.813	127	14	14	100	104	65	.800	2	2	-1	-3		0.8
1985	Mon-N	91	312	31	78	18	0	6	25	33	29	.250	.326	.365	.691	99	-3	-0	94	77	36	.619	2	2	-1	5	1	0.1
	SF-N	54	181	22	42	8	0	3	22	17	22	.232	.302	.326	.627	81	-6	-4	93	131	19	.546	0	0	0	-1	1	-0.7
	Yr	145	493	53	120	26	0	9	47	50	51	.243	.317	.351	.668	93	-9	-5	93	98	58	.605	2	2	-1	4		-0.6
1986	SF-N	15	16	2	3	2	0	0	0	4	4	.188	.350	.313	.663	88	-0	-0	96	0	2	.692	0	0	0	0	/1	0.0
	Hou-N	17	24	5	7	1	0	1	3	5	2	.292	.414	.458	.872	137	2	1	103	85	5	.941	0	0	0	0	1	0.1
	Yr	32	40	7	10	3	0	1	3	9	6	.250	.388	.400	.788	118	1	1	99	45	7	.833	0	0	0	0		0.1
1987	StL-N	24	60	5	14	2	0	1	11	7	8	.233	.313	.317	.630	69	-3	-3	99	200	6	.542	0	0	0	-1	1	-0.4
Total	15	1732	5479	746	1464	282	23	153	763	761	719	.267	.359	.411	.770	114	111	113	100	112	830	.783	154	63	8	-47	*13/O	1.2
LEW DRILL Drill, Lewis L b: 5/9/1877, Browerville, Minn. d: 7/4/69, St.Paul, Minn. BR/TR, 5'6", 186 lbs. Deb: 4/23/02																												
1902	Was-A	38	123	21	34	7	2	1	16	16		.276	.360	.390	.750	111	2	2	99	105	18	.719	0			-1	C/2O3	0.3
	Bal-A	2	8	2	2	0	0	0	0	0		.250	.250	.250	.500	39	-1	-1	102	0	1	.333	0			0	/C1	0.0

YEAR	TM/L	G	AB	R	H	2B	3B	HR	RBI	BB	SO	AVG	OBP	SLG	PRO	/A	BR	/A	PF	CHI	RC	TA	SB	CS	SBR	FR	POS	TPR
	Was-A	33	98	12	24	3	2	0	13	10		.245	.315	.316	.631	78	-3	-3	99	138	12	.622	5			-1	C/O2	-0.1
	Yr	73	229	35	60	10	4	1	29	26		.262	.337	.354	.691	95	-2	-1	99	119	30	.663	5			-2		0.2
1903	Was-A	51	154	11	39	9	3	0	23	15		.253	.320	.351	.670	98	1	-0	105	153	19	.635	4			-0	C/1	0.5
1904	Was-A	46	142	17	38	7	2	1	11	21		.268	.362	.366	.728	144	6	7	93	76	20	.731	3			3	C1	1.5
	Det-A	51	160	7	39	6	1	0	13	20		.244	.328	.294	.622	105	1	2	96	105	16	.570	2			2	C/1	0.9
	Yr	97	302	24	77	13	3	1	24	41		.255	.344	.328	.672	123	7	9	94	92	37	.644	5			5		2.4
1905	Det-A	72	211	17	55	9	0	0	24	32		.261	.358	.303	.661	115	5	5	98	134	26	.660	7			1	C	1.5
Total	4	293	896	87	231	41	10	2	100	114		.258	.342	.333	.674	109	11	13	98	118	112	.651	21			3	C/1O23	4.6
■ **JIM DRISCOLL** Driscoll, James Bernard b: 5/14/44, Medford, Mass. BL/TR, 5'11", 175 lbs. Deb: 6/17/70																												
1970	Oak-A	21	52	2	10	0	0	1	2	2	15	.192	.236	.250	.486	35	-5	-4	97	51	3	.372	0	0	0	-1	/2S	-0.3
1972	Tex-A	15	18	0	0	0	0	0	0	2	3	.000	.100	.000	.100	-73	-4	-4	94	0	0	.105	0	0	0	0	/23	-0.3
Total	2	36	70	2	10	0	0	1	2	4	18	.143	.200	.186	.386	9	-8	-8	96	37	3	.295	0	0	0	-1	/2S3	-0.6
■ **PADDY DRISCOLL** Driscoll, John Leo b: 1/11/1895, Evanston, Ill. d: 6/29/68, Chicago, Ill. BR/TR, 5'8.5", 155 lbs. Deb: 6/12/17																												
1917	Chi-N	13	28	2	3	1	0	0	3	2	6	.107	.167	.143	.310	-4	-3	-4	105	289	1	.320	2			0	/23S	-0.2
■ **MIKE DRISSEL** Drissel, Michael F. b: 12/19/1864, St.Louis, Mo. d: 2/26/13, St.Louis, Mo. BR/TR, 5'11", Deb: 1885																												
1885	StL-a	6	20	0	1	0	0	0		0		.050	.050	.050	.100	-73	-4	-3	93	0	0	.053				0	/C	-0.2
■ **WALT DROPO** Dropo, Walter "Moose" b: 1/23, Moosup, Conn. BR/TR, 6'5", 220 lbs. Deb: 4/19/49																												
1949	Bos-A	11	41	3	6	2	0	0	1	3	7	.146	.205	.195	.400	6	-6	-6	107	43	1	.297	0	0	0	-0	1	-0.5
1950	Bos-A	136	559	101	180	28	8	34	**144**	45	75	.322	.378	.583	.961	125	32	20	114	123	122	.952	0	0	0	-4	*1	0.9
1951	Bos-A	99	360	37	86	14	0	11	57	38	52	.239	.312	.369	.681	78	-9	-13	108	123	40	.590	0	0	0	-4	1	-1.7
1952	Bos-A	37	132	13	35	7	1	6	27	11	22	.265	.331	.470	.801	113	3	2	107	129	18	.708	0	0	0	-0	1	0.0
	Det-A	115	459	56	128	17	3	23	70	26	63	.279	.320	.479	.800	122	9	10	99	96	66	.714	2	2	-1	0	*1	0.2
	Yr	152	591	69	163	24	4	29	97	37	85	.276	.323	.477	.800	119	12	12	101	105	88	.727	2	2	-1	0		0.2
1953	Det-A	152	606	61	150	30	3	13	96	29	69	.248	.289	.371	.660	79	-22	-20	98	**143**	61	.548	2	0	1	12	*1	-1.0
1954	Det-A	107	320	27	90	14	2	4	44	24	41	.281	.331	.375	.706	93	-3	-3	100	126	37	.590	0	1	-1	1	1	-0.5
1955	Chi-A	141	453	55	127	15	2	19	79	42	71	.280	.344	.448	.792	111	6	5	101	113	66	.722	0	1	-1	-7	*1	-0.8
1956	Chi-A	125	361	42	96	13	1	8	52	37	51	.266	.339	.374	.713	85	-6	-8	104	122	44	.629	1	0	0	-5	*1	-1.6
1957	Chi-A	93	223	24	57	2	0	13	49	16	40	.256	.305	.439	.745	102	-1	-0	99	141	26	.644	0	1	-1	-3	1	-0.4
1958	Chi-A	28	52	3	10	1	0	2	8	5	11	.192	.276	.327	.603	66	-3	-2	98	139	4	.511	0	0	0	-0	1	-0.2
	Cin-N	63	162	18	47	7	2	7	31	12	31	.290	.343	.488	.831	109	3	2	107	128	25	.754	0	0	0	0	1	0.0
1959	Cin-N	26	39	4	4	1	0	1	2	4	7	.103	.205	.205	.410	9	-5	-5	103	73	1	.342	0	0	0	0	1	-0.6
	Bal-A	62	151	17	42	9	0	6	21	12	20	.278	.331	.457	.788	118	2	3	97	95	21	.704	0	0	0	-4	1/3	0.0
1960	Bal-A	79	179	16	48	8	0	4	21	20	19	.268	.345	.380	.725	94	-1	-1	102	103	22	.631	0	1	-1	-2	1/3	-0.8
1961	Bal-A	14	27	1	7	0	0	1	2	4	3	.259	.355	.370	.725	97	-0	-0	97	60	3	.609	0	0	0	0	1	0.0
Total	13	1288	4124	478	1113	168	22	152	704	328	582	.270	.327	.432	.759	100	0	-18	103	120	559	.708	5	6	-2	-15	*1/3	-7.0
■ **KEITH DRUMRIGHT** Drumright, Keith Alan b: 10/21/54, Springfield, Mo. BL/TR, 5'10", 170 lbs. Deb: 9/01/78																												
1978	Hou-N	17	55	5	9	0	0	0	2	3	4	.164	.207	.164	.371	5	-7	-7	95	88	2	.245	0	1	-1	-1	2	-0.7
1981	Oak-A	31	86	8	25	1	1	0	11	4	4	.291	.322	.326	.648	91	-1	-1	96	154	9	.500	0	0	0	-4	2/D	-0.4
Total	2	48	141	13	34	1	1	0	13	7	8	.241	.277	.262	.539	57	-8	-8	95	128	10	.396	0	1	-1	-5	/2D	-1.1
■ **JEAN DUBUC** Dubuc, Jean Joseph Octave Arthur "Chauncey" b: 9/15/1888, St.Johnsbury, Vt. d: 8/28/58, Fort Myers, Fla. BR/TR, 5'10.5", 185 lbs. Deb: 6/25/08 C																												
1908	Cin-N	15	29	2	4	1	0	0	2	0		.138	.138	.172	.310	-0	-3	-3	103	154	1	.200	0			1	P	0.0
1909	Cin-N	19	18	1	3	0	0	0	0	2		.167	.250	.167	.417	32	-1	-1	94	0	1	.333	0			0	P	0.0
1912	Det-A	40	108	16	29	6	2	1	9	3		.269	.295	.389	.684	100	-1	-1	95	67	12	.582	0			4	P/O	0.0
1913	Det-A	68	135	17	36	5	3	2	11	2	17	.267	.277	.393	.670	97	-2	-2	99	66	14	.566	1			6	P/O	0.0
1914	Det-A	70	124	9	28	8	1	1	11	7	11	.226	.273	.331	.603	80	-3	-4	102	94	12	.521	1			3	P	0.0
1915	Det-A	60	112	7	23	2	1	0	14	8	15	.205	.258	.241	.499	46	-7	-8	108	176	7	.393	0			1	P	0.0
1916	Det-A	52	78	3	20	0	2	0	7	7	12	.256	.318	.308	.625	84	-1	-2	105	104	8	.534	0			4	P	0.0
1918	Bos-A	5	6	0	1	0	0	0	0	1	2	.167	.286	.167	.452	38	-0	-0	95	0	0	.400	0			0	/P	0.0
1919	NY-N	37	42	2	6	1	1	0	2	0	6	.143	.143	.214	.357	7	-5	-5	100	86	1	.250	0			2	P	0.0
Total	9	366	652	57	150	23	10	4	56	30	63	.230	.266	.314	.580	72	-25	-26	101	98	56	.476	2			21	P/O	0.0
■ **ROB DUCEY** Ducey, Robert Thomas b: 5/24/65, Toronto, Ont., Can. BL/TR, 6'2", 175 lbs. Deb: 5/01/87																												
1987	Tor-A	34	48	12	9	1	0	1	6	8	10	.188	.304	.271	.574	54	-3	-3	101	150	5	.590	2	0	1	-6	O/D	-0.7
1988	Tor-A	27	54	15	17	4	1	0	6	5	7	.315	.373	.426	.799	124	2	2	100	104	9	.763	1	0	0	-4	O	-0.1
Total	2	61	102	27	26	5	1	1	12	13	17	.255	.339	.353	.692	89	-1	-1	100	126	14	.675	3	0	1	-9	/OD	-0.8
■ **JOHN DUDRA** Dudra, John Joseph b: 5/27/16, Assumption, Ill. d: 10/24/65, Pana, Ill. BR/TR, 5'11.5", 175 lbs. Deb: 9/07/41																												
1941	Bos-N	14	25	3	9	3	1	0	3	3	4	.360	.429	.560	.989	190	3	3	93	77	6	1.063	0			-0	/231S	0.3
■ **PAT DUFF** Duff, Patrick Henry b: 5/6/1875, Providence, R.I. d: 9/11/25, Providence, R.I. TR , Deb: 4/16/06																												
1906	Was-A	1	1	0	0	0	0	0	0	0		.000	.000	.000	.000	-99	-0	-0	91	0	0	.000	0			0	H	0.0
■ **CHARLIE DUFFEE** Duffee, Charles Edward "Home Run" b: 1/27/1866, Mobile, Ala. d: 12/24/1894, Mobile, Ala. BR , Deb: 4/17/1889																												
1889	StL-a	137	509	93	124	15	12	15	86	60	81	.244	.327	.409	.736	99	6	-5	112	99	77	.758	21			17	*O/32	0.6
1890	StL-a	98	378	68	104	11	7	3		37		.275	.343	.365	.708	96	5	-5	116	0	56	.719	20			9	O3/S	0.1
1891	Col-a	137	552	86	166	28	4	10	90	42	36	.301	.353	.420	.774	139	15	25	89	95	99	.824	41			11	*O/3S	2.6
1892	Was-N	132	492	64	122	12	11	6	51	36	33	.248	.302	.354	.656	95	-1	-5	105	83	63	.649	28			15	*O/31	0.6
1893	Cin-N	4	12	3	2	1	0	0	0	5	0	.167	.412	.250	.662	78	-0	-0	101	0	1	.800	0			0	/O	0.0
Total	5	508	1943	314	518	67	34	34	227	180	150	.267	.332	.389	.721	107	25	11	105	74	295	.740	110			52	O/31S2	3.9
■ **ED DUFFY** Duffy, Edward Charles b: 1844, Ireland 5'7.5", 152 lbs. Deb: 5/08/1871																												
1871	Chi-n	25	121	31	28							.231															S/3	
■ **FRANK DUFFY** Duffy, Frank Thomas b: 10/14/46, Oakland, Cal. BR/TR, 6'1", 180 lbs. Deb: 9/04/70																												
1970	Cin-N	6	11	1	2	2	0	0	0	1	2	.182	.250	.364	.614	60	-1	-1	104	0	1	.667	1	0	0	0	/S	0.0
1971	Cin-N	13	16	0	3	1	0	0	1	1	2	.188	.235	.250	.485	39	-1	-1	96	102	1	.385	0	0	0	-0	S	0.0
	SF-N	21	28	4	5	0	0	0	2	0	10	.179	.179	.179	.357	1	-4	-4	100	163	1	.208	0	0	0	-0	/S23	-0.2
	Yr	34	44	4	8	1	0	0	3	1	12	.182	.200	.205	.405	15	-5	-5	98	142	2	.270	0	0	0	-0		-0.2
1972	Cle-A	130	385	23	92	16	4	3	27	31	54	.239	.297	.325	.622	79	-7	-10	107	84	36	.531	6	2	1	-6	*S	-0.2
1973	Cle-A	116	361	34	95	16	4	8	50	25	41	.263	.314	.396	.711	102	-1	-0	97	118	41	.620	6	6	-2	1	*S	1.5
1974	Cle-A	158	549	62	128	18	0	8	48	30	64	.233	.273	.310	.583	67	-24	-24	101	99	45	.472	7	8	-3	-12	*S	-2.8
1975	Cle-A	146	482	44	117	22	2	1	47	27	60	.243	.286	.303	.589	67	-22	-21	100	121	39	.478	10	10	-3	14	*S	0.4
1976	Cle-A	133	392	38	83	11	2	2	30	29	50	.212	.270	.265	.535	57	-21	-21	100	105	29	.450	10	0	3	-3	*S	-1.4
1977	Cle-A	122	334	30	67	13	2	4	31	21	47	.201	.248	.287	.535	47	-26	-24	98	114	24	.450	8	3	1	-15	*S	-2.4
1978	Bos-A	64	104	12	27	5	0	0	4	6	11	.260	.306	.308	.614	68	-4	-5	107	49	10	.506	1	1	-0	1	3S2/D	0.0
1979	Bos-A	6	3	0	0	0	0	0	0	0	1	.000	.000	.000	.000	-93	-1	-1	107	0	0	.000	0	0	0	0	/21	0.0
Total	10	915	2665	248	619	104	14	26	240	171	342	.232	.281	.311	.592	68	-111	-112	101	104	227	.509	49	30	-3	-21	S/32D1	-5.1
■ **HUGH DUFFY** Duffy, Hugh b: 11/26/1866, Cranston, R.I. d: 10/19/54, Boston, Mass. BR/TR, 5'7", 168 lbs. Deb: 1888 MCH																												
1888	Chi-N	71	298	60	84	10	4	7	41	9	32	.282	.305	.413	.718	121	9	6	107	90	43	.682	13			5	O/S3	1.0
1889	Chi-N	136	584	144	172	21	7	12	89	46	30	.295	.348	.416	.764	116	10	11	99	84	105	.833	52			-8	*OS	-0.1
1890	Chi-P	138	596	**161**	**191**	36	16	7	82	59	20	.320	.384	.470	.853	124	24	19	104	66	**141**	1.035	78			12	*O	2.0
1891	Bos-a	127	536	134	180	20	8	8	108	61	29	.336	.408	.448	.855	150	34	35	99	104	136	1.096	85			-3	*O/3S	2.3
1892	Bos-N	147	612	125	184	28	12	5	81	60	37	.301	.364	.410	.774	120	26	14	113	83	113	.848	51			-12	*O/3	-0.1
1893	Bos-N	131	560	147	203	23	7	6	118	50	13	.363	.416	.461	.876	131	28	25	103	113	129	.989	44			-5	*O	1.3

YEAR	TM/L	G	AB	R	H	2B	3B	HR	RBI	BB	SO	AVG	OBP	SLG	PRO	/A	BR	/A	PF	CHI	RC	TA	SB	CS	SBR	FR	POS	TPR
1894	Bos-N	125	539	161	**237**	**51**	15	**18**	**145**	66	15	**.440**	.502	**.690**	**1.192**	165	**77**	62	113	90	**216**	**1.613**	48			3	*O/S	4.3
1895	Bos-N	130	531	110	187	30	6	9	100	63	16	.352	.425	.482	.907	132	30	27	103	95	130	1.061	42			2	*O	1.4
1896	Bos-N	131	527	97	158	16	8	5	112	52	19	.300	.365	.389	.754	93	1	-6	108	156	91	.808	39			3	*O/2S	-0.9
1897	Bos-N	134	550	130	187	25	10	**11**	129	52		.340	.403	.482	.885	126	28	21	107	134	126	1.003	41			-1	*O/2S	0.9
1898	Bos-N	152	568	97	169	13	3	8	108	59		.298	.365	.373	.738	110	12	9	104	147	90	.754	29			2	*O/31C	0.1
1899	Bos-N	147	588	103	164	29	7	5	102	39		.279	.327	.378	.705	91	-5	-9	105	140	83	.684	26			-7	*O	-2.3
1900	Bos-N	55	181	27	55	5	4	2	31	16		.304	.360	.409	.769	95	4	-2	120	121	31	.802	11			-2	O/2	-0.7
1901	Mil-A	79	285	40	86	15	9	2	45	16		.302	.339	.439	.777	122	5	8	95	111	48	.769	12			-18	OM	-0.9
1904	Phi-N	18	46	10	13	1	1	0	5	13		.283	.441	.348	.789	159	4	4	93	114	9	.970	3			1	OM	0.4
1905	Phi-N	15	40	7	12	2	1	0	3	1		.300	.317	.400	.717	110	1	0	104	65	5	.607	0			0	/OM	0.0
1906	Phi-N	1	1	0	0	0	0	0	0	0		.000	.000	.000	.000	-99	-0	-0	92	0	0	.000	0			0	HM	0.0
Total	17	1737	7042	1553	2282	325	118	105	1299	662	211	.324	.384	.448	.833	123	286	225	105	109	1495	.929	574			-28	*O/S23C1	8.7
■ **JOE DUGAN**	Dugan, Joseph Anthony "Jumping Joe" b: 5/12/1897, Mahanoy City, Pa. d: 7/7/82, Norwood, Mass. BR/TR, 5'11", 160 lbs. Deb: 7/05/17																											
1917	Phi-A	43	134	9	26	8	0	0	16	3	16	.194	.229	.254	.482	50	-9	-8	94	169	8	.370	0			1	S/2	-0.5
1918	Phi-A	121	411	26	80	11	3	3	34	16	55	.195	.230	.258	.488	45	-28	-30	104	110	25	.390	4			7	S2	-1.6
1919	Phi-A	104	387	25	105	17	2	1	30	11	30	.271	.300	.333	.634	74	-12	-15	106	84	40	.546	9			2	S/23	-0.3
1920	Phi-A	123	491	65	158	40	5	3	60	19	51	.322	.351	.442	.793	116	5	9	94	99	73	.716	5	8	-3	3	3S2	1.5
1921	Phi-A	119	461	54	136	22	6	10	58	28	45	.295	.342	.434	.776	94	-4	-6	103	92	69	.730	5	1	1	-19	*3	-1.3
1922	Bos-A	84	341	45	98	22	3	3	38	9	28	.287	.308	.396	.704	85	-10	-8	96	100	40	.598	2	3	-1	-6	3S	-0.6
	NY-A	60	252	44	72	9	1	3	25	13	21	.286	.331	.365	.696	80	-7	-8	102	76	31	.611	1	0	0	-7	3	-0.7
	Yr	144	593	89	170	31	4	6	63	22	49	.287	.318	.383	.701	83	-17	-16	98	91	72	.603	3	3	-1	-13		-1.3
1923	NY-A	146	644	111	182	30	7	7	67	25	41	.283	.311	.384	.695	79	-19	-23	104	75	76	.599	4	2	0	-11	*3	-1.5
1924	NY-A	148	610	105	184	31	7	3	56	31	32	.302	.341	.390	.731	89	-12	-11	99	66	81	.641	1	3	-2	-10	*3/2	-0.9
1925	NY-A	102	404	50	118	19	4	0	31	19	20	.292	.330	.359	.689	78	-16	-14	96	76	47	.586	2	4	-2	0	3	-0.8
1926	NY-A	123	434	39	125	19	5	1	64	25	16	.288	.328	.362	.690	80	-13	-13	99	136	52	.591	2	4	-2	-15	*3	-1.7
1927	NY-A	112	387	44	104	24	3	2	43	27	37	.269	.321	.362	.683	77	-14	-14	100	98	45	.604	1	0	0	-15	*3	-1.9
1928	NY-A	94	312	33	86	15	0	6	34	16	15	.276	.317	.381	.699	90	-8	-5	92	85	38	.615	1	0	0	-14	3/2	-1.6
1929	Bos-N	60	125	14	38	10	0	0	15	8	8	.304	.346	.384	.730	86	-4	-3	94	107	16	.644	0			-3	3/S2O	-0.2
1931	Det-A	8	17	1	4	0	0	0	0	0	3	.235	.235	.235	.471	23	-2	-2	104	0	1	.308	0	0	0	0	/3	0.0
Total	14	1447	5410	665	1516	277	46	42	571	250	418	.280	.317	.372	.689	82	-154	-150	100	93	642	.597	37	25		-86	*3S/2O	-12.1
■ **BILL DUGAN**	Dugan, William H. b: 1864, Kingston, N.Y. Deb: 8/05/1884																											
1884	Ric-a	9	28	4	2	1	0	0		0		.071	.103	.107	.211	-31	-4	-4	99	0	0	.154				0	/C	-0.2
	KC-U	3	6	0	0	0	0	0		0		.000	.000	.000	.000	-99	-1	-1	87	0	0	.000	0			0	/O	0.0
Total	1	12	34	4	2	1	0	0		0		.059	.086	.088	.174	-44	-5	-5	97	0	0	.125	0			0	/CO	-0.2
■ **GUS DUGAS**	Dugas, Augustin Joseph b: 3/24/07, St.Jean Dematha, Que., Canada BL/TL, 5'9", 165 lbs. Deb: 9/17/30																											
1930	Pit-N	9	31	8	9	2	0	0	1	7	4	.290	.421	.355	.776	93	-0	0	97	33	5	.818	0			-1	/O	0.0
1932	Pit-N	55	97	13	23	3	3	3	12	7	11	.237	.288	.423	.711	89	-2	-2	99	89	12	.649	0			-3	O	-0.5
1933	Phi-N	37	71	4	12	3	0	0	9	1	9	.169	.181	.211	.392	10	-8	-10	118	226	2	.262	0			0	1/O	-0.9
1934	Was-A	24	19	2	1	1	0	0	1	3	3	.053	.182	.105	.287	-24	-4	-4	101	167	0	.278	0	0	0	-0	/O	-0.3
Total	4	125	218	27	45	9	3	3	23	18	27	.206	.267	.317	.583	53	-14	-15	105	129	20	.503	0	0		-4	/O1	-1.7
■ **DAN DUGDALE**	Dugdale, Daniel Edward b: 10/28/1864, Peoria, Ill. d: 3/9/34, Seattle, Wash. Deb: 5/20/1886																											
1886	KC-N	12	40	4	7	0	0	0	2	2	13	.175	.214	.175	.389	18	-4	-4	107	93	2	.303	1			0	/CO	-0.3
1894	Was-N	38	134	19	32	4	2	0	16	13	14	.239	.306	.299	.605	49	-11	-11	98	110	15	.588	7			-5	C/3O	-0.9
Total	2	50	174	23	39	4	2	0	18	15	27	.224	.286	.270	.556	42	-15	-15	100	106	17	.519	8			-5	/CO3	-1.2
■ **OSCAR DUGEY**	Dugey, Oscar Joseph "Jake" b: 10/25/1887, Palestine, Tex. d: 1/1/66, Dallas, Tex. BR/TR, 5'8", 160 lbs. Deb: 9/13/13 C																											
1913	Bos-N	5	8	1	2	0	0	0	0	1	1	.250	.333	.250	.583	72	-0	-0	95	0	1	.500	0			0	/32S	0.0
1914	Bos-N	58	109	17	21	2	0	1	10	10	15	.193	.267	.239	.505	49	-7	-7	104	125	9	.534	10			-1	O2/3	-0.8
1915	Phi-N	42	39	4	6	1	0	0	0	7	5	.154	.283	.179	.462	38	-2	-3	107	0	2	.471	2	1	0	0	2	-0.2
1916	Phi-N	41	50	9	11	3	0	0	1	9	8	.220	.339	.280	.619	95	-0	0	96	28	6	.667	3			0	2	0.1
1917	Phi-N	44	72	12	14	4	1	0	9	4	9	.194	.237	.278	.515	53	-4	-4	108	174	5	.448	2			3	2/O	0.0
1920	Bos-N	5	0	2	0	0	0	0	0	0	0	—	—	—	—	—	0	0	96	—	—	—	0	0	0	0	R	0.0
Total	6	195	278	45	54	10	1	1	20	31	38	.194	.277	.248	.526	57	-13	-14	104	96	28	.524	17	1		2	/2O3S	-0.9
■ **JIM DUGGAN**	Duggan, James Elmer "Mer" b: 6/3/1884, Whiteland, Ind. d: 12/5/51, Indianapolis, Ind. BL/TL, 5'10", 165 lbs. Deb: 6/29/11																											
1911	StL-A	1	4	1	0	0	0	0	0	1	1	.000	.200	.000	.200	-45	-1	-1	95	0	0	.250	0			0	/1	0.0
■ **TOM DUNBAR**	Dunbar, Thomas Jerome b: 11/24/59, Graniteville, S.C. BL/TL, 6'2", 192 lbs. Deb: 9/07/83																											
1983	Tex-A	12	24	3	6	0	0	0	3	5	7	.250	.379	.250	.629	76	-0	-0	101	195	3	.700	3	1	0	-3	/OD	-0.2
1984	Tex-A	34	97	9	25	2	0	2	10	6	16	.258	.301	.340	.641	77	-3	-3	100	102	10	.548	1	0	0	-3	O/D	-0.6
1985	Tex-A	45	104	7	21	4	0	1	5	12	9	.202	.291	.269	.560	50	-6	-7	108	64	7	.451	0	3	-2	-4	DO	-1.2
Total	3	91	225	19	52	6	0	3	18	23	32	.231	.305	.298	.603	64	-10	-11	104	95	20	.522	4	4	-1	-10	/OD	-2.0
■ **DAVE DUNCAN**	Duncan, David Edwin b: 9/26/45, Dallas, Tex. BR/TR, 6'2", 190 lbs. Deb: 5/06/64 C																											
1964	KC-A	25	53	2	9	0	1	1	5	2	20	.170	.200	.264	.464	27	-5	-5	105	125	3	.356	0	0	0	-1	C	-0.5
1967	KC-A	34	101	9	19	4	0	5	11	4	50	.188	.219	.376	.595	73	-4	-4	100	87	8	.500	0	1	-1	-2	C	-0.4
1968	Oak-A	82	246	15	47	4	0	7	28	25	68	.191	.268	.293	.561	71	-9	-8	98	129	19	.478	1	2	-1	-9	C	-1.6
1969	Oak-A	58	127	11	16	3	0	3	22	19	41	.126	.240	.220	.460	32	-12	-11	92	239	7	.416	0	0	0	-11	C	-1.9
1970	Oak-A	86	232	21	60	7	0	10	29	22	38	.259	.323	.418	.741	106	0	1	97	92	31	.672	0	0	0	3	C	0.6
1971	Oak-A	103	363	39	92	13	1	15	40	28	77	.253	.309	.419	.727	104	1	1	101	84	47	.655	1	1	-0	1	*C	0.6
1972	Oak-A	121	403	39	88	13	0	19	59	34	68	.218	.287	.392	.679	104	-1	1	97	115	43	.597	0	2	-1	2	*C	0.3
1973	Cle-A	95	344	43	80	11	1	17	43	35	86	.233	.309	.419	.728	106	1	2	97	88	44	.678	3	3	-1	4	C/D	0.7
1974	Cle-A	136	425	45	85	10	1	16	46	42	91	.200	.275	.341	.616	76	-14	-14	101	94	38	.531	0	4	-2	0	*C/1D	-1.2
1975	Bal-A	96	307	30	63	7	0	12	41	16	82	.205	.247	.345	.592	73	-15	-12	91	111	25	.488	0	0	0	-4	C	-1.2
1976	Bal-A	93	284	20	58	7	0	4	17	25	56	.204	.271	.271	.542	60	-15	-14	98	73	21	.440	0	0	0	3	C	-0.7
Total	11	929	2885	274	617	79	4	109	341	252	677	.214	.280	.357	.638	84	-72	-64	97	105	285	.569	5	13	-6	-14	C/D1	-5.3
■ **JIM DUNCAN**	Duncan, James William b: 7/1/1871, Saltsburg, Pa. d: 10/16/01, Foxburg, Pa. BR/TR, 5'8", 140 lbs. Deb: 7/18/1899																											
1899	Was-N	15	47	5	11	2	0	0	5	4		.234	.294	.277	.571	62	-3	-2	96	118	4	.500	1			0	C	-0.1
	Cle-N	31	105	9	24	2	3	2	9	4		.229	.257	.362	.619	79	-5	-3	89	63	10	.519	0			0	1C	-0.2
	Yr	46	152	14	35	4	3	2	14	8		.230	.269	.336	.604	74	-7	-5	91	83	14	.513	1			0		-0.3
Total	1	46	152	14	35	4	3	2	14	8		.230	.269	.336	.604	74	-7	-5	91	80	14	.513	1			0	/C1	-0.3
■ **PAT DUNCAN**	Duncan, Louis Baird b: 10/6/1893, Coalton, Ohio d: 7/17/60, Columbus, Ohio BR/TR, 5'10", 170 lbs. Deb: 7/16/15																											
1915	Pit-N	3	5	0	1	0	0	0	0	0	1	.200	.200	.200	.400	21	-0	-0	99	0	0	.250	0			-0	/O	0.0
1919	Cin-N	31	90	9	22	3	3	2	17	8	7	.244	.306	.411	.717	109	1	1	105	154	12	.691	2			-1	O	-0.1
1920	Cin-N	154	576	75	170	16	11	2	83	42	42	.295	.350	.372	.722	120	6	13	90	155	74	.663	18	18	-5	3	*O	0.2
1921	Cin-N	145	532	57	164	27	10	2	60	44	33	.308	.367	.408	.775	104	4	4	101	105	76	.707	7	18	-9	9	*O	-0.1
1922	Cin-N	151	607	94	199	44	12	8	94	40	31	.328	.370	.479	.850	123	14	18	96	100	97	.789	12	28	-13	1	*O	0.0
1923	Cin-N	147	566	92	185	26	8	7	83	30	27	.327	.363	.438	.801	113	8	10	98	115	87	.749	15	13	-3	-5	*O	-0.3
1924	Cin-N	96	319	34	86	21	6	2	37	20	23	.270	.313	.392	.705	87	-6	-6	101	103	37	.608	1	7	-4	-16	O	-2.8
Total	7	727	2695	361	827	137	50	23	374	184	164	.307	.355	.420	.775	111	27	39	97	118	383	.711	55	84		-10	O	-3.1
■ **MARIANO DUNCAN**	Duncan, Mariano (Nalasco) b: 3/13/63, San Pedro De Macoris, D.R. BB/TR, 6', 160 lbs. Deb: 4/09/85																											
1985	LA-N	142	562	74	137	24	6	6	39	38	113	.244	.295	.340	.635	83	-18	-13	93	79	60	.611	38	8	7	1	*S2	0.4
1986	LA-N	109	407	47	93	7	0	8	30	30	78	.229	.285	.305	.589	66	-21	-18	94	86	38	.613	48	13	7	-1	*S	-0.1

YEAR	TM/L	G	AB	R	H	2B	3B	HR	RBI	BB	SO	AVG	OBP	SLG	PRO	/A	BR	/A	PF	CHI	RC	TA	SB	CS	SBR	FR	POS	TPR
1987	LA-N	76	261	31	56	8	1	6	18	17	62	.215	.268	.322	.590	60	-17	-14	92	72	24	.543	11	1	3	1	S/2O	-0.2
Total	3	327	1230	152	286	39	7	20	87	85	253	.233	.286	.324	.610	73	-56	-45	93	79	122	.606	97	22	16	1	S/2O	0.1
■ **TAYLOR DUNCAN**	Duncan, Taylor Mc Dowell b: 5/12/53, Memphis, Tenn. BR/TR, 6', 170 lbs. Deb: 9/15/77																											
1977	StL-N	8	12	2	4	0	0	1	2	2	1	.333	.429	.583	1.012	176	1	1	96	80	3	1.125	0	0	0	0	/3	0.1
1978	Oak-A	104	319	25	82	15	2	2	37	19	38	.257	.299	.335	.634	77	-10	-10	101	129	32	.520	1	2	-1	-11	32/SD	-2.2
Total	2	112	331	27	86	15	2	3	39	21	39	.260	.304	.344	.648	81	-8	-9	101	127	35	.540	1	2	-1	-11	/32DS	-2.1
■ **VERN DUNCAN**	Duncan, Vernon Van Duke b: 1/6/1890, Clayton, N.C. d: 6/1/54, Daytona Beach, Fla BL/TR, 5'9", 155 lbs. Deb: 9/11/13																											
1913	Phi-N	8	12	3	5	1	0	0	1	0	3	.417	.417	.500	.917	144	1	1	112	61	2	.857	0			-0	/O	0.0
1914	Bal-F	157	557	99	160	20	8	2	53	67	55	.287	.364	.363	.726	109	8	9	99	88	84	.710	13			1	*O/32	0.2
1915	Bal-F	146	531	68	142	18	4	2	43	54	40	.267	.335	.328	.663	90	-1	-6	107	83	71	.635	19			-1	*O3/2	-1.2
Total	3	311	1100	170	307	39	12	4	97	121	98	.279	.351	.347	.698	100	8	3	103	85	157	.675	32			0	O/32	-1.0
■ **GUS DUNDON**	Dundon, Augustus Joseph b: 7/10/1874, Columbus, Ohio d: 9/1/40, Pittsburgh, Pa. BR/TR, 5'10", 165 lbs. Deb: 4/14/04																											
1904	Chi-A	108	373	40	85	9	3	0	36	30		.228	.285	.268	.553	78	-8	-8	99	137	35	.517	19			-17	*2/3S	-2.7
1905	Chi-A	106	364	30	70	7	3	0	22	23		.192	.240	.228	.468	52	-20	-18	97	96	24	.408	14			5	*2/S	-1.4
1906	Chi-A	33	96	7	13	1	0	0	4	11		.135	.224	.146	.370	20	-9	-8	92	104	4	.349	4			-1	2S	-0.9
Total	3	247	833	77	168	17	6	0	62	64		.202	.259	.236	.495	61	-37	-34	97	115	63	.448	37			-13	2/S3	-5.0
■ **SAM DUNGAN**	Dungan, Samuel Morrison b: 1/29/1866, Ferndale, Cal. d: 3/16/39, Santa Ana, Cal. BR, 5'11", 180 lbs. Deb: 4/12/1892																											
1892	Chi-N	113	433	46	123	19	7	0	53	35	19	.284	.346	.360	.706	125	8	13	92	111	61	.684	15			-6	*O	0.3
1893	Chi-N	107	465	86	138	23	7	2	64	29	8	.297	.350	.389	.739	95	-2	-5	104	90	69	.703	11			2	*O	-0.5
1894	Chi-N	10	39	5	9	2	0	0	3	7	1	.231	.348	.282	.630	51	-3	-3	108	80	4	.633	1			0	O	-0.2
	Lou-N	8	32	6	11	1	0	0	3	4	1	.344	.417	.375	.792	107	-0	1	88	61	6	.857	2			0	/O	0.1
	Yr	18	71	11	20	3	0	0	6	11	2	.282	.378	.324	.702	73	-3	-3	99	76	10	.725	3			0		-0.1
1900	Chi-N	6	15	1	4	0	0	0	1	1		.267	.313	.267	.579	68	-1	-1	93	78	1	.455	0			0	/O	0.0
1901	Was-A	138	559	70	179	26	12	1	72	40		.320	.366	.415	.781	120	14	15	99	93	90	.739	9			-1	*O1	1.0
Total	5	382	1543	214	464	71	26	3	196	116	29	.301	.355	.386	.742	110	17	20	98	96	231	.709	38			-5	O/1	0.7
■ **LEE DUNHAM**	Dunham, Leland Huffield b: 6/9/02, Atlanta, Ill. d: 5/11/61, Atlanta, Ill. BL/TL, 5'11", 185 lbs. Deb: 4/17/26																											
1926	Phi-N	5	4	0	1	0	0	0	1	0	1	.250	.250	.250	.500	34	-0	-0	103	346	0	.333	0			0	/1	0.0
■ **FRED DUNLAP**	Dunlap, Frederick C. "Sure Shot" b: 5/21/1859, Philadelphia, Pa. d: 12/1/02, Philadelphia, Pa. BR/TR, 5'8", 165 lbs. Deb: 5/01/1880 M																											
1880	Cle-N	85	373	61	103	**27**	9	4	30	7	32	.276	.289	.429	.718	142	15	15	99	55	47	.619				6	*2	2.4
1881	Cle-N	80	351	60	114	25	4	3	24	18	24	.325	.358	.444	.802	157	20	22	96	44	57	.734				4	*2/3	2.6
1882	Cle-N	84	364	68	102	19	4	0	28	23	26	.280	.323	.354	.677	131	7	13	90	63	43	.580				17	*2M	2.8
1883	Cle-N	93	396	81	129	34	2	4	37	22	21	.326	.361	.452	.813	139	21	19	105	58	66	.753				7	*2/O	1.8
1884	StL-U	101	449	**160**	**185**	39	8	**13**		29		**.412**	**.448**	**.621**	**1.069**	**249**	**72**	**70**	104	0	**128**	**1.167**	0			**25**	*2/OPM	**7.6**
1885	StL-N	106	423	70	114	11	5	2	25	41	24	.270	.334	.333	.667	126	9	14	92	51	48	.589				**20**	*2M	**4.2**
1886	StL-N	71	285	53	76	15	2	3	32	28	30	.267	.332	.365	.697	118	5	7	95	80	38	.665	7			20	2	2.6
	Det-N	51	196	32	56	8	3	4	37	16	21	.286	.340	.418	.758	119	7	4	109	131	33	.793	13			-0	2/O	0.5
	Yr	122	481	85	132	23	5	7	69	44	51	.274	.335	.387	.722	118	11	11	101	102	71	.716	20			20		3.1
1887	Det-N	65	272	60	72	13	10	5	45	25	12	.265	.327	.441	.768	111	4	4	102	99	45	.800	15			16	2/P	1.9
1888	Pit-N	82	321	41	84	12	4	1	36	16	30	.262	.303	.333	.636	111	2	4	95	113	41	.633	24			11	2	1.8
1889	Pit-N	121	451	59	106	19	0	2	65	46	33	.235	.309	.290	.599	78	-18	-9	89	144	48	.580	21			-1	*2M	0.0
1890	Pit-N	17	64	9	11	1	1	0	3	7	6	.172	.264	.219	.483	49	-4	-3	88	69	4	.453	2			0	2	-0.2
	NY-P	1	4	1	2	0	0	0	0	0	0	.500	.500	.500	1.000	156	0	0	109	0	1	1.000	0			0	/2	0.0
1891	Was-a	8	25	4	5	1	1	0	4	5	4	.200	.355	.320	.675	101	0	0	95	147	4	.850	3			0	/2	0.0
Total	12	965	3974	759	1159	224	53	41	366	283	263	.292	.340	.406	.745	135	140	159	97	73	604	.706	85			125	2/OP3	28.0
■ **GRANT DUNLAP**	Dunlap, Grant Lester "Snap" b: 12/20/23, Stockton, Cal. BR/TR, 6'2", 180 lbs. Deb: 4/21/53																											
1953	StL-N	16	17	2	6	0	1	1	3	0	2	.353	.353	.647	1.000	151	1	1	102	84	3	.917	0	0	0	-0	/O	0.1
■ **BILL DUNLAP**	Dunlap, William James b: 5/1/09, Three Rivers, Mass. d: 11/29/80, Reading, Pa. BR/TR, 5'11", 170 lbs. Deb: 9/02/29																											
1929	Bos-N	10	29	6	12	0	1	1	4	4	4	.414	.485	.586	1.071	175	3	3	94	68	8	1.235	0			-2	/O	0.1
1930	Bos-N	16	29	3	2	1	0	0	0	0	6	.069	.069	.103	.172	-61	-7	-7	97	0	0	.111	0			-1	/O	-0.7
Total	2	26	58	9	14	1	1	1	4	4	10	.241	.290	.345	.635	57	-4	-4	95	36	8	.545	0			-2	/O	-0.6
■ **JACK DUNLEAVY**	Dunleavy, John Francis b: 9/14/1879, Harrison, N.J. d: 4/12/44, S.Norwalk, Conn. TL, 5'6", 167 lbs. Deb: 03																											
1903	StL-N	61	193	23	48	3	3	0	10	13		.249	.296	.295	.591	73	-7	-6	96	56	20	.552	10			6	OP	0.1
1904	StL-N	51	172	23	40	7	3	1	14	16		.233	.298	.326	.623	95	-1	-1	99	89	20	.606	8			4	O/P	0.3
1905	StL-N	119	435	52	105	8	8	1	25	55		.241	.327	.303	.630	99	-3	2	91	62	49	.612	15			4	*O/2	-0.2
Total	3	231	800	98	193	18	14	2	49	84		.241	.313	.306	.620	92	-12	-6	94	66	89	.596	33			14	O/P2	0.2
■ **GEORGE DUNLOP**	Dunlop, George Henry b: 7/19/1888, Meriden, Conn. d: 12/12/72, Meriden, Conn. BR/TR, 5'10", 170 lbs. Deb: 9/09/13																											
1913	Cle-A	7	17	3	4	1	0	0	0	0	5	.235	.235	.294	.529	52	-1	-1	106	0	1	.385	0			0	/S3	0.0
1914	Cle-A	1	3	0	0	0	0	0	0	1	1	.000	.250	.000	.250	-24	-0	-0	102	0	0	.333	0			0	/S	0.0
Total	2	8	20	3	4	1	0	0	0	1	6	.200	.238	.250	.488	41	-1	-2	105	0	1	.375	0			0	/S3	0.0
■ **JACK DUNN**	Dunn, John Joseph b: 10/6/1872, Meadville, Pa. d: 10/22/28, Towson, Md. BR/TR, 5'9", Deb: 5/06/1897																											
1897	Bro-N	36	131	20	29	4	0	0	17	4		.221	.244	.252	.496	32	-13	-13	102	151	9	.382	2			0	P/2O3S	0.0
1898	Bro-N	51	167	21	41	0	1	0	19	7		.246	.280	.257	.537	60	-9	-8	95	134	13	.429	3			-1	P/OS3	0.0
1899	Bro-N	43	122	21	30	2	1	0	16	3		.246	.264	.279	.543	49	-8	-9	105	144	10	.435	3			3	P/S	0.0
1900	Bro-N	10	26	2	6	0	0	0	1	1		.231	.259	.231	.490	35	-2	-2	108	52	2	.350	0			0	P	0.0
	Phi-N	10	33	3	10	1	0	0	5	0		.303	.303	.333	.636	79	-1	-1	98	142	4	.522	1			0	P	0.0
	Yr	20	59	5	16	1	0	0	6	1		.271	.283	.288	.571	58	-3	-3	103	100	5	.442	1			0	P	0.0
1901	Phi-N	2	1	1	1	0	0	0	0	0		1.000	1.000	1.000	2.000	474	0	0	103	0	2	—	1			0	/P	0.0
	Bal-A	96	362	41	90	9	4	0	36	21		.249	.290	.296	.585	60	-17	-21	107	112	35	.507	10			-17	3S/P2O	-3.2
1902	NY-N	100	342	26	72	11	1	0	14	20		.211	.254	.249	.503	57	-17	-17	100	58	26	.437	13			-45	OS3/P2	-6.7
1903	NY-N	78	257	35	62	15	1	0	37	15		.241	.283	.307	.590	66	-10	-13	106	151	26	.544	12			-2	S32/O	-1.0
1904	NY-N	64	181	27	56	12	2	1	19	11		.309	.349	.414	.763	131	7	6	105	89	31	.776	11			3	3S/2OP	1.1
Total	8	490	1622	197	397	54	10	1	164	82		.245	.282	.292	.574	65	-69	-76	103	111	157	.500	56			-58	3P/SO2	-9.8
■ **JOE DUNN**	Dunn, Joseph Edward b: 3/11/1885, Springfield, Ohio d: 3/19/44, Springfield, Ohio BR/TR, 5'9", 160 lbs. Deb: 9/12/08																											
1908	Bro-N	20	64	3	11	3	0	0	5	0		.172	.172	.219	.391	27	-5	-5	95	137	2	.264	0			3	C	-0.1
1909	Bro-N	10	25	1	4	1	0	0	2	0		.160	.192	.200	.392	23	-2	-2	99	145	1	.286	0			1	/C	0.0
Total	2	30	89	4	15	4	0	0	7	0		.169	.178	.213	.391	26	-8	-7	96	139	3	.270	0			4	/C	-0.1
■ **RON DUNN**	Dunn, Ronald Ray b: 1/24/50, Oklahoma City, Okla. BR/TR, 5'11", 180 lbs. Deb: 9/03/74																											
1974	Chi-N	23	68	6	20	7	0	2	15	12	8	.294	.400	.485	.885	147	5	5	100	148	12	.849	0	0	0	-2	2/3	0.4
1975	Chi-N	32	44	2	7	3	0	1	6	6	17	.159	.260	.295	.555	52	-3	-3	104	145	4	.514	0	0	0	-1	3/O2	-0.4
Total	2	55	112	8	27	10	0	3	21	18	25	.241	.346	.411	.757	109	2	1	102	147	16	.753	0	0	0	-3	/23O	0.0
■ **STEVE DUNN**	Dunn, Stephen b: 12/21/1858, London, Ont., Can. d: 5/5/33, London, Ont., Can. Deb: 9/27/1884																											
1884	StP-U	9	32	2	8	2	0	0		0		.250	.250	.313	.563	89	-0	-0	100	0	3	.417	0			0	/13	0.0
■ **SHAWON DUNSTON**	Dunston, Shawon Donnell b: 3/21/63, Brooklyn, N.Y. BR/TR, 6'1", 175 lbs. Deb: 4/09/85																											
1985	Chi-N	74	250	40	65	12	4	4	18	19	42	.260	.312	.388	.700	82	-2	-7	116	66	31	.665	11	3	2	14	S	1.4
1986	Chi-N	150	581	66	145	37	3	17	68	21	114	.250	.279	.411	.691	83	-12	-16	107	95	64	.611	13	11	-3	23	*S	1.8
1987	Chi-N	95	346	40	85	18	3	5	22	10	68	.246	.269	.358	.627	64	-18	-19	101	63	32	.544	12	3	2	3	S	-0.2
1988	Chi-N	155	575	69	143	23	6	9	56	16	108	.249	.272	.357	.628	76	-17	-20	104	98	55	.566	30	9	4	11	*S	0.6

YEAR	TM/L	G	AB	R	H	2B	3B	HR	RBI	BB	SO	AVG	OBP	SLG	PRO	/A	BR	/A	PF	CHI	RC	TA	SB	CS	SBR	FR	POS	TPR
Total	4	474	1752	215	438	90	16	35	164	66	332	.250	.280	.380	.659	77	-50	-62	106	86	182	.597	66	26	4	51	S	3.6
■ DAN DURAN	Duran, Daniel James b: 3/16/54, Palo Alto, Cal. BL/TL, 5'11", 190 lbs. Deb: 4/17/81																											
1981	Tex-A	13	16	1	4	0	0	0	0	1	1	.250	.294	.250	.544	64	-1	-1	91	0	1	.385	0	0	0	-1	/O1	-0.1
■ KID DURBIN	Durbin, Blaine Alphonsus b: 9/10/1886, Kansas d: 9/11/43, Kirkwood, Mo. BL/TL, 5'8", 155 lbs. Deb: 4/24/07																											
1907	Chi-N	11	18	2	6	0	0	0	0	1		.333	.368	.333	.702	115	0	0	106	0	2	.583	0			0	/PO	0.2
1908	Chi-N	14	28	3	7	1	0	0	0	2		.250	.300	.286	.586	84	-0	-0	106	0	2	.476	0			0	O	0.0
1909	Cin-N	6	5	1	1	0	0	0	0	1		.200	.333	.200	.533	71	-0	-0	94	0	0	.500	0			0	H	0.0
	Pit-N	1	0	0	0	0	0	0	0	0		—	—	—	—	—	0	0	105	—	—	—	0			0	R	0.0
	Yr	7	5	1	1	0	0	0	0	1		.200	.333	.200	.533	70	-0	-0	95	0	0	.500	0			0		0.0
Total	3	32	51	6	14	1	0	0	0	4		.275	.327	.294	.621	94	0	-0	105	0	5	.514	0			0	/OP	0.2
■ JOE DURHAM	Durham, Joseph Vann "Pop" b: 7/31/31, Newport News, Va. BR/TR, 6'1", 186 lbs. Deb: 9/10/54																											
1954	Bal-A	10	40	4	9	0	0	1	3	4	7	.225	.295	.300	.595	66	-2	-2	95	73	4	.516	0	0	0	-1	O	-0.2
1957	Bal-A	77	157	19	29	2	0	4	17	16	42	.185	.260	.274	.534	49	-12	-10	93	122	11	.451	1	1	-0	-10	O	-2.5
1959	StL-N	6	5	2	0	0	0	0	0	0	1	.000	.000	.000	.000	-96	-1	-1	105	0	0	.000	0	0	0	0	/O	0.0
Total	3	93	202	25	38	2	0	5	20	20	50	.188	.261	.272	.534	49	-15	-14	94	110	15	.461	1	1	-0	-11	/O	-2.7
■ LEON DURHAM	Durham, Leon b: 7/31/57, Cincinnati, Ohio BL/TL, 6'1", 185 lbs. Deb: 5/27/80																											
1980	StL-N	96	303	42	82	15	4	8	42	18	55	.271	.314	.426	.739	102	1	-0	103	109	40	.681	8	5	-1	3	O/1	-0.1
1981	Chi-N	87	328	42	95	14	6	10	35	27	53	.290	.344	.460	.804	122	10	9	104	80	50	.812	25	11	1	-3	O/1	0.5
1982	Chi-N	148	539	84	168	33	7	22	90	66	77	.312	.389	.521	.910	148	38	36	103	108	108	.952	28	14	0	-10	*O/1	2.5
1983	Chi-N	100	337	58	87	18	8	12	55	66	83	.258	.384	.466	.850	133	17	17	101	115	64	.915	12	6	0	-6	O/1	1.0
1984	Chi-N	137	473	86	132	30	4	23	96	69	86	.279	.372	.505	.877	131	28	22	110	125	90	.910	16	8	0	4	*1	2.3
1985	Chi-N	153	542	58	153	32	2	21	75	64	99	.282	.358	.465	.823	111	20	10	116	97	90	.808	7	6	-2	2	*1	0.6
1986	Chi-N	141	484	66	127	18	7	20	65	67	98	.262	.353	.452	.806	113	14	10	107	95	78	.797	8	7	-2	-7	*1	-0.4
1987	Chi-N	131	439	70	120	22	1	27	63	51	92	.273	.349	.513	.862	124	15	14	101	82	79	.850	2	2	-1	-8	*1	-0.1
1988	Chi-N	24	73	10	16	6	1	3	6	9	20	.219	.305	.452	.757	110	1	1	104	57	10	.724	0	1	-1	-0	1	0.0
	Cin-N	21	51	4	11	3	0	1	2	5	12	.216	.286	.333	.619	73	-2	-2	105	40	5	.550	0	0	0	-1	1	-0.3
	Yr	45	124	14	27	9	1	4	8	14	32	.218	.297	.403	.700	95	-0	-1	105	50	15	.653	0	1	-1	-1		-0.3
Total	9	1038	3569	520	991	191	40	147	529	442	675	.278	.359	.477	.836	123	143	116	106	100	615	.856	106	60	-4	-26	1O	6.0
■ BOBBY DURNBAUGH	Durnbaugh, Robert Eugene "Scroggy" b: 1/15/33, Dayton, Ohio BR/TR, 5'8", 170 lbs. Deb: 9/22/57																											
1957	Cin-N	2	1	0	0	0	0	0	0	0	0	.000	.000	.000	.000	-95	-0	-0	105	0	0	.000	0	0	0	0	/S	0.0
■ GEORGE DURNING	Durning, George Dewey b: 5/9/1898, Philadelphia, Pa. d: 4/18/86, Tampa, Fla. BR/TR, 5'11", 175 lbs. Deb: 9/12/25																											
1925	Phi-N	5	14	3	5	0	0	0	1	2	1	.357	.438	.357	.795	91	0	-0	116	71	2	.778	0	0	0	2	/O	0.2
■ LEO DUROCHER	Durocher, Leo Ernest "Lippy" b: 7/27/05, W.Springfield, Mass. BR/TR, 5'10", 160 lbs. Deb: 10/02/25 MC																											
1925	NY-A	2	1	1	0	0	0	0	0	0	0	.000	.000	.000	.000	-99	-0	-0	96	0	0	.000	0	0	0	0	H	0.0
1928	NY-A	102	296	46	80	8	6	0	31	22	52	.270	.327	.338	.665	81	-11	-7	92	106	33	.573	1	4	-2	-3	2S	-0.5
1929	NY-A	106	341	53	84	4	5	0	32	34	33	.246	.320	.287	.607	58	-21	-20	99	112	34	.535	3	1	0	11	S2	0.0
1930	Cin-N	119	354	31	86	15	3	3	32	20	45	.243	.287	.328	.615	53	-30	-25	90	88	33	.515	0			3	*S2	-0.9
1931	Cin-N	121	361	26	82	11	5	1	29	18	32	.227	.264	.294	.557	52	-26	-24	95	95	29	.444	0			-4	*S	-1.8
1932	Cin-N	143	457	43	99	22	5	1	33	36	40	.217	.275	.293	.569	55	-30	-28	96	90	39	.486	3			-14	*S	-2.9
1933	Cin-N	16	51	6	11	1	0	1	3	4	5	.216	.273	.294	.567	63	-3	-2	99	63	4	.442	0			-2	S	-0.3
	StL-N	123	395	45	102	18	4	2	41	26	32	.258	.306	.339	.645	82	-8	-9	102	110	40	.536	3			-4	*S	-0.5
	Yr	139	446	51	113	19	4	3	44	30	37	.253	.302	.334	.636	80	-11	-12	102	105	45	.529	3			-6		-0.8
1934	StL-N	146	500	62	130	26	5	3	70	33	40	.260	.308	.350	.658	67	-17	-26	114	137	53	.549	2			-4	*S	-2.7
1935	StL-N	143	513	62	136	23	5	8	78	29	46	.265	.304	.376	.681	79	-14	-16	104	130	57	.575	4			7	*S	-0.2
1936	StL-N	136	510	57	146	22	3	1	58	29	47	.286	.327	.347	.674	86	-13	-9	94	116	56	.552	3			-11	*S	-1.1
1937	StL-N	135	477	46	97	11	3	1	47	38	36	.203	.262	.245	.507	38	-40	-41	101	144	30	.406	6			-18	*S	-4.8
1938	Bro-N	141	479	41	105	18	5	1	56	47	30	.219	.293	.284	.577	62	-26	-23	96	**146**	42	.493	3			-10	*S	-2.3
1939	Bro-N	116	390	42	108	21	6	1	34	27	24	.277	.325	.369	.695	80	-8	-11	107	85	46	.598	2			-12	*S/3M	-1.5
1940	Bro-N	62	160	10	37	9	1	1	14	12	13	.231	.285	.319	.604	61	-7	-9	108	96	14	.496	1			-5	S/2M	-0.8
1941	Bro-N	18	42	2	12	1	0	0	6	1	3	.286	.302	.310	.612	70	-2	-2	103	167	4	.452	0			0	S/2M	0.0
1943	Bro-N	6	18	1	4	0	0	0	1	1	2	.222	.263	.222	.485	41	-1	-1	100	90	1	.333	0			-1	/SM	-0.1
1945	Bro-N	2	5	1	1	0	0	0	2	0	0	.200	.200	.200	.400	12	-1	-1	96	694	0	.250	0			0	/2M	0.0
Total	17	1637	5350	575	1320	210	56	24	567	377	480	.247	.299	.320	.619	66	-257	-255	100	115	513	.530	31	5		-66	*S/23	-20.4
■ RED DURRETT	Durrett, Elmer Charles b: 2/3/21, Sherman, Tex. BL/TL, 5'10", 170 lbs. Deb: 9/14/44																											
1944	Bro-N	11	32	3	5	1	0	1	1	7	10	.156	.308	.281	.589	67	-1	-1	99	30	3	.571	0			2	/O	0.0
1945	Bro-N	8	16	2	2	0	0	0	0	3	3	.125	.263	.125	.388	10	-2	-2	96	0	1	.357	0			-0	/O	-0.1
Total	2	19	48	5	7	1	0	1	1	10	13	.146	.293	.229	.522	49	-3	-3	98	20	4	.512	0			1	/O	-0.1
■ CEDRIC DURST	Durst, Cedric Montgomery b: 8/23/1896, Austin, Tex. d: 2/16/71, San Diego, Cal. BL/TL, 5'11", 160 lbs. Deb: 5/30/22																											
1922	StL-A	15	12	5	4	1	0	0	0	0	1	.333	.333	.417	.750	89	-0	-0	106	0	2	.625	0	0	0	-2	/O	-0.2
1923	StL-A	45	85	12	18	2	0	5	11	8	14	.212	.280	.412	.691	77	-3	-4	104	75	10	.642	0	0	0	-1	O/1	-0.4
1926	StL-A	80	219	32	52	7	5	3	16	22	19	.237	.310	.356	.666	73	-9	-9	101	62	24	.587	0	5	-3	3	O/1	-1.3
1927	NY-A	65	129	18	32	4	3	0	25	6	7	.248	.281	.326	.607	57	-8	-8	100	198	12	.495	0	0	0	-8	O/1	-1.7
1928	NY-A	74	135	18	34	2	1	2	10	7	9	.252	.289	.326	.615	66	-8	-6	92	69	13	.515	1	0	0	-4	O/1	-1.1
1929	NY-A	92	202	32	52	3	3	4	31	15	25	.257	.309	.361	.670	73	-9	-8	99	125	23	.599	3	2	-0	-2	O/1	-1.2
1930	NY-A	8	19	0	3	1	0	0	5	0	1	.158	.158	.211	.368	-8	-3	-3	90	415	1	.250	0	0	0	-1	/O	-0.2
	Bos-A	102	302	29	74	19	5	1	24	17	24	.245	.290	.351	.641	66	-18	-15	93	73	31	.559	3	1	0	-5	O	-2.0
	Yr	110	321	29	77	20	5	1	29	17	25	.240	.282	.343	.625	62	-21	-18	93	102	32	.539	3	1	0	-5		-2.2
Total	7	481	1103	146	269	39	17	15	122	75	100	.244	.294	.351	.645	68	-59	-54	97	99	115	.561	7	8	-3	-19	O/1	-8.1
■ ERV DUSAK	Dusak, Ervin Frank "Four Sack" b: 7/29/20, Chicago, Ill. BR/TR, 6'2", 185 lbs. Deb: 9/18/41																											
1941	StL-N	6	14	1	2	0	0	0	3	2	6	.143	.250	.143	.393	11	-2	-2	110	542	1	.417	1			1	/O	0.0
1942	StL-N	12	27	4	5	3	0	0	3	3	7	.185	.267	.296	.563	60	-1	-1	108	139	2	.478	0			-1	/O3	-0.2
1946	StL-N	100	275	38	66	9	1	9	42	33	63	.240	.321	.378	.700	92	-1	-3	107	120	34	.670	7			1	O3/2	-0.3
1947	StL-N	111	328	56	93	7	3	6	28	50	34	.284	.378	.378	.756	95	2	-1	106	73	50	.729	1			3	O/3	-0.1
1948	StL-N	114	311	60	65	9	2	6	19	49	55	.209	.317	.309	.625	69	-12	-13	101	62	34	.597	3			-3	O2/3PS	-1.7
1949	StL-N	1	0	1	0	0	0	0	0	0	0	—	—	—	—	—	0	0	110	—	—	—	0			0	R	0.0
1950	StL-N	23	12	0	1	1	0	0	0	0	3	.083	.083	.167	.250	-35	-2	-2	103	0	0	.182	0			0	P/O	0.0
1951	StL-N	5	2	1	1	0	0	1	1	0	1	.500	.500	2.000	2.500	535	1	1	101	55	2	4.000	0	0	0	0	/P	0.0
	Pit-N	21	39	6	12	3	0	1	7	3	11	.308	.357	.462	.819	111	1	1	107	129	7	.778	0	0	0	-4	O/P23	-0.2
	Yr	26	41	7	13	3	0	2	8	3	12	.317	.364	.537	.900	132	2	2	106	117	8	.893	0	0	0	-4		-0.2
1952	Pit-N	20	27	1	6	0	0	1	3	2	8	.222	.276	.333	.609	68	-1	-1	100	98	2	.478	0	0	0	-2	O	-0.3
Total	9	413	1035	168	251	32	6	24	106	142	188	.243	.334	.355	.688	84	-16	-22	104	92	167	.663	12	0		-4	O/23PS	-2.8
■ AL DWIGHT	Dwight, Albert Ward b: 1/4/1856, New York, N.Y. d: 2/20/03, San Francisco, Cal Deb: 6/19/1884																											
1884	KC-U	12	43	8	10	2	0	0		2		.233	.267	.279	.546	97	-1	0	87	0	3	.424	0			0	C/O2	0.0
■ JIM DWYER	Dwyer, James Edward b: 1/3/50, Evergreen Park, Ill. BL/TL, 5'10", 165 lbs. Deb: 6/10/73																											
1973	StL-N	28	57	7	11	1	1	0	0	1	5	.193	.207	.246	.453	27	-6	-5	91	0	2	.300	0	0	0	-2	O	-0.8
1974	StL-N	74	86	13	24	1	0	2	11	11	16	.279	.367	.360	.728	101	1	0	104	115	12	.683	0	0	0	-5	O/1	-0.5
1975	StL-N	21	31	4	6	1	0	0	1	4	6	.194	.286	.226	.512	42	-2	-2	103	55	2	.423	0	0	0	-0	/O	-0.2
	Mon-N	60	175	22	50	7	1	3	20	23	30	.286	.369	.389	.757	102	3	1	108	100	28	.754	4	1	1	0	O	0.0

YEAR	TM/L	G	AB	R	H	2B	3B	HR	RBI	BB	SO	AVG	OBP	SLG	PRO	/A	BR	/A	PF	CHI	RC	TA	SB	CS	SBR	FR	POS	TPR
	Yr	81	206	26	56	8	1	3	21	27	36	.272	.356	.364	.720	94	1	-1	107	89	30	.702	4	1	1	0		-0.2
1976	Mon-N	50	92	7	17	3	1	0	5	11	10	.185	.272	.239	.511	46	-6	-6	100	87	6	.423	0	0	0	-2	O	-0.9
	NY-N	11	13	2	2	0	0	0	0	2	1	.154	.267	.154	.421	23	-1	-1	92	0	1	.364	0	0	0	-0	/O	-0.1
	Yr	61	105	9	19	3	1	0	5	13	11	.181	.271	.229	.500	43	-8	-7	99	73	7	.430	0	0	0	-2		-1.0
1977	StL-N	13	31	3	7	1	0	0	2	4	5	.226	.351	.258	.609	69	-1	-1	96	100	3	.583	0	0	0	-2	O	-0.2
1978	StL-N	34	65	8	14	3	0	1	4	9	3	.215	.320	.308	.628	80	-2	-1	95	69	7	.596	1	0	0	-5	O	-0.6
	SF-N	73	173	22	39	9	2	5	22	28	29	.225	.333	.387	.721	110	0	2	92	106	25	.748	6	0	2	2	O1	0.4
	Yr	107	238	30	53	12	2	6	26	37	32	.223	.330	.366	.695	102	-1	1	93	95	33	.710	7	0	2	-2		-0.2
1979	Bos-A	76	113	19	30	7	0	2	14	17	9	.265	.366	.381	.747	95	1	-0	107	110	15	.703	3	1	0	-2	1O	-0.3
1980	Bos-A	93	260	41	74	11	1	9	38	28	23	.285	.359	.438	.797	115	6	6	102	105	41	.766	3	2	-0	-3	OD/1	0.1
1981	Bal-A	68	134	16	30	0	1	3	10	20	19	.224	.325	.306	.631	83	-2	-2	99	78	14	.565	0	2	-1	-9	O/1D	-1.4
1982	Bal-A	71	148	28	45	4	3	6	15	27	24	.304	.411	.493	.905	147	11	11	100	66	33	.990	2	0	1	-7	O/1D	0.2
1983	Bal-A	100	196	37	56	17	1	8	38	31	29	.286	.383	.505	.888	142	12	12	100	121	39	.910	1	1	-0	-9	OD/1	0.2
1984	Bal-A	76	161	22	41	9	1	2	21	23	24	.255	.348	.360	.708	102	-0	1	94	131	21	.653	0	2	-1	-6	O/D	-0.7
1985	Bal-A	101	233	35	58	8	3	7	36	37	31	.249	.354	.399	.753	107	3	3	99	125	33	.716	0	3	-2	-6	O/D	-0.5
1986	Bal-A	94	160	18	39	13	1	8	31	23	31	.244	.346	.488	.833	126	6	6	99	121	27	.824	0	2	-1	-1	OD/1	0.3
1987	Bal-A	92	241	54	66	7	1	15	33	37	57	.274	.373	.498	.871	132	11	11	98	80	46	.900	4	1	1	-1	DO	0.9
1988	Bal-A	35	53	3	12	0	0	0	3	12	11	.226	.369	.226	.596	75	-1	-1	95	99	5	.585	0	0	0	-0	D/O	0.0
	Min-A	20	41	6	12	1	0	2	15	13	8	.293	.473	.463	.936	154	5	4	106	239	10	1.100	0	0	0	0	D	0.4
	Yr	55	94	9	24	1	0	2	18	25	19	.255	.417	.330	.746	113	3	3	99	152	15	.803	0	0	0	-0		0.4
Total	16	1190	2463	367	633	103	17	73	319	361	371	.257	.355	.402	.756	109	34	36	99	102	374	.751	24	15	-2	-57	OD/1	-3.7

■ JOHN DWYER Dwyer, John E. Deb: 5/16/1882

YEAR	TM/L	G	AB	R	H	2B	3B	HR	RBI	BB	SO	AVG	OBP	SLG	PRO	/A	BR	/A	PF	CHI	RC	TA	SB	CS	SBR	FR	POS	TPR
1882	Cle-N	1	3	0	0	0	0	0	1	0	0	.000	.000	.000	.000	-99	-1	-1	90	0	0	.000				0	/OC	0.0

■ DOUBLE JOE DWYER Dwyer, Joseph Michael b: 3/27/04, Orange, N.J. BL/TL, 5'9", 186 lbs. Deb: 4/20/37

YEAR	TM/L	G	AB	R	H	2B	3B	HR	RBI	BB	SO	AVG	OBP	SLG	PRO	/A	BR	/A	PF	CHI	RC	TA	SB	CS	SBR	FR	POS	TPR
1937	Cin-N	12	11	2	3	0	0	0	1	1	0	.273	.333	.273	.606	73	-0	-0	91	120	1	.500	0			0	H	0.0

■ JERRY DYBZINSKI Dybzinski, Jerome Matthew b: 7/7/55, Cleveland, Ohio BR/TR, 6'2", 180 lbs. Deb: 4/11/80

YEAR	TM/L	G	AB	R	H	2B	3B	HR	RBI	BB	SO	AVG	OBP	SLG	PRO	/A	BR	/A	PF	CHI	RC	TA	SB	CS	SBR	FR	POS	TPR
1980	Cle-A	114	248	32	57	11	1	1	23	13	35	.230	.274	.294	.568	54	-15	-16	102	118	21	.467	4	1	1	4	S2/3D	-0.3
1981	Cle-A	48	57	10	17	0	0	0	6	5	8	.298	.355	.298	.653	96	-1	-0	93	138	8	.707	7	1	2	-1	S/23D	0.4
1982	Cle-A	80	212	19	49	6	2	0	22	21	25	.231	.309	.278	.588	63	-10	-10	100	149	18	.491	3	5	-2	2	S/3	-0.3
1983	Chi-A	127	256	30	59	10	1	1	32	18	29	.230	.286	.289	.575	57	-14	-15	103	162	21	.502	11	4	1	8	*S/3	0.0
1984	Chi-A	94	132	17	31	5	1	1	10	13	12	.235	.313	.311	.624	66	-5	-6	111	91	14	.594	7	2	1	5	S3/2D	0.5
1985	Pit-N	5	4	0	0	0	0	0	0	0	0	.000	.000	.000	.000	-97	-1	-1	103	0	0	.000	0	0	0	0	/S	0.0
Total	6	468	909	108	213	32	5	3	93	70	109	.234	.296	.290	.586	61	-46	-49	103	135	81	.529	32	13	2	19	S/32D	0.3

■ JIM DYCK Dyck, James Robert b: 2/3/22, Omaha, Neb. BR/TR, 6'2", 200 lbs. Deb: 9/27/51

YEAR	TM/L	G	AB	R	H	2B	3B	HR	RBI	BB	SO	AVG	OBP	SLG	PRO	/A	BR	/A	PF	CHI	RC	TA	SB	CS	SBR	FR	POS	TPR
1951	StL-A	4	15	1	1	0	0	0	0	1	1	.067	.125	.067	.192	-45	-3	-3	105	0	0	.143	0	0	0	0	/3	-0.3
1952	StL-A	122	402	60	108	22	3	15	64	50	68	.269	.354	.450	.804	126	12	13	97	106	67	.775	0	4	-2	7	3O	1.6
1953	StL-A	112	334	38	71	15	1	9	27	38	40	.213	.299	.344	.643	69	-13	-16	107	70	33	.568	3	2	-0	-5	O3	-2.5
1954	Cle-A	2	1	0	1	0	0	0	1	1	0	1.000	1.000	1.000	2.000	423	1	1	106	379	1	—	0	0	0	0	H	0.1
1955	Bal-A	61	197	32	55	13	1	2	22	28	21	.279	.372	.386	.757	116	2	4	90	100	29	.711	1	0	0	-2	O3	0.0
1956	Bal-A	11	23	3	5	2	0	0	0	10	5	.217	.455	.304	.759	110	1	1	94	0	4	.944	0	0	0	-1	/O	0.0
	Cin-N	18	11	5	1	0	0	0	0	3	5	.091	.286	.091	.377	7	-1	-2	108	0	0	.364	0	0	0	0	/13	-0.1
Total	6	330	983	139	242	52	5	26	114	131	140	.246	.339	.389	.728	99	-3	-1	99	87	135	.701	4	6	-2	-2	O3/1	-1.2

■ BEN DYER Dyer, Benjamin Franklin b: 2/13/1893, Chicago, Ill. d: 8/7/59, Kenosha, Wis. BR/TR, 5'10", 170 lbs. Deb: 5/23/14

YEAR	TM/L	G	AB	R	H	2B	3B	HR	RBI	BB	SO	AVG	OBP	SLG	PRO	/A	BR	/A	PF	CHI	RC	TA	SB	CS	SBR	FR	POS	TPR
1914	NY-N	7	4	1	1	0	0	0	0	0	1	.250	.250	.250	.500	51	-0	-0	96	0	0	.667	1			0	/S2	0.0
1915	NY-N	7	19	4	4	0	1	0	0	4	3	.211	.375	.316	.691	120	1	1	91	0	2	.733	0			0	/3S	0.1
1916	Det-A	4	14	4	4	1	0	0	1	1	1	.286	.333	.357	.690	103	0	0	105	71	2	.600	0			-0	/S	0.0
1917	Det-A	30	67	6	14	5	0	0	0	2	17	.209	.232	.284	.515	59	-4	-4	98	0	5	.453	3			-2	S/3	-0.4
1918	Det-A	13	18	1	5	0	0	0	2	0	6	.278	.278	.278	.556	70	-1	-1	97	146	1	.385	0			-0	/P1O2	0.0
1919	Det-A	44	85	11	21	4	0	0	15	8	19	.247	.312	.294	.606	76	-3	-3	93	218	8	.516	0			-3	3S/O	-0.2
Total	6	105	207	27	49	10	1	0	18	15	47	.237	.291	.295	.586	76	-7	-6	96	107	18	.513	4			-5	/3SO1P2	-0.5

■ DUFFY DYER Dyer, Don Robert b: 8/15/45, Dayton, Ohio BR/TR, 6', 187 lbs. Deb: 9/21/68 C

YEAR	TM/L	G	AB	R	H	2B	3B	HR	RBI	BB	SO	AVG	OBP	SLG	PRO	/A	BR	/A	PF	CHI	RC	TA	SB	CS	SBR	FR	POS	TPR
1968	NY-N	1	3	0	1	0	0	0	0	1	1	.333	.500	.333	.833	151	0	0	102	0	1	1.000	0	0	0	0	/C	0.1
1969	NY-N	29	74	5	19	3	1	3	12	4	22	.257	.295	.446	.741	105	0	0	100	115	9	.638	0	0	0	0	C	0.2
1970	NY-N	59	148	8	31	1	0	2	12	21	32	.209	.308	.257	.564	51	-9	-10	104	106	12	.488	1	1	-0	1	C	-0.6
1971	NY-N	59	169	13	39	7	1	2	18	14	45	.231	.293	.320	.613	76	-6	-5	96	122	16	.522	1	0	0	-0	C	-0.4
1972	NY-N	94	325	33	75	17	3	8	36	28	71	.231	.302	.375	.677	96	-4	-2	95	103	36	.598	0	1	-1	22	C/O	2.6
1973	NY-N	70	189	9	35	6	1	1	9	13	40	.185	.245	.243	.488	36	-16	-17	101	74	11	.381	0	1	-1	-1	C	-1.5
1974	NY-N	63	142	14	30	1	1	0	10	18	15	.211	.304	.232	.537	52	-9	-8	99	117	10	.441	0	0	0	-3	C	-0.9
1975	Pit-N	48	132	8	30	5	2	3	16	6	22	.227	.266	.364	.630	74	-5	-5	99	109	12	.519	0	0	0	2	C	-0.1
1976	Pit-N	69	184	12	41	8	0	3	9	29	35	.223	.338	.315	.653	86	-2	-2	100	52	21	.616	0	0	0	3	C	0.3
1977	Pit-N	94	270	27	65	11	1	3	19	54	49	.241	.373	.322	.695	86	-2	-3	103	79	36	.708	6	0	2	0	C	-0.1
1978	Pit-N	58	175	7	37	8	1	0	13	18	32	.211	.296	.269	.564	56	-9	-10	105	110	14	.486	2	1	0	5	C	-0.4
1979	Mon-N	28	74	4	18	6	0	1	8	9	17	.243	.325	.365	.690	86	-1	-1	102	106	9	.632	0	0	0	4	C	0.3
1980	Det-A	48	108	11	20	1	0	4	11	13	34	.185	.273	.306	.578	55	-6	-7	105	95	9	.505	0	0	0	2	CD	-0.2
1981	Det-A	2	0	0	0	0	0	0	0	0	0	—	—	—	—	—	0	0	105	—	—	—	0	0	0	0	/C	0.0
Total	14	722	1993	151	441	74	11	30	173	228	415	.221	.307	.315	.622	73	-71	-72	100	96	204	.568	10	4	1	35	C/DO	-0.7

■ JIMMY DYKES Dykes, James Joseph b: 11/10/1896, Philadelphia, Pa. d: 6/15/76, Philadelphia, Pa. BR/TR, 5'9", 185 lbs. Deb: 5/06/18 MC

YEAR	TM/L	G	AB	R	H	2B	3B	HR	RBI	BB	SO	AVG	OBP	SLG	PRO	/A	BR	/A	PF	CHI	RC	TA	SB	CS	SBR	FR	POS	TPR
1918	Phi-A	59	186	13	35	3	3	0	13	19	32	.188	.267	.237	.504	50	-11	-12	104	108	13	.444	3			5	2/3	-0.3
1919	Phi-A	17	49	4	9	1	0	0	1	7	11	.184	.286	.204	.490	37	-4	-4	106	36	3	.425	0			-0	2	-0.2
1920	Phi-A	142	546	81	140	25	4	8	35	55	73	.256	.334	.361	.695	90	-12	-7	94	48	68	.643	6	9	-4	13	*23	0.7
1921	Phi-A	155	613	88	168	32	13	17	77	60	75	.274	.353	.452	.805	101	2	-1	103	77	100	.796	6	5	-1	26	*2	2.6
1922	Phi-A	145	501	66	138	23	7	12	68	55	98	.275	.359	.421	.780	98	2	-1	104	100	79	.773	6	2	1	-9	*3/2	0.5
1923	Phi-A	124	416	50	105	28	1	4	43	35	40	.252	.318	.353	.671	76	-15	-15	100	94	48	.613	6	4	-1	-2	*2S/3	-1.0
1924	Phi-A	110	410	68	128	26	6	3	50	38	59	.312	.372	.427	.799	106	3	3	99	95	65	.752	1	4	-2	10	23/S	1.5
1925	Phi-A	122	465	93	150	32	11	5	55	46	49	.323	.393	.471	.864	115	13	11	103	83	88	.873	3	1	0	4	32/S	2.0
1926	Phi-A	124	429	54	123	32	5	1	44	49	34	.287	.370	.392	.762	84	0	-11	118	89	66	.750	6	2	1	10	32/S	0.9
1927	Phi-A	121	417	61	135	33	6	3	60	44	23	.324	.394	.453	.847	123	12	14	97	103	74	.848	2	0	1	-2	13/SO2P	1.1
1928	Phi-A	85	242	39	67	11	0	5	30	27	21	.277	.361	.384	.746	93	-1	-2	103	95	36	.722	2	1	0	-3	2S3/1O	0.0
1929	Phi-A	119	401	76	131	34	6	13	79	51	25	.327	.412	.539	.950	131	26	20	109	108	91	1.033	8	3	1	-14	S32	1.5
1930	Phi-A	125	435	69	131	28	4	6	73	74	53	.301	.414	.425	.840	114	13	13	99	122	82	.886	3	3	-1	-13	*3/O	0.4
1931	Phi-A	101	355	48	97	28	2	3	46	49	47	.273	.371	.389	.759	95	1	-1	105	105	54	.746	1	2	-1	1	3S	0.4
1932	Phi-A	153	558	71	148	29	5	7	90	77	65	.265	.358	.373	.731	79	-7	-19	114	134	80	.721	8	2	1	-7	*3S/2	-1.3
1933	Chi-A	151	554	49	144	22	6	1	68	69	37	.260	.354	.327	.681	81	-12	-13	101	126	67	.635	3	7	-3	-1	*3	-0.4
1934	Chi-A	127	456	52	122	17	4	7	82	64	28	.268	.363	.368	.731	90	-6	-6	99	148	65	.707	1	1	-0	-4	312M	-1.2
1935	Chi-A	117	403	45	116	24	2	4	61	59	28	.288	.381	.387	.769	91	1	-4	109	126	63	.762	4	3	-1	-9	31/2M	-1.3
1936	Chi-A	127	435	62	116	16	3	7	60	61	36	.267	.362	.366	.728	81	-13	-12	99	108	61	.699	1	3	-2	-8	*3M	-1.7
1937	Chi-A	30	85	10	26	5	0	1	23	9	7	.306	.372	.400	.772	92	-1	-1	103	213	13	.729	0	0	0	-1	13M	-0.2
1938	Chi-A	26	89	9	27	4	2	2	13	10	8	.303	.374	.461	.834	110	1	1	98	93	16	.823	0	0	0	-2	2/S3M	0.0
1939	Chi-A	2	1	0	0	0	0	0	0	0	0	.000	.000	.000	.000	-94	-0	-0	107	0	0	.000	0	0	0	0	/3M	0.0
Total	22	2282	8046	1108	2256	453	90	109	1071	958	849	.280	.365	.400	.765	95	-6	-46	103	104	1232	.746	70	52		-5	*321S/OP	4.0

YEAR	TM/L	G	AB	R	H	2B	3B	HR	RBI	BB	SO	AVG	OBP	SLG	PRO	/A	BR	/A	PF	CHI	RC	TA	SB	CS	SBR	FR	POS	TPR
■ **LENNY DYKSTRA** Dykstra, Leonard Kyle b: 2/10/63, Santa Ana, Cal. BL/TL, 5'10", 160 lbs. Deb: 5/03/85																												
1985	NY-N	83	236	40	60	9	3	1	19	30	24	.254	.341	.331	.671	91	-3	-2	97	93	30	.681	15	2	3	9	O	0.9
1986	NY-N	147	431	77	127	27	7	8	45	58	55	.295	.378	.445	.824	132	16	19	96	83	80	.892	31	7	5	-3	*O	1.9
1987	NY-N	132	431	86	123	37	3	10	43	40	67	.285	.352	.455	.806	113	7	8	99	76	74	.845	27	7	4	-7	*O	0.0
1988	NY-N	126	429	57	116	19	3	8	33	30	43	.270	.323	.385	.707	113	1	6	90	70	56	.704	30	8	4	1	*O	0.8
Total	4	488	1527	260	426	92	16	27	140	158	189	.279	.350	.413	.763	115	21	30	95	79	240	.798	103	24	17	0	O	3.6
■ **JOHN DYLER** Dyler, John F. b: 6/1852, Louisville, Ky. Deb: 7/22/1882																												
1882	Lou-a	1	4	0	0	0	0	0		0		.000	.000	.000	.000	-99	-1	-1	94	0	0	.000				0	/O	0.0
■ **DON EADDY** Eaddy, Donald Johnson b: 2/16/34, Grand Rapids, Mich BR/TR, 5'11", 165 lbs. Deb: 4/24/59																												
1959	Chi-N	15	1	3	0	0	0	0	0	0	1	.000	.000	.000	.000	-99	-0	-0	98	0	0	.000	0	0	0	0	/3	0.0
■ **TRUCK EAGAN** Eagan, Charles Eugene b: 8/10/1877, San Francisco, Cal d: 3/19/49, San Francisco, Cal 5'11", 190 lbs. Deb: 5/01/01																												
1901	Pit-N	4	12	0	1	0	0	0	2	0		.083	.083	.083	.167	-51	-2	-2	101	669	0	.182	1			0	/S	-0.1
	Cle-A	5	18	2	3	0	1	0	2	1		.167	.211	.278	.488	38	-2	-1	95	129	1	.400	0			0	/23	-0.1
Total	1	9	30	2	4	0	1	0	4	1		.133	.161	.200	.361	3	-4	-4	97	338	1	.308	1			0	/2S3	-0.2
■ **BILL EAGAN** Eagan, William "Bad Bill" b: 6/1/1869, Camden, N.J. d: 2/14/05, Denver, Colo. Deb: 4/08/1891																												
1891	StL-a	83	302	49	65	11	4	4	43	44	54	.215	.321	.318	.639	75	-5	-12	114	117	38	.692	21			14	2	0.6
1893	Chi-N	6	19	3	5	0	0	0	2	5	5	.263	.417	.263	.680	81	-0	-0	104	109	4	1.000	4			0	/2	0.0
1898	Pit-N	19	61	14	20	2	3	0	5	8		.328	.431	.459	.890	162	5	5	98	55	13	.976	1			0	2	0.5
Total	3	108	382	66	90	13	7	4	50	57	59	.236	.344	.338	.682	88	0	-7	111	107	55	.747	26			14	2	1.1
■ **BILL EAGLE** Eagle, William Lycurgus b: 7/25/1877, Rockville, Md. d: 4/27/51, Churchton, Md. Deb: 8/20/1898																												
1898	Was-N	4	13	0	4	1	0	0	2	0		.308	.308	.385	.692	99	-0	-0	102	121	2	.556	0			0	/O	0.0
■ **CHARLIE EAKLE** Eakle, Charles Emory b: 9/27/1887, Maryland d: 6/15/59, Baltimore, Md. Deb: 8/20/15																												
1915	Bal-F	2	7	0	2	1	0	0	0	0	0	.286	.286	.429	.714	103	0	-0	107	0	1	.800	1			0	/2	0.0
■ **HOWARD EARL** Earl, Howard J. "Slim Jim" b: 2/27/1869, Massachusetts d: 12/22/16, North Bay, N.Y. 6'1", Deb: 4/19/1890																												
1890	Chi-N	92	384	57	95	10	3	7	51	18	47	.247	.285	.344	.628	78	-9	-14	109	107	43	.585	17			-5	O2/S1	-1.6
1891	CM-a	31	129	21	32	5	2	1	17	5	13	.248	.281	.341	.623	72	-4	-6	112	111	14	.546	3			0	O/1	-0.4
Total	2	123	513	78	127	15	5	8	68	23	60	.248	.284	.343	.627	76	-13	-20	110	108	57	.575	20			-5	/O21S	-2.0
■ **SCOTT EARL** Earl, William Scott b: 9/18/60, Seymour, Ind. BR/TR, 5'11", 165 lbs. Deb: 9/10/84																												
1984	Det-A	14	35	3	4	0	1	0	1	0	9	.114	.114	.171	.286	-23	-6	-6	96	66	1	.226	1	0	0	0	2	-0.4
■ **BILLY EARLE** Earle, William Moffat "The Little Globetrotter" b: 11/10/1867, Philadelphia, Pa. d: 5/30/46, Omaha, Neb. BR/TR, 5'10.5", 170 lbs. Deb: 4/27/1889																												
1889	Cin-a	53	169	37	45	4	7	4	31	30	24	.266	.386	.444	.830	132	9	8	105	104	40	1.081	26			0	OC/1	0.6
1890	StL-a	22	73	16	17	3	1	0		7		.233	.317	.301	.618	73	-1	-3	116	0	9	.661	6			0	C/OS32	-0.2
1892	Pit-N	5	13	5	7	2	0	0	3	4	1	.538	.647	.692	1.339	330	4	4	94	102	7	2.500	2			0	/C	0.3
1893	Pit-N	27	95	21	24	4	4	2	15	7	6	.253	.304	.442	.746	93	-1	-2	106	86	13	.704	1			0	C	-0.1
1894	Lou-N	21	65	10	23	1	0	0	7	9	3	.354	.432	.369	.802	110	0	2	88	80	12	.833	2			0	C/123O	0.2
	Bro-N	14	50	13	17	6	0	0	6	6	2	.340	.421	.460	.881	121	1	2	94	73	12	1.030	4			0	C/2	0.2
	Yr	35	115	23	40	7	0	0	13	15	5	.348	.427	.409	.836	115	2	4	91	80	23	.920	6			0		0.4
Total	5	142	465	102	133	20	12	6	62	63	36	.286	.378	.419	.798	114	13	10	103	78	93	.919	41			0	C/O123S	1.0
■ **JAKE EARLY** Early, Jacob Willard b: 5/19/15, King's Mountain, N.C. d: 5/31/85, Melbourne, Fla. BL/TR, 5'11", 168 lbs. Deb: 5/04/39																												
1939	Was-A	32	84	8	22	7	2	0	14	5	14	.262	.303	.393	.696	85	-3	-2	90	143	10	.603	0	0	0	0	C	0.0
1940	Was-A	80	206	26	53	8	4	5	14	23	22	.257	.335	.408	.743	98	-3	-1	93	51	29	.688	0	1	-1	4	C	0.6
1941	Was-A	104	355	42	102	20	7	10	54	24	38	.287	.338	.468	.805	114	4	5	98	98	57	.742	0	1	-1	-4	*C	0.6
1942	Was-A	104	353	31	72	14	2	3	46	37	37	.204	.281	.280	.562	61	-20	-18	96	150	30	.479	0	0	0	9	C	0.3
1943	Was-A	126	423	37	109	23	3	5	60	53	43	.258	.346	.362	.708	103	4	3	104	130	57	.666	5	3	-0	-5	*C	0.4
1946	Was-A	64	189	13	38	6	0	4	18	23	27	.201	.288	.296	.584	69	-9	-7	92	101	17	.513	0	0	0	1	C	-0.3
1947	StL-A	87	214	25	48	9	3	3	19	54	34	.224	.381	.336	.717	98	2	2	102	86	32	.741	0	1	-1	-0	C	0.8
1948	Was-A	97	246	22	54	7	2	1	28	36	33	.220	.322	.276	.598	58	-14	-15	103	133	25	.552	2	1	0	0	C	-0.7
1949	Was-A	53	138	12	34	4	0	1	11	26	11	.246	.370	.297	.667	85	-3	-2	91	86	17	.618	0	1	-1	-1	C	0.0
Total	9	747	2208	216	532	98	23	32	264	281	259	.241	.330	.350	.679	88	-41	-35	98	112	275	.634	7	8	-3	4	C	1.7
■ **MIKE EASLER** Easler, Michael Anthony b: 11/29/50, Cleveland, Ohio BL/TR, 6', 190 lbs. Deb: 9/05/73																												
1973	Hou-N	6	7	1	0	0	0	0	0	2	4	.000	.222	.000	.222	-35	-1	-1	95	0	0	.286	0	0	0	-1	/O	-0.1
1974	Hou-N	15	15	0	1	0	0	0	0	0	5	.067	.067	.067	.133	-64	-3	-3	98	0	0	.067	0	0	0	0	H	-0.2
1975	Hou-N	5	5	0	0	0	0	0	0	0	1	.000	.000	.000	.000	-99	-1	-1	94	0	0	.000	0	0	0	0	H	0.0
1976	Cal-A	21	54	6	13	1	1	0	4	2	11	.241	.268	.296	.564	71	-2	-2	92	96	4	.442	1	1	-0	0	D	-0.1
1977	Pit-N	10	18	3	8	2	0	1	5	0	1	.444	.444	.722	1.167	202	3	2	103	125	6	1.300	0	0	0	-0	/O	0.2
1979	Pit-N	55	54	8	15	1	1	2	11	8	13	.278	.371	.444	.815	115	2	1	106	145	9	.800	0	1	-1	-2	/O	0.0
1980	Pit-N	132	393	66	133	27	3	21	74	43	65	.338	.404	.583	.986	167	37	36	103	100	88	1.004	5	9	-4	-8	*O	1.9
1981	Pit-N	95	339	43	97	18	5	7	42	24	45	.286	.333	.431	.764	120	6	7	96	101	44	.672	4	7	-3	6	O	0.9
1982	Pit-N	142	475	52	131	27	2	15	58	40	85	.276	.340	.436	.776	105	9	3	110	90	69	.713	1	1	-0	-3	*O	-0.1
1983	Pit-N	115	381	44	117	17	2	10	54	22	64	.307	.350	.441	.791	114	8	7	103	108	57	.714	4	2	0	-6	*O	0.0
1984	Bos-A	156	601	87	188	31	5	27	91	58	134	.313	.377	.516	.893	131	36	28	110	98	118	.884	1	1	-0	2	*D1	2.7
1985	Bos-A	155	568	71	149	29	4	16	74	53	129	.262	.329	.412	.740	99	1	-1	102	106	75	.667	0	1	-1	-3	*DO	-0.4
1986	NY-A	146	490	64	148	26	2	14	78	49	87	.302	.365	.449	.814	118	15	13	103	119	76	.753	3	2	-0	-1	*DO	1.1
1987	Phi-N	33	110	7	31	4	0	1	10	6	20	.282	.319	.345	.664	73	-4	-4	104	97	12	.543	0	1	-1	1	O	-0.4
	NY-A	65	167	13	47	6	0	4	21	14	32	.281	.341	.389	.730	96	-1	-1	98	109	22	.653	1	0	0	-1	DO	-0.1
Total	14	1151	3677	465	1078	189	25	118	522	321	696	.293	.353	.454	.807	117	103	84	104	103	581	.772	20	26	-10	-15	OD/1	5.4
■ **CARL EAST** East, Carlton William b: 8/27/1894, Marietta, Ga. d: 1/15/53, Whitesburg, Ga. BL/TR, 6'2", 178 lbs. Deb: 8/24/15																												
1915	StL-A	1	1	0	0	0	0	0	0	0	0	.000	.000	.000	.000	-99	-0	-0	96	0	0	.000	0			-0	/P	0.0
1924	Was-A	2	6	1	2	1	0	0	2	2	1	.333	.500	.500	1.000	161	1	1	98	225	2	1.250	0	0	0	-0	/O	0.0
Total	2	3	7	1	2	1	0	0	2	2	1	.286	.444	.429	.873	132	0	0	98	200	2	1.000	0	0		-0	/OP	0.0
■ **HARRY EAST** East, Henry H. b: 4/1863, St.Louis, Mo. Deb: 6/17/1882																												
1882	Bal-a	1	4	0	0	0	0	0		0		.000	.000	.000	.000	-99	-1	-1	92	0	0	.000				0	/3	0.0
■ **LUKE EASTER** Easter, Luscious Luke b: 8/4/15, St.Louis, Mo. d: 3/29/79, Euclid, Ohio BL/TR, 6'4.5", 240 lbs. Deb: 8/11/49 C																												
1949	Cle-A	21	45	6	10	3	0	0	2	8	6	.222	.340	.289	.629	69	-2	-2	98	53	4	.553	0	1	-1	-4	O	-0.6
1950	Cle-A	141	540	96	151	20	4	28	107	70	95	.280	.373	.487	.860	121	14	15	98	113	100	.843	0	3	-2	-2	*1O	0.5
1951	Cle-A	128	486	65	131	12	5	27	103	37	71	.270	.333	.481	.814	125	9	13	95	124	77	.757	0	1	-1	-7	*1	0.3
1952	Cle-A	127	437	63	115	10	3	31	97	44	84	.263	.337	.513	.850	148	17	22	91	114	79	.835	1	1	-0	0	*1	1.5
1953	Cle-A	68	211	26	64	9	0	7	31	15	35	.303	.361	.445	.806	122	5	6	95	100	30	.698	0	2	-1	1	1	0.4
1954	Cle-A	6	6	0	1	0	0	0	0	0	2	.167	.167	.167	.333	-8	-1	-1	106	0	0	.200	0	0	0	0	H	0.0
Total	6	491	1725	256	472	54	12	93	340	174	293	.274	.350	.481	.830	127	42	54	95	113	290	.818	1	8	-5	-12	1/O	2.1
■ **HENRY EASTERDAY** Easterday, Henry P. b: 9/16/1864, Philadelphia, Pa. d: 3/30/1895, Philadelphia, Pa. BR/TR, 5'6", 145 lbs. Deb: 6/23/1884																												
1884	Phi-U	28	115	12	28	5	0	0		5		.243	.275	.287	.562	97	-1	0	93	0	9	.437	0			5	S	0.5
1888	KC-a	115	401	42	76	7	6	3	37	31		.190	.256	.259	.516	64	-13	-17	106	100	33	.502	23			21	*S	0.9
1889	Col-a	95	324	43	56	5	8	4	34	41	57	.173	.270	.275	.544	63	-18	-13	91	98	27	.530	10			20	S/23	1.2
1890	Col-a	58	197	25	31	5	2	0		23		.157	.249	.203	.452	35	-15	-15	99	0	11	.416	5			3	S	-0.7
	Phi-a	19	68	17	10	1	0	1		10		.147	.256	.206	.462	39	-5	-5	97	0	5	.483	4			0	S	-0.3
	Lou-a	7	24	2	2	0	0	0		2		.083	.185	.083	.269	-18	-3	-4	107	0	1	.273	1			0	/S3	-0.2

YEAR	TM/L	G	AB	R	H	2B	3B	HR	RBI	BB	SO	AVG	OBP	SLG	PRO	/A	BR	/A	PF	CHI	RC	TA	SB	CS	SBR	FR	POS	TPR
	Yr	84	289	44	43	6	2	1		35		.149	.245	.194	.439	32	-24	-24	99	0	17	.419	10			3		-1.2
Total	4	322	1129	141	203	23	16	8	71	112	57	.180	.259	.250	.509	58	-56	-53	99	64	87	.482	43			49	S/23	1.4
■ **PAUL EASTERLING** Easterling, Paul b: 9/28/05, Reidsville, Ga. BR/TR, 5'11", 180 lbs. Deb: 4/11/28																												
1928	Det-A	43	114	17	37	7	1	3	12	8	24	.325	.374	.482	.856	124	4	4	99	64	21	.846	2	1	0	-3	O	0.0
1930	Det-A	29	79	7	16	6	0	1	14	6	18	.203	.259	.316	.575	43	-7	-7	105	166	6	.484	0	1	-1	-2	O	-1.0
1938	Phi-A	4	7	1	2	0	0	0	0	1	2	.286	.375	.286	.661	67	-0	-0	101	0	1	.600	0	0	0	0	/O	0.0
Total	3	76	200	25	55	13	1	4	26	15	44	.275	.329	.410	.739	89	-4	-4	101	102	28	.680	2	2	-1	-5	/O	-1.0
■ **TED EASTERLY** Easterly, Theodore Harrison b: 4/20/1885, Lincoln, Neb. d: 7/6/51, Clear Lake Highlands, Cal. BL/TR, 5'8", 165 lbs. Deb: 4/17/09																												
1909	Cle-A	98	287	32	75	14	10	1	27	13		.261	.293	.390	.684	113	3	3	102	90	34	.627	8			2	C	1.2
1910	Cle-A	110	363	34	111	16	6	0	55	21		.306	.344	.363	.727	128	10	10	100	146	51	.675	10			-3	CO	1.4
1911	Cle-A	99	287	34	93	19	5	1	37	8		.324	.345	.436	.780	114	5	4	103	98	45	.722	6			-5	OC	-0.2
1912	Cle-A	63	186	17	55	4	0	1	21	7		.296	.328	.333	.662	88	-3	-3	101	108	21	.565	3			4	C	0.6
	Chi-A	30	55	5	20	2	0	0	14	2		.364	.386	.400	.786	126	2	2	99	212	9	.714	1			-1	C/O	0.2
	Yr	93	241	22	75	6	0	1	35	9		.311	.341	.349	.690	97	-1	-1	100	143	30	.596	4			3		0.8
1913	Chi-A	60	97	3	23	1	0	0	8	4	9	.237	.267	.247	.515	53	-6	-6	95	118	7	.405	2			0	C	-0.3
1914	KC-F	134	436	58	146	20	12	1	67	31	25	.335	.379	.443	.822	142	19	22	95	123	80	.807	10			-7	*C	2.1
1915	KC-F	110	309	32	84	12	5	3	32	21	15	.272	.318	.372	.690	108	1	2	97	93	39	.613	2			-6	C	-0.2
Total	7	704	2020	215	607	88	38	7	261	107	49	.300	.337	.392	.729	116	31	34	99	115	285	.668	42			-17	C/O	4.8
■ **ROY EASTERWOOD** Easterwood, Roy Charles "Shag" b: 1/12/15, Waxahachie, Tex. d: 8/24/84, Graham, Tex. BR/TR, 6'0.5", 196 lbs. Deb: 4/21/44																												
1944	Chi-N	17	33	1	7	2	0	1	2	1	11	.212	.235	.364	.599	66	-2	-2	101	48	2	.464	0			-0	C	0.0
■ **JOHN EASTON** Easton, John David "Goose" b: 3/4/33, Trenton, N.J. BR/TR, 6'2", 185 lbs. Deb: 6/19/55																												
1955	Phi-N	1	0	0	0	0	0	0	0	0	0	—	—	—	—	—	0	0	102	—	—	—	0	0	0	0	R	0.0
1959	Phi-N	3	3	0	0	0	0	0	0	0	3	.000	.000	.000	.000	-99	-1	-1	99	0	0	.000	0	0	0	0	H	0.0
Total	2	4	3	0	0	0	0	0	0	0	3	.000	.000	.000	.000	-99	-1	-1	99	0	2	.000	0	0	0	0		0.0
■ **EDDIE EAYRS** Eayrs, Edwin b: 11/10/1890, Blackstone, Mass. d: 11/30/69, Warwick, R.I. BL/TL, 5'7", 160 lbs. Deb: 6/30/13																												
1913	Pit-N	4	6	0	1	0	0	0	0	0	1	.167	.167	.167	.333	-5	-1	-1	96	0	0	.200	0			0	/P	0.0
1920	Bos-N	87	244	31	80	5	2	1	24	30	18	.328	.410	.377	.787	132	10	12	96	98	40	.778	4	3	-1	-6	O/P	0.2
1921	Bos-N	15	15	0	1	0	0	0	1	0	4	.067	.067	.067	.133	-70	-3	-3	93	367	0	.071	0	0	0	-0	/P	-0.2
	Bro-N	8	6	1	1	0	0	0	1	2	0	.167	.375	.167	.542	46	-0	-0	105	367	1	.600	0	0	0	-0	/O	0.0
	Yr	23	21	1	2	0	0	0	2	2	4	.095	.174	.095	.269	-28	-4	-4	97	383	0	.211	0	0	0	-1		-0.2
Total	3	114	271	32	83	5	2	1	26	32	23	.306	.388	.351	.738	116	6	7	96	116	41	.707	4	3		-6	/OP	0.0
■ **HI EBRIGHT** Ebright, Hiram C. "Buck" b: 6/12/1859, Lancaster Co., Pa d: 10/24/16, Milwaukee, Wis. BR/TR, Deb: 4/24/1889																												
1889	Was-N	16	59	7	15	2	2	1	6	3	8	.254	.302	.407	.708	107	-0	0	92	68	8	.659	1			0	/COS	0.0
■ **JOHNNY ECHOLS** Echols, John Gresham b: 1/9/17, Atlanta, Ga. d: 11/13/72, Atlanta, Ga. BR/TR, 5'10.5", 175 lbs. Deb: 5/24/39																												
1939	StL-N	2	0	0	0	0	0	0	0	0	0	—	—	—	—	—	0	0	105	—	—	—	0			0	R	0.0
■ **OX ECKHARDT** Eckhardt, Oscar George b: 12/23/01, Yorktown, Tex. d: 4/22/51, Yorktown, Tex. BL/TR, 6'1", 185 lbs. Deb: 4/16/32																												
1932	Bos-N	8	8	1	2	0	0	0	1	0	1	.250	.250	.250	.500	37	-1	-1	93	186	0	.333	0			0	H	0.0
1936	Bro-N	16	44	5	8	1	0	1	6	5	2	.182	.265	.273	.538	43	-3	-4	105	142	4	.472	0			1	O	-0.3
Total	2	24	52	6	10	1	0	1	7	5	3	.192	.263	.269	.532	42	-4	-4	103	148	4	.452	0			1	/O	-0.3
■ **CHARLIE EDEN** Eden, Charles M. b: 1/18/1855, Lexington, Ky. d: 9/17/20, Cincinnati, Ohio BR/TR, Deb: 8/17/1877																												
1877	Chi-N	15	55	9	12	0	1	0	5	3	6	.218	.259	.255	.513	63	-2	-2	98	121	4	.395				-2	O	-0.3
1879	Cle-N	81	353	40	96	**31**	7	3	34	6	20	.272	.284	.425	.709	131	11	11	99	65	44	.607				-5	*O/1C	0.3
1884	Pit-a	32	122	12	33	7	4	1		7		.270	.341	.418	.759	154	7	7	97	0	18	.719				-4	O/P	0.3
1885	Pit-a	98	405	57	103	18	6	0		17		.254	.298	.328	.626	94	0	-4	106	0	41	.523				-14	*O/P3	-2.0
Total	4	226	935	118	244	56	18	4	39	33	26	.261	.296	.372	.669	113	16	13	102	31	106	.572				-24	O/P13C	-1.7
■ **MIKE EDEN** Eden, Edward Michael b: 5/22/49, Fort Clayton, Canal Zone BB/TR, 5'10", 170 lbs. Deb: 8/02/76																												
1976	Atl-N	5	8	0	0	0	0	0	1	0	0	.000	.000	.000	.000	-90	-2	-2	111	0	0	.000	0	0	0	0	/2	-0.1
1978	Chi-A	10	17	1	2	0	0	0	0	4	0	.118	.286	.118	.403	17	-2	-2	101	0	1	.375	0	0	0	-1	/S2	-0.1
Total	2	15	25	1	2	0	0	0	1	4	0	.080	.207	.080	.287	-16	-4	-4	104	0	1	.250	0	0	0	-1	/2S	-0.2
■ **STUMP EDINGTON** Edington, Jacob Frank b: 7/4/1891, Roleen, Ind. d: 11/11/69, Bastrop, La. BL/TL, 5'8", 170 lbs. Deb: 6/20/12																												
1912	Pit-N	15	53	4	16	0	2	0	12	3	1	.302	.339	.377	.717	97	-0	-0	99	206	7	.622	0			-0	O	0.0
■ **DAVE EDLER** Edler, David Delmar b: 8/5/56, Sioux City, Iowa BR/TR, 6', 185 lbs. Deb: 9/04/80																												
1980	Sea-A	28	89	11	20	1	0	3	9	8	16	.225	.289	.337	.626	69	-4	-4	103	90	8	.533	2	3	-1	0	3	-0.4
1981	Sea-A	29	78	7	11	3	0	0	5	11	13	.141	.256	.179	.435	27	-7	-7	100	140	4	.408	3	3	-1	0	3/S	-0.7
1982	Sea-A	40	104	14	29	2	2	2	18	11	13	.279	.348	.394	.742	95	1	-1	109	153	14	.700	4	2	0	-1	3/OD	-0.1
1983	Sea-A	29	63	2	12	1	1	1	4	5	11	.190	.261	.286	.547	51	-4	-4	100	74	4	.482	3	3	-1	-0	3/1OD	-0.5
Total	4	126	334	34	72	7	3	6	36	35	53	.216	.294	.308	.602	65	-14	-16	104	119	30	.553	12	11	-3	-1	/3D1OS	-1.7
■ **BOB EDMONDSON** Edmondson, Robert E. b: 4/30/1879, Paris, Ky. d: 8/14/31, Lawrence, Kan. BR/TR, 5'11", 185 lbs. Deb: 9/15/06																												
1906	Was-A	3	3	1	1	0	0	0	0	0		.333	.333	.333	.667	122	0	0	91	0	0	.500	0			0	/PO	0.0
1908	Was-A	26	80	5	15	4	1	0	2	7		.188	.253	.262	.515	73	-3	-2	95	36	5	.431	0			2	O	-0.1
Total	2	29	83	6	16	4	1	0	2	7		.193	.256	.265	.521	74	-3	-2	95	35	5	.433	0			2	/OP	-0.1
■ **EDDIE EDMONSON** Edmonson, Earl Edward b: 11/20/1889, Hopewell, Pa. d: 5/10/71, Leesburg, Fla. BL/TR, 6', 175 lbs. Deb: 10/04/13																												
1913	Cle-A	2	5	0	0	0	0	0	0	0	0	.000	.000	.000	.000	-95	-1	-1	106	0	0	.000	0			-0	/1O	-0.1
■ **AL EDWARDS** Edwards, Albert b: 1896, Freeport, L.I., N.Y. TR, Deb: 9/17/15																												
1915	Phi-A	2	5	0	0	0	0	0	0	0	3	.000	.000	.000	.000	-99	-1	-1	96	0	0	.000	0			0	/2	0.0
■ **BRUCE EDWARDS** Edwards, Charles Bruce "Bull" b: 7/15/23, Quincy, Ill. d: 4/25/75, Sacramento, Cal. BR/TR, 5'8", 180 lbs. Deb: 6/23/46																												
1946	Bro-N	92	292	24	78	13	5	1	25	34	20	.267	.348	.356	.704	97	0	-1	103	87	37	.632	1			-1	C	0.1
1947	Bro-N	130	471	53	139	15	8	9	80	49	55	.295	.364	.418	.782	102	5	2	105	135	73	.731	2			3	*C	0.8
1948	Bro-N	96	286	36	79	17	2	8	54	26	28	.276	.341	.434	.774	104	3	1	104	137	41	.719	4			-0	CO3/1	0.3
1949	Bro-N	64	148	24	31	3	0	8	25	25	15	.209	.324	.392	.716	90	-2	-2	102	115	19	.675	0			-1	C/O3	-0.1
1950	Bro-N	50	142	16	26	4	1	8	16	13	22	.183	.256	.394	.651	64	-7	-9	107	77	13	.582	1			2	C/1	-0.5
1951	Bro-N	17	36	6	9	2	0	1	8	1	3	.250	.270	.389	.659	77	-1	-1	98	182	4	.536	0	0	0	0	/C	0.0
	Chi-N	51	141	19	33	9	2	3	17	16	14	.234	.316	.390	.707	91	-2	-2	97	103	17	.640	1	2	-1	-0	C/1	-0.2
	Yr	68	177	25	42	11	2	4	25	17	17	.237	.308	.390	.698	89	-4	-3	97	125	21	.624	1	2	-1	0		-0.2
1952	Chi-N	50	94	7	23	2	2	1	12	8	12	.245	.304	.340	.644	76	-3	-3	103	134	9	.533	0	0	0	-0	C/2	-0.2
1954	Chi-N	4	3	1	0	0	0	0	1	2	2	.000	.400	.000	.400	15	-0	-0	101	0	0	.667	0	0	0	0	H	0.0
1955	Was-A	30	57	5	10	2	0	0	3	16	6	.175	.356	.211	.567	61	-3	-2	91	93	5	.549	0	1	-1	0	C/3	0.0
1956	Cin-N	7	5	0	1	0	0	0	0	0	2	.200	.200	.200	.400	7	-1	-1	108	0	0	.250	0	0	0	0	/C23	0.0
Total	10	591	1675	191	429	67	20	39	241	190	179	.256	.335	.390	.725	93	-11	-17	103	116	217	.689	9	3		3	C/O312	0.2
■ **DAVE EDWARDS** Edwards, David Leonard b: 2/24/54, Los Angeles, Cal. BR/TR, 6', 170 lbs. Deb: 9/11/78																												
1978	Min-A	15	44	7	11	3	0	1	3	7	13	.250	.377	.386	.764	122	1	2	94	59	7	.794	1	1	-0	2	O	0.3
1979	Min-A	96	229	42	57	8	0	8	35	24	45	.249	.323	.389	.711	84	-3	-6	109	119	29	.667	6	3	0	-2	O	-1.0
1980	Min-A	81	200	26	50	9	1	2	20	12	51	.250	.296	.335	.631	67	-8	-10	109	107	19	.522	2	1	0	-1	O/D	-1.1
1981	SD-N	58	112	13	24	4	1	2	13	11	24	.214	.285	.321	.606	77	-4	-3	93	121	10	.543	3	1	0	-5	O	-1.0
1982	SD-N	71	55	7	10	2	0	1	2	1	14	.182	.196	.273	.469	33	-5	-5	92	44	2	.340	0	0	0	-13	O/1	-1.9
Total	5	321	640	95	152	26	2	14	73	55	147	.237	.302	.350	.652	76	-19	-22	103	105	67	.595	12	6	0	-19	O/D1	-4.7

YEAR	TM/L	G	AB	R	H	2B	3B	HR	RBI	BB	SO	AVG	OBP	SLG	PRO	/A	BR	/A	PF	CHI	RC	TA	SB	CS	SBR	FR	POS	TPR
■ **HANK EDWARDS**	Edwards, Henry Albert b: 1/29/19, Elmwood Place, O. d: 6/22/88, Santa Ana, Cal. BL/TL, 6', 190 lbs. Deb: 9/10/41																											
1941	Cle-A	16	68	10	15	1	1	1	6	2	4	.221	.243	.309	.552	45	-6	-6	101	78	5	.434	0	0	0	-1	O	-0.7
1942	Cle-A	13	48	6	12	2	1	0	7	5	8	.250	.321	.333	.654	92	-1	-1	92	157	6	.622	2	1	0	-0	O	-0.1
1943	Cle-A	92	297	38	82	18	6	3	28	30	34	.276	.343	.407	.750	132	6	10	90	79	41	.680	4	8	-4	-1	O	0.3
1946	Cle-A	124	458	62	138	33	**16**	10	54	43	48	.301	.361	.509	.870	159	23	29	89	80	88	.850	1	3	-2	-0	*O	2.2
1947	Cle-A	108	393	54	102	12	3	15	59	31	55	.260	.315	.420	.735	108	-0	2	96	105	53	.664	1	3	-2	-6	*O	-0.9
1948	Cle-A	55	160	27	43	9	2	3	18	18	18	.269	.346	.406	.753	101	-0	-0	99	82	24	.708	1	1	-0	-5	O	-0.6
1949	Cle-A	5	15	3	4	0	0	1	1	1	2	.267	.313	.467	.779	107	-0	-0	98	34	2	.667	0	0	0	-1	/O	0.0
	Chi-N	58	176	25	51	8	4	7	21	19	22	.290	.359	.500	.859	136	6	8	94	73	31	.829	0			-5	O	0.0
1950	Chi-N	41	110	13	40	11	1	2	21	10	13	.364	.417	.536	.953	142	8	7	105	125	25	.958	0			-5	O	0.1
1951	Bro-N	35	31	1	7	3	0	0	3	4	9	.226	.314	.323	.637	73	-1	-1	98	116	3	.538	0	0	0	0	H	0.0
	Cin-N	41	127	14	40	9	1	3	20	13	17	.315	.379	.472	.851	127	5	5	101	112	22	.793	0	2	-1	-4	O	-0.1
	Yr	76	158	15	47	12	1	3	23	17	26	.297	.366	.443	.809	117	4	4	99	115	26	.750	0	2	-1	-4		-0.1
1952	Cin-N	74	184	24	52	7	6	6	28	19	22	.283	.350	.484	.833	130	7	7	100	102	31	.788	0	3	-2	-7	O	-0.2
	Chi-A	8	18	2	6	0	0	0	1	0	2	.333	.333	.333	.667	86	-0	-0	100	62	2	.462	0	0	0	0	/O	0.0
1953	StL-A	65	106	6	21	3	0	0	9	13	10	.198	.286	.226	.512	37	-9	-10	107	139	8	.425	0	1	-1	-1	O	-1.1
Total	11	735	2191	285	613	116	41	51	276	208	264	.280	.343	.440	.783	120	38	50	95	94	340	.739	9	22	-7	-37	O	-1.1
■ **DOC EDWARDS**	Edwards, Howard Rodney b: 12/10/36, Red Jacket, W.Va. BR/TR, 6'2", 215 lbs. Deb: 4/21/62 MC																											
1962	Cle-A	53	143	13	39	6	0	3	9	9	14	.273	.325	.378	.702	90	-2	-2	98	57	18	.613	0	0	0	5	C	0.5
1963	Cle-A	10	31	6	8	2	0	0	0	2	6	.258	.303	.323	.626	78	-1	-1	97	0	3	.522	0	0	0	0	C	0.0
	KC-A	71	240	16	60	12	0	6	35	11	23	.250	.289	.375	.664	78	-5	-8	108	136	24	.554	0	1	-1	4	C	-0.3
	Yr	81	271	22	68	14	0	6	35	13	29	.251	.290	.369	.659	78	-6	-8	106	119	28	.550	0	1	-1	4		-0.3
1964	KC-A	97	294	25	66	10	0	5	28	13	40	.224	.265	.310	.574	57	-16	-18	105	112	21	.444	0	1	-1	-4	C/1	-2.0
1965	KC-A	6	20	1	3	0	0	0	0	1	2	.150	.190	.150	.340	-2	-3	-3	97	0	0	.211	0	0	0	0	/C	-0.1
	NY-A	45	100	3	19	3	0	1	9	13	14	.190	.289	.250	.539	54	-6	-6	101	133	6	.449	1	2	-1	1	C	-0.2
	Yr	51	120	4	22	3	0	1	9	14	16	.183	.274	.233	.507	45	-8	-8	101	118	7	.415	1	2	-1	2		-0.3
1970	Phi-N	35	78	5	21	0	0	0	6	4	10	.269	.313	.269	.582	60	-4	-4	96	111	6	.426	0	0	0	-1	C	-0.3
Total	5	317	906	69	216	33	0	15	87	53	109	.238	.287	.325	.612	67	-38	-41	103	105	79	.511	1	4	-2	5	C/1	-2.4
■ **JOHNNY EDWARDS**	Edwards, John Alban b: 6/10/38, Columbus, Ohio BL/TR, 6'4", 220 lbs. Deb: 6/27/61																											
1961	Cin-N	52	145	14	27	5	0	2	14	18	28	.186	.280	.262	.543	43	-11	-12	104	128	11	.479	1	0	0	-1	C	-0.8
1962	Cin-N	133	452	47	115	28	5	8	50	45	70	.254	.323	.392	.715	89	-6	-7	102	98	58	.653	1	1	-0	25	*C	1.9
1963	Cin-N	148	495	46	128	19	4	11	67	45	93	.259	.325	.380	.705	98	2	-1	104	130	61	.626	1	5	-3	17	*C	1.9
1964	Cin-N	126	423	47	119	23	1	7	55	34	65	.281	.336	.390	.726	101	2	1	103	121	56	.646	1	2	-1	11	*C	1.5
1965	Cin-N	114	371	47	99	22	2	17	51	50	45	.267	.355	.474	.830	127	16	14	104	93	64	.819	0	0	0	12	*C	3.1
1966	Cin-N	98	282	24	54	8	0	6	39	31	42	.191	.272	.284	.555	48	-17	-22	114	167	21	.473	1	3	-2	-2	C	-2.3
1967	Cin-N	80	209	10	43	6	0	2	20	16	28	.206	.262	.263	.525	47	-13	-15	109	136	14	.416	1	4	-2	-4	C	-1.8
1968	StL-N	85	230	14	55	9	1	3	29	16	20	.239	.291	.326	.618	89	-4	-3	95	145	21	.511	1	1	-0	6	C	0.5
1969	Hou-N	151	496	52	115	20	6	6	50	53	69	.232	.309	.333	.641	78	-13	-14	102	110	49	.556	2	1	0	-8	*C	-1.2
1970	Hou-N	140	458	46	101	16	4	7	49	51	63	.221	.300	.319	.619	70	-22	-18	94	114	44	.544	1	0	0	5	*C	-0.6
1971	Hou-N	106	317	18	74	13	4	1	23	26	38	.233	.292	.309	.601	76	-12	-10	93	93	30	.512	1	1	-0	-4	*C	-1.2
1972	Hou-N	108	332	33	89	16	2	5	40	50	39	.268	.366	.373	.739	104	6	4	106	118	47	.702	2	4	-2	-13	*C	-0.5
1973	Hou-N	79	250	24	61	10	2	5	27	19	23	.244	.303	.360	.663	87	-6	-5	95	103	27	.580	1	0	0	-5	C	-0.4
1974	Hou-N	50	117	8	26	7	1	1	10	11	12	.222	.295	.325	.619	75	-4	-4	98	94	11	.548	1	1	-0	2	C	-0.1
Total	14	1470	4577	430	1106	202	32	81	524	465	635	.242	.314	.353	.667	85	-84	-92	101	117	515	.604	15	23	-9	39	*C	-0.0
■ **MARSHALL EDWARDS**	Edwards, Marshall Lynn b: 8/27/52, Fort Lewis, Wash. BL/TL, 5'9", 157 lbs. Deb: 4/11/81																											
1981	Mil-A	40	58	10	14	1	1	0	4	0	2	.241	.241	.293	.534	56	-4	-3	96	92	4	.489	6	2	1	-7	O/D	-1.1
1982	Mil-A	69	178	24	44	4	1	2	14	4	8	.247	.264	.315	.578	62	-10	-9	94	90	14	.490	10	4	1	-0	O/D	-1.0
1983	Mil-A	51	74	14	22	1	1	0	5	1	9	.297	.307	.338	.645	84	-2	-2	92	78	6	.534	5	5	-2	-2	O/D	-0.4
Total	3	160	310	48	80	6	3	2	23	5	19	.258	.270	.316	.586	66	-16	-14	94	88	24	.512	21	11	-0	-9	O/D	-2.5
■ **MIKE EDWARDS**	Edwards, Michael Lewis b: 8/27/52, Fort Lewis, Wash. BR/TR, 5'10", 154 lbs. Deb: 9/10/77																											
1977	Pit-N	7	6	1	0	0	0	0	0	0	3	.000	.143	.000	.143	-56	-1	-1	103	0	-0	.125	0	2	-1	-0	/2	-0.2
1978	Oak-A	142	414	48	113	16	2	1	23	16	32	.273	.303	.329	.632	77	-13	-13	101	65	37	.550	27	21	-5	-20	*2/SD	-3.0
1979	Oak-A	122	400	35	93	12	2	1	23	15	37	.233	.264	.280	.544	53	-30	-24	89	77	27	.429	10	6	-1	-16	*2/S	-3.4
1980	Oak-A	46	59	10	14	0	0	0	3	1	5	.237	.250	.237	.487	36	-5	-5	95	84	3	.340	1	1	-0	-2	2/OD	-0.6
Total	4	317	879	94	220	28	4	2	49	32	77	.250	.281	.298	.579	63	-49	-43	95	71	68	.488	38	30	-7	-38	2/SDO	-7.2
■ **BEN EGAN**	Egan, Arthur Augustus b: 11/20/1883, Augusta, N.Y. d: 2/18/68, Sherrill, N.Y. BR/TR, 6', 195 lbs. Deb: 9/29/08 C																											
1908	Phi-A	2	6	1	1	1	0	0	0	1		.167	.286	.333	.619	96	0	-0	108	0	1	.600	0			0	/C	0.0
1912	Phi-A	48	138	9	24	3	4	0	13	6		.174	.208	.254	.462	32	-13	-13	99	124	7	.386	3			-1	C	-0.8
1914	Cle-A	29	88	7	20	2	1	0	11	3	20	.227	.277	.273	.549	64	-4	-4	102	172	7	.435	0	1	-1	3	C	0.0
1915	Cle-A	42	120	4	13	3	0	0	6	8	14	.108	.164	.133	.297	-11	-16	-17	104	128	3	.224	0			6	C	-0.7
Total	4	121	352	21	58	9	5	0	30	18	34	.165	.212	.219	.431	26	-33	-34	102	135	18	.342	3	1		8	C	-1.5
■ **JIM EGAN**	Egan, James K. "Troy Terrier" b: 1858, Ansonia, Conn. d: 9/26/1884, New Haven, Conn. TL, Deb: 5/15/1882																											
1882	Tro-N	30	115	15	23	3	2	0	10	1	21	.200	.207	.261	.468	51	-6	-6	95	114	6	.337				0	OP/C	-0.4
■ **DICK EGAN**	Egan, Richard Joseph b: 6/23/1884, Portland, Ore. d: 7/7/47, Oakland, Cal. BR/TR, 5'11", 162 lbs. Deb: 9/15/08																											
1908	Cin-N	18	68	8	14	3	1	0	5	2		.206	.229	.279	.508	62	-3	-3	103	97	6	.519	7			0	2	-0.3
1909	Cin-N	127	480	59	132	14	3	2	53	37		.275	.329	.329	.659	113	3	6	94	125	63	.678	39			**22**	*2S	2.9
1910	Cin-N	135	474	70	116	11	5	0	46	53	38	.245	.322	.289	.611	78	-12	-13	101	124	59	.648	41			-12	*2/S	-2.2
1911	Cin-N	153	558	80	139	11	5	1	56	59	50	.249	.322	.292	.614	79	-20	-13	92	121	65	.621	37			14	*2	-0.2
1912	Cin-N	149	507	69	125	14	5	0	52	56	26	.247	.324	.294	.618	75	-20	-14	92	120	58	.605	24			-2	*2	-2.1
1913	Cin-N	60	195	15	55	7	3	0	22	15	13	.282	.333	.349	.682	93	-1	-2	102	120	25	.636	6			4	2S/3	0.2
1914	Bro-N	106	337	30	76	10	3	1	21	22	25	.226	.273	.282	.555	64	-15	-15	101	78	28	.479	8			-11	S3/021	-2.5
1915	Bro-N	3	3	0	0	0	0	0	0	0	0	.000	.000	.000	.000	-99	-1	-1	101	0	0	.000	0			0	H	0.0
	Bos-N	83	220	20	57	9	1	0	21	28	18	.259	.343	.309	.652	100	0	1	98	118	24	.593	3	4	-2	-2	O2S/13	-0.2
	Yr	86	223	20	57	9	1	0	21	28	18	.256	.339	.305	.644	97	-0	0	98	114	24	.582	3	4	-2	-2		-0.2
1916	Bos-N	83	238	23	53	8	3	0	16	19	21	.223	.280	.282	.562	78	-8	-6	93	95	21	.476	2			-14	2S/3	-1.9
Total	9	917	3080	374	767	87	29	4	292	291	191	.249	.315	.300	.615	83	-76	-60	96	114	349	.599	167	4		-1	2S/031	-6.3
■ **TOM EGAN**	Egan, Thomas Patrick b: 6/9/46, Los Angeles, Cal. BR/TR, 6'4", 218 lbs. Deb: 5/27/65																											
1965	Cal-A	18	38	3	10	0	1	0	1	3	12	.263	.317	.316	.633	82	-1	-1	98	35	4	.517	0	0	0	1	C	0.1
1966	Cal-A	7	11	0	0	0	0	0	0	1	5	.000	.083	.000	.083	-74	-2	-2	99	0	0	.091	0	0	0	0	/C	-0.1
1967	Cal-A	1	1	0	0	0	0	0	0	0	0	.000	.000	.000	.000	-99	-0	-0	96	0	0	.000	0	0	0	0	/C	0.0
1968	Cal-A	16	43	2	5	1	0	1	4	2	15	.116	.156	.209	.365	10	-5	-4	94	143	1	.268	0	0	0	-1	C	-0.4
1969	Cal-A	46	120	7	17	1	0	5	16	17	41	.142	.254	.275	.529	48	-9	-8	99	134	9	.481	0	1	-1	4	C	-0.1
1970	Cal-A	79	210	14	50	6	0	4	20	14	67	.238	.289	.324	.613	75	-9	-7	92	101	20	.506	0	0	0	-9	C	-1.5
1971	Chi-A	85	251	29	60	11	1	10	34	26	94	.239	.320	.410	.731	108	1	2	98	104	35	.694	1	0	0	-1	C/1	0.5
1972	Chi-A	50	141	8	27	3	0	2	9	4	48	.191	.224	.255	.480	40	-10	-11	106	90	7	.353	0	0	0	-3	C	-1.5
1974	Cal-A	43	94	4	11	0	0	0	4	8	40	.117	.194	.117	.311	-10	-13	-12	92	143	3	.244	1	0	0	2	C	-0.8
1975	Cal-A	28	70	7	16	3	1	0	3	5	14	.229	.280	.300	.580	68	-3	-3	95	55	6	.456	0	0	0	-4	C	-0.5
Total	10	373	979	74	196	25	3	22	91	80	336	.200	.267	.299	.566	63	-51	-47	97	103	83	.488	2	1	0	-10	C/1	-4.3
■ **ELMER EGGERT**	Eggert, Elmer Albert "Mose" b: 1/29/02, Rochester, N.Y. d: 4/9/71, Rochester, N.Y. BR/TR, 5'9", 160 lbs. Deb: 4/27/27																											
1927	Bos-A	5	3	0	0	0	0	0	0	1	1	.000	.250	.000	.250	-33	-1	-1	95	0	0	.333	0	0	0	0	/2	0.0

1088 **EGGLER-ELLICK** Player Register

YEAR	TM/L	G	AB	R	H	2B	3B	HR	RBI	BB	SO	AVG	OBP	SLG	PRO	/A	BR	/A	PF	CHI	RC	TA	SB	CS	SBR	FR	POS	TPR
■ **DAVE EGGLER**	Eggler, David Daniel b: 4/30/1851, Brooklyn, N.Y. d: 4/5/02, Buffalo, N.Y. BR/TR, 5'9", 165 lbs. Deb: 5/18/1871																											
1871	Mut-n	33	150	37	47							.313															*O	
1872	Mut-n	56	295	95	102							.346															*O	
1873	Mut-n	53	281	83	92							.327															*O	
1874	Phi-n	58	306	70	96							.314															*O/2	
1875	Ath-n	66	302	65	87							.288															*O	
1876	Phi-N	39	174	28	52	4	0	0	19	2	4	.299	.307	.322	.629	111	2	2	99	121	18	.475				4	O	0.5
1877	Chi-N	33	136	20	36	3	0	0	20	1	5	.265	.270	.287	.557	77	-4	-3	98	177	11	.400				2	O	-0.1
1879	Buf-N	78	317	41	66	5	7	0	27	11	41	.208	.235	.268	.503	57	-11	-18	114	118	20	.382				-7	*O	-2.5
1883	Bal-a	53	202	15	38	2	0	0		1		.188	.192	.198	.390	24	-16	-18	107	0	8	.250				-1	O	-1.6
	Buf-N	38	153	13	38	2	1	0	13	2	29	.248	.258	.275	.533	62	-7	-7	100	109	11	.383				-2	O	-0.6
1884	Buf-N	63	241	25	47	3	1	0	20	6	54	.195	.215	.216	.430	34	-17	-20	107	135	11	.299				-1	O	-1.9
1885	Buf-N	6	24	0	2	0	0	0	0	2	4	.083	.154	.083	.237	-22	-3	-3	99	0	0	.182				0	/O	-0.2
Total	5 n	266	1334	350	424							.318															/O	
Total	6	310	1247	142	279	19	9	0	99	25	137	.224	.239	.253	.492	55	-57	-67	106	106	80	.352				-6	O/2	-6.4
■ **HACK EIBEL**	Eibel, Henry Hack b: 12/6/1893, Brooklyn, N.Y. d: 10/16/45, Macon, Ga. BL/TL, 5'11", 220 lbs. Deb: 6/13/12																											
1912	Cle-A	1	3	0	0	0	0	0	0	0		.000	.000	.000	.000	-99	-1	-1	101	0	0	.000				-0	/O	0.0
1920	Bos-A	29	43	4	8	2	0	0	6	3	6	.186	.239	.233	.472	26	-5	-4	96	211	2	.389	1	1	-0	-2	/OP1	-0.6
Total	2	30	46	4	8	2	0	0	6	3	6	.174	.224	.217	.442	19	-5	-5	96	198	2	.359	1	1		-2	/OP1	-0.6
■ **IKE EICHRODT**	Eichrodt, Frederick George b: 1/6/03, Chicago, Ill. d: 7/14/65, Indianapolis, Ind BR/TR, 5'11.5", 167 lbs. Deb: 9/07/25																											
1925	Cle-A	15	52	4	12	3	1	0	4	2	7	.231	.259	.327	.586	45	-4	-5	106	79	4	.475	0	0	0	-1	O	-0.6
1926	Cle-A	37	80	14	25	7	1	0	7	2	11	.313	.329	.425	.754	96	-1	-1	100	70	11	.673	1	0	0	-4	O	-0.5
1927	Cle-A	85	267	24	59	19	2	0	25	16	25	.221	.265	.307	.572	50	-21	-20	97	101	22	.481	2	0	1	6	O	-1.8
1931	Chi-A	34	117	9	25	5	1	0	15	1	8	.214	.220	.274	.494	32	-12	-11	92	155	7	.359	0	0	0	-2	O	-1.3
Total	4	171	516	51	121	34	5	0	51	21	51	.234	.264	.320	.584	53	-39	-37	97	106	44	.478	3	0	1	-0	O	-4.2
■ **JIM EISENREICH**	Eisenreich, James Michael b: 4/18/59, St.Cloud, Minn. BL/TL, 5'11", 180 lbs. Deb: 4/06/82																											
1982	Min-A	34	99	10	30	6	0	2	9	11	13	.303	.378	.424	.803	120	3	3	100	75	17	.771	0	0	0	0	O	0.2
1983	Min-A	2	7	1	2	1	0	0	0	1	1	.286	.375	.429	.804	115	0	0	105	0	1	.800	0	0	0	1	/O	0.1
1984	Min-A	12	32	1	7	1	0	0	3	2	4	.219	.265	.250	.515	41	-2	-3	106	150	2	.462	2	0	1	-0	/OD	-0.2
1987	KC-A	44	105	10	25	8	2	4	21	7	13	.238	.286	.467	.752	92	-1	-2	104	137	13	.687	1	1	-0	0	D	-0.1
1988	KC-A	82	202	26	44	8	1	1	19	6	31	.218	.240	.282	.523	44	-15	-16	103	126	14	.442	9	3	1	-8	OD	-2.3
Total	5	174	445	48	108	24	3	7	52	27	62	.243	.288	.357	.645	74	-15	-17	103	116	47	.580	12	4	1	-7	/OD	-2.3
■ **ELAND**	Eland Deb:4/14/1873																											
1873	Mar-n	1	4	0	0							.000															/O	
■ **KID ELBERFELD**	Elberfeld, Norman Arthur "The Tabasco Kid" b: 4/13/1875, Pomeroy, Ohio d: 1/13/44, Chattanooga, Tenn. BR/TR, 5'7", 158 lbs. Deb: 5/30/1898 M																											
1898	Phi-N	14	38	1	9	4	0	0	7	5		.237	.356	.342	.698	109	0	1	95	163	5	.690	0			0	3	0.1
1899	Cin-N	41	138	23	36	4	2	0	22	15		.261	.350	.319	.669	82	-2	-3	106	156	18	.667	5			0	S3	-0.2
1901	Det-A	121	432	76	133	21	11	3	76	57		.308	.389	.428	.817	117	18	11	110	131	83	.886	23			**23**	*S	3.6
1902	Det-A	130	488	70	127	17	6	1	64	55		.260	.335	.326	.661	86	-8	-7	99	125	61	.645	19			8	*S	1.2
1903	Det-A	35	132	29	45	5	3	0	19	11		.341	.392	.424	.816	152	8	8	97	117	25	.839	6			-2	S/3	0.7
	NY-A	90	349	49	100	18	5	0	45	22		.287	.329	.367	.696	110	4	4	100	122	49	.667	16			0	S	0.9
	Yr	125	481	78	145	23	8	0	64	33		.301	.346	.383	.729	122	12	13	99	121	73	.711	22			-2		1.6
1904	NY-A	122	445	55	117	13	5	2	46	37		.263	.320	.328	.648	96	4	-2	112	120	54	.613	18			6	*S	0.6
1905	NY-A	111	390	48	102	18	2	0	53	23		.262	.303	.318	.621	97	-1	-1	102	156	44	.573	18			3	*S	0.5
1906	NY-A	99	346	59	106	12	4	2	31	30		.306	.362	.382	.743	112	14	6	120	87	56	.754	19			-5	S	0.3
1907	NY-A	120	447	61	121	17	6	0	51	36		.271	.325	.336	.661	104	7	2	109	117	57	.638	22			13	*S	2.0
1908	NY-A	19	56	11	11	3	0	0	5	6		.196	.274	.250	.524	76	-1	-1	95	134	4	.467	1			-1	SM	-0.1
1909	NY-A	106	379	47	90	9	5	0	26	28		.237	.314	.288	.601	91	-3	-3	99	97	40	.602	23			1	S3	0.1
1910	Was-A	127	455	53	114	9	2	2	42	35		.251	.322	.292	.614	92	-3	-3	101	118	49	.587	19			-3	*32/S	-0.2
1911	Was-A	127	404	58	110	19	4	0	47	65		.272	.405	.339	.744	112	10	12	97	118	66	.854	24			1	23	1.2
1914	Bro-N	30	62	7	14	1	0	0	1	2	4	.226	.304	.242	.546	63	-3	-3	101	24	4	.458	0			-2	S/2	-0.4
Total	14	1292	4561	647	1235	170	55	10	535	427	4	.271	.342	.339	.680	102	45	22	104	120	614	.676	213			42	S3/2	10.3
■ **GEORGE ELDER**	Elder, George Rezin b: 3/10/21, Lebanon, Ky. BL/TR, 5'11", 180 lbs. Deb: 7/22/49																											
1949	StL-A	41	44	9	11	3	0	0	2	4	11	.250	.313	.318	.631	67	-2	-2	100	49	5	.545	0	0	0	-1	O	-0.3
■ **LEE ELIA**	Elia, Lee Constantine b: 7/16/37, Philadelphia, Pa. BR/TR, 5'11", 175 lbs. Deb: 4/23/66 MC																											
1966	Chi-A	80	195	16	40	5	2	3	22	15	39	.205	.269	.297	.566	66	-9	-8	94	138	14	.460	0	1	-1	4	S	0.0
1968	Chi-N	15	17	1	3	0	0	0	3	0	6	.176	.222	.176	.399	19	-2	-2	112	421	1	.286	0	0	0	0	/S23	0.0
Total	2	95	212	17	43	5	2	3	25	15	45	.203	.265	.288	.553	62	-11	-10	96	160	15	.465	0	1	-1	4	/S32	0.0
■ **PETE ELKO**	Elko, Peter "Piccolo Pete" b: 6/17/18, Wilkes-Barre, Pa. BR/TR, 5'11", 185 lbs. Deb: 9/17/43																											
1943	Chi-N	9	30	1	4	0	0	0	0	4	5	.133	.235	.133	.369	8	-3	-3	99	0	1	.286	0			-1	/3	-0.3
1944	Chi-N	7	22	2	5	1	0	0	0	0	0	.227	.227	.273	.500	40	-2	-2	101	0	1	.353	0			1	/3	0.0
Total	2	16	52	3	9	1	0	0	0	4	5	.173	.232	.192	.424	22	-5	-5	100	0	2	.326	0			0	/3	-0.3
■ **ROY ELLAM**	Ellam, Roy "Whitey" or "Slippery" b: 2/8/1886, W.Conshohocken, Pa. d: 10/28/48, Conshohocken, Pa. BR/TR, 5'10.5", 203 lbs. Deb: 09																											
1909	Cin-N	10	21	4	4	0	1	1	4	7		.190	.393	.429	.821	167	2	2	94	121	4	1.000	1			-0	/S	0.2
1918	Pit-N	26	77	9	10	1	1	0	2	17	17	.130	.302	.169	.471	42	-4	-5	106	59	5	.507	2			-3	S	-0.7
Total	2	36	98	13	14	1	2	1	6	24	17	.143	.323	.224	.547	66	-2	-3	103	73	9	.607	3			-3	/S	-0.5
■ **FRANK ELLERBE**	Ellerbe, Francis Rogers "Governor" b: 12/25/1895, Marion, S.C. d: 7/7/88, BR/TR, 5'10.5", 165 lbs. Deb: 8/28/19																											
1919	Was-A	28	105	13	29	4	1	0	16	2	15	.276	.290	.333	.623	76	-4	-4	98	176	12	.553	5			-3	S	-0.4
1920	Was-A	101	336	38	98	14	2	0	36	19	23	.292	.331	.345	.677	84	-10	-8	95	109	39	.583	5	4	-1	-3	3S/O	-0.4
1921	Was-A	10	10	1	2	0	1	0	1	0	2	.200	.200	.400	.600	51	-1	-1	99	86	1	.500	0	0	0	0	H	0.0
	StL-A	105	430	65	124	20	12	2	49	22	42	.288	.327	.405	.732	85	-10	-11	101	90	56	.641	1	6	-3	-2	*3	-0.6
	Yr	115	440	66	126	20	13	2	50	22	44	.286	.325	.405	.729	85	-11	-12	101	90	56	.637	1	6	-3	-2		-0.6
1922	StL-A	91	342	42	84	16	3	1	33	25	37	.246	.303	.319	.621	59	-19	-22	106	107	35	.535	1	0	0	8	3	-0.3
1923	StL-A	18	49	6	9	0	0	0	1	1	5	.184	.200	.184	.384	1	-7	-7	104	38	2	.244	0	1	-1	-1	3	-0.6
1924	StL-A	21	61	7	12	3	0	0	2	2	3	.197	.222	.246	.468	19	-7	-8	107	44	3	.340	0	1	-1	-1	3	-0.7
	Cle-A	46	120	7	31	1	3	1	14	1	9	.258	.270	.342	.612	59	-8	-8	97	105	11	.483	0	0	0	4	3/2	0.0
	Yr	67	181	14	43	4	3	1	16	3	12	.238	.254	.309	.563	45	-16	-15	100	87	14	.432	0	1	-1	3		-0.7
Total	6	420	1453	179	389	58	22	4	152	72	136	.268	.306	.346	.652	70	-67	-68	100	102	158	.553	12	12		2	3/S2O	-3.0
■ **JOE ELLICK**	Ellick, Joseph J. b: 4/3/1854, Cincinnati, Ohio d: 4/21/23, Kansas City, Kan. 5'10", 162 lbs. Deb: 5/13/1875 M																											
1875	RS-n	6	24	1	5							.208															/3OS	
1878	Mil-N	3	13	2	2	0	0	0	1	0	1	.154	.154	.154	.308	1	-1	-1	107	163	0	.182				0	/C3P	0.0
1880	Wor-N	5	18	1	1	0	0	0	0	1	2	.056	.105	.056	.161	-39	-3	-3	113	0	0	.118				0	/3	-0.2
1884	CP-U	92	394	71	93	11	0	0		16		.236	.266	.264	.530	80	-8	-8	99	0	28	.399	0			-2	OS/2M	-0.8
	KC-U	2	8	0	0	0	0	0		0		.000	.000	.000	.000	-99	-2	-1	87	0	0	.000	0			0	/2O	0.0
	Bal-U	7	27	2	4	0	0	0		2		.148	.207	.148	.355	20	-2	-3	110	0	1	.261	0			0	/SO	-0.1
	Yr	101	429	73	97	11	0	0		18		.226	.257	.252	.509	73	-12	-11	100	0	28	.380	0			-2		-0.9
Total	3	109	460	76	100	11	0	0	1	19	3	.217	.248	.241	.490	66	-15	-16	101	4	30	.361	0			-2	/OS32CP	-1.1

YEAR	TM/L	G	AB	R	H	2B	3B	HR	RBI	BB	SO	AVG	OBP	SLG	PRO	/A	BR	/A	PF	CHI	RC	TA	SB	CS	SBR	FR	POS	TPR
■ **LARRY ELLIOT**	Elliot, Lawrence Lee b: 3/5/38, San Diego, Cal. BL/TL, 6'2", 200 lbs. Deb: 4/19/62																											
1962	Pit-N	8	10	2	3	0	0	1	2	0	1	.300	.300	.600	.900	132	0	0	102	88	2	.857	0	0	0	-1	/O	0.0
1963	Pit-N	4	4	0	0	0	0	0	0	0	3	.000	.000	.000	.000	-99	-1	-1	99	0	0	.000	0	0	0	0	H	0.0
1964	NY-N	80	224	27	51	8	0	9	22	28	55	.228	.322	.384	.705	103	-0	1	95	80	27	.652	1	2	-1	3	O	0.1
1966	NY-N	65	199	24	49	14	2	5	32	17	46	.246	.306	.412	.718	103	-1	0	94	139	25	.643	0	1	-1	-0	O	-0.1
Total	4	157	437	53	103	22	2	15	56	45	105	.236	.311	.398	.710	102	-2	1	95	105	54	.656	1	3	-2	2	O	0.0
■ **ALLEN ELLIOTT**	Elliott, Allen Clifford "Ace" b: 12/25/1897, St.Louis, Mo. d: 5/6/79, St.Louis, Mo. BL/TR, 6', 170 lbs. Deb: 6/14/23																											
1923	Chi-N	53	168	21	42	8	2	2	29	2	12	.250	.267	.357	.625	61	-9	-10	104	155	15	.519	3	3	-1	-1	1	-1.5
1924	Chi-N	10	14	0	2	0	0	0	0	0	1	.143	.143	.143	.286	-23	-2	-2	101	0	0	.167	0	0	0	0	1	-0.2
Total	2	63	182	21	44	8	2	2	29	2	13	.242	.258	.341	.599	55	-12	-13	104	143	16	.489	3	3	-1	-1	/1	-1.7
■ **CARTER ELLIOTT**	Elliott, Carter Ward b: 11/29/1893, Atchison, Kan. d: 5/21/59, Palm Springs, Cal. BL/TR, 5'11", 165 lbs. Deb: 9/10/21																											
1921	Chi-N	12	28	5	7	2	0	0	0	5	3	.250	.364	.321	.685	78	-0	-1	107	0	4	.667	0	0	0	1	S	0.1
■ **GENE ELLIOTT**	Elliott, Eugene Birminghouse b: 2/8/1889, Fayette Co., Pa. d: 1/5/76, Huntingdon, Pa. BL/TR, 5'7", 150 lbs. Deb: 4/13/11																											
1911	NY-A	5	13	1	1	1	0	0	1	2		.077	.200	.154	.354	-1	-2	-2	111	169	0	.333	0			-1	/O3	-0.2
■ **ROWDY ELLIOTT**	Elliott, Harold B. b: 7/8/1890, Kokomo, Ind. d: 2/12/34, San Francisco, Cal BR/TR, 5'9", 160 lbs. Deb: 9/24/10																											
1910	Bos-N	3	2	0	0	0	0	0	0	0	0	.000	.000	.000	.000	-88	-1	-1	114	0	0	.000	0			0	/C	0.0
1916	Chi-N	23	55	5	14	3	0	0	3	3	5	.255	.293	.309	.602	73	-1	-2	117	70	6	.512	1			-1	C	-0.1
1917	Chi-N	85	223	18	56	8	5	0	28	11	11	.251	.292	.332	.624	87	-3	-4	105	146	22	.545	4			2	C	0.2
1918	Chi-N	5	10	0	0	0	0	0	0	2	1	.000	.167	.000	.167	-47	-2	-2	102	0	0	.200	0			-0	/C	-0.1
1920	Bro-N	41	112	13	27	4	0	1	13	3	6	.241	.267	.304	.571	57	-5	-7	111	136	9	.447	0	0	0	-3	C	-0.7
Total	5	157	402	36	97	15	5	1	44	19	23	.241	.281	.311	.592	72	-11	-15	108	128	37	.498	5	0		-2	C	-0.7
■ **HARRY ELLIOTT**	Elliott, Harry Lewis b: 12/30/23, San Francisco, Cal BR/TR, 5'9", 175 lbs. Deb: 8/01/53																											
1953	StL-N	24	59	6	15	6	1	1	6	3	8	.254	.302	.441	.742	89	-1	-1	102	81	7	.638	0	0	0	-0	O	-0.1
1955	StL-N	68	117	9	30	4	0	1	12	11	9	.256	.326	.316	.642	71	-5	-5	101	121	10	.505	0	2	-1	-3	O	-0.9
Total	2	92	176	15	45	10	1	2	18	14	17	.256	.318	.358	.676	77	-6	-6	101	108	17	.560	0	2	-1	-3	/O	-1.0
■ **RANDY ELLIOTT**	Elliott, Randy Lee b: 6/5/51, Oxnard, Cal. BR/TR, 6'2", 190 lbs. Deb: 9/10/72																											
1972	SD-N	14	49	5	10	3	1	0	6	2	11	.204	.235	.306	.541	60	-3	-3	88	164	3	.425	0	0	0	0	O	-0.2
1974	SD-N	13	33	5	7	1	0	1	2	7	9	.212	.350	.333	.683	98	-0	0	93	55	4	.667	0	1	-1	-3	O/1	-0.3
1977	SF-N	73	167	17	40	5	1	7	26	8	24	.240	.278	.407	.686	78	-5	-6	104	117	17	.575	0	2	-1	-2	O	-1.0
1980	Oak-A	14	39	4	5	3	0	0	1	1	13	.128	.150	.205	.355	-4	-6	-5	95	49	1	.257	0	0	0	0	D	-0.4
Total	4	114	288	31	62	12	2	8	35	18	57	.215	.264	.354	.618	68	-14	-14	99	108	25	.526	0	3	-2	-4	/OD1	-1.9
■ **BOB ELLIOTT**	Elliott, Robert Irving "Mr. Team" b: 11/26/16, San Francisco, Cal d: 5/4/66, San Diego, Cal. BR/TR, 6', 185 lbs. Deb: 9/02/39 MC																											
1939	Pit-N	32	129	18	43	10	3	3	19	9	4	.333	.377	.527	.904	141	7	7	100	96	24	.856	0			4	O	1.0
1940	Pit-N	148	551	88	161	34	11	5	64	45	28	.292	.348	.421	.769	117	8	11	95	98	81	.728	13			-10	*O	-0.4
1941	Pit-N	141	527	74	144	24	10	3	76	64	52	.273	.353	.374	.727	102	4	3	103	141	72	.678	6			-4	*O	-0.7
1942	Pit-N	143	560	75	166	26	7	9	89	52	35	.296	.358	.416	.774	125	18	17	101	134	84	.712	2			-3	*3/O	1.5
1943	Pit-N	156	581	82	183	30	12	7	101	56	24	.315	.376	.444	.820	131	26	24	104	133	96	.771	4			-6	*3/2S	1.8
1944	Pit-N	143	538	85	160	28	16	10	108	75	42	.297	.383	.465	.848	131	28	24	105	**147**	100	.865	9			3	*3/S	3.5
1945	Pit-N	144	541	80	157	36	6	8	108	64	38	.290	.366	.423	.790	115	14	12	103	157	84	.748	5			11	3O	1.8
1946	Pit-N	140	486	50	128	25	3	5	68	64	44	.263	.351	.358	.709	98	2	0	103	137	62	.660	6			5	O3	0.3
1947	Bos-N	150	555	93	176	35	5	22	113	87	60	.317	.410	.517	.927	149	37	39	97	126	120	.957	3			-4	*3	3.0
1948	Bos-N	151	540	99	153	24	5	23	100	**131**	57	.283	.423	.474	.897	140	38	37	102	122	117	.980	6			-11	*3	2.2
1949	Bos-N	139	482	77	135	29	5	17	76	90	38	.280	.395	.467	.862	135	23	25	97	106	92	.873	0			12	*3	3.8
1950	Bos-N	142	531	94	162	28	5	24	107	68	67	.305	.386	.512	.898	156	26	36	86	127	103	.889	2			-16	*3	1.9
1951	Bos-N	136	480	73	137	29	2	15	70	65	56	.285	.371	.448	.819	122	14	15	98	106	81	.786	2	0	1	-5	*3	0.9
1952	NY-N	98	272	33	62	6	2	10	35	36	20	.228	.323	.375	.698	91	-3	-3	102	103	35	.650	1	0	0	-9	O3	-1.3
1953	StL-A	48	160	19	40	7	1	5	29	30	18	.250	.368	.400	.768	101	2	1	107	139	25	.752	0	1	-1	-3	3	-0.3
	Chi-A	67	208	24	54	11	1	4	32	31	21	.260	.358	.380	.738	94	0	-1	106	130	31	.709	1	1	-0	-2	3/O	-0.5
	Yr	115	368	43	94	18	2	9	61	61	39	.255	.363	.389	.751	97	3	-0	106	135	57	.738	1	2	-1	-5		-0.8
Total	15	1978	7141	1064	2061	382	94	170	1195	967	604	.289	.375	.440	.815	124	245	246	100	127	1206	.823	60	2		-40	*3O/S2	18.5
■ **BEN ELLIS**	Ellis, Benjamin Franklin b: Pottsville, Pa. Deb: 7/16/1896																											
1896	Phi-N	4	16	0	1	0	0	0	0	3	6	.063	.211	.063	.273	-25	-3	-3	102	0	0	.267	0			0	/S3	-0.2
■ **RUBE ELLIS**	Ellis, George William b: 11/17/1885, Downey, Cal. d: 3/13/38, Rivera, Cal. BL/TL, 6', 170 lbs. Deb: 09																											
1909	StL-N	149	575	76	154	10	9	3	46	54		.268	.334	.332	.666	112	6	8	96	89	67	.627	16			14	*O	1.8
1910	StL-N	142	550	87	142	18	8	4	54	62	70	.258	.339	.342	.681	108	-1	5	92	83	72	.686	25			6	*O	0.6
1911	StL-N	155	555	69	139	20	10	3	66	66	64	.250	.332	.339	.671	87	-9	-9	101	120	66	.637	9			2	*O	-1.1
1912	StL-N	109	305	47	82	18	2	4	33	34	36	.269	.342	.380	.723	98	-1	-1	100	87	42	.700	6			2	O	-0.1
Total	4	555	1985	279	517	66	29	14	199	216	170	.260	.336	.344	.680	101	-5	3	97	96	247	.657	56			24	O	1.2
■ **JOHN ELLIS**	Ellis, John Charles b: 8/21/48, New London, Conn. BR/TR, 6'2.5", 225 lbs. Deb: 5/17/69																											
1969	NY-A	22	62	2	18	4	0	1	8	1	11	.290	.313	.403	.716	104	-0	-0	95	115	7	.587	0	2	-1	2	C	0.2
1970	NY-A	78	226	24	56	12	1	7	29	18	47	.248	.309	.403	.712	103	-2	-0	92	105	27	.631	0	1	-1	0	1/3C	-0.2
1971	NY-A	83	238	16	58	12	1	3	34	23	42	.244	.326	.340	.666	92	-3	-2	97	154	25	.573	0	0	0	1	1/C	-0.3
1972	NY-A	52	136	13	40	5	1	5	25	8	22	.294	.333	.456	.789	144	5	6	92	136	17	.667	0	0	0	4	C/1	1.0
1973	Cle-A	127	437	59	118	12	2	14	68	46	57	.270	.344	.403	.746	113	6	7	97	125	60	.678	0	0	0	3	CD1	1.2
1974	Cle-A	128	477	58	136	23	6	10	64	32	53	.285	.331	.421	.753	114	8	8	101	111	62	.655	1	2	-1	-2	1CD	0.3
1975	Cle-A	92	296	22	68	11	1	7	32	14	33	.230	.269	.345	.614	73	-12	-11	100	100	24	.488	0	1	-1	0	C/1D	-0.9
1976	Tex-A	11	31	4	13	2	0	1	8	0	4	.419	.419	.581	1.000	187	3	3	102	146	7	.947	0	0	0	1	/CD	0.4
1977	Tex-A	49	119	7	28	7	0	4	15	8	26	.235	.283	.395	.678	79	-3	-4	105	101	13	.598	0	0	0	0	CD/1	-0.3
1978	Tex-A	34	94	7	23	4	0	3	17	6	20	.245	.290	.383	.673	91	-2	-1	96	149	11	.583	0	1	-1	2	C/D	0.0
1979	Tex-A	111	316	33	90	12	0	12	61	15	55	.285	.321	.437	.758	102	0	0	100	135	44	.680	2	2	-1	0	D1/C	0.0
1980	Tex-A	73	182	12	43	9	1	1	23	14	23	.236	.294	.313	.608	66	-8	-8	100	149	17	.517	3	0	1	-0	1D/C	-0.9
1981	Tex-A	23	58	2	8	3	0	1	7	5	10	.138	.219	.241	.460	36	-5	-4	91	161	2	.370	0	1	-1	1	1/D	-0.4
Total	13	883	2672	259	699	116	13	69	391	190	403	.262	.315	.392	.707	100	-14	-8	98	125	317	.636	6	10	-4	12	1CD/3	0.1
■ **ROB ELLIS**	Ellis, Robert Walter b: 7/3/50, Grand Rapids, Mich. BR/TR, 5'11", 180 lbs. Deb: 6/18/71																											
1971	Mil-A	36	111	9	22	2	0	0	6	12	24	.198	.282	.216	.498	42	-8	-8	103	102	7	.385	0	2	-1	-4	3O	-1.5
1974	Mil-A	22	48	4	14	2	0	0	4	4	11	.292	.346	.333	.679	94	-0	-0	102	98	6	.588	0	0	0	-0	O/3D	0.0
1975	Mil-A	6	7	3	2	0	0	0	0	0	0	.286	.286	.286	.571	62	-0	-0	100	0	0	.333	0	0	0	-2	/OD	-0.2
Total	3	64	166	16	38	4	0	0	10	16	35	.229	.301	.253	.554	57	-9	-9	103	97	13	.450	0	2	-1	-6	/O3D	-1.7
■ **BABE ELLISON**	Ellison, Herbert Spencer "Bert" b: 11/15/1895, Rutland, Ark. d: 8/11/55, San Francisco, Cal BR/TR, 5'11", 170 lbs. Deb: 9/18/16																											
1916	Det-A	2	7	0	1	0	0	0	1	0	1	.143	.143	.143	.286	-14	-1	-1	105	357	0	.167	0			1	/3	0.0
1917	Det-A	9	29	2	5	1	2	1	4	6	3	.172	.333	.448	.782	142	1	1	98	95	4	.833	0			-0	/1	0.1
1918	Det-A	7	23	1	6	1	0	0	2	3	1	.261	.346	.304	.651	100	-0	0	97	104	3	.647	1			-1	/O2	0.0
1919	Det-A	56	134	18	29	4	0	0	11	13	24	.216	.291	.246	.537	55	-8	-7	93	121	11	.486	4			-1	2O/S	-0.6
1920	Det-A	61	155	11	34	7	2	0	21	8	26	.219	.258	.290	.548	44	-13	-13	103	164	12	.467	4	1	1	1	1/O3	-1.1
Total	5	135	348	32	75	13	4	1	39	30	55	.216	.282	.284	.566	58	-21	-20	98	140	30	.511	9	1		-1	/12O3S	-1.6
■ **VERDO ELMORE**	Elmore, Verdo Wilson "Ellie" b: 12/10/1899, Gordo, Ala. d: 8/5/69, Birmingham, Ala. BL/TR, 5'11", 185 lbs. Deb: 9/11/24																											
1924	StL-A	7	17	2	3	3	0	0	0	1	3	.176	.222	.353	.575	44	-2	-2	107	0	1	.500	0	0	0	-2	/O	-0.3

YEAR	TM/L	G	AB	R	H	2B	3B	HR	RBI	BB	SO	AVG	OBP	SLG	PRO	/A	BR	/A	PF	CHI	RC	TA	SB	CS	SBR	FR	POS	TPR
■ **ROY ELSH** Elsh, Eugene Reybold b: 3/1/1892, Penns Grove, N.J. d: 11/12/78, Philadelphia, Pa. BR/TR, 5'9", 165 lbs. Deb: 4/19/23																												
1923	Chi-A	81	209	28	52	7	2	0	24	16	23	.249	.305	.301	.607	61	-12	-12	98	130	20	.576	15	8	-0	1	O	-1.5
1924	Chi-A	60	147	21	45	9	1	0	11	10	14	.306	.350	.381	.731	91	-3	-2	97	65	20	.692	6	2	1	-7	O/1	-0.9
1925	Chi-A	32	48	6	9	1	0	0	4	5	7	.188	.264	.208	.472	22	-6	-5	96	134	3	.436	2	0	1	-1	O/1	-0.6
Total	3	173	404	55	106	17	3	0	39	31	44	.262	.317	.319	.636	67	-20	-19	97	107	43	.597	23	10	1	-7	O/1	-3.0
■ **KEVIN ELSTER** Elster, Kevin Daniel b: 8/3/64, San Pedro, Cal. BR/TR, 6'2", 180 lbs. Deb: 9/02/86																												
1986	NY-N	19	30	3	5	1	0	0	0	3	8	.167	.242	.200	.442	24	-3	-3	96	0	2	.360	0	0	0	1	S	0.0
1987	NY-N	5	10	1	4	2	0	0	1	0	1	.400	.400	.600	1.000	163	1	1	99	66	2	.857	0	0	0	0	/S	0.1
1988	NY-N	149	406	41	87	11	1	9	37	35	47	.214	.282	.313	.594	78	-16	-11	90	96	37	.515	2	0	1	-4	*S	-0.4
Total	3	173	446	45	96	14	1	9	38	38	56	.215	.281	.312	.593	76	-18	-13	91	89	40	.513	2	0	1	-3	S	-0.3
■ **BONES ELY** Ely, Frederick William b: 6/7/1863, N.Girard, Pa. d: 1/10/52, Berkeley, Cal. BR/TR, 6'1", 155 lbs. Deb: 6/19/1884																												
1884	Buf-N	1	4	0	0	0	0	0	0	0	2	.000	.000	.000	.000	-94	-1	-1	107	0	0	.000				0	/OP	0.0
1886	Lou-a	10	32	5	5	0	0	0		2		.156	.206	.156	.362	14	-3	-3	108	0	1	.296	1			0	/PO	0.0
1890	Syr-a	119	496	72	130	16	6	0		31		.262	.307	.319	.625	96	-9	-2	90	0	64	.639	44			19	OS/123P	1.3
1891	Bro-N	31	111	9	17	0	1	0	11	7	9	.153	.203	.171	.375	11	-12	-12	97	169	5	.319	4			0	S/32	-1.0
1893	StL-N	44	178	25	45	1	6	0	16	17	13	.253	.318	.326	.644	73	-7	-7	99	80	20	.579	2			-5	S	-0.8
1894	StL-N	127	510	85	156	20	12	12	89	30	34	.306	.344	.463	.807	93	-7	-8	101	96	91	.816	23			-1	*S/2P	-0.1
1895	StL-N	117	467	68	121	16	2	1	46	19	17	.259	.288	.308	.596	56	-31	-31	100	89	51	.552	28			1	*S	-1.6
1896	Pit-N	128	537	85	153	15	9	3	77	33	33	.285	.326	.363	.689	89	-13	-7	93	115	71	.641	18			-6	*S	-1.0
1897	Pit-N	133	516	63	146	20	8	2	74	25		.283	.317	.364	.682	83	-14	-13	98	118	64	.605	10			4	*S	-0.4
1898	Pit-N	148	519	49	110	14	5	2	44	24		.212	.247	.270	.517	51	-34	-32	98	93	37	.416	6			3	*S	-1.9
1899	Pit-N	138	522	66	145	18	6	3	72	22		.278	.313	.352	.666	86	-12	-10	99	117	62	.581	8			-5	*S/2	-0.6
1900	Pit-N	130	475	60	116	6	6	0	51	17		.244	.270	.282	.552	53	-29	-31	103	121	39	.437	6			8	*S	-0.8
1901	Pit-N	65	240	18	50	6	3	0	28	6		.208	.228	.258	.486	42	-17	-18	101	154	16	.384	5			-1	S/3	-1.4
	Phi-A	45	171	11	37	6	2	0	16	3		.216	.230	.275	.505	41	-14	-14	100	110	12	.418	6			1	S	-0.8
1902	Was-A	105	381	39	100	11	2	1	62	21		.262	.301	.310	.611	72	-15	-14	99	172	37	.505	3			-8	*S	-1.1
Total	14	1341	5159	655	1331	149	68	24	586	257	108	.258	.294	.327	.621	72	-218	-202	98	103	570	.553	164			11	*S/O2P31	-10.2
■ **CHESTER EMERSON** Emerson, Chester Arthur "Chuck" b: 10/27/1889, Stow, Me. d: 7/2/71, Augusta, Me. BL/TR, 5'8", 165 lbs. Deb: 9/27/11																												
1911	Phi-A	7	18	2	4	0	0	0	0	6		.222	.417	.222	.639	86	0	0	93	0	2	.786	1			0	/O	0.0
1912	Phi-A	1	1	0	0	0	0	0	0	0		.000	.000	.000	.000	-99	-0	-0	99	0	0	.000	0			0	H	0.0
Total	2	8	19	2	4	0	0	0	0	6		.211	.400	.211	.611	78	-0	-0	93	0	2	.733	1			0	/O	0.0
■ **CAL EMERY** Emery, Calvin Wayne b: 6/28/37, Centre Hall, Pa. BL/TL, 6'2", 205 lbs. Deb: 7/15/63 C																												
1963	Phi-N	16	19	0	3	1	0	0	0	0	2	.158	.158	.211	.368	5	-2	-2	103	0	1	.250	0	0	0	0	/1	-0.2
■ **SPOKE EMERY** Emery, Herrick Smith b: 12/10/1898, Bay City, Mich. d: 6/2/75, Cape Canaveral, Fla. BR/TR, 5'9", 165 lbs. Deb: 7/18/24																												
1924	Phi-N	5	3	3	2	0	0	0	0	0	0	.667	.667	.667	1.333	240	1	1	108	0	1	1.000	0	1	-1	0	/O	0.0
■ **FRANK EMMER** Emmer, Frank William b: 2/17/1896, Crestline, Ohio d: 10/18/63, Homestead, Fla. BR/TR, 5'8", 150 lbs. Deb: 4/25/16																												
1916	Cin-N	42	89	8	13	3	1	0	2	7	27	.146	.208	.202	.411	27	-8	-8	98	44	4	.342	1			-2	S/O23	-0.8
1926	Cin-N	80	224	22	44	7	6	0	18	13	30	.196	.244	.281	.525	43	-19	-17	95	99	16	.433	1			-5	S	-1.6
Total	2	122	313	30	57	10	7	0	20	20	57	.182	.234	.259	.492	39	-27	-25	96	83	20	.406	2			-7	S/O32	-2.4
■ **BOB EMMERICH** Emmerich, Robert G. b: 8/1/1897, New York, N.Y. d: 11/22/48, Bridgeport, Conn. BR/TR, 5'3", 155 lbs. Deb: 9/22/23																												
1923	Bos-N	13	24	3	2	0	0	0	0	2	3	.083	.154	.083	.237	-36	-5	-5	100	0	0	.217	1	1	-0	-1	/O	-0.5
■ **BILL ENDICOTT** Endicott, William Franklin b: 9/4/18, Acorn, Mo. BL/TL, 5'11.5", 175 lbs. Deb: 4/21/46																												
1946	StL-N	20	20	2	4	3	0	0	3	4	4	.200	.333	.350	.683	88	-0	-0	107	160	2	.647	0			-0	/O	0.0
■ **CLYDE ENGLE** Engle, Arthur Clyde "Hack" b: 3/19/1884, Dayton, Ohio d: 12/26/39, Boston, Mass. BR/TR, 5'10", 190 lbs. Deb: 4/12/09																												
1909	NY-A	135	492	66	137	20	5	3	71	47		.278	.347	.358	.705	124	13	14	99	**157**	65	.693	18			-6	*O	0.2
1910	NY-A	5	13	0	3	0	0	0	0	2		.231	.333	.231	.564	72	-0	-0	107	0	1	.600	1			-0	/O	0.0
	Bos-A	106	363	59	96	18	7	2	38	31		.264	.326	.369	.695	119	7	7	99	102	46	.670	12			-3	32O/S	0.4
	Yr	111	376	59	99	18	7	2	38	33		.263	.326	.364	.690	117	6	7	99	98	47	.668	13			-3		0.4
1911	Bos-A	146	514	58	139	13	3	2	48	51		.270	.343	.319	.662	86	-9	-8	99	97	65	.653	24			1	132O	-0.6
1912	Bos-A	57	171	32	40	5	3	0	18	28		.234	.348	.298	.647	80	-2	-4	107	118	22	.710	12			-2	123/SO	-0.5
1913	Bos-A	143	498	75	144	17	12	2	50	53	41	.289	.363	.384	.747	115	12	10	103	92	76	.782	28			-9	*1/O	0.1
1914	Bos-A	55	134	14	26	2	0	0	9	14	11	.194	.275	.209	.484	47	-9	-8	98	121	7	.402	4	9	-4	-1	1/23	-1.4
	Buf-F	32	110	12	28	4	1	0	12	11	18	.255	.322	.309	.631	78	-2	-3	104	135	14	.610	5			-1	3/O	-0.3
1915	Buf-F	141	501	56	131	22	8	3	71	34	43	.261	.308	.355	.664	96	-3	-3	100	140	65	.638	24			-5	*O23/1	-1.3
1916	Cle-A	11	26	1	4	0	0	0	1	0	6	.154	.154	.154	.308	-8	-3	-3	100	89	1	.182	0			0	/31O	-0.3
Total	8	831	2822	373	748	101	39	12	318	271	119	.265	.334	.341	.675	100	3	0	101	118	362	.664	128	9		-28	O13/2S	-3.7
■ **CHARLIE ENGLE** Engle, Charlie August "Cholly" b: 8/27/03, New York, N.Y. d: 10/12/83, San Antonio, Tex. BR/TR, 5'8", 145 lbs. Deb: 9/14/25																												
1925	Phi-A	1	0	0	0	0	0	0	0	0	0	—	—	—	—	—	0	0	103	—	—	—	0	0	0	0	/S	0.0
1926	Phi-A	19	19	7	2	0	0	0	0	10	6	.105	.433	.105	.539	39	-1	-1	118	0	2	.765	0	0	0	-1	S	0.0
1930	Pit-N	67	216	34	57	10	1	0	15	22	20	.264	.335	.319	.654	61	-14	-13	97	75	24	.585	1			0	3S2	-0.7
Total	3	87	235	41	59	10	1	0	15	32	26	.251	.346	.302	.648	60	-14	-14	99	67	388	.602	1	0		-0	/S32	-0.7
■ **DAVE ENGLE** Engle, Ralph David b: 11/30/56, San Diego, Cal. BR/TR, 6'3", 210 lbs. Deb: 4/14/81																												
1981	Min-A	82	248	29	64	14	4	5	32	13	37	.258	.298	.407	.705	97	-0	-2	105	108	27	.593	0	1	-1	-4	O/3D	-0.8
1982	Min-A	58	186	20	42	7	2	4	16	10	22	.226	.269	.349	.618	68	-8	-8	100	83	16	.507	0	0	0	-0	OD	-0.9
1983	Min-A	120	374	46	114	22	4	8	43	28	39	.305	.355	.449	.804	114	10	7	105	88	57	.726	2	1	0	3	CD/O	1.3
1984	Min-A	109	391	56	104	20	1	4	38	26	22	.266	.312	.353	.665	79	-9	-11	106	103	39	.536	0	1	-1	4	CD	-0.2
1985	Min-A	70	172	28	44	8	2	7	25	21	28	.256	.337	.448	.784	109	3	2	103	101	26	.752	2	2	-1	0	DC/O	0.2
1986	Det-A	35	86	6	22	7	0	0	4	7	13	.256	.312	.337	.649	81	-3	-2	95	55	9	.545	0	0	0	0	1/OCD	-0.2
1987	Mon-N	59	84	7	19	4	0	1	14	6	11	.226	.278	.310	.587	52	-5	-6	106	193	6	.471	1	0	0	0	O/C13	-0.5
1988	Mon-N	34	37	4	8	3	0	0	1	5	5	.216	.310	.297	.607	71	-1	-1	106	36	3	.516	0	0	0	-1	/CO3	-0.1
Total	8	567	1578	196	417	85	13	29	173	116	177	.264	.316	.390	.706	91	-14	-22	104	98	183	.633	5	5	-2	2	COD/13	-1.2
■ **CHARLIE ENGLISH** English, Charles Dewie b: 4/8/10, Darlington, S.C. BR/TR, 5'9.5", 160 lbs. Deb: 7/23/32																												
1932	Chi-A	24	63	7	20	3	1	1	8	3	7	.317	.348	.444	.793	119	0	1	87	86	10	.721	0	0	0	-1	3/S	0.1
1933	Chi-A	3	9	2	4	2	0	0	1	1	1	.444	.500	.667	1.167	205	1	1	101	56	3	1.400	0	0	0	0	/2	0.1
1936	NY-N	6	1	0	0	0	0	0	0	0	0	.000	.000	.000	.000	-99	-0	-0	100	0	0	.000	0			0	/2	0.0
1937	Cin-N	17	63	1	15	3	1	0	4	0	2	.238	.238	.317	.556	54	-5	-4	91	73	4	.392	0			3	3/2	0.0
Total	4	50	136	10	39	8	2	1	13	4	10	.287	.307	.397	.704	95	-3	-1	90	78	17	.580	0	0		2	/32S	0.2
■ **WOODY ENGLISH** English, Elwood George b: 3/2/07, Fredonia, Ohio BR/TR, 5'10", 155 lbs. Deb: 4/26/27																												
1927	Chi-N	87	334	46	97	14	4	1	28	16	26	.290	.325	.365	.690	84	-8	-8	100	83	39	.591	1			4	S/3	0.4
1928	Chi-N	116	475	68	142	22	4	2	34	30	28	.299	.343	.375	.718	93	-9	-5	95	63	60	.643	4			9	*S/3	1.8
1929	Chi-N	144	608	131	168	29	3	1	52	68	50	.276	.352	.339	.691	71	-25	-26	101	74	74	.659	13			17	*S	0.9
1930	Chi-N	156	638	152	214	36	17	14	59	100	72	.335	.430	.511	.941	120	31	26	105	49	141	1.026	3			-7	3S	2.3
1931	Chi-N	156	634	117	202	38	8	2	53	68	80	.319	.391	.413	.804	121	17	21	96	62	108	.808	12			-1	*S3	3.1
1932	Chi-N	127	522	70	142	23	7	3	47	55	73	.272	.344	.360	.704	86	-6	-9	104	78	68	.658	5			2	3S	0.3
1933	Chi-N	105	398	54	104	19	2	3	41	53	44	.261	.348	.342	.690	100	0	2	97	102	51	.645	5			-4	*3/S	0.0
1934	Chi-N	109	421	65	117	26	5	3	31	48	65	.278	.353	.385	.738	100	-1	1	98	69	61	.700	6			6	S3/2	1.2
1935	Chi-N	34	84	11	17	2	0	2	8	20	4	.202	.368	.298	.666	82	-1	-1	99	93	12	.716	1			2	3S	0.2
1936	Chi-N	64	182	33	45	9	0	0	20	40	28	.247	.394	.297	.691	84	-0	-2	105	131	26	.707	1			3	S3/2	0.5

YEAR	TM/L	G	AB	R	H	2B	3B	HR	RBI	BB	SO	AVG	OBP	SLG	PRO	/A	BR	/A	PF	CHI	RC	TA	SB	CS	SBR	FR	POS	TPR
1937	Bro-N	129	378	45	90	16	2	1	42	65	55	.238	.350	.299	.649	75	-9	-11	104	130	42	.603	4			-16	*S2	-1.7
1938	Bro-N	34	72	9	18	2	0	0	7	8	11	.250	.333	.278	.611	73	-3	-2	96	126	7	.554	2			-1	3/2S	-0.3
Total	12	1261	4746	801	1356	236	52	32	422	571	536	.286	.366	.378	.743	95	-13	-15	100	79	690	.722	57			11	S3/2	8.7
■ GIL ENGLISH	English, Gilbert Raymond b: 7/2/09, Glenola, N.C. BR/TR, 5'11", 180 lbs. Deb: 9/20/31																											
1931	NY-N	3	8	0	0	0	0	0	0	1	3	.000	.111	.000	.111	-70	-2	-2	97	0	0	.125	0			0	/3	-0.1
1932	NY-N	59	204	22	46	7	5	2	19	5	20	.225	.244	.338	.582	55	-13	-13	99	94	17	.468	0			1	3S	-0.6
1936	Det-A	1	1	0	0	0	0	0	0	0	1	.000	.000	.000	.000	-99	-0	-0	95	0	0	.000	0	0	0	0	/3	0.0
1937	Det-A	18	65	6	17	1	0	1	6	6	4	.262	.333	.323	.656	61	-3	-4	109	86	7	.592	1	1	-0	-0	2/3	-0.2
	Bos-N	79	269	25	78	5	2	2	37	23	27	.290	.348	.346	.694	98	-3	-0	90	135	32	.594	3			-6	3	-0.2
1938	Bos-N	53	165	17	41	6	0	2	21	15	16	.248	.315	.321	.636	86	-5	-3	88	129	16	.534	1			-1	3/O2S	-0.4
1944	Bro-N	27	79	4	12	3	0	1	7	6	7	.152	.212	.228	.440	24	-8	-8	99	120	4	.348	0			-4	S3/2	-0.9
Total	6	240	791	74	194	22	7	8	90	56	78	.245	.298	.321	.619	71	-36	-30	94	116	76	.530	5	1		-9	3/S2O	-2.4
■ DEL ENNIS	Ennis, Delmer b: 6/8/25, Philadelphia, Pa. BR/TR, 6', 195 lbs. Deb: 4/28/46																											
1946	Phi-N	141	540	70	169	30	6	17	73	39	65	.313	.364	.485	.849	147	25	29	95	92	96	.818	5			12	*O	4.0
1947	Phi-N	139	541	71	149	25	6	12	81	37	51	.275	.325	.410	.736	94	-6	-6	100	123	69	.663	9			7	*O	-0.3
1948	Phi-N	152	589	86	171	40	4	30	95	47	58	.290	.345	.525	.869	141	23	28	94	95	106	.841	2			-2	*O	1.5
1949	Phi-N	154	610	92	184	39	11	25	110	59	61	.302	.367	.525	.892	136	29	29	101	101	118	.883	2			4	*O	2.3
1950	Phi-N	153	595	92	185	34	8	31	**126**	56	59	.311	.372	.551	.923	143	32	34	97	122	115	.892	2			-4	*O	2.4
1951	Phi-N	144	532	76	142	20	5	15	73	68	42	.267	.352	.408	.760	107	4	6	97	110	77	.710	4	2	0	-1	*O	0.1
1952	Phi-N	151	592	90	171	30	10	20	107	47	65	.289	.341	.475	.816	123	17	16	101	130	94	.756	6	4	-1	-5	*O	0.7
1953	Phi-N	152	578	79	165	22	3	29	125	57	53	.285	.355	.484	.839	117	13	14	99	141	100	.798	1	3	-2	3	*O	0.8
1954	Phi-N	145	556	73	145	23	2	25	119	50	60	.261	.324	.444	.768	99	-3	-2	99	**154**	75	.692	2	1	0	2	*O/1	-0.4
1955	Phi-N	146	564	82	167	24	7	29	120	46	46	.296	.351	.518	.869	124	20	19	102	136	99	.833	4	2	0	3	*O	1.8
1956	Phi-N	153	630	80	164	23	3	26	95	33	62	.260	.300	.430	.730	99	-8	-3	94	111	77	.649	7	3	0	-7	*O	-1.5
1957	StL-N	136	490	61	140	24	3	24	105	37	50	.286	.337	.494	.831	119	12	12	101	**141**	73	.749	1	3	-2	-19	*O	-1.2
1958	StL-N	106	329	22	86	18	1	3	47	15	35	.261	.296	.350	.645	66	-14	-17	106	157	29	.502	0	1	-1	-2	O	-2.1
1959	Cin-N	5	12	1	4	0	0	0	1	2	2	.333	.429	.333	.762	103	0	0	103	101	2	.750	0	0	0	-0	/O	0.0
	Chi-A	26	96	10	21	6	0	2	7	4	10	.219	.250	.344	.594	63	-5	-5	97	71	8	.481	0	0	0	-4	O	-1.0
Total	14	1903	7254	985	2063	358	69	288	1284	597	719	.284	.341	.472	.813	117	139	152	99	122	1137	.786	45	19		-12	*O/1	7.1
■ RUSS ENNIS	Ennis, Russell Elwood "Hack" b: 3/10/1897, Superior, Wis. d: 1/21/49, Superior, Wis. BR/TR, 5'11.5", 160 lbs. Deb: 9/19/26																											
1926	Was-A	1	0	0	0	0	0	0	0	0	0	—	—	—	—	—	0	0	98	—	—	—	0	0	0	0	/C	0.0
■ GEORGE ENRIGHT	Enright, George Albert b: 5/9/54, New Britain, Conn. BR/TR, 5'11", 175 lbs. Deb: 8/08/76																											
1976	Chi-A	2	1	0	0	0	0	0	0	0	0	.000	.000	.000	.000	-99	-0	-0	99	0	0	.000	0	0	0	0	/C	0.0
■ MUTZ ENS	Ens, Anton b: 11/8/1884, St.Louis, Mo. d: 6/28/50, St.Louis, Mo. BL/TL, 6'1", 180 lbs. Deb: 9/02/12																											
1912	Chi-A	3	6	0	0	0	0	0	0	0		.000	.000	.000	.000	-99	-2	-2	99	0	0	.000	0			0	/1	0.0
■ JEWEL ENS	Ens, Jewel Winklemeyer b: 8/24/1889, St.Louis, Mo. d: 1/17/50, Syracuse, N.Y. BR/TR, 5'10.5", 165 lbs. Deb: 4/29/22 MC																											
1922	Pit-N	47	142	18	42	7	3	0	17	7	9	.296	.338	.387	.725	84	-3	-4	104	108	19	.670	3	0	1	-7	2/31S	-0.9
1923	Pit-N	12	29	3	8	1	1	0	5	0	3	.276	.276	.379	.655	74	-1	-1	97	160	3	.619	2	0	1	0	/13	0.0
1924	Pit-N	5	10	2	3	0	0	0	0	0	3	.300	.300	.300	.600	58	-1	-1	106	0	1	.429	0	0	0	0	/1	0.0
1925	Pit-N	3	5	2	1	0	0	1	2	0	1	.200	.200	.800	1.000	140	0	0	102	102	1	1.000	0	0	0	0	/1	0.0
Total	4	67	186	25	54	8	4	1	24	7	16	.290	.323	.392	.716	82	-5	-5	103	110	24	.659	5	0	2	-7	/213S	-0.9
■ CHARLIE ENWRIGHT	Enwright, Charles Massey b: 10/6/1887, Sacramento, Cal. d: 1/19/17, Sacramento, Cal. BL/TR, 5'10", Deb: 09																											
1909	StL-N	3	7	1	1	0	0	0	1	0		.143	.143	.143	.286	-11	-1	-1	96	364	0	.500	2			0	/S	0.0
■ JACK ENZENROTH	Enzenroth, Clarence Herman b: 11/4/1885, Mineral Point, Wis. d: 2/21/44, Detroit, Mich. BR/TR, 5'10", 164 lbs. Deb: 5/01/14																											
1914	StL-A	3	6	0	1	0	0	0	0	2	3	.167	.444	.167	.611	87	0	0	98	0	0	.667	0	1	-1	0	/C	0.0
	KC-F	26	67	7	12	4	1	0	5	5	19	.179	.236	.269	.505	47	-5	-5	95	100	4	.418	0			-1	C	-0.4
1915	KC-F	14	19	3	3	0	0	0	3	6	0	.158	.360	.158	.518	58	-1	-1	97	361	1	.563	0			0	/C	0.0
Total	2	43	92	10	16	4	1	0	8	13	22	.174	.283	.239	.522	54	-5	-5	96	153	6	.468	0	1		-1	/C	-0.4
■ JIM EPPARD	Eppard, James Gerhard b: 4/27/60, South Bend, Ind. BL/TL, 6'2", 180 lbs. Deb: 9/08/87																											
1987	Cal-A	8	9	2	3	0	0	0	0	2	0	.333	.455	.333	.788	116	0	0	99	0	1	.714	0	0	0	-0	/O	0.0
1988	Cal-A	56	113	7	32	3	1	0	14	11	15	.283	.347	.327	.674	96	-1	-0	94	150	13	.565	0	0	0	-1	OD/1	-0.1
Total	2	64	122	9	35	3	1	0	14	13	15	.287	.356	.328	.683	97	-1	0	95	138	14	.582	0	0	0	-1	/OD1	-0.1
■ AUBREY EPPS	Epps, Aubrey Lee "Yo-Yo" b: 3/3/12, Memphis, Tenn. d: 11/13/84, Ackerman, Miss. BR/TR, 5'10", 170 lbs. Deb: 9/29/35																											
1935	Pit-N	1	4	1	3	0	1	0	3	0	0	.750	.750	1.250	2.000	400	2	2	107	221	4	5.000	0			0	/C	0.2
■ HAL EPPS	Epps, Harold Franklin b: 3/26/14, Athens, Ga. BL/TL, 6', 175 lbs. Deb: 9/09/38																											
1938	StL-N	17	50	8	15	0	0	1	3	2	4	.300	.327	.360	.687	80	-1	-2	111	52	6	.629	2			0	O	-0.1
1940	StL-N	11	15	6	3	0	0	0	1	0	3	.200	.200	.200	.400	10	-2	-2	102	124	1	.250	0			-1	/O	-0.2
1943	StL-A	8	35	2	10	4	0	0	1	3	4	.286	.342	.400	.742	116	1	1	100	22	4	.643	1	1	-0	-0	/O	0.0
1944	StL-A	22	62	15	11	1	1	0	3	14	14	.177	.338	.226	.563	61	-2	-2	102	77	6	.547	0	1	-1	3	O	0.0
	Phi-A	67	229	27	60	8	8	0	13	18	18	.262	.316	.367	.683	94	-2	-2	101	56	28	.601	2	1	0	0	O	-0.3
	Yr	89	291	42	71	9	9	0	16	32	32	.244	.321	.337	.658	87	-4	-5	101	62	34	.591	2	2	-1	3		-0.3
Total	4	125	391	58	99	13	9	1	21	37	43	.253	.319	.340	.660	86	-6	-7	102	59	44	.591	5	3		2	/O	-0.6
■ MIKE EPSTEIN	Epstein, Michael Peter "Superjew" b: 4/4/43, Bronx, N.Y. BL/TL, 6'3.5", 230 lbs. Deb: 9/16/66																											
1966	Bal-A	6	11	1	2	0	1	0	3	1	3	.182	.250	.364	.614	73	-0	-0	101	315	1	.556	0	0	0	-0	/1	0.0
1967	Bal-A	9	13	0	2	0	0	0	0	3	5	.154	.313	.154	.466	44	-1	-1	95	0	1	.417	0	0	0	0	/1	0.0
	Was-A	96	284	32	65	7	4	9	29	38	74	.229	.332	.377	.709	107	4	3	102	90	37	.673	1	4	-2	0	1	-0.5
	Yr	105	297	32	67	7	4	9	29	41	79	.226	.331	.367	.698	105	3	3	102	82	38	.662	1	4	-2	0		-0.5
1968	Was-A	123	385	40	90	8	2	13	33	48	91	.234	.339	.366	.705	124	8	11	91	79	48	.657	1	1	-0	2	*1	0.9
1969	Was-A	131	403	73	112	18	1	30	85	85	99	.278	.416	.551	.967	174	40	41	97	111	96	1.049	2	5	-2	-4	*1	2.8
1970	Was-A	140	430	55	110	15	3	20	56	73	117	.256	.375	.444	.819	130	16	19	96	90	76	.833	2	3	-1	-4	*1	0.7
1971	Was-A	24	85	6	21	1	1	1	9	12	31	.247	.366	.318	.684	103	0	1	92	130	12	.688	1	0	0	2	1	0.2
	Oak-A	104	329	43	77	13	0	18	51	62	71	.234	.368	.438	.806	127	14	13	101	107	57	.829	0	3	-2	4	1	1.1
	Yr	128	414	49	98	14	1	19	60	74	102	.237	.368	.413	.781	122	14	14	99	112	69	.801	1	3	-2	5		1.3
1972	Oak-A	138	455	63	123	18	2	26	70	68	68	.270	.378	.490	.868	162	33	35	97	99	88	.888	0	1	-1	-1	*1	2.1
1973	Tex-A	27	85	9	16	3	0	1	6	14	19	.188	.324	.259	.582	68	-3	-3	97	96	8	.549	0	0	0	1	1	-0.3
	Cal-A	91	312	30	67	8	2	8	32	34	54	.215	.302	.330	.632	81	-9	-7	96	101	31	.559	0	0	0	-1	1	-1.3
	Yr	118	397	39	83	11	2	9	38	48	73	.209	.307	.315	.622	78	-12	-10	96	101	40	.560	0	0	0	-0		-1.6
1974	Cal-A	18	62	10	10	2	0	4	6	10	13	.161	.288	.387	.675	100	-1	-0	92	69	8	.673	0	0	0	-0	1	0.0
Total	9	907	2854	362	695	93	16	130	380	448	645	.244	.360	.424	.784	129	100	112	97	98	461	.797	7	17	-8	-3	1	5.7
■ JOE ERAUTT	Erautt, Joseph Michael "Stubby" b: 9/1/21, Vibank, Sask., Can. d: 10/6/76, Portland, Ore. BR/TR, 5'9", 175 lbs. Deb: 5/09/50																											
1950	Chi-A	16	18	0	4	0	0	0	1	1	3	.222	.263	.222	.485	26	-2	-2	97	86	1	.357	0	0	0	0	/C	0.0
1951	Chi-A	16	25	3	4	1	0	0	0	3	2	.160	.276	.200	.476	31	-2	-2	97	0	1	.375	0	0	0	-0	C	-0.1
Total	2	32	43	3	8	1	0	0	1	4	5	.186	.271	.209	.480	29	-4	-4	97	34	2	.368	0	0	0	-0	/C	-0.1
■ HANK ERICKSON	Erickson, Henry Nels "Popeye" b: 11/11/07, Chicago, Ill. d: 12/13/64, Louisville, Ky. BR/TR, 6'1", 185 lbs. Deb: 4/17/35																											
1935	Cin-N	37	88	9	23	3	2	1	4	6	4	.261	.323	.375	.698	93	-2	-1	93	40	11	.621	0			1	C	0.0
■ CAL ERMER	Ermer, Calvin Coolidge b: 11/10/23, Baltimore, Md. BR/TR, 6'0.5", 175 lbs. Deb: 9/26/47 MC																											
1947	Was-A	1	3	0	0	0	0	0	0	0	0	.000	.000	.000	.000	-99	-1	-1	97	0	0	.000	0	0	0	0	/2	0.0

YEAR	TM/L	G	AB	R	H	2B	3B	HR	RBI	BB	SO	AVG	OBP	SLG	PRO	/A	BR	/A	PF	CHI	RC	TA	SB	CS	SBR	FR	POS	TPR
■ **FRANK ERNAGA** Ernaga, Frank John b: 8/22/30, Susanville, Cal. BR/TR, 6'1", 195 lbs. Deb: 5/24/57																												
1957	Chi-N	20	35	9	11	3	2	2	7	9	14	.314	.455	.686	1.140	209	5	6	96	97	12	1.375	0	0	0	-1	O	0.4
1958	Chi-N	9	8	0	1	0	0	0	0	0	2	.125	.125	.125	.250	-33	-2	-2	101	0	0	.143	0	0	0	0	H	-0.1
Total	2	29	43	9	12	3	2	2	7	9	16	.279	.404	.581	.985	165	4	4	97	82	12	1.097	0	0	0	-1	/O	0.3
■ **TEX ERWIN** Erwin, Ross Emil b: 12/22/1885, Forney, Tex. d: 4/5/53, Rochester, N.Y. BL/TR, 6', 185 lbs. Deb: 8/26/07																												
1907	Det-A	4	5	0	1	0	0	0	1	1		.200	.333	.200	.533	72	-0	-0	102	358	0	.500	0			0	/C	0.0
1910	Bro-N	81	202	15	38	3	1	1	10	24	12	.188	.278	.228	.505	50	-13	-12	95	71	14	.451	3			7	C	-0.1
1911	Bro-N	91	218	30	59	13	2	7	34	31	23	.271	.367	.445	.811	131	8	9	97	97	37	.849	5			3	C	1.7
1912	Bro-N	59	133	14	28	3	0	2	14	18	16	.211	.305	.278	.583	63	-7	-6	95	110	12	.533	1			5	C	0.1
1913	Bro-N	20	31	6	8	1	0	0	3	4	5	.258	.343	.290	.633	78	-1	-1	104	121	3	.565	0			-2	C	-0.1
1914	Bro-N	9	11	0	5	0	0	0	1	2	1	.455	.538	.455	.993	194	2	2	101	72	3	1.333	1			0	/C	0.2
	Cin-N	12	35	5	11	3	0	1	7	2	3	.314	.351	.486	.837	141	2	2	105	127	6	.792	0			-1	C	0.2
	Yr	21	46	5	16	3	0	1	8	4	4	.348	.400	.478	.878	156	3	3	103	107	9	.900	1			-1		0.4
Total	6	276	635	70	150	23	3	11	70	82	60	.236	.326	.334	.660	90	-10	-7	97	96	75	.633	10			13	C	2.0
■ **NICK ESASKY** Esasky, Nicholas Andrew b: 2/24/60, Hialeah, Fla. BR/TR, 6'3", 200 lbs. Deb: 6/19/83																												
1983	Cin-N	85	302	41	80	10	5	12	46	27	99	.265	.331	.450	.782	112	5	4	103	108	46	.751	6	2	1	-8	3	-0.6
1984	Cin-N	113	322	30	62	10	5	10	45	52	103	.193	.305	.348	.653	79	-7	-9	106	124	36	.616	1	2	-1	-5	31	-1.6
1985	Cin-N	125	413	61	108	21	0	21	66	41	102	.262	.334	.465	.799	115	11	8	105	103	63	.755	3	4	-2	-5	3O1	0.0
1986	Cin-N	102	330	35	76	17	2	12	41	47	97	.230	.328	.403	.731	96	0	-2	104	97	44	.686	0	2	-1	-2	1O/3	-0.8
1987	Cin-N	100	346	48	94	19	2	22	59	29	76	.272	.328	.529	.857	118	9	8	104	95	57	.809	0	0	0	-4	1/3O	-0.1
1988	Cin-N	122	391	40	95	17	2	15	62	48	104	.243	.332	.412	.744	107	6	4	105	120	56	.724	7	2	1	-9	*1	-1.0
Total	6	647	2104	255	515	94	16	92	319	244	581	.245	.327	.436	.763	105	25	13	105	108	301	.741	17	12	-2	-33	13/O	-4.1
■ **NINO ESCALERA** Escalera, Saturnino Cuadrado b: 12/1/29, Santurce, P.R. BL/TR, 5'10", 165 lbs. Deb: 4/17/54																												
1954	Cin-N	73	69	15	11	1	1	0	3	7	11	.159	.237	.203	.440	15	-9	-9	104	84	4	.373	1	0	0	0	O/1S	-0.8
■ **JIM ESCHEN** Eschen, James Godrich b: 8/21/1891, Brooklyn, N.Y. d: 9/27/60, Sloatsburg, N.Y. BR/TR, 5'10.5", 160 lbs. Deb: 7/10/15																												
1915	Cle-A	15	42	11	10	1	0	0	2	5	9	.238	.319	.262	.581	71	-1	-1	104	62	4	.485	0	1	-1	2	O	0.0
■ **LARRY ESCHEN** Eschen, Lawrence Edward b: 9/22/20, Suffern, N.Y. BR/TR, 6', 180 lbs. Deb: 6/16/42																												
1942	Phi-A	12	11	0	0	0	0	0	0	4	6	.000	.267	.000	.267	-22	-2	-2	96	0	0	.364	0	0	0	-1	/S2	-0.1
■ **ANGEL ESCOBAR** Escobar, Angel Rubenque (Rivas) b: 5/12/65, La Sabana, Venez. BB/TR, 6', 160 lbs. Deb: 5/17/1988																												
1988	SF-N	3	3	1	1	0	0	0	0	0	0	.333	.333	.333	.667	98	-0	-0	94	0	0	.500	0	0	0	0	/S3	0.0
■ **JIMMY ESMOND** Esmond, James J. b: 10/8/1889, Albany, N.Y. d: 6/26/48, Troy, N.Y. BR/TR, 5'11", 167 lbs. Deb: 4/20/11																												
1911	Cin-N	73	198	27	54	4	6	1	11	17	30	.273	.330	.369	.699	104	-2	1	92	49	26	.674	7			-5	S3/2	-0.2
1912	Cin-N	82	231	24	45	5	3	1	40	20	31	.195	.259	.255	.514	44	-19	-17	92	217	19	.484	11			-7	S	-1.6
1914	Ind-F	151	542	74	160	23	**15**	2	49	40	48	.295	.344	.404	.748	103	9	1	111	80	88	.743	25			3	*S	1.5
1915	New-F	155	569	79	147	20	10	5	62	59	54	.258	.328	.355	.683	108	2	6	94	99	78	.661	18			18	*S	3.7
Total	4	461	1540	204	406	52	34	9	162	136	163	.264	.323	.359	.682	96	-10	-9	99	104	211	.661	61			9	S/32	3.4
■ **JUAN ESPINO** Espino, Juan (Reyes) b: 3/16/56, Bonao, D.R. BR/TR, 6'1", 190 lbs. Deb: 6/25/82																												
1982	NY-A	3	2	0	0	0	0	0	0	0	1	.000	.000	.000	.000	-99	-1	-1	96	0	0	.000	0	0	0	0	/C	0.0
1983	NY-A	10	23	1	6	0	0	1	3	1	5	.261	.292	.391	.683	87	-0	-0	99	98	3	.588	0	0	0	-0	C	0.0
1985	NY-A	9	11	0	4	0	0	0	0	0	0	.364	.364	.364	.727	104	-0	0	96	0	1	.571	0	0	0	0	/C	0.1
1986	NY-A	27	37	1	6	2	0	0	5	2	9	.162	.205	.216	.421	15	-4	-4	103	249	2	.323	0	0	0	0	C	-0.2
Total	4	49	73	2	16	2	0	1	8	3	15	.219	.250	.288	.538	47	-5	-5	100	159	6	.421	0	0	0	0	/C	-0.1
■ **ALVARO ESPINOZA** Espinoza, Alvaro Alberto b: 2/19/62, Valencia, Venez. BR/TR, 6', 170 lbs. Deb: 9/14/84																												
1984	Min-A	1	0	0	0	0	0	0	0	0	0	—	—	—	—	—	0	0	106	—	—	—	0	0	0	0	/S	0.0
1985	Min-A	32	57	5	15	2	0	0	9	1	9	.263	.288	.298	.586	59	-3	-3	103	210	4	.422	0	1	-1	-1	S	-0.2
1986	Min-A	37	42	4	9	1	0	0	1	1	10	.214	.233	.238	.471	27	-4	-4	108	40	2	.324	0	1	-1	-1	2S	-0.3
1988	NY-A	3	3	0	0	0	0	0	0	0	0	.000	.000	.000	.000	-99	-1	-1	96	0	0	.000	0	0	0	0	/2S	0.0
Total	4	73	102	9	24	3	0	0	10	2	19	.235	.257	.265	.522	41	-8	-9	105	134	13	.375	0	2	-1	-2	/S2	-0.5
■ **SAMMY ESPOSITO** Esposito, Samuel b: 12/15/31, Chicago, Ill. BR/TR, 5'9", 165 lbs. Deb: 9/28/52																												
1952	Chi-A	1	4	0	1	0	0	0	0	0	2	.250	.250	.250	.500	39	-0	-0	100	0	0	.250	0	1	-1	0	/S	0.0
1955	Chi-A	3	4	3	0	0	0	0	0	1	0	.000	.200	.000	.200	-42	-1	-1	101	0	0	.250	0	0	0	0	/3	0.0
1956	Chi-A	81	184	30	42	8	2	3	25	41	19	.228	.374	.342	.717	87	-1	-2	104	130	26	.723	1	2	-1	1	3S/2	0.1
1957	Chi-A	94	176	26	36	3	0	2	15	38	27	.205	.346	.256	.601	67	-7	-6	99	116	19	.599	5	1	1	6	3S/2O	0.4
1958	Chi-A	98	81	16	20	3	0	0	3	12	6	.247	.358	.284	.642	81	-2	-1	98	52	9	.603	1	1	-0	0	3S/2O	0.4
1959	Chi-A	69	66	12	11	1	0	1	5	11	16	.167	.286	.227	.513	44	-5	-5	97	109	5	.456	0	1	-1	1	3S/2	-0.3
1960	Chi-A	57	77	14	14	5	0	1	11	10	20	.182	.276	.286	.562	52	-5	-5	101	172	6	.485	0	0	0	0	3S/2	-0.2
1961	Chi-A	63	94	12	16	5	0	1	8	12	21	.170	.264	.255	.519	40	-8	-8	99	116	7	.444	0	0	0	1	3S2	-0.2
1962	Chi-A	75	81	14	19	1	0	0	4	17	13	.235	.367	.247	.614	73	-3	-2	95	79	8	.561	0	1	-1	0	3S/2	0.0
1963	Chi-A	1	0	0	0	0	0	0	0	0	0	—	—	—	—	—	0	0	104	—	—	—	0	0	0	0	R	0.0
	KC-A	18	25	3	5	1	0	0	2	3	3	.200	.286	.240	.526	46	-2	-2	108	139	2	.409	0	0	0	0	/2S3	0.0
	Yr	19	25	3	5	1	0	0	2	3	3	.200	.286	.240	.526	46	-2	-2	107	132	2	.409	0	0	0	0		0.0
Total	10	560	792	130	164	27	2	8	73	145	127	.207	.333	.277	.609	66	-33	-33	100	113	89	.589	7	7	-2	9	3S/2O	0.2
■ **CECIL ESPY** Espy, Cecil Edward b: 1/20/63, San Diego, Cal. BB/TR, 6'3", 195 lbs. Deb: 9/02/83																												
1983	LA-N	20	11	4	3	1	0	0	1	1	2	.273	.333	.364	.697	93	-0	-0	100	99	1	.625	0	0	0	-4	O	-0.3
1987	Tex-A	14	8	1	0	0	0	0	0	1	3	.000	.111	.000	.111	-64	-2	-2	104	0	0	.333	2	0	1	-0	/O	-0.1
1988	Tex-A	123	347	46	86	17	6	2	39	20	83	.248	.291	.349	.639	77	-10	-11	101	122	37	.641	33	10	4	3	OD/SC12	-0.5
Total	3	157	366	51	89	18	6	2	40	22	88	.243	.288	.342	.629	74	-13	-13	101	118	39	.633	35	10	5	-2	O/DSC21	-0.9
■ **CHUCK ESSEGIAN** Essegian, Charles Abraham b: 8/9/31, Boston, Mass. BR/TR, 5'11", 200 lbs. Deb: 4/15/58																												
1958	Phi-N	39	114	15	28	5	2	5	16	12	34	.246	.317	.456	.774	104	-0	0	98	99	17	.727	0	0	0	-1	O	-0.1
1959	StL-N	17	39	2	7	2	1	0	5	1	13	.179	.200	.282	.482	25	-4	-4	105	184	1	.343	0	0	0	-1	/O	-0.5
	LA-N	24	46	6	14	6	0	1	5	4	11	.304	.360	.500	.860	124	2	2	102	78	8	.818	0	0	0	-2	O	0.0
	Yr	41	85	8	21	8	1	1	10	5	24	.247	.289	.400	.689	79	-3	-3	103	126	10	.600	0	0	0	-3		-0.5
1960	LA-N	52	79	8	17	3	0	3	11	8	24	.215	.287	.367	.654	67	-3	-4	115	117	9	.597	0	0	0	-1	O	-0.5
1961	Bal-A	1	1	0	0	0	0	0	0	0	0	.000	.000	.000	.000	-99	-0	-0	97	0	0	.000	0	0	0	0	H	0.0
	KC-A	4	6	1	2	1	0	0	0	1	2	.333	.429	.500	.929	145	0	0	102	131	1	1.000	0	0	0	0	/O	0.1
	Cle-A	60	166	25	48	7	1	12	35	10	33	.289	.333	.560	.894	139	7	8	96	106	29	.839	0	0	0	-0	O	0.5
	Yr	65	173	26	50	8	1	12	36	11	35	.289	.335	.555	.890	138	7	8	97	108	30	.837	0	0	0	0		0.6
1962	Cle-A	106	336	59	92	12	0	21	50	42	68	.274	.366	.497	.863	133	14	15	98	86	62	.854	0	0	0	-6	O	0.6
1963	KC-A	101	231	23	52	9	0	5	27	19	48	.225	.287	.329	.616	67	-9	-11	108	124	21	.516	0	0	0	-2	O	-1.4
Total	6	404	1018	139	260	45	4	47	150	97	233	.255	.326	.446	.772	105	7	6	102	105	148	.732	0	0	0	-12	O	-1.3
■ **JIM ESSIAN** Essian, James Sarkis b: 1/2/51, Detroit, Mich. BR/TR, 6'2", 195 lbs. Deb: 9/15/73																												
1973	Phi-N	2	3	0	0	0	0	0	0	0	1	.000	.000	.000	.000	-93	-1	-1	108	0	0	.000	0	0	0	0	/C	0.0
1974	Phi-N	17	20	1	2	0	0	0	0	2	1	.100	.182	.100	.282	-19	-3	-3	103	0	0	.211	0	0	0	-0	C/13	-0.2
1975	Phi-N	2	1	1	1	0	0	0	1	1	0	1.000	1.000	1.000	2.000	450	1	1	101	387	1	—	0	0	0	0	/C	0.1
1976	Chi-A	78	199	20	49	7	0	0	21	23	28	.246	.327	.281	.609	80	-4	-4	99	144	19	.522	2	1	0	-1	C/13	-0.2
1977	Chi-A	114	322	50	88	18	2	10	44	52	35	.273	.376	.435	.811	121	10	11	99	103	53	.785	1	4	-2	11	*C/3	2.2
1978	Oak-A	126	278	21	62	9	1	3	26	44	22	.223	.329	.295	.624	76	-7	-8	101	113	28	.559	2	1	0	-11	*C/12D	-1.4
1979	Oak-A	98	313	34	76	16	0	8	40	25	29	.243	.303	.371	.674	91	-9	-4	89	110	33	.572	0	1	-1	11	C3/10D	0.8

YEAR	TM/L	G	AB	R	H	2B	3B	HR	RBI	BB	SO	AVG	OBP	SLG	PRO	/A	BR	/A	PF	CHI	RC	TA	SB	CS	SBR	FR	POS	TPR
1980	Oak-A	87	285	19	66	11	0	5	29	30	18	.232	.305	.323	.628	76	-11	-9	95	106	25	.521	1	3	-2	9	CD/1	0.1
1981	Chi-A	27	52	6	16	3	0	0	5	4	5	.308	.357	.365	.723	109	1	1	100	103	6	.590	0	1	-1	-2	C/3	0.0
1982	Sea-A	48	153	14	42	8	0	3	20	11	7	.275	.327	.386	.713	87	-1	-3	109	118	20	.640	2	0	1	-5	C	-0.4
1983	Cle-A	48	93	11	19	4	0	2	11	16	8	.204	.321	.312	.633	71	-3	-4	105	123	10	.592	0	1	-1	-2	C/3	-0.3
1984	Oak-A	63	136	17	32	9	0	2	10	23	17	.235	.350	.346	.696	102	-1	1	92	75	18	.667	1	1	-0	2	C/3D	0.6
Total	12	710	1855	194	453	85	3	33	207	231	171	.244	.330	.347	.676	89	-28	-22	98	109	214	.627	9	13	-5	11	C/3D1O2	1.3

■ **BOBBY ESTALELLA** Estalella, Roberto (Ventoza) b: 4/25/11, Cardenas, Cuba BR/TR, 5'8", 180 lbs. Deb: 9/07/35

YEAR	TM/L	G	AB	R	H	2B	3B	HR	RBI	BB	SO	AVG	OBP	SLG	PRO	/A	BR	/A	PF	CHI	RC	TA	SB	CS	SBR	FR	POS	TPR
1935	Was-A	15	51	7	16	2	0	2	10	17	7	.314	.485	.471	.956	162	5	6	92	120	13	1.200	1	0	0	2	3	0.7
1936	Was-A	13	9	2	2	0	2	0	0	4	5	.222	.462	.667	1.128	180	1	1	98	0	3	1.429	0	0	0	0	H	0.1
1939	Was-A	82	280	51	77	18	6	8	41	40	27	.275	.368	.468	.835	124	5	9	90	91	48	.813	2	3	-1	-5	O	0.1
1941	StL-A	46	83	7	20	6	1	0	14	18	13	.241	.376	.337	.714	90	-1	-1	100	177	11	.687	0	1	-1	-4	O	-0.5
1942	Was-A	133	429	68	119	24	5	8	65	85	42	.277	.400	.413	.813	135	20	22	96	114	74	.816	5	2	0	-3	3O	1.9
1943	Phi-A	117	367	43	95	14	4	11	63	52	44	.259	.352	.409	.761	121	11	10	101	126	52	.701	1	3	-2	-1	O	0.5
1944	Phi-A	140	506	54	151	17	9	7	60	59	60	.298	.374	.409	.783	122	16	16	101	101	80	.730	3	3	-1	-8	*O/1	0.3
1945	Phi-A	126	451	45	135	25	6	8	52	74	46	.299	.399	.435	.834	**152**	26	30	94	91	79	.807	1	6	-3	-2	*O	2.0
1949	Phi-A	8	20	2	5	0	0	0	3	1	2	.250	.286	.250	.536	43	-2	-2	99	206	0	.300	0	0	0	0	/O	-0.1
Total	9	680	2196	279	620	106	33	44	308	350	246	.282	.383	.421	.804	130	82	92	97	108	361	.810	13	18	-7	-20	O/31	5.0

■ **DUDE ESTERBROOK** Esterbrook, Thomas John b: 6/29/1857, Staten Is., N.Y. d: 4/30/01, Middletown, N.Y. BR/TR, 5'11", 167 lbs. Deb: 5/01/1880 M

YEAR	TM/L	G	AB	R	H	2B	3B	HR	RBI	BB	SO	AVG	OBP	SLG	PRO	/A	BR	/A	PF	CHI	RC	TA	SB	CS	SBR	FR	POS	TPR
1880	Buf-N	64	253	20	61	12	1	0	35	0	15	.241	.241	.296	.538	89	-5	-2	91	180	19	.391				-0	1O/2SC	-0.4
1882	Cle-N	45	179	13	44	4	3	0	19	5	12	.246	.266	.302	.568	91	-4	-1	90	125	15	.437				10	O/1	0.7
1883	NY-a	97	407	55	103	9	7	0		15		.253	.280	.310	.589	83	-5	-9	108	0	36	.464				-5	*3	-1.1
1884	NY-a	112	477	110	150	29	11	1		12		.314	.345	.428	.772	154	27	27	100	0	72	.691				6	*3	3.0
1885	NY-N	88	359	48	92	14	5	2	44	4	28	.256	.264	.340	.604	86	-3	-8	109	127	33	.472				2	*3/O	-0.4
1886	NY-N	123	473	62	125	20	6	3	43	8	43	.264	.277	.351	.627	101	-7	1	89	82	51	.537	13			-9	*3	-0.2
1887	NY-a	26	101	11	17	1	0	0		6		.168	.222	.178	.400	16	-11	-9	88	0	6	.393	8			0	/1OS2	-0.6
1888	Ind-N	64	246	21	54	8	0	0	17	2	20	.220	.232	.252	.484	59	-12	-11	95	104	17	.401	11			-2	1/3	-1.7
	Lou-a	23	93	9	21	6	0	0	7	3		.226	.265	.290	.556	89	-2	-1	91	82	9	.514	5			0	1	0.0
1889	Lou-a	11	44	8	14	3	0	0	9	5	2	.318	.400	.386	.786	132	2	2	96	134	9	.967	6			0	/1OSM	0.2
1890	NY-N	45	197	29	57	14	1	0	29	10	8	.289	.333	.371	.704	113	1	3	95	104	29	.700	12			0	1	0.0
1891	Bro-N	3	8	1	3	0	0	0	0	0	1	.375	.444	.375	.819	146	0	1	97	0	1	.800	0			0	/O2	0.0
Total	11	701	2837	387	741	120	34	6	203	70	129	.261	.284	.334	.618	98	-18	-7	97	74	297	.521	55			1	31/O2SC	-0.5

■ **FRANK ESTRADA** Estrada, Francisco (Soto) b: 2/12/48, Navojoa, Sonora, Mex BR/TR, 5'8", 182 lbs. Deb: 9/14/71

YEAR	TM/L	G	AB	R	H	2B	3B	HR	RBI	BB	SO	AVG	OBP	SLG	PRO	/A	BR	/A	PF	CHI	RC	TA	SB	CS	SBR	FR	POS	TPR
1971	NY-N	1	2	0	1	0	0	0	0	0	0	.500	.500	.500	1.000	191	0	0	96	0	1	1.000	0	0	0	0	/C	0.0

■ **ANDY ETCHEBARREN** Etchebarren, Andrew Auguste b: 6/20/43, Whittier, Cal. BR/TR, 6'1", 190 lbs. Deb: 9/26/62 C

YEAR	TM/L	G	AB	R	H	2B	3B	HR	RBI	BB	SO	AVG	OBP	SLG	PRO	/A	BR	/A	PF	CHI	RC	TA	SB	CS	SBR	FR	POS	TPR
1962	Bal-A	2	6	0	2	0	0	0	1	0	2	.333	.333	.333	.667	85	-0	-0	95	198	1	.500	0	0	0	0	/C	0.0
1965	Bal-A	5	6	1	1	0	0	1	4	0	2	.167	.167	.667	.833	125	0	0	100	237	1	.800	0	0	0	0	/C	0.0
1966	Bal-A	121	412	49	91	14	6	11	50	38	106	.221	.295	.364	.659	87	-7	-7	101	115	42	.578	0	1	-1	3	*C	0.1
1967	Bal-A	112	330	29	71	13	0	7	35	38	80	.215	.300	.318	.618	88	-7	-5	95	116	31	.539	1	0	0	0	*C	0.3
1968	Bal-A	74	189	20	44	11	2	5	20	19	46	.233	.313	.392	.704	110	3	2	102	96	23	.644	0	0	0	-8	C	-0.2
1969	Bal-A	73	217	29	54	9	2	3	26	28	42	.249	.353	.350	.703	94	0	-1	104	123	25	.636	1	2	-1	1	C	0.4
1970	Bal-A	78	230	19	56	10	1	4	28	21	41	.243	.315	.348	.663	85	-5	-5	97	123	24	.584	4	1	1	-4	C	-0.6
1971	Bal-A	70	222	21	60	8	0	9	29	16	40	.270	.322	.428	.750	108	2	2	103	97	28	.661	1	4	-2	-3	C	0.0
1972	Bal-A	71	188	11	38	6	1	2	21	17	43	.202	.279	.277	.555	67	-8	-7	98	151	14	.459	0	2	-1	-3	C	-1.1
1973	Bal-A	54	152	16	39	9	1	2	23	12	21	.257	.319	.368	.688	87	-1	-3	107	146	16	.587	1	1	-0	-3	C	-0.4
1974	Bal-A	62	180	13	40	8	0	2	15	6	26	.222	.251	.300	.551	63	-10	-9	93	98	13	.434	1	0	0	-2	C	-0.8
1975	Bal-A	8	20	0	4	1	0	0	3	0	3	.200	.200	.250	.450	29	-2	-2	91	230	1	.313	0	0	0	-0	/C	-0.1
	Cal-A	31	100	10	28	0	1	3	17	14	19	.280	.368	.390	.758	121	2	3	95	136	15	.720	1	0	0	-5	C	0.0
	Yr	39	120	10	32	1	1	3	20	14	22	.267	.343	.367	.710	107	0	1	94	161	15	.648	1	0	0	-5		-0.1
1976	Cal-A	103	247	15	56	9	1	0	21	24	37	.227	.305	.271	.577	76	-9	-6	92	120	20	.470	0	2	-1	-22	*C	-2.7
1977	Cal-A	80	114	11	29	2	2	0	14	12	19	.254	.325	.307	.632	78	-4	-3	95	159	12	.562	3	1	0	-22	C	-2.2
1978	Mil-A	4	5	1	2	1	0	0	2	1	2	.400	.500	.600	1.100	197	1	1	106	263	2	1.333	0	0	0	0	/C	0.1
Total	15	948	2618	245	615	101	17	49	309	246	529	.235	.308	.343	.651	88	-44	-39	98	122	268	.588	13	14	-5	-67	C	-7.2

■ **BUCK ETCHISON** Etchison, Clarence Hampton b: 1/27/15, Baltimore, Md. d: 1/24/80, E.New Market, Md. BL/TL, 6'1", 190 lbs. Deb: 9/22/43

YEAR	TM/L	G	AB	R	H	2B	3B	HR	RBI	BB	SO	AVG	OBP	SLG	PRO	/A	BR	/A	PF	CHI	RC	TA	SB	CS	SBR	FR	POS	TPR
1943	Bos-N	10	19	2	6	3	0	0	2	2	2	.316	.381	.474	.855	138	1	1	106	80	4	.846	0			0	/1	0.1
1944	Bos-N	109	308	30	66	16	0	8	33	33	50	.214	.292	.344	.637	83	-9	-7	95	91	32	.569	1			-0	1	-1.4
Total	2	119	327	32	72	19	0	8	35	35	52	.220	.298	.352	.649	87	-8	-6	95	90	35	.582	1			-0	/1	-1.3

■ **BOBBY ETHERIDGE** Etheridge, Bobby Lamar "Luke" b: 11/25/42, Greenville, Miss. BR/TR, 5'9", 170 lbs. Deb: 7/16/67

YEAR	TM/L	G	AB	R	H	2B	3B	HR	RBI	BB	SO	AVG	OBP	SLG	PRO	/A	BR	/A	PF	CHI	RC	TA	SB	CS	SBR	FR	POS	TPR
1967	SF-N	40	115	13	26	7	2	1	15	7	12	.226	.299	.348	.647	84	-2	-2	101	145	12	.559	0	0	0	-1	3	-0.5
1969	SF-N	56	131	13	34	9	0	1	10	19	26	.260	.358	.351	.709	98	0	0	101	82	15	.623	0	0	0	-1	3/S	0.0
Total	2	96	246	26	60	16	2	2	25	26	38	.244	.331	.350	.681	92	-2	-2	101	110	27	.605	0	0	0	-2	/3S	-0.5

■ **NICK ETTEN** Etten, Nicholas Raymond Thomas b: 9/19/13, Spring Grove, Ill BL/TL, 6'2", 198 lbs. Deb: 9/08/38

YEAR	TM/L	G	AB	R	H	2B	3B	HR	RBI	BB	SO	AVG	OBP	SLG	PRO	/A	BR	/A	PF	CHI	RC	TA	SB	CS	SBR	FR	POS	TPR
1938	Phi-A	22	81	6	21	6	2	0	11	9	7	.259	.333	.383	.716	78	-3	-3	101	122	11	.683	1	0	0	-1	1	-0.5
1939	Phi-A	43	155	20	39	11	2	3	29	16	11	.252	.322	.406	.728	87	-4	-3	97	139	20	.658	0	0	0	0	1	-0.6
1941	Phi-N	151	540	78	168	27	4	14	79	82	33	.311	.405	.454	.859	146	32	34	97	105	104	.887	9			-2	*1	1.1
1942	Phi-N	139	459	37	121	21	3	8	41	67	26	.264	.357	.375	.732	121	10	13	94	79	65	.699	3			-1	*1	0.1
1943	NY-A	154	583	78	158	35	5	14	107	76	31	.271	.355	.420	.775	131	19	22	96	144	89	.728	3	7	-3	-11	*1	0.3
1944	NY-A	154	573	88	168	25	4	**22**	91	**97**	29	.293	.399	.466	.865	138	37	33	106	104	114	.884	4	2	0	4	*1	2.8
1945	NY-A	152	565	77	161	24	4	18	**111**	90	23	.285	.387	.437	.824	130	30	25	107	141	98	.801	2	3	-1	-9	*1	1.0
1946	NY-A	108	323	37	75	14	1	9	49	38	35	.232	.315	.365	.680	89	-5	-5	100	129	39	.618	0	1	-1	-4	1	-1.4
1947	Phi-N	14	41	5	10	4	0	1	8	5	4	.244	.326	.415	.741	95	-0	-0	100	148	5	.667	0			-0	1	0.0
Total	9	937	3320	426	921	167	25	89	526	480	199	.277	.371	.423	.794	125	116	115	100	119	544	.795	22	13		-24	1	2.8

■ **FRED EUNICK** Eunick, Fernandas Bowen b: 4/22/1892, Baltimore, Md. d: 12/9/59, Baltimore, Md. BR/TR, 5'6", 148 lbs. Deb: 8/29/17

YEAR	TM/L	G	AB	R	H	2B	3B	HR	RBI	BB	SO	AVG	OBP	SLG	PRO	/A	BR	/A	PF	CHI	RC	TA	SB	CS	SBR	FR	POS	TPR
1917	Cle-A	1	2	0	0	0	0	0	0	0	0	.000	.000	.000	.000	-87	-0	-1	114	0	0	.000	0			0	/3	0.0

■ **FRANK EUSTACE** Eustace, Frank John b: 11/7/1873, New York, N.Y. d: 10/20/32, Pottsville, Pa. 5'9", 160 lbs. Deb: 4/17/1896

YEAR	TM/L	G	AB	R	H	2B	3B	HR	RBI	BB	SO	AVG	OBP	SLG	PRO	/A	BR	/A	PF	CHI	RC	TA	SB	CS	SBR	FR	POS	TPR
1896	Lou-N	25	100	18	17	2	2	1	11	6	14	.170	.217	.260	.477	27	-11	-10	98	116	7	.434	4			0	S/2	-0.8

■ **AL EVANS** Evans, Alfred Hubert b: 9/28/16, Kenly, N.C. d: 4/6/79, Wilson, N.C. BR/TR, 5'11", 190 lbs. Deb: 9/13/39

YEAR	TM/L	G	AB	R	H	2B	3B	HR	RBI	BB	SO	AVG	OBP	SLG	PRO	/A	BR	/A	PF	CHI	RC	TA	SB	CS	SBR	FR	POS	TPR
1939	Was-A	7	21	2	7	0	0	0	1	5	2	.333	.462	.333	.795	118	1	1	90	48	4	.857	0	0	0	0	/C	0.1
1940	Was-A	14	25	1	8	2	0	0	7	6	7	.320	.452	.400	.852	132	1	2	93	253	6	1.000	1	0	0	1	/C	0.3
1941	Was-A	53	159	16	44	8	4	1	19	9	18	.277	.315	.396	.712	89	-3	-3	98	102	19	.600	0	3	-2	-2	C	-0.3
1942	Was-A	74	223	22	51	4	1	0	10	25	36	.229	.309	.256	.565	63	-11	-10	96	62	19	.486	3	0	1	6	C	0.5
1944	Was-A	14	22	5	2	0	0	0	0	2	6	.091	.167	.091	.258	-28	-4	-3	90	0	0	.190	0	0	0	0	/C	-0.2
1945	Was-A	51	150	19	39	11	2	2	19	17	22	.260	.339	.400	.739	123	3	4	93	104	21	.696	2	1	0	1	C	0.8
1946	Was-A	88	272	30	69	10	4	2	30	30	28	.254	.332	.342	.674	96	-4	-1	92	115	32	.597	1	2	-1	2	C	0.3
1947	Was-A	99	319	17	77	8	3	2	23	28	25	.241	.303	.304	.607	71	-13	-12	97	82	29	.500	2	1	0	7	C	0.3
1948	Was-A	93	228	19	59	6	3	2	28	38	20	.259	.367	.338	.705	85	-3	-4	103	114	29	.650	1	1	-0	0	C	0.2
1949	Was-A	109	321	32	87	12	3	2	42	50	19	.271	.369	.346	.715	98	-4	0	91	123	45	.679	4	1	1	-2	*C	0.4
1950	Was-A	90	289	24	68	8	3	2	30	29	21	.235	.309	.304	.614	58	-19	-18	99	110	28	.522	0	0	0	-2	C	-1.5
1951	Bos-A	12	24	1	3	1	0	0	2	4	2	.125	.250	.167	.417	13	-3	-3	108	179	1	.381	0	0	0	-1	C	-0.2
Total	12	704	2053	188	514	70	23	13	211	243	206	.250	.332	.326	.658	82	-59	-48	96	104	234	.603	14	9	-1	9	C	0.7

YEAR	TM/L	G	AB	R	H	2B	3B	HR	RBI	BB	SO	AVG	OBP	SLG	PRO	/A	BR	/A	PF	CHI	RC	TA	SB	CS	SBR	FR	POS	TPR
■ BARRY EVANS	Evans, Barry Steven b: 11/30/56, Atlanta, Ga. BR/TR, 6'1", 180 lbs. Deb: 9/04/78																											
1978	SD-N	24	90	7	24	1	1	0	4	4	10	.267	.298	.300	.598	73	-4	-3	93	60	8	.470	0	0	0	0	3	-0.3
1979	SD-N	56	162	9	35	5	0	1	14	5	16	.216	.240	.265	.505	39	-14	-13	96	121	10	.366	0	2	-1	5	3/S2	-1.1
1980	SD-N	73	125	11	29	3	2	1	14	17	21	.232	.324	.312	.636	84	-3	-2	93	132	14	.576	1	1	-0	1	32/S1	0.0
1981	SD-N	54	93	11	30	5	0	0	7	9	9	.323	.382	.376	.759	124	2	3	93	78	12	.667	2	2	-1	-0	31/2S	0.1
1982	NY-A	17	31	2	8	3	0	0	2	6	6	.258	.395	.355	.750	112	1	1	96	73	5	.783	0	0	0	0	/23S	0.2
Total	5	224	501	40	126	17	3	2	41	41	62	.251	.309	.309	.619	77	-18	-15	94	102	49	.526	3	5	-2	6	3/2S1	-1.1
■ DARRELL EVANS	Evans, Darrell Wayne b: 5/26/47, Pasadena, Cal. BL/TR, 6'2", 200 lbs. Deb: 4/20/69																											
1969	Atl-N	12	26	3	6	0	0	0	1	1	8	.231	.259	.231	.490	37	-2	-2	104	67	2	.350	0	0	0	0	/3	-0.1
1970	Atl-N	12	44	4	14	1	1	0	9	7	5	.318	.423	.386	.809	114	2	1	104	218	7	.781	0	0	0	1	3	0.2
1971	Atl-N	89	260	42	63	11	1	12	38	39	54	.242	.343	.431	.774	107	6	3	110	104	39	.755	2	3	-1	3	3/O	0.6
1972	Atl-N	125	418	67	106	12	0	19	71	90	58	.254	.391	.419	.809	124	20	18	105	133	76	.853	4	2	0	6	*3	2.4
1973	Atl-N	161	595	114	167	25	8	41	104	**124**	104	.281	.407	.556	.964	146	55	44	113	88	**143**	1.055	6	3	0	7	*31	4.8
1974	Atl-N	160	571	99	137	21	3	25	79	**126**	88	.240	.383	.419	.801	118	23	19	105	93	100	.839	4	2	0	16	*3	3.3
1975	Atl-N	156	567	82	138	22	2	22	73	105	106	.243	.364	.406	.769	119	12	16	95	92	91	.790	12	3	2	23	*3/1	4.1
1976	Atl-N	44	139	11	24	0	0	1	10	30	33	.173	.320	.194	.514	43	-8	-10	111	131	11	.508	3	0	1	-1	1/3	-1.2
	SF-N	92	257	42	57	9	1	10	36	42	38	.222	.331	.381	.712	99	1	-0	103	108	36	.719	6	1	1	4	1/3	0.1
	Yr	136	396	53	81	9	1	11	46	72	71	.205	.327	.316	.643	78	-7	-10	106	116	47	.648	9	1	2	3		-1.1
1977	SF-N	144	461	64	117	18	3	17	72	69	50	.254	.355	.416	.771	102	5	2	104	119	71	.763	9	6	-1	-8	O13	-1.1
1978	SF-N	159	547	82	133	24	2	20	78	105	64	.243	.365	.404	.769	125	13	20	92	117	87	.778	4	5	-2	11	*3	2.8
1979	SF-N	160	562	68	142	23	2	17	70	91	80	.253	.359	.391	.750	113	6	11	92	108	83	.737	6	7	-2	20	*3	2.3
1980	SF-N	154	556	69	147	23	0	20	78	83	65	.264	.362	.414	.776	121	14	17	96	113	87	.779	17	5	2	17	*31	3.6
1981	SF-N	102	357	51	92	13	4	12	48	54	33	.258	.358	.417	.776	114	10	8	105	104	56	.761	2	3	-1	1	31	0.3
1982	SF-N	141	465	64	119	20	4	16	61	77	64	.256	.364	.419	.783	127	13	17	94	100	74	.779	5	4	-1	-1	31S	1.2
1983	SF-N	142	523	94	145	29	3	30	82	84	81	.277	.379	.516	.896	145	33	32	101	95	104	.923	6	6	-2	1	*13/S	2.7
1984	Det-A	131	401	60	93	11	1	16	63	77	70	.232	.356	.384	.740	109	5	7	96	124	58	.735	2	2	-1	3	D13	0.6
1985	Det-A	151	505	81	125	17	0	**40**	94	85	85	.248	.357	.519	.876	128	25	21	106	100	96	.895	0	4	-2	10	*1D/3	2.0
1986	Det-A	151	507	78	122	15	0	29	85	91	105	.241	.357	.442	.799	123	14	17	95	111	85	.812	3	2	-0	8	*1D/3	1.7
1987	Det-A	150	499	90	128	20	0	34	99	100	84	.257	.383	.501	.884	137	26	28	97	115	103	.947	6	5	-1	6	*1D/3	2.1
1988	Det-A	144	437	48	91	9	0	22	64	84	89	.208	.337	.380	.717	106	2	5	94	110	57	.692	1	4	-2	2	D1	0.1
Total	20	2580	8697	1313	2166	323	35	403	1315	1564	1364	.249	.366	.433	.799	120	274	274	100	108	1466	.827	98	67	-11	129	*31D/OS	32.5
■ DWIGHT EVANS	Evans, Dwight Michael "Dewey" b: 11/3/51, Santa Monica, Cal. BR/TR, 6'2", 180 lbs. Deb: 9/16/72																											
1972	Bos-A	18	57	2	15	3	1	1	6	7	13	.263	.344	.404	.747	116	2	1	105	96	8	.682	0	0	0	0	O	0.1
1973	Bos-A	119	282	46	63	13	1	10	32	40	52	.223	.322	.383	.705	92	-1	-3	106	91	36	.678	5	0	2	-11	*O/D	-1.5
1974	Bos-A	133	463	60	130	19	8	10	70	38	77	.281	.338	.421	.759	110	10	6	107	125	65	.691	4	4	-1	10	*O/D	1.2
1975	Bos-A	128	412	61	113	24	6	13	56	47	60	.274	.354	.456	.811	117	15	10	109	95	66	.773	3	4	-2	18	*O/D	2.4
1976	Bos-A	146	501	61	121	34	5	17	62	57	92	.242	.326	.431	.757	109	12	6	110	91	69	.716	6	7	-2	8	*O/D	0.9
1977	Bos-A	73	230	39	66	9	2	14	36	28	58	.287	.364	.526	.890	119	12	7	117	87	45	.905	4	2	0	-1	O/D	0.3
1978	Bos-A	147	497	75	123	24	2	24	63	65	119	.247	.337	.449	.786	111	12	7	107	86	74	.756	8	5	-1	6	*O/D	0.9
1979	Bos-A	152	489	69	134	24	1	21	58	69	76	.274	.365	.456	.821	112	14	9	107	78	79	.791	6	9	-4	7	*O	0.6
1980	Bos-A	148	463	72	123	37	5	18	60	64	98	.266	.361	.484	.845	127	19	18	102	84	85	.855	3	1	0	-4	*O/D	1.0
1981	Bos-A	108	412	84	122	19	4	**22**	71	**85**	85	.296	.418	.522	**.940**	**159**	**40**	**36**	106	87	**95**	**1.013**	3	2	-0	-3	*O	3.2
1982	Bos-A	162	609	122	178	37	7	32	98	112	125	.292	**.403**	.534	.937	140	48	40	110	89	134	.980	3	2	-0	1	*O/D	3.5
1983	Bos-A	126	470	74	112	19	4	22	58	70	97	.238	.339	.436	.776	110	8	7	101	89	71	.757	3	0	1	2	OD	0.9
1984	Bos-A	162	630	**121**	186	37	8	32	104	96	115	.295	.392	.532	**.924**	138	47	38	110	85	**132**	.944	3	1	0	-3	*O/D	3.0
1985	Bos-A	159	617	110	162	29	1	29	78	**114**	105	.263	.382	.454	.836	125	27	25	102	74	112	.858	7	2	1	-3	*O/D	2.0
1986	Bos-A	152	529	86	137	33	2	26	97	97	117	.259	.380	.476	.856	133	26	27	100	124	100	.882	3	3	-1	0	*O/D	2.1
1987	Bos-A	154	541	109	165	37	2	34	123	**106**	98	.305	.422	.569	.991	162	51	51	99	127	134	1.074	4	6	-2	-4	1O/D	3.3
1988	Bos-A	149	559	96	164	31	7	21	111	76	99	.293	.379	.487	.866	129	31	24	109	**140**	104	.859	5	1	1	-8	O1/D	1.3
Total	17	2236	7761	1287	2114	429	66	346	1183	1171	1486	.272	.371	.478	.849	126	373	309	106	98	1408	.875	70	49	-8	14	*O1/D	25.2
■ JAKE EVANS	Evans, Jacob "Bloody Jake" b: Baltimore, Md. d: 2/3/07, Baltimore, Md. TR , 5'8", 154 lbs. Deb: 1879																											
1879	Tro-N	72	280	30	65	9	5	0	17	5	18	.232	.246	.300	.546	84	-6	-4	93	72	21	.414				17	*O	1.0
1880	Tro-N	47	180	31	46	8	1	0	22	7	15	.256	.283	.311	.595	92	0	-2	110	146	16	.470				-1	O/P	-0.4
1881	Tro-N	83	315	35	76	11	5	0	28	14	30	.241	.274	.308	.581	82	-6	-6	100	102	27	.464				10	*O	0.2
1882	Wor-N	80	334	33	71	10	4	0	25	7	22	.213	.229	.266	.495	58	-15	-15	100	91	21	.365				14	*OS/32P	-0.1
1883	Cle-N	90	332	36	79	13	2	0	31	8	38	.238	.256	.289	.545	63	-13	-16	105	114	25	.411				4	*O/S32P	-0.8
1884	Cle-N	80	313	32	81	18	3	1	38	15	49	.259	.293	.345	.638	98	-0	-1	102	125	32	.530				4	*O/2S	0.2
1885	Bal-a	20	77	18	17	1	1	0		7		.221	.318	.260	.578	82	-1	-1	106	0	7	.517				0	O	0.0
Total	7	472	1831	215	435	70	21	1	161	63	172	.238	.264	.300	.565	78	-42	-46	101	101	150	.442				48	O/S23P	0.1
■ JOE EVANS	Evans, Joseph Patton "Doc" b: 5/15/1895, Meridian, Miss. d: 8/9/53, Gulfport, Miss. BR/TR, 5'9", 160 lbs. Deb: 7/03/15																											
1915	Cle-A	42	109	17	28	4	2	0	11	22	18	.257	.382	.330	.712	109	3	2	104	104	17	.780	6	1	1	2	3/2	0.7
1916	Cle-A	33	82	4	12	1	0	0	1	7	12	.146	.213	.159	.372	12	-9	-9	100	27	4	.343	4			2	3	-0.5
1917	Cle-A	132	385	36	73	4	5	2	33	42	44	.190	.271	.242	.513	49	-20	-26	114	120	31	.474	12			-1	*3	-2.3
1918	Cle-A	79	243	38	64	6	7	1	22	30	29	.263	.344	.358	.702	103	4	1	108	89	32	.693	7			-1	3	0.1
1919	Cle-A	21	14	9	1	0	0	0	0	2	1	.071	.188	.071	.259	-24	-2	-2	107	0	0	.308	1			0	/S	-0.1
1920	Cle-A	56	172	32	60	9	9	0	23	15	3	.349	.404	.506	.910	135	10	9	104	93	36	.956	6	2	1	-1	O/S	0.5
1921	Cle-A	57	153	36	51	11	0	0	21	19	5	.333	.410	.405	.816	110	3	3	99	116	27	.835	4	1	1	0	O	0.0
1922	Cle-A	75	145	35	39	6	2	0	22	8	4	.269	.307	.338	.645	67	-7	-7	102	161	16	.630	11	2	2	-6	O	-1.3
1923	Was-A	106	372	42	98	15	3	0	38	27	18	.263	.313	.320	.633	71	-18	-15	95	111	38	.545	6	5	-1	0	O3/1	-1.9
1924	StL-A	77	209	30	53	3	3	0	19	24	12	.254	.330	.297	.627	58	-11	-13	107	101	21	.544	1	4	-2	1	O	-1.7
1925	StL-A	55	159	27	50	12	0	0	20	16	6	.314	.377	.390	.767	88	-1	-3	108	108	25	.757	6	2	1	-2	O	-0.7
Total	11	733	2043	306	529	71	31	3	210	212	152	.259	.329	.328	.658	78	-49	-61	105	106	247	.621	64	17		-6	O3/S12	-7.2
■ STEVE EVANS	Evans, Louis Richard b: 2/17/1885, Cleveland, Ohio d: 12/28/43, Cleveland, Ohio BL/TL, 5'10", 175 lbs. Deb: 4/16/08																											
1908	NY-N	2	2	0	1	0	0	0	0	0		.500	.500	.500	1.000	214	0	0	104	0	0	1.000	0			0	/O	0.0
1909	StL-N	143	498	67	129	17	6	2	56	66		.259	.362	.329	.691	120	12	14	96	127	63	.699	14			-7	*O/1	0.3
1910	StL-N	151	506	73	122	21	8	2	73	78	63	.241	.376	.326	.702	115	8	14	92	158	66	.740	10			-7	*O1	0.1
1911	StL-N	154	547	74	161	24	13	5	71	46	52	.294	.369	.413	.782	118	14	13	101	102	88	.788	13			-7	*O	0.2
1912	StL-N	135	491	59	139	23	9	6	72	36	51	.283	.353	.403	.756	107	4	4	100	119	73	.744	11			-8	*O	-0.7
1913	StL-N	97	245	18	61	15	6	1	31	20	28	.249	.321	.371	.692	105	-1	1	93	120	29	.663	5			-9	O/1	-0.9
1914	Bro-F	145	514	93	179	41	**15**	12	96	50	49	.348	.406	**.556**	.962	**173**	48	47	101	110	127	1.057	18			-9	*O1	3.4
1915	Bro-F	63	216	44	64	14	4	3	30	35	0	.296	.394	.440	.834	150	14	14	98	106	41	.901	7			-6	O/1	0.6
	Bal-F	88	340	50	107	20	6	1	37	28	0	.315	.367	.418	.784	123	13	10	107	97	56	.764	8			-10	O/1	-0.4
	Yr	151	556	94	171	**34**	10	4	67	63	0	.308	.378	.426	.804	134	27	25	103	102	98	.818	15			-16		0.2
Total	8	978	3359	478	963	175	67	32	466	359	243	.287	.370	.407	.778	127	111	119	98	119	544	.793	86			-62	O/1	2.6
■ BILL EVERETT	Everett, William L. "Wild Bill" b: 12/13/1868, Ft.Wayne, Ind. d: 1/19/38, Denver, Colo. BL/TR, 6'.5 ", 185 lbs. Deb: 4/18/1895																											
1895	Chi-N	133	550	129	197	16	10	3	88	33	42	.358	.399	.440	.839	115	15	12	103	104	118	.924	47			-9	*3/2	0.4
1896	Chi-N	132	575	130	184	16	13	2	46	41	43	.320	.367	.403	.771	97	4	-4	108	48	105	.821	46			-11	*3O	-0.9
1897	Chi-N	92	379	63	119	14	7	5	39	36		.314	.373	.427	.801	113	7	7	100	57	72	.862	26			-7	3/O	0.0
1898	Chi-N	149	596	102	190	15	6	0	69	53		.319	.377	.364	.741	112	14	11	103	92	95	.741	28			-3	*1	0.8
1899	Chi-N	136	536	87	166	17	5	1	74	31		.310	.351	.366	.717	103	-0	3	96	121	81	.703	30			7	*1	1.1
1900	Chi-N	23	91	10	24	4	0	0	17	3		.264	.287	.308	.595	71	-4	-3	93	201	9	.493	2			0	1	-0.2

YEAR	TM/L	G	AB	R	H	2B	3B	HR	RBI	BB	SO	AVG	OBP	SLG	PRO	/A	BR	/A	PF	CHI	RC	TA	SB	CS	SBR	FR	POS	TPR
1901	Was-A	33	115	14	22	3	2	0	8	15		.191	.285	.252	.537	52	-7	-7	99	89	11	.548	7			0	1	-0.7
Total	7	698	2842	535	902	85	43	11	341	212	85	.317	.367	.389	.756	104	28	19	102	89	490	.781	186			-23	13/O2	0.5

■ **JOHNNY EVERS** Evers, John Joseph "Crab" or "Trojan" b: 7/22/1883, Troy, N.Y. d: 3/28/47, Albany, N.Y. BL/TR, 5'9", 125 lbs. Deb: 9/01/02 MCH

YEAR	TM/L	G	AB	R	H	2B	3B	HR	RBI	BB	SO	AVG	OBP	SLG	PRO	/A	BR	/A	PF	CHI	RC	TA	SB	CS	SBR	FR	POS	TPR
1902	Chi-N	26	90	7	20	0	0	0	2	3		.222	.247	.222	.470	48	-6	-5	96	35	5	.343	1			2	2/S	0.0
1903	Chi-N	124	464	70	136	27	7	0	52	19		.293	.321	.381	.702	107	-0	3	95	96	66	.674	25			-7	*2S/3	0.2
1904	Chi-N	152	532	49	141	14	7	0	47	28		.265	.302	.318	.619	93	-5	-5	101	104	60	.570	26			31	*2	3.1
1905	Chi-N	99	340	44	94	11	2	1	37	27		.276	.330	.329	.659	94	-0	-2	105	114	44	.642	19			4	2	0.7
1906	Chi-N	154	533	65	136	17	6	1	51	36		.255	.302	.315	.617	89	-4	-8	107	111	67	.637	49			5	*2/3	-0.2
1907	Chi-N	151	508	66	127	18	4	2	51	39		.250	.303	.313	.616	89	-3	-6	106	119	64	.640	46			**28**	*2	2.7
1908	Chi-N	126	416	83	125	19	6	0	37	66		.300	.396	.375	.771	141	26	23	106	97	75	.887	36			-3	*2/O	2.2
1909	Chi-N	127	463	88	122	19	6	1	24	73		.263	.369	.337	.705	120	14	14	101	47	66	.765	28			1	*2	1.4
1910	Chi-N	125	433	87	114	11	7	0	28	108	18	.263	.413	.321	.734	114	15	15	101	62	70	.868	28			-4	*2	1.4
1911	Chi-N	46	155	29	35	4	3	0	7	34	10	.226	.372	.290	.662	89	-1	-0	97	56	19	.725	6			0	23	0.0
1912	Chi-N	143	478	73	163	23	11	1	63	74	18	.341	**.431**	.441	.873	134	29	27	104	101	98	.962	16			5	*2	2.6
1913	Chi-N	136	446	81	127	20	5	3	49	50	14	.285	.361	.372	.733	111	7	7	99	104	64	.721	11			20	*2M	2.5
1914	Bos-N	139	491	81	137	20	3	1	40	87	26	.279	.390	.338	.728	112	15	12	104	83	72	.754	12			5	*2	1.7
1915	Bos-N	83	278	38	73	4	1	1	22	50	16	.263	.375	.295	.670	106	4	5	98	105	35	.653	7	8	-3	0	2	0.3
1916	Bos-N	71	241	33	52	4	1	0	15	40	19	.216	.330	.241	.570	82	-5	-3	93	109	23	.550	5			-17	2	-1.9
1917	Bos-N	24	83	5	16	0	0	0	0	13	8	.193	.302	.193	.495	55	-4	-4	96	0	5	.448	1			-2	2	-0.4
	Phi-N	56	183	20	41	5	1	1	12	30	13	.224	.333	.279	.612	82	-1	-3	108	87	19	.627	8			2	2/3	0.3
	Yr	80	266	25	57	5	1	1	12	43	21	.214	.324	.252	.576	74	-5	-6	104	61	24	.569	9			0		-0.1
1922	Chi-A	1	3	0	0	0	0	0	1	2	0	.000	.400	.000	.400	12	-0	-0	101	0	0	.667	0	0	0	0	/2	0.0
1929	Bos-N	1	0	0	0	0	0	0	0	0	0	—	—	—	—	—	0	0	94	—	—	—	0			0	/2	0.0
Total	18	1784	6137	919	1659	216	70	12	538	779	142	.270	.354	.334	.688	106	82	70	102	91	854	.707	324	8		71	*2/3SO	16.6

■ **JOE EVERS** Evers, Joseph Francis b: 9/10/1891, Troy, N.Y. d: 1/4/49, Albany, N.Y. BR/TR, 5'9", 135 lbs. Deb: 4/24/13

YEAR	TM/L	G	AB	R	H	2B	3B	HR	RBI	BB	SO	AVG	OBP	SLG	PRO	/A	BR	/A	PF	CHI	RC	TA	SB	CS	SBR	FR	POS	TPR
1913	NY-N	1	0	0	0	0	0	0	0	0	0	—	—	—	—	—	0	0	103	—	—	—	0			0	R	0.0

■ **TOM EVERS** Evers, Thomas Francis b: 3/31/1852, Troy, N.Y. d: 3/23/25, Washington, D.C. Deb: 5/25/1882

YEAR	TM/L	G	AB	R	H	2B	3B	HR	RBI	BB	SO	AVG	OBP	SLG	PRO	/A	BR	/A	PF	CHI	RC	TA	SB	CS	SBR	FR	POS	TPR
1882	Bal-a	1	4	0	0	0	0	0		0		.000	.000	.000	.000	-99	-1	-1	92	0	0	.000				0	/2	0.0
1884	Was-U	109	427	54	99	6	1	0		7		.232	.244	.251	.495	70	-14	-12	97	0	27	.348	0			10	*2	-0.5
Total	2	110	431	54	99	6	1	0		7		.230	.242	.248	.490	68	-15	-13	97	0	27	.343	0			10	2	-0.5

■ **HOOT EVERS** Evers, Walter Arthur b: 2/8/21, St.Louis, Mo. BR/TR, 6'2", 180 lbs. Deb: 9/16/41 C

YEAR	TM/L	G	AB	R	H	2B	3B	HR	RBI	BB	SO	AVG	OBP	SLG	PRO	/A	BR	/A	PF	CHI	RC	TA	SB	CS	SBR	FR	POS	TPR
1941	Det-A	1	4	0	0	0	0	0	0	0	2	.000	.000	.000	.000	-94	-1	-1	106	0	0	.000	0	0	0	-0	/O	-0.1
1946	Det-A	81	304	42	81	8	4	4	33	34	43	.266	.344	.359	.703	89	-1	-4	108	106	41	.664	7	1	2	-2	O	-0.8
1947	Det-A	126	460	67	136	24	5	10	67	45	49	.296	.366	.435	.801	117	13	11	104	109	73	.753	8	7	-2	3	*O	0.7
1948	Det-A	139	538	81	169	33	6	10	103	51	31	.314	.378	.454	.831	125	15	17	96	135	92	.776	3	4	-2	-3	*O	0.7
1949	Det-A	132	432	68	131	21	6	7	72	70	38	.303	.403	.428	.831	111	14	9	108	120	76	.812	6	7	-2	3	*O	0.7
1950	Det-A	143	526	100	170	35	**11**	21	103	71	40	.323	.408	.551	.959	149	34	36	97	103	116	.969	5	9	-4	9	*O	3.6
1951	Det-A	116	393	47	88	15	2	11	46	40	47	.224	.297	.356	.653	72	-14	-17	106	95	40	.576	5	3	-0	4	*O	-1.7
1952	Det-A	1	1	0	1	0	0	0	0	0	0	1.000	1.000	1.000	2.000	462	0	0	99	0	1	—	0	0	0	0	H	0.0
	Bos-A	106	401	53	105	17	4	14	59	29	55	.262	.318	.429	.747	100	2	-2	107	109	54	.680	5	2	0	3	*O	0.0
	Yr	107	402	53	106	17	4	14	59	29	55	.264	.320	.430	.750	100	2	-1	107	108	55	.683	5	2	0	3		0.0
1953	Bos-A	99	300	39	72	10	1	11	31	23	41	.240	.301	.390	.691	78	-7	-11	109	76	35	.609	2	1	0	-8	O	-2.0
1954	Bos-A	6	8	1	0	0	0	0	0	0	2	.000	.000	.000	.000	-99	-2	-2	100	0	0	.000	0	0	0	-0	/O	-0.2
	NY-N	12	11	1	1	0	0	1	3	0	6	.091	.091	.364	.455	11	-2	-2	105	169	0	.400	0	0	0	-1	/O	-0.2
	Det-A	30	60	5	11	4	0	0	5	5	8	.183	.258	.250	.508	39	-5	-5	100	126	4	.431	1	0	0	-4	O	-0.9
1955	Bal-A	60	185	21	44	10	1	6	30	19	28	.238	.309	.400	.709	100	-3	-1	90	122	21	.625	2	1	0	-4	O	-0.7
	Cle-A	39	66	10	19	7	1	2	9	3	12	.288	.319	.515	.834	117	1	1	104	84	10	.755	0	1	-1	-3	O	-0.3
	Yr	99	251	31	63	17	2	8	39	22	40	.251	.311	.430	.742	103	-2	-1	95	108	35	.691	2	2	-1	-7		-1.0
1956	Cle-A	3	0	1	0	0	0	0	0	1	0	—	1.000	—	1.430	286	0	0	101	0	0	—	0	0	0	0	H	0.0
	Bal-A	48	112	20	27	3	0	1	4	24	18	.241	.375	.295	.670	84	-2	-1	94	41	15	.682	1	0	0	-2	O	-0.4
	Yr	51	112	21	27	3	0	1	4	25	18	.241	.380	.295	.674	85	-2	-1	95	39	15	.694	1	0	0	-2		-0.4
Total	12	1142	3801	556	1055	187	41	98	565	415	420	.278	.353	.426	.778	106	41	29	102	107	578	.757	45	36	-8	-5	*O	-1.6

■ **G. EWELL** Ewell, G. b: Washington, D.C. Deb: 6/26/1871

YEAR	TM/L	G	AB	R	H	2B	3B	HR	RBI	BB	SO	AVG	OBP	SLG	PRO	/A	BR	/A	PF	CHI	RC	TA	SB	CS	SBR	FR	POS	TPR
1871	Cle-n	1	4	0	0							.000															/O	

■ **REUBEN EWING** Ewing, Reuben (born Reuben Cohen) b: 11/30/1899, Odessa, Russia d: 10/5/70, W.Hartford, Conn. 5'4.5", 150 lbs. Deb: 6/21/21

YEAR	TM/L	G	AB	R	H	2B	3B	HR	RBI	BB	SO	AVG	OBP	SLG	PRO	/A	BR	/A	PF	CHI	RC	TA	SB	CS	SBR	FR	POS	TPR
1921	StL-N	3	1	0	0	0	0	0	0	0	1	.000	.000	.000	.000	-99	-0	-0	95	0	0	.000	0	0	0	0	/S	0.0

■ **SAM EWING** Ewing, Samuel James b: 4/9/49, Lewisburg, Tenn. BL/TL, 6'3", 200 lbs. Deb: 9/11/73

YEAR	TM/L	G	AB	R	H	2B	3B	HR	RBI	BB	SO	AVG	OBP	SLG	PRO	/A	BR	/A	PF	CHI	RC	TA	SB	CS	SBR	FR	POS	TPR
1973	Chi-A	11	20	1	3	1	0	0	2	2	6	.150	.227	.200	.427	21	-2	-2	102	196	1	.333	0	0	0	0	/1	-0.1
1976	Chi-A	19	41	3	9	2	1	0	2	2	8	.220	.256	.317	.573	68	-2	-2	99	59	3	.469	0	0	0	0	D/1	-0.1
1977	Tor-A	97	244	24	70	8	2	4	34	19	42	.287	.338	.385	.724	94	-1	-2	103	127	30	.623	1	1	-0	-7	OD/1	-1.0
1978	Tor-A	40	56	3	10	0	0	2	9	5	9	.179	.246	.286	.532	49	-4	-4	100	162	4	.457	0	0	0	-1	/OD	-0.4
Total	4	167	361	31	92	11	3	6	47	28	65	.255	.308	.352	.660	81	-9	-10	102	129	39	.578	1	1	-0	-7	/OD1	-1.6

■ **BUCK EWING** Ewing, William b: 10/17/1859, Hoaglands, Ohio d: 10/20/06, Cincinnati, Ohio BR/TR, 5'10", 188 lbs. Deb: 9/09/1880 MH

YEAR	TM/L	G	AB	R	H	2B	3B	HR	RBI	BB	SO	AVG	OBP	SLG	PRO	/A	BR	/A	PF	CHI	RC	TA	SB	CS	SBR	FR	POS	TPR
1880	Tro-N	13	45	1	8	1	0	0	5	1	3	.178	.196	.200	.396	31	-3	-4	110	203	2	.270				0	C/O	-0.3
1881	Tro-N	67	272	40	68	14	7	0	25	7	8	.250	.269	.353	.622	94	-2	-2	100	96	26	.505				22	CS/O3	2.0
1882	Tro-N	74	328	67	89	16	11	2	29	10	15	.271	.293	.405	.698	127	7	10	95	61	40	.598				12	3C/2O1P	2.1
1883	NY-N	88	376	90	114	11	13	**10**	41	20	14	.303	.338	.481	.820	146	20	20	100	58	63	.767				11	CO2/S3	2.9
1884	NY-N	94	382	90	106	15	**20**	3	41	28	22	.277	.327	.445	.772	143	17	19	98	76	57	.717				8	*CO/S3P	2.9
1885	NY-N	81	342	81	104	15	12	6	63	13	17	.304	.330	.471	.800	143	20	15	109	118	54	.731				2	CO/3S1P	2.1
1886	NY-N	73	275	59	85	11	7	4	31	16	17	.309	.347	.444	.791	157	12	17	89	80	50	.821	18			6	CO/1	2.3
1887	NY-N	77	318	83	97	17	13	6	44	30	33	.305	.370	.497	.867	131	17	13	107	68	70	.982	26			-1	32/C	1.1
1888	NY-N	103	415	83	127	18	15	6	58	24	28	.306	.348	.465	.813	173	27	31	93	95	88	.948	53			6	C3/SP	3.8
1889	NY-N	99	407	91	133	23	13	4	87	37	32	.327	.383	.477	.860	134	21	18	105	134	89	.967	34			14	*C/PO	2.8
1890	NY-P	83	352	98	119	19	15	8	72	39	12	.338	.406	.545	.951	142	26	20	109	88	95	1.150	36			8	C/2PM	2.5
1891	NY-N	14	49	8	17	2	1	0	18	5	5	.347	.407	.429	.836	156	3	3	94	250	11	.969	5			0	/2C	0.3
1892	NY-N	105	393	58	122	10	15	8	76	38	26	.310	.371	.473	.845	160	26	27	98	113	87	.982	42			4	1C/2	2.3
1893	Cle-N	116	500	117	172	28	15	6	122	41	18	.344	.394	.496	.890	133	25	22	104	133	119	1.024	47			-1	*O/21C	1.3
1894	Cle-N	53	211	32	53	12	4	2	39	24	9	.251	.328	.374	.702	63	-11	-15	111	134	33	.766	18			-3	O/2	-1.6
1895	Cin-N	105	434	90	138	24	13	5	94	30	22	.318	.363	.468	.831	107	8	2	108	128	88	.905	34			7	*1M	1.0
1896	Cin-N	69	263	41	73	14	4	1	38	29	13	.278	.349	.373	.722	88	-3	-5	105	115	50	.884	41			5	1M	0.1
1897	Cin-N	1	1	0	0	0	0	0	0	0	0	.000	.500	.000	.500	39	0	0	107	0	0	1.000	0			0	/1M	0.0
Total	18	1315	5363	1129	1625	250	178	71	883	392	294	.303	.351	.456	.807	130	212	191	102	103	1021	.856	354			100	C103/2SP	27.6

■ **ART EWOLDT** Ewoldt, Arthur Lee "Sheriff" b: 1/8/1894, Paullina, Iowa BR/TR, 5'10", 165 lbs. Deb: 9/17/19

YEAR	TM/L	G	AB	R	H	2B	3B	HR	RBI	BB	SO	AVG	OBP	SLG	PRO	/A	BR	/A	PF	CHI	RC	TA	SB	CS	SBR	FR	POS	TPR
1919	Phi-A	9	32	2	7	1	0	0	2	1	5	.219	.242	.250	.492	36	-3	-3	106	91	2	.360	0			-0	/3	-0.2

■ **HOMER EZZELL** Ezzell, Homer Estell b: 2/28/1896, Victoria, Tex. d: 8/3/76, San Antonio, Tex. BR/TR, 5'10", 158 lbs. Deb: 4/22/23

YEAR	TM/L	G	AB	R	H	2B	3B	HR	RBI	BB	SO	AVG	OBP	SLG	PRO	/A	BR	/A	PF	CHI	RC	TA	SB	CS	SBR	FR	POS	TPR
1923	StL-A	88	279	31	68	6	0	0	14	15	20	.244	.287	.265	.552	44	-22	-23	104	65	22	.444	4	3	-1	-6	3/2	-1.9
1924	Bos-A	90	277	35	75	8	4	0	32	14	21	.271	.311	.329	.639	63	-15	-16	104	116	29	.575	12	5	1	5	3S/C	-0.2
1925	Bos-A	58	186	40	53	6	4	0	15	19	18	.285	.351	.360	.711	85	-5	-4	95	75	24	.679	9	7	-2	-2	3/2	-0.3
Total	3	236	742	106	196	20	8	0	61	48	59	.264	.312	.313	.625	61	-42	-43	102	86	75	.551	25	15	-1	-3	3/S2C	-2.4

YEAR	TM/L	G	AB	R	H	2B	3B	HR	RBI	BB	SO	AVG	OBP	SLG	PRO	/A	BR	/A	PF	CHI	RC	TA	SB	CS	SBR	FR	POS	TPR
■ **JAY FAATZ** Faatz, Jayson S. b: 10/24/1860, Weedsport, N.Y. d: 4/10/23, Syracuse, N.Y. BR/TR, 6'4", Deb: 8/22/1884 M																												
1884	Pit-a	29	112	18	27	2	3	0		1		.241	.274	.313	.586	96	-1	-0	97	0	10	.471				-1	1	-0.2
1888	Cle-a	120	470	73	124	10	2	0	51	12		.264	.312	.294	.606	100	-1	1	97	117	65	.679	64			1	*1	-0.4
1889	Cle-N	117	442	50	102	12	5	2	38	17	28	.231	.275	.294	.569	58	-24	-26	103	85	44	.541	27			6	*1	-2.5
1890	Buf-P	32	111	18	21	0	2	1	16	9	5	.189	.297	.252	.549	53	-8	-6	92	141	9	.522	2			0	1	-0.4
Total	4	298	1135	159	274	24	12	3	105	39	33	.241	.293	.292	.584	77	-33	-31	99	96	128	.588	93			6	1	-3.5
■ **BUNNY FABRIQUE** Fabrique, Albert La Verne b: 12/23/1887, Clinton, Mich. d: 1/10/60, Ann Arbor, Mich. BB/TR, 5'8.5", 150 lbs. Deb: 10/04/16																												
1916	Bro-N	2	2	0	0	0	0	0	0	0	1	.000	.000	.000	.000	-97	-0	-0	103	0	0	.000	0			0	/S	0.0
1917	Bro-N	25	88	8	18	3	0	1	3	8	9	.205	.271	.273	.544	65	-3	-4	104	44	6	.457	0			-1	S	-0.4
Total	2	27	90	8	18	3	0	1	3	8	10	.200	.265	.267	.532	61	-4	-4	104	43	6	.444	0			-1	/S	-0.4
■ **LENNY FAEDO** Faedo, Leonardo Lago b: 5/13/60, Tampa, Fla. BR/TR, 6', 170 lbs. Deb: 9/06/80																												
1980	Min-A	5	8	1	2	1	0	0	0	0	0	.250	.250	.375	.625	63	-0	-0	109	0	1	.500	0	0	0	1	/S	0.0
1981	Min-A	12	41	3	8	0	1	0	6	1	5	.195	.214	.244	.458	30	-4	-4	105	235	2	.333	0	0	0	-2	S	-0.4
1982	Min-A	90	255	16	62	8	0	3	22	16	22	.243	.290	.310	.600	65	-12	-12	100	100	22	.480	1	0	0	-15	S/D	-1.9
1983	Min-A	51	173	16	48	7	0	1	18	4	19	.277	.294	.335	.629	69	-7	-8	105	115	16	.481	0	0	0	-8	S	-1.2
1984	Min-A	16	52	6	13	1	0	1	6	4	3	.250	.304	.327	.630	71	-2	-2	106	120	5	.525	0	0	0	-3	S/D	-0.3
Total	5	174	529	42	133	17	1	5	52	25	49	.251	.286	.316	.602	64	-24	-26	103	116	46	.489	1	0	0	-27	S/D	-3.8
■ **FRED FAGIN** Fagin, Frederick H. b: Cincinnati, Ohio Deb: 6/25/1895																												
1895	StL-N	1	3	0	1	0	0	0	2	0	0	.333	.333	.333	.667	74	-0	-0	100	559	0	.500	0			0	/C	0.0
■ **FRANK FAHEY** Fahey, Francis Raymond b: 1/22/1896, Milford, Mass. d: 3/19/54, Boston, Mass. BB/TR, 6'1", 190 lbs. Deb: 4/25/18																												
1918	Phi-A	10	17	2	3	1	0	0	1	0	3	.176	.176	.235	.412	23	-2	-2	104	91	1	.286	0			-2	/OP	-0.3
■ **HOWARD FAHEY** Fahey, Howard Simpson "Cap" or "Kid" b: 6/24/1892, Medford, Mass. d: 10/24/71, Clearwater, Fla. BR/TR, 5'7.5", 145 lbs. Deb: 7/23/12																												
1912	Phi-A	5	8	0	0	0	0	0	0	0		.000	.000	.000	.000	-99	-2	-2	99	0	0	.000	0			0	/32S	-0.1
■ **BILL FAHEY** Fahey, William Roger b: 6/14/50, Detroit, Mich. BL/TR, 6', 200 lbs. Deb: 9/26/71 C																												
1971	Was-A	2	8	0	0	0	0	0	0	0	0	.000	.000	.000	.000	-99	-2	-2	92	0	0	.000	0	0	0	0	/C	-0.1
1972	Tex-A	39	119	8	20	2	0	1	10	12	23	.168	.250	.210	.460	40	-9	-8	94	149	7	.412	4	0	1	-1	C	-0.8
1974	Tex-A	6	16	1	4	0	0	0	0	0	1	.250	.250	.250	.500	46	-1	-1	96	0	1	.333	0	0	0	0	/C	0.0
1975	Tex-A	21	37	3	11	1	1	0	3	1	10	.297	.316	.378	.694	96	-0	-0	100	82	4	.556	0	0	0	0	C	0.1
1976	Tex-A	38	80	12	20	2	0	1	9	11	6	.250	.348	.313	.660	92	-0	-0	102	123	9	.613	1	0	0	3	C	0.4
1977	Tex-A	37	68	3	15	4	0	0	5	1	8	.221	.232	.279	.511	37	-6	-6	105	104	4	.370	0	0	0	0	C	-0.4
1979	SD-N	73	209	14	60	8	1	3	19	21	17	.287	.352	.378	.730	103	0	1	96	85	28	.656	1	1	-0	-3	C	0.0
1980	SD-N	93	241	18	62	4	0	1	22	21	16	.257	.317	.286	.603	75	-9	-7	93	121	23	.503	2	0	1	-9	C	-1.4
1981	Det-A	27	67	5	17	2	0	1	9	2	4	.254	.275	.328	.604	70	-2	-3	105	141	6	.462	0	1	-1	0	C	-0.1
1982	Det-A	28	67	7	10	2	0	0	4	0	5	.149	.149	.179	.328	-10	-10	-10	100	133	2	.228	1	0	0	1	C	-0.6
1983	Det-A	19	22	4	6	1	0	0	2	5	3	.273	.407	.318	.726	108	0	1	96	112	3	.750	0	0	0	0	C	0.1
Total	11	383	934	75	225	26	2	7	83	74	93	.241	.298	.296	.594	69	-40	-37	97	113	87	.508	9	2	2	-7	C	-2.8
■ **FERRIS FAIN** Fain, Ferris Roy "Burrhead" b: 5/29/21, San Antonio, Tex. BL/TL, 5'11", 180 lbs. Deb: 4/15/47																												
1947	Phi-A	136	461	70	134	28	6	7	71	95	34	.291	.414	.423	.837	133	25	25	100	128	86	.853	4	5	-2	2	*1	2.2
1948	Phi-A	145	520	81	146	27	6	7	88	113	37	.281	.412	.396	.808	114	17	15	102	139	93	.838	10	5	0	8	*1	2.9
1949	Phi-A	150	525	81	138	21	5	3	78	136	51	.263	.415	.339	.754	102	8	9	99	137	87	.799	8	1	**2**	3	*1	1.5
1950	Phi-A	151	522	83	147	25	4	10	83	133	26	.282	.430	.402	.832	127	18	27	90	127	101	.889	8	5	-1	9	*1	2.6
1951	Phi-A	117	425	63	146	30	3	6	57	80	20	**.344**	.451	.471	.921	141	34	30	106	99	96	.969	0	3	-2	9	*1O	3.4
1952	Phi-A	145	538	82	176	**43**	3	2	59	105	26	**.327**	**.438**	.429	.867	128	36	29	111	89	107	.881	3	5	-2	16	*1	3.5
1953	Chi-A	128	446	73	114	18	2	6	52	108	28	.256	.405	.345	.750	98	9	5	106	108	72	.780	3	2	-0	7	*1	0.9
1954	Chi-A	65	235	30	71	10	1	5	51	40	14	.302	.406	.417	.823	121	10	9	104	181	44	.862	5	1	1	-6	1	0.2
1955	Det-A	58	140	23	37	8	0	2	23	52	12	.264	.464	.364	.828	129	9	10	97	151	28	.963	2	1	0	-1	1	0.7
	Cle-A	56	118	9	30	3	0	0	8	42	13	.254	.453	.280	.733	97	4	3	104	90	19	.849	3	0	1	0	1	0.2
	Yr	114	258	32	67	11	0	2	31	94	25	.260	.459	.326	.785	113	13	13	100	122	50	.934	5	1	1	-0		0.9
Total	9	1151	3930	595	1139	213	30	48	570	904	261	.290	.425	.396	.821	120	169	162	102	123	735	.894	46	28	-3	47	*1/O	18.1
■ **GEORGE FAIR** Fair, George T. b: 1/14/1856, Boston, Mass. d: 2/12/39, Roslindale, Mass. 5'7.5", 140 lbs. Deb: 7/29/1876																												
1876	NY-N	1	4	0	0	0	0	0	0	0	0	.000	.000	.000	.000	-99	-1	-1	87	0	0	.000				0	/2	0.0
■ **JIM FAIREY** Fairey, James Burke b: 9/22/44, Orangeburg, S.C. BL/TL, 5'10", 190 lbs. Deb: 4/14/68																												
1968	LA-N	99	156	17	31	3	3	1	10	9	32	.199	.242	.276	.518	61	-9	-7	91	92	10	.414	1	1	-0	-10	O	-2.3
1969	Mon-N	20	49	6	14	1	0	1	6	1	7	.286	.300	.367	.667	86	-1	-1	100	115	4	.487	0	2	-1	-0	O	-0.3
1970	Mon-N	92	211	35	51	9	3	3	25	14	38	.242	.295	.355	.651	73	-8	-8	100	115	21	.548	1	3	-2	-5	O	-1.7
1971	Mon-N	92	200	19	49	8	1	1	19	12	23	.245	.288	.310	.598	70	-8	-8	99	119	18	.494	3	3	-1	-2	O	-1.2
1972	Mon-N	86	141	9	33	7	0	1	15	10	21	.234	.285	.305	.590	66	-6	-6	102	134	12	.482	1	3	-2	-7	O	-1.8
1973	LA-N	10	9	0	2	0	0	0	0	1	1	.222	.300	.222	.522	47	-1	-1	100	0	1	.429	0	0	0	0	H	0.0
Total	6	399	766	86	180	28	7	7	75	47	122	.235	.281	.317	.598	69	-33	-31	98	113	65	.498	6	12	-5	-24	O	-7.3
■ **RON FAIRLY** Fairly, Ronald Ray b: 7/12/38, Macon, Ga. BL/TL, 5'10", 175 lbs. Deb: 9/09/58																												
1958	LA-N	15	53	6	15	1	0	2	8	6	7	.283	.356	.415	.771	99	0	0	105	120	8	.718	0	0	0	0	O	0.0
1959	LA-N	118	244	27	58	12	1	4	23	31	29	.238	.326	.344	.670	77	-7	-8	102	97	28	.601	0	4	-2	-9	O	-2.0
1960	LA-N	14	37	6	4	0	3	1	3	7	12	.108	.250	.351	.601	54	-2	-3	115	76	3	.588	0	0	0	-1	O	-0.4
1961	LA-N	111	245	42	79	15	2	10	48	48	22	.322	.435	.522	.958	149	21	20	102	123	60	1.047	0	0	0	-4	O1	1.0
1962	LA-N	147	460	80	128	15	7	14	71	75	59	.278	.383	.433	.816	128	14	19	93	116	80	.810	1	1	-0	-20	*1O	-0.7
1963	LA-N	152	490	62	133	21	0	12	77	58	69	.271	.350	.388	.737	118	9	12	95	146	68	.685	5	2	0	-8	*1O	0.0
1964	LA-N	150	454	62	116	19	5	10	74	65	59	.256	.351	.385	.737	117	6	11	92	**148**	66	.715	4	0	1	1	*1	0.8
1965	LA-N	158	555	73	152	28	1	9	70	76	72	.274	.364	.377	.741	119	9	15	91	130	82	.707	2	0	1	3	*O1	1.4
1966	LA-N	117	351	53	101	20	0	14	61	52	38	.288	.383	.464	.847	138	18	19	97	125	63	.843	3	2	-0	-12	O1	0.2
1967	LA-N	153	486	45	107	19	0	10	55	54	51	.220	.299	.321	.620	88	-14	-7	88	123	46	.535	1	4	-2	-3	O1	-2.1
1968	LA-N	141	441	32	103	15	1	4	43	41	61	.234	.305	.299	.604	90	-9	-5	91	126	40	.504	0	2	-1	3	*O1	-1.0
1969	LA-N	30	64	3	14	3	2	0	8	9	6	.219	.315	.328	.643	82	-2	-1	99	153	7	.588	0	0	0	-1	1O	-0.4
	Mon-N	70	253	35	73	13	4	12	39	28	22	.289	.359	.514	.873	142	13	13	100	96	46	.855	1	0	0	2	1O	1.1
	Yr	100	317	38	87	16	6	12	47	37	28	.274	.350	.476	.827	130	12	12	100	114	54	.801	1	0	0	1		0.7
1970	Mon-N	119	385	54	111	19	0	15	61	72	64	.288	.406	.455	.860	130	19	19	100	110	76	.916	10	2	2	8	*1/O	1.8
1971	Mon-N	146	447	58	115	23	0	13	71	81	65	.257	.377	.396	.773	121	14	15	99	134	71	.772	1	3	-2	5	*1O	0.8
1972	Mon-N	140	446	51	124	15	1	17	68	46	45	.278	.349	.430	.780	118	12	11	102	115	66	.726	3	4	-2	5	O1	0.7
1973	Mon-N	142	413	70	123	13	1	17	49	86	33	.298	.422	.458	.880	138	29	26	104	82	85	.933	2	2	-1	-13	*O/1	0.7
1974	Mon-N	101	282	35	69	9	1	12	43	57	28	.245	.374	.411	.785	114	9	7	104	109	46	.796	2	1	0	2	1O	0.5
1975	StL-N	107	229	32	69	13	2	7	37	45	22	.301	.422	.467	.890	142	16	16	103	112	46	.917	0	1	-1	-2	1O	1.0
1976	StL-N	73	110	13	29	4	0	0	21	23	12	.264	.391	.300	.691	94	1	1	104	245	14	.651	0	0	0	2	1	0.2
	Oak-A	15	46	9	11	1	0	3	10	9	12	.239	.364	.457	.820	140	2	2	100	128	8	.833	0	0	0	-1	1	0.1
1977	Tor-A	132	458	60	128	24	2	19	64	58	58	.279	.363	.465	.828	121	16	14	103	96	75	.789	0	4	-2	2	D1O	1.0
1978	Cal-A	91	235	23	51	5	0	10	40	25	31	.217	.295	.366	.661	84	-5	-5	102	136	25	.583	0	1	-1	1	1/D	-0.8
Total	21	2442	7184	931	1913	307	33	215	1044	1052	877	.266	.363	.408	.771	118	170	191	98	121	1107	.764	35	33	-9	-41	*1O/D	3.9
■ **ANTON FALCH** Falch, Anton C. b: 12/4/1860, Milwaukee, Wis. d: 3/31/36, Wauwatosa, Wis. 6'6", 220 lbs. Deb: 9/30/1884																												
1884	Mil-U	5	18	0	2	0	0	0		0		.111	.111	.111	.222	-25	-2	-2	100	0	0	.125	0			0	/OC	-0.1

YEAR	TM/L	G	AB	R	H	2B	3B	HR	RBI	BB	SO	AVG	OBP	SLG	PRO	/A	BR	/A	PF	CHI	RC	TA	SB	CS	SBR	FR	POS	TPR
■ BIBB FALK	Falk, Bibb August "Jockey" b: 1/27/1899, Austin, Tex. BL/TL, 6', 175 lbs. Deb: 9/17/20 MC																											
1920	Chi-A	7	17	1	5	1	1	0	2	0	5	.294	.294	.471	.765	105	-0	-0	96	88	2	.667	0	0	0	-1	/O	0.0
1921	Chi-A	152	585	62	167	31	11	5	82	37	69	.285	.330	.402	.732	87	-14	-13	99	119	78	.659	4	4	-1	-11	*O	-3.5
1922	Chi-A	131	483	58	144	27	1	12	79	27	55	.298	.335	.433	.768	98	-3	-3	101	118	68	.690	2	6	-3	-5	*O	-1.9
1923	Chi-A	87	274	44	84	18	6	5	38	25	12	.307	.367	.471	.837	121	7	7	98	90	47	.815	4	5	-2	-7	O	-0.7
1924	Chi-A	138	526	77	185	37	8	6	99	47	21	.352	.406	.487	.893	134	23	25	97	122	103	.893	6	6	-2	10	*O	2.1
1925	Chi-A	154	602	80	181	35	9	4	99	51	25	.301	.357	.409	.766	98	-6	-2	96	136	89	.711	4	5	-2	-2	*O	-1.8
1926	Chi-A	155	566	86	195	43	4	8	108	66	22	.345	.415	.477	.892	144	28	35	92	132	112	.911	9	10	-3	5	*O	2.4
1927	Chi-A	145	535	76	175	35	6	9	83	52	19	.327	.391	.465	.856	119	17	15	102	106	96	.861	5	0	2	**22**	*O	2.6
1928	Chi-A	98	286	42	83	18	4	1	37	25	16	.290	.347	.392	.739	95	-3	-2	99	110	40	.696	5	1	1	2	O	-0.2
1929	Cle-A	125	426	65	133	30	7	13	93	42	14	.312	.374	.507	.881	124	15	14	100	127	80	.882	4	4	-1	-6	*O	0.2
1930	Cle-A	82	191	34	62	12	1	4	36	23	8	.325	.397	.461	.858	111	5	4	105	119	36	.876	2	0	1	1	O	0.3
1931	Cle-A	79	161	30	49	13	1	2	28	17	13	.304	.371	.435	.806	104	3	1	106	122	26	.779	1	1	-0	-5	O	-0.5
Total	12	1353	4652	655	1463	300	59	69	784	412	279	.314	.372	.449	.821	113	71	81	99	120	778	.792	46	42	-11	3	*O	-1.0
■ CHARLIE FALLON	Fallon, Charles Augustus b: 3/7/1881, New York, N.Y. d: 6/10/60, Kings Park, N.Y. BR/TR, 5'6", Deb: 6/30/05																											
1905	NY-A	1	0	0	0	0	0	0	0	0		—	—	—	—	—	0	0	102	—	—	—	0			0	R	0.0
■ GEORGE FALLON	Fallon, George Decatur "Flash" b: 7/8/16, Jersey City, N.J. BR/TR, 5'9", 155 lbs. Deb: 9/27/37																											
1937	Bro-N	4	8	0	2	1	0	0	0	1	0	.250	.333	.375	.708	88	-0	-0	104	0	0	.500	0			-0	/2	0.0
1943	StL-N	36	78	6	18	1	0	0	5	2	9	.231	.259	.244	.503	44	-5	-6	105	95	5	.349	0			2	2	-0.3
1944	StL-N	69	141	16	28	6	0	1	9	16	11	.199	.285	.262	.547	54	-8	-8	101	81	11	.466	1			0	2S/3	0.0
1945	StL-N	24	55	4	13	2	1	0	7	6	6	.236	.311	.309	.621	73	-2	-2	100	143	6	.571	1			-1	S/2	0.0
Total	4	133	282	26	61	10	1	1	21	25	26	.216	.285	.270	.554	56	-16	-16	102	94	22	.475	2			-0	/2S3	-0.3
■ PETE FALSEY	Falsey, Peter James b: 4/24/1891, New Haven, Conn. d: 5/23/76, Los Angeles, Cal. BL/TL, 5'6.5", 132 lbs. Deb: 7/16/14																											
1914	Pit-N	3	1	0	0	0	0	0	0	0	1	.000	.000	.000	.000	-99	-0	-0	92	0	0	.000	0			0	H	0.0
■ JIM FANNING	Fanning, William James b: 9/14/27, Chicago, Ill. BR/TR, 5'11", 180 lbs. Deb: 9/11/54 M																											
1954	Chi-N	11	38	2	7	0	0	0	1	1	7	.184	.205	.184	.389	2	-5	-5	101	56	1	.229	0	0	0	-0	C	-0.5
1955	Chi-N	5	10	0	0	0	0	0	0	1	2	.000	.091	.000	.091	-73	-3	-3	100	0	0	.091	0	0	0	-0	/C	-0.2
1956	Chi-N	1	4	0	1	0	0	0	0	0	0	.250	.250	.250	.500	36	-0	-0	99	0	0	.250	0	0	0	0	/C	0.0
1957	Chi-N	47	89	3	16	2	0	0	4	4	17	.180	.223	.202	.426	16	-11	-10	96	92	4	.303	0	0	0	1	C	-0.7
Total	4	64	141	5	24	2	0	0	5	6	26	.170	.209	.184	.394	6	-19	-18	98	73	4	.275	0	0	0	0	/C	-1.4
■ CARMEN FANZONE	Fanzone, Carmen Ronald b: 8/30/43, Detroit, Mich. BR/TR, 6', 200 lbs. Deb: 7/21/70																											
1970	Bos-A	10	15	0	3	1	0	0	3	2	2	.200	.333	.267	.600	61	-1	-1	111	304	1	.538	0	0	0	-0	/3	0.0
1971	Chi-N	12	43	5	8	2	0	2	5	2	7	.186	.222	.372	.594	60	-2	-3	110	92	3	.500	0	0	0	-1	/O31	-0.3
1972	Chi-N	86	222	26	50	11	0	8	42	35	45	.225	.338	.383	.721	92	2	-2	114	158	28	.687	2	3	-1	5	312/SO	0.1
1973	Chi-N	64	150	22	41	7	0	6	22	20	38	.273	.359	.440	.799	111	4	3	108	105	24	.763	1	2	-1	-1	31/O	0.0
1974	Chi-N	65	158	13	30	6	0	4	22	15	27	.190	.269	.304	.572	60	-9	-9	100	142	13	.496	0	1	-1	-3	32/1O	-1.3
Total	5	237	588	66	132	27	0	20	94	74	119	.224	.317	.372	.690	86	-5	-11	108	140	70	.651	3	6	-3	0	3/12OS	-1.5
■ BOB FARLEY	Farley, Robert Jacob b: 11/15/37, Watsontown, Pa. BL/TL, 6'2", 200 lbs. Deb: 4/15/61																											
1961	SF-N	13	20	3	2	0	0	0	1	3	5	.100	.217	.100	.317	-12	-3	-3	98	202	1	.278	0	0	0	-1	/O1	-0.3
1962	Chi-A	35	53	7	10	1	1	1	4	13	13	.189	.348	.302	.650	81	-1	-1	95	84	6	.659	0	1	-1	-0	1	-0.2
	Det-A	36	50	9	8	2	0	1	4	14	10	.160	.344	.260	.604	59	-2	-3	111	99	6	.643	0	0	0	-3	O/1	-0.6
	Yr	71	103	16	18	3	1	2	8	27	23	.175	.346	.282	.628	69	-3	-4	103	93	12	.651	0	1	-1	-4		-0.8
Total	2	84	123	19	20	3	1	2	9	30	28	.163	.327	.252	.579	57	-7	-7	102	108	13	.587	0	1	-1	-4	/1O	-1.1
■ TOM FARLEY	Farley, Thomas T. b: Chicago, Ill. Deb: 6/24/1884																											
1884	Was-a	14	52	5	11	4	0	0		1		.212	.241	.288	.529	84	-1	-1	88	0	4	.415				1	O	0.0
■ ALEX FARMER	Farmer, Alexander Johnson b: 5/9/1880, New York, N.Y. d: 3/5/20, New York, N.Y. BR/TR, 6', 175 lbs. Deb: 9/01/08																											
1908	Bro-N	12	30	1	5	1	0	0	2	1		.167	.194	.200	.394	28	-2	-2	95	128	1	.280	0			1	C	0.0
■ JACK FARMER	Farmer, Floyd Haskell b: 7/14/1892, Granville, Tenn. d: 5/21/70, Columbia, La. BR/TR, 6', 180 lbs. Deb: 7/08/16																											
1916	Pit-N	55	166	10	45	6	4	0	14	7	24	.271	.309	.355	.664	99	0	-0	105	94	19	.570	1			-11	2O/S3	-1.1
1918	Cle-A	7	9	1	2	0	0	0	1	0	3	.222	.300	.222	.522	53	-0	-1	108	182	1	.714	2			-2	/O	-0.2
Total	2	62	175	11	47	6	4	0	15	7	27	.269	.308	.349	.657	97	-0	-1	105	99	20	.578	3			-12	/2OS3	-1.3
■ BILL FARMER	Farmer, William b: 12/27/1870, BR/TR, 5'11.5", Deb: 1888																											
1888	Pit-N	2	4	0	0	0	0	0	0	0	1	.000	.000	.000	.000	-99	-1	-1	95	0	0	.000	0			0	/CO	0.0
	Phi-a	3	12	0	2	0	0	0	1	0		.167	.167	.167	.333	9	-1	-1	101	152	0	.200	0			0	/C	0.0
Total	1	5	16	0	2	0	0	0	1	0	1	.125	.125	.125	.250	-19	-2	-2	99	114	0	.143	0			0	/CO	0.0
■ SID FARRAR	Farrar, Sidney Douglas b: 8/10/1859, Paris Hill, Me. d: 5/7/35, New York, N.Y. TR , 5'10", Deb: 5/01/1883																											
1883	Phi-N	99	377	41	88	19	8	0	29	4	37	.233	.241	.326	.568	78	-13	-8	90	83	30	.439				-0	*1	-1.7
1884	Phi-N	111	428	62	105	16	6	1	45	9	25	.245	.261	.318	.579	88	-10	-5	92	114	36	.449				3	*1	-1.1
1885	Phi-N	111	420	49	103	20	3	3	36	28	34	.245	.292	.329	.621	97	0	-2	104	82	41	.524				2	*1	-1.7
1886	Phi-N	118	439	55	109	19	7	5	50	16	47	.248	.275	.358	.632	93	-6	-4	98	97	47	.555	10			3	*1	-2.1
1887	Phi-N	116	443	83	125	20	9	4	72	42	29	.282	.358	.395	.753	115	8	10	97	121	73	.789	24			2	*1	-0.5
1888	Phi-N	131	508	53	124	24	7	1	53	31	38	.244	.304	.325	.629	90	2	-7	114	120	58	.599	21			2	*1	-1.7
1889	Phi-N	130	477	70	128	22	2	3	58	52	36	.268	.348	.342	.689	91	-2	-6	104	103	68	.713	28			-5	*1	-1.7
1890	Phi-P	127	481	84	122	17	11	1	69	51	23	.254	.331	.341	.672	80	-12	-14	102	115	59	.638	9			-2	*1	-2.2
Total	8	943	3573	497	904	157	53	18	412	233	269	.253	.305	.342	.647	92	-32	-35	101	105	413	.592	92			4	1	-12.7
■ DUKE FARRELL	Farrell, Charles Andrew b: 8/31/1866, Oakdale, Mass. d: 2/15/25, Boston, Mass. BB/TR, 6'1", 208 lbs. Deb: 1888																											
1888	Chi-N	64	241	34	56	6	3	3	19	4	41	.232	.245	.320	.564	75	-6	-8	107	81	21	.481	8			0	CO/1	-0.7
1889	Chi-N	101	407	66	101	19	7	11	75	41	21	.248	.318	.410	.729	105	1	2	99	119	59	.725	13			4	CO	0.6
1890	Chi-P	117	451	79	131	21	12	2	84	42	28	.290	.352	.404	.756	99	2	-2	104	125	69	.728	8			18	C1O	1.6
1891	Bos-a	122	473	108	143	19	13	**12**	**110**	59	48	.302	.384	.474	.858	151	29	30	99	130	97	.933	21			9	3CO/1	3.6
1892	Pit-N	152	605	96	130	10	13	8	77	46	53	.215	.276	.314	.590	85	-16	-10	94	117	59	.549	20			-6	*3O	-0.7
1893	Was-N	124	511	84	143	13	13	4	75	47	12	.280	.346	.380	.726	106	-4	5	90	106	73	.698	11			21	C3/1	2.8
1894	NY-N	114	401	47	114	20	12	4	66	35	15	.284	.346	.424	.770	87	-10	-10	100	100	64	.756	9			17	*C/31	1.3
1895	NY-N	90	312	38	90	16	9	1	58	38	18	.288	.371	.407	.778	108	2	5	95	127	52	.806	11			7	C3/1	1.4
1896	NY-N	58	191	23	54	7	3	1	37	19	7	.283	.351	.366	.717	92	-2	-2	99	146	26	.672	2			-1	CS/3	0.0
	Was-N	37	130	18	39	7	3	1	30	7	3	.300	.345	.423	.768	109	0	1	95	149	20	.725	2			2	C3	0.5
	Yr	95	321	41	93	14	6	2	67	26	10	.290	.349	.389	.738	99	-2	-0	97	149	46	.693	4			1		0.5
1897	Was-N	78	261	41	84	9	6	0	53	17		.322	.366	.402	.768	103	2	1	101	148	42	.740	8			8	C/1	1.5
1898	Was-N	99	338	47	106	12	6	1	53	34		.314	.383	.393	.776	123	12	11	102	120	57	.789	12			1	C1	1.5
1899	Was-N	5	12	2	4	1	0	0	1	2		.333	.429	.417	.845	141	1	1	96	61	3	1.000	1			-0	/C	0.0
	Bro-N	80	254	40	76	10	7	2	55	35		.299	.390	.417	.808	119	10	8	105	154	45	.843	6			6	C	1.7
	Yr	85	266	42	80	11	7	2	56	37		.301	.392	.417	.809	120	10	8	104	149	47	.849	7			6		1.7
1900	Bro-N	76	273	33	75	11	5	0	39	11		.275	.303	.352	.654	77	-7	-10	108	129	31	.556	3			0	C	-0.2
1901	Bro-N	80	284	38	84	10	6	1	31	7		.296	.313	.384	.697	98	0	-2	106	93	37	.615	7			1	C1	0.7
1902	Bro-N	74	264	14	64	5	2	0	24	12		.242	.275	.277	.552	76	-9	-7	95	116	22	.455	6			-2	C1	-0.4
1903	Bos-A	17	52	5	21	5	1	0	8	5		.404	.456	.538	.995	179	6	6	112	103	14	1.097	1			1	C	0.9
1904	Bos-A	68	198	11	42	9	2	0	15	15		.212	.268	.278	.545	71	-5	-6	105	102	15	.455	1			0	C	0.0
1905	Bos-A	7	21	2	6	1	0	0	2	1		.286	.318	.333	.652	109	0	0	100	102	2	.533	0			0	/C	0.1

YEAR	TM/L	G	AB	R	H	2B	3B	HR	RBI	BB	SO	AVG	OBP	SLG	PRO	/A	BR	/A	PF	CHI	RC	TA	SB	CS	SBR	FR	POS	TPR
Total	18	1563	5679	826	1563	211	123	51	912	477	246	.275	.335	.383	.718	102	6	14	99	119	808	.688	150			87	*C301/S	16.2
■ **DOC FARRELL**	Farrell, Edward Stephen b: 12/26/01, Johnson City, N.Y. d: 12/20/66, Livingston, N.J. BR/TR, 5'8", 160 lbs. Deb: 6/23/25																											
1925	NY-N	27	56	6	12	1	0	0	4	4	6	.214	.267	.232	.499	29	-6	-6	99	109	3	.378	0	1	-1	0	S/32	-0.4
1926	NY-N	67	171	19	49	10	1	2	23	12	17	.287	.341	.392	.732	99	-1	-0	98	109	22	.697	4			-3	S/2	0.1
1927	NY-N	42	142	13	55	10	1	3	34	12	11	.387	.442	.535	.978	161	12	12	100	140	33	1.034	0			6	S/3	2.1
	Bos-N	110	424	44	124	13	2	1	58	14	21	.292	.315	.340	.655	81	-15	-11	93	146	44	.540	4			-5	S23	-0.9
	Yr	152	566	57	179	23	3	4	92	26	32	.316	.348	.389	.737	102	-3	1	95	145	74	.651	4			1		1.2
1928	Bos-N	134	483	36	104	14	2	3	43	26	26	.215	.263	.271	.534	41	-43	-41	97	112	35	.435	3			-18	*S/2	-4.0
1929	Bos-N	5	8	0	1	0	0	0	2	0	1	.125	.125	.125	.250	-40	-2	-2	94	685	0	.143	0			0	/2S	0.0
	NY-N	63	178	18	38	6	0	0	16	9	17	.213	.251	.247	.499	24	-21	-21	100	124	11	.393	2			4	32/S	-1.1
	Yr	68	186	18	39	6	0	0	18	9	18	.210	.246	.242	.488	22	-23	-23	99	176	11	.381	2			4		-1.1
1930	StL-N	23	61	3	13	1	1	0	6	4	2	.213	.262	.262	.524	26	-7	-8	105	129	4	.438	1			1	S/21	-0.3
	Chi-N	46	113	21	33	6	0	1	16	9	5	.292	.344	.372	.716	70	-5	-6	105	123	14	.637	0			-2	S/2	-0.2
	Yr	69	174	24	46	7	1	1	22	13	7	.264	.316	.333	.649	54	-12	-13	105	127	18	.563	1			-0		-0.5
1932	NY-A	26	63	4	11	1	1	0	4	2	8	.175	.212	.222	.434	13	-8	-8	95	96	3	.327	0	0	0	0	2/S13	-0.5
1933	NY-A	44	93	16	25	0	0	0	6	16	6	.269	.376	.269	.645	81	-3	-1	91	80	11	.603	0	0	0	-3	S2	-0.1
1935	Bos-A	4	7	1	2	1	0	0	1	1	0	.286	.375	.429	.804	99	0	0	108	113	1	.800	0	0	0	0	/2	0.0
Total	9	591	1799	181	467	63	8	10	213	109	120	.260	.306	.320	.626	65	-98	-91	97	124	182	.532	14	1		-17	S2/31	-5.3
■ **JACK FARRELL**	Farrell, John "Hartford Jack" d: 11/15/16, Hartford, Conn. Deb: 10/27/1874																											
1874	Har-n	3	15	3	5							.333															/O	
■ **JACK FARRELL**	Farrell, John A. "Moose" b: 7/5/1857, Newark, N.J. d: 2/10/14, Overbrook, N.J. BR/TR, 5'9", 165 lbs. Deb: 5/01/1879 M																											
1879	Syr-N	54	241	40	73	6	2	1	21	3	13	.303	.311	.357	.668	135	5	9	89	71	27	.530				-6	2	0.7
	Pro-N	12	51	5	13	2	0	0	5	0	0	.255	.255	.294	.549	79	-1	-1	102	119	4	.395				9	2	0.8
	Yr	66	292	45	86	8	2	1	26	3	13	.295	.302	.346	.648	124	4	7	91	81	31	.505				3		1.5
1880	Pro-N	80	339	46	92	12	5	3	36	10	6	.271	.292	.363	.655	126	7	9	96	96	37	.538				-10	*2	0.1
1881	Pro-N	84	345	69	82	16	5	5	36	29	23	.238	.297	.357	.653	112	2	6	93	80	37	.578				-4	*2/OM	0.4
1882	Pro-N	84	366	67	93	21	6	2	31	16	23	.254	.285	.361	.646	100	2	-1	106	67	39	.542				-3	*2	-0.1
1883	Pro-N	95	420	92	128	24	11	3	61	15	21	.305	.329	.436	.764	129	14	14	101	97	62	.678				**22**	*2	2.7
1884	Pro-N	111	469	70	102	13	6	1	37	35	44	.217	.272	.277	.549	72	-14	-15	102	84	36	.450				-7	*2/3	-1.7
1885	Pro-N	68	257	27	53	7	1	1	19	10	25	.206	.236	.253	.489	64	-12	-9	91	103	16	.368				-18	2	-1.7
1886	Phi-N	17	60	7	11	0	1	0	3	3	11	.183	.222	.217	.439	35	-5	-5	98	77	3	.347	1			0	2	-0.3
	Was-N	47	171	24	41	11	4	2	18	15	12	.240	.301	.386	.687	115	1	3	94	86	24	.715	12			-11	2	-0.4
	Yr	64	231	31	52	11	5	2	21	18	23	.225	.281	.342	.623	93	-3	-1	95	85	27	.615	13			-11		-0.7
1887	Was-N	87	339	40	75	14	9	0	41	20	12	.221	.267	.316	.582	66	-17	-14	95	125	38	.602	31			-8	S2	-1.8
1888	Bal-a	103	398	72	81	19	5	3	36	26		.204	.256	.299	.555	83	-9	-6	96	89	39	.555	29			6	S2	0.3
1889	Bal-a	42	157	25	33	3	0	1	26	15	15	.210	.287	.248	.536	55	-9	-9	100	187	16	.565	14			0	S	-0.4
Total	11	884	3613	584	877	148	55	22	370	197	205	.243	.283	.332	.615	95	-34	-19	97	95	377	.545	87			-28	2S/3O	-1.4
■ **JACK FARRELL**	Farrell, John J. b: 6/16/1892, Chicago, Ill. d: 3/24/18, Chicago, Ill. BB/TR, 5'8", 145 lbs. Deb: 4/16/14																											
1914	Chi-F	156	524	58	123	23	4	0	35	52	65	.235	.304	.294	.598	79	-18	-12	91	84	54	.544	12			15	*2/S	0.5
1915	Chi-F	70	222	27	48	10	1	0	14	25	18	.216	.296	.270	.566	70	-8	-8	97	84	22	.534	8			-0	2/S	-0.7
Total	2	226	746	85	171	33	5	0	49	77	83	.229	.301	.287	.588	76	-27	-20	93	84	76	.541	20			15	2/S	-0.2
■ **JOHN FARRELL**	Farrell, John Sebastian b: 12/4/1876, Covington, Ky. d: 5/13/21, Kansas City, Mo. BR/TR, 5'10", 160 lbs. Deb: 4/26/01																											
1901	Was-A	135	555	100	151	32	11	3	63	52		.272	.334	.386	.720	102	1	2	99	77	82	.720	25			-2	2O/3	-0.3
1902	StL-N	138	565	68	141	13	5	0	25	43		.250	.303	.290	.593	89	-9	-6	95	46	54	.509	9			**23**	*2S	2.7
1903	StL-N	130	519	83	141	25	8	1	32	48		.272	.333	.356	.690	102	-1	2	96	47	69	.661	17			17	*2/O	2.4
1904	StL-N	131	509	72	130	23	3	0	20	46		.255	.317	.312	.629	98	-1	-0	99	41	57	.583	16			17	*2	2.0
1905	StL-N	7	24	6	4	0	1	0	1	4		.167	.286	.250	.536	68	-1	-1	91	61	2	.550	1			-1	/2	-0.1
Total	5	541	2172	329	567	93	28	4	141	193		.261	.321	.335	.657	98	-11	-3	97	53	264	.616	68			53	2/OS3	6.7
■ **JOE FARRELL**	Farrell, Joseph F. b: 1857, Brooklyn, N.Y. d: 4/18/1893, Brooklyn, N.Y. R , 5'6", 160 lbs. Deb: 5/01/1882																											
1882	Det-N	69	283	34	70	12	2	1	24	4	20	.247	.258	.314	.572	81	-6	-6	102	93	24	.437				-13	32/S	-1.6
1883	Det-N	101	444	58	108	13	5	0	36	5	29	.243	.252	.295	.547	72	-18	-12	91	92	34	.405				14	*3	0.2
1884	Det-N	110	461	59	104	10	5	3	41	14	66	.226	.248	.289	.537	73	-17	-12	94	88	34	.412				-7	*3/O	-2.1
1886	Bal-a	73	301	36	63	8	3	1		12		.209	.240	.266	.505	66	-14	-10	91	0	21	.408	5			-13	23/O	-1.9
Total	4	353	1489	187	345	43	15	5	101	35	115	.232	.249	.291	.540	73	-54	-40	94	72	112	.413	5			-19	3/2SO	-5.4
■ **KERBY FARRELL**	Farrell, Major Kerby b: 9/3/13, Leapwood, Tenn. d: 12/17/75, Nashville, Tenn. BL/TL, 5'11", 172 lbs. Deb: 4/24/43 MC																											
1943	Bos-N	85	280	11	75	14	1	0	21	16	15	.268	.307	.325	.632	78	-7	-8	106	83	26	.502	1			1	1/P	-0.9
1945	Chi-A	103	396	44	102	11	3	0	34	24	18	.258	.300	.301	.601	78	-13	-11	95	109	35	.476	4	9	-4	-2	1	-2.2
Total	2	188	676	55	177	25	4	0	55	40	33	.262	.303	.311	.614	78	-20	-20	100	99	61	.496	5	9		-1	1/P	-3.1
■ **BILL FARRELL**	Farrell, William Deb: 5/03/1882																											
1882	Phi-a	2	7	2	2	1	0	0		1		.286	.375	.429	.804	152	1	0	112	0	1	.800				0	/OC	0.0
1883	Bal-a	2	7	0	0	0	0	0		1		.000	.125	.000	.125	-53	-1	-1	107	0	0	.143				0	/S	0.0
Total	2	4	14	2	2	1	0	0		2		.143	.250	.214	.464	50	-1	-1	109	0	1	.417				0	/SOC	0.0
■ **JOHN FARROW**	Farrow, John Jacob b: Verplanck's Point, N.Y. d: 12/31/14, Perth Amboy, N.J. BL/TR, Deb: 4/28/1873																											
1873	Res-n	12	51	2	8							.157															/CSO1	
1874	Atl-n	27	125	16	26							.208															C2	
1884	Bro-a	16	58	7	11	2	0	0		3		.190	.230	.224	.454	52	-3	-3	98	0	3	.340				0	C	-0.2
Total	2 n	39	176	18	34							.193															C	
■ **BUCK FAUSETT**	Fausett, Robert Shaw "Leaky" b: 4/8/08, Sheridan, Ark. BL/TR, 5'10", 170 lbs. Deb: 4/18/44																											
1944	Cin-N	13	31	2	3	0	1	0	1	1	2	.097	.125	.161	.286	-21	-5	-5	95	72	0	.200	0			-0	/3P	-0.4
■ **JOE FAUTSCH**	Fautsch, Joseph Roamon b: 2/28/1887, Minneapolis, Minn. d: 3/16/71, New Hope, Minn. BR/TR, 5'10", 162 lbs. Deb: 4/24/16																											
1916	Chi-A	1	1	0	0	0	0	0	0	0	0	.000	.000	.000	.000	-93	-0	-0	108	0	0	.000	0			0	H	0.0
◘ **ERNIE FAZIO**	Fazio, Ernest Joseph b: 1/25/42, Oakland, Cal. BR/TR, 5'7", 165 lbs. Deb: 7/03/62																											
1962	Hou-N	12	12	3	1	0	0	0	1	2	5	.083	.214	.083	.298	-18	-2	-2	93	394	0	.273	0	0	0	0	S	0.0
1963	Hou-N	102	228	31	42	10	3	2	5	27	70	.184	.273	.281	.554	65	-12	-9	92	30	18	.500	4	4	-1	-12	2/S3	-1.8
1966	KC-A	27	34	3	7	0	1	0	2	4	10	.206	.289	.265	.554	64	-2	-1	94	93	3	.519	1	0	0	0	2/S	0.0
Total	3	141	274	37	50	10	4	2	8	33	85	.182	.273	.270	.543	61	-15	-13	92	54	22	.496	5	4	-1	-12	/2S3	-1.8
■ **AL FEDEROFF**	Federoff, Alfred "Whitey" b: 7/11/24, Bairdford, Pa. BR/TR, 5'10.5", 165 lbs. Deb: 9/27/51																											
1951	Det-A	2	4	0	0	0	0	0	0	0	0	.000	.000	.000	.000	-95	-1	-1	106	0	0	.000	0	0	0	0	/2	0.0
1952	Det-A	74	231	14	56	4	2	0	14	16	13	.242	.294	.277	.571	60	-12	-12	99	82	20	.458	1	0	0	-2	2/S	-1.0
Total	2	76	235	14	56	4	2	0	14	16	13	.238	.290	.272	.562	57	-14	-13	99	80	20	.448	1	0	0	-2	/2S	-1.0
■ **BILL FEHRING**	Fehring, William Paul "Dutch" b: 5/31/12, Columbus, Ind. BB/TR, 6', 195 lbs. Deb: 6/25/34																											
1934	Chi-A	1	1	0	0	0	0	0	0	0	1	.000	.000	.000	.000	-99	-0	-0	99	0	0	.000	0	0	0	0	/C	0.0
■ **EDDIE FEINBERG**	Feinberg, Edward Isadore "Itzzy" b: 9/29/17, Philadelphia, Pa. d: 4/20/86, Hollywood, Fla. BB/TR, 5'9", 165 lbs. Deb: 9/11/38																											
1938	Phi-N	10	20	0	3	0	0	0	0	0	1	.150	.150	.150	.300	-17	-3	-3	100	0	0	.176	0			0	/SO	-0.2
1939	Phi-N	6	18	2	4	1	0	0	0	2	0	.222	.300	.278	.578	60	-1	-1	94	0	2	.500	0			-0	/2S	0.0
Total	2	16	38	2	7	1	0	0	0	2	1	.184	.225	.211	.436	20	-4	-4	97	0	2	.323	0			0	/S2O	-0.2

YEAR	TM/L	G	AB	R	H	2B	3B	HR	RBI	BB	SO	AVG	OBP	SLG	PRO	/A	BR	/A	PF	CHI	RC	TA	SB	CS	SBR	FR	POS	TPR
■ **MIKE FELDER**	Felder, Michael Otis b: 11/18/61, Vallejo, Cal. BB/TR, 5'8", 160 lbs. Deb: 9/11/85																											
1985	Mil-A	15	56	8	11	1	0	0	0	5	6	.196	.262	.214	.477	31	-5	-5	105	0	3	.438	4	1	1	1	O	-0.3
1986	Mil-A	44	155	24	37	2	4	1	13	13	16	.239	.298	.323	.620	68	-6	-7	102	100	17	.648	16	2	4	1	O/D	-0.2
1987	Mil-A	108	289	48	77	5	7	2	31	28	23	.266	.331	.353	.684	81	-7	-8	102	115	38	.735	34	8	5	1	O/2D	-0.3
1988	Mil-A	50	81	14	14	1	0	0	5	0	11	.173	.183	.185	.368	3	-10	-11	103	132	3	.343	8	2	1	-5	OD/2	-1.4
Total	4	217	581	94	139	9	11	3	49	46	56	.239	.296	.308	.604	62	-28	-31	103	102	61	.632	62	13	11	-2	O/D2	-2.2
■ **MARV FELDERMAN**	Felderman, Marvin Wilfred "Coonie" b: 12/20/15, Bellevue, Iowa BR/TR, 6'1", 187 lbs. Deb: 4/19/42																											
1942	Chi-N	3	6	0	1	0	0	0	0	1	4	.167	.286	.167	.452	35	-0	-0	96	0	0	.400	0			0	/C	0.0
■ **GUS FELIX**	Felix, August Guenther b: 5/24/1895, Cincinnati, Ohio d: 5/12/60, Montgomery, Ala. BR/TR, 6', 180 lbs. Deb: 4/19/23																											
1923	Bos-N	139	506	64	138	17	2	6	44	51	65	.273	.348	.350	.697	85	-10	-10	100	81	62	.638	8	13	-5	-1	*O/23	-1.9
1924	Bos-N	59	204	25	43	7	1	1	10	18	16	.211	.275	.270	.544	49	-15	-14	94	64	15	.445	0	3	-2	2	O	-1.3
1925	Bos-N	121	459	60	141	25	7	2	66	30	34	.307	.356	.405	.762	100	-4	0	94	125	66	.700	5	5	-2	15	*O	0.9
1926	Bro-N	134	432	64	121	21	7	3	53	51	32	.280	.360	.382	.742	100	1	1	99	105	60	.733	9			-9	*O	-1.1
1927	Bro-N	130	445	43	118	21	8	0	57	39	47	.265	.327	.348	.675	79	-12	-13	103	131	51	.618	6			-6	*O	-2.3
Total	5	583	2046	256	561	91	25	12	230	189	194	.274	.341	.361	.701	87	-40	-35	98	105	254	.645	28	21		2	O/23	-5.7
■ **JACK FELLER**	Feller, Jack Leland b: 12/10/36, Adrian, Mich. BR/TR, 5'10.5", 185 lbs. Deb: 9/13/58																											
1958	Det-A	1	0	0	0	0	0	0	0	0	0	—	—	—	—	—	0	0	104	—	—	—	0	0	0	0	/C	0.0
■ **HAPPY FELSCH**	Felsch, Oscar Emil b: 8/22/1891, Milwaukee, Wis. d: 8/17/64, Milwaukee, Wis. BR/TR, 5'11", 175 lbs. Deb: 4/14/15																											
1915	Chi-A	121	427	65	106	18	11	3	53	51	59	.248	.334	.363	.697	111	4	5	98	116	52	.667	16	18	-6	-10	*O	-1.8
1916	Chi-A	146	546	73	164	24	12	7	70	31	67	.300	.341	.427	.768	121	17	12	108	104	85	.733	13			2	*O	0.7
1917	Chi-A	152	575	75	177	17	10	6	102	33	52	.308	.352	.403	.755	134	19	20	98	155	87	.746	26			16	*O	2.9
1918	Chi-A	53	206	16	52	2	5	1	20	15	13	.252	.306	.325	.632	90	-3	-3	101	110	22	.578	6			4	O	-0.1
1919	Chi-A	135	502	68	138	34	11	7	86	40	35	.275	.336	.428	.764	109	7	4	105	140	76	.769	19			19	*O	1.5
1920	Chi-A	142	556	88	188	40	15	14	115	37	25	.338	.384	.540	.923	149	31	34	96	125	109	.916	8	13	-5	14	*O	2.9
Total	6	749	2812	385	825	135	64	38	446	207	251	.293	.347	.427	.774	123	75	73	101	127	431	.754	88	31		45	O	6.1
■ **JOHN FELSKE**	Felske, John Frederick b: 5/30/42, Chicago, Ill. BR/TR, 6'3", 195 lbs. Deb: 7/26/68 MC																											
1968	Chi-N	4	2	0	0	0	0	0	0	0	1	.000	.000	.000	.000	-89	-0	-0	112	0	0	.000	0	0	0	0	/C	0.0
1972	Mil-A	37	80	6	11	3	0	1	5	8	23	.138	.216	.213	.428	29	-7	-7	95	104	4	.352	0	0	0	0	C/1	-0.7
1973	Mil-A	13	22	1	3	0	1	0	4	1	11	.136	.174	.227	.401	13	-3	-2	96	314	1	.316	0	0	0	0	/C1	-0.1
Total	3	54	104	7	14	3	1	1	9	9	35	.135	.204	.212	.415	23	-10	-10	96	145	5	.344	0	0	0	1	/C1	-0.8
■ **FRANK FENNELLY**	Fennelly, Francis John b: 2/18/1860, Fall River, Mass. d: 8/4/20, Fall River, Mass. BR/TR, 5'8", 168 lbs. Deb: 5/01/1884																											
1884	Was-a	62	257	52	75	17	7	2		20		.292	.343	.436	.779	176	15	20	88	0	39	.725				12	S/2	2.7
	Cin-a	28	122	42	43	5	8	2		11		.352	.415	.574	.989	211	16	15	106	0	30	1.051				-6	S	0.8
	Yr	90	379	94	118	22	15	4		31		.311	.367	.480	.847	189	32	35	94	0	68	.824				6		3.5
1885	Cin-a	112	454	82	124	14	17	10		38		.273	.333	.445	.778	142	24	21	104	0	69	.736				-13	*S	0.9
1886	Cin-a	132	497	113	124	13	17	6		60		.249	.351	.380	.732	137	20	23	96	0	80	.802	32			12	*S	3.7
1887	Cin-a	134	526	133	140	15	16	8		82		.266	.369	.401	.770	108	14	6	108	0	108	.961	74			-8	*S	-0.3
1888	Cin-a	120	448	64	88	8	7	2	56	63		.196	.297	.259	.556	81	-6	-7	101	145	48	.619	43			15	*S/2O	1.2
	Phi-a	15	47	13	11	2	2	1	12	9		.234	.357	.426	.783	153	3	3	101	156	9	.944	5			-1	S	0.2
	Yr	135	495	77	99	10	9	3	68	72		.200	.303	.275	.578	88	-3	-4	101	148	57	.649	48			14		1.4
1889	Phi-a	138	513	70	132	20	5	1	64	65	78	.257	.344	.322	.666	94	-3	-1	98	111	64	.651	15			-6	*S	0.3
1890	BB-a	45	178	40	44	8	3	2		30		.247	.356	.360	.715	113	4	4	100	0	26	.746	6			-3	S/3	0.2
Total	7	786	3042	609	781	102	82	34	132	378	78	.257	.345	.378	.723	121	87	84	100	43	472	.766	175			2	S/23O	9.7
■ **BOBBY FENWICK**	Fenwick, Robert Richard b: 12/10/46, Okinawa BR/TR, 5'9", 165 lbs. Deb: 4/26/72																											
1972	Hou-N	36	50	7	9	3	0	0	4	3	13	.180	.226	.240	.466	31	-4	-5	106	137	2	.349	0	1	-1	2	2/S3	-0.1
1973	StL-N	5	6	0	1	0	0	0	1	0	2	.167	.167	.167	.333	-8	-1	-1	91	402	0	.200	0	0	0	0	/2	0.0
Total	2	41	56	7	10	3	0	0	5	3	15	.179	.220	.232	.452	27	-5	-6	105	164	3	.340	0	1	-1	2	/2S3	-0.1
■ **JOE FERGUSON**	Ferguson, Joseph Vance b: 9/19/46, San Francisco, Cal. BR/TR, 6'2", 200 lbs. Deb: 9/12/70 C																											
1970	LA-N	5	4	0	1	0	0	0	1	2	2	.250	.500	.250	.750	120	0	0	90	388	1	1.000	0	0	0	-0	/C	0.0
1971	LA-N	36	102	13	22	3	0	2	7	12	15	.216	.304	.304	.608	74	-3	-3	99	77	10	.542	1	0	0	-2	C	-0.4
1972	LA-N	8	24	2	7	3	0	1	5	2	4	.292	.346	.542	.888	159	1	2	94	128	4	.789	0	0	0	-0	/CO	0.2
1973	LA-N	136	487	84	128	26	0	25	88	87	81	.263	.376	.470	.846	133	23	23	100	123	92	.871	1	1	-0	-6	*CO	2.4
1974	LA-N	111	349	54	88	14	1	16	57	75	73	.252	.384	.436	.820	139	16	19	93	110	60	.836	2	2	-1	-2	CO	1.9
1975	LA-N	66	202	15	42	2	1	5	23	35	47	.208	.328	.302	.630	80	-6	-4	95	117	22	.600	2	1	0	3	CO	-0.1
1976	LA-N	54	185	24	41	7	0	6	18	25	41	.222	.318	.357	.674	91	-2	-2	100	84	22	.639	2	0	1	0	OC	-0.1
	StL-N	71	189	22	38	8	4	4	21	32	40	.201	.320	.349	.669	86	-2	-3	104	104	22	.648	4	2	1	0	CO	0.0
	Yr	125	374	46	79	15	4	10	39	57	81	.211	.319	.353	.672	89	-4	-5	102	96	45	.650	6	2	1	1		-0.1
1977	Hou-N	132	421	59	108	21	3	16	61	85	79	.257	.381	.435	.816	128	13	18	93	108	74	.840	6	2	1	9	*C/1	2.5
1978	Hou-N	51	150	20	31	5	0	7	22	37	30	.207	.367	.380	.747	115	3	4	95	114	22	.760	0	0	0	-1	C	0.5
	LA-N	67	198	20	47	11	0	7	28	34	41	.237	.352	.399	.751	110	3	3	99	111	27	.710	1	2	-1	-6	C/O	-0.1
	Yr	118	348	40	78	16	0	14	50	71	71	.224	.359	.391	.749	113	6	8	97	113	52	.747	1	2	-1	-7		0.4
1979	LA-N	122	363	54	95	14	0	20	69	70	68	.262	.384	.466	.849	131	17	17	100	119	68	.871	1	0	0	-1	CO	1.7
1980	LA-N	77	172	20	41	3	2	9	29	38	46	.238	.376	.436	.812	130	7	8	97	113	27	.816	2	2	-1	-10	C/O	-0.1
1981	LA-N	17	14	2	2	1	0	0	1	2	5	.143	.250	.214	.464	33	-1	-1	98	131	1	.417	0	0	0	-0	/O	-0.1
	Cal-A	12	30	5	7	1	0	1	5	9	8	.233	.410	.367	.777	120	2	1	104	140	5	.833	0	0	0	0	/CO	0.2
1982	Cal-A	36	84	10	19	2	0	3	8	12	19	.226	.323	.357	.680	86	-1	-1	100	82	9	.609	0	0	0	3	C/O	0.3
1983	Cal-A	12	27	3	2	0	0	0	2	5	8	.074	.219	.074	.293	-16	-4	-4	96	391	0	.250	0	0	0	0	/CO	-0.3
Total	14	1013	3001	407	719	121	11	122	445	562	607	.240	.361	.409	.770	116	66	77	97	114	465	.793	22	12	-1	-13	CO/1	8.5
■ **BOB FERGUSON**	Ferguson, Robert V. "Death To Flying Things" b: 1/31/1845, Brooklyn, N.Y. d: 5/3/1894, Brooklyn, N.Y. BB/TR, 5'9.5", 149 lbs. Deb: 5/18/1871 M																											
1871	Mut-n	33	156	30	34							.218															32/CM	
1872	Atl-n	35	164	34	43							.262															*3M	
1873	Atl-n	51	238	36	59							.248															*3/PM	
1874	Atl-n	56	249	34	64							.257															*3/CP	
1875	Har-n	84	373	65	87							.233															*3M	
1876	Har-N	69	310	48	82	8	5	0	32	2	11	.265	.269	.323	.592	89	-1	-5	108	104	28	.447				2	*3M	-0.3
1877	Har-N	58	254	40	65	7	2	0	35	3	10	.256	.265	.299	.564	86	-6	-2	89	**165**	21	.418				19	*3/PM	1.7
1878	Chi-N	61	259	44	91	10	2	0	39	10	12	.351	**.375**	.405	.781	145	16	13	108	133	40	.685				19	*S/2CM	**3.2**
1879	Tro-N	30	123	18	31	5	2	0	4	4	3	.252	.276	.325	.601	104	-0	1	93	37	11	.478				1	3/2M	0.2
1880	Tro-N	82	332	55	87	9	0	0	22	**24**	24	.262	.312	.289	.601	95	3	-2	110	80	31	.490				-3	*2M	-0.2
1881	Tro-N	85	339	56	96	13	5	1	35	29	12	.283	.340	.360	.700	120	8	8	100	93	42	.621				-10	*2M	0.1
1882	Tro-N	81	319	44	82	15	2	0	32	23	21	.257	.307	.317	.624	106	1	3	95	113	32	.523				-12	*2/SM	-0.6
1883	Phi-N	86	329	39	85	9	2	0	27	18	21	.258	.297	.298	.595	90	-7	-2	90	98	30	.475				-7	*2/PM	-1.1
1884	Pit-a	10	41	2	6	0	0	0		0		.146	.146	.146	.293	-3	-4	-4	97	0	1	.171				0	/O13M	-0.3
Total	5 n	259	1180	199	287							.243															/O13M	
Total	9	562	2306	346	625	76	20	1	226	113	114	.271	.305	.323	.628	102	8	9	100	104	236	.510				8	32/SOC1P	2.7
■ **FELIX FERMIN**	Fermin, Felix Jose (Minaya) b: 10/9/63, Mao Valverde, D.R. BR/TR, 5'11", 160 lbs. Deb: 7/08/87																											
1987	Pit-N	23	68	6	17	0	0	0	4	4	9	.250	.301	.250	.551	46	-5	-5	104	94	5	.407	0	0	0	-1	S	-0.3
1988	Pit-N	43	87	9	24	0	2	0	2	8	10	.276	.357	.322	.679	98	0	0	98	29	10	.627	3	1	0	-3	S	0.0
Total	2	66	155	15	41	0	2	0	6	12	19	.265	.333	.290	.624	74	-5	-5	100	56	15	.542	3	1	0	-4	/S	-0.3

YEAR	TM/L	G	AB	R	H	2B	3B	HR	RBI	BB	SO	AVG	OBP	SLG	PRO	/A	BR	/A	PF	CHI	RC	TA	SB	CS	SBR	FR	POS	TPR
■ **ED FERNANDES**	Fernandes, Edward Paul b: 3/11/18, Oakland, Cal. d: 11/27/68, Hayward, Cal. BB/TR, 5'9", 185 lbs. Deb: 6/09/40																											
1940	Pit-N	28	33	1	4	1	0	0	2	7	6	.121	.275	.152	.427	22	-3	-3	95	148	2	.414	0			-0	C	-0.1
1946	Chi-A	14	32	4	8	2	0	0	4	8	7	.250	.400	.313	.712	104	1	1	97	152	5	.720	0	0	0	1	C	0.2
Total	2	42	65	5	12	3	0	0	6	15	13	.185	.338	.231	.568	62	-3	-3	96	150	6	.556	0	0		1	/C	0.1
■ **FRANK FERNANDEZ**	Fernandez, Frank b: 4/16/43, Staten Island, N.Y. BR/TR, 6', 185 lbs. Deb: 9/12/67																											
1967	NY-A	9	28	1	6	2	0	1	4	2	7	.214	.290	.393	.683	106	-0	0	94	119	3	.625	1	1	-0	2	/CO	0.2
1968	NY-A	51	135	15	23	6	1	7	30	35	50	.170	.341	.385	.726	118	4	4	101	176	20	.765	1	0	0	5	C/O	1.3
1969	NY-A	89	229	34	51	6	1	12	29	65	68	.223	.401	.415	.816	135	12	13	95	89	42	.886	1	3	-2	6	CO	2.3
1970	Oak-A	94	252	30	54	5	0	15	44	40	76	.214	.327	.413	.739	106	1	2	97	119	35	.721	1	0	0	3	C/O	0.7
1971	Oak-A	2	4	0	0	0	0	0	0	1	2	.000	.200	.000	.200	-39	-1	-1	101	0	0	.250	0	0	0	0	/C	0.0
	Was-A	18	30	0	3	0	0	0	4	4	10	.100	.206	.100	.306	-12	-4	-4	92	544	1	.241	0	0	0	-0	/OC	-0.4
	Oak-A	2	5	1	1	1	0	0	1	0	1	.200	.200	.400	.600	66	-0	-0	101	204	0	.500	0	0	0	0	/C	0.0
	Yr	22	39	1	4	1	0	0	5	5	13	.103	.205	.128	.333	-4	-5	-5	94	489	2	.286	0	0	0	-0		-0.4
	Chi-N	17	41	11	7	1	0	4	4	17	15	.171	.414	.488	.902	141	4	3	110	51	10	1.088	0	0	0	-0	C	0.3
1972	Chi-N	3	3	0	0	0	0	0	0	0	2	.000	.000	.000	.000	-88	-1	-1	114	0	0	.000	0	0	0	0	/C	0.0
Total	6	285	727	92	145	21	2	39	116	164	231	.199	.351	.395	.746	113	15	17	98	131	111	.787	4	4	-1	16	C/O	4.4
■ **NANNY FERNANDEZ**	Fernandez, Froilan b: 10/25/18, Wilmington, Cal. BR/TR, 5'9", 170 lbs. Deb: 4/14/42																											
1942	Bos-N	145	577	63	147	29	3	6	55	38	61	.255	.303	.347	.650	94	-9	-6	95	99	58	.572	15			4	3O	-0.2
1946	Bos-N	115	372	37	95	15	2	2	42	30	44	.255	.313	.323	.635	85	-10	-7	95	124	37	.528	1			-0	3SO	-0.6
1947	Bos-N	83	209	16	43	4	0	2	21	22	20	.206	.281	.254	.535	44	-17	-16	97	132	16	.450	2			-7	S/O3	-1.8
1950	Pit-N	65	198	23	51	11	0	6	27	19	17	.258	.326	.404	.730	88	-3	-4	103	106	24	.654	2			0	3	-0.2
Total	4	408	1356	139	336	59	5	16	145	109	142	.248	.306	.334	.640	83	-38	-33	96	112	135	.569	20			-4	3/SO	-2.8
■ **CHICO FERNANDEZ**	Fernandez, Humberto (Perez) b: 3/2/32, Havana, Cuba BR/TR, 6', 165 lbs. Deb: 7/14/56																											
1956	Bro-N	34	66	11	15	2	0	1	9	3	10	.227	.261	.303	.564	50	-5	-5	103	165	4	.446	2	3	-1	-0	S	-0.4
1957	Phi-N	149	500	42	131	14	4	5	51	31	64	.262	.306	.336	.642	74	-19	-18	98	116	48	.552	18	5	2	-24	*S	-3.4
1958	Phi-N	148	522	38	120	18	5	6	51	37	48	.230	.283	.318	.601	60	-31	-30	98	115	45	.513	12	6	0	-14	*S	-3.3
1959	Phi-N	45	123	15	26	5	1	0	3	10	11	.211	.271	.268	.539	44	-10	-10	99	37	9	.441	2	1	0	-1	S/2	-0.8
1960	Det-A	133	435	44	105	13	3	4	35	39	50	.241	.305	.313	.618	66	-20	-20	102	93	41	.540	13	4	2	-1	*S	-0.9
1961	Det-A	133	435	41	108	15	4	3	40	36	45	.248	.306	.322	.628	71	-20	-17	96	105	41	.532	8	5	-1	-19	*S/3	-2.8
1962	Det-A	141	503	64	125	17	2	20	59	42	69	.249	.306	.410	.716	82	-8	-15	111	90	62	.656	10	3	1	-25	*S/31	-3.0
1963	Det-A	15	49	3	7	1	0	0	2	6	11	.143	.236	.163	.400	14	-6	-6	104	105	1	.298	0	1	-1	-2	S	-0.7
	NY-N	58	145	12	29	6	0	1	9	9	30	.200	.247	.262	.509	47	-10	-10	99	92	10	.431	3	0	1	0	S/32	-0.4
Total	8	856	2778	270	666	91	19	40	259	213	338	.240	.295	.329	.624	67	-127	-131	101	102	262	.561	68	28	4	-85	S/321	-15.7
■ **CHICO FERNANDEZ**	Fernandez, Lorenzo Marto (Mosquera) b: 4/23/39, Havana, Cuba BR/TR, 5'10", 160 lbs. Deb: 4/20/68																											
1968	Bal-A	24	18	0	2	0	0	0	0	1	2	.111	.158	.111	.269	-17	-3	-3	102	0	0	.188	0	0	0	0	/S2	-0.1
■ **TONY FERNANDEZ**	Fernandez, Octavio Antonio (Castro) b: 8/6/62, San Pedro De Macoris, D.R. BB/TR, 6'2", 165 lbs. Deb: 9/02/83																											
1983	Tor-A	15	34	5	9	1	1	0	2	2	2	.265	.324	.353	.677	80	-1	-1	108	65	4	.556	0	1	-1	-0	S/D	0.0
1984	Tor-A	88	233	29	63	5	3	3	19	17	15	.270	.320	.356	.676	86	-4	-5	102	82	25	.583	5	7	-3	-3	S3/D	-0.4
1985	Tor-A	161	564	71	163	31	10	2	51	43	41	.289	.342	.390	.732	99	0	-1	101	91	75	.663	13	6	0	9	*S	2.0
1986	Tor-A	163	687	91	213	33	9	10	65	27	52	.310	.340	.428	.768	103	7	3	105	77	99	.709	25	12	0	3	*S	1.4
1987	Tor-A	146	578	90	186	29	8	5	67	51	48	.322	.382	.426	.807	114	14	13	101	109	94	.799	32	12	2	16	*S	3.5
1988	Tor-A	154	648	76	186	41	4	5	70	45	65	.287	.337	.386	.723	102	2	2	100	93	86	.660	15	5	2	11	*S	2.2
Total	6	727	2744	362	820	140	35	25	274	185	223	.299	.347	.403	.749	103	18	11	102	91	382	.706	90	43	1	36	S/3D	8.7
■ **AL FERRARA**	Ferrara, Alfred John "The Bull" b: 12/22/39, Brooklyn, N.Y. BR/TR, 6'1", 200 lbs. Deb: 7/30/63																											
1963	LA-N	21	44	2	7	0	0	1	1	6	9	.159	.275	.227	.502	49	-3	-3	95	32	3	.459	0	0	0	0	O	-0.2
1965	LA-N	41	81	5	17	2	1	1	10	9	20	.210	.297	.296	.593	74	-3	-2	91	154	8	.523	0	0	0	-3	O	-0.6
1966	LA-N	63	115	15	31	4	0	5	23	9	35	.270	.339	.435	.773	117	2	2	97	149	17	.713	0	0	0	-4	O	-0.1
1967	LA-N	122	347	41	96	16	1	16	50	33	73	.277	.345	.467	.812	148	13	18	88	99	56	.770	0	1	-1	-9	O	0.4
1968	LA-N	2	7	0	1	0	0	0	0	0	2	.143	.143	.143	.286	-16	-1	-1	91	0	0	.167	0	0	0	-1	/O	-0.1
1969	SD-N	138	366	39	95	22	1	14	56	45	69	.260	.352	.440	.792	125	10	12	97	111	58	.766	0	0	0	-8	O	-0.1
1970	SD-N	138	372	44	103	15	4	13	51	46	63	.277	.373	.444	.817	124	10	13	95	97	64	.801	0	0	0	-13	O	-0.4
1971	SD-N	17	17	0	2	1	0	0	2	5	5	.118	.318	.176	.495	45	-1	-1	96	271	1	.471	0	0	0	-1	/O	-0.1
	Cin-N	32	33	2	6	0	0	1	5	3	10	.182	.270	.273	.543	56	-2	-2	96	170	2	.464	0	0	0	-1	/O	-0.2
	Yr	49	50	2	8	1	0	1	7	8	15	.160	.288	.240	.528	53	-3	-3	96	210	4	.488	0	0	0	-1		-0.3
Total	8	574	1382	148	358	60	7	51	198	156	286	.259	.346	.423	.769	120	25	36	94	110	209	.749	0	1	-1	-38	O	-1.4
■ **MIKE FERRARO**	Ferraro, Michael Dennis b: 8/18/44, Kingston, N.Y. BR/TR, 5'11", 175 lbs. Deb: 9/06/66 MC																											
1966	NY-A	10	28	4	5	0	0	0	0	3	3	.179	.281	.179	.460	38	-2	-2	94	0	2	.375	0	0	0	1	3	0.0
1968	NY-A	23	87	5	14	0	1	0	1	2	17	.161	.180	.184	.364	10	-9	-9	101	27	2	.237	0	0	0	0	3	-0.9
1969	Sea-A	5	4	0	0	0	0	0	0	1	0	.000	.200	.000	.200	-41	-1	-1	98	0	0	.250	0	0	0	0	H	0.0
1972	Mil-A	124	381	19	97	18	1	2	29	17	41	.255	.286	.323	.609	85	-10	-8	95	94	29	.456	0	5	-3	-15	*3/S	-2.5
Total	4	162	500	28	116	18	2	2	30	23	61	.232	.267	.288	.555	68	-22	-20	96	76	33	.413	0	5	-3	-14	3/S	-3.4
■ **RICK FERRELL**	Ferrell, Richard Benjamin b: 10/12/05, Durham, N.C. BR/TR, 5'10", 160 lbs. Deb: 4/19/29 CH																											
1929	StL-A	64	144	21	33	6	1	0	20	32	10	.229	.373	.285	.658	72	-5	-5	100	167	18	.664	1	2	-1	1	C	0.0
1930	StL-A	101	314	43	84	18	4	1	41	46	10	.268	.363	.360	.723	78	-6	-11	108	117	43	.688	1	4	-2	5	*C	0.1
1931	StL-A	117	386	47	118	30	4	3	57	56	12	.306	.394	.427	.821	113	10	9	102	108	67	.823	2	3	-1	9	*C	2.3
1932	StL-A	126	438	67	138	30	5	2	65	66	18	.315	.406	.420	.826	114	12	12	100	117	78	.839	5	5	-2	8	*C	2.2
1933	StL-A	22	72	8	18	2	0	1	5	12	4	.250	.357	.319	.677	70	-2	-3	115	65	9	.685	2	0	1	3	C	0.1
	Bos-A	118	421	50	125	19	4	3	72	58	19	.297	.385	.382	.767	103	4	4	101	144	66	.748	2	2	-1	12	*C	1.9
	Yr	140	493	58	143	21	4	4	77	70	23	.290	.381	.373	.754	97	3	0	103	132	75	.739	4	2	0	15		2.0
1934	Bos-A	132	437	50	130	29	4	1	48	66	20	.297	.390	.389	.779	96	3	-1	106	93	70	.769	0	0	0	2	*C	1.3
1935	Bos-A	133	458	54	138	34	4	3	61	65	15	.301	.388	.413	.801	99	7	1	108	107	75	.790	5	8	-3	4	*C	0.6
1936	Bos-A	121	410	59	128	27	5	8	55	65	17	.312	.406	.461	.867	107	10	6	106	85	80	.898	0	1	-1	6	*C	1.9
1937	Bos-A	18	65	8	20	2	0	1	4	15	4	.308	.438	.385	.822	106	2	2	103	52	12	.889	0	0	0	0	C	0.2
	Was-A	86	279	31	64	6	0	1	32	50	18	.229	.348	.262	.610	59	-17	-14	94	144	29	.579	1	1	-0	-0	C	-0.7
	Yr	104	344	39	84	8	0	2	36	65	22	.244	.366	.285	.651	69	-15	-13	96	129	41	.632	1	1	-0	-0		-0.5
1938	Was-A	135	411	55	120	24	5	1	58	75	17	.292	.401	.382	.783	102	1	5	95	123	69	.801	1	0	0	-4	*C	0.3
1939	Was-A	87	274	32	77	13	1	0	31	41	12	.281	.377	.336	.712	93	-5	-1	90	114	38	.668	1	1	-0	1	C	0.5
1940	Was-A	103	326	35	89	18	2	0	28	47	15	.273	.365	.340	.705	90	-6	-3	93	91	44	.649	1	1	-0	6	C	0.9
1941	Was-A	21	66	8	18	5	0	0	13	15	4	.273	.407	.348	.756	104	1	1	98	204	10	.765	1	0	0	-1	C	0.2
	StL-A	100	321	30	81	14	3	2	23	52	22	.252	.357	.333	.690	83	-6	-6	100	72	41	.644	2	1	0	-3	C	-0.3
	Yr	121	387	38	99	19	3	2	36	67	26	.256	.366	.336	.702	87	-5	-5	100	97	52	.671	3	1	0	-4		-0.1
1942	StL-A	99	273	20	61	6	1	0	26	33	13	.223	.307	.253	.560	56	-14	-16	104	133	23	.468	0	1	-1	-2	C	-0.6
1943	StL-A	74	209	12	50	7	0	0	20	34	14	.239	.348	.273	.621	82	-3	-3	100	128	23	.568	0	0	0	0	C	0.1
1944	Was-A	99	339	14	94	11	1	0	25	46	13	.277	.364	.316	.679	106	-0	4	90	86	41	.605	2	1	0	6	C	1.8
1945	Was-A	91	286	33	76	12	1	1	38	43	13	.266	.366	.325	.691	108	2	5	93	143	35	.625	2	4	-2	2	C	1.2
1947	Was-A	37	99	10	30	11	0	0	12	14	7	.303	.389	.414	.804	127	3	4	97	108	16	.753	0	0	0	3	C	1.0
Total	18	1884	6028	687	1692	324	45	28	734	931	277	.281	.378	.363	.741	95	-8	-10	100	113	888	.722	29	35	-12	58	*C	15.0
■ **WES FERRELL**	Ferrell, Wesley Cheek b: 2/2/08, Greensboro, N.C. d: 12/9/76, Sarasota, Fla. BR/TR, 6'2", 195 lbs. Deb: 9/09/27																											
1927	Cle-A	1	0	0	0	0	0	0	0	0	0	—	—	—	—	—	0	0	97	—	—	—	0	0	0	0	/P	0.0
1928	Cle-A	2	4	0	1	0	1	0	0	0	0	.250	.250	.750	1.000	145	0	0	106	0	1	1.000	0	0	0	0	/P	0.0

YEAR	TM/L	G	AB	R	H	2B	3B	HR	RBI	BB	SO	AVG	OBP	SLG	PRO	/A	BR	/A	PF	CHI	RC	TA	SB	CS	SBR	FR	POS	TPR
1929	Cle-A	47	93	12	22	5	3	1	12	6	28	.237	.283	.387	.670	71	-4	-4	100	105	10	.606	1	0	0	3	P	0.0
1930	Cle-A	53	118	19	35	8	3	0	14	12	15	.297	.362	.415	.777	92	-1	-1	105	95	18	.735	0	0	0	-3	P	0.0
1931	Cle-A	48	116	24	37	6	1	9	30	10	21	.319	.373	.621	.994	148	9	8	106	100	27	1.038	0	0	0	5	P	0.0
1932	Cle-A	55	128	14	31	5	2	2	18	6	21	.242	.276	.359	.635	58	-7	-9	108	116	13	.536	0	0	0	1	P	0.0
1933	Cle-A	61	140	26	38	7	0	7	26	20	22	.271	.363	.471	.834	114	4	3	105	100	25	.843	0	0	0	2	PO	0.9
1934	Bos-A	34	78	12	22	4	0	4	17	7	15	.282	.341	.487	.828	105	1	0	106	113	13	.821	1	0	0	-2	P	0.0
1935	Bos-A	75	150	25	52	5	1	7	32	21	16	.347	.427	.533	.960	136	11	9	108	108	35	1.031	0	0	0	2	P	0.0
1936	Bos-A	61	135	20	36	6	1	5	24	14	10	.267	.336	.437	.773	84	-3	-4	106	105	20	.737	0	0	0	-3	P	0.0
1937	Bos-A	18	33	7	12	2	0	1	9	7	3	.364	.475	.515	.990	145	3	3	103	154	9	1.143	0	0	0	2	P	0.0
	Was-A	53	106	7	27	5	0	0	16	9	18	.255	.313	.302	.615	59	-7	-6	94	171	10	.519	0	0	0	-1	P	-0.2
	Yr	71	139	14	39	7	0	1	25	16	21	.281	.355	.353	.707	82	-4	-3	97	169	18	.650	0	0	0	1		-0.2
1938	Was-A	26	49	6	11	2	0	1	6	15	7	.224	.406	.327	.733	90	-0	0	95	107	8	.816	0	0	0	1	P	0.0
	NY-A	5	12	1	2	1	0	0	1	1	4	.167	.231	.250	.481	19	-2	-2	105	113	1	.400	0	0	0	1	/P	0.0
	Yr	31	61	7	13	3	0	1	7	16	11	.213	.377	.311	.688	77	-2	-1	96	111	9	.729	0	0	0	2		0.0
1939	NY-A	3	8	0	1	1	0	0	1	0	2	.125	.125	.250	.375	-7	-1	-1	91	169	0	.286	0	0	0	0	/P	0.0
1940	Bro-N	2	2	0	0	0	0	0	0	0	2	.000	.000	.000	.000	-93	-1	-1	108	0	0	.000	0			1	/P	0.0
1941	Bos-N	4	4	2	2	0	0	1	2	1	1	.500	.600	1.250	1.850	443	2	2	93	90	3	3.000	0			-0	/P	0.0
Total	15	548	1176	175	329	57	12	38	208	129	185	.280	.351	.446	.797	99	3	-4	104	112	1082	.773	2	0		6	P/O	0.7

■ **SERGIO FERRER** Ferrer, Sergio (Marrero) b: 1/29/51, Santurce, P.R. BB/TR, 5'7", 145 lbs. Deb: 4/05/74

YEAR	TM/L	G	AB	R	H	2B	3B	HR	RBI	BB	SO	AVG	OBP	SLG	PRO	/A	BR	/A	PF	CHI	RC	TA	SB	CS	SBR	FR	POS	TPR
1974	Min-A	24	57	12	16	0	2	0	0	8	6	.281	.379	.351	.730	110	1	1	101	0	8	.744	3	2	-0	-0	S/2	0.2
1975	Min-A	32	81	14	20	3	1	0	2	3	11	.247	.282	.309	.591	62	-4	-4	107	31	7	.492	3	4	-2	-0	S2/D	-0.3
1978	NY-N	37	33	8	7	0	1	0	1	4	7	.212	.316	.273	.589	67	-1	-1	98	44	3	.536	1	0	0	-1	S/23	0.1
1979	NY-N	32	7	7	0	0	0	0	0	2	3	.000	.222	.000	.222	-36	-1	-1	95	0	0	.222	0	2	-1	-0	3/S2	-0.2
Total	4	125	178	41	43	3	4	0	3	17	27	.242	.318	.303	.622	75	-5	-6	103	22	18	.566	7	8	-3	-1	/S23D	-0.2

■ **HOBE FERRIS** Ferris, Albert Sayles b: 12/7/1877, Providence, R.I. d: 3/18/38, Detroit, Mich. BR/TR, 5'8", 162 lbs. Deb: 4/26/01

YEAR	TM/L	G	AB	R	H	2B	3B	HR	RBI	BB	SO	AVG	OBP	SLG	PRO	/A	BR	/A	PF	CHI	RC	TA	SB	CS	SBR	FR	POS	TPR
1901	Bos-A	138	523	68	131	16	15	2	63	23		.250	.282	.350	.632	78	-18	-15	97	107	57	.559	13			8	*2/S	-1.1
1902	Bos-A	134	499	57	122	16	14	8	63	21		.244	.275	.381	.656	82	-14	-13	99	99	57	.589	11			**25**	*2	1.6
1903	Bos-A	141	525	69	132	19	7	9	66	25		.251	.285	.366	.651	86	-3	-11	112	111	59	.580	11			14	*2/S	0.6
1904	Bos-A	156	563	50	120	23	10	3	63	23		.213	.244	.306	.550	72	-16	-19	105	133	45	.456	7			-0	*2	-2.0
1905	Bos-A	142	523	51	115	24	16	6	59	23		.220	.253	.361	.614	96	-4	-5	100	104	52	.547	11			15	*2	1.0
1906	Bos-A	130	495	47	121	25	13	2	44	10		.244	.259	.360	.619	96	-5	-4	98	92	49	.524	8			7	*2/3	0.0
1907	Bos-A	150	561	41	135	25	2	4	60	10		.241	.254	.314	.568	82	-13	-13	101	116	49	.462	11			15	*2	0.1
1908	StL-A	148	555	54	150	26	7	2	74	14		.270	.288	.353	.641	107	4	2	103	146	56	.533	6			12	*3	2.6
1909	StL-A	148	556	36	120	18	5	4	58	12		.216	.232	.288	.520	70	-25	-20	92	138	37	.420	11			5	*32	-1.2
Total	9	1287	4800	473	1146	192	89	40	550	161		.239	.263	.341	.604	85	-94	-99	101	117	460	.516	89			99	*23/S	1.6

■ **WILLY FETZER** Fetzer, William Mc Kinnon b: 6/24/1884, Concord, N.C. d: 5/3/59, Butner, N.C. 5'10.5", 180 lbs. Deb: 9/04/06

YEAR	TM/L	G	AB	R	H	2B	3B	HR	RBI	BB	SO	AVG	OBP	SLG	PRO	/A	BR	/A	PF	CHI	RC	TA	SB	CS	SBR	FR	POS	TPR
1906	Phi-A	1	1	0	0	0	0	0	0	0		.000	.000	.000	.000	-99	-0	-0	94	0	0	.000	0			0	H	0.0

■ **CHICK FEWSTER** Fewster, Wilson Lloyd b: 11/10/1895, Baltimore, Md. d: 4/16/45, Baltimore, Md. BR/TR, 5'11", 160 lbs. Deb: 9/19/17

YEAR	TM/L	G	AB	R	H	2B	3B	HR	RBI	BB	SO	AVG	OBP	SLG	PRO	/A	BR	/A	PF	CHI	RC	TA	SB	CS	SBR	FR	POS	TPR
1917	NY-A	11	36	2	8	0	0	0	1	5	5	.222	.317	.222	.539	61	-1	-2	107	45	3	.500	1			-0	2	0.0
1918	NY-A	5	2	1	1	0	0	0	0	0	0	.500	.500	.500	1.000	213	0	0	95	0	0	1.000	0			0	/2	0.0
1919	NY-A	81	244	38	69	9	3	1	15	34	36	.283	.386	.357	.743	103	5	3	106	60	36	.777	8			11	OS/23	1.4
1920	NY-A	21	21	8	6	1	0	0	1	7	2	.286	.464	.333	.798	111	1	1	102	50	4	.875	0	1	-1	0	/S2	0.1
1921	NY-A	66	207	44	58	19	0	1	19	28	43	.280	.382	.386	.768	94	-0	-1	103	78	32	.771	4	4	-1	-3	O2	-0.7
1922	NY-A	44	132	20	32	4	1	1	9	16	23	.242	.324	.311	.635	65	-6	-7	102	73	14	.567	2	4	-2	2	O/2	-0.8
	Bos-A	23	83	8	24	4	1	0	9	6	10	.289	.344	.361	.706	87	-2	-1	96	109	11	.726	8	3	1	-1	3	0.0
	Yr	67	215	28	56	8	2	1	18	22	33	.260	.332	.330	.662	73	-8	-8	100	87	24	.627	10	7	-1	1		-0.8
1923	Bos-A	90	284	32	67	10	1	0	15	39	35	.236	.334	.278	.613	61	-14	-15	102	65	26	.554	7	14	-6	-6	2S/3	-2.0
1924	Cle-A	101	322	36	86	12	2	0	36	24	36	.267	.324	.317	.641	68	-16	-15	97	117	32	.569	12	12	-4	-21	2/3	-3.4
1925	Cle-A	93	294	39	73	16	1	1	38	36	25	.248	.330	.320	.650	62	-15	-18	106	131	32	.591	6	9	-4	-12	23/O	-2.6
1926	Bro-N	105	337	53	82	16	3	2	24	45	49	.243	.341	.326	.667	81	-8	-8	99	73	39	.663	9			-10	*2	-1.1
1927	Bro-N	4	1	1	0	0	0	0	0	0	0	.000	.000	.000	.000	-97	-0	-0	103	0	0	.000	0			0	H	0.0
Total	11	644	1963	282	506	91	12	6	167	240	264	.258	.346	.326	.672	76	-58	-62	102	87	230	.639	57	47		-39	2O/S3	-9.1

■ **NEIL FIALA** Fiala, Neil Stephen b: 8/24/56, St.Louis, Mo. BL/TR, 6'1", 185 lbs. Deb: 9/03/81

YEAR	TM/L	G	AB	R	H	2B	3B	HR	RBI	BB	SO	AVG	OBP	SLG	PRO	/A	BR	/A	PF	CHI	RC	TA	SB	CS	SBR	FR	POS	TPR
1981	StL-N	3	3	0	0	0	0	0	0	0	1	.000	.000	.000	.000	-98	-1	-1	102	0	0	.000	0	0	0	0	/H	0.0
	Cin-N	2	2	1	1	0	0	0	1	0	1	.500	.500	.500	1.000	183	0	0	101	393	1	1.000	0	0	0	0	/H	0.0
	Yr	5	5	1	1	0	0	0	1	0	2	.200	.200	.200	.400	14	-1	-1	101	157	0	.250	0	0	0	0		0.0
Total	1	5	5	1	1	0	0	0	1	0	2	.200	.200	.200	.400	14	-1	-1	101	157	1	.250	0	0	0	0		0.0

■ **JIM FIELD** Field, James C. b: 4/24/1863, Philadelphia, Pa. d: 5/13/53, Atlantic City, N.J Deb: 1883

YEAR	TM/L	G	AB	R	H	2B	3B	HR	RBI	BB	SO	AVG	OBP	SLG	PRO	/A	BR	/A	PF	CHI	RC	TA	SB	CS	SBR	FR	POS	TPR
1883	Col-a	76	295	31	75	10	6	1		7		.254	.272	.339	.611	109	-2	4	87	0	28	.486				-7	*1	-0.8
1884	Col-a	105	417	74	97	9	7	4		23		.233	.292	.317	.609	104	1	3	97	0	40	.522				-4	*1	-0.5
1885	Pit-a	56	209	28	50	9	1	1		13		.239	.306	.306	.612	91	-0	-2	106	0	20	.528				-0	1	-0.6
	Bal-a	38	144	16	30	3	2	0		13		.208	.278	.257	.535	68	-4	-5	106	0	11	.447				1	1	-0.6
	Yr	94	353	44	80	12	3	1		26		.227	.295	.286	.581	82	-4	-8	106	0	30	.495				1		-1.2
1890	Roc-a	52	188	30	38	7	5	4		21		.202	.309	.356	.665	106	-1	2	93	0	24	.693	8			-5	1/P	-0.4
1898	Was-N	5	21	1	2	0	0	0	0	0		.095	.095	.095	.190	-44	-4	-4	102	0	0	.158	1			0	/1	-0.3
Total	5	332	1274	180	292	38	21	10	0	77		.229	.288	.316	.603	96	-9	-2	97	0	122	.525	9			-16	1/P	-3.2

■ **SAM FIELD** Field, Samuel Jay b: 10/12/1848, Philadelphia, Pa. d: 10/28/04, Sinking Spring, Pa BR/TR, 5'9.5", 182 lbs. Deb: 5/19/1875 M

YEAR	TM/L	G	AB	R	H	2B	3B	HR	RBI	BB	SO	AVG	OBP	SLG	PRO	/A	BR	/A	PF	CHI	RC	TA	SB	CS	SBR	FR	POS	TPR
1875	Cen-n	3	11	2	1							.091															/CO	
	Nat-n	5	17	0	4							.235															/COM	
	Yr	8	28	2	5							.179																
1876	Cin-N	4	14	2	0	0	0	0	0	1	3	.000	.067	.000	.067	-85	-3	-2	90	0	0	.071				0	/C2	-0.1
Total		4	14	2	0	0	0	0	0	1	3	.000	.067	.000	.067	-85	-3	-2	90	0	0	.071				0	/C2O	-0.1

■ **CECIL FIELDER** Fielder, Cecil Grant b: 9/21/63, Los Angeles, Cal. BR/TR, 6'3", 230 lbs. Deb: 7/20/85

YEAR	TM/L	G	AB	R	H	2B	3B	HR	RBI	BB	SO	AVG	OBP	SLG	PRO	/A	BR	/A	PF	CHI	RC	TA	SB	CS	SBR	FR	POS	TPR
1985	Tor-A	30	74	6	23	4	0	4	16	6	16	.311	.363	.527	.890	139	4	4	101	124	14	.849	0	0	0	0	1	0.2
1986	Tor-A	34	83	7	13	2	0	4	13	6	27	.157	.222	.325	.548	45	-6	-7	105	133	5	.466	0	0	0	-0	D/13O	-0.7
1987	Tor-A	82	175	30	47	7	1	14	32	20	48	.269	.347	.560	.907	135	9	8	101	91	32	.881	0	1	-1	1	D1/3	0.6
1988	Tor-A	74	174	24	40	6	1	9	23	14	53	.230	.291	.431	.722	100	-1	-1	100	90	20	.638	0	1	-1	0	D1/23	-0.1
Total	4	220	506	67	123	19	2	31	84	46	144	.243	.310	.472	.782	109	6	5	101	102	71	.737	0	2	-1	1	D/132O	0.0

■ **BRUCE FIELDS** Fields, Bruce Alan b: 10/6/60, Cleveland, Ohio BL/TR, 6', 185 lbs. Deb: 9/03/86

YEAR	TM/L	G	AB	R	H	2B	3B	HR	RBI	BB	SO	AVG	OBP	SLG	PRO	/A	BR	/A	PF	CHI	RC	TA	SB	CS	SBR	FR	POS	TPR
1986	Det-A	16	43	4	12	1	1	0	6	1	6	.279	.295	.349	.644	79	-1	-1	95	159	4	.531	1	1	-0	-1	O/D	-0.2
1988	Sea-A	38	67	8	18	5	0	1	5	4	11	.269	.310	.388	.698	88	-1	-1	108	69	7	.577	0	1	-1	-5	O/D	-0.7
Total	2	54	110	12	30	6	1	1	11	5	17	.273	.304	.373	.677	84	-2	-2	103	103	12	.560	1	2	-1	-7	/OD	-0.9

■ **GEORGE FIELDS** Fields, George W. b: 1851, Waterbury, Conn. d: 9/22/33, Waterbury, Conn. Deb: 5/02/1872

YEAR	TM/L	G	AB	R	H	2B	3B	HR	RBI	BB	SO	AVG	OBP	SLG	PRO	/A	BR	/A	PF	CHI	RC	TA	SB	CS	SBR	FR	POS	TPR
1872	Man-n	17	71	18	20							.282															3/O6	

■ **JOCKO FIELDS** Fields, John Joseph b: 10/20/1864, Cork, Ireland d: 10/14/50, Jersey City, N.J. BR/TR, 5'10", 160 lbs. Deb: 5/31/1887

YEAR	TM/L	G	AB	R	H	2B	3B	HR	RBI	BB	SO	AVG	OBP	SLG	PRO	/A	BR	/A	PF	CHI	RC	TA	SB	CS	SBR	FR	POS	TPR
1887	Pit-N	43	164	26	44	9	2	0	17	7	13	.268	.306	.348	.654	89	-4	-2	93	94	20	.608	7			0	OC/13P	-0.1
1888	Pit-N	45	169	22	33	7	2	1	15	8	19	.195	.232	.278	.510	67	-7	-6	95	114	13	.471	9			0	OC/3	-0.5
1889	Pit-N	75	289	41	90	22	5	2	43	29	30	.311	.376	.443	.819	146	11	17	89	101	52	.829	7			-3	OC	0.9
1890	Pit-P	126	526	101	149	18	20	9	86	57	52	.283	.357	.445	.802	126	10	18	92	87	94	.844	24			7	O2C/S	1.7

YEAR	TM/L	G	AB	R	H	2B	3B	HR	RBI	BB	SO	AVG	OBP	SLG	PRO	/A	BR	/A	PF	CHI	RC	TA	SB	CS	SBR	FR	POS	TPR
1891	Pit-N	23	75	10	18	3	0	0	5	10	13	.240	.337	.280	.617	81	-1	-1	101	69	8	.579	1			0	C/S	0.0
	Phi-N	8	30	4	7	2	1	0	5	4	2	.233	.324	.367	.690	108	0	0	95	135	4	.652	0			0	/C	0.0
	Yr	31	105	14	25	5	1	0	10	14	15	.238	.333	.305	.638	88	-1	-1	100	89	11	.600	1			0		0.0
1892	NY-N	21	66	8	18	4	2	0	5	9	10	.273	.368	.394	.762	135	3	3	98	59	11	.792	2			0	OC	0.3
Total	6	341	1319	212	359	65	32	12	176	124	139	.272	.338	.397	.736	116	13	29	93	93	202	.735	50			3	O/C2S31P	2.3
■ **JESUS FIGUEROA** Figueroa, Jesus Maria (Figueroa) b: 2/57, Santo Domingo, P.R. BL/TL, 5'10", 160 lbs. Deb: 4/22/80																												
1980	Chi-N	115	198	20	50	5	0	1	11	14	16	.253	.308	.293	.601	65	-8	-9	106	71	18	.500	2	1	0	-1	O	-1.3
■ **SAM FILE** File, Lawrence Samuel b: 5/18/22, Chester, Pa. BR/TR, 5'11", 160 lbs. Deb: 9/10/40																												
1940	Phi-N	7	13	0	1	0	0	0	1	0	1	.077	.077	.077	.154	-59	-3	-3	97	371	0	.077	0			0	/S3	-0.1
■ **STEVE FILIPOWICZ** Filipowicz, Stephen Charles "Flip" b: 6/28/21, Donora, Pa. d: 2/21/75, Wilkes-Barre, Pa. BR/TR, 5'8", 195 lbs. Deb: 9/03/44																												
1944	NY-N	15	41	10	8	2	1	0	7	3	7	.195	.250	.293	.543	51	-3	-3	104	209	3	.429	0			-1	O/C	-0.4
1945	NY-N	35	112	14	23	5	0	2	16	4	13	.205	.239	.304	.543	50	-8	-8	100	139	8	.433	0			-7	O	-1.6
1948	Cin-N	7	26	0	9	0	1	0	3	2	1	.346	.393	.423	.816	117	1	1	103	104	5	.765	0			-0	/O	0.0
Total	3	57	179	24	40	7	2	2	26	9	21	.223	.265	.318	.583	61	-10	-10	101	150	15	.482	0			-8	/OC	-2.0
■ **JACK FIMPLE** Fimple, John Joseph b: 2/10/59, Darby, Pa. BR/TR, 6'2", 185 lbs. Deb: 7/30/83																												
1983	LA-N	54	148	16	37	8	1	2	22	11	39	.250	.302	.358	.660	82	-4	-4	100	148	16	.565	1	0	0	-5	C	-0.6
1984	LA-N	12	26	2	5	1	0	0	3	1	6	.192	.222	.231	.453	26	-3	-3	104	196	1	.292	0	0	0	-0	C	-0.2
1986	LA-N	13	13	2	1	0	0	0	2	6	6	.077	.368	.077	.445	32	-1	-1	94	798	1	.583	0	0	0	0	/C12	0.0
1987	Cal-A	13	10	1	2	0	0	0	1	1	2	.200	.273	.200	.473	29	-1	-1	99	200	1	.375	0	0	0	0	C	0.0
Total	4	92	197	21	45	9	1	2	28	19	53	.228	.296	.315	.611	69	-8	-8	100	213	18	.539	1	0	0	-6	/C21	-0.8
■ **JIM FINIGAN** Finigan, James Leroy b: 8/19/28, Quincy, Ill. d: 5/16/81, Quincy, Ill. BR/TR, 5'11", 175 lbs. Deb: 4/25/54																												
1954	Phi-A	136	487	57	147	25	6	7	51	64	66	.302	.383	.421	.804	122	14	15	98	91	76	.742	2	8	-4	6	*3	1.1
1955	KC-A	150	545	72	139	30	7	9	68	61	49	.255	.333	.385	.719	92	-6	-7	101	109	68	.644	1	3	-2	-1	23	-0.3
1956	KC-A	91	250	29	54	7	2	2	21	30	28	.216	.302	.284	.586	55	-16	-16	101	102	23	.517	3	1	0	4	23	-0.7
1957	Det-A	64	174	20	47	4	2	0	17	23	18	.270	.359	.316	.675	80	-2	-4	107	122	21	.611	1	1	-0	-4	3/2	-0.7
1958	SF-N	23	25	3	5	2	0	0	1	3	5	.200	.310	.280	.590	58	-1	-1	100	59	2	.524	0	0	0	0	/23	0.0
1959	Bal-A	48	119	14	30	6	0	1	10	9	10	.252	.305	.328	.632	76	-4	-4	97	94	11	.516	1	0	0	2	3/2S	-0.1
Total	6	512	1600	195	422	74	17	19	168	190	176	.264	.344	.367	.711	92	-16	-17	101	102	200	.661	8	13	-5	6	32/S	-0.7
■ **BOB FINLEY** Finley, Robert Edward b: 11/25/15, Ennis, Tex. d: 1/2/86, W.Covina, Cal. BR/TR, 6'1", 200 lbs. Deb: 7/04/43																												
1943	Phi-N	28	81	9	21	2	0	1	7	4	10	.259	.294	.321	.615	83	-2	-2	94	87	7	.476	0			2	C	0.1
1944	Phi-N	94	281	18	70	11	1	1	21	12	25	.249	.292	.306	.598	68	-12	-12	100	85	24	.473	1			3	C	-0.4
Total	2	122	362	27	91	13	1	2	28	16	35	.251	.292	.309	.602	71	-14	-14	99	85	31	.479	1			5	/C	-0.3
■ **BILL FINLEY** Finley, William James b: 10/4/1863, New York, N.Y. d: 10/6/12, Asbury Park, N.J. Deb: 7/12/1886																												
1886	NY-N	13	44	2	8	0	0	0	5	1	8	.182	.200	.182	.382	19	-4	-4	89	204	2	.306	2			0	/OC	-0.2
■ **NEAL FINN** Finn, Cornelius Francis "Mickey" b: 1/24/04, Brooklyn, N.Y. d: 7/7/33, Allentown, Pa. BR/TR, 5'11", 168 lbs. Deb: 4/21/30																												
1930	Bro-N	87	273	42	76	13	0	3	30	26	18	.278	.350	.359	.709	72	-12	-12	101	97	35	.665	3			-4	2	-0.5
1931	Bro-N	118	413	46	113	22	2	0	45	21	42	.274	.314	.337	.650	74	-15	-15	101	118	45	.550	2			-2	*2	-1.1
1932	Bro-N	65	189	22	45	5	2	0	14	11	15	.238	.284	.286	.569	56	-12	-11	96	96	16	.472	2			6	3/2S	0.0
1933	Phi-N	51	169	15	40	4	1	0	13	10	14	.237	.287	.272	.559	51	-8	-12	118	106	14	.451	2			-1	2	-0.9
Total	4	321	1044	125	274	44	5	3	102	68	89	.262	.314	.323	.637	66	-47	-50	103	106	109	.548	9			-1	2/3S	-2.5
■ **HAL FINNEY** Finney, Harold Wilson b: 7/7/05, Lafayette, Ala. BR/TR, 5'11", 170 lbs. Deb: 6/24/31																												
1931	Pit-N	10	26	2	8	1	0	0	2	0	1	.308	.333	.346	.679	82	-1	-1	101	79	3	.611	1			0	/C	0.0
1932	Pit-N	31	33	14	7	3	0	0	4	3	4	.212	.297	.303	.600	62	-2	-2	99	149	3	.538	0			0	C	0.0
1933	Pit-N	56	133	17	31	4	1	1	18	3	19	.233	.250	.301	.551	60	-8	-7	95	157	9	.402	0			1	C	-0.4
1934	Pit-N	5	0	3	0	0	0	0	0	0	0	—	1.000	—	1.301	253	0	0	105	0	0	—	0			0	/C	0.0
1936	Pit-N	21	35	3	0	0	0	0	3	0	8	.000	.000	.000	.000	-99	-10	-10	98	0	0	.000	0			1	C	-0.8
Total	5	123	227	39	46	8	1	1	27	6	32	.203	.233	.260	.493	38	-19	-18	97	123	16	.381	1			1	/C	-1.2
■ **LOU FINNEY** Finney, Louis Klopsche b: 8/13/10, Buffalo, Ala. d: 4/22/66, Lafayette, Ala. BL/TR, 6', 180 lbs. Deb: 9/12/31																												
1931	Phi-A	9	24	7	9	0	1	0	3	6	1	.375	.516	.458	.974	150	3	3	105	90	6	1.200	0	0	0	1	/O	0.3
1933	Phi-A	74	240	26	64	12	2	3	32	13	17	.267	.307	.371	.678	86	-8	-5	92	109	27	.581	1	3	-2	0	O	-0.7
1934	Phi-A	92	272	32	76	11	4	1	28	14	17	.279	.315	.360	.675	76	-11	-10	97	93	31	.583	4	3	-1	-1	O1	-1.3
1935	Phi-A	109	410	45	112	11	6	0	31	18	18	.273	.307	.329	.636	65	-22	-22	100	79	42	.540	7	2	1	-6	O1	-2.7
1936	Phi-A	151	653	100	197	26	10	1	41	47	22	.302	.351	.377	.728	79	-21	-21	101	46	85	.652	7	9	-3	-2	1O	-3.4
1937	Phi-A	92	379	53	95	14	9	1	20	20	16	.251	.288	.343	.631	62	-25	-22	94	49	36	.526	2	5	-2	-2	1O/2	-3.1
1938	Phi-A	122	454	61	125	21	12	10	48	39	25	.275	.333	.441	.773	91	-8	-8	101	72	65	.724	5	8	-3	1	1O	-1.7
1939	Phi-A	9	22	1	3	0	0	0	1	2	0	.136	.208	.136	.345	-10	-4	-4	97	113	1	.263	0	0	0	0	/O	-0.2
	Bos-A	95	249	43	81	18	3	1	46	24	11	.325	.385	.434	.818	100	4	0	108	140	41	.757	2	5	-2	-1	1O	-0.5
	Yr	104	271	44	84	18	3	1	47	26	11	.310	.370	.410	.780	92	-0	-3	107	139	41	.709	2	5	-2	-1		-0.7
1940	Bos-A	130	534	73	171	31	15	5	73	33	13	.320	.360	.463	.822	111	8	7	101	107	87	.748	5	2	0	4	O1	0.4
1941	Bos-A	127	497	83	143	24	10	4	53	38	17	.288	.340	.400	.740	92	-4	-6	103	91	66	.645	2	5	-2	-3	O1	-1.7
1942	Bos-A	113	397	58	113	16	7	3	61	29	11	.285	.335	.383	.718	98	-0	-2	104	134	51	.625	3	3	-1	1	O/1	-0.8
1944	Bos-A	68	251	37	72	11	2	0	32	23	7	.287	.347	.347	.693	100	-0	0	98	135	31	.594	1	0	0	-1	1/O	-0.3
1945	Bos-A	2	2	0	0	0	0	0	0	0	1	.000	.000	.000	.000	-99	-1	-0	95	0	0	.000	0	0	0	0	H	0.0
	StL-A	57	213	24	59	8	4	2	22	21	6	.277	.345	.380	.725	96	3	-1	115	97	27	.632	0	0	0	-1	O1/3	-0.3
	Yr	59	215	24	59	8	4	2	22	21	7	.274	.342	.377	.719	95	2	-1	115	94	27	.624	0	0	0	-1		-0.3
1946	StL-A	16	30	0	9	0	0	0	3	2	4	.300	.344	.300	.644	83	-1	-1	98	127	3	.524	0	0	0	0	/O	0.0
1947	Phi-N	4	4	0	0	0	0	0	0	0	0	.000	.000	.000	.000	-99	-1	-1	100	0	0	.000	0			0	H	0.0
Total	15	1270	4631	643	1329	203	85	31	494	329	186	.287	.336	.388	.723	87	-88	-92	101	90	599	.649	39	45		-9	O1/32	-16.0
■ **MIKE FIORE** Fiore, Michael Gary Joseph b: 10/11/44, Brooklyn, N.Y. BL/TL, 6', 175 lbs. Deb: 9/21/68																												
1968	Bal-A	6	17	2	1	0	0	0	0	4	4	.059	.273	.059	.332	5	-2	-2	102	0	1	.375	0	0	0	-0	/1O	-0.2
1969	KC-A	107	339	53	93	14	1	12	35	84	63	.274	.421	.428	.849	134	22	20	103	79	66	.907	4	4	-1	5	1O	1.8
1970	KC-A	25	72	6	13	2	0	0	4	13	24	.181	.306	.208	.514	45	-5	-5	98	108	5	.475	1	1	-0	-0	1	-0.6
	Bos-A	41	50	5	7	0	0	0	4	8	4	.140	.259	.140	.399	12	-6	-6	111	231	2	.341	0	0	0	-1	1/O	-0.8
	Yr	66	122	11	20	2	0	0	8	21	28	.164	.287	.180	.467	30	-11	-12	106	186	8	.423	1	1	-0	-1		-1.4
1971	Bos-A	51	62	9	11	2	0	1	6	12	14	.177	.311	.258	.569	59	-3	-3	106	129	5	.509	0	3	-2	-0	1	-0.6
1972	StL-N	17	10	0	1	0	0	0	1	2	3	.100	.250	.100	.350	3	-1	-1	105	411	0	.300	0	0	0	-0	/1O	-0.1
	SD-N	7	6	0	0	0	0	0	0	1	3	.000	.143	.000	.143	-64	-1	-1	88	0	0	.167	0	0	0	0	H	0.0
	Yr	24	16	0	1	0	0	0	1	3	6	.063	.211	.063	.273	-19	-2	-2	100	308	0	.267	0	0	0	-0		-0.1
Total	5	254	556	75	126	18	1	13	50	124	115	.227	.370	.333	.703	95	4	2	103	103	79	.724	5	8	-3	3	1/O	-0.5
■ **DAN FIROVA** Firova, Daniel Michael b: 10/16/56, Refugio, Tex. BR/TR, 6', 185 lbs. Deb: 9/01/81																												
1981	Sea-A	13	2	0	0	0	0	0	0	0	1	.000	.000	.000	.000	-99	-1	-1	100	0	0	.000	0	0	0	-0	C	0.0
1982	Sea-A	3	5	0	0	0	0	0	0	0	0	.000	.000	.000	.000	-91	-1	-1	109	0	0	.000	0	0	0	0	/C	0.0
1988	Cle-A	1	0	0	0	0	0	0	0	0	0	—	—	—	—	—	0	0	102	—	—	—	0	0	0	0	/C	0.0
Total	3	17	7	0	0	0	0	0	0	0	1	.000	.000	.000	.000	-94	-2	-2	107	0	0	.000	0	0	0	-0	/C	0.0
■ **WILLIAM FISCHER** Fischer, William Charles b: 3/2/1891, New York, N.Y. d: 9/4/45, Richmond, Va. BL/TR, 6', 174 lbs. Deb: 6/11/13																												
1913	Bro-N	62	165	16	44	9	4	1	12	10	5	.267	.313	.388	.700	95	-1	-2	104	65	19	.620	0			-11	C	-0.9
1914	Bro-N	43	105	12	27	1	2	0	8	8	12	.257	.310	.305	.614	82	-2	-2	101	91	10	.526	1			3	C	0.2
1915	Chi-F	105	292	30	96	15	4	4	50	24	19	.329	.380	.449	.828	149	16	17	97	126	54	.816	5			-8	C	1.1

YEAR	TM/L	G	AB	R	H	2B	3B	HR	RBI	BB	SO	AVG	OBP	SLG	PRO	/A	BR	/A	PF	CHI	RC	TA	SB	CS	SBR	FR	POS	TPR
1916	Chi-N	65	179	15	35	9	2	1	14	11	8	.196	.246	.285	.531	54	-8	-11	117	103	14	.451	2			-3	C	-1.2
	Pit-N	42	113	11	29	7	1	1	6	10	3	.257	.323	.363	.685	105	1	1	105	54	14	.631	1			3	C	0.6
	Yr	107	292	26	64	16	3	2	20	21	11	.219	.276	.315	.591	73	-7	-11	112	85	27	.518	3			0		-0.6
1917	Pit-N	95	245	25	70	9	2	3	25	27	19	.286	.359	.376	.734	126	8	8	100	95	35	.749	11			4	C/1	1.7
Total	5	412	1099	109	301	50	15	10	115	90	66	.274	.331	.374	.705	108	14	10	103	95	146	.658	20			-13	C/1	1.5
■ **MIKE FISCHLIN** Fischlin, Michael Thomas b: 9/13/55, Sacramento, Cal. BR/TR, 6'1", 165 lbs. Deb: 9/03/77																												
1977	Hou-N	13	15	0	3	0	0	0	0	0	2	.200	.200	.200	.400	8	-2	-2	93	0	1	.250	0	0	0	-0	S	0.0
1978	Hou-N	44	86	3	10	1	0	0	0	4	9	.116	.165	.128	.293	-18	-13	-13	95	0	2	.221	1	0	0	-7	S	-1.6
1980	Hou-N	1	1	0	0	0	0	0	0	0	1	.000	.000	.000	.000	-99	-0	-0	98	0	0	.000	0	0	0	0	/S	0.0
1981	Cle-A	22	43	3	10	1	0	0	5	3	6	.233	.283	.256	.538	60	-2	-2	93	178	3	.486	3	2	-0	-0	S/2	0.0
1982	Cle-A	112	276	34	74	12	1	0	21	34	36	.268	.353	.319	.671	86	-4	-4	100	95	34	.633	9	5	-0	2	*S/32C	0.7
1983	Cle-A	95	225	31	47	5	2	2	23	26	32	.209	.296	.276	.572	56	-12	-14	105	132	22	.544	9	2	2	10	2S/3D	0.1
1984	Cle-A	85	133	17	30	4	2	1	14	12	20	.226	.290	.308	.598	62	-6	-7	106	127	12	.514	2	2	-1	1	23S	-0.2
1985	Cle-A	73	60	12	12	4	1	0	2	5	7	.200	.262	.300	.562	57	-4	-3	94	44	5	.469	0	1	-1	-2	2S/13D	-0.3
1986	NY-A	71	102	9	21	2	0	0	3	8	29	.206	.264	.225	.489	35	-9	-9	103	52	6	.365	0	1	-1	1	S2	-0.4
1987	Atl-N	1	0	0	0	0	0	0	0	0	0	—	—	—	—	—	0	0	108	—	—	—	0	0	0	0	/R	0.0
Total	10	517	941	109	207	29	6	3	68	92	142	.220	.293	.273	.566	56	-53	-55	101	95	91	.506	24	13	-1	4	S2/31DC	-1.7
■ **SAM FISHBURN** Fishburn, Samuel E. b: 5/15/1893, Haverhill, Mass. d: 4/11/65, Bethlehem, Pa. BR/TR, 5'9", 157 lbs. Deb: 9/30/19																												
1919	StL-N	9	6	0	2	1	0	0	2	0	0	.333	.333	.500	.833	158	0	0	94	259	1	.750	0			0	/12	0.1
■ **JOHN FISHEL** Fishel, John Alan b: 11/8/63, Fullerton, Cal. BR/TR, 5'11", 185 lbs. Deb: 7/14/88																												
1988	Hou-N	19	26	1	6	0	0	1	2	3	6	.231	.310	.346	.656	95	-0	-0	93	67	3	.600	0	0	0	-2	/O	-0.2
■ **FISHER** Fisher b:Johnstown, Pa. Deb: 7/17/1884																												
1884	Phi-U	10	36	7	8	2	0	0		3		.222	.282	.278	.560	97	-0	0	93	0	3	.464	0			0	/P1	0.0
	WiL-U	8	29	0	2	0	0	0		0		.069	.069	.069	.138	-52	-4	-5	103	0	0	.074	0			0	/OS	-0.3
	Yr	18	65	7	10	2	0	0		3		.154	.191	.185	.376	28	-5	-4	97	0	2	.273	0			0		-0.3
1885	Buf-N	1	4	0	0	0	0	0	0	0	0	.000	.000	.000	.000	-99	-1	-1	99	0	0	.000				0	/P	0.0
Total	2	19	69	7	10	2	0	0	0	3	0	.145	.181	.174	.354	21	-6	-5	97	0	3	.254				0	/POS1	-0.3
■ **GUS FISHER** Fisher, August Harris b: 10/21/1885, Pottsborough, Tex. d: 4/8/72, Portland, Ore. BL/TR, 5'10", 175 lbs. Deb: 4/18/11																												
1911	Cle-A	70	203	20	53	6	3	0	12	7		.261	.302	.320	.623	72	-7	-8	103	62	21	.553	6			6	C/1	0.4
1912	NY-A	4	10	1	1	0	0	0	0	0		.100	.100	.100	.200	-42	-2	-2	101	0	0	.111	0			0	/C	0.0
Total	2	74	213	21	54	6	3	0	12	7		.254	.293	.310	.603	67	-9	-10	103	60	21	.528	6			6	/C1	0.4
■ **SHOWBOAT FISHER** Fisher, George Aloys b: 1/16/1899, Jennings, Iowa BL/TR, 5'10", 170 lbs. Deb: 4/24/23																												
1923	Was-A	13	23	4	6	2	0	0	2	4	3	.261	.370	.348	.718	95	-0	-0	95	85	3	.706	0	0	0	0	/O	0.0
1924	Was-A	15	41	7	9	1	0	0	6	6	6	.220	.319	.244	.563	47	-3	-3	98	198	4	.563	2	0	1	-3	O	-0.5
1930	StL-N	92	254	49	95	18	6	8	61	25	21	.374	.432	.587	1.019	137	18	16	105	122	62	1.126	4			-4	O	0.6
1932	StL-A	18	22	2	4	0	0	0	2	2	5	.182	.250	.182	.432	14	-3	-3	100	167	1	.333	0	0	0	-1	/O	-0.3
Total	4	138	340	62	114	21	6	8	71	37	35	.335	.402	.503	.905	117	12	10	103	131	71	.951	6	0		-8	/O	-0.2
■ **HARRY FISHER** Fisher, Harry C. b: Philadelphia, Pa. Deb: 6/07/1884																												
1884	KC-U	10	40	3	8	2	0	0		0		.200	.200	.250	.450	59	-2	-1	87	0	2	.313	0			0	/3S	0.0
	CP-U	1	3	1	2	0	0	0		1		.667	.750	.667	1.417	385	1	1	99	0	2	3.000	0			0	/3	0.1
	Yr	11	43	4	10	2	0	0		1		.233	.250	.279	.529	89	-1	-0	88	0	3	.394	0			0		0.1
	Cle-N	6	24	2	3	0	0	0	0	0	3	.125	.125	.125	.250	-21	-3	-3	102	0	0	.143				0	/2C	-0.2
1889	Lou-a	1	2	0	1	0	0	0	0	0	0	.500	.500	.500	1.000	197	0	0	96	0	1	1.000	0			0	/O	0.0
Total	2	18	69	6	14	2	0	0	0	1	3	.203	.214	.232	.446	50	-4	-3	93	0	4	.309	0			0	/32OCS	-0.1
■ **HARRY FISHER** Fisher, Harry Devereux b: 1/3/26, Newbury, Ont., Can. d: 9/20/81, Waterloo, Ont., Ca BL/TR, 6', 180 lbs. Deb: 9/16/51																												
1951	Pit-N	3	3	0	0	0	0	0	0	0	0	.000	.000	.000	.000	-94	-1	-1	107	0	0	.000	0	0	0	0	H	0.0
1952	Pit-N	15	15	0	5	1	0	0	1	0	3	.333	.333	.400	.733	103	-0	0	100	65	2	.545	0	0	0	-0	/P	0.0
Total	2	18	18	0	5	1	0	0	1	0	3	.278	.278	.333	.611	67	-1	-1	101	54	2	.429	0	0	0	-0	/P	0.0
■ **RED FISHER** Fisher, John Gus b: 6/22/1887, Pittsburgh, Pa. d: 1/31/40, Louisville, Ky. TR , Deb: 4/25/10																												
1910	StL-A	23	72	5	9	2	1	0	3	8		.125	.222	.181	.403	28	-6	-6	94	87	4	.429	5			-2	O	-0.8
■ **NEWT FISHER** Fisher, Newton "Ike" b: 6/18/1871, Nashville, Tenn. d: 2/28/47, Norwood Park, Ill. BR/TR, 5'9.5 ", 171 lbs. Deb: 5/17/1898																												
1898	Phi-N	9	26	0	3	1	0	0	0	0		.115	.148	.154	.302	-13	-4	-4	95	0	1	.261	1			0	/C3	-0.2
■ **TOM FISHER** Fisher, Robert Taylor b: 11/3/1886, Nashville, Tenn. d: 8/4/63, Jacksonville, Fla. BR/TR, 5'9.5", 170 lbs. Deb: 6/03/12																												
1912	Bro-N	82	257	27	60	10	3	0	26	14	32	.233	.273	.296	.569	58	-16	-15	95	115	23	.492	7			-13	S/23	-1.9
1913	Bro-N	132	474	42	124	11	10	4	54	10	43	.262	.278	.352	.631	76	-15	-17	104	112	49	.554	16			-17	*S	-2.6
1914	Chi-N	15	50	5	15	2	2	0	5	3	4	.300	.340	.420	.760	128	1	1	98	88	8	.743	2			-2	S	0.0
1915	Chi-N	147	568	70	163	22	5	5	53	30	51	.287	.326	.370	.696	108	6	5	102	79	69	.593	9	20	-9	-16	*S	-1.8
1916	Cin-N	61	136	9	37	4	3	0	11	8	14	.272	.313	.346	.658	104	0	0	98	93	17	.626	7			-1	S/2O	0.1
1918	StL-N	63	246	36	78	11	3	2	20	15	11	.317	.356	.411	.767	143	9	11	93	75	37	.732	7			11	2	2.7
1919	StL-N	3	11	0	3	1	0	0	1	0	2	.273	.273	.364	.636	96	-0	-0	94	103	1	.500	0			0	/2	0.0
Total	7	503	1742	189	480	61	26	11	170	80	157	.276	.309	.359	.668	96	-14	-14	100	94	203	.591	48	20		-37	S/2O3	-3.5
■ **WILBUR FISHER** Fisher, Wilbur Mc Cullough b: 7/18/1894, Greenbottom, W.Va d: 10/24/60, Welch, W.Va. BL/TR, 6', 174 lbs. Deb: 6/13/16																												
1916	Pit-N	1	1	0	0	0	0	0	0	0	0	.000	.000	.000	.000	-96	-0	-0	105	0	0	.000	0			0	H	0.0
■ **CHEROKEE FISHER** Fisher, William Charles b: 12/1845, Philadelphia, Pa. d: 9/26/12, New York, N.Y. BR/TR, 5'9", 164 lbs. Deb: 5/06/1871																												
1871	Rok-n	25	124	24	28							.226															*P/S	
1872	Bal-n	44	234	39	48							.205															3OP	
1873	Ath-n	51	259	51	66							.255															*O/P1	
1874	Har-n	52	231	29	53							.229															PO/3S	
1875	Phi-n	41	169	26	39							.231															P/O	
1876	Cin-N	35	129	12	32	1	0	0	4	0	8	.248	.248	.256	.504	76	-4	-2	90	42	8	.340				-2	PO/S1	0.0
1877	Chi-N	1	4	0	0	0	0	0	0	0	2	.000	.000	.000	.000	-99	-1	-1	98	0	0	.000				0	/3	0.0
1878	Pro-N	1	3	0	0	0	0	0	0	0	0	.000	.000	.000	.000	-99	-1	-1	98	0	0	.000				0	/P	0.0
Total	5 n	213	1017	169	234							.230															/P	
Total	3	37	136	12	32	1	0	0	4	0	10	.235	.235	.243	.478	66	-6	-4	90	40	8	.317				-2	P/O3S1	0.0
■ **CARLTON FISK** Fisk, Carlton Ernest "Pudge" b: 12/26/47, Bellows Falls, Vt. BR/TR, 6'3", 200 lbs. Deb: 9/18/69																												
1969	Bos-A	2	5	0	0	0	0	0	0	0	2	.000	.000	.000	.000	-95	-1	-1	105	0	0	.000	0	0	0	0	/C	0.0
1971	Bos-A	14	48	7	15	2	1	2	6	1	10	.313	.327	.521	.847	130	2	2	106	79	8	.765	0	0	0	0	C	0.2
1972	Bos-A	131	457	74	134	28	**9**	22	61	52	83	.293	.370	.538	.909	160	37	35	105	83	90	.914	5	2	0	17	*C	**5.9**
1973	Bos-A	135	508	65	125	21	0	26	71	37	99	.246	.310	.441	.751	103	4	1	106	94	69	.702	7	2	1	17	*C/D	2.2
1974	Bos-A	52	187	36	56	12	1	11	26	24	23	.299	.385	.551	.936	156	16	14	107	80	40	.978	5	1	1	1	C/D	1.8
1975	Bos-A	79	263	47	87	14	4	10	52	27	32	.331	.397	.529	.926	147	20	17	109	118	54	.925	4	3	-1	0	C/D	1.9
1976	Bos-A	134	487	76	124	17	5	17	58	56	71	.255	.339	.415	.754	109	12	6	110	93	70	.728	12	5	1	**18**	*C/D	3.1
1977	Bos-A	152	536	106	169	26	3	26	102	75	85	.315	.408	.521	.929	129	40	27	117	120	117	.969	7	6	-2	16	*C	4.4
1978	Bos-A	157	571	94	162	39	5	20	88	71	83	.284	.370	.475	.844	126	28	22	107	107	103	.846	7	2	1	16	*C/OD	4.4
1979	Bos-A	91	320	49	87	23	2	10	42	10	38	.272	.307	.450	.757	94	-1	-4	107	93	42	.674	3	0	1	-9	DC/O	-1.0
1980	Bos-A	131	478	73	138	25	3	18	62	36	62	.289	.355	.467	.821	121	15	14	102	89	77	.793	11	5	0	12	*C/O13D	3.0
1981	Chi-A	96	338	44	89	12	0	7	45	38	37	.263	.358	.361	.719	108	5	5	100	126	45	.673	3	2	-0	-8	C/13O	0.1

YEAR	TM/L	G	AB	R	H	2B	3B	HR	RBI	BB	SO	AVG	OBP	SLG	PRO	/A	BR	/A	PF	CHI	RC	TA	SB	CS	SBR	FR	POS	TPR
1982	Chi-A	135	476	66	127	17	3	14	65	46	60	.267	.339	.403	.742	106	2	4	97	113	67	.719	17	2	4	-4	*C/1	1.1
1983	Chi-A	138	488	85	141	26	4	26	86	46	88	.289	.357	.518	.876	133	24	22	103	104	90	.870	9	6	-1	-6	*C/D	2.1
1984	Chi-A	102	359	54	83	20	1	21	43	26	60	.231	.292	.468	.760	96	2	-3	111	76	49	.724	6	0	2	-9	C/D	-0.4
1985	Chi-A	153	543	85	129	23	1	37	107	52	81	.238	.324	.488	.812	119	13	13	100	120	85	.813	17	9	-0	3	*CD	2.0
1986	Chi-A	125	457	42	101	11	0	14	63	22	92	.221	.266	.337	.603	63	-23	-24	101	131	39	.497	2	4	-2	4	CO/D	-1.8
1987	Chi-A	135	454	68	116	22	1	23	71	39	72	.256	.325	.460	.786	98	3	-2	109	102	66	.732	1	4	-2	15	*C/1OD	1.8
1988	Chi-A	76	253	37	70	8	1	19	50	37	40	.277	.380	.542	.921	159	19	20	97	104	52	.947	0	0	0	4	C	2.6
Total	19	2038	7228	1108	1953	346	44	323	1098	695	1118	.270	.344	.464	.809	117	216	166	105	104	1161	.804	116	53	3	86	*CD/O13	33.4

■ **WES FISLER** Fisler, Weston Dickson b: 7/5/1841, Camden, N.J. d: 12/25/22, Philadelphia, Pa. 5'6", 137 lbs. Deb: 5/20/1871

YEAR	TM/L	G	AB	R	H	2B	3B	HR	RBI	BB	SO	AVG	OBP	SLG	PRO	/A	BR	/A	PF	CHI	RC	TA	SB	CS	SBR	FR	POS	TPR
1871	Ath-n	28	150	43	44							.293															*1/2	
1872	Ath-n	46	248	50	81							.327															*2	
1873	Ath-n	43	227	42	71							.313															*2/1	
1874	Ath-n	37	175	27	67							.383															1/2	
1875	Ath-n	57	272	54	75							.276															1/O2	
1876	Phi-N	59	278	42	80	15	1	1	30	2	4	.288	.293	.360	.653	117	4	5	99	87	30	.515				-4	O21/S	0.0
Total	5 n	211	1072	216	338							.315															O21/S	

■ **CHARLIE FITZBERGER** Fitzberger, Charles Casper b: 2/13/04, Baltimore, Md. d: 1/25/65, Baltimore, Md. BL/TL, 6'1.5", 170 lbs. Deb: 9/11/28

YEAR	TM/L	G	AB	R	H	2B	3B	HR	RBI	BB	SO	AVG	OBP	SLG	PRO	/A	BR	/A	PF	CHI	RC	TA	SB	CS	SBR	FR	POS	TPR
1928	Bos-N	7	7	0	2	0	0	0	0	0	3	.286	.286	.286	.571	51	-1	-0	97	0	1	.400	0			0	H	0.0

■ **DENNIS FITZGERALD** Fitzgerald, Dennis S. b: 3/18/ 1865 England d: 10/16/36, New Haven, Conn. 5'10", 160 lbs. Deb: 4/17/1890

YEAR	TM/L	G	AB	R	H	2B	3B	HR	RBI	BB	SO	AVG	OBP	SLG	PRO	/A	BR	/A	PF	CHI	RC	TA	SB	CS	SBR	FR	POS	TPR
1890	Phi-a	2	8	0	2	0	0	0		0		.250	.250	.250	.500	51	-1	-0	97	0	1	.333	0			0	/S	0.0

■ **DENNIS FITZGERALD** Fitzgerald, Dennis S. b: 3/1865 England d: 10/16/36, New Haven, Conn. 5'10", 160 lbs. Deb: 4/17/1890

YEAR	TM/L	G	AB	R	H	2B	3B	HR	RBI	BB	SO	AVG	OBP	SLG	PRO	/A	BR	/A	PF	CHI	RC	TA	SB	CS	SBR	FR	POS	TPR
1948	Pit-N	102	262	31	70	9	3	1	35	32	37	.267	.349	.336	.685	82	-4	-6	104	144	33	.636	3			-5	C	-0.3
1949	Pit-N	75	160	16	42	7	0	2	18	8	27	.262	.302	.344	.646	72	-6	-7	101	111	16	.528	1			-1	C	-0.5
1950	Pit-N	6	15	1	1	1	0	0	0	0	3	.067	.067	.133	.200	-48	-3	-3	103	0	0	.133	0			-0	/C	-0.2
1951	Pit-N	55	97	8	22	6	0	0	13	7	10	.227	.286	.289	.574	52	-6	-7	107	180	7	.451	1	1	-0	1	C	-0.5
1952	Pit-N	51	73	4	17	1	0	1	7	7	15	.233	.300	.288	.588	64	-3	-3	100	114	5	.452	0	2	-1	0	C/3	-0.3
1953	Pit-N	6	17	2	2	1	0	0	1	0	2	.118	.118	.176	.294	-24	-3	-3	102	130	0	.200	0	0	0	0	/C	-0.2
	Was-A	88	288	23	72	13	0	3	39	19	34	.250	.299	.326	.625	73	-13	-11	94	140	27	.511	2	1	0	3	C	-0.3
1954	Was-A	115	360	33	104	13	5	4	40	33	22	.289	.352	.386	.738	104	1	2	98	100	48	.647	0	1	-1	-2	*C	0.4
1955	Was-A	74	236	28	56	3	1	4	19	25	23	.237	.318	.309	.628	76	-10	-7	91	83	23	.534	0	1	-1	1	C	-0.3
1956	Was-A	64	148	15	45	8	0	2	12	20	16	.304	.387	.399	.786	106	2	2	102	69	23	.738	0	0	0	0	C	0.3
1957	Was-A	45	125	14	34	8	0	1	13	10	9	.272	.331	.360	.691	91	-2	-2	98	107	13	.580	2	0	1	2	C	0.3
1958	Was-A	58	114	7	30	3	0	0	11	8	15	.263	.311	.289	.601	69	-5	-5	97	134	9	.446	0	0	0	1	C/1	-0.3
1959	Was-A	19	62	5	12	3	0	0	5	4	8	.194	.242	.242	.484	33	-6	-6	100	131	4	.373	0	0	0	-1	C	-0.5
	Cle-A	49	129	12	35	6	1	1	4	12	14	.271	.343	.357	.699	96	-1	-1	97	32	15	.606	0	0	0	-1	C	0.0
	Yr	68	191	17	47	9	1	1	9	16	22	.246	.311	.319	.630	75	-7	-6	97	62	19	.530	0	0	0	-2		-0.5
Total	12	807	2086	199	542	82	10	19	217	185	235	.260	.324	.336	.660	80	-60	-56	98	110	223	.583	9	6		-2	C/13	-2.4

■ **HOWIE FITZGERALD** Fitzgerald, Howard Chumney "Lefty" b: 5/16/02, Eagle Lake, Tex. d: 2/27/59, Eagle Falls, Tex. BL/TL, 5'11.5", 163 lbs. Deb: 9/17/22

YEAR	TM/L	G	AB	R	H	2B	3B	HR	RBI	BB	SO	AVG	OBP	SLG	PRO	/A	BR	/A	PF	CHI	RC	TA	SB	CS	SBR	FR	POS	TPR
1922	Chi-N	10	24	3	8	1	0	0	4	3	2	.333	.407	.375	.782	109	0	0	95	155	4	.813	1	0	0	-2	/O	0.0
1924	Chi-N	7	19	1	3	0	0	0	2	0	2	.158	.158	.158	.316	-15	-3	-3	101	243	0	.188	0	0	0	-2	/O	-0.4
1926	Bos-A	31	97	11	25	2	0	0	8	5	7	.258	.294	.278	.572	49	-7	-7	101	101	7	.434	1	4	-2	-5	O	-1.5
Total	3	48	140	15	36	3	0	0	14	8	11	.257	.297	.279	.576	51	-10	-10	100	129	12	.454	2	4	-2	-9	/O	-1.9

■ **MIKE FITZGERALD** Fitzgerald, Justin Howard b: 6/22/1890, San Mateo, Cal. d: 1/17/45, San Mateo, Cal. BL/TR, 5'8", 160 lbs. Deb: 6/20/11

YEAR	TM/L	G	AB	R	H	2B	3B	HR	RBI	BB	SO	AVG	OBP	SLG	PRO	/A	BR	/A	PF	CHI	RC	TA	SB	CS	SBR	FR	POS	TPR
1911	NY-A	16	37	6	10	1	0	0	6	4		.270	.341	.297	.639	71	-1	-1	111	184	5	.704	4			-2	/O	-0.3
1918	Phi-N	66	133	21	39	8	0	0	6	13	6	.293	.361	.353	.714	108	3	2	109	48	18	.681	3			-18	O	-2.1
Total	2	82	170	27	49	9	0	0	12	17	6	.288	.356	.341	.698	99	2	0	109	78	23	.686	7			-19	/O	-2.4

■ **MATTY FITZGERALD** Fitzgerald, Matthew William b: 8/31/1880, Albany, N.Y. d: 9/22/49, Albany, N.Y. TR , 6', 185 lbs. Deb: 9/15/06

YEAR	TM/L	G	AB	R	H	2B	3B	HR	RBI	BB	SO	AVG	OBP	SLG	PRO	/A	BR	/A	PF	CHI	RC	TA	SB	CS	SBR	FR	POS	TPR
1906	NY-N	4	6	2	4	0	0	0	2	0		.667	.667	.667	1.333	320	1	1	100	182	3	2.500	1			0	/C	0.2
1907	NY-N	7	15	1	2	1	0	0	1	0		.133	.133	.200	.333	5	-2	-2	105	126	0	.231	0			-0	/C	-0.1
Total	2	11	21	3	6	1	0	0	3	0		.286	.286	.333	.619	92	-0	-0	104	142	4	.533	1			-0	/C	0.1

■ **MIKE FITZGERALD** Fitzgerald, Michael Patrick b: 3/28/64, Savannah, Ga. BR/TR, 6'1", 200 lbs. Deb: 6/23/88

YEAR	TM/L	G	AB	R	H	2B	3B	HR	RBI	BB	SO	AVG	OBP	SLG	PRO	/A	BR	/A	PF	CHI	RC	TA	SB	CS	SBR	FR	POS	TPR
1988	StL-N	13	46	4	9	1	0	0	1	0	9	.196	.213	.217	.430	23	-5	-5	104	40	2	.297	0	0	0	0	1	-0.5

■ **MIKE FITZGERALD** Fitzgerald, Michael Roy b: 7/13/60, Long Beach, Cal. BR/TR, 6', 185 lbs. Deb: 9/13/83

YEAR	TM/L	G	AB	R	H	2B	3B	HR	RBI	BB	SO	AVG	OBP	SLG	PRO	/A	BR	/A	PF	CHI	RC	TA	SB	CS	SBR	FR	POS	TPR
1983	NY-N	8	20	1	2	0	0	1	2	3	6	.100	.217	.250	.467	30	-2	-2	99	99	1	.444	0	0	0	-0	/C	-0.1
1984	NY-N	112	360	20	87	15	1	2	33	24	71	.242	.291	.306	.596	68	-15	-15	100	111	29	.469	1	0	0	-2	*C	-1.4
1985	Mon-N	108	295	25	61	7	1	5	34	38	55	.207	.301	.288	.590	70	-13	-11	94	135	26	.531	5	3	-0	-22	*C	-3.0
1986	Mon-N	73	209	20	59	13	1	6	37	27	34	.282	.367	.440	.807	125	6	7	98	134	34	.788	3	2	-0	-11	C	-0.2
1987	Mon-N	107	287	32	69	11	0	3	36	42	54	.240	.339	.310	.649	69	-10	-12	106	147	30	.582	3	4	-2	-15	*C/12	-2.0
1988	Mon-N	63	155	17	42	6	1	5	23	19	22	.271	.351	.419	.770	114	4	3	106	115	23	.723	2	2	-1	2	C/O	0.7
Total	6	471	1326	115	320	52	4	22	165	153	242	.241	.322	.336	.658	82	-29	-30	100	128	143	.605	14	11	-2	-49	C/O21	-6.0

■ **RAY FITZGERALD** Fitzgerald, Raymond Francis b: 12/5/04, Chicopee, Mass. d: 9/6/77, Westfield, Mass. BR/TR, 5'9", 168 lbs. Deb: 4/18/31

YEAR	TM/L	G	AB	R	H	2B	3B	HR	RBI	BB	SO	AVG	OBP	SLG	PRO	/A	BR	/A	PF	CHI	RC	TA	SB	CS	SBR	FR	POS	TPR
1931	Cin-N	1	1	0	0	0	0	0	0	0	0	.000	.000	.000	.000	-99	-0	-0	95	0	0	.000	0			0	H	0.0

■ **SHAUN FITZMAURICE** Fitzmaurice, Shaun Earle b: 8/25/42, Worcester, Mass. BR/TR, 6', 180 lbs. Deb: 9/09/66

YEAR	TM/L	G	AB	R	H	2B	3B	HR	RBI	BB	SO	AVG	OBP	SLG	PRO	/A	BR	/A	PF	CHI	RC	TA	SB	CS	SBR	FR	POS	TPR
1966	NY-N	9	13	2	2	0	0	0	0	2	6	.154	.267	.154	.421	22	-1	-1	94	0	1	.455	1	0	0	1	/O	0.0

■ **ED FITZPATRICK** Fitzpatrick, Edward Henry b: 12/9/1889, Lewiston, Pa. d: 10/23/65, Bethlehem, Pa. BR/TR, 5'8", 165 lbs. Deb: 4/17/15

YEAR	TM/L	G	AB	R	H	2B	3B	HR	RBI	BB	SO	AVG	OBP	SLG	PRO	/A	BR	/A	PF	CHI	RC	TA	SB	CS	SBR	FR	POS	TPR
1915	Bos-N	105	303	54	67	19	3	0	24	43	36	.221	.344	.304	.648	99	1	2	98	100	36	.664	13	8	-1	-4	2O	-0.3
1916	Bos-N	83	216	17	46	8	0	1	18	15	26	.213	.280	.264	.544	73	-8	-6	93	119	19	.482	5			-18	2O	-2.7
1917	Bos-N	63	178	20	45	8	4	0	17	12	22	.253	.318	.343	.661	107	1	1	96	107	20	.617	4			-4	2O3	-0.1
Total	3	251	697	91	158	35	7	1	59	70	84	.227	.319	.301	.620	93	-6	-3	96	107	75	.596	22	8		-26	2/O3	-3.1

■ **TOM FITZSIMMONS** Fitzsimmons, Thomas William b: 4/6/1890, Oakland, Cal. d: 12/20/71, Oakland, Cal. BR/TR, 6'1", 190 lbs. Deb: 6/12/19

YEAR	TM/L	G	AB	R	H	2B	3B	HR	RBI	BB	SO	AVG	OBP	SLG	PRO	/A	BR	/A	PF	CHI	RC	TA	SB	CS	SBR	FR	POS	TPR
1919	Bro-N	4	4	1	0	0	0	0	0	1	2	.000	.200	.000	.200	-40	-1	-1	94	0	0	.250	0			0	/3	0.0

■ **MAX FLACK** Flack, Max John b: 2/5/1890, Belleville, Ill. d: 7/31/75, Belleville, Ill. BL/TL, 5'7", 148 lbs. Deb: 4/16/14

YEAR	TM/L	G	AB	R	H	2B	3B	HR	RBI	BB	SO	AVG	OBP	SLG	PRO	/A	BR	/A	PF	CHI	RC	TA	SB	CS	SBR	FR	POS	TPR
1914	Chi-F	134	502	66	124	15	3	2	39	51	48	.247	.316	.301	.617	85	-14	-8	91	95	62	.632	37			-0	*O	-1.5
1915	Chi-F	141	523	88	164	20	14	3	45	40	21	.314	.362	.423	.785	136	20	22	97	75	98	.830	37			0	*O	1.6
1916	Chi-N	141	465	65	120	14	3	3	20	42	43	.258	.320	.320	.640	83	-1	-10	117	51	53	.591	24	19	-4	-5	*O	-2.1
1917	Chi-N	131	447	65	111	18	7	0	21	51	34	.248	.325	.320	.645	94	0	-2	105	58	50	.628	17			-3	*O	-0.9
1918	Chi-N	123	478	74	123	17	10	4	41	56	19	.257	.343	.360	.702	112	9	8	102	74	63	.707	17			-1	*O	0.0
1919	Chi-N	116	469	71	138	20	4	6	35	34	13	.294	.346	.392	.738	121	12	12	100	58	67	.722	18			-3	*O	0.5
1920	Chi-N	135	520	85	157	30	6	4	49	52	15	.302	.373	.406	.779	125	17	18	99	82	77	.741	13	19	-8	-7	*O	-0.4
1921	Chi-N	133	572	80	172	31	4	6	37	32	15	.301	.342	.400	.742	90	-4	-9	107	47	77	.686	17	11	-2	-2	*O	-1.7
1922	Chi-N	17	54	7	12	1	0	0	6	2	4	.222	.250	.241	.491	29	-6	-5	95	161	3	.395	2	1	0	-3	O	-0.7
	StL-N	66	267	46	78	12	1	2	21	31	11	.292	.368	.367	.735	89	-3	-3	101	68	37	.686	3	5	-2	-6	O	-1.2
	Yr	83	321	53	90	13	1	2	27	33	15	.280	.349	.346	.695	80	-9	-9	100	89	39	.633	5	6	-2	-8		-1.9
1923	StL-N	128	505	82	147	16	9	3	28	41	16	.291	.348	.376	.724	101	-6	1	90	53	66	.658	7	8	-3	-8	*O	-1.2
1924	StL-N	67	209	31	55	11	3	2	21	21	5	.263	.330	.373	.704	86	-3	-4	103	91	25	.642	3	5	-2	-1	O	-0.8
1925	StL-N	79	241	23	60	7	8	0	28	21	9	.249	.309	.344	.654	65	-12	-13	102	120	26	.592	5	3	-0	-3	O	-1.6
Total	12	1411	5252	783	1461	212	72	35	391	474	253	.278	.341	.366	.707	100	9	6	101	71	704	.678	200	71		-41	*O	-10.0

YEAR	TM/L	G	AB	R	H	2B	3B	HR	RBI	BB	SO	AVG	OBP	SLG	PRO	/A	BR	/A	PF	CHI	RC	TA	SB	CS	SBR	FR	POS	TPR
■ WALLY FLAGER	Flager, Walter Leonard b: 11/3/21, Chicago Heights, Ill. BL/TR, 5'11", 160 lbs. Deb: 4/17/45																											
1945	Cin-N	21	52	5	11	1	0	0	6	8	5	.212	.317	.231	.547	57	-3	-3	94	174	4	.476	0			0	S	0.0
	Phi-N	49	168	21	42	4	1	2	15	17	15	.250	.323	.321	.644	82	-5	-4	96	88	18	.570	1			5	S/2	0.6
	Yr	70	220	26	53	5	1	2	21	25	20	.241	.321	.300	.621	76	-7	-6	96	116	23	.550	1			5		0.6
Total	1	70	220	26	53	5	1	2	21	25	20	.241	.321	.300	.621	76	-7	-6	96	109	23	.550	1			5	/S2	0.6
■ IRA FLAGSTEAD	Flagstead, Ira James "Pete" b: 9/22/1893, Montague, Mich. d: 3/13/40, Olympia, Wash. BR/TR, 5'9", 165 lbs. Deb: 7/20/17																											
1917	Det-A	4	4	0	0	0	0	0	0	0	1	.000	.000	.000	.000	-99	-1	-1	98	0	0	.000	0			-1	/O	-0.1
1919	Det-A	97	287	43	95	22	3	5	41	35	39	.331	.416	.481	.897	162	21	23	93	97	59	.969	6			-2	O	1.5
1920	Det-A	110	311	40	73	13	5	3	35	37	27	.235	.318	.338	.656	72	-12	-13	103	108	35	.603	3	4	-2	3	O	-1.7
1921	Det-A	85	259	40	79	15	1	1	31	21	21	.305	.371	.382	.753	96	-2	-1	96	104	38	.723	7	4	-0	-4	SO/23	0.1
1922	Det-A	44	91	21	28	5	3	3	8	14	16	.308	.411	.527	.939	146	6	6	98	50	20	1.000	0	1	-1	-2	O	0.1
1923	Det-A	1	1	0	0	0	0	0	0	0	0	.000	.000	.000	.000	-99	-0	-0	97	0	0	.000	0	0	0	0	H	0.0
	Bos-A	109	382	55	119	23	4	8	53	37	26	.312	.380	.455	.835	117	10	9	102	93	65	.821	8	10	-4	19	*O	1.5
	Yr	110	383	55	119	23	4	8	53	37	26	.311	.379	.454	.833	117	10	9	102	92	65	.818	8	10	-4	19		1.5
1924	Bos-A	149	560	106	172	35	7	5	43	77	41	.307	.401	.421	.823	108	13	9	104	60	97	.833	10	13	-5	-5	*O	-0.9
1925	Bos-A	148	572	84	160	38	2	6	61	63	30	.280	.356	.385	.741	93	-10	-6	95	82	81	.701	5	6	-2	14	*O	-0.6
1926	Bos-A	98	415	65	124	31	7	3	31	36	22	.299	.363	.429	.792	105	3	3	101	49	64	.754	4	6	-2	5	O	-0.1
1927	Bos-A	131	466	63	133	26	8	4	69	57	25	.285	.374	.401	.775	107	2	6	95	122	72	.796	12	0	4	7	*O	0.5
1928	Bos-A	140	510	84	148	41	4	1	39	60	23	.290	.366	.392	.758	101	1	2	98	70	75	.736	12	9	-2	-1	*O	-0.7
1929	Bos-A	14	36	9	11	2	0	0	3	5	1	.306	.390	.361	.751	93	-0	-0	102	79	5	.679	1	3	-2	-3	O	-0.4
	Was-A	18	39	5	7	1	0	0	9	4	5	.179	.256	.205	.461	20	-5	-5	100	385	3	.406	1	0	0	4	O	0.0
	Yr	32	75	14	18	3	0	0	12	9	6	.240	.321	.280	.601	56	-5	-5	100	254	7	.533	2	3	-1	1		-0.4
	Pit-N	26	50	8	14	2	1	0	6	4	2	.280	.333	.360	.693	69	-2	-2	103	114	6	.639	1			0	/O	-0.2
1930	Pit-N	44	156	21	39	7	4	2	21	17	9	.250	.324	.385	.708	73	-8	-7	97	112	20	.667	1			-4	O	-1.1
Total	13	1218	4139	644	1202	261	49	41	450	467	288	.290	.370	.407	.776	103	15	24	99	88	639	.760	71	56		32	*O/S23	-2.1
■ MARTIN FLAHERTY	Flaherty, Martin b: Worcester, Mass. BL/TL, Deb: 8/18/1881																											
1881	Wor-N	1	2	0	0	0	0	0	0	0	2	.000	.000	.000	.000	-95	-0	-0	105	0	0	.000				0	/O	0.0
■ PAT FLAHERTY	Flaherty, Patrick Henry b: 1/31/1876, St.Louis, Mo. d: 1/28/46, Chicago, Ill. 5'9", 166 lbs. Deb: 7/11/1894																											
1894	Lou-N	38	145	15	43	5	3	0	15	9	6	.297	.342	.372	.714	84	-6	-3	88	81	20	.647	2			-4	3	-0.5
■ AL FLAIR	Flair, Albert Dell "Broadway" b: 7/24/16, New Orleans, La. d: 7/25/88, New Orleans, La. BL/TL, 6'4", 195 lbs. Deb: 9/06/41																											
1941	Bos-A	10	30	3	6	2	1	0	2	1	1	.200	.226	.333	.559	45	-2	-3	103	71	2	.462	1	1	-0	0	/1	-0.2
■ CHARLIE FLANAGAN	Flanagan, Charles James b: 12/31/1891, Oakland, Cal. d: 1/8/30, San Francisco, Cal. BR/TR, 6', 175 lbs. Deb: 7/09/13																											
1913	StL-A	4	3	0	0	0	0	0	0	1	0	.000	.250	.000	.250	-27	-0	-0	95	0	0	.333	0			-0	/3O	0.0
■ ED FLANAGAN	Flanagan, Edward J. "Sleepy" b: 9/15/1861, Lowell, Mass. d: 11/10/26, Lowell, Mass. 6'1", 190 lbs. Deb: 4/16/1887																											
1887	Phi-a	19	80	12	20	5	0	1		3		.250	.286	.350	.636	79	-2	-2	99	0	9	.583	3			0	1	-0.1
1889	Lou-a	23	88	11	22	7	3	0	8	7	11	.250	.305	.398	.703	106	-0	0	96	69	11	.652	1			0	1	0.0
Total	2	42	168	23	42	12	3	1	8	10	11	.250	.296	.375	.671	93	-3	-2	97	37	20	.619	4			0	/1	-0.1
■ STEAMER FLANAGAN	Flanagan, James Paul b: 4/20/1881, Kingston, Pa. d: 4/21/47, Wilkes-Barre, Pa. 6'1", 185 lbs. Deb: 9/25/05																											
1905	Pit-N	7	25	7	7	1	1	0	3	1		.280	.308	.400	.708	108	0	0	104	106	4	.778	3			1	/O	0.0
■ JOHN FLANNERY	Flannery, John Michael b: 1/25/57, Long Beach, Cal. BR/TR, 6'3", 173 lbs. Deb: 9/02/77																											
1977	Chi-A	7	2	1	0	0	0	0	0	1	1	.000	.333	.000	.333	0	-0	-0	99	0	0	.500	0	0	0	0	/S3D	0.0
■ TIM FLANNERY	Flannery, Timothy Earl b: 9/29/57, Tulsa, Okla. BL/TR, 5'11", 175 lbs. Deb: 9/03/79																											
1979	SD-N	22	65	2	10	0	1	0	4	4	5	.154	.225	.185	.410	14	-8	-7	96	132	3	.310	0	0	0	-1	2	-0.6
1980	SD-N	95	292	15	70	12	0	0	25	18	30	.240	.284	.281	.565	62	-16	-14	93	121	23	.445	2	2	-1	1	23	-0.9
1981	SD-N	37	67	4	17	4	1	0	6	2	4	.254	.275	.343	.619	80	-2	-2	93	102	6	.510	1	0	0	-0	3/2	-0.1
1982	SD-N	122	379	40	100	11	7	0	30	30	32	.264	.321	.330	.651	90	-9	-5	92	94	42	.558	1	0	0	-22	*2/3S	-2.2
1983	SD-N	92	214	24	50	7	3	3	19	20	23	.234	.314	.336	.650	81	-6	-5	99	93	23	.582	2	2	-1	3	32/S	-0.3
1984	SD-N	86	128	24	35	3	3	2	10	12	17	.273	.350	.391	.740	109	1	2	99	70	19	.726	4	1	1	-3	23S	0.2
1985	SD-N	126	384	50	108	14	3	1	40	58	39	.281	.388	.341	.729	104	6	5	102	119	55	.702	2	5	-2	-13	*2/3	-0.9
1986	SD-N	134	368	48	103	11	2	3	28	54	61	.280	.379	.345	.724	106	3	5	95	82	50	.677	3	6	-3	-3	*23/S	0.2
1987	SD-N	106	276	23	63	5	1	0	20	42	30	.228	.334	.254	.588	61	-15	-14	97	114	25	.520	2	4	-2	2	2/3S	-1.1
1988	SD-N	79	170	16	45	5	4	0	19	24	32	.265	.369	.341	.710	108	2	3	97	131	22	.669	3	2	-0	-1	3/2S	0.2
Total	10	899	2343	246	601	72	25	9	201	264	273	.257	.340	.320	.660	87	-42	-31	96	104	267	.602	20	22	-7	-36	23/S	-5.5
■ ROY FLASKAMPER	Flaskamper, Raymond Harold "Flash" b: 10/31/01, St.Louis, Mo. d: 2/3/78, San Antonio, Tex. BB/TR, 5'7", 140 lbs. Deb: 8/16/27																											
1927	Chi-A	26	95	12	21	5	0	0	6	3	8	.221	.260	.274	.534	38	-9	-9	102	78	7	.419	0	0	0	-2	S	-0.8
■ FRANK FLEET	Fleet, Frank H. b: 1848, New York, N.Y. d: 6/13/1900, New York, N.Y. Deb: 10/18/1871																											
1871	Mut-n	1	5	1	2							.400															/P	
1872	Eck-n	13	58	10	11							.190															3/2O	
1873	Res-n	22	96	11	22							.229															/2SP31	
1874	Atl-n	20	94	18	22							.234															C/2O	
1875	StL-n	3	12	1	1							.083															/P	
	Atl-n	26	116	13	25							.216															2C/SP	
	Yr	29	128	14	26							.203																
Total	5 n	85	381	54	83							.218															2C/SP	
■ ANGEL FLEITAS	Fleitas, Angel Felix Husta b: 11/10/14, Los Abreus, Cuba BR/TR, 5'9", 160 lbs. Deb: 7/05/48																											
1948	Was-A	15	13	1	1	0	0	0	1	3	5	.077	.250	.077	.327	-10	-2	-2	103	338	0	.286	0	2	-1	-1	/S	-0.3
■ LES FLEMING	Fleming, Leslie Harvey "Moe" b: 8/7/15, Singleton, Tex. d: 3/5/80, Cleveland, Tex. BL/TL, 5'10", 185 lbs. Deb: 4/22/39																											
1939	Det-A	8	16	0	0	0	0	0	1	0	4	.000	.000	.000	.000	-90	-5	-5	111	0	0	.000	0	0	0	-0	/O	-0.4
1941	Cle-A	2	8	0	2	1	0	0	2	0	0	.250	.250	.375	.625	63	-0	-0	101	241	1	.500	0	0	0	0	/1	0.0
1942	Cle-A	156	548	71	160	27	4	14	82	106	57	.292	.412	.432	.845	150	32	38	92	110	105	.868	6	8	-3	-9	*1	2.4
1945	Cle-A	42	140	18	46	10	2	3	22	11	5	.329	.382	.493	.874	155	9	9	99	102	27	.835	0	0	0	-3	O/1	0.5
1946	Cle-A	99	306	40	85	17	5	8	42	50	42	.278	.383	.444	.827	147	14	18	89	100	55	.825	1	0	0	3	1/O	1.7
1947	Cle-A	103	281	39	68	14	2	4	43	53	42	.242	.362	.349	.711	102	1	2	96	144	40	.689	0	0	0	1	1	0.1
1949	Pit-N	24	31	0	8	0	2	0	7	6	2	.258	.395	.387	.782	110	1	1	101	220	5	.826	0			0	/1	0.1
Total	7	434	1330	168	369	69	15	29	199	226	152	.277	.386	.417	.804	135	51	63	93	116	232	.824	7	8		-8	1/O	4.4
■ TOM FLEMING	Fleming, Thomas Vincent "Sleuth" b: 11/20/1873, Philadelphia, Pa. d: 12/26/57, Boston, Mass. BL , 5'11", 155 lbs. Deb: 9/19/1899																											
1899	NY-N	22	77	9	16	1	1	0	4	1		.208	.218	.247	.465	30	-7	-7	97	65	4	.344	1			0	O	-0.6
1902	Phi-N	5	16	2	6	0	0	0	2	1		.375	.412	.375	.787	138	1	1	105	115	3	.700	0			-0	/O	0.0
1904	Phi-N	3	6	0	0	0	0	0	0	0		.000	.000	.000	.000	-99	-1	-1	93	0	0	.000	0			0	/O	0.0
Total	3	30	99	11	22	1	1	0	6	2		.222	.238	.253	.490	40	-8	-8	98	69	7	.364	1			-0	/O	-0.6
■ FLETCHER	Fletcher Deb:6/21/1872																											
1872	Eck-n	2	8	1	2							.250															/O	
■ ART FLETCHER	Fletcher, Arthur b: 1/5/1885, Collinsville, Ill. d: 2/6/50, Los Angeles, Cal. BR/TR, 5'10.5", 170 lbs. Deb: 09 C																											
1909	NY-N	29	98	7	21	0	1	0	6	1		.214	.238	.235	.472	45	-6	-7	105	95	5	.338	0			0	S/23	-0.6
1910	NY-N	51	125	12	28	2	1	0	13	4	9	.224	.248	.256	.504	49	-9	-8	95	142	10	.464	9			-0	S23	-0.7
1911	NY-N	112	326	73	104	17	8	1	37	30	27	.319	.400	.429	.829	129	15	14	102	87	64	.919	20			2	S32	1.9

YEAR	TM/L	G	AB	R	H	2B	3B	HR	RBI	BB	SO	AVG	OBP	SLG	PRO	/A	BR	/A	PF	CHI	RC	TA	SB	CS	SBR	FR	POS	TPR
1912	NY-N	129	419	64	118	17	9	1	57	16	29	.282	.330	.372	.702	88	-6	-8	104	121	56	.671	16			6	*S/23	1.0
1913	NY-N	136	538	76	160	20	9	4	71	24	35	.297	.345	.390	.735	107	6	4	103	112	80	.743	32			-12	*S	0.1
1914	NY-N	135	514	62	147	26	8	2	79	22	37	.286	.332	.379	.711	116	6	8	96	**151**	68	.668	15			4	*S	1.8
1915	NY-N	149	562	59	143	17	7	3	74	6	36	.254	.280	.326	.606	91	-13	-8	91	**156**	50	.492	12	18	-7	**33**	*S	2.3
1916	NY-N	133	500	53	143	23	8	3	66	13	36	.286	.323	.382	.705	121	8	10	96	139	68	.653	15			21	*S	**4.3**
1917	NY-N	151	557	70	145	24	5	4	56	23	28	.260	.312	.343	.655	104	0	2	97	113	60	.595	12			25	*S	3.2
1918	NY-N	124	468	51	123	20	2	0	47	18	26	.263	.311	.314	.625	93	-5	-4	98	128	48	.557	12			**22**	*S	2.3
1919	NY-N	127	488	54	135	20	5	3	54	9	28	.277	.300	.357	.656	97	-3	-3	100	122	52	.555	6			27	*S	3.1
1920	NY-N	41	171	21	44	7	2	0	24	1	15	.257	.282	.322	.604	74	-6	-6	100	149	15	.496	3	2	-0	7	S	0.3
	Phi-N	102	379	36	112	25	7	4	38	15	28	.296	.329	.430	.759	108	7	3	109	86	52	.681	4	6	-2	13	*S	2.0
	Yr	143	550	57	156	32	9	4	62	16	43	.284	.315	.396	.711	97	1	-3	106	105	66	.622	7	8	-3	20		2.3
1922	Phi-N	110	396	46	111	20	5	7	53	21	14	.280	.325	.409	.734	78	-8	-16	113	101	53	.666	3	2	-0	9	*S	0.0
Total	13	1529	5541	684	1534	238	77	32	675	203	348	.277	.319	.365	.684	99	-14	-17	100	123	680	.626	159	28		155	*S/32	21.0
■ **ELBIE FLETCHER** Fletcher, Elburt Preston b: 3/18/16, Milton, Mass. BL/TL, 6', 180 lbs. Deb: 9/16/34																												
1934	Bos-N	8	4	4	2	0	0	0	0	0	2	.500	.500	.500	1.000	197	0	0	86	0	1	1.500	1			0	/1	0.0
1935	Bos-N	39	148	12	35	7	1	1	9	7	13	.236	.271	.318	.589	60	-9	-8	96	66	13	.474	1			0	1	-0.7
1937	Bos-N	148	539	56	133	22	4	1	38	56	64	.247	.321	.308	.629	79	-20	-13	90	86	56	.543	3			-0	*1	-2.1
1938	Bos-N	147	529	71	144	24	7	6	48	60	40	.272	.351	.378	.729	114	1	10	88	81	73	.676	5			7	*1	0.4
1939	Bos-N	35	106	14	26	2	0	0	6	19	5	.245	.365	.264	.629	78	-3	-2	92	79	12	.605	1			1	1	-0.3
	Pit-N	102	370	49	112	23	4	12	71	48	28	.303	.386	.484	.869	133	17	17	100	128	69	.862	3			-5	*1	0.0
	Yr	137	476	63	138	25	4	12	77	67	33	.290	.381	.435	.816	122	14	16	98	116	82	.805	4			-4		-0.3
1940	Pit-N	147	510	94	139	22	7	16	104	**119**	54	.273	**.418**	.437	.856	143	32	35	95	151	103	.930	5			5	*1	2.7
1941	Pit-N	151	521	95	150	29	13	11	74	**118**	54	.288	**.421**	.457	.878	143	38	36	103	104	111	.965	5			9	*1	2.5
1942	Pit-N	145	506	86	146	22	5	7	57	105	60	.289	**.417**	.393	.810	136	30	30	101	102	94	.852	0			11	*1	3.1
1943	Pit-N	154	544	91	154	24	5	9	70	95	49	.283	.395	.395	.791	123	24	21	104	111	91	.789	1			2	*1	1.7
1946	Pit-N	148	532	72	136	25	8	4	66	111	37	.256	.384	.355	.739	107	12	10	103	118	82	.754	4			1	*1	-0.1
1947	Pit-N	69	157	22	38	9	1	1	22	29	24	.242	.364	.331	.695	85	-2	-2	101	148	20	.677	2			0	1	-0.4
1949	Bos-N	122	413	57	108	19	3	11	51	84	65	.262	.396	.402	.798	118	12	14	97	102	72	.822	1			0	*1	1.4
Total	12	1415	4879	723	1323	228	58	79	616	851	495	.271	.384	.390	.774	118	133	149	98	108	796	.793	32			30	*1	8.2
■ **FRANK FLETCHER** Fletcher, Oliver Frank b: 3/6/1891, Hildreth, Ill. d: 10/7/74, St.Petersburg, Fla. BR/TR, 5'10", 165 lbs. Deb: 7/14/14																												
1914	Phi-N	1	1	0	0	0	0	0	0	0	1	.000	.000	.000	.000	-99	-0	-0	100	0	0	.000	0			0	H	0.0
■ **SCOTT FLETCHER** Fletcher, Scott Brian b: 7/30/58, Fort Walton Beach Fla. BR/TR, 5'11", 168 lbs. Deb: 4/25/81																												
1981	Chi-N	19	46	6	10	4	0	0	1	2	4	.217	.250	.304	.554	54	-3	-3	104	28	4	.444	0	0	0	2	2/S3	0.1
1982	Chi-N	11	24	4	4	0	0	0	1	4	5	.167	.286	.167	.452	28	-2	-2	103	98	2	.450	1	0	0	-1	S	-0.2
1983	Chi-A	114	262	42	62	16	5	3	31	29	22	.237	.317	.370	.688	86	-4	-5	103	114	31	.636	5	1	1	7	*S2/3D	0.9
1984	Chi-A	149	456	46	114	13	3	3	35	46	46	.250	.329	.311	.641	71	-12	-18	111	92	51	.587	10	4	1	16	*S2/3	1.0
1985	Chi-A	119	301	38	77	8	1	2	31	35	47	.256	.333	.309	.642	77	-8	-8	100	124	31	.559	5	5	-2	5	3S2/D	-0.2
1986	Tex-A	147	530	82	159	34	5	3	50	47	59	.300	.361	.400	.761	113	7	10	96	92	76	.702	12	11	-3	2	*S32/D	1.6
1987	Tex-A	156	588	82	169	28	4	5	63	61	66	.287	.359	.374	.733	93	-1	-4	104	113	78	.672	13	12	-3	9	*S	0.8
1988	Tex-A	140	515	59	142	19	4	0	47	62	34	.276	.367	.328	.695	95	0	-0	101	117	66	.642	8	5	-1	8	*S/C	1.3
Total	8	855	2722	359	737	122	22	16	259	286	283	.271	.347	.349	.696	90	-23	-31	102	106	339	.649	54	38	-7	48	S2/3DC	5.3
■ **ELMER FLICK** Flick, Elmer Harrison b: 1/11/1876, Bedford, Ohio d: 1/9/71, Bedford, Ohio BL/TR, 5'9", 168 lbs. Deb: 5/02/1898 H																												
1898	Phi-N	134	453	84	137	16	13	8	81	86		.302	.424	.448	.873	162	36	40	95	114	98	1.019	23			7	*O	3.5
1899	Phi-N	127	485	98	166	22	11	2	98	42		.342	.405	.445	.850	140	25	27	97	143	102	.934	31			7	*O	2.3
1900	Phi-N	138	545	106	200	32	16	11	**110**	56		.367	.426	.545	.971	**173**	51	**52**	98	110	145	1.125	35			7	*O	4.2
1901	Phi-N	138	540	112	180	32	17	8	88	52		.333	.392	.500	.892	156	40	38	103	96	121	.978	30			17	*O	3.9
1902	Phi-A	11	37	15	11	2	1	0	3	6		.297	.395	.405	.801	115	1	1	108	67	8	.962	4			0	O	0.0
	Cle-A	110	424	70	126	20	11	2	61	47		.297	.367	.410	.778	121	11	13	97	118	73	.809	20			-12	*O	-0.5
	Yr	121	461	85	137	22	12	2	64	53		.297	.370	.410	.780	120	12	14	98	114	81	.821	24			-12		-0.5
1903	Cle-A	140	523	81	155	23	16	2	51	51		.296	.359	.413	.772	138	22	24	96	88	88	.791	24			2	*O	1.7
1904	Cle-A	150	579	97	177	31	17	6	56	51		.306	.362	.449	.811	156	36	37	102	66	111	.868	**38**			9	*O/2	4.0
1905	Cle-A	132	500	72	154	29	**18**	4	65	53		**.308**	.374	**.462**	**.836**	**168**	**38**	**38**	100	84	**102**	**.922**	35			-4	*O/2	3.0
1906	Cle-A	157	624	**98**	194	33	**22**	1	62	54		.311	.366	.439	.805	149	38	35	103	72	117	.853	**39**			-1	*O/2	3.1
1907	Cle-A	147	549	78	166	15	**18**	3	58	64		.302	.375	.412	.787	164	34	38	93	76	103	.864	41			2	*O	3.5
1908	Cle-A	9	35	4	8	1	1	0	2	3		.229	.289	.314	.604	93	-0	-0	106	59	3	.519	0			0	/O	0.0
1909	Cle-A	66	235	28	60	10	2	0	15	22		.255	.322	.315	.637	99	1	0	102	83	26	.606	9			2	O	0.0
1910	Cle-A	24	68	5	18	2	1	1	7	10		.265	.359	.368	.727	128	2	2	100	92	9	.720	1			-4	O	-0.2
Total	13	1483	5597	948	1752	268	164	48	757	597		.313	.381	.445	.826	150	335	345	99	94	1106	.894	330			32	*O/2	28.5
■ **LEW FLICK** Flick, Lewis Miller "Noisy" b: 2/18/15, Bristol, Tenn. BL/TL, 5'9", 155 lbs. Deb: 9/28/43																												
1943	Phi-A	1	5	2	3	0	0	0	0	0	0	.600	.600	.600	1.200	248	1	1	101	0	2	1.500	0	0	0	0	/O	0.1
1944	Phi-A	19	35	1	4	0	0	0	2	1	2	.114	.139	.114	.253	-27	-6	-6	101	180	0	.176	1	0	0	-1	/O	-0.6
Total	2	20	40	3	7	0	0	0	2	1	2	.175	.195	.175	.370	6	-5	-5	101	158	2	.250	1	0	0	-1	/O	-0.5
■ **DON FLINN** Flinn, Don Raphael b: 11/17/1892, Bluffdale, Tex. d: 3/9/59, Waco, Tex. BR/TR, 6'1", 185 lbs. Deb: 9/02/17																												
1917	Pit-N	14	37	1	11	1	1	0	1	1	6	.297	.316	.378	.694	113	0	0	100	28	4	.615	1			-0	O	0.0
■ **SILVER FLINT** Flint, Frank Sylvester b: 8/3/1855, Philadelphia, Pa. d: 1/14/1892, Chicago, Ill. BR/TR, 6', 180 lbs. Deb: 5/04/1875 M																												
1875	RS-n	16	58	3	5							.086															C/3	
1878	Ind-N	63	254	23	57	7	0	0	18	2	15	.224	.230	.252	.482	67	-11	-6	87	101	15	.335				3	*C/O	0.0
1879	Chi-N	79	324	46	92	22	6	1	41	6	44	.284	.297	.398	.695	121	9	7	105	115	39	.582				3	*C/OM	0.8
1880	Chi-N	74	284	30	46	10	4	0	17	5	32	.162	.176	.225	.402	33	-18	-20	105	99	12	.290				2	*CO	-1.2
1881	Chi-N	80	306	46	95	18	0	1	34	6	39	.310	.324	.379	.703	111	6	3	108	101	38	.578				-14	*C/O1	-1.0
1882	Chi-N	81	331	48	83	18	8	4	44	2	50	.251	.255	.390	.645	102	1	0	101	107	34	.528				-5	*CO	0.1
1883	Chi-N	85	332	57	88	23	4	0	32	3	69	.265	.272	.358	.630	82	-4	-9	109	95	33	.500				-9	*CO	-1.2
1884	Chi-N	73	279	35	57	5	2	9	45	7	57	.204	.224	.333	.557	67	-9	-12	108	129	21	.450				-8	C	-1.2
1885	Chi-N	68	249	27	52	8	2	1	17	2	52	.209	.215	.269	.484	49	-12	-17	114	84	15	.350				2	C/O	-0.7
1886	Chi-N	54	173	30	35	6	2	1	13	12	36	.202	.254	.277	.532	53	-8	-12	116	83	13	.442	1			-3	C/1	-0.9
1887	Chi-N	49	187	22	50	8	6	3	21	4	28	.267	.283	.422	.705	82	-2	-7	116	75	25	.657	7			-1	C/1	-0.1
1888	Chi-N	22	77	6	14	3	0	0	3	1	21	.182	.203	.221	.423	34	-5	-6	107	63	4	.317	1			0	C	-0.5
1889	Chi-N	15	56	6	13	1	0	1	9	3	18	.232	.271	.304	.575	62	-3	-3	99	134	5	.488	1			0	C	-0.1
Total	12	743	2852	376	682	129	34	21	294	53	461	.239	.253	.330	.584	78	-57	-83	106	101	254	.464	10			-30	C/O13	-6.0
■ **CURT FLOOD** Flood, Curtis Charles b: 1/18/38, Houston, Tex. BR/TR, 5'9", 165 lbs. Deb: 9/09/56																												
1956	Cin-N	5	1	0	0	0	0	0	0	0	1	.000	.000	.000	.000	-92	-0	-0	108	0	0	.000	0	0	0	0	H	0.0
1957	Cin-N	3	3	2	1	0	0	1	1	0	0	.333	.333	1.333	1.667	304	1	1	105	59	1	2.000	0	0	0	0	/32	0.1
1958	StL-N	121	422	50	110	17	2	10	41	31	56	.261	.317	.382	.699	79	-10	-13	106	90	44	.581	2	12	-7	14	*O/3	-0.9
1959	StL-N	121	208	24	53	7	3	7	26	16	35	.255	.308	.418	.726	87	-3	-4	105	97	26	.648	2	1	0	-13	*O/2	-1.9
1960	StL-N	140	396	37	94	20	1	8	38	35	54	.237	.306	.354	.659	74	-11	-15	108	94	41	.565	0	3	-2	-5	*O/3	-2.7
1961	StL-N	132	335	53	108	15	5	2	21	35	33	.322	.391	.415	.806	101	8	2	113	58	56	.779	6	2	1	-3	*O	-0.6
1962	StL-N	151	635	99	188	30	5	12	70	42	57	.296	.349	.416	.765	96	4	-3	109	79	92	.698	8	6	-1	10	*O	-0.2
1963	StL-N	158	662	112	200	34	9	5	63	42	57	.302	.346	.403	.749	107	12	7	107	90	92	.685	17	12	-2	10	*O	0.7
1964	StL-N	162	679	97	**211**	25	3	5	46	43	53	.311	.356	.378	.735	95	7	-3	112	61	90	.641	8	11	-4	7	*O	-0.4
1965	StL-N	156	617	90	191	30	3	11	83	51	50	.310	.368	.421	.789	114	18	14	107	113	97	.743	9	3	1	2	*O	1.2

YEAR	TM/L	G	AB	R	H	2B	3B	HR	RBI	BB	SO	AVG	OBP	SLG	PRO	/A	BR	/A	PF	CHI	RC	TA	SB	CS	SBR	FR	POS	TPR
1966	StL-N	160	626	64	167	21	5	10	78	26	50	.267	.300	.364	.665	84	-14	-14	100	135	67	.570	14	7	0	2	*O	-1.7
1967	StL-N	134	514	68	172	24	1	5	50	37	46	.335	.382	.414	.796	126	19	18	101	96	82	.722	2	2	-1	6	*O	1.9
1968	StL-N	150	618	71	186	17	4	5	60	33	58	.301	.341	.366	.707	118	9	12	95	93	78	.617	11	6	-0	13	*O	1.9
1969	StL-N	153	606	80	173	31	3	4	57	48	57	.285	.345	.366	.711	100	0	0	100	94	76	.631	9	7	-2	10	*O	0.0
1971	Was-A	13	35	4	7	0	0	0	2	5	2	.200	.300	.200	.500	48	-2	-2	92	117	2	.400	0	1	-1	-1	O	-0.4
Total	15	1759	6357	851	1861	271	44	85	636	444	609	.293	.344	.389	.733	99	38	-1	105	92	844	.669	88	73	-17	50	*O/32	-3.0
■ **TIM FLOOD** Flood, Timothy A. b: 3/13/1877, Montgomery City, Mo. d: 6/15/29, St.Loius, Mo. BR/TR, Deb: 9/24/1899																												
1899	StL-N	10	31	0	9	0	0	0	3	4		.290	.371	.290	.662	79	-0	-1	108	102	4	.636	1			0	2	0.0
1902	Bro-N	132	476	43	104	11	4	3	51	23		.218	.255	.277	.532	69	-19	-17	95	128	37	.438	8			-15	*2/O	-2.4
1903	Bro-N	89	309	27	77	15	2	0	32	15		.249	.284	.311	.595	70	-12	-12	101	109	32	.539	14			-16	2/SO	-2.2
Total	3	231	816	70	190	26	6	3	86	42		.233	.270	.290	.561	70	-32	-30	98	120	72	.482	23			-31	2/SO	-4.6
■ **PAUL FLORENCE** Florence, Paul Robert "Pep" b: 4/22/1900, Chicago, Ill. d: 5/28/86, Gainesville, Fla. BB/TR, 6'1", 185 lbs. Deb: 5/22/26																												
1926	NY-N	76	188	19	43	4	3	2	14	23	12	.229	.322	.314	.636	73	-7	-6	98	74	20	.600	2			-10	C	-1.3
■ **GIL FLORES** Flores, Gilberto (Garcia) b: 10/27/52, Ponce, P.R. BR/TR, 6', 185 lbs. Deb: 5/08/77																												
1977	Cal-A	104	342	41	95	19	4	1	26	23	39	.278	.325	.365	.691	93	-6	-3	95	80	36	.596	12	10	-2	-6	O/D	-1.4
1978	NY-N	11	29	8	8	0	1	0	1	3	5	.276	.344	.345	.689	95	-0	-0	98	40	4	.667	1	0	0	-0	/O	0.0
1979	NY-N	70	93	9	18	1	1	1	10	8	17	.194	.265	.258	.523	46	-7	-7	95	147	7	.461	2	0	1	-6	O	-1.3
Total	3	185	464	58	121	20	6	2	37	34	61	.261	.314	.343	.657	83	-13	-10	95	91	47	.593	15	10	-2	-13	O/D	-2.7
■ **DICKIE FLOWERS** Flowers, Charles Richard b: 1850, Philadelphia, Pa. d: 10/5/1892, Philadelphia, Pa. Deb: 6/03/1871																												
1871	Tro-n	21	109	40	33							.303															*S/2	
1872	Ath-n	3	17	1	4							.235															/S	
Total	2 n	24	126	41	37							.294															/S	
■ **JAKE FLOWERS** Flowers, D'Arcy Raymond b: 3/16/02, Cambridge, Md. d: 12/27/62, Clearwater, Fla. BR/TR, 5'11.5", 170 lbs. Deb: 9/07/23 C																												
1923	StL-N	13	32	0	3	1	0	0	2	2	7	.094	.147	.125	.272	-31	-6	-5	90	176	0	.226	1	2	-1	-1	/S23	-0.5
1926	StL-N	40	74	13	20	1	0	3	9	5	9	.270	.325	.405	.730	93	-1	-1	102	80	10	.685	1			-2	2/1S	-0.2
1927	Bro-N	67	231	26	54	5	5	2	20	21	25	.234	.300	.325	.625	66	-11	-12	103	88	23	.565	3			-5	S/2	-0.9
1928	Bro-N	103	339	51	93	11	6	2	44	47	30	.274	.366	.360	.726	91	-3	-3	99	125	47	.736	10			-5	2/S	-0.5
1929	Bro-N	46	130	16	26	6	0	1	16	22	6	.200	.316	.269	.585	49	-11	-9	94	144	12	.635	9			-7	2	-1.3
1930	Bro-N	89	253	37	81	18	3	2	50	21	18	.320	.372	.439	.811	95	-2	-2	101	147	40	.797	5			-4	2/O	0.1
1931	Bro-N	22	31	3	7	0	0	0	1	7	4	.226	.368	.226	.594	62	-1	-1	101	51	3	.625	1			0	/2S	0.0
	StL-N	45	137	19	34	11	1	2	19	9	6	.248	.295	.387	.681	77	-4	-5	107	115	16	.670	7			3	S2/3	0.1
	Yr	67	168	22	41	11	1	2	20	16	10	.244	.310	.357	.667	75	-5	-6	105	94	19	.661	8			3		0.1
1932	StL-N	67	247	35	63	11	1	2	18	31	18	.255	.341	.332	.672	82	-5	-5	100	81	30	.658	7			-2	3/S2	-0.1
1933	Bro-N	78	210	28	49	11	2	2	22	24	15	.233	.312	.333	.645	87	-4	-3	97	109	23	.645	13			-6	S2/3O	-0.5
1934	Cin-N	13	9	1	3	0	0	0	0	1	1	.333	.455	.333	.788	114	0	0	101	0	2	1.000	1			0	H	0.0
Total	10	583	1693	229	433	75	18	16	201	190	139	.256	.333	.350	.683	80	-47	-46	100	112	206	.670	58	2		-28	2S/310	-3.8
■ **BUBBA FLOYD** Floyd, Leslie Roe b: 6/23/17, Dallas, Tex. BR/TR, 5'11", 160 lbs. Deb: 6/16/44																												
1944	Det-A	3	9	1	4	1	0	0	0	1	0	.444	.500	.556	1.056	191	1	1	105	0	3	1.200	0	0	0	0	/S	0.1
■ **BOBBY FLOYD** Floyd, Robert Nathan b: 10/20/43, Hawthorne, Cal. BR/TR, 6'1", 180 lbs. Deb: 9/18/68																												
1968	Bal-A	5	9	0	1	1	0	0	1	0	3	.111	.111	.222	.333	-1	-1	-1	102	214	0	.250	0	0	0	0	/S	0.0
1969	Bal-A	39	84	7	17	4	0	0	1	6	17	.202	.256	.250	.506	40	-7	-7	104	19	5	.380	0	0	0	-1	2S/3	-0.6
1970	Bal-A	3	2	0	0	0	0	0	0	0	2	.000	.000	.000	.000	-99	-1	-1	97	0	0	.000	0	0	0	0	/S2	0.0
	KC-A	14	43	5	14	4	0	0	9	4	9	.326	.383	.419	.802	123	1	1	98	202	7	.733	0	1	-1	-1	/S3	0.1
	Yr	17	45	5	14	4	0	0	9	4	11	.311	.367	.400	.767	114	1	1	98	167	7	.688	0	1	-1	-1		0.1
1971	KC-A	31	66	8	10	3	0	0	2	7	21	.152	.233	.197	.430	23	-7	-7	99	63	3	.357	0	0	0	1	S/23	-0.3
1972	KC-A	61	134	9	24	3	0	0	5	5	29	.179	.209	.201	.410	22	-13	-13	100	77	5	.289	1	0	0	-0	3S/2	-0.9
1973	KC-A	51	78	10	26	3	1	0	8	4	14	.333	.366	.397	.763	105	1	1	109	101	10	.643	1	1	-0	5	2S	0.9
1974	KC-A	10	9	1	1	0	0	0	0	2	4	.111	.273	.111	.384	13	-1	-1	106	0	0	.375	0	0	0	0	/23S	0.0
Total	7	214	425	40	93	18	1	0	26	28	99	.219	.267	.266	.533	52	-26	-27	102	81	32	.428	2	2	-1	4	/S23	-0.8
■ **JOHN FLUHRER** Fluhrer, John L. (Also Played Under Name Of Wm. G. Morris 1 Game In 1915) b: 1/3/1894, Adrian, Mich. d: 7/17/46, Columbus, Ohio BR/TR, 5'9", 165 lbs. Deb: 9/05/15																												
1915	Chi-N	6	6	0	2	0	0	0	0	1	0	.333	.429	.333	.762	129	0	0	102	0	1	1.000	1			-1	/O	0.0
■ **ED FLYNN** Flynn, Edward J. b: 1864, Chicago, Ill. BL, 5'9", 165 lbs. Deb: 5/05/1887																												
1887	Cle-a	7	27	0	5	1	0	0		1		.185	.214	.222	.437	24	-3	-3	98	0	2	.455	3			0	/3O	-0.1
■ **GEORGE FLYNN** Flynn, George A. "Dibby" b: 5/24/1871, Chicago, Ill. d: 12/28/01, Chicago, Ill. Deb: 4/17/1896																												
1896	Chi-N	29	106	15	27	1	2	0	4	11	9	.255	.336	.302	.638	65	-4	-6	108	37	15	.722	12			0	O	-0.4
■ **JOHN FLYNN** Flynn, John Anthony b: 9/7/1883, Providence, R.I. d: 3/23/35, Providence, R.I. BR/TR, 6'0.5", 175 lbs. Deb: 4/22/10																												
1910	Pit-N	96	332	32	91	10	2	6	52	30	47	.274	.336	.370	.707	95	2	-3	112	131	44	.664	6			1	1	-0.2
1911	Pit-N	33	59	5	12	0	1	0	3	9	8	.203	.309	.237	.546	53	-3	-3	101	72	4	.489	0			-1	1/O	-0.4
1912	Was-A	20	71	9	12	4	1	0	5	7		.169	.253	.254	.507	45	-5	-5	99	94	5	.475	2			0	1	-0.4
Total	3	149	462	46	115	14	4	6	60	46	55	.249	.320	.335	.655	83	-7	-12	108	118	53	.608	8			1	1/O	-1.0
■ **JOE FLYNN** Flynn, Joseph b: Philadelphia, Pa. Deb: 4/18/1884																												
1884	Phi-U	52	209	38	52	9	4	4		11		.249	.286	.388	.674	136	6	8	93	0	24	.586	0			-5	OC/1S	0.2
	Bos-U	9	31	4	7	2	0	0		2		.226	.273	.290	.563	92	-0	-0	98	0	3	.458	0			0	/CO1	0.0
	Yr	61	240	42	59	11	4	4		13		.246	.285	.375	.660	130	5	8	93	0	26	.569	0			-5		0.2
Total	1	61	240	42	59	11	4	4		13		.246	.285	.375	.660	130	5	8	93	0	26	.569	0			-5	/OC1S	0.2
■ **MIKE FLYNN** Flynn, Michael E. b: Lowell, Mass. Deb: 8/31/1891																												
1891	Bos-a	1	2	0	0	0	0	0	0	0	1	.000	.000	.000	.000	-99	-1	-0	99	0	0	.000	0			0	/C	0.0
■ **DOUG FLYNN** Flynn, Robert Douglas b: 4/18/51, Lexington, Ky. BR/TR, 5'11", 165 lbs. Deb: 4/09/75																												
1975	Cin-N	89	127	17	34	7	0	1	20	11	13	.268	.326	.346	.673	83	-2	-3	104	165	14	.592	3	0	1	1	32S	0.2
1976	Cin-N	93	219	20	62	5	2	1	20	10	24	.283	.314	.338	.652	83	-4	-5	103	100	24	.538	2	0	1	-3	23S	-0.3
1977	Cin-N	36	32	0	8	1	1	0	5	0	6	.250	.250	.344	.594	57	-2	-2	100	182	3	.458	0	0	0	-1	3/2S	-0.1
	NY-N	90	282	14	54	6	1	0	14	11	23	.191	.222	.220	.442	20	-32	-31	96	90	13	.315	1	3	-2	-11	S2/3	-3.3
	Yr	126	314	14	62	7	2	0	19	11	29	.197	.225	.232	.457	24	-34	-33	97	118	16	.328	1	3	-2	-12		-3.4
1978	NY-N	156	532	37	126	12	8	0	36	30	50	.237	.279	.289	.568	60	-29	-28	98	93	40	.442	3	5	-2	-4	*2S	-2.2
1979	NY-N	157	555	35	135	19	5	4	61	17	46	.243	.266	.317	.583	61	-33	-29	95	129	42	.441	0	3	-2	-7	*2S	-2.7
1980	NY-N	128	443	46	113	9	8	0	24	22	20	.255	.290	.312	.602	71	-19	-17	96	69	36	.467	2	2	-1	-3	*2/S	-1.2
1981	NY-N	105	325	24	72	12	4	1	20	11	19	.222	.247	.292	.539	52	-21	-21	101	80	20	.401	1	2	-1	6	*2/S	-0.8
1982	Tex-A	88	270	13	57	6	2	0	19	4	14	.211	.223	.248	.471	31	-26	-24	93	113	15	.353	6	2	1	2	2S	-1.5
	Mon-N	58	193	13	47	6	2	0	20	4	23	.244	.259	.295	.554	52	-12	-13	105	138	13	.396	0	2	-1	-5	2	-1.6
1983	Mon-N	143	452	44	107	18	4	0	26	19	38	.237	.268	.294	.562	55	-28	-28	102	77	33	.430	2	1	0	-11	*2S	-3.4
1984	Mon-N	124	366	23	89	12	1	0	17	12	41	.243	.267	.281	.549	59	-22	-19	91	65	27	.408	0	0	0	-17	2S	-3.1
1985	Mon-N	9	6	0	1	0	0	0	0	0	0	.167	.167	.167	.333	-7	-1	-1	94	0	0	.200	0	0	0	0	/2S	0.0
	Det-A	32	51	2	13	2	1	0	2	0	3	.255	.255	.333	.588	56	-3	-3	106	47	4	.436	0	0	0	-1	2/S3	-0.2
Total	11	1308	3853	288	918	115	39	7	284	151	320	.238	.267	.294	.561	57	-234	-225	98	96	285	.441	20	20	-6	-54	2S/3	-20.2
■ **CLIPPER FLYNN** Flynn, William b: 4/29/1849, Lansingburgh, N.Y. d: 11/11/1881, Lansingburgh, N.Y. 5'7", 140 lbs. Deb: 5/09/1871																												
1871	Tro-n	29	148	44	46							.311															1/O3	
1872	Oly-n	9	41	4	9							.220															/1	

YEAR	TM/L	G	AB	R	H	2B	3B	HR	RBI	BB	SO	AVG	OBP	SLG	PRO	/A	BR	/A	PF	CHI	RC	TA	SB	CS	SBR	FR	POS	TPR
Total	2 n	38	189	48	55							.291															/1	
■ **JIM FOGARTY**	Fogarty, James G. b: 2/12/1864, San Francisco, Cal d: 5/20/1891, Philadelphia, Pa. BR , 5'10.5", 180 lbs. Deb: 5/01/1884 M																											
1884	Phi-N	97	378	42	80	12	6	1	37	20	54	.212	.251	.283	.534	74	-14	-9	92	123	28	.426				6	*O3/2SP	-0.2
1885	Phi-N	111	427	49	99	13	3	0	39	30	37	.232	.282	.276	.559	78	-8	-10	104	111	34	.451				19	*O2/S3	0.6
1886	Phi-N	77	280	54	82	13	5	3	47	42	16	.293	.385	.407	.792	144	15	16	98	120	57	.939	30			2	O2/S3P	1.7
1887	Phi-N	126	495	113	129	26	12	8	50	**82**	44	.261	.376	.410	.787	125	17	20	97	60	118	1.085	102			29	*O/S32P	4.1
1888	Phi-N	121	454	72	107	14	6	1	35	53	66	.236	.325	.300	.624	90	4	-5	114	87	65	.732	58			14	*O/3S	0.7
1889	Phi-N	128	499	107	129	15	17	3	54	65	60	.259	.352	.375	.727	100	4	1	104	87	103	.968	**99**			17	*O/P	1.1
1890	Phi-P	91	347	71	83	17	6	4	58	59	50	.239	.364	.357	.721	93	-1	-2	102	124	60	.864	36			9	O/3M	0.2
Total	7	751	2880	508	709	110	55	20	320	351	327	.246	.335	.343	.678	100	18	10	102	98	464	.782	325			95	O/32SP	8.2
■ **JOE FOGARTY**	Fogarty, Joseph J. b: San Francisco, Cal. Deb: 1885																											
1885	StL-N	2	8	1	1	0	0	0	0	0	1	.125	.125	.125	.250	-21	-1	-1	92	0	0	.143				0	/O	0.0
■ **LEE FOHL**	Fohl, Leo Alexander b: 11/28/1876, Lowell, Ohio d: 10/30/65, Cleveland, Ohio BL/TR, 5'10", 175 lbs. Deb: 8/29/02 M																											
1902	Pit-N	1	3	0	0	0	0	0	1	0		.000	.000	.000	.000	-95	-1	-1	105	0	0	.000	0			0	/C	0.0
1903	Cin-N	4	14	3	5	1	1	0	2	0		.357	.357	.571	.929	151	1	1	109	80	3	.889	0			-0	/C	0.1
Total	2	5	17	3	5	1	1	0	3	0		.294	.294	.471	.765	112	0	0	108	66	3	.667	0			-0	/C	0.1
■ **HANK FOILES**	Foiles, Henry Lee b: 6/10/29, Richmond, Va. BR/TR, 6', 195 lbs. Deb: 4/21/53																											
1953	Cin-N	5	13	1	2	0	0	0	0	1	2	.154	.214	.154	.368	-2	-2	-2	99	0	0	.273	0	0	0	0	/C	-0.1
	Cle-A	7	7	2	1	0	0	0	0	1	1	.143	.250	.143	.393	9	-1	-1	95	0	0	.333	0	0	0	-0	/C	0.0
1955	Cle-A	62	111	13	29	9	0	1	7	17	18	.261	.359	.369	.729	93	-0	-1	104	59	15	.674	0	0	0	-6	C	-0.4
1956	Cle-A	1	0	0	0	0	0	0	0	0	0	—	—	—	—	—	0	0	101	—	—	—	0	0	0	0	/C	0.0
	Pit-N	79	222	24	47	10	2	7	25	17	56	.212	.268	.369	.637	68	-10	-11	102	103	21	.547	0	1	-1	-3	C	-1.3
1957	Pit-N	109	281	32	76	10	4	9	36	37	53	.270	.355	.431	.786	117	4	7	94	101	43	.746	1	3	-2	-10	*C	0.1
1958	Pit-N	104	264	31	54	10	2	8	30	45	53	.205	.323	.348	.671	82	-8	-6	95	107	31	.642	0	1	-1	-3	*C	-0.4
1959	Pit-N	53	80	10	18	3	0	3	4	7	16	.225	.287	.375	.662	72	-3	-3	103	41	8	.578	0	0	0	-3	C	-0.2
1960	KC-A	6	7	1	4	0	0	0	1	3	2	.571	.700	.571	1.271	251	2	2	99	98	3	2.333	0	0	0	0	/C	0.2
	Cle-A	24	68	9	19	1	0	1	6	7	5	.279	.347	.338	.685	88	-1	-1	98	90	9	.612	0	0	0	0	C	0.0
	Det-A	26	56	5	14	3	0	0	3	1	8	.250	.263	.304	.567	52	-4	-4	102	69	4	.432	1	0	0	-1	C	-0.2
	Yr	56	131	15	37	4	0	1	10	11	15	.282	.338	.336	.674	83	-3	-3	100	85	16	.583	1	0	0	-1		0.0
1961	Bal-A	43	124	18	34	6	0	6	19	12	27	.274	.338	.468	.806	116	2	2	97	98	18	.729	0	2	-1	-1	C	0.0
1962	Cin-N	43	131	17	36	6	1	7	25	13	39	.275	.340	.496	.836	119	4	3	102	115	22	.804	0	0	0	8	C	1.1
1963	Cin-N	1	3	0	0	0	0	0	0	1	0	.000	.250	.000	.250	-21	-0	-0	104	0	0	.667	1	0	0	0	/C	0.0
	LA-A	41	84	8	18	1	1	4	10	8	13	.214	.290	.393	.683	98	-1	-0	91	93	9	.609	0	0	0	-0	C	0.0
1964	LA-A	4	4	0	1	0	0	0	0	0	2	.250	.250	.250	.500	45	-0	-0	89	0	0	.333	0	0	0	0	H	0.0
Total	11	608	1455	171	353	59	10	46	166	170	295	.243	.323	.392	.714	93	-20	-16	98	93	200	.672	3	7	-3	-19	C	-1.2
■ **CURRY FOLEY**	Foley, Charles Joseph b: 1/14/1856, Milltown, Ireland d: 10/20/1898, Boston, Mass. TL , 180 lbs. Deb: 5/13/1879																											
1879	Bos-N	35	146	16	46	3	1	0	17	3	4	.315	.329	.349	.678	115	4	2	107	119	17	.540				0	PO/1	0.0
1880	Bos-N	80	332	44	97	13	2	2	31	8	14	.292	.309	.361	.670	138	9	12	92	86	38	.545				-5	PO1	0.4
1881	Buf-N	83	375	58	96	20	2	1	25	7	27	.256	.270	.328	.598	86	-6	-7	101	59	34	.466				-4	O1P	-1.3
1882	Buf-N	84	341	51	104	16	4	3	49	12	26	.305	.329	.402	.730	127	12	10	104	120	46	.629				-2	*O/P	0.6
1883	Buf-N	23	111	23	30	5	3	0	6	4	12	.270	.296	.369	.665	101	0	0	100	44	12	.556				0	O/P	0.0
Total	5	305	1305	192	373	57	12	6	128	34	83	.286	.304	.362	.666	114	18	18	100	87	148	.543				-11	O/P1	-0.3
■ **MARV FOLEY**	Foley, Marvis Edwin b: 8/29/53, Stanford, Ky. BL/TR, 6', 195 lbs. Deb: 9/11/78																											
1978	Chi-A	11	34	3	12	0	0	0	6	4	6	.353	.421	.353	.774	119	1	1	101	198	5	.667	0	1	-1	0	C	0.1
1979	Chi-A	34	97	6	24	3	0	2	10	7	5	.247	.298	.340	.638	70	-4	-4	102	99	9	.519	0	0	0	-1	C	-0.3
1980	Chi-A	68	137	14	29	5	0	4	15	9	22	.212	.270	.336	.606	67	-7	-6	97	101	13	.528	0	0	0	-8	C/1	-1.1
1982	Chi-A	27	36	1	4	0	0	0	1	6	4	.111	.238	.111	.349	-0	-5	-5	97	100	1	.313	0	0	0	-0	C/31D	-0.3
1984	Tex-A	63	115	13	25	2	0	6	19	15	24	.217	.313	.391	.704	93	-1	-1	100	120	15	.670	0	0	0	-2	C/13D	0.0
Total	5	203	419	37	94	10	0	12	51	41	61	.224	.298	.334	.632	74	-15	-15	99	114	44	.563	0	1	-1	-11	C/D13	-1.6
■ **RAY FOLEY**	Foley, Raymond Kirwin b: 6/23/06, Naugatuck, Conn. d: 3/22/80, Vero Beach, Fla. BL/TR, 5'11", 173 lbs. Deb: 7/04/28																											
1928	NY-N	2	1	1	0	0	0	0	0	1	1	.000	.500	.000	.500	40	0	0	102	0	0	1.000	0			0	H	0.0
■ **TOM FOLEY**	Foley, Thomas J. b: 8/16/1842, Cashel, Ireland d: 11/3/26, Chicago, Ill. 5'9.5", 157 lbs. Deb: 5/08/1871																											
1871	Chi-n	18	84	18	21							.250															O/C3	
■ **TOM FOLEY**	Foley, Thomas Michael b: 9/9/59, Columbus, Ga. BL/TR, 6'1", 175 lbs. Deb: 4/09/83																											
1983	Cin-N	68	98	7	20	4	1	0	9	13	17	.204	.297	.265	.563	55	-5	-6	103	137	9	.506	1	0	0	-3	S/2	-0.4
1984	Cin-N	106	277	26	70	8	3	5	27	24	36	.253	.312	.357	.670	83	-5	-6	106	93	32	.597	3	2	-0	-13	S2/3	-1.0
1985	Cin-N	43	92	7	18	5	1	0	6	6	16	.196	.245	.272	.517	42	-7	-7	105	96	7	.432	1	0	0	-3	2S/3	-0.8
	Phi-N	46	158	17	42	8	0	3	17	13	18	.266	.322	.373	.695	92	-1	-2	102	100	18	.603	1	3	-2	-2	S	-0.1
	Yr	89	250	24	60	13	1	3	23	19	34	.240	.294	.336	.630	73	-8	-9	104	99	24	.538	2	3	-1	-5		-0.9
1986	Phi-N	39	61	8	18	2	1	0	5	10	11	.295	.394	.361	.755	105	1	1	104	91	10	.773	2	0	1	-1	S/23	0.3
	Mon-N	64	202	18	52	13	2	1	18	20	26	.257	.324	.356	.681	90	-3	-3	98	96	24	.641	8	3	1	1	S23	0.1
	Yr	103	263	26	70	15	3	1	23	30	37	.266	.341	.357	.699	93	-2	-2	100	95	34	.673	10	3	1	-0		0.4
1987	Mon-N	106	280	35	82	18	3	5	28	11	40	.293	.322	.432	.754	92	-2	-4	106	82	34	.650	6	10	-4	-9	S2/3	-1.0
1988	Mon-N	127	377	33	100	21	3	5	43	30	49	.265	.321	.377	.698	94	-0	-3	106	110	41	.593	2	7	-4	5	2S/3	0.3
Total	6	599	1545	151	402	79	14	19	153	127	213	.260	.317	.366	.684	86	-23	-30	104	99	174	.610	24	25	-8	-25	S2/3	-2.6
■ **WILL FOLEY**	Foley, William Brown b: 11/15/1855, Chicago, Ill. d: 11/12/16, Chicago, Ill. BR/TR, 5'9.5", 150 lbs. Deb: 8/23/1875																											
1875	Chi-n	3	14	0	3							.214															/3	
1876	Cin-N	58	221	19	50	3	2	0	9	0	14	.226	.226	.258	.484	68	-9	-5	90	54	13	.333				-7	3C	-1.0
1877	Cin-N	56	216	23	41	5	1	0	18	4	13	.190	.205	.222	.427	42	-16	-10	82	130	10	.297				8	*3	0.2
1878	Mil-N	56	229	33	62	8	5	0	22	7	14	.271	.292	.349	.642	103	2	0	107	99	24	.521				-13	*3/C	-0.9
1879	Cin-N	56	218	22	46	5	1	0	25	2	16	.211	.218	.243	.461	55	-11	-9	95	169	12	.320				2	3O/2	-0.6
1881	Det-N	5	15	0	2	0	0	0	1	2	3	.133	.235	.133	.369	17	-1	-1	106	174	0	.308				0	/3	0.0
1884	CP-U	19	71	15	20	1	1	0		5		.282	.329	.324	.653	122	2	2	99	0	8	.549	0			-4	3	0.0
Total	6	250	970	112	221	22	10	0	75	20	60	.228	.243	.271	.515	72	-33	-24	94	105	67	.378	0			-14	3/CO2	-2.3
■ **TIM FOLI**	Foli, Timothy John b: 12/8/50, Culver City, Cal. BR/TR, 6', 179 lbs. Deb: 9/11/70 C																											
1970	NY-N	5	11	0	4	0	0	0	1	0	2	.364	.364	.364	.727	92	-0	-0	104	97	1	.571	0	0	0	-0	/S3	0.0
1971	NY-N	97	288	32	65	12	2	0	24	18	50	.226	.274	.281	.555	60	-16	-15	96	121	22	.457	5	0	2	-9	23S/O	-1.9
1972	Mon-N	149	540	45	130	12	2	2	35	25	43	.241	.282	.281	.563	59	-28	-29	102	93	44	.459	11	7	-1	13	*S/2	0.0
1973	Mon-N	126	458	37	110	11	0	2	36	28	40	.240	.285	.277	.563	54	-27	-29	104	111	33	.439	6	3	0	15	*S/2O	0.3
1974	Mon-N	121	441	41	112	10	3	0	39	28	27	.254	.303	.290	.593	64	-19	-22	104	120	40	.490	8	2	1	18	*S/3	1.0
1975	Mon-N	152	572	64	136	25	2	1	29	36	49	.238	.285	.294	.579	56	-31	-36	108	67	49	.487	13	3	2	14	*S/2	-0.2
1976	Mon-N	149	546	41	144	36	1	6	54	16	33	.264	.285	.366	.651	83	-14	-14	100	97	52	.526	6	5	-1	13	*S/3	1.2
1977	Mon-N	13	57	2	10	5	1	0	3	0	4	.175	.175	.298	.474	25	-6	-6	98	68	3	.354	0	0	0	-1	S	-0.4
	SF-N	104	368	30	84	17	3	4	27	11	16	.228	.251	.323	.574	50	-25	-27	104	82	28	.449	2	4	-2	4	*S/23O	-1.0
	Yr	117	425	32	94	22	4	4	30	11	20	.221	.241	.320	.561	47	-31	-33	104	81	31	.437	2	4	-2	3		-1.4
1978	NY-N	113	413	37	106	21	1	1	27	14	30	.257	.284	.320	.604	70	-18	-17	98	81	35	.466	2	5	-2	-6	*S	-1.7
1979	NY-N	3	7	0	0	0	0	0	0	0	0	.000	.000	.000	.000	-99	-2	-2	95	0	0	.000	0	0	0	-0	/S	-0.1
	Pit-N	133	525	70	153	23	1	1	65	28	14	.291	.338	.345	.683	82	-9	-13	106	148	63	.583	6	5	-1	-2	*S	-0.2
	Yr	136	532	70	153	23	1	1	65	28	14	.288	.334	.340	.674	80	-11	-15	105	**145**	62	.573	6	5	-1	-2		-0.3

YEAR	TM/L	G	AB	R	H	2B	3B	HR	RBI	BB	SO	AVG	OBP	SLG	PRO	/A	BR	/A	PF	CHI	RC	TA	SB	CS	SBR	FR	POS	TPR
1980	Pit-N	127	495	61	131	22	0	3	38	19	23	.265	.300	.327	.627	73	-17	-19	103	93	49	.527	11	7	-1	-0	*S	-0.5
1981	Pit-N	86	316	32	78	12	2	0	20	17	10	.247	.287	.297	.585	69	-14	-13	96	85	28	.482	7	7	-2	-7	S	-1.3
1982	Cal-A	150	480	46	121	14	2	3	56	14	22	.252	.276	.308	.585	60	-26	-26	100	143	40	.449	2	4	-2	14	*S/23	-0.1
1983	Cal-A	88	330	29	83	10	0	2	29	5	18	.252	.265	.300	.565	58	-20	-19	96	110	25	.420	2	3	-1	16	S3	0.0
1984	NY-A	61	163	8	41	11	0	0	16	2	16	.252	.265	.319	.584	65	-9	-8	94	123	13	.437	0	0	0	3	S23/1	-0.1
1985	Pit-N	19	37	1	7	0	0	0	2	4	2	.189	.268	.189	.457	29	-3	-3	103	114	1	.324	0	0	0	1	S	0.0
Total	16	1696	6047	576	1515	241	20	25	501	265	399	.251	.286	.309	.595	64	-284	-297	102	104	527	.491	81	55	-9	84	*S/2301	-5.0
■ DEE FONDY	Fondy, Dee Virgil b: 10/31/24, Slaton, Tex. BL/TL, 6'3", 195 lbs. Deb: 4/17/51																											
1951	Chi-N	49	170	23	46	7	2	3	20	11	20	.271	.319	.388	.707	92	-3	-2	97	103	20	.629	5	6	-2	0	1	-0.4
1952	Chi-N	145	554	69	166	21	9	10	67	28	60	.300	.334	.424	.759	106	5	3	103	101	75	.671	13	11	-3	2	*1	-0.2
1953	Chi-N	150	595	79	184	24	11	18	78	44	106	.309	.358	.477	.835	112	12	10	103	95	104	.800	10	7	-1	2	*1	0.7
1954	Chi-N	141	568	77	162	30	4	9	49	35	84	.285	.328	.400	.727	88	-10	-11	101	80	75	.674	20	5	**3**	12	*1	-0.1
1955	Chi-N	150	574	69	152	23	8	17	65	35	87	.265	.309	.422	.731	92	-8	-8	100	95	71	.652	8	9	-3	1	*1	-2.0
1956	Chi-N	137	543	52	146	22	9	9	46	20	74	.269	.295	.392	.687	84	-14	-13	99	86	62	.593	9	7	-2	-0	*1	-2.1
1957	Chi-N	11	51	3	16	3	1	0	2	0	9	.314	.314	.412	.725	97	-1	-0	96	34	5	.579	1	2	-1	0	1	-0.1
	Pit-N	95	323	42	101	13	2	2	35	25	59	.313	.364	.384	.748	108	1	4	94	112	46	.694	11	5	0	-2	1	-0.4
	Yr	106	374	45	117	16	3	2	37	25	68	.313	.357	.388	.745	106	1	3	94	104	52	.680	12	7	-1	-2		-0.5
1958	Cin-N	89	124	23	27	1	1	1	11	5	27	.218	.248	.266	.514	34	-11	-12	107	126	9	.455	7	1	2	-5	1O	-1.8
Total	8	967	3502	437	1000	144	47	69	373	203	526	.286	.326	.413	.739	95	-29	-30	100	94	467	.680	84	53	-7	9	1/O	-6.4
■ LEW FONSECA	Fonseca, Lewis Albert b: 1/21/1899, Oakland, Cal. BR/TR, 5'10.5", 180 lbs. Deb: 4/13/21 M																											
1921	Cin-N	82	297	38	82	10	3	1	41	8	13	.276	.304	.340	.644	70	-13	-13	101	147	30	.528	2	3	-1	-2	21O	-1.6
1922	Cin-N	81	291	55	105	20	3	4	45	14	18	.361	.390	.491	.882	132	11	12	96	103	53	.845	7	8	-3	11	2	1.8
1923	Cin-N	65	237	33	66	11	4	3	28	9	16	.278	.310	.397	.707	87	-6	-5	98	98	30	.637	4	0	1	6	21	0.2
1924	Cin-N	20	57	5	13	2	1	0	9	4	4	.228	.279	.298	.577	54	-4	-4	101	193	5	.500	1	0	0	0	2/1	-0.3
1925	Phi-N	126	467	78	149	30	5	7	60	21	42	.319	.352	.450	.802	89	1	-9	116	94	74	.750	6	2	1	-4	21	-1.7
1927	Cle-A	112	428	60	133	20	7	2	40	12	17	.311	.333	.404	.737	93	-7	-5	97	76	55	.675	12	0	4	-2	21	-0.3
1928	Cle-A	75	263	38	86	19	4	3	36	13	17	.327	.361	.464	.825	109	5	3	106	94	44	.782	4	2	0	2	13/S2	0.2
1929	Cle-A	148	566	97	209	44	15	6	103	50	23	**.369**	.426	.532	.958	145	39	38	100	117	127	1.022	19	11	-1	6	*1	2.1
1930	Cle-A	40	129	20	36	9	2	0	17	7	7	.279	.316	.380	.696	72	-5	-6	105	115	16	.613	1	0	0	1	1/3	-0.6
1931	Cle-A	26	108	21	40	9	1	1	14	8	7	.370	.419	.500	.919	132	6	5	106	71	22	.943	3	2	-0	1	1	0.3
	Chi-A	121	465	65	139	26	5	2	71	32	22	.299	.348	.389	.737	101	-4	1	92	128	63	.667	4	4	-1	-6	O2/13	-1.0
	Yr	147	573	86	179	35	6	3	85	40	29	.312	.361	.410	.772	108	2	6	95	118	85	.715	7	6	-2	-6		-0.7
1932	Chi-A	18	37	0	5	1	0	0	6	1	7	.135	.158	.162	.320	-19	-6	-6	87	335	1	.219	0	0	0	1	/OPM	-0.4
1933	Chi-A	23	59	8	12	2	0	2	15	7	6	.203	.288	.339	.627	65	-3	-3	101	192	6	.596	1	0	0	-0	1M	-0.3
Total	12	937	3404	518	1075	203	50	31	485	186	199	.316	.355	.432	.787	103	14	9	101	112	525	.738	64	32	0	13	12O/3SP	-1.6
■ BARRY FOOTE	Foote, Barry Clifton b: 2/16/52, Smithfield, N.C. BR/TR, 6'3", 205 lbs. Deb: 9/14/73																											
1973	Mon-N	6	6	0	4	0	1	0	1	0	0	.667	.667	1.000	1.667	342	2	2	104	67	4	3.000	0	0	0	0	H	0.2
1974	Mon-N	125	420	44	110	23	4	11	60	35	74	.262	.323	.414	.737	101	2	-1	104	112	52	.650	2	1	0	13	*C	1.8
1975	Mon-N	118	387	25	75	16	1	7	30	17	48	.194	.230	.295	.524	41	-30	-34	108	86	24	.410	0	1	-1	-0	*C	-3.2
1976	Mon-N	105	350	32	82	12	2	7	27	17	32	.234	.272	.340	.612	73	-13	-14	100	74	31	.502	2	1	0	8	C/31	0.0
1977	Mon-N	15	49	4	12	3	1	2	8	4	10	.245	.302	.469	.771	105	0	0	98	110	7	.711	0	0	0	1	C	0.1
	Phi-N	18	32	3	7	1	0	1	3	3	6	.219	.286	.344	.629	68	-1	-2	100	86	1	.452	0	0	0	0	C	-0.1
	Yr	33	81	7	19	4	1	3	11	7	16	.235	.295	.420	.715	90	-1	-1	99	100	8	.603	0	0	0	1		0.0
1978	Phi-N	39	57	4	9	0	0	1	4	1	11	.158	.172	.211	.383	6	-7	-7	105	106	2	.260	0	0	0	-1	C	-0.7
1979	Chi-N	132	429	47	109	26	0	16	56	34	49	.254	.316	.427	.743	90	-1	-7	112	96	56	.680	5	2	0	-16	*C	-2.0
1980	Chi-N	63	202	16	48	13	1	6	28	13	18	.238	.284	.401	.685	84	-4	-5	106	112	21	.586	1	1	-0	8	C	0.4
1981	Chi-N	9	22	0	0	0	0	0	1	3	7	.000	.120	.000	.120	-61	-5	-5	104	0	0	.130	0	0	0	0	/C	-0.4
	NY-A	40	125	12	26	4	0	6	10	8	21	.208	.256	.384	.640	82	-3	-3	100	59	10	.528	0	0	0	1	C/1D	-0.1
1982	NY-A	17	48	4	7	5	0	0	2	1	11	.146	.163	.250	.413	12	-6	-6	96	67	2	.302	0	0	0	-0	C	-0.4
Total	10	687	2127	191	489	103	10	57	230	136	287	.230	.279	.368	.647	75	-67	-81	105	92	209	.570	10	6	-1	14	C/D13	-4.4
■ JIM FORAN	Foran, James H. b: 1848, New York 5'6.5", 159 lbs. Deb: 5/04/1871																											
1871	Kek-n	19	90	20	31							.344															1/O	
■ DAVY FORCE	Force, David W. "Wee Davy" or "Tom Thumb" b: 7/27/1849, New York, N.Y. d: 6/21/18, Englewood, N.J. BR/TR, 5'4", 130 lbs. Deb: 5/05/1871																											
1871	Oly-n	32	166	45	44							.265															*S/3	
1872	Tro-n	25	133	39	55							.414															3/S	
	Bal-n	18	93	30	38							.409															3	
	Yr	43	226	69	93							.412																
1873	Bal-n	48	250	75	85							.340															3S/P	
1874	Chi-n	59	305	61	92							.302															3S/O	
1875	Ath-n	77	391	77	122							.312															*S	
1876	Phi-N	60	284	48	66	6	0	0	17	5	3	.232	.246	.254	.499	67	-10	-9	99	69	18	.353				20	*S/3	0.9
	NY-N	1	3	0	0	0	0	0	0	0	0	.000	.000	.000	.000	-99	-1	-1	87	0	0	.000				0	/S	0.0
	Yr	61	287	48	66	6	0	0	17	5	3	.230	.243	.251	.494	66	-10	-10	99	69	18	.348				20		0.9
1877	StL-N	58	225	24	59	5	3	0	22	11	15	.262	.297	.311	.608	90	-2	-2	102	113	21	.488				6	*S/3	0.4
1879	Buf-N	79	316	36	66	5	2	0	8	13	37	.209	.240	.237	.477	51	-14	-20	114	40	18	.352				2	*S/3	-1.1
1880	Buf-N	81	290	22	49	10	0	0	17	10	35	.169	.197	.203	.400	40	-19	-15	91	107	12	.286				29	2S	1.7
1881	Buf-N	75	278	21	50	9	1	0	15	11	29	.180	.211	.219	.430	35	-20	-20	101	87	13	.316				**25**	2S/O3	0.8
1882	Buf-N	73	278	39	67	10	1	1	28	12	17	.241	.272	.295	.567	79	-5	-7	104	113	23	.445				6	*S3/2	0.5
1883	Buf-N	96	378	40	82	11	3	0	35	12	39	.217	.241	.262	.503	53	-21	-21	100	125	24	.375				-6	*S3/2	-1.9
1884	Buf-N	106	403	47	83	13	3	0	36	27	41	.206	.256	.253	.509	57	-17	-22	107	124	27	.403				-3	*S/2	-1.3
1885	Buf-N	71	253	20	57	6	1	0	15	13	19	.225	.263	.257	.520	69	-8	-8	99	82	18	.398				-1	2S/3	-0.4
1886	Was-N	68	242	26	44	5	1	0	16	17	26	.182	.236	.211	.446	39	-18	-16	94	104	14	.389	9			15	S/23	0.0
Total	5 n	259	1338	327	436							.326															S/23	
Total	10	768	2950	323	623	80	15	1	209	131	261	.211	.245	.249	.494	57	-134	-141	101	98	189	.376	9			94	S23/OP	-0.4
■ CURT FORD	Ford, Curtis Glenn b: 10/11/60, Jackson, Miss. BL/TR, 5'10", 150 lbs. Deb: 6/22/85																											
1985	StL-N	11	12	2	6	2	0	0	3	4	1	.500	.625	.667	1.292	273	3	3	96	149	6	2.167	1	0	0	-1	/O	0.2
1986	StL-N	85	214	30	53	15	2	2	29	23	29	.248	.321	.364	.685	86	-3	-4	103	138	27	.683	13	5	1	1	O	-0.3
1987	StL-N	89	228	32	65	9	5	3	26	14	32	.285	.329	.408	.737	95	-2	-2	99	102	28	.676	11	8	-2	1	O	-0.5
1988	StL-N	92	128	11	25	6	0	1	18	8	26	.195	.243	.266	.508	44	-9	-10	104	195	8	.444	6	1	1	-5	O/1	-1.5
Total	4	277	582	75	149	32	7	6	76	49	88	.256	.315	.366	.681	85	-11	-12	101	136	69	.652	31	14	1	-5	O/1	-2.1
■ DAN FORD	Ford, Darnell Glenn b: 5/19/52, Los Angeles, Cal. BR/TR, 6'1", 185 lbs. Deb: 4/12/75																											
1975	Min-A	130	440	72	123	21	1	15	59	30	79	.280	.333	.434	.767	108	8	4	107	96	60	.695	6	7	-2	-15	*O/D	-1.7
1976	Min-A	145	514	87	137	24	7	20	86	36	118	.267	.327	.457	.784	130	16	17	98	114	75	.754	17	6	2	-9	*O/D	0.7
1977	Min-A	144	453	66	121	25	7	11	60	41	79	.267	.341	.426	.767	105	5	3	103	105	65	.718	6	4	-1	-14	*O/D	-1.6
1978	Min-A	151	592	78	162	36	10	11	82	48	88	.274	.333	.424	.757	118	8	12	94	121	80	.688	7	7	-2	-10	*O/D	-0.3
1979	Cal-A	142	569	100	165	26	5	21	101	40	86	.290	.340	.464	.804	124	10	16	93	126	85	.739	8	5	-1	12	*O	2.0
1980	Cal-A	65	226	22	63	11	0	7	26	19	45	.279	.340	.420	.760	112	2	3	96	89	28	.648	0	1	-1	-4	OD	-0.2
1981	Cal-A	97	375	53	104	14	1	15	48	23	71	.277	.328	.440	.768	115	8	6	104	95	49	.675	2	2	-1	-8	O	-0.4
1982	Bal-A	123	421	46	99	21	3	10	43	23	71	.235	.281	.371	.652	77	-14	-14	100	92	43	.565	5	2	0	0	*O/D	-1.7
1983	Bal-A	103	407	63	114	30	4	9	55	29	55	.280	.333	.440	.772	110	5	5	100	111	59	.724	9	2	2	-4	*O	0.1
1984	Bal-A	25	91	7	21	4	0	1	5	7	13	.231	.286	.308	.593	68	-4	-4	94	66	8	.493	1	0	0	1	O/D	-0.2

YEAR	TM/L	G	AB	R	H	2B	3B	HR	RBI	BB	SO	AVG	OBP	SLG	PRO	/A	BR	/A	PF	CHI	RC	TA	SB	CS	SBR	FR	POS	TPR
1985	Bal-A	28	75	4	14	2	0	1	1	7	17	.187	.256	.253	.509	41	-6	-6	99	18	4	.400	0	1	-1	0	D	-0.6
Total	11	1153	4163	598	1123	214	38	121	566	303	722	.270	.326	.427	.753	109	38	44	99	105	556	.710	61	37	-4	-53	*O/D	-3.9
■ ED FORD	Ford, Edward L. b: 1862, Richmond, Va. 5'9.5", 160 lbs. Deb: 10/09/1884																											
1884	Ric-a	2	5	0	0	0	0	0		0		.000	.000	.000	.000	-99	-1	-1	99	0	0	.000				0	/S1	0.0
■ HOD FORD	Ford, Horace Hills b: 7/23/1897, New Haven, Conn. d: 1/29/77, Winchester, Mass. BR/TR, 5'10", 165 lbs. Deb: 9/08/19																											
1919	Bos-N	10	28	4	6	0	1	0	3	2	6	.214	.290	.286	.576	75	-1	-1	98	146	2	.500	0			1	/S3	0.0
1920	Bos-N	88	257	16	62	12	5	1	30	18	25	.241	.296	.339	.635	85	-6	-5	96	129	26	.556	3	3	-1	4	2S/1	0.1
1921	Bos-N	152	555	50	155	29	5	2	61	36	49	.279	.328	.360	.688	88	-14	-9	93	111	64	.589	2	11	-6	-4	*2S	-1.4
1922	Bos-N	143	515	58	140	23	9	2	60	30	36	.272	.317	.363	.680	80	-20	-15	94	111	61	.593	2	1	0	-8	*S2	-1.4
1923	Bos-N	111	380	27	103	16	7	2	50	31	30	.271	.326	.366	.692	82	-10	-10	100	124	46	.615	1	1	-0	-6	2S	-1.2
1924	Phi-N	145	530	58	144	27	5	3	53	27	40	.272	.308	.358	.667	73	-17	-22	108	99	56	.554	1	9	-5	10	*2	-2.5
1925	Bro-N	66	216	32	59	11	0	1	15	26	15	.273	.357	.338	.695	84	-6	-4	94	70	27	.631	0	3	-2	0	S	0.0
1926	Cin-N	57	197	14	55	6	1	0	18	14	12	.279	.336	.320	.656	81	-6	-4	95	101	21	.570	1			-5	S	-0.5
1927	Cin-N	115	409	45	112	16	2	1	46	33	34	.274	.331	.330	.661	78	-12	-12	100	119	45	.572	0			-7	*S2	-0.9
1928	Cin-N	149	506	49	122	17	4	0	54	47	31	.241	.308	.291	.599	60	-31	-28	96	133	47	.513	1			16	*S	0.8
1929	Cin-N	148	529	68	146	14	6	3	50	41	25	.276	.329	.342	.671	67	-27	-27	99	92	59	.603	8			4	*S2	-0.5
1930	Cin-N	132	424	36	98	16	7	1	34	24	28	.231	.272	.309	.581	44	-42	-35	90	87	36	.482	2			-2	S2	-2.0
1931	Cin-N	84	175	18	40	8	1	0	13	13	13	.229	.286	.286	.571	57	-11	-10	95	93	15	.474	0			-2	S/23	-0.5
1932	StL-N	1	2	0	0	0	0	0	0	0	0	.000	.000	.000	.000	-99	-1	-1	100	0	0	.000	0			0	/S	0.0
	Bos-N	40	95	9	26	5	2	0	6	6	9	.274	.324	.368	.692	92	-2	-1	93	64	12	.609	0			0	2S/3	0.2
	Yr	41	97	9	26	5	2	0	6	6	9	.268	.317	.361	.678	88	-2	-2	93	62	12	.592	0			0		0.2
1933	Bos-N	5	15	0	1	0	0	0	1	3	1	.067	.222	.067	.289	-15	-2	-2	96	376	0	.222	0			0	/S	-0.1
Total	15	1446	4833	484	1269	200	55	16	494	351	354	.263	.316	.337	.652	73	-207	-186	97	108	517	.563	21	28		-0	S2/31	-9.9
■ TED FORD	Ford, Theodore Henry b: 2/7/47, Vineland, N.J. BR/TR, 5'10", 180 lbs. Deb: 4/07/70																											
1970	Cle-A	26	46	5	8	1	0	1	1	3	13	.174	.224	.261	.485	29	-4	-5	115	27	3	.395	0	0	0	1	O	-0.4
1971	Cle-A	74	196	15	38	6	0	2	14	9	34	.194	.229	.255	.484	35	-16	-18	106	102	10	.370	2	2	-1	2	O	-1.9
1972	Tex-A	129	429	43	101	19	1	14	50	37	80	.235	.301	.382	.683	108	0	3	94	104	50	.617	4	3	-1	8	*O	0.8
1973	Cle-A	11	40	3	9	0	1	0	3	2	7	.225	.262	.275	.537	53	-3	-2	97	109	3	.438	1	0	0	-3	O	-0.5
Total	4	240	711	66	156	26	2	17	68	51	134	.219	.275	.333	.608	77	-23	-22	99	99	66	.531	7	5	-1	8	O	-2.0
■ TOM FORSTER	Forster, Thomas W. b: 5/1/1859, New York, N.Y. d: 7/17/46, New York, N.Y. Deb: 8/04/1882																											
1882	Det-N	21	76	5	7	0	0	0	2	5	12	.092	.148	.092	.240	-20	-10	-10	102	98	1	.174				-8	2	-1.6
1884	Pit-a	35	126	10	28	5	0	0		7		.222	.263	.262	.525	77	-3	-3	97	0	9	.408				8	S/32	0.4
1885	NY-a	57	213	28	47	7	2	0		17		.221	.281	.272	.554	93	-5	1	84	0	17	.458				-10	2/O	-0.6
1886	NY-a	67	251	33	49	3	2	1		20		.195	.263	.235	.498	56	-11	-13	104	0	18	.450	9			-7	2/OS	-1.7
Total	4	180	666	76	131	15	4	1	2	49	12	.197	.256	.236	.492	61	-29	-25	96	11	45	.409	9			-18	2/SO3	-3.5
■ CLARENCE FORSYTHE	Forsythe, Clarence D. b: 1888, St.Louis, Mo. TR , Deb: 10/02/15																											
1915	Bal-F	1	3	0	0	0	0	0	0	1	0	.000	.250	.000	.250	-22	-0	-0	107	0	0	.333	0			0	/3	0.0
■ GEORGE FOSS	Foss, George Dueward "Deeby" b: 6/13/1897, Register, Va. d: 11/10/69, Brandon, Fla. BR/TR, 5'10.5", 170 lbs. Deb: 4/16/21																											
1921	Was-A	4	7	0	0	0	0	0	0	0	1	.000	.000	.000	.000	-99	-2	-2	99	0	0	.000	0	0	0	0	/3	-0.1
■ RAY FOSSE	Fosse, Raymond Earl b: 4/4/47, Marion, Ill. BR/TR, 6'2", 215 lbs. Deb: 9/08/67																											
1967	Cle-A	7	16	0	1	0	0	0	0	0	5	.063	.063	.063	.125	-63	-3	-3	100	0	0	.067	0	0	0	1	/C	-0.1
1968	Cle-A	1	0	0	0	0	0	0	0	0	0	—	—	—	—	—	0	0	101	—	—	—	0	0	0	0	/C	0.0
1969	Cle-A	37	116	11	20	3	0	2	9	8	29	.172	.232	.250	.482	37	-10	-10	94	103	7	.394	1	0	0	3	C	-0.3
1970	Cle-A	120	450	62	138	17	1	18	61	39	55	.307	.363	.469	.832	111	16	8	115	99	74	.773	1	5	-3	19	*C	2.7
1971	Cle-A	133	486	53	134	21	1	12	62	36	62	.276	.331	.397	.728	100	3	-0	106	113	61	.644	4	1	1	9	*C/1	1.6
1972	Cle-A	134	457	42	110	20	1	10	41	45	46	.241	.313	.354	.667	92	-1	-4	107	91	48	.587	5	1	1	14	*C/1	1.2
1973	Oak-A	143	492	37	126	23	2	7	52	25	62	.256	.293	.354	.647	94	-13	-5	87	105	49	.534	2	2	-1	-7	*C/D	-1.0
1974	Oak-A	69	204	20	40	8	3	4	23	11	31	.196	.244	.324	.568	62	-11	-11	100	116	15	.468	1	1	-0	-13	C/D	-2.2
1975	Oak-A	82	136	14	19	3	2	0	12	8	19	.140	.193	.191	.384	10	-16	-15	93	177	4	.285	0	1	-1	-18	C/12	-3.2
1976	Cle-A	90	276	26	83	9	1	2	30	20	20	.301	.348	.362	.710	109	3	3	100	109	33	.596	1	2	-1	2	C/1D	0.7
1977	Cle-A	78	238	25	63	7	1	6	27	7	26	.265	.294	.378	.673	84	-6	-6	98	99	24	.541	0	5	-3	1	C/1D	-0.5
	Sea-A	11	34	3	12	3	0	0	5	2	2	.353	.389	.441	.830	131	1	1	96	132	5	.680	0	1	-1	0	/CD	0.1
	Yr	89	272	28	75	10	1	6	32	9	28	.276	.306	.386	.692	90	-5	-4	97	104	30	.571	0	6	-4	1		-0.4
1979	Mil-A	19	52	6	12	3	1	0	2	2	6	.231	.286	.327	.613	65	-3	-3	100	45	5	.512	0	0	0	0	C/1D	-0.1
Total	12	924	2957	299	758	117	13	61	324	203	363	.256	.308	.367	.675	89	-41	-45	101	106	325	.595	15	19	-7	11	C/1D2	-1.1
■ POP FOSTER	Foster, Clarence Francis b: 4/8/1878, New Haven, Conn. d: 4/16/44, Princeton, N.J. BR/TR, 5'8.5", Deb: 9/13/1898																											
1898	NY-N	32	112	10	30	6	1	0	9	0		.268	.268	.339	.607	80	-4	-3	95	72	10	.463	0			0	O3/S	-0.2
1899	NY-N	84	301	48	89	9	7	3	57	20		.296	.348	.402	.750	111	3	4	97	137	46	.717	7			-10	O/S3	-0.9
1900	NY-N	31	84	19	22	3	1	0	11	11		.262	.347	.321	.669	90	-1	-1	97	127	10	.613	0			0	O/S2	0.0
1901	Was-A	103	392	65	109	16	9	6	54	41		.278	.346	.411	.757	113	6	7	99	101	61	.749	10			-3	*O/S	0.2
	Chi-A	12	35	4	10	2	2	1	6	4		.286	.359	.543	.902	151	2	2	99	86	7	.920	0			0	/O	0.2
	Yr	115	427	69	119	18	11	7	60	45		.279	.347	.422	.769	116	8	9	99	100	68	.763	10			-3		0.4
Total	4	262	924	146	260	36	20	10	137	76		.281	.339	.396	.735	108	6	9	98	111	133	.697	17			-12	O/S32	-0.7
■ EDDIE FOSTER	Foster, Edward Cunningham "Kid" b: 2/13/1887, Chicago, Ill. d: 1/15/37, Washington, D.C. BR/TR, 5'6.5", 145 lbs. Deb: 4/14/10																											
1910	NY-A	30	83	5	11	2	0	0	1	8		.133	.217	.157	.374	16	-8	-8	107	28	3	.333	2			-1	S	-0.9
1912	Was-A	154	618	98	176	34	9	2	70	53		.285	.345	.379	.724	108	5	5	99	86	88	.719	27			12	*3	1.5
1913	Was-A	106	409	56	101	11	5	1	41	36	31	.247	.309	.306	.615	76	-10	-13	106	109	42	.597	22			5	*3	-0.5
1914	Was-A	156	616	82	174	16	10	2	50	60	47	.282	.348	.351	.699	109	8	7	101	75	79	.672	31	18	-2	-17	*3	-0.8
1915	Was-A	154	618	75	170	25	10	0	52	48	30	.275	.329	.348	.677	102	0	-0	101	73	76	.628	20	6	2	-6	32	0.0
1916	Was-A	158	606	75	153	18	9	1	44	68	26	.252	.332	.317	.649	95	-3	-3	100	71	66	.612	23	16	-3	-18	32	-1.6
1917	Was-A	143	554	66	130	16	8	0	43	46	23	.235	.293	.292	.586	85	-15	-10	92	92	50	.517	11			-7	32	-1.0
1918	Was-A	129	519	70	147	13	3	0	29	41	20	.283	.339	.320	.659	95	-1	-3	104	61	59	.597	12			5	*3/2	0.3
1919	Was-A	120	478	57	126	12	5	0	26	33	21	.264	.314	.310	.623	77	-16	-14	98	61	51	.577	20			6	*3	0.0
1920	Bos-A	117	386	48	100	17	6	0	41	42	17	.259	.336	.334	.671	81	-11	-9	96	112	46	.634	10	4	1	6	32	0.4
1921	Bos-A	120	412	51	117	18	6	0	35	57	15	.284	.371	.357	.728	87	-7	-6	100	83	58	.719	13	7	-0	-6	32	-0.3
1922	Bos-A	48	109	11	23	3	0	0	3	9	10	.211	.277	.239	.516	37	-10	-10	96	41	8	.425	1	1	-0	-1	3/S	-0.7
	StL-A	37	144	29	44	4	0	0	12	20	8	.306	.394	.333	.727	86	-1	-2	106	86	21	.713	3	1	0	2	3	0.4
	Yr	85	253	40	67	7	0	0	15	29	18	.265	.345	.292	.638	67	-11	-11	100	61	28	.580	4	2	0	1		-0.3
1923	StL-A	27	100	9	18	2	0	0	4	7	7	.180	.241	.200	.441	16	-12	-13	104	72	6	.341	0	0	0	-1	2/3	-1.1
Total	13	1499	5652	732	1490	191	71	6	451	528	255	.264	.329	.326	.655	89	-80	-80	100	79	652	.614	195	53		-19	*32/S	-4.3
■ ELMER FOSTER	Foster, Elmer Ellsworth b: 8/15/1861, Minneapolis, Minn. d: 7/22/46, Deephaven, Minn. BR/TL, Deb: 6/18/1884																											
1884	Phi-a	4	11	4	2	0	0	0		3		.182	.357	.182	.539	74	0	-0	114	0	1	.556				0	/CO	0.0
	Phi-U	1	3	0	1	0	1	0		0		.333	.333	1.000	1.333	362	1	1	93	0	1	1.500	0			0	/C	0.1
1886	NY-a	35	125	16	23	0	1	0		7		.184	.239	.200	.439	38	-8	-9	104	0	7	.363	3			0	2O	-0.7
1888	NY-N	37	136	15	20	3	2	0	10	9	20	.147	.216	.199	.415	37	-10	-8	93	140	9	.448	13			-3	O/3	-1.1
1889	NY-N	2	4	2	0	0	0	0	0	3	1	.000	.429	.000	.429	25	-0	-0	105	0	1	1.250	2			0	/O	0.0
1890	Chi-N	27	105	20	26	4	2	5	23	9	21	.248	.325	.467	.791	121	4	2	109	115	22	1.000	18			0	O	0.2
1891	Chi-N	4	16	3	3	0	0	1	1	1	2	.188	.235	.375	.610	73	-1	-1	106	33	2	.615	1			0	/O	0.0
Total	6	110	400	60	75	7	6	6	34	32	44	.188	.261	.280	.541	67	-14	-16	102	79	42	.582	37			-3	/O2C3	-1.5

■ GEORGE FOSTER Foster, George Arthur b: 12/1/48, Tuscaloosa, Ala. BR/TR, 6'1.5", 180 lbs. Deb: 9/10/69

YEAR	TM/L	G	AB	R	H	2B	3B	HR	RBI	BB	SO	AVG	OBP	SLG	PRO	/A	BR	/A	PF	CHI	RC	TA	SB	CS	SBR	FR	POS	TPR
1969	SF-N	9	5	1	2	0	0	0	1	0	1	.400	.400	.400	.800	123	0	0	101	200	1	.667	0	0	0	-3	/O	-0.2
1970	SF-N	9	19	2	6	1	1	1	4	2	5	.316	.381	.632	1.013	174	2	2	96	103	4	1.000	0	0	0	-1	/O	0.1
1971	SF-N	36	105	11	28	5	0	3	8	6	27	.267	.306	.400	.706	99	-1	-0	100	64	11	.585	0	1	-1	-2	O	-0.4
	Cin-N	104	368	39	86	18	4	10	50	23	93	.234	.291	.386	.677	94	-6	-4	96	121	36	.589	7	6	-2	7	*O	-0.1
	Yr	140	473	50	114	23	4	13	58	29	120	.241	.295	.389	.684	95	-6	-5	97	106	49	.594	7	7	-2	5		-0.5
1972	Cin-N	59	145	15	29	4	1	2	12	5	44	.200	.232	.283	.515	49	-11	-10	93	105	8	.398	2	1	0	-6	O	-1.8
1973	Cin-N	17	39	6	11	3	0	4	9	4	7	.282	.349	.667	1.016	188	4	4	93	95	8	1.000	0	1	-1	-1	O	0.2
1974	Cin-N	106	276	31	73	18	0	7	41	30	52	.264	.345	.406	.751	112	3	4	98	119	38	.700	3	2	-0	-4	O	-0.3
1975	Cin-N	134	463	71	139	24	4	23	78	40	73	.300	.360	.518	.878	135	24	21	104	98	82	.841	2	1	0	14	*O/1	3.1
1976	Cin-N	144	562	86	172	21	9	29	**121**	52	89	.306	.369	.530	.899	149	37	35	103	123	111	.918	17	3	3	9	*O/1	4.3
1977	Cin-N	158	615	**124**	197	31	2	**52**	**149**	61	107	.320	.386	**.631**	**1.017**	**168**	**56**	**56**	100	116	**144**	1.048	6	4	-1	13	*O	6.2
1978	Cin-N	158	604	97	170	26	7	**40**	**120**	70	138	.281	.363	.546	.909	147	39	37	103	112	115	.901	4	4	-1	3	*O	3.4
1979	Cin-N	121	440	68	133	18	3	30	98	59	105	.302	.388	.561	.950	160	34	35	97	118	95	.966	0	2	-1	-2	*O	2.8
1980	Cin-N	144	528	79	144	21	5	25	93	75	99	.273	.364	.473	.838	130	23	22	102	120	91	.822	1	0	0	1	*O	1.9
1981	Cin-N	108	414	64	122	23	2	22	90	51	75	.295	.376	.519	.895	151	28	27	101	121	81	.898	4	0	1	4	*O	3.1
1982	NY-N	151	550	64	136	23	2	13	70	50	123	.247	.312	.367	.680	91	-8	-7	99	116	62	.596	1	1	-0	8	*O	0.0
1983	NY-N	157	601	74	145	19	2	28	90	38	111	.241	.291	.419	.710	96	-7	-6	99	112	68	.620	1	1	-0	5	*O	-0.3
1984	NY-N	146	553	67	149	22	1	24	86	30	122	.269	.314	.443	.757	111	6	6	100	113	73	.674	2	2	-1	3	*O	0.3
1985	NY-N	129	452	57	119	24	1	21	77	46	87	.263	.334	.460	.794	124	11	13	97	115	69	.749	0	1	-1	-6	*O	0.3
1986	NY-N	72	233	28	53	6	1	13	38	21	53	.227	.291	.429	.721	101	-2	-1	96	109	28	.649	1	1	-0	-2	O	-0.4
	Chi-A	15	51	2	11	0	2	1	4	3	8	.216	.259	.353	.612	65	-3	-3	101	76	4	.500	0	0	0	1	O/D	-0.1
Total	18	1977	7023	986	1925	307	47	348	1239	666	1419	.274	.341	.480	.821	127	229	231	100	114	1129	.807	51	31	-3	41	*O/D1	22.1

■ LEO FOSTER Foster, Leonard Norris b: 2/2/51, Covington, Ky. BR/TR, 5'11", 165 lbs. Deb: 7/09/71

YEAR	TM/L	G	AB	R	H	2B	3B	HR	RBI	BB	SO	AVG	OBP	SLG	PRO	/A	BR	/A	PF	CHI	RC	TA	SB	CS	SBR	FR	POS	TPR
1971	Atl-N	9	10	1	0	0	0	0	0	0	1	.000	.000	.000	.000	-91	-3	-3	110	0	0	.000	0	0	0	0	/S	-0.2
1973	Atl-N	3	6	1	1	1	0	0	0	0	2	.167	.167	.333	.500	31	-1	-1	113	0	0	.400	0	0	0	-0	/S	0.0
1974	Atl-N	72	112	16	22	2	0	1	5	9	22	.196	.256	.241	.497	38	-9	-10	105	64	7	.389	1	2	-1	-3	S2/3O	-0.8
1976	NY-N	24	59	11	12	2	0	1	15	8	5	.203	.299	.288	.587	73	-2	-2	92	289	6	.596	3	0	1	1	/3S2	0.0
1977	NY-N	36	75	6	17	3	0	0	6	5	14	.227	.284	.267	.551	51	-5	-5	96	120	6	.475	3	1	0	-2	2/S3	-0.4
Total	5	144	262	35	52	8	0	2	26	22	44	.198	.263	.252	.515	44	-20	-20	100	129	19	.447	7	3	0	-5	/S23O	-1.4

■ REDDY FOSTER Foster, Oscar E. b: 1867, Richmond, Va. d: 12/19/08, Richmond, Va. Deb: 6/03/1896

YEAR	TM/L	G	AB	R	H	2B	3B	HR	RBI	BB	SO	AVG	OBP	SLG	PRO	/A	BR	/A	PF	CHI	RC	TA	SB	CS	SBR	FR	POS	TPR
1896	NY-N	1	1	0	0	0	0	0	0	0	0	.000	.000	.000	.000	-99	-0	-0	99	0	0	.000	0			0		0.0

■ ROY FOSTER Foster, Roy b: 7/29/45, Bixby, Miss. BR/TR, 6', 185 lbs. Deb: 4/07/70

YEAR	TM/L	G	AB	R	H	2B	3B	HR	RBI	BB	SO	AVG	OBP	SLG	PRO	/A	BR	/A	PF	CHI	RC	TA	SB	CS	SBR	FR	POS	TPR
1970	Cle-A	139	477	66	128	26	0	23	60	54	75	.268	.357	.468	.825	109	17	8	115	85	78	.796	3	3	-1	-8	*O	-0.6
1971	Cle-A	125	396	51	97	21	1	18	45	35	48	.245	.316	.439	.755	106	5	2	106	81	54	.708	6	1	1	-2	*O	-0.1
1972	Cle-A	73	143	19	32	4	0	4	13	21	23	.224	.331	.336	.667	92	0	-1	107	91	16	.602	0	2	-1	-7	O	-1.1
Total	3	337	1016	136	257	51	1	45	118	110	146	.253	.338	.438	.776	106	22	9	110	84	147	.758	9	6	-1	-16	O	-1.8

■ BOB FOTHERGILL Fothergill, Robert Roy "Fats" b: 8/16/1897, Massillon, Ohio d: 3/20/38, Detroit, Mich. BR/TR, 5'10.5", 230 lbs. Deb: 4/18/22

YEAR	TM/L	G	AB	R	H	2B	3B	HR	RBI	BB	SO	AVG	OBP	SLG	PRO	/A	BR	/A	PF	CHI	RC	TA	SB	CS	SBR	FR	POS	TPR
1922	Det-A	42	152	20	49	12	4	0	29	8	9	.322	.356	.454	.810	112	2	2	98	150	22	.722	1	5	-3	-8	O	-1.0
1923	Det-A	101	241	34	76	18	2	1	49	12	19	.315	.358	.419	.777	108	1	2	97	161	36	.716	4	4	-1	-8	O	-1.2
1924	Det-A	54	166	28	50	8	3	0	15	5	13	.301	.326	.386	.711	83	-5	-5	100	77	20	.605	2	3	-1	-4	O	-1.2
1925	Det-A	71	204	38	72	14	0	2	28	6	3	.353	.377	.451	.828	110	2	3	99	96	34	.761	2	2	-1	-1	O	-0.3
1926	Det-A	110	387	63	142	31	7	3	73	33	23	.367	.421	.506	.927	146	23	25	97	123	78	.918	4	12	-6	-11	*O	0.0
1927	Det-A	143	527	93	189	38	9	9	114	47	31	.359	.413	.516	.929	130	31	24	108	129	109	.976	9	0	3	-4	*O	1.1
1928	Det-A	111	347	49	110	28	10	3	63	24	19	.317	.366	.481	.848	122	10	10	99	123	61	.842	8	3	1	-3	O	0.2
1929	Det-A	115	277	42	98	24	9	6	62	11	11	.354	.378	.570	.949	145	15	16	97	121	58	.956	3	1	0	-6	O	0.8
1930	Det-A	55	143	14	37	9	3	2	14	6	10	.259	.289	.406	.694	70	-6	-7	105	73	16	.607	1	1	-0	-6	O	-1.3
	Chi-A	52	135	10	40	9	0	0	24	4	8	.296	.326	.363	.689	73	-5	-6	103	162	16	.579	0	0	0	-5	O	-1.0
	Yr	107	278	24	77	18	3	2	38	10	18	.277	.307	.385	.692	71	-11	-13	104	117	32	.594	1	1	-0	-11		-2.3
1931	Chi-A	108	312	25	88	9	4	3	56	17	17	.282	.323	.365	.689	87	-9	-6	92	150	37	.597	2	2	-1	-3	O	-1.2
1932	Chi-A	116	346	36	102	24	1	7	50	27	10	.295	.348	.431	.778	115	-0	6	87	98	51	.730	4	4	-1	-14	O	-1.1
1933	Bos-A	28	32	1	11	1	0	0	5	2	4	.344	.382	.375	.757	100	0	0	101	139	5	.667	0	0	0	-1	/O	0.0
Total	12	1106	3269	453	1064	225	52	36	582	202	177	.325	.368	.459	.828	115	58	65	98	124	544	.786	40	37	-10	-73	O	-6.2

■ JACK FOURNIER Fournier, Jacques Frank b: 9/29/1892, Au Sable, Mich. d: 9/5/73, Tacoma, Wash. BL/TR, 6', 195 lbs. Deb: 4/13/12

YEAR	TM/L	G	AB	R	H	2B	3B	HR	RBI	BB	SO	AVG	OBP	SLG	PRO	/A	BR	/A	PF	CHI	RC	TA	SB	CS	SBR	FR	POS	TPR
1912	Chi-A	35	73	5	14	5	2	0	2	4		.192	.262	.315	.578	66	-4	-4	99	29	6	.525	1			1	1	-0.1
1913	Chi-A	68	172	20	40	8	5	1	23	21	23	.233	.323	.355	.678	103	-0	1	95	128	21	.705	9			3	1O	0.2
1914	Chi-A	109	379	44	118	14	9	6	44	31	44	.311	.368	.443	.811	139	19	17	103	90	61	.774	10	13	-5	4	1/O	1.8
1915	Chi-A	126	422	86	136	20	18	5	77	64	37	.322	.429	**.491**	.920	**179**	41	42	98	125	91	1.017	21	16	-3	2	1O	3.7
1916	Chi-A	105	313	36	75	13	9	3	44	36	40	.240	.328	.367	.695	101	3	-0	108	127	44	.735	19			-3	1/O	-0.4
1917	Chi-A	1	1	0	0	0	0	0	0	0	1	.000	.000	.000	.000	-99	-0	-0	98	0	0	.000	0			0	H	0.0
1918	NY-A	27	100	9	35	6	1	0	12	7	7	.350	.393	.430	.823	157	6	6	95	104	19	.877	7			-0	1	0.4
1920	StL-N	141	530	77	162	33	14	3	61	42	42	.306	.370	.438	.808	134	22	23	98	104	84	.804	26	20	-4	1	*1	1.9
1921	StL-N	149	574	103	197	27	9	16	86	56	48	.343	.409	.505	.914	148	34	39	95	90	114	.937	20	22	-7	-4	*1	2.3
1922	StL-N	128	404	64	119	23	9	10	61	40	21	.295	.368	.470	.838	114	8	8	101	97	69	.829	6	8	-3	-1	*1/P	0.3
1923	Bro-N	133	515	91	181	30	13	22	102	43	28	.351	.411	.588	.999	165	44	45	98	103	**125**	1.083	11	4	1	6	*1	4.1
1924	Bro-N	154	563	93	188	25	4	**27**	116	83	46	.334	.428	.536	.965	159	48	49	99	117	133	1.058	7	5	-1	7	*1	4.7
1925	Bro-N	145	545	99	191	21	16	22	130	**86**	39	.350	.446	.569	1.015	168	50	56	94	130	141	1.133	4	6	-2	3	*1	3.8
1926	Bro-N	87	243	39	69	9	2	11	48	30	16	.284	.365	.473	.838	125	8	8	99	112	42	.839	0			0	1	0.6
1927	Bos-N	122	374	55	106	18	2	10	53	44	16	.283	.368	.422	.790	119	7	10	93	99	59	.791	4			1	*1	0.4
Total	15	1530	5208	821	1631	252	113	136	859	587	408	.313	.392	.483	.875	142	285	301	98	108	1010	.909	145	94		18	*1/OP	23.7

■ BILL FOUSER Fouser, William C. b: 1855, Philadelphia, Pa. d: 3/1/19, Philadelphia, Pa. Deb: 4/22/1876

YEAR	TM/L	G	AB	R	H	2B	3B	HR	RBI	BB	SO	AVG	OBP	SLG	PRO	/A	BR	/A	PF	CHI	RC	TA	SB	CS	SBR	FR	POS	TPR
1876	Phi-N	21	89	11	12	0	1	0	2	0	0	.135	.135	.157	.292	-3	-9	-9	99	49	2	.182				0	2/O1	-0.7

■ DAVE FOUTZ Foutz, David Luther "Scissors" b: 9/7/1856, Carroll Co., Md. d: 3/5/1897, Waverly, Ind. BR/TR, 6'2", 161 lbs. Deb: 7/29/1884 M

YEAR	TM/L	G	AB	R	H	2B	3B	HR	RBI	BB	SO	AVG	OBP	SLG	PRO	/A	BR	/A	PF	CHI	RC	TA	SB	CS	SBR	FR	POS	TPR
1884	StL-a	33	119	17	27	4	0	0		8		.227	.276	.261	.536	71	-3	-4	110	0	9	.424				0	PO	0.0
1885	StL-a	65	238	42	59	6	4	0		11		.248	.281	.307	.588	94	-3	-1	93	0	21	.469				7	P1/O	0.0
1886	StL-a	102	414	66	116	18	9	3		9		.280	.297	.389	.686	104	6	-2	111	0	54	.631	17			3	PO1	0.0
1887	StL-a	102	423	79	151	26	13	4		23		.357	.393	.508	.901	139	28	21	110	0	95	.963	22			-4	OP1	1.7
1888	Bro-a	140	563	91	156	20	13	3	99	28		.277	.314	.375	.688	118	13	10	105	129	79	.678	35			-1	O1P	0.2
1889	Bro-a	138	553	118	153	19	8	7	113	64	23	.277	.355	.378	.733	115	9	13	96	135	92	.798	43			-4	*1P	-0.2
1890	Bro-N	129	509	106	154	25	13	5	98	52	25	.303	.368	.432	.801	135	22	22	100	133	99	.887	42			0	*1O/P	1.2
1891	Bro-N	130	521	87	134	26	8	2	73	40	25	.257	.313	.349	.662	97	-4	-2	97	120	74	.703	48			-4	*1/PS	-0.8
1892	Bro-N	61	220	33	41	5	3	1	26	14	14	.186	.235	.250	.485	47	-14	-14	101	138	18	.492	19			0	OP/1	-1.2
1893	Bro-N	130	557	91	137	20	10	7	67	32	34	.246	.287	.355	.642	79	-25	-16	91	74	70	.640	39			-7	O1/PM	-2.1
1894	Bro-N	72	293	40	90	12	9	0	51	14	13	.307	.341	.410	.750	87	-9	-6	94	119	47	.734	14			-2	1/PM	-0.5
1895	Bro-N	31	115	14	34	4	1	0	21	4	2	.296	.319	.348	.667	78	-5	-3	94	147	13	.556	1			0	O/1M	-0.2
1896	Bro-N	2	8	0	2	1	0	0	0	1	0	.250	.333	.375	.708	101	-0	0	87	0	1	.667	0			0	/O1M	0.0
Total	13	1135	4533	784	1254	186	91	32	548	300	136	.277	.323	.379	.702	104	15	16	100	89	672	.704	280			-13	1OP/S	-1.9

■ FRANK FOUTZ Foutz, Frank Hayes b: 4/8/1877, Baltimore, Md. d: 12/25/61, Lima, Ohio BR/TR, Deb: 4/26/01

YEAR	TM/L	G	AB	R	H	2B	3B	HR	RBI	BB	SO	AVG	OBP	SLG	PRO	/A	BR	/A	PF	CHI	RC	TA	SB	CS	SBR	FR	POS	TPR
1901	Bal-A	20	72	13	17	4	1	2	14	8		.236	.313	.403	.715	93	-0	-1	107	134	9	.673	0			-1	1	-0.2

YEAR	TM/L	G	AB	R	H	2B	3B	HR	RBI	BB	SO	AVG	OBP	SLG	PRO	/A	BR	/A	PF	CHI	RC	TA	SB	CS	SBR	FR	POS	TPR

■ BOOB FOWLER Fowler, Joseph Chester "Gink" b: 11/11/1900, Waco, Tex. BL/TR, 5'11.5", 180 lbs. Deb: 5/06/23

YEAR	TM/L	G	AB	R	H	2B	3B	HR	RBI	BB	SO	AVG	OBP	SLG	PRO	/A	BR	/A	PF	CHI	RC	TA	SB	CS	SBR	FR	POS	TPR
1923	Cin-N	11	33	9	11	0	1	1	6	1	3	.333	.353	.485	.838	122	1	1	98	111	6	.818	1	0	0	-0	S	0.2
1924	Cin-N	59	129	20	43	6	1	0	9	5	15	.333	.358	.395	.754	101	0	0	101	64	18	.659	2	2	-1	-1	S/23	0.1
1925	Cin-N	6	5	0	2	1	0	0	2	0	1	.400	.400	.600	1.000	156	0	0	97	237	1	1.000	0	0	0	0	H	0.0
1926	Bos-A	2	8	1	1	0	0	0	1	0	0	.125	.125	.125	.250	-34	-2	-2	101	347	0	.143	0	0	0	0	/3	0.0
Total	4	78	175	30	57	7	2	1	18	6	19	.326	.348	.406	.754	100	-0	-0	100	90	25	.667	3	2	-0	-1	/S32	0.3

■ CHARLIE FOX Fox, Charles Francis "Irish" b: 10/7/21, New York, N.Y. BR/TR, 5'11", 180 lbs. Deb: 9/24/42 MC

YEAR	TM/L	G	AB	R	H	2B	3B	HR	RBI	BB	SO	AVG	OBP	SLG	PRO	/A	BR	/A	PF	CHI	RC	TA	SB	CS	SBR	FR	POS	TPR
1942	NY-N	3	7	1	3	0	0	0	1	1	2	.429	.500	.429	.929	169	1	1	103	124	2	1.000	0			0	/C	0.1

■ PETE FOX Fox, Ervin b: 3/8/09, Evansville, Ind. d: 7/5/66, Detroit, Mich. BR/TR, 5'11", 165 lbs. Deb: 4/12/33

YEAR	TM/L	G	AB	R	H	2B	3B	HR	RBI	BB	SO	AVG	OBP	SLG	PRO	/A	BR	/A	PF	CHI	RC	TA	SB	CS	SBR	FR	POS	TPR
1933	Det-A	128	535	82	154	26	13	7	57	23	38	.288	.320	.424	.744	90	-6	-10	107	81	71	.674	9	6	-1	-4	*O	-1.7
1934	Det-A	128	516	101	147	31	2	2	45	49	53	.285	.351	.364	.716	87	-11	-9	98	82	69	.702	25	10	2	6	*O	-0.2
1935	Det-A	131	517	116	166	38	8	15	73	45	52	.321	.382	.513	.895	134	21	24	97	85	103	.930	14	4	2	-2	*O	2.1
1936	Det-A	73	220	46	67	12	1	4	26	34	23	.305	.405	.423	.827	109	3	5	95	80	39	.840	1	3	-2	-2	O	0.0
1937	Det-A	148	628	116	208	39	8	12	82	41	43	.331	.372	.476	.848	103	10	2	109	89	109	.822	12	8	-1	-3	*O	-0.6
1938	Det-A	155	634	91	186	35	10	7	96	31	39	.293	.328	.413	.742	84	-17	-17	100	122	85	.684	16	7	1	-2	*O	-1.6
1939	Det-A	141	519	69	153	24	6	7	66	35	41	.295	.342	.405	.746	81	-8	-17	111	98	69	.691	23	12	-0	5	*O	-1.4
1940	Det-A	93	350	49	101	17	4	5	48	21	30	.289	.329	.403	.732	80	-6	-12	111	113	46	.650	7	7	-2	-1	O	-1.9
1941	Bos-A	73	268	38	81	12	7	0	31	21	32	.302	.357	.399	.757	97	-0	-1	103	105	41	.720	9	2	2	-2	O	-0.5
1942	Bos-A	77	256	42	67	15	5	3	42	20	28	.262	.323	.395	.717	97	-0	-2	104	135	31	.647	8	7	-2	-13	O	-2.1
1943	Bos-A	127	489	54	141	24	4	2	44	34	40	.288	.337	.366	.703	102	3	1	104	92	62	.646	22	8	2	-6	*O	-0.7
1944	Bos-A	121	496	70	156	37	6	1	64	27	34	.315	.354	.419	.773	123	12	13	98	116	75	.703	10	5	0	-5	*O	0.5
1945	Bos-A	66	208	21	51	4	1	0	20	11	18	.245	.296	.274	.570	69	-9	-8	95	127	18	.465	2	2	-1	-8	O	-1.9
Total	13	1461	5636	895	1678	314	75	65	694	392	471	.298	.347	.415	.762	97	-9	-32	103	100	819	.723	158	81	-1	-36	*O	-10.0

■ PADDY FOX Fox, George B. b: 12/1/1868, Pottstown, Pa. d: 5/8/14, Philadelphia, Pa. Deb: 7/13/1891

YEAR	TM/L	G	AB	R	H	2B	3B	HR	RBI	BB	SO	AVG	OBP	SLG	PRO	/A	BR	/A	PF	CHI	RC	TA	SB	CS	SBR	FR	POS	TPR
1891	Lou-a	6	19	1	2	0	1	0	2	2	3	.105	.261	.211	.471	41	-1	-1	90	147	1	.471	0			0	/3	0.0
1899	Pit-N	13	41	4	10	0	1	1	3	3		.244	.311	.366	.677	89	-1	-1	99	51	5	.677	2			0	/1C	0.0
Total	2	19	60	5	12	0	2	1	5	5	3	.200	.294	.317	.611	75	-2	-2	96	84	6	.604	2			0	/13C	0.0

■ NELLIE FOX Fox, Jacob Nelson b: 12/25/27, St.Thomas, Pa. d: 12/1/75, Baltimore, Md. BL/TR, 5'10", 160 lbs. Deb: 6/08/47 C

YEAR	TM/L	G	AB	R	H	2B	3B	HR	RBI	BB	SO	AVG	OBP	SLG	PRO	/A	BR	/A	PF	CHI	RC	TA	SB	CS	SBR	FR	POS	TPR
1947	Phi-A	7	3	2	0	0	0	0	0	1	0	.000	.250	.000	.250	-27	-0	-0	100	0	0	.333	0	0	0	0	/2	0.0
1948	Phi-A	3	13	0	2	0	0	0	0	1	0	.154	.214	.154	.368	-1	-2	-2	102	0	1	.364	1	0	0	0	/2	-0.1
1949	Phi-A	88	247	42	63	6	2	0	21	32	9	.255	.354	.296	.650	74	-9	-8	99	99	28	.577	2	2	-1	1	2	-0.5
1950	Chi-A	130	457	45	113	12	7	0	30	35	17	.247	.304	.304	.608	58	-31	-29	97	76	45	.510	4	3	-1	-3	*2	-2.2
1951	Chi-A	147	604	93	189	32	12	4	55	43	11	.313	.372	.425	.798	119	13	15	97	65	98	.744	9	12	-5	-3	*2	1.3
1952	Chi-A	152	648	76	**192**	25	10	0	39	34	14	.296	.334	.366	.700	95	-6	-5	100	54	80	.591	5	5	-2	11	*2	1.1
1953	Chi-A	154	624	92	178	31	8	3	72	49	18	.285	.344	.375	.719	89	-5	-10	106	97	81	.631	4	5	-2	6	*2	0.3
1954	Chi-A	155	631	111	**201**	24	8	2	47	51	12	.319	.374	.391	.766	106	9	6	104	62	93	.706	16	9	-1	-5	*2	0.7
1955	Chi-A	154	636	100	198	28	7	6	59	38	15	.311	.366	.406	.772	106	6	6	101	70	95	.703	7	9	-3	**29**	*2	4.0
1956	Chi-A	154	649	109	192	20	10	4	52	44	14	.296	.350	.376	.726	88	-8	-11	104	67	84	.637	8	4	0	3	*2	0.3
1957	Chi-A	155	619	110	**196**	27	8	6	61	75	13	.317	.404	.415	.819	125	24	25	99	77	109	.810	5	6	-2	**21**	*2	5.3
1958	Chi-A	155	623	82	**187**	21	6	0	49	47	11	.300	.360	.353	.713	99	-1	1	98	79	79	.622	5	6	-2	2	*2	1.1
1959	Chi-A	156	624	84	191	34	6	2	70	71	13	.306	.383	.389	.773	116	13	16	97	98	97	.733	5	6	-2	-3	*2	1.6
1960	Chi-A	150	605	85	175	24	**10**	2	59	50	13	.289	.353	.372	.725	95	-2	-3	101	88	81	.645	2	4	-2	14	*2	1.9
1961	Chi-A	159	606	67	152	11	5	2	51	59	12	.251	.326	.295	.622	68	-26	-25	99	114	60	.525	2	3	-1	-3	*2	-1.0
1962	Chi-A	157	621	79	166	27	7	2	54	38	12	.267	.317	.343	.660	82	-19	-15	95	104	67	.551	1	2	-1	7	*2	0.1
1963	Chi-A	137	539	54	140	19	0	2	42	24	17	.260	.300	.306	.606	67	-21	-24	104	109	49	.477	0	2	-1	1	*2	-1.4
1964	Hou-N	133	442	45	117	12	6	0	28	27	13	.265	.322	.319	.641	84	-10	-8	96	83	47	.531	0	2	-1	1	*2	0.1
1965	Hou-N	21	41	3	11	2	0	0	1	0	2	.268	.286	.317	.603	78	-2	-1	89	32	3	.452	0	0	0	0	/312	-0.1
Total	19	2367	9232	1279	2663	355	112	35	790	719	216	.288	.349	.363	.712	93	-75	-74	100	83	1197	.644	76	80	-25	78	*2/31	12.5

■ JACK FOX Fox, John Paul b: 5/21/1885, Reading, Pa. d: 6/28/63, Reading, Pa. BR/TR, 5'10", 185 lbs. Deb: 6/02/08

YEAR	TM/L	G	AB	R	H	2B	3B	HR	RBI	BB	SO	AVG	OBP	SLG	PRO	/A	BR	/A	PF	CHI	RC	TA	SB	CS	SBR	FR	POS	TPR
1908	Phi-A	9	30	2	6	0	0	0	0	0		.200	.200	.200	.400	29	-2	-2	108	0	1	.333	2			1	/O	-0.1

■ BILL FOX Fox, William Henry b: 1/15/1872, Fiskdale, Mass. d: 5/7/46, Minneapolis, Minn. BB/TR, 5'10", 160 lbs. Deb: 8/20/1897

YEAR	TM/L	G	AB	R	H	2B	3B	HR	RBI	BB	SO	AVG	OBP	SLG	PRO	/A	BR	/A	PF	CHI	RC	TA	SB	CS	SBR	FR	POS	TPR
1897	Was-N	4	14	4	4	0	0	0	0	1		.286	.333	.286	.619	65	-1	-1	101	0	1	.500	0			0	/S2	0.0
1901	Cin-N	44	163	9	29	2	1	0	7	4		.178	.198	.202	.400	18	-17	-16	95	72	9	.343	9			3	2	-0.8
Total	2	48	177	13	33	2	1	0	7	5		.186	.209	.209	.418	23	-17	-16	95	66	10	.354	9			3	/2S	-0.8

■ JIMMIE FOXX Foxx, James Emory "Beast" or "Double X" b: 10/22/07, Sudlersville, Md. d: 7/21/67, Miami, Fla. BR/TR, 6', 195 lbs. Deb: 5/01/25 H

YEAR	TM/L	G	AB	R	H	2B	3B	HR	RBI	BB	SO	AVG	OBP	SLG	PRO	/A	BR	/A	PF	CHI	RC	TA	SB	CS	SBR	FR	POS	TPR
1925	Phi-A	10	9	2	6	1	0	0	0	0	1	.667	.667	.778	1.444	258	2	2	103	0	4	2.333	0	0	0	0	/C	0.2
1926	Phi-A	26	32	8	10	2	1	0	5	1	6	.313	.333	.438	.771	85	-0	-1	118	121	5	.727	1	0	0	-0	C/O	0.0
1927	Phi-A	61	130	23	42	6	5	3	20	14	11	.323	.393	.515	.908	139	6	7	97	88	26	.955	2	0	1	-1	1/C	0.5
1928	Phi-A	118	400	85	131	29	10	13	79	60	43	.327	.416	.548	.964	147	30	29	103	107	91	1.022	3	8	-4	3	31C	2.7
1929	Phi-A	149	517	123	183	23	9	33	118	103	70	.354	**.463**	.625	1.088	163	**63**	56	109	98	**154**	1.282	9	7	-2	-4	*1/3	2.8
1930	Phi-A	153	562	127	188	33	13	37	156	93	66	.335	.429	.637	1.066	167	57	58	99	117	154	1.202	7	7	-2	-2	*1	3.1
1931	Phi-A	139	515	93	150	32	10	30	120	73	84	.291	.380	.567	.947	139	33	29	105	110	113	1.005	4	3	-1	-5	*13/O	1.3
1932	Phi-A	154	585	**151**	213	33	9	**58**	**169**	116	96	**.364**	.469	**.749**	**1.218**	185	**97**	**84**	114	98	**207**	**1.470**	3	7	-3	-3	*13	**5.7**
1933	Phi-A	149	573	125	204	37	9	**48**	**163**	96	93	**.356**	.449	**.703**	**1.153**	**219**	**83**	**90**	92	105	**184**	**1.353**	2	2	-1	5	*1/S	**7.6**
1934	Phi-A	150	539	120	180	28	6	44	130	**111**	75	.334	.449	.653	1.102	186	66	69	97	95	165	1.316	11	2	2	4	*1/3	4.6
1935	Phi-A	147	535	118	185	33	7	**36**	115	114	99	.346	.461	**.636**	**1.096**	181	**67**	67	100	92	**163**	**1.299**	6	4	-1	5	*1C/3	**5.5**
1936	Bos-A	155	585	130	198	32	8	41	143	105	119	.338	.440	.631	1.071	152	57	51	106	100	168	1.248	13	4	2	-2	*1O/3	2.7
1937	Bos-A	150	569	111	162	24	6	36	127	99	96	.285	.392	.538	.929	128	27	25	103	111	123	1.002	10	8	-2	9	*1/C	1.2
1938	Bos-A	149	565	139	197	33	9	50	**175**	**119**	76	**.349**	**.462**	**.704**	**1.166**	**184**	**78**	**76**	102	104	**189**	**1.403**	5	4	-1	5	*1	**5.3**
1939	Bos-A	124	467	130	168	31	10	**35**	105	89	72	.360	**.464**	**.694**	**1.158**	177	**66**	60	108	79	150	**1.313**	4	3	-1	3	*1/P	4.6
1940	Bos-A	144	515	106	153	30	4	36	119	101	87	.297	.412	.581	.993	153	43	42	101	108	124	1.044	4	7	-3	-1	1C/3	3.4
1941	Bos-A	135	487	87	146	27	8	19	105	93	103	.300	.412	.505	.917	137	31	29	103	125	102	.929	2	5	-2	6	*1/3O	2.8
1942	Bos-A	30	100	18	27	4	0	5	14	18	15	.270	.392	.460	.852	134	6	5	104	82	20	.892	0	0	0	-0	1	0.5
	Chi-N	70	205	25	42	8	0	3	19	22	55	.205	.282	.288	.570	70	-9	-8	96	104	16	.477	1			-1	1/C	-1.3
1944	Chi-N	15	20	0	1	1	0	0	2	2	5	.050	.136	.100	.236	-33	-4	-4	101	359	0	.211	0			0	/3C	-0.2
1945	Phi-N	89	224	30	60	11	1	7	38	23	39	.268	.336	.420	.756	113	2	3	96	115	32	.701	0			-1	13/P	0.2
Total	20	2317	8134	1751	2646	458	125	534	1922	1452	1311	.325	.428	.609	1.038	162	803	768	103	104	2190	1.170	87	71		20	*13C/OPS	53.2

■ JOE FOY Foy, Joseph Anthony b: 2/21/43, New York, N.Y. BR/TR, 6', 215 lbs. Deb: 4/13/66

YEAR	TM/L	G	AB	R	H	2B	3B	HR	RBI	BB	SO	AVG	OBP	SLG	PRO	/A	BR	/A	PF	CHI	RC	TA	SB	CS	SBR	FR	POS	TPR
1966	Bos-A	151	554	97	145	23	8	15	63	91	80	.262	.368	.413	.781	114	20	14	109	93	86	.757	2	5	-2	4	*3S	1.3
1967	Bos-A	130	446	70	112	22	4	16	49	46	87	.251	.325	.426	.751	105	11	3	115	88	59	.698	8	6	-1	-11	*3/O	-0.6
1968	Bos-A	150	515	65	116	18	2	10	60	84	91	.225	.338	.326	.665	102	4	4	101	**138**	64	.678	26	8	3	1	*3/O	1.3
1969	KC-A	145	519	72	136	19	2	11	71	74	75	.262	.360	.370	.729	102	5	3	103	134	73	.751	37	15	2	-15	*31O/S2	-0.9
1970	NY-N	99	322	39	76	12	0	6	37	68	58	.236	.376	.329	.705	87	-1	-3	104	118	45	.760	22	13	-1	-4	3	-1.1
1971	Was-A	41	128	12	30	8	0	0	11	27	14	.234	.368	.297	.665	97	-0	1	92	120	16	.670	4	1	1	-3	3/2S	-0.2
Total	6	716	2484	355	615	102	16	58	291	390	405	.248	.354	.372	.725	103	38	22	105	115	343	.744	99	48	1	-29	3/OS12	-0.2

■ JULIO FRANCO Franco, Julio Cesar b: 8/23/58, San Pedro De Macoris, D.R. BR/TR, 6', 160 lbs. Deb: 4/23/82

YEAR	TM/L	G	AB	R	H	2B	3B	HR	RBI	BB	SO	AVG	OBP	SLG	PRO	/A	BR	/A	PF	CHI	RC	TA	SB	CS	SBR	FR	POS	TPR
1982	Phi-N	16	29	3	8	1	0	0	3	2	4	.276	.323	.310	.633	83	-1	-1	94	131	2	.458	0	2	-1	-0	S/3	0.0
1983	Cle-A	149	560	68	153	24	8	8	80	27	50	.273	.309	.387	.696	86	-8	-12	105	132	61	.632	32	12	2	-6	*S	-0.6
1984	Cle-A	160	658	82	188	22	5	3	79	43	68	.286	.335	.348	.683	84	-9	-14	106	127	73	.590	19	10	-0	3	*S/D	0.1
1985	Cle-A	160	636	97	183	33	4	6	90	54	74	.288	.347	.381	.728	105	0	5	94	132	79	.641	13	9	-2	-8	*S/2D	0.7

YEAR	TM/L	G	AB	R	H	2B	3B	HR	RBI	BB	SO	AVG	OBP	SLG	PRO	/A	BR	/A	PF	CHI	RC	TA	SB	CS	SBR	FR	POS	TPR
1986	Cle-A	149	599	80	183	30	5	10	74	32	66	.306	.341	.422	.763	110	6	7	98	110	76	.654	10	7	-1	-7	*S2/D	0.6
1987	Cle-A	128	495	86	158	24	3	8	52	57	56	.319	.393	.428	.821	116	15	13	103	85	82	.824	32	9	4	-16	*S/2D	0.6
1988	Cle-A	152	613	88	186	23	6	10	54	56	72	.303	.364	.409	.773	114	14	13	102	67	90	.734	25	11	1	-1	*2/D	2.2
Total	7	914	3590	504	1059	157	31	45	432	271	390	.295	.347	.394	.741	102	17	12	101	110	462	.702	131	60	3	-37	S2/D3	3.6
■ **TITO FRANCONA** Francona, John Patsy b: 11/4/33, Aliquippa, Pa. BL/TL, 5'11", 190 lbs. Deb: 4/17/56																												
1956	Bal-A	139	445	62	115	16	4	9	57	51	60	.258	.336	.373	.709	92	-8	-5	94	110	58	.672	11	5	0	2	*O1	-0.8
1957	Bal-A	97	279	35	65	8	3	7	38	29	48	.233	.312	.358	.670	89	-7	-4	93	124	31	.621	7	3	0	-8	O/1	-1.6
1958	Chi-A	41	128	10	33	3	2	1	10	14	24	.258	.331	.336	.667	86	-3	-2	98	87	13	.578	2	3	-1	-2	O	-0.7
	Det-A	45	69	11	17	5	0	0	10	15	16	.246	.381	.319	.700	91	0	-0	104	182	9	.685	0	0	0	-3	O/1	-0.4
	Yr	86	197	21	50	8	2	1	20	29	40	.254	.350	.330	.680	87	-2	-3	101	138	24	.632	2	3	-1	-5		-1.1
1959	Cle-A	122	399	68	145	17	2	20	79	35	42	.363	.419	.566	.985	174	37	38	97	109	93	1.004	2	0	1	4	O1	4.0
1960	Cle-A	147	544	84	159	**36**	2	17	79	67	67	.292	.375	.460	.835	127	19	21	98	109	96	.821	4	1	1	3	*O1	1.8
1961	Cle-A	155	592	87	178	30	8	16	85	56	52	.301	.365	.459	.824	123	15	18	96	110	100	.784	2	1	0	1	*O1	1.3
1962	Cle-A	158	621	82	169	28	5	14	70	47	74	.272	.330	.401	.731	98	-4	-2	98	92	84	.662	3	2	-0	2	*1	-1.1
1963	Cle-A	142	500	57	114	29	0	10	41	47	77	.228	.297	.346	.643	82	-14	-12	97	86	52	.582	9	1	2	-7	*O1	-2.2
1964	Cle-A	111	270	35	67	13	2	8	24	44	46	.248	.362	.400	.762	109	6	5	103	77	41	.751	1	3	-2	-12	O1	-1.2
1965	StL-N	81	174	15	45	6	2	5	19	17	30	.259	.325	.402	.727	97	1	-1	107	93	23	.654	0	0	0	-6	O1	-0.8
1966	StL-N	83	156	14	33	4	1	4	17	7	27	.212	.250	.327	.577	59	-9	-9	100	113	13	.476	0	0	0	-1	1/O	-1.2
1967	Phi-N	27	73	7	15	1	0	0	3	7	10	.205	.275	.219	.494	41	-5	-6	104	78	4	.377	0	1	-1	0	1/O	-0.7
	Atl-N	82	254	28	63	5	1	6	25	20	34	.248	.305	.346	.652	83	-5	-6	104	98	27	.558	1	0	0	-3	1/O	-1.2
	Yr	109	327	35	78	6	1	6	28	27	44	.239	.299	.318	.617	73	-10	-11	104	93	31	.520	1	1	-0	-3		-1.9
1968	Atl-N	122	346	32	99	13	1	2	47	51	45	.286	.378	.347	.725	128	10	13	93	157	47	.672	3	0	1	-8	O1	0.1
1969	Atl-N	51	88	5	26	1	0	2	22	13	10	.295	.386	.375	.761	110	2	2	104	226	13	.719	0	1	-1	-1	O/1	0.0
	Oak-A	32	85	12	29	6	1	3	20	12	11	.341	.423	.541	.964	182	8	9	92	146	21	1.036	0	0	0	1	1/O	0.8
1970	Oak-A	32	33	2	8	0	0	1	6	6	6	.242	.375	.333	.708	100	0	0	97	173	4	.621	0	0	0	0	/1O	0.0
	Mil-A	52	65	4	15	3	0	0	4	6	15	.231	.296	.277	.573	60	-4	-3	98	90	6	.500	1	0	0	1	1	-0.2
	Yr	84	98	6	23	3	0	1	10	12	21	.235	.324	.296	.620	74	-3	-3	98	124	11	.573	1	0	0	1		-0.2
Total	15	1719	5121	650	1395	224	34	125	656	544	694	.272	.346	.403	.749	108	40	56	98	109	734	.716	46	21	1	-37	O1	-4.1
■ **TERRY FRANCONA** Francona, Terry Jon b: 4/22/59, Aberdeen, S.D. BL/TL, 6'1", 190 lbs. Deb: 8/19/81																												
1981	Mon-N	34	95	11	26	0	1	1	8	5	6	.274	.317	.326	.643	84	-2	-2	99	92	11	.551	1	0	0	0	O/1	-0.1
1982	Mon-N	46	131	14	42	3	0	0	9	8	11	.321	.360	.344	.703	93	-0	-1	105	78	16	.585	2	3	-1	-5	O1	-0.8
1983	Mon-N	120	230	21	59	11	1	3	22	6	20	.257	.275	.352	.628	72	-9	-10	102	97	20	.483	0	2	-1	-2	O1	-1.6
1984	Mon-N	58	214	18	74	19	2	1	18	5	12	.346	.364	.467	.831	144	8	10	91	70	35	.736	0	0	0	2	1/O	1.1
1985	Mon-N	107	281	19	75	15	1	2	31	12	12	.267	.299	.349	.648	86	-8	-6	94	119	29	.547	5	5	-2	2	1O/3	-0.7
1986	Chi-N	86	124	13	31	3	0	2	8	6	8	.250	.290	.323	.613	64	-5	-6	107	69	11	.485	0	1	-1	-7	O1	-1.6
1987	Cin-N	102	207	16	47	5	0	3	12	10	12	.227	.266	.295	.561	47	-15	-16	104	68	16	.448	2	0	1	-4	1/O	-2.3
1988	Cle-A	62	212	24	66	8	0	1	12	5	18	.311	.327	.363	.690	92	-2	-3	102	60	24	.547	0	0	0	1	D/1O	-0.1
Total	8	615	1494	136	420	64	5	13	120	57	99	.281	.310	.357	.667	85	-34	-33	99	84	161	.556	10	11	-4	-14	1O/D3	-6.1
■ **CHARLIE FRANK** Frank, Charles b: 5/30/1870, Mobile, Ala. d: 5/24/22, Memphis, Tenn. Deb: 8/18/1893																												
1893	StL-N	40	164	29	55	6	3	1	17	18	8	.335	.408	.427	.834	125	6	6	99	67	33	.899	8			2	O	0.6
1894	StL-N	80	319	52	89	12	7	4	42	44	13	.279	.372	.398	.770	86	-6	-7	101	73	54	.817	14			-2	O/1P	-1.0
Total	2	120	483	81	144	18	10	5	59	62	21	.298	.384	.408	.792	98	0	-0	100	71	86	.844	22			0	O/1P	-0.4
■ **FRED FRANK** Frank, Frederick b: 3/11/1874, Louisa, Ky. d: 3/27/50, Ashland, Ky. Deb: 9/27/1898																												
1898	Cle-N	17	53	3	11	1	1	0	3	4		.208	.276	.264	.540	60	-3	-3	96	65	4	.476	1			0	O	-0.1
■ **FRANKLIN** Franklin Deb:9/27/1884																												
1884	Was-U	1	3	0	0	0	0	0		0		.000	.000	.000	.000	-99	-1	-1	97	0	0	.000	0			0	/O	0.0
■ **MOE FRANKLIN** Franklin, Murray Asher b: 4/1/14, Chicago, Ill. d: 3/16/78, Harbor City, Cal. BR/TR, 6', 175 lbs. Deb: 8/12/41																												
1941	Det-A	13	10	1	3	1	0	0	0	2	2	.300	.417	.400	.817	110	0	0	106	0	2	.750	0	0	0	0	/S3	0.0
1942	Det-A	48	154	24	40	7	0	2	16	7	5	.260	.301	.344	.645	72	-4	-7	113	96	16	.530	0	0	0	-1	S/2	-0.5
Total	2	61	164	25	43	8	0	2	16	9	7	.262	.309	.348	.656	74	-4	-6	112	89	18	.548	0	0	0	-1	/S23	-0.5
■ **HERMAN FRANKS** Franks, Herman Louis b: 1/4/14, Price, Utah BL/TR, 5'10.5", 187 lbs. Deb: 4/27/39 MC																												
1939	StL-N	17	17	1	1	0	0	0	3	3	3	.059	.200	.059	.259	-26	-3	-3	105	0	0	.235	0			-1	C	-0.3
1940	Bro-N	65	131	11	24	4	0	1	14	20	6	.183	.296	.237	.533	45	-9	-10	108	153	10	.486	2			-2	C	-1.0
1941	Bro-N	57	139	10	28	7	0	1	11	14	13	.201	.275	.273	.548	53	-8	-9	103	97	11	.464	0			-1	C/O	-0.4
1947	Phi-A	8	15	2	3	0	1	0	1	4	4	.200	.368	.333	.702	96	0	0	100	74	2	.692	0	0	0	0	/C	0.1
1948	Phi-A	40	98	10	22	7	1	1	14	16	11	.224	.345	.347	.692	83	-2	-2	102	128	12	.650	0	0	0	2	C	0.2
1949	NY-N	1	3	1	2	0	0	0	0	0	0	.667	.667	.667	1.333	255	1	1	102	0	1	2.000	0			0	/C	0.1
Total	6	188	403	35	80	18	2	3	43	57	37	.199	.302	.275	.578	57	-21	-24	104	117	37	.536	2	0		-2	C/O	-1.3
■ **JOE FRAZIER** Frazier, Joseph Filmore b: 10/6/22, Liberty, N.C. BL/TR, 6', 180 lbs. Deb: 8/31/47 M																												
1947	Cle-A	9	14	1	1	1	0	0	0	1	1	.071	.133	.143	.276	-24	-2	-2	96	0	0	.214	0	0	0	-1	/O	-0.3
1954	StL-N	81	88	8	26	5	2	3	18	13	17	.295	.392	.500	.892	130	4	4	100	134	18	.921	0	0	0	-2	O/1	0.1
1955	StL-N	58	70	12	14	1	0	4	9	6	12	.200	.273	.386	.658	72	-3	-3	101	93	7	.576	0	0	0	-3	O	-0.6
1956	StL-N	14	19	1	4	2	0	1	4	3	3	.211	.318	.474	.792	110	0	0	99	141	3	.750	0	1	-1	-1	/O	0.0
	Cin-N	10	17	2	4	0	0	1	2	1	7	.235	.278	.412	.690	76	-0	-1	108	84	2	.571	0	0	0	-2	/O	-0.2
	Yr	24	36	3	8	2	0	2	6	4	10	.222	.300	.444	.744	94	-0	-0	103	123	4	.667	0	1	-1	-2		-0.2
	Bal-A	45	74	7	19	6	0	1	12	11	6	.257	.360	.378	.739	101	-0	0	94	145	10	.702	0	0	0	-1	O	0.0
Total	4	217	282	31	68	15	2	10	45	35	46	.241	.331	.415	.746	97	-2	-1	99	118	40	.714	0	1	-1	-10	/O1	-1.0
■ **JOHNNY FREDERICK** Frederick, John Henry b: 1/26/02, Denver, Colo. d: 6/18/77, Tigard, Ore. BL/TL, 5'11", 165 lbs. Deb: 4/18/29																												
1929	Bro-N	148	628	127	206	**52**	6	24	75	39	34	.328	.372	.545	.917	131	21	26	94	55	122	.929	6			3	*O	1.4
1930	Bro-N	142	616	120	206	44	11	17	76	46	34	.334	.383	.524	.908	116	16	15	101	60	120	.910	1			3	*O	0.7
1931	Bro-N	146	611	81	165	34	8	17	71	31	46	.270	.312	.435	.747	97	-3	-4	101	71	84	.684	2			-4	*O	-1.5
1932	Bro-N	118	384	54	115	28	2	16	56	25	35	.299	.349	.508	.856	132	14	16	96	86	69	.836	1			-1	O	0.8
1933	Bro-N	147	556	65	171	22	7	7	64	36	14	.308	.355	.410	.765	122	13	15	97	102	84	.709	9			-6	*O	0.0
1934	Bro-N	104	307	51	91	20	1	4	35	33	13	.296	.370	.407	.777	114	4	7	95	92	49	.747	4			-5	O/1	-0.1
Total	6	805	3102	498	954	200	35	85	377	210	176	.308	.357	.477	.833	118	64	74	98	75	527	.807	23			-11	O/1	1.3
■ **ED FREED** Freed, Edwin Charles b: 8/22/19, Centre Valley, Pa. BR/TR, 5'6", 165 lbs. Deb: 9/11/42																												
1942	Phi-N	13	33	3	10	3	1	0	1	4	3	.303	.378	.455	.833	152	2	2	94	25	6	.833	1			-1	O	0.1
■ **ROGER FREED** Freed, Roger Vernon b: 6/2/46, Los Angeles, Cal. BR/TR, 6', 190 lbs. Deb: 9/18/70																												
1970	Bal-A	4	13	0	2	0	0	0	1	3	4	.154	.313	.154	.466	34	-1	-1	97	206	1	.455	0	0	0	0	/1O	0.0
1971	Phi-N	118	348	23	77	12	1	6	37	44	86	.221	.314	.313	.627	76	-9	-10	103	119	35	.555	0	3	-2	-7	*O/C	-2.4
1972	Phi-N	73	129	10	29	4	0	6	18	23	39	.225	.346	.395	.742	114	2	3	97	107	18	.721	0	1	-1	-3	O	-0.2
1974	Cin-N	6	6	1	2	0	0	1	3	1	1	.333	.429	.833	1.262	252	1	1	98	145	2	1.200	0	0	0	0	/1	0.1
1976	Mon-N	8	15	0	3	1	0	0	1	0	3	.200	.200	.267	.467	31	-1	-1	100	96	1	.333	0	0	0	0	/1O	-0.1
1977	StL-N	49	83	10	33	2	1	5	21	11	9	.398	.468	.627	1.095	199	11	11	96	125	24	1.212	0	0	0	-1	1/O	0.9
1978	StL-N	52	92	3	22	6	0	2	20	8	17	.239	.300	.370	.670	91	-2	-1	95	198	10	.597	1	0	0	-2	1/O	-0.3
1979	StL-N	34	31	2	8	2	0	2	8	5	7	.258	.361	.516	.877	130	2	1	105	144	6	.875	0	0	0	0	/1	0.1
Total	8	344	717	49	176	27	2	22	109	95	166	.245	.337	.381	.718	101	2	2	100	130	97	.683	1	4	-2	-12	O/1C	-1.9

YEAR	TM/L	G	AB	R	H	2B	3B	HR	RBI	BB	SO	AVG	OBP	SLG	PRO	/A	BR	/A	PF	CHI	RC	TA	SB	CS	SBR	FR	POS	TPR
■ **BILL FREEHAN**	Freehan, William Ashley b: 11/29/41, Detroit, Mich. BR/TR, 6'3", 203 lbs. Deb: 9/26/61																											
1961	Det-A	4	10	1	4	0	0	0	4	1	0	.400	.455	.400	.855	136	1	1	96	392	2	.833	0	0	0	-0	/C	0.0
1963	Det-A	100	300	37	73	12	2	9	36	39	56	.243	.334	.387	.721	98	1	-0	104	105	40	.677	2	0	1	1	C1	0.2
1964	Det-A	144	520	69	156	14	8	18	80	36	68	.300	.355	.462	.816	131	17	20	96	118	86	.775	5	1	1	24	*C/1	**5.1**
1965	Det-A	130	431	45	101	15	0	10	43	39	63	.234	.308	.339	.647	79	-9	-12	105	103	45	.573	4	2	0	16	*C	1.4
1966	Det-A	136	492	47	115	22	0	12	46	40	72	.234	.295	.352	.647	83	-10	-11	102	94	50	.567	5	2	0	**23**	*C/1	2.0
1967	Det-A	155	517	66	146	23	1	20	74	73	71	.282	.392	.447	.839	148	34	34	99	108	94	.851	1	2	-1	8	*C1	5.4
1968	Det-A	155	540	73	142	24	2	25	84	65	64	.263	.367	.454	.821	139	33	29	106	119	94	.819	0	1	-1	8	*C1/O	4.7
1969	Det-A	143	489	61	128	16	3	16	49	53	55	.262	.344	.405	.749	105	6	4	103	82	68	.693	1	2	-1	17	*C1	2.7
1970	Det-A	117	395	44	95	17	3	16	52	52	48	.241	.335	.420	.755	104	4	2	103	100	55	.707	0	3	-2	3	*C	0.5
1971	Det-A	148	516	57	143	26	4	21	71	54	48	.277	.356	.465	.821	137	20	23	96	98	82	.776	2	7	-4	-8	*C/O	2.0
1972	Det-A	111	374	51	98	18	2	10	56	48	51	.262	.355	.401	.756	110	12	7	113	133	55	.718	0	1	-1	6	*C/1	1.5
1973	Det-A	110	380	33	89	10	1	6	29	40	30	.234	.325	.313	.638	80	-9	-9	101	85	39	.559	0	0	0	12	C/1D	0.5
1974	Det-A	130	445	58	132	17	5	18	60	42	44	.297	.364	.479	.842	133	23	19	106	90	77	.806	2	0	1	-6	1C/D	1.4
1975	Det-A	120	427	42	105	17	3	14	47	32	56	.246	.308	.398	.706	95	-2	-4	104	87	51	.631	2	0	1	14	*C/1	1.4
1976	Det-A	71	237	22	64	10	1	5	27	12	27	.270	.308	.384	.692	98	-0	-1	104	98	28	.588	0	0	0	0	C/1D	0.1
Total	15	1774	6073	706	1591	241	35	200	758	626	753	.262	.342	.412	.754	112	120	101	103	102	867	.725	24	21	-5	120	*C1/DO	28.9
■ **JERRY FREEMAN**	Freeman, Frank Ellsworth "Buck" b: 12/26/1879, Placerville, Cal. d: 9/30/52, Los Angeles, Cal. BL/TR, 6'2", 220 lbs. Deb: 4/14/08																											
1908	Was-A	154	531	45	134	15	5	1	45	36		.252	.300	.305	.605	104	-1	2	95	105	48	.514	6			-12	*1	-1.5
1909	Was-A	19	48	2	8	0	1	0	3	4		.167	.245	.208	.454	48	-3	-2	90	116	3	.450	3			-0	1/O	-0.2
Total	2	173	579	47	142	15	6	1	48	40		.245	.295	.297	.592	99	-4	-0	95	105	51	.508	9			-12	1/O	-1.7
■ **JOHN FREEMAN**	Freeman, John Edward b: 1/24/01, Boston, Mass. d: 4/14/58, Washington, D.C. BR/TR, 5'8", 160 lbs. Deb: 6/17/27																											
1927	Bos-A	4	2	0	0	0	0	0	0	0	0	.000	.000	.000	.000	-99	-1	-1	95	0	0	.000	0	0	0	-1	/O	-0.1
■ **BUCK FREEMAN**	Freeman, John Frank b: 10/30/1871, Catasauqua, Pa. d: 6/25/49, Wilkes-Barre, Pa. BL/TL, 5'9", 169 lbs. Deb: 6/27/1891																											
1891	Was-a	5	18	1	4	1	0	0	1	2	2	.222	.300	.278	.578	71	-1	-1	95	59	2	.500	0			0	/P	0.0
1898	Was-N	29	107	19	39	2	3	3	21	7		.364	.424	.523	.947	171	10	10	102	103	25	1.015	2			0	O	0.9
1899	Was-N	155	588	107	187	19	25	**25**	122	23		.318	.361	.563	.924	161	38	42	96	98	130	.978	21			-13	*O/P	1.7
1900	Bos-N	117	418	58	126	19	13	6	65	25		.301	.341	.452	.793	100	10	-3	120	100	70	.767	10			-8	O1	-1.6
1901	Bos-A	129	490	88	166	23	15	12	114	44		.339	.393	.520	.914	159	35	37	97	131	110	.975	17			-5	*1/2O	2.3
1902	Bos-A	138	564	75	174	38	19	11	**121**	32		.309	.346	.502	.847	135	23	24	99	121	106	.851	17			-4	*O	1.0
1903	Bos-A	141	567	74	163	39	20	**13**	**104**	30		.287	.323	.496	.819	129	28	20	112	113	95	.782	5			-5	*O	0.6
1904	Bos-A	157	597	64	167	20	**19**	7	84	32		.280	.316	.412	.728	126	20	17	105	124	82	.663	7			-4	*O	0.3
1905	Bos-A	130	455	59	109	20	8	3	49	46		.240	.309	.338	.648	107	4	4	100	109	51	.601	8			-4	1O/3	-0.4
1906	Bos-A	121	392	42	98	18	9	1	30	28		.250	.300	.349	.649	107	2	3	98	78	44	.578	5			2	O1/3	0.1
1907	Bos-A	4	12	1	2	0	0	1	2	3		.167	.333	.417	.750	140	1	1	101	91	2	.800	0			1	/O	0.1
Total	11	1126	4208	588	1235	199	131	82	713	272	<u>2</u>	.293	.339	.462	.801	131	170	153	103	110	716	.783	92			-41	O1/P32	5.0
■ **GENE FREESE**	Freese, Eugene Lewis "Augie" b: 1/8/34, Wheeling, W.Va. BR/TR, 5'11", 175 lbs. Deb: 4/13/55																											
1955	Pit-N	134	455	69	115	21	8	14	44	34	57	.253	.310	.426	.737	96	-6	-4	97	77	60	.675	5	1	1	-3	32	0.0
1956	Pit-N	65	207	17	43	9	0	3	14	16	45	.208	.274	.295	.569	52	-14	-14	102	84	18	.497	2	1	0	-3	32	-1.5
1957	Pit-N	114	346	44	98	18	2	6	31	17	42	.283	.321	.399	.719	98	-4	-2	94	82	44	.648	9	4	0	-3	32O	-0.2
1958	Pit-N	17	18	1	3	0	0	1	2	1	2	.167	.211	.333	.544	43	-2	-1	95	92	1	.438	0	0	0	0	/3	-0.1
	StL-N	62	191	28	49	11	1	6	16	10	32	.257	.294	.419	.712	81	-4	-6	106	67	24	.632	1	1	-0	-4	S2/3	-0.7
	Yr	79	209	29	52	11	1	7	18	11	34	.249	.286	.411	.698	79	-6	-7	104	74	25	.616	1	1	-0	-4		-0.8
1959	Phi-N	132	400	60	107	14	5	23	70	43	61	.268	.346	.500	.846	123	12	12	99	105	69	.839	8	4	0	-18	*3/2	-0.8
1960	Chi-A	127	455	60	124	32	6	17	79	29	65	.273	.318	.481	.799	112	6	5	101	117	64	.736	10	6	-1	1	*3	0.8
1961	Cin-N	152	575	78	159	27	2	26	87	27	78	.277	.309	.466	.775	98	-0	-3	104	103	77	.697	8	2	1	-18	*3/2	-2.5
1962	Cin-N	18	42	2	6	1	0	0	1	6	8	.143	.250	.167	.417	14	-5	-5	102	56	2	.342	0	0	0	-1	3	-0.5
1963	Cin-N	66	217	20	53	9	1	6	26	17	42	.244	.305	.378	.683	92	-1	-2	104	109	26	.625	4	2	0	-2	3/O	-0.4
1964	Pit-N	99	289	33	65	13	2	9	40	19	45	.225	.273	.377	.650	80	-8	-8	101	121	28	.551	1	2	-1	1	3	-1.2
1965	Pit-N	43	80	6	21	4	0	0	8	6	18	.262	.330	.313	.642	82	-2	-2	100	133	7	.500	0	2	-1	-1	3	-0.4
	Chi-A	17	32	2	9	0	1	1	4	5	9	.281	.378	.438	.816	143	1	2	92	98	6	.826	0	0	0	0	/3	0.2
1966	Chi-A	48	106	8	22	2	0	3	10	8	20	.208	.270	.311	.581	70	-5	-4	94	100	9	.512	2	1	0	1	3	-0.3
	Hou-N	21	33	1	3	0	0	0	0	5	11	.091	.211	.091	.301	-13	-5	-5	97	0	1	.290	1	0	0	-0	/32O	-0.4
Total	12	1115	3446	429	877	161	28	115	432	243	535	.254	.307	.418	.725	94	-37	-38	100	97	434	.675	51	26	-0	-49	32/SO	-8.0
■ **GEORGE FREESE**	Freese, George Walter "Bud" b: 9/12/26, Wheeling, W.Va. BR/TR, 6', 190 lbs. Deb: 4/29/53																											
1953	Det-A	1	1	0	0	0	0	0	0	0	0	.000	.000	.000	.000	-99	-0	-0	98	0	0	.000	0	0	0	0	H	0.0
1955	Pit-N	51	179	17	46	8	2	3	22	17	18	.257	.328	.374	.703	89	-3	-3	97	119	21	.617	1	1	-0	-4	3	-0.7
1961	Chi-N	9	7	0	2	0	0	0	1	1	4	.286	.375	.286	.661	79	-0	-0	100	202	1	.600	0	0	0	0	H	0.0
Total	3	61	187	17	48	8	2	3	23	18	22	.257	.329	.369	.697	87	-4	-3	97	122	22	.643	1	1	-0	-4	/3	-0.7
■ **JIM FREGOSI**	Fregosi, James Louis b: 4/4/42, San Francisco, Cal. BR/TR, 6'1", 190 lbs. Deb: 9/14/61 M																											
1961	LA-A	11	27	7	6	0	0	0	3	1	4	.222	.250	.222	.472	25	-3	-3	111	196	1	.304	0	0	0	0	S	-0.1
1962	LA-A	58	175	15	51	3	4	3	23	18	27	.291	.358	.406	.763	103	1	1	102	114	25	.705	2	1	0	3	S	0.7
1963	LA-A	154	592	83	170	29	12	9	50	36	104	.287	.328	.422	.750	119	6	12	91	80	81	.664	2	2	-1	5	*S	2.4
1964	LA-A	147	505	86	140	22	9	18	72	72	87	.277	.372	.463	.835	147	22	29	89	112	89	.835	8	3	1	12	*S	4.3
1965	Cal-A	161	602	66	167	19	7	15	64	54	107	.277	.341	.407	.748	114	9	11	98	88	85	.702	13	5	1	9	*S	2.9
1966	Cal-A	162	611	78	154	32	7	13	67	67	89	.252	.328	.391	.719	107	5	6	99	97	80	.681	17	8	0	19	*S/1	3.6
1967	Cal-A	151	590	75	171	23	6	9	56	49	77	.290	.349	.395	.744	125	14	17	96	79	82	.680	9	6	-1	-6	*S	2.2
1968	Cal-A	159	614	77	150	21	**13**	9	49	60	101	.244	.317	.365	.681	113	4	8	94	74	72	.621	9	4	0	-15	*S	0.5
1969	Cal-A	161	580	78	151	22	6	12	47	93	86	.260	.364	.381	.745	109	9	9	99	71	86	.735	9	2	2	-9	*S	0.9
1970	Cal-A	158	601	95	167	33	5	22	82	69	92	.278	.355	.459	.814	134	18	25	92	103	101	.786	0	2	-1	0	*S/1	3.6
1971	Cal-A	107	347	31	81	15	1	5	33	39	61	.233	.320	.326	.645	84	-7	-6	99	107	39	.587	2	1	0	-4	S1/O	-0.3
1972	NY-N	101	340	31	79	15	4	5	32	38	71	.232	.311	.344	.655	90	-6	-4	95	102	37	.582	0	1	-1	0	3/S1	-0.4
1973	NY-N	45	124	7	29	4	1	0	11	20	25	.234	.340	.282	.623	74	-4	-4	101	126	12	.566	1	2	-1	0	S3/1O	-0.2
	Tex-A	45	157	25	42	6	2	6	16	12	31	.268	.324	.446	.769	118	3	3	97	73	23	.709	0	1	-1	-4	31/S	-0.1
1974	Tex-A	78	230	31	60	5	0	12	34	22	41	.261	.325	.439	.765	123	5	6	96	98	29	.676	0	1	-1	2	13	0.6
1975	Tex-A	77	191	25	50	5	0	7	33	20	39	.262	.335	.398	.733	107	2	2	100	131	24	.655	0	1	-1	3	1D/3	0.1
1976	Tex-A	58	133	17	31	7	0	2	12	23	33	.233	.346	.331	.677	97	1	0	102	92	17	.651	2	0	1	0	1D/3	0.0
1977	Tex-A	13	28	4	7	1	0	1	5	3	4	.250	.323	.393	.715	90	-0	-0	105	142	4	.667	0	0	0	0	/1D	0.0
	Pit-N	36	56	10	16	1	1	3	16	13	10	.286	.420	.500	.920	142	4	4	103	173	13	1.049	2	0	1	-1	1/3	0.3
1978	Pit-N	20	20	3	4	1	0	0	1	6	8	.200	.385	.250	.635	76	-0	-0	105	79	3	.688	0	0	0	0	/312	0.0
Total	18	1902	6523	844	1726	264	78	151	706	715	1097	.265	.340	.398	.739	114	83	115	96	94	904	.707	76	40	-1	14	*S13/DO2	21.0
■ **VERN FREIBERGER**	Freiberger, Vern Donald b: 12/19/23, Detroit, Mich. BR/TL, 6'1", 170 lbs. Deb: 9/06/41																											
1941	Cle-A	2	8	0	1	0	0	0	1	0	2	.125	.125	.125	.250	-34	-2	-2	101	361	0	.125	0	0	0	0	/1	-0.1
■ **HOWARD FREIGAU**	Freigau, Howard Earl "Ty" b: 8/1/02, Dayton, Ohio d: 7/18/32, Chattanooga, Tenn BR/TR, 5'10.5", 160 lbs. Deb: 9/13/22																											
1922	StL-N	3	1	0	0	0	0	0	0	0	0	.000	.000	.000	.000	-99	-0	-0	101	0	0	.000	0	0	0	0	/S3	0.0
1923	StL-N	113	358	30	94	18	1	1	35	25	36	.263	.314	.327	.641	77	-16	-11	90	103	37	.556	5	4	-1	-7	S2/13O	-1.1
1924	StL-N	98	376	35	101	17	6	2	39	19	24	.269	.306	.362	.667	76	-12	-13	103	102	42	.597	10	3	1	-8	3/S	-1.2
1925	StL-N	9	26	2	4	0	0	0	0	2	1	.154	.214	.154	.368	-4	-4	-4	102	0	1	.273	0	0	0	-0	/S2	-0.3
	Chi-N	117	476	77	146	22	10	8	71	30	31	.307	.349	.445	.794	104	0	2	97	103	73	.753	10	6	-1	2	3S/1	0.9
	Yr	126	502	79	150	22	10	8	71	32	32	.299	.342	.430	.772	98	-4	-2	98	95	73	.723	10	6	-1	1		0.6

YEAR	TM/L	G	AB	R	H	2B	3B	HR	RBI	BB	SO	AVG	OBP	SLG	PRO	/A	BR	/A	PF	CHI	RC	TA	SB	CS	SBR	FR	POS	TPR
1926	Chi-N	140	508	51	137	27	7	3	51	43	42	.270	.327	.368	.695	82	-10	-14	106	92	61	.636	6			-3	*3/SO	-1.4
1927	Chi-N	30	86	12	20	5	0	0	10	9	10	.233	.313	.291	.603	62	-4	-4	100	140	8	.530	0			0	3	-0.1
1928	Bro-N	17	34	6	7	2	0	0	3	1	3	.206	.229	.265	.493	29	-4	-4	99	119	2	.370	0			0	3/S	-0.2
	Bos-N	52	109	11	28	8	1	1	17	9	14	.257	.319	.376	.695	83	-3	-3	97	138	13	.642	1			-3	S2	-0.3
	Yr	69	143	17	35	10	1	1	20	10	17	.245	.299	.350	.648	71	-7	-6	98	135	15	.574	1			-3		-0.5
Total	7	579	1974	224	537	99	25	15	226	138	161	.272	.322	.370	.692	82	-53	-51	99	102	238	.626	32	13		-20	3S/210	-3.7
■ **CHARLIE FRENCH**	French, Charles Calvin b: 10/12/1883, Indianapolis, Ind. d: 3/30/62, Indianapolis, Ind. BL/TR, 5'6", 140 lbs. Deb: 5/23/09																											
1909	Bos-A	51	167	15	42	3	1	0	13	15		.251	.324	.281	.606	84	-1	-3	109	109	17	.584	8			2	2S	0.0
1910	Bos-A	9	40	4	8	1	0	0	3	1		.200	.220	.225	.445	40	-3	-3	99	106	2	.313	0			-0	/2	-0.3
	Chi-A	45	170	17	28	1	1	0	4	10		.165	.224	.182	.406	29	-14	-13	95	50	8	.345	5			-5	2O	-2.2
	Yr	54	210	21	36	2	1	0	7	11		.171	.223	.190	.414	31	-17	-16	96	62	9	.339	5			-5		-2.5
Total	2	105	377	36	78	5	2	0	20	26		.207	.269	.231	.500	56	-18	-19	102	82	27	.441	13			-3	/2SO	-2.5
■ **PAT FRENCH**	French, Frank Alexander b: 9/22/1893, Dover, N.H. d: 7/13/69, Bath, Maine BR/TR, 6'1", 180 lbs. Deb: 7/02/17																											
1917	Phi-A	3	2	0	0	0	0	0	0	0	0	.000	.000	.000	.000	-99	-0	-0	94	0	0	.000	0			-0	/O	0.0
■ **RAY FRENCH**	French, Raymond Edward b: 1/9/1895, Alameda, Cal. d: 4/3/78, Alameda, Cal. BR/TR, 5'9.5", 158 lbs. Deb: 9/17/20																											
1920	NY-A	2	2	2	0	0	0	0	1	0	1	.000	.000	.000	.000	-98	-1	-1	102	0	0	.000	0	0	0	0	/S	0.0
1923	Bro-N	43	73	14	16	2	1	0	7	4	7	.219	.269	.274	.543	45	-6	-6	98	123	6	.439	0	0	0	0	S	-0.2
1924	Chi-A	37	112	13	20	4	0	0	11	10	13	.179	.246	.214	.460	20	-14	-13	97	151	7	.398	3	1	0	-3	S/2	-1.2
Total	3	82	187	29	36	6	1	0	19	14	21	.193	.252	.235	.488	28	-20	-19	97	139	12	.408	3	1	0	-3	/S2	-1.4
■ **JIM FRENCH**	French, Richard James b: 8/13/41, Warren, Ohio BL/TR, 5'8", 180 lbs. Deb: 9/12/65																											
1965	Was-A	13	37	4	11	0	0	1	7	9	5	.297	.435	.378	.813	133	2	2	100	171	7	.889	1	0	0	1	C	0.5
1966	Was-A	10	24	0	5	1	0	0	3	4	5	.208	.321	.250	.571	70	-1	-1	95	210	2	.500	0	1	-1	0	C	0.0
1967	Was-A	6	16	0	1	0	0	0	1	3	4	.063	.211	.063	.273	-16	-2	-2	102	417	0	.267	0	0	0	1	/C	0.0
1968	Was-A	59	165	9	32	5	0	1	10	19	19	.194	.281	.242	.524	65	-8	-6	91	100	13	.449	1	2	-1	6	C	0.1
1969	Was-A	63	158	14	29	6	3	2	13	41	15	.184	.352	.297	.649	86	-2	-1	97	98	20	.690	1	0	0	5	C	0.8
1970	Was-A	69	166	20	35	3	1	1	13	38	23	.211	.358	.259	.617	76	-4	-4	96	114	17	.591	0	1	-1	-6	C/O	-0.9
1971	Was-A	14	41	6	6	2	0	0	4	7	7	.146	.271	.195	.466	37	-3	-3	92	204	2	.375	0	2	-1	1	C	-0.2
Total	7	234	607	53	119	17	4	5	51	121	78	.196	.331	.262	.593	75	-18	-15	95	127	61	.571	3	6	-3	7	C/O	0.3
■ **WALT FRENCH**	French, Walter Edward "Piggy" or "Fitz" b: 7/12/1899, Moorestown, N.J. d: 5/13/84, Mountain Home, Ark BL/TR, 5'7.5", 155 lbs. Deb: 9/15/23																											
1923	Phi-A	16	39	7	9	3	0	0	2	5	7	.231	.318	.308	.626	65	-2	-2	100	57	4	.548	0	1	-1	-1	O	-0.3
1925	Phi-A	67	100	20	37	9	0	0	14	1	9	.370	.376	.460	.836	108	1	1	103	102	16	.750	1	1	-0	-1	O	-0.1
1926	Phi-A	112	397	51	121	18	7	1	36	18	24	.305	.340	.393	.733	77	-6	-16	118	78	53	.642	2	3	-1	1	O	-2.2
1927	Phi-A	109	326	48	99	10	5	0	41	16	14	.304	.338	.365	.703	85	-9	-7	97	115	39	.639	9	0	3	-3	O	-1.4
1928	Phi-A	48	74	9	19	4	0	0	7	2	5	.257	.286	.311	.597	55	-5	-5	103	104	6	.482	1	1	-0	-2	O	-0.7
1929	Phi-A	45	45	7	12	1	0	1	9	2	3	.267	.298	.356	.653	62	-2	-3	109	162	5	.545	0	0	0	-3	O	-0.5
Total	6	397	981	142	297	45	12	2	109	44	62	.303	.336	.379	.715	80	-22	-32	107	98	123	.629	13	6	0	-9	O	-5.2
■ **BILL FRENCH**	French, William b: Baltimore, Md. Deb: 4/14/1873																											
1873	Mar-n	5	19	3	4							.211															/1OP1	
■ **LONNY FREY**	Frey, Linus Reinhard "Junior" b: 8/23/10, St.Louis, Mo. BL/TR, 5'10", 160 lbs. Deb: 8/29/33																											
1933	Bro-N	34	135	25	43	5	3	0	12	13	13	.319	.378	.400	.778	127	4	5	97	74	21	.740	4			-3	S	0.5
1934	Bro-N	125	490	77	139	24	5	8	57	52	54	.284	.358	.402	.760	109	3	7	95	99	75	.740	11			5	*S3	1.4
1935	Bro-N	131	515	88	135	35	11	11	77	66	68	.262	.352	.437	.788	118	8	13	94	104	82	.768	6			3	*S/2	2.0
1936	Bro-N	148	524	63	146	29	4	4	60	71	56	.279	.369	.372	.741	95	2	-1	105	105	77	.708	7			-27	*S2/O	-1.8
1937	Chi-N	78	198	33	55	9	3	1	22	33	15	.278	.381	.369	.750	102	3	2	103	104	31	.762	6			-4	S2/3O	0.1
1938	Cin-N	124	501	76	133	26	6	4	36	49	50	.265	.331	.365	.696	93	-6	-4	98	64	66	.640	4			-6	*2/S	-0.1
1939	Cin-N	125	484	95	141	27	9	11	55	72	46	.291	.387	.452	.840	121	19	17	103	71	91	.860	5			12	*2	3.3
1940	Cin-N	150	563	102	150	23	6	8	54	80	48	.266	.361	.371	.732	101	4	3	101	83	82	.749	**22**			18	*2	3.1
1941	Cin-N	146	543	78	138	29	5	6	59	72	37	.254	.345	.359	.704	99	0	1	99	106	72	.694	16			-2	*2	0.9
1942	Cin-N	141	523	66	139	23	6	2	39	87	38	.266	.373	.344	.717	109	10	10	101	75	75	.716	9			12	*2	3.4
1943	Cin-N	144	586	78	154	20	8	2	43	76	56	.263	.347	.334	.682	98	-0	0	99	66	75	.643	7			14	*2	1.9
1946	Cin-N	111	333	46	82	10	3	3	24	63	31	.246	.368	.321	.689	93	1	-1	104	77	44	.688	5			14	2O	1.6
1947	Chi-N	24	43	4	9	0	0	0	3	4	6	.209	.277	.209	.486	30	-4	-4	101	123	3	.382	0			0	/2	-0.2
	NY-A	24	28	10	5	2	0	0	2	10	1	.179	.410	.250	.660	89	0	0	97	105	5	.875	3	0	1	-0	/2	0.1
1948	NY-A	1	0	1	0	0	0	0	0	0	0	—	—	—	—	—	0	0	100	—	—	—	0	0	0	0	R	0.0
	NY-N	29	51	6	13	1	0	1	6	4	6	.255	.309	.333	.642	74	-2	-2	100	112	6	.553	0			0	2	0.0
Total	14	1535	5517	848	1482	263	69	61	549	752	525	.269	.359	.374	.734	103	43	45	100	86	808	.731	105	0		35	2S/O3	16.2
■ **PEPE FRIAS**	Frias, Jesus Maria (Andujar) b: 7/14/48, San De Pedro De Macoris, D.R. BR/TR, 5'10", 159 lbs. Deb: 4/06/73																											
1973	Mon-N	100	225	19	52	10	1	0	22	10	24	.231	.267	.284	.551	51	-14	-16	104	138	16	.420	1	3	-2	1	S2/3O	-0.8
1974	Mon-N	75	112	12	24	4	1	0	7	7	10	.214	.261	.268	.528	46	-8	-8	104	90	8	.432	1	0	0	2	S32/O	-0.2
1975	Mon-N	51	64	4	8	2	0	0	4	3	13	.125	.164	.156	.320	-10	-10	-10	108	155	2	.224	0	1	-1	3	S3/2	-0.4
1976	Mon-N	76	113	7	28	5	0	0	8	4	14	.248	.274	.292	.566	60	-6	-6	100	93	9	.432	1	1	-0	3	2S/3O	0.1
1977	Mon-N	53	70	10	18	1	0	0	5	0	10	.257	.257	.271	.529	43	-6	-6	98	105	5	.377	1	0	0	-0	2S/3	-0.2
1978	Mon-N	73	15	5	4	2	1	0	5	0	3	.267	.267	.533	.800	124	0	0	96	248	2	.727	0	0	0	-1	2/S	0.4
1979	Atl-N	140	475	41	123	18	4	1	44	20	36	.259	.292	.320	.612	61	-22	-27	109	113	42	.482	3	2	-0	-3	*S	-1.7
1980	Tex-A	116	227	27	55	5	1	0	10	4	23	.242	.259	.273	.532	46	-17	-17	100	63	15	.398	5	1	1	-1	*S/32	-0.7
	LA-N	14	9	1	2	1	0	0	0	0	0	.222	.222	.333	.556	55	-1	-1	97	0	0	.375	0	0	0	-0	S	0.0
1981	LA-N	25	36	6	9	1	0	0	3	1	3	.250	.289	.278	.567	63	-2	-2	98	118	3	.444	0	0	0	0	S/23	0.0
Total	9	723	1346	132	323	49	8	1	108	49	136	.240	.269	.290	.560	52	-85	-92	105	108	102	.443	12	8	-1	3	S2/3O	-3.5
■ **BERNIE FRIBERG**	Friberg, Bernard Albert (born Gustaf Bernhard Friberg) b: 8/18/1899, Manchester, N.H. d: 12/8/58, Lynn, Mass. BR/TR, 5'11.", 178 lbs. Deb: 8/20/19																											
1919	Chi-N	8	20	0	4	1	0	0	1	0	2	.200	.200	.250	.450	35	-2	-2	100	78	1	.313	0			-1	/O	-0.2
1920	Chi-N	50	114	11	24	5	1	0	7	6	20	.211	.250	.272	.522	50	-7	-7	99	87	8	.424	2	2	-1	-5	2O	-1.4
1922	Chi-N	97	296	51	92	8	2	0	23	37	37	.311	.391	.351	.742	98	-1	1	95	77	41	.706	8	10	-4	-2	O/132	-0.6
1923	Chi-N	146	547	91	174	27	11	12	88	45	49	.318	.372	.473	.846	117	16	13	104	111	91	.814	13	19	-8	4	*3	1.2
1924	Chi-N	142	495	67	138	19	3	5	82	66	53	.279	.369	.360	.729	95	-0	-1	101	**164**	65	.698	19	27	-11	3	*3	0.2
1925	Chi-N	44	152	12	39	5	3	1	16	14	22	.257	.327	.349	.676	75	-6	-5	97	104	18	.605	0	1	-1	-1	3O/1S	-0.5
	Phi-N	91	304	41	82	12	1	5	22	39	35	.270	.353	.365	.718	72	-7	-14	116	62	41	.677	1	1	-0	-6	23/PC	-1.8
	Yr	135	456	53	121	17	4	6	38	53	57	.265	.344	.360	.704	73	-13	-19	110	76	59	.653	1	2	-1	-8		-2.3
1926	Phi-N	144	478	38	128	21	3	1	51	57	77	.268	.346	.331	.676	80	-10	-12	103	112	56	.620	2			19	*2	1.4
1927	Phi-N	111	335	31	78	8	2	1	28	41	49	.233	.322	.278	.600	64	-17	-15	96	102	32	.545	3			15	*3/2	0.5
1928	Phi-N	52	94	11	19	3	0	1	7	12	16	.202	.292	.266	.558	45	-7	-8	104	89	8	.493	0			-1	S/3201	-0.4
1929	Phi-N	128	455	74	137	21	10	7	55	49	54	.301	.370	.437	.808	91	-0	-7	110	87	73	.786	1			-6	SO/21	-0.5
1930	Phi-N	105	331	62	113	21	1	4	42	47	35	.341	.425	.447	.872	105	8	5	106	90	64	.904	1			-2	2OS/3	0.6
1931	Phi-N	103	353	33	92	19	5	1	26	33	25	.261	.324	.351	.675	77	-9	-12	106	73	42	.605	1			4	23/1S	-0.3
1932	Phi-N	61	154	17	37	8	2	0	14	19	23	.240	.324	.318	.642	66	-5	-8	112	106	17	.581	0			-9	2	-1.2
1933	Bos-A	17	41	5	13	3	0	0	9	6	1	.317	.404	.390	.794	110	1	1	101	188	7	.786	0	0	0	-0	/23S	0.1
Total	14	1299	4169	544	1170	181	44	38	471	471	498	.281	.356	.373	.728	87	-46	-71	104	102	564	.684	51	60		12	32OS/1CP	-2.9
■ **JIM FRIDLEY**	Fridley, James Riley "Big Jim" b: 9/6/24, Philippi, W.Va. BR/TR, 6'2", 205 lbs. Deb: 4/15/52																											
1952	Cle-A	62	175	23	44	2	0	4	16	14	40	.251	.311	.331	.642	87	-5	-3	91	85	18	.555	3	3	-1	-6	O	-1.2
1954	Bal-A	85	240	25	59	8	5	4	36	21	41	.246	.312	.371	.683	91	-5	-4	95	135	25	.574	0	1	-1	-5	O	-1.0

YEAR	TM/L	G	AB	R	H	2B	3B	HR	RBI	BB	SO	AVG	OBP	SLG	PRO	/A	BR	/A	PF	CHI	RC	TA	SB	CS	SBR	FR	POS	TPR
1958	Cin-N	5	9	2	2	2	0	0	1	0	2	.222	.222	.444	.667	66	-0	-0	107	103	1	.571	0	0	0	-1	/O	0.0
Total	3	152	424	50	105	12	5	8	53	35	83	.248	.310	.356	.666	89	-11	-7	94	114	44	.594	3	4	-2	-11	O	-2.2
■ PAT FRIEL Friel, Patrick Henry b: 6/11/1860, Lewsburg, W.Va. d: 1/15/24, Providence, R.I. BB , 5'11", 170 lbs. Deb: 7/13/1890																												
1890	Syr-a	62	261	51	65	8	2	3		17		.249	.302	.330	.632	98	-4	-0	90	0	37	.714	34			-7	O	-0.8
1891	Phi-a	2	8	2	2	1	0	0	0	0	0	.250	.250	.375	.625	78	-0	-0	103	0	1	.500	0			0	/O	0.0
Total	2	64	269	53	67	9	2	3	0	17	0	.249	.301	.331	.632	97	-5	-1	91	0	38	.708	34			-7	/O	-0.8
■ BILL FRIEL Friel, William Edward b: 4/1/1876, Renovo, Pa. d: 12/24/59, St.Louis, Mo. BL/TR, 5'10", 215 lbs. Deb: 5/03/01																												
1901	Mil-A	106	376	51	100	13	7	4	35	23		.266	.308	.370	.678	94	-6	-3	95	75	49	.641	15			-8	3O/2S	-1.1
1902	StL-A	80	267	26	64	9	2	2	20	14		.240	.278	.311	.588	63	-13	-14	102	74	25	.498	4			1	O21/3SPC	-1.2
1903	StL-A	97	351	46	80	11	8	0	25	23		.228	.275	.305	.580	80	-10	-8	95	89	31	.494	4			-7	23/O	-1.5
Total	3	283	994	123	244	33	17	6	80	60		.245	.288	.331	.619	80	-29	-25	97	80	105	.549	23			-15	/32O1SCP	-3.8
■ FRANK FRIEND Friend, Frank B. b: Washington, D.C. d: 9/8/1897, Atlantic City, N.J Deb: 8/02/1896																												
1896	Lou-N	2	5	1	1	0	0	0	0	1	1	.200	.333	.200	.533	45	-0	-0	98	0	0	.500	0			0	/C	0.0
■ OWEN FRIEND Friend, Owen Lacey "Red" b: 3/21/27, Granite City, Ill. BR/TR, 6'1", 180 lbs. Deb: 10/02/49 C																												
1949	StL-A	2	8	1	3	0	0	0	1	0	0	.375	.375	.375	.750	99	-0	-0	100	116	1	.600	0	0	0	0	/2	0.0
1950	StL-A	119	372	48	88	15	2	8	50	40	68	.237	.312	.352	.664	65	-18	-22	107	111	41	.582	2	1	0	-6	23/S	-2.0
1953	Det-A	31	96	10	17	4	0	3	10	6	9	.177	.233	.313	.546	47	-8	-7	98	95	6	.435	0	1	-1	-1	2	-0.7
	Cle-A	34	68	7	16	2	0	2	13	5	16	.235	.288	.353	.641	76	-3	-2	95	160	7	.537	0	0	0	2	2/S3	0.1
	Yr	65	164	17	33	6	0	5	23	11	25	.201	.256	.329	.585	59	-11	-10	96	131	14	.493	0	1	-1	1		-0.6
1955	Bos-A	14	42	3	11	3	0	0	2	4	11	.262	.326	.333	.659	62	-1	-3	124	53	4	.545	0	0	0	0	S/2	0.0
	Chi-N	6	10	0	1	0	0	0	0	0	3	.100	.100	.100	.200	-47	-2	-2	100	0	0	.111	0	0	0	0	/3S	-0.1
1956	Chi-N	2	2	0	0	0	0	0	0	0	2	.000	.000	.000	.000	-99	-1	-1	99	0	0	.000	0	0	0	0	H	0.0
Total	5	208	598	69	136	24	2	13	76	55	109	.227	.295	.339	.634	62	-32	-37	105	108	59	.565	2	2	-1	-6	2/3S	-2.7
■ BUCK FRIERSON Frierson, Robert Lawrence b: 7/29/17, Chicota, Tex. BR/TR, 6'3", 195 lbs. Deb: 9/09/41																												
1941	Cle-A	5	11	2	3	1	0	0	2	1	1	.273	.333	.364	.697	84	-0	-0	101	177	1	.625	0	0	0	-1	/O	-0.1
■ FRED FRINK Frink, Fred Ferdinand b: 8/25/11, Macon, Ga. BR/TR, 6'1", 180 lbs. Deb: 7/01/34																												
1934	Phi-N	2	0	0	0	0	0	0	0	0	0	—	—	—	—	—	0	0	108	—	—	—	0			-0	/O	0.0
■ CHARLIE FRISBEE Frisbee, Charles Augustus "Bunt" b: 2/2/1874, Dows, Iowa d: 11/7/54, Alden, Iowa BB/TR, 5'9", 175 lbs. Deb: 6/22/1899																												
1899	Bos-N	42	152	22	50	4	2	0	20	9		.329	.366	.382	.748	103	2	1	105	108	26	.755	10			-3	O	-0.3
1900	NY-N	4	13	2	2	1	0	0	3	2		.154	.267	.231	.497	41	-1	-1	97	319	1	.455	0			0	/O	0.0
Total	2	46	165	24	52	5	2	0	23	11		.315	.358	.370	.728	98	1	-0	104	126	26	.726	10			-3	/O	-0.3
■ FRANKIE FRISCH Frisch, Frank Francis "The Fordham Flash" b: 9/9/1898, Bronx, N.Y. d: 3/12/73, Wilmington, Del. BB/TR, 5'11", 165 lbs. Deb: 6/14/19 MCH																												
1919	NY-N	54	190	21	43	3	2	2	24	4	14	.226	.242	.295	.537	61	-9	-9	100	150	16	.510	15			3	23/S	-0.5
1920	NY-N	110	440	57	123	10	10	4	77	20	18	.280	.311	.375	.686	97	-3	-3	100	178	52	.668	34	11	4	6	*3/S	1.3
1921	NY-N	153	618	121	211	31	17	8	100	42	28	.341	.384	.485	.870	132	25	27	98	109	118	.933	**49**	13	**7**	12	32	4.5
1922	NY-N	132	514	101	168	16	13	5	51	47	13	.327	.387	.438	.824	108	10	7	104	79	87	.843	31	17	-1	5	23/S	1.3
1923	NY-N	151	641	116	**223**	32	10	12	111	46	12	.348	.395	.485	.880	129	28	27	101	99	123	.907	29	12	2	4	*23	3.3
1924	NY-N	145	603	**121**	198	33	15	7	69	56	24	.328	.387	.468	.855	140	24	31	91	73	111	.874	22	9	1	**26**	*2S/3	4.9
1925	NY-N	120	502	89	166	26	6	11	48	32	14	.331	.374	.472	.846	116	11	11	99	56	87	.842	21	12	-1	6	32S	2.0
1926	NY-N	135	545	75	171	29	4	5	44	33	16	.314	.353	.409	.762	107	3	5	98	62	76	.746	23			8	*2/3	1.8
1927	StL-N	153	617	112	208	31	11	10	78	43	10	.337	.387	.472	.858	120	25	19	107	75	109	.951	**48**			**49**	*2/S	**6.3**
1928	StL-N	141	547	107	164	29	9	10	86	64	17	.300	.374	.441	.815	112	10	10	100	120	90	.875	29			-2	*2	1.0
1929	StL-N	138	527	93	176	40	12	5	74	53	12	.334	.397	.484	.881	119	15	16	98	99	99	.952	24			-12	*23/S	0.7
1930	StL-N	133	540	121	187	46	9	10	114	55	16	.346	.407	.520	.927	116	20	16	105	121	111	.994	15			23	*23	4.6
1931	StL-N	131	518	96	161	24	4	4	82	45	13	.311	.368	.396	.764	99	5	0	107	143	78	.784	**28**			15	*2	2.1
1932	StL-N	115	486	59	142	26	2	3	60	25	13	.292	.327	.372	.699	87	-8	-8	100	113	60	.651	18			14	23/S	1.4
1933	StL-N	147	585	74	177	32	6	4	66	48	16	.303	.358	.398	.757	114	13	11	102	97	83	.706	18			-3	*2SM	1.9
1934	StL-N	140	550	74	168	30	6	3	75	45	10	.305	.359	.398	.757	90	3	-7	114	126	79	.692	11			7	*23M	1.3
1935	StL-N	103	354	52	104	16	2	1	55	35	16	.294	.359	.359	.718	90	-2	-4	104	156	48	.642	2			-1	2/3M	0.2
1936	StL-N	93	303	40	83	10	0	1	26	36	10	.274	.353	.317	.670	86	-6	-4	94	93	36	.590	2			-9	23/SM	-0.7
1937	StL-N	17	32	3	7	2	0	0	4	1	0	.219	.242	.281	.524	42	-3	-3	101	160	2	.370	0			-0	/2M	-0.2
Total	19	2311	9112	1532	2880	466	138	105	1244	730	272	.316	.369	.432	.801	110	159	142	101	105	1465	.811	419	74		150	*23/S	37.2
■ EMIL FRISK Frisk, John Emil b: 10/15/1874, Kalkaska, Mich. d: 1/27/22, Seattle, Wash. BL/TR, 6'1", 190 lbs. Deb: 9/02/1899																												
1899	Cin-N	9	25	5	7	1	0	0	2	2		.280	.333	.320	.653	78	-1	-1	106	77	3	.556	0			0	/P	0.0
1901	Det-A	20	48	10	15	3	0	1	7	3		.313	.353	.438	.790	109	1	0	110	92	8	.727	0			2	P/O	0.0
1905	StL-A	124	429	58	112	11	6	3	36	42		.261	.327	.336	.663	123	7	11	91	86	51	.609	7			-2	*O	0.3
1907	StL-A	5	4	0	1	0	0	0	0	1		.250	.400	.250	.650	113	0	0	98	0	0	.667	0			0	H	0.0
Total	4	158	506	73	135	15	6	4	45	48		.267	.330	.344	.674	119	8	11	94	85	61	.617	7			-0	O/P	0.3
■ HARRY FRITZ Fritz, Harry Koch "Dutchman" b: 9/30/1890, Philadelphia, Pa. d: 11/4/74, Columbus, Ohio BR/TR, 5'8", 170 lbs. Deb: 9/29/13																												
1913	Phi-A	5	13	1	0	0	0	0	0	2	4	.000	.188	.000	.188	-46	-2	-2	97	0	0	.231	0			0	/3	-0.1
1914	Chi-F	65	174	16	37	5	1	0	13	18	18	.213	.286	.253	.539	61	-10	-8	91	107	15	.467	2			-0	3/S2	-0.7
1915	Chi-F	79	236	27	59	8	4	3	26	13	27	.250	.289	.356	.645	93	-4	-3	97	101	27	.571	4			1	3/2S	0.0
Total	3	149	423	44	96	13	5	3	39	33	49	.227	.284	.303	.587	75	-16	-13	95	100	42	.514	6			1	3/S2	-0.8
■ LARRY FRITZ Fritz, Lawrence Joseph b: 2/14/49, E.Chicago, Ind. BL/TL, 6'2", 225 lbs. Deb: 5/30/75																												
1975	Phi-N	1	1	0	0	0	0	0	0	0	0	.000	.000	.000	.000	-99	-0	-0	101	0	0	.000	0	0	0	0	H	0.0
■ DOUG FROBEL Frobel, Douglas Steven b: 6/6/59, Ottawa, Ont., Can. BL/TR, 6'4", 196 lbs. Deb: 9/05/82																												
1982	Pit-N	16	34	5	7	2	0	2	3	1	11	.206	.229	.441	.670	76	-1	-1	110	56	3	.607	1	1	-0	-1	O	-0.2
1983	Pit-N	32	60	10	17	4	1	3	11	4	17	.283	.328	.533	.861	131	2	2	103	106	9	.804	1	1	-0	-4	O	-0.2
1984	Pit-N	126	276	33	56	9	3	12	28	24	84	.203	.272	.388	.659	88	-7	-5	94	77	27	.603	7	5	-1	-2	*O	-1.2
1985	Pit-N	53	109	14	22	5	0	0	7	19	24	.202	.320	.248	.568	59	-5	-5	103	103	9	.543	4	3	-1	-4	O	-1.0
	Mon-N	12	23	3	3	1	0	1	4	2	6	.130	.200	.304	.504	42	-2	-2	94	159	1	.409	0	0	0	-0	/O	-0.1
	Yr	65	132	17	25	6	0	1	11	21	30	.189	.301	.258	.558	57	-7	-7	101	115	11	.527	4	3	-1	-4		-1.1
1987	Cle-A	29	40	5	4	0	0	2	5	5	13	.100	.200	.250	.450	18	-5	-5	103	125	2	.405	0	0	0	-4	O/D	-0.8
Total	5	268	542	70	109	21	4	20	58	55	155	.201	.277	.365	.642	79	-18	-17	99	91	52	.604	13	10	-2	-15	O/D	-3.5
■ BEN FROELICH Froelich, William Palmer b: 11/12/1887, Pittsburgh, Pa. d: 9/16 Pittsburgh, Pa. TR , Deb: 09																												
1909	Phi-N	1	1	0	0	0	0	0	0	0	0	.000	.000	.000	.000	-94	-0	-0	106	0	0	.000	0			0	/C	0.0
■ JERRY FRY Fry, Jerry Ray b: 2/29/56, Salinas, Cal. BR/TR, 6', 185 lbs. Deb: 9/04/78																												
1978	Mon-N	4	9	0	0	0	0	0	0	1	5	.000	.100	.000	.100	-73	-2	-2	96	0	0	.111	0	0	0	1	/C	-0.1
■ MIKE FUENTES Fuentes, Michael Jay b: 7/11/58, Miami, Fla. BR/TR, 6'3", 190 lbs. Deb: 9/02/83																												
1983	Mon-N	6	4	1	1	0	0	0	0	0	2	.250	.250	.250	.500	38	-0	-0	102	0	0	.333	0	0	0	0	/H	0.0
1984	Mon-N	3	4	0	1	0	0	0	0	1	2	.250	.400	.250	.650	94	-0	0	91	0	1	.667	0	0	0	0	/O	0.0
Total	2	9	8	1	2	0	0	0	0	1	4	.250	.333	.250	.583	68	-0	-0	96	0	1	.500	0	0	0	0	/O	0.0
■ TITO FUENTES Fuentes, Rigoberto (Peat) b: 1/4/44, Havana, Cuba BB/TR, 5'11", 175 lbs. Deb: 8/18/65																												
1965	SF-N	26	72	12	15	1	0	0	1	5	14	.208	.269	.222	.491	36	-6	-6	111	26	4	.367	0	1	-1	-2	S/23	-0.6
1966	SF-N	133	541	63	141	21	3	9	40	9	57	.261	.277	.360	.637	77	-19	-17	97	80	53	.521	6	3	0	-0	S2	-0.7
1967	SF-N	133	344	27	72	12	1	5	29	27	61	.209	.267	.294	.560	60	-18	-18	101	104	26	.468	4	3	-1	12	*2/S	0.2

YEAR	TM/L	G	AB	R	H	2B	3B	HR	RBI	BB	SO	AVG	OBP	SLG	PRO	/A	BR	/A	PF	CHI	RC	TA	SB	CS	SBR	FR	POS	TPR
1969	SF-N	67	183	28	54	4	3	1	14	15	25	.295	.352	.366	.718	100	1	0	101	80	24	.639	2	4	-2	1	3S	0.4
1970	SF-N	123	435	49	116	13	7	2	32	36	52	.267	.327	.343	.670	83	-12	-10	96	80	49	.580	4	5	-2	-11	2S3	-0.9
1971	SF-N	152	630	63	172	28	6	4	52	18	46	.273	.300	.356	.655	85	-14	-13	100	86	65	.547	12	2	2	3	*2	0.0
1972	SF-N	152	572	64	151	33	6	7	53	39	56	.264	.314	.379	.694	96	-4	-4	100	97	69	.632	16	5	2	-20	*2	-1.1
1973	SF-N	160	656	78	182	25	5	6	63	45	62	.277	.331	.358	.689	87	-8	-12	105	88	79	.609	12	6	0	-3	*2/3	-0.9
1974	SF-N	108	390	33	97	15	2	0	22	22	32	.249	.294	.297	.591	61	-18	-22	108	75	33	.481	7	3	0	-4	*2	-2.0
1975	SD-N	146	565	57	158	21	3	4	43	25	51	.280	.314	.349	.662	84	-13	-13	100	84	58	.542	8	8	-2	2	*2	-0.7
1976	SD-N	135	520	48	137	18	0	2	36	18	38	.263	.289	.310	.599	79	-21	-14	89	88	45	.465	5	3	-0	-6	*2	-1.5
1977	Det-A	151	615	83	190	19	10	5	51	38	61	.309	.351	.397	.748	99	3	-1	105	75	85	.655	4	4	-1	3	*2/D	1.3
1978	Oak-A	13	43	5	6	1	0	0	2	1	6	.140	.159	.163	.322	-9	-6	-6	101	113	1	.216	0	0	0	-1	2	-0.6
Total	13	1499	5566	610	1491	211	46	45	438	298	561	.268	.309	.347	.656	82	-135	-136	100	85	593	.568	80	47	-4	-26	*2S/3D	-7.1
■ **OLLIE FUHRMAN**	Fuhrman, Alfred George b: 7/20/1896, Jordan, Minn. d: 1/11/69, Peoria, Ill. BB/TR, 5'11", 185 lbs. Deb: 4/13/22																											
1922	Phi-A	6	6	1	2	1	0	0	0	0	0	.333	.333	.500	.833	110	0	0	104	0	1	.750	0	0	0	0	/C	0.0
■ **DOT FULGHUM**	Fulghum, James Lavoisier b: 7/4/1900, Valdosta, Ga. d: 11/11/67, Miami, Fla. BR/TR, 5'8.5", 165 lbs. Deb: 9/15/21																											
1921	Phi-A	2	2	0	0	0	0	0	0	1	1	.000	.333	.000	.333	-8	-0	-0	103	0	0	.500	0	0	0	0	/S	0.0
■ **NIG FULLER**	Fuller, Charles F. b: 3/30/1879, Toledo, Ohio d: 11/12/47, Toledo, Ohio BR/TR, Deb: 7/01/02																											
1902	Bro-N	3	9	0	0	0	0	0	1	0		.000	.000	.000	.000	-99	-2	-2	95	0	0	.000	0			0	/C	-0.1
■ **FRANK FULLER**	Fuller, Frank Edward "Rabbit" b: 1/1/1893, Detroit, Mich. d: 10/29/65, Warren, Mich. BB/TR, 5'7", 150 lbs. Deb: 4/14/15																											
1915	Det-A	14	32	6	5	0	0	0	2	9	7	.156	.341	.156	.498	45	-1	-2	108	136	2	.533	2	3	-1	-0	/2S	-0.2
1916	Det-A	20	10	2	1	0	0	0	1	1	4	.100	.182	.100	.282	-15	-1	-1	105	357	1	.556	3			0	/2S	0.0
1923	Bos-A	6	21	3	5	0	0	0	0	1	1	.238	.273	.238	.511	35	-2	-2	102	0	1	.412	1	1	-0	-1	/2	-0.2
Total	3	40	63	11	11	0	0	0	3	11	12	.175	.297	.175	.472	34	-5	-5	106	128	4	.500	6	4		-1	/2S	-0.4
■ **HARRY FULLER**	Fuller, Henry W. b: 12/5/1862, Cincinnati, Ohio d: 12/12/1895, Cincinnati, Ohio Deb: 4/08/1891																											
1891	StL-a	1	2	0	0	0	0	0	0	0	1	.000	.000	.000	.000	-88	-1	-1	114	0	0	.000	0			0	/3	0.0
■ **JIM FULLER**	Fuller, James Hardy b: 11/28/50, Bethesda, Md. BR/TR, 6'3", 215 lbs. Deb: 9/10/73																											
1973	Bal-A	9	26	2	3	0	0	2	4	1	17	.115	.148	.346	.494	33	-2	-3	107	105	1	.435	0	0	0	1	/O1D	-0.1
1974	Bal-A	64	189	17	42	11	0	7	28	8	68	.222	.265	.392	.657	94	-4	-2	93	116	19	.570	1	0	0	-3	O/1D	-0.7
1977	Hou-N	34	100	5	16	6	0	2	9	10	45	.160	.243	.280	.523	43	-9	-8	93	106	7	.459	0	1	-1	4	O/1	-0.5
Total	3	107	315	24	61	17	0	11	41	19	130	.194	.249	.352	.601	71	-15	-13	94	112	27	.529	1	1	-0	1	/O1D	-1.3
■ **JOHN FULLER**	Fuller, John Edward b: 1/29/50, Lynwood, Cal. BL/TL, 6'2", 180 lbs. Deb: 5/09/74																											
1974	Atl-N	3	3	1	1	0	0	0	0	0	0	.333	.333	.333	.667	83	-0	-0	105	0	0	.500	0	0	0	-0	/O	0.0
■ **VERN FULLER**	Fuller, Vernon Gordon b: 3/1/44, Menomonie, Wis. BR/TR, 6'1", 170 lbs. Deb: 9/05/64																											
1964	Cle-A	2	1	0	0	0	0	0	0	0	0	.000	.000	.000	.000	-97	-0	-0	103	0	0	.000	0	0	0	0	H	0.0
1966	Cle-A	16	47	7	11	2	1	2	2	7	6	.234	.357	.447	.804	128	2	2	101	31	8	.833	0	0	0	0	2	0.3
1967	Cle-A	73	206	18	46	10	0	7	21	19	55	.223	.301	.374	.675	98	-1	-1	100	89	24	.618	2	3	-1	1	2/S	0.1
1968	Cle-A	97	244	14	59	8	2	0	18	24	49	.242	.320	.291	.611	85	-3	-4	101	109	24	.526	2	2	-1	-9	23/S	-1.1
1969	Cle-A	108	254	25	60	11	1	4	22	20	53	.236	.297	.335	.632	81	-8	-7	94	91	24	.534	2	1	0	-1	*2/3	-0.3
1970	Cle-A	29	33	3	6	2	0	1	2	3	9	.182	.250	.333	.583	52	-2	-3	115	58	3	.519	0	0	0	1	2/31	0.0
Total	6	325	785	67	182	33	4	14	65	73	172	.232	.307	.338	.644	88	-12	-12	99	91	82	.585	6	6	-2	-9	2/3S1	-1.0
■ **SHORTY FULLER**	Fuller, William Benjamin b: 10/10/1867, Cincinnati, Ohio d: 4/11/04, Cincinnati, Ohio BR/TR, Deb: 1888																											
1888	Was-N	49	170	11	31	5	2	0	12	10	14	.182	.232	.235	.467	53	-9	-8	96	110	11	.410	6			-3	S/2	-0.8
1889	StL-a	140	517	91	117	18	6	0	51	52	56	.226	.303	.284	.587	62	-19	-30	112	101	57	.605	38			15	*S	-0.3
1890	StL-a	130	526	118	146	9	9	1		73		.278	.377	.335	.712	97	12	-2	116	0	91	.842	60			7	*S	1.0
1891	StL-a	137	586	107	127	15	7	2	63	67	28	.217	.301	.276	.578	60	-23	-37	114	96	63	.599	42			-11	*S2	-3.5
1892	NY-N	141	508	74	115	11	4	1	48	52	22	.226	.298	.270	.568	75	-15	-14	98	107	53	.575	37			-7	*S	-1.1
1893	NY-N	130	474	78	112	14	8	0	51	60	21	.236	.325	.300	.624	66	-21	-24	104	100	56	.635	26			9	*S	-0.8
1894	NY-N	93	368	81	104	14	4	2	46	52	16	.283	.374	.359	.733	79	-11	-11	100	81	63	.826	32			-7	*S/O32	-0.9
1895	NY-N	126	458	82	103	11	3	0	32	64	34	.225	.323	.262	.585	57	-29	-25	95	76	45	.566	15			29	*S	1.1
1896	NY-N	18	72	10	12	0	0	0	7	14	5	.167	.310	.167	.477	30	-7	-6	99	145	5	.517	4			0	S	-0.5
Total	9	964	3679	652	867	97	43	6	310	444	196	.236	.323	.290	.613	69	-122	-157	106	82	444	.640	260			33	S/23O	-5.8
■ **CHICK FULLIS**	Fullis, Charles Philip b: 2/27/04, Girardville, Pa. d: 3/28/46, Ashland, Pa. BR/TR, 5'9", 170 lbs. Deb: 4/13/28																											
1928	NY-N	11	1	5	0	0	0	0	0	1	1	.000	.500	.000	.500	40	0	0	102	0	0	1.000	0			0	H	0.0
1929	NY-N	86	274	67	79	11	1	7	29	30	26	.288	.365	.412	.777	93	-3	-3	100	74	41	.785	7			-8	O	-1.5
1930	NY-N	13	6	2	0	0	0	0	0	0	1	.000	.000	.000	.000	-99	-2	-2	98	0	0	.167	1			-1	/O	-0.2
1931	NY-N	89	302	61	99	15	2	3	28	23	13	.328	.383	.421	.804	120	7	9	97	73	50	.823	13			2	O/2	0.8
1932	NY-N	96	235	35	70	14	3	1	21	11	12	.298	.332	.396	.728	96	-2	-1	99	81	31	.642	1			-9	O/2	-1.3
1933	Phi-N	151	647	91	200	31	6	1	45	36	34	.309	.350	.380	.731	92	7	-6	118	59	87	.660	18			5	*O/3	-0.9
1934	Phi-N	28	102	8	23	6	0	0	12	10	4	.225	.301	.284	.585	53	-6	-7	108	152	10	.525	2			-4	O	-1.2
	StL-N	69	199	21	52	9	1	0	26	14	11	.261	.310	.317	.626	60	-9	-12	114	149	19	.529	4			-1	O	-1.5
	Yr	97	301	29	75	15	1	0	38	24	15	.249	.307	.306	.612	58	-15	-20	112	151	29	.530	6			-5		-2.7
1936	StL-N	47	89	15	25	6	1	0	6	7	11	.281	.333	.371	.704	95	-1	-1	94	64	12	.625	0			0	O	-0.1
Total	8	590	1855	305	548	92	14	12	167	132	113	.295	.347	.380	.726	90	-8	-23	107	81	250	.686	46			-15	O/23	-5.9
■ **CHICK FULMER**	Fulmer, Charles John b: 2/12/1851, Philadelphia, Pa. d: 2/15/40, Philadelphia, Pa. TR , 6', 158 lbs. Deb: 8/23/1871																											
1871	Rok-n	16	70	12	17							.243															S/1	
1872	Mut-n	36	169	29	51							.302															3S	
1873	Phi-n	49	244	41	64							.262															*S/C	
1874	Phi-n	57	265	49	70							.264															S3	
1875	Phi-n	68	288	49	64							.222															*S3	
1876	Lou-N	66	267	28	73	9	5	1	29	1	10	.273	.276	.356	.632	105	2	1	104	102	27	.495				-2	*S	-0.1
1879	Buf-N	76	306	30	82	11	5	0	28	5	34	.268	.280	.337	.616	89	1	-6	114	101	30	.482				**30**	*2	2.8
1880	Buf-N	11	44	3	7	0	0	0	1	2	4	.159	.196	.159	.355	24	-3	-3	91	50	1	.243				0	2	-0.2
1882	Cin-a	79	324	54	91	13	4	0		10		.281	.302	.346	.648	108	6	2	109	0	35	.524				-13	*S	-0.8
1883	Cin-a	92	361	52	93	13	5	5		13		.258	.283	.363	.646	103	2	1	103	0	38	.537				-2	*S	-0.3
1884	Cin-a	31	114	13	20	2	1	0		1		.175	.183	.211	.393	28	-8	-9	106	0	4	.266				-16	S/O3	-2.4
	StL-a	1	5	0	0	0	0	0		0		.000	.000	.000	.000	-91	-1	-1	110	0	0	.000				0	/2	0.0
	Yr	32	119	13	20	2	1	0		1		.168	.175	.202	.377	23	-9	-10	106	0	4	.253				-16		-2.4
Total	5 n	226	1036	180	266							.257															/2	
Total	6	356	1421	180	366	48	20	6	58	32	48	.258	.274	.332	.606	93	-2	-16	107	42	135	.478				-4	S/23OC1	-1.0
■ **CHRIS FULMER**	Fulmer, Christopher b: 7/4/1858, Tamaqua, Pa. d: 11/9/31, Tamaqua, Pa. BR/TR, 5'8", 165 lbs. Deb: 8/04/1884																											
1884	Was-U	48	181	39	50	9	0	0		11		.276	.318	.326	.644	122	4	5	97	0	19	.534	0			-7	CO/1	0.0
1886	Bal-a	80	270	54	66	9	3	1		48		.244	.363	.311	.674	126	7	11	91	0	42	.799	29			1	CO/P	1.4
1887	Bal-a	56	201	52	54	11	4	0		36		.269	.382	.363	.746	115	5	6	96	0	42	.986	35			-12	C/O	0.2
1888	Bal-a	52	166	20	31	5	1	0	10	21		.187	.286	.229	.515	71	-5	-4	96	80	14	.526	10			-14	C/O	-1.1
1889	Bal-a	16	58	11	15	3	1	0	13	6	12	.259	.338	.345	.683	97	-0	-0	100	190	8	.674	2			0	O/C	0.0
Total	5	252	876	176	216	37	9	1	23	122	12	.247	.343	.313	.655	111	10	18	95	27	125	.724	76			-32	C/O1P	0.5
■ **W. FULMER**	Fulmer, W. b: Philadelphia, Pa. Deb: 7/19/1875																											
1875	Atl-n	1	4	1	2							.500															/3	

YEAR	TM/L	G	AB	R	H	2B	3B	HR	RBI	BB	SO	AVG	OBP	SLG	PRO	/A	BR	/A	PF	CHI	RC	TA	SB	CS	SBR	FR	POS	TPR
■ **DAVE FULTZ**	Fultz, David Lewis b: 5/29/1875, Staunton, Va. d: 10/29/59, De Land, Fla. BR/TR, 5'11", 170 lbs. Deb: 7/01/1898																											
1898	Phi-N	19	55	7	10	2	2	0	5	6		.182	.262	.291	.553	64	-3	-2	95	94	5	.511	1			0	O/2S	-0.1
1899	Phi-N	2	5	0	2	0	0	0	0	0		.400	.400	.400	.800	126	0	0	97	0	1	1.000	1			0	/2S	0.0
	Bal-N	57	210	31	62	3	2	0	18	13		.295	.342	.329	.671	81	-3	-6	108	82	30	.682	17			0	O3/21	-0.4
	Yr	59	215	31	64	3	2	0	18	13		.298	.343	.330	.674	82	-3	-6	107	79	31	.689	18			0		-0.4
1901	Phi-A	132	561	95	164	17	9	0	52	32		.292	.331	.355	.685	92	-6	-6	100	73	80	.673	36			-19	*O2/S	-2.3
1902	Phi-A	129	506	**109**	153	20	5	1	49	62		.302	.379	.368	.746	101	9	3	108	76	89	.827	44			-14	*O2	-1.6
1903	NY-A	79	295	39	66	12	1	0	25	25		.224	.284	.271	.556	69	-10	-10	100	119	32	.585	29			5	O/3	-1.0
1904	NY-A	97	339	39	93	17	4	2	32	24		.274	.322	.366	.688	107	8	3	112	94	47	.671	17			10	O	0.8
1905	NY-A	129	422	49	98	13	3	0	42	39		.232	.297	.277	.574	83	-6	-7	102	131	49	.617	44			-10	*O	-2.5
Total	7	644	2393	369	648	84	26	3	223	201		.271	.328	.331	.659	90	-12	-26	104	93	332	.679	189			-28	O/23S1	-7.1
■ **MARK FUNDERBURK**	Funderburk, Mark Clifford b: 5/16/57, Charlotte, N.C. BR/TR, 6'4", 226 lbs. Deb: 9/04/81																											
1981	Min-A	8	15	2	3	1	0	0	2	2	1	.200	.294	.267	.561	60	-1	-1	105	196	1	.500	0	0	0	-1	/OD	-0.1
1985	Min-A	23	70	7	22	7	1	2	13	5	12	.314	.360	.529	.889	135	4	3	103	120	11	.792	0	1	-1	-1	D/O1	0.2
Total	2	31	85	9	25	8	1	2	15	7	13	.294	.348	.482	.830	122	3	3	103	134	13	.738	0	1	-1	-2	/DO1	0.1
■ **LIZ FUNK**	Funk, Elias Calvin b: 10/28/04, La Cygne, Kan. d: 1/16/68, Norman, Okla. BL/TL, 5'8.5", 160 lbs. Deb: 4/26/29																											
1929	NY-A	1	0	0	0	0	0	0	0	0	0	—	—	—	—	—	0	0	99	—	—	—	0	0	0	0	R	0.0
1930	Det-A	140	527	74	145	26	11	4	65	29	39	.275	.319	.389	.708	75	-18	-22	105	105	66	.647	12	6	0	2	*O	-2.2
1932	Chi-A	122	440	59	114	21	5	2	40	43	19	.259	.325	.343	.668	84	-17	-9	87	87	49	.619	17	15	-4	1	*O	-1.5
1933	Chi-A	10	9	1	2	0	0	0	0	1	0	.222	.300	.222	.522	40	-1	-1	101	0	1	.429	0	0	0	-1	/O	-0.1
Total	4	273	976	134	261	47	16	6	105	73	58	.267	.322	.367	.688	78	-36	-32	97	96	128	.632	29	21	-4	2	O	-3.8
■ **CARL FURILLO**	Furillo, Carl Anthony "Skoonj" or "The Reading Rifle" b: 3/8/22, Stony Creek Mills, Pa. BR/TR, 6', 190 lbs. Deb: 4/16/46																											
1946	Bro-N	117	335	29	95	18	6	3	35	31	20	.284	.346	.400	.746	108	4	3	103	91	46	.688	6			4	*O	0.5
1947	Bro-N	124	437	61	129	24	7	8	88	34	24	.295	.347	.437	.785	102	3	1	105	152	62	.717	7			-3	*O	-0.6
1948	Bro-N	108	364	55	103	20	4	4	44	43	32	.297	.374	.407	.781	107	7	4	104	103	57	.757	6			6	*O	0.3
1949	Bro-N	142	549	95	177	27	10	18	106	37	29	.322	.368	.506	.875	130	23	22	102	123	98	.830	4			-2	*O	1.2
1950	Bro-N	153	620	99	189	30	6	18	106	41	40	.305	.353	.460	.813	105	9	4	107	128	96	.753	8			-3	*O	-0.3
1951	Bro-N	158	667	93	197	32	4	16	91	43	33	.295	.344	.427	.772	109	5	7	98	102	97	.697	8	7	-2	13	*O	1.3
1952	Bro-N	134	425	52	105	18	1	8	59	31	33	.247	.304	.351	.655	80	-11	-12	102	133	42	.544	1	4	-2	-2	*O	-2.0
1953	Bro-N	132	479	82	165	38	6	21	92	34	32	**.344**	.393	.580	.973	144	33	31	104	105	107	.961	1	1	-0	1	*O	2.4
1954	Bro-N	150	547	56	161	23	1	19	96	49	35	.294	.358	.444	.802	106	6	5	101	129	83	.735	2	4	-2	4	*O	0.2
1955	Bro-N	140	523	83	164	24	3	26	95	43	43	.314	.373	.520	.894	128	25	22	104	112	97	.860	4	5	-2	-2	*O	1.5
1956	Bro-N	149	523	66	151	30	0	21	83	57	41	.289	.360	.467	.826	117	15	13	103	117	80	.757	1	1	-0	-7	*O	0.0
1957	Bro-N	119	395	61	121	17	4	12	66	29	33	.306	.361	.461	.822	102	10	2	116	125	62	.747	0	2	-1	-8	*O	-1.0
1958	LA-N	122	411	54	119	19	3	18	83	35	28	.290	.348	.482	.830	112	9	7	105	139	64	.761	0	2	-1	-8	*O	-0.5
1959	LA-N	50	93	8	27	4	0	0	13	7	11	.290	.340	.333	.673	79	-2	-3	102	169	10	.535	0	0	0	-6	O	-0.8
1960	LA-N	8	10	1	2	0	1	0	1	0	2	.200	.200	.400	.600	52	-1	-1	115	101	1	.500	0	0	0	-0	/O	0.0
Total	15	1806	6378	895	1910	324	56	192	1058	514	436	.299	.356	.458	.814	112	136	106	104	120	1004	.786	48	26		-14	*O	2.2
■ **EDDIE FUSSELBACK**	Fusselback, Edward L. b: 7/17/1856, Philadelphia, Pa. d: 4/14/26, Philadelphia, Pa. 5'6", 156 lbs. Deb: 5/03/1882																											
1882	StL-a	35	136	13	31	2	0	0		5		.228	.255	.243	.498	69	-4	-4	100	0	9	.362				0	CO/P	-0.3
1884	Bal-U	68	303	60	86	16	3	1		3		.284	.291	.366	.657	109	6	1	110	0	33	.525	0			16	C/3SO	1.7
1885	Phi-a	5	19	2	6	1	0	0		0		.316	.316	.368	.684	115	0	0	103	0	2	.538				0	/C	0.0
1888	Lou-a	1	4	0	1	0	0	0	1	0		.250	.250	.250	.500	69	-0	-0	91	305	0	.333	0			0	/O	0.0
Total	4	109	462	75	124	19	3	1	1	8		.268	.281	.329	.610	98	2	-3	107	3	44	.473	0			16	/CO3SP	1.4
■ **LES FUSSELMAN**	Fusselman, Lester Leroy b: 3/7/21, Pryor, Okla. d: 5/21/70, Cleveland, Ohio BR/TR, 6'1", 195 lbs. Deb: 4/16/52																											
1952	StL-N	32	63	5	10	3	0	1	3	0	9	.159	.159	.254	.413	13	-8	-7	98	62	2	.291	0	0	0	-1	C	-0.7
1953	StL-N	11	8	1	2	1	0	0	0	0	0	.250	.250	.375	.625	59	-0	-1	102	0	0	.429	0	0	0	-0	C	0.0
Total	2	43	71	6	12	4	0	1	3	0	9	.169	.169	.268	.437	19	-8	-8	98	55	3	.317	0	0	0	-1	/C	-0.7
■ **GABE GABLER**	Gabler, William Louis b: 8/4/30, St.Louis, Mo. BL/TR, 6'1", 190 lbs. Deb: 9/16/58																											
1958	Chi-N	3	3	0	0	0	0	0	0	0	3	.000	.000	.000	.000	-99	-1	-1	101	0	0	.000	0	0	0	0	H	0.0
■ **LEN GABRIELSON**	Gabrielson, Leonard Gary b: 2/14/40, Oakland, Cal. BL/TR, 6'4", 210 lbs. Deb: 9/09/60																											
1960	Mil-N	4	3	1	0	0	0	0	0	1	0	.000	.250	.000	.250	-27	-1	-0	91	0	0	.333	0	0	0	-0	/O	0.0
1963	Mil-N	46	120	14	26	5	0	3	15	8	23	.217	.266	.333	.599	71	-5	-5	101	129	11	.516	1	1	-0	-2	O1/3	-0.9
1964	Mil-N	24	38	0	7	2	0	0	1	1	8	.184	.205	.237	.442	25	-4	-4	97	46	2	.355	1	0	0	-0	1/O	-0.4
	Chi-N	89	272	22	67	11	2	5	23	19	37	.246	.298	.357	.655	79	-6	-8	105	84	30	.600	9	4	0	0	O/1	-0.9
	Yr	113	310	22	74	13	2	5	24	20	45	.239	.287	.342	.629	74	-10	-11	103	76	32	.568	10	4	1	-0		-1.3
1965	Chi-N	28	48	4	12	0	0	3	5	7	16	.250	.345	.438	.783	117	1	1	102	69	7	.737	0	2	-1	-3	O/1	-0.2
	SF-N	88	269	36	81	6	5	4	26	26	48	.301	.367	.405	.772	106	7	3	111	89	42	.738	4	0	1	-4	O/1	-0.1
	Yr	116	317	40	93	6	5	7	31	33	64	.293	.364	.410	.774	108	8	5	108	85	49	.738	4	2	0	-6		-0.3
1966	SF-N	94	240	27	52	7	0	4	16	21	51	.217	.280	.296	.576	62	-13	-12	97	81	21	.482	0	1	-1	-12	O/1	-2.8
1967	Cal-A	11	12	2	1	0	0	0	2	2	4	.083	.214	.083	.298	-9	-2	-2	96	834	0	.273	0	0	0	-0	/O	-0.1
	LA-N	90	238	20	62	10	3	7	29	15	41	.261	.307	.416	.723	119	1	4	88	100	30	.652	3	1	0	-3	O	-0.1
1968	LA-N	108	304	38	82	16	1	10	35	32	47	.270	.339	.428	.767	143	11	14	91	92	44	.709	1	1	-0	-6	O	0.3
1969	LA-N	83	178	13	48	5	1	1	18	12	25	.270	.316	.326	.642	81	-5	-4	99	118	18	.522	1	2	-1	-7	O/1	-1.5
1970	LA-N	43	42	1	8	2	0	0	6	1	15	.190	.209	.238	.447	22	-5	-4	90	233	2	.324	0	0	0	-1	/O1	-0.4
Total	9	708	1764	178	446	64	12	37	176	145	315	.253	.311	.366	.677	93	-19	-17	98	102	206	.612	20	12	-1	-38	O/13	-7.1
■ **LEN GABRIELSON**	Gabrielson, Leonard Hilbourne b: 9/8/15, Oakland, Cal. BL/TL, 6'3", 210 lbs. Deb: 4/21/39																											
1939	Phi-N	5	18	3	4	0	0	0	1	2	3	.222	.300	.222	.522	45	-1	-1	94	93	1	.429	0			0	/1	-0.1
■ **EDDIE GAEDEL**	Gaedel, Edward Carl b: 6/8/25, Chicago, Ill. d: 6/18/61, Chicago, Ill. BR, 3'7", 065 lbs. Deb: 8/19/51																											
1951	StL-A	1	0	0	0	0	0	0	0	1	0	—	1.000	—	1.222	233	0	0	105	0	0	—	0	0	0	0	H	0.0
■ **GARY GAETTI**	Gaetti, Gary Joseph b: 8/19/58, Centralia, Ill. BR/TR, 6', 180 lbs. Deb: 9/20/81																											
1981	Min-A	9	26	4	5	0	0	2	3	0	6	.192	.192	.423	.615	70	-1	-1	105	69	2	.500	0	0	0	1	/3D	0.0
1982	Min-A	145	508	59	117	25	4	25	84	37	107	.230	.286	.443	.729	97	-4	-4	100	114	59	.645	0	4	-2	1	*3/SD	-0.7
1983	Min-A	157	584	81	143	30	3	21	78	54	121	.245	.313	.414	.727	93	-2	-6	105	106	74	.667	7	1	2	16	*3/SD	1.2
1984	Min-A	162	588	55	154	29	4	5	65	44	81	.262	.318	.350	.668	80	-12	-16	106	120	67	.592	11	5	0	14	*3/OS	0.0
1985	Min-A	160	560	71	138	31	0	20	63	37	89	.246	.301	.409	.710	89	-7	-9	103	88	66	.647	13	5	1	21	*3/O1D	0.7
1986	Min-A	157	596	91	171	34	1	34	108	52	108	.287	.350	.518	.869	124	27	20	108	111	99	.832	14	15	-5	21	*3/S2O	3.1
1987	Min-A	154	584	95	150	36	2	31	109	37	92	.257	.304	.485	.789	110	3	6	96	123	75	.715	10	7	-1	-6	*3/D	-0.3
1988	Min-A	133	468	66	141	29	2	28	88	36	85	.301	.358	.551	.909	142	30	26	106	104	89	.897	7	4	-0	-5	*3S/D	2.1
Total	8	1077	3914	522	1019	214	16	166	598	297	689	.260	.318	.450	.768	104	33	15	104	109	531	.731	62	41	-6	63	*3/SOD21	6.1
■ **FABIAN GAFFKE**	Gaffke, Fabian Sebastian b: 8/5/13, Milwaukee, Wis. BR/TR, 5'10", 185 lbs. Deb: 9/09/36																											
1936	Bos-A	15	55	5	7	2	0	1	3	4	5	.127	.200	.218	.418	3	-9	-9	106	66	3	.354	0	0	0	-2	O	-0.9
1937	Bos-A	54	184	32	53	10	4	6	34	15	25	.288	.342	.484	.825	102	1	-0	103	109	30	.789	1	2	-1	-7	O	-0.8
1938	Bos-A	15	10	2	1	0	0	0	1	3	2	.100	.308	.100	.408	6	-1	-1	102	338	1	.444	0	0	0	-1	/OC	-0.1
1939	Bos-A	1	1	0	0	0	0	0	1	0	0	.000	.000	.000	.000	-92	-0	-0	108	0	0	.000	0	0	0	0	H	0.0
1941	Cle-A	4	4	0	1	0	0	0	0	2	2	.250	.500	.250	.750	103	0	0	101	0	1	1.000	0	0	0	-1	/O	0.0
1942	Cle-A	40	67	4	11	2	0	0	3	6	13	.164	.243	.194	.437	26	-7	-6	92	81	3	.350	1	0	0	-2	O	-0.9
Total	6	129	321	43	73	14	4	7	42	30	47	.227	.297	.361	.659	68	-16	-17	101	102	37	.591	2	2	-1	-12	/OC	-2.7

YEAR	TM/L	G	AB	R	H	2B	3B	HR	RBI	BB	SO	AVG	OBP	SLG	PRO	/A	BR	/A	PF	CHI	RC	TA	SB	CS	SBR	FR	POS	TPR
■ PHIL GAGLIANO	Gagliano, Philip Joseph b: 12/27/41, Memphis, Tenn. BR/TR, 6'1", 180 lbs. Deb: 4/16/63																											
1963	StL-N	10	5	1	2	0	0	0	1	1	1	.400	.500	.400	.900	152	0	0	107	210	1	1.000	0	0	0	0	/23	0.1
1964	StL-N	40	58	5	15	4	0	1	9	3	10	.259	.295	.379	.674	79	-1	-2	112	148	6	.556	0	1	-1	0	2/O13	-0.1
1965	StL-N	122	363	46	87	14	2	8	53	40	45	.240	.317	.355	.672	84	-5	-8	107	144	41	.597	2	1	0	-2	2O3	-0.8
1966	StL-N	90	213	23	54	8	2	2	15	24	29	.254	.332	.338	.670	87	-3	-3	100	81	24	.596	2	1	0	-3	3/1O2	-0.7
1967	StL-N	73	217	20	48	7	0	2	21	19	26	.221	.287	.281	.568	62	-10	-10	101	130	17	.463	0	0	0	-6	23/1S	-1.7
1968	StL-N	53	105	13	24	4	2	0	13	7	12	.229	.283	.305	.588	80	-3	-2	95	171	9	.482	0	0	0	-2	23/O	-0.4
1969	StL-N	62	128	7	29	2	0	1	10	14	12	.227	.303	.266	.568	61	-6	-6	100	108	10	.457	0	0	0	-4	2/13O	-1.0
1970	StL-N	18	32	0	6	0	0	0	2	1	3	.188	.212	.188	.400	8	-4	-4	106	129	1	.259	0	1	-1	-0	/312	-0.5
	Chi-N	26	40	5	6	0	0	0	5	5	5	.150	.244	.150	.394	7	-5	-6	120	323	2	.314	0	0	0	0	2/13	-0.3
	Yr	44	72	5	12	0	0	0	7	6	8	.167	.231	.167	.397	7	-9	-11	114	247	3	.290	0	1	-1	0		-0.8
1971	Bos-A	47	68	11	22	5	0	0	13	11	5	.324	.418	.397	.815	125	3	3	106	197	12	.809	0	0	0	-2	O/23	0.0
1972	Bos-A	52	82	9	21	4	1	0	10	10	13	.256	.337	.329	.666	94	0	-0	105	155	10	.613	1	0	0	2	O/321	0.2
1973	Cin-N	63	69	8	20	2	0	0	7	13	16	.290	.402	.319	.721	110	1	2	93	128	10	.714	0	0	0	0	/321O	0.2
1974	Cin-N	46	31	2	2	0	0	0	0	15	7	.065	.370	.065	.434	27	-2	-2	98	0	2	.586	0	0	0	0	/213	-0.1
Total	12	702	1411	150	336	50	7	14	159	163	184	.238	.319	.313	.632	77	-35	-40	103	134	146	.569	5	4	-1	-18	23/O1S	-5.1
■ RALPH GAGLIANO	Gagliano, Ralph Michael b: 10/8/46, Memphis, Tenn. BL/TR, 5'11", 170 lbs. Deb: 9/21/65																											
1965	Cle-A	1	0	0	0	0	0	0	0	0	0	—	—	—	—	—	0	0	98	—	—	—	0	0	0	0	R	0.0
■ GREG GAGNE	Gagne, Gregory Carpenter b: 11/12/61, Fall River, Mass. BR/TR, 5'11", 185 lbs. Deb: 6/05/83																											
1983	Min-A	10	27	2	3	1	0	0	3	0	6	.111	.111	.148	.259	-28	-5	-5	105	293	1	.167	0	0	0	-1	S	-0.5
1984	Min-A	2	1	0	0	0	0	0	0	0	0	.000	.000	.000	.000	-95	-0	-0	106	0	0	.000	0	0	0	0	/H	0.0
1985	Min-A	114	293	37	66	15	3	2	23	20	57	.225	.282	.317	.599	62	-15	-16	103	92	27	.534	10	4	1	-7	*S/D	-1.4
1986	Min-A	156	472	63	118	22	6	12	54	30	108	.250	.303	.398	.701	83	-7	-12	108	96	57	.641	12	10	-2	-17	*S/2	-2.2
1987	Min-A	137	437	68	116	28	7	10	40	25	84	.265	.311	.430	.741	99	-4	-1	96	73	58	.676	6	6	-2	9	*S/O2D	1.1
1988	Min-A	149	461	70	109	20	6	14	48	27	110	.236	.289	.397	.686	85	-7	-11	106	85	50	.624	15	7	0	-13	*S/O23	-1.6
Total	6	568	1691	240	412	86	22	38	168	102	365	.244	.295	.388	.682	82	-38	-46	104	89	192	.622	43	27	-3	-29	S/O2D3	-4.6
■ ED GAGNIER	Gagnier, Edward J. b: 4/16/1883, Paris, France d: 9/13/46, Detroit, Mich. BR/TR, 5'9", 170 lbs. Deb: 4/14/14																											
1914	Bro-F	94	337	22	63	12	2	0	25	13	24	.187	.217	.234	.452	29	-31	-31	101	116	20	.365	8			6	S/3	-2.0
1915	Bro-F	20	50	8	13	1	0	0	4	10	0	.260	.383	.280	.663	100	1	1	98	103	6	.703	2			0	S/2	0.1
	Buf-F	1	2	0	0	0	0	0	0	0	0	.000	.000	.000	.000	-99	-0	-0	100	0	0	.000	0			0	/2	0.0
	Yr	21	52	8	13	1	0	0	4	10	0	.250	.371	.269	.640	93	0	0	98	103	6	.667	2			0		0.1
Total	2	115	389	30	76	13	2	0	29	23	24	.195	.240	.239	.479	38	-31	-31	100	114	27	.403	10			6	S/23	-1.9
■ CHICK GAGNON	Gagnon, Harold Dennis b: 9/27/1897, Millbury, Mass. d: 4/30/70, Wilmington, Del. BR/TR, 5'7.5", 158 lbs. Deb: 6/27/22																											
1922	Det-A	10	4	2	1	0	0	0	0	0	2	.250	.250	.250	.500	31	-0	-0	98	0	0	.333	0	0	0	0	/S3	0.0
1924	Was-A	4	5	1	1	0	0	0	1	0	0	.200	.200	.200	.400	3	-1	-1	98	331	0	.250	0	0	0	0	/S	0.0
Total	2	14	9	3	2	0	0	0	1	0	2	.222	.222	.222	.444	16	-1	-1	98	184	0	.286	0	0	0	0	/S3	0.0
■ DEL GAINER	Gainer, Dellos Clinton "Sheriff" b: 11/10/1886, Montrose, W.Va. d: 1/29/47, Elkins, W.Va. BR/TR, 6', 180 lbs. Deb: 10/02/09																											
1909	Det-A	2	5	0	1	0	0	0	0	0		.200	.200	.200	.400	24	-0	-0	110	0	0	.250	0			0	/1	0.0
1911	Det-A	70	248	32	75	11	4	2	25	20		.302	.366	.403	.770	106	5	2	108	81	40	.780	10			-6	1	-0.1
1912	Det-A	51	179	28	43	5	6	0	20	18		.240	.320	.335	.655	92	-3	-2	95	113	24	.699	14			-4	1	-0.4
1913	Det-A	105	363	47	97	16	8	2	25	30	45	.267	.333	.372	.705	107	2	3	99	64	46	.680	10			-5	*1	-0.2
1914	Det-A	1	0	0	0	0	0	0	0	0	0	—	—	—	—	—	0	0	102	—	—	—	0			0	/1	0.0
	Bos-A	38	84	11	20	9	2	2	13	8	14	.238	.312	.464	.776	136	3	3	98	108	12	.758	2	2	-1	-2	12/O	0.0
	Yr	39	84	11	20	9	2	2	13	8	14	.238	.312	.464	.776	136	3	3	98	106	12	.758	2	2	-1	-2		0.0
1915	Bos-A	82	200	30	59	5	8	1	29	21	31	.295	.371	.415	.786	136	8	9	99	115	35	.797	7	2	1	-1	1/O	0.6
1916	Bos-A	56	142	14	36	6	0	3	18	10	24	.254	.303	.359	.662	105	-1	0	94	107	18	.623	5			0	1/2	0.0
1917	Bos-A	52	172	28	53	10	2	2	19	15	21	.308	.374	.424	.798	133	9	7	108	88	27	.773	1			-2	1	0.3
1919	Bos-A	47	118	9	28	6	2	0	13	13	15	.237	.318	.322	.640	87	-3	-2	91	124	13	.633	5			-3	1O	-0.7
1922	StL-N	43	97	19	26	7	4	2	23	14	6	.268	.360	.485	.845	115	2	2	101	152	17	.836	0	2	-1	-1	1O	0.0
Total	10	547	1608	218	438	75	36	14	185	149	156	.272	.342	.390	.732	112	21	21	100	97	278	.724	54	6		-23	1/O2	-0.5
■ JOE GAINES	Gaines, Arnesta Joe b: 11/22/36, Bryan, Tex. BR/TR, 6'1", 190 lbs. Deb: 6/29/60																											
1960	Cin-N	11	15	2	3	0	0	0	1	0	1	.200	.200	.200	.400	10	-2	-2	98	135	1	.250	0	0	0	0	/O	-0.1
1961	Cin-N	5	3	2	0	0	0	0	0	2	1	.000	.400	.000	.400	17	-0	-0	104	0	0	.667	0	0	0	-1	/O	-0.1
1962	Cin-N	64	52	12	12	3	0	1	7	8	16	.231	.333	.346	.679	81	-1	-1	102	131	6	.634	0	0	0	-3	O	-0.4
1963	Bal-A	66	126	24	36	4	1	6	20	20	39	.286	.384	.476	.860	149	7	8	94	107	23	.863	2	1	0	-6	O	0.0
1964	Bal-A	16	26	2	4	0	0	1	2	3	7	.154	.241	.269	.511	40	-2	-2	105	85	2	.455	0	0	0	-0	/O	-0.2
	Hou-N	89	307	37	78	9	7	7	34	27	69	.254	.318	.397	.716	104	0	1	96	99	39	.668	8	2	1	-3	O	-0.2
1965	Hou-N	100	229	21	52	8	1	6	31	18	59	.227	.292	.349	.641	90	-6	-3	89	131	24	.577	4	1	1	-9	O	-1.4
1966	Hou-N	11	13	4	1	1	0	0	0	3	5	.077	.250	.154	.404	16	-1	-1	97	0	1	.417	0	0	0	-1	/O	-0.2
Total	7	362	771	104	186	25	9	21	95	81	197	.241	.317	.379	.696	100	-6	-1	94	110	96	.666	14	4	2	-23	O	-2.6
■ TY GAINEY	Gainey, Telmanch b: 12/25/60, Cheraw, N.C. BL/TR, 6'1", 190 lbs. Deb: 4/24/85																											
1985	Hou-N	13	37	5	6	0	0	0	0	2	9	.162	.244	.162	.406	16	-4	-4	96	0	2	.323	0	0	0	0	/O	-0.3
1986	Hou-N	26	50	6	15	3	1	1	6	6	19	.300	.375	.460	.835	126	2	2	103	92	9	.889	3	1	0	-1	O	0.1
1987	Hou-N	18	24	1	3	0	0	0	1	2	9	.125	.192	.125	.317	-15	-4	-4	93	133	1	.286	1	0	0	-0	/O	-0.3
Total	3	57	111	12	24	3	1	1	7	10	37	.216	.293	.288	.581	61	-6	-6	98	70	12	.545	4	1	1	-1	/O	-0.5
■ AUGIE GALAN	Galan, August John b: 5/25/12, Berkeley, Cal. BB/TR, 6', 175 lbs. Deb: 4/29/34 C																											
1934	Chi-N	66	192	31	50	6	2	5	22	16	15	.260	.317	.391	.708	90	-3	-3	98	88	25	.660	4			1	2/3S	0.3
1935	Chi-N	154	646	**133**	203	41	11	12	79	87	53	.314	.399	.467	.866	133	32	32	99	73	133	.937	**22**			-9	*O	1.6
1936	Chi-N	145	575	74	152	26	4	8	81	67	50	.264	.344	.365	.709	87	-6	-10	105	130	77	.685	16			-0	*O	-1.5
1937	Chi-N	147	611	104	154	24	10	18	78	79	48	.252	.339	.412	.751	101	3	1	103	79	92	.765	**23**			-5	*O/2S	-1.0
1938	Chi-N	110	395	52	113	16	9	6	69	49	17	.286	.368	.418	.785	110	9	7	105	139	64	.775	8			4	*O	0.9
1939	Chi-N	148	549	104	167	36	8	6	71	75	26	.304	.392	.432	.823	120	18	18	101	108	97	.827	8			-6	*O	0.9
1940	Chi-N	68	209	33	48	14	2	3	22	37	23	.230	.346	.359	.704	95	-1	-1	100	97	29	.742	9			3	O/2	0.0
1941	Chi-N	65	120	18	25	3	0	1	13	22	10	.208	.331	.258	.589	72	-4	-3	94	138	12	.552	0			-4	O	-0.8
	Bro-N	17	27	3	7	3	0	0	4	3	1	.259	.333	.370	.704	95	-0	-0	103	144	4	.650	0			0	/O	0.0
	Yr	82	147	21	32	6	0	1	17	25	11	.218	.331	.279	.610	76	-4	-4	96	141	16	.574	0			-4		-0.8
1942	Bro-N	69	209	24	55	16	0	0	22	24	12	.263	.339	.340	.679	97	0	-0	102	115	25	.618	2			-4	O/12	-0.6
1943	Bro-N	139	495	83	142	26	3	9	67	**103**	39	.287	.412	.406	.818	137	28	29	100	112	93	.876	6			6	*O1	3.1
1944	Bro-N	151	547	96	174	43	9	12	93	**101**	23	.318	.426	.495	.922	160	47	47	99	115	123	.992	4			2	*O/2	3.8
1945	Bro-N	152	576	114	177	36	7	9	92	114	27	.307	.423	.441	.864	147	37	40	96	109	116	.936	13			-6	1O3	2.8
1946	Bro-N	99	274	53	85	22	5	3	38	68	21	.310	.451	.460	.910	155	25	24	103	105	65	1.074	8			-8	O31	1.6
1947	Cin-N	124	392	60	123	18	2	6	61	94	19	.314	**.449**	.416	.865	144	24	29	91	127	83	.945	8			-6	*O	1.8
1948	Cin-N	54	77	18	22	3	2	2	16	26	4	.286	.471	.455	.926	147	8	7	103	146	19	1.088	0			-3	O	0.3
1949	NY-N	22	17	0	1	1	0	0	2	5	3	.059	.273	.118	.390	8	-2	-2	102	377	1	.412	0			-0	/1O	-0.2
	Phi-A	12	26	4	8	2	0	0	0	9	2	.308	.486	.385	.870	133	2	2	99	0	6	1.000	0	0	0	-1	/O	0.0
Total	16	1742	5937	1004	1706	336	74	100	830	979	393	.287	.390	.419	.810	123	216	217	100	109	1064	.855	123	0		-37	*O/132S	13.0
■ ANDRES GALARRAGA	Galarraga, Andres Jose (born Padovani (Galarraga)) b: 6/18/61, Caracas, Venez. BR/TR, 6'3", 235 lbs. Deb: 8/23/85																											
1985	Mon-N	24	75	9	14	1	0	2	4	3	18	.187	.228	.280	.508	44	-6	-5	94	59	5	.413	1	2	-1	1	1	-0.5
1986	Mon-N	105	321	39	87	13	0	10	42	30	79	.271	.339	.405	.744	107	2	3	98	105	43	.684	6	5	-1	-5	*1	-0.7
1987	Mon-N	147	551	72	168	40	3	13	90	41	127	.305	.364	.459	.823	110	13	8	106	130	88	.770	7	10	-4	-1	*1	-0.4

YEAR	TM/L	G	AB	R	H	2B	3B	HR	RBI	BB	SO	AVG	OBP	SLG	PRO	/A	BR	/A	PF	CHI	RC	TA	SB	CS	SBR	FR	POS	TPR
1988	Mon-N	157	609	99	**184**	**42**	8	29	92	39	153	.302	.354	.540	.894	145	39	35	106	94	114	.887	13	4	2	-3	*1	2.8
Total	4	433	1556	219	453	96	11	54	228	113	377	.291	.348	.471	.820	120	48	41	103	107	249	.790	27	21	-5	-8	1	1.2
■ MILT GALATZER	Galatzer, Milton b: 5/4/07, Chicago, Il.. d: 1/29/76, San Francisco, Cal BL/TL, 5'10", 168 lbs. Deb: 6/25/33																											
1933	Cle-A	57	160	19	38	2	1	1	17	23	21	.237	.333	.281	.615	61	-8	-9	105	118	16	.560	2	3	-1	-2	O/1	-1.2
1934	Cle-A	49	196	29	53	10	2	0	15	21	8	.270	.344	.342	.686	77	-6	-6	101	72	24	.634	3	2	-0	0	O	-0.6
1935	Cle-A	93	259	45	78	9	3	0	19	35	8	.301	.389	.359	.748	95	-1	-0	99	69	38	.720	4	5	-2	-8	O	-0.9
1936	Cle-A	49	97	12	23	4	1	0	6	13	8	.237	.333	.299	.632	54	-6	-7	106	67	10	.579	1	2	-1	-8	O/P1	-1.5
1939	Cin-N	3	5	0	0	0	0	0	0	0	1	.000	.000	.000	.000	-97	-1	-1	103	0	0	.000	0			0	/1	-0.1
Total	5	251	717	105	192	25	7	1	57	92	46	.268	.354	.326	.681	75	-22	-24	102	80	88	.633	10	12		-18	O/1P	-4.3
■ ARCHIE GALBRAITH	Galbraith, Archibald Victor b: 9/22/1877, Boxford, Mass. d: 12/25/71, Northampton, Mass Deb: 8/29/02																											
1902	Pit-N	1	0	0	0	0	0	0	0	0		—	—	—	—	—	0	0	105	—	—	—	0			0	/3	0.0
■ AL GALLAGHER	Gallagher, Alan Mitchell Edward George Patrick Henry b: 10/19/45, San Francisco, Cal. BR/TR, 6', 180 lbs. Deb: 4/07/70																											
1970	SF-N	109	282	31	75	15	2	4	28	30	37	.266	.337	.376	.712	95	-4	-2	96	92	35	.636	2	1	0	-10	3	-1.4
1971	SF-N	136	429	47	119	18	5	5	57	40	57	.277	.342	.378	.719	104	2	3	100	131	53	.632	2	1	0	-12	*3	-0.9
1972	SF-N	82	233	19	52	3	1	2	18	33	39	.223	.322	.270	.592	70	-8	-8	100	107	21	.518	2	1	0	-1	3	-1.0
1973	SF-N	5	9	1	2	0	0	0	1	0	0	.222	.300	.222	.522	45	-1	-1	105	201	0	.375	0	0	0	-0	/3	0.0
	Cal-A	110	311	16	85	6	1	0	26	35	31	.273	.349	.299	.648	87	-5	-4	96	110	32	.546	1	3	-2	1	3/2S	-0.5
Total	4	442	1264	114	333	42	9	11	130	138	164	.263	.338	.337	.675	91	-15	-12	98	113	142	.609	7	6	-2	-22	3/S2	-3.8
■ SHORTY GALLAGHER	Gallagher, Charles William b: 4/30/1872, Detroit, Mich. d: 6/23/24, Detroit, Mich. Deb: 8/13/01																											
1901	Cle-A	2	4	0	0	0	0	0	0	0		.000	.000	.000	.000	-99	-1	-1	95	0	0	.000	0			0	/O	0.0
■ DAVE GALLAGHER	Gallagher, David Thomas b: 9/20/60, Trenton, N.J. BR/TR, 6' ", 180 lbs. Deb: 4/12/87																											
1987	Cle-A	15	36	2	4	1	1	0	1	2	5	.111	.158	.194	.352	-7	-6	-6	103	57	1	.333	2	0	1	2	O	-0.3
1988	Chi-A	101	347	59	105	15	3	5	31	29	40	.303	.356	.406	.763	116	6	7	97	81	49	.689	5	4	-1	-5	O/D	0.0
Total	2	116	383	61	109	16	4	5	32	31	45	.285	.338	.386	.725	104	1	2	98	78	50	.650	7	4	-0	-3	O/D	-0.3
■ JIM GALLAGHER	Gallagher, James E. b: Findlay, Ohio d: 3/29/1894, Scranton, Pa. Deb: 9/04/1886																											
1886	Was-N	1	5	1	1	0	0	0	0	0	2	.200	.200	.200	.400	23	-0	-0	94	0	0	.250	0			0	/S	0.0
■ JOHN GALLAGHER	Gallagher, John Carroll b: 2/18/1892, Pittsburgh, Pa. d: 3/30/52, Norfolk, Va. BR/TR, 5'10.5", 156 lbs. Deb: 8/20/15																											
1915	Bal-F	40	126	11	25	4	0	0	4	5	22	.198	.229	.230	.459	34	-10	-11	107	50	8	.347	1			-2	2/S3	-1.2
■ JACKIE GALLAGHER	Gallagher, John Laurence b: 1/28/02, Providence, R.I. d: 9/10/84, Gladwyn, Pa. BL/TR, 5'10", 175 lbs. Deb: 8/24/23																											
1923	Cle-A	1	1	0	1	0	0	0	0	0	0	1.000	1.000	1.000	2.000	423	0	0	101	0	1	—	0	0	0	-0	/O	0.0
■ JOE GALLAGHER	Gallagher, Joseph Emmett "Muscles" b: 3/7/14, Buffalo, N.Y. BR/TR, 6'2", 210 lbs. Deb: 4/20/39																											
1939	NY-A	14	41	8	10	0	1	2	9	3	8	.244	.311	.439	.750	98	-1	-0	91	127	6	.742	1	0	0	-2	O	-0.1
	StL-A	71	266	41	75	17	2	9	40	17	42	.282	.327	.462	.790	99	-1	-2	100	92	38	.709	0	1	-1	1	O	-0.2
	Yr	85	307	49	85	17	3	11	49	20	50	.277	.325	.459	.785	99	-2	-2	99	99	44	.713	1	1	-0	-0		-0.3
1940	StL-A	23	70	14	19	3	1	2	8	4	12	.271	.311	.429	.739	85	-1	-2	106	80	9	.667	2	0	1	-1	O	-0.3
	Bro-N	57	110	10	29	6	1	3	16	2	14	.264	.283	.418	.701	84	-2	-3	108	108	13	.610	1			-3	O	-0.6
Total	2	165	487	73	133	26	5	16	73	26	76	.273	.314	.446	.760	94	-5	-7	102	97	66	.702	4	1		-4	O	-1.2
■ GIL GALLAGHER	Gallagher, Lawrence Kirby b: 9/5/1896, Washington, D.C. d: 1/6/57, Washington, D.C. BB/TR, 5'8", 155 lbs. Deb: 9/13/22																											
1922	Bos-N	7	22	1	1	1	0	0	2	1	7	.045	.087	.091	.178	-57	-5	-5	94	350	0	.143	0	0	0	0	/S	-0.4
■ BOB GALLAGHER	Gallagher, Robert Collins b: 7/7/48, Newton, Mass. BL/TL, 6'3", 185 lbs. Deb: 5/17/72																											
1972	Bos-A	7	5	0	0	0	0	0	0	0	3	.000	.000	.000	.000	-95	-1	-1	105	0	0	.000	0	0	0	0	H	0.0
1973	Hou-N	71	148	16	39	3	1	2	10	3	27	.264	.278	.338	.616	74	-6	-5	95	72	13	.477	0	1	-1	-2	O/1	-0.9
1974	Hou-N	102	87	13	15	2	0	0	3	12	23	.172	.280	.195	.475	35	-7	-7	98	68	6	.425	1	0	0	-18	O/1	-2.8
1975	NY-N	33	15	5	2	1	0	0	0	1	3	.133	.188	.200	.387	8	-2	-2	95	0	0	.286	0	0	0	-5	O	-0.7
Total	4	213	255	34	56	6	1	2	13	16	56	.220	.268	.275	.543	53	-17	-16	96	65	20	.438	1	1	-0	-25	O/1	-4.4
■ WILLIAM GALLAGHER	Gallagher, William H. b: 1875, Lowell, Mass. Deb: 8/19/1896																											
1896	Phi-N	14	49	9	15	2	0	0	6	10	0	.306	.433	.347	.780	107	1	1	102	108	8	.824	0			0	S	0.1
■ WILLIAM GALLAGHER	Gallagher, William John b: Philadelphia, Pa. TL , Deb: 5/02/1883																											
1883	Bal-a	16	61	9	10	3	1	0		3		.164	.203	.246	.449	41	-4	-4	107	0	3	.353				0	/OPS	-0.3
	Phi-N	2	8	1	0	0	0	0	0	0	4	.000	.000	.000	.000	-99	-2	-2	90	0	0	.000				0	/O	-0.1
1884	Phi-U	3	11	1	1	0	0	0		0		.091	.091	.091	.182	-41	-2	-1	93	0	0	.100	0			0	/P	0.0
Total	2	21	80	11	11	3	1	0	0	3	4	.138	.169	.200	.369	18	-7	-7	103	0	3	.275	0			0	/OPS	-0.4
■ STAN GALLE	Galle, Stanley Joseph (born Stanley Joseph Galazewski) b: 2/7/19, Milwaukee, Wis. BR/TR, 5'7", 165 lbs. Deb: 4/14/42																											
1942	Was-A	13	18	3	2	0	0	0	1	1	0	.111	.158	.111	.269	-25	-3	-3	96	176	0	.158	0	0	0	0	/3	-0.2
■ MIKE GALLEGO	Gallego, Michael Anthon b: 10/31/60, Whittier, Cal. BR/TR, 5'8", 160 lbs. Deb: 4/11/85																											
1985	Oak-A	76	77	13	16	5	1	1	9	12	14	.208	.322	.338	.660	87	-2	-1	93	123	9	.625	1	1	-0	-5	2S3	-0.3
1986	Oak-A	20	37	2	10	2	0	0	4	1	6	.270	.289	.324	.614	72	-2	-1	94	133	3	.448	0	2	-1	1	2/3S	0.0
1987	Oak-A	72	124	18	31	6	0	2	14	12	21	.250	.321	.347	.668	86	-4	-2	91	114	13	.566	0	1	-1	-0	23S	0.0
1988	Oak-A	129	277	38	58	8	0	2	20	34	53	.209	.298	.260	.558	61	-15	-13	95	102	23	.478	2	3	-1	0	2S3	-0.6
Total	4	297	515	71	115	21	1	5	47	59	94	.223	.307	.297	.604	72	-22	-17	94	110	48	.528	3	7	-3	-5	2/S3	-0.9
■ JIM GALLIGAN	Galligan, James M. b: 1862, Easton, Pa. d: 7/17/01, New York, N.Y. 5'10", 160 lbs. Deb: 9/02/1889																											
1889	Lou-a	31	120	6	20	0	2	0	7	6	17	.167	.213	.200	.413	20	-13	-12	96	85	5	.320	1			0	O	-0.9
■ CHICK GALLOWAY	Galloway, Clarence Edward b: 8/4/1896, Clinton, S.C. d: 11/7/69, Clinton, S.C. BR/TR, 5'8", 160 lbs. Deb: 9/09/19																											
1919	Phi-A	17	63	2	9	0	0	0	4	1	8	.143	.156	.143	.299	-15	-10	-10	106	164	1	.185	0			1	S	-0.8
1920	Phi-A	98	298	28	60	9	3	0	18	22	22	.201	.259	.252	.510	38	-28	-25	94	84	21	.417	2	2	-1	1	S/23	-1.6
1921	Phi-A	131	465	42	123	28	5	3	47	29	43	.265	.310	.366	.676	70	-21	-23	103	90	53	.610	12	7	-1	-22	*S3/2	-2.7
1922	Phi-A	155	571	83	185	26	9	6	69	39	38	.324	.368	.433	.801	104	6	3	104	95	92	.762	10	4	1	4	*S	2.3
1923	Phi-A	134	504	64	140	18	9	2	62	37	30	.278	.327	.361	.688	81	-15	-15	100	119	59	.618	12	10	-2	1	*S	-0.2
1924	Phi-A	129	464	41	128	16	4	2	48	23	23	.276	.311	.341	.652	69	-23	-22	99	99	48	.555	11	12	-4	-9	*S	-2.0
1925	Phi-A	149	481	52	116	11	4	3	71	59	28	.241	.324	.299	.623	57	-29	-32	103	**155**	51	.586	16	9	-1	-0	*S	-0.9
1926	Phi-A	133	408	37	98	13	6	0	49	31	20	.240	.295	.301	.597	48	-27	-37	118	135	38	.516	8	6	-1	-13	*S	-3.9
1927	Phi-A	77	181	25	48	10	4	0	22	18	9	.265	.332	.365	.696	83	-5	-4	97	111	22	.639	1	0	0	-3	S/3	-0.1
1928	Det-A	53	148	17	39	5	2	1	17	15	3	.264	.331	.345	.676	78	-5	-4	99	108	18	.658	7	2	1	2	S3/1O	0.0
Total	10	1076	3583	391	946	136	46	17	407	274	224	.264	.317	.342	.659	69	-155	-170	103	113	402	.589	79	52		-38	S/3201	-9.9
■ JIM GALLOWAY	Galloway, James Cato "Bad News" b: 9/16/1887, Iredell, Tex. d: 5/3/50, Fort Worth, Tex. BB/TR, 6'3", 187 lbs. Deb: 8/24/12																											
1912	StL-N	21	54	4	10	2	0	0	4	5	8	.185	.254	.222	.476	31	-5	-5	100	112	4	.432	2			-0	2/S	-0.5
■ JIM GALVIN	Galvin, James Joseph b: 8/11/07, Somerville, Mass. d: 9/30/69, Marietta, Ga. BR/TR, 5'11.5", 180 lbs. Deb: 9/27/30																											
1930	Bos-A	2	2	0	0	0	0	0	0	0	0	.000	.000	.000	.000	-99	-1	-1	93	0	0	.000	0	0	0	0	H	0.0
■ JOHN GALVIN	Galvin, John b: Brooklyn, N.Y. d: 4/20/04, Brooklyn, N.Y. Deb: 5/07/1872																											
1872	Atl-n	1	4	0	0							.000															/2	
1874	Atl-n	1	4	1	0							.000															/2	
Total	2 n	2	8	1	0							.000															/2	
■ JOHN GAMBLE	Gamble, John Robert b: 2/10/48, Reno, Nev. BR/TR, 5'10", 165 lbs. Deb: 9/07/72																											
1972	Det-A	6	3	0	0	0	0	0	0	0	0	.000	.000	.000	.000	-88	-1	-1	113	0	0	.000	0	0	0	0	/S	0.0

YEAR	TM/L	G	AB	R	H	2B	3B	HR	RBI	BB	SO	AVG	OBP	SLG	PRO	/A	BR	/A	PF	CHI	RC	TA	SB	CS	SBR	FR	POS	TPR
1973	Det-A	7	0	1	0	0	0	0	0	0	0	—	—	—	—	—	0	0	101	—	—	—	0	0	0	0	R	0.0
Total	2	13	3	1	0	0	0	0	0	0	0	.000	.000	.000	.000	-88	-1	-1	113	0	0	.000	0	0	0	0	/S	0.0
■ **LEE GAMBLE**	Gamble, Lee Jesse b: 6/28/10, Renovo, Pa. BL/TR, 6'1", 170 lbs. Deb: 9/15/35																											
1935	Cin-N	2	4	2	2	1	0	0	2	1	0	.500	.600	.750	1.350	279	1	1	93	241	2	2.500	1			-0	/O	0.1
1938	Cin-N	53	75	13	24	3	1	0	5	0	6	.320	.320	.387	.707	96	-1	-1	98	62	9	.558	0			-0	/O	0.0
1939	Cin-N	72	221	24	59	7	2	0	14	9	14	.267	.296	.317	.612	63	-11	-12	103	73	21	.515	5			-5	O	-1.7
1940	Cin-N	38	42	12	6	1	0	0	0	0	1	.143	.143	.167	.310	-15	-7	-7	101	0	1	.189	0			-0	O	-0.6
Total	4	165	342	51	91	12	3	0	21	10	21	.266	.287	.319	.606	63	-17	-18	101	64	34	.496	6			-6	/O	-2.2
■ **OSCAR GAMBLE**	Gamble, Oscar Charles b: 12/20/49, Ramer, Ala. BL/TR, 5'11", 160 lbs. Deb: 8/27/69																											
1969	Chi-N	24	71	6	16	1	1	1	5	10	12	.225	.321	.310	.631	73	-2	-3	107	80	7	.552	0	2	-1	-1	O	-0.5
1970	Phi-N	88	275	31	72	12	4	1	19	27	37	.262	.330	.345	.675	84	-7	-6	96	75	30	.595	5	4	-1	3	O	-0.6
1971	Phi-N	92	280	24	62	11	1	6	23	21	35	.221	.278	.332	.610	70	-11	-12	103	84	27	.543	5	2	0	-8	O	-2.3
1972	Phi-N	74	135	17	32	5	2	1	13	19	16	.237	.335	.326	.661	91	-2	-1	97	114	15	.593	0	1	-1	-2	O/1	-0.5
1973	Cle-A	113	390	56	104	11	3	20	44	34	37	.267	.330	.464	.794	125	10	11	97	73	60	.752	3	4	-2	-2	DO	0.6
1974	Cle-A	135	454	74	132	16	4	19	59	48	51	.291	.365	.469	.834	137	22	22	101	88	77	.809	5	6	-2	-2	*DO	1.9
1975	Cle-A	121	348	60	91	16	3	15	45	53	39	.261	.362	.454	.816	130	14	14	100	85	58	.830	11	5	0	-2	OD	1.1
1976	NY-A	110	340	43	79	13	1	17	57	38	38	.232	.317	.426	.743	117	6	6	99	112	47	.716	5	3	-0	-3	*O/D	0.1
1977	Chi-A	137	408	75	121	22	2	31	83	54	54	.297	.387	.588	.975	162	34	35	99	99	96	1.031	1	2	-1	-6	DO	2.6
1978	SD-N	126	375	46	103	15	3	7	47	51	45	.275	.370	.387	.757	121	8	11	93	112	57	.736	1	2	-1	-3	*O	0.3
1979	Tex-A	64	161	27	54	6	0	8	32	37	15	.335	.462	.522	.984	165	17	17	100	114	39	1.088	2	1	0	1	DO	1.7
	NY-A	36	113	21	44	4	1	11	32	13	13	.389	.452	.735	1.187	224	18	18	96	106	38	1.371	0	0	0	-1	O/D	1.6
	Yr	100	274	48	98	10	1	19	64	50	28	.358	.458	.609	1.068	188	35	35	98	112	82	1.236	2	1	0	1		3.3
1980	NY-A	78	194	40	54	10	2	14	50	28	21	.278	.381	.567	.948	157	15	15	99	128	44	1.014	2	0	1	-7	OD	0.7
1981	NY-A	80	189	24	45	8	0	10	27	35	23	.238	.360	.439	.799	129	8	8	100	93	31	.793	0	2	-1	-3	OD	0.2
1982	NY-A	108	316	49	86	21	2	18	57	58	47	.272	.392	.522	.914	154	22	24	96	104	69	.983	6	3	0	4	DO	2.7
1983	NY-A	74	180	26	47	10	2	7	26	25	23	.261	.361	.456	.816	125	6	6	99	99	31	.809	0	0	0	-1	OD	0.5
1984	NY-A	54	125	17	23	2	0	10	27	25	18	.184	.320	.440	.760	115	1	2	94	127	19	.786	1	0	0	-2	DO	0.1
1985	Chi-A	70	148	20	30	5	0	4	20	34	22	.203	.355	.318	.673	86	-2	-2	100	134	19	.689	0	0	0	0	D	-0.1
Total	17	1584	4502	656	1195	188	31	200	666	610	546	.265	.358	.454	.813	128	159	168	98	99	766	.821	47	37	-8	-33	OD/1	10.1
■ **DAFF GAMMONS**	Gammons, John Ashley b: 3/17/1876, New Bedford, Mass. d: 9/24/63, E.Greenwich, R.I. 5'11", 170 lbs. Deb: 4/23/01																											
1901	Bos-N	28	93	10	18	0	1	0	1	3		.194	.219	.215	.434	25	-8	-10	112	17	6	.373	5			2	O/23	-0.9
■ **CHICK GANDIL**	Gandil, Charles Arnold b: 1/19/1887, St.Paul, Minn. d: 12/13/70, Calistoga, Cal. BR/TR, 6'1.5", 190 lbs. Deb: 4/14/10																											
1910	Chi-A	77	275	21	53	7	3	2	21	24		.193	.267	.262	.529	69	-11	-9	95	105	22	.505	12			6	1/O	0.0
1912	Was-A	117	443	59	135	20	15	2	81	27		.305	.350	.431	.781	124	11	12	99	145	74	.789	21			1	*1	1.5
1913	Was-A	148	550	61	175	25	8	1	72	36	33	.318	.363	.398	.762	116	14	11	106	122	84	.747	22			7	*1	1.9
1914	Was-A	145	526	48	136	24	10	3	74	44	44	.259	.324	.359	.683	104	2	2	101	135	67	.660	30	19	-2	21	*1	2.3
1915	Was-A	136	485	53	141	20	15	2	64	29	33	.291	.340	.406	.746	122	11	11	101	109	70	.709	20	13	-2	2	*1	0.5
1916	Cle-A	146	533	51	138	26	9	0	72	36	48	.259	.312	.341	.653	96	-4	-4	100	150	64	.597	13			10	*1	0.3
1917	Chi-A	149	553	53	151	9	7	0	57	30	36	.273	.316	.315	.631	95	-6	-4	98	120	58	.560	16			-5	*1	-1.7
1918	Chi-A	114	439	49	119	18	4	0	55	27	19	.271	.319	.330	.649	95	-3	-3	101	147	47	.578	9			-4	*1	-1.6
1919	Chi-A	115	441	54	128	24	7	1	60	20	20	.290	.325	.383	.709	94	-2	-5	105	134	57	.645	10			-4	*1	-1.7
Total	9	1147	4245	449	1176	173	78	11	556	273	233	.277	.327	.362	.689	104	13	9	101	130	543	.647	153	32		34	*1/O	1.5
■ **BOB GANDY**	Gandy, Robert Brinkley "String" b: 8/25/1893, Jacksonville, Fla. d: 6/19/45, Jacksonville, Fla BL/TR, 6'3", 180 lbs. Deb: 10/05/16																											
1916	Phi-N	1	2	0	0	0	0	0	0	0	1	.000	.000	.000	.000	-99	-0	-0	96	0	0	.000	0			0	/O	0.0
■ **BOB GANLEY**	Ganley, Robert Stephen b: 4/23/1875, Lowell, Mass. d: 10/9/45, Lowell, Mass. BL/TL, 5'7", 156 lbs. Deb: 9/01/05																											
1905	Pit-N	32	127	12	40	1	2	0	7	8		.315	.356	.354	.710	110	2	2	104	52	17	.644	3			-1	O	-0.1
1906	Pit-N	137	511	63	132	7	6	0	31	41		.258	.313	.295	.609	88	-4	-7	104	79	55	.557	19			-4	*O	-1.4
1907	Was-A	154	605	73	167	10	5	1	35	54		.276	.335	.314	.649	121	8	14	90	57	79	.648	40			20	*O	2.8
1908	Was-A	150	549	61	131	19	9	1	36	45		.239	.296	.311	.608	105	0	3	95	82	57	.589	30			-0	*O	-0.5
1909	Was-A	19	63	5	16	3	0	0	5	1		.254	.266	.302	.567	88	-2	-1	90	103	6	.511	4			1	O	0.0
	Phi-A	80	274	32	54	4	2	0	9	28		.197	.272	.226	.498	56	-13	-13	102	57	20	.482	16			8	O	-0.8
	Yr	99	337	37	70	7	2	0	14	29		.208	.270	.240	.511	62	-14	-14	100	67	26	.487	20			8		-0.8
Total	5	572	2129	246	540	44	24	2	123	177		.254	.311	.300	.611	98	-9	-2	97	70	234	.583	112			23	O	-0.0
■ **BILL GANNON**	Gannon, William G. b: 1876, New Haven, Conn. d: 4/26/27, Fort Worth, Tex. Deb: 8/28/1898																											
1898	StL-N	1	3	0	0	0	0	0	0	0		.000	.000	.000	.000	-95	-1	-1	106	0	0	.000	0			0	/P	0.0
1901	Chi-N	15	61	2	9	0	0	0	0	1		.148	.161	.148	.309	-9	-8	-8	100	0	2	.288	5			0	O	-0.9
Total	2	16	64	2	9	0	0	0	0	1		.141	.154	.141	.294	-13	-9	-9	100	0	2	.273	5			0	/OP	-0.9
■ **RON GANT**	Gant, Ronald Edwin b: 3/2/65, Victoria, Tex. BR/TR, 6' ", 172 lbs. Deb: 9/06/87																											
1987	Atl-N	21	83	9	22	4	0	2	9	1	11	.265	.274	.386	.659	67	-4	-4	108	96	7	.561	4	2	0	4	2	0.0
1988	Atl-N	146	563	85	146	28	8	19	60	46	118	.259	.319	.439	.757	110	10	7	104	84	78	.726	19	10	-0	2	*23	1.3
Total	2	167	646	94	168	32	8	21	69	47	129	.260	.313	.432	.745	104	6	3	105	85	86	.708	23	12	-0	6	2/3	1.3
■ **JOE GANTENBEIN**	Gantenbein, Joseph Stephen "Sep" b: 8/25/16, San Francisco, Cal BL/TR, 5'9", 168 lbs. Deb: 4/20/39																											
1939	Phi-A	111	348	47	101	14	4	4	36	32	22	.290	.353	.388	.741	92	-5	-4	97	83	48	.664	1	5	-3	-20	23/S	-2.1
1940	Phi-A	75	197	21	47	6	2	4	23	11	21	.239	.282	.350	.633	66	-11	-10	96	103	20	.539	1	0	0	-3	3/1SO	-0.9
Total	2	186	545	68	148	20	6	8	59	43	43	.272	.328	.374	.703	83	-17	-14	97	90	68	.624	2	5	-2	-22	/23S1O	-3.0
■ **JIM GANTNER**	Gantner, James Elmer b: 1/5/53, Fond Du Lac, Wis. BL/TR, 6', 180 lbs. Deb: 9/03/76																											
1976	Mil-A	26	69	6	17	1	0	0	7	6	11	.246	.316	.261	.577	71	-2	-2	99	149	6	.491	1	0	0	-1	3/D	-0.3
1977	Mil-A	14	47	4	14	1	0	1	2	2	5	.298	.327	.383	.710	97	-1	-0	95	38	6	.629	2	1	0	0	3	0.0
1978	Mil-A	43	97	14	21	1	0	1	8	5	10	.216	.269	.258	.527	46	-7	-7	106	113	8	.447	2	0	1	-1	23/1S	-0.5
1979	Mil-A	70	208	29	59	10	3	2	22	16	17	.284	.341	.389	.730	96	-1	-1	100	97	27	.650	3	5	-2	-1	32/SP	-0.1
1980	Mil-A	132	415	47	117	21	3	4	40	30	29	.282	.332	.376	.708	99	-4	-1	95	93	50	.627	11	10	-3	-1	32/S	-0.1
1981	Mil-A	107	352	35	94	14	1	2	33	29	29	.267	.328	.330	.658	94	-4	-2	96	106	38	.559	3	6	-3	19	*2	1.8
1982	Mil-A	132	447	48	132	17	2	4	43	26	36	.295	.337	.369	.706	100	-4	-0	94	97	56	.614	6	3	0	5	*2	1.2
1983	Mil-A	161	603	85	170	23	8	11	74	38	46	.282	.331	.401	.732	110	-0	7	92	107	79	.648	5	6	-2	8	*2	1.7
1984	Mil-A	153	613	61	173	27	1	3	56	30	51	.282	.319	.344	.663	91	-14	-7	92	98	64	.542	6	5	-1	12	*2	1.0
1985	Mil-A	143	523	63	133	15	4	5	44	33	42	.254	.302	.327	.629	69	-20	-23	105	96	49	.530	11	8	-2	11	*23/S	-0.8
1986	Mil-A	139	497	58	136	25	1	7	38	26	50	.274	.318	.370	.688	86	-9	-10	102	75	56	.601	13	7	-0	-10	*2/3SD	-1.2
1987	Mil-A	81	265	37	72	14	0	4	30	19	22	.272	.332	.370	.702	85	-5	-6	102	109	32	.634	6	2	1	-4	23/D	-0.4
1988	Mil-A	155	539	67	149	28	2	0	47	34	50	.276	.323	.336	.659	82	-11	-13	103	105	60	.585	20	8	1	-5	*2/3	-0.6
Total	13	1356	4675	554	1287	197	25	44	444	294	398	.275	.323	.356	.680	89	-79	-66	98	98	530	.603	89	61	-10	32	*23/SDP1	1.7
■ **CHARLIE GANZEL**	Ganzel, Charles William b: 6/18/1862, Waterford, Wis. d: 4/7/14, Quincy, Mass. BR/TR, 6', 161 lbs. Deb: 9/27/1884																											
1884	StP-U	7	23	2	5	0	0	0		0		.217	.217	.217	.435	47	-1	-1	100	0	1	.278	0			0	/CO	0.0
1885	Phi-N	34	125	15	21	3	1	0	6	4	13	.168	.194	.208	.402	29	-10	-10	104	85	5	.288				0	C/O	-0.6
1886	Phi-N	1	3	0	0	0	0	0	0	0	1	.000	.000	.000	.000	-99	-1	-1	98	0	0	.000	0			-1	/C	-0.1
	Det-N	57	213	28	58	7	2	1	31	7	22	.272	.295	.338	.633	85	-2	-5	109	137	23	.542	5			3	C/O1	0.1
	Yr	58	216	28	58	7	2	1	31	7	23	.269	.291	.333	.625	83	-3	-6	109	135	23	.532	5			2		0.0
1887	Det-N	57	227	40	59	6	5	0	20	8	2	.260	.288	.330	.619	72	-8	-9	102	84	23	.518	3			9	C/O13	0.5
1888	Det-N	95	386	45	96	13	5	1	46	14	15	.249	.277	.316	.593	92	-4	-3	98	140	38	.514	12			-3	2C/3OS1	-0.3
1889	Bos-N	73	275	30	73	3	5	1	43	15	11	.265	.308	.324	.632	77	-8	-9	102	142	32	.589	13			3	CO/1S3	-0.4

YEAR	TM/L	G	AB	R	H	2B	3B	HR	RBI	BB	SO	AVG	OBP	SLG	PRO	/A	BR	/A	PF	CHI	RC	TA	SB	CS	SBR	FR	POS	TPR
1890	Bos-N	38	163	21	44	7	3	0	24	5	6	.270	.300	.350	.650	82	-2	-5	111	135	18	.546	1			0	CO/S2	-0.3
1891	Bos-N	70	263	33	68	18	5	1	29	12	13	.259	.304	.376	.680	89	-1	-6	112	84	33	.631	7			-3	CO	-0.3
1892	Bos-N	54	198	25	53	9	3	0	25	18	12	.268	.332	.343	.675	94	2	-2	113	115	26	.648	7			-11	C/O1	-0.8
1893	Bos-N	73	281	50	75	10	2	1	48	22	9	.267	.325	.327	.652	73	-10	-11	103	141	33	.592	6			-5	CO1	-0.9
1894	Bos-N	70	266	51	74	7	6	3	56	19	6	.278	.326	.383	.710	64	-13	-19	113	139	34	.635	1			-5	C/1OS2	-1.4
1895	Bos-N	80	277	38	73	2	5	1	52	24	6	.264	.325	.318	.642	66	-13	-14	103	160	30	.559	1			0	C/S1	-0.5
1896	Bos-N	47	179	28	47	2	0	1	18	9	5	.263	.305	.291	.596	55	-10	-13	108	96	17	.492	2			5	C/1S	-0.2
1897	Bos-N	30	105	15	28	4	3	0	14	4		.267	.300	.362	.662	71	-4	-5	107	108	12	.584	2			0	C/1	-0.3
Total	14	786	2984	421	774	91	45	10	412	161	121	.259	.301	.330	.631	75	-86	-114	106	124	325	.554	60			-7	CO/21S3	-5.5
■ **BABE GANZEL** Ganzel, Foster Pirie b: 5/22/01, Malden, Mass. d: 2/6/78, Jacksonville, Fla. BR/TR, 5'10.5", 172 lbs. Deb: 9/19/27																												
1927	Was-A	13	48	7	21	4	2	1	13	7	3	.438	.509	.667	1.176	210	8	8	97	119	16	1.444	0	0	0	1	O	0.7
1928	Was-A	10	26	2	2	1	0	0	4	1	4	.077	.111	.115	.226	-40	-5	-5	102	458	0	.167	0	0	0	-1	/O	-0.5
Total	2	23	74	9	23	5	2	1	17	8	7	.311	.378	.473	.851	122	2	2	98	230	16	.843	0	0	0	0	/O	0.2
■ **JOHN GANZEL** Ganzel, John Henry b: 4/7/1874, Kalamazoo, Mich. d: 1/14/59, Orlando, Fla. BR/TR, 6'0.5", 195 lbs. Deb: 4/21/1898 M																												
1898	Pit-N	15	45	5	6	0	0	0	2	4		.133	.204	.133	.337	-1	-6	-6	98	101	1	.256	0			0	1	-0.4
1900	Chi-N	78	284	29	78	14	4	4	32	10		.275	.299	.394	.694	100	-4	-1	93	82	36	.617	5			-4	1	-0.3
1901	NY-N	138	526	42	113	13	3	2	66	20		.215	.244	.262	.506	53	-34	-28	91	**162**	36	.397	6			3	*1	-2.4
1903	NY-A	129	476	62	132	25	7	3	71	30		.277	.320	.378	.698	111	6	6	100	143	62	.637	9			7	*1	1.4
1904	NY-A	130	465	50	121	16	10	6	48	24		.260	.297	.376	.673	102	7	0	112	95	57	.616	13			2	*1/2S	0.5
1907	Cin-N	145	531	61	135	20	**16**	2	64	29		.254	.293	.363	.656	113	2	5	95	129	61	.583	9			-2	*1	0.0
1908	Cin-N	112	388	32	97	16	10	1	53	19		.250	.285	.351	.636	102	1	-0	103	149	39	.553	6			-2	*1M	-0.5
Total	7	747	2715	281	682	104	50	18	336	136		.251	.287	.346	.633	94	-28	-23	99	130	292	.553	48			2	1/2S	-1.7
■ **JOE GARAGIOLA** Garagiola, Joseph Henry b: 2/12/26, St.Louis, Mo. BL/TR, 6', 190 lbs. Deb: 5/26/46																												
1946	StL-N	74	211	21	50	4	1	3	22	23	25	.237	.312	.308	.620	72	-6	-8	107	111	21	.533	0			-6	C	-1.2
1947	StL-N	77	183	20	47	10	2	5	25	40	14	.257	.398	.415	.814	109	6	4	106	102	33	.844	0			-10	C	-0.3
1948	StL-N	24	56	9	6	1	0	2	7	12	9	.107	.275	.232	.508	38	-5	-5	101	138	5	.520	0			0	C	-0.2
1949	StL-N	81	241	25	63	14	0	3	26	31	19	.261	.348	.357	.705	81	-3	-6	110	103	31	.641	0			-6	C	-0.9
1950	StL-N	34	88	8	28	6	1	2	20	10	7	.318	.388	.477	.865	122	3	3	103	161	15	.800	0			0	C	0.4
1951	StL-N	27	72	9	14	3	2	2	9	9	7	.194	.284	.375	.659	75	-3	-3	101	105	7	.590	0	0	0	-0	C	-0.2
	Pit-N	72	212	24	54	8	2	9	35	32	20	.255	.358	.439	.796	106	4	2	107	113	36	.804	4	1	1	1	C	0.5
	Yr	99	284	33	68	11	4	11	44	41	27	.239	.339	.423	.762	99	1	-0	105	112	44	.756	4	1	1	1		0.3
1952	Pit-N	118	344	35	94	15	4	8	54	50	24	.273	.369	.410	.779	116	8	9	100	128	55	.748	0	1	-1	4	*C	1.4
1953	Pit-N	27	73	9	17	5	0	2	14	10	11	.233	.341	.384	.725	87	-1	-1	102	161	10	.707	1	0	0	0	C	0.1
	Chi-N	74	228	21	62	9	4	1	21	21	23	.272	.336	.360	.696	79	-6	-7	103	96	27	.598	0	0	0	2	C	0.0
	Yr	101	301	30	79	14	4	3	35	31	34	.262	.337	.365	.703	81	-7	-8	103	115	38	.630	1	0	0	2		0.1
1954	Chi-N	63	153	16	43	5	0	5	21	28	12	.281	.405	.412	.817	113	4	4	101	106	27	.833	0	0	0	-2	C	0.3
	NY-N	5	11	1	3	2	0	0	1	1	2	.273	.333	.455	.788	98	0	-0	105	79	2	.750	0	0	0	-1	/C	0.0
	Yr	68	164	17	46	7	0	5	22	29	14	.280	.401	.415	.816	112	4	4	101	105	31	.856	0	0	0	-2		0.3
Total	9	676	1872	198	481	82	16	42	255	267	173	.257	.355	.385	.740	95	2	-8	104	115	270	.724	5	2		-17	C	-0.1
■ **MIKE GARBARK** Garbark, Nathaniel Michael (born Nathaniel Michael Garbach) b: 2/2/16, Houston, Tex. BR/TR, 6', 200 lbs. Deb: 4/18/44																												
1944	NY-A	89	299	23	78	9	4	1	33	25	27	.261	.320	.328	.648	80	-6	-8	106	118	30	.530	0	1	-1	6	C	0.3
1945	NY-A	60	176	23	38	5	3	1	26	23	12	.216	.310	.295	.605	71	-5	-7	107	171	16	.524	0	1	-1	-1	C	-0.3
Total	2	149	475	46	116	14	7	2	59	48	39	.244	.316	.316	.632	77	-11	-14	107	138	47	.545	0	2	-1	5	C	0.0
■ **BOB GARBARK** Garbark, Robert Michael (born Robert Michael Garbach) b: 11/13/09, Houston, Tex. BR/TR, 5'11", 178 lbs. Deb: 9/03/34																												
1934	Cle-A	5	11	1	0	0	0	0	0	1	3	.000	.083	.000	.083	-77	-3	-3	101	0	0	.091	0	0	0	0	/C	-0.1
1935	Cle-A	6	18	4	6	1	0	0	4	5	1	.333	.478	.389	.867	127	1	1	99	194	4	1.000	0	0	0	-1	/C	0.0
1937	Chi-N	1	1	0	0	0	0	0	0	0	0	.000	.000	.000	.000	-98	-0	-0	103	0	0	.000	0			0	H	0.0
1938	Chi-N	23	54	2	14	0	0	0	5	1	0	.259	.273	.259	.532	45	-4	-4	105	129	3	.333	0			-0	C/1	-0.3
1939	Chi-N	24	21	1	3	0	0	0	0	0	3	.143	.143	.143	.286	-23	-4	-4	101	0	0	.158	0			0	C	-0.2
1944	Phi-A	18	23	2	6	2	0	0	2	1	0	.261	.292	.348	.639	81	-1	-1	101	90	2	.500	0	0	0	0	C	0.0
1945	Bos-A	68	199	21	52	6	0	0	17	18	10	.261	.329	.291	.620	85	-4	-3	95	106	20	.506	0	1	-1	-2	C	0.0
Total	7	145	327	31	81	9	0	0	28	26	17	.248	.307	.275	.582	67	-15	-14	98	104	29	.466	0	1		-4	C/1	-0.6
■ **BARBARO GARBEY** Garbey, Barbaro (Garbey) b: 12/4/56, Santiago, Cuba BR/TR, 5'10", 170 lbs. Deb: 4/03/84																												
1984	Det-A	110	327	45	94	17	1	5	52	17	35	.287	.327	.391	.718	102	-1	0	96	145	38	.617	6	7	-2	1	13DO/2	-0.4
1985	Det-A	86	237	27	61	9	1	6	29	15	37	.257	.310	.380	.690	82	-4	-6	106	106	27	.600	3	2	-0	-1	1OD/3	-0.9
1988	Tex-A	30	62	4	12	2	0	0	5	4	11	.194	.242	.226	.468	32	-6	-6	101	142	3	.340	0	0	0	-1	/O13D	-0.7
Total	3	226	626	76	167	28	2	11	86	36	83	.267	.312	.371	.682	87	-11	-12	101	130	68	.599	9	9	-3	-2	1/DO32	-2.0
■ **ALEX GARBOWSKI** Garbowski, Alexander b: 6/25/25, Yonkers, N.Y BR/TR, 6'1", 185 lbs. Deb: 4/16/52																												
1952	Det-A	2	0	0	0	0	0	0	0	0	0	—	—	—	—	—	0	0	99	—	—	—	0	0	0	0	R	0.0
■ **KIKO GARCIA** Garcia, Alfonso Rafael b: 10/14/53, Martinez, Cal. BR/TR, 5'11", 180 lbs. Deb: 9/11/76																												
1976	Bal-A	11	32	2	7	1	1	1	4	0	4	.219	.219	.406	.625	82	-1	-1	98	96	3	.577	2	1	0	1	S	0.1
1977	Bal-A	65	131	20	29	6	0	2	10	6	31	.221	.255	.313	.568	58	-8	-7	93	84	9	.450	2	3	-1	10	S/2	0.9
1978	Bal-A	79	186	17	49	6	4	0	13	7	43	.263	.290	.339	.629	84	-6	-4	91	81	18	.538	7	1	2	12	S/2	1.6
1979	Bal-A	126	417	54	103	15	9	5	24	32	87	.247	.304	.362	.666	81	-13	-11	97	56	42	.582	11	9	-2	-9	*S2/3O	-0.7
1980	Bal-A	111	311	27	62	8	0	1	27	24	57	.199	.257	.235	.491	35	-27	-27	101	139	18	.398	8	4	0	-1	S2/O	-1.9
1981	Hou-N	48	136	9	37	6	1	0	15	10	16	.272	.327	.331	.657	98	-2	-0	88	131	15	.563	2	2	-1	-1	S3/2	0.1
1982	Hou-N	34	76	5	16	5	0	1	5	3	15	.211	.241	.316	.556	55	-5	-5	99	73	5	.452	1	0	0	2	S/32	0.0
1983	Phi-N	84	118	22	34	7	1	2	9	9	20	.288	.344	.415	.759	108	1	1	101	65	15	.652	1	2	-1	4	2S3	0.8
1984	Phi-N	57	60	6	14	2	0	0	5	4	11	.233	.281	.267	.548	54	-4	-4	102	122	4	.400	0	0	0	0	S3/2	0.0
1985	Phi-N	4	3	0	0	0	0	0	0	0	1	.000	.000	.000	.000	-98	-1	-1	102	0	0	.000	0	0	0	0	/S3	0.0
Total	10	619	1470	162	351	56	16	12	112	95	285	.239	.287	.323	.610	70	-66	-59	97	91	128	.533	34	22	-3	18	S2/3O	0.9
■ **DAMASO GARCIA** Garcia, Damaso Domingo (Sanchez) b: 2/7/55, Moca, D.R. BR/TR, 6'1", 165 lbs. Deb: 6/24/78																												
1978	NY-A	18	41	5	8	0	0	0	1	2	6	.195	.233	.195	.428	22	-4	-4	99	49	2	.324	1	0	0	0	2/S	-0.1
1979	NY-A	11	38	3	10	1	0	0	4	0	2	.263	.263	.289	.553	51	-3	-2	96	140	3	.448	2	0	1	1	S/3	0.1
1980	Tor-A	140	543	50	151	30	7	4	46	12	55	.278	.297	.381	.679	85	-13	-13	100	84	54	.561	13	13	-4	20	*2/D	1.0
1981	Tor-A	64	250	24	63	8	1	1	13	9	32	.252	.278	.304	.582	61	-11	-14	111	68	21	.500	13	3	2	-9	2/D	-1.9
1982	Tor-A	147	597	89	185	32	3	5	42	21	44	.310	.339	.399	.737	94	1	-6	109	64	81	.724	54	20	4	11	*2/D	1.8
1983	Tor-A	131	525	84	161	23	6	3	38	24	34	.307	.339	.390	.730	92	-0	-6	108	74	66	.670	31	17	-1	-11	*2	-1.3
1984	Tor-A	152	633	79	180	32	5	5	46	16	46	.284	.312	.374	.686	88	-10	-12	102	77	76	.654	46	12	7	-7	*2/D	-0.4
1985	Tor-A	146	600	70	169	25	4	8	65	15	41	.282	.304	.377	.680	84	-13	-14	101	109	64	.595	28	15	-1	-13	*2	-2.1
1986	Tor-A	122	424	57	119	22	0	6	46	13	32	.281	.308	.375	.683	82	-9	-11	105	103	44	.569	9	6	-1	-10	*2D/1	-1.6
1988	Atl-N	21	60	3	7	1	0	1	4	3	10	.117	.159	.183	.342	-2	-8	-8	104	114	1	.263	1	0	0	0	2	-0.7
Total	10	952	3711	464	1053	174	26	33	305	115	302	.284	.310	.371	.681	83	-70	-89	104	84	412	.625	198	86	8	-17	2/DS13	-5.2
■ **DANNY GARCIA** Garcia, Daniel Raphael b: 4/29/54, Brooklyn, N.Y. BL/TL, 6'1", 182 lbs. Deb: 4/26/81																												
1981	KC-A	12	14	4	2	0	0	0	0	0	2	.143	.143	.143	.286	-18	-2	-2	99	0	0	.167	0	0	0	-2	/O1	-0.3
■ **LEO GARCIA** Garcia, Leonardo Antonio (Peralt b: 11/6/62, Santiago, D.R. BL/TL, 5'8", 160 lbs. Deb: 4/06/87																												
1987	Cin-N	31	30	8	6	0	0	1	2	4	8	.200	.294	.300	.594	56	-2	-2	104	66	3	.640	3	1	0	-2	O	-0.3
1988	Cin-N	23	28	2	4	1	0	0	0	4	5	.143	.250	.179	.429	24	-3	-3	105	0	1	.360	0	1	-1	-1	/O	-0.5
Total	2	54	58	10	10	1	0	1	2	8	13	.172	.273	.241	.514	41	-4	-5	104	34	4	.500	3	2	-0	-3	/O	-0.8

YEAR	TM/L	G	AB	R	H	2B	3B	HR	RBI	BB	SO	AVG	OBP	SLG	PRO	/A	BR	/A	PF	CHI	RC	TA	SB	CS	SBR	FR	POS	TPR
■ **PEDRO GARCIA**	Garcia, Pedro Modesto (Delfi) b: 4/17/50, Guayama, P.R. BR/TR, 5'10", 175 lbs. Deb: 4/06/73																											
1973	Mil-A	160	580	67	142	**32**	5	15	54	40	119	.245	.299	.395	.694	98	-6	-3	96	79	66	.621	11	10	-3	-11	*2	-1.0
1974	Mil-A	141	452	46	90	15	4	12	54	26	67	.199	.251	.330	.580	64	-21	-23	102	115	37	.505	8	5	-1	-9	*2	-2.7
1975	Mil-A	98	302	40	68	15	2	6	38	18	59	.225	.273	.348	.621	74	-11	-11	100	119	27	.550	12	6	0	7	2/D	0.0
1976	Mil-A	41	106	12	23	7	1	1	9	4	23	.217	.259	.330	.589	72	-4	-4	99	91	9	.500	2	2	-1	-4	2	-0.6
	Det-A	77	227	21	45	10	2	3	20	9	40	.198	.242	.300	.541	56	-13	-14	104	100	16	.441	2	3	-1	5	2	-0.5
	Yr	118	333	33	68	17	3	4	29	13	63	.204	.247	.309	.556	61	-17	-17	102	97	25	.462	4	5	-2	1		-1.1
1977	Tor-A	41	130	10	27	10	1	0	9	5	21	.208	.254	.300	.554	49	-9	-10	103	91	10	.448	0	0	0	-3	2/D	-0.9
Total	5	558	1797	196	395	89	15	37	184	102	329	.220	.270	.348	.618	75	-64	-64	100	99	164	.548	35	26	-5	-15	2/D	-5.7
■ **CHICO GARCIA**	Garcia, Vinicio Uzcanga b: 12/24/24, Verzcruz, Mexico BR/TR, 5'8", 170 lbs. Deb: 4/24/54																											
1954	Bal-A	39	62	6	7	0	2	0	5	8	3	.113	.214	.177	.392	8	-8	-8	95	172	3	.345	0	0	0	-2	2	-0.8
■ **AL GARDELLA**	Gardella, Alfred Stephan b: 1/11/18, New York, N.Y. BL/TL, 5'10", 172 lbs. Deb: 5/17/45																											
1945	NY-N	16	26	2	2	0	0	0	1	4	3	.077	.226	.077	.303	-14	-4	-4	100	174	1	.292	0			-0	/1O	-0.4
■ **DANNY GARDELLA**	Gardella, Daniel Lewis b: 2/26/20, New York, N.Y. BL/TL, 5'7.5", 160 lbs. Deb: 5/14/44																											
1944	NY-N	47	112	20	28	2	2	6	14	11	13	.250	.323	.464	.787	116	2	2	104	72	17	.744	0			1	O	0.1
1945	NY-N	121	430	54	117	10	1	18	71	46	55	.272	.349	.426	.775	115	8	8	100	106	65	.733	2			-5	O1	-0.1
1950	StL-N	1	1	0	0	0	0	0	0	0	0	.000	.000	.000	.000	-97	-0	-0	103	0	0	.000	0			0	H	0.0
Total	3	169	543	74	145	12	3	24	85	57	68	.267	.343	.433	.776	115	10	10	100	99	82	.754	2			-4	O/1	0.0
■ **RON GARDENHIRE**	Gardenhire, Ronald Clyde b: 10/24/57, Butzbach, Germany BR/TR, 6', 175 lbs. Deb: 9/01/81																											
1981	NY-N	27	48	2	13	1	0	0	3	5	9	.271	.340	.292	.631	80	-1	-1	101	84	5	.568	2	2	-1	-2	S/23	0.0
1982	NY-N	141	384	29	92	17	1	3	33	23	55	.240	.283	.313	.595	67	-18	-17	99	100	32	.479	5	6	-2	0	*S/23	-0.8
1983	NY-N	17	32	1	2	0	0	0	1	1	4	.063	.091	.063	.153	-58	-7	-7	99	198	0	.097	0	0	0	0	S	-0.5
1984	NY-N	74	207	20	51	7	1	1	10	9	43	.246	.278	.304	.582	63	-10	-10	100	59	17	.476	6	1	1	-3	S2/3	-0.6
1985	NY-N	26	39	5	7	2	1	0	2	8	11	.179	.319	.282	.601	72	-1	-1	97	72	4	.559	0	0	0	-1	S/23	0.0
Total	5	285	710	57	165	27	3	4	49	46	122	.232	.279	.296	.575	62	-37	-36	99	90	57	.484	13	9	-2	-5	S/23	-1.9
■ **ALEX GARDNER**	Gardner, Alexander b: 4/28/1861, Toronto, Ont., Can. d: 6/18/26, Danvers, Mass. Deb: 5/10/1884																											
1884	Was-a	1	3	0	0	0	0	0		0		.000	.000	.000	.000	-99	-1	-1	88	0	0	.000				0	/C	0.0
■ **ART GARDNER**	Gardner, Arthur Junior b: 9/21/52, Madden, Miss. BL/TL, 5'11", 175 lbs. Deb: 9/02/75																											
1975	Hou-N	13	31	3	6	0	0	0	2	1	8	.194	.242	.194	.436	23	-3	-3	94	129	1	.333	1	0	0	-1	/O	-0.3
1977	Hou-N	66	65	7	10	0	0	0	3	3	15	.154	.203	.154	.357	-3	-9	-9	93	120	2	.241	0	0	0	-3	O	-1.3
1978	SF-N	7	3	2	0	0	0	0	0	0	2	.000	.000	.000	.000	-99	-1	-1	92	0	0	.000	0	1	-1	0	H	0.0
Total	3	86	99	12	16	0	0	0	5	4	25	.162	.210	.162	.371	2	-13	-13	93	119	3	.274	1	1	-0	-4	/O	-1.6
■ **EARLE GARDNER**	Gardner, Earle Mc Clurkin b: 1/24/1884, Sparta, Ill. d: 3/2/43, Sparta, Ill. BR/TR, 5'11", 160 lbs. Deb: 9/18/08																											
1908	NY-A	20	75	7	16	2	0	0	4	1		.213	.224	.240	.464	55	-4	-4	95	88	4	.322	0			-3	2	-0.7
1909	NY-A	22	85	12	28	4	0	0	15	3		.329	.352	.376	.729	131	3	3	99	191	12	.684	4			-5	2	-0.2
1910	NY-A	86	271	36	66	4	2	1	24	21		.244	.303	.284	.587	78	-5	-7	107	111	26	.532	9			-1	2	-1.3
1911	NY-A	102	357	36	94	13	2	0	39	20		.263	.312	.311	.622	67	-13	-18	111	121	39	.570	14			-1	*2	-1.9
1912	NY-A	43	160	14	45	3	1	0	26	5		.281	.303	.313	.616	75	-5	-6	101	177	18	.574	11			-10	2	-1.5
Total	5	273	948	105	249	26	5	1	108	50		.263	.304	.304	.608	76	-24	-32	106	131	100	.548	38			-19	2	-5.6
■ **GID GARDNER**	Gardner, Frank Washington b: 1859, E.Cambridge, Mass. d: 8/1/14, Cambridge, Mass. Deb: 8/23/1879																											
1879	Tro-N	2	6	1	1	0	0	0	0	0	0	.167	.167	.167	.333	11	-1	-1	93	0	0	.200				0	/P	0.0
1880	Cle-N	10	32	0	6	1	1	0	4	2	4	.188	.235	.281	.517	75	-1	-1	99	162	2	.423				0	/PO	0.0
1883	Bal-a	42	161	28	44	10	3	1		18		.273	.346	.391	.738	128	7	5	107	0	22	.692				-1	O/23P	0.4
1884	Bal-a	41	173	32	37	6	8	2		14		.214	.280	.376	.656	116	3	3	99	0	19	.596				1	O/1	0.4
	CP-U	38	149	22	38	10	2	0		10		.255	.302	.349	.651	120	3	3	99	0	16	.559	0			-3	O/3P2	0.0
	Bal-U	1	4	0	1	0	0	0		0		.250	.250	.250	.500	63	-0	-0	110	0	0	.333	0			0	/S	0.0
	Yr	39	153	22	39	10	2	0		10		.255	.301	.346	.647	119	3	3	100	0	16	.553	0			-3		0.0
1885	Bal-a	44	170	22	37	5	4	0		12		.218	.269	.294	.563	76	-4	-5	106	0	14	.466				2	2/O1P	0.0
1887	Ind-N	18	63	8	11	1	0	1	8	12	11	.175	.307	.238	.545	57	-3	-3	96	145	7	.654	7			0	O/2	-0.1
1888	Was-N	1	3	0	1	0	0	0	0	1	1	.333	.500	.333	.833	181	0	0	96	0	1	1.000	0			0	/S	0.0
	Phi-N	1	3	0	2	0	0	0	1	0	0	.667	.667	.667	1.333	291	1	1	114	179	1	2.000	0			0	/2	0.1
	Was-N	1	1	0	0	0	0	0	0	0	0	.000	.000	.000	.000	-99	-0	-0	96	0	0	.000	0			0	/2	0.0
	Yr	3	7	0	3	0	0	0	1	1	1	.429	.500	.429	.929	198	1	1	102	119	2	1.000	0			0		0.1
Total	7	199	765	113	178	33	18	4	13	69	16	.233	.298	.339	.636	103	6	3	102	20	82	.574	7			-1	O/2P31S	0.8
■ **RAY GARDNER**	Gardner, Raymond Vincent b: 10/25/01, Frederick, Md. d: 5/3/68, Frederick, Md. BR/TR, 5'8", 145 lbs. Deb: 4/16/29																											
1929	Cle-A	82	256	28	67	3	2	1	24	29	16	.262	.337	.301	.638	65	-12	-12	100	103	26	.574	10	13	-5	18	S	0.8
1930	Cle-A	33	13	7	1	0	0	0	1	0	0	.077	.077	.077	.154	-58	-3	-3	105	332	0	.077	0	1	-1	1	S/23	0.0
Total	2	115	269	35	68	3	2	1	25	29	16	.253	.326	.290	.615	59	-15	-16	100	113	26	.544	10	14	-5	19	S/23	0.8
■ **BILLY GARDNER**	Gardner, William Frederick "Shotgun" b: 7/19/27, Waterford, Conn. BR/TR, 6', 170 lbs. Deb: 4/22/54 MC																											
1954	NY-N	62	108	10	23	5	0	1	7	6	19	.213	.261	.287	.548	41	-9	-10	105	81	8	.437	0	1	-1	0	32/S	-0.8
1955	NY-N	59	187	26	38	10	1	3	17	13	19	.203	.262	.316	.578	53	-13	-13	99	101	16	.490	0	0	0	-1	S3/2	-1.1
1956	Bal-A	144	515	53	119	16	2	11	50	29	53	.231	.281	.334	.615	66	-30	-26	94	93	45	.512	5	5	-2	-15	*2S/3	-2.9
1957	Bal-A	154	644	79	169	**36**	3	6	55	53	67	.262	.326	.356	.682	93	-12	-7	93	76	75	.606	10	7	-1	9	*2/S	1.0
1958	Bal-A	151	560	32	126	28	2	3	33	34	53	.225	.273	.298	.571	61	-33	-29	94	80	45	.460	2	3	-1	-20	*2S	-3.9
1959	Bal-A	140	401	34	87	13	2	6	27	38	61	.217	.286	.304	.591	64	-21	-19	97	76	34	.498	2	1	0	**15**	*2/S3	0.1
1960	Was-A	145	592	71	152	26	5	9	56	43	76	.257	.314	.363	.677	81	-15	-16	102	87	66	.578	0	4	-2	1	*2S	-0.6
1961	Min-A	45	154	13	36	9	0	1	11	10	14	.234	.280	.312	.592	55	-9	-11	106	84	12	.464	0	0	0	-3	2/3	-0.8
	NY-A	41	99	11	21	5	0	1	2	6	18	.212	.278	.293	.571	55	-7	-6	96	24	8	.463	0	0	0	5	3/2	0.2
	Yr	86	253	24	57	14	0	2	13	16	32	.225	.279	.304	.584	55	-16	-16	101	57	22	.480	0	0	0	2		-0.6
1962	NY-A	4	1	1	0	0	0	0	0	0	1	.000	.000	.000	.000	-99	-0	-0	94	0	0	.000	0	0	0	0	/23	0.0
	Bos-A	53	199	22	54	9	2	0	12	10	39	.271	.310	.337	.646	72	-7	-8	102	72	20	.520	0	1	-1	0	2/3S	-0.4
	Yr	57	200	23	54	9	2	0	12	10	40	.270	.308	.335	.643	72	-8	-8	102	67	20	.517	0	1	-1	0		-0.4
1963	Bos-A	36	84	4	16	2	1	0	1	4	19	.190	.236	.238	.474	31	-7	-8	106	21	5	.362	0	0	0	-1	2/3	-0.7
Total	10	1034	3544	356	841	159	18	41	271	246	439	.237	.293	.327	.620	69	-164	-152	97	80	334	.534	19	22	-8	-8	2S/3	-9.9
■ **LARRY GARDNER**	Gardner, William Lawrence b: 5/13/1886, Enosburg Falls, Vt d: 3/11/76, St.George, Vt. BL/TR, 5'8", 165 lbs. Deb: 6/25/08																											
1908	Bos-A	3	10	0	3	1	0	0	1	0		.300	.300	.400	.700	132	0	0	98	94	1	.571	0			0	/3	0.0
1909	Bos-A	19	37	7	11	1	2	0	5	4		.297	.381	.432	.813	144	2	2	109	120	6	.846	1			0	/3S	0.3
1910	Bos-A	113	413	55	117	12	10	2	36	41		.283	.354	.375	.729	130	14	14	99	87	58	.703	8			-6	*2	0.1
1911	Bos-A	138	492	80	140	17	8	4	44	64		.285	.373	.376	.749	110	8	8	99	80	81	.798	27			7	32	1.5
1912	Bos-A	143	517	88	163	24	18	3	86	56		.315	.383	.449	.832	129	25	20	107	126	98	.887	25			-3	*3	1.4
1913	Bos-A	131	473	64	133	17	10	0	63	47	34	.281	.347	.359	.707	104	4	2	103	140	63	.694	18			-14	*3	-0.8
1914	Bos-A	155	553	50	143	23	19	3	68	35	39	.259	.303	.385	.688	109	1	3	98	117	61	.610	16	23	-9	-1	*3	-0.3
1915	Bos-A	127	430	51	111	14	6	1	55	39	24	.258	.327	.326	.653	96	-3	-2	99	133	49	.589	11	12	-4	-8	*3	-0.8
1916	Bos-A	148	493	47	152	19	7	2	62	48	27	.308	.372	.387	.759	137	17	20	94	115	79	.742	12			-11	*3	1.7
1917	Bos-A	146	501	53	133	23	7	1	61	54	37	.265	.341	.345	.686	101	6	1	108	132	66	.668	16			-4	*3	0.4
1918	Phi-A	127	463	50	132	22	6	1	52	43	22	.285	.346	.365	.711	110	7	5	104	117	60	.668	9			11	*3	1.8
1919	Cle-A	139	524	67	157	29	7	2	79	39	29	.300	.352	.393	.745	102	6	1	107	143	75	.695	7			-6	*3	0.5
1920	Cle-A	154	597	72	185	31	11	3	118	53	25	.310	.367	.414	.781	103	6	2	104	**171**	86	.704	3	20	-11	-2	*3	0.0
1921	Cle-A	153	586	101	187	32	14	3	120	65	16	.319	.391	.437	.828	112	11	12	99	**164**	103	.816	3	3	-1	1	*3	2.2

YEAR	TM/L	G	AB	R	H	2B	3B	HR	RBI	BB	SO	AVG	OBP	SLG	PRO	/A	BR	/A	PF	CHI	RC	TA	SB	CS	SBR	FR	POS	TPR
1922	Cle-A	137	470	74	134	31	3	2	68	49	21	.285	.355	.377	.732	89	-6	-7	102	136	64	.689	9	8	-2	-7	*3	-0.2
1923	Cle-A	52	79	4	20	5	1	0	12	12	7	.253	.352	.342	.693	82	-2	-2	101	152	10	.650	0	1	-1	1	3	0.1
1924	Cle-A	38	50	3	10	0	0	0	4	5	1	.200	.273	.200	.473	24	-6	-5	97	132	3	.357	0	2	-1	-1	/32	-0.5
Total	17	1923	6688	866	1931	301	129	27	934	654	282	.289	.355	.384	.739	109	90	75	102	129	965	.709	165	69		-41	*32/S	7.4
■ ART GARIBALDI	Garibaldi, Arthur Edward b: 8/20/07, San Francisco, Cal d: 10/19/67, Sacramento, Cal. BR/TR, 5'8", 165 lbs. Deb: 6/20/36																											
1936	StL-N	71	232	30	64	12	0	1	20	16	30	.276	.323	.341	.663	83	-7	-5	94	86	26	.570	3			-5	32	-0.4
■ DEBS GARMS	Garms, Debs C. "Tex" b: 6/26/08, Bangs, Tex. d: 12/16/84, Glen Rose, Tex. BL/TR, 5'8.5", 165 lbs. Deb: 8/10/32																											
1932	StL-A	34	134	20	38	7	1	1	8	17	7	.284	.364	.373	.737	91	-1	-1	100	53	19	.717	4	3	-1	2	O	-0.1
1933	StL-A	78	189	35	60	10	2	4	24	30	21	.317	.416	.455	.871	114	10	5	115	82	36	.896	2	5	-2	-1	O	0.0
1934	StL-A	91	232	25	68	14	4	0	31	27	19	.293	.372	.388	.760	92	-1	-2	104	115	35	.726	0	0	0	-4	O	-0.5
1935	StL-A	10	15	1	4	0	0	0	0	2	2	.267	.353	.267	.620	58	-1	-1	107	0	2	.545	0	0	0	-0	/O	0.0
1937	Bos-N	125	478	60	124	15	8	2	37	37	33	.259	.317	.337	.653	86	-15	-9	90	85	54	.567	2			-9	O3	-1.9
1938	Bos-N	117	428	62	135	19	1	0	47	34	22	.315	.371	.364	.736	117	3	10	88	111	60	.653	4			-3	O3/2	0.4
1939	Bos-N	132	513	68	153	24	9	2	37	39	20	.298	.350	.392	.742	108	-1	5	92	69	73	.670	2			-2	O3	0.2
1940	Pit-N	103	358	76	127	23	7	5	57	23	6	.355	.395	.500	.895	153	21	24	95	109	72	.880	3			2	3O	2.4
1941	Pit-N	83	220	25	58	9	3	3	42	22	12	.264	.331	.373	.703	95	-1	-1	103	167	28	.634	0			-4	3O	-0.5
1943	StL-N	90	249	26	64	10	2	0	22	13	8	.257	.299	.313	.612	74	-8	-9	105	102	24	.497	1			-3	O3/S	-1.4
1944	StL-N	73	149	17	30	3	0	0	5	13	8	.201	.265	.221	.487	38	-12	-12	101	54	9	.380	0			-5	O3	-1.7
1945	StL-N	74	146	23	49	7	2	0	18	31	3	.336	.452	.411	.863	141	10	10	100	104	30	.910	0			-4	3O	0.6
Total	12	1010	3111	438	910	141	39	17	328	288	161	.293	.355	.379	.735	104	6	18	97	95	442	.679	18	8		-30	O3/S2	-2.5
■ PHIL GARNER	Garner, Philip Mason b: 4/30/49, Jefferson City, Tenn. BR/TR, 5'10", 175 lbs. Deb: 9/10/73																											
1973	Oak-A	9	5	0	0	0	0	0	0	0	3	.000	.000	.000	.000	-99	-1	-1	87	0	0	.000	0	0	0	-0	/3	-0.1
1974	Oak-A	30	28	4	5	1	0	0	1	1	5	.179	.207	.214	.421	21	-3	-3	100	65	1	.333	1	1	-0	-0	3/S2D	-0.2
1975	Oak-A	160	488	46	120	21	5	6	54	30	65	.246	.296	.346	.643	87	-13	-9	93	111	48	.539	4	6	-2	-11	*2/S	-1.6
1976	Oak-A	159	555	54	145	29	12	8	74	36	71	.261	.309	.400	.709	107	3	3	100	118	67	.680	35	13	3	-11	*2	0.4
1977	Pit-N	153	585	99	152	35	10	17	77	55	65	.260	.326	.441	.767	101	2	-0	103	106	84	.763	32	9	4	1	*32S	0.8
1978	Pit-N	154	528	66	138	25	9	10	66	66	71	.261	.349	.400	.749	103	7	3	105	111	71	.732	27	14	-0	-3	23/S	0.5
1979	Pit-N	150	549	76	161	32	8	11	59	55	74	.293	.361	.441	.802	111	13	9	106	87	89	.789	17	8	0	1	23S	1.5
1980	Pit-N	151	548	62	142	27	6	5	58	46	53	.259	.319	.358	.676	86	-8	-11	103	111	64	.649	32	7	5	12	*2/S	1.7
1981	Pit-N	56	181	22	46	6	2	1	20	21	21	.254	.332	.326	.658	91	-3	-2	96	127	19	.583	4	6	-2	1	2	0.0
	Hou-N	31	113	13	27	3	1	0	6	15	11	.239	.328	.283	.611	84	-3	-2	88	78	12	.596	6	2	1	-5	2	-0.3
	Yr	87	294	35	73	9	3	1	26	36	32	.248	.330	.310	.640	88	-6	-3	93	111	32	.596	10	8	-2	-4		-0.3
1982	Hou-N	155	588	65	161	33	8	13	83	40	92	.274	.323	.423	.747	108	4	5	99	120	78	.701	24	13	-1	-2	*23	0.9
1983	Hou-N	154	567	76	135	24	2	14	79	63	84	.238	.320	.362	.681	98	-9	-2	90	134	68	.650	18	12	-2	4	*3	-0.4
1984	Hou-N	128	374	60	104	17	6	4	45	43	63	.278	.359	.388	.746	119	6	9	93	112	53	.694	3	2	-0	11	32	2.1
1985	Hou-N	135	463	65	124	23	10	6	51	34	72	.268	.321	.400	.720	104	-1	2	96	100	57	.634	4	4	-1	-3	*32	-0.2
1986	Hou-N	107	313	43	83	14	3	9	41	30	45	.265	.331	.415	.747	102	2	1	103	104	39	.692	12	6	0	0	3/2	0.0
1987	Hou-N	43	112	15	25	5	0	3	15	8	20	.223	.275	.348	.623	69	-6	-5	93	125	11	.539	1	0	0	1	3/2	-0.3
	LA-N	70	126	14	24	4	0	2	8	20	24	.190	.301	.270	.571	58	-8	-7	92	80	11	.557	5	1	1	2	32/S	-0.2
	Yr	113	238	29	49	9	0	5	23	28	44	.206	.289	.307	.596	63	-14	-12	92	98	23	.554	6	1	1	3		-0.5
1988	SF-N	15	13	0	2	0	0	0	1	1	3	.154	.214	.154	.368	8	-2	-1	94	200	0	.250	0	1	-1	0	/3	-0.1
Total	16	1860	6136	780	1594	299	82	109	738	564	842	.260	.326	.389	.714	99	-21	-10	99	110	774	.690	225	105	4	-2	23/SD	4.5
■ RALPH GARR	Garr, Ralph Allen "Road Runner" b: 12/12/45, Monroe, La. BL/TR, 5'11", 185 lbs. Deb: 9/03/68																											
1968	Atl-N	11	7	3	2	0	0	0	0	1	0	.286	.375	.286	.661	108	0	0	93	0	1	.800	1	0	0	0	H	0.0
1969	Atl-N	22	27	6	6	1	0	0	2	2	4	.222	.276	.259	.535	49	-2	-2	104	115	2	.455	1	1	-0	-2	/O	-0.4
1970	Atl-N	37	96	18	27	3	0	0	8	5	12	.281	.317	.313	.629	66	-4	-5	104	103	9	.541	5	2	0	1	O	-0.4
1971	Atl-N	154	639	101	219	24	6	9	44	30	68	.343	.374	.441	.815	118	24	17	110	51	105	.780	30	14	1	6	*O	1.9
1972	Atl-N	134	554	87	180	22	0	12	53	25	41	.325	.361	.430	.790	118	16	13	105	76	86	.750	25	9	2	-1	*O	0.8
1973	Atl-N	148	668	94	200	32	6	11	55	22	64	.299	.324	.415	.738	91	1	-9	113	62	87	.684	35	11	4	-1	*O	-1.3
1974	Atl-N	143	606	87	**214**	24	**17**	11	54	28	52	**.353**	.384	.503	.887	140	35	31	105	54	113	.872	26	16	-2	-3	*O	2.2
1975	Atl-N	151	625	74	174	26	**11**	6	31	44	50	.278	.329	.384	.713	102	-3	0	95	41	78	.643	14	9	-1	3	*O	-0.2
1976	Chi-A	136	527	63	158	22	6	4	36	17	41	.300	.324	.387	.711	108	3	4	99	65	66	.624	14	5	1	-2	*O/D	0.0
1977	Chi-A	134	543	78	163	29	7	10	54	27	44	.300	.333	.435	.768	108	4	5	99	85	77	.698	12	7	-1	-2	*O/D	-0.1
1978	Chi-A	118	443	67	122	18	9	3	29	24	41	.275	.314	.377	.691	93	-5	-5	101	69	51	.594	7	5	-1	-5	*O/D	-1.3
1979	Chi-A	102	307	34	86	10	2	9	39	17	19	.280	.320	.414	.734	94	-2	-3	102	97	39	.639	2	4	-2	-10	OD	-1.7
	Cal-A	6	24	0	3	0	0	0	0	0	3	.125	.125	.125	.250	-35	-4	-4	93	0	0	.143	0	0	0	0	/D	-0.3
	Yr	108	331	34	89	10	2	9	39	17	22	.269	.307	.393	.699	85	-7	-7	102	93	40	.610	2	4	-2	-10		-2.0
1980	Cal-A	21	42	5	8	1	0	0	3	4	6	.190	.261	.214	.475	33	-4	-4	96	130	2	.382	0	0	0	-0	/OD	-0.3
Total	13	1317	5108	717	1562	212	64	75	408	246	445	.306	.340	.416	.756	107	59	39	103	65	716	.707	172	83	2	-16	*O/D	-1.1
■ ADRIAN GARRETT	Garrett, Henry Adrian "Pat" b: 1/3/43, Brooksville, Fla. BL/TR, 6'3", 185 lbs. Deb: 4/13/66 C																											
1966	Atl-N	4	3	0	0	0	0	0	0	0	2	.000	.000	.000	.000	-99	-1	-1	99	0	0	.000	0	0	0	-0	/O	0.0
1970	Chi-N	3	3	0	0	0	0	0	0	0	3	.000	.000	.000	.000	-83	-1	-1	120	0	0	.000	0	0	0	0	H	0.0
1971	Oak-A	14	21	1	3	0	0	1	2	5	7	.143	.308	.286	.593	69	-1	-1	101	91	2	.611	0	0	0	-0	/O	0.0
1972	Oak-A	14	11	0	0	0	0	0	0	1	4	.000	.083	.000	.083	-76	-2	-2	97	0	0	.091	0	0	0	-1	/O	-0.2
1973	Chi-N	36	54	7	12	0	0	3	8	4	18	.222	.276	.389	.665	76	-2	-2	108	107	6	.605	1	0	0	-1	/OC	-0.2
1974	Chi-N	10	8	0	0	0	0	0	0	1	1	.000	.111	.000	.111	-67	-2	-2	100	0	0	.111	0	0	0	0	/C1O	0.0
1975	Chi-N	16	21	1	2	0	0	1	6	1	8	.095	.136	.238	.374	2	-3	-3	104	290	1	.316	0	0	0	0	/1	-0.2
	Cal-A	37	107	17	28	5	0	6	18	14	28	.262	.347	.477	.824	138	4	5	95	100	20	.861	3	0	1	-1	D1/OC	0.4
1976	Cal-A	29	48	4	6	3	0	0	3	5	16	.125	.208	.188	.395	18	-5	-5	92	128	2	.318	0	0	0	-1	C/1D	-0.5
Total	8	163	276	30	51	8	0	11	37	31	87	.185	.267	.333	.600	70	-12	-11	98	110	30	.559	4	0	1	-5	/DCO1	-0.7
■ WAYNE GARRETT	Garrett, Ronald Wayne b: 12/3/47, Brooksville, Fla. BL/TR, 5'11", 175 lbs. Deb: 4/12/69																											
1969	NY-N	124	400	38	87	11	3	1	39	40	75	.218	.293	.268	.561	58	-22	-22	100	142	34	.481	4	2	0	-6	32/S	-2.3
1970	NY-N	114	366	74	93	17	4	12	45	81	60	.254	.392	.421	.813	113	12	10	104	94	68	.871	5	1	1	-10	32/S	0.4
1971	NY-N	56	202	20	43	2	0	1	11	28	31	.213	.312	.238	.549	60	-10	-9	96	93	15	.464	1	3	-2	-2	3/2	-1.2
1972	NY-N	111	298	41	69	13	3	2	29	70	58	.232	.378	.315	.693	104	3	5	95	119	41	.708	3	2	-0	-5	32	0.0
1973	NY-N	140	504	76	129	20	3	16	58	72	74	.256	.350	.403	.753	107	6	6	101	98	74	.727	6	5	-1	11	*3/S2	1.4
1974	NY-N	151	522	55	117	14	3	13	53	89	96	.224	.339	.337	.676	90	-5	-5	99	97	64	.650	4	6	-2	14	*3/S	0.5
1975	NY-N	107	274	49	73	8	3	6	34	50	45	.266	.382	.383	.765	118	6	8	95	107	44	.772	3	2	-0	6	3/S2	1.4
1976	NY-N	80	251	36	56	8	1	4	26	52	26	.223	.359	.311	.669	99	-1	2	92	113	31	.673	7	5	-1	9	32/S	1.0
	Mon-N	59	177	15	43	4	1	2	11	30	20	.243	.353	.311	.663	89	-1	-1	100	69	21	.635	2	2	-1	2	2/3	0.3
	Yr	139	428	51	99	12	2	6	37	82	46	.231	.356	.311	.667	95	-2	1	95	96	54	.668	9	7	-2	11		1.3
1977	Mon-N	68	159	17	43	6	1	2	22	30	18	.270	.389	.358	.748	104	2	2	98	140	24	.750	2	2	-1	-3	3/2	0.0
1978	Mon-N	49	69	6	12	0	0	1	2	8	10	.174	.260	.217	.477	36	-6	-6	96	44	4	.390	0	0	0	-0	3	-0.5
	StL-N	33	63	11	21	4	0	1	10	11	16	.333	.432	.444	.877	153	4	5	95	128	12	.889	1	0	0	-0	3	0.5
	Yr	82	132	17	33	4	0	2	12	19	26	.250	.344	.326	.670	92	-2	-1	95	78	16	.618	1	0	0	-0		0.0
Total	10	1092	3285	438	786	107	22	61	340	561	529	.239	.352	.341	.693	95	-11	-5	98	106	432	.684	38	30	-7	16	32/S	1.5
■ GIL GARRIDO	Garrido, Gil Gonzalo b: 6/26/41, Panama City, Pan. BR/TR, 5'9", 150 lbs. Deb: 4/24/64																											
1964	SF-N	14	25	1	2	0	0	0	1	2	7	.080	.148	.080	.228	-34	-4	-4	100	205	0	.208	1	0	0	-0	S	-0.3
1968	Atl-N	18	53	5	11	0	0	0	2	2	2	.208	.236	.208	.444	37	-4	-4	93	77	3	.302	0	0	0	-2	S	-0.3
1969	Atl-N	82	227	18	50	5	1	0	10	16	11	.220	.272	.251	.523	46	-16	-17	104	70	14	.390	0	0	0	-13	S	-2.1
1970	Atl-N	101	367	38	97	5	4	1	19	15	16	.264	.293	.308	.601	59	-20	-22	104	65	28	.441	0	2	-1	-13	S2	-2.3

YEAR	TM/L	G	AB	R	H	2B	3B	HR	RBI	BB	SO	AVG	OBP	SLG	PRO	/A	BR	/A	PF	CHI	RC	TA	SB	CS	SBR	FR	POS	TPR
1971	Atl-N	79	125	8	27	3	0	0	12	15	12	.216	.300	.240	.540	50	-7	-8	110	163	9	.441	0	1	-1	-2	S32	-0.5
1972	Atl-N	40	75	11	20	1	0	0	7	11	6	.267	.368	.280	.648	82	-1	-1	105	137	8	.576	1	1	-0	-1	2S/3	0.0
Total	6	334	872	81	207	14	5	1	51	61	54	.237	.288	.268	.556	53	-52	-57	104	92	63	.443	2	4	-2	-32	S/23	-5.5
■ CECIL GARRIOTT	Garriott, Virgil Cecil b: 8/15/16, Harristown, Ill. BL/TR, 5'8", 165 lbs. Deb: 9/04/46																											
1946	Chi-N	6	5	1	0	0	0	0	0	0	2	.000	.167	.000	.167	-54	-1	-1	94	0	0	.200	0			0	H	0.0
■ FORD GARRISON	Garrison, Robert Ford "Rocky" or "Snapper" b: 8/29/15, Greenville, S.C. BR/TR, 5'10.5", 180 lbs. Deb: 4/22/43 C																											
1943	Bos-A	36	129	13	36	5	1	1	11	5	14	.279	.306	.357	.663	90	-2	-2	104	82	13	.526	0	1	-1	-0	O	-0.3
1944	Bos-A	13	49	5	12	3	0	0	2	6	4	.245	.327	.306	.633	83	-1	-1	98	51	6	.568	0	0	0	0	O	-0.1
	Phi-A	121	449	58	121	13	2	4	37	22	40	.269	.307	.334	.641	82	-11	-11	101	84	47	.538	10	4	1	6	*O	-0.8
	Yr	134	498	63	133	16	2	4	39	28	44	.267	.309	.331	.640	82	-12	-12	101	81	52	.541	10	4	1	6		-0.9
1945	Phi-A	6	23	3	7	1	0	1	6	4	3	.304	.407	.478	.886	167	2	2	94	137	5	1.000	1	0	0	1	/O	0.3
1946	Phi-A	9	37	1	4	0	0	0	0	0	6	.108	.108	.108	.216	-38	-7	-7	104	0	0	.114	0	0	0	-2	/O	-1.0
Total	4	185	687	80	180	22	3	6	56	37	67	.262	.302	.329	.631	80	-18	-19	101	79	71	.537	11	5	0	4	O	-1.9
■ HANK GARRITY	Garrity, Francis Joseph b: 2/4/08, Boston, Mass. d: 9/1/62, Boston, Mass. BR/TR, 6'1", 185 lbs. Deb: 7/26/31																											
1931	Chi-A	8	14	0	3	1	0	0	2	1	2	.214	.267	.286	.552	49	-1	-1	92	165	1	.455	0	0	0	0	/C	0.0
■ STEVE GARVEY	Garvey, Steven Patrick b: 12/22/48, Tampa, Fla. BR/TR, 5'10", 192 lbs. Deb: 9/01/69																											
1969	LA-N	3	3	0	1	0	0	0	0	0	1	.333	.333	.333	.667	89	-0	-0	99	0	0	.500	0	0	0	0	H	0.0
1970	LA-N	34	93	8	25	5	0	1	6	6	17	.269	.313	.355	.668	88	-3	-2	90	65	10	.556	1	1	-0	2	3/2	0.0
1971	LA-N	81	225	27	51	12	1	7	26	21	33	.227	.293	.382	.675	91	-4	-3	99	99	24	.593	1	2	-1	9	3	0.6
1972	LA-N	96	294	36	79	14	2	9	30	19	36	.269	.315	.422	.737	115	2	4	94	82	37	.658	4	2	0	5	3/1	0.9
1973	LA-N	114	349	37	106	17	3	8	50	11	42	.304	.331	.438	.769	111	4	4	100	113	47	.660	0	2	-1	-6	1O	-0.6
1974	LA-N	156	642	95	200	32	3	21	111	31	66	.312	.346	.469	.815	136	19	25	93	125	102	.749	5	4	-1	-13	*1	0.3
1975	LA-N	160	659	85	210	38	6	18	95	33	66	.319	.354	.476	.830	136	22	27	95	96	106	.768	11	2	2	-9	*1	1.1
1976	LA-N	162	631	85	200	37	4	13	80	50	69	.317	.368	.450	.818	132	25	25	100	101	100	.771	19	8	1	-16	*1	0.3
1977	LA-N	162	646	91	192	25	3	33	115	38	90	.297	.337	.498	.836	121	16	16	100	116	103	.779	9	6	-1	-15	*1	-0.7
1978	LA-N	162	639	89	**202**	36	9	21	113	40	70	.316	.357	.499	.857	138	29	30	99	124	108	.806	10	5	0	-9	*1	1.6
1979	LA-N	162	648	92	204	32	1	28	110	37	59	.315	.354	.497	.851	130	24	24	100	114	102	.766	3	6	-3	-2	*1	1.2
1980	LA-N	163	658	78	**200**	27	1	26	106	36	67	.304	.343	.467	.809	128	19	21	97	115	97	.724	6	11	-5	4	*1	1.3
1981	LA-N	110	431	63	122	23	1	10	64	25	49	.283	.324	.411	.735	110	3	4	98	129	54	.640	3	5	-2	-6	*1	-0.8
1982	LA-N	162	625	66	176	35	1	16	86	20	86	.282	.305	.418	.723	106	-2	2	95	111	76	.621	5	3	-0	0	*1	-0.6
1983	SD-N	100	388	76	114	22	0	14	59	29	39	.294	.348	.459	.806	123	10	11	99	112	57	.735	4	1	1	-7	*1	0.0
1984	SD-N	161	617	72	175	27	2	8	86	24	64	.284	.312	.373	.684	93	-8	-7	99	135	64	.546	1	2	-1	-5	*1	-1.8
1985	SD-N	162	654	80	184	34	6	17	81	35	67	.281	.321	.430	.750	106	5	4	102	103	82	.644	0	0	0	-7	*1	-0.8
1986	SD-N	155	557	58	142	22	0	21	81	23	72	.255	.286	.408	.693	93	-11	-8	95	114	59	.579	1	2	-1	-16	*1	-3.0
1987	SD-N	27	76	5	16	2	0	1	9	1	10	.211	.231	.276	.507	35	-7	-7	97	150	4	.365	0	0	0	0	1	-0.7
Total	19	2332	8835	1143	2599	440	43	272	1308	479	1003	.294	.333	.446	.779	118	144	170	98	113	1233	.719	83	62	-12	-89	*13/O2	-1.7
■ ROD GASPAR	Gaspar, Rodney Earl b: 4/3/46, Long Beach, Cal. BB/TR, 5'11", 165 lbs. Deb: 4/08/69																											
1969	NY-N	118	215	26	49	6	1	1	14	25	19	.228	.314	.279	.593	67	-9	-9	100	89	21	.553	7	3	0	-2	O	-1.6
1970	NY-N	11	14	4	0	0	0	0	0	1	4	.000	.067	.000	.067	-77	-4	-4	104	0	0	.143	1	0	0	-0	/O	-0.3
1971	SD-N	16	17	1	2	0	0	0	2	3	3	.118	.250	.118	.368	7	-2	-2	96	407	1	.313	0	1	-1	0	/O	-0.2
1974	SD-N	33	14	4	3	0	0	0	1	4	3	.214	.389	.214	.603	77	-0	-0	93	129	2	.636	0	0	0	-2	/O1	-0.2
Total	4	178	260	35	54	6	1	1	17	33	29	.208	.302	.250	.552	56	-15	-15	100	108	24	.514	8	4	0	-5	O/1	-2.3
■ TOM GASTALL	Gastall, Thomas Everett b: 6/13/32, Fall River, Mass. d: 9/20/56, Rivera Beach, Md. BR/TR, 6'2", 187 lbs. Deb: 6/21/55																											
1955	Bal-A	20	27	4	4	1	0	0	0	3	5	.148	.233	.185	.419	15	-3	-3	90	0	1	.333	0	0	0	0	C	-0.1
1956	Bal-A	32	56	3	11	2	0	0	4	3	8	.196	.250	.232	.482	30	-6	-5	94	115	3	.362	0	0	0	0	C	-0.4
Total	2	52	83	7	15	3	0	0	4	6	13	.181	.244	.217	.461	25	-9	-8	93	77	4	.357	0	0	0	0	/C	-0.5
■ ED GASTFIELD	Gastfield, Edward b: 8/1/1865, Chicago, Ill. d: 12/1/1899, Chicago, Ill. Deb: 8/13/1884																											
1884	Det-N	23	82	6	6	1	0	0	2	2	34	.073	.095	.085	.181	-46	-13	-12	94	100	1	.118				0	C/O1	-1.0
1885	Det-N	1	3	0	0	0	0	0	0	0	2	.000	.000	.000	.000	-99	-1	-1	97	0	0	.000				0	/C	0.0
	Chi-N	1	3	0	0	0	0	0	0	0	1	.000	.000	.000	.000	-88	-1	-1	114	0	0	.000				0	/C	0.0
	Yr	2	6	0	0	0	0	0	0	0	3	.000	.000	.000	.000	-95	-1	-1	106	0	0	.000				0		0.0
Total	2	25	88	6	6	1	0	0	2	2	37	.068	.089	.080	.168	-49	-14	-14	94	93	1	.110				0	/C1O	-1.0
■ ALEX GASTON	Gaston, Alexander Nathaniel b: 3/12/1893, New York, N.Y. d: 2/8/79, Santa Monica, Cal. BR/TR, 5'9", 170 lbs. Deb: 9/26/20																											
1920	NY-N	4	10	2	1	0	0	0	1	1	2	.100	.182	.100	.282	-18	-1	-1	100	387	0	.222	0	0	0	0	/C	-0.1
1921	NY-N	20	22	1	5	1	1	0	3	1	9	.227	.261	.364	.625	65	-1	-1	98	138	2	.529	0	0	0	-0	C	0.0
1922	NY-N	16	26	1	5	0	0	0	1	0	3	.192	.192	.192	.385	-1	-4	-4	104	70	1	.286	1	0	0	-1	C	-0.3
1923	NY-N	22	39	3	8	2	0	1	5	0	6	.205	.225	.333	.558	45	-3	-3	101	110	3	.452	0	0	0	-1	C	-0.2
1926	Bos-A	98	301	37	67	5	3	0	21	21	28	.223	.282	.259	.541	41	-26	-26	101	91	24	.453	3	0	1	1	C	-1.7
1929	Bos-A	55	116	14	26	5	2	2	9	6	8	.224	.262	.353	.616	56	-8	-8	102	65	11	.533	1	0	0	-0	C	-0.2
Total	6	215	514	58	112	13	6	3	40	29	56	.218	.266	.284	.550	43	-43	-44	101	94	41	.460	5	0	2	-0	C	-2.5
■ CITO GASTON	Gaston, Clarence Edwin b: 3/17/44, San Antonio, Tex. BR/TR, 6'3", 190 lbs. Deb: 9/14/67 C																											
1967	Atl-N	9	25	1	3	0	1	0	1	0	5	.120	.120	.200	.320	-10	-4	-4	104	83	0	.250	1	0	0	-1	/O	-0.4
1969	SD-N	129	391	20	90	11	7	2	28	24	117	.230	.276	.309	.586	66	-19	-18	97	88	32	.476	4	4	-1	1	*O	-2.5
1970	SD-N	146	584	92	186	26	9	29	93	41	142	.318	.365	.543	.908	147	30	34	95	95	111	.877	4	1	1	-1	*O	2.7
1971	SD-N	141	518	57	118	13	9	17	61	24	121	.228	.265	.386	.651	85	-14	-12	96	101	51	.554	1	0	0	-6	*O	-2.3
1972	SD-N	111	379	30	102	14	0	7	44	22	76	.269	.313	.361	.674	103	-5	0	88	114	39	.551	0	2	-1	0	O	-0.5
1973	SD-N	133	476	51	119	18	4	16	57	20	88	.250	.282	.405	.687	94	-10	-6	94	97	52	.583	0	0	0	1	*O	-1.0
1974	SD-N	106	267	19	57	11	0	6	33	16	51	.213	.261	.322	.583	67	-14	-12	93	122	22	.477	0	0	0	3	O	-1.1
1975	Atl-N	64	141	17	34	4	0	6	15	17	33	.241	.323	.397	.720	104	-0	0	95	78	18	.661	1	0	0	0	O/1	0.0
1976	Atl-N	69	134	15	39	4	0	4	25	13	21	.291	.354	.410	.764	105	3	1	111	144	18	.683	1	0	0	-3	O/1	-0.2
1977	Atl-N	56	85	6	23	4	0	3	21	5	19	.271	.311	.424	.735	84	-1	-2	113	187	11	.646	1	0	0	-1	/O1	-0.2
1978	Atl-N	60	118	5	27	1	0	1	9	3	20	.229	.248	.263	.511	38	-9	-11	112	105	7	.358	0	0	0	-3	O/1	-1.6
	Pit-N	2	2	1	1	0	0	0	0	0	0	.500	.500	.500	1.000	171	0	0	105	0	1	1.000	0	0	0	-0	/O	0.0
	Yr	62	120	6	28	1	0	1	9	3	20	.233	.252	.267	.519	40	-9	-10	112	103	8	.380	0	0	0	-4		-1.6
Total	11	1026	3120	314	799	106	30	91	387	185	693	.256	.300	.397	.696	96	-43	-29	96	104	361	.621	13	7	-0	-10	O/1	-7.1
■ JOE GATES	Gates, Joseph Daniel b: 10/3/54, Gary, Ind. BL/TR, 5'7", 175 lbs. Deb: 9/12/78																											
1978	Chi-A	8	24	6	6	0	0	0	1	4	6	.250	.379	.250	.629	80	-0	-0	101	67	3	.632	1	0	0	-1	/2	0.0
1979	Chi-A	16	16	5	1	0	1	0	1	2	3	.063	.167	.188	.354	-5	-2	-2	102	128	0	.375	1	1	-0	-1	/23	-0.2
Total	2	24	40	11	7	0	1	0	2	6	9	.175	.298	.225	.523	46	-3	-3	101	90	3	.529	2	1	0	-2	/23	-0.2
■ MIKE GATES	Gates, Michael Grant b: 9/20/56, Culver City, Cal. BL/TR, 6', 165 lbs. Deb: 5/06/81																											
1981	Mon-N	1	2	1	1	0	1	0	1	0	1	.500	.500	1.500	2.000	456	1	1	99	131	2	3.000	0	0	0	0	/2	0.1
1982	Mon-N	36	121	16	28	2	3	0	8	9	19	.231	.285	.298	.582	60	-6	-7	105	87	11	.479	0	0	0	-2	2	-0.6
Total	2	37	123	17	29	2	4	0	9	9	20	.236	.288	.317	.605	66	-5	-6	105	88	12	.505	0	0	0	-2	/2	-0.5
■ FRANK GATINS	Gatins, Frank Anthony (born Frank Anthony Gestino) b: 3/6/1871, Johnstown, Pa. d: 11/8/11, Johnstown, Pa. Deb: 9/21/1898																											
1898	Was-N	17	58	6	13	2	0	0	5	3		.224	.274	.259	.533	54	-3	-3	102	103	5	.467	2			0	S	-0.2
1901	Bro-N	50	197	21	45	7	2	1	21	5		.228	.248	.299	.547	56	-10	-12	106	116	16	.461	6			-6	3/S	-1.3
Total	2	67	255	27	58	9	2	1	26	8		.227	.254	.290	.544	56	-13	-15	105	112	21	.462	8			-6	/3S	-1.5

YEAR	TM/L	G	AB	R	H	2B	3B	HR	RBI	BB	SO	AVG	OBP	SLG	PRO	/A	BR	/A	PF	CHI	RC	TA	SB	CS	SBR	FR	POS	TPR
■ **JIM GAUDET**	Gaudet, James Jennings b: 6/3/55, New Orleans, La. BR/TR, 6', 185 lbs. Deb: 9/10/78																											
1978	KC-A	3	8	0	0	0	0	0	0	0	3	.000	.000	.000	.000	-98	-2	-2	102	0	0	.000	0	0	0	0	/C	-0.1
1979	KC-A	3	6	0	1	0	0	0	0	0	0	.167	.167	.167	.333	-9	-1	-1	105	0	0	.200	0	0	0	0	/C	0.0
Total	2	6	14	0	1	0	0	0	0	0	3	.071	.071	.071	.143	-58	-3	-3	103	0	0	.077	0	0	0	0	/C	-0.1
■ **MIKE GAULE**	Gaule, Michael John b: 8/4/1869, Baltimore, Md. d: 1/24/18, Baltimore, Md. BL/TL, 6'2", Deb: 6/15/1889																											
1889	Lou-a	1	2	0	0	0	0	0	0	0	1	.000	.000	.000	.000	-99	-1	-0	96	0	0	.000	0			0	/O	0.0
■ **DOC GAUTREAU**	Gautreau, Walter Paul "Punk" b: 7/26/01, Cambridge, Mass. d: 8/23/70, Salt Lake City, Ut BR/TR, 5'4", 129 lbs. Deb: 6/22/25																											
1925	Phi-A	4	7	0	0	0	0	0	0	0	3	.000	.000	.000	.000	-97	-2	-2	103	0	0	.000	0	0	0	0	/2	-0.1
	Bos-N	68	279	45	73	13	3	0	23	35	13	.262	.346	.330	.676	79	-10	-7	94	77	33	.653	11	7	-1	-15	2	-2.2
1926	Bos-N	79	266	36	71	9	4	0	8	35	24	.267	.356	.331	.687	99	-4	1	86	32	33	.728	17			-14	2	-0.9
1927	Bos-N	87	236	38	58	12	2	0	20	25	20	.246	.321	.314	.634	75	-9	-7	93	95	24	.624	11			-5	2	-1.2
1928	Bos-N	23	18	3	5	0	1	0	1	4	3	.278	.409	.389	.798	113	0	1	97	51	3	.923	1			-0	/2S	0.1
Total	4	261	806	122	207	34	10	0	52	99	63	.257	.341	.324	.665	83	-25	-15	91	66	94	.667	40	7		-34	2/S	-4.3
■ **SID GAUTREAUX**	Gautreaux, Sidney Allen "Pudge" b: 5/4/12, Schriever, La. d: 4/19/80, Morgan City, La. BB/TR, 5'8", 190 lbs. Deb: 4/15/36																											
1936	Bro-N	75	71	8	19	3	0	0	16	9	7	.268	.358	.310	.668	77	-1	-2	105	258	9	.604	0			-1	C	-0.1
1937	Bro-N	11	10	0	1	1	0	0	2	1	1	.100	.182	.200	.382	3	-1	-1	104	360	0	.333	0			0	H	0.0
Total	2	86	81	8	20	4	0	0	18	10	8	.247	.337	.296	.633	69	-3	-3	105	270	9	.574	0			-1	/C	-0.1
■ **MIKE GAZELLA**	Gazella, Michael b: 10/13/1896, Olyphant, Pa. d: 9/11/78, Odessa, Tex. BR/TR, 5'7.5", 165 lbs. Deb: 7/02/23																											
1923	NY-A	8	13	2	1	0	0	0	1	2	3	.077	.200	.077	.277	-24	-2	-2	104	342	0	.250	0	0	0	0	/S23	-0.1
1926	NY-A	66	168	21	39	6	0	0	21	25	24	.232	.335	.268	.603	59	-9	-9	99	159	17	.557	2	2	-1	-4	3S	-0.8
1927	NY-A	54	115	17	32	8	4	0	9	23	16	.278	.403	.417	.820	113	3	3	100	62	21	.916	4	0	1	-6	3/S	0.0
1928	NY-A	32	56	11	13	0	0	0	2	6	7	.232	.317	.232	.550	50	-4	-3	92	53	5	.500	2	1	0	-2	3/2S	-0.3
Total	4	160	352	51	85	14	4	0	33	56	50	.241	.350	.304	.654	73	-13	-12	99	116	43	.644	8	3	1	-12	3/S2	-1.2
■ **DALE GEAR**	Gear, Dale Dudley b: 2/2/1872, Lone Elm, Kan. d: 9/23/51, Topeka, Kan. 5'11", 165 lbs. Deb: 8/15/1896																											
1896	Cle-N	4	15	5	6	1	1	0	3	1	1	.400	.438	.600	1.038	159	2	1	110	98	4	1.111	0			0	/P1	0.0
1897	Cle-N	7	24	3	4	1	0	0	2	3		.167	.286	.208	.494	30	-2	-3	111	119	2	.550	2			0	/O	-0.1
1901	Was-A	58	199	17	47	9	2	0	20	4		.236	.251	.302	.553	55	-12	-12	99	105	16	.434	2			1	OP	-0.5
Total	3	69	238	25	57	11	3	0	25	8	1	.239	.267	.311	.578	60	-13	-13	101	106	22	.481	4			1	/OP1	-0.6
■ **GARY GEARHART**	Gearhart, Lloyd William b: 8/10/23, New Lebanon, Ohio BR/TL, 5'11", 180 lbs. Deb: 4/18/47																											
1947	NY-N	73	179	26	44	9	0	6	17	17	30	.246	.315	.397	.711	87	-4	-4	101	71	22	.647	1			1	O	-0.4
■ **HUCK GEARY**	Geary, Eugene Francis Joseph b: 1/22/17, Buffalo, N.Y. d: 1/27/81, Cuba, N.Y. BL/TR, 5'10.5", 170 lbs. Deb: 7/17/42																											
1942	Pit-N	9	22	3	5	0	0	0	2	2	3	.227	.292	.227	.519	52	-1	-1	101	148	2	.412	0			-1	/S	-0.1
1943	Pit-N	46	166	17	25	4	0	1	13	18	6	.151	.234	.193	.426	23	-16	-17	104	137	8	.373	3			-1	S	-1.4
Total	2	55	188	20	30	4	0	1	15	20	9	.160	.240	.197	.437	26	-17	-18	104	138	10	.377	3			-3	/S	-1.5
■ **ELMER GEDEON**	Gedeon, Elmer John b: 4/15/17, Cleveland, Ohio d: 4/15/44, France BR/TR, 6'4", 196 lbs. Deb: 9/18/39																											
1939	Was-A	5	15	1	3	0	0	0	1	2	5	.200	.294	.200	.494	32	-2	-1	90	113	1	.417	0	0	0	1	/O	0.0
■ **JOE GEDEON**	Gedeon, Elmer Joseph b: 12/5/1893, Sacramento, Cal. d: 5/19/41, San Francisco, Cal BR/TR, 6', 167 lbs. Deb: 5/13/13																											
1913	Was-A	29	71	3	13	1	2	1	6	1	6	.183	.205	.296	.501	44	-5	-6	106	89	4	.448	3			0	O/32SP	-0.5
1914	Was-A	4	2	0	0	0	0	0	1	0	1	.000	.333	.000	.333	1	-0	-0	101	0	0	.500	0			-2	/O	-0.1
1916	NY-A	122	435	50	92	14	4	0	27	40	61	.211	.282	.262	.544	63	-19	-20	101	86	38	.499	14			-11	*2	-3.0
1917	NY-A	33	117	15	28	7	0	0	8	7	13	.239	.288	.299	.587	74	-3	-4	107	84	11	.528	4			-1	2	-0.3
1918	StL-A	123	441	39	94	14	3	1	41	27	29	.213	.271	.265	.536	62	-21	-21	99	127	34	.458	7			16	*2	0.1
1919	StL-A	120	437	57	111	13	4	0	27	50	35	.254	.340	.302	.642	83	-9	-7	97	66	51	.592	4			-5	*2	-0.1
1920	StL-A	153	606	95	177	33	6	0	61	55	36	.292	.355	.366	.721	82	-7	-17	111	85	82	.653	1	3	-2	-28	*2	-4.1
Total	7	584	2109	259	515	82	19	2	171	180	181	.244	.311	.304	.615	73	-65	-75	103	90	220	.550	33	3		-31	2/O3SP	-8.0
■ **RICH GEDMAN**	Gedman, Richard Leo b: 9/26/59, Worcester, Mass. BL/TR, 6', 210 lbs. Deb: 9/07/80																											
1980	Bos-A	9	24	2	5	0	0	0	1	0	5	.208	.208	.208	.417	14	-3	-3	102	78	1	.250	0	0	0	0	/CD	-0.1
1981	Bos-A	62	205	22	59	15	0	5	26	9	31	.288	.321	.434	.755	109	3	2	106	98	26	.639	0	0	0	-2	C	0.3
1982	Bos-A	92	289	30	72	17	2	4	26	10	37	.249	.279	.363	.642	68	-10	-14	110	89	25	.506	0	1	-1	-2	C	-1.1
1983	Bos-A	81	204	21	60	16	1	2	18	15	37	.294	.345	.412	.757	106	2	2	101	78	28	.671	0	1	-1	-2	C	0.2
1984	Bos-A	133	449	54	121	26	4	24	72	29	72	.269	.315	.506	.821	111	12	6	110	96	71	.772	0	0	0	-3	*C	1.1
1985	Bos-A	144	498	66	147	30	5	18	80	50	79	.295	.363	.484	.847	127	20	19	102	108	86	.815	2	0	1	7	*C	3.1
1986	Bos-A	135	462	49	119	29	0	16	65	37	61	.258	.318	.424	.742	101	0	0	100	106	59	.665	1	0	0	14	*C	2.2
1987	Bos-A	52	151	11	31	8	0	1	13	10	24	.205	.255	.278	.533	42	-12	-12	99	115	11	.426	0	0	0	0	C	-0.7
1988	Bos-A	95	299	33	69	14	0	9	39	18	49	.231	.281	.368	.649	74	-9	-12	109	113	31	.555	0	0	0	-2	C/D	-0.9
Total	9	803	2581	288	683	155	12	79	340	178	395	.265	.316	.426	.742	98	3	-13	105	101	338	.679	3	2	-0	12	C/D	4.1
■ **COUNT GEDNEY**	Gedney, Alfred W., b: 5/10/1849, Brooklyn, N.Y. d: 3/26/22, Hackensack, N.J. 5'9", 140 lbs. Deb: 4/27/1872																											
1872	Tro-n	9	46	15	19							.413															/O	
	Eck-n	18	76	8	12							.158															O	
	Yr	27	122	23	31							.254																
1873	Mut-n	52	236	41	60							.254															*O	
1874	Ath-n	54	235	48	76							.323															*O/1	
1875	Mut-n	67	263	29	52							.198															*O/P	
Total	4 n	200	856	141	219							.256															*O/P	
■ **BILLY GEER**	Geer, William Henry Harrison (born George Harrison Geer) b: 8/13/1849, Syracuse, N.Y. TR , 5'8", 160 lbs. Deb: 10/15/1874																											
1874	Mut-n	2	8	0	2							.250															/O	
1875	NH-n	37	173	20	39							.225															O2//	
1878	Cin-N	61	237	31	52	13	2	0	20	10	18	.219	.251	.291	.542	81	-5	-4	95	100	18	.427				-4	*S/2	-0.3
1880	Wor-N	2	6	0	0	0	0	0	0	0	0	.000	.000	.000	.000	-89	-1	-1	113	0	0	.000				0	/OS	0.0
1884	Phi-U	9	36	7	9	2	1	0		4		.250	.325	.361	.686	142	1	2	93	0	4	.630	0			0	/S	0.2
	Bro-a	107	391	68	82	15	7	0		38		.210	.281	.284	.565	90	-4	-2	98	0	32	.485				15	*S/P2	1.0
1885	Lou-a	14	51	2	6	2	0	0		2		.118	.167	.157	.324	4	-5	-6	102	0	1	.244				0	S	-0.4
Total	2 n	39	181	20	41							.227															S	
Total	4	193	721	108	149	32	10	0	20	54	18	.207	.264	.279	.543	82	-15	-11	97	32	55	.449				11	S/O2P	0.5
■ **LOU GEHRIG**	Gehrig, Henry Louis "The Iron Horse" b: 6/19/03, New York, N.Y. d: 6/2/41, Riverdale, N.Y. BL/TL, 6', 200 lbs. Deb: 6/15/23 H																											
1923	NY-A	13	26	6	11	4	1	1	9	2	5	.423	.464	.769	1.234	212	4	4	104	134	9	1.467	0	0	0	-0	/1	0.3
1924	NY-A	10	12	2	6	1	0	0	5	1	3	.500	.538	.583	1.122	191	2	2	99	236	4	1.333	0	0	0	-0	/1O	0.1
1925	NY-A	126	437	73	129	23	10	20	68	46	49	.295	.365	.531	.896	130	14	17	96	80	85	.920	6	3	0	-5	*1/O	0.8
1926	NY-A	155	572	135	179	47	**20**	16	107	105	72	.313	.420	.549	.969	152	44	45	99	97	137	1.070	6	5	-1	-8	*1	2.7
1927	NY-A	155	584	149	218	**52**	18	47	**175**	109	84	.373	.474	.765	1.240	218	**101**	**101**	100	95	**208**	1.555	10	0	3	-6	*1	8.2
1928	NY-A	154	562	139	210	**47**	13	27	**142**	95	69	.374	**.467**	.648	1.115	207	76	83	92	116	169	1.287	4	11	-5	-8	*1	5.7
1929	NY-A	154	553	127	166	32	10	35	126	122	68	.300	.431	.584	1.015	161	52	53	99	107	146	1.161	4	4	-1	-5	*1	2.3
1930	NY-A	154	581	143	220	42	17	41	**174**	101	63	.379	.473	.721	1.194	221	88	99	90	113	**195**	1.427	12	14	-5	2	*1/O	6.8
1931	NY-A	155	619	**163**	**211**	31	15	**46**	**184**	117	56	.341	.446	.662	1.108	191	80	82	98	107	185	1.295	17	12	-2	-10	*1/O	5.0
1932	NY-A	156	596	138	208	42	9	34	151	108	38	.349	.451	.621	1.072	183	69	73	95	114	168	1.216	4	11	-5	-6	*1	4.1
1933	NY-A	152	593	**138**	198	41	12	32	139	92	42	.334	.424	.605	1.030	187	60	68	91	108	151	1.130	9	13	-5	-4	*1	4.4
1934	NY-A	154	579	128	210	40	6	**49**	**165**	109	31	**.363**	**.465**	**.706**	**1.172**	**208**	**86**	**90**	96	105	**195**	**1.414**	9	5	-0	1	*1/S	**5.8**
1935	NY-A	149	535	**125**	176	26	10	30	119	**132**	38	.329	**.466**	.583	1.049	**183**	62	**68**	93	107	154	1.249	8	7	-2	1	*1	4.7

YEAR	TM/L	G	AB	R	H	2B	3B	HR	RBI	BB	SO	AVG	OBP	SLG	PRO	/A	BR	/A	PF	CHI	RC	TA	SB	CS	SBR	FR	POS	TPR
1936	NY-A	155	579	**167**	205	37	7	**49**	152	**130**	46	.354	**.478**	**.696**	**1.174**	**197**	**82**	**88**	95	95	**199**	**1.437**	3	4	-2	1	*1	5.7
1937	NY-A	157	569	138	200	37	9	37	159	**127**	49	.351	**.473**	.643	**1.116**	**175**	**73**	**72**	102	121	**181**	**1.347**	4	3	-1	-5	*1	4.2
1938	NY-A	157	576	115	170	32	6	29	114	107	75	.295	.410	.523	.932	125	30	25	105	105	131	1.029	6	1	1	-0	*1	0.3
1939	NY-A	8	28	2	4	0	0	0	1	5	1	.143	.273	.143	.416	10	-4	-3	91	86	1	.346	0	0	0	-0	/1	-0.3
Total	17	2164	8001	1888	2721	534	163	493	1990	1508	789	.340	.447	.632	1.080	181	918	963	97	105	2317	1.249	102	93	-25	-52	*1/OS	60.8
■ **CHARLIE GEHRINGER** Gehringer, Charles Leonard "The Mechanical Man" b: 5/11/03, Fowlerville, Mich. BL/TR, 5'11", 180 lbs. Deb: 9/22/24 CH																												
1924	Det-A	5	13	2	6	0	0	0	1	0	2	.462	.462	.462	.923	139	1	1	100	55	2	.875	1	1	-0	0	/2	0.1
1925	Det-A	8	18	3	3	0	0	0	0	2	0	.167	.250	.167	.417	7	-3	-3	99	0	1	.313	0	1	-1	0	/2	-0.1
1926	Det-A	123	459	62	127	19	17	1	48	30	42	.277	.322	.399	.721	90	-10	-8	97	89	59	.658	9	7	-2	-1	*2/3	-0.5
1927	Det-A	133	508	110	161	29	11	4	61	52	31	.317	.383	.441	.824	105	10	4	108	91	85	.850	17	0	5	16	*2	2.4
1928	Det-A	154	603	108	193	29	16	6	74	69	22	.320	.395	.451	.846	123	21	21	99	84	110	.864	15	9	-1	2	*2	2.9
1929	Det-A	155	634	**131**	**215**	**45**	**19**	13	106	64	19	.339	.405	.532	.936	143	37	39	97	93	139	1.014	**27**	9	**3**	-3	*2	3.9
1930	Det-A	154	610	144	201	47	15	16	98	69	17	.330	.404	.534	.938	129	33	29	105	77	130	.993	19	15	-3	2	*2	2.6
1931	Det-A	101	383	67	119	24	5	4	53	29	15	.311	.359	.431	.790	103	3	1	104	101	60	.772	13	4	2	-6	2/1	0.1
1932	Det-A	152	618	112	184	44	11	19	107	68	34	.298	.370	.497	.867	120	19	18	102	95	114	.876	9	8	-2	-1	*2	1.9
1933	Det-A	155	628	103	204	42	6	12	105	68	27	.325	.393	.468	.862	120	25	19	107	102	117	.864	5	4	-1	6	*2	2.1
1934	Det-A	154	601	**134**	**214**	50	7	11	127	99	25	.356	.450	.517	.967	153	48	50	98	131	144	1.073	11	8	-2	8	*2	5.8
1935	Det-A	150	610	123	201	32	8	19	108	79	16	.330	.409	.502	.911	139	32	35	97	97	129	.966	11	4	1	5	*2	4.3
1936	Det-A	154	641	144	227	**60**	12	15	116	83	13	.354	.431	.555	.987	149	43	48	95	83	157	1.077	4	1	1	16	*2	**6.4**
1937	Det-A	144	564	133	209	40	1	14	96	90	25	**.371**	.458	.520	.978	134	44	36	109	104	140	1.100	11	4	1	-1	*2	4.5
1938	Det-A	152	568	133	174	32	5	20	107	113	21	.306	.425	.486	.911	127	28	28	100	104	128	1.030	14	1	**4**	2	*2	3.5
1939	Det-A	118	406	86	132	29	6	16	86	68	16	.325	.423	.544	.967	131	29	22	111	110	97	1.035	4	3	-1	4	*2	2.7
1940	Det-A	139	515	108	161	33	3	10	81	101	17	.313	.428	.447	.875	114	26	17	111	119	111	.948	10	0	3	-15	*2	1.1
1941	Det-A	127	436	65	96	19	4	3	46	95	26	.220	.363	.303	.666	73	-10	-14	106	118	55	.654	1	2	-1	2	*2	-0.2
1942	Det-A	45	45	6	12	0	0	1	7	7	4	.267	.365	.333	.699	86	0	-1	113	137	6	.667	0	0	0	0	/2	0.0
Total	19	2323	8860	1774	2839	574	146	184	1427	1186	372	.320	.404	.480	.884	124	376	342	103	99	1785	.930	181	81	6	36	*2/13	43.5
■ **PHIL GEIER** Geier, Philip Louis "Little Phil" b: 11/3/1875, Washington, D.C. d: 9/25/67, Spokane, Wash. BL/TR, 5'7", 145 lbs. Deb: 8/17/1896																												
1896	Phi-N	17	56	12	13	0	1	0	6	6	7	.232	.317	.268	.585	56	-3	-3	102	115	6	.581	3			0	O/2C	-0.2
1897	Phi-N	92	316	51	88	6	2	1	35	56		.278	.392	.320	.712	96	-0	2	96	100	48	.785	19			-1	O2/S3	0.1
1900	Cin-N	30	113	18	29	1	4	0	10	7		.257	.300	.336	.636	84	-4	-2	92	84	13	.571	3			0	O/3	-0.1
1901	Phi-A	50	211	42	49	5	2	0	23	24		.232	.311	.275	.586	65	-9	-9	100	108	21	.549	7			0	O/S3	-0.8
	Mil-A	11	39	4	7	1	1	0	1	5		.179	.273	.256	.529	51	-3	-2	95	33	4	.594	4			0	/O3	-0.1
	Yr	61	250	46	56	6	3	0	24	29		.224	.305	.272	.577	63	-12	-11	99	96	25	.557	11			1		-0.9
1904	Bos-N	149	580	70	141	17	2	1	27	56		.243	.310	.284	.594	89	-8	-6	97	51	58	.544	18			-6	*O/32S	-1.6
Total	5	349	1315	197	327	30	12	2	102	154	7	.249	.329	.294	.624	84	-27	-20	97	77	149	.606	54			-5	O/23SC	-2.7
■ **GARY GEIGER** Geiger, Gary Merle b: 4/4/37, Sand Ridge, Ill. BL/TR, 6', 168 lbs. Deb: 4/15/58																												
1958	Cle-A	91	195	28	45	3	1	1	6	27	43	.231	.333	.272	.605	73	-7	-6	94	43	20	.556	2	2	-1	7	O/3P	-0.2
1959	Bos-A	120	335	45	82	10	4	11	48	21	55	.245	.289	.397	.686	82	-7	-10	106	114	38	.625	9	3	1	-1	O	-1.4
1960	Bos-A	77	245	32	74	13	3	9	33	23	38	.302	.369	.490	.859	126	10	9	103	88	43	.822	2	2	-1	5	O	1.0
1961	Bos-A	140	499	82	116	21	6	18	64	87	91	.232	.351	.407	.758	100	2	1	102	103	78	.787	16	4	2	3	*O	0.1
1962	Bos-A	131	466	67	116	18	4	16	54	67	66	.249	.346	.408	.754	100	2	1	102	92	69	.757	18	11	-1	0	*O	-0.4
1963	Bos-A	121	399	67	105	13	5	16	44	36	63	.263	.329	.441	.770	107	7	4	106	82	59	.739	9	4	0	8	O/1	0.9
1964	Bos-A	5	13	3	5	0	1	0	1	2	2	.385	.467	.538	1.005	176	1	1	102	61	4	1.125	0	0	0	-0	/O	0.1
1965	Bos-A	24	45	5	9	3	0	1	2	13	10	.200	.379	.333	.713	97	1	0	107	46	7	.861	3	0	1	0	O	0.1
1966	Atl-N	78	126	23	33	5	3	4	10	21	29	.262	.372	.444	.816	127	5	5	99	62	22	.821	0	1	-1	-5	O	-0.1
1967	Atl-N	69	117	17	19	1	1	1	5	20	35	.162	.285	.214	.498	43	-8	-8	104	74	8	.455	1	1	-0	-4	O	-1.5
1969	Hou-N	93	125	19	28	4	1	0	16	24	34	.224	.353	.272	.625	76	-3	-3	102	189	14	.616	2	1	0	-9	O	-1.6
1970	Hou-N	5	4	0	1	0	0	0	0	0	0	.250	.250	.250	.500	37	-0	-0	94	0	0	.333	0	0	0	-1	/O	0.0
Total	12	954	2569	388	633	91	29	77	283	341	466	.246	.339	.394	.733	97	3	-6	103	93	363	.729	62	29	1	2	O/13P	-3.0
■ **BILL GEIS** Geis, William J. (born William J. Geiss) b: 7/15/1858, Chicago, Ill. d: 9/18/24, Chicago, Ill. 5'10", 164 lbs. Deb: 5/01/1884																												
1884	Det-N	75	283	23	50	11	4	2	16	6	60	.177	.194	.265	.459	46	-18	-16	94	69	15	.348				-12	2/O1P	-2.3
■ **EMIL GEISS** Geiss, Emil August b: 3/20/1867, Chicago, Ill. d: 10/4/11, Chicago, Ill. Deb: 5/18/1887																												
1887	Chi-N	3	12	0	1	0	0	0	0	0	7	.083	.083	.083	.167	-46	-2	-3	116	0	0	.091	0			0	/21P	-0.1
■ **CHARLIE GELBERT** Gelbert, Charles Magnus b: 1/26/06, Scranton, Pa. d: 1/13/67, Easton, Pa. BR/TR, 5'11", 170 lbs. Deb: 4/16/29																												
1929	StL-N	146	512	60	134	29	8	3	65	51	46	.262	.329	.367	.696	73	-23	-21	98	115	62	.653	8			5	*S	0.3
1930	StL-N	139	513	92	156	39	11	3	72	43	41	.304	.360	.441	.801	88	-6	-10	105	108	80	.776	6			6	*S	0.7
1931	StL-N	131	447	61	129	29	5	1	62	54	31	.289	.365	.383	.748	95	2	-2	107	127	66	.730	7			8	*S	1.7
1932	StL-N	122	455	60	122	28	9	1	45	39	30	.268	.330	.376	.706	89	-6	-6	100	98	59	.664	8			-7	*S	-0.3
1935	StL-N	62	168	24	49	7	2	2	21	17	18	.292	.357	.393	.750	97	1	-0	104	105	25	.686	0			-1	3S/2	0.1
1936	StL-N	93	280	33	64	15	2	3	27	25	26	.229	.292	.329	.620	71	-13	-11	94	95	25	.520	2			-4	3S/2	-0.7
1937	Cin-N	43	114	12	22	4	0	1	13	15	12	.193	.287	.254	.541	53	-8	-7	91	146	9	.479	1			3	S/23	0.0
	Det-A	20	47	4	4	2	0	0	1	4	11	.085	.157	.128	.285	-25	-9	-10	109	57	1	.233	0	0	0	0	S	-0.7
1939	Was-A	68	188	36	48	7	5	3	29	30	11	.255	.361	.394	.754	103	-2	1	90	118	28	.738	2	0	1	1	S3/2	0.5
1940	Was-A	22	54	7	20	7	1	0	7	4	3	.370	.424	.537	.961	158	4	4	93	87	13	.971	0	0	0	-0	S/P2	0.5
	Bos-A	30	91	9	18	2	0	0	8	8	16	.198	.263	.220	.482	26	-10	-10	101	145	6	.378	0	0	0	1	3/S	-0.5
	Yr	52	145	16	38	9	1	0	15	12	19	.262	.323	.338	.661	73	-6	-5	97	122	17	.574	0	0	0	1		0.0
Total	9	876	2869	398	766	169	43	17	350	290	245	.267	.336	.374	.709	83	-71	-72	100	111	373	.667	34	0		12	S3/2P	1.6
■ **FRANK GENINS** Genins, C. Frank "Frenchy" b: 11/2/1866, St.Louis, Mo. d: 9/30/22, St.Louis, Mo. TR , Deb: 7/05/1892																												
1892	Cin-N	35	110	12	20	4	0	0	7	12	12	.182	.262	.218	.480	46	-7	-7	103	90	8	.478	7			0	SO/3	-0.6
	StL-N	15	51	5	10	1	0	0	4	1	11	.196	.212	.216	.427	32	-4	-4	95	112	3	.366	3			0	S/O	-0.3
	Yr	50	161	17	30	5	0	0	11	13	23	.186	.247	.217	.465	42	-11	-11	101	98	11	.443	10			0		-0.9
1895	Pit-N	73	252	43	63	8	0	2	24	22	14	.250	.315	.306	.621	64	-14	-12	97	82	31	.635	19			0	O32/S1	-0.9
1901	Cle-A	26	101	15	23	5	0	0	9	8		.228	.284	.277	.562	61	-6	-5	95	107	9	.500	3			4	O	0.0
Total	3	149	514	75	116	18	0	2	44	43	37	.226	.288	.272	.560	57	-30	-28	97	91	51	.545	32			4	/OS321	-1.8
■ **GEORGE GENOVESE** Genovese, George Michael b: 2/22/22, Staten Island, N.Y BL/TR, 5'6.5", 160 lbs. Deb: 4/29/50																												
1950	Was-A	3	1	1	0	0	0	0	0	1	0	.000	.500	.000	.500	37	0	0	99	0	0	1.000	0	0	0	0	H	0.0
■ **JIM GENTILE** Gentile, James Edward "Diamond Jim" b: 6/3/34, San Francisco, Cal. BL/TL, 6'3.5", 210 lbs. Deb: 9/10/57																												
1957	Bro-N	4	6	1	1	0	0	1	1	1	1	.167	.286	.667	.952	125	0	0	116	59	1	1.000	0	0	0	0	/1	0.0
1958	LA-N	12	30	0	4	1	0	0	4	4	6	.133	.235	.167	.402	8	-4	-4	105	331	1	.333	0	0	0	0	/1	-0.4
1960	Bal-A	138	384	67	112	17	0	21	98	68	72	.292	.407	.500	.907	141	26	25	102	150	82	.954	0	0	0	-5	*1	1.2
1961	Bal-A	148	486	96	147	25	2	46	141	96	106	.302	.428	.646	1.074	188	59	61	97	125	138	1.199	1	1	-0	3	*1	4.9
1962	Bal-A	152	545	80	137	21	1	33	87	77	100	.251	.351	.475	.827	127	15	19	95	102	92	.817	1	0	0	5	*1	1.4
1963	Bal-A	145	496	65	123	16	1	24	72	76	101	.248	.355	.429	.784	126	14	18	94	108	77	.765	1	0	0	4	*1	1.9
1964	KC-A	136	439	71	110	10	0	28	71	84	122	.251	.376	.465	.840	127	21	19	105	107	81	.864	0	0	0	1	*1	1.6
1965	KC-A	38	118	14	29	5	0	10	22	9	26	.246	.305	.542	.847	140	5	5	97	97	19	.804	0	0	0	-1	1	0.3
	Hou-N	81	227	22	55	11	1	7	31	34	72	.242	.353	.392	.745	124	4	7	89	117	33	.723	0	0	0	1	1	0.4
1966	Hou-N	49	144	16	35	6	1	7	18	21	39	.243	.355	.444	.799	124	4	5	97	89	24	.795	0	0	0	1	1	0.4
	Cle-A	33	47	2	6	1	0	2	4	5	18	.128	.212	.277	.488	38	-4	-4	101	88	3	.429	0	0	0	-0	/1	-0.4
Total	9	936	2922	434	759	113	6	179	549	475	663	.260	.372	.486	.858	137	141	151	97	116	550	.898	3	1	0	10	1	11.3

YEAR	TM/L	G	AB	R	H	2B	3B	HR	RBI	BB	SO	AVG	OBP	SLG	PRO	/A	BR	/A	PF	CHI	RC	TA	SB	CS	SBR	FR	POS	TPR
■ **SAM GENTILE**	Gentile, Samuel Christopher b: 10/12/16, Charlestown, Mass. BL/TR, 5'11", 180 lbs. Deb: 4/24/43																											
1943	Bos-N	8	4	1	1	1	0	0	0	1	0	.250	.400	.500	.900	151	0	0	106	0	1	1.000	0			0	H	0.0
■ **HARVEY GENTRY**	Gentry, Harvey William b: 5/27/26, Winston-Salem, N.C BL/TR, 6', 170 lbs. Deb: 4/14/54																											
1954	NY-N	5	4	0	1	0	0	0	1	1	0	.250	.400	.250	.650	70	-0	-0	105	394	1	.667	0	0	0	0	H	0.0
■ **ALEX GEORGE**	George, Alex Thomas M. b: 9/27/38, Kansas City, Mo. BL/TR, 5'11.5", 170 lbs. Deb: 9/16/55																											
1955	KC-A	5	10	0	1	0	0	0	0	1	7	.100	.182	.100	.282	-22	-2	-2	101	0	0	.222	0	0	0	-0	/S	-0.1
■ **GREEK GEORGE**	George, Charles Peter b: 12/25/12, Waycross, Ga. BR/TR, 6'2", 200 lbs. Deb: 6/30/35																											
1935	Cle-A	2	0	0	0	0	0	0	0	0	0	—	—	—	—	—	0	0	99	—	—	—	0	0	0	0	/C	0.0
1936	Cle-A	23	77	3	15	3	0	0	5	9	16	.195	.279	.234	.513	26	-9	-9	106	90	5	.435	0	0	0	1	C	-0.5
1938	Bro-N	7	20	0	4	0	1	0	2	0	4	.200	.200	.300	.500	37	-2	-2	96	120	1	.353	0			-0	/C	-0.1
1941	Chi-N	35	64	4	10	2	0	0	6	2	10	.156	.182	.188	.369	4	-8	-8	94	181	2	.255	0			1	C	-0.4
1945	Phi-A	51	138	8	24	4	1	0	11	17	29	.174	.265	.217	.482	43	-10	-9	94	133	8	.392	0	0	0	-0	C	-0.5
Total	5	118	299	15	53	9	2	0	24	28	59	.177	.248	.221	.468	30	-29	-28	97	130	17	.373	0	0		2	/C	-1.5
■ **BEN GERAGHTY**	Geraghty, Benjamin Raymond b: 7/19/12, Jersey City, N.J. d: 6/18/63, Jacksonville, Fla BR/TR, 5'11", 175 lbs. Deb: 4/17/36																											
1936	Bro-N	51	129	11	25	4	0	0	9	8	16	.194	.241	.225	.466	25	-13	-14	105	110	7	.376	4			-6	S/23	-1.7
1943	Bos-N	8	1	2	0	0	0	0	0	0	0	.000	.000	.000	.000	-95	-0	-0	106	0	0	.000	0			0	/2S3	0.0
1944	Bos-N	11	16	3	4	0	0	0	0	1	2	.250	.294	.250	.544	57	-1	-1	95	0	1	.417	0			0	/23	0.0
Total	3	70	146	16	29	4	0	0	9	9	18	.199	.245	.226	.471	27	-15	-15	104	97	8	.393	4			-6	/S23	-1.7
■ **CRAIG GERBER**	Gerber, Craig Stuart b: 1/8/59, Chicago, Ill. BL/TR, 6', 175 lbs. Deb: 4/11/85																											
1985	Cal-A	65	91	8	24	1	2	0	6	2	3	.264	.280	.319	.598	63	-5	-5	101	82	7	.431	0	3	-2	3	S/32D	0.0
■ **WALLY GERBER**	Gerber, Walter "Spooks" b: 8/18/1891, Columbus, Ohio d: 6/19/51, Columbus, Ohio BR/TR, 5'10", 152 lbs. Deb: 9/23/14																											
1914	Pit-N	17	54	5	13	1	1	0	5	2	8	.241	.281	.296	.577	77	-2	-2	92	113	4	.463	0			1	S	0.0
1915	Pit-N	56	144	8	28	2	0	0	7	9	16	.194	.252	.208	.460	40	-10	-10	99	89	9	.402	6	1	1	-1	3S/2	-0.8
1917	StL-A	14	39	2	12	1	1	0	2	3	2	.308	.357	.385	.742	133	1	1	95	48	6	.704	1			1	S/2	0.3
1918	StL-A	56	171	10	41	4	0	0	10	19	11	.240	.316	.263	.579	75	-5	-5	99	81	15	.508	2			-12	S	-1.4
1919	StL-A	140	462	43	105	14	6	1	37	49	36	.227	.308	.290	.598	70	-19	-17	97	100	44	.529	1			-10	*S	-1.5
1920	StL-A	154	584	70	163	26	2	2	60	58	32	.279	.346	.341	.687	74	-13	-23	111	109	69	.606	4	13	-7	7	*S	-0.8
1921	StL-A	114	436	55	121	12	9	2	48	34	19	.278	.337	.360	.697	77	-14	-15	101	107	53	.618	3	7	-3	-3	*S	-0.5
1922	StL-A	153	604	81	161	22	8	1	51	52	34	.267	.326	.334	.660	68	-24	-29	106	94	69	.584	6	4	-1	-0	*S	-1.1
1923	StL-A	154	605	85	170	26	3	1	62	54	50	.281	.342	.339	.681	76	-17	-21	104	98	72	.601	4	6	-2	7	*S	0.0
1924	StL-A	148	496	61	135	20	4	0	55	43	34	.272	.341	.329	.670	68	-19	-24	107	114	58	.598	4	5	-2	-5	*S	-1.4
1925	StL-A	72	246	29	67	13	1	0	19	26	15	.272	.344	.333	.678	67	-10	-13	108	78	29	.608	1	2	-1	3	S	0.0
1926	StL-A	131	411	37	111	8	0	0	42	40	29	.270	.339	.290	.629	65	-20	-20	101	120	43	.536	0	2	-1	-1	*S	-1.0
1927	StL-A	142	438	44	98	13	9	0	45	35	25	.224	.284	.295	.579	48	-33	-36	106	116	38	.494	2	0	1	6	*S/3	-1.7
1928	StL-A	6	18	1	5	1	0	0	0	1	3	.278	.316	.333	.649	68	-1	-1	104	0	2	.538	0	0	0	-0	/S	0.0
	Bos-A	104	300	21	64	6	1	0	28	32	31	.213	.289	.240	.529	41	-25	-25	98	133	24	.464	6	1	1	13	*S	0.0
	Yr	110	318	22	69	7	1	0	28	33	34	.217	.291	.245	.536	43	-26	-25	98	126	26	.468	6	1	1	13		0.0
1929	Bos-A	61	91	6	15	3	1	0	5	8	12	.165	.232	.220	.452	17	-11	-12	102	86	5	.382	1	0	0	-3	S2	-0.9
Total	15	1522	5099	558	1309	172	46	7	476	465	357	.257	.323	.313	.635	66	-222	-250	104	104	539	.557	41	41		2	*S/23	-10.8
■ **BOB GEREN**	Geren, Robert Peter b: 9/22/61, San Diego, Cal. BR/TR, 6'3", 205 lbs. Deb: 5/17/88																											
1988	NY-A	10	10	0	1	0	0	0	0	2	3	.100	.250	.100	.350	2	-1	-1	96	0	0	.333	0	0	0	-0	C	0.0
■ **JOE GERHARDT**	Gerhardt, John Joseph "Move Up Joe" b: 2/14/1855, Washington, D.C. d: 3/11/22, Middletown, N.Y. BR/TR, 6', 160 lbs. Deb: 9/01/1873 M																											
1873	Nat-n	13	56	6	11							.196															S	
1874	Bal-n	14	65	10	20							.308															S	
1875	Mut-n	57	254	29	54							.213															32/S	
1876	Lou-N	65	292	33	76	10	3	2	18	3	5	.260	.268	.336	.603	96	-0	-2	104	51	27	.468				0	*1/2S03	0.0
1877	Lou-N	59	250	41	76	6	5	1	35	5	8	.304	.318	.380	.698	90	5	-7	132	128	31	.575				19	*2/OS1	1.2
1878	Cin-N	60	259	46	77	7	2	0	28	7	14	.297	.316	.340	.656	121	4	6	95	104	28	.522				3	*2	1.3
1879	Cin-N	79	313	22	62	12	3	1	39	3	19	.198	.206	.265	.471	57	-15	-13	95	**162**	17	.343				6	23/1S	-0.1
1881	Det-N	80	297	35	72	13	6	0	36	7	31	.242	.260	.327	.586	78	-6	-9	106	131	26	.462				7	*2/3	0.1
1883	Lou-a	78	319	56	84	11	9	0		14		.263	.294	.354	.649	115	3	6	94	0	34	.540				19	*2M	2.2
1884	Lou-a	106	404	39	89	7	8	0		13		.220	.254	.277	.531	85	-10	-4	89	0	29	.413				26	*2/S	2.2
1885	NY-N	112	399	43	62	12	2	0	33	24	47	.155	.203	.195	.399	27	-30	-36	109	150	16	.303				8	*2	-1.3
1886	NY-N	123	426	44	81	11	7	0	40	22	63	.190	.230	.249	.479	51	-28	-20	89	125	27	.394	8			0	*2	-1.3
1887	NY-N	1	4	0	0	0	0	0	0	0	0	.000	.000	.000	.000	-93	-1	-1	107	0	0	.000	0			0	/3	0.0
	NY-a	85	307	40	68	13	2	0		24		.221	.280	.277	.557	65	-17	-10	88	0	29	.523	15			10	2/3	0.0
1890	BB-a	99	369	34	75	10	3	3		30		.203	.270	.271	.541	61	-18	-18	100	0	30	.486	9			33	*2	1.7
	StL-a	37	125	15	32	0	0	1		9		.256	.321	.280	.601	69	-3	-6	116	0	13	.559	5			1	23M	-0.3
	Yr	136	494	49	107	10	3	4	0	39		.217	.283	.273	.557	63	-21	-24	104	0	43	.504	14			**34**		1.4
1891	Lou-a	2	6	0	0	0	0	0	0	1	0	.000	.143	.000	.143	-64	-1	-1	90	0	0	.167	0			0	/2	0.0
Total	3 n	84	375	45	85							.227															/2	
Total	12	986	3770	448	854	112	50	8	229	162	187	.227	.261	.289	.550	73	-117	-114	100	72	308	.447	37			132	2/31S0	5.7
■ **KEN GERHART**	Gerhart, Harold Kenneth b: 5/19/61, Charleston, S.C. BR/TR, 6', 190 lbs. Deb: 9/14/86																											
1986	Bal-A	20	69	4	16	2	0	1	7	4	18	.232	.274	.304	.578	59	-4	-4	99	116	6	.455	0	1	-1	-2	O	-0.6
1987	Bal-A	92	284	41	69	10	2	14	34	17	53	.243	.288	.440	.728	92	-5	-4	98	81	35	.679	9	2	2	-4	O	-0.8
1988	Bal-A	103	262	27	51	10	1	9	23	21	57	.195	.260	.344	.603	71	-12	-10	95	78	24	.553	7	3	0	-3	O/D	-1.4
Total	3	215	615	72	136	22	3	24	64	42	128	.221	.274	.384	.658	80	-21	-18	97	84	64	.609	16	6	1	-9	O/D	-2.8
■ **GEORGE GERKEN**	Gerken, George Herbert "Pickles" b: 7/28/03, Chicago, Ill. d: 10/23/77, Arcadia, Cal. BR/TR, 5'11.5", 175 lbs. Deb: 4/19/27																											
1927	Cle-A	6	14	1	3	0	0	0	2	1	3	.214	.267	.214	.481	27	-2	-1	97	222	1	.364	0	0	0	0	/O	-0.1
1928	Cle-A	38	115	16	26	7	2	0	9	12	22	.226	.305	.322	.626	61	-6	-7	106	83	12	.582	3	2	-0	-1	O	-0.9
Total	2	44	129	17	29	7	2	0	11	13	25	.225	.301	.310	.611	58	-7	-8	105	98	13	.559	3	2	-0	-1	/O	-1.0
■ **JOHNNY GERLACH**	Gerlach, John Glenn b: 5/11/17, Shullsburg, Wis. BR/TR, 5'9", 165 lbs. Deb: 9/03/38																											
1938	Chi-A	9	25	2	7	0	0	0	1	4	2	.280	.379	.280	.659	69	-1	-1	98	48	3	.611	0	0	0	0	/S	0.0
1939	Chi-A	3	2	0	2	0	0	0	0	0	0	1.000	1.000	1.000	2.000	388	1	1	107	0	2	—	0	0	0	0	/3	0.1
Total	2	12	27	2	9	0	0	0	1	4	2	.333	.419	.333	.753	93	-0	-0	98	45	5	.722	0	0	0	0	/S3	0.1
■ **DICK GERNERT**	Gernert, Richard Edward b: 9/28/28, Reading, Pa. BR/TR, 6'3", 209 lbs. Deb: 4/16/52 C																											
1952	Bos-A	102	367	58	89	20	2	19	67	35	83	.243	.317	.463	.780	108	5	2	107	112	56	.751	4	1	1	-1	1	-0.3
1953	Bos-A	139	494	73	125	15	1	21	71	88	82	.253	.371	.415	.786	103	10	4	109	104	81	.774	0	7	-4	-3	*1	-0.5
1954	Bos-A	14	23	2	6	2	0	0	1	6	4	.261	.414	.348	.762	110	1	1	100	47	3	.737	0	0	0	0	/1	0.1
1955	Bos-A	7	20	6	4	2	0	0	1	1	5	.200	.238	.300	.538	35	-2	-2	124	62	1	.412	0	0	0	0	/1	-0.1
1956	Bos-A	106	306	53	89	11	0	16	68	56	57	.291	.404	.484	.888	130	16	15	103	130	63	.924	1	0	0	-6	O1	0.5
1957	Bos-A	99	316	45	75	13	3	14	58	39	62	.237	.327	.430	.757	96	2	-2	110	129	44	.716	1	1	-0	-2	1O	-0.5
1958	Bos-A	122	431	59	102	19	1	20	69	59	78	.237	.331	.425	.756	101	4	1	105	116	60	.713	2	0	1	3	*1	0.0
1959	Bos-A	117	298	41	78	14	1	11	42	52	49	.262	.371	.426	.798	112	9	6	106	103	47	.773	1	2	-1	1	1O	0.6
1960	Chi-N	52	96	8	24	3	0	0	11	10	19	.250	.321	.281	.602	68	-4	-4	98	165	8	.494	1	0	0	1	1/O	-0.3
	Det-A	21	50	6	15	4	0	1	5	4	5	.300	.352	.440	.792	111	1	1	102	78	8	.722	0	0	0	-1	1/O	-0.1
1961	Det-A	6	5	1	1	0	0	1	1	1	2	.200	.333	.800	1.133	201	1	1	96	56	1	1.000	0	0	0	0	H	0.1
	Cin-N	40	63	4	19	1	0	0	7	7	9	.302	.371	.317	.689	82	-1	-1	104	141	8	.614	0	0	0	1	1	-0.1

YEAR	TM/L	G	AB	R	H	2B	3B	HR	RBI	BB	SO	AVG	OBP	SLG	PRO	/A	BR	/A	PF	CHI	RC	TA	SB	CS	SBR	FR	POS	TPR
1962	Hou-N	10	24	1	5	0	0	0	1	5	7	.208	.345	.208	.553	56	-1	-1	93	79	2	.526	0	0	0	0	/1	0.0
Total	11	835	2493	357	632	104	8	103	402	363	462	.254	.352	.426	.778	105	40	20	106	115	382	.775	10	11	-4	-8	1O	-0.6
■ **CESAR GERONIMO** Geronimo, Cesar Francisco (Zorrilla) b: 3/11/48, El Seibo, D.R. BL/TL, 6', 165 lbs. Deb: 4/16/69																												
1969	Hou-N	28	8	8	2	1	0	0	0	0	3	.250	.250	.375	.625	72	-0	-0	102	0	1	.500	0	0	0	-3	/O	-0.3
1970	Hou-N	47	37	5	9	0	0	0	2	2	5	.243	.300	.243	.543	51	-3	-2	94	86	3	.400	0	0	0	-6	O	-0.9
1971	Hou-N	94	82	13	18	2	2	1	6	5	31	.220	.264	.329	.594	73	-4	-3	93	81	7	.515	2	2	-1	-18	O	-2.5
1972	Cin-N	120	255	32	70	9	7	4	29	24	64	.275	.344	.412	.756	122	5	7	93	102	34	.680	2	7	-4	-8	*O	-1.0
1973	Cin-N	139	324	35	68	14	3	4	33	23	74	.210	.269	.309	.577	64	-18	-15	93	118	26	.492	5	5	-2	-2	*O	-2.5
1974	Cin-N	150	474	73	133	17	8	7	54	46	96	.281	.347	.395	.741	109	4	5	98	100	65	.689	9	5	-0	3	*O	0.2
1975	Cin-N	148	501	69	129	25	5	6	53	48	97	.257	.327	.363	.691	88	-6	-9	104	103	61	.643	13	5	1	9	*O	-0.3
1976	Cin-N	149	486	59	149	24	11	2	49	56	95	.307	.385	.414	.799	123	19	17	103	91	82	.819	22	5	4	-3	*O	1.3
1977	Cin-N	149	492	54	131	22	4	10	52	35	89	.266	.321	.388	.710	89	-8	-8	100	94	60	.641	10	4	1	4	*O	-0.7
1978	Cin-N	122	296	28	67	15	1	5	27	43	67	.226	.330	.334	.665	84	-5	-6	103	94	35	.646	8	3	1	-5	*O	-1.4
1979	Cin-N	123	356	38	85	17	4	4	38	37	56	.239	.314	.343	.657	81	-10	-9	97	112	38	.579	1	1	-0	1	*O	-1.1
1980	Cin-N	103	145	16	37	5	0	2	9	14	24	.255	.321	.331	.652	81	-3	-4	102	66	16	.577	2	1	0	-13	O	-2.0
1981	KC-A	59	118	14	29	0	2	2	13	11	16	.246	.310	.331	.641	86	-2	-2	99	113	13	.602	6	1	1	-8	O	-1.0
1982	KC-A	53	119	14	32	6	3	4	23	8	16	.269	.315	.471	.786	112	2	2	100	135	16	.717	2	0	1	0	O/D	0.1
1983	KC-A	38	87	2	18	4	0	0	4	2	13	.207	.242	.253	.495	36	-8	-8	101	71	5	.366	0	1	-1	-2	O	-1.0
Total	15	1522	3780	460	977	161	50	51	392	354	746	.258	.327	.368	.695	93	-37	-35	99	100	462	.653	82	40	1	-49	*O/D	-13.1
■ **LOU GERTENRICH** Gertenrich, Louis Wilhelm b: 5/4/1875, Chicago, Ill. d: 10/23/33, Chicago, Ill. 5'8", 175 lbs. Deb: 9/15/01																												
1901	Mil-A	2	3	1	1	0	0	0	0	0		.333	.333	.333	.667	92	-0	-0	95	0	0	.500	0			0	/O	0.0
1903	Pit-N	1	3	0	0	0	0	0	0	0		.000	.000	.000	.000	-96	-1	-1	105	0	0	.000	0			0	/O	0.0
Total	2	3	6	1	1	0	0	0	0	0		.167	.167	.167	.333	-5	-1	-1	100	0	0	.200	0			0	/O	0.0
■ **DOC GESSLER** Gessler, Harry Homer "Brownie" b: 12/23/1880, Indiana, Pa. d: 12/26/24, Indiana, Pa. BL/TR, 5'10", 180 lbs. Deb: 4/23/03 M																												
1903	Det-A	29	105	9	25	5	4	0	12	3		.238	.259	.362	.621	89	-2	-2	97	116	10	.525	1			2	O	0.0
	Bro-N	49	154	20	38	8	3	0	18	17		.247	.322	.338	.659	89	-2	-2	101	111	20	.672	9			1	O	-0.2
1904	Bro-N	104	341	41	99	18	4	2	28	30		.290	.348	.384	.732	134	11	13	95	76	51	.719	13			6	O/12	1.6
1905	Bro-N	126	431	44	125	17	4	3	46	38		.290	.348	.369	.716	121	9	11	96	97	66	.729	26			2	*1O	0.8
1906	Bro-N	9	33	3	8	1	2	0	4	3		.242	.306	.394	.699	139	1	1	87	108	5	.760	3			-1	/1	0.0
	Chi-N	34	83	8	21	3	0	0	10	12		.253	.347	.289	.637	95	1	-0	107	152	10	.645	4			1	O/1	0.1
	Yr	43	116	11	29	4	2	0	14	15		.250	.336	.319	.655	104	1	1	102	145	15	.678	7			1		0.1
1908	Bos-A	128	435	55	134	13	14	3	63	51		.308	.381	.423	.804	167	31	32	98	130	75	.844	19			-9	*O	1.8
1909	Bos-A	111	396	56	115	24	1	0	46	31		.290	.354	.356	.710	114	11	7	109	133	54	.698	16			-5	*O	-0.1
	Was-A	17	54	10	13	2	1	0	8	12		.241	.406	.315	.721	142	3	4	90	160	8	.878	4			-2	O/1	0.1
	Yr	128	450	66	128	26	2	0	54	43		.284	.361	.351	.712	117	14	11	107	138	63	.720	20			-8		0.0
1910	Was-A	145	487	58	126	17	11	2	50	62		.259	.361	.351	.712	122	16	15	101	111	68	.740	18			-7	*O	0.2
1911	Was-A	128	450	65	127	19	5	4	78	74		.282	.406	.373	.780	122	16	18	97	141	80	.901	29			-15	*O/1	-0.6
Total	8	880	2969	369	831	127	49	14	363	333		.280	.362	.370	.731	125	94	97	99	118	449	.758	142			-26	O1/2	3.7
■ **CHARLIE GETTIG** Gettig, Charles Henry b: 1871, Baltimore, Md. d: 4/11/35, Baltimore, Md. 5'10", 172 lbs. Deb: 8/05/1896																												
1896	NY-N	6	9	3	3	1	0	0	0	0	0	.333	.333	.444	.778	107	0	0	99	0	1	.667	0			0	/P	0.0
1897	NY-N	22	75	8	15	6	0	0	12	6		.200	.277	.280	.557	50	-5	-5	98	167	7	.533	3			0	/32OSP	-0.4
1898	NY-N	64	196	30	49	6	2	0	26	15		.250	.310	.301	.611	82	-5	-4	95	133	20	.551	5			0	OP2/S31C	-0.3
1899	NY-N	34	97	7	24	3	0	0	9	7		.247	.305	.278	.583	64	-5	-4	97	102	10	.534	4			0	P/321O	0.0
Total	4	126	377	48	91	16	2	0	47	28	0	.241	.302	.294	.597	71	-15	-13	96	129	38	.545	12			0	/PO23S1C	-0.7
■ **TOM GETTINGER** Gettinger, Thomas L. b: 1870, Mobile, Ala. BL/TL, 5'10", 180 lbs. Deb: 9/21/1889																												
1889	StL-a	4	16	2	7	0	0	1	2	2	1	.438	.500	.625	1.125	198	3	2	112	42	5	1.333	0			0	/O	0.2
1890	StL-a	58	227	31	54	7	5	3		20		.238	.302	.352	.655	82	-2	-8	116	0	27	.630	8			-6	O	-1.4
1895	Lou-N	63	260	28	70	11	5	2	32	8	15	.269	.296	.373	.669	77	-11	-9	95	92	31	.595	6			1	O/P	-1.0
Total	3	125	503	61	131	18	10	6	34	30	16	.260	.306	.372	.678	83	-10	-14	105	48	64	.629	14			-5	O/P	-2.2
■ **JAKE GETTMAN** Gettman, Jacob John b: 10/25/1876, Frank, Russia d: 10/4/56, Denver, Colo. BB/TL, 5'11", 185 lbs. Deb: 8/20/1897																												
1897	Was-N	36	143	28	45	7	3	3	29	7		.315	.359	.469	.828	118	4	3	101	118	28	.867	8			-3	O	-0.1
1898	Was-N	142	567	75	157	16	5	5	47	29		.277	.319	.349	.668	92	-5	-7	102	64	75	.646	32			3	*O/1	-1.1
1899	Was-N	19	62	5	13	1	0	0	2	4		.210	.258	.226	.483	36	-5	-5	96	44	5	.449	4			0	O/1	-0.4
Total	3	197	772	108	215	24	8	8	78	40		.278	.322	.361	.683	93	-7	-8	101	73	108	.668	44			-0	O/1	-1.6
■ **GUS GETZ** Getz, Gustave "Gee-Gee" b: 8/3/1889, Pittsburgh, Pa. d: 5/28/69, Keansburg, N.J. BR/TR, 5'11", 165 lbs. Deb: 09																												
1909	Bos-N	40	148	6	33	2	0	0	9	1		.223	.228	.236	.465	47	-10	-9	96	95	8	.330	2			1	3/2S	-0.8
1910	Bos-N	54	144	14	28	0	1	0	7	6	10	.194	.232	.208	.440	25	-13	-16	114	81	7	.336	2			2	32/OS	-1.3
1914	Bro-N	55	210	13	52	8	1	0	20	2	15	.248	.255	.295	.550	63	-10	-10	101	119	17	.462	9			8	3	0.0
1915	Bro-N	130	477	39	123	10	5	2	46	8	14	.258	.275	.312	.587	76	-14	-15	101	116	41	.485	19	15	-3	4	*3/S	-0.9
1916	Bro-N	40	96	9	21	1	2	0	8	0	5	.219	.219	.271	.490	48	-6	-6	103	122	8	.467	9			-1	3/S1	-0.6
1917	Cin-N	7	14	2	4	0	0	0	3	3	0	.286	.412	.286	.697	125	0	1	92	289	2	.700	0			0	/23	0.1
1918	Cle-A	6	15	2	2	1	0	0	0	4	1	.133	.350	.200	.550	61	-0	-0	108	0	1	.615	0			0	/3	0.0
	Pit-N	7	10	0	2	0	0	0	0	0	1	.200	.200	.200	.400	21	-1	-1	106	0	0	.250	0			0	/3	0.0
Total	7	339	1114	85	265	22	9	2	93	24	46	.238	.257	.279	.536	60	-54	-57	102	109	85	.441	41	15		14	3/2S01	-3.5
■ **CHAPPIE GEYGAN** Geygan, James Edward b: 6/3/03, Ironton, Ohio d: 3/15/66, Columbus, Ohio BR/TR, 5'11", 170 lbs. Deb: 7/16/24																												
1924	Bos-A	33	82	7	21	5	2	0	4	4	16	.256	.307	.366	.673	70	-4	-4	104	44	9	.571	0	2	-1	-1	S	-0.2
1925	Bos-A	3	11	0	2	0	0	0	0	0	2	.182	.182	.182	.364	-8	-2	-2	95	0	0	.222	0	0	0	0	/S	0.0
1926	Bos-A	4	10	0	3	0	0	0	0	1	1	.300	.364	.300	.664	74	-0	-0	101	0	1	.571	0	0	0	0	/3	0.0
Total	3	40	103	7	26	5	2	0	4	5	19	.252	.300	.340	.640	63	-6	-6	103	35	10	.532	0	2	-1	-0	/S3	-0.2
■ **PATSY GHARRITY** Gharrity, Edward Patrick b: 3/13/1892, Parnell, Iowa d: 10/10/66, Beloit, Wis. BR/TR, 5'10", 170 lbs. Deb: 5/16/16 C																												
1916	Was-A	39	92	8	21	5	1	0	9	8	18	.228	.297	.304	.601	81	-2	-2	100	115	9	.549	2			-1	C1	-0.2
1917	Was-A	76	176	15	50	5	0	0	18	14	18	.284	.337	.313	.649	106	-0	1	92	117	20	.603	7			0	1/CO	0.0
1918	Was-A	4	4	0	1	1	0	0	2	0	1	.250	.250	.500	.750	121	0	0	104	365	0	.667	0			0	H	0.0
1919	Was-A	111	347	35	94	19	4	2	43	25	39	.271	.325	.366	.691	96	-3	-3	98	117	42	.628	4			2	CO/1	0.0
1920	Was-A	131	428	51	105	18	3	3	44	37	52	.245	.307	.322	.629	70	-21	-18	95	105	44	.555	6	5	-1	10	*C/1O	0.1
1921	Was-A	121	387	62	120	19	8	7	55	45	44	.310	.386	.455	.841	115	8	9	99	96	70	.844	4	3	-1	4	*C	1.5
1922	Was-A	96	273	40	70	16	6	5	45	36	30	.256	.351	.414	.765	108	-0	3	92	126	41	.757	3	3	-1	4	C	0.8
1923	Was-A	93	251	26	52	9	4	3	33	22	27	.207	.276	.311	.587	57	-17	-15	95	130	23	.537	6	2	1	6	C1	-0.7
1929	Was-A	3	2	0	0	0	0	0	0	1	2	.000	.333	.000	.333	-7	-0	-0	100	0	0	.500	0	0	0	0	H	0.0
1930	Was-A	2	1	0	0	0	0	0	0	0	0	.000	.000	.000	.000	-99	-0	-0	101	0	0	.000	0	0	0	0	/1	0.0
Total	10	676	1961	237	513	92	26	20	249	188	231	.262	.331	.366	.696	91	-36	-25	96	113	250	.651	32	13		24	C1/O	1.5
■ **JOE GIANNINI** Giannini, Joseph Francis b: 9/8/1888, San Francisco, Cal d: 9/26/42, San Francisco, Cal. BL/TR, 5'8", 155 lbs. Deb: 8/07/11																												
1911	Bos-A	1	2	0	1	1	0	0	0	0		.500	.500	1.000	1.500	318	1	1	99	0	1	2.000	0			0	/S	0.1
■ **JOHN GIBBONS** Gibbons, John Michael b: 6/8/62, Great Falls, Mont. BR/TR, 5'11", 187 lbs. Deb: 4/11/84																												
1984	NY-N	10	31	1	2	0	0	0	1	3	11	.065	.171	.065	.236	-31	-5	-5	100	196	0	.207	0	0	0	-0	/C	-0.5
1986	NY-N	8	19	4	9	4	0	1	1	3	5	.474	.545	.842	1.388	290	5	5	96	21	8	1.727	0	0	0	0	/C	0.5
Total	2	18	50	5	11	4	0	1	2	6	16	.220	.316	.360	.676	90	-1	-1	98	128	9	.625	0	0	0	0	/C	0.0

YEAR	TM/L	G	AB	R	H	2B	3B	HR	RBI	BB	SO	AVG	OBP	SLG	PRO	/A	BR	/A	PF	CHI	RC	TA	SB	CS	SBR	FR	POS	TPR
■ **JAKE GIBBS**	Gibbs, Jerry Dean b: 11/7/38, Grenada, Miss. BL/TR, 6', 180 lbs. Deb: 9/11/62																											
1962	NY-A	2	0	2	0	0	0	0	0	0	0	—	—	—	—	—	0	0	94	—	—	—	0	0	0	0	/3	0.0
1963	NY-A	4	8	1	2	0	0	0	0	0	1	.250	.250	.250	.500	40	-1	-1	101	0	1	.333	0	0	0	0	/C	0.0
1964	NY-A	3	6	1	1	0	0	0	0	0	2	.167	.167	.167	.333	-7	-1	-1	103	0	0	.200	0	0	0	0	/C	0.0
1965	NY-A	37	68	6	15	1	0	2	7	4	20	.221	.274	.324	.598	68	-3	-3	101	104	7	.509	0	0	0	1	C	0.0
1966	NY-A	62	182	19	47	6	0	3	20	19	16	.258	.328	.341	.669	99	-1	-0	94	118	20	.601	5	2	0	8	C	1.2
1967	NY-A	116	374	33	87	7	1	4	25	28	57	.233	.293	.289	.582	77	-12	-10	94	87	31	.488	7	6	-2	18	C	1.5
1968	NY-A	124	423	31	90	12	3	3	29	27	68	.213	.270	.277	.546	65	-17	-18	101	101	30	.456	9	8	-2	14	*C	0.0
1969	NY-A	71	219	18	49	9	2	0	18	23	30	.224	.298	.283	.581	66	-11	-9	95	117	18	.497	3	4	-2	10	C	0.3
1970	NY-A	49	153	23	46	9	2	8	26	7	14	.301	.335	.542	.878	150	7	8	92	98	27	.838	2	0	1	6	C	1.5
1971	NY-A	70	206	23	45	9	0	5	21	12	23	.218	.271	.335	.606	73	-8	-8	97	102	18	.518	2	2	-1	4	C	-0.1
Total	10	538	1639	157	382	53	8	25	146	120	231	.233	.291	.321	.612	80	-48	-41	97	101	161	.537	28	22	-5	61	C/3	4.4
■ **CHARLIE GIBSON**	Gibson, Charles Ellsworth "Gibby" b: 11/17/1879, Sharon, Pa. d: 11/22/54, Sharon, Pa. TR , 6', 160 lbs. Deb: 9/23/05																											
1905	StL-A	1	3	0	0	0	0	0	0	0		.000	.000	.000	.000	-99	-1	-1	91	0	0	.000	0			0	/C	0.0
■ **CHARLIE GIBSON**	Gibson, Charles Griffin b: 11/21/1899, Lagrange, Ga. BR/TR, 5'8", 160 lbs. Deb: 5/30/24																											
1924	Phi-A	12	15	1	2	0	0	0	1	2	0	.133	.235	.133	.369	-3	-2	-2	99	165	1	.308	0	0	0	-0	C	-0.1
■ **FRANK GIBSON**	Gibson, Frank Gilbert b: 9/27/1890, Omaha, Neb. d: 4/27/61, Austin, Tex. BB/TR, 6'0.5", 172 lbs. Deb: 4/22/13																											
1913	Det-A	23	57	8	8	1	0	0	2	3	9	.140	.197	.158	.355	4	-7	-7	99	79	2	.306	2			-2	C/O	-0.7
1921	Bos-N	63	125	14	33	5	4	2	13	3	17	.264	.292	.416	.708	92	-3	-2	93	82	15	.620	0	0	0	2	C	0.2
1922	Bos-N	66	164	15	49	7	2	3	20	10	27	.299	.339	.421	.760	101	-2	-0	94	90	24	.716	4	1	1	1	C1	0.1
1923	Bos-N	41	50	13	15	1	0	0	5	7	7	.300	.386	.320	.706	88	-0	-0	100	110	6	.622	0	2	-1	1	C	0.0
1924	Bos-N	90	229	25	71	15	6	1	30	10	23	.310	.342	.441	.783	115	2	4	94	105	34	.711	1	1	-0	6	C1/3	1.0
1925	Bos-N	104	316	36	88	23	5	2	50	15	28	.278	.313	.402	.715	87	-10	-7	94	134	39	.632	3	3	-1	-2	C/1	-0.4
1926	Bos-N	24	47	3	16	4	0	0	7	4	6	.340	.392	.426	.818	139	1	2	86	121	8	.774	0			1	C	0.4
1927	Bos-N	60	167	7	37	1	2	0	19	3	10	.222	.235	.251	.487	33	-16	-15	93	158	9	.362	2			4	C	-0.7
Total	8	471	1155	121	317	57	19	8	146	55	127	.274	.310	.377	.688	86	-35	-25	94	115	137	.601	12	7		11	C/13O	-0.1
■ **GEORGE GIBSON**	Gibson, George C. "Moon" b: 7/22/1880, London, Ont., Can. d: 1/25/67, London, Ont., Can. BR/TR, 5'11.5", 190 lbs. Deb: 7/02/05 MC																											
1905	Pit-N	46	135	14	24	2	2	2	14	15		.178	.260	.267	.527	56	-7	-7	104	116	10	.477	2			-3	C	-0.5
1906	Pit-N	81	259	8	46	6	1	0	20	16		.178	.225	.208	.434	35	-19	-20	104	135	13	.333	1			-6	C	-2.1
1907	Pit-N	113	382	28	84	8	7	3	25	18		.220	.255	.301	.556	72	-12	-14	105	78	31	.453	2			-7	*C/1	-1.3
1908	Pit-N	143	486	37	111	19	4	2	45	19		.228	.257	.296	.554	83	-13	-10	95	118	36	.445	4			-14	*C	-1.9
1909	Pit-N	150	510	42	135	25	9	2	52	44		.265	.326	.361	.686	109	7	5	105	102	61	.637	9			-6	*C	1.0
1910	Pit-N	143	482	53	125	22	6	3	44	47	31	.259	.333	.349	.681	88	-1	-8	112	88	58	.639	7			6	*C	0.5
1911	Pit-N	100	311	32	65	12	2	0	19	29	16	.209	.281	.260	.541	51	-20	-20	101	79	23	.467	3			1	C	-1.1
1912	Pit-N	95	300	23	72	14	3	2	35	20	16	.240	.290	.327	.616	69	-14	-13	99	113	28	.522	0			-7	C	-1.4
1913	Pit-N	48	118	6	33	4	2	0	12	10	8	.280	.341	.347	.689	101	-0	0	96	106	15	.635	2			1	C	0.4
1914	Pit-N	102	274	19	78	9	5	0	30	27	27	.285	.359	.354	.713	122	5	7	92	112	36	.679	4			-7	*C	0.4
1915	Pit-N	120	351	28	88	15	6	1	30	31	25	.251	.313	.336	.649	98	-1	-1	99	95	40	.585	5	2	0	-1	*C	0.5
1916	Pit-N	33	84	4	17	2	2	0	4	3	7	.202	.239	.274	.512	55	-4	-5	105	69	6	.403	0			2	C	0.0
1917	NY-N	35	82	1	14	3	0	0	5	7	2	.171	.236	.207	.443	38	-6	-6	97	113	4	.368	1			-6	C	-1.1
1918	NY-N	4	2	0	1	1	0	0	0	0	0	.500	.500	1.000	1.500	362	1	1	98	0	1	2.000	0			0	/C	0.1
Total	14	1213	3776	295	893	142	49	15	335	286	132	.236	.294	.312	.606	81	-84	-91	102	101	361	.528	40	2		-47	*C/1	-6.5
■ **RUSS GIBSON**	Gibson, John Russell b: 5/6/39, Fall River, Mass. BR/TR, 6'1", 195 lbs. Deb: 4/14/67																											
1967	Bos-A	49	138	8	28	7	0	1	15	12	31	.203	.267	.275	.542	53	-7	-9	115	153	9	.427	0	0	0	-2	C	-0.8
1968	Bos-A	76	231	15	52	11	1	3	20	8	38	.225	.251	.320	.571	72	-8	-8	101	103	17	.446	1	2	-1	-3	C/1	-0.9
1969	Bos-A	85	287	21	72	9	1	3	27	15	25	.251	.290	.321	.611	67	-12	-13	105	107	24	.480	1	1	-0	-0	C	-0.8
1970	SF-N	24	69	3	16	6	0	0	6	7	12	.232	.303	.319	.621	70	-3	-3	96	106	6	.509	0	0	0	2	C	0.0
1971	SF-N	25	57	2	11	1	1	1	7	2	13	.193	.220	.298	.519	46	-4	-4	100	142	3	.396	0	0	0	-1	C	-0.4
1972	SF-N	5	12	0	2	0	1	0	3	0	4	.167	.167	.333	.500	39	-1	-1	100	308	0	.333	0	0	0	0	/C	0.0
Total	6	264	794	49	181	34	4	8	78	44	123	.228	.269	.311	.580	64	-35	-39	104	119	60	.476	2	3	-1	-5	C/1	-2.9
■ **KIRK GIBSON**	Gibson, Kirk Harold b: 5/28/57, Pontiac, Mich. BL/TL, 6'3", 215 lbs. Deb: 9/08/79																											
1979	Det-A	12	38	3	9	3	0	1	4	1	3	.237	.256	.395	.651	75	-2	-1	96	85	3	.594	3	3	-1	-1	O	-0.3
1980	Det-A	51	175	23	46	2	1	9	16	10	45	.263	.306	.440	.746	97	-0	-1	105	60	22	.676	4	7	-3	2	O/D	-0.2
1981	Det-A	83	290	41	95	11	3	9	40	18	64	.328	.371	.479	.850	136	15	14	105	96	50	.842	17	5	2	-3	O/D	1.2
1982	Det-A	69	266	34	74	16	2	8	35	25	41	.278	.342	.444	.786	113	5	5	100	104	40	.761	9	7	-2	8	O/D	0.9
1983	Det-A	128	401	60	91	12	9	15	51	53	96	.227	.323	.414	.737	106	1	3	96	94	59	.752	14	3	2	-0	DO	0.4
1984	Det-A	149	531	92	150	23	10	27	91	63	103	.282	.367	.516	.883	147	30	32	96	104	106	.949	29	9	3	-12	*O/D	1.9
1985	Det-A	154	581	96	167	37	5	29	97	71	137	.287	.370	.518	.888	132	32	27	106	105	118	.962	30	4	7	-9	*O/D	2.2
1986	Det-A	119	441	84	118	11	2	28	86	68	107	.268	.374	.492	.866	141	22	25	95	121	88	.967	34	6	7	-12	*O/D	1.6
1987	Det-A	128	487	95	135	25	3	24	79	71	117	.277	.375	.489	.863	132	21	23	97	108	95	.934	26	7	4	1	*O/D	2.3
1988	LA-N	150	542	106	157	28	1	25	76	73	120	.290	.381	.483	.864	138	34	30	106	96	107	.940	31	4	7	4	*O	3.9
Total	10	1043	3752	634	1042	168	36	175	575	453	833	.278	.362	.482	.843	130	158	156	101	102	688	.900	197	55	26	-23	OD	13.9
■ **WHITEY GIBSON**	Gibson, Leighton P. b: 10/6/1868, Lancaster, Pa. d: 10/11/07, Talmadge, Pa. TR , 5'9", 178 lbs. Deb: 1888																											
1888	Phi-a	1	3	0	0	0	0	0	0	0		.000	.000	.000	.000	-99	-1	-1	101	0	0	.000	0			0	/C	0.0
■ **JOE GIEBEL**	Giebel, Joseph Henry b: 11/30/1891, Washington, D.C. d: 3/17/81, Silver Spring, Md. BR/TR, 5'10.5", 175 lbs. Deb: 9/30/13																											
1913	Phi-A	1	3	0	1	0	0	0	0	0	1	.333	.333	.333	.667	99	-0	-0	97	0	0	.500	0			0	/C	0.0
■ **NORM GIGON**	Gigon, Norman Phillip b: 5/12/38, Teaneck, N.J. BR/TR, 6', 195 lbs. Deb: 4/12/67																											
1967	Chi-N	34	70	8	12	3	1	1	6	4	14	.171	.237	.286	.523	48	-5	-5	102	108	5	.433	0	0	0	-1	2/O3	-0.5
■ **GUS GIL**	Gil, Tomas Gustavo (Guillen) b: 4/19/39, Caracas, Venez. BR/TR, 5'10", 180 lbs. Deb: 4/11/67																											
1967	Cle-A	51	96	11	11	4	0	0	5	9	18	.115	.198	.156	.354	6	-11	-11	100	139	3	.287	0	0	0	0	2/1	-1.0
1969	Sea-A	92	221	20	49	7	0	0	17	16	28	.222	.274	.253	.528	49	-15	-15	98	122	16	.418	2	0	1	1	32S	-1.1
1970	Mil-A	64	119	12	22	4	0	1	12	21	12	.185	.307	.244	.551	55	-7	-7	98	152	10	.520	2	0	1	-2	23	-0.4
1971	Mil-A	14	32	3	5	1	0	0	3	10	5	.156	.357	.188	.545	56	-1	-1	103	204	3	.630	1	0	0	0	/23	0.0
Total	4	221	468	46	87	16	0	1	37	56	63	.186	.274	.226	.501	43	-34	-34	99	140	33	.441	5	0	2	-1	2/3S1	-2.5
■ **ANDY GILBERT**	Gilbert, Andrew b: 7/18/14, Latrobe, Pa. BR/TR, 6', 203 lbs. Deb: 9/14/42 C																											
1942	Bos-A	6	11	0	1	0	0	0	1	1	3	.091	.167	.091	.258	-26	-2	-2	104	352	0	.200	0	0	0	-1	/O	-0.3
1946	Bos-A	2	1	1	0	0	0	0	0	0	0	.000	.000	.000	.000	-87	-0	-0	114	0	0	.000	0	0	0	-0	/O	0.0
Total	2	8	12	1	1	0	0	0	1	1	3	.083	.154	.083	.237	-31	-2	-2	104	325	0	.182	0	0	0	-2	/O	-0.3
■ **CHARLIE GILBERT**	Gilbert, Charles Mader b: 7/8/19, New Orleans, La. d: 8/13/83, New Orleans, La. BL/TL, 5'9", 165 lbs. Deb: 4/16/40																											
1940	Bro-N	57	142	23	35	9	1	2	8	8	13	.246	.287	.366	.653	73	-4	-6	108	51	16	.561	0			1	O	-0.6
1941	Chi-N	39	86	11	24	2	1	0	12	11	6	.279	.361	.326	.686	101	-0	0	94	155	11	.625	1			0	O	0.0
1942	Chi-N	74	179	18	33	6	3	0	7	25	24	.184	.284	.251	.536	60	-9	-8	96	58	14	.480	1			2	O	-0.7
1943	Chi-N	8	20	1	3	0	0	0	0	3	3	.150	.261	.150	.411	20	-2	-2	99	0	1	.412	1			-0	/O	-0.2
1946	Chi-N	15	13	2	1	0	0	0	1	1	4	.077	.143	.077	.220	-39	-2	-2	94	373	0	.154	0			0	/O	-0.1
	Phi-N	88	260	34	63	5	2	1	17	25	18	.242	.314	.288	.602	75	-9	-8	95	81	26	.528	3			6	O	-0.2
	Yr	103	273	36	64	5	2	1	18	26	22	.234	.306	.278	.584	70	-12	-10	95	127	25	.507	3			6		-0.3
1947	Phi-N	83	152	20	36	5	2	2	10	13	14	.237	.301	.336	.637	69	-7	-7	100	65	15	.545	1			-0	O	-0.8
Total	6	364	852	109	195	27	9	5	55	86	82	.229	.302	.299	.601	70	-34	-33	98	78	82	.530	7			9	O	-2.6

YEAR	TM/L	G	AB	R	H	2B	3B	HR	RBI	BB	SO	AVG	OBP	SLG	PRO	/A	BR	/A	PF	CHI	RC	TA	SB	CS	SBR	FR	POS	TPR
■ BUDDY GILBERT	Gilbert, Drew Edward b: 7/26/35, Knoxville, Tenn. BL/TR, 6'3", 195 lbs. Deb: 9/09/59																											
1959	Cin-N	7	20	4	3	0	0	2	2	3	4	.150	.261	.450	.711	82	-1	-1	103	54	3	.706	0	0	0	1	/O	0.0
■ TOOKIE GILBERT	Gilbert, Harold Joseph b: 4/4/29, New Orleans, La. d: 6/23/67, New Orleans, La. BL/TR, 6'2.5", 185 lbs. Deb: 5/05/50																											
1950	NY-N	113	322	40	71	12	2	4	32	43	36	.220	.314	.307	.622	65	-16	-15	98	111	33	.568	3			3	*1	-1.6
1953	NY-N	70	160	12	27	3	0	3	16	22	21	.169	.269	.244	.513	36	-15	-15	98	130	12	.459	1	0	0	2	1	-1.2
Total	2	183	482	52	98	15	2	7	48	65	57	.203	.299	.286	.586	55	-31	-30	98	117	45	.539	4	0		4	1	-2.8
■ HARRY GILBERT	Gilbert, Harry L. b: Pottstown, Pa. d: 4/10/06, Pottstown, Pa. Deb: 6/23/1890																											
1890	Pit-N	2	8	1	2	0	0	0	0	0	3	.250	.250	.250	.500	54	-1	-0	88	0	1	.333	0			0	/2	0.0
■ JOHN GILBERT	Gilbert, John G. b: 1/8/1864, Pottstown, Pa. d: 11/12/03, Pottstown, Pa. Deb: 6/23/1890																											
1890	Pit-N	2	8	0	0	0	0	0	0	0	2	.000	.000	.000	.000	-99	-2	-2	88	0	0	.000	0			0	/S	-0.1
■ JACK GILBERT	Gilbert, John Robert "Jackrabbit" b: 9/4/1875, Rhinecliff, N.Y. d: 7/7/41, Albany, N.Y. Deb: 9/11/1898																											
1898	Was-N	2	5	0	1	0	0	0	1	1		.200	.429	.200	.629	83	0	0	102	302	1	1.000	1			0	/O	0.0
	NY-N	1	4	0	1	0	0	0	0	0		.250	.250	.250	.500	48	-0	-0	95	0	1	.667	1			0	/O	0.0
	Yr	3	9	0	2	0	0	0	1	1		.222	.364	.222	.586	72	-0	-0	100	302	1	.857	2			0		0.0
1904	Pit-N	25	87	13	21	0	0	0	3	12		.241	.333	.241	.575	81	-1	-1	99	55	8	.545	3			-1	O	-0.2
Total	2	28	96	13	23	0	0	0	4	13		.240	.336	.240	.576	80	-1	-1	99	69	10	.575	5			-1	/O	-0.2
■ LARRY GILBERT	Gilbert, Lawrence William b: 12/3/1891, New Orleans, La. d: 2/17/65, New Orleans, La. BL/TL, 5'9", 158 lbs. Deb: 4/14/14																											
1914	Bos-N	72	224	32	60	6	1	5	25	26	34	.268	.347	.371	.717	109	4	3	104	92	30	.689	3			-1	O	0.0
1915	Bos-N	45	106	11	16	4	0	0	4	11	13	.151	.231	.189	.419	28	-9	-9	98	76	6	.385	4	1	1	-3	O	-1.3
Total	2	117	330	43	76	10	1	5	29	37	47	.230	.310	.312	.622	84	-5	-6	102	87	35	.580	7	1		-4	/O	-1.3
■ MARK GILBERT	Gilbert, Mark David b: 8/22/56, Atlanta, Ga. BB/TR, 6', 175 lbs. Deb: 7/21/85																											
1985	Chi-A	7	22	3	6	1	0	0	3	4	5	.273	.385	.318	.703	95	0	0	100	173	3	.647	0	0	0	-0	/O	0.0
■ PETE GILBERT	Gilbert, Peter b: 9/6/1867, Baltic, Conn. d: 1/1/12, Springfield, Mass. TR , Deb: 9/06/1890																											
1890	BB-a	29	100	25	28	2	1	1		10		.280	.363	.350	.713	113	2	2	100	0	17	.833	12			0	3	0.2
1891	Bal-a	139	513	81	118	15	7	3	72	37	77	.230	.317	.304	.621	79	-12	-13	101	129	61	.638	31			-2	*3	-0.8
1892	Bal-N	4	15	0	3	0	0	0	0	1	3	.200	.250	.200	.450	38	-1	-1	100	0	1	.417	1			0	/3	0.0
1894	Bro-N	6	25	1	2	0	0	0	1	1	3	.080	.148	.080	.228	-46	-6	-6	94	146	1	.261	2			0	/23	-0.3
	Lou-N	28	108	13	33	3	1	1	14	5	4	.306	.353	.380	.733	89	-4	-1	88	93	16	.680	2			0	3	0.0
	Yr	34	133	14	35	3	1	1	15	6	7	.263	.315	.323	.638	62	-10	-7	89	106	15	.582	4			0		-0.3
Total	4	206	761	120	184	20	9	5	87	54	87	.242	.321	.311	.633	79	-21	-19	99	105	95	.648	48			-2	3/2	-0.9
■ WALLY GILBERT	Gilbert, Walter John b: 12/19/1900, Oscoda, Mich. d: 9/7/58, Duluth, Minn. BR/TR, 6', 180 lbs. Deb: 8/18/28																											
1928	Bro-N	39	153	26	31	4	0	0	3	14	8	.203	.274	.229	.503	33	-15	-15	99	32	10	.426	2			0	3	-1.3
1929	Bro-N	143	569	88	173	31	4	3	58	42	29	.304	.359	.388	.748	90	-12	-7	94	83	79	.699	7			9	*3	1.1
1930	Bro-N	150	623	92	183	34	5	3	67	47	33	.294	.345	.379	.724	75	-25	-25	101	91	80	.664	7			10	*3	-1.0
1931	Bro-N	145	552	60	147	25	6	0	46	39	38	.266	.322	.333	.655	75	-18	-19	101	94	62	.573	3			6	*3	-0.2
1932	Cin-N	114	420	35	90	18	2	1	40	20	23	.214	.252	.274	.526	43	-35	-33	96	129	30	.418	2			-9	*3	-3.1
Total	5	591	2317	301	624	112	17	7	214	162	131	.269	.322	.341	.663	71	-104	-98	98	92	261	.585	21			16	3	-4.5
■ BILLY GILBERT	Gilbert, William Oliver b: 6/21/1876, Tullytown, Pa. d: 8/8/27, New York, N.Y. BR/TR, 5'4", 153 lbs. Deb: 4/25/01																											
1901	Mil-A	127	492	77	133	14	7	0	43	31		.270	.314	.327	.641	84	-13	-9	95	89	58	.588	19			-3	*2	-1.5
1902	Bal-A	129	445	74	109	12	3	2	38	45		.245	.314	.299	.613	71	-15	-17	102	92	55	.643	38			-6	*S	-1.0
1903	NY-N	128	413	62	104	9	0	1	40	41		.252	.319	.281	.600	69	-13	-17	106	108	50	.628	37			7	*2	-0.2
1904	NY-N	146	478	57	121	13	3	1	54	46		.253	.319	.299	.618	89	-3	-6	105	138	57	.622	33			7	*2	0.5
1905	NY-N	115	376	45	93	11	3	0	24	41		.247	.321	.293	.614	84	-5	-6	101	77	40	.572	11			13	*2	1.4
1906	NY-N	104	307	44	71	6	1	1	27	42		.231	.324	.267	.591	86	-3	-3	100	116	35	.619	22			19	2	1.7
1908	StL-N	89	276	12	59	7	0	0	10	20		.214	.267	.239	.506	68	-11	-9	94	58	18	.424	6			-3	2	-1.3
1909	StL-N	12	29	4	5	0	0	0	1	4		.172	.333	.172	.506	60	-1	-1	96	73	2	.542	1			-1	2	-0.1
Total	8	850	2816	375	695	72	17	5	237	270		.247	.313	.290	.603	79	-64	-67	101	99	315	.592	167			33	2S	-0.5
■ ROD GILBREATH	Gilbreath, Rodney Joe b: 9/24/52, Laurel, Miss. BR/TR, 6'2", 180 lbs. Deb: 6/17/72																											
1972	Atl-N	18	38	2	9	1	0	0	1	2	10	.237	.293	.263	.556	56	-2	-2	105	41	3	.452	1	1	-0	-0	/23	-0.1
1973	Atl-N	29	74	10	21	2	1	0	2	6	10	.284	.346	.338	.684	80	-1	-2	113	32	9	.607	2	1	0	1	3	-0.1
1974	Atl-N	3	6	2	2	0	0	0	0	2	0	.333	.500	.333	.833	130	1	0	105	0	1	1.000	0	0	0	0	/2	0.1
1975	Atl-N	90	202	24	49	3	1	2	16	24	26	.243	.326	.297	.623	78	-7	-5	95	94	21	.563	5	5	-2	-0	23/S	-0.4
1976	Atl-N	116	383	57	96	11	8	1	32	42	36	.251	.331	.329	.660	79	-5	-11	111	97	43	.591	7	7	-2	2	*2/3S	-0.5
1977	Atl-N	128	407	47	99	15	2	8	43	45	79	.243	.322	.349	.670	71	-11	-18	113	104	44	.587	3	9	-5	-0	*2/3	-1.5
1978	Atl-N	116	326	22	80	13	3	3	31	26	51	.245	.301	.331	.632	68	-10	-15	112	105	32	.547	7	6	-2	1	32	-1.4
Total	7	500	1436	164	356	45	15	14	125	147	212	.248	.322	.329	.651	74	-36	-53	109	95	152	.587	25	29	-10	3	23/S	-3.9
■ DON GILE	Gile, Donald Loren "Bear" b: 4/19/35, Modesto, Cal. BR/TR, 6'6", 220 lbs. Deb: 9/25/59																											
1959	Bos-A	3	10	1	2	1	0	0	1	0	2	.200	.273	.300	.573	54	-1	-1	106	134	1	.444	0	0	0	0	/C	0.0
1960	Bos-A	29	51	6	9	1	1	1	4	1	13	.176	.192	.294	.486	29	-5	-5	103	87	3	.372	0	0	0	-0	C1	-0.5
1961	Bos-A	8	18	2	5	0	0	1	1	1	5	.278	.316	.444	.760	99	-0	-0	102	36	3	.692	0	0	0	0	/1C	0.0
1962	Bos-A	18	41	3	2	0	0	1	3	3	15	.049	.133	.122	.255	-30	-8	-8	102	149	0	.214	0	0	0	0	1	-0.8
Total	4	58	120	12	18	2	1	3	9	5	35	.150	.197	.258	.455	21	-14	-14	103	105	6	.362	0	0	0	-0	/1C	-1.3
■ BRIAN GILES	Giles, Brian Jeffrey b: 4/27/60, Manhattan, Kan. BR/TR, 6'1", 165 lbs. Deb: 9/12/81																											
1981	NY-N	9	7	0	0	0	0	0	0	0	3	.000	.000	.000	.000	-99	-2	-2	101	0	0	.000	0	0	0	-0	/2S	-0.1
1982	NY-N	45	138	14	29	5	0	3	10	12	29	.210	.273	.312	.585	64	-7	-7	99	75	13	.555	6	1	1	-0	2/S	-0.3
1983	NY-N	145	400	39	98	15	0	2	27	36	77	.245	.311	.298	.608	70	-16	-15	99	85	37	.544	17	10	-1	9	*2S	0.0
1985	Mil-A	34	58	6	10	1	0	1	1	7	16	.172	.262	.241	.503	37	-5	-5	105	23	4	.460	2	1	0	0	S2/D	-0.2
1986	Chi-A	9	11	0	3	0	0	0	1	0	2	.273	.273	.273	.545	50	-1	-1	101	133	1	.333	0	0	0	-0	/2S	0.0
Total	5	242	614	59	140	21	0	6	39	55	127	.228	.294	.292	.585	63	-30	-30	99	77	55	.536	25	12	0	9	2/SD	-0.6
■ GEORGE GILHAM	Gilham, George Louis b: 9/17/1899, Shamokin, Pa. d: 4/25/37, Lansdowne, Pa. BR/TR, 5'11", 164 lbs. Deb: 9/24/20																											
1920	StL-N	1	3	0	0	0	0	0	0	0	1	.000	.000	.000	.000	-99	-1	-1	98	0	0	.000	0	0	0	0	/C	0.0
1921	StL-N	1	1	0	0	0	0	0	0	0	0	.000	.000	.000	.000	-99	-0	-0	95	0	0	.000	0	0	0	0	H	0.0
Total	2	2	4	0	0	0	0	0	0	0	1	.000	.000	.000	.000	-99	-1	-1	97	0	0	.000	0	0	0	0	/C	0.0
■ FRANK GILHOOLEY	Gilhooley, Frank Patrick "Flash" b: 6/10/1892, Toledo, Ohio d: 7/11/59, Toledo, Ohio BL/TR, 5'8", 155 lbs. Deb: 9/18/11																											
1911	StL-N	1	0	0	0	0	0	0	0	0	0	—	—	—	—	—	0	0	101	—	—	—	0			-0	/O	0.0
1912	StL-N	13	49	5	11	0	0	0	2	3	8	.224	.269	.224	.494	36	-4	-4	100	62	3	.368	0			-2	O	-0.5
1913	NY-A	24	85	10	29	2	1	0	14	4	9	.341	.378	.388	.766	123	2	2	101	154	14	.786	6			-2	O	0.0
1914	NY-A	1	3	0	2	0	0	0	0	1	0	.667	.750	.667	1.417	327	1	1	100	0	2	3.000	0			-0	/O	0.1
1915	NY-A	1	4	0	0	0	0	0	0	0	1	.000	.000	.000	.000	-99	-1	-1	98	0	0	.000	0			-0	/O	0.0
1916	NY-A	58	223	40	62	5	3	1	10	37	17	.278	.383	.341	.724	116	6	6	101	40	35	.807	16			-1	O	0.2
1917	NY-A	54	165	14	40	6	1	0	8	30	13	.242	.362	.291	.653	93	1	0	107	60	19	.680	6			-4	O	-0.7
1918	NY-A	112	427	59	118	13	5	1	23	53	24	.276	.358	.337	.695	116	6	9	95	55	53	.663	7			-5	*O	-0.1
1919	Bos-A	48	112	14	27	4	0	0	1	12	8	.241	.315	.277	.591	73	-5	-3	91	12	10	.529	2			-6	O	-1.2
Total	9	312	1068	142	289	30	10	2	58	140	80	.271	.357	.323	.680	104	8	10	98	55	136	.675	37			-21	O	-2.2
■ BOB GILKS	Gilks, Robert James b: 7/2/1864, Cincinnati, Ohio d: 8/21/44, Brunswick, Ga. BR/TR, 5'8", 178 lbs. Deb: 8/25/1887																											
1887	Cle-a	22	83	12	26	2	0	0		3		.313	.352	.337	.690	97	-0	-0	98	0	12	.667	5			0	P/1O2	0.0
1888	Cle-a	119	484	59	111	14	4	1	63	7		.229	.245	.281	.526	73	-16	-14	97	144	38	.434	16			2	O3/SP2	-1.4

YEAR	TM/L	G	AB	R	H	2B	3B	HR	RBI	BB	SO	AVG	OBP	SLG	PRO	/A	BR	/A	PF	CHI	RC	TA	SB	CS	SBR	FR	POS	TPR
1889	Cle-N	53	210	17	50	5	2	0	18	7	20	.238	.273	.281	.554	54	-12	-13	103	96	18	.469	6			0	OS1/2	-1.1
1890	Cle-N	130	544	65	116	10	3	0	41	32	38	.213	.265	.243	.507	53	-34	-29	94	83	40	.437	17			2	*O/PS2	-2.5
1893	Bal-N	15	64	10	17	2	0	0	7	0	3	.266	.277	.297	.574	50	-4	-5	107	103	6	.489	3			0	O	-0.3
Total	5	339	1385	163	320	33	9	1	129	49	61	.231	.265	.270	.535	62	-67	-62	97	101	115	.455	47			4	O/3PS12	-5.3
JIM GILL Gill, James C. b: St.Louis, Mo. Deb: 6/27/1889																												
1889	StL-a	2	8	2	2	1	0	0	1	1	2	.250	.333	.375	.708	92	0	-0	112	92	1	.833	1			0	/O2	0.0
JOHNNY GILL Gill, John Wesley "Patcheye" b: 3/27/05, Nashville, Tenn. d: 12/26/84, Nashville, Tenn. BL/TR, 6'2", 190 lbs. Deb: 8/28/27																												
1927	Cle-A	21	60	8	13	3	0	1	4	7	13	.217	.319	.317	.636	67	-3	-3	97	60	6	.617	1	0	0	-2	O	-0.4
1928	Cle-A	2	2	0	0	0	0	0	0	0	1	.000	.000	.000	.000	-95	-1	-1	106	0	0	.000	0	0	0	0	H	0.0
1931	Was-A	8	30	2	8	2	1	0	5	1	6	.267	.313	.400	.712	86	-1	-1	101	146	3	.609	0	1	-1	3	/O	0.1
1934	Was-A	13	53	7	13	3	0	2	7	2	3	.245	.286	.415	.701	78	-2	-2	101	85	6	.625	0	0	0	-1	O	-0.2
1935	Chi-N	3	3	2	1	1	0	0	1	0	1	.333	.333	.667	1.000	163	0	0	99	180	1	1.000	0			0	H	0.0
1936	Chi-N	71	174	20	44	8	0	7	28	13	19	.253	.309	.420	.728	90	-2	-3	105	106	23	.659	0			-4	O	-0.8
Total	6	118	322	39	79	17	1	10	45	23	43	.245	.306	.398	.703	83	-8	-9	102	97	40	.638	1	1		-3	/O	-1.3
WARREN GILL Gill, Warren Darst "Doc" b: 12/21/1878, Ladoga, Ind. d: 11/26/52, Laguna Beach, Cal. BR/TR, 6'1", 175 lbs. Deb: 8/26/08																												
1908	Pit-N	27	76	10	17	0	1	0	14	11		.224	.322	.250	.572	90	-1	-0	95	283	7	.559	3			-2	1	-0.3
SAM GILLEN Gillen, Samuel (born Samuel Gilleland) b: 1870, Pittsburgh, Pa. d: 5/13/05, Pittsburgh, Pa. Deb: 8/19/1893																												
1893	Pit-N	3	6	0	0	0	0	0	0	0	1	.000	.000	.000	.000	-94	-2	-2	106	0	0	.000	0			0	/S	0.0
1897	Phi-N	75	270	32	70	10	3	0	27	35		.259	.353	.319	.671	84	-6	-4	96	94	32	.635	2			-28	S/3	-2.6
Total	2	78	276	32	70	10	3	0	27	35	1	.254	.346	.312	.658	80	-8	-6	96	92	32	.617	2			-28	/S3	-2.6
TOM GILLEN Gillen, Thomas J. b: 5/18/1862, Philadelphia, Pa. d: 1/26/1889, Philadelphia, Pa. 5'8", 160 lbs. Deb: 4/18/1884																												
1884	Phi-U	29	116	5	18	2	0	0		1		.155	.162	.172	.335	14	-10	-9	93	0	3	.214	0			0	C/O	-0.5
1886	Det-N	2	10	2	4	0	0	0	4	0	1	.400	.400	.400	.800	132	0	0	109	281	2	.667	0			0	/C	0.0
Total	2	31	126	7	22	2	0	0	4	1	1	.175	.181	.190	.372	26	-10	-8	94	22	5	.240	0			0	/CO	-0.5
CARDEN GILLENWATER Gillenwater, Carden Edison b: 5/13/18, Riceville, Tenn. BR/TR, 6'1", 175 lbs. Deb: 9/22/40																												
1940	StL-N	7	25	1	4	1	0	0	5	0	2	.160	.160	.200	.360	-1	-3	-3	102	371	1	.238	0			-1	/O	-0.4
1943	Bro-N	8	17	1	3	0	0	0	2	2	3	.176	.263	.176	.440	28	-2	-1	100	241	1	.357	0			-0	/O	-0.1
1945	Bos-N	144	517	74	149	20	2	7	72	73	70	.288	.379	.375	.755	98	10	1	112	119	75	.735	13			19	*O	1.4
1946	Bos-N	99	224	30	51	10	1	1	14	39	27	.228	.342	.295	.637	86	-4	-3	95	76	25	.610	3			-3	O	-0.7
1948	Was-A	77	221	23	54	10	4	3	21	39	36	.244	.358	.367	.724	90	-2	-3	103	79	30	.697	4	2	0	-4	O	-0.8
Total	5	335	1004	129	261	41	7	11	114	153	138	.260	.359	.348	.707	91	-1	-9	106	107	133	.696	20	2		11	O	-0.6
JIM GILLESPIE Gillespie, James b: Buffalo, N.Y. Deb: 10/01/1890																												
1890	Buf-P	1	3	0	0	0	0	0	0	0	2	.000	.000	.000	.000	-99	-1	-1	92	0	0	.000	0			0	/O	0.0
PAUL GILLESPIE Gillespie, Paul Allen b: 9/18/20, Sugar Valley, Ga. d: 8/11/70, Anniston, Ala. BL/TR, 6'3", 195 lbs. Deb: 9/11/42																												
1942	Chi-N	5	16	3	4	0	0	2	4	1	2	.250	.294	.625	.919	172	1	1	96	93	3	.917	0			0	/C	0.1
1944	Chi-N	9	26	2	7	1	0	1	2	3	3	.269	.345	.423	.768	114	1	0	101	51	4	.700	0			-0	/C	0.1
1945	Chi-N	75	163	12	47	6	0	3	25	18	9	.288	.366	.380	.746	109	2	2	99	122	24	.718	2			-5	C/O	-0.1
Total	3	89	205	17	58	7	0	6	31	22	14	.283	.358	.405	.763	114	4	4	99	111	31	.736	2			-5	/CO	0.1
PETE GILLESPIE Gillespie, Peter Patrick b: 11/30/1851, Carbondale, Pa. d: 5/5/10, Carbondale, Pa. BL/TR, 6'1.5", 178 lbs. Deb: 5/01/1880																												
1880	Tro-N	82	346	50	84	20	5	2	24	17	35	.243	.278	.347	.625	100	4	-1	110	61	34	.523				6	*O	0.2
1881	Tro-N	84	348	43	96	14	3	0	41	9	24	.276	.294	.333	.627	96	-2	-2	100	130	35	.496				3	*O	0.0
1882	Tro-N	74	298	46	82	5	4	2	33	9	14	.275	.296	.339	.635	108	1	3	95	110	31	.509				-7	*O	-0.4
1883	NY-N	98	411	64	129	23	12	1	62	9	27	.314	.329	.436	.764	130	14	14	100	114	60	.667				6	*O	1.9
1884	NY-N	101	413	75	109	7	4	2	44	19	35	.264	.296	.315	.611	94	-4	-2	98	118	39	.490				-3	*O	-0.5
1885	NY-N	102	420	67	123	17	6	0	52	15	32	.293	.317	.362	.679	109	8	3	109	126	49	.562				-4	*O	-0.3
1886	NY-N	97	396	65	108	13	8	0	58	16	30	.273	.301	.346	.647	109	-2	5	89	133	48	.590	17			-13	*O	-0.6
1887	NY-N	76	295	40	78	9	3	3	37	12	21	.264	.304	.346	.650	76	-7	-11	107	105	43	.719	37			-2	O/3	-1.0
Total	8	714	2927	450	809	108	45	10	351	106	218	.276	.303	.354	.657	103	12	9	101	113	340	.568	54			-15	O/3	-0.7
JIM GILLIAM Gilliam, James William "Junior" b: 10/17/28, Nashville, Tenn. d: 10/8/78, Inglewood, Cal. BB/TR, 5'10.5", 175 lbs. Deb: 4/14/53 C																												
1953	Bro-N	151	605	125	168	31	**17**	6	63	100	38	.278	.383	.415	.798	104	10	7	104	81	104	.819	21	14	-2	5	*2	1.5
1954	Bro-N	146	607	107	171	28	8	13	52	76	30	.282	.364	.418	.782	102	4	3	101	60	95	.751	8	7	-2	-9	*2/O	0.0
1955	Bro-N	147	538	110	134	20	8	7	40	70	37	.249	.342	.355	.697	82	-10	-13	104	81	67	.660	15	15	-5	0	2O	-0.9
1956	Bro-N	153	594	102	178	23	8	6	43	95	39	.300	.400	.396	.795	112	17	15	103	62	103	.826	21	9	1	13	*2O	3.5
1957	Bro-N	149	617	89	154	26	4	2	37	64	31	.250	.324	.314	.639	62	-22	-35	116	66	69	.603	26	10	2	5	*2/O	-1.6
1958	LA-N	147	555	81	145	25	5	2	43	78	22	.261	.352	.335	.687	80	-11	-14	105	89	71	.662	18	11	-1	10	O32	-0.5
1959	LA-N	145	553	91	156	18	4	3	34	**96**	25	.282	.388	.345	.734	96	3	1	102	66	84	.756	23	10	1	11	*3/2O	0.9
1960	LA-N	151	557	96	138	20	2	5	40	96	28	.248	.361	.318	.679	76	-5	-17	115	81	72	.664	12	9	-2	13	*32	-0.5
1961	LA-N	144	439	74	107	26	3	4	32	79	34	.244	.359	.344	.703	86	-5	-7	102	79	60	.694	8	4	0	2	32O	0.0
1962	LA-N	160	588	83	159	24	1	4	43	93	35	.270	.372	.335	.707	99	-3	3	93	86	81	.693	17	7	1	1	*23/O	1.7
1963	LA-N	148	525	77	148	27	4	6	49	60	28	.282	.358	.383	.741	119	10	14	95	100	76	.718	19	5	3	-2	*23	2.3
1964	LA-N	116	334	44	76	8	3	2	27	42	21	.228	.319	.287	.607	79	-11	-8	92	109	32	.539	4	4	-1	-11	32/O	-2.3
1965	LA-N	111	372	54	104	19	4	4	39	53	31	.280	.375	.384	.760	125	9	13	91	106	58	.763	9	5	-0	1	3O/2	1.0
1966	LA-N	88	235	30	51	9	0	1	16	34	17	.217	.316	.268	.584	66	-10	-9	97	102	21	.521	2	1	0	-1	3/12	-1.1
Total	14	1956	7119	1163	1889	304	71	65	558	1036	416	.265	.361	.355	.717	92	-25	-48	102	81	992	.711	203	111	-6	35	*23O/1	4.0
BARNEY GILLIGAN Gilligan, Andrew Bernard b: 1/3/1856, Cambridge, Mass. d: 4/1/34, Lynn, Mass. BR/TR, 5'6.5", 130 lbs. Deb: 9/25/1875																												
1875	Atl-n	2	8	2	2							.250															/CO	
1879	Cle-N	52	205	20	35	6	2	0	11	0	13	.171	.171	.220	.390	28	-15	-15	99	87	8	.265				-3	CO/S	-1.7
1880	Cle-N	30	99	9	17	4	3	1	13	6	12	.172	.219	.303	.522	76	-2	-2	99	144	7	.439				0	C/OS	0.0
1881	Pro-N	46	183	19	40	7	2	0	20	9	24	.219	.255	.279	.534	73	-7	-5	93	144	13	.420				-1	CS/O	-0.4
1882	Pro-N	56	201	32	45	7	6	0	26	4	26	.224	.239	.318	.557	73	-5	-7	106	137	16	.436				6	C/S	0.3
1883	Pro-N	74	263	34	52	13	3	0	24	26	32	.198	.270	.270	.540	64	-10	-11	101	120	20	.460				9	*C	0.2
1884	Pro-N	82	294	47	72	13	2	1	38	35	41	.245	.325	.313	.638	100	2	1	102	140	31	.572				9	*C/31	1.4
1885	Pro-N	71	252	23	54	7	3	0	12	23	33	.214	.280	.266	.546	85	-6	-2	91	63	19	.455				-3	C/SO2	0.0
1886	Was-N	81	273	23	52	9	2	0	17	39	35	.190	.292	.238	.530	67	-11	-8	94	90	21	.498	6			1	CO/S3	-0.1
1887	Was-N	28	90	7	18	2	0	1	6	5	18	.200	.242	.256	.498	42	-7	-6	95	71	6	.417	2			0	C/SO	-0.5
1888	Det-N	1	5	1	1	0	0	0	0	0	1	.200	.200	.200	.400	30	-0	-0	98	0	0	.250	0			0	/C	0.0
Total	10	521	1865	215	386	68	23	3	167	147	235	.207	.265	.273	.538	71	-62	-56	98	110	141	.449	8			18	C/OS321	-0.8
GRANT GILLIS Gillis, Grant b: 1/24/01, Grove Hill, Ala. d: 2/4/81, Thomasville, Ala. BR/TR, 5'10", 165 lbs. Deb: 9/19/27																												
1927	Was-A	10	36	8	8	3	1	0	2	2	0	.222	.263	.361	.624	63	-2	-2	97	51	3	.536	0	0	0	-1	S	-0.1
1928	Was-A	24	87	13	22	5	1	0	10	4	5	.253	.309	.333	.642	68	-4	-4	102	121	9	.545	0	1	-1	1	S/23	-0.1
1929	Bos-A	28	73	5	18	4	0	0	11	6	8	.247	.304	.301	.605	55	-5	-5	102	171	7	.500	0	1	-1	-2	2	-0.6
Total	3	62	196	26	48	12	2	0	23	12	13	.245	.299	.327	.625	62	-11	-11	101	127	19	.527	0	2	-1	-2	/2S3	-0.8
JIM GILMAN Gilman, James Deb: 7/10/1893																												
1893	Cle-N	2	7	1	2	0	0	0	1	0	2	.286	.286	.286	.571	51	-0	-1	104	137	1	.400	0			0	/3	0.0
PIT GILMAN Gilman, Pitkin Clark b: 3/14/1864, Laporte, Ohio d: 8/17/50, Elyria, Ohio BL/TL, Deb: 9/18/1884																												
1884	Cle-N	2	10	0	1	0	0	0	0	0	3	.100	.100	.100	.200	-36	-2	-2	102	0	0	.111				0	/O	0.0

YEAR	TM/L	G	AB	R	H	2B	3B	HR	RBI	BB	SO	AVG	OBP	SLG	PRO	/A	BR	/A	PF	CHI	RC	TA	SB	CS	SBR	FR	POS	TPR
■ **GROVER GILMORE** Gilmore, Ernest Grover b: 11/1/1888, Chicago, Ill. d: 11/25/19, Sioux City, Iowa BL/TL, 5'9.5", 170 lbs. Deb: 4/18/14																												
1914	KC-F	139	530	91	152	25	5	1	32	37	108	.287	.333	.358	.692	103	-1	2	95	58	75	.661	23			1	*O	-0.4
1915	KC-F	119	411	53	117	22	15	1	47	26	50	.285	.327	.418	.746	124	9	10	97	99	66	.738	19			2	*O	0.7
Total	2	258	941	144	269	47	20	2	79	63	158	.286	.331	.385	.715	112	7	12	96	75	141	.695	42			3	O	0.3
■ **JIM GILMORE** Gilmore, James b: 5/1853, Baltimore, Md. d: 11/18/28, Baltimore, Md. Deb: 4/26/1875																												
1875	Nat-n	4	15	4	5							.333															/C23	
■ **GILROY** Gilroy Deb:9/07/1874																												
1874	Chi-n	8	39	4	8							.205															/C	
1875	Ath-n	2	8	0	2							.250															/CO	
Total	2 n	10	47	4	10							.213															/CO	
■ **TINSLEY GINN** Ginn, Tinsley Rucker b: 9/26/1891, Royston, Ga. d: 8/30/31, Atlanta, Ga. BL/TR, 5'9", 180 lbs. Deb: 6/27/14																												
1914	Cle-A	2	1	0	0	0	0	0	0	0	0	.000	.000	.000	.000	-98	-0	-0	102	0	0	.000	0			-1	/O	0.0
■ **JOE GINSBERG** Ginsberg, Myron Nathan b: 10/11/26, New York, N.Y. BL/TR, 5'11", 180 lbs. Deb: 9/15/48																												
1948	Det-A	11	36	7	13	0	0	0	1	3	1	.361	.410	.361	.771	110	0	1	96	26	5	.667	0	0	0	-1	C	0.0
1950	Det-A	36	95	12	22	6	0	0	12	11	6	.232	.318	.295	.612	60	-6	-5	97	148	10	.547	1	0	0	-4	C	-0.6
1951	Det-A	102	304	44	79	10	2	8	37	43	21	.260	.355	.385	.740	95	0	-2	106	94	43	.689	0	2	-1	-7	C	-0.2
1952	Det-A	113	307	29	68	13	2	6	36	51	21	.221	.338	.336	.673	89	-4	-4	99	111	37	.635	1	1	-0	-2	*C	0.0
1953	Det-A	18	53	6	16	2	0	0	3	10	1	.302	.422	.340	.761	110	1	1	98	62	9	.784	0	0	0	1	C	0.3
	Cle-A	46	109	10	31	4	0	0	10	14	4	.284	.371	.321	.692	93	-1	-0	95	106	14	.610	0	0	0	-5	C	-0.3
	Yr	64	162	16	47	6	0	0	13	24	5	.290	.388	.327	.715	99	0	1	96	94	23	.664	0	0	0	-4		0.0
1954	Cle-A	3	2	0	1	0	1	0	1	0	0	.500	.667	1.500	2.167	453	1	1	106	126	2	4.000	0	0	0	0	/C	0.1
1956	KC-A	71	195	15	48	8	1	1	12	23	17	.246	.326	.313	.639	69	-8	-9	101	70	19	.548	1	1	-0	7	C	0.0
	Bal-A	15	28	0	2	0	0	0	2	2	4	.071	.133	.071	.205	-47	-6	-6	94	374	0	.143	0	0	0	0	/C	-0.4
	Yr	86	223	15	50	8	1	1	14	25	21	.224	.302	.283	.585	55	-14	-14	100	124	21	.506	1	1	-0	7		-0.4
1957	Bal-A	85	175	15	48	8	2	1	18	18	19	.274	.349	.360	.709	101	-1	0	93	108	23	.644	2	1	0	-6	C	-0.2
1958	Bal-A	61	109	4	23	1	0	3	16	13	14	.211	.306	.303	.609	73	-5	-4	94	153	11	.558	0	0	0	0	C	-0.2
1959	Bal-A	65	166	14	30	2	0	1	14	21	13	.181	.273	.211	.484	36	-14	-14	97	145	10	.401	1	0	0	-2	C	-1.2
1960	Bal-A	14	30	3	8	1	0	0	6	6	1	.267	.389	.300	.689	87	-0	-0	102	261	4	.652	0	0	0	-1	C	0.0
	Chi-A	28	75	8	19	4	0	0	9	10	8	.253	.349	.307	.656	78	-2	-2	101	153	9	.614	1	0	0	2	C	0.1
	Yr	42	105	11	27	5	0	0	15	16	9	.257	.361	.305	.665	81	-2	-2	101	195	13	.633	1	0	0	1		0.1
1961	Chi-A	6	3	0	0	0	0	0	0	1	2	.000	.250	.000	.250	-27	-1	-1	99	0	0	.333	0	0	0	0	/C	0.0
	Bos-A	19	24	1	6	0	0	0	5	0	2	.250	.250	.250	.500	34	-2	-2	102	326	1	.316	0	0	0	0	/C	-0.1
	Yr	25	27	1	6	0	0	0	5	1	4	.222	.250	.222	.472	27	-3	-3	101	248	1	.318	0	0	0	0		-0.1
1962	NY-N	2	5	0	0	0	0	0	0	0	1	.000	.000	.000	.000	-96	-1	-1	104	0	0	.000	0	0	0	0	/C	-0.1
Total	13	695	1716	168	414	59	8	20	182	226	135	.241	.334	.320	.654	79	-48	-46	99	118	198	.609	7	5	-1	-17	C	-2.8
■ **AL GIONFRIDDO** Gionfriddo, Albert Francis b: 3/8/22, Dysart, Pa. BL/TL, 5'6", 165 lbs. Deb: 9/23/44																												
1944	Pit-N	4	6	0	1	0	0	0	0	1	1	.167	.286	.167	.452	28	-1	-1	105	0	0	.400	0			0	/O	0.0
1945	Pit-N	122	409	74	116	18	9	2	42	60	22	.284	.377	.386	.763	109	8	7	103	91	64	.778	12			-1	*O	0.1
1946	Pit-N	64	102	11	26	2	2	0	10	14	5	.255	.345	.314	.659	85	-1	-2	103	117	12	.610	1			-5	O	-0.7
1947	Pit-N	1	1	0	0	0	0	0	0	0	0	.000	.000	.000	.000	-99	-0	-0	101	0	0	.000	0			0	H	0.0
	Bro-N	37	62	10	11	2	1	0	6	16	11	.177	.346	.242	.588	56	-3	-4	105	148	7	.635	2			-2	O	-0.5
	Yr	38	63	10	11	2	1	0	6	16	11	.175	.342	.238	.580	54	-3	-4	105	144	7	.623	2			-2		-0.5
Total	4	228	580	95	154	22	12	2	58	91	39	.266	.366	.355	.721	97	3	1	104	101	83	.733	15			-8	O	-1.1
■ **TOMMY GIORDANO** Giordano, Thomas Arthur "T-Bone" b: 10/9/25, Newark, N.J. BR/TR, 6', 175 lbs. Deb: 9/11/53																												
1953	Phi-A	11	40	6	7	2	0	2	5	5	6	.175	.267	.375	.642	70	-2	-2	102	90	4	.588	0	1	-1	-1	2	-0.2
■ **TONY GIULIANI** Giuliani, Angelo John b: 11/24/12, St.Paul, Minn. BR/TR, 5'11", 175 lbs. Deb: 4/18/36																												
1936	StL-A	71	198	17	43	3	0	0	13	11	13	.217	.258	.232	.491	21	-24	-25	103	91	12	.368	0	0	0	3	C	-1.4
1937	StL-A	19	53	6	16	1	0	0	3	3	3	.302	.339	.321	.660	68	-3	-2	99	60	6	.541	0	0	0	1	C	0.0
1938	Was-A	46	115	10	25	4	0	0	15	8	3	.217	.268	.252	.520	33	-12	-11	95	175	8	.422	1	0	0	-1	C	-0.9
1939	Was-A	54	172	20	43	6	2	0	18	4	7	.250	.267	.308	.575	52	-14	-12	90	115	13	.419	0	1	-1	1	C	-0.7
1940	Bro-N	1	1	0	0	0	0	0	0	0	0	.000	.000	.000	.000	-93	-0	-0	108	0	0	.000	0			0	/C	0.0
1941	Bro-N	3	2	0	0	0	0	0	0	0	0	.000	.000	.000	.000	-97	-1	-1	103	0	0	.000	0			0	/C	0.0
1943	Was-A	49	133	5	30	4	1	0	20	12	14	.226	.290	.271	.560	62	-6	-7	104	203	11	.453	0	1	-1	-2	C	-0.6
Total	7	243	674	58	157	18	3	0	69	38	40	.233	.274	.269	.542	41	-60	-58	98	131	50	.422	1	2		2	C	-3.6
■ **JIM GLADD** Gladd, James Walter b: 10/2/22, Ft.Gibson, Okla. d: 11/8/77, Long Beach, Cal. BR/TR, 6'2", 190 lbs. Deb: 9/09/46																												
1946	NY-N	4	11	0	1	0	0	0	0	1	4	.091	.167	.091	.258	-26	-2	-2	102	0	0	.200	0			0	/C	-0.1
■ **DAN GLADDEN** Gladden, Clinton Daniel b: 7/7/57, San Jose, Cal. BB/TR, 5'11", 180 lbs. Deb: 9/05/83																												
1983	SF-N	18	63	6	14	2	0	1	9	5	11	.222	.279	.302	.581	60	-3	-3	101	165	4	.509	4	3	-1	3	O	0.0
1984	SF-N	86	342	71	120	17	2	4	31	33	37	.351	.411	.447	.859	147	20	21	96	71	64	.909	31	16	-0	5	O	2.3
1985	SF-N	142	502	64	122	15	8	7	41	40	78	.243	.308	.347	.654	89	-12	-8	93	85	54	.625	32	15	1	5	*O	-0.5
1986	SF-N	102	351	55	97	16	1	4	29	39	59	.276	.357	.362	.719	103	1	2	96	85	49	.736	27	10	2	8	O	1.1
1987	Min-A	121	438	69	109	21	2	8	38	38	72	.249	.313	.361	.674	82	-13	-10	96	85	50	.647	25	9	2	5	*O/D	-0.5
1988	Min-A	141	576	91	155	32	6	11	62	46	74	.269	.327	.403	.730	97	2	-2	106	82	78	.708	28	8	4	13	*O/23P	1.2
Total	6	610	2272	356	617	103	19	35	210	201	331	.272	.336	.380	.716	100	-6	-0	98	84	299	.714	147	61	8	39	O/DP32	3.6
■ **BUCK GLADMAN** Gladman, John H. b: 1864, Washington, D.C. Deb: 7/07/1883																												
1883	Phi-N	1	4	1	0	0	0	0	0	0	2	.000	.000	.000	.000	-99	-1	-1	90	0	0	.000				0	/3	0.0
1884	Was-a	56	224	17	35	5	3	1		3		.156	.178	.219	.397	35	-16	-12	88	0	9	.291				-7	3/OS	-1.6
1886	Was-N	44	152	17	21	5	3	1	15	12	30	.138	.201	.230	.431	33	-13	-11	94	131	8	.397	5			-5	3	-1.2
Total	3	101	380	35	56	10	6	2	15	15	32	.147	.186	.221	.407	32	-30	-24	91	54	17	.330	5			-12	/3OS	-2.8
■ **ROLAND GLADU** Gladu, Roland Edouard b: 5/10/13, Montreal, Que., Can BL/TR, 5'8.5", 185 lbs. Deb: 4/18/44																												
1944	Bos-N	21	66	5	16	2	1	1	7	3	8	.242	.275	.348	.624	79	-2	-2	95	97	6	.500	0			-1	3/O	-0.2
■ **JACK GLASSCOCK** Glasscock, John Wesley "Pebbly Jack" b: 7/22/1859, Wheeling, W.Va. d: 2/24/47, Wheeling, W.Va. BR/TR, 5'8", 160 lbs. Deb: 5/01/1879 M																												
1879	Cle-N	80	325	31	68	9	3	0	29	6	24	.209	.224	.255	.479	58	-14	-14	99	130	19	.346				1	*23	-0.5
1880	Cle-N	77	296	37	72	13	3	0	27	2	21	.243	.248	.307	.556	88	-4	-4	99	111	23	.415				7	*S	0.7
1881	Cle-N	85	335	49	86	9	5	0	33	15	8	.257	.289	.313	.602	93	-4	-2	96	111	31	.482				8	*S/2	1.1
1882	Cle-N	84	358	66	104	27	9	4	46	13	9	.291	.315	.450	.765	158	16	22	90	79	52	.685				**20**	*S/3	**4.4**
1883	Cle-N	96	383	67	110	19	6	0	46	13	23	.287	.311	.368	.679	101	2	-0	105	109	45	.564				16	*S/2	1.7
1884	Cle-N	72	281	45	70	4	4	1	22	25	16	.249	.310	.302	.613	92	-1	-2	102	83	27	.521				27	S/2P	2.8
	Cin-U	38	172	48	72	9	5	2		8		.419	.444	.564	1.008	221	24	22	108	0	44	1.050	0			0	S/2	2.0
1885	StL-N	111	446	66	125	18	3	1	40	29	10	.280	.324	.341	.665	125	8	13	92	79	51	.564				12	*S/2	2.8
1886	StL-N	121	486	96	158	29	7	3	40	38	13	.325	.374	.432	.806	153	26	30	95	51	95	.872	38			21	*S/O	4.3
1887	Ind-N	122	483	91	142	18	7	0	40	41	8	.294	.361	.360	.722	108	4	7	96	63	87	.842	62			**35**	*S/P	3.1
1888	Ind-N	113	442	63	119	17	3	1	45	14	17	.269	.302	.328	.630	108	1	4	95	115	60	.663	48			9	*S/2P	1.6
1889	Ind-N	134	582	128	**205**	40	3	7	85	31	10	.352	.390	.467	.857	130	30	22	109	76	132	.968	57			**31**	*S/2PM	**4.9**
1890	NY-N	124	512	91	**172**	32	9	1	66	41	8	**.336**	.395	.439	.834	153	29	33	95	77	113	.968	54			15	*S	**4.0**
1891	NY-N	97	369	46	89	12	6	0	55	36	11	.241	.317	.306	.623	89	-7	-3	94	150	46	.654	29			-10	*S	-0.7
1892	StL-N	139	566	83	151	27	5	3	72	44	19	.267	.327	.348	.675	112	4	8	95	103	75	.660	26			1	*SM	1.5
1893	StL-N	48	195	32	56	8	1	1	26	25	3	.287	.382	.354	.736	99	1	1	99	95	35	.856	20			-6	S	-0.2

YEAR	TM/L	G	AB	R	H	2B	3B	HR	RBI	BB	SO	AVG	OBP	SLG	PRO	/A	BR	/A	PF	CHI	RC	TA	SB	CS	SBR	FR	POS	TPR
	Pit-N	66	293	49	100	7	11	1	74	17	4	.341	.385	.451	.836	116	9	6	106	144	58	.876	16			11	S	1.6
	Yr	114	488	81	156	15	12	2	100	42	7	.320	.384	.412	.796	110	10	7	103	124	93	.867	36			5		1.4
1894	Pit-N	86	332	46	93	10	7	1	63	31	4	.280	.349	.361	.710	77	-14	-10	94	150	49	.724	18			3	S	-0.2
1895	Lou-N	18	74	9	25	3	1	1	6	3	1	.338	.387	.446	.833	123	2	2	95	45	14	.816	1			0	S/1	0.2
	Was-N	25	100	20	23	2	0	0	10	7	3	.230	.300	.250	.550	43	-8	-9	103	118	9	.494	3			0	S	-0.6
	Yr	43	174	29	48	5	1	1	16	10	4	.276	.337	.333	.670	75	-6	-6	100	89	21	.619	4			0		-0.4
Total	17	1736	7030	1163	2040	313	98	27	825	439	212	.290	.337	.374	.712	114	103	125	98	95	1064	.702	372			200	*S/231PO	34.5

■ TOMMY GLAVIANO Glaviano, Thomas Giatano "Rabbit" b: 10/26/23, Sacramento, Cal. BR/TR, 5'9", 175 lbs. Deb: 4/19/49

YEAR	TM/L	G	AB	R	H	2B	3B	HR	RBI	BB	SO	AVG	OBP	SLG	PRO	/A	BR	/A	PF	CHI	RC	TA	SB	CS	SBR	FR	POS	TPR
1949	StL-N	87	258	32	69	16	1	6	36	41	35	.267	.380	.407	.787	101	5	2	110	110	42	.776	0			6	3/2	0.8
1950	StL-N	115	410	92	117	29	2	11	44	90	74	.285	.421	.446	.867	125	21	19	103	76	85	.953	6			7	*3/2S	2.5
1951	StL-N	54	104	20	19	4	0	1	4	26	18	.183	.356	.250	.606	65	-4	-4	101	53	12	.640	3	0	1	-1	O/2	-0.3
1952	StL-N	80	162	30	39	5	1	3	19	27	26	.241	.366	.340	.705	99	0	1	98	116	21	.669	0	0	0	4	3/2	0.6
1953	Phi-N	53	74	17	15	1	2	3	5	24	20	.203	.410	.392	.802	112	2	3	99	51	14	.905	2	0	1	-0	32/S	0.3
Total	5	389	1008	191	259	55	6	24	108	208	173	.257	.395	.395	.789	108	26	21	103	86	174	.847	11	0		15	3/2OS	3.9

■ HARRY GLEASON Gleason, Harry Gilbert b: 3/28/1875, Camden, N.J. d: 10/21/61, Camden, N.J. TR, 5'6", 160 lbs. Deb: 9/27/01

YEAR	TM/L	G	AB	R	H	2B	3B	HR	RBI	BB	SO	AVG	OBP	SLG	PRO	/A	BR	/A	PF	CHI	RC	TA	SB	CS	SBR	FR	POS	TPR
1901	Bos-A	1	1	0	1	0	0	0	0	0		1.000	1.000	1.000	2.000	476	0	0	97	0	2	—	1			0	/3	0.0
1902	Bos-A	71	240	30	54	5	5	2	25	10		.225	.256	.313	.569	59	-14	-14	99	102	21	.489	6			3	3O/2	-1.2
1903	Bos-A	6	13	3	2	1	0	0	2	0		.154	.154	.231	.385	13	-1	-1	112	240	0	.273	0			0	/3	-0.1
1904	StL-A	46	155	10	33	7	1	0	6	4		.213	.233	.271	.504	64	-7	-6	95	53	10	.385	1			-3	S3/2O	-0.8
1905	StL-A	150	535	45	116	11	5	1	57	34		.217	.264	.262	.525	75	-19	-13	91	145	44	.470	23			-16	*3/2	-2.6
Total	5	274	944	88	206	24	11	3	90	48		.218	.256	.276	.533	68	-40	-34	94	121	78	.461	31			-16	3/OS2	-4.7

■ JACK GLEASON Gleason, John Day b: 7/14/1854, St.Louis, Mo. d: 9/4/44, St.Louis, Mo. BR/TR, 170 lbs. Deb: 10/02/1877

YEAR	TM/L	G	AB	R	H	2B	3B	HR	RBI	BB	SO	AVG	OBP	SLG	PRO	/A	BR	/A	PF	CHI	RC	TA	SB	CS	SBR	FR	POS	TPR
1877	StL-N	1	4	0	1	0	0	0	0	0	1	.250	.250	.250	.500	57	-0	-0	102	0	0	.333				0	/O	0.0
1882	StL-a	78	331	53	84	10	1	2		27		.254	.310	.308	.618	109	4	4	100	0	32	.522				3	*3/O2	0.4
1883	StL-a	9	34	2	8	0	0	0		4		.235	.316	.235	.551	74	-1	-1	108	0	3	.462				1	/O3	0.0
	Lou-a	84	355	69	105	11	4	2		25		.296	.342	.366	.708	136	12	15	94	0	46	.620				-33	*3/S	-1.4
	Yr	93	389	71	113	11	4	2		29		.290	.340	.355	.694	130	11	14	95	0	48	.605				-32		-1.4
1884	StL-U	92	395	90	128	30	2	3		23		.324	.361	.433	.794	162	27	25	104	0	63	.727	0			-9	*3	1.5
1885	StL-N	2	7	0	1	0	0	0	0	0	1	.143	.143	.143	.286	-8	-1	-1	92	0	0	.167				0	/3	0.0
1886	Phi-a	77	299	39	56	8	7	1		16		.187	.255	.271	.526	66	-11	-11	100	0	23	.477	8			-7	3	-1.2
Total	6	343	1425	253	383	59	14	8	0	95	2	.269	.319	.347	.666	119	30	31	100	0	168	.583	8			-45	3/OS2	-0.7

■ ROY GLEASON Gleason, Roy William b: 4/9/43, Melrose Park, Ill. BB/TR, 6'5.5", 220 lbs. Deb: 9/03/63

YEAR	TM/L	G	AB	R	H	2B	3B	HR	RBI	BB	SO	AVG	OBP	SLG	PRO	/A	BR	/A	PF	CHI	RC	TA	SB	CS	SBR	FR	POS	TPR
1963	LA-N	8	1	3	1	1	0	0	0	0	0	1.000	1.000	2.000	3.000	780	1	1	95	0	2	—	0	0	0	0	H	0.1

■ BILL GLEASON Gleason, William G. "Will" b: 11/12/1858, St.Louis, Mo. d: 7/21/32, St.Louis, Mo. BR/TR, 170 lbs. Deb: 5/02/1882

YEAR	TM/L	G	AB	R	H	2B	3B	HR	RBI	BB	SO	AVG	OBP	SLG	PRO	/A	BR	/A	PF	CHI	RC	TA	SB	CS	SBR	FR	POS	TPR
1882	StL-a	79	347	63	100	11	6	1		6		.288	.300	.363	.663	123	7	8	100	0	39	.534				11	*S	1.9
1883	StL-a	98	425	81	122	21	9	2		16		.287	.313	.393	.706	116	12	6	108	0	54	.604				-3	*S	0.0
1884	StL-a	110	472	97	127	21	7	1		28		.269	.326	.350	.676	112	13	6	110	0	55	.594				-17	*S/3	-1.2
1885	StL-a	112	472	79	119	9	5	3		29		.252	.316	.311	.627	109	2	7	93	0	48	.541				-43	*S	-3.1
1886	StL-a	125	524	97	141	18	5	0		43		.269	.333	.323	.655	97	6	-4	111	0	64	.621	19			-29	*S	-2.3
1887	StL-a	135	598	135	172	19	1	0		41		.288	.342	.323	.664	80	-8	-19	110	0	76	.622	23			-9	*S	-2.3
1888	Phi-a	123	499	55	112	10	2	0	61	12		.224	.256	.253	.508	65	-19	-19	101	**153**	40	.450	27			-17	*S/31	-2.8
1889	Lou-a	16	58	6	14	2	0	0	5	4	1	.241	.302	.276	.577	70	-2	-2	96	91	5	.500	1			0	S	-0.1
Total	8	798	3395	613	907	111	35	7	66	179	1	.267	.314	.327	.641	97	11	-17	105	24	380	.567	70			-107	S/31	-9.9

■ KID GLEASON Gleason, William J. b: 10/26/1866, Camden, N.J. d: 1/2/33, Philadelphia, Pa. BB/TR, 5'7", 158 lbs. Deb: 1888 MC

YEAR	TM/L	G	AB	R	H	2B	3B	HR	RBI	BB	SO	AVG	OBP	SLG	PRO	/A	BR	/A	PF	CHI	RC	TA	SB	CS	SBR	FR	POS	TPR
1888	Phi-N	24	83	4	17	2	0	0	5	3	16	.205	.233	.229	.461	43	-5	-6	114	94	5	.379	3			0	P/O	0.0
1889	Phi-N	30	99	11	25	5	0	0	8	8	12	.253	.308	.303	.611	70	-4	-4	104	80	11	.568	4			0	P/O2	0.0
1890	Phi-N	63	224	22	47	3	0	0	17	12	21	.210	.250	.223	.473	37	-17	-19	108	103	15	.407	10			0	P/2	0.0
1891	Phi-N	65	214	31	53	5	2	0	17	20	17	.248	.318	.290	.608	83	-5	-3	95	80	22	.559	6			-2	P/OS	0.0
1892	StL-N	66	233	35	50	4	2	3	25	34	23	.215	.315	.288	.602	88	-4	-2	95	103	24	.590	7			5	PO/21	0.0
1893	StL-N	59	199	25	51	6	4	0	20	19	8	.256	.327	.327	.654	76	-7	-6	99	84	22	.595	2			3	PO/S	0.0
1894	StL-N	9	28	3	7	0	1	0	1	2	1	.250	.300	.321	.621	51	-2	-2	101	31	3	.524	0			0	/P1	0.0
	Bal-N	26	86	22	30	5	1	0	17	7	2	.349	.398	.430	.828	102	0	0	99	127	15	.804	1			0	P/1	0.0
	Yr	35	114	25	37	5	2	0	18	9	3	.325	.374	.404	.777	89	-2	-2	100	103	18	.727	1			0		0.0
1895	Bal-N	112	421	90	130	14	12	0	74	33	18	.309	.366	.399	.765	93	-0	-6	107	126	70	.773	19			-15	23/PO	-1.2
1896	NY-N	133	541	79	162	17	5	4	89	42	13	.299	.352	.372	.724	94	-5	-4	99	128	89	.768	46			2	*2/3O	0.1
1897	NY-N	131	540	85	172	16	4	1	106	26		.319	.353	.369	.722	94	-5	-4	98	**163**	88	.736	43			-2	*2/S	0.4
1898	NY-N	150	570	78	126	8	5	0	62	39		.221	.278	.253	.531	57	-32	-28	95	138	47	.473	21			20	*2/S	-0.1
1899	NY-N	146	576	72	152	14	4	0	59	24		.264	.293	.302	.595	67	-27	-25	97	110	61	.535	29			24	*2	0.7
1900	NY-N	111	420	60	104	11	3	1	29	17		.248	.277	.295	.572	61	-23	-21	97	76	42	.519	23			12	*2/S	-0.2
1901	Det-A	135	547	82	150	16	12	3	75	41		.274	.325	.364	.689	84	-5	-14	110	100	77	.685	32			6	*2	-1.1
1902	Det-A	118	441	42	109	11	4	1	38	25		.247	.288	.297	.585	64	-21	-20	99	99	44	.521	17			2	*2	-1.2
1903	Phi-N	106	412	65	117	19	6	1	49	23		.284	.322	.367	.688	106	-2	2	92	108	54	.631	12			-6	*2/O	0.2
1904	Phi-N	153	587	61	161	23	6	0	42	37		.274	.317	.334	.651	111	2	7	93	75	69	.587	17			1	*2/3	1.2
1905	Phi-N	155	608	95	150	17	7	1	50	45		.247	.299	.303	.601	78	-14	-17	104	89	61	.535	16			-8	*2	-1.5
1906	Phi-N	135	494	47	112	17	2	0	34	36		.227	.279	.269	.548	79	-15	-11	92	99	43	.487	17			-31	*2	-4.6
1907	Phi-N	36	126	11	18	3	0	0	6	7		.143	.188	.167	.355	12	-12	-13	104	110	5	.287	3			0	2/1SO	-1.4
1908	Phi-N	2	1	0	0	0	0	0	0	0		.000	.000	.000	.000	-99	-0	-0	100	0	0	.000	0			0	/2O	0.0
1912	Chi-A	1	2	0	1	0	0	0	0	0		.500	.500	.500	1.000	188	0	0	99	0	0	1.000	0			0	/2	0.0
Total	22	1966	7452	1020	1944	216	80	15	823	500	131	.261	.309	.317	.626	80	-203	-196	99	107	868	.583	328			10	*2P/OS31	-8.7

■ BILLY GLEASON Gleason, William Patrick b: 9/6/1894, Chicago, Ill. d: 1/9/57, Holyoke, Mass. BR/TR, 5'6.5", 157 lbs. Deb: 9/25/16

YEAR	TM/L	G	AB	R	H	2B	3B	HR	RBI	BB	SO	AVG	OBP	SLG	PRO	/A	BR	/A	PF	CHI	RC	TA	SB	CS	SBR	FR	POS	TPR
1916	Pit-N	1	2	0	0	0	0	0	0	0	0	.000	.000	.000	.000	-96	-0	-0	105	0	0	.000	0			-0	/2	0.0
1917	Pit-N	13	42	3	7	1	0	0	0	5	5	.167	.255	.190	.446	38	-3	-3	100	0	2	.400	1			-1	2	-0.3
1921	StL-A	26	74	6	19	0	1	0	8	6	6	.257	.329	.284	.613	57	-4	-5	101	131	7	.518	0	1	-1	-3	2	-0.6
Total	3	40	118	9	26	1	1	0	8	11	11	.220	.298	.246	.543	49	-8	-8	100	82	9	.462	1	1		-3	/2	-0.9

■ JIM GLEESON Gleeson, James Joseph "Gee Gee" b: 3/5/12, Kansas City, Mo. BB/TR, 6'1", 191 lbs. Deb: 4/25/36 C

YEAR	TM/L	G	AB	R	H	2B	3B	HR	RBI	BB	SO	AVG	OBP	SLG	PRO	/A	BR	/A	PF	CHI	RC	TA	SB	CS	SBR	FR	POS	TPR
1936	Cle-A	41	139	26	36	9	2	4	12	18	17	.259	.344	.439	.783	87	-2	-3	106	53	22	.779	2	1	0	-2	O	-0.5
1939	Chi-N	111	332	43	74	19	6	4	45	39	46	.223	.308	.352	.661	77	-11	-11	101	128	38	.627	7			-4	O	-1.6
1940	Chi-N	129	485	76	152	39	11	5	61	54	52	.313	.389	.470	.859	137	24	25	100	99	91	.856	4			0	*O	2.0
1941	Cin-N	102	301	47	70	10	0	3	34	45	30	.233	.340	.296	.636	81	-6	-6	99	125	33	.607	7			-8	O	-1.7
1942	Cin-N	9	20	3	4	0	0	0	2	2	2	.200	.304	.200	.504	48	-1	-1	101	185	2	.438	0			-0	/O	-0.1
Total	5	392	1277	195	336	77	19	16	154	158	147	.263	.350	.391	.741	101	4	3	100	109	185	.732	20	1		-15	O	-1.9

■ FRANK GLEICH Gleich, Frank Elmer "Inch" b: 3/7/1894, Columbus, Ohio d: 3/27/49, Columbus, Ohio BL/TR, 5'11", 175 lbs. Deb: 9/17/19

YEAR	TM/L	G	AB	R	H	2B	3B	HR	RBI	BB	SO	AVG	OBP	SLG	PRO	/A	BR	/A	PF	CHI	RC	TA	SB	CS	SBR	FR	POS	TPR
1919	NY-A	5	4	0	1	0	0	0	1	1	0	.250	.400	.250	.650	80	-0	-0	106	363	0	.667	0			-2	/O	-0.2
1920	NY-A	24	41	6	5	0	0	0	3	6	10	.122	.234	.122	.356	-4	-6	-6	102	211	2	.306	0	0	0	-4	O	-1.1
Total	2	29	45	6	6	0	0	0	4	7	10	.133	.250	.133	.383	4	-6	-6	103	225	2	.333	0	0		-6	/O	-1.3

■ BOB GLENALVIN Glenalvin, Robert J. (born Robert J. Dowling) b: 1/17/1867, Indianapolis, Ind. d: 3/24/44, Detroit, Mich. TR, Deb: 7/12/1890

YEAR	TM/L	G	AB	R	H	2B	3B	HR	RBI	BB	SO	AVG	OBP	SLG	PRO	/A	BR	/A	PF	CHI	RC	TA	SB	CS	SBR	FR	POS	TPR
1890	Chi-N	66	250	43	67	10	3	4	26	19	31	.268	.337	.380	.717	102	3	-0	109	75	43	.825	30			-13	2	-0.9
1893	Chi-N	16	61	11	21	3	1	0	12	7	3	.344	.412	.426	.838	121	2	2	104	129	14	1.000	7			0	2	0.2
Total	2	82	311	54	88	13	4	4	38	26	34	.283	.352	.389	.741	106	6	2	108	85	57	.857	37			-13	/2	-0.7

YEAR	TM/L	G	AB	R	H	2B	3B	HR	RBI	BB	SO	AVG	OBP	SLG	PRO	/A	BR	/A	PF	CHI	RC	TA	SB	CS	SBR	FR	POS	TPR
■ ED GLENN	Glenn, Edward C. "Mouse" b: 9/19/1860, Richmond, Va. d: 2/10/1892, Richmond, Va. BR/TR, 5'10", 160 lbs. Deb: 8/05/1884																											
1884	Ric-a	43	175	26	43	2	4	1		5		.246	.271	.320	.591	96	-1	-1	99	0	16	.470				4	O	0.3
1886	Pit-a	71	277	32	53	6	5	0		17		.191	.241	.249	.490	59	-14	-11	93	0	22	.473	19			-1	O	-1.1
1888	KC-a	3	8	0	0	0	0	0	0	0		.000	.200	.000	.200	-30	-1	-1	106	0	0	.375	1			0	/O	0.0
	Bos-N	20	65	8	10	0	2	0	3	2	8	.154	.203	.215	.418	33	-5	-5	106	77	3	.327	0			0	O/3	-0.4
Total	3	137	525	66	106	8	11	1	3	24	8	.202	.245	.265	.510	66	-21	-18	96	10	40	.451	20			4	O/3	-1.2
■ ED GLENN	Glenn, Edward D. b: 1874, Ludlow, Ky. d: 12/6/11, Ludlow, Ky. Deb: 9/07/1898																											
1898	Was-N	1	4	0	0	0	0	0	0	0		.000	.000	.000	.000	-98	-1	-1	102	0	0	.000	0			0	/S	0.0
	NY-N	2	4	1	1	0	0	0	0	3		.250	.571	.250	.821	150	1	1	95	0	1	1.667	1			0	/S	0.1
	Yr	3	8	1	1	0	0	0	0	3		.125	.364	.125	.489	46	-0	-0	97	0	1	.714	1			0		0.1
1902	Chi-N	2	7	0	0	0	0	0	0	1		.000	.125	.000	.125	-63	-1	-1	96	0	0	.143	0			0	/S	0.0
Total	2	5	15	1	1	0	0	0	0	4		.067	.263	.067	.330	0	-2	-2	97	0	1	.429	1			0	/S	0.1
■ HARRY GLENN	Glenn, Harry Melville "Husky" b: 6/9/1890, Shelburn, Ind. d: 10/12/18, St.Paul, Minn. BR/TR, 6'1", 200 lbs. Deb: 4/14/15																											
1915	StL-N	6	16	1	5	0	0	0	1	3	0	.313	.421	.313	.734	123	1	1	100	76	2	.727	0			0	/C	0.2
■ JOHN GLENN	Glenn, John b: 7/10/28, Moultrie, Ga. BR/TR, 6'3", 180 lbs. Deb: 6/16/60																											
1960	StL-N	32	31	4	8	0	1	0	5	0	9	.258	.258	.323	.581	53	-2	-2	108	203	3	.435	0	0	0	-8	O	-1.0
■ JOHN GLENN	Glenn, John W. b: 1849, Rochester, N.Y. d: 11/10/1888, Sandy Hill, N.Y. BR/TR, 5'8.5", 169 lbs. Deb: 5/13/1871																											
1871	Oly-n	26	123	24	37							.301															*O	
1872	Oly-n	9	40	5	6							.150															/O	
	Nat-n	1	4	0	2							.500															/O	
	Yr	10	44	5	8							.182																
1873	Nat-n	39	194	39	49							.253															*1	
1874	Chi-n	55	245	34	64							.261															1O	
1875	Chi-n	70	325	48	76							.234															O1	
1876	Chi-N	66	276	55	84	9	2	0	32	12	6	.304	.333	.351	.685	102	8	-2	125	114	33	.568				0	*O1	-0.2
1877	Chi-N	50	202	31	46	6	1	0	20	8	16	.228	.257	.267	.524	67	-8	-7	98	128	14	.397				2	O1	-0.5
Total	5 n	200	931	150	234							.251															O1	
Total	2	116	478	86	130	15	3	0	52	20	22	.272	.301	.316	.617	89	1	-10	114	120	47	.491				2	O1/0	-0.7
■ JOE GLENN	Glenn, Joseph Charles "Gabby" (born Joseph Charles Gurzensky) b: 11/19/08, Dickson City, Pa. d: 5/6/85, Tunkhannock, Pa. BR/TR, 5'11", 175 lbs. Deb: 9/15/32																											
1932	NY-A	6	16	0	2	0	0	0	0	1	5	.125	.222	.125	.347	-8	-3	-2	95	0	1	.286	0	0	0	-0	/C	-0.1
1933	NY-A	5	21	1	3	0	0	0	1	0	3	.143	.143	.143	.286	-26	-4	-3	91	113	0	.167	0	0	0	0	/C	-0.2
1935	NY-A	17	43	7	10	4	0	0	6	4	1	.233	.298	.326	.623	66	-3	-2	93	146	4	.545	0	0	0	-0	C	-0.1
1936	NY-A	44	129	21	35	7	0	1	20	20	10	.271	.373	.349	.722	84	-4	-2	95	135	18	.705	1	1	-0	-2	C	0.0
1937	NY-A	25	53	6	15	2	2	0	4	10	11	.283	.397	.396	.793	99	0	0	102	65	9	.816	0	0	0	0	C	0.2
1938	NY-A	41	123	10	32	7	2	0	25	10	14	.260	.316	.350	.665	63	-7	-8	105	197	14	.593	1	0	0	-1	C	-0.6
1939	StL-A	88	286	29	78	13	1	4	29	31	40	.273	.344	.367	.711	81	-8	-8	100	84	36	.642	4	4	-1	2	C	-0.1
1940	Bos-A	22	47	3	6	1	0	0	4	5	7	.128	.212	.149	.360	-5	-7	-7	101	206	1	.267	0	0	0	-2	C	-0.6
Total	8	248	718	77	181	34	5	5	89	81	91	.252	.330	.334	.664	69	-33	-33	99	121	84	.603	6	5	-1	-2	C	-1.5
■ NORM GLOCKSON	Glockson, Norman Stanley b: 6/15/1894, Blue Island, Ill. d: 8/5/55, Maywood, Ill. BR/TR, 6'2", 200 lbs. Deb: 9/16/14																											
1914	Cin-N	7	12	0	0	0	0	0	0	1	6	.000	.077	.000	.077	-73	-3	-3	105	0	0	.083	0			-0	/C	-0.2
■ AL GLOSSOP	Glossop, Alban b: 7/23/15, Christopher, Ill. BB/TR, 6', 170 lbs. Deb: 9/23/39																											
1939	NY-N	10	32	3	6	0	0	1	3	4	2	.188	.278	.281	.559	51	-2	-2	99	92	3	.481	0			1	2	0.0
1940	NY-N	27	91	16	19	3	0	4	8	10	16	.209	.294	.374	.668	83	-2	-2	100	64	10	.630	1			4	2	0.3
	Bos-N	60	148	17	35	2	1	3	14	17	22	.236	.315	.324	.639	78	-4	-4	99	91	16	.574	1			1	23/S	-0.1
	Yr	87	239	33	54	5	1	7	22	27	38	.226	.307	.343	.650	80	-7	-7	99	83	27	.599	2			4		0.2
1942	Phi-N	121	454	33	102	15	1	4	40	29	35	.225	.273	.289	.561	68	-21	-18	94	110	36	.458	3			14	*2/3	0.5
1943	Bro-N	87	217	28	37	9	0	3	21	28	27	.171	.268	.253	.522	51	-14	-13	100	118	17	.464	0			-6	S23/O	-1.6
1946	Chi-N	4	10	2	0	0	0	0	0	1	3	.000	.231	.000	.231	-34	-2	-2	94	0	0	.300	0			0	/2S	-0.1
Total	5	309	952	99	199	29	2	15	86	89	105	.209	.280	.291	.571	66	-45	-42	97	102	83	.499	5			14	2/S3O	-1.0
■ BILL GLYNN	Glynn, William Vincent b: 7/30/25, Sussex, N.J. BL/TL, 6', 190 lbs. Deb: 9/16/49																											
1949	Phi-N	8	10	0	2	0	0	0	1	0	3	.200	.200	.200	.400	8	-1	-1	101	188	0	.250	0			0	/1	0.0
1952	Cle-A	44	92	15	25	5	0	2	7	5	16	.272	.309	.391	.701	104	-1	-0	91	62	11	.600	1	0	0	0	1	-0.1
1953	Cle-A	147	411	60	100	14	2	3	30	44	65	.243	.324	.309	.633	75	-16	-13	95	82	45	.555	1	3	-2	2	*1/O	-1.5
1954	Cle-A	111	171	19	43	3	2	5	18	12	21	.251	.301	.380	.681	81	-4	-5	106	85	19	.597	3	2	-0	2	1/O	-0.6
Total	4	310	684	94	170	22	4	10	56	61	105	.249	.315	.336	.651	79	-22	-20	97	81	75	.576	5	5		4	1/O	-2.2
■ JOHN GOCHNAUER	Gochnauer, John Peter b: 9/12/1875, Altoona, Pa. d: 9/27/29, Altoona, Pa. BR/TR, 5'9", 160 lbs. Deb: 9/29/01																											
1901	Bro-N	3	11	1	4	0	0	0	2	1		.364	.417	.364	.780	123	0	0	106	171	2	.857	1			0	/S	0.1
1902	Cle-A	127	459	45	85	16	4	0	37	38		.185	.247	.237	.485	37	-39	-37	97	114	29	.412	7			-15	*S	-3.9
1903	Cle-A	134	438	48	81	16	4	0	48	48		.185	.265	.240	.505	56	-23	-21	96	**168**	31	.457	10			-22	*S	-3.7
Total	3	264	908	94	170	32	8	0	87	87		.187	.258	.240	.498	47	-61	-57	97	141	63	.438	18			-37	S	-7.5
■ JOHN GODAR	Godar, John Michael b: 10/25/1864, Cincinnati, Ohio d: 6/23/49, Park Ridge, Ill. 5'9", 170 lbs. Deb: 7/08/1892																											
1892	Bal-N	5	14	2	3	0	0	0	1	2	1	.214	.353	.214	.567	75	-0	-0	100	102	1	.636	1			0	/O	0.0
■ DANNY GODBY	Godby, Danny Ray b: 11/4/46, Logan, W.Va. BR/TR, 6', 185 lbs. Deb: 8/10/74																											
1974	StL-N	13	13	2	2	0	0	0	1	3	4	.154	.313	.154	.466	32	-1	-1	104	193	1	.455	0	0	0	1	/O	0.0
■ JOE GODDARD	Goddard, Joseph Harold b: 7/23/50, Beckley, W.Va. BR/TR, 5'11", 181 lbs. Deb: 7/31/72																											
1972	SD-N	12	35	0	7	2	0	0	2	5	9	.200	.300	.257	.557	67	-2	-1	88	91	3	.467	0	0	0	-0	C	0.0
■ JOHN GODWIN	Godwin, John Henry "Bunny" b: 3/10/1877, E.Liverpool, Ohio d: 5/5/56, E.Liverpool, Ohio BR/TR, 6', 190 lbs. Deb: 8/14/05																											
1905	Bos-A	15	43	4	14	1	0	0	10	3		.326	.370	.349	.718	130	2	2	100	238	7	.724	3			0	/O2	0.1
1906	Bos-A	66	193	11	36	2	1	0	15	6		.187	.211	.207	.418	33	-15	-14	98	136	10	.331	6			-1	3SO/21	-1.5
Total	2	81	236	15	50	3	1	0	25	9		.212	.241	.233	.474	51	-13	-13	99	155	17	.392	9			-1	/3OS21	-1.4
■ ED GOEBEL	Goebel, Edwin b: 9/1/1899, Brooklyn, N.Y. d: 8/12/59, Brooklyn, N.Y. BR/TR, 5'11", 170 lbs. Deb: 5/13/22																											
1922	Was-A	37	59	13	16	1	0	1	3	8	16	.271	.358	.339	.697	90	-1	-1	92	47	7	.659	1	1	-0	-1	O	-0.2
■ BILLY GOECKEL	Goeckel, William John b: 9/3/1871, Wilkes-Barre, Pa. d: 11/1/22, Philadelphia, Pa. BL/TL, Deb: 8/10/1899																											
1899	Phi-N	37	141	17	37	3	1	0	16	1		.262	.283	.298	.581	63	-7	-7	97	119	14	.500	6			0	1	-0.5
■ CHUCK GOGGIN	Goggin, Charles Francis b: 7/7/45, Pompano Beach, Fla. BB/TR, 5'11", 175 lbs. Deb: 9/08/72																											
1972	Pit-N	5	7	0	2	0	0	0	0	1	1	.286	.375	.286	.661	88	-0	-0	103	0	1	.600	0	0	0	0	/2	0.0
1973	Pit-N	1	1	1	1	0	0	0	0	0	0	1.000	1.000	1.000	2.000	496	0	0	92	0	1	—	0	0	0	0	/C	0.1
	Atl-N	64	90	18	26	5	0	0	7	9	19	.289	.354	.344	.698	83	-0	-2	113	91	11	.597	0	1	-1	-3	2/OSC	-0.3
	Yr	65	91	19	27	5	0	0	7	9	19	.297	.360	.352	.712	87	-0	-1	113	89	11	.612	0	1	-1	-3		-0.2
1974	Bos-A	2	1	0	0	0	0	0	0	0	1	.000	.000	.000	.000	-94	-0	-0	107	0	0	.000	0	0	0	0	/2	0.0
Total	3	72	99	19	29	5	0	0	7	10	21	.293	.358	.343	.701	85	-0	-2	112	82	13	.620	0	1	-1	-3	/2OSC	-0.2
■ MIKE GOLDEN	Golden, Michael Henry b: 9/11/1851, Shirley, Mass. d: 1/11/29, Rockford, Ill. BR/TR, 5'7", 166 lbs. Deb: 5/05/1875																											
1875	Wes-n	13	50	3	7							.140															P	
	Chi-n	39	161	18	39							.242															OP/1	
	Yr	52	211	21	46							.218																
1878	Mil-N	55	214	16	44	6	3	0	20	3	35	.206	.217	.262	.478	53	-10	-12	107	123	12	.347				-3	OP/1	-1.6

YEAR	TM/L	G	AB	R	H	2B	3B	HR	RBI	BB	SO	AVG	OBP	SLG	PRO	/A	BR	/A	PF	CHI	RC	TA	SB	CS	SBR	FR	POS	TPR
Total		55	214	16	44	6	3	0	20	3	35	.206	.217	.262	.478	53	-10	-12	107	123	12	.347				-3	/OP1	-1.6
■ JONAH GOLDMAN	Goldman, Jonah John b: 8/29/06, New York, N.Y. d: 8/17/80, Palm Beach, Fla. BR/TR, 5'7", 170 lbs. Deb: 9/22/28																											
1928	Cle-A	7	21	1	5	1	0	0	2	3	0	.238	.333	.286	.619	61	-1	-1	106	114	2	.563	0	0	0	1	/S	0.0
1930	Cle-A	111	306	32	74	18	0	1	44	28	25	.242	.312	.310	.622	56	-19	-22	105	149	31	.544	3	5	-2	10	S3	-0.2
1931	Cle-A	30	62	0	8	1	0	0	3	4	6	.129	.182	.145	.327	-12	-10	-11	106	110	2	.255	1	1	-0	2	S	-0.5
Total	3	148	389	33	87	20	0	1	49	35	31	.224	.293	.283	.576	45	-30	-34	105	141	35	.494	4	6	-2	12	S/3	-0.7
■ GORDON GOLDSBERRY	Goldsberry, Gordon Frederick b: 8/30/27, Sacramento, Cal. BL/TL, 6', 170 lbs. Deb: 4/20/49																											
1949	Chi-A	39	145	25	36	3	2	1	13	18	9	.248	.331	.317	.649	74	-6	-5	98	93	17	.589	2	0	1	0	1	-0.3
1950	Chi-A	82	127	19	34	8	2	2	25	26	18	.268	.392	.409	.802	109	2	2	97	149	22	.796	0	2	-1	-1	1/O	-0.1
1951	Chi-A	10	11	4	1	0	0	0	1	2	2	.091	.231	.091	.322	-11	-2	-2	97	357	0	.300	0	0	0	0	/1	-0.1
1952	StL-A	86	227	30	52	9	3	3	17	34	37	.229	.330	.335	.664	88	-4	-3	97	75	27	.611	0	2	-1	-3	1/O	-1.2
Total	4	217	510	78	123	20	7	6	56	80	66	.241	.344	.343	.687	87	-10	-8	97	105	66	.652	2	4	-2	-5	1/O	-1.7
■ WALT GOLDSBY	Goldsby, Walton Hugh b: 12/31/1861, Louisiana d: 1/11/14, Dallas, Tex. Deb: 5/28/1884																											
1884	StL-a	5	20	2	4	0	0	0		0		.200	.200	.200	.400	30	-1	-2	110	0	1	.250				0	/O	-0.1
	Was-a	6	24	4	9	0	0	0		1		.375	.400	.375	.775	179	1	2	88	0	4	.667				0	/O	0.2
	Ric-a	11	40	4	9	1	0	0		1		.225	.262	.250	.512	71	-1	-1	99	0	3	.387				0	O	0.0
	Yr	22	84	10	22	1	0	0		2		.262	.287	.274	.561	88	-1	-1	99	0	7	.419				0		0.1
1886	Was-N	6	18	0	4	1	0	0	1	2	3	.222	.300	.278	.578	82	-0	-0	94	65	2	.500	0			0	/O	0.0
1888	Bal-a	45	165	13	39	1	1	0	14	8		.236	.288	.255	.543	81	-4	-3	96	102	17	.563	17			-7	O	-0.9
Total	3	73	267	23	65	3	1	0	15	12	3	.243	.289	.262	.551	83	-5	-4	97	68	26	.515	17			-7	/O	-0.8
■ WALLY GOLDSMITH	Goldsmith, Wallace b: 1849, Baltimore, Md. 5'7", 146 lbs. Deb: 5/04/1871																											
1871	Kek-n	19	91	9	19							.209															S/3C2	
1872	Oly-n	9	40	4	9							.225															/S2	
1873	Mar-n	1	4	0	0							.000															/2	
1875	Wes-n	13	53	3	6							.113															3	
Total	4 n	42	188	16	34							.181															3	
■ LONNIE GOLDSTEIN	Goldstein, Leslie Elmer b: 5/13/18, Austin, Tex. BL/TL, 6'2.5", 190 lbs. Deb: 9/11/43																											
1943	Cin-N	5	5	1	1	0	0	0	0	2	1	.200	.429	.200	.629	85	0	0	99	0	0	.600	0			0	/1	0.0
1946	Cin-N	6	5	1	0	0	0	0	0	1	1	.000	.167	.000	.167	-49	-1	-1	104	0	0	.200	0			0	H	0.0
Total	2	11	10	2	1	0	0	0	0	3	2	.100	.308	.100	.408	19	-1	-1	101	0	0	.444	0			0	/1	0.0
■ PURNAL GOLDY	Goldy, Purnal William b: 11/28/37, Camden, N.J. BR/TR, 6'5", 200 lbs. Deb: 4/12/62																											
1962	Det-A	20	70	8	16	1	1	3	12	0	12	.229	.239	.400	.639	62	-3	-4	111	129	6	.509	0	0	0	-0	O	-0.4
1963	Det-A	9	8	1	2	0	0	0	0	0	4	.250	.250	.250	.500	39	-1	-1	104	0	1	.333	0	0	0	0	H	0.0
Total	2	29	78	9	18	1	1	3	12	0	16	.231	.241	.385	.625	60	-4	-5	110	116	6	.517	0	0	0	-0	/O	-0.4
■ STAN GOLETZ	Goletz, Stanley "Stash" b: 5/21/18, Crescent, Ohio BL/TL, 6'3", 200 lbs. Deb: 9/09/41																											
1941	Chi-A	5	5	0	3	0	0	0	0	0	2	.600	.600	.600	1.200	233	1	1	94	0	2	1.500	0	0	0	0	H	0.1
■ MIKE GOLIAT	Goliat, Mike Mitchel b: 11/5/25, Yatesboro, Pa. BR/TR, 6', 180 lbs. Deb: 8/03/49																											
1949	Phi-N	55	189	24	40	6	3	3	19	20	32	.212	.290	.323	.613	64	-10	-10	101	104	17	.522	0			-5	2/1	-1.2
1950	Phi-N	145	483	49	113	13	6	13	64	53	75	.234	.314	.366	.680	80	-16	-14	97	114	53	.605	3			-10	*2	-1.9
1951	Phi-N	41	138	14	31	2	1	4	15	9	18	.225	.277	.341	.618	67	-7	-7	97	98	13	.523	0	1	-1	-7	2/3	-1.2
	StL-A	5	11	0	2	0	0	0	1	0	1	.182	.182	.182	.364	-1	-2	-2	105	179	0	.222	0	0	0	0	/2	-0.1
1952	StL-A	3	4	0	0	0	0	0	0	1	1	.000	.200	.000	.200	-42	-1	-1	97	0	0	.250	0	0	0	0	/2	0.0
Total	4	249	825	87	186	21	10	20	99	83	127	.225	.300	.348	.648	73	-35	-33	98	110	84	.591	3	1		-22	2/13	-4.4
■ WALT GOLVIN	Golvin, Walter George b: 2/1/1894, Hershey, Neb. d: 6/11/73, Gardena, Cal. BL/TL, 6', 165 lbs. Deb: 4/15/22																											
1922	Chi-N	2	2	0	0	0	0	0	1	0	0	.000	.000	.000	.000	-99	-1	-1	95	0	0	.000	0	0	0	0	/1	0.0
■ CHILE GOMEZ	Gomez, Jose Luis (Rodriguez) b: 5/23/09, Villaunion, Mex. BR/TR, 5'10", 165 lbs. Deb: 7/27/35																											
1935	Phi-N	67	222	24	51	3	0	0	16	17	34	.230	.285	.243	.528	38	-17	-21	114	107	15	.406	2			2	S2	-1.4
1936	Phi-N	108	332	24	77	4	1	0	28	14	32	.232	.265	.250	.515	36	-28	-31	108	120	22	.373	0			0	2S	-2.3
1942	Was-A	25	73	8	14	2	2	0	6	9	7	.192	.280	.274	.554	59	-4	-4	96	106	6	.484	1	0	0	-2	2/3	-0.4
Total	3	200	627	56	142	9	3	0	50	40	73	.226	.274	.250	.524	39	-49	-57	109	113	43	.412	3	0		-0	2/S3	-4.1
■ LUIS GOMEZ	Gomez, Jose Luis (Sanchez) b: 8/19/51, Guadalajara, Mex. BR/TR, 5'9", 150 lbs. Deb: 4/28/74																											
1974	Min-A	82	168	18	35	1	0	0	3	12	16	.208	.261	.214	.475	38	-13	-13	101	33	10	.362	2	3	-1	-2	S/2D	-1.1
1975	Min-A	89	72	7	10	0	0	0	5	4	12	.139	.184	.139	.323	-7	-10	-11	107	192	2	.215	0	2	-1	-2	S/2D	-0.6
1976	Min-A	38	57	5	11	1	0	0	3	3	3	.193	.233	.211	.444	31	-5	-5	98	96	3	.327	1	0	0	1	S/230D	-0.1
1977	Min-A	32	65	6	16	4	2	0	11	4	9	.246	.290	.369	.659	76	-2	-2	103	182	7	.549	0	2	-1	2	2/S30D	0.1
1978	Tor-A	153	413	39	92	7	3	0	32	34	41	.223	.282	.254	.536	52	-26	-26	100	120	28	.413	2	10	-5	-8	*S	-2.7
1979	Tor-A	59	163	11	39	7	0	0	11	6	17	.239	.266	.282	.548	47	-12	-13	103	92	11	.405	1	0	0	1	32S	-0.7
1980	Atl-N	121	278	18	53	6	0	0	24	17	27	.191	.240	.212	.452	27	-27	-27	101	161	13	.324	0	4	-2	-1	*S	-1.7
1981	Atl-N	35	35	4	7	0	0	0	1	6	4	.200	.317	.200	.517	49	-2	-2	100	56	3	.448	0	1	-1	-1	S/32P	-0.1
Total	8	609	1251	108	263	26	5	0	90	86	129	.210	.262	.239	.501	41	-97	-99	101	118	76	.388	6	22	-11	-10	S/23DOP	-6.9
■ PRESTON GOMEZ	Gomez, Pedro (Martinez) b: 4/20/23, Preston, Cuba BR/TR, 5'11", 170 lbs. Deb: 5/05/44 MC																											
1944	Was-A	8	7	2	2	1	0	0	2	0	4	.286	.286	.429	.714	114	-0	0	90	241	1	.600	0	0	0	-0	/2S	0.0
■ RANDY GOMEZ	Gomez, Randell Scott b: 2/4/58, San Mateo, Cal. BR/TR, 5'10", 185 lbs. Deb: 8/21/84																											
1984	SF-N	14	30	0	5	1	0	0	0	8	3	.167	.342	.200	.542	58	-1	-1	96	0	2	.519	0	0	0	-0	C	0.0
■ JESSE GONDER	Gonder, Jesse Lemar b: 1/20/36, Monticello, Ark. BL/TR, 5'10", 180 lbs. Deb: 9/23/60																											
1960	NY-A	7	7	1	2	0	0	1	3	1	1	.286	.375	.714	1.089	199	1	1	94	147	2	1.200	0	0	0	0	/C	0.1
1961	NY-A	15	12	2	4	1	0	0	3	3	1	.333	.467	.417	.883	143	1	1	96	235	2	.889	0	0	0	0	H	0.1
1962	Cin-N	4	4	0	0	0	0	0	0	0	3	.000	.000	.000	.000	-98	-1	-1	102	0	0	.000	0	0	0	0	H	0.0
1963	Cin-N	31	32	5	10	2	0	3	5	1	12	.313	.333	.656	.990	171	3	3	104	70	7	1.000	0	0	0	0	/C	0.4
	NY-N	42	126	12	38	4	0	3	15	6	25	.302	.333	.405	.738	112	2	2	99	105	16	.624	1	2	-1	-2	C	0.0
	Yr	73	158	17	48	6	0	6	20	7	37	.304	.333	.456	.789	123	5	4	101	91	23	.696	1	2	-1	-1		0.4
1964	NY-N	131	341	28	92	11	1	7	35	29	65	.270	.331	.370	.700	102	-1	1	95	98	38	.592	0	0	0	6	C	1.0
1965	NY-N	53	105	6	25	4	0	4	9	11	20	.238	.310	.390	.701	96	-1	-1	100	70	11	.605	0	0	0	-3	C	-0.1
	Mil-N	31	53	2	8	2	0	1	5	4	9	.151	.211	.245	.456	27	-5	-5	104	130	2	.362	0	0	0	1	C	-0.3
	Yr	84	158	8	33	6	0	5	14	15	29	.209	.277	.342	.619	72	-6	-6	102	93	15	.543	0	0	0	-2		-0.4
1966	Pit-N	59	160	13	36	3	1	7	16	12	39	.225	.287	.387	.675	85	-3	-3	101	81	16	.585	0	0	0	-7	C	-0.9
1967	Pit-N	22	36	4	5	1	0	0	3	5	9	.139	.279	.167	.446	31	-3	-3	100	207	2	.394	0	0	0	0	C	-0.1
Total	8	395	876	73	220	28	2	26	94	72	184	.251	.312	.377	.689	95	-8	-6	98	100	97	.620	1	2	-1	-4	C	0.2
■ DAN GONZALES	Gonzales, Daniel David b: 9/30/53, Whittier, Cal. BL/TR, 6'1", 195 lbs. Deb: 4/07/79																											
1979	Det-A	7	18	1	4	1	0	0	2	0	2	.222	.222	.278	.500	35	-2	-2	96	154	1	.375	1	0	0	-1	/O	-0.1
1980	Det-A	2	7	1	1	0	0	0	0	0	1	.143	.143	.143	.286	-20	-1	-1	105	0	0	.167	0	0	0	0	/OD	0.0
Total	2	9	25	2	5	1	0	0	2	0	3	.200	.200	.240	.440	19	-3	-3	99	111	1	.350	1	0	0	-1	/OD	-0.1
■ RENE GONZALES	Gonzales, Rene Adrian b: 9/3/60, Austin, Tex. BR/TR, 6'3", 180 lbs. Deb: 7/27/84																											
1984	Mon-N	29	30	5	7	1	0	0	2	2	4	.233	.303	.267	.570	67	-1	-1	91	98	3	.478	0	0	0	-2	S	0.0
1986	Mon-N	11	26	1	3	0	0	0	0	2	7	.115	.179	.115	.294	-18	-4	-4	98	0	0	.200	0	2	-1	0	/S3	-0.4
1987	Bal-A	37	60	14	16	2	1	1	7	3	11	.267	.302	.383	.685	83	-2	-2	98	107	7	.587	1	0	0	2	3/2S	0.1

YEAR	TM/L	G	AB	R	H	2B	3B	HR	RBI	BB	SO	AVG	OBP	SLG	PRO	/A	BR	/A	PF	CHI	RC	TA	SB	CS	SBR	FR	POS	TPR
1988	Bal-A	92	237	13	51	6	0	2	15	13	32	.215	.265	.266	.531	52	-16	-15	95	86	17	.424	2	0	1	1	32/1SO	-1.1
Total	4	169	353	33	77	9	1	3	24	20	54	.218	.268	.275	.543	53	-23	-21	95	84	27	.438	3	2	-0	1	3/S2O1	-1.4
■ **TONY GONZALEZ**	Gonzalez, Andres Antonio (Gonzalez) b: 8/28/36, Central Cunagua, Cuba BL/TR, 5'9", 170 lbs. Deb: 4/12/60																											
1960	Cin-N	39	99	10	21	5	1	3	14	4	27	.212	.250	.374	.624	69	-5	-4	98	123	9	.538	1	0	0	-4	O	-0.9
	Phi-N	78	241	27	72	17	5	6	33	11	47	.299	.337	.485	.823	114	7	4	107	99	38	.760	2	2	-1	4	O	0.6
	Yr	117	340	37	93	22	6	9	47	15	74	.274	.312	.453	.765	102	2	0	104	108	47	.696	3	2	-0	0		-0.3
1961	Phi-N	126	426	58	118	16	8	12	58	49	66	.277	.360	.437	.796	117	7	10	94	108	68	.793	15	5	2	7	*O	1.2
1962	Phi-N	118	437	76	132	16	4	20	63	40	82	.302	.372	.494	.867	138	19	22	95	95	80	.879	17	8	0	2	*O	1.7
1963	Phi-N	155	555	78	170	36	12	4	66	53	68	.306	.375	.436	.811	129	24	23	103	111	91	.782	13	8	-1	6	*O	2.1
1964	Phi-N	131	421	55	117	25	3	4	40	44	74	.278	.355	.380	.735	108	5	6	99	95	56	.660	0	5	-3	-4	*O	-0.4
1965	Phi-N	108	370	48	109	19	1	13	41	31	52	.295	.354	.457	.811	134	13	15	95	82	54	.733	3	4	-2	-3	*O	0.8
1966	Phi-N	132	384	53	110	20	4	6	40	26	60	.286	.337	.406	.743	104	3	2	101	97	51	.656	2	6	-3	0	*O	-0.3
1967	Phi-N	149	508	74	172	23	9	9	59	47	58	.339	.400	.472	.872	143	33	30	104	93	94	.853	10	9	-2	5	*O	2.9
1968	Phi-N	121	416	45	110	13	4	3	38	40	42	.264	.339	.337	.676	106	3	4	97	110	47	.594	6	5	-1	-8	*O	-1.2
1969	SD-N	53	182	17	41	4	0	2	8	19	24	.225	.309	.280	.589	68	-8	-7	97	57	16	.503	1	0	0	5	O	-0.4
	Atl-N	89	320	51	94	15	2	10	50	27	22	.294	.358	.447	.805	120	10	9	104	118	51	.761	3	1	0	3	O	0.8
	Yr	142	502	68	135	19	2	12	58	46	46	.269	.340	.386	.726	102	2	2	101	96	69	.672	4	1	1	7		0.4
1970	Atl-N	123	430	57	114	18	2	7	55	46	45	.265	.347	.365	.712	87	-5	-7	104	122	54	.647	3	5	-2	-7	*O	-2.1
	Cal-A	26	92	9	28	2	0	1	12	2	11	.304	.326	.359	.685	97	-2	-1	92	135	10	.565	3	2	-0	1	O	0.0
1971	Cal-A	111	314	32	77	9	2	3	38	28	28	.245	.313	.315	.628	80	-9	-8	99	144	30	.524	0	1	-1	-5	O	-1.8
Total	12	1559	5195	690	1485	238	57	103	615	467	706	.286	.353	.413	.766	114	95	98	100	105	749	.731	79	61	-13	1	*O	3.0
■ **DENNY GONZALEZ**	Gonzalez, Denio Mariano (Manzueta) b: 7/22/63, Sabana Grande Boya, D.R. BR/TR, 5'11", 165 lbs. Deb: 8/06/84																											
1984	Pit-N	26	82	9	15	3	1	0	4	7	21	.183	.247	.244	.491	41	-7	-6	94	78	4	.389	1	1	-0	-0	3S/O	-0.5
1985	Pit-N	35	124	11	28	4	0	4	12	13	27	.226	.299	.355	.654	80	-3	-3	103	87	13	.584	2	4	-2	-5	3O/2	-1.0
1987	Pit-N	5	7	1	0	0	0	0	0	1	2	.000	.125	.000	.125	-61	-2	-2	104	0	0	.143	0	0	0	0	/S	-0.1
1988	Pit-N	24	32	5	6	1	0	0	1	6	10	.188	.316	.219	.535	57	-2	-1	98	57	3	.481	0	0	0	-0	S/23	0.0
Total	4	90	245	26	49	8	1	4	17	27	60	.200	.279	.290	.569	60	-13	-13	99	77	20	.500	3	5	-2	-5	/3SO2	-1.6
■ **EUSEBIO GONZALEZ**	Gonzalez, Eusebio Miguel (Lopez) "Papo" b: 7/13/1892, Havana, Cuba d: 2/14/76, Havana, Cuba BR/TR, 5'10", 165 lbs. Deb: 7/26/18																											
1918	Bos-A	3	5	2	2	0	1	0	0	1	1	.400	.571	.800	1.371	329	1	1	95	0	2	2.000	0			0	/S3	0.2
■ **FERNANDO GONZALEZ**	Gonzalez, Jose Fernando (Quinones) b: 6/19/50, Arecibo, P.R. BR/TR, 5'10", 165 lbs. Deb: 9/15/72																											
1972	Pit-N	3	2	0	0	0	0	0	0	0	2	.000	.000	.000	.000	-97	-1	-1	103	0	0	.000	0	0	0	0	/3	0.0
1973	Pit-N	37	49	5	11	0	1	1	5	1	11	.224	.255	.327	.581	65	-3	-2	92	106	4	.462	0	0	0	-0	/3	-0.2
1974	KC-A	9	21	1	3	1	0	0	2	0	4	.143	.143	.190	.333	-5	-3	-3	106	197	1	.278	1	0	0	-1	/3D	-0.2
	NY-A	51	121	11	26	5	1	1	7	7	7	.215	.258	.298	.555	62	-6	-6	96	71	9	.439	0	0	0	-1	2/3S	-0.4
	Yr	60	142	12	29	6	1	1	9	7	11	.204	.242	.282	.523	51	-9	-9	97	93	9	.414	1	0	0	-1		-0.6
1977	Pit-N	80	181	17	50	10	0	4	27	13	21	.276	.325	.398	.723	90	-2	-3	103	129	20	.620	3	3	-1	-3	3O/2S	-0.6
1978	Pit-N	9	21	2	4	1	0	0	0	1	3	.190	.227	.238	.465	29	-2	-2	105	0	1	.353	0	0	0	0	/23	-0.1
	SD-N	101	320	27	80	10	2	2	29	18	32	.250	.290	.313	.602	74	-14	-11	93	108	29	.492	4	4	-1	4	2	-0.1
	Yr	110	341	29	84	11	2	2	29	19	35	.246	.286	.308	.594	70	-16	-13	94	100	30	.483	4	4	-1	4		-0.2
1979	SD-N	114	323	22	70	13	3	9	34	18	34	.217	.258	.359	.617	69	-16	-15	96	94	28	.513	0	0	0	-4	*2/3	-1.2
Total	6	404	1038	85	244	40	7	17	104	58	114	.235	.276	.336	.612	71	-46	-42	96	102	92	.514	8	7	-2	-4	2/3OSD	-2.8
■ **JOSE GONZALEZ**	Gonzalez, Jose Rafael (Gutierrez) b: 11/23/64, Puerto Plata, D.R. BR/TR, 6'2", 190 lbs. Deb: 9/02/85																											
1985	LA-N	23	11	6	3	2	0	0	0	1	3	.273	.333	.455	.788	127	0	0	93	0	1	.700	1	1	-0	-5	O	-0.5
1986	LA-N	57	93	15	20	5	1	2	6	7	29	.215	.270	.355	.625	75	-4	-3	94	61	9	.579	4	3	-1	-9	O	-1.3
1987	LA-N	19	16	2	3	2	0	0	1	1	2	.188	.235	.313	.548	48	-1	-1	92	80	2	.846	5	0	2	-1	O	-0.1
1988	LA-N	37	24	7	2	1	0	0	0	2	10	.083	.154	.125	.279	-18	-4	-4	106	0	1	.364	3	0	1	-7	O	-1.0
Total	4	136	144	30	28	10	1	2	7	11	44	.194	.252	.319	.571	59	-9	-8	96	48	13	.583	13	4	2	-22	O	-2.9
■ **JULIO GONZALEZ**	Gonzalez, Julio Cesar (Hernandez) b: 12/25/52, Caguas, P.R. BR/TR, 5'11", 162 lbs. Deb: 4/08/77																											
1977	Hou-N	110	383	34	94	18	3	1	27	19	45	.245	.288	.316	.604	67	-21	-17	93	87	34	.492	3	3	-1	-10	S2	-1.7
1978	Hou-N	78	223	24	52	3	1	1	16	8	31	.233	.263	.269	.532	52	-15	-14	95	101	15	.419	6	1	1	-6	2S/3	-1.4
1979	Hou-N	68	181	16	45	5	2	0	10	5	14	.249	.280	.298	.579	64	-11	-8	90	73	15	.454	2	1	0	-0	2S/3	-0.4
1980	Hou-N	40	52	5	6	1	0	0	1	1	8	.115	.132	.135	.267	-26	-9	-9	98	57	1	.191	1	0	0	0	S3/2	-0.6
1981	StL-N	20	22	2	7	1	0	1	3	1	3	.318	.348	.500	.848	136	1	1	102	84	3	.706	0	0	0	0	/S23	0.2
1982	StL-N	42	87	9	21	3	2	1	7	1	24	.241	.258	.356	.615	68	-4	-4	103	81	7	.493	1	1	-0	1	3/2S	-0.2
1983	Det-A	12	21	0	3	1	0	0	2	1	7	.143	.182	.190	.372	3	-3	-3	96	195	1	.263	0	0	0	-0	/S23	-0.2
Total	7	370	969	90	228	32	8	4	66	36	132	.235	.269	.297	.566	58	-61	-54	94	88	76	.463	13	6	0	-15	2S/3	-4.3
■ **MIKE GONZALEZ**	Gonzalez, Miguel Angel (Cordero) b: 9/24/1890, Havana, Cuba d: 2/19/77, Havana, Cuba BR/TR, 6'1", 200 lbs. Deb: 9/28/12 MC																											
1912	Bos-N	1	2	0	0	0	0	0	0	1	1	.000	.333	.000	.333	-4	-0	-0	107	0	0	.500	0			0	/C	0.0
1914	Cin-N	95	176	19	41	6	0	0	10	13	16	.233	.293	.267	.560	64	-7	-8	105	77	14	.474	2			-3	C	-0.7
1915	StL-N	51	97	12	22	2	2	0	10	8	9	.227	.306	.289	.594	80	-2	-2	100	136	9	.558	4	2	0	2	C/1	0.1
1916	StL-N	118	331	33	79	15	4	0	29	28	18	.239	.304	.308	.612	91	-4	-3	97	113	34	.548	5			12	C1	1.5
1917	StL-N	106	290	28	76	8	1	1	28	22	24	.262	.316	.307	.623	90	-3	-3	102	117	31	.579	12			4	C1/O	0.4
1918	StL-N	117	349	33	88	13	4	3	20	39	30	.252	.327	.338	.665	110	2	4	93	60	41	.655	14			4	*C/O1	1.8
1919	NY-N	58	158	18	30	6	0	0	8	20	9	.190	.293	.228	.521	58	-7	-7	100	86	11	.484	3			-6	C/1	-1.1
1920	NY-N	11	13	1	3	0	0	0	0	3	1	.231	.375	.231	.606	77	-0	-0	100	0	2	.700	1	0	0	0	/C	0.1
1921	NY-N	13	24	3	9	1	0	0	0	1	0	.375	.400	.417	.817	119	1	1	98	0	4	.733	0	0	0	0	/1C	0.1
1924	StL-N	120	402	34	119	27	1	3	53	24	22	.296	.337	.391	.728	92	-3	-5	103	116	52	.635	1	5	-3	-7	*C	-1.1
1925	StL-N	22	71	9	22	3	0	0	4	6	2	.310	.380	.352	.732	86	-1	-1	102	57	9	.667	1	2	-1	1	C	0.0
	Chi-N	70	197	26	52	13	1	3	18	13	15	.264	.316	.386	.702	80	-7	-6	97	75	24	.637	2	1	0	4	C/1	0.0
	Yr	92	268	35	74	16	1	3	22	19	17	.276	.333	.377	.710	82	-8	-7	99	71	34	.645	3	3	-1	5		0.0
1926	Chi-N	80	253	24	63	13	3	1	23	13	17	.249	.288	.336	.624	64	-12	-14	106	90	24	.537	3			5	C	-0.6
1927	Chi-N	39	108	15	26	4	1	1	15	10	8	.241	.311	.324	.635	70	-4	-5	100	138	11	.573	1			4	C	0.2
1928	Chi-N	49	158	12	43	9	2	1	21	12	7	.272	.324	.373	.697	86	-4	-3	95	121	19	.635	2			5	C	0.5
1929	Chi-N	60	167	15	40	3	0	0	18	18	14	.240	.317	.257	.575	44	-14	-14	101	143	14	.496	1			-0	C	-0.8
1931	StL-N	15	19	1	2	0	0	0	3	0	3	.105	.105	.105	.211	-41	-4	-4	107	535	0	.118	0			0	C	-0.2
1932	StL-N	17	14	0	2	0	0	0	3	0	2	.143	.143	.143	.286	-23	-2	-2	100	558	0	.167	0			0	/C	-0.1
Total	17	1042	2829	283	717	123	19	13	263	231	198	.253	.314	.324	.638	80	-73	-73	100	104	300	.575	52	10		26	C/1O	0.1
■ **ORLANDO GONZALEZ**	Gonzalez, Orlando Eugene b: 11/15/51, Havana, Cuba BL/TL, 6'2", 180 lbs. Deb: 6/07/76																											
1976	Cle-A	28	68	5	17	2	0	0	4	5	7	.250	.301	.279	.581	71	-2	-2	100	81	5	.455	1	2	-1	-2	1/OD	-0.6
1978	Phi-N	26	26	1	5	0	0	0	0	1	1	.192	.222	.192	.415	16	-3	-3	105	0	1	.286	0	0	0	-2	O/1	-0.5
1980	Oak-A	25	70	10	17	0	0	0	1	9	8	.243	.329	.243	.572	63	-4	-3	95	23	6	.473	0	2	-1	1	1/OD	-0.4
Total	3	79	164	16	39	2	0	0	5	15	16	.238	.302	.250	.552	58	-9	-8	98	43	12	.442	1	4	-2	-4	/1OD	-1.5
■ **PEDRO GONZALEZ**	Gonzalez, Pedro (Olivares) b: 12/12/37, San Pedro De Macoris, D.R. BR/TR, 6', 176 lbs. Deb: 4/11/63																											
1963	NY-A	14	26	3	5	1	0	0	1	0	5	.192	.192	.231	.423	18	-3	-3	101	70	1	.273	0	1	-1	0	/2	-0.2
1964	NY-A	80	112	18	31	8	1	0	5	7	22	.277	.331	.366	.697	91	-1	-1	103	52	13	.609	3	4	-2	-2	1O/32	-0.6
1965	NY-A	7	5	0	2	1	0	0	0	0	2	.400	.400	.600	1.000	178	0	0	101	0	1	1.000	0	0	0	0	H	0.1
	Cle-A	116	400	38	101	14	3	5	39	18	57	.253	.290	.340	.630	80	-12	-11	98	107	38	.529	7	4	-0	2	*2/O3	-0.3
	Yr	123	405	38	103	15	3	5	39	18	59	.254	.291	.343	.634	81	-11	-11	98	101	39	.534	7	4	-0	2		-0.2
1966	Cle-A	110	352	21	82	9	2	2	17	15	54	.233	.268	.287	.555	59	-18	-19	101	67	27	.450	8	5	-1	-0	*2/3O	-1.1
1967	Cle-A	80	189	19	43	6	0	1	8	12	36	.228	.277	.275	.552	64	-8	-9	100	61	13	.437	4	6	-2	0	2/13S	-0.9

YEAR	TM/L	G	AB	R	H	2B	3B	HR	RBI	BB	SO	AVG	OBP	SLG	PRO	/A	BR	/A	PF	CHI	RC	TA	SB	CS	SBR	FR	POS	TPR
Total	5	407	1084	99	264	39	6	8	70	52	176	.244	.283	.313	.596	70	-42	-42	100	79	93	.498	22	20	-5	-0	2/103S	-3.0
■ CHARLIE GOOCH	Gooch, Charles Furman b: 6/5/02, Smyrna, Tenn. d: 5/30/82, Lanham, Md. BR/TR, 5'9", 170 lbs. Deb: 4/18/29																											
1929	Was-A	39	57	6	16	2	1	0	5	7	8	.281	.359	.351	.710	84	-1	-1	100	86	7	.643	0	1	-1	0	/13S	-0.1
■ JOHNNY GOOCH	Gooch, John Beverley b: 11/9/1897, Smyrna, Tenn. d: 3/15/75, Nashville, Tenn. BB/TR, 5'11", 175 lbs. Deb: 9/09/21 C																											
1921	Pit-N	13	38	2	9	0	0	0	3	3	3	.237	.293	.237	.530	40	-3	-3	103	122	3	.448	1	0	0	0	C	-0.1
1922	Pit-N	105	353	45	116	15	3	1	42	39	15	.329	.403	.397	.800	103	6	4	104	103	59	.777	1	1	-0	-3	*C	0.1
1923	Pit-N	66	202	16	56	10	2	1	20	17	13	.277	.336	.361	.698	87	-4	-4	97	93	25	.633	2	1	0	-1	C	0.0
1924	Pit-N	70	224	26	65	6	5	0	25	16	12	.290	.343	.362	.705	84	-3	-5	106	113	27	.617	1	3	-2	-1	C	-0.6
1925	Pit-N	79	215	24	64	8	4	0	30	20	16	.298	.357	.372	.730	85	-4	-4	102	133	30	.669	1	0	0	-3	C	-0.2
1926	Pit-N	86	218	19	59	15	1	1	42	20	14	.271	.340	.362	.703	79	-3	-7	112	177	27	.648	1			-3	C	-0.5
1927	Pit-N	101	291	22	75	17	2	2	48	19	21	.258	.305	.351	.656	74	-11	-11	102	155	31	.565	0			-5	C	-0.9
1928	Pit-N	31	80	7	19	2	1	0	5	3	6	.237	.265	.287	.553	42	-7	-7	107	77	6	.426	0			-1	C	-0.6
	Bro-N	42	101	9	32	1	2	0	12	7	9	.317	.361	.366	.727	91	-1	-1	99	115	13	.638	0			-1	C	0.0
	Yr	73	181	16	51	3	3	0	17	10	15	.282	.319	.331	.651	69	-8	-8	102	100	19	.538	0			-2		-0.6
1929	Bro-N	1	1	0	0	0	0	0	0	0	0	.000	.000	.000	.000	-99	-0	-0	94	0	0	.000	0			0	H	0.0
	Cin-N	92	287	22	86	13	5	0	34	24	10	.300	.356	.380	.736	83	-8	-7	99	107	38	.687	4			4	C	0.3
	Yr	93	288	22	86	13	5	0	34	24	10	.299	.355	.378	.733	82	-8	-8	99	106	38	.683	4			4		0.3
1930	Cin-N	82	276	29	67	10	3	2	30	27	15	.243	.315	.322	.637	60	-20	-16	90	109	28	.565	0			1	C	-0.9
1933	Bos-A	37	77	6	14	1	1	0	2	11	7	.182	.284	.221	.505	35	-7	-7	101	39	5	.444	0	0	0	2	C	-0.3
Total	11	805	2363	227	662	98	29	7	293	206	141	.280	.342	.355	.697	79	-65	-69	101	118	292	.628	11	5		-10	C	-3.7
■ LEE GOOCH	Gooch, Lee Currin b: 2/23/1890, Oxford, N.C. d: 5/18/66, Raleigh, N.C. BR/TR, 6', 190 lbs. Deb: 8/17/15																											
1915	Cle-A	2	2	0	1	0	0	0	0	0	0	.500	.500	.500	1.000	192	0	0	104	0	1	1.000	0			0	H	0.0
1917	Phi-A	17	59	4	17	2	0	1	8	4	10	.288	.333	.373	.706	123	1	1	94	117	7	.619	0			-3	O	-0.2
Total	2	19	61	4	18	2	0	1	8	4	10	.295	.338	.377	.716	126	1	2	94	113	8	.628	0			-3	/O	-0.2
■ GENE GOOD	Good, Eugene J. b: 12/13/1882, Roxbury, Mass. d: 8/6/47, Boston, Mass. 5'6", 130 lbs. Deb: 4/12/06																											
1906	Bos-N	34	119	4	18	0	0	0	0	13		.151	.235	.151	.386	22	-10	-10	100	0	5	.327	2			-3	O	-1.5
■ WILBUR GOOD	Good, Wilbur David "Lefty" b: 9/28/1885, Punxsutawney, Pa. d: 12/30/63, Brooksville, Fla. BL/TL, 5'6", 165 lbs. Deb: 8/18/05																											
1905	NY-A	5	8	2	3	0	0	0	0	0		.375	.375	.375	.750	138	0	0	102	0	1	.600	0			0	/P	0.0
1908	Cle-A	46	154	23	43	1	3	1	14	13		.279	.335	.344	.679	116	4	3	106	96	19	.658	7			2	O	0.3
1909	Cle-A	94	318	33	68	6	5	0	17	28		.214	.296	.264	.560	75	-7	-8	102	83	28	.536	13			3	O	-0.9
1910	Bos-N	23	86	15	29	5	4	0	11	6	13	.337	.394	.488	.882	138	6	4	114	88	18	.965	5			5	O	0.9
1911	Bos-N	43	165	21	44	9	3	0	15	12	22	.267	.316	.358	.674	85	-3	-4	103	91	19	.612	3			6	O	0.1
	Chi-N	58	145	27	39	5	4	2	21	11	17	.269	.329	.400	.729	107	0	1	97	111	22	.764	10			-4	O	-0.3
	Yr	101	310	48	83	14	7	2	36	23	39	.268	.322	.377	.700	96	-3	-3	99	103	41	.683	13			2		-0.2
1912	Chi-N	39	35	7	5	0	0	0	1	3	7	.143	.211	.143	.353	-2	-5	-5	104	67	2	.367	3			-3	O	-0.7
1913	Chi-N	49	91	11	23	3	2	1	12	11	16	.253	.340	.363	.702	102	0	0	99	121	12	.735	5			-4	O	-0.4
1914	Chi-N	154	580	70	158	24	7	2	43	53	74	.272	.341	.348	.689	107	4	5	98	72	77	.694	31			-3	*O	-0.1
1915	Chi-N	128	498	66	126	18	9	2	27	34	65	.253	.307	.337	.645	93	-3	-5	102	57	52	.581	19	17	-5	-7	*O	-2.1
1916	Phi-N	75	136	25	34	4	3	1	15	8	13	.250	.306	.346	.652	104	-0	0	96	119	17	.637	7			-7	O	-0.8
1918	Chi-A	35	148	24	37	9	4	0	11	11	16	.250	.315	.365	.680	105	0	0	101	64	16	.622	1			6	O	0.5
Total	11	749	2364	324	609	84	44	9	187	190	243	.258	.321	.342	.663	98	-4	-7	101	80	284	.640	104	17		-6	O/P	-3.5
■ BILL GOODENOUGH	Goodenough, William B. b: 1863, St.Louis, Mo. d: 5/24/05, St.Louis, Mo. 6'1", 170 lbs. Deb: 8/31/1893																											
1893	StL-N	10	31	4	5	1	0	0	2	3	4	.161	.297	.194	.491	33	-3	-3	99	91	2	.538	2			0	O	-0.1
■ MIKE GOODFELLOW	Goodfellow, Michael J. b: 10/3/1866, Port Jervis, N.Y. d: 2/12/20, Newark, N.J. 6', 180 lbs. Deb: 6/13/1887																											
1887	StL-a	1	4	0	0	0	0	0		0		.000	.000	.000	.000	-91	-1	-1	110	0	0	.000	0			0	/C	0.0
1888	Cle-a	68	269	24	66	7	0	0	29	11		.245	.283	.271	.554	83	-6	-4	97	126	23	.463	7			-3	O/C1S	-0.8
Total	2	69	273	24	66	7	0	0	29	11		.242	.279	.267	.546	80	-7	-6	98	124	23	.454	7			-3	/OC1S	-0.8
■ IVAL GOODMAN	Goodman, Ival Richard "Goodie" b: 7/23/08, Northview, Mo. d: 11/25/84, Cincinnati, Ohio BL/TR, 5'11", 170 lbs. Deb: 4/16/35																											
1935	Cin-N	148	592	86	159	23	**18**	12	72	35	50	.269	.314	.429	.743	104	-4	2	93	86	83	.701	14			5	*O	0.1
1936	Cin-N	136	489	81	139	15	**14**	17	71	38	53	.284	.347	.476	.823	124	12	14	97	90	82	.790	6			1	*O	1.0
1937	Cin-N	147	549	86	150	25	12	12	55	55	58	.273	.347	.428	.775	120	7	13	91	78	85	.751	10			3	*O	1.0
1938	Cin-N	145	568	103	166	27	10	30	92	53	51	.292	.368	.533	.901	149	33	35	98	81	116	.908	3			4	*O	3.6
1939	Cin-N	124	470	85	152	37	16	7	84	54	32	.323	.401	.515	.916	140	30	28	103	124	101	.941	2			6	*O	3.1
1940	Cin-N	136	519	78	134	20	6	12	63	60	54	.258	.335	.389	.724	98	-0	-1	101	104	72	.698	9			-10	*O	-1.5
1941	Cin-N	42	149	14	40	5	2	1	12	16	15	.268	.343	.349	.692	96	-1	-0	99	80	18	.619	1			-2	O	-0.3
1942	Cin-N	87	226	21	55	18	1	0	15	24	32	.243	.319	.332	.651	89	-3	-3	101	74	24	.562	0			-1	O	-0.4
1943	Chi-N	80	225	31	72	10	5	3	45	24	20	.320	.390	.449	.839	144	12	13	99	148	40	.834	4			-5	O	0.6
1944	Chi-N	62	141	24	37	8	1	1	16	23	15	.262	.377	.355	.732	106	2	2	101	108	20	.704	0			-5	O	-0.4
Total	10	1107	3928	609	1104	188	85	95	525	382	380	.281	.352	.445	.797	120	90	103	98	95	641	.787	49			-2	O	6.8
■ JAKE GOODMAN	Goodman, Jacob b: 9/14/1853, Lancaster, Pa. d: 3/9/1890, Reading, Pa. Deb: 5/02/1878																											
1878	Mil-N	60	252	28	62	4	3	1	27	7	33	.246	.266	.298	.564	80	-4	-6	107	113	20	.432				-4	*1	-0.7
1882	Pit-a	10	41	5	13	2	2	0		2		.317	.349	.463	.812	177	3	3	97	0	7	.750				0	1	0.3
Total	2	70	293	33	75	6	5	1	27	9	33	.256	.278	.321	.599	92	-1	-3	105	97	27	.472				-4	/1	-0.4
■ BILLY GOODMAN	Goodman, William Dale b: 3/22/26, Concord, N.C. d: 10/1/84, Sarasota, Fla. BL/TR, 5'11", 165 lbs. Deb: 4/19/47 C																											
1947	Bos-A	12	11	1	2	0	0	0	1	1	2	.182	.250	.182	.432	20	-1	-1	108	184	1	.333	0	0	0	0	/O	0.0
1948	Bos-A	127	445	65	138	27	2	1	66	74	44	.310	.414	.387	.801	113	12	12	100	130	75	.780	5	3	-0	-2	*1/23	1.5
1949	Bos-A	122	443	54	132	23	3	0	56	58	21	.298	.382	.363	.745	91	0	-4	107	122	65	.686	2	0	1	-3	*1	-0.5
1950	Bos-A	110	424	91	150	25	3	4	68	52	25	**.354**	.427	.455	.882	110	18	9	114	117	86	.871	2	4	-2	2	O31/2S	0.7
1951	Bos-A	141	546	92	162	34	4	0	50	79	37	.297	.388	.374	.761	99	8	2	108	93	85	.730	7	4	-0	2	12O/3	0.3
1952	Bos-A	138	513	79	157	27	3	4	56	48	23	.306	.370	.394	.764	105	9	5	107	104	80	.718	8	2	1	18	*21/3O	2.8
1953	Bos-A	128	514	73	161	33	5	2	41	57	11	.313	.384	.409	.793	105	11	5	109	62	87	.752	1	4	-2	7	*21	1.6
1954	Bos-A	127	489	71	148	25	4	1	36	51	15	.303	.371	.376	.747	105	4	4	100	77	70	.678	3	3	-1	6	21O3	1.1
1955	Bos-A	149	599	100	176	31	2	0	52	99	44	.294	.397	.352	.749	83	7	-13	124	79	90	.721	5	5	-2	-21	*2/1O	-2.6
1956	Bos-A	105	399	61	117	22	8	2	38	40	22	.293	.358	.404	.761	98	0	-1	103	87	59	.698	0	3	-2	1	2	0.5
1957	Bos-A	18	16	1	1	1	0	0	0	2	1	.063	.167	.125	.292	-17	-3	-3	110	0	0	.267	0	0	0	0	H	-0.2
	Bal-A	73	263	36	81	10	3	3	33	21	18	.308	.366	.403	.769	118	4	6	93	116	36	.667	0	2	-1	-3	3/O12S	0.3
	Yr	91	279	37	82	11	3	3	33	23	19	.294	.354	.387	.741	106	1	2	96	93	36	.638	0	2	-1	-3		0.1
1958	Chi-A	116	425	41	127	15	5	0	40	37	21	.299	.358	.358	.715	99	-0	1	98	108	55	.623	1	0	0	-5	*3/12S	0.1
1959	Chi-A	104	268	21	67	14	1	1	28	19	20	.250	.304	.321	.625	74	-10	-9	97	124	27	.537	3	0	1	2	3/2	-0.6
1960	Chi-A	30	77	5	18	4	0	0	6	12	8	.234	.337	.286	.623	69	-3	-3	101	107	8	.557	0	0	0	1	3/2	-0.1
1961	Chi-A	41	51	4	13	4	0	1	10	7	6	.255	.345	.392	.737	97	-0	-0	99	170	7	.692	0	0	0	0	/312	0.0
1962	Hou-N	82	161	12	41	4	1	0	10	12	11	.255	.306	.292	.598	66	-8	-7	93	84	14	.468	0	0	0	-0	23/1	-0.3
Total	16	1623	5644	807	1691	299	44	19	591	669	329	.300	.377	.378	.755	98	49	3	106	99	844	.719	37	30	-7	7	213O/S	4.6
■ ED GOODSON	Goodson, James Edward b: 1/25/48, Pulaski, Va. BL/TR, 6'3", 180 lbs. Deb: 9/05/70																											
1970	SF-N	7	11	1	3	0	0	0	0	0	2	.273	.273	.273	.545	49	-1	-1	96	0	1	.375	0	0	0	0	/1	0.0
1971	SF-N	20	42	4	8	1	0	0	1	2	4	.190	.227	.214	.442	26	-4	-4	100	45	2	.297	0	0	0	-0	1	-0.5
1972	SF-N	58	150	15	42	1	1	6	30	8	12	.280	.321	.420	.741	109	1	1	100	152	18	.632	0	0	0	-2	1	-0.2
1973	SF-N	102	384	37	116	20	1	12	53	15	44	.302	.332	.453	.785	110	6	4	105	103	54	.685	0	1	-1	-5	3	-0.3
1974	SF-N	98	298	25	81	15	0	6	48	18	22	.272	.320	.383	.702	89	-2	-5	108	140	35	.607	1	0	0	1	1/3	-0.6

YEAR	TM/L	G	AB	R	H	2B	3B	HR	RBI	BB	SO	AVG	OBP	SLG	PRO	/A	BR	/A	PF	CHI	RC	TA	SB	CS	SBR	FR	POS	TPR
1975	SF-N	39	121	10	25	7	0	1	8	7	14	.207	.250	.289	.539	49	-9	-9	102	81	8	.416	0	1	-1	1	13	-0.9
	Atl-N	47	76	5	16	2	0	1	8	2	8	.211	.231	.276	.507	42	-6	-6	95	129	4	.354	0	0	0	-0	1/3	-0.6
	Yr	86	197	15	41	9	0	2	16	9	22	.208	.243	.284	.527	47	-15	-14	98	108	13	.401	0	1	-1	0		-1.5
1976	LA-N	83	118	8	27	4	0	3	17	8	19	.229	.278	.339	.617	75	-4	-4	100	134	9	.490	0	0	0	0	3/1O2	-0.4
1977	LA-N	61	66	3	11	1	0	1	5	3	10	.167	.203	.227	.430	15	-8	-8	100	111	2	.310	0	1	-1	0	1/3	-0.8
Total	8	515	1266	108	329	51	2	30	170	63	135	.260	.298	.374	.673	84	-27	-31	103	118	133	.577	1	3	-2	-5	13/O2	-4.3
■ **PEP GOODWIN** Goodwin, Claire Vernon b: 12/19/1891, Pocatello, Idaho d: 2/15/72, Oakland, Cal. BL/TR, 5'10.5", 160 lbs. Deb: 4/16/14																												
1914	KC-F	112	374	38	88	15	6	1	32	27	23	.235	.287	.316	.602	76	-14	-11	95	97	37	.521	4			-4	S3/1	-1.0
1915	KC-F	81	229	22	54	5	1	0	16	15	23	.236	.283	.266	.549	65	-10	-9	97	95	21	.469	6			1	S2	-0.5
Total	2	193	603	60	142	20	7	1	48	42	46	.235	.285	.297	.582	72	-24	-21	96	96	58	.501	10			-4	S/321	-1.5
■ **DANNY GOODWIN** Goodwin, Danny Kay b: 9/2/53, St.Louis, Mo. BL/TR, 6'1", 195 lbs. Deb: 9/03/75																												
1975	Cal-A	4	10	0	1	0	0	0	0	0	5	.100	.100	.100	.200	-46	-2	-2	95	0	-0	.091	0	0	0	0	/D	-0.1
1977	Cal-A	35	91	5	19	6	1	1	8	5	19	.209	.250	.330	.580	60	-6	-5	95	96	7	.473	0	0	0	0	D	-0.4
1978	Cal-A	24	58	9	16	5	0	2	10	10	13	.276	.382	.466	.848	135	3	3	102	120	11	.860	0	0	0	0	D	0.3
1979	Min-A	58	159	22	46	8	5	5	27	11	23	.289	.335	.497	.832	112	4	2	109	110	25	.763	0	0	0	0	D/1	0.2
1980	Min-A	55	115	12	23	5	0	1	11	17	32	.200	.303	.270	.573	54	-6	-8	109	126	10	.500	0	0	0	0	D1	-0.7
1981	Min-A	59	151	18	34	6	1	2	17	16	32	.225	.299	.318	.617	74	-4	-5	105	123	15	.554	3	1	0	-1	1/OD	-0.6
1982	Oak-A	17	52	6	11	2	1	2	8	2	13	.212	.241	.404	.645	77	-2	-2	95	118	4	.523	0	0	0	0	D	-0.1
Total	7	252	636	72	150	32	8	13	81	61	137	.236	.303	.373	.675	83	-13	-16	104	114	72	.614	3	1	0	-0	D/1O	-1.4
■ **RAY GOOLSBY** Goolsby, Raymond Daniel "Ox" b: 9/5/19, Florala, Ala. BR/TR, 6'1", 185 lbs. Deb: 4/18/46																												
1946	Was-A	3	4	0	0	0	0	0	0	1	1	.000	.200	.000	.200	-44	-1	-1	92	0	0	.250	0	0	0	-0	/O	0.0
■ **GREG GOOSSEN** Goossen, Gregory Bryant b: 12/14/45, Los Angeles, Cal. BR/TR, 6'1.5", 210 lbs. Deb: 9/03/65																												
1965	NY-N	11	31	2	9	0	0	1	2	1	5	.290	.313	.387	.700	96	-0	-0	100	55	4	.591	0	0	0	-1	/C	0.0
1966	NY-N	13	32	1	6	2	0	1	5	1	11	.188	.235	.344	.579	62	-2	-2	94	150	2	.448	0	0	0	-0	C	-0.1
1967	NY-N	37	69	2	11	1	0	0	3	4	26	.159	.216	.174	.390	13	-8	-8	99	104	3	.288	0	0	0	-2	C	-0.8
1968	NY-N	38	106	4	22	7	0	0	6	10	21	.208	.288	.274	.562	68	-4	-4	102	87	8	.466	0	0	0	1	1/C	-0.4
1969	Sea-A	52	139	19	43	8	1	10	24	14	29	.309	.385	.597	.982	174	13	13	98	85	30	.990	1	1	-0	2	1/O	1.3
1970	Mil-A	21	47	3	12	3	0	1	3	10	12	.255	.407	.383	.790	121	2	2	98	58	8	.833	0	0	0	1	1	0.2
	Was-A	21	36	2	8	3	0	0	1	2	8	.222	.263	.306	.569	59	-2	-2	96	37	3	.448	0	0	0	-1	/O1	-0.3
	Yr	42	83	5	20	6	0	1	4	12	20	.241	.351	.349	.700	96	-0	-0	97	49	11	.672	0	0	0	-1		-0.1
Total	6	193	460	33	111	24	1	13	44	42	112	.241	.317	.383	.700	99	-1	-1	99	84	58	.650	1	1	-0	-1	/1CO	-0.1
■ **GLEN GORBOUS** Gorbous, Glen Edward b: 7/8/30, Drumheller, Alt., Can. BL/TR, 6'2", 175 lbs. Deb: 4/11/55																												
1955	Cin-N	8	18	2	6	3	0	0	4	3	1	.333	.429	.500	.929	138	1	1	106	180	4	1.000	0	0	0	-0	/O	0.1
	Phi-N	91	224	25	53	9	1	4	23	21	17	.237	.302	.339	.641	68	-10	-10	102	106	22	.539	0	3	-2	5	O	-0.7
	Yr	99	242	27	59	12	1	4	27	24	18	.244	.312	.351	.663	74	-8	-9	102	114	25	.568	0	3	-2	5		-0.6
1956	Phi-N	15	33	1	6	0	0	0	1	0	1	.182	.182	.182	.364	-2	-5	-4	94	70	1	.222	0	0	0	-2	/O	-0.6
1957	Phi-N	3	2	1	1	1	0	0	1	1	0	.500	.667	1.000	1.667	346	1	1	98	207	2	3.000	0	0	0	0	H	0.1
Total	3	117	277	29	66	13	1	4	29	25	19	.238	.301	.336	.637	68	-12	-13	101	108	28	.551	0	3	-2	3	/O	-1.1
■ **JOE GORDON** Gordon, Joseph Lowell "Flash" b: 2/18/15, Los Angeles, Cal. d: 4/14/78, Sacramento, Cal. BR/TR, 5'10", 180 lbs. Deb: 4/18/38 MC																												
1938	NY-A	127	458	83	117	24	7	25	97	56	72	.255	.340	.502	.843	103	3	-1	105	110	81	.872	11	3	2	17	*2	2.0
1939	NY-A	151	567	92	161	32	5	28	111	75	57	.284	.370	.506	.876	133	17	25	91	103	103	.870	11	10	-3	6	*2	3.1
1940	NY-A	155	616	112	173	32	10	30	103	52	57	.281	.340	.511	.851	119	13	14	99	97	107	.838	18	8	1	14	*2	3.4
1941	NY-A	156	588	104	162	26	7	24	87	72	80	.276	.358	.466	.824	119	13	15	98	94	98	.798	10	9	-2	10	*21	3.2
1942	NY-A	147	538	88	173	29	4	18	103	79	95	.322	.409	.491	.900	153	39	39	99	121	108	.906	12	6	0	8	*2	5.2
1943	NY-A	152	543	82	135	28	5	17	69	98	75	.249	.365	.413	.778	132	21	23	96	97	84	.758	4	7	-3	25	*2	5.4
1946	NY-A	112	376	35	79	15	0	11	47	49	72	.210	.308	.338	.645	80	-10	-10	100	114	38	.576	2	5	-2	14	*2	1.1
1947	Cle-A	155	562	89	153	27	6	29	93	62	49	.272	.346	.496	.842	138	21	24	96	95	96	.815	7	3	0	-3	*2	2.9
1948	Cle-A	144	550	96	154	21	4	32	124	77	68	.280	.371	.507	.879	134	23	24	99	118	106	.879	5	2	0	-5	*2/S	2.2
1949	Cle-A	148	541	74	136	18	3	20	84	83	33	.251	.355	.407	.762	104	0	2	98	109	79	.724	5	6	-2	-5	*2	-0.3
1950	Cle-A	119	368	59	87	12	1	19	57	56	44	.236	.340	.429	.770	98	-3	-2	98	92	56	.753	4	1	1	-13	*2	-0.6
Total	11	1566	5707	914	1530	264	52	253	975	759	702	.268	.357	.466	.822	121	136	153	98	104	959	.832	89	60	-9	68	*2/1S	27.6
■ **MIKE GORDON** Gordon, Michael William b: 9/11/53, Leominster, Mass. BB/TR, 6'3", 215 lbs. Deb: 4/07/77																												
1977	Chi-N	8	23	0	1	0	0	0	2	2	8	.043	.120	.043	.163	-47	-5	-5	114	800	0	.136	0	0	0	0	/C	-0.5
1978	Chi-N	4	5	0	1	0	0	0	0	3	2	.200	.556	.200	.756	108	1	1	110	0	1	1.250	0	0	0	-0	/C	0.0
Total	2	12	28	0	2	0	0	0	2	5	10	.071	.235	.071	.307	-11	-4	-5	113	589	1	.308	0	0	0	-0	/C	-0.5
■ **SID GORDON** Gordon, Sidney b: 8/13/17, Brooklyn, N.Y. d: 6/17/75, New York, N.Y. BR/TR, 5'10", 185 lbs. Deb: 9/11/41																												
1941	NY-N	9	31	4	8	1	1	0	4	6	1	.258	.378	.355	.733	104	1	0	103	134	5	.739	0			-1	/O	0.0
1942	NY-N	6	19	4	6	0	1	0	2	3	2	.316	.409	.421	.830	139	1	1	103	93	3	.786	0			1	/3	0.2
1943	NY-N	131	474	50	119	9	11	9	63	43	32	.251	.315	.373	.688	102	-2	0	96	114	50	.585	2			6	31O/2	0.3
1946	NY-N	135	450	64	132	15	4	5	45	60	27	.293	.380	.378	.758	114	11	10	102	93	66	.703	1			-1	*O3	0.7
1947	NY-N	130	437	57	119	19	8	13	57	50	21	.272	.347	.442	.789	107	4	4	101	91	67	.745	2			-0	*O/3	0.0
1948	NY-N	142	521	100	156	26	4	30	107	74	39	.299	.390	.537	.927	149	35	35	100	115	108	.953	8			-8	*3O	2.3
1949	NY-N	141	489	87	139	26	2	26	90	95	37	.284	.404	.505	.909	140	32	31	102	111	99	.925	1			-19	*3O/1	1.1
1950	Bos-N	134	481	78	146	33	4	27	103	78	31	.304	.403	.557	.960	**174**	35	45	86	116	109	1.003	2			7	*O3	**4.5**
1951	Bos-N	150	550	96	158	28	1	29	109	80	32	.287	.383	.500	.883	138	28	30	98	123	103	.862	2	0	1	-7	*O3	1.9
1952	Bos-N	144	522	69	151	22	2	25	75	77	49	.289	.384	.483	.866	146	28	32	95	95	101	.862	0	4	-2	-4	*O/3	2.2
1953	Mil-N	140	464	67	127	22	4	19	75	71	40	.274	.372	.461	.834	123	12	16	94	110	82	.818	1	1	-0	-2	*O	0.7
1954	Pit-N	131	363	38	111	12	0	12	49	67	24	.306	.414	.438	.852	126	15	17	97	99	70	.863	0	0	0	-4	O3	1.0
1955	Pit-N	16	47	2	8	1	0	0	1	2	6	.170	.204	.191	.396	6	-6	-6	97	45	1	.262	0	0	0	-1	/3O	-0.6
	NY-N	66	144	19	35	6	1	7	25	25	15	.243	.355	.444	.799	112	2	3	99	119	25	.817	0	0	0	2	3O	0.4
	Yr	82	191	21	43	7	1	7	26	27	21	.225	.321	.382	.703	87	-4	-3	98	105	26	.676	0	0	0	1		-0.2
Total	13	1475	4992	735	1415	220	43	202	805	731	356	.283	.377	.466	.844	131	196	217	97	107	889	.865	19	5		-32	O3/12	14.7
■ **GEORGE GORE** Gore, George F. "Piano Legs" b: 5/3/1857, Saccarappa, Me. d: 9/16/33, Utica, N.Y. BL/TR, 5'11", 195 lbs. Deb: 5/01/1879 M																												
1879	Chi-N	63	266	43	70	17	4	0	32	8	30	.263	.285	.357	.642	105	3	1	105	125	28	.526				-3	O/1	-0.2
1880	Chi-N	77	322	70	116	23	2	2	47	21	10	**.360**	**.399**	**.463**	**.862**	**182**	**30**	**28**	105	98	**61**	**.825**				3	*O/1	2.7
1881	Chi-N	73	309	**86**	92	18	9	1	44	27	23	.298	.354	.424	.778	132	16	12	108	101	48	.728				1	*O/31	1.1
1882	Chi-N	84	367	**99**	117	15	7	3	51	**29**	19	.319	.369	.422	.791	151	22	22	101	92	59	.736				3	*O	2.1
1883	Chi-N	92	392	105	131	30	9	2	16	27	13	.334	.377	.472	.849	143	26	21	109	26	72	.812				7	*O	2.6
1884	Chi-N	103	422	104	134	18	4	5	34	**61**	26	.318	.404	.415	.818	146	31	25	108	54	72	.819				0	*O	2.2
1885	Chi-N	109	441	115	138	21	13	5	57	68	25	.313	.405	.454	.858	156	41	31	114	81	83	.884				-7	*O	2.0
1886	Chi-N	118	444	150	135	20	12	6	63	**102**	30	.304	.434	.444	.878	144	42	30	116	82	98	1.042	23			-5	*O	2.4
1887	NY-N	111	459	95	133	16	5	1	49	42	18	.290	.358	.353	.711	93	2	-4	107	79	74	.767	39			-1	*O	-0.3
1888	NY-N	64	254	37	56	4	4	2	17	30	31	.220	.308	.291	.599	102	-1	2	93	66	27	.591	11			-7	O	-0.4
1889	NY-N	120	488	132	149	21	7	7	54	84	28	.305	.416	.420	.836	129	27	23	105	62	99	.959	28			-10	*O	0.7
1890	NY-P	93	399	132	127	26	8	10	55	77	23	.318	.432	.499	.931	138	31	24	109	57	101	1.129	28			-20	O	0.0
1891	NY-N	130	528	103	150	22	7	2	48	74	34	.284	.379	.364	.743	127	16	21	94	61	82	.772	19			-10	*O	0.4
1892	NY-N	53	193	47	49	11	2	0	11	49	16	.254	.412	.332	.744	130	10	11	98	45	35	.944	20			0	O	0.8
	StL-N	20	73	9	15	0	1	0	4	18	6	.205	.363	.233	.596	87	-0	0	95	64	7	.638	2			-2	OM	-0.1
	Yr	73	266	56	64	11	3	0	15	67	22	.241	.399	.305	.703	119	10	11	97	51	42	.856	22			-2		0.7
Total	14	1310	5357	1327	1612	262	94	46	582	717	332	.301	.386	.411	.797	134	297	247	105	72	945	.832	170			-50	*O/13	16.0

YEAR	TM/L	G	AB	R	H	2B	3B	HR	RBI	BB	SO	AVG	OBP	SLG	PRO	/A	BR	/A	PF	CHI	RC	TA	SB	CS	SBR	FR	POS	TPR
■ **BOB GORINSKI**	Gorinski, Robert John b: 1/7/52, Latrobe, Pa. BR/TR, 6'3", 215 lbs. Deb: 4/10/77																											
1977	Min-A	54	118	14	23	4	1	3	22	5	29	.195	.228	.322	.550	47	-9	-9	103	185	9	.458	1	0	0	-8	O/D	-1.8
■ **HERB GORMAN**	Gorman, Herbert Allen b: 12/18/24, San Francisco, Cal d: 4/5/53, San Diego, Cal. BL/TL, 5'11", 180 lbs. Deb: 4/19/52																											
1952	StL-N	1	1	0	0	0	0	0	0	0	0	.000	.000	.000	.000	-99	-0	-0	98	0	0	.000	0	0	0	0	H	0.0
■ **HOWIE GORMAN**	Gorman, Howard Paul "Lefty" b: 5/14/13, Pittsburgh, Pa. d: 4/29/84, Harrisburg, Pa. BL/TL, 6'2", 160 lbs. Deb: 8/07/37																											
1937	Phi-N	13	19	3	4	1	0	0	1	1	1	.211	.250	.263	.513	37	-2	-2	108	72	1	.467	1			-3	/O	-0.5
1938	Phi-N	1	1	0	0	0	0	0	0	0	0	.000	.000	.000	.000	-99	-0	-0	100	0	0	.000	0			0	H	0.0
Total	2	14	20	3	4	1	0	0	1	1	1	.200	.238	.250	.488	30	-2	-2	108	69	1	.438	1			-3	/O	-0.5
■ **JACK GORMAN**	Gorman, John F. "Stooping Jack" b: 1859, St.Louis, Mo. d: 9/9/1889, St.Louis, Mo. Deb: 1883																											
1883	StL-a	1	4	0	0	0	0	0		0		.000	.000	.000	.000	-93	-1	-1	108	0	0	.000				0	/O	0.0
1884	KC-U	33	137	25	38	5	2	0		4		.277	.298	.343	.641	133	2	5	87	0	14	.515	0			0	1/O3	0.4
	Pit-a	8	27	3	4	0	1	0		1		.148	.179	.222	.401	33	-2	-2	97	0	1	.304				0	/PO3	-0.1
Total	2	42	168	28	42	5	3	0		5		.250	.272	.315	.587	109	-1	2	89	0	15	.460				0	/1O3P	0.3
■ **JOHNNY GORYL**	Goryl, John Albert b: 10/21/33, Cumberland, R.I. BR/TR, 5'10", 175 lbs. Deb: 9/20/57 MC																											
1957	Chi-N	9	38	7	8	2	0	0	1	5	9	.211	.318	.263	.581	61	-2	-2	96	36	3	.516	0	1	-1	-1	/3	-0.2
1958	Chi-N	83	219	27	53	9	3	4	14	27	34	.242	.331	.365	.696	84	-5	-5	101	63	24	.602	0	1	-1	2	32	0.0
1959	Chi-N	25	48	1	9	3	1	1	6	5	3	.188	.264	.354	.618	64	-3	-3	98	121	4	.535	1	1	-0	0	2/3	-0.1
1962	Min-A	37	26	6	5	0	1	2	2	2	6	.192	.250	.500	.750	92	-0	-1	105	42	3	.682	0	0	0	0	/2S	0.0
1963	Min-A	64	150	29	43	5	3	9	24	15	29	.287	.355	.540	.895	146	9	9	100	93	28	.874	0	0	0	-7	23/S	0.5
1964	Min-A	58	114	9	16	0	2	0	1	10	25	.140	.216	.175	.391	10	-14	-14	101	21	5	.317	1	0	0	-2	23	-1.2
Total	6	276	595	79	134	19	10	16	48	64	106	.225	.306	.371	.677	83	-15	-15	100	64	66	.625	2	3	-1	-6	2/3S	-1.0
■ **JIM GOSGER**	Gosger, James Charles b: 11/6/42, Port Huron, Mich. BL/TL, 5'11", 185 lbs. Deb: 5/04/63																											
1963	Bos-A	19	16	3	1	0	0	0	0	3	5	.063	.211	.063	.273	-18	-3	-3	106	0	0	.267	0	0	0	-0	/O	-0.2
1965	Bos-A	81	324	45	83	15	4	9	35	29	61	.256	.321	.410	.732	99	2	-1	107	87	43	.671	3	1	0	12	O	0.9
1966	Bos-A	40	126	16	32	4	0	5	17	15	20	.254	.333	.405	.738	102	2	0	109	108	18	.688	0	1	-1	0	O	0.0
	KC-A	88	272	34	61	14	1	5	27	37	53	.224	.322	.338	.660	95	-3	-1	94	106	32	.630	5	3	-0	4	O	0.0
	Yr	128	398	50	93	18	1	10	44	52	73	.234	.325	.359	.685	98	-1	-0	99	107	50	.650	5	4	-1	4		0.0
1967	KC-A	134	356	31	86	14	5	5	36	53	69	.242	.340	.351	.691	105	3	3	100	107	44	.654	5	7	-3	2	*O	0.0
1968	Oak-A	88	150	7	27	1	1	0	5	17	21	.180	.263	.200	.463	43	-10	-10	98	71	8	.398	4	0	1	0	O	-1.2
1969	Sea-A	39	55	4	6	2	1	1	1	6	11	.109	.197	.236	.433	21	-6	-6	98	25	3	.412	2	1	0	-2	O	-0.9
	NY-N	10	15	0	2	2	0	0	1	1	6	.133	.188	.267	.454	26	-2	-2	100	100	1	.385	0	0	0	-1	/O	-0.2
1970	Mon-N	91	274	38	72	11	2	5	37	35	35	.263	.348	.372	.721	93	-2	-2	100	123	37	.684	5	3	-0	2	O1	-0.5
1971	Mon-N	51	102	7	16	2	2	0	8	9	17	.157	.232	.216	.448	28	-10	-10	99	148	5	.367	1	1	-0	-1	O/1	-1.2
1973	NY-N	38	92	9	22	2	0	0	10	9	16	.239	.307	.261	.568	58	-5	-5	101	167	7	.458	0	1	-1	-5	O	-1.2
1974	NY-N	26	33	3	3	0	0	0	0	3	2	.091	.167	.091	.258	-27	-6	-6	99	0	0	.188	0	0	0	-7	O	-1.3
Total	10	705	1815	197	411	67	16	30	177	217	316	.226	.311	.331	.642	82	-38	-39	101	103	199	.596	25	18	-3	4	O/1	-5.8
■ **GOOSE GOSLIN**	Goslin, Leon Allen b: 10/16/1900, Salem, N.J. d: 5/15/71, Bridgeton, N.J. BL/TR, 5'11.5", 185 lbs. Deb: 9/16/21 H																											
1921	Was-A	14	50	8	13	1	1	1	6	5	5	.260	.339	.380	.719	84	-1	-1	99	95	7	.676	0	0	0	-0	O	-0.2
1922	Was-A	101	358	44	116	19	7	3	53	25	26	.324	.373	.441	.814	121	6	10	92	116	58	.772	4	4	-1	-0	O	0.1
1923	Was-A	150	600	86	180	29	**18**	9	99	40	53	.300	.347	.453	.800	116	5	10	95	120	95	.763	7	2	1	7	*O	0.3
1924	Was-A	154	579	100	199	30	17	12	**129**	68	29	.344	.421	.516	.937	143	36	37	98	135	126	.995	16	14	-4	-9	*O	1.2
1925	Was-A	150	601	116	201	34	**20**	18	113	53	50	.334	.394	.547	.941	140	31	33	98	105	131	1.015	26	8	**3**	0	*O	2.1
1926	Was-A	147	568	105	201	26	15	17	108	63	38	.354	.425	.542	.967	154	42	44	98	108	131	1.029	8	8	-2	8	*O	3.6
1927	Was-A	148	581	96	194	37	15	13	120	50	28	.334	.392	.516	.908	138	28	30	97	113	114	.972	21	0	6	-7	*O	1.2
1928	Was-A	135	456	80	173	36	10	17	102	48	19	**.379**	.442	.614	1.056	172	49	48	102	108	125	1.213	16	3	**3**	5	*O	4.6
1929	Was-A	145	553	82	159	28	7	18	91	66	33	.288	.366	.461	.827	112	9	9	100	107	97	.839	10	3	1	-5	*O	0.0
1930	Was-A	47	188	34	51	11	5	7	38	19	19	.271	.344	.495	.839	109	2	2	101	106	32	.842	3	2	-0	-7	O	-0.5
	StL-A	101	396	81	129	25	7	30	100	48	35	.326	.400	.652	1.052	150	35	30	108	92	101	1.163	14	9	-1	11	*O	3.2
	Yr	148	584	115	180	36	12	37	138	67	54	.308	.382	.601	.983	137	37	32	106	97	132	1.055	17	11	-2	4		2.7
1931	StL-A	151	591	114	194	42	10	24	105	80	41	.328	.412	.555	.967	148	45	43	102	83	137	1.045	9	6	-1	2	*O	3.2
1932	StL-A	150	572	88	171	28	9	17	104	92	35	.299	.398	.469	.866	124	22	22	100	116	110	.912	12	9	-2	7	*O/3	1.9
1933	Was-A	132	549	97	163	35	10	10	64	42	32	.297	.348	.452	.800	115	7	10	96	81	87	.763	5	2	0	4	*O	0.9
1934	Det-A	151	614	106	187	38	7	13	100	65	38	.305	.373	.453	.826	115	11	13	98	112	105	.812	5	4	-1	2	*O	1.1
1935	Det-A	147	590	88	172	34	6	9	109	56	31	.292	.355	.415	.770	102	-2	1	97	**144**	88	.730	5	4	-1	2	*O	0.1
1936	Det-A	147	572	122	180	33	8	24	125	85	50	.315	.403	.526	.930	134	25	29	95	115	126	1.010	14	4	2	-9	*O	1.5
1937	Det-A	79	181	30	43	11	1	4	35	35	18	.238	.367	.376	.743	80	-3	-5	109	150	27	.755	0	1	-1	-3	O/1	-0.9
1938	Was-A	38	57	6	9	3	0	2	8	8	5	.158	.262	.316	.577	46	-5	-5	95	113	5	.542	0	0	0	-2	O	-0.5
Total	18	2287	8656	1483	2735	500	173	248	1609	948	585	.316	.387	.500	.887	129	340	359	99	111	1702	.917	175	83	3	4	*O/13	22.9
■ **HOWIE GOSS**	Goss, Howard Wayne b: 11/1/34, Wewoka, Okla. BR/TR, 6'4", 204 lbs. Deb: 4/10/62																											
1962	Pit-N	89	111	19	27	6	0	2	10	9	36	.243	.306	.351	.657	74	-4	-4	102	88	12	.614	5	2	0	-12	O	-1.8
1963	Hou-N	133	411	37	86	18	2	9	44	31	128	.209	.265	.328	.593	76	-16	-13	92	114	36	.509	4	6	-2	-1	*O	-2.4
Total	2	222	522	56	113	24	2	11	54	40	164	.216	.274	.333	.607	75	-20	-17	94	108	48	.533	9	8	-2	-12	O	-4.2
■ **DICK GOSSETT**	Gossett, John Star b: 8/21/1891, Dennison, Ohio d: 10/6/62, Massillon, Ohio BR/TR, 5'11", 185 lbs. Deb: 4/30/13																											
1913	NY-A	39	105	9	17	2	0	0	9	10	22	.162	.254	.181	.435	28	-9	-9	101	168	5	.375	1			2	C	-0.3
1914	NY-A	10	21	3	3	0	0	0	1	5	5	.143	.333	.143	.476	44	-1	-1	100	125	1	.500	0			1	C	0.1
Total	2	49	126	12	20	2	0	0	10	15	27	.159	.269	.175	.444	31	-10	-10	101	160	6	.396	1			4	/C	-0.2
■ **JULIO GOTAY**	Gotay, Julio Enrique (Sanchez) b: 6/9/39, Fajardo, P.R. BR/TR, 6', 180 lbs. Deb: 8/06/60																											
1960	StL-N	3	8	1	3	0	0	0	0	0	2	.375	.375	.375	.750	98	0	-0	108	0	1	.800	1	0	0	0	/S3	0.0
1961	StL-N	10	45	5	11	4	0	0	5	3	5	.244	.292	.333	.625	58	-2	-3	113	116	4	.514	0	0	0	-0	S	-0.1
1962	StL-N	127	369	47	94	12	1	2	27	27	47	.255	.316	.309	.625	63	-16	-20	109	89	34	.527	7	3	0	1	*S/2O3	-0.6
1963	Pit-N	4	2	0	1	0	0	0	0	0	0	.500	.500	.500	1.000	192	0	0	99	0	1	1.000	0	0	0	0	/2	0.1
1964	Pit-N	3	2	1	1	0	0	0	0	1	0	.500	.667	.500	1.167	232	1	1	101	0	1	2.000	0	0	0	0	H	0.1
1965	Cal-A	40	77	6	19	4	0	1	3	4	9	.247	.284	.338	.622	78	-3	-2	98	43	7	.500	0	0	0	1	2/3S	0.0
1966	Hou-N	4	5	0	0	0	0	0	0	0	0	.000	.000	.000	.000	-99	-1	-1	97	0	0	.000	0	0	0	0	/3	0.0
1967	Hou-N	77	234	30	66	10	2	2	15	15	30	.282	.331	.368	.698	107	-0	2	94	68	28	.594	1	1	-0	-2	2S/3	0.3
1968	Hou-N	75	165	9	41	3	0	1	11	4	21	.248	.271	.285	.555	67	-7	-7	99	93	11	.402	1	2	-1	-2	2/3	-0.8
1969	Hou-N	46	81	7	21	5	0	0	9	7	13	.259	.318	.321	.639	78	-2	-2	102	139	7	.538	2	1	0	1	2/3	0.0
Total	10	389	988	106	257	38	3	6	70	61	127	.260	.309	.323	.632	75	-30	-33	102	85	94	.540	12	7	-1	-2	S2/3O	-1.0
■ **CHARLES GOULD**	Gould, Charles Harvey b: 8/21/1847, Cincinnati, Ohio d: 4/10/17, Flushing, N.Y. BR/TR, 6', 172 lbs. Deb: 5/05/1871 M																											
1871	Bos-n	31	156	38	42							.269															*1/O	
1872	Bos-n	45	223	41	57							.256															*1/O	
1874	Bal-n	33	151	20	34							.225															1/C	
1875	NH-n	27	115	9	29							.252															1OM	
1876	Cin-N	61	258	27	65	7	0	0	11	6	11	.252	.269	.279	.548	92	-4	-0	90	50	20	.404				1	*1/PM	0.1
1877	Cin-N	24	91	5	25	2	1	0	13	5	5	.275	.313	.319	.631	121	0	3	82	155	9	.515				-1	1/O	0.1
Total	4 n	136	645	108	162							.251															1/O	
Total	2	85	349	32	90	9	1	0	24	11	16	.258	.281	.289	.570	100	-4	2	87	78	29	.432				0	1/OPC	0.2
■ **NICK GOULISH**	Goulish, Nicholas Edward b: 11/13/17, Punxsutawney, Pa. d: 5/15/84, Youngstown, Ohio BL/TL, 6'1", 179 lbs. Deb: 4/19/44																											
1944	Phi-N	1	1	0	0	0	0	0	0	0	0	.000	.000	.000	.000	-99	-0	-0	100	0	0	.000	0			0	H	0.0

YEAR	TM/L	G	AB	R	H	2B	3B	HR	RBI	BB	SO	AVG	OBP	SLG	PRO	/A	BR	/A	PF	CHI	RC	TA	SB	CS	SBR	FR	POS	TPR
1945	Phi-N	13	11	4	3	0	0	0	2	1	3	.273	.333	.273	.606	72	-0	-0	96	231	1	.500	0			-1	/O	0.0
Total	2	14	12	4	3	0	0	0	2	1	3	.250	.308	.250	.558	58	-1	-1	97	214	1	.444	0			-1	/O	0.0
■ **CLAUDE GOUZZIE**	Gouzzie, Claude b: 1881, Pennsylvania d: 9/21/07, Denver, Colo. BR/TR, 5'9", 170 lbs. Deb: 03																											
1903	StL-A	1	1	0	0	0	0	0	0	0	0	.000	.000	.000	.000	-99	-0	-0	95	0	0	.000	0			0	/2	0.0
■ **HANK GOWDY**	Gowdy, Henry Morgan b: 8/24/1889, Columbus, Ohio d: 8/1/66, Columbus, Ohio BR/TR, 6'2", 182 lbs. Deb: 9/13/10 MC																											
1910	NY-N	7	14	1	3	1	0	0	2	2	3	.214	.313	.286	.598	78	-0	-0	95	174	2	.636	1			0	/1	0.0
1911	NY-N	4	4	1	1	1	0	0	0	2	0	.250	.500	.500	1.000	176	1	1	102	0	1	1.333	0			0	/1	0.1
	Bos-N	29	97	9	28	4	2	0	16	4	19	.289	.324	.371	.695	91	-1	-2	103	150	12	.623	2			1	1/C	-0.1
	Yr	33	101	10	29	5	2	0	16	6	19	.287	.333	.376	.710	95	-0	-1	103	132	13	.653	2			1		0.0
1912	Bos-N	44	96	16	26	6	1	3	10	16	13	.271	.386	.448	.834	119	4	3	107	65	18	.914	3			2	C/1	0.5
1913	Bos-N	3	5	0	3	1	0	0	2	3	2	.600	.750	.800	1.550	362	2	2	95	182	3	3.500	0			0	/C	0.2
1914	Bos-N	128	366	42	89	17	6	3	46	48	40	.243	.337	.347	.684	99	3	1	104	123	46	.697	14			9	*C/1	1.5
1915	Bos-N	118	316	27	78	15	3	2	30	41	34	.247	.339	.332	.671	105	3	3	98	103	38	.657	10	4	1	-3	*C	0.8
1916	Bos-N	118	349	32	88	14	1	1	34	24	33	.252	.311	.307	.618	97	-4	-1	93	123	38	.556	8			-5	*C	0.0
1917	Bos-N	49	154	12	33	7	0	0	14	15	13	.214	.288	.260	.548	71	-5	-5	96	135	12	.479	2			2	C	0.0
1919	Bos-N	78	219	18	61	8	1	1	22	19	16	.279	.339	.338	.677	106	1	2	98	111	26	.627	5			5	C/1	1.2
1920	Bos-N	80	214	14	52	11	2	0	18	20	15	.243	.314	.313	.627	83	-5	-4	96	104	23	.583	6	1	1	12	C	1.4
1921	Bos-N	64	164	17	49	7	2	2	17	16	11	.299	.368	.402	.771	112	1	3	93	87	26	.748	2	0	1	3	C	0.9
1922	Bos-N	92	221	23	70	11	1	1	27	24	13	.317	.391	.389	.780	108	2	4	94	106	35	.757	2	1	0	2	C/1	0.6
1923	Bos-N	23	48	5	6	1	1	0	5	15	5	.125	.354	.188	.541	47	-3	-3	100	196	5	.628	1	1	-0	1	C	-0.1
	NY-N	53	122	13	40	6	3	1	18	21	9	.328	.427	.451	.877	130	7	6	101	109	25	.951	2	0	1	-2	C	0.7
	Yr	76	170	18	46	7	4	1	23	36	14	.271	.404	.376	.780	106	4	3	101	138	29	.840	3	1	0	-1		0.6
1924	NY-N	87	191	25	62	9	1	4	37	26	11	.325	.411	.445	.856	142	9	11	91	139	37	.884	1	0	0	-9	C	0.4
1925	NY-N	47	114	14	37	4	3	3	19	12	7	.325	.389	.491	.880	125	4	4	99	104	22	.883	0	0	0	-1	C	0.5
1929	Bos-N	10	16	1	7	0	0	0	3	0	2	.438	.438	.438	.875	125	0	1	94	147	3	.778	0			0	/C	0.1
1930	Bos-N	16	25	0	5	1	0	0	2	3	1	.200	.310	.240	.550	37	-3	-2	97	115	2	.500	0			-1	C	-0.1
Total	17	1050	2735	270	738	124	27	21	322	311	247	.270	.351	.358	.709	104	15	24	98	116	372	.688	59	7		15	C/1	8.6
■ **BILLY GRABARKEWITZ**	Grabarkewitz, Billy Cordell b: 1/18/46, Lockhart, Tex. BR/TR, 5'10", 165 lbs. Deb: 4/22/69																											
1969	LA-N	34	65	4	6	1	1	0	5	4	19	.092	.145	.138	.283	-21	-10	-10	99	223	1	.226	1	0	0	0	S/32	-0.7
1970	LA-N	156	529	92	153	20	8	17	84	95	149	.289	.403	.454	.857	144	25	33	90	114	103	.916	19	9	0	3	3S2	4.1
1971	LA-N	44	71	9	16	5	0	0	6	19	16	.225	.389	.296	.685	98	1	1	99	116	9	.695	1	2	-1	0	23/S	0.1
1972	LA-N	53	144	17	24	4	0	4	16	18	53	.167	.268	.278	.546	59	-8	-7	94	126	12	.516	3	0	1	0	32/S	-0.5
1973	Cal-A	61	129	27	21	6	1	3	9	28	27	.163	.316	.295	.611	76	-4	-3	96	75	13	.600	2	2	-1	-1	23/SOD	-0.3
	Phi-N	25	66	12	19	2	0	2	7	12	18	.288	.397	.409	.807	115	3	2	108	85	12	.875	3	1	0	0	2/3O	0.3
1974	Phi-N	34	30	7	4	0	0	1	2	5	10	.133	.257	.233	.490	37	-2	-3	103	77	2	.556	3	1	0	-0	/O3	-0.2
	Chi-N	53	125	21	31	3	2	1	12	21	28	.248	.361	.328	.689	94	-0	-0	100	105	16	.667	1	2	-1	-3	2/S3	-0.1
	Yr	87	155	28	35	3	2	2	14	26	38	.226	.341	.310	.650	82	-3	-3	101	95	18	.642	4	3	-1	-4		-0.3
1975	Oak-A	6	2	0	0	0	0	0	0	0	1	.000	.000	.000	.000	-99	-1	-1	93	0	0	.000	0	0	0	0	/2D	0.0
Total	7	466	1161	189	274	41	12	28	141	202	321	.236	.354	.364	.718	104	3	12	94	113	169	.739	33	17	-0	-1	32/SOD	2.7
■ **ROD GRABER**	Graber, Rodney Blaine b: 6/20/31, Marshallville, O. BL/TL, 5'11", 175 lbs. Deb: 9/09/58																											
1958	Cle-A	4	8	0	1	0	0	0	0	1	2	.125	.222	.125	.347	-2	-1	-1	94	0	0	.286	0	0	0	0	/O	0.0
■ **JOHNNY GRABOWSKI**	Grabowski, John Patrick "Nig b: 1/7/1900, Ware, Mass. d: 5/23/46, Albany, N.Y. BR/TR, 5'10", 185 lbs. Deb: 7/11/24																											
1924	Chi-A	20	56	10	14	3	0	0	3	2	4	.250	.276	.304	.579	51	-4	-4	97	58	5	.452	0	0	0	2	C	0.0
1925	Chi-A	21	46	5	14	4	1	0	10	2	4	.304	.333	.435	.768	98	-1	-0	96	167	6	.667	0	1	-1	-0	C	0.0
1926	Chi-A	48	122	6	32	1	1	1	11	4	15	.262	.286	.311	.597	61	-8	-7	92	91	11	.462	0	1	-1	-3	C/1	-0.7
1927	NY-A	70	195	29	54	2	4	0	25	20	15	.277	.350	.328	.678	77	-6	-6	100	130	23	.610	0	0	0	-2	C	-0.4
1928	NY-A	75	202	21	48	7	1	1	21	10	21	.238	.274	.297	.571	54	-15	-13	92	114	17	.455	0	0	0	-7	C	-1.3
1929	NY-A	22	59	4	12	1	0	0	2	3	6	.203	.242	.220	.462	20	-7	-7	99	53	3	.333	0	1	-1	-0	C	-0.5
1931	Det-A	40	136	9	32	7	1	1	14	6	19	.235	.268	.324	.591	53	-9	-10	104	98	12	.481	0	0	0	2	C	-0.4
Total	7	296	816	84	206	25	8	3	86	47	84	.252	.295	.314	.609	60	-50	-47	97	107	76	.498	0	3	-2	-9	C/1	-3.3
■ **JOE GRACE**	Grace, Joseph Laverne b: 1/5/14, Gorham, Ill. d: 9/18/69, Murphysboro, Ill. BL/TR, 6'1", 180 lbs. Deb: 9/24/38																											
1938	StL-A	12	47	7	16	1	0	0	4	2	3	.340	.367	.362	.729	83	-1	-1	100	81	6	.594	0	1	-1	-3	O	-0.3
1939	StL-A	74	207	35	63	11	2	3	22	19	24	.304	.363	.420	.783	99	-0	-0	100	77	33	.741	3	2	-0	-4	O	-0.4
1940	StL-A	80	229	45	59	14	2	5	25	26	23	.258	.336	.402	.738	85	-3	-5	106	84	32	.684	2	2	-1	-6	OC	-1.3
1941	StL-A	115	362	53	112	17	4	6	60	57	31	.309	.410	.428	.839	122	14	14	100	123	69	.845	1	3	-2	-3	O/C	0.4
1946	StL-A	48	161	21	37	7	2	1	13	16	20	.230	.307	.317	.624	76	-5	-5	98	93	16	.534	1	3	-2	-0	O	-0.9
	Was-A	77	321	39	97	17	4	2	31	24	19	.302	.358	.399	.757	121	5	8	92	78	46	.671	1	4	-2	4	O	0.5
	Yr	125	482	60	134	24	6	3	44	40	39	.278	.341	.371	.712	105	-1	3	94	84	62	.629	2	7	-4	3		-0.4
1947	Was-A	78	234	25	58	9	4	3	17	35	15	.248	.348	.359	.707	100	-0	0	97	67	31	.658	1	2	-1	3	O	0.0
Total	6	484	1561	225	442	76	18	20	172	179	135	.283	.362	.393	.755	104	8	10	99	90	231	.714	9	17	-8	-8	O/C	-2.0
■ **MIKE GRACE**	Grace, Michael Lee b: 6/14/56, Pontiac, Mich. BR/TR, 6', 175 lbs. Deb: 4/18/78																											
1978	Cin-N	5	3	0	0	0	0	0	0	0	2	.000	.000	.000	.000	-97	-1	-1	103	0	0	.000	0	0	0	0	/3	0.0
■ **EARL GRACE**	Grace, Robert Earl b: 2/24/07, Barlow, Ky. d: 12/22/80, Phoenix, Ariz. BL/TR, 6', 175 lbs. Deb: 4/23/29																											
1929	Chi-N	27	80	7	20	1	0	2	17	9	7	.250	.333	.338	.671	66	-4	-4	101	176	9	.617	0			-0	C	-0.1
1931	Chi-N	7	9	2	1	0	0	0	1	4	1	.111	.385	.111	.496	41	-1	-0	96	356	1	.625	0			0	/C	0.0
	Pit-N	47	150	8	42	6	1	1	20	13	5	.280	.337	.353	.691	85	-3	-3	101	127	19	.611	0			0	C	0.0
	Yr	54	159	10	43	6	1	1	21	17	6	.270	.341	.340	.681	84	-3	-3	100	164	20	.612	0			1		0.0
1932	Pit-N	115	390	41	107	17	5	8	55	14	23	.274	.305	.405	.710	89	-7	-6	99	112	48	.618	0			1	*C	-0.1
1933	Pit-N	93	291	22	84	13	1	3	44	26	23	.289	.349	.371	.720	111	3	4	95	141	40	.646	0			2	C	0.9
1934	Pit-N	95	289	27	78	17	1	4	24	20	19	.270	.317	.377	.694	81	-6	-8	105	71	35	.594	0			-4	C/1	-0.8
1935	Pit-N	77	224	19	59	8	1	3	29	32	17	.263	.355	.348	.704	84	-2	-4	107	120	27	.627	1			5	C	0.0
1936	Phi-N	86	221	24	55	11	0	4	32	34	20	.249	.352	.353	.705	83	-2	-5	108	126	30	.665	0			-2	C	-0.4
1937	Phi-N	80	223	19	47	10	1	6	29	33	15	.211	.313	.345	.658	73	-6	-9	108	110	25	.601	0			-1	C	-0.7
Total	8	627	1877	169	493	83	10	31	251	185	130	.263	.331	.367	.698	86	-29	-36	103	119	235	.633	1			1	C/1	-1.2
■ **MARK GRACE**	Grace, Mark Eugene b: 6/28/64, Winston-Salem, N.C BL/TL, 6'2", 190 lbs. Deb: 5/02/88																											
1988	Chi-N	134	486	65	144	23	4	7	57	60	43	.296	.374	.403	.777	118	16	13	104	107	74	.725	3	3	-1	-3	*1	0.3
■ **JOHN GRADY**	Grady, John J. b: 6/18/1860, Lowell, Mass. d: 7/15/1893, Lowell, Mass. 5'7", 150 lbs. Deb: 5/10/1884																											
1884	Alt-U	9	36	5	11	3	0	0		2		.306	.342	.389	.731	145	2	2	101	0	5	.640	0			0	/1O	0.1
■ **MIKE GRADY**	Grady, Michael William b: 12/23/1869, Kennett Square, Pa d: 12/3/43, Kennett Square, Pa. BR/TR, 5'11", 190 lbs. Deb: 4/24/1894																											
1894	Phi-N	60	190	45	69	13	8	0	40	14	13	.363	.427	.516	.942	135	9	11	95	113	44	1.008	3			-15	C1/O	0.0
1895	Phi-N	46	123	21	40	3	1	1	23	14	8	.325	.407	.390	.797	110	2	3	99	126	22	.843	5			-16	C/O31	-0.8
1896	Phi-N	71	242	49	77	20	7	1	44	16	19	.318	.382	.471	.853	124	9	8	102	108	49	.903	10			-2	C/3	1.0
1897	Phi-N	4	13	1	2	0	0	0	0	1		.154	.214	.154	.368	-1	-2	-2	96	0	0	.273	0			0	/C	-0.1
	StL-N	83	322	48	90	11	3	7	45	26		.280	.352	.398	.749	107	0	4	93	94	49	.737	7			-1	1/O	0.1
	Yr	87	335	49	92	11	3	7	45	27		.275	.347	.388	.735	103	-2	2	94	89	49	.716	7			-1		0.0
1898	NY-N	93	287	64	85	19	5	3	49	38		.296	.399	.429	.827	148	16	19	95	112	58	.950	20			-14	CO/1S	0.8
1899	NY-N	86	311	47	104	18	8	2	54	29		.334	.402	.463	.865	144	17	18	97	117	68	.961	20			-4	C3/O1	1.5
1900	NY-N	83	251	36	55	8	4	0	27	34		.219	.312	.283	.595	69	-10	-9	97	119	26	.582	9			-5	C1S/3O2	-0.8
1901	Was-A	94	347	57	99	17	10	9	56	27		.285	.337	.470	.807	125	10	11	99	95	61	.823	14			-1	1C/O	0.8

YEAR	TM/L	G	AB	R	H	2B	3B	HR	RBI	BB	SO	AVG	OBP	SLG	PRO	/A	BR	/A	PF	CHI	RC	TA	SB	CS	SBR	FR	POS	TPR
1904	StL-N	101	323	44	101	15	11	5	43	31		.313	.373	.474	.847	165	23	24	99	95	61	.856	6			-11	C1/23	1.9
1905	StL-N	100	311	41	89	20	7	4	41	33		.286	.355	.434	.789	150	14	17	91	97	55	.824	15			-4	C1	2.0
1906	StL-N	97	280	33	70	11	3	3	27	48		.250	.360	.343	.703	121	9	9	101	94	37	.710	5			-5	C1	0.8
Total	11	918	3000	486	881	155	67	35	449	311	40	.294	.369	.425	.794	128	97	111	97	104	529	.824	114			-78	C1/30S2	7.2
■ FRED GRAFF	Graff, Frederick Gottleib b: 8/25/1889, Canton, Ohio d: 10/4/79, Chattanooga, Tenn. BR/TR, 5'10.5", 164 lbs. Deb: 5/14/13																											
1913	StL-A	4	5	1	2	1	0	0	2	3	3	.400	.625	.600	1.225	272	1	1	95	237	2	2.000	0			0	/3	0.2
■ LOUIS GRAFF	Graff, Louis George "Chappie" b: 7/25/1866, Philadelphia, Pa. d: 4/16/55, Bryn Mawr, Pa. TR , Deb: 6/23/1890																											
1890	Syr-a	1	5	0	2	1	0	0		0		.400	.400	.600	1.000	218	1	1	90	0	1	1.000	0			0	/C	0.1
■ MILT GRAFF	Graff, Milton Edward b: 12/30/30, Jefferson Center, Pa. BL/TR, 5'7.5", 158 lbs. Deb: 4/16/57 C																											
1957	KC-A	56	155	16	28	4	3	0	10	15	10	.181	.262	.245	.507	40	-13	-13	99	104	10	.429	2	5	-2	-7	2	-2.0
1958	KC-A	5	1	0	0	0	0	0	0	0	0	.000	.000	.000	.000	-95	-0	-0	106	0	0	.000	0	0	0	0	/2	0.0
Total	2	61	156	16	28	4	3	0	10	15	10	.179	.260	.244	.504	39	-13	-13	99	103	10	.429	2	5	-2	-7	/2	-2.0
■ MOONLIGHT GRAHAM	Graham, Archibald Wright b: 11/9/1876, Fayetteville, N.C. d: 8/25/65, Chisolm, Minn. 5'10.5", 170 lbs. Deb: 6/29/05																											
1905	NY-N	1	0	0	0	0	0	0	0	0		—	—	—	—	—	0	0	101	—	—	—	0			0	/O	0.0
■ SKINNY GRAHAM	Graham, Arthur William b: 8/12/09, Somerville, Mass. d: 7/10/67, Cambridge, Mass. BL/TR, 5'7", 162 lbs. Deb: 9/14/34																											
1934	Bos-A	13	47	7	11	2	1	0	3	6	13	.234	.321	.319	.640	62	-2	-3	106	68	5	.605	2	2	-1	-1	O	-0.4
1935	Bos-A	8	10	1	3	0	0	0	1	1	3	.300	.364	.300	.664	68	-0	-0	108	113	1	.714	1	0	0	-1	/O	0.0
Total	2	21	57	8	14	2	1	0	4	7	16	.246	.328	.316	.644	63	-3	-3	106	76	6	.622	3	2	-0	-2	/O	-0.4
■ BARNEY GRAHAM	Graham, Barney b: Philadelphia, Pa. d: 12/31/1896, Mobile, Ala. Deb: 9/04/1889																											
1889	Phi-a	4	18	0	3	0	0	0	0	0	0	.167	.167	.167	.333	-4	-2	-2	98	0	1	.200	0			0	/3	-0.1
■ BERNIE GRAHAM	Graham, Bernard b: 1860, Beloit, Wis. d: 10/30/1886, Mobile, Ala. Deb: 7/11/1884																											
1884	CP-U	1	5	2	1	0	0	0		0		.200	.200	.200	.400	36	-0	-0	99	0	0	.250	0			-0	/O	0.0
	Bal-U	41	167	21	45	11	0	0		2		.269	.278	.335	.613	96	1	-2	110	0	16	.475	0			2	O/1	0.0
	Yr	42	172	23	46	11	0	0		2		.267	.276	.331	.607	95	1	-2	110	0	16	.468	0			2		0.0
Total	1	42	172	23	46	11	0	0		2		.267	.276	.331	.607	95	1	-2	110	0	16	.468	0			2	/O1	0.0
■ BERT GRAHAM	Graham, Bert "B.G." b: 4/3/1886, Tilton, Ill. d: 6/19/71, Cottonwood, Ariz. BB/TR, 5'11.5", 187 lbs. Deb: 9/09/10																											
1910	StL-A	8	26	1	3	2	1	0	5	1		.115	.148	.269	.417	32	-2	-2	94	264	1	.348	0			-0	/12	-0.1
■ CHARLIE GRAHAM	Graham, Charles Henry b: 4/25/1878, Santa Clara, Cal. d: 8/29/48, San Francisco, Cal BR/TR, 5'11", 180 lbs. Deb: 4/16/06																											
1906	Bos-A	30	90	10	21	1	0	1	12	10		.233	.310	.278	.588	88	-1	-1	98	156	8	.522	1			3	C	0.5
■ DAN GRAHAM	Graham, Daniel Jay b: 7/19/54, Ray, Ariz. BL/TR, 6'1", 205 lbs. Deb: 6/08/79																											
1979	Min-A	2	4	0	0	0	0	0	0	0	0	.000	.000	.000	.000	-92	-1	-1	109	0	0	.000	0	0	0	0	/H	0.0
1980	Bal-A	86	266	32	74	7	1	15	54	14	40	.278	.314	.481	.795	114	4	4	101	122	40	.724	0	0	0	5	C/3OD	1.2
1981	Bal-A	55	142	7	25	3	0	2	11	13	32	.176	.245	.239	.485	41	-11	-11	99	108	8	.392	0	0	0	-3	C/3D	-1.2
Total	3	143	412	39	99	10	1	17	65	27	72	.240	.287	.393	.680	88	-8	-8	100	116	48	.598	0	0	0	2	C/3DO	0.0
■ TINY GRAHAM	Graham, Dawson Francis b: 9/9/1892, Nashville, Tenn. d: 12/29/62, Nashville, Tenn. BR/TR, 6'2", 185 lbs. Deb: 8/30/14																											
1914	Cin-N	25	61	5	14	1	0	0	3	3	10	.230	.266	.246	.512	50	-4	-4	105	72	4	.404	1			-1	1	-0.5
■ PEACHES GRAHAM	Graham, George Frederick b: 3/23/1877, Aledo, Ill. d: 7/25/39, Long Beach, Cal. BR/TR, 5'9", 180 lbs. Deb: 9/14/02																											
1902	Cle-A	2	6	0	2	0	0	0	1	1		.333	.429	.333	.762	119	0	0	97	165	1	.750	0			0	/2	0.0
1903	Chi-N	1	2	0	0	0	0	0	0	0		.000	.000	.000	.000	-99	-1	-0	95	0	0	.000	0			0	/P	0.0
1908	Bos-N	75	215	22	59	5	0	0	22	23		.274	.345	.298	.642	104	3	2	104	132	23	.583	4			1	C/2	0.7
1909	Bos-N	92	267	27	64	6	3	0	17	24		.240	.302	.285	.587	87	-5	-4	96	81	24	.527	7			5	C/OS3	0.6
1910	Bos-N	110	291	31	82	13	2	0	21	33	15	.282	.359	.340	.699	91	2	-3	114	74	38	.665	5			-1	C/31O	0.0
1911	Bos-N	33	88	7	24	6	1	0	12	14	5	.273	.373	.364	.736	103	1	1	103	127	13	.750	2			4	C	0.7
	Chi-N	36	71	6	17	3	0	0	8	11	8	.239	.365	.282	.646	85	-1	-1	97	135	8	.667	2			0	C	0.2
	Yr	69	159	13	41	9	1	0	20	25	13	.258	.369	.327	.696	96	0	0	100	133	21	.712	4			4		0.9
1912	Phi-N	24	59	6	17	1	0	1	4	8	5	.288	.373	.356	.729	100	0	0	100	56	8	.714	1			1	C	0.2
Total	7	373	999	99	265	34	6	1	85	114	33	.265	.343	.314	.658	94	-0	-5	104	97	114	.619	21			10	C/O231SP	2.4
■ JACK GRAHAM	Graham, John Bernard b: 12/24/16, Minneapolis, Minn. BL/TR, 6'2", 200 lbs. Deb: 4/16/46																											
1946	Bro-N	2	5	0	1	0	0	0	0	0	0	.200	.200	.200	.400	13	-1	-1	103	0	0	.250	0			0	/1	0.0
	NY-N	100	270	34	59	6	4	14	47	23	37	.219	.282	.426	.708	98	-2	-3	102	112	32	.648	1			-4	O/1	-0.8
	Yr	102	275	34	60	6	4	14	47	23	37	.218	.281	.422	.703	97	-3	-3	102	109	32	.641	1			-4		-0.8
1949	StL-A	137	500	71	119	22	1	24	79	61	62	.238	.326	.430	.756	99	-4	-4	100	100	72	.711	0	1	-1	-5	*1	-0.7
Total	2	239	775	105	179	28	5	38	126	84	99	.231	.310	.427	.737	98	-7	-7	100	103	104	.691	1	1		-8	1/O	-1.5
■ LEE GRAHAM	Graham, Lee Willard b: 9/12/59, Summerfield, Fla. BL/TL, 5'10", 170 lbs. Deb: 9/03/83																											
1983	Bos-A	5	6	2	0	0	0	0	1	0	0	.000	.000	.000	.000	-99	-2	-2	101	0	-0	.000	0	1	-1	1	/O	-0.1
■ ROY GRAHAM	Graham, Roy Vincent b: 2/22/1895, San Francisco, Cal d: 4/26/33, Manila, Phillipines BR/TR, 5'10.5", 175 lbs. Deb: 5/28/22																											
1922	Chi-A	5	3	0	0	0	0	0	0	0	0	.000	.400	.000	.400	12	-0	-0	101	0	0	.667	0	0	0	0	/C	0.0
1923	Chi-A	36	82	3	16	2	0	0	6	9	6	.195	.290	.220	.510	36	-7	-7	98	114	6	.439	0	0	0	-0	C	-0.4
Total	2	41	85	3	16	2	0	0	6	9	6	.188	.296	.212	.508	36	-8	-8	98	108	6	.449	0	0	0	0	/C	-0.4
■ WAYNE GRAHAM	Graham, Wayne Leon b: 4/6/37, Yoakum, Tex. BR/TR, 6', 200 lbs. Deb: 4/10/63																											
1963	Phi-N	10	22	1	4	0	0	0	0	3	1	.182	.280	.182	.462	35	-2	-2	103	0	1	.389	0	0	0	-1	/O	-0.3
1964	NY-N	20	33	1	3	1	0	0	0	0	5	.091	.091	.121	.212	-43	-6	-6	95	0	0	.133	0	0	0	0	3	-0.6
Total	2	30	55	2	7	1	0	0	0	3	6	.127	.172	.145	.318	-9	-8	-8	98	0	2	.229	0	0	0	-1	/3O	-0.9
■ ALEX GRAMMAS	Grammas, Alexander Peter b: 4/3/26, Birmingham, Ala. BR/TR, 6', 175 lbs. Deb: 4/13/54 MC																											
1954	StL-N	142	401	57	106	17	4	2	29	40	29	.264	.339	.342	.680	77	-12	-12	100	80	47	.610	6	1	1	21	*S/3	1.8
1955	StL-N	128	366	32	88	19	2	3	25	33	36	.240	.308	.328	.636	69	-16	-16	101	78	37	.556	4	1	1	4	*S	-0.7
1956	StL-N	6	12	1	3	0	0	0	1	1	1	.250	.308	.250	.558	53	-1	-1	99	141	1	.444	0	0	0	0	/S	0.0
	Cin-N	77	140	17	34	11	0	0	16	16	18	.243	.325	.321	.646	69	-5	-6	108	150	16	.579	0	1	-1	-3	3S/2	-0.8
	Yr	83	152	18	37	11	0	0	17	17	19	.243	.324	.316	.639	68	-5	-7	108	151	17	.569	0	1	-1	-3		-0.8
1957	Cin-N	73	99	14	30	4	0	0	8	10	6	.303	.367	.343	.710	88	-1	-1	105	98	11	.592	1	3	-2	-2	S2/3	0.0
1958	Cin-N	105	216	25	47	8	0	0	12	34	24	.218	.329	.255	.584	53	-12	-14	107	90	20	.525	2	2	-1	-0	S32	-0.9
1959	StL-N	131	368	43	99	14	2	3	30	38	26	.269	.339	.342	.681	78	-8	-11	105	90	43	.598	3	3	-1	-4	*S	-1.0
1960	StL-N	102	196	20	48	4	1	4	17	12	15	.245	.292	.337	.629	66	-8	-10	108	88	17	.503	0	1	-1	-1	S23	-0.6
1961	StL-N	89	170	23	36	10	1	0	21	19	21	.212	.295	.282	.577	48	-11	-14	113	176	15	.489	0	1	-1	-1	S2/3	-0.7
1962	StL-N	21	18	0	2	0	0	0	1	1	6	.111	.158	.111	.269	-24	-3	-3	109	197	0	.176	0	0	0	0	S/2	-0.1
	Chi-N	23	60	3	14	3	0	0	3	2	7	.233	.270	.283	.553	46	-4	-5	106	70	4	.420	1	1	-0	1	S/23	-0.2
	Yr	44	78	3	16	3	0	0	4	3	13	.205	.244	.244	.487	29	-8	-8	107	135	4	.364	1	1	-0	1		-0.3
1963	Chi-N	16	27	1	5	0	0	0	0	0	3	.185	.185	.185	.370	7	-3	-3	105	0	1	.227	0	0	0	-0	S	-0.1
Total	10	913	2073	236	512	90	10	12	163	206	192	.247	.320	.317	.637	67	-84	-97	105	97	212	.569	17	14	-3	14	S32	-3.3
■ JACK GRANEY	Graney, John Gladstone b: 6/10/1886, St.Thomas, Ont., Can. d: 4/20/78, Louisiana, Mo. BL/TL, 5'9", 180 lbs. Deb: 4/30/08																											
1908	Cle-A	2	0	0	0	0	0	0	0	0		—	—	—	—	—	0	0	106	—	—	—	0			-0	/P	0.0
1910	Cle-A	116	454	62	107	13	9	1	31	37		.236	.293	.311	.604	89	-6	-6	100	77	46	.565	18			6	*O	-0.5
1911	Cle-A	146	527	84	142	25	5	1	45	66		.269	.363	.342	.704	94	0	-2	103	88	73	.722	21			5	*O	-0.8
1912	Cle-A	78	264	44	64	13	2	0	20	50		.242	.367	.307	.674	92	0	-0	101	87	33	.710	9			4	O	0.0
1913	Cle-A	148	517	56	138	18	12	3	68	48	55	.267	.335	.366	.701	99	3	-1	106	125	69	.710	27			1	*O	-0.7

YEAR	TM/L	G	AB	R	H	2B	3B	HR	RBI	BB	SO	AVG	OBP	SLG	PRO	/A	BR	/A	PF	CHI	RC	TA	SB	CS	SBR	FR	POS	TPR
1914	Cle-A	130	460	63	122	17	10	1	39	67	46	.265	.362	.352	.714	112	10	9	102	94	60	.708	20	18	-5	-5	*O	-0.8
1915	Cle-A	116	404	42	105	20	7	1	56	59	29	.260	.357	.351	.708	108	7	5	104	139	51	.685	12	15	-5	7	*O	0.0
1916	Cle-A	155	589	106	142	**41**	14	5	54	102	72	.241	.355	.384	.739	122	17	17	100	69	85	.761	10			3	*O	1.3
1917	Cle-A	146	535	87	122	29	7	3	35	**94**	49	.228	.348	.325	.673	92	6	-3	114	61	65	.697	16			-4	*O	-1.7
1918	Cle-A	70	177	27	42	7	4	0	9	28	13	.237	.351	.322	.673	95	2	-0	108	58	20	.674	3			-6	O	-0.9
1919	Cle-A	128	461	79	108	22	8	1	30	**105**	39	.234	.380	.323	.703	92	4	-0	107	63	60	.748	7			4	*O	-0.4
1920	Cle-A	62	152	31	45	11	1	0	13	27	21	.296	.412	.382	.794	107	4	3	104	79	27	.844	4	2	0	-6	O	-0.6
1921	Cle-A	68	107	19	32	3	0	2	18	20	9	.299	.414	.383	.797	105	2	2	99	131	19	.829	1	1	-0	-8	O	-0.8
1922	Cle-A	37	58	6	9	0	0	0	2	9	12	.155	.279	.155	.435	15	-7	-7	102	79	3	.388	0	0	0	-2	O	-0.9
Total	14	1402	4705	706	1178	219	79	18	420	712	345	.250	.354	.342	.696	100	42	17	104	87	823	.704	148	36		-1	*O/P	-6.8
■ EDDIE GRANT	Grant, Edward Leslie "Harvard Eddie" b: 5/21/1883, Franklin, Mass. d: 10/5/18, Argonne Forest, France BL/TR, 5'11.5", 168 lbs. Deb: 8/04/05																											
1905	Cle-A	2	8	1	3	0	0	0	0	0		.375	.375	.375	.750	141	0	0	100	0	1	.600	0			0	/2	0.0
1907	Phi-N	74	268	26	65	4	3	0	19	10		.243	.270	.280	.550	71	-8	-9	104	102	24	.468	10			-5	3	-1.6
1908	Phi-N	147	598	69	146	13	8	0	32	35		.244	.286	.293	.579	87	-9	-9	100	61	55	.524	27			-2	*3S	-0.8
1909	Phi-N	154	631	75	170	18	4	1	37	35		.269	.311	.315	.626	90	-4	-9	106	58	68	.575	28			4	*3	-0.2
1910	Phi-N	152	579	70	155	15	5	1	67	39	54	.268	.315	.316	.631	88	-12	-9	96	133	67	.585	25			-12	*3	-2.2
1911	Cin-N	136	458	49	102	12	7	1	53	51	47	.223	.301	.286	.587	70	-22	-16	92	136	49	.590	28			-4	*3S	-1.4
1912	Cin-N	96	255	37	61	6	1	2	20	18	27	.239	.292	.294	.586	65	-14	-11	92	83	25	.541	11			-5	S3	-1.0
1913	Cin-N	27	94	12	20	1	0	0	9	11	10	.213	.295	.223	.519	48	-6	-6	102	159	8	.527	7			-1	3	-0.7
	NY-N	27	20	8	4	1	0	0	1	2	2	.200	.273	.250	.523	48	-1	-1	103	73	1	.500	1			0	/32S	-0.1
	Yr	54	114	20	24	2	0	0	10	13	12	.211	.291	.228	.519	48	-7	-7	102	119	9	.522	8			-1		-0.8
1914	NY-N	88	282	34	78	7	1	0	29	23	21	.277	.333	.309	.642	96	-3	-1	96	121	32	.598	11			3	3S2	0.5
1915	NY-N	87	192	18	40	2	1	0	10	9	20	.208	.248	.229	.477	49	-13	-11	91	87	11	.373	5	6	-2	-2	3/21S	-1.4
Total	10	990	3385	399	844	79	30	5	277	233	181	.249	.299	.295	.594	80	-92	-83	98	97	341	.546	153	6		-23	3S/21	-8.9
■ JIMMY GRANT	Grant, James Charles b: 10/6/18, Racine, Wis. d: 7/8/70, Rochester, Minn. BL/TR, 5'8", 166 lbs. Deb: 9/08/42																											
1942	Chi-A	12	36	0	6	1	1	0	1	5	6	.167	.268	.250	.518	47	-3	-3	99	39	3	.467	0	0	0	1	3	0.0
1943	Chi-A	58	197	23	51	9	2	4	22	18	34	.259	.321	.386	.707	105	1	1	101	91	23	.620	4	3	-1	-1	3	0.0
	Cle-A	15	22	3	3	2	0	0	1	4	7	.136	.269	.227	.497	51	-1	-1	90	73	2	.474	0	0	0	0	/3	0.0
	Yr	73	219	26	54	11	2	4	23	22	41	.247	.315	.370	.685	101	-0	-0	99	89	28	.637	4	3	-1	-1		0.0
1944	Cle-A	61	99	12	27	4	3	1	12	11	20	.273	.357	.404	.761	117	2	2	100	101	16	.750	1	0	0	1	2/3	0.4
Total	3	146	354	38	87	16	6	5	36	38	67	.246	.322	.367	.690	100	-1	-1	100	87	43	.648	5	3	-0	1	/32	0.4
■ TOM GRANT	Grant, Thomas Raymond b: 5/28/57, Worcester, Mass. BL/TR, 6'2", 190 lbs. Deb: 6/17/83																											
1983	Chi-N	16	20	2	3	1	0	0	2	3	4	.150	.261	.200	.461	29	-2	-2	101	198	1	.412	0	0	0	-2	O	-0.4
■ GEORGE GRANTHAM	Grantham, George Farley "Boots" b: 5/20/1900, Galena, Kan. d: 3/16/54, Kingman, Ariz. BL/TR, 5'10", 170 lbs. Deb: 9/20/22																											
1922	Chi-N	7	23	3	4	1	1	0	3	1	3	.174	.208	.304	.513	32	-2	-2	95	150	2	.526	2	0	1	0	/3	0.0
1923	Chi-N	152	570	81	160	36	8	8	70	71	92	.281	.360	.414	.774	99	4	0	104	91	85	.799	43	28	-4	1	*2	-0.1
1924	Chi-N	127	469	85	148	19	6	12	60	55	63	.316	.390	.458	.848	125	19	18	101	92	81	.857	21	21	-6	1	*2/3	0.6
1925	Pit-N	114	359	74	117	24	6	8	52	50	29	.326	.413	.493	.906	128	18	17	102	92	77	.992	14	4	2	-3	*1	0.5
1926	Pit-N	141	449	66	143	27	13	8	70	60	42	.318	.400	.490	.890	123	25	17	112	99	88	.938	6			-2	*1	1.0
1927	Pit-N	151	531	96	162	33	11	8	66	74	39	.305	.396	.454	.850	125	22	21	102	89	97	.894	9			-20	*21	-0.2
1928	Pit-N	124	440	93	142	24	9	10	85	59	37	.323	.408	.486	.894	124	22	18	107	127	87	.960	9			-0	*1/23	0.5
1929	Pit-N	110	349	85	107	23	10	12	90	93	38	.307	.454	.533	.987	139	28	26	103	141	89	1.198	10			-0	2O1	2.3
1930	Pit-N	146	552	120	179	34	14	18	99	81	66	.324	.413	.534	.947	131	25	28	97	104	121	1.027	5			-15	*2/1	2.5
1931	Pit-N	127	465	91	142	26	6	10	46	71	50	.305	.400	.452	.851	128	21	21	101	72	89	.892	5			-10	12	0.6
1932	Cin-N	126	493	81	144	29	6	6	39	56	40	.292	.364	.412	.776	112	7	9	96	63	77	.754	4			-15	*21	0.2
1933	Cin-N	87	260	32	53	14	3	4	28	38	21	.204	.310	.327	.637	83	-5	-5	99	108	29	.608	4			-1	21	-0.1
1934	NY-N	32	29	5	7	2	0	1	4	8	6	.241	.405	.414	.819	122	1	1	98	96	6	.909	0			0	/13	0.1
Total	13	1444	4989	912	1508	292	93	105	712	717	526	.302	.392	.461	.854	121	185	169	102	97	927	.898	132	53		-64	21/O3	7.9
■ MICKEY GRASSO	Grasso, Newton Michael b: 5/10/20, Newark, N.J. d: 10/15/75, Miami, Fla. BR/TR, 6', 195 lbs. Deb: 9/18/46																											
1946	NY-N	7	22	1	3	0	0	0	1	0	3	.136	.136	.136	.273	-22	-4	-4	102	124	0	.136	0			0	/C	-0.3
1950	Was-A	75	195	25	56	4	1	1	22	25	31	.287	.374	.333	.707	83	-4	-4	99	112	26	.646	1	1	-0	-2	C	-0.2
1951	Was-A	52	175	16	36	3	0	1	14	14	17	.206	.268	.240	.508	40	-15	-14	95	111	10	.385	0	0	0	-2	C	-1.2
1952	Was-A	115	361	22	78	9	0	0	27	29	36	.216	.276	.241	.517	45	-27	-27	100	116	24	.400	1	0	0	-1	*C	-2.1
1953	Was-A	61	196	13	41	7	0	2	22	9	20	.209	.251	.276	.527	45	-16	-15	94	136	12	.399	0	0	0	2	C	-1.0
1954	Cle-A	4	6	1	2	0	0	1	1	1	1	.333	.500	.833	1.333	246	1	1	106	47	3	1.750	0	0	0	-0	/C	0.1
1955	NY-N	8	2	0	0	0	0	0	0	3	0	.000	.600	.000	.600	78	0	0	99	0	0	1.000	0	0	0	-0	/C	0.0
Total	7	322	957	78	216	23	1	5	87	81	108	.226	.291	.268	.558	53	-64	-61	98	117	76	.466	2	1		-3	C	-4.7
■ LEW GRAULICH	Graulich, Lewis b: Camden, N.J. Deb: 9/17/1891																											
1891	Phi-N	7	26	2	8	0	0	0	3	1	2	.308	.333	.308	.641	94	-0	-0	95	109	3	.500	0			0	/C1	0.0
■ FRANK GRAVES	Graves, Frank M. b: 11/2/1860, Cincinnati, Ohio 6', 163 lbs. Deb: 5/10/1886																											
1886	StL-N	43	138	7	21	2	0	0	9	7	48	.152	.193	.167	.360	11	-15	-13	95	128	7	.350	11			4	C/OP	-0.5
■ JOE GRAVES	Graves, Joseph Ebenezer b: 2/27/06, Marblehead, Mass. d: 12/22/80, Salem, Mass. BR/TR, 5'10", 160 lbs. Deb: 9/26/26																											
1926	Chi-N	2	5	0	0	0	0	0	0	0	1	.000	.000	.000	.000	-94	-1	-1	106	0	0	.000	0			0	/3	0.0
■ SID GRAVES	Graves, Samuel Sidney "Whitey" b: 11/30/01, Marblehead, Mass. d: 12/26/83, Biddeford, Maine BR/TR, 6', 170 lbs. Deb: 7/23/27																											
1927	Bos-N	7	20	5	5	1	1	0	2	0	1	.250	.250	.400	.650	77	-1	-1	93	87	2	.600	1			1	/O	0.0
■ GARY GRAY	Gray, Gary George b: 9/21/52, New Orleans, La. BR/TR, 6', 187 lbs. Deb: 6/23/77																											
1977	Tex-A	1	2	0	0	0	0	0	0	0	1	.000	.000	.000	.000	-96	-1	-1	105	0	0	.000	0	0	0	-0	/O	0.0
1978	Tex-A	17	50	4	12	1	0	2	6	1	12	.240	.255	.380	.635	79	-2	-2	96	95	5	.538	1	0	0	0	D	0.0
1979	Tex-A	16	42	4	10	0	0	0	1	2	8	.238	.273	.238	.511	39	-4	-3	100	38	2	.371	1	1	-0	0	D	-0.3
1980	Cle-A	28	54	4	8	1	0	2	4	3	13	.148	.193	.278	.471	27	-6	-6	102	74	2	.375	0	0	0	-2	/1OD	-0.8
1981	Sea-A	69	208	27	51	7	1	13	31	4	44	.245	.259	.476	.735	108	1	1	100	88	22	.633	2	0	1	-2	1D/O	-0.1
1982	Sea-A	80	269	26	69	14	2	7	29	24	59	.257	.322	.401	.724	89	-1	-4	109	90	35	.659	1	1	-0	-0	1D	-0.5
Total	6	211	625	65	150	23	3	24	71	34	137	.240	.281	.402	.683	85	-12	-15	104	84	66	.607	5	2	0	-4	1/DO	-1.7
■ REDDY GRAY	Gray, James D. TR , Deb: 6/17/1890																											
1890	Pit-P	2	9	3	2	0	0	1	3	0	2	.222	.222	.556	.778	115	-0	0	92	109	1	.714	0			0	/2	0.0
	Pit-N	1	3	0	0	0	0	0	0	0	1	.000	.000	.000	.000	-99	-1	-1	88	0	0	.000	0			0	/S	0.0
1893	Pit-N	2	9	0	4	1	0	0	2	0	1	.444	.444	.556	1.000	157	1	1	106	116	2	1.000	0			0	/S	0.1
Total	2	5	21	3	6	1	0	1	5	0	4	.286	.286	.476	.762	108	-0	0	98	96	3	.667	0			0	/S2	0.1
■ JIM GRAY	Gray, James W. b: 8/7/1862, Pittsburgh, Pa. d: 1/31/38, Allegheny, Pa. Deb: 10/09/1884																											
1884	Pit-a	1	2	0	1	0	0	0		0		.500	.500	.500	1.000	240	0	0	97	0	1	1.000				0	/3	0.0
■ LORENZO GRAY	Gray, Lorenzo b: 3/4/58, Mound Bayou, Miss. BR/TR, 6'1", 180 lbs. Deb: 7/08/82																											
1982	Chi-A	17	28	4	8	1	0	0	0	2	4	.286	.333	.321	.655	83	-1	-1	97	0	3	.600	1	0	0	-0	3	0.0
1983	Chi-A	41	78	18	14	3	0	1	4	8	16	.179	.256	.256	.512	40	-6	-7	103	68	5	.433	1	0	0	2	3/D	-0.3
Total	2	58	106	22	22	4	0	1	4	10	20	.208	.276	.274	.549	51	-7	-7	102	50	8	.471	2	0	1	2	/3D	-0.3
■ MILT GRAY	Gray, Milton Marshall b: 2/21/14, Louisville, Ky. d: 6/30/69, Quincy, Fla. BR/TR, 6'1", 170 lbs. Deb: 5/27/37																											
1937	Was-A	2	6	0	0	0	0	0	0	0	1	.000	.000	.000	.000	-99	-2	-2	94	0	0	.000	0	0	0	0	/C	-0.1

YEAR	TM/L	G	AB	R	H	2B	3B	HR	RBI	BB	SO	AVG	OBP	SLG	PRO	/A	BR	/A	PF	CHI	RC	TA	SB	CS	SBR	FR	POS	TPR
■ **PETE GRAY**	Gray, Peter J. (born Peter Wyshner) b: 3/6/15, Nanticoke, Pa. BL/TL, 6'1", 169 lbs. Deb: 4/17/45																											
1945	StL-A	77	234	26	51	6	2	0	13	13	11	.218	.259	.261	.520	44	-15	-19	115	77	16	.414	5	6	-2	3	O	-2.1
■ **DICK GRAY**	Gray, Richard Benjamin b: 7/11/31, Jefferson, Pa. BR/TR, 5'11", 165 lbs. Deb: 4/15/58																											
1958	LA-N	58	197	25	49	5	6	9	30	19	30	.249	.327	.472	.799	104	2	1	105	105	29	.755	1	1	-0	10	3	1.1
1959	LA-N	21	52	8	8	1	0	2	4	6	12	.154	.241	.288	.530	40	-5	-5	102	77	4	.467	0	0	0	0	3	-0.4
	StL-N	36	51	9	16	1	0	1	6	6	8	.314	.386	.392	.778	103	1	0	105	105	9	.806	3	0	1	-0	S/32O	0.1
	Yr	57	103	17	24	2	0	3	10	12	20	.233	.313	.340	.653	71	-4	-4	104	96	12	.625	3	0	1	-0		-0.3
1960	StL-N	9	5	1	0	0	0	0	1	2	2	.000	.286	.000	.286	-13	-1	-1	108	0	0	.400	0	0	0	0	/23	0.0
Total	3	124	305	43	73	7	6	12	41	33	52	.239	.322	.420	.741	91	-3	-4	104	98	42	.725	4	1	1	10	/3S2O	0.8
■ **STAN GRAY**	Gray, Stanley Oscar "Dolly" b: 12/10/1888, Ladonia, Tex. d: 10/11/64, Snyder, Tex. 6'0.5", 184 lbs. Deb: 9/17/12																											
1912	Pit-N	6	20	4	5	0	1	0	2	0	3	.250	.250	.350	.600	64	-1	-1	99	96	2	.467	0			0	/1	0.0
■ **DAVID GREEN**	Green, David Alejandro (Casaya) b: 12/4/60, Managua, Nicaragua BR/TR, 6'3", 170 lbs. Deb: 9/04/81																											
1981	StL-N	21	34	6	5	1	0	0	2	6	5	.147	.275	.176	.451	30	-3	-3	102	131	2	.400	0	1	-1	-2	O	-0.5
1982	StL-N	76	166	21	47	7	1	2	23	8	29	.283	.320	.373	.693	90	-2	-2	103	133	20	.661	11	3	2	-4	O	-0.5
1983	StL-N	146	422	52	120	14	10	8	69	26	76	.284	.327	.422	.749	108	2	3	98	135	53	.722	34	16	1	-10	*O	-0.8
1984	StL-N	126	452	49	121	14	4	15	65	20	105	.268	.300	.416	.716	101	-2	-2	99	111	53	.649	17	9	-0	-5	*1O	-1.1
1985	SF-N	106	294	36	73	10	2	5	20	22	58	.248	.303	.347	.650	87	-8	-5	93	68	28	.550	6	5	-1	-4	1O	-1.2
1987	StL-N	14	30	4	8	2	1	1	1	2	5	.267	.313	.500	.813	113	0	0	99	22	4	.739	0	1	-1	-1	O/1	-0.1
Total	6	489	1398	168	374	48	18	31	180	84	278	.268	.311	.394	.705	98	-12	-8	98	110	161	.668	68	35	-1	-25	O1	-4.2
■ **DANNY GREEN**	Green, Edward b: 11/6/1876, Burlington, N.J. d: 11/9/14, Camden, N.J. BL , Deb: 8/17/1898																											
1898	Chi-N	47	188	26	59	4	3	4	27	7		.314	.342	.431	.773	120	5	4	103	93	33	.783	12			7	O	0.7
1899	Chi-N	117	475	90	140	12	11	6	56	35		.295	.351	.404	.755	114	6	8	96	72	76	.749	18			2	*O	0.2
1900	Chi-N	103	389	63	116	21	5	5	49	17		.298	.328	.416	.744	115	2	6	93	92	64	.758	28			-6	*O	-0.7
1901	Chi-N	133	537	82	168	16	12	6	61	40		.313	.360	.421	.781	128	19	19	100	74	95	.805	31			6	*O	1.1
1902	Chi-A	129	481	77	150	16	11	0	62	53		.312	.380	.391	.771	121	12	15	95	115	87	.834	35			-1	*O	0.6
1903	Chi-A	135	499	75	154	26	7	6	62	47		.309	.368	.425	.793	151	25	29	92	103	91	.835	29			2	*O	2.3
1904	Chi-A	147	536	83	142	16	10	2	62	63		.265	.342	.343	.686	121	14	14	99	108	74	.698	28			-1	*O	0.5
1905	Chi-A	112	379	56	92	13	6	0	44	53		.243	.336	.309	.644	111	5	7	97	142	44	.631	11			-8	*O	-0.6
Total	8	923	3484	552	1021	124	65	29	423	315		.293	.353	.391	.744	124	87	103	97	99	563	.762	192			0	O	4.1
■ **PUMPSIE GREEN**	Green, Elijah Jerry b: 10/27/33, Oakland, Cal. BB/TR, 6', 175 lbs. Deb: 7/21/59																											
1959	Bos-A	50	172	30	40	6	3	1	10	29	22	.233	.350	.320	.670	81	-3	-4	106	69	22	.667	4	2	0	2	2/S	0.0
1960	Bos-A	133	260	36	63	10	3	3	21	44	47	.242	.354	.338	.693	86	-3	-4	103	85	32	.651	3	4	-2	-1	2S	0.1
1961	Bos-A	88	219	33	57	12	3	6	27	42	32	.260	.379	.425	.804	113	6	5	102	95	38	.827	4	2	0	-1	S/2	0.9
1962	Bos-A	56	91	12	21	2	1	2	11	11	18	.231	.314	.341	.654	74	-3	-3	102	118	11	.614	1	0	0	0	2/S	0.0
1963	NY-N	17	54	8	15	1	2	1	5	12	13	.278	.409	.426	.835	142	3	3	99	82	9	.833	0	2	-1	1	3	0.3
Total	5	344	796	119	196	31	12	13	74	138	132	.246	.360	.364	.724	94	1	-3	103	88	112	.725	12	10	-2	1	2S/3	1.3
■ **GARY GREEN**	Green, Gary Allan b: 1/14/62, Pittsburgh, Pa. BR/TR, 6'3", 175 lbs. Deb: 9/14/86																											
1986	SD-N	13	33	2	7	1	0	0	2	1	11	.212	.235	.242	.478	34	-3	-3	95	100	2	.346	0	0	0	-2	S	-0.2
■ **GENE GREEN**	Green, Gene Leroy b: 6/26/33, Los Angeles, Cal. d: 5/23/81, St.Louis, Mo. BR/TR, 6'2.5", 200 lbs. Deb: 9/10/57																											
1957	StL-N	6	15	0	3	1	0	0	2	0	3	.200	.200	.267	.467	24	-2	-2	101	207	1	.308	0	0	0	-1	/O	-0.2
1958	StL-N	137	442	47	124	18	3	13	55	37	48	.281	.338	.423	.761	94	-0	-4	106	101	56	.662	2	1	0	7	OC	0.3
1959	StL-N	30	74	8	14	6	0	1	3	5	18	.189	.241	.311	.551	43	-6	-6	105	47	5	.459	0	0	0	3	OC	-0.3
1960	Bal-A	1	4	0	1	0	0	0	0	0	0	.250	.250	.250	.500	35	-0	-0	102	0	0	.333	0	0	0	0	/O	0.0
1961	Was-A	110	364	52	102	16	3	18	62	35	65	.280	.345	.489	.834	126	9	12	95	105	51	.738	0	2	-1	-4	CO	0.5
1962	Cle-A	66	143	16	40	4	1	11	28	8	21	.280	.318	.552	.870	132	5	5	98	99	23	.798	0	0	0	-2	O/1	0.2
1963	Cle-A	43	78	4	16	3	0	2	7	4	22	.205	.262	.321	.582	64	-4	-4	97	94	6	.470	0	0	0	-3	O	-0.7
	Cin-N	15	31	3	7	1	0	1	3	0	8	.226	.250	.355	.605	69	-1	-1	104	90	2	.480	0	0	0	1	/C	0.0
Total	7	408	1151	130	307	49	7	46	160	89	185	.267	.322	.441	.763	101	1	-0	101	99	145	.712	2	3	-1	0	OC/1	-0.2
■ **JIM GREEN**	Green, James R. b: Cleveland, Ohio Deb: 7/19/1884																											
1884	Was-U	10	36	4	5	1	0	0		0		.139	.139	.167	.306	3	-4	-3	97	0	1	.194	0			0	/3O	-0.2
■ **JOE GREEN**	Green, Joseph Henry (Also Played Under Name Of Joseph Henry Greene) b: 9/17/1897, Philadelphia, Pa. d: 2/4/72, Bryn Mawr, Pa. TR , 6'2", 170 lbs. Deb: 7/02/24																											
1924	Phi-A	1	1	0	0	0	0	0	0	0	0	.000	.000	.000	.000	-99	-0	-0	99	0	0	.000	0	0	0	0	H	0.0
■ **LENNY GREEN**	Green, Leonard Charles b: 1/6/33, Detroit, Mich. BL/TL, 5'11", 170 lbs. Deb: 8/25/57																											
1957	Bal-A	19	33	2	6	1	1	1	5	1	4	.182	.206	.364	.570	56	-2	-2	93	132	2	.464	0	1	-1	-3	O	-0.6
1958	Bal-A	69	91	10	21	4	0	0	4	9	10	.231	.300	.275	.575	63	-5	-4	94	64	8	.466	0	2	-1	-6	O	-1.5
1959	Bal-A	27	24	3	7	0	0	1	2	1	3	.292	.346	.417	.763	112	0	0	97	61	4	.706	0	0	0	-6	O	-0.7
	Was-A	88	190	29	46	6	1	2	15	20	15	.242	.314	.316	.630	73	-7	-7	100	89	20	.593	9	5	-0	-4	O	-1.3
	Yr	115	214	32	53	6	1	3	17	21	18	.248	.318	.327	.645	78	-6	-6	99	83	24	.605	9	5	-0	-10		-2.0
1960	Was-A	127	330	62	97	16	7	5	33	43	25	.294	.385	.430	.816	118	11	10	102	82	58	.862	21	8	2	-6	*O	0.1
1961	Min-A	156	600	92	171	28	7	9	50	81	50	.285	.376	.400	.776	101	9	3	106	71	96	.773	17	11	-2	-6	*O	-0.9
1962	Min-A	158	619	97	168	33	3	14	63	88	36	.271	.369	.402	.771	103	9	5	105	76	98	.762	8	4	0	3	*O	0.2
1963	Min-A	145	280	41	67	10	1	4	27	31	21	.239	.319	.325	.644	81	-6	-7	100	110	32	.616	11	5	0	-16	*O	-2.7
1964	Min-A	26	15	3	0	0	0	0	0	4	6	.000	.211	.000	.211	-35	-3	-3	101	0	0	.250	0	1	-1	-2	/O	-0.5
	LA-A	39	92	13	23	2	0	2	4	10	8	.250	.330	.337	.667	97	-2	-0	89	46	11	.611	2	0	1	-0	O	0.0
	Bal-A	14	21	0	4	0	0	0	1	7	3	.190	.393	.190	.583	65	-0	-1	105	106	2	.706	1	0	0	1	/O	0.1
	Yr	79	128	16	27	2	0	2	5	21	17	.211	.327	.273	.600	72	-5	-4	96	42	14	.588	3	1	0	-1		-0.4
1965	Bos-A	119	373	69	103	24	6	7	24	48	43	.276	.363	.429	.792	116	13	9	107	55	60	.779	8	2	1	-1	O	0.6
1966	Bos-A	85	133	18	32	6	0	1	12	15	19	.241	.327	.308	.635	77	-2	-4	109	114	13	.532	0	1	-1	-0	O	-0.5
1967	Det-A	58	151	22	42	8	1	1	13	9	17	.278	.319	.364	.683	102	0	0	99	93	17	.580	1	1	-0	-5	O	-0.6
1968	Det-A	6	4	0	1	0	0	0	0	1	0	.250	.400	.250	.650	94	0	0	106	0	0	.500	0	0	0	-1	/O	0.0
Total	12	1136	2956	461	788	138	27	47	253	368	260	.267	.353	.379	.733	98	14	1	103	78	421	.722	78	41	-1	-52	O	-8.3
■ **DICK GREEN**	Green, Richard Larry b: 4/21/41, Sioux City, Iowa BR/TR, 5'10", 180 lbs. Deb: 9/09/63																											
1963	KC-A	13	37	5	10	2	0	1	4	2	10	.270	.325	.405	.730	96	0	-0	108	93	5	.643	0	0	0	0	/S2	0.1
1964	KC-A	130	435	48	115	14	5	11	37	27	87	.264	.312	.395	.707	91	-3	-6	105	76	52	.619	3	3	-1	11	*2	1.8
1965	KC-A	133	474	64	110	15	1	15	55	50	110	.232	.309	.363	.672	93	-6	-4	97	107	53	.594	0	2	-1	-12	*2	-1.1
1966	KC-A	140	507	58	127	24	3	9	62	27	101	.250	.298	.363	.661	94	-8	-5	94	126	54	.571	6	1	1	-3	*2/3	0.6
1967	KC-A	122	349	26	69	12	4	5	37	30	68	.198	.261	.298	.559	65	-16	-15	100	130	28	.488	6	3	0	-9	32/1S	-2.4
1968	Oak-A	76	202	19	47	6	0	6	18	21	41	.233	.308	.351	.660	101	-0	0	98	87	23	.611	3	1	0	2	2/C3	0.6
1969	Oak-A	136	483	61	133	25	6	12	64	53	94	.275	.357	.427	.783	128	12	17	92	108	72	.731	2	3	-1	5	*2	2.7
1970	Oak-A	135	384	34	73	7	0	4	29	38	73	.190	.268	.240	.508	42	-30	-29	97	113	25	.420	3	0	1	-3	*2/3C	-1.8
1971	Oak-A	144	475	58	116	14	1	12	49	51	83	.244	.321	.354	.675	91	-5	-6	101	98	53	.596	1	1	-0	6	*2/S	0.7
1972	Oak-A	26	42	1	12	1	1	0	3	3	5	.286	.348	.357	.705	114	1	1	97	84	5	.594	0	1	-1	-1	2	0.1
1973	Oak-A	133	332	33	87	17	0	3	42	21	63	.262	.310	.340	.650	95	-8	-2	87	135	33	.529	0	2	-1	-6	*2/S3	-0.4
1974	Oak-A	100	287	20	61	8	2	2	22	22	50	.213	.269	.275	.544	56	-16	-16	100	102	20	.435	2	3	-1	-3	*2	-1.6
Total	12	1288	4007	427	960	145	23	80	422	345	785	.240	.305	.347	.652	88	-80	-65	97	108	424	.583	26	20	-4	-12	*2/3SC1	-0.7
■ **HANK GREENBERG**	Greenberg, Henry Benjamin "Hammerin' Hank" b: 1/1/11, New York, N.Y. d: 9/4/86, Beverly Hills, Cal BR/TR, 6'3.5", 210 lbs. Deb: 9/14/30 H																											
1930	Det-A	1	1	0	0	0	0	0	0	0	0	.000	.000	.000	.000	-95	-0	-0	105	0	0	.000	0	0	0	0	H	0.0
1933	Det-A	117	449	59	135	33	3	12	87	46	78	.301	.367	.468	.835	113	12	8	107	125	79	.832	6	2	1	-3	*1	-0.2

YEAR	TM/L	G	AB	R	H	2B	3B	HR	RBI	BB	SO	AVG	OBP	SLG	PRO	/A	BR	/A	PF	CHI	RC	TA	SB	CS	SBR	FR	POS	TPR
1934	Det-A	153	593	118	201	**63**	7	26	139	63	93	.339	.404	.600	1.005	160	47	49	98	109	144	1.083	9	5	-0	1	*1	2.1
1935	Det-A	152	619	121	203	46	16	**36**	**170**	87	91	.328	.411	.628	1.039	171	58	61	97	112	161	1.146	4	3	-1	6	*1	4.6
1936	Det-A	12	46	10	16	6	2	1	16	9	6	.348	.455	.630	1.085	173	5	5	95	171	14	1.300	1	0	0	0	1	0.4
1937	Det-A	154	594	137	200	49	14	40	**183**	102	101	.337	.436	.668	1.105	160	67	59	109	129	178	1.285	8	3	1	6	*1	4.2
1938	Det-A	155	556	**144**	175	23	4	**58**	146	**119**	92	.315	.438	.683	1.122	176	66	66	100	94	172	1.319	7	5	-1	7	*1	4.4
1939	Det-A	138	500	112	156	42	7	33	112	91	95	.312	.420	.622	1.042	147	47	38	111	98	136	1.161	8	3	1	-4	*1	2.1
1940	Det-A	148	573	129	195	**50**	8	**41**	**150**	93	75	.340	.433	**.670**	**1.103**	163	**69**	**59**	111	113	**171**	**1.222**	6	3	0	1	*O	**4.6**
1941	Det-A	19	67	12	18	5	1	2	12	16	12	.269	.410	.463	.872	123	3	3	106	122	14	.960	1	0	0	-3	O	-0.1
1945	Det-A	78	270	47	84	20	2	13	60	42	40	.311	.404	.544	.948	164	25	23	106	119	61	.980	3	1	0	-8	O	1.4
1946	Det-A	142	523	91	145	29	5	**44**	**127**	80	88	.277	.373	.604	.977	157	46	41	108	114	119	1.013	5	1	1	3	*1	3.8
1947	Pit-N	125	402	71	100	13	2	25	74	**104**	73	.249	.408	.478	.885	133	23	23	101	105	83	.943	0			1	*1	1.6
Total	13	1394	5193	1051	1628	379	71	331	1276	852	844	.313	.412	.605	1.017	155	468	434	104	112	1331	1.128	58	26		8	*1O	28.9

■ **AL GREENE** Greene, Altar Alphonse b: 11/9/54, Detroit, Mich. BL/TR, 5'11", 190 lbs. Deb: 7/23/79

YEAR	TM/L	G	AB	R	H	2B	3B	HR	RBI	BB	SO	AVG	OBP	SLG	PRO	/A	BR	/A	PF	CHI	RC	TA	SB	CS	SBR	FR	POS	TPR
1979	Det-A	29	59	9	8	1	0	3	6	10	15	.136	.261	.305	.566	54	-4	-4	96	85	5	.528	0	1	-1	0	D/O	-0.3

■ **JUNE GREENE** Greene, Julius Foust b: 6/25/1899, Ramseur, N.C. d: 3/19/74, Glendora, Cal. BL/TR, 6'2.5", 185 lbs. Deb: 4/20/28

YEAR	TM/L	G	AB	R	H	2B	3B	HR	RBI	BB	SO	AVG	OBP	SLG	PRO	/A	BR	/A	PF	CHI	RC	TA	SB	CS	SBR	FR	POS	TPR
1928	Phi-N	11	6	0	3	0	0	0	0	3	1	.500	.667	.500	1.167	201	1	1	104	0	2	2.000	0			0	/P	0.2
1929	Phi-N	21	19	1	4	1	0	0	0	2	4	.211	.286	.263	.549	34	-2	-2	110	0	1	.467	0			0	/P	0.0
Total	2	32	25	1	7	1	0	0	0	5	5	.280	.400	.320	.720	77	-0	-1	108	0	4	.722	0			1	/P	0.2

■ **PADDY GREENE** Greene, Patrick Joseph "Patsy" (a.k.a. Patrick Foley In 1902) b: 3/20/1875, Providence, R.I. d: 10/20/34, Providence, R.I. BR/TR, 5'8", 150 lbs. Deb: 9/10/02

YEAR	TM/L	G	AB	R	H	2B	3B	HR	RBI	BB	SO	AVG	OBP	SLG	PRO	/A	BR	/A	PF	CHI	RC	TA	SB	CS	SBR	FR	POS	TPR
1902	Phi-N	19	65	6	11	1	0	0	1	2		.169	.194	.185	.379	17	-6	-7	105	29	3	.296	2			0	3	-0.5
1903	NY-A	4	13	1	4	1	0	0	0	0		.308	.308	.385	.692	108	0	0	100	0	2	.556	0			0	/3S	0.0
	Det-A	1	3	0	0	0	0	0	0	0		.000	.000	.000	.000	-99	-1	-1	97	0	0	.000	0			-0	/3	0.0
	Yr	5	16	1	4	1	0	0	0	0		.250	.250	.313	.563	70	-1	-1	99	0	1	.417	0			-0		0.0
Total	2	24	81	7	15	2	0	0	1	2		.185	.205	.210	.415	27	-7	-7	104	23	4	.318	2			0	/3S	-0.5

■ **JIM GREENGRASS** Greengrass, James Raymond b: 10/24/27, Addison, N.Y. BR/TR, 6'1", 200 lbs. Deb: 9/09/52

YEAR	TM/L	G	AB	R	H	2B	3B	HR	RBI	BB	SO	AVG	OBP	SLG	PRO	/A	BR	/A	PF	CHI	RC	TA	SB	CS	SBR	FR	POS	TPR
1952	Cin-N	18	68	10	21	2	1	5	24	7	12	.309	.373	.588	.962	164	5	5	100	180	15	.979	0	0	0	3	O	0.8
1953	Cin-N	154	606	86	173	22	7	20	100	47	83	.285	.340	.444	.784	103	1	2	99	126	89	.714	6	4	-1	6	*O	0.1
1954	Cin-N	139	542	79	152	27	4	27	95	41	81	.280	.331	.494	.826	108	7	4	104	114	82	.752	0	3	-2	3	*O	0.1
1955	Cin-N	13	39	1	4	2	0	0	1	9	9	.103	.271	.154	.425	16	-5	-5	106	67	2	.417	0	0	0	2	O	-0.3
	Phi-N	94	323	43	88	20	2	12	37	33	43	.272	.342	.458	.800	108	4	3	102	83	48	.737	0	2	-1	3	O/3	0.3
	Yr	107	362	44	92	22	2	12	38	42	52	.254	.333	.425	.759	97	-0	-2	102	82	50	.699	0	2	-1	4		0.0
1956	Phi-N	86	215	24	44	9	2	5	25	28	43	.205	.296	.335	.631	73	-9	-8	94	121	20	.549	0	0	0	-4	O	-1.4
Total	5	504	1793	243	482	82	16	69	282	165	271	.269	.332	.448	.780	102	4	3	101	114	257	.735	6	9	-4	12	O/3	-0.4

■ **MIKE GREENWELL** Greenwell, Michael Lewis b: 7/18/63, Louisville, Ky. BL/TR, 6', 170 lbs. Deb: 9/05/85

YEAR	TM/L	G	AB	R	H	2B	3B	HR	RBI	BB	SO	AVG	OBP	SLG	PRO	/A	BR	/A	PF	CHI	RC	TA	SB	CS	SBR	FR	POS	TPR
1985	Bos-A	17	31	7	10	1	0	4	8	3	4	.323	.382	.742	1.124	194	4	4	102	91	9	1.286	1	0	0	-5	O	0.0
1986	Bos-A	31	35	4	11	2	0	0	4	5	7	.314	.400	.371	.771	113	1	1	100	123	5	.720	0	0	0	-2	O/D	0.0
1987	Bos-A	125	412	71	135	31	6	19	89	35	40	.328	.389	.570	.959	152	30	30	99	122	90	.976	5	4	-1	-0	OD/C	2.5
1988	Bos-A	158	590	86	192	39	8	22	119	87	38	.325	.420	.531	.950	151	53	46	109	132	134	1.019	16	8	0	4	*OD	4.7
Total	4	331	1068	168	348	73	14	45	220	130	89	.326	.406	.547	.953	151	88	81	105	127	239	1.011	22	12	-1	-3	O/DC	7.2

■ **BILL GREENWOOD** Greenwood, William F. b: 1857, Philadelphia, Pa. d: 5/2/02, Philadelphia, Pa. BB/TL, 5'7.5", 180 lbs. Deb: 9/16/1882

YEAR	TM/L	G	AB	R	H	2B	3B	HR	RBI	BB	SO	AVG	OBP	SLG	PRO	/A	BR	/A	PF	CHI	RC	TA	SB	CS	SBR	FR	POS	TPR
1882	Phi-a	7	30	8	9	1	0	0		1		.300	.323	.333	.656	109	1	0	112	0	3	.524				0	/O2	0.0
1884	Bro-a	92	385	52	83	8	3	3		10		.216	.237	.275	.513	71	-13	-11	98	0	26	.387				-10	*2/S	-1.6
1887	Bal-a	118	495	114	130	16	6	0		54		.263	.336	.319	.656	89	-8	-4	96	0	79	.778	71			5	*2/O	0.1
1888	Bal-a	115	409	69	78	13	1	0	29	30		.191	.256	.227	.484	60	-18	-15	96	95	36	.529	46			-20	2S/O	-2.9
1889	Col-a	118	414	62	93	7	10	3	49	58	71	.225	.327	.312	.639	93	-7	-0	91	104	56	.713	37			-4	*2	-0.1
1890	Roc-a	124	437	76	97	11	6	2		48		.222	.310	.288	.599	85	-11	-5	93	0	53	.653	40			-9	*2/S	-0.8
Total	6	574	2170	381	490	56	26	8	78	201	71	.226	.298	.287	.584	81	-55	-36	95	38	253	.618	194			-38	2/SO	-5.3

■ **BRIAN GREER** Greer, Brian Keith b: 5/14/59, Lynwood, Cal. BR/TR, 6'3", 210 lbs. Deb: 9/13/77

YEAR	TM/L	G	AB	R	H	2B	3B	HR	RBI	BB	SO	AVG	OBP	SLG	PRO	/A	BR	/A	PF	CHI	RC	TA	SB	CS	SBR	FR	POS	TPR
1977	SD-N	1	1	0	0	0	0	0	0	0	1	.000	.000	.000	.000	-99	-0	-0	88	0	0	.000	0	0	0	0	H	0.0
1979	SD-N	4	3	0	0	0	0	0	0	0	1	.000	.000	.000	.000	-99	-1	-1	96	0	0	.000	0	0	0	-1	/O	-0.1
Total	2	5	4	0	0	0	0	0	0	0	2	.000	.000	.000	.000	-99	-1	-1	94	0	0	.000	0	0	0	-1	/O	-0.1

■ **ED GREER** Greer, Edward C. b: 1865, Philadelphia, Pa. d: 2/4/1890, Philadelphia, Pa. BR , Deb: 1885

YEAR	TM/L	G	AB	R	H	2B	3B	HR	RBI	BB	SO	AVG	OBP	SLG	PRO	/A	BR	/A	PF	CHI	RC	TA	SB	CS	SBR	FR	POS	TPR
1885	Bal-a	56	211	32	42	7	0	0		8		.199	.235	.232	.468	47	-11	-13	106	0	12	.349				-1	OC	-1.4
1886	Bal-a	11	38	2	5	1	0	0		2		.132	.175	.158	.333	6	-4	-3	91	0	2	.364	4			-1	/OC	-0.3
	Phi-a	71	264	33	51	5	3	1		8		.193	.223	.246	.469	48	-16	-16	100	0	18	.408	12			4	O/C	-1.2
	Yr	82	302	35	56	6	3	1		10		.185	.217	.235	.452	43	-20	-19	99	0	19	.402	16			3		-1.5
1887	Phi-a	3	11	1	2	0	0	0		0		.182	.182	.182	.364	3	-1	-1	99	0	1	.444	2			0	/O	0.0
	Bro-a	91	327	49	83	13	2	2		25		.254	.318	.324	.643	83	-8	-7	99	0	45	.697	33			-1	OC	-0.8
	Yr	94	338	50	85	13	2	2		25		.251	.314	.320	.634	80	-9	-8	99	0	46	.688	35			-1		-0.8
Total	3	232	851	117	183	26	5	3		43		.215	.261	.268	.529	60	-40	-41	100	0	77	.497	51			1	O/C	-3.7

■ **TOMMY GREGG** Gregg, William Thomas b: 7/29/63, Boone, N.C. BL/TL, 6'1", 190 lbs. Deb: 9/14/87

YEAR	TM/L	G	AB	R	H	2B	3B	HR	RBI	BB	SO	AVG	OBP	SLG	PRO	/A	BR	/A	PF	CHI	RC	TA	SB	CS	SBR	FR	POS	TPR
1987	Pit-N	10	8	3	2	1	0	0	0	0	2	.250	.250	.375	.625	60	-0	-0	104	0	0	.375	0	0	0	-1	/O	-0.1
1988	Pit-N	14	15	4	3	1	0	1	3	1	4	.200	.250	.467	.717	104	-0	-0	98	120	1	.615	0	1	-1	-2	/O	-0.2
	Atl-N	11	29	1	10	3	0	0	4	2	2	.345	.387	.448	.835	133	1	1	104	123	5	.750	0	0	0	3	/O	0.4
	Yr	25	44	5	13	4	0	1	7	3	6	.295	.340	.455	.795	126	1	1	101	126	6	.697	0	1	-1	1		0.2
Total	2	35	52	8	15	5	0	1	7	3	8	.288	.327	.442	.770	113	1	1	102	104	6	.667	0	1	-1	-0	/O	0.1

■ **ED GREMMINGER** Gremminger, Lorenzo Edward "Battleship" b: 3/30/1874, Canton, Ohio d: 5/26/42, Canton, Ohio TR , 6'1", 200 lbs. Deb: 4/21/1895

YEAR	TM/L	G	AB	R	H	2B	3B	HR	RBI	BB	SO	AVG	OBP	SLG	PRO	/A	BR	/A	PF	CHI	RC	TA	SB	CS	SBR	FR	POS	TPR
1895	Cle-N	20	78	10	21	1	0	0	15	5	13	.269	.313	.282	.595	58	-5	-4	97	194	7	.474	0			0	3	-0.3
1902	Bos-N	140	522	55	134	20	12	1	65	39		.257	.308	.347	.655	109	2	5	95	130	59	.585	7			3	*3	1.5
1903	Bos-N	140	511	57	135	24	9	5	56	31		.264	.306	.376	.682	100	-4	-2	96	89	64	.625	12			20	*3	1.8
1904	Det-A	83	309	18	66	13	3	1	28	14		.214	.248	.285	.532	73	-10	-9	96	122	23	.432	3			-12	3	-2.0
Total	4	383	1420	140	356	58	24	7	164	89	13	.251	.295	.340	.635	95	-18	-10	96	117	154	.558	22			11	3	1.0

■ **BUDDY GREMP** Gremp, Lewis Edward b: 8/5/19, Denver, Col. BR/TR, 6'1", 175 lbs. Deb: 9/13/40

YEAR	TM/L	G	AB	R	H	2B	3B	HR	RBI	BB	SO	AVG	OBP	SLG	PRO	/A	BR	/A	PF	CHI	RC	TA	SB	CS	SBR	FR	POS	TPR
1940	Bos-N	4	9	0	2	0	0	0	2	0	0	.222	.222	.222	.444	23	-1	-1	99	371	0	.250	0			0	/1	0.0
1941	Bos-N	37	75	7	18	3	0	0	10	5	3	.240	.287	.280	.568	65	-4	-3	93	172	5	.413	0			1	1/2C	-0.4
1942	Bos-N	72	207	12	45	11	0	3	19	13	21	.217	.267	.314	.581	73	-8	-7	95	95	17	.479	1			-0	1/3	-1.3
Total	3	113	291	19	65	14	0	3	31	18	24	.223	.271	.302	.573	69	-13	-12	95	123	22	.468	1			0	/12C3	-1.7

■ **REDDY GREY** Grey, Romer Carl (born Romer Carl Gray) b: 4/8/1875, Zanesville, Ohio d: 11/9/34, Altadena, Cal. TL , 5'11", 175 lbs. Deb: 5/28/03

YEAR	TM/L	G	AB	R	H	2B	3B	HR	RBI	BB	SO	AVG	OBP	SLG	PRO	/A	BR	/A	PF	CHI	RC	TA	SB	CS	SBR	FR	POS	TPR
1903	Pit-N	1	3	1	1	0	0	0	1	1		.333	.500	.333	.833	136	0	0	105	328	1	1.000	0			0	/O	0.0

■ **BILL GREY** Grey, William Tobin b: 4/5/1871, Philadelphia, Pa. d: 12/8/32, Philadelphia, Pa. 5'11", 175 lbs. Deb: 5/14/1890

YEAR	TM/L	G	AB	R	H	2B	3B	HR	RBI	BB	SO	AVG	OBP	SLG	PRO	/A	BR	/A	PF	CHI	RC	TA	SB	CS	SBR	FR	POS	TPR
1890	Phi-N	34	128	20	31	8	4	0	21	6	3	.242	.287	.367	.654	85	-2	-3	108	138	15	.619	5			0	O/32C1	-0.2
1891	Phi-N	23	75	11	18	0	0	0	7	3	10	.240	.296	.240	.536	62	-4	-3	95	113	6	.474	3			0	CO/S3	-0.2
1895	Cin-N	52	181	24	55	17	4	1	29	15	8	.304	.364	.459	.822	105	3	1	108	94	32	.825	4			0	32/SCO	0.0
1896	Cin-N	46	121	15	25	2	1	0	17	19	11	.207	.314	.240	.554	47	-8	-9	105	169	11	.563	6			0	2C/SO13	-0.7
1898	Pit-N	137	528	56	121	17	5	0	67	28		.229	.281	.280	.561	65	-25	-23	98	132	44	.469	5			-22	*3	-3.8
Total	5	292	1033	126	250	44	14	1	141	71	32	.242	.302	.315	.616	73	-35	-38	101	129	109	.557	23			-22	3/2COS1	-4.9

YEAR	TM/L	G	AB	R	H	2B	3B	HR	RBI	BB	SO	AVG	OBP	SLG	PRO	/A	BR	/A	PF	CHI	RC	TA	SB	CS	SBR	FR	POS	TPR
■ **BOBBY GRICH**	Grich, Robert Anthony b: 1/15/49, Muskegon, Mich. BR/TR, 6'2", 180 lbs. Deb: 6/29/70																											
1970	Bal-A	30	95	11	20	1	3	0	8	9	21	.211	.279	.284	.563	57	-6	-5	97	120	7	.474	1	1	-0	-1	S/23	-0.3
1971	Bal-A	7	30	7	9	0	0	1	6	5	8	.300	.400	.400	.800	123	1	1	103	141	6	.857	1	0	0	0	/S2	0.2
1972	Bal-A	133	460	66	128	21	3	12	50	53	96	.278	.362	.415	.777	134	18	19	98	94	71	.763	13	6	0	1	S21/3	3.4
1973	Bal-A	162	581	82	146	29	7	12	50	107	91	.251	.374	.387	.761	107	15	9	107	80	92	.789	17	9	-0	22	*2	3.8
1974	Bal-A	160	582	92	153	29	6	19	82	90	117	.263	.380	.431	.811	143	28	34	93	101	99	.831	17	11	-2	9	*2	5.0
1975	Bal-A	150	524	81	136	26	4	13	57	107	88	.260	.393	.399	.792	137	22	29	91	94	90	.830	14	10	-2	25	*2	5.7
1976	Bal-A	144	518	93	138	31	4	13	54	86	99	.266	.374	.417	.791	135	23	24	98	86	87	.810	14	6	1	1	*2/3D	3.6
1977	Cal-A	52	181	24	44	6	0	7	23	37	40	.243	.374	.392	.767	116	4	5	95	95	27	.777	6	6	-2	-0	S	0.9
1978	Cal-A	144	487	68	122	16	2	6	42	75	83	.251	.359	.329	.687	93	-1	-2	102	95	64	.658	4	3	-1	1	*2	0.7
1979	Cal-A	153	534	78	157	30	5	30	101	59	84	.294	.366	.537	.904	152	29	35	93	105	103	.893	1	0	0	4	*2	4.3
1980	Cal-A	150	498	60	135	22	2	14	62	84	108	.271	.381	.408	.788	121	14	17	96	101	78	.762	3	7	-3	-2	*2/1	1.9
1981	Cal-A	100	352	56	107	14	2	**22**	61	40	71	.304	.381	**.543**	.924	157	28	26	104	95	73	.933	2	4	-2	10	*2	3.9
1982	Cal-A	145	506	74	132	28	5	19	65	82	109	.261	.372	.449	.821	124	19	19	100	93	87	.821	3	3	-1	20	*2/D	4.5
1983	Cal-A	120	387	65	113	17	0	16	62	76	62	.292	.417	.460	.877	147	26	28	96	109	77	.910	2	4	-2	21	*2/S	5.0
1984	Cal-A	116	363	60	93	15	1	18	58	57	70	.256	.360	.452	.812	121	12	12	101	106	58	.787	2	5	-2	5	213	1.7
1985	Cal-A	144	479	74	116	17	3	13	53	81	77	.242	.355	.372	.727	99	2	1	101	99	63	.687	3	5	-2	22	*213/D	2.3
1986	Cal-A	98	313	42	84	18	0	9	30	39	54	.268	.355	.412	.767	113	5	6	96	77	45	.714	1	3	-2	0	21/3	0.8
Total	17	2008	6890	1033	1833	320	47	224	864	1087	1278	.266	.373	.424	.796	125	239	259	98	96	1129	.815	104	83	-19	139	*2S/13D	47.4
■ **TIM GRIESENBECK**	Griesenbeck, Carlos Phillipe Timothy b: 12/10/1897, San Antonio, Tex. d: 3/25/53, San Antonio, Tex. BR/TR, 5'10.5", 190 lbs. Deb: 9/11/20																											
1920	StL-N	5	3	1	1	0	0	0	0	0	0	.333	.333	.333	.667	94	-0	-0	98	0	0	.500	0	0	0	0	/C	0.0
■ **TOM GRIEVE**	Grieve, Thomas Alan b: 3/4/48, Pittsfield, Mass. BR/TR, 6'2", 190 lbs. Deb: 7/05/70																											
1970	Was-A	47	116	12	23	5	1	3	10	14	38	.198	.290	.336	.626	75	-5	-4	96	84	12	.574	0	0	0	-7	O	-1.3
1972	Tex-A	64	142	12	29	2	1	3	11	11	39	.204	.271	.296	.567	73	-6	-5	94	90	11	.479	1	3	-2	-4	O	-1.2
1973	Tex-A	66	123	22	38	6	0	7	21	7	25	.309	.351	.528	.880	149	7	7	97	96	22	.831	1	0	0	-12	O/D	-0.5
1974	Tex-A	84	259	30	66	10	4	9	32	20	48	.255	.313	.429	.742	116	3	4	96	91	33	.658	0	0	0	0	DO/1	0.3
1975	Tex-A	118	369	46	102	17	1	14	61	22	74	.276	.317	.442	.759	113	4	5	100	114	48	.661	0	2	-1	-8	OD	-0.6
1976	Tex-A	149	546	57	139	23	3	20	81	35	119	.255	.304	.418	.722	108	5	3	102	110	65	.636	4	1	1	1	DO	0.4
1977	Tex-A	79	236	24	53	9	0	7	30	13	57	.225	.274	.352	.626	66	-11	-12	105	114	23	.535	1	0	0	-7	OD	-2.0
1978	NY-N	54	101	5	21	3	0	2	8	9	23	.208	.273	.297	.570	60	-6	-5	98	88	8	.464	0	1	-1	-0	O/1	-0.7
1979	StL-N	9	15	1	3	1	0	0	0	4	1	.200	.368	.267	.635	73	-0	-0	105	0	2	.667	0	0	0	-1	/O	-0.1
Total	9	670	1907	209	474	76	10	65	254	135	424	.249	.303	.401	.704	100	-8	-7	100	103	224	.639	7	7	-2	-39	OD/1	-5.7
■ **KEN GRIFFEY**	Griffey, George Kenneth b: 4/10/50, Donora, Pa. BL/TL, 5'11", 190 lbs. Deb: 8/25/73																											
1973	Cin-N	25	86	19	33	5	1	3	14	6	10	.384	.424	.570	.994	186	8	9	93	97	21	1.073	4	2	0	-3	O	0.5
1974	Cin-N	88	227	24	57	9	5	2	19	27	43	.251	.333	.361	.695	96	-2	-1	98	83	29	.676	9	4	0	-2	O	-0.5
1975	Cin-N	132	463	95	141	15	9	4	46	67	67	.305	.394	.402	.795	116	16	13	104	92	77	.796	16	7	1	-9	*O	0.0
1976	Cin-N	148	562	111	189	28	9	6	74	62	65	.336	.403	.450	.853	138	32	30	103	107	109	.904	34	11	4	-3	*O	2.7
1977	Cin-N	154	585	117	186	35	8	12	57	69	84	.318	.390	.467	.857	129	25	25	100	78	108	.857	17	8	0	6	*O	2.6
1978	Cin-N	158	614	90	177	33	8	10	63	54	70	.288	.346	.417	.763	109	9	7	103	93	93	.743	23	5	4	2	*O	0.8
1979	Cin-N	95	380	62	120	27	4	8	32	36	39	.316	.376	.471	.848	133	16	17	97	60	68	.838	12	5	1	1	O	1.6
1980	Cin-N	146	544	89	160	28	10	13	85	62	77	.294	.367	.454	.821	126	21	20	102	125	99	.856	23	1	6	-4	*O	1.7
1981	Cin-N	101	396	65	123	21	6	2	34	39	42	.311	.374	.409	.783	121	12	12	101	76	61	.748	12	4	1	5	O	1.5
1982	NY-A	127	484	70	134	23	2	12	54	39	58	.277	.331	.407	.738	105	1	3	96	95	65	.676	10	4	1	6	*O	0.6
1983	NY-A	118	458	60	140	21	3	11	46	34	45	.306	.356	.437	.793	119	10	11	99	82	74	.752	6	1	1	-4	*1/OD	0.4
1984	NY-A	120	399	44	109	20	1	7	56	29	32	.273	.324	.381	.705	100	-3	-0	94	129	49	.615	2	2	-1	5	O1/D	0.0
1985	NY-A	127	438	68	120	28	4	10	69	41	51	.274	.336	.425	.761	111	4	6	96	127	63	.716	7	7	-2	1	*O/1D	0.4
1986	NY-A	59	198	33	60	7	0	9	26	15	24	.303	.355	.475	.830	121	7	6	103	86	31	.762	2	2	-1	0	O/D	0.4
	Atl-N	80	292	36	90	15	3	12	32	20	43	.308	.353	.503	.856	131	12	11	102	71	51	.848	12	7	-1	-4	O/1	0.5
1987	Atl-N	122	399	65	114	24	1	14	64	46	54	.286	.361	.456	.817	106	9	4	108	114	62	.766	4	7	-3	-3	*O/1	-0.5
1988	Atl-N	69	193	21	48	5	0	2	19	17	26	.249	.310	.306	.615	74	-5	-6	104	117	17	.503	1	3	-2	-5	O1	-1.5
	Cin-N	25	50	5	14	1	0	2	4	2	5	.280	.308	.420	.728	102	0	-0	105	59	7	.639	0	0	0	-1	1	0.0
	Yr	94	243	26	62	6	0	4	23	19	31	.255	.309	.329	.638	80	-5	-6	105	103	25	.543	1	3	-2	-5		-1.5
Total	16	1894	6768	1074	2015	345	74	139	794	665	835	.298	.361	.432	.794	118	170	166	101	96	1083	.785	194	80	10	-11	*O1/D	11.2
■ **ALFREDO GRIFFIN**	Griffin, Alfredo Claudino (born Baptist (Griffin)) b: 10/6/57, Santo Domingo, D.R. BB/TR, 5'11", 160 lbs. Deb: 9/04/76																											
1976	Cle-A	12	4	0	1	0	0	0	0	0	2	.250	.250	.250	.500	47	-0	-0	100	0	0	.250	0	1	-1	0	/SD	0.0
1977	Cle-A	14	41	5	6	1	0	0	3	3	5	.146	.205	.171	.375	4	-5	-5	98	170	1	.316	2	2	-1	-2	S/D	-0.5
1978	Cle-A	5	4	1	2	1	0	0	0	2	1	.500	.667	.750	1.417	319	1	1	93	0	2	2.500	0	0	0	-0	/S	0.1
1979	Tor-A	153	624	81	179	22	10	2	31	40	59	.287	.335	.364	.699	86	-10	-13	103	44	75	.622	21	16	-3	6	*S	1.0
1980	Tor-A	155	653	63	166	26	**15**	2	41	24	58	.254	.285	.349	.634	73	-25	-25	100	60	59	.530	18	23	-8	6	*S	-1.4
1981	Tor-A	101	388	30	81	19	6	0	21	17	38	.209	.244	.289	.533	48	-24	-29	111	78	24	.425	8	12	-5	-14	S/32	-4.3
1982	Tor-A	162	539	57	130	20	8	1	48	22	48	.241	.271	.314	.584	55	-30	-36	109	112	45	.474	10	8	-2	5	*S	-1.8
1983	Tor-A	162	528	62	132	22	9	4	47	27	44	.250	.290	.348	.639	69	-19	-24	108	94	52	.539	8	11	-4	-7	*S/2D	-2.5
1984	Tor-A	140	419	53	101	8	2	4	30	4	33	.241	.250	.298	.548	50	-28	-29	102	87	31	.433	11	3	2	-5	*S2/D	-2.2
1985	Oak-A	162	614	75	166	18	7	2	64	20	50	.270	.293	.332	.626	76	-25	-19	93	123	60	.536	24	9	2	-10	*S	-1.5
1986	Oak-A	162	594	74	169	23	6	4	51	35	52	.285	.326	.364	.690	95	-9	-4	94	91	71	.641	33	16	0	-12	*S	-0.6
1987	Oak-A	144	494	69	130	23	5	3	60	28	41	.263	.308	.348	.656	82	-18	-12	91	**132**	52	.596	26	13	0	4	*S/2	-0.1
1988	LA-N	95	316	39	63	8	3	1	27	24	30	.199	.260	.253	.513	45	-21	-23	106	133	22	.433	7	5	-1	8	S	-0.9
Total	13	1467	5218	609	1326	191	71	23	423	246	461	.254	.291	.331	.622	70	-213	-218	101	93	495	.539	168	119	-21	-18	*S/2D3	-14.7
■ **DOUG GRIFFIN**	Griffin, Douglas Lee b: 6/4/47, South Gate, Cal. BR/TR, 6', 160 lbs. Deb: 9/11/70																											
1970	Cal-A	18	55	2	7	1	0	0	4	6	5	.127	.213	.145	.359	1	-7	-7	92	202	2	.275	0	0	0	1	2/3	-0.4
1971	Bos-A	125	483	51	118	23	2	3	27	31	45	.244	.293	.319	.611	69	-17	-20	106	72	44	.518	11	5	0	-2	*2	-1.8
1972	Bos-A	129	470	43	122	12	1	2	35	45	48	.260	.327	.302	.629	84	-6	-9	105	105	50	.555	9	2	2	2	*2	0.3
1973	Bos-A	113	396	43	101	14	5	1	33	21	42	.255	.298	.323	.621	71	-13	-16	106	101	36	.510	7	5	-1	-10	*2	-2.3
1974	Bos-A	93	312	35	83	12	4	0	33	28	21	.266	.330	.330	.661	85	-3	-6	107	126	32	.553	2	8	-4	-9	2/S	-1.4
1975	Bos-A	100	287	21	69	6	0	1	29	18	29	.240	.290	.272	.562	55	-15	-18	109	138	22	.439	2	2	-1	-21	2/S	-3.7
1976	Bos-A	49	127	14	24	2	0	0	4	9	14	.189	.248	.205	.453	30	-10	-12	110	59	7	.352	2	1	0	-6	2/D	-1.6
1977	Bos-A	5	6	0	0	0	0	0	0	0	0	.000	.000	.000	.000	-85	-2	-2	117	0	0	.000	0	0	0	0	/2	-0.1
Total	8	632	2136	209	524	70	12	7	165	158	204	.245	.301	.299	.600	68	-75	-90	106	104	193	.515	33	23	-4	-45	2/3DS	-11.0
■ **PUG GRIFFIN**	Griffin, Francis Arthur b: 4/24/1896, Lincoln, Neb. d: 10/12/51, Colorado Springs, Colo. BR/TR, 5'11.5", 187 lbs. Deb: 7/27/17																											
1917	Phi-A	18	25	4	5	1	0	1	3	1	9	.200	.231	.360	.591	85	-1	-1	94	90	2	.550	1			0	/1	0.0
1920	NY-N	5	4	0	1	0	0	0	0	1	2	.250	.400	.250	.650	90	0	0	100	0	0	.667	0	0	0	-1	/O	0.0
Total	2	23	29	4	6	1	0	1	3	2	11	.207	.258	.345	.603	87	-1	-1	95	75	3	.565	1	0		-1	/1O	0.0
■ **IVY GRIFFIN**	Griffin, Ivy Moore b: 12/25/1896, Tomashville, Ala. d: 8/25/57, Gainesville, Fla. BL/TR, 5'11", 180 lbs. Deb: 9/09/19																											
1919	Phi-A	17	68	5	20	2	2	0	6	3	10	.294	.333	.382	.716	95	-0	-1	106	89	8	.625	0			1	1	0.0
1920	Phi-A	129	467	46	111	15	1	0	20	17	49	.238	.281	.274	.555	50	-35	-31	94	56	37	.443	3	3	-1	5	*1/2	-2.6
1921	Phi-A	39	103	14	33	4	2	0	13	5	6	.320	.369	.398	.767	93	-1	-1	103	109	15	.694	1	2	-1	-1	1	-0.2
Total	3	185	638	65	164	21	5	0	39	25	65	.257	.301	.306	.607	63	-36	-33	97	68	60	.499	4	5		4	1/2	-2.8
■ **MIKE GRIFFIN**	Griffin, Michael Joseph b: 3/20/1865, Utica, N.Y. d: 4/10/08, Utica, N.Y. BL/TR, 5'7", 160 lbs. Deb: 4/16/1887 M																											
1887	Bal-a	136	532	142	160	32	13	3		55		.301	.375	.427	.801	131	19	23	96	0	123	1.032	94			-18	*O	0.0
1888	Bal-a	137	542	103	139	21	11	0	46	55		.256	.331	.336	.666	122	12	15	96	67	77	.715	46			4	*O	1.3

YEAR	TM/L	G	AB	R	H	2B	3B	HR	RBI	BB	SO	AVG	OBP	SLG	PRO	/A	BR	/A	PF	CHI	RC	TA	SB	CS	SBR	FR	POS	TPR
1889	Bal-a	137	531	**152**	148	21	14	4	48	91	29	.279	.387	.394	.781	125	21	21	100	54	98	.893	39			-2	*OS/2	1.3
1890	Phi-P	115	489	127	140	29	6	6	54	64	19	.286	.377	.407	.784	109	9	7	102	59	88	.860	30			15	*O	1.3
1891	Bro-N	134	521	106	139	**36**	9	3	65	57	31	.267	.340	.388	.728	117	9	11	97	95	93	.851	65			23	*O	2.4
1892	Bro-N	129	452	103	125	17	11	3	66	68	36	.277	.376	.383	.759	130	19	18	101	114	86	.899	49			9	*O/S	2.2
1893	Bro-N	95	362	85	103	21	7	6	59	59	23	.285	.396	.431	.827	135	13	19	91	89	76	.977	30			8	*O/2	1.9
1894	Bro-N	107	402	122	144	28	4	5	75	78	14	.358	.467	.485	.952	140	26	31	94	95	112	1.225	39			5	*O	2.2
1895	Bro-N	131	519	140	173	38	7	4	65	93	29	.333	.444	.457	.900	143	32	38	94	63	120	1.061	27			12	*O/S	3.2
1896	Bro-N	122	493	101	152	27	9	4	51	48	25	.308	.380	.424	.804	130	10	21	87	57	90	.848	23			1	*O	1.2
1897	Bro-N	134	534	136	169	25	11	2	56	81		.316	.416	.416	.832	121	21	20	102	62	101	.901	16			4	*O	1.2
1898	Bro-N	134	537	88	161	18	6	2	40	60		.300	.379	.367	.745	123	14	18	95	51	82	.745	15			7	*OM	1.5
Total	12	1511	5914	1405	1753	313	108	42	625	809	206	.296	.388	.407	.795	127	205	244	96	66	1148	.905	473			69	*O/S2	19.7
■ THOMAS GRIFFIN	Griffin, Thomas William b: 1/1857, Titusville, Pa. d: 4/17/33, Rockford, Ill. Deb: 9/27/1884																											
1884	Mil-U	11	41	5	9	2	0	0		3		.220	.273	.268	.541	84	-1	-1	100	0	3	.438	0			0	1	0.0
■ SANDY GRIFFIN	Griffin, Tobias Charles b: 7/19/1858, Fayetteville, N.Y d: 6/5/26, Fayetteville, N.Y. 5'10", 160 lbs. Deb: 5/26/1884 M																											
1884	NY-N	16	62	7	11	2	0	0	6	1	19	.177	.190	.210	.400	26	-5	-5	98	162	3	.275				0	O	-0.4
1890	Roc-a	107	407	85	125	28	4	5		50		.307	.388	.432	.821	156	23	28	93	0	78	.890	21			-20	*O/2	0.2
1891	Was-a	20	69	15	19	4	2	0	10	10	3	.275	.398	.391	.789	135	3	4	95	113	12	.860	2			0	OM	0.3
1893	StL-N	23	92	9	18	1	1	0	9	16	2	.196	.315	.228	.543	47	-6	-6	99	113	7	.527	2			0	O	-0.4
Total	4	166	630	116	173	35	7	5	25	77	24	.275	.361	.376	.737	124	14	20	94	44	100	.759	25			-20	O/2	-0.3
■ BERT GRIFFITH	Griffith, Bartholomew Joseph "Buck" b: 3/30/1896, St.Louis, Mo. d: 5/5/73, Bishop, Cal. BR/TR, 5'11", 185 lbs. Deb: 4/13/22																											
1922	Bro-N	106	325	45	100	22	8	2	35	5	11	.308	.322	.443	.765	100	-4	-1	95	82	43	.672	5	7	-3	-3	O/1	-0.9
1923	Bro-N	79	248	23	73	8	4	2	37	13	16	.294	.332	.383	.715	90	-4	-4	98	129	31	.621	1	2	-1	-9	O	-1.4
1924	Was-A	6	8	1	1	0	0	0	0	0	1	.125	.125	.125	.250	-36	-2	-2	98	0	0	.143	0	0	0	0	/O	0.0
Total	3	191	581	69	174	30	12	4	72	18	28	.299	.324	.413	.737	94	-10	-7	96	101	74	.642	6	9	-4	-12	O/1	-2.3
■ DERRELL GRIFFITH	Griffith, Robert Derrell b: 12/12/43, Anadarko, Okla. BL/TR, 6', 168 lbs. Deb: 9/26/63																											
1963	LA-N	1	2	0	0	0	0	0	0	0	0	.000	.000	.000	.000	-99	-1	-0	95	0	0	.000	0	0	0	0	/2	0.0
1964	LA-N	78	238	27	69	16	2	4	23	5	21	.290	.307	.424	.732	113	0	3	92	83	29	.633	5	1	1	-4	3O	-0.2
1965	LA-N	22	41	3	7	0	0	1	2	0	9	.171	.171	.244	.415	17	-5	-4	91	64	1	.286	0	0	0	-1	O	-0.5
1966	LA-N	23	15	3	1	0	0	0	2	2	3	.067	.176	.067	.243	-30	-3	-3	97	841	0	.214	0	0	0	-2	/O	-0.4
Total	4	124	296	33	77	16	2	5	27	7	33	.260	.280	.378	.658	90	-7	-5	92	123	31	.568	5	1	1	-6	/O32	-1.1
■ TOMMY GRIFFITH	Griffith, Thomas Herman b: 10/26/1889, Prospect, Ohio d: 4/13/67, Cincinnati, Ohio BL/TR, 5'10", 175 lbs. Deb: 8/28/13																											
1913	Bos-N	37	127	16	32	4	1	1	12	9	8	.252	.301	.323	.624	83	-4	-3	95	99	12	.537	1			-1	O	-0.4
1914	Bos-N	16	48	3	5	0	0	0	1	2	6	.104	.140	.104	.244	-26	-7	-8	104	72	1	.163	0			3	O	-0.4
1915	Cin-N	160	583	59	179	31	16	4	85	41	34	.307	.355	.436	.790	135	25	24	103	129	85	.708	6	24	-13	-20	*O	-1.4
1916	Cin-N	155	595	50	158	28	7	2	61	36	37	.266	.310	.346	.656	103	0	1	98	121	69	.595	16			-1	*O	-0.5
1917	Cin-N	115	363	45	98	18	7	1	45	19	23	.270	.308	.366	.674	115	2	5	92	128	41	.596	5			1	*O	0.3
1918	Cin-N	118	427	47	113	10	4	2	48	39	30	.265	.326	.321	.647	101	-1	1	97	134	47	.592	10			-3	*O	-0.9
1919	Bro-N	125	484	65	136	18	4	6	57	23	32	.281	.315	.372	.687	113	2	6	94	119	57	.609	8			-4	*O	-0.3
1920	Bro-N	93	334	41	87	9	4	2	30	15	18	.260	.292	.329	.622	70	-10	-14	111	102	32	.512	3	3	-1	-15	O	-3.7
1921	Bro-N	129	455	66	142	21	6	12	71	36	13	.312	.364	.464	.828	112	11	8	105	108	77	.794	3	3	-1	2	*O	0.4
1922	Bro-N	99	329	44	104	17	8	4	49	23	10	.316	.361	.453	.814	114	4	6	95	106	55	.792	7	1	2	3	O	0.7
1923	Bro-N	131	481	70	141	21	9	8	66	50	19	.293	.361	.424	.785	109	5	6	98	104	76	.769	8	2	1	-9	*O	-0.5
1924	Bro-N	140	482	43	121	19	5	3	67	34	19	.251	.300	.330	.630	69	-21	-21	99	146	48	.527	0	5	-3	-14	*O	-4.0
1925	Bro-N	7	4	2	0	0	0	0	0	3	2	.000	.429	.000	.429	21	-0	-0	94	0	1	1.000	1	0	0	-1	/O	0.0
	Chi-N	76	235	38	67	12	1	7	27	21	11	.285	.346	.434	.780	101	-1	-0	97	78	35	.733	2	4	-2	-4	O	-0.6
	Yr	83	239	40	67	12	1	7	27	24	13	.280	.348	.427	.775	100	-1	-0	97	71	35	.739	3	4	-2	-4		-0.6
Total	13	1401	4947	589	1383	208	72	52	619	351	262	.280	.328	.382	.711	103	5	11	99	117	634	.644	70	42		-61	*O	-11.3
■ ART GRIGGS	Griggs, Art Carle b: 12/10/1883, Topeka, Kan. d: 12/19/38, Los Angeles, Cal. BR/TR, 5'11", 185 lbs. Deb: 5/02/09																											
1909	StL-A	108	364	38	102	17	5	0	43	24		.280	.330	.354	.684	127	6	9	92	131	45	.637	11			-2	1O/2S	0.6
1910	StL-A	123	416	28	98	22	5	2	30	25		.236	.281	.327	.607	96	-6	-3	94	80	40	.544	11			-9	O21/S3	-1.8
1911	Cle-A	27	68	7	17	3	2	1	7	5		.250	.301	.397	.698	92	-1	-1	103	79	8	.647	1			-1	2/O31	-0.2
1912	Cle-A	89	273	29	83	16	7	0	39	33		.304	.381	.414	.795	126	10	10	101	115	47	.826	10			0	1	1.1
1914	Bro-F	40	112	10	32	6	1	1	15	5	11	.286	.316	.384	.700	99	-0	-0	101	118	15	.613	1			0	1/O	0.0
1915	Bro-F	27	38	4	11	1	0	1	2	3	7	.289	.341	.395	.736	120	1	1	98	40	5	.667	0			0	/1O	0.1
1918	Det-A	28	99	11	36	8	0	0	16	10	5	.364	.422	.444	.866	167	7	8	97	135	19	.889	2			-2	1	0.4
Total	7	442	1370	127	379	73	20	5	152	105	23	.277	.330	.370	.700	116	17	22	96	106	178	.659	36			-14	1/O23S	0.2
■ DENVER GRIGSBY	Grigsby, Denver Clarence b: 3/25/01, Jackson, Ky. d: 11/10/73, Sapulpa, Okla. BL/TR, 5'9", 155 lbs. Deb: 9/01/23																											
1923	Chi-N	24	72	8	21	5	2	0	5	7	5	.292	.363	.417	.779	101	1	0	104	59	10	.722	1	3	-2	-2	O	-0.3
1924	Chi-N	124	411	58	123	18	2	3	48	31	47	.299	.357	.375	.732	95	-1	-2	101	107	51	.655	10	19	-8	3	*O	-0.8
1925	Chi-N	51	137	20	35	5	0	0	20	19	12	.255	.346	.292	.638	67	-7	-6	97	178	16	.583	1	1	-0	-1	O	-0.7
Total	3	199	620	86	179	28	4	3	73	57	64	.289	.355	.361	.717	89	-7	-8	101	118	77	.647	12	23	-10	0	O	-1.8
■ JOHN GRIM	Grim, John Helm b: 8/9/1867, Lebanon, Ky. d: 7/28/61, Indianapolis, Ind TR , 6'2", 175 lbs. Deb: 1888																											
1888	Phi-N	2	7	0	1	0	0	0	0	0	0	.143	.143	.143	.286	-7	-1	-1	114	0	0	.167	0			0	/O2	0.0
1890	Roc-a	50	192	30	51	6	9	2		7		.266	.299	.422	.720	124	2	4	93	0	29	.738	14			0	SC/32O1P	0.4
1891	CM-a	29	119	14	28	5	1	1	14	2	5	.235	.248	.319	.567	57	-6	-8	112	101	10	.451	1			0	C3/2	-0.6
1892	Lou-N	97	370	40	90	16	4	1	36	13	24	.243	.280	.316	.596	89	-9	-5	92	94	39	.550	18			-3	C12/OS3	-0.2
1893	Lou-N	99	415	68	111	19	8	3	54	12	10	.267	.303	.373	.676	84	-13	-10	96	96	53	.628	15			11	*C/12OS	0.7
1894	Lou-N	108	410	66	122	27	7	7	70	16	15	.298	.339	.449	.788	102	-8	1	88	96	69	.778	14			13	C2/13	1.6
1895	Bro-N	93	329	54	92	17	5	0	44	13	9	.280	.321	.362	.683	82	-11	-8	94	103	42	.624	9			0	*C/O1	0.0
1896	Bro-N	81	281	32	75	13	1	2	35	12	14	.267	.311	.342	.653	84	-11	-5	87	101	33	.587	7			3	C/1	0.4
1897	Bro-N	80	290	26	72	10	1	0	25	1		.248	.259	.290	.548	45	-22	-23	102	87	23	.417	3			6	C	-0.5
1898	Bro-N	52	178	17	50	5	1	0	11	8		.281	.323	.320	.643	92	-3	-2	95	58	19	.539	1			-4	C	-0.1
1899	Bro-N	15	47	3	13	1	0	0	7	1		.277	.306	.298	.604	65	-2	-2	105	153	4	.471	0			0	C	-0.1
Total	11	706	2638	350	705	119	37	16	296	85	77	.267	.302	.359	.661	84	-85	-59	94	88	321	.600	82			26	C/21S3OP	1.6
■ ED GRIMES	Grimes, Edward Adelbert b: 9/8/05, Chicago, Ill. d: 10/5/74, Chicago, Ill. BR/TR, 5'10", 165 lbs. Deb: 4/19/31																											
1931	StL-A	43	57	9	15	1	2	0	5	9	3	.263	.364	.351	.715	86	-1	-1	102	82	8	.714	1	0	0	0	3/2S	0.1
1932	StL-A	31	68	7	16	0	1	0	13	6	12	.235	.297	.265	.562	47	-5	-5	100	242	5	.453	0	1	-1	1	3/2S	-0.2
Total	2	74	125	16	31	1	3	0	18	15	15	.248	.329	.304	.633	65	-6	-6	101	167	14	.568	1	1	-0	1	/32S	-0.1
■ ROY GRIMES	Grimes, Austin Roy "Bummer" b: 9/11/1893, Bergholz, Ohio d: 9/13/54, Gilford Lake, O. BR/TR, 6'1", 176 lbs. Deb: 7/31/20																											
1920	NY-N	26	57	5	9	1	0	0	3	3	8	.158	.200	.175	.375	8	-7	-7	100	116	2	.286	1	1	-0	-2	2	-0.8
■ OSCAR GRIMES	Grimes, Oscar Ray Jr. b: 4/13/15, Minerva, Ohio BR/TR, 5'11", 178 lbs. Deb: 9/28/38																											
1938	Cle-A	4	10	2	2	0	1	0	2	2	0	.200	.333	.400	.733	84	-0	-0	99	169	1	.750	0	0	0	0	/21	0.0
1939	Cle-A	119	364	51	98	20	5	4	56	56	61	.269	.368	.385	.753	95	-3	-2	98	124	55	.743	8	3	1	-2	21S/3	-0.1
1940	Cle-A	11	13	3	0	0	0	0	0	0	5	.000	.000	.000	.000	-99	-4	-4	93	0	0	.000	0	0	0	0	/13	-0.3
1941	Cle-A	77	244	28	58	9	3	4	24	39	47	.238	.345	.348	.693	83	-5	-5	101	88	34	.690	4	0	1	-3	12/3	-0.7
1942	Cle-A	51	84	10	15	2	0	0	2	13	17	.179	.289	.202	.491	43	-6	-5	92	41	6	.458	3	2	-0	-0	2/31S	-0.4
1943	NY-A	9	20	4	3	0	0	0	1	3	7	.150	.261	.150	.411	22	-2	-2	96	122	1	.353	0	0	0	0	/S1	-0.1
1944	NY-A	116	387	44	108	17	8	5	46	59	57	.279	.377	.403	.780	116	13	10	106	99	67	.794	6	0	2	-12	3S	0.0
1945	NY-A	142	480	64	127	19	7	4	45	97	73	.265	.395	.358	.753	111	17	12	107	90	77	.764	7	6	-2	3	*3/1	1.8

YEAR	TM/L	G	AB	R	H	2B	3B	HR	RBI	BB	SO	AVG	OBP	SLG	PRO	/A	BR	/A	PF	CHI	RC	TA	SB	CS	SBR	FR	POS	TPR
1946	NY-A	14	39	1	8	1	0	0	4	1	7	.205	.225	.231	.456	27	-4	-4	100	169	2	.313	0	1	-1	2	/S2	-0.2
	Phi-A	59	191	28	50	5	0	1	20	27	29	.262	.356	.304	.660	82	-3	-4	104	127	23	.595	2	0	1	-8	2/3S	-0.7
	Yr	73	230	29	58	6	0	1	24	28	36	.252	.336	.291	.627	74	-6	-7	104	137	24	.544	2	1	0	-7		-0.9
Total	9	602	1832	235	469	73	24	18	200	297	303	.256	.363	.352	.715	95	3	-3	103	102	266	.711	30	12	2	-22	321/S	-0.7
■ RAY GRIMES	Grimes, Oscar Ray Sr. b: 9/11/1893, Bergholz, Ohio d: 5/25/53, Minerva, Ohio BR/TR, 5'11", 168 lbs. Deb: 9/24/20																											
1920	Bos-A	1	4	1	1	0	0	0	0	0	1	.250	.400	.250	.650	78	-0	-0	96	0	0	.667	0	0	0	0	/1	0.0
1921	Chi-N	147	530	91	170	38	6	6	79	70	55	.321	.406	.449	.855	118	23	17	107	120	99	.867	5	8	-3	-5	*1	0.6
1922	Chi-N	138	509	99	180	45	12	14	99	75	33	.354	.442	.572	1.014	168	47	51	95	110	130	1.128	7	7	-2	-2	*1	4.1
1923	Chi-N	64	216	32	71	7	2	2	36	24	17	.329	.401	.407	.808	109	5	4	104	137	38	.821	5	0	2	-1	1	0.0
1924	Chi-N	51	177	33	53	6	5	5	34	28	15	.299	.401	.475	.876	132	9	9	101	133	35	.937	4	2	0	-1	1	0.5
1926	Phi-N	32	101	13	30	5	0	0	15	6	13	.297	.343	.347	.689	83	-2	-2	103	148	12	.592	0			-1	1	-0.3
Total	6	433	1537	269	505	101	25	27	263	204	133	.329	.413	.480	.892	132	82	79	101	122	314	.933	21	17		-10	1	4.9
■ CHARLIE GRIMM	Grimm, Charles John "Jolly Cholly" b: 8/25/1896, St.Louis, Mo. d: 11/15/83, Scottsdale, Ariz. BL/TL, 5'11.5", 173 lbs. Deb: 7/30/16 MC																											
1916	Phi-A	12	22	0	2	0	0	0	0	2	4	.091	.167	.091	.258	-23	-3	-3	98	0	0	.200	0			-2	/O	-0.5
1918	StL-N	50	141	11	31	7	0	0	12	6	15	.220	.262	.270	.531	66	-6	-5	93	119	10	.436	2			0	1/O3	-0.6
1919	Pit-N	14	44	6	14	1	3	0	6	2	4	.318	.348	.477	.825	140	2	2	105	111	7	.800	1			-1	1	0.1
1920	Pit-N	148	533	38	121	13	7	2	54	30	40	.227	.273	.289	.562	61	-27	-27	101	133	42	.464	7	8	-3	4	*1	-2.9
1921	Pit-N	151	562	62	154	21	17	7	71	31	38	.274	.314	.409	.724	87	-9	-12	103	106	70	.647	6	8	-3	-5	*1	-2.2
1922	Pit-N	154	593	64	173	28	13	0	76	43	15	.292	.343	.383	.726	84	-12	-15	104	119	76	.649	6	10	-4	-4	*1	-2.2
1923	Pit-N	152	563	78	194	29	13	7	99	41	43	.345	.389	.480	.869	132	22	25	97	122	102	.839	6	9	-4	2	*1	1.2
1924	Pit-N	151	542	53	156	25	12	2	63	37	22	.288	.336	.389	.725	88	-5	-10	106	108	70	.645	3	6	-3	-3	*1	-2.1
1925	Chi-N	141	519	73	159	29	5	10	76	38	25	.306	.354	.439	.793	104	0	2	97	107	80	.744	4	3	-1	-0	*1	-1.1
1926	Chi-N	147	524	58	145	30	6	8	82	49	25	.277	.342	.403	.745	94	-0	-5	106	123	72	.702	3			-5	*1	-1.4
1927	Chi-N	147	543	68	169	29	6	2	74	45	21	.311	.367	.398	.765	105	4	4	100	119	79	.714	3			3	*1	-0.2
1928	Chi-N	147	547	67	161	25	5	5	62	39	20	.294	.342	.386	.728	95	-8	-4	95	100	71	.668	7			-2	*1	-2.1
1929	Chi-N	120	463	66	138	28	3	10	91	42	25	.298	.358	.436	.794	94	-4	-4	101	137	71	.763	3			-1	*1	-1.0
1930	Chi-N	114	429	58	124	27	2	6	66	41	26	.289	.359	.403	.763	80	-11	-14	105	122	62	.725	1			4	*1	-1.3
1931	Chi-N	146	531	65	176	33	11	4	66	53	29	.331	.393	.458	.851	134	22	25	96	94	99	.839	1			0	*1	1.3
1932	Chi-N	149	570	66	175	42	2	7	80	35	22	.307	.349	.425	.774	103	5	2	104	115	86	.711	2			9	*1M	0.3
1933	Chi-N	107	384	38	95	15	2	3	37	23	15	.247	.290	.320	.610	76	-13	-12	97	107	33	.482	1			7	*1M	-0.6
1934	Chi-N	75	267	24	79	8	1	5	47	16	12	.296	.338	.390	.728	96	-2	-1	98	142	34	.619	1			0	1M	-0.6
1935	Chi-N	2	8	0	0	0	0	0	0	0	1	.000	.000	.000	.000	-99	-2	-2	99	0	0	.000	0			0	/1M	-0.1
1936	Chi-N	39	132	13	33	4	0	1	16	5	8	.250	.277	.303	.580	54	-8	-9	105	132	10	.433	0			1	1M	-1.0
Total	20	2166	7917	908	2299	394	108	79	1078	578	410	.290	.341	.397	.738	95	-54	-63	101	116	1077	.673	57	44		7	*1/O3	-17.0
■ MOOSE GRIMSHAW	Grimshaw, Myron Frederick b: 11/30/1875, St.Johnsville, N.Y d: 12/11/36, Canajoharie, N.Y. BB/TR, 6'1", 173 lbs. Deb: 4/25/05																											
1905	Bos-A	85	285	39	68	8	2	4	35	21		.239	.291	.323	.614	96	-1	-1	100	122	29	.539	4			-6	1	-0.9
1906	Bos-A	110	428	46	124	16	12	0	48	23		.290	.326	.383	.709	126	11	11	98	102	56	.632	5			1	*1	1.0
1907	Bos-A	64	181	19	37	7	2	0	33	16		.204	.269	.265	.534	71	-5	-6	101	246	15	.486	6			-1	O1/S	-0.8
Total	3	259	894	104	229	31	16	4	116	60		.256	.303	.340	.643	105	4	5	99	138	100	.570	15			-6	1/OS	-0.7
■ DICK GROAT	Groat, Richard Morrow b: 11/4/30, Wilkinsburg, Pa. BR/TR, 5'11.5", 180 lbs. Deb: 6/19/52																											
1952	Pit-N	95	384	38	109	6	1	1	29	19	27	.284	.319	.313	.632	76	-12	-12	100	81	35	.478	2	4	-2	12	S	0.1
1955	Pit-N	151	521	45	139	28	2	4	51	38	26	.267	.318	.351	.669	80	-17	-15	97	108	54	.550	0	2	-1	16	*S	0.4
1956	Pit-N	142	520	40	142	19	3	0	37	35	25	.273	.319	.321	.640	71	-19	-21	102	99	52	.511	0	3	-2	7	*S/3	-0.5
1957	Pit-N	125	501	58	158	30	5	7	54	27	28	.315	.354	.437	.791	118	7	11	94	90	74	.692	0	1	-1	1	*S/3	1.6
1958	Pit-N	151	584	67	175	36	9	3	66	23	32	.300	.331	.408	.738	99	-6	-2	95	117	72	.618	2	2	-1	4	*S	1.1
1959	Pit-N	147	593	74	163	22	7	5	51	32	35	.275	.314	.361	.675	77	-18	-20	103	95	62	.547	0	2	-1	3	*S	-1.2
1960	Pit-N	138	573	85	186	26	4	2	50	39	35	**.325**	.372	.394	.766	111	9	9	99	77	85	.679	0	2	-1	15	*S	2.8
1961	Pit-N	148	596	71	164	25	6	6	55	40	44	.275	.322	.367	.689	83	-15	-14	99	90	65	.568	0	4	-2	13	*S/3	1.0
1962	Pit-N	161	678	76	199	34	3	2	61	31	61	.294	.327	.361	.689	83	-15	-17	102	85	78	.569	2	1	0	14	*S	1.2
1963	StL-N	158	631	85	201	**43**	11	6	73	56	58	.319	.380	.450	.830	128	31	26	107	98	106	.777	3	1	0	-9	*S	3.5
1964	StL-N	161	636	70	186	35	6	1	70	44	42	.292	.338	.371	.709	89	0	-9	112	127	78	.603	2	3	-1	-7	*S	-0.6
1965	StL-N	153	587	55	149	26	5	0	52	56	50	.254	.320	.315	.635	75	-15	-19	107	123	61	.540	1	1	-0	-1	*S/3	-0.4
1966	Phi-N	155	584	58	152	21	4	2	53	40	38	.260	.313	.320	.633	76	-18	-18	101	118	56	.517	2	1	0	18	*S3/1	1.1
1967	Phi-N	10	26	3	3	0	0	0	1	4	4	.115	.233	.115	.349	3	-3	-3	104	138	1	.304	0	0	0	1	/S	-0.1
	SF-N	34	70	4	12	1	1	0	4	6	7	.171	.237	.214	.451	30	-6	-6	101	110	3	.344	0	0	0	1	S/2	-0.1
	Yr	44	96	7	15	1	1	0	5	10	11	.156	.236	.188	.423	22	-9	-10	102	120	4	.333	0	0	0	2		-0.2
Total	14	1929	7484	829	2138	352	67	39	707	490	512	.286	.332	.366	.698	89	-95	-111	102	101	882	.609	14	27	-12	86	*S/321	9.9
■ HEINIE GROH	Groh, Henry Knight b: 9/18/1889, Rochester, N.Y. d: 8/22/68, Cincinnati, Ohio BR/TR, 5'8", 158 lbs. Deb: 4/12/12 M																											
1912	NY-N	27	48	8	13	2	1	0	3	8	7	.271	.375	.354	.729	96	0	0	104	59	8	.886	6			0	2/S3	0.0
1913	NY-N	4	2	0	0	0	0	0	0	0	1	.000	.000	.000	.000	-97	-1	-1	103	0	0	.000	0			0	/3S	0.0
	Cin-N	117	397	51	112	19	5	3	48	38	36	.282	.351	.378	.729	106	5	4	102	112	59	.758	24			6	*2/S	0.7
	Yr	121	399	51	112	19	5	3	48	38	37	.281	.349	.376	.725	105	4	3	102	108	59	.753	24			6		0.7
1914	Cin-N	139	455	59	131	18	4	2	32	64	28	.288	.391	.358	.749	118	17	14	105	73	72	.815	24			-4	*2/S	1.0
1915	Cin-N	160	587	72	170	32	9	3	50	50	33	.290	.354	.390	.745	122	18	16	103	77	83	.691	12	17	-7	11	*32	2.9
1916	Cin-N	149	553	85	149	24	14	2	28	**84**	34	.269	.370	.374	.744	131	22	23	98	46	83	.762	13			13	*32/S	4.3
1917	Cin-N	156	599	91	**182**	**39**	11	1	53	71	30	.304	**.385**	.411	.796	156	33	39	92	71	96	.815	15			4	*3/2	4.5
1918	Cin-N	126	493	**86**	158	**28**	3	1	37	54	24	.320	**.395**	.396	.791	146	**26**	**28**	97	61	79	.797	11			1	*3M	**3.5**
1919	Cin-N	122	448	79	139	17	11	5	63	56	26	.310	.392	.431	**.823**	140	27	25	105	113	81	.887	21			5	*3	3.3
1920	Cin-N	145	550	86	164	28	12	0	49	60	29	.298	.375	.393	.768	135	17	24	90	84	81	.741	16	19	-7	-6	*3/S	1.9
1921	Cin-N	97	357	54	118	19	6	0	48	36	17	.331	.398	.417	.815	115	10	9	101	114	60	.834	22	14	-2	6	3	1.3
1922	NY-N	115	426	63	113	21	3	3	51	53	21	.265	.353	.350	.703	79	-10	-12	104	120	55	.665	5	6	-2	6	*3	0.0
1923	NY-N	123	465	91	135	22	5	4	48	60	22	.290	.379	.385	.763	100	3	2	101	94	71	.743	3	4	-2	6	*3	0.9
1924	NY-N	145	559	82	157	32	3	2	46	52	29	.281	.354	.360	.713	100	-5	2	91	86	74	.667	8	6	-1	7	*3	1.7
1925	NY-N	25	65	7	15	4	0	0	4	6	3	.231	.296	.292	.588	51	-5	-5	99	75	6	.500	0	0	0	-0	3/2	-0.3
1926	NY-N	12	35	2	8	2	0	0	3	2	3	.229	.270	.286	.556	51	-2	-2	98	104	3	.444	0			0	/3	-0.1
1927	Pit-N	14	35	2	10	1	0	0	3	2	2	.286	.324	.314	.639	70	-1	-1	102	95	3	.520	0			1	3	0.0
Total	16	1676	6074	918	1774	308	87	26	566	696	345	.292	.373	.384	.757	119	155	164	99	85	915	.754	180	66		55	*32/S	25.6
■ LEW GROH	Groh, Lewis Carl "Silver" b: 10/16/1883, Rochester, N.Y. d: 10/20/60, Rochester, N.Y. BR/TR, Deb: 8/02/19																											
1919	Phi-A	2	4	0	0	0	0	0	0	0	2	.000	.000	.000	.000	-95	-1	-1	106	0	0	.000	0			0	/3	0.0
■ GEORGE GROSART	Grosart, George Albert b: 1879, Meadville, Pa. D, Apr.18, 1902 Homestead, Pa. Deb: 6/07/01																											
1901	Bos-N	7	26	4	3	0	0	0	1	0		.115	.115	.115	.231	-29	-4	-5	112	114	0	.130	0			3	/O	-0.2
■ HOWDIE GROSKLOSS	Groskloss, Howard Hoffman b: 4/9/07, Pittsburgh, Pa. BR/TR, 5'9", 176 lbs. Deb: 6/23/30																											
1930	Pit-N	2	3	0	1	0	0	0	1	0	0	.333	.333	.333	.667	64	-0	-0	97	345	0	.500	0			0	/S	0.0
1931	Pit-N	53	161	13	45	7	2	0	20	11	16	.280	.326	.348	.673	81	-4	-4	101	127	19	.586	1			-5	2/S	-0.6
1932	Pit-N	17	20	1	2	0	0	0	0	0	3	.100	.100	.100	.200	-46	-4	-4	99	0	0	.111	0			-0	/S	-0.3
Total	3	72	184	14	48	7	2	0	21	11	19	.261	.303	.321	.623	67	-8	-8	100	118	19	.522	1			-5	/2S	-0.9
■ EMIL GROSS	Gross, Emil Michael b: 3/3/1858, Chicago, Ill. d: 8/24/21, Eagle River, Wis. BR/TR, 6', 190 lbs. Deb: 8/13/1879																											
1879	Pro-N	30	132	31	46	9	5	0	24	4	8	.348	.368	.492	.860	178	11	11	102	137	24	.802				-5	C	0.5
1880	Pro-N	87	347	43	90	18	3	1	34	16	15	.259	.292	.337	.629	117	5	6	96	110	35	.518				-17	*C	-0.3
1881	Pro-N	51	182	15	50	9	4	1	24	13	11	.275	.323	.385	.708	130	5	6	93	116	23	.629				-5	C/O	0.1

YEAR	TM/L	G	AB	R	H	2B	3B	HR	RBI	BB	SO	AVG	OBP	SLG	PRO	/A	BR	/A	PF	CHI	RC	TA	SB	CS	SBR	FR	POS	TPR
1883	Phi-N	57	231	39	71	25	7	1	25	12	18	.307	.342	.489	.831	165	13	17	90	79	40	.781				-8	C/O	1.0
1884	CP-U	23	95	13	34	6	2	4		6		.358	.396	.589	.986	231	13	13	99	0	23	1.016	0			0	C/O	1.1
Total	5	248	987	141	291	67	21	7	107	51	52	.295	.329	.427	.756	150	46	53	95	97	145	.678	0			-35	C/O	2.4
■ TURKEY GROSS	Gross, Ewell b: 2/21/1896, Mesquite, Tex. d: 1/11/36, Dallas, Tex. BR/TR, 6', 165 lbs. Deb: 4/14/25																											
1925	Bos-A	9	32	2	3	0	1	0	2	2	2	.094	.171	.156	.328	-17	-6	-6	95	136	1	.276	0	0	0	0	/S	-0.3
■ GREG GROSS	Gross, Gregory Eugene b: 8/1/52, York, Pa. BL/TL, 5'10", 160 lbs. Deb: 9/05/73																											
1973	Hou-N	14	39	5	9	2	1	0	1	4	4	.231	.302	.333	.636	80	-1	-1	95	31	4	.576	2	1	0	0	/O	0.0
1974	Hou-N	156	589	78	185	21	8	0	36	76	39	.314	.393	.377	.770	119	16	17	98	60	86	.712	12	20	-8	8	*O	1.2
1975	Hou-N	132	483	67	142	14	10	0	41	63	37	.294	.375	.364	.740	112	6	9	94	95	69	.681	2	2	-1	2	*O	0.7
1976	Hou-N	128	426	52	122	12	3	0	27	64	39	.286	.380	.329	.708	118	4	12	86	76	56	.648	2	6	-3	2	*O	0.7
1977	Chi-N	115	239	43	77	10	4	5	32	33	19	.322	.404	.460	.865	115	12	7	114	102	45	.846	0	1	-1	-6	O	-0.1
1978	Chi-N	124	347	34	92	12	7	1	39	33	19	.265	.329	.349	.678	81	-5	-9	110	125	41	.599	3	1	0	-9	*O	-2.2
1979	Phi-N	111	174	21	58	6	3	0	15	29	5	.333	.429	.402	.831	132	8	9	97	85	32	.860	5	2	0	-11	O	-0.3
1980	Phi-N	127	154	19	37	7	2	0	12	24	7	.240	.346	.312	.658	79	-2	-4	107	99	18	.607	1	1	-0	-21	O/1	-3.0
1981	Phi-N	83	102	14	23	6	1	0	7	15	5	.225	.325	.304	.629	71	-2	-4	112	89	10	.565	2	2	-1	-8	O	-1.4
1982	Phi-N	119	134	14	40	4	0	0	10	19	8	.299	.386	.328	.714	108	1	2	94	89	17	.650	4	3	-1	-15	O	-1.4
1983	Phi-N	136	245	25	74	12	3	0	29	34	16	.302	.389	.376	.765	112	6	5	101	125	36	.714	3	5	-2	-22	*O/1	-2.1
1984	Phi-N	112	202	19	65	9	1	0	16	24	11	.322	.396	.376	.773	116	6	6	102	82	31	.723	1	0	0	-5	O1	-0.1
1985	Phi-N	93	169	21	44	5	2	0	14	32	9	.260	.378	.314	.692	94	1	0	102	105	22	.662	1	0	0	-8	O/1	-0.9
1986	Phi-N	87	101	11	25	5	0	0	8	21	11	.248	.382	.297	.679	86	-0	-1	104	106	12	.663	1	0	0	-4	O/1P	-0.4
1987	Phi-N	114	133	14	38	4	1	1	12	25	12	.286	.403	.353	.756	98	2	1	104	96	21	.753	0	0	0	-13	O1	-1.4
1988	Phi-N	98	133	10	27	1	0	0	5	16	3	.203	.293	.211	.504	46	-9	-9	101	71	9	.413	0	0	0	-11	O1	-2.2
Total	16	1749	3670	447	1058	130	46	7	304	512	244	.288	.376	.354	.731	104	42	42	100	90	506	.699	39	44	-15	-120	*O/1P	-12.9
■ WAYNE GROSS	Gross, Wayne Dale b: 1/14/52, Riverside, Cal. BL/TR, 6'2", 210 lbs. Deb: 8/21/76																											
1976	Oak-A	10	18	0	4	0	0	0	1	2	1	.222	.300	.222	.522	55	-1	-1	100	96	1	.429	0	0	0	-0	/1OD	-0.1
1977	Oak-A	146	485	66	113	21	1	22	63	86	84	.233	.354	.416	.771	115	8	11	95	95	76	.778	5	4	-1	-21	*3/1	-1.3
1978	Oak-A	118	285	18	57	10	2	7	23	40	63	.200	.309	.323	.632	77	-8	-8	101	80	31	.588	0	2	-1	-12	*31	-2.2
1979	Oak-A	138	442	54	99	19	1	14	50	72	62	.224	.334	.367	.700	100	-6	1	89	96	57	.675	4	3	-1	-9	*31/O	-0.7
1980	Oak-A	113	366	45	103	20	3	14	61	44	39	.281	.360	.467	.827	132	13	15	95	112	64	.825	5	3	-0	-13	31/D	0.1
1981	Oak-A	82	243	29	50	7	1	10	31	34	28	.206	.308	.366	.674	98	-2	-1	96	102	28	.632	2	1	0	-8	3/1D	-0.8
1982	Oak-A	129	386	43	97	14	0	9	41	53	50	.251	.345	.358	.702	98	-2	0	95	99	52	.667	3	1	0	-5	*31/D	-0.7
1983	Oak-A	137	339	34	79	18	0	12	44	36	52	.233	.312	.392	.704	97	-4	-2	96	102	41	.648	3	5	-2	-9	13/PD	-1.5
1984	Bal-A	127	342	53	74	9	1	22	64	68	69	.216	.348	.442	.789	124	9	12	94	118	55	.801	3	2	-1	5	*3/1D	1.7
1985	Bal-A	103	217	31	51	8	0	11	18	46	48	.235	.369	.424	.793	118	6	7	99	57	37	.818	1	1	-0	0	3D/1	0.4
1986	Oak-A	3	2	0	0	0	0	0	0	1	0	.000	.333	.000	.333	2	-0	-0	94	0	0	.500	0	0	0	0	/3	0.0
Total	11	1106	3125	373	727	126	9	121	396	482	496	.233	.339	.395	.734	107	13	35	95	97	443	.727	24	22	-6	-73	31/DOP	-5.1
■ JERRY GROTE	Grote, Gerald Wayne b: 10/6/42, San Antonio, Tex. BR/TR, 5'10", 185 lbs. Deb: 9/21/63																											
1963	Hou-N	3	5	0	1	0	0	0	1	1	3	.200	.333	.200	.533	62	-0	-0	92	420	1	.500	0	0	0	0	/C	0.0
1964	Hou-N	100	298	26	54	9	3	3	24	20	75	.181	.242	.262	.504	44	-23	-22	96	113	18	.405	0	2	-1	8	C	-1.1
1966	NY-N	120	317	26	75	12	2	3	31	40	81	.237	.328	.315	.643	85	-7	-5	94	120	33	.579	4	3	-1	-9	*C/3	-1.2
1967	NY-N	120	344	25	67	8	0	4	23	14	65	.195	.228	.253	.481	38	-28	-28	99	96	19	.366	2	2	-1	-13	*C	-3.7
1968	NY-N	124	404	29	114	18	0	3	31	44	81	.282	.357	.349	.706	110	8	7	102	87	50	.628	1	5	-3	12	*C	2.3
1969	NY-N	113	365	38	92	12	3	6	40	32	59	.252	.314	.351	.665	86	-7	-7	100	110	39	.574	2	1	0	3	*C	0.3
1970	NY-N	126	415	38	106	14	1	2	34	36	39	.255	.316	.308	.625	66	-18	-20	104	98	39	.515	2	1	0	3	*C	-1.1
1971	NY-N	125	403	35	109	25	0	2	35	40	47	.270	.339	.347	.687	98	-2	-0	96	98	44	.577	1	4	-2	-1	*C	0.0
1972	NY-N	64	205	15	43	5	1	3	21	26	27	.210	.308	.288	.595	74	-7	-6	95	129	19	.533	1	0	0	13	C/3O	1.1
1973	NY-N	84	285	17	73	10	2	1	32	13	23	.256	.291	.316	.607	68	-12	-13	101	138	24	.466	0	0	0	-2	C/3	-0.9
1974	NY-N	97	319	25	82	8	1	5	36	33	33	.257	.331	.335	.666	87	-5	-5	99	114	35	.570	0	1	-1	-8	C	-0.9
1975	NY-N	119	386	28	114	14	5	2	39	38	23	.295	.360	.373	.733	109	3	5	95	101	51	.644	0	1	-1	14	*C	2.2
1976	NY-N	101	323	30	88	14	2	4	28	38	19	.272	.351	.365	.716	113	2	5	92	83	39	.627	1	2	-1	1	C/O	1.1
1977	NY-N	42	115	8	31	3	1	0	7	9	12	.270	.333	.313	.646	78	-4	-3	96	78	11	.528	0	0	0	1	C3	-0.1
	LA-N	18	27	3	7	0	0	0	4	2	5	.259	.310	.259	.570	55	-2	-2	100	229	2	.391	0	1	-1	0	C/3	-0.1
	Yr	60	142	11	38	3	1	0	11	11	17	.268	.329	.303	.632	73	-5	-5	97	124	14	.523	0	1	-1	2		-0.2
1978	LA-N	41	70	5	19	5	0	0	9	10	5	.271	.363	.343	.705	99	0	0	99	149	10	.667	0	0	0	-2	C/3	0.0
1981	KC-A	22	56	4	17	3	1	1	9	3	2	.304	.350	.446	.796	130	2	2	99	126	9	.750	1	0	0	-1	C	0.3
	LA-N	2	2	0	0	0	0	0	0	0	1	.000	.000	.000	.000	-99	-1	-1	98	0	0	.000	0	0	0	0	/C	0.0
Total	16	1421	4339	352	1092	160	22	39	404	399	600	.252	.318	.326	.644	83	-102	-92	98	107	443	.566	15	23	-9	19	*C/3O	-1.8
■ JOHNNY GROTH	Groth, John Thomas b: 7/23/26, Chicago, Ill. BR/TR, 6', 182 lbs. Deb: 9/05/46																											
1946	Det-A	4	9	1	0	0	0	0	0	0	3	.000	.000	.000	.000	-92	-2	-2	108	0	0	.000	0	0	0	-1	/O	-0.3
1947	Det-A	2	4	1	1	0	0	0	0	2	1	.250	.500	.250	.750	108	0	0	104	0	0	.600	0	0	0	1	/O	0.1
1948	Det-A	6	17	3	8	3	0	1	5	1	1	.471	.500	.824	1.324	258	3	3	96	99	7	1.667	0	0	0	1	/O	0.4
1949	Det-A	103	348	60	102	19	5	11	73	65	27	.293	.407	.471	.878	123	17	13	108	130	66	.873	3	7	-3	6	O	1.3
1950	Det-A	157	566	95	173	30	8	12	85	95	27	.306	.407	.451	.858	124	19	22	97	103	106	.842	1	5	-3	-16	*O	0.0
1951	Det-A	118	428	41	128	29	1	3	49	31	32	.299	.349	.393	.742	95	-0	-4	106	101	57	.637	1	1	-0	-5	*O	-1.2
1952	Det-A	141	524	56	149	22	2	4	51	51	39	.284	.348	.357	.705	97	-2	-2	99	101	64	.606	2	10	-5	-7	*O	-1.8
1953	StL-A	141	557	65	141	27	4	10	57	42	53	.253	.308	.370	.678	77	-15	-20	107	95	62	.585	5	6	-2	13	*O	-1.3
1954	Chi-A	125	422	41	116	20	0	7	60	42	37	.275	.343	.372	.715	93	-2	-4	104	128	49	.611	3	9	-5	-5	*O	-1.6
1955	Chi-A	32	77	13	26	7	0	2	11	6	13	.338	.386	.506	.892	137	4	4	101	91	15	.868	1	0	0	1	O	0.4
	Was-A	63	183	22	40	4	5	2	17	18	18	.219	.289	.328	.616	72	-9	-7	91	96	18	.541	2	0	1	4	O	-0.4
	Yr	95	260	35	66	11	5	4	28	24	31	.254	.317	.381	.698	92	-5	-3	94	95	32	.633	3	0	1	6		0.0
1956	KC-A	95	244	22	63	13	3	5	37	30	31	.258	.339	.398	.737	93	-2	-3	101	123	32	.667	1	2	-1	-2	O	-0.9
1957	KC-A	55	59	10	15	0	0	0	2	7	6	.254	.333	.254	.588	64	-3	-3	99	53	5	.478	0	0	0	-14	O	-2.0
	Det-A	38	103	11	30	10	0	0	16	6	7	.291	.336	.388	.725	91	-0	-1	107	158	14	.635	0	0	0	-1	O	-0.4
	Yr	93	162	21	45	10	0	0	18	13	13	.278	.335	.340	.675	83	-3	-4	102	96	20	.585	0	0	0	-15		-2.4
1958	Det-A	88	146	24	41	5	2	2	11	13	19	.281	.340	.384	.723	95	-0	-1	104	71	18	.627	0	1	-1	-12	O	-1.9
1959	Det-A	55	102	12	24	7	1	1	10	7	14	.235	.284	.353	.637	67	-4	-5	111	101	11	.551	0	0	0	-5	O	-1.2
1960	Det-A	25	19	3	7	1	0	0	2	3	1	.368	.455	.421	.876	136	1	1	102	98	4	.846	0	1	-1	-2	/O	-0.1
Total	15	1248	3808	480	1064	197	31	60	486	419	329	.279	.353	.395	.747	98	3	-8	102	106	528	.701	19	42	-20	-45	*O	-10.9
■ ROY GROVER	Grover, Roy Arthur b: 1/17/1892, Snohomish, Wash. d: 2/7/78, Milwaukie, Ore. BR/TR, 5'8", 150 lbs. Deb: 9/13/16																											
1916	Phi-A	20	77	8	21	1	2	0	7	6	10	.273	.325	.338	.663	101	-0	-0	98	83	11	.661	5			1	2	0.2
1917	Phi-A	141	482	45	108	15	7	0	34	43	53	.224	.292	.284	.576	81	-14	-10	94	91	46	.521	12			2	*2	0.0
1919	Phi-A	22	56	8	13	1	0	0	2	5	6	.232	.295	.250	.545	51	-3	-4	106	52	5	.442	0			-0	2/3	-0.2
	Was-A	24	75	6	14	0	0	0	7	6	10	.187	.256	.187	.443	26	-7	-7	98	181	4	.377	2			-7	2	-1.2
	Yr	46	131	14	27	1	0	0	9	11	16	.206	.273	.214	.486	37	-11	-11	102	120	9	.404	2			-7		-1.4
Total	3	207	690	67	156	17	9	0	50	60	79	.226	.292	.277	.569	74	-25	-21	96	97	66	.513	19			-4	2/3	-1.2
■ HARVEY GRUBB	Grubb, Harvey Harrison b: 9/18/1890, Lexington, N.C. d: 1/25/70, Corpus Christi, Tex. BR/TR, 6', 165 lbs. Deb: 9/27/12																											
1912	Cle-A	1	0	0	0	0	0	0	0	0		—	1.000	—	1.277	267	0	0	101	0	0	—	0			-0	/O	0.0
■ JOHN GRUBB	Grubb, John Maywood b: 8/4/48, Richmond, Va. BL/TR, 6'3", 175 lbs. Deb: 9/10/72																											
1972	SD-N	7	21	4	7	1	1	0	1	1	3	.333	.364	.476	.840	155	1	1	88	41	3	.688	0	1	-1	1	/O	0.1
1973	SD-N	113	389	52	121	22	3	8	37	37	50	.311	.374	.445	.819	134	14	17	94	77	66	.798	9	3	1	4	*O/3	1.7

YEAR	TM/L	G	AB	R	H	2B	3B	HR	RBI	BB	SO	AVG	OBP	SLG	PRO	/A	BR	/A	PF	CHI	RC	TA	SB	CS	SBR	FR	POS	TPR
1974	SD-N	140	444	53	127	20	4	8	42	46	47	.286	.358	.403	.761	121	8	11	93	80	68	.726	4	0	1	4	*O/3	1.2
1975	SD-N	144	553	72	149	36	2	4	38	59	59	.269	.345	.363	.709	97	-2	-1	100	66	71	.639	2	7	-4	-9	*O	-1.9
1976	SD-N	109	384	54	109	22	1	5	27	65	53	.284	.393	.385	.778	137	14	20	89	68	62	.773	1	2	-1	-6	O/13	0.9
1977	Cle-A	34	93	8	28	3	3	2	14	19	18	.301	.425	.462	.887	145	6	7	98	113	18	.887	0	3	-2	-1	O/D	0.3
1978	Cle-A	113	378	54	100	16	6	14	61	59	60	.265	.367	.450	.816	138	15	19	93	116	66	.831	5	1	1	2	*O	1.9
	Tex-A	21	33	8	13	3	0	1	6	11	5	.394	.545	.576	1.121	224	6	6	96	108	12	1.476	1	1	-0	-1	O/D	0.5
	Yr	134	411	62	113	19	6	15	67	70	65	.275	.383	.460	.843	145	21	25	94	115	80	.890	6	2	1	1		2.4
1979	Tex-A	102	289	42	79	14	0	10	37	34	44	.273	.352	.426	.777	109	4	4	100	93	43	.727	2	4	-2	-3	O	-0.3
1980	Tex-A	110	274	40	76	12	1	9	32	42	35	.277	.377	.427	.804	120	9	9	100	87	43	.769	2	3	-1	-8	O/D	-0.1
1981	Tex-A	67	199	26	46	9	1	3	26	23	25	.231	.317	.332	.649	96	-3	-1	91	136	20	.562	0	3	-2	-6	O	-1.0
1982	Tex-A	103	308	35	86	13	3	3	26	39	37	.279	.371	.370	.741	112	3	6	93	84	44	.691	0	3	-2	-6	OD	-0.3
1983	Det-A	57	134	20	34	5	2	4	22	28	17	.254	.390	.410	.801	126	5	6	96	128	23	.810	0	0	0	-4	OD	0.1
1984	Det-A	86	176	25	47	5	0	8	17	36	36	.267	.397	.432	.829	135	9	10	96	68	33	.885	1	0	0	-7	OD	0.2
1985	Det-A	78	155	19	38	7	1	5	25	24	25	.245	.350	.400	.750	99	2	0	106	129	22	.707	0	1	-1	-3	DO	-0.3
1986	Det-A	81	210	32	70	13	1	13	51	28	28	.333	.417	.590	1.007	180	21	23	95	125	54	1.092	0	1	-1	-3	DO	1.8
1987	Det-A	59	114	9	23	6	0	2	13	15	16	.202	.295	.307	.602	63	-6	-6	97	127	10	.526	0	0	0	-4	OD/3	-0.9
Total	16	1424	4154	553	1153	207	29	99	475	566	558	.278	.369	.413	.782	122	105	130	96	92	658	.772	27	33	-12	-52	*OD/13	3.9

■ **FRANK GRUBE** Grube, Franklin Thomas "Hans" b: 1/7/05, Easton, Pa. d: 7/2/45, New York, N.Y. BR/TR, 5'9", 190 lbs. Deb: 5/12/31

YEAR	TM/L	G	AB	R	H	2B	3B	HR	RBI	BB	SO	AVG	OBP	SLG	PRO	/A	BR	/A	PF	CHI	RC	TA	SB	CS	SBR	FR	POS	TPR
1931	Chi-A	88	265	29	58	13	2	1	24	22	22	.219	.284	.294	.578	56	-19	-16	92	98	23	.498	2	2	-1	5	C	-0.4
1932	Chi-A	93	277	36	78	16	2	0	31	33	13	.282	.362	.354	.716	99	-5	1	87	106	38	.695	6	1	1	5	C	1.1
1933	Chi-A	85	256	23	59	13	0	0	23	38	20	.230	.334	.281	.616	64	-12	-12	101	107	27	.571	1	1	-0	-7	C	-1.4
1934	StL-A	65	170	22	49	10	0	0	11	24	11	.288	.379	.347	.727	85	-2	-3	104	62	24	.705	2	1	0	6	C	0.7
1935	StL-A	3	6	3	2	1	0	0	0	0	1	.333	.333	.500	.833	106	0	0	107	0	1	.750	0	0	0	0	/C	0.0
	Chi-A	9	19	1	7	2	0	0	6	3	2	.368	.455	.474	.928	129	1	1	109	226	4	1.000	0	0	0	1	/C	0.2
	Yr	12	25	4	9	3	0	0	6	3	3	.360	.429	.480	.909	124	1	1	108	170	5	.938	0	0	0	1		0.2
1936	Chi-A	33	93	6	15	2	1	0	11	9	15	.161	.235	.204	.440	9	-14	-13	99	187	5	.372	1	0	0	2	C	-0.6
1941	StL-A	18	39	1	6	2	0	0	1	2	4	.154	.195	.205	.400	6	-5	-5	100	44	2	.303	0	0	0	-0	C	-0.4
Total	7	394	1125	121	274	59	5	1	107	131	88	.244	.326	.308	.634	68	-54	-48	96	104	124	.579	12	5	1	12	C	-0.8

■ **KELLY GRUBER** Gruber, Kelly Wayne b: 2/26/62, Houston, Tex. BR/TR, 6', 180 lbs. Deb: 4/20/84

YEAR	TM/L	G	AB	R	H	2B	3B	HR	RBI	BB	SO	AVG	OBP	SLG	PRO	/A	BR	/A	PF	CHI	RC	TA	SB	CS	SBR	FR	POS	TPR
1984	Tor-A	15	16	1	1	0	0	1	2	0	5	.063	.063	.250	.313	-18	-3	-3	102	114	0	.250	0	0	0	-1	3/OS	-0.2
1985	Tor-A	5	13	0	3	0	0	0	1	0	3	.231	.231	.231	.462	27	-1	-1	101	132	1	.300	0	0	0	-0	/32	-0.1
1986	Tor-A	87	143	20	28	4	1	5	15	5	27	.196	.223	.343	.566	49	-10	-11	105	93	8	.452	2	5	-2	-3	32D/OS	-1.5
1987	Tor-A	138	341	50	80	14	3	12	36	17	70	.235	.285	.399	.684	79	-11	-11	101	83	37	.628	12	2	2	0	*3S/2OD	-0.8
1988	Tor-A	158	569	75	158	33	5	16	81	38	92	.278	.331	.438	.768	114	9	9	100	111	79	.727	23	5	4	24	*3/2OS	3.8
Total	5	403	1082	146	270	51	9	34	135	60	197	.250	.298	.408	.705	91	-15	-16	101	100	125	.654	37	12	4	21	3/2SDO	1.2

■ **SIG GRYSKA** Gryska, Sigmund Stanley b: 11/4/15, Chicago, Ill. BR/TR, 5'11.5", 173 lbs. Deb: 9/28/38

YEAR	TM/L	G	AB	R	H	2B	3B	HR	RBI	BB	SO	AVG	OBP	SLG	PRO	/A	BR	/A	PF	CHI	RC	TA	SB	CS	SBR	FR	POS	TPR
1938	StL-A	7	21	3	10	2	1	0	4	3	3	.476	.542	.667	1.208	201	3	3	100	97	8	1.545	0	0	0	-1	/S	0.3
1939	StL-A	18	49	4	13	2	0	0	8	6	10	.265	.345	.306	.652	68	-2	-2	100	180	6	.632	3	1	0	1	S	0.0
Total	2	25	70	7	23	4	1	0	12	9	13	.329	.405	.414	.819	108	1	1	100	155	13	.837	3	1	0	0	/S	0.3

■ **MARV GUDAT** Gudat, Marvin John b: 8/27/05, Goliad, Tex. d: 3/1/54, Los Angeles, Cal. BL/TL, 5'11", 162 lbs. Deb: 5/21/29

YEAR	TM/L	G	AB	R	H	2B	3B	HR	RBI	BB	SO	AVG	OBP	SLG	PRO	/A	BR	/A	PF	CHI	RC	TA	SB	CS	SBR	FR	POS	TPR
1929	Cin-N	9	10	0	2	0	0	0	0	0	0	.200	.200	.200	.400	-1	-2	-2	99	0	0	.250	0			-1	/P	0.0
1932	Chi-N	60	94	15	24	4	1	1	15	16	10	.255	.369	.351	.720	91	0	-1	104	155	13	.714	0			-4	O/1P	-0.5
Total	2	69	104	15	26	4	1	1	15	16	10	.250	.355	.337	.692	83	-2	-2	104	142	14	.667	0			-5	/O1P	-0.5

■ **MIKE GUERRA** Guerra, Fermin (Romero) b: 10/11/12, Havana, Cuba BR/TR, 5'9", 150 lbs. Deb: 9/19/37

YEAR	TM/L	G	AB	R	H	2B	3B	HR	RBI	BB	SO	AVG	OBP	SLG	PRO	/A	BR	/A	PF	CHI	RC	TA	SB	CS	SBR	FR	POS	TPR
1937	Was-A	1	3	0	0	0	0	0	0	0	2	.000	.000	.000	.000	-99	-1	-1	94	0	0	.000	0	0	0	0	/C	0.0
1944	Was-A	75	210	29	59	7	2	1	29	13	14	.281	.323	.348	.670	102	-3	-0	90	138	25	.599	8	2	1	3	C/O	0.8
1945	Was-A	56	138	11	29	1	1	1	15	10	12	.210	.268	.254	.522	56	-9	-7	93	143	9	.431	4	1	1	1	C	-0.2
1946	Was-A	41	83	3	21	2	1	0	4	5	6	.253	.295	.301	.597	73	-4	-3	92	61	7	.477	1	0	0	0	C	0.0
1947	Phi-A	72	209	20	45	2	2	0	18	10	15	.215	.251	.244	.495	38	-18	-18	100	130	13	.365	1	2	-1	8	C	-0.5
1948	Phi-A	53	142	18	30	4	2	1	23	18	13	.211	.300	.289	.589	56	-9	-9	102	177	12	.504	2	3	-1	3	C	-0.3
1949	Phi-A	98	298	41	79	14	1	3	31	37	26	.265	.346	.349	.695	85	-7	-6	99	94	37	.626	3	0	1	4	C	0.3
1950	Phi-A	87	252	25	71	10	4	2	26	16	12	.282	.325	.377	.702	88	-9	-5	90	89	31	.599	1	0	0	1	C	0.0
1951	Bos-A	10	32	1	5	0	0	0	2	6	5	.156	.289	.156	.446	21	-3	-4	108	143	2	.400	1	0	0	-1	C	-0.3
	Was-A	72	214	20	43	2	1	1	20	16	18	.201	.257	.234	.490	35	-20	-19	95	135	13	.389	4	4	-1	-2	C	-1.7
	Yr	82	246	21	48	2	1	1	22	22	23	.195	.261	.224	.485	33	-23	-22	97	138	15	.396	5	4	-1	-3		-2.0
Total	9	565	1581	168	382	42	14	9	168	131	123	.242	.300	.303	.603	67	-81	-72	95	120	148	.523	25	12	0	16	C/O	-1.9

■ **MARIO GUERRERO** Guerrero, Mario Miguel (Abud) b: 9/28/49, Santo Domingo, D.R. BR/TR, 5'10", 155 lbs. Deb: 4/08/73

YEAR	TM/L	G	AB	R	H	2B	3B	HR	RBI	BB	SO	AVG	OBP	SLG	PRO	/A	BR	/A	PF	CHI	RC	TA	SB	CS	SBR	FR	POS	TPR
1973	Bos-A	66	219	19	51	5	2	0	11	10	21	.233	.273	.274	.547	51	-13	-15	106	72	16	.423	2	2	-1	-4	S2	-1.2
1974	Bos-A	93	284	18	70	6	2	0	23	13	22	.246	.284	.282	.566	59	-13	-16	107	113	21	.432	3	1	0	-3	S	-1.1
1975	StL-N	64	184	17	44	9	0	0	11	10	7	.239	.286	.288	.574	58	-10	-11	103	80	14	.436	0	0	0	-0	S	-0.3
1976	Cal-A	83	268	24	76	12	0	1	18	7	12	.284	.309	.340	.649	98	-4	-1	92	74	27	.510	0	0	0	2	2S/D	0.5
1977	Cal-A	86	244	17	69	8	2	1	28	4	16	.283	.294	.344	.639	78	-9	-8	95	128	24	.492	0	0	0	-0	SD2	-0.2
1978	Oak-A	143	505	27	139	18	4	3	38	15	35	.275	.304	.345	.649	81	-13	-13	101	84	49	.508	0	5	-3	-25	*S	-3.0
1979	Oak-A	46	166	12	38	5	0	0	18	6	7	.229	.256	.259	.515	44	-14	-12	89	164	10	.366	0	1	-1	-4	S	-1.0
1980	Oak-A	116	381	32	91	16	2	2	23	19	32	.239	.277	.307	.584	63	-21	-18	95	73	29	.455	3	3	-1	-34	*S	-4.4
Total	8	697	2251	166	578	79	12	7	170	84	152	.257	.288	.312	.600	69	-98	-93	99	93	190	.476	8	12	-5	-70	S/2D	-10.7

■ **PEDRO GUERRERO** Guerrero, Pedro b: 6/29/56, San Pedro De Macoris, D.R. BR/TR, 5'11", 176 lbs. Deb: 9/22/78

YEAR	TM/L	G	AB	R	H	2B	3B	HR	RBI	BB	SO	AVG	OBP	SLG	PRO	/A	BR	/A	PF	CHI	RC	TA	SB	CS	SBR	FR	POS	TPR
1978	LA-N	5	8	3	5	0	1	0	1	0	0	.625	.625	.875	1.500	318	2	2	99	57	4	2.333	0	0	0	0	/1	0.2
1979	LA-N	25	62	7	15	2	0	2	9	1	14	.242	.254	.371	.625	69	-3	-3	100	123	6	.542	2	0	1	-1	O/13	-0.4
1980	LA-N	75	183	27	59	9	1	7	31	12	31	.322	.364	.497	.861	143	9	9	97	110	33	.827	2	1	0	-2	O2/31	0.7
1981	LA-N	98	347	46	104	17	2	12	48	34	57	.300	.366	.464	.830	137	15	16	98	98	54	.765	5	9	-4	-0	O3/1	0.9
1982	LA-N	150	575	87	175	27	5	32	100	65	89	.304	.380	.536	.915	162	40	44	95	103	120	.971	22	5	4	7	*O3	5.4
1983	LA-N	160	584	87	174	28	6	32	103	72	110	.298	.377	.531	.908	149	38	38	100	106	118	.951	23	7	3	9	*3/1	4.5
1984	LA-N	144	535	85	162	29	4	16	72	49	105	.303	.362	.462	.824	125	21	18	104	101	89	.789	9	8	-2	6	3O1	2.0
1985	LA-N	137	487	99	156	22	2	33	87	83	68	.320	**.425**	**.577**	**1.002**	**191**	**53**	**57**	93	97	121	**1.098**	12	4	1	6	O31	**6.4**
1986	LA-N	31	61	7	15	3	0	5	10	2	19	.246	.281	.541	.822	129	1	2	94	83	9	.766	0	0	0	-1	O/1	0.0
1987	LA-N	152	545	89	184	25	2	27	89	74	85	.338	.421	.539	.960	166	43	49	92	100	121	.992	9	7	-2	-4	*O1	3.6
1988	LA-N	59	215	24	64	7	1	5	35	25	33	.298	.379	.409	.788	119	8	6	106	144	35	.766	2	1	0	-3	31/O	0.2
	StL-N	44	149	16	40	7	1	5	30	21	26	.268	.366	.430	.796	123	6	5	104	155	24	.795	2	0	1	-1	1/O	0.2
	Yr	103	364	40	104	14	2	10	65	46	59	.286	.373	.418	.791	120	14	12	105	150	61	.784	4	1	1	-5		0.4
Total	11	1080	3751	577	1153	176	25	176	615	438	637	.307	.384	.508	.892	150	232	244	98	106	735	.930	88	42	1	15	O31/2	23.7

■ **OZZIE GUILLEN** Guillen, Oswaldo Jose (Barrios) b: 1/20/64, Oculare Del Tuy, Venezuela BL/TR, 5'11", 150 lbs. Deb: 4/09/85

YEAR	TM/L	G	AB	R	H	2B	3B	HR	RBI	BB	SO	AVG	OBP	SLG	PRO	/A	BR	/A	PF	CHI	RC	TA	SB	CS	SBR	FR	POS	TPR
1985	Chi-A	150	491	71	134	21	9	1	33	12	36	.273	.292	.358	.650	77	-16	-16	100	73	50	.536	7	4	-0	9	*S	0.4
1986	Chi-A	159	547	58	137	19	4	2	47	12	52	.250	.268	.311	.579	57	-32	-32	101	106	43	.446	8	4	0	12	*S/D	-1.1
1987	Chi-A	149	560	64	156	22	7	2	51	22	52	.279	.307	.354	.661	70	-19	-26	109	102	61	.583	25	8	3	17	*S	0.1
1988	Chi-A	156	566	58	148	16	7	0	39	25	40	.261	.295	.314	.610	73	-22	-20	97	89	50	.517	25	13	-0	**43**	*S	3.0
Total	4	614	2164	251	575	78	27	5	170	71	180	.266	.291	.334	.624	69	-90	-95	102	93	203	.529	65	29	2	81	S/D	2.4

■ **BOBBY GUINDON** Guindon, Robert Joseph b: 9/4/43, Brookline, Mass. BL/TL, 6'2", 185 lbs. Deb: 9/19/64

YEAR	TM/L	G	AB	R	H	2B	3B	HR	RBI	BB	SO	AVG	OBP	SLG	PRO	/A	BR	/A	PF	CHI	RC	TA	SB	CS	SBR	FR	POS	TPR
1964	Bos-A	5	8	0	1	1	0	0	0	1	4	.125	.222	.250	.472	31	-1	-1	102	0	1	.429	0	0	0	-0	/1O	0.0

YEAR	TM/L	G	AB	R	H	2B	3B	HR	RBI	BB	SO	AVG	OBP	SLG	PRO	/A	BR	/A	PF	CHI	RC	TA	SB	CS	SBR	FR	POS	TPR
■ BEN GUINEY	Guiney, Benjamin Franklin b: 11/16/1858, Detroit, Mich. d: 12/5/30, Detroit, Mich. BB/TR, 6', 170 lbs. Deb: 9/04/1883																											
1883	Det-N	1	5	1	1	0	0	0	0	0	1	.200	.200	.200	.400	24	-0	-0	91	0	0	.250				0	/O	0.0
1884	Det-N	2	7	0	0	0	0	0	0	0	3	.000	.000	.000	.000	-99	-2	-1	94	0	0	.000				0	/C	0.0
Total	2	3	12	1	1	0	0	0	0	0	4	.083	.083	.083	.167	-52	-2	-2	93	0	0	.091				0	/CO	0.0
■ BEN GUINTINI	Guintini, Benjamin John b: 1/13/20, Los Banos, Cal. BR/TR, 6'1.5", 190 lbs. Deb: 4/21/46																											
1946	Pit-N	2	3	0	0	0	0	0	0	0	0	.000	.000	.000	.000	-97	-1	-1	103	0	0	.000	0			-0	/O	0.0
1950	Phi-A	3	4	0	0	0	0	0	0	0	1	.000	.000	.000	.000	-99	-1	-1	90	0	0	.000	0	0	0	0	/O	0.0
Total	2	5	7	0	0	0	0	0	0	0	1	.000	.000	.000	.000	-99	-2	-2	95	0	0	.000	0	0		0	/O	0.0
■ LOU GUISTO	Guisto, Louis Joseph b: 1/16/1894, Napa, Cal. BR/TR, 5'11", 193 lbs. Deb: 9/10/16																											
1916	Cle-A	6	19	2	3	0	0	0	2	4	3	.158	.304	.158	.462	39	-1	-1	100	243	1	.500	1			0	/1	0.0
1917	Cle-A	73	200	9	37	4	2	0	29	25	18	.185	.282	.225	.507	48	-10	-14	114	231	14	.460	3			3	1	-1.3
1921	Cle-A	2	2	0	1	0	0	0	1	0	1	.500	.500	.500	1.000	157	0	0	99	343	0	1.000	0	0	0	0	/1	0.0
1922	Cle-A	35	84	7	21	10	1	0	9	2	7	.250	.276	.393	.669	71	-4	-4	102	98	9	.571	0	0	0	-1	1	-0.5
1923	Cle-A	40	144	17	26	5	0	0	18	15	15	.181	.262	.215	.478	26	-15	-15	101	202	9	.403	1	1	-0	0	1	-1.6
Total	5	156	449	35	88	19	3	0	59	46	44	.196	.277	.252	.528	46	-30	-34	107	200	33	.464	5	1		3	1	-3.4
■ BRAD GULDEN	Gulden, Bradley Lee b: 6/10/56, New Ulm, Minn. BL/TR, 5'10", 175 lbs. Deb: 9/22/78																											
1978	LA-N	3	4	0	0	0	0	0	0	0	2	.000	.000	.000	.000	-99	-1	-1	99	0	0	.000	0	0	0	0	/C	0.0
1979	NY-A	40	92	10	15	4	0	0	6	9	16	.163	.238	.207	.444	22	-10	-10	96	121	4	.346	0	1	-1	-2	C	-1.0
1980	NY-A	2	3	1	1	0	0	1	2	0	0	.333	.333	1.333	1.667	337	1	1	99	111	1	2.000	0	0	0	0	/C	0.1
1981	Sea-A	8	16	0	3	2	0	0	1	0	2	.188	.188	.313	.500	42	-1	-1	100	78	1	.385	0	0	0	-1	/C	-0.1
1982	Mon-N	5	6	1	0	0	0	0	0	1	1	.000	.143	.000	.143	-54	-1	-1	105	0	0	.167	0	0	0	0	/C	0.0
1984	Cin-N	107	292	31	66	8	2	4	33	33	35	.226	.309	.308	.617	70	-10	-12	106	127	28	.540	2	2	-1	-11	*C	-2.1
1986	SF-N	17	22	2	2	0	0	0	1	2	5	.091	.167	.091	.258	-28	-4	-4	96	199	0	.190	0	0	0	-0	C	-0.3
Total	7	182	435	45	87	14	2	5	43	45	61	.200	.278	.276	.554	53	-26	-28	103	125	35	.480	2	3	-1	-14	C	-3.4
■ TOM GULLEY	Gulley, Thomas Jefferson b: 12/25/1899, Garner, N.C. d: 11/24/66, St.Charles, Ark. BL/TR, 5'11", 178 lbs. Deb: 8/24/23																											
1923	Cle-A	2	3	1	1	1	0	0	0	0	0	.333	.333	.667	1.000	157	0	0	101	0	1	1.000	0	0	0	-0	/O	0.0
1924	Cle-A	8	20	4	3	0	1	0	1	3	2	.150	.261	.250	.511	33	-2	-2	97	66	1	.471	0	0	0	0	/O	-0.1
1926	Chi-A	16	35	5	8	3	1	0	8	5	2	.229	.325	.371	.696	89	-1	-1	92	209	5	.667	0	0	0	-2	O	-0.3
Total	3	26	58	10	12	4	2	0	9	8	4	.207	.303	.345	.648	73	-3	-2	94	150	7	.609	0	0	0	-2	/O	-0.4
■ TED GULLIC	Gullic, Theodore Jasper b: 1/2/07, Koshkonong, Mo. BR/TR, 6'2", 175 lbs. Deb: 4/15/30																											
1930	StL-A	92	308	39	77	7	5	4	44	27	43	.250	.310	.344	.655	61	-16	-20	108	124	35	.593	4	0	1	0	O/1	-2.0
1933	StL-A	104	304	34	74	18	3	5	35	15	38	.243	.281	.372	.653	63	-14	-20	115	91	32	.571	3	1	0	9	O31	-0.9
Total	2	196	612	73	151	25	8	9	79	42	81	.247	.296	.358	.654	62	-30	-40	111	108	67	.582	7	1	2	9	O/31	-2.9
■ GLENN GULLIVER	Gulliver, Glenn James b: 10/15/54, Detroit, Mich. BL/TR, 5'11", 175 lbs. Deb: 7/17/82																											
1982	Bal-A	50	145	24	29	7	0	1	5	37	18	.200	.363	.269	.632	77	-3	-3	100	48	17	.644	0	0	0	1	3	-0.2
1983	Bal-A	23	47	5	10	3	0	0	2	9	5	.213	.339	.277	.616	72	-1	-1	100	60	5	.564	0	1	-1	-1	3	-0.2
Total	2	73	192	29	39	10	0	1	7	46	23	.203	.357	.271	.628	76	-4	-4	100	50	22	.632	0	1	-1	0	/3	-0.4
■ FRED GUNKLE	Gunkle, Frederick W. b: Dubuque, Iowa Deb: 5/17/1879																											
1879	Cle-N	1	3	1	0	0	0	0	0	0	1	.000	.000	.000	.000	-99	-1	-1	99	0	0	.000				0	/OC	0.0
■ HY GUNNING	Gunning, Hyland b: 8/6/1888, Maplewood, N.J. d: 3/28/75, Togus, Me. BL/TR, 6'1.5", 189 lbs. Deb: 8/08/11																											
1911	Bos-A	4	9	0	1	0	0	0	2	2		.111	.273	.111	.384	9	-1	-1	99	676	0	.375	0			0	/1	0.0
■ TOM GUNNING	Gunning, Thomas Francis b: 3/4/1862, Newmarket, N.H. d: 3/17/31, Fall River, Mass. BR/TR, 5'10", 160 lbs. Deb: 7/26/1884																											
1884	Bos-N	12	45	4	5	1	1	0	2	1	12	.111	.130	.178	.308	-4	-5	-5	98	88	1	.225				0	C	-0.4
1885	Bos-N	48	174	17	32	3	0	0	15	5	29	.184	.207	.201	.408	35	-13	-11	94	152	7	.282				-5	C	-1.0
1886	Bos-N	27	98	15	22	2	1	0	7	3	19	.224	.248	.265	.513	58	-5	-5	97	89	7	.421	3			0	C	-0.3
1887	Phi-N	28	104	22	27	6	1	1	16	5	6	.260	.306	.365	.672	90	-2	-1	97	123	18	.818	18			0	C	0.0
1888	Phi-a	23	92	18	18	0	0	0	5	2		.196	.237	.196	.433	41	-6	-6	101	88	8	.500	14			0	C	-0.4
1889	Phi-a	8	24	3	6	0	1	1	1	0	4	.250	.250	.458	.708	104	-0	-0	98	20	4	.778	3			0	/C	0.0
Total	6	146	537	79	110	12	4	2	46	16	70	.205	.235	.253	.488	52	-31	-28	97	113	45	.457	38			-5	C	-2.1
■ JOE GUNSON	Gunson, Joseph Brook b: 3/23/1863, Philadelphia, Pa. d: 11/15/42, Philadelphia, Pa. BR/TR, 5'6", 160 lbs. Deb: 6/14/1884																											
1884	Was-U	45	166	15	23	2	0	0		3		.139	.154	.151	.304	3	-16	-15	97	0	4	.196	0			-8	CO	-1.8
1889	KC-a	34	122	15	24	3	1	0	12	3	17	.197	.228	.238	.466	32	-10	-12	106	118	7	.367	2			0	C/O3	-0.9
1892	Bal-N	89	314	35	67	10	5	0	32	16	17	.213	.267	.277	.544	66	-13	-13	100	113	24	.453	2			4	CO/12	-0.3
1893	StL-N	40	151	20	41	5	0	0	15	6	6	.272	.321	.305	.626	69	-7	-6	99	89	15	.518	0			0	C/O	-0.2
	Cle-N	21	73	11	19	1	0	0	9	6	0	.260	.316	.274	.590	57	-4	-5	104	123	6	.481	0			-1	C	-0.2
	Yr	61	224	31	60	6	0	0	24	12	6	.268	.320	.295	.614	65	-11	-11	101	102	22	.506	0			-1		-0.4
Total	4	229	826	96	174	21	6	0	68	34	40	.211	.254	.251	.505	50	-50	-51	100	88	57	.397	4			-4	C/O123	-3.4
■ ERNIE GUST	Gust, Ernest Herman Frank "Red" b: 1/24/1888, Bay City, Mich. d: 10/26/45, Maupin, Ore. BR/TR, 6', 170 lbs. Deb: 8/17/11																											
1911	StL-A	3	12	0	0	0	0	0	0	0		.000	.000	.000	.000	-99	-3	-3	95	0	0	.000	0			-0	/1	-0.2
■ FRANKIE GUSTINE	Gustine, Frank William b: 2/20/20, Hoopeston, Ill. BR/TR, 6', 175 lbs. Deb: 9/13/39																											
1939	Pit-N	22	70	5	13	3	0	0	3	9	4	.186	.278	.229	.507	38	-6	-6	100	69	5	.417	0			0	3	-0.4
1940	Pit-N	133	524	59	147	32	7	1	55	35	39	.281	.328	.374	.702	98	-5	-2	95	109	63	.615	7			-12	*2	-0.4
1941	Pit-N	121	463	46	125	24	7	1	46	28	38	.270	.313	.359	.672	87	-8	-9	103	100	51	.576	5			-4	*23	-0.5
1942	Pit-N	115	388	34	89	11	4	2	35	29	27	.229	.286	.294	.580	69	-15	-15	101	108	31	.479	5			-17	*2/S3C	-2.6
1943	Pit-N	112	414	40	120	21	3	0	43	32	36	.290	.341	.355	.696	97	0	-2	104	108	51	.632	12			-4	S2/1	0.2
1944	Pit-N	127	405	42	93	18	3	2	42	33	41	.230	.288	.304	.591	63	-18	-21	105	117	34	.503	8			-15	*S2/3	-1.9
1945	Pit-N	128	478	67	134	27	5	2	66	37	33	.280	.335	.370	.705	93	-3	-5	103	128	58	.626	8			-4	*S2/C	0.4
1946	Pit-N	131	495	60	128	23	6	8	52	40	52	.259	.318	.378	.696	94	-3	-5	103	97	59	.611	2			1	*2S/3	0.0
1947	Pit-N	156	616	102	183	30	6	9	67	63	65	.297	.364	.409	.773	104	5	4	101	86	92	.719	5			15	*3	1.4
1948	Pit-N	131	449	68	120	19	2	9	42	42	62	.267	.333	.379	.711	88	-5	-8	104	82	56	.642	5			12	*3	0.2
1949	Chi-N	76	261	29	59	13	4	4	27	18	22	.226	.279	.352	.631	72	-12	-11	94	100	24	.540	3			-0	32	-0.9
1950	StL-A	9	19	1	3	1	0	0	2	3	8	.158	.273	.211	.483	23	-2	-2	107	173	1	.389	0	1	-1	-1	/3	-0.3
Total	12	1261	4582	553	1214	222	47	38	480	369	427	.265	.322	.359	.681	87	-73	-82	102	102	525	.620	60	1		-29	23S/C1	-4.8
■ BUCKY GUTH	Guth, Charles Henry b: 8/18/47, Baltimore, Md. BR/TR, 6'1", 180 lbs. Deb: 9/12/72																											
1972	Min-A	3	3	1	0	0	0	0	0	0	0	.000	.000	.000	.000	-93	-1	-1	107	0	0	.000	0	0	0	0	/S	0.0
■ CESAR GUTIERREZ	Gutierrez, Cesar Dario "Coca" b: 1/26/43, Coro, Venez. BR/TR, 5'9", 155 lbs. Deb: 4/16/67																											
1967	SF-N	18	21	4	3	0	0	0	0	1	4	.143	.217	.143	.360	5	-3	-3	101	0	1	.333	1	0	0	1	S/2	0.1
1969	SF-N	15	23	4	5	1	0	0	0	6	2	.217	.379	.261	.640	81	-0	-0	101	0	3	.722	1	0	0	0	/3S	0.0
	Det-A	17	49	5	12	1	0	0	0	5	3	.245	.315	.265	.580	62	-2	-2	103	0	4	.463	1	2	-1	-2	S	-0.4
1970	Det-A	135	415	40	101	11	6	0	22	18	39	.243	.276	.299	.575	57	-24	-25	103	72	33	.452	4	3	-1	-12	*S	-2.6
1971	Det-A	38	37	8	7	0	0	0	4	0	3	.189	.211	.189	.400	15	-4	-4	96	233	2	.267	0	0	0	1	S/32	-0.1
Total	4	223	545	61	128	13	6	0	26	30	51	.235	.279	.281	.559	54	-33	-34	102	69	43	.457	7	5	-1	-12	S/32	-3.0
■ JACKIE GUTIERREZ	Gutierrez, Joaquin Fernando b: 6/27/60, Cartagena, Columbia BR/TR, 5'11", 175 lbs. Deb: 9/06/83																											
1983	Bos-A	5	10	2	3	0	0	0	0	1	1	.300	.364	.300	.664	84	-0	-0	101	0	1	.444	0	1	-1	0	/S	0.0
1984	Bos-A	151	449	55	118	12	3	2	29	15	49	.263	.287	.316	.603	60	-20	-26	110	78	37	.477	12	5	1	-24	*S	-3.8
1985	Bos-A	103	275	33	60	5	2	2	21	12	37	.218	.251	.273	.524	42	-21	-22	102	103	18	.429	10	2	2	3	S	-0.9
1986	Bal-A	61	145	8	27	3	0	0	4	3	27	.186	.208	.207	.415	14	-17	-17	99	53	6	.303	3	1	0	-4	2/3D	-1.7

YEAR	TM/L	G	AB	R	H	2B	3B	HR	RBI	BB	SO	AVG	OBP	SLG	PRO	/A	BR	/A	PF	CHI	RC	TA	SB	CS	SBR	FR	POS	TPR
1987	Bal-A	3	1	0	0	0	0	0	0	0	0	.000	.000	.000	.000	-99	-0	-0	98	0	0	.000	0	0	0	0	/23	0.0
1988	Phi-N	33	77	8	19	4	0	0	9	2	9	.247	.266	.299	.565	61	-4	-4	101	156	6	.417	0	0	0	-1	S3	-0.3
Total	6	356	957	106	227	24	5	4	63	33	123	.237	.263	.285	.549	49	-63	-70	105	87	67	.448	25	9	2	-26	S/23D	-6.7

■ **DON GUTTERIDGE** Gutteridge, Donald Joseph b: 6/19/12, Pittsburg, Kan. BR/TR, 5'10.5", 165 lbs. Deb: 9/07/36 MC

YEAR	TM/L	G	AB	R	H	2B	3B	HR	RBI	BB	SO	AVG	OBP	SLG	PRO	/A	BR	/A	PF	CHI	RC	TA	SB	CS	SBR	FR	POS	TPR
1936	StL-N	23	91	13	29	3	4	3	16	1	14	.319	.326	.538	.865	137	3	4	94	100	16	.841	3			-1	3	0.4
1937	StL-N	119	447	66	121	26	10	7	61	25	66	.271	.311	.421	.731	96	-3	-4	101	107	59	.681	12			-3	*3/S	0.0
1938	StL-N	142	552	61	141	21	15	9	64	29	49	.255	.293	.397	.689	79	-11	-19	111	96	64	.624	14			-6	3S	-2.1
1939	StL-N	148	524	71	141	27	4	7	54	27	70	.269	.309	.376	.685	79	-14	-17	105	91	61	.595	5			-17	*3/S	-2.9
1940	StL-N	69	108	19	29	5	0	3	14	5	15	.269	.301	.398	.699	89	-2	-2	102	100	13	.630	3			-4	3	-0.5
1942	StL-A	147	616	90	157	27	11	1	50	59	54	.255	.320	.339	.659	82	-12	-15	104	73	69	.592	16	13	-3	5	*2/3	-0.8
1943	StL-A	132	538	77	147	35	6	1	36	50	46	.273	.335	.366	.701	105	3	3	100	58	68	.631	10	9	-2	-26	*2	-2.1
1944	StL-A	148	603	89	148	27	11	3	36	51	63	.245	.304	.342	.646	83	-13	-14	102	58	67	.593	20	8	1	-9	*2	-1.7
1945	StL-A	143	543	72	129	24	3	2	49	43	46	.238	.295	.304	.599	64	-19	-28	115	110	51	.512	9	6	-1	-25	*2O	-5.7
1946	Bos-A	22	47	8	11	3	0	1	6	2	7	.234	.265	.362	.627	65	-2	-3	114	114	5	.514	0	0	0	0	/23	0.0
1947	Bos-A	54	131	20	22	2	0	2	5	17	13	.168	.264	.229	.493	35	-11	-12	108	51	9	.450	3	1	0	2	23	-0.8
1948	Pit-N	4	2	0	0	0	0	0	0	0	1	.000	.000	.000	.000	-96	-1	-1	104	0	0	.000	0			0	H	0.0
Total	12	1151	4202	586	1075	200	64	39	391	309	444	.256	.308	.362	.669	83	-81	-108	105	83	484	.610	95	37		-83	23/SO	-16.2

■ **DOUG GWOSDZ** Gwosdz, Douglas Wayne b: 6/20/60, Houston, Tex. BR/TR, 5'11", 185 lbs. Deb: 8/17/81

YEAR	TM/L	G	AB	R	H	2B	3B	HR	RBI	BB	SO	AVG	OBP	SLG	PRO	/A	BR	/A	PF	CHI	RC	TA	SB	CS	SBR	FR	POS	TPR
1981	SD-N	16	24	1	4	2	0	0	3	3	6	.167	.259	.250	.509	48	-2	-2	93	196	2	.450	0	0	0	1	C	0.0
1982	SD-N	7	17	1	3	0	0	0	0	2	7	.176	.263	.176	.440	27	-2	-1	92	0	1	.357	0	0	0	-0	/C	-0.1
1983	SD-N	39	55	7	6	1	0	1	4	7	19	.109	.210	.182	.391	9	-7	-7	99	122	2	.333	0	0	0	0	C	-0.5
1984	SD-N	7	8	0	2	0	0	0	1	2	5	.250	.400	.250	.650	87	-0	0	99	196	1	.667	0	0	0	-0	/C	0.0
Total	4	69	104	9	15	3	0	1	8	14	37	.144	.246	.202	.448	27	-10	-10	97	125	6	.393	0	0	0	1	/C	-0.6

■ **TONY GWYNN** Gwynn, Anthony Keith b: 5/9/60, Los Angeles, Cal. BL/TL, 5'11", 185 lbs. Deb: 7/19/82

YEAR	TM/L	G	AB	R	H	2B	3B	HR	RBI	BB	SO	AVG	OBP	SLG	PRO	/A	BR	/A	PF	CHI	RC	TA	SB	CS	SBR	FR	POS	TPR
1982	SD-N	54	190	33	55	12	2	1	17	14	16	.289	.338	.389	.728	112	1	3	92	88	25	.671	8	3	1	0	O	0.3
1983	SD-N	86	304	34	94	12	2	1	37	23	21	.309	.358	.372	.730	103	1	2	99	129	39	.641	7	4	-0	6	O	0.6
1984	SD-N	158	606	88	**213**	21	10	5	71	59	23	**.351**	.411	.444	.855	142	34	35	99	104	108	.852	33	18	-1	11	*O	4.1
1985	SD-N	154	622	90	197	29	5	6	46	45	33	.317	.365	.408	.773	114	13	12	102	65	88	.695	14	11	-2	11	*O	1.8
1986	SD-N	160	642	**107**	**211**	33	7	14	59	52	35	.329	.382	.467	.849	140	28	32	95	66	113	.852	37	9	6	17	*O	5.2
1987	SD-N	157	589	119	**218**	36	13	7	54	82	35	**.370**	.450	.511	.961	159	50	52	97	71	143	1.116	56	12	10	5	*O	5.9
1988	SD-N	133	521	64	163	22	5	7	70	51	40	**.313**	.374	.415	.789	130	18	20	97	114	81	.771	26	11	1	2	*O	2.0
Total	7	902	3474	535	1151	165	44	41	354	326	203	.331	.390	.440	.830	133	146	155	98	87	595	.851	181	68	14	52	O	19.9

■ **CHRIS GWYNN** Gwynn, Christopher Karlton b: 10/13/64, Los Angeles, Cal. BL/TL, 6' ", 200 lbs. Deb: 8/14/87

YEAR	TM/L	G	AB	R	H	2B	3B	HR	RBI	BB	SO	AVG	OBP	SLG	PRO	/A	BR	/A	PF	CHI	RC	TA	SB	CS	SBR	FR	POS	TPR
1987	LA-N	17	32	2	7	1	0	0	2	1	7	.219	.242	.250	.492	34	-3	-3	92	100	2	.360	0	0	0	-1	O	-0.4
1988	LA-N	12	11	1	2	0	0	0	0	1	2	.182	.250	.182	.432	24	-1	-1	106	0	1	.333	0	0	0	-2	/O	-0.2
Total	2	29	43	3	9	1	0	0	2	2	9	.209	.244	.233	.477	31	-4	-4	96	73	3	.353	0	0	0	-3	/O	-0.6

■ **DICK GYSELMAN** Gyselman, Richard Renald b: 4/6/08, San Francisco, Cal. BR/TR, 6'2", 170 lbs. Deb: 4/20/33

YEAR	TM/L	G	AB	R	H	2B	3B	HR	RBI	BB	SO	AVG	OBP	SLG	PRO	/A	BR	/A	PF	CHI	RC	TA	SB	CS	SBR	FR	POS	TPR
1933	Bos-N	58	155	10	37	6	2	0	12	7	21	.239	.272	.303	.575	66	-7	-7	96	96	12	.435	0			2	3/2S	-0.2
1934	Bos-N	24	36	7	6	1	1	0	4	2	11	.167	.211	.250	.461	27	-4	-3	86	160	2	.367	0			0	3/2	-0.1
Total	2	82	191	17	43	7	3	0	16	9	32	.225	.260	.293	.553	59	-11	-10	94	108	14	.439	0			2	/32S	-0.3

■ **BERT HAAS** Haas, Berthold John b: 2/8/14, Naperville, Ill. BR/TR, 5'11", 178 lbs. Deb: 9/09/37

YEAR	TM/L	G	AB	R	H	2B	3B	HR	RBI	BB	SO	AVG	OBP	SLG	PRO	/A	BR	/A	PF	CHI	RC	TA	SB	CS	SBR	FR	POS	TPR
1937	Bro-N	16	25	2	10	3	0	0	2	1	1	.400	.423	.520	.943	149	2	2	104	55	5	.875	0			-1	/O1	0.1
1938	Bro-N	1	0	0	0	0	0	0	0	0	0	—	—	—	—	—	0	0	96	—	—	—	0			0	H	0.0
1942	Cin-N	154	585	59	140	21	6	6	54	59	54	.239	.310	.326	.637	85	-10	-11	101	101	61	.565	6			-10	*3/1O	-2.2
1943	Cin-N	101	332	39	87	17	6	4	44	22	26	.262	.308	.386	.693	100	-1	-1	99	113	38	.617	6			3	13O	0.0
1946	Cin-N	140	535	57	141	24	7	3	50	33	42	.264	.310	.351	.661	84	-10	-13	104	100	58	.609	22			-3	*1/3	-2.9
1947	Cin-N	135	482	58	138	17	7	3	67	42	27	.286	.346	.369	.715	99	-7	-1	91	135	63	.658	9			-6	O1	-1.2
1948	Phi-N	95	333	35	94	9	2	4	34	36	25	.282	.354	.357	.711	99	-2	0	94	99	42	.661	8			-2	31	-0.2
1949	Phi-N	2	1	0	0	0	0	0	0	1	1	.000	.500	.000	.500	45	0	0	101	0	0	1.000	0			0	H	0.0
	NY-N	54	104	12	27	2	3	1	10	5	8	.260	.294	.365	.659	75	-4	-4	102	92	11	.544	0			-1	13	-0.4
	Yr	56	105	12	27	2	3	1	10	6	9	.257	.297	.362	.659	75	-4	-4	101	89	11	.550	0			-1		-0.4
1951	Chi-A	23	43	1	7	0	1	1	2	5	4	.163	.250	.279	.529	44	-4	-3	97	48	3	.459	0	0	0	-2	/1O3	-0.4
Total	9	721	2440	263	644	93	32	22	263	204	188	.264	.323	.355	.678	91	-36	-31	98	107	288	.628	51	0		-21	13/O	-7.2

■ **BRUNO HAAS** Haas, Bruno Philip "Boon" b: 5/5/1891, Worcester, Mass. d: 6/5/52, Sarasota, Fla. BB/TL, 5'10", 180 lbs. Deb: 6/23/15

YEAR	TM/L	G	AB	R	H	2B	3B	HR	RBI	BB	SO	AVG	OBP	SLG	PRO	/A	BR	/A	PF	CHI	RC	TA	SB	CS	SBR	FR	POS	TPR
1915	Phi-A	12	18	1	1	0	0	0	0	1	7	.056	.105	.056	.161	-54	-3	-3	96	0	0	.118	0			1	/PO	-0.1

■ **EDDIE HAAS** Haas, George Edwin b: 5/26/35, Paducah, Ky. BL/TR, 5'11", 178 lbs. Deb: 9/08/57 MC

YEAR	TM/L	G	AB	R	H	2B	3B	HR	RBI	BB	SO	AVG	OBP	SLG	PRO	/A	BR	/A	PF	CHI	RC	TA	SB	CS	SBR	FR	POS	TPR
1957	Chi-N	14	24	1	5	1	0	0	4	1	5	.208	.240	.250	.490	33	-2	-2	96	276	2	.368	0	0	0	-1	/O	-0.2
1958	Mil-N	9	14	2	5	0	0	0	1	2	1	.357	.438	.357	.795	127	0	1	89	83	2	.778	0	0	0	-0	/O	0.0
1960	Mil-N	32	32	4	7	2	0	1	5	5	14	.219	.324	.375	.699	100	-0	0	91	135	4	.680	0	0	0	-0	/O	0.0
Total	3	55	70	7	17	3	0	1	10	8	20	.243	.321	.329	.649	82	-2	-2	92	170	8	.585	0	0	0	-1	/O	-0.2

■ **MULE HAAS** Haas, George William b: 10/15/03, Montclair, N.J. d: 6/30/74, New Orleans, La. BL/TR, 6'1", 175 lbs. Deb: 8/15/25 C

YEAR	TM/L	G	AB	R	H	2B	3B	HR	RBI	BB	SO	AVG	OBP	SLG	PRO	/A	BR	/A	PF	CHI	RC	TA	SB	CS	SBR	FR	POS	TPR
1925	Pit-N	4	3	1	0	0	0	0	0	0	1	.000	.000	.000	.000	-98	-1	-1	102	0	0	.000	0	0	0	-1	/O	-0.1
1928	Phi-A	91	332	41	93	21	4	6	39	23	20	.280	.331	.422	.752	94	-3	-4	103	86	46	.690	2	3	-1	5	O	-0.4
1929	Phi-A	139	578	115	181	41	9	16	82	34	38	.313	.356	.498	.854	108	13	5	109	74	100	.813	0	4	-2	-1	*O	-0.4
1930	Phi-A	132	532	91	159	33	7	2	68	43	33	.299	.352	.398	.751	90	-8	-7	99	99	76	.688	2	2	-1	6	*O	-0.5
1931	Phi-A	102	440	82	142	29	7	8	56	30	29	.323	.366	.475	.841	114	11	8	105	68	77	.802	0	0	0	-0	*O	0.1
1932	Phi-A	143	558	91	170	28	5	6	65	62	49	.305	.376	.405	.781	90	3	-9	114	95	89	.750	1	0	0	-3	*O	-1.5
1933	Chi-A	146	585	97	168	33	4	1	51	65	41	.287	.360	.362	.723	91	-5	-6	101	70	79	.661	0	5	-3	5	*O	-0.8
1934	Chi-A	106	351	54	94	16	3	2	22	47	22	.268	.354	.348	.702	82	-9	-8	99	58	47	.661	1	0	0	-5	O	-1.2
1935	Chi-A	92	327	44	95	22	1	2	40	37	17	.291	.363	.382	.745	85	-3	-7	109	106	48	.712	4	1	1	-0	O	-0.6
1936	Chi-A	119	408	75	116	26	2	0	46	64	29	.284	.383	.358	.741	84	-8	-8	99	104	61	.724	1	1	-0	-8	O/1	-1.7
1937	Chi-A	54	111	8	23	3	3	0	15	16	10	.207	.313	.288	.601	51	-8	-8	103	161	11	.568	1	1	0	-1	1/O	-1.1
1938	Phi-A	40	78	7	16	2	0	0	12	12	10	.205	.311	.231	.542	37	-7	-7	101	225	7	.484	0	0	0	-1	O/1	-0.8
Total	12	1168	4303	706	1257	254	45	43	496	433	299	.292	.359	.402	.761	92	-24	-53	104	89	642	.715	12	16	-6	-4	*O/1	-9.0

■ **EMIL HABERER** Haberer, Emil Karl b: 2/2/1878, Cincinnati, Ohio d: 10/19/51, Louisville, Ky. BR/TR, 6'1", 204 lbs. Deb: 7/09/01

YEAR	TM/L	G	AB	R	H	2B	3B	HR	RBI	BB	SO	AVG	OBP	SLG	PRO	/A	BR	/A	PF	CHI	RC	TA	SB	CS	SBR	FR	POS	TPR
1901	Cin-N	6	18	2	3	0	1	0	1	3		.167	.286	.278	.563	69	-1	-1	95	67	1	.533	0			0	/31	0.0
1903	Cin-N	5	13	1	1	0	0	0	0	2		.077	.200	.077	.277	-17	-2	-2	109	0	0	.250	0			0	/C	-0.1
1909	Cin-N	5	16	1	3	1	0	0	2	0		.188	.188	.250	.438	39	-1	-1	94	182	1	.308	0			-0	/C	0.0
Total	3	16	47	4	7	1	1	0	3	5		.149	.231	.213	.444	33	-4	-4	99	83	2	.375	0			-0	/C31	-0.1

■ **IRV HACH** Hach, Irvin William "Major" b: 6/6/1873, Louisville, Ky. d: 8/13/36, Louisville, Ky. Deb: 7/01/1897

YEAR	TM/L	G	AB	R	H	2B	3B	HR	RBI	BB	SO	AVG	OBP	SLG	PRO	/A	BR	/A	PF	CHI	RC	TA	SB	CS	SBR	FR	POS	TPR
1897	Lou-N	16	51	5	11	2	0	0	3	5		.216	.322	.255	.577	58	-3	-3	95	69	5	.550	1			0	/23	-0.1

■ **STAN HACK** Hack, Stanley Camfield "Smiling Stan" b: 12/6/09, Sacramento, Cal d: 12/15/79, Dixon, Ill. BL/TR, 6', 170 lbs. Deb: 4/12/32 MC

YEAR	TM/L	G	AB	R	H	2B	3B	HR	RBI	BB	SO	AVG	OBP	SLG	PRO	/A	BR	/A	PF	CHI	RC	TA	SB	CS	SBR	FR	POS	TPR
1932	Chi-N	72	178	32	42	5	6	2	19	17	16	.236	.306	.365	.671	76	-5	-6	104	100	21	.647	5			-2	3	-0.3
1933	Chi-N	20	60	10	21	3	1	1	2	8	3	.350	.451	.483	.934	172	6	6	97	23	15	1.128	4			-1	3	0.6
1934	Chi-N	111	402	54	116	16	6	1	21	45	42	.289	.363	.366	.729	98	-1	0	98	51	57	.697	11			15	*3	2.2
1935	Chi-N	124	427	75	133	23	9	4	64	65	17	.311	.406	.436	.842	127	19	19	99	119	83	.896	14			1	*3/1	2.3
1936	Chi-N	149	561	102	167	27	4	6	78	89	39	.298	.396	.392	.788	108	14	10	105	123	94	.804	17			-11	*31	0.9
1937	Chi-N	154	582	106	173	27	6	2	63	83	42	.297	.388	.375	.762	105	10	8	103	107	94	.771	16			-11	*3/1	0.4

YEAR	TM/L	G	AB	R	H	2B	3B	HR	RBI	BB	SO	AVG	OBP	SLG	PRO	/A	BR	/A	PF	CHI	RC	TA	SB	CS	SBR	FR	POS	TPR
1938	Chi-N	152	609	109	195	34	11	4	67	94	39	.320	.411	.432	.843	126	31	27	105	76	119	.888	**16**			5	*3	2.8
1939	Chi-N	156	641	112	191	28	6	8	56	65	35	.298	.364	.398	.762	104	5	5	101	64	97	.742	**17**			-7	*3	0.2
1940	Chi-N	149	603	101	**191**	38	6	8	40	75	24	**.317**	.395	.439	.834	130	27	27	100	45	112	.877	21			11	*3/1	3.6
1941	Chi-N	151	586	111	**186**	33	5	7	45	99	40	.317	.417	.427	.844	147	34	39	94	52	114	.893	10			-14	*3/1	2.6
1942	Chi-N	140	553	91	166	36	3	6	39	94	40	.300	.402	.409	.811	143	30	32	96	51	100	.846	9			-14	*3	1.9
1943	Chi-N	144	533	78	154	24	4	3	35	82	27	.289	.384	.366	.750	118	15	16	99	66	83	.738	5			-11	*3	0.4
1944	Chi-N	98	383	65	108	16	1	3	32	53	21	.282	.369	.352	.722	103	4	3	101	77	53	.684	5			9	31	1.5
1945	Chi-N	150	597	110	193	29	7	2	43	99	30	.323	.420	.405	.826	132	29	30	99	52	111	.868	12			16	*3/1	4.3
1946	Chi-N	92	323	55	92	13	4	0	26	83	32	.285	.431	.350	.781	130	16	18	94	82	56	.840	3			-1	3	1.9
1947	Chi-N	76	240	28	65	11	2	0	12	41	19	.271	.377	.333	.711	89	-2	-2	101	56	33	.676	0			9	3	0.5
Total	16	1938	7278	1239	2193	363	81	57	642	1092	466	.301	.394	.397	.791	119	231	233	100	73	1241	.819	165			-7	*3/1	25.8

■ **RICH HACKER** Hacker, Richard Warren b: 10/6/47, Belleville, Ill. BB/TR, 6', 160 lbs. Deb: 7/02/71 C

YEAR	TM/L	G	AB	R	H	2B	3B	HR	RBI	BB	SO	AVG	OBP	SLG	PRO	/A	BR	/A	PF	CHI	RC	TA	SB	CS	SBR	FR	POS	TPR
1971	Mon-N	16	33	2	4	1	0	0	2	3	12	.121	.194	.152	.346	-1	-4	-4	99	163	1	.276	0	0	0	0	S	-0.1

■ **JIM HACKETT** Hackett, James Joseph "Sunny Jim" b: 10/1/1877, Jacksonville, Ill. d: 3/28/61, Douglas, Mich. BR/TR, 6'2", 185 lbs. Deb: 9/14/02

YEAR	TM/L	G	AB	R	H	2B	3B	HR	RBI	BB	SO	AVG	OBP	SLG	PRO	/A	BR	/A	PF	CHI	RC	TA	SB	CS	SBR	FR	POS	TPR
1902	StL-N	6	21	2	6	1	0	0	4	2		.286	.348	.333	.681	118	0	0	95	202	3	.667	1			-1	/PO	0.0
1903	StL-N	99	351	24	80	13	8	0	36	19		.228	.268	.311	.578	69	-16	-14	96	108	30	.480	2			-8	1/P	-2.1
Total	2	105	372	26	86	14	8	0	40	21		.231	.272	.312	.584	71	-16	-14	96	114	33	.490	3			-8	/1PO	-2.1

■ **MERT HACKETT** Hackett, Mortimer Martin b: 11/11/1859, Cambridge, Mass. d: 2/22/38, Cambridge, Mass. BR/TR, 5'10.5", 175 lbs. Deb: 5/02/1883

YEAR	TM/L	G	AB	R	H	2B	3B	HR	RBI	BB	SO	AVG	OBP	SLG	PRO	/A	BR	/A	PF	CHI	RC	TA	SB	CS	SBR	FR	POS	TPR
1883	Bos-N	46	179	20	42	8	6	2	24	1	48	.235	.239	.380	.619	79	-3	-5	106	115	17	.504				-11	C/O	-1.2
1884	Bos-N	72	268	28	55	13	2	1	20	2	66	.205	.211	.280	.491	54	-14	-14	98	88	16	.362				3	C/3	-0.3
1885	Bos-N	34	115	9	21	7	1	0	4	2	28	.183	.197	.261	.457	50	-7	-6	94	46	6	.340				4	C	0.1
1886	KC-N	62	230	18	50	8	3	3	25	4	59	.217	.231	.317	.548	61	-10	-12	107	101	18	.433	1			-6	CO	-1.2
1887	Ind-N	42	147	12	35	6	3	2	10	7	24	.238	.282	.361	.643	82	-4	-3	96	53	16	.589	4			-5	C/O1	-0.2
Total	5	256	939	87	203	42	15	8	83	16	225	.216	.231	.318	.549	65	-39	-40	101	85	73	.438	5			-16	C/O13	-2.8

■ **WALTER HACKETT** Hackett, Walter Henry b: 8/15/1857, Cambridge, Mass. d: 10/2/20, Cambridge, Mass. Deb: 4/17/1884

YEAR	TM/L	G	AB	R	H	2B	3B	HR	RBI	BB	SO	AVG	OBP	SLG	PRO	/A	BR	/A	PF	CHI	RC	TA	SB	CS	SBR	FR	POS	TPR
1884	Bos-U	103	415	71	101	19	0	1		7		.243	.256	.296	.552	88	-6	-5	98	0	32	.414	0			8	*S	0.5
1885	Bos-N	35	125	8	23	3	0	0	9	3	22	.184	.203	.208	.411	35	-9	-8	94	123	5	.284				0	2S	-0.7
Total	2	138	540	79	124	22	0	1	9	10	22	.230	.244	.276	.520	76	-15	-13	97	29	38	.382				8	S/2	-0.2

■ **KENT HADLEY** Hadley, Kent William b: 12/17/34, Pocatello, Idaho BL/TL, 6'3", 190 lbs. Deb: 9/14/58

YEAR	TM/L	G	AB	R	H	2B	3B	HR	RBI	BB	SO	AVG	OBP	SLG	PRO	/A	BR	/A	PF	CHI	RC	TA	SB	CS	SBR	FR	POS	TPR
1958	KC-A	3	11	1	2	0	0	0	0	0	4	.182	.182	.182	.364	0	-1	-2	106	0	0	.222	0	0	0	0	/1	-0.1
1959	KC-A	113	288	40	73	11	1	10	39	24	74	.253	.313	.403	.716	94	-3	-3	101	105	36	.637	1	2	-1	-2	1	-0.5
1960	NY-A	55	64	8	13	2	0	4	11	6	19	.203	.271	.422	.693	90	-2	-1	94	110	7	.635	0	0	0	1	1	-0.1
Total	3	171	363	49	88	13	1	14	50	30	97	.242	.302	.399	.701	90	-6	-6	100	103	43	.637	1	2	-1	-1	1	-0.7

■ **CHICK HAFEY** Hafey, Charles James b: 2/12/03, Berkeley, Cal. d: 7/2/73, Calistoga, Cal. BR/TR, 6', 185 lbs. Deb: 8/28/24 H

YEAR	TM/L	G	AB	R	H	2B	3B	HR	RBI	BB	SO	AVG	OBP	SLG	PRO	/A	BR	/A	PF	CHI	RC	TA	SB	CS	SBR	FR	POS	TPR
1924	StL-N	24	91	10	23	5	2	2	22	4	8	.253	.292	.418	.709	86	-2	-2	103	193	11	.647	1	0	0	-0	O	-0.2
1925	StL-N	93	358	36	108	25	2	5	57	10	29	.302	.321	.425	.745	87	-7	-8	102	124	45	.642	3	7	-3	-4	O	-1.6
1926	StL-N	78	225	30	61	19	2	4	38	11	36	.271	.311	.427	.738	95	-2	-3	102	122	29	.677	2			-8	O	-1.2
1927	StL-N	103	346	62	114	26	5	18	63	36	41	.329	.401	.590	.990	151	29	26	107	85	80	1.108	12			5	O	2.6
1928	StL-N	138	520	101	175	46	6	27	111	40	53	.337	.386	.604	.990	155	39	39	100	102	116	1.055	8			1	*O	3.3
1929	StL-N	134	517	101	175	47	9	29	125	45	42	.338	.394	.632	1.026	152	37	38	98	110	124	1.114	7			-3	*O	2.1
1930	StL-N	120	446	108	150	39	12	26	107	46	51	.336	.407	.652	1.059	144	35	31	105	102	114	1.203	12			-7	*O	1.4
1931	StL-N	122	450	94	157	35	8	16	95	39	43	**.349**	**.404**	.569	.973	149	36	32	107	114	105	**1.055**	11			-9	*O	1.7
1932	Cin-N	83	253	34	87	19	3	2	36	22	20	.344	.403	.466	.869	138	12	14	96	108	49	.886	4			-6	O	0.3
1933	Cin-N	144	568	77	172	34	6	7	62	40	44	.303	.351	.421	.772	121	14	15	99	86	85	.698	3			2	*O	0.8
1934	Cin-N	140	535	75	157	29	6	18	67	52	63	.293	.359	.471	.830	119	15	14	101	84	93	.802	4			-1	*O	0.7
1935	Cin-N	15	59	10	20	6	1	1	9	4	5	.339	.400	.525	.925	157	4	4	93	92	13	.950	1			-2	O	0.2
1937	Cin-N	89	257	39	67	11	5	9	41	23	42	.261	.324	.447	.771	118	2	5	91	104	38	.719	2			-1	O	0.1
Total	13	1283	4625	777	1466	341	67	164	833	372	477	.317	.372	.526	.898	133	212	206	101	103	902	.917	70	7		-32	*O	10.2

■ **BUD HAFEY** Hafey, Daniel Albert b: 8/6/12, Berkeley, Cal. d: 7/27/86, Sacramento, Cal. BR/TR, 6', 185 lbs. Deb: 4/21/35

YEAR	TM/L	G	AB	R	H	2B	3B	HR	RBI	BB	SO	AVG	OBP	SLG	PRO	/A	BR	/A	PF	CHI	RC	TA	SB	CS	SBR	FR	POS	TPR
1935	Chi-A	2	0	1	0	0	0	0	0	0	0	—	—	—	—	—	0	0	109	—	—	—	0	0	0	0	R	0.0
	Pit-N	58	184	29	42	11	2	6	16	16	48	.228	.290	.408	.698	80	-4	-6	107	62	22	.619	0			6	O	-0.1
1936	Pit-N	39	118	19	25	6	1	4	13	10	27	.212	.273	.381	.655	76	-5	-4	98	81	12	.567	0			0	O	-0.4
1939	Cin-N	6	13	1	2	1	0	0	1	1	4	.154	.214	.231	.445	19	-1	-2	103	122	1	.455	1			-0	/O	-0.1
	Phi-N	18	51	3	9	1	0	0	3	3	12	.176	.222	.196	.418	14	-6	-6	94	110	2	.318	1			1	O/P	-0.4
	Yr	24	64	4	11	2	0	0	4	4	16	.172	.221	.203	.424	15	-8	-7	96	118	3	.345	2			0		-0.5
Total	3	123	366	53	78	19	3	10	33	30	91	.213	.273	.363	.636	68	-17	-18	102	77	938	.569	2	0		6	/OP	-1.0

■ **TOM HAFEY** Hafey, Thomas Francis "Heave-O" or "The Arm" b: 7/12/13, Berkeley, Cal. BR/TR, 6'1", 180 lbs. Deb: 7/21/39

YEAR	TM/L	G	AB	R	H	2B	3B	HR	RBI	BB	SO	AVG	OBP	SLG	PRO	/A	BR	/A	PF	CHI	RC	TA	SB	CS	SBR	FR	POS	TPR
1939	NY-N	70	256	37	62	10	1	6	26	10	44	.242	.271	.359	.630	69	-12	-12	99	88	24	.515	1			-3	3	-1.3
1944	StL-A	8	14	1	5	2	0	0	2	1	4	.357	.400	.500	.900	153	1	1	102	103	3	.889	0	0	0	-1	/O1	0.0
Total	2	78	270	38	67	12	1	6	28	11	48	.248	.278	.367	.644	73	-11	-11	99	89	27	.547	1	0		-4	/3O1	-1.3

■ **JOE HAGUE** Hague, Joe Clarence b: 4/25/44, Huntington, W.Va. BL/TL, 6', 195 lbs. Deb: 9/19/68

YEAR	TM/L	G	AB	R	H	2B	3B	HR	RBI	BB	SO	AVG	OBP	SLG	PRO	/A	BR	/A	PF	CHI	RC	TA	SB	CS	SBR	FR	POS	TPR
1968	StL-N	7	17	2	4	0	0	1	1	2	2	.235	.316	.412	.728	123	0	0	95	42	2	.692	0	0	0	-1	/O1	0.0
1969	StL-N	40	100	8	17	2	1	2	8	12	23	.170	.259	.270	.529	49	-7	-7	100	97	7	.448	0	2	-1	-1	O/1	-1.0
1970	StL-N	139	451	58	122	16	4	14	68	63	87	.271	.361	.417	.778	101	6	2	106	115	69	.743	2	1	0	-6	1O	-1.2
1971	StL-N	129	380	46	86	9	3	16	54	58	69	.226	.332	.392	.724	104	3	2	101	112	51	.690	0	3	-2	-6	1O	-1.3
1972	StL-N	27	76	8	18	5	1	3	11	17	18	.237	.376	.447	.824	127	4	3	105	105	13	.836	0	1	-1	1	1/O	0.2
	Cin-N	69	138	17	34	7	1	4	20	20	18	.246	.342	.399	.740	118	2	3	93	123	18	.697	1	1	-0	-1	1O	0.0
	Yr	96	214	25	52	12	2	7	31	37	36	.243	.355	.416	.770	122	6	7	97	119	33	.756	1	2	-1	-1		0.2
1973	Cin-N	19	33	2	5	2	0	0	1	5	5	.152	.263	.212	.475	36	-3	-3	93	57	2	.464	1	0	0	-1	/O1	-0.3
Total	6	430	1195	141	286	41	10	40	163	177	222	.239	.339	.391	.730	100	5	2	102	110	163	.710	4	8	-4	-15	1O	-3.6

■ **BILL HAGUE** Hague, William L. (born William L. Haug) b: 1852, Philadelphia, Pa. BR/TR, 5'9", 164 lbs. Deb: 5/04/1875

YEAR	TM/L	G	AB	R	H	2B	3B	HR	RBI	BB	SO	AVG	OBP	SLG	PRO	/A	BR	/A	PF	CHI	RC	TA	SB	CS	SBR	FR	POS	TPR
1875	StL-n	62	261	24	59							.226															*3/1	
1876	Lou-N	67	294	31	78	8	0	1	22	2	10	.265	.270	.303	.573	87	-3	-5	104	71	25	.421				-26	*3/S	-2.8
1877	Lou-N	59	263	38	70	7	1	1	24	7	18	.266	.285	.312	.597	67	-3	-16	132	92	24	.461				-17	*3	-2.5
1878	Pro-N	62	250	21	51	3	0	0	25	5	34	.204	.220	.216	.436	45	-15	-14	98	166	12	.296				19	*3	0.8
1879	Pro-N	51	209	20	47	3	1	0	21	3	19	.225	.236	.249	.485	59	-9	-9	102	144	13	.340				4	3	-0.3
Total	4	239	1016	110	246	21	2	2	92	17	81	.242	.255	.273	.527	66	-30	-44	109	115	73	.382				-19	3/S1	-4.8

■ **DON HAHN** Hahn, Donald Antone b: 11/16/48, San Francisco, Cal. BR/TR, 6'1", 180 lbs. Deb: 4/08/69

YEAR	TM/L	G	AB	R	H	2B	3B	HR	RBI	BB	SO	AVG	OBP	SLG	PRO	/A	BR	/A	PF	CHI	RC	TA	SB	CS	SBR	FR	POS	TPR
1969	Mon-N	4	9	0	1	0	0	0	2	0	5	.111	.111	.111	.222	-37	-2	-2	100	802	0	.125	0	0	0	0	/O	-0.1
1970	Mon-N	82	149	22	38	8	0	0	8	27	27	.255	.376	.309	.685	86	-2	-2	100	67	21	.693	4	2	0	-6	O	-1.0
1971	NY-N	98	178	16	42	5	1	1	11	21	32	.236	.320	.292	.612	77	-5	-5	96	81	17	.531	2	3	-1	-2	O	-1.0
1972	NY-N	17	37	0	6	0	0	0	1	4	12	.162	.244	.162	.406	18	-4	-4	95	68	2	.313	0	0	0	-2	O	-0.6
1973	NY-N	93	262	22	60	10	0	2	21	22	43	.229	.289	.290	.579	60	-14	-14	101	103	22	.476	2	1	0	-6	O	-2.5
1974	NY-N	110	323	34	81	14	1	4	28	37	34	.251	.330	.337	.667	87	-5	-5	99	89	36	.591	2	0	1	-8	*O	-1.7
1975	Phi-N	9	5	0	0	0	0	0	0	0	2	.000	.000	.000	.000	-99	-1	-1	101	0	0	.000	0	0	0	-1	/O	-0.2
	StL-N	7	8	3	1	0	0	0	0	1	1	.125	.222	.125	.347	-2	-1	-1	103	0	0	.250	0	0	0	-1	/O	-0.1
	SD-N	34	26	7	6	1	2	0	3	10	2	.231	.444	.423	.868	142	2	2	100	105	5	1.000	1	0	0	-6	O	-0.4
	Yr	50	39	10	7	1	2	0	3	11	5	.179	.360	.308	.668	86	-0	-0	100	72	5	.706	1	0	0	-8		-0.7
Total	7	454	997	104	235	38	4	7	74	122	158	.236	.321	.303	.624	75	-32	-31	99	92	103	.570	11	6	-0	-32	O	-7.6

YEAR	TM/L	G	AB	R	H	2B	3B	HR	RBI	BB	SO	AVG	OBP	SLG	PRO	/A	BR	/A	PF	CHI	RC	TA	SB	CS	SBR	FR	POS	TPR
■ DICK HAHN	Hahn, Richard Frederick b: 7/24/16, Canton, Ohio BR/TR, 5'11", 176 lbs. Deb: 9/07/40																											
1940	Was-A	1	3	0	0	0	0	0	0	0	0	.000	.000	.000	.000	-99	-1	-1	93	0	0	.000	0	0	0	0	/C	0.0
■ ED HAHN	Hahn, William Edgar b: 8/27/1875, Nevada, Ohio d: 11/29/41, Des Moines, Iowa BL/TR, 160 lbs. Deb: 8/31/05																											
1905	NY-A	43	160	32	51	5	0	0	11	25		.319	.411	.350	.761	142	10	9	102	60	24	.752	1			2	O	1.0
1906	NY-A	11	22	2	2	1	0	0	1	3		.091	.200	.136	.336	6	-2	-3	120	121	1	.400	2			0	/O	-0.2
	Chi-A	130	484	80	110	7	5	0	27	69		.227	.324	.262	.586	94	-4	0	92	67	48	.575	19			14	*O	1.1
	Yr	141	506	82	112	8	5	0	28	72		.221	.318	.257	.575	88	-7	-3	94	72	49	.566	21			14		0.9
1907	Chi-A	156	592	87	151	9	7	0	45	84		.255	.348	.294	.642	103	9	6	104	80	68	.624	17			-4	*O	-0.6
1908	Chi-A	122	447	58	112	12	8	0	21	39		.251	.311	.313	.624	111	3	6	94	60	45	.567	11			-21	*O	-2.4
1909	Chi-A	76	287	30	52	6	0	1	16	31		.181	.268	.213	.480	53	-15	-14	97	83	18	.443	9			5	O	-1.2
1910	Chi-A	15	53	2	6	2	0	0	1	7		.113	.217	.151	.368	16	-5	-5	95	40	2	.319	0			-4	O	-1.0
Total	6	553	2045	291	484	42	20	1	122	258		.237	.323	.278	.601	95	-5	0	98	71	207	.570	59			-7	O	-3.3
■ ED HAIGH	Haigh, Edward E. b: 2/7/1867, Philadelphia, Pa. d: 2/13/53, Atlantic City, N.J Deb: 8/14/1892																											
1892	StL-N	1	4	0	1	0	0	0	0	0	2	.250	.250	.250	.500	55	-0	-0	95	0	0	.333	0			0	/O	0.0
■ HINKEY HAINES	Haines, Henry Luther b: 12/23/1898, Red Lion, Pa. d: 1/9/79, Sharon Hill, Pa. BR/TR, 5'10", 170 lbs. Deb: 8/20/23																											
1923	NY-A	28	25	9	4	2	0	0	3	4	5	.160	.276	.240	.516	35	-2	-2	104	171	2	.591	3	1	0	-3	O	-0.5
■ JERRY HAIRSTON	Hairston, Jerry Wayne b: 2/16/52, Birmingham, Ala. BB/TR, 5'10", 170 lbs. Deb: 7/26/73																											
1973	Chi-A	60	210	25	57	11	1	0	23	33	30	.271	.373	.333	.706	98	2	1	102	132	29	.667	0	0	0	0	O1/D	0.0
1974	Chi-A	45	109	8	25	7	0	0	8	13	18	.229	.311	.294	.605	74	-3	-3	102	98	10	.511	0	2	-1	-5	OD	-1.0
1975	Chi-A	69	219	26	62	8	0	0	23	46	23	.283	.410	.320	.729	105	5	4	103	129	33	.733	1	0	0	-1	O/D	0.2
1976	Chi-A	44	119	20	27	2	2	0	10	24	19	.227	.357	.277	.634	88	-1	-1	99	116	14	.624	1	1	-0	-4	O	-0.5
1977	Chi-A	13	26	3	8	2	0	0	4	5	7	.308	.419	.385	.804	122	1	1	99	159	4	.750	0	0	0	-1	O	0.0
	Pit-N	51	52	5	10	2	0	2	6	6	10	.192	.276	.346	.622	64	-3	-3	103	100	5	.558	0	0	0	-4	O/2	-0.6
1981	Chi-A	9	25	5	7	1	0	1	6	2	4	.280	.357	.440	.797	129	1	1	100	168	4	.778	0	0	0	-1	/O	0.0
1982	Chi-A	85	90	11	21	5	0	5	18	9	15	.233	.303	.456	.759	108	0	1	97	128	12	.694	0	0	0	-8	O/D	-0.7
1983	Chi-A	101	126	17	37	9	1	5	22	23	16	.294	.403	.500	.903	142	9	8	103	110	26	.945	0	1	-1	-8	O/D	0.0
1984	Chi-A	115	227	41	59	13	2	5	19	41	29	.260	.375	.401	.776	104	6	3	111	71	37	.785	2	1	0	-5	OD	-0.2
1985	Chi-A	95	140	9	34	8	0	2	20	29	18	.243	.380	.343	.723	100	1	1	100	147	20	.725	0	0	0	-1	D/O	0.0
1986	Chi-A	101	225	32	61	15	0	5	26	26	26	.271	.349	.404	.754	105	2	2	101	98	31	.682	0	0	0	-2	D1O	-0.2
1987	Chi-A	66	126	14	29	8	0	5	20	25	25	.230	.362	.413	.775	98	2	0	109	119	20	.772	0	0	0	-1	OD/1	-0.1
1988	Chi-A	2	2	0	0	0	0	0	0	0	0	.000	.000	.000	.000	-99	-1	-1	97	0	0	.000	0	0	0	0	/H	0.0
Total	13	856	1696	216	437	91	6	30	205	282	240	.258	.366	.371	.738	102	22	15	103	114	245	.731	4	5	-2	-40	OD/12	-3.1
■ JOHNNY HAIRSTON	Hairston, John Louis b: 8/29/45, Birmingham, Ala. BR/TR, 6'2", 200 lbs. Deb: 9/06/69																											
1969	Chi-N	3	4	0	1	0	0	0	0	0	2	.250	.250	.250	.500	38	-0	-0	107	0	0	.333	0	0	0	-0	/CO	0.0
■ SAMMY HAIRSTON	Hairston, Samuel b: 1/28/20, Crawford, Miss. BR/TR, 5'10.5", 187 lbs. Deb: 7/21/51 C																											
1951	Chi-A	4	5	1	2	1	0	0	1	2	0	.400	.571	.600	1.171	224	1	1	97	119	2	1.667	0	0	0	0	/C	0.1
■ CHET HAJDUK	Hajduk, Chester b: 7/21/18, Chicago, Ill. BR/TR, 6', 195 lbs. Deb: 4/16/41																											
1941	Chi-A	1	1	0	0	0	0	0	0	0	0	.000	.000	.000	.000	-99	-0	-0	94	0	0	.000	0	0	0	0	H	0.0
■ GEORGE HALAS	Halas, George Stanley b: 2/2/1895, Chicago, Ill. d: 10/31/83, Chicago, Ill. BB/TR, 6', 164 lbs. Deb: 5/06/19																											
1919	NY-A	12	22	0	2	0	0	0	0	0	8	.091	.091	.091	.182	-46	-4	-4	106	0	0	.100	0			-1	/O	-0.6
■ JOHN HALDEMAN	Haldeman, John Avery b: 12/2/1855, Pee Wee Valley, Ky. d: 9/17/1899, Louisville, Ky. BL/TR, 5'10", 175 lbs. Deb: 7/03/1877																											
1877	Lou-N	1	4	0	0	0	0	0	0	0	0	.000	.000	.000	.000	-76	-1	-1	132	0	0	.000				0	/2	0.0
■ ODELL HALE	Hale, Arvel Odell "Bad News" b: 8/10/08, Hosston, La. d: 6/9/80, El Dorado, Ark. BR/TR, 5'10", 175 lbs. Deb: 8/01/31																											
1931	Cle-A	25	92	14	26	2	4	1	5	8	8	.283	.340	.424	.764	94	-0	-1	106	40	14	.742	2	0	1	0	32/S	0.1
1933	Cle-A	98	351	49	97	19	8	10	64	30	37	.276	.333	.462	.795	104	3	1	105	113	53	.755	2	3	-1	-3	23	-0.2
1934	Cle-A	143	563	82	170	44	6	13	101	48	50	.302	.357	.471	.827	111	8	8	101	118	91	.793	8	12	-5	**23**	*2/3	2.9
1935	Cle-A	150	589	80	179	37	11	16	101	52	55	.304	.361	.486	.847	118	13	13	99	109	101	.837	15	13	-3	3	*3/2	1.3
1936	Cle-A	153	620	126	196	50	13	14	87	64	43	.316	.380	.506	.887	111	15	9	106	84	120	.900	8	5	-1	**16**	*3/2	2.3
1937	Cle-A	154	561	74	150	32	4	6	82	56	41	.267	.335	.371	.706	80	-19	-17	98	127	71	.657	9	6	-1	16	32	0.5
1938	Cle-A	130	496	69	138	32	2	8	69	44	39	.278	.338	.399	.737	85	-13	-12	99	111	70	.699	8	1	2	-2	*2	-0.7
1939	Cle-A	108	253	36	79	16	2	4	48	25	18	.312	.374	.439	.813	110	3	4	98	132	39	.745	4	5	-2	-5	2/3	0.0
1940	Cle-A	48	50	3	11	3	1	0	6	5	7	.220	.291	.320	.611	63	-3	-3	93	135	5	.525	0	0	0	0	/3	-0.1
1941	Bos-A	12	24	5	5	2	0	1	1	3	4	.208	.296	.417	.713	84	-1	-1	103	27	3	.650	0	0	0	-0	/32	0.0
	NY-N	41	102	13	20	3	0	0	9	18	13	.196	.317	.225	.542	53	-5	-6	103	141	9	.512	1			1	2	-0.2
Total	10	1062	3701	551	1071	240	51	73	573	353	315	.289	.352	.441	.793	101	-1	-5	101	110	576	.764	57	45		49	23/S	5.9
■ GEORGE HALE	Hale, George Wagner "Ducky" b: 8/3/1894, Dexter, Kan. d: 11/1/45, Wichita, Kan. BR/TR, 5'10", 160 lbs. Deb: 8/24/14																											
1914	StL-A	6	11	1	2	0	0	0	0	0	3	.182	.182	.182	.364	10	-1	-1	98	0	0	.222	0			0	/C	0.0
1916	StL-A	4	1	0	0	0	0	0	0	0	1	.000	.500	.000	.500	54	0	0	95	0	0	1.000	0			0	/C	0.0
1917	StL-A	38	61	4	12	2	1	0	8	10	12	.197	.310	.262	.572	79	-2	-1	95	179	5	.531	0			0	C	0.1
1918	StL-A	12	30	0	4	1	0	0	1	1	5	.133	.161	.167	.328	-1	-4	-4	99	73	1	.231	0			0	C	-0.2
Total	4	60	103	5	18	3	1	0	9	11	21	.175	.261	.223	.484	49	-6	-6	96	130	6	.412	0			0	/C	-0.1
■ JOHN HALE	Hale, John Steven b: 8/5/53, Fresno, Cal. BL/TR, 6'2", 195 lbs. Deb: 9/08/74																											
1974	LA-N	4	4	2	4	1	0	0	2	0	0	1.000	1.000	1.250	2.250	568	2	2	93	154	5	—	0	0	0	-1	/O	0.1
1975	LA-N	71	204	20	43	7	0	6	22	26	51	.211	.306	.333	.639	82	-6	-5	95	99	22	.591	1	2	-1	-3	O	-1.1
1976	LA-N	44	91	4	14	2	1	0	8	16	14	.154	.294	.198	.491	42	-6	-6	100	171	7	.513	4	1	1	-4	O	-1.1
1977	LA-N	79	108	10	26	4	1	2	11	15	28	.241	.333	.352	.685	84	-2	-2	100	100	14	.663	2	1	0	-16	O	-2.1
1978	Sea-A	107	211	24	36	8	0	4	22	34	64	.171	.286	.265	.551	55	-12	-12	102	128	18	.514	3	4	-2	-13	O/D	-3.0
1979	Sea-A	54	63	6	14	3	0	2	7	12	26	.222	.347	.365	.712	92	-0	-0	100	93	8	.686	0	0	0	-13	O	-1.4
Total	6	359	681	66	137	25	2	14	72	103	183	.201	.310	.305	.615	72	-25	-24	99	118	74	.587	10	8	-2	-49	O/D	-8.6
■ BOB HALE	Hale, Robert Houston b: 11/7/33, Sarasota, Fla. BL/TL, 5'10", 195 lbs. Deb: 7/04/55																											
1955	Bal-A	67	182	13	65	7	1	0	29	5	19	.357	.378	.407	.784	124	3	5	90	146	25	.640	0	2	-1	0	1	0.2
1956	Bal-A	85	207	18	49	10	1	1	24	11	10	.237	.279	.309	.588	58	-14	-12	94	134	16	.458	0	2	-1	0	1	-1.4
1957	Bal-A	42	44	2	11	0	0	0	7	2	2	.250	.283	.250	.533	50	-3	-3	93	251	2	.342	0	0	0	0	/1	-0.2
1958	Bal-A	19	20	2	7	2	0	0	3	2	1	.350	.409	.450	.859	145	1	1	94	134	3	.733	0	0	0	0	/1	0.1
1959	Bal-A	40	54	2	10	3	0	0	7	2	6	.185	.214	.241	.455	25	-6	-5	97	212	3	.333	0	0	0	-0	/1	-0.5
1960	Cle-A	70	70	2	21	7	0	0	12	3	6	.300	.329	.400	.729	98	-1	-0	98	168	10	.633	0	0	0	0	/1	0.0
1961	Cle-A	42	36	0	6	0	0	0	6	1	7	.167	.211	.167	.377	2	-5	-5	96	392	2	.267	0	0	0	0	H	-0.4
	NY-A	11	13	2	2	0	0	0	1	1	0	.154	.154	.385	.538	40	-1	-1	96	49	0	.417	0	0	0	0	/1	-0.1
	Yr	53	49	2	8	0	0	0	7	1	7	.163	.196	.224	.421	13	-6	-6	96	328	2	.310	0	0	0	0		-0.5
Total	7	376	626	41	171	29	2	2	89	26	51	.273	.305	.335	.641	77	-26	-21	94	169	61	.520	0	4	-2	0	1	-2.3
■ SAMMY HALE	Hale, Samuel Douglas b: 9/10/1896, Glen Rose, Tex. d: 9/6/74, Wheeler, Tex. BR/TR, 5'8.5", 160 lbs. Deb: 4/20/20																											
1920	Det-A	76	116	13	34	3	3	1	14	5	15	.293	.322	.397	.719	87	-2	-3	103	100	15	.646	2	0	1	1	3/O2	0.0
1921	Det-A	9	2	2	0	0	0	0	0	0	1	.000	.000	.000	.000	-99	-1	-1	96	0	0	.000	0	1	-1	0	H	0.0
1923	Phi-A	115	434	68	125	22	8	3	51	17	31	.288	.327	.396	.723	89	-8	-8	100	98	57	.657	8	3	1	-10	*3	-0.3
1924	Phi-A	80	261	41	83	14	2	2	17	17	19	.318	.367	.410	.777	101	-0	0	99	50	39	.722	3	2	-0	-0	3/OS	0.3
1925	Phi-A	110	391	62	135	30	11	8	63	17	27	.345	.376	.540	.915	126	15	13	103	90	77	.912	7	4	-0	-1	3/2	1.6
1926	Phi-A	111	327	49	92	22	9	4	43	13	36	.281	.311	.440	.751	80	-5	-13	118	94	43	.665	1	4	-2	5	3/O	-0.2

YEAR	TM/L	G	AB	R	H	2B	3B	HR	RBI	BB	SO	AVG	OBP	SLG	PRO	/A	BR	/A	PF	CHI	RC	TA	SB	CS	SBR	FR	POS	TPR
1927	Phi-A	131	501	77	157	24	8	5	81	32	32	.313	.358	.423	.781	106	1	3	97	126	74	.750	11	0	3	4	*3	1.5
1928	Phi-A	88	314	38	97	20	9	4	58	9	21	.309	.334	.468	.803	106	2	1	103	125	49	.742	2	0	1	7	3	1.0
1929	Phi-A	101	379	51	105	14	3	1	40	12	18	.277	.303	.338	.641	59	-20	-25	109	107	40	.536	6	2	1	-4	3/2	-2.0
1930	StL-A	62	190	21	52	8	1	2	25	8	18	.274	.303	.358	.661	62	-10	-12	108	112	20	.554	1	1	-0	-0	3	-0.9
Total	10	883	2915	422	880	157	54	30	392	130	218	.302	.336	.424	.760	92	-27	-43	104	102	414	.696	41	17	2	-0	3/O2S	1.0
■ FRED HALEY	Haley, Fred b: Wheeling, W.Va. TR , Deb: 6/22/1880																											
1880	Tro-N	2	7	0	0	0	0	0	0	1	2	.000	.125	.000	.125	-49	-1	-1	110	0	0	.143				0	/C	0.0
■ RAY HALEY	Haley, Raymond Timothy "Pat" b: 1/23/1891, Danbury, Iowa d: 10/8/73, Bradenton, Fla. BR/TR, 5'11", 180 lbs. Deb: 4/21/15																											
1915	Bos-A	5	7	2	1	1	0	0	0	1	0	.143	.250	.286	.536	61	-0	-0	99	0	1	.500	0			-0	/C	0.0
1916	Bos-A	1	1	0	0	0	0	0	0	0	1	.000	.000	.000	.000	-99	-0	-0	94	0	0	.000	0			0	H	0.0
	Phi-A	34	108	8	25	5	0	0	4	6	19	.231	.278	.278	.556	68	-5	-4	98	48	8	.446	0			7	C	0.5
	Yr	35	109	8	25	5	0	0	4	6	20	.229	.276	.275	.551	67	-5	-5	98	46	8	.440	0			7		0.5
1917	Phi-A	41	98	7	27	2	1	0	11	4	12	.276	.311	.316	.627	98	-1	-1	94	127	10	.535	2			0	C	0.3
Total	3	81	214	17	53	8	1	0	15	11	32	.248	.291	.294	.585	80	-6	-5	96	82	19	.484	2			7	/C	0.8
■ ALBERT HALL	Hall, Albert b: 3/7/58, Birmingham, Ala. BB/TR, 5'11", 155 lbs. Deb: 9/12/81																											
1981	Atl-N	6	2	1	0	0	0	0	0	1	1	.000	.333	.000	.333	1	-0	-0	100	0	0	.500	0	0	0	-1	/O	0.0
1982	Atl-N	5	0	1	0	0	0	0	0	0	0	—	—	—	—	—	0	0	107	—	—	—	0	0	0	0	/R	0.0
1983	Atl-N	10	8	2	0	0	0	0	0	2	2	.000	.200	.000	.200	-38	-2	-2	106	0	0	.333	1	1	-0	-1	/O	-0.2
1984	Atl-N	87	142	25	37	6	1	1	9	10	18	.261	.309	.338	.647	75	-3	-5	110	69	15	.577	6	4	-1	-12	O	-2.1
1985	Atl-N	54	47	5	7	0	1	0	3	9	12	.149	.286	.191	.477	34	-4	-4	106	133	3	.432	1	1	-0	-3	O	-0.7
1986	Atl-N	16	50	6	12	2	0	0	1	5	6	.240	.309	.280	.589	62	-2	-2	102	28	5	.659	8	3	1	0	O	-0.1
1987	Atl-N	92	292	54	83	20	4	3	24	38	36	.284	.370	.411	.781	99	4	0	108	74	48	.862	33	10	4	5	O	0.7
1988	Atl-N	85	231	27	57	7	1	1	15	21	35	.247	.315	.299	.614	74	-6	-8	104	83	22	.569	15	10	-2	5	O	-0.5
Total	8	355	772	121	196	35	7	5	52	86	110	.254	.332	.337	.669	80	-14	-21	107	76	92	.680	64	29	2	-6	O	-2.9
■ AL HALL	Hall, Archibald W. b: Worcester, Mass. d: 2/10/1885, Warren, Pa. Deb: 5/01/1879																											
1879	Tro-N	67	306	30	79	7	3	0	14	3	13	.258	.265	.301	.566	92	-5	-2	93	46	25	.419				4	*O	0.0
1880	Cle-N	3	8	1	1	0	0	0	0	0	0	.125	.125	.125	.250	-15	-1	-1	99	0	0	.143				0	/O	0.0
Total	2	70	314	31	80	7	3	0	14	3	13	.255	.262	.296	.558	90	-5	-3	93	45	25	.410				4	/O	0.0
■ CHARLIE HALL	Hall, Charles Walter "Doc" b: 8/24/1863, Toulon, Ill. d: 6/24/21, Tacoma, Wash. Deb: 5/03/1887																											
1887	NY-a	3	12	1	1	0	0	0		2		.083	.214	.083	.298	-16	-2	-1	88	0	0	.364	1			0	/O	0.0
■ GEORGE HALL	Hall, George William b: 6/22/1849, England d: 6/11/23, Ridgewood, N.J. BL , 5'7", 142 lbs. Deb: 5/05/1871																											
1871	Oly-n	32	146	31	38							.260															*O	
1872	Bal-n	54	263	69	79							.300															*O/1	
1873	Bal-n	34	169	43	54							.320															O	
1874	Bos-n	47	209	58	67							.321															*O	
1875	Ath-n	77	362	70	108							.298															*O	
1876	Phi-N	60	268	51	98	7	13	**5**	45	8	4	.366	.384	.545	.929	**208**	29	29	99	91	57	.906				-0	*O	2.5
1877	Lou-N	61	269	53	87	15	8	0	26	12	19	.323	.352	.439	.791	112	14	1	132	72	43	.714				-6	*O	-0.5
Total	5 n	244	1149	271	346							.301															*O	
Total	2	121	537	104	185	22	21	5	71	20	23	.345	.368	.492	.860	152	43	31	116	81	100	.807				-6	O/1	2.0
■ IRV HALL	Hall, Irvin Gladstone b: 10/7/18, Alberton, Md. BR/TR, 5'10.5", 160 lbs. Deb: 4/20/43																											
1943	Phi-A	151	544	37	139	15	4	0	54	22	42	.256	.292	.298	.590	72	-20	-20	101	124	47	.473	10	7	-1	-13	*S/23	-3.6
1944	Phi-A	143	559	60	150	20	8	0	45	31	46	.268	.309	.333	.642	83	-13	-13	101	93	56	.516	2	5	-2	-12	2S/1	-2.3
1945	Phi-A	151	616	62	161	17	5	0	50	35	42	.261	.307	.305	.613	83	-18	-13	94	92	58	.490	3	10	-5	25	*2	0.9
1946	Phi-A	63	185	19	46	6	2	0	19	9	18	.249	.287	.303	.590	62	-9	-10	104	129	16	.459	1	1	-0	-9	2/S	-1.6
Total	4	508	1904	178	496	58	19	0	168	97	148	.261	.302	.311	.613	78	-59	-57	99	105	176	.501	16	23	-9	-10	2S/13	-6.6
■ JIM HALL	Hall, James d: 1/30/1886, Brooklyn, N.Y. Deb: 5/20/1872																											
1872	Atl-n	13	57	8	14							.246															2/O	
1874	Atl-n	2	8	0	1							.125															/2	
1875	Wes-n	1	4	0	1							.250															/O	
Total	3 n	16	69	8	16							.232															/O	
■ JIMMIE HALL	Hall, Jimmie Randolph b: 3/17/38, Mt.Holly, N.C. BL/TR, 6', 175 lbs. Deb: 4/09/63																											
1963	Min-A	156	497	88	129	21	5	33	80	63	101	.260	.343	.521	.864	138	24	24	100	94	89	.858	3	3	-1	12	*O	3.2
1964	Min-A	149	510	61	144	20	3	25	75	44	112	.282	.341	.480	.821	124	16	16	101	99	83	.780	5	2	0	5	*O	1.6
1965	Min-A	148	522	81	149	25	4	20	86	51	79	.285	.350	.464	.814	128	19	19	101	121	86	.798	14	7	0	-3	*O	1.1
1966	Min-A	120	356	52	85	7	4	20	47	33	66	.239	.303	.449	.753	102	5	0	111	90	44	.676	1	2	-1	1	*O	-0.3
1967	Cal-A	129	401	54	100	8	3	16	55	42	65	.249	.321	.404	.725	118	6	8	96	109	52	.669	4	1	1	-3	*O	0.3
1968	Cal-A	46	126	15	27	3	0	1	8	16	19	.214	.303	.262	.565	77	-4	-3	94	95	10	.485	1	0	0	-5	O	-1.0
	Cle-A	53	111	4	22	4	0	1	8	10	19	.198	.264	.261	.526	59	-5	-5	101	107	8	.440	1	0	0	2	O	-0.4
	Yr	99	237	19	49	7	0	2	16	26	38	.207	.285	.262	.547	68	-9	-9	98	102	19	.474	2	0	1	-4		-1.4
1969	Cle-A	4	10	1	0	0	0	0	0	2	3	.000	.167	.000	.167	-53	-2	-2	94	0	0	.273	1	0	0	-0	/O	-0.1
	NY-A	80	212	21	50	8	5	3	26	19	34	.236	.299	.363	.662	88	-5	-4	95	121	24	.627	8	3	1	-5	O/1	-0.9
	Yr	84	222	22	50	8	5	3	26	21	37	.225	.292	.347	.639	82	-7	-6	95	116	24	.608	9	3	1	-5		-1.0
	Chi-N	11	24	1	5	1	0	0	1	1	5	.208	.240	.250	.490	35	-2	-2	107	67	2	.368	0	0	0	-1	/O	-0.3
1970	Chi-N	28	32	2	3	1	0	0	1	4	12	.094	.194	.125	.319	-10	-5	-6	120	97	1	.276	0	0	0	-1	/O	-0.6
	Atl-N	39	47	7	10	2	0	2	4	2	14	.213	.245	.383	.628	63	-3	-3	104	65	4	.526	0	0	0	-6	O	-1.0
	Yr	67	79	9	13	3	0	2	5	6	26	.165	.224	.278	.502	30	-8	-9	111	80	5	.418	0	0	0	-7		-1.6
Total	8	963	2848	387	724	100	24	121	391	287	529	.254	.323	.434	.757	112	45	42	101	103	402	.729	38	18	1	-4	O/1	1.6
■ MEL HALL	Hall, Melvin b: 9/16/60, Lyons, N.Y. BL/TL, 6', 185 lbs. Deb: 9/03/81																											
1981	Chi-N	10	11	1	1	0	0	1	2	1	4	.091	.167	.364	.530	45	-1	-1	104	112	1	.500	0	0	0	-1	/O	-0.2
1982	Chi-N	24	80	6	21	3	2	0	4	5	17	.262	.322	.350	.672	85	-1	-2	103	56	9	.583	0	1	-1	2	O	0.0
1983	Chi-N	112	410	60	116	23	5	17	56	42	101	.283	.354	.488	.842	130	16	16	101	90	71	.826	6	6	-2	-6	*O	0.6
1984	Chi-N	48	150	25	42	11	3	4	22	12	23	.280	.333	.473	.807	113	4	3	110	104	23	.766	2	1	0	-1	O	0.0
	Cle-A	83	257	43	66	13	1	7	30	35	55	.257	.350	.397	.747	100	3	1	106	97	38	.718	1	1	-0	-1	O/D	-0.2
1985	Cle-A	23	66	7	21	6	0	0	12	8	12	.318	.392	.409	.801	127	2	3	94	176	10	.729	0	1	-1	-3	O/D	-0.1
1986	Cle-A	140	442	68	131	29	2	18	77	33	65	.296	.348	.493	.841	130	16	17	98	113	75	.807	6	2	1	-8	*O/D	0.6
1987	Cle-A	142	485	57	136	21	1	18	76	20	68	.280	.310	.439	.749	94	-3	-5	103	114	63	.664	5	4	-1	2	*OD	-0.6
1988	Cle-A	150	515	69	144	32	4	6	71	28	50	.280	.317	.392	.709	96	-3	-4	102	128	63	.620	7	3	0	-5	*O/D	-1.1
Total	8	732	2416	336	678	138	18	71	350	184	395	.281	.334	.441	.775	109	33	28	102	110	353	.729	27	19	-3	-22	O/D	-1.0
■ DICK HALL	Hall, Richard Wallace b: 9/27/30, St.Louis, Mo. BR/TR, 6'6", 200 lbs. Deb: 4/15/52																											
1952	Pit-N	26	80	6	11	1	0	0	2	2	17	.138	.159	.150	.309	-14	-12	-12	100	65	2	.200	0	1	-1	1	O/3	-1.2
1953	Pit-N	7	24	2	4	0	0	0	1	1	3	.167	.200	.167	.367	-3	-4	-4	102	97	1	.286	1	1	-0	0	/2	-0.2
1954	Pit-N	112	310	38	74	8	4	2	27	33	46	.239	.312	.310	.622	65	-17	-15	97	104	29	.528	3	0	1	4	*O	-1.3
1955	Pit-N	21	40	3	7	1	0	1	3	6	5	.175	.283	.275	.558	50	-3	-3	97	87	3	.472	0	0	0	-3	P/O	0.0
1956	Pit-N	33	29	5	10	0	0	0	1	5	7	.345	.441	.345	.786	113	1	1	102	42	5	.750	0	0	0	-1	P/1	0.0
1957	Pit-N	10	1	0	0	0	0	0	0	0	1	.000	.000	.000	.000	-99	-0	-0	94	0	0	.000	0	0	0	-0	/P	0.0
1959	Pit-N	2	2	0	0	0	0	0	0	0	0	.000	.000	.000	.000	-97	-1	-1	103	0	0	.000	0	0	0	-0	/P	0.0
1960	KC-A	32	56	5	6	0	0	0	4	4	15	.107	.167	.107	.274	-25	-10	-10	99	261	2	.220	1	0	0	-1	P	0.0
1961	Bal-A	30	36	4	5	0	0	0	1	3	13	.139	.205	.139	.344	-6	-5	-5	97	78	1	.250	0	0	0	1	P	0.0

YEAR	TM/L	G	AB	R	H	2B	3B	HR	RBI	BB	SO	AVG	OBP	SLG	PRO	/A	BR	/A	PF	CHI	RC	TA	SB	CS	SBR	FR	POS	TPR
1962	Bal-A	44	24	3	4	1	0	0	1	4	9	.167	.286	.208	.494	38	-2	-2	95	79	2	.450	0	0	0	-0	P	0.0
1963	Bal-A	48	28	7	13	1	0	1	4	0	8	.464	.464	.607	1.071	211	3	4	94	84	8	1.133	0	0	0	1	P	0.0
1964	Bal-A	45	16	1	2	0	0	0	3	1	3	.125	.176	.125	.301	-14	-2	-3	105	636	0	.200	0	0	0	0	P	0.0
1965	Bal-A	49	15	1	5	2	0	0	4	1	4	.333	.412	.467	.878	149	1	1	100	237	3	.900	0	0	0	-1	P	0.0
1966	Bal-A	32	12	0	2	0	0	0	2	0	5	.167	.231	.167	.397	16	-1	-1	101	420	1	.300	0	0	0	0	P	0.0
1967	Phi-N	48	14	1	1	0	0	0	0	0	5	.071	.071	.071	.143	-57	-3	-3	104	0	0	.071	0	0	0	1	P	0.0
1968	Phi-N	32	3	0	1	0	0	0	0	0	1	.333	.333	.333	.667	103	-0	0	97	0	0	.500	0	0	0	-0	P	0.0
1969	Bal-A	39	7	1	2	0	0	0	2	1	1	.286	.375	.286	.661	84	-0	-0	104	401	1	.800	1	0	0	-1	P	0.0
1970	Bal-A	32	12	2	1	0	0	0	1	0	3	.083	.083	.083	.167	-56	-2	-2	97	405	0	.083	0	0	0	-1	P	0.0
1971	Bal-A	27	5	0	2	1	0	0	0	0	1	.400	.400	.600	1.000	175	0	0	103	0	1	1.000	0	0	0	-1	P	0.0
Total	19	669	714	79	150	15	4	4	56	61	147	.210	.274	.259	.533	44	-57	-55	98	129	59	.449	6	2	1	-2	PO/231	-2.7
■ BOB HALL	Hall, Robert Prill b: 12/20/1878, Baltimore, Md. d: 12/1/50, Wellesley, Mass. TR , 5'10", 158 lbs. Deb: 4/18/04																											
1904	Phi-N	46	163	11	26	4	0	0	17	14		.160	.226	.184	.410	31	-13	-12	93	220	8	.358	5			-3	3S1	-1.5
1905	NY-N	1	3	1	1	0	0	0	0	0		.333	.333	.333	.667	100	-0	-0	101	0	0	.500	0			0	/O	0.0
	Bro-N	56	203	21	48	4	1	2	15	11		.236	.276	.296	.571	75	-7	-6	96	84	19	.510	8			10	O/21	0.1
	Yr	57	206	22	49	4	1	2	15	11		.238	.276	.296	.573	75	-7	-6	96	82	20	.510	8			10		0.1
Total	2	103	369	33	75	8	1	2	32	25		.203	.254	.247	.500	56	-20	-18	94	144	28	.439	13			6	/O3S12	-1.4
■ RUSS HALL	Hall, Robert Russell b: 9/29/1871, Shelbyville, Ky. d: 7/1/37, Los Angeles, Cal. TL , Deb: 4/15/1898																											
1898	StL-N	39	143	13	35	2	1	0	10	7		.245	.285	.273	.557	59	-7	-8	106	79	12	.444	1			0	S/3O	-0.7
1901	Cle-A	1	4	2	2	0	0	0	0	0		.500	.500	.500	1.000	191	0	0	95	0	1	1.000	0			0	/S	0.0
Total	2	40	147	15	37	2	1	0	10	7		.252	.290	.279	.569	62	-6	-8	105	77	13	.455	1			0	/S3O	-0.7
■ BILL HALL	Hall, William Lemuel b: 7/30/28, Moultrie, Ga. d: 1/1/86, Moultrie, Ga. BL/TR, 5'11", 165 lbs. Deb: 4/18/54																											
1954	Pit-N	5	7	0	0	0	0	0	0	0	0	.000	.000	.000	.000	-99	-2	-2	97	0	0	.000	0	0	0	0	/C	-0.1
1956	Pit-N	1	3	0	0	0	0	0	0	0	1	.000	.000	.000	.000	-98	-1	-1	102	0	0	.000	0	0	0	0	/C	0.0
1958	Pit-N	51	116	15	33	6	0	1	15	15	13	.284	.366	.362	.728	99	-1	0	95	138	15	.671	0	0	0	-1	C	0.1
Total	3	57	126	15	33	6	0	1	15	15	14	.262	.340	.333	.674	83	-3	-3	95	128	15	.600	0	0	0	-1	/C	0.0
■ TOM HALLER	Haller, Thomas Frank b: 6/23/37, Lockport, Ill. BL/TR, 6'4", 195 lbs. Deb: 4/11/61 C																											
1961	SF-N	30	62	5	9	1	0	2	8	9	23	.145	.264	.258	.522	40	-5	-5	98	147	4	.473	0	1	-1	0	C	-0.3
1962	SF-N	99	272	53	71	13	1	18	55	51	59	.261	.385	.515	.900	138	16	16	101	112	56	.942	1	4	-2	2	C	1.6
1963	SF-N	98	298	32	76	8	1	14	44	34	45	.255	.335	.430	.765	124	7	9	96	109	41	.715	4	6	-2	6	C/O	1.6
1964	SF-N	117	388	43	98	14	3	16	48	55	51	.253	.348	.428	.776	117	10	10	100	94	58	.754	4	2	0	5	*C/O	1.9
1965	SF-N	134	422	40	106	4	3	16	49	47	67	.251	.338	.389	.726	94	3	-3	111	96	56	.676	0	0	0	-6	*C	-0.3
1966	SF-N	142	471	74	113	19	2	27	67	53	74	.240	.325	.461	.785	118	9	11	97	96	69	.747	1	3	-2	-11	*C/1	0.1
1967	SF-N	141	455	54	114	23	5	14	49	62	61	.251	.345	.415	.761	116	11	10	101	88	68	.733	0	4	-2	-4	*C/O	1.3
1968	LA-N	144	474	37	135	27	5	4	53	46	76	.285	.351	.388	.739	134	13	18	91	116	66	.673	1	4	-2	11	*C	3.6
1969	LA-N	134	445	46	117	18	3	6	39	48	58	.263	.337	.357	.695	96	-2	-2	99	88	55	.624	0	3	-2	-5	*C	0.0
1970	LA-N	112	325	47	93	16	6	10	47	32	35	.286	.354	.465	.818	131	7	12	90	101	54	.790	3	0	1	-18	*C	0.0
1971	LA-N	84	202	23	54	5	0	5	32	25	30	.267	.354	.366	.720	106	2	2	99	146	26	.652	0	2	-1	-4	C	-0.1
1972	Det-A	59	121	7	25	5	2	2	13	15	14	.207	.294	.331	.625	76	-2	-4	113	118	12	.561	0	1	-1	2	C	-0.1
Total	12	1294	3935	461	1011	153	31	134	504	477	593	.257	.342	.414	.756	114	68	74	99	103	567	.729	14	30	-14	-21	*C/O1	9.3
■ NEWT HALLIDAY	Halliday, Newton Reese b: 6/18/1896, Chicago, Ill. d: 4/6/18, Great Lakes, Ill. BR/TR, 6'1", 175 lbs. Deb: 8/19/16																											
1916	Pit-N	1	1	0	0	0	0	0	0	0	1	.000	.000	.000	.000	-96	-0	-0	105	0	0	.000	0			0	/1	0.0
■ JOCKO HALLIGAN	Halligan, William E. b: 12/8/1868, Avon, N.Y. d: 2/13/45, Buffalo, N.Y. 5'9", 166 lbs. Deb: 5/13/1890																											
1890	Buf-P	57	211	28	53	9	2	3	33	20	19	.251	.319	.355	.674	89	-6	-2	92	110	27	.652	7			1	OC	-0.2
1891	Cin-N	61	247	43	77	13	6	3	44	24	25	.312	.375	.449	.824	156	13	16	91	94	45	.829	5			-3	O	0.8
1892	Cin-N	26	101	14	29	4	0	2	12	12	9	.287	.363	.386	.749	124	4	3	103	79	16	.750	3			0	O	0.3
	Bal-N	46	178	38	47	4	7	2	43	30	24	.264	.376	.399	.775	137	9	9	100	151	30	.847	8			0	O1/C	0.8
	Yr	72	279	52	76	8	7	4	55	42	33	.272	.372	.394	.766	132	12	12	101	126	46	.813	11			0		1.1
Total	3	190	737	123	206	30	15	10	132	86	77	.280	.358	.402	.760	127	19	26	95	111	117	.770	23			-3	O/C1	1.7
■ ED HALLINAN	Hallinan, Edward S. b: 8/23/1888, San Francisco, Cal d: 8/24/40, San Francisco, Cal BR/TR, 5'9", 168 lbs. Deb: 5/13/11																											
1911	StL-A	52	169	15	35	3	1	0	14	14		.207	.268	.237	.504	43	-13	-12	95	118	11	.433	4			-1	S2/3	-0.9
1912	StL-A	28	86	11	19	2	0	0	1	5		.221	.272	.244	.516	48	-6	-6	99	16	7	.448	3			-1	S	-0.3
Total	2	80	255	26	54	5	1	0	15	19		.212	.269	.239	.508	45	-19	-18	96	84	18	.438	7			-2	/S23	-1.2
■ JIMMY HALLINAN	Hallinan, James H. b: 5/27/1849, Ireland d: 10/28/1879, Chicago, Ill. BL/TL, 5'9", 172 lbs. Deb: 7/26/1871																											
1871	Kek-n	5	25	7	5							.200															/S	
1875	Wes-n	13	58	11	14							.241															S	
	Mut-n	44	204	30	61							.299															S/3	
	Yr	57	262	41	75							.286																
1876	NY-N	54	240	45	67	7	6	2	36	2	4	.279	.285	.383	.668	139	5	10	87	119	27	.543				-10	*S/2O	0.0
1877	Cin-N	16	73	18	27	1	1	0	7	1	1	.370	.378	.411	.789	182	4	6	82	68	12	.674				-7	2	0.0
	Chi-N	19	89	17	25	4	1	0	11	4	2	.281	.312	.348	.660	109	1	1	98	104	10	.547				1	O	0.1
	Yr	35	162	35	52	5	2	0	18	5	3	.321	.341	.377	.718	139	5	7	91	89	21	.600				-6		0.1
1878	Chi-N	16	67	14	19	3	0	0	2	5	6	.284	.333	.328	.662	109	1	1	108	33	8	.563				0	O/2	0.1
	Ind-N	3	12	0	3	2	0	0	1	0	2	.250	.250	.417	.667	134	0	0	87	69	1	.556				0	/O	0.0
	Yr	19	79	14	22	5	0	0	3	5	8	.278	.321	.342	.663	113	2	1	105	40	9	.561				0		0.1
Total	2 n	62	287	48	80							.279															/O	
Total	3	108	481	94	141	17	8	2	57	12	15	.293	.310	.374	.685	134	11	18	91	95	57	.565				-16	S/O23	0.2
■ BILL HALLMAN	Hallman, William Harry b: 3/15/1876, Philadelphia, Pa. d: 4/23/50, Philadelphia, Pa. Deb: 4/25/01																											
1901	Mil-A	139	549	70	135	27	6	2	47	41		.246	.298	.328	.626	79	-18	-14	95	77	59	.563	12			2	*O	-1.1
1903	Chi-A	63	207	29	43	7	4	0	18	31		.208	.311	.280	.591	87	-4	-2	92	114	22	.610	11			3	O	-0.1
1906	Pit-N	23	89	12	24	3	1	1	6	15		.270	.375	.360	.735	126	4	3	104	54	13	.769	3			1	O	0.4
1907	Pit-N	94	302	39	67	6	2	0	15	33		.222	.299	.255	.553	72	-7	-9	105	75	30	.557	21			8	O	-0.4
Total	4	319	1147	150	269	43	13	3	86	120		.235	.307	.303	.610	82	-25	-21	98	81	124	.585	47			14	O	-1.2
■ BILL HALLMAN	Hallman, William Wilson b: 3/31/1867, Pittsburgh, Pa. d: 9/11/20, Philadelphia, Pa. BR/TR, 5'8", Deb: 1888 M																											
1888	Phi-N	18	63	5	13	4	1	0	6	1	12	.206	.219	.302	.520	58	-2	-3	114	113	4	.420	1			0	C/2OS3	-0.2
1889	Phi-N	119	462	67	117	21	8	2	60	36	54	.253	.313	.346	.659	82	-9	-13	104	110	58	.638	20			8	*S2/C	0.0
1890	Phi-P	84	356	59	95	16	7	1	37	33	24	.267	.338	.360	.697	86	-6	-7	102	74	46	.659	6			0	OC23/S	-0.5
1891	Phi-a	141	587	112	166	21	13	6	69	38	56	.283	.332	.394	.725	107	5	3	103	77	85	.694	18			-1	*2	1.0
1892	Phi-N	138	586	106	171	27	10	2	84	32	52	.292	.335	.382	.717	114	11	8	104	99	83	.677	19			-25	*2	-1.4
1893	Phi-N	132	596	119	183	28	7	5	76	51	27	.307	.367	.403	.769	107	5	5	100	78	98	.770	22			-18	*21	-1.0
1894	Phi-N	119	505	107	156	19	7	0	66	36	15	.309	.360	.374	.734	83	-17	-12	95	102	83	.759	36			-22	*2	-1.9
1895	Phi-N	124	539	94	169	26	5	1	91	34	20	.314	.359	.386	.745	95	-5	-3	99	128	82	.708	16			3	*2/S	0.5
1896	Phi-N	120	469	82	150	21	3	2	83	45	23	.320	.382	.390	.772	104	5	4	102	134	78	.771	16			5	*2/P	1.0
1897	Phi-N	31	126	16	33	3	0	0	15	8		.262	.326	.286	.612	67	-6	-5	96	117	12	.527	1			-7	2	-0.8
	StL-N	79	298	31	66	6	2	0	26	24		.221	.288	.255	.543	49	-22	-19	93	102	26	.500	12			-3	2/1M	-1.2
	Yr	110	424	47	99	9	2	0	41	32		.233	.300	.264	.564	55	-28	-24	94	107	38	.508	13			-10		-2.0
1898	Bro-N	134	509	57	124	10	7	2	63	29		.244	.291	.303	.594	77	-18	-14	95	126	49	.512	9			-2	*23	-1.0
1901	Cle-A	5	19	2	4	0	0	0	3	2		.211	.286	.211	.496	43	-1	-1	95	251	1	.400	0			-1	/S	-0.1
	Phi-N	123	445	46	82	13	5	0	38	26		.184	.229	.236	.465	36	-35	-37	103	124	28	.397	13			-9	23	-3.6

YEAR	TM/L	G	AB	R	H	2B	3B	HR	RBI	BB	SO	AVG	OBP	SLG	PRO	/A	BR	/A	PF	CHI	RC	TA	SB	CS	SBR	FR	POS	TPR
1902	Phi-N	73	254	14	63	8	4	0	35	14		.248	.287	.311	.598	82	-4	-6	105	156	26	.534	9			1	3	-0.1
1903	Phi-N	63	198	20	42	11	2	0	17	16		.212	.271	.288	.559	66	-10	-8	92	96	16	.481	2			-1	23/1OS	-0.6
Total	14	1503	6012	937	1634	234	81	21	769	425	283	.272	.325	.348	.673	87	-109	-110	100	107	776	.632	200			-71	*23S/OC1P	-9.9
■ **JIM HALPIN**	Halpin, James Nathaniel b: 10/4/1863, England d: 1/4/1893, Boston, Mass. Deb: 6/15/1882																											
1882	Wor-N	2	8	0	0	0	0	0	0	0	2	.000	.000	.000	.000	-99	-2	-2	100	0	0	.000				0	/3	-0.1
1884	Was-U	46	168	24	31	3	0	0		2		.185	.194	.202	.396	35	-11	-10	97	0	7	.263	0			-7	S/3	-1.4
1885	Det-N	15	54	3	7	2	0	0	1	1	12	.130	.145	.167	.312	1	-6	-6	97	39	1	.213				0	S	-0.4
Total	3	63	230	27	38	5	0	0	1	3	14	.165	.176	.187	.363	22	-19	-18	97	9	8	.240				-7	/S3	-1.9
■ **AL HALT**	Halt, Alva William b: 11/23/1890, Sandusky, Ohio d: 1/22/73, Sandusky, Ohio BR/TR, 6', 180 lbs. Deb: 5/29/14																											
1914	Bro-F	80	261	26	61	6	2	3	25	13	39	.234	.270	.307	.577	64	-12	-12	101	101	26	.520	11			4	S/2O	-0.3
1915	Bro-F	151	524	41	131	22	7	3	64	39	79	.250	.302	.336	.638	91	-8	-7	98	127	62	.598	20			-5	*3S	-0.5
1918	Cle-A	26	69	9	12	2	0	0	1	9	12	.174	.269	.203	.472	39	-5	-5	108	26	4	.474	4			0	3/2S1	-0.5
Total	3	257	854	76	204	30	9	6	90	61	130	.239	.290	.316	.606	78	-25	-24	99	111	92	.563	35			-0	3S/21O	-1.3
■ **RALPH HAM**	Ham, Ralph A. b: 1850, Troy, N.Y. d: 2/13/05, Troy, N.Y. 5'8", 158 lbs. Deb: 5/06/1871																											
1871	Rok-n	25	118	25	26							.220															O/2S	
1872	Man-n	1	6	0	2							.333															/S	
Total	2 n	26	124	25	28							.226															/S	
■ **CHARLIE HAMBURG**	Hamburg, Charles M. (born Charles M. Hambrick) b: 11/22/1863, Louisville, Ky. d: 5/18/31, Union, N.J. 6', 175 lbs. Deb: 4/18/1890																											
1890	Lou-a	133	485	93	132	22	2	3		69		.272	.370	.344	.714	106	11	5	107	0	81	.816	46			-0	*O	-0.1
■ **JIM HAMBY**	Hamby, James Sanford "Cracker" b: 7/29/1897, Wilkesboro, N.C. BR/TR, 6', 170 lbs. Deb: 9/20/26																											
1926	NY-N	1	3	0	0	0	0	0	0	0	0	.000	.000	.000	.000	-99	-1	-1	98	0	0	.000	0			0	/C	0.0
1927	NY-N	21	52	6	10	0	1	0	5	7	7	.192	.288	.231	.519	40	-4	-4	100	146	4	.476	1			-2	C	-0.4
Total	2	22	55	6	10	0	1	0	5	7	7	.182	.274	.218	.492	33	-5	-5	100	139	4	.444	1			-2	/C	-0.4
■ **DARRYL HAMILTON**	Hamilton, Darryl Quinn b: 12/3/64, Baton Rouge, La. BL/TR, 6', 180 lbs. Deb: 6/03/88																											
1988	Mil-A	44	103	14	19	4	0	1	11	12	9	.184	.276	.252	.528	47	-7	-7	103	151	8	.517	7	3	0	-1	O/D	-0.8
■ **JEFF HAMILTON**	Hamilton, Jeffrey Robert b: 3/19/64, Flint, Mich. BR/TR, 6'3", 190 lbs. Deb: 6/28/86																											
1986	LA-N	71	147	22	33	5	0	5	19	2	43	.224	.235	.361	.595	66	-8	-7	94	111	12	.470	0	0	0	3	3/S	-0.5
1987	LA-N	35	83	5	18	3	0	0	1	7	22	.217	.286	.253	.539	48	-7	-6	92	19	6	.439	0	1	-1	2	3/S	-0.3
1988	LA-N	111	309	34	73	14	2	6	33	10	51	.236	.269	.353	.622	73	-10	-12	106	104	27	.500	0	2	-1	-11	*3/1S	-2.5
Total	3	217	539	61	124	22	2	11	53	19	116	.230	.263	.340	.602	67	-25	-25	101	92	45	.486	0	3	-2	-6	3/S1	-3.3
■ **TOM HAMILTON**	Hamilton, Thomas Ball "Ham" b: 9/29/25, Altoona, Kan. d: 11/29/73, Tyler, Tex. BL/TR, 6'4", 213 lbs. Deb: 9/04/52																											
1952	Phi-A	9	10	1	2	1	0	0	1	1	1	.200	.273	.300	.573	54	-1	-1	111	124	1	.500	0	0	0	0	/1	0.0
1953	Phi-A	58	56	8	11	2	0	0	5	7	11	.196	.286	.232	.518	40	-5	-5	102	142	4	.426	0	0	0	-1	/1O	-0.5
Total	2	67	66	9	13	3	0	0	6	8	12	.197	.284	.242	.526	42	-5	-5	103	140	5	.436	0	0	0	-1	/1O	-0.5
■ **BILLY HAMILTON**	Hamilton, William Robert "Sliding Billy" b: 2/16/1866, Newark, N.J. d: 12/16/40, Worcester, Mass. BL/TR, 5'6", 165 lbs. Deb: 1888																											
1888	KC-a	35	129	21	34	4	4	0	11	4		.264	.307	.357	.663	109	2	1	106	73	20	.768	19			-3	O	-0.2
1889	KC-a	137	534	144	161	17	12	3	77	87	41	.301	.413	.395	.808	126	28	22	106	88	136	1.134	**111**			-8	*O	0.7
1890	Phi-N	123	496	133	161	13	9	2	49	83	37	.325	.430	.399	.829	134	33	27	108	63	**132**	**1.170**	**102**			3	*O	2.4
1891	Phi-N	133	527	**141**	**179**	23	7	2	60	**102**	28	**.340**	**.453**	.421	.874	166	**46**	**50**	95	66	**155**	**1.270**	**111**			5	*O	4.2
1892	Phi-N	139	554	132	183	21	7	3	53	81	29	.330	.423	.410	.833	148	40	37	104	61	123	1.005	57			13	*O	4.1
1893	Phi-N	82	355	110	135	22	7	5	44	63	7	**.380**	**.490**	.524	**1.014**	**172**	41	41	100	52	115	**1.386**	43			2	O	3.2
1894	Phi-N	129	544	**192**	220	25	15	4	87	**126**	17	.404	**.523**	.528	1.050	164	61	**68**	95	69	206	1.605	**98**			4	*O	4.7
1895	Phi-N	123	517	**166**	201	22	6	7	74	**96**	30	.389	.490	.495	.985	159	51	52	99	64	**177**	1.443	**97**			-4	*O	3.0
1896	Bos-N	131	523	152	191	24	9	3	52	**110**	29	.365	**.477**	.463	.940	140	47	39	108	52	159	1.316	83			-13	*O	1.4
1897	Bos-N	127	507	**152**	174	17	5	3	61	**105**		.343	.461	.414	.875	126	34	27	107	70	130	1.162	66			-6	*O	1.0
1898	Bos-N	110	417	110	154	16	5	3	50	87		.369	**.480**	.453	**.933**	**165**	45	43	104	66	120	**1.262**	54			-18	*O	1.7
1899	Bos-N	84	297	63	92	7	1	1	33	72		.310	.446	.350	.796	117	15	13	105	91	56	.956	19			-3	O	0.4
1900	Bos-N	136	520	103	173	20	5	1	47	107		.333	**.447**	.396	.843	114	33	16	120	61	109	.994	32			1	*O	0.4
1901	Bos-N	102	348	71	100	11	2	3	38	64		.287	.398	.356	.754	109	13	8	112	101	59	.839	20			-18	O	-2.0
Total	14	1591	6268	1690	2158	242	94	40	736	1187	218	.344	.455	.432	.887	141	491	442	105	68	1698	1.190	912			-46	*O	25.0
■ **KEN HAMLIN**	Hamlin, Kenneth Lee b: 5/18/35, Detroit, Mich. BR/TR, 5'10", 170 lbs. Deb: 6/17/57																											
1957	Pit-N	2	1	0	0	0	0	0	0	0	0	.000	.000	.000	.000	-99	-0	-0	94	0	0	.000	0	0	0	0	/S	0.0
1959	Pit-N	3	8	1	1	0	0	0	0	2	1	.125	.300	.125	.425	18	-1	-1	103	0	0	.429	0	0	0	0	/S	0.0
1960	KC-A	140	428	51	96	10	2	2	24	44	48	.224	.298	.271	.569	56	-26	-25	99	77	35	.468	1	1	-0	-33	*S	-4.9
1961	LA-A	42	91	4	19	3	0	1	5	11	9	.209	.301	.275	.576	49	-6	-7	111	70	7	.468	0	1	-1	2	S	-0.2
1962	Was-A	98	292	29	74	12	0	3	22	22	22	.253	.306	.325	.631	69	-12	-13	101	84	28	.537	7	7	-2	-8	S/2	-1.7
1965	Was-A	117	362	45	99	21	1	4	22	33	45	.273	.336	.370	.706	100	0	0	100	62	47	.649	8	2	1	-6	2S/3	0.1
1966	Was-A	66	158	13	34	7	1	1	16	13	21	.215	.275	.291	.566	66	-8	-7	95	137	12	.458	1	0	0	-2	2/3	-0.4
Total	7	468	1340	143	323	53	4	11	89	125	146	.241	.307	.311	.618	71	-52	-52	100	80	129	.543	17	11	-2	-47	S2/3	-7.1
■ **STEVE HAMMOND**	Hammond, Steven Benjamin b: 5/9/57, Atlanta, Ga. BL/TR, 6'2", 190 lbs. Deb: 6/28/82																											
1982	KC-A	46	126	14	29	5	1	1	11	4	18	.230	.254	.310	.563	54	-8	-8	100	105	8	.410	0	1	-1	2	O/D	-0.8
■ **JACK HAMMOND**	Hammond, Walter Charles "Wobby" b: 2/26/1891, Amsterdam, N.Y. d: 3/4/42, Kenosha, Wis. BR/TR, 5'11", 170 lbs. Deb: 4/15/15																											
1915	Cle-A	35	84	9	18	2	1	0	4	1	19	.214	.224	.262	.485	44	-6	-6	104	62	5	.343	0	1	-1	-2	2	-0.9
1922	Cle-A	1	4	1	1	0	0	0	0	0	0	.250	.250	.250	.500	30	-0	-0	102	0	0	.333	0	0	0	0	/2	0.0
	Pit-N	9	11	3	3	0	0	0	0	1	0	.273	.333	.273	.606	56	-1	-1	104	0	1	.500	0	0	0	-1	/2	-0.1
Total	2	45	99	13	22	2	1	0	4	2	19	.222	.238	.263	.500	44	-7	-7	104	52	7	.359	0	1	-1	-3	/2	-1.0
■ **GRANNY HAMNER**	Hamner, Granville Wilbur b: 4/26/27, Richmond, Va. BR/TR, 5'10", 163 lbs. Deb: 9/14/44																											
1944	Phi-N	21	77	6	19	1	0	0	5	3	7	.247	.275	.260	.535	51	-5	-5	100	91	6	.390	0			2	S	0.0
1945	Phi-N	14	41	3	7	2	0	0	6	1	3	.171	.190	.220	.410	14	-5	-5	96	231	2	.286	0			2	S	-0.1
1946	Phi-N	2	7	0	1	0	0	0	0	0	3	.143	.143	.143	.286	-20	-1	-1	95	0	0	.167	0			0	/S	0.0
1947	Phi-N	2	7	1	2	0	0	0	0	1	0	.286	.375	.286	.661	78	-0	-0	100	0	1	.500	0			0	/S	0.0
1948	Phi-N	129	446	42	116	21	5	3	48	22	39	.260	.298	.350	.648	79	-17	-13	94	109	45	.535	2			-10	2S/3	-1.3
1949	Phi-N	154	662	83	174	32	5	6	53	25	47	.263	.290	.353	.643	71	-28	-28	101	70	63	.522	6			-1	*S	-1.1
1950	Phi-N	157	637	78	172	27	5	11	82	39	35	.270	.314	.380	.694	84	-18	-16	97	122	74	.595	2			-5	*S	-0.4
1951	Phi-N	150	589	61	150	23	7	9	72	29	32	.255	.290	.363	.653	77	-22	-20	97	118	58	.545	10	5	0	-4	*S	-1.1
1952	Phi-N	151	596	74	164	30	5	17	87	27	51	.275	.307	.428	.734	101	-1	-2	101	118	75	.638	7	3	0	-1	*S	0.1
1953	Phi-N	154	609	90	168	30	8	21	92	32	28	.276	.313	.455	.768	98	-5	-4	99	112	84	.680	2	1	0	-10	2S	-0.3
1954	Phi-N	152	596	83	178	39	11	13	89	53	44	.299	.356	.466	.822	114	10	11	99	117	98	.767	1	2	-1	-21	*2/S	-0.1
1955	Phi-N	104	405	57	104	12	4	5	43	41	30	.257	.327	.343	.670	76	-12	-13	102	109	46	.580	0	1	-1	-20	2S	-2.5
1956	Phi-N	122	401	42	90	24	3	4	42	30	42	.224	.278	.329	.608	66	-21	-19	94	123	35	.506	2	0	1	-10	*S2/P	-1.8
1957	Phi-N	133	502	59	114	19	5	10	62	34	42	.227	.276	.345	.621	67	-25	-24	98	134	43	.510	3	1	0	-34	*2/SP	-4.7
1958	Phi-N	35	133	18	40	7	3	2	18	8	16	.301	.340	.444	.784	107	1	1	98	117	17	.663	0	0	0	-3	32/S	0.0
1959	Phi-N	21	64	10	19	4	0	2	6	5	5	.297	.348	.453	.801	112	1	1	99	69	9	.708	0	1	-1	-0	S/3	0.1
	Cle-A	27	67	4	11	1	1	1	3	1	8	.164	.176	.254	.430	17	-8	-7	97	59	3	.310	0	0	0	-2	S/23	-0.8
1962	KC-A	3	0	0	0	0	0	0	0	0	0	—	—	—	—	—	0	0	100	—	—	—	0	0	0	0	/P	0.0
Total	17	1531	5839	711	1529	272	62	104	708	351	432	.262	.304	.383	.688	84	-157	-144	98	112	660	.608	35	14		-117	S2/3P	-14.0

YEAR	TM/L	G	AB	R	H	2B	3B	HR	RBI	BB	SO	AVG	OBP	SLG	PRO	/A	BR	/A	PF	CHI	RC	TA	SB	CS	SBR	FR	POS	TPR
■ **GARVIN HAMNER**	Hamner, Wesley Garvin b: 3/18/24, Richmond, Va. BR/TR, 5'11", 172 lbs. Deb: 4/17/45																											
1945	Phi-N	32	101	12	20	3	0	0	5	7	9	.198	.250	.228	.478	35	-9	-9	96	75	6	.381	2			0	2/S3	-0.5
■ **IKE HAMPTON**	Hampton, Isaac Bernard b: 8/22/51, Camden, S.C. BB/TR, 6', 165 lbs. Deb: 9/12/74																											
1974	NY-N	4	4	0	0	0	0	0	1	0	1	.000	.000	.000	.000	-99	-1	-1	99	0	0	.000	0	0	0	0	/C	0.0
1975	Cal-A	31	66	8	10	3	0	0	4	7	19	.152	.243	.197	.440	27	-6	-6	95	118	4	.368	0	0	0	-3	C/S3	-0.7
1976	Cal-A	3	2	0	0	0	0	0	0	0	0	.000	.000	.000	.000	-99	-0	-0	92	0	0	.000	0	0	0	0	/CS	0.0
1977	Cal-A	52	44	5	13	1	0	3	9	2	10	.295	.340	.523	.863	139	2	2	95	111	7	.788	0	0	0	-7	C/D	-0.2
1978	Cal-A	19	14	2	3	0	1	1	4	2	7	.214	.313	.571	.884	141	1	1	102	144	3	1.000	1	0	0	-0	C/1D	0.1
1979	Cal-A	4	5	0	2	0	0	0	0	0	1	.400	.400	.400	.800	126	0	0	93	0	1	.667	0	0	0	0	/1	0.0
Total	6	113	135	15	28	4	1	4	18	11	38	.207	.277	.341	.618	75	-5	-5	95	110	14	.561	1	0	0	-10	/CD1S3	-0.8
■ **BERT HAMRIC**	Hamric, Odbert Herman b: 3/1/28, Clarksburg, W.Va. d: 8/8/84, Springboro, Ohio BL/TR, 6', 165 lbs. Deb: 4/24/55																											
1955	Bro-N	2	1	0	0	0	0	0	0	0	1	.000	.000	.000	.000	-96	-0	-0	104	0	0	.000	0	0	0	0	H	0.0
1958	Bal-A	8	8	0	1	0	0	0	0	0	6	.125	.125	.125	.250	-33	-1	-1	94	0	0	.143	0	0	0	0	H	0.0
Total	2	10	9	0	1	0	0	0	0	0	7	.111	.111	.111	.222	-41	-2	-2	95	0	0	.125	0	0	0	0		0.0
■ **RAY HAMRICK**	Hamrick, Raymond Bernard b: 8/1/21, Nashville, Tenn. BR/TR, 5'11.5", 160 lbs. Deb: 8/14/43																											
1943	Phi-N	44	160	12	32	3	1	0	9	8	28	.200	.238	.231	.469	38	-13	-12	94	89	9	.344	0			-4	2S	-1.4
1944	Phi-N	74	292	22	60	10	1	1	23	23	34	.205	.268	.257	.525	48	-20	-20	100	112	20	.423	1			11	S	0.1
Total	2	118	452	34	92	13	2	1	32	31	62	.204	.258	.248	.506	45	-33	-32	98	104	29	.398	1			8	/S2	-1.3
■ **BUDDY HANCKEN**	Hancken, Morris Medlock b: 8/30/14, Birmingham, Ala. BR/TR, 6'1", 175 lbs. Deb: 5/14/40 C																											
1940	Phi-A	1	0	0	0	0	0	0	0	0	0	—	—	—	—	—	0	0	96	—	—	—	0	0	0	0	/C	0.0
■ **FRED HANCOCK**	Hancock, Fred James b: 3/28/20, Allenport, Pa. d: 3/12/86, Clearwater, Fla. BR/TR, 5'8", 170 lbs. Deb: 4/26/49																											
1949	Chi-A	39	52	7	7	2	1	0	9	8	9	.135	.262	.212	.474	27	-6	-5	98	281	3	.417	0	1	-1	-0	S/3O	-0.5
■ **GARRY HANCOCK**	Hancock, Ronald Garry b: 1/23/54, Tampa, Fla. BL/TL, 6', 175 lbs. Deb: 7/16/78																											
1978	Bos-A	38	80	10	18	3	0	0	4	1	12	.225	.235	.262	.497	37	-6	-7	107	75	5	.349	0	0	0	-0	OD	-0.7
1980	Bos-A	46	115	9	33	6	0	4	19	3	11	.287	.305	.443	.749	100	-0	-0	102	118	14	.628	0	3	-2	-1	OD	-0.3
1981	Bos-A	26	45	4	7	3	0	0	3	2	4	.156	.191	.222	.414	18	-5	-5	106	117	2	.300	0	0	0	0	/OD	-0.4
1982	Bos-A	11	14	3	0	0	0	0	0	1	1	.000	.067	.000	.067	-72	-3	-4	110	0	0	.071	0	0	0	-2	/O	-0.5
1983	Oak-A	101	256	29	70	7	3	8	30	5	13	.273	.290	.418	.708	96	-4	-2	96	90	30	.608	2	0	1	-10	O1/D	-1.2
1984	Oak-A	51	60	2	13	2	0	0	8	0	1	.217	.217	.250	.467	31	-6	-5	92	213	2	.294	0	0	0	-5	O/1PD	-1.0
Total	6	273	570	57	141	21	3	12	64	12	42	.247	.264	.358	.622	71	-24	-24	99	106	53	.502	2	3	-1	-18	O/D1P	-4.1
■ **MIKE HANDIBOE**	Handiboe, Aloysius James "Coalyard Mike" b: 7/21/1887, Washington, D.C. d: 1/31/53, Savannah, Ga. BL/TL, 5'10", 155 lbs. Deb: 9/08/11																											
1911	NY-A	5	15	0	1	0	0	0	0	2		.067	.176	.067	.243	-28	-3	-3	111	0	0	.214	0			-0	/O	-0.3
■ **GENE HANDLEY**	Handley, Eugene Louis b: 11/25/14, Kennett, Mo. BR/TR, 5'10.5", 165 lbs. Deb: 4/16/46																											
1946	Phi-A	89	251	31	63	8	5	0	21	22	25	.251	.311	.323	.634	74	-8	-9	104	99	26	.563	8	3	1	-13	2/3S	-1.6
1947	Phi-A	36	90	10	23	2	1	0	8	10	2	.256	.330	.300	.630	76	-3	-3	100	109	9	.543	1	0	0	-2	23/S	-0.3
Total	2	125	341	41	86	10	6	0	29	32	27	.252	.316	.317	.633	75	-10	-12	103	101	35	.571	9	3	1	-15	/23S	-1.9
■ **LEE HANDLEY**	Handley, Lee Elmer "Jeep" b: 7/31/13, Clarion, Iowa d: 4/8/70, Pittsburgh, Pa. BR/TR, 5'7", 160 lbs. Deb: 4/15/36																											
1936	Cin-N	24	78	10	24	1	0	2	8	7	16	.308	.365	.397	.762	109	1	1	97	77	12	.732	3			2	2/3	0.5
1937	Pit-N	127	480	59	120	21	12	3	37	37	40	.250	.305	.363	.668	79	-14	-15	102	74	55	.591	5			-9	*2/3	-1.8
1938	Pit-N	139	570	91	153	25	8	6	51	53	31	.268	.332	.372	.704	93	-5	-5	100	77	72	.635	7			8	*3	0.0
1939	Pit-N	101	376	43	107	14	5	1	42	32	20	.285	.341	.356	.697	88	-6	-6	100	115	45	.651	**17**			0	*3	-0.2
1940	Pit-N	98	302	50	85	7	4	1	19	27	16	.281	.340	.341	.681	93	-4	-2	95	66	37	.626	7			3	3/2	0.0
1941	Pit-N	124	459	59	132	18	4	0	33	35	22	.288	.338	.344	.682	90	-4	-6	103	77	53	.615	16			-4	*3	-0.8
1944	Pit-N	40	86	7	19	2	0	0	5	3	5	.221	.247	.244	.491	37	-7	-8	105	85	4	.342	1			-1	23/S	-0.5
1945	Pit-N	98	312	39	93	16	2	1	32	20	16	.298	.340	.372	.712	95	-1	-3	103	93	40	.638	7			10	3	0.6
1946	Pit-N	116	416	43	99	8	7	1	28	29	20	.238	.289	.298	.587	65	-19	-20	103	84	36	.483	4			9	*3/2	-1.0
1947	Phi-N	101	277	17	70	10	3	0	42	24	18	.253	.312	.310	.623	66	-13	-13	100	181	26	.514	1			-5	3/2S	-2.0
Total	10	968	3356	418	902	122	45	15	297	267	204	.269	.323	.345	.669	83	-73	-77	101	91	380	.608	68			13	32/S	-5.2
■ **HARRY HANEBRINK**	Hanebrink, Harry Aloysius b: 11/12/27, St.Louis, Mo. BL/TR, 6', 165 lbs. Deb: 5/03/53																											
1953	Mil-N	51	80	8	19	1	1	1	8	6	8	.237	.291	.313	.603	61	-5	-4	94	111	8	.525	1	0	0	-3	2/3	-0.5
1957	Mil-N	6	7	0	2	0	0	0	0	1	2	.286	.375	.286	.661	90	-0	-0	90	0	1	.600	0	0	0	0	/3	0.0
1958	Mil-N	63	133	14	25	3	0	4	10	13	9	.188	.270	.301	.571	57	-10	-8	89	79	10	.482	0	1	-1	-1	O/3	-1.0
1959	Phi-N	57	97	10	25	3	1	1	7	2	12	.258	.273	.340	.613	62	-5	-5	99	79	8	.467	0	0	0	-1	2/3O	-0.5
Total	4	177	317	32	71	7	2	6	25	22	31	.224	.279	.315	.594	61	-20	-17	93	85	27	.500	1	1	-0	-5	/2O3	-2.0
■ **FRED HANEY**	Haney, Fred Girard "Pudge" b: 4/25/1898, Albuquerque, N.Mex d: 11/9/77, Beverly Hills, Cal. BR/TR, 5'6", 170 lbs. Deb: 4/18/22 MC																											
1922	Det-A	81	213	41	75	7	4	0	25	32	14	.352	.439	.423	.862	128	10	11	98	99	40	.869	3	7	-3	3	31/S	1.5
1923	Det-A	142	503	85	142	13	4	4	67	45	23	.282	.347	.348	.695	86	-11	-9	97	125	64	.648	12	5	1	-1	23S	0.1
1924	Det-A	86	256	54	79	11	1	1	30	39	13	.309	.400	.371	.771	100	2	2	100	101	41	.779	7	4	-0	0	3/S2	0.7
1925	Det-A	114	398	84	111	15	3	0	40	66	29	.279	.384	.332	.716	84	-7	-7	99	103	58	.733	11	1	3	3	*3	0.4
1926	Bos-A	138	462	47	102	15	7	0	52	74	28	.221	.330	.284	.613	60	-25	-26	101	138	50	.598	13	6	0	6	*3	-0.6
1927	Bos-A	47	116	23	32	4	1	3	12	25	14	.276	.404	.405	.809	117	3	4	95	71	20	.905	4	0	1	-1	3/O	0.5
	Chi-N	4	3	0	0	0	0	0	0	0	0	.000	.000	.000	.000	-99	-1	-1	100	0	0	.000	0			0	H	0.0
1929	StL-N	10	26	4	3	1	1	0	2	1	2	.115	.179	.231	.409	1	-4	-4	98	114	1	.348	0			-1	/3	-0.3
Total	7	622	1977	338	544	66	21	8	228	282	123	.275	.368	.342	.710	86	-35	-30	99	114	274	.699	50	23		9	3/2S10	2.3
■ **LARRY HANEY**	Haney, Wallace Larry b: 11/19/42, Charlottesville, Va BR/TR, 6'2", 195 lbs. Deb: 7/27/66 C																											
1966	Bal-A	20	56	3	9	1	0	1	3	1	15	.161	.190	.232	.422	20	-6	-6	101	79	3	.319	0	0	0	0	C	-0.4
1967	Bal-A	58	164	13	44	11	0	3	20	6	28	.268	.294	.390	.684	106	-0	1	95	114	18	.573	1	0	0	0	C	0.5
1968	Bal-A	38	89	5	21	3	1	1	5	0	19	.236	.236	.326	.562	67	-4	-4	102	67	6	.414	0	0	0	-3	C	-0.5
1969	Sea-A	22	59	3	15	3	0	2	7	6	12	.254	.323	.407	.730	105	0	0	98	94	7	.660	1	1	-0	0	C	0.1
	Oak-A	53	86	8	13	4	0	2	12	7	19	.151	.223	.267	.491	40	-8	-7	92	166	4	.392	0	0	0	-8	C	-1.1
	Yr	75	145	11	28	7	0	4	19	13	31	.193	.264	.324	.588	68	-7	-6	94	146	11	.500	1	1	-0	-8		-1.0
1970	Oak-A	2	2	2	0	0	0	0	0	2	1	.000	.500	.000	.500	51	0	0	97	0	0	1.000	0	0	0	0	/C	0.0
1972	Oak-A	5	4	0	0	0	0	0	0	0	1	.000	.000	.000	.000	-99	-1	-1	97	0	0	.000	0	0	0	0	/C2	0.0
1973	Oak-A	2	2	0	1	0	0	0	0	0	0	.500	.500	.500	1.000	209	0	0	87	0	0	.500	0	0	0	0	/C	0.0
	StL-N	2	1	0	0	0	0	0	0	0	1	.000	.000	.000	.000	-99	-0	-0	91	0	0	.000	0	0	0	0	/C	0.0
1974	Oak-A	76	121	12	20	4	0	2	3	3	18	.165	.185	.248	.433	24	-12	-12	100	33	5	.330	1	0	0	-9	C/31	-1.9
1975	Oak-A	47	26	3	5	0	0	1	2	1	4	.192	.222	.308	.530	52	-2	-2	93	70	2	.429	0	0	0	-5	C/3	-0.5
1976	Oak-A	88	177	12	40	2	0	0	10	13	26	.226	.283	.237	.520	53	-10	-10	100	91	12	.392	0	1	-1	-14	C	-2.2
1977	Mil-A	63	127	7	29	2	0	0	10	5	30	.228	.258	.244	.502	40	-11	-10	95	128	8	.360	0	0	0	0	C	-0.7
1978	Mil-A	4	5	0	1	0	0	0	1	0	1	.200	.200	.200	.400	12	-1	-1	106	395	0	.250	0	0	0	0	/C	0.0
Total	12	480	919	68	198	30	1	12	73	44	175	.215	.254	.289	.543	57	-54	-51	97	97	66	.437	3	2	-0	-38	C/312	-6.7
■ **CHARLIE HANFORD**	Hanford, Charles Joseph b: 6/3/1881, Tunstall, England d: 7/19/63, Trenton, N.J. BR/TR, 5'6.5", 145 lbs. Deb: 4/13/14																											
1914	Buf-F	155	597	83	174	28	13	13	90	32	81	.291	.328	.447	.775	116	13	10	104	112	103	.794	37			4	*O	0.5
1915	Chi-F	77	179	27	43	4	5	0	22	12	28	.240	.288	.318	.606	82	-5	-4	97	139	20	.581	10			-6	O	-1.3
Total	2	232	776	110	217	32	18	13	112	44	109	.280	.318	.418	.736	108	8	6	103	119	123	.742	47			-3	O	-0.8
■ **PAT HANIFIN**	Hanifin, Patrick James b: 1868, Nova Scotia, Canada d: 11/5/08, Springfield, Mass. Deb: 4/29/1897																											
1897	Bro-N	10	20	4	5	0	0	0	2	1		.250	.375	.250	.625	68	-1	-1	102	117	3	.867	4			0	/O2	0.0

YEAR	TM/L	G	AB	R	H	2B	3B	HR	RBI	BB	SO	AVG	OBP	SLG	PRO	/A	BR	/A	PF	CHI	RC	TA	SB	CS	SBR	FR	POS	TPR
■ **JAY HANKINS**	Hankins, Jay Nelson b: 11/7/35, St.Louis Co., Mo. BL/TR, 5'7", 170 lbs. Deb: 4/15/61																											
1961	KC-A	76	173	23	32	0	3	3	6	8	17	.185	.225	.272	.497	32	-17	-17	102	42	11	.403	2	0	1	-9	O	-2.7
1963	KC-A	10	34	2	6	0	1	1	4	0	3	.176	.176	.324	.500	34	-3	-3	108	120	2	.379	0	1	-1	1	/O	-0.2
Total	2	86	207	25	38	0	4	4	10	8	20	.184	.218	.280	.498	32	-20	-21	103	54	13	.406	2	1	0	-8	/O	-2.9
■ **FRANK HANKINSON**	Hankinson, Frank Edward b: 4/29/1856, New York, N.Y. d: 4/5/11, Palisades Park, N.J BR/TR, 5'11", 168 lbs. Deb: 5/01/1878																											
1878	Chi-N	58	240	38	64	8	3	1	27	5	36	.267	.282	.338	.619	95	1	-2	108	111	23	.489				10	*3/P	0.9
1879	Chi-N	44	171	14	31	4	0	0	8	2	14	.181	.191	.205	.395	29	-12	-14	105	82	7	.264				0	PO/3	0.0
1880	Cle-N	69	263	32	55	7	4	1	19	1	23	.209	.212	.278	.490	65	-10	-9	99	93	16	.356				-10	*3O/P	-1.8
1881	Tro-N	85	321	34	62	15	0	1	19	10	41	.193	.218	.249	.467	46	-19	-19	100	81	18	.347				4	*3/S	-0.7
1883	NY-N	94	337	40	74	13	6	2	30	19	38	.220	.261	.312	.573	73	-10	-10	100	96	28	.471				-5	*3/O	-1.2
1884	NY-N	105	389	44	90	16	7	2	43	23	59	.231	.274	.324	.598	89	-5	-4	98	114	35	.498				-4	*3/O	-1.1
1885	NY-a	94	362	43	81	12	2	2		12		.224	.251	.285	.535	85	-12	-3	84	0	26	.413				18	*3/P	1.8
1886	NY-a	136	522	66	126	14	5	2		49		.241	.306	.299	.605	89	-4	-7	104	0	52	.543	10			24	*3	2.0
1887	NY-a	127	512	79	137	29	11	1		38		.268	.318	.373	.691	108	-4	7	88	0	68	.661	19			5	*3	0.6
1888	KC-a	37	155	20	27	4	1	1	20	11		.174	.229	.232	.461	47	-8	-10	106	132	9	.383	2			0	2/SO31	-0.8
Total	10	849	3272	410	747	122	39	13	166	170	211	.228	.267	.301	.568	79	-85	-71	98	57	283	.470	31			42	3/OP2S1	-0.3
■ **NED HANLON**	Hanlon, Edward Hugh b: 8/22/1857, Montville, Conn. d: 4/14/37, Baltimore, Md. BL/TR, 5'9.5", 170 lbs. Deb: 5/01/1880 M																											
1880	Cle-N	73	280	30	69	10	3	0	32	11	30	.246	.275	.304	.578	97	-1	-1	99	146	24	.455				-3	*O/S	-0.5
1881	Det-N	76	305	63	85	14	8	2	28	22	11	.279	.327	.397	.724	118	9	6	106	74	41	.650				-3	*O/S	0.2
1882	Det-N	82	347	68	80	18	6	5	38	26	25	.231	.284	.360	.644	103	2	2	102	81	36	.566				12	*O/2	1.1
1883	Det-N	100	413	65	100	13	2	1	40	34	44	.242	.300	.291	.590	88	-8	-3	91	108	37	.492				2	*O2	0.2
1884	Det-N	114	450	86	119	18	6	5	39	40	52	.264	.324	.364	.689	124	9	14	94	66	55	.616				11	*O	2.1
1885	Det-N	105	424	93	128	18	8	1	29	47	18	.302	.372	.389	.761	150	23	25	97	52	63	.716				0	*O	2.0
1886	Det-N	126	494	105	116	6	6	4	60	57	39	.235	.314	.296	.610	79	-6	-13	109	131	63	.669	50			-5	*O/2	-1.4
1887	Det-N	118	471	79	129	13	7	4	69	30	24	.274	.320	.357	.677	88	-6	-8	102	121	78	.787	69			-2	*O	-0.6
1888	Det-N	109	459	64	122	6	8	5	39	15	32	.266	.295	.346	.641	108	3	4	98	85	60	.641	38			-8	*O	-0.4
1889	Pit-N	116	461	81	110	14	10	2	37	58	25	.239	.326	.325	.652	94	-9	-0	89	68	68	.749	53			-2	*OM	-0.5
1890	Pit-P	118	472	106	131	16	6	1	44	80	24	.278	.389	.343	.732	107	3	11	92	70	90	.918	65			-5	*OM	0.1
1891	Pit-N	119	455	87	121	12	8	0	60	48	30	.266	.341	.327	.669	96	-0	-1	101	124	71	.763	54			-5	*O/SM	-1.1
1892	Bal-N	11	43	3	7	1	1	0	2	3	3	.163	.217	.233	.450	37	-3	-3	100	65	2	.361	0			0	OM	-0.2
Total	13	1267	5074	930	1317	159	79	30	517	471	357	.260	.325	.340	.664	103	15	32	98	93	687	.677	329			-9	*O/2S	1.0
■ **BILL HANLON**	Hanlon, William Henry "Big Bill" b: 3/16/1865, Sacramento, Cal. d: 3/18/51, Sacramento, Cal. Deb: 4/16/03																											
1903	Chi-N	8	21	4	2	0	0	0	2	6		.095	.296	.095	.392	16	-2	-2	95	322	1	.474	1			-0	/1	-0.1
■ **JOHN HANNA**	Hanna, John b: 11/3/1863, Philadelphia, Pa. d: 11/7/30, Philadelphia, Pa. Deb: 5/23/1884																											
1884	Was-a	23	76	8	5	0	0	0		6		.066	.134	.066	.200	-36	-10	-9	88	0	1	.155				-2	C/O	-0.8
	Ric-a	22	67	6	13	2	1	0		0		.194	.206	.254	.460	52	-3	-3	99	0	4	.333				4	C/S	0.2
	Yr	45	143	14	18	2	1	0		6		.126	.167	.154	.321	7	-14	-12	93	0	4	.232				2		-0.6
Total	1	45	143	14	18	2	1	0		6		.126	.167	.154	.321	7	-14	-12	93	0	4	.232				2	/COS	-0.6
■ **TRUCK HANNAH**	Hannah, James Harrison b: 6/5/1889, Larimore, N.D. d: 4/27/82, Fountain Valley, Cal. BR/TR, 6'1", 190 lbs. Deb: 4/15/18																											
1918	NY-A	90	250	24	55	6	0	2	21	51	25	.220	.361	.268	.629	95	-0	2	95	105	26	.651	5			-0	C	1.0
1919	NY-A	75	227	14	54	8	3	1	20	22	19	.238	.313	.313	.626	72	-7	-9	106	98	22	.555	0			-4	C/1	-0.8
1920	NY-A	79	259	24	64	11	1	2	25	24	35	.247	.313	.320	.634	67	-12	-13	102	99	28	.564	2	0	1	-8	C	-1.3
Total	3	244	736	62	173	25	4	5	66	97	79	.235	.331	.300	.631	78	-19	-20	100	101	76	.591	7	0		-13	C/1	-1.1
■ **JACK HANNIFIN**	Hannifin, John Joseph b: 2/25/1883, Holyoke, Mass. d: 10/27/45, Northampton, Mass. BR/TR, 5'11", 167 lbs. Deb: 4/19/06																											
1906	Phi-A	1	1	0	1	0	0	0	0	0		1.000	1.000	1.000	2.000	569	0	0	94	0	1	—	0			0	H	0.1
	NY-N	10	30	4	6	0	1	0	3	2		.200	.250	.267	.517	63	-1	-1	100	137	2	.458	1			0	/S32	0.0
1907	NY-N	56	149	16	34	7	3	1	15	15		.228	.299	.336	.634	96	0	-1	105	107	17	.617	6			0	13/SO	0.0
1908	NY-N	1	2	0	0	0	0	0	0	0		.000	.000	.000	.000	-96	-0	-0	104	0	0	.000	0			0	/O	0.0
	Bos-N	90	257	30	53	6	2	2	22	28		.206	.284	.268	.553	76	-5	-6	104	113	21	.510	7			6	32S/O	0.0
	Yr	91	259	30	53	6	2	2	22	28		.205	.282	.266	.549	74	-6	-7	104	111	21	.505	7			6		0.0
Total	3	158	439	50	94	13	6	3	40	45		.214	.287	.292	.579	82	-7	-9	104	112	41	.542	14			6	/3S12O	0.1
■ **DOUG HANSEN**	Hansen, Douglas William b: 12/16/28, Los Angeles, Cal. BR/TR, 6', 180 lbs. Deb: 9/04/51																											
1951	Cle-A	3	0	2	0	0	0	0	0	0	0	—	—	—	—	—	0	0	95	—	—	—	0	0	0	0	R	0.0
■ **BOB HANSEN**	Hansen, Robert Joseph b: 5/26/48, Boston, Mass. BL/TL, 6', 195 lbs. Deb: 5/10/74																											
1974	Mil-A	58	88	8	26	4	1	2	9	3	16	.295	.319	.432	.750	112	1	1	102	80	12	.683	2	1	0	0	D/1	0.1
1976	Mil-A	24	61	4	10	1	0	0	4	6	8	.164	.239	.180	.419	24	-6	-6	99	140	3	.327	0	0	0	0	D/1	-0.5
Total	2	82	149	12	36	5	1	2	13	9	24	.242	.285	.329	.614	77	-4	-5	101	105	15	.522	2	1	0	0	/D1	-0.4
■ **RON HANSEN**	Hansen, Ronald Lavern b: 4/5/38, Oxford, Neb. BR/TR, 6'3", 190 lbs. Deb: 4/15/58 C																											
1958	Bal-A	12	19	1	0	0	0	0	1	0	7	.000	.050	.000	.050	-90	-5	-5	94	0	0	.053	0	0	0	-1	S	-0.3
1959	Bal-A	2	4	0	0	0	0	0	0	1	1	.000	.200	.000	.200	-41	-1	-1	97	0	0	.250	0	0	0	0	/S	0.0
1960	Bal-A	153	530	72	135	22	5	22	86	69	94	.255	.343	.440	.782	108	7	6	102	115	78	.738	3	3	-1	8	*S	2.5
1961	Bal-A	155	533	51	132	13	2	12	51	66	96	.248	.332	.347	.679	84	-13	-11	97	92	60	.598	1	3	-2	9	*S/2	0.7
1962	Bal-A	71	196	12	34	7	0	3	17	30	36	.173	.289	.255	.545	51	-14	-13	95	114	14	.480	0	1	-1	-1	S	-1.0
1963	Chi-A	144	482	55	109	17	2	13	67	78	74	.226	.334	.351	.685	88	-3	-6	104	**138**	57	.631	1	1	-0	**27**	*S	2.9
1964	Chi-A	158	575	85	150	25	3	20	68	73	73	.261	.350	.419	.769	118	11	14	96	101	86	.730	1	0	0	14	*S	3.0
1965	Chi-A	162	587	61	138	23	4	11	66	60	73	.235	.308	.344	.652	92	-11	-6	92	119	60	.563	1	1	-0	18	*S/2	2.1
1966	Chi-A	23	74	3	13	1	0	0	4	15	10	.176	.322	.189	.511	54	-4	-3	94	127	6	.484	0	1	-1	2	S	0.0
1967	Chi-A	157	498	35	116	20	0	8	51	64	51	.233	.320	.321	.642	96	-5	-1	94	116	53	.570	0	3	-2	7	*S	1.6
1968	Was-A	86	275	28	51	12	0	8	28	35	49	.185	.282	.316	.598	89	-6	-4	91	108	23	.521	0	0	0	0	S/3	0.3
	Chi-A	40	87	7	20	3	0	1	4	11	12	.230	.316	.299	.615	86	-1	-1	101	59	8	.521	0	0	0	1	3/S2	0.1
	Yr	126	362	35	71	15	0	9	32	46	61	.196	.290	.312	.602	87	-7	-5	94	93	35	.546	0	0	0	1		0.4
1969	Chi-A	85	185	15	48	6	1	2	22	18	25	.259	.328	.335	.664	79	-3	-5	108	130	20	.572	2	0	1	5	21/S3	0.0
1970	NY-A	59	91	13	27	4	0	4	14	19	9	.297	.423	.473	.896	159	7	8	92	103	20	.955	0	1	-1	1	S3/2	0.9
1971	NY-A	61	145	6	30	3	0	2	20	9	27	.207	.253	.269	.522	49	-10	-10	97	181	9	.400	0	0	0	1	3/2S	-0.8
1972	KC-A	16	30	2	4	0	0	0	2	3	6	.133	.212	.133	.345	4	-3	-3	100	209	1	.259	0	0	0	0	/S32	-0.2
Total	15	1384	4311	446	1007	156	17	106	501	551	643	.234	.323	.351	.675	92	-55	-41	97	115	494	.631	9	14	-6	92	*S/321	11.8
■ **DON HANSKI**	Hanski, Donald Thomas (born Donald Thomas Hanyzewski) b: 2/27/16, Laporte, Ind. d: 9/2/57, Worth, Ill. BL/TL, 5'11", 180 lbs. Deb: 5/06/43																											
1943	Chi-A	9	21	1	5	1	0	0	2	0	5	.238	.238	.286	.524	52	-1	-1	101	122	1	.353	0	1	-1	0	/1P	-0.1
1944	Chi-A	2	1	0	0	0	0	0	0	0	0	.000	.000	.000	.000	-99	-0	-0	100	0	0	.000	0	0	0	0	/P	0.0
Total	2	11	22	1	5	1	0	0	2	0	5	.227	.227	.273	.500	45	-2	-2	101	116	1	.333	0	1	-1	0	/1P	-0.1
■ **JOE HANSON**	Hanson, Joseph b: St.Louis, Mo. TR, Deb: 7/14/13																											
1913	NY-A	1	2	0	0	0	0	0	0	0	0	.000	.000	.000	.000	-99	-0	-1	101	0	0	.000	0			0	/C	0.0
■ **JOHN HAPPENNY**	Happenny, John Clifford "Cliff" b: 5/18/01, Waltham, Mass. BR/TR, 5'11", 165 lbs. Deb: 7/02/23																											
1923	Chi-A	32	86	7	19	5	0	0	10	3	13	.221	.256	.279	.535	41	-8	-7	98	142	6	.418	0	0	0	-1	2/S3	-0.6
■ **BILL HARBIDGE**	Harbidge, William Arthur "Yaller Bill" b: 3/29/1855, Philadelphia, Pa. d: 3/17/24, Philadelphia, Pa. BL/TL, 162 lbs. Deb: 5/15/1875																											
1875	Har-n	51	227	32	49							.216															CO2/1	
1876	Har-N	30	106	11	23	2	1	0	6	3	2	.217	.239	.255	.493	59	-4	-5	108	75	7	.361				-2	C/O1	-0.4
1877	Har-N	41	167	18	37	5	2	0	8	3	6	.222	.235	.275	.511	68	-7	-5	89	60	11	.377				-3	C/O23	-0.5

YEAR	TM/L	G	AB	R	H	2B	3B	HR	RBI	BB	SO	AVG	OBP	SLG	PRO	/A	BR	/A	PF	CHI	RC	TA	SB	CS	SBR	FR	POS	TPR
1878	Chi-N	54	240	32	71	12	0	0	37	6	13	.296	.313	.346	.659	108	4	1	108	145	27	.527				-10	*C/O	-0.6
1879	Chi-N	4	18	2	2	0	0	0	1	0	5	.111	.111	.111	.222	-25	-2	-2	105	155	0	.125				0	/O	-0.1
1880	Tro-N	9	27	3	10	0	1	0	2	0	3	.370	.370	.444	.815	158	2	2	110	61	5	.706				0	/CO	0.2
1882	Tro-N	32	123	11	23	1	1	0	13	10	17	.187	.248	.211	.460	52	-7	-6	95	178	7	.360				-2	O/1C	-0.6
1883	Phi-N	73	280	32	62	12	3	0	21	24	20	.221	.283	.286	.569	82	-8	-4	90	96	23	.477				-6	OS/2C3	-0.6
1884	Cin-U	82	341	59	95	12	5	2		25		.279	.328	.361	.689	123	12	8	108	0	41	.602	0			4	*O/S1	0.9
Total	8	325	1302	168	323	44	13	2	88	71	66	.248	.287	.306	.593	91	-10	-11	101	81	120	.480	0			-18	OC/2S13	-1.7

■ **SCOTT HARDESTY** Hardesty, Scott Durbin b: 1/26/1870, Bellville, Ohio d: 10/29/44, Fostoria, Ohio Deb: 8/17/1899

YEAR	TM/L	G	AB	R	H	2B	3B	HR	RBI	BB	SO	AVG	OBP	SLG	PRO	/A	BR	/A	PF	CHI	RC	TA	SB	CS	SBR	FR	POS	TPR
1899	NY-N	22	72	4	16	0	0	0	4	1		.222	.243	.222	.465	31	-7	-6	97	77	4	.357	2			0	S/1	-0.5

■ **PAT HARDGROVE** Hardgrove, William Henry b: 5/10/1895, Palmyra, Kan. d: 1/26/73, Jackson, Miss. BR/TR, 5'10", 158 lbs. Deb: 6/08/18

YEAR	TM/L	G	AB	R	H	2B	3B	HR	RBI	BB	SO	AVG	OBP	SLG	PRO	/A	BR	/A	PF	CHI	RC	TA	SB	CS	SBR	FR	POS	TPR
1918	Chi-A	2	2	0	0	0	0	0	0	0	0	.000	.000	.000	.000	-99	-0	-0	101	0	0	.000	0			0	H	0.0

■ **LOU HARDIE** Hardie, Louis W. b: 8/24/1864, New York, N.Y. d: 3/5/29, Oakland, Cal. 5'11", 180 lbs. Deb: 5/22/1884

YEAR	TM/L	G	AB	R	H	2B	3B	HR	RBI	BB	SO	AVG	OBP	SLG	PRO	/A	BR	/A	PF	CHI	RC	TA	SB	CS	SBR	FR	POS	TPR
1884	Phi-N	3	8	0	3	2	0	0	0	0	2	.375	.375	.625	1.000	226	1	1	92	0	2	1.000				0	/C	0.1
1886	Chi-N	16	51	4	9	0	0	0	3	4	10	.176	.236	.176	.413	23	-4	-6	116	109	2	.333	1			0	C/O3	-0.4
1890	Bos-N	47	185	17	42	8	0	3	17	18	36	.227	.296	.319	.614	73	-5	-8	111	80	19	.566	4			0	CO/3S1	-0.6
1891	Bal-a	15	56	7	13	0	3	0	1	8	8	.232	.328	.339	.667	93	-0	-0	101	16	7	.698	3			0	O	0.0
Total	4	81	300	28	67	10	3	3	21	30	56	.223	.294	.307	.601	71	-8	-13	109	70	31	.558	8			0	/CO31S	-0.9

■ **BUD HARDIN** Hardin, William Edgar b: 6/14/22, Shelby, N.C. BR/TR, 5'10", 165 lbs. Deb: 4/15/52

YEAR	TM/L	G	AB	R	H	2B	3B	HR	RBI	BB	SO	AVG	OBP	SLG	PRO	/A	BR	/A	PF	CHI	RC	TA	SB	CS	SBR	FR	POS	TPR
1952	Chi-N	3	7	1	1	0	0	0	0	0	0	.143	.143	.143	.286	-20	-1	-1	103	0	0	.167	0	0	0	-0	/S2	-0.1

■ **LOU HARDING** Harding, Louis Edward "Jumbo" b: San Francisco, Cal. 5'9.5", 213 lbs. Deb: 10/05/1886

YEAR	TM/L	G	AB	R	H	2B	3B	HR	RBI	BB	SO	AVG	OBP	SLG	PRO	/A	BR	/A	PF	CHI	RC	TA	SB	CS	SBR	FR	POS	TPR
1886	StL-a	1	3	0	1	1	0	0		0		.333	.333	.667	1.000	191	0	0	111	0	1	1.000	0			0	/C	0.0

■ **CARROLL HARDY** Hardy, Carroll William b: 5/18/33, Sturgis, S.Dak. BR/TR, 6', 185 lbs. Deb: 4/15/58

YEAR	TM/L	G	AB	R	H	2B	3B	HR	RBI	BB	SO	AVG	OBP	SLG	PRO	/A	BR	/A	PF	CHI	RC	TA	SB	CS	SBR	FR	POS	TPR
1958	Cle-A	27	49	10	10	3	0	1	6	6	14	.204	.304	.327	.630	78	-2	-1	94	127	5	.585	1	2	-1	1	O	-0.1
1959	Cle-A	32	53	12	11	1	0	0	2	3	7	.208	.250	.226	.476	33	-5	-5	97	66	3	.372	1	1	-0	2	O	-0.3
1960	Cle-A	29	18	7	2	1	0	0	1	2	2	.111	.200	.167	.367	0	-3	-2	98	131	1	.294	0	0	0	-4	O	-0.6
	Bos-A	73	145	26	34	5	2	2	15	17	40	.234	.315	.338	.653	74	-5	-5	103	107	14	.575	3	2	-0	-4	O	-1.2
	Yr	102	163	33	36	6	2	2	16	19	42	.221	.302	.319	.621	67	-7	-8	102	115	15	.544	3	2	-0	-8		-1.8
1961	Bos-A	85	281	46	74	20	2	3	36	26	53	.263	.330	.381	.711	88	-4	-5	102	122	36	.653	4	2	0	2	O	-0.5
1962	Bos-A	115	362	52	78	13	5	8	36	54	68	.215	.321	.345	.666	77	-10	-11	102	96	40	.613	3	7	-3	4	*O	-1.3
1963	Hou-N	15	44	5	10	3	0	0	3	3	7	.227	.277	.295	.572	70	-2	-2	92	97	4	.486	1	0	0	0	O	-0.1
1964	Hou-N	46	157	13	29	1	1	2	12	8	30	.185	.234	.242	.476	35	-14	-13	96	114	8	.361	0	0	0	7	O	-0.7
1967	Min-A	11	8	1	3	0	0	1	2	1	1	.375	.444	.750	1.194	231	1	1	107	93	3	1.400	0	0	0	-1	/O	0.0
Total	8	433	1117	172	251	47	10	17	113	120	222	.225	.304	.330	.634	72	-42	-43	100	107	114	.578	13	14	-5	7	O	-4.8

■ **JACK HARDY** Hardy, John Doolittle b: 6/23/1877, Cleveland, Ohio d: 10/20/21, Cleveland, Ohio TR , 6', 185 lbs. Deb: 8/29/03

YEAR	TM/L	G	AB	R	H	2B	3B	HR	RBI	BB	SO	AVG	OBP	SLG	PRO	/A	BR	/A	PF	CHI	RC	TA	SB	CS	SBR	FR	POS	TPR
1903	Cle-A	5	19	1	3	1	0	0	1	1		.158	.200	.211	.411	25	-2	-2	96	95	1	.375	1			-0	/O	-0.1
1907	Chi-N	1	4	0	1	0	0	0	0	0		.250	.250	.250	.500	55	-0	-0	106	0	0	.333	0			0	/C	0.0
1909	Was-A	10	24	3	4	0	0	0	4	1		.167	.200	.167	.367	18	-2	-2	90	386	1	.250	0			0	/C2	0.0
1910	Was-A	7	8	1	2	0	0	0	0	0		.250	.250	.250	.500	56	-0	-0	101	0	0	.333	0			-0	/CO	0.0
Total	4	23	55	5	10	1	0	0	5	2		.182	.211	.200	.411	29	-5	-4	95	203	2	.311	1			-0	/CO2	-0.1

■ **GARY HARGIS** Hargis, Gary Lynn b: 11/2/56, Minneapolis, Minn. BR/TR, 5'11", 165 lbs. Deb: 9/29/79

YEAR	TM/L	G	AB	R	H	2B	3B	HR	RBI	BB	SO	AVG	OBP	SLG	PRO	/A	BR	/A	PF	CHI	RC	TA	SB	CS	SBR	FR	POS	TPR
1979	Pit-N	1	0	0	0	0	0	0	0	0	0	—	—	—	—	—	0	0	106	—	—	—	0	0	0	0	/R	0.0

■ **BUBBLES HARGRAVE** Hargrave, Eugene Franklin b: 7/15/1892, New Haven, Ind. d: 2/23/69, Cincinnati, Ohio BR/TR, 5'10.5", 174 lbs. Deb: 9/18/13

YEAR	TM/L	G	AB	R	H	2B	3B	HR	RBI	BB	SO	AVG	OBP	SLG	PRO	/A	BR	/A	PF	CHI	RC	TA	SB	CS	SBR	FR	POS	TPR
1913	Chi-N	3	3	0	1	0	0	0	1	0	0	.333	.333	.333	.667	92	-0	-0	99	363	0	.500	0			0	/C	0.0
1914	Chi-N	23	36	3	8	2	0	0	2	0	4	.222	.222	.278	.500	49	-2	-2	98	72	2	.429	2			0	C	-0.1
1915	Chi-N	15	19	2	3	0	1	0	2	1	5	.158	.200	.263	.463	39	-1	-1	102	153	1	.375	0			0	/C	0.0
1921	Cin-N	93	263	28	76	17	8	1	38	12	15	.289	.327	.426	.753	97	-1	-2	101	121	36	.693	4	2	0	2	C	0.5
1922	Cin-N	98	320	49	101	22	10	7	57	26	18	.316	.371	.512	.883	131	11	13	96	108	60	.892	7	4	-0	-2	C	1.1
1923	Cin-N	118	378	54	126	23	9	10	78	44	22	.333	.419	.521	.941	150	27	28	98	121	84	1.000	4	5	-2	-2	*C	2.8
1924	Cin-N	98	312	42	94	19	10	3	33	30	20	.301	.370	.455	.825	119	9	9	101	80	53	.809	2	2	-1	-5	C	0.5
1925	Cin-N	87	273	28	82	13	6	2	33	25	23	.300	.361	.414	.775	100	-1	0	97	99	41	.737	4	3	-1	-12	C	-0.7
1926	Cin-N	105	326	42	115	22	8	6	62	25	17	.353	.406	.525	.930	157	22	24	95	113	67	.957	2			-9	C	1.8
1927	Cin-N	102	305	36	94	18	3	0	35	31	18	.308	.376	.387	.763	105	3	3	100	104	45	.716	0			-3	C	0.6
1928	Cin-N	65	190	19	56	12	3	0	23	13	14	.295	.353	.389	.742	98	-2	-1	96	111	26	.709	4			1	C	0.4
1930	NY-A	45	108	11	30	7	0	0	12	10	9	.278	.339	.343	.682	82	-4	-2	90	108	13	.603	0	0	0	-2	C	0.0
Total	12	852	2533	314	786	155	58	29	376	217	165	.310	.372	.452	.824	119	60	69	98	107	429	.807	29	16		-31	C	6.9

■ **PINKY HARGRAVE** Hargrave, William Kc Kinley b: 1/31/1896, New Haven, Ind. d: 10/3/42, Ft.Wayne, Ind. BB/TR, 5'8.5", 180 lbs. Deb: 5/18/23

YEAR	TM/L	G	AB	R	H	2B	3B	HR	RBI	BB	SO	AVG	OBP	SLG	PRO	/A	BR	/A	PF	CHI	RC	TA	SB	CS	SBR	FR	POS	TPR
1923	Was-A	33	59	4	17	2	0	0	8	2	6	.288	.311	.322	.634	71	-3	-2	95	144	6	.500	0	0	0	0	/3CO	0.0
1924	Was-A	24	33	3	5	1	1	0	5	1	4	.152	.176	.242	.419	7	-5	-5	98	207	1	.321	0	0	0	0	/C	-0.3
1925	Was-A	5	6	0	3	0	0	0	0	1	2	.500	.571	.500	1.071	177	1	1	98	0	2	1.333	0	0	0	0	/C	0.1
	StL-A	67	225	34	64	15	2	8	43	13	13	.284	.326	.476	.802	94	-1	-4	108	110	35	.764	2	0	1	2	C	0.3
	Yr	72	231	34	67	15	2	8	43	14	15	.290	.333	.476	.810	97	-0	-3	107	102	37	.774	2	0	1	3		0.4
1926	StL-A	92	235	20	66	16	3	7	37	10	38	.281	.319	.464	.782	102	-1	-1	101	97	35	.740	3	0	1	5	C	0.8
1928	Det-A	121	320	38	88	13	5	10	63	32	28	.275	.343	.441	.783	105	1	2	99	126	50	.764	4	1	1	-1	C	0.7
1929	Det-A	76	185	26	61	12	0	3	26	20	24	.330	.401	.443	.844	120	5	6	97	98	33	.841	2	2	-1	1	C	1.0
1930	Det-A	55	137	18	39	8	0	5	18	20	12	.285	.380	.453	.832	105	2	1	105	78	25	.867	2	0	1	-3	C	0.2
	Was-A	10	31	3	6	2	2	1	7	3	1	.194	.265	.484	.749	84	-1	-1	101	129	4	.760	1	0	0	0	/C	0.0
	Yr	65	168	21	45	10	2	6	25	23	13	.268	.359	.458	.818	101	1	0	104	87	29	.846	3	0	1	-2		0.2
1931	Was-A	40	80	6	26	8	0	1	19	9	12	.325	.393	.463	.856	123	3	3	101	157	15	.870	1	0	0	-2	C	0.3
1932	Bos-N	82	217	20	57	14	3	4	33	24	18	.263	.336	.410	.746	107	-0	2	93	122	31	.712	1			1	C	0.6
1933	Bos-N	45	73	5	13	0	0	0	6	5	7	.178	.241	.178	.419	22	-7	-7	96	173	3	.323	1			-1	C	-0.7
Total	10	650	1601	177	445	91	16	39	265	140	165	.278	.339	.428	.767	99	-5	-5	100	117	241	.733	17	3		5	C/3O	3.0

■ **CHARLIE HARGREAVES** Hargreaves, Charles Russell b: 12/14/1896, Trenton, N.J. d: 5/9/79, Neptune, N.J. BR/TR, 6', 170 lbs. Deb: 7/15/23

YEAR	TM/L	G	AB	R	H	2B	3B	HR	RBI	BB	SO	AVG	OBP	SLG	PRO	/A	BR	/A	PF	CHI	RC	TA	SB	CS	SBR	FR	POS	TPR
1923	Bro-N	20	57	5	16	0	0	0	4	1	2	.281	.293	.281	.574	53	-4	-4	98	88	5	.415	0	0	0	2	C	0.0
1924	Bro-N	15	27	4	11	2	0	0	5	1	1	.407	.429	.481	.910	145	2	2	99	140	5	.824	0	1	-1	1	/C	0.2
1925	Bro-N	45	83	9	23	3	1	0	13	6	1	.277	.326	.337	.663	74	-4	-3	94	165	9	.574	1	1	-0	2	C/1	0.0
1926	Bro-N	85	208	14	52	13	2	2	23	19	10	.250	.316	.361	.676	82	-6	-5	99	98	24	.615	1			2	C	0.0
1927	Bro-N	46	133	9	38	3	1	0	11	14	7	.286	.362	.323	.686	83	-2	-3	103	89	16	.632	1			3	C	0.3
1928	Bro-N	20	61	3	12	2	0	0	5	6	6	.197	.269	.230	.498	32	-6	-6	99	127	4	.429	1			-1	C	-0.4
	Pit-N	79	260	15	74	8	2	1	32	12	9	.285	.319	.342	.661	68	-10	-13	107	124	28	.554	1			-3	C	-1.0
	Yr	99	321	18	86	10	2	1	37	18	15	.268	.309	.321	.630	62	-16	-19	105	126	31	.528	2			-4		-1.4
1929	Pit-N	102	328	33	88	12	5	1	44	16	12	.268	.306	.345	.651	59	-20	-22	103	130	34	.550	1			2	*C	-1.0
1930	Pit-N	11	31	4	7	1	0	0	2	2	1	.226	.273	.258	.531	30	-4	-3	97	86	2	.417	0			1	C	0.0
Total	8	423	1188	96	321	44	11	4	139	77	49	.270	.318	.336	.654	68	-54	-57	102	118	126	.562	6	2		8	C/1	-1.9

■ **MIKE HARGROVE** Hargrove, Dudley Michael b: 10/26/49, Perryton, Tex. BL/TL, 6', 195 lbs. Deb: 4/07/74

YEAR	TM/L	G	AB	R	H	2B	3B	HR	RBI	BB	SO	AVG	OBP	SLG	PRO	/A	BR	/A	PF	CHI	RC	TA	SB	CS	SBR	FR	POS	TPR
1974	Tex-A	131	415	57	134	18	6	4	66	49	42	.323	.400	.424	.824	143	21	24	96	138	71	.784	0	0	0	4	1D/O	2.4
1975	Tex-A	145	519	82	157	22	2	11	62	79	66	.303	.399	.416	.815	131	24	24	100	98	88	.799	4	3	-1	-3	O1D	1.5
1976	Tex-A	151	541	80	155	30	1	7	58	**97**	64	.287	.401	.384	.785	128	26	25	102	103	91	.794	2	3	-1	1	*1/D	1.8
1977	Tex-A	153	525	98	160	28	4	18	69	103	59	.305	.424	.476	.900	139	38	34	105	92	110	.943	2	5	-2	0	*1	2.3

YEAR	TM/L	G	AB	R	H	2B	3B	HR	RBI	BB	SO	AVG	OBP	SLG	PRO	/A	BR	/A	PF	CHI	RC	TA	SB	CS	SBR	FR	POS	TPR
1978	Tex-A	146	494	63	124	24	1	7	40	**107**	47	.251	.391	.346	.738	113	12	14	96	87	73	.744	2	5	-2	12	*1/D	1.8
1979	SD-N	52	125	15	24	5	0	0	8	25	15	.192	.327	.232	.559	57	-7	-6	96	109	11	.519	0	2	-1	-0	1	-0.9
	Cle-A	100	338	60	110	21	4	10	56	63	40	.325	.438	.500	.938	144	28	25	106	110	76	.992	2	3	-1	-1	O1/D	1.8
1980	Cle-A	160	589	86	179	22	2	11	85	111	36	.304	.421	.404	.825	124	29	27	102	118	105	.832	4	2	0	-5	*1	1.1
1981	Cle-A	94	322	43	102	21	0	2	49	60	16	.317	**.432**	.401	.832	151	21	24	93	**150**	57	.836	5	4	-1	7	1/D	2.9
1982	Cle-A	160	591	67	160	26	1	4	65	101	58	.271	.380	.338	.718	99	4	4	100	130	79	.673	2	2	-1	10	*1/D	0.9
1983	Cle-A	134	469	57	134	21	4	3	57	78	40	.286	.393	.367	.760	105	11	7	105	130	71	.724	0	6	-4	9	*1/D	0.7
1984	Cle-A	133	352	44	94	14	2	2	44	53	38	.267	.363	.335	.698	89	-1	-3	106	141	43	.629	0	2	-1	2	*1	-0.9
1985	Cle-A	107	284	31	81	14	1	1	27	39	29	.285	.372	.352	.724	106	1	4	94	104	38	.664	1	0	0	3	1/OD	0.1
Total	12	1666	5564	783	1614	266	28	80	686	965	550	.290	.400	.391	.791	121	208	202	101	115	914	.806	24	37	-15	38	*1O/D	15.5
■ TIM HARKNESS	Harkness, Thomas William b: 12/23/37, Lachine, Que., Can. BL/TL, 6'2", 182 lbs. Deb: 9/12/61																											
1961	LA-N	5	8	4	4	2	0	0	0	3	1	.500	.636	.750	1.386	260	2	2	102	0	5	2.500	1	0	0	0	/1	0.2
1962	LA-N	92	62	9	16	2	0	2	7	10	20	.258	.370	.387	.757	112	1	1	93	92	10	.783	1	0	0	-1	1	-0.1
1963	NY-N	123	375	35	79	12	3	10	41	36	79	.211	.292	.339	.631	81	-9	-9	99	110	38	.572	4	3	-1	10	*1	-0.1
1964	NY-N	39	117	11	33	2	1	2	13	9	18	.282	.339	.368	.706	104	-0	1	95	109	13	.600	1	1	-0	1	1	0.1
Total	4	259	562	59	132	18	4	14	61	58	118	.235	.316	.356	.672	92	-6	-5	98	106	66	.624	7	4	-0	10	1	0.1
■ DICK HARLEY	Harley, Richard Joseph b: 9/25/1872, Philadelphia, Pa. d: 4/3/52, Philadelphia, Pa. BL/TR, 5'10.5", 165 lbs. Deb: 6/02/1897																											
1897	StL-N	89	330	43	96	6	4	3	35	36		.291	.379	.361	.740	105	1	5	93	85	55	.808	23			-1	*O	-0.1
1898	StL-N	142	549	74	135	6	5	0	42	34		.246	.313	.275	.588	68	-18	-23	106	81	53	.527	13			7	*O	-2.3
1899	Cle-N	142	567	70	142	15	7	1	50	40		.250	.315	.307	.621	82	-20	-11	89	77	61	.569	15			3	*O	-1.5
1900	Cin-N	5	21	2	9	1	0	0	5	1		.429	.455	.476	.931	174	2	2	92	138	7	1.250	4			0	/O	0.2
1901	Cin-N	133	535	69	146	13	2	4	27	31		.273	.313	.327	.640	92	-8	-5	95	46	68	.625	37			-8	*O	-2.5
1902	Det-A	125	491	59	138	9	8	2	44	36		.281	.330	.344	.674	90	-7	-6	99	80	64	.637	20			-0	*O	-1.3
1903	Chi-N	104	386	72	89	9	1	0	33	45		.231	.311	.259	.570	68	-16	-13	95	112	40	.579	27			-0	*O	-1.8
Total	7	740	2879	389	755	59	27	10	236	223		.262	.325	.312	.637	84	-66	-50	96	79	348	.614	139			0	O	-9.3
■ LARRY HARLOW	Harlow, Larry Duane b: 11/13/51, Colorado Springs, Colo. BL/TL, 6'2", 185 lbs. Deb: 9/20/75																											
1975	Bal-A	4	3	1	1	0	0	0	0	0	1	.333	.333	.333	.667	98	-0	-0	91	0	0	.500	0	0	0	-1	/O	-0.1
1977	Bal-A	46	48	4	10	0	1	0	0	5	8	.208	.283	.250	.533	50	-3	-3	93	0	4	.590	6	1	1	-9	O	-1.1
1978	Bal-A	147	460	67	112	25	1	8	26	55	72	.243	.326	.354	.680	100	-5	1	91	55	53	.633	14	11	-2	-13	*O/P	-1.7
1979	Bal-A	38	41	5	11	1	0	0	1	7	4	.268	.375	.293	.668	85	-1	-0	97	32	4	.606	1	3	-2	-8	O	-1.0
	Cal-A	62	159	22	37	8	2	0	14	25	34	.233	.344	.308	.652	84	-4	-2	93	110	18	.606	1	3	-2	0	O	-0.5
	Yr	100	200	27	48	9	2	0	15	32	38	.240	.350	.305	.655	83	-5	-3	94	80	22	.606	2	6	-3	-8		-1.5
1980	Cal-A	109	301	47	83	13	4	4	27	48	61	.276	.377	.385	.763	114	6	7	96	82	45	.730	3	2	-0	12	O/1D	1.7
1981	Cal-A	43	82	13	17	1	0	0	4	16	25	.207	.337	.220	.556	61	-3	-4	104	87	7	.507	1	1	-0	-7	O	-1.2
Total	6	449	1094	159	271	48	8	12	72	156	205	.248	.344	.339	.683	96	-11	-1	94	70	132	.658	26	21	-5	-26	O/D1P	-3.9
■ BILL HARMAN	Harman, William Bell b: 1/2/19, Bridgewater, Va. BR/TR, 6'4", 200 lbs. Deb: 6/17/41																											
1941	Phi-N	15	14	1	1	0	0	0	0	0	3	.071	.071	.071	.143	-61	-3	-3	97	0	0	.077	0			-0	/PC	-0.1
■ CHUCK HARMON	Harmon, Charles Byron b: 4/23/26, Washington, Ind. BR/TR, 6'2", 175 lbs. Deb: 4/17/54																											
1954	Cin-N	94	286	39	68	7	3	2	25	17	27	.238	.283	.304	.587	51	-20	-21	104	106	26	.500	7	3	0	3	3/1	-1.7
1955	Cin-N	96	198	31	50	6	3	5	28	26	24	.253	.348	.389	.737	90	-1	-2	106	123	27	.723	9	9	-3	2	3O/1	-0.4
1956	Cin-N	13	4	2	0	0	0	0	0	0	0	.000	.000	.000	.000	-92	-1	-1	108	0	0	.250	1	0	0	-2	/O1	-0.2
	StL-N	20	15	2	0	0	0	0	0	2	2	.000	.118	.000	.118	-65	-4	-4	99	0	0	.133	0	0	0	-3	O/13	-0.7
	Yr	33	19	4	0	0	0	0	0	2	2	.000	.095	.000	.095	-70	-5	-5	103	0	0	.158	1	0	0	-5		-0.9
1957	StL-N	9	3	2	1	0	1	0	1	0	0	.333	.333	1.000	1.333	239	1	1	101	138	1	2.000	1	0	0	-3	/O	-0.1
	Phi-N	57	86	14	22	2	1	0	5	1	4	.256	.264	.302	.567	53	-6	-6	98	80	6	.493	7	2	1	-4	O/31	-0.8
	Yr	66	89	16	23	2	2	0	6	1	4	.258	.267	.326	.593	59	-5	-5	99	90	7	.535	8	2	1	-6		-0.9
Total	4	289	592	90	141	15	8	7	59	46	57	.238	.298	.326	.624	62	-31	-33	104	105	60	.573	25	14	-1	-7	3/O1	-3.9
■ TERRY HARMON	Harmon, Terry Walter b: 4/12/44, Toledo, Ohio BR/TR, 6'2", 180 lbs. Deb: 7/23/67																											
1967	Phi-N	2	0	0	0	0	0	0	0	0	0	—	—	—	—	—	0	0	104	—	—	—	0	0	0	0	R	0.0
1969	Phi-N	87	201	25	48	8	1	0	16	22	31	.239	.323	.289	.612	74	-7	-6	98	111	20	.532	1	2	-1	4	S2/3	0.3
1970	Phi-N	71	129	16	32	2	4	0	7	12	22	.248	.317	.326	.642	75	-5	-4	96	65	14	.610	6	3	0	-5	S2/3	-0.2
1971	Phi-N	79	221	27	45	4	2	0	12	20	45	.204	.282	.240	.521	48	-14	-15	103	92	17	.449	3	2	-0	5	2/S31	-0.6
1972	Phi-N	73	218	35	62	8	2	2	13	29	28	.284	.373	.367	.740	115	4	5	97	62	32	.712	3	2	-0	-2	2S/3	0.8
1973	Phi-N	72	148	17	31	3	0	0	8	13	14	.209	.278	.230	.508	39	-11	-13	108	95	10	.408	1	0	0	1	2S/3	-0.6
1974	Phi-N	27	15	5	2	0	0	0	0	3	3	.133	.278	.133	.411	17	-2	-2	103	0	1	.385	0	0	0	-0	/S2	0.0
1975	Phi-N	48	72	14	13	1	2	0	5	9	13	.181	.280	.250	.530	47	-5	-5	101	107	5	.452	0	0	0	-2	S/23	-0.3
1976	Phi-N	42	61	12	18	4	1	0	6	3	10	.295	.328	.393	.722	97	0	-0	107	96	8	.682	3	0	1	-1	S2/3	0.2
1977	Phi-N	46	60	13	11	1	0	2	5	6	9	.183	.269	.300	.569	52	-4	-4	100	83	4	.472	0	2	-1	2	2S/3	0.0
Total	10	547	1125	164	262	31	12	4	72	117	175	.233	.312	.292	.605	69	-43	-44	101	86	172	.543	17	11	-2	3	2S/31	-0.4
■ BRIAN HARPER	Harper, Brian David b: 10/16/59, Los Angeles, Cal. BR/TR, 6'2", 195 lbs. Deb: 9/29/79																											
1979	Cal-A	1	2	0	0	0	0	0	0	0	1	.000	.000	.000	.000	-99	-1	-1	93	0	0	.000	0	0	0	0	/H	0.0
1981	Cal-A	4	11	1	3	0	0	0	1	0	0	.273	.273	.273	.545	55	-1	-1	104	130	1	.500	1	0	0	0	/OD	0.0
1982	Pit-N	20	29	4	8	1	0	2	4	1	4	.276	.300	.517	.817	113	1	0	110	75	4	.727	0	0	0	-1	/O	0.0
1983	Pit-N	61	131	16	29	4	1	7	20	2	15	.221	.239	.427	.666	79	-4	-5	103	103	12	.562	0	0	0	-6	O/1	-1.1
1984	Pit-N	46	112	4	29	4	0	2	11	5	11	.259	.303	.348	.651	87	-3	-2	94	96	11	.529	0	0	0	-3	O/C	-0.6
1985	StL-N	43	52	5	13	4	0	0	8	2	3	.250	.278	.327	.605	72	-2	-2	96	187	4	.463	0	0	0	-3	O/3C1	-0.4
1986	Det-A	19	36	2	5	1	0	0	3	3	3	.139	.205	.167	.372	4	-5	-5	95	199	1	.281	0	0	0	-2	O/C1D	-0.6
1987	Oak-A	11	17	1	4	1	0	0	3	0	4	.235	.235	.294	.529	44	-1	-1	91	239	1	.357	0	0	0	-0	/OD	-0.1
1988	Min-A	60	166	15	49	11	1	3	20	10	12	.295	.346	.428	.774	109	3	2	106	99	20	.636	0	3	-2	0	C/3D	0.2
Total	9	265	556	48	140	26	2	14	70	23	53	.252	.289	.381	.670	84	-13	-13	101	117	55	.561	1	3	-2	-15	O/CD31	-2.6
■ GEORGE HARPER	Harper, George Washington b: 6/24/1892, Arlington, Ky. d: 8/18/78, Magnolia, Ark. BL/TR, 5'8", 167 lbs. Deb: 4/15/16																											
1916	Det-A	44	56	4	9	1	0	0	3	5	8	.161	.230	.179	.408	22	-5	-6	105	107	2	.319	0			-4	O	-1.1
1917	Det-A	47	117	6	24	3	0	0	12	11	15	.205	.290	.231	.521	60	-5	-5	98	160	9	.462	2			-5	O	-1.2
1918	Det-A	69	227	19	55	5	2	0	16	18	14	.242	.301	.282	.583	78	-7	-6	97	91	21	.500	3			-5	O	-1.5
1922	Cin-N	128	430	67	146	22	8	2	68	35	22	.340	.397	.442	.839	121	11	14	96	121	75	.823	11	10	-3	-1	*O	0.5
1923	Cin-N	61	125	14	32	4	2	3	16	11	9	.256	.316	.392	.708	88	-3	-2	98	97	15	.632	0	2	-1	-2	O	-0.5
1924	Cin-N	28	74	7	20	3	0	0	3	13	5	.270	.393	.311	.704	90	-0	-0	101	48	10	.684	1	3	-2	1	O	0.0
	Phi-N	109	411	68	121	26	6	16	55	38	23	.294	.361	.504	.865	120	16	12	108	83	72	.864	10	11	-4	2	*O	0.8
	Yr	137	485	75	141	29	6	16	58	51	28	.291	.366	.474	.841	117	16	12	106	76	82	.835	11	14	-5	3		0.8
1925	Phi-N	132	495	86	173	35	7	18	97	28	32	.349	.391	.558	.949	121	28	16	116	107	105	.970	10	8	-2	9	*O	1.9
1926	Phi-N	56	194	32	61	6	5	7	38	16	7	.314	.367	.505	.872	128	8	7	103	113	35	.902	6			-5	O	0.0
1927	NY-N	145	483	85	160	19	6	16	87	84	27	.331	.435	.495	.930	149	37	37	100	108	106	1.037	7			-2	*O	2.9
1928	NY-N	19	57	11	13	1	0	2	7	10	4	.228	.353	.351	.704	83	-1	-1	102	96	8	.727	1			2	O	0.0
	StL-N	99	272	41	83	8	2	17	58	51	15	.305	.418	.537	.955	148	20	20	100	105	62	1.063	2			0	O	1.7
	Yr	118	329	52	96	9	2	19	65	61	19	.292	.407	.505	.912	137	19	19	100	104	69	1.000	3			2	O	1.7
1929	Bos-N	136	457	65	133	25	5	10	68	69	27	.291	.389	.433	.822	110	4	9	94	104	79	.852	5			-7	*O	-0.8
Total	11	1073	3398	505	1030	158	43	91	528	389	208	.303	.380	.455	.836	118	103	96	102	105	597	.845	58	<u>34</u>		-15	O	2.7
■ TERRY HARPER	Harper, Terry Joe b: 8/19/55, Douglasville, Ga. BR/TR, 6'4", 195 lbs. Deb: 9/12/80																											
1980	Atl-N	21	54	3	10	2	1	0	3	6	5	.185	.279	.259	.538	50	-3	-4	101	85	4	.500	2	1	0	-2	O	-0.6
1981	Atl-N	40	73	9	19	1	0	2	8	11	17	.260	.357	.356	.713	103	1	1	100	98	10	.737	5	1	1	-3	O	-0.1

YEAR	TM/L	G	AB	R	H	2B	3B	HR	RBI	BB	SO	AVG	OBP	SLG	PRO	/A	BR	/A	PF	CHI	RC	TA	SB	CS	SBR	FR	POS	TPR
1982	Atl-N	48	150	16	43	3	0	2	16	14	28	.287	.352	.347	.698	90	-0	-2	107	108	19	.649	7	4	-0	1	O	-0.1
1983	Atl-N	80	201	19	53	13	1	3	26	20	43	.264	.333	.383	.716	93	-1	-2	106	120	24	.654	6	5	-1	-3	O	-0.6
1984	Atl-N	40	102	4	16	3	1	0	8	4	21	.157	.196	.206	.402	12	-12	-13	110	149	3	.323	4	1	1	2	O	-1.1
1985	Atl-N	138	492	58	130	15	2	17	72	44	76	.264	.328	.407	.735	98	2	-1	106	117	62	.667	9	9	-3	-7	*O	-1.5
1986	Atl-N	106	265	26	68	12	0	8	30	29	39	.257	.332	.392	.725	97	-0	-1	102	93	30	.634	3	6	-3	-11	O	-1.6
1987	Det-A	31	64	4	13	3	0	3	10	9	8	.203	.301	.391	.692	85	-2	-1	97	117	8	.660	1	0	0	-2	DO	-0.3
	Pit-N	36	66	8	19	3	0	1	7	7	11	.288	.356	.379	.735	91	-0	-1	104	100	7	.593	0	1	-1	-3	O	-0.4
Total	8	540	1467	147	371	55	5	36	180	144	248	.253	.323	.371	.694	88	-16	-24	105	111	167	.649	37	28	-6	-27	O/D	-6.3
■ **TOMMY HARPER**	Harper, Tommy b: 10/14/40, Oak Grove, La. BR/TR, 5'9", 165 lbs. Deb: 4/09/62 C																											
1962	Cin-N	6	23	1	4	0	0	0	1	2	6	.174	.240	.174	.414	13	-3	-3	102	100	1	.350	1	0	0	-0	/3	-0.2
1963	Cin-N	129	408	67	106	12	3	10	37	44	72	.260	.336	.377	.714	101	3	1	104	84	54	.681	12	1	3	7	*O/3	0.6
1964	Cin-N	102	317	42	77	5	2	4	22	39	56	.243	.328	.309	.637	78	-7	-8	103	82	37	.648	24	3	5	0	O/3	-0.5
1965	Cin-N	159	646	**126**	166	28	3	18	64	78	127	.257	.342	.393	.735	103	7	4	104	76	94	.747	35	6	7	2	*O/32	0.8
1966	Cin-N	149	553	85	154	22	5	5	31	57	85	.278	.349	.363	.713	87	0	-9	114	64	74	.697	29	10	3	2	*O	-0.8
1967	Cin-N	103	365	55	82	17	3	7	22	43	51	.225	.306	.345	.652	79	-6	-10	109	66	42	.655	23	8	2	9	*O	-0.3
1968	Cle-A	130	235	26	51	15	2	6	26	26	56	.217	.298	.374	.672	102	1	0	101	105	26	.649	11	7	-1	-18	*O/2	-2.6
1969	Sea-A	148	537	78	126	10	2	9	41	95	90	.235	.351	.311	.662	88	-7	-5	98	90	71	.769	**73**	18	11	-2	23O	0.7
1970	Mil-A	154	604	104	179	35	4	31	82	77	107	.296	.380	.522	.901	149	37	39	98	72	122	.967	38	16	2	7	*32O	5.0
1971	Mil-A	152	585	79	151	26	3	14	52	65	92	.258	.333	.385	.718	100	2	0	103	76	82	.718	25	3	6	-16	O3/2	-1.6
1972	Bos-A	144	556	92	141	29	2	14	49	67	104	.254	.343	.388	.732	112	13	10	105	70	81	.744	25	7	3	-4	*O	0.5
1973	Bos-A	147	566	92	159	23	3	17	71	61	93	.281	.352	.422	.774	111	13	9	106	102	91	.831	**54**	14	**8**	0	*O/D	1.3
1974	Bos-A	118	443	66	105	15	3	5	24	46	65	.237	.313	.318	.631	77	-10	-13	107	64	47	.612	28	12	1	-6	OD	-2.0
1975	Cal-A	89	285	40	68	10	1	3	31	38	51	.239	.332	.312	.645	88	-5	-3	95	121	32	.641	19	8	1	-1	D1/O	-0.4
	Oak-A	34	69	11	22	4	0	2	7	5	9	.319	.373	.464	.837	146	3	4	93	71	12	.900	7	0	2	-2	1/O3D	0.3
	Yr	123	354	51	90	14	1	5	38	43	60	.254	.340	.342	.682	99	-2	0	94	108	46	.702	26	8	3	-3		-0.1
1976	Bal-A	46	77	8	18	5	0	1	7	10	16	.234	.322	.338	.660	95	-1	-0	98	93	9	.635	4	3	-1	-0	D/1O	-0.1
Total	15	1810	6269	972	1609	256	36	146	567	753	1080	.257	.340	.379	.719	100	41	14	104	80	876	.748	408	116	53	-22	*O3D/21	0.7
■ **TOBY HARRAH**	Harrah, Colbert Dale b: 10/26/48, Sissonville, W.Va. BR/TR, 6', 175 lbs. Deb: 9/05/69																											
1969	Was-A	8	1	4	0	0	0	0	0	0	0	.000	.000	.000	.000	-99	-0	-0	97	0	0	.000	0	0	0	0	/S	0.0
1971	Was-A	127	383	45	88	11	3	2	22	40	48	.230	.303	.290	.592	74	-15	-12	92	77	33	.516	10	9	-2	-1	*S/3	-0.3
1972	Tex-A	116	374	47	97	14	3	1	31	34	31	.259	.321	.321	.642	97	-4	-1	94	105	41	.592	16	7	1	-13	*S	-0.2
1973	Tex-A	118	461	64	120	16	1	10	50	46	49	.260	.330	.364	.694	98	-3	-1	97	95	56	.637	10	3	1	-5	S3	0.5
1974	Tex-A	161	573	79	149	23	2	21	74	50	65	.260	.322	.417	.739	116	7	10	96	98	72	.677	15	14	-4	-0	*S/3	1.8
1975	Tex-A	151	522	81	153	24	1	20	93	98	71	.293	.406	.458	.864	144	34	34	100	122	105	.938	23	9	2	14	*S32	**6.2**
1976	Tex-A	155	584	64	152	21	1	15	67	91	59	.260	.363	.377	.740	114	15	14	102	93	82	.709	8	5	-1	2	*S/3D	2.5
1977	Tex-A	159	539	90	142	25	5	27	87	**109**	73	.263	.397	.479	.875	131	32	28	105	104	112	.976	27	5	5	-24	*3/S	0.5
1978	Tex-A	139	450	56	103	17	3	12	59	83	66	.229	.351	.360	.711	104	3	5	96	120	65	.766	31	8	5	-6	3S	0.7
1979	Cle-A	149	527	99	147	25	1	20	77	89	60	.279	.391	.444	.835	118	21	17	106	107	98	.884	20	9	1	-30	*3S/D	-0.6
1980	Cle-A	160	561	100	150	22	4	11	72	98	60	.267	.383	.380	.763	107	12	10	102	116	89	.781	17	2	4	4	*3/SD	1.7
1981	Cle-A	103	361	64	105	12	4	5	44	57	44	.291	.389	.388	.777	133	14	17	93	113	60	.802	12	1	3	-9	*3/SD	1.1
1982	Cle-A	162	602	100	183	29	4	25	78	84	52	.304	.400	.490	.890	143	38	38	100	89	123	.938	17	3	3	-17	*3/2S	2.1
1983	Cle-A	138	526	81	140	23	1	9	53	75	49	.266	.365	.365	.730	97	4	0	105	91	73	.709	16	10	-1	-10	*3/2D	-1.0
1984	NY-A	88	253	40	55	9	4	1	26	42	28	.217	.333	.296	.630	81	-7	-5	94	133	27	.589	3	0	1	5	3/2OD	0.2
1985	Tex-A	126	396	65	107	18	1	9	44	113	60	.270	.437	.389	.826	119	23	18	108	102	80	.949	11	4	1	-3	*2/SD	2.0
1986	Tex-A	95	289	36	63	18	2	7	41	44	53	.218	.325	.367	.692	93	-4	-2	96	129	35	.647	2	5	-2	-8	2	-0.6
Total	17	2155	7402	1115	1954	307	40	195	918	1153	868	.264	.368	.395	.763	114	170	169	100	105	1152	.789	238	94	15	-101	*3S2/DO	16.6
■ **JOHN HARRELL**	Harrell, John Robert b: 11/27/47, Long Beach, Cal. BR/TR, 6'2", 190 lbs. Deb: 10/01/69																											
1969	SF-N	2	6	0	3	0	0	0	2	2	1	.500	.625	.500	1.125	216	1	1	101	272	2	1.667	0	0	0	-0	/C	0.1
■ **BILLY HARRELL**	Harrell, William b: 7/18/28, Norristown, Pa. BR/TR, 6'1.5", 180 lbs. Deb: 9/02/55																											
1955	Cle-A	13	19	2	8	0	0	0	1	3	3	.421	.500	.421	.921	144	2	2	104	47	5	1.091	1	0	0	0	S	0.3
1957	Cle-A	22	57	6	15	1	1	1	5	4	7	.263	.311	.368	.680	84	-1	-1	102	82	7	.651	3	1	0	-1	S/32	0.0
1958	Cle-A	101	229	36	50	4	0	7	19	15	36	.218	.272	.328	.600	68	-12	-10	94	79	22	.565	12	2	2	-5	S3/2O	-0.3
1961	Bos-A	37	37	10	6	2	0	0	1	1	8	.162	.184	.216	.400	6	-5	-5	102	49	1	.313	1	0	0	0	3/S1	-0.3
Total	4	173	342	54	79	7	1	8	26	23	54	.231	.283	.327	.611	69	-16	-15	97	75	35	.577	17	3	3	-5	/S321O	-0.3
■ **BUD HARRELSON**	Harrelson, Derrel Mc Kinley b: 6/6/44, Niles, Cal. BB/TR, 5'11", 160 lbs. Deb: 9/02/65 C																											
1965	NY-N	19	37	3	4	1	1	0	0	2	11	.108	.154	.189	.343	-4	-5	-5	100	0	1	.273	0	0	0	0	S	-0.2
1966	NY-N	33	99	20	22	2	4	0	4	13	23	.222	.313	.323	.636	82	-3	-2	94	53	11	.642	7	3	0	2	S	0.3
1967	NY-N	151	540	59	137	16	4	1	28	48	64	.254	.319	.304	.623	80	-13	-13	99	74	54	.542	12	13	-4	6	*S	0.6
1968	NY-N	111	402	38	88	7	3	0	14	29	68	.219	.273	.251	.524	57	-20	-21	102	59	28	.419	4	5	-2	-4	*S	-1.5
1969	NY-N	123	395	42	98	11	6	0	24	54	54	.248	.341	.306	.648	82	-7	-8	100	79	44	.584	1	3	-2	-4	*S	0.1
1970	NY-N	157	564	72	137	18	8	1	42	95	74	.243	.355	.309	.663	76	-13	-16	104	98	72	.670	23	4	5	-23	*S	-1.4
1971	NY-N	142	547	55	138	16	6	0	32	53	59	.252	.321	.303	.624	80	-15	-13	96	75	59	.590	28	7	4	11	*S	2.2
1972	NY-N	115	418	54	90	10	4	1	24	58	57	.215	.315	.266	.581	70	-17	-14	95	92	40	.544	12	4	1	-3	*S	-0.2
1973	NY-N	106	356	35	92	12	3	0	20	48	49	.258	.348	.309	.657	83	-6	-6	101	74	42	.610	5	1	1	-10	*S	-0.1
1974	NY-N	106	331	48	75	10	0	1	13	71	39	.227	.366	.266	.632	79	-6	-5	99	56	39	.642	9	4	0	18	S	2.4
1975	NY-N	34	73	5	16	2	0	0	3	12	13	.219	.329	.247	.576	65	-3	-3	95	64	7	.517	0	0	0	-1	S	0.0
1976	NY-N	118	359	34	84	12	4	1	26	63	56	.234	.351	.298	.649	93	-4	-0	92	91	44	.649	9	3	1	-10	*S	0.1
1977	NY-N	107	269	25	48	6	2	1	12	27	28	.178	.256	.227	.483	32	-26	-25	96	75	17	.412	5	4	-1	-11	S	-2.3
1978	Phi-N	71	103	16	22	1	0	0	9	18	21	.214	.331	.223	.554	54	-5	-6	105	155	10	.554	5	2	0	4	2S	0.2
1979	Phi-N	53	71	7	20	6	0	0	7	13	14	.282	.400	.366	.766	114	2	2	97	107	11	.782	3	3	-1	0	2S/3O	0.4
1980	Tex-A	87	180	26	49	6	0	1	9	29	23	.272	.373	.322	.695	92	-1	-1	100	58	24	.659	4	4	-1	-1	S/2	0.4
Total	16	1533	4744	539	1120	136	45	7	267	633	653	.236	.329	.288	.617	75	-142	-135	99	78	502	.583	127	60	2	-29	*S/23O	1.0
■ **KEN HARRELSON**	Harrelson, Kenneth Smith "Hawk" b: 9/4/41, Woodruff, S.C. BR/TR, 6'2", 190 lbs. Deb: 6/09/63																											
1963	KC-A	79	226	16	52	10	1	6	23	23	58	.230	.301	.363	.664	79	-5	-7	108	96	23	.573	1	1	-0	-2	1O	-1.1
1964	KC-A	49	139	15	27	5	0	7	12	13	34	.194	.263	.381	.644	73	-5	-6	105	69	12	.555	0	1	-1	0	O1	-0.7
1965	KC-A	150	483	61	115	17	3	23	66	66	112	.238	.331	.429	.759	118	9	11	97	99	65	.720	9	7	-2	-3	*1/O	0.0
1966	KC-A	63	210	24	47	5	0	5	22	27	59	.224	.312	.319	.631	87	-4	-3	94	115	23	.613	9	2	2	-1	1/O	-0.4
	Was-A	71	250	25	62	8	1	7	28	26	53	.248	.321	.372	.693	104	-0	1	95	105	30	.629	4	1	1	-3	1	-0.3
	Yr	134	460	49	109	13	1	12	50	53	112	.237	.317	.348	.665	96	-5	-2	94	111	54	.627	13	3	2	-4		-0.7
1967	Was-A	26	79	10	16	0	0	3	10	7	15	.203	.267	.316	.584	70	-3	-3	102	123	6	.500	1	0	0	0	1	-0.4
	KC-A	61	174	23	53	11	0	6	30	17	17	.305	.366	.471	.838	147	10	10	100	125	31	.849	8	2	1	-1	1	0.7
	Bos-A	23	80	9	16	4	1	3	14	5	12	.200	.247	.387	.635	74	-2	-3	115	146	7	.552	1	1	-0	-3	O/1	-0.8
	Yr	110	333	42	85	15	1	12	54	29	44	.255	.315	.414	.729	110	5	4	103	131	45	.700	10	3	1	-5		-0.5
1968	Bos-A	150	535	79	147	17	4	35	**109**	69	90	.275	.360	.518	.877	163	40	40	101	130	94	.850	2	6	-3	5	*O1	4.0
1969	Bos-A	10	46	6	10	1	0	3	8	4	6	.217	.280	.435	.715	93	-0	-1	105	96	5	.632	0	1	-1	0	1	-0.1
	Cle-A	149	519	83	115	13	4	27	84	95	96	.222	.344	.418	.762	119	9	13	94	120	76	.770	17	8	0	1	*O1	0.9
	Yr	159	565	89	125	14	4	30	92	99	102	.221	.339	.419	.759	117	9	13	95	119	81	.760	17	9	-0	1		0.8
1970	Cle-A	17	39	3	11	1	0	1	1	6	4	.282	.378	.385	.762	96	1	0	115	22	6	.724	0	0	0	0	1	0.0
1971	Cle-A	52	161	20	32	2	0	5	14	24	21	.199	.303	.304	.607	68	-6	-7	106	89	16	.556	1	0	0	-3	1/O	-1.1
Total	9	900	2941	374	703	94	14	131	421	382	577	.239	.328	.414	.742	112	44	46	99	110	393	.730	53	30	-2	-11	1O	0.7

YEAR	TM/L	G	AB	R	H	2B	3B	HR	RBI	BB	SO	AVG	OBP	SLG	PRO	/A	BR	/A	PF	CHI	RC	TA	SB	CS	SBR	FR	POS	TPR
■ **ANDY HARRINGTON**	Harrington, Andrew Matthew b: 2/12/03, Mountain View, Cal d: 1/26/79, Boise, Idaho BR/TR, 5'11", 170 lbs. Deb: 4/18/25																											
1925	Det-A	1	1	0	0	0	0	0	0	0	0	.000	.000	.000	.000	-99	-0	-0	99	0	0	.000	0	0	0	0	H	0.0
■ **MICKEY HARRINGTON**	Harrington, Charles Michael b: 10/8/34, Hattiesburg, Miss. BR/TR, 6'4", 205 lbs. Deb: 7/10/63																											
1963	Phi-N	1	0	0	0	0	0	0	0	0	0	—	—	—	—	—	0	0	103	—	—	—	0	0	0	0	R	0.0
■ **JERRY HARRINGTON**	Harrington, Jeremiah Peter b: 8/12/1869, Keokuk, Iowa d: 4/16/13, Keokuk, Iowa TR, 5'11", 220 lbs. Deb: 4/30/1890																											
1890	Cin-N	65	236	25	58	7	1	1	23	15	29	.246	.299	.297	.596	70	-7	-10	108	97	23	.517	4			2	C	-0.2
1891	Cin-N	92	333	25	76	10	5	2	41	19	34	.228	.272	.306	.578	77	-13	-9	91	113	30	.490	4			-3	C/3	-0.2
1892	Cin-N	22	61	6	13	1	0	0	3	6	1	.213	.284	.230	.513	55	-3	-3	103	66	4	.417	0			0	C/1	-0.2
1893	Lou-N	10	36	4	4	1	0	0	6	3	9	.111	.179	.139	.318	-15	-6	-6	96	329	1	.250	0			0	C	-0.4
Total	4	189	666	60	151	19	6	3	73	43	73	.227	.278	.287	.564	67	-29	-28	98	115	57	.478	8			-1	C/13	-1.0
■ **JOE HARRINGTON**	Harrington, Joseph C. b: 12/21/1869, Fall River, Mass. d: 9/13/33, Fall River, Mass. 5'8.5", 162 lbs. Deb: 9/10/1895																											
1895	Bos-N	18	65	21	18	0	2	2	13	7	5	.277	.356	.431	.787	101	0	-0	103	109	11	.830	3			0	2	0.0
1896	Bos-N	54	198	25	39	5	3	1	25	19	17	.197	.271	.268	.538	40	-16	-19	108	131	15	.472	2			-8	3/S2	-2.0
Total	2	72	263	46	57	5	5	3	38	26	22	.217	.292	.308	.600	55	-16	-19	106	126	27	.553	5			-8	/32S	-2.0
■ **CANDY HARRIS**	Harris, Alonzo b: 9/17/47, Selma, Ala. BB/TR, 6', 160 lbs. Deb: 4/13/67																											
1967	Hou-N	6	1	0	0	0	0	0	0	0	1	.000	.000	.000	.000	-99	-0	-0	94	0	0	.000	0	0	0	0	H	0.0
■ **GAIL HARRIS**	Harris, Boyd Gail b: 10/15/31, Abingdon, Va. BL/TL, 6', 195 lbs. Deb: 6/03/55																											
1955	NY-N	79	263	27	61	9	0	12	36	20	46	.232	.291	.403	.694	83	-8	-7	99	103	30	.615	0	0	0	-3	1	-1.5
1956	NY-N	12	38	2	5	0	1	1	1	3	10	.132	.233	.263	.496	34	-4	-4	97	32	3	.455	0	0	0	0	1	-0.3
1957	NY-N	90	225	28	54	7	3	9	31	16	28	.240	.308	.418	.725	91	-3	-3	102	106	29	.669	1	0	0	-1	1	-0.9
1958	Det-A	134	451	63	123	18	8	20	83	36	60	.273	.332	.481	.813	116	11	9	104	120	70	.759	1	2	-1	0	*1	0.5
1959	Det-A	114	349	39	77	4	3	9	39	29	49	.221	.292	.327	.618	63	-15	-20	111	109	33	.532	0	1	-1	-1	1	-2.0
1960	Det-A	8	5	0	0	0	0	0	0	2	1	.000	.286	.000	.286	-16	-1	-1	102	0	0	.400	0	0	0	0	/1	0.0
Total	6	437	1331	159	320	38	15	51	190	106	194	.240	.306	.406	.713	88	-18	-25	104	108	165	.660	2	3	-1	-4	1	-4.2
■ **CHARLIE HARRIS**	Harris, Charles Jenkins b: 10/21/1877, Macon, Ga. d: 3/14/63, Gainesville, Fla. 5'8", 200 lbs. Deb: 5/25/1899																											
1899	Bal-N	30	68	16	19	3	0	0	1	3		.279	.319	.324	.643	73	-2	-3	108	14	9	.612	4			0	3/O2S	-0.1
■ **DAVE HARRIS**	Harris, David Stanley "Sheriff" b: 7/14/1900, Summerfield, N.C. d: 9/18/73, Atlanta, Ga. BR/TR, 5'11", 170 lbs. Deb: 4/14/25																											
1925	Bos-N	92	340	49	90	8	7	5	36	27	44	.265	.321	.374	.694	82	-12	-9	94	92	41	.634	6	4	-1	4	O	-0.7
1928	Bos-N	7	17	2	2	1	0	0	0	2	6	.118	.211	.176	.387	2	-2	-2	97	0	1	.333	0			-1	/O	-0.3
1930	Chi-A	33	86	16	21	2	1	5	13	7	22	.244	.309	.465	.774	91	-1	-2	103	78	13	.738	0	0	0	-1	O/2	-0.2
	Was-A	73	205	40	65	19	8	4	44	28	35	.317	.399	.546	.945	135	12	11	101	118	45	1.021	6	3	0	1	O	0.8
	Yr	106	291	56	86	21	9	9	57	35	57	.296	.373	.522	.895	122	10	9	102	106	57	.933	6	3	0	-0		0.6
1931	Was-A	77	231	49	72	14	8	5	50	49	38	.312	.434	.506	.941	146	18	17	101	125	53	1.055	7	6	-2	-4	O	0.7
1932	Was-A	81	156	26	51	7	4	6	29	19	34	.327	.400	.538	.938	141	9	9	100	95	33	.982	4	4	-1	-2	O	0.4
1933	Was-A	82	177	33	46	9	2	5	38	25	26	.260	.358	.418	.776	109	1	3	96	142	28	.788	3	1	0	-7	O/13	-0.5
1934	Was-A	97	235	28	59	14	3	2	37	39	40	.251	.358	.362	.719	85	-4	-5	101	136	32	.704	2	3	-1	-4	O/3	-1.0
Total	7	542	1447	243	406	74	33	32	247	196	245	.281	.368	.444	.812	110	20	23	99	113	246	.820	28	21		-15	O/312	-0.8
■ **FRANK HARRIS**	Harris, Frank W. b: 11/2/1858, Pittsburgh, Pa. d: 11/26/39, E.Moline, Ill. Deb: 4/17/1884																											
1884	Alt-U	24	95	10	25	2	1	0		3		.263	.286	.305	.591	98	-0	-0	101	0	8	.457	0			0	1/O	0.0
■ **BILLY HARRIS**	Harris, James William b: 11/24/43, Hamlet, N.C. BL/TR, 6', 175 lbs. Deb: 6/16/68																											
1968	Cle-A	38	94	10	20	5	1	0	3	8	22	.213	.275	.287	.562	70	-3	-3	101	48	7	.474	2	0	1	-2	23/S	-0.4
1969	KC-A	5	7	1	2	1	0	0	0	0	1	.286	.286	.429	.714	95	-0	-0	103	0	1	.600	0	0	0	0	/2	0.0
Total	2	43	101	11	22	6	1	0	3	8	23	.218	.275	.297	.572	72	-3	-4	101	44	8	.506	2	0	1	-2	/23S	-0.4
■ **JOHN HARRIS**	Harris, John Thomas b: 9/13/54, Portland, Ore. BL/TL, 6'3", 205 lbs. Deb: 9/26/79																											
1979	Cal-A	1	2	0	0	0	0	0	0	0	1	.000	.000	.000	.000	-99	-1	-1	93	0	0	.000	0	0	0	0	/1	0.0
1980	Cal-A	19	41	8	12	5	0	2	7	7	4	.293	.396	.561	.957	166	3	4	96	94	8	.938	0	1	-1	0	1/O	0.3
1981	Cal-A	36	77	5	19	3	0	3	9	3	11	.247	.275	.403	.678	89	-1	-1	104	88	7	.548	0	0	0	-3	1O/D	-0.5
Total	3	56	120	13	31	8	0	5	16	10	16	.258	.315	.450	.765	113	2	2	101	89	15	.681	0	1	-1	-3	/1OD	-0.2
■ **JOE HARRIS**	Harris, Joseph "Moon" b: 5/30/1891, Coulters, Pa. d: 12/10/59, Renton, Pa. BR/TR, 5'9", 170 lbs. Deb: 6/09/14																											
1914	NY-A	2	1	0	0	0	0	0	0	3	1	.000	.800	.000	.800	143	1	1	100	0	0	4.000	0			-0	/1O	0.1
1917	Cle-A	112	369	40	112	22	4	0	65	55	32	.304	.398	.385	.783	122	19	13	114	168	59	.821	11			7	1/O3	1.8
1919	Cle-A	62	184	30	69	16	1	1	46	33	21	.375	.472	.489	.962	160	19	18	107	179	43	1.096	2			-0	1/S	1.5
1922	Bos-A	119	408	53	129	30	9	6	54	30	15	.316	.364	.478	.842	123	9	12	96	91	69	.800	2	6	-3	5	O1	0.6
1923	Bos-A	142	483	82	162	28	11	13	76	52	27	.335	.406	.520	.925	140	29	28	102	91	104	.972	7	3	0	-13	*O/1	0.2
1924	Bos-A	133	491	82	148	36	9	3	77	81	25	.301	.406	.430	.835	111	14	11	104	123	92	.881	6	1	1	4	*1/O	0.9
1925	Bos-A	8	19	4	3	0	1	1	2	5	5	.158	.333	.421	.754	95	-0	-0	95	61	3	.813	0	0	0	0	/1	0.0
	Was-A	100	300	60	97	21	9	12	59	51	28	.323	.430	.573	1.003	156	25	26	98	95	76	1.131	5	3	-0	-3	1O	1.6
	Yr	108	319	64	100	21	10	13	61	56	33	.313	.424	.564	.988	153	24	25	98	93	79	1.108	5	3	-0	-3		1.6
1926	Was-A	92	257	43	79	13	9	5	55	37	9	.307	.405	.486	.891	134	12	13	98	133	52	.934	2	3	-1	-2	1O	0.6
1927	Pit-N	129	411	57	134	27	9	5	73	48	19	.326	.402	.472	.874	131	20	19	102	122	78	.888	0			-2	*1/O	0.9
1928	Pit-N	16	23	2	9	2	1	0	2	4	2	.391	.500	.565	1.065	167	3	3	107	55	7	1.286	0			0	/1	0.2
	Bro-N	55	89	8	21	6	1	1	8	14	4	.236	.340	.360	.699	84	-2	-2	99	81	11	.676	0			-2	O	-0.3
	Yr	71	112	10	30	8	2	1	10	18	6	.268	.374	.402	.776	102	1	1	101	76	17	.780	0			-2		-0.1
Total	10	970	3035	461	963	201	64	47	517	413	188	.317	.404	.472	.877	130	150	141	102	118	594	.916	35	16		-5	1O/S3	8.1
■ **LENNY HARRIS**	Harris, Leonard Anthony b: 10/28/64, Miami, Fla. BL/TR, 5'10", 195 lbs. Deb: 9/07/88																											
1988	Cin-N	16	43	7	16	1	0	0	8	5	4	.372	.438	.395	.833	133	3	2	105	188	9	.929	4	1	1	1	/32	0.4
■ **NED HARRIS**	Harris, Robert Ned b: 7/9/16, Ames, Iowa d: 12/18/76, W.Palm Beach, Fla. BL/TL, 5'11", 175 lbs. Deb: 4/20/41																											
1941	Det-A	26	61	11	13	3	1	1	4	6	13	.213	.284	.344	.628	61	-3	-4	106	59	7	.583	1	0	0	-3	O	-0.6
1942	Det-A	121	398	53	108	16	10	9	45	49	35	.271	.351	.430	.781	106	9	3	113	80	63	.750	5	4	-1	-12	*O	-1.6
1943	Det-A	114	354	43	90	14	3	6	32	47	29	.254	.343	.362	.705	101	3	1	106	80	46	.655	6	8	-3	-4	O	-0.9
1946	Det-A	1	1	0	0	0	0	0	0	0	0	.000	.000	.000	.000	-92	-0	-0	108	0	0	.000	0	0	0	0	H	0.0
Total	4	262	814	107	211	33	14	16	81	102	77	.259	.342	.393	.736	100	9	-0	109	78	115	.707	12	12	-4	-19	O	-3.1
■ **SPENCER HARRIS**	Harris, Spencer Anthony b: 8/12/1900, Duluth, Minn. d: 7/3/82, Minneapolis, Minn. BL/TL, 5'9", 145 lbs. Deb: 4/14/25																											
1925	Chi-A	56	92	12	26	2	0	1	13	14	13	.283	.383	.337	.720	88	-2	-1	96	128	12	.681	1	3	-2	-4	O	-0.7
1926	Chi-A	80	222	36	56	11	3	2	27	20	15	.252	.317	.356	.673	82	-8	-6	92	108	26	.639	8	3	1	-6	O	-1.4
1929	Was-A	6	14	1	3	1	0	0	1	0	3	.214	.214	.286	.500	28	-2	-2	100	86	1	.455	1	0	0	-1	/O	-0.1
1930	Phi-A	22	49	4	9	1	0	0	5	5	2	.184	.259	.204	.463	19	-6	-6	99	166	3	.375	0	0	0	0	O	-0.5
Total	4	164	377	53	94	15	3	3	46	39	33	.249	.323	.329	.652	73	-18	-14	94	120	43	.606	10	6	-1	-10	O	-2.7
■ **BUCKY HARRIS**	Harris, Stanley Raymond b: 11/8/1896, Port Jervis, N.Y. d: 11/8/77, Bethesda, Md. BR/TR, 5'9.5", 156 lbs. Deb: 8/28/19 M																											
1919	Was-A	8	28	0	6	2	0	0	4	1	3	.214	.267	.286	.552	56	-2	-2	98	185	2	.455	0			-3	/2	-0.3
1920	Was-A	136	506	76	152	26	6	1	68	41	36	.300	.377	.381	.758	106	3	6	95	129	73	.730	16	17	-5	-14	*2	-0.9
1921	Was-A	154	584	82	169	22	8	0	54	54	39	.289	.367	.354	.722	86	-11	-10	99	95	83	.726	29	9	3	12	*2	0.9
1922	Was-A	154	602	95	162	24	8	2	40	52	38	.269	.341	.346	.687	86	-17	-10	92	64	75	.663	25	11	1	**26**	*2	2.7
1923	Was-A	145	532	60	150	21	13	2	70	50	29	.282	.358	.382	.740	100	-4	1	95	121	74	.726	23	16	-3	18	*2/S	2.0
1924	Was-A	143	544	88	146	28	9	1	58	56	41	.268	.344	.358	.703	83	-15	-14	98	85	72	.679	19	10	-0	-16	*2M	-2.4
1925	Was-A	144	551	91	158	30	3	1	66	64	21	.287	.370	.358	.728	87	-10	-8	98	98	77	.701	14	12	-3	3	*2M	-0.1
1926	Was-A	141	537	94	152	39	9	1	63	58	41	.283	.363	.395	.757	100	-2	0	98	106	80	.745	16	11	-2	-5	*2M	0.0

YEAR	TM/L	G	AB	R	H	2B	3B	HR	RBI	BB	SO	AVG	OBP	SLG	PRO	/A	BR	/A	PF	CHI	RC	TA	SB	CS	SBR	FR	POS	TPR
1927	Was-A	128	475	98	127	20	3	1	55	66	33	.267	.363	.328	.691	83	-11	-9	97	111	60	.704	18	0	5	2	*2M	-0.1
1928	Was-A	99	358	34	73	11	5	0	28	27	26	.204	.264	.263	.526	38	-32	-33	102	104	26	.446	5	2	0	5	2/3OM	-2.1
1929	Det-A	7	11	3	1	0	0	0	0	2	2	.091	.231	.091	.322	-14	-2	-2	97	0	1	.400	1	0	0	0	/2SM	0.0
1931	Det-A	4	8	1	1	1	0	0	0	1	1	.125	.222	.250	.472	23	-1	-1	104	0	0	.429	0	0	0	0	/2M	0.0
Total	12	1263	4736	722	1297	224	64	9	506	472	310	.274	.352	.354	.706	86	-104	-81	97	100	624	.684	166	88		28	*2/SO3	-0.3
■ **VIC HARRIS**	Harris, Victor Lanier b: 3/27/50, Los Angeles, Cal. BB/TR, 5'11", 165 lbs. Deb: 7/21/72																											
1972	Tex-A	61	186	8	26	5	1	0	10	12	39	.140	.192	.177	.369	11	-20	-19	94	127	7	.319	7	3	0	-1	2/S	-1.9
1973	Tex-A	152	555	71	138	14	7	8	44	55	81	.249	.319	.342	.661	89	-10	-8	97	82	58	.584	13	12	-3	-4	*O32	-1.8
1974	Chi-N	62	200	18	39	6	3	0	11	29	26	.195	.297	.255	.552	55	-11	-11	100	83	18	.536	9	3	1	-6	2	-1.3
1975	Chi-N	51	56	6	10	0	0	0	5	6	7	.179	.258	.179	.437	22	-6	-6	104	193	3	.348	0	0	0	-3	O/32	-0.8
1976	StL-N	97	259	21	59	12	3	1	19	16	55	.228	.275	.309	.584	63	-12	-13	104	88	21	.471	1	2	-1	-0	2O3/S	-1.4
1977	SF-N	69	165	28	43	12	0	2	14	19	36	.261	.337	.370	.707	86	-2	-3	104	84	22	.661	2	1	0	-5	2S/3O	-0.4
1978	SF-N	53	100	8	15	4	0	1	11	11	24	.150	.234	.220	.454	30	-10	-9	92	174	6	.388	0	0	0	-3	S2/O	-0.9
1980	Mil-A	34	89	8	19	4	1	1	7	12	13	.213	.307	.315	.622	75	-3	-3	95	88	10	.611	4	1	1	-3	O/32	-0.4
Total	8	579	1610	168	349	57	15	13	121	160	281	.217	.289	.295	.584	65	-75	-72	99	98	145	.525	36	22	-2	-24	2O/3S	-8.9
■ **CHUCK HARRISON**	Harrison, Charles William b: 4/25/41, Abilene, Tex. BR/TR, 5'10", 185 lbs. Deb: 9/15/65																											
1965	Hou-N	15	45	2	9	4	0	1	9	8	9	.200	.321	.356	.676	102	-0	0	89	196	6	.667	0	0	0	0	1	0.0
1966	Hou-N	119	434	52	111	23	2	9	52	37	69	.256	.317	.380	.697	95	-4	-3	97	116	51	.615	2	0	1	3	*1	-0.4
1967	Hou-N	70	177	13	43	7	3	2	26	13	30	.243	.295	.350	.645	90	-4	-3	94	158	18	.540	0	0	0	-1	1	-0.6
1969	KC-A	75	213	18	47	5	1	3	18	16	20	.221	.278	.296	.574	59	-11	-12	103	100	17	.474	1	2	-1	5	1	-1.2
1971	KC-A	49	143	9	31	4	0	2	21	11	19	.217	.273	.287	.559	59	-8	-8	99	182	12	.460	0	0	0	0	1	-0.9
Total	5	328	1012	94	241	43	6	17	126	85	147	.238	.299	.343	.642	82	-28	-25	98	133	104	.566	3	2	-0	7	1	-3.1
■ **BEN HARRISON**	Harrison, Leo J. BR , Deb: 9/27/01																											
1901	Was-A	1	2	0	0	0	0	0	0	1		.000	.333	.000	.333	-0	-0	-0	99	0	0	.500	0			0	/O	0.0
■ **TOM HARRISON**	Harrison, Thomas James b: 1/18/45, Trail, B.C., Canada BR/TR, 6'3", 200 lbs. Deb: 5/07/65																											
1965	KC-A	2	0	0	0	0	0	0	0	0	0	—	—	—	—	—	0	0	97	—	—	—	0	0	0	0	/P	0.0
■ **RIT HARRISON**	Harrison, Washington Ritter b: 9/16/1848, Waterbury, Conn. d: 11/7/1888, Bridgeport, Conn. Deb: 5/20/1875																											
1875	NH-n	1	4	0	2							.500															/C	
■ **SAM HARSHANY**	Harshany, Samuel b: 5/1/10, Madison, Ill. BR/TR, 6', 180 lbs. Deb: 9/28/37																											
1937	StL-A	5	11	0	1	1	0	0	0	3	0	.091	.286	.182	.468	21	-1	-1	99	0	1	.500	0	0	0	0	/C	0.0
1938	StL-A	11	24	2	7	0	0	0	0	3	2	.292	.370	.292	.662	68	-1	-1	100	0	3	.588	0	0	0	1	C	0.0
1939	StL-A	42	145	15	35	2	0	0	15	9	8	.241	.290	.255	.545	40	-13	-13	100	137	10	.409	0	1	-1	1	C	-0.8
1940	StL-A	3	1	0	0	0	0	0	0	1	0	.000	.500	.000	.500	40	0	0	106	0	0	1.000	0	0	0	0	/C	0.0
Total	4	61	181	17	43	3	0	0	15	16	10	.238	.303	.254	.557	43	-15	-15	100	107	14	.453	0	1	-1	2	/C	-0.8
■ **BURT HART**	Hart, James Burton b: 6/28/1873, Brown Co., Minn. d: 1/29/21, Sacramento, Cal. BB , 6'3", 200 lbs. Deb: 6/06/01																											
1901	Bal-A	58	206	33	64	3	5	0	23	20		.311	.372	.374	.745	102	3	1	107	96	32	.732	7			-5	1	-0.5
■ **HUB HART**	Hart, James Henry b: 2/2/1878, Everett, Mass. d: 10/10/60, Fort Wayne, Ind. BL/TR, 5'11", 170 lbs. Deb: 7/16/05																											
1905	Chi-A	11	20	2	2	0	0	0	4	3		.100	.217	.100	.317	3	-2	-2	97	714	0	.278	0			0	/C	-0.1
1906	Chi-A	17	37	1	6	0	0	0	0	2		.162	.205	.162	.367	18	-3	-3	92	0	1	.258	0			-1	C	-0.2
1907	Chi-A	29	70	6	19	1	0	0	7	5		.271	.320	.286	.606	92	-0	-1	104	125	7	.510	1			-1	C	0.1
Total	3	57	127	9	27	1	0	0	11	10		.213	.270	.220	.491	58	-6	-6	99	188	9	.390	1			-2	/C	-0.2
■ **MIKE HART**	Hart, James Michael b: 12/20/51, Kalamazoo, Mich. BB/TR, 6'3", 185 lbs. Deb: 6/12/80																											
1980	Tex-A	5	4	1	1	0	0	0	0	1	1	.250	.400	.250	.650	82	-0	-0	100	0	1	.667	0	0	0	-1	/O	0.0
■ **JIM RAY HART**	Hart, James Ray b: 10/30/41, Hookerton, N.C. BR/TR, 5'11", 185 lbs. Deb: 7/07/63																											
1963	SF-N	7	20	1	4	1	0	0	2	3	6	.200	.360	.250	.610	83	-0	-0	96	168	2	.588	0	0	0	-1	/3	-0.1
1964	SF-N	153	566	71	162	15	6	31	81	47	94	.286	.345	.498	.843	134	25	24	100	90	95	.807	5	2	0	8	*3/O	2.5
1965	SF-N	160	591	91	177	30	6	23	96	47	75	.299	.353	.487	.840	121	25	18	111	114	98	.792	6	4	-1	-12	*3O	0.0
1966	SF-N	156	578	88	165	23	4	33	93	48	75	.285	.344	.510	.855	137	25	27	97	101	92	.791	2	5	-2	-7	*3O	1.5
1967	SF-N	158	578	98	167	26	7	29	99	77	100	.289	.376	.509	.885	150	39	38	101	114	111	.883	1	1	-0	-13	3O	1.8
1968	SF-N	136	480	67	124	14	3	23	78	46	74	.258	.327	.444	.771	133	17	18	98	119	66	.710	3	1	0	-10	3O	0.6
1969	SF-N	95	236	27	60	9	0	3	26	28	49	.254	.346	.331	.676	89	-2	-2	101	120	27	.603	0	0	0	-10	O/3	-1.6
1970	SF-N	76	255	30	72	12	1	8	37	30	29	.282	.365	.431	.796	117	5	6	96	107	38	.730	0	0	0	-7	3O	-0.2
1971	SF-N	31	39	5	10	0	0	2	5	6	8	.256	.356	.410	.766	117	1	1	100	92	5	.710	0	1	-1	-0	/3O	0.0
1972	SF-N	24	79	10	24	5	0	5	8	6	10	.304	.360	.557	.917	158	6	6	100	56	14	.864	0	1	-1	-0	3	0.5
1973	SF-N	5	3	0	0	0	0	0	1	3	1	.000	.500	.000	.500	47	0	0	105	0	1	1.000	0	0	0	0	/3	0.0
	NY-A	114	339	29	86	13	2	13	52	36	45	.254	.325	.419	.744	108	3	3	101	113	42	.657	0	2	-1	0	*D	0.2
1974	NY-A	10	19	1	1	0	0	0	0	3	7	.053	.182	.053	.234	-31	-3	-3	96	0	0	.222	0	0	0	0	/D	-0.2
Total	12	1125	3783	518	1052	148	29	170	578	380	573	.278	.348	.467	.816	128	139	135	101	107	592	.798	17	17	-5	-52	3OD	5.0
■ **MIKE HART**	Hart, Michael Lawrence b: 2/17/58, Milwaukee, Wis. BL/TL, 5'11", 185 lbs. Deb: 5/08/84																											
1984	Min-A	13	29	0	5	0	0	0	5	1	2	.172	.200	.172	.372	4	-4	-4	106	399	1	.240	0	1	-1	0	O	-0.4
1987	Bal-A	34	76	7	12	2	0	4	12	6	19	.158	.220	.342	.562	48	-6	-6	98	126	5	.478	1	4	-2	1	O	-0.7
Total	2	47	105	7	17	2	0	4	17	7	21	.162	.214	.295	.510	35	-10	-10	100	199	5	.415	1	5	-3	1	/O	-1.1
■ **TOM HART**	Hart, Thomas Henry "Bushy" b: 6/15/1869, Canaan, N.Y. d: 9/17/39, Gardner, Mass. Deb: 4/15/1891																											
1891	Was-a	8	24	1	3	0	0	0	2	2	1	.125	.192	.125	.317	-8	-3	-3	95	193	1	.286	1			0	/CO	-0.2
■ **BILL HART**	Hart, William Woodrow b: 3/4/13, Wiconisco, Pa. d: 7/29/68, Lykins, Pa. BR/TR, 6', 175 lbs. Deb: 9/18/43																											
1943	Bro-N	8	19	0	3	0	0	0	1	1	2	.158	.200	.158	.358	4	-2	-2	100	120	0	.235	0			-1	/3S	-0.2
1944	Bro-N	29	90	8	16	4	2	0	4	9	7	.178	.253	.267	.519	47	-7	-6	99	60	7	.453	1			-4	S/3	-0.7
1945	Bro-N	58	161	27	37	6	2	3	27	14	21	.230	.291	.348	.639	81	-5	-5	96	144	17	.611	7			-8	3/S	-1.1
Total	3	95	270	35	56	10	4	3	32	24	30	.207	.272	.307	.580	64	-14	-13	97	114	24	.532	8			-12	/3S	-2.0
■ **BRUCE HARTFORD**	Hartford, Bruce Daniel b: 5/14/1892, Chicago, Ill. d: 5/25/75, Los Angeles, Cal. BR/TR, 6'0.5", 190 lbs. Deb: 6/03/14																											
1914	Cle-A	8	22	5	4	1	0	0	0	4	9	.182	.308	.227	.535	60	-1	-1	102	0	2	.500	0			-0	/S	0.0
■ **CHRIS HARTJE**	Hartje, Christian Henry b: 3/25/15, San Francisco, Cal d: 6/26/46, Seattle, Wash. BR/TR, 5'10.5", 165 lbs. Deb: 9/09/39																											
1939	Bro-N	9	16	2	5	1	0	0	5	1	0	.313	.353	.375	.728	89	-0	-0	107	305	2	.583	0			0	/C	0.0
■ **GROVER HARTLEY**	Hartley, Grover Allen "Slick" b: 7/2/1888, Osgood, Ind. d: 10/19/64, Daytona Beach, Fla BR/TR, 5'11", 175 lbs. Deb: 5/13/11 C																											
1911	NY-N	11	18	1	4	2	0	0	1	1	1	.222	.263	.333	.596	65	-1	-1	102	56	2	.571	1			-2	C	-0.1
1912	NY-N	25	34	3	8	2	1	0	7	0	4	.235	.257	.353	.610	64	-2	-2	104	196	3	.577	2			-3	C	-0.3
1913	NY-N	23	19	4	6	0	0	0	0	1	2	.316	.350	.316	.666	88	-0	-0	103	0	3	.846	4			-1	C/1	0.0
1914	StL-F	86	212	24	61	13	2	1	25	12	26	.288	.326	.382	.708	97	0	-1	106	107	29	.642	4			4	C2/13O	0.4
1915	StL-F	120	394	47	108	21	6	1	50	42	21	.274	.344	.365	.710	105	5	3	105	125	56	.685	10			2	*C/1	0.9
1916	StL-A	89	222	19	50	8	0	0	12	30	24	.225	.325	.261	.587	80	-5	-4	95	74	21	.552	4			-4	C	-0.4
1917	StL-A	19	13	2	3	0	0	0	0	2	1	.231	.333	.231	.564	76	-0	-0	95	0	1	.500	0			0	/CS3	0.0
1924	NY-N	4	7	1	2	1	0	0	1	1	0	.286	.375	.429	.804	126	0	0	91	122	1	1.000	1	0	0	-0	/C	0.0
1925	NY-N	46	95	9	30	1	1	0	8	8	3	.316	.375	.347	.722	87	-2	-1	99	86	13	.677	2	0	1	-0	C/1	0.0
1926	NY-N	13	21	0	1	0	0	0	0	5	0	.048	.231	.048	.278	-22	-4	-3	98	0	0	.300	0			-1	C	-0.4
1927	Bos-A	103	244	23	67	11	0	1	31	22	14	.275	.337	.332	.669	78	-9	-7	95	123	28	.593	1	0	0	-7	C	-0.9
1929	Cle-A	24	33	2	9	0	1	0	8	2	1	.273	.314	.333	.648	67	-2	-2	100	249	3	.542	0	0	0	0	C	0.0

YEAR	TM/L	G	AB	R	H	2B	3B	HR	RBI	BB	SO	AVG	OBP	SLG	PRO	/A	BR	/A	PF	CHI	RC	TA	SB	CS	SBR	FR	POS	TPR
1930	Cle-A	1	4	0	3	0	0	0	1	0	0	.750	.750	.750	1.500	268	1	1	105	113	2	3.000	0	0	0	0	/C	0.1
1934	StL-A	5	3	0	1	1	0	0	0	1	0	.333	.500	.667	1.167	191	0	0	104	0	1	1.500	0	0	0	0	/C	0.1
Total	14	569	1319	135	353	60	11	3	144	127	97	.268	.335	.337	.671	89	-17	-17	100	108	164	.627	29	0		-12	C/123OS	-0.6
■ CHICK HARTLEY	Hartley, Walter Scott b: 8/22/1880, Philadelphia, Pa. d: 7/18/48, Philadelphia, Pa. BR/TR, 5'8", 180 lbs. Deb: 6/04/02																											
1902	NY-N	1	4	0	0	0	0	0	0	0	0	.000	.000	.000	.000	-99	-1	-1	100	0	0	.000	0			0	/O	0.0
■ FRED HARTMAN	Hartman, Frederick Orrin "Dutch" b: 4/25/1868, Allegheny, Pa. d: 11/11/38, Mc Keesport, Pa. BR/TR, Deb: 7/26/1894																											
1894	Pit-N	49	182	41	58	4	7	2	20	16	11	.319	.389	.451	.840	110	1	3	94	64	37	.927	12			-3	3	0.0
1897	StL-N	124	516	67	158	21	8	2	67	26		.306	.350	.390	.740	104	-2	3	93	91	79	.709	18			-4	*3	0.0
1898	NY-N	123	475	57	129	16	11	2	88	25		.272	.312	.364	.676	101	-4	0	95	158	59	.613	11			7	*3	0.9
1899	NY-N	50	174	25	41	3	5	1	16	12		.236	.307	.328	.635	78	-6	-5	97	83	19	.579	2			-4	3	-0.7
1901	Chi-A	120	473	77	146	23	13	3	89	25		.309	.343	.431	.775	117	9	10	99	140	83	.795	31			-5	*3	0.2
1902	StL-N	114	416	30	90	10	3	0	52	14		.216	.242	.255	.497	58	-22	-20	95	173	30	.411	14			-6	*3/S1	-2.1
Total	6	580	2236	297	622	77	47	10	332	118	11	.278	.321	.368	.689	97	-23	-8	96	127	306	.652	88			-15	3/S1	-1.7
■ J. C. HARTMAN	Hartman, J C b: 4/15/34, Cottonton, Ala. BR/TR, 6', 175 lbs. Deb: 7/21/62																											
1962	Hou-N	51	148	11	33	5	0	0	5	4	16	.223	.248	.257	.505	39	-13	-12	93	52	9	.367	1	1	-0	3	S	-0.4
1963	Hou-N	39	90	2	11	1	0	0	3	2	13	.122	.151	.133	.284	-19	-13	-13	92	105	2	.195	1	0	0	-2	S	-1.2
Total	2	90	238	13	44	6	0	0	8	6	29	.185	.211	.210	.421	18	-27	-25	93	72	10	.303	2	1	0	1	/S	-1.6
■ GABBY HARTNETT	Hartnett, Charles Leo b: 12/20/1900, Woonsocket, R.I. d: 12/20/72, Park Ridge, Ill. BR/TR, 6'1", 195 lbs. Deb: 4/12/22 MCH																											
1922	Chi-N	31	72	4	14	1	1	0	4	6	8	.194	.256	.236	.493	29	-8	-7	95	82	5	.414	1	0	0	3	C	-0.3
1923	Chi-N	85	231	28	62	12	2	8	39	25	22	.268	.347	.442	.789	102	2	1	104	109	37	.793	4	0	1	2	C1	0.3
1924	Chi-N	111	354	56	106	17	7	16	67	39	37	.299	.377	.523	.899	137	19	18	101	105	72	.956	10	2	2	1	*C	2.2
1925	Chi-N	117	398	61	115	28	3	24	67	36	77	.289	.351	.555	.906	131	14	16	97	81	75	.903	1	5	-3	11	*C	2.7
1926	Chi-N	93	284	35	78	25	3	8	41	32	37	.275	.352	.468	.821	112	7	5	106	90	46	.811	0			5	C	1.2
1927	Chi-N	127	449	56	132	32	5	10	80	44	42	.294	.361	.454	.815	117	10	10	100	122	73	.798	2			13	*C	3.1
1928	Chi-N	120	388	61	117	26	9	14	57	65	32	.302	.404	.523	.928	149	24	27	95	83	83	1.007	3			12	*C	4.5
1929	Chi-N	25	22	2	6	2	1	1	9	5	5	.273	.407	.591	.998	142	2	1	101	193	5	1.188	1			0	/C	0.1
1930	Chi-N	141	508	84	172	31	3	37	122	55	62	.339	.404	.630	1.034	138	35	31	105	100	125	1.119	0			7	*C	3.9
1931	Chi-N	116	380	53	107	32	1	8	70	52	48	.282	.370	.434	.804	120	9	11	96	132	64	.810	3			11	*C	2.7
1932	Chi-N	121	406	52	110	25	3	12	52	51	59	.271	.354	.436	.790	107	7	5	104	91	66	.774	0			3	*C/1	1.2
1933	Chi-N	140	490	55	135	21	4	16	88	37	51	.276	.326	.433	.759	119	9	10	97	130	67	.672	1			1	*C	1.7
1934	Chi-N	130	438	58	131	21	1	22	90	37	46	.299	.358	.502	.860	131	16	17	98	113	77	.807	0			5	*C	2.6
1935	Chi-N	116	413	67	142	32	6	13	91	41	46	.344	.404	.545	.949	154	30	31	99	124	91	.944	1			-0	*C	2.9
1936	Chi-N	121	424	49	130	25	6	7	64	30	36	.307	.361	.443	.804	110	9	6	105	108	68	.732	0			2	*C	1.1
1937	Chi-N	110	356	47	126	21	6	12	82	43	19	.354	.424	.548	.971	158	31	30	103	128	85	1.000	0			-8	*C	2.5
1938	Chi-N	88	299	40	82	19	1	10	59	48	17	.274	.380	.445	.825	120	12	10	105	133	53	.819	1			-3	CM	1.0
1939	Chi-N	97	306	36	85	18	2	12	59	37	32	.278	.358	.467	.825	119	8	8	101	121	50	.780	0			-0	CM	1.0
1940	Chi-N	37	64	3	17	3	0	1	12	8	7	.266	.347	.359	.707	96	-0	-0	100	171	8	.620	0			0	C/1M	0.1
1941	NY-N	64	150	20	45	5	0	5	26	12	14	.300	.356	.433	.789	118	4	3	103	117	22	.709	0			5	C	1.2
Total	20	1990	6432	867	1912	396	64	236	1179	703	697	.297	.370	.489	.858	126	241	234	101	111	1173	.863	28	7		69	*C/1	35.7
■ PAT HARTNETT	Hartnett, Patrick J. "Happy" b: 10/20/1863, Boston, Mass. d: 4/10/35, Boston, Mass. 6'1", 175 lbs. Deb: 4/18/1890																											
1890	StL-a	14	53	6	10	2	1	0		6		.189	.283	.264	.547	55	-2	-4	116	0	4	.512	1			0	1	-0.2
■ GREG HARTS	Harts, Gregory Rudolph b: 4/21/50, Atlanta, Ga. BL/TL, 6', 168 lbs. Deb: 9/15/73																											
1973	NY-N	3	2	0	1	0	0	0	0	0	0	.500	.500	.500	1.000	177	0	0	101	0	1	1.000	0	0	0	0	H	0.0
■ TOPSY HARTSEL	Hartsel, Tully Frederick b: 6/26/1874, Polk, Ohio d: 10/14/44, Toledo, Ohio BL/TL, 5'5", 155 lbs. Deb: 9/14/1898																											
1898	Lou-N	22	71	11	23	0	0	0	9	11		.324	.422	.324	.746	122	3	3	96	121	11	.771	2			0	O	0.3
1899	Lou-N	30	75	8	18	1	1	1	7	11		.240	.345	.320	.665	83	-1	-2	103	79	9	.649	1			0	O	0.0
1900	Cin-N	18	64	10	21	2	1	2	5	8		.328	.403	.484	.887	160	4	5	92	43	16	1.070	7			0	O	0.4
1901	Chi-N	140	558	111	187	25	16	7	54	74		.335	.413	.475	.888	160	44	44	100	55	130	1.024	41			0	*O	2.8
1902	Phi-A	137	545	**109**	154	20	12	5	58	**87**		.283	.381	.391	.772	107	15	8	108	72	102	.887	**47**			2	*O	0.1
1903	Phi-A	98	373	65	116	19	14	5	26	49		.311	.391	.477	.868	156	29	27	104	43	77	.934	13			3	O	2.4
1904	Phi-A	147	534	79	135	17	12	2	25	75		.253	.345	.341	.686	118	15	14	102	44	71	.692	19			4	*O	1.0
1905	Phi-A	149	533	87	147	22	8	0	28	**121**		.276	**.410**	.347	.757	131	35	28	109	47	93	.886	36			-13	*O	0.8
1906	Phi-A	144	533	96	136	21	9	1	30	**88**		.255	.361	.334	.695	128	16	21	94	52	77	.748	31			5	*O	2.2
1907	Phi-A	143	507	93	142	23	6	3	29	**106**		.280	**.405**	.367	.771	140	34	31	106	47	85	.855	20			-14	*O	0.9
1908	Phi-A	129	460	73	112	16	6	4	29	**93**		.243	.371	.330	.701	122	21	17	108	57	61	.747	15			-18	*O	-0.8
1909	Phi-A	83	267	30	72	4	4	1	18	48		.270	.381	.326	.707	121	10	9	102	82	34	.708	3			6	O	1.4
1910	Phi-A	90	285	45	63	10	3	0	22	58		.221	.353	.277	.630	96	2	1	102	105	32	.667	11			-7	O	-1.0
1911	Phi-A	25	38	8	9	2	0	0	1	8		.237	.396	.289	.685	99	0	1	93	31	5	.724	0			0	/O	0.0
Total	14	1355	4843	825	1335	182	92	31	341	837		.276	.383	.370	.753	128	227	207	103	58	801	.821	246			-33	*O	10.5
■ ROY HARTSFIELD	Hartsfield, Roy Thomas "Spec" b: 10/25/25, Chattahoochee, Ga. BR/TR, 5'9", 165 lbs. Deb: 4/28/50 MC																											
1950	Bos-N	107	419	62	116	15	2	7	24	27	61	.277	.322	.372	.694	95	-11	-4	86	53	52	.624	7			-11	2	-1.1
1951	Bos-N	120	450	63	122	11	2	6	31	41	73	.271	.333	.344	.678	84	-10	-9	98	71	56	.609	7	2	1	-7	*2	-1.0
1952	Bos-N	38	107	13	28	4	3	0	4	5	12	.262	.295	.355	.650	84	-3	-3	95	41	11	.531	0	0	0	-1	2	-0.2
Total	3	265	976	138	266	30	7	13	59	73	146	.273	.324	.358	.682	89	-25	-15	93	60	119	.613	14	2		-19	2	-2.3
■ ROY HARTZELL	Hartzell, Roy Allen b: 7/6/1881, Golden, Colo. d: 11/6/61, Golden, Colo. BL/TR, 5'8.5", 155 lbs. Deb: 4/17/06																											
1906	StL-A	113	404	43	86	7	0	0	24	21		.213	.252	.230	.482	54	-21	-20	98	96	29	.418	19			-4	*3/S2	-1.8
1907	StL-A	60	220	20	52	3	5	0	13	11		.236	.273	.295	.568	85	-4	-4	98	73	20	.494	7			0	32/SO	-0.1
1908	StL-A	115	422	41	112	5	6	2	32	19		.265	.297	.320	.617	99	1	-1	103	90	45	.574	24			-13	OS/32	-1.8
1909	StL-A	152	595	64	161	12	5	0	32	29		.271	.312	.308	.620	105	-3	2	92	60	59	.537	14			5	OS/2	0.5
1910	StL-A	151	542	52	118	13	5	2	30	49		.218	.290	.271	.561	80	-15	-11	94	77	48	.519	18			5	3SO	-0.2
1911	NY-A	144	527	67	156	17	11	3	91	63		.296	.375	.387	.763	102	10	2	111	153	86	.790	22			-11	*3S/O	-0.7
1912	NY-A	123	416	50	113	10	11	1	38	64		.272	.370	.356	.726	106	6	5	101	86	63	.769	20			-5	3OS/2	-0.2
1913	NY-A	141	490	60	127	18	1	0	38	67	40	.259	.353	.300	.653	91	-3	-3	101	97	60	.672	26			4	2O3/S	-0.1
1914	NY-A	137	481	55	112	15	9	1	32	68	38	.233	.335	.308	.643	93	-2	-2	100	76	52	.619	22	25	-8	4	*O/2	-1.5
1915	NY-A	119	387	39	97	11	2	3	60	57	37	.251	.351	.313	.664	100	1	2	98	160	42	.608	7	19	-9	-1	*O/23	-1.4
1916	NY-A	33	64	12	12	1	0	0	7	9	3	.188	.297	.203	.500	50	-3	-4	101	192	5	.462	1			-7	O	-1.3
Total	11	1288	4548	503	1146	112	55	12	397	457	118	.252	.325	.309	.633	93	-33	-33	100	98	508	.602	180	44		-23	O3S2	-8.6
■ LUTHER HARVEL	Harvel, Luther Raymond "Red" b: 9/30/05, Cambria, Ill. d: 4/10/86, Kansas City, Mo. BR/TR, 5'11", 180 lbs. Deb: 7/31/28																											
1928	Cle-A	40	136	12	30	6	1	0	12	4	17	.221	.264	.279	.543	40	-11	-12	106	108	10	.439	1	1	-0	1	O	-1.2
■ ERWIN HARVEY	Harvey, Ervin King "Zaza" b: 1/5/1879, Saratoga, Cal. d: 6/3/54, Santa Monica, Cal. BL , Deb: 5/03/00																											
1900	Chi-N	2	3	0	0	0	0	0	0	0		.000	.000	.000	.000	-99	-1	-1	93	0	0	.000	0			0	/P	0.0
1901	Chi-A	17	40	11	10	3	1	0	3	2		.250	.286	.375	.661	84	-1	-1	99	63	5	.600	1			2	P	0.0
	Cle-A	45	170	21	60	5	5	1	24	9		.353	.385	.459	.844	143	8	9	95	95	37	.927	15			1	O	0.8
	Yr	62	210	32	70	8	6	1	27	11		.333	.367	.443	.809	131	7	8	96	87	41	.857	16			3		0.8
1902	Cle-A	12	46	5	16	2	0	0	5	3		.348	.388	.391	.779	122	1	1	97	97	8	.733	1			-1	O	0.0
Total	3	76	259	37	86	10	6	1	32	14		.332	.366	.429	.795	127	7	9	96	90	49	.821	17			1	/OP	0.8
■ ZIGGY HASBROOK	Hasbrook, Robert Lyndon "Ziggy" b: 11/21/1893, Grundy Center, Ia. d: 2/9/76, Garland, Tex. BR/TR, 6'1", 180 lbs. Deb: 9/06/16																											
1916	Chi-A	9	8	1	1	0	0	0	0	1	2	.125	.222	.125	.347	4	-1	-1	108	0	0	.286	0			0	/1	0.0

YEAR	TM/L	G	AB	R	H	2B	3B	HR	RBI	BB	SO	AVG	OBP	SLG	PRO	/A	BR	/A	PF	CHI	RC	TA	SB	CS	SBR	FR	POS	TPR
1917	Chi-A	2	1	1	0	0	0	0	0	0	0	.000	.000	.000	.000	-99	-0	-0	98	0	0	.000	0			0	/2	0.0
Total	2	11	9	2	1	0	0	0	0	1	2	.111	.200	.111	.311	-6	-1	-1	107	0	0	.250	0			0	/12	0.0
■ **DON HASENMAYER** Hasenmayer, Donald Irvin b: 4/4/27, Roslyn, Pa. BR/TR, 5'10.5", 180 lbs. Deb: 5/02/45																												
1945	Phi-N	5	18	1	2	0	0	0	1	2	1	.111	.200	.111	.311	-13	-3	-3	96	177	1	.250	0			-0	/23	-0.2
1946	Phi-N	6	12	0	1	1	0	0	0	0	2	.083	.083	.167	.250	-32	-2	-2	95	0	0	.182	0			0	/3	-0.1
Total	2	11	30	1	3	1	0	0	1	2	3	.100	.156	.133	.290	-19	-5	-5	96	111	1	.222	0			-0	/32	-0.3
■ **MICKEY HASLIN** Haslin, Michael Joseph b: 10/31/10, Wilkes-Barre, Pa. BR/TR, 5'8", 165 lbs. Deb: 9/07/33																												
1933	Phi-N	26	89	3	21	2	0	0	9	3	5	.236	.261	.258	.519	41	-6	-8	118	147	6	.391	1			-0	2	-0.6
1934	Phi-N	72	166	28	44	8	2	1	11	16	13	.265	.330	.355	.685	77	-4	-6	108	64	19	.594	1			-4	32/S	-0.4
1935	Phi-N	110	407	53	108	17	3	3	52	19	25	.265	.300	.344	.644	64	-16	-23	114	128	42	.534	5			-1	S3/2	-1.8
1936	Phi-N	16	64	6	22	1	1	0	6	3	5	.344	.373	.391	.764	98	1	-0	108	90	9	.636	0			0	2/3	0.1
	Bos-N	36	104	14	29	1	2	2	11	5	9	.279	.312	.385	.697	91	-2	-1	95	85	11	.563	0			1	3/2	0.1
	Yr	52	168	20	51	2	3	2	17	8	14	.304	.335	.387	.722	95	-2	-1	99	88	21	.598	0			1		0.2
1937	NY-N	27	42	8	8	1	0	0	5	9	3	.190	.333	.214	.548	52	-2	-2	100	200	3	.514	1			1	/S23	0.0
1938	NY-N	31	102	13	33	3	0	3	15	4	4	.324	.361	.441	.802	116	3	2	103	100	16	.718	0			1	32	0.4
Total	6	318	974	125	265	33	8	9	109	59	64	.272	.316	.350	.666	73	-27	-39	109	112	108	.578	8			-2	S/23	-2.2
■ **PETE HASNEY** Hasney, Peter James b: 5/26/1865, England d: 5/24/08, Philadelphia, Pa. Deb: 9/13/1890																												
1890	Phi-a	2	7	1	1	0	0	0		1		.143	.250	.143	.393	18	-1	-1	97	0	0	.333	0			0	/O	0.0
■ **BILL HASSAMAER** Hassamaer, William Louis "Roaring Bill" b: 7/26/1864, St.Louis, Mo. d: 5/29/10, St.Louis, Mo. 6', 180 lbs. Deb: 4/19/1894																												
1894	Was-N	118	494	106	159	33	17	4	90	41	20	.322	.375	.482	.857	109	4	6	98	105	98	.884	16			-2	O32/S	0.0
1895	Was-N	85	358	42	100	18	4	1	60	26	13	.279	.328	.360	.688	77	-11	-13	103	122	46	.632	8			-8	O	-2.2
	Lou-N	23	96	7	20	2	2	0	14	3	4	.208	.232	.271	.503	32	-10	-9	95	159	6	.382	0			0	1/2S	-0.7
	Yr	108	454	49	120	20	6	1	74	29	17	.264	.308	.341	.650	68	-21	-22	101	131	52	.575	8			-8		-2.9
1896	Lou-N	30	106	8	26	5	0	2	14	14	7	.245	.333	.349	.682	83	-3	-2	98	96	13	.650	1			0	1	-0.1
Total	3	256	1054	163	305	58	23	7	178	84	44	.289	.342	.408	.750	89	-20	-18	99	115	163	.721	25			-9	O/132S	-3.0
■ **BUDDY HASSETT** Hassett, John Aloysius b: 9/5/11, New York, N.Y. BL/TL, 5'11", 180 lbs. Deb: 4/14/36																												
1936	Bro-N	156	635	79	197	29	11	3	82	35	17	.310	.350	.405	.755	98	2	-2	105	116	92	.673	5			5	*1	-0.9
1937	Bro-N	137	556	71	169	31	6	1	53	20	19	.304	.334	.387	.721	91	-4	-7	104	84	71	.632	13			5	*1/O	-0.9
1938	Bro-N	115	335	49	98	11	6	0	40	32	19	.293	.356	.361	.717	102	-0	2	96	119	44	.638	3			-3	O/1	-0.3
1939	Bos-N	147	590	72	182	15	3	2	60	29	14	.308	.342	.354	.696	95	-10	-4	92	108	72	.603	13			2	*1O	-1.6
1940	Bos-N	124	458	59	107	19	4	0	27	25	16	.234	.273	.293	.566	57	-28	-27	99	76	34	.447	4			3	1O	-3.3
1941	Bos-N	118	405	59	120	9	4	1	33	36	15	.296	.354	.346	.699	105	-1	3	93	83	51	.639	10			3	1	-0.7
1942	NY-A	132	538	80	153	16	6	5	48	32	16	.284	.325	.364	.689	94	-6	-5	99	85	65	.588	5	5	-2	8	*1	0.0
Total	7	929	3517	469	1026	130	40	12	343	209	116	.292	.333	.362	.695	92	-47	-41	99	96	431	.618	53	5		23	1O	-7.7
■ **RON HASSEY** Hassey, Ronald William b: 2/27/53, Tucson, Ariz. BL/TR, 6'2", 200 lbs. Deb: 4/23/78																												
1978	Cle-A	25	74	5	15	0	0	2	9	5	7	.203	.262	.284	.546	57	-5	-4	93	132	6	.483	2	0	1	-2	C	-0.4
1979	Cle-A	75	223	20	64	14	0	4	32	19	19	.287	.343	.404	.747	95	0	-2	106	121	30	.659	1	0	0	-3	C/1	-0.1
1980	Cle-A	130	390	43	124	18	4	8	65	49	51	.318	.395	.446	.842	127	18	16	102	128	68	.797	0	2	-1	-7	*C/1D	1.3
1981	Cle-A	61	190	8	44	4	0	1	25	17	11	.232	.301	.268	.570	70	-8	-6	93	181	16	.461	0	1	-1	-1	C/1D	-0.5
1982	Cle-A	113	323	33	81	18	0	5	34	53	32	.251	.358	.353	.711	96	0	-0	100	105	42	.673	3	2	-0	-13	*C/1D	-0.7
1983	Cle-A	117	341	48	92	21	0	6	42	38	35	.270	.346	.384	.731	96	1	-1	105	110	45	.660	2	2	-1	-5	*C/D	-0.1
1984	Cle-A	48	149	11	38	5	1	0	19	15	26	.255	.323	.302	.625	70	-5	-6	106	168	15	.530	1	0	0	1	C/1D	-0.1
	Chi-N	19	33	5	11	0	0	2	5	4	6	.333	.405	.515	.921	143	3	2	110	85	6	.875	0	1	-1	0	/C1	0.2
1985	NY-A	92	267	31	79	16	1	13	42	28	21	.296	.369	.509	.878	144	14	15	96	95	49	.856	0	0	0	4	C/1D	2.1
1986	NY-A	64	191	23	57	14	0	6	29	24	16	.298	.382	.466	.848	127	9	8	103	108	33	.811	1	1	-0	0	C/D	1.0
	Chi-A	49	150	22	53	11	1	3	20	22	11	.353	.439	.500	.939	155	13	13	101	95	32	.942	0	0	0	0	DC	1.3
	Yr	113	341	45	110	25	1	9	49	46	27	.323	.408	.481	.889	139	21	20	102	103	69	.895	1	1	-0	0		2.3
1987	Chi-A	49	145	15	31	9	0	3	12	17	11	.214	.305	.338	.643	66	-6	-8	109	83	13	.553	0	0	0	3	CD	-0.2
1988	Oak-A	107	323	32	83	15	0	7	45	30	42	.257	.328	.368	.696	100	-2	0	95	128	39	.622	2	0	1	-7	C/D	-0.2
Total	11	949	2799	296	772	145	7	60	379	321	288	.276	.354	.397	.751	106	31	27	101	119	394	.715	12	9	-2	-29	C/D1	3.6
■ **JOE HASSLER** Hassler, Joseph Frederick b: 4/7/05, Ft.Smith, Ark. d: 9/4/71, Duncan, Okla. BR/TR, 6', 165 lbs. Deb: 5/26/28																												
1928	Phi-A	28	34	5	9	2	0	0	3	2	4	.265	.306	.324	.629	64	-2	-2	103	94	3	.500	0	1	-1	-2	S	-0.1
1929	Phi-A	4	4	1	0	0	0	0	0	0	2	.000	.000	.000	.000	-92	-1	-1	109	0	0	.000	0	0	0	0	/S	0.0
1930	StL-A	5	8	3	2	0	0	0	1	0	1	.250	.250	.250	.500	25	-1	-1	108	166	0	.333	0	0	0	0	/S	0.0
Total	3	37	46	9	11	2	0	0	4	2	7	.239	.271	.283	.553	43	-4	-4	104	98	4	.417	0	1	-1	-2	/S	-0.1
■ **GENE HASSON** Hasson, Charles Eugene b: 7/20/15, Connellsville, Pa BL/TL, 6', 197 lbs. Deb: 9/09/37																												
1937	Phi-A	28	98	12	30	6	3	3	14	13	14	.306	.387	.520	.908	135	4	5	94	82	20	.941	0	0	0	-1	1	0.0
1938	Phi-A	19	69	10	19	6	2	1	12	12	7	.275	.383	.464	.846	110	1	1	101	123	13	.880	0	0	0	-1	1	-0.1
Total	2	47	167	22	49	12	5	4	26	25	21	.293	.385	.497	.882	124	5	6	97	99	33	.915	0	0	0	-2	/1	-0.1
■ **SCOTT HASTINGS** Hastings, Winfield Scott b: 8/10/1846, Hillsboro, Ohio d: 8/14/07, Sawtelle, Cal. BR/TR, 5'8", 161 lbs. Deb: 5/06/1871 M																												
1871	Rok-n	25	120	27	28							.233															*C/2OM	
1872	Cle-n	21	116	33	49							.422															C/O2M	
	Bal-n	11	56	19	11							.196															/C2	
	Yr	32	172	52	60							.349																
1873	Bal-n	31	160	42	41							.256															CO/2	
1874	Har-n	52	237	60	88							.371															CO/2	
1875	Chi-n	66	298	43	74							.248															CO/2	
1876	Lou-N	67	283	36	73	6	1	0	21	5	11	.258	.271	.286	.557	82	-4	-6	104	84	22	.410				-7	*O/C	-1.1
1877	Cin-N	20	71	7	10	1	0	0	3	3	6	.141	.176	.155	.331	6	-7	-5	82	92	2	.230				-6	C/O	-0.9
Total	5 n	206	987	224	291							.295															C/O	
Total	2	87	354	43	83	7	1	0	24	8	17	.234	.251	.260	.511	69	-11	-11	99	86	24	.369				-13	CO/2	-2.0
■ **MICKEY HATCHER** Hatcher, Michael Vaughn b: 3/15/55, Cleveland, Ohio BR/TR, 6'2", 200 lbs. Deb: 8/03/79																												
1979	LA-N	33	93	9	25	4	1	1	5	7	12	.269	.327	.366	.692	89	-1	-1	100	53	9	.566	1	3	-2	-1	O3	-0.4
1980	LA-N	57	84	4	19	2	0	1	5	2	12	.226	.244	.286	.530	49	-6	-6	97	73	4	.356	0	2	-1	-6	O3	-1.4
1981	Min-A	99	377	36	96	23	2	3	37	15	29	.255	.287	.350	.637	79	-9	-11	105	109	36	.521	3	1	0	-2	O/13D	-1.5
1982	Min-A	84	277	23	69	13	2	3	26	8	27	.249	.270	.343	.613	67	-13	-13	100	100	21	.464	0	2	-1	-0	OD/3	-1.5
1983	Min-A	106	375	50	119	15	3	9	47	14	19	.317	.344	.445	.789	110	7	5	105	95	54	.687	2	0	1	4	OD/13	0.8
1984	Min-A	152	576	61	174	35	5	5	69	37	34	.302	.346	.406	.753	102	6	2	106	117	78	.650	0	1	-1	10	*OD1/3	0.7
1985	Min-A	116	444	46	125	28	0	3	49	16	23	.282	.310	.365	.674	81	-10	-12	103	116	46	.539	0	0	0	4	OD/1	-0.9
1986	Min-A	115	317	40	88	13	3	3	32	19	26	.278	.318	.366	.684	80	-6	-9	108	102	36	.576	2	1	0	-3	OD1/3	-1.4
1987	LA-N	101	287	27	81	19	1	7	42	20	19	.282	.331	.429	.760	108	-1	2	92	116	39	.679	2	3	-1	4	31/O	0.2
1988	LA-N	87	191	22	56	8	0	1	25	7	7	.293	.325	.351	.676	88	-2	-3	106	143	20	.535	0	0	0	-2	O1/3	-0.6
Total	10	950	3021	318	852	160	17	36	337	145	208	.282	.317	.382	.699	89	-35	-47	103	108	343	.603	10	13	-5	9	OD1/3	-6.0
■ **WILLIAM HATCHER** Hatcher, William Augustus "Billy" b: 10/4/60, Williams, Ariz. BR/TR, 5'9", 175 lbs. Deb: 9/10/84																												
1984	Chi-N	8	9	1	1	0	0	0	0	1	0	.111	.200	.111	.311	-10	-1	-1	110	0	0	.500	2	0	1	-0	/O	-0.1
1985	Chi-N	53	163	24	40	12	1	2	10	8	12	.245	.293	.368	.661	72	-4	-7	116	60	14	.537	2	4	-2	-1	O	-1.1
1986	Hou-N	127	419	55	108	15	4	6	36	22	52	.258	.303	.356	.658	79	-11	-13	103	86	47	.652	38	14	3	3	*O	-0.9
1987	Hou-N	141	564	96	167	28	3	11	63	42	70	.296	.354	.415	.769	111	3	8	93	83	89	.811	53	9	11	4	*O	1.7
1988	Hou-N	145	530	79	142	25	4	7	52	37	56	.268	.325	.370	.695	106	-1	3	93	98	66	.671	32	13	2	2	*O	0.4

YEAR	TM/L	G	AB	R	H	2B	3B	HR	RBI	BB	SO	AVG	OBP	SLG	PRO	/A	BR	/A	PF	CHI	RC	TA	SB	CS	SBR	FR	POS	TPR
Total	5	474	1685	255	458	80	12	26	161	110	190	.272	.326	.380	.706	96	-15	-10	98	86	216	.709	127	40	14	8	O	0.0

■ FRED HATFIELD Hatfield, Fred James b: 3/18/25, Lanett, Ala. BL/TR, 6'1", 171 lbs. Deb: 8/31/50 C

YEAR	TM/L	G	AB	R	H	2B	3B	HR	RBI	BB	SO	AVG	OBP	SLG	PRO	/A	BR	/A	PF	CHI	RC	TA	SB	CS	SBR	FR	POS	TPR
1950	Bos-A	10	12	3	3	0	0	0	2	3	1	.250	.400	.250	.650	61	-0	-1	114	230	2	.667	0	0	0	0	/3	0.0
1951	Bos-A	80	163	23	28	4	2	2	14	22	27	.172	.274	.258	.532	41	-13	-15	108	104	13	.485	1	0	0	8	3	-0.7
1952	Bos-A	19	25	6	8	1	1	1	3	4	2	.320	.433	.560	.993	164	3	2	107	66	4	.864	0	3	-2	-0	3	0.0
	Det-A	112	441	42	104	12	2	2	25	35	52	.236	.301	.286	.587	64	-21	-21	99	68	38	.480	2	2	-1	10	*3/S	-1.1
	Yr	131	466	48	112	13	3	3	28	39	54	.240	.309	.300	.609	70	-19	-19	100	68	43	.505	2	5	-2	9		-1.1
1953	Det-A	109	311	41	79	11	1	3	19	40	34	.254	.341	.325	.666	82	-8	-7	98	64	36	.594	3	5	-2	2	32/S	-0.7
1954	Det-A	81	218	31	64	12	0	2	25	28	24	.294	.386	.376	.763	110	4	4	100	108	33	.739	4	2	0	-6	23	0.0
1955	Det-A	122	413	51	96	15	3	8	33	61	49	.232	.338	.341	.680	86	-9	-7	97	76	51	.644	3	2	-0	1	23S	0.1
1956	Det-A	8	12	2	3	0	0	0	2	2	1	.250	.400	.250	.650	78	-0	-0	97	249	2	.667	0	0	0	0	/2	0.0
	Chi-A	106	321	46	84	9	1	7	33	37	36	.262	.352	.361	.714	85	-4	-6	104	90	43	.664	1	0	0	1	*3/S	-0.2
	Yr	114	333	48	87	9	1	7	35	39	37	.261	.354	.357	.712	85	-5	-6	104	103	44	.664	1	0	0	1		-0.2
1957	Chi-A	69	114	14	23	3	0	0	8	15	20	.202	.321	.228	.549	53	-7	-7	99	122	10	.505	1	0	0	3	3	-0.2
1958	Cle-A	3	8	0	1	0	0	0	1	1	1	.125	.222	.125	.347	-2	-1	-1	94	401	0	.286	0	0	0	0	/3	0.0
	Cin-N	3	1	0	0	0	0	0	0	0	0	.000	.000	.000	.000	-93	-0	-0	107	0	0	.000	0	0	0	0	/23	0.0
Total	9	722	2039	259	493	67	10	25	165	248	247	.242	.334	.321	.655	78	-57	-58	100	86	233	.610	15	14	-4	18	32/S	-2.8

■ GIL HATFIELD Hatfield, Gilbert "Colonel" b: 1/27/1855, Hoboken, N.J. d: 5/27/21, Hoboken, N.J. TR, 5'9.5", 168 lbs. Deb: 1885

YEAR	TM/L	G	AB	R	H	2B	3B	HR	RBI	BB	SO	AVG	OBP	SLG	PRO	/A	BR	/A	PF	CHI	RC	TA	SB	CS	SBR	FR	POS	TPR
1885	Buf-N	11	30	1	4	0	1	0	0	0	11	.133	.133	.200	.333	7	-3	-3	99	0	1	.231				0	/32	-0.2
1887	NY-N	2	7	2	3	1	0	0	3	0	1	.429	.429	.571	1.000	166	1	1	107	231	2	1.000	0			0	/3	0.1
1888	NY-N	28	105	7	19	1	0	0	9	2	18	.181	.211	.190	.401	33	-8	-7	93	164	6	.372	8			0	3S/O2	-0.6
1889	NY-N	32	125	21	23	2	0	1	12	9	15	.184	.250	.224	.474	32	-11	-12	105	118	9	.471	9			0	S/P3	-0.9
1890	NY-P	71	287	32	80	13	6	1	37	17	19	.279	.328	.376	.704	82	-5	-9	109	93	40	.681	12			-4	3S/PO	-0.7
1891	Was-a	134	500	83	128	11	8	1	48	50	39	.256	.335	.316	.651	93	-6	-2	95	91	69	.699	43			4	*S3/PO	0.5
1893	Bro-N	34	120	24	35	3	3	2	19	17	5	.292	.388	.417	.805	128	3	5	91	95	23	.918	9			-7	3	0.0
1895	Lou-N	5	16	3	3	0	0	0	1	1	1	.188	.278	.188	.465	24	-2	-2	95	93	1	.385	0			0	/3S	0.0
Total	8	317	1190	173	295	31	18	5	129	96	109	.248	.315	.317	.632	81	-31	-29	99	100	152	.641	81			-6	S3/PO2	-1.8

■ JOHN HATFIELD Hatfield, John Van Buskirk b: 7/20/1847, New Jersey d: 2/20/09, Long Island City, N.Y. 5'10", 165 lbs. Deb: 5/18/1871 M

YEAR	TM/L	G	AB	R	H	2B	3B	HR	RBI	BB	SO	AVG	OBP	SLG	PRO	/A	BR	/A	PF	CHI	RC	TA	SB	CS	SBR	FR	POS	TPR
1871	Mut-n	33	168	41	44							.262															*O/23	
1872	Mut-n	56	297	75	90							.303															*2	
1873	Mut-n	52	260	54	76							.292															*32M	
1874	Mut-n	64	299	47	67							.224															*O/3P1	
1875	Mut-n	2	9	2	4							.444															/O	
1876	NY-N	1	4	0	1	0	0	0	1	0	0	.250	.250	.250	.500	77	-0	-0	87	345	0	.333				0	/2	0.0
Total	5 n	207	1033	219	281							.272															/2	

■ GRADY HATTON Hatton, Grady Edgebert b: 10/7/22, Beaumont, Tex. BL/TR, 5'8.5", 170 lbs. Deb: 4/16/46 MC

YEAR	TM/L	G	AB	R	H	2B	3B	HR	RBI	BB	SO	AVG	OBP	SLG	PRO	/A	BR	/A	PF	CHI	RC	TA	SB	CS	SBR	FR	POS	TPR
1946	Cin-N	116	436	56	118	18	3	14	69	66	53	.271	.369	.422	.791	119	15	12	104	110	73	.804	6			-11	*3/O	0.3
1947	Cin-N	146	524	91	147	24	8	16	77	81	50	.281	.377	.448	.825	130	15	21	91	103	92	.835	7			-4	*3	1.3
1948	Cin-N	133	458	58	110	17	2	9	44	72	50	.240	.343	.345	.688	84	-7	-9	103	91	59	.669	7			7	*3/2SO	-0.3
1949	Cin-N	137	537	71	141	38	5	11	69	62	48	.263	.342	.413	.756	106	1	4	96	98	79	.720	4			-2	*3	0.3
1950	Cin-N	130	438	67	114	17	1	11	54	70	39	.260	.366	.379	.745	92	-0	-3	105	107	67	.749	6			-6	*3/2S	-0.8
1951	Cin-N	96	331	41	84	9	3	4	37	33	32	.254	.321	.335	.657	76	-10	-11	101	119	38	.585	4	2	0	1	3/O	-0.9
1952	Cin-N	128	433	48	92	14	1	9	57	66	60	.212	.319	.312	.631	76	-13	-13	100	140	48	.594	5	4	-1	-6	*2	-1.4
1953	Cin-N	83	159	22	37	3	1	7	22	29	24	.233	.351	.396	.747	95	-1	-1	99	102	24	.730	0	1	-1	1	21/3	0.1
1954	Cin-N	1	1	0	0	0	0	0	0	0	0	.000	.000	.000	.000	-96	-0	-0	104	0	0	.000	0	0	0	0	H	0.0
	Chi-A	13	30	3	5	1	0	0	3	5	3	.167	.286	.200	.486	34	-3	-3	104	190	2	.462	1	0	0	0	3/1	-0.2
	Bos-A	99	302	40	85	12	3	5	33	58	25	.281	.401	.391	.791	117	10	10	100	94	51	.799	1	1	-0	2	3/1S	0.6
	Yr	112	332	43	90	13	3	5	36	63	28	.271	.390	.373	.764	109	7	7	101	107	53	.767	2	1	0	2		0.4
1955	Bos-A	126	380	48	93	11	4	4	49	76	28	.245	.371	.326	.697	71	-3	-16	124	134	51	.676	0	1	-1	4	*3/2	-1.0
1956	Bos-A	5	5	0	2	0	0	0	2	0	0	.400	.400	.400	.800	109	0	0	103	374	1	.667	0	0	0	0	H	0.0
	StL-N	44	73	10	18	1	2	0	7	13	7	.247	.360	.315	.676	85	-1	-1	99	129	9	.638	1	0	0	1	2/3	0.1
	Bal-A	27	61	4	9	1	0	1	3	13	6	.148	.297	.213	.510	39	-5	-5	94	70	5	.500	0	0	0	-1	23	-0.4
1960	Chi-N	28	38	3	13	0	0	0	7	2	5	.342	.390	.342	.732	105	0	0	98	219	5	.593	0	0	0	1	/2	0.2
Total	12	1312	4206	562	1068	166	33	91	533	646	430	.254	.355	.374	.729	95	-4	-14	102	111	604	.722	42	9		-13	32/1OS	-2.1

■ ARTHUR HAUGER Hauger, John Arthur b: 11/18/1893, Delhi, Ohio d: 8/2/44, Redwood City, Cal BL/TR, 5'11", 168 lbs. Deb: 7/17/12

YEAR	TM/L	G	AB	R	H	2B	3B	HR	RBI	BB	SO	AVG	OBP	SLG	PRO	/A	BR	/A	PF	CHI	RC	TA	SB	CS	SBR	FR	POS	TPR
1912	Cle-A	15	18	0	1	0	0	0	0	1		.056	.105	.056	.161	-53	-4	-4	101	0	0	.118	0			-1	/O	-0.5

■ ARNOLD HAUSER Hauser, Arnold George "Peewee" or "Stub" b: 9/25/1888, Chicago, Ill. d: 5/22/66, Aurora, Ill. BR/TR, 5'6", 145 lbs. Deb: 4/21/10

YEAR	TM/L	G	AB	R	H	2B	3B	HR	RBI	BB	SO	AVG	OBP	SLG	PRO	/A	BR	/A	PF	CHI	RC	TA	SB	CS	SBR	FR	POS	TPR
1910	StL-N	119	375	37	77	7	2	2	36	49	39	.205	.312	.251	.562	70	-15	-11	92	125	34	.560	15			-15	*S/3	-2.2
1911	StL-N	136	515	61	124	11	8	3	46	26	67	.241	.286	.311	.597	66	-24	-25	101	98	53	.555	24			-12	*S/3	-3.2
1912	StL-N	133	479	73	124	14	7	1	42	39	69	.259	.319	.324	.642	76	-16	-16	100	91	58	.628	26			7	*S	0.4
1913	StL-N	22	45	3	13	0	3	0	9	2	2	.289	.347	.422	.769	128	1	1	93	172	7	.750	1			-0	/S2	0.1
1915	Chi-F	23	54	6	11	1	0	0	4	5	7	.204	.271	.222	.493	48	-3	-3	97	120	4	.442	2			-1	S/3	-0.3
Total	5	433	1468	180	349	33	20	6	137	121	184	.238	.305	.300	.605	72	-58	-53	98	106	157	.581	68			-22	S/32	-5.2

■ JOE HAUSER Hauser, Joseph John "Unser Choe" b: 1/12/1899, Milwaukee, Wis. BL/TL, 5'10.5", 175 lbs. Deb: 4/18/22

YEAR	TM/L	G	AB	R	H	2B	3B	HR	RBI	BB	SO	AVG	OBP	SLG	PRO	/A	BR	/A	PF	CHI	RC	TA	SB	CS	SBR	FR	POS	TPR
1922	Phi-A	111	368	61	119	21	5	9	43	30	37	.323	.378	.481	.858	117	11	9	104	75	65	.827	1	5	-3	-5	1	-0.5
1923	Phi-A	146	537	93	165	21	9	17	94	69	52	.307	.398	.475	.873	129	23	23	100	111	104	.905	6	6	-2	-4	*1	1.1
1924	Phi-A	149	562	97	162	31	8	27	115	56	52	.288	.358	.516	.874	125	16	16	99	109	104	.884	7	5	-1	-2	*1	0.6
1926	Phi-A	91	229	31	44	10	0	8	36	39	34	.192	.312	.341	.653	60	-10	-16	118	120	26	.636	1	2	-1	0	1	-1.8
1928	Phi-A	95	300	61	78	19	5	16	59	52	45	.260	.369	.517	.886	127	13	12	103	100	60	.942	4	2	0	-6	1	0.1
1929	Cle-A	37	48	8	12	1	1	3	9	4	8	.250	.308	.500	.808	104	-0	-0	100	93	7	.778	0	0	0	0	/1	0.0
Total	6	629	2044	351	580	103	28	80	356	250	228	.284	.367	.479	.846	116	53	44	103	103	367	.854	19	20	-6	-16	1	-0.5

■ GEORGE HAUSMANN Hausmann, George John b: 2/11/16, St.Louis, Mo. BR/TR, 5'5", 145 lbs. Deb: 4/18/44

YEAR	TM/L	G	AB	R	H	2B	3B	HR	RBI	BB	SO	AVG	OBP	SLG	PRO	/A	BR	/A	PF	CHI	RC	TA	SB	CS	SBR	FR	POS	TPR
1944	NY-N	131	466	70	124	20	4	1	30	40	25	.266	.324	.333	.657	82	-9	-11	104	69	52	.564	3			1	*2	0.2
1945	NY-N	154	623	98	174	15	8	2	45	73	46	.279	.356	.339	.694	94	-3	-3	100	64	81	.640	7			6	*2	1.5
1949	NY-N	16	47	5	6	0	1	0	3	7	6	.128	.241	.170	.411	12	-6	-6	102	141	3	.366	0			-0	2	-0.5
Total	3	301	1136	173	304	35	13	3	78	120	77	.268	.338	.329	.667	86	-18	-20	101	69	135	.607	10			7	2	1.2

■ CHARLIE HAUTZ Hautz, Charles A. b: 2/5/1852, St.Louis, Mo. d: 1/24/29, St.Louis, Mo. 5'7", 150 lbs. Deb: 5/04/1875

YEAR	TM/L	G	AB	R	H	2B	3B	HR	RBI	BB	SO	AVG	OBP	SLG	PRO	/A	BR	/A	PF	CHI	RC	TA	SB	CS	SBR	FR	POS	TPR
1875	RS-n	18	75	5	23							.307															1	
1884	Pit-a	7	24	0	5	0	0	0		3		.208	.296	.208	.505	73	-1	-1	97	0	2	.421				0	/1O	0.0

■ ROY HAWES Hawes, Roy Lee b: 7/5/26, Shiloh, Ill. BL/TL, 6'2", 190 lbs. Deb: 9/23/51

YEAR	TM/L	G	AB	R	H	2B	3B	HR	RBI	BB	SO	AVG	OBP	SLG	PRO	/A	BR	/A	PF	CHI	RC	TA	SB	CS	SBR	FR	POS	TPR
1951	Was-A	3	6	0	1	0	0	0	0	0	1	.167	.167	.167	.333	-10	-1	-1	95	0	0	.200	0	0	0	0	/1	0.0

■ BILL HAWES Hawes, William Hildreth b: 11/17/1853, Nashua, N.H. d: 6/16/40, Lowell, Mass. BR/TR, 5'10", 155 lbs. Deb: 5/01/1879

YEAR	TM/L	G	AB	R	H	2B	3B	HR	RBI	BB	SO	AVG	OBP	SLG	PRO	/A	BR	/A	PF	CHI	RC	TA	SB	CS	SBR	FR	POS	TPR
1879	Bos-N	38	155	19	31	3	3	0	9	2	13	.200	.210	.258	.468	50	-8	-9	107	80	9	.339				-2	O/C	-1.0
1884	Cin-U	79	349	80	97	7	4	4		5		.278	.288	.355	.643	108	5	1	108	0	37	.512	0			-7	O1	-0.5
Total	2	117	504	99	128	10	7	4	9	7	13	.254	.264	.325	.590	90	-2	-8	108	25	45	.455	0			-8	/O1C	-1.5

■ THORNY HAWKES Hawkes, Thorndike Proctor b: 10/15/1852, Danvers, Mass. d: 2/3/29, Danvers, Mass. BR/TR, 5'8", 135 lbs. Deb: 5/01/1879

YEAR	TM/L	G	AB	R	H	2B	3B	HR	RBI	BB	SO	AVG	OBP	SLG	PRO	/A	BR	/A	PF	CHI	RC	TA	SB	CS	SBR	FR	POS	TPR
1879	Tro-N	64	250	24	52	6	1	0	20	4	14	.208	.220	.240	.460	55	-13	-10	93	119	14	.323				25	*2	1.9
1884	Was-a	38	151	16	42	4	2	0		4		.278	.297	.331	.628	121	1	4	88	0	15	.495				-5	2/O	0.0

YEAR	TM/L	G	AB	R	H	2B	3B	HR	RBI	BB	SO	AVG	OBP	SLG	PRO	/A	BR	/A	PF	CHI	RC	TA	SB	CS	SBR	FR	POS	TPR
Total	2	102	401	40	94	10	3	0	20	8	14	.234	.249	.274	.524	80	-11	-7	91	74	29	.384				19	2/O	1.9
■ CHICKEN HAWKS	Hawks, Nelson Louis b: 2/3/1896, San Francisco, Cal. d: 5/26/73, San Rafael, Cal. BL/TL, 5'11", 167 lbs. Deb: 4/14/21																											
1921	NY-A	41	73	16	21	2	3	2	15	5	12	.288	.333	.479	.813	102	0	-0	103	125	11	.755	0	1	-1	-1	O	-0.2
1925	Phi-N	105	320	52	103	15	5	5	45	32	33	.322	.387	.447	.834	97	7	-1	116	101	55	.807	3	6	-3	0	1	-1.1
Total	2	146	393	68	124	17	8	7	60	37	45	.316	.377	.453	.830	98	7	-1	113	106	66	.797	3	7	-3	-1	/1O	-1.3
■ HOWIE HAWORTH	Haworth, Homer Howard "Cully" b: 8/27/1893, Newberg, Ore. d: 1/28/53, Troutdale, Ore. BL/TR, 5'10.5", 165 lbs. Deb: 8/14/15																											
1915	Cle-A	7	7	0	1	0	0	0	1	2	2	.143	.333	.143	.476	41	-0	-0	104	340	0	.500	0			0	/C	0.0
■ JACK HAYDEN	Hayden, John Francis b: 10/21/1880, Bryn Mawr, Pa. d: 8/3/42, Haverford, Pa. BR/TL, 5'9", Deb: 4/26/01																											
1901	Phi-A	51	211	35	56	6	4	0	17	18		.265	.323	.332	.655	83	-4	-4	100	68	25	.594	4			-2	O	-0.5
1906	Bos-A	85	322	22	80	6	4	1	14	17		.248	.286	.301	.587	87	-5	-5	98	54	30	.496	6			3	O	-0.5
1908	Chi-N	11	45	3	9	2	0	0	2	1		.200	.217	.244	.462	46	-3	-3	106	62	2	.361	1			1	O	-0.2
Total	3	147	578	60	145	14	8	1	33	36		.251	.295	.308	.603	83	-12	-12	100	60	57	.520	11			2	O	-1.2
■ CHARLIE HAYES	Hayes, Charles De Wayne b: 5/29/65, Hattiesburg, Miss. BR/TR, 6', 190 lbs. Deb: 9/11/88																											
1988	SF-N	7	11	0	1	0	0	0	0	0	3	.091	.091	.091	.182	-51	-2	-2	94	0	0	.100	0	0	0	-1	/O3	-0.2
■ FRANKIE HAYES	Hayes, Frank Witman "Blimp" b: 10/13/14, Jamesburg, N.J. d: 6/22/55, Point Pleasant, N.J. BR/TR, 6'1", 190 lbs. Deb: 9/21/33																											
1933	Phi-A	3	5	0	0	0	0	0	0	0	2	.000	.000	.000	.000	-99	-1	-1	92	0	0	.000	0	0	0	0	/C	0.0
1934	Phi-A	92	248	24	56	10	0	6	30	20	44	.226	.286	.339	.625	62	-15	-14	97	98	25	.554	2	1	0	-6	C	-1.0
1936	Phi-A	144	505	39	137	25	2	10	67	46	58	.271	.335	.388	.723	77	-19	-19	101	96	66	.662	3	5	-2	-4	*C	-1.1
1937	Phi-A	60	188	24	49	11	1	10	38	29	34	.261	.359	.489	.849	119	3	5	94	107	34	.871	0	0	0	-2	C	0.6
1938	Phi-A	99	316	56	92	19	3	11	55	54	51	.291	.396	.475	.871	116	9	9	101	102	62	.912	2	3	-1	-2	C	0.7
1939	Phi-A	124	431	66	122	28	5	20	83	40	55	.283	.348	.510	.859	120	9	10	97	102	76	.834	4	1	1	4	*C	2.0
1940	Phi-A	136	465	73	143	23	4	16	70	61	59	.308	.389	.477	.866	129	17	20	96	96	89	.867	9	3	1	4	*C/1	3.1
1941	Phi-A	126	439	66	123	27	4	12	63	62	56	.280	.369	.442	.811	113	9	8	101	99	70	.761	2	0	1	5	*C	2.0
1942	Phi-A	21	63	8	15	4	0	0	5	9	8	.238	.333	.302	.635	82	-2	-1	96	93	6	.558	1	1	-0	0	C	0.1
	StL-A	56	159	14	40	6	0	2	17	28	39	.252	.364	.327	.691	91	-0	-1	104	103	22	.672	0	0	0	-1	C	0.4
	Yr	77	222	22	55	10	0	2	22	37	47	.248	.355	.320	.675	89	-2	-2	102	102	29	.649	1	1	-0	-1		0.5
1943	StL-A	88	250	16	47	7	0	5	30	37	36	.188	.295	.276	.571	67	-10	-10	100	130	22	.512	1	0	0	0	C/1	-0.5
1944	Phi-A	155	581	62	144	18	6	13	78	57	59	.248	.315	.367	.682	93	-5	-6	101	118	68	.600	2	1	0	-1	*C/1	0.4
1945	Phi-A	32	110	12	25	2	1	3	14	18	14	.227	.336	.345	.681	105	-0	1	94	110	14	.655	1	0	0	-0	C	0.4
	Cle-A	119	385	39	91	15	6	6	43	53	52	.236	.335	.353	.688	101	0	1	99	103	49	.640	1	1	-0	10	*C	2.1
	Yr	151	495	51	116	17	7	9	57	71	66	.234	.335	.352	.687	102	0	2	97	105	64	.647	2	1	0	9		2.5
1946	Cle-A	51	156	11	40	12	0	3	18	21	26	.256	.345	.391	.736	119	1	3	89	98	20	.659	1	3	-2	-1	C	0.3
	Chi-A	53	179	15	38	6	0	2	16	29	33	.212	.322	.279	.601	71	-7	-6	97	111	17	.537	1	1	-0	4	C	0.0
	Yr	104	335	26	78	18	0	5	34	50	59	.233	.332	.331	.664	92	-5	-2	93	105	39	.608	2	4	-2	3		0.3
1947	Bos-A	5	13	0	2	0	0	0	1	0	1	.154	.154	.154	.308	-13	-2	-2	108	184	0	.182	0	0	0	0	/C	-0.1
Total	14	1364	4493	525	1164	213	32	119	628	564	627	.259	.343	.400	.744	100	-13	-3	98	104	640	.718	30	20	-3	9	*C/1	9.4
■ JACKIE HAYES	Hayes, John J. b: 6/27/1861, Brooklyn, N.Y. TR , Deb: 5/02/1882																											
1882	Wor-N	78	326	27	88	22	4	4	54	6	26	.270	.283	.399	.682	116	5	5	100	123	38	.571				-3	*OC/3S	0.1
1883	Pit-a	85	351	41	92	23	5	3		15		.262	.292	.382	.674	123	6	9	94	0	40	.575				-8	CO/S12	0.5
1884	Pit-a	33	124	11	28	6	1	0		4		.226	.256	.290	.546	83	-3	-2	97	0	9	.427				1	C/1O2	0.1
	Bro-a	16	51	4	12	3	0	0		3		.235	.278	.294	.572	92	-1	-0	98	0	4	.462				4	C/O	0.4
	Yr	49	175	15	40	9	1	0		7		.229	.262	.291	.554	85	-3	-2	97	0	14	.437				5		0.5
1885	Bro-a	42	137	10	18	3	0	0		5		.131	.179	.153	.333	7	-14	-15	104	0	4	.244				-8	C	-1.4
1886	Was-N	26	89	8	17	3	0	3	9	4	23	.191	.226	.326	.552	71	-4	-3	94	79	7	.458	0			0	CO/2	-0.2
1887	Bal-a	8	28	2	4	3	0	0		0		.143	.143	.250	.393	10	-3	-3	96	0	1	.292	0			0	/O3C	-0.2
1890	Bro-P	12	42	3	8	0	0	0	5	2	4	.190	.227	.190	.418	13	-5	-6	106	171	2	.294	0			0	/OSC2	-0.3
Total	7	300	1148	106	267	63	10	10	68	39	53	.233	.260	.331	.591	89	-18	-14	98	47	105	.480	0			-14	CO/1S32	-1.0
■ MIKE HAYES	Hayes, Michael b: 1853, Cleveland, Ohio 5'7.5", 170 lbs. Deb: 9/09/1876																											
1876	NY-N	5	21	1	3	0	2	0	2	0	0	.143	.143	.333	.476	63	-1	-1	87	102	1	.389				0	/O	0.0
■ JACKIE HAYES	Hayes, Minter Carney b: 7/19/06, Clanton, Ala. d: 2/9/83, Birmingham, Ala. BR/TR, 5'10.5", 165 lbs. Deb: 8/05/27																											
1927	Was-A	10	29	2	7	0	0	0	2	1	2	.241	.267	.241	.508	34	-3	-3	97	95	2	.364	0	0	0	-0	/S3	-0.1
1928	Was-A	60	210	30	54	7	3	0	22	5	10	.257	.274	.319	.593	55	-14	-14	102	113	19	.481	3	0	1	3	2S/3	-0.6
1929	Was-A	123	424	52	117	20	3	2	57	24	29	.276	.316	.351	.668	72	-18	-18	100	126	47	.571	4	5	-2	-1	32/S	-1.4
1930	Was-A	51	166	25	47	7	2	1	20	7	8	.283	.312	.367	.680	71	-7	-8	101	104	18	.574	2	3	-1	-2	2/31	-0.9
1931	Was-A	38	108	11	24	2	1	0	8	6	4	.222	.263	.259	.522	37	-10	-10	101	94	8	.429	2	0	1	-3	2/3S	-0.8
1932	Chi-A	117	475	53	122	20	5	2	54	30	28	.257	.302	.333	.635	74	-25	-17	87	117	48	.549	7	4	-0	7	2S3	-0.3
1933	Chi-A	138	535	65	138	23	5	2	47	55	36	.258	.331	.331	.661	75	-18	-19	101	91	61	.592	2	3	-1	13	*2	-0.8
1934	Chi-A	62	226	19	58	9	1	1	31	23	20	.257	.325	.319	.644	67	-11	-11	99	141	25	.576	3	2	-0	-14	2	-2.0
1935	Chi-A	89	329	45	88	14	0	4	45	29	15	.267	.327	.347	.673	68	-13	-17	109	124	39	.603	3	1	0	-1	2	-1.3
1936	Chi-A	108	417	53	130	34	3	5	84	35	25	.312	.366	.444	.810	100	-1	-1	99	139	69	.779	4	2	0	16	2S/3	2.0
1937	Chi-A	143	573	63	131	27	4	2	79	41	37	.229	.282	.300	.583	46	-47	-50	103	**146**	49	.482	1	6	-3	23	*2	-1.4
1938	Chi-A	62	238	40	78	21	2	1	20	24	6	.328	.389	.445	.835	111	3	4	98	66	42	.821	3	2	-0	-4	2	0.2
1939	Chi-A	72	269	34	67	12	3	0	23	27	10	.249	.320	.316	.636	59	-15	-17	107	97	28	.538	0	3	-2	-1	2	-1.5
1940	Chi-A	18	41	2	8	0	1	0	1	2	11	.195	.233	.244	.476	23	-5	-5	104	36	3	.364	0	0	0	-2	2	-0.5
Total	14	1091	4040	494	1069	196	33	20	493	309	241	.265	.318	.344	.663	70	-183	-184	100	116	456	.581	34	31	-8	34	2/3S1	-9.4
■ VON HAYES	Hayes, Von Francis b: 8/31/58, Stockton, Cal. BL/TR, 6'5", 185 lbs. Deb: 4/14/81																											
1981	Cle-A	43	109	21	28	8	2	1	17	14	10	.257	.352	.394	.746	123	2	3	93	145	17	.798	8	1	2	1	DO/3	0.6
1982	Cle-A	150	527	65	132	25	3	14	82	42	63	.250	.311	.389	.700	91	-7	-7	100	133	63	.677	32	13	2	5	*O/31	-0.5
1983	Phi-N	124	351	45	93	9	5	6	32	36	55	.265	.338	.370	.709	95	-1	-2	101	86	42	.673	20	12	-1	-3	*O	-0.8
1984	Phi-N	152	561	85	164	27	6	16	67	59	84	.292	.360	.447	.807	123	19	18	102	90	94	.852	48	13	7	7	*O	2.7
1985	Phi-N	152	570	76	150	30	4	13	70	61	99	.263	.334	.398	.733	102	3	2	102	111	79	.712	21	8	2	5	*O	0.5
1986	Phi-N	158	610	**107**	186	**46**	2	19	98	74	77	.305	.381	.480	.861	130	30	27	104	118	111	.871	24	12	0	1	*1O	2.3
1987	Phi-N	158	556	84	154	36	5	21	84	121	77	.277	.406	.473	.879	127	30	27	104	109	113	.950	16	7	1	-11	*1O	0.6
1988	Phi-N	104	367	43	100	28	2	6	45	49	59	.272	.360	.409	.768	119	11	10	101	113	57	.789	20	9	1	-3	1O/3	0.3
Total	8	1041	3651	526	1007	209	29	96	495	456	524	.276	.358	.428	.786	114	86	77	102	111	576	.815	189	75	12	2	O1/D3	5.7
■ BILL HAYES	Hayes, William Ernest b: 10/24/57, Cheverly, Md. BR/TR, 6', 195 lbs. Deb: 9/30/80																											
1980	Chi-N	4	9	0	2	1	0	0	0	0	3	.222	.222	.333	.556	50	-1	-1	106	0	1	.429	0	0	0	0	/C	0.0
1981	Chi-N	1	0	0	0	0	0	0	0	0	0	—	—	—	—	—	0	0	104	—	—	—	0	0	0	0	/C	0.0
Total	2	5	9	0	2	1	0	0	0	0	3	.222	.222	.333	.556	50	-1	-1	106	0	1	.429	0	0	0	0	/C	0.0
■ RED HAYWORTH	Hayworth, Myron Claude b: 5/14/15, High Point, N.C. BR/TR, 6'1.5", 200 lbs. Deb: 4/21/44																											
1944	StL-A	90	270	20	60	11	1	1	0	0	0	.222	.222	.281	.504	43	-21	-21	102	0	17	.362	0	0	0	-13	C	-2.9
1945	StL-A	56	160	7	31	4	0	0	17	7	6	.194	.228	.219	.446	26	-14	-17	115	176	7	.311	0	2	-1	-2	C	-1.7
Total	2	146	430	27	91	15	1	1	17	7	6	.212	.224	.258	.482	36	-35	-38	107	67	25	.342	0	2	-1	-15	C	-4.6
■ RAY HAYWORTH	Hayworth, Raymond Hall b: 1/29/04, High Point, N.C. BR/TR, 6', 180 lbs. Deb: 6/27/26 C																											
1926	Det-A	12	11	1	3	0	0	0	5	1	1	.273	.333	.273	.606	61	-1	-1	97	566	1	.500	0	0	0	0	/C	0.0
1929	Det-A	14	43	5	11	0	0	0	4	3	8	.256	.304	.256	.560	47	-3	-3	97	124	4	.438	0	0	0	0	C	-0.1
1930	Det-A	77	227	24	63	15	4	0	22	20	19	.278	.336	.379	.715	77	-7	-8	105	85	29	.639	0	2	-1	-4	C	-0.5
1931	Det-A	88	273	28	70	10	3	0	25	19	27	.256	.307	.315	.622	61	-14	-16	104	96	27	.520	0	1	-1	4	C	-0.4

YEAR	TM/L	G	AB	R	H	2B	3B	HR	RBI	BB	SO	AVG	OBP	SLG	PRO	/A	BR	/A	PF	CHI	RC	TA	SB	CS	SBR	FR	POS	TPR
1932	Det-A	109	338	41	99	20	2	2	44	31	22	.293	.354	.382	.736	89	-4	-5	102	109	47	.675	1	1	-0	-3	*C	-0.2
1933	Det-A	134	425	37	104	14	3	1	45	35	28	.245	.302	.299	.601	56	-24	-28	107	115	40	.505	0	0	0	-16	*C	-3.6
1934	Det-A	54	167	20	49	5	2	0	27	16	22	.293	.355	.347	.702	84	-4	-4	98	155	21	.617	0	2	-1	-3	C	-0.1
1935	Det-A	51	175	22	54	14	2	0	22	9	14	.309	.342	.411	.754	97	-2	-1	97	104	25	.669	0	0	0	1	C	0.2
1936	Det-A	81	250	31	60	10	0	1	30	39	18	.240	.347	.292	.639	62	-15	-13	95	128	28	.600	0	0	0	-8	C	-1.2
1937	Det-A	30	78	9	21	2	0	1	8	14	15	.269	.394	.333	.727	78	-1	-2	109	95	12	.737	0	0	0	-1	C	0.0
1938	Det-A	8	19	1	4	0	0	0	5	3	4	.211	.318	.211	.529	35	-2	-2	100	423	2	.533	1	0	0	-0	/C	0.0
	Bro-N	5	4	0	0	0	0	0	0	1	1	.000	.200	.000	.200	-43	-1	-1	96	0	0	.250	0			0	/C	0.0
1939	Bro-N	21	26	0	4	2	0	0	1	4	7	.154	.267	.231	.497	32	-2	-3	107	61	2	.417	0			0	C	-0.1
	NY-N	5	13	1	3	0	0	0	0	0	1	.231	.231	.231	.462	25	-1	-1	99	0	1	.300	0			1	/C	0.0
	Yr	26	39	1	7	2	0	0	1	4	8	.179	.256	.231	.487	30	-4	-4	106	52	3	.406	0			1		-0.1
1942	StL-A	1	1	0	1	0	0	0	0	0	0	1.000	1.000	1.000	2.000	445	0	0	104	0	1	—	0	0	0	0	H	0.0
1944	Bro-N	7	10	0	0	0	0	0	0	2	1	.000	.167	.000	.167	-51	-2	-2	99	0	0	.182	0			0	/C	0.0
1945	Bro-N	2	2	0	0	0	0	0	0	1	0	.000	.333	.000	.333	-3	-0	-0	96	0	0	.500	0			0	/C	0.0
Total	15	699	2062	220	546	92	16	5	238	198	188	.265	.331	.332	.663	70	-84	-89	102	115	237	.585	2	6		-29	C	-6.0

■ **DRUNGO HAZEWOOD** Hazewood, Drungo La Rue b: 9/2/59, Mobile, Ala. BR/TR, 6'3", 210 lbs. Deb: 9/19/80

YEAR	TM/L	G	AB	R	H	2B	3B	HR	RBI	BB	SO	AVG	OBP	SLG	PRO	/A	BR	/A	PF	CHI	RC	TA	SB	CS	SBR	FR	POS	TPR
1980	Bal-A	6	5	1	0	0	0	0	0	0	4	.000	.000	.000	.000	-99	-1	-1	101	0	0	.000	0	0	0	-1	/O	-0.2

■ **BOB HAZLE** Hazle, Robert Sidney "Hurricane" b: 12/9/30, Laurens, S.C. BL/TR, 6', 190 lbs. Deb: 9/08/55

YEAR	TM/L	G	AB	R	H	2B	3B	HR	RBI	BB	SO	AVG	OBP	SLG	PRO	/A	BR	/A	PF	CHI	RC	TA	SB	CS	SBR	FR	POS	TPR
1955	Cin-N	6	13	0	3	0	0	0	0	0	3	.231	.231	.231	.462	22	-1	-1	106	0	1	.300	0	0	0	2	/O	0.0
1957	Mil-N	41	134	26	54	12	0	7	27	18	15	.403	.477	.649	1.126	220	19	21	90	104	41	1.274	1	3	-2	-7	O	1.1
1958	Mil-N	20	56	6	10	0	0	0	5	9	4	.179	.303	.179	.482	35	-5	-4	89	207	4	.435	0	0	0	-2	O	-0.6
	Det-A	43	58	5	14	2	0	2	5	5	13	.241	.302	.379	.681	83	-1	-1	104	72	7	.614	0	0	0	-2	O	-0.4
Total	3	110	261	37	81	14	0	9	37	32	35	.310	.390	.467	.857	138	12	14	94	115	53	.858	1	3	-2	-10	/O	0.1

■ **DOC HAZLETON** Hazleton, Willard Carpenter b: 8/28/1876, Strafford, Vt. d: 3/17/41, Burlington, Vt. Deb: 4/17/02

YEAR	TM/L	G	AB	R	H	2B	3B	HR	RBI	BB	SO	AVG	OBP	SLG	PRO	/A	BR	/A	PF	CHI	RC	TA	SB	CS	SBR	FR	POS	TPR
1902	StL-N	7	23	0	3	0	0	0	0	2		.130	.200	.130	.330	4	-2	-2	95	0	1	.250	0			-0	/1	-0.2

■ **FRAN HEALY** Healy, Francis Xavier b: 9/6/46, Holyoke, Mass. BR/TR, 6'5", 220 lbs. Deb: 9/03/69

YEAR	TM/L	G	AB	R	H	2B	3B	HR	RBI	BB	SO	AVG	OBP	SLG	PRO	/A	BR	/A	PF	CHI	RC	TA	SB	CS	SBR	FR	POS	TPR
1969	KC-A	6	10	0	4	1	0	0	0	0	5	.400	.400	.500	.900	146	1	1	103	0	2	.833	0	0	0	0	/C	0.1
1971	SF-N	47	93	10	26	3	0	2	11	15	24	.280	.380	.376	.756	115	2	2	100	109	14	.739	1	0	0	-1	C	0.2
1972	SF-N	45	99	12	15	4	0	1	8	13	24	.152	.257	.222	.479	37	-8	-8	100	131	6	.419	0	1	-1	0	C	-0.6
1973	KC-A	95	279	25	77	15	2	6	34	31	56	.276	.348	.409	.757	103	5	1	109	101	40	.705	3	4	-2	-6	C/D	-0.3
1974	KC-A	139	445	59	112	24	2	9	53	62	73	.252	.344	.375	.720	101	5	2	106	107	59	.697	16	8	0	0	*C	0.7
1975	KC-A	56	188	16	48	5	2	2	18	14	19	.255	.307	.335	.642	80	-5	-5	102	100	18	.547	4	3	-1	-1	C/D	-0.4
1976	KC-A	8	24	2	3	0	0	0	1	4	10	.125	.250	.125	.375	12	-3	-3	100	128	1	.409	2	0	1	-0	/CD	-0.1
	NY-A	46	120	10	32	3	0	0	9	9	17	.267	.318	.292	.609	80	-3	-3	99	99	11	.511	3	1	0	2	C/D	0.0
	Yr	54	144	12	35	3	0	0	10	13	27	.243	.306	.264	.570	68	-5	-5	99	105	12	.496	5	1	1	1		-0.1
1977	NY-A	27	67	10	15	5	0	0	7	6	13	.224	.288	.299	.586	61	-4	-4	99	139	6	.509	1	0	0	0	C	-0.1
1978	NY-A	1	1	0	0	0	0	0	0	0	1	.000	.000	.000	.000	-99	-0	-0	99	0	0	.000	0	0	0	0	/C	0.0
Total	9	470	1326	144	332	60	6	20	141	154	242	.250	.329	.350	.679	90	-9	-16	104	107	158	.643	30	17	-1	-7	C/D	-0.5

■ **FRANCIS HEALY** Healy, Francis Xavier Paul b: 6/29/10, Holyoke, Mass. BR/TR, 5'9.5", 175 lbs. Deb: 4/29/30

YEAR	TM/L	G	AB	R	H	2B	3B	HR	RBI	BB	SO	AVG	OBP	SLG	PRO	/A	BR	/A	PF	CHI	RC	TA	SB	CS	SBR	FR	POS	TPR
1930	NY-N	7	2	2	0	0	0	0	0	0	0	.000	.000	.000	.000	-99	-1	-1	98	0	0	.000	0			0	/C	0.0
1931	NY-N	6	7	1	1	0	0	0	0	0	0	.143	.143	.143	.286	-24	-1	-1	97	0	0	.167	0			-0	/C	0.0
1932	NY-N	14	32	5	8	2	0	0	4	2	8	.250	.294	.313	.607	64	-2	-2	99	149	3	.500	0			-1	C	-0.1
1934	StL-N	15	13	1	4	1	0	0	1	0	2	.308	.308	.385	.692	74	-0	-1	114	72	1	.500	0			-0	/C3O	0.0
Total	4	42	54	9	13	3	0	0	5	2	10	.241	.268	.296	.564	50	-4	-4	102	107	4	.429	0			-1	/CO3	-0.1

■ **THOMAS HEALY** Healy, Thomas Fitzgerald b: 10/30/1895, Altoona, Pa. d: 1/15/74, Cleveland, Ohio BR/TR, 6', 172 lbs. Deb: 7/13/15

YEAR	TM/L	G	AB	R	H	2B	3B	HR	RBI	BB	SO	AVG	OBP	SLG	PRO	/A	BR	/A	PF	CHI	RC	TA	SB	CS	SBR	FR	POS	TPR
1915	Phi-A	23	77	11	17	1	0	0	5	6	4	.221	.310	.234	.544	65	-3	-3	96	96	5	.438	0	4	-2	0	3/S	-0.3
1916	Phi-A	6	23	4	6	1	1	0	2	1	2	.261	.320	.391	.711	116	0	0	98	76	3	.706	1			0	/3	0.1
Total	2	29	100	15	23	2	1	0	7	7	6	.230	.313	.270	.582	77	-3	-2	97	92	8	.494	1	4		0	/3S	-0.2

■ **CHARLIE HEARD** Heard, Charles b: 1/30/1872, Philadelphia, Pa. d: 2/20/45, Philadelphia, Pa. BR/TR, 6'2", 190 lbs. Deb: 7/14/1890

YEAR	TM/L	G	AB	R	H	2B	3B	HR	RBI	BB	SO	AVG	OBP	SLG	PRO	/A	BR	/A	PF	CHI	RC	TA	SB	CS	SBR	FR	POS	TPR
1890	Pit-N	12	43	2	8	2	0	0	0	1	15	.186	.205	.233	.437	33	-4	-3	88	0	2	.314	0			0	/OP	-0.2

■ **HEARN** Hearn Deb:4/18/1872

YEAR	TM/L	G	AB	R	H	2B	3B	HR	RBI	BB	SO	AVG	OBP	SLG	PRO	/A	BR	/A	PF	CHI	RC	TA	SB	CS	SBR	FR	POS	TPR
1872	Oly-n	1	3	0	1							.333															/S	

■ **ED HEARN** Hearn, Edmund b: 9/17/1888, Ventura, Cal. d: 9/8/52, Sawtelle, Cal. TR , 5'9", 160 lbs. Deb: 6/09/10

YEAR	TM/L	G	AB	R	H	2B	3B	HR	RBI	BB	SO	AVG	OBP	SLG	PRO	/A	BR	/A	PF	CHI	RC	TA	SB	CS	SBR	FR	POS	TPR
1910	Bos-A	2	2	0	0	0	0	0	0	0		.000	.000	.000	.000	-99	-0	-0	99	0	0	.000	0			-0	/S	0.0

■ **ED HEARN** Hearn, Edward John b: 8/23/60, Stuart, Fla. BR/TR, 6'3", 215 lbs. Deb: 5/17/86

YEAR	TM/L	G	AB	R	H	2B	3B	HR	RBI	BB	SO	AVG	OBP	SLG	PRO	/A	BR	/A	PF	CHI	RC	TA	SB	CS	SBR	FR	POS	TPR
1986	NY-N	49	136	16	36	5	0	4	10	12	19	.265	.324	.390	.714	100	-1	-0	96	61	16	.619	0	1	-1	2	C	0.2
1987	KC-A	6	17	2	5	2	0	0	3	4	2	.294	.429	.412	.840	121	1	1	104	171	3	.846	0	0	0	0	/C	0.1
1988	KC-A	7	18	1	4	2	0	0	1	0	1	.222	.222	.333	.556	52	-1	-1	103	66	1	.400	0	0	0	-0	/CD	0.0
Total	3	62	171	19	45	9	0	4	14	16	22	.263	.326	.386	.712	98	-1	-1	97	74	20	.641	0	1	-1	2	/CD	0.3

■ **HUGHIE HEARNE** Hearne, Hugh Joseph b: 4/18/1873, Troy, N.Y. d: 9/22/32, Troy, N.Y. BR/TR, 5'8", 182 lbs. Deb: 8/29/01

YEAR	TM/L	G	AB	R	H	2B	3B	HR	RBI	BB	SO	AVG	OBP	SLG	PRO	/A	BR	/A	PF	CHI	RC	TA	SB	CS	SBR	FR	POS	TPR
1901	Bro-N	2	5	1	2	0	0	0	3	0		.400	.400	.400	.800	127	0	0	106	502	1	.667	0			0	/C	0.0
1902	Bro-N	66	231	22	65	10	0	0	28	16		.281	.328	.325	.653	109	1	2	95	132	26	.566	3			-2	C	0.7
1903	Bro-N	26	57	8	16	3	2	0	4	3		.281	.317	.404	.720	105	0	0	101	56	8	.683	2			-2	C/1	0.0
Total	3	94	293	31	83	13	2	0	35	19		.283	.327	.341	.668	109	2	3	96	123	35	.590	5			-4	/C1	0.7

■ **JEFF HEARRON** Hearron, Jeffrey Vernon b: 11/19/61, Lomg Beach, Cal. BR/TR, 6'1", 195 lbs. Deb: 8/25/85

YEAR	TM/L	G	AB	R	H	2B	3B	HR	RBI	BB	SO	AVG	OBP	SLG	PRO	/A	BR	/A	PF	CHI	RC	TA	SB	CS	SBR	FR	POS	TPR
1985	Tor-A	4	7	0	1	0	0	0	0	0	2	.143	.143	.143	.286	-21	-1	-1	101	0	0	.167	0	0	0	-0	/C	0.0
1986	Tor-A	12	23	2	5	1	0	0	4	3	7	.217	.308	.261	.569	55	-1	-1	105	266	2	.474	0	0	0	-2	C	-0.1
Total	2	16	30	2	6	1	0	0	4	3	9	.200	.273	.233	.506	39	-2	-3	104	209	2	.400	0	0	0	-2	/C	-0.1

■ **JEFF HEATH** Heath, John Geoffrey b: 4/1/15, Ft.William, Ont., Canada d: 12/9/75, Seattle, Wash. BL/TR, 5'11.5", 200 lbs. Deb: 9/13/36

YEAR	TM/L	G	AB	R	H	2B	3B	HR	RBI	BB	SO	AVG	OBP	SLG	PRO	/A	BR	/A	PF	CHI	RC	TA	SB	CS	SBR	FR	POS	TPR
1936	Cle-A	12	41	6	14	3	3	1	8	3	4	.341	.386	.634	1.021	140	3	2	106	89	10	1.111	1	0	0	-3	O	0.0
1937	Cle-A	20	61	8	14	1	4	0	8	0	9	.230	.230	.377	.607	51	-5	-5	98	119	5	.479	0	1	-1	-1	O	-0.6
1938	Cle-A	126	502	104	172	31	**18**	21	112	33	55	.343	.383	.602	.985	145	29	30	99	110	114	1.021	3	1	0	0	*O	2.7
1939	Cle-A	121	431	64	126	31	7	14	69	41	64	.292	.354	.494	.848	117	8	9	98	93	75	.829	8	4	0	6	*O	1.1
1940	Cle-A	100	356	55	78	16	3	14	50	40	62	.219	.298	.399	.697	85	-12	-9	93	100	45	.661	5	3	-0	2	O	-1.2
1941	Cle-A	151	585	89	199	32	**20**	24	123	50	69	.340	.396	.586	.982	156	45	44	101	111	138	1.030	18	12	-2	-7	*O	2.5
1942	Cle-A	147	568	82	158	37	13	10	76	62	66	.278	.350	.442	.792	133	15	21	92	101	89	.753	9	9	-3	4	*O	1.2
1943	Cle-A	118	424	58	116	22	6	18	79	63	58	.274	.369	.481	.850	164	25	30	90	114	79	.853	5	8	-3	-2	*O	2.3
1944	Cle-A	60	151	20	50	5	2	5	33	18	12	.331	.402	.490	.892	154	11	11	100	134	31	.885	0	1	-1	-1	O	0.8
1945	Cle-A	102	370	60	113	16	7	15	61	56	39	.305	.398	.508	.906	165	29	30	99	100	80	.939	3	1	0	-5	*O	2.2
1946	Was-A	48	166	23	47	12	3	4	27	36	36	.283	.411	.464	.875	156	11	13	92	122	34	.911	0	4	-2	-4	O	0.4
	StL-A	86	316	46	87	20	4	12	57	37	37	.275	.353	.478	.831	133	12	13	98	123	56	.811	0	2	-1	-8	O	0.0
	Yr	134	482	69	134	32	7	16	84	73	73	.278	.374	.473	.847	141	23	26	96	123	91	.848	0	6	-4	-12		0.4
1947	StL-A	141	491	81	123	20	7	27	85	88	87	.251	.366	.485	.850	133	23	22	102	104	91	.859	2	1	0	-1	*O	1.5
1948	Bos-N	115	364	64	116	26	5	20	76	51	46	.319	.404	.582	.986	162	32	31	102	105	89	1.056	2			-2	*O	2.2
1949	Bos-N	36	111	17	34	7	0	9	23	15	26	.306	.389	.613	1.002	170	10	10	97	91	27	1.051	0			-2	O	0.6
Total	14	1383	4937	777	1447	279	102	194	887	593	670	.293	.370	.509	.879	140	235	253	97	107	964	.896	56	47		-24	*O	15.7

YEAR	TM/L	G	AB	R	H	2B	3B	HR	RBI	BB	SO	AVG	OBP	SLG	PRO	/A	BR	/A	PF	CHI	RC	TA	SB	CS	SBR	FR	POS	TPR
■ KELLY HEATH	Heath, Kelly Mark b: 9/4/57, Plattsburg, N.Y. BR/TR, 5'7", 155 lbs. Deb: 4/20/82																											
1982	KC-A	1	1	0	0	0	0	0	0	0	0	.000	.000	.000	.000	-99	-0	-0	100	0	0	.000	0	0	0	0	/2	0.0
■ MIKE HEATH	Heath, Michael Thomas b: 2/5/55, Tampa, Fla. BR/TR, 5'11", 180 lbs. Deb: 6/03/78																											
1978	NY-A	33	92	6	21	3	1	0	8	4	9	.228	.268	.283	.551	56	-6	-5	99	122	7	.431	0	0	0	-1	C	-0.4
1979	Oak-A	74	258	19	66	8	0	3	27	17	18	.256	.309	.322	.631	80	-10	-6	89	115	23	.505	1	0	0	3	OC/3D	-0.3
1980	Oak-A	92	305	27	74	10	2	1	33	16	28	.243	.280	.298	.579	62	-17	-15	95	137	24	.456	3	3	-1	9	CD/O	-0.4
1981	Oak-A	84	301	26	71	7	1	8	30	13	36	.236	.270	.346	.615	79	-10	-9	96	93	25	.500	3	3	-1	9	C/O	0.3
1982	Oak-A	101	318	43	77	18	4	3	39	27	36	.242	.301	.352	.654	83	-9	-7	95	129	35	.595	8	3	1	7	CO/3	0.5
1983	Oak-A	96	345	45	97	17	0	6	33	18	59	.281	.319	.383	.701	96	-4	-2	96	88	39	.590	3	4	-2	-2	CO/3D	-0.2
1984	Oak-A	140	475	49	118	21	5	13	64	26	72	.248	.289	.396	.685	95	-9	-4	92	112	50	.592	7	4	-0	-3	*CO/3S	-0.2
1985	Oak-A	138	436	71	109	18	6	13	55	41	63	.250	.316	.408	.724	104	-3	2	93	100	53	.654	7	7	-2	-9	*CO3	-0.4
1986	StL-N	65	190	19	39	8	1	4	25	23	36	.205	.294	.321	.615	68	-8	-9	103	137	17	.547	2	3	-1	-4	C/O	-1.2
	Det-A	30	98	11	26	3	0	4	11	4	17	.265	.294	.418	.712	97	-1	-1	95	83	12	.662	4	1	1	3	C/3	0.4
1987	Det-A	93	270	34	76	16	0	8	33	21	42	.281	.340	.430	.770	107	1	2	97	94	38	.691	1	5	-3	-5	CO/13S2D	0.0
1988	Det-A	86	219	24	54	7	2	5	18	18	32	.247	.307	.365	.672	93	-4	-2	94	75	24	.585	1	0	0	-3	C/O	-0.1
Total	11	1032	3307	374	828	136	22	68	376	228	448	.250	.301	.366	.668	88	-80	-57	95	107	349	.593	40	33	-8	5	CO/D31S2	-2.0
■ MICKEY HEATH	Heath, Minor Wilson b: 10/30/03, Toledo, Ohio d: 7/30/86, Dallas, Tex. BL/TL, 6', 175 lbs. Deb: 4/18/31																											
1931	Cin-N	7	26	2	7	0	0	0	3	2	5	.269	.321	.269	.591	63	-1	-1	95	162	2	.474	0			-0	/1	-0.1
1932	Cin-N	39	134	14	27	1	3	0	15	20	23	.201	.310	.254	.563	56	-8	-7	96	167	12	.514	0			-1	1	-1.0
Total	2	46	160	16	34	1	3	0	18	22	28	.213	.311	.256	.568	57	-10	-9	96	166	15	.508	0			-1	/1	-1.1
■ TOMMY HEATH	Heath, Thomas George b: 8/18/13, Akron, Col. d: 2/26/67, Los Gatos, Cal. BR/TR, 5'10", 185 lbs. Deb: 4/23/35																											
1935	StL-A	47	93	10	22	3	0	0	9	20	13	.237	.372	.269	.640	64	-3	-4	107	122	11	.634	0	0	0	2	C	0.0
1937	StL-A	17	43	4	10	0	2	1	3	10	3	.233	.377	.395	.773	96	-0	-0	99	51	7	.818	0	0	0	1	C	0.1
1938	StL-A	70	194	22	44	13	0	2	22	35	24	.227	.345	.325	.670	69	-9	-9	100	108	24	.649	0	1	-1	6	C	-0.1
Total	3	134	330	36	76	16	2	3	34	65	40	.230	.357	.318	.675	71	-12	-13	102	104	42	.667	0	1	-1	9	C	0.0
■ BILL HEATH	Heath, William Chris b: 3/10/39, Yuba City, Cal. BL/TR, 5'8", 175 lbs. Deb: 10/03/65																											
1965	Chi-A	1	1	0	0	0	0	0	0	0	0	.000	.000	.000	.000	-99	-0	-0	92	0	0	.000	0	0	0	0	H	0.0
1966	Hou-N	55	123	12	37	6	0	0	8	9	11	.301	.353	.350	.703	99	-0	0	97	78	15	.600	1	0	0	2	C	0.4
1967	Hou-N	9	11	0	1	0	0	0	0	4	3	.091	.333	.091	.424	29	-1	-1	94	0	1	.500	0	0	0	0	/C	0.0
	Det-A	20	32	0	4	0	0	0	4	1	4	.125	.152	.125	.277	-18	-5	-5	99	417	1	.179	0	0	0	0	/C	-0.3
1969	Chi-N	27	32	1	5	0	1	0	1	12	4	.156	.386	.219	.605	69	-0	-1	107	57	4	.679	0	0	0	0	/C	0.0
Total	4	112	199	13	47	6	1	0	13	26	22	.236	.327	.276	.604	72	-6	-6	99	118	20	.542	1	0	0	3	/C	0.1
■ CLIFF HEATHCOTE	Heathcote, Clifton Earl b: 1/24/1898, Glen Rock, Pa. d: 1/19/39, York, Pa. BL/TL, 5'10.5", 160 lbs. Deb: 6/04/18																											
1918	StL-N	88	348	37	90	12	3	4	32	20	40	.259	.301	.345	.646	103	-2	0	93	88	38	.593	12			-8	O	-1.3
1919	StL-N	114	401	53	112	13	4	1	29	20	41	.279	.315	.339	.654	102	-2	0	94	83	49	.637	27			-6	*O/1	-1.0
1920	StL-N	133	489	55	139	18	8	3	56	25	31	.284	.320	.372	.693	101	-2	-0	98	116	57	.629	21	14	-2	2	*O	-0.8
1921	StL-N	62	156	18	38	6	2	0	9	10	9	.244	.293	.308	.601	62	-9	-8	95	69	14	.537	7	5	-1	-7	O	-1.7
1922	StL-N	34	98	11	24	5	2	0	14	9	4	.245	.315	.337	.652	67	-5	-5	101	148	10	.566	0	2	-1	3	O	-0.3
	Chi-N	76	243	37	68	8	7	1	34	18	15	.280	.330	.383	.712	88	-6	-5	95	124	31	.655	5	2	0	-0	O	-0.6
	Yr	110	341	48	92	13	9	1	48	27	19	.270	.325	.370	.695	81	-11	-9	97	133	41	.628	5	4	-1	3		-0.9
1923	Chi-N	117	393	48	98	14	3	1	27	25	22	.249	.298	.308	.606	57	-23	-25	104	77	36	.577	32	17	-1	2	*O	-2.6
1924	Chi-N	113	392	66	121	19	7	0	30	28	28	.309	.356	.393	.749	100	1	0	101	72	51	.708	26	24	-7	-2	*O	-1.0
1925	Chi-N	109	380	57	100	14	5	5	39	39	26	.263	.343	.366	.709	83	-10	-9	97	92	49	.687	15	11	-2	14	O	0.0
1926	Chi-N	139	510	98	141	33	3	10	53	58	30	.276	.353	.412	.764	99	4	-0	106	81	74	.780	18			15	*O	0.9
1927	Chi-N	83	228	28	67	12	4	2	25	20	16	.294	.359	.408	.766	105	2	2	100	88	33	.758	6			10	O	0.9
1928	Chi-N	67	137	26	39	8	0	3	18	17	12	.285	.364	.409	.772	107	1	2	95	99	21	.806	6			-2	O	-0.1
1929	Chi-N	82	224	45	70	17	0	2	31	25	17	.313	.384	.415	.799	97	-0	-0	101	107	36	.831	9			3	O	-0.1
1930	Chi-N	70	150	30	39	10	1	9	18	18	15	.260	.343	.520	.863	100	0	-1	105	59	26	.910	4			-1	O	-0.3
1931	Cin-N	90	252	34	65	15	6	0	28	32	16	.258	.342	.365	.707	95	-3	-1	95	108	33	.679	3			13	O	0.8
1932	Cin-N	8	3	3	0	0	0	0	0	0	0	.000	.000	.000	.000	-99	-1	-1	96	0	0	.000	0			0	H	0.0
	Phi-N	30	39	7	11	2	0	1	5	3	3	.282	.333	.410	.744	88	-0	-1	112	98	6	.679	0			0	/1	0.0
	Yr	38	42	10	11	2	0	1	5	3	3	.262	.311	.381	.692	78	-1	-1	109	77	5	.613	0			0		0.0
Total	15	1415	4443	653	1222	206	55	42	448	367	325	.275	.333	.375	.708	92	-55	-52	99	92	563	.681	191	75		35	*O/1	-7.2
■ RICHIE HEBNER	Hebner, Richard Joseph b: 11/26/47, Boston, Mass. BL/TR, 6'1", 195 lbs. Deb: 9/23/68																											
1968	Pit-N	2	1	0	0	0	0	0	0	0	0	.000	.000	.000	.000	-99	-0	-0	101	0	0	.000	0	0	0	0	H	0.0
1969	Pit-N	129	459	72	138	23	4	8	47	53	53	.301	.383	.420	.803	132	17	20	95	89	77	.784	4	1	1	0	*3/1	2.2
1970	Pit-N	120	420	60	122	24	8	11	46	42	48	.290	.365	.464	.829	125	12	14	97	80	71	.796	2	3	-1	-0	*3	0.9
1971	Pit-N	112	388	50	105	17	8	17	67	32	68	.271	.331	.487	.818	130	13	14	99	116	62	.777	2	2	-1	-7	*3	0.7
1972	Pit-N	124	427	63	128	24	4	19	72	52	54	.300	.384	.508	.892	147	29	28	103	110	85	.896	0	0	0	-17	*3	1.0
1973	Pit-N	144	509	73	138	28	1	25	74	56	60	.271	.348	.477	.825	138	17	22	92	95	85	.797	0	1	-1	-10	*3	0.9
1974	Pit-N	146	550	97	160	21	6	18	68	60	53	.291	.367	.449	.816	130	20	22	98	92	90	.771	0	3	-2	-2	*3	1.5
1975	Pit-N	128	472	65	116	16	4	15	57	43	48	.246	.322	.392	.714	98	-2	-2	99	102	61	.654	0	1	-1	-10	*3	-1.3
1976	Pit-N	132	434	60	108	21	3	8	51	47	39	.249	.328	.366	.694	96	-2	-2	100	107	54	.632	1	3	-2	-14	*3	-1.9
1977	Phi-N	118	397	67	113	17	4	18	62	61	46	.285	.384	.484	.868	130	18	18	100	103	74	.880	7	8	-3	3	*13/2	1.3
1978	Phi-N	137	435	61	123	22	3	17	71	53	58	.283	.372	.464	.837	126	19	16	105	111	74	.820	4	7	-3	-5	*13/2	0.5
1979	NY-N	136	473	54	127	25	2	10	79	59	59	.268	.359	.393	.752	111	5	8	95	148	71	.723	3	1	0	-3	*3/1	0.0
1980	Det-A	104	341	48	99	10	7	12	82	38	45	.290	.365	.466	.831	120	12	10	105	164	57	.790	0	3	-2	1	13/D	0.5
1981	Det-A	78	226	19	51	8	2	5	28	27	28	.226	.314	.345	.659	85	-3	-4	105	118	24	.593	1	2	-1	-2	1D	-0.9
1982	Det-A	68	179	25	49	6	0	8	18	25	21	.274	.363	.441	.804	119	5	5	100	70	30	.795	1	1	-0	0	1D	0.4
	Pit-N	25	70	6	21	2	0	2	12	5	3	.300	.347	.414	.761	102	1	0	110	134	11	.760	4	0	1	-2	O/13	0.0
1983	Pit-N	78	162	23	43	4	1	5	26	17	28	.265	.339	.395	.734	100	1	0	103	130	22	.720	8	3	1	-5	3/1O	-0.6
1984	Chi-N	44	81	12	27	3	0	2	8	10	15	.333	.407	.444	.851	126	4	4	110	75	15	.839	1	0	0	-1	3/1O	0.2
1985	Chi-N	83	120	10	26	2	0	3	22	7	15	.217	.266	.308	.574	52	-7	-9	116	191	9	.464	0	1	-1	-1	1/3O	-1.0
Total	18	1908	6144	865	1694	273	57	203	890	687	741	.276	.356	.438	.793	119	161	163	100	109	972	.777	38	40	-13	-75	*31/DO2	4.4
■ MIKE HECHINGER	Hechinger, Michael Vincent b: 2/14/1890, Chicago, Ill. d: 8/13/67, Chicago, Ill. BR/TR, 6', 175 lbs. Deb: 9/27/12																											
1912	Chi-N	2	3	0	0	0	0	0	0	2	0	.000	.400	.000	.400	14	-0	-0	104	0	0	.667	0			0	/C	0.0
1913	Chi-N	2	2	0	0	0	0	0	0	0	0	.000	.000	.000	.000	-99	-1	-1	99	0	0	.000	0			0	H	0.0
	Bro-N	9	11	1	2	1	0	0	0	0	2	.182	.182	.273	.455	28	-1	-1	104	0	0	.333	0			-0	/C	0.0
	Yr	11	13	1	2	1	0	0	0	0	2	.154	.154	.231	.385	9	-2	-2	103	0	0	.273	0			-0		0.0
Total	2	13	16	1	2	1	0	0	0	2	2	.125	.222	.188	.410	16	-2	-2	104	0	0	.357	0			-0	/C	0.0
■ GUY HECKER	Hecker, Guy Jackson b: 4/3/1856, Youngville, Pa. d: 12/3/38, Wooster, Ohio BR/TR, 6', 190 lbs. Deb: 5/02/1882 M																											
1882	Lou-a	78	340	62	94	14	4	3		5		.276	.287	.368	.655	127	6	9	94	0	37	.528				2	*1P/O	1.0
1883	Lou-a	79	322	56	88	6	6	1		10		.273	.295	.339	.634	110	1	4	94	0	33	.509				3	PO1	0.0
1884	Lou-a	78	316	53	94	14	8	4		10		.297	.323	.430	.754	165	15	20	89	0	45	.667				7	*P/O	0.0
1885	Lou-a	70	297	48	81	9	2	2		5		.273	.287	.337	.624	97	-1	-2	102	0	29	.491				5	P1/O	0.0
1886	Lou-a	84	343	76	117	14	5	4		32		.341	.402	.446	.848	156	27	22	108	0	73	.942	25			1	P1O	0.0
1887	Lou-a	91	370	89	118	21	6	4		31		.319	.381	.441	.821	123	15	11	107	0	82	.984	48			-5	1PO	0.4
1888	Lou-a	56	211	32	48	9	2	0	29	11		.227	.285	.289	.574	96	-3	0	91	145	24	.601	20			0	1P/O	0.0
1889	Lou-a	81	327	42	93	17	5	1	36	18	27	.284	.333	.376	.709	109	1	4	96	78	48	.701	17			-0	1P/O	-0.1
1890	Pit-N	86	340	43	77	13	9	0	38	19	17	.226	.285	.318	.603	88	-10	-4	88	113	35	.567	13			2	1P/OM	-0.5

YEAR	TM/L	G	AB	R	H	2B	3B	HR	RBI	BB	SO	AVG	OBP	SLG	PRO	/A	BR	/A	PF	CHI	RC	TA	SB	CS	SBR	FR	POS	TPR
Total	9	703	2866	501	810	117	47	19	103	141	44	.283	.324	.376	.700	120	52	65	97	34	407	.669	123			15	P1/O	0.8
■ DANNY HEEP Heep, Daniel William b: 7/3/57, San Antonio, Tex. BL/TL, 5'11", 185 lbs. Deb: 8/31/79																												
1979	Hou-N	14	14	0	2	0	0	0	2	1	4	.143	.200	.143	.343	-5	-2	-2	90	396	1	.250	0	0	0	1	/O	0.0
1980	Hou-N	33	87	6	24	8	0	0	6	8	9	.276	.344	.368	.712	101	-0	0	98	74	12	.651	0	0	0	0	1	0.0
1981	Hou-N	33	96	6	24	3	0	0	11	10	11	.250	.321	.281	.602	81	-3	-2	88	160	9	.493	0	0	0	-1	1/O	-0.3
1982	Hou-N	85	198	16	47	14	1	4	22	21	31	.237	.314	.379	.692	94	-2	-2	99	99	23	.614	0	2	-1	-2	O1	-0.6
1983	NY-N	115	253	30	64	12	0	8	21	29	40	.253	.332	.395	.727	102	0	1	99	67	33	.675	3	3	-1	-5	O1	-0.6
1984	NY-N	99	199	36	46	9	2	1	12	27	22	.231	.326	.312	.638	80	-5	-5	100	72	20	.571	3	1	0	-0	O1	-0.6
1985	NY-N	95	271	26	76	17	0	7	42	27	27	.280	.348	.421	.768	117	5	6	97	124	37	.689	2	2	-1	-5	O/1	-0.1
1986	NY-N	86	195	24	55	8	2	5	33	30	31	.282	.381	.421	.801	126	6	7	96	136	31	.776	1	4	-2	-3	O	0.1
1987	LA-N	60	98	7	16	4	0	0	9	8	10	.163	.226	.204	.430	16	-12	-11	92	180	4	.330	1	0	0	-2	O/1	-1.3
1988	LA-N	95	149	14	36	2	0	0	11	22	13	.242	.343	.255	.598	70	-4	-5	106	116	14	.538	2	0	1	-3	O1/P	-0.8
Total	10	715	1560	165	390	77	5	25	169	183	198	.250	.331	.354	.685	93	-16	-12	98	111	183	.636	12	12	-4	-21	O1/P	-4.2
■ DON HEFFNER Heffner, Donald Henry "Jeep" b: 2/8/11, Rouzerville, Pa. BR/TR, 5'10", 155 lbs. Deb: 4/17/34 MC																												
1934	NY-A	72	241	29	63	8	3	0	25	25	18	.261	.331	.320	.650	72	-11	-9	96	108	27	.575	1	1	-0	-9	2	-1.4
1935	NY-A	10	36	3	11	3	1	0	8	4	1	.306	.375	.444	.819	120	1	1	93	173	6	.800	0	0	0	-2	2	0.0
1936	NY-A	19	48	7	11	2	1	0	6	6	5	.229	.315	.313	.627	58	-3	-3	95	129	5	.568	0	0	0	0	/32S	-0.1
1937	NY-A	60	201	23	50	6	5	0	21	19	19	.249	.314	.328	.642	61	-12	-12	102	109	20	.555	1	4	-2	-5	2S/310	-1.3
1938	StL-A	141	473	47	116	23	3	2	69	65	53	.245	.341	.319	.661	66	-23	-23	100	152	56	.617	1	1	-0	-6	*2	-2.2
1939	StL-A	110	375	45	100	10	2	1	35	48	39	.267	.350	.312	.662	70	-15	-15	100	100	41	.567	1	7	-4	4	S2	-0.5
1940	StL-A	126	487	52	115	23	2	3	53	39	37	.236	.295	.310	.606	54	-31	-35	106	127	45	.510	5	5	-2	**17**	*2	-1.1
1941	StL-A	110	399	48	93	14	2	0	17	38	27	.233	.303	.278	.581	55	-26	-26	100	55	36	.495	5	6	-2	-2	*2	-1.9
1942	StL-A	19	36	2	6	2	0	0	3	1	4	.167	.189	.222	.411	15	-4	-4	104	132	1	.313	1	0	0	0	/21	-0.3
1943	StL-A	18	33	2	4	1	0	0	2	2	2	.121	.171	.152	.323	-5	-4	-4	100	146	1	.233	0	0	0	-2	2/1	-0.5
	Phi-A	52	178	17	37	6	0	0	8	18	12	.208	.284	.242	.526	54	-10	-10	101	69	13	.442	3	2	-0	-4	2/1	-1.3
	Yr	70	211	19	41	7	0	0	10	20	14	.194	.267	.227	.495	45	-14	-15	101	91	14	.409	3	2	-0	-6		-1.8
1944	Det-A	6	19	0	4	1	0	0	1	5	1	.211	.375	.263	.638	80	-0	-0	105	74	2	.667	0	0	0	1	/2	0.1
Total	11	743	2526	275	610	99	19	6	248	270	218	.241	.317	.303	.620	61	-139	-142	101	110	254	.547	18	26	-10	-7	2/S310	-10.5
■ JIM HEGAN Hegan, James Edward b: 8/3/20, Lynn, Mass. d: 6/17/84, Swampscott, Mass. BR/TR, 6'2", 195 lbs. Deb: 9/09/41 C																												
1941	Cle-A	16	47	4	15	2	0	1	5	4	7	.319	.373	.426	.798	110	1	1	101	77	8	.727	0	0	0	-0	C	0.1
1942	Cle-A	68	170	10	33	5	0	0	11	11	31	.194	.243	.224	.467	35	-15	-14	92	102	9	.350	1	3	-2	-5	C	-1.1
1946	Cle-A	88	271	29	64	11	5	0	17	17	44	.236	.284	.314	.597	75	-12	-9	89	76	23	.475	1	4	-2	-2	C	-0.8
1947	Cle-A	135	378	38	94	14	5	4	42	41	49	.249	.324	.344	.668	89	-7	-6	96	109	44	.597	3	1	0	-9	*C	-0.3
1948	Cle-A	144	472	60	117	21	6	14	61	48	74	.248	.317	.407	.724	93	-8	-7	99	88	62	.668	6	3	0	5	*C	0.7
1949	Cle-A	152	468	54	105	19	5	8	55	49	89	.224	.298	.338	.635	70	-24	-22	98	104	49	.555	1	0	0	-7	*C	-2.0
1950	Cle-A	131	415	53	91	16	5	14	58	42	52	.219	.291	.383	.674	73	-20	-19	98	100	47	.603	1	0	0	9	*C	-0.4
1951	Cle-A	133	416	60	99	17	5	6	43	38	72	.238	.302	.346	.648	79	-16	-13	95	95	45	.558	0	3	-2	3	*C	-0.2
1952	Cle-A	112	333	39	75	17	2	4	41	29	47	.225	.287	.324	.612	77	-14	-10	91	128	32	.519	0	2	-1	-5	*C	-1.1
1953	Cle-A	112	299	37	65	10	1	9	37	25	41	.217	.280	.348	.628	72	-14	-12	95	105	29	.537	1	2	-1	-16	*C	-2.5
1954	Cle-A	139	423	56	99	12	7	11	40	34	48	.234	.291	.374	.665	76	-13	-16	106	79	43	.565	0	1	-1	-11	*C	-2.1
1955	Cle-A	116	304	30	67	5	2	9	40	34	33	.220	.299	.339	.638	68	-13	-15	104	115	31	.559	0	1	-1	-15	*C	-2.6
1956	Cle-A	122	315	42	70	15	2	6	34	49	54	.222	.327	.340	.667	75	-11	-11	101	102	36	.618	1	1	-0	-22	*C	-3.1
1957	Cle-A	58	148	14	32	7	0	4	15	16	23	.216	.293	.345	.637	72	-6	-6	102	94	15	.554	0	1	-1	-4	C	-0.7
1958	Det-A	45	130	14	25	6	0	1	7	10	32	.192	.250	.262	.512	39	-11	-11	104	76	8	.400	0	0	0	-2	C	-1.2
	Phi-N	25	59	5	13	6	0	0	6	4	16	.220	.270	.322	.592	57	-4	-4	98	130	5	.500	0	0	0	0	C	-0.1
1959	Phi-N	25	51	1	10	1	0	0	8	3	10	.196	.241	.216	.456	23	-6	-6	99	294	3	.333	0	1	-1	-2	C	-0.5
	SF-N	21	30	0	4	1	0	0	0	1	10	.133	.161	.167	.328	-13	-5	-5	95	0	1	.214	0	1	-1	-1	C	-0.4
	Yr	46	81	1	14	2	0	0	8	4	20	.173	.212	.198	.409	10	-10	-10	98	166	3	.286	0	2	-1	-3		-0.9
1960	Chi-N	24	43	4	9	2	1	1	5	1	10	.209	.244	.372	.617	67	-2	-2	98	107	3	.500	0	0	0	-3	C	-0.3
Total	17	1666	4772	550	1087	187	46	92	525	456	742	.228	.296	.344	.640	74	-199	-185	98	100	491	.570	15	24	-10	-86	*C	-18.6
■ MIKE HEGAN Hegan, James Michael b: 7/21/42, Cleveland, Ohio BL/TL, 6'1", 188 lbs. Deb: 9/13/64																												
1964	NY-A	5	5	0	0	0	0	0	0	1	2	.000	.167	.000	.167	-47	-1	-1	103	0	0	.200	0	0	0	0	/1	0.0
1966	NY-A	13	39	7	8	0	1	0	2	7	11	.205	.326	.256	.582	75	-1	-1	94	86	3	.529	1	1	-0	1	1	0.0
1967	NY-A	68	118	12	16	4	1	1	3	20	40	.136	.266	.212	.478	45	-8	-7	94	45	9	.510	7	1	2	0	1O	-1.0
1969	Sea-A	95	267	54	78	9	6	8	37	62	61	.292	.427	.461	.888	151	20	21	98	101	58	.985	6	5	-1	0	O1	1.8
1970	Mil-A	148	476	70	116	21	2	11	52	67	116	.244	.338	.366	.704	96	-3	-2	98	102	61	.668	9	7	-2	6	*1/O	-0.3
1971	Mil-A	46	122	19	27	4	1	4	11	26	19	.221	.358	.369	.727	103	2	1	103	79	18	.735	1	1	-0	2	1	0.1
	Oak-A	65	55	5	13	3	0	0	3	5	13	.236	.300	.291	.591	68	-2	-2	101	77	5	.524	1	0	0	0	1/O	-0.4
	Yr	111	177	24	40	7	1	4	14	31	32	.226	.341	.345	.686	93	-0	-1	102	78	24	.681	2	1	0	2		-0.3
1972	Oak-A	98	79	13	26	3	1	1	5	7	20	.329	.384	.430	.814	147	4	4	97	56	14	.778	1	0	0	0	1/O	-0.1
1973	Oak-A	75	71	8	13	2	0	1	5	5	17	.183	.237	.254	.490	44	-6	-5	87	94	4	.390	0	0	0	-2	1/OD	-1.0
	NY-A	37	131	12	36	3	2	6	14	7	34	.275	.312	.466	.777	116	2	2	101	71	19	.701	0	0	0	-1	1	0.0
	Yr	112	202	20	49	5	2	7	19	12	51	.243	.285	.391	.676	97	-4	-2	92	87	23	.587	0	0	0	-3		-1.0
1974	NY-A	18	53	3	12	2	0	2	9	5	9	.226	.317	.377	.694	103	-0	0	96	136	6	.636	1	1	-0	1	1	0.0
	Mil-A	89	190	21	45	7	1	7	32	33	34	.237	.350	.395	.745	111	4	3	102	131	27	.720	0	4	-2	-1	D1O	0.0
	Yr	107	243	24	57	9	1	9	41	38	43	.235	.343	.391	.734	109	4	4	101	133	34	.708	1	5	-3	-0		0.0
1975	Mil-A	93	203	19	51	11	0	5	22	31	42	.251	.350	.379	.730	106	2	2	100	92	28	.699	1	1	-0	-6	O1/D	-0.6
1976	Mil-A	80	218	30	54	4	3	5	31	25	54	.248	.328	.362	.690	103	1	1	99	127	27	.625	0	0	0	-3	DO1	-0.3
1977	Mil-A	35	53	8	9	0	0	2	3	10	17	.170	.313	.283	.596	67	-2	-2	95	57	6	.591	0	0	0	-3	/O1D	-0.5
Total	12	965	2080	281	504	73	18	53	229	311	489	.242	.343	.371	.714	104	12	16	99	96	285	.700	28	21	-4	-6	1O/D	-2.3
■ BOB HEGMAN Hegman, Robert Hilmer b: 2/26/58, Springfield, Minn. BR/TR, 6'1", 180 lbs. Deb: 8/08/85																												
1985	KC-A	1	0	0	0	0	0	0	0	0	0	—	—	—	—	—	0	0	102	—	—	—	0	0	0	0	/2	0.0
■ JACK HEIDEMANN Heidemann, Jack Seale b: 7/11/49, Brenham, Tex. BR/TR, 6', 175 lbs. Deb: 5/02/69																												
1969	Cle-A	3	3	0	0	0	0	0	0	0	2	.000	.250	.000	.250	-26	-0	-0	94	0	0	.333	0	0	0	0	/S	0.0
1970	Cle-A	133	445	44	94	14	2	6	37	34	88	.211	.270	.292	.562	48	-28	-36	115	101	35	.464	2	4	-2	-6	*S	-3.3
1971	Cle-A	81	240	16	50	7	0	0	9	12	46	.208	.252	.237	.489	37	-19	-21	106	64	14	.364	1	3	-2	-7	S	-2.2
1972	Cle-A	10	20	0	3	0	0	0	0	2	3	.150	.261	.150	.411	23	-2	-2	107	0	1	.333	0	0	0	-0	S	0.0
1974	Cle-A	12	11	2	1	0	0	0	0	0	2	.091	.091	.091	.182	-47	-2	-2	101	0	0	.091	0	0	0	0	/3S12	-0.1
	StL-N	47	70	8	19	1	0	0	3	5	10	.271	.320	.286	.606	68	-3	-3	104	58	7	.481	0	0	0	-1	S/3	0.1
1975	NY-N	61	145	12	31	4	2	1	16	17	28	.214	.296	.290	.586	66	-7	-6	95	137	13	.517	1	0	0	-2	S/32	-0.2
1976	NY-N	5	12	0	1	0	0	0	0	0	0	.083	.083	.083	.167	-57	-2	-2	92	0	0	.091	0	0	0	0	/S2	-0.1
	Mil-A	69	146	11	32	1	0	2	10	7	24	.219	.255	.267	.522	53	-9	-9	99	85	10	.395	1	3	-2	-5	32/D	-1.4
1977	Mil-A	5	1	1	0	0	0	0	0	1	0	.000	.500	.000	.500	53	0	0	95	0	0	1.000	0	0	0	0	/2D	0.0
Total	8	426	1093	94	231	27	4	9	75	78	203	.211	.268	.268	.536	47	-72	-81	107	89	80	.438	5	10	-5	-22	S/32D1	-7.2
■ EMMETT HEIDRICK Heidrick, R. Emmet "Snags" b: 7/9/1876, Queenstown, Pa. d: 1/20/16, Clarion, Pa. BL/TR, 6', 185 lbs. Deb: 9/14/1898																												
1898	Cle-N	19	76	10	23	2	2	0	8	3		.303	.329	.382	.711	111	0	1	96	88	11	.660	3			0	O	0.1
1899	StL-N	146	591	109	194	21	14	2	82	34		.328	.368	.421	.789	110	14	7	108	95	115	.859	55			1	*O	0.0
1900	StL-N	85	339	51	102	6	8	2	45	18		.301	.336	.383	.720	108	-0	3	93	109	52	.717	22			15	O	1.0
1901	StL-N	118	502	94	170	24	12	6	67	21		.339	.365	.470	.835	149	25	28	97	78	100	.870	32			9	*O	2.3
1902	StL-A	110	447	75	129	19	10	3	56	34		.289	.339	.396	.735	103	3	1	102	88	67	.717	17			-12	*O/PS3	-1.6
1903	StL-A	120	461	55	129	20	15	1	42	19		.280	.308	.395	.703	117	6	8	95	87	64	.663	19			-11	*O/C	-1.0

YEAR	TM/L	G	AB	R	H	2B	3B	HR	RBI	BB	SO	AVG	OBP	SLG	PRO	/A	BR	/A	PF	CHI	RC	TA	SB	CS	SBR	FR	POS	TPR
1904	StL-A	133	538	66	147	14	10	1	36	16		.273	.294	.342	.636	109	1	4	95	69	66	.601	35			-3	*O	-0.7
1908	StL-A	26	93	8	20	2	2	1	6	1		.215	.223	.312	.535	73	-3	-3	103	72	7	.452	3			1	O	-0.3
Total	8	757	3047	468	914	108	73	16	342	146		.300	.333	.399	.732	115	46	49	99	86	482	.727	186			0	O/C3SP	-0.2
■ **FRANK HEIFER**	Heifer, Franklin "Heck" b: 1/18/1854, Reading, Pa. d: 8/29/1893, Reading, Pa. 5'10.5", 175 lbs. Deb: 6/04/1875																											
1875	Bos-n	11	48	11	16							.333															/1OP	
■ **CHINK HEILEMAN**	Heileman, John George b: 8/10/1872, Cincinnati, Ohio d: 7/19/40, Cincinnati, Ohio TR , 5'8", 155 lbs. Deb: 7/08/01																											
1901	Cin-N	5	15	1	2	1	0	0	1	0		.133	.133	.200	.333	-3	-2	-2	95	112	0	.231	0			0	/32	0.0
■ **HARRY HEILMANN**	Heilmann, Harry Edwin "Slug" b: 8/3/1894, San Francisco, Cal. d: 7/9/51, Southfield, Mich. BR/TR, 6'1", 195 lbs. Deb: 5/16/14 CH																											
1914	Det-A	67	182	25	41	8	1	2	18	22	29	.225	.316	.313	.629	87	-2	-3	102	107	18	.550	1	8	-5	-5	O1/2	-1.4
1916	Det-A	136	451	57	127	30	11	2	73	42	40	.282	.349	.410	.760	123	14	12	105	137	70	.744	9			-11	O1/2	-0.4
1917	Det-A	150	556	57	156	22	11	5	86	41	54	.281	.333	.387	.720	123	11	12	98	142	73	.675	11			-8	*O1	-0.4
1918	Det-A	79	286	34	79	10	6	5	39	35	10	.276	.359	.406	.765	135	10	12	97	115	45	.802	13			-7	O1/2	0.0
1919	Det-A	140	537	74	172	30	15	8	93	37	41	.320	.366	.477	.843	145	23	27	93	128	93	.827	7			-10	*1	0.7
1920	Det-A	145	543	66	168	28	5	9	89	39	32	.309	.358	.429	.787	105	5	3	103	127	82	.725	3	7	-3	0	*1O	-0.1
1921	Det-A	149	602	114	**237**	43	14	19	139	53	37	**.394**	.444	.606	1.051	173	59	62	96	120	159	1.137	2	6	-3	-19	*O/1	2.5
1922	Det-A	118	455	92	162	27	10	21	92	58	28	.356	.432	.598	1.030	170	44	45	98	104	119	1.148	8	4	0	-17	*O/1	1.9
1923	Det-A	144	524	121	211	44	11	18	115	74	40	**.403**	.481	.632	1.113	198	71	73	97	108	159	1.306	8	7	-2	-0	*O1	5.6
1924	Det-A	153	570	107	197	**45**	16	10	113	78	41	.346	.428	.533	.961	148	40	41	100	118	134	1.056	13	5	1	3	*O/1	3.2
1925	Det-A	150	573	97	225	40	11	13	134	67	27	**.393**	.457	.569	1.026	160	**52**	**53**	99	130	149	1.130	6	6	-2	-11	*O	2.5
1926	Det-A	141	502	90	184	41	8	9	103	67	19	.367	.445	.534	.979	159	42	44	97	121	120	1.062	6	7	-2	-6	*O	2.5
1927	Det-A	141	505	106	201	50	9	14	120	72	16	**.398**	.475	.616	1.091	168	62	56	108	115	145	1.303	11	0	3	-13	*O	3.2
1928	Det-A	151	558	83	183	38	10	14	107	57	45	.328	.390	.507	.897	135	27	28	99	120	112	.918	7	3	0	-2	*O1	1.7
1929	Det-A	125	453	86	156	41	7	15	120	50	39	.344	.412	.565	.977	153	33	34	97	139	104	1.033	5	6	-2	-12	*O/1	1.4
1930	Cin-N	142	459	79	153	43	6	19	91	64	50	.333	.416	.577	.993	151	28	36	90	97	109	1.085	2			3	*O1	2.6
1932	Cin-N	15	31	3	8	2	0	0	6	0	2	.258	.258	.323	.581	57	-2	-2	96	223	3	.435	0			0	/1	-0.1
Total	17	2146	7787	1291	2660	542	151	183	1538	856	550	.342	.410	.520	.930	149	517	534	99	122	1693	.976	112	59		-114	*O1/2	25.4
■ **VAL HEIM**	Heim, Val Raymond b: 11/4/20, Plymouth, Wis. BL/TR, 5'11", 170 lbs. Deb: 8/31/42																											
1942	Chi-A	13	45	6	9	1	1	0	7	5	3	.200	.294	.267	.561	59	-2	-2	99	210	4	.514	1	0	0	-2	O	-0.4
■ **BUD HEINE**	Heine, William Henry b: 9/22/1900, Elmira, N.Y. d: 9/2/76, Ft.Lauderdale, Fla BL/TR, 5'8", 145 lbs. Deb: 10/01/21																											
1921	NY-N	1	2	0	0	0	0	0	0	0	0	.000	.000	.000	.000	-99	-1	-1	98	0	0	.000	0	0	0	0	/2	0.0
■ **TOM HEINTZELMAN**	Heintzelman, Thomas Kenneth b: 11/3/46, St.Charles, Mo. BR/TR, 6'1", 180 lbs. Deb: 8/12/73																											
1973	StL-N	23	29	5	9	0	0	0	0	3	3	.310	.375	.310	.685	101	-0	0	91	0	3	.571	0	0	0	0	/2	0.1
1974	StL-N	38	74	10	17	4	0	1	6	9	14	.230	.313	.324	.638	76	-2	-2	104	86	8	.579	0	0	0	2	2/3S	0.1
1977	SF-N	2	2	0	0	0	0	0	0	0	0	.000	.000	.000	.000	-96	-1	-1	104	0	0	.000	0	0	0	0	H	0.0
1978	SF-N	27	35	2	8	1	0	2	6	2	5	.229	.270	.429	.699	101	-1	-0	92	113	4	.630	0	0	0	0	/231	0.0
Total	4	90	140	17	34	5	0	3	12	14	22	.243	.312	.343	.655	84	-3	-3	98	73	16	.585	0	0	0	2	/231S	0.2
■ **JACK HEINZMAN**	Heinzman, John Peter b: 9/27/1863, New Albany, Ind. d: 11/10/14, Louisville, Ky. BR/TR, Deb: 10/02/1886																											
1886	Lou-a	1	5	1	0	0	0			0		.000	.000	.000	.000	-93	-1	-1	108	0	0	.000	0			0	/1	0.0
■ **BOB HEISE**	Heise, Robert Lowell b: 5/12/47, San Antonio, Tex. BR/TR, 6', 175 lbs. Deb: 9/12/67																											
1967	NY-N	16	62	7	20	4	0	0	3	3	1	.323	.354	.387	.741	113	1	1	99	55	8	.600	0	1	-1	1	2/S3	0.2
1968	NY-N	6	23	3	5	0	0	0	1	1	1	.217	.250	.217	.467	40	-2	-2	102	89	1	.316	0	0	0	0	/S2	0.0
1969	NY-N	4	10	1	3	1	0	0	0	3	2	.300	.462	.400	.862	143	1	1	100	0	2	.875	0	0	0	0	/S	0.1
1970	SF-N	67	154	15	36	5	1	1	22	5	13	.234	.258	.299	.557	51	-11	-11	96	174	11	.418	0	1	-1	-3	S2/3	-0.6
1971	SF-N	13	11	2	0	0	0	0	0	0	1	.000	.000	.000	.000	-99	-3	-3	100	0	0	.000	0	0	0	0	/S32	-0.2
	Mil-A	68	189	10	48	7	0	0	7	7	15	.254	.281	.291	.572	60	-10	-10	103	52	14	.429	1	1	-0	-4	S3/2O	-0.9
1972	Mil-A	95	271	23	72	10	1	0	12	12	14	.266	.302	.310	.612	86	-6	-5	95	60	25	.478	1	1	-0	-6	23/S	-0.6
1973	Mil-A	49	98	8	20	2	0	0	4	4	4	.204	.235	.224	.460	31	-9	-9	96	71	5	.329	1	0	0	-3	S/312D	-0.7
1974	StL-N	3	7	0	1	0	0	0	0	0	0	.143	.143	.143	.286	-19	-1	-1	104	0	0	.143	0	0	0	0	/2	0.0
	Cal-A	29	75	7	20	7	0	0	6	5	10	.267	.313	.360	.673	101	-1	-0	92	87	8	.561	0	1	-1	1	2/3S	0.1
1975	Bos-A	63	126	12	27	3	0	0	21	4	6	.214	.250	.238	.488	35	-10	-12	109	269	8	.360	0	0	0	-4	32/S1	-1.4
1976	Bos-A	32	56	5	15	2	0	0	5	1	2	.268	.293	.304	.597	68	-2	-3	110	113	5	.442	0	1	-1	-1	3/S2	-0.3
1977	KC-A	54	62	11	16	2	1	0	5	2	8	.258	.292	.323	.615	67	-3	-3	100	99	6	.489	0	1	-1	-1	2S3/1	0.0
Total	11	499	1144	104	283	43	3	1	86	47	77	.247	.281	.293	.574	64	-55	-55	99	103	92	.450	3	7	-3	-20	S23/1DO	-4.3
■ **AL HEIST**	Heist, Alfred Michael b: 10/5/27, Brooklyn, N.Y. BR/TR, 6'2", 185 lbs. Deb: 7/17/60 C																											
1960	Chi-N	41	102	11	28	5	3	1	6	10	12	.275	.339	.412	.751	107	1	1	98	54	14	.714	3	1	0	0	O	0.0
1961	Chi-N	109	321	48	82	14	3	7	37	39	51	.255	.338	.383	.721	91	-4	-4	100	104	42	.667	3	3	-1	-5	O	-1.5
1962	Hou-N	27	72	4	16	1	0	0	3	3	9	.222	.263	.236	.499	38	-6	-6	93	70	4	.344	0	0	0	-1	O	-0.7
Total	3	177	495	63	126	20	6	8	46	52	72	.255	.328	.368	.696	87	-10	-9	99	89	60	.640	6	4	-1	-6	O	-2.2
■ **HEINIE HEITMULLER**	Heitmuller, William Frederick b: 1883, San Francisco, Cal. d: 10/8/12, Los Angeles, Cal. 6'2", 215 lbs. Deb: 4/26/09																											
1909	Phi-A	64	210	36	60	9	8	0	15	18		.286	.351	.405	.755	136	9	9	102	69	31	.753	7			5	O	1.2
1910	Phi-A	31	111	11	27	2	2	0	7	7		.243	.288	.297	.585	82	-2	-3	102	80	11	.548	6			0	O	-0.3
Total	2	95	321	47	87	11	10	0	22	25		.271	.330	.368	.697	117	7	6	102	73	42	.679	13			5	/O	0.9
■ **WOODIE HELD**	Held, Woodson George b: 3/25/32, Sacramento, Cal. BR/TR, 5'10.5", 167 lbs. Deb: 9/05/54																											
1954	NY-A	4	3	2	0	0	0	0	0	2	1	.000	.400	.000	.400	17	-0	-0	99	0	0	.667	0	0	0	0	/S3	0.0
1957	NY-A	1	1	0	0	0	0	0	0	0	0	.000	.000	.000	.000	-99	-0	-0	94	0	0	.000	0	0	0	0	H	0.0
	KC-A	92	326	48	78	14	3	20	50	37	81	.239	.322	.485	.807	119	7	7	99	96	52	.795	4	0	1	12	O	1.5
	Yr	93	327	48	78	14	3	20	50	37	81	.239	.322	.483	.805	118	6	7	99	95	52	.792	4	0	1	12		1.5
1958	KC-A	47	131	13	28	2	0	4	16	10	28	.214	.280	.321	.600	61	-6	-7	106	119	11	.495	0	1	-1	-2	O/3S	-1.2
	Cle-A	67	144	12	28	4	1	3	17	15	36	.194	.288	.299	.587	65	-7	-6	94	131	12	.516	1	2	-1	-1	OS/3	-0.8
	Yr	114	275	25	56	6	1	7	33	25	64	.204	.284	.309	.593	64	-14	-13	99	127	25	.518	1	3	-2	-3		-2.0
1959	Cle-A	143	525	82	132	19	3	29	71	47	118	.251	.315	.465	.780	115	6	8	97	86	75	.722	1	2	-1	-11	*S3/O2	0.4
1960	Cle-A	109	376	45	97	15	1	21	67	44	73	.258	.344	.471	.814	121	9	10	98	111	62	.793	0	1	-1	-0	*S	1.7
1961	Cle-A	146	509	67	136	23	5	23	78	69	111	.267	.358	.468	.826	123	13	16	96	102	85	.801	0	0	0	-8	*S	1.8
1962	Cle-A	139	466	55	116	12	2	19	58	73	107	.249	.364	.406	.769	109	6	8	98	96	72	.764	5	1	1	-5	*S/3O	1.1
1963	Cle-A	133	416	61	103	19	4	17	61	61	96	.248	.355	.435	.790	124	12	14	97	110	66	.778	2	2	-1	4	2O/S3	2.5
1964	Cle-A	118	364	50	86	13	0	18	49	43	88	.236	.329	.420	.749	104	3	2	103	100	51	.716	1	0	0	0	2O3	0.7
1965	Was-A	122	332	46	82	16	2	16	54	49	74	.247	.349	.452	.801	126	12	12	100	113	53	.780	0	0	0	-2	*O/32S	0.6
1966	Bal-A	56	82	6	17	3	1	1	7	12	30	.207	.309	.305	.613	76	-2	-2	101	105	9	.569	0	0	0	-1	O/2S3	-0.3
1967	Bal-A	26	41	4	6	3	0	1	6	6	12	.146	.286	.293	.578	75	-1	-1	95	167	4	.571	0	0	0	0	/23O	0.0
	Cal-A	58	141	15	31	3	0	4	17	18	41	.220	.317	.326	.643	94	-1	-1	96	122	14	.559	0	2	-1	-3	3OS/2	-0.4
	Yr	84	182	19	37	6	0	5	23	24	53	.203	.310	.319	.628	90	-3	-2	95	138	18	.562	0	2	-1	-3		-0.4
1968	Cal-A	33	45	4	5	1	0	0	0	5	15	.111	.231	.133	.364	13	-5	-4	94	0	2	.325	0	0	0	-1	/2S3O	-0.4
	Chi-A	40	54	5	9	1	0	0	2	5	14	.167	.250	.185	.435	33	-4	-4	101	86	3	.348	0	0	0	-6	O/32	-1.2
	Yr	73	99	9	14	2	0	0	2	10	29	.141	.241	.162	.403	24	-9	-9	98	47	5	.337	0	0	0	-6		-1.6
1969	Chi-A	56	63	9	9	2	0	3	6	13	19	.143	.299	.317	.616	67	-2	-3	108	83	7	.618	0	0	0	-3	O/S32	-0.6
Total	14	1390	4019	524	963	150	22	179	559	509	944	.240	.333	.421	.755	109	38	47	98	102	578	.741	14	11	-2	-27	SO23	5.4
■ **HANK HELF**	Helf, Henry Hartz b: 8/26/13, Austin, Tex. d: 10/27/84, Austin, Tex. BR/TR, 6'1", 196 lbs. Deb: 5/05/38																											
1938	Cle-A	6	13	1	1	0	0	0	1	1	1	.077	.143	.077	.220	-44	-3	-3	99	338	0	.167	0	0	0	0	/C	-0.1

YEAR	TM/L	G	AB	R	H	2B	3B	HR	RBI	BB	SO	AVG	OBP	SLG	PRO	/A	BR	/A	PF	CHI	RC	TA	SB	CS	SBR	FR	POS	TPR
1940	Cle-A	1	1	0	0	0	0	0	0	0	0	.000	.000	.000	.000	-99	-0	-0	93	0	0	.000	0	0	0	0	/C	0.0
1946	StL-A	71	182	17	35	11	0	6	21	9	40	.192	.234	.352	.586	63	-10	-10	98	97	14	.484	0	1	-1	-4	C	-1.1
Total	3	78	196	18	36	11	0	6	22	10	41	.184	.227	.332	.559	54	-14	-13	98	113	14	.458	0	1	-1	-4	/C	-1.2
■ **TY HELFRICH** Helfrich, Emory Wilbur b: 10/9/1890, Pleasantville, N.J. d: 3/18/55, Pleasantville, N.J BR/TR, 5'10", 178 lbs. Deb: 6/30/15																												
1915	Bro-F	43	104	12	25	6	0	0	5	15	21	.240	.336	.298	.634	91	-1	-1	98	58	12	.608	2			-3	2/O	-0.2
■ **HELLINGS** Hellings b:Philadelphia, Pa. Deb: 7/19/1875																												
1875	Atl-n	1	4	0	1							.250															/2	
■ **TONY HELLMAN** Hellman, Anthony J. b: 1861, Cincinnati, Ohio d: 3/29/1898, Cincinnati, Ohio Deb: 10/10/1886																												
1886	Bal-a	1	3	0	0	0	0	0		0		.000	.000	.000	.000	-99	-1	-1	91	0	0	.000	0			0	/C	0.0
■ **TOMMY HELMS** Helms, Tommy Vann b: 5/5/41, Charlotte, N.C. BR/TR, 5'10", 165 lbs. Deb: 9/23/64 MC																												
1964	Cin-N	2	1	0	0	0	0	0	0	0	1	.000	.000	.000	.000	-97	-0	-0	103	0	0	.000	0	0	0	0	H	0.0
1965	Cin-N	21	42	4	16	2	2	0	6	3	7	.381	.435	.524	.959	163	4	4	104	113	10	1.038	1	0	0	-0	/S32	0.5
1966	Cin-N	138	542	72	154	23	1	9	49	24	31	.284	.317	.380	.697	81	-6	-14	114	94	61	.576	3	4	-2	-8	*32	-2.5
1967	Cin-N	137	497	40	136	27	4	2	35	24	41	.274	.307	.356	.663	82	-8	-12	109	81	49	.539	5	10	-5	-6	2S	-1.2
1968	Cin-N	127	507	35	146	28	2	2	47	12	27	.288	.307	.363	.670	90	-1	-7	111	106	53	.541	5	6	-2	10	*2/S3	1.0
1969	Cin-N	126	480	38	129	18	1	1	40	18	33	.269	.297	.317	.613	73	-18	-18	99	106	39	.464	4	6	-2	-5	*2/S	-1.4
1970	Cin-N	150	575	42	136	21	1	1	45	21	33	.237	.263	.282	.545	44	-44	-47	104	108	39	.403	2	2	-1	7	*2S	-2.2
1971	Cin-N	150	547	40	141	26	1	3	52	26	33	.258	.293	.325	.618	78	-19	-16	96	115	48	.487	3	4	-2	14	*2	0.3
1972	Hou-N	139	518	45	134	20	5	5	60	24	27	.259	.297	.346	.642	77	-13	-17	106	130	52	.534	4	3	-1	25	*2	1.8
1973	Hou-N	146	543	44	156	28	2	4	61	32	21	.287	.327	.368	.695	97	-6	-3	95	118	63	.584	1	1	-0	-4	*2	-0.1
1974	Hou-N	137	452	32	126	21	1	5	50	23	27	.279	.315	.363	.678	91	-7	-6	98	108	48	.563	5	4	-1	6	*2	0.6
1975	Hou-N	64	135	7	28	2	0	0	14	10	8	.207	.267	.222	.489	39	-11	-10	94	180	8	.373	0	0	0	1	2/3S	-0.6
1976	Pit-N	62	87	10	24	5	1	1	13	10	5	.276	.357	.391	.748	112	2	2	100	135	13	.714	0	0	0	-0	32/S	0.2
1977	Pit-N	15	12	0	0	0	0	0	0	0	3	.000	.000	.000	.000	-97	-3	-3	103	0	0	.000	0	0	0	0	H	-0.2
	Bos-A	21	59	5	16	2	0	1	5	4	4	.271	.328	.356	.684	74	-1	-2	117	83	7	.591	0	0	0	0	D/32	-0.1
Total	14	1435	4997	414	1342	223	21	34	477	231	301	.269	.303	.342	.645	78	-132	-152	103	109	491	.538	33	40	-14	41	*23/SD	-3.9
■ **HEINIE HELTZEL** Heltzel, William Wade b: 12/21/13, York, Pa. BR/TR, 5'10", 150 lbs. Deb: 7/27/43																												
1943	Bos-N	29	86	6	13	3	0	0	5	7	13	.151	.215	.186	.401	15	-9	-10	106	113	4	.311	0			2	3	-0.8
1944	Phi-N	11	22	1	4	1	0	0	0	2	3	.182	.280	.227	.507	44	-2	-2	100	0	1	.421	0			1	S	0.1
Total	2	40	108	7	17	4	0	0	5	9	16	.157	.229	.194	.423	21	-11	-11	104	89	5	.337	0			3	/3S	-0.7
■ **ED HEMINGWAY** Hemingway, Edson Marshall b: 5/8/1893, Sheridan, Mich. d: 7/5/69, Grand Rapids, Mich BB/TR, 5'11.5", 165 lbs. Deb: 9/17/14																												
1914	StL-A	3	5	0	0	0	0	0	0	1	1	.000	.167	.000	.167	-51	-1	-1	98	0	0	.400	1			0	/3	0.0
1917	NY-N	7	25	3	8	1	1	0	1	2	1	.320	.370	.440	.810	153	1	1	97	36	4	.882	2			1	/3	0.2
1918	Phi-N	33	108	7	23	4	1	0	12	7	9	.213	.267	.269	.536	58	-5	-6	109	160	9	.482	4			-1	2/31	-0.5
Total	3	43	138	10	31	5	2	0	13	10	11	.225	.282	.290	.572	70	-4	-5	106	131	14	.542	7			-0	/231	-0.3
■ **DUCKY HEMP** Hemp, William H. b: 12/27/1867, St.Louis, Mo. d: 3/6/23, St.Louis, Mo. Deb: 10/06/1887																												
1887	Lou-a	1	3	1	1	1	0	0		1		.333	.500	.667	1.167	212	1	1	107	0	1	1.500	0			0	/O	0.0
1890	Pit-N	21	81	9	19	0	2	0	4	8	12	.235	.311	.284	.595	86	-2	-1	88	56	8	.565	3			0	O	0.0
	Syr-a	9	33	1	5	1	0	0		0		.152	.152	.182	.333	-1	-4	-4	90	0	1	.250	1			0	/O	-0.2
Total	2	31	117	11	25	2	2	0	4	9	12	.214	.276	.265	.541	67	-6	-4	89	39	10	.489	4			0	/O	-0.2
■ **CHARLIE HEMPHILL** Hemphill, Charles Judson "Eagle Eye" b: 4/20/1876, Greenville, Mich. d: 6/22/53, Detroit, Mich. BL/TL, 5'9", 160 lbs. Deb: 6/27/1899																												
1899	StL-N	11	37	4	9	0	0	1	3	6		.243	.364	.324	.688	85	-0	-1	108	63	4	.679	0			-2	O	-0.2
	Cle-N	55	202	23	56	3	5	2	23	6		.277	.298	.371	.669	95	-5	-2	89	89	24	.575	3			-9	O	-1.2
	Yr	66	239	27	65	3	5	3	26	12		.272	.310	.364	.674	94	-5	-2	92	85	29	.592	3			-11		-1.4
1901	Bos-A	136	545	71	142	10	10	3	62	39		.261	.310	.332	.642	82	-14	-12	97	109	61	.573	11			-3	*O	-1.4
1902	Cle-A	25	94	14	25	2	0	0	11	5		.266	.303	.287	.590	68	-4	-4	97	137	10	.522	4			-1	O	-0.4
	StL-A	103	416	67	132	14	11	6	58	44		.317	.383	.447	.830	129	18	17	102	81	82	.891	23			1	*O/2	1.0
	Yr	128	510	81	157	16	11	6	69	49		.308	.369	.418	.786	118	14	13	101	93	91	.819	27			-0		0.6
1903	StL-A	105	383	36	94	6	3	3	29	23		.245	.288	.300	.588	83	-10	-7	95	89	39	.533	16			9	*O	-0.4
1904	StL-A	114	438	47	112	13	2	2	45	35		.256	.311	.308	.619	104	2	2	95	114	50	.592	23			-1	*O/2	-0.5
1906	StL-A	154	585	90	169	19	12	4	62	43		.289	.338	.383	.720	130	18	19	98	92	89	.721	33			3	*O	1.8
1907	StL-A	153	603	66	156	20	9	0	38	51		.259	.317	.322	.638	108	4	6	98	62	67	.579	14			-9	*O	-1.2
1908	NY-A	142	505	62	150	12	9	0	44	59		.297	.371	.356	.727	146	24	26	95	88	80	.792	42			-2	*O	1.9
1909	NY-A	73	181	23	44	5	1	0	10	32		.243	.357	.282	.639	103	2	2	99	76	21	.679	10			6	O	0.8
1910	NY-A	102	351	45	84	9	4	0	21	55		.239	.350	.288	.638	93	3	-0	107	81	42	.674	19			-1	O	-0.5
1911	NY-A	69	201	32	57	4	2	1	15	37		.284	.397	.338	.736	96	4	0	111	71	31	.799	9			-5	O	-0.7
Total	11	1242	4541	580	1230	117	68	22	421	435		.271	.336	.341	.677	107	40	48	99	88	601	.664	207			-12	*O/2	-1.0
■ **FRANK HEMPHILL** Hemphill, Frank Vernon b: 5/13/1878, Greenville, Mich. d: 11/16/50, Chicago, Ill. BR/TR, 5'11", 165 lbs. Deb: 4/17/06																												
1906	Chi-A	13	40	0	3	0	0	0	2	9		.075	.245	.075	.320	3	-4	-4	92	257	1	.351	1			-5	O	-0.9
1909	Was-A	1	3	0	0	0	0	0	0	0		.000	.000	.000	.000	-99	-1	-1	90	0	0	.000	0			0	/O	0.0
Total	2	14	43	0	3	0	0	0	2	9		.070	.231	.070	.301	-4	-5	-4	92	242	1	.325	1			-4	/O	-0.9
■ **ROLLIE HEMSLEY** Hemsley, Ralston Burdett b: 6/24/07, Syracuse, Ohio d: 7/31/72, Washington, D.C. BR/TR, 5'10", 170 lbs. Deb: 4/13/28 C																												
1928	Pit-N	50	133	14	36	2	3	0	18	4	10	.271	.292	.331	.623	58	-7	-9	107	146	12	.505	1			-2	C	-0.6
1929	Pit-N	88	235	31	68	13	7	0	37	11	22	.289	.321	.404	.725	76	-8	-10	103	133	29	.641	1			1	C	-0.1
1930	Pit-N	104	324	45	82	19	6	2	45	22	21	.253	.301	.367	.668	62	-21	-20	97	124	35	.595	3			9	C	-0.5
1931	Pit-N	10	35	3	6	3	0	0	1	3	3	.171	.237	.257	.494	33	-3	-3	101	40	2	.414	0			0	/C	-0.2
	Chi-N	66	204	28	63	17	4	3	31	17	30	.309	.362	.475	.837	129	6	7	96	104	36	.837	4			6	C	1.5
	Yr	76	239	31	69	20	4	3	32	20	33	.289	.344	.444	.787	114	3	4	96	96	37	.765	4			6		1.3
1932	Chi-N	60	151	27	36	10	3	4	20	10	16	.238	.286	.424	.710	84	-3	-4	104	98	19	.661	2			2	C/O	0.0
1933	Cin-N	49	116	9	22	8	0	0	7	6	8	.190	.230	.259	.488	40	-9	-9	99	88	6	.360	0			0	C	-0.7
	StL-A	32	95	7	23	2	1	1	15	11	12	.242	.321	.316	.637	60	-4	-6	115	152	10	.569	0	0	0	3	C	-0.1
1934	StL-A	123	431	47	133	31	7	2	52	29	37	.309	.355	.427	.782	97	-0	-3	104	93	66	.737	6	2	1	14	*C/O	2.1
1935	StL-A	144	504	57	146	32	7	0	48	44	41	.290	.349	.381	.730	83	-8	-13	107	85	69	.669	3	2	-0	12	*C	0.3
1936	StL-A	116	377	43	99	24	2	2	39	46	30	.263	.343	.353	.696	70	-16	-18	103	91	47	.644	2	3	-1	5	*C	-0.4
1937	StL-A	100	334	30	74	12	3	3	28	25	29	.222	.276	.302	.578	46	-29	-28	99	87	29	.485	0	0	0	3	C/1	-1.6
1938	Cle-A	66	203	27	60	11	3	2	28	23	14	.296	.367	.409	.776	95	-2	-1	99	106	31	.743	1	1	-0	4	C	0.3
1939	Cle-A	107	395	58	104	17	4	2	36	26	26	.263	.309	.342	.651	68	-21	-19	98	88	41	.540	2	4	-2	1	*C	-1.2
1940	Cle-A	119	416	46	111	20	5	4	42	22	25	.267	.304	.368	.671	79	-17	-13	93	92	45	.555	1	3	-2	3	*C	-0.3
1941	Cle-A	98	288	29	69	10	5	2	24	18	19	.240	.284	.330	.614	62	-16	-17	101	84	27	.507	2	0	1	-3	C	-1.2
1942	Cin-N	36	115	7	13	1	2	0	7	4	11	.113	.143	.157	.299	-12	-16	-17	101	144	3	.214	0			0	C	-1.6
	NY-A	31	85	12	25	3	1	0	15	5	9	.294	.333	.353	.686	94	-1	-1	99	176	10	.581	1	0	0	0	C	0.3
1943	NY-A	62	180	12	43	6	3	2	24	13	9	.239	.290	.339	.629	87	-4	-4	96	131	18	.521	0	1	-1	-1	C	-0.2
1944	NY-A	81	284	23	76	12	5	2	26	9	13	.268	.290	.366	.656	82	-6	-8	106	85	25	.502	0	2	-1	5	C	0.1
1946	Phi-N	49	139	7	31	4	1	0	11	9	10	.223	.270	.266	.536	55	-9	-8	95	111	10	.418	0			6	C	0.0
1947	Phi-N	2	3	0	1	0	0	0	1	0	0	.333	.333	.333	.667	77	-0	-0	100	370	0	.500	0			0	/C	0.0
Total	19	1593	5047	562	1321	257	72	31	555	357	395	.262	.311	.360	.671	74	-196	-203	101	102	571	.589	29	18		68	*C/O1	-4.1
■ **SOLLY HEMUS** Hemus, Solomon Joseph b: 4/17/23, Phoenix, Ariz. BL/TR, 5'9", 165 lbs. Deb: 4/27/49 MC																												
1949	StL-N	20	33	8	11	1	0	0	2	7	3	.333	.450	.364	.814	109	2	1	110	63	6	.826	0			2	2	0.3
1950	StL-N	11	15	1	2	1	0	0	0	2	4	.133	.235	.200	.435	15	-2	-2	103	0	1	.385	0			0	/3	-0.1

YEAR	TM/L	G	AB	R	H	2B	3B	HR	RBI	BB	SO	AVG	OBP	SLG	PRO	/A	BR	/A	PF	CHI	RC	TA	SB	CS	SBR	FR	POS	TPR
1951	StL-N	120	420	68	118	18	9	2	32	75	31	.281	.395	.381	.776	109	9	9	101	79	70	.781	7	7	-2	13	*S2	2.8
1952	StL-N	151	570	**105**	153	28	8	15	52	96	55	.268	.392	.425	.817	129	25	26	98	61	103	.829	1	5	-3	5	*S/3	3.3
1953	StL-N	154	585	110	163	32	11	14	61	86	40	.279	.382	.443	.825	113	15	13	102	76	107	.829	2	1	0	16	*S/2	3.9
1954	StL-N	124	214	43	65	15	3	2	27	55	27	.304	.456	.430	.886	132	14	14	100	108	50	1.040	5	1	1	6	S32	2.5
1955	StL-N	96	206	36	50	10	2	5	21	27	22	.243	.336	.383	.720	90	-3	-3	101	90	28	.686	1	1	-0	0	32/S	-0.1
1956	StL-N	8	5	1	1	0	0	0	2	1	1	.200	.429	.200	.629	77	-0	-0	99	845	1	.750	0	0	0	0	H	0.0
	Phi-N	78	187	24	54	10	4	5	24	28	21	.289	.401	.465	.866	140	10	11	94	99	36	.879	1	1	-0	-9	2/3	0.6
	Yr	86	192	25	55	10	4	5	26	29	22	.286	.402	.458	.860	138	10	11	95	179	36	.875	1	1	-0	-9		0.6
1957	Phi-N	70	108	8	20	6	1	0	5	20	8	.185	.323	.259	.582	60	-6	-5	98	74	8	.526	1	1	-0	-6	2	-1.0
1958	Phi-N	105	334	53	95	14	3	8	36	51	34	.284	.392	.416	.808	116	9	10	98	91	59	.824	3	1	0	-13	2/3	0.2
1959	StL-N	24	17	2	4	2	0	0	1	8	2	.235	.500	.353	.853	126	2	2	105	67	4	1.154	0	0	0	0	/23M	0.2
Total	11	961	2694	459	736	137	41	51	263	456	248	.273	.390	.411	.802	115	74	76	100	82	472	.834	21	18		13	S2/3	12.6
■ **DAVE HENDERSON** Henderson, David Lee b: 7/21/58, Merced, Cal. BR/TR, 6'2", 210 lbs. Deb: 4/09/81																												
1981	Sea-A	59	126	17	21	3	0	6	13	16	24	.167	.266	.333	.599	72	-5	-5	100	85	11	.555	2	1	0	-3	O	-0.9
1982	Sea-A	104	324	47	82	17	1	14	48	36	67	.253	.328	.441	.769	100	4	-0	109	104	46	.718	2	5	-2	4	*O	-0.1
1983	Sea-A	137	484	50	130	24	5	17	55	28	93	.269	.310	.444	.754	105	2	2	100	82	67	.699	9	3	1	16	*O/D	1.7
1984	Sea-A	112	350	42	98	23	0	14	43	19	56	.280	.321	.466	.786	112	6	5	102	84	51	.724	5	5	-2	3	OD	0.3
1985	Sea-A	139	502	70	121	28	2	14	68	48	104	.241	.311	.388	.699	95	-7	-3	95	116	61	.641	6	1	1	-6	*O	-0.9
1986	Sea-A	103	337	51	93	19	4	14	44	37	95	.276	.351	.481	.832	119	11	9	105	86	57	.802	1	3	-2	-2	OD	0.3
	Bos-A	36	51	8	10	3	0	1	3	2	15	.196	.226	.314	.540	46	-4	-4	100	63	4	.452	1	0	0	-2	O	-0.6
	Yr	139	388	59	103	22	4	15	47	39	110	.265	.336	.459	.794	111	8	6	104	80	62	.765	2	3	-1	-4		-0.3
1987	Bos-A	75	184	30	43	10	0	8	25	22	48	.234	.316	.418	.734	94	-2	-2	99	99	25	.690	1	1	-0	-5	O/D	-0.7
	SF-N	15	21	2	5	2	0	0	1	8	5	.238	.448	.333	.782	116	1	1	96	57	5	1.063	2	0	1	-1	/O	0.1
1988	Oak-A	146	507	100	154	38	1	24	94	47	92	.304	.367	.525	.892	155	31	34	95	111	94	.860	2	4	-2	-1	*O	2.8
Total	8	926	2886	417	757	167	13	112	394	263	599	.262	.327	.446	.772	111	36	37	100	97	419	.735	31	23	-5	3	O/D	2.0
■ **KEN HENDERSON** Henderson, Kenneth Joseph b: 6/15/46, Carroll, Iowa BB/TR, 6'2", 180 lbs. Deb: 4/23/65																												
1965	SF-N	63	73	10	14	1	1	0	7	9	19	.192	.280	.233	.513	42	-5	-6	111	171	4	.429	1	1	-0	-6	O	-1.4
1966	SF-N	11	29	4	9	1	1	1	1	2	3	.310	.375	.517	.892	149	2	2	97	23	6	.900	0	0	0	-2	O	0.0
1967	SF-N	65	179	15	34	3	0	4	14	19	52	.190	.275	.274	.549	57	-10	-10	101	95	14	.467	0	1	-1	-1	O	-1.5
1968	SF-N	3	3	1	1	0	0	0	0	2	1	.333	.600	.333	.933	190	1	1	98	0	1	1.500	0	0	0	-0	/O	0.0
1969	SF-N	113	374	42	84	14	4	6	44	42	64	.225	.311	.332	.643	79	-10	-10	101	124	39	.584	6	4	-1	-2	*O/3	-1.9
1970	SF-N	148	554	104	163	35	3	17	88	87	78	.294	.395	.460	.855	134	25	28	96	118	106	.900	20	3	4	6	*O	3.0
1971	SF-N	141	504	80	133	26	6	15	65	84	76	.264	.372	.429	.801	127	19	20	100	107	86	.838	18	3	4	-4	*O/1	1.5
1972	SF-N	130	439	60	113	21	2	18	51	38	66	.257	.319	.437	.757	113	6	6	100	85	61	.724	14	7	0	9	*O	1.0
1973	Chi-A	73	262	32	68	13	0	6	32	27	49	.260	.331	.378	.709	97	-0	-1	102	110	30	.625	3	4	-2	1	OD	-0.1
1974	Chi-A	162	602	76	176	35	5	20	95	66	112	.292	.364	.467	.831	135	29	28	102	116	100	.804	12	7	-1	1	*O	2.4
1975	Chi-A	140	513	65	129	20	3	9	53	74	65	.251	.350	.355	.705	96	2	-1	103	103	64	.654	5	3	-0	5	*O/D	0.0
1976	Atl-N	133	435	52	114	19	0	13	61	62	68	.262	.355	.395	.751	101	8	2	111	114	60	.706	5	7	-3	-7	*O	-1.2
1977	Tex-A	75	244	23	63	14	0	5	23	18	37	.258	.317	.377	.694	84	-4	-6	105	85	28	.605	2	1	0	-7	O/D	-1.3
1978	NY-N	7	22	2	5	2	0	1	4	4	4	.227	.346	.455	.801	124	1	1	98	122	3	.778	0	1	-1	0	/O	0.0
	Cin-N	64	144	10	24	6	1	3	19	23	32	.167	.281	.285	.566	57	-8	-8	103	151	11	.500	0	0	0	-0	O	-1.0
	Yr	71	166	12	29	8	1	4	23	27	36	.175	.290	.307	.597	65	-7	-8	102	149	14	.534	0	1	-1	-0		-1.0
1979	Cin-N	10	13	1	3	1	0	0	2	0	2	.231	.231	.308	.538	47	-1	-1	97	198	1	.400	0	0	0	-0	/O	-0.1
	Chi-N	62	81	11	19	2	0	2	8	15	16	.235	.361	.333	.694	81	-0	-2	112	96	11	.683	0	0	0	-6	O	-0.8
	Yr	72	94	12	22	3	0	2	10	15	18	.234	.345	.330	.675	77	-1	-3	110	113	12	.644	0	0	0	-7		-0.9
1980	Chi-N	44	82	7	16	3	0	2	9	17	19	.195	.333	.305	.638	75	-2	-2	106	115	9	.609	0	0	0	-1	O	-0.3
Total	16	1444	4553	595	1168	216	26	122	576	589	763	.257	.346	.396	.741	105	53	40	102	110	634	.731	86	42	1	-15	*O/D31	-1.7
■ **RICKEY HENDERSON** Henderson, Rickey Henley b: 12/25/58, Chicago, Ill. BR/TL, 5'10", 180 lbs. Deb: 6/24/79																												
1979	Oak-A	89	351	49	96	13	3	1	26	34	39	.274	.341	.336	.677	94	-7	-2	89	71	44	.693	33	11	3	6	O	0.4
1980	Oak-A	158	591	111	179	22	4	9	53	117	54	.303	.422	.399	.821	134	29	33	95	68	120	1.032	**100**	26	14	18	*O/D	6.1
1981	Oak-A	108	423	**89**	**135**	18	7	6	35	64	68	.319	.411	.437	.848	151	27	29	96	58	81	.968	**56**	22	4	18	*O	**5.0**
1982	Oak-A	149	536	119	143	24	4	10	51	**116**	94	.267	.399	.382	.782	122	17	21	95	83	99	**1.030**	**130**	42	**14**	6	*O/D	3.6
1983	Oak-A	145	513	105	150	25	7	9	48	**103**	80	.292	.415	.421	.836	137	27	30	96	82	109	**1.097**	**108**	19	**21**	8	*O/D	5.6
1984	Oak-A	142	502	113	147	27	4	16	58	86	81	.293	.401	.458	.860	150	29	35	92	88	103	**1.018**	**66**	18	9	6	*O	4.5
1985	NY-A	143	547	**146**	172	28	5	24	72	99	65	.314	.422	.516	.938	162	45	49	96	71	138	**1.181**	**80**	10	**18**	12	*O/D	**7.4**
1986	NY-A	153	608	**130**	160	31	5	28	74	89	81	.263	.359	.469	.828	121	21	19	103	71	112	.969	**87**	18	**15**	3	*O/D	3.2
1987	NY-A	95	358	78	104	17	3	17	37	80	52	.291	.423	.497	.920	148	26	28	98	56	84	1.107	41	8	8	3	OD	3.3
1988	NY-A	140	554	118	169	30	2	6	50	82	54	.305	.397	.399	.796	129	21	24	96	73	107	.988	**93**	13	**20**	7	*O/D	4.9
Total	10	1322	4983	1058	1455	235	44	126	504	870	668	.292	.400	.433	.833	135	236	266	96	73	998	1.035	794	187	126	88	*O/D	44.0
■ **STEVE HENDERSON** Henderson, Stephen Curtis b: 11/18/52, Houston, Tex. BR/TR, 6'2", 190 lbs. Deb: 6/16/77																												
1977	NY-N	99	350	67	104	16	6	12	65	43	79	.297	.376	.480	.856	133	14	16	96	130	61	.832	6	3	0	0	O	1.3
1978	NY-N	157	587	83	156	30	9	10	65	60	109	.266	.336	.399	.735	106	3	5	98	103	74	.669	13	7	-0	7	*O	0.6
1979	NY-N	98	350	42	107	16	8	5	39	38	58	.306	.380	.440	.820	130	12	14	95	93	59	.820	13	5	1	4	O	1.7
1980	NY-N	143	513	75	149	17	8	8	58	62	90	.290	.370	.402	.772	120	12	15	96	102	75	.748	23	12	-0	5	*O	1.5
1981	Chi-N	82	287	32	84	9	5	5	35	42	61	.293	.387	.411	.798	122	11	10	104	109	45	.770	5	7	-3	-12	O	-0.6
1982	Chi-N	92	257	23	60	12	4	2	29	22	64	.233	.294	.335	.629	73	-9	-10	103	124	25	.553	6	5	-1	-2	O	-1.3
1983	Sea-A	121	436	50	128	32	3	10	54	44	82	.294	.358	.450	.808	121	12	13	100	99	66	.755	10	14	-5	-2	*O/D	0.4
1984	Sea-A	109	325	42	85	12	3	10	35	38	62	.262	.341	.409	.750	104	3	2	102	86	45	.696	2	4	-2	-5	OD	-0.5
1985	Oak-A	85	193	25	58	8	3	3	31	18	34	.301	.360	.420	.780	122	4	5	93	137	27	.683	0	0	0	-9	O/D	-0.4
1986	Oak-A	11	26	2	2	1	0	0	3	0	5	.077	.077	.115	.192	-52	-5	-5	94	398	-0	.111	0	0	0	-2	/OD	-0.6
1987	Oak-A	46	114	14	33	7	0	3	9	12	19	.289	.357	.430	.787	119	2	3	91	62	16	.693	0	0	0	-7	O/D	-0.4
1988	Hou-N	42	46	4	10	2	0	0	5	7	14	.217	.321	.261	.582	74	-2	-1	93	167	4	.526	1	1	-0	0	/O1	-0.1
Total	12	1085	3484	459	976	162	49	68	428	386	677	.280	.354	.413	.767	114	58	67	98	108	497	.747	79	58	-11	-21	O/D1	1.6
■ **GEORGE HENDRICK** Hendrick, George Andrew b: 10/18/49, Los Angeles, Cal. BR/TR, 6'3", 195 lbs. Deb: 6/04/71																												
1971	Oak-A	42	114	8	27	4	1	0	8	3	20	.237	.256	.289	.546	54	-7	-7	101	99	7	.383	0	1	-1	-4	O	-1.3
1972	Oak-A	58	121	10	22	1	1	4	15	3	22	.182	.208	.306	.514	53	-8	-7	97	128	7	.423	3	2	-0	-4	O	-1.4
1973	Cle-A	113	440	64	118	18	0	21	61	25	71	.268	.310	.452	.763	116	5	7	97	97	58	.691	7	6	-2	-8	*O	-0.5
1974	Cle-A	139	495	65	138	23	1	19	67	33	73	.279	.325	.444	.770	119	11	10	101	97	66	.688	6	4	-1	-5	*O/D	0.2
1975	Cle-A	145	561	82	145	21	2	24	86	40	78	.258	.308	.431	.739	107	3	3	100	111	65	.643	6	7	-2	6	*O	0.3
1976	Cle-A	149	551	72	146	20	3	25	81	51	82	.265	.327	.448	.776	126	16	16	100	99	77	.711	4	4	-1	4	*O/D	1.7
1977	SD-N	152	541	75	168	25	2	23	81	61	74	.311	.382	.492	.874	151	25	34	88	99	102	.876	11	6	-0	7	*O	3.5
1978	SD-N	36	111	9	27	4	0	3	8	12	16	.243	.317	.360	.677	96	-2	-1	93	65	13	.609	1	1	-0	1	O	-0.1
	StL-N	102	382	55	110	27	1	17	67	28	44	.288	.340	.497	.837	138	14	16	95	117	63	.786	1	0	0	0	*O	1.4
	Yr	138	493	64	137	31	1	20	75	40	60	.278	.335	.467	.801	129	13	16	94	104	76	.749	2	1	0	1		1.3
1979	StL-N	140	493	67	148	27	1	16	75	49	62	.300	.363	.456	.820	117	15	12	105	111	78	.756	2	3	-1	8	*O	1.5
1980	StL-N	150	572	73	173	33	2	25	109	32	67	.302	.344	.498	.842	129	22	20	103	122	94	.790	6	1	1	4	*O	2.0
1981	StL-N	101	394	67	112	19	3	18	61	41	44	.284	.358	.485	.842	135	18	18	102	104	67	.816	4	2	0	1	*O	1.6
1982	StL-N	136	515	65	145	20	5	19	104	37	80	.282	.331	.450	.781	113	10	8	103	150	74	.709	3	2	-0	-8	*O	-0.1
1983	StL-N	144	529	73	168	33	3	18	97	51	76	.318	.380	.493	.873	143	28	30	98	124	96	.841	3	4	-2	-2	1O	2.2
1984	StL-N	120	441	57	122	28	1	9	69	32	75	.277	.327	.406	.733	106	2	3	99	134	55	.635	0	2	-1	-5	*O/1	-0.7
1985	Pit-N	69	256	23	59	15	0	2	25	18	42	.230	.281	.313	.594	64	-12	-13	103	118	21	.476	1	0	0	1	O	-1.3
	Cal-A	16	41	5	5	1	0	2	6	4	8	.122	.200	.293	.493	33	-4	-4	101	132	1	.400	0	0	0	-1	O/D	-0.4

YEAR	TM/L	G	AB	R	H	2B	3B	HR	RBI	BB	SO	AVG	OBP	SLG	PRO	/A	BR	/A	PF	CHI	RC	TA	SB	CS	SBR	FR	POS	TPR
1986	Cal-A	102	283	45	77	13	1	14	47	26	41	.272	.335	.473	.809	123	7	8	96	106	42	.743	1	1	-0	-8	O/1D	-0.2
1987	Cal-A	65	162	14	39	10	0	5	25	14	18	.241	.301	.395	.696	84	-4	-4	99	126	17	.595	0	0	0	-8	O/1D	-1.2
1988	Cal-A	69	127	12	31	1	0	3	19	7	20	.244	.289	.323	.612	75	-5	-4	94	151	12	.495	0	1	-1	-2	O1/3D	-0.7
Total	18	2048	7129	941	1980	343	27	267	1111	567	1013	.278	.333	.446	.779	117	135	145	99	114	1015	.736	59	47	-11	-24	*O1/D3	6.5

■ HARVEY HENDRICK Hendrick, Harvey "Gink" b: 11/9/1897, Mason, Tenn. d: 10/29/41, Covington, Tenn. BL/TR, 6'2", 190 lbs. Deb: 8/20/23

YEAR	TM/L	G	AB	R	H	2B	3B	HR	RBI	BB	SO	AVG	OBP	SLG	PRO	/A	BR	/A	PF	CHI	RC	TA	SB	CS	SBR	FR	POS	TPR
1923	NY-A	37	66	9	18	3	1	3	12	2	8	.273	.294	.485	.779	98	-0	-1	104	100	10	.771	3	0	1	-2	O	-0.2
1924	NY-A	40	76	7	20	0	0	1	11	2	7	.263	.291	.303	.594	54	-5	-5	99	140	7	.482	1	0	0	-0	O	-0.5
1925	Cle-A	25	28	2	8	1	2	0	9	3	5	.286	.355	.464	.819	100	0	-0	106	232	5	.800	0	0	0	0	/1	0.0
1927	Bro-N	128	458	55	142	18	11	4	50	24	40	.310	.350	.424	.773	103	3	2	103	87	66	.794	29			-11	O1/2	-1.4
1928	Bro-N	126	425	83	135	15	10	11	59	54	34	.318	.397	.478	.875	129	18	19	99	91	80	.948	16			1	3O	1.9
1929	Bro-N	110	384	69	136	25	6	14	82	31	20	.354	.404	.560	.964	144	21	24	94	109	84	1.052	14			-5	O1/3S	1.3
1930	Bro-N	68	167	29	43	10	1	5	28	20	19	.257	.344	.419	.763	83	-5	-5	101	114	24	.758	2			-4	O/1	-1.0
1931	Bro-N	1	1	0	0	0	0	0	0	0	0	.000	.000	.000	.000	-99	-0	-0	101	0	0	.000	0			0	H	0.0
	Cin-N	137	530	74	167	32	9	1	75	53	40	.315	.379	.415	.795	119	11	15	95	127	87	.766	3			-4	*1	0.0
	Yr	138	531	74	167	32	9	1	75	53	40	.315	.379	.414	.793	119	11	14	95	126	87	.764	3			-4		0.0
1932	StL-N	28	72	8	18	2	0	1	5	5	9	.250	.299	.319	.618	66	-3	-3	100	72	7	.519	0			-1	3/O	-0.2
	Cin-N	94	398	56	120	30	3	4	40	23	29	.302	.341	.422	.763	108	2	4	96	73	58	.701	3			-2	1	-0.3
	Yr	122	470	64	138	32	3	5	45	28	38	.294	.335	.406	.741	101	-1	0	97	73	65	.672	3			-3		-0.5
1933	Chi-N	69	189	30	55	13	3	4	23	13	17	.291	.346	.455	.801	131	6	7	97	88	31	.779	4			2	1/O3	0.8
1934	Phi-N	59	116	12	34	8	0	0	19	9	15	.293	.344	.362	.706	82	-2	-3	108	163	15	.600	0			-1	O/13	-0.3
Total	11	922	2910	434	896	157	46	48	413	239	243	.308	.364	.443	.807	113	46	52	98	103	473	.803	75	0		-28	1O3/S2	0.1

■ ELLIE HENDRICKS Hendricks, Elrod Jerome b: 12/22/40, Charlotte Amalie, V.I. BL/TR, 6'1", 175 lbs. Deb: 4/13/68 C

YEAR	TM/L	G	AB	R	H	2B	3B	HR	RBI	BB	SO	AVG	OBP	SLG	PRO	/A	BR	/A	PF	CHI	RC	TA	SB	CS	SBR	FR	POS	TPR
1968	Bal-A	79	183	19	37	8	1	7	23	19	51	.202	.281	.372	.652	94	-1	-2	102	111	19	.587	0	0	0	-6	C	-0.5
1969	Bal-A	105	295	36	72	5	0	12	38	39	44	.244	.336	.383	.719	97	1	-1	104	102	40	.678	0	1	-1	1	C/1	0.5
1970	Bal-A	106	322	32	78	9	0	12	41	33	44	.242	.320	.382	.702	96	-3	-2	97	104	41	.649	1	0	0	-5	C	-0.5
1971	Bal-A	101	316	33	79	14	1	9	42	39	38	.250	.336	.386	.722	101	2	1	103	115	41	.663	0	0	0	-4	C/1	0.1
1972	Bal-A	33	84	6	13	4	0	0	4	12	19	.155	.260	.202	.463	40	-6	-6	98	98	5	.397	0	1	-1	-1	C	-0.7
	Chi-N	17	43	7	5	1	0	2	6	13	8	.116	.321	.279	.600	63	-1	-2	114	137	4	.625	0	1	-1	-1	C	-0.2
1973	Bal-A	41	101	9	18	5	1	3	15	10	22	.178	.259	.337	.596	62	-5	-6	107	137	9	.529	0	0	0	-2	C/D	-0.6
1974	Bal-A	66	159	18	33	8	2	3	8	17	25	.208	.288	.340	.628	86	-4	-3	93	50	16	.563	0	0	0	-1	C/1D	-0.2
1975	Bal-A	85	223	32	48	8	2	8	38	34	40	.215	.322	.377	.698	107	-1	2	91	135	28	.665	0	1	-1	-3	C	0.1
1976	Bal-A	28	79	2	11	1	0	1	4	7	13	.139	.209	.190	.399	18	-8	-8	98	85	3	.319	0	1	-1	1	C	-0.7
	NY-A	26	53	6	12	1	0	3	5	3	10	.226	.268	.415	.683	99	-0	-0	99	62	6	.595	0	0	0	1	C	0.1
	Yr	54	132	8	23	2	0	4	9	10	23	.174	.232	.280	.513	50	-9	-8	98	76	9	.423	0	1	-1	2		-0.6
1977	NY-A	10	11	1	3	1	0	1	5	0	2	.273	.273	.636	.909	141	0	0	99	198	2	.875	0	0	0	0	/C	0.1
1978	Bal-A	13	18	4	6	1	0	1	1	3	3	.333	.429	.556	.984	192	2	2	91	30	4	1.083	0	0	0	0	/CPD	0.2
1979	Bal-A	1	1	0	0	0	0	0	0	0	0	.000	.000	.000	.000	-99	-0	-0	97	0	0	.000	0	0	0	0	/C	0.0
Total	12	711	1888	205	415	66	7	62	230	229	319	.220	.308	.361	.669	90	-26	-24	99	106	218	.624	1	5	-3	-20	C/1DP	-2.3

■ JACK HENDRICKS Hendricks, John Charles b: 4/9/1875, Joliet, Ill. d: 5/13/43, Chicago, Ill. BL/TL, 5'11.5", 160 lbs. Deb: 6/12/02 M

YEAR	TM/L	G	AB	R	H	2B	3B	HR	RBI	BB	SO	AVG	OBP	SLG	PRO	/A	BR	/A	PF	CHI	RC	TA	SB	CS	SBR	FR	POS	TPR
1902	NY-N	8	26	1	6	2	0	0	0	2		.231	.286	.308	.593	85	-0	-0	100	0	3	.600	2			3	/O	0.2
	Chi-N	2	7	0	4	0	1	0	0	0		.571	.571	.857	1.429	358	2	2	96	0	4	2.000	0			0	/O	0.2
	Yr	10	33	1	10	2	1	0	0	2		.303	.343	.424	.767	140	1	1	99	0	6	.783	2			3		0.4
1903	Was-A	32	112	10	20	1	3	0	4	13		.179	.264	.241	.505	51	-6	-7	105	56	8	.467	3			-3	O	-1.1
Total	2	42	145	11	30	3	4	0	4	15		.207	.281	.283	.564	69	-4	-5	104	44	15	.530	5			-0	/O	-0.7

■ TIM HENDRYX Hendryx, Timothy Green b: 1/31/1891, Leroy, Ill d: 8/14/57, Corpus Christi, Tex. BR/TR, 5'9", 170 lbs. Deb: 9/28/11

YEAR	TM/L	G	AB	R	H	2B	3B	HR	RBI	BB	SO	AVG	OBP	SLG	PRO	/A	BR	/A	PF	CHI	RC	TA	SB	CS	SBR	FR	POS	TPR
1911	Cle-A	3	7	0	2	0	0	0	0	0		.286	.286	.286	.571	58	-0	-0	103	0	1	.400	0			0	/3	0.0
1912	Cle-A	23	70	9	17	2	4	1	14	8		.243	.329	.429	.758	115	1	1	101	144	11	.792	3			-1	O	0.0
1915	NY-A	13	40	4	8	2	0	0	1	4	2	.200	.289	.250	.539	62	-2	-2	98	34	2	.429	0	3	-2	1	O	-0.2
1916	NY-A	15	62	10	18	7	1	0	5	8	6	.290	.380	.435	.816	143	3	3	101	57	12	.909	4			-3	O	0.0
1917	NY-A	125	393	43	98	14	7	5	44	62	45	.249	.359	.359	.717	111	11	7	107	103	53	.725	6			-9	*O	-0.8
1918	StL-A	88	219	22	61	14	3	0	33	37	35	.279	.388	.370	.757	130	9	9	99	149	34	.791	5			-8	O	-0.2
1920	Bos-A	99	363	54	119	21	5	0	73	42	27	.328	.400	.413	.814	121	10	12	96	181	60	.794	7	9	-3	-14	O	-1.3
1921	Bos-A	49	137	10	33	8	2	0	22	24	13	.241	.362	.328	.690	77	-4	-4	100	168	18	.686	1	1	-0	-6	O	-1.2
Total	8	415	1291	152	356	68	22	6	192	185	128	.276	.372	.376	.749	112	28	27	101	137	191	.750	26	13		-39	O/3	-3.7

■ DAVE HENGEL Hengel, David Lee b: 12/18/61, Oakland, Cal. BR/TR, 6', 185 lbs. Deb: 9/03/86

YEAR	TM/L	G	AB	R	H	2B	3B	HR	RBI	BB	SO	AVG	OBP	SLG	PRO	/A	BR	/A	PF	CHI	RC	TA	SB	CS	SBR	FR	POS	TPR
1986	Sea-A	21	63	3	12	1	0	1	6	1	13	.190	.215	.254	.469	27	-6	-7	105	126	3	.346	0	0	0	-1	D/O	-0.7
1987	Sea-A	10	19	2	6	0	0	1	4	0	4	.316	.316	.474	.789	104	0	0	103	133	2	.600	0	0	0	-2	/OD	-0.1
1988	Sea-A	26	60	3	10	1	0	2	7	1	15	.167	.180	.283	.464	26	-6	-6	108	121	3	.360	0	0	0	-1	OD	-0.7
Total	3	57	142	8	28	2	0	4	17	2	32	.197	.214	.296	.510	36	-12	-13	106	125	8	.395	0	0	0	-4	/OD	-1.5

■ MOXIE HENGLE Hengle, Emery J. b: 10/7/1857, Chicago, Ill. d: 12/11/24, Forest River, Ill. 5'8", 144 lbs. Deb: 4/20/1884

YEAR	TM/L	G	AB	R	H	2B	3B	HR	RBI	BB	SO	AVG	OBP	SLG	PRO	/A	BR	/A	PF	CHI	RC	TA	SB	CS	SBR	FR	POS	TPR
1884	CP-U	19	74	9	15	2	1	0		3		.203	.234	.257	.491	66	-3	-2	99	0	5	.373	0			-6	2	-0.8
	StP-U	9	33	2	5	1	1	0		0		.152	.152	.242	.394	31	-2	-2	100	0	1	.286	0			1	/2	0.0
	Yr	28	107	11	20	3	2	0		3		.187	.209	.252	.461	56	-5	-5	100	0	6	.345	0			-5		-0.8
1885	Buf-N	7	26	2	4	0	0	0	0	1	2	.154	.185	.154	.339	11	-2	-2	99	0	1	.227				0	/2O	-0.1
Total	2	35	133	13	24	3	2	0	0	4	2	.180	.204	.233	.437	47	-7	-7	99	0	7	.321				-5	/2O	-0.9

■ GAIL HENLEY Henley, Gail Curtice b: 10/15/28, Wichita, Kan. BL/TR, 5'9", 180 lbs. Deb: 4/13/54

YEAR	TM/L	G	AB	R	H	2B	3B	HR	RBI	BB	SO	AVG	OBP	SLG	PRO	/A	BR	/A	PF	CHI	RC	TA	SB	CS	SBR	FR	POS	TPR
1954	Pit-N	14	30	7	9	1	0	1	2	4	4	.300	.382	.433	.816	116	1	1	97	49	5	.810	0	0	0	-1	/O	0.0

■ BUTCH HENLINE Henline, Walter John b: 12/20/1894, Ft.Wayne, Ind. d: 10/9/57, Sarasota, Fla. BR/TR, 5'10", 175 lbs. Deb: 4/13/21 U

YEAR	TM/L	G	AB	R	H	2B	3B	HR	RBI	BB	SO	AVG	OBP	SLG	PRO	/A	BR	/A	PF	CHI	RC	TA	SB	CS	SBR	FR	POS	TPR
1921	NY-N	1	1	0	0	0	0	0	0	0	1	.000	.000	.000	.000	-99	-0	-0	98	0	0	.000	0	0	0	0	H	0.0
	Phi-N	33	111	8	34	2	0	0	8	2	6	.306	.319	.324	.643	69	-5	-5	102	82	11	.506	1	0	0	1	C	-0.1
	Yr	34	112	8	34	2	0	0	8	2	7	.304	.316	.321	.637	68	-5	-5	102	79	11	.500	1	0	0	1		-0.1
1922	Phi-N	125	430	57	136	20	4	14	64	36	33	.316	.380	.479	.859	106	13	4	113	90	79	.851	2	2	-1	3	*C	0.7
1923	Phi-N	111	330	45	107	14	3	7	46	37	33	.324	.407	.448	.855	110	14	7	114	96	62	.882	7	5	-1	-3	C/O	0.8
1924	Phi-N	115	289	41	82	18	4	5	35	27	15	.284	.361	.426	.787	102	4	1	108	92	45	.761	1	2	-1	4	C/O	0.6
1925	Phi-N	93	263	43	80	12	5	8	48	24	16	.304	.380	.479	.859	102	7	1	116	114	49	.875	3	1	0	-1	C/O	0.3
1926	Phi-N	99	283	32	80	14	1	2	30	21	18	.283	.339	.360	.699	85	-4	-6	103	96	35	.626	1			3	C/1O	0.0
1927	Bro-N	67	177	12	47	10	3	1	18	17	10	.266	.337	.373	.710	87	-2	-3	103	91	22	.662	1			4	C	0.5
1928	Bro-N	55	132	12	28	3	1	2	8	17	8	.212	.302	.295	.597	57	-8	-8	99	63	12	.558	2			-1	C	-0.5
1929	Bro-N	27	62	5	15	2	0	1	7	9	9	.242	.338	.323	.661	68	-3	-3	94	104	7	.617	0			1	C	0.0
1930	Chi-A	3	8	1	1	0	0	0	2	0	3	.125	.125	.125	.250	-35	-2	-2	103	664	0	.143	0	0	0	0	/C	0.0
1931	Chi-A	11	15	2	1	1	0	0	2	2	4	.067	.176	.133	.310	-19	-3	-3	92	330	0	.286	0	0	0	0	/C	-0.1
Total	11	740	2101	258	611	96	21	40	268	192	156	.291	.361	.414	.774	95	10	-15	108	97	324	.745	18	10		11	C/O1	2.2

■ LES HENNESSEY Hennessey, Lester Baker b: 12/12/1893, Lynn, Mass. d: 11/20/76, New York, N.Y. BR/TR, 6', 190 lbs. Deb: 6/04/13

YEAR	TM/L	G	AB	R	H	2B	3B	HR	RBI	BB	SO	AVG	OBP	SLG	PRO	/A	BR	/A	PF	CHI	RC	TA	SB	CS	SBR	FR	POS	TPR
1913	Det-A	14	22	2	3	0	0	0	0	3	6	.136	.240	.136	.376	11	-2	-2	99	0	1	.421	2			-0	/2	-0.2

■ FRITZ HENRICH Henrich, Frank Wilde b: 5/8/1899, Cincinnati, Ohio d: 5/1/59, Philadelphia, Pa. BL/TL, 5'10", 160 lbs. Deb: 4/21/24

YEAR	TM/L	G	AB	R	H	2B	3B	HR	RBI	BB	SO	AVG	OBP	SLG	PRO	/A	BR	/A	PF	CHI	RC	TA	SB	CS	SBR	FR	POS	TPR
1924	Phi-N	36	90	4	19	4	0	0	4	2	12	.211	.228	.256	.484	27	-9	-10	108	63	5	.352	0	0	0	-7	O	-1.6

■ BOBBY HENRICH Henrich, Robert Edward b: 12/24/38, Lawrence, Kan. BR/TR, 6'1", 185 lbs. Deb: 5/03/57

YEAR	TM/L	G	AB	R	H	2B	3B	HR	RBI	BB	SO	AVG	OBP	SLG	PRO	/A	BR	/A	PF	CHI	RC	TA	SB	CS	SBR	FR	POS	TPR
1957	Cin-N	29	10	8	2	0	0	0	1	1	4	.200	.273	.200	.473	28	-1	-1	105	207	1	.375	0	0	0	-3	/SO32	-0.3
1958	Cin-N	5	3	2	0	0	0	0	0	0	2	.000	.000	.000	.000	-93	-1	-1	107	0	0	.000	0	0	0	0	/S	0.0

YEAR	TM/L	G	AB	R	H	2B	3B	HR	RBI	BB	SO	AVG	OBP	SLG	PRO	/A	BR	/A	PF	CHI	RC	TA	SB	CS	SBR	FR	POS	TPR
1959	Cin-N	14	3	3	0	0	0	0	0	0	1	.000	.000	.000	.000	-97	-1	-1	103	0	0	.000	0	0	0	0	/S3	0.0
Total	3	48	16	13	2	0	0	0	1	1	7	.125	.176	.125	.301	-17	-3	-3	105	134	1	.214	0	0	0	-3	/SO32	-0.3
■ **TOMMY HENRICH** Henrich, Thomas David "The Clutch" or "Old Reliable" b: 2/20/13, Massillon, Ohio BL/TL, 6', 180 lbs. Deb: 5/11/37 C																												
1937	NY-A	67	206	39	66	14	5	8	42	35	17	.320	.419	.553	.972	140	14	13	102	104	50	1.093	4	0	1	-7	O	0.5
1938	NY-A	131	471	109	127	24	7	22	91	92	32	.270	.391	.490	.882	113	15	11	105	110	96	.957	6	2	1	-2	*O	0.9
1939	NY-A	99	347	64	96	18	4	9	57	51	23	.277	.371	.429	.800	114	3	7	91	111	60	.816	7	0	2	2	O/1	0.8
1940	NY-A	90	293	57	90	28	5	10	53	48	30	.307	.408	.539	.947	145	20	20	99	102	68	.991	1	2	-1	-1	O/1	1.2
1941	NY-A	144	538	106	149	27	5	31	85	81	40	.277	.377	.519	.895	137	26	28	98	86	113	.929	3	1	0	-1	*O	1.7
1942	NY-A	127	483	77	129	30	5	13	67	58	42	.267	.352	.431	.782	120	12	12	99	101	79	.762	4	4	-1	-2	*O/1	0.1
1946	NY-A	150	565	92	142	25	4	19	83	87	63	.251	.358	.411	.769	114	12	12	100	96	92	.768	5	2	0	2	*O1	0.6
1947	NY-A	142	550	109	158	35	**13**	16	98	71	54	.287	.372	.485	.857	142	26	29	97	121	104	.854	3	2	-0	5	*O/1	2.9
1948	NY-A	146	588	**138**	181	42	**14**	25	100	76	42	.308	.391	.554	.945	149	39	39	100	74	130	.962	2	3	-1	0	*O1	3.5
1949	NY-A	115	411	90	118	20	3	24	85	86	34	.287	.416	.526	.942	148	30	29	100	107	98	1.023	2	2	-1	-6	O1	2.1
1950	NY-A	73	151	20	41	6	8	6	34	27	6	.272	.382	.536	.918	134	7	7	99	119	30	.915	0	1	-1	-1	1	0.3
Total	11	1284	4603	901	1297	269	73	183	795	712	383	.282	.382	.491	.873	132	203	207	99	101	922	.914	37	19	-0	-10	*O1	14.6
■ **OLAF HENRIKSEN** Henriksen, Olaf "Swede" b: 4/26/1888, Kirkerup, Denmark d: 10/17/62, Norwood, Mass. BL/TL, 5'7.5", 158 lbs. Deb: 8/11/11																												
1911	Bos-A	27	93	17	34	2	1	0	8	14		.366	.449	.409	.857	141	6	6	99	73	19	.949	4			-1	O	0.3
1912	Bos-A	37	56	20	18	3	1	0	8	14		.321	.457	.411	.868	139	5	4	107	116	11	.974	0			-3	O	0.1
1913	Bos-A	31	40	8	15	1	0	0	2	7	5	.375	.468	.400	.868	150	3	3	103	44	8	1.040	3			-1	/O	0.1
1914	Bos-A	61	95	16	25	2	1	1	5	22	12	.263	.407	.337	.744	127	4	4	98	54	14	.811	5	4	-1	-6	O	-0.3
1915	Bos-A	73	92	9	18	2	2	0	13	18	7	.196	.333	.261	.594	78	-2	-2	99	184	8	.557	1	5	-3	-4	O	-0.9
1916	Bos-A	68	99	13	20	2	2	0	11	19	15	.202	.331	.263	.593	84	-2	-1	94	151	10	.595	2			-5	O	-0.8
1917	Bos-A	15	12	1	1	0	0	0	1	3	4	.083	.267	.083	.350	7	-1	-1	108	359	0	.364	0			0	H	0.0
Total	7	312	487	84	131	12	7	1	48	97	43	.269	.392	.329	.721	113	13	14	99	116	70	.751	15	9		-19	O	-1.5
■ **SNAKE HENRY** Henry, Frederick Marshall b: 7/19/1895, Waynesville, N.C. BL/TL, 6', 170 lbs. Deb: 9/15/22																												
1922	Bos-N	18	66	5	13	4	1	0	5	2	8	.197	.221	.288	.508	32	-7	-6	94	94	4	.418	2	2	-1	-0	1	-0.6
1923	Bos-N	11	9	1	1	0	0	0	2	1	1	.111	.200	.111	.311	-16	-2	-1	100	704	0	.250	0	0	0	0	H	0.0
Total	2	29	75	6	14	4	1	0	7	3	9	.187	.218	.267	.485	26	-9	-8	95	172	4	.397	2	2	-1	-0	/1	-0.6
■ **GEORGE HENRY** Henry, George Washington b: 8/10/1863, Philadelphia, Pa. d: 12/30/34, Lynn, Mass. BR/TR, 5'9", 180 lbs. Deb: 4/27/1893																												
1893	Cin-N	21	83	11	23	3	0	0	13	11	12	.277	.375	.313	.688	84	-1	-1	101	131	11	.683	2			0	O	0.0
■ **JOHN HENRY** Henry, John Michael b: 9/2/1863, Springfield, Mass. d: 6/11/39, Hartford, Conn. Deb: 8/13/1884																												
1884	Cle-N	9	26	2	4	0	0	0	0	0	12	.154	.154	.154	.308	-3	-3	-3	102	0	1	.182				0	/PO	0.0
1885	Bal-a	10	34	4	9	3	0	0		1		.265	.286	.353	.639	98	0	-0	106	0	4	.520				0	/PO	0.0
1886	Was-N	4	14	3	5	0	0	0	0	0	3	.357	.357	.357	.714	126	0	0	94	0	2	.556	0			0	/P	0.0
1890	NY-N	37	144	19	35	6	0	0	16	7	12	.243	.283	.285	.568	71	-6	-5	95	120	15	.560	12			-3	O	-0.7
Total	4	60	218	28	53	9	0	0	16	8	27	.243	.273	.284	.558	70	-9	-8	97	80	21	.503	12			-3	/OP	-0.7
■ **JOHN HENRY** Henry, John Park "Bull" b: 12/26/1889, Amherst, Mass. d: 11/24/41, Fort Huachuca, Ariz. BR/TR, 6', 180 lbs. Deb: 7/08/10																												
1910	Was-A	29	87	2	13	1	1	0	5	2		.149	.169	.184	.352	10	-9	-9	101	116	3	.270	2			1	C1	-0.6
1911	Was-A	85	261	24	53	5	0	0	21	25		.203	.273	.222	.495	40	-21	-20	97	122	18	.438	8			9	C1	-0.3
1912	Was-A	63	191	23	37	4	1	0	9	31		.194	.309	.225	.535	54	-10	-10	99	70	16	.552	10			8	C	0.4
1913	Was-A	96	273	26	61	8	4	1	26	30	43	.223	.309	.293	.602	72	-8	-10	106	111	26	.561	5			-7	C	-0.9
1914	Was-A	91	261	22	44	7	4	0	20	37	47	.169	.274	.226	.500	50	-15	-15	101	127	19	.473	7	3	0	-1	C	-1.0
1915	Was-A	95	277	20	61	9	2	1	22	36	28	.220	.323	.278	.601	79	-6	-6	101	94	29	.592	10	2	2	4	C	0.7
1916	Was-A	117	305	28	76	12	3	0	46	49	40	.249	.364	.308	.672	102	3	3	100	175	40	.703	12			-5	*C	0.3
1917	Was-A	65	163	10	31	6	0	0	18	24	16	.190	.302	.227	.529	67	-7	-5	92	175	12	.485	1			4	C	0.3
1918	Bos-N	43	102	6	21	2	0	0	4	10	15	.206	.283	.225	.509	59	-5	-4	94	66	6	.420	0			-3	C	-0.3
Total	9	684	1920	161	397	54	15	2	171	244	189	.207	.303	.254	.557	65	-78	-77	100	122	169	.528	55	5		8	C/1	-1.4
■ **RON HENRY** Henry, Ronald Baxter b: 8/7/36, Chester, Pa. BR/TR, 6'1", 180 lbs. Deb: 4/15/61																												
1961	Min-A	20	28	1	4	0	0	0	3	2	7	.143	.200	.143	.343	-6	-4	-4	106	294	0	.222	0	0	0	0	/C1	-0.3
1964	Min-A	22	41	4	5	1	1	2	5	2	17	.122	.163	.341	.504	36	-4	-4	101	106	2	.432	0	0	0	-2	C	-0.4
Total	2	42	69	5	9	1	1	2	8	4	24	.130	.178	.261	.439	18	-8	-8	103	183	3	.361	0	0	0	-1	/C1	-0.7
■ **BABE HERMAN** Herman, Floyd Caves b: 6/26/03, Buffalo, N.Y. d: 11/27/87, Glendale, Cal. BL/TL, 6'4", 190 lbs. Deb: 4/14/26 C																												
1926	Bro-N	137	496	64	158	35	11	11	81	44	53	.319	.375	.500	.875	135	22	23	99	106	91	.891	8			-2	*1O	1.5
1927	Bro-N	130	412	65	112	26	9	14	73	39	41	.272	.336	.481	.817	114	8	6	103	106	65	.807	4			0	*1/O	0.0
1928	Bro-N	134	486	64	165	37	6	12	91	38	36	.340	.390	.514	.904	136	23	24	99	116	94	.907	1			-7	*O	1.2
1929	Bro-N	146	569	105	217	42	13	21	113	55	45	.381	.436	.612	1.047	166	50	55	94	100	146	1.205	21			-13	*O/1	2.6
1930	Bro-N	153	614	143	241	48	11	35	130	66	56	.393	.455	.678	1.132	168	69	68	101	83	183	1.351	18			-12	*O	3.9
1931	Bro-N	151	610	93	191	43	16	18	97	50	65	.313	.365	.525	.890	135	29	28	101	89	118	.924	17			4	*O	2.4
1932	Cin-N	148	577	87	188	38	**19**	16	87	60	45	.326	.389	.541	.930	153	38	41	96	95	124	.974	7			15	*O	4.4
1933	Chi-N	137	508	77	147	36	12	16	93	50	57	.289	.353	.502	.855	146	26	28	97	122	90	.827	6			-6	*O	1.5
1934	Chi-N	125	467	65	142	34	5	14	84	35	71	.304	.353	.488	.841	126	14	15	98	114	81	.790	1			-10	*O/1	0.0
1935	Pit-N	26	81	8	19	8	1	0	7	3	10	.235	.271	.358	.629	63	-4	-5	107	87	7	.500	0			-3	O1	-0.7
	Cin-N	92	349	44	117	23	5	10	58	35	25	.335	.396	.516	.912	153	21	24	93	105	75	.936	5			-3	O1	1.7
	Yr	118	430	52	136	31	6	10	65	38	35	.316	.373	.486	.859	134	17	19	96	102	82	.852	5			-5		1.0
1936	Cin-N	119	380	59	106	25	2	13	71	39	36	.279	.348	.458	.806	119	7	9	97	118	61	.765	4			-8	O/1	-0.2
1937	Det-A	17	20	2	6	3	0	0	3	1	6	.300	.364	.450	.814	95	0	-0	109	114	4	.929	2	0	1	-0	/O	0.0
1945	Bro-N	37	34	6	9	1	0	1	9	5	7	.265	.359	.382	.741	111	0	1	96	195	5	.692	0			-1	/O	0.0
Total	13	1552	5603	882	1818	399	110	181	997	520	553	.324	.383	.532	.915	141	304	318	98	104	1143	.952	94	0		-47	*O1	18.3
■ **BILLY HERMAN** Herman, William Jennings Bryan b: 7/7/09, New Albany, Ind. BR/TR, 5'11", 180 lbs. Deb: 8/29/31 MCH																												
1931	Chi-N	25	98	14	32	7	0	0	16	13	6	.327	.405	.398	.803	122	3	4	96	140	17	.818	2			-3	2	0.2
1932	Chi-N	154	656	102	206	42	7	1	51	40	33	.314	.358	.404	.762	100	5	1	104	61	97	.720	14			19	*2	3.1
1933	Chi-N	153	619	82	173	35	2	0	44	45	34	.279	.332	.342	.675	96	-5	-3	97	69	70	.570	5			29	*2	3.9
1934	Chi-N	113	456	79	138	21	6	3	42	34	31	.303	.355	.395	.750	103	1	2	98	77	66	.684	6			4	*2	1.7
1935	Chi-N	154	666	113	**227**	**57**	6	7	83	42	29	.341	.383	.476	.859	130	27	28	99	76	121	.807	6			19	*2	5.6
1936	Chi-N	153	632	101	211	57	7	5	93	59	30	.334	.392	.470	.862	125	28	24	105	93	118	.828	5			15	*2	4.7
1937	Chi-N	138	564	106	189	35	11	8	65	56	22	.335	.396	.479	.875	133	29	27	103	70	112	.861	2			19	*2	5.1
1938	Chi-N	152	624	86	173	34	7	1	56	59	31	.277	.342	.359	.701	88	-5	-9	105	79	76	.606	3			25	*2	2.6
1939	Chi-N	156	623	111	191	34	**18**	7	70	66	31	.307	.378	.453	.830	121	20	19	101	75	104	.794	9			-3	*2	2.2
1940	Chi-N	135	558	77	163	24	4	5	57	47	30	.292	.347	.376	.723	100	0	0	100	83	72	.628	1			16	*2	2.5
1941	Chi-N	11	36	4	7	0	1	0	0	9	5	.194	.356	.250	.606	77	-1	-1	94	0	4	.621	0			2	2	0.2
	Bro-N	133	536	77	156	30	4	3	41	58	38	.291	.361	.379	.740	105	7	5	103	67	75	.669	1			-18	*2	-0.4
	Yr	144	572	81	163	30	5	3	41	67	43	.285	.361	.371	.732	104	6	4	103	62	79	.666	1			-17		-0.2
1942	Bro-N	155	571	76	146	34	2	2	65	72	52	.256	.339	.333	.672	95	-1	-2	102	125	68	.618	6			-9	*2/1	0.1
1943	Bro-N	153	585	76	193	41	2	2	100	66	26	.330	.398	.417	.815	136	28	28	100	**153**	97	.764	4			-20	*23	1.1
1946	Bro-N	47	184	24	53	8	4	0	28	26	10	.288	.376	.375	.751	111	4	3	103	145	26	.708	2			-1	32	0.4
	Bos-N	75	252	32	77	23	1	3	22	43	13	.306	.409	.440	.849	149	15	17	95	70	47	.852	1			-4	21/3	1.3
	Yr	122	436	56	130	31	5	3	50	69	23	.298	.395	.413	.808	133	19	20	98	100	75	.806	3			-5		1.7
1947	Pit-N	15	47	3	10	4	0	0	6	2	7	.213	.245	.298	.543	43	-4	-4	101	159	3	.400	0			-1	2/1M	-0.3
Total	15	1922	7707	1163	2345	486	82	47	839	737	428	.304	.367	.407	.774	112	151	140	101	87	1173	.739	67			89	*2/31	34.0

YEAR	TM/L	G	AB	R	H	2B	3B	HR	RBI	BB	SO	AVG	OBP	SLG	PRO	/A	BR	/A	PF	CHI	RC	TA	SB	CS	SBR	FR	POS	TPR
■ **AL HERMANN**	Hermann, Albert Bartel b: 3/28/1899, Milltown, N.J. d: 8/20/80, Lewes, Del. BR/TR, 6', 180 lbs. Deb: 7/17/23																											
1923	Bos-N	31	93	2	22	4	0	0	11	0	7	.237	.237	.280	.516	36	-9	-9	100	149	6	.397	3	2	-0	-1	2/31	-0.9
1924	Bos-N	1	1	0	0	0	0	0	0	0	1	.000	.000	.000	.000	-99	-0	-0	94	0	0	.000	0	0	0	0	H	0.0
Total	2	32	94	2	22	4	0	0	11	0	8	.234	.234	.277	.511	34	-9	-9	100	147	6	.392	3	2	-0	-1	/231	-0.9
■ **GENE HERMANSKI**	Hermanski, Eugene Victor b: 5/11/20, Pittsfield, Mass. BL/TR, 5'11.5", 185 lbs. Deb: 8/15/43																											
1943	Bro-N	18	60	6	18	2	1	0	12	11	7	.300	.417	.367	.783	127	3	3	100	201	10	.795	1			2	O	0.5
1946	Bro-N	64	110	15	22	2	2	0	8	17	10	.200	.313	.255	.567	60	-5	-5	103	107	9	.516	2			-8	O	-1.4
1947	Bro-N	79	189	36	52	7	1	7	39	28	7	.275	.377	.434	.811	110	5	3	105	140	33	.843	5			-7	O	-0.5
1948	Bro-N	133	400	63	116	22	7	15	60	64	46	.290	.391	.493	.883	132	22	19	104	93	81	.955	15			-2	*O	0.9
1949	Bro-N	87	224	48	67	12	3	8	42	47	21	.299	.431	.487	.918	143	17	16	102	119	50	1.061	12			-4	O	0.8
1950	Bro-N	94	289	36	86	17	3	7	34	36	26	.298	.381	.450	.831	110	8	5	107	87	50	.807	2			5	O	0.7
1951	Bro-N	31	80	8	20	4	0	1	5	10	12	.250	.333	.338	.671	83	-2	-2	98	64	9	.578	0	2	-1	1	O	-0.2
	Chi-N	75	231	28	65	12	1	3	20	35	30	.281	.385	.381	.766	110	4	5	97	80	37	.756	3	0	1	2	O	0.5
	Yr	106	311	36	85	16	1	4	25	45	42	.273	.372	.370	.742	103	2	3	97	76	46	.714	3	2	-0	3		0.3
1952	Chi-N	99	275	28	70	6	0	4	34	29	32	.255	.330	.320	.650	78	-6	-8	103	133	32	.579	2	0	1	-0	O	-0.8
1953	Chi-N	18	40	1	6	1	0	0	1	4	7	.150	.227	.175	.402	7	-5	-6	103	56	2	.343	1	0	0	-2	O	-0.7
	Pit-N	41	62	7	11	0	0	1	4	8	14	.177	.282	.226	.507	34	-6	-6	102	92	4	.434	0	0	0	-1	O	-0.6
	Yr	59	102	8	17	1	0	1	5	12	21	.167	.261	.206	.467	23	-11	-12	102	82	6	.402	1	0	0	-3		-1.3
Total	9	739	1960	276	533	85	18	46	259	289	212	.272	.372	.404	.776	106	33	26	103	106	316	.801	43	2		-13	O	-0.8
■ **REMY HERMOSO**	Hermoso, Angel Remigio b: 10/1/46, Carabobo, Venezuela BR/TR, 5'8", 155 lbs. Deb: 9/14/67																											
1967	Atl-N	11	26	3	8	0	0	0	0	2	4	.308	.357	.308	.665	88	-0	-0	104	0	3	.611	1	0	0	-1	/S2	0.0
1969	Mon-N	28	74	6	12	0	0	0	3	5	10	.162	.225	.162	.387	10	-9	-9	100	100	3	.318	3	1	0	1	2/S	-0.5
1970	Mon-N	4	1	1	0	0	0	0	0	0	0	.000	.000	.000	.000	-99	-0	-0	100	0	0	.000	0	0	0	0	/23	0.0
1974	Cle-A	48	122	15	27	3	1	0	5	7	7	.221	.264	.262	.526	51	-8	-8	101	61	9	.418	2	2	-1	3	2	-0.3
Total	4	91	223	25	47	3	1	0	8	14	21	.211	.261	.233	.494	41	-17	-17	101	67	15	.406	6	3	0	3	/2S3	-0.8
■ **ENZO HERNANDEZ**	Hernandez, Enzo Octavio b: 2/12/49, Valle De Guanape, Venez. BR/TR, 5'8", 155 lbs. Deb: 4/17/71																											
1971	SD-N	143	549	58	122	9	3	0	12	54	34	.222	.295	.250	.545	58	-31	-28	96	32	46	.491	21	5	3	-5	*S	-1.1
1972	SD-N	114	329	33	64	11	2	1	15	22	25	.195	.245	.249	.494	46	-26	-21	88	72	23	.469	24	3	5	-8	*S/O	-1.1
1973	SD-N	70	247	26	55	2	1	0	9	17	14	.223	.273	.239	.512	46	-19	-17	94	62	17	.455	15	4	2	0	S	-0.5
1974	SD-N	147	512	55	119	19	2	0	34	38	36	.232	.285	.277	.563	62	-29	-25	93	94	45	.533	37	10	5	-7	*S	-1.0
1975	SD-N	116	344	37	75	12	2	0	19	26	25	.218	.277	.265	.541	51	-23	-23	100	81	28	.496	20	4	4	13	*S	0.7
1976	SD-N	113	340	31	87	13	3	1	24	32	16	.256	.320	.321	.640	93	-8	-3	89	82	36	.577	12	7	-1	-7	*S	0.0
1977	SD-N	7	3	1	0	0	0	0	0	0	0	.000	.000	.000	.000	-99	-1	-1	88	0	0	.000	0	0	0	0	/S	0.0
1978	LA-N	4	3	0	0	0	0	0	0	0	1	.000	.000	.000	.000	-99	-1	-1	99	0	0	.000	0	0	0	0	/S	0.0
Total	8	714	2327	241	522	66	13	2	113	189	151	.224	.284	.266	.550	59	-136	-118	94	69	196	.513	129	33	19	-13	S/O	-3.0
■ **JACKIE HERNANDEZ**	Hernandez, Jacinto (Zulueta) b: 9/11/40, Central Tinguaro, Cuba BR/TR, 5'11", 165 lbs. Deb: 9/14/65																											
1965	Cal-A	6	6	2	2	1	0	0	1	0	1	.333	.333	.500	.833	137	0	0	98	138	1	1.000	1	0	0	0	/S3	0.1
1966	Cal-A	58	23	19	1	0	0	0	2	1	4	.043	.083	.043	.127	-63	-5	-5	99	840	0	.130	1	1	-0	0	3/2SO	-0.4
1967	Min-A	29	28	1	4	0	0	0	3	0	6	.143	.143	.143	.286	-14	-4	-4	107	313	1	.167	0	0	0	-0	S3	-0.3
1968	Min-A	83	199	13	35	3	0	2	17	9	52	.176	.219	.221	.440	32	-16	-17	106	146	10	.355	5	2	0	-4	S/1	-1.7
1969	KC-A	145	504	54	112	14	2	4	40	38	111	.222	.279	.282	.561	56	-29	-30	103	106	42	.495	17	7	1	-18	*S	-4.3
1970	KC-A	83	238	14	55	4	1	2	10	15	50	.231	.282	.282	.564	57	-14	-14	98	55	18	.445	1	3	-2	2	S	-0.6
1971	Pit-N	88	233	30	48	7	3	3	26	17	45	.206	.260	.300	.560	59	-13	-13	99	134	18	.455	0	2	-1	-3	S/3	-0.7
1972	Pit-N	72	176	12	33	7	1	1	14	9	43	.188	.227	.256	.483	36	-15	-15	103	120	10	.367	0	0	0	4	S/3	-0.3
1973	Pit-N	54	73	8	18	1	2	0	8	4	12	.247	.286	.315	.601	72	-3	-3	92	140	6	.474	0	0	0	2	S	0.6
Total	9	618	1480	153	308	37	9	12	121	93	324	.208	.258	.270	.527	49	-99	-101	101	126	106	.440	25	15	-1	-18	S/3201	-7.6
■ **KEITH HERNANDEZ**	Hernandez, Keith b: 10/20/53, San Francisco, Cal. BL/TL, 6', 180 lbs. Deb: 8/30/74																											
1974	StL-N	14	34	3	10	1	2	0	2	7	8	.294	.415	.441	.856	135	2	2	104	51	7	.880	0	0	0	0	/1	0.2
1975	StL-N	64	188	20	47	8	2	3	20	17	26	.250	.312	.362	.674	84	-4	-4	103	100	20	.578	0	1	-1	1	1	-0.7
1976	StL-N	129	374	54	108	21	5	7	46	49	53	.289	.376	.428	.803	123	14	13	104	98	61	.783	4	2	0	12	*1	2.0
1977	StL-N	161	560	90	163	41	4	15	91	79	88	.291	.380	.459	.839	129	20	23	96	123	95	.817	7	7	-2	4	*1	1.7
1978	StL-N	159	542	90	138	32	4	11	64	82	68	.255	.355	.389	.744	113	7	11	95	110	78	.732	13	5	1	3	*1	0.9
1979	StL-N	161	610	**116**	210	**48**	11	11	105	80	78	**.344**	**.421**	.513	.934	147	47	43	105	127	**135**	.976	11	6	-0	18	*1	5.4
1980	StL-N	159	595	**111**	191	39	8	16	99	86	73	.321	**.410**	.494	.904	147	43	41	103	121	122	.934	14	8	-1	5	*1	4.0
1981	StL-N	103	376	65	115	27	4	8	48	61	45	.306	.405	.463	.868	143	25	24	102	101	73	.905	12	5	1	6	1/O	2.8
1982	StL-N	160	579	79	173	33	6	7	94	100	67	.299	.404	.413	.817	125	27	24	103	**150**	101	.843	19	11	-1	6	*1/O	2.2
1983	StL-N	55	218	34	62	15	4	3	26	24	30	.284	.355	.431	.787	119	5	6	98	96	34	.748	1	1	-0	2	1	0.4
	NY-N	95	320	43	98	8	3	9	37	64	42	.306	.425	.434	.859	140	20	21	99	93	64	.922	8	4	0	4	1	2.1
	Yr	150	538	77	160	23	7	12	63	88	72	.297	.398	.433	.831	132	25	26	98	95	99	.856	9	5	-0	5		2.5
1984	NY-N	154	550	83	171	31	0	15	94	97	89	.311	.415	.449	.864	143	35	36	100	134	108	.887	2	3	-1	18	*1	4.9
1985	NY-N	158	593	87	183	34	4	10	91	77	59	.309	.390	.430	.820	133	25	27	97	135	100	.789	3	3	-1	15	*1	3.8
1986	NY-N	149	551	94	171	34	1	13	83	**94**	69	.310	.414	.446	.861	144	32	35	96	123	106	.876	2	1	0	16	*1	4.6
1987	NY-N	154	587	87	170	28	2	18	89	81	104	.290	.379	.436	.816	117	15	16	99	121	98	.786	0	2	-1	15	*1	2.1
1988	NY-N	95	348	43	96	16	0	11	55	31	57	.276	.337	.417	.754	128	7	10	90	126	47	.678	2	1	0	3	1	0.9
Total	15	1970	7025	1099	2106	416	60	157	1044	1029	956	.300	.391	.443	.835	132	322	328	99	121	1250	.856	98	60	-7	126	*1/O	37.3
■ **LEONARDO HERNANDEZ**	Hernandez, Leonardo Jesus b: 11/6/59, Santa Lucia, Venz. BR/TR, 5'11", 170 lbs. Deb: 9/19/82																											
1982	Bal-A	2	2	0	0	0	0	0	0	0	2	.000	.000	.000	.000	-99	-1	-1	100	0	0	.000	0	0	0	0	/H	0.0
1983	Bal-A	64	203	21	50	6	1	6	26	12	19	.246	.288	.374	.663	81	-6	-6	100	108	21	.567	1	0	0	-2	3	-0.7
1985	Bal-A	12	21	0	1	0	0	0	0	0	4	.048	.048	.048	.095	-75	-5	-5	99	0	-0	.045	0	0	0	-0	/1OD	-0.4
1986	NY-A	7	22	2	5	2	0	1	4	1	8	.227	.261	.455	.715	88	-0	-0	103	123	3	.647	0	0	0	0	/32	0.0
Total	4	85	248	23	56	8	1	7	30	13	33	.226	.264	.351	.615	67	-12	-12	100	100	24	.526	1	0	0	-2	/3D201	-1.1
■ **PEDRO HERNANDEZ**	Hernandez, Pedro Julio (born Pedro Julio Montas (Hernandez)) b: 4/4/59, La Romana, D.R. BR/TR, 6'1", 160 lbs. Deb: 9/08/79																											
1979	Tor-A	3	0	1	0	0	0	0	0	0	0	—	—	—	—	—	0	0	103	—	—	—	0	0	0	0	/R	0.0
1982	Tor-A	8	9	1	0	0	0	0	0	0	3	.000	.000	.000	.000	-92	-2	-3	109	0	0	.000	0	0	0	-0	/3OD	-0.2
Total	2	11	9	2	0	0	0	0	0	0	3	.000	.000	.000	.000	-92	-2	-3	109	0	24	.000	0	0	0	-0	/D3O	-0.2
■ **TOBY HERNANDEZ**	Hernandez, Rafael Tobias (Alvarado) b: 11/30/58, Calabozo, Venz. BR/TR, 6'1", 160 lbs. Deb: 6/22/84																											
1984	Tor-A	3	2	1	1	0	0	0	0	0	0	.500	.500	.500	1.000	175	0	0	102	0	1	1.000	0	0	0	0	/C	0.0
■ **RUDY HERNANDEZ**	Hernandez, Rodolfo (Acosta) b: 10/18/51, Enpalme, Mexico BR/TR, 5'9", 150 lbs. Deb: 9/06/72																											
1972	Chi-A	8	21	0	4	0	0	0	1	0	3	.190	.190	.190	.381	13	-2	-2	106	104	1	.235	0	0	0	-0	/S	-0.1
■ **CHICO HERNANDEZ**	Hernandez, Salvador Jose (Ramos) b: 1/3/16, Havana, Cuba d: 1/3/86, Havana, Cuba BR/TR, 6', 195 lbs. Deb: 4/16/42																											
1942	Chi-N	47	118	6	27	5	0	0	7	11	13	.229	.295	.271	.566	69	-5	-4	96	81	10	.467	0			2	C	-0.1
1943	Chi-N	43	126	10	34	4	0	0	9	9	9	.270	.324	.302	.625	82	-3	-3	99	85	12	.500	0			-4	C	-0.5
Total	2	90	244	16	61	9	0	0	16	20	22	.250	.309	.287	.596	76	-8	-7	97	83	22	.487	0			-3	/C	-0.6
■ **LARRY HERNDON**	Herndon, Larry Darnell b: 11/3/53, Sunflower, Miss. BR/TR, 6'3", 190 lbs. Deb: 9/04/74																											
1974	StL-N	12	1	3	1	0	0	0	0	0	0	1.000	1.000	1.000	2.000	445	0	0	104	0	1	—	0	0	0	-0	/O	0.0
1976	SF-N	115	337	42	97	11	3	2	23	23	45	.288	.337	.356	.693	94	-1	-3	103	70	40	.618	12	10	-2	-11	*O	-2.0
1977	SF-N	49	109	13	26	4	3	1	5	5	20	.239	.278	.358	.636	66	-5	-6	104	48	10	.551	4	2	0	-0	O	-0.7
1978	SF-N	151	471	52	122	15	9	1	32	35	71	.259	.312	.335	.647	88	-12	-7	92	79	48	.561	13	8	-1	-4	*O	-1.8
1979	SF-N	132	354	35	91	14	5	7	36	29	70	.257	.315	.384	.699	97	-5	-2	92	91	43	.640	8	6	-1	-5	*O	-1.1

YEAR	TM/L	G	AB	R	H	2B	3B	HR	RBI	BB	SO	AVG	OBP	SLG	PRO	/A	BR	/A	PF	CHI	RC	TA	SB	CS	SBR	FR	POS	TPR
1980	SF-N	139	493	54	127	17	11	8	49	19	91	.258	.287	.385	.672	90	-11	-8	96	92	50	.568	8	8	-2	-1	*O	-1.7
1981	SF-N	96	364	48	105	15	8	5	41	20	55	.288	.327	.415	.742	104	3	1	105	99	46	.675	15	6	1	-7	O	-0.7
1982	Det-A	157	614	92	179	21	13	23	88	38	92	.292	.334	.480	.814	120	15	15	100	102	90	.746	12	9	-2	1	*O/D	0.9
1983	Det-A	153	603	88	182	28	9	20	92	46	95	.302	.354	.478	.832	132	21	24	96	110	97	.779	9	3	1	-3	*OD	2.1
1984	Det-A	125	407	52	114	18	5	7	43	32	63	.280	.336	.400	.736	107	1	3	96	93	55	.670	6	2	1	-8	*O/D	-0.7
1985	Det-A	137	442	45	108	12	7	12	37	33	79	.244	.298	.385	.683	80	-10	-13	106	71	50	.599	2	1	0	-1	*O	-1.5
1986	Det-A	106	283	33	70	13	1	8	37	27	40	.247	.315	.385	.700	95	-4	-2	95	111	36	.641	2	1	0	-5	OD	-0.8
1987	Det-A	89	225	32	73	13	2	9	47	23	35	.324	.387	.520	.907	143	13	14	97	130	42	.860	1	0	0	-5	OD	0.7
1988	Det-A	76	174	16	39	5	0	4	20	23	37	.224	.318	.322	.640	85	-4	-3	94	117	17	.556	0	1	-1	-3	DO	-0.6
Total	14	1537	4877	605	1334	186	76	107	550	353	793	.274	.325	.409	.733	103	2	14	98	94	624	.680	92	57	-7	-50	*OD	-7.9

■ TOM HERNON Hernon, Thomas H. b: 11/4/1866, E.Bridgewater, Mass d: 2/4/02, New Bedford, Mass. BR/TR, Deb: 9/13/1897

YEAR	TM/L	G	AB	R	H	2B	3B	HR	RBI	BB	SO	AVG	OBP	SLG	PRO	/A	BR	/A	PF	CHI	RC	TA	SB	CS	SBR	FR	POS	TPR
1897	Chi-N	4	16	2	1	0	0	0	2	0		.063	.063	.063	.125	-66	-4	-4	100	597	0	.133	1			0	/O	-0.2

■ ED HERR Herr, Edward Joseph b: 5/18/1862, St.Louis, Mo. d: 7/18/43, St.Louis, Mo. BR/TR, 5'9.5", 179 lbs. Deb: 4/16/1887

YEAR	TM/L	G	AB	R	H	2B	3B	HR	RBI	BB	SO	AVG	OBP	SLG	PRO	/A	BR	/A	PF	CHI	RC	TA	SB	CS	SBR	FR	POS	TPR
1887	Cle-a	11	44	6	12	2	0	0		6		.273	.360	.318	.678	95	-0	0	98	0	6	.688	2			0	3	0.0
1888	StL-a	43	172	21	46	7	1	3	43	11		.267	.323	.372	.695	113	5	2	111	187	24	.690	9			0	SO/3	0.2
1890	StL-a	12	41	5	9	2	1	0		5		.220	.347	.317	.664	85	0	-1	116	0	5	.719	2			0	/2O3	0.0
Total	3	66	257	32	67	11	2	3	43	22		.261	.333	.354	.687	105	5	1	109	122	35	.695	13			0	/S3O2	0.2

■ TOM HERR Herr, Thomas Mitchell b: 4/4/56, Lancaster, Pa. BB/TR, 6', 175 lbs. Deb: 8/13/79

YEAR	TM/L	G	AB	R	H	2B	3B	HR	RBI	BB	SO	AVG	OBP	SLG	PRO	/A	BR	/A	PF	CHI	RC	TA	SB	CS	SBR	FR	POS	TPR
1979	StL-N	14	10	4	2	0	0	0	1	2	2	.200	.333	.200	.533	47	-1	-1	105	198	1	.625	1	0	0	0	/2	0.0
1980	StL-N	76	222	29	55	12	5	0	15	16	21	.248	.301	.347	.648	78	-6	-7	103	77	22	.582	9	2	2	0	2S	0.1
1981	StL-N	103	411	50	110	14	9	0	46	39	30	.268	.333	.345	.678	91	-4	-4	102	122	49	.647	23	7	3	4	*2	1.0
1982	StL-N	135	493	83	131	19	4	0	36	57	56	.266	.344	.320	.665	84	-7	-9	103	95	59	.639	25	12	0	6	*2	0.3
1983	StL-N	89	313	43	101	14	4	2	31	43	27	.323	.406	.412	.818	130	13	14	98	93	53	.789	6	8	-3	-8	2	0.6
1984	StL-N	145	558	67	154	23	2	4	49	49	56	.276	.337	.346	.682	93	-5	-4	99	90	66	.609	13	7	-0	11	*2	1.0
1985	StL-N	159	596	97	180	38	3	8	110	80	55	.302	.386	.416	.803	130	22	25	96	**155**	107	.849	31	3	8	-27	*2	0.7
1986	StL-N	152	559	48	141	30	4	2	61	73	75	.252	.344	.331	.675	84	-8	-10	103	135	69	.657	22	8	2	-22	*2	-2.8
1987	StL-N	141	510	73	134	29	0	2	83	68	62	.263	.353	.331	.684	84	-11	-9	99	**200**	65	.661	19	4	3	-10	*2	-1.3
1988	StL-N	15	50	4	13	0	0	1	3	11	4	.260	.393	.320	.713	103	1	1	104	67	8	.789	3	0	1	0	2/O	0.2
	Min-A	86	304	42	80	16	0	1	21	40	47	.263	.349	.326	.674	85	-3	-5	106	83	36	.631	10	3	1	-8	2/SD	-0.6
Total	10	1115	4026	540	1101	195	31	20	456	478	435	.273	.353	.352	.705	96	-7	-9	101	123	533	.694	162	54	16	-54	*2/SDO	-0.8

■ JOSE HERRERA Herrera, Jose Concepcion (Ontiveros) "Loco" b: 4/8/42, San Lorenzo, Venez. BR/TR, 5'8", 165 lbs. Deb: 6/03/67

YEAR	TM/L	G	AB	R	H	2B	3B	HR	RBI	BB	SO	AVG	OBP	SLG	PRO	/A	BR	/A	PF	CHI	RC	TA	SB	CS	SBR	FR	POS	TPR
1967	Hou-N	5	4	0	1	0	0	0	1	0	1	.250	.250	.250	.500	47	-0	-0	94	414	0	.333	0	0	0	0	H	0.0
1968	Hou-N	27	100	9	24	5	0	0	7	4	12	.240	.269	.290	.559	69	-4	-4	99	108	7	.418	0	2	-1	-2	O/2	-0.8
1969	Mon-N	47	126	7	36	5	0	2	12	3	14	.286	.302	.373	.675	88	-2	-2	100	91	13	.537	1	2	-1	-1	O/23	-0.5
1970	Mon-N	1	1	0	0	0	0	0	0	0	1	.000	.000	.000	.000	-99	-0	-0	100	0	0	.000	0	0	0	0	H	0.0
Total	4	80	231	16	61	10	0	2	20	7	28	.264	.286	.333	.619	78	-7	-7	100	103	21	.489	1	4	-2	-3	/O23	-1.3

■ PANCHO HERRERA Herrera, Juan Francisco (Willavicencio) b: 6/16/34, Santiago, Cuba BR/TR, 6'3", 220 lbs. Deb: 4/15/58

YEAR	TM/L	G	AB	R	H	2B	3B	HR	RBI	BB	SO	AVG	OBP	SLG	PRO	/A	BR	/A	PF	CHI	RC	TA	SB	CS	SBR	FR	POS	TPR
1958	Phi-N	29	63	5	17	3	0	1	6	7	15	.270	.352	.365	.717	92	-1	-1	98	95	8	.640	1	2	-1	-2	31	-0.3
1960	Phi-N	145	512	61	144	26	6	17	71	51	136	.281	.352	.455	.807	111	13	9	107	104	78	.750	2	3	-1	5	*12	0.8
1961	Phi-N	126	400	56	103	17	2	13	51	55	120	.257	.353	.408	.760	108	2	5	94	102	58	.732	5	1	1	5	*1	0.3
Total	3	300	975	122	264	46	8	31	128	113	271	.271	.352	.430	.782	108	14	13	101	102	145	.754	8	6	-1	8	1/23	0.8

■ MIKE HERRERA Herrera, Ramon b: 12/19/1897, Havana, Cuba d: 2/3/78, Havana, Cuba BR/TR, 5'6", 147 lbs. Deb: 9/22/25

YEAR	TM/L	G	AB	R	H	2B	3B	HR	RBI	BB	SO	AVG	OBP	SLG	PRO	/A	BR	/A	PF	CHI	RC	TA	SB	CS	SBR	FR	POS	TPR
1925	Bos-A	10	39	2	15	0	0	0	8	2	2	.385	.415	.385	.799	109	0	1	95	189	6	.750	1	0	0	1	2	0.2
1926	Bos-A	74	237	20	61	14	1	0	19	15	13	.257	.304	.325	.629	63	-13	-13	101	84	23	.514	0	5	-3	7	23/S	-0.4
Total	2	84	276	22	76	14	1	0	27	17	15	.275	.320	.333	.653	70	-12	-12	100	98	29	.541	1	5	-3	7	/23S	-0.2

■ LEFTY HERRING Herring, Silas Clarke b: 3/4/1880, Philadelphia, Pa. d: 2/11/65, Massapequa, N.Y. BL/TL, 5'11", 160 lbs. Deb: 5/16/1899

YEAR	TM/L	G	AB	R	H	2B	3B	HR	RBI	BB	SO	AVG	OBP	SLG	PRO	/A	BR	/A	PF	CHI	RC	TA	SB	CS	SBR	FR	POS	TPR
1899	Was-N	2	1	1	1	0	0	0	0	1		1.000	1.000	1.000	2.000	477	1	1	96	0	1	—	0			0	/P	0.0
1904	Was-A	15	46	3	8	1	0	0	2	7		.174	.283	.196	.479	59	-2	-2	93	85	3	.421	0			-1	1/O	-0.2
Total	2	17	47	4	9	1	0	0	2	8		.191	.309	.213	.522	74	-1	-1	93	81	4	.474	0			-1	/1OP	-0.2

■ ED HERRMANN Herrmann, Edward Martin b: 8/27/46, San Diego, Cal. BL/TR, 6'1", 195 lbs. Deb: 9/01/67

YEAR	TM/L	G	AB	R	H	2B	3B	HR	RBI	BB	SO	AVG	OBP	SLG	PRO	/A	BR	/A	PF	CHI	RC	TA	SB	CS	SBR	FR	POS	TPR
1967	Chi-A	2	3	1	2	1	0	0	1	1	0	.667	.750	1.000	1.750	440	1	1	94	139	2	4.000	0	0	0	-0	/C	0.1
1969	Chi-A	102	290	31	67	8	0	8	31	30	35	.231	.320	.341	.662	78	-6	-9	108	101	32	.591	0	2	-1	-7	C	-1.0
1970	Chi-A	96	297	42	84	9	0	19	52	31	41	.283	.356	.505	.862	128	13	11	106	102	54	.840	0	1	-1	2	C	1.4
1971	Chi-A	101	294	32	63	6	0	11	35	44	48	.214	.321	.347	.668	91	-4	-3	98	106	33	.628	2	0	1	-2	C	0.0
1972	Chi-A	116	354	23	88	9	0	10	40	43	37	.249	.337	.359	.695	101	4	1	106	106	41	.624	0	0	0	-7	*C	-0.4
1973	Chi-A	119	379	42	85	17	1	10	39	31	55	.224	.295	.354	.649	80	-10	-11	102	93	37	.561	2	4	-2	2	*C/D	-0.7
1974	Chi-A	107	367	32	95	13	1	10	39	16	49	.259	.290	.381	.671	90	-5	-6	102	90	37	.551	1	0	0	4	*C	0.1
1975	NY-A	80	200	16	51	9	2	6	30	16	23	.255	.310	.410	.720	103	-0	0	99	115	24	.632	0	0	0	4	DC	0.5
1976	Cal-A	29	46	5	8	3	0	2	8	7	8	.174	.283	.370	.653	98	-1	-0	92	134	5	.632	0	0	0	-3	C	-0.1
	Hou-N	79	265	14	54	8	0	3	25	22	40	.204	.275	.268	.543	63	-16	-11	86	120	20	.447	0	0	0	-1	C	-0.8
1977	Hou-N	56	158	7	46	7	0	1	17	15	18	.291	.356	.354	.711	99	-1	0	93	115	20	.629	1	1	-0	4	C	0.3
1978	Hou-N	16	36	1	4	1	0	0	0	3	3	.111	.179	.139	.318	-11	-5	-5	95	0	1	.242	0	0	0	-0	C	-0.4
	Mon-N	19	40	1	7	1	0	0	3	1	4	.175	.195	.200	.395	11	-5	-5	96	149	1	.257	0	0	0	1	C	-0.2
	Yr	35	76	2	11	2	0	0	3	4	7	.145	.188	.171	.359	1	-10	-10	95	81	2	.254	0	0	0	1		-0.6
Total	11	922	2729	247	654	92	4	80	320	260	361	.240	.312	.364	.677	91	-33	-35	100	104	308	.618	6	8	-3	-3	C/D	-1.2

■ RICK HERRSCHER Herrscher, Richard Franklin b: 11/3/36, St.Louis, Mo. BR/TR, 6'2.5", 187 lbs. Deb: 8/01/62

YEAR	TM/L	G	AB	R	H	2B	3B	HR	RBI	BB	SO	AVG	OBP	SLG	PRO	/A	BR	/A	PF	CHI	RC	TA	SB	CS	SBR	FR	POS	TPR
1962	NY-N	35	50	5	11	3	0	1	6	5	11	.220	.291	.340	.631	66	-2	-3	104	118	5	.564	0	0	0	-1	1/3OS	-0.2

■ JOHN HERRNSTEIN Herrnstein, John Ellett b: 5/31/38, Hampton, Va. BL/TL, 6'3", 215 lbs. Deb: 9/15/62

YEAR	TM/L	G	AB	R	H	2B	3B	HR	RBI	BB	SO	AVG	OBP	SLG	PRO	/A	BR	/A	PF	CHI	RC	TA	SB	CS	SBR	FR	POS	TPR
1962	Phi-N	6	5	0	1	0	0	0	1	1	3	.200	.333	.200	.533	50	-0	-0	95	394	0	.500	0	0	0	-0	/O	0.0
1963	Phi-N	15	12	1	2	0	0	1	1	1	5	.167	.231	.417	.647	80	-0	-0	103	52	1	.600	0	0	0	-0	/O1	0.0
1964	Phi-N	125	303	38	71	12	4	6	25	22	67	.234	.291	.360	.650	83	-7	-7	99	81	31	.554	1	2	-1	-19	O1	-3.3
1965	Phi-N	63	85	8	17	2	0	1	5	2	18	.200	.227	.259	.486	39	-7	-7	95	83	4	.352	0	0	0	-3	1O	-1.0
1966	Phi-N	4	10	0	1	0	0	0	1	0	7	.100	.100	.100	.200	-44	-2	-2	101	420	0	.111	0	0	0	-0	/O	-0.1
	Chi-N	9	17	3	3	0	0	0	0	3	8	.176	.300	.176	.476	36	-1	-1	100	0	1	.429	0	0	0	-0	/1O	-0.1
	Atl-N	17	18	2	4	0	0	0	1	0	7	.222	.222	.222	.444	24	-2	-2	99	105	1	.286	0	0	0	-1	/O	-0.2
	Yr	30	45	5	8	0	0	0	2	3	22	.178	.229	.178	.407	15	-5	-5	99	130	2	.297	0	0	0	-1	/O	-0.4
Total	5	239	450	52	99	14	4	8	34	29	115	.220	.272	.322	.594	67	-20	-19	98	89	39	.504	1	2	-1	-24	/O1	-4.7

■ EARL HERSH Hersh, Earl Walter b: 5/21/32, Ebbvale, Md. BL/TL, 6', 205 lbs. Deb: 9/04/56

YEAR	TM/L	G	AB	R	H	2B	3B	HR	RBI	BB	SO	AVG	OBP	SLG	PRO	/A	BR	/A	PF	CHI	RC	TA	SB	CS	SBR	FR	POS	TPR
1956	Mil-N	7	13	0	3	3	0	0	0	0	5	.231	.231	.462	.692	81	-0	-0	99	0	1	.600	0	0	0	-1	/O	-0.1

■ MIKE HERSHBERGER Hershberger, Norman Michael b: 10/9/39, Massillon, Ohio BR/TR, 5'10", 175 lbs. Deb: 9/05/61

YEAR	TM/L	G	AB	R	H	2B	3B	HR	RBI	BB	SO	AVG	OBP	SLG	PRO	/A	BR	/A	PF	CHI	RC	TA	SB	CS	SBR	FR	POS	TPR
1961	Chi-A	15	55	9	17	3	0	0	5	2	2	.309	.333	.364	.697	87	-1	-1	99	100	6	.575	1	1	-0	2	O	0.0
1962	Chi-A	148	427	54	112	14	2	4	46	37	36	.262	.325	.333	.658	82	-13	-10	95	119	43	.563	10	6	-1	-4	*O	-1.9
1963	Chi-A	135	476	64	133	26	2	3	45	39	39	.279	.339	.361	.700	92	-2	-4	104	106	60	.633	9	3	1	6	*O	-0.1
1964	Chi-A	141	452	55	104	15	3	2	31	48	47	.230	.310	.290	.599	71	-18	-16	96	96	42	.525	8	6	-1	3	*O	-2.0
1965	KC-A	150	494	43	114	15	5	5	48	37	42	.231	.291	.312	.603	74	-19	-17	97	118	42	.505	7	3	0	6	*O	-1.6
1966	KC-A	146	538	55	136	27	7	2	57	47	37	.253	.316	.340	.656	94	-7	-4	94	**134**	58	.584	13	5	1	12	*O	0.4
1967	KC-A	142	480	55	122	25	1	1	49	38	40	.254	.318	.317	.635	89	-6	-6	100	**135**	49	.553	10	3	1	6	*O	-0.3
1968	Oak-A	99	246	23	67	9	2	5	32	21	22	.272	.332	.386	.718	119	5	5	98	125	32	.672	8	3	1	-5	O	-0.2

YEAR	TM/L	G	AB	R	H	2B	3B	HR	RBI	BB	SO	AVG	OBP	SLG	PRO	/A	BR	/A	PF	CHI	RC	TA	SB	CS	SBR	FR	POS	TPR
1969	Oak-A	51	129	11	26	2	0	1	10	10	15	.202	.259	.240	.499	44	-10	-9	92	118	8	.393	1	2	-1	-5	O	-1.6
1970	Mil-A	49	98	7	23	5	0	1	6	10	8	.235	.306	.316	.622	73	-4	-4	98	71	9	.519	1	2	-1	-7	O	-1.2
1971	Chi-A	74	177	22	46	9	0	2	15	30	23	.260	.379	.345	.724	109	3	4	98	91	25	.732	6	2	1	-5	O	-0.2
Total	11	1150	3572	398	900	150	22	26	344	319	311	.252	.319	.328	.647	86	-73	-61	97	116	374	.588	74	36	1	9	*O	-8.7

■ WILLARD HERSHBERGER Hershberger, Willard Mc Kee "Bill" b: 5/28/10, Lemon Cove, Cal. d: 8/3/40, Boston, Mass. BR/TR, 5'10.5", 167 lbs. Deb: 4/19/38

YEAR	TM/L	G	AB	R	H	2B	3B	HR	RBI	BB	SO	AVG	OBP	SLG	PRO	/A	BR	/A	PF	CHI	RC	TA	SB	CS	SBR	FR	POS	TPR
1938	Cin-N	49	105	12	29	3	1	0	12	5	6	.276	.315	.324	.639	78	-3	-3	98	128	11	.532	1			-1	C/2	-0.1
1939	Cin-N	63	174	23	60	9	2	0	32	9	4	.345	.384	.420	.803	112	4	3	103	161	27	.708	1			-1	C	0.4
1940	Cin-N	48	123	6	38	4	2	0	26	6	6	.309	.351	.374	.725	99	0	-0	101	210	15	.600	0			-2	C	0.0
Total	3	160	402	41	127	16	5	0	70	20	16	.316	.356	.381	.737	100	1	0	101	167	53	.643	2			-3	C/2	0.3

■ NEAL HERTWECK Hertweck, Neal Charles b: 11/22/31, St.Louis, Mo. BL/TL, 6'1.5", 175 lbs. Deb: 9/27/52

YEAR	TM/L	G	AB	R	H	2B	3B	HR	RBI	BB	SO	AVG	OBP	SLG	PRO	/A	BR	/A	PF	CHI	RC	TA	SB	CS	SBR	FR	POS	TPR
1952	StL-N	2	6	0	0	0	0	0	0	1	1	.000	.143	.000	.143	-59	-1	-1	98	0	0	.167	0	0	0	0	/1	0.0

■ STEVE HERTZ Hertz, Stephen Allan b: 2/26/45, Farfield, Ohio BR/TR, 6'1", 195 lbs. Deb: 4/21/64

YEAR	TM/L	G	AB	R	H	2B	3B	HR	RBI	BB	SO	AVG	OBP	SLG	PRO	/A	BR	/A	PF	CHI	RC	TA	SB	CS	SBR	FR	POS	TPR
1964	Hou-N	5	4	2	0	0	0	0	0	0	3	.000	.000	.000	.000	-99	-1	-1	96	0	0	.000	0	0	0	0	/3	0.0

■ BUCK HERZOG Herzog, Charles Lincoln b: 7/9/1885, Baltimore, Md. d: 9/4/53, Baltimore, Md. BR/TR, 5'11", 160 lbs. Deb: 4/17/08 M

YEAR	TM/L	G	AB	R	H	2B	3B	HR	RBI	BB	SO	AVG	OBP	SLG	PRO	/A	BR	/A	PF	CHI	RC	TA	SB	CS	SBR	FR	POS	TPR
1908	NY-N	64	160	38	48	6	2	0	11	36		.300	.429	.363	.791	150	13	12	104	73	31	.982	16			-1	2S/3O	1.1
1909	NY-N	42	130	16	24	2	0	0	8	13		.185	.264	.200	.464	43	-8	-9	105	112	7	.396	2			-3	O/23S	-1.3
1910	Bos-N	106	380	51	95	20	3	3	32	30	34	.250	.329	.342	.672	84	-2	-9	114	77	48	.660	13			9	*3	0.0
1911	Bos-N	79	294	53	91	19	5	5	41	33	21	.310	.398	.459	.857	135	16	14	103	89	65	1.005	26			-4	S/3	1.3
	NY-N	69	247	37	66	14	4	1	26	14	19	.267	.325	.368	.693	92	-3	-4	102	95	36	.740	22			8	3/2S	0.7
	Yr	148	541	90	157	33	9	6	67	47	40	.290	.365	.418	.783	115	13	11	103	92	100	.880	48			4		2.0
1912	NY-N	140	482	72	127	20	9	2	47	57	34	.263	.350	.355	.705	90	-4	-6	104	91	73	.766	37			7	*3	0.2
1913	NY-N	96	290	46	83	15	3	3	31	22	12	.286	.349	.390	.739	108	4	3	103	92	45	.792	23			1	3/2	0.3
1914	Cin-N	138	498	54	140	14	8	1	40	42	27	.281	.348	.347	.695	102	5	2	105	87	72	.754	46			31	*S/1M	3.9
1915	Cin-N	155	579	61	153	14	10	1	42	34	21	.264	.314	.328	.642	92	-4	-6	103	88	66	.604	35	16	1	31	*S/1M	3.2
1916	Cin-N	79	281	30	75	14	2	1	24	21	12	.267	.329	.342	.671	108	2	3	98	102	38	.665	15			-2	S3/OM	0.5
	NY-N	77	280	40	73	10	4	0	25	22	24	.261	.326	.325	.651	105	0	2	96	115	37	.662	19			7	23/S	1.2
	Yr	156	561	70	148	24	6	1	49	43	36	.264	.327	.333	.661	106	3	5	97	109	74	.663	34			5		1.7
1917	NY-N	114	417	69	98	10	8	2	31	31	36	.235	.308	.312	.620	93	-4	-3	97	84	43	.583	12			-9	*2	-0.5
1918	Bos-N	118	473	57	108	12	6	0	26	29	28	.228	.280	.279	.559	75	-16	-13	94	66	39	.482	10			1	21/S	-0.7
1919	Bos-N	73	275	27	77	8	5	1	25	13	11	.280	.327	.356	.683	108	2	2	98	102	36	.672	16			-11	2/1	-0.6
	Chi-N	52	193	15	53	4	4	0	17	10	7	.275	.336	.337	.673	102	1	1	100	98	25	.679	12			-0	2	0.3
	Yr	125	468	42	130	12	9	1	42	23	18	.278	.331	.348	.679	105	3	3	99	101	61	.675	28			-11		-0.3
1920	Chi-N	91	305	39	59	9	2	0	19	20	21	.193	.261	.236	.497	44	-22	-21	99	104	20	.424	8	9	-3	2	23/1	-2.1
Total	13	1493	5284	705	1370	191	75	20	445	427	307	.259	.328	.335	.663	95	-20	-31	102	90	681	.666	312	25		65	23S/01	7.5

■ WHITEY HERZOG Herzog, Dorrel Norman Elvert b: 11/9/31, New Athens, Ill. BL/TL, 5'11", 182 lbs. Deb: 4/17/56 MC

YEAR	TM/L	G	AB	R	H	2B	3B	HR	RBI	BB	SO	AVG	OBP	SLG	PRO	/A	BR	/A	PF	CHI	RC	TA	SB	CS	SBR	FR	POS	TPR
1956	Was-A	117	421	49	103	13	7	4	35	35	74	.245	.303	.337	.640	67	-20	-21	102	87	44	.564	8	5	-1	-4	*O/1	-3.0
1957	Was-A	36	78	7	13	3	0	0	4	13	12	.167	.301	.205	.506	42	-6	-6	98	99	6	.478	1	2	-1	-1	O	-0.9
1958	Was-A	8	5	0	0	0	0	0	0	1	5	.000	.167	.000	.167	-52	-1	-1	97	0	0	.200	0	0	0	-2	/O	-0.3
	KC-A	88	96	11	23	1	2	0	9	16	21	.240	.348	.292	.640	74	-2	-3	106	129	10	.579	0	3	-2	-10	O1	-1.8
	Yr	96	101	11	23	1	2	0	9	17	26	.228	.339	.277	.616	68	-3	-4	105	118	10	.556	0	3	-2	-12		-2.1
1959	KC-A	38	123	25	36	7	1	1	9	34	23	.293	.446	.390	.836	130	8	8	101	74	25	.933	1	0	0	2	O/1	0.8
1960	KC-A	83	252	43	67	10	2	8	38	40	32	.266	.366	.417	.783	113	5	5	99	115	39	.755	0	1	-1	-1	O/1	0.1
1961	Bal-A	113	323	39	94	11	6	5	35	50	41	.291	.388	.409	.796	116	8	9	97	93	53	.770	1	4	-2	-12	O	-0.8
1962	Bal-A	99	263	34	70	13	1	7	35	41	36	.266	.371	.403	.774	115	4	6	95	109	41	.752	2	3	-1	1	O	0.3
1963	Det-A	52	53	5	8	2	1	0	7	11	17	.151	.308	.226	.534	51	-3	-3	104	244	5	.533	0	0	0	-1	/1O	-0.4
Total	8	634	1614	213	414	60	20	25	172	241	261	.257	.356	.365	.720	95	-8	-6	99	103	222	.698	13	18	-7	-28	O/1	-6.0

■ TOM HESS Hess, Thomas (born Thomas Heslin) b: 8/15/1875, Brooklyn, N.Y. d: 12/15/45, Albany, N.Y. Deb: 6/06/1892

YEAR	TM/L	G	AB	R	H	2B	3B	HR	RBI	BB	SO	AVG	OBP	SLG	PRO	/A	BR	/A	PF	CHI	RC	TA	SB	CS	SBR	FR	POS	TPR
1892	Bal-N	1	2	0	0	0	0	0	0	0	0	.000	.000	.000	.000	-99	-0	-0	100	0	0	.000	0			0	/C	0.0

■ GUS HETLING Hetling, August Julius b: 11/21/1885, St.Louis, Mo. d: 10/13/62, Wichita, Kan. BR/TR, 5'10", 165 lbs. Deb: 10/06/06

YEAR	TM/L	G	AB	R	H	2B	3B	HR	RBI	BB	SO	AVG	OBP	SLG	PRO	/A	BR	/A	PF	CHI	RC	TA	SB	CS	SBR	FR	POS	TPR
1906	Det-A	2	7	0	1	0	0	0	0	0	0	.143	.143	.143	.286	-9	-1	-1	108	0	0	.167	0			-0	/3	0.0

■ GEORGE HEUBEL Heubel, George A. b: 1849, Paterson, N.J. d: 1/22/1896, Philadelphia, Pa. 5'11.5", 178 lbs. Deb: 5/20/1871

YEAR	TM/L	G	AB	R	H	2B	3B	HR	RBI	BB	SO	AVG	OBP	SLG	PRO	/A	BR	/A	PF	CHI	RC	TA	SB	CS	SBR	FR	POS	TPR
1871	Ath-n	17	78	10	25							.321															O/1	
1872	Oly-n	5	24	2	3							.125															/O	
1876	NY-N	1	4	0	0	0	0	0	0	0	0	.000	.000	.000	.000	-99	-1	-1	87	0	0	.000				0	/1	0.0
Total	2 n	22	102	12	28							.275															/1	

■ JOHNNY HEVING Heving, John Aloysius b: 4/29/1896, Covington, Ky. d: 12/24/68, Salisbury, N.C. BR/TR, 6', 175 lbs. Deb: 9/24/20

YEAR	TM/L	G	AB	R	H	2B	3B	HR	RBI	BB	SO	AVG	OBP	SLG	PRO	/A	BR	/A	PF	CHI	RC	TA	SB	CS	SBR	FR	POS	TPR
1920	StL-A	1	1	0	0	0	0	0	0	0	0	.000	.000	.000	.000	-90	-0	-0	111	0	0	.000	0	0	0	0	H	0.0
1924	Bos-A	45	109	15	31	5	1	0	11	10	7	.284	.345	.349	.693	76	-3	-4	104	96	14	.615	0	0	0	1	C	0.0
1925	Bos-A	45	119	14	20	7	0	0	6	12	7	.168	.244	.227	.471	21	-15	-14	95	74	7	.390	0	1	-1	3	C	-0.8
1928	Bos-A	82	158	11	41	7	2	0	11	11	10	.259	.308	.329	.637	69	-8	-7	98	73	16	.542	1	1	-0	-5	C	-0.7
1929	Bos-A	76	188	26	60	4	3	0	23	8	7	.319	.354	.372	.726	86	-3	-4	102	112	24	.623	1	2	-1	-0	C	0.0
1930	Bos-A	75	220	15	61	5	3	0	17	11	14	.277	.312	.327	.639	67	-12	-10	93	78	23	.535	2	0	1	3	C	0.0
1931	Phi-A	42	113	8	27	3	2	1	12	6	8	.239	.277	.327	.605	56	-7	-8	105	99	10	.500	0	0	0	-1	C	-0.5
1932	Phi-A	33	77	14	21	6	1	0	10	7	6	.273	.333	.377	.710	73	-2	-3	114	115	10	.643	0	0	0	1	C	0.0
Total	8	399	985	103	261	37	12	1	90	65	59	.265	.312	.330	.642	65	-51	-51	100	90	104	.544	4	4	-1	2	C	-2.0

■ MIKE HEYDON Heydon, Michael Edward "Ed" b: 7/15/1874, Missouri d: 10/13/13, Indianapolis, Ind. BL/TR, 6', Deb: 10/12/1898

YEAR	TM/L	G	AB	R	H	2B	3B	HR	RBI	BB	SO	AVG	OBP	SLG	PRO	/A	BR	/A	PF	CHI	RC	TA	SB	CS	SBR	FR	POS	TPR
1898	Bal-N	3	9	2	1	0	0	0	1	2		.111	.333	.111	.444	30	-1	-1	103	308	0	.500	0			0	/C	0.0
1899	Was-N	3	3	0	0	0	0	0	0	2		.000	.400	.000	.400	17	-0	-0	96	0	0	.667	0			0	/C	0.0
1901	StL-N	16	43	2	9	1	1	1	6	5		.209	.292	.349	.641	90	-1	-0	97	112	5	.647	2			1	C/O	0.1
1904	Chi-A	4	10	0	1	1	0	0	1	1		.100	.182	.200	.382	22	-1	-1	99	187	0	.333	0			-0	/C	0.0
1905	Was-A	77	245	20	47	7	4	1	26	21		.192	.256	.265	.521	64	-9	-10	104	139	18	.460	5			13	C	1.1
1906	Was-A	49	145	14	23	7	1	0	10	14		.159	.233	.221	.453	48	-9	-8	91	114	8	.393	2			0	C	-0.3
1907	Was-A	62	164	14	30	3	0	0	9	25		.183	.291	.201	.492	66	-6	-4	90	98	11	.455	3			-6	C	-0.5
Total	7	214	619	52	111	19	6	2	53	70		.179	.264	.239	.503	62	-26	-24	97	123	43	.455	12			8	C/O	0.4

■ JACK HIATT Hiatt, Jack E b: 7/27/42, Bakersfield, Cal. BR/TR, 6'2", 190 lbs. Deb: 9/07/64 C

YEAR	TM/L	G	AB	R	H	2B	3B	HR	RBI	BB	SO	AVG	OBP	SLG	PRO	/A	BR	/A	PF	CHI	RC	TA	SB	CS	SBR	FR	POS	TPR
1964	LA-A	9	16	2	6	0	0	0	2	2	3	.375	.444	.375	.819	147	1	1	89	141	3	.800	0	0	0	0	/C1	0.1
1965	SF-N	40	67	5	19	4	0	1	7	12	14	.284	.392	.388	.780	109	2	1	111	100	10	.745	0	0	0	-0	C/1	0.1
1966	SF-N	18	23	2	7	2	0	0	1	4	5	.304	.407	.391	.799	127	1	1	97	47	4	.813	0	0	0	0	/1	0.1
1967	SF-N	73	153	24	42	6	0	6	26	27	37	.275	.387	.431	.818	133	8	8	101	128	27	.825	0	0	0	-1	1/CO	0.6
1968	SF-N	90	224	14	52	10	2	4	34	41	61	.232	.353	.348	.702	114	5	5	98	159	29	.674	0	0	0	-4	C1	0.4
1969	SF-N	69	194	18	38	4	0	7	34	48	58	.196	.355	.325	.680	91	-0	-1	101	162	25	.685	0	0	0	-7	C/1	-0.3
1970	Mon-N	17	43	4	14	2	0	0	7	14	14	.326	.491	.372	.863	135	3	3	100	170	9	1.000	0	0	0	1	C/1	0.4
	Chi-N	66	178	19	43	12	1	2	22	31	48	.242	.354	.354	.708	75	-2	-7	120	124	23	.667	0	0	0	-3	C/1	-0.6
	Yr	83	221	23	57	14	1	2	29	45	62	.258	.383	.357	.741	86	2	-3	116	135	33	.729	0	0	0	-2		-0.2
1971	Hou-N	69	174	16	48	8	1	1	16	35	39	.276	.403	.351	.753	124	6	7	93	102	28	.766	0	1	-1	-2	C/1	0.6
1972	Hou-N	10	25	2	5	3	0	0	0	5	5	.200	.333	.320	.653	81	-0	-1	106	0	3	.619	0	0	0	-1	C	0.0
	Cal-A	22	45	4	13	0	1	1	5	5	11	.289	.360	.400	.760	142	1	2	88	99	7	.697	0	0	0	-1	C	0.1
Total	9	483	1142	110	287	51	5	22	154	224	295	.251	.376	.363	.738	108	25	21	102	130	168	.749	0	1	-1	-18	C/1O	1.5

YEAR	TM/L	G	AB	R	H	2B	3B	HR	RBI	BB	SO	AVG	OBP	SLG	PRO	/A	BR	/A	PF	CHI	RC	TA	SB	CS	SBR	FR	POS	TPR
■ **JIM HIBBS** Hibbs, James Kerr b: 9/10/44, Klamath Falls, Ore. BR/TR, 6', 190 lbs. Deb: 4/12/67																												
1967	Cal-A	3	3	0	0	0	0	0	0	0	2	.000	.000	.000	.000	-99	-1	-1	96	0	0	.000	0	0	0	0	H	0.0
■ **EDDIE HICKEY** Hickey, Edward A. b: 8/18/1872, Cleveland, Ohio d: 3/25/41, Tacoma, Wash. Deb: 9/03/01																												
1901	Chi-N	10	37	4	6	0	0	0	3	2		.162	.205	.162	.367	8	-4	-4	100	171	1	.290	1			-1	3	-0.3
■ **MIKE HICKEY** Hickey, Michael Francis b: 12/25/1871, Chicopee, Mass. d: 6/11/18, Springfield, Mass BR/TR, 5'10.5", 150 lbs. Deb: 9/14/1899																												
1899	Bos-N	1	3	0	1	0	0	0	0	0		.333	.333	.333	.667	81	-0	-0	105	0	0	.500	0			0	/2	0.0
■ **CHARLIE HICKMAN** Hickman, Charles Taylor "Cheerful Charlie" or "Piano Legs" b: 5/4/1876, Taylortown, Pa. d: 4/19/34, Morgantown, W.Va. BR/TR, 5'11.5", 215 lbs. Deb: 9/08/1897																												
1897	Bos-N	2	3	1	2	0	0	1	2	0		.667	.667	1.667	2.333	475	2	2	107	73	3	5.000	0			0	/P	0.0
1898	Bos-N	19	58	4	15	2	0	0	7	1		.259	.271	.293	.564	61	-3	-3	104	125	5	.419	0			0	/O1P	-0.2
1899	Bos-N	19	63	15	25	2	7	0	15	2		.397	.433	.651	1.084	189	8	7	105	112	19	1.211	1			0	P/O1	0.0
1900	NY-N	127	473	65	148	19	17	9	91	17		.313	.337	.482	.819	130	14	16	97	114	82	.785	10			-8	*3/O	0.8
1901	NY-N	112	406	44	113	20	6	4	62	15		.278	.304	.387	.691	111	-0	4	91	125	50	.604	5			0	OS3/P21	0.4
1902	Bos-A	28	108	13	32	6	2	3	16	3		.296	.315	.472	.788	118	2	2	99	90	17	.724	1			-3	O	-0.1
	Cle-A	102	426	60	161	30	11	8	94	12		.378	.395	.559	.954	170	34	36	97	114	100	.974	8			-6	1/2P	3.0
	Yr	130	534	73	**193**	36	13	11	110	15		.361	.379	.541	.920	159	36	38	97	109	116	.918	9			-8		2.9
1903	Cle-A	131	522	64	154	31	11	12	97	17		.295	.317	.466	.783	139	19	22	96	120	84	.745	14			-6	*1/2	1.7
1904	Cle-A	86	337	34	97	22	10	4	45	13		.288	.314	.448	.762	140	14	14	102	99	52	.721	9			0	21/O	1.6
	Det-A	42	144	18	35	6	6	2	22	11		.243	.297	.410	.706	130	4	4	96	129	19	.670	3			3	1	0.9
	Yr	128	481	52	132	28	16	6	67	24		.274	.309	.437	.746	137	18	18	100	109	70	.705	12			3		2.5
1905	Det-A	59	213	21	47	12	3	2	20	12		.221	.262	.333	.596	92	-3	-2	98	98	20	.518	3			4	O1	0.0
	Was-A	88	360	48	112	25	9	2	46	9		.311	.328	.447	.775	141	17	15	104	85	55	.698	3			2	2/1	1.8
	Yr	147	573	69	159	37	12	4	66	21		.277	.303	.405	.708	124	14	13	102	91	74	.626	6			6		1.8
1906	Was-A	120	451	53	128	25	5	9	57	14		.284	.305	.421	.727	141	12	17	91	101	62	.659	9			3	O1/32	1.7
1907	Was-A	60	198	20	55	9	4	1	23	14		.278	.325	.379	.704	140	5	8	90	108	26	.650	4			1	1O/2P	0.8
	Chi-A	21	23	1	6	2	0	0	1	4		.261	.370	.348	.718	127	1	1	104	45	3	.706	0			0	/O	0.1
	Yr	81	221	21	61	11	4	1	24	18		.276	.331	.376	.706	136	6	8	94	93	29	.656	4			1		0.9
1908	Cle-A	65	197	16	46	6	1	2	16	9		.234	.267	.305	.572	83	-3	-4	106	91	16	.470	2			2	O1/2	-0.4
Total	12	1081	3982	477	1176	217	92	59	614	153		.295	.322	.441	.762	133	123	137	97	108	612	.706	72			-8	1O23/PS	12.1
■ **JIM HICKMAN** Hickman, David James b: 5/19/1894, Johnson City, Tenn d: 12/30/58, Brooklyn, N.Y. BR/TR, 5'7.5", 170 lbs. Deb: 9/17/15																												
1915	Bal-F	20	81	7	17	4	1	1	7	4	14	.210	.247	.321	.568	63	-4	-4	107	84	8	.547	5			5	O	0.0
1916	Bro-N	9	5	3	1	0	0	0	0	2	0	.200	.429	.200	.629	93	0	0	103	0	1	1.000	1			-1	/O	0.0
1917	Bro-N	114	370	46	81	15	4	6	36	17	66	.219	.253	.330	.583	75	-11	-12	104	99	33	.529	14			14	*O	-0.1
1918	Bro-N	53	167	14	39	4	7	1	16	8	31	.234	.281	.359	.640	93	-2	-2	101	96	17	.594	5			-1	O	-0.5
1919	Bro-N	57	104	14	20	3	1	0	11	6	17	.192	.236	.240	.477	46	-7	-6	94	171	6	.393	2			-3	O	-1.1
Total	5	253	727	84	158	26	13	8	70	37	128	.217	.258	.322	.580	74	-23	-25	102	106	65	.529	27			14	O	-1.7
■ **JIM HICKMAN** Hickman, James Lucius b: 5/10/37, Henning, Tenn. BR/TR, 6'3", 192 lbs. Deb: 4/14/62																												
1962	NY-N	140	392	54	96	18	2	13	46	47	96	.245	.330	.401	.731	92	-3	-5	104	92	52	.683	4	4	-1	-9	*O	-2.1
1963	NY-N	146	494	53	113	21	6	17	51	44	120	.229	.293	.399	.692	98	-3	-2	99	88	56	.614	0	5	-3	-6	O3	-1.6
1964	NY-N	139	409	48	105	14	1	11	57	36	90	.257	.320	.377	.696	100	-2	-0	95	125	48	.608	0	1	-1	-4	*O/3	-0.8
1965	NY-N	141	369	32	87	18	0	15	40	27	76	.236	.291	.407	.698	94	-4	-4	100	85	42	.623	3	1	0	-6	O13	-1.5
1966	NY-N	58	160	15	38	7	0	4	16	13	34	.237	.299	.356	.655	86	-4	-3	94	97	17	.575	2	1	0	-0	O1	-0.5
1967	LA-N	65	98	7	16	6	1	0	10	14	28	.163	.268	.245	.513	54	-6	-5	88	173	6	.448	1	1	-0	-2	O/13P	-0.9
1968	Chi-N	75	188	22	42	6	3	5	23	18	38	.223	.295	.367	.662	87	-1	-3	112	115	20	.582	1	1	-0	-1	O	-0.8
1969	Chi-N	134	338	38	80	11	2	21	54	47	74	.237	.330	.467	.797	114	9	6	107	98	52	.775	2	1	0	-13	*O	-1.3
1970	Chi-N	149	514	102	162	33	4	32	115	93	99	.315	.421	.582	1.003	138	50	35	120	115	129	1.083	0	1	-1	-3	O1	2.2
1971	Chi-N	117	383	50	98	13	2	19	60	50	61	.256	.346	.449	.795	113	12	7	110	109	58	.755	0	1	-1	-3	O1	-0.2
1972	Chi-N	115	368	65	100	15	2	17	64	52	64	.272	.365	.462	.827	117	17	10	114	119	64	.822	3	1	0	0	1O	0.5
1973	Chi-N	92	201	27	49	1	2	3	20	42	42	.244	.374	.313	.688	85	-0	-2	108	112	25	.658	1	1	-0	1	1O	-0.4
1974	StL-N	50	60	5	16	0	0	2	4	8	10	.267	.353	.367	.720	98	0	0	104	55	7	.638	0	0	0	0	1/3	0.0
Total	13	1421	3974	518	1002	163	25	159	560	491	832	.252	.337	.426	.763	106	64	34	106	106	578	.740	17	19	-6	-46	O1/3P	-7.4
■ **BUDDY HICKS** Hicks, Clarence Walter b: 2/15/27, Belvedere, Cal. BB/TR, 5'10", 170 lbs. Deb: 4/17/56																												
1956	Det-A	26	47	5	10	2	0	0	5	3	2	.213	.260	.255	.515	38	-4	-4	97	156	3	.385	0	1	-1	-0	S/23	-0.2
■ **JIM HICKS** Hicks, James Edward b: 5/18/40, East Chicago, Ind. BR/TR, 6'3", 205 lbs. Deb: 10/02/64																												
1964	Chi-A	2	0	0	0	0	0	0	0	0	0	—	—	—	—	—	0	0	96	—	—	—	0	0	0	0	R	0.0
1965	Chi-A	13	19	2	5	1	0	1	2	0	9	.263	.263	.474	.737	114	-0	0	92	69	2	.600	0	0	0	-2	/O	-0.1
1966	Chi-A	18	26	3	5	0	1	0	1	1	5	.192	.222	.269	.491	43	-2	-2	94	60	1	.364	0	0	0	-1	O/1	-0.3
1969	StL-N	19	44	5	8	0	2	1	3	4	14	.182	.250	.341	.591	64	-2	-2	100	67	4	.528	0	0	0	1	O	-0.2
	Cal-A	37	48	6	4	0	0	3	8	13	18	.083	.279	.271	.550	55	-3	-3	99	146	4	.578	0	1	-1	-2	O/1	-0.6
1970	Cal-A	4	4	0	1	0	0	0	0	0	2	.250	.250	.250	.500	42	-0	-0	92	0	0	.333	0	0	0	0	H	0.0
Total	5	93	141	16	23	1	3	5	14	18	48	.163	.258	.319	.577	63	-8	-7	97	95	15	.529	0	1	-1	-4	/O1	-1.2
■ **NAT HICKS** Hicks, Nathaniel Woodhull b: 4/19/1845, Hempstead, N.Y. d: 4/21/07, Hoboken, N.J. BR/TR, 6'1", 186 lbs. Deb: 4/22/1872 M																												
1872	Mut-n	56	276	54	85							.308															*C/O	
1873	Mut-n	28	132	12	28							.212															C	
1874	Phi-n	58	284	51	73							.257															*C/O	
1875	Mut-n	62	270	32	63							.233															*C/OM	
1876	NY-N	45	188	20	44	4	1	0	15	3	4	.234	.246	.266	.512	81	-6	-2	87	107	13	.368				-1	C	0.0
1877	Cin-N	8	32	3	6	0	0	0	3	1	2	.188	.212	.188	.400	33	-3	-2	82	173	1	.269				0	/C	-0.1
Total	4 n	204	962	149	249							.259															/C	
Total	2	53	220	23	50	4	1	0	18	4	6	.227	.241	.255	.496	74	-8	-4	86	117	14	.353				-1	C/O	-0.1
■ **JOE HICKS** Hicks, William Joseph b: 4/7/33, Ivy, Va. BL/TR, 6', 180 lbs. Deb: 9/18/59																												
1959	Chi-A	6	7	0	3	0	0	0	0	1	1	.429	.500	.429	.929	163	1	1	97	0	1	.800	0	1	-1	-0	/O	0.0
1960	Chi-A	36	47	3	9	1	0	0	2	6	3	.191	.296	.213	.509	40	-4	-4	101	78	3	.425	0	1	-1	-3	O	-0.7
1961	Was-A	12	29	2	5	0	0	1	1	0	4	.172	.172	.276	.448	19	-3	-3	95	36	1	.320	0	1	-1	1	/O	-0.3
1962	Was-A	102	174	20	39	4	2	6	14	15	34	.224	.286	.374	.659	75	-6	-6	101	67	19	.597	3	1	0	-2	O	-0.9
1963	NY-N	56	159	16	36	6	1	5	22	7	31	.226	.272	.371	.643	84	-4	-4	99	125	16	.548	0	2	-1	1	O	-0.6
Total	5	212	416	41	92	11	3	12	39	29	73	.221	.278	.349	.627	72	-17	-17	100	87	40	.547	3	6	-3	-4	O	-2.5
■ **MAHLON HIGBEE** Higbee, Mahlon Jesse b: 8/16/01, Louisville, Ky. d: 4/7/68, De Pauw, Ind. 5'11", 165 lbs. Deb: 9/27/22																												
1922	NY-N	3	10	2	4	0	0	1	5	0	2	.400	.400	.700	1.100	172	1	1	104	175	3	1.167	0	0	0	-1	/O	0.0
■ **HIGBY** Higby Deb:9/18/1872																												
1872	Atl-n	1	4	0	0							.000															/O	
■ **BILL HIGDON** Higdon, William Travis b: 4/27/24, Camp Hill, Ala. d: 8/30/86, Pascagoula, Miss. BL/TR, 6'1", 193 lbs. Deb: 9/10/49																												
1949	Chi-A	11	23	3	7	3	0	0	1	6	3	.304	.448	.435	.883	137	1	2	98	34	6	1.063	1	0	0	-0	/O	0.1
■ **MIKE HIGGINS** Higgins, Michael Franklin "Pinky" b: 5/27/09, Red Oak, Tex. d: 3/21/69, Dallas, Tex. BR/TR, 6'1", 185 lbs. Deb: 6/25/30 M																												
1930	Phi-A	14	24	1	6	2	0	0	0	4	5	.250	.357	.333	.690	77	-1	-1	99	0	3	.667	0	0	0	-0	/32S	0.0
1933	Phi-A	152	567	85	178	35	11	13	99	61	53	.314	.383	.483	.866	140	22	29	92	108	104	.856	2	7	-4	-5	*3	3.0
1934	Phi-A	144	543	89	179	37	6	16	90	56	70	.330	.392	.508	.901	135	24	26	97	98	110	.929	9	3	1	-18	*3	0.8
1935	Phi-A	133	524	69	155	32	4	23	94	42	62	.296	.350	.504	.854	119	12	12	100	102	93	.846	6	2	1	-11	*3	0.2
1936	Phi-A	146	550	89	159	32	2	12	80	67	61	.289	.366	.420	.786	93	-6	-6	101	103	87	.772	7	4	-0	-11	*3	-1.3

YEAR	TM/L	G	AB	R	H	2B	3B	HR	RBI	BB	SO	AVG	OBP	SLG	PRO	/A	BR	/A	PF	CHI	RC	TA	SB	CS	SBR	FR	POS	TPR
1937	Bos-A	153	570	88	172	33	5	9	106	76	51	.302	.385	.425	.809	101	5	2	103	138	95	.795	2	6	-3	-17	*3	-1.3
1938	Bos-A	139	524	77	159	29	5	5	106	71	55	.303	.388	.406	.794	97	1	-1	102	**167**	85	.789	10	9	-2	-8	*3	-0.5
1939	Det-A	132	489	57	135	23	2	8	76	56	41	.276	.353	.380	.733	79	-9	-17	111	125	66	.675	7	4	-0	-8	*3	-2.5
1940	Det-A	131	480	70	130	24	3	13	76	61	31	.271	.357	.415	.771	89	-0	-8	111	118	73	.730	4	2	0	-6	*3	-0.5
1941	Det-A	147	540	79	161	28	3	11	73	67	45	.298	.378	.422	.800	105	10	5	106	101	86	.749	5	4	-1	-0	*3	1.1
1942	Det-A	143	499	65	133	34	2	11	79	72	21	.267	.362	.409	.771	103	12	4	113	120	72	.716	3	7	-3	-17	*3	-1.4
1943	Det-A	138	523	62	145	20	1	10	84	57	31	.277	.349	.377	.726	106	8	5	106	143	68	.642	2	5	-2	-9	*3	-0.4
1944	Det-A	148	543	79	161	32	4	7	76	81	34	.297	.392	.409	.801	122	23	20	105	120	91	.772	4	4	-1	-5	*3	1.3
1946	Det-A	18	60	2	13	3	1	0	8	5	6	.217	.277	.300	.577	56	-3	-4	108	169	5	.469	0	1	-1	-0	3	-0.2
	Bos-A	64	200	18	55	11	1	2	28	24	24	.275	.356	.370	.726	90	1	-2	114	133	26	.639	0	2	-1	-1	3	0.0
	Yr	82	260	20	68	14	2	2	36	29	30	.262	.338	.354	.692	83	-2	-6	113	143	31	.601	0	3	-2	-1		-0.2
Total	14	1802	6636	930	1941	375	50	140	1075	800	590	.292	.370	.427	.798	106	100	63	104	120	1065	.781	61	60	-18	-115	*3/2S	-1.7

■ BOB HIGGINS Higgins, Robert Stone b: 9/23/1886, Fayetteville, Tenn. d: 5/25/41, Chattanooga, Tenn. BR/TR, 5'8", 176 lbs. Deb: 9/13/09

YEAR	TM/L	G	AB	R	H	2B	3B	HR	RBI	BB	SO	AVG	OBP	SLG	PRO	/A	BR	/A	PF	CHI	RC	TA	SB	CS	SBR	FR	POS	TPR
1909	Cle-A	8	23	0	2	0	0	0	0	0		.087	.087	.087	.174	-44	-4	-4	102	0	0	.095	0			0	/C	-0.2
1911	Bro-N	4	10	1	3	0	0	0	2	1	0	.300	.364	.300	.664	89	-0	-0	97	225	1	.714	1			0	/C3	0.0
1912	Bro-N	1	2	0	0	0	0	0	0	0	1	.000	.000	.000	.000	-99	-1	-1	95	0	0	.000	0			0	/C	0.0
Total	3	13	35	1	5	0	0	0	2	1	1	.143	.167	.143	.310	-6	-4	-4	100	69	2	.233	1			0	/C3	-0.2

■ BILL HIGGINS Higgins, William Edward b: 9/8/1861, Wilmington, Del. d: 4/25/19, Wilmington, Del. TR, Deb: 1888

YEAR	TM/L	G	AB	R	H	2B	3B	HR	RBI	BB	SO	AVG	OBP	SLG	PRO	/A	BR	/A	PF	CHI	RC	TA	SB	CS	SBR	FR	POS	TPR
1888	Bos-N	14	54	5	10	1	0	0	4	1	3	.185	.200	.204	.404	29	-4	-4	106	133	2	.295	1			0	2	-0.3
1890	StL-a	67	258	39	65	6	2	0		24		.252	.316	.291	.606	70	-6	-12	116	0	27	.549	7			13	2	0.3
	Syr-a	1	4	1	1	1	0	0		0		.250	.250	.500	.750	135	0	0	90	0	1	.667	0			1	/2	0.1
	Yr	68	262	40	66	7	2	0	0	24		.252	.315	.294	.609	71	-6	-12	116	0	27	.551	7			14		0.4
Total	2	82	316	45	76	8	2	0	4	25	3	.241	.296	.278	.575	65	-10	-17	114	21	29	.504	8			14	/2	0.1

■ ANDY HIGH High, Andrew Aird "Handy Andy" b: 11/21/1897, Ava, Ill. d: 2/22/81, Toledo, Ohio BL/TR, 5'6", 155 lbs. Deb: 4/12/22 C

YEAR	TM/L	G	AB	R	H	2B	3B	HR	RBI	BB	SO	AVG	OBP	SLG	PRO	/A	BR	/A	PF	CHI	RC	TA	SB	CS	SBR	FR	POS	TPR
1922	Bro-N	153	579	82	164	27	10	6	65	59	26	.283	.354	.396	.749	98	-6	-1	95	97	80	.691	3	12	-6	-1	*3S/2	0.2
1923	Bro-N	123	426	51	115	23	9	3	37	47	13	.270	.344	.387	.731	95	-4	-3	98	76	60	.696	4	1	1	1	3S/2	0.4
1924	Bro-N	144	582	98	191	26	13	6	61	57	16	.328	.390	.448	.838	125	21	22	99	70	102	.814	3	6	-3	-11	*2S/3	0.1
1925	Bro-N	44	115	11	23	4	1	0	6	14	5	.200	.287	.252	.539	42	-10	-9	94	74	9	.462	0	1	-1	-1	23/S	-0.9
	Bos-N	60	219	31	63	11	1	4	28	24	2	.288	.361	.402	.762	101	-1	1	94	101	32	.720	3	5	-2	-3	3/2	0.0
	Yr	104	334	42	86	15	2	4	34	38	7	.257	.335	.350	.685	80	-12	-9	94	90	40	.626	3	6	-3	-4		-0.9
1926	Bos-N	130	476	55	141	17	10	2	66	39	9	.296	.351	.387	.737	114	-1	8	86	123	64	.681	4			-11	32	0.0
1927	Bos-N	113	384	59	116	15	9	4	46	26	11	.302	.350	.419	.769	113	2	6	93	93	55	.720	4			-17	3/2S	-0.5
1928	StL-N	111	368	58	105	14	3	6	37	37	10	.285	.355	.389	.744	94	-3	-3	100	82	51	.703	2			-9	32	-0.9
1929	StL-N	146	603	95	178	32	4	10	63	38	18	.295	.340	.411	.751	87	-15	-13	98	75	82	.696	7			-10	*32	-1.1
1930	StL-N	72	215	34	60	12	2	2	29	23	6	.279	.349	.381	.730	73	-8	-10	105	114	29	.684	1			-6	3/2	-1.2
1931	StL-N	63	131	20	35	6	1	0	19	24	4	.267	.389	.328	.717	89	0	-1	107	157	19	.719	0			0	32	0.1
1932	Cin-N	84	191	16	36	4	2	0	12	23	6	.188	.276	.230	.506	39	-16	-15	96	101	14	.439	1			-4	32	-1.3
1933	Cin-N	24	43	4	9	2	0	1	6	5	1	.209	.292	.326	.617	77	-1	-1	99	133	4	.528	0			-0	3/2	0.0
1934	Phi-N	47	68	4	14	2	0	0	7	9	3	.206	.299	.235	.534	41	-5	-6	108	158	4	.433	1			-2	3/2	-0.5
Total	13	1314	4400	618	1250	195	65	44	482	425	130	.284	.350	.388	.738	95	-47	-26	97	94	603	.687	33	25		-72	32/S	-5.6

■ CHARLIE HIGH High, Charles Edwin b: 12/1/1898, Ava, Ill. d: 9/11/60, Oak Grove, Ore. BL/TR, 5'9", 170 lbs. Deb: 9/05/19

YEAR	TM/L	G	AB	R	H	2B	3B	HR	RBI	BB	SO	AVG	OBP	SLG	PRO	/A	BR	/A	PF	CHI	RC	TA	SB	CS	SBR	FR	POS	TPR
1919	Phi-A	11	29	2	2	0	0	0	1	3	4	.069	.182	.069	.251	-27	-5	-5	106	181	1	.296	2			-1	/O	-0.6
1920	Phi-A	17	65	7	20	2	1	1	6	3	6	.308	.375	.415	.790	116	1	2	94	67	10	.723	0	2	-1	-1	O	-0.2
Total	2	28	94	9	22	2	1	1	7	6	10	.234	.314	.309	.623	70	-4	-4	98	103	11	.568	2	2		-2	/O	-0.8

■ HUGH HIGH High, Hugh Jenken "Bunny" b: 10/24/1887, Pottstown, Pa. d: 11/16/62, St.Louis, Mo. BL/TL, 5'7.5", 155 lbs. Deb: 4/11/13

YEAR	TM/L	G	AB	R	H	2B	3B	HR	RBI	BB	SO	AVG	OBP	SLG	PRO	/A	BR	/A	PF	CHI	RC	TA	SB	CS	SBR	FR	POS	TPR
1913	Det-A	87	183	18	42	6	1	0	16	28	24	.230	.335	.273	.608	79	-4	-4	99	114	18	.603	6			1	O	-0.4
1914	Det-A	80	184	25	49	5	3	0	17	26	21	.266	.363	.326	.689	105	3	2	102	106	24	.674	7	6	-2	-5	O	-0.8
1915	NY-A	119	427	51	110	19	7	1	43	62	47	.258	.356	.342	.698	111	6	7	98	104	56	.706	22	13	-1	-7	*O	-0.8
1916	NY-A	116	377	44	99	13	4	1	28	47	44	.263	.349	.326	.675	101	2	2	101	81	51	.669	13			-1	*O	-0.5
1917	NY-A	103	365	37	86	11	6	1	19	48	31	.236	.329	.307	.636	88	-1	-4	107	63	39	.613	8			2	*O	-0.8
1918	NY-A	7	10	1	0	0	0	0	0	1	1	.000	.091	.000	.091	-77	-2	-2	95	0	0	.100	0			0	/O	-0.1
Total	6	512	1546	176	386	54	21	3	123	212	168	.250	.345	.318	.662	97	4	1	102	89	189	.654	56	19		-9	O	-3.4

■ DICK HIGHAM Higham, Richard b: 1852, England d: 3/18/05, Chicago, Ill. BL/TR, Deb: 6/01/1871 MU

YEAR	TM/L	G	AB	R	H	2B	3B	HR	RBI	BB	SO	AVG	OBP	SLG	PRO	/A	BR	/A	PF	CHI	RC	TA	SB	CS	SBR	FR	POS	TPR
1871	Mut-n	21	97	21	32							.330															2/OC3	
1872	Bal-n	46	242	67	82							.339															CO/21	
1873	Mut-n	49	247	57	75							.304															O2C/3	
1874	Mut-n	65	342	58	87							.254															*CO/2M	
1875	Chi-n	43	214	44	50							.234															C2/O	
	Mut-n	15	66	11	22							.333															/C2O1	
	Yr	58	280	55	72							.257																
1876	Har-N	67	312	59	102	**21**	2	0	35	2	7	.327	.331	.407	.738	134	14	10	108	80	43	.614				1	*OC/S2	0.9
1878	Pro-N	62	281	**60**	90	**22**	1	1	29	5	16	.320	.332	.416	.749	148	13	14	98	71	40	.639				1	*O/C	0.9
1880	Tro-N	1	5	1	1	0	0	0	0	0	0	.200	.200	.200	.400	33	-0	-0	110	0	0	.250				0	/OC	0.0
Total	5 n	239	1208	258	348							.288															/OC	
Total	3	130	598	120	193	43	3	1	64	7	23	.323	.331	.410	.740	139	26	23	103	75	83	.622				2	OC/213S	1.8

■ JOHN HILAND Hiland, John William b: 1861, Philadelphia, Pa. d: 4/10/01, Philadelphia, Pa. TL, Deb: 1885

YEAR	TM/L	G	AB	R	H	2B	3B	HR	RBI	BB	SO	AVG	OBP	SLG	PRO	/A	BR	/A	PF	CHI	RC	TA	SB	CS	SBR	FR	POS	TPR
1885	Phi-N	3	9	0	0	0	0	0	0	0	4	.000	.000	.000	.000	-97	-2	-2	104	0	0	.000				0	/2	-0.1

■ GEORGE HILDEBRAND Hildebrand, George Albert b: 9/6/1878, San Francisco, Cal d: 5/30/60, Woodland Hills, Cal. 5'8", 170 lbs. Deb: 4/17/02 U

YEAR	TM/L	G	AB	R	H	2B	3B	HR	RBI	BB	SO	AVG	OBP	SLG	PRO	/A	BR	/A	PF	CHI	RC	TA	SB	CS	SBR	FR	POS	TPR
1902	Bro-N	11	41	3	9	1	0	0	5	3		.220	.273	.244	.517	65	-2	-2	95	183	3	.406	0			1	O	-0.1

■ PALMER HILDEBRAND Hildebrand, Palmer Marion "Pete" b: 12/23/1884, Shauck, Ohio d: 1/25/60, N.Canton, Ohio BR/TR, 5'10", 170 lbs. Deb: 5/14/13

YEAR	TM/L	G	AB	R	H	2B	3B	HR	RBI	BB	SO	AVG	OBP	SLG	PRO	/A	BR	/A	PF	CHI	RC	TA	SB	CS	SBR	FR	POS	TPR
1913	StL-N	26	55	3	9	2	0	0	1	1	10	.164	.207	.200	.407	18	-6	-6	93	33	2	.326	1			1	C/O	-0.2

■ R. E. HILDEBRAND Hildebrand, R. E. Deb: 8/29/02

YEAR	TM/L	G	AB	R	H	2B	3B	HR	RBI	BB	SO	AVG	OBP	SLG	PRO	/A	BR	/A	PF	CHI	RC	TA	SB	CS	SBR	FR	POS	TPR
1902	Chi-N	1	4	1	0	0	0	0	0	1		.000	.200	.000	.200	-38	-1	-1	96	0	0	.250	0			0	/O	0.0

■ BELDEN HILL Hill, Belden L. b: 8/24/1864, Kewanee, Ill. d: 10/22/34, Cedar Rapids, Iowa BR/TR, 6', Deb: 8/27/1890

YEAR	TM/L	G	AB	R	H	2B	3B	HR	RBI	BB	SO	AVG	OBP	SLG	PRO	/A	BR	/A	PF	CHI	RC	TA	SB	CS	SBR	FR	POS	TPR
1890	BB-a	9	30	3	5	2	0	0		3		.167	.306	.233	.539	61	-1	-1	100	0	4	.760	6			0	/3	0.0

■ DON HILL Hill, Donald Earl b: 11/12/60, Pomona, Cal. BB/TR, 5'10", 160 lbs. Deb: 7/25/83

YEAR	TM/L	G	AB	R	H	2B	3B	HR	RBI	BB	SO	AVG	OBP	SLG	PRO	/A	BR	/A	PF	CHI	RC	TA	SB	CS	SBR	FR	POS	TPR
1983	Oak-A	53	158	20	42	7	0	2	15	4	21	.266	.284	.348	.632	76	-6	-5	96	96	15	.500	1	1	-0	-5	S	-0.6
1984	Oak-A	73	174	21	40	6	0	2	16	5	12	.230	.251	.299	.550	56	-12	-10	92	110	13	.420	1	1	-0	-6	S/23D	-1.0
1985	Oak-A	123	393	45	112	13	2	3	48	23	33	.285	.325	.351	.676	92	-8	-4	93	129	45	.582	9	4	0	-22	*2	-2.1
1986	Oak-A	108	339	37	96	16	2	4	29	23	38	.283	.329	.378	.706	99	-3	-1	94	82	41	.614	5	2	0	0	23/SD	0.3
1987	Chi-A	111	410	57	98	14	6	9	46	30	35	.239	.293	.368	.661	69	-15	-20	109	105	43	.567	1	0	0	-6	23/D	-1.9
1988	Chi-A	83	221	17	48	6	1	2	20	26	32	.217	.300	.281	.580	65	-10	-10	97	117	20	.514	3	1	0	2	23/D	-0.3
Total	6	551	1695	197	436	62	11	22	174	111	171	.257	.303	.346	.649	79	-54	-49	98	107	177	.565	20	9	1	-37	2S/3D	-5.6

■ HERMAN HILL Hill, Herman Alexander b: 10/12/45, Tuskegee, Ala. d: 12/14/70, Valencia, Venez. BL/TR, 6'2", 190 lbs. Deb: 9/02/69

YEAR	TM/L	G	AB	R	H	2B	3B	HR	RBI	BB	SO	AVG	OBP	SLG	PRO	/A	BR	/A	PF	CHI	RC	TA	SB	CS	SBR	FR	POS	TPR
1969	Min-A	16	2	4	0	0	0	0	0	0	1	.000	.000	.000	.000	-98	-1	-1	102	0	-1	.250	1	2	-1	-1	/O	-0.1
1970	Min-A	27	22	8	2	0	0	0	0	0	6	.091	.091	.091	.182	-51	-4	-4	98	0	0	.100	0	0	0	-2	O	-0.6
Total	2	43	24	12	2	0	0	0	0	0	7	.083	.083	.083	.167	-55	-5	-5	99	0	-0	.125	1	2	-1	-2	/O	-0.7

YEAR	TM/L	G	AB	R	H	2B	3B	HR	RBI	BB	SO	AVG	OBP	SLG	PRO	/A	BR	/A	PF	CHI	RC	TA	SB	CS	SBR	FR	POS	TPR
■ HUGH HILL	Hill, Hugh Ellis b: 7/21/1879, Ringgold, Ga. d: 9/6/58, Cincinnati, Ohio BL/TR, 5'11.5", 168 lbs. Deb: 5/01/03																											
1903	Cle-A	1	1	0	0	0	0	0	0	0		.000	.000	.000	.000	-99	-0	-0	96	0	0	.000	0			0	H	0.0
1904	StL-N	23	93	13	21	2	1	3	4	2		.226	.242	.366	.608	89	-2	-2	99	30	9	.542	3			-3	O	-0.5
Total	2	24	94	13	21	2	1	3	4	2		.223	.240	.362	.601	87	-2	-2	99	30	9	.534	3			-3	/O	-0.5
■ HUNTER HILL	Hill, Hunter Benjamin b: 6/21/1879, Austin, Tex. d: 2/22/59, Austin, Tex. BR/TR, Deb: 03																											
1903	StL-A	86	317	30	77	11	3	0	25	8		.243	.262	.297	.558	72	-12	-10	95	98	26	.433	2			2	3	-0.8
1904	StL-A	58	219	19	47	3	0	0	14	6		.215	.236	.228	.464	51	-12	-11	95	107	13	.349	4			-9	3/O	-2.0
	Was-A	77	290	18	57	6	1	0	17	11		.197	.226	.224	.450	48	-18	-15	93	103	17	.369	10			0	3/O	-1.4
	Yr	135	509	37	104	9	1	0	31	17		.204	.230	.226	.456	49	-30	-27	94	105	30	.360	14			-8		-3.4
1905	Was-A	104	374	37	78	12	1	1	24	32		.209	.271	.254	.525	66	-12	-14	104	93	29	.463	10			-2	*3	-1.3
Total	3	325	1200	104	259	32	5	1	80	57		.216	.251	.253	.505	61	-55	-51	97	99	85	.411	26			-8	3/O	-5.5
■ JESSE HILL	Hill, Jesse Terrill b: 1/20/07, Yates, Mo. BR/TR, 5'9", 165 lbs. Deb: 4/17/35																											
1935	NY-A	107	392	69	115	20	3	4	33	42	32	.293	.362	.390	.752	102	-3	1	93	69	58	.744	14	4	2	3	O	0.5
1936	Was-A	85	233	50	71	19	5	0	34	29	23	.305	.384	.429	.813	103	1	2	98	110	42	.870	11	0	3	-10	O	-0.5
1937	Was-A	33	92	24	20	2	1	1	4	13	16	.217	.314	.293	.608	57	-6	-6	94	46	9	.575	2	1	0	4	O	-0.1
	Phi-A	70	242	32	71	12	3	1	37	31	20	.293	.374	.380	.754	96	-3	-0	94	136	38	.799	16	3	3	-8	O	-0.7
	Yr	103	334	56	91	14	4	2	41	44	36	.272	.357	.356	.713	85	-9	-6	94	107	47	.733	18	4	3	-4		-0.8
Total	3	295	959	175	277	53	12	6	108	115	91	.289	.366	.388	.753	96	-11	-3	94	94	147	.770	43	8	8	-11	O	-0.8
■ MARC HILL	Hill, Marc Kevin b: 2/18/52, Elsberry, Mo. BR/TR, 6'3", 205 lbs. Deb: 9/28/73 C																											
1973	StL-N	1	3	0	0	0	0	0	0	0	1	.000	.000	.000	.000	-99	-1	-1	91	0	0	.000	0	0	0	0	/C	0.0
1974	StL-N	10	21	2	5	1	0	0	2	4	5	.238	.360	.286	.646	79	-0	-0	104	129	2	.588	0	0	0	1	/C	0.1
1975	SF-N	72	182	14	39	4	0	5	23	25	27	.214	.309	.319	.628	73	-6	-6	102	122	18	.553	0	0	0	-2	C/3	-0.6
1976	SF-N	54	131	11	24	5	0	3	15	10	19	.183	.246	.290	.537	50	-9	-9	103	123	9	.441	0	1	-1	-4	C/1	-1.1
1977	SF-N	108	320	28	80	10	0	9	50	34	34	.250	.322	.366	.688	81	-7	-9	104	139	36	.597	0	1	-1	-7	*C	-1.8
1978	SF-N	117	358	20	87	15	1	3	36	45	39	.243	.329	.316	.645	88	-8	-4	92	117	36	.561	1	2	-1	3	*C/1	0.1
1979	SF-N	63	169	20	35	3	0	3	15	26	25	.207	.313	.278	.591	68	-8	-6	92	106	15	.521	0	1	-1	-2	C/1	-0.7
1980	SF-N	17	41	1	7	2	0	0	0	1	7	.171	.190	.220	.410	15	-5	-5	96	0	2	.286	0	0	0	0	C	-0.3
	Sea-A	29	70	8	16	2	1	2	9	3	10	.229	.260	.371	.632	69	-3	-3	103	110	6	.509	0	0	0	-3	C	-0.4
1981	Chi-A	16	6	0	0	0	0	0	0	0	1	.000	.000	.000	.000	-99	-2	-2	100	0	0	.000	0	0	0	-0	C/13	0.0
1982	Chi-A	53	88	9	23	2	0	3	13	6	13	.261	.316	.386	.702	94	-1	-1	97	121	10	.594	0	0	0	-1	C/13	0.1
1983	Chi-A	58	133	11	30	6	0	1	11	9	24	.226	.275	.293	.568	55	-8	-8	103	102	10	.444	0	1	-1	-2	C/1D	-0.8
1984	Chi-A	77	193	15	45	10	1	5	20	9	26	.233	.275	.373	.648	70	-6	-9	111	92	16	.516	0	1	-1	-7	C/1	-1.1
1985	Chi-A	40	75	5	10	2	0	0	4	12	9	.133	.253	.160	.413	16	-8	-8	100	132	4	.358	0	0	0	1	C/3	-0.5
1986	Chi-A	22	19	2	3	0	0	0	0	1	3	.158	.238	.158	.396	11	-2	-2	101	0	1	.313	0	0	0	0	C	0.0
Total	14	737	1809	146	404	62	3	34	198	185	243	.223	.298	.317	.615	69	-75	-75	100	114	165	.542	1	7	-4	-23	C/13D	-7.0
■ OLIVER HILL	Hill, Oliver Clinton b: 10/16/12, Powder Springs, Ga d: 9/20/70, Decatur, Ga. BL/TR, 5'11", 178 lbs. Deb: 4/19/39																											
1939	Bos-N	2	2	1	1	1	0	0	0	0	0	.500	.500	1.000	1.500	321	1	1	92	0	1	2.000	0			0	H	0.1
■ HOMER HILLEBRAND	Hillebrand, Homer Hiller Henry "Doc" b: 10/10/1879, Freeport, Ill. d: 1/20/74, Elsinore, Cal. 5'8", 165 lbs. Deb: 4/24/05																											
1905	Pit-N	39	110	9	26	3	2	0	7	6		.236	.276	.300	.576	70	-4	-4	104	74	10	.476	1			-2	1P/OC	-0.4
1906	Pit-N	7	21	1	5	1	0	0	3	1		.238	.273	.286	.558	73	-1	-1	104	182	2	.438	0			1	/P	0.0
1908	Pit-N	1	0	0	0	0	0	0	0	0		—	—	—	—	—	0	0	95	—	—	—	0			0	/P	0.0
Total	3	47	131	10	31	4	2	0	10	7		.237	.275	.298	.573	71	-4	-5	104	91	13	.470	1			-1	/P1OC	-0.4
■ CHUCK HILLER	Hiller, Charles Joseph b: 10/1/34, Johnsburg, Ill. BL/TR, 5'11", 170 lbs. Deb: 4/11/61 C																											
1961	SF-N	70	240	38	57	12	1	2	12	32	30	.237	.330	.321	.651	75	-8	-8	98	59	28	.606	4	4	-1	-14	2	-1.4
1962	SF-N	161	602	94	166	22	2	3	48	55	49	.276	.344	.334	.678	82	-13	-14	101	95	71	.596	5	4	-1	-15	*2	-1.5
1963	SF-N	111	417	44	93	10	2	6	33	20	23	.223	.262	.300	.562	64	-21	-19	96	99	31	.442	3	2	-0	-12	*2	-2.6
1964	SF-N	80	205	21	37	8	1	1	17	17	23	.180	.247	.244	.491	39	-16	-17	100	132	13	.401	1	1	-0	5	2/3	-0.7
1965	SF-N	7	7	1	1	0	0	1	1	0	1	.143	.143	.571	.714	82	-0	-0	111	59	0	.571	0	0	0	0	/2	0.0
	NY-N	100	286	24	68	11	1	5	21	14	24	.238	.276	.336	.611	71	-11	-11	100	78	25	.498	1	1	-0	-2	2/O3	-1.0
	Yr	107	293	25	69	11	1	6	22	14	25	.235	.273	.341	.614	71	-11	-12	101	78	26	.502	1	1	-0	-2		-1.0
1966	NY-N	108	254	25	71	8	2	2	14	15	22	.280	.332	.350	.683	96	-3	-1	94	62	31	.589	0	0	0	4	23/O	0.5
1967	NY-N	25	54	0	5	3	0	0	3	2	11	.093	.125	.148	.273	-22	-9	-8	99	155	1	.200	0	0	0	0	2	-0.7
	Phi-N	31	43	4	13	1	0	0	2	2	4	.302	.333	.326	.659	86	-1	-1	104	59	4	.500	0	2	-1	-0	/2	-0.1
	Yr	56	97	4	18	4	0	0	5	4	15	.186	.218	.227	.445	27	-9	-9	102	105	5	.321	0	2	-1	-0		-0.8
1968	Pit-N	11	13	2	5	1	0	0	1	0	0	.385	.385	.462	.846	152	1	1	101	70	2	.667	0	0	0	0	/2	0.1
Total	8	704	2121	253	516	76	9	20	152	157	187	.243	.301	.316	.617	72	-81	-78	99	90	206	.530	14	14	-4	-34	2/3O	-7.4
■ HOB HILLER	Hiller, Harvey Max b: 5/12/1893, E.Mauch Chunk, Pa. d: 12/27/56, Leighton, Pa. BR/TR, 5'8", 162 lbs. Deb: 4/22/20																											
1920	Bos-A	17	29	4	5	1	1	0	2	2	5	.172	.226	.276	.502	34	-3	-3	96	88	1	.370	0	3	-2	1	/3S2O	-0.2
1921	Bos-A	1	1	0	0	0	0	0	0	0	0	.000	.000	.000	.000	-99	-0	-0	100	0	0	.000	0	0	0	0	H	0.0
Total	2	18	30	4	5	1	1	0	2	2	5	.167	.219	.267	.485	29	-3	-3	96	85	1	.357	0	3	-2	1	/3S2O	-0.2
■ ED HILLEY	Hilley, Edward Garfield "Whitey" b: 6/17/1879, Cleveland, Ohio d: 11/14/56, Cleveland, Ohio BR/TR, 5'10.5", 170 lbs. Deb: 03																											
1903	Phi-A	1	3	1	1	0	0	0	0	1		.333	.500	.333	.833	151	0	0	104	0	1	1.000	0			0	/3	0.0
■ MACK HILLIS	Hillis, Malcolm David b: 7/23/01, Cambridge, Mass. d: 6/16/61, Cambridge, Mass. BR/TR, 5'10", 165 lbs. Deb: 9/13/24																											
1924	NY-A	1	1	1	0	0	0	0	0	0	0	.000	.000	.000	.000	-99	-0	-0	99	0	0	.000	0	0	0	0	/2	0.0
1928	Pit-N	11	36	6	9	2	3	1	7	0	6	.250	.250	.556	.806	98	-0	-0	107	108	5	.778	1			-0	/23	0.0
Total	2	12	37	7	9	2	3	1	7	0	6	.243	.243	.541	.784	93	-0	-1	107	105	5	.750	1	0		-0	/23	0.0
■ PAT HILLY	Hilly, William Edward (born William Edward Hilgerink) b: 2/24/1887, Fostoria, Ohio d: 7/25/53, Eureka, Mo. BR/TR, 5'11", 180 lbs. Deb: 5/07/14																											
1914	Phi-N	8	10	2	3	0	0	0	1	1	5	.300	.364	.300	.664	98	0	0	100	121	1	.571	0			-1	/O	0.0
■ DAVE HILTON	Hilton, John David b: 9/15/50, Uvalde, Tex. BR/TR, 5'11", 191 lbs. Deb: 9/10/72 C																											
1972	SD-N	13	47	2	10	2	1	0	5	3	6	.213	.260	.298	.558	66	-3	-2	88	150	4	.486	1	0	0	-1	3	-0.2
1973	SD-N	70	234	21	46	9	0	5	16	19	35	.197	.260	.299	.559	58	-15	-13	94	77	18	.477	2	1	0	2	32	-1.1
1974	SD-N	74	217	17	52	8	2	1	12	13	28	.240	.283	.309	.591	70	-10	-9	93	66	17	.474	3	5	-2	-3	32	-1.4
1975	SD-N	4	8	0	0	0	0	0	0	0	0	.000	.000	.000	.000	-99	-2	-2	100	0	0	.000	0	0	0	0	/3	-0.1
Total	4	161	506	40	108	19	3	6	33	35	69	.213	.266	.298	.564	61	-30	-26	93	78	40	.477	6	6	-2	-2	3/2	-2.8
■ JACK HIMES	Himes, John Herb b: 9/22/1878, Bryan, Ohio d: 12/16/49, Joliet, Ill. BL/TR, 6'2", 180 lbs. Deb: 9/18/05																											
1905	StL-N	12	41	3	6	0	0	0	0	1		.146	.167	.146	.313	-6	-5	-5	91	0	1	.200	0			0	O	-0.4
1906	StL-N	40	155	10	42	5	2	0	14	7		.271	.302	.329	.632	98	-1	-1	101	96	17	.549	4			-1	O	-0.2
Total	2	52	196	13	48	5	2	0	14	8		.245	.275	.291	.565	77	-6	-5	99	76	18	.466	4			-0	/O	-0.6
■ HARRY HINCHMAN	Hinchman, Harry Sibley b: 8/4/1878, Philadelphia, Pa. d: 1/19/33, Toledo, Ohio BB/TR, 5'11", 165 lbs. Deb: 7/29/07																											
1907	Cle-A	15	51	3	11	3	1	0	9	5		.216	.286	.314	.599	100	-0	0	93	213	5	.575	2			3	2	0.3
■ BILL HINCHMAN	Hinchman, William White b: 4/4/1883, Philadelphia, Pa. d: 2/21/63, Columbus, Ohio BR/TR, 5'11", 190 lbs. Deb: 9/24/05 C																											
1905	Cin-N	17	51	10	13	4	1	0	10	13		.255	.406	.373	.779	131	3	3	103	187	10	.947	4			-3	O/31	0.0
1906	Cin-N	18	54	7	11	1	1	0	1	8		.204	.306	.259	.566	68	-1	-2	115	27	5	.558	2			2	O	0.0
1907	Cle-A	152	514	62	117	19	9	1	50	47		.228	.292	.305	.598	99	-4	0	93	118	52	.552	15			-2	*O/12	-1.0
1908	Cle-A	137	464	55	107	23	8	6	59	38		.231	.289	.353	.642	104	5	2	106	124	48	.591	9			-7	OS/1	-0.8
1909	Cle-A	139	457	57	118	20	13	2	53	41		.258	.331	.372	.703	119	11	10	102	118	62	.714	22			9	*O/S	1.6
1915	Pit-N	156	577	72	177	33	14	5	77	48	75	.307	.368	.438	.807	145	30	31	99	116	94	.782	17	17	-5	-3	*O	1.9

YEAR	TM/L	G	AB	R	H	2B	3B	HR	RBI	BB	SO	AVG	OBP	SLG	PRO	/A	BR	/A	PF	CHI	RC	TA	SB	CS	SBR	FR	POS	TPR
1916	Pit-N	152	555	64	175	18	**16**	4	76	54	61	.315	.378	.427	.805	140	31	28	105	128	96	.797	10			-7	*O1	1.7
1917	Pit-N	69	244	27	46	5	5	2	29	33	27	.189	.288	.275	.562	73	-7	-7	100	162	20	.535	5			-1	O1	-1.1
1918	Pit-N	50	111	10	26	5	2	0	13	15	8	.234	.336	.315	.651	93	0	-0	106	140	12	.624	1			-8	O/1	-1.1
1920	Pit-N	18	16	0	3	0	0	0	1	1	3	.188	.278	.188	.465	35	-1	-1	101	129	1	.385	0	0	0	0	H	0.0
Total	10	908	3043	364	793	128	69	20	369	298	174	.261	.331	.368	.699	117	67	63	101	125	398	.673	85	17		-21	O/1S32	1.2
■ **HUNKEY HINES**	Hines, Henry Fred b: 9/29/1867, Elgin, Ill. d: 1/2/28, Rockford, Ill. BR/TR, 5'7", 165 lbs. Deb: 5/16/1895																											
1895	Bro-N	2	8	3	2	0	0	0	1	2	0	.250	.400	.250	.650	77	-0	-0	94	121	1	.667	0			0	/O	0.0
■ **MIKE HINES**	Hines, Michael P. b: 1864, Ireland d: 3/14/10, New Bedford, Mass. BR/TL, 5'10", 176 lbs. Deb: 5/01/1883																											
1883	Bos-N	63	231	38	52	13	1	0	16	7	36	.225	.248	.290	.538	59	-10	-12	106	83	17	.413				5	C/O	-0.3
1884	Bos-N	35	132	16	23	3	0	0	3	3	24	.174	.193	.197	.390	23	-11	-11	98	40	5	.266				5	C	-0.2
1885	Bos-N	14	56	11	13	4	0	0	4	4	5	.232	.283	.304	.587	96	-1	-0	94	79	5	.488				0	O	0.0
	Bro-a	3	13	1	1	0	1	0		0		.077	.077	.231	.308	-5	-1	-2	104	0	0	.250				0	/C	0.0
	Pro-N	1	3	0	0	0	0	0	0	0	2	.000	.000	.000	.000	-99	-1	-1	91	0	0	.000				0	/C	0.0
1888	Bos-N	4	16	3	2	0	1	0	2	2	0	.125	.222	.250	.472	49	-1	-1	106	158	1	.429	0			0	/OC	0.0
Total	4	120	451	69	91	20	3	0	25	16	67	.202	.229	.259	.489	50	-25	-26	102	70	28	.369	0			10	/CO	-0.5
■ **PAUL HINES**	Hines, Paul A. b: 3/1/1852, Washington, D.C. d: 7/10/35, Hyattsville, Md. BR/TR, 5'9.5", 173 lbs. Deb: 4/20/1872																											
1872	Nat-n	11	49	10	14							.286															1/3	
1873	Nat-n	39	186	33	61							.328															*O/2C	
1874	Chi-n	59	283	47	78							.276															*O2/S	
1875	Chi-n	69	322	42	101							.314															O2	
1876	Chi-N	64	305	62	101	**21**	3	2	59	1	3	.331	.333	.439	.773	124	17	5	125	151	46	.662				4	*O/2	0.7
1877	Chi-N	60	261	44	73	11	7	0	23	1	8	.280	.282	.375	.658	107	1	2	98	84	28	.527				-4	*O2	-0.2
1878	Pro-N	62	257	42	92	13	4	**4**	**50**	2	10	**.358**	.363	**.486**	**.849**	181	**20**	21	98	131	**47**	**.770**				3	*O/S	1.7
1879	Pro-N	85	409	81	**146**	25	10	2	52	8	16	**.357**	.369	.482	.851	175	33	**32**	102	78	**75**	.779				5	*O	3.1
1880	Pro-N	85	374	64	115	20	2	3	35	13	17	.307	.331	.396	.726	151	17	19	96	70	50	.622				5	*O/21	2.1
1881	Pro-N	80	361	65	103	**27**	5	2	31	13	12	.285	.310	.404	.715	132	9	12	93	61	46	.616				-1	*O/21	0.9
1882	Pro-N	84	379	73	117	28	10	4	34	10	14	.309	.326	.467	.793	143	21	17	106	52	59	.714				-1	*O/1	1.4
1883	Pro-N	97	442	94	132	32	4	4	45	18	23	.299	.326	.416	.742	123	12	12	101	69	61	.652				1	*O/1	1.3
1884	Pro-N	114	490	94	148	**36**	10	3	41	44	28	.302	.360	.435	.794	146	28	27	102	55	78	.751				0	*O/1P	2.3
1885	Pro-N	98	411	63	111	20	4	1	35	19	18	.270	.302	.345	.648	119	4	9	91	72	44	.537				1	*O/1S32	0.7
1886	Was-N	121	487	80	152	30	8	9	56	35	21	.312	.358	.462	.820	158	27	32	94	63	90	.839	21			2	*O31/S2	3.1
1887	Was-N	123	478	83	147	32	5	10	72	48	24	.308	.380	.458	.838	140	23	27	95	86	103	.970	46			-13	*O/12S	1.2
1888	Ind-N	133	513	84	144	26	3	4	58	41	45	.281	.343	.366	.710	135	18	21	95	100	77	.726	31			-8	*O/1S	1.1
1889	Ind-N	121	486	77	148	27	1	6	72	49	22	.305	.374	.401	.775	109	13	6	109	107	88	.837	34			1	*1O	-0.1
1890	Pit-N	31	121	11	22	1	0	0	9	11	7	.182	.256	.190	.446	37	-10	-8	88	125	8	.414	6			0	1O	-0.6
	Bos-N	69	273	41	72	12	3	2	48	32	20	.264	.350	.352	.701	97	3	-2	111	151	38	.701	9			-10	O	-1.1
	Yr	100	394	52	94	13	3	2	57	43	27	.239	.321	.302	.623	81	-7	-9	104	**144**	44	.607	15			-10		-1.7
1891	Was-a	54	206	25	58	7	5	0	31	21	16	.282	.376	.364	.740	120	5	6	95	115	31	.757	6			-3	O/1	0.1
Total	4 n	178	840	132	254							.302															O/1	
Total	16	1481	6253	1083	1881	368	84	56	751	366	304	.301	.343	.413	.756	133	239	238	100	87	970	.718	153			-18	*O1/23SPC	17.7
■ **GORDIE HINKLE**	Hinkle, Daniel Gordon b: 4/3/05, Toronto, Ohio d: 3/19/72, Houston, Tex. BR/TR, 6', 185 lbs. Deb: 4/19/34																											
1934	Bos-A	27	75	7	13	6	1	0	9	7	23	.173	.244	.280	.524	33	-8	-8	106	143	5	.452	0	0	0	1	C	-0.4
■ **GEORGE HINSHAW**	Hinshaw, George Addison b: 10/23/59, Los Angeles, Cal. BR/TR, 6', 185 lbs. Deb: 9/19/82																											
1982	SD-N	6	15	1	4	0	0	0	1	3	5	.267	.389	.267	.656	94	-0	0	92	98	2	.636	0	0	0	0	/O	0.0
1983	SD-N	7	16	1	7	1	0	0	4	0	4	.438	.438	.500	.938	161	1	1	99	198	4	1.000	1	0	0	1	/3	0.2
Total	2	13	31	2	11	1	0	0	5	3	9	.355	.412	.387	.799	130	1	1	95	145	5	.800	1	0	0	1	/O3	0.2
■ **PAUL HINSON**	Hinson, James Paul b: 5/9/04, Van Leer, Tenn. d: 9/23/60, Muskogee, Okla. BR/TR, 5'10", 150 lbs. Deb: 4/19/28																											
1928	Bos-A	3	0	1	0	0	0	0	0	0	0	—	—	—	—	—	0	0	98	—	—	—	0	0	0	0	R	0.0
■ **CHUCK HINTON**	Hinton, Charles Edward b: 5/3/34, Rocky Mount, N.C. BR/TR, 6'1", 180 lbs. Deb: 5/14/61																											
1961	Was-A	106	339	51	88	13	5	6	34	40	81	.260	.339	.381	.720	97	-4	-1	95	91	47	.736	22	5	4	-2	O	-0.2
1962	Was-A	151	542	73	168	25	6	17	75	47	66	.310	.365	.472	.837	122	17	17	101	99	92	.834	28	10	2	-4	*O2/S	1.1
1963	Was-A	150	566	80	152	20	12	15	55	64	79	.269	.344	.426	.770	117	11	13	98	77	84	.757	25	9	2	6	*O3/1S	1.7
1964	Was-A	138	514	71	141	25	7	11	53	57	77	.274	.348	.414	.762	110	8	8	101	97	71	.720	17	6	2	6	*O/3	1.1
1965	Cle-A	133	431	59	110	17	6	18	54	53	65	.255	.338	.448	.786	123	12	13	98	91	68	.795	17	3	3	-1	O12/3	1.3
1966	Cle-A	123	348	46	89	9	3	12	50	35	66	.256	.326	.402	.728	106	3	3	101	119	45	.684	10	6	-1	-0	*O/12	-0.1
1967	Cle-A	147	498	55	122	19	3	10	37	43	100	.245	.306	.355	.662	95	-3	-4	100	76	53	.581	6	8	-3	-11	*O/2	-2.3
1968	Cal-A	116	267	28	52	10	3	7	23	24	61	.195	.261	.333	.595	84	-7	-6	94	90	22	.518	3	1	0	-6	1O3/2	-1.5
1969	Cle-A	94	121	18	31	3	2	3	19	8	22	.256	.308	.388	.696	99	-1	-1	94	136	15	.630	2	0	1	-10	O3	-1.0
1970	Cle-A	107	195	24	62	4	0	9	29	25	34	.318	.395	.477	.872	122	11	7	115	98	37	.855	0	2	-1	-2	1O/C23	0.1
1971	Cle-A	88	147	13	33	7	0	5	14	20	34	.224	.317	.374	.692	90	-1	-2	106	82	18	.641	0	0	0	-5	1O/C	-0.8
Total	11	1353	3968	518	1048	152	47	113	443	416	685	.264	.335	.412	.747	109	46	47	100	93	553	.735	130	50	9	-27	O1/23CS	-0.6
■ **JOHN HINTON**	Hinton, John Robert "Red" b: 6/20/1876, Pittsburgh, Pa. d: 7/19/20, Braddock, Pa. BR/TR, 6', 200 lbs. Deb: 6/03/01																											
1901	Bos-N	4	13	0	1	0	0	0	0	2		.077	.200	.077	.277	-15	-2	-2	112	0	0	.250	0			0	/3	-0.1
■ **TOMMY HINZO**	Hinzo, Thomas Lee b: 6/18/64, San Diego, Cal. BB/TR, 5'10", 170 lbs. Deb: 7/16/87																											
1987	Cle-A	67	257	31	68	9	3	3	21	10	47	.265	.297	.358	.655	72	-10	-11	103	88	26	.568	9	4	0	-7	2	-1.1
■ **GENE HISER**	Hiser, Gene Taylor b: 12/11/48, Baltimore, Md. BL/TL, 5'11", 175 lbs. Deb: 8/20/71																											
1971	Chi-N	17	29	4	6	0	0	0	1	4	8	.207	.303	.207	.510	43	-2	-2	110	68	2	.478	1	0	0	0	/O	-0.1
1972	Chi-N	32	46	2	9	0	0	0	4	6	8	.196	.288	.196	.484	35	-3	-4	114	183	3	.421	1	0	0	-0	/O	-0.4
1973	Chi-N	100	109	15	19	3	0	1	6	11	17	.174	.256	.229	.486	33	-9	-11	108	86	7	.427	4	5	-2	-17	O	-3.4
1974	Chi-N	12	17	2	4	1	0	0	1	0	3	.235	.235	.294	.529	47	-1	-1	100	77	1	.385	0	0	0	-2	/O	-0.3
1975	Chi-N	45	62	11	15	3	0	0	6	11	7	.242	.356	.290	.646	78	-1	-1	104	129	7	.592	0	1	-1	-3	O/1	-0.5
Total	5	206	263	34	53	7	0	1	18	32	43	.202	.291	.240	.530	46	-17	-20	108	111	20	.470	6	6	-2	-22	O/1	-4.7
■ **LARRY HISLE**	Hisle, Larry Eugene b: 5/5/47, Portsmouth, Ohio BR/TR, 6'2", 193 lbs. Deb: 4/10/68																											
1968	Phi-N	7	11	1	4	1	0	0	1	1	4	.364	.417	.455	.871	166	1	1	97	84	2	.857	0	0	0	-1	/O	0.0
1969	Phi-N	145	482	75	128	23	5	20	56	48	152	.266	.338	.459	.797	124	13	14	98	80	75	.791	18	8	1	5	*O	1.2
1970	Phi-N	126	405	52	83	22	4	10	44	53	139	.205	.302	.353	.655	78	-15	-13	96	99	44	.607	5	5	-2	-0	*O	-2.0
1971	Phi-N	36	76	7	15	3	0	0	3	6	22	.197	.256	.237	.493	39	-6	-6	103	68	4	.391	1	0	0	-1	O	-0.7
1973	Min-A	143	545	88	148	25	6	15	64	64	128	.272	.352	.422	.774	113	13	10	104	97	82	.746	11	4	1	15	*O	2.2
1974	Min-A	143	510	68	146	20	7	19	79	48	112	.286	.357	.465	.822	134	22	22	101	108	83	.794	12	6	0	0	*O	1.9
1975	Min-A	80	255	37	80	9	2	11	51	27	39	.314	.382	.494	.876	136	15	13	107	123	50	.934	17	3	3	-1	OD	1.3
1976	Min-A	155	581	81	158	19	5	14	96	56	93	.272	.346	.394	.740	118	12	14	98	144	79	.721	31	18	-2	11	*O	2.1
1977	Min-A	141	546	95	165	36	3	28	**119**	56	106	.302	.373	.533	.906	140	32	30	103	133	107	.930	21	10	0	5	*O/D	3.0
1978	Mil-A	142	520	96	151	24	0	34	115	67	90	.290	.377	.533	.909	145	36	32	106	127	103	.923	10	6	-1	-2	OD	2.8
1979	Mil-A	26	96	18	27	7	0	3	14	11	19	.281	.355	.448	.803	115	2	2	100	105	15	.753	1	0	0	0	DO	0.2
1980	Mil-A	17	60	16	17	0	0	6	16	14	7	.283	.427	.583	1.010	184	7	7	95	113	16	1.133	1	1	-0	0	D	0.7
1981	Mil-A	27	87	11	20	4	0	4	11	6	17	.230	.295	.414	.709	107	-0	0	96	90	11	.647	0	0	0	0	D	0.0
1982	Mil-A	9	31	7	4	0	0	2	5	5	13	.129	.250	.323	.573	59	-2	-2	94	127	2	.517	0	0	0	0	/D	-0.1
Total	14	1197	4205	652	1146	193	32	166	674	462	941	.273	.351	.452	.803	122	131	124	101	113	673	.812	128	61	2	31	*OD	12.6

YEAR	TM/L	G	AB	R	H	2B	3B	HR	RBI	BB	SO	AVG	OBP	SLG	PRO	/A	BR	/A	PF	CHI	RC	TA	SB	CS	SBR	FR	POS	TPR
■ **JIM HITCHCOCK** Hitchcock, James Franklin b: 6/28/11, Inverness, Ala. d: 6/23/59, Montgomery, Ala. BR/TR, 5'11", 175 lbs. Deb: 8/24/38																												
1938	Bos-N	28	76	2	13	0	0	0	7	2	11	.171	.192	.171	.363	1	-10	-9	88	195	2	.246	1			-1	S/3	-0.8
■ **BILLY HITCHCOCK** Hitchcock, William Clyde b: 7/31/16, Inverness, Ala. BR/TR, 6'1.5", 185 lbs. Deb: 4/14/42 MC																												
1942	Det-A	85	280	27	59	8	1	0	29	26	21	.211	.280	.246	.527	43	-19	-23	113	148	20	.424	2	2	-1	-4	S/3	-2.3
1946	Det-A	3	3	0	0	0	0	0	0	1	0	.000	.250	.000	.250	-24	-0	-1	108	0	0	.333	0	0	0	0	/2	0.0
	Was-A	98	354	27	75	8	3	0	25	26	52	.212	.268	.251	.519	49	-26	-22	92	109	23	.403	2	4	-2	-10	S3	-3.1
	Yr	101	357	27	75	8	3	0	25	27	52	.210	.268	.249	.517	49	-26	-23	92	106	23	.402	2	4	-2	-10		-3.1
1947	StL-A	80	275	25	61	2	2	1	28	21	34	.222	.277	.255	.532	47	-19	-20	102	144	20	.422	3	0	1	3	23/S1	-1.4
1948	Bos-A	49	124	15	37	3	2	1	20	7	9	.298	.341	.379	.720	91	-2	-2	100	135	16	.604	0	0	0	3	23	0.1
1949	Bos-A	55	147	22	30	6	1	0	9	17	11	.204	.291	.259	.549	43	-12	-13	107	81	11	.457	2	3	-1	0	1/2	-1.2
1950	Phi-A	115	399	35	109	22	5	1	54	45	32	.273	.347	.361	.708	91	-11	-5	90	129	45	.598	3	1	0	-1	*2/S	0.1
1951	Phi-A	77	222	27	68	10	4	1	36	21	23	.306	.371	.401	.772	103	3	1	106	140	36	.731	2	0	1	7	32/1	0.7
1952	Phi-A	119	407	45	100	8	4	1	56	39	45	.246	.318	.292	.610	64	-15	-21	111	175	40	.516	1	1	-0	2	*31	-2.0
1953	Det-A	22	38	8	8	0	0	0	0	3	3	.211	.268	.211	.479	31	-4	-4	98	0	2	.324	0	0	0	0	3/2S	-0.3
Total	9	703	2249	231	547	67	22	5	257	206	230	.243	.310	.299	.609	65	-105	-109	102	134	212	.526	15	11	-2	-0	32S/1	-9.4
■ **MYRIL HOAG** Hoag, Myril Oliver b: 3/9/08, Davis, Cal. d: 7/28/71, High Springs, Fla BR/TR, 5'11", 180 lbs. Deb: 4/15/31																												
1931	NY-A	44	28	6	4	2	0	0	3	1	8	.143	.172	.214	.387	1	-4	-4	98	165	1	.292	0	0	0	-8	O/3	-1.1
1932	NY-A	46	54	18	20	5	0	1	7	7	13	.370	.443	.519	.961	155	4	4	95	76	13	1.059	1	0	0	-10	O/1	-0.5
1934	NY-A	97	251	45	67	8	2	3	34	21	21	.267	.324	.351	.674	77	-10	-8	96	117	28	.588	1	3	-2	-6	O	-1.5
1935	NY-A	48	110	13	28	4	1	1	13	12	19	.255	.328	.336	.664	77	-4	-3	93	110	13	.631	4	2	0	-3	O/3	-0.6
1936	NY-A	45	156	23	47	9	4	3	34	7	16	.301	.343	.468	.811	104	-1	0	95	134	25	.782	3	1	0	-2	O	-0.1
1937	NY-A	106	362	48	109	19	8	3	46	33	33	.301	.364	.423	.787	96	-1	-2	102	97	55	.742	4	7	-3	-5	O	-1.2
1938	NY-A	85	267	28	74	14	3	0	48	25	31	.277	.344	.352	.696	71	-10	-12	105	173	33	.638	4	3	-1	-4	O	-1.5
1939	StL-A	129	482	58	142	23	4	10	75	24	35	.295	.329	.421	.751	90	-8	-9	100	111	62	.657	9	5	-0	-3	*O/P	-1.3
1940	StL-A	76	191	20	50	11	0	3	26	13	30	.262	.309	.366	.675	70	-8	-9	106	119	22	.586	2	0	1	-8	O	-1.8
1941	StL-A	1	1	0	0	0	0	0	0	0	0	.000	.000	.000	.000	-99	-0	-0	100	0	0	.000	0	0	0	0	H	0.0
	Chi-A	106	380	30	97	13	3	1	44	27	29	.255	.306	.313	.620	69	-20	-16	94	130	34	.503	6	10	-4	-3	O	-2.9
	Yr	107	381	30	97	13	3	1	44	27	29	.255	.306	.312	.618	68	-20	-17	94	129	34	.502	6	10	-4	-3		-2.9
1942	Chi-A	113	412	47	99	18	2	2	37	36	21	.240	.301	.308	.610	72	-16	-15	99	100	38	.537	17	8	0	-4	*O	-2.7
1944	Chi-A	17	48	5	11	1	0	0	4	10	1	.229	.362	.250	.612	77	-1	-1	100	120	5	.561	1	3	-2	0	O	-0.2
	Cle-A	67	277	33	79	9	3	1	27	25	23	.285	.347	.350	.697	99	0	0	100	94	35	.623	6	4	-1	6	O	0.4
	Yr	84	325	38	90	10	3	1	31	35	24	.277	.349	.335	.684	96	-1	-1	100	100	40	.615	7	7	-2	6		0.2
1945	Cle-A	40	128	10	27	5	3	0	3	11	18	.211	.279	.297	.575	68	-6	-5	99	29	11	.490	1	2	-1	2	O/P	-0.5
Total	13	1020	3147	384	854	141	33	28	401	252	298	.271	.328	.364	.692	83	-85	-81	99	113	375	.627	59	48	-11	-47	O/P31	-15.5
■ **DON HOAK** Hoak, Donald Albert "Tiger" b: 2/5/28, Roulette, Pa. d: 10/9/69, Pittsburgh, Pa. BR/TR, 6'1", 170 lbs. Deb: 4/18/54 C																												
1954	Bro-N	88	261	41	64	9	5	7	26	25	39	.245	.321	.398	.719	85	-6	-6	101	82	33	.681	8	3	1	2	3	-0.2
1955	Bro-N	94	279	50	67	13	3	5	19	46	50	.240	.350	.362	.712	86	-3	-5	104	66	36	.695	9	5	-0	14	3	0.8
1956	Chi-N	121	424	51	91	18	4	5	37	41	46	.215	.285	.311	.597	61	-24	-23	99	108	40	.535	8	3	1	-10	*3	-3.3
1957	Cin-N	149	529	78	155	**39**	2	19	89	74	54	.293	.384	.482	.866	124	24	21	105	121	94	.848	8	15	-7	2	*3/2	1.9
1958	Cin-N	114	417	51	109	30	0	6	50	43	36	.261	.333	.376	.710	81	-7	-11	107	120	50	.636	6	8	-3	1	*3/S	-1.1
1959	Pit-N	155	564	60	166	29	3	8	65	71	75	.294	.377	.399	.776	104	8	6	103	112	86	.739	9	2	2	9	*3	1.1
1960	Pit-N	155	553	97	156	24	9	16	79	74	74	.282	.368	.445	.813	122	17	18	99	111	90	.779	3	2	-0	6	*3	2.2
1961	Pit-N	145	503	72	150	27	7	12	61	73	53	.298	.390	.451	.842	123	18	19	99	95	90	.832	4	2	0	1	*3	1.3
1962	Pit-N	121	411	63	99	14	8	5	48	49	49	.241	.323	.350	.674	79	-11	-12	102	121	44	.596	4	2	0	-4	*3	-1.3
1963	Phi-N	115	377	35	87	11	3	6	24	27	52	.231	.284	.324	.608	73	-12	-14	103	72	32	.507	5	5	-2	8	*3	-0.6
1964	Phi-N	6	4	0	0	0	0	0	0	0	2	.000	.000	.000	.000	-99	-1	-1	99	0	0	.000	0	0	0	0	H	0.0
Total	11	1263	4322	598	1144	214	44	89	498	523	530	.265	.347	.396	.743	97	4	-9	102	104	597	.720	64	47	-9	29	*3/S2	0.8
■ **BILL HOBBS** Hobbs, William Lee "Smokey" b: 5/7/1893, Grant'S Lick, Ky. d: 1/5/45, Hamilton, Ohio BR/TR, 5'9.5", 155 lbs. Deb: 8/09/13																												
1913	Cin-N	4	4	0	0	0	0	0	0	0	3	.000	.000	.000	.000	-98	-1	-1	102	0	0	.000	0			0	/23	0.0
1916	Cin-N	6	11	1	2	1	0	0	1	2	0	.182	.308	.273	.580	80	-0	-0	98	132	1	.667	1			0	/S	0.0
Total	2	10	15	1	2	1	0	0	1	2	3	.133	.235	.200	.435	32	-1	-1	99	101	1	.462	1			0	/S32	0.0
■ **DOC HOBLITZEL** Hoblitzel, Richard Carleton (born Richard Carleton Hoblitzell) b: 10/26/1888, Waverly, W.Va. d: 11/14/62, Parkersburg, W.Va. BR/TR, 6', 172 lbs. Deb: 9/05/08																												
1908	Cin-N	32	114	8	29	3	2	0	8	7		.254	.298	.316	.613	95	-0	-1	103	90	11	.529	2			-1	1	-0.2
1909	Cin-N	142	517	59	159	23	11	4	67	44		.308	.364	.418	.782	154	25	29	94	113	83	.779	17			-2	*1	2.5
1910	Cin-N	155	611	85	170	24	13	4	70	47	32	.278	.332	.380	.712	106	4	3	101	96	85	.701	28			-8	*1/2	-0.6
1911	Cin-N	158	622	81	180	19	13	11	91	42	44	.289	.342	.415	.757	121	7	14	92	102	98	.769	32			1	*1	0.9
1912	Cin-N	148	558	73	164	32	12	2	85	48	28	.294	.352	.405	.757	116	4	10	92	119	88	.759	23			0	*1	0.5
1913	Cin-N	137	502	59	143	23	7	3	62	35	26	.285	.334	.376	.710	101	1	0	102	121	67	.680	18			-6	*1	-1.2
1914	Cin-N	78	248	31	52	8	7	0	26	26	26	.210	.287	.298	.586	71	-8	-9	105	130	24	.551	7			-3	1	-1.4
	Bos-A	68	229	31	73	10	3	0	33	19	21	.319	.386	.389	.774	136	9	10	98	142	35	.750	12	12	-4	-2	1	0.4
1915	Bos-A	124	399	54	113	15	12	2	61	38	26	.283	.351	.396	.747	125	11	11	99	129	57	.697	9	14	-6	1	*1	0.0
1916	Bos-A	130	417	57	108	17	1	0	39	47	28	.259	.338	.305	.643	99	-2	1	94	112	50	.605	10			1	*1	0.0
1917	Bos-A	120	420	49	108	19	7	1	47	46	22	.257	.336	.343	.679	99	4	-0	108	122	53	.660	12			-7	*1	-1.2
1918	Bos-A	25	69	4	11	1	0	0	4	8	3	.159	.266	.174	.440	34	-5	-5	95	122	4	.431	3			1	1	-0.5
Total	11	1317	4706	591	1310	194	88	27	593	407	256	.278	.340	.374	.715	112	49	63	98	115	655	.695	173	26		-25	*1/2	-0.8
■ **BUTCH HOBSON** Hobson, Clell Lavern b: 8/17/51, Tuscaloosa, Ala. BR/TR, 6'1", 193 lbs. Deb: 9/07/75																												
1975	Bos-A	2	4	0	1	0	0	0	0	0	2	.250	.250	.250	.500	38	-0	-0	109	0	0	.333	0	0	0	0	/3	0.0
1976	Bos-A	76	269	34	63	7	5	8	34	15	62	.234	.275	.387	.661	83	-4	-7	110	104	26	.553	0	1	-1	-5	3	-1.3
1977	Bos-A	159	593	77	157	33	5	30	112	27	162	.265	.301	.489	.790	95	6	-7	117	119	80	.713	5	4	-1	-29	*3	-4.0
1978	Bos-A	147	512	65	128	26	2	17	80	50	122	.250	.317	.408	.725	95	1	-4	107	124	65	.652	1	0	0	-11	*3D	-1.5
1979	Bos-A	146	528	74	138	26	7	28	93	30	78	.261	.301	.496	.797	103	5	-0	107	105	70	.711	3	2	-0	-15	*3/2	-1.2
1980	Bos-A	93	324	35	74	6	0	11	39	25	69	.228	.284	.349	.632	71	-13	-14	102	104	30	.533	1	1	-0	-4	3D	-1.7
1981	Cal-A	85	268	27	63	7	4	4	36	35	60	.235	.326	.336	.661	87	-2	-4	104	138	31	.605	1	1	-0	-11	3/D	-1.4
1982	NY-A	30	58	2	10	2	0	0	3	1	14	.172	.186	.207	.393	8	-7	-7	96	100	2	.260	0	0	0	-0	D1	-0.7
Total	8	738	2556	314	634	107	23	98	397	183	569	.248	.300	.423	.722	90	-15	-43	109	115	305	.662	11	9	-2	-75	3/D12	-11.8
■ **ED HOCK** Hock, Edward Francis b: 3/27/1899, Franklin Furnace, Ohio d: 11/21/63, Portsmouth, Ohio BL/TL, 5'10.5", 165 lbs. Deb: 7/08/20																												
1920	StL-N	1	0	0	0	0	0	0	0	0	0	—	—	—	—	—	0	0	98	—	—	—	0	0	0	-0	/O	0.0
1923	Cin-N	2	0	0	0	0	0	0	0	0	0	—	—	—	—	—	0	0	98	—	—	—	0	0	0	0	R	0.0
1924	Cin-N	16	10	7	1	0	0	0	0	0	2	.100	.182	.100	.282	-22	-2	-2	101	0	0	.222	0	0	0	0	/O	-0.1
Total	3	19	10	7	1	0	0	0	0	0	2	.100	.182	.100	.282	-22	-2	-2	101	0	610	.222	0	0	0	-0	/O	-0.1
■ **ORIS HOCKETT** Hockett, Oris Leon "Brown" b: 9/29/09, Amboy, Ind. d: 3/23/69, Torrance, Cal. BL/TR, 5'9", 182 lbs. Deb: 9/04/38																												
1938	Bro-N	21	70	8	23	5	1	1	8	4	9	.329	.365	.471	.836	134	3	3	96	80	13	.787	0			-3	O	0.0
1939	Bro-N	9	13	3	3	0	0	0	1	1	1	.231	.286	.231	.516	38	-1	-1	107	122	1	.400	0			1	/O	0.0
1941	Cle-A	2	6	0	2	0	0	0	1	2	0	.333	.500	.333	.833	123	0	0	101	181	1	1.000	0	0	0	-1	/O	0.0
1942	Cle-A	148	601	85	150	22	7	7	48	45	45	.250	.305	.344	.650	90	-15	-9	92	71	63	.564	12	12	-4	-4	*O	-2.7
1943	Cle-A	141	601	70	166	33	4	2	51	45	45	.276	.331	.354	.685	111	-0	6	90	75	69	.597	13	18	-7	-5	*O	-0.9
1944	Cle-A	124	457	47	132	29	5	1	50	35	27	.289	.339	.381	.720	105	3	3	100	104	59	.636	8	9	-3	-12	*O	-1.6
1945	Chi-A	106	417	46	122	23	4	2	55	27	30	.293	.340	.381	.721	115	4	6	95	128	52	.630	10	9	-2	-2	*O	-0.2
Total	7	551	2165	259	598	112	21	13	214	159	157	.276	.329	.365	.694	105	-7	8	94	91	258	.616	43	48		-25	O	-5.4

YEAR	TM/L	G	AB	R	H	2B	3B	HR	RBI	BB	SO	AVG	OBP	SLG	PRO	/A	BR	/A	PF	CH!	RC	TA	SB	CS	SBR	FR	POS	TPR
■ JOHNNY HODAPP	Hodapp, Urban John b: 9/26/05, Cincinnati, Ohio d: 6/14/80, Cincinnati, Ohio BR/TR, 6', 185 lbs. Deb: 8/19/25																											
1925	Cle-A	37	130	12	31	5	1	0	14	11	7	.238	.298	.292	.590	47	-10	-11	106	123	12	.505	2	2	-1	1	3	-0.7
1926	Cle-A	3	5	0	1	0	0	0	0	0	1	.200	.200	.200	.400	5	-1	-1	100	0	0	.250	0	0	0	0	/3	0.0
1927	Cle-A	79	240	25	73	15	3	5	40	14	23	.304	.343	.454	.797	109	1	2	97	107	36	.749	2	0	1	3	3/1	0.8
1928	Cle-A	116	449	51	145	31	6	2	73	20	20	.323	.352	.432	.784	99	2	-1	106	128	68	.708	2	1	0	9	*31	0.8
1929	Cle-A	90	294	30	96	12	7	4	51	15	14	.327	.361	.456	.817	109	3	3	100	120	47	.761	3	3	-1	6	2	0.9
1930	Cle-A	154	635	111	**225**	**51**	8	9	121	32	29	.354	.386	.502	.889	118	21	17	105	123	120	.863	6	5	-1	13	*2	2.7
1931	Cle-A	122	468	71	138	19	4	2	56	27	23	.295	.336	.365	.701	79	-11	-15	106	107	56	.600	1	5	-3	7	*2	-0.2
1932	Cle-A	7	16	2	2	1	0	0	0	0	2	.125	.125	.188	.313	-19	-3	-3	108	0	0	.214	0	0	0	0	/2	-0.2
	Chi-A	68	176	21	40	8	0	3	20	11	3	.227	.273	.324	.597	62	-12	-9	87	101	16	.507	1	0	0	-4	O/23	-1.2
	Yr	75	192	23	42	9	0	3	20	11	5	.219	.261	.313	.574	54	-15	-12	89	92	16	.480	1	0	0	-4		-1.4
1933	Bos-A	115	413	55	129	27	5	3	54	33	14	.312	.365	.424	.788	107	5	4	101	100	64	.737	1	1	-0	-3	*21	-0.1
Total	9	791	2826	378	880	169	34	28	429	163	136	.311	.350	.425	.775	98	-4	-15	103	114	420	.707	18	17	-5	33	23/O1	2.8
■ MEL HODERLEIN	Hoderlein, Melvin Anthony b: 6/24/23, Mt.Carmel, Ohio BB/TR, 5'10", 185 lbs. Deb: 8/16/51																											
1951	Bos-A	9	14	1	5	1	1	0	1	6	2	.357	.550	.571	1.121	189	3	2	108	45	4	1.273	0	1	-1	1	/23	0.2
1952	Was-A	72	208	16	56	8	2	0	17	18	22	.269	.333	.327	.660	84	-4	-4	100	93	20	.533	2	0	1	-3	2	-0.4
1953	Was-A	23	47	5	9	0	0	0	5	6	9	.191	.283	.191	.475	32	-4	-4	94	206	3	.375	0	0	0	0	2/S	-0.2
1954	Was-A	14	25	0	4	1	0	0	1	1	4	.160	.192	.200	.392	8	-3	-3	98	76	1	.286	0	0	0	-0	/S2	-0.2
Total	4	118	294	22	74	10	3	0	24	31	37	.252	.327	.306	.633	76	-9	-9	99	107	28	.566	2	1	0	-3	/2S3	-0.6
■ CHARLIE HODES	Hodes, Charles b: 1848, New York, N.Y. d: 2/14/1875, Brooklyn, N.Y. 5'11.5", 175 lbs. Deb: 5/08/1871																											
1871	Chi-n	28	138	32	34							.246															C/3OS	
1872	Tro-n	13	65	17	15							.231															/SOC3	
1874	Atl-n	21	84	8	12							.143															O/2	
Total	3 n	62	287	57	61							.213															O/2	
■ BERT HODGE	Hodge, Edward Burton b: 5/25/17, Knoxville, Tenn. BL/TR, 5'11", 170 lbs. Deb: 4/14/42																											
1942	Phi-N	8	11	0	2	0	0	0	0	1	0	.182	.250	.182	.432	29	-1	-1	94	0	0	.300	0			0	/3	0.0
■ GOMER HODGE	Hodge, Harold Morris b: 4/3/44, Rutherfordton, N.C. BB/TR, 6'2", 185 lbs. Deb: 4/06/71																											
1971	Cle-A	80	83	3	17	3	0	1	9	4	19	.205	.258	.277	.536	49	-5	-6	106	141	6	.426	0	0	0	1	/132	-0.5
■ GIL HODGES	Hodges, Gilbert Raymond (born b: 4/4/24, Princeton, Ind. d: 4/2/72, West Palm Beach, Fla BR/TR, 6'1.5", 200 lbs. Deb: 10/03/43 M																											
1943	Bro-N	1	2	0	0	0	0	0	0	1	2	.000	.333	.000	.333	-0	-0	-0	100	0	0	1.000	1			0	/3	0.0
1947	Bro-N	28	77	9	12	3	1	1	7	14	19	.156	.286	.260	.545	44	-6	-6	105	113	6	.500	0			0	C	-0.5
1948	Bro-N	134	481	48	120	18	5	11	70	43	61	.249	.311	.376	.687	82	-11	-13	104	125	56	.621	7			-0	1C	-1.1
1949	Bro-N	156	596	94	170	23	4	23	115	66	64	.285	.360	.453	.813	115	14	13	102	135	99	.797	10			-3	*1	0.9
1950	Bro-N	153	561	98	159	26	2	32	113	73	73	.283	.367	.508	.875	120	22	16	107	117	105	.877	6			0	*1	1.0
1951	Bro-N	158	582	118	156	25	3	40	103	93	99	.268	.374	.527	.901	143	32	34	98	99	119	.928	9	7	-2	7	*1	3.6
1952	Bro-N	153	508	87	129	27	1	32	102	107	90	.254	.386	.500	.886	142	32	31	102	116	106	.931	2	4	-2	5	*1	2.9
1953	Bro-N	141	520	101	157	22	7	31	122	75	84	.302	.393	.550	.943	137	33	30	104	128	119	.984	1	4	-2	5	*1O	2.8
1954	Bro-N	154	579	106	176	23	5	42	130	74	84	.304	.384	.579	.962	145	38	37	101	118	128	.986	3	3	-1	9	*1	3.8
1955	Bro-N	150	546	75	158	24	5	27	102	80	91	.289	.383	.500	.883	126	26	23	104	124	105	.884	2	1	0	-0	*1O	1.1
1956	Bro-N	153	550	86	146	29	4	32	87	76	91	.265	.355	.507	.862	125	22	20	103	104	97	.846	3	3	-1	1	*1O/C	1.2
1957	Bro-N	150	579	94	173	28	7	27	98	63	91	.299	.370	.511	.881	115	27	15	116	114	109	.871	5	3	-0	2	*1/32	0.3
1958	LA-N	141	475	68	123	15	1	22	64	52	87	.259	.332	.434	.766	96	0	-3	105	99	67	.721	8	2	1	0	*13/OC	-0.9
1959	LA-N	124	413	57	114	19	2	25	80	58	92	.276	.369	.513	.883	130	19	18	102	115	77	.879	3	2	-0	2	*1/3	1.0
1960	LA-N	101	197	22	39	8	1	8	30	26	37	.198	.295	.371	.665	70	-5	-9	115	125	22	.610	0	1	-1	3	13	-1.1
1961	LA-N	109	215	25	52	4	0	8	31	24	43	.242	.318	.372	.690	81	-5	-6	102	120	26	.633	3	1	0	0	*1	-1.1
1962	NY-N	54	127	15	32	1	0	9	17	15	27	.252	.331	.472	.803	109	2	1	104	77	19	.758	0	0	0	3	1	0.2
1963	NY-N	11	22	2	5	0	0	0	3	3	2	.227	.320	.227	.547	61	-1	-1	99	252	2	.471	0	0	0	1	1	0.0
Total	18	2071	7030	1105	1921	295	48	370	1274	943	1137	.273	.361	.487	.848	119	238	199	104	116	1261	.866	63	31		33	*1/OC32	14.1
■ RON HODGES	Hodges, Ronald Wray b: 6/22/49, Rocky Mount, Va. BL/TR, 6'1", 185 lbs. Deb: 6/13/73																											
1973	NY-N	45	127	5	33	2	0	1	18	11	19	.260	.319	.299	.618	72	-5	-5	101	176	11	.485	0	1	-1	-1	C	-0.3
1974	NY-N	59	136	16	30	4	0	4	14	19	11	.221	.316	.338	.654	84	-3	-3	99	93	15	.602	0	0	0	-3	C	-0.3
1975	NY-N	9	34	3	7	1	0	2	4	1	6	.206	.229	.412	.640	79	-1	-1	95	79	3	.536	0	0	0	1	/C	0.0
1976	NY-N	56	155	21	35	6	0	4	24	27	16	.226	.341	.342	.683	103	-1	1	92	142	19	.661	2	0	1	0	C	0.5
1977	NY-N	66	117	6	31	4	0	1	5	9	17	.265	.317	.325	.642	76	-4	-4	96	49	12	.534	0	2	-1	1	C	-0.4
1978	NY-N	47	102	4	26	4	1	0	7	10	11	.255	.327	.314	.641	81	-3	-2	98	87	10	.537	1	2	-1	5	C	0.3
1979	NY-N	59	86	4	14	4	0	0	5	19	16	.163	.314	.209	.524	48	-6	-5	95	110	7	.514	0	0	0	3	C	-0.1
1980	NY-N	36	42	4	10	2	0	0	5	10	13	.238	.385	.286	.670	94	0	0	96	165	5	.676	1	1	-0	1	/C	0.1
1981	NY-N	35	43	5	13	2	0	1	6	5	8	.302	.375	.419	.794	124	1	1	101	112	7	.800	1	0	0	0	/C	0.2
1982	NY-N	80	228	26	56	12	1	5	27	41	40	.246	.361	.373	.733	107	3	3	99	106	32	.722	4	3	-1	8	C	1.2
1983	NY-N	110	250	20	65	12	0	0	21	49	42	.260	.385	.308	.693	96	1	1	99	108	31	.653	0	3	-2	-3	C	0.0
1984	NY-N	64	106	5	22	3	0	1	11	23	18	.208	.354	.264	.618	76	-2	-2	100	139	11	.602	1	1	-0	-0	C	-0.1
Total	12	666	1426	119	342	56	2	19	147	224	217	.240	.345	.322	.666	88	-19	-15	98	114	165	.634	10	13	-5	12	C	1.1
■ RALPH HODGIN	Hodgin, Elmer Ralph b: 2/10/16, Greensboro, N.C. BL/TR, 5'10", 167 lbs. Deb: 4/19/39																											
1939	Bos-N	32	48	4	10	1	0	0	4	3	4	.208	.255	.229	.484	34	-5	-4	92	133	2	.341	0			-1	/O	-0.5
1943	Chi-A	117	407	52	128	22	8	1	50	20	24	.314	.356	.415	.771	124	12	11	101	106	59	.678	3	5	-2	-4	3O	0.5
1944	Chi-A	121	465	56	137	25	7	1	51	21	14	.295	.333	.385	.718	105	2	2	100	107	60	.615	3	1	0	7	3O	0.8
1946	Chi-A	87	258	32	65	10	1	0	25	19	6	.252	.308	.298	.607	72	-10	-9	97	123	23	.480	0	1	-1	-4	O	-1.7
1947	Chi-A	59	180	26	53	10	3	1	24	13	4	.294	.352	.400	.752	113	2	3	97	118	25	.669	1	0	0	0	O	0.1
1948	Chi-A	114	331	28	88	11	5	1	34	21	11	.266	.310	.338	.648	76	-14	-12	95	100	33	.522	0	3	-2	2	O	-1.4
Total	6	530	1689	198	481	79	24	4	188	97	63	.285	.330	.367	.697	97	-13	-10	98	110	203	.604	7	10		-1	O3	-2.2
■ PAUL HODGSON	Hodgson, Paul Joseph Denis b: 4/14/60, Montreal, Que., Can. BR/TR, 6'2", 190 lbs. Deb: 8/31/80																											
1980	Tor-A	20	41	5	9	0	1	1	5	3	12	.220	.273	.341	.614	67	-2	-2	100	115	3	.486	0	1	-1	-1	O/D	-0.2
■ ART HOELSKOETTER	Hoelskoetter, Arthur "Holley" or "Hoss" (a.k.a. Arthur H. Hostetter) b: 9/30/1882, St.Louis, Mo. d: 8/3/54, St.Louis, Mo. BR/TR, 6'2", Deb: 9/10/05																											
1905	StL-N	24	83	7	20	2	1	0	5	3		.241	.267	.289	.557	74	-3	-2	91	74	7	.444	1			0	3/2P	0.0
1906	StL-N	94	317	21	71	6	3	0	14	4		.224	.234	.262	.495	56	-17	-17	101	61	20	.362	2			7	3SPO/2	-1.0
1907	StL-N	119	397	21	98	6	3	2	28	27		.247	.295	.292	.587	90	-7	-5	96	89	37	.495	5			-3	21/CP3	-0.6
1908	StL-N	62	155	10	36	7	1	0	6	6		.232	.261	.290	.551	83	-4	-3	94	51	11	.437	1			1	C/312	0.0
Total	4	299	952	59	225	21	8	2	53	40		.236	.267	.282	.549	76	-31	-27	97	72	75	.436	9			6	/23C1SPO	-1.6
■ JACK HOEY	Hoey, John Bernard b: 11/10/1881, Watertown, Mass. d: 11/14/47, Waterbury, Conn. BL/TL, 5'9", 185 lbs. Deb: 6/27/06																											
1906	Bos-A	94	361	27	88	8	4	0	24	14		.244	.272	.288	.560	78	-10	-9	98	89	32	.469	10			-1	O	-1.4
1907	Bos-A	39	96	7	21	2	1	0	8	1		.219	.227	.260	.487	56	-5	-5	101	114	6	.373	2			1	O	-0.5
1908	Bos-A	13	43	5	7	0	0	0	3	0		.163	.163	.163	.326	7	-4	-4	98	161	1	.222	1			-1	O	-0.5
Total	3	146	500	39	116	10	5	0	35	15		.232	.254	.272	.526	68	-19	-18	99	100	39	.427	13			-0	O	-2.4
■ STEW HOFFERTH	Hofferth, Stewart Edward b: 1/27/13, Logansport, Ind. BR/TR, 6'2", 195 lbs. Deb: 4/19/44																											
1944	Bos-N	66	180	14	36	8	0	1	26	11	5	.200	.246	.261	.507	45	-14	-13	95	186	10	.384	0			2	C	-0.8
1945	Bos-N	50	170	13	40	2	0	3	15	14	11	.235	.297	.300	.597	59	-8	-10	112	87	15	.504	1			7	C	-0.2
1946	Bos-N	20	58	3	12	1	1	0	10	3	6	.207	.246	.259	.505	46	-4	-4	95	249	4	.383	0			-1	C	-0.4
Total	3	136	408	30	88	11	1	4	51	28	22	.216	.268	.277	.545	52	-26	-27	102	153	30	.445	1			7	C	-1.4

YEAR	TM/L	G	AB	R	H	2B	3B	HR	RBI	BB	SO	AVG	OBP	SLG	PRO	/A	BR	/A	PF	CHI	RC	TA	SB	CS	SBR	FR	POS	TPR
■ **DUTCH HOFFMAN** Hoffman, Clarence Casper "Red" b: 1/28/04, Freeburg, Ill. d: 12/6/62, Belleville, Ill. BR/TR, 6', 175 lbs. Deb: 4/23/29																												
1929	Chi-A	107	337	27	87	16	5	3	37	24	28	.258	.307	.362	.669	76	-15	-12	95	97	38	.601	6	3	0	-5	O	-2.0
■ **DANNY HOFFMAN** Hoffman, Daniel John b: 3/2/1880, Canaan, Conn. d: 3/14/22, Manchester, Conn. BL/TL, 5'9", 175 lbs. Deb: 4/20/03																												
1903	Phi-A	74	248	29	61	5	7	2	22	6		.246	.264	.347	.611	81	-5	-6	104	86	25	.529	7			2	O/P	-0.8
1904	Phi-A	53	204	31	61	7	5	3	24	5		.299	.316	.426	.742	134	7	7	102	99	31	.706	9			1	O	0.5
1905	Phi-A	119	454	64	119	10	10	1	35	33		.262	.312	.335	.647	98	4	-1	109	85	63	.690	**46**			4	*O	-0.2
1906	Phi-A	7	22	4	5	0	0	0	0	3		.227	.320	.227	.547	79	-0	-0	94	0	2	.529	1			3	/O	0.2
	NY-A	100	320	34	82	10	6	0	23	27		.256	.314	.325	.639	85	1	-6	120	82	44	.685	32			-0	O	-1.1
	Yr	107	342	38	87	10	6	0	23	30		.254	.315	.319	.633	85	1	-7	118	77	46	.675	33			2		-0.9
1907	NY-A	136	517	81	131	10	3	5	46	42		.253	.309	.313	.623	93	1	-4	109	89	61	.606	30			-1	*O	-1.3
1908	StL-A	99	363	41	91	9	7	1	25	23		.251	.295	.322	.618	100	1	-0	103	83	38	.577	17			17	O	1.3
1909	StL-A	110	387	44	104	6	7	2	26	41		.269	.349	.336	.685	127	9	12	92	78	52	.714	24			13	*O	2.4
1910	StL-A	106	380	20	90	11	5	0	27	34		.237	.306	.292	.598	93	-5	-3	94	95	38	.569	16			-6	*O	-1.4
1911	StL-A	24	81	11	17	3	2	0	7	12		.210	.326	.296	.623	78	-2	-2	95	104	9	.641	3			5	O	0.1
Total	9	828	2976	359	761	71	52	14	235	226		.256	.311	.329	.640	99	9	-4	104	86	364	.633	185			37	O/P	-0.3
■ **TEX HOFFMAN** Hoffman, Edward Adolph b: 11/30/1893, San Antonio, Tex. d: 5/19/47, New Orleans, La. BL/TR, 5'9", 195 lbs. Deb: 7/11/15																												
1915	Cle-A	9	13	1	2	0	0	0	2	1	5	.154	.214	.154	.368	10	-1	-1	104	340	1	.273	0			0	/3	0.0
■ **GLENN HOFFMAN** Hoffman, Glenn Edward b: 7/7/58, Orange, Cal. BR/TR, 6'1", 175 lbs. Deb: 4/12/80																												
1980	Bos-A	114	312	37	89	15	4	4	42	19	41	.285	.330	.397	.728	97	-1	-2	102	120	39	.626	2	4	-2	-5	*3/S2	-0.7
1981	Bos-A	78	242	28	56	10	0	1	20	12	25	.231	.271	.285	.556	57	-12	-14	106	109	18	.423	0	1	-1	1	S/3	-0.8
1982	Bos-A	150	469	53	98	23	2	7	49	30	69	.209	.264	.311	.575	52	-28	-34	110	117	35	.464	0	4	-2	16	*S	-0.6
1983	Bos-A	143	473	56	123	24	1	4	41	30	76	.260	.307	.340	.647	77	-14	-15	101	93	51	.545	1	1	-0	-3	*S	-0.9
1984	Bos-A	64	74	8	14	4	0	0	4	5	10	.189	.241	.243	.484	31	-7	-8	110	89	4	.359	0	1	-1	-4	S/32	-0.7
1985	Bos-A	96	279	40	77	17	2	6	34	25	40	.276	.346	.416	.762	105	3	2	102	101	40	.705	2	2	-1	3	S/23	1.1
1986	Bos-A	12	23	1	5	2	0	0	1	2	3	.217	.280	.304	.584	60	-1	-1	100	57	2	.474	0	0	0	-1	S/3	-0.1
1987	Bos-A	21	55	5	11	3	0	0	6	3	9	.200	.267	.255	.521	41	-5	-5	99	171	4	.413	0	0	0	-1	S/32	-0.3
	LA-N	40	132	10	29	5	0	0	10	7	23	.220	.270	.258	.527	44	-11	-10	92	117	9	.398	0	1	-1	1	S	-0.4
Total	8	718	2059	238	502	103	9	22	207	133	296	.244	.296	.335	.630	71	-76	-86	104	109	201	.537	5	14	-7	8	S3/2	-3.4
■ **IZZY HOFFMAN** Hoffman, Harry C. b: 1/5/1875, Bridgeport, N.J. d: 11/13/42, Philadelphia, Pa. BL/TL, Deb: 4/14/04																												
1904	Was-A	10	30	1	3	1	0	0	1	2		.100	.156	.133	.290	-7	-4	-3	93	93	1	.222	0			-1	/O	-0.4
1907	Bos-N	19	86	17	24	3	1	0	3	6		.279	.326	.337	.663	115	1	1	95	34	10	.597	2			-1	O	0.0
Total	2	29	116	18	27	4	1	0	4	8		.233	.282	.284	.567	85	-3	-2	95	49	11	.483	2			-2	/O	-0.4
■ **JOHN HOFFMAN** Hoffman, John Edward "Pork Chop" b: 10/31/43, Aberdeen, S.D. BL/TR, 6', 190 lbs. Deb: 7/30/64																												
1964	Hou-N	6	15	1	1	0	0	0	0	1	7	.067	.125	.067	.192	-46	-3	-3	96	0	0	.133	0	0	0	0	/C	-0.2
1965	Hou-N	2	6	1	2	0	0	0	1	0	3	.333	.333	.333	.667	100	-0	-0	89	207	1	.500	0	0	0	0	/C	0.0
Total	2	8	21	2	3	0	0	0	1	1	10	.143	.182	.143	.325	-8	-3	-3	94	57	1	.222	0	0	0	1	/C	-0.2
■ **LARRY HOFFMAN** Hoffman, Lawrence Charles b: 7/18/1878, Chicago, Ill. d: 12/29/48, Chicago, Ill. BR/TR, Deb: 7/09/01																												
1901	Chi-N	6	22	2	7	1	0	0	6	0		.318	.318	.364	.682	99	-0	-0	100	256	3	.600	1			-0	/32	0.0
■ **HICKEY HOFFMAN** Hoffman, Otto Charles b: 10/27/1856, Cleveland, Ohio d: 10/27/15, Peoria, Ill. Deb: 5/10/1879																												
1879	Cle-N	2	6	0	0	0	0	0	0	0	3	.000	.000	.000	.000	-99	-1	-1	99	0	0	.000				0	/CO	0.0
■ **RAY HOFFMAN** Hoffman, Raymond Lamont b: 6/14/17, Detroit, Mich. BL/TR, 6'0.5", 175 lbs. Deb: 8/30/42																												
1942	Was-A	7	19	2	1	0	0	0	2	1	1	.053	.100	.053	.153	-59	-4	-4	96	705	0	.111	0	0	0	0	/3	-0.3
■ **JESSE HOFFMEISTER** Hoffmeister, Jesse H. b: Toledo, Ohio Deb: 7/24/1897																												
1897	Pit-N	48	188	33	58	6	9	3	36	8		.309	.337	.484	.821	119	3	4	98	111	33	.808	6			-15	3	-0.8
■ **SOLLY HOFMAN** Hofman, Arthur Frederick "Circus Solly" b: 10/29/1882, St.Louis, Mo. d: 3/10/56, St.Louis, Mo. BR/TR, 6', 160 lbs. Deb: 03																												
1903	Pit-N	3	2	1	0	0	0	0	0	0		.000	.000	.000	.000	-96	-1	-1	105	0	0	.000	0			0	/O	0.0
1904	Chi-N	7	26	7	7	0	0	1	4	1		.269	.296	.385	.681	111	0	0	101	119	4	.684	2			-0	/OS	0.0
1905	Chi-N	86	287	43	68	14	4	1	38	20		.237	.287	.324	.611	80	-6	-8	105	140	32	.584	15			3	2/1S3O	-0.1
1906	Chi-N	64	195	30	50	2	3	2	20	20		.256	.326	.328	.654	99	2	0	107	104	26	.669	13			1	O1/S23	0.0
1907	Chi-N	134	470	67	126	11	3	1	36	41		.268	.327	.311	.637	96	2	-2	106	97	59	.628	29			12	OS1/32	1.0
1908	Chi-N	120	411	55	100	15	5	2	42	33		.243	.300	.319	.618	94	-0	-3	106	120	42	.576	15			1	O12/3	-0.3
1909	Chi-N	153	527	60	150	21	4	2	58	53		.285	.351	.351	.702	119	12	12	101	117	70	.687	20			-3	*O	0.4
1910	Chi-N	136	477	83	155	24	16	3	86	65	34	.325	.406	.461	.867	152	32	32	101	139	102	.975	29			2	*O1/3	3.1
1911	Chi-N	143	512	66	129	17	2	2	70	66	40	.252	.341	.305	.645	84	-11	-9	97	**155**	65	.666	30			-9	*O1	-2.1
1912	Chi-N	36	125	28	34	11	0	0	18	22	13	.272	.385	.360	.745	101	2	1	104	143	19	.802	5			6	O/1	0.6
	Pit-N	17	53	7	15	4	1	0	2	5	6	.283	.345	.396	.741	104	0	0	99	32	7	.684	0			3	O	0.2
	Yr	53	178	35	49	15	1	0	20	27	19	.275	.374	.371	.745	102	2	1	102	110	26	.767	5			9		0.8
1913	Pit-N	28	83	11	19	5	2	0	7	8	6	.229	.297	.337	.634	84	-2	-2	96	91	9	.609	3			1	O	-0.1
1914	Bro-F	147	515	65	148	25	12	5	83	54	41	.287	.355	.412	.767	118	13	12	101	135	91	.817	34			3	*21O/S	1.6
1915	Buf-F	109	346	29	81	10	6	0	27	30	28	.234	.295	.298	.593	76	-10	-10	100	94	36	.547	12			1	O1/32S	-1.3
1916	NY-A	6	27	0	8	1	1	0	2	1	1	.296	.321	.407	.729	117	0	0	101	56	4	.684	1			2	/O	0.2
	Chi-N	5	16	2	5	2	1	0	2	2	2	.313	.389	.563	.951	163	2	1	117	88	4	1.000	0			0	/O	0.2
Total	14	1194	4072	554	1095	162	60	19	495	421	171	.269	.338	.352	.690	104	34	26	102	122	568	.695	208			23	O21/S3	3.4
■ **BOBBY HOFMAN** Hofman, Robert George b: 10/5/25, St.Louis, Mo. BR/TR, 5'10", 160 lbs. Deb: 4/19/49 C																												
1949	NY-N	19	48	4	10	0	0	0	3	5	6	.208	.296	.208	.505	37	-4	-4	102	113	3	.410	0			-0	2	-0.3
1952	NY-N	32	63	11	18	2	2	2	4	8	10	.286	.375	.476	.851	131	3	3	102	43	11	.830	0	0	0	-1	2/31	0.3
1953	NY-N	74	169	21	45	7	2	12	34	12	23	.266	.315	.544	.859	121	4	4	98	104	27	.795	1	1	-0	-1	32	0.3
1954	NY-N	71	125	12	28	5	0	8	30	17	15	.224	.322	.456	.778	95	-0	-1	105	146	19	.750	0	0	0	-1	12/3	-0.1
1955	NY-N	96	207	32	55	7	2	10	28	22	31	.266	.339	.464	.803	112	3	3	99	90	30	.735	0	2	-1	-1	1C2/3	0.1
1956	NY-N	47	56	1	10	1	0	0	2	6	8	.179	.270	.196	.466	29	-6	-5	97	77	3	.375	0	0	0	-0	/C312	-0.5
1957	NY-N	2	2	0	0	0	0	0	0	0	1	.000	.000	.000	.000	-98	-1	-1	102	0	0	.000	0	0	0	0	H	0.0
Total	7	341	670	81	166	22	6	32	101	70	94	.248	.323	.442	.765	100	-1	-1	100	100	93	.734	1	3		-5	/213C	-0.2
■ **FRED HOFMANN** Hofmann, Fred "Bootnose" b: 6/10/1894, St.Louis, Mo. d: 11/19/64, St.Helena, Cal. BR/TR, 5'11.5", 175 lbs. Deb: 9/26/19 C																												
1919	NY-A	1	1	0	0	0	0	0	0	0	0	.000	.000	.000	.000	-95	-0	-0	106	0	0	.000	0			0	/C	0.0
1920	NY-A	15	24	3	7	0	0	0	1	1	2	.292	.346	.292	.638	69	-1	-1	102	50	2	.529	0	0	0	-0	C	0.0
1921	NY-A	23	62	7	11	1	1	1	5	5	13	.177	.250	.274	.524	33	-6	-7	103	86	4	.451	0	0	0	-1	C/1	-0.6
1922	NY-A	37	91	13	27	5	3	2	10	9	12	.297	.360	.484	.844	116	2	2	102	71	16	.828	0	0	0	-1	C	0.2
1923	NY-A	72	238	24	69	10	4	3	26	18	27	.290	.350	.403	.753	94	-1	-2	104	85	34	.706	2	1	0	-6	C	-0.3
1924	NY-A	62	166	17	29	6	1	1	11	12	15	.175	.239	.241	.480	24	-19	-19	99	85	10	.406	2	1	0	-1	C	-1.5
1925	NY-A	3	2	0	0	0	0	0	0	0	0	.000	.000	.000	.000	-99	-1	-1	96	0	0	.000	0	0	0	0	/C	0.0
1927	Bos-A	87	217	20	59	19	1	0	24	21	26	.272	.342	.369	.710	89	-5	-3	95	100	28	.665	2	0	1	-8	C	-0.6
1928	Bos-A	78	199	14	45	8	1	0	16	11	25	.226	.270	.276	.547	45	-16	-16	98	100	15	.432	0	1	-1	-7	C	-1.7
Total	9	378	1000	98	247	49	11	7	93	77	120	.247	.308	.339	.647	69	-48	-47	100	89	110	.573	6	3		-24	C/1	-4.5
■ **HARRY HOGAN** Hogan, Harry S. b: 11/1/1875, Syracuse, N.Y. d: 1/24/34, Syracuse, N.Y. Deb: 8/13/01																												
1901	Cle-A	1	4	0	0	0	0	0	0	0		.000	.000	.000	.000	-99	-1	-1	95	0	0	.000	0			0	/O	0.0
■ **SHANTY HOGAN** Hogan, James Francis b: 3/21/06, Somerville, Mass. d: 4/7/67, Boston, Mass. BR/TR, 6'1", 240 lbs. Deb: 6/23/25																												
1925	Bos-N	9	21	2	6	1	1	0	3	1	3	.286	.318	.429	.747	95	-0	-0	94	119	3	.667	0	0	0	-1	/O	0.0

YEAR	TM/L	G	AB	R	H	2B	3B	HR	RBI	BB	SO	AVG	OBP	SLG	PRO	/A	BR	/A	PF	CHI	RC	TA	SB	CS	SBR	FR	POS	TPR
1926	Bos-N	4	14	1	4	1	1	0	5	0	0	.286	.286	.500	.786	125	0	0	86	247	2	.700	0			1	/C	0.1
1927	Bos-N	71	229	24	66	17	1	3	32	9	23	.288	.324	.410	.734	102	-2	-0	93	109	29	.663	2			7	C	1.0
1928	NY-N	131	411	48	137	25	2	10	71	42	25	.333	.406	.477	.883	127	19	18	102	112	79	.898	0			-14	*C	1.1
1929	NY-N	102	317	19	95	13	0	5	45	25	22	.300	.362	.388	.750	86	-6	-6	100	112	44	.698	1			-9	C	-0.6
1930	NY-N	122	389	60	132	26	2	13	75	21	24	.339	.378	.517	.894	116	8	9	98	108	73	.883	2			-0	C	1.2
1931	NY-N	123	396	42	119	17	1	12	65	29	29	.301	.354	.439	.794	116	6	8	97	110	63	.751	1			-15	*C	-0.1
1932	NY-N	140	502	36	144	18	2	8	77	26	22	.287	.323	.378	.702	89	-9	-8	99	134	62	.606	0			-7	*C	-0.9
1933	Bos-N	96	328	15	83	7	0	3	30	13	9	.253	.288	.302	.590	71	-13	-12	96	104	25	.439	0			-4	C	-1.3
1934	Bos-N	92	279	20	73	5	2	4	34	16	13	.262	.316	.337	.653	87	-10	-4	86	116	27	.523	0			0	C	0.0
1935	Bos-N	59	163	9	49	8	0	2	25	21	8	.301	.394	.387	.780	116	4	5	96	131	27	.759	0			-1	C	0.4
1936	Was-A	19	65	8	21	4	0	1	7	11	2	.323	.421	.431	.852	113	2	2	98	75	12	.867	0	1	-1	-1	C	0.2
1937	Was-A	21	66	4	10	4	0	0	5	6	8	.152	.222	.212	.434	11	-9	-9	94	122	3	.351	0	1	-1	0	C	-0.6
Total	13	989	3180	288	939	146	12	61	474	220	188	.295	.348	.406	.754	101	-12	3	97	115	449	.694	6	2		-44	C/O	0.5
■ **KENNY HOGAN**	Hogan, Kenneth Sylvester b: 10/9/02, Cleveland, Ohio d: 1/2/80, Cleveland, Ohio BL/TR, 5'9", 145 lbs. Deb: 10/02/21																											
1921	Cin-N	1	2	0	0	0	0	0	0	0	1	.000	.000	.000	.000	-99	-1	-1	101	0	0	.000	0	0	0	-0	/O	0.0
1923	Cle-A	1	0	0	0	0	0	0	0	0	0	—	—	—	—	—	0	0	101	—	—	—	0	0	0	0	R	0.0
1924	Cle-A	2	1	0	0	0	0	0	0	0	0	.000	.000	.000	.000	-99	-0	-0	97	0	0	.000	0	0	0	0	H	0.0
Total	3	4	3	0	0	0	0	0	0	0	1	.000	.000	.000	.000	-99	-1	-1	99	0	0	.000	0	0	0	-0	/O	0.0
■ **MARTY HOGAN**	Hogan, Martin F. b: 10/15/1869, Wensbury, England d: 8/15/23, Youngstown, Ohio 5'8", 145 lbs. Deb: 8/06/1894																											
1894	Cin-N	6	23	4	3	0	0	0	3	1	4	.130	.167	.130	.297	-27	-5	-5	100	281	1	.300	2			0	/O	-0.3
	StL-N	29	100	11	28	3	4	0	13	3	13	.280	.308	.390	.698	68	-5	-6	101	92	15	.694	7			0	O	-0.3
	Yr	35	123	15	31	3	4	0	16	4	17	.252	.281	.341	.623	50	-10	-10	101	132	15	.609	9			0		-0.6
1895	StL-N	5	18	2	3	1	0	0	2	3	0	.167	.286	.222	.508	34	-2	-2	100	148	2	.600	2			0	/O	0.0
Total	2	40	141	17	34	4	4	0	18	7	17	.241	.282	.326	.608	48	-12	-12	101	130	17	.607	11			0	/O	-0.6
■ **EDDIE HOGAN**	Hogan, Robert Edward b: 4/1860, St.Louis, Mo. BR, 5'7", 153 lbs. Deb: 7/05/1882																											
1882	StL-a	1	3	1	1	0	0	0		0		.333	.333	.333	.667	126	0	0	100	0	0	.500				0	/P	0.0
1884	Mil-U	11	37	6	3	1	0	0		7		.081	.227	.108	.335	17	-3	-3	100	0	1	.324	0			0	O	-0.2
1887	NY-a	32	120	22	24	6	1	0		30		.200	.373	.267	.639	94	-1	2	88	0	17	.802	12			0	O/S3	0.2
1888	Cle-a	78	269	60	61	16	6	0	24	50		.227	.368	.331	.699	132	12	13	97	85	45	.861	30			-6	O	0.3
Total	4	122	429	89	89	23	7	0	24	87		.207	.357	.294	.651	111	8	12	95	53	63	.788	42			-6	O/S3P	0.3
■ **WILLIE HOGAN**	Hogan, William Henry "Happy" b: 9/14/1884, N.San Juan, Cal. d: 9/28/74, San Jose, Cal. BR/TR, 5'10", 175 lbs. Deb: 4/12/11																											
1911	Phi-A	7	19	1	2	1	0	0	2	0		.105	.105	.158	.263	-29	-3	-3	93	225	0	.176	0			0	/O	-0.3
	StL-A	123	443	53	115	17	8	2	62	43		.260	.328	.348	.675	93	-7	-4	95	134	55	.662	18			16	*O/1	0.2
	Yr	130	462	54	117	18	8	2	64	43		.253	.320	.340	.659	88	-10	-7	95	140	54	.638	18			16		-0.1
1912	StL-A	107	360	32	77	10	2	1	36	34		.214	.284	.261	.545	57	-20	-20	99	126	32	.516	17			14	O	-1.1
Total	2	237	822	86	194	28	10	3	100	77		.236	.304	.305	.609	74	-31	-27	97	132	87	.583	35			29	O/1	-1.2
■ **BERT HOGG**	Hogg, Wilbert George "Sonny" b: 4/21/13, Detroit, Mich. d: 11/5/73, Detroit, Mich. BR/TR, 5'11.5", 162 lbs. Deb: 6/01/34																											
1934	Bro-N	2	1	0	0	0	0	0	0	0	0	.000	.000	.000	.000	-99	-0	-0	95	0	0	.000	0			0	/3	0.0
■ **GEORGE HOGRIEVER**	Hogriever, George C. b: 3/17/1869, Cincinnati, Ohio d: 1/26/61, Appleton, Wis. BR/TR, 5'8", 160 lbs. Deb: 4/24/1895																											
1895	Cin-N	69	239	61	65	8	7	2	34	36	17	.272	.374	.389	.763	92	1	-3	108	98	51	.994	41			2	O/2	-0.4
1901	Mil-A	54	221	25	52	10	2	0	16	30		.235	.327	.299	.625	80	-6	-4	95	66	24	.609	7			3	O	-0.1
Total	2	123	460	86	117	18	9	2	50	66	17	.254	.352	.346	.697	87	-5	-7	102	83	76	.805	48			5	O/2	-0.5
■ **BILL HOHMAN**	Hohman, William Henry b: 11/27/03, Brooklyn, Md. d: 10/29/68, Baltimore, Md. BR/TR, 6', 178 lbs. Deb: 8/24/27																											
1927	Phi-N	7	18	1	5	0	0	0	0	2	3	.278	.350	.278	.628	72	-1	-1	96	0	2	.538	0			-1	/O	0.0
■ **EDDIE HOHNHORST**	Hohnhorst, Edward Hicks b: 1/31/1885, Kentucky d: 3/28/16, Covington, Ky. BL/TL, 6'1", 175 lbs. Deb: 9/14/10																											
1910	Cle-A	17	62	8	20	3	1	0	6	4		.323	.364	.403	.767	141	3	3	100	90	10	.762	3			1	1	0.5
1912	Cle-A	15	54	5	11	1	0	0	2	2		.204	.232	.222	.454	30	-5	-5	101	57	4	.442	5			0	1	-0.4
Total	2	32	116	13	31	4	1	0	8	6		.267	.303	.319	.622	86	-2	-2	100	75	14	.600	8			1	/1	0.1
■ **BILL HOLBERT**	Holbert, William H. b: 3/14/1855, Baltimore, Md. d: 3/1/35, Laurel, Md. BR/TR, Deb: 9/05/1876 M																											
1876	Lou-N	12	43	3	11	0	0	0	5	0	3	.256	.256	.256	.512	68	-1	-2	104	154	3	.344				0	C	0.0
1878	Mil-N	45	173	10	32	2	0	0	12	3	14	.185	.199	.197	.395	28	-13	-14	107	122	7	.262				-2	OC	-1.6
1879	Syr-N	59	229	11	46	0	0	0	21	1	20	.201	.204	.201	.405	39	-16	-12	89	163	10	.257				5	*C/O	-0.6
	Tro-N	4	15	1	4	0	0	0	2	0	1	.267	.267	.267	.533	82	-0	-0	93	179	1	.364				1	/CM	0.0
	Yr	63	244	12	50	0	0	0	23	1	21	.205	.208	.205	.413	41	-16	-12	89	167	11	.263				6		-0.6
1880	Tro-N	60	212	18	40	5	1	0	8	9	18	.189	.222	.222	.443	46	-10	-13	110	62	11	.326				12	*C/O	0.3
1881	Tro-N	46	180	16	49	3	0	0	14	3	13	.272	.284	.289	.573	80	-4	-4	100	95	15	.420				7	C/O	0.2
1882	Tro-N	71	251	24	46	5	0	0	23	11	22	.183	.218	.203	.421	38	-17	-16	95	152	11	.302				15	*C3/O	0.4
1883	NY-a	73	299	26	71	9	1	0		1		.237	.240	.274	.514	61	-11	-15	108	0	20	.364				37	*C/O2	2.3
1884	NY-a	65	255	28	53	5	0	0		7		.208	.235	.227	.462	54	-12	-12	100	0	14	.332				14	C/OS	0.6
1885	NY-a	56	202	13	35	3	0	0		8		.173	.205	.188	.393	32	-16	-11	84	0	8	.275				12	CO/3	0.6
1886	NY-a	48	171	8	35	4	2	0		6		.205	.232	.251	.483	51	-9	-10	104	0	11	.390	4			18	C/OS	0.9
1887	NY-a	69	255	20	58	4	3	0		7		.227	.248	.267	.515	51	-19	-13	88	0	20	.442	12			0	C/1S2	-0.1
1888	Bro-a	15	50	4	6	1	0	0	1	2		.120	.170	.140	.310	1	-5	-6	105	43	1	.227	0			0	C	-0.4
Total	12	623	2335	182	486	41	7	0	86	58	91	.208	.228	.232	.460	48	-135	-128	98	59	133	.334	16			119	C/O31S2	2.6
■ **SAMMY HOLBROOK**	Holbrook, James Marbury b: 7/17/10, Meridian, Miss. BR/TR, 5'11", 189 lbs. Deb: 4/25/35																											
1935	Was-A	52	135	20	35	2	2	2	25	30	16	.259	.408	.348	.756	106	1	3	92	160	22	.810	0	0	0	-5	C	0.0
■ **JOE HOLDEN**	Holden, Joseph Francis "Socks" b: 6/4/13, St.Clair, Pa. BL/TR, 5'8", 175 lbs. Deb: 6/14/34																											
1934	Phi-N	10	14	1	1	0	0	0	0	0	2	.071	.071	.071	.143	-57	-3	-3	108	0	0	.071	0			0	/C	-0.2
1935	Phi-N	6	9	0	1	0	0	0	0	0	3	.111	.111	.111	.222	-35	-2	-2	114	0	-0	.182	1			0	/C	-0.1
1936	Phi-N	1	1	0	0	0	0	0	0	0	0	.000	.000	.000	.000	-93	-0	-0	108	0	0	.000	0			0	H	0.0
Total	3	17	24	1	2	0	0	0	0	0	5	.083	.083	.083	.167	-50	-5	-5	110	0	-0	.136	1			0	/C	-0.3
■ **BILL HOLDEN**	Holden, William Paul b: 9/7/1889, Birmingham, Ala. d: 9/14/71, Pensacola, Fla. BR/TR, 6', 170 lbs. Deb: 9/11/13																											
1913	NY-A	18	53	6	16	3	1	0	8	8	5	.302	.393	.396	.790	130	2	2	101	138	9	.784	0			4	O	0.5
1914	NY-A	50	165	12	30	3	2	0	12	16	26	.182	.254	.224	.478	44	-11	-11	100	124	9	.396	2	4	-2	1	O	-1.6
	Cin-N	11	28	2	6	0	0	0	1	3	5	.214	.290	.214	.505	49	-2	-2	105	60	2	.409	0			-1	O	-0.3
Total	2	79	246	20	52	6	3	0	21	27	36	.211	.289	.260	.550	64	-11	-11	101	120	20	.470	2	4		3	/O	-1.4
■ **JIM HOLDSWORTH**	Holdsworth, James "Long Jim" b: 7/14/1850, New York, N.Y. d: 3/22/18, New York, N.Y. BR/TR, Deb: 5/14/1872																											
1872	Cle-n	21	109	18	35							.321															*S	
	Eck-n	2	8	1	2							.250															/S	
	Yr	23	117	19	37							.316																
1873	Mut-n	53	232	45	71							.306															*S	
1874	Phi-n	58	302	59	99							.328															3S/O	
1875	Mut-n	71	339	47	92							.271															OS	
1876	NY-N	52	241	23	64	3	2	0	19	1	2	.266	.269	.295	.563	101	-3	2	87	78	20	.407				1	*O/2	0.2
1877	Har-N	55	260	26	66	5	2	0	20	2	8	.254	.260	.288	.548	81	-8	-4	89	78	20	.397				-5	*O	-0.9
1882	Tro-N	1	3	0	0	0	0	0	0	0	1	.000	.000	.000	.000	-99	-1	-1	95	0	0	.000				0	/O	0.0
1884	Ind-a	5	18	1	2	0	0	0		2		.111	.200	.111	.311	6	-2	-2	96	0	0	.250				0	/O	-0.1
Total	4 n	205	990	170	299							.302															/O	

YEAR	TM/L	G	AB	R	H	2B	3B	HR	RBI	BB	SO	AVG	OBP	SLG	PRO	/A	BR	/A	PF	CHI	RC	TA	SB	CS	SBR	FR	POS	TPR
Total	4	113	522	50	132	8	4	0	39	5	11	.253	.260	.284	.543	86	-14	-5	89	75	40	.392				-4	OS/32	-0.8
■ WALTER HOLKE	Holke, Walter Henry "Union Man" b: 12/25/1892, St.Louis, Mo. d: 10/12/54, St.Louis, Mo. BB/TL, 6'1.5", 185 lbs. Deb: 10/06/14 C																											
1914	NY-N	2	6	0	2	0	0	0	0	0	0	.333	.333	.333	.667	103	-0	-0	96	0	1	.500	0			0	/1	0.0
1916	NY-N	34	111	16	39	4	2	0	13	6	16	.351	.390	.423	.813	156	6	7	96	110	22	.889	10			-0	1	0.6
1917	NY-N	153	527	55	146	12	7	2	55	34	54	.277	.327	.338	.665	107	3	4	97	118	61	.604	13			-6	*1	-0.3
1918	NY-N	88	326	38	82	17	4	1	27	10	26	.252	.276	.337	.613	89	-6	-5	98	92	32	.537	10			4	1	-0.3
1919	Bos-N	137	518	48	151	14	6	0	48	21	25	.292	.325	.342	.667	103	0	1	98	112	63	.605	19			5	*1	0.5
1920	Bos-N	144	551	53	162	15	11	3	64	28	31	.294	.329	.377	.707	106	1	3	96	121	66	.603	4	11	-5	-4	*1	-0.7
1921	Bos-N	150	579	60	151	15	10	3	63	17	41	.261	.284	.337	.621	69	-31	-25	93	116	53	.506	8	11	-4	3	*1	-2.9
1922	Bos-N	105	395	35	115	9	4	0	46	14	23	.291	.317	.334	.651	72	-19	-15	94	129	40	.531	6	8	-3	-1	*1	-1.9
1923	Phi-N	147	562	64	175	31	4	7	70	16	37	.311	.330	.418	.749	85	-5	-15	114	98	74	.652	7	9	-3	-1	*1/P	-2.7
1924	Phi-N	148	563	60	169	23	6	6	64	25	33	.300	.330	.394	.724	87	-6	-12	108	99	70	.622	3	8	-4	3	*1	-1.8
1925	Phi-N	39	86	11	21	5	0	1	17	3	6	.244	.270	.337	.607	47	-6	-8	116	189	8	.492	0	0	0	0	1	-0.9
	Cin-N	65	232	24	65	8	4	1	20	17	12	.280	.329	.362	.691	79	-8	-7	97	83	28	.600	1	3	-2	-0	1	-1.4
	Yr	104	318	35	86	13	4	2	37	20	18	.270	.314	.355	.669	68	-14	-16	104	125	35	.570	1	3	-2	0		-2.3
Total	11	1212	4456	464	1278	153	58	24	487	191	304	.287	.318	.363	.682	89	-71	-72	100	111	517	.591	81	50		3	*1/P	-11.8
■ BILL HOLLAHAN	Hollahan, William James "Happy" b: 11/22/1896, New York, N.Y. BR/TR, 5'8", 165 lbs. Deb: 9/27/20																											
1920	Was-A	3	4	0	1	0	0	0	1	1	2	.250	.400	.250	.650	79	-0	-0	95	351	1	1.000	1	0	0	0	/3	0.0
■ DUTCH HOLLAND	Holland, Robert Clyde b: 10/12/03, Middlesex, N.C. d: 6/16/67, Lumberton, N.C. BR/TR, 6'1", 190 lbs. Deb: 8/16/32																											
1932	Bos-N	39	156	15	46	11	1	1	18	12	20	.295	.345	.397	.743	106	-0	1	93	109	22	.673	0			0	O	-0.1
1933	Bos-N	13	31	3	8	3	0	0	3	3	8	.258	.324	.355	.678	97	-0	-0	96	102	4	.652	1			-1	/O	-0.1
1934	Cle-A	50	128	19	32	12	1	2	13	13	11	.250	.319	.406	.725	86	-3	-3	101	75	17	.677	0	0	0	-5	O	-0.7
Total	3	102	315	37	86	26	2	3	34	28	39	.273	.332	.397	.729	96	-3	-2	97	94	43	.672	1	0		-7	/O	-0.9
■ WILL HOLLAND	Holland, Willard A. b: Georgetown, Del. d: 7/19/30, Philadelphia, Pa. 5'10", 180 lbs. Deb: 7/10/1889																											
1889	Bal-a	40	143	13	27	1	2	0	16	9	28	.189	.247	.224	.471	36	-12	-12	100	146	9	.405	4			-13	S/O	-1.8
■ GARY HOLLE	Holle, Gary Charles b: 8/11/54, Albany, N.Y. BR/TL, 6'6", 210 lbs. Deb: 6/02/79																											
1979	Tex-A	5	6	0	1	1	0	0	0	1	0	.167	.286	.333	.619	66	-0	-0	100	0	1	.600	0	0	0	0	/1	0.0
■ BUG HOLLIDAY	Holliday, James Wear b: 2/8/1867, St.Louis, Mo. d: 2/15/10, Cincinnati, Ohio BR/TR, 5'11", 151 lbs. Deb: 4/17/1889																											
1889	Cin-a	135	563	107	181	28	7	**19**	104	43	59	.321	.372	.497	.869	142	33	28	105	78	124	.971	46			-10	*O	1.1
1890	Cin-N	131	518	93	140	18	14	4	75	49	36	.270	.341	.382	.724	105	8	2	108	104	87	.804	50			-2	*O	-0.2
1891	Cin-N	111	442	74	141	21	10	9	84	37	28	.319	.376	.473	.848	163	26	32	91	100	92	.927	30			-14	*O	1.0
1892	Cin-N	152	602	114	176	23	16	**13**	91	57	39	.292	.355	.449	.803	140	30	27	103	87	114	.871	43			4	*O/P	2.4
1893	Cin-N	126	500	108	155	24	10	5	89	73	22	.310	.401	.428	.829	121	18	16	101	102	101	.933	32			-12	*O/1	0.0
1894	Cin-N	121	511	119	190	24	7	13	119	40	20	.372	.420	.523	.942	128	23	23	100	103	127	1.053	29			0	*O/1	1.1
1895	Cin-N	32	127	25	38	9	2	0	20	10	3	.299	.350	.402	.752	89	-1	-3	108	116	20	.753	6			0	O	-0.1
1896	Cin-N	29	84	17	27	4	0	0	8	9	4	.321	.394	.369	.763	99	1	0	105	74	13	.737	1			0	O/1SP	0.0
1897	Cin-N	61	195	50	61	9	4	2	20	27		.313	.399	.431	.830	113	7	4	107	65	37	.881	6			-5	O/S21	-0.2
1898	Cin-N	30	106	21	25	2	1	0	7	14		.236	.325	.274	.599	69	-3	-4	108	74	11	.593	5			0	O	-0.3
Total	10	928	3648	728	1134	162	71	65	617	359	211	.311	.376	.448	.823	126	141	126	103	93	727	.899	248			-39	O/1S2P	4.8
■ HOLLY HOLLINGSHEAD	Hollingshead, John Samuel (Also Played Under Name Of Samuel John Holly) b: 1/17/1853, Washington, D.C. d: 10/6/26, Washington, D.C. Deb: 4/20/1872 M																											
1872	Nat-n	9	45	12	14							.311															/2	
1873	Nat-n	30	137	25	35							.255															O/2	
1875	Nat-n	19	88	8	20							.227															O	
Total	3 n	58	270	45	69							.256															O	
■ STAN HOLLMIG	Hollmig, Stanley Ernest "Hondo" b: 1/2/26, Fredericksburg, Tex d: 12/4/81, San Antonio, Tex. BR/TR, 6'2.5", 190 lbs. Deb: 4/19/49																											
1949	Phi-N	81	251	28	64	11	6	2	26	20	43	.255	.315	.371	.686	83	-6	-6	101	99	28	.595	1			-9	O	-1.8
1950	Phi-N	11	12	1	3	2	0	0	1	0	3	.250	.250	.417	.667	74	-1	-1	97	77	1	.500	0			-1	/O	0.0
1951	Phi-N	2	2	0	0	0	0	0	0	0	0	.000	.000	.000	.000	-99	-1	-1	97	0	0	.000	0	0	0	0	H	0.0
Total	3	94	265	29	67	13	6	2	27	20	46	.253	.310	.370	.680	81	-7	-7	100	97	29	.611	1	0		-9	/O	-1.8
■ CHARLIE HOLLOCHER	Hollocher, Charles Jacob b: 6/11/1896, St.Louis, Mo. d: 8/14/40, Frontenac, Mo. BL/TR, 5'7", 154 lbs. Deb: 4/16/18																											
1918	Chi-N	131	509	72	**161**	23	6	2	38	47	30	.316	.379	.397	.775	134	23	22	102	61	**85**	.802	26			-18	*S	0.7
1919	Chi-N	115	430	51	116	14	5	3	26	44	19	.270	.347	.347	.694	108	6	6	100	57	57	.688	16			-1	*S	1.0
1920	Chi-N	80	301	53	96	17	2	0	22	41	15	.319	.406	.389	.795	130	13	14	99	63	49	.826	20	14	-2	9	S	2.6
1921	Chi-N	140	558	71	161	28	8	3	37	43	13	.289	.342	.384	.725	86	-6	-12	107	59	70	.639	5	16	-8	7	*S	0.1
1922	Chi-N	152	592	90	201	37	8	3	69	58	5	.340	.403	.444	.847	125	18	23	95	85	100	.821	19	29	-12	-4	*S	1.5
1923	Chi-N	66	260	46	89	14	2	1	28	26	5	.342	.410	.423	.833	115	9	7	104	77	44	.823	9	10	-3	-7	S	0.2
1924	Chi-N	76	286	28	70	12	4	2	21	18	7	.245	.292	.336	.627	67	-13	-14	101	79	26	.524	4	11	-5	-3	S	-1.5
Total	7	760	2936	411	894	145	35	14	241	277	94	.304	.370	.392	.762	110	50	46	101	68	432	.732	99	80		-17	S	4.6
■ ED HOLLY	Holly, Edward William (born Edward William Ruthlavy) b: 7/6/1879, Chicago, Ill. d: 11/27/73, Williamsport, Pa. BR/TR, 5'10", 165 lbs. Deb: 7/18/06																											
1906	StL-N	10	34	1	2	0	0	0	7	5		.059	.179	.059	.238	-24	-5	-5	101	0	0	.219	0			-0	S	-0.4
1907	StL-N	150	545	55	125	18	3	1	40	36		.229	.277	.279	.556	79	-15	-13	96	104	48	.486	16			11	*S/2	0.5
1914	Pit-F	100	350	28	86	9	4	0	26	17	52	.246	.281	.294	.575	69	-16	-14	94	93	35	.508	14			-10	S/O2	-1.8
1915	Pit-F	16	42	8	11	2	0	0	5	5	6	.262	.340	.310	.650	89	-0	-0	104	139	6	.677	3			0	S/3	0.0
Total	4	276	971	92	224	29	7	1	78	63	58	.231	.278	.278	.556	72	-36	-32	96	97	89	.490	33			1	S/23O	-1.7
■ WATTIE HOLM	Holm, Roscoe Albert b: 12/28/01, Peterson, Iowa d: 5/19/50, Everly, Iowa BR/TR, 5'9.5", 160 lbs. Deb: 4/15/24																											
1924	StL-N	81	293	40	86	10	4	0	23	8	16	.294	.317	.355	.672	78	-9	-9	103	82	32	.545	1	4	-2	2	O/C3	-1.0
1925	StL-N	13	58	10	12	1	1	0	2	3	1	.207	.246	.259	.505	28	-6	-6	102	41	4	.413	1	0	0	2	O	-0.3
1926	StL-N	55	144	18	41	5	1	0	21	18	14	.285	.364	.333	.698	87	-2	-2	102	151	18	.670	3			-5	O	-0.7
1927	StL-N	110	419	55	120	27	8	3	66	24	29	.286	.327	.411	.737	90	-3	-7	107	135	54	.672	4			-9	O/3	-1.9
1928	StL-N	102	386	61	107	24	6	3	47	32	17	.277	.334	.394	.728	90	-6	-6	100	106	50	.667	1			-16	3/O	-2.0
1929	StL-N	64	176	21	41	5	6	0	14	12	8	.233	,282	.330	.611	52	-14	-14	98	83	16	.526	1			3	O/3	-1.3
1932	StL-N	11	17	2	3	1	0	0	1	3	1	.176	.333	.235	.569	56	-1	-1	100	93	2	.571	0			-0	/O	0.0
Total	7	436	1493	207	410	73	26	6	174	100	86	.275	.322	.370	.693	80	-41	-46	103	109	176	.615	11	4		-23	O/3C	-7.2
■ BILLY HOLM	Holm, William Frederick Henry b: 7/21/12, Chicago, Ill. d: 7/27/77, East Chicago, Ind. BR/TR, 5'10.5", 168 lbs. Deb: 9/24/43																											
1943	Chi-N	7	15	0	1	0	0	0	0	2	4	.067	.176	.067	.243	-29	-2	-2	99	0	0	.214	0			-1	/C	-0.2
1944	Chi-N	54	132	10	18	2	0	0	6	16	19	.136	.235	.152	.386	10	-15	-16	101	108	6	.328	1			-1	C	-1.4
1945	Bos-A	58	135	12	25	2	1	0	9	23	17	.185	.317	.215	.532	58	-7	-6	95	112	11	.491	1	1	-0	-2	C	-0.2
Total	3	119	282	22	44	4	1	0	15	41	40	.156	.272	.177	.449	31	-24	-24	98	104	17	.401	2	1		-4	C	-1.8
■ GARY HOLMAN	Holman, Gary Richard b: 1/25/44, Long Beach, Cal. BL/TL, 6'1", 200 lbs. Deb: 6/26/68																											
1968	Was-A	75	85	10	25	5	1	0	7	13	15	.294	.388	.376	.764	145	4	5	91	94	13	.738	0	0	0	1	1O	0.5
1969	Was-A	41	31	1	5	1	0	0	2	4	7	.161	.257	.194	.451	28	-3	-3	97	134	2	.385	0	0	0	-1	1/O	-0.4
Total	2	116	116	11	30	6	1	0	9	17	22	.259	.353	.328	.681	111	1	2	93	104	15	.640	0	0	0	0	/1O	0.1
■ FRED HOLMES	Holmes, Frederick C. b: 7/1/1878, Chicago, Ill. d: 2/13/56, Norwood Park, Ill. TR , Deb: 03																											
1903	NY-A	1	0	0	0	0	0	0	0	0	1	—	1.000	—	1.328	318	0	0	100	0	0	—	0			0	/1	0.0
1904	Chi-N	1	3	1	1	1	0	0	0	0	0	.333	.333	.667	1.000	207	0	0	101	0	1	1.000	0			0	/C	0.0
Total	2	2	3	1	1	1	0	0	0	0	1	.333	.500	.667	1.167	262	1	1	100	0	1	1.500	0			0	/C1	0.0

YEAR	TM/L	G	AB	R	H	2B	3B	HR	RBI	BB	SO	AVG	OBP	SLG	PRO	/A	BR	/A	PF	CHI	RC	TA	SB	CS	SBR	FR	POS	TPR
■ **DUCKY HOLMES**	Holmes, Howard Elbert b: 7/8/1883, Dayton, Ohio d: 9/18/45, Dayton, Ohio BR/TR, 5'10", 160 lbs. Deb: 4/18/06																											
1906	StL-N	9	27	2	5	0	0	0	2	2		.185	.241	.185	.427	34	-2	-2	101	146	1	.318	0			-1	/C	-0.2
■ **DUCKY HOLMES**	Holmes, James William b: 1/28/1869, Des Moines, Iowa d: 8/6/32, Truro, Iowa BL/TR, 5'6", 170 lbs. Deb: 8/08/1895																											
1895	Lou-N	40	161	33	60	10	2	3	20	12	9	.373	.426	.516	.942	152	11	12	95	64	40	1.059	9			0	O/S3P	1.0
1896	Lou-N	47	141	22	38	3	2	0	18	13	5	.270	.360	.319	.679	83	-3	-2	98	115	20	.709	8			-7	O/PS2	-0.9
1897	Lou-N	2	4	0	0	0	0	0	0	1		.000	.200	.000	.200	-46	-1	-1	95	0	0	.250	0			0	/S	0.0
	NY-N	79	306	51	82	8	6	1	44	18		.268	.317	.343	.660	77	-10	-10	98	122	44	.701	30			-7	O/S	-1.9
	Yr	81	310	51	82	8	6	1	44	19		.265	.315	.339	.654	76	-11	-10	98	119	44	.693	30			-7		-1.9
1898	StL-N	23	101	9	24	1	1	0	0	2		.238	.260	.267	.527	50	-6	-7	106	0	8	.442	4			2	O	-0.5
	Bal-N	113	442	54	126	10	9	1	64	23		.285	.332	.355	.687	97	-1	-2	103	128	62	.674	25			2	*O	-0.6
	Yr	136	543	63	150	11	10	1	64	25		.276	.319	.339	.658	88	-7	-9	103	106	70	.628	29			4		-1.1
1899	Bal-N	138	553	80	177	31	7	4	66	39		.320	.380	.423	.803	114	17	11	108	73	110	.896	50			4	*O	0.5
1901	Det-A	131	537	90	158	28	10	4	62	37		.294	.340	.406	.746	98	5	-3	110	75	88	.765	35			-2	*O	-0.5
1902	Det-A	92	362	50	93	15	4	2	33	28		.257	.310	.337	.647	82	-9	-9	99	82	44	.617	16			0	O	-1.2
1903	Was-A	21	71	13	16	3	1	1	8	5		.225	.276	.338	.614	81	-1	-2	105	109	10	.709	10			-2	O/32	-0.4
	Chi-A	86	344	53	96	7	5	0	18	25		.279	.328	.328	.656	108	0	4	92	51	46	.657	25			4	O/3	0.2
	Yr	107	415	66	112	10	6	1	26	30		.270	.319	.330	.649	102	-1	2	95	63	56	.667	35			2		-0.2
1904	Chi-A	68	251	42	78	11	9	1	19	14		.311	.347	.438	.785	151	13	14	99	66	44	.792	13			1	O	1.2
1905	Chi-A	92	328	42	66	15	2	0	22	19		.201	.245	.259	.504	64	-14	-13	97	94	24	.439	11			-2	O	-2.0
Total	10	932	3601	539	1014	142	58	17	374	236	14	.282	.332	.367	.700	99	2	-8	102	84	540	.708	236			-6	O/3SP2	-5.1
■ **TOMMY HOLMES**	Holmes, Thomas Francis "Kelly" b: 3/29/17, Brooklyn, N.Y. BL/TL, 5'10", 180 lbs. Deb: 4/14/42 M																											
1942	Bos-N	141	558	56	155	24	4	4	41	64	10	.278	.353	.357	.710	113	7	10	95	64	76	.657	2			10	*O	1.7
1943	Bos-N	152	629	75	170	33	10	5	41	58	20	.270	.334	.378	.712	100	4	-0	106	51	82	.655	7			1	*O	-0.4
1944	Bos-N	155	631	93	195	42	6	13	73	61	11	.309	.372	.456	.828	140	26	31	95	69	110	.801	4			2	*O	2.1
1945	Bos-N	154	636	125	**224**	**47**	6	**28**	117	70	9	.352	.420	**.577**	**.997**	156	**63**	**53**	112	80	**156**	**1.078**	15			-0	*O	**4.5**
1946	Bos-N	149	568	80	176	35	6	6	79	58	14	.310	.377	.424	.801	134	20	24	95	121	91	.759	7			5	*O	2.7
1947	Bos-N	150	618	90	**191**	33	3	9	53	44	16	.309	.360	.416	.776	109	4	7	97	66	91	.699	3			5	*O	0.6
1948	Bos-N	139	585	85	190	35	7	6	61	46	20	.325	.375	.439	.814	118	16	15	102	80	94	.738	1			-3	*O	0.2
1949	Bos-N	117	380	47	101	20	4	8	59	39	6	.266	.337	.403	.740	101	-2	0	97	126	51	.675	1			0	*O	-0.5
1950	Bos-N	105	322	44	96	20	1	9	51	33	8	.298	.370	.450	.821	133	7	13	86	114	53	.771	0			-4	O	0.6
1951	Bos-N	27	29	1	5	2	0	0	5	3	4	.172	.250	.241	.491	33	-3	-3	98	276	2	.417	0	0	0	-1	/OM	-0.3
1952	Bro-N	31	36	2	4	1	0	0	1	4	4	.111	.200	.139	.339	-4	-5	-5	102	78	1	.273	0	0	0	-1	/O	-0.5
Total	11	1320	4992	698	1507	292	47	88	581	480	122	.302	.366	.432	.798	122	138	144	99	83	809	.775	40	0		13	*O	10.7
■ **RED HOLT**	Holt, James Emmett Madison b: 7/25/1894, Dayton, Tenn. d: 2/2/61, Birmingham, Ala. BL/TL, 5'11", 175 lbs. Deb: 9/05/25																											
1925	Phi-A	27	88	13	24	7	0	1	8	12	9	.273	.360	.386	.746	87	-1	-2	103	72	13	.719	0	0	0	-1	1	-0.3
■ **JIM HOLT**	Holt, James William b: 5/27/44, Graham, N.C. BL/TR, 6', 180 lbs. Deb: 4/17/68																											
1968	Min-A	70	106	9	22	2	1	0	8	4	20	.208	.236	.245	.482	43	-7	-8	106	132	5	.341	0	1	-1	-6	O/1	-1.8
1969	Min-A	12	14	3	5	0	0	1	2	0	4	.357	.357	.571	.929	153	1	1	102	73	3	.889	0	0	0	-2	/O1	0.0
1970	Min-A	142	319	37	85	9	3	3	40	17	32	.266	.304	.342	.645	79	-10	-9	98	137	32	.529	3	1	0	-8	*O/1	-2.3
1971	Min-A	126	340	35	88	11	3	1	29	16	28	.259	.294	.318	.612	70	-12	-14	104	107	30	.492	5	1	1	2	*O/1	-1.4
1972	Min-A	10	27	6	12	1	0	1	6	0	1	.444	.444	.593	1.037	193	3	3	107	132	6	1.000	0	0	0	-0	/O1	0.3
1973	Min-A	132	441	52	131	25	3	11	58	29	43	.297	.343	.442	.785	115	10	8	104	100	63	.695	0	3	-2	1	*O1	0.3
1974	Min-A	79	197	24	50	11	0	0	16	14	16	.254	.307	.310	.616	77	-6	-6	101	103	18	.497	0	0	0	4	1/O	-0.5
	Oak-A	30	42	1	6	0	0	0	0	1	9	.143	.182	.143	.325	-6	-6	-6	100	0	1	.222	0	0	0	-0	1/D	-0.6
	Yr	109	239	25	56	11	0	0	16	15	25	.234	.285	.280	.565	63	-11	-11	101	76	21	.459	0	0	0	3		-1.1
1975	Oak-A	102	123	7	27	3	0	2	16	11	11	.220	.294	.293	.587	71	-5	-4	93	146	10	.485	0	0	0	-3	1/OCD	-0.9
1976	Oak-A	4	7	0	2	2	0	0	2	1	2	.286	.375	.571	.946	175	1	1	100	192	2	1.000	0	0	0	0	/D	0.1
Total	9	707	1616	174	428	64	10	19	177	93	166	.265	.308	.352	.660	85	-31	-34	102	113	170	.567	8	6	-1	-12	O1/DC	-6.8
■ **ROGER HOLT**	Holt, Roger Boyd b: 4/8/56, Daytona Beach, Fla. BB/TR, 5'11", 165 lbs. Deb: 10/04/80																											
1980	NY-A	2	6	0	1	0	0	0	1	1	2	.167	.286	.167	.452	27	-1	-1	99	390	0	.400	0	0	0	0	/2	0.0
■ **MARTY HONAN**	Honan, Martin Weldon b: Chicago, Ill. d: 8/20/08, Chicago, Ill. Deb: 10/03/1890																											
1890	Chi-N	1	3	0	0	0	0	0	1	0	2	.000	.000	.000	.000	-92	-1	-1	109	0	0	.000	0			0	/C	0.0
1891	Chi-N	5	12	1	2	0	1	0	3	1	3	.167	.231	.333	.564	61	-1	-1	106	219	1	.500	0			0	/C	0.0
Total	2	6	15	1	2	0	1	0	4	1	5	.133	.188	.267	.454	31	-1	-1	107	178	1	.385	0			0	/C	0.0
■ **ABIE HOOD**	Hood, Albie Larrison b: 1/31/03, Sanford, N.C. BL/TR, 5'7", 152 lbs. Deb: 7/15/25																											
1925	Bos-N	5	21	2	6	2	0	1	2	1	0	.286	.318	.524	.842	119	0	0	94	45	3	.800	0	0	0	-1	/2	0.0
■ **WALLY HOOD**	Hood, Wallace James Sr. b: 2/9/1895, Whittier, Cal. d: 5/2/65, Hollywood, Cal. BR/TR, 5'11.5", 160 lbs. Deb: 4/15/20																											
1920	Bro-N	7	14	4	2	1	0	0	1	4	4	.143	.333	.214	.548	53	-1	-1	111	129	2	.750	2	0	1	1	/O	0.1
	Pit-N	2	1	1	0	0	0	0	0	1	0	.000	.500	.000	.500	51	0	0	101	0	0	2.000	1	0	0	0	H	0.0
	Yr	9	15	5	2	1	0	0	1	5	4	.133	.350	.200	.550	56	-0	-1	109	115	2	.846	3	0	1	1		0.1
1921	Bro-N	56	65	16	17	1	2	1	4	9	14	.262	.360	.385	.745	93	-0	-0	105	52	9	.740	2	2	-1	-10	O	-1.1
1922	Bro-N	2	0	2	0	0	0	0	0	0	0	—	—	—	—	—	0	0	95	—	—	—	0	0	0	0	R	0.0
Total	3	67	80	23	19	2	2	1	5	14	18	.237	.358	.350	.708	86	-1	-1	106	66	20	.762	5	2	0	-9	/O	-1.0
■ **ALEX HOOKS**	Hooks, Alexander Marcus b: 8/29/06, Edgewood, Tex. BL/TL, 6'1", 183 lbs. Deb: 4/17/35																											
1935	Phi-A	15	44	4	10	3	0	0	4	3	10	.227	.277	.295	.572	48	-3	-3	100	104	4	.471	0	0	0	0	1	-0.3
■ **HARRY HOOPER**	Hooper, Harry Bartholomew b: 8/24/1887, Bell Station, Cal. d: 12/18/74, Santa Cruz, Cal. BL/TR, 5'10", 168 lbs. Deb: 4/16/09 H																											
1909	Bos-A	81	255	29	72	3	4	0	12	16		.282	.337	.325	.662	100	3	0	109	56	32	.650	15			6	O	0.4
1910	Bos-A	155	584	81	156	9	10	2	27	62		.267	.346	.327	.673	112	9	10	99	45	82	.703	40			8	*O	1.1
1911	Bos-A	130	524	93	163	20	6	4	45	73		.311	.399	.395	.794	123	18	19	99	60	98	.892	38			1	*O	0.9
1912	Bos-A	147	590	98	143	20	12	2	53	66		.242	.326	.327	.653	81	-9	-15	107	77	73	.660	29			-2	*O	-2.5
1913	Bos-A	148	586	100	169	29	12	4	40	60	51	.288	.359	.399	.759	118	16	13	103	50	90	.779	26			5	*O/P	1.1
1914	Bos-A	141	530	85	137	23	15	1	41	58	47	.258	.336	.364	.700	113	6	8	98	75	66	.673	19	14	-3	3	*O	0.0
1915	Bos-A	149	566	90	133	20	13	2	51	89	36	.235	.342	.327	.669	101	2	2	99	80	66	.660	22	20	-5	4	*O	-0.7
1916	Bos-A	151	575	75	156	20	11	1	37	80	35	.271	.361	.350	.711	121	11	16	94	56	80	.719	27	11	2	-5	*O	0.2
1917	Bos-A	151	559	89	143	21	11	3	45	80	40	.256	.355	.349	.704	106	12	6	108	70	76	.726	21			-10	*O	-1.3
1918	Bos-A	126	474	81	137	26	13	1	44	75	25	.289	.391	.405	.796	147	25	28	95	71	82	.875	24			-6	*O	1.7
1919	Bos-A	128	491	76	131	25	6	3	49	79	28	.267	.374	.360	.734	117	7	13	91	82	72	.789	23			5	*O	0.9
1920	Bos-A	139	536	91	167	30	17	7	53	88	27	.312	.411	.470	.881	138	28	31	96	66	104	.925	16	18	-6	2	*O	1.4
1921	Chi-A	108	419	74	137	26	5	8	58	55	21	.327	.406	.470	.876	124	16	16	99	86	82	.920	13	7	-0	-9	*O	-0.1
1922	Chi-A	152	602	111	183	35	8	11	80	68	33	.304	.379	.444	.823	113	13	12	101	92	102	.826	16	12	-2	1	*O	0.0
1923	Chi-A	145	576	87	166	32	4	10	65	68	22	.288	.370	.410	.780	107	5	6	98	74	88	.769	18	18	-5	-8	*O	-1.9
1924	Chi-A	130	476	107	156	27	8	10	62	65	26	.328	.413	.481	.894	134	22	25	97	81	95	.943	16	13	-3	7	*O	1.8
1925	Chi-A	127	442	62	117	23	5	6	55	54	21	.265	.351	.380	.731	89	-10	-6	96	101	62	.718	12	8	-1	-3	*O	-1.9
Total	17	2308	8785	1429	2466	389	160	75	817	1136	412	.281	.368	.387	.755	114	174	184	99	72	1349	.774	375	121		-1	*O/P	1.1
■ **MIKE HOOPER**	Hooper, Michael H. b: 2/7/1850, Baltimore, Md. d: 12/1/17, Baltimore, Md. 5'6", 165 lbs. Deb: 6/27/1873																											
1873	Mar-n	2	9	0	0							.000															/CO	
■ **CHARLIE HOOVER**	Hoover, Charles E. b: 9/21/1865, Mound City, Ill. TR , Deb: 1888																											
1888	KC-a	3	10	0	3	0	0	0	1	0		.300	.300	.300	.600	90	-0	-0	106	100	1	.429	0			0	/C	0.0

YEAR	TM/L	G	AB	R	H	2B	3B	HR	RBI	BB	SO	AVG	OBP	SLG	PRO	/A	BR	/A	PF	CHI	RC	TA	SB	CS	SBR	FR	POS	TPR
1889	KC-a	71	258	44	64	2	5	1	25	29	38	.248	.329	.306	.635	79	-5	-7	106	89	30	.613	9			-2	C/3O	-0.2
Total	2	74	268	44	67	2	5	1	26	29	38	.250	.328	.306	.634	79	-5	-8	106	89	31	.607	9			-2	/C3O	-0.2
■ JOE HOOVER	Hoover, Robert Joseph b: 4/15/15, Brawley, Tex. d: 9/2/65, Los Angeles, Cal. BR/TR, 5'11", 175 lbs. Deb: 4/21/43																											
1943	Det-A	144	575	78	140	15	8	4	38	36	101	.243	.289	.318	.607	74	-18	-21	106	68	54	.502	6	5	-1	-7	*S	-3.0
1944	Det-A	120	441	67	104	20	2	0	29	35	66	.236	.301	.290	.591	66	-17	-20	105	83	40	.501	7	10	-4	15	*S/2	-0.1
1945	Det-A	74	222	33	57	10	5	1	17	21	35	.257	.324	.360	.684	93	-1	-2	106	74	28	.635	6	2	1	5	S	0.6
Total	3	338	1238	178	301	45	15	5	84	92	202	.243	.300	.316	.616	74	-36	-43	105	75	122	.533	19	17	-5	13	S/2	-2.5
■ BUSTER HOOVER	Hoover, William J. b: 1863, Philadelphia, Pa. BR/TR, 6'1", 178 lbs. Deb: 4/17/1884																											
1884	Phi-U	63	275	76	100	20	8	0		12		.364	.390	.495	.885	213	27	30	93	0	54	.846	0			2	OS/123	2.7
	Phi-N	10	42	6	8	1	0	1	4	4	9	.190	.261	.286	.547	78	-1	-1	92	79	3	.471				0	O	0.0
1886	Bal-a	40	157	25	34	2	6	0		16		.217	.297	.306	.603	100	-1	1	91	0	19	.659	15			-2	O	-0.1
1892	Cin-N	14	51	7	9	0	0	0	2	5	4	.176	.250	.176	.426	30	-4	-4	103	70	3	.357	1			0	O	-0.3
Total	3	127	525	114	151	23	14	1	6	37	13	.288	.337	.390	.727	147	20	26	93	13	79	.695	16			-0	O/S213	2.3
■ DON HOPKINS	Hopkins, Donald b: 1/9/52, West Point, Miss. BL/TR, 6', 175 lbs. Deb: 4/08/75																											
1975	Oak-A	82	6	25	1	0	0	0	0	2	0	.167	.375	.167	.542	62	-0	-0	93	0	-9	1.714	21	9	1	-2	D/OR	0.0
1976	Oak-A	3	0	0	0	0	0	0	0	0	0	—	—	—	—	—	0	0	100	—	-9	.000	0	1	-1	0	R	0.0
Total	2	85	6	25	1	0	0	0	0	2	0	.167	.375	.167	.542	62	-0	-0	93	0	-19	1.600	21	10	0	-2	/DO	0.0
■ GAIL HOPKINS	Hopkins, Gail Eason b: 2/19/43, Tulsa, Okla. BL/TR, 5'10", 198 lbs. Deb: 6/29/68																											
1968	Chi-A	29	37	4	8	2	0	0	2	6	3	.216	.326	.270	.596	81	-1	-1	101	86	4	.552	0	0	0	0	/1	0.0
1969	Chi-A	124	373	52	99	13	3	8	46	50	28	.265	.354	.381	.734	97	4	-0	108	111	51	.684	2	1	0	-4	*1	-1.1
1970	Chi-A	116	287	32	82	8	1	6	29	28	19	.286	.351	.383	.735	97	1	-1	106	92	39	.662	0	0	0	3	1/C	-0.1
1971	KC-A	103	295	35	82	16	1	9	47	37	13	.278	.366	.431	.797	127	10	11	99	125	47	.770	3	1	0	1	1	0.8
1972	KC-A	53	71	1	15	2	0	0	5	7	4	.211	.282	.239	.521	56	-4	-4	100	123	5	.414	0	0	0	-0	1/3	-0.5
1973	KC-A	74	138	17	34	6	1	2	16	29	15	.246	.385	.348	.732	99	3	1	109	116	18	.702	1	2	-1	0	D1	0.0
1974	LA-N	15	18	1	4	0	0	0	0	3	1	.222	.333	.222	.556	62	-1	-1	93	0	1	.500	0	0	0	0	/C1	0.0
Total	7	514	1219	142	324	47	6	25	145	160	83	.266	.355	.376	.730	101	13	6	105	109	165	.703	6	4	-1	-1	1/DC3	-0.9
■ BUCK HOPKINS	Hopkins, John Winton "Sis" b: 1/3/1883, Grafton, Va. d: 10/2/29, Phoebus, Va. BR/TR, 5'10", 165 lbs. Deb: 7/22/07																											
1907	StL-N	15	44	7	6	3	0	0	3	10		.136	.296	.205	.501	62	-2	-1	96	129	3	.553	2			-1	O	-0.2
■ MARTY HOPKINS	Hopkins, Meredith Hilliard b: 2/22/07, Wolfe City, Tex. d: 11/20/63, Dallas, Tex. BR/TR, 5'11", 175 lbs. Deb: 4/17/34																											
1934	Phi-N	10	25	6	3	2	0	0	3	7	5	.120	.313	.200	.512	37	-2	-2	108	216	2	.522	0			-1	/3	-0.1
	Chi-A	67	210	22	45	7	0	2	28	42	26	.214	.348	.276	.624	63	-10	-10	99	146	23	.601	0	3	-2	2	3	-0.9
1935	Chi-A	59	144	20	32	3	0	2	17	36	23	.222	.378	.285	.663	68	-4	-6	109	123	19	.696	1	0	0	-3	3/2	-0.6
Total	2	136	379	48	80	12	0	4	48	85	54	.211	.357	.274	.631	63	-16	-19	104	142	44	.632	1	3		-2	3/2	-1.6
■ MIKE HOPKINS	Hopkins, Michael Joseph "Skinner" b: 11/1/1872, Glasgow, Scotland d: 2/5/52, Pittsburgh, Pa. BR/TR, 5'8", 160 lbs. Deb: 8/24/02																											
1902	Pit-N	1	2	0	2	1	0	0	0	0		1.000	1.000	1.500	2.500	641	1	1	105	0	3	—	0			0	/C	0.1
■ JOHNNY HOPP	Hopp, John Leonard "Hippity" b: 7/18/16, Hastings, Neb. BL/TL, 5'10", 170 lbs. Deb: 9/18/39 C																											
1939	StL-N	6	4	1	2	1	0	0	2	1	1	.500	.600	.750	1.350	248	1	1	105	244	2	2.000	0			0	/1	0.1
1940	StL-N	80	152	24	41	7	4	1	14	9	21	.270	.315	.388	.703	91	-2	-2	102	84	18	.626	3			-1	O1	-0.5
1941	StL-N	134	445	83	135	25	11	4	50	50	63	.303	.378	.436	.813	117	17	12	110	88	77	.832	15			3	O1	0.6
1942	StL-N	95	314	41	81	16	7	3	37	36	40	.258	.334	.382	.716	101	4	1	108	106	43	.730	14			-4	1	-1.0
1943	StL-N	91	241	33	54	10	2	2	25	24	22	.224	.297	.307	.604	71	-8	-9	105	113	24	.566	8			-3	O1	-1.6
1944	StL-N	139	527	106	177	35	9	11	72	58	47	.336	.404	.499	.903	152	37	37	101	89	110	.949	15			2	*O/1	2.8
1945	StL-N	124	446	67	129	22	8	3	44	49	24	.289	.363	.395	.758	111	7	7	100	84	68	.754	14			1	*O1	0.2
1946	Bos-N	129	445	71	148	23	8	3	48	34	34	.333	.386	.440	.827	142	20	22	95	87	77	.842	21			2	1O	1.8
1947	Bos-N	134	430	74	124	20	2	2	32	58	30	.288	.376	.358	.734	99	-0	1	97	74	62	.723	13			-12	*O	-1.4
1948	Pit-N	120	392	64	109	15	12	1	31	40	25	.278	.345	.385	.730	93	-1	-4	104	75	53	.676	5			4	O1	-0.4
1949	Pit-N	20	55	5	12	3	1	0	3	7	3	.218	.306	.309	.616	65	-3	-3	101	66	5	.545	0			0	/O1	-0.2
	Bro-N	8	14	0	0	0	0	0	0	0	3	.000	.000	.000	.000	-99	-4	-4	102	0	0	.000	0			0	/O1	-0.3
	Pit-N	85	316	50	106	11	4	5	36	30	26	.335	.393	.443	.836	123	11	11	101	89	56	.829	9			4	1/O	1.4
	Yr	113	385	55	118	14	5	5	39	37	32	.306	.367	.408	.775	107	5	4	101	79	59	.744	9			4	1/O	0.9
1950	Pit-N	106	318	51	108	24	5	8	47	43	17	.340	.420	.522	.942	143	22	21	103	95	71	1.000	7			-0	1/O	1.7
	NY-A	19	27	9	9	2	1	1	8	8	1	.333	.486	.593	1.078	176	3	4	99	145	8	1.200	0	1	-1	-1	1/O	0.1
1951	NY-A	46	63	10	13	1	0	2	4	9	11	.206	.306	.317	.623	75	-3	-2	92	55	7	.620	2	0	1	0	1	-0.1
1952	NY-A	15	25	4	4	0	0	0	2	2	3	.160	.250	.160	.410	16	-3	-3	98	187	1	.409	2	0	1	0	1	-0.2
	Det-A	42	46	5	10	1	0	0	3	6	7	.217	.308	.239	.547	54	-3	-3	99	102	4	.459	0	0	0	-1	/O1	-0.3
	Yr	57	71	9	14	1	0	0	5	8	10	.197	.287	.211	.499	41	-5	-5	99	127	5	.448	2	0	1	-1		-0.5
Total	14	1393	4260	698	1262	216	74	46	458	464	378	.296	.368	.414	.782	114	96	87	102	89	685	.792	128	1		-6	O1	2.7
■ SHAGS HORAN	Horan, Joseph Patrick b: 9/6/1895, St.Louis, Mo. d: 2/13/69, Torrance, Cal. BR/TR, 5'10", 170 lbs. Deb: 7/14/24																											
1924	NY-A	22	31	4	9	1	0	0	7	1	5	.290	.313	.323	.635	65	-2	-2	99	231	3	.500	0	0	0	-4	O	-0.6
■ SAM HORN	Horn, Samuel Lee b: 11/2/63, Dallas, Tex. BL/TL, 6'5", 215 lbs. Deb: 7/25/87																											
1987	Bos-A	46	158	31	44	7	0	14	34	17	55	.278	.356	.589	.945	147	10	10	99	100	32	.933	0	1	-1	0	D	0.9
1988	Bos-A	24	61	4	9	0	0	2	8	11	20	.148	.278	.246	.524	44	-4	-5	109	151	5	.491	0	0	0	0	D	-0.4
Total	2	70	219	35	53	7	0	16	42	28	75	.242	.333	.493	.826	117	6	5	102	115	36	.821	0	1	-1	0	/D	0.5
■ BOB HORNER	Horner, James Robert b: 8/6/57, Junction City, Kan. BR/TR, 6'1", 195 lbs. Deb: 6/16/78																											
1978	Atl-N	89	323	50	86	17	1	23	63	24	42	.266	.321	.539	.860	122	13	9	112	105	54	.820	0	0	0	5	3	1.3
1979	Atl-N	121	487	66	153	15	1	33	98	22	74	.314	.348	.552	.900	130	25	20	109	112	89	.852	0	2	-1	2	31	1.6
1980	Atl-N	124	463	81	124	14	1	35	89	27	50	.268	.310	.529	.839	129	15	15	101	103	70	.775	3	1	0	12	*3/1	2.7
1981	Atl-N	79	300	42	83	10	0	15	42	32	39	.277	.348	.460	.808	128	10	11	100	95	47	.765	2	3	-1	-9	3	-0.3
1982	Atl-N	140	499	85	130	24	0	32	97	66	75	.261	.351	.501	.852	127	23	19	107	112	86	.835	3	5	-2	-17	*3	-0.2
1983	Atl-N	104	386	75	117	25	1	20	68	50	63	.303	.384	.528	.913	143	26	23	106	108	76	.909	4	2	0	-1	*3/1	2.0
1984	Atl-N	32	113	15	31	8	0	3	19	14	17	.274	.354	.425	.779	108	3	1	110	133	17	.729	0	0	0	-0	3	0.1
1985	Atl-N	130	483	61	129	25	3	27	89	50	57	.267	.337	.499	.836	123	18	15	106	117	77	.786	1	1	-0	-2	13	1.0
1986	Atl-N	141	517	70	141	22	0	27	87	52	72	.273	.342	.472	.813	120	14	13	102	113	79	.755	1	4	-2	-0	*1	0.6
1988	StL-N	60	206	15	53	9	1	3	33	32	23	.257	.360	.354	.714	102	3	2	104	164	26	.654	0	0	0	-0	1	-0.1
Total	10	1020	3777	560	1047	169	8	218	685	369	512	.277	.344	.499	.843	126	151	127	105	113	621	.829	14	18	-7	-11	31	8.7
■ ROGERS HORNSBY	Hornsby, Rogers "Rajah" b: 4/27/1896, Winters, Tex. d: 1/5/63, Chicago, Ill. BR/TR, 5'11", 175 lbs. Deb: 9/10/15 MCH																											
1915	StL-N	18	57	5	14	2	0	0	4	2	6	.246	.271	.281	.552	67	-2	-2	100	95	4	.400	0	2	-1	-6	S	-1.0
1916	StL-N	139	495	63	155	17	15	6	65	40	63	.313	.369	.444	.814	155	28	30	97	115	88	.826	17			-2	3S1/2	3.4
1917	StL-N	145	523	86	171	24	**17**	8	66	45	34	.327	.385	**.484**	**.868**	163	**40**	**39**	102	97	100	**.906**	17			17	*S	**6.2**
1918	StL-N	115	416	51	117	19	11	5	60	40	43	.281	.349	.416	.764	142	16	19	93	128	60	.749	8			8	*S/O	3.2
1919	StL-N	138	512	68	163	15	9	8	71	48	41	.318	.384	.430	.814	**153**	29	**32**	94	109	87	.837	17			6	3S2/1	4.3
1920	StL-N	149	589	96	**218**	**44**	20	9	**94**	60	50	**.370**	**.431**	**.559**	**.990**	**187**	**63**	**64**	98	108	**138**	**1.047**	12	15	-5	16	*2	**8.0**
1921	StL-N	154	592	**131**	**235**	**44**	**18**	21	**126**	60	48	**.397**	**.458**	**.639**	**1.097**	**197**	**74**	**79**	95	111	**169**	**1.238**	13	13	-4	-1	*2/OS31	7.2
1922	StL-N	154	623	**141**	**250**	**46**	14	**42**	**152**	65	50	**.401**	**.459**	**.722**	**1.181**	**198**	**90**	**89**	101	89	**200**	**1.384**	17	12	-2	-7	*2	**7.2**
1923	StL-N	107	424	89	163	32	10	17	83	55	29	**.384**	**.459**	**.627**	**1.086**	**204**	**52**	**58**	90	89	120	**1.220**	3	7	-3	-14	21	3.9
1924	StL-N	143	536	**121**	**227**	**43**	14	25	94	**89**	32	**.424**	**.507**	**.696**	**1.203**	**214**	**94**	**92**	103	74	**186**	**1.461**	5	12	-6	-8	*2	**6.8**
1925	StL-N	138	504	133	203	41	10	**39**	**143**	83	39	**.403**	**.489**	**.756**	**1.245**	**209**	**87**	**86**	102	108	**187**	**1.549**	5	3	-0	-20	*2M	**5.8**
1926	StL-N	134	527	96	167	34	5	11	93	61	39	.317	.388	.463	.851	125	21	20	102	112	94	.856	3			-32	*2M	-0.5

YEAR	TM/L	G	AB	R	H	2B	3B	HR	RBI	BB	SO	AVG	OBP	SLG	PRO	/A	BR	/A	PF	CHI	RC	TA	SB	CS	SBR	FR	POS	TPR
1927	NY-N	155	568	**133**	205	32	9	26	125	**86**	38	.361	**.448**	**.586**	**1.035**	**176**	**63**	**63**	100	113	**148**	**1.190**	9			3	*2	6.1
1928	Bos-N	140	486	99	188	42	7	21	94	**107**	41	**.387**	**.498**	**.632**	**1.130**	**199**	**72**	**75**	97	87	**154**	**1.409**	5			-26	*2M	**4.8**
1929	Chi-N	156	602	**156**	229	47	8	39	149	87	65	.380	.459	**.679**	**1.139**	**176**	**74**	**73**	101	93	**183**	**1.338**	2			2	*2	**7.0**
1930	Chi-N	42	104	15	32	5	1	2	18	12	12	.308	.385	.433	.817	93	-0	-1	105	122	17	.806	0			1	2M	0.3
1931	Chi-N	100	357	64	118	37	1	16	90	56	23	.331	.421	.574	.996	172	34	36	96	129	90	1.096	1			-2	23M	3.7
1932	Chi-N	19	58	10	13	2	0	1	7	10	4	.224	.357	.310	.667	78	-1	-1	104	124	7	.667	0			-2	O/3M	-0.3
1933	StL-N	46	83	9	27	6	0	2	21	12	6	.325	.423	.470	.893	151	7	6	102	175	17	.915	1			-0	2	0.8
	StL-A	11	9	2	3	1	0	1	2	2	1	.333	.455	.778	1.232	193	2	1	115	67	3	1.500	0	0	0	0	HM	0.1
1934	StL-A	24	23	2	7	2	0	1	11	7	4	.304	.484	.522	1.006	153	3	2	104	245	7	1.250	0	0	0	-0	/3OM	0.2
1935	StL-A	10	24	1	5	3	0	0	3	3	6	.208	.296	.333	.630	59	-1	-2	107	127	2	.579	0	0	0	-0	/123M	-0.1
1936	StL-A	2	5	1	2	0	0	0	2	1	0	.400	.500	.400	.900	121	0	0	103	324	1	1.000	0	0	0	0	/1M	0.0
1937	StL-A	20	56	7	18	3	0	1	11	7	5	.321	.397	.429	.825	109	1	1	99	140	10	.816	0	0	0	-1	2M	0.2
Total	23	2259	8173	1579	2930	541	169	301	1584	1038	679	.358	.434	.577	1.010	176	843	858	99	105	2074	1.118	135	64		-69	*2S3/10	77.3

■ MIKE HORNUNG Hornung, Michael Joseph "Ubbo Ubbo" b: 6/12/1857, Carthage, N.Y. d: 10/30/31, Howard Beach, N.Y. BR/TR, 5'8.5", 164 lbs. Deb: 5/01/1879

YEAR	TM/L	G	AB	R	H	2B	3B	HR	RBI	BB	SO	AVG	OBP	SLG	PRO	/A	BR	/A	PF	CHI	RC	TA	SB	CS	SBR	FR	POS	TPR
1879	Buf-N	78	319	46	85	18	7	0	38	2	27	.266	.271	.367	.638	94	2	-4	114	121	33	.509				-2	*O/1	-0.6
1880	Buf-N	85	342	47	91	8	11	1	42	8	29	.266	.283	.363	.645	129	6	10	91	116	36	.526				0	*O1/2P	0.7
1881	Bos-N	83	324	40	78	12	8	2	25	5	25	.241	.252	.346	.598	94	-6	-2	91	78	29	.476				12	*O	0.8
1882	Bos-N	85	388	67	117	14	11	1	50	2	25	.302	.305	.402	.707	121	10	8	103	91	49	.583				10	*O/1	1.5
1883	Bos-N	98	446	**107**	124	25	13	8	66	8	54	.278	.291	.446	.737	113	10	5	106	89	59	.643				7	*O/3	1.3
1884	Bos-N	115	518	119	139	27	10	7	51	17	80	.268	.292	.400	.691	118	8	10	98	66	62	.591				5	*O/1	1.2
1885	Bos-N	25	109	14	22	4	1	1	7	1	20	.202	.209	.284	.493	62	-5	-4	94	63	7	.368				0	O	-0.3
1886	Bos-N	94	424	67	109	12	2	2	40	10	62	.257	.274	.309	.583	79	-12	-10	97	82	41	.498	16			5	*O	-0.2
1887	Bos-N	98	437	85	118	10	6	5	49	17	28	.270	.302	.355	.657	85	-10	-8	98	77	61	.677	41			13	*O	0.4
1888	Bos-N	107	431	61	103	11	7	3	53	16	39	.239	.269	.318	.587	84	-6	-9	106	138	46	.561	29			-7	*O	-1.7
1889	Bal-a	135	533	73	122	13	9	1	78	22	72	.229	.269	.293	.561	62	-27	-27	100	**149**	52	.533	34			11	*O/3	-1.7
1890	NY-N	120	513	62	122	18	5	0	65	12	37	.238	.258	.292	.550	65	-26	-22	95	139	50	.519	39			-1	O1/3S	-2.3
Total	12	1123	4784	788	1230	172	90	31	564	120	498	.257	.277	.350	.627	92	-56	-53	100	104	524	.554	159			51	*O/132SP	-0.9

■ TONY HORTON Horton, Anthony Darrin b: 12/6/44, Santa Monica, Cal. BR/TR, 6'3", 210 lbs. Deb: 7/31/64

YEAR	TM/L	G	AB	R	H	2B	3B	HR	RBI	BB	SO	AVG	OBP	SLG	PRO	/A	BR	/A	PF	CHI	RC	TA	SB	CS	SBR	FR	POS	TPR
1964	Bos-A	36	126	9	28	5	0	1	8	3	20	.222	.240	.286	.526	45	-9	-10	102	87	7	.371	0	0	0	1	O/1	-1.0
1965	Bos-A	60	163	23	48	8	1	7	23	18	36	.294	.365	.485	.849	130	8	7	107	95	29	.815	0	2	-1	1	1	0.5
1966	Bos-A	6	22	0	3	0	0	0	2	0	5	.136	.136	.136	.273	-20	-3	-4	109	285	0	.143	0	0	0	0	/1	-0.3
1967	Bos-A	21	39	2	12	3	0	0	9	0	5	.308	.308	.385	.692	90	0	-1	115	250	4	.517	0	0	0	0	/1	0.0
	Cle-A	106	363	35	102	13	4	10	44	18	52	.281	.322	.421	.744	118	7	7	100	100	48	.662	3	0	1	-2	1	-0.1
	Yr	127	402	37	114	16	4	10	53	18	57	.284	.321	.418	.739	114	7	6	103	127	53	.652	3	0	1	-2		-0.1
1968	Cle-A	133	477	57	119	29	3	14	59	34	56	.249	.304	.411	.714	114	7	7	101	108	59	.643	3	1	0	-3	*1	-0.1
1969	Cle-A	159	625	77	174	25	4	27	93	37	91	.278	.321	.461	.782	123	10	15	94	107	85	.695	3	3	-1	0	*1	0.3
1970	Cle-A	115	413	48	111	19	3	17	59	30	54	.269	.324	.453	.777	98	5	-2	115	102	55	.696	3	2	-0	2	*1	-0.5
Total	7	636	2228	251	597	102	15	76	297	140	319	.268	.315	.430	.745	109	25	19	102	107	287	.677	12	8	-1	-2	1/O	-1.2

■ WILLIE HORTON Horton, Willie Watterson b: 10/18/42, Arno, Va. BR/TR, 5'11", 209 lbs. Deb: 9/10/63 C

YEAR	TM/L	G	AB	R	H	2B	3B	HR	RBI	BB	SO	AVG	OBP	SLG	PRO	/A	BR	/A	PF	CHI	RC	TA	SB	CS	SBR	FR	POS	TPR
1963	Det-A	15	43	6	14	2	1	1	4	0	8	.326	.326	.488	.814	120	1	1	104	70	7	.793	2	0	1	-1	/O	0.0
1964	Det-A	25	80	6	13	1	3	1	10	11	20	.162	.272	.287	.559	58	-5	-4	96	163	7	.522	0	0	0	-3	O	-0.7
1965	Det-A	143	512	69	140	20	2	29	104	48	101	.273	.343	.490	.833	127	21	18	105	130	81	.789	5	9	-4	3	*O/3	1.3
1966	Det-A	146	526	72	138	22	6	27	100	44	103	.262	.323	.481	.804	125	17	16	102	128	80	.753	1	1	-0	-2	*O	0.9
1967	Det-A	122	401	47	110	20	3	19	67	36	80	.274	.340	.481	.821	141	19	19	99	112	64	.769	0	0	0	-4	*O	1.3
1968	Det-A	143	512	68	146	20	2	36	85	49	110	.285	.357	.543	.900	159	41	38	106	96	95	.875	0	3	-2	-5	*O	2.9
1969	Det-A	141	508	66	133	17	1	28	91	52	93	.262	.334	.465	.798	117	13	11	103	116	78	.762	3	3	-1	6	*O	1.3
1970	Det-A	96	371	53	113	18	2	17	69	28	43	.305	.357	.501	.858	130	16	14	103	125	65	.812	0	1	-1	2	*O	1.2
1971	Det-A	119	450	64	130	25	1	22	72	37	75	.289	.352	.496	.848	144	21	23	96	108	73	.788	1	5	-3	-8	*O	0.9
1972	Det-A	108	333	44	77	9	5	11	36	27	47	.231	.295	.387	.682	90	-0	-5	113	93	37	.602	0	0	0	-8	O	-1.7
1973	Det-A	111	411	42	130	19	3	17	53	23	57	.316	.363	.501	.864	140	21	20	101	83	69	.793	1	4	-2	-12	*O/D	0.3
1974	Det-A	72	238	32	71	8	1	15	47	21	36	.298	.363	.529	.892	145	16	14	106	108	44	.862	0	1	-1	-7	O/D	0.5
1975	Det-A	159	615	62	169	13	1	25	92	44	109	.275	.323	.421	.744	105	5	3	104	112	79	.652	1	2	-1	0	*D	0.2
1976	Det-A	114	401	40	105	17	0	14	56	49	63	.262	.345	.409	.754	116	10	9	104	106	55	.689	0	0	0	0	*D	0.9
1977	Det-A	1	4	0	1	0	0	0	0	0	0	.250	.250	.250	.500	35	-0	-0	105	0	0	.333	0	0	0	-0	/O	0.0
	Tex-A	139	519	55	150	23	3	15	75	42	117	.289	.342	.432	.774	105	6	3	105	113	73	.693	2	3	-1	-2	*DO	0.0
	Yr	140	523	55	151	23	3	15	75	42	117	.289	.342	.430	.772	104	6	3	105	112	73	.690	2	3	-1	-2		0.0
1978	Cle-A	50	169	15	42	7	0	5	22	15	25	.249	.314	.379	.692	101	-2	-0	93	110	19	.619	3	0	1	0	D	0.1
	Oak-A	32	102	11	32	8	0	3	19	9	15	.314	.369	.480	.850	136	5	5	101	129	18	.806	0	1	-1	-1	D/O	0.4
	Tor-A	33	122	12	25	6	0	3	19	4	29	.205	.230	.328	.558	55	-8	-8	100	156	8	.427	0	0	0	0	D	-0.7
	Yr	115	393	38	99	21	0	11	60	28	69	.252	.303	.389	.693	96	-4	-3	97	131	47	.615	3	1	0	-1		-0.2
1979	Sea-A	162	646	77	180	19	5	29	106	42	112	.279	.327	.458	.785	109	6	6	100	113	91	.704	1	1	-0	0	*D	0.6
1980	Sea-A	97	335	32	74	10	1	8	36	39	70	.221	.310	.328	.638	73	-11	-13	103	107	35	.567	0	4	-2	0	D	-1.4
Total	18	2028	7298	873	1993	284	40	325	1163	620	1313	.273	.335	.457	.791	119	194	170	103	112	1077	.754	20	38	-17	-42	*OD/3	8.3

■ TIM HOSLEY Hosley, Timothy Kenneth b: 5/10/47, Spartanburg, S.C. BR/TR, 5'11", 185 lbs. Deb: 9/08/70

YEAR	TM/L	G	AB	R	H	2B	3B	HR	RBI	BB	SO	AVG	OBP	SLG	PRO	/A	BR	/A	PF	CHI	RC	TA	SB	CS	SBR	FR	POS	TPR
1970	Det-A	7	12	1	2	0	0	1	2	0	6	.167	.167	.417	.583	54	-1	-1	103	101	1	.500	0	0	0	0	/C	0.0
1971	Det-A	7	16	2	3	0	0	2	6	0	1	.188	.188	.563	.750	110	-0	-0	96	163	1	.643	0	0	0	-0	/C1	0.0
1973	Oak-A	13	14	3	3	0	0	0	2	2	3	.214	.313	.214	.527	58	-1	-1	87	262	1	.455	0	0	0	-0	C	0.0
1974	Oak-A	11	7	3	2	0	0	0	1	1	2	.286	.375	.286	.661	92	-0	-0	100	197	1	.600	0	0	0	-0	/C1	0.0
1975	Chi-N	62	141	22	36	7	0	6	20	27	25	.255	.382	.433	.815	121	6	5	104	98	24	.820	1	1	-0	-6	C	0.1
1976	Oak-A	37	55	4	9	2	0	1	4	8	12	.164	.270	.255	.524	54	-3	-3	100	90	4	.468	0	0	0	-4	C	-0.5
	Chi-N	1	1	0	0	0	0	0	0	0	0	.000	.000	.000	.000	-91	-0	-0	109	0	0	.000	0	0	0	0	H	0.0
1977	Oak-A	39	78	5	15	0	0	1	10	16	13	.192	.337	.231	.568	61	-4	-3	95	189	7	.547	0	0	0	-3	CD/1	-0.5
1978	Oak-A	13	23	1	7	2	0	0	3	1	6	.304	.360	.391	.751	110	0	0	101	132	3	.688	0	0	0	-0	/CD	0.0
1981	Oak-A	18	21	2	2	0	0	1	5	2	5	.095	.174	.238	.412	18	-2	-2	96	245	1	.368	0	0	0	0	/1D	-0.1
Total	9	208	368	43	79	11	0	12	53	57	73	.215	.326	.342	.669	88	-5	-5	100	137	44	.648	1	1	-0	-13	C/D1	-1.0

■ CHUCK HOSTETLER Hostetler, Charles Cloyd b: 9/22/03, Mc Clellandtown, Pa. d: 2/18/71, Fort Collins, Colo BL/TR, 6', 175 lbs. Deb: 4/18/44

YEAR	TM/L	G	AB	R	H	2B	3B	HR	RBI	BB	SO	AVG	OBP	SLG	PRO	/A	BR	/A	PF	CHI	RC	TA	SB	CS	SBR	FR	POS	TPR
1944	Det-A	90	265	42	79	9	2	0	20	21	31	.298	.350	.347	.697	94	0	-2	105	78	33	.603	4	4	-1	-3	O	-0.7
1945	Det-A	42	44	3	7	3	0	0	2	7	8	.159	.275	.227	.502	44	-3	-3	106	72	3	.459	0	0	0	-3	/O	-0.6
Total	2	132	309	45	86	12	2	0	22	28	39	.278	.338	.330	.668	87	-3	-5	105	77	36	.590	4	4	-1	-6	/O	-1.3

■ DAVE HOSTETLER Hostetler, David Alan b: 3/27/56, Pasadena, Cal. BR/TR, 6'4", 215 lbs. Deb: 9/15/81

YEAR	TM/L	G	AB	R	H	2B	3B	HR	RBI	BB	SO	AVG	OBP	SLG	PRO	/A	BR	/A	PF	CHI	RC	TA	SB	CS	SBR	FR	POS	TPR
1981	Mon-N	5	6	1	3	0	0	1	1	0	2	.500	.500	1.000	1.500	321	2	2	99	44	3	2.000	0	0	0	0	/1	0.2
1982	Tex-A	113	418	53	97	12	3	22	67	42	113	.232	.304	.433	.737	107	-1	3	93	115	52	.671	2	2	-1	-8	*1/D	-0.8
1983	Tex-A	94	304	31	67	9	2	11	46	42	103	.220	.325	.372	.696	90	-3	-4	101	126	36	.643	0	2	-1	0	D/1	-0.4
1984	Tex-A	37	82	7	18	2	1	3	10	13	27	.220	.326	.378	.704	94	-0	-1	100	100	9	.638	0	0	0	0	1D	0.0
1988	Pit-N	6	8	0	2	0	0	0	0	0	3	.250	.250	.250	.500	45	-1	-1	98	0	1	.333	0	0	0	0	/1C	0.0
Total	5	255	818	92	187	23	6	37	124	97	248	.229	.315	.407	.722	100	-4	-0	97	116	101	.690	2	4	-2	-8	1D/C	-1.0

■ PETE HOTALING Hotaling, Peter James "Monkey" b: 12/16/1856, Mohawk, N.Y. d: 7/3/28, Cleveland, Ohio BR/TR, 5'8", 166 lbs. Deb: 5/01/1879

YEAR	TM/L	G	AB	R	H	2B	3B	HR	RBI	BB	SO	AVG	OBP	SLG	PRO	/A	BR	/A	PF	CHI	RC	TA	SB	CS	SBR	FR	POS	TPR
1879	Cin-N	81	369	64	103	20	9	1	27	12	17	.279	.302	.390	.692	133	10	13	95	56	45	.586				0	*O/C23	1.0
1880	Cle-N	78	325	40	78	17	8	0	41	10	30	.240	.263	.342	.604	104	1	2	99	119	30	.490				-4	*O/C	-0.4
1881	Wor-N	77	317	51	98	15	3	1	35	18	12	.309	.346	.385	.731	123	11	9	105	103	43	.639				-2	*O/C	0.5
1882	Bos-N	84	378	64	98	16	5	0	28	16	21	.259	.289	.328	.617	95	-1	-3	103	66	37	.500				1	*O	-0.2

YEAR	TM/L	G	AB	R	H	2B	3B	HR	RBI	BB	SO	AVG	OBP	SLG	PRO	/A	BR	/A	PF	CHI	RC	TA	SB	CS	SBR	FR	POS	TPR
1883	Cle-N	100	417	54	108	20	8	0	30	12	31	.259	.280	.345	.625	85	-6	-9	105	64	41	.505				-2	*O	-0.6
1884	Cle-N	102	408	69	99	16	6	3	27	28	50	.243	.291	.333	.625	94	-2	-3	102	57	41	.531				-3	*O/2	-0.5
1885	Bro-a	94	370	73	95	9	5	1		49		.257	.350	.316	.666	110	9	6	104	0	42	.618				-1	*O	0.0
1887	Cle-a	126	505	108	151	28	13	3		53		.299	.373	.424	.797	128	17	20	98	0	98	.895	43			-4	*O	0.9
1888	Cle-a	98	403	67	101	7	6	0	55	26		.251	.307	.298	.605	100	-0	1	97	118	49	.623	35			-10	*O	-1.1
Total	9	840	3492	590	931	148	63	9	243	224	161	.267	.314	.353	.667	108	39	36	101	60	426	.606	78			-26	O/C23	-0.4
■ **KEN HOTTMAN**	Hottman, Kenneth Roger b: 5/7/48, Stockton, Cal. BR/TR, 5'11", 190 lbs. Deb: 9/11/71																											
1971	Chi-A	6	16	1	2	0	0	0	0	1	2	.125	.176	.125	.301	-14	-2	-2	98	0	0	.200	0	0	0	-1	/O	-0.3
■ **SADIE HOUCK**	Houck, Sargent Perry b: 1856, Washington, D.C. d: 5/26/19, Washington, D.C. BR/TR, 5'7", 151 lbs. Deb: 5/01/1879																											
1879	Bos-N	80	356	69	95	24	9	2	49	4	11	.267	.275	.402	.677	112	7	4	107	111	40	.563				-9	OS	-0.3
1880	Bos-N	12	47	2	7	0	0	0	2	0	6	.149	.149	.149	.298	1	-5	-4	92	106	1	.175				-2	O	-0.5
	Pro-N	49	184	27	37	7	7	1	22	3	6	.201	.214	.332	.545	85	-3	-2	96	128	13	.435				-1	O	-0.4
	Yr	61	231	29	44	7	7	1	24	3	12	.190	.201	.294	.495	69	-8	-7	95	125	14	.380				-3		-0.9
1881	Det-N	75	308	43	86	16	6	1	36	6	6	.279	.293	.380	.673	103	3	0	106	110	35	.554				-1	*S	0.5
1883	Det-N	101	416	52	105	18	12	0	40	9	18	.252	.268	.353	.622	95	-7	-1	91	100	40	.502				2	*S	0.5
1884	Phi-a	108	472	93	140	19	14	0		7		.297	.318	.396	.714	118	17	7	114	0	61	.608				22	*S/2	2.4
1885	Phi-a	93	388	74	99	10	9	0		10		.255	.286	.327	.614	93	-2	-4	103	0	37	.498				21	*S	1.6
1886	Bal-a	61	260	29	50	8	1	0		4		.192	.216	.231	.447	46	-17	-14	91	0	19	.443	25			-6	S/2O	-1.4
	Was-N	52	195	14	42	3	0	0	14	2	28	.215	.223	.231	.454	41	-14	-12	94	103	11	.333	4			-3	S/2	-1.4
1887	NY-a	10	33	3	5	1	0	0		3		.152	.243	.182	.425	24	-3	-3	88	0	2	.429	2			0	S/2	-0.1
Total	8	641	2659	406	666	106	58	4	163	48	75	.250	.269	.338	.608	91	-25	-30	101	61	261	.501	31			24	SO/2	0.9
■ **RALPH HOUK**	Houk, Ralph George b: 8/9/19, Lawrence, Kan. BR/TR, 5'11", 193 lbs. Deb: 4/26/47 MC																											
1947	NY-A	41	92	7	25	3	1	0	12	11	5	.272	.350	.326	.676	92	-1	-1	97	147	11	.594	0	0	0	-2	C	0.1
1948	NY-A	14	29	3	8	2	0	0	3	0	0	.276	.276	.345	.621	64	-2	-2	100	101	3	.476	0	0	0	-0	C	0.0
1949	NY-A	5	7	0	4	0	0	0	1	0	1	.571	.571	.571	1.143	202	1	1	100	86	2	1.333	0	0	0	0	/C	0.1
1950	NY-A	10	9	0	1	1	0	0	1	0	2	.111	.111	.222	.333	-16	-2	-2	99	173	0	.250	0	0	0	0	/C	0.0
1951	NY-A	3	5	0	1	0	0	0	2	0	1	.200	.200	.200	.400	9	-1	-1	92	715	0	.250	0	0	0	0	/C	0.0
1952	NY-A	9	6	0	2	0	0	0	0	1	0	.333	.429	.333	.762	116	0	0	98	0	1	.750	0	0	0	0	/C	0.1
1953	NY-A	8	9	2	2	0	0	0	1	0	1	.222	.222	.222	.444	22	-1	-1	93	185	0	.250	0	0	0	0	/C	0.0
1954	NY-A	1	1	0	0	0	0	0	0	0	0	.000	.000	.000	.000	-99	-0	-0	99	0	0	.000	0	0	0	0	H	0.0
Total	8	91	158	12	43	6	1	0	20	12	10	.272	.324	.323	.646	79	-5	-5	97	150	18	.548	0	0	0	-2	/C	0.3
■ **FRANK HOUSE**	House, Henry Franklin "Pig" b: 2/18/30, Bessemer, Ala. BL/TR, 6'1.5", 190 lbs. Deb: 7/21/50																											
1950	Det-A	5	5	1	2	1	0	0	0	0	1	.400	.400	.600	1.000	159	0	0	97	0	1	1.000	0	0	0	-0	/C	0.0
1951	Det-A	18	41	3	9	2	0	1	4	6	2	.220	.319	.341	.661	74	-1	-2	106	84	4	.583	1	1	-0	-1	C	-0.1
1954	Det-A	114	352	35	88	12	1	9	38	31	34	.250	.313	.366	.679	86	-8	-8	100	92	41	.599	2	1	0	4	*C	0.1
1955	Det-A	102	328	37	85	11	1	15	53	22	25	.259	.312	.436	.748	103	-2	-1	97	105	45	.680	0	0	0	2	C	0.5
1956	Det-A	94	321	44	77	6	2	10	44	21	19	.240	.293	.364	.657	75	-14	-12	97	112	31	.546	1	1	-0	1	C	-1.0
1957	Det-A	106	348	31	90	9	0	7	36	35	26	.259	.328	.345	.673	78	-7	-10	107	101	38	.579	1	1	-0	8	C	0.1
1958	KC-A	76	202	16	51	6	3	4	24	12	13	.252	.298	.371	.669	79	-5	-6	106	111	20	.556	1	0	0	2	C	-0.3
1959	KC-A	98	347	32	82	14	3	1	30	20	23	.236	.282	.303	.584	60	-19	-19	101	109	27	.457	0	3	-2	7	C	-0.8
1960	Cin-N	23	28	0	5	2	0	0	3	0	2	.179	.179	.250	.429	16	-3	-3	98	174	1	.280	0	0	0	0	/C	-0.2
1961	Det-A	17	22	3	5	1	1	0	3	4	2	.227	.346	.364	.710	94	-0	-0	96	147	3	.667	0	0	0	-1	C	0.0
Total	10	653	1994	202	494	64	11	47	235	151	147	.248	.304	.362	.666	79	-59	-62	101	105	210	.590	6	7	-2	22	C	-1.7
■ **CHARLIE HOUSEHOLDER**	Householder, Charles F. b: 1856, Harrisburg, Pa. 5'7", 150 lbs. Deb: 4/20/1884																											
1884	CP-U	83	310	32	74	12	5	1		12		.239	.267	.319	.586	98	-1	-0	99	0	27	.470	0			-9	3O/SP	-0.7
■ **CHARLIE HOUSEHOLDER**	Householder, Charles W. b: 1856, Harrisburg, Pa. d: 12/26/08, Harrisburg, Pa. BL/TL, 5'11", 158 lbs. Deb: 5/02/1882																											
1882	Bal-a	74	307	42	78	10	7	1		4		.254	.264	.342	.606	111	0	4	92	0	28	.476				3	*1/C	0.6
1884	Bro-a	76	273	28	66	15	3	3		12		.242	.279	.352	.630	110	2	3	98	0	27	.531				-7	1C/O2	-0.2
Total	2	150	580	70	144	25	10	4		16		.248	.271	.347	.617	111	3	7	95	0	56	.502				-4	1/CO2	0.4
■ **ED HOUSEHOLDER**	Householder, Edward H. b: 10/12/1869, Pittsburgh, Pa. d: 7/3/24, Los Angeles, Cal. Deb: 4/17/03																											
1903	Bro-N	12	43	5	9	0	0	0	9	2		.209	.244	.209	.454	31	-4	-4	101	328	3	.412	3			1	O	-0.2
■ **PAUL HOUSEHOLDER**	Householder, Paul Wesley b: 9/4/58, Columbus, Ohio BB/TR, 6', 180 lbs. Deb: 8/26/80																											
1980	Cin-N	20	45	3	11	1	1	0	7	1	13	.244	.261	.311	.572	58	-3	-3	102	198	4	.471	1	0	0	-1	O	-0.3
1981	Cin-N	23	69	12	19	4	0	2	9	10	16	.275	.367	.420	.787	122	2	2	101	101	11	.792	3	1	0	-1	O	0.1
1982	Cin-N	138	417	40	88	11	5	9	34	30	77	.211	.267	.326	.593	64	-20	-21	102	82	35	.535	17	11	-2	3	*O	-2.1
1983	Cin-N	123	380	40	97	24	4	6	43	44	60	.255	.336	.387	.723	97	0	-1	103	103	48	.679	12	12	-4	2	*O	-0.4
1984	Cin-N	14	12	3	1	1	0	0	0	3	3	.083	.267	.167	.433	23	-1	-1	106	0	1	.500	1	1	-0	-2	O	-0.3
	StL-N	13	14	1	2	0	0	0	0	0	3	.143	.143	.143	.286	-20	-2	-2	99	0	0	.154	0	0	0	-3	/O	-0.5
	Yr	27	26	4	3	1	0	0	0	3	6	.115	.207	.154	.361	3	-3	-3	102	0	1	.320	1	1	-0	-5		-0.8
1985	Mil-A	95	299	41	77	15	0	11	34	27	60	.258	.321	.418	.739	96	-0	-2	105	85	40	.672	1	2	-1	1	O/D	-0.2
1986	Mil-A	26	78	4	17	3	1	1	16	7	16	.218	.291	.321	.611	66	-3	-4	102	228	7	.531	1	2	-1	-1	O/D	-0.6
1987	Hou-N	14	12	2	1	1	0	0	1	4	2	.083	.313	.167	.479	34	-1	-1	93	200	1	.545	0	0	0	-2	/O	-0.2
Total	8	466	1326	146	313	60	11	29	144	126	250	.236	.305	.363	.669	82	-28	-33	103	102	146	.624	36	29	-7	-4	O/D	-4.5
■ **JOHN HOUSEMAN**	Houseman, John Franklin b: 1/10/1870, Holland d: 11/4/22, Chicago, Ill. Deb: 9/11/1894																											
1894	Chi-N	4	15	5	6	3	1	0	4	5	3	.400	.571	.733	1.305	200	3	3	108	86	8	2.111	2			0	/S2	0.2
1897	StL-N	80	278	34	68	6	6	0	21	28		.245	.329	.309	.638	76	-11	-7	93	73	34	.652	16			-9	2O/S3	-1.2
Total	2	84	293	39	74	9	7	0	25	33	3	.253	.344	.331	.675	85	-7	-4	94	74	42	.712	18			-9	/2OS3	-1.0
■ **BEN HOUSER**	Houser, Benjamin Franklin b: 11/30/1883, Shenandoah, Pa. d: 1/15/52, Augusta, Maine BL/TL, 6'1", 185 lbs. Deb: 5/02/10																											
1910	Phi-A	34	69	9	13	3	2	0	7	7		.188	.263	.290	.553	72	-2	-2	102	129	5	.482	0			-0	1	-0.1
1911	Bos-N	20	71	11	18	1	0	1	9	8	6	.254	.329	.310	.639	77	-2	-2	103	124	8	.604	2			0	1	-0.2
1912	Bos-N	108	332	38	95	17	3	8	52	22	29	.286	.332	.428	.760	100	2	-2	107	105	47	.700	1			-2	1	-0.5
Total	3	162	472	58	126	21	5	9	68	37	35	.267	.322	.390	.711	93	-2	-6	106	112	60	.650	3			-2	1	-0.8
■ **LEFTY HOUTZ**	Houtz, Fred Fritz b: 9/4/1875, Connersville, Ind. d: 2/15/59, Wapakoneta, Ohio BL/TL, 5'10", 170 lbs. Deb: 7/23/1899																											
1899	Cin-N	5	17	1	4	0	1	0	0	4		.235	.381	.353	.734	99	0	0	106	0	3	.846	1			0	/O	0.0
■ **STEVE HOVLEY**	Hovley, Stephen Eugene b: 12/18/44, Ventura, Cal. BL/TL, 5'10", 188 lbs. Deb: 6/26/69																											
1969	Sea-A	91	329	41	91	14	3	3	20	30	34	.277	.339	.365	.704	98	-1	-1	98	63	43	.660	10	4	1	1	O	0.0
1970	Mil-A	40	135	17	38	9	0	0	16	17	11	.281	.366	.348	.714	100	0	1	98	140	18	.686	5	1	1	-1	O	-0.1
	Oak-A	72	100	8	19	1	0	0	1	5	11	.190	.229	.200	.429	20	-11	-11	97	20	5	.337	3	0	1	-4	O	-1.5
	Yr	112	235	25	57	10	0	0	17	22	22	.243	.310	.285	.595	67	-11	-10	97	64	23	.541	8	1	2	-5		-1.6
1971	Oak-A	24	27	3	3	2	0	0	3	7	9	.111	.314	.185	.499	44	-2	-2	101	245	3	.625	2	0	1	-1	O	-0.1
1972	KC-A	105	196	24	53	5	1	3	24	24	29	.270	.353	.352	.705	110	3	3	100	129	26	.655	3	3	-1	-4	O	-0.3
1973	KC-A	104	232	29	59	8	1	2	24	33	34	.254	.347	.323	.670	82	-2	-5	109	116	28	.633	6	4	-1	-9	OD	-1.6
Total	5	436	1019	122	263	39	5	8	88	116	128	.258	.336	.330	.666	88	-13	-14	101	100	122	.629	29	12	2	-18	O/D	-3.6
■ **DAVE HOWARD**	Howard, David Austin "Del" b: 5/1/1889, Washington, D.C. d: 1/26/56, Dallas, Tex. BR/TR, 5'11", 165 lbs. Deb: 5/08/12																											
1912	Was-A	1	0	0	0	0	0	0	0	0		—	—	—	—	—	0	0	99	—	—	—	0			0	R	0.0
1915	Bro-F	24	36	5	8	1	0	0	1	1	8	.222	.243	.250	.493	47	-2	-2	98	40	2	.357	0			0	2/OS3	-0.2
Total	2	25	36	5	8	1	0	0	1	1	8	.222	.243	.250	.493	47	-2	-2	98	40	124	.357	0			0	/2O3S	-0.2

YEAR	TM/L	G	AB	R	H	2B	3B	HR	RBI	BB	SO	AVG	OBP	SLG	PRO	/A	BR	/A	PF	CHI	RC	TA	SB	CS	SBR	FR	POS	TPR
■ **DOUG HOWARD**	Howard, Douglas Lynn b: 2/6/48, Salt Lake City, Utah BR/TR, 6'3", 185 lbs. Deb: 9/06/72																											
1972	Cal-A	11	38	4	10	1	0	0	2	1	3	.263	.300	.289	.589	86	-1	-1	88	77	3	.433	0	0	0	0	/O13	0.0
1973	Cal-A	8	21	2	2	0	0	0	1	1	6	.095	.136	.095	.232	-35	-4	-4	96	196	0	.158	0	0	0	-1	/O13	-0.4
1974	Cal-A	22	39	5	9	0	1	0	5	2	1	.231	.268	.282	.550	63	-2	-2	92	179	2	.424	1	0	0	-2	/O1D	-0.3
1975	StL-N	17	29	1	6	0	0	1	1	0	7	.207	.207	.310	.517	41	-2	-2	103	32	2	.391	0	0	0	0	/1	-0.2
1976	Cle-A	39	90	7	19	4	0	0	13	3	13	.211	.245	.256	.500	47	-6	-6	100	217	5	.373	1	1	-0	-1	1/OD	-0.9
Total	5	97	217	19	46	5	1	1	22	7	30	.212	.243	.258	.501	47	-15	-15	96	160	13	.383	2	1	0	-4	/1OD3	-1.8
■ **ELSTON HOWARD**	Howard, Elston Gene b: 2/23/29, St.Louis, Mo. d: 12/14/80, New York, N.Y. BR/TR, 6'2", 196 lbs. Deb: 4/14/55 C																											
1955	NY-A	97	279	33	81	8	7	10	43	20	36	.290	.340	.477	.817	120	5	6	98	98	45	.762	0	0	0	0	O/C	0.3
1956	NY-A	98	290	35	76	8	3	5	34	21	30	.262	.314	.362	.676	79	-10	-9	99	106	30	.562	0	1	-1	-6	OC	-1.8
1957	NY-A	110	356	33	90	13	4	8	44	16	43	.253	.285	.379	.664	85	-11	-8	94	109	31	.529	2	5	-2	-10	OC/1	-2.4
1958	NY-A	103	376	45	118	19	5	11	66	22	60	.314	.352	.479	.830	123	12	11	103	127	60	.757	1	1	-0	7	CO/1	1.7
1959	NY-A	125	443	59	121	24	6	18	73	20	57	.273	.309	.476	.785	121	5	9	93	108	61	.699	0	1	-1	-0	1CO	0.9
1960	NY-A	107	323	29	79	11	3	6	39	28	43	.245	.305	.353	.658	82	-11	-8	94	116	35	.575	3	0	1	-0	C/O	-0.1
1961	NY-A	129	446	64	155	17	5	21	77	28	65	.348	.390	.549	.939	154	29	31	96	98	94	.923	0	3	-2	8	*C/1	3.4
1962	NY-A	136	494	63	138	23	5	21	91	31	76	.279	.323	.474	.797	119	6	10	94	124	69	.708	1	1	-0	7	*C	2.4
1963	NY-A	135	487	75	140	21	6	28	85	35	68	.287	.343	.528	.871	139	24	24	101	106	83	.819	0	0	0	12	*C	3.9
1964	NY-A	150	550	63	172	27	3	15	84	48	73	.313	.373	.455	.828	125	22	20	103	123	93	.781	1	1	-0	20	*C	4.6
1965	NY-A	110	391	38	91	15	1	9	45	24	65	.233	.279	.345	.624	75	-13	-13	101	117	34	.506	0	0	0	4	C/1O	-0.3
1966	NY-A	126	410	38	105	19	2	6	35	37	65	.256	.319	.356	.675	100	-3	-0	94	90	45	.580	0	0	0	16	*C1	2.2
1967	NY-A	66	199	13	39	6	0	3	17	12	36	.196	.249	.271	.520	57	-12	-10	94	113	13	.410	0	0	0	9	C/1	0.2
	Bos-A	42	116	9	17	3	0	1	11	9	24	.147	.214	.198	.413	20	-11	-13	115	176	5	.320	0	0	0	-2	C	-1.3
	Yr	108	315	22	56	9	0	4	28	21	60	.178	.236	.244	.480	41	-23	-23	102	138	19	.384	0	0	0	7		-1.1
1968	Bos-A	71	203	22	49	4	0	5	18	22	45	.241	.319	.335	.654	98	-0	-0	101	93	21	.575	1	1	-0	-2	C	0.0
Total	14	1605	5363	619	1471	218	50	167	762	373	786	.274	.325	.427	.752	109	34	48	98	112	718	.690	9	14	-6	62	*CO/1	13.7
■ **FRANK HOWARD**	Howard, Frank Oliver "Hondo" or "The Capital Punisher" b: 8/8/36, Columbus, Ohio BR/TR, 6'7", 255 lbs. Deb: 9/10/58 MC																											
1958	LA-N	8	29	3	7	1	0	1	2	1	11	.241	.267	.379	.646	65	-1	-2	105	60	3	.522	0	0	0	0	/O	-0.1
1959	LA-N	9	21	2	3	0	1	1	6	2	9	.143	.217	.381	.598	54	-1	-2	102	220	2	.556	0	0	0	-0	/O	-0.1
1960	LA-N	117	448	54	120	15	2	23	77	32	108	.268	.321	.464	.785	97	6	-2	115	115	66	.721	0	1	-1	-4	*O/1	-1.0
1961	LA-N	92	267	36	79	10	2	15	45	21	50	.296	.349	.517	.866	123	9	8	102	99	44	.796	0	1	-1	-5	O/1	-0.1
1962	LA-N	141	493	80	146	25	6	31	119	39	108	.296	.349	.560	.909	150	25	30	93	127	90	.868	1	0	0	3	*O	2.5
1963	LA-N	123	417	58	114	16	1	28	64	33	116	.273	.333	.518	.851	148	21	23	95	91	70	.814	1	2	-1	-1	*O	1.6
1964	LA-N	134	433	60	98	13	2	24	69	51	113	.226	.308	.432	.740	115	3	7	92	109	56	.685	1	0	0	-8	*O	-0.4
1965	Was-A	149	516	53	149	22	6	21	84	55	112	.289	.360	.477	.836	135	24	24	100	115	90	.806	0	0	0	-9	*O	1.0
1966	Was-A	146	493	52	137	19	4	18	71	53	104	.278	.349	.442	.791	133	16	20	95	112	74	.736	1	1	-0	-6	*O	0.9
1967	Was-A	149	519	71	133	20	2	36	89	60	155	.256	.339	.511	.850	145	30	28	102	102	88	.823	0	1	-1	-11	*O/1	1.3
1968	Was-A	158	598	79	164	28	3	**44**	106	54	141	.274	.340	**.552**	.892	**182**	45	50	91	104	110	.872	0	0	0	-2	*O1	4.7
1969	Was-A	161	592	111	175	17	2	48	111	102	96	.296	.403	.574	.978	176	57	59	97	98	132	1.004	1	0	0	-18	*O1	3.5
1970	Was-A	161	566	90	160	15	1	**44**	**126**	**132**	125	.283	.420	.546	.966	**171**	54	57	96	111	130	1.030	1	2	-1	-10	*O1	3.9
1971	Was-A	153	549	60	153	25	2	26	83	77	121	.279	.369	.474	.843	149	27	32	92	106	89	.800	1	0	0	-6	*O1	2.1
1972	Tex-A	95	287	28	70	9	0	9	31	42	55	.244	.342	.369	.712	118	5	7	94	97	34	.644	1	0	0	-2	1O	-0.1
	Det-A	14	33	1	8	1	0	1	7	4	8	.242	.324	.364	.688	92	0	-0	113	195	4	.640	0	0	0	-0	1/O	-0.1
	Yr	109	320	29	78	10	0	10	38	46	63	.244	.341	.369	.709	115	5	6	97	111	45	.686	1	0	0	-2		-0.2
1973	Det-A	85	227	26	58	9	1	12	29	24	28	.256	.327	.463	.789	119	5	5	101	81	30	.709	0	1	-1	0	D/1	0.4
Total	16	1895	6488	864	1774	245	35	382	1119	782	1460	.273	.355	.499	.853	143	324	345	97	107	1110	.857	8	9	-3	-79	*O1/D	20.0
■ **DEL HOWARD**	Howard, George Elmer b: 12/24/1877, Kenney, Ill. d: 12/24/56, Seattle, Wash. BL/TR, 6', 180 lbs. Deb: 4/15/05																											
1905	Pit-N	123	435	56	127	18	5	2	63	27		.292	.333	.370	.703	107	6	3	104	134	62	.672	19			-6	1O/P	-0.7
1906	Bos-N	147	545	46	142	19	8	1	54	26		.261	.294	.330	.624	96	-4	-4	100	114	59	.553	17			-11	O2S/1	-1.7
1907	Bos-N	50	187	20	51	4	2	1	13	11		.273	.313	.332	.645	109	1	1	95	80	23	.618	11			-2	O/2	-0.1
	Chi-N	51	148	10	34	2	2	0	13	6		.230	.260	.270	.530	64	-6	-7	106	123	11	.430	3			1	1/O	-0.6
	Yr	101	335	30	85	6	4	1	26	17		.254	.290	.304	.594	87	-5	-5	101	103	34	.532	14			-0		-0.7
1908	Chi-N	96	315	42	88	7	3	1	26	23		.279	.328	.330	.659	106	4	2	106	95	37	.608	11			4	O/1	0.6
1909	Chi-N	69	203	25	40	4	2	1	24	18		.197	.282	.251	.533	66	-7	-8	101	162	15	.497	6			-1	1	-1.0
Total	5	536	1833	199	482	54	22	6	193	111		.263	.307	.326	.633	96	-6	-11	102	118	208	.579	67			-14	O1/2SP	-3.5
■ **IVON HOWARD**	Howard, Ivon Chester b: 10/12/1882, Kenney, Ill. d: 3/30/67, Medford, Ore. BB/TR, 5'10", 170 lbs. Deb: 4/25/14																											
1914	StL-A	81	209	21	51	6	2	0	20	28	42	.244	.342	.292	.634	93	-1	-1	98	123	23	.631	14	10	-2	-2	31/OS	-0.4
1915	StL-A	113	324	43	90	10	7	2	43	43	48	.278	.368	.370	.738	126	9	11	96	116	50	.793	29	12	2	1	13O/2S	1.2
1916	Cle-A	81	246	20	46	11	5	0	23	30	34	.187	.298	.272	.571	72	-8	-8	100	123	24	.575	9			2	2/1	-0.4
1917	Cle-A	27	39	7	4	0	0	0	0	3	5	.103	.167	.103	.269	-16	-5	-6	114	0	1	.229	1			1	/32O	-0.5
Total	4	302	818	91	191	27	14	2	86	104	129	.233	.331	.308	.639	93	-6	-4	98	115	98	.653	53	22		2	/123OS	-0.1
■ **LARRY HOWARD**	Howard, Lawrence Rayford b: 6/6/45, Columbus, Ohio BR/TR, 6'3", 200 lbs. Deb: 8/09/70																											
1970	Hou-N	31	88	11	27	6	0	2	16	10	23	.307	.378	.443	.821	127	2	3	94	138	15	.778	0	0	0	0	C/1O	0.4
1971	Hou-N	24	64	6	15	3	0	2	14	3	17	.234	.269	.375	.644	87	-2	-1	93	190	6	.519	0	1	-1	-1	C	-0.1
1972	Hou-N	54	157	16	35	7	0	2	13	17	30	.223	.299	.306	.605	68	-6	-7	106	99	14	.512	0	0	0	-7	C/O	-1.1
1973	Hou-N	20	48	3	8	3	0	0	4	5	12	.167	.245	.229	.474	34	-4	-4	95	146	3	.390	0	0	0	-1	C	-0.3
	Atl-N	4	8	0	1	0	0	0	0	2	3	.125	.300	.125	.425	19	-1	-1	113	0	0	.429	0	0	0	0	/C	0.0
	Yr	24	56	3	9	3	0	0	4	7	15	.161	.254	.214	.468	32	-5	-5	98	128	4	.404	0	0	0	-1		-0.3
Total	4	133	365	36	86	19	0	6	47	37	85	.236	.306	.337	.643	79	-10	-10	99	127	37	.571	0	1	-1	-8	C/O1	-1.1
■ **MIKE HOWARD**	Howard, Michael Fredric b: 4/2/58, Seattle, Wash. BB/TR, 6'2", 185 lbs. Deb: 9/12/81																											
1981	NY-N	14	24	4	4	1	0	0	3	4	6	.167	.286	.208	.494	42	-2	-2	101	236	2	.550	2	0	1	-1	O	-0.2
1982	NY-N	33	39	5	7	0	0	1	3	6	7	.179	.304	.256	.561	59	-2	-2	99	90	4	.594	2	0	1	-2	O/2	-0.3
1983	NY-N	1	3	0	1	0	0	0	1	0	1	.333	.333	.333	.667	86	-0	-0	99	396	0	.500	0	0	0	-0	/O	0.0
Total	3	48	66	9	12	1	0	1	7	10	14	.182	.299	.242	.541	54	-4	-4	99	155	6	.574	4	0	1	-4	/O2	-0.5
■ **PAUL HOWARD**	Howard, Paul Joseph "Del" b: 5/20/1884, Boston, Mass. d: 8/29/68, Miami, Fla. BR/TR, 5'8", 170 lbs. Deb: 9/16/09																											
1909	Bos-A	6	15	2	3	1	0	0	2	3		.200	.368	.267	.635	92	0	0	109	193	1	.667	0			0	/O	0.0
■ **WILBUR HOWARD**	Howard, Wilbur Leon b: 1/8/49, Lowell, N.C. BB/TR, 6'2", 170 lbs. Deb: 9/04/73																											
1973	Mil-A	16	39	3	8	0	0	0	1	2	10	.205	.244	.205	.449	29	-4	-3	96	49	2	.313	0	1	-1	2	O/D	-0.2
1974	Hou-N	64	111	19	24	4	0	2	5	5	18	.216	.250	.306	.556	56	-7	-7	98	48	7	.453	4	5	-2	-6	O	-1.6
1975	Hou-N	121	392	62	111	16	8	0	21	21	67	.283	.325	.365	.689	96	-5	-3	94	57	49	.677	32	11	3	4	O	0.1
1976	Hou-N	94	191	26	42	7	2	1	18	7	28	.220	.247	.293	.541	61	-12	-9	86	117	12	.440	7	5	-1	-7	O/2	-2.0
1977	Hou-N	87	187	22	48	6	0	2	13	5	30	.257	.276	.321	.597	64	-11	-9	93	79	17	.528	11	1	3	-4	O/2	-1.2
1978	Hou-N	84	148	17	34	4	1	1	13	5	22	.230	.269	.291	.560	60	-9	-8	95	112	12	.479	6	2	1	3	O/C2	-0.4
Total	6	466	1068	149	267	37	11	6	71	45	175	.250	.284	.322	.606	73	-48	-39	93	78	98	.549	60	25	3	-8	O/2CD	-5.3
■ **JIM HOWARTH**	Howarth, James Eugene b: 3/7/47, Biloxi, Miss. BL/TL, 5'11", 175 lbs. Deb: 9/05/71																											
1971	SF-N	7	13	3	3	1	0	0	2	3	3	.231	.375	.308	.683	96	0	0	100	204	2	.700	0	0	0	-1	/O	0.0
1972	SF-N	74	119	16	28	4	0	1	7	16	18	.235	.326	.294	.620	77	-3	-3	100	76	12	.563	3	2	-0	-2	O/1	-0.7
1973	SF-N	65	90	8	18	1	1	0	7	7	8	.200	.258	.233	.491	35	-8	-8	105	134	6	.384	0	0	0	-4	O/1	-1.4
1974	SF-N	6	4	0	0	0	0	0	0	0	0	.000	.000	.000	.000	-93	-1	-1	108	0	0	.000	0	0	0	-0	/O	-0.1
Total	4	152	226	27	49	6	1	1	16	26	29	.217	.298	.265	.563	58	-12	-12	102	105	19	.497	3	2	-0	-7	/O1	-2.2

YEAR	TM/L	G	AB	R	H	2B	3B	HR	RBI	BB	SO	AVG	OBP	SLG	PRO	/A	BR	/A	PF	CHI	RC	TA	SB	CS	SBR	FR	POS	TPR
■ **ART HOWE**	Howe, Arthur Henry b: 12/15/46, Pittsburgh, Pa. BR/TR, 6'2", 190 lbs. Deb: 7/10/74 C																											
1974	Pit-N	29	74	10	18	4	1	1	5	9	13	.243	.325	.365	.690	95	-1	-0	98	64	9	.632	0	0	0	-0	3/S	0.0
1975	Pit-N	63	146	13	25	9	0	1	10	15	15	.171	.248	.253	.502	40	-12	-12	99	97	9	.421	1	0	0	-2	3/S	-1.3
1976	Hou-N	21	29	0	4	1	0	0	0	6	6	.138	.286	.172	.458	37	-2	-2	86	0	2	.423	0	0	0	-0	/32	-0.2
1977	Hou-N	125	413	44	109	23	7	8	58	41	60	.264	.338	.412	.749	108	-0	4	93	120	57	.686	0	1	-1	1	23S	1.2
1978	Hou-N	119	420	46	123	33	3	7	55	34	41	.293	.347	.436	.783	124	9	12	95	109	60	.703	2	3	-1	-11	*23/1	0.6
1979	Hou-N	118	355	32	88	15	2	6	33	36	37	.248	.319	.352	.671	92	-8	-4	90	91	41	.600	3	1	0	-6	23/1	-0.7
1980	Hou-N	110	321	34	91	12	5	10	46	34	29	.283	.354	.445	.799	125	9	10	98	105	50	.749	1	0	0	-2	13/S2	0.6
1981	Hou-N	103	361	43	107	22	4	3	36	41	23	.296	.368	.404	.773	135	10	15	88	93	53	.709	1	3	-2	4	3/1	1.4
1982	Hou-N	110	365	29	87	15	1	5	38	41	45	.238	.317	.326	.643	81	-9	-9	99	113	38	.566	2	0	1	3	31	-0.8
1984	StL-N	89	139	17	30	5	0	2	12	18	18	.216	.306	.295	.601	70	-5	-5	99	100	12	.504	0	2	-1	4	31/2S	-0.1
1985	StL-N	4	3	0	0	0	0	0	0	0	0	.000	.000	.000	.000	-99	-1	-1	96	0	0	.000	0	0	0	0	/13	0.0
Total	11	891	2626	268	682	139	23	43	293	275	287	.260	.332	.379	.711	103	-11	8	94	102	330	.660	10	10	-3	-8	321/S	0.7
■ **SHORTY HOWE**	Howe, John b: New York, N.Y. Deb: 6/17/1890																											
1890	NY-N	19	64	4	11	0	0	0	4	3	2	.172	.221	.172	.392	17	-7	-6	95	110	3	.340	3			0	2/3	-0.5
1893	NY-N	1	5	1	3	0	0	0	2	0	0	.600	.600	.600	1.200	215	1	1	104	157	2	2.000	1			0	/3	0.1
Total	2	20	69	5	14	0	0	0	6	3	2	.203	.247	.203	.449	34	-6	-5	95	113	6	.400	4			0	/23	-0.4
■ **HARRY HOWELL**	Howell, Henry Harry b: 11/14/1876, New Jersey d: 5/22/56, Spokane, Wash. BR/TR, 5'9", Deb: 10/10/1898																											
1898	Bro-N	2	8	1	2	0	0	0	1	1		.250	.333	.250	.583	74	-0	-0	95	130	1	.500	0			0	/P	0.0
1899	Bal-N	28	82	4	12	2	2	0	3	3		.146	.195	.220	.415	14	-10	-10	108	51	4	.329	0			0	P	0.0
1900	Bro-N	22	42	6	12	2	0	1	6	6		.286	.375	.405	.780	109	1	1	108	94	7	.800	1			0	P	0.0
1901	Bal-A	53	188	26	41	10	5	2	26	5		.218	.238	.356	.595	61	-10	-11	107	115	18	.537	7			-3	P/OS12	0.0
1902	Bal-A	96	347	42	93	16	11	2	42	18		.268	.304	.395	.699	92	-4	-5	102	99	45	.638	7			1	P2O3S/1D	0.3
1903	NY-A	40	106	14	23	3	2	1	12	5		.217	.252	.311	.564	70	-4	-4	100	120	9	.470	1			4	P/3S12	0.0
1904	StL-A	36	113	9	25	5	2	1	6	4		.221	.248	.327	.575	88	-2	-2	95	56	9	.466	0			9	P	0.0
1905	StL-A	42	135	9	26	6	2	1	10	3		.193	.210	.289	.499	65	-6	-5	91	85	8	.385	0			18	P/O	0.0
1906	StL-A	35	103	5	13	3	1	0	6	6		.126	.174	.175	.349	11	-10	-10	98	121	4	.289	2			7	P	0.0
1907	StL-A	44	114	12	27	5	1	1	7	7		.237	.281	.325	.606	97	-1	-1	98	63	11	.529	2			9	P/O	0.0
1908	StL-A	41	120	10	22	7	0	1	9	4		.183	.210	.267	.476	54	-6	-6	103	97	6	.367	0			0	P	0.0
1909	StL-A	18	34	5	6	1	0	0	3	2		.176	.222	.206	.428	39	-3	-2	92	165	1	.321	0			0	P/3O	0.0
1910	StL-A	1	2	0	0	0	0	0	0	0		.000	.000	.000	.000	-99	-0	-0	94	0	0	.000	0			0	/P	0.0
Total	13	458	1394	143	302	60	26	10	131	64		.217	.252	.319	.571	69	-55	-57	101	95	123	.485	20			45	P/O32S1D	0.3
■ **DIXIE HOWELL**	Howell, Homer Elliott b: 4/24/19, Louisville, Ky. BR/TR, 5'11.5", 190 lbs. Deb: 5/06/47																											
1947	Pit-N	76	214	23	59	11	0	4	25	27	34	.276	.357	.383	.740	96	-1	-1	101	98	31	.701	1			0	C	0.1
1949	Cin-N	64	172	17	42	6	1	2	18	8	21	.244	.286	.326	.611	66	-9	-8	96	109	15	.489	0			1	C	-0.5
1950	Cin-N	82	224	30	50	9	1	2	22	32	31	.223	.326	.299	.625	63	-11	-12	105	116	23	.558	0			-5	C	-1.3
1951	Cin-N	77	207	22	52	6	1	2	18	15	34	.251	.302	.319	.621	67	-10	-10	101	97	20	.506	0	2	-1	-5	C	-1.4
1952	Cin-N	17	37	4	7	1	1	2	4	3	9	.189	.250	.432	.682	86	-1	-1	100	71	3	.576	0	0	0	0	C	0.0
1953	Bro-N	1	1	0	0	0	0	0	0	0	1	.000	.000	.000	.000	-96	-0	-0	104	0	0	.000	0	0	0	0	H	0.0
1955	Bro-N	16	42	2	11	4	0	0	5	1	7	.262	.279	.357	.636	64	-2	-2	104	135	4	.516	0	0	0	0	C	-0.1
1956	Bro-N	7	13	0	3	2	0	0	1	1	3	.231	.286	.385	.670	76	-0	-0	103	84	2	.600	0	0	0	0	/C	0.0
Total	8	340	910	98	224	39	4	12	93	87	140	.246	.315	.337	.652	73	-34	-35	101	105	98	.580	1	2		-8	C	-3.2
■ **JACK HOWELL**	Howell, Jack Robert b: 8/18/61, Tucson, Ariz. BL/TR, 6', 180 lbs. Deb: 5/20/85																											
1985	Cal-A	43	137	19	27	4	0	5	18	16	33	.197	.281	.336	.617	68	-6	-6	101	117	14	.563	1	1	-0	-3	3	-1.0
1986	Cal-A	63	151	26	41	14	2	4	21	19	28	.272	.353	.470	.823	128	5	6	96	101	27	.829	2	0	1	-2	3/OD	0.3
1987	Cal-A	138	449	64	110	18	5	23	64	57	118	.245	.333	.461	.794	109	5	6	99	93	70	.774	4	3	-1	-7	O32	-0.4
1988	Cal-A	154	500	59	127	32	2	16	63	46	130	.254	.324	.422	.746	114	4	8	94	97	67	.685	2	6	-3	-20	*3/O	-1.4
Total	4	398	1237	168	305	68	9	48	166	138	309	.247	.326	.432	.759	109	8	13	97	98	178	.726	9	10	-3	-32	3/O2D	-2.5
■ **RED HOWELL**	Howell, Murray Donald "Porky" b: 1/29/09, Atlanta, Ga. d: 10/1/50, Travelers Rest, S.C BR/TR, 6', 215 lbs. Deb: 4/24/41																											
1941	Cle-A	11	7	0	2	0	0	0	2	4	2	.286	.545	.286	.831	124	1	1	101	354	2	1.200	0	0	0	0	H	0.1
■ **ROY HOWELL**	Howell, Roy Lee b: 12/18/53, Lompoc, Cal. BL/TR, 6'1", 190 lbs. Deb: 9/09/74																											
1974	Tex-A	13	44	2	11	1	0	1	3	2	10	.250	.283	.341	.624	82	-1	-1	96	65	4	.515	0	0	0	0	3	0.0
1975	Tex-A	125	383	43	96	15	2	10	51	39	79	.251	.325	.379	.703	99	-1	-1	100	112	48	.643	2	2	-1	2	*3/D	0.2
1976	Tex-A	140	491	55	124	28	2	8	53	30	106	.253	.297	.367	.664	92	-5	-6	102	100	51	.559	1	0	0	-11	*3/D	-1.7
1977	Tex-A	7	17	0	0	0	0	0	0	2	4	.000	.105	.000	.105	-65	-4	-4	105	0	0	.118	0	0	0	0	/O13D	-0.3
	Tor-A	96	364	41	115	17	1	10	44	42	76	.316	.388	.451	.839	125	15	14	103	86	61	.793	4	1	1	-1	3/D	1.2
	Yr	103	381	41	115	17	1	10	44	44	80	.302	.376	.430	.806	116	11	10	103	80	60	.753	4	1	1	-1		0.9
1978	Tor-A	140	551	67	149	28	3	8	61	44	78	.270	.326	.376	.701	96	-3	-3	100	100	67	.610	0	1	-1	11	*3/OD	0.6
1979	Tor-A	138	511	60	126	28	4	15	72	42	91	.247	.311	.405	.716	89	-7	-9	103	116	62	.638	1	4	-2	2	*3/D	-0.6
1980	Tor-A	142	528	51	142	28	9	10	57	50	92	.269	.338	.413	.751	105	3	3	100	95	74	.689	0	0	0	-11	*3/D	-0.7
1981	Mil-A	76	244	37	58	13	1	6	33	23	39	.238	.309	.373	.682	100	-2	-0	96	118	28	.604	0	0	0	-5	3D/1O	-0.5
1982	Mil-A	98	300	31	78	11	2	4	38	21	39	.260	.308	.350	.658	86	-8	-6	94	130	33	.558	0	2	-1	-0	D/1O	-0.7
1983	Mil-A	69	194	23	54	9	6	4	25	15	29	.278	.330	.448	.779	122	3	5	92	99	27	.701	1	3	-2	0	D/1	0.3
1984	Mil-A	68	164	12	38	5	1	4	17	8	32	.232	.284	.348	.632	80	-6	-4	92	98	14	.507	0	1	-1	2	3/1D	-0.1
Total	11	1112	3791	422	991	183	31	80	454	318	675	.261	.322	.389	.712	98	-16	-13	99	104	470	.647	9	14	-6	-12	3D/1O	-2.3
■ **BILL HOWERTON**	Howerton, William Ray "Hopalong" b: 12/12/21, Lompoc, Cal. BL/TR, 5'11", 185 lbs. Deb: 9/11/49																											
1949	StL-N	9	13	1	4	1	0	0	1	0	2	.308	.308	.385	.692	77	-0	-0	110	75	2	.556	0			-1	/O	-0.1
1950	StL-N	110	313	50	88	20	8	10	59	47	60	.281	.375	.492	.867	122	12	11	103	124	61	.882	0			-5	O	0.3
1951	StL-N	24	65	10	17	4	1	1	4	10	12	.262	.360	.400	.760	103	1	0	101	53	9	.706	0	1	-1	0	O	0.0
	Pit-N	80	219	29	60	12	2	11	37	26	44	.274	.351	.498	.849	118	7	5	107	101	37	.810	1	0	0	-6	O/3	-0.1
	Yr	104	284	39	77	16	3	12	41	36	56	.271	.353	.475	.828	115	8	6	105	90	48	.793	1	1	-0	-6		-0.1
1952	Pit-N	13	25	3	8	1	1	0	4	6	5	.320	.452	.440	.892	149	2	2	100	142	5	.944	0	0	0	-1	/O3	0.1
	NY-N	11	15	2	1	1	0	0	1	3	2	.067	.222	.133	.356	1	-2	-2	102	195	1	.357	0	0	0	-0	/O	-0.1
	Yr	24	40	5	9	2	1	0	5	9	7	.225	.367	.325	.692	93	0	-0	101	172	6	.710	0	0	0	-1		0.0
Total	4	247	650	95	178	39	12	22	106	92	125	.274	.364	.472	.836	116	20	16	104	111	115	.846	1	1		-12	O/3	0.1
■ **DAN HOWLEY**	Howley, Daniel Philip "Howling Dan" or "Dapper Dan" b: 10/16/1885, E.Weymouth, Mass. d: 3/10/44, E.Weymouth, Mass. TR, 6', 187 lbs. Deb: 5/15/13 MC																											
1913	Phi-N	26	32	5	4	2	0	0	2	4	4	.125	.222	.188	.410	16	-3	-4	112	121	2	.464	3			0	C	-0.1
■ **DICK HOWSER**	Howser, Richard Dalton b: 5/14/36, Miami, Fla. d: 6/17/87, Kansas City, Mo. BR/TR, 5'8", 155 lbs. Deb: 4/11/61 MC																											
1961	KC-A	158	611	108	171	29	6	3	45	92	38	.280	.379	.362	.740	97	3	1	102	68	95	.777	37	9	6	-14	*S	0.4
1962	KC-A	83	286	53	68	8	3	6	34	38	8	.238	.329	.350	.679	83	-6	-6	100	117	37	.702	19	2	5	-5	S	-0.1
1963	KC-A	15	41	4	8	0	0	0	1	7	3	.195	.313	.195	.508	43	-3	-3	108	52	3	.455	0	0	0	0	S	-0.2
	Cle-A	49	162	25	40	5	0	1	10	22	18	.247	.337	.296	.633	82	-4	-3	97	84	17	.608	9	3	1	-10	S	-1.0
	Yr	64	203	29	48	5	0	1	11	29	21	.236	.332	.276	.608	73	-6	-6	99	77	21	.577	9	3	1	-10		-1.2
1964	Cle-A	162	637	101	163	23	4	3	52	76	39	.256	.337	.319	.656	81	-12	-14	103	92	74	.611	20	7	2	4	*S	-0.7
1965	Cle-A	107	307	47	72	8	2	1	6	57	25	.235	.356	.283	.640	86	-4	-3	98	28	38	.664	17	4	3	1	S2	0.5
1966	Cle-A	67	140	18	32	9	1	2	4	15	23	.229	.303	.350	.653	86	-2	-3	101	30	14	.569	2	4	-2	-1	2S	-0.1
1967	NY-A	63	149	18	40	6	0	0	10	25	15	.268	.381	.309	.689	112	3	4	94	91	19	.655	1	4	-2	2	23/S	0.5
1968	NY-A	85	150	24	23	2	1	0	3	35	17	.153	.321	.180	.501	54	-6	-7	101	48	11	.485	0	1	-1	5	2/3S	0.0
Total	8	789	2483	398	617	90	17	16	165	367	186	.248	.348	.318	.666	86	-32	-34	101	73	308	.669	105	34	11	-18	S/23	-0.7

YEAR	TM/L	G	AB	R	H	2B	3B	HR	RBI	BB	SO	AVG	OBP	SLG	PRO	/A	BR	/A	PF	CHI	RC	TA	SB	CS	SBR	FR	POS	TPR
■ **DUMMY HOY**	Hoy, William Ellsworth b: 5/23/1862, Houckstown, Ohio d: 12/15/61, Cincinnati, Ohio BL/TR, 5'4", 148 lbs. Deb: 1888																											
1888	Was-N	136	503	77	138	10	8	2	29	69	48	.274	.374	.338	.712	136	21	24	96	51	97	.910	**82**			5	*O	2.7
1889	Was-N	127	507	98	139	11	6	0	39	75	30	.274	.374	.320	.694	105	2	9	92	62	76	.755	35			-6	*O	-0.1
1890	Buf-P	122	493	107	147	17	8	1	53	94	36	.298	.418	.371	.790	124	16	24	92	67	95	.936	39			3	*O/2	1.7
1891	StL-a	141	567	136	165	14	5	5	66	119	25	.291	.424	.360	.784	112	29	14	114	75	114	.980	59			-5	*O	0.3
1892	Was-N	152	593	108	166	19	8	3	75	86	23	.280	.375	.354	.729	117	20	15	105	93	104	.843	60			-16	*O	-0.5
1893	Was-N	130	564	106	138	12	6	0	45	66	9	.245	.337	.287	.625	76	-23	-12	90	66	73	.678	48			-3	*O	-1.6
1894	Cin-N	126	495	114	148	22	13	5	70	87	18	.299	.416	.426	.842	105	8	8	100	75	101	.971	27			-0	*O	0.0
1895	Cin-N	107	429	93	119	21	12	3	55	52	8	.277	.363	.403	.767	92	0	-6	108	75	83	.906	50			-2	*O	-1.3
1896	Cin-N	121	443	120	132	23	7	4	57	65	13	.298	.403	.409	.812	111	14	10	105	82	95	.994	50			3	*O	0.4
1897	Cin-N	128	497	87	145	24	6	2	42	54		.292	.371	.376	.748	93	2	-4	107	56	85	.815	37			6	*O	-0.6
1898	Lou-N	148	582	104	177	15	16	6	66	49		.304	.367	.416	.783	132	20	23	96	68	105	.832	37			2	*O	1.5
1899	Lou-N	154	633	116	194	17	13	5	49	61		.306	.373	.398	.771	110	13	10	103	49	109	.800	32			-6	*O	-0.4
1901	Chi-A	132	527	112	155	28	11	2	60	**86**		.294	.393	.400	.794	124	20	20	99	75	96	.871	27			-3	*O	1.4
1902	Cin-N	72	279	48	81	15	2	2	20	41		.290	.381	.380	.761	125	14	10	110	53	46	.798	11			-1	O	0.4
Total	14	1796	7112	1426	2044	248	121	40	726	1004	210	.287	.384	.373	.757	111	155	146	101	68	1278	.860	594			-21	*O/2	3.9
■ **KENT HRBEK**	Hrbek, Kent Alan b: 5/21/60, Minneapolis, Minn. BL/TR, 6'4", 200 lbs. Deb: 8/24/81																											
1981	Min-A	24	67	5	16	5	0	1	7	5	9	.239	.301	.358	.660	85	-1	-1	105	101	8	.588	0	0	0	-0	1/D	-0.1
1982	Min-A	140	532	82	160	21	4	23	92	54	80	.301	.365	.485	.850	131	22	22	100	119	91	.808	3	1	0	-3	*1/D	1.6
1983	Min-A	141	515	75	153	41	5	16	84	57	71	.297	.370	.489	.860	128	24	21	105	116	91	.832	4	6	-2	-3	*1/D	0.9
1984	Min-A	149	559	80	174	31	3	27	107	65	87	.311	.387	.522	.909	141	37	33	106	121	110	.898	1	1	-0	-6	*1/D	1.7
1985	Min-A	158	593	78	165	31	2	21	93	67	87	.278	.353	.444	.797	113	14	11	103	120	93	.755	1	1	-0	1	*1/D	0.2
1986	Min-A	149	550	85	147	27	1	29	91	71	81	.267	.357	.478	.835	116	20	14	108	110	93	.814	2	2	-1	-5	*1/D	-0.1
1987	Min-A	143	477	85	136	20	1	34	90	84	60	.285	.392	.545	.937	152	33	36	96	101	103	.980	5	2	0	-11	*1/D	1.1
1988	Min-A	143	510	75	159	31	0	25	76	67	54	.312	.392	.520	.911	144	37	32	106	91	104	.915	0	3	-2	-7	*1D/O	1.8
Total	8	1047	3803	565	1110	207	16	176	640	470	529	.292	.372	.494	.866	131	187	169	104	111	692	.875	16	16	-5	-33	1/DO	7.1
■ **WALT HRINIAK**	Hriniak, Walter John b: 5/22/43, Natick, Mass. BL/TR, 5'11", 180 lbs. Deb: 9/10/68 C																											
1968	Atl-N	9	26	0	9	0	0	0	3	0	3	.346	.346	.346	.692	116	0	0	93	140	3	.529	0	0	0	-1	/C	0.0
1969	Atl-N	7	7	0	1	0	0	0	0	2	1	.143	.333	.143	.476	36	-0	-1	104	0	0	.429	0	0	0	-0	/C	0.0
	SD-N	31	66	4	15	0	0	0	1	8	11	.227	.329	.227	.556	60	-3	-3	97	27	5	.472	0	0	0	1	C	0.0
	Yr	38	73	4	16	0	0	0	1	10	12	.219	.329	.219	.549	58	-4	-4	98	22	6	.475	0	0	0	0		0.0
Total	2	47	99	4	25	0	0	0	4	10	15	.253	.333	.253	.586	72	-4	-3	96	51	9	.487	0	0	0	-0	/C	0.0
■ **AL HUBBARD**	Hubbard, Allen (Player Under Name Of Al West For 1 Game In 1883) b: 12/9/1860, Westfield, Mass. d: 12/14/30, Newton, Mass. Deb: 1883																											
1883	Phi-a	2	6	2	2	0	0	0		1		.333	.429	.333	.762	145	0	0	103	0	1	.750				0	/SC	0.0
■ **GLENN HUBBARD**	Hubbard, Glenn Dee b: 9/25/57, Hahn Afb, Germany BR/TR, 5'9", 150 lbs. Deb: 7/14/78																											
1978	Atl-N	44	163	15	42	4	0	2	13	10	20	.258	.309	.319	.628	68	-5	-8	112	94	17	.532	2	1	0	-2	2	-0.6
1979	Atl-N	97	325	34	75	12	0	3	29	27	43	.231	.292	.295	.587	55	-17	-21	109	109	28	.479	0	6	-4	4	2	-1.5
1980	Atl-N	117	431	55	107	21	3	9	43	49	69	.248	.325	.374	.699	93	-3	-4	101	96	53	.646	7	5	-1	7	*2	1.0
1981	Atl-N	99	361	39	85	13	5	6	33	33	59	.235	.303	.349	.652	85	-8	-7	100	92	39	.579	4	2	0	-2	2	-0.2
1982	Atl-N	145	532	75	132	25	1	9	59	59	62	.248	.327	.350	.676	83	-7	-12	107	115	65	.618	4	3	-1	23	*2	1.8
1983	Atl-N	148	517	65	136	24	6	12	70	55	71	.263	.339	.402	.741	99	3	-1	106	116	68	.672	3	9	-5	21	*2	2.2
1984	Atl-N	120	397	53	93	27	2	9	43	55	61	.234	.333	.380	.714	91	1	-4	110	97	53	.684	4	1	1	22	*2	2.3
1985	Atl-N	142	439	51	102	21	0	5	39	56	54	.232	.325	.314	.639	75	-11	-14	106	102	47	.575	4	3	-1	**57**	*2	4.4
1986	Atl-N	143	408	42	94	16	1	4	36	66	74	.230	.343	.304	.647	78	-9	-10	102	106	47	.614	3	2	-0	**34**	*2	2.6
1987	Atl-N	141	443	69	117	33	2	5	38	77	57	.264	.380	.381	.762	95	5	-1	108	82	67	.749	1	1	-0	**23**	*2	2.4
1988	Oak-A	105	294	35	75	12	2	3	33	33	50	.255	.336	.340	.676	95	-3	-1	95	120	34	.593	1	3	-2	-1	*2/D	0.3
Total	11	1301	4310	533	1058	208	22	67	436	520	620	.245	.331	.351	.682	85	-55	-82	105	103	516	.636	33	36	-12	185	*2/D	14.7
■ **KEN HUBBS**	Hubbs, Kenneth Douglas b: 12/23/41, Riverside, Cal. d: 2/13/64, Provo, Utah BR/TR, 6'2", 175 lbs. Deb: 9/10/61																											
1961	Chi-N	10	28	4	5	1	1	1	2	0	8	.179	.179	.393	.571	46	-2	-2	100	58	2	.478	0	0	0	0	/2	0.0
1962	Chi-N	160	661	90	172	24	9	5	49	35	129	.260	.300	.346	.647	69	-26	-30	106	70	64	.523	3	7	-3	6	*2	-1.3
1963	Chi-N	154	566	54	133	19	3	8	47	39	93	.235	.287	.322	.608	71	-18	-22	105	98	48	.503	8	9	-3	24	*2	0.9
Total	3	324	1255	148	310	44	13	14	98	74	230	.247	.292	.336	.628	70	-46	-54	105	82	114	.524	11	16	-6	29	2	-0.4
■ **CLARENCE HUBER**	Huber, Clarence Bill "Gilly" b: 10/27/1896, Tyler, Tex. d: 2/22/65, Laredo, Tex. BR/TR, 5'10", 165 lbs. Deb: 9/17/20																											
1920	Det-A	11	42	4	9	2	1	0	0	0	5	.214	.214	.310	.524	36	-4	-4	103	0	3	.394	0	0	0	2	3	-0.1
1921	Det-A	1	0	0	0	0	0	0	0	0	0	—	—	—	—	—	0	0	96	—	—	—	0	0	0	0	/3	0.0
1925	Phi-N	124	436	46	124	28	5	5	54	17	33	.284	.311	.406	.717	71	-13	-23	116	100	53	.621	3	5	-2	-9	*3	-2.3
1926	Phi-N	118	376	45	92	17	7	1	34	42	29	.245	.324	.335	.659	75	-11	-13	103	91	42	.630	9			7	*3	-0.4
Total	4	254	854	95	225	47	13	6	88	59	67	.263	.313	.370	.683	71	-28	-40	109	91	100	.614	12	5		-0	3	-2.8
■ **OTTO HUBER**	Huber, Otto b: 3/12/14, Garfield, N.J. BR/TR, 5'10", 165 lbs. Deb: 6/10/39																											
1939	Bos-N	11	22	2	6	1	0	0	3	0	1	.273	.273	.318	.591	64	-1	-1	92	157	2	.438	0			0	/23	0.0
■ **DAVE HUDGENS**	Hudgens, David Mark b: 12/5/56, Oroville, Cal. BL/TL, 6'2", 210 lbs. Deb: 9/04/83																											
1983	Oak-A	6	7	0	1	0	0	0	0	0	3	.143	.143	.143	.286	-22	-1	-1	96	0	0	.167	0	0	0	0	/1D	0.0
■ **JIMMY HUDGENS**	Hudgens, James Price b: 8/24/02, Newburg, Mo. d: 8/26/55, St.Louis, Mo. BB/TR, 6', 180 lbs. Deb: 9/14/23																											
1923	StL-N	6	12	2	3	1	0	0	0	3	3	.250	.400	.333	.733	106	0	0	90	0	2	.778	0	0	0	-1	/12	0.0
1925	Cin-N	3	7	0	3	1	1	0	0	1	1	.429	.500	.857	1.357	246	1	1	97	0	3	1.750	0	0	0	0	/1	0.1
1926	Cin-N	17	20	2	5	1	0	0	1	1	0	.250	.286	.300	.586	61	-1	-1	95	58	2	.467	0			0	/1	0.0
Total	3	26	39	4	11	3	1	0	1	5	4	.282	.364	.410	.774	112	0	1	94	27	7	.750	0	0		-1	/12	0.1
■ **REX HUDLER**	Hudler, Rex Allen b: 9/2/60, Tempe, Ariz. BR/TR, 6'1", 180 lbs. Deb: 9/09/84																											
1984	NY-A	9	7	2	1	1	0	0	0	1	5	.143	.333	.286	.619	78	-0	-0	94	0	1	.667	0	0	0	0	/2	0.0
1985	NY-A	20	51	4	8	0	1	0	1	1	9	.157	.173	.196	.369	1	-7	-7	96	40	2	.250	0	1	-1	1	2/1S	-0.5
1986	Bal-A	14	1	1	0	0	0	0	0	0	0	.000	.000	.000	.000	-99	-0	-0	99	0	0	1.000	1	0	0	0	2/3	0.1
1988	Mon-N	77	216	38	59	14	2	4	14	10	34	.273	.305	.412	.717	99	0	-1	106	55	28	.771	29	7	5	0	2S/O	0.7
Total	4	120	275	45	68	15	3	4	15	12	48	.247	.281	.367	.649	80	-7	-8	103	51	31	.664	30	8	4	1	/2S031	0.3
■ **JOHNNY HUDSON**	Hudson, John Wilson "Mr. Chips" b: 6/30/12, Bryan, Tex. d: 11/7/70, Bryan, Tex. BR/TR, 5'10", 160 lbs. Deb: 6/20/36																											
1936	Bro-N	6	12	1	2	0	0	0	0	2	1	.167	.286	.167	.452	23	-1	-1	105	0	1	.400	0			-1	/S2	-0.1
1937	Bro-N	13	27	3	5	4	0	0	2	3	9	.185	.267	.333	.600	60	-1	-2	104	80	2	.522	0			-1	S/2	0.0
1938	Bro-N	135	498	59	130	21	5	2	37	39	76	.261	.315	.335	.650	82	-14	-12	96	79	51	.549	7			-0	*2/S	-0.2
1939	Bro-N	109	343	46	87	17	3	2	32	30	36	.254	.317	.338	.656	71	-11	-15	107	96	36	.575	5			-8	S2/3	-1.7
1940	Bro-N	85	179	13	39	4	3	0	19	9	26	.218	.255	.274	.529	43	-13	-15	108	144	12	.411	2			-6	S2/3	-1.5
1941	Chi-N	50	99	8	20	4	0	0	6	3	15	.202	.225	.242	.468	34	-9	-8	94	90	5	.366	3			0	S23	-0.5
1945	NY-N	28	11	8	0	0	0	0	0	1	1	.000	.083	.000	.083	-76	-3	-3	100	0	0	.083	0			0	/32	-0.1
Total	7	426	1169	138	283	50	11	4	96	87	164	.242	.296	.314	.610	66	-53	-55	101	93	107	.533	17			-15	2S/3	-4.1
■ **FRANK HUELSMAN**	Huelsman, Frank Elmer b: 6/5/1874, St.Louis, Mo. d: 6/9/59, Affton, Mo. BR/TR, 6'2", 210 lbs. Deb: 10/03/1897																											
1897	StL-N	2	7	0	2	1	0	0	0	0		.286	.286	.429	.714	95	-0	-0	93	0	1	.600	0			0	/O	0.0
1904	Chi-A	3	6	0	1	1	0	0	0	0		.167	.167	.333	.500	58	-0	-0	99	0	0	.400	0			0	/O	0.0
	Det-A	4	18	1	6	1	0	0	4	1		.333	.368	.389	.757	149	1	1	96	184	3	.750	1			1	/O	0.1
	Chi-A	1	1	0	0	0	0	0	0	0		.000	.000	.000	.000	-99	-0	-0	99	0	0	.000	0			0	H	0.0
	StL-A	20	68	6	15	2	1	0	1	6		.221	.284	.279	.563	85	-1	-1	95	20	6	.472	0			1	O	0.0

YEAR	TM/L	G	AB	R	H	2B	3B	HR	RBI	BB	SO	AVG	OBP	SLG	PRO	/A	BR	/A	PF	CHI	RC	TA	SB	CS	SBR	FR	POS	TPR
	Was-A	84	303	21	75	19	4	2	30	24		.248	.303	.356	.659	119	4	6	93	104	35	.605	6			-1	O	0.0
	Yr	112	396	28	97	23	5	2	35	31		.245	.300	.343	.643	113	3	5	93	90	44	.582	7			1		0.1
1905	Was-A	121	421	48	114	28	8	3	62	31		.271	.321	.397	.717	124	13	11	104	133	59	.681	11			-12	*O	-0.6
Total	3	235	824	76	213	52	13	5	97	62		.258	.310	.371	.682	119	15	16	99	112	104	.632	18			-11	O	-0.5
■ **BEN HUFFMAN** Huffman, Benjamin Franklin b: 6/26/14, Rileyville, Va. BL/TR, 5'11.5", 175 lbs. Deb: 4/23/37																												
1937	StL-A	76	176	18	48	9	0	1	24	10	7	.273	.323	.341	.664	68	-9	-8	99	131	20	.578	1	0	0	1	C	-0.3
■ **ED HUG** Hug, Edward Ambrose b: 7/14/1880, Fayetteville, O. d: 5/11/53, Cincinnati, Ohio BR/TR, Deb: 03																												
1903	Bro-N	1	0	0	0	0	0	0	0	1		—	1.000	—	1.341	290	0	0	101	0	0	—	0			0	/C	0.0
■ **MILLER HUGGINS** Huggins, Miller James "Hug" or "Mighty Mite" b: 3/27/1879, Cincinnati, Ohio d: 9/25/29, New York, N.Y. BB/TR, 5'6.5", 140 lbs. Deb: 4/15/04 MH																												
1904	Cin-N	140	491	96	129	12	7	2	30	88		.263	.375	.328	.703	105	16	7	114	63	67	.724	13			-0	*2	1.1
1905	Cin-N	149	564	117	154	11	8	1	38	**103**		.273	.385	.326	.712	112	16	14	103	61	83	.766	27			**36**	*2	6.0
1906	Cin-N	146	545	81	159	11	7	0	26	71		.292	.373	.338	.711	108	18	9	115	45	86	.767	41			21	*2	3.2
1907	Cin-N	156	561	64	139	12	4	1	31	**83**		.248	.345	.289	.633	106	4	7	95	63	67	.647	28			0	*2	1.1
1908	Cin-N	135	498	65	119	14	5	0	23	58		.239	.318	.287	.605	93	-0	-2	103	53	53	.609	30			0	*2	-0.2
1909	Cin-N	57	159	18	34	3	1	0	6	28		.214	.335	.245	.580	87	-2	-1	94	56	16	.632	11			4	23	0.3
1910	StL-N	151	547	101	145	15	6	1	36	**116**	46	.265	.399	.320	.719	120	14	21	92	61	85	.823	34			1	*2	2.6
1911	StL-N	138	509	106	133	19	2	1	24	96	52	.261	.385	.312	.697	95	3	2	101	43	76	.793	37			4	*2	0.3
1912	StL-N	120	431	82	131	15	4	0	29	87	31	.304	.422	.357	.779	115	14	14	100	61	80	.923	35			-3	*2	0.7
1913	StL-N	121	382	74	109	12	0	0	27	92	49	.285	**.432**	.317	.749	125	16	20	93	86	62	.890	23			4	*2M	2.2
1914	StL-N	148	509	85	134	17	4	1	24	**105**	63	.263	.396	.318	.714	109	15	13	104	47	75	.816	32			-4	*2M	0.8
1915	StL-N	107	353	57	85	5	2	2	24	74	68	.241	.377	.283	.660	101	5	5	100	92	40	.679	13	12	-3	4	*2M	0.7
1916	StL-N	18	9	2	3	0	0	0	0	2	3	.333	.500	.333	.833	164	1	1	97	0	2	1.000	0			1	/2M	0.2
Total	13	1586	5558	948	1474	146	50	9	318	1003	312	.265	.381	.314	.695	107	121	110	102	60	793	.758	324	12		67	*2/3	19.0
■ **JOE HUGHES** Hughes, Joseph Thompson b: 2/21/1880, Pardo, Pa. d: 3/13/51, Cleveland, Ohio BR/TR, 5'10", 165 lbs. Deb: 8/30/02																												
1902	Chi-N	1	3	0	0	0	0	0	0	0	0	.000	.000	.000	.000	-99	-1	-1	96	0	0	.000	0			0	/O	0.0
■ **KEITH HUGHES** Hughes, Keith Wills b: 9/12/63, Bryn Mawr, Pa. BL/TL, 6'3", 210 lbs. Deb: 5/19/87																												
1987	NY-A	4	4	0	0	0	0	0	0	0	2	.000	.000	.000	.000	-99	-1	-1	98	0	0	.000	0	0	0	0	/H	0.0
	Phi-N	37	76	8	20	2	0	0	10	7	11	.263	.333	.289	.623	64	-3	-4	104	181	8	.526	0	0	0	-3	O	-0.6
1988	Bal-A	41	108	10	21	4	2	2	14	16	27	.194	.298	.324	.622	78	-4	-3	95	136	11	.578	1	0	0	1	O/D	-0.1
Total	2	82	188	18	41	6	2	2	24	23	40	.218	.307	.303	.610	68	-8	-8	99	151	19	.547	1	0	0	-2	/OD	-0.7
■ **ROY HUGHES** Hughes, Roy John "Jeep" or "Sage" b: 1/11/11, Cincinnati, Ohio BR/TR, 5'10.5", 167 lbs. Deb: 4/16/35																												
1935	Cle-A	82	266	40	78	15	3	0	14	18	17	.293	.340	.372	.713	85	-6	-6	99	48	35	.686	13	3	2	5	2S/3	0.4
1936	Cle-A	152	638	112	188	35	9	0	63	57	40	.295	.356	.378	.734	77	-18	-24	106	75	88	.702	20	9	1	9	*2	-0.3
1937	Cle-A	104	346	57	96	12	6	1	40	40	22	.277	.352	.355	.708	81	-11	-9	98	109	45	.680	11	6	-0	9	32	0.3
1938	StL-A	58	96	16	27	3	0	2	13	12	11	.281	.361	.375	.736	85	-2	-2	100	105	14	.739	3	0	1	-0	2/3S	0.0
1939	StL-A	17	23	6	2	0	0	0	1	4	4	.087	.222	.087	.309	-18	-4	-4	100	169	1	.273	0	0	0	-0	/2S	-0.3
	Phi-N	65	237	22	54	5	1	1	16	21	18	.228	.291	.270	.561	55	-16	-14	94	93	18	.464	4			-8	2	-1.9
1940	Phi-N	1	0	0	0	0	0	0	0	0	0	—	—	—	—	—	0	0	97	—	—	—	0			0	/2	0.0
1944	Chi-N	126	478	86	137	16	6	1	28	35	30	.287	.337	.351	.688	93	-4	-4	101	62	58	.632	16			10	3S	1.6
1945	Chi-N	69	222	34	58	8	1	0	8	16	18	.261	.311	.306	.617	73	-8	-8	99	41	22	.536	6			1	S2/31	0.0
1946	Phi-N	89	276	23	65	11	1	0	22	19	15	.236	.287	.283	.570	65	-14	-12	95	105	23	.484	7			-4	S3/21	-1.3
Total	9	763	2582	396	705	105	27	5	205	222	175	.273	.332	.340	.673	77	-83	-84	100	78	323	.625	80	18		23	23S/1	-1.5
■ **TERRY HUGHES** Hughes, Terry Wayne b: 5/13/49, Spartanburg, S.C. BR/TR, 6'1", 185 lbs. Deb: 9/02/70																												
1970	Chi-N	2	3	0	1	0	0	0	0	0	0	.333	.333	.333	.667	66	-0	-0	120	0	0	.500	0	0	0	-0	/3O	0.0
1973	StL-N	11	14	1	3	1	0	0	1	1	4	.214	.267	.286	.552	59	-1	-1	91	100	1	.417	0	0	0	-0	/31	0.0
1974	Bos-A	41	69	5	14	2	0	1	6	6	18	.203	.286	.275	.561	58	-3	-4	107	107	6	.491	0	0	0	-3	3/D	-0.6
Total	3	54	86	6	18	3	0	1	7	7	22	.209	.284	.279	.563	59	-4	-5	104	103	7	.485	0	0	0	-3	/3D1O	-0.6
■ **TOM HUGHES** Hughes, Thomas Franklin b: 8/6/07, Emmet, Ark. BL/TR, 6'1", 190 lbs. Deb: 9/09/30																												
1930	Det-A	17	59	8	22	2	3	0	5	4	8	.373	.413	.508	.921	126	3	2	105	55	12	.895	0	1	-1	-3	O	0.0
■ **BILL HUGHES** Hughes, William R. b: 11/25/1866, Bladensville, Ill. d: 8/25/43, Santa Ana, Cal. BL/TL, Deb: 9/28/1884																												
1884	Was-U	14	49	5	6	0	0	0		2		.122	.157	.122	.279	-5	-5	-5	97	0	1	.186	0			0	/1O	-0.3
1885	Phi-a	4	16	3	3	1	1	0		1		.188	.278	.375	.653	104	0	0	103	0	2	.615				0	/OP	0.0
Total	2	18	65	8	9	1	1	0		3		.138	.188	.185	.373	25	-5	-5	98	0	3	.286				0	/1OP	-0.3
■ **EMIL HUHN** Huhn, Emil Hugo "Hap" b: 3/10/1892, North Vernon, Ind. d: 9/5/25, Camden, S.C. BR/TR, 6', 180 lbs. Deb: 4/10/15																												
1915	New-F	124	415	34	94	18	1	1	41	28	40	.227	.275	.282	.557	69	-18	-15	94	126	38	.492	13			0	*1C	-1.4
1916	Cin-N	37	94	4	24	3	2	0	3	2	11	.255	.271	.330	.601	86	-2	-2	98	38	8	.471	0			0	C1/O	-0.1
1917	Cin-N	23	51	2	10	1	2	0	3	2	5	.196	.226	.294	.521	64	-3	-2	92	77	3	.439	1			0	C/1	-0.1
Total	3	184	560	40	128	22	5	1	47	32	56	.229	.270	.291	.561	71	-23	-19	95	107	50	.484	14			0	1/CO	-1.6
■ **TIM HULETT** Hulett, Timothy Craig b: 1/12/60, Springfield, Ill. BR/TR, 6', 185 lbs. Deb: 9/15/83																												
1983	Chi-A	6	5	0	1	0	0	0	0	0	0	.200	.200	.200	.400	10	-1	-1	103	0	0	.500	1	0	0	0	/2	0.0
1984	Chi-A	8	7	1	0	0	0	0	0	1	4	.000	.125	.000	.125	-56	-2	-2	111	0	0	.286	1	0	0	0	/32	0.0
1985	Chi-A	141	395	52	106	19	4	5	37	30	81	.268	.326	.375	.701	91	-5	-4	100	90	48	.625	6	4	-1	4	*32/O	-0.3
1986	Chi-A	150	520	53	120	16	5	17	44	21	91	.231	.262	.379	.641	72	-21	-21	101	71	49	.541	4	1	1	-9	32	-2.8
1987	Chi-A	68	240	20	52	10	0	7	28	10	41	.217	.248	.346	.594	52	-15	-18	109	107	19	.474	0	2	-1	-0	3/2	-1.9
Total	5	373	1167	126	279	45	9	29	109	62	217	.239	.280	.368	.648	73	-43	-46	102	84	117	.564	12	7	-1	-5	32/O	-5.0
■ **BILLY HULEN** Hulen, William Franklin b: 3/12/1870, Dixon, Cal. d: 10/2/47, Santa Rosa, Cal. BL/TL, 5'8", 148 lbs. Deb: 5/02/1896																												
1896	Phi-N	88	339	87	90	18	7	0	38	55	20	.265	.368	.360	.728	92	-1	-2	102	95	55	.803	23			-22	SO/2	-1.9
1899	Was-N	19	68	10	10	1	0	0	3	10		.147	.256	.162	.418	18	-7	-7	96	89	4	.448	5			0	S	-0.5
Total	2	107	407	97	100	19	7	0	41	65	20	.246	.350	.327	.676	81	-8	-9	101	94	59	.736	28			-22	/SO2	-2.4
■ **RUDY HULSWITT** Hulswitt, Rudolph Edward b: 2/23/1877, Newport, Ky. d: 1/16/50, Louisville, Ky. BR/TR, 5'8.5", 165 lbs. Deb: 6/16/1899 C																												
1899	Lou-N	1	0	0	0	0	0	0	0	0		—	—	—	—	—	0	0	103	—	—	—	0			0	/S	0.0
1902	Phi-N	128	497	59	135	11	7	0	38	30		.272	.313	.322	.635	93	-1	-4	105	79	55	.558	12			4	*S/3	0.6
1903	Phi-N	138	519	56	128	22	9	1	58	28		.247	.285	.329	.615	83	-17	-11	92	109	53	.535	10			-4	*S	-0.7
1904	Phi-N	113	406	36	99	11	4	1	36	16		.244	.273	.298	.571	84	-11	-7	93	108	36	.472	8			-19	*S	-2.7
1908	Cin-N	119	386	27	88	5	7	1	28	30		.228	.284	.285	.569	82	-7	-8	103	97	32	.493	7			-15	*S/2	-2.8
1909	StL-N	82	289	21	81	8	3	0	29	19		.280	.329	.329	.658	110	2	3	96	113	32	.591	7			-10	S2	-0.7
1910	StL-N	63	133	9	33	7	2	0	14	13	10	.248	.320	.331	.651	98	-2	-0	92	111	15	.630	5			-3	S/2	-0.1
Total	7	644	2230	208	564	64	32	3	203	136	10	.253	.297	.314	.611	89	-36	-29	97	101	283	.534	49			-46	S/23	-6.4
■ **JOHN HUMMEL** Hummel, John Edwin "Silent John" b: 4/4/1883, Bloomsburg, Pa. d: 5/18/59, Springfield, Mass. BR/TR, 5'11", 160 lbs. Deb: 9/12/05																												
1905	Bro-N	30	109	19	29	3	4	0	7	9		.266	.322	.367	.689	112	1	1	96	64	15	.688	6			-1	2	0.3
1906	Bro-N	97	286	20	57	6	4	1	21	36		.199	.289	.259	.548	84	-8	-4	87	99	25	.524	10			0	2O1	-0.4
1907	Bro-N	107	342	41	80	12	3	3	31	26		.234	.288	.313	.601	95	-4	-2	94	103	33	.531	6			9	2O1/S	0.7
1908	Bro-N	154	594	51	143	11	12	4	41	34		.241	.282	.320	.602	99	-5	-2	95	69	57	.541	20			21	O2/S1	2.0
1909	Bro-N	146	542	54	152	15	9	4	52	22		.280	.311	.363	.674	112	4	5	99	96	64	.608	16			0	12SO	0.3
1910	Bro-N	153	578	67	141	21	13	5	74	57	81	.244	.314	.351	.665	99	-6	-2	95	114	69	.648	21			-14	*2	-1.3
1911	Bro-N	137	477	54	129	21	11	5	58	67	66	.270	.360	.392	.752	114	7	9	97	103	73	.776	16			-3	*2/1S	0.3
1912	Bro-N	122	411	55	116	21	7	5	54	49	55	.282	.359	.404	.763	114	5	7	95	102	62	.753	7			-11	2O1	-0.6

YEAR	TM/L	G	AB	R	H	2B	3B	HR	RBI	BB	SO	AVG	OBP	SLG	PRO	/A	BR	/A	PF	CHI	RC	TA	SB	CS	SBR	FR	POS	TPR
1913	Bro-N	67	198	20	48	7	7	2	24	13	23	.242	.292	.379	.671	87	-3	-4	104	108	22	.620	4			-3	OS/12	-0.6
1914	Bro-N	73	208	25	55	8	9	0	20	16	25	.264	.317	.389	.706	109	2	2	101	89	26	.667	5			-1	1O/2S	0.0
1915	Bro-N	53	100	6	23	2	3	0	8	6	11	.230	.274	.310	.584	75	-3	-3	101	99	9	.487	1	1	-0	-4	O1/S	-0.9
1918	NY-A	22	61	9	18	1	2	0	4	11	8	.295	.411	.377	.788	146	3	4	95	63	10	.884	3			-3	O/12	0.0
Total	12	1161	3906	421	991	128	84	29	394	346	269	.254	.315	.352	.667	104	-8	10	96	96	465	.631	115	1		-9	2O1/S	-0.2
■ AL HUMPHREY	Humphrey, Albert b: 2/28/1886, Ashtabula, Ohio d: 5/13/61, Ashtabula, Ohio BL/TR, 5'11", 180 lbs. Deb: 9/01/11																											
1911	Bro-N	8	27	4	5	0	0	0	0	3	7	.185	.267	.185	.452	28	-3	-2	97	0	1	.364	0			-2	/O	-0.4
■ TERRY HUMPHREY	Humphrey, Terryal Gene b: 8/4/49, Chickasha, Okla. BR/TR, 6'3", 185 lbs. Deb: 9/05/71																											
1971	Mon-N	9	26	1	5	1	0	0	1	0	4	.192	.192	.231	.423	20	-3	-3	99	68	1	.273	0	0	0	0	/C	-0.2
1972	Mon-N	69	215	13	40	8	0	1	9	16	38	.186	.249	.237	.486	38	-17	-18	102	68	12	.397	4	1	1	-4	C	-1.8
1973	Mon-N	43	90	5	15	2	0	1	9	5	16	.167	.211	.222	.433	19	-10	-10	104	157	4	.321	0	1	-1	-0	C	-0.9
1974	Mon-N	20	52	3	10	3	0	0	3	4	9	.192	.250	.250	.500	38	-4	-4	104	89	4	.405	0	0	0	2	C	-0.1
1975	Det-A	18	41	0	10	0	0	0	1	2	6	.244	.279	.244	.523	47	-3	-3	104	38	3	.375	0	0	0	2	C	0.0
1976	Cal-A	71	196	17	48	10	0	1	19	13	30	.245	.308	.311	.620	89	-4	-2	92	114	18	.506	0	1	-1	-16	C	-1.7
1977	Cal-A	123	304	17	69	11	0	2	34	21	58	.227	.286	.283	.569	59	-18	-16	95	146	24	.457	1	1	-0	-51	*C	-6.5
1978	Cal-A	53	114	11	25	4	1	1	9	6	12	.219	.270	.298	.569	59	-6	-6	102	96	9	.457	0	1	-1	-3	C/23	-0.8
1979	Cal-A	9	17	2	1	0	0	0	0	1	2	.059	.111	.059	.170	-57	-4	-3	93	0	0	.125	0	0	0	-1	/C	-0.3
Total	9	415	1055	69	223	39	1	6	85	68	175	.211	.268	.267	.535	52	-69	-67	98	109	75	.440	5	5	-2	-71	C/32	-12.3
■ JOHN HUMPHRIES	Humphries, John Henry b: 11/12/1861, N.Gower, Ont., Can. d: 11/29/33, Salinas, Cal. TL , 6', 185 lbs. Deb: 7/07/1883																											
1883	NY-N	29	107	5	12	1	0	0	4	1	22	.112	.120	.121	.242	-26	-16	-16	100	109	2	.147				0	CO	-1.3
1884	Was-a	49	193	23	34	2	0	0		9		.176	.217	.187	.403	39	-13	-10	88	0	8	.289				-0	CO/1	-0.6
	NY-N	20	64	6	6	0	0	0	2	9	19	.094	.205	.094	.299	-3	-7	-7	98	115	1	.259				0	C	-0.5
Total	2	98	364	34	52	3	0	0	6	19	41	.143	.188	.151	.339	10	-36	-32	93	52	11	.240				-0	/CO1	-2.4
■ RANDY HUNDLEY	Hundley, Cecil Randolph b: 6/1/42, Martinsville, Va. BR/TR, 5'11", 170 lbs. Deb: 9/27/64 C																											
1964	SF-N	2	1	1	0	0	0	0	0	0	1	.000	.000	.000	.000	-99	-0	-0	100	0	0	.000	0	0	0	0	/C	0.0
1965	SF-N	6	15	0	1	0	0	0	0	0	4	.067	.067	.067	.133	-56	-3	-3	111	0	0	.067	0	0	0	-0	/C	-0.3
1966	Chi-N	149	526	50	124	22	3	19	63	35	113	.236	.287	.397	.685	88	-10	-10	100	102	58	.596	1	3	-2	19	*C	1.1
1967	Chi-N	152	539	68	144	25	3	14	60	44	75	.267	.325	.403	.727	105	4	3	102	98	68	.645	2	4	-2	15	*C	2.7
1968	Chi-N	160	553	41	125	18	4	7	65	39	69	.226	.282	.311	.593	69	-15	-22	112	**145**	46	.483	1	0	0	2	*C	-1.5
1969	Chi-N	151	522	67	133	15	1	18	64	61	90	.255	.336	.391	.727	97	2	-2	107	101	69	.670	2	3	-1	5	*C	1.2
1970	Chi-N	73	250	13	61	5	0	7	36	16	52	.244	.289	.348	.637	58	-11	-18	120	129	25	.528	0	1	-1	-4	C	-1.8
1971	Chi-N	9	21	1	7	1	0	0	2	0	2	.333	.333	.381	.714	93	-0	-0	110	102	3	.571	0	0	0	-0	/C	0.0
1972	Chi-N	114	357	23	78	12	0	5	30	22	62	.218	.264	.294	.558	51	-20	-25	114	103	25	.435	1	0	0	-6	*C	-2.6
1973	Chi-N	124	368	35	83	11	1	10	43	30	51	.226	.284	.342	.626	67	-14	-18	108	111	33	.537	5	6	-2	-7	*C	-2.0
1974	Min-A	32	88	2	17	2	0	0	3	4	12	.193	.228	.216	.444	28	-8	-8	101	62	4	.307	0	0	0	-2	C	-0.8
1975	SD-N	74	180	7	37	5	1	2	14	19	29	.206	.285	.278	.563	57	-10	-10	100	97	14	.473	0	0	0	0	C	-0.8
1976	Chi-N	13	18	3	3	2	0	0	1	1	4	.167	.211	.278	.488	34	-2	-2	109	77	1	.400	0	0	0	0	/C	0.0
1977	Chi-N	2	4	0	0	0	0	0	0	0	1	.000	.000	.000	.000	-88	-1	-1	114	0	0	.000	0	0	0	0	/C	0.0
Total	14	1061	3442	311	813	118	13	82	381	271	565	.236	.294	.350	.644	76	-87	-116	107	109	346	.567	12	17	-7	22	*C	-4.8
■ BERNIE HUNGLING	Hungling, Bernard Herman "Bud" b: 3/5/1896, Dayton, Ohio d: 3/30/68, Dayton, Ohio BR/TR, 6'2", 180 lbs. Deb: 4/14/22																											
1922	Bro-N	39	102	9	23	1	2	1	13	6	20	.225	.269	.304	.572	50	-8	-7	95	134	9	.494	2	0	1	-0	C	-0.6
1923	Bro-N	2	4	0	0	0	0	0	0	0	2	.000	.000	.000	.000	-99	-1	-1	98	0	0	.000	0	1	-1	0	/C	-0.1
1930	StL-A	10	31	4	10	2	0	0	2	5	3	.323	.417	.387	.804	97	1	0	108	55	5	.810	0	0	0	0	C	0.1
Total	3	51	137	13	33	3	2	1	15	11	25	.241	.297	.314	.611	58	-9	-8	98	111	14	.533	2	1	0	0	/C	-0.6
■ BILL HUNNEFIELD	Hunnefield, William Fenton "Wild Bill" b: 1/5/1899, Dedham, Mass. d: 8/28/76, Nantucket, Mass. BB/TR, 5'10", 165 lbs. Deb: 4/17/26																											
1926	Chi-A	131	470	81	129	26	4	3	48	37	28	.274	.329	.366	.695	88	-14	-8	92	92	59	.669	24	9	2	2	S32	0.5
1927	Chi-A	112	365	45	104	25	1	2	36	25	24	.285	.332	.375	.708	82	-9	-10	102	84	45	.674	13	0	4	-10	S2/3	-1.1
1928	Chi-A	94	333	42	98	8	3	2	24	26	24	.294	.351	.354	.705	87	-6	-6	99	68	43	.676	16	6	1	-6	2/S3	-0.5
1929	Chi-A	47	127	13	23	5	0	0	9	7	3	.181	.224	.220	.444	16	-16	-15	95	110	7	.396	7	2	1	3	2/3S	-0.9
1930	Chi-A	31	81	11	22	2	0	1	5	4	10	.272	.314	.333	.647	63	-4	-5	103	55	9	.550	1	1	-0	-2	S/1	-0.4
1931	Cle-A	21	71	13	17	4	1	0	4	9	4	.239	.325	.324	.649	67	-3	-4	106	57	8	.636	3	1	0	-2	S/2	0.0
	Bos-N	11	21	2	6	0	0	0	1	0	2	.286	.286	.286	.571	55	-1	-1	99	59	2	.400	0			0	/32	0.0
	NY-N	64	196	23	53	5	0	1	17	9	16	.270	.302	.311	.614	68	-9	-9	97	95	19	.510	3			-1	2/S	-0.6
	Yr	75	217	25	59	5	0	1	18	9	18	.272	.301	.309	.610	66	-11	-10	97	90	20	.500	3			-1		-0.6
Total	6	511	1664	230	452	75	9	9	144	117	111	.272	.322	.344	.666	76	-64	-58	97	83	191	.619	67	19		-13	S2/31	-3.0
■ RANDY HUNT	Hunt, James Randall b: 1/3/60, Prattville, Ala. BR/TR, 6', 185 lbs. Deb: 6/04/85																											
1985	StL-N	14	19	1	3	0	0	0	1	0	5	.158	.158	.158	.316	-12	-3	-3	96	133	0	.176	0	1	-1	-1	C	-0.3
1986	Mon-N	21	48	4	10	0	0	2	5	5	16	.208	.283	.333	.616	71	-2	-2	98	91	4	.525	0	0	0	-3	C	-0.4
Total	2	35	67	5	13	0	0	2	6	5	21	.194	.250	.284	.534	49	-5	-5	97	102	4	.421	0	1	-1	-4	/C	-0.7
■ KEN HUNT	Hunt, Kenneth Lawrence b: 7/13/34, Grand Forks, N.Dak BR/TR, 6'1", 205 lbs. Deb: 9/10/59																											
1959	NY-A	6	12	2	4	1	0	0	1	0	3	.333	.333	.417	.750	113	0	0	93	79	2	.625	0	0	0	-0	/O	0.0
1960	NY-A	25	22	4	6	2	0	0	1	4	4	.273	.407	.364	.771	117	1	1	94	49	4	.813	0	0	0	-6	O	-0.5
1961	LA-A	149	479	70	122	29	3	25	84	49	120	.255	.329	.484	.813	103	8	1	111	107	76	.790	8	2	1	-1	*O/2	-0.3
1962	LA-A	13	11	4	2	0	0	1	1	1	5	.182	.250	.455	.705	83	-0	-0	102	50	1	.700	1	0	0	0	/1	0.0
1963	LA-A	59	142	17	26	6	1	5	16	15	49	.183	.261	.345	.606	75	-6	-5	91	105	12	.533	0	1	-1	-7	O	-1.4
	Was-A	7	20	1	4	0	0	1	4	2	6	.200	.273	.350	.623	75	-1	-1	98	167	1	.500	0	0	0	0	/O	0.0
	Yr	66	162	18	30	6	1	6	20	17	55	.185	.263	.346	.608	75	-7	-5	92	113	15	.541	0	1	-1	-7		-1.4
1964	Was-A	51	96	9	13	4	0	1	4	14	35	.135	.245	.208	.454	27	-9	-9	101	74	5	.391	0	1	-1	0	O	-1.1
Total	6	310	782	107	177	42	4	33	111	85	222	.226	.306	.417	.723	89	-8	-14	105	101	101	.694	9	4	0	-14	O/12	-3.3
■ JOEL HUNT	Hunt, Oliver Joel "Jodie" b: 10/11/05, Texico, N.Mex. BR/TR, 5'10", 165 lbs. Deb: 4/27/31																											
1931	StL-N	4	1	2	0	0	0	0	0	0	1	.000	.000	.000	.000	-94	-0	-0	107	0	0	.000	0			-0	/O	0.0
1932	StL-N	12	21	0	4	1	0	0	3	4	3	.190	.320	.238	.558	53	-1	-1	100	223	2	.529	0			0	/O	-0.1
Total	2	16	22	2	4	1	0	0	3	4	4	.182	.308	.227	.535	46	-2	-2	100	215	2	.500	0			-0	/O	-0.1
■ DICK HUNT	Hunt, Richard M. b: 1847, New York d: 11/20/1895, Brooklyn, N.Y. 5'9", 145 lbs. Deb: 5/07/1872																											
1872	Eck-n	11	52	11	15							.288															/O2	
■ RON HUNT	Hunt, Ronald Kenneth b: 2/23/41, St.Louis, Mo. BR/TR, 6', 186 lbs. Deb: 4/16/63																											
1963	NY-N	143	533	64	145	28	4	10	42	40	50	.272	.338	.396	.734	111	8	8	99	70	71	.664	5	4	-1	4	*2/3	2.2
1964	NY-N	127	475	59	144	19	6	6	42	29	30	.303	.357	.406	.764	120	10	12	95	87	66	.685	6	2	1	6	*23	2.8
1965	NY-N	57	196	21	47	12	1	1	10	14	19	.240	.310	.327	.637	80	-5	-5	100	63	18	.534	2	7	-4	-1	2/3	-0.7
1966	NY-N	132	479	63	138	19	2	3	33	41	34	.288	.358	.355	.713	105	1	5	94	82	61	.637	8	10	-4	13	*2/S3	2.2
1967	LA-N	110	388	44	102	17	3	3	33	39	24	.263	.346	.345	.691	112	0	6	88	97	48	.625	2	1	0	-0	2/3	1.2
1968	SF-N	148	529	79	132	19	0	2	28	78	41	.250	.372	.297	.669	105	7	9	98	70	66	.646	6	6	-2	-15	*2	0.0
1969	SF-N	128	478	72	125	23	3	3	41	51	47	.262	.363	.341	.704	97	2	1	101	101	66	.683	9	2	2	1	*2/3	1.4
1970	SF-N	117	367	70	103	17	1	6	41	44	29	.281	.396	.381	.777	114	8	10	96	101	59	.767	1	2	-1	-12	23	0.6
1971	Mon-N	152	520	89	145	20	3	5	38	58	41	.279	.403	.358	.761	118	18	18	99	82	85	.781	5	7	-3	1	*23	2.4
1972	Mon-N	129	443	56	112	20	0	0	18	51	29	.253	.363	.298	.661	88	-2	-4	102	59	55	.643	9	2	2	2	*2/3	0.8
1973	Mon-N	113	401	61	124	14	0	0	18	52	19	.309	.419	.344	.763	109	12	10	104	55	63	.765	10	7	-1	-11	*23	0.2
1974	Mon-N	115	403	66	108	15	0	0	26	55	17	.268	.375	.305	.680	88	-1	-3	104	86	51	.636	2	5	-2	-4	32/S	-0.9
	StL-N	12	23	1	4	0	0	0	0	3	2	.174	.321	.174	.495	40	-2	-2	104	0	2	.474	0	0	0	1	/2	0.0

YEAR	TM/L	G	AB	R	H	2B	3B	HR	RBI	BB	SO	AVG	OBP	SLG	PRO	/A	BR	/A	PF	CHI	RC	TA	SB	CS	SBR	FR	POS	TPR
	Yr	127	426	67	112	15	0	0	26	58	19	.263	.372	.298	.670	85	-3	-5	104	79	54	.636	2	5	-2	-4		-0.9
Total	12	1483	5235	745	1429	223	23	39	370	555	382	.273	.369	.347	.716	105	56	66	98	79	711	.694	65	55	-14	-16	*23/S	12.2
■ **EDDIE HUNTER** Hunter, Edison Franklin b: 2/6/05, Bellevue, Ky. d: 3/14/67, Collrain Turnpike Ohio BR/TR, 5'7.5", 150 lbs. Deb: 8/05/33																												
1933	Cin-N	1	0	0	0	0	0	0	0	0	0	—	—	—	—	—	0	0	99	—	—	—	0			0	/3	0.0
■ **NEWT HUNTER** Hunter, Frederick Creighton b: 1/5/1880, Chillicothe, Ohio d: 10/26/63, Columbus, Ohio BR/TR, 6', 180 lbs. Deb: 4/12/11 C																												
1911	Pit-N	65	209	35	53	10	6	2	24	25	43	.254	.345	.388	.732	104	1	1	101	95	31	.763	9			-2	1	-0.2
■ **GEORGE HUNTER** Hunter, George Henry b: 7/8/1887, Buffalo, N.Y. d: 1/11/68, Harrisburg, Pa. BB , 5'8.5", 165 lbs. Deb: 09																												
1909	Bro-N	44	123	8	28	7	0	0	8	9		.228	.286	.285	.570	79	-3	-3	99	83	10	.484	1			0	OP	0.0
1910	Bro-N	1	0	0	0	0	0	0	0	0	0	—	—	—	—	—	0	0	95	—	—	—	0			-0	/O	0.0
Total	2	45	123	8	28	7	0	0	8	9	0	.228	.286	.285	.570	79	-3	-3	99	83	20	.484	1			-0	/OP	0.0
■ **BILLY HUNTER** Hunter, Gordon William b: 6/4/28, Punxsutawney, Pa. BR/TR, 6', 180 lbs. Deb: 4/14/53 MC																												
1953	StL-A	154	567	50	124	18	1	1	37	24	45	.219	.253	.259	.512	36	-49	-54	107	93	37	.386	3	1	0	**17**	*S	-2.4
1954	Bal-A	125	411	28	100	9	5	2	27	21	38	.243	.283	.304	.588	64	-23	-20	95	78	33	.465	5	4	-1	-4	*S	-1.5
1955	NY-A	98	255	14	58	7	1	3	20	15	18	.227	.270	.298	.568	54	-17	-17	98	88	20	.485	9	2	2	-5	S	-0.9
1956	NY-A	39	75	8	21	3	4	0	11	2	4	.280	.299	.427	.725	91	-2	-1	99	128	8	.586	0	1	-1	3	S/3	0.4
1957	KC-A	116	319	39	61	10	4	8	29	27	43	.191	.261	.323	.584	59	-19	-19	99	90	27	.506	1	2	-1	-9	2S3	-2.2
1958	KC-A	22	58	6	9	1	1	2	11	5	7	.155	.222	.310	.533	43	-5	-5	106	184	4	.471	1	1	-0	0	S/23	-0.2
	Cle-A	76	190	21	37	10	2	0	9	17	37	.195	.264	.268	.533	50	-14	-12	94	71	14	.465	4	1	1	-12	S/3	-1.3
	Yr	98	248	27	46	11	3	2	20	22	44	.185	.255	.278	.533	48	-18	-17	97	98	19	.469	5	2	0	-12		-1.5
Total	6	630	1875	166	410	58	18	16	144	111	192	.219	.265	.294	.560	52	-128	-128	100	90	144	.469	23	12	-0	-9	S/23	-8.1
■ **BUDDY HUNTER** Hunter, Harold James b: 8/9/47, Omaha, Neb. BR/TR, 5'10", 170 lbs. Deb: 7/01/71																												
1971	Bos-A	8	9	2	2	1	0	0	0	2	1	.222	.364	.333	.697	93	0	-0	106	0	1	.714	0	0	0	0	/2	0.0
1973	Bos-A	13	7	3	3	1	0	0	2	3	1	.429	.636	.571	1.208	229	2	2	106	196	3	2.000	0	0	0	-0	/32D	0.2
1975	Bos-A	1	1	0	0	0	0	0	0	0	0	.000	.000	.000	.000	-92	-0	-0	109	0	0	.000	0	0	0	-0	/2	0.0
Total	3	22	17	5	5	2	0	0	2	5	2	.294	.478	.412	.890	145	2	2	106	94	5	1.083	0	0	0	-0	/23D	0.2
■ **HERB HUNTER** Hunter, Herbert Harrison b: 12/25/1896, Boston, Mass. d: 7/25/70, Orlando, Fla. BL/TR, 6'0.5", 165 lbs. Deb: 4/29/16																												
1916	NY-N	21	28	3	7	0	0	1	4	0	5	.250	.250	.357	.607	89	-1	-1	96	122	3	.476	0			0	/31	0.0
	Chi-N	2	4	0	0	0	0	0	0	0	0	.000	.000	.000	.000	-86	-1	-1	117	0	0	.000	0			0	/3	0.0
	Yr	23	32	3	7	0	0	1	4	0	5	.219	.219	.313	.531	64	-2	-1	98	117	2	.400	0			0		0.0
1917	Chi-N	3	3	0	0	0	0	0	0	0	0	.000	.000	.000	.000	-96	-1	-1	105	0	0	.000	0			0	/23	0.0
1920	Bos-A	4	12	2	1	0	0	0	0	1	1	.083	.154	.083	.237	-37	-2	-2	96	0	0	.182	0	0	0	-0	/O	-0.2
1921	StL-N	9	2	3	0	0	0	0	0	1	0	.000	.333	.000	.333	-5	-0	-0	95	0	-0	.200	0	3	-2	0	/1	-0.1
Total	4	39	49	8	8	0	0	1	4	2	6	.163	.196	.224	.421	24	-5	-5	98	67	3	.295	0	3		0	/3O12	-0.3
■ **BILL HUNTER** Hunter, William Ellsworth b: 7/8/1887, Buffalo, N.Y. d: 4/10/34, Buffalo, N.Y. BL/TL, 5'7.5", 155 lbs. Deb: 8/06/12																												
1912	Cle-A	21	55	6	9	2	0	0	2	10		.164	.303	.200	.503	44	-4	-4	101	61	4	.478	0			1	O	-0.3
■ **BILL HUNTER** Hunter, William Robert b: St.Thomas, Ont., Can. 5'7.5", 160 lbs. Deb: 5/02/1884																												
1884	Lou-a	2	7	1	1	0	0	0		0		.143	.143	.143	.286	-6	-1	-1	89	0	0	.167				0	/C	0.0
■ **STEVE HUNTZ** Huntz, Stephen Michael b: 12/3/45, Cleveland, Ohio BB/TR, 6'1", 204 lbs. Deb: 9/19/67																												
1967	StL-N	3	6	1	1	0	0	0	0	1	2	.167	.286	.167	.452	32	-0	-0	101	0	0	.400	0	0	0	-0	/2	0.0
1969	StL-N	71	139	13	27	4	0	3	13	27	34	.194	.325	.288	.613	73	-4	-4	100	106	13	.573	0	0	0	3	S2/3	0.6
1970	SD-N	106	352	54	77	8	0	11	37	66	69	.219	.344	.335	.679	87	-7	-5	95	97	44	.654	0	3	-2	3	S3	0.2
1971	Chi-A	35	86	10	18	3	1	2	6	7	9	.209	.269	.337	.606	73	-4	-3	98	70	8	.536	1	0	0	1	2/S3	0.0
1975	SD-N	22	53	3	8	4	0	0	4	7	8	.151	.250	.226	.476	33	-5	-5	100	129	3	.413	0	0	0	-1	3/2	-0.5
Total	5	237	636	81	131	19	1	16	60	108	122	.206	.322	.314	.637	77	-20	-17	97	97	70	.609	1	3	-2	6	S/32	0.3
■ **DAVE HUPPERT** Huppert, David Blain b: 4/1/57, Southgate, Cal. BR/TR, 6'1", 190 lbs. Deb: 9/15/83																												
1983	Bal-A	2	0	0	0	0	0	0	0	0	0	—	—	—	—	—	0	0	100	—	—	—	0	0	0	0	/C	0.0
1985	Mil-A	15	21	1	1	0	0	0	0	2	7	.048	.130	.048	.178	-47	-4	-4	105	0	0	.143	0	0	0	1	C	-0.2
Total	2	17	21	1	1	0	0	0	0	2	7	.048	.130	.048	.178	-47	-4	-4	105	0	70	.143	0	0	0	1	/C	-0.2
■ **CLINT HURDLE** Hurdle, Clinton Merrick b: 7/30/57, Big Rapids, Mich. BL/TR, 6'3", 195 lbs. Deb: 9/18/77																												
1977	KC-A	9	26	5	8	0	0	2	7	2	7	.308	.357	.538	.896	140	1	1	100	139	5	.889	0	0	0	-1	/O	0.0
1978	KC-A	133	417	48	110	25	5	7	56	56	84	.264	.352	.398	.750	108	7	6	102	118	61	.709	1	3	-2	-9	O1/3D	-0.9
1979	KC-A	59	171	16	41	10	3	3	30	28	24	.240	.350	.386	.736	93	0	-1	105	154	24	.704	0	1	-1	-5	O/3D	-0.8
1980	KC-A	130	395	50	116	31	2	10	60	34	61	.294	.353	.458	.811	122	11	11	98	111	62	.748	0	0	0	-10	*O	0.0
1981	KC-A	28	76	12	25	3	1	4	15	13	10	.329	.427	.553	.980	183	8	8	99	109	18	1.038	0	0	0	-1	O	0.7
1982	Cin-N	19	34	2	7	1	0	0	1	2	6	.206	.270	.235	.506	42	-3	-3	102	49	2	.379	0	1	-1	-2	O	-0.5
1983	NY-N	13	33	3	6	2	0	0	2	2	10	.182	.229	.242	.471	31	-3	-3	99	99	2	.357	0	0	0	-0	/3O	-0.3
1985	NY-N	43	82	7	16	4	0	3	7	13	20	.195	.313	.354	.666	89	-1	-1	97	73	9	.632	0	1	-1	-1	CO	-0.1
1986	StL-N	78	154	18	30	5	1	3	15	26	38	.195	.315	.299	.614	68	-6	-6	103	109	16	.579	0	0	0	-2	1O/C3	-1.0
1987	NY-N	3	3	1	1	0	0	0	0	0	1	.333	.333	.333	.667	78	-0	-0	99	0	0	.500	0	0	0	0	/1	0.0
Total	10	515	1391	162	360	81	12	32	193	176	261	.259	.345	.403	.748	105	14	12	101	114	199	.718	1	6	-3	-31	O/1C3D	-2.9
■ **JERRY HURLEY** Hurley, Jeremiah Joseph b: 6/15/1863, Boston, Mass. d: 9/17/50, Boston, Mass. TR , 6', 190 lbs. Deb: 5/01/1889																												
1889	Bos-N	1	4	0	0	0	0	0	0	0	0	.000	.000	.000	.000	-98	-1	-1	102	0	0	.000	0			0	/OC	0.0
1890	Pit-P	8	22	5	6	1	0	0	2	2	5	.273	.333	.318	.652	83	-1	-0	92	78	2	.563	0			0	/CO	0.0
1891	CM-a	24	66	10	14	3	2	0	6	12	13	.212	.333	.318	.652	80	-1	-2	112	83	8	.673	2			0	C/O1	-0.1
Total	3	33	92	15	20	4	2	0	8	14	18	.217	.321	.304	.625	73	-2	-3	107	78	10	.611	2			0	/CO1	-0.1
■ **JERRY HURLEY** Hurley, Jeremiah b: 4/1875, New York, N.Y. d: 12/27/19, New York, N.Y. BR/TR, Deb: 9/23/01																												
1901	Cin-N	9	21	1	1	0	0	0	0	1		.048	.091	.048	.139	-62	-4	-4	95	0	0	.150	1			1	/C	-0.2
1907	Bro-N	1	2	0	0	0	0	0	0	1		.000	.333	.000	.333	7	-0	-0	94	0	0	.500	0			0	/C	0.0
Total	2	10	23	1	1	0	0	0	0	2		.043	.120	.043	.163	-53	-4	-4	95	0	0	.182	1			1	/C	-0.2
■ **DICK HURLEY** Hurley, William F. b: 1847, Honesdale, Pa. 5'7", 160 lbs. Deb: 4/18/1872																												
1872	Oly-n	2	8	0	0							.000															/O	
■ **DON HURST** Hurst, Frank O'Donnell b: 8/12/05, Maysville, Ky. d: 12/6/52, Los Angeles, Cal. BL/TL, 6', 215 lbs. Deb: 5/13/28																												
1928	Phi-N	107	396	73	113	23	4	19	64	68	40	.285	.391	.508	.899	128	20	17	104	85	80	.965	3			5	*1	1.1
1929	Phi-N	154	589	100	179	29	4	31	125	80	36	.304	.390	.525	.914	113	22	13	110	113	120	.980	10			5	*1	0.9
1930	Phi-N	119	391	78	128	19	3	17	78	46	22	.327	.401	.522	.923	114	14	10	106	105	81	.981	6			0	1/O	0.4
1931	Phi-N	137	489	63	149	37	5	11	91	64	28	.305	.386	.468	.855	121	21	17	106	126	93	.888	8			11	*1	1.6
1932	Phi-N	150	579	109	196	41	4	24	**143**	65	27	.339	.412	.547	.959	139	46	37	112	145	134	1.042	10			-3	*1	2.5
1933	Phi-N	147	550	58	147	27	8	8	76	48	32	.267	.327	.389	.716	88	3	-9	118	127	72	.641	3			7	*1	-0.4
1934	Phi-N	40	130	16	34	9	0	2	21	12	7	.262	.324	.377	.701	80	-2	-4	108	138	17	.639	1			-2	1	-0.7
	Chi-N	51	151	13	30	5	0	3	12	8	18	.199	.239	.291	.530	42	-13	-12	98	82	10	.419	0			0	1	-1.5
	Yr	91	281	29	64	14	0	5	33	20	25	.228	.279	.331	.610	61	-15	-16	102	108	27	.518	1			-1		-2.2
Total	7	905	3275	510	976	190	28	115	610	391	210	.298	.375	.478	.854	112	110	68	109	118	606	.875	41			24	1/O	3.9
■ **JEFF HUSON** Huson, Jeffrey Kent b: 8/15/64, Scottsdale, Ariz. BL/TR, 6'3", 170 lbs. Deb: 9/02/88																												
1988	Mon-N	20	42	7	13	2	0	0	3	4	3	.310	.370	.357	.727	104	1	0	106	80	5	.656	2	1	0	-1	S/23O	0.0
■ **CARL HUSTA** Husta, Carl Lawrence "Sox" b: 4/8/02, Egg Harbor, N.J. d: 11/6/51, Kingston, N.Y. BR/TR, 5'11", 176 lbs. Deb: 9/24/25																												
1925	Phi-A	6	22	2	3	0	0	0	2	2	3	.136	.208	.136	.345	-11	-4	-4	103	228	1	.263	0	0	0	0	/S	-0.2

YEAR	TM/L	G	AB	R	H	2B	3B	HR	RBI	BB	SO	AVG	OBP	SLG	PRO	/A	BR	/A	PF	CHI	RC	TA	SB	CS	SBR	FR	POS	TPR
■ **HARRY HUSTON**	Huston, Harry Emanuel Kress b: 10/14/1883, Bellefontaine, O. d: 10/13/69, Blackwell, Okla. TR , 5'9", 168 lbs. Deb: 9/03/06																											
1906	Phi-N	2	4	0	0	0	0	0	0	0	1	.000	.200	.000	.200	-39	-1	-1	92	0	0	.250	0			0	/C	0.0
■ **WARREN HUSTON**	Huston, Warren Llewellyn b: 10/31/13, Newtonville, Mass. BR/TR, 6', 170 lbs. Deb: 6/24/37																											
1937	Phi-A	38	54	5	7	3	0	0	3	2	9	.130	.161	.185	.346	-14	-10	-9	94	103	1	.250	0	1	-1	-0	2S/3	-0.6
1944	Bos-N	33	55	7	11	1	0	0	1	8	5	.200	.313	.218	.531	54	-3	-3	95	30	4	.447	0			1	3/2S	0.0
Total	2	71	109	12	18	4	0	0	4	10	14	.165	.242	.202	.444	20	-13	-12	94	64	5	.347	0	1		0	/32S	-0.6
■ **JOE HUTCHESON**	Hutcheson, Joseph Johnson "Slug" or "Poodles" b: 2/5/05, Springtown, Tex. BL/TR, 6'2", 200 lbs. Deb: 7/08/33																											
1933	Bro-N	55	184	19	43	4	1	6	21	15	13	.234	.295	.364	.659	90	-3	-2	97	93	20	.575	1			1	O	-0.4
■ **ED HUTCHINSON**	Hutchinson, Edwin Forrest b: 5/19/1867, Pittsburgh, Pa. d: 1930, California BL, 5'11", 175 lbs. Deb: 6/17/1890																											
1890	Chi-N	4	17	0	1	1	0	0	0	0	0	.059	.059	.118	.176	-44	-3	-3	109	0	0	.125	0			0	/2	-0.2
■ **FRED HUTCHINSON**	Hutchinson, Frederick Charles b: 8/12/19, Seattle, Wash. d: 11/12/64, Bradenton, Fla. BL/TR, 6'2", 190 lbs. Deb: 5/02/39 M																											
1939	Det-A	13	34	5	13	1	0	0	6	2	0	.382	.417	.412	.828	101	1	0	111	145	5	.696	0	0	0	0	P	0.0
1940	Det-A	17	30	1	8	1	0	0	2	0	0	.267	.267	.300	.567	42	-2	-3	111	80	2	.409	0	0	0	0	P	0.0
1941	Det-A	2	2	0	0	0	0	0	0	0	2	.000	.000	.000	.000	-94	-1	-1	106	0	0	.000	0	0	0	0	H	0.0
1946	Det-A	40	89	11	28	4	0	0	13	6	1	.315	.358	.360	.717	93	0	-1	108	155	12	.613	0	0	0	3	P	0.0
1947	Det-A	56	106	8	32	5	2	2	15	6	6	.302	.339	.443	.783	112	2	1	104	104	15	.705	2	0	1	2	P	0.0
1948	Det-A	76	112	11	23	1	0	1	12	23	9	.205	.341	.241	.582	58	-6	-6	96	135	11	.576	3	0	1	3	P	0.2
1949	Det-A	38	73	12	18	2	1	0	7	8	5	.247	.329	.301	.631	63	-3	-4	108	109	7	.542	1	0	0	2	P	0.0
1950	Det-A	44	95	15	31	7	0	0	20	12	3	.326	.407	.400	.807	111	2	2	97	182	17	.773	0	0	0	2	P	0.0
1951	Det-A	47	85	7	16	2	0	0	7	7	4	.188	.250	.212	.462	24	-9	-9	106	139	5	.347	0	1	-1	2	P	0.0
1952	Det-A	17	18	0	1	0	0	0	0	3	0	.056	.190	.056	.246	-30	-3	-3	99	0	0	.222	0	0	0	2	PM	0.0
1953	Det-A	4	6	1	1	0	0	1	1	0	0	.167	.167	.667	.833	119	0	0	98	53	1	.800	0	0	0	0	/P1M	0.0
Total	11	354	650	71	171	23	3	4	83	67	30	.263	.334	.326	.660	75	-20	-23	103	131	76	.598	6	1	1	15	P/1	0.2
■ **ROY HUTSON**	Hutson, Roy Lee b: 2/27/02, Luray, Mo. d: 5/20/57, La Mesa, Cal. BL/TR, 5'9", 165 lbs. Deb: 9/20/25																											
1925	Bro-N	7	8	1	4	0	0	0	1	1	1	.500	.556	.500	1.056	183	1	1	94	89	2	1.250	0	0	0	-1	/O	0.0
■ **JIM HUTTO**	Hutto, James Neamon b: 10/17/47, Norfolk, Va. BR/TR, 5'11", 195 lbs. Deb: 4/17/70																											
1970	Phi-N	57	92	7	17	2	0	3	12	5	20	.185	.227	.304	.531	43	-8	-8	96	126	6	.423	0	0	0	-2	O1/C3	-1.1
1975	Bal-A	4	5	0	0	0	0	0	0	0	2	.000	.000	.000	.000	-99	-1	-1	91	0	0	.000	0	0	0	0	/C	0.0
Total	2	61	97	7	17	2	0	3	12	5	22	.175	.216	.289	.504	36	-9	-9	96	120	6	.412	0	0	0	-2	/O1C3	-1.1
■ **TOM HUTTON**	Hutton, Thomas George b: 4/20/46, Los Angeles, Cal. BL/TL, 5'11", 180 lbs. Deb: 9/16/66																											
1966	LA-N	3	2	0	0	0	0	0	0	0	0	.000	.000	.000	.000	-99	-1	-1	97	0	0	.000	0	0	0	0	/1	0.0
1969	LA-N	16	48	2	13	0	0	0	4	5	7	.271	.340	.271	.610	74	-2	-1	99	123	5	.500	0	0	0	1	1	-0.1
1972	Phi-N	134	381	40	99	16	2	4	38	56	24	.260	.355	.344	.699	102	1	3	97	109	47	.642	5	8	-3	-2	1O	-1.0
1973	Phi-N	106	247	31	65	11	0	5	29	32	31	.263	.348	.368	.716	91	0	-2	108	110	31	.660	3	1	0	1	1	-0.4
1974	Phi-N	96	208	32	50	6	3	4	33	30	13	.240	.336	.356	.692	91	-1	-2	103	148	25	.642	2	2	-1	-4	1O	-1.0
1975	Phi-N	113	165	24	41	6	0	3	24	27	10	.248	.354	.339	.694	92	-1	-1	101	143	19	.625	2	5	-2	-1	1O	-0.9
1976	Phi-N	95	124	15	25	5	1	1	13	27	11	.202	.344	.282	.627	74	-2	-3	107	132	13	.600	1	2	-1	-1	1/O	-0.9
1977	Phi-N	107	81	12	25	3	0	2	11	12	10	.309	.398	.420	.818	119	3	3	100	110	13	.783	1	1	-0	-2	1/O	-0.3
1978	Tor-A	64	173	19	44	9	0	2	9	19	11	.254	.328	.341	.669	88	-2	-2	100	55	19	.581	1	2	-1	-7	O/1	-1.1
	Mon-N	39	59	4	12	3	0	0	5	10	5	.203	.319	.254	.573	65	-3	-2	96	132	5	.500	0	0	0	-2	1/O	-0.5
1979	Mon-N	86	83	14	21	2	1	1	13	10	7	.253	.333	.337	.671	82	-2	-2	102	166	9	.576	0	0	0	-2	1/O	-0.5
1980	Mon-N	62	55	2	12	2	0	0	5	4	10	.218	.271	.255	.526	48	-4	-4	99	141	4	.409	0	0	0	-2	/1OP	-0.5
1981	Mon-N	31	29	1	3	0	0	0	2	2	1	.103	.161	.103	.265	-24	-5	-5	99	262	1	.192	0	0	0	-1	/1O	-0.5
Total	12	952	1655	196	410	63	7	22	186	234	140	.248	.341	.334	.675	88	-18	-21	101	121	190	.633	15	21	-8	-22	1O/P	-7.7
■ **HAM HYATT**	Hyatt, Robert Hamilton b: 11/1/1884, Buncombe Co., N.C. d: 9/11/63, Liberty Lake, Wash. BL/TR, 6'1", 185 lbs. Deb: 09																											
1909	Pit-N	49	67	9	20	3	4	0	7	3		.299	.329	.463	.791	140	3	3	105	82	10	.745	1			0	/O1	0.3
1910	Pit-N	74	175	19	46	5	6	1	30	8	14	.263	.306	.377	.684	89	-1	-4	112	152	20	.620	3			-1	1/O	-0.4
1912	Pit-N	46	97	13	28	3	1	0	22	6	8	.289	.330	.340	.670	85	-2	-2	99	225	11	.594	2			-3	O/1	-0.5
1913	Pit-N	63	81	8	27	6	2	4	16	3	8	.333	.372	.605	.977	184	7	8	96	95	18	1.000	0			-0	/1O	0.7
1914	Pit-N	74	79	2	17	3	1	1	15	7	14	.215	.295	.316	.612	89	-2	-1	92	194	7	.565	1			0	/1C	0.0
1915	StL-N	106	295	23	79	8	9	2	46	28	24	.268	.337	.376	.714	116	6	6	100	150	38	.662	3	3	-1	-3	1O	-0.2
1918	NY-A	53	131	11	30	8	0	2	10	8	8	.229	.273	.336	.609	89	-3	-3	95	73	12	.525	1			-2	O/1	-0.6
Total	7	465	925	85	247	36	23	10	146	63	76	.267	.321	.388	.709	109	7	7	101	142	117	.651	11	3		-9	1/OC	-0.7
■ **PAT HYNES**	Hynes, Patrick J. b: 3/12/1884, St.Louis, Mo. d: 3/12/07, St.Louis, Mo. TL , Deb: 03																											
1903	StL-N	1	3	0	0	0	0	0	0	0		.000	.000	.000	.000	-99	-1	-1	96	0	0	.000	0			-1	/P	0.0
1904	StL-A	66	254	23	60	7	3	0	15	3		.236	.245	.287	.533	74	-9	-8	95	81	19	.407	3			-1	O/P	-1.3
Total	2	67	257	23	60	7	3	0	15	3		.233	.242	.284	.526	71	-10	-8	95	80	19	.401	3			-2	/OP	-1.3
■ **PETE INCAVIGLIA**	Incaviglia, Peter Joseph b: 4/2/64, Pebble Beach, Cal. BR/TR, 6'1", 225 lbs. Deb: 4/08/86																											
1986	Tex-A	153	540	82	135	21	2	30	88	55	185	.250	.324	.463	.787	117	8	12	96	105	82	.750	3	2	-0	-15	*OD	-0.7
1987	Tex-A	139	509	85	138	26	4	27	80	48	168	.271	.335	.497	.832	114	12	10	104	98	85	.814	9	3	1	-8	*O/D	0.0
1988	Tex-A	116	418	59	104	19	3	22	54	39	153	.249	.323	.467	.790	117	9	9	101	84	63	.762	6	4	-1	2	OD	0.9
Total	3	408	1467	226	377	66	9	79	222	142	506	.257	.328	.476	.803	116	29	30	100	96	230	.787	18	9	0	-20	O/D	0.2
■ **ALEXIS INFANTE**	Infante, Fermin Alexis (Carpio) b: 12/4/61, Barquisimeto, Venez. BR/TR, 5'10", 175 lbs. Deb: 9/27/87																											
1987	Tor-A	1	0	0	0	0	0	0	0	0	0	—	—	—	—	—	0	0	101	—	—	—	0	0	0	0	/R	0.0
1988	Tor-A	19	15	7	3	0	0	0	0	2	4	.200	.294	.200	.494	41	-1	-1	100	0	1	.385	0	0	0	1	/3SD	0.0
Total	2	20	15	7	3	0	0	0	0	2	4	.200	.294	.200	.494	41	-1	-1	100	0	231	.385	0	0	0	1	/3DS	0.0
■ **SCOTTY INGERTON**	Ingerton, William John b: 4/19/1886, Peninsula, Ohio d: 6/15/56, Cleveland, Ohio BR/TR, 6'1", 172 lbs. Deb: 4/12/11																											
1911	Bos-N	136	521	63	130	24	4	5	61	39	68	.250	.304	.340	.644	77	-15	-18	103	114	55	.573	6			11	3O12/S	-0.6
■ **CHARLIE INGRAHAM**	Ingraham, Charles b: 4/1860 Illinois 5'11", 170 lbs. Deb: 1883																											
1883	Bal-a	1	4	0	1	0	0	0		0		.250	.250	.250	.500	58	-0	-0	107	0	0	.333				0	/C	0.0
■ **MEL INGRAM**	Ingram, Melvin David b: 7/4/04, Asheville, N.C. d: 10/28/79, Medford, Ore. BR/TR, 5'11.5", 175 lbs. Deb: 7/24/29																											
1929	Pit-N	3	0	1	0	0	0	0	0	0	0	—	—	—	—	—	0	0	103	—	—	—	0			0	R	0.0
■ **DANE IORG**	Iorg, Dane Charles b: 5/11/50, Eureka, Cal. BL/TR, 6', 180 lbs. Deb: 4/09/77																											
1977	Phi-N	12	30	3	5	1	0	0	2	1	3	.167	.194	.200	.394	6	-4	-4	100	133	1	.280	0	0	0	0	/1	-0.4
	StL-N	30	32	2	10	1	0	0	4	5	4	.313	.405	.344	.749	108	0	1	96	145	4	.667	0	1	-1	-2	/O	-0.1
	Yr	42	62	5	15	2	0	0	6	6	7	.242	.309	.274	.583	60	-4	-3	97	145	5	.469	0	1	-1	-2		-0.5
1978	StL-N	35	85	6	23	4	1	0	4	4	10	.271	.303	.341	.645	84	-2	-2	95	55	8	.516	0	0	0	0	O	-0.2
1979	StL-N	79	179	12	52	11	1	1	21	12	28	.291	.339	.380	.718	91	-1	-2	105	117	22	.612	1	2	-1	-5	O1	-0.9
1980	StL-N	105	251	33	76	23	1	3	36	20	34	.303	.354	.438	.792	117	6	6	103	120	38	.724	1	1	-0	-5	O/13	-0.2
1981	StL-N	75	217	23	71	11	2	2	39	7	9	.327	.348	.424	.772	116	4	4	102	156	30	.660	2	0	1	-12	O/13	-0.9
1982	StL-N	102	238	17	70	14	1	0	34	23	23	.294	.356	.361	.718	98	1	-0	103	155	28	.606	0	1	-1	-6	O1/3	-0.8
1983	StL-N	58	116	6	31	9	1	0	11	10	11	.267	.331	.362	.693	94	-1	-1	98	104	13	.593	1	0	0	-2	O1	-0.3
1984	StL-N	15	28	3	4	2	0	0	3	2	6	.143	.200	.214	.414	17	-3	-3	99	196	1	.308	0	0	0	-0	/1O	-0.3
	KC-A	78	235	27	60	16	2	5	30	13	15	.255	.294	.404	.699	92	-3	-3	99	109	26	.590	0	1	-1	-4	1O/3D	-1.0
1985	KC-A	64	130	7	29	9	1	1	21	8	16	.223	.268	.331	.599	62	-7	-7	102	181	10	.472	0	1	-1	-6	O/13D	-1.4
1986	SD-N	90	106	10	24	2	1	2	11	2	21	.226	.241	.321	.561	56	-7	-6	95	110	8	.429	0	0	0	-1	1/3OP	-0.7
Total	10	743	1647	149	455	103	11	14	216	107	180	.276	.321	.378	.699	92	-17	-19	101	130	190	.613	5	7	-3	-43	O1/3DP	-7.2

YEAR	TM/L	G	AB	R	H	2B	3B	HR	RBI	BB	SO	AVG	OBP	SLG	PRO	/A	BR	/A	PF	CHI	RC	TA	SB	CS	SBR	FR	POS	TPR
■ **GARTH IORG**	Iorg, Garth Ray b: 10/12/54, Arcata, Cal. BR/TR, 5'11", 170 lbs. Deb: 4/09/78																											
1978	Tor-A	19	49	3	8	0	0	0	3	3	4	.163	.226	.163	.390	11	-6	-6	100	148	2	.273	0	0	0	0	2	-0.4
1980	Tor-A	80	222	24	55	10	1	2	14	12	39	.248	.286	.329	.615	68	-10	-10	100	69	20	.503	2	1	0	-1	23O1/SD	-1.0
1981	Tor-A	70	215	17	52	11	0	0	10	7	31	.242	.269	.293	.562	56	-11	-13	111	62	16	.432	2	3	-1	-6	23/S1D	-2.0
1982	Tor-A	129	417	45	119	20	5	1	36	12	38	.285	.312	.365	.676	78	-9	-13	109	93	47	.559	3	2	-0	-8	*32/D	-2.1
1983	Tor-A	122	375	40	103	22	5	2	39	13	45	.275	.301	.376	.677	78	-8	-12	108	104	41	.574	7	0	2	-11	32/S	-1.9
1984	Tor-A	121	247	24	56	10	3	1	25	5	16	.227	.245	.304	.549	50	-17	-17	102	128	16	.408	1	3	-2	-4	*3/2SD	-2.0
1985	Tor-A	131	288	33	90	22	1	7	37	21	26	.313	.359	.469	.828	123	9	9	101	94	45	.757	3	6	-3	-5	*32	0.0
1986	Tor-A	137	327	30	85	19	1	3	44	20	47	.260	.305	.352	.656	75	-9	-12	105	141	35	.558	3	0	1	-1	32/S	-1.1
1987	Tor-A	122	310	35	65	11	0	4	30	21	52	.210	.264	.284	.548	46	-24	-24	101	120	23	.443	2	2	-1	-6	23/D	-2.3
Total	9	931	2450	251	633	125	16	20	238	114	298	.258	.294	.347	.641	72	-84	-98	105	104	244	.542	23	17	-3	-42	32/O1DS	-12.8
■ **HAPPY IOTT**	Iott, Frederick "Happy Jack" or "Biddo" (born Frederick Hoyot) b: 7/7/1876, Houlton, Me. d: 2/17/41, Island Falls, Me. BR/TR, 5'10", 175 lbs. Deb: 9/16/03																											
1903	Cle-A	3	10	1	2	0	0	0	0	2		.200	.333	.200	.533	67	-0	-0	96	0	1	.625	1			-0	/O	0.0
■ **HAL IRELAN**	Irelan, Harold "Grump" b: 8/5/1890, Burnettsville, Ind. d: 7/16/44, Carmel, Ind. BB/TR, 5'7", 165 lbs. Deb: 4/23/14																											
1914	Phi-N	67	165	16	39	8	0	1	16	21	22	.236	.326	.303	.629	87	-2	-2	100	109	17	.595	3			3	2/S13	0.1
■ **TIM IRELAND**	Ireland, Timothy Neal b: 3/14/53, Oakland, Cal. BB/TR, 6', 180 lbs. Deb: 9/20/81																											
1981	KC-A	4	0	1	0	0	0	0	0	0	0	—	—	—	—	—	0	0	99	—	17	.000	0	1	-1	0	/1	0.0
1982	KC-A	7	7	2	1	0	0	0	0	1	1	.143	.250	.143	.393	11	-1	-1	100	0	0	.333	0	0	0	-1	/2O3	0.0
Total	2	11	7	3	1	0	0	0	0	1	1	.143	.250	.143	.393	11	-1	-1	100	0	17	.286	0	1	-1	-1	/21O3	0.0
■ **MONTE IRVIN**	Irvin, Montford b: 2/25/19, Columbia, Ala. BR/TR, 6'1", 195 lbs. Deb: 7/08/49 H																											
1949	NY-N	36	76	7	17	3	2	0	7	17	11	.224	.366	.316	.681	83	-1	-1	102	110	10	.672	0			0	O/13	0.0
1950	NY-N	110	374	61	112	19	5	15	66	52	41	.299	.392	.497	.889	134	18	19	98	112	76	.914	3			2	1O/3	1.6
1951	NY-N	151	558	94	174	19	11	24	**121**	89	44	.312	.415	.514	.929	146	41	39	102	138	127	.990	12	2	2	5	*O1	4.2
1952	NY-N	46	126	10	39	2	1	4	21	10	11	.310	.365	.437	.801	118	4	3	102	122	20	.725	0	1	-1	-3	O	-0.1
1953	NY-N	124	444	72	146	21	5	21	97	55	34	.329	.406	.541	.947	147	29	31	98	127	96	.943	2	0	1	8	*O	3.2
1954	NY-N	135	432	62	113	13	3	19	64	70	23	.262	.367	.438	.805	103	6	3	105	102	69	.786	7	4	-0	3	*O/13	0.1
1955	NY-N	51	150	16	38	7	1	1	17	17	15	.253	.341	.333	.675	81	-4	-4	99	130	18	.624	3	0	1	0	O	-0.2
1956	Chi-N	111	339	44	92	13	3	15	50	41	41	.271	.350	.460	.810	117	7	8	99	105	53	.767	1	0	0	7	O	1.2
Total	8	764	2499	366	731	97	31	99	443	351	220	.293	.385	.475	.860	126	101	99	101	120	468	.890	28	7		21	O1/3	10.0
■ **ED IRVIN**	Irvin, William Edward b: 1882, Philadelphia, Pa. d: 2/18/16, Philadelphia, Pa. TR , Deb: 5/18/12																											
1912	Det-A	1	3	0	2	0	2	0	0	0		.667	.667	2.000	2.667	690	2	2	95	0	4	6.000	0			0	/3	0.2
■ **ARTHUR IRWIN**	Irwin, Arthur Albert "Doc" or "Sandy" b: 2/14/1858, Toronto, Ont., Can. d: 7/16/21, Atlantic Ocean BL/TR, 5'8.5", 158 lbs. Deb: 5/01/1880 M																											
1880	Wor-N	85	352	53	91	19	4	1	35	11	27	.259	.281	.344	.625	98	4	-2	113	99	35	.506				**31**	*S/3C	3.2
1881	Wor-N	50	206	27	55	8	2	0	24	7	4	.267	.291	.325	.616	89	-2	-3	105	132	20	.490				-11	S	-0.8
1882	Wor-N	84	333	30	73	12	4	0	30	14	34	.219	.251	.279	.530	70	-11	-11	100	115	24	.412				16	3S	0.9
1883	Pro-N	98	406	67	116	22	7	0	44	12	38	.286	.306	.374	.681	105	2	2	101	106	48	.566				-9	*S/2	-0.2
1884	Pro-N	102	404	73	97	14	3	2	44	28	52	.240	.289	.304	.594	86	-6	-6	102	124	36	.492				-5	*S/P	-0.1
1885	Pro-N	59	218	16	39	2	1	0	14	14	29	.179	.228	.197	.426	42	-14	-12	91	120	10	.318				2	S/32	-0.5
1886	Phi-N	101	373	51	87	6	6	0	34	35	39	.233	.299	.282	.581	79	-9	-8	98	112	40	.573	24			3	*S/3	-0.5
1887	Phi-N	100	374	65	95	14	8	2	56	48	26	.254	.344	.350	.694	98	-1	1	97	129	53	.720	19			-11	*S	-1.0
1888	Phi-N	125	448	51	98	12	4	0	28	33	56	.219	.277	.263	.540	66	-11	-20	114	87	39	.494	19			11	*S/2	-0.4
1889	Phi-N	18	73	9	16	5	0	0	10	6	6	.219	.278	.288	.566	57	-4	-4	104	150	8	.579	6			0	S	-0.3
	Was-N	85	313	49	73	10	5	0	32	42	37	.233	.326	.297	.623	83	-9	-4	92	109	34	.604	9			8	S/P2M	0.6
	Yr	103	386	58	89	15	5	0	42	48	43	.231	.317	.295	.613	78	-13	-9	94	117	42	.599	15			8		0.3
1890	Bos-P	96	354	60	92	17	1	0	45	57	29	.260	.364	.314	.678	78	-6	-10	107	113	47	.706	16			-6	*S	-0.7
1891	Bos-a	6	17	1	2	0	0	0	0	2	1	.118	.286	.118	.403	19	-2	-2	99	0	1	.400	0			0	/SM	0.0
1894	Phi-N	1	0	0	0	0	0	0	0	0	0	—	—	—	—	—	0	0	95	—	—	—	0			0	/SM	0.0
Total	13	1010	3871	552	934	141	45	5	396	309	378	.241	.299	.305	.604	82	-68	-79	102	112	395	.542	93			30	S/32PC	0.2
■ **CHARLIE IRWIN**	Irwin, Charles Edwin b: 2/15/1869, Clinton, Ill. d: 9/21/25, Chicago, Ill. BL/TR, 5'10", 160 lbs. Deb: 9/03/1893																											
1893	Chi-N	21	82	14	25	6	2	0	13	10	1	.305	.394	.427	.820	116	3	2	104	108	16	.895	4			0	S	0.2
1894	Chi-N	128	498	84	144	24	9	8	95	63	23	.289	.379	.422	.801	88	-4	-12	108	119	95	.895	35			-9	3S	-1.3
1895	Chi-N	3	10	4	2	0	0	0	0	2	1	.200	.333	.200	.533	40	-1	-1	103	0	1	.500	0			0	/S	0.0
1896	Cin-N	127	476	77	141	16	6	1	67	26	17	.296	.338	.361	.699	82	-9	-13	105	113	70	.696	31			6	*3	0.0
1897	Cin-N	134	505	89	146	26	6	0	74	47		.289	.359	.364	.723	87	-3	-10	107	125	78	.741	27			-7	*3	-1.3
1898	Cin-N	136	501	77	120	14	5	3	55	31		.240	.292	.305	.597	68	-17	-23	108	105	51	.546	18			10	*3	-0.8
1899	Cin-N	90	314	42	73	4	8	1	52	26		.232	.295	.306	.601	63	-14	-17	106	164	37	.622	26			-13	3/S21	-2.6
1900	Cin-N	87	333	59	91	15	6	1	44	14		.273	.303	.363	.666	93	-7	-3	92	113	40	.595	9			-7	3S/O2	-0.8
1901	Cin-N	67	260	25	62	12	2	0	25	14		.238	.277	.300	.577	73	-10	-8	95	114	26	.530	13			2	3	-0.1
	Bro-N	65	242	25	52	13	2	0	20	14		.215	.258	.285	.543	56	-13	-14	106	99	19	.458	4			-10	3	-2.0
	Yr	132	502	50	114	25	4	0	45	28		.227	.268	.293	.561	64	-23	-23	100	107	45	.495	17			-8		-2.1
1902	Bro-N	131	458	59	125	14	0	2	43	39		.273	.330	.317	.647	107	2	5	95	101	53	.592	13			-9	*3/S	0.1
Total	10	989	3679	555	981	144	46	16	488	286	42	.267	.325	.344	.669	82	-74	-94	103	116	487	.653	180			-36	3S/O21	-8.6
■ **JOHN IRWIN**	Irwin, John b: 7/21/1861, Toronto, Ont., Can d: 2/28/34, Boston, Mass. BL/TR, 5'10", 168 lbs. Deb: 5/31/1882																											
1882	Wor-N	1	4	0	0	0	0	0	0	0	2	.000	.000	.000	.000	-99	-1	-1	100	0	0	.000				0	/1	0.0
1884	Bos-U	105	432	81	101	22	6	1		15		.234	.260	.319	.579	96	-2	-1	98	0	37	.462	0			0	*3	0.1
1886	Phi-a	3	13	4	3	1	0	0		0		.231	.231	.308	.538	69	-0	-0	100	0	1	.400	0			0	/S3	0.0
1887	Was-N	8	31	6	11	2	0	2	3	3	6	.355	.429	.613	1.041	197	4	4	95	35	11	1.450	6			0	/S3	0.3
1888	Was-N	37	126	14	28	5	2	0	8	5	18	.222	.263	.294	.557	82	-3	-2	96	79	14	.602	15			0	S3	-0.1
1889	Was-N	58	228	42	66	11	4	0	25	25	14	.289	.370	.373	.742	119	4	7	92	84	36	.765	10			2	3	1.1
1890	Buf-P	77	308	62	72	11	4	0	34	43	19	.234	.335	.295	.631	77	-11	-6	92	108	37	.661	18			2	31/2	0.0
1891	Bos-a	19	72	6	16	2	2	0	15	6	9	.222	.282	.306	.588	72	-3	-3	99	201	8	.607	6			0	O/3S	-0.1
	Lou-a	14	55	7	15	1	1	0	7	5	6	.273	.344	.327	.672	105	-0	1	90	119	7	.625	1			0	3	0.1
	Yr	33	127	13	31	3	3	0		11	15	.244	.309	.315	.624	85	-3	-2	95	172	15	.615	7			0		0.0
Total	8	322	1269	222	312	55	19	3	92	102	74	.246	.308	.326	.634	95	-14	-2	95	68	151	.610	56			3	3/SO12	1.4
■ **TOMMY IRWIN**	Irwin, Thomas Andrew b: 12/20/12, Altoona, Pa. BR/TR, 5'11", 165 lbs. Deb: 10/01/38																											
1938	Cle-A	3	9	1	1	0	0	0	0	3	1	.111	.333	.111	.444	16	-1	-1	99	0	1	.500	0	0	0	0	/S	0.0
■ **WALT IRWIN**	Irwin, Walter Kingsley b: 9/23/1897, Henrietta, Pa. d: 8/18/76, Spring Lake, Mich. BR/TR, 5'10.5", 170 lbs. Deb: 4/24/21																											
1921	StL-N	4	1	1	0	0	0	0	0	0	1	.000	.000	.000	.000	-99	-0	-0	95	0	0	.000	0	0	0	0	H	0.0
■ **ORLANDO ISALES**	Isales, Orlando (Pizarro) b: 12/22/59, Santurce, P.R. BR/TR, 5'9", 175 lbs. Deb: 9/11/80																											
1980	Phi-N	3	5	1	2	0	1	0	3	1	0	.400	.500	.800	1.300	240	1	1	107	297	2	1.667	0	0	0	-0	/O	0.1
■ **FRANK ISBELL**	Isbell, William Frank "Bald Eagle" b: 8/21/1875, Delevan, N.Y. d: 7/15/41, Wichita, Kan. BL/TR, 5'11", 190 lbs. Deb: 5/01/1898																											
1898	Chi-N	45	159	17	37	4	0	0	8	3		.233	.252	.258	.509	47	-11	-11	103	59	11	.393	3			0	OP/32S	-1.0
1901	Chi-A	137	556	93	143	15	8	3	70	36		.257	.302	.329	.632	77	-17	-16	99	122	73	.656	**52**			14	*1/2PS3	-0.7
1902	Chi-A	137	515	62	130	14	4	4	59	14		.252	.272	.318	.591	68	-25	-22	95	113	56	.561	38			10	*1/SPC	-0.8
1903	Chi-A	138	546	52	132	25	9	2	59	12		.242	.258	.332	.590	84	-16	-11	92	120	55	.529	26			5	*13/2SO	-0.5
1904	Chi-A	96	314	27	66	10	3	1	34	16		.210	.248	.271	.519	67	-12	-12	99	147	26	.484	19			-1	12/OS	-1.2
1905	Chi-A	94	341	55	101	21	11	2	45	15		.296	.326	.440	.766	149	15	16	97	105	55	.750	15			-2	2O/1S	1.3
1906	Chi-A	143	549	71	153	18	11	0	57	30		.279	.316	.352	.668	121	6	11	92	103	75	.657	37			-12	*2O/PC	-0.5

YEAR	TM/L	G	AB	R	H	2B	3B	HR	RBI	BB	SO	AVG	OBP	SLG	PRO	/A	BR	/A	PF	CHI	RC	TA	SB	CS	SBR	FR	POS	TPR
1907	Chi-A	125	486	60	118	19	7	0	41	22		.243	.276	.311	.586	85	-7	-9	104	93	49	.530	22			5	*2/OPS	-0.4
1908	Chi-A	84	320	31	79	15	3	1	49	19		.247	.289	.322	.611	107	-0	2	94	167	34	.581	18			4	12	0.4
1909	Chi-A	120	433	33	97	17	6	0	33	23		.224	.265	.291	.556	78	-13	-12	97	107	38	.515	23			6	*1/O2	-0.7
Total	10	1119	4219	501	1056	158	62	13	455	190		.250	.283	.326	.609	89	-79	-63	97	115	471	.576	253			27	12O/3PSC	-4.1

■ **MIKE IVIE** Ivie, Michael Wilson b: 8/8/52, Atlanta, Ga. BR/TR, 6'3", 205 lbs. Deb: 9/04/71

YEAR	TM/L	G	AB	R	H	2B	3B	HR	RBI	BB	SO	AVG	OBP	SLG	PRO	/A	BR	/A	PF	CHI	RC	TA	SB	CS	SBR	FR	POS	TPR
1971	SD-N	6	17	0	8	0	0	0	3	1	1	.471	.526	.471	.997	191	2	2	96	153	3	.833	0	0	0	0	/C	0.3
1974	SD-N	12	34	1	3	0	0	1	3	2	8	.088	.139	.176	.315	-13	-5	-5	93	129	1	.258	0	0	0	0	1	-0.5
1975	SD-N	111	377	36	94	16	2	8	46	20	63	.249	.294	.366	.660	83	-10	-10	100	110	37	.555	4	4	-1	-1	13/C	-1.7
1976	SD-N	140	405	51	118	19	5	7	70	30	41	.291	.348	.415	.763	131	8	13	89	143	56	.690	6	6	-2	3	*1/C3	0.9
1977	SD-N	134	489	66	133	29	2	9	66	39	57	.272	.328	.395	.723	106	-5	3	88	122	64	.651	3	2	-0	3	*13	0.0
1978	SF-N	117	318	34	98	14	3	11	55	27	45	.308	.366	.475	.841	146	14	17	92	119	55	.810	3	0	1	-8	1O	0.7
1979	SF-N	133	402	58	115	18	3	27	89	47	80	.286	.362	.547	.909	157	24	27	92	117	79	.916	5	1	1	-5	1O/32	1.9
1980	SF-N	79	286	21	69	16	1	4	25	19	40	.241	.289	.346	.635	80	-9	-8	96	91	27	.527	1	2	-1	-3	1	-1.5
1981	SF-N	7	17	1	5	2	0	0	3	0	1	.294	.294	.412	.706	94	-0	-0	105	168	2	.583	0	0	0	0	/1	0.0
	Hou-N	19	42	2	10	3	0	0	6	2	11	.238	.273	.310	.582	73	-2	-1	88	181	3	.455	0	1	-1	-0	1	-0.2
	Yr	26	59	3	15	5	0	0	9	2	12	.254	.279	.339	.618	80	-2	-2	93	184	5	.489	0	1	-1	0		-0.2
1982	Hou-N	7	6	0	2	0	0	0	0	1	0	.333	.429	.333	.762	117	0	0	99	0	1	.750	0	0	0	0	/H	0.0
	Det-A	80	259	35	60	12	1	14	38	24	51	.232	.302	.448	.750	102	0	0	100	96	35	.696	0	0	0	0	D	0.0
1983	Det-A	12	42	4	9	4	0	0	7	2	4	.214	.250	.310	.560	55	-3	-3	96	211	3	.429	0	0	0	1	1	-0.1
Total	11	857	2694	309	724	133	17	81	411	214	402	.269	.326	.421	.747	113	13	35	93	119	366	.698	22	16	-3	-9	1/3DOC2	-0.2

■ **HANK IZQUIERDO** Izquierdo, Enrique Roberto (Valdes) b: 3/20/31, Matanzas, Cuba BR/TR, 5'11", 175 lbs. Deb: 8/09/67

YEAR	TM/L	G	AB	R	H	2B	3B	HR	RBI	BB	SO	AVG	OBP	SLG	PRO	/A	BR	/A	PF	CHI	RC	TA	SB	CS	SBR	FR	POS	TPR
1967	Min-A	16	26	4	7	2	0	0	2	1	2	.269	.296	.346	.642	84	-0	-1	107	93	3	.526	0	0	0	-3	C	-0.2

■ **RAY JABLONSKI** Jablonski, Raymond Leo "Jabbo" b: 12/17/26, Chicago, Ill. d: 11/25/85, Chicago, Ill. BR/TR, 5'10", 175 lbs. Deb: 4/14/53

YEAR	TM/L	G	AB	R	H	2B	3B	HR	RBI	BB	SO	AVG	OBP	SLG	PRO	/A	BR	/A	PF	CHI	RC	TA	SB	CS	SBR	FR	POS	TPR
1953	StL-N	157	604	64	162	23	5	21	112	34	61	.268	.308	.427	.735	88	-11	-12	102	139	77	.643	2	2	-1	-9	*3	-2.6
1954	StL-N	152	611	80	181	33	3	12	104	49	42	.296	.350	.419	.769	99	-1	-1	100	149	88	.701	9	4	0	-7	*3/1	-0.6
1955	Cin-N	74	221	28	53	9	0	9	28	13	35	.240	.291	.403	.694	77	-6	-8	106	98	25	.607	0	1	-1	-3	3O	-1.1
1956	Cin-N	130	407	42	104	25	1	15	66	37	57	.256	.328	.432	.761	94	1	-3	108	126	54	.692	2	4	-2	-12	*3/2	-1.7
1957	NY-N	107	305	37	88	15	1	9	57	31	47	.289	.354	.433	.787	108	5	4	102	149	46	.718	0	2	-1	4	3/1O	0.8
1958	SF-N	82	230	28	53	15	1	12	46	17	50	.230	.289	.461	.750	94	-3	-3	100	134	27	.676	2	0	1	-4	3	-0.5
1959	StL-N	60	87	11	22	4	0	3	14	8	19	.253	.316	.402	.718	86	-1	-2	105	129	11	.647	1	0	0	1	3/S	-0.1
	KC-A	25	65	4	17	1	0	2	8	3	11	.262	.294	.369	.663	80	-2	-2	101	105	7	.563	0	0	0	-0	3	-0.1
1960	KC-A	21	32	3	7	1	0	0	3	4	8	.219	.306	.250	.556	53	-2	-2	99	147	3	.462	0	0	0	0	/3	-0.1
Total	8	808	2562	297	687	126	11	83	438	196	330	.268	.324	.423	.747	93	-21	-30	103	135	338	.694	16	13	-3	-30	3/O1S2	-6.0

■ **FRED JACKLITSCH** Jacklitsch, Frederick Lawrence b: 5/24/1876, Brooklyn, N.Y. d: 7/18/37, Brooklyn, N.Y. BR/TR, 5'9", 180 lbs. Deb: 6/06/00

YEAR	TM/L	G	AB	R	H	2B	3B	HR	RBI	BB	SO	AVG	OBP	SLG	PRO	/A	BR	/A	PF	CHI	RC	TA	SB	CS	SBR	FR	POS	TPR
1900	Phi-N	5	11	0	2	1	0	0	3	0		.182	.182	.273	.455	26	-1	-1	98	313	1	.333	0			0	/C	0.0
1901	Phi-N	33	120	14	30	4	3	0	24	12		.250	.318	.333	.652	89	-1	-2	103	205	14	.600	2			-1	C/3	0.1
1902	Phi-N	38	114	8	23	4	0	0	8	9		.202	.260	.237	.497	52	-6	-6	105	103	8	.418	2			-1	C/O	-0.3
1903	Bro-N	60	176	31	47	8	3	1	21	33		.267	.383	.364	.746	114	5	5	101	101	27	.783	4			-5	C/2O	0.4
1904	Bro-N	26	77	8	18	3	1	0	8	7		.234	.298	.299	.596	90	-1	-1	95	127	9	.627	7			-1	1/2C	-0.1
1905	NY-A	1	3	1	0	0	0	0	1	1		.000	.250	.000	.250	-17	-0	-0	102	0	0	.333	0			0	/C	0.0
1907	Phi-N	73	202	19	43	7	0	0	17	27		.213	.306	.248	.553	73	-5	-6	104	129	18	.528	7			7	C/1O	0.6
1908	Phi-N	37	86	6	19	3	0	0	7	14		.221	.330	.256	.586	90	-0	-0	100	122	8	.582	3			3	C	0.5
1909	Phi-N	20	32	6	10	1	1	0	1	10		.313	.476	.406	.882	165	4	3	106	28	7	1.091	1			0	C/2	0.5
1910	Phi-N	25	51	7	10	3	0	0	2	5	9	.196	.268	.255	.523	55	-3	-3	96	54	3	.439	0			1	C/123	-0.1
1914	Bal-F	122	337	40	93	21	4	2	48	52	66	.276	.373	.380	.753	117	9	9	99	129	52	.766	7			-17	*C	-0.2
1915	Bal-F	49	135	20	32	9	0	2	13	31	25	.237	.380	.348	.728	108	4	3	107	88	19	.777	2			0	C/S	0.5
1917	Bos-N	1	0	0	0	0	0	0	0	0	0	—	—	—	—	—	0	0	96	—	—	—	0			0	/C	0.0
Total	13	490	1344	160	327	64	12	5	153	201	100	.243	.342	.320	.662	96	4	1	102	120	185	.655	35			-14	C/12O3S	1.9

■ **CHARLIE JACKSON** Jackson, Charles Herbert "Lefty" b: 2/7/1894, Granite City, Ill. d: 5/27/68, Radford, Va. BL/TL, 5'9", 150 lbs. Deb: 8/20/15

YEAR	TM/L	G	AB	R	H	2B	3B	HR	RBI	BB	SO	AVG	OBP	SLG	PRO	/A	BR	/A	PF	CHI	RC	TA	SB	CS	SBR	FR	POS	TPR
1915	Chi-A	1	1	0	0	0	0	0	0	0	1	.000	.000	.000	.000	-99	-0	-0	98	0	0	.000	0			0	H	0.0
1917	Pit-N	41	121	7	29	3	2	0	1	10	22	.240	.303	.298	.601	85	-2	-2	100	11	12	.554	4			-1	O	-0.4
Total	2	42	122	7	29	3	2	0	1	10	23	.238	.301	.295	.596	83	-2	-2	99	11	12	.548	4			-1	/O	-0.4

■ **CHUCK JACKSON** Jackson, Charles Leo b: 3/19/63, Seattle, Wash. BR/TR, 6', 185 lbs. Deb: 5/26/87

YEAR	TM/L	G	AB	R	H	2B	3B	HR	RBI	BB	SO	AVG	OBP	SLG	PRO	/A	BR	/A	PF	CHI	RC	TA	SB	CS	SBR	FR	POS	TPR
1987	Hou-N	35	71	3	15	3	0	1	6	7	19	.211	.282	.296	.578	57	-5	-4	93	100	6	.500	1	1	-0	-3	3O/S	-0.8
1988	Hou-N	45	83	7	19	5	1	1	8	7	16	.229	.289	.349	.638	88	-2	-1	93	100	8	.552	1	1	-0	-2	3/SO	-0.2
Total	2	80	154	10	34	8	1	2	14	14	35	.221	.286	.325	.610	73	-7	-5	93	100	14	.532	2	2	-1	-5	/3OS	-1.0

■ **DARRIN JACKSON** Jackson, Darrin Jay b: 8/22/62, Los Angeles, Cal. BR/TR, 6'1", 170 lbs. Deb: 6/17/85

YEAR	TM/L	G	AB	R	H	2B	3B	HR	RBI	BB	SO	AVG	OBP	SLG	PRO	/A	BR	/A	PF	CHI	RC	TA	SB	CS	SBR	FR	POS	TPR
1985	Chi-N	5	11	0	1	0	0	0	0	0	3	.091	.091	.091	.182	-42	-2	-2	116	0	0	.100	0	0	0	-0	/O	-0.2
1987	Chi-N	7	5	2	4	1	0	0	0	0	0	.800	.800	1.000	1.800	371	2	2	101	0	4	5.000	0	0	0	-2	/O	0.0
1988	Chi-N	100	188	29	50	11	3	6	20	5	28	.266	.289	.452	.741	105	1	0	104	78	24	.669	4	1	1	-8	O	-0.8
Total	3	112	204	31	55	12	3	6	20	5	31	.270	.290	.446	.737	103	1	-0	105	72	28	.660	4	1	1	-9	/O	-1.0

■ **GEORGE JACKSON** Jackson, George Christopher "Hickory" b: 10/14/1882, Springfield, Mo. d: 11/25/72, Cleburne, Tex. BR/TR, 6'0.5", 180 lbs. Deb: 8/02/11

YEAR	TM/L	G	AB	R	H	2B	3B	HR	RBI	BB	SO	AVG	OBP	SLG	PRO	/A	BR	/A	PF	CHI	RC	TA	SB	CS	SBR	FR	POS	TPR
1911	Bos-N	39	147	28	51	11	2	0	25	12	21	.347	.404	.449	.853	134	8	7	103	136	31	.958	12			-2	O	0.3
1912	Bos-N	110	397	55	104	13	5	4	48	38	72	.262	.342	.350	.692	83	-5	-9	107	109	55	.713	22			6	*O	-0.5
1913	Bos-N	3	10	2	3	0	0	0	0	0	2	.300	.300	.300	.600	76	-0	-0	95	0	1	.429	0			0	/O	0.0
Total	3	152	554	85	158	24	7	4	73	50	95	.285	.357	.375	.733	96	2	-3	106	114	87	.768	34			4	O	-0.2

■ **HENRY JACKSON** Jackson, Henry Everett b: 6/23/1861, Union City, Ind. d: 9/14/32, Chicago, Ill. BR/TR, 6'2", 185 lbs. Deb: 9/13/1887

YEAR	TM/L	G	AB	R	H	2B	3B	HR	RBI	BB	SO	AVG	OBP	SLG	PRO	/A	BR	/A	PF	CHI	RC	TA	SB	CS	SBR	FR	POS	TPR
1887	Ind-N	10	38	1	10	1	0	0	3	0	12	.263	.263	.289	.553	57	-2	-2	96	86	4	.464	2			0	1	-0.1

■ **JIM JACKSON** Jackson, James Benner b: 11/28/1877, Philadelphia, Pa. d: 10/9/55, Philadelphia, Pa. BR/TR, Deb: 4/26/01

YEAR	TM/L	G	AB	R	H	2B	3B	HR	RBI	BB	SO	AVG	OBP	SLG	PRO	/A	BR	/A	PF	CHI	RC	TA	SB	CS	SBR	FR	POS	TPR
1901	Bal-A	99	364	42	91	17	3	2	50	20		.250	.289	.330	.619	68	-13	-17	107	128	39	.553	11			10	O	-0.7
1902	NY-N	35	110	14	20	5	1	0	13	15		.182	.280	.245	.525	64	-4	-4	100	170	9	.533	6			1	O	-0.5
1905	Cle-A	109	426	59	109	12	4	2	31	34		.256	.311	.317	.628	102	1	1	100	68	48	.580	15			6	*O/3	0.2
1906	Cle-A	105	374	44	80	13	2	0	38	38		.214	.286	.259	.546	71	-10	-12	103	145	36	.544	25			-6	*O	-2.3
Total	4	348	1274	159	300	47	10	4	132	107		.235	.295	.297	.592	79	-27	-32	103	117	132	.557	57			11	O/3	-3.3

■ **JOE JACKSON** Jackson, Joseph Jefferson "Shoeless Joe" b: 7/16/1889, Brandon Mills, S.C. d: 12/5/51, Greenville, S.C. BL/TR, 6'1", 200 lbs. Deb: 8/25/08

YEAR	TM/L	G	AB	R	H	2B	3B	HR	RBI	BB	SO	AVG	OBP	SLG	PRO	/A	BR	/A	PF	CHI	RC	TA	SB	CS	SBR	FR	POS	TPR
1908	Phi-A	5	23	0	3	0	0	0	3	0		.130	.130	.130	.261	-13	-3	-3	108	324	0	.150	0			0	/O	-0.3
1909	Phi-A	5	17	3	3	0	0	0	3	1		.176	.222	.176	.399	26	-1	-1	102	393	1	.286	0			0	/O	0.0
1910	Cle-A	20	75	15	29	2	5	1	11	8		.387	.446	.587	1.032	224	10	10	100	83	21	1.217	4			1	O	1.1
1911	Cle-A	147	571	126	233	45	19	7	83	56		.408	**.468**	.590	1.058	**189**	72	69	103	75	175	1.308	41			10	*O	**6.5**
1912	Cle-A	152	572	121	226	44	**26**	3	90	54		.395	.458	.579	1.036	193	70	69	101	85	166	1.249	35			10	*O	6.9
1913	Cle-A	148	528	109	**197**	**39**	17	7	71	80	26	.373	.460	**.551**	**1.011**	185	**66**	**62**	106	78	**140**	1.215	26			-4	*O	5.2
1914	Cle-A	122	453	61	153	22	13	3	53	41	34	.338	.399	.464	.862	156	32	30	102	96	86	.883	22	15	-2	-0	*O	2.2
1915	Cle-A	83	303	42	99	16	9	3	45	28	11	.327	.389	.469	.858	151	20	19	104	107	54	.855	10	10	-3	-5	O1	0.6
	Chi-A	45	158	21	43	4	5	2	36	24	12	.272	.378	.399	.777	136	7	7	98	188	23	.768	6	10	-4	-0	O	0.0
	Yr	128	461	63	142	20	14	5	81	52	23	.308	.385	.445	.830	146	27	26	102	136	77	.823	16	20	-7	-6		0.6
1916	Chi-A	155	592	91	202	40	**21**	3	78	46	25	.341	.393	.495	.888	154	45	40	108	98	119	.911	24	14	-1	-2	*O	3.1
1917	Chi-A	146	538	91	162	20	17	5	75	57	25	.301	.375	.429	.805	149	29	30	98	116	89	.819	13			11	*O	3.5
1918	Chi-A	17	65	9	23	2	2	1	20	8	1	.354	.425	.492	.917	176	6	6	101	180	15	1.024	3			-1	O	0.5
1919	Chi-A	139	516	79	181	31	14	7	96	60	10	.351	.422	.506	.928	153	42	39	105	131	111	.997	9			-6	*O	2.4

YEAR	TM/L	G	AB	R	H	2B	3B	HR	RBI	BB	SO	AVG	OBP	SLG	PRO	/A	BR	/A	PF	CHI	RC	TA	SB	CS	SBR	FR	POS	TPR
1920	Chi-A	146	570	105	218	42	**20**	12	121	56	14	.382	.444	.589	1.033	179	58	62	96	121	145	1.121	9	12	-5	2	*O	4.4
Total	13	1330	4981	873	1772	307	168	54	785	519	158	.356	.423	.517	.940	168	452	439	102	106	1146	1.027	202	61		17	*O/1	36.1

■ **KEN JACKSON** Jackson, Kenneth Bernard b: 8/21/63, Shreveport, La. BR/TR, 6'1", 190 lbs. Deb: 9/12/87

YEAR	TM/L	G	AB	R	H	2B	3B	HR	RBI	BB	SO	AVG	OBP	SLG	PRO	/A	BR	/A	PF	CHI	RC	TA	SB	CS	SBR	FR	POS	TPR
1987	Phi-N	8	16	1	4	2	0	0	2	1	4	.250	.333	.375	.708	84	-0	-0	104	133	2	.667	0	0	0	-0	/S	0.0

■ **LOU JACKSON** Jackson, Louis Clarence b: 7/26/35, Riverton, La. d: 5/27/69, Tokyo, Japan BL/TR, 5'10", 168 lbs. Deb: 7/23/58

YEAR	TM/L	G	AB	R	H	2B	3B	HR	RBI	BB	SO	AVG	OBP	SLG	PRO	/A	BR	/A	PF	CHI	RC	TA	SB	CS	SBR	FR	POS	TPR
1958	Chi-N	24	35	5	6	2	1	1	6	1	9	.171	.194	.371	.566	45	-3	-3	101	155	2	.452	0	1	-1	-3	O	-0.6
1959	Chi-N	6	4	2	1	0	0	0	1	0	2	.250	.250	.250	.500	34	-0	-0	98	404	0	.333	0	0	0	0	H	0.0
1964	Bal-A	4	8	0	3	0	0	0	0	0	2	.375	.375	.375	.750	104	0	0	105	0	1	.600	0	0	0	0	/O	0.0
Total	3	34	47	7	10	2	1	1	7	1	13	.213	.229	.362	.591	54	-3	-3	101	150	3	.474	0	1	-1	-3	/O	-0.6

■ **RANDY JACKSON** Jackson, Ransom Joseph "Handsome Ransom" b: 2/10/26, Little Rock, Ark. BR/TR, 6'1.5", 180 lbs. Deb: 5/02/50

YEAR	TM/L	G	AB	R	H	2B	3B	HR	RBI	BB	SO	AVG	OBP	SLG	PRO	/A	BR	/A	PF	CHI	RC	TA	SB	CS	SBR	FR	POS	TPR
1950	Chi-N	34	111	13	25	4	3	3	6	7	25	.225	.271	.396	.668	70	-5	-6	105	44	11	.611	4			-1	3	-0.6
1951	Chi-N	145	557	78	153	24	6	16	76	47	44	.275	.332	.425	.758	105	1	3	97	109	77	.699	14	3	2	4	*3	0.8
1952	Chi-N	116	379	44	88	8	5	9	34	27	42	.232	.285	.351	.636	73	-13	-15	103	83	36	.542	6	5	-1	-4	*3/O	-1.7
1953	Chi-N	139	498	61	142	22	8	19	66	42	61	.285	.341	.476	.817	107	6	4	103	89	77	.755	8	4	0	1	*3	0.1
1954	Chi-N	126	484	77	132	17	6	19	67	44	55	.273	.336	.450	.786	102	1	0	101	102	74	.735	2	1	0	-6	*3	-0.3
1955	Chi-N	138	499	73	132	13	7	21	70	58	58	.265	.342	.445	.787	107	5	5	100	105	75	.739	0	2	-1	-8	*3	-0.4
1956	Bro-N	101	307	37	84	15	7	8	53	28	38	.274	.338	.446	.785	106	4	2	103	139	43	.713	2	1	0	20	3	2.2
1957	Bro-N	48	131	7	26	1	0	2	16	9	20	.198	.250	.252	.502	30	-12	-15	116	170	8	.378	0	0	0	2	3	-1.1
1958	LA-N	35	65	8	12	3	0	1	4	5	10	.185	.243	.277	.520	36	-6	-6	105	79	4	.411	0	0	0	2	3	-0.3
	Cle-A	29	91	7	22	3	1	4	13	3	18	.242	.266	.429	.695	93	-2	-1	94	102	9	.583	0	0	0	1	3	0.0
1959	Cle-A	3	7	0	1	0	0	0	0	0	1	.143	.143	.143	.286	-22	-1	-1	97	0	0	.143	0	0	0	0	/3	0.0
	Chi-N	41	74	7	18	5	1	1	10	11	10	.243	.341	.378	.720	93	-1	-1	98	130	9	.639	0	0	0	-0	3/O	-0.1
Total	10	955	3203	412	835	115	44	103	415	281	382	.261	.322	.421	.742	95	-24	-30	101	104	422	.699	36	16		11	3/O	-1.4

■ **REGGIE JACKSON** Jackson, Reginald Martinez b: 5/18/46, Wyncote, Pa. BL/TL, 6', 195 lbs. Deb: 6/09/67

YEAR	TM/L	G	AB	R	H	2B	3B	HR	RBI	BB	SO	AVG	OBP	SLG	PRO	/A	BR	/A	PF	CHI	RC	TA	SB	CS	SBR	FR	POS	TPR
1967	KC-A	35	118	13	21	4	4	1	6	10	46	.178	.271	.305	.576	70	-4	-4	100	65	10	.525	1	1	-0	-2	O	-0.7
1968	Oak-A	154	553	82	138	13	6	29	74	50	171	.250	.317	.452	.770	133	19	20	98	96	83	.756	14	4	2	8	*O	2.7
1969	Oak-A	152	549	**123**	151	36	3	47	118	114	142	.275	.410	**.608**	**1.019**	**197**	62	**68**	92	106	144	1.151	13	5	1	3	*O	**6.9**
1970	Oak-A	149	426	57	101	21	2	23	66	75	135	.237	.361	.458	.819	129	15	17	97	101	70	.864	26	17	-2	-2	*O	0.7
1971	Oak-A	150	567	87	157	29	3	32	80	63	161	.277	.355	.508	.863	141	30	30	101	90	103	.874	16	10	-1	10	*O	3.5
1972	Oak-A	135	499	72	132	25	2	25	75	59	125	.265	.352	.473	.825	148	26	28	97	107	84	.821	9	8	-2	7	*O	3.3
1973	Oak-A	151	539	**99**	158	28	2	**32**	**117**	76	111	.293	.387	**.531**	**.918**	**179**	41	**50**	87	123	112	.973	22	8	2	-0	*O/D	4.7
1974	Oak-A	148	506	90	146	25	1	29	93	86	105	.289	.396	.514	.910	159	41	41	100	112	109	**1.005**	25	5	**5**	8	*OD	5.1
1975	Oak-A	157	593	91	150	39	3	**36**	104	67	133	.253	.332	.511	.843	145	25	30	93	103	100	.846	17	8	0	7	*O/D	3.4
1976	Bal-A	134	498	84	138	27	2	27	91	54	108	.277	.353	**.502**	.855	152	29	30	98	112	86	.875	28	7	4	3	*OD	3.6
1977	NY-A	146	525	93	150	39	2	32	110	74	129	.286	.377	.550	.928	151	36	37	99	116	116	1.005	17	3	3	-7	*OD	2.8
1978	NY-A	139	511	82	140	13	5	27	97	58	133	.274	.358	.477	.836	135	22	23	99	125	87	.833	14	11	-2	0	*OD	1.9
1979	NY-A	131	465	78	138	24	2	29	89	65	107	.297	.385	.544	.929	154	31	34	96	107	93	.935	9	8	-2	3	*O/D	2.9
1980	NY-A	143	514	94	154	22	4	**41**	111	83	122	.300	.399	.597	.996	170	49	50	99	103	125	1.065	1	2	-1	-7	OD	3.9
1981	NY-A	94	334	33	79	17	1	15	54	46	82	.237	.331	.428	.759	117	7	7	100	119	47	.714	0	3	-2	-3	OD	0.1
1982	Cal-A	153	530	92	146	17	1	**39**	101	85	156	.275	.378	.532	.910	146	35	34	100	103	107	.935	4	5	-2	-23	*O/D	0.5
1983	Cal-A	116	397	43	77	14	1	14	49	52	140	.194	.294	.340	.634	77	-14	-12	96	110	42	.584	0	2	-1	-7	DO	-1.9
1984	Cal-A	143	525	67	117	17	2	25	81	55	141	.223	.300	.406	.706	92	-6	-7	101	114	64	.661	8	4	0	-0	*D/O	-0.6
1985	Cal-A	143	460	64	116	27	0	27	85	78	138	.252	.362	.487	.849	129	20	19	101	111	79	.840	1	2	-1	-12	OD	0.5
1986	Cal-A	132	419	65	101	12	2	18	58	92	115	.241	.381	.408	.789	121	13	15	96	105	68	.802	1	1	-0	-0	*D/O	1.3
1987	Oak-A	115	336	42	74	14	1	15	43	33	97	.220	.298	.402	.699	92	-8	-4	91	95	42	.654	2	1	0	-2	DO	-0.6
Total	21	2820	9864	1551	2584	463	49	563	1702	1375	2597	.262	.358	.490	.848	140	468	507	97	107	1772	.883	228	115	-1	-15	*OD	44.0

■ **SONNY JACKSON** Jackson, Roland Thomas b: 7/9/44, Washington, D.C. BL/TR, 5'9", 150 lbs. Deb: 9/27/63 C

YEAR	TM/L	G	AB	R	H	2B	3B	HR	RBI	BB	SO	AVG	OBP	SLG	PRO	/A	BR	/A	PF	CHI	RC	TA	SB	CS	SBR	FR	POS	TPR
1963	Hou-N	1	3	0	0	0	0	0	0	0	1	.000	.000	.000	.000	-99	-1	-1	92	0	0	.000	0	0	0	0	/S	0.0
1964	Hou-N	9	23	3	8	1	0	0	1	2	3	.348	.400	.391	.791	129	1	1	96	46	4	.800	1	0	0	0	/S	0.2
1965	Hou-N	10	23	1	3	0	0	0	0	1	1	.130	.167	.130	.297	-17	-3	-3	89	0	0	.238	1	1	-0	-1	/S3	-0.3
1966	Hou-N	150	596	80	174	6	5	3	25	42	53	.292	.342	.334	.676	91	-8	-6	97	45	74	.658	49	14	6	-10	*S	0.2
1967	Hou-N	129	520	67	123	18	3	0	25	36	45	.237	.286	.283	.569	68	-24	-21	94	68	42	.488	22	9	1	-3	*S	-0.8
1968	Atl-N	105	358	37	81	8	2	1	19	25	35	.226	.282	.268	.551	71	-14	-12	93	82	27	.478	16	6	1	-9	S	-0.7
1969	Atl-N	98	318	41	76	3	5	1	27	35	33	.239	.318	.289	.608	69	-11	-13	104	114	32	.560	12	7	-1	-21	S	-2.4
1970	Atl-N	103	328	60	85	14	3	0	20	45	27	.259	.350	.320	.670	78	-7	-9	104	74	41	.648	11	4	1	-12	S	-0.8
1971	Atl-N	149	547	58	141	20	5	2	25	35	45	.258	.304	.324	.627	71	-16	-22	110	57	54	.524	7	6	-2	-4	*O	-3.4
1972	Atl-N	60	126	20	30	6	3	0	8	7	9	.238	.278	.333	.612	70	-5	-5	105	78	11	.500	1	0	0	-6	SO/3	-1.0
1973	Atl-N	117	206	29	43	5	2	0	12	22	13	.209	.288	.252	.541	45	-13	-17	113	93	17	.485	6	3	0	-16	OS	-3.1
1974	Atl-N	5	7	0	3	0	0	0	0	0	0	.429	.429	.429	.857	134	0	0	105	0	1	.600	0	1	-1	0	/O	0.0
Total	12	936	3055	396	767	81	28	7	162	250	265	.251	.310	.303	.613	73	-102	-107	101	70	301	.561	126	51	7	-82	SO/3	-12.1

■ **RON JACKSON** Jackson, Ronald Harris b: 10/22/33, Kalamazoo, Mich. BR/TR, 6'7", 225 lbs. Deb: 6/15/54

YEAR	TM/L	G	AB	R	H	2B	3B	HR	RBI	BB	SO	AVG	OBP	SLG	PRO	/A	BR	/A	PF	CHI	RC	TA	SB	CS	SBR	FR	POS	TPR
1954	Chi-A	40	93	10	26	4	0	4	10	6	20	.280	.337	.452	.788	111	1	1	104	70	14	.754	2	1	0	-2	1	-0.1
1955	Chi-A	40	74	10	15	1	1	2	7	8	22	.203	.280	.324	.605	62	-4	-4	101	87	7	.550	1	0	0	-1	1	-0.5
1956	Chi-A	22	56	7	12	3	0	1	4	10	13	.214	.333	.321	.655	71	-2	-2	104	71	6	.630	1	0	0	-1	1	-0.2
1957	Chi-A	13	60	4	19	3	0	2	8	1	12	.317	.328	.467	.795	116	1	1	99	82	9	.690	0	0	0	-1	1	0.0
1958	Chi-A	61	146	19	34	4	0	7	21	18	46	.233	.325	.404	.729	101	-0	0	98	105	20	.698	2	0	1	-1	1	0.0
1959	Chi-A	10	14	3	3	1	0	1	2	1	0	.214	.313	.500	.813	123	0	0	97	79	2	.750	0	0	0	-0	/1	0.0
1960	Bos-A	10	31	1	7	2	0	0	0	1	6	.226	.250	.290	.540	44	-2	-3	103	0	2	.385	0	0	0	0	/1	-0.2
Total	7	196	474	54	116	18	1	17	52	45	119	.245	.317	.395	.711	92	-6	-6	101	81	60	.673	6	1	1	-5	1	-1.0

■ **RON JACKSON** Jackson, Ronnie Damien b: 5/9/53, Birmingham, Ala. BR/TR, 6', 200 lbs. Deb: 9/12/75

YEAR	TM/L	G	AB	R	H	2B	3B	HR	RBI	BB	SO	AVG	OBP	SLG	PRO	/A	BR	/A	PF	CHI	RC	TA	SB	CS	SBR	FR	POS	TPR
1975	Cal-A	13	39	2	9	2	0	0	2	2	10	.231	.268	.282	.550	59	-2	-2	95	70	3	.452	1	1	-0	0	/O3D	-0.2
1976	Cal-A	127	410	44	93	18	3	8	40	30	58	.227	.291	.344	.635	93	-8	-4	92	93	40	.553	5	4	-1	3	*3/2OD	-0.1
1977	Cal-A	106	292	38	71	15	2	8	28	24	42	.243	.303	.390	.693	92	-6	-3	95	80	34	.620	3	2	-0	0	13D/OS	-0.6
1978	Cal-A	105	387	49	115	18	6	6	57	16	31	.297	.340	.421	.761	111	6	5	102	127	53	.669	2	3	-1	-7	13/OD	-0.5
1979	Min-A	159	583	85	158	40	5	14	68	51	59	.271	.339	.429	.768	97	4	-3	109	91	84	.711	3	1	0	10	*1/S3O	0.0
1980	Min-A	131	396	48	105	29	3	5	42	28	41	.265	.319	.391	.710	86	-4	-8	109	96	43	.596	1	8	-5	1	*1O/3D	-1.9
1981	Min-A	54	175	17	46	9	0	4	28	10	15	.263	.306	.383	.689	93	-1	-2	105	139	20	.597	2	2	-1	1	1/O3D	-0.2
	Det-A	31	95	12	27	8	1	1	12	8	11	.284	.340	.421	.761	112	2	2	105	109	15	.754	4	1	1	-1	1	0.0
	Yr	85	270	29	73	17	1	5	40	18	26	.270	.318	.396	.715	100	1	-0	105	129	36	.660	6	3	0	-0		-0.2
1982	Cal-A	53	142	15	47	6	0	2	19	10	12	.331	.383	.415	.799	119	4	4	100	117	22	.717	0	1	-1	1	1/3	0.3
1983	Cal-A	102	348	41	80	16	1	8	39	27	33	.230	.291	.351	.642	79	-12	-10	96	104	34	.550	2	2	-1	3	31DO	-0.9
1984	Cal-A	33	91	5	15	2	1	0	5	7	13	.165	.224	.209	.433	20	-10	-10	101	105	4	.329	0	0	0	-1	1/3O	-1.2
	Bal-A	12	28	0	8	2	0	0	2	0	4	.286	.286	.357	.643	81	-1	-1	94	80	2	.455	0	2	-1	1	3	0.0
	Yr	45	119	5	23	4	1	0	7	7	17	.193	.238	.244	.482	34	-11	-11	100	101	7	.367	0	2	-1	-0		-1.2
Total	10	926	2986	356	774	165	22	56	342	213	329	.259	.316	.385	.701	93	-27	-33	101	102	355	.635	23	27	-9	10	13/OD2S	-5.3

■ **SAM JACKSON** Jackson, Samuel b: 3/24/1849, Ripon, England d: 8/4/1893, Chilton Springs, N.Y. BR/TR, 5'5.5", 160 lbs. Deb: 5/16/1871

YEAR	TM/L	G	AB	R	H	2B	3B	HR	RBI	BB	SO	AVG	OBP	SLG	PRO	/A	BR	/A	PF	CHI	RC	TA	SB	CS	SBR	FR	POS	TPR
1871	Bos-n	15	77	15	15							.195															2/O	
1872	Atl-n	3	13	0	2							.154															/O	
Total	2 n	18	90	15	17							.189															/O	

YEAR	TM/L	G	AB	R	H	2B	3B	HR	RBI	BB	SO	AVG	OBP	SLG	PRO	/A	BR	/A	PF	CHI	RC	TA	SB	CS	SBR	FR	POS	TPR
■ **TRAVIS JACKSON**	Jackson, Travis Calvin "Stonewall" b: 11/2/03, Waldo, Ark. d: 6/27/87, Waldo, Ark. BR/TR, 5'10.5", 160 lbs. Deb: 9/27/22 CH																											
1922	NY-N	3	8	1	0	0	0	0	0	0	2	.000	.000	.000	.000	-97	-2	-2	104	0	0	.000	0	0	0	0	/S	-0.1
1923	NY-N	96	327	45	90	12	7	4	37	22	40	.275	.321	.391	.712	86	-7	-7	101	93	41	.637	3	3	-1	5	S3/2	0.2
1924	NY-N	151	596	81	180	26	8	11	76	21	56	.302	.326	.428	.754	110	-1	5	91	98	80	.667	6	7	-2	-0	*S	1.4
1925	NY-N	112	411	51	117	15	2	9	59	24	43	.285	.327	.397	.724	85	-10	-10	99	113	54	.663	8	3	1	2	*S	0.2
1926	NY-N	111	385	64	126	24	8	8	51	20	26	.327	.362	.494	.856	131	14	15	98	84	66	.822	2			-6	*S/O	1.6
1927	NY-N	127	469	67	149	29	4	14	98	32	30	.318	.363	.486	.849	126	15	16	100	130	80	.841	8			22	*S/3	4.7
1928	NY-N	150	537	73	145	35	6	14	77	56	46	.270	.339	.436	.775	99	-0	-2	102	101	79	.760	8			28	*S	4.4
1929	NY-N	149	551	92	162	21	12	21	94	64	56	.294	.367	.490	.857	111	8	8	100	99	98	.884	10			19	*S	4.2
1930	NY-N	116	431	70	146	27	8	13	82	32	25	.339	.386	.529	.915	121	12	14	98	108	85	.937	6			5	*S	2.5
1931	NY-N	145	555	65	172	26	10	5	71	36	23	.310	.353	.420	.773	111	5	7	97	104	83	.739	13			9	*S	2.7
1932	NY-N	52	195	23	50	17	1	4	38	13	16	.256	.310	.415	.725	94	-2	-2	99	155	26	.669	1			-3	S	0.0
1933	NY-N	53	122	11	30	5	0	0	12	8	11	.246	.292	.287	.579	67	-5	-5	99	129	10	.474	2			1	S3	-0.2
1934	NY-N	137	523	75	140	26	7	16	101	37	71	.268	.316	.436	.752	101	-2	-1	98	135	71	.668	1			7	*S/3	0.9
1935	NY-N	128	511	74	154	20	12	9	80	29	64	.301	.340	.440	.780	112	5	7	96	121	76	.699	3			-7	*3	0.5
1936	NY-N	126	465	41	107	8	1	7	53	18	56	.230	.260	.297	.557	49	-33	-34	100	120	36	.428	0			3	*3/S	-2.0
Total	15	1656	6086	833	1768	291	86	135	929	412	565	.291	.337	.433	.770	103	-5	10	98	111	883	.721	71	13		83	*S3/O2	21.0
■ **BO JACKSON**	Jackson, Vincent Edward b: 11/30/62, Bessemer, Ala. BR/TR, 6'1", 220 lbs. Deb: 9/02/86																											
1986	KC-A	25	82	9	17	2	1	2	9	7	34	.207	.286	.329	.615	68	-4	-4	100	109	8	.582	3	1	0	-4	O/D	-0.7
1987	KC-A	116	396	46	93	17	2	22	53	30	158	.235	.297	.455	.752	93	-3	-5	104	86	55	.726	10	4	1	-7	*O/D	-1.3
1988	KC-A	124	439	63	108	16	4	25	68	25	146	.246	.288	.472	.760	106	3	1	103	98	59	.758	27	6	5	4	*O/D	0.7
Total	3	265	917	118	218	35	7	49	130	62	338	.238	.292	.451	.743	96	-4	-8	103	94	122	.732	40	11	5	-7	O/D	-1.3
■ **BILL JACKSON**	Jackson, William Riley b: 4/4/1881, Pittsburgh, Pa. d: 9/24/58, Peoria, Ill. BL/TL, 5'11.5", 160 lbs. Deb: 4/30/14																											
1914	Chi-F	26	25	2	1	0	0	0	1	3	5	.040	.143	.040	.183	-51	-5	-4	91	361	0	.167	0			0	/O1	-0.4
1915	Chi-F	50	98	15	16	1	0	1	12	14	15	.163	.268	.204	.472	42	-7	-7	97	188	7	.451	3			-1	1/O	-0.7
Total	2	76	123	17	17	1	0	1	13	17	20	.138	.243	.171	.414	24	-12	-11	96	223	7	.387	3			-1	/1O	-1.1
■ **SPOOK JACOBS**	Jacobs, Forrest Vandergrift b: 11/4/25, Cheswold, Del. BR/TR, 5'8.5", 155 lbs. Deb: 4/13/54																											
1954	Phi-A	132	508	63	131	11	1	0	26	60	22	.258	.336	.283	.620	72	-18	-17	98	66	55	.574	17	3	3	-12	*2	-2.1
1955	KC-A	13	23	7	6	0	0	0	1	3	0	.261	.370	.261	.631	71	-1	-1	101	62	2	.550	1	2	-1	-0	/2	-0.1
1956	KC-A	32	97	13	21	3	0	0	5	15	5	.216	.321	.247	.569	52	-6	-6	101	78	8	.531	4	1	1	1	2	-0.1
	Pit-N	11	37	4	6	2	0	0	1	2	5	.162	.225	.216	.441	19	-4	-4	102	54	2	.333	0	2	-1	0	2	-0.4
Total	3	188	665	87	164	16	1	0	33	80	32	.247	.329	.274	.603	66	-29	-29	99	67	67	.562	22	8	2	-11	2	-2.7
■ **JAKE JACOBS**	Jacobs, Lamar Gary b: 6/9/37, Youngstown, Ohio BR/TR, 6', 175 lbs. Deb: 9/13/60																											
1960	Was-A	6	2	0	0	0	0	0	0	0	0	.000	.000	.000	.000	-98	-1	-1	102	0	0	.000	0	0	0	0	H	0.0
1961	Min-A	4	8	0	2	0	0	0	0	0	2	.250	.250	.250	.500	32	-1	-1	106	0	1	.333	0	0	0	-1	/O	-0.1
Total	2	10	10	0	2	0	0	0	0	0	2	.200	.200	.200	.400	7	-1	-1	105	0	1	.250	0	0	0	-1	/O	-0.1
■ **MIKE JACOBS**	Jacobs, Morris Elmore b: 1877, d: 3/21/49, Louisville, Ky. Deb: 7/16/02																											
1902	Chi-N	5	19	1	4	0	0	0	2	0		.211	.211	.211	.421	33	-2	-1	96	176	1	.267	0			0	/S	0.0
■ **OTTO JACOBS**	Jacobs, Otto Albert b: 4/19/1889, Chicago, Ill. d: 11/19/55, Chicago, Ill. BR/TR, 5'9", 180 lbs. Deb: 6/13/18																											
1918	Chi-A	29	73	4	15	3	1	0	3	5	8	.205	.256	.274	.530	60	-4	-4	101	55	5	.431	0			-1	C	-0.2
■ **RAY JACOBS**	Jacobs, Raymond F. b: 1/2/02, Salt Lake City, Utah d: 4/5/52, Los Angeles, Cal. BR/TR, 6', 160 lbs. Deb: 4/20/28																											
1928	Chi-N	2	2	0	0	0	0	0	0	0	1	.000	.000	.000	.000	-99	-1	-1	95	0	0	.000	0			0	H	0.0
■ **MERWIN JACOBSON**	Jacobson, Merwin John William "Jake" b: 3/7/1894, New Britain, Conn. d: 1/13/78, Baltimore, Md. BL/TL, 5'11.5", 165 lbs. Deb: 9/08/15																											
1915	NY-N	8	24	0	2	0	0	0	0	1	5	.083	.120	.083	.203	-42	-4	-4	91	0	0	.136	0			0	/O	-0.3
1916	Chi-N	4	13	2	3	0	0	0	0	1	4	.231	.286	.231	.516	51	-1	-1	117	0	1	.600	2			-0	/O	0.0
1926	Bro-N	110	288	41	71	9	2	0	23	36	24	.247	.330	.292	.622	69	-12	-11	99	95	29	.576	5			0	O	-1.4
1927	Bro-N	11	6	4	0	0	0	0	1	0	1	.000	.000	.000	.000	-97	-2	-2	103	0	0	.000	0			-1	/O	-0.2
Total	4	133	331	47	76	9	2	0	24	38	34	.230	.309	.269	.578	59	-18	-18	99	83	31	.525	7			-1	/O	-1.9
■ **BABY DOLL JACOBSON**	Jacobson, William Chester b: 8/16/1890, Cable, Ill. d: 1/16/77, Orion, Ill. BR/TR, 6'3", 215 lbs. Deb: 4/14/15																											
1915	Det-A	37	65	5	14	6	2	0	4	5	14	.215	.282	.369	.651	87	-1	-2	108	57	6	.566	0	2	-1	-1	1/O	-0.4
	StL-A	34	115	13	24	6	1	1	9	10	26	.209	.295	.304	.599	83	-3	-2	96	82	10	.553	3	3	-1	-3	O	-0.8
	Yr	71	180	18	38	12	3	1	13	15	40	.211	.290	.328	.618	83	-4	-4	102	70	17	.558	3	5	-2	-4		-1.2
1917	StL-A	148	529	53	131	23	7	4	55	31	67	.248	.294	.340	.635	99	-6	-3	95	105	53	.565	10			9	*O1	-0.2
1919	StL-A	120	455	70	147	31	8	4	51	24	47	.323	.362	.453	.815	132	15	17	97	90	75	.789	9			8	*O/1	1.7
1920	StL-A	154	609	97	216	34	14	9	122	46	37	.355	.402	.501	.903	124	32	22	111	137	121	.910	11	7	-1	1	*O/1	0.9
1921	StL-A	151	599	90	211	38	14	5	90	42	30	.352	.398	.487	.885	124	22	21	101	106	114	.871	8	8	-2	-4	*O1	0.2
1922	StL-A	145	555	88	176	22	16	9	102	46	36	.317	.379	.463	.842	112	15	10	106	136	100	.860	19	6	2	1	*O/1	0.2
1923	StL-A	147	592	76	183	29	6	8	81	29	27	.309	.343	.419	.762	96	-2	-5	104	108	84	.687	6	6	-2	4	*O	-1.5
1924	StL-A	152	579	103	184	41	12	19	97	35	45	.318	.361	.528	.889	119	19	13	107	94	107	.871	6	8	-3	13	*O	1.1
1925	StL-A	142	540	103	184	30	9	15	76	45	26	.341	.392	.513	.905	119	21	15	108	81	105	.902	8	11	-4	-4	*O	-0.4
1926	StL-A	50	182	18	52	15	1	2	21	9	14	.286	.319	.412	.731	89	-4	-4	101	90	23	.644	1	2	-1	-4	O	-1.1
	Bos-A	98	394	44	120	36	1	6	69	22	22	.305	.344	.447	.791	104	1	1	101	107	61	.742	4	1	1	-6	O	-1.0
	Yr	148	576	62	172	51	2	8	90	31	36	.299	.337	.436	.772	99	-2	-3	101	102	84	.710	5	3	-0	-9		-2.1
1927	Bos-A	45	155	11	38	9	3	0	24	5	12	.245	.278	.342	.620	64	-10	-8	95	151	14	.521	1	0	0	1	O	-0.8
	Cle-A	32	103	13	26	5	0	0	13	6	4	.252	.300	.301	.601	58	-7	-6	97	140	9	.494	0	0	0	0	O	-0.7
	Phi-A	17	35	3	8	3	0	1	5	0	3	.229	.229	.400	.629	63	-2	-2	97	98	3	.519	0	0		-5	O	-0.7
	Yr	94	293	27	72	17	3	1	42	11	19	.246	.280	.334	.615	62	-19	-17	96	140	27	.511	1	0	0	-4		-2.2
Total	11	1472	5507	787	1714	328	94	83	819	355	410	.311	.357	.450	.807	111	91	66	103	108	886	.769	86	54		10	*O/1	-3.5
■ **BROOK JACOBY**	Jacoby, Brook Wallace b: 11/23/59, Philadelphia, Pa. BR/TR, 5'11", 175 lbs. Deb: 9/13/81																											
1981	Atl-N	11	10	0	2	0	0	0	1	0	3	.200	.200	.200	.400	14	-1	-1	100	196	0	.222	0	0	0	-1	/3	-0.1
1983	Atl-N	4	8	0	0	0	0	0	0	0	1	.000	.000	.000	.000	-95	-2	-2	106	0	0	.000	0	0	0	0	/3	-0.1
1984	Cle-A	126	439	64	116	19	3	7	40	32	73	.264	.319	.369	.688	85	-6	-10	106	87	50	.592	3	2	-0	-19	*3/S	-2.7
1985	Cle-A	161	606	72	166	26	3	20	87	48	120	.274	.327	.426	.753	111	3	7	94	115	81	.670	2	3	-1	-7	*3/2	-0.5
1986	Cle-A	158	583	83	168	30	4	17	80	56	137	.288	.351	.441	.791	118	12	14	98	106	88	.731	2	1	0	-13	*3	-0.2
1987	Cle-A	155	540	73	162	26	4	32	69	75	73	.300	.388	.541	.929	140	35	33	103	72	110	.930	2	3	-1	-5	*3/1D	2.1
1988	Cle-A	152	552	59	133	25	0	9	49	48	101	.241	.303	.335	.638	77	-16	-17	102	94	55	.544	2	3	-1	2	*3	-1.5
Total	7	767	2738	351	747	126	14	85	326	259	508	.273	.337	.422	.759	107	25	24	100	95	385	.711	11	12	-4	-42	3/1D2S	-3.0
■ **HARRY JACOBY**	Jacoby, Harry b: Philadelphia, Pa. Deb: 5/02/1882																											
1882	Bal-a	31	121	17	21	1	1	1		7		.174	.219	.223	.442	53	-6	-5	92	0	6	.340				0	3O	-0.3
1885	Bal-a	11	43	4	6	2	0	0		2		.140	.178	.186	.364	16	-4	-4	106	0	1	.270				0	2	-0.3
Total	2	42	164	21	27	3	1	1		9		.165	.208	.213	.422	42	-10	-9	96	0	8	.321				0	/3O2	-0.6
■ **ART JAHN**	Jahn, Arthur Charles b: 12/2/1895, Struble, Iowa d: 1/9/48, Little Rock, Ark. BR/TR, 6', 180 lbs. Deb: 7/02/25																											
1925	Chi-N	58	226	30	68	10	8	0	37	11	20	.301	.336	.416	.752	93	-3	-3	97	148	31	.675	2	2	-1	-1	O	-0.5
1928	NY-N	10	29	7	8	1	0	1	7	2	5	.276	.323	.414	.736	89	-0	-1	102	166	4	.667	0			1	/O	0.0
	Phi-N	36	94	8	21	4	0	0	11	4	11	.223	.270	.266	.536	39	-8	-9	104	157	7	.425	0			-5	O	-1.4
	Yr	46	123	15	29	5	0	1	18	6	16	.236	.282	.301	.583	51	-9	-9	104	162	10	.479	0			-4		-1.4
Total	2	104	349	45	97	15	8	1	55	17	36	.278	.317	.375	.692	78	-12	-12	100	152	41	.602	2	2		-5	/O	-1.9

YEAR	TM/L	G	AB	R	H	2B	3B	HR	RBI	BB	SO	AVG	OBP	SLG	PRO	/A	BR	/A	PF	CHI	RC	TA	SB	CS	SBR	FR	POS	TPR
■ **ART JAMES**	James, Arthur b: 8/2/52, Detroit, Mich. BL/TL, 6', 170 lbs. Deb: 4/10/75																											
1975	Det-A	11	40	2	9	2	0	0	1	1	3	.225	.244	.275	.519	45	-3	-3	104	36	2	.382	1	2	-1	2	O	-0.2
■ **BERT JAMES**	James, Berton Hulon "Jesse" b: 7/7/1886, Coopertown, Tenn. d: 1/2/59, Adairville, Ky. BL/TR, 5'11", 175 lbs. Deb: 09																											
1909	StL-N	6	21	1	6	0	0	0	0	4		.286	.400	.286	.686	119	1	1	96	0	3	.733	1			1	/O	0.2
■ **CHARLIE JAMES**	James, Charles Wesley b: 12/22/37, St.Louis, Mo. BR/TR, 6'1", 195 lbs. Deb: 8/02/60																											
1960	StL-N	43	50	5	9	1	0	2	5	1	12	.180	.196	.320	.516	36	-4	-5	108	92	3	.415	0	0	0	-10	O	-1.6
1961	StL-N	108	349	43	89	19	2	4	44	15	59	.255	.292	.355	.647	62	-15	-21	113	130	34	.531	2	2	-1	-4	O	-3.0
1962	StL-N	129	388	50	107	13	4	8	59	10	58	.276	.301	.392	.693	78	-9	-14	109	132	42	.573	3	4	-2	-9	*O	-3.0
1963	StL-N	116	347	34	93	14	2	10	45	10	64	.268	.292	.406	.699	92	-2	-4	107	111	37	.581	2	1	0	-1	*O	-1.0
1964	StL-N	88	233	24	52	9	1	5	17	11	58	.223	.261	.335	.596	59	-11	-14	112	75	19	.481	0	0	0	-6	O	-2.2
1965	Cin-N	26	39	2	8	0	0	0	2	1	9	.205	.225	.205	.430	21	-4	-4	104	104	1	.265	0	0	0	-1	/O	-0.4
Total	6	510	1406	158	358	56	9	29	172	48	260	.255	.284	.369	.653	71	-45	-62	110	115	137	.552	7	7	-2	-31	O	-11.2
■ **CLEO JAMES**	James, Cleo Joel b: 8/31/40, Clarksdale, Miss. BR/TR, 5'10", 176 lbs. Deb: 4/15/68																											
1968	LA-N	10	10	2	2	1	0	0	0	0	6	.200	.200	.300	.500	54	-1	-1	91	0	1	.375	0	0	0	-0	/O	0.0
1970	Chi-N	100	176	33	37	7	2	3	14	17	24	.210	.298	.324	.622	55	-8	-13	120	82	18	.592	5	0	2	-6	O	-2.1
1971	Chi-N	54	150	25	43	7	0	2	13	10	16	.287	.355	.373	.729	97	2	-0	110	85	21	.696	6	2	1	2	O/3	0.1
1973	Chi-N	44	45	9	5	0	0	0	0	1	6	.111	.130	.111	.242	-30	-8	-8	108	0	1	.262	5	0	2	-4	O	-1.2
Total	4	208	381	69	87	15	2	5	27	28	52	.228	.300	.318	.618	62	-15	-22	114	72	40	.591	16	2	4	-9	O/3	-3.2
■ **DION JAMES**	James, Dion b: 11/9/62, Philadelphia, Pa. BL/TL, 6'1", 170 lbs. Deb: 9/16/83																											
1983	Mil-A	11	20	1	2	0	0	0	1	2	2	.100	.182	.100	.282	-22	-3	-3	92	195	1	.278	1	0	0	-1	/OD	-0.3
1984	Mil-A	128	387	52	114	19	5	1	30	32	41	.295	.353	.377	.730	111	2	6	92	80	50	.659	10	10	-3	-16	*O	-1.6
1985	Mil-A	18	49	5	11	1	0	0	3	6	6	.224	.309	.245	.554	52	-3	-3	105	99	4	.474	0	0	0	-1	O/D	-0.3
1987	Atl-N	134	494	80	154	37	6	10	61	70	63	.312	.399	.472	.871	120	23	17	108	98	95	.885	10	8	-2	-8	*O	0.2
1988	Atl-N	132	386	46	99	17	5	3	30	58	59	.256	.355	.350	.705	99	3	1	104	83	48	.659	9	9	-3	-5	*O	-0.9
Total	5	423	1336	184	380	74	16	14	125	168	171	.284	.367	.395	.762	107	22	18	102	90	198	.736	30	27	-7	-31	O/D	-2.9
■ **CHRIS JAMES**	James, Donald Chris b: 10/4/62, Rusk, Tex. BR/TR, 6'1", 195 lbs. Deb: 4/23/86																											
1986	Phi-N	16	46	5	13	3	0	1	5	1	13	.283	.298	.413	.711	90	-1	-1	104	91	5	.588	0	0	0	-1	O	-0.1
1987	Phi-N	115	358	48	105	20	6	17	54	27	67	.293	.346	.525	.871	122	12	11	104	90	66	.853	3	1	0	-2	*O	0.5
1988	Phi-N	150	566	57	137	24	1	19	66	31	73	.242	.285	.389	.674	91	-8	-9	101	97	59	.583	7	4	-0	7	*O/3	-0.4
Total	3	281	970	110	255	47	7	37	125	59	153	.263	.309	.440	.749	103	4	1	102	94	130	.682	10	5	0	5	O/3	0.0
■ **SKIP JAMES**	James, Philip Robert b: 10/21/49, Elmhurst, Ill. BL/TL, 6', 185 lbs. Deb: 9/12/77																											
1977	SF-N	10	15	3	4	1	0	0	3	2	3	.267	.353	.333	.686	82	-0	-0	104	240	2	.583	0	0	0	-0	/1	0.0
1978	SF-N	41	21	5	2	1	0	0	3	4	5	.095	.240	.143	.383	10	-3	-2	92	397	1	.381	1	0	0	-0	1	-0.3
Total	2	51	36	8	6	2	0	0	6	6	8	.167	.286	.222	.508	43	-3	-3	97	333	2	.469	1	0	0	-0	/1	-0.3
■ **BERNIE JAMES**	James, Robert Byrne b: 9/2/05, Angleton, Tex. BB/TR, 5'9.5", 150 lbs. Deb: 5/06/29																											
1929	Bos-N	46	101	12	31	3	2	0	9	9	13	.307	.369	.376	.746	91	-2	-1	94	81	14	.729	3			-1	2/O	0.0
1930	Bos-N	8	11	1	2	1	0	0	1	0	1	.182	.182	.273	.455	8	-2	-2	97	115	1	.333	0			0	/2	0.0
1933	NY-N	60	125	22	28	2	1	1	10	8	12	.224	.271	.280	.551	58	-7	-7	99	99	10	.495	5			9	2/S3	0.5
Total	3	114	237	35	61	6	3	1	20	17	26	.257	.310	.321	.630	70	-11	-9	96	92	25	.580	8			8	/2S3O	0.5
■ **CHARLIE JAMIESON**	Jamieson, Charles Devine "Cuckoo" b: 2/7/1893, Paterson, N.J. d: 10/27/69, Paterson, N.J. BL/TL, 5'8.5", 165 lbs. Deb: 9/20/15																											
1915	Was-A	17	68	9	19	3	2	0	7	6	9	.279	.338	.382	.720	114	1	1	101	79	9	.653	0			4	O	0.4
1916	Was-A	64	145	16	36	4	0	0	13	18	18	.248	.331	.276	.607	83	-3	-3	100	116	16	.578	5			-4	O/1P	-0.9
1917	Was-A	20	35	4	6	2	0	0	2	6	5	.171	.293	.229	.521	64	-2	-1	92	90	2	.483	0			-2	/OP	-0.3
	Phi-A	85	345	41	92	6	2	0	27	37	36	.267	.341	.296	.637	101	-1	1	94	82	36	.589	8			-6	O	-1.0
	Yr	105	380	45	98	8	2	0	29	43	41	.258	.336	.289	.626	98	-3	0	93	84	38	.578	8			-8		-1.3
1918	Phi-A	110	416	50	84	11	2	0	11	54	30	.202	.297	.238	.535	59	-18	-20	104	39	30	.500	11			-6	*O/P	-3.3
1919	Cle-A	26	17	3	6	2	1	0	2	0	2	.353	.353	.588	.941	152	1	1	107	73	4	1.091	2			-1	/PO	0.0
1920	Cle-A	108	370	69	118	17	7	1	40	41	26	.319	.388	.411	.799	108	7	5	104	92	58	.751	2	9	-5	0	O/1	-0.7
1921	Cle-A	140	536	94	166	33	10	1	46	67	27	.310	.387	.414	.802	105	5	6	99	71	89	.797	8	4	0	1	*O	-0.4
1922	Cle-A	145	567	87	183	29	11	3	57	54	22	.323	.388	.429	.816	111	11	10	102	86	96	.811	15	8	-0	4	*O/P	0.3
1923	Cle-A	152	644	130	**222**	36	12	2	51	80	37	.345	.422	.447	.869	127	30	29	101	51	125	.906	19	12	-2	7	*O	1.9
1924	Cle-A	143	594	98	213	34	8	3	53	47	15	.359	.407	.458	.865	127	20	23	97	55	111	.872	21	11	-0	4	*O	1.5
1925	Cle-A	138	557	109	165	24	5	4	42	72	26	.296	.380	.379	.759	87	-4	-10	106	56	81	.732	14	18	-7	8	*O	-1.7
1926	Cle-A	143	555	89	166	33	7	2	45	53	22	.299	.361	.395	.756	97	-2	-2	100	72	80	.710	9	8	-2	-2	*O	-1.6
1927	Cle-A	127	489	73	151	23	6	0	36	64	14	.309	.394	.380	.775	105	4	6	97	57	75	.775	7	0	2	-3	*O	-0.4
1928	Cle-A	112	433	63	133	18	4	1	37	56	20	.307	.388	.374	.762	95	3	-1	106	74	63	.712	3	12	-6	3	*O	-0.9
1929	Cle-A	102	364	56	106	22	1	0	26	50	12	.291	.378	.357	.735	90	-3	-3	100	70	48	.675	2	13	-7	-2	O	-1.5
1930	Cle-A	103	366	64	110	22	1	1	52	36	20	.301	.368	.374	.742	85	-5	-8	105	126	53	.702	5	2	0	-7	O	-1.6
1931	Cle-A	28	43	7	13	2	1	0	4	5	1	.302	.375	.395	.770	96	0	-0	106	78	6	.742	1	1	-0	-2	/O	-0.1
1932	Cle-A	16	16	0	1	1	0	0	0	2	3	.063	.211	.125	.336	-10	-3	-3	108	0	1	.333	0	0	0	0	/O	-0.1
Total	18	1779	6560	1062	1990	322	80	18	551	748	345	.303	.378	.385	.763	101	43	33	101	70	983	.737	132	98		-4	*O/P1	-10.4
■ **VIC JANOWICZ**	Janowicz, Victor Felix b: 2/26/30, Elyria, Ohio BR/TR, 5'9", 185 lbs. Deb: 5/31/53																											
1953	Pit-N	42	123	10	31	3	1	2	8	5	31	.252	.287	.341	.628	62	-7	-7	102	65	11	.500	0	1	-1	0	C	-0.4
1954	Pit-N	41	73	10	11	3	0	0	2	7	23	.151	.235	.192	.426	13	-9	-9	97	56	4	.355	0	0	0	-1	3/O	-0.9
Total	2	83	196	20	42	6	1	2	10	12	54	.214	.267	.286	.552	44	-16	-16	100	62	15	.452	0	1	-1	-0	/C3O	-1.3
■ **RAY JANSEN**	Jansen, Raymond William b: 1/16/1889, St.Louis, Mo. d: 3/19/34, St.Louis, Mo. BR/TR, 5'11", 155 lbs. Deb: 9/30/10																											
1910	StL-A	1	5	0	4	0	0	0	0	0		.800	.800	.800	1.600	426	2	2	94	0	3	4.000	0			0	/3	0.2
■ **HEINIE JANTZEN**	Jantzen, Walter C. b: 4/9/1890, Chicago, Ill. d: 4/1/48, Hines, Ill. BR/TR, 5'11.5", 170 lbs. Deb: 6/29/12																											
1912	StL-A	31	119	10	22	0	1	1	8	4		.185	.218	.227	.445	28	-11	-11	99	94	6	.361	3			2	O	-1.1
■ **HAL JANVRIN**	Janvrin, Harold Chandler "Childe Harold" b: 8/27/1892, Haverhill, Mass. d: 3/1/62, Boston, Mass. BR/TR, 5'11.5", 168 lbs. Deb: 7/09/11																											
1911	Bos-A	9	27	2	4	1	0	0	1	3		.148	.233	.185	.419	17	-3	-3	99	68	1	.348	0			0	/31	-0.2
1913	Bos-A	87	276	18	57	5	1	3	25	23	27	.207	.272	.264	.537	55	-15	-16	103	108	24	.525	17			-5	S3/21	-1.7
1914	Bos-A	143	492	65	117	18	6	1	51	38	50	.238	.296	.305	.601	83	-12	-11	98	128	48	.557	29	20	-3	-10	21S/3	-2.4
1915	Bos-A	99	316	41	85	9	1	0	37	14	27	.269	.317	.304	.620	86	-6	-6	99	131	31	.514	8	14	-6	-6	S3/2	-1.1
1916	Bos-A	117	310	32	69	11	4	0	26	32	32	.223	.299	.284	.583	80	-9	-7	94	105	31	.531	6			-1	S2/13	-0.1
1917	Bos-A	55	127	21	25	3	0	0	8	11	13	.197	.266	.220	.487	45	-8	-9	108	103	9	.412	2			-0	2S/1	-0.6
1919	Was-A	61	208	17	37	4	1	1	13	19	17	.178	.253	.221	.474	34	-18	-18	98	98	13	.439	8			-14	2/S	-2.7
	StL-N	7	14	1	3	1	0	0	1	2	2	.214	.313	.286	.598	85	-0	-0	94	97	1	.545	0			0	/2S3	0.0
1920	StL-N	87	270	33	74	8	4	1	28	17	19	.274	.317	.344	.662	92	-4	-3	98	113	29	.569	5	6	-2	-0	S1O/2	-0.5
1921	StL-N	18	32	5	9	1	0	0	5	1	0	.281	.303	.313	.616	67	-2	-1	95	183	3	.522	1	0	0	-0	/12	-0.1
	Bro-N	44	92	8	18	4	0	0	14	7	6	.196	.253	.239	.492	29	-9	-10	105	233	6	.427	3	1	0	1	S2/13O	-0.6
	Yr	62	124	13	27	5	0	0	19	8	6	.218	.265	.258	.523	38	-11	-11	102	222	9	.449	4	1	1	1		-0.7
1922	Bro-N	30	57	7	17	3	1	0	1	4	4	.298	.344	.386	.730	93	-1	-1	95	16	8	.650	0	0	0	-0	2/S3I0	0.0
Total	10	757	2221	250	515	68	18	6	210	171	197	.232	.292	.287	.579	70	-87	-84	99	118	204	.518	79	41		-34	S21/3O	-10.0
■ **ROY JARVIS**	Jarvis, Leroy Gilbert b: 6/27/26, Shawnee, Okla. BR/TR, 5'9", 160 lbs. Deb: 4/30/44																											
1944	Bro-N	1	1	0	0	0	0	0	0	0	1	.000	.000	.000	.000	-99	-0	-0	99	0	0	.000	0			0	/C	0.0
1946	Pit-N	2	4	0	1	0	0	0	0	1	1	.250	.400	.250	.650	84	0	-0	103	0	1	.667	0			0	/C	0.0
1947	Pit-N	18	45	4	7	1	0	1	4	6	5	.156	.255	.244	.499	33	-4	-4	101	106	3	.436	0			0	C	-0.3

YEAR	TM/L	G	AB	R	H	2B	3B	HR	RBI	BB	SO	AVG	OBP	SLG	PRO	/A	BR	/A	PF	CHI	RC	TA	SB	CS	SBR	FR	POS	TPR
Total	3	21	50	4	8	1	0	1	4	7	7	.160	.263	.240	.503	35	-5	-5	101	95	3	.442	0			0	/C	-0.3
■ PAUL JATA Jata, Paul b: 9/4/49, Astoria, N.Y. BR/TR, 6'1", 190 lbs. Deb: 4/19/72																												
1972	Det-A	32	74	8	17	2	0	0	3	7	14	.230	.296	.257	.553	58	-3	-4	113	66	6	.441	0	1	-1	-1	1O/C	-0.7
■ AL JAVIER Javier, Ignacio Alfred (born Wilkes (Javier)) b: 2/4/54, San Pedro De Macoris, D.R. BR/TR, 5'11", 170 lbs. Deb: 9/09/76																												
1976	Hou-N	8	24	1	5	0	0	0	0	2	5	.208	.269	.208	.478	43	-2	-2	86	0	1	.350	0	0	0	-2	/O	-0.3
■ JULIAN JAVIER Javier, Manuel Julian (Liranzo) b: 8/9/36, San Francisco De Macoris, D.R. BR/TR, 6'1", 175 lbs. Deb: 5/28/60																												
1960	StL-N	119	451	55	107	19	8	4	21	21	72	.237	.273	.341	.614	62	-21	-26	108	54	43	.549	19	4	3	13	*2	0.1
1961	StL-N	113	445	58	124	14	3	2	41	30	51	.279	.327	.337	.664	68	-14	-22	113	112	51	.585	11	4	1	2	*2	-0.5
1962	StL-N	155	598	97	157	25	5	7	39	47	73	.263	.317	.356	.674	74	-16	-23	109	70	70	.625	26	9	2	3	*2/S	-0.3
1963	StL-N	161	609	82	160	27	9	9	46	24	86	.263	.297	.381	.678	87	-6	-11	107	76	68	.600	18	10	-1	-9	*2	-1.0
1964	StL-N	155	535	66	129	19	5	12	65	30	82	.241	.283	.363	.645	72	-15	-22	112	116	52	.555	9	7	-2	2	*2	-0.9
1965	StL-N	77	229	34	52	6	4	2	23	8	44	.227	.262	.314	.577	58	-12	-14	107	122	17	.468	5	5	-2	-0	2	-1.2
1966	StL-N	147	460	52	105	13	5	7	31	26	63	.228	.271	.324	.595	65	-22	-22	100	77	40	.510	11	5	0	1	*2	-1.1
1967	StL-N	140	520	68	146	16	3	14	64	25	92	.281	.315	.404	.719	103	2	1	101	107	63	.622	6	7	-2	-22	*2	-1.5
1968	StL-N	139	519	54	135	25	4	4	52	24	61	.260	.294	.347	.641	96	-6	-4	95	116	52	.542	10	3	1	-16	*2	-1.1
1969	StL-N	143	493	59	139	28	2	10	42	40	74	.282	.337	.408	.745	108	4	5	100	74	67	.683	8	4	0	-15	*2	0.0
1970	StL-N	139	513	62	129	16	3	2	42	24	70	.251	.286	.306	.592	55	-30	-34	106	102	42	.468	6	4	-1	17	*2	-0.1
1971	StL-N	90	259	32	67	6	4	3	28	9	33	.259	.289	.347	.636	79	-8	-8	101	115	25	.530	5	1	1	-1	2/3	-0.3
1972	Cin-N	44	91	3	19	2	0	2	12	6	11	.209	.258	.297	.554	61	-5	-5	93	149	7	.459	1	0	0	-1	3/21	-0.4
Total	13	1622	5722	722	1469	216	55	78	506	314	812	.257	.298	.355	.652	78	-150	-184	105	94	597	.579	135	63	3	-25	*2/3S1	-8.3
■ STAN JAVIER Javier, Stanley Julian Antonio (De Javier) b: 1/9/64, San Francisco De Macoris, D.R. BB/TR, 6', 185 lbs. Deb: 4/15/84																												
1984	NY-A	7	7	1	1	0	0	0	0	0	1	.143	.143	.143	.286	-22	-1	-1	94	0	0	.167	0	0	0	-2	/O	-0.2
1986	Oak-A	59	114	13	23	8	0	0	8	16	27	.202	.305	.272	.577	64	-6	-5	94	103	11	.602	8	0	2	2	O/D	-0.1
1987	Oak-A	81	151	22	28	3	1	2	9	19	33	.185	.276	.258	.535	48	-12	-10	91	80	12	.480	3	2	-0	-4	O/1D	-1.6
1988	Oak-A	125	397	49	102	13	3	2	35	32	63	.257	.316	.320	.635	83	-11	-8	95	105	42	.586	20	1	5	0	*O/1D	-0.4
Total	4	272	669	85	154	24	4	4	52	67	124	.230	.303	.296	.599	70	-30	-24	94	97	65	.563	31	3	8	-3	O/1D	-2.3
■ TEX JEANES Jeanes, Ernest Lee b: 12/19/1900, Maypearl, Tex. d: 4/5/73, Longview, Tex. BR/TR, 6', 176 lbs. Deb: 4/20/21																												
1921	Cle-A	4	2	1	1	0	0	0	4	1	0	.500	.667	.500	1.167	203	0	0	99	0	1	2.000	0	0	0	0	/O	0.1
1922	Cle-A	1	1	0	0	0	0	0	0	1	0	.000	.500	.000	.500	39	0	0	102	0	0	1.000	0	0	0	-0	/PO	0.0
1925	Was-A	15	19	2	5	1	0	1	4	3	2	.263	.364	.474	.837	114	0	0	98	112	4	.929	1	0	0	-5	O	-0.4
1926	Was-A	21	30	6	7	2	0	0	3	0	3	.233	.233	.300	.533	39	-3	-3	98	113	2	.391	0	0	0	-3	O	-0.6
1927	NY-N	11	20	5	6	0	0	0	0	2	2	.300	.364	.300	.664	80	-0	-0	100	0	2	.571	0			1	/OP	0.0
Total	5	52	72	14	19	3	0	1	11	7	7	.264	.329	.347	.676	77	-3	-2	99	74	9	.623	1	0		-7	/OP	-0.9
■ HAL JEFFCOAT Jeffcoat, Harold Bentley b: 9/6/24, W.Columbia, S.C. BR/TR, 5'10.5", 185 lbs. Deb: 4/20/48																												
1948	Chi-N	134	473	53	132	16	4	4	42	24	68	.279	.315	.355	.670	87	-13	-9	93	89	54	.579	8			4	*O	-1.2
1949	Chi-N	108	363	43	89	18	6	2	26	20	48	.245	.286	.344	.631	73	-17	-14	94	75	36	.566	12			-1	*O	-2.1
1950	Chi-N	66	179	21	42	13	1	2	18	6	23	.235	.259	.352	.611	56	-11	-12	105	101	13	.514	7			-4	O	-1.7
1951	Chi-N	113	278	44	76	20	2	4	27	16	23	.273	.315	.403	.718	94	-4	-3	97	84	35	.649	8	4	0	2	O	-0.3
1952	Chi-N	102	297	29	65	17	2	4	30	15	40	.219	.259	.330	.589	60	-16	-17	103	106	22	.482	7	2	1	15	O	-0.3
1953	Chi-N	106	183	22	43	3	1	4	22	21	26	.235	.314	.328	.642	66	-9	-9	103	119	20	.593	5	0	2	-7	*O	-1.8
1954	Chi-N	56	31	13	8	2	1	1	6	1	7	.258	.281	.484	.765	94	-0	-0	101	131	4	.750	2	0	1	-1	P/O	0.0
1955	Chi-N	52	23	3	4	0	0	1	1	2	9	.174	.240	.304	.544	43	-2	-2	100	40	1	.429	0	0	0	1	P	0.0
1956	Cin-N	49	54	5	8	2	0	0	5	3	20	.148	.193	.185	.378	2	-7	-8	108	211	2	.271	0	1	-1	3	P	0.0
1957	Cin-N	53	69	13	14	3	1	4	11	5	20	.203	.267	.449	.716	83	-2	-2	105	106	8	.649	0	0	0	-1	P	0.0
1958	Cin-N	50	9	2	5	0	0	0	0	1	2	.556	.600	.556	1.156	194	2	1	107	0	3	1.500	0	0	0	2	P/O	0.0
1959	Cin-N	17	1	1	1	1	0	0	0	0	0	1.000	1.000	2.000	3.000	654	1	1	103	0	2	—	0	0	0	0	P	0.0
	StL-N	12	3	0	0	0	0	0	0	0	3	.000	.000	.000	.000	-96	-1	-1	105	0	0	.000	0	0	0	0	P	0.0
	Yr	29	4	1	1	1	0	0	0	0	3	.250	.250	.500	.750	90	-0	-0	104	0	1	.667	0	0	0	0		0.0
Total	12	918	1963	249	487	95	18	26	188	114	289	.248	.291	.355	.646	74	-79	-76	99	96	200	.583	49	7		12	OP	-7.4
■ GREGG JEFFERIES Jefferies, Gregory Scott b: 8/1/67, Burlingame, Cal. BB/TR, 5'11", 175 lbs. Deb: 9/06/87																												
1987	NY-N	6	6	0	3	1	0	0	2	0	0	.500	.500	.667	1.167	209	1	1	99	200	2	1.333	0	0	0	0	/H	0.1
1988	NY-N	29	109	19	35	8	2	6	17	8	10	.321	.368	.596	.964	191	10	11	90	83	24	1.026	5	1	1	-2	32	1.1
Total	2	35	115	19	38	9	2	6	19	8	10	.330	.374	.600	.974	192	10	12	91	89	26	1.038	5	1	1	-2	/32	1.2
■ STAN JEFFERSON Jefferson, Stanley b: 12/4/62, New York, N.Y. BB/TR, 5'11", 175 lbs. Deb: 9/07/86																												
1986	NY-N	14	24	6	5	1	0	1	3	2	8	.208	.296	.375	.671	88	-1	-0	96	100	3	.600	0	0	0	0	/O	0.0
1987	SD-N	116	422	59	97	8	7	8	29	39	92	.230	.298	.339	.637	71	-19	-18	97	71	45	.637	34	11	4	-5	*O	-2.2
1988	SD-N	49	111	16	16	1	2	1	4	9	22	.144	.215	.216	.431	25	-11	-11	97	59	6	.394	5	1	1	-4	O	-1.5
Total	3	179	557	81	118	10	9	10	36	50	122	.212	.282	.316	.597	63	-31	-29	97	70	53	.593	39	12	5	-8	O	-3.7
■ IRV JEFFRIES Jeffries, Irvine Franklin b: 9/10/05, Louisville, Ky. d: 6/8/82, Louisville, Ky. BR/TR, 5'10", 175 lbs. Deb: 4/30/30																												
1930	Chi-A	40	97	14	23	3	0	2	11	3	2	.237	.275	.330	.604	51	-7	-8	103	96	9	.500	1	2	-1	1	3S	-0.4
1931	Chi-A	79	223	29	50	10	0	2	16	14	9	.224	.270	.296	.566	53	-17	-14	92	73	19	.480	3	0	1	-3	3/2SO	-1.0
1934	Phi-N	56	175	28	43	6	0	4	19	15	10	.246	.305	.349	.654	69	-6	-8	108	94	18	.565	2			-5	2/3	-0.7
Total	3	175	495	71	116	19	0	8	46	32	21	.234	.284	.321	.605	58	-30	-30	100	85	46	.514	6	2		-7	/32SO	-2.1
■ FRANK JELINICH Jelinich, Frank Anthony "Jelly" b: 9/3/19, San Jose, Cal. BR/TR, 6'2", 198 lbs. Deb: 9/06/41																												
1941	Chi-N	4	8	0	1	0	0	0	2	1	2	.125	.222	.125	.347	-1	-1	-1	94	722	0	.286	0			-1	/O	-0.1
■ GREG JELKS Jelks, Gregory Dion b: 8/16/61, Cherokee, Ala. BR/TR, 6'2", 190 lbs. Deb: 8/20/87																												
1987	Phi-N	10	11	2	1	1	0	0	0	3	4	.091	.286	.182	.468	26	-1	-1	104	0	1	.500	0	0	0	0	/31O	0.0
■ STEVE JELTZ Jeltz, Larry Steven b: 5/28/59, Paris, France BB/TR, 5'11", 180 lbs. Deb: 7/17/83																												
1983	Phi-N	13	8	0	1	0	1	0	1	1	2	.125	.222	.375	.597	62	-0	-0	101	132	0	.444	0	0	0	0	/2S3	0.0
1984	Phi-N	28	68	7	14	0	1	1	7	7	11	.206	.280	.279	.559	57	-4	-4	102	125	5	.483	2	1	0	-2	S/3	-0.2
1985	Phi-N	89	196	17	37	4	1	0	12	26	55	.189	.284	.219	.503	42	-14	-15	102	111	13	.422	1	1	-0	-4	S	-1.2
1986	Phi-N	145	439	44	96	11	4	0	36	65	97	.219	.321	.262	.583	60	-20	-23	104	125	40	.527	6	3	0	-5	*S	-1.4
1987	Phi-N	114	293	37	68	9	6	0	12	39	54	.232	.324	.304	.628	65	-13	-14	104	54	28	.542	1	2	-1	-6	*S/O	-0.7
1988	Phi-N	148	379	39	71	11	4	0	27	59	58	.187	.297	.237	.534	54	-20	-21	101	120	29	.476	3	0	1	-4	*S	-1.3
Total	6	537	1383	144	287	35	17	1	95	197	277	.208	.307	.260	.567	57	-72	-77	103	107	115	.513	13	7	-0	-19	S/23O	-4.8
■ JOHN JENKINS Jenkins, John Robert b: 7/7/1896, Bosworth, Mo. d: 8/3/68, Columbia, Mo. BR/TR, 5'8", 160 lbs. Deb: 8/05/22																												
1922	Chi-A	5	3	0	0	0	0	0	1	0	2	.000	.000	.000	.000	-99	-1	-1	101	0	0	.000	0	0	0	0	/2S	0.0
■ JOE JENKINS Jenkins, Joseph Daniel b: 10/12/1890, Shelbyville, Tenn. d: 6/21/74, Fresno, Cal. BR/TR, 5'11", 170 lbs. Deb: 4/30/14																												
1914	StL-A	19	32	0	4	1	1	0	0	1	11	.125	.152	.219	.370	11	-4	-4	98	0	1	.357	2			-0	/C	-0.2
1917	Chi-A	10	9	0	1	0	0	0	2	0	5	.111	.111	.111	.222	-33	-1	-1	98	718	0	.125	0			0	/C	0.0
1919	Chi-A	11	19	0	3	1	0	0	1	1	1	.158	.200	.211	.411	15	-2	-2	105	91	1	.375	1			0	/C	-0.1
Total	3	40	60	0	8	2	1	0	3	2	17	.133	.161	.200	.361	6	-7	-7	100	133	2	.327	3			-0	/C	-0.3
■ TOM JENKINS Jenkins, Thomas Griffith "Tut" b: 4/10/1898, Camden, Ala. d: 5/3/79, Weymouth, Mass. BL/TR, 6'1.5", 174 lbs. Deb: 9/15/25																												
1925	Bos-A	15	64	9	19	2	1	0	5	3	4	.297	.338	.359	.698	81	-2	-2	95	63	8	.600	0	0	0	-2	O	-0.4
1926	Bos-A	21	50	3	9	1	1	0	6	3	7	.180	.226	.240	.466	21	-6	-6	101	170	3	.366	0	0	0	-2	O	-0.7
	Phi-A	6	23	3	4	2	0	0	0	0	2	.174	.174	.261	.435	10	-3	-4	118	0	1	.316	0	0	0	0	/O	-0.3
	Yr	27	73	6	13	3	1	0	6	3	9	.178	.211	.247	.457	18	-9	-9	105	138	4	.350	0	0	0	-2		-1.0

YEAR	TM/L	G	AB	R	H	2B	3B	HR	RBI	BB	SO	AVG	OBP	SLG	PRO	/A	BR	/A	PF	CHI	RC	TA	SB	CS	SBR	FR	POS	TPR
1929	StL-A	21	22	1	4	0	1	0	0	4	8	.182	.308	.273	.580	51	-2	-2	100	0	2	.556	0	0	0	-1	/O	-0.2
1930	StL-A	2	8	1	2	1	1	0	3	0	1	.250	.250	.625	.875	105	0	-0	108	203	1	.833	0	0	0	-0	/O	0.0
1931	StL-A	81	230	20	61	7	2	3	25	17	25	.265	.316	.352	.668	74	-8	-9	102	92	25	.576	1	3	-2	-6	O	-1.8
1932	StL-A	25	62	5	20	1	0	0	5	1	6	.323	.333	.339	.672	74	-2	-2	100	80	7	.524	0	0	0	1	O	-0.1
Total	6	171	459	42	119	14	6	3	44	28	53	.259	.303	.336	.639	65	-23	-24	102	87	47	.536	1	3	-2	-9	O	-3.5

■ **ALAMAZOO JENNINGS** Jennings, Alfred Gorden b: 11/30/1850, Newport, Ky. d: 11/2/1894, Cincinnati, Ohio BR , Deb: 8/15/1878

YEAR	TM/L	G	AB	R	H	2B	3B	HR	RBI	BB	SO	AVG	OBP	SLG	PRO	/A	BR	/A	PF	CHI	RC	TA	SB	CS	SBR	FR	POS	TPR
1878	Mil-N	1	2	0	0	0	0	0	0	1	0	.000	.333	.000	.333	16	-0	-0	107	0	0	.500				0	/C	0.0

■ **HUGHIE JENNINGS** Jennings, Hugh Ambrose "Ee-Yah" b: 4/2/1869, Pittston, Pa. d: 2/1/28, Scranton, Pa. BR/TR, 5'8.5", 165 lbs. Deb: 6/01/1891 MCH

YEAR	TM/L	G	AB	R	H	2B	3B	HR	RBI	BB	SO	AVG	OBP	SLG	PRO	/A	BR	/A	PF	CHI	RC	TA	SB	CS	SBR	FR	POS	TPR
1891	Lou-a	90	360	53	105	10	8	1	58	17	36	.292	.339	.372	.712	118	2	8	90	130	51	.675	12			10	S1/3	1.7
1892	Lou-N	152	594	65	132	16	4	2	61	30	30	.222	.270	.273	.543	71	-25	-18	92	118	53	.496	28			11	*S	0.0
1893	Lou-N	23	88	6	12	3	0	0	9	3	3	.136	.174	.170	.344	-8	-14	-13	96	164	3	.250	0			0	S	-1.0
	Bal-N	16	55	6	14	0	0	1	6	4	3	.255	.339	.309	.648	70	-2	-3	107	82	6	.585	0			0	S/O	-0.1
	Yr	39	143	12	26	3	0	1	15	7	6	.182	.240	.224	.464	25	-15	-16	101	135	8	.368	0			0		-1.1
1894	Bal-N	128	501	134	168	28	16	4	109	37	17	.335	.411	.479	.890	116	14	14	99	122	117	1.024	37			32	*S	4.0
1895	Bal-N	131	529	159	204	41	7	4	125	24	17	.386	.444	.512	.957	139	39	32	107	131	148	1.169	53			**30**	*S	**5.8**
1896	Bal-N	130	521	125	209	27	9	0	121	19	11	.401	.472	.488	.960	153	46	44	102	132	157	1.263	70			30	*S	6.2
1897	Bal-N	117	439	133	156	26	9	2	79	42		.355	.463	.469	.932	157	37	41	95	116	126	1.251	60			26	*S	**5.8**
1898	Bal-N	143	534	135	175	25	11	1	87	78		.328	.451	.421	.872	149	45	43	103	102	117	1.039	28			1	*S2/O	4.5
1899	Bro-N	16	41	7	7	0	2	0	6	9		.171	.346	.268	.614	69	-1	-1	105	167	5	.765	4			0	S/1	0.0
	Bal-N	2	8	2	3	0	2	0	2	0		.375	.375	.875	1.250	224	1	1	108	93	3	1.400	0			0	/2	0.1
	Bro-N	51	175	35	57	3	8	0	34	13		.326	.389	.434	.823	123	7	6	105	140	36	.915	14			2	1/2S	0.7
	Yr	69	224	44	67	3	12	0	42	22		.299	.379	.420	.799	116	7	5	105	149	44	.898	18			2		0.8
1900	Bro-N	115	441	61	120	18	6	1	69	31		.272	.320	.347	.667	80	-8	-13	108	146	60	.670	31			5	*1/2	-0.5
1901	Phi-N	82	302	38	79	21	2	1	39	25		.262	.318	.354	.672	94	-1	-2	103	121	39	.650	13			-4	1/2S	-0.5
1902	Phi-N	78	290	32	79	13	4	1	32	14		.272	.306	.355	.661	100	1	-1	105	111	35	.592	8			1	1/S2	-0.1
1903	Bro-N	6	17	2	4	0	0	0	1	1		.235	.278	.235	.513	48	-1	-1	101	80	1	.462	1			0	/O	0.0
1907	Det-A	1	4	0	1	1	0	0	0	0		.250	.250	.500	.750	138	0	0	102	0	1	.667	0			0	/2SM	0.0
1909	Det-A	2	4	1	2	0	0	0	2	0		.500	.500	.500	1.000	196	0	0	110	386	1	1.000	0			0	/1M	0.0
1912	Det-A	1	1	0	0	0	0	0	0	0		.000	.000	.000	.000	-99	-0	-0	95	0	0	.000	0			0	HM	0.0
1918	Det-A	1	0	0	0	0	0	0	0	0	0	—	—	—	—	—	0	0	97	—	—	—	0			0	/1M	0.0
Total	17	1285	4904	994	1527	232	88	18	840	347	<u>117</u>	.311	.384	.406	.789	118	141	137	101	124	957	.865	359			142	S1/203	26.6

■ **DOUG JENNINGS** Jennings, James Douglas b: 9/30/64, Atlanta, Ga. BL/TL, 5'10", 165 lbs. Deb: 4/08/88

YEAR	TM/L	G	AB	R	H	2B	3B	HR	RBI	BB	SO	AVG	OBP	SLG	PRO	/A	BR	/A	PF	CHI	RC	TA	SB	CS	SBR	FR	POS	TPR
1988	Oak-A	71	101	9	21	6	0	1	15	21	28	.208	.355	.297	.652	89	-1	-0	95	181	12	.646	0	1	-1	-4	O1/SD	-0.5

■ **BILL JENNINGS** Jennings, William Lee b: 9/28/25, St.Louis, Mo. BR/TR, 6'2", 175 lbs. Deb: 7/19/51

YEAR	TM/L	G	AB	R	H	2B	3B	HR	RBI	BB	SO	AVG	OBP	SLG	PRO	/A	BR	/A	PF	CHI	RC	TA	SB	CS	SBR	FR	POS	TPR
1951	StL-A	64	195	20	35	10	2	0	13	26	42	.179	.276	.251	.527	41	-16	-17	105	95	15	.463	1	0	0	-7	S	-1.9

■ **WOODY JENSEN** Jensen, Forrest Docenus b: 8/11/07, Bremerton, Wash. BL/TL, 5'10.5", 160 lbs. Deb: 4/20/31

YEAR	TM/L	G	AB	R	H	2B	3B	HR	RBI	BB	SO	AVG	OBP	SLG	PRO	/A	BR	/A	PF	CHI	RC	TA	SB	CS	SBR	FR	POS	TPR
1931	Pit-N	73	267	43	65	5	4	3	17	10	18	.243	.276	.326	.602	61	-15	-15	101	64	25	.510	4			1	O	-1.7
1932	Pit-N	7	5	2	0	0	0	0	0	0	2	.000	.000	.000	.000	-99	-1	-1	99	0	0	.000	0			-0	/O	-0.1
1933	Pit-N	70	196	29	58	7	3	0	15	8	2	.296	.330	.362	.692	103	-1	0	95	79	25	.590	1			-1	O	-0.3
1934	Pit-N	88	283	34	82	13	4	0	27	4	13	.290	.304	.364	.668	74	-9	-11	105	94	30	.531	2			-3	O	-1.6
1935	Pit-N	143	627	97	203	28	7	8	62	15	14	.324	.344	.429	.773	99	4	-1	107	67	90	.677	9			-7	*O	-1.3
1936	Pit-N	153	696	98	197	34	10	10	58	16	19	.283	.305	.404	.709	92	-13	-11	98	57	84	.595	2			-1	*O	-1.8
1937	Pit-N	124	509	77	142	23	9	5	45	15	29	.279	.301	.389	.690	84	-11	-13	102	81	58	.568	2			-0	*O	-1.8
1938	Pit-N	68	125	12	25	4	0	0	10	1	3	.200	.213	.232	.445	22	-13	-13	100	125	6	.301	0			-11	O	-2.4
1939	Pit-N	12	12	0	2	0	0	0	1	0	0	.167	.167	.167	.333	-10	-2	-2	100	183	0	.182	0			-1	/O	-0.2
Total	9	738	2720	392	774	114	37	26	235	69	100	.285	.307	.382	.689	84	-61	-67	102	74	318	.589	20			-23	O	-11.2

■ **JACKIE JENSEN** Jensen, Jack Eugene b: 3/9/27, San Francisco, Cal. d: 7/14/82, Charlottesville, Va. BR/TR, 5'11", 190 lbs. Deb: 4/18/50

YEAR	TM/L	G	AB	R	H	2B	3B	HR	RBI	BB	SO	AVG	OBP	SLG	PRO	/A	BR	/A	PF	CHI	RC	TA	SB	CS	SBR	FR	POS	TPR
1950	NY-A	45	70	13	12	2	2	1	5	7	8	.171	.247	.300	.547	40	-7	-7	99	72	5	.525	4	0	1	-5	O	-0.9
1951	NY-A	56	168	30	50	8	1	8	25	18	18	.298	.369	.500	.869	146	7	9	92	83	34	.917	8	2	1	3	O	1.1
1952	NY-A	7	19	3	2	1	1	0	2	4	4	.105	.261	.263	.524	47	-1	-1	98	149	1	.556	1	0	0	-1	/O	-0.1
	Was-A	144	570	80	163	29	5	10	80	63	40	.286	.360	.407	.767	113	10	10	100	110	86	.736	17	6	2	3	*O	1.1
	Yr	151	589	83	165	30	6	10	82	67	44	.280	.357	.402	.759	111	9	9	100	112	88	.730	18	6	**2**	2		1.0
1953	Was-A	147	552	87	147	32	8	10	84	73	51	.266	.357	.408	.765	112	5	9	94	129	82	.743	18	8	1	-6	*O	0.0
1954	Bos-A	152	580	92	160	25	7	25	117	79	52	.276	.365	.472	.837	128	21	21	100	135	94	.821	**22**	7	2	-16	*O	0.4
1955	Bos-A	152	574	95	158	27	6	26	**116**	89	63	.275	.375	.479	.854	103	23	4	124	130	102	.865	16	7	1	-2	*O	-0.4
1956	Bos-A	151	578	80	182	23	**11**	20	97	89	43	.315	.407	.497	.904	134	33	31	103	111	116	.919	11	3	2	-1	*O	2.3
1957	Bos-A	145	544	82	153	29	2	23	103	75	66	.281	.370	.469	.839	116	21	14	110	133	91	.813	8	5	-1	1	*O	0.6
1958	Bos-A	154	548	83	157	31	0	35	**122**	99	65	.286	.398	.535	.933	147	43	39	105	130	120	.990	9	4	0	4	*O	3.4
1959	Bos-A	148	535	101	148	31	0	28	**112**	88	67	.277	.379	.492	.870	130	28	24	106	135	100	.900	20	5	3	11	*O	3.1
1961	Bos-A	137	498	64	131	21	2	13	66	66	69	.263	.353	.392	.744	97	0	-1	102	113	68	.698	9	8	-2	9	*O	0.1
Total	11	1438	5236	810	1463	259	45	199	929	750	546	.279	.372	.460	.832	119	184	152	104	123	900	.865	143	55	10	1	*O	10.7

■ **DAN JESSEE** Jessee, Daniel Edward b: 2/22/01, Olive Hill, Ky. d: 4/30/70, Venice, Fla. BL/TR, 5'10", 165 lbs. Deb: 8/14/29

YEAR	TM/L	G	AB	R	H	2B	3B	HR	RBI	BB	SO	AVG	OBP	SLG	PRO	/A	BR	/A	PF	CHI	RC	TA	SB	CS	SBR	FR	POS	TPR
1929	Cle-A	1	0	0	0	0	0	0	0	0	0	—	—	—	—	—	0	0	100	—	—	—	0	0	0	0	R	0.0

■ **GARRY JESTADT** Jestadt, Garry Arthur b: 3/19/47, Chicago, Ill. BR/TR, 6'2", 188 lbs. Deb: 9/17/69

YEAR	TM/L	G	AB	R	H	2B	3B	HR	RBI	BB	SO	AVG	OBP	SLG	PRO	/A	BR	/A	PF	CHI	RC	TA	SB	CS	SBR	FR	POS	TPR
1969	Mon-N	6	6	1	0	0	0	0	1	0	0	.000	.000	.000	.000	-99	-2	-2	100	0	0	.000	0	0	0	0	/S	0.0
1971	Chi-N	3	3	0	0	0	0	0	0	0	0	.000	.000	.000	.000	-91	-1	-1	110	0	0	.000	0	0	0	0	/3	0.0
	SD-N	75	189	17	55	13	0	0	13	11	24	.291	.330	.360	.690	99	-1	-0	96	78	19	.548	1	3	-2	1	32/S	0.0
	Yr	78	192	17	55	13	0	0	13	11	24	.286	.325	.354	.679	95	-2	-1	97	75	19	.537	1	3	-2	1		0.0
1972	SD-N	92	256	15	63	5	1	6	22	13	21	.246	.283	.344	.626	87	-8	-5	88	85	24	.510	0	0	0	-5	23/S	-0.6
Total	3	176	454	33	118	18	1	6	36	24	45	.260	.297	.344	.641	88	-12	-8	92	80	44	.526	1	3	-2	-4	/32S	-0.6

■ **JOHNNY JETER** Jeter, John b: 10/24/44, Shreveport, La. BR/TR, 6'1", 180 lbs. Deb: 6/14/69

YEAR	TM/L	G	AB	R	H	2B	3B	HR	RBI	BB	SO	AVG	OBP	SLG	PRO	/A	BR	/A	PF	CHI	RC	TA	SB	CS	SBR	FR	POS	TPR
1969	Pit-N	28	29	7	9	1	1	1	6	3	15	.310	.375	.517	.892	156	2	2	95	134	6	.905	1	1	-0	-4	O	-0.3
1970	Pit-N	85	126	27	30	3	2	2	12	13	34	.238	.314	.341	.656	78	-4	-4	97	95	13	.635	9	5	-0	-9	O	-1.5
1971	SD-N	18	75	8	24	4	0	1	3	2	16	.320	.338	.413	.751	116	1	1	96	32	11	.673	2	0	1	5	O	0.7
1972	SD-N	110	326	25	72	4	3	7	21	18	92	.221	.266	.316	.582	73	-16	-11	88	70	25	.500	11	5	0	-3	O	-1.9
1973	Chi-A	89	300	38	72	14	4	7	26	9	74	.240	.262	.383	.645	78	-9	-10	102	75	28	.542	4	3	-1	-1	O/D	-1.3
1974	Cle-A	6	17	3	6	1	0	0	1	1	6	.353	.389	.412	.801	129	1	1	101	56	2	.643	1	2	-1	-2	/O	-0.2
Total	6	336	873	108	213	27	10	18	69	46	237	.244	.284	.360	.644	83	-26	-21	95	74	85	.578	28	16	-1	-13	O/D	-4.5

■ **SAM JETHROE** Jethroe, Samuel "Jet" b: 1/20/22, E.St.Louis, Ill. BB/TR, 6'1", 178 lbs. Deb: 4/18/50

YEAR	TM/L	G	AB	R	H	2B	3B	HR	RBI	BB	SO	AVG	OBP	SLG	PRO	/A	BR	/A	PF	CHI	RC	TA	SB	CS	SBR	FR	POS	TPR
1950	Bos-N	141	582	100	159	28	8	18	58	52	93	.273	.338	.442	.780	120	2	13	86	64	89	.810	**35**			5	*O	1.2
1951	Bos-N	148	572	101	160	29	10	18	65	57	88	.280	.356	.460	.816	120	14	15	98	84	103	.863	**35**	5	**8**	-0	*O	1.8
1952	Bos-N	151	608	79	141	23	7	13	58	68	112	.232	.318	.357	.675	92	-11	-7	95	76	76	.665	28	9	3	2	*O	-0.5
1954	Pit-N	2	1	0	0	0	0	0	0	0	0	.000	.000	.000	.000	-99	-0	-0	97	0	0	.000	0	0	0	-0	/O	0.0
Total	4	442	1763	280	460	80	25	49	181	177	293	.261	.337	.418	.755	110	5	21	93	75	267	.787	98	<u>14</u>		6	O	2.5

■ **NAT JEWETT** Jewett, Nathan W. b: 12/25/1842, New York, N.Y. d: 2/23/14, Bronx, N.Y. 5'6", 137 lbs. Deb: 7/04/1872

YEAR	TM/L	G	AB	R	H	2B	3B	HR	RBI	BB	SO	AVG	OBP	SLG	PRO	/A	BR	/A	PF	CHI	RC	TA	SB	CS	SBR	FR	POS	TPR
1872	Eck-n	2	8	1	1							.125															/C	

■ **HOUSTON JIMENEZ** Jimenez, Alfonso (Gonzalez) b: 10/30/57, Navojoa, Sonora, Mex BR/TR, 5'8", 144 lbs. Deb: 6/13/83

YEAR	TM/L	G	AB	R	H	2B	3B	HR	RBI	BB	SO	AVG	OBP	SLG	PRO	/A	BR	/A	PF	CHI	RC	TA	SB	CS	SBR	FR	POS	TPR
1983	Min-A	36	86	5	15	5	1	0	9	4	11	.174	.211	.256	.467	26	-9	-9	105	160	5	.361	0	1	-1	-6	S	-1.3

YEAR	TM/L	G	AB	R	H	2B	3B	HR	RBI	BB	SO	AVG	OBP	SLG	PRO	/A	BR	/A	PF	CHI	RC	TA	SB	CS	SBR	FR	POS	TPR
1984	Min-A	108	298	28	60	11	1	0	19	15	34	.201	.240	.245	.485	33	-26	-28	106	104	17	.358	0	1	-1	-18	*S	-3.8
1987	Pit-N	5	6	0	0	0	0	0	0	1	2	.000	.143	.000	.143	-56	-1	-1	104	0	0	.167	0	0	0	0	/2S	0.0
1988	Cle-A	9	21	1	1	0	0	0	1	0	2	.048	.048	.048	.095	-72	-5	-5	102	398	0	.048	0	0	0	-0	/2S	-0.4
Total	4	158	411	34	76	16	2	0	29	20	49	.185	.223	.234	.456	25	-41	-44	105	128	21	.343	0	2	-1	-24	S/2	-5.5
■ **ELVIO JIMENEZ**	Jimenez, Felix Elvio (Rivera) b: 1/6/40, San Pedro De Macoris, D.R. BR/TR, 5'9", 170 lbs. Deb: 10/04/64																											
1964	NY-A	1	6	0	2	0	0	0	0	0	0	.333	.333	.333	.667	84	-0	-0	103	0	1	.500	0	0	0	0	/O	0.0
■ **MANNY JIMENEZ**	Jimenez, Manuel Emilio (Rivera) b: 11/19/38, San Pedro De Macoris, D.R. BL/TR, 6'1", 185 lbs. Deb: 4/11/62																											
1962	KC-A	139	479	48	144	24	2	11	69	31	34	.301	.357	.428	.785	110	7	7	100	115	72	.710	0	1	-1	-7	*O	-0.5
1963	KC-A	60	157	12	44	9	0	0	15	16	14	.280	.365	.338	.703	92	0	-1	108	118	19	.617	0	1	-1	1	O	-0.2
1964	KC-A	95	204	19	46	7	0	12	38	15	24	.225	.295	.436	.731	96	-1	-2	105	129	21	.630	0	0	0	-5	O	-0.8
1966	KC-A	13	35	1	4	0	1	0	1	6	4	.114	.244	.171	.415	23	-3	-3	94	70	2	.375	0	0	0	-2	O	-0.6
1967	Pit-N	50	56	3	14	2	0	2	10	1	4	.250	.276	.393	.669	89	-1	-1	100	148	5	.522	0	0	0	-2	/O	-0.2
1968	Pit-N	66	66	7	20	1	1	1	11	6	15	.303	.403	.394	.797	138	4	4	101	160	11	.787	0	0	0	-1	/O	0.3
1969	Chi-N	6	6	0	1	0	0	0	0	0	2	.167	.167	.167	.333	-6	-1	-1	107	0	0	.167	0	0	0	0	H	0.0
Total	7	429	1003	90	273	43	4	26	144	75	97	.272	.339	.401	.740	101	5	3	102	121	130	.688	0	2	-1	-17	O	-2.0
■ **TOMMY JOHNS**	Johns, Thomas Pearce b: 9/7/1851, Baltimore, Md. d: 4/13/27, Baltimore, Md. Deb: 5/14/1873																											
1873	Mar-n	1	5	0	0							.000															/O	
■ **PETE JOHNS**	Johns, William R. b: 1/17/1889, Cleveland, Ohio d: 8/9/64, Cleveland, Ohio BR/TR, 5'10", 165 lbs. Deb: 8/25/15																											
1915	Chi-A	28	100	7	21	2	1	0	11	8	11	.210	.275	.250	.525	59	-5	-5	98	153	6	.419	2	7	-4	-5	3	-1.2
1918	StL-A	46	89	5	16	1	1	0	11	4	6	.180	.215	.213	.429	30	-8	-8	99	211	4	.315	0			1	1/S302	-0.8
Total	2	74	189	12	37	3	2	0	22	12	17	.196	.248	.233	.480	45	-13	-13	98	180	10	.371	2	7		-4	/310S2	-2.0
■ **ABBIE JOHNSON**	Johnson, Albert J. b: 7/26/1872, Sweden d: 5/2/24, Oak Forest, Ill. Deb: 9/01/1896																											
1896	Lou-N	25	87	10	20	2	1	0	14	4	6	.230	.264	.276	.540	45	-7	-7	98	168	6	.418	0			0	2	-0.5
1897	Lou-N	48	161	16	39	6	1	0	23	13		.242	.303	.292	.595	62	-9	-8	95	143	15	.516	2			-11	2S	-1.3
Total	2	73	248	26	59	8	2	0	37	17	6	.238	.289	.286	.576	56	-16	-15	96	152	22	.481	2			-11	/2S	-1.8
■ **ALEX JOHNSON**	Johnson, Alexander b: 12/7/42, Helena, Ark. BR/TR, 6', 205 lbs. Deb: 7/25/64																											
1964	Phi-N	43	109	18	33	7	1	4	18	6	26	.303	.345	.495	.840	135	5	5	99	112	18	.785	1	2	-1	-3	O	0.0
1965	Phi-N	97	262	27	77	9	3	8	28	15	60	.294	.337	.443	.780	124	6	7	95	83	37	.706	4	4	-1	-7	O	-0.3
1966	StL-N	25	86	7	16	0	1	2	6	5	18	.186	.231	.279	.510	41	-7	-7	100	84	4	.400	1	1	-0	-3	O	-1.0
1967	StL-N	81	175	20	39	9	2	1	12	9	26	.223	.273	.314	.587	67	-7	-8	101	86	15	.514	6	3	0	2	O	-0.9
1968	Cin-N	149	603	79	188	32	6	2	58	26	71	.312	.343	.395	.738	109	14	8	111	106	77	.645	16	6	1	-4	*O	-0.1
1969	Cin-N	139	523	86	165	18	4	17	88	25	69	.315	.357	.463	.820	130	18	19	99	123	82	.755	11	8	-2	-8	*O	0.2
1970	Cal-A	156	614	85	202	26	6	14	86	35	68	**.329**	.372	.459	.831	140	22	29	92	114	99	.777	17	2	4	-1	*O	2.5
1971	Cal-A	65	242	19	63	8	0	2	21	15	34	.260	.309	.318	.627	79	-7	-7	99	105	22	.518	5	2	0	-8	O	-1.7
1972	Cle-A	108	356	31	85	10	1	8	37	22	40	.239	.285	.340	.625	80	-7	-10	107	107	30	.519	6	8	-3	-9	O	-2.7
1973	Tex-A	158	624	62	179	26	3	8	68	32	82	.287	.324	.377	.700	100	-4	-2	97	109	72	.597	10	5	0	-0	*DO	-0.2
1974	Tex-A	114	453	57	132	14	3	4	41	28	59	.291	.338	.362	.700	106	1	3	96	97	52	.622	20	9	1	1	OD	0.3
	NY-A	10	28	3	6	1	0	1	2	0	3	.214	.214	.357	.571	65	-1	-1	96	60	2	.455	0	0	0	-0	/OD	-0.1
	Yr	124	481	60	138	15	3	5	43	28	62	.287	.331	.362	.693	104	-1	2	96	95	61	.642	20	9	1	1		0.2
1975	NY-A	52	119	15	31	5	1	1	15	7	21	.261	.302	.345	.646	83	-3	-3	99	131	11	.526	2	3	-1	-1	D/O	-0.5
1976	Det-A	125	429	41	115	15	2	6	45	19	49	.268	.302	.354	.657	89	-5	-7	104	102	41	.552	14	10	-2	-6	OD	-1.7
Total	13	1322	4623	550	1331	180	33	78	525	244	626	.288	.329	.392	.720	105	23	26	100	106	563	.654	113	63	-4	-47	OD	-6.2
■ **TONY JOHNSON**	Johnson, Anthony Clair b: 6/23/56, Memphis, Tenn. BR/TR, 6'3", 145 lbs. Deb: 9/28/81																											
1981	Mon-N	2	1	0	0	0	0	0	0	0	0	.000	.000	.000	.000	-99	-0	-0	99	0	0	.000	0	0	0	-0	/O	0.0
1982	Tor-A	70	98	17	23	2	1	3	14	11	26	.235	.312	.367	.679	79	-2	-3	109	124	7	.562	3	13	-7	-3	OD	-1.2
Total	2	72	99	17	23	2	1	3	14	11	26	.232	.309	.364	.673	78	-2	-3	108	123	7	.556	3	13	-7	-3	/OD	-1.2
■ **BOB JOHNSON**	Johnson, Bobby Earl b: 7/31/59, Dallas, Tex. BR/TR, 6'3", 195 lbs. Deb: 9/01/81																											
1981	Tex-A	6	18	2	5	0	0	2	4	1	3	.278	.316	.611	.927	178	1	1	91	92	3	.857	0	0	0	1	/C1	0.2
1982	Tex-A	20	56	4	7	2	0	2	7	3	22	.125	.183	.268	.451	24	-6	-6	93	133	2	.358	0	1	-1	2	C/1	-0.2
1983	Tex-A	72	175	18	37	6	1	5	16	16	55	.211	.281	.343	.624	70	-7	-7	101	83	16	.552	3	0	1	-0	C1	-0.4
Total	3	98	249	24	49	8	1	9	27	20	80	.197	.262	.345	.607	67	-12	-12	99	95	21	.534	3	1	0	2	/C1	-0.4
■ **CALEB JOHNSON**	Johnson, Caleb Clark b: 5/23/1844, Fulton, Ill. d: 3/7/25, Sterling, Ill. Deb: 5/24/1871																											
1871	Cle-n	16	65	10	16							.246															/2OS	
■ **CHARLIE JOHNSON**	Johnson, Charles Cleveland "Home Run" b: 3/12/1885, Slatington, Pa. d: 8/28/40, Marcus Hook, Pa. 5'9", 150 lbs. Deb: 9/21/08																											
1908	Phi-N	6	16	2	4	0	1	0	2	1		.250	.294	.375	.669	116	0	0	100	128	2	.583	0			0	/O	0.0
■ **CLIFF JOHNSON**	Johnson, Clifford b: 7/22/47, San Antonio, Tex. BR/TR, 6'4", 215 lbs. Deb: 9/13/72																											
1972	Hou-N	5	4	0	1	0	0	0	0	2	0	.250	.500	.250	.750	112	0	0	106	0	1	1.000	0	0	0	0	/C	0.0
1973	Hou-N	7	20	6	6	2	0	2	6	1	7	.300	.364	.700	1.064	198	2	2	95	121	5	1.143	0	0	0	-0	/1	0.2
1974	Hou-N	83	171	26	39	4	1	10	29	33	45	.228	.362	.439	.801	126	6	6	98	107	28	.804	0	1	-1	1	C1	0.7
1975	Hou-N	122	340	52	94	16	1	20	65	46	64	.276	.371	.506	.877	150	19	21	94	108	65	.885	1	0	0	-0	1C/O	2.0
1976	Hou-N	108	318	36	72	21	2	10	49	62	59	.226	.359	.399	.759	133	8	14	86	120	48	.757	0	0	0	-2	CO1	1.4
1977	Hou-N	51	144	22	43	8	0	10	23	23	30	.299	.409	.563	.972	170	12	14	93	83	35	1.049	0	1	-1	-1	O1	1.0
	NY-A	56	142	24	42	8	0	12	31	20	23	.296	.405	.606	1.010	174	14	15	99	101	36	1.087	0	1	-1	0	DC1	1.3
1978	NY-A	76	174	20	32	9	1	6	19	30	32	.184	.307	.351	.658	86	-3	-3	99	95	19	.622	0	0	0	-0	DC/1	-0.2
1979	NY-A	28	64	11	17	6	0	2	6	10	7	.266	.365	.453	.818	125	2	2	96	66	11	.830	0	0	0	0	D/C	0.2
	Cle-A	72	240	37	65	10	0	18	61	24	39	.271	.349	.538	.887	128	11	9	106	128	45	.884	2	0	1	0	D/C	1.0
	Yr	100	304	48	82	16	0	20	67	34	46	.270	.353	.520	.873	128	13	12	103	111	57	.873	2	0	1	0		1.2
1980	Cle-A	54	174	25	40	3	1	6	28	25	30	.230	.327	.362	.689	86	-2	-3	102	135	19	.615	0	1	-1	0	D	-0.3
	Chi-N	68	196	28	46	8	0	10	34	29	35	.235	.336	.429	.765	106	3	2	106	118	29	.740	0	0	0	-0	1/OC	0.0
1981	Oak-A	84	273	40	71	8	0	17	59	28	60	.260	.336	.476	.812	137	10	12	96	128	44	.798	5	3	-0	0	D/1	1.2
1982	Oak-A	73	214	19	51	10	0	7	31	26	41	.238	.326	.383	.710	99	-2	-0	95	120	27	.661	1	2	-1	-0	D1	-0.1
1983	Tor-A	142	407	59	108	23	1	22	76	67	69	.265	.376	.489	.865	125	21	16	108	112	76	.874	0	1	-1	0	*D/1	1.6
1984	Tor-A	127	359	51	109	23	1	16	61	50	62	.304	.393	.507	.900	145	24	23	102	106	72	.904	0	1	-1	0	*D/1	2.2
1985	Tex-A	82	296	31	76	17	1	12	56	31	44	.257	.333	.443	.776	102	4	1	108	141	45	.740	0	0	0	0	D	0.1
	Tor-A	24	73	4	20	0	0	1	10	9	15	.274	.354	.315	.669	84	-1	-1	101	153	9	.593	0	0	0	0	D/1	0.0
	Yr	106	369	35	96	17	1	13	66	40	59	.260	.337	.417	.755	99	3	-0	107	145	56	.719	0	0	0	0		0.1
1986	Tor-A	107	336	48	84	12	1	15	55	52	57	.250	.357	.426	.783	108	7	5	105	117	52	.760	0	1	-1	0	D/1	0.3
Total	15	1369	3945	539	1016	188	10	196	699	568	719	.258	.358	.459	.817	124	136	135	100	115	667	.827	9	12	-5	-3	D1C/O	12.6
■ **DARRELL JOHNSON**	Johnson, Darrell Dean b: 8/25/28, Horace, Neb. BR/TR, 6'1", 180 lbs. Deb: 4/20/52 MC																											
1952	StL-A	29	78	9	22	2	1	0	9	11	4	.282	.371	.333	.704	100	0	0	97	129	10	.638	0	0	0	1	C	0.3
	Chi-A	22	37	3	4	0	0	0	1	5	9	.108	.214	.108	.322	-9	-5	-5	100	93	1	.294	1	0	0	-2	C	-0.6
	Yr	51	115	12	26	2	1	0	10	16	13	.226	.321	.261	.581	64	-5	-5	98	116	11	.522	1	0	0	-1		-0.3
1957	NY-A	21	46	4	10	1	0	1	8	3	10	.217	.280	.304	.584	64	-3	-2	94	186	4	.486	0	0	0	1	C	0.0
1958	NY-A	5	16	1	4	0	0	0	0	0	2	.250	.250	.250	.500	37	-1	-1	103	0	1	.333	0	0	0	0	/C	0.0
1960	StL-N	8	2	0	0	0	0	0	0	1	0	.000	.333	.000	.333	1	-0	-0	108	0	0	.500	0	0	0	-0	/C	0.0
1961	Phi-N	21	61	4	14	1	0	0	3	3	8	.230	.277	.246	.523	43	-5	-5	94	81	4	.388	0	0	0	1	C	-0.1
	Cin-N	20	54	3	17	2	0	1	6	1	2	.315	.327	.407	.735	90	-1	-1	104	97	7	.605	0	0	0	-0	C	0.0
	Yr	41	115	7	31	3	0	1	9	4	10	.270	.300	.322	.622	66	-6	-6	99	90	11	.494	0	0	0	0		-0.1

YEAR	TM/L	G	AB	R	H	2B	3B	HR	RBI	BB	SO	AVG	OBP	SLG	PRO	/A	BR	/A	PF	CHI	RC	TA	SB	CS	SBR	FR	POS	TPR
1962	Cin-N	2	4	0	0	0	0	0	0	2	0	.000	.333	.000	.333	-2	-0	-1	102	0	0	.500	0	0	0	1	/C	0.0
	Bal-A	6	22	0	4	0	0	0	1	0	4	.182	.182	.182	.364	-2	-3	-3	95	99	1	.222	0	0	0	-0	/C	-0.2
Total	6	134	320	24	75	6	1	2	28	26	39	.234	.296	.278	.574	58	-19	-18	98	108	28	.482	1	0	0	1	C	-0.6

■ **DAVE JOHNSON** Johnson, David Allen b: 1/30/43, Orlando, Fla. BR/TR, 6'1", 170 lbs. Deb: 4/13/65 M

YEAR	TM/L	G	AB	R	H	2B	3B	HR	RBI	BB	SO	AVG	OBP	SLG	PRO	/A	BR	/A	PF	CHI	RC	TA	SB	CS	SBR	FR	POS	TPR
1965	Bal-A	20	47	5	8	3	0	0	1	5	6	.170	.250	.234	.484	38	-4	-4	100	38	3	.452	3	0	1	0	/32S	-0.2
1966	Bal-A	131	501	47	129	20	3	7	56	31	64	.257	.302	.351	.653	86	-9	-9	101	122	52	.549	3	4	-2	-1	*2/S	0.0
1967	Bal-A	148	510	62	126	30	3	10	64	59	82	.247	.330	.376	.706	115	6	9	95	123	63	.646	4	5	-2	2	*2/3	1.5
1968	Bal-A	145	504	50	122	24	4	9	56	44	80	.242	.309	.359	.668	100	1	-0	102	118	53	.588	7	3	0	2	*2S	1.0
1969	Bal-A	142	511	52	143	34	1	7	57	57	52	.280	.356	.391	.747	105	7	4	104	106	70	.678	3	4	-2	-4	*2/S	0.5
1970	Bal-A	149	530	68	149	27	1	10	53	66	68	.281	.361	.392	.753	111	7	9	97	92	77	.702	2	1	0	-4	*2/S	2.0
1971	Bal-A	142	510	67	144	26	1	18	72	51	55	.282	.353	.443	.796	121	16	14	103	107	79	.746	3	1	0	-5	*2	1.7
1972	Bal-A	118	376	31	83	22	3	5	32	52	68	.221	.322	.335	.657	98	-1	0	98	97	41	.602	1	1	-0	2	*2	0.9
1973	Atl-N	157	559	84	151	25	0	43	99	81	93	.270	.371	.546	.917	134	38	29	113	94	116	.955	5	3	-0	-9	*2	2.6
1974	Atl-N	136	454	56	114	18	0	15	62	75	59	.251	.361	.390	.751	105	8	5	105	110	64	.713	1	2	-1	-0	12	0.4
1975	Atl-N	1	1	0	1	1	0	0	1	0	0	1.000	1.000	2.000	3.000	754	1	1	95	193	2	—	0	0	0	0	H	0.1
1977	Phi-N	78	156	23	50	9	1	8	36	23	20	.321	.414	.545	.959	154	13	13	100	132	35	.991	1	1	-0	1	1/23	1.1
1978	Phi-N	44	89	14	17	2	0	2	14	10	19	.191	.287	.281	.568	56	-5	-5	105	179	8	.500	0	0	0	1	2/31	-0.3
	Chi-N	24	49	5	15	1	1	2	6	5	9	.306	.393	.490	.883	132	3	2	110	79	10	.886	0	0	0	1	3	0.3
	Yr	68	138	19	32	3	1	4	20	15	28	.232	.325	.355	.680	84	-2	-3	107	146	17	.636	0	0	0	2		0.0
Total	13	1435	4797	564	1252	242	18	136	609	559	675	.261	.343	.404	.747	110	80	67	102	108	673	.720	33	25	-5	-13	*21/S3	11.6

■ **DERON JOHNSON** Johnson, Deron Roger b: 7/17/38, San Diego, Cal. BR/TR, 6'2", 200 lbs. Deb: 9/20/60 C

YEAR	TM/L	G	AB	R	H	2B	3B	HR	RBI	BB	SO	AVG	OBP	SLG	PRO	/A	BR	/A	PF	CHI	RC	TA	SB	CS	SBR	FR	POS	TPR
1960	NY-A	6	4	0	2	1	0	0	0	0	0	.500	.500	.750	1.250	247	1	1	94	0	2	1.500	0	0	0	0	/3	0.1
1961	NY-A	13	19	1	2	0	0	0	2	2	5	.105	.190	.105	.296	-19	-3	-3	96	392	0	.211	0	0	0	0	/3	-0.1
	KC-A	83	283	31	61	11	3	8	42	14	44	.216	.255	.360	.615	61	-16	-17	102	131	24	.504	0	1	-1	1	O3/1	-1.7
	Yr	96	302	32	63	11	3	8	44	16	49	.209	.251	.344	.595	57	-19	-20	101	170	24	.486	0	1	-1	1		-1.8
1962	KC-A	17	19	1	2	1	0	0	0	3	8	.105	.227	.158	.385	6	-3	-3	100	0	1	.333	0	0	0	-0	/13O	-0.2
1964	Cin-N	140	477	63	130	24	4	21	79	37	98	.273	.328	.472	.799	118	13	11	103	113	71	.740	4	3	-1	2	*1O/3	0.8
1965	Cin-N	159	616	92	177	30	7	32	**130**	52	97	.287	.345	.515	.859	133	30	27	104	**138**	105	.814	0	4	-2	-10	*3	0.8
1966	Cin-N	142	505	75	130	25	3	24	81	39	87	.257	.313	.461	.775	98	7	-1	114	114	70	.705	1	2	-1	-10	*O13	-1.9
1967	Cin-N	108	361	39	81	18	1	13	53	22	104	.224	.273	.388	.661	80	-7	-11	109	123	36	.567	0	1	-1	-4	13	-2.2
1968	Atl-N	127	342	29	71	11	1	8	33	35	79	.208	.287	.316	.603	87	-8	-5	93	105	31	.520	0	1	-1	-3	13	-1.4
1969	Phi-N	138	475	51	121	19	4	17	80	60	111	.255	.338	.419	.757	113	7	8	98	131	66	.709	4	2	0	-9	O31	-0.6
1970	Phi-N	159	574	66	147	28	3	27	93	72	132	.256	.339	.456	.795	115	8	11	96	107	89	.759	0	0	0	-12	*1/3	-1.3
1971	Phi-N	158	582	74	154	29	0	34	95	72	146	.265	.348	.490	.837	131	26	24	103	106	96	.803	0	1	-1	5	*13	1.8
1972	Phi-N	96	230	19	49	4	1	9	31	26	69	.213	.301	.357	.658	89	-4	-3	97	117	24	.587	0	1	-1	-2	1	-1.0
1973	Phi-N	12	36	3	6	2	0	1	5	5	10	.167	.286	.306	.591	59	-2	-2	108	143	3	.548	0	0	0	0	1	-0.2
	Oak-A	131	464	61	114	14	2	19	81	59	116	.246	.332	.407	.739	123	4	12	87	132	63	.688	0	1	-1	-2	*D1	0.9
1974	Oak-A	50	174	16	34	1	2	7	23	11	37	.195	.243	.345	.588	67	-8	-8	100	114	13	.490	1	0	0	-1	1D	-1.0
	Mil-A	49	152	14	23	3	0	6	18	21	41	.151	.254	.289	.544	55	-9	-9	102	114	11	.496	1	0	0	0	D/1	-0.8
	Bos-A	11	25	0	3	0	0	0	2	0	6	.120	.120	.120	.240	-29	-4	-4	107	262	0	.136	0	0	0	0	/D	-0.4
	Yr	110	351	30	60	4	2	13	43	32	84	.171	.240	.305	.545	55	-21	-22	102	131	28	.485	2	0	1	-1		-2.2
1975	Chi-A	148	555	66	129	25	1	18	72	48	117	.232	.295	.378	.673	86	-9	-12	103	107	58	.581	0	1	-1	-1	D1	-1.6
	Bos-A	3	10	2	6	0	0	1	3	2	0	.600	.667	.900	1.567	312	3	3	109	98	6	2.750	0	0	0	0	/1D	0.3
	Yr	151	565	68	135	25	1	19	75	50	117	.239	.302	.388	.690	91	-6	-9	103	107	70	.626	0	1	-1	-1		-1.3
1976	Bos-A	15	38	3	5	1	1	0	0	5	11	.132	.233	.211	.443	27	-3	-4	110	0	2	.371	0	0	0	0	/1D	-0.4
Total	16	1765	5941	706	1447	247	33	245	923	585	1318	.244	.313	.420	.733	103	21	14	101	118	772	.689	11	18	-8	-46	13DO	-10.1

■ **DON JOHNSON** Johnson, Donald Spore "Pep" b: 12/7/11, Chicago, Ill. BR/TR, 6', 170 lbs. Deb: 9/26/43

YEAR	TM/L	G	AB	R	H	2B	3B	HR	RBI	BB	SO	AVG	OBP	SLG	PRO	/A	BR	/A	PF	CHI	RC	TA	SB	CS	SBR	FR	POS	TPR
1943	Chi-N	10	42	5	8	2	0	0	1	2	4	.190	.227	.238	.465	35	-4	-4	99	35	2	.353	0			2	2	-0.1
1944	Chi-N	154	608	50	169	37	1	2	71	28	48	.278	.311	.352	.663	86	-12	-13	101	118	65	.558	8			0	*2	0.3
1945	Chi-N	138	557	94	168	23	2	2	58	32	34	.302	.343	.361	.704	97	-4	-3	99	94	70	.614	9			10	*2	1.9
1946	Chi-N	83	314	37	76	10	1	1	19	26	39	.242	.306	.290	.596	74	-12	-10	94	80	29	.514	6			-8	2	-1.6
1947	Chi-N	120	402	33	104	17	2	3	26	24	45	.259	.302	.333	.635	68	-18	-19	101	67	41	.531	2			3	*2/3	-0.3
1948	Chi-N	6	12	0	3	0	0	0	0	0	1	.250	.250	.250	.500	38	-1	-1	93	0	1	.400	1			0	/23	0.0
Total	6	511	1935	219	528	89	6	8	175	112	171	.273	.315	.337	.653	82	-51	-49	99	92	208	.567	26			7	2/3	0.2

■ **ED JOHNSON** Johnson, Edwin Cyril b: 3/31/1899, Morganfield, Ky. d: 7/3/75, Morganfield, Ky. BL/TR, 5'9", 160 lbs. Deb: 9/26/20

YEAR	TM/L	G	AB	R	H	2B	3B	HR	RBI	BB	SO	AVG	OBP	SLG	PRO	/A	BR	/A	PF	CHI	RC	TA	SB	CS	SBR	FR	POS	TPR
1920	Was-A	4	13	1	3	0	0	0	2	3	2	.231	.375	.231	.606	66	-1	-0	95	248	1	.600	0	0	0	-2	/O	-0.1

■ **ELMER JOHNSON** Johnson, Elmer Ellsworth "Hickory" b: 6/12/1884, Beard, Ind. d: 10/31/66, Hollywood, Fla. BR/TR, 5'9", 185 lbs. Deb: 4/24/14

YEAR	TM/L	G	AB	R	H	2B	3B	HR	RBI	BB	SO	AVG	OBP	SLG	PRO	/A	BR	/A	PF	CHI	RC	TA	SB	CS	SBR	FR	POS	TPR
1914	NY-N	11	12	0	2	1	0	0	0	1	3	.167	.231	.250	.481	45	-1	-1	96	0	1	.400	0			-0	C	0.0

■ **ERNIE JOHNSON** Johnson, Ernest Rudolph b: 4/29/1888, Chicago, Ill. d: 5/1/52, Monrovia, Cal. BL/TR, 5'9", 151 lbs. Deb: 8/05/12

YEAR	TM/L	G	AB	R	H	2B	3B	HR	RBI	BB	SO	AVG	OBP	SLG	PRO	/A	BR	/A	PF	CHI	RC	TA	SB	CS	SBR	FR	POS	TPR
1912	Chi-A	18	42	7	11	0	1	0	5	1		.262	.279	.310	.589	69	-2	-2	99	128	4	.452	0			-0	S	0.0
1915	StL-F	152	512	58	123	18	10	7	67	46	35	.240	.303	.355	.658	90	-4	-7	105	121	69	.668	32			19	*S	2.5
1916	StL-A	74	236	29	54	9	3	0	19	30	23	.229	.323	.292	.616	89	-4	-2	95	98	27	.632	13			10	S3	1.4
1917	StL-A	80	199	28	49	6	2	2	20	12	16	.246	.296	.327	.622	95	-3	-2	95	101	23	.613	13			5	S23	0.7
1918	StL-A	29	34	7	9	1	0	0	0	0	2	.265	.286	.294	.580	76	-1	-1	99	0	4	.600	4			-1	S/3	0.0
1921	Chi-A	142	613	93	181	28	7	1	51	29	24	.295	.328	.369	.697	78	-21	-21	99	66	73	.625	22	13	-1	25	*S	1.9
1922	Chi-A	144	603	85	153	17	3	0	56	40	30	.254	.304	.292	.596	55	-38	-39	101	98	54	.515	21	18	-5	-1	*S	-2.8
1923	Chi-A	12	53	5	10	2	0	0	1	3	5	.189	.246	.226	.472	25	-6	-6	98	25	3	.409	2	1	0	-2	S	-0.5
	NY-A	19	38	6	17	1	1	1	8	1	1	.447	.462	.605	1.067	172	4	4	104	105	10	1.143	0	0	0	-1	S/3	0.4
	Yr	31	91	11	27	3	1	1	9	4	6	.297	.333	.385	.718	87	-2	-2	102	75	12	.646	2	1	0	-3		-0.1
1924	NY-A	64	119	24	42	4	8	3	12	11	7	.353	.412	.597	1.009	160	10	10	99	50	26	1.012	1	6	-3	1	2/S3	0.9
1925	NY-A	76	170	30	48	5	1	5	17	8	10	.282	.315	.412	.726	86	-5	-4	96	67	22	.672	6	3	0	-4	2S/3	-0.1
Total	10	810	2619	372	697	91	36	19	256	181	153	.266	.317	.350	.667	81	-71	-71	100	89	314	.624	114	41		52	S/23	4.4

■ **FRANK JOHNSON** Johnson, Frank Herbert b: 7/22/42, El Paso, Tex. BR/TR, 6'1", 155 lbs. Deb: 9/07/66

YEAR	TM/L	G	AB	R	H	2B	3B	HR	RBI	BB	SO	AVG	OBP	SLG	PRO	/A	BR	/A	PF	CHI	RC	TA	SB	CS	SBR	FR	POS	TPR
1966	SF-N	15	32	2	7	0	0	0	0	2	7	.219	.265	.219	.483	37	-3	-3	97	0	2	.346	0	1	-1	-2	O	-0.5
1967	SF-N	8	10	3	3	0	0	0	0	1	2	.300	.364	.300	.664	91	-0	-0	101	0	1	.500	0	0	0	0	/O	0.0
1968	SF-N	67	174	11	33	2	0	1	7	12	23	.190	.246	.218	.464	41	-12	-12	98	72	10	.361	1	0	0	-3	3/OS2	-1.5
1969	SF-N	7	10	2	1	0	0	0	0	0	1	.100	.100	.100	.200	-43	-2	-2	101	0	0	.100	0	0	0	-1	/O	-0.3
1970	SF-N	67	161	25	44	1	2	3	31	19	18	.273	.357	.360	.717	97	-1	-0	96	180	18	.615	1	1	-0	-1	O1	-0.4
1971	SF-N	32	49	4	4	1	0	0	5	3	9	.082	.135	.102	.237	-32	-8	-8	100	407	1	.174	0	0	0	-1	/1O	-1.1
Total	6	196	436	47	92	4	2	4	43	37	60	.211	.277	.257	.534	54	-27	-25	97	141	31	.444	2	2	-1	-8	/O13S2	-3.8

■ **HOWARD JOHNSON** Johnson, Howard Michael b: 11/29/60, Clearwater, Fla. BB/TR, 5'11", 178 lbs. Deb: 4/14/82

YEAR	TM/L	G	AB	R	H	2B	3B	HR	RBI	BB	SO	AVG	OBP	SLG	PRO	/A	BR	/A	PF	CHI	RC	TA	SB	CS	SBR	FR	POS	TPR
1982	Det-A	54	155	23	49	5	0	4	14	16	30	.316	.384	.426	.810	122	5	5	100	72	25	.796	7	4	-0	-3	3D/O	0.1
1983	Det-A	27	66	11	14	0	0	3	5	7	10	.212	.297	.348	.646	81	-2	-2	96	61	7	.585	0	0	0	-1	3/D	-0.2
1984	Det-A	116	355	43	88	14	1	12	50	40	67	.248	.326	.394	.720	102	-1	1	96	113	46	.685	10	6	-1	-11	*3/S1OD	-0.8
1985	NY-N	126	389	38	94	18	4	11	46	34	78	.242	.303	.393	.696	96	-4	-3	97	98	45	.633	6	4	-1	-13	*3/SO	-1.6
1986	NY-N	88	220	30	54	14	0	10	39	31	64	.245	.341	.445	.787	121	4	6	96	121	36	.817	8	1	2	-1	3S/O	0.9
1987	NY-N	157	554	93	147	22	1	36	99	83	113	.265	.366	.504	.870	129	22	23	99	104	106	.939	32	10	4	-7	*3S/O	2.3
1988	NY-N	148	495	85	114	21	1	24	68	86	104	.230	.348	.422	.770	133	14	20	90	99	78	.815	23	7	3	-7	*3/S	1.8
Total	7	716	2234	323	560	94	7	100	321	297	466	.251	.342	.433	.775	117	39	51	96	102	344	.796	86	32	7	-44	3S/D01	2.5

YEAR	TM/L	G	AB	R	H	2B	3B	HR	RBI	BB	SO	AVG	OBP	SLG	PRO	/A	BR	/A	PF	CHI	RC	TA	SB	CS	SBR	FR	POS	TPR
■ **SPUD JOHNSON**	Johnson, John Ralph b: 1860, Canada BL/TL, 5'9", 175 lbs. Deb: 4/18/1889																											
1889	Col-a	116	459	91	130	14	10	2	79	39	47	.283	.355	.370	.725	120	6	13	91	123	74	.775	34			-11	O3/1S	0.0
1890	Col-a	135	538	106	186	23	18	1		48		.346	.409	.461	.870	161	39	40	99	0	122	.991	43			-16	*O	1.4
1891	Cle-N	80	327	49	84	8	3	1	46	22	23	.257	.319	.309	.628	81	-6	-8	105	137	38	.605	16			-5	O/1	-1.5
Total	3	331	1324	246	400	45	31	4	125	109	70	.302	.368	.392	.760	126	40	45	98	76	235	.813	93			-33	O/31S	-0.1
■ **LANCE JOHNSON**	Johnson, Kenneth Lance b: 7/6/63, Cincinnati, Ohio BL/TL, 5'10", 160 lbs. Deb: 7/10/87																											
1987	StL-N	33	59	4	13	2	1	0	7	4	6	.220	.270	.288	.558	49	-4	-4	99	164	5	.551	6	1	1	-5	O	-0.9
1988	Chi-A	33	124	11	23	4	1	0	6	6	11	.185	.223	.234	.457	29	-12	-11	97	84	7	.394	6	2	1	-2	O/D	-1.2
Total	2	66	183	15	36	6	2	0	13	10	17	.197	.238	.251	.490	36	-16	-16	98	110	11	.450	12	3	2	-7	/OD	-2.1
■ **LAMAR JOHNSON**	Johnson, Lamar b: 9/2/50, Bessemer, Ala. BR/TR, 6'2", 215 lbs. Deb: 5/18/74																											
1974	Chi-A	10	29	1	10	0	0	0	2	0	3	.345	.345	.345	.690	97	-0	-0	102	79	2	.455	0	0	0	-0	/1D	0.0
1975	Chi-A	8	30	2	6	3	0	1	1	1	5	.200	.226	.400	.626	71	-1	-1	103	26	3	.542	0	0	0	0	/1D	-0.1
1976	Chi-A	82	222	29	71	11	1	4	33	19	37	.320	.379	.432	.811	138	10	11	99	117	34	.730	2	1	0	1	D1/O	1.0
1977	Chi-A	118	374	52	113	12	5	18	65	24	53	.302	.344	.505	.850	129	13	14	99	106	59	.773	1	1	-0	1	D1	1.2
1978	Chi-A	148	498	52	136	23	2	8	72	43	46	.273	.333	.376	.709	98	-1	-1	101	**138**	59	.620	6	5	-1	-2	*1D	-0.8
1979	Chi-A	133	479	60	148	29	1	12	74	41	56	.309	.366	.449	.815	116	12	11	102	116	73	.747	8	2	1	1	1D	0.8
1980	Chi-A	147	541	51	150	26	3	13	81	47	53	.277	.335	.409	.744	106	2	4	97	129	71	.660	2	3	-1	3	1D	0.1
1981	Chi-A	41	134	10	37	7	0	1	15	5	14	.276	.302	.351	.653	88	-2	-2	100	117	12	.500	0	2	-1	0	1/D	-0.4
1982	Tex-A	105	324	37	84	11	0	7	38	31	40	.259	.326	.358	.684	94	-5	-2	93	111	35	.585	3	5	-2	-1	D1	-0.4
Total	9	792	2631	294	755	122	12	64	381	211	307	.287	.342	.415	.757	110	28	32	99	119	349	.699	22	19	-5	3	1D/O	1.4
■ **LARRY JOHNSON**	Johnson, Larry Doby b: 8/17/50, Cleveland, Ohio BR/TR, 6', 185 lbs. Deb: 10/03/72																											
1972	Cle-A	1	2	0	1	0	0	0	0	0	1	.500	.500	.500	1.000	185	0	0	107	0	1	1.000	0	0	0	0	/C	0.0
1974	Cle-A	1	0	1	0	0	0	0	0	0	0	—	—	—	—	—	0	0	101	—	—	—	0	0	0	0	R	0.0
1975	Mon-N	1	3	0	1	1	0	0	1	1	1	.333	.500	.667	1.167	205	1	1	108	197	1	1.500	0	0	0	0	/C	0.1
1976	Mon-N	6	13	0	2	1	0	0	0	0	2	.154	.154	.231	.385	8	-2	-2	100	0	1	.273	0	0	0	0	/C	0.0
1978	Chi-A	3	8	0	1	0	0	0	0	1	4	.125	.222	.125	.347	0	-1	-1	101	0	0	.286	0	0	0	0	/CD	0.0
Total	5	12	26	1	5	2	0	0	1	2	8	.192	.250	.269	.519	46	-2	-2	102	28	3	.429	0	0	0	1	/CD	0.1
■ **LOU JOHNSON**	Johnson, Louis Brown "Slick" b: 9/22/34, Lexington, Ky. BR/TR, 5'11", 170 lbs. Deb: 4/17/60																											
1960	Chi-N	34	68	6	14	2	1	0	1	5	19	.206	.270	.265	.535	48	-5	-5	98	22	5	.474	3	1	0	1	O	-0.3
1961	LA-A	1	0	0	0	0	0	0	0	0	0	—	—	—	—	—	0	0	111	—	—	—	0	0	0	-0	/O	0.0
1962	Mil-N	61	117	22	33	4	5	2	13	11	27	.282	.349	.453	.802	114	2	2	99	87	20	.826	6	1	1	-9	O	-0.7
1965	LA-N	131	468	57	121	24	1	12	58	24	81	.259	.317	.391	.708	107	-1	3	91	112	58	.661	15	6	1	-5	*O	-0.4
1966	LA-N	152	526	71	143	20	2	17	73	21	75	.272	.317	.414	.732	105	0	2	97	116	63	.638	8	10	-4	2	*O	-0.3
1967	LA-N	104	330	39	89	14	1	11	41	24	52	.270	.332	.418	.751	129	5	10	88	99	44	.684	4	3	-1	0	O	0.6
1968	Chi-N	62	205	14	50	14	3	1	14	6	23	.244	.289	.356	.645	83	-2	-5	112	78	20	.549	3	1	0	-4	O	-1.2
	Cle-A	65	202	25	52	11	1	5	23	9	24	.257	.302	.396	.698	109	2	2	101	104	24	.639	6	1	1	0	O	0.1
1969	Cal-A	67	133	10	27	8	0	0	9	10	19	.203	.274	.263	.537	51	-9	-9	99	103	10	.486	5	1	1	-5	O	-1.4
Total	8	677	2049	244	529	97	14	48	232	110	320	.258	.313	.389	.702	102	-7	2	96	102	249	.654	50	24	1	-19	O	-3.6
■ **OTIS JOHNSON**	Johnson, Otis L. b: 11/5/1883, Fowler, Ind. d: 11/9/15, Johnson City, N.Y. BB/TR, 5'9", 185 lbs. Deb: 4/12/11																											
1911	NY-A	71	209	21	49	9	6	3	36	39		.234	.363	.378	.741	96	3	-1	111	138	34	.831	12			-5	S2/3	0.0
■ **PAUL JOHNSON**	Johnson, Paul Oscar b: 9/2/1896, N.Grosvenordale, Conn. d: 2/14/73, Mc Allen, Tex. BR/TR, 5'8", 160 lbs. Deb: 9/13/20																											
1920	Phi-A	18	72	6	15	0	0	0	5	4	8	.208	.250	.208	.458	24	-8	-7	94	112	4	.345	1	1	-0	-3	O	-1.1
1921	Phi-A	48	127	17	40	6	2	1	10	9	17	.315	.360	.417	.778	95	-0	-1	103	61	18	.697	0	2	-1	-3	O	-0.7
Total	2	66	199	23	55	6	2	1	15	13	25	.276	.321	.342	.662	71	-8	-8	100	79	22	.558	1	3	-2	-6	/O	-1.8
■ **RANDY JOHNSON**	Johnson, Randall Glenn b: 6/10/56, Escondido, Cal. BR/TR, 6'1", 190 lbs. Deb: 4/27/82																											
1982	Atl-N	27	46	5	11	5	0	0	6	6	4	.239	.352	.348	.700	90	0	-0	107	147	6	.649	0	1	-1	1	2/3	0.1
1983	Atl-N	86	144	22	36	3	0	1	17	20	27	.250	.345	.292	.637	74	-3	-4	106	149	15	.557	1	3	-2	0	3/2	-0.7
1984	Atl-N	91	294	28	82	13	0	5	30	21	21	.279	.329	.374	.703	89	-1	-5	110	94	35	.615	4	7	-3	-1	3	-0.9
Total	3	204	484	55	129	21	0	6	53	47	52	.267	.336	.347	.684	85	-5	-9	108	116	56	.609	5	11	-5	0	3/2	-1.5
■ **RANDY JOHNSON**	Johnson, Randall Stuart b: 8/15/58, Miami, Fla. BL/TL, 6'2", 195 lbs. Deb: 7/05/80																											
1980	Chi-A	12	20	0	4	0	0	0	3	2	4	.200	.304	.200	.504	43	-2	-1	97	293	2	.438	0	0	0	0	/1OD	-0.1
1982	Min-A	89	234	26	58	10	0	10	33	30	46	.248	.333	.419	.752	105	2	2	100	103	34	.715	0	0	0	-0	D/O	0.1
Total	2	101	254	26	62	10	0	10	36	32	50	.244	.331	.402	.733	100	0	0	100	118	36	.692	0	0	0	-0	/DO1	0.0
■ **FOOTER JOHNSON**	Johnson, Richard Allan "Treads" b: 2/15/32, Dayton, Ohio BL/TL, 5'11", 175 lbs. Deb: 6/22/58																											
1958	Chi-N	8	5	1	0	0	0	0	0	0	1	.000	.000	.000	.000	-99	-1	-1	101	0	0	.000	0	0	0	0	H	0.0
■ **BOB JOHNSON**	Johnson, Robert Lee "Indian Bob" b: 11/26/06, Pryor, Okla. d: 7/6/82, Tacoma, Wash. BR/TR, 6', 180 lbs. Deb: 4/12/33																											
1933	Phi-A	142	535	103	155	44	4	21	93	85	74	.290	.387	.505	.892	147	27	33	92	99	109	.948	8	3	1	3	*O	3.0
1934	Phi-A	141	547	111	168	26	6	34	92	58	60	.307	.375	.563	.938	143	29	31	97	79	114	.979	12	8	-1	11	*O	3.5
1935	Phi-A	147	582	103	174	29	5	28	109	78	76	.299	.384	.510	.894	130	25	25	100	93	116	.920	2	4	-2	6	*O	2.5
1936	Phi-A	153	566	91	165	29	14	25	121	88	71	.292	.389	.525	.913	123	20	19	101	112	118	.966	6	6	-2	4	*O2/1	1.7
1937	Phi-A	138	477	91	146	32	6	25	108	98	65	.306	.425	.556	.981	155	35	40	94	115	117	1.104	9	7	-2	10	*O/2	3.9
1938	Phi-A	152	563	114	176	27	9	30	113	87	73	.313	.406	.552	.959	137	33	32	101	101	128	1.035	9	8	-2	4	*O/23	3.0
1939	Phi-A	150	544	115	184	30	9	23	114	99	59	.338	.440	.553	.993	157	46	48	97	110	138	1.101	15	5	2	10	*O/2	5.0
1940	Phi-A	138	512	93	137	25	4	31	103	83	64	.268	.374	.514	.888	134	21	24	96	111	100	.902	8	2	1	8	*O	2.2
1941	Phi-A	149	552	98	152	30	8	22	107	95	75	.275	.385	.478	.863	126	22	22	101	122	106	.876	6	4	-1	9	*O1	2.0
1942	Phi-A	149	550	78	160	35	7	13	80	82	61	.291	.384	.451	.835	139	26	29	96	104	99	.819	3	2	-0	6	*O	2.4
1943	Was-A	117	438	65	116	22	8	7	63	64	50	.265	.362	.400	.762	118	14	12	104	124	67	.749	11	5	0	4	O31	1.5
1944	Bos-A	144	525	106	170	40	8	17	106	95	67	.324	**.431**	.528	**.959**	**177**	**53**	**54**	98	124	124	**1.005**	2	7	-4	6	*O	5.4
1945	Bos-A	143	529	71	148	27	7	12	74	63	56	.280	.358	.425	.783	134	17	21	95	105	83	.741	5	3	-0	2	*O	1.7
Total	13	1863	6920	1239	2051	396	95	288	1283	1075	851	.296	.393	.506	.899	140	366	389	98	107	1418	.949	96	64	-10	81	*O/123	37.8
■ **BOB JOHNSON**	Johnson, Robert Wallace b: 3/4/36, Omaha, Neb. BR/TR, 5'10", 175 lbs. Deb: 4/19/60																											
1960	KC-A	76	146	12	30	4	0	1	9	19	23	.205	.301	.253	.555	52	-9	-9	99	88	11	.480	2	0	1	-3	S23	-0.7
1961	Was-A	61	224	27	66	13	1	6	28	19	26	.295	.352	.442	.794	117	3	5	95	96	32	.724	4	2	0	2	S/23	1.1
1962	Was-A	135	466	58	134	20	2	12	43	32	50	.288	.335	.416	.751	100	-0	-1	101	76	59	.661	9	6	-1	-1	3S/2O	0.1
1963	Bal-A	82	254	34	75	10	0	8	32	18	35	.295	.347	.429	.776	124	5	7	94	101	39	.732	5	1	1	1	2/1S3	1.3
1964	Bal-A	93	210	18	52	8	2	3	29	9	37	.248	.282	.348	.629	70	-8	-9	105	150	19	.500	0	0	0	0	S12/30	-0.7
1965	Bal-A	87	273	36	66	13	2	5	27	15	34	.242	.284	.359	.643	81	-7	-7	100	99	26	.535	1	0	0	0	1S3/2	-0.6
1966	Bal-A	71	157	13	34	5	0	1	10	12	24	.217	.276	.268	.544	57	-9	-9	101	93	11	.430	0	1	-1	-1	21/3	-0.9
1967	Bal-A	4	3	1	1	0	0	0	0	1	1	.333	.500	.333	.833	159	0	0	95	0	1	1.000	0	0	0	0	H	0.0
	NY-N	90	230	26	80	8	3	5	27	12	29	.348	.380	.474	.854	144	12	13	99	90	39	.767	1	1	-0	1	21S/3	1.8
1968	Cin-N	16	15	2	4	0	0	0	1	1	2	.267	.313	.267	.579	67	-0	-1	111	105	1	.455	0	0	0	0	/S1	0.0
	Atl-N	59	187	15	49	5	1	0	11	10	20	.262	.299	.299	.599	86	-4	-3	93	83	16	.462	0	0	0	-0	3/2	-0.3
	Yr	75	202	17	53	5	1	0	12	11	22	.262	.300	.297	.597	82	-5	-4	97	89	17	.461	0	0	0	-0		-0.3
1969	StL-N	19	29	1	6	0	0	1	2	2	4	.207	.258	.310	.568	59	-2	-2	100	67	2	.440	0	0	0	-0	/31	-0.1
	Oak-A	51	67	5	23	1	0	1	9	3	4	.343	.380	.403	.783	129	2	2	92	120	11	.705	0	0	0	0	/12	0.2
1970	Oak-A	30	46	6	8	1	0	1	2	3	2	.174	.240	.261	.501	39	-4	-4	97	54	3	.439	2	1	0	-0	/31	-0.4
Total	11	874	2307	254	628	88	11	44	230	156	291	.272	.321	.377	.698	95	-21	-17	99	95	269	.626	24	12	0	-1	S231/O	0.8

YEAR	TM/L	G	AB	R	H	2B	3B	HR	RBI	BB	SO	AVG	OBP	SLG	PRO	/A	BR	/A	PF	CHI	RC	TA	SB	CS	SBR	FR	POS	TPR
■ **RON JOHNSON**	Johnson, Ronald David b: 3/23/56, Long Beach, Cal. BR/TR, 6'3", 215 lbs. Deb: 9/12/82																											
1982	KC-A	8	14	2	4	2	0	0	0	4	3	.286	.444	.429	.873	141	1	1	100	0	3	1.000	0	0	0	0	/1	0.1
1983	KC-A	9	27	2	7	0	0	0	1	3	1	.259	.333	.259	.593	65	-1	-1	101	56	3	.500	0	0	0	0	/1C	-0.1
1984	Mon-N	5	5	0	1	0	0	0	1	0	2	.200	.200	.200	.400	14	-1	-1	91	392	0	.250	0	0	0	-0	/1O	0.0
Total	3	22	46	4	12	2	0	0	2	7	6	.261	.358	.304	.663	85	-1	-1	100	69	6	.618	0	0	0	-0	/1CO	0.0
■ **RONDIN JOHNSON**	Johnson, Rondin Allen b: 12/16/58, Bremerton, Wash. BB/TR, 5'10", 160 lbs. Deb: 9/03/86																											
1986	KC-A	11	31	1	8	0	1	0	2	0	3	.258	.258	.323	.581	58	-2	-2	100	80	3	.435	0	0	0	0	2	0.0
■ **ROY JOHNSON**	Johnson, Roy Cleveland b: 2/23/03, Pryor, Okla. d: 9/10/73, Tacoma, Wash. BL/TR, 5'9", 175 lbs. Deb: 4/18/29																											
1929	Det-A	148	640	128	201	**45**	14	10	69	67	60	.314	.379	.475	.854	122	17	20	97	61	114	.861	20	15	-3	**19**	*O	2.7
1930	Det-A	125	462	84	127	30	13	2	35	40	46	.275	.333	.409	.742	83	-10	-13	105	61	63	.713	17	10	-1	3	*O	-1.3
1931	Det-A	151	621	107	173	37	**19**	8	55	72	51	.279	.355	.438	.793	104	6	3	104	54	96	.808	33	21	-3	17	*O	0.7
1932	Det-A	49	195	33	49	14	2	3	22	20	26	.251	.324	.390	.714	83	-5	-5	102	92	26	.703	7	2	1	-2	O	-0.7
	Bos-A	94	349	70	104	24	4	11	47	44	41	.298	.378	.484	.862	126	11	13	97	82	66	.912	13	4	2	-6	O	0.5
	Yr	143	544	103	153	38	6	14	69	64	67	.281	.359	.450	.809	110	6	7	99	86	91	.834	20	6	2	-8		-0.2
1933	Bos-A	133	483	88	151	30	7	10	95	55	36	.313	.387	.466	.853	124	18	17	101	127	88	.868	13	10	-2	-7	*O	0.4
1934	Bos-A	143	569	85	182	43	10	7	119	54	36	.320	.379	.467	.846	111	14	9	106	147	102	.844	11	5	0	-3	*O	0.4
1935	Bos-A	145	553	70	174	33	9	3	66	74	34	.315	.398	.423	.822	104	13	6	108	98	95	.824	11	12	-4	-0	*O	0.0
1936	NY-A	63	147	21	39	8	2	1	19	21	14	.265	.361	.367	.728	85	-4	-3	95	108	21	.725	3	1	0	-2	O	-0.4
1937	NY-A	12	51	5	15	3	0	0	6	3	2	.294	.333	.353	.686	72	-2	-2	102	121	6	.611	1	0	0	-2	O	-0.4
	Bos-N	85	260	24	72	8	3	3	22	38	29	.277	.369	.365	.735	111	1	5	90	76	37	.711	5			-2	O/3	0.0
1938	Bos-N	7	29	2	5	0	0	0	1	1	5	.172	.200	.172	.372	4	-4	-3	88	77	1	.292	1			-2	/O	-0.5
Total	10	1155	4359	717	1292	275	83	58	556	489	380	.296	.369	.437	.806	107	55	45	102	89	715	.808	135	80		12	*O/3	1.4
■ **ROY JOHNSON**	Johnson, Roy Edward b: 6/27/59, Parkin, Ark. BL/TL, 6'4", 205 lbs. Deb: 7/03/82																											
1982	Mon-N	17	32	2	7	2	0	0	2	1	6	.219	.242	.281	.524	44	-2	-3	105	87	2	.400	0	0	0	-1	O	-0.3
1984	Mon-N	16	33	2	5	2	0	1	2	7	10	.152	.300	.303	.603	76	-1	-1	91	60	4	.643	1	0	0	-1	O	-0.1
1985	Mon-N	3	5	0	0	0	0	0	0	0	3	.000	.000	.000	.000	-99	-1	-1	94	0	0	.000	0	0	0	-1	/O	-0.2
Total	3	36	70	4	12	4	0	1	4	8	19	.171	.256	.271	.528	49	-5	-5	97	68	6	.483	1	0	0	-3	/O	-0.6
■ **STAN JOHNSON**	Johnson, Stanley Lucius b: 2/12/37, Dallas, Tex. BL/TL, 5'10", 180 lbs. Deb: 9/18/60																											
1960	Chi-A	5	6	1	1	0	0	1	1	0	1	.167	.167	.667	.833	113	0	0	101	56	0	.667	0	1	-1	-1	/O	0.0
1961	KC-A	3	3	1	0	0	0	0	0	2	1	.000	.400	.000	.400	17	-0	-0	102	0	0	.500	0	0	0	-1	/O	0.0
Total	2	8	9	2	1	0	0	1	1	2	2	.111	.273	.444	.717	88	-0	-0	101	30	0	.600	0	1	-1	-1	/O	0.0
■ **TIM JOHNSON**	Johnson, Timothy Evald b: 7/22/49, Grand Forks, N.D. BL/TR, 6'1", 170 lbs. Deb: 4/24/73																											
1973	Mil-A	136	465	39	99	10	2	0	32	29	93	.213	.261	.243	.504	44	-35	-33	96	111	30	.393	6	3	0	-17	*S	-3.2
1974	Mil-A	93	245	25	60	7	7	0	25	11	48	.245	.280	.331	.611	73	-8	-9	102	121	23	.511	4	3	-1	-6	S2/3OD	-0.9
1975	Mil-A	38	85	6	12	1	0	0	2	6	17	.141	.198	.153	.351	0	-11	-11	100	59	3	.293	3	0	1	-1	23S/1D	-0.9
1976	Mil-A	105	273	25	75	4	3	0	14	19	32	.275	.327	.311	.638	88	-4	-4	99	63	28	.534	4	1	1	-9	*23/1S	-0.6
1977	Mil-A	30	33	5	2	1	0	0	2	5	10	.061	.184	.091	.275	-23	-6	-5	95	264	1	.290	1	0	0	0	2/S3OD	-0.3
1978	Mil-A	3	3	1	0	0	0	0	0	2	0	.000	.400	.000	.400	20	-0	-0	106	0	0	.667	0	0	0	0	/S	0.0
	Tor-A	68	79	9	19	2	0	0	3	8	16	.241	.318	.266	.584	66	-3	-3	100	56	7	.492	0	1	-1	-1	S2	0.0
	Yr	71	82	10	19	2	0	0	3	10	16	.232	.323	.256	.579	64	-3	-3	100	54	8	.500	0	1	-1	-1		0.0
1979	Tor-A	43	86	6	16	2	1	0	6	8	15	.186	.255	.233	.488	32	-8	-8	103	115	5	.384	0	1	-1	1	2/31	-0.6
Total	7	516	1269	116	283	27	13	0	84	88	231	.223	.276	.265	.541	55	-76	-74	99	100	98	.448	18	9	0	-33	S2/31DO	-6.5
■ **WALLACE JOHNSON**	Johnson, Wallace Darnell b: 12/25/56, Gary, Ind. BB/TR, 6', 173 lbs. Deb: 9/08/81																											
1981	Mon-N	11	9	1	2	0	1	0	3	1	1	.222	.300	.444	.744	110	0	0	99	294	0	.667	1	1	-0	0	/2	0.0
1982	Mon-N	36	57	5	11	0	2	0	2	5	5	.193	.258	.263	.521	44	-4	-4	105	52	4	.511	4	1	1	-1	2	-0.3
1983	Mon-N	3	2	1	1	0	0	0	0	1	0	.500	.667	.500	1.167	224	1	1	102	0	1	3.000	1	0	0	0	/H	0.1
	SF-N	7	8	0	1	0	0	0	1	0	0	.125	.125	.125	.250	-30	-1	-1	101	396	0	.143	0	0	0	-0	/2	-0.1
	Yr	10	10	1	2	0	0	0	1	1	0	.200	.273	.200	.473	33	-1	-1	101	277	1	.500	1	0	0	-0		0.0
1984	Mon-N	17	24	3	5	0	0	0	4	5	4	.208	.345	.208	.553	64	-1	-1	91	314	2	.526	0	0	0	0	/1	0.0
1986	Mon-N	61	127	13	36	3	1	1	10	7	9	.283	.321	.346	.667	86	-3	-2	98	85	14	.594	6	3	0	-1	1	-0.4
1987	Mon-N	75	85	7	21	5	0	1	14	7	6	.247	.304	.341	.646	67	-4	-4	106	175	10	.641	5	0	2	0	/1	-0.2
1988	Mon-N	86	94	7	29	5	1	0	3	12	15	.309	.387	.383	.770	115	3	2	106	33	14	.696	0	2	-1	-0	1/2	0.1
Total	7	296	406	37	106	13	5	2	37	38	40	.261	.324	.333	.657	81	-9	-10	102	111	46	.615	17	7	1	-2	/12	-0.8
■ **WALTER JOHNSON**	Johnson, Walter Perry "Barney" or "The Big Train" b: 11/6/1887, Humboldt, Kan. d: 12/10/46, Washington, D.C. BR/TR, 6'1", 200 lbs. Deb: 8/02/07 MH																											
1907	Was-A	14	36	3	4	0	1	0	1	1		.111	.135	.167	.302	-3	-4	-4	90	60	1	.219	0			-2	P	0.0
1908	Was-A	36	79	7	13	3	2	0	5	6		.165	.224	.253	.477	59	-4	-3	95	94	4	.394	0			-4	P	0.0
1909	Was-A	40	101	6	13	3	0	1	6	1		.129	.137	.188	.325	3	-11	-10	90	105	2	.227	0			-1	P	0.0
1910	Was-A	45	137	14	24	6	1	2	12	4		.175	.199	.277	.476	48	-9	-9	101	101	7	.389	2			-2	P	0.0
1911	Was-A	42	128	18	30	5	3	1	15	0		.234	.234	.344	.578	63	-8	-7	97	108	10	.459	1			3	P	0.0
1912	Was-A	55	144	16	38	6	4	2	20	7		.264	.298	.403	.701	101	-1	-1	99	104	18	.632	2			1	P	0.0
1913	Was-A	54	134	12	35	5	6	2	14	5	14	.261	.293	.433	.726	106	1	-0	106	0	16	.667	2			-1	P/O	0.0
1914	Was-A	55	136	23	30	4	1	3	16	10	27	.221	.274	.331	.605	81	-4	-4	101	111	13	.538	2			2	P/O	0.0
1915	Was-A	64	147	14	34	7	4	2	17	8	34	.231	.276	.374	.650	93	-2	-2	101	95	15	.557	0	2	-1	0	P/O	0.0
1916	Was-A	58	142	13	32	2	4	1	7	11	28	.225	.286	.317	.603	81	-4	-4	100	52	13	.518	0			-5	P	0.0
1917	Was-A	57	130	15	33	12	1	0	15	9	30	.254	.312	.362	.674	114	0	2	92	115	14	.608	1			-0	P	0.0
1918	Was-A	65	150	10	40	4	4	1	18	9	18	.267	.321	.367	.688	103	1	0	104	113	18	.627	2			-2	P/O	0.0
1919	Was-A	56	125	13	24	1	3	1	8	12	17	.192	.263	.272	.535	51	-8	-8	98	78	9	.465	1			0	P/O	0.0
1920	Was-A	33	64	7	17	1	3	1	8	3	12	.266	.299	.422	.720	94	-1	-1	95	94	8	.638	0	0	0	-1	P	0.0
1921	Was-A	38	111	10	30	7	0	0	10	6	14	.270	.308	.333	.641	64	-6	-6	99	93	11	.531	0	0	0	-3	P	0.0
1922	Was-A	43	108	8	22	3	0	1	15	2	12	.204	.218	.259	.477	26	-12	-11	92	173	6	.349	0	0	0	0	P	0.0
1923	Was-A	42	93	11	18	3	3	0	13	4	15	.194	.227	.290	.517	37	-9	-8	95	165	6	.413	0	0	0	-2	P	0.0
1924	Was-A	39	113	18	32	9	0	1	14	3	11	.283	.308	.389	.697	80	-4	-4	98	98	13	.593	0	0	0	-1	P	0.0
1925	Was-A	36	97	12	42	6	1	2	20	3	6	.433	.455	.577	1.033	164	9	9	98	108	24	1.071	0	1	-1	-4	P	0.0
1926	Was-A	35	103	6	20	5	0	1	12	3	11	.194	.217	.272	.489	27	-11	-11	98	132	6	.373	0	0	0	-5	P	0.0
1927	Was-A	26	46	6	16	2	0	2	10	3	4	.348	.388	.522	.909	139	2	2	97	111	9	.900	0	0	0	0	P	0.0
Total	21	933	2324	242	547	94	41	24	256	110	253	.235	.273	.342	.615	76	-86	-81	98	99	227	.521	13	3		-25	P/O	0.0
■ **BILL JOHNSON**	Johnson, William Lawrence b: 10/18/1892, Chicago, Ill. d: 11/3/50, Los Angeles, Cal. BL/TR, 5'11", 170 lbs. Deb: 9/22/16																											
1916	Phi-A	4	15	1	4	1	0	0	1	0	4	.267	.267	.333	.600	82	-0	-0	98	73	1	.455	0			-1	/O	-0.1
1917	Phi-A	48	109	7	19	2	2	1	8	8	14	.174	.237	.257	.494	54	-7	-6	94	93	8	.456	4			-5	O	-1.3
Total	2	52	124	8	23	3	2	1	9	8	18	.185	.241	.266	.507	58	-7	-6	94	90	9	.455	4			-6	/O	-1.4
■ **BILL JOHNSON**	Johnson, William Russell "Bull" b: 8/30/18, Montclair, N.J. BR/TR, 5'10", 180 lbs. Deb: 4/22/43																											
1943	NY-A	155	592	70	166	24	6	5	94	53	30	.280	.344	.367	.710	112	6	8	96	157	71	.605	3	5	-2	12	*3	2.1
1946	NY-A	85	296	51	77	14	5	4	35	31	42	.260	.334	.382	.716	99	-0	-0	100	109	40	.656	1	0	0	3	3	0.9
1947	NY-A	132	494	67	141	19	8	10	95	44	43	.285	.351	.417	.768	117	8	10	97	**151**	69	.684	1	2	-1	-21	*3	-0.9
1948	NY-A	127	446	59	131	20	6	12	64	41	30	.294	.358	.446	.805	113	7	7	100	92	68	.724	0	0	0	0	*3	0.2
1949	NY-A	113	329	48	82	11	3	8	56	48	44	.249	.348	.374	.722	91	-4	-5	100	131	43	.664	1	0	0	-3	31/2	-0.6
1950	NY-A	108	327	44	85	16	2	6	40	42	30	.260	.346	.376	.722	85	-8	-7	99	98	43	.657	1	0	0	-2	*3/1	-1.2
1951	NY-A	15	40	5	12	3	0	0	4	7	0	.300	.404	.375	.779	122	1	1	92	95	6	.710	0	1	-1	-1	3	0.0
	StL-N	124	442	52	116	23	1	14	64	46	49	.262	.340	.414	.754	101	1	0	101	112	63	.704	5	3	-0	10	*3	0.9
1952	StL-N	94	282	23	71	10	2	2	34	34	21	.252	.339	.323	.661	86	-5	-4	98	137	32	.586	1	0	0	5	3	0.3

YEAR	TM/L	G	AB	R	H	2B	3B	HR	RBI	BB	SO	AVG	OBP	SLG	PRO	/A	BR	/A	PF	CHI	RC	TA	SB	CS	SBR	FR	POS	TPR
1953	StL-N	11	5	0	1	1	0	0	1	1	1	.200	.333	.400	.733	89	-0	-0	102	195	1	.750	0	0	0	0	3	0.0
Total	9	964	3253	419	882	141	33	61	487	347	290	.271	.346	.391	.737	103	5	10	99	125	437	.697	13	11	-3	3	3/12	1.7
■ **BILL JOHNSON** Johnson, William T. "Sleepy Bill" b: Chester, Pa. d: 21, BL/TL, Deb: 6/27/1884																												
1884	Phi-U	1	4	0	0	0	0	0		0		.000	.000	.000	.000	-99	-1	-1	93	0	0	.000	0			0	/O	0.0
1887	Ind-N	11	42	3	8	0	0	0	3	0	6	.190	.209	.190	.400	13	-5	-4	96	118	3	.412	5			0	O	-0.3
1890	BB-a	24	95	15	28	2	3	0		7		.295	.350	.379	.728	117	2	2	100	0	16	.776	8			0	O	0.2
1891	Bal-a	129	480	101	130	13	14	2	79	89	55	.271	.389	.369	.758	119	16	15	101	132	83	.863	32			8	*O	1.5
1892	Bal-N	4	15	2	2	0	0	0	2	2	0	.133	.235	.133	.369	13	-1	-1	100	325	0	.308	0			0	/O	0.0
Total	5	169	636	121	168	15	17	2	84	98	61	.264	.368	.351	.718	109	11	10	101	117	102	.795	45			8	O	1.4
■ **GREGORY JOHNSTON** Johnston, Gregory Bernard b: 2/12/55, Los Angeles, Cal. BL/TL, 6', 175 lbs. Deb: 7/27/79																												
1979	SF-N	42	74	5	15	2	0	1	7	2	17	.203	.224	.270	.494	37	-7	-6	92	121	4	.367	0	0	0	-1	O	-0.7
1980	Min-A	14	27	3	5	3	0	0	1	2	4	.185	.241	.296	.538	43	-2	-2	109	49	1	.400	0	0	0	-1	O	-0.3
1981	Min-A	7	16	2	2	0	0	0	0	2	5	.125	.222	.125	.347	2	-2	-2	105	0	1	.286	0	0	0	1	/O	-0.1
Total	3	63	117	10	22	5	0	1	8	6	26	.188	.228	.256	.484	34	-11	-11	98	86	6	.379	0	0	0	-2	/O	-1.1
■ **JIMMY JOHNSTON** Johnston, James Harle b: 12/10/1889, Cleveland, Tenn. d: 2/14/67, Chattanooga, Tenn. BR/TR, 5'10", 160 lbs. Deb: 5/03/11 C																												
1911	Chi-A	1	2	0	0	0	0	0	2	0		.000	.000	.000	.000	-99	-1	-1	97	0	0	.000	0			-0	/O	0.0
1914	Chi-N	50	101	9	23	3	2	1	8	4	9	.228	.264	.327	.591	77	-3	-3	98	81	9	.526	3			5	O/2	0.1
1916	Bro-N	118	425	58	107	13	8	1	26	35	38	.252	.313	.327	.640	94	-1	-3	103	74	44	.591	22	19	-5	9	*O	0.3
1917	Bro-N	103	330	33	89	10	4	0	25	23	28	.270	.321	.324	.645	95	-1	-2	104	90	39	.614	16			-9	O1/S23	-1.5
1918	Bro-N	123	484	54	136	16	8	0	27	33	31	.281	.328	.347	.675	104	3	2	101	54	59	.644	22			4	O1/32	0.1
1919	Bro-N	117	405	56	114	11	4	1	23	29	26	.281	.334	.336	.670	108	1	4	94	66	48	.615	11			-3	2O/1S	0.3
1920	Bro-N	155	635	87	185	17	12	1	52	43	23	.291	.338	.361	.699	91	1	-8	111	77	77	.630	19	15	-3	-6	*3/OS	-1.0
1921	Bro-N	152	624	104	203	41	14	5	56	45	26	.325	.372	.460	.832	114	16	13	105	60	105	.826	28	16	-1	10	*3/S	2.2
1922	Bro-N	138	567	110	181	20	7	4	49	38	17	.319	.364	.400	.764	102	-2	2	95	69	83	.722	18	9	0	-2	2S3	0.4
1923	Bro-N	151	625	111	203	29	11	4	60	53	15	.325	.378	.426	.803	114	11	13	98	67	100	.770	16	13	-3	5	2S3	2.0
1924	Bro-N	86	315	51	94	11	2	2	29	27	10	.298	.356	.365	.721	95	-2	-2	99	89	41	.652	5	6	-2	-5	S3/1O	-0.2
1925	Bro-N	123	431	63	128	13	3	2	43	45	15	.297	.369	.355	.724	92	-7	-3	94	98	59	.679	7	5	-1	-14	3O/1S	-1.3
1926	Bos-N	23	57	7	14	1	0	1	5	10	3	.246	.358	.316	.674	96	-1	0	86	82	7	.698	2			-1	3/2O	0.0
	NY-N	37	69	11	16	0	0	0	5	6	5	.232	.293	.232	.525	44	-5	-5	98	108	5	.415	0			-4	O	-0.9
	Yr	60	126	18	30	1	0	1	10	16	8	.238	.324	.270	.594	65	-6	-5	93	100	11	.542	2			-5		-0.9
Total	13	1377	5070	754	1493	185	75	22	410	391	246	.294	.347	.374	.721	100	9	8	100	73	676	.676	169	83		-11	3O2S/1	0.5
■ **JOHNNY JOHNSTON** Johnston, John Thomas b: 3/28/1890, Longview, Tex. d: 3/7/40, San Diego, Cal. BL/TR, 5'11", 172 lbs. Deb: 4/10/13																												
1913	StL-A	111	380	37	85	14	4	2	27	42	51	.224	.308	.297	.605	81	-11	-8	95	85	38	.576	11			11	*O	-0.2
■ **REX JOHNSTON** Johnston, Rex David b: 11/8/37, Colton, Cal. BB/TR, 6'1.5", 202 lbs. Deb: 4/15/64																												
1964	Pit-N	14	7	1	0	0	0	0	0	3	0	.000	.300	.000	.300	-7	-1	-1	101	0	0	.429	0	0	0	-3	/O	-0.3
■ **RICHARD JOHNSTON** Johnston, Richard Frederick b: 4/6/1863, Kingston, N.Y. d: 4/4/34, Detroit, Mich. BR/TR, 5'8", 155 lbs. Deb: 8/12/1884																												
1884	Ric-a	39	146	23	41	5	5	2		2		.281	.291	.425	.715	135	5	5	99	0	18	.610				10	O/S	1.3
1885	Bos-N	26	111	17	26	6	3	1	23	0	15	.234	.234	.369	.604	99	-1	-0	94	175	10	.482				0	O	0.0
1886	Bos-N	109	413	48	99	18	9	1	57	3	70	.240	.245	.334	.579	77	-13	-12	97	134	37	.484	11			15	*O	0.5
1887	Bos-N	127	507	87	131	13	20	5	77	16	35	.258	.281	.393	.674	89	-10	-8	98	113	72	.710	52			23	*O	1.3
1888	Bos-N	135	585	102	173	31	**18**	12	68	15	33	.296	.314	.472	.786	142	30	26	106	69	100	.794	35			5	*O	2.8
1889	Bos-N	132	539	80	123	16	4	5	67	41	60	.228	.285	.301	.586	64	-25	-27	102	109	57	.575	34			-8	*O	-3.4
1890	Bos-P	2	9	0	1	0	0	0	0	0	1	.111	.111	.111	.222	-37	-2	-2	107	0	0	.125	0			0	/O	-0.1
	NY-P	77	306	37	74	9	7	1	43	18	25	.242	.288	.327	.615	60	-16	-20	109	116	32	.547	7			-0	O/S	-1.8
	Yr	79	315	37	75	9	7	1	43	18	26	.238	.284	.321	.604	58	-17	-22	109	113	31	.533	7			-0		-1.9
1891	CM-a	99	376	59	83	11	2	6	51	38	44	.221	.301	.309	.609	69	-11	-19	112	112	39	.584	12			-2	*O	-2.0
Total	8	746	2992	453	751	109	68	33	386	133	283	.251	.285	.366	.651	88	-44	-57	103	103	367	.620	151			42	O/S	-1.4
■ **DOC JOHNSTON** Johnston, Wheeler Roger b: 9/9/1887, Cleveland, Tenn. d: 2/17/61, Chattanooga, Tenn. BL/TL, 6', 170 lbs. Deb: 09																												
1909	Cin-N	3	10	1	0	0	0	0	1	0		.000	.000	.000	.000	-99	-2	-2	94	0	0	.000	0			0	/1	-0.2
1912	Cle-A	43	164	22	46	7	4	1	11	11		.280	.326	.390	.716	103	0	0	101	58	23	.703	8			0	1	0.1
1913	Cle-A	133	530	74	135	19	12	2	39	35	65	.255	.309	.347	.657	87	-7	-11	106	64	60	.620	19			-2	*1	-1.3
1914	Cle-A	103	340	43	83	15	1	0	23	28	46	.244	.311	.294	.605	80	-7	-8	102	88	34	.553	14	9	-1	-4	1/O	-1.4
1915	Pit-N	147	543	71	144	19	12	5	64	38	40	.265	.328	.372	.700	113	7	8	99	108	72	.671	26	17	-2	-10	*1	-1.2
1916	Pit-N	114	404	33	86	10	10	0	39	20	42	.213	.262	.287	.549	66	-15	-17	105	136	37	.503	17			-2	*1	-2.7
1918	Cle-A	74	273	30	62	12	2	0	25	26	19	.227	.301	.286	.587	71	-8	-10	108	124	27	.564	12			-2	1	-1.8
1919	Cle-A	102	331	42	101	17	3	1	33	25	18	.305	.359	.384	.743	102	4	1	107	92	53	.765	21			-0	1	-0.6
1920	Cle-A	147	535	68	156	24	10	2	71	28	32	.292	.333	.385	.718	87	-9	-12	104	120	69	.655	13	6	0	1	*1	-0.9
1921	Cle-A	118	384	53	114	20	7	2	46	29	15	.297	.353	.401	.754	93	-5	-4	99	98	53	.677	2	9	-5	1	*1	-0.8
1922	Phi-A	71	260	41	65	11	7	1	29	24	15	.250	.316	.358	.673	72	-10	-11	104	114	30	.622	7	6	-2	-3	1	-2.0
Total	11	1055	3774	478	992	154	68	14	381	264	292	.263	.319	.351	.670	88	-51	-67	103	102	457	.627	139	47		-23	*1/O	-12.8
■ **FRED JOHNSTON** Johnston, Wilfred Ivy b: 7/9/1900, Pineville, N.C. d: 7/14/59, Tyler, Tex. BR/TR, 5'11.5", 170 lbs. Deb: 6/29/24																												
1924	Bro-N	4	4	1	1	0	0	0	0	0	1	.250	.250	.250	.500	35	-0	-0	99	0	0	.333	0	0	0	0	/23	0.0
■ **JAY JOHNSTONE** Johnstone, John William b: 11/20/45, Manchester, Conn. BL/TR, 6'1", 175 lbs. Deb: 7/30/66																												
1966	Cal-A	61	254	35	67	12	4	3	17	11	36	.264	.297	.378	.675	93	-3	-3	99	60	28	.575	3	3	-1	-1	O	-0.6
1967	Cal-A	79	230	18	48	7	1	2	10	5	37	.209	.226	.274	.499	49	-16	-14	96	60	13	.378	3	2	-0	5	O	-1.2
1968	Cal-A	41	115	11	30	4	1	0	3	7	15	.261	.303	.313	.616	93	-2	-1	94	36	12	.523	2	1	0	4	O	0.1
1969	Cal-A	148	540	64	146	20	5	10	59	38	75	.270	.324	.381	.706	97	-3	-3	99	106	65	.615	3	9	-5	5	*O	-0.5
1970	Cal-A	119	320	34	76	10	5	11	39	24	53	.237	.293	.403	.696	98	-6	-2	92	97	37	.618	1	0	0	-8	*O	-1.4
1971	Chi-A	124	388	53	101	14	1	16	40	38	50	.260	.331	.425	.756	116	6	7	98	77	56	.730	10	5	0	-8	*O	-0.4
1972	Chi-A	113	261	27	49	9	0	4	17	25	42	.188	.259	.268	.527	54	-14	-16	106	87	19	.451	2	1	0	-5	O	-2.6
1973	Oak-A	23	28	1	3	1	0	0	3	2	4	.107	.167	.143	.310	-14	-4	-4	87	295	1	.231	0	1	-1	-2	/O2D	-0.5
1974	Phi-N	64	200	30	59	10	4	6	30	24	28	.295	.371	.475	.846	131	9	8	103	102	35	.838	5	5	-2	-4	O	0.1
1975	Phi-N	122	350	50	115	19	2	7	54	42	39	.329	.401	.454	.855	135	18	17	101	116	64	.846	7	3	0	-4	*O	1.0
1976	Phi-N	129	440	62	140	38	4	5	53	41	39	.318	.379	.457	.836	127	21	17	107	94	75	.793	5	5	-2	7	*O/1	1.8
1977	Phi-N	112	363	64	103	18	4	15	59	38	38	.284	.355	.479	.834	121	11	10	100	108	59	.786	3	7	-3	1	O1	0.4
1978	Phi-N	35	56	3	10	2	0	0	4	6	9	.179	.258	.214	.472	32	-5	-5	105	132	3	.360	0	2	-1	-3	/1O	-0.9
	NY-A	36	65	6	17	0	0	1	6	4	1	.262	.333	.308	.641	82	-1	-1	99	103	7	.551	0	1	-1	-4	O/D	-0.5
1979	NY-A	23	48	7	10	1	0	1	7	2	7	.208	.240	.292	.532	45	-4	-4	96	158	4	.447	1	0	0	-2	O	-0.5
	SD-N	75	201	10	59	8	2	0	32	18	21	.294	.352	.353	.705	96	-2	-1	96	179	24	.596	1	3	-2	-5	O1	-0.9
1980	LA-N	109	251	31	77	15	2	2	20	24	29	.307	.372	.406	.778	121	6	7	97	73	39	.732	3	2	-0	0	O	0.5
1981	LA-N	61	83	8	17	3	0	3	6	7	13	.205	.267	.349	.616	75	-3	-3	98	62	7	.514	0	1	-1	-1	O/1	-0.5
1982	LA-N	21	13	1	1	1	0	0	2	5	2	.077	.333	.154	.487	43	-1	-1	95	392	1	.583	0	0	0	0	H	0.0
	Chi-N	98	269	39	67	13	1	10	43	40	41	.249	.346	.416	.763	109	5	4	103	119	40	.734	0	2	-1	0	O	0.2
	Yr	119	282	40	68	14	1	10	45	45	43	.241	.346	.404	.750	107	4	3	102	170	41	.726	0	2	-1	0		0.2
1983	Chi-N	86	140	16	36	7	0	6	22	20	24	.257	.362	.436	.798	119	4	4	101	110	22	.780	1	1	-0	-5	O	-0.2
1984	Chi-N	52	73	8	21	2	2	0	3	7	18	.288	.350	.370	.720	93	0	-1	110	44	9	.630	0	0	0	-4	O	-0.4
1985	LA-N	17	15	0	2	1	0	0	2	1	2	.133	.188	.200	.387	9	-2	-2	93	266	0	.267	0	0	0	0	H	-0.1
Total	20	1748	4703	578	1254	215	38	102	531	429	623	.267	.331	.394	.724	103	15	16	100	99	618	.671	50	54	-17	-32	*O/1D2	-7.1

YEAR	TM/L	G	AB	R	H	2B	3B	HR	RBI	BB	SO	AVG	OBP	SLG	PRO	/A	BR	/A	PF	CHI	RC	TA	SB	CS	SBR	FR	POS	TPR
■ STAN JOK	Jok, Stanley Edward "Tucker" b: 5/3/26, Buffalo, N.Y. d: 3/6/72, Buffalo, N.Y. BR/TR, 6', 190 lbs. Deb: 4/13/54																											
1954	Phi-N	3	3	0	0	0	0	0	0	0	2	.000	.000	.000	.000	-99	-1	-1	99	0	0	.000	0	0	0	0	H	0.0
	Chi-A	3	12	1	2	0	0	0	2	1	2	.167	.231	.167	.397	10	-1	-2	104	402	0	.273	0	0	0	0	/3	-0.1
1955	Chi-A	6	4	3	1	0	0	1	2	1	1	.250	.400	1.000	1.400	265	1	1	101	107	2	1.667	0	0	0	-1	/3O	0.0
Total	2	12	19	4	3	0	0	1	4	2	5	.158	.238	.316	.554	48	-1	-2	102	274	2	.500	0	0	0	-1	/3O	-0.1
■ SMEAD JOLLEY	Jolley, Smead Powell "Guinea" or "Smudge" b: 1/14/02, Wesson, Ark. BL/TR, 6'3.5", 210 lbs. Deb: 4/17/30																											
1930	Chi-A	152	616	76	193	38	12	16	114	28	52	.313	.346	.492	.838	107	7	4	103	114	103	.795	3	1	0	-6	*O	-0.6
1931	Chi-A	54	110	5	33	11	0	3	28	7	4	.300	.353	.482	.835	127	2	4	92	149	19	.805	0	0	0	-5	O	-0.2
1932	Chi-A	12	42	3	15	3	0	0	7	3	0	.357	.413	.429	.842	136	1	2	87	130	8	.852	1	0	0	-3	O	0.0
	Bos-A	137	531	57	164	27	5	18	99	27	29	.309	.345	.480	.825	115	7	9	97	109	85	.763	0	5	-3	-6	*O/C	-0.4
	Yr	149	573	60	179	30	5	18	106	30	29	.312	.350	.476	.826	116	8	11	96	112	93	.769	1	5	-3	-9		-0.4
1933	Bos-A	118	411	47	116	32	4	9	65	24	20	.282	.325	.445	.770	101	-0	-1	101	103	59	.709	1	1	-0	-5	*O	-0.8
Total	4	473	1710	188	521	111	21	46	313	89	105	.305	.343	.475	.818	110	17	18	99	113	274	.766	5	7	-3	-24	O/C	-2.0
■ JONES	Jones Deb:5/14/1873																											
1873	Mar-n	1	5	0	3							.600															/O	
1874	Bal-n	2	7	0	1							.143															/CO	
1875	Har-n	1	5	1	0							.000															/O	
Total	3 n	4	17	1	4							.235															/O	
■ JONES	Jones b:Johnstown, Pa. Deb: 7/14/1884																											
1884	Was-a	4	17	2	5	0	0	0		1		.294	.333	.294	.627	124	0	0	88	0	2	.500				0	/O	0.0
■ CHARLIE JONES	Jones, Charles C. "Casey" b: 6/2/1876, Butler, Pa. d: 4/2/47, Two Harbors, Minn. BR/TR, 6'1", Deb: 5/03/01																											
1901	Bos-A	10	41	6	6	2	0	0	6	1		.146	.167	.195	.362	1	-5	-5	97	251	2	.314	2			-3	O	-0.7
1904	Chi-A	5	17	2	4	0	1	0	1	1		.235	.278	.353	.631	102	-0	0	99	63	2	.538	0			-0	/O	0.0
1905	Was-A	142	544	68	113	18	4	2	41	31		.208	.250	.267	.517	63	-21	-24	104	93	43	.464	24			12	*O	-1.9
1906	Was-A	131	497	56	120	11	11	3	42	24		.241	.276	.326	.602	99	-7	-2	91	95	56	.584	34			-4	*O/2	-1.1
1907	Was-A	121	437	48	116	14	10	0	37	22		.265	.301	.343	.644	119	3	7	90	90	54	.617	26			3	*O/21S	0.5
1908	StL-A	74	263	37	61	11	2	0	17	14		.232	.271	.289	.560	81	-5	-6	103	86	23	.515	14			10	O	0.1
Total	6	483	1799	217	420	56	28	5	144	93		.233	.271	.304	.575	86	-35	-29	97	95	180	.537	100			19	O/21S	-3.1
■ CHARLIE JONES	Jones, Charles F. b: New York, N.Y. Deb: 6/28/1884																											
1884	Bro-a	25	90	10	16	1	0	0		5		.178	.221	.189	.410	38	-6	-6	98	0	4	.297				0	23/O	-0.4
1885	NY-a	1	4	0	1	0	0	0		0		.250	.250	.250	.500	72	-0	-0	84	0	0	.333				0	/3	0.0
Total	2	26	94	10	17	1	0	0		5		.181	.222	.191	.414	39	-6	-6	97	0	4	.299				0	/23O	-0.4
■ CHARLEY JONES	Jones, Charles Wesley "Baby" (born Benjamin Wesley Rippay) b: 4/30/1850, Alamance Co., N.C. BR/TR, Deb: N/A.																											
1875	Wes-n	12	52	4	13							.250															O	
1876	Cin-N	64	276	40	79	17	4	4	38	7	17	.286	.304	.420	.724	155	11	15	90	89	36	.624				1	*O	1.4
1877	Cin-N	17	69	16	21	3	3	1	10	4	8	.304	.342	.478	.821	191	4	6	82	100	12	.771				1	1/O	0.6
	Chi-N	2	8	1	3	1	0	0	2	1	0	.375	.444	.500	.944	200	1	1	98	163	2	1.000				1	/O	0.2
	Cin-N	38	163	36	51	8	7	1	26	10	17	.313	.353	.466	.819	191	10	15	82	98	27	.768				10	O	2.1
	Yr	57	240	53	75	12	10	2	38	15	25	.313	.353	.471	.824	191	16	22	82	106	41	.776				12		2.9
1878	Cin-N	61	261	50	81	11	7	3	39	4	17	.310	.321	.441	.761	155	13	14	95	113	38	.661				6	*O	1.4
1879	Bos-N	83	355	**85**	112	22	10	**9**	**62**	**29**	38	.315	.367	.510	.877	173	**33**	29	107	92	68	**.864**				12	*O	3.5
1880	Bos-N	66	280	44	84	15	3	5	37	11	27	.300	.326	.429	.755	167	15	18	92	88	40	.668				-5	*O	1.1
1883	Cin-a	90	391	84	115	15	11	11		20		.294	.328	.473	.802	150	23	21	103	0	62	.743				-0	*O	1.8
1884	Cin-a	112	472	117	148	19	17	7		37		.314	**.376**	.470	.846	168	40	36	106	0	85	.830				4	*O	3.5
1885	Cin-a	112	487	108	157	19	17	4		21		.322	.362	.456	.818	154	32	29	104	0	82	.764				13	*O	3.2
1886	Cin-a	127	500	87	135	22	11	5		61		.270	.356	.388	.744	141	22	25	96	0	72	.723	3			1	*O	1.9
1887	Cin-a	41	153	28	48	7	4	2		19		.314	.400	.451	.851	129	9	6	108	0	31	.933	7			-0	O	0.4
	NY-a	62	247	30	63	11	3	3		12		.255	.306	.360	.666	99	-5	1	88	0	30	.625	8			1	O/P1	0.0
	Yr	103	400	58	111	18	7	5		31		.278	.343	.395	.738	112	4	7	96	0	61	.737	15			1		0.4
1888	KC-a	6	25	2	4	0	1	0	5	1		.160	.192	.240	.432	38	-2	-2	106	239	1	.381	1			0	/O	-0.1
Total	11	881	3687	728	1101	170	98	55	219	237	124	.299	.347	.443	.789	153	207	216	99	37	588	.743	19			44	O/1P	21.0
■ CHRIS JONES	Jones, Christopher Dale b: 7/13/57, Los Angeles, Cal. BL/TL, 6', 183 lbs. Deb: 6/08/85																											
1985	Hou-N	31	25	0	5	0	0	0	1	3	7	.200	.286	.200	.486	40	-2	-2	96	80	2	.400	0	0	0	-3	O	-0.5
1986	SF-N	3	1	0	0	0	0	0	0	0	0	.000	.000	.000	.000	-99	-0	-0	96	0	0	1.000	1	0	0	0	/H	0.0
Total	2	34	26	0	5	0	0	0	1	3	7	.192	.276	.192	.468	35	-2	-2	96	77	2	.429	1	0	0	-3	/O	-0.5
■ CLARENCE JONES	Jones, Clarence Woodrow b: 11/7/41, Zanesville, Ohio BL/TL, 6'2", 185 lbs. Deb: 4/20/67 C																											
1967	Chi-N	53	135	13	34	7	0	2	16	14	33	.252	.322	.348	.670	90	-1	-2	102	125	16	.592	0	0	0	-3	O1	-0.7
1968	Chi-N	5	2	0	0	0	0	0	0	2	1	.000	.500	.000	.500	54	0	0	112	0	0	1.000	0	0	0	0	/1	0.0
Total	2	58	137	13	34	7	0	2	16	16	34	.248	.327	.343	.670	90	-1	-1	102	122	16	.612	0	0	0	-3	/O1	-0.7
■ CLEON JONES	Jones, Cleon Joseph b: 8/4/42, Plateau, Ala. BR/TL, 6', 185 lbs. Deb: 9/14/63																											
1963	NY-N	6	15	1	2	0	0	0	1	0	4	.133	.133	.133	.267	-23	-2	-2	99	210	0	.154	0	0	0	-1	/O	-0.3
1965	NY-N	30	74	2	11	1	0	1	9	2	23	.149	.171	.203	.374	5	-9	-9	100	207	3	.286	1	0	0	-0	O	-1.0
1966	NY-N	139	495	74	136	16	4	8	57	30	62	.275	.320	.372	.692	97	-6	-2	94	118	57	.613	16	8	0	-3	*O	-0.9
1967	NY-N	129	411	46	101	10	5	5	30	19	57	.246	.286	.331	.617	77	-13	-13	99	82	39	.534	12	2	2	-7	*O	-2.4
1968	NY-N	147	509	63	151	29	4	14	55	31	98	.297	.343	.452	.795	134	22	21	102	87	77	.765	23	12	-0	-6	*O	0.8
1969	NY-N	137	483	92	164	25	4	12	75	64	60	.340	.424	.482	.907	153	37	37	100	114	100	.947	16	8	0	0	*O1	3.0
1970	NY-N	134	506	71	140	25	8	10	63	57	87	.277	.356	.417	.773	102	5	2	104	107	71	.722	12	3	2	6	*O	0.4
1971	NY-N	136	505	63	161	24	6	14	69	53	87	.319	.386	.473	.859	147	28	30	96	106	92	.838	6	5	-1	-1	*O	2.5
1972	NY-N	106	375	39	92	15	1	5	52	30	83	.245	.308	.331	.639	86	-9	-7	95	157	36	.532	1	6	-3	0	O1	-1.6
1973	NY-N	92	339	48	88	13	0	11	48	28	51	.260	.322	.395	.717	97	-2	-2	101	118	41	.631	1	1	-0	-1	O	-0.7
1974	NY-N	124	461	62	130	23	1	13	60	38	79	.282	.345	.421	.765	114	7	8	99	101	66	.699	3	3	-1	-0	*O	0.2
1975	NY-N	21	50	2	12	1	0	0	2	3	6	.240	.283	.260	.543	54	-3	-3	95	59	4	.421	0	0	0	-3	O	-0.6
1976	Chi-A	12	40	2	8	1	0	0	3	5	5	.200	.304	.225	.529	57	-2	-2	99	131	3	.455	0	0	0	-2	/OD	-0.4
Total	13	1213	4263	565	1196	183	33	93	524	360	702	.281	.342	.404	.747	111	53	57	99	111	589	.711	91	48	-2	-19	*O/1D	-1.0
■ COBE JONES	Jones, Coburn Dyas b: 8/21/07, Denver, Colo. d: 6/3/69, Denver, Colo. BB/TR, 5'7", 155 lbs. Deb: 9/27/28																											
1928	Pit-N	1	2	0	1	0	0	0	0	0	0	.500	.500	.500	1.000	152	0	0	107	0	0	1.000	0			0	/S	0.0
1929	Pit-N	25	63	6	16	5	1	0	4	1	5	.254	.266	.365	.631	53	-5	-5	103	60	6	.532	1			-3	S	-0.4
Total	2	26	65	6	17	5	1	0	4	1	5	.262	.273	.369	.642	56	-5	-5	104	58	6	.542	1			-3	/S	-0.4
■ DARRYL JONES	Jones, Darryl Lee b: 6/5/51, Meadville, Pa. BR/TR, 5'10", 175 lbs. Deb: 6/06/79																											
1979	NY-A	18	47	6	12	5	1	0	6	2	7	.255	.286	.404	.690	88	-1	-1	96	121	5	.583	0	0	0	-1	D/O	-0.1
■ DAVY JONES	Jones, David Jefferson "Kangaroo" b: 6/30/1880, Cambria, Wis. d: 3/31/72, Mankato, Minn. BL/TR, 5'10", 165 lbs. Deb: 9/15/01																											
1901	Mil-A	14	52	12	9	0	0	3	5	11		.173	.317	.346	.664	90	-1	-0	95	50	7	.767	4			1	O	0.0
1902	StL-A	15	49	4	11	1	1	0	3	6		.224	.309	.286	.595	66	-2	-2	102	72	6	.658	5			7	O	0.3
	Chi-N	64	243	41	74	12	3	0	14	38		.305	.399	.379	.777	148	14	15	96	46	42	.840	12			8	O	1.9
1903	Chi-N	130	497	64	140	18	3	1	62	53		.282	.351	.336	.687	103	0	4	95	124	65	.658	15			11	*O	0.7
1904	Chi-N	98	336	44	82	11	5	3	39	41		.244	.326	.333	.660	105	3	3	101	125	42	.657	14			-5	O	-0.5
1906	Det-A	84	323	41	84	12	2	0	24	41		.260	.343	.310	.653	99	4	1	108	75	43	.678	21			8	O	0.7
1907	Det-A	126	491	101	134	10	6	0	27	60		.273	.352	.318	.670	114	11	10	102	53	67	.689	30			19	*O	2.5

YEAR	TM/L	G	AB	R	H	2B	3B	HR	RBI	BB	SO	AVG	OBP	SLG	PRO	/A	BR	/A	PF	CHI	RC	TA	SB	CS	SBR	FR	POS	TPR
1908	Det-A	56	121	17	25	2	1	0	10	13		.207	.284	.240	.523	72	-3	-3	101	130	11	.552	11			-1	O	-0.6
1909	Det-A	69	204	44	57	2	2	0	10	28		.279	.369	.309	.678	104	5	2	110	61	27	.707	12			-2	O	-0.1
1910	Det-A	113	377	77	100	6	6	0	24	51		.265	.362	.313	.675	109	7	7	102	77	52	.722	25			3	*O	0.6
1911	Det-A	98	341	78	93	10	0	0	19	41		.273	.354	.302	.656	78	-6	-10	108	64	45	.690	25			0	O	-1.5
1912	Det-A	97	316	54	93	5	2	0	24	38		.294	.370	.323	.693	104	1	3	95	78	44	.700	16			1	O	0.0
1913	Chi-A	12	21	2	6	0	0	0	0	9	0	.286	.500	.286	.786	138	2	2	95	0	3	1.067	1			-1	/O	0.1
1914	Pit-F	97	352	58	96	9	8	2	24	42	16	.273	.350	.361	.711	110	3	5	94	69	53	.719	15			1	O	0.1
1915	Pit-F	14	49	6	16	0	1	0	4	6	0	.327	.400	.367	.767	123	2	2	104	82	8	.758	1			0	O	0.2
Total	14	1087	3772	643	1020	98	40	9	289	478	16	.270	.354	.325	.679	105	41	40	101	80	516	.697	207			51	*O	4.4

■ FIELDER JONES Jones, Fielder Allison b: 8/13/1871, Shinglehouse, Pa. d: 3/13/34, Portland, Ore. BL/TR, 5'11", 180 lbs. Deb: 4/18/1896 M

YEAR	TM/L	G	AB	R	H	2B	3B	HR	RBI	BB	SO	AVG	OBP	SLG	PRO	/A	BR	/A	PF	CHI	RC	TA	SB	CS	SBR	FR	POS	TPR
1896	Bro-N	104	395	82	140	10	8	3	46	48	15	.354	.427	.443	.870	151	20	29	87	69	84	.953	18			-5	*O	1.4
1897	Bro-N	135	548	134	172	15	10	0	49	61		.314	.392	.378	.769	104	8	6	102	61	102	.864	48			5	*O	0.1
1898	Bro-N	146	596	89	181	15	9	1	69	46		.304	.362	.364	.726	117	9	14	95	82	94	.740	36			-2	*O/S	0.3
1899	Bro-N	102	365	75	104	8	2	2	38	54		.285	.386	.334	.720	97	4	1	105	96	55	.766	18			-3	O	-0.7
1900	Bro-N	136	552	106	171	26	4	4	54	57		.310	.374	.393	.768	106	12	6	108	64	96	.806	33			-1	*O	-0.6
1901	Chi-A	133	521	120	162	16	3	2	65	84		.311	.407	.365	.771	118	17	18	99	92	95	.869	38			1	*O	1.5
1902	Chi-A	135	532	98	171	16	5	0	54	57		.321	.387	.370	.757	118	11	15	95	80	91	.795	33			13	*O	1.8
1903	Chi-A	136	530	71	152	18	5	0	45	47		.287	.345	.340	.685	117	7	12	92	87	71	.656	21			-4	*O	-0.1
1904	Chi-A	149	547	72	133	14	5	3	42	53		.243	.310	.303	.613	98	-0	0	99	86	61	.589	25			-0	*OM	-1.0
1905	Chi-A	153	568	91	139	17	12	2	38	73		.245	.331	.327	.658	115	9	12	97	62	70	.650	20			7	*OM	1.2
1906	Chi-A	144	496	77	114	22	4	2	34	83		.230	.340	.302	.643	113	6	11	92	76	61	.678	26			-8	*OM	-0.3
1907	Chi-A	154	559	72	146	18	1	0	47	67		.261	.340	.297	.637	102	6	4	104	97	64	.605	17			1	*OM	-0.3
1908	Chi-A	149	529	92	134	11	7	1	50	86		.253	.358	.306	.664	126	15	19	94	109	66	.694	26			-11	*OM	0.0
1914	StL-F	5	3	0	1	0	0	0	0	1	0	.333	.500	.333	.833	134	0	0	106	0	1	1.000	0			0	HM	0.0
1915	StL-F	7	6	1	0	0	0	0	0	0	0	.000	.000	.000	.000	-96	-1	-1	105	0	0	.000	0			0	/OM	-0.1
Total	15	1788	6747	1180	1920	206	75	20	631	817	15	.285	.364	.346	.710	113	123	144	98	81	1011	.733	359			-8	*O/S	3.2

■ FRANK JONES Jones, Frank M. b: 8/25/1858, Princeton, Ill. d: 2/4/36, Marietta, Ohio Deb: 7/02/1884

YEAR	TM/L	G	AB	R	H	2B	3B	HR	RBI	BB	SO	AVG	OBP	SLG	PRO	/A	BR	/A	PF	CHI	RC	TA	SB	CS	SBR	FR	POS	TPR
1884	Det-N	2	6	1	2	0	0	0	0	0	0	.333	.333	.333	.667	118	0	0	94	0	1	.500				0	/SO	0.0

■ DEACON JONES Jones, Grover William b: 4/18/34, White Plains, N.Y. BL/TR, 5'10", 185 lbs. Deb: 9/08/62 C

YEAR	TM/L	G	AB	R	H	2B	3B	HR	RBI	BB	SO	AVG	OBP	SLG	PRO	/A	BR	/A	PF	CHI	RC	TA	SB	CS	SBR	FR	POS	TPR
1962	Chi-A	18	28	3	9	2	0	0	8	4	6	.321	.406	.393	.799	122	1	1	95	289	5	.789	0	0	0	-0	/1	0.0
1963	Chi-A	17	16	4	3	0	1	1	2	2	2	.188	.316	.500	.816	119	0	0	104	76	2	.786	0	0	0	0	/1	0.0
1966	Chi-A	5	5	0	2	0	0	0	0	0	0	.400	.400	.400	.800	139	0	0	94	0	1	.667	0	0	0	0	H	0.0
Total	3	40	49	7	14	2	1	1	10	6	8	.286	.375	.429	.804	122	2	2	98	191	8	.800	0	0	0	-0	/1	0.0

■ HAL JONES Jones, Harold Marion b: 4/9/36, Louisiana, Mo. BR/TR, 6'2", 194 lbs. Deb: 9/15/61

YEAR	TM/L	G	AB	R	H	2B	3B	HR	RBI	BB	SO	AVG	OBP	SLG	PRO	/A	BR	/A	PF	CHI	RC	TA	SB	CS	SBR	FR	POS	TPR
1961	Cle-A	12	35	2	6	0	0	2	4	2	12	.171	.216	.343	.559	49	-3	-3	96	87	2	.467	0	0	0	1	1	-0.2
1962	Cle-A	5	16	2	5	1	0	0	1	0	4	.313	.353	.375	.728	98	-0	-0	98	66	2	.636	0	0	0	0	/1	0.0
Total	2	17	51	4	11	1	0	2	5	2	16	.216	.259	.353	.612	64	-3	-3	97	80	5	.525	0	0	0	1	/1	-0.2

■ HENRY JONES Jones, Henry M. "Baldy" b: Cadillac, Mich. Deb: 8/20/1884

YEAR	TM/L	G	AB	R	H	2B	3B	HR	RBI	BB	SO	AVG	OBP	SLG	PRO	/A	BR	/A	PF	CHI	RC	TA	SB	CS	SBR	FR	POS	TPR
1884	Det-N	34	129	23	27	3	1	0	3	16	19	.209	.297	.248	.545	78	-3	-2	94	31	10	.471				0	2O/S	-0.1
1890	Pit-N	5	9	0	2	0	0	0	0	0	0	.222	.222	.222	.444	35	-1	-1	88	0	1	.429	1			0	/P	0.0
Total	2	39	138	23	29	3	1	0	3	16	19	.210	.292	.246	.539	76	-4	-3	93	29	10	.468	1			0	/2OSP	-0.1

■ HOWIE JONES Jones, Howard "Cotton" (born Howard Painter) b: 3/1/1897, Irwin, Pa. d: 7/15/72, Jeanette, Pa. BL/TL, 5'11", 165 lbs. Deb: 9/05/21

YEAR	TM/L	G	AB	R	H	2B	3B	HR	RBI	BB	SO	AVG	OBP	SLG	PRO	/A	BR	/A	PF	CHI	RC	TA	SB	CS	SBR	FR	POS	TPR
1921	StL-N	3	2	0	0	0	0	0	0	0	1	.000	.000	.000	.000	-99	-1	-1	95	0	0	.000	0	0	0	-0	/O	0.0

■ DALTON JONES Jones, James Dalton b: 12/10/43, Mc Comb, Miss. BL/TR, 6'1", 180 lbs. Deb: 4/17/64

YEAR	TM/L	G	AB	R	H	2B	3B	HR	RBI	BB	SO	AVG	OBP	SLG	PRO	/A	BR	/A	PF	CHI	RC	TA	SB	CS	SBR	FR	POS	TPR
1964	Bos-A	118	374	37	86	16	4	6	39	22	38	.230	.275	.342	.617	69	-15	-16	102	113	36	.536	6	3	0	-4	2/S3	-1.1
1965	Bos-A	112	367	41	99	13	5	5	37	28	45	.270	.325	.373	.698	91	-1	-4	107	101	46	.634	8	1	2	-3	3/2	-0.4
1966	Bos-A	115	252	26	59	11	5	4	23	22	27	.234	.303	.365	.668	83	-3	-6	109	93	27	.590	1	2	-1	1	2/3	0.0
1967	Bos-A	89	159	18	46	6	2	3	25	11	23	.289	.335	.409	.744	104	3	1	115	141	21	.655	0	1	-1	-2	32/1	0.0
1968	Bos-A	111	354	38	83	13	0	5	29	17	53	.234	.272	.314	.585	76	-10	-11	101	99	28	.459	1	1	-0	-1	12/3	-1.4
1969	Bos-A	111	336	50	74	18	3	3	33	39	36	.220	.305	.318	.623	71	-11	-13	105	114	34	.552	1	1	-0	1	1/32	-1.8
1970	Det-A	89	191	29	42	7	0	6	21	33	33	.220	.338	.351	.689	87	-2	-3	103	100	24	.667	1	1	-0	-1	231	0.0
1971	Det-A	83	138	15	35	5	0	5	11	9	21	.254	.304	.399	.703	102	-1	-0	96	64	15	.606	1	3	-2	-3	O3/12	-0.5
1972	Det-A	7	7	0	0	0	0	0	0	0	2	.000	.000	.000	.000	-88	-2	-2	113	0	0	.000	0	0	0	0	H	-0.1
	Tex-A	72	151	14	24	2	0	4	19	10	31	.159	.211	.252	.463	40	-12	-11	94	159	8	.380	1	0	0	-2	32/1O	-1.3
	Yr	79	158	14	24	2	0	4	19	10	33	.152	.202	.241	.443	33	-14	-13	96	145	8	.360	1	0	0	-2		-1.4
Total	9	907	2329	268	548	91	19	41	237	191	309	.235	.296	.343	.640	80	-54	-65	104	107	240	.569	20	13	-2	-12	231/OS	-6.6

■ JAKE JONES Jones, James Murrell b: 11/23/20, Epps, La. BR/TR, 6'3", 197 lbs. Deb: 9/20/41

YEAR	TM/L	G	AB	R	H	2B	3B	HR	RBI	BB	SO	AVG	OBP	SLG	PRO	/A	BR	/A	PF	CHI	RC	TA	SB	CS	SBR	FR	POS	TPR
1941	Chi-A	3	11	0	0	0	0	0	0	0	4	.000	.000	.000	.000	-99	-3	-3	94	0	0	.000	0	0	0	0	/1	-0.2
1942	Chi-A	7	20	2	3	1	0	0	0	2	2	.150	.227	.200	.427	21	-2	-2	99	0	1	.412	1	0	0	-0	/1	-0.1
1946	Chi-A	24	79	10	21	5	1	3	13	2	13	.266	.284	.468	.752	111	0	0	97	107	10	.639	0	0	0	-2	1	-0.2
1947	Chi-A	45	171	15	41	7	1	3	20	13	25	.240	.297	.345	.642	81	-5	-5	97	115	18	.552	1	0	0	-0	1	-0.5
	Bos-A	109	404	50	95	14	3	16	76	41	60	.235	.310	.403	.714	91	-3	-7	108	135	52	.663	5	4	-1	-1	*1	-1.1
	Yr	154	575	65	136	21	4	19	96	54	85	.237	.306	.386	.693	88	-9	-12	104	130	71	.636	6	4	-1	-1		-1.6
1948	Bos-A	36	105	3	21	4	0	1	8	11	26	.200	.276	.267	.543	45	-8	-9	100	87	8	.455	1	0	0	-0	1	-0.6
Total	5	224	790	80	181	31	5	23	117	69	130	.229	.294	.368	.663	80	-22	-25	103	116	88	.603	8	4	0	-3	1	-2.7

■ JIM JONES Jones, James Tilford "Sheriff" b: 12/25/1876, London, Ky. d: 5/6/53, London, Ky. TR , 5'10", 162 lbs. Deb: 6/29/1897

YEAR	TM/L	G	AB	R	H	2B	3B	HR	RBI	BB	SO	AVG	OBP	SLG	PRO	/A	BR	/A	PF	CHI	RC	TA	SB	CS	SBR	FR	POS	TPR
1897	Lou-N	2	4	2	1	1	0	0	0	1		.250	.400	.500	.900	146	0	0	95	0	1	1.000	0			0	/P	0.0
1901	NY-N	21	91	10	19	4	3	0	5	4		.209	.242	.319	.561	70	-4	-3	91	50	8	.486	2			-1	O/P	-0.5
1902	NY-N	67	249	16	59	11	1	0	19	13		.237	.275	.289	.564	76	-7	-7	100	97	22	.484	7			3	O	-0.9
Total	3	90	344	28	79	16	4	0	24	18		.230	.268	.299	.567	75	-11	-10	98	83	31	.491	9			2	/OP	-1.4

■ JEFF JONES Jones, Jeffrey Raymond b: 10/22/57, Philadelphia, Pa. BR/TR, 6'2", 200 lbs. Deb: 4/04/83

YEAR	TM/L	G	AB	R	H	2B	3B	HR	RBI	BB	SO	AVG	OBP	SLG	PRO	/A	BR	/A	PF	CHI	RC	TA	SB	CS	SBR	FR	POS	TPR
1983	Cin-N	16	44	6	10	3	0	0	5	11	13	.227	.393	.295	.688	91	0	0	103	152	7	.794	2	0	1	1	O/1	0.1

■ BINKY JONES Jones, John Joseph b: 7/11/1899, St.Louis, Mo. d: 5/13/61, St.Louis, Mo. BR/TR, 5'9", 154 lbs. Deb: 4/15/24

YEAR	TM/L	G	AB	R	H	2B	3B	HR	RBI	BB	SO	AVG	OBP	SLG	PRO	/A	BR	/A	PF	CHI	RC	TA	SB	CS	SBR	FR	POS	TPR
1924	Bro-N	10	37	0	4	1	0	0	2	0	3	.108	.108	.135	.243	-36	-7	-7	99	149	1	.152	0	0	0	-0	S	-0.6

■ JOHN JONES Jones, John William "Skins" b: 5/13/01, Coatesville, Pa. d: 11/3/56, Baltimore, Md. BL/TL, 5'11", 185 lbs. Deb: 9/26/23

YEAR	TM/L	G	AB	R	H	2B	3B	HR	RBI	BB	SO	AVG	OBP	SLG	PRO	/A	BR	/A	PF	CHI	RC	TA	SB	CS	SBR	FR	POS	TPR
1923	Phi-A	1	4	0	1	0	0	0	1	0	1	.250	.250	.250	.500	32	-0	-0	100	349	0	.333	0	0	0	0	/O	0.0
1932	Phi-A	4	6	0	1	0	0	0	0	0	3	.167	.167	.167	.333	-12	-1	-1	114	0	0	.200	0	0	0	-0	/O	0.0
Total	2	5	10	0	2	0	0	0	1	0	4	.200	.200	.200	.400	4	-1	-2	109	139	0	.250	0	0	0	0	/O	0.0

■ LYNN JONES Jones, Lynn Morris b: 1/1/53, Meadville, Pa. BR/TR, 5'9", 175 lbs. Deb: 4/13/79

YEAR	TM/L	G	AB	R	H	2B	3B	HR	RBI	BB	SO	AVG	OBP	SLG	PRO	/A	BR	/A	PF	CHI	RC	TA	SB	CS	SBR	FR	POS	TPR
1979	Det-A	95	213	33	63	8	0	4	26	17	22	.296	.351	.390	.740	103	0	1	96	105	28	.683	9	6	-1	-7	O	-0.9
1980	Det-A	30	55	9	14	2	2	0	6	10	5	.255	.369	.364	.733	96	0	0	105	117	8	.705	1	0	0	-2	O/D	-0.1
1981	Det-A	71	174	19	45	5	0	2	19	18	10	.259	.332	.322	.653	85	-2	-3	105	120	18	.555	1	2	-1	-6	O/D	-1.1
1982	Det-A	58	139	15	31	3	1	0	14	7	14	.223	.260	.259	.519	43	-11	-11	100	155	9	.384	0	2	-1	-6	O/D	-1.9
1983	Det-A	49	64	9	17	1	2	0	6	3	6	.266	.299	.344	.642	80	-2	-2	96	107	7	.542	1	0	0	-7	O/D	-0.8
1984	KC-A	47	103	11	31	6	0	1	10	4	9	.301	.333	.388	.722	100	-0	-0	99	93	11	.582	1	3	-2	-12	O	-1.4
1985	KC-A	110	152	12	32	7	0	0	9	8	15	.211	.264	.257	.520	43	-12	-12	102	91	10	.394	0	1	-1	-21	*O/D	-3.5
1986	KC-A	67	47	1	6	2	0	0	1	6	5	.128	.226	.170	.397	11	-6	-6	100	50	2	.326	0	0	0	-21	O/2D	-2.8
Total	8	527	947	109	239	34	5	7	91	73	86	.252	.310	.321	.631	74	-32	-33	100	110	92	.547	13	14	-5	-82	O/D2	-12.5

YEAR	TM/L	G	AB	R	H	2B	3B	HR	RBI	BB	SO	AVG	OBP	SLG	PRO	/A	BR	/A	PF	CHI	RC	TA	SB	CS	SBR	FR	POS	TPR
■ MACK JONES	Jones, Mack "Mack The Knife" b: 11/6/38, Atlanta, Ga. BL/TR, 6'1", 180 lbs. Deb: 7/13/61																											
1961	Mil-N	28	104	13	24	3	2	0	12	12	28	.231	.322	.298	.620	72	-5	-4	92	165	10	.583	4	4	-1	-0	O	-0.6
1962	Mil-N	91	333	51	85	17	4	10	36	44	100	.255	.354	.420	.775	108	4	4	99	88	52	.766	5	1	1	-7	O	-0.6
1963	Mil-N	93	228	36	50	11	4	3	22	26	59	.219	.318	.342	.660	89	-2	-3	101	106	26	.647	8	4	0	-3	O	-1.0
1965	Mil-N	143	504	78	132	18	7	31	75	29	122	.262	.314	.510	.824	123	16	14	104	91	81	.799	8	2	1	-0	*O	1.1
1966	Atl-N	118	417	60	110	14	1	23	66	39	85	.264	.338	.468	.806	123	12	12	99	107	65	.796	16	10	-1	-7	*O/1	0.1
1967	Atl-N	140	454	72	115	23	4	17	50	64	108	.253	.357	.434	.791	120	16	14	104	85	73	.795	10	6	-1	6	*O	1.4
1968	Cin-N	103	234	40	59	9	1	10	34	28	46	.252	.345	.427	.772	117	9	6	111	110	34	.730	2	3	-1	-7	O	-0.5
1969	Mon-N	135	455	73	123	23	5	22	79	67	110	.270	.382	.488	.870	141	27	27	100	112	85	.886	6	7	-2	-1	*O	1.7
1970	Mon-N	108	271	51	65	11	3	14	32	59	74	.240	.399	.458	.857	129	14	14	100	75	56	.953	5	3	-0	-8	O	0.1
1971	Mon-N	43	91	11	15	3	0	3	9	15	24	.165	.296	.297	.593	69	-4	-3	99	102	9	.584	1	0	0	-3	O	-0.7
Total	10	1002	3091	485	778	132	31	133	415	383	756	.252	.349	.444	.792	118	87	81	102	99	492	.805	65	40	-5	-30	O/1	1.0
■ RED JONES	Jones, Maurice Morris b: 11/2/14, Timpson, Tex. d: 6/30/75, Lincoln, Cal. BL/TR, 6'3", 190 lbs. Deb: 4/16/40																											
1940	StL-N	12	11	0	1	0	0	0	1	1	2	.091	.167	.091	.258	-27	-2	-2	102	371	0	.200	0			-0	/O	-0.1
■ RICKY JONES	Jones, Ricky Miron b: 6/4/58, Tupelo, Miss. BR/TR, 6'3", 186 lbs. Deb: 9/03/86																											
1986	Bal-A	16	33	2	6	2	0	0	4	6	8	.182	.308	.242	.550	54	-2	-2	99	199	3	.519	0	0	0	-1	2/3	-0.1
■ BOB JONES	Jones, Robert Oliver b: 10/11/49, Elkton, Md. BL/TL, 6'2", 195 lbs. Deb: 10/01/74																											
1974	Tex-A	2	5	0	0	0	0	0	0	0	1	.000	.000	.000	.000	-99	-1	-1	96	0	0	.000	0	0	0	0	/O	0.0
1975	Tex-A	9	11	2	1	0	0	0	0	3	3	.091	.286	.091	.377	11	-1	-1	100	0	1	.400	0	0	0	-1	/OD	-0.2
1976	Cal-A	78	166	22	35	6	0	6	17	14	30	.211	.276	.355	.632	91	-4	-2	92	85	16	.566	3	0	1	-4	O/D	-0.6
1977	Cal-A	14	17	3	3	0	0	1	3	4	5	.176	.333	.353	.686	92	-0	-0	95	132	2	.667	0	0	0	0	/D	0.0
1981	Tex-A	10	34	4	9	1	0	3	7	1	7	.265	.286	.559	.845	152	1	2	91	98	5	.769	0	1	-1	3	O	0.4
1983	Tex-A	41	72	5	16	4	0	1	11	5	17	.222	.291	.319	.611	67	-3	-3	101	165	6	.500	0	2	-1	-0	OD/1	-0.4
1984	Tex-A	64	143	14	37	4	0	4	22	10	19	.259	.312	.371	.682	88	-2	-2	100	135	17	.607	1	1	-0	0	O1/D	-0.3
1985	Tex-A	83	134	14	30	2	0	5	23	11	30	.224	.288	.351	.638	68	-5	-6	108	147	14	.571	1	0	0	-7	OD/1	-1.3
1986	Tex-A	13	21	1	2	0	0	0	3	2	5	.095	.174	.095	.269	-25	-4	-3	96	598	0	.211	0	0	0	-2	/O1	-0.5
Total	9	314	603	65	133	17	0	20	86	50	117	.221	.286	.348	.634	78	-19	-18	99	138	62	.570	5	4	-1	-11	O/D1	-2.9
■ BOB JONES	Jones, Robert Walter "Ducky" b: 12/2/1889, Clayton, Cal. d: 8/30/64, San Diego, Cal. BL/TR, 6', 170 lbs. Deb: 4/11/17																											
1917	Det-A	46	77	16	12	1	2	0	2	4	8	.156	.198	.221	.418	28	-7	-7	98	42	4	.369	3			-0	2/3	-0.5
1918	Det-A	74	287	43	79	14	4	0	21	17	16	.275	.320	.352	.672	106	-0	1	97	80	34	.611	7			-1	3/1O	0.0
1919	Det-A	127	439	37	114	18	6	1	57	34	39	.260	.314	.335	.649	88	-11	-7	93	141	50	.594	11			-18	*3	-1.6
1920	Det-A	81	265	35	66	6	3	1	18	22	13	.249	.309	.306	.615	61	-14	-15	103	75	26	.527	3	4	-2	6	3/2S	-0.5
1921	Det-A	141	554	82	168	23	9	1	72	37	24	.303	.348	.383	.731	90	-11	-8	96	117	73	.653	8	9	-3	12	*3	1.1
1922	Det-A	124	455	65	117	10	6	3	44	36	18	.257	.314	.325	.640	68	-22	-21	98	102	48	.564	8	6	-1	12	*3	0.2
1923	Det-A	100	372	51	93	15	4	1	40	29	13	.250	.306	.320	.626	67	-19	-17	97	114	38	.547	7	6	-2	6	3	0.0
1924	Det-A	110	393	52	107	27	4	0	47	20	20	.272	.308	.361	.669	72	-18	-17	100	109	43	.560	1	5	-3	-0	*3	-1.0
1925	Det-A	50	148	18	35	6	0	0	15	9	5	.236	.280	.277	.557	42	-13	-13	99	122	12	.447	1	1	-0	1	3	-0.8
Total	9	853	2990	399	791	120	38	7	316	208	156	.265	.314	.337	.651	76	-115	-104	97	108	327	.571	49	31		17	3/21SO	-3.1
■ RON JONES	Jones, Ronald Glen b: 6/11/64, Seguin, Tex. BL/TR, 5'10", 200 lbs. Deb: 8/26/88																											
1988	Phi-N	33	124	15	36	6	1	8	26	2	14	.290	.302	.548	.850	138	5	5	101	115	20	.778	0	0	0	1	O	0.6
■ ROSS JONES	Jones, Ross A. b: 1/14/60, Miami, Fla. BR/TR, 6'2", 185 lbs. Deb: 4/02/84																											
1984	NY-N	17	10	2	1	1	0	0	1	3	4	.100	.308	.200	.508	45	-1	-1	100	196	1	.556	0	0	0	0	/S23	0.0
1986	Sea-A	11	21	0	2	0	0	0	0	0	4	.095	.095	.095	.190	-45	-4	-4	105	0	0	.100	0	1	-1	1	/S23D	-0.3
1987	KC-A	39	114	10	29	4	2	0	10	5	15	.254	.292	.325	.616	62	-6	-6	104	108	10	.489	1	0	0	5	S/2	0.1
Total	3	67	145	12	32	5	2	0	11	8	23	.221	.266	.283	.549	46	-11	-11	104	101	11	.429	1	1	-0	6	/S23D	-0.2
■ RUPPERT JONES	Jones, Ruppert Sanderson b: 3/12/55, Dallas, Tex. BL/TL, 5'10", 170 lbs. Deb: 8/01/76																											
1976	KC-A	28	51	9	11	1	1	1	7	3	16	.216	.259	.333	.593	73	-2	-2	100	134	4	.476	0	2	-1	-4	O/D	-0.7
1977	Sea-A	160	597	85	157	26	8	24	76	55	120	.263	.327	.454	.781	115	7	10	96	93	89	.748	13	9	-2	13	*O/D	1.7
1978	Sea-A	129	472	48	111	24	3	6	46	55	85	.235	.315	.337	.652	82	-10	-11	102	109	51	.618	22	6	3	9	*O	-0.1
1979	Sea-A	162	622	109	166	29	9	21	78	85	78	.267	.358	.444	.801	115	14	14	100	85	99	.815	33	12	3	8	*O	1.8
1980	NY-A	83	328	38	73	11	3	9	42	34	50	.223	.301	.357	.658	80	-9	-9	99	109	36	.642	18	8	1	5	O	-0.4
1981	SD-N	105	397	53	99	34	1	4	39	43	66	.249	.323	.370	.693	103	-2	1	93	102	47	.627	7	9	-3	5	*O	0.0
1982	SD-N	116	424	69	120	20	2	12	61	62	90	.283	.376	.425	.800	134	15	19	92	117	69	.808	18	15	-4	2	*O	1.7
1983	SD-N	133	335	42	78	12	3	12	49	35	58	.233	.305	.394	.699	93	-4	-4	99	115	37	.645	11	11	-3	4	*O/1	-0.4
1984	Det-A	79	215	26	61	12	1	12	37	21	47	.284	.347	.516	.864	141	10	11	96	100	36	.822	2	4	-2	0	O/D	0.7
1985	Cal-A	125	389	66	90	17	2	21	67	57	82	.231	.330	.447	.777	109	5	5	101	112	60	.773	7	4	-0	13	OD	1.6
1986	Cal-A	126	393	73	90	21	3	17	49	64	87	.229	.341	.427	.769	113	6	8	96	89	60	.780	10	3	1	-10	*O	-0.4
1987	Cal-A	85	192	25	47	8	2	8	28	20	38	.245	.316	.432	.748	98	-1	-1	99	104	26	.700	2	1	0	-12	O/D	-1.4
Total	12	1331	4415	643	1103	215	38	147	579	534	817	.250	.332	.416	.748	107	28	41	98	102	614	.742	143	84	-8	33	*O/D1	4.1
■ JACK JONES	Jones, Ryerson L. "Ri" or "Angel Sleeves" b: Cincinnati, Ohio TR , Deb: 1883																											
1883	Lou-a	2	7	1	0	0	0	0		0		.000	.000	.000	.000	-99	-1	-1	94	0	0	.000				0	/OS	0.0
1884	Cin-U	69	272	36	71	5	1	2		12		.261	.292	.309	.601	96	1	-2	108	0	25	.478	0			7	S23	0.5
Total	2	71	279	37	71	5	1	2		12		.254	.285	.301	.586	91	-0	-4	108	0	25	.462	0			7	/S23O	0.5
■ TOM JONES	Jones, Thomas b: 1/22/1877, Honesdale, Pa. d: 6/21/23, Danville, Pa. BR/TR, 6'1", 195 lbs. Deb: 8/25/02																											
1902	Bal-A	37	159	22	45	8	4	0	14	2		.283	.292	.384	.676	86	-3	-4	102	67	19	.561	1			-0	1/2	-0.2
1904	StL-A	156	625	53	152	15	10	2	68	15		.243	.261	.309	.570	86	-14	-10	95	135	56	.474	16			-1	*12/O	-0.8
1905	StL-A	135	504	44	122	16	2	0	48	30		.242	.285	.282	.566	89	-10	-5	91	128	43	.463	5			5	*1	-0.3
1906	StL-A	144	539	51	136	22	6	0	30	24		.252	.284	.315	.600	91	-7	-6	98	68	57	.548	27			8	*1	-0.2
1907	StL-A	155	549	53	137	17	3	0	34	34		.250	.293	.291	.585	90	-7	-6	98	78	55	.529	24			2	*1	-0.6
1908	StL-A	155	549	43	135	14	2	1	50	30		.246	.285	.284	.569	84	-8	-10	103	121	47	.493	18			-2	*1	-1.6
1909	StL-A	97	337	60	84	9	3	0	29	18		.249	.299	.294	.593	95	-5	-2	92	115	32	.538	13			4	1/3	0.2
	Det-A	44	153	13	43	9	0	0	18	5		.281	.317	.340	.657	97	1	-1	110	136	19	.627	9			-1	1	-0.1
	Yr	141	490	73	127	18	3	0	47	23		.259	.305	.308	.613	96	-4	-3	97	122	51	.565	22			3		0.1
1910	Det-A	135	432	32	110	13	4	0	45	35		.255	.325	.303	.628	95	-1	-2	102	130	52	.615	22			-3	*1	0.0
Total	8	1058	3847	371	964	123	34	3	336	193		.251	.290	.303	.592	90	-54	-45	98	109	380	.524	135			11	*1/2O3	-3.6
■ TRACY JONES	Jones, Tracy Donald b: 3/31/61, Hawthorne, Cal. BR/TR, 6'3", 180 lbs. Deb: 4/07/86																											
1986	Cin-N	46	86	16	30	3	0	2	10	9	5	.349	.411	.453	.864	132	5	4	104	89	17	.932	7	1	2	-0	O/1	0.5
1987	Cin-N	117	359	53	104	17	3	10	44	23	40	.290	.338	.437	.775	100	1	-0	104	94	52	.784	31	8	5	-0	O	0.0
1988	Cin-N	37	83	9	19	1	0	1	9	8	6	.229	.304	.277	.581	64	-3	-4	105	138	8	.603	9	0	3	-2	O	-0.4
	Mon-N	53	141	20	47	5	1	2	15	12	12	.333	.390	.426	.815	127	6	5	106	91	23	.812	9	6	-1	-6	O	-0.2
	Yr	90	224	29	66	6	1	3	24	20	18	.295	.358	.371	.728	104	3	2	105	112	32	.745	18	6	2	-8		-0.6
Total	3	253	669	98	200	26	4	15	78	52	63	.299	.354	.417	.771	105	9	6	104	98	100	.808	56	15	8	-9	O/1	-0.1
■ NIPPY JONES	Jones, Vernal Leroy b: 6/29/25, Los Angeles, Cal. BR/TR, 6'1", 185 lbs. Deb: 6/08/46																											
1946	StL-N	16	12	3	4	0	0	0	1	2	2	.333	.429	.333	.762	110	0	0	107	93	1	.600	0			0	/2	0.0
1947	StL-N	23	73	6	18	4	0	1	5	2	10	.247	.267	.342	.609	57	-4	-5	106	66	6	.474	0			-1	2/O	-0.3
1948	StL-N	132	481	58	122	21	9	10	81	36	45	.254	.307	.397	.704	89	-9	-9	101	140	52	.599	2			-10	*1	-2.0
1949	StL-N	110	380	51	114	20	2	8	62	16	20	.300	.330	.426	.756	92	-0	-5	110	126	50	.650	1			-7	1	-1.1
1950	StL-N	13	26	0	6	1	0	0	6	3	1	.231	.310	.269	.580	52	-2	-2	103	331	2	.435	0			0	/1	-0.1
1951	StL-N	80	300	20	79	12	0	3	41	9	13	.263	.287	.333	.620	66	-15	-15	101	148	25	.470	1	2	-1	-3	1	-1.9

YEAR	TM/L	G	AB	R	H	2B	3B	HR	RBI	BB	SO	AVG	OBP	SLG	PRO	/A	BR	/A	PF	CHI	RC	TA	SB	CS	SBR	FR	POS	TPR
1952	Phi-N	8	30	3	5	0	0	1	5	0	4	.167	.167	.267	.433	18	-3	-3	101	177	1	.296	0	0	0	0	/1	-0.3
1957	Mil-N	30	79	5	21	2	1	2	8	3	7	.266	.293	.392	.685	91	-2	-1	90	90	9	.586	0	0	0	-0	1/O	-0.3
Total	8	412	1381	146	369	60	12	25	209	71	102	.267	.304	.382	.687	81	-35	-40	103	135	147	.598	4	2		-21	1/2O	-6.0
■ BILL JONES	Jones, William b: Syracuse, N.Y. Deb: 5/17/1882																											
1882	Bal-a	4	15	1	1	0	0	0		0		.067	.067	.067	.133	-59	-2	-2	92	0	0	.071				0	/OC	-0.1
1884	Phi-U	4	14	2	2	0	0	0		1		.143	.200	.143	.343	19	-1	-1	93	0	0	.250	0			0	/CO	0.0
Total	2	8	29	3	3	0	0	0		1		.103	.133	.103	.237	-21	-3	-3	93	0	0	.154	0			0	/CO	-0.1
■ BILL JONES	Jones, William Dennis "Midget" b: 4/8/1887, Hartland, N.B., Can. d: 10/10/46, Boston, Mass. BL/TR, 5'6.5", 157 lbs. Deb: 6/20/11																											
1911	Bos-N	24	51	6	11	2	1	0	3	15	7	.216	.394	.294	.688	91	0	0	103	68	6	.775	1			-1	O	0.0
1912	Bos-N	3	2	0	1	0	0	0	2	0	1	.500	.500	.500	1.000	162	0	0	107	674	0	1.000	0			0	H	0.0
Total	2	27	53	6	12	2	1	0	5	15	8	.226	.397	.302	.699	93	1	0	104	85	7	.780	1			-1	/O	0.0
■ TEX JONES	Jones, William Roderick b: 8/4/1885, Marion, Kan. d: 2/26/38, Wichita, Kan. BR/TR, 6', 192 lbs. Deb: 4/13/11																											
1911	Chi-A	9	31	4	6	1	0	0	4	3		.194	.265	.226	.491	39	-3	-2	97	193	2	.440	1			1	/1	-0.1
■ TIM JONES	Jones, William Timothy b: 12/1/62, Sumter, S.C. BL/TR, 5'10", 172 lbs. Deb: 7/26/88																											
1988	StL-N	31	52	2	14	0	0	0	3	4	10	.269	.321	.269	.591	68	-2	-2	104	86	5	.550	4	1	1	1	/S23	0.0
■ PUDDIN' HEAD JONES	Jones, Willie Edward b: 8/16/25, Dillon, S.C. d: 10/18/83, Cincinnati, Ohio BR/TR, 6'1", 188 lbs. Deb: 9/10/47																											
1947	Phi-N	18	62	5	14	0	1	0	10	7	0	.226	.304	.258	.562	51	-4	-4	100	236	5	.490	2			-1	3	-0.5
1948	Phi-N	17	60	9	20	2	0	2	9	3	5	.333	.365	.467	.832	131	2	2	94	101	9	.721	0			-0	3	0.2
1949	Phi-N	149	532	71	130	35	1	19	77	65	66	.244	.328	.421	.749	99	-1	-2	101	105	71	.694	3			-7	*3	-0.6
1950	Phi-N	157	610	100	163	28	6	25	88	61	40	.267	.337	.456	.793	109	4	6	97	102	93	.751	5			-5	*3	0.1
1951	Phi-N	148	564	79	161	28	5	22	81	60	47	.285	.358	.470	.828	125	16	18	97	100	100	.809	6	2	1	-8	*3	1.0
1952	Phi-N	147	541	60	135	12	3	18	72	53	36	.250	.323	.383	.706	94	-4	-5	101	114	68	.641	5	3	-0	4	*3	0.3
1953	Phi-N	149	481	61	108	16	2	19	70	85	45	.225	.342	.385	.727	90	-7	-6	99	115	69	.708	1	1	-0	-5	*3	-1.4
1954	Phi-N	142	535	64	145	28	3	12	56	61	54	.271	.346	.402	.748	95	-4	-3	99	93	77	.698	4	1	1	1	*3	0.0
1955	Phi-N	146	516	65	133	20	3	16	81	77	51	.258	.357	.401	.759	99	2	1	102	**136**	77	.736	6	2	1	-12	*3	-1.1
1956	Phi-N	149	520	88	144	20	4	17	78	92	49	.277	.387	.429	.815	126	17	21	94	127	89	.813	5	4	-1	1	*3	2.1
1957	Phi-N	133	440	58	96	19	2	9	47	61	41	.218	.313	.332	.645	75	-16	-15	98	115	47	.581	1	0	0	-5	*3	-1.6
1958	Phi-N	118	398	52	108	15	1	14	60	49	45	.271	.354	.420	.774	106	3	4	98	119	60	.730	1	2	-1	-12	*3/1	-0.8
1959	Phi-N	47	160	23	43	9	1	7	24	19	14	.269	.346	.469	.815	115	3	3	99	103	26	.777	0	0	0	-9	3	-0.6
	Cle-A	11	18	1	4	1	0	0	1	1	3	.222	.263	.278	.541	50	-1	-1	97	79	1	.429	0	0	0	-0	/3	0.0
	Cin-N	72	233	33	58	12	1	7	31	28	26	.249	.332	.399	.731	91	-2	-3	103	110	30	.659	0	2	-1	-4	3	-1.0
1960	Cin-N	79	149	16	40	7	0	3	27	31	16	.268	.394	.376	.770	114	4	4	98	169	25	.793	1	0	0	2	3/2	0.6
1961	Cin-N	9	7	1	0	0	0	0	0	2	3	.000	.222	.000	.222	-33	-1	-1	104	0	0	.286	0	0	0	0	/3	0.0
Total	15	1691	5826	786	1502	252	33	190	812	755	541	.258	.345	.410	.755	102	10	20	99	114	845	.739	40	17		-59	*3/21	-3.3
■ BUBBER JONNARD	Jonnard, Clarence James b: 11/23/1897, Nashville, Tenn. d: 8/23/77, New York, N.Y. BR/TR, 6'1", 185 lbs. Deb: 10/01/20 C																											
1920	Chi-A	2	5	0	0	0	0	0	0	0	1	.000	.000	.000	.000	-99	-1	-1	96	0	0	.000	0	0	0	0	/C	0.0
1922	Pit-N	10	21	4	5	0	1	0	2	2	4	.238	.304	.333	.638	62	-1	-1	104	100	2	.563	0	0	0	-0	C	0.0
1926	Phi-N	19	34	3	4	1	0	0	2	3	4	.118	.189	.147	.336	-8	-5	-5	103	138	1	.267	0			1	C	-0.3
1927	Phi-N	53	143	18	42	6	0	0	14	7	7	.294	.327	.336	.662	80	-4	-4	96	102	15	.545	0			-1	C	-0.1
1929	StL-N	18	31	1	3	0	0	0	2	0	6	.097	.097	.097	.194	-53	-7	-7	98	228	0	.107	0			0	C	-0.4
1935	Phi-N	1	1	0	0	0	0	0	0	0	1	.000	.000	.000	.000	-88	-0	-0	114	0	0	.000	0			0	/C	0.0
Total	6	103	235	26	54	7	1	0	20	12	23	.230	.267	.268	.535	42	-20	-19	98	121	19	.414	0	0		-0	/C	-0.8
■ EDDIE JOOST	Joost, Edwin David b: 6/5/16, San Francisco, Cal BR/TR, 6', 175 lbs. Deb: 9/11/36 M																											
1936	Cin-N	13	26	1	4	1	0	0	1	2	5	.154	.214	.192	.407	11	-3	-3	97	71	1	.318	0			0	/S2	-0.1
1937	Cin-N	6	12	0	1	0	0	0	0	0	0	.083	.083	.083	.167	-60	-3	-2	91	0	0	.091	0			0	/2	-0.1
1939	Cin-N	42	143	23	36	6	3	0	14	12	15	.252	.310	.336	.645	71	-5	-6	103	109	15	.550	1			3	2/S	0.0
1940	Cin-N	88	278	24	60	7	2	1	24	32	40	.216	.301	.266	.567	57	-15	-16	101	116	24	.498	4			-3	S/23	-1.0
1941	Cin-N	152	537	67	136	25	4	4	40	69	59	.253	.340	.337	.678	92	-5	-4	99	76	66	.637	9			-7	*S/213	0.2
1942	Cin-N	142	562	65	126	30	3	6	41	62	57	.224	.307	.320	.627	83	-11	-12	101	68	59	.578	9			-5	*S2	-0.7
1943	Bos-N	124	421	34	78	16	3	2	20	68	80	.185	.299	.252	.550	56	-20	-23	106	66	35	.510	5			0	32/S	-2.2
1945	Bos-N	35	141	16	35	7	1	0	9	13	7	.248	.312	.312	.624	66	-5	-7	112	68	14	.523	0			-3	23	-0.8
1947	Phi-A	151	540	76	111	22	3	13	64	114	110	.206	.348	.330	.678	89	-5	-5	100	96	73	.686	6	6	-2	0	*S	-0.7
1948	Phi-A	135	509	99	127	22	2	16	55	119	87	.250	.393	.395	.788	108	11	10	102	64	91	.828	2	4	-2	9	*S	1.7
1949	Phi-A	144	525	128	138	25	3	23	81	149	80	.263	.429	.453	.883	135	32	33	99	78	119	.997	2	1	0	7	*S	3.9
1950	Phi-A	131	476	79	111	12	3	18	58	103	68	.233	.373	.384	.757	105	-2	6	90	81	77	.780	5	1	1	-2	*S	1.0
1951	Phi-A	140	553	107	160	28	5	19	78	106	70	.289	.409	.461	.870	127	30	26	106	77	115	.926	10	8	-2	5	*S	3.7
1952	Phi-A	146	540	94	132	26	3	20	75	122	94	.244	.388	.415	.803	112	21	14	111	87	98	.844	5	8	-3	-3	*S	1.6
1953	Phi-A	51	177	39	44	6	0	6	15	45	24	.249	.401	.384	.785	110	5	5	102	62	32	.853	3	2	-0	-8	S	0.0
1954	Phi-A	19	47	7	17	3	0	1	9	10	10	.362	.474	.489	.963	167	5	5	98	131	10	.943	0	1	-1	-0	/S32M	0.5
1955	Bos-A	55	119	15	23	2	0	5	17	17	21	.193	.299	.336	.635	57	-5	-9	124	115	13	.592	0	0	0	-1	S2/3	-0.6
Total	17	1574	5606	874	1339	238	35	134	601	1043	827	.239	.361	.366	.727	98	25	10	102	80	842	.741	61	31		-7	*S2/31	6.4
■ DUTCH JORDAN	Jordan, Adolf Otto b: 1/5/1880, Pittsburgh, Pa. d: 12/23/72, W.Allegheny, Pa. BR/TR, 5'10", 185 lbs. Deb: 4/25/03																											
1903	Bro-N	78	267	27	63	11	1	0	21	19		.236	.287	.285	.571	64	-12	-13	101	91	25	.510	9			-9	23/O1	-1.7
1904	Bro-N	87	252	21	45	10	2	0	19	13		.179	.219	.234	.453	43	-17	-16	95	118	15	.382	7			-29	23/1	-4.6
Total	2	165	519	48	108	21	3	0	40	32		.208	.254	.260	.514	55	-29	-28	98	104	40	.445	16			-39	2/31O	-6.3
■ BUCK JORDAN	Jordan, Baxter Byerly b: 1/16/07, Cooleemee, N.C. BL/TR, 6', 170 lbs. Deb: 9/15/27																											
1927	NY-N	5	5	0	1	0	0	0	0	0	3	.200	.200	.200	.400	7	-1	-1	100	0	0	.250	0			0	H	0.0
1929	NY-N	2	2	1	1	1	0	0	0	0	0	.500	.500	1.000	1.500	262	0	0	100	0	1	2.000	0			0	/1	0.0
1931	Was-A	9	18	3	4	2	0	0	1	1	3	.222	.263	.333	.596	55	-1	-1	101	55	2	.500	0	0	0	-0	/1	-0.1
1932	Bos-N	49	212	27	68	12	3	2	29	4	5	.321	.333	.434	.767	112	1	3	93	106	30	.674	1			-1	1	0.0
1933	Bos-N	152	588	77	168	29	9	4	46	34	22	.286	.327	.386	.713	107	2	4	96	70	74	.615	4			-5	*1	-0.3
1934	Bos-N	124	489	68	152	26	9	2	58	35	19	.311	.358	.413	.771	123	4	14	86	106	74	.695	3			-5	*1	0.0
1935	Bos-N	130	470	62	131	24	5	5	35	19	17	.279	.307	.383	.690	88	-11	-8	96	66	54	.579	3			1	1/3O	-0.8
1936	Bos-N	138	555	81	179	27	5	3	66	45	22	.323	.375	.405	.781	116	9	13	95	96	83	.692	2			1	*1	0.2
1937	Bos-N	8	8	1	2	0	0	0	0	0	0	.250	.250	.250	.500	40	-1	-1	90	0	0	.286	0			0	H	0.0
	Cin-N	98	316	45	89	14	3	1	28	25	14	.282	.334	.354	.689	96	-5	-2	91	88	39	.614	6			-1	1	-0.6
	Yr	106	324	46	91	14	3	1	28	25	14	.281	.332	.352	.684	94	-6	-2	91	81	39	.607	6			-1		-0.6
1938	Cin-N	9	7	0	2	0	0	0	0	2	0	.286	.444	.286	.730	107	0	0	98	0	1	.800	0			0	H	0.0
	Phi-N	87	310	31	93	18	1	0	18	17	4	.300	.336	.365	.701	92	-3	-3	100	59	38	.585	1			-2	31	-0.7
	Yr	96	317	31	95	18	1	0	18	19	4	.300	.339	.363	.702	93	-3	-3	100	53	39	.590	1			-2		-0.7
Total	10	811	2980	396	890	153	35	17	281	182	109	.299	.340	.391	.731	105	-6	18	94	83	397	.654	20	0		-12	1/3O	-2.3
■ SLATS JORDAN	Jordan, Clarence Veasey b: 9/26/1879, Baltimore, Md. d: 12/7/53, Catonsville, Md. BL/TL, 6'1", 190 lbs. Deb: 9/28/01																											
1901	Bal-A	1	3	0	0	0	0	0	0	0		.000	.000	.000	.000	-94	-1	-1	107	0	0	.000	0			0	/1	0.0
1902	Bal-A	1	4	0	0	0	0	0	0	0		.000	.000	.000	.000	-98	-1	-1	102	0	0	.000	0			0	/O	0.0
Total	2	2	7	0	0	0	0	0	0	0		.000	.000	.000	.000	-96	-2	-2	104	0	0	.000	0			0	/O1	0.0
■ JIMMY JORDAN	Jordan, James William "Lord" b: 1/13/08, Tucapau, S.C. d: 12/4/57, Gastonia, N.C. BR/TR, 5'9", 157 lbs. Deb: 4/20/33																											
1933	Bro-N	70	211	16	54	12	1	0	17	4	6	.256	.270	.322	.592	71	-9	-8	97	94	18	.466	3			-5	S2	-0.9
1934	Bro-N	97	369	34	98	17	2	0	43	9	32	.266	.285	.322	.607	66	-20	-17	95	130	33	.464	1			3	S2/3	-0.7
1935	Bro-N	94	295	26	82	7	0	0	30	9	17	.278	.302	.302	.603	67	-15	-13	94	122	27	.466	3			6	2S/3	-0.1

YEAR	TM/L	G	AB	R	H	2B	3B	HR	RBI	BB	SO	AVG	OBP	SLG	PRO	/A	BR	/A	PF	CHI	RC	TA	SB	CS	SBR	FR	POS	TPR
1936	Bro-N	115	398	26	93	15	1	2	28	15	21	.234	.262	.291	.553	46	-29	-31	105	81	31	.426	1			-20	2/S3	-4.3
Total	4	376	1273	102	327	51	4	2	118	37	76	.257	.279	.308	.587	60	-73	-70	98	107	108	.462	8			-16	2S/3	-6.0
■ MIKE JORDAN	Jordan, Michael Henry "Mitty" b: 2/7/1863, Lawrence, Mass. d: 9/25/40, Lawrence, Mass. Deb: 8/21/1890																											
1890	Pit-N	37	125	8	12	1	0	0	6	15	19	.096	.210	.104	.314	-7	-16	-14	88	142	4	.319	5			2	O	-1.0
■ RICKY JORDAN	Jordan, Paul Scott b: 5/26/65, Richmond, Cal. BR/TR, 6'5", 210 lbs. Deb: 7/17/88																											
1988	Phi-N	69	273	41	84	15	1	11	43	7	39	.308	.325	.491	.816	130	9	9	101	109	41	.728	1	1	-0	-3	1	0.2
■ SCOTT JORDAN	Jordan, Scott Alan b: 5/27/63, Waco, Tex. BR/TR, 6', 178 lbs. Deb: 9/02/88																											
1988	Cle-A	7	9	0	1	0	0	0	1	0	3	.111	.111	.111	.222	-37	-2	-2	102	398	0	.125	0	0	0	-1	/O	-0.2
■ TOM JORDAN	Jordan, Thomas Jefferson b: 9/5/19, Lawton, Okla. BR/TR, 6'1.5", 195 lbs. Deb: 9/04/44																											
1944	Chi-A	14	45	2	12	1	1	0	3	1	0	.267	.283	.333	.616	76	-2	-2	100	72	4	.471	0	0	0	0	C	0.0
1946	Chi-A	10	15	1	4	2	1	0	0	0	1	.267	.267	.533	.800	124	0	0	97	0	1	.571	0	0	0	0	/C	0.1
	Cle-A	14	35	2	7	1	0	1	3	3	1	.200	.263	.314	.577	69	-2	-1	89	81	2	.484	1	1	-0	0	C	0.0
	Yr	24	50	3	11	3	1	1	3	3	2	.220	.264	.380	.644	85	-2	-1	92	47	4	.548	1	1	-0	0		0.1
1948	StL-A	1	1	0	0	0	0	0	0	0	0	.000	.000	.000	.000	-94	-0	-0	106	0	0	.000	0	0	0	0	H	0.0
Total	3	39	96	5	23	4	2	1	6	4	2	.240	.270	.354	.624	79	-4	-3	95	64	7	.527	1	1	-0	0	/C	0.1
■ TIM JORDAN	Jordan, Timothy Joseph b: 2/14/1879, New York, N.Y. d: 9/13/49, Bronx, N.Y. BL/TL, 6'1", 170 lbs. Deb: 8/10/01																											
1901	Was-A	6	20	2	4	1	0	0	2	3		.200	.304	.250	.554	57	-1	-1	99	129	2	.500	0			0	/1	0.0
1903	NY-A	2	8	2	1	0	0	0	0	0		.125	.125	.125	.250	-24	-1	-1	100	0	0	.143	0			0	/1	0.0
1906	Bro-N	129	450	67	118	20	8	**12**	78	59		.262	.348	.422	.770	164	22	29	87	133	73	.798	16			-9	*1	1.5
1907	Bro-N	147	485	43	133	15	8	4	53	74		.274	.370	.363	.733	140	20	24	94	113	71	.739	10			-6	*1	1.6
1908	Bro-N	148	515	58	127	18	5	**12**	60	59		.247	.324	.371	.695	130	14	17	95	98	63	.668	9			-14	*1	0.0
1909	Bro-N	103	330	47	90	20	3	3	36	59		.273	.386	.379	.765	141	17	18	99	103	52	.829	13			-9	1	0.8
1910	Bro-N	5	5	1	1	0	0	1	3	0	2	.200	.200	.800	1.000	198	0	0	95	149	1	1.000	0			0	H	0.0
Total	7	540	1813	220	474	74	24	32	232	254	2	.261	.353	.382	.735	141	72	85	94	112	261	.744	48			-37	1	3.9
■ ART JORGENS	Jorgens, Arndt Ludwig b: 5/18/05, Modum, Norway d: 3/1/80, Wilmette, Ill. BR/TR, 5'9", 160 lbs. Deb: 4/26/29																											
1929	NY-A	18	34	6	11	3	0	0	4	6	7	.324	.425	.412	.837	118	1	1	99	98	6	.800	0	2	-1	-0	C	0.1
1930	NY-A	16	30	7	11	3	0	0	1	2	4	.367	.406	.467	.873	135	1	2	90	24	6	.842	0	0	0	-1	C	0.2
1931	NY-A	46	100	12	27	1	2	0	14	9	3	.270	.330	.320	.650	73	-4	-4	98	144	11	.554	0	1	-1	-1	C	-0.2
1932	NY-A	56	151	13	33	7	1	2	19	14	11	.219	.285	.318	.603	59	-10	-9	95	118	14	.525	0	0	0	-3	C	-0.7
1933	NY-A	21	50	9	11	3	0	2	13	12	3	.220	.371	.400	.771	115	1	1	91	167	8	.846	1	0	0	2	C	0.4
1934	NY-A	58	183	14	38	6	1	0	20	23	24	.208	.296	.251	.547	44	-15	-14	96	145	15	.490	2	0	1	3	C	-0.4
1935	NY-A	36	84	6	20	2	0	0	8	12	10	.238	.333	.262	.595	60	-5	-4	93	123	8	.531	0	0	0	-1	C	-0.3
1936	NY-A	31	66	5	18	3	1	0	5	2	3	.273	.294	.348	.643	61	-5	-4	95	70	7	.521	0	0	0	-1	C	-0.1
1937	NY-A	13	23	3	3	1	0	0	3	2	5	.130	.200	.174	.374	-5	-4	-4	102	257	1	.300	0	0	0	0	C	-0.2
1938	NY-A	9	17	3	4	2	0	0	2	3	3	.235	.350	.353	.703	73	-1	-1	105	113	2	.692	0	0	0	0	/C	0.0
1939	NY-A	3	0	1	0	0	0	0	0	0	0	—	—	—	—	—	0	0	91	—	—	—	0	0	0	0	/C	0.0
Total	11	307	738	79	176	31	5	4	89	85	73	.238	.317	.310	.627	65	-41	-36	96	128	80	.561	3	3	-1	-2	C	-1.2
■ PINKY JORGENSEN	Jorgensen, Carl b: 11/21/14, Laton, Cal. BR/TR, 6'1", 195 lbs. Deb: 9/14/37																											
1937	Cin-N	6	14	1	4	0	0	0	1	1	2	.286	.333	.286	.619	76	-1	-0	91	90	2	.500	0			0	/O	0.0
■ SPIDER JORGENSEN	Jorgensen, John Donald b: 11/3/19, Folsom, Cal. BL/TR, 5'9", 155 lbs. Deb: 4/15/47																											
1947	Bro-N	129	441	57	121	29	8	5	67	58	45	.274	.360	.410	.770	100	3	0	105	127	69	.751	4			0	*3	-0.2
1948	Bro-N	31	90	15	27	6	2	1	13	16	13	.300	.411	.444	.856	126	5	4	104	113	18	.906	1			-2	3	0.2
1949	Bro-N	53	134	15	36	5	1	1	14	23	13	.269	.376	.343	.719	93	-0	-0	102	108	19	.697	0			1	3	0.1
1950	Bro-N	2	2	0	0	0	0	0	1	1	0	.000	.333	.000	.333	-4	-0	-0	107	0	0	.500	0			0	/3	0.0
	NY-N	24	37	5	5	0	0	0	4	5	2	.135	.238	.135	.373	1	-5	-5	98	309	2	.313	0			0	/3	-0.4
	Yr	26	39	5	5	0	0	0	5	6	2	.128	.244	.128	.373	1	-6	-5	99	285	2	.324	0			0		-0.4
1951	NY-N	28	51	5	12	0	0	2	8	3	2	.235	.291	.353	.644	71	-2	-2	102	129	6	.564	0	0	0	-3	O/3	-0.4
Total	5	267	755	97	201	40	11	9	107	106	75	.266	.359	.384	.743	95	-0	-4	104	130	114	.729	5	0		-2	3/O	-0.7
■ MIKE JORGENSEN	Jorgensen, Michael b: 8/16/48, Passaic, N.J. BL/TL, 6', 195 lbs. Deb: 9/10/68																											
1968	NY-N	8	14	0	2	1	0	0	0	0	4	.143	.143	.214	.357	6	-2	-2	102	0	0	.250	0	0	0	0	/1	-0.1
1970	NY-N	76	87	15	17	3	1	3	4	10	23	.195	.278	.356	.635	66	-4	-5	104	39	9	.597	2	2	-1	2	1O	-0.7
1971	NY-N	45	118	16	26	1	1	5	11	11	24	.220	.303	.373	.676	94	-2	-1	96	76	12	.602	1	2	-1	-1	O/1	-0.3
1972	Mon-N	113	372	48	86	12	3	13	47	53	75	.231	.333	.384	.718	101	2	1	102	108	47	.693	12	13	-4	1	1O	-0.9
1973	Mon-N	138	413	49	95	16	2	9	47	64	49	.230	.338	.344	.681	86	-5	-7	104	112	52	.680	16	7	1	4	*1O	-0.8
1974	Mon-N	131	287	45	89	16	1	11	59	70	39	.310	.448	.488	.936	155	28	26	104	132	68	1.039	3	5	-2	3	1O	2.2
1975	Mon-N	144	445	58	116	18	0	18	67	79	75	.261	.380	.422	.803	113	16	11	108	107	76	.815	3	3	-1	4	*1/O	0.7
1976	Mon-N	125	343	36	87	13	0	6	23	52	48	.254	.352	.344	.696	98	1	1	100	65	45	.676	7	1	2	-1	1O	-0.4
1977	Mon-N	19	20	3	4	1	0	0	0	3	4	.200	.304	.250	.554	51	-1	-1	98	0	2	.471	0	0	0	0	/1	0.0
	Oak-A	66	203	18	50	4	1	8	32	25	44	.246	.335	.394	.729	103	-0	1	95	122	28	.696	3	2	-0	-2	1O/D	-0.4
1978	Tex-A	96	97	20	19	3	0	1	9	18	10	.196	.322	.258	.579	67	-4	-3	96	127	9	.561	3	1	0	2	1/OD	-0.3
1979	Tex-A	90	157	21	35	7	0	6	16	14	29	.223	.295	.382	.677	81	-4	-4	100	79	17	.598	0	2	-1	-1	1O	-1.0
1980	NY-N	119	321	43	82	11	0	7	43	46	55	.255	.349	.355	.704	101	-0	1	96	126	39	.635	0	3	-2	-2	1O	-0.6
1981	NY-N	86	122	8	25	5	2	3	15	12	24	.205	.276	.352	.629	77	-4	-4	101	113	13	.596	4	0	1	-1	1O	-0.5
1982	NY-N	120	114	16	29	6	0	2	14	21	24	.254	.370	.360	.730	107	2	2	99	117	17	.736	2	0	1	-3	1O	-0.3
1983	NY-N	38	24	5	6	3	0	1	3	2	4	.250	.333	.500	.833	130	1	1	99	79	3	.750	0	1	-1	0	1	0.0
	Atl-N	57	48	5	12	1	0	1	8	8	8	.250	.357	.333	.690	87	-0	-1	106	167	6	.649	0	0	0	-1	1/O	-0.1
	Yr	95	72	10	18	4	0	2	11	10	12	.250	.349	.389	.738	101	1	0	103	132	10	.696	0	1	-1	-0		-0.1
1984	Atl-N	31	26	4	7	1	0	0	5	3	6	.269	.345	.308	.653	77	-0	-1	110	245	3	.550	0	1	-1	-1	/1O	-0.2
	StL-N	59	98	5	24	4	2	1	12	10	17	.245	.315	.357	.672	90	-2	-1	99	124	11	.600	0	0	0	-1	1	-0.2
	Yr	90	124	9	31	5	2	1	17	13	23	.250	.321	.347	.668	86	-2	-2	102	168	14	.589	0	1	-1	-2		-0.4
1985	StL-N	72	112	14	22	6	0	0	11	31	27	.196	.375	.250	.625	82	-1	-1	96	156	13	.660	2	1	0	-3	1/O	-0.5
Total	17	1633	3421	429	833	132	13	95	426	532	589	.243	.349	.373	.722	100	19	13	101	108	470	.718	58	44	-9	0	*1O/D	-4.4
■ FELIX JOSE	Jose, Domingo Felix b: 5/8/65, Santo Domingo, D.R. BL/TR, 6'1", 190 lbs. Deb: 9/02/88																											
1988	Oak-A	8	6	2	2	1	0	0	1	0	1	.333	.333	.500	.833	137	0	0	95	132	1	1.000	1	0	0	-1	/O	0.0
■ RICK JOSEPH	Joseph, Ricardo Emelindo b: 8/24/39, San Pedro De Macoris, D.R. d: 9/8/79, Santiago, D.R. BR/TR, 6'1", 192 lbs. Deb: 6/18/64																											
1964	KC-A	17	54	3	12	2	0	0	1	3	11	.222	.263	.259	.522	44	-4	-4	105	30	3	.386	0	1	-1	-0	1/3	-0.5
1967	Phi-N	17	41	4	9	2	0	1	5	4	10	.220	.289	.341	.630	76	-1	-1	104	122	4	.563	0	0	0	0	1	-0.1
1968	Phi-N	66	155	20	34	5	0	3	12	16	35	.219	.297	.310	.606	84	-3	-3	97	89	14	.520	0	1	-1	2	13/O	-0.2
1969	Phi-N	99	264	35	72	15	0	6	37	22	57	.273	.331	.398	.729	105	1	1	98	121	34	.653	2	1	0	1	31/2	0.1
1970	Phi-N	71	119	7	27	2	1	3	10	6	28	.227	.264	.336	.600	62	-7	-7	96	79	9	.474	0	0	0	-3	O1/3	-1.0
Total	5	270	633	69	154	26	1	13	65	51	141	.243	.302	.349	.651	85	-14	-13	99	98	66	.567	2	3	-1	0	/31O2	-1.7
■ DUANE JOSEPHSON	Josephson, Duane Charles b: 6/3/42, New Hampton, Iowa BR/TR, 6', 190 lbs. Deb: 9/15/65																											
1965	Chi-A	4	9	2	1	0	0	0	0	2	4	.111	.273	.111	.384	15	-1	-1	92	0	0	.375	0	0	0	-1	/C	-0.1
1966	Chi-A	11	38	3	9	1	0	0	3	3	3	.237	.293	.263	.556	65	-2	-2	94	128	3	.419	0	0	0	-1	C	-0.2
1967	Chi-A	62	189	11	45	5	1	1	9	6	24	.238	.262	.291	.553	67	-9	-8	94	65	13	.401	0	3	-2	-4	C	-1.0
1968	Chi-A	128	434	35	107	16	6	6	45	18	52	.247	.286	.353	.639	92	-5	-5	101	113	41	.525	2	4	-2	16	*C	1.6
1969	Chi-A	52	162	19	39	6	2	1	20	13	17	.241	.301	.321	.622	68	-6	-7	108	146	16	.524	0	0	0	-4	C	-0.7
1970	Chi-A	96	285	28	90	12	1	4	41	24	28	.316	.375	.407	.782	109	6	4	106	130	42	.694	0	1	-1	1	C	0.7

YEAR	TM/L	G	AB	R	H	2B	3B	HR	RBI	BB	SO	AVG	OBP	SLG	PRO	/A	BR	/A	PF	CHI	RC	TA	SB	CS	SBR	FR	POS	TPR
1971	Bos-A	91	306	38	75	14	1	10	39	22	35	.245	.296	.395	.691	89	-3	-5	106	105	31	.582	2	0	1	0	C	0.0
1972	Bos-A	26	82	11	22	4	1	1	7	4	11	.268	.310	.378	.688	99	0	-0	105	86	7	.537	0	2	-1	1	1/C	-0.1
Total	8	470	1505	147	388	58	12	23	164	92	174	.258	.305	.358	.663	89	-19	-24	103	110	153	.571	4	10	-5	8	C/1	0.2
■ **VON JOSHUA**	Joshua, Von Everett b: 5/1/48, Oakland, Cal. BL/TL, 5'10", 170 lbs. Deb: 9/02/69																											
1969	LA-N	14	8	2	2	0	0	0	0	0	2	.250	.250	.250	.500	41	-1	-1	99	0	1	.500	1	0	0	-2	/O	-0.2
1970	LA-N	72	109	23	29	1	3	1	8	6	24	.266	.304	.358	.662	86	-4	-2	90	74	12	.573	2	2	-1	-6	O	-1.0
1971	LA-N	11	7	2	0	0	0	0	0	0	1	.000	.000	.000	.000	-99	-2	-2	99	0	0	.000	0	0	0	-1	/O	-0.2
1973	LA-N	75	159	19	40	4	1	2	17	8	29	.252	.292	.327	.619	71	-6	-6	100	118	16	.553	7	2	1	-6	O	-1.3
1974	LA-N	81	124	11	29	5	1	1	16	7	17	.234	.280	.315	.595	71	-6	-5	93	147	10	.500	3	2	-0	-8	O	-1.5
1975	SF-N	129	507	75	161	25	10	7	43	32	75	.318	.359	.448	.807	121	14	13	102	71	81	.773	20	10	0	3	*O	1.2
1976	SF-N	42	156	13	41	5	2	0	2	4	20	.263	.281	.321	.602	68	-6	-7	103	16	13	.455	1	3	-2	0	O	-0.9
	Mil-A	107	423	44	113	13	5	5	28	18	58	.267	.297	.357	.654	92	-6	-6	99	69	42	.545	8	10	-4	0	*O/D	-1.1
1977	Mil-A	144	536	58	140	25	7	9	49	21	74	.261	.289	.384	.673	86	-15	-11	95	85	53	.566	12	9	-2	-14	*O	-3.1
1979	LA-N	94	142	22	40	7	1	3	14	7	23	.282	.315	.408	.724	96	-1	-1	100	83	17	.611	1	1	-0	-8	O	-1.0
1980	SD-N	53	63	8	15	2	1	2	7	5	15	.238	.294	.397	.691	98	-1	-0	93	89	7	.588	0	1	-1	-2	O/1	-0.3
Total	10	822	2234	277	610	87	31	30	184	108	338	.273	.307	.380	.687	92	-33	-28	98	79	250	.609	55	40	-8	-44	O/1D	-9.4
■ **TED JOURDAN**	Jourdan, Theodore Charles b: 9/5/1895, New Orleans, La. d: 9/23/61, New Orleans, La. BL/TL, 6', 175 lbs. Deb: 9/18/16																											
1916	Chi-A	3	2	0	0	0	0	0	0	1	1	.000	.333	.000	.333	1	-0	-0	108	0	1	1.500	2			0	H	0.0
1917	Chi-A	17	34	2	5	0	1	0	2	1	3	.147	.171	.206	.377	15	-4	-3	98	103	1	.276	0			-0	1	-0.4
1918	Chi-A	7	10	1	1	0	0	0	1	0	0	.100	.100	.100	.200	-39	-2	-2	101	365	0	.111	0			0	/1	-0.1
1920	Chi-A	48	150	16	36	5	2	0	8	17	17	.240	.337	.300	.637	73	-6	-5	96	62	17	.603	3	2	-0	-2	1	-0.7
Total	4	75	196	19	42	5	3	0	11	19	21	.214	.300	.270	.570	58	-11	-10	97	82	18	.526	5	2		-3	/1	-1.2
■ **POP JOY**	Joy, Aloysius C. b: 6/11/1860, Washington, D.C. d: 6/28/37, Washington, D.C. Deb: 6/03/1884																											
1884	Was-U	36	130	12	28	0	0	0		2		.215	.227	.215	.443	52	-7	-6	97	0	7	.294	0			0	1	-0.5
■ **JOYCE**	Joyce Deb:8/14/1886																											
1886	Was-N	1	0	0	0	0	0	0	0	0	0	—	—	—	—	—	0	0	94	—	—	—	0			0	/O	0.0
■ **BILL JOYCE**	Joyce, William Michael "Scrappy Bill" b: 9/21/1865, St.Louis, Mo. d: 5/8/41, St.Louis, Mo. BL/TR, 5'11", 185 lbs. Deb: 4/19/1890 M																											
1890	Bro-P	133	489	121	123	18	18	1	78	**123**	77	.252	.413	.368	.782	105	16	9	106	112	95	.978	43			-12	*3	0.5
1891	Bos-a	65	243	76	75	9	15	3	51	63	27	.309	.460	.506	.966	183	29	30	99	99	75	1.351	36			-2	3/1	2.5
1892	Bro-N	97	372	89	91	15	12	6	45	82	55	.245	.392	.398	.790	139	23	22	101	72	69	.929	23			-18	3/O	0.9
1894	Was-N	99	355	103	126	25	14	17	89	87	33	.355	.496	.648	1.143	180	48	50	98	84	128	1.528	21			-4	*3	3.3
1895	Was-N	126	474	110	148	25	13	17	95	**96**	54	.312	.442	.527	.969	147	40	37	103	78	126	1.193	29			-11	*3	2.2
1896	Was-N	81	310	85	97	16	10	9	51	67	20	.313	.454	.516	.970	166	30	33	95	68	89	1.277	32			-7	32	2.4
	NY-N	49	165	36	61	9	2	5	43	34	14	.370	.500	.539	1.039	179	21	22	99	126	52	1.394	13			1	3M	2.1
	Yr	130	475	121	158	25	12	**14**	94	101	34	.333	.470	.524	.994	170	51	54	96	90	142	1.315	45			-6		4.5
1897	NY-N	109	388	109	118	15	13	3	64	78		.304	.441	.433	.874	136	25	26	98	102	91	1.096	33			1	*3/1M	2.2
1898	NY-N	145	508	91	131	20	9	10	91	88		.258	.385	.392	.777	133	21	25	95	127	92	.897	34			7	*13/2M	3.0
Total	8	904	3304	820	970	152	106	71	607	718	280	.294	.435	.468	.903	146	252	253	100	96	816	1.129	264			-45	31/2O	19.1
■ **WALLY JOYNER**	Joyner, Wallace Keith b: 6/16/62, Atlanta, Ga. BL/TL, 6'2", 185 lbs. Deb: 4/08/86																											
1986	Cal-A	154	593	82	172	27	3	22	100	57	58	.290	.354	.457	.811	125	16	19	96	125	96	.772	5	2	0	8	*1	1.7
1987	Cal-A	149	564	100	161	33	1	34	117	72	64	.285	.371	.528	.900	137	29	30	99	124	111	.914	8	2	1	-8	*1	0.8
1988	Cal-A	158	597	81	176	31	2	13	85	55	51	.295	.359	.419	.778	124	14	19	94	124	89	.724	8	2	1	14	*1	2.4
Total	3	461	1754	263	509	91	6	69	302	184	173	.290	.362	.467	.828	129	60	68	97	124	296	.818	21	6	3	14	1	4.9
■ **FRANK JUDE**	Jude, Frank b: 1884, Libby, Minn. d: 5/4/61, Brownsville, Tex. BR/TR, 5'7", 150 lbs. Deb: 7/09/06																											
1906	Cin-N	80	308	31	64	6	4	1	31	16		.208	.247	.263	.510	53	-14	-19	115	129	22	.426	7			-3	O	-2.6
■ **JOE JUDGE**	Judge, Joseph Ignatius b: 5/25/1894, Brooklyn, N.Y. d: 3/11/63, Washington, D.C. BL/TL, 5'8.5", 155 lbs. Deb: 9/20/15 C																											
1915	Was-A	12	41	7	17	2	0	0	9	4	6	.415	.500	.463	.963	186	5	5	101	155	10	1.037	2	3	-1	-1	1/O	0.3
1916	Was-A	103	336	42	74	10	8	0	28	54	44	.220	.333	.298	.631	90	-3	-3	100	102	40	.668	18			-3	*1	-0.7
1917	Was-A	102	393	62	112	15	15	2	30	50	40	.285	.369	.415	.783	151	18	22	92	56	63	.826	17			1	*1	2.1
1918	Was-A	130	502	56	131	23	7	1	46	49	32	.261	.332	.341	.672	99	1	-1	104	93	63	.658	20			2	*1	-0.7
1919	Was-A	135	521	83	150	33	12	2	31	81	35	.288	.386	.409	.795	125	18	20	98	45	87	.860	23			-5	*1	0.4
1920	Was-A	126	493	103	164	19	15	5	51	65	34	.333	.416	.462	.878	139	25	29	95	65	96	.909	12	12	-4	-8	*1	1.6
1921	Was-A	153	622	87	187	26	11	7	72	68	35	.301	.372	.412	.784	101	1	2	99	77	100	.789	21	6	3	-2	*1	0.1
1922	Was-A	148	591	84	174	32	15	10	81	50	20	.294	.355	.450	.806	118	6	13	92	86	91	.757	5	15	-8	3	*1	-0.2
1923	Was-A	113	405	56	127	24	6	2	63	58	20	.314	.406	.417	.823	124	12	16	95	130	72	.853	11	7	-1	5	*1	1.4
1924	Was-A	140	516	71	167	38	9	3	79	53	21	.324	.393	.450	.843	119	13	14	98	115	93	.852	13	8	-1	-2	*1	0.5
1925	Was-A	112	376	65	118	31	5	8	66	55	21	.314	.406	.487	.892	128	15	17	98	109	73	.919	7	12	-5	4	*1	1.2
1926	Was-A	134	453	70	132	25	11	7	92	53	25	.291	.367	.442	.808	112	6	8	98	**144**	75	.801	7	5	-1	6	*1	0.7
1927	Was-A	137	522	68	161	29	11	2	71	45	22	.308	.366	.418	.783	106	2	4	97	112	79	.762	10	0	3	-5	*1	-0.5
1928	Was-A	153	542	78	166	31	10	3	93	80	19	.306	.396	.417	.813	112	14	12	102	144	96	.850	16	4	2	-1	*1	0.5
1929	Was-A	143	543	83	171	35	8	6	71	73	33	.315	.397	.442	.839	116	15	15	100	100	100	.865	12	5	1	3	*1	-0.1
1930	Was-A	126	442	83	144	29	11	10	80	60	29	.326	.410	.509	.919	130	22	22	101	106	95	.990	13	6	0	2	*1	0.9
1931	Was-A	35	74	11	21	3	0	0	9	8	8	.284	.354	.324	.678	79	-2	-2	101	124	9	.604	0	0	0	-1	1	-0.3
1932	Was-A	82	291	45	75	16	3	3	29	37	19	.258	.343	.364	.708	84	-7	-7	100	86	38	.671	3	3	-1	-0	1	-1.4
1933	Bro-N	42	112	7	24	2	1	0	9	7	10	.214	.261	.250	.511	48	-8	-7	97	121	7	.396	1			-1	1	-0.9
	Bos-A	35	108	20	32	8	1	0	0	0	0	.296	.296	.389	.685	79	-3	-4	101	0	12	.571	2	1	0	0	1	-0.5
1934	Bos-A	10	15	3	5	2	0	0	2	2	1	.333	.412	.467	.878	119	1	0	106	95	3	.900	0	0	0	0	/1	0.0
Total	20	2171	7898	1184	2352	433	159	71	1012	952	474	.298	.377	.420	.797	115	153	175	98	97	1301	.805	213	87		-2	*1/O	4.4
■ **WALLY JUDNICH**	Judnich, Walter Franklin b: 1/24/17, San Francisco, Cal d: 7/12/71, Glendale, Cal. BL/TL, 6'1", 205 lbs. Deb: 4/16/40																											
1940	StL-A	137	519	97	157	27	7	24	89	54	71	.303	.368	.520	.888	120	20	15	106	100	102	.888	8	5	-1	-4	*O	0.1
1941	StL-A	146	546	90	155	40	6	14	83	80	45	.284	.377	.456	.833	119	16	16	100	103	98	.824	5	5	-2	-1	*O	0.4
1942	StL-A	132	457	78	143	22	6	17	82	74	41	.313	.413	.499	.912	150	35	33	104	106	101	.957	3	2	-0	-5	*O	2.0
1946	StL-A	142	511	60	134	23	4	15	72	60	54	.262	.340	.411	.751	111	6	7	98	110	74	.694	0	4	-2	7	*O	0.4
1947	StL-A	144	500	58	129	24	3	18	64	60	62	.258	.338	.426	.763	109	6	5	102	90	75	.720	2	5	-2	-6	*1O	-0.6
1948	Cle-A	79	218	36	56	13	3	2	29	56	23	.257	.411	.372	.782	111	6	6	99	113	38	.824	2	3	-1	-4	O1	0.0
1949	Pit-N	10	35	5	8	1	0	0	1	1	2	.229	.250	.257	.507	36	-3	-3	101	42	2	.370	0			2	/O	-0.1
Total	7	790	2786	424	782	150	29	90	420	385	298	.281	.369	.452	.822	120	85	79	102	102	491	.824	20	24		-11	O1	2.2
■ **LYLE JUDY**	Judy, Lyle Leroy "Punch" b: 11/15/13, Lawrenceville, Ill BR/TR, 5'10", 150 lbs. Deb: 9/17/35																											
1935	StL-N	8	11	2	0	0	0	0	0	2	2	.000	.154	.000	.154	-53	-2	-2	104	0	0	.308	2			0	/2	-0.1
■ **RED JUELICH**	Juelich, John Samuel b: 9/20/16, St.Louis, Mo. d: 12/25/70, St.Louis, Mo. BR/TR, 5'11.5", 170 lbs. Deb: 5/30/39																											
1939	Pit-N	17	46	5	11	0	2	0	4	2	4	.239	.271	.326	.597	60	-3	-3	100	98	3	.436	0			0	2/3	-0.1
■ **GEORGE JUMONVILLE**	Jumonville, George Benedict b: 5/16/17, Mobile, Ala. BR/TR, 6', 175 lbs. Deb: 9/13/40																											
1940	Phi-N	11	34	0	3	0	0	0	0	1	6	.088	.139	.088	.227	-37	-6	-6	97	0	0	.161	0			0	S/3	-0.4
1941	Phi-N	6	7	1	3	0	0	1	2	0	0	.429	.429	.857	1.286	264	1	1	97	80	3	1.500	0			0	/2S	0.2
Total	2	17	41	1	6	0	0	1	2	1	6	.146	.186	.220	.406	12	-5	-5	97	13	3	.314	0			0	/S23	-0.2
■ **ED JURAK**	Jurak, Edward James b: 10/24/57, Los Angeles, Cal. BR/TR, 6'2", 185 lbs. Deb: 6/30/82																											
1982	Bos-A	12	21	3	7	0	0	0	7	2	4	.333	.391	.333	.725	92	0	-0	110	400	3	.643	0	0	0	-0	3/O	0.0
1983	Bos-A	75	159	19	44	8	4	0	18	18	25	.277	.354	.377	.731	100	1	1	101	117	21	.661	1	2	-1	0	S13/2D	0.1

YEAR	TM/L	G	AB	R	H	2B	3B	HR	RBI	BB	SO	AVG	OBP	SLG	PRO	/A	BR	/A	PF	CHI	RC	TA	SB	CS	SBR	FR	POS	TPR
1984	Bos-A	47	66	6	16	3	1	1	7	12	12	.242	.359	.364	.723	91	0	-1	110	103	9	.679	0	2	-1	2	12/3S	0.0
1985	Bos-A	26	13	4	3	0	0	0	0	1	3	.231	.286	.231	.516	43	-1	-1	102	0	1	.364	0	0	0	-0	/3S1OD	0.0
1988	Oak-A	3	1	1	0	0	0	0	0	0	0	.000	.000	.000	.000	-99	-0	-0	95	0	0	.000	0	0	0	0	/3D	0.0
Total	5	163	260	33	70	11	5	1	32	33	44	.269	.354	.362	.715	94	0	-1	104	130	34	.665	1	4	-2	2	/S312DO	0.1
■ **BILLY JURGES**	Jurges, William Frederick b: 5/9/08, Bronx, N.Y. BR/TR, 5'11", 175 lbs. Deb: 5/04/31 MC																											
1931	Chi-N	88	293	34	59	15	5	0	23	25	41	.201	.264	.287	.551	50	-22	-20	96	98	24	.474	2			2	32/S	-1.2
1932	Chi-N	115	396	40	100	24	4	2	52	19	26	.253	.288	.348	.637	68	-17	-19	104	134	41	.537	1			**26**	*S/3	1.6
1933	Chi-N	143	487	49	131	17	6	5	50	26	39	.269	.313	.359	.672	94	-6	-4	97	99	52	.557	3			21	*S	2.7
1934	Chi-N	100	358	43	88	15	2	8	33	19	34	.246	.289	.366	.655	76	-14	-13	98	78	37	.550	1			-15	S	-2.4
1935	Chi-N	146	519	69	125	33	1	1	59	42	39	.241	.304	.314	.618	67	-24	-23	99	131	50	.520	3			**28**	*S	1.0
1936	Chi-N	118	429	51	120	25	1	1	42	23	25	.280	.321	.350	.671	77	-12	-14	105	97	46	.554	4			13	*S	0.5
1937	Chi-N	129	450	53	134	18	10	1	65	42	41	.298	.365	.389	.754	102	4	3	103	134	66	.686	2			-19	*S	-0.5
1938	Chi-N	137	465	53	114	18	3	1	47	58	53	.245	.335	.303	.638	73	-13	-16	105	120	48	.555	3			-7	*S	-1.3
1939	NY-N	138	543	84	155	21	11	6	63	47	34	.285	.349	.398	.747	101	0	1	99	95	71	.657	3			18	*S	2.7
1940	NY-N	63	214	23	54	3	3	2	36	25	14	.252	.347	.322	.669	85	-3	-3	100	182	23	.596	2			5	S	0.8
1941	NY-N	134	471	50	138	25	2	5	61	47	36	.293	.361	.386	.747	107	7	5	103	114	66	.671	0			6	*S	2.3
1942	NY-N	127	464	45	119	7	1	2	30	43	42	.256	.324	.289	.612	78	-11	-12	103	81	42	.496	1			-1	*S	-0.4
1943	NY-N	136	481	46	110	8	2	4	29	53	38	.229	.310	.279	.589	74	-17	-15	96	73	44	.505	2			9	S3	0.4
1944	NY-N	85	246	28	52	2	1	1	23	23	20	.211	.279	.240	.519	45	-17	-18	104	133	17	.426	4			5	3S/2	-0.7
1945	NY-N	61	176	22	57	3	1	3	24	24	11	.324	.405	.403	.808	126	7	7	100	104	30	.795	2			2	3/S	0.9
1946	Chi-N	82	221	26	49	9	2	0	17	43	28	.222	.351	.281	.631	85	-4	-2	94	102	24	.606	3			0	S/32	0.4
1947	Chi-N	14	40	5	8	2	0	1	2	9	9	.200	.347	.325	.672	79	-1	-1	101	46	5	.688	0			1	S	0.1
Total	17	1816	6253	721	1613	245	55	43	656	568	530	.258	.325	.335	.660	82	-140	-145	100	108	686	.593	36			94	*S3/2	6.9
■ **JOE JUST**	Just, Joseph Erwin (born Joseph Erwin Juszczak) b: 1/8/16, Milwaukee, Wis. BR/TR, 5'11", 185 lbs. Deb: 5/13/44																											
1944	Cin-N	11	11	0	2	0	0	0	0	0	2	.182	.250	.182	.432	24	-1	-1	95	0	0	.300	0			0	C	0.0
1945	Cin-N	14	34	2	5	0	0	0	2	4	7	.147	.237	.147	.384	9	-4	-4	94	139	1	.300	0			0	C	-0.2
Total	2	25	45	2	7	0	0	0	2	4	9	.156	.240	.156	.396	12	-5	-5	94	105	2	.308	0			0	/C	-0.2
■ **SKIP JUTZE**	Jutze, Alfred Henry b: 5/28/46, Queens, N.Y. BR/TR, 5'11", 190 lbs. Deb: 9/01/72																											
1972	StL-N	21	71	1	17	2	0	0	5	1	16	.239	.250	.268	.518	45	-5	-5	105	108	4	.351	0	1	-1	2	C	-0.2
1973	Hou-N	90	278	18	62	6	0	0	18	19	37	.223	.275	.245	.520	47	-20	-19	95	106	17	.381	0	1	-1	-5	C	-2.0
1974	Hou-N	8	13	0	3	0	0	0	1	1	1	.231	.286	.231	.516	47	-1	-1	98	129	1	.333	0	0	0	0	/C	0.0
1975	Hou-N	51	93	9	21	2	0	0	6	2	4	.226	.242	.247	.489	38	-8	-7	94	101	6	.356	1	0	0	0	C	-0.5
1976	Hou-N	42	92	7	14	2	3	0	6	4	16	.152	.188	.239	.427	24	-10	-8	86	105	4	.325	0	0	0	-0	C	-0.6
1977	Sea-A	42	109	10	24	2	0	3	15	7	12	.220	.267	.321	.588	62	-6	-6	96	135	8	.457	0	4	-2	0	C	-0.6
Total	6	254	656	45	141	14	3	3	51	34	86	.215	.255	.259	.514	45	-50	-46	95	111	39	.393	1	6	-3	-3	C	-3.9
■ **JIM KAAT**	Kaat, James Lee b: 11/7/38, Zeeland, Mich. BL/TL, 6'4.5", 205 lbs. Deb: 8/02/59 C																											
1959	Was-A	3	1	0	0	0	0	0	0	0	1	.000	.000	.000	.000	-99	-0	-0	100	0	0	.000	0	0	0	0	/P	0.0
1960	Was-A	13	14	0	2	0	0	0	0	0	6	.143	.143	.143	.286	-22	-2	-2	102	0	0	.167	0	0	0	0	P	0.0
1961	Min-A	47	63	10	15	3	1	0	1	4	13	.238	.294	.317	.612	60	-3	-4	106	20	6	.500	0	0	0	3	P	0.0
1962	Min-A	48	100	9	18	3	1	1	10	8	40	.180	.241	.260	.501	33	-9	-10	105	137	7	.415	0	0	0	6	P	0.0
1963	Min-A	36	61	2	8	1	0	1	8	2	19	.131	.185	.197	.381	7	-8	-8	100	223	2	.296	0	0	0	4	P	0.0
1964	Min-A	46	83	11	14	1	0	3	11	11	31	.169	.266	.289	.555	54	-5	-5	101	141	7	.500	0	0	0	3	P	0.0
1965	Min-A	56	93	6	23	4	0	1	9	3	29	.247	.271	.323	.593	67	-4	-4	101	113	9	.493	2	0	1	3	P	0.0
1966	Min-A	47	118	12	23	2	1	2	13	5	41	.195	.228	.280	.507	40	-8	-10	111	140	8	.396	0	0	0	0	P	0.0
1967	Min-A	45	99	7	17	3	1	1	4	7	26	.172	.226	.253	.479	39	-7	-8	107	60	6	.381	0	0	0	1	P	0.0
1968	Min-A	36	77	7	12	3	0	0	5	2	18	.156	.177	.195	.372	12	-8	-9	106	143	2	.254	0	0	0	-0	P	0.0
1969	Min-A	43	87	8	18	8	0	2	10	4	20	.207	.250	.368	.618	70	-4	-4	102	106	8	.536	0	0	0	-3	P	0.0
1970	Min-A	56	76	17	15	1	0	1	8	6	20	.197	.265	.250	.515	43	-6	-6	98	147	5	.413	0	0	0	2	P	0.0
1971	Min-A	54	93	6	15	3	0	0	5	2	16	.161	.179	.194	.372	5	-12	-12	104	113	4	.282	2	0	1	-0	P	0.0
1972	Min-A	24	45	3	13	3	0	2	4	1	16	.289	.304	.489	.793	124	1	1	107	60	6	.697	0	1	-1	0	P	0.0
1973	Min-A	31	0	1	0	0	0	0	0	0	0	—	—	—	—	—	0	0	104	—	—	—	0	0	0	-1	P	0.0
	Chi-A	7	0	0	0	0	0	0	0	0	0	—	—	—	—	—	0	0	102	—	—	—	0	0	0	-1	/P	0.0
	Yr	38	0	1	0	0	0	0	0	0	0	—	—	—	—	—	0	0	103	—	—	—	0	0	0	-2		0.0
1974	Chi-A	42	1	0	0	0	0	0	0	0	0	.000	.000	.000	.000	-98	-0	-0	102	0	0	.000	0	0	0	-2	P	0.0
1975	Chi-A	43	0	0	0	0	0	0	0	0	0	—	—	—	—	—	0	0	103	—	—	—	0	0	0	-2	P	0.0
1976	Phi-N	42	79	4	14	3	1	1	8	2	24	.177	.198	.278	.476	32	-7	-8	107	123	5	.369	0	0	0	-3	P	0.0
1977	Phi-N	36	53	4	10	3	0	0	2	2	12	.189	.218	.245	.463	24	-6	-6	100	62	3	.341	0	0	0	-2	P	0.0
1978	Phi-N	26	48	4	7	1	0	0	4	0	15	.146	.163	.167	.330	-7	-7	-7	105	198	1	.214	0	0	0	-2	P	0.0
1979	Phi-N	3	1	0	0	0	0	0	0	0	1	.000	.500	.000	.500	50	0	0	97	0	0	1.000	0	0	0	0	/P	0.0
	NY-A	40	0	0	0	0	0	0	0	0	0	—	—	—	—	—	0	0	96	—	—	—	0	0	0	-1	P	0.0
1980	NY-A	4	0	0	0	0	0	0	0	0	0	—	—	—	—	—	0	0	99	—	—	—	0	0	0	1	/P	0.0
	StL-N	49	35	4	5	1	0	1	2	2	13	.143	.189	.257	.446	23	-4	-4	103	66	2	.400	1	0	0	-2	P	0.0
1981	StL-N	41	8	2	3	1	0	0	2	1	0	.375	.444	.500	.944	164	1	1	102	196	2	1.000	0	0	0	1	P	0.0
1982	StL-N	62	12	0	0	0	0	0	0	1	4	.000	.077	.000	.077	-74	-3	-3	103	0	0	.083	0	0	0	1	P	0.0
1983	StL-N	24	4	0	0	0	0	0	0	0	2	.000	.000	.000	.000	-99	-1	-1	98	0	0	.000	0	0	0	0	P	0.0
Total	25	1004	1251	117	232	44	5	16	106	63	367	.185	.229	.267	.496	38	-102	-108	104	115	96	.401	5	1	1	6	P	0.0
■ **JACK KADING**	Kading, John Frederick b: 11/17/1884, Waukesha, Wis. d: 6/2/64, Chicago, Ill. 6'3", 190 lbs. Deb: 9/12/10																											
1910	Pit-N	8	23	5	7	2	1	0	4	4	5	.304	.407	.478	.886	142	2	1	112	127	5	.938	0			0	/1	0.1
1914	Chi-F	3	3	0	0	0	0	0	0	0	0	.000	.000	.000	.000	-99	-1	-1	91	0	0	.000	0			0	H	0.0
Total	2	11	26	5	7	2	1	0	4	4	5	.269	.367	.423	.790	118	1	1	110	114	5	.789	0			0	/1	0.1
■ **JAKE KAFORA**	Kafora, Frank Jacob "Tomatoes" b: 10/16/1888, Chicago, Ill. d: 3/23/28, Chicago, Ill. BR/TR, 6', 180 lbs. Deb: 10/05/13																											
1913	Pit-N	1	1	1	0	0	0	0	0	0	1	.000	.500	.000	.500	52	0	0	96	0	0	1.000	0			0	/C	0.0
1914	Pit-N	21	23	2	3	0	0	0	0	0	6	.130	.200	.130	.330	-1	-3	-3	92	0	1	.250	0			-0	C	-0.2
Total	2	22	24	3	3	0	0	0	0	0	7	.125	.222	.125	.347	4	-3	-3	93	0	1	.286	0			-0	/C	-0.2
■ **IKE KAHDOT**	Kahdot, Isaac Leonard "Chief" b: 10/22/01, Georgetown, Okla. BR/TR, 5'5.5", 145 lbs. Deb: 9/05/22																											
1922	Cle-A	4	2	0	0	0	0	0	0	0	1	.000	.000	.000	.000	-98	-1	-1	102	0	0	.000	0	0	0	0	/3	0.0
■ **NICK KAHL**	Kahl, Nicholas Alexander b: 4/10/1879, Coulterville, Ill. d: 7/13/59, Sparta, Ill. BR/TR, 5'9", 185 lbs. Deb: 5/02/05																											
1905	Cle-A	40	135	16	29	4	1	0	21	4		.215	.237	.259	.497	59	-6	-6	100	218	9	.377	1			0	2/SO	-0.6
■ **BOB KAHLE**	Kahle, Robert Wayne b: 11/23/15, Newcastle, Ind. BR/TR, 6', 170 lbs. Deb: 4/21/38																											
1938	Bos-N	8	3	2	1	0	0	0	0	0	0	.333	.333	.333	.667	95	-0	-0	88	0	0	.500	0			0	H	0.0
■ **OWEN KAHN**	Kahn, Owen Earle "Jack" b: 6/5/05, Richmond, Va. d: 1/17/81, Richmond, Va. BR/TR, 5'11", 160 lbs. Deb: 5/24/30																											
1930	Bos-N	1	0	1	0	0	0	0	0	0	0	—	—	—	—	—	0	0	97	—	—	—	0			0	R	0.0
■ **MIKE KAHOE**	Kahoe, Michael Joseph b: 9/3/1873, Yellow Springs, O d: 5/14/49, Akron, Ohio BR/TR, 6', 185 lbs. Deb: 9/22/1895																											
1895	Cin-N	3	4	0	0	0	0	0	0	0	0	.000	.000	.000	.000	-93	-1	-1	108	0	0	.000	0			0	/C	0.0
1899	Cin-N	14	42	2	7	1	1	0	4	0		.167	.167	.238	.405	11	-5	-5	106	123	2	.314	1			0	C	-0.4
1900	Cin-N	52	175	18	33	3	3	1	9	4		.189	.207	.257	.464	32	-17	-15	92	59	10	.366	3			7	C/S	-0.2
1901	Cin-N	4	13	0	4	0	0	0	0	1		.308	.357	.308	.665	101	-0	0	95	0	1	.556	0			0	/C	0.1
	Chi-N	67	237	21	53	12	2	1	21	8		.224	.249	.304	.553	61	-12	-12	100	96	20	.462	5			0	C/1	-0.3
	Yr	71	250	21	57	12	2	1	21	9		.228	.255	.304	.559	63	-12	-12	100	90	21	.466	5			0		-0.2

YEAR	TM/L	G	AB	R	H	2B	3B	HR	RBI	BB	SO	AVG	OBP	SLG	PRO	/A	BR	/A	PF	CHI	RC	TA	SB	CS	SBR	FR	POS	TPR
1902	Chi-N	7	18	0	4	1	0	0	2	0		.222	.222	.278	.500	58	-1	-1	96	138	1	.357	0			0	/C3S	0.0
	StL-A	55	197	21	48	9	2	2	28	6		.244	.266	.340	.606	67	-9	-9	102	129	19	.517	4			-3	C	-0.7
1903	StL-A	77	244	26	46	7	5	0	23	11		.189	.224	.258	.482	48	-16	-14	95	132	15	.379	1			1	C/O	-0.4
1904	StL-A	72	236	9	51	6	1	0	12	8		.216	.242	.250	.492	61	-11	-10	95	76	16	.384	4			2	C	0.0
1905	Phi-N	16	51	2	13	2	0	0	4	1		.255	.269	.294	.563	67	-2	-2	104	93	4	.447	1			1	C	0.0
1907	Chi-N	5	10	0	4	0	0	0	1	0		.400	.400	.400	.800	144	1	0	106	95	2	.667	0			0	/C1	0.1
	Was-A	17	47	3	9	1	0	0	1	0		.191	.191	.213	.404	33	-4	-3	90	36	2	.263	0			-1	C	-0.3
1908	Was-A	17	27	1	5	1	0	0	0	0		.185	.185	.222	.407	35	-2	-2	95	0	1	.273	0			0	C	0.0
1909	Was-A	4	8	0	1	0	0	0	0	0		.125	.125	.125	.250	-23	-1	-1	90	0	0	.429	2			0	/C	0.0
Total	11	410	1309	103	278	43	14	4	105	39	0	.212	.235	.276	.511	53	-80	-76	97	94	93	.408	21			7	C/103S	-2.1

■ **AL KAISER** Kaiser, Alfred Edward "Deerfoot" b: 8/3/1886, Cincinnati, Ohio d: 4/11/69, Cincinnati, Ohio BR/TR, 5'9", 165 lbs. Deb: 4/18/11

YEAR	TM/L	G	AB	R	H	2B	3B	HR	RBI	BB	SO	AVG	OBP	SLG	PRO	/A	BR	/A	PF	CHI	RC	TA	SB	CS	SBR	FR	POS	TPR
1911	Chi-N	26	84	16	21	0	5	0	7	7	12	.250	.308	.369	.677	92	-2	-1	97	76	11	.698	6			-2	O	-0.3
	Bos-N	66	197	20	40	5	2	2	15	10	26	.203	.249	.279	.528	46	-14	-15	103	83	15	.452	4			-5	O	-2.1
	Yr	92	281	36	61	5	7	2	22	17	38	.217	.267	.306	.573	59	-16	-17	101	82	26	.523	10			-7		-2.4
1912	Bos-N	4	13	0	0	0	0	0	0	0	3	.000	.000	.000	.000	-93	-4	-4	107	0	-0	.000	0			0	/O	-0.3
1914	Ind-F	59	187	22	43	10	0	1	16	17	41	.230	.294	.299	.594	63	-7	-10	111	98	20	.549	6			-2	O/1	-1.5
Total	3	155	481	58	104	15	7	3	38	34	82	.216	.271	.295	.566	57	-27	-30	105	86	46	.515	16			-9	O/1	-4.2

■ **JOHN KALAHAN** Kalahan, John Joseph b: 9/30/1878, Philadelphia, Pa. d: 6/20/52, Philadelphia, Pa. TR , 6', 165 lbs. Deb: 03

YEAR	TM/L	G	AB	R	H	2B	3B	HR	RBI	BB	SO	AVG	OBP	SLG	PRO	/A	BR	/A	PF	CHI	RC	TA	SB	CS	SBR	FR	POS	TPR
1903	Phi-A	1	5	0	0	0	0	0	0	0		.000	.000	.000	.000	-96	-1	-1	104	0	0	.000	0			0	/C	0.0

■ **CHARLIE KALBFUS** Kalbfus, Charles Henry "Skinny" b: 12/28/1864, Washington, D.C. d: 11/18/41, Washington, D.C. BR/TR, 5'11", 145 lbs. Deb: 4/18/1884

YEAR	TM/L	G	AB	R	H	2B	3B	HR	RBI	BB	SO	AVG	OBP	SLG	PRO	/A	BR	/A	PF	CHI	RC	TA	SB	CS	SBR	FR	POS	TPR
1884	Was-U	1	5	1	1	0	0	0		0		.200	.200	.200	.400	37	-0	-0	97	0	0	.250	0			0	/O	0.0

■ **FRANK KALIN** Kalin, Frank Bruno "Fats" (born Frank Bruno Kalinkiewicz) b: 10/3/17, Steubenvillie, Ohio d: 1/12/75, Weirton, W.Va. BR/TR, 6', 200 lbs. Deb: 9/25/40

YEAR	TM/L	G	AB	R	H	2B	3B	HR	RBI	BB	SO	AVG	OBP	SLG	PRO	/A	BR	/A	PF	CHI	RC	TA	SB	CS	SBR	FR	POS	TPR
1940	Pit-N	3	3	0	0	0	0	0	1	2	0	.000	.400	.000	.400	20	-0	-0	95	0	0	.500	0			-1	/O	0.0
1943	Chi-A	4	4	0	0	0	0	0	0	0	0	.000	.000	.000	.000	-99	-1	-1	101	0	0	.000	0	0	0	0	H	0.0
Total	2	7	7	0	0	0	0	0	1	2	0	.000	.222	.000	.222	-34	-1	-1	98	0	0	.250	0	0		-1	/O	0.0

■ **AL KALINE** Kaline, Albert William b: 12/19/34, Baltimore, Md. BR/TR, 6'1.5", 175 lbs. Deb: 6/25/53 H

YEAR	TM/L	G	AB	R	H	2B	3B	HR	RBI	BB	SO	AVG	OBP	SLG	PRO	/A	BR	/A	PF	CHI	RC	TA	SB	CS	SBR	FR	POS	TPR
1953	Det-A	30	28	9	7	0	0	1	2	1	5	.250	.300	.357	.657	79	-1	-1	98	57	3	.591	1	0	0	-7	O	-0.7
1954	Det-A	138	504	42	139	18	3	4	43	22	45	.276	.306	.347	.653	79	-16	-16	100	89	48	.527	9	5	-0	5	*O	-1.5
1955	Det-A	152	588	121	**200**	24	8	27	102	82	57	**.340**	.425	.546	.971	165	50	53	97	100	135	1.012	6	8	-3	4	*O	4.5
1956	Det-A	153	617	96	194	32	10	27	128	70	55	.314	.385	.530	.915	144	33	36	97	113	129	.933	7	1	2	**18**	*O	4.6
1957	Det-A	149	577	83	170	29	4	23	90	43	38	.295	.347	.478	.825	115	16	11	107	109	92	.782	11	9	-2	11	*O	1.2
1958	Det-A	146	543	84	170	34	7	16	85	54	47	.313	.377	.490	.867	132	27	24	104	115	96	.833	7	4	-0	**23**	*O	3.8
1959	Det-A	136	511	86	167	19	2	27	94	72	42	.327	.414	**.530**	**.944**	142	**42**	34	111	111	114	**.994**	10	4	1	4	*O	3.2
1960	Det-A	147	551	77	153	29	4	15	68	65	47	.278	.357	.426	.784	109	9	8	102	101	84	.767	19	4	3	2	*O	0.8
1961	Det-A	153	586	116	190	**41**	7	19	82	66	42	.324	.396	.515	.912	148	35	38	96	95	121	.935	14	1	4	19	*O/3	5.3
1962	Det-A	100	398	78	121	16	6	29	94	47	39	.304	.379	.593	.972	141	31	25	111	111	85	.980	4	0	1	10	*O	3.2
1963	Det-A	145	551	89	172	24	3	27	101	54	48	.312	.378	.514	.891	142	34	32	104	123	105	.878	6	4	-1	-4	*O	2.3
1964	Det-A	146	525	77	154	31	5	17	68	75	51	.293	.385	.469	.853	142	27	30	96	103	97	.854	4	1	1	-9	*O	1.7
1965	Det-A	125	399	72	112	18	2	18	72	72	49	.281	.391	.471	.862	136	25	22	105	126	77	.899	6	0	2	-2	*O/3	1.9
1966	Det-A	142	479	85	138	29	1	29	88	81	66	.288	.396	.534	.931	161	42	41	102	110	105	.983	5	5	-2	10	*O	4.7
1967	Det-A	131	458	94	141	28	2	25	78	83	47	.308	.415	.541	.957	182	48	49	99	107	104	1.015	8	2	1	6	*O	5.6
1968	Det-A	102	327	49	94	14	1	10	53	55	39	.287	.395	.428	.823	140	22	19	106	136	59	.846	6	4	-1	-1	O1	1.6
1969	Det-A	131	456	74	124	17	0	21	69	54	61	.272	.350	.447	.798	118	13	11	103	106	71	.754	1	2	-1	-0	*O/1	0.6
1970	Det-A	131	467	64	130	24	4	16	71	77	49	.278	.382	.450	.831	124	20	18	103	118	79	.808	2	2	-1	0	O1	1.1
1971	Det-A	133	405	69	119	19	2	15	54	82	57	.294	.421	.462	.883	157	31	33	96	95	81	.921	4	6	-2	-6	*O/1	2.1
1972	Det-A	106	278	46	87	11	2	10	32	28	33	.313	.380	.475	.855	136	18	14	113	83	48	.807	1	0	0	-8	O1	0.4
1973	Det-A	91	310	40	79	13	0	10	45	29	28	.255	.325	.394	.718	100	0	-0	101	119	39	.653	4	1	1	-6	O1	-0.8
1974	Det-A	147	558	71	146	28	2	13	64	65	75	.262	.340	.389	.729	103	7	3	106	104	75	.669	2	2	-1	0	*D	0.3
Total	22	2834	10116	1622	3007	498	75	399	1583	1277	1020	.297	.379	.480	.859	134	513	484	102	108	1846	.880	137	65	2	69	*OD1/3	45.9

■ **WILLIE KAMM** Kamm, William Edward b: 2/2/1900, San Francisco, Cal. BR/TR, 5'10.5", 170 lbs. Deb: 4/18/23

YEAR	TM/L	G	AB	R	H	2B	3B	HR	RBI	BB	SO	AVG	OBP	SLG	PRO	/A	BR	/A	PF	CHI	RC	TA	SB	CS	SBR	FR	POS	TPR
1923	Chi-A	149	544	57	159	39	9	6	87	62	82	.292	.366	.430	.796	111	7	8	98	120	86	.789	17	13	-3	7	*3	2.9
1924	Chi-A	147	528	58	134	28	6	6	93	64	59	.254	.337	.364	.700	83	-16	-13	97	**149**	68	.664	9	8	-2	8	*3	0.4
1925	Chi-A	152	509	82	142	32	4	6	83	**90**	36	.279	.391	.393	.784	104	2	6	96	130	83	.803	11	13	-5	-0	*3	0.9
1926	Chi-A	143	480	63	141	24	10	0	62	77	24	.294	.396	.385	.781	114	6	12	92	116	80	.816	14	4	2	13	*3	3.7
1927	Chi-A	148	540	85	146	32	13	0	59	70	18	.270	.354	.378	.732	88	-7	-9	102	102	74	.713	7	0	2	1	*3	0.2
1928	Chi-A	155	552	70	170	30	12	1	84	73	22	.308	.391	.411	.802	112	11	12	99	133	93	.816	17	9	-0	-3	*3	1.1
1929	Chi-A	147	523	72	140	33	6	3	63	75	23	.268	.363	.371	.734	94	-7	-2	95	113	76	.734	12	4	1	2	*3	0.9
1930	Chi-A	112	331	49	89	21	6	3	47	51	20	.269	.368	.396	.764	91	-2	-4	103	111	51	.764	5	4	-1	14	*3	1.2
1931	Chi-A	18	59	9	15	4	1	0	9	7	6	.254	.333	.356	.689	88	-2	-1	92	141	7	.644	1	1	-0	-1	3	0.0
	Cle-A	114	410	68	121	31	4	0	66	64	13	.295	.392	.390	.782	100	6	2	106	139	66	.799	13	9	-2	-1	*3	0.6
	Yr	132	469	77	136	35	5	0	75	71	19	.290	.384	.386	.770	99	5	1	104	**140**	73	.778	14	10	-2	-1		0.6
1932	Cle-A	148	524	76	150	34	9	3	83	75	36	.286	.379	.403	.781	95	4	-3	108	129	85	.782	6	3	0	6	*3	1.2
1933	Cle-A	133	447	59	126	17	2	1	47	54	27	.282	.359	.336	.695	81	-8	-11	105	105	58	.651	7	3	0	-4	*3	-0.3
1934	Cle-A	121	386	52	104	23	3	0	42	62	38	.269	.372	.345	.716	85	-6	-6	101	105	55	.717	7	1	2	4	*3	0.0
1935	Cle-A	6	18	2	6	0	0	0	1	0	1	.333	.333	.333	.667	73	-1	-1	99	57	2	.462	0	1	-1	0	/3	0.0
Total	13	1693	5851	802	1643	348	85	29	826	824	405	.281	.372	.384	.756	97	-12	-9	100	122	884	.752	126	73	-6	47	*3	12.8

■ **ALEX KAMPOURIS** Kampouris, Alexis William b: 11/13/12, Sacramento, Cal. BR/TR, 5'8", 155 lbs. Deb: 7/31/34

YEAR	TM/L	G	AB	R	H	2B	3B	HR	RBI	BB	SO	AVG	OBP	SLG	PRO	/A	BR	/A	PF	CHI	RC	TA	SB	CS	SBR	FR	POS	TPR
1934	Cin-N	19	66	6	13	1	0	0	3	3	18	.197	.254	.212	.466	26	-7	-7	101	79	4	.389	2			-0	2	-0.4
1935	Cin-N	148	499	46	123	26	5	7	62	32	84	.246	.295	.361	.655	80	-18	-14	93	111	55	.578	8			-6	*2/S	-0.7
1936	Cin-N	122	355	43	85	10	4	5	46	24	46	.239	.289	.332	.622	69	-17	-15	97	123	35	.527	3			8	*2/O	0.1
1937	Cin-N	146	458	62	114	21	4	17	71	60	65	.249	.342	.424	.766	117	4	10	91	105	67	.723	2			2	*2	1.8
1938	Cin-N	21	74	13	19	1	0	2	7	10	13	.257	.353	.351	.704	96	-0	-0	98	81	9	.627	0			-1	2	0.0
	NY-N	82	268	35	66	9	1	5	37	27	50	.246	.318	.343	.661	79	-7	-8	103	125	30	.574	0			8	2	0.5
	Yr	103	342	48	85	10	1	7	44	37	63	.249	.325	.345	.670	83	-7	-8	102	117	40	.595	0			7		0.5
1939	NY-N	74	201	23	50	12	2	5	29	30	41	.249	.349	.403	.752	103	1	1	99	111	29	.709	0			10	23	1.4
1941	Bro-N	16	51	8	16	4	2	2	9	11	8	.314	.444	.588	1.033	183	6	6	103	92	15	1.200	0			-2	2	0.5
1942	Bro-N	10	21	3	5	2	1	0	3	0	4	.238	.238	.429	.667	91	-0	-0	102	124	2	.563	0			-0	/2	0.0
1943	Bro-N	19	44	9	10	4	1	0	4	17	6	.227	.452	.364	.815	137	4	4	100	90	9	.944	0			-2	2	0.2
	Was-A	51	145	24	30	4	0	2	13	30	25	.207	.361	.276	.637	84	-1	-1	104	103	19	.695	7	1	2	-2	32/O	0.0
Total	9	708	2182	272	531	94	20	45	284	244	360	.243	.325	.367	.692	91	-34	-24	97	110	272	.657	22	1		15	2/3SO	3.4

■ **FRANK KANE** Kane, Francis Thomas "Sugar" b: 3/9/1895, Whitman, Mass. d: 12/2/62, Brockton, Mass. BL/TR, 5'11.5", 175 lbs. Deb: 9/13/15

YEAR	TM/L	G	AB	R	H	2B	3B	HR	RBI	BB	SO	AVG	OBP	SLG	PRO	/A	BR	/A	PF	CHI	RC	TA	SB	CS	SBR	FR	POS	TPR
1915	Bro-F	3	10	2	2	0	1	0	2	0	0	.200	.200	.400	.600	77	-0	-0	98	180	1	.500	0			0	/O	0.0
1919	NY-A	1	1	0	0	0	0	0	0	0	0	.000	.000	.000	.000	-95	-0	-0	106	0	0	.000	0			0	H	0.0
Total	2	4	11	2	2	0	1	0	2	0	0	.182	.182	.364	.545	60	-1	-1	98	164	1	.444	0			0	/O	0.0

■ **JIM KANE** Kane, James Joseph "Shamus" b: 11/27/1881, Scranton, Pa. d: 10/2/47, Omaha, Neb. BL/TL, 6'2", 225 lbs. Deb: 4/21/08

YEAR	TM/L	G	AB	R	H	2B	3B	HR	RBI	BB	SO	AVG	OBP	SLG	PRO	/A	BR	/A	PF	CHI	RC	TA	SB	CS	SBR	FR	POS	TPR
1908	Pit-N	55	145	16	35	3	3	0	22	12		.241	.299	.303	.603	100	-1	-0	95	192	14	.555	5			-3	1	-0.4

■ **JOHN KANE** Kane, John Francis b: 9/24/1882, Chicago, Ill. d: 1/28/34, St.Anthony, Idaho BR/TR, 5'6", 138 lbs. Deb: 4/11/07

YEAR	TM/L	G	AB	R	H	2B	3B	HR	RBI	BB	SO	AVG	OBP	SLG	PRO	/A	BR	/A	PF	CHI	RC	TA	SB	CS	SBR	FR	POS	TPR
1907	Cin-N	79	262	40	65	9	4	3	19	22		.248	.306	.347	.654	112	2	3	95	73	35	.675	20			-3	O3/S2	-0.1
1908	Cin-N	130	455	61	97	11	7	3	23	43		.213	.281	.288	.569	82	-8	-9	103	67	43	.570	30			-4	*O/2	-1.6

YEAR	TM/L	G	AB	R	H	2B	3B	HR	RBI	BB	SO	AVG	OBP	SLG	PRO	/A	BR	/A	PF	CHI	RC	TA	SB	CS	SBR	FR	POS	TPR
1909	Chi-N	20	45	6	4	1	0	0	5	2		.089	.146	.111	.257	-20	-6	-6	101	364	1	.220	1			0	/OS32	-0.6
1910	Chi-N	32	62	11	15	0	0	1	12	9	10	.242	.338	.290	.628	83	-1	-1	101	199	7	.617	2			-5	O/23S	-0.5
Total	4	261	824	118	181	21	11	7	59	76	10	.220	.286	.297	.584	85	-13	-13	100	95	86	.583	53			-11	O/32S	-2.8
■ JOHN KANE	Kane, John Francis b: 2/19/1900, Chicago, Ill. d: 7/25/56, Chicago, Ill. BB/TR, 5'10.5", 162 lbs. Deb: 9/03/25																											
1925	Chi-A	14	56	6	10	1	0	0	3	0	3	.179	.193	.196	.389	-1	-9	-8	96	97	2	.261	0	0	0	0	/S2	-0.5
■ TOM KANE	Kane, Thomas Joseph "Sugar" b: 12/15/06, Chicago, Ill. d: 6/30/75, Lincoln, Cal. BR/TR, 5'10.5", 160 lbs. Deb: 8/03/38																											
1938	Bos-N	2	2	0	0	0	0	0	0	2	0	.000	.500	.000	.500	54	0	0	88	0	0	.667	0			-0	/2	0.0
■ JERRY KANE	Kane, William b: 1867, Collinsville, Ill. BR/TR, 6', 175 lbs. Deb: 5/02/1890																											
1890	StL-a	8	25	3	5	0	0	0		2		.200	.259	.200	.459	32	-2	-3	116	0	1	.350	0			0	/1C	-0.1
■ ROD KANEHL	Kanehl, Roderick Edwin "Hot Rod" b: 4/1/34, Wichita, Kan. BR/TR, 6'1", 180 lbs. Deb: 4/15/62																											
1962	NY-N	133	351	52	87	10	2	4	27	23	36	.248	.296	.322	.618	63	-17	-19	104	85	32	.523	8	6	-1	-0	23O/1S	-1.4
1963	NY-N	109	191	26	46	6	0	1	9	5	26	.241	.268	.288	.556	60	-10	-10	99	65	13	.439	6	3	0	-3	O32/1	-1.6
1964	NY-N	98	254	25	59	7	1	1	11	7	18	.232	.256	.280	.535	53	-17	-15	95	61	19	.416	3	1	0	7	2O3/1	-0.6
Total	3	340	796	103	192	23	3	6	47	35	80	.241	.277	.300	.577	60	-43	-44	100	73	64	.480	17	10	-1	4	2O/31S	-3.6
■ HEINIE KAPPEL	Kappel, Henry b: 1862, Philadelphia, Pa. d: 8/27/05, Philadelphia, Pa. BR/TR, 5'8", 160 lbs. Deb: 5/22/1887																											
1887	Cin-a	23	78	11	22	3	2	0		2		.282	.309	.372	.680	84	-1	-2	108	0	10	.625	3			0	/3O2S	-0.1
1888	Cin-a	36	143	18	37	4	4	1	15	2		.259	.274	.364	.638	106	0	0	101	83	20	.708	20			0	S2/3	0.0
1889	Col-a	46	173	25	47	7	5	3	21	21	28	.272	.354	.422	.776	135	5	8	91	78	30	.833	10			0	S3	0.7
Total	3	105	394	54	106	14	11	4	36	25	28	.269	.318	.391	.708	114	4	6	98	65	60	.747	33			0	/S32O	0.6
■ JOE KAPPEL	Kappel, Joseph b: 4/27/1857, Philadelphia, Pa. d: 7/8/29, Philadelphia, Pa. BR, 5'10", 165 lbs. Deb: 5/26/1884																											
1884	Phi-N	4	15	1	1	0	0	0	0	0	2	.067	.067	.067	.133	-63	-3	-2	92	0	0	.071				0	/C	-0.1
1890	Phi-a	56	208	29	50	8	1	1		20		.240	.310	.303	.613	85	-4	-3	97	0	24	.608	12			0	OS3/C2	-0.2
Total	2	60	223	30	51	8	1	1	0	20	2	.229	.295	.287	.582	77	-7	-6	97	0	24	.564	12			0	/OS3C2	-0.3
■ RON KARKOVICE	Karkovice, Ronald Joseph b: 8/8/63, Union, N.J. BR/TR, 6'1", 210 lbs. Deb: 8/17/86																											
1986	Chi-A	37	97	13	24	7	0	4	13	9	37	.247	.318	.443	.761	105	1	0	101	94	13	.711	1	0	0	1	C	0.4
1987	Chi-A	39	85	7	6	0	0	2	7	7	40	.071	.160	.141	.301	-17	-15	-16	109	155	2	.296	3	0	1	4	C/D	-0.6
1988	Chi-A	46	115	10	20	4	0	3	9	7	30	.174	.228	.287	.515	44	-9	-9	97	85	8	.459	4	2	0	2	C	-0.4
Total	3	122	297	30	50	11	0	9	29	23	107	.168	.238	.296	.534	44	-23	-24	102	108	23	.492	8	2	1	7	C/D	-0.6
■ BILL KARLON	Karlon, William John "Hank" b: 1/21/09, Palmer, Mass. d: 12/7/64, Ware, Mass. BR/TR, 6'1", 190 lbs. Deb: 4/28/30																											
1930	NY-A	2	5	0	0	0	0	0	0	0	1	.000	.000	.000	.000	-99	-2	-1	90	0	0	.000	0	0	0	-0	/O	-0.1
■ MARTY KAROW	Karow, Martin Gregory (born Martin Gregory Karowsky) b: 7/18/04, Braddock, Pa. d: 4/27/86, Bryan, Texas BR/TR, 5'10.5", 170 lbs. Deb: 6/21/27																											
1927	Bos-A	6	10	0	2	1	0	0	0	0	2	.200	.200	.300	.500	30	-1	-1	95	0	1	.375	0	0	0	0	/S3	0.0
■ JOHN KARST	Karst, John Gottlieb "King" b: 10/15/1893, Philadelphia, Pa. d: 5/21/76, Cape May Court House, N.J. TR, 5'11.5", 175 lbs. Deb: 10/06/15																											
1915	Bro-N	1	0	0	0	0	0	0	0	0	0	—	—	—	—	—	0	0	101	—	—	—	0			0	/3	0.0
■ EDDIE KASKO	Kasko, Edward Michael b: 6/27/32, Linden, N.J. BR/TR, 6', 180 lbs. Deb: 4/18/57 M																											
1957	StL-N	134	479	59	131	16	5	1	35	33	53	.273	.320	.334	.654	76	-16	-16	101	89	52	.559	6	1	1	2	*3S/2	-1.0
1958	StL-N	104	259	20	57	8	1	2	22	21	25	.220	.279	.282	.560	46	-19	-21	106	115	19	.446	1	2	-1	-11	S2/3	-2.7
1959	Cin-N	118	329	39	93	14	1	2	31	14	38	.283	.312	.350	.661	74	-11	-13	103	104	35	.539	2	2	-1	3	S3/2	-0.7
1960	Cin-N	126	479	56	140	21	1	6	51	46	37	.292	.362	.378	.739	105	3	4	98	110	66	.678	9	9	-3	2	32S	0.6
1961	Cin-N	126	469	64	127	22	1	2	27	32	36	.271	.323	.335	.658	72	-16	-19	104	68	52	.564	4	3	-1	-16	*S3/2	-2.4
1962	Cin-N	134	533	74	148	26	2	4	41	35	44	.278	.328	.356	.685	82	-12	-13	102	85	59	.575	3	3	-1	-7	*3S	-1.6
1963	Cin-N	76	199	25	48	9	0	3	10	21	29	.241	.314	.332	.645	83	-3	-4	104	56	21	.558	0	2	-1	-2	3S/2	-0.5
1964	Hou-N	133	448	45	109	16	1	0	22	37	52	.243	.302	.283	.586	69	-19	-17	96	72	38	.477	4	6	-2	4	*S/3	-0.7
1965	Hou-N	68	215	18	53	7	1	1	10	11	20	.247	.296	.302	.598	78	-9	-6	89	61	17	.466	1	3	-2	-8	S/3	-0.8
1966	Bos-A	58	136	11	29	7	0	1	12	15	19	.213	.291	.287	.578	61	-6	-7	109	120	11	.491	1	0	0	1	S3/2	-0.4
Total	10	1077	3546	411	935	146	13	22	261	265	353	.264	.318	.331	.649	77	-108	-112	101	87	370	.563	31	31	-9	-33	S3/2	-10.2
■ RAY KATT	Katt, Raymond Frederick b: 5/9/27, New Braunfels, Tex. BR/TR, 6'2", 190 lbs. Deb: 9/16/52 C																											
1952	NY-N	9	27	4	6	0	0	0	0	1	5	.222	.250	.222	.472	31	-2	-3	102	65	1	.304	0	0	0	-0	/C	-0.2
1953	NY-N	8	29	2	5	1	0	0	1	1	3	.172	.200	.207	.407	6	-4	-4	98	66	1	.292	0	0	0	-1	/C	-0.3
1954	NY-N	86	200	26	51	7	1	9	33	19	29	.255	.320	.435	.755	90	-2	-4	105	114	28	.699	1	0	0	-9	C	-0.9
1955	NY-N	124	326	27	70	7	2	7	28	22	38	.215	.269	.313	.581	55	-22	-21	99	92	25	.468	0	0	0	-24	*C	-4.2
1956	NY-N	37	101	10	23	4	0	7	14	6	16	.228	.278	.475	.753	100	-1	-1	97	86	13	.688	0	1	-1	-4	C	-0.3
	StL-N	47	158	11	41	4	0	6	20	6	24	.259	.291	.399	.690	84	-4	-4	99	104	18	.583	0	1	-1	2	C	0.0
	Yr	84	259	21	64	8	0	13	34	12	40	.247	.286	.429	.714	90	-5	-4	98	97	31	.628	0	2	-1	-1		-0.3
1957	NY-N	72	165	11	38	3	1	2	17	15	35	.230	.302	.297	.599	60	-9	-9	102	128	15	.500	1	0	0	-8	C	-1.3
1958	StL-N	19	41	1	7	1	0	1	4	4	6	.171	.244	.268	.513	33	-4	-4	106	118	2	.405	0	0	0	0	C	-0.2
1959	StL-N	15	24	0	7	2	0	0	2	0	8	.292	.292	.375	.667	73	-1	-1	105	90	2	.474	0	0	0	-1	C	0.0
Total	8	417	1071	92	248	29	4	32	120	74	164	.232	.285	.356	.641	69	-49	-50	101	103	105	.560	2	2	-1	-44	C	-7.4
■ BENNY KAUFF	Kauff, Benjamin Michael b: 1/5/1890, Pomeroy, Ohio d: 11/17/61, Columbus, Ohio BL/TL, 5'8", 157 lbs. Deb: 4/20/12																											
1912	NY-A	5	11	4	3	0	0	0	2	3		.273	.429	.273	.701	100	0	0	101	223	2	.875	1			-1	/O	0.0
1914	Ind-F	154	571	**120**	**211**	**44**	13	8	95	72	55	**.370**	**.440**	.534	**.974**	161	**59**	**51**	111	100	**172**	**1.256**	**75**			5	*O	4.9
1915	Bro-F	136	483	92	165	23	11	12	83	85	50	**.342**	**.440**	**.509**	**.949**	**185**	**52**	**53**	98	102	**136**	**1.214**	**55**			13	*O	**6.3**
1916	NY-N	154	552	71	146	22	15	9	74	68	65	.264	.348	.408	.756	138	21	24	96	124	81	.778	40	26	-4	-3	*O	1.7
1917	NY-N	153	559	89	172	22	4	5	68	59	54	.308	.379	.388	.767	140	25	27	97	109	91	.804	30			-8	*O	1.6
1918	NY-N	67	270	41	85	19	4	2	39	16	30	.315	.355	.437	.792	145	12	13	98	105	43	.778	9			5	O	1.6
1919	NY-N	135	491	73	136	27	7	10	67	39	45	.277	.334	.422	.756	127	15	15	100	116	72	.761	21			-8	*O	0.1
1920	NY-N	55	157	31	43	12	3	3	26	25	14	.274	.380	.446	.826	137	8	8	100	127	26	.826	3	7	-3	3	O	0.5
Total	8	859	3094	521	961	169	57	49	454	367	313	.311	.386	.450	.836	149	193	191	100	111	624	.926	234	33		6	O	16.7
■ DICK KAUFFMAN	Kauffman, Howard Richard b: 6/22/1888, E.Lewisburg, Pa. d: 4/16/48, Mifflinburg, Pa. BB/TR, 6'3", 190 lbs. Deb: 9/17/14																											
1914	StL-A	7	15	1	4	1	0	0	2	0	3	.267	.267	.333	.600	82	-0	-0	98	150	1	.455	0			0	/1	0.0
1915	StL-A	37	124	9	32	8	2	0	14	5	27	.258	.298	.355	.653	100	-1	-1	96	108	12	.537	0	3	-2	1	1/O	-0.3
Total	2	44	139	10	36	9	2	0	16	5	30	.259	.295	.353	.647	98	-2	-1	96	112	14	.528	0	3		1	/1O	-0.3
■ CHARLIE KAVANAGH	Kavanagh, Charles Hugh "Silk" b: 6/9/1893, Chicago, Ill. BR/TR, 5'9", 165 lbs. Deb: 6/11/14																											
1914	Chi-A	6	5	0	1	0	0	0	0	0	2	.200	.333	.200	.533	59	-0	-0	103	0	0	.500	0			0	H	0.0
■ LEO KAVANAGH	Kavanagh, Leo Daniel b: 8/9/1894, Chicago, Ill. d: 8/10/50, Chicago, Ill. BR/TR, 5'9", 180 lbs. Deb: 4/22/14																											
1914	Chi-F	5	11	0	3	0	0	0	1	1	0	.273	.333	.273	.606	82	-0	-0	91	120	1	.500	0			0	/S	0.0
■ MARTY KAVANAGH	Kavanagh, Martin Joseph b: 6/13/1891, Harrison, N.J. d: 7/28/60, Eloise, Mich. BR/TR, 6', 187 lbs. Deb: 4/18/14																											
1914	Det-A	127	439	60	109	21	6	4	35	41	42	.248	.318	.351	.669	99	-0	-1	102	81	51	.625	16	14	-4	-7	*2/1	-1.3
1915	Det-A	113	332	55	98	14	13	3	49	42	44	.295	.378	.443	.820	134	18	15	108	107	56	.822	8	8	-2	-4	12/SO3	0.6
1916	Det-A	58	78	6	11	4	0	0	5	9	15	.141	.239	.192	.431	28	-7	-7	105	119	4	.373	0			-1	O/23	-0.8
	Cle-A	19	44	4	11	2	1	1	10	2	5	.250	.283	.409	.692	108	0	0	100	170	5	.606	0			0	/213	0.1
	Yr	77	122	10	22	6	1	1	15	11	20	.180	.254	.270	.524	56	-7	-7	103	133	9	.450	0			-0		-0.7
1917	Cle-A	14	14	1	0	0	0	0	0	3	2	.000	.176	.000	.176	-40	-2	-3	114	0	0	.214	0			1	/O	-0.1
1918	Cle-A	13	38	4	8	2	0	0	6	7	7	.211	.348	.263	.611	78	-0	-1	108	219	4	.633	1			-0	1	-0.1
	StL-N	12	44	6	8	1	0	1	8	3	1	.182	.234	.273	.507	58	-2	-2	93	214	3	.444	1			-0	/O2	-0.2
	Det-A	13	44	2	12	3	0	0	9	11	6	.273	.418	.341	.759	133	2	2	97	232	6	.813	0			-1	1	0.1

YEAR	TM/L	G	AB	R	H	2B	3B	HR	RBI	BB	SO	AVG	OBP	SLG	PRO	/A	BR	/A	PF	CHI	RC	TA	SB	CS	SBR	FR	POS	TPR
Total	5	369	1033	138	257	47	20	9	122	118	122	.249	.330	.359	.690	103	8	3	104	112	129	.655	26	22		-12	2/103S	-1.7
■ KAVANAUGH Kavanaugh Deb:9/11/1872																												
1872	Eck-n	5	22	5	4							.182															/1O	
■ BILL KAY Kay, Walter Brocton "King Bill" b: 2/14/1878, New Castle, Va. d: 12/3/45, Roanoke, Va. BL/TR, 6'2", 180 lbs. Deb: 8/12/07																												
1907	Was-A	25	60	8	20	1	1	0	7	0		.333	.333	.383	.717	145	2	2	90	109	8	.575	0			1	O	0.3
■ EDDIE KAZAK Kazak, Edward Terrance (born Edward Terrance Tkaczuk) b: 7/18/20, Steubenville, O. BR/TR, 6', 175 lbs. Deb: 9/29/48																												
1948	StL-N	6	22	1	6	3	0	0	2	0	2	.273	.273	.409	.682	82	-1	-1	101	83	2	.529	0			0	/3	0.0
1949	StL-N	92	326	43	99	15	3	6	42	29	17	.304	.362	.423	.786	100	5	0	110	103	49	.712	0			5	3/2	0.6
1950	StL-N	93	207	21	53	2	2	5	23	18	19	.256	.319	.357	.676	75	-7	-8	103	100	23	.581	0			2	3	-0.4
1951	StL-N	11	33	2	6	2	0	0	4	5	5	.182	.289	.242	.532	44	-2	-3	101	193	3	.464	0	0	0	1	3	-0.1
1952	StL-N	3	2	1	0	0	0	0	0	0	0	.000	.000	.000	.000	-99	-1	-1	98	0	0	.000	0	0	0	0	/3	0.0
	Cin-N	13	15	1	1	0	1	0	0	0	2	.067	.067	.200	.267	-29	-3	-3	100	0	0	.214	0	0	0	0	/31	-0.2
	Yr	16	17	2	1	0	1	0	0	0	2	.059	.059	.176	.235	-37	-3	-3	99	0	0	.188	0	0	0	0		-0.2
Total	5	218	605	69	165	22	6	11	71	52	45	.273	.332	.383	.716	85	-9	-14	107	104	77	.650	0	0		9	3/21	-0.1
■ TED KAZANSKI Kazanski, Theodore Stanley b: 1/25/34, Hamtramck, Mich. BR/TR, 6'1", 175 lbs. Deb: 6/25/53																												
1953	Phi-N	95	360	39	78	17	5	2	27	26	53	.217	.275	.308	.583	52	-26	-25	99	95	31	.486	1	1	-0	-21	S	-3.8
1954	Phi-N	39	104	7	14	2	0	1	8	4	14	.135	.167	.183	.349	-9	-17	-17	99	143	2	.242	0	1	-1	-4	S	-1.8
1955	Phi-N	9	12	1	1	0	0	1	1	1	1	.083	.154	.333	.487	24	-1	-1	102	58	1	.455	0	0	0	-0	/S3	-0.1
1956	Phi-N	117	379	35	80	11	1	4	34	20	41	.211	.253	.277	.530	45	-31	-28	94	123	25	.408	0	2	-1	-24	*2/S	-4.5
1957	Phi-N	62	185	15	49	7	1	3	11	17	20	.265	.327	.362	.689	86	-4	-3	98	60	21	.590	1	1	-0	-5	32/S	-0.5
1958	Phi-N	95	289	21	66	12	2	3	35	22	34	.228	.292	.315	.607	62	-16	-16	98	145	25	.506	2	3	-1	-10	2S3	-2.1
Total	6	417	1329	118	288	49	9	14	116	90	163	.217	.270	.299	.569	52	-95	-90	97	112	105	.472	4	8	-4	-64	2S/3	-12.8
■ BOB KEARNEY Kearney, Robert Henry b: 10/3/56, San Antonio, Tex. BR/TR, 6', 190 lbs. Deb: 9/25/79																												
1979	SF-N	2	0	0	0	0	0	0	0	1	0	—	1.000	—	1.299	294	0	0	92	0	0	—	0	0	0	0	/C	0.0
1981	Oak-A	1	0	0	0	0	0	0	0	0	0	—	—	—	—	—	0	0	96	—	—	—	0	0	0	0	/C	0.0
1982	Oak-A	22	71	7	12	3	0	0	5	3	10	.169	.224	.211	.435	21	-8	-7	95	133	4	.333	0	0	0	3	C	-0.2
1983	Oak-A	108	298	33	76	11	0	8	32	21	50	.255	.313	.372	.685	92	-5	-3	96	93	32	.578	1	4	-2	1	*C/D	0.0
1984	Sea-A	133	431	39	97	24	1	7	43	18	72	.225	.259	.334	.594	61	-22	-24	102	104	36	.494	7	5	-1	2	*C	-1.3
1985	Sea-A	108	305	24	74	14	1	6	27	11	59	.243	.278	.354	.632	76	-12	-10	95	85	29	.519	1	1	-0	-10	*C	-1.5
1986	Sea-A	81	204	23	49	10	0	6	25	12	35	.240	.282	.377	.660	75	-6	-8	105	105	20	.546	0	2	-1	-0	C	-0.4
1987	Sea-A	24	47	5	8	4	1	0	1	1	9	.170	.188	.298	.485	26	-5	-5	103	28	3	.385	0	0	0	1	C	-0.1
Total	8	479	1356	131	316	66	3	27	133	67	235	.233	.275	.346	.621	70	-59	-57	99	96	123	.529	9	12	-5	-3	C/D	-3.5
■ TEDDY KEARNS Kearns, Edward Joseph b: 1/1/1900, Trenton, N.J. d: 12/21/49, Trenton, N.J. BR/TR, 5'11", 180 lbs. Deb: 9/18/24																												
1924	Chi-N	4	16	0	4	0	1	0	1	1	1	.250	.294	.375	.669	77	-1	-1	101	64	2	.583	0	0	0	0	/1	0.0
1925	Chi-N	3	2	0	1	0	0	0	0	0	0	.500	.500	.500	1.000	160	0	0	97	0	0	1.000	0	0	0	0	/1	0.0
Total	2	7	18	0	5	0	1	0	1	1	1	.278	.316	.389	.705	86	-0	-0	101	58	2	.615	0	0	0	0	/1	0.0
■ TOM KEARNS Kearns, Thomas J. "Dasher" b: 11/9/1859, Rochester, N.Y. d: 12/7/38, Buffalo, N.Y. TR, 5'7", 160 lbs. Deb: 8/26/1880																												
1880	Buf-N	2	7	0	0	0	0	0	0	0	0	.000	.000	.000	.000	-99	-1	-1	91	0	0	.000				0	/C	0.0
1882	Det-N	4	13	2	4	2	0	0	1	0	4	.308	.308	.462	.769	140	1	1	102	56	2	.667				0	/2	0.0
1884	Det-N	21	79	9	16	0	1	0	7	2	10	.203	.222	.228	.450	45	-5	-4	94	136	4	.317				0	2	-0.3
Total	3	27	99	11	20	2	1	0	8	2	14	.202	.218	.242	.460	48	-6	-5	94	117	6	.329				0	/2C	-0.3
■ EDDIE KEARSE Kearse, Edward Paul "Truck" b: 2/23/16, San Francisco, Cal d: 7/15/68, Eureka, Cal. BR/TR, 6'1", 195 lbs. Deb: 6/13/42																												
1942	NY-A	11	26	2	5	0	0	0	2	3	1	.192	.276	.192	.468	33	-2	-2	99	141	2	.409	1	0	0	0	C	0.0
■ CHICK KEATING Keating, Walter Francis b: 8/8/1891, Philadelphia, Pa. d: 7/13/59, Philadelphia, Pa. BR/TR, 5'9.5", 155 lbs. Deb: 9/26/13																												
1913	Chi-N	2	5	0	1	1	0	0	0	0	1	.200	.200	.400	.600	70	-0	-0	99	0	0	.500	0			0	/S	0.0
1914	Chi-N	20	30	3	3	0	1	0	0	6	9	.100	.250	.167	.417	25	-3	-3	98	0	1	.407	0			-2	S	-0.3
1915	Chi-N	4	8	1	0	0	0	0	0	0	3	.000	.000	.000	.000	-98	-2	-2	102	0	0	.125	1			-0	/S	-0.1
1926	Phi-N	4	2	0	0	0	0	0	0	0	0	.000	.000	.000	.000	-97	-1	-1	103	0	0	.000	0			0	/2S3	0.0
Total	4	30	45	4	4	1	1	0	0	6	13	.089	.196	.156	.352	4	-5	-5	99	0	2	.341	1			-2	/S23	-0.4
■ GREG KEATLEY Keatley, Gregory Steven b: 9/12/53, Princeton, W.Va. BR/TR, 6'2", 200 lbs. Deb: 9/27/81																												
1981	KC-A	2	0	0	0	0	0	0	0	0	0	—	—	—	—	—	0	0	99	—	—	—	0	0	0	0	/C	0.0
■ PAT KEEDY Keedy, Charles Patrick b: 1/40/58, Birmingham, Ala. BR/TR, 6'4", 205 lbs. Deb: 9/10/85																												
1985	Cal-A	3	4	1	2	1	0	1	1	0	0	.500	.500	1.500	2.000	418	2	2	101	44	2	2.000	0	1	-1	-0	/3O	0.1
1987	Chi-A	17	41	6	7	1	0	2	2	2	14	.171	.209	.341	.551	40	-3	-4	109	40	3	.500	1	0	0	-0	3/12SOD	-0.3
Total	2	20	45	7	9	2	0	3	3	2	14	.200	.234	.444	.678	70	-2	-2	108	40	5	.622	1	1	-0	-1	/31ODS2	-0.2
■ WILLIE KEELER Keeler, William Henry "Wee Willie" b: 3/3/1872, Brooklyn, N.Y. d: 1/1/23, Brooklyn, N.Y. BL/TL, 5'4.5", 140 lbs. Deb: 9/30/1892 H																												
1892	NY-N	14	53	7	17	3	0	0	6	3	3	.321	.368	.377	.746	130	2	2	98	94	9	.806	5			0	3	0.2
1893	NY-N	7	24	5	8	2	1	1	7	5	1	.333	.448	.625	1.073	180	3	3	104	109	8	1.438	3			0	/O2S	0.2
	Bro-N	20	80	14	25	1	1	1	9	4	4	.313	.353	.387	.740	109	-0	1	91	77	12	.691	2			0	3/O	0.1
	Yr	27	104	19	33	3	2	2	16	9	5	.317	.377	.442	.820	127	3	4	94	89	20	.859	5			0		0.3
1894	Bal-N	129	590	165	219	27	22	5	94	40	6	.371	.427	.517	.944	130	28	29	99	70	148	1.065	32			2	*O/2	1.7
1895	Bal-N	131	565	162	213	24	15	4	78	37	12	.377	.429	.494	.922	130	34	26	107	65	143	1.071	47			-2	*O	1.1
1896	Bal-N	126	544	153	210	22	13	4	82	37	9	.386	.432	.496	.928	144	37	35	102	74	149	1.141	67			4	*O	2.5
1897	Bal-N	129	564	145	**239**	27	19	1	74	35		**.424**	.464	.544	**1.008**	**177**	**55**	**60**	95	62	**176**	**1.271**	64			-3	*O	4.0
1898	Bal-N	129	561	126	**216**	7	2	1	44	31		**.385**	.420	.410	.830	137	30	28	103	49	111	.846	28			0	*O/3	1.8
1899	Bro-N	141	570	**140**	216	12	13	1	61	37		.379	.423	.451	.874	137	34	30	105	64	131	.977	45			-4	*O	1.5
1900	Bro-N	136	563	106	**204**	13	12	4	68	30		.362	.395	.449	.844	126	26	20	108	71	119	.903	41			9	*O/2	1.5
1901	Bro-N	136	595	123	202	18	12	2	43	21		.339	.362	.420	.782	122	20	15	106	50	101	.748	23			-4	*O3/2	0.0
1902	Bro-N	133	559	86	186	20	5	0	38	21		.333	.357	.386	.743	139	19	22	95	54	86	.686	19			0	*O	1.3
1903	NY-A	132	512	95	160	14	7	0	32	32		.313	.353	.367	.720	118	12	12	100	59	77	.693	24			-9	*O/3	-0.5
1904	NY-A	143	543	78	186	14	8	2	40	35		.343	.382	.409	.791	136	32	25	112	69	95	.779	21			-6	*O	1.1
1905	NY-A	149	560	81	169	14	4	4	38	43		.302	.352	.363	.714	127	18	17	102	61	80	.678	19			-4	*O2/3	0.8
1906	NY-A	152	592	96	180	9	3	2	33	40		.304	.348	.340	.688	98	12	-1	120	51	80	.641	23			2	*O	-0.5
1907	NY-A	107	423	50	99	5	2	0	17	15		.234	.260	.255	.516	61	-16	-20	109	54	31	.401	7			-19	*O	-5.0
1908	NY-A	91	323	38	85	3	1	1	14	31		.263	.328	.288	.616	108	2	4	95	58	34	.580	14			-0	O	0.0
1909	NY-A	99	360	44	95	7	5	1	32	24		.264	.327	.319	.647	105	2	2	99	111	40	.600	10			-18	O	-2.1
1910	NY-N	19	10	5	3	0	0	0	0	3	1	.300	.462	.300	.762	129	1	1	95	0	2	1.000	1			-1	/O	0.0
Total	19	2123	8591	1719	2932	242	145	34	810	524	36	.341	.384	.415	.799	127	350	310	104	63	1633	.822	495			-52	*O/32S	9.7
■ BOB KEELY Keely, Robert William b: 8/22/09, St.Louis, Mo. BR/TR, 6', 175 lbs. Deb: 7/25/44 C																												
1944	StL-N	1	0	0	0	0	0	0	0	0	0	—	—	—	—	—	0	0	101	—	—	—	0			0	/C	0.0
1945	StL-N	1	1	0	0	0	0	0	0	0	0	.000	.000	.000	.000	-99	-0	-0	100	0	0	.000	0			0	/C	0.0
Total	2	2	1	0	0	0	0	0	0	0	0	.000	.000	.000	.000	-99	-0	-0	100	0	1633	.000	0			0	/C	0.0
■ BILL KEEN Keen, William Brown "Buster" b: 8/16/1892, Oglethorpe, Ga. d: 7/16/47, South Point, Ohio BR/TR, 6', 181 lbs. Deb: 8/08/11																												
1911	Pit-N	6	7	0	0	0	0	0	0	1	4	.000	.125	.000	.125	-63	-2	-2	101	0	0	.143	0			0	/1	-0.1
■ JIM KEENAN Keenan, James W. b: 2/10/1858, New Haven, Conn. d: 9/21/26, Cincinnati, Ohio BR/TR, 5'10", 186 lbs. Deb: 5/17/1875																												
1875	NH-n	3	12	1	1							.083															/3C	
1880	Buf-N	2	7	1	1	0	0	0	0	1	1	.143	.250	.143	.393	41	-0	-0	91	0	0	.333				0	/C	0.0

YEAR	TM/L	G	AB	R	H	2B	3B	HR	RBI	BB	SO	AVG	OBP	SLG	PRO	/A	BR	/A	PF	CHI	RC	TA	SB	CS	SBR	FR	POS	TPR
1882	Pit-a	25	96	10	21	7	0	1		1		.219	.227	.323	.550	86	-2	-1	97	0	7	.427				1	C/OS	0.0
1884	Ind-a	68	249	36	73	14	4	3		16		.293	.343	.418	.761	156	14	15	96	0	37	.699				4	C/1OSP	2.1
1885	Cin-a	36	132	16	35	2	2	1		8		.265	.307	.333	.640	101	1	0	104	0	14	.536				-1	C/1P	0.3
1886	Cin-a	44	148	31	40	4	3	3		18		.270	.357	.399	.756	145	7	8	96	0	22	.731	0			0	C/O31P	0.7
1887	Cin-a	47	174	19	44	4	1	0		11		.253	.301	.287	.588	61	-8	-10	108	0	18	.531	7			3	C1	0.0
1888	Cin-a	85	313	38	73	9	8	1	40	22		.233	.294	.323	.617	100	0	0	101	117	33	.571	9			0	C1	0.7
1889	Cin-a	87	300	52	86	10	11	6	60	48	35	.287	.395	.453	.849	137	18	16	105	114	62	.972	18			-1	C1/3	1.8
1890	Cin-N	54	202	21	28	4	2	3	19	19	36	.139	.216	.223	.439	27	-18	-21	108	108	11	.402	5			1	C/1O3	-1.4
1891	Cin-N	75	252	30	51	7	5	4	33	33	39	.202	.302	.317	.620	90	-5	-2	91	107	25	.587	2			1	1C/3	0.0
Total	10	523	1873	254	452	61	36	22	152	177	111	.241	.314	.348	.661	102	7	5	101	65	229	.626	41			9	C1/O3PS	4.2

■ GEORGE KEERL Keerl, George Henry b: 4/10/1847, Baltimore, Md. d: 9/13/23, Menominee, Mich. 5'7", 145 lbs. Deb: 5/05/1875

YEAR	TM/L	G	AB	R	H	2B	3B	HR	RBI	BB	SO	AVG	OBP	SLG	PRO	/A	BR	/A	PF	CHI	RC	TA	SB	CS	SBR	FR	POS	TPR
1875	Chi-n	6	26	2	3							.115															/2	

■ JIM KEESEY Keesey, James Ward b: 10/27/02, Perryville, Md. d: 9/5/51, Boise, Idaho BR/TR, 6'0.5", 170 lbs. Deb: 9/06/25

YEAR	TM/L	G	AB	R	H	2B	3B	HR	RBI	BB	SO	AVG	OBP	SLG	PRO	/A	BR	/A	PF	CHI	RC	TA	SB	CS	SBR	FR	POS	TPR
1925	Phi-A	5	5	1	2	0	0	0	1	0	2	.400	.400	.400	.800	100	0	0	103	167	1	.667	0	0	0	0	/1	0.0
1930	Phi-A	11	12	2	3	1	0	0	2	1	2	.250	.308	.333	.641	63	-1	-1	99	166	1	.556	0	0	0	0	/1	0.0
Total	2	16	17	3	5	1	0	0	3	1	4	.294	.333	.353	.686	74	-1	-1	100	166	2	.583	0	0	0	0	/1	0.0

■ BILL KEISTER Keister, William Hoffman "Wagon Tongue" b: 8/17/1874, Baltimore, Md. d: 8/19/24, Baltimore, Md. BL/TR, 5'5.5", 168 lbs. Deb: 5/20/1896

YEAR	TM/L	G	AB	R	H	2B	3B	HR	RBI	BB	SO	AVG	OBP	SLG	PRO	/A	BR	/A	PF	CHI	RC	TA	SB	CS	SBR	FR	POS	TPR
1896	Bal-N	15	58	8	14	3	0	0	5	3	5	.241	.302	.293	.595	58	-3	-4	102	86	6	.591	4			0	/23	-0.2
1898	Bos-N	10	30	5	5	2	0	0	4	0		.167	.167	.233	.400	15	-3	-3	104	173	1	.280	0			0	/S2O	-0.2
1899	Bal-N	136	523	96	172	22	16	3	73	16		.329	.368	.449	.817	117	17	11	108	97	101	.855	33			-22	S2/O	-0.5
1900	StL-N	126	497	78	149	26	10	1	72	25		.300	.333	.398	.732	111	1	6	93	119	79	.733	32			-25	*2/S3	-1.1
1901	Bal-A	115	442	78	145	20	**21**	2	93	18		.328	.354	.482	.836	124	17	13	107	**142**	86	.859	24			-21	*S	-0.1
1902	Was-A	119	483	82	145	33	9	9	90	14		.300	.320	.462	.782	118	8	9	99	126	82	.781	27			0	O23/S	0.6
1903	Phi-N	100	400	53	128	27	7	3	63	14		.320	.343	.445	.788	137	11	15	92	115	66	.746	11			-1	*O	.7
Total	7	621	2433	400	758	133	63	18	400	90	5	.312	.341	.440	.781	118	48	48	100	119	422	.782	131			-69	S2O/3	-.8

■ MICKEY KELIHER Keliher, Maurice Michael b: 1/11/1890, Washington, D.C. d: 9/7/30, Washington, D.C. BL/TL, 6', 175 lbs. Deb: 9/09/11

YEAR	TM/L	G	AB	R	H	2B	3B	HR	RBI	BB	SO	AVG	OBP	SLG	PRO	/A	BR	/A	PF	CHI	RC	TA	SB	CS	SBR	FR	POS	TPR
1911	Pit-N	3	7	0	0	0	0	0	0	0	5	.000	.000	.000	.000	-99	-2	-2	101	0	0	.000	0			0	/1	-0.1
1912	Pit-N	2	0	1	0	0	0	0	0	0	0	—	—	—	—	—	0	0	99	—	—	—	0			0	R	0.0
Total	2	5	7	1	0	0	0	0	0	0	5	.000	.000	.000	.000	-99	-2	-2	101	0	0	.000	0			0	/1	-0.1

■ SKEETER KELL Kell, Everett Lee b: 10/11/29, Swifton, Ark. BR/TR, 5'9", 160 lbs. Deb: 4/19/52

YEAR	TM/L	G	AB	R	H	2B	3B	HR	RBI	BB	SO	AVG	OBP	SLG	PRO	/A	BR	/A	PF	CHI	RC	TA	SB	CS	SBR	FR	POS	TPR
1952	Phi-A	75	213	24	47	8	3	0	17	14	18	.221	.275	.286	.561	51	-13	-16	111	104	18	.480	5	1	1	-7	2	-1.9

■ GEORGE KELL Kell, George Clyde b: 8/23/22, Swifton, Ark. BR/TR, 5'9", 175 lbs. Deb: 9/28/43 H

YEAR	TM/L	G	AB	R	H	2B	3B	HR	RBI	BB	SO	AVG	OBP	SLG	PRO	/A	BR	/A	PF	CHI	RC	TA	SB	CS	SBR	FR	POS	TPR
1943	Phi-A	1	5	1	1	0	1	0	1	0	0	.200	.200	.600	.800	129	0	0	101	105	1	.750	0	0	0	0	/3	0.0
1944	Phi-A	139	514	51	138	15	3	0	44	22	23	.268	.300	.309	.609	73	-18	-18	101	102	43	.461	5	2	0	-8	*3	-2.7
1945	Phi-A	147	567	50	154	30	3	4	56	27	15	.272	.306	.356	.662	98	-8	-4	94	97	61	.545	2	0	1	20	*3	2.1
1946	Phi-A	26	87	3	26	6	1	0	11	10	6	.299	.378	.391	.768	110	2	2	104	125	14	.726	0	0	0	2	3	0.6
	Det-A	105	434	67	142	19	9	4	41	30	14	.327	.371	.440	.811	116	14	10	108	74	71	.734	3	2	-0	-1	*3/1	1.7
	Yr	131	521	70	168	25	10	4	52	40	20	.322	.372	.432	.804	115	16	11	107	85	85	.735	3	2	-0	1		2.3
1947	Det-A	152	588	75	188	29	5	5	93	61	16	.320	.387	.412	.798	117	18	15	104	141	95	.743	9	11	-4	16	*3	3.2
1948	Det-A	92	368	47	112	24	3	2	44	33	15	.304	.369	.402	.772	109	3	4	96	93	56	.701	2	2	-1	-5	3	-0.3
1949	Det-A	134	522	97	179	38	9	3	59	71	13	**.343**	.424	.467	.892	126	28	23	108	77	106	.890	7	5	-1	-2	*3	1.9
1950	Det-A	157	641	114	**218**	**56**	6	8	101	66	18	.340	.403	.484	.886	131	25	28	97	100	123	.846	3	3	-1	-3	*3	1.7
1951	Det-A	147	598	92	**191**	**36**	3	2	59	61	18	.319	.386	.400	.786	107	12	7	106	76	97	.742	10	3	1	9	*3	1.2
1952	Det-A	39	152	11	45	8	0	1	17	15	13	.296	.359	.368	.728	104	1	1	99	103	21	.645	0	1	-1	3	3	0.4
	Bos-A	75	276	41	88	15	2	6	40	31	10	.319	.390	.453	.843	125	13	10	107	111	48	.785	0	1	-1	-3	3	0.7
	Yr	114	428	52	133	23	2	7	57	46	23	.311	.379	.423	.802	118	13	11	104	109	70	.740	0	2	-1	0		1.1
1953	Bos-A	134	460	68	141	41	2	12	73	52	22	.307	.383	.483	.866	122	21	15	109	107	88	.858	5	2	0	-10	*3/O	0.0
1954	Bos-A	26	93	15	24	3	0	0	10	15	3	.258	.361	.290	.651	80	-2	-2	100	143	11	.592	0	0	0	1	3	-0.2
	Chi-A	71	233	25	66	10	0	5	48	18	12	.283	.335	.391	.725	95	-1	-2	104	172	30	.636	1	1	-0	-2	13/O	-0.7
	Yr	97	326	40	90	13	0	5	58	33	15	.276	.343	.362	.705	91	-3	-4	103	166	42	.628	1	1	-0	-2		-0.9
1955	Chi-A	128	429	44	134	24	1	8	81	51	36	.312	.393	.429	.822	120	14	13	101	**148**	75	.799	2	2	-1	-11	*31/O	0.3
1956	Chi-A	21	80	7	25	5	0	1	11	8	6	.313	.375	.412	.788	103	1	1	104	121	12	.707	0	0	0	0	3/1	0.1
	Bal-A	102	345	45	90	17	2	8	37	25	31	.261	.316	.391	.708	91	-8	-5	94	89	42	.617	0	1	-1	-5	3/12	-0.7
	Yr	123	425	52	115	22	2	9	48	33	37	.271	.328	.395	.723	94	-7	-5	96	95	55	.639	0	1	-1	-5		-0.6
1957	Bal-A	99	310	28	92	9	0	9	44	25	16	.297	.353	.413	.766	117	4	6	93	112	44	.686	2	0	1	-2	31	0.6
Total	15	1795	6702	881	2054	385	50	78	870	621	287	.306	.368	.414	.782	111	118	105	102	105	1038	.741	51	36	-6	-1	*3/1O2	9.9

■ DUKE KELLEHER Kelleher, Albert Aloysius b: 9/30/1893, New York, N.Y. d: 9/28/47, Staten Island, N.Y. TR , Deb: 8/18/16

YEAR	TM/L	G	AB	R	H	2B	3B	HR	RBI	BB	SO	AVG	OBP	SLG	PRO	/A	BR	/A	PF	CHI	RC	TA	SB	CS	SBR	FR	POS	TPR
1916	NY-N	1	0	0	0	0	0	0	0	0	0	—	—	—	—	—	0	0	96	—	—	—	0			0	/C	0.0

■ FRANKIE KELLEHER Kelleher, Francis Eugene b: 8/22/16, San Francisco, Cal d: 4/13/79, Stockton, Cal. BR/TR, 6'1", 195 lbs. Deb: 7/18/42

YEAR	TM/L	G	AB	R	H	2B	3B	HR	RBI	BB	SO	AVG	OBP	SLG	PRO	/A	BR	/A	PF	CHI	RC	TA	SB	CS	SBR	FR	POS	TPR
1942	Cin-N	38	110	13	20	3	1	3	12	16	20	.182	.286	.309	.595	73	-4	-4	101	103	10	.543	0			0	O	-0.4
1943	Cin-N	9	10	1	0	0	0	0	0	2	0	.000	.167	.000	.167	-50	-2	-2	99	0	0	.200	0			0	/O	-0.1
Total	2	47	120	14	20	3	1	3	12	18	20	.167	.275	.283	.559	63	-6	-6	101	94	10	.520	0			0	/O	-0.5

■ JOHN KELLEHER Kelleher, John Patrick b: 9/13/1893, Brookline, Mass. d: 8/21/60, Brighton, Mass. BR/TR, 5'11", 150 lbs. Deb: 7/31/12

YEAR	TM/L	G	AB	R	H	2B	3B	HR	RBI	BB	SO	AVG	OBP	SLG	PRO	/A	BR	/A	PF	CHI	RC	TA	SB	CS	SBR	FR	POS	TPR
1912	StL-N	8	12	0	4	1	0	0	1	0	2	.333	.333	.417	.750	105	0	0	100	67	2	.625	0			0	/3	0.0
1916	Bro-N	2	3	0	0	0	0	0	0	0	0	.000	.000	.000	.000	-97	-1	-1	103	0	0	.000	0			0	/S3	0.0
1921	Chi-N	95	301	31	93	11	7	4	47	16	16	.309	.346	.432	.778	98	2	-1	107	121	44	.700	2	5	-2	4	321S/O	0.1
1922	Chi-N	63	193	23	50	7	1	0	20	15	14	.259	.316	.306	.621	64	-11	-9	95	118	18	.533	5	7	-3	-1	3/S1	-0.8
1923	Chi-N	66	193	27	59	10	0	6	21	14	9	.306	.353	.451	.803	106	3	1	104	70	29	.746	2	4	-2	-2	1S3/2	-0.1
1924	Bos-N	1	1	0	0	0	0	0	0	0	1	.000	.000	.000	.000	-99	-0	-0	94	0	0	.000	0	0	0	0	H	0.0
Total	6	235	703	81	206	29	8	10	89	45	42	.293	.337	.400	.737	91	-8	-10	103	105	93	.657	9	16		1	/312SO	-0.8

■ MICK KELLEHER Kelleher, Michael Dennis b: 7/25/47, Seattle, Wash. BR/TR, 5'9", 176 lbs. Deb: 9/01/72 C

YEAR	TM/L	G	AB	R	H	2B	3B	HR	RBI	BB	SO	AVG	OBP	SLG	PRO	/A	BR	/A	PF	CHI	RC	TA	SB	CS	SBR	FR	POS	TPR
1972	StL-N	23	63	5	10	2	1	0	1	6	15	.159	.232	.222	.454	28	-6	-6	105	29	4	.370	0	0	0	0	S	-0.2
1973	StL-N	43	38	4	7	2	0	0	2	4	11	.184	.279	.237	.516	49	-3	-2	91	89	3	.452	0	0	0	-2	S	0.1
1974	Hou-N	19	57	4	9	0	0	0	2	5	10	.158	.226	.158	.384	9	-7	-7	98	86	2	.300	1	1	-0	-0	S	-0.5
1975	StL-N	7	4	0	0	0	0	0	0	0	1	.000	.000	.000	.000	-97	-1	-1	103	0	0	.000	0	0	0	0	/S	0.0
1976	Chi-N	124	337	28	77	12	1	0	22	15	32	.228	.266	.270	.536	48	-21	-25	109	93	22	.397	0	4	-2	-2	*S3/2	-2.0
1977	Chi-N	63	122	14	28	5	2	0	11	9	12	.230	.288	.303	.591	52	-7	-9	114	119	10	.485	0	0	0	9	2S/3	0.4
1978	Chi-N	68	95	8	24	1	0	0	6	7	11	.253	.304	.263	.567	54	-5	-6	110	95	7	.468	4	1	1	5	32S	0.1
1979	Chi-N	73	142	14	36	4	1	0	10	7	9	.254	.298	.296	.594	56	-7	-9	112	94	13	.482	2	0	1	6	32S	0.0
1980	Chi-N	105	96	12	14	1	1	0	4	9	17	.146	.219	.177	.396	11	-11	-12	106	93	3	.300	1	3	-2	4	23S	-0.3
1981	Det-A	61	77	10	17	4	0	0	6	7	10	.221	.286	.273	.558	59	-4	-4	105	112	6	.431	0	0	0	0	32/S	-0.2
1982	Det-A	2	1	0	0	0	0	0	0	0	0	.000	.000	.000	.000	-99	-0	-0	100	0	0	.000	0	0	0	0	/23	0.0
	Cal-A	34	49	9	8	1	0	0	1	5	5	.163	.255	.184	.438	23	-5	-5	100	44	2	.340	1	1	-0	2	S/3	0.0
	Yr	36	50	9	8	1	0	0	1	5	5	.160	.250	.180	.430	20	-5	-5	100	42	2	.333	1	1	-0	2		0.0
Total	11	622	1081	108	230	32	6	0	65	74	133	.213	.268	.253	.521	43	-77	-87	108	91	72	.420	9	10	-3	22	S32	-2.6

■ CHARLIE KELLER Keller, Charles Ernest "King Kong" b: 9/12/16, Middletown, Md. BL/TR, 5'10", 185 lbs. Deb: 4/22/39

YEAR	TM/L	G	AB	R	H	2B	3B	HR	RBI	BB	SO	AVG	OBP	SLG	PRO	/A	BR	/A	PF	CHI	RC	TA	SB	CS	SBR	FR	POS	TPR
1939	NY-A	111	398	87	133	21	6	11	83	81	49	.334	.447	.500	.947	155	29	34	91	128	97	1.051	6	3	0	-5	*O	2.4
1940	NY-A	138	500	102	143	18	15	21	93	**106**	65	.286	.411	.508	.919	139	30	31	99	112	114	.995	8	2	1	1	*O	2.2
1941	NY-A	140	507	102	151	24	10	33	122	102	65	.298	.416	.580	.996	164	46	47	98	116	134	1.110	6	4	-1	4	*O	4.0

YEAR	TM/L	G	AB	R	H	2B	3B	HR	RBI	BB	SO	AVG	OBP	SLG	PRO	/A	BR	/A	PF	CHI	RC	TA	SB	CS	SBR	FR	POS	TPR
1942	NY-A	152	544	106	159	24	9	26	108	114	61	.292	.417	.513	.930	161	47	47	99	113	131	1.043	14	2	3	1	*O	4.1
1943	NY-A	141	512	97	139	15	11	31	86	**106**	60	.271	.396	.525	**.922**	**175**	**46**	**48**	96	92	**116**	**.992**	7	5	-1	4	*O	4.9
1945	NY-A	44	163	26	49	7	4	10	34	31	21	.301	.412	.577	.989	173	18	16	107	105	41	1.059	0	2	-1	3	O	1.7
1946	NY-A	150	538	98	148	29	10	30	101	113	101	.275	.405	.533	.938	160	46	46	100	98	127	1.015	1	4	-2	-2	*O	3.5
1947	NY-A	45	151	36	36	6	1	13	36	41	18	.238	.404	.550	.954	169	14	15	97	115	37	1.059	0	0	0	-3	O	1.0
1948	NY-A	83	247	41	66	15	2	6	44	41	25	.267	.372	.417	.789	109	4	4	100	123	40	.767	1	1	-0	-7	O	-0.5
1949	NY-A	60	116	17	29	4	1	3	16	25	15	.250	.392	.379	.771	104	2	2	100	103	20	.811	2	0	1	-7	O	-0.4
1950	Det-A	50	51	7	16	1	3	2	16	13	6	.314	.453	.569	1.022	166	5	5	97	158	15	1.200	0	0	0	-1	/O	0.4
1951	Det-A	54	62	6	16	2	0	3	21	11	12	.258	.370	.435	.805	111	2	1	106	208	11	.826	0	0	0	1	/O	0.1
1952	NY-A	2	1	0	0	0	0	0	0	0	1	.000	.000	.000	.000	-99	-0	-0	98	0	0	.000	0	0	0	-0	/O	0.0
Total	13	1170	3790	725	1085	166	72	189	760	784	499	.286	.410	.518	.928	154	286	296	98	112	883	1.027	45	23	-0	-12	*O	23.4
■ HAL KELLER	Keller, Harold Kefauver b: 7/7/27, Middletown, Md. BL/TR, 6'1", 200 lbs. Deb: 9/13/49																											
1949	Was-A	3	3	1	1	0	0	0	0	0	0	.333	.333	.333	.667	84	-0	-0	91	0	0	.500	0	0	0	0	H	0.0
1950	Was-A	11	28	1	6	3	0	1	5	2	2	.214	.267	.429	.695	76	-1	-1	99	115	3	.609	0	0	0	-0	/C	0.0
1952	Was-A	11	23	2	4	2	0	0	0	1	1	.174	.208	.261	.469	30	-2	-2	100	0	1	.368	0	0	0	0	C	-0.1
Total	3	25	54	4	11	5	0	1	5	3	3	.204	.246	.352	.597	58	-4	-4	99	61	5	.512	0	0	0	-0	/C	-0.1
■ FRANK KELLERT	Kellert, Frank William b: 7/6/24, Oklahoma City, Okla. d: 11/19/76, Oklahoma City, Okla. BR/TR, 6'2.5", 185 lbs. Deb: 4/18/53																											
1953	StL-A	2	4	0	0	0	0	0	0	0	0	.000	.000	.000	.000	-94	-1	-1	107	0	0	.000	0	0	0	0	/1	0.0
1954	Bal-A	10	34	3	7	2	0	0	1	5	4	.206	.308	.265	.572	61	-2	-2	95	43	3	.519	0	0	0	0	/1	-0.1
1955	Bro-N	39	80	12	26	4	2	4	19	9	10	.325	.393	.575	.968	146	6	5	104	133	18	.982	0	1	-1	0	1	0.4
1956	Chi-N	71	129	10	24	3	1	4	17	12	22	.186	.255	.318	.573	54	-9	-9	99	136	9	.469	0	0	0	0	1	-0.9
Total	4	122	247	25	57	9	3	8	37	26	36	.231	.304	.389	.693	84	-6	-6	100	119	30	.613	0	1	-1	1	/1	-0.6
■ RED KELLETT	Kellett, Donald Stafford b: 7/15/09, Brooklyn, N.Y. d: 11/5/70, Ft.Lauderdale, Fla. BR/TR, 6', 185 lbs. Deb: 7/02/34																											
1934	Bos-A	9	9	0	0	0	0	0	0	1	5	.000	.100	.000	.100	-68	-2	-2	106	0	0	.111	0	0	0	0	/S23	-0.1
■ JOE KELLEY	Kelley, Joseph James b: 12/9/1871, Cambridge, Mass. d: 8/14/43, Baltimore, Md. BR/TR, 5'11", 190 lbs. Deb: 7/27/1891 MH																											
1891	Bos-N	12	45	7	11	1	1	0	3	2	7	.244	.277	.311	.588	65	-2	-2	112	62	4	.471	0			0	O	-0.1
1892	Pit-N	56	205	26	49	7	7	0	28	17	21	.239	.297	.341	.639	101	-2	0	94	125	24	.609	8			1	O	0.0
	Bal-N	10	33	3	7	0	0	0	4	4	7	.212	.316	.212	.528	62	-1	-1	100	175	3	.538	2			-3	O	-0.3
	Yr	66	238	29	56	7	7	0	32	21	28	.235	.300	.324	.624	95	-3	-1	95	135	27	.599	10			-2		-0.3
1893	Bal-N	125	502	120	153	27	16	9	76	77	44	.305	.401	.476	.877	126	26	19	107	75	112	1.011	33			4	*O	1.5
1894	Bal-N	129	507	165	199	48	20	6	111	107	36	.393	.502	.602	1.104	169	62	63	99	91	181	1.503	46			-0	*O	4.0
1895	Bal-N	131	518	148	189	26	19	10	134	77	29	.365	.456	.546	1.003	150	49	42	107	106	158	1.289	54			10	*O	3.2
1896	Bal-N	131	519	148	189	31	19	8	100	91	19	.364	.469	.543	1.013	166	56	54	102	81	**178**	**1.430**	**87**			4	*O	4.1
1897	Bal-N	131	505	113	183	31	9	5	118	70		.362	.447	.489	.936	158	39	44	95	140	133	1.143	44			-0	*O/S3	2.8
1898	Bal-N	124	464	71	149	18	15	2	110	56		.321	.398	.438	.835	138	26	24	103	**169**	93	.908	24			-2	*O/3	1.4
1899	Bro-N	143	538	108	175	21	14	6	93	70		.325	.406	.450	.856	131	29	25	105	105	114	.953	31			6	*O	2.0
1900	Bro-N	121	454	90	145	23	17	6	91	53		.319	.391	.485	.875	133	27	21	108	127	98	.968	26			1	O13	1.4
1901	Bro-N	120	492	77	151	22	12	4	65	40		.307	.359	.425	.784	122	18	14	106	87	84	.783	18			4	*1/3	1.8
1902	Bal-A	60	222	50	69	17	7	1	34	34		.311	.402	.464	.866	139	13	13	102	102	47	.974	12			-3	O/31	0.6
	Cin-N	40	156	24	50	9	2	1	12	15		.321	.380	.423	.803	137	9	7	110	58	27	.792	3			1	O2/3SM	0.8
1903	Cin-N	105	383	85	121	22	4	3	45	51		.316	.396	.418	.814	123	19	13	109	91	72	.874	18			6	OS2/31M	1.6
1904	Cin-N	123	449	75	126	21	13	0	63	49		.281	.351	.385	.737	113	16	8	114	141	68	.734	15			1	*1/O2M	0.4
1905	Cin-N	90	321	43	89	7	6	1	37	27		.277	.333	.346	.679	101	2	1	103	115	41	.629	8			-21	O/1M	-2.7
1906	Cin-N	129	465	43	106	19	11	1	53	44		.228	.295	.323	.617	82	-3	-11	115	134	48	.565	9			15	*O/1S3	0.2
1908	Bos-N	73	228	25	59	8	2	2	17	27		.259	.337	.338	.675	114	5	4	104	79	27	.645	5			0	O1M	0.4
Total	17	1853	7006	1421	2220	358	194	65	1194	911	163	.317	.399	.451	.850	132	388	338	105	109	1510	.953	443			24	*O1/32S	23.1
■ MIKE KELLEY	Kelley, Michael Joseph b: 12/2/1876, Otter River, Mass. d: 6/6/55, Minneapolis, Minn. BR/TR, 6', 210 lbs. Deb: 7/15/1899																											
1899	Lou-N	76	282	48	68	11	2	3	33	21		.241	.305	.326	.631	73	-9	-11	103	102	32	.598	10			-1	1	-0.9
■ BILL KELLEY	Kelley, William J. b: New York, N.Y. Deb: 5/04/1871																											
1871	Kek-n	18	71	17	15							.211															O/1	
■ FRANK KELLIHER	Kelliher, Francis Mortimer "Yucka" b: 5/23/1899, Somerville, Mass. d: 3/4/56, Somerville, Mass. BL/TL, 5'9.5", 175 lbs. Deb: 9/19/19																											
1919	Was-A	1	1	0	0	0	0	0	0	0	0	.000	.000	.000	.000	-99	-0	-0	98	0	0	.000	0			0	H	0.0
■ NATE KELLOGG	Kellogg, Nathaniel Monroe b: 9/28/1858, Rochester, Iowa d: 15, 5'9", 175 lbs. Deb: 1885																											
1885	Det-N	5	17	4	2	1	0	0	0	1	5	.118	.167	.176	.343	11	-2	-2	97	0	1	.267				0	/S	-0.1
■ BILL KELLOGG	Kellogg, William Dearstyne b: 5/25/1884, Albany, N.Y. d: 12/12/71, Baltimore, Md. BR/TR, 5'10", 153 lbs. Deb: 4/14/14																											
1914	Cin-N	71	126	14	22	0	1	0	7	14	28	.175	.262	.190	.453	34	-10	-10	105	106	8	.442	7			-2	12/O3	-1.4
■ RED KELLY	Kelly, Albert Michael b: 11/15/1884, Union, Ill. d: 2/4/61, Zephyr Hills, Fla. TR , 5'11.5", 165 lbs. Deb: 6/18/10																											
1910	Chi-A	14	45	6	7	0	1	0	1	7		.156	.296	.200	.496	59	-2	-2	95	42	3	.474	0			-1	O	-0.3
■ CHARLIE KELLY	Kelly, Charles H. Deb: 6/14/1883																											
1883	Phi-N	2	7	1	1	0	1	0	0	0	3	.143	.143	.429	.571	72	-0	-0	90	0	0	.500				0	/3	0.0
1886	Phi-a	1	3	0	0	0	0	0		0		.000	.000	.000	.000	-99	-1	-1	100	0	0	.000	0			0	/S	0.0
Total	2	3	10	1	1	0	1	0	0	0	3	.100	.100	.300	.400	19	-1	-1	93	0	0	.333	0			0	/3S	0.0
■ PAT KELLY	Kelly, Dale Patrick b: 8/27/55, Santa Maria, Cal. BR/TR, 6'3", 210 lbs. Deb: 5/28/80																											
1980	Tor-A	3	7	0	2	0	0	0	0	0	4	.286	.286	.286	.571	57	-0	-0	100	0	1	.400	0	0	0	0	/C	0.0
■ GEORGE KELLY	Kelly, George Lange "Highpockets" b: 9/10/1895, San Francisco, Cal. d: 10/13/84, Burlingame, Cal. BR/TR, 6'4", 190 lbs. Deb: 8/18/15 CH																											
1915	NY-N	17	38	2	6	0	0	1	4	1	9	.158	.179	.237	.416	28	-3	-3	91	127	1	.303	0	1	-1	0	/1O	-0.4
1916	NY-N	49	76	4	12	2	1	0	3	6	24	.158	.220	.211	.430	34	-6	-6	96	74	4	.359	1			-4	1O/3	-1.1
1917	NY-N	11	7	0	0	0	0	0	0	0	3	.000	.000	.000	.000	-99	-2	-2	97	0	0	.000	0			-0	/OP12	-0.1
	Pit-N	8	23	2	2	0	1	0	0	1	9	.087	.125	.174	.299	-9	-3	-3	100	0	0	.238	0			0	/1	-0.3
	Yr	19	30	2	2	0	1	0	0	1	12	.067	.097	.133	.230	-30	-5	-5	98	0	0	.179	0			-0		-0.4
1919	NY-N	32	107	12	31	6	2	1	14	3	15	.290	.315	.411	.727	118	2	2	100	116	14	.645	1			-1	1	0.1
1920	NY-N	155	590	69	157	22	11	11	**94**	41	92	.266	.320	.397	.717	106	3	3	100	144	71	.639	6	16	-8	4	*1	-0.1
1921	NY-N	149	587	95	181	42	9	**23**	122	40	73	.308	.356	.528	.884	134	23	25	98	125	104	.854	4	12	-6	11	*1	2.7
1922	NY-N	151	592	96	194	33	8	17	107	30	65	.328	.363	.497	.860	116	15	12	104	111	106	.845	12	3	2	9	*1	2.0
1923	NY-N	145	560	82	172	23	5	16	103	47	64	.307	.362	.452	.814	112	10	9	101	123	92	.797	14	7	0	-6	*1	-0.6
1924	NY-N	144	571	91	185	37	9	21	**136**	38	52	.324	.371	.531	.902	152	29	36	91	144	112	.910	7	2	1	-1	*1O/23	2.9
1925	NY-N	147	586	87	181	29	3	20	99	35	54	.309	.350	.471	.821	109	5	6	99	111	96	.781	5	2	0	15	*21O	1.5
1926	NY-N	136	499	70	151	24	4	13	80	36	52	.303	.352	.445	.797	116	8	10	98	108	76	.759	4			8	*12	1.4
1927	Cin-N	61	222	27	60	16	4	5	21	11	23	.270	.308	.446	.754	100	-1	-1	100	66	29	.691	1			-1	12/O	-0.4
1928	Cin-N	116	402	46	119	33	7	3	58	28	35	.296	.345	.435	.780	107	1	3	96	114	59	.731	2			6	1O	-0.2
1929	Cin-N	147	577	73	169	45	9	5	103	33	61	.293	.332	.428	.760	87	-13	-13	99	143	79	.706	7			2	*1	-1.5
1930	Cin-N	51	188	18	54	10	1	5	35	7	20	.287	.313	.431	.744	86	-7	-4	90	128	24	.664	1			0	1	-0.5
	Chi-N	39	166	22	55	6	1	3	19	7	16	.331	.362	.434	.796	87	-2	-4	105	86	25	.721	0			2	1	-0.2
	Yr	90	354	40	109	16	2	8	54	14	36	.308	.336	.432	.768	87	-10	-8	97	111	49	.690	1			2		-0.7
1932	Bro-N	64	202	23	49	9	1	4	22	22	27	.243	.317	.356	.673	84	-5	-4	96	97	24	.614	0			1	1/O	-0.6
Total	16	1622	5993	819	1778	337	76	148	1020	386	694	.297	.342	.452	.794	110	53	67	98	120	918	.749	65	43		45	*12/O3P	4.6

YEAR	TM/L	G	AB	R	H	2B	3B	HR	RBI	BB	SO	AVG	OBP	SLG	PRO	/A	BR	/A	PF	CHI	RC	TA	SB	CS	SBR	FR	POS	TPR
■ **PAT KELLY**	Kelly, Harold Patrick b: 7/30/44, Philadelphia, Pa. BL/TL, 6'1", 185 lbs. Deb: 9/06/67																											
1967	Min-A	8	1	1	0	0	0	0	0	0	1	.000	.000	.000	.000	-94	-0	-0	107	0	0	.000	0	0	0	0	H	0.0
1968	Min-A	12	35	2	4	2	0	1	2	3	10	.114	.205	.257	.462	37	-3	-3	106	71	1	.382	0	2	-1	1	O	-0.3
1969	KC-A	112	417	61	110	20	4	8	32	49	70	.264	.348	.388	.737	103	4	2	103	73	61	.788	40	13	4	3	*O	0.7
1970	KC-A	136	452	56	106	16	1	6	38	76	105	.235	.347	.314	.661	85	-8	-7	98	98	55	.690	34	16	1	10	*O	-0.1
1971	Chi-A	67	213	32	62	6	3	3	22	36	29	.291	.396	.390	.786	126	8	9	98	100	34	.822	14	9	-1	0	O	0.6
1972	Chi-A	119	402	57	105	14	7	5	24	55	69	.261	.356	.368	.724	109	9	7	106	63	59	.768	32	9	4	-3	*O	0.5
1973	Chi-A	144	550	77	154	24	5	1	44	65	91	.280	.358	.347	.705	97	2	-0	102	86	67	.653	22	15	-2	-2	*O/D	-0.8
1974	Chi-A	122	424	60	119	16	3	4	21	46	58	.281	.354	.361	.715	104	4	3	102	51	54	.672	18	11	-1	-6	DO	-0.5
1975	Chi-A	133	471	73	129	21	7	9	45	58	69	.274	.356	.406	.761	111	10	8	103	81	67	.733	18	10	-1	-4	*OD	0.0
1976	Chi-A	107	311	42	79	20	3	5	34	45	45	.254	.354	.386	.740	117	7	8	99	97	44	.741	15	7	0	-4	DO	0.3
1977	Bal-A	120	360	50	92	13	0	10	49	53	75	.256	.357	.375	.732	107	1	5	93	118	53	.770	25	7	3	-12	*O/D	-0.6
1978	Bal-A	100	274	38	75	12	1	11	40	34	58	.274	.358	.445	.803	137	9	12	91	102	41	.778	10	8	-2	-10	O/D	0.0
1979	Bal-A	68	153	25	44	11	0	9	25	20	25	.288	.374	.536	.910	146	9	9	97	88	30	.922	4	5	-2	-4	OD	0.3
1980	Bal-A	89	200	38	52	10	1	3	26	34	54	.260	.368	.365	.733	101	2	1	101	124	31	.799	16	2	4	-4	OD	0.0
1981	Cle-A	48	75	8	16	4	0	1	16	14	9	.213	.337	.307	.644	93	-1	-0	93	241	7	.582	2	4	-2	-2	D/O	-0.4
Total	15	1385	4338	620	1147	189	35	76	418	588	768	.264	.356	.377	.733	107	54	55	100	90	604	.755	250	118	4	-37	OD	-0.3
■ **JIM KELLY**	Kelly, James Robert (a.k.a. real name of Robert John Taggert in 1918) b: 2/1/1884, Bloomfield, N.J. d: 4/10/61, Kingsport, Tenn. BL/TR, 5'10.5", 180 lbs. Deb: 4/26/14																											
1914	Pit-N	32	44	4	10	2	1	0	3	2	3	.227	.261	.318	.579	78	-2	-1	92	78	4	.471	0			-0	/O	-0.1
1915	Pit-F	148	524	68	154	12	17	4	50	35	46	.294	.338	.405	.743	115	11	9	104	82	88	.770	38			10	*O	1.2
1918	Bos-N	35	146	19	48	1	4	0	4	9	9	.329	.376	.390	.766	143	6	7	94	23	22	.735	4			-0	O	0.5
Total	3	215	714	91	212	15	22	4	57	46	58	.297	.341	.396	.738	118	15	14	101	70	114	.743	42			10	O	1.6
■ **TOM KELLY**	Kelly, Jay Thomas b: 8/15/50, Graceville, Minn. BL/TL, 5'11", 188 lbs. Deb: 5/11/75 M																											
1975	Min-A	49	127	11	23	5	0	1	11	15	22	.181	.268	.244	.512	42	-9	-10	107	124	9	.430	0	0	0	2	1/O	-1.0
■ **JOHN KELLY**	Kelly, John B. b: 3/13/1879, Clifton Heights, Pa. d: 3/19/44, Baltimore, Md. 5'9", 165 lbs. Deb: 4/11/07																											
1907	StL-N	53	197	12	37	5	0	0	6	13		.188	.238	.213	.451	45	-13	-12	96	52	12	.387	7			-9	O	-2.6
■ **JOHN KELLY**	Kelly, John Francis "Honest John" or "Father" b: 1859, Paterson, N.J. d: 4/13/08, Paterson, N.J. BR/TR, 6', 185 lbs. Deb: 1882																											
1882	Cle-N	30	104	6	14	2	0	0	5	1	24	.135	.143	.154	.297	-5	-12	-10	90	105	2	.189				-16	C	-2.1
1883	Bal-a	48	202	18	46	9	2	0		3		.228	.239	.292	.531	66	-7	-9	107	0	14	.397				-17	CO	-1.9
	Phi-N	1	3	0	0	0	0	0	0	0	2	.000	.000	.000	.000	-99	-1	-1	90	0	0	.000				0	/O	0.0
1884	Cin-U	38	142	23	40	5	1	1		6		.282	.311	.352	.663	115	3	2	108	0	16	.549	0			-8	C/O	-0.2
	Was-U	4	14	1	5	1	0	0		0		.357	.357	.429	.786	170	1	1	97	0	2	.667	0			0	/CO	0.1
	Yr	42	156	24	45	6	1	1		6		.288	.315	.359	.674	119	4	3	107	0	18	.559	0			-8		-0.1
Total	3	121	465	48	105	17	3	1	5	10	26	.226	.242	.282	.524	69	-15	-17	103	23	35	.392	0			-40	C/O	-4.1
■ **KICK KELLY**	Kelly, John O. "Diamond John" b: 10/31/1856, New York, N.Y. d: 3/27/26, Malba, N.Y. 6'0.5", 185 lbs. Deb: 5/01/1879 M																											
1879	Syr-N	10	36	4	4	1	0	0	2	0	6	.111	.111	.139	.250	-20	-4	-4	89	140	1	.156				0	/C1	-0.3
	Tro-N	6	22	1	5	0	0	0	0	0	1	.227	.227	.227	.455	54	-1	-1	93	0	1	.294				0	/CO3	0.0
	Yr	16	58	5	9	1	0	0	2	0	7	.155	.155	.172	.328	9	-6	-5	90	96	2	.204				0		-0.3
Total	1	16	58	5	9	1	0	0	2	0	7	.155	.155	.172	.328	9	-6	-5	91	87	2	.204				0	/CO13	-0.3
■ **JOE KELLY**	Kelly, Joseph Henry b: 9/23/1886, Weir City, Kan. d: 8/16/77, St.Joseph, Mo. BR/TR, 5'10", 175 lbs. Deb: 4/14/14																											
1914	Pit-N	141	508	47	113	19	9	1	48	39	59	.222	.283	.301	.584	80	-17	-12	92	118	48	.549	21			-6	*O	-2.4
1916	Chi-N	54	169	18	43	7	1	2	15	9	16	.254	.296	.343	.639	82	-1	-4	117	93	20	.619	10			0	O	-0.5
1917	Bos-N	116	445	41	99	9	8	3	36	26	45	.222	.268	.299	.567	77	-14	-12	96	104	40	.526	21			15	*O	0.0
1918	Bos-N	47	155	20	36	2	4	0	15	6	12	.232	.265	.297	.562	76	-6	-5	94	123	14	.546	12			-2	O	-0.9
1919	Bos-N	18	64	3	9	1	0	0	3	0	11	.141	.154	.156	.310	-7	-8	-8	98	117	2	.236	2			-0	O	-0.9
Total	5	376	1341	129	300	38	22	6	117	80	143	.224	.272	.298	.570	75	-46	-41	97	111	123	.533	66			7	O	-4.7
■ **JOE KELLY**	Kelly, Joseph James b: 4/23/1900, New York, N.Y. d: 11/24/67, Lynbrook, N.Y. BL/TL, 6', 180 lbs. Deb: 4/13/26																											
1926	Chi-N	65	176	16	59	15	3	0	32	7	11	.335	.361	.455	.815	111	4	3	106	138	27	.744	0			-6	O	-0.4
1928	Chi-N	32	52	3	11	1	0	1	7	1	3	.212	.255	.288	.543	44	-5	-4	95	138	4	.439	0			-0	1	-0.4
Total	2	97	228	19	70	16	3	1	39	8	14	.307	.336	.417	.753	97	-1	-2	103	138	31	.665	0			-6	/O1	-0.8
■ **KING KELLY**	Kelly, Michael Joseph b: 12/31/1857, Troy, N.Y. d: 11/8/1894, Boston, Mass. BR/TR, 5'10", 170 lbs. Deb: 5/01/1878 MH																											
1878	Cin-N	60	237	29	67	7	1	0	27	7	7	.283	.303	.321	.624	110	1	3	95	123	24	.488				7	*OC/3	0.6
1879	Cin-N	77	345	78	120	20	12	2	47	8	14	.348	.363	.493	.855	**189**	28	31	95	83	63	.791				6	3OC/2	3.2
1880	Chi-N	84	344	72	100	17	9	1	60	12	22	.291	.315	.401	.716	134	14	12	105	165	45	.615				4	*OC3/S2P	1.3
1881	Chi-N	82	353	84	114	**27**	3	2	55	16	14	.323	.352	.433	.786	134	18	14	108	115	55	.707				2	*OC/3	1.4
1882	Chi-N	84	377	81	115	**37**	4	1	55	10	27	.305	.323	.432	.755	138	16	15	101	107	54	.660				-3	SOC/31	1.5
1883	Chi-N	98	428	92	109	28	10	3	61	16	35	.255	.282	.388	.669	92	0	-6	109	107	48	.571				-14	*OC/23P	-1.3
1884	Chi-N	108	452	**120**	160	28	5	13	95	46	24	**.354**	**.414**	.524	.938	179	**49**	**43**	108	114	**100**	**.969**				-3	OCS3/1P	3.7
1885	Chi-N	107	438	**124**	126	24	7	9	75	46	24	.288	.355	.436	.791	136	27	18	114	115	70	.760				-0	OC/231	1.8
1886	Chi-N	118	451	**155**	175	32	11	4	79	83	33	**.388**	**.483**	.534	1.018	180	64	52	116	90	**146**	**1.366**	53			-3	OC/132S	4.7
1887	Bos-N	116	484	120	156	34	11	8	63	55	40	.322	.393	.488	.880	149	30	32	98	65	129	1.146	84			-6	O2C/PS3M	2.2
1888	Bos-N	107	440	85	140	22	11	9	71	31	39	.318	.368	.480	.848	162	34	31	106	94	101	1.007	56			6	CO	3.8
1889	Bos-N	125	507	120	149	**41**	5	9	78	65	40	.294	.376	.448	.824	129	22	20	102	81	114	1.011	68			-2	*OC	1.2
1890	Bos-P	89	340	83	111	18	6	4	66	52	22	.326	.419	.450	.869	126	18	14	107	112	88	1.127	51			-5	CS/O13PM	0.9
1891	CM-a	82	283	56	84	15	7	1	53	51	28	.297	.408	.410	.818	123	16	10	112	131	58	.960	22			-4	C/3O21PS	0.7
	Bos-a	4	15	2	4	0	0	1	4	0	2	.267	.267	.467	.733	113	0	0	99	116	2	.727	1			-1	/C	0.0
	Yr	86	298	58	88	15	7	2		51	30	.295	.402	.413	.814	123	16	10	111	132	60	.948	23			-5		0.7
	Bos-N	16	52	7	12	1	0	0	5	6	10	.231	.322	.250	.572	62	-2	-3	112	112	6	.650	6			0	C/O	-0.1
1892	Bos-N	78	281	40	53	7	0	2	41	39	31	.189	.287	.235	.522	53	-12	-18	113	178	27	.566	24			0	C/O31P	-1.2
1893	NY-N	20	67	9	18	1	0	0	15	6	5	.269	.329	.284	.612	63	-3	-4	104	216	7	.571	3			0	C/O	-0.2
Total	16	1455	5894	1357	1813	359	102	69	950	549	417	.308	.368	.438	.806	136	321	265	106	109	1135	.861	368			-16	OC/3S21P	24.2
■ **SPEED KELLY**	Kelly, R B b: 8/12/1884, Brian, Ohio d: 5/6/49, Goshen, Ind. BR/TR, 6'2", 185 lbs. Deb: 7/13/09																											
1909	Was-A	17	42	3	6	2	1	0	1	3		.143	.200	.238	.438	43	-3	-3	90	39	2	.389	1			0	3/2O	-0.1
■ **BOBBY KELLY**	Kelly, Roberto Conrado (Gray) b: 10/1/64, Panama City, Pan. BR/TR, 6'2", 180 lbs. Deb: 7/29/87																											
1987	NY-A	23	52	12	14	3	0	1	7	5	15	.269	.333	.385	.718	93	-1	-0	98	121	7	.829	9	3	1	1	O/D	0.0
1988	NY-A	38	77	9	19	4	1	1	7	3	15	.247	.275	.364	.639	81	-3	-2	96	90	8	.600	5	2	0	1	O/D	-0.1
Total	2	61	129	21	33	7	1	2	14	8	30	.256	.299	.372	.671	86	-3	-3	96	103	15	.693	14	5	1	1	/OD	-0.1
■ **VAN KELLY**	Kelly, Van Howard b: 3/18/46, Charlotte, N.C. BL/TR, 5'11", 180 lbs. Deb: 6/13/69																											
1969	SD-N	73	209	16	51	7	1	3	15	12	24	.244	.285	.330	.615	74	-8	-7	97	77	19	.503	0	1	-1	-1	32	-0.7
1970	SD-N	38	89	9	15	3	0	1	9	15	21	.169	.288	.236	.524	44	-7	-6	95	145	7	.474	0	1	-1	-0	3/2	-0.7
Total	2	111	298	25	66	10	1	4	24	27	45	.221	.286	.302	.588	65	-15	-14	96	99	26	.498	0	2	-1	-1	/32	-1.4
■ **BILL KELLY**	Kelly, William Henry "Big Bill" b: 12/28/1899, Syracuse, N.Y. BR/TR, 6', 190 lbs. Deb: 9/06/20																											
1920	Phi-A	9	13	0	3	1	0	0	0	0	2	.231	.231	.308	.538	44	-1	-1	94	0	1	.400	0	0	0	0	/1	0.0
1928	Phi-N	23	71	6	12	1	1	0	5	7	20	.169	.244	.211	.455	19	-8	-9	104	119	4	.373	0			1	1	-0.9
Total	2	32	84	6	15	2	1	0	5	7	22	.179	.242	.226	.468	23	-9	-10	103	102	5	.377	0	0		1	/1	-0.9
■ **BILLY KELLY**	Kelly, William Joseph b: 5/1/1886, Baltimore, Md. d: 6/3/40, Detroit, Mich. BR/TR, 6'0.5", 183 lbs. Deb: 5/02/10																											
1910	StL-N	2	2	1	0	0	0	0	0	1	0	.000	.333	.000	.333	-1	-0	-0	92	0	0	.500	0			0	/C	0.0
1911	Pit-N	6	8	0	1	0	0	0	0	0	2	.125	.125	.125	.250	-30	-1	-1	101	0	0	.143	0			0	/C	0.0

YEAR	TM/L	G	AB	R	H	2B	3B	HR	RBI	BB	SO	AVG	OBP	SLG	PRO	/A	BR	/A	PF	CHI	RC	TA	SB	CS	SBR	FR	POS	TPR
1912	Pit-N	48	132	20	42	3	2	1	11	2	16	.318	.328	.394	.722	98	-1	-1	99	67	20	.689	8			-3	C	0.0
1913	Pit-N	48	82	11	22	2	2	0	9	2	12	.268	.302	.341	.644	87	-2	-2	96	117	8	.550	1			1	C	0.1
Total	4	104	224	32	65	5	4	1	20	5	30	.290	.312	.362	.673	89	-5	-4	98	82	28	.610	9			-2	/C	0.1
■ **BILLY KELSEY**	Kelsey, George William b: 8/24/1881, Covington, Ohio d: 4/25/68, Springfield, Ohio BR/TR, 5'10", 150 lbs. Deb: 10/04/07																											
1907	Pit-N	2	5	1	2	0	0	0	0	0	0	.400	.400	.400	.800	146	0	0	105	0	1	.667	0			0	/C	0.0
■ **KEN KELTNER**	Keltner, Kenneth Frederick "Butch" b: 10/31/16, Milwaukee, Wis. BR/TR, 6', 190 lbs. Deb: 10/02/37																											
1937	Cle-A	1	1	0	0	0	0	0	0	1	0	0	.000	.000	.000	.000	-99	-0	-0	98	0	0	.000	0	0	0	0	/3	0.0
1938	Cle-A	149	576	86	159	31	9	26	113	33	75	.276	.319	.497	.815	103	-4	-2	99	107	90	.776	4	3	-1	-9	*3	-0.6
1939	Cle-A	154	587	84	191	35	11	13	97	51	41	.325	.379	.489	.868	123	17	19	98	103	105	.825	6	6	-2	5	*3	1.7
1940	Cle-A	149	543	67	138	24	10	15	77	51	56	.254	.322	.418	.740	97	-9	-4	93	104	75	.691	10	5	0	-5	*3	0.0
1941	Cle-A	149	581	83	156	31	13	23	84	51	56	.269	.330	.485	.815	112	8	7	101	90	95	.773	2	2	-1	**22**	*3	3.5
1942	Cle-A	152	624	72	179	34	4	6	78	20	36	.287	.312	.383	.695	104	-7	-1	92	103	72	.573	4	3	-1	16	*3	1.7
1943	Cle-A	110	427	47	111	31	3	4	39	36	20	.260	.317	.375	.692	113	-0	5	90	88	50	.598	2	2	-1	2	*3	0.8
1944	Cle-A	149	573	74	169	41	9	13	91	53	29	.295	.355	.466	.821	133	23	23	100	109	91	.753	4	3	-1	15	*3	3.8
1946	Cle-A	116	398	47	96	17	1	13	45	30	38	.241	.294	.387	.681	101	-7	-2	89	90	42	.577	0	3	-2	-8	*3	-0.3
1947	Cle-A	151	541	49	139	29	3	11	76	59	45	.257	.331	.383	.714	102	-2	0	96	119	72	.657	5	4	-1	-4	*3	0.0
1948	Cle-A	153	558	91	166	24	4	31	119	89	52	.297	.395	.522	.917	145	33	34	99	107	116	.921	2	1	0	-1	*3	2.7
1949	Cle-A	80	246	35	57	9	2	8	30	38	26	.232	.335	.382	.717	91	-4	-4	98	87	32	.660	0	1	-1	-2	3	-0.5
1950	Bos-A	13	28	2	9	2	0	0	2	3	6	.321	.387	.393	.780	87	0	-1	114	63	4	.667	0	0	0	1	/31	0.0
Total	13	1526	5683	737	1570	308	69	163	852	514	480	.276	.338	.441	.778	113	46	75	96	102	843	.740	39	33	-8	33	*3/1	12.8
■ **JOHN KELTY**	Kelty, John James "Chief" b: 1867, Jersey City, N.J. 5'10", 175 lbs. Deb: 4/19/1890																											
1890	Pit-N	59	207	24	49	10	2	1	27	22	42	.237	.322	.319	.641	101	-2	2	88	121	25	.646	10			-4	O	-0.2
■ **RUDY KEMLER**	Kemler, Rudolph b: 1860, Chicago, Ill. d: 6/20/09, Chicago, Ill. BR/TR, Deb: 7/26/1879																											
1879	Pro-N	2	7	0	1	0	0	0	0	0	1	.143	.143	.143	.286	-5	-1	-1	102	0	0	.167				0	/C	0.0
1881	Cle-N	1	3	0	0	0	0	0	0	0	1	.000	.000	.000	.000	-99	-1	-1	96	0	0	.000				0	/C	0.0
1882	Cin-a	3	11	0	1	1	0	0		0		.091	.091	.182	.273	-9	-1	-1	109	0	0	.200				-1	/CO	-0.2
	Pit-a	24	99	7	25	4	0	0		1		.253	.260	.293	.553	89	-2	-1	97	0	8	.405				4	C/O	0.3
	Yr	27	110	7	26	5	0	0		1		.236	.243	.282	.525	78	-3	-2	98	0	8	.381				3		0.1
1883	Col-a	84	318	27	66	6	2	0		13		.208	.239	.239	.478	62	-16	-9	87	0	19	.353				0	*C/O	-0.1
1884	Col-a	61	211	28	42	3	3	0		15		.199	.252	.242	.494	66	-8	-7	97	0	13	.391				-24	C/1O	-2.4
1885	Pit-a	18	64	2	13	2	1	0		2		.203	.239	.266	.504	58	-3	-3	106	0	4	.392				0	C	-0.2
1886	StL-a	35	123	13	17	2	0	0		8		.138	.197	.154	.351	11	-12	-14	111	0	4	.264	0			0	C/1	-1.2
1889	Col-a	8	26	2	3	0	0	0	0	3	3	.115	.207	.115	.322	-7	-3	-3	91	0	1	.261	0			0	/C	-0.2
Total	8	236	862	79	168	18	6	0	0	42	5	.195	.234	.230	.464	53	-46	-41	96	0	48	.349	0			-21	C/1O	-4.0
■ **BILL KEMMER**	Kemmer, William E. BR, 6'2", Deb: 6/03/1895																											
1895	Lou-N	11	38	5	7	0	0	1	3	2	4	.184	.225	.263	.488	28	-4	-4	95	64	2	.387	0			0	/31	-0.2
■ **STEVE KEMP**	Kemp, Steven F b: 8/7/54, San Angelo, Tex. BL/TL, 6', 195 lbs. Deb: 4/07/77																											
1977	Det-A	151	552	75	142	29	4	18	88	71	93	.257	.347	.422	.769	104	7	4	105	129	83	.736	3	3	-1	-8	*O	-1.0
1978	Det-A	159	582	75	161	18	4	15	79	97	87	.277	.381	.399	.780	111	18	12	108	119	94	.767	2	3	-1	0	*O	0.8
1979	Det-A	134	490	88	156	26	3	26	105	68	70	.318	.404	.543	.946	158	37	40	96	124	106	.966	5	6	-2	2	*OD	3.3
1980	Det-A	135	508	88	149	23	3	21	101	69	64	.293	.382	.474	.857	126	24	21	105	**137**	89	.831	5	1	1	4	OD	2.3
1981	Det-A	105	372	52	103	18	4	9	49	70	48	.277	.393	.419	.812	128	19	17	105	111	64	.828	9	3	1	-9	OD	0.7
1982	Chi-A	160	580	91	166	23	1	19	98	89	83	.286	.384	.428	.812	126	21	23	97	136	99	.809	7	7	-2	-12	*O/D	0.4
1983	NY-A	109	373	53	90	17	3	12	49	41	37	.241	.320	.399	.719	98	-2	-1	99	104	45	.643	1	0	0	1	*O/D	0.0
1984	NY-A	94	313	37	91	12	1	7	41	40	54	.291	.373	.403	.775	122	7	10	94	111	47	.728	4	1	1	-5	OD	0.3
1985	Pit-N	92	236	19	59	13	2	2	21	25	54	.250	.322	.347	.669	85	-4	-5	103	95	27	.593	1	0	0	-3	O	-0.9
1986	Pit-N	13	16	1	3	0	0	1	1	4	6	.188	.350	.375	.725	100	0	0	100	44	2	.786	1	0	0	0	/O	0.1
1988	Tex-A	16	36	2	8	0	0	0	2	2	9	.222	.263	.222	.485	37	-3	-3	101	99	2	.379	1	0	0	-1	/O1D	-0.3
Total	11	1168	4058	581	1128	179	25	130	634	576	605	.278	.370	.431	.801	119	126	117	102	121	658	.806	39	24	-3	-32	*O/D1	5.7
■ **FRED KENDALL**	Kendall, Fred Lyn b: 1/31/49, Torrance, Cal. BR/TR, 6'1", 185 lbs. Deb: 9/08/69																											
1969	SD-N	10	26	2	4	0	0	0	0	2	5	.154	.214	.154	.368	5	-3	-3	97	0	1	.250	0	0	0	0	/C	-0.2
1970	SD-N	4	9	0	0	0	0	0	1	0	0	.000	.000	.000	.000	-99	-3	-2	95	0	0	.000	0	0	0	-0	/C1O	-0.2
1971	SD-N	49	111	2	19	1	0	1	7	7	16	.171	.220	.207	.428	23	-11	-11	96	110	5	.323	1	0	0	1	C/13	-0.8
1972	SD-N	91	273	18	59	3	4	6	18	11	42	.216	.249	.322	.571	69	-15	-11	88	70	21	.457	0	0	0	-2	C/1	-0.9
1973	SD-N	145	507	39	143	22	3	10	59	30	35	.282	.323	.396	.720	105	-2	2	94	105	61	.615	3	1	0	7	*C	1.8
1974	SD-N	141	424	32	98	15	2	8	45	49	33	.231	.311	.333	.643	86	-11	-8	93	105	43	.559	0	1	-1	2	*C	0.0
1975	SD-N	103	286	16	57	12	1	0	24	26	28	.199	.266	.248	.514	43	-22	-22	100	131	18	.404	0	1	-1	0	C	-1.9
1976	SD-N	146	456	30	112	17	0	2	39	36	42	.246	.305	.296	.601	80	-17	-11	89	107	39	.479	1	1	-0	-9	*C	-1.3
1977	Cle-A	103	317	18	79	13	1	3	39	16	27	.249	.287	.325	.612	68	-15	-14	98	138	29	.486	0	1	-1	1	*C/D	-1.0
1978	Bos-A	20	41	3	8	1	0	0	4	1	2	.195	.214	.220	.434	21	-4	-5	107	176	2	.303	0	0	0	0	1/CD	-0.4
1979	SD-N	46	102	8	17	2	0	1	6	11	7	.167	.248	.216	.463	29	-10	-10	96	95	5	.371	0	0	0	-1	C/1	-1.0
1980	SD-N	19	24	2	7	0	0	0	2	0	3	.292	.292	.292	.583	68	-1	-1	93	113	2	.412	0	0	0	-1	C/1	-0.1
Total	12	877	2576	170	603	86	11	31	244	189	240	.234	.288	.312	.600	72	-114	-95	94	108	225	.508	5	5	-2	-2	C/1D3O	-6.0
■ **AL KENDERS**	Kenders, Albert Daniel George b: 4/4/37, Barrington, N.J. BR/TR, 6', 185 lbs. Deb: 8/14/61																											
1961	Phi-N	10	23	0	4	1	0	0	1	1	0	.174	.208	.217	.426	14	-3	-3	94	81	1	.286	0	0	0	0	C	-0.1
■ **EDDIE KENNA**	Kenna, Edward Aloysius "Scrap Iron" b: 9/30/1897, San Francisco, Cal. d: 8/21/72, San Francisco, Cal BR/TR, 5'7.5", 150 lbs. Deb: 6/02/28																											
1928	Was-A	41	118	14	35	4	2	1	20	14	8	.297	.376	.390	.766	100	1	0	102	140	16	.705	1	5	-3	2	C	0.2
■ **ED KENNEDY**	Kennedy, Edward b: 4/1/1856, Carbondale, Pa. d: 5/20/05, New York, N.Y. Deb: 5/02/1883																											
1883	NY-a	94	356	57	78	6	7	2		17		.219	.255	.292	.547	70	-9	-13	108	0	27	.435				-8	*O	-1.7
1884	NY-a	103	378	49	72	6	2	1		16		.190	.225	.225	.450	49	-20	-20	100	0	20	.333				4	*O/S2C	-1.5
1885	NY-a	96	349	35	71	8	4	2		12		.203	.238	.266	.505	73	-15	-6	84	0	23	.392				1	*O	-0.8
1886	Bro-a	6	22	1	4	0	0	0		2		.182	.250	.182	.432	37	-1	-1	100	0	1	.389	1			0	/O	0.0
Total	4	299	1105	142	225	20	13	5		47		.204	.239	.259	.498	63	-45	-41	97	0	71	.385	1			-2	O/C2S	-4.0
■ **JIM KENNEDY**	Kennedy, James Earl b: 11/1/46, Tulsa, Okla. BL/TR, 5'9", 160 lbs. Deb: 6/14/70																											
1970	StL-N	12	24	1	3	0	0	0	0	0	0	.125	.125	.125	.250	-31	-4	-5	106	0	0	.143	0	0	0	2	/S2	-0.1
■ **JOHN KENNEDY**	Kennedy, John Edward b: 5/29/41, Chicago, Ill. BR/TR, 6', 185 lbs. Deb: 9/05/62																											
1962	Was-A	14	42	6	11	0	1	1	2	2	7	.262	.295	.381	.676	80	-1	-1	101	42	5	.563	0	1	-1	-1	/S3	-0.1
1963	Was-A	36	62	3	11	1	1	0	4	6	22	.177	.261	.226	.487	39	-5	-5	98	120	4	.434	2	0	1	0	3/S	-0.3
1964	Was-A	148	482	55	111	16	4	7	35	29	119	.230	.281	.324	.605	67	-21	-22	101	84	41	.496	3	3	-1	-3	*3S/2	-2.4
1965	LA-N	104	105	12	18	3	0	1	5	8	33	.171	.243	.229	.472	37	-9	-8	91	77	6	.389	1	0	0	3	3/S	-0.7
1966	LA-N	125	274	15	55	9	2	3	24	10	64	.201	.242	.281	.523	46	-20	-19	97	117	18	.412	1	2	-1	0	3S2	-1.8
1967	NY-A	78	179	22	35	4	0	1	17	17	35	.196	.269	.235	.504	53	-11	-10	94	158	12	.416	2	1	0	3	S3/2	-0.3
1969	Sea-A	61	128	18	30	3	1	4	14	14	25	.234	.315	.367	.682	92	-2	-2	98	95	16	.653	4	0	1	-1	S3	0.1
1970	Mil-A	25	55	8	14	2	0	2	6	5	9	.255	.317	.400	.717	98	-0	-0	98	87	6	.614	0	1	-1	-1	2/3S1	0.0
	Bos-A	43	129	15	33	7	1	4	17	6	14	.256	.294	.419	.713	85	-2	-3	111	104	16	.622	0	0	0	-2	3/2	-0.4
	Yr	68	184	23	47	9	1	6	23	11	23	.255	.301	.413	.714	90	-2	-3	106	99	23	.629	0	1	-1	-3		-0.4
1971	Bos-A	74	272	41	75	12	5	5	22	14	42	.276	.321	.412	.732	101	1	-0	106	72	36	.649	1	1	-0	-6	2S/3	-0.1
1972	Bos-A	71	212	22	52	11	1	2	22	18	40	.245	.313	.335	.648	88	-2	-3	105	119	23	.561	0	1	-1	-2	2S3	0.0

YEAR	TM/L	G	AB	R	H	2B	3B	HR	RBI	BB	SO	AVG	OBP	SLG	PRO	/A	BR	/A	PF	CHI	RC	TA	SB	CS	SBR	FR	POS	TPR
1973	Bos-A	67	155	17	28	9	1	1	16	12	45	.181	.249	.271	.519	44	-11	-12	106	140	11	.431	0	0	0	-1	23/D	-1.2
1974	Bos-A	10	15	3	2	0	0	1	1	1	6	.133	.188	.333	.521	44	-1	-1	107	49	0	.400	0	0	0	-0	/23	0.0
Total	12	856	2110	237	475	77	17	32	185	142	461	.225	.282	.323	.605	70	-84	-87	101	102	193	.524	14	10	-2	-11	3S2/D1	-7.2
■ **JOHN KENNEDY** Kennedy, John Irvin b: 11/23/34, Sumter, S.C. BR/TR, 5'10", 175 lbs. Deb: 4/22/57																												
1957	Phi-N	5	2	1	0	0	0	0	0	0	1	.000	.000	.000	.000	-99	-1	-1	98	0	0	.000	0	0	0	0	/3	0.0
■ **JUNIOR KENNEDY** Kennedy, Junior Raymond b: 8/9/50, Fort Gibson, Okla. BR/TR, 5'11", 175 lbs. Deb: 8/09/74																												
1974	Cin-N	22	19	2	3	0	0	0	0	6	4	.158	.360	.158	.518	49	-1	-1	98	0	1	.529	0	0	0	-1	2/3	0.0
1978	Cin-N	89	157	22	40	2	2	0	11	31	28	.255	.381	.293	.674	88	-0	-1	103	95	20	.672	4	1	1	-5	2/3	0.0
1979	Cin-N	83	220	29	60	7	0	1	17	28	31	.273	.355	.318	.673	87	-3	-3	97	92	26	.611	4	3	-1	-3	2/S3	-0.1
1980	Cin-N	104	337	31	88	16	3	1	34	36	34	.261	.332	.335	.668	85	-5	-6	102	116	39	.596	3	1	0	-7	*2	-0.5
1981	Cin-N	27	44	5	11	1	0	0	5	1	5	.250	.267	.273	.539	53	-3	-3	101	164	3	.394	0	0	0	0	2/3	-0.1
1982	Chi-N	105	242	22	53	3	1	2	25	21	34	.219	.281	.264	.546	52	-15	-16	103	140	17	.426	1	4	-2	-2	2S/3	-1.5
1983	Chi-N	17	22	3	3	0	0	0	3	1	6	.136	.174	.136	.310	-13	-3	-3	101	396	0	.190	0	0	0	1	/23S	-0.1
Total	7	447	1041	114	258	29	6	4	95	124	142	.248	.328	.299	.627	75	-31	-32	101	118	107	.564	12	9	-2	-16	2/S3	-2.3
■ **DOC KENNEDY** Kennedy, Michael Joseph b: 8/11/1853, Brooklyn, N.Y. d: 5/23/20, Grove, N.Y. BR/TR, Deb: 5/01/1879																												
1879	Cle-N	49	193	19	56	8	2	1	18	2	10	.290	.297	.368	.665	119	3	4	99	87	22	.533				0	C/1	0.3
1880	Cle-N	66	250	26	50	10	1	0	18	5	12	.200	.216	.248	.464	57	-11	-10	99	108	14	.335				-3	*C/O	-0.8
1881	Cle-N	39	150	19	47	7	1	0	15	5	13	.313	.335	.373	.709	127	4	5	96	95	19	.592				3	C/O3	0.7
1882	Cle-N	1	3	0	1	0	0	0	0	1	0	.333	.500	.333	.833	194	0	0	90	0	1	1.000				0	/C	0.0
1883	Buf-N	5	19	3	6	0	0	0	2	2	2	.316	.381	.316	.697	115	0	0	100	118	2	.615				0	/O1	0.0
Total	5	160	615	67	160	25	4	1	53	15	37	.260	.278	.319	.596	97	-3	-1	98	98	57	.464				-0	C/O13	0.2
■ **RAY KENNEDY** Kennedy, Raymond Lincoln b: 5/19/1895, Pittsburgh, Pa. d: 1/18/69, Casselberry, Fla. BR/TR, 5'9", 165 lbs. Deb: 9/08/16																												
1916	StL-A	1	1	0	0	0	0	0	0	0	0	.000	.000	.000	.000	-99	-0	-0	95	0	0	.000	0			0	H	0.0
■ **BOB KENNEDY** Kennedy, Robert Daniel b: 8/18/20, Chicago, Ill. BR/TR, 6'2", 193 lbs. Deb: 9/14/39 MC																												
1939	Chi-A	3	8	0	2	0	0	0	1	0	0	.250	.250	.250	.500	26	-1	-1	107	169	0	.286	0	0	0	0	/3	0.0
1940	Chi-A	154	606	74	153	23	3	3	52	42	58	.252	.301	.315	.616	58	-36	-39	104	100	55	.495	3	7	-3	-4	*3	-3.5
1941	Chi-A	76	257	16	53	9	3	1	29	17	23	.206	.255	.276	.532	43	-22	-20	94	139	19	.441	5	3	-0	4	3	-1.2
1942	Chi-A	113	412	37	95	18	5	0	38	22	41	.231	.270	.299	.568	60	-23	-22	99	111	31	.463	11	7	-1	7	3O	-1.5
1946	Chi-A	113	411	43	106	13	5	5	34	24	42	.258	.300	.350	.651	84	-11	-10	97	83	40	.540	6	8	-3	4	O3	-1.0
1947	Chi-A	115	428	47	112	19	3	6	48	18	38	.262	.291	.362	.654	84	-13	-11	97	104	42	.530	3	4	-2	-4	*O/3	-2.2
1948	Chi-A	30	113	4	28	8	1	0	14	4	17	.248	.274	.336	.610	65	-7	-6	95	127	9	.457	0	2	-1	-1	O	-0.9
	Cle-A	66	73	10	22	3	2	0	5	4	6	.301	.338	.397	.735	96	-1	-1	99	58	10	.635	0	0	0	-17	O/21	-1.8
	Yr	96	186	14	50	11	3	0	19	8	23	.269	.299	.360	.659	77	-7	-7	98	81	20	.540	0	2	-1	-18		-2.7
1949	Cle-A	121	424	49	117	23	5	9	57	37	40	.276	.334	.417	.752	101	-3	-2	98	98	57	.672	5	5	-2	-0	O3	-0.5
1950	Cle-A	146	540	79	157	27	5	9	54	53	31	.291	.355	.409	.764	97	-5	-3	98	77	79	.692	3	4	-2	1	*O	-0.5
1951	Cle-A	108	321	30	79	15	4	7	29	34	33	.246	.320	.383	.703	95	-5	-3	95	72	38	.630	4	2	0	-7	*O	-1.3
1952	Cle-A	22	40	6	12	3	1	0	12	9	5	.300	.429	.425	.854	152	3	3	91	264	9	.964	1	0	0	-1	O/3	0.1
1953	Cle-A	100	161	22	38	5	0	3	22	19	11	.236	.320	.323	.643	78	-6	-5	95	134	16	.545	0	2	-1	-23	O	-3.1
1954	Cle-A	1	0	0	0	0	0	0	0	0	0	—	—	—	—	—	0	0	106	—	—	—	0	0	0	-0	/O	0.0
	Bal-A	106	323	37	81	13	2	6	45	28	43	.251	.311	.359	.670	87	-8	-6	95	127	33	.564	2	1	0	-7	3O	-1.8
	Yr	107	323	37	81	13	2	6	45	28	43	.251	.311	.359	.670	87	-8	-6	95	126	33	.564	2	1	0	-7		-1.8
1955	Bal-A	26	70	10	10	1	0	0	5	10	10	.143	.250	.157	.407	13	-9	-8	90	170	3	.328	0	1	-1	-1	O/13	-1.0
	Chi-A	83	214	28	65	10	2	9	43	16	16	.304	.352	.495	.848	125	7	6	101	121	35	.772	0	2	-1	-9	3O/1	-0.3
	Yr	109	284	38	75	11	2	9	48	26	26	.264	.326	.412	.738	99	-2	-1	98	134	36	.653	0	3	-2	-10		-1.3
1956	Chi-A	8	13	0	1	0	0	0	0	2	4	.077	.200	.077	.277	-23	-2	-2	104	0	0	.250	0	0	0	0	/3	-0.1
	Det-A	69	177	17	41	5	0	4	22	24	19	.232	.330	.328	.658	77	-6	-5	97	117	18	.581	2	2	-1	-3	O3	-0.9
	Yr	77	190	17	42	5	0	4	22	26	23	.221	.321	.311	.632	69	-9	-8	97	105	18	.556	2	2	-1	-3		-1.0
1957	Chi-A	4	2	0	0	0	0	0	0	0	1	.000	.000	.000	.000	-99	-1	-1	99	0	0	.000	0	0	0	0	H	0.0
	Bro-N	19	31	5	4	1	0	1	4	1	5	.129	.156	.258	.414	8	-4	-5	116	151	1	.321	0	0	0	-3	/O3	-0.7
Total	16	1483	4624	514	1176	196	41	63	514	364	443	.254	.310	.355	.665	80	-153	-140	98	104	511	.588	45	50	-17	-65	O3/12	-22.2
■ **SNAPPER KENNEDY** Kennedy, Sherman Montgomery b: 11/1/1878, Conneaut, Ohio d: 8/15/45, Pasadena, Tex. BB/TR, 5'10", 165 lbs. Deb: 5/01/02																												
1902	Chi-N	1	5	0	0	0	0	0	0	0		.000	.000	.000	.000	-99	-1	-1	96	0	0	.000	0			0	/O	0.0
■ **TERRY KENNEDY** Kennedy, Terrence Edward b: 6/4/56, Euclid, Ohio BL/TR, 6'3", 220 lbs. Deb: 9/04/78																												
1978	StL-N	10	29	0	5	0	0	0	2	4	3	.172	.273	.172	.445	28	-3	-3	95	159	1	.346	0	0	0	1	C	-0.1
1979	StL-N	33	109	11	31	7	0	2	17	6	20	.284	.322	.404	.725	92	-1	-1	105	135	14	.625	0	0	0	-1	C	0.0
1980	StL-N	84	248	28	63	12	3	4	34	28	34	.254	.330	.375	.705	94	-1	-2	103	128	30	.624	0	0	0	0	CO	-0.1
1981	SD-N	101	382	32	115	24	1	2	41	22	53	.301	.342	.385	.727	114	3	6	93	107	49	.620	0	2	-1	6	*C	1.2
1982	SD-N	153	562	75	166	42	1	21	97	26	91	.295	.332	.486	.818	137	17	22	92	116	90	.757	1	0	0	-5	*C1	1.9
1983	SD-N	149	549	47	156	27	2	17	98	51	89	.284	.347	.434	.781	116	11	11	99	**142**	81	.719	1	3	-2	3	*C/1	1.7
1984	SD-N	148	530	54	127	16	1	14	57	33	99	.240	.287	.353	.640	80	-16	-15	99	100	50	.530	1	2	-1	-6	*C	-1.8
1985	SD-N	143	532	54	139	27	1	10	74	31	102	.261	.302	.372	.674	86	-10	-11	102	132	55	.556	0	0	0	9	*C/1	0.3
1986	SD-N	141	432	46	114	22	1	12	57	37	74	.264	.325	.403	.728	104	-1	2	95	108	54	.644	0	3	-2	2	*C	0.5
1987	Bal-A	143	512	51	128	13	1	18	62	35	112	.250	.299	.385	.684	82	-15	-13	98	101	57	.589	1	0	0	17	*C	1.4
1988	Bal-A	85	265	20	60	10	0	3	16	15	53	.226	.270	.298	.569	62	-15	-13	95	72	19	.436	0	0	0	8	C	-0.1
Total	11	1190	4150	418	1104	200	11	103	555	288	730	.266	.316	.394	.710	98	-30	-17	97	115	499	.633	4	10	-5	33	*C/O1	4.9
■ **ED KENNEDY** Kennedy, William Edward b: 4/5/1861, Bellevue, Ky. d: 12/22/12, Cheyenne, Wyoming BR/TR, 5'7", 160 lbs. Deb: 5/17/1884																												
1884	Cin-U	13	48	6	10	1	1	0		1		.208	.224	.271	.495	62	-2	-2	108	0	3	.368	0			0	/3SO	-0.1
■ **JERRY KENNEY** Kenney, Gerald T b: 6/30/45, St.Louis, Mo. BL/TR, 6'1", 170 lbs. Deb: 9/05/67																												
1967	NY-A	20	58	4	18	2	0	1	5	10	8	.310	.412	.397	.808	148	3	4	94	80	11	.854	2	1	0	1	S	0.6
1969	NY-A	130	447	49	115	14	2	2	34	48	36	.257	.331	.311	.642	84	-11	-8	95	96	47	.597	25	14	-1	13	3OS	0.4
1970	NY-A	140	404	46	78	10	7	4	35	52	44	.193	.285	.282	.567	62	-23	-20	92	112	34	.542	20	6	2	9	*3/2	-0.8
1971	NY-A	120	325	50	85	10	3	0	20	56	38	.262	.372	.311	.682	98	1	2	97	81	40	.647	9	8	-2	4	*3/S1	0.1
1972	NY-A	50	119	16	25	2	0	0	7	16	13	.210	.304	.227	.531	64	-5	-4	92	108	8	.455	3	0	1	6	S/3	0.8
1973	Cle-A	5	16	0	4	0	1	0	2	2	0	.250	.333	.375	.708	102	-0	0	97	134	2	.667	0	0	0	1	/2	0.1
Total	6	465	1369	165	325	38	13	7	103	184	139	.237	.329	.299	.628	82	-36	-26	95	98	142	.610	59	29	0	33	3/SO21	1.2
■ **JOHN KENNEY** Kenney, John Deb: 5/02/1872																												
1872	Atl-n	5	21	0	0							.000															/2O	
■ **DICK KENWORTHY** Kenworthy, Richard Lee b: 4/1/41, Red Oak, Iowa BR/TR, 5'9", 170 lbs. Deb: 9/08/62																												
1962	Chi-A	3	4	0	0	0	0	0	0	0	3	.000	.000	.000	.000	-99	-1	-1	95	0	0	.000	0	0	0	0	/2	0.0
1964	Chi-A	2	2	0	0	0	0	0	0	0	1	.000	.000	.000	.000	-99	-1	-1	96	0	0	.000	0	0	0	0	H	0.0
1965	Chi-A	3	1	0	0	0	0	0	0	1	0	.000	.667	.000	.667	116	0	0	92	0	0	2.000	0	0	0	0	H	0.0
1966	Chi-A	9	25	1	5	0	0	0	0	0	0	.200	.200	.200	.400	16	-3	-3	94	0	1	.250	0	0	0	0	/3	-0.2
1967	Chi-A	50	97	9	22	4	1	4	11	4	17	.227	.265	.412	.677	104	-1	-0	94	88	9	.570	0	2	-1	1	3	0.0
1968	Chi-A	58	122	2	27	2	0	0	2	5	21	.221	.252	.238	.490	49	-7	-8	101	30	7	.347	0	1	-1	1	3	-0.6
Total	6	125	251	12	54	6	1	4	13	10	42	.215	.251	.295	.546	64	-12	-11	97	48	18	.426	0	3	-2	1	/32	-0.8
■ **DUKE KENWORTHY** Kenworthy, William Jennings "Iron Duke" b: 7/4/1886, Cambridge, Ohio d: 9/21/50, Eureka, Cal. BB/TR, 5'7", 165 lbs. Deb: 8/28/12																												
1912	Was-A	12	38	6	9	1	0	0	2	2		.237	.293	.263	.556	60	-2	-2	99	67	4	.552	3			-0	O	-0.2
1914	KC-F	146	545	93	173	40	14	**15**	91	36	44	.317	.360	.525	.884	159	33	36	95	105	120	.965	37			**24**	*2	**6.3**

YEAR	TM/L	G	AB	R	H	2B	3B	HR	RBI	BB	SO	AVG	OBP	SLG	PRO	/A	BR	/A	PF	CHI	RC	TA	SB	CS	SBR	FR	POS	TPR
1915	KC-F	122	396	59	118	30	7	3	52	28	32	.298	.344	.432	.776	133	13	15	97	106	69	.788	20			5	*2/O	2.2
1917	StL-A	5	10	1	1	0	0	0	1	1	1	.100	.182	.100	.282	-15	-1	-1	95	359	0	.333	1			0	/2	0.0
Total	4	285	989	159	301	71	21	18	146	67	77	.304	.349	.473	.822	143	42	48	96	107	193	.868	61			29	2/O	8.3
■ **JOE KEOUGH**	Keough, Joseph William b: 1/7/46, Pomona, Cal. BL/TL, 6', 185 lbs. Deb: 8/07/68																											
1968	Oak-A	34	98	7	21	2	1	2	18	8	11	.214	.274	.316	.590	80	-3	-2	98	208	9	.506	1	0	0	-0	O/1	-0.3
1969	KC-A	70	166	17	31	2	0	0	7	13	13	.187	.254	.199	.453	27	-16	-16	103	85	10	.384	5	2	0	-1	O/1	-1.9
1970	KC-A	57	183	28	59	6	2	4	21	23	18	.322	.398	.443	.841	134	8	9	98	91	32	.802	1	1	-0	0	O1	0.6
1971	KC-A	110	351	34	87	14	2	3	30	35	26	.248	.318	.325	.643	83	-8	-7	99	100	34	.536	0	6	-4	-6	*O	-2.1
1972	KC-A	56	64	8	14	2	0	0	5	8	7	.219	.324	.250	.574	72	-2	-2	100	131	6	.560	2	0	1	-3	O	-0.5
1973	Chi-A	5	1	1	0	0	0	0	0	0	0	.000	.000	.000	.000	-98	-0	-0	102	0	0	.000	0	0	0	0	H	0.0
Total	6	332	863	95	212	26	5	9	81	87	75	.246	.318	.319	.637	82	-20	-19	99	109	90	.569	9	9	-3	-11	O/1	-4.2
■ **MARTY KEOUGH**	Keough, Richard Martin b: 4/14/35, Oakland, Cal. BL/TL, 6', 180 lbs. Deb: 4/21/56																											
1956	Bos-A	3	2	1	0	0	0	0	1	1	0	.000	.333	.000	.333	-5	-0	-0	103	0	0	.500	0	0	0	0	H	0.0
1957	Bos-A	9	17	1	1	0	0	0	0	4	3	.059	.238	.059	.297	-13	-3	-3	110	0	0	.313	0	0	0	0	/O	-0.2
1958	Bos-A	68	118	21	26	3	3	1	9	7	29	.220	.264	.322	.586	58	-7	-7	105	88	10	.484	1	1	-0	-3	O/1	-1.2
1959	Bos-A	96	251	40	61	13	5	7	27	26	40	.243	.321	.418	.740	96	0	-2	106	84	35	.706	3	1	0	-4	O/1	-0.8
1960	Bos-A	38	105	15	26	6	1	1	9	8	8	.248	.301	.352	.653	74	-4	-4	103	88	11	.573	2	2	-1	2	O	-0.3
	Cle-A	65	149	19	37	5	0	3	11	9	23	.248	.296	.342	.638	74	-6	-6	98	72	15	.543	2	3	-1	-3	O	-1.0
	Yr	103	254	34	63	11	1	4	20	17	31	.248	.298	.346	.644	74	-10	-10	100	79	26	.558	4	5	-2	-1		-1.3
1961	Was-A	135	390	57	97	18	9	9	34	32	60	.249	.309	.410	.719	95	-6	-4	95	71	50	.678	12	5	1	2	*O1	-0.5
1962	Cin-N	111	230	34	64	8	2	7	27	21	31	.278	.349	.422	.771	104	2	1	102	90	35	.740	3	1	0	-8	O1	-1.1
1963	Cin-N	95	172	21	39	8	2	6	21	25	37	.227	.338	.401	.739	108	3	2	104	101	24	.712	1	4	-2	-5	1O	-0.7
1964	Cin-N	109	276	29	71	9	1	9	28	22	58	.257	.314	.395	.709	95	-1	-2	103	84	35	.639	1	2	-1	-4	O/1	-0.9
1965	Cin-N	62	43	14	5	0	0	0	3	3	14	.116	.191	.116	.308	-11	-6	-6	104	249	1	.231	0	0	0	-1	1/O	-0.9
1966	Atl-N	17	17	1	1	0	0	0	1	1	6	.059	.111	.059	.170	-52	-3	-3	99	420	0	.125	0	0	0	-1	/1O	-0.4
	Chi-N	33	26	3	6	1	0	0	5	5	9	.231	.375	.269	.644	83	-0	-0	100	300	3	.700	1	0	0	-2	/O	-0.1
	Yr	50	43	4	7	1	0	0	6	6	15	.163	.280	.186	.466	33	-4	-4	100	349	3	.444	1	0	0	-3		-0.5
Total	11	841	1796	256	434	71	23	43	176	164	318	.242	.311	.379	.690	87	-31	-34	101	93	220	.642	26	19	-4	-27	O1	-8.1
■ **JOHN KERINS**	Kerins, John Nelson b: 7/15/1858, Indianapolis, Ind d: 9/8/19, Louisville, Ky. BR/TR, 5'10", 177 lbs. Deb: 5/01/1884 M																											
1884	Ind-a	94	364	58	78	10	3	6		6		.214	.229	.308	.537	79	-9	-8	96	0	26	.416				7	*1/CO3	-0.3
1885	Lou-a	112	456	65	111	9	16	3		20		.243	.281	.353	.634	100	1	-1	102	0	46	.536				-3	*1C/O3	-1.0
1886	Lou-a	120	487	113	131	19	9	4		66		.269	.360	.370	.729	121	19	13	108	0	76	.772	26			**38**	C1/OS	4.5
1887	Lou-a	112	476	101	140	18	19	5		38		.294	.349	.443	.792	114	13	7	107	0	93	.893	49			23	1C/O	2.8
1888	Lou-a	83	319	38	75	11	4	2	41	25		.235	.297	.313	.610	109	-0	4	91	122	35	.590	16			-7	OC/132M	-0.3
1889	Lou-a	2	9	2	3	1	0	0	3	0	1	.333	.333	.444	.778	128	0	0	96	189	1	.667	0			0	/OC	0.0
	Bal-a	16	53	7	15	2	0	0	12	2	4	.283	.321	.321	.642	85	-1	-1	100	202	6	.579	2			0	/1COS	0.0
	Yr	18	62	9	18	3	0	0	15	2	5	.290	.323	.339	.662	91	-1	-1	99	211	8	.591	2			0		0.0
1890	StL-a	18	63	8	8	2	0	0		8		.127	.225	.159	.384	13	-6	-8	116	0	3	.364	2			0	1/CM	-0.6
Total	7	557	2227	392	561	72	51	20	56	165	5	.252	.308	.357	.665	104	16	7	102	23	287	.642	95			59	1C/O3S2	5.1
■ **ORIE KERLIN**	Kerlin, Orie Milton "Cy" b: 1/23/1891, Summerfield, La. d: 10/29/74, Shreveport, La. BL/TR, 5'7", 149 lbs. Deb: 6/06/15																											
1915	Pit-F	3	1	0	0	0	0	0	0	0	0	.000	.000	.000	.000	-96	-0	-0	104	0	0	.000	0			0	/C	0.0
■ **BILL KERN**	Kern, William George b: 2/28/33, Coplay, Pa. BR/TR, 6'2", 184 lbs. Deb: 9/19/62																											
1962	KC-A	8	16	1	4	0	0	1	1	0	3	.250	.250	.438	.688	81	-1	-1	100	40	2	.583	0	0	0	1	/O	0.0
■ **JOE KERNAN**	Kernan, Joseph b: Baltimore, Md. Deb: 4/14/1873																											
1873	Mar-n	2	8	1	3							.375															/2O	
■ **GEORGE KERNEK**	Kernek, George Boyd b: 1/12/40, Holdenville, Okla. BL/TL, 6'3", 170 lbs. Deb: 9/05/65																											
1965	StL-N	10	31	6	9	3	1	0	3	2	4	.290	.333	.452	.785	111	1	0	107	89	5	.727	0	0	0	0	/1	0.0
1966	StL-N	20	50	5	12	0	1	0	3	4	9	.240	.309	.280	.589	65	-2	-2	100	90	5	.513	1	0	0	-0	1	-0.2
Total	2	30	81	11	21	3	2	0	6	6	13	.259	.318	.346	.664	83	-2	-2	102	90	9	.590	1	0	0	-0	/1	-0.2
■ **DAN KERNS**	Kerns, Daniel P. b: Philadelphia, Pa. Deb: 10/01/20																											
1920	Phi-A	1	1	0	0	0	0	0	0	0	0	.000	.000	.000	.000	-99	-0	-0	94	0	0	.000	0	0	0	0	H	0.0
■ **RUSS KERNS**	Kerns, Russell Eldon b: 11/10/20, Fremont, Ohio BL/TR, 6', 188 lbs. Deb: 8/18/45																											
1945	Det-A	1	1	0	0	0	0	0	0	0	0	.000	.000	.000	.000	-94	-0	-0	106	0	0	.000	0	0	0	0	H	0.0
■ **JOHN KERR**	Kerr, John Francis b: 11/26/1898, San Francisco, Cal BR/TR, 5'8", 158 lbs. Deb: 5/01/23																											
1923	Det-A	19	42	4	9	1	0	0	1	4	5	.214	.283	.238	.521	39	-4	-4	97	34	3	.424	0	0	0	-1	S	-0.2
1924	Det-A	17	11	3	3	0	0	0	1	0	0	.273	.273	.273	.545	41	-1	-1	100	110	1	.375	0	0	0	-1	/3O	-0.1
1929	Chi-A	127	419	50	108	20	4	1	39	31	24	.258	.310	.332	.642	69	-22	-18	95	94	44	.566	9	7	-2	13	*2/S	-0.3
1930	Chi-A	70	266	37	77	11	6	3	27	21	23	.289	.351	.410	.760	90	-3	-4	103	80	39	.723	4	2	0	-8	2S	-0.8
1931	Chi-A	128	444	51	119	17	2	2	50	35	22	.268	.324	.329	.653	78	-18	-13	92	109	50	.585	9	3	1	-5	*2/3S	-0.8
1932	Was-A	51	132	14	36	6	1	0	15	13	3	.273	.338	.333	.671	75	-5	-5	100	114	15	.612	3	2	-0	-1	2S/3	-0.3
1933	Was-A	28	40	5	8	0	0	0	0	3	2	.200	.256	.200	.456	23	-4	-4	96	0	2	.344	0	0	0	0	2/3	-0.3
1934	Was-A	31	103	8	28	4	0	0	12	8	13	.272	.324	.311	.635	64	-5	-5	101	125	11	.539	1	1	-0	2	32	-0.2
Total	8	471	1457	172	388	59	13	6	145	115	92	.266	.323	.337	.660	74	-62	-54	96	96	165	.589	26	15	-1	-1	2/S3O	-3.0
■ **DOC KERR**	Kerr, John Jonas b: 1/17/1882, Del Roy, Ohio d: 6/9/37, Baltimore, Md. BB/TR, 5'10.5", 190 lbs. Deb: 4/22/14																											
1914	Pit-F	42	71	3	17	4	2	1	7	10	0	.239	.333	.394	.728	114	1	1	94	81	10	.704	0			0	C	0.1
	Bal-F	14	34	4	9	1	1	0	1	1	0	.265	.286	.353	.639	83	-1	-1	99	30	4	.560	1			0	C/1	0.0
	Yr	56	105	7	26	5	3	1	8	11	0	.248	.319	.381	.700	105	-0	0	96	70	13	.658	1			0		0.1
1915	Bal-F	3	6	1	2	0	0	0	0	1	0	.333	.429	.333	.762	119	0	0	107	0	1	.750	0			0	/C1	0.0
Total	2	59	111	8	28	5	3	1	8	12	0	.252	.325	.378	.704	105	0	1	96	62	14	.663	1			0	/C1	0.1
■ **BUDDY KERR**	Kerr, John Joseph b: 11/6/22, Astoria, N.Y. BR/TR, 6'2", 175 lbs. Deb: 9/08/43																											
1943	NY-N	27	98	14	28	3	0	2	12	8	5	.286	.352	.378	.729	115	1	2	96	103	13	.667	1			2	S	0.6
1944	NY-N	150	548	68	146	31	4	9	63	37	32	.266	.316	.387	.703	94	-3	-6	104	96	65	.639	14			**16**	*S	2.9
1945	NY-N	149	546	53	136	20	3	4	40	41	34	.249	.304	.319	.623	73	-20	-20	100	76	54	.527	5			**28**	*S	2.3
1946	NY-N	145	497	50	124	20	3	6	40	53	31	.249	.324	.338	.662	87	-8	-9	102	82	57	.601	7			2	*S3	0.3
1947	NY-N	138	547	73	157	23	5	7	49	36	49	.287	.331	.386	.717	89	-9	-9	101	83	69	.619	2			8	*S	1.0
1948	NY-N	144	496	41	119	16	4	0	46	56	36	.240	.317	.288	.605	65	-23	-23	100	123	48	.542	9			1	*S	-0.6
1949	NY-N	90	220	16	46	4	0	0	19	21	23	.209	.284	.227	.511	38	-19	-19	102	143	16	.417	0			-5	S	-1.4
1950	Bos-N	155	507	45	115	24	6	2	46	50	50	.227	.296	.310	.606	69	-30	-20	86	109	45	.501	0			2	*S	-0.2
1951	Bos-N	69	172	18	32	4	0	1	18	22	20	.186	.282	.227	.509	39	-14	-14	98	166	13	.437	0	0	0	0	S/2	-0.8
Total	9	1067	3631	378	903	145	25	31	333	324	280	.249	.312	.328	.640	76	-125	-118	99	101	380	.573	38	0		54	*S/32	4.1
■ **MEL KERR**	Kerr, John Melville b: 5/22/03, Souris, Man., Can. BL/TL, 5'11.5", 155 lbs. Deb: 9/16/25 C																											
1925	Chi-N	1	0	1	0	0	0	0	0	0	0	—	—	—	—	—	0	0	97	—	—	—	0	0	0	0	R	0.0
■ **DAN KERWIN**	Kerwin, Daniel Patrick (born Daniel Patrick Kervin) b: 7/9/1879, Philadelphia, Pa. d: 7/13/60, Philadelphia, Pa. BL/TL, 5'9", 164 lbs. Deb: 03																											
1903	Cin-N	2	6	1	4	1	0	0	1	2		.667	.750	.833	1.583	326	2	2	109	66	4	3.500	0			0	/O	0.2
■ **DON KESSINGER**	Kessinger, Donald Eulon b: 7/17/42, Forrest City, Ark. BB/TR, 6'1", 170 lbs. Deb: 9/07/64 M																											
1964	Chi-N	4	12	1	2	0	0	0	0	0	1	.167	.167	.167	.333	-5	-2	-2	105	0	0	.200	0	0	0	0	/S	0.0
1965	Chi-N	106	309	19	62	4	3	0	14	20	44	.201	.254	.233	.487	37	-25	-26	102	81	18	.374	1	2	-1	0	*S	-1.5

YEAR	TM/L	G	AB	R	H	2B	3B	HR	RBI	BB	SO	AVG	OBP	SLG	PRO	/A	BR	/A	PF	CHI	RC	TA	SB	CS	SBR	FR	POS	TPR
1966	Chi-N	150	533	50	146	8	2	1	43	26	46	.274	.308	.302	.610	70	-21	-21	100	112	49	.494	13	7	-0	-8	*S	-1.7
1967	Chi-N	145	580	61	134	10	7	0	42	33	80	.231	.277	.272	.550	57	-31	-32	102	106	43	.435	6	13	-6	-6	*S	-3.0
1968	Chi-N	160	655	63	157	14	7	1	32	38	86	.240	.283	.287	.570	64	-22	-31	112	62	54	.461	9	9	-3	20	*S	0.7
1969	Chi-N	158	664	109	181	38	6	4	53	61	70	.273	.335	.366	.701	90	-3	-8	107	72	84	.637	11	8	-2	**25**	*S	3.5
1970	Chi-N	154	631	100	168	21	14	1	39	66	59	.266	.338	.349	.686	70	-13	-30	120	59	76	.624	12	6	0	7	*S	-0.2
1971	Chi-N	155	617	77	159	18	6	2	38	52	54	.258	.318	.316	.634	73	-15	-22	110	68	63	.556	15	8	-0	4	*S	0.3
1972	Chi-N	149	577	77	158	20	6	1	39	67	44	.274	.351	.334	.686	84	-1	-11	114	79	70	.618	8	7	-2	11	*S	1.7
1973	Chi-N	160	577	52	151	22	3	0	43	57	44	.262	.328	.310	.638	72	-16	-22	108	98	57	.541	6	6	-2	18	*S	1.6
1974	Chi-N	153	599	83	155	20	7	1	42	62	54	.259	.332	.321	.653	83	-12	-12	100	88	64	.570	7	7	-2	4	*S	0.7
1975	Chi-N	154	601	77	146	26	10	0	46	68	47	.243	.321	.319	.640	75	-17	-20	104	89	66	.569	4	7	-3	2	*S3	-0.4
1976	StL-N	145	502	55	120	22	6	1	40	61	51	.239	.323	.313	.635	78	-11	-14	104	98	53	.562	3	0	1	4	*S2/3	0.3
1977	StL-N	59	134	14	32	4	0	0	7	14	26	.239	.311	.269	.579	60	-8	-7	96	78	12	.476	0	0	0	3	S2/3	0.1
	Chi-A	39	119	12	28	3	2	0	11	13	7	.235	.311	.294	.605	66	-5	-5	99	125	11	.526	2	1	0	-7	S2/3	-0.8
1978	Chi-A	131	431	35	110	18	1	1	31	36	34	.255	.313	.309	.621	75	-14	-14	101	90	41	.510	2	4	-2	-10	*S/2	-1.5
1979	Chi-A	56	110	14	22	6	0	1	7	10	12	.200	.267	.282	.548	47	-8	-8	102	79	8	.452	1	0	0	-2	S/12	-0.2
Total	16	2078	7651	899	1931	254	80	14	527	684	759	.252	.316	.312	.628	72	-225	-285	107	84	769	.550	100	85	-21	65	*S/231	-0.4

■ **HENRY KESSLER** Kessler, Henry "Lucky" b: 1847, Brooklyn, N.Y. d: 1/9/1900, Franklin, Pa. BR/TR, 5'10", 144 lbs. Deb: 8/04/1873

YEAR	TM/L	G	AB	R	H	2B	3B	HR	RBI	BB	SO	AVG	OBP	SLG	PRO	/A	BR	/A	PF	CHI	RC	TA	SB	CS	SBR	FR	POS	TPR
1873	Atl-n	1	6	0	1							.167															/1	
1874	Atl-n	14	57	8	16							.281															/C2O3	
1875	Atl-n	25	108	17	26							.241															S/OC2	
1876	Cin-N	59	248	26	64	5	0	0	11	7	10	.258	.278	.278	.557	96	-3	1	90	52	20	.413				-16	SO	-1.3
1877	Cin-N	6	20	0	2	0	0	0	0	2	1	.100	.182	.100	.282	-11	-2	-2	82	0	0	.222				0	/C1	-0.1
Total	3 n	40	171	25	43							.251															/C1	
Total	2	65	268	26	66	5	0	0	11	9	11	.246	.271	.265	.536	88	-6	-1	89	48	20	.396				-16	/SOC213	-1.4

■ **FRED KETCHUM** Ketchum, Frederick L. b: 7/27/1875, Elmira, N.Y. d: 3/12/08, Cortland, N.Y. BL/TR, Deb: 9/12/1899

YEAR	TM/L	G	AB	R	H	2B	3B	HR	RBI	BB	SO	AVG	OBP	SLG	PRO	/A	BR	/A	PF	CHI	RC	TA	SB	CS	SBR	FR	POS	TPR
1899	Lou-N	15	61	13	18	1	0	0	5	0		.295	.306	.311	.618	70	-2	-3	103	85	7	.512	2			0	O	-0.1
1901	Phi-A	5	22	5	5	0	0	0	2	0		.227	.227	.227	.455	28	-2	-2	100	121	1	.294	0			1	/O	0.0
Total	2	20	83	18	23	1	0	0	7	0		.277	.286	.289	.575	59	-4	-5	103	95	8	.450	2			1	/O	-0.1

■ **PHIL KETTER** Ketter, Philip b: Hutchinson, Kan. TR , Deb: 5/23/12

YEAR	TM/L	G	AB	R	H	2B	3B	HR	RBI	BB	SO	AVG	OBP	SLG	PRO	/A	BR	/A	PF	CHI	RC	TA	SB	CS	SBR	FR	POS	TPR
1912	StL-A	2	6	1	2	0	0	0	0	0		.333	.333	.333	.667	92	-0	-0	99	0	1	.500	0			0	/C	0.0

■ **SAM KHALIFA** Khalifa, Sam b: 12/5/63, Fontana, Cal. BR/TR, 5'11", 170 lbs. Deb: 6/25/85

YEAR	TM/L	G	AB	R	H	2B	3B	HR	RBI	BB	SO	AVG	OBP	SLG	PRO	/A	BR	/A	PF	CHI	RC	TA	SB	CS	SBR	FR	POS	TPR
1985	Pit-N	95	320	30	76	14	3	2	31	34	56	.237	.311	.319	.629	74	-10	-11	103	117	32	.553	5	2	0	12	S	0.9
1986	Pit-N	64	151	8	28	6	0	0	4	19	28	.185	.276	.225	.502	40	-12	-12	100	47	9	.408	0	2	-1	4	S/2	-0.3
1987	Pit-N	5	17	1	3	0	0	0	2	0	2	.176	.176	.176	.353	-6	-3	-3	104	266	1	.214	0	0	0	-0	/S	-0.1
Total	3	164	488	39	107	20	3	2	37	53	86	.219	.296	.285	.581	61	-24	-25	102	99	41	.512	5	4	-1	15	S/2	0.5

■ **HOD KIBBIE** Kibbie, Horace Kent b: 7/18/03, Ft.Worth, Tex. d: 10/19/75, Ft.Worth, Tex. BR/TR, 5'10", 150 lbs. Deb: 6/13/25

YEAR	TM/L	G	AB	R	H	2B	3B	HR	RBI	BB	SO	AVG	OBP	SLG	PRO	/A	BR	/A	PF	CHI	RC	TA	SB	CS	SBR	FR	POS	TPR
1925	Bos-N	11	41	5	11	2	0	0	2	5	6	.268	.348	.317	.665	76	-2	-1	94	56	5	.600	0	0	0	-1	/2S	-0.1

■ **JACK KIBBLE** Kibble, John Westly "Happy" b: 1/2/1892, Seatonville, Ill. d: 12/13/69, Roundup, Mont. BB/TR, 5'9.5", 154 lbs. Deb: 9/10/12

YEAR	TM/L	G	AB	R	H	2B	3B	HR	RBI	BB	SO	AVG	OBP	SLG	PRO	/A	BR	/A	PF	CHI	RC	TA	SB	CS	SBR	FR	POS	TPR
1912	Cle-A	5	8	1	0	0	0	0	0	0		.000	.111	.000	.111	-67	-2	-2	101	0	0	.125	0			0	/32	-0.1

■ **STEVE KIEFER** Kiefer, Steven George b: 10/18/60, Chicago, Ill. BR/TR, 6'1", 175 lbs. Deb: 9/03/84

YEAR	TM/L	G	AB	R	H	2B	3B	HR	RBI	BB	SO	AVG	OBP	SLG	PRO	/A	BR	/A	PF	CHI	RC	TA	SB	CS	SBR	FR	POS	TPR
1984	Oak-A	23	40	7	7	1	2	0	2	2	10	.175	.214	.300	.514	44	-3	-3	92	66	3	.471	2	1	0	-1	S/3D	-0.1
1985	Oak-A	40	66	8	13	1	1	1	10	1	18	.197	.209	.288	.497	37	-6	-5	93	180	4	.370	0	0	0	-2	3/D	-0.8
1986	Mil-A	2	6	0	0	0	0	0	0	0	4	.000	.000	.000	.000	-98	-2	-2	102	0	0	.000	0	0	0	-1	/S	-0.1
1987	Mil-A	28	99	17	20	4	0	5	17	7	28	.202	.262	.394	.656	70	-4	-5	102	128	10	.573	0	0	0	-2	3/2	-0.6
1988	Mil-A	7	10	2	3	1	0	1	1	2	3	.300	.462	.700	1.162	213	2	2	103	40	4	1.429	0	0	0	0	/23	0.2
Total	5	100	221	34	43	7	3	7	30	12	63	.195	.243	.348	.591	59	-13	-13	98	124	20	.520	2	1	0	-6	/3S2D	-1.4

■ **BILL KIENZLE** Kienzle, William H. b: Philadelphia, Pa. BL/TL, Deb: 9/15/1882

YEAR	TM/L	G	AB	R	H	2B	3B	HR	RBI	BB	SO	AVG	OBP	SLG	PRO	/A	BR	/A	PF	CHI	RC	TA	SB	CS	SBR	FR	POS	TPR
1882	Phi-a	9	33	8	11	3	2	0		5		.333	.421	.545	.967	200	4	4	112	0	8	1.045				0	/O	0.3
1884	Phi-U	67	299	76	76	13	8	0		21		.254	.303	.351	.654	130	7	10	93	0	33	.565	0			-2	O	0.6
Total	2	76	332	84	87	16	10	0		26		.262	.316	.370	.686	139	11	14	95	0	40	.608	0			-2	/O	0.9

■ **PETE KILDUFF** Kilduff, Peter John b: 4/4/1893, Weir City, Kan. d: 2/14/30, Pittsburg, Kan. BR/TR, 5'7", 155 lbs. Deb: 4/18/17

YEAR	TM/L	G	AB	R	H	2B	3B	HR	RBI	BB	SO	AVG	OBP	SLG	PRO	/A	BR	/A	PF	CHI	RC	TA	SB	CS	SBR	FR	POS	TPR
1917	NY-N	31	78	12	16	3	0	1	12	4	11	.205	.253	.282	.535	66	-3	-3	97	185	6	.468	2			-1	2/S3	-0.2
	Chi-N	56	202	23	56	9	5	0	15	12	19	.277	.324	.371	.695	108	3	2	105	82	27	.685	11			-17	S/2	-1.6
	Yr	87	280	35	72	12	5	1	27	16	30	.257	.304	.346	.651	98	-1	-1	102	121	32	.620	13			-18		-1.8
1918	Chi-N	30	93	7	19	2	2	0	13	7	7	.204	.267	.269	.536	62	-4	-4	102	197	8	.459	1			-2	2	-0.4
1919	Chi-N	31	88	5	24	4	2	0	8	10	5	.273	.360	.364	.724	117	2	2	100	97	12	.703	1			0	3/2S	0.3
	Bro-N	32	73	9	22	3	1	0	8	12	11	.301	.407	.370	.777	143	4	4	94	115	13	.882	5			-2	3/2	0.3
	Yr	63	161	14	46	7	3	0	16	22	16	.286	.382	.366	.748	129	6	7	97	108	24	.783	6			-2		0.6
1920	Bro-N	141	478	62	130	26	8	0	58	58	43	.272	.351	.360	.711	94	4	-3	111	133	61	.650	2	9	-5	11	*2/3	0.7
1921	Bro-N	107	372	45	107	15	10	3	45	31	36	.288	.344	.406	.750	93	-1	-4	105	105	52	.697	6	6	-2	6	*2/3	0.1
Total	5	428	1384	163	374	62	28	4	159	134	132	.270	.338	.364	.702	96	4	-5	105	122	178	.658	28	15		-5	2/S3	-0.8

■ **JOHN KILEY** Kiley, John Frederick b: 7/1/1859, S.Dedham, Mass. d: 12/18/40, Norwood, Mass. BL/TL, Deb: 5/01/1884

YEAR	TM/L	G	AB	R	H	2B	3B	HR	RBI	BB	SO	AVG	OBP	SLG	PRO	/A	BR	/A	PF	CHI	RC	TA	SB	CS	SBR	FR	POS	TPR
1884	Was-a	14	56	9	12	2	2	0		3		.214	.267	.321	.588	106	-0	1	88	0	5	.500				0	O	0.1
1891	Bos-N	1	2	0	0	0	0	0	0	1	1	.000	.500	.000	.500	47	0	0	112	0	0	1.000	0			0	/P	0.0
Total	2	15	58	9	12	2	2	0	0	4	1	.207	.281	.310	.592	105	-0	1	90	0	5	.522	0			0	/OP	0.1

■ **PAT KILHULLEN** Kilhullen, Joseph Isadore b: 8/10/1890, Carbondale, Pa. d: 11/2/22, Oakland, Cal. BR/TR, 5'9", 175 lbs. Deb: 6/10/14

YEAR	TM/L	G	AB	R	H	2B	3B	HR	RBI	BB	SO	AVG	OBP	SLG	PRO	/A	BR	/A	PF	CHI	RC	TA	SB	CS	SBR	FR	POS	TPR
1914	Pit-N	1	1	0	0	0	0	0	0	0	0	.000	.000	.000	.000	-99	-0	-0	92	0	0	.000	0			0	/C	0.0

■ **HARMON KILLEBREW** Killebrew, Harmon Clayton "Killer" b: 6/29/36, Payette, Idaho BR/TR, 6', 195 lbs. Deb: 6/23/54 H

YEAR	TM/L	G	AB	R	H	2B	3B	HR	RBI	BB	SO	AVG	OBP	SLG	PRO	/A	BR	/A	PF	CHI	RC	TA	SB	CS	SBR	FR	POS	TPR
1954	Was-A	9	13	1	4	1	0	0	3	2	3	.308	.400	.385	.785	118	0	0	98	228	2	.700	0	0	0	0	/2	0.0
1955	Was-A	38	80	12	16	1	0	4	7	9	31	.200	.281	.363	.643	79	-4	-3	91	64	8	.567	0	0	0	1	3/2	0.0
1956	Was-A	44	99	10	22	2	0	5	13	10	39	.222	.294	.394	.688	79	-3	-4	102	90	11	.620	0	0	0	1	3/2	-0.1
1957	Was-A	9	31	4	9	2	0	2	5	2	8	.290	.333	.548	.882	140	1	1	98	86	6	.864	0	0	0	0	/32	0.2
1958	Was-A	13	31	2	6	0	0	0	2	0	12	.194	.219	.194	.412	15	-4	-3	97	134	1	.280	0	0	0	-1	/3	-0.4
1959	Was-A	153	546	98	132	20	2	**42**	105	90	116	.242	.356	.516	.873	136	27	27	100	107	103	.893	3	2	-0	-8	*3/O	1.8
1960	Was-A	124	442	84	122	19	1	31	80	71	106	.276	.377	.534	.911	141	27	26	102	97	91	.936	1	0	0	-6	13	1.7
1961	Min-A	150	541	94	156	20	7	46	122	107	109	.288	.409	.606	1.015	158	53	48	106	99	138	1.103	1	2	-1	-9	*13/O	2.9
1962	Min-A	155	552	85	134	21	1	**48**	**126**	106	142	.243	.369	.545	.914	136	33	29	105	119	113	.949	1	2	-1	-13	*O/1	1.0
1963	Min-A	142	515	88	133	18	0	**45**	96	72	105	.258	.353	**.555**	.908	149	33	33	100	101	99	.907	0	0	0	-9	*O	2.1
1964	Min-A	158	577	95	156	11	1	**49**	111	93	135	.270	.379	.548	.927	153	43	43	101	108	122	.956	0	0	0	-12	*O	2.5
1965	Min-A	113	401	78	108	16	1	25	75	72	69	.269	.386	.501	.887	148	28	27	101	119	79	.914	0	0	0	-5	13/O	2.1
1966	Min-A	162	569	89	160	27	1	39	110	**103**	98	.281	.393	.538	.931	148	50	42	111	116	122	.972	0	2	-1	-11	*31O	2.6
1967	Min-A	163	547	105	147	24	1	**44**	113	**131**	111	.269	.413	.558	.970	173	62	58	107	114	131	1.058	1	0	0	-8	*1/3	4.1
1968	Min-A	100	295	40	62	7	2	17	40	70	70	.210	.365	.420	.785	130	16	14	106	100	46	.797	0	0	0	2	13	1.4
1969	Min-A	162	555	106	153	20	2	**49**	**140**	**145**	84	.276	**.430**	.584	1.014	178	**66**	64	102	126	**146**	**1.148**	8	2	1	-10	*31	5.2
1970	Min-A	157	527	96	143	20	1	41	113	128	84	.271	.416	.546	.962	166	50	51	98	118	116	1.007	0	3	-2	-21	*31	2.8
1971	Min-A	147	500	61	127	19	1	28	**119**	**114**	96	.254	.393	.464	.857	136	31	29	104	**163**	92	.881	3	2	-0	-10	13	1.3
1972	Min-A	139	433	53	100	13	2	26	74	94	91	.231	.369	.450	.820	133	26	22	107	116	73	.829	0	1	-1	10	*1	2.1
1973	Min-A	69	248	29	60	9	1	5	32	41	59	.242	.352	.347	.698	94	0	-1	104	127	31	.646	0	0	0	3	1/D	-0.1

YEAR	TM/L	G	AB	R	H	2B	3B	HR	RBI	BB	SO	AVG	OBP	SLG	PRO	/A	BR	/A	PF	CHI	RC	TA	SB	CS	SBR	FR	POS	TPR
1974	Min-A	122	333	28	74	7	0	13	54	45	61	.222	.315	.360	.675	93	-2	-3	101	134	37	.609	0	0	0	2	D1	-0.1
1975	KC-A	106	312	25	62	13	0	14	44	54	70	.199	.319	.375	.694	94	-2	-2	102	106	39	.673	1	2	-1	0	D/1	-0.3
Total	22	2435	8147	1283	2086	290	24	573	1584	1559	1699	.256	.379	.509	.887	142	532	498	103	115	1609	.948	19	18	-5	-102	13OD/2	32.8
■ **RED KILLEFER**	Killefer, Wade Hampton b: 4/13/1884, Bloomingdale, Mich d: 9/4/58, Los Angeles, Cal. BR/TR, 5′9″, 175 lbs. Deb: 9/16/07																											
1907	Det-A	1	4	0	0	0	0	0	0	0		.000	.000	.000	.000	-99	-1	-1	102	0	0	.000	0			0	/O	0.0
1908	Det-A	28	75	9	16	1	0	0	11	3		.213	.244	.227	.470	54	-4	-4	101	243	5	.407	4			-1	2/S3	-0.5
1909	Det-A	23	61	6	17	2	2	1	4	3		.279	.343	.426	.770	130	3	2	110	53	9	.773	2			0	2/O	0.2
	Was-A	40	121	11	21	1	0	0	5	13		.174	.265	.182	.447	46	-8	-6	90	89	7	.410	4			1	O/3C2S	-0.6
	Yr	63	182	17	38	3	2	1	9	16		.209	.291	.264	.554	77	-5	-4	97	77	15	.521	6			1		-0.4
1910	Was-A	106	345	35	79	17	1	0	24	29		.229	.318	.284	.602	88	-3	-4	101	96	39	.602	17			-6	2O	-1.7
1914	Cin-N	42	141	16	39	6	1	0	12	20	18	.277	.386	.333	.719	109	4	3	105	98	22	.814	11			-2	O/23	0.0
1915	Cin-N	155	555	75	151	25	11	1	41	38	33	.272	.340	.362	.702	110	9	7	103	81	69	.640	12	18	-7	-3	*O/1	-0.7
1916	Cin-N	70	234	29	57	9	1	1	18	21	8	.244	.327	.303	.630	96	-1	-0	98	98	26	.605	7			0	O	-0.2
	NY-N	2	1	0	1	0	0	0	1	1	0	1.000	1.000	1.000	2.000	538	1	1	96	397	1	—	0			0	H	0.1
	Yr	72	235	29	58	9	1	1	19	22	8	.247	.332	.306	.638	99	0	1	98	108	27	.616	7			0		-0.1
Total	7	467	1537	181	381	61	16	3	116	128	59	.248	.327	.314	.641	97	0	-2	101	96	178	.614	57	18		-11	O2/3SC1	-3.4
■ **BILL KILLEFER**	Killefer, William Lavier b: 10/10/1887, Bloomingdale, Mich d: 7/3/60, Elsmere, Del. BR/TR, 5′10.5″, 200 lbs. Deb: 9/13/09 MC																											
1909	StL-A	11	29	0	4	0	0	0	1	0		.138	.138	.138	.276	-14	-4	-3	92	96	1	.240	2			1	C	-0.1
1910	StL-A	74	193	14	24	2	2	0	7	12		.124	.184	.155	.339	7	-21	-20	94	86	6	.260	0			7	C	-0.5
1911	Phi-N	6	16	3	3	0	0	0	2	0	2	.188	.188	.188	.375	5	-2	-2	108	225	1	.231	0			0	/C	-0.1
1912	Phi-N	85	268	18	60	6	3	1	21	4	14	.224	.241	.280	.521	42	-22	-22	100	91	20	.418	6			3	C	-1.4
1913	Phi-N	120	360	25	88	14	3	0	24	4	17	.244	.255	.300	.555	52	-20	-26	112	81	27	.423	2			4	*C/1	-1.4
1914	Phi-N	98	299	27	70	10	1	0	27	8	17	.234	.261	.274	.536	59	-16	-16	100	119	22	.419	3			10	C	-0.2
1915	Phi-N	105	320	26	76	9	2	0	24	18	14	.237	.287	.278	.565	66	-11	-14	107	103	26	.470	5	3	-0	-10	*C	-1.9
1916	Phi-N	97	286	22	62	5	4	3	27	8	14	.217	.246	.294	.539	68	-12	-11	96	115	22	.433	2			-8	C	-1.5
1917	Phi-N	125	409	28	112	12	0	0	31	15	21	.274	.306	.303	.609	81	-6	-10	108	96	38	.495	4			5	*C/O	0.1
1918	Chi-N	104	331	30	77	10	3	0	22	17	10	.233	.276	.281	.557	69	-12	-13	102	89	27	.465	5			-9	*C	-1.4
1919	Chi-N	103	315	17	90	10	2	0	22	15	8	.286	.322	.330	.652	96	-1	-2	100	82	35	.560	5			1	*C	0.6
1920	Chi-N	62	191	16	42	7	1	0	16	8	5	.220	.280	.267	.547	58	-10	-10	99	121	15	.457	2	2	-1	4	C	-0.2
1921	Chi-N	45	133	11	43	1	0	0	16	4	4	.323	.357	.331	.688	78	-3	-4	107	133	15	.581	3	3	-1	1	CM	0.0
Total	13	1035	3150	237	751	86	21	4	240	113	126	.238	.273	.283	.555	63	-141	-151	103	100	255	.448	39	8		9	*C/O1	-8.0
■ **GENE KIMBALL**	Kimball, Eugene B. b: 8/31/1850, Rochester, N.Y. d: 8/2/1882, Rochester, N.Y. 5′10″, 160 lbs. Deb: 5/04/1871																											
1871	Cle-n	29	136	18	25							.184															2/SO	
■ **DICK KIMBLE**	Kimble, Richard Lewis b: 7/27/15, Buchtel, Ohio BL/TR, 5′9″, 160 lbs. Deb: 8/20/45																											
1945	Was-A	20	49	5	12	1	1	0	1	5	2	.245	.315	.306	.621	86	-1	-1	93	24	5	.513	0	0	0	-2	S	-0.1
■ **BRUCE KIMM**	Kimm, Bruce Edward b: 6/29/51, Cedar Rapids, Iowa BR/TR, 5′11″, 175 lbs. Deb: 5/04/76 C																											
1976	Det-A	63	152	13	40	8	0	1	6	15	20	.263	.329	.336	.665	92	-1	-1	104	43	17	.598	4	3	-1	0	C/D	0.0
1977	Det-A	14	25	2	2	1	0	0	1	0	4	.080	.115	.120	.235	-34	-5	-5	105	132	0	.160	0	1	-1	1	C/D	-0.3
1979	Chi-N	9	11	0	1	0	0	0	0	0	0	.091	.091	.091	.182	-45	-2	-2	112	0	0	.091	0	1	-1	-1	/C	-0.3
1980	Chi-A	100	251	20	61	10	1	0	19	17	26	.243	.291	.291	.582	62	-14	-12	97	101	19	.448	1	3	-2	-14	C	-2.3
Total	4	186	439	35	104	19	1	1	26	32	50	.237	.290	.292	.582	63	-21	-21	100	80	37	.470	5	8	-3	-13	C/D	-2.9
■ **WALLY KIMMICK**	Kimmick, Walter Lyons b: 5/30/1897, Turtle Creek, Pa. BR/TR, 5′11″, 174 lbs. Deb: 9/13/19																											
1919	StL-N	2	1	1	0	0	0	0	0	1	0	.000	.500	.000	.500	60	0	0	94	0	0	2.000	1			0	/S	0.0
1921	Cin-N	3	6	0	1	0	0	0	1	0	1	.167	.167	.167	.333	-11	-1	-1	101	367	0	.200	0	0	0	0	/3	0.0
1922	Cin-N	39	89	11	22	2	1	0	12	3	12	.247	.272	.292	.564	47	-7	-7	96	161	7	.433	0	0	0	-0	S/23	-0.4
1923	Cin-N	29	80	11	18	2	1	0	6	5	15	.225	.271	.275	.546	45	-6	-6	98	96	7	.484	3	0	1	2	2/3S	-0.2
1925	Phi-N	70	141	16	43	3	2	1	10	22	26	.305	.399	.376	.775	86	1	-3	116	63	21	.743	0	3	-2	-3	S32	-0.2
1926	Phi-N	20	28	0	6	2	1	0	2	3	7	.214	.290	.357	.647	71	-1	-1	103	69	3	.591	0			0	/1S32	0.0
Total	6	163	345	39	90	9	5	1	31	34	61	.261	.327	.325	.652	66	-15	-18	105	99	39	.581	4	3		-1	/S231	-0.8
■ **JERRY KINDALL**	Kindall, Gerald Donald "Slim" b: 5/27/35, St.Paul, Minn. BR/TR, 6′2.5″, 175 lbs. Deb: 7/01/56																											
1956	Chi-N	32	55	7	9	1	1	0	0	6	17	.164	.246	.218	.464	27	-6	-6	99	0	3	.396	1	0	0	-2	S	-0.5
1957	Chi-N	72	181	18	29	3	0	6	12	8	48	.160	.196	.276	.472	26	-19	-19	96	73	9	.378	1	0	0	-0	23/S	-1.5
1958	Chi-N	3	6	0	1	1	0	0	0	0	3	.167	.167	.333	.500	28	-1	-1	101	0	0	.400	0	0	0	0	/2	0.0
1960	Chi-N	89	246	17	59	16	2	2	23	5	52	.240	.255	.346	.601	64	-13	-13	98	103	19	.477	4	3	-1	7	2/S	0.1
1961	Chi-N	96	310	37	75	22	3	9	44	18	89	.242	.288	.419	.707	85	-8	-8	100	113	36	.628	2	2	-1	6	2S	0.8
1962	Cle-A	154	530	51	123	21	1	13	55	45	107	.232	.292	.349	.641	73	-22	-20	98	99	53	.553	4	3	-1	21	*2	1.1
1963	Cle-A	86	234	27	48	4	1	5	20	18	71	.205	.268	.295	.563	59	-13	-12	97	100	19	.479	3	1	0	-6	S2/1	-1.3
1964	Cle-A	23	25	5	9	1	0	2	2	2	7	.360	.407	.640	1.047	181	3	3	103	38	6	1.059	0	0	0	-1	1	0.1
	Min-A	62	128	8	19	2	0	1	6	7	44	.148	.199	.188	.386	8	-16	-16	101	94	5	.288	0	0	0	-3	2/S1	-1.3
	Yr	85	153	13	28	3	0	3	8	9	51	.183	.233	.261	.495	37	-13	-13	101	79	10	.394	0	0	0	-3		-1.2
1965	Min-A	125	342	41	67	12	1	6	36	36	97	.196	.278	.289	.568	61	-17	-18	101	128	29	.495	2	2	-1	-3	*23/S	-1.5
Total	9	742	2057	211	439	83	9	44	198	145	535	.213	.268	.327	.595	62	-112	-108	99	100	180	.515	17	11	-2	21	2S/31	-4.0
■ **RALPH KINER**	Kiner, Ralph Mc Pherran b: 10/27/22, Santa Rita, N.Mex. BR/TR, 6′2″, 195 lbs. Deb: 4/16/46 H																											
1946	Pit-N	144	502	63	124	17	3	**23**	81	74	109	.247	.345	.430	.775	116	12	10	103	108	75	.748	3			-9	*O	-0.1
1947	Pit-N	152	565	118	177	23	4	**51**	127	98	81	.313	.417	**.639**	**1.055**	**175**	**61**	**61**	101	97	**154**	**1.155**	1			9	*O	**6.2**
1948	Pit-N	156	555	104	147	19	5	**40**	123	112	61	.265	.391	.533	.924	142	38	35	104	117	120	.974	1			-9	*O	1.5
1949	Pit-N	152	549	116	170	19	5	**54**	**127**	**117**	61	.310	.432	**.658**	**1.089**	**187**	70	**69**	101	88	163	**1.247**	6			-3	*O	**5.6**
1950	Pit-N	150	547	112	149	21	6	**47**	118	122	79	.272	.408	.590	.998	155	49	47	103	94	133	1.071	2			-1	*O	3.9
1951	Pit-N	151	531	**124**	164	31	6	**42**	109	**137**	57	.309	**.452**	**.627**	**1.079**	176	**71**	66	107	88	165	**1.254**	2	1	0	-2	O1	5.8
1952	Pit-N	149	516	90	126	17	2	**37**	87	**110**	77	.244	.384	.500	.884	144	33	33	100	97	111	.955	3	0	1	-11	*O	1.9
1953	Pit-N	41	148	27	40	6	1	7	29	25	21	.270	.383	.466	.849	118	5	5	102	133	30	.890	1	0	0	-1	O	0.2
	Chi-N	117	414	73	117	14	2	28	87	75	67	.283	.394	.529	.923	134	24	22	103	119	91	.961	1	1	-0	-5	*O	1.2
	Yr	158	562	100	157	20	3	35	116	100	88	.279	.391	.512	.903	130	29	27	103	123	121	.945	2	1	0	-5		1.4
1954	Chi-N	147	557	88	159	36	5	22	73	76	90	.285	.373	.487	.860	121	18	18	101	90	101	.846	2	0	1	-2	*O	1.1
1955	Cle-A	113	321	56	78	13	0	18	54	65	46	.243	.370	.452	.822	116	10	8	104	101	57	.837	0	0	0	-7	O	-0.3
Total	10	1472	5205	971	1451	216	39	369	1015	1011	749	.279	.398	.548	.946	148	391	373	102	100	1201	1.039	22	2		-41	*O/1	27.0
■ **CHICK KING**	King, Charles Gilbert b: 11/10/30, Paris, Tenn. BR/TR, 6′2″, 190 lbs. Deb: 8/27/54																											
1954	Det-A	11	28	4	6	0	1	0	3	3	8	.214	.290	.286	.576	58	-2	-2	100	142	2	.478	0	0	0	2	/O	0.0
1955	Det-A	7	21	3	5	0	0	0	0	1	2	.238	.273	.238	.511	40	-2	-2	97	0	1	.375	0	0	0	-1	/O	-0.2
1956	Det-A	7	9	0	2	0	0	0	0	1	4	.222	.300	.222	.522	41	-1	-1	97	0	1	.429	0	0	0	-1	/O	-0.1
1958	Chi-N	8	8	1	2	0	0	0	1	3	1	.250	.455	.250	.705	93	0	0	101	207	1	.833	0	0	0	-2	/O	-0.1
1959	Chi-N	7	3	3	0	0	0	0	0	0	1	.000	.000	.000	.000	-99	-1	-1	98	0	0	.000	0	0	0	0	/O	0.0
	StL-N	5	7	0	3	0	0	0	1	0	2	.429	.429	.429	.857	123	0	0	105	135	1	.750	0	0	0	-0	/O	0.0
	Yr	12	10	3	3	0	0	0	1	0	3	.300	.300	.300	.600	60	-1	-1	101	56	1	.429	0	0	0	-0		0.0
Total	5	45	76	11	18	0	1	0	5	8	18	.237	.310	.263	.573	56	-5	-4	99	91	7	.483	0	0	0	-1	/O	-0.4
■ **LEE KING**	King, Edward Lee b: 3/28/1894, Waltham, Mass. d: 9/7/38, Newton Centre, Mass. BR/TR, 5′10″, 160 lbs. Deb: 6/24/16																											
1916	Phi-A	42	144	13	27	1	2	0	8	7	15	.188	.230	.222	.452	37	-11	-11	98	91	9	.376	4			-5	OS/32	-1.7
1919	Bos-N	2	1	0	0	0	0	0	0	0	0	.000	.000	.000	.000	-99	-0	-0	98	0	0	.000	0			0	H	0.0
Total	2	44	145	13	27	1	2	0	8	7	15	.186	.229	.221	.449	36	-12	-11	98	90	9	.373	4			-5	/OS32	-1.7

YEAR	TM/L	G	AB	R	H	2B	3B	HR	RBI	BB	SO	AVG	OBP	SLG	PRO	/A	BR	/A	PF	CHI	RC	TA	SB	CS	SBR	FR	POS	TPR
■ HAL KING	King, Harold b: 2/1/44, Oviedo, Fla. BL/TR, 6'1", 200 lbs. Deb: 9/06/67																											
1967	Hou-N	15	44	2	11	1	2	0	6	2	9	.250	.283	.364	.646	89	-1	-1	94	155	5	.545	0	0	0	1	C	0.0
1968	Hou-N	27	55	4	8	2	1	0	2	7	16	.145	.242	.218	.460	39	-4	-4	99	70	3	.396	0	0	0	-1	C	-0.4
1970	Atl-N	89	204	29	53	8	0	11	30	32	41	.260	.366	.461	.826	115	6	5	104	92	35	.827	1	0	0	-5	C	0.3
1971	Atl-N	86	198	14	41	9	0	5	19	29	43	.207	.320	.328	.649	76	-4	-6	110	97	20	.590	0	0	0	-1	C	-0.5
1972	Tex-A	50	122	12	22	5	0	4	12	25	35	.180	.333	.320	.653	101	0	1	94	98	14	.650	0	0	0	-1	C	0.0
1973	Cin-N	35	43	5	8	0	0	4	10	6	10	.186	.286	.465	.751	112	0	0	93	126	6	.743	0	0	0	0	/C	0.1
1974	Cin-N	20	17	1	3	1	0	0	3	3	4	.176	.300	.235	.535	52	-1	-1	98	290	1	.500	0	0	0	0	/C	0.0
Total	7	322	683	67	146	26	3	24	82	104	158	.214	.325	.366	.691	93	-3	-5	102	103	85	.678	1	0	0	-7	C	-0.5
■ JIM KING	King, James Hubert b: 8/27/32, Elkins, Ark. BL/TR, 6', 185 lbs. Deb: 4/17/55																											
1955	Chi-N	113	301	43	77	12	3	11	45	24	39	.256	.315	.425	.740	94	-3	-3	100	113	41	.684	2	1	0	4	O	0.0
1956	Chi-N	118	317	32	79	13	2	15	54	30	40	.249	.316	.445	.761	103	0	1	99	123	44	.709	1	2	-1	10	O	0.6
1957	StL-N	22	35	1	11	0	0	0	2	4	2	.314	.385	.314	.699	90	-0	-0	101	75	4	.625	0	0	0	-2	/O	-0.2
1958	SF-N	34	56	8	12	2	1	2	8	10	8	.214	.343	.393	.736	94	-0	-0	100	118	8	.733	0	1	-1	-3	O	-0.3
1961	Was-A	110	263	43	71	12	1	11	46	38	45	.270	.366	.449	.815	123	7	8	95	119	46	.831	4	0	1	-7	O/C	0.0
1962	Was-A	132	333	39	81	15	0	11	35	55	37	.243	.355	.387	.743	99	1	1	101	86	49	.737	4	2	0	1	*O	-0.1
1963	Was-A	136	459	61	106	16	5	24	62	45	43	.231	.301	.444	.745	108	2	4	98	96	60	.693	3	0	1	-1	*O	0.0
1964	Was-A	134	415	46	100	15	1	18	56	55	65	.241	.337	.412	.749	106	4	4	101	105	60	.727	3	1	0	7	*O	0.7
1965	Was-A	120	258	46	55	10	2	14	49	44	50	.213	.339	.430	.769	117	6	6	100	133	38	.759	1	0	0	-3	O	0.0
1966	Was-A	117	310	41	77	14	2	10	30	38	41	.248	.330	.403	.734	116	4	6	95	81	41	.687	4	0	1	-2	O	0.2
1967	Was-A	47	100	10	21	2	2	1	12	15	13	.210	.331	.300	.631	86	-1	-1	102	152	11	.598	1	1	-0	-3	O/C	-0.5
	Chi-A	23	50	2	6	1	0	0	2	4	16	.120	.185	.140	.325	-3	-6	-6	94	119	1	.244	0	0	0	-2	O	-0.8
	Cle-A	19	21	2	3	0	0	0	0	1	2	.143	.182	.143	.325	-3	-3	-3	100	0	1	.222	0	0	0	-0	/O	-0.2
	Yr	89	171	14	30	3	2	1	14	20	31	.175	.273	.234	.507	51	-10	-10	100	114	13	.451	1	1	-0	-5	O	-1.5
Total	11	1125	2918	374	699	112	19	117	401	363	401	.240	.328	.411	.740	104	11	16	99	107	406	.722	23	8	2	0	O/C	-0.6
■ LEE KING	King, Lee b: 12/26/1892, Hundred, W.Va. d: 9/16/67, Shinnstown, W.Va. BR/TR, 5'10", 175 lbs. Deb: 9/20/16																											
1916	Pit-N	8	18	0	2	0	0	0	1	0	7	.111	.111	.111	.222	-30	-3	-3	105	199	0	.125	0			-2	/O	-0.6
1917	Pit-N	111	381	32	95	14	5	1	35	15	58	.249	.281	.320	.602	85	-8	-8	100	110	35	.514	8			5	*O	-0.6
1918	Pit-N	36	112	9	26	3	2	1	11	11	15	.232	.301	.321	.622	85	-1	-2	106	107	11	.581	3			-9	O	-1.4
1919	NY-N	21	20	5	2	1	0	0	1	1	6	.100	.143	.150	.293	-12	-3	-3	100	130	0	.222	0			-3	/O	-0.6
1920	NY-N	93	261	32	72	11	4	7	42	21	38	.276	.335	.429	.764	119	6	6	100	122	36	.704	3	7	-3	-3	O	-0.5
1921	NY-N	39	94	17	21	4	2	0	7	13	6	.223	.324	.309	.633	70	-4	-4	98	89	10	.573	0	2	-1	-4	O/1	-1.0
	Phi-N	64	216	25	58	19	4	4	32	8	37	.269	.298	.449	.747	93	-3	-3	102	108	27	.660	1	4	-2	-3	O	-0.9
	Yr	103	310	42	79	23	6	4	39	21	43	.255	.306	.406	.713	87	-7	-7	100	101	37	.633	1	6	-3	-7		-1.9
1922	Phi-N	19	53	8	12	5	1	2	13	8	6	.226	.328	.472	.800	92	0	-1	113	147	9	.805	0	0	0	-0	O	-0.1
	NY-N	20	34	6	6	3	0	0	2	5	2	.176	.282	.265	.547	40	-3	-3	104	78	3	.536	1	0	0	1	/1O	-0.1
	Yr	39	87	14	18	8	1	2	15	13	8	.207	.310	.391	.701	74	-3	-4	108	115	11	.696	1	0	0	0		-0.2
Total	7	411	1189	134	294	60	18	15	144	82	175	.247	.299	.366	.665	88	-19	-20	101	112	131	.594	16	13		-20	O/1	-5.8
■ LYNN KING	King, Lynn Paul "Dig" b: 11/28/07, Villisca, Iowa d: 5/11/72, Atlantic, Iowa BL/TR, 5'9", 165 lbs. Deb: 9/21/35																											
1935	StL-N	8	22	6	4	0	0	0	0	4	1	.182	.308	.182	.490	34	-2	-2	104	0	1	.500	2			2	/O	0.0
1936	StL-N	78	100	12	19	2	1	0	10	9	14	.190	.257	.230	.487	34	-9	-9	94	154	6	.405	2			-4	O	-1.3
1939	StL-N	89	85	10	20	2	0	0	11	15	3	.235	.350	.259	.609	63	-3	-4	105	183	9	.591	2			-9	O	-1.3
Total	3	175	207	28	43	4	1	0	21	28	18	.208	.302	.237	.539	47	-15	-15	100	149	16	.503	6			-11	/O	-2.6
■ MART KING	King, Marshal Ney b: 1849, Troy, N.Y. d: 10/19/11, Troy, N.Y. 5'9.5", 176 lbs. Deb: 5/08/1871																											
1871	Chi-n	20	109	23	16							.147															O/CS	
1872	Tro-n	3	12	0	0							.000															O	
Total	2 n	23	121	23	16							.132															O	
■ SAM KING	King, Samuel Warren b: 5/17/1852, Peabody, Mass. d: 8/11/22, Peabody, Mass. TL , Deb: 5/01/1884																											
1884	Was-a	12	45	3	8	2	0	0		1		.178	.213	.222	.435	50	-3	-2	88	0	2	.324				0	1	-0.1
■ STEVE KING	King, Stephen F. b: 1845, Troy, N.Y. d: 7/8/1895, Troy, N.Y. 5'9", 175 lbs. Deb: 5/09/1871																											
1871	Tro-n	29	144	45	57							.396															*O	
1872	Tro-n	25	128	31	38							.297															O	
Total	2 n	54	272	76	95							.349															O	
■ WES KINGDON	Kingdon, Westcott William b: 7/4/1900, Los Angeles, Cal. d: 4/19/75, Capistrano, Cal. BR/TR, 5'8", 148 lbs. Deb: 6/12/32																											
1932	Was-A	18	34	10	11	3	1	0	3	5	2	.324	.410	.471	.881	128	2	2	100	63	7	.913	0	0	0	0	/3S	0.2
■ MIKE KINGERY	Kingery, Michael Scott b: 3/29/61, St.James, Minn. BL/TL, 6', 180 lbs. Deb: 7/07/86																											
1986	KC-A	62	209	25	54	8	5	3	14	12	30	.258	.299	.388	.686	86	-4	-4	100	62	23	.617	7	3	0	-1	O	-0.6
1987	Sea-A	120	354	38	99	25	4	9	52	27	43	.280	.334	.449	.783	104	3	2	103	112	51	.728	7	9	-3	9	*O/D	0.4
1988	Sea-A	57	123	21	25	6	0	1	9	19	23	.203	.315	.276	.591	62	-5	-6	108	97	12	.570	3	1	0	0	O1	-0.6
Total	3	239	686	84	178	39	9	13	75	58	96	.259	.320	.399	.719	91	-6	-9	103	94	87	.674	17	13	-3	8	O/1D	-0.8
■ DAVE KINGMAN	Kingman, David Arthur b: 12/21/48, Pendleton, Ore. BR/TR, 6'6", 210 lbs. Deb: 7/30/71																											
1971	SF-N	41	115	17	32	10	2	6	24	9	35	.278	.336	.557	.893	149	7	7	100	119	22	.929	5	0	2	-3	1O	0.3
1972	SF-N	135	472	65	106	17	4	29	83	51	140	.225	.306	.462	.767	116	8	8	100	114	67	.759	16	6	1	-4	31O	0.0
1973	SF-N	112	305	54	62	10	1	24	55	41	122	.203	.302	.479	.780	108	4	2	105	101	42	.770	8	5	-1	-4	31/P	-0.5
1974	SF-N	121	350	41	78	18	2	18	55	37	125	.223	.303	.440	.743	98	1	-2	108	102	44	.701	8	8	-2	2	13/O	-0.7
1975	NY-N	134	502	65	116	22	1	36	88	34	153	.231	.285	.494	.779	119	4	7	95	98	66	.725	7	5	-1	1	O13	0.2
1976	NY-N	123	474	70	113	14	1	37	86	28	135	.238	.288	.506	.794	133	10	14	92	100	65	.745	7	4	-0	1	*O1	1.0
1977	NY-N	58	211	22	44	7	0	9	28	13	66	.209	.264	.370	.634	71	-10	-9	96	109	20	.564	3	2	-0	-3	O1	-1.5
	SD-N	56	168	16	40	9	0	11	39	12	48	.238	.297	.488	.785	121	1	3	88	136	23	.731	2	3	-1	1	O1/3	0.1
	Yr	114	379	38	84	16	0	20	67	25	114	.222	.279	.422	.701	92	-10	-6	92	123	44	.644	5	5	-2	-3		-1.4
	Cal-A	10	36	4	7	2	0	2	4	1	16	.194	.237	.417	.654	78	-1	-1	95	77	4	.586	0	0	0	0	/1O	-0.1
	NY-A	8	24	5	6	2	0	4	7	2	13	.250	.333	.833	1.167	209	3	3	99	87	6	1.211	0	1	-1	0	/D	0.3
	Yr	18	60	9	13	4	0	6	11	3	29	.217	.277	.583	.860	132	2	2	96	85	9	.833	0	1	-1	0		0.2
1978	Chi-N	119	395	65	105	17	4	28	79	39	111	.266	.341	.542	.883	130	21	16	110	105	73	.882	3	4	-2	-13	*O/1	-0.2
1979	Chi-N	145	532	97	153	19	5	**48**	115	45	131	.288	.348	**.613**	**.960**	140	38	30	112	99	112	.977	4	2	0	-2	*O	2.4
1980	Chi-N	81	255	31	71	8	0	18	57	21	44	.278	.333	.522	.855	127	11	9	106	121	40	.796	2	2	-1	-1	O/1	0.4
1981	NY-N	100	353	40	78	11	3	22	59	55	105	.221	.328	.456	.784	120	9	9	101	108	54	.785	6	0	2	-5	1O	0.2
1982	NY-N	149	535	80	109	9	1	**37**	99	59	156	.204	.288	.432	.719	100	-3	-2	99	116	67	.682	4	0	1	-12	*1	-2.0
1983	NY-N	100	248	25	49	7	0	13	29	22	57	.198	.266	.383	.649	79	-9	-8	99	86	26	.594	2	1	0	1	1/O	-0.9
1984	Oak-A	147	549	68	147	23	1	35	118	44	119	.268	.329	.505	.833	139	18	24	92	130	91	.802	2	1	0	-1	*D/1	2.3
1985	Oak-A	158	592	66	141	16	0	30	91	62	114	.238	.313	.417	.730	105	-3	3	93	113	75	.668	3	2	-0	-0	*D/1	0.2
1986	Oak-A	144	561	70	118	19	0	35	94	33	126	.210	.258	.431	.689	90	-14	-10	94	114	57	.608	3	3	-1	0	*D/1	-1.1
Total	16	1941	6677	901	1575	240	25	442	1210	608	1816	.236	.305	.478	.783	115	93	102	99	109	955	.762	85	49	-4	-43	O1D3/P	0.4
■ HARRY KINGMAN	Kingman, Henry Lees b: 4/3/1892, Tientsin, China d: 12/27/82, Oakland, Cal. BL/TL, 6'1.5", 165 lbs. Deb: 7/01/14																											
1914	NY-A	4	3	0	0	0	0	0	0	1	2	.000	.250	.000	.250	-24	-0	-0	100	0	0	.333	0			0	/1	0.0
■ WALT KINLOCK	Kinlock, Walter b: 1878, St.Joseph, Mo. Deb: 8/01/1895																											
1895	StL-N	1	3	0	1	0	0	0	0	0	2	.333	.333	.333	.667	74	-0	-0	100	0	0	.500	0			0	/3	0.0

YEAR	TM/L	G	AB	R	H	2B	3B	HR	RBI	BB	SO	AVG	OBP	SLG	PRO	/A	BR	/A	PF	CHI	RC	TA	SB	CS	SBR	FR	POS	TPR
■ **BOB KINSELLA**	Kinsella, Robert Francis "Red" b: 1/5/1899, Springfield, Ill. d: 12/30/51, Los Angeles, Cal. BL/TR, 5'9.5", 165 lbs. Deb: 9/20/19																											
1919	NY-N	3	9	1	2	0	0	0	0	0	3	.222	.222	.222	.444	34	-1	-1	100	0	1	.429	1			-2	/O	-0.2
1920	NY-N	1	3	0	1	0	0	0	1	0	2	.333	.333	.333	.667	92	-0	-0	100	387	0	.500	0	0	0	-0	/O	0.0
Total	2	4	12	1	3	0	0	0	1	0	5	.250	.250	.250	.500	49	-1	-1	100	97	1	.444	1	0		-2	/O	-0.2
■ **KINSLER**	Kinsler b:Staten Island, N.Y. Deb: 6/08/1893																											
1893	NY-N	1	3	1	0	0	0	0	0	1	1	.000	.250	.000	.250	-29	-1	-1	104	0	0	.333	0			0	/O	0.0
■ **TOM KINSLOW**	Kinslow, Thomas F. b: 1/12/1866, Washington, D.C. d: 2/22/01, Washington, D.C. BR/TR, 5'10", 160 lbs. Deb: 6/04/1886																											
1886	Was-N	3	8	1	2	0	0	0	1	0	1	.250	.250	.250	.500	56	-0	-0	94	163	1	.333	0			0	/C	0.0
1887	NY-a	2	6	0	0	0	0	0		0		.000	.000	.000	.000	-99	-2	-1	88	0	0	.000	0			0	/C	0.0
1890	Bro-P	64	242	30	64	11	6	4	46	10	22	.264	.299	.409	.708	85	-5	-7	106	113	31	.635	2			7	C	0.1
1891	Bro-N	61	228	22	54	6	0	0	33	9	22	.237	.266	.263	.529	57	-13	-12	97	163	17	.414	3			-8	C	-1.3
1892	Bro-N	66	246	37	75	6	11	2	40	13	16	.305	.342	.443	.785	137	10	10	101	109	40	.743	4			7	C	1.9
1893	Bro-N	78	312	38	76	8	4	4	45	11	13	.244	.272	.333	.605	68	-18	-13	91	108	30	.508	4			2	C/O	-0.3
1894	Bro-N	62	223	39	68	5	6	2	41	20	11	.305	.362	.408	.770	92	-5	-2	94	117	35	.742	4			-5	C/1	-0.1
1895	Pit-N	19	62	10	14	2	0	0	5	2	2	.226	.250	.258	.508	34	-6	-6	97	87	4	.396	1			0	C	-0.4
1896	Lou-N	8	25	4	7	0	1	0	7	1	5	.280	.308	.360	.668	79	-1	-1	98	224	3	.556	0			0	/C1	0.0
1898	Was-N	3	9	0	1	0	0	0	0	0		.111	.111	.111	.222	-35	-2	-2	102	0	0	.125	0			0	/C1	0.0
	StL-N	14	53	5	15	2	1	0	4	1		.283	.309	.358	.668	88	-1	-1	106	65	6	.553	0			0	C	0.0
	Yr	17	62	5	16	2	1	0	4	1		.258	.281	.323	.604	71	-2	-3	105	53	6	.478	0			0		0.0
Total	10	380	1414	186	376	40	29	12	222	67	92	.266	.301	.361	.662	83	-42	-36	98	118	167	.578	18			2	C/1O	-0.1
■ **WALT KINZIE**	Kinzie, Walter Harris b: 3/1858 Kansas d: 11/5/09, 5'10.5", 161 lbs. Deb: 7/17/1882																											
1882	Det-N	13	53	5	5	0	1	0	2	0	8	.094	.094	.132	.226	-28	-7	-7	102	98	1	.146				0	S	-0.6
1884	Chi-N	19	82	4	13	3	0	2	8	0	13	.159	.159	.268	.427	29	-6	-7	108	104	4	.319				0	S/3	-0.6
	StL-a	2	9	0	1	0	0	0		0		.111	.111	.111	.222	-24	-1	-1	110	0	0	.125				0	/2	0.0
Total	2	34	144	9	19	3	1	2	10	0	21	.132	.132	.208	.340	6	-15	-16	106	95	4	.240				0	/S23	-1.2
■ **ED KIPPERT**	Kippert, Edward August "Kickapoo" b: 1/3/1880, Detroit, Mich. d: 6/3/60, Detroit, Mich. BR/TR, 5'10.5", 180 lbs. Deb: 4/14/14																											
1914	Cin-N	2	2	0	0	0	0	0	0	0	0	.000	.000	.000	.000	-96	-0	-0	105	0	0	.000	0			-1	/O	0.0
■ **JIM KIRBY**	Kirby, James Herschel b: 5/5/23, Nashville, Tenn. BR/TR, 5'11", 175 lbs. Deb: 5/01/49																											
1949	Chi-N	3	2	0	1	0	0	0	0	0	0	.500	.500	.500	1.000	179	0	0	94	0	1	1.000	0			0	H	0.0
■ **LA RUE KIRBY**	Kirby, La Rue b: 12/30/1889, Eureka, Mich. d: 6/10/61, Lansing, Mich. BB/TR, 6', 185 lbs. Deb: 8/07/12																											
1912	NY-N	3	5	1	1	1	0	0	0	0	0	.200	.200	.400	.600	60	-0	-0	104	0	0	.500	0			0	/P	0.0
1914	StL-F	52	195	21	48	6	3	2	18	14	30	.246	.297	.338	.635	77	-5	-6	106	95	22	.578	5			3	O	-0.5
1915	StL-F	61	178	15	38	7	2	0	16	17	31	.213	.282	.275	.557	62	-8	-9	105	118	16	.493	3			-0	O/P	-1.1
Total	3	116	378	37	87	14	5	2	34	31	61	.230	.289	.310	.598	70	-13	-15	105	105	39	.536	8			3	O/P	-1.6
■ **TOM KIRK**	Kirk, Thomas Daniel b: 9/27/27, Philadelphia, Pa. d: 8/1/74, Philadelphia, Pa. BL/TL, 5'10.5", 182 lbs. Deb: 6/24/47																											
1947	Phi-A	1	1	0	0	0	0	0	0	0	0	.000	.000	.000	.000	-99	-0	-0	100	0	0	.000	0	0	0	0	H	0.0
■ **JAY KIRKE**	Kirke, Judson Fabian b: 6/16/1888, Fleischmann's, N.Y. d: 8/31/68, New Orleans, La. BL/TR, 6', 195 lbs. Deb: 9/28/10																											
1910	Det-A	8	25	3	5	1	0	0	3	1		.200	.231	.240	.471	47	-2	-2	102	185	2	.400	1			-1	/2O	-0.3
1911	Bos-N	20	89	9	32	5	5	0	12	2	6	.360	.380	.528	.909	148	6	5	103	74	19	.930	3			-1	O/12S3	0.3
1912	Bos-N	103	359	53	115	11	4	4	62	9	46	.320	.339	.407	.745	96	0	-3	107	132	51	.668	7			2	O3/1	-0.2
1913	Bos-N	18	38	3	9	2	0	0	3	1	6	.237	.293	.289	.582	70	-2	-1	95	99	3	.483	0			1	O	0.0
1914	Cle-A	67	242	18	66	10	2	1	25	7	30	.273	.296	.343	.639	90	-4	-4	102	111	23	.516	5	10	-5	-2	O1	-1.4
1915	Cle-A	87	339	35	105	19	2	2	40	14	21	.310	.346	.395	.742	118	7	6	104	103	47	.658	5	6	-2	-2	1	-0.1
1918	NY-N	17	56	1	14	1	0	0	3	1	3	.250	.263	.268	.531	64	-3	-2	98	76	4	.381	0			1	1	-0.1
Total	7	320	1148	122	346	49	13	7	148	35	112	.301	.328	.385	.713	102	4	-2	104	112	148	.621	21	16		-3	O1/32S	-1.8
■ **WILLIE KIRKLAND**	Kirkland, Willie Charles b: 2/17/34, Siluria, Ala. BL/TR, 6'1", 206 lbs. Deb: 4/15/58																											
1958	SF-N	122	418	48	108	25	6	14	56	43	69	.258	.335	.447	.782	105	2	2	100	101	64	.751	3	2	-0	-2	*O	-0.3
1959	SF-N	126	463	64	126	22	3	22	68	42	84	.272	.337	.475	.812	119	8	11	95	98	75	.780	5	3	-0	-0	*O	0.8
1960	SF-N	146	515	59	130	21	10	21	65	44	86	.252	.316	.454	.771	120	4	11	90	91	74	.742	12	7	-1	4	*O	1.0
1961	Cle-A	146	525	84	136	22	5	27	95	48	77	.259	.322	.474	.797	114	5	8	96	115	84	.778	7	0	2	7	*O	1.1
1962	Cle-A	137	419	56	84	9	1	21	72	43	62	.200	.275	.377	.652	75	-17	-16	98	129	44	.607	9	1	2	2	*O	-1.6
1963	Cle-A	127	427	51	98	13	2	15	47	45	99	.230	.304	.375	.679	92	-6	-5	97	96	50	.631	8	2	1	9	*O	0.2
1964	Bal-A	66	150	14	30	5	0	3	22	17	26	.200	.286	.293	.579	58	-8	-9	105	176	14	.533	3	2	-0	1	O	-1.0
	Was-A	32	102	8	22	6	0	5	13	6	30	.216	.259	.422	.681	85	-2	-3	101	95	11	.605	0	0	0	-4	O	-0.7
	Yr	98	252	22	52	11	0	8	35	23	56	.206	.275	.345	.621	69	-10	-11	104	151	25	.562	3	2	-0	-3		-1.7
1965	Was-A	123	312	38	72	9	1	14	54	19	65	.231	.275	.401	.676	89	-5	-5	100	134	33	.595	3	2	-0	-3	O	-1.3
1966	Was-A	124	163	21	31	2	1	6	17	16	50	.190	.263	.325	.588	72	-7	-6	95	100	14	.526	2	0	1	-14	O	-2.3
Total	9	1149	3494	443	837	134	29	148	509	323	648	.240	.307	.422	.728	100	-26	-11	97	110	463	.695	52	19	4	-1	O	-4.1
■ **ED KIRKPATRICK**	Kirkpatrick, Edgar Leon b: 10/8/44, Spokane, Wash. BL/TR, 5'11.5", 195 lbs. Deb: 9/13/62																											
1962	LA-A	3	6	0	0	0	0	0	0	0	2	.000	.000	.000	.000	-98	-2	-2	102	0	0	.000	0	0	0	0	/C	-0.1
1963	LA-A	34	77	4	15	5	0	2	7	6	19	.195	.262	.338	.600	73	-4	-3	91	92	7	.540	1	0	0	-1	CO	-0.3
1964	LA-A	75	219	20	53	13	3	2	22	23	30	.242	.320	.356	.676	99	-3	-0	89	111	24	.600	2	2	-1	-5	O	-0.8
1965	Cal-A	19	73	8	19	5	0	3	8	3	9	.260	.289	.452	.742	110	0	1	98	84	8	.627	1	2	-1	0	O	0.0
1966	Cal-A	117	312	31	60	7	4	9	44	51	67	.192	.315	.327	.642	86	-5	-5	99	143	35	.635	7	4	-0	-7	*O/1	-1.6
1967	Cal-A	3	8	0	0	0	0	0	0	0	2	.000	.000	.000	.000	-99	-2	-2	96	0	0	.000	0	0	0	-0	/CO	-0.2
1968	Cal-A	89	161	23	37	4	0	1	15	25	32	.230	.337	.273	.610	92	-2	-0	94	137	16	.555	1	3	-2	-5	O/C1	-1.0
1969	KC-A	120	315	40	81	11	4	14	49	43	42	.257	.352	.451	.803	120	10	9	103	107	52	.793	3	5	-2	9	O/C132	1.4
1970	KC-A	134	424	59	97	17	2	18	62	55	65	.229	.319	.406	.724	100	-1	-1	98	111	54	.682	4	4	-1	1	CO1	0.0
1971	KC-A	120	365	46	80	12	1	9	46	48	60	.219	.313	.332	.645	84	-8	-7	99	127	37	.580	3	4	-2	-0	OC	-0.8
1972	KC-A	113	364	43	100	15	1	9	43	51	50	.275	.368	.396	.764	127	14	14	100	105	55	.736	3	5	-2	1	*C/1	1.5
1973	KC-A	126	429	61	113	24	3	6	45	46	48	.263	.336	.375	.711	92	0	-5	109	99	52	.630	3	7	-3	-5	*OC/D	-1.6
1974	Pit-N	116	271	32	67	9	0	6	38	51	30	.247	.370	.347	.717	104	3	3	98	131	37	.705	1	2	-1	-2	1O/C	-0.2
1975	Pit-N	89	144	15	34	5	0	5	16	18	22	.236	.321	.375	.696	93	-2	-1	99	90	17	.635	1	0	0	-2	1O	-0.4
1976	Pit-N	83	146	14	34	9	0	0	16	14	15	.233	.300	.295	.595	69	-6	-6	100	143	13	.504	1	0	0	-2	1/O3	-0.8
1977	Pit-N	21	28	5	4	2	0	1	4	8	6	.143	.333	.321	.655	75	-1	-1	103	133	3	.692	1	0	0	-1	1/O3	-0.1
	Tex-A	20	48	2	9	1	0	0	3	4	11	.188	.250	.208	.458	25	-5	-5	105	119	3	.390	2	0	1	0	/O1CD	-0.4
	Mil-A	29	77	8	21	4	0	0	6	10	8	.273	.364	.325	.688	94	-1	-0	95	95	10	.632	0	1	-1	-3	O/3D	-0.3
	Yr	49	125	10	30	5	0	0	9	14	19	.240	.321	.280	.601	66	-5	-5	99	107	12	.542	2	1	0	-3		-0.7
Total	16	1311	3467	411	824	143	18	85	424	456	518	.238	.330	.363	.693	96	-13	-12	100	115	424	.660	34	39	-13	-21	OC1/D32	-5.7
■ **ENOS KIRKPATRICK**	Kirkpatrick, Enos Claire b: 12/8/1885, Pittsburgh, Pa. d: 4/14/64, Pittsburgh, Pa. BR/TR, 5'10", 175 lbs. Deb: 8/24/12																											
1912	Bro-N	32	94	13	18	1	1	0	6	9	15	.191	.269	.223	.493	37	-8	-8	95	96	7	.474	5			2	3/S	-0.5
1913	Bro-N	48	89	13	22	4	1	1	5	3	18	.247	.287	.348	.636	77	-2	-3	104	53	10	.612	5			-0	S/123	-0.2
1914	Bal-F	55	174	22	44	7	2	2	16	18	30	.253	.323	.351	.673	94	-2	-1	99	86	24	.685	10			-2	3S/O1	-0.2
1915	Bal-F	68	171	22	41	8	2	0	19	24	15	.240	.333	.310	.643	85	-1	-3	107	129	23	.685	12			-2	32/1S	-0.4
Total	4	203	528	70	125	20	6	3	46	54	78	.237	.311	.314	.626	78	-13	-15	102	97	64	.633	32			-3	/3S21O	-1.3
■ **JOE KIRRENE**	Kirrene, Joseph John b: 10/4/31, San Francisco, Cal. BR/TR, 6'2", 195 lbs. Deb: 10/01/50																											
1950	Chi-A	1	4	0	1	0	0	0	0	0	1	.250	.250	.250	.500	29	-0	-0	97	0	0	.333	0	0	0	0	/3	0.0
1954	Chi-A	9	23	4	7	1	0	0	4	5	2	.304	.448	.348	.796	116	1	1	104	190	4	.882	1	0	0	0	/3	0.1

YEAR	TM/L	G	AB	R	H	2B	3B	HR	RBI	BB	SO	AVG	OBP	SLG	PRO	/A	BR	/A	PF	CHI	RC	TA	SB	CS	SBR	FR	POS	TPR
Total	2	10	27	4	8	1	0	0	4	5	3	.296	.424	.333	.758	105	1	1	103	167	4	.800	1	0	0	0	/3	0.1
■ **ERNIE KISH** Kish, Ernest Alexander b: 2/6/18, Washington, D.C. BL/TR, 5'9.5", 170 lbs. Deb: 7/29/45																												
1945	Phi-A	43	110	10	27	5	1	0	10	9	9	.245	.320	.309	.629	88	-2	-1	94	106	11	.523	0	3	-2	-3	O	-0.7
■ **CHRIS KITSOS** Kitsos, Christopher Anestos b: 2/11/28, New York, N.Y. BB/TR, 5'9", 165 lbs. Deb: 4/21/54																												
1954	Chi-N	1	0	0	0	0	0	0	0	0	0	—	—	—	—	—	0	0	101	—	—	—	0	0	0	0	/S	0.0
■ **RON KITTLE** Kittle, Ronald Dale b: 1/5/58, Gary, Indiana BR/TR, 6'4", 200 lbs. Deb: 9/02/82																												
1982	Chi-A	20	29	3	7	2	0	1	7	3	12	.241	.313	.414	.726	100	-0	-0	97	187	4	.682	0	0	0	-2	/OD	-0.1
1983	Chi-A	145	520	75	132	19	3	35	100	39	150	.254	.316	.504	.820	118	13	11	103	109	81	.791	8	3	1	-13	*O/D	-0.2
1984	Chi-A	139	466	67	100	15	0	32	74	49	137	.215	.298	.453	.750	94	1	-5	111	96	62	.710	3	6	-3	-1	*O/D	-1.2
1985	Chi-A	116	379	51	87	12	0	26	58	31	92	.230	.296	.467	.763	105	1	1	100	90	48	.695	1	4	-2	-5	OD	-0.6
1986	Chi-A	86	296	34	63	11	0	17	48	28	87	.213	.287	.422	.710	90	-4	-5	101	111	34	.648	2	1	0	1	DO	-0.4
	NY-A	30	80	8	19	2	0	4	12	7	23	.237	.299	.412	.711	89	-1	-1	103	106	11	.689	2	0	1	0	D/O	0.0
	Yr	116	376	42	82	13	0	21	60	35	110	.218	.290	.420	.710	90	-5	-6	101	110	49	.678	4	1	1	1		-0.4
1987	NY-A	59	159	21	44	5	0	12	28	10	36	.277	.324	.535	.858	126	5	5	98	92	26	.800	0	1	-1	1	D/O	0.5
1988	Cle-A	75	225	31	58	8	0	18	43	16	65	.258	.329	.533	.863	135	10	10	102	98	42	.862	0	0	0	0	D	1.0
Total	7	670	2154	290	510	74	3	145	370	183	602	.237	.306	.476	.782	107	25	16	103	102	307	.756	16	15	-4	-19	OD	-1.0
■ **MALACHI KITTRIDGE** Kittridge, Malachi Jedediah "Jedediah" b: 10/12/1869, Clinton, Mass. d: 6/23/28, Gary, Ind. BR/TR, 5'7", 170 lbs. Deb: 4/19/1890 M																												
1890	Chi-N	96	333	46	67	8	3	3	35	39	53	.201	.287	.270	.557	59	-14	-19	109	107	29	.515	7			-5	*C	-1.4
1891	Chi-N	79	296	26	62	8	5	2	27	17	28	.209	.252	.291	.543	56	-16	-19	106	86	23	.457	4			0	C	-0.9
1892	Chi-N	69	229	19	41	5	0	0	10	11	27	.179	.217	.201	.418	30	-20	-17	92	67	11	.314	2			11	C	-0.2
1893	Chi-N	70	255	32	59	9	5	2	30	17	15	.231	.279	.329	.609	61	-14	-16	104	91	25	.531	3			6	C	-0.2
1894	Chi-N	51	168	36	53	8	2	0	23	26	20	.315	.407	.387	.794	87	-0	-3	108	98	28	.809	2			1	C	0.2
1895	Chi-N	60	212	30	48	6	3	3	29	16	9	.226	.284	.325	.609	57	-13	-15	103	104	22	.561	6			-6	C	-1.2
1896	Chi-N	65	215	17	48	4	1	1	19	14	14	.223	.274	.265	.539	41	-17	-20	108	91	18	.467	6			1	C/P	-1.0
1897	Chi-N	79	262	25	53	5	5	1	30	22		.202	.264	.271	.535	43	-21	-21	100	119	22	.488	9			1	C	-0.7
1898	Lou-N	86	287	27	70	8	5	1	31	15		.244	.281	.317	.599	76	-10	-9	96	100	29	.530	9			-7	C	-0.8
1899	Lou-N	45	129	11	26	2	1	0	12	26		.202	.335	.233	.568	57	-6	-7	103	123	11	.573	3			5	C	0.1
	Was-N	44	133	14	20	3	0	0	11	10		.150	.215	.173	.388	9	-16	-15	96	147	6	.319	2			4	C	-0.7
	Yr	89	262	25	46	5	1	0	23	36		.176	.278	.202	.480	35	-22	-22	100	136	17	.440	5			8		-0.6
1901	Bos-N	114	381	24	96	14	0	2	40	32		.252	.310	.304	.614	72	-9	-15	112	112	37	.526	2			3	*C	0.2
1902	Bos-N	80	255	18	60	7	0	2	30	24		.235	.301	.286	.587	87	-4	-3	95	131	24	.518	4			4	C	0.8
1903	Bos-N	32	99	10	21	2	0	0	6	11		.212	.291	.232	.523	54	-6	-5	96	84	7	.449	1			4	C	0.1
	Was-A	60	192	8	41	4	1	0	16	10		.214	.252	.245	.497	49	-11	-12	105	123	12	.384	1			-0	C	-0.4
1904	Was-A	81	265	11	64	7	0	0	24	8		.242	.264	.268	.532	76	-9	-7	93	126	20	.403	2			8	CM	1.0
1905	Was-A	77	238	16	39	8	0	0	14	15		.164	.213	.197	.411	31	-18	-19	104	106	11	.317	1			11	C	0.0
1906	Was-A	22	68	5	13	0	0	0	3	1		.191	.203	.191	.394	27	-6	-5	91	84	3	.255	0			0	C	-0.3
	Cle-A	5	10	0	1	0	0	0	0	0		.100	.100	.100	.200	-36	-2	-2	103	0	0	.111	0			-0	/C	-0.1
	Yr	27	78	5	14	0	0	0	3	1		.179	.190	.179	.369	18	-7	-7	93	71	3	.234	0			-0		-0.4
Total	16	1215	4027	375	882	108	31	17	390	314	166	.219	.276	.274	.550	57	-213	-229	102	106	336	.472	64			40	*C/P	-5.5
■ **BOBBY KLAUS** Klaus, Robert Francis b: 12/27/37, Spring Grove, Ill. BR/TR, 5'10", 170 lbs. Deb: 4/21/64																												
1964	Cin-N	40	93	10	17	5	1	2	6	4	13	.183	.216	.323	.539	48	-6	-7	103	68	7	.455	1	0	0	-1	23/S	-0.6
	NY-N	56	209	25	51	8	3	2	11	25	30	.244	.325	.340	.664	92	-3	-2	95	62	24	.604	3	4	-2	1	23/S	0.0
	Yr	96	302	35	68	13	4	4	17	29	43	.225	.293	.334	.627	77	-9	-9	98	65	31	.558	4	4	-1	0		-0.6
1965	NY-N	119	288	30	55	12	0	2	12	45	49	.191	.302	.253	.556	58	-15	-15	100	63	24	.494	1	6	-3	-0	2S3	-1.2
Total	2	215	590	65	123	25	4	6	29	74	92	.208	.298	.295	.593	68	-24	-23	99	63	54	.528	5	10	-5	-0	2/3S	-1.8
■ **BILLY KLAUS** Klaus, William Joseph b: 12/9/28, Fox Lake, Ill. BL/TR, 5'9", 160 lbs. Deb: 4/16/52																												
1952	Bos-N	7	4	3	0	0	0	0	0	1	1	.000	.200	.000	.200	-42	-1	-1	95	0	0	.250	0	0	0	0	/S	0.0
1953	Mil-N	2	2	1	0	0	0	0	1	0	0	.000	.000	.000	.000	-99	-1	-1	94	0	0	.000	0	0	0	0	H	0.0
1955	Bos-A	135	541	83	153	26	2	7	60	60	44	.283	.354	.377	.731	78	-2	-19	124	105	78	.689	6	0	2	1	*S/3	-0.2
1956	Bos-A	135	520	91	141	29	5	7	59	90	43	.271	.380	.387	.766	100	5	3	103	95	83	.759	1	0	0	6	*3S	1.3
1957	Bos-A	127	477	76	120	18	4	10	42	55	53	.252	.329	.369	.698	82	-6	-12	110	85	59	.631	2	0	1	17	*S	1.5
1958	Bos-A	61	88	5	14	4	0	1	7	5	16	.159	.204	.239	.443	20	-10	-10	105	117	4	.342	0	0	0	1	S	-0.5
1959	Bal-A	104	321	33	80	11	0	3	25	51	38	.249	.352	.312	.664	86	-5	-4	97	90	37	.610	2	4	-2	2	S3/2	0.0
1960	Bal-A	46	43	8	9	2	0	1	6	9	9	.209	.346	.326	.672	81	-1	-1	102	138	5	.657	0	0	0	1	2S/3	0.3
1961	Was-A	91	251	26	57	8	2	7	30	30	34	.227	.314	.359	.673	83	-7	-6	95	106	30	.629	2	2	-1	2	3S/2O	0.0
1962	Phi-N	102	248	30	51	8	2	4	20	29	43	.206	.291	.302	.594	63	-14	-12	95	91	23	.525	1	1	-0	-2	3S2	-0.8
1963	Phi-N	11	18	1	1	0	0	0	0	1	4	.056	.105	.056	.161	-51	-3	-4	103	0	0	.118	0	0	0	0	/S3	-0.2
Total	11	821	2513	357	626	106	15	40	250	331	285	.249	.337	.351	.688	81	-45	-66	106	96	320	.650	14	7	0	27	S3/2O	1.4
■ **OLLIE KLEE** Klee, Ollie Chester "Babe" b: 5/20/1900, Piqua, Ohio d: 2/9/77, Toledo, Ohio BL/TL, 5'9.5", 160 lbs. Deb: 8/10/25																												
1925	Cin-N	3	1	0	0	0	0	0	0	0	1	.000	.000	.000	.000	-99	-0	-0	97	0	0	.000	0	0	0	-0	/O	0.0
■ **CHUCK KLEIN** Klein, Charles Herbert b: 10/7/04, Indianapolis, Ind. d: 3/28/58, Indianapolis, Ind. BL/TR, 6', 185 lbs. Deb: 7/30/28 CH																												
1928	Phi-N	64	253	41	91	14	4	11	34	14	22	.360	.396	.577	.973	145	18	16	104	72	55	.994	0			1	O	1.4
1929	Phi-N	149	616	126	219	45	6	**43**	145	54	61	.356	.407	.657	1.065	145	53	44	110	99	158	1.169	5			4	*O	3.1
1930	Phi-N	156	648	**158**	250	**59**	8	40	170	54	50	.386	.436	.687	1.123	157	67	61	106	100	186	1.274	4			**33**	*O	**7.2**
1931	Phi-N	148	594	**121**	200	34	10	**31**	**121**	59	49	.337	.398	**.584**	**.982**	151	**49**	**44**	106	94	**140**	1.051	7			-5	*O	3.1
1932	Phi-N	154	650	**152**	**226**	50	15	**38**	137	60	49	.348	.404	**.646**	**1.050**	158	**68**	58	112	92	**171**	**1.182**	**20**			8	*O	**5.3**
1933	Phi-N	152	606	101	**223**	**44**	7	**28**	**120**	56	36	**.368**	**.422**	**.602**	**1.025**	161	**69**	**56**	118	97	**162**	**1.132**	15			8	*O	**5.8**
1934	Chi-N	115	435	78	131	27	2	20	80	47	38	.301	.372	.510	.882	137	20	22	98	108	86	.884	3			-4	*O	1.2
1935	Chi-N	119	434	71	127	14	4	21	73	41	42	.293	.355	.488	.844	125	14	15	99	98	76	.814	4			-2	*O	0.7
1936	Chi-N	29	109	19	32	5	0	5	18	16	14	.294	.384	.477	.861	125	5	4	105	101	21	.861	0			-0	O	0.2
	Phi-N	117	492	83	152	30	7	20	86	33	45	.309	.352	.520	.873	122	20	15	108	93	92	.853	6			-8	*O	0.1
	Yr	146	601	102	184	35	7	25	104	49	59	.306	.358	.512	.871	123	25	19	107	95	115	.858	6			-8		0.3
1937	Phi-N	115	406	74	132	20	2	15	57	39	21	.325	.386	.495	.881	127	21	17	108	85	81	.871	3			-4	*O	0.7
1938	Phi-N	129	458	53	113	22	2	8	61	38	30	.247	.304	.356	.660	81	-12	-13	100	120	52	.591	7			-3	*O	-1.7
1939	Phi-N	25	47	8	9	2	1	1	9	10	4	.191	.333	.340	.674	87	-1	-1	94	174	6	.711	1			0	O/1	0.0
	Pit-N	85	270	37	81	16	4	11	47	26	17	.300	.361	.511	.873	133	11	11	100	101	50	.855	1			-3	O	0.7
	Yr	110	317	45	90	18	5	12	56	36	21	.284	.357	.486	.843	127	10	11	98	119	57	.831	2			-3		0.7
1940	Phi-N	116	354	39	77	16	2	7	37	44	30	.218	.304	.333	.637	78	-12	-10	97	99	37	.575	2			-5	O	-1.9
1941	Phi-N	50	73	6	9	0	0	1	3	10	6	.123	.229	.164	.393	12	-8	-8	97	72	3	.333	0			-1	O	-1.0
1942	Phi-N	14	14	0	1	0	0	0	0	0	2	.071	.071	.071	.143	-62	-3	-3	94	0	0	.071	0			0	H	-0.2
1943	Phi-N	12	20	0	2	0	0	0	3	0	3	.100	.100	.100	.200	-45	-4	-3	94	542	0	.167	1			-1	/O	-0.4
1944	Phi-N	4	7	1	1	0	0	0	0	0	2	.143	.143	.143	.286	-19	-1	-1	100	0	0	.167	0			1	/O	0.0
Total	17	1753	6486	1168	2076	398	74	300	1201	601	521	.320	.379	.543	.922	135	375	324	106	99	1378	.956	79			17	*O/1	24.3
■ **LOU KLEIN** Klein, Louis Frank b: 10/22/18, New Orleans, La. d: 6/20/76, Metaire, La. BR/TR, 5'11", 167 lbs. Deb: 4/21/43 MC																												
1943	StL-N	154	627	91	180	28	14	7	62	50	70	.287	.342	.410	.752	111	12	8	105	77	91	.705	9			9	*2S	2.8
1945	StL-N	19	57	12	13	4	1	1	6	14	9	.228	.389	.386	.775	116	2	2	100	83	10	.841	0			1	/SO32	0.3
1946	StL-N	23	93	12	18	3	0	1	4	9	7	.194	.265	.258	.523	46	-6	-7	107	49	7	.453	1			-0	2	-0.6
1949	StL-N	58	114	25	25	6	0	2	12	22	20	.219	.355	.325	.680	76	-2	-4	110	105	15	.670	0			2	S/23	0.1
1951	Cle-A	2	2	0	0	0	0	0	0	0	1	.000	.000	.000	.000	-99	-1	-1	95	0	0	.000	0	0	0	0	H	0.0
	Phi-A	49	144	22	33	7	0	5	17	10	12	.229	.279	.382	.661	73	-5	-6	106	87	15	.565	0	0	0	1	2	-0.3

YEAR	TM/L	G	AB	R	H	2B	3B	HR	RBI	BB	SO	AVG	OBP	SLG	PRO	/A	BR	/A	PF	CHI	RC	TA	SB	CS	SBR	FR	POS	TPR
	Yr	51	146	22	33	7	0	5	17	10	13	.226	.276	.377	.652	71	-6	-7	105	83	15	.556	0	0	0	1		-0.3
Total	5	305	1037	162	269	48	15	16	101	105	119	.259	.330	.381	.711	95	-1	-8	105	80	139	.667	10	0		12	2/S3O	2.3
■ **RED KLEINOW**	Kleinow, John Peter b: 7/20/1879, Milwaukee, Wis. d: 10/9/29, New York, N.Y. BR/TR, 5'10", 165 lbs. Deb: 5/03/04																											
1904	NY-A	68	209	12	43	8	4	0	16	15		.206	.259	.282	.541	65	-6	-9	112	101	17	.470	4			-1	C/3O	-0.2
1905	NY-A	88	253	23	56	6	3	1	24	20		.221	.278	.281	.559	78	-6	-6	102	116	22	.497	7			-7	C/1	-0.4
1906	NY-A	96	268	30	59	9	3	0	31	24		.220	.284	.276	.560	64	-6	-13	120	152	24	.507	8			-11	C/1	-1.7
1907	NY-A	90	269	30	71	6	4	0	26	24		.264	.324	.316	.640	98	2	-0	109	109	30	.576	5			2	C/1	1.0
1908	NY-A	96	279	16	47	3	2	1	13	22		.168	.229	.204	.434	45	-17	-15	95	81	13	.362	5			-8	C/2	-1.6
1909	NY-A	78	206	34	47	11	4	0	15	25		.228	.315	.320	.635	101	1	1	99	88	22	.623	7			-6	C	0.1
1910	NY-A	6	12	2	5	0	0	0	2	1		.417	.462	.417	.878	163	1	1	107	148	3	1.143	2			-0	/C	0.1
	Bos-A	50	147	9	22	1	0	1	8	20		.150	.251	.177	.428	35	-11	-10	99	102	7	.392	3			-6	C	-1.2
	Yr	56	159	11	27	1	0	1	10	21		.170	.267	.195	.462	45	-9	-9	100	109	9	.432	5			-6		-1.1
1911	Bos-A	8	14	0	3	0	0	0	0	2		.214	.313	.214	.527	48	-1	-1	99	0	1	.545	1			0	/C	0.0
	Phi-N	4	8	0	1	1	0	0	0	0	1	.125	.125	.250	.375	4	-1	-1	108	0	0	.286	0			0	/C	0.0
Total	8	584	1665	156	354	45	20	3	135	153	1	.213	.279	.269	.548	71	-43	-54	106	107	140	.491	42			-37	C/123O	-3.9
■ **JAY KLEVEN**	Kleven, Jay Allen b: 12/2/49, Oakland, Cal. BR/TR, 6'2", 190 lbs. Deb: 6/20/76																											
1976	NY-N	2	5	0	1	0	0	0	2	0	1	.200	.200	.200	.400	15	-1	-1	92	770	0	.200	0	0	0	0	/C	0.0
■ **LOU KLIMCHOCK**	Klimchock, Louis Stephen b: 10/15/39, Hostetter, Pa. BL/TR, 5'11", 180 lbs. Deb: 9/27/58																											
1958	KC-A	2	10	2	2	0	0	1	1	0	1	.200	.200	.500	.700	81	-0	-0	106	43	1	.625	0	0	0	0	/2	0.0
1959	KC-A	17	66	10	18	1	0	4	13	1	6	.273	.284	.470	.753	102	-0	-0	101	121	8	.640	0	0	0	0	2	0.1
1960	KC-A	10	10	0	3	0	0	0	0	0	0	.300	.300	.300	.600	64	-1	-1	99	0	1	.429	0	0	0	0	/2	0.0
1961	KC-A	57	121	8	26	4	1	1	16	5	13	.215	.246	.289	.535	42	-10	-10	102	165	9	.417	0	0	0	-0	1/O32	-1.1
1962	Mil-N	8	8	0	0	0	0	0	0	0	2	.000	.000	.000	.000	-99	-2	-2	99	0	0	.000	0	0	0	0	H	-0.1
1963	Was-A	9	14	1	2	0	0	0	2	0	1	.143	.143	.143	.286	-20	-2	-2	98	419	0	.167	0	0	0	0	/2	-0.1
	Mil-N	24	46	6	9	1	0	0	1	0	12	.196	.196	.217	.413	19	-5	-5	101	42	2	.263	0	1	-1	0	1	-0.5
1964	Mil-N	10	21	3	7	2	0	0	2	1	2	.333	.364	.429	.792	126	1	1	97	91	3	.667	0	0	0	0	/32	0.1
1965	Mil-N	34	39	3	3	0	0	0	3	2	8	.077	.122	.077	.199	-41	-7	-7	104	415	0	.135	0	0	0	0	/1	-0.7
1966	NY-N	5	5	0	0	0	0	0	0	0	3	.000	.000	.000	.000	-99	-1	-1	94	0	0	.000	0	0	0	0	H	0.0
1968	Cle-A	11	15	0	2	0	0	0	3	1	0	.133	.188	.133	.321	-1	-2	-2	101	643	0	.231	0	0	0	0	/312	-0.1
1969	Cle-A	90	258	26	74	13	2	6	26	18	14	.287	.333	.422	.756	117	3	4	94	82	36	.676	0	0	0	-4	32/C	0.2
1970	Cle-A	41	56	5	9	0	0	1	2	3	9	.161	.217	.214	.431	17	-6	-7	115	54	3	.333	0	0	0	0	/12	-0.6
Total	12	318	669	64	155	21	3	13	69	31	71	.232	.267	.330	.597	65	-33	-33	100	132	63	.490	0	1	-1	-4	/3210C	-2.8
■ **BOBBY KLINE**	Kline, John Robert b: 1/27/29, St.Petersburg, Fla BR/TR, 6', 179 lbs. Deb: 4/11/55																											
1955	Was-A	77	140	12	31	5	0	0	9	11	27	.221	.288	.257	.545	52	-10	-9	91	93	11	.438	0	0	0	6	S/23P	0.5
■ **JOHNNY KLING**	Kling, John "Noisy" b: 2/25/1875, Kansas City, Mo. d: 1/31/47, Kansas City, Mo. BR/TR, 5'9.5", 160 lbs. Deb: 9/11/00 M																											
1900	Chi-N	15	51	8	15	3	1	0	7	2		.294	.321	.392	.713	106	-0	0	93	109	7	.611	0			0	C	0.0
1901	Chi-N	74	256	26	70	6	3	0	21	9		.273	.298	.320	.618	81	-6	-6	100	86	28	.532	8			-1	C/1O	0.1
1902	Chi-N	114	431	49	123	19	3	0	57	29		.285	.330	.343	.674	115	5	7	96	141	58	.653	24			-1	*C/S	1.8
1903	Chi-N	132	491	67	146	29	13	3	68	22		.297	.327	.428	.755	122	8	11	95	102	78	.739	23			-5	*C	1.6
1904	Chi-N	123	452	41	110	18	0	2	46	16		.243	.269	.296	.566	76	-13	-13	101	123	39	.459	7			-3	*CO/1	-0.8
1905	Chi-N	111	380	26	83	8	6	1	52	28		.218	.272	.279	.551	63	-16	-18	105	169	33	.495	13			-2	*C/O1	-0.8
1906	Chi-N	107	343	45	107	15	8	2	46	23		.312	.355	.420	.775	135	16	14	107	112	58	.767	14			0	C/O	2.4
1907	Chi-N	104	334	44	95	15	8	1	43	27		.284	.338	.386	.724	121	10	8	106	126	48	.690	9			-4	C/1	1.3
1908	Chi-N	126	424	51	117	23	5	4	59	21		.276	.310	.382	.692	116	9	7	106	133	53	.648	16			2	*C/O1	1.6
1910	Chi-N	91	297	31	80	17	2	2	32	37	27	.269	.354	.360	.714	108	4	3	101	101	39	.687	3			3	C	1.1
1911	Chi-N	27	80	8	14	3	2	1	5	8	14	.175	.250	.300	.550	56	-5	-5	97	63	6	.500	1			1	C	-0.2
	Bos-N	75	241	32	54	8	1	2	24	30	29	.224	.310	.290	.600	66	-10	-11	103	107	22	.535	0			12	C/3	0.6
	Yr	102	321	40	68	11	3	3	29	38	43	.212	.295	.293	.588	64	-15	-16	102	96	28	.526	1			12		0.4
1912	Bos-N	81	252	26	80	10	3	2	30	15	30	.317	.356	.405	.761	101	2	-0	107	94	37	.698	3			7	CM	1.1
1913	Cin-N	80	209	20	57	7	6	0	23	14	14	.273	.318	.364	.682	93	-2	-2	102	110	24	.605	2			6	CM	0.8
Total	13	1260	4241	474	1151	181	61	20	513	281	114	.271	.317	.357	.674	100	2	-6	102	118	529	.621	123			14	*C/O13S	10.6
■ **RUDY KLING**	Kling, Rudolph A. b: 3/23/1870, St.Louis, Mo. d: 3/14/37, St.Louis, Mo. TR , 5'10", 178 lbs. Deb: 9/21/02																											
1902	StL-N	4	10	1	2	0	0	0	0	4		.200	.429	.200	.629	102	0	0	95	0	1	.875	1			0	/S	0.1
■ **JOE KLINGER**	Klinger, Joseph John b: 8/2/02, Canonsburg, Pa. d: 7/31/60, Little Rock, Ark. BR/TR, 6', 190 lbs. Deb: 9/13/27																											
1927	NY-N	3	5	0	2	0	0	0	0	0	2	.400	.400	.400	.800	115	0	0	100	0	1	.667	0			0	/O	0.0
1930	Chi-A	4	8	0	3	0	0	0	1	0	0	.375	.375	.375	.750	88	-0	-0	103	111	1	.600	0	0	0	0	/C1	0.0
Total	2	7	13	0	5	0	0	0	1	0	2	.385	.385	.385	.769	98	0	-0	102	68	2	.625	0	0		0	/1CO	0.0
■ **NAP KLOZA**	Kloza, John Clarence b: 9/7/03, Poland d: 6/11/62, Milwaukee, Wis. BR/TR, 5'11", 180 lbs. Deb: 8/16/31																											
1931	StL-A	3	7	1	1	0	0	0	0	1	4	.143	.250	.143	.393	5	-1	-1	102	0	0	.333	0	0	0	-0	/O	-0.1
1932	StL-A	19	13	4	2	0	1	0	2	4	4	.154	.353	.308	.661	73	-0	-0	100	167	2	.727	0	0	0	-1	/O	-0.1
Total	2	22	20	5	3	0	1	0	2	5	8	.150	.320	.250	.570	50	-1	-1	101	114	2	.588	0	0	0	-1	/O	-0.2
■ **JOE KLUGMANN**	Klugmann, Joe b: 3/26/1895, St.Louis, Mo. d: 7/18/51, Moberly, Mo. BR/TR, 5'11", 175 lbs. Deb: 9/23/21																											
1921	Chi-N	6	21	3	6	0	0	0	2	1	2	.286	.348	.286	.634	65	-1	-1	107	125	2	.500	0	1	-1	0	/2	0.0
1922	Chi-N	2	2	0	0	0	0	0	0	0	0	.000	.000	.000	.000	-99	-1	-1	95	0	0	.000	0	0	0	0	/2	0.0
1924	Bro-N	31	79	7	13	2	1	0	3	2	9	.165	.185	.215	.400	7	-10	-10	99	64	3	.288	0	0	0	-2	2/S	-1.3
1925	Cle-A	38	85	12	28	9	2	0	12	8	4	.329	.387	.482	.869	112	2	2	106	98	16	.897	3	1	0	-3	2/13	0.0
Total	4	77	187	22	47	11	3	0	17	11	15	.251	.296	.342	.639	64	-9	-10	103	86	21	.556	3	2	-0	-4	/213S	-1.3
■ **ELMER KLUMPP**	Klumpp, Elmer Edward b: 8/26/06, St.Louis, Mo. BR/TR, 6', 184 lbs. Deb: 4/17/34																											
1934	Was-A	12	15	2	2	0	0	0	0	0	1	.133	.188	.133	.321	-16	-3	-3	101	0	0	.231	0	0	0	-0	C	-0.1
1937	Bro-N	5	11	0	1	0	0	0	2	1	4	.091	.167	.091	.258	-27	-2	-2	104	721	0	.182	0			-0	/C	-0.1
Total	2	17	26	2	3	0	0	0	2	1	5	.115	.179	.115	.294	-21	-5	-5	102	309	1	.208	0	0		-0	/C	-0.2
■ **BILLY KLUSMAN**	Klusman, William F. b: 3/24/1865, Cincinnati, Ohio d: 6/24/07, Cincinnati, Ohio BR/TR, 5'10.5", 185 lbs. Deb: 1888																											
1888	Bos-N	28	107	9	18	4	0	2	11	5	13	.168	.205	.262	.467	47	-6	-7	106	118	7	.404	3			0	2	-0.6
1890	StL-a	15	65	9	18	4	1	1		1		.277	.288	.415	.703	94	0	-1	116	0	8	.617	1			0	2	0.0
Total	2	43	172	18	36	8	1	3	11	6	13	.209	.236	.320	.556	66	-6	-8	110	74	15	.478	4			0	/2	-0.6
■ **TED KLUSZEWSKI**	Kluszewski, Theodore Bernard "Big Klu" b: 9/10/24, Argo, Ill. d: 3/29/88, Cincinnati, Ohio BL/TL, 6'2", 225 lbs. Deb: 4/18/47 C																											
1947	Cin-N	9	10	1	1	0	0	0	2	1	2	.100	.182	.100	.282	-26	-2	-2	91	741	0	.222	0			0	/1	-0.1
1948	Cin-N	113	379	49	104	23	4	12	57	18	32	.274	.307	.451	.758	100	-1	-2	103	103	48	.657	1			-0	1	-0.2
1949	Cin-N	136	531	63	164	26	2	8	68	19	24	.309	.333	.411	.743	103	-3	0	96	108	70	.637	3			-4	*1	-0.3
1950	Cin-N	134	538	76	165	37	0	25	111	33	28	.307	.348	.515	.863	118	16	13	105	129	89	.799	3			-10	*1	-0.2
1951	Cin-N	154	607	74	157	35	2	13	77	35	33	.259	.301	.387	.688	83	-15	-16	101	115	69	.594	6	2	1	-6	*1	-2.3
1952	Cin-N	135	497	62	159	24	11	16	86	47	28	.320	.383	.509	.892	146	30	30	100	118	97	.867	3	3	-1	-11	*1	1.4
1953	Cin-N	149	570	97	180	25	0	40	108	55	34	.316	.380	.570	.950	145	35	36	99	100	126	.958	2	0	1	-19	*1	1.4
1954	Cin-N	149	573	104	187	28	3	**49**	**141**	78	35	.326	.410	.642	1.052	163	57	54	104	104	151	1.122	0	2	-1	-3	*1	4.3
1955	Cin-N	153	612	116	**192**	25	0	47	113	66	40	.314	.384	.585	.969	144	45	40	106	88	136	.995	1	1	-0	-9	*1	1.9
1956	Cin-N	138	517	91	156	14	1	35	102	49	31	.302	.366	.536	.901	128	27	22	108	115	99	.887	1	0	0	-2	*1	1.4
1957	Cin-N	69	127	12	34	7	0	6	21	5	5	.268	.301	.465	.765	96	-0	-1	105	113	17	.684	0	0	0	0	1	-0.2
1958	Pit-N	100	301	29	88	13	4	4	37	26	16	.292	.351	.402	.753	104	-0	2	95	115	41	.670	0	0	0	-1	1	-0.3

YEAR	TM/L	G	AB	R	H	2B	3B	HR	RBI	BB	SO	AVG	OBP	SLG	PRO	/A	BR	/A	PF	CHI	RC	TA	SB	CS	SBR	FR	POS	TPR
1959	Pit-N	60	122	11	32	10	1	2	17	5	14	.262	.291	.410	.701	82	-3	-4	103	123	14	.591	0	0	0	-0	1	-0.4
	Chi-A	31	101	11	30	2	1	2	10	9	10	.297	.355	.396	.751	109	1	1	97	86	13	.645	0	1	-1	-1	1	0.0
1960	Chi-A	81	181	20	53	9	0	5	39	22	10	.293	.369	.425	.795	113	4	4	101	166	29	.750	0	1	-1	-2	1	0.0
1961	LA-A	107	263	32	64	12	0	15	39	24	23	.243	.307	.460	.767	91	-1	-4	111	92	37	.714	0	0	0	-2	1	-1.2
Total	15	1718	5929	848	1766	290	29	279	1028	492	365	.298	.354	.498	.852	122	190	173	102	111	1036	.835	20	10		-69	*1	5.2
■ **MICKEY KLUTTS** Klutts, Gene Ellis b: 9/20/54, Montebello, Cal. BR/TR, 5'11", 170 lbs. Deb: 7/07/76																												
1976	NY-A	2	3	0	0	0	0	0	0	0	1	.000	.000	.000	.000	-99	-1	-1	99	0	0	.000	0	0	0	-0	/S	0.0
1977	NY-A	5	15	3	4	1	0	1	4	2	1	.267	.389	.533	.922	151	1	1	99	144	3	.917	0	1	-1	0	/3S	0.0
1978	NY-A	1	2	1	2	1	0	0	0	0	0	1.000	1.000	1.500	2.500	602	2	2	99	0	3	—	0	0	0	0	/3	0.1
1979	Oak-A	24	73	3	14	2	1	1	4	7	20	.192	.262	.288	.550	54	-5	-4	89	64	5	.459	0	1	-1	-2	S/23	-0.4
1980	Oak-A	75	197	20	53	14	0	4	21	13	41	.269	.314	.401	.715	100	-2	-0	95	90	22	.608	1	4	-2	-11	3/S2D	-1.2
1981	Oak-A	15	46	9	17	0	0	5	11	2	9	.370	.396	.696	1.091	218	6	6	96	92	13	1.172	0	0	0	-1	3	0.5
1982	Oak-A	55	157	10	28	8	0	0	14	9	18	.178	.223	.229	.452	26	-16	-15	95	155	8	.338	0	0	0	-2	3	-1.7
1983	Tor-A	22	43	3	11	0	0	3	5	1	11	.256	.289	.465	.754	96	0	-0	108	67	5	.667	0	1	-1	-1	3/D	-0.1
Total	8	199	536	49	129	26	1	14	59	34	101	.241	.290	.371	.661	84	-16	-12	95	104	60	.572	1	7	-4	-17	3/S2D	-2.8
■ **CLYDE KLUTTZ** Kluttz, Clyde Franklin b: 12/12/17, Rockwell, N.C. d: 5/12/79, Salisbury, N.C. BR/TR, 6', 193 lbs. Deb: 4/20/42																												
1942	Bos-N	72	210	21	56	10	1	1	31	7	13	.267	.294	.338	.632	89	-5	-4	95	155	20	.500	0			-3	C	-0.5
1943	Bos-N	66	207	13	51	7	0	0	20	15	9	.246	.297	.280	.577	64	-9	-10	106	124	17	.453	0			-0	C	-0.8
1944	Bos-N	81	229	20	64	12	2	2	19	13	14	.279	.318	.376	.694	100	-2	-1	95	74	28	.589	0			2	C	0.4
1945	Bos-N	25	81	9	24	4	1	0	10	2	6	.296	.313	.370	.684	80	-1	-3	112	116	8	.533	0			3	C	0.0
	NY-N	73	222	25	62	14	0	4	21	15	10	.279	.331	.396	.727	102	-0	-0	100	73	29	.642	1			1	C	0.2
	Yr	98	303	34	86	18	1	4	31	17	16	.284	.326	.389	.716	96	-2	-3	103	85	38	.622	1			4		0.2
1946	NY-N	5	8	0	3	0	0	0	1	0	1	.375	.375	.375	.750	111	0	0	102	124	1	.600	0			0	/C	0.0
	StL-N	52	136	8	36	7	0	0	14	10	10	.265	.315	.316	.631	74	-4	-5	107	121	14	.525	0			-4	C	-0.7
	Yr	57	144	8	39	7	0	0	15	10	11	.271	.318	.319	.638	77	-4	-5	106	124	15	.528	0			-4		-0.7
1947	Pit-N	73	232	26	70	9	2	6	42	17	18	.302	.355	.435	.790	108	3	2	101	131	37	.738	1			0	C	0.4
1948	Pit-N	94	271	26	60	12	2	4	20	20	19	.221	.275	.325	.600	59	-15	-17	104	75	25	.516	3			-4	C	-1.3
1951	StL-A	4	4	2	2	1	0	0	1	1	0	.500	.600	.750	1.350	252	1	1	105	119	2	2.000	0	0	0	0	/C	0.1
	Was-A	53	159	15	49	9	0	1	22	20	8	.308	.389	.384	.773	115	3	4	95	123	26	.732	0	0	0	-2	C	0.5
	Yr	57	163	17	51	10	0	1	23	21	8	.313	.395	.393	.787	118	4	5	96	125	27	.754	0	0	0	-2		0.6
1952	Was-A	58	144	7	33	5	0	1	11	12	11	.229	.293	.285	.578	61	-8	-8	100	93	11	.458	0	0	0	-0	C	-0.4
Total	9	656	1903	172	510	90	8	19	212	132	119	.268	.318	.354	.671	86	-37	-39	101	106	218	.584	5	0		-7	C	-2.1
■ **OTTO KNABE** Knabe, Franz Otto "Dutch" b: 6/2/1884, Carrick, Pa. d: 5/17/61, Philadelphia, Pa. BR/TR, 5'8", 175 lbs. Deb: 10/03/05 M																												
1905	Pit-N	3	10	0	3	1	0	0	2	3		.300	.462	.400	.862	154	1	1	104	153	2	1.000	0			0	/3	0.1
1907	Phi-N	129	444	67	113	16	9	1	34	52		.255	.333	.338	.670	108	7	5	104	89	57	.665	18			-1	*2/O	0.7
1908	Phi-N	151	555	63	121	26	8	0	27	49		.218	.281	.294	.575	86	-9	-8	100	61	51	.551	27			11	*2	0.1
1909	Phi-N	113	402	40	94	13	3	0	34	35		.234	.308	.281	.589	79	-7	-10	106	116	36	.536	9			2	*2/O	-0.9
1910	Phi-N	137	510	73	133	18	6	1	44	47	42	.261	.327	.325	.652	94	-6	-4	96	87	62	.613	15			17	*2	1.7
1911	Phi-N	142	528	99	125	15	6	1	42	94	35	.237	.352	.294	.646	76	-10	-15	108	78	64	.675	23			-13	*2	-3.1
1912	Phi-N	126	426	56	120	11	4	0	46	55	20	.282	.366	.326	.693	90	-4	-4	100	114	57	.693	16			1	*2	-0.6
1913	Phi-N	148	571	70	150	25	7	2	53	45	26	.263	.320	.342	.661	79	-8	-17	112	85	68	.610	14			9	*2	-1.2
1914	Bal-F	147	469	45	106	26	2	2	42	53	28	.226	.305	.303	.607	75	-15	-14	99	104	51	.565	10			15	*2M	0.3
1915	Bal-F	103	320	38	81	16	2	1	25	37	16	.253	.331	.325	.656	88	-2	-4	107	84	39	.619	7			-6	2/OM	-0.9
1916	Pit-N	28	89	4	17	3	1	0	9	6	6	.191	.258	.247	.505	53	-5	-5	105	166	7	.431	1			-7	2	-1.2
	Chi-N	51	145	17	40	8	0	0	7	9	18	.276	.327	.331	.658	87	0	-2	117	58	17	.590	3			1	2/S3O	0.0
	Yr	79	234	21	57	11	1	0	16	15	24	.244	.300	.299	.600	75	-4	-7	113	98	24	.525	4			-6		-1.2
Total	11	1278	4469	572	1103	178	48	8	365	485	191	.247	.323	.313	.637	85	-56	-78	104	90	512	.609	143			29	*2/O3S	-5.0
■ **COTTON KNAUPP** Knaupp, Henry Antone b: 8/13/1889, San Antonio, Tex. d: 7/6/67, New Orleans, La. BR/TR, 5'9", 165 lbs. Deb: 8/30/10																												
1910	Cle-A	18	59	3	14	3	1	0	11	8		.237	.338	.322	.660	107	1	1	100	218	7	.644	1			-1	S	0.1
1911	Cle-A	13	39	2	4	1	0	0	0	0		.103	.103	.128	.231	-35	-7	-7	103	0	0	.143	0			-1	S	-0.6
Total	2	31	98	5	18	4	1	0	11	8		.184	.252	.245	.497	48	-6	-6	101	139	7	.425	1			-1	/S	-0.5
■ **ALAN KNICELY** Knicely, Alan Lee b: 5/19/55, Harrisonburg, Va. BR/TR, 6', 190 lbs. Deb: 8/12/79																												
1979	Hou-N	7	6	0	0	0	0	0	0	2	3	.000	.250	.000	.250	-29	-1	-1	90	0	0	.250	0	0	0	0	/C3	0.0
1980	Hou-N	1	1	0	0	0	0	0	0	0	1	.000	.000	.000	.000	-99	-0	-0	98	0	0	.000	0	0	0	0	/H	0.0
1981	Hou-N	3	7	2	4	0	0	2	2	0	1	.571	.571	1.429	2.000	513	3	3	88	49	6	3.333	0	0	0	-0	/CO	0.3
1982	Hou-N	59	133	10	25	2	0	2	12	14	30	.188	.270	.248	.518	46	-9	-9	99	121	9	.425	0	1	-1	-4	CO/3	-1.4
1983	Cin-N	59	98	11	22	3	0	2	10	16	28	.224	.333	.316	.650	79	-2	-2	103	107	9	.566	0	2	-1	-1	C/O1	-0.3
1984	Cin-N	10	29	0	4	0	0	0	5	3	6	.138	.219	.138	.357	2	-4	-4	106	490	1	.269	0	0	0	-1	/1C	-0.4
1985	Cin-N	48	158	17	40	9	0	5	26	16	34	.253	.326	.405	.731	98	1	-0	105	131	20	.653	0	0	0	-5	C	-0.3
	Phi-N	7	7	0	0	0	0	0	0	0	4	.000	.000	.000	.000	-98	-2	-2	102	0	0	.000	0	0	0	0	/1	-0.1
	Yr	55	165	17	40	9	0	5	26	16	38	.242	.313	.388	.701	91	-1	-2	105	117	22	.648	0	0	0	-5		-0.4
1986	StL-N	34	82	8	16	3	0	1	6	17	21	.195	.333	.268	.602	66	-3	-3	103	96	9	.588	1	1	-0	-0	1/C	-0.4
Total	8	228	521	48	111	17	0	12	61	68	128	.213	.306	.315	.621	72	-18	-19	102	133	53	.566	1	4	-2	-11	C/1O3	-2.6
■ **AUSTIN KNICKERBOCKER** Knickerbocker, Austin Jay b: 10/15/18, Bangall, N.Y. BR/TR, 5'11", 185 lbs. Deb: 4/19/47																												
1947	Phi-A	21	48	8	12	3	2	0	2	3	4	.250	.294	.396	.690	90	-1	-1	100	39	5	.579	0	1	-1	-0	O	-0.2
■ **BILL KNICKERBOCKER** Knickerbocker, William Hart b: 12/29/11, Los Angeles, Cal. d: 9/8/63, Sebastopol, Cal. BR/TR, 5'11", 170 lbs. Deb: 4/12/33																												
1933	Cle-A	80	279	20	63	16	3	2	32	11	30	.226	.255	.326	.581	51	-20	-21	105	110	22	.468	1	4	-2	1	S	-1.4
1934	Cle-A	146	593	82	188	32	5	4	67	25	40	.317	.347	.408	.755	94	-6	-7	101	93	82	.669	6	6	-2	-8	*S	-0.5
1935	Cle-A	132	540	77	161	34	5	0	55	27	31	.298	.332	.380	.711	84	-14	-13	99	97	64	.598	2	12	-7	6	*S	-0.6
1936	Cle-A	155	618	81	182	35	3	8	73	56	30	.294	.354	.400	.754	81	-14	-20	106	92	85	.687	5	14	-7	-1	*S	-1.5
1937	StL-A	121	491	53	128	29	5	4	61	30	32	.261	.303	.365	.668	68	-26	-25	99	116	55	.581	3	2	-0	-4	*S/2	-2.0
1938	NY-A	46	128	15	32	8	3	1	21	11	10	.250	.309	.383	.692	69	-6	-7	105	137	16	.625	0	0	0	5	2/S	0.0
1939	NY-A	6	13	2	2	1	0	0	1	0	0	.154	.154	.231	.385	-3	-2	-2	91	113	0	.250	0	0	0	0	/2S	0.0
1940	NY-A	45	124	17	30	8	1	1	10	14	8	.242	.333	.347	.680	78	-4	-4	99	79	15	.622	1	1	-0	-1	S3	-0.2
1941	Chi-A	89	343	51	84	23	2	7	29	41	27	.245	.329	.385	.714	94	-6	-3	94	64	46	.675	6	5	-1	-10	2	-0.5
1942	Phi-A	87	289	25	73	12	0	1	19	29	30	.253	.323	.304	.627	80	-8	-7	96	75	28	.520	1	2	-1	-5	2/S	-1.0
Total	10	907	3418	423	943	198	27	28	368	244	238	.276	.326	.374	.700	80	-107	-109	100	95	413	.615	25	46	-20	-18	S2/3	-7.7
■ **LON KNIGHT** Knight, Alonzo P. b: 6/16/1853, Philadelphia, Pa. d: 4/23/32, Philadelphia, Pa. BR/TR, 5'11.5", 165 lbs. Deb: 9/04/1875 M																												
1875	Ath-n	13	51	5	6							.118															P	
1876	Phi-N	55	240	32	60	9	3	0	24	2	2	.250	.256	.313	.569	89	-3	-3	99	115	20	.428				0	P1/O2	0.0
1880	Wor-N	49	201	31	48	11	3	0	21	5	8	.239	.257	.323	.581	85	-1	-4	113	113	17	.458				3	O	-0.2
1881	Det-N	83	340	67	92	16	3	1	52	23	21	.271	.317	.344	.661	101	3	0	106	133	38	.565				-1	*O/21	-0.1
1882	Det-N	86	347	39	72	12	6	0	24	16	21	.207	.242	.277	.519	65	-13	-14	102	89	24	.407				-2	*O/1	-1.5
1883	Phi-a	97	429	98	108	23	9	1		21		.252	.287	.354	.641	103	3	1	103	0	45	.539				-3	*O/32M	-0.1
1884	Phi-a	108	484	94	131	18	12	1		10		.271	.287	.364	.651	99	6	-4	114	0	52	.530				8	*O/P1M	0.2
1885	Phi-a	29	119	17	25	1	1	0		9		.210	.271	.235	.507	61	-4	-5	103	0	8	.404				4	O/P	-0.2
	Pro-N	25	81	8	13	1	0	0	8	11	17	.160	.261	.173	.434	46	-5	-4	91	203	4	.368				0	O/P	-0.2
Total	7	532	2241	386	549	91	37	3	129	97	69	.245	.277	.323	.600	89	-14	-32	106	64	207	.486				8	O/P123	-2.1
■ **RAY KNIGHT** Knight, Charles Ray b: 12/28/52, Albany, Ga. BR/TR, 6'1", 185 lbs. Deb: 9/10/74																												
1974	Cin-N	14	11	1	2	1	0	0	2	1	2	.182	.250	.273	.523	47	-1	-1	98	257	1	.400	0	0	0	-0	3	-0.1

YEAR	TM/L	G	AB	R	H	2B	3B	HR	RBI	BB	SO	AVG	OBP	SLG	PRO	/A	BR	/A	PF	CHI	RC	TA	SB	CS	SBR	FR	POS	TPR
1977	Cin-N	80	92	8	24	5	1	1	13	9	16	.261	.327	.370	.696	86	-2	-2	100	141	12	.638	1	1	-0	-3	32/OS	-0.4
1978	Cin-N	83	65	7	13	3	0	1	4	3	13	.200	.235	.292	.528	45	-5	-5	103	72	3	.393	0	0	0	-1	3/201S	-0.6
1979	Cin-N	150	551	64	175	37	4	10	79	38	57	.318	.365	.454	.819	125	16	18	97	114	85	.738	4	4	-1	-14	*3	-0.3
1980	Cin-N	162	618	71	163	39	7	14	78	36	62	.264	.309	.417	.726	99	-1	-2	102	105	72	.622	1	2	-1	-16	*3	-2.0
1981	Cin-N	106	386	43	100	23	1	6	34	33	51	.259	.324	.370	.694	96	-2	-2	101	85	42	.591	2	4	-2	-12	*3	-2.2
1982	Hou-N	158	609	72	179	36	6	6	70	48	58	.294	.350	.402	.753	111	8	9	99	100	83	.665	2	5	-2	-0	13	0.0
1983	Hou-N	145	507	43	154	36	4	9	70	42	62	.304	.362	.444	.805	136	15	21	90	112	77	.727	0	3	-2	-10	*1	0.2
1984	Hou-N	88	278	15	62	10	0	2	29	14	30	.223	.263	.281	.543	57	-18	-15	93	135	20	.417	0	3	-2	4	31	-1.4
	NY-N	27	93	13	26	4	0	1	6	7	13	.280	.337	.355	.691	94	-1	-1	100	67	11	.603	0	0	0	-3	3/1	-0.3
	Yr	115	371	28	88	14	0	3	35	21	43	.237	.282	.299	.581	67	-18	-16	94	120	32	.467	0	3	-2	1		-1.7
1985	NY-N	90	271	22	59	12	0	6	36	13	32	.218	.256	.328	.585	64	-14	-13	97	134	18	.452	1	1	-0	-10	3/21	-2.4
1986	NY-N	137	486	51	145	24	2	11	76	40	63	.298	.357	.424	.780	120	9	12	96	129	70	.698	2	1	0	-9	*3/1	0.0
1987	Bal-A	150	563	46	144	24	0	14	65	39	90	.256	.311	.373	.684	83	-15	-13	98	105	63	.586	0	0	0	14	*3D/1	-0.2
1988	Det-A	105	299	34	65	12	2	3	33	20	30	.217	.273	.301	.574	64	-16	-14	94	132	23	.462	1	1	-0	0	1D3/O	-1.7
Total	13	1495	4829	490	1311	266	27	84	595	343	579	.271	.325	.390	.714	100	-25	-9	97	112	579	.640	14	25	-11	-61	*31/D2OS	-11.4

■ **GEORGE KNIGHT** Knight, George Henry b: 11/24/1855, Lakeville, Conn. d: 10/4/12, Lakeville, Conn. Deb: 9/28/1875

YEAR	TM/L	G	AB	R	H	2B	3B	HR	RBI	BB	SO	AVG	OBP	SLG	PRO	/A	BR	/A	PF	CHI	RC	TA	SB	CS	SBR	FR	POS	TPR
1875	NH-n	1	4	0	0							.000															/P	

■ **JOHN KNIGHT** Knight, John Wesley "Schoolboy" b: 10/6/1885, Philadelphia, Pa. d: 12/19/65, Walnut Creek, Cal. BR/TR, 6'2.5", 180 lbs. Deb: 4/14/05

YEAR	TM/L	G	AB	R	H	2B	3B	HR	RBI	BB	SO	AVG	OBP	SLG	PRO	/A	BR	/A	PF	CHI	RC	TA	SB	CS	SBR	FR	POS	TPR
1905	Phi-A	88	325	28	66	12	1	3	29	9		.203	.225	.274	.498	54	-15	-19	109	108	21	.394	4			-19	S/3	-3.8
1906	Phi-A	74	253	29	49	7	2	3	20	19		.194	.250	.273	.523	70	-10	-8	94	95	19	.461	6			2	3/2	-0.1
1907	Phi-A	40	139	9	29	6	1	0	12	10		.209	.262	.266	.528	66	-5	-5	106	118	10	.436	1			-2	3	-0.5
	Bos-A	98	360	28	78	10	3	2	29	19		.217	.256	.278	.534	71	-12	-12	101	104	28	.450	8			1	3/2	-0.5
	Yr	138	499	37	107	16	4	2	41	29		.214	.258	.275	.532	70	-16	-17	102	109	39	.446	9			-1		-1.0
1909	NY-A	116	360	46	85	8	5	0	40	37		.236	.311	.286	.597	89	-4	-4	99	150	35	.571	15			-8	S12	-1.1
1910	NY-A	117	414	58	129	25	4	3	45	34		.312	.372	.413	.785	136	21	18	107	98	72	.821	23			-4	S1/23O	1.7
1911	NY-A	132	470	69	126	16	7	3	62	42		.268	.342	.351	.693	85	-4	-11	111	128	63	.686	18			-10	S12/3	-1.2
1912	Was-A	32	93	10	15	2	1	0	9	16		.161	.284	.204	.489	41	-7	-7	99	158	6	.500	4			-3	2/1	-1.0
1913	NY-A	70	250	24	59	10	0	0	24	25	27	.236	.310	.276	.586	71	-8	-9	101	131	23	.539	7			3	12	-0.6
Total	8	767	2664	301	636	96	24	14	270	211	27	.239	.300	.309	.608	83	-43	-56	104	118	279	.562	86			-41	S312/O	-7.1

■ **JOE KNIGHT** Knight, Jonas William "Quiet Joe" b: 9/28/1859, Point Stanley, Ont., Canada d: 10/18/38, St.Thomas, Ont., Can. BL/TL, 5'11", 185 lbs. Deb: 5/16/1884

YEAR	TM/L	G	AB	R	H	2B	3B	HR	RBI	BB	SO	AVG	OBP	SLG	PRO	/A	BR	/A	PF	CHI	RC	TA	SB	CS	SBR	FR	POS	TPR
1884	Phi-N	6	24	2	6	3	0	0	2	0	2	.250	.250	.375	.625	102	-0	0	92	78	2	.500				0	/P	0.0
1890	Cin-N	127	481	67	150	26	8	4	67	38	31	.312	.367	.424	.791	123	19	13	108	96	83	.795	17			-8	*O	0.2
Total	2	133	505	69	156	29	8	4	69	38	33	.309	.362	.422	.784	122	19	13	107	95	85	.779	17			-8	O/P	0.2

■ **PETE KNISELY** Knisely, Peter Cole b: 8/11/1887, Waynesburg, Pa. d: 7/1/48, Brownsville, Pa. BR/TR, Deb: N/A.

YEAR	TM/L	G	AB	R	H	2B	3B	HR	RBI	BB	SO	AVG	OBP	SLG	PRO	/A	BR	/A	PF	CHI	RC	TA	SB	CS	SBR	FR	POS	TPR
1912	Cin-N	21	67	10	22	7	3	0	7	4	5	.328	.375	.522	.897	156	4	4	92	67	14	.956	3			2	O/2S	0.6
1913	Chi-N	2	2	0	0	0	0	0	0	0	1	.000	.000	.000	.000	-99	-1	-1	99	0	0	.000	0			0	H	0.0
1914	Chi-N	37	69	5	9	0	1	0	5	5	6	.130	.200	.159	.359	7	-8	-8	98	165	2	.283	0			3	O	-0.5
1915	Chi-N	64	134	12	33	9	0	0	17	15	18	.246	.331	.313	.645	94	-0	-1	102	155	14	.583	1	2	-1	-4	O/2	-0.6
Total	4	124	272	27	64	16	4	0	29	24	30	.235	.307	.324	.630	86	-5	-4	99	135	30	.571	4	2		1	/O2S	-0.5

■ **MIKE KNODE** Knode, Kenneth Thomson b: 11/8/1895, Westminster, Md. d: 12/20/80, South Bend, Ind. BR/TR, 5'10", 160 lbs. Deb: 6/28/20

YEAR	TM/L	G	AB	R	H	2B	3B	HR	RBI	BB	SO	AVG	OBP	SLG	PRO	/A	BR	/A	PF	CHI	RC	TA	SB	CS	SBR	FR	POS	TPR
1920	StL-N	42	65	11	15	1	1	0	12	5	6	.231	.306	.277	.582	70	-2	-2	98	258	6	.490	0	1	-1	-1	/O2S3	-0.4

■ **RAY KNODE** Knode, Robert Troxell "Bob" b: 1/28/01, Westminster, Md. d: 4/13/82, Battle Creek, Mich BL/TL, 5'10", 160 lbs. Deb: 6/30/23

YEAR	TM/L	G	AB	R	H	2B	3B	HR	RBI	BB	SO	AVG	OBP	SLG	PRO	/A	BR	/A	PF	CHI	RC	TA	SB	CS	SBR	FR	POS	TPR
1923	Cle-A	22	38	7	11	0	0	2	4	2	4	.289	.325	.447	.772	101	-0	-0	101	59	6	.741	1	0	0	0	1	0.0
1924	Cle-A	11	37	6	9	1	0	0	4	3	0	.243	.300	.270	.570	49	-3	-3	97	132	3	.517	2	1	0	1	1	-0.1
1925	Cle-A	45	108	13	27	5	0	0	11	10	4	.250	.314	.296	.610	52	-7	-8	106	115	10	.536	3	3	-1	0	1	-0.8
1926	Cle-A	31	24	6	8	1	1	0	4	3	4	.333	.407	.458	.866	126	1	1	100	124	5	.875	0	0	0	0	1	0.1
Total	4	109	207	32	55	7	1	2	23	18	12	.266	.324	.338	.663	68	-9	-10	103	109	24	.603	6	4	-1	1	/1	-0.8

■ **PUNCH KNOLL** Knoll, Charles Elmer b: 10/7/1881, Evansville, Ind. d: 2/7/60, Evansville, Ind. BR/TR, 5'7.5", 170 lbs. Deb: 4/27/05

YEAR	TM/L	G	AB	R	H	2B	3B	HR	RBI	BB	SO	AVG	OBP	SLG	PRO	/A	BR	/A	PF	CHI	RC	TA	SB	CS	SBR	FR	POS	TPR
1905	Was-A	79	244	24	52	10	5	0	29	9		.213	.241	.295	.536	68	-8	-9	104	144	19	.438	3			5	O/C1	-0.7

■ **BOBBY KNOOP** Knoop, Robert Frank b: 10/18/38, Sioux City, Iowa BR/TR, 6'1", 170 lbs. Deb: 4/13/64 C

YEAR	TM/L	G	AB	R	H	2B	3B	HR	RBI	BB	SO	AVG	OBP	SLG	PRO	/A	BR	/A	PF	CHI	RC	TA	SB	CS	SBR	FR	POS	TPR
1964	LA-A	162	486	42	105	8	1	7	38	46	109	.216	.291	.280	.570	67	-26	-19	89	103	39	.475	3	2	-0	**37**	*2	3.5
1965	Cal-A	142	465	47	125	24	4	7	43	31	101	.269	.315	.383	.697	99	-2	-1	98	90	56	.609	3	2	-0	19	*2	2.6
1966	Cal-A	161	590	54	137	18	**11**	17	72	43	144	.232	.285	.386	.672	92	-8	-7	99	115	61	.578	1	5	-3	23	*2	2.9
1967	Cal-A	159	511	51	125	18	5	9	38	44	136	.245	.306	.352	.658	98	-4	-2	96	77	54	.570	2	2	-1	5	*2	0.8
1968	Cal-A	152	494	48	123	20	4	3	39	35	128	.249	.303	.324	.627	96	-6	-3	94	99	47	.521	3	2	-0	12	*2	1.5
1969	Cal-A	27	71	5	14	1	0	1	6	13	16	.197	.321	.254	.575	63	-3	-3	99	115	6	.516	1	3	-2	-1	2	-0.4
	Chi-A	104	345	34	79	14	1	6	41	35	68	.229	.304	.328	.631	71	-11	-14	108	126	34	.549	2	0	1	20	*2	1.0
	Yr	131	416	39	93	15	1	7	47	48	84	.224	.307	.315	.622	70	-14	-17	107	124	40	.546	3	3	-1	18		0.6
1970	Chi-A	130	402	34	92	13	2	5	36	34	79	.229	.292	.308	.601	62	-19	-22	106	105	37	.503	0	1	-1	23	*2	1.3
1971	KC-A	72	161	14	33	8	1	1	11	15	36	.205	.273	.286	.558	59	-9	-9	99	92	12	.463	1	0	0	-2	2/3	-0.8
1972	KC-A	44	97	8	23	5	0	0	7	9	16	.237	.302	.289	.591	76	-3	-3	100	104	8	.468	0	0	0	1	2/3	0.0
Total	9	1153	3622	337	856	129	29	56	331	305	833	.236	.298	.334	.632	83	-91	-83	98	101	353	.555	16	17	-5	135	*2/3	12.4

■ **GEORGE KNOTHE** Knothe, George Bertram b: 1/12/1898, Bayonne, N.J. d: 7/3/81, Dover, N.J. BR/TR, 5'10", 165 lbs. Deb: 4/25/32

YEAR	TM/L	G	AB	R	H	2B	3B	HR	RBI	BB	SO	AVG	OBP	SLG	PRO	/A	BR	/A	PF	CHI	RC	TA	SB	CS	SBR	FR	POS	TPR
1932	Phi-N	6	12	2	1	1	0	0	0	0	0	.083	.083	.167	.250	-31	-2	-2	112	0	0	.182	0			-0	/2	-0.1

■ **FRITZ KNOTHE** Knothe, Wilfred Edgar b: 5/1/03, Passaic, N.J. d: 3/27/63, Passaic, N.J. BR/TR, 5'10.5", 180 lbs. Deb: 4/12/32

YEAR	TM/L	G	AB	R	H	2B	3B	HR	RBI	BB	SO	AVG	OBP	SLG	PRO	/A	BR	/A	PF	CHI	RC	TA	SB	CS	SBR	FR	POS	TPR
1932	Bos-N	89	344	45	82	19	1	1	36	39	37	.238	.318	.308	.626	74	-14	-11	93	130	36	.576	5			-4	3	-0.6
1933	Bos-N	44	158	15	36	5	2	1	6	13	25	.228	.291	.304	.594	72	-6	-5	96	47	15	.508	1			2	3/S	-0.2
	Phi-N	41	113	10	17	2	0	0	11	6	19	.150	.193	.168	.361	3	-14	-16	118	218	3	.270	2			3	3/2	-1.2
	Yr	85	271	25	53	7	2	1	17	19	44	.196	.251	.247	.498	40	-20	-22	107	130	18	.405	3			4		-1.4
Total	2	174	615	70	135	26	3	2	53	58	81	.220	.289	.281	.570	59	-34	-32	98	124	55	.498	8			1	3/S2	-2.0

■ **JOE KNOTTS** Knotts, Joseph Steven b: 3/3/1884, Greensboro, Pa. d: 9/15/50, Philadelphia, Pa. BR/TR, Deb: 9/18/07

YEAR	TM/L	G	AB	R	H	2B	3B	HR	RBI	BB	SO	AVG	OBP	SLG	PRO	/A	BR	/A	PF	CHI	RC	TA	SB	CS	SBR	FR	POS	TPR
1907	Bos-N	3	8	0	0	0	0	0	0	1		.000	.111	.000	.111	-68	-1	-1	95	0	0	.125	0			0	/C	0.0

■ **JAKE KNOWDELL** Knowdell, Jacob Augustus b: 7/27/1840, Brooklyn, N.Y. 5'7.5", 148 lbs. Deb: 6/20/1874

YEAR	TM/L	G	AB	R	H	2B	3B	HR	RBI	BB	SO	AVG	OBP	SLG	PRO	/A	BR	/A	PF	CHI	RC	TA	SB	CS	SBR	FR	POS	TPR
1874	Atl-n	23	90	8	12							.133															C/O	
1875	Atl-n	43	165	17	32							.194															C/SO	
1878	Mil-N	4	14	2	3	1	0	0	2	0	3	.214	.214	.286	.500	59	-1	-1	107	169	1	.364				0	/COS	0.0
Total	2 n	66	255	25	44							.173															/COS	

■ **JIMMY KNOWLES** Knowles, James "Darby" b: 1859, Toronto, Ont., Canada d: 3/1/04, Chicago, Ill. 5'9", 160 lbs. Deb: 5/02/1884

YEAR	TM/L	G	AB	R	H	2B	3B	HR	RBI	BB	SO	AVG	OBP	SLG	PRO	/A	BR	/A	PF	CHI	RC	TA	SB	CS	SBR	FR	POS	TPR
1884	Pit-a	46	182	19	42	5	7	0		5		.231	.259	.335	.594	98	-1	-0	97	0	16	.486				-0	1	-0.2
	Bro-a	41	153	19	36	5	1	1		3		.235	.255	.301	.555	85	-3	-2	98	0	12	.427				2	13	0.0
	Yr	87	335	38	78	10	8	1		8		.233	.257	.319	.577	92	-4	-2	97	0	28	.459				2		-0.2
1886	Was-N	115	443	43	94	16	11	3	35	15	73	.212	.238	.318	.556	73	-18	-14	94	81	39	.504	20			24	23	1.4
1887	NY-a	16	60	12	15	1	1	0		1		.250	.262	.300	.562	66	-3	-2	88	0	6	.556	6			0	2/3	-0.1
1890	Roc-a	123	491	83	138	12	8	5		59		.281	.359	.369	.728	127	11	17	93	0	87	.839	55			3	*3	1.6
1892	NY-N	16	59	9	9	1	0	0	7	6	8	.153	.231	.169	.400	23	-5	-5	98	219	3	.360	2			0	3/S	-0.4
Total	5	357	1388	185	334	40	28	9	42	89	81	.241	.288	.329	.618	95	-19	-6	94	35	164	.601	83			29	3/21S	2.3

■ ANDY KNOX Knox, Andrew Jackson "Dasher" b: 1/6/1864, Philadelphia, Pa. d: 9/14/40, Philadelphia, Pa. BR/TR, Deb: 9/19/1890

YEAR	TM/L	G	AB	R	H	2B	3B	HR	RBI	BB	SO	AVG	OBP	SLG	PRO	/A	BR	/A	PF	CHI	RC	TA	SB	CS	SBR	FR	POS	TPR
1890	Phi-a	21	75	6	19	3	0	0		9		.253	.333	.293	.627	90	-1	-1	97	0	9	.643	5			0	1	0.0

■ CLIFF KNOX Knox, Clifford Hiram "Bud" b: 1/7/02, Coalville, Iowa d: 9/24/65, Oskaloosa, Iowa BB/TR, 5'11.5", 178 lbs. Deb: 7/01/24

YEAR	TM/L	G	AB	R	H	2B	3B	HR	RBI	BB	SO	AVG	OBP	SLG	PRO	/A	BR	/A	PF	CHI	RC	TA	SB	CS	SBR	FR	POS	TPR
1924	Pit-N	6	18	1	4	0	0	0	2	2	0	.222	.300	.222	.522	39	-1	-2	106	182	1	.429	0	0	0	0	/C	-0.1

■ JOHN KNOX Knox, John Clinton b: 7/26/48, Newark, N.J. BL/TR, 6', 170 lbs. Deb: 8/01/72

YEAR	TM/L	G	AB	R	H	2B	3B	HR	RBI	BB	SO	AVG	OBP	SLG	PRO	/A	BR	/A	PF	CHI	RC	TA	SB	CS	SBR	FR	POS	TPR
1972	Det-A	14	13	1	1	1	0	0	0	1	2	.077	.143	.154	.297	-10	-2	-2	113	0	0	.250	0	0	0	0	/2	-0.1
1973	Det-A	12	32	1	9	1	0	0	3	3	3	.281	.343	.313	.655	85	-1	-1	101	118	4	.583	1	1	-0	-0	/2	0.0
1974	Det-A	55	88	11	27	1	1	0	6	6	13	.307	.351	.341	.692	94	0	-1	106	79	9	.594	5	4	-1	-2	2/3D	-0.1
1975	Det-A	43	86	8	23	1	0	0	2	10	9	.267	.344	.279	.623	75	-2	-3	104	32	8	.507	1	2	-1	-0	2/3D	-0.2
Total	4	124	219	21	60	4	1	0	11	20	27	.274	.335	.301	.636	79	-4	-6	105	61	21	.547	7	7	-2	-3	/2D3	-0.4

■ NICK KOBACK Koback, Nicholas Nicholie b: 7/19/35, Hartford, Conn. BR/TR, 6', 187 lbs. Deb: 7/29/53

YEAR	TM/L	G	AB	R	H	2B	3B	HR	RBI	BB	SO	AVG	OBP	SLG	PRO	/A	BR	/A	PF	CHI	RC	TA	SB	CS	SBR	FR	POS	TPR
1953	Pit-N	7	16	1	2	0	1	0	0	1	4	.125	.176	.250	.426	9	-2	-2	102	0	0	.313	0	0	0	0	/C	-0.1
1954	Pit-N	4	10	0	0	0	0	0	0	0	8	.000	.000	.000	.000	-99	-3	-3	97	0	0	.000	0	0	0	1	/C	-0.1
1955	Pit-N	5	7	0	2	0	0	0	0	0	1	.286	.286	.286	.571	54	-0	-0	97	0	1	.400	0	0	0	0	/C	0.0
Total	3	16	33	1	4	0	1	0	0	1	13	.121	.147	.182	.329	-15	-6	-6	99	0	1	.241	0	0	0	1	/C	-0.2

■ BARNEY KOCH Koch, Barnett b: 3/23/23, Campbell, Neb. d: 6/6/87, Tacoma, Wash. BR/TR, 5'8", 140 lbs. Deb: 7/23/44

YEAR	TM/L	G	AB	R	H	2B	3B	HR	RBI	BB	SO	AVG	OBP	SLG	PRO	/A	BR	/A	PF	CHI	RC	TA	SB	CS	SBR	FR	POS	TPR
1944	Bro-N	33	96	11	21	2	0	0	1	3	9	.219	.242	.240	.482	36	-8	-8	99	16	6	.342	0			-4	2/S	-0.9

■ BRAD KOCHER Kocher, Bradley Wilson b: 1/16/1888, White Haven, Pa. d: 1/13/65, White Haven, Pa. BR/TR, 5'11", 188 lbs. Deb: 4/24/12

YEAR	TM/L	G	AB	R	H	2B	3B	HR	RBI	BB	SO	AVG	OBP	SLG	PRO	/A	BR	/A	PF	CHI	RC	TA	SB	CS	SBR	FR	POS	TPR
1912	Det-A	24	63	5	13	3	1	0	9	2		.206	.231	.286	.516	50	-5	-4	95	167	4	.400	0			-2	C	-0.2
1915	NY-N	4	11	3	5	0	1	0	2	0	1	.455	.455	.636	1.091	250	2	2	91	109	3	1.167	0			-0	/C	0.2
1916	NY-N	34	65	1	7	2	0	0	1	2	10	.108	.134	.138	.273	-17	-9	-9	96	44	1	.190	0			-2	C	-0.9
Total	3	62	139	9	25	5	2	0	12	4	11	.180	.203	.245	.447	34	-12	-11	95	105	9	.333	0			-4	/C	-0.9

■ PETE KOEGEL Koegel, Peter John b: 7/31/47, Mineola, N.Y. BR/TR, 6'6.5", 230 lbs. Deb: 9/01/70

YEAR	TM/L	G	AB	R	H	2B	3B	HR	RBI	BB	SO	AVG	OBP	SLG	PRO	/A	BR	/A	PF	CHI	RC	TA	SB	CS	SBR	FR	POS	TPR
1970	Mil-A	7	8	2	2	0	0	1	1	1	3	.250	.333	.625	.958	161	1	1	98	51	2	1.000	0	0	0	-0	/O	0.0
1971	Mil-A	2	3	0	0	0	0	0	0	2	2	.000	.400	.000	.400	21	-0	-0	103	0	0	.667	0	0	0	0	/1	0.0
	Phi-N	12	26	1	6	1	0	0	3	2	7	.231	.286	.269	.555	56	-1	-1	103	174	2	.429	0	0	0	0	/CO	0.0
1972	Phi-N	41	49	3	7	2	0	0	1	6	16	.143	.236	.184	.420	21	-5	-5	97	46	2	.349	0	0	0	-1	/1C3O	-0.6
Total	3	62	86	6	15	3	0	1	5	11	28	.174	.268	.244	.512	46	-6	-6	99	81	6	.444	0	0	0	-1	/C13O	-0.6

■ BEN KOEHLER Koehler, Benard James b: 1/26/1877, Schoerndorn, Germany d: 5/21/61, South Bend, Ind. BR/TR, 5'10.5", 175 lbs. Deb: 4/23/05

YEAR	TM/L	G	AB	R	H	2B	3B	HR	RBI	BB	SO	AVG	OBP	SLG	PRO	/A	BR	/A	PF	CHI	RC	TA	SB	CS	SBR	FR	POS	TPR
1905	StL-A	142	536	55	127	14	6	2	47	32		.237	.280	.297	.577	93	-9	-4	91	108	52	.521	22			-7	*O1/2	-1.9
1906	StL-A	66	186	27	41	1	1	0	15	24		.220	.310	.237	.546	75	-4	-4	98	124	17	.531	9			-1	O/2S3	-0.7
Total	2	208	722	82	168	15	7	2	62	56		.233	.288	.281	.569	88	-14	-8	93	112	69	.523	31			-8	O/213S	-2.6

■ PIP KOEHLER Koehler, Horace Levering b: 1/16/02, Gilbert, Pa. d: 12/8/86, Tacoma, Wash. BR/TR, 5'10", 165 lbs. Deb: 4/22/25

YEAR	TM/L	G	AB	R	H	2B	3B	HR	RBI	BB	SO	AVG	OBP	SLG	PRO	/A	BR	/A	PF	CHI	RC	TA	SB	CS	SBR	FR	POS	TPR
1925	NY-N	12	2	1	0	0	0	0	0	0	1	.000	.000	.000	.000	-99	-1	-1	99	0	0	.000	0	0	0	-1	/O	-0.1

■ LEN KOENECKE Koenecke, Leonard George b: 1/18/04, Baraboo, Wis. d: 9/17/35, Toronto, Ont., Can BL/TR, 5'11", 180 lbs. Deb: 4/12/32

YEAR	TM/L	G	AB	R	H	2B	3B	HR	RBI	BB	SO	AVG	OBP	SLG	PRO	/A	BR	/A	PF	CHI	RC	TA	SB	CS	SBR	FR	POS	TPR
1932	NY-N	42	137	33	35	5	0	4	14	11	13	.255	.320	.380	.700	89	-2	-2	99	81	17	.667	3			-7	O	-1.1
1934	Bro-N	123	460	79	147	31	7	14	73	70	38	.320	.411	.509	.919	153	31	34	95	101	103	.981	8			-1	*O	2.6
1935	Bro-N	100	325	43	92	13	2	4	27	43	45	.283	.369	.372	.741	106	1	4	94	73	49	.696	0			-8	O	-0.6
Total	3	265	922	155	274	49	9	22	114	124	96	.297	.383	.441	.824	127	30	37	95	88	169	.837	11			-16	O	0.9

■ MARK KOENIG Koenig, Mark Anthony b: 7/19/02, San Francisco, Cal BB/TR, 6', 180 lbs. Deb: 9/08/25

YEAR	TM/L	G	AB	R	H	2B	3B	HR	RBI	BB	SO	AVG	OBP	SLG	PRO	/A	BR	/A	PF	CHI	RC	TA	SB	CS	SBR	FR	POS	TPR
1925	NY-A	28	110	14	23	6	1	0	4	5	4	.209	.243	.282	.525	34	-12	-11	96	46	7	.409	0	1	-1	-1	S	-0.7
1926	NY-A	147	617	93	167	26	8	5	62	43	37	.271	.319	.363	.682	78	-22	-21	99	78	72	.600	4	3	-1	-1	*S	-1.0
1927	NY-A	123	526	99	150	20	11	3	62	25	21	.285	.320	.382	.702	82	-16	-15	100	94	62	.614	3	0	1	13	*S	0.7
1928	NY-A	132	533	89	170	19	10	4	63	32	19	.319	.360	.415	.774	112	2	8	92	98	78	.701	3	5	-2	-14	*S	0.3
1929	NY-A	116	373	44	109	27	5	3	41	23	17	.292	.335	.416	.751	93	-5	-4	99	86	52	.679	1	1	-0	4	S3/2	0.6
1930	NY-A	21	74	9	17	5	0	0	9	6	5	.230	.296	.297	.594	57	-5	-4	90	138	7	.509	0	0	0	0	S	-0.1
	Det-A	76	267	37	64	9	2	1	16	20	15	.240	.295	.300	.595	49	-20	-22	105	65	25	.507	2	0	1	-2	S/P3O	-1.3
	Yr	97	341	46	81	14	2	1	25	26	20	.238	.295	.299	.595	50	-25	-26	102	82	32	.508	2	0	1	-2		-1.4
1931	Det-A	106	364	33	92	24	4	1	39	14	12	.253	.282	.349	.631	63	-19	-21	104	99	36	.547	8	2	1	-5	2S/P	-1.6
1932	Chi-N	33	102	15	36	5	1	3	11	3	5	.353	.377	.510	.887	130	5	4	104	67	19	.848	0			7	S	1.3
1933	Chi-N	80	218	32	62	12	1	3	25	15	9	.284	.330	.390	.720	108	1	2	97	100	28	.644	5			1	3S/2	0.6
1934	Cin-N	151	633	60	172	26	6	1	67	15	24	.272	.289	.336	.625	66	-30	-31	101	107	59	.487	5			-2	3S2/1	-2.3
1935	NY-N	107	396	40	112	12	0	3	37	13	18	.283	.306	.336	.641	75	-15	-14	96	94	39	.493	0			0	2S3	-0.6
1936	NY-N	42	58	7	16	4	0	1	7	8	4	.276	.373	.397	.770	107	1	1	100	95	10	.762	0			2	S/23	0.4
Total	12	1162	4271	572	1190	195	49	28	443	222	190	.279	.316	.367	.683	80	-135	-128	99	91	495	.592	31	12		1	S32/P10	-3.7

■ HENRY KOHLER Kohler, Henry C. b: 5/5/1852, Baltimore, Md. d: 8/27/34, Baltimore, Md. Deb: 7/12/1871

YEAR	TM/L	G	AB	R	H	2B	3B	HR	RBI	BB	SO	AVG	OBP	SLG	PRO	/A	BR	/A	PF	CHI	RC	TA	SB	CS	SBR	FR	POS	TPR
1871	Kek-n	3	12	0	2							.167															/13	
1873	Mar-n	6	22	2	3							.136															/3C	
1874	Bal-n	1	4	0	0							.000															/1	
Total	3 n	10	38	2	5							.132															/1	

■ DICK KOKOS Kokos, Richard Jerome (born Richard Jerome Kokoszka) b: 2/28/28, Chicago, Ill. d: 4/9/86, Chicago, Ill. BL/TL, 5'8.5", 170 lbs. Deb: 7/08/48

YEAR	TM/L	G	AB	R	H	2B	3B	HR	RBI	BB	SO	AVG	OBP	SLG	PRO	/A	BR	/A	PF	CHI	RC	TA	SB	CS	SBR	FR	POS	TPR
1948	StL-A	71	258	40	77	15	3	4	40	28	32	.298	.374	.426	.800	106	4	2	106	113	44	.784	4	3	-1	-5	O	-0.5
1949	StL-A	143	501	80	131	28	1	23	77	66	91	.261	.351	.459	.810	114	7	7	100	90	86	.797	3	5	-2	3	*O	0.4
1950	StL-A	143	490	77	128	27	5	18	67	88	73	.261	.375	.447	.822	102	7	2	107	86	87	.832	8	8	-2	9	*O	0.6
1953	StL-A	107	299	41	72	12	0	13	38	56	53	.241	.361	.411	.772	101	4	1	107	87	47	.758	0	5	-3	-4	O	-0.7
1954	Bal-A	11	10	1	2	0	0	1	1	4	3	.200	.429	.500	.929	161	1	1	95	47	2	1.000	0	0	0	0	/O	0.1
Total	5	475	1558	239	410	82	9	59	223	242	252	.263	.365	.441	.806	107	24	14	104	92	266	.813	15	21	-8	3	O	-0.1

■ GARY KOLB Kolb, Gary Alan b: 3/13/40, Rock Falls, Ill. BL/TR, 6', 194 lbs. Deb: 9/07/60

YEAR	TM/L	G	AB	R	H	2B	3B	HR	RBI	BB	SO	AVG	OBP	SLG	PRO	/A	BR	/A	PF	CHI	RC	TA	SB	CS	SBR	FR	POS	TPR
1960	StL-N	9	3	1	0	0	0	0	0	0	0	.000	.000	.000	.000	-93	-1	-1	108	0	0	.000	0	0	0	0	/O	0.0
1962	StL-N	6	14	1	5	0	0	0	0	1	3	.357	.400	.357	.757	97	0	0	109	0	2	.600	0	0	0	-1	/O	0.0
1963	StL-N	75	96	23	26	1	5	3	10	22	26	.271	.407	.479	.886	144	8	7	107	76	21	.972	2	1	0	-11	O/C3	-0.7
1964	Mil-N	36	64	7	12	1	0	0	2	6	10	.188	.257	.203	.460	33	-6	-5	97	63	4	.407	3	2	-0	-3	O/32C	-0.9
1965	Mil-N	24	27	3	7	0	0	0	1	1	6	.259	.286	.259	.545	53	-2	-2	104	59	2	.364	0	0	0	-3	O	-0.4
	NY-N	40	90	8	15	2	0	1	7	3	28	.167	.194	.222	.416	17	-10	-10	100	126	4	.338	3	0	1	-1	O/13	-1.1
	Yr	64	117	11	22	2	0	1	8	4	34	.188	.215	.231	.446	25	-11	-12	102	102	6	.351	3	0	1	-3		-1.5
1968	Pit-N	74	119	16	26	4	1	2	6	11	17	.218	.285	.319	.604	80	-3	-3	101	57	11	.531	2	1	0	-3	OC/32	-0.6
1969	Pit-N	29	37	4	3	1	0	0	3	2	14	.081	.128	.108	.236	-35	-7	-6	95	301	1	.176	0	0	0	0	/C	-0.5
Total	7	293	450	63	94	9	6	6	29	46	104	.209	.282	.296	.578	65	-19	-20	102	93	43	.525	10	4	1	-20	O/C321	-4.2

■ DON KOLLOWAY Kolloway, Donald Martin "Butch" or "Cab" b: 8/4/18, Posen, Ill. BR/TR, 6'3", 200 lbs. Deb: 9/16/40

YEAR	TM/L	G	AB	R	H	2B	3B	HR	RBI	BB	SO	AVG	OBP	SLG	PRO	/A	BR	/A	PF	CHI	RC	TA	SB	CS	SBR	FR	POS	TPR
1940	Chi-A	10	40	5	9	1	0	0	3	0	3	.225	.225	.250	.475	22	-5	-5	104	111	2	.344	1	0	0	-2	2	-0.4
1941	Chi-A	71	280	33	76	8	3	3	24	6	12	.271	.292	.354	.645	75	-13	-11	94	80	27	.546	11	4	1	-6	2/1	-0.9
1942	Chi-A	147	601	72	164	**40**	4	3	60	30	39	.273	.311	.368	.678	91	-10	-9	99	88	66	.582	16	14	-4	-4	*21	-1.3
1943	Chi-A	85	348	29	75	14	4	1	33	9	30	.216	.235	.287	.523	52	-22	-22	101	124	22	.418	11	7	-1	2	2	-1.8
1946	Chi-A	123	482	45	135	23	4	3	53	9	29	.280	.293	.363	.656	85	-13	-11	97	112	52	.553	14	6	1	3	23	0.2
1947	Chi-A	124	485	49	135	25	4	2	35	17	34	.278	.303	.359	.662	86	-13	-11	97	76	48	.537	11	4	1	10	21/3	0.5
1948	Chi-A	119	417	60	114	14	4	6	38	18	18	.273	.303	.369	.673	82	-15	-12	95	75	44	.549	2	4	-2	13	23	0.0
1949	Chi-A	4	4	0	0	0	0	0	0	0	1	.000	.000	.000	.000	-99	-1	-1	98	0	0	.000	0	0	0	0	/3	0.0

YEAR	TM/L	G	AB	R	H	2B	3B	HR	RBI	BB	SO	AVG	OBP	SLG	PRO	/A	BR	/A	PF	CHI	RC	TA	SB	CS	SBR	FR	POS	TPR
	Det-A	126	483	71	142	19	3	2	47	49	25	.294	.361	.358	.720	84	-6	-11	108	92	62	.633	7	7	-2	-9	21/3	-1.9
	Yr	130	487	71	142	19	3	2	47	49	26	.292	.359	.355	.714	83	-7	-12	107	89	61	.626	7	7	-2	-9		-1.9
1950	Det-A	125	467	55	135	20	4	6	62	29	28	.289	.331	.388	.718	86	-13	-11	97	110	57	.603	1	3	-2	2	*1/2	-1.4
1951	Det-A	78	212	28	54	7	0	1	17	15	12	.255	.307	.302	.609	62	-10	-12	106	91	19	.488	2	3	-1	3	1	-1.0
1952	Det-A	65	173	19	42	9	0	2	21	7	19	.243	.280	.329	.610	70	-8	-7	99	124	15	.478	0	2	-1	-0	1/2	-1.0
1953	Phi-A	2	1	0	0	0	0	0	0	0	1	.000	.000	.000	.000	-98	-0	-0	102	0	0	.000	0	0	0	0	/3	0.0
Total	12	1079	3993	466	1081	180	30	29	393	189	251	.271	.305	.353	.658	80	-128	-123	99	95	413	.567	76	54	-10	12	21/3	-9.0
■ **KARL KOLSETH** Kolseth, Karl Dickey "Koley" b: 12/25/1892, Cambridge, Mass. d: 5/3/56, Cumberland, Md. BL/TR, 6', 182 lbs. Deb: 9/30/15																												
1915	Bal-F	6	23	1	6	1	1	0	1	1	0	.261	.292	.391	.683	95	-0	-0	107	41	3	.588	0			0	/1	0.0
■ **FRED KOMMERS** Kommers, Frederick Raymond "Bugs" b: 3/31/1886, Chicago, Ill. d: 6/14/43, Chicago, Ill. BL/TR, 6', 175 lbs. Deb: 6/25/13																												
1913	Pit-N	40	155	14	36	5	4	0	22	10	29	.232	.279	.316	.595	73	-6	-6	96	173	13	.504	1			-0	O	-0.6
1914	StL-F	76	244	33	75	9	8	3	41	24	0	.307	.369	.447	.816	126	10	8	106	125	44	.828	7			-2	O	0.4
	Bal-F	16	42	5	9	1	0	1	1	7	0	.214	.327	.310	.636	83	-1	-1	99	23	4	.606	0			0	O	0.0
	Yr	92	286	38	84	10	8	4	42	31	0	.294	.363	.427	.789	120	10	8	105	109	48	.792	7			-2		0.4
Total	2	132	441	52	120	15	12	4	64	41	29	.272	.334	.388	.722	104	3	2	102	131	62	.685	8			-2	O	-0.2
■ **BRAD KOMMINSK** Komminsk, Brad Lynn b: 4/4/61, Lima, Ohio BR/TR, 6'2", 202 lbs. Deb: 9/28/83																												
1983	Atl-N	19	36	2	8	2	0	0	4	5	7	.222	.317	.278	.595	63	-2	-2	106	158	3	.517	0	0	0	-1	O	-0.3
1984	Atl-N	90	301	37	61	10	0	8	36	29	77	.203	.277	.316	.593	60	-14	-17	110	119	27	.569	18	8	1	-5	O	-2.5
1985	Atl-N	106	300	52	68	12	3	4	21	38	71	.227	.316	.327	.642	75	-8	-10	106	76	32	.602	10	8	-2	-8	O	-2.2
1986	Atl-N	5	5	1	2	0	0	0	1	0	1	.400	.400	.400	.800	119	0	0	102	199	0	.500	0	1	-1	-1	/3O	0.0
1987	Mil-A	7	15	0	1	0	0	0	0	1	7	.067	.125	.067	.192	-46	-3	-3	102	0	0	.214	1	0	0	0	/OD	-0.2
Total	5	227	657	92	140	24	3	12	62	73	163	.213	.295	.314	.608	65	-26	-32	108	99	63	.582	29	17	-2	-15	O/3D	-5.2
■ **ED KONETCHY** Konetchy, Edward Joseph "Big Ed" b: 9/3/1885, Lacrosse, Wis. d: 5/27/47, Ft.Worth, Tex. BR/TR, 6'2.5", 195 lbs. Deb: 6/29/07																												
1907	StL-N	91	331	34	83	11	8	3	30	26		.251	.305	.360	.665	115	3	5	96	94	41	.637	13			2	1	0.5
1908	StL-N	154	545	46	135	19	12	5	50	38		.248	.297	.354	.651	117	5	8	94	98	60	.602	16			11	*1	1.8
1909	StL-N	152	576	88	165	23	14	4	80	65		.286	.366	.396	.762	143	26	28	96	117	90	.791	25			4	*1	3.1
1910	StL-N	144	520	87	157	23	16	3	78	78	59	.302	.397	.425	.822	153	28	34	92	125	94	.884	18			6	*1/P	4.0
1911	StL-N	158	571	90	165	**38**	13	6	88	81	63	.289	.384	.433	.816	127	23	22	101	119	105	.892	27			-6	*1	1.0
1912	StL-N	143	538	81	169	26	13	8	82	62	66	.314	.389	.455	.844	131	23	23	100	99	105	.911	25			6	*1/O	2.3
1913	StL-N	140	504	75	139	18	17	8	68	53	41	.276	.353	.427	.779	132	14	19	93	110	82	.827	27			9	*1/P	2.2
1914	Pit-N	154	563	56	140	23	9	4	51	32	48	.249	.291	.343	.634	96	-10	-5	92	96	61	.584	20			4	*1	-0.3
1915	Pit-F	152	576	79	181	31	18	10	93	41	52	.314	.360	.483	.842	143	32	29	104	105	114	.876	27			2	*1	3.5
1916	Bos-N	158	566	76	147	29	13	3	70	43	46	.260	.320	.373	.693	121	8	12	93	134	74	.654	13			10	*1	1.7
1917	Bos-N	130	474	56	129	19	13	2	54	36	40	.272	.330	.380	.710	122	9	11	96	119	62	.687	16			1	*1	1.2
1918	Bos-N	119	437	33	103	15	5	2	56	32	35	.236	.291	.307	.598	88	-9	-6	94	160	40	.518	5			-2	*1/OP	-1.2
1919	Bro-N	132	486	46	145	24	9	1	47	29	39	.298	.342	.391	.733	128	11	15	94	100	68	.692	14			7	*1	2.1
1920	Bro-N	131	497	62	153	22	12	5	63	33	18	.308	.352	.431	.783	111	14	8	111	113	75	.725	3	2	-0	3	*1	1.0
1921	Bro-N	55	197	25	53	6	5	3	23	19	21	.269	.336	.396	.732	89	-2	-3	105	99	26	.687	3	3	-1	-1	1	-0.5
	Phi-N	72	268	38	86	17	4	8	59	21	17	.321	.379	.504	.883	129	12	11	102	144	52	.896	3	0	1	1	1	1.1
	Yr	127	465	63	139	23	9	11	82	40	38	.299	.361	.458	.819	112	10	8	103	125	78	.802	6	3	0	0		0.6
Total	15	2085	7649	972	2150	344	181	75	992	689	545	.281	.345	.403	.748	124	186	210	97	114	1150	.741	255	5		56	*1/OP	23.5
■ **MIKE KONNICK** Konnick, Michael Aloysius b: 1/13/1889, Glen Lyon, Pa. d: 7/9/71, Wilkes-Barre, Pa. BR/TR, 5'9", 180 lbs. Deb: 09																												
1909	Cin-N	2	5	0	2	1	0	0	1	0		.400	.400	.600	1.000	226	1	1	94	121	1	1.000	0			0	/C	0.1
1910	Cin-N	1	3	0	0	0	0	0	0	1	0	.000	.250	.000	.250	-26	-0	-0	101	0	0	.333	0			0	/S	0.0
Total	2	3	8	0	2	1	0	0	1	1	0	.250	.333	.375	.708	119	0	0	97	67	1	.667	0			0	/CS	0.1
■ **BRUCE KONOPKA** Konopka, Bruno Bruce b: 9/16/19, Hammond, Ind. BL/TL, 6'2", 190 lbs. Deb: 6/07/42																												
1942	Phi-A	5	10	2	3	0	0	0	1	1	0	.300	.364	.300	.664	91	-0	-0	96	117	1	.571	0	0	0	0	/1	0.0
1943	Phi-A	2	2	0	0	0	0	0	0	0	1	.000	.000	.000	.000	-99	-0	-0	101	0	0	.000	0	0	0	0	H	0.0
1946	Phi-A	38	93	7	22	4	1	0	9	4	8	.237	.268	.301	.569	56	-5	-6	104	122	7	.432	0	0	0	0	1/O	-0.6
Total	3	45	105	9	25	4	1	0	10	5	9	.238	.273	.295	.568	57	-6	-6	103	119	8	.434	0	0	0	0	/1O	-0.6
■ **HARRY KOONS** Koons, Henry M. b: 1863, Philadelphia, Pa. BR/TR, 5'8", 174 lbs. Deb: 4/17/1884																												
1884	Alt-U	21	78	8	18	2	1	0		2		.231	.250	.282	.532	78	-2	-2	101	0	6	.400	0			0	3/C	-0.1
	CP-U	1	3	0	0	0	0	0		0		.000	.000	.000	.000	-99	-1	-1	99	0	0	.000	0			0	/3	0.0
	Yr	22	81	8	18	2	1	0		2		.222	.241	.272	.513	72	-2	-2	101	0	5	.381	0			0		-0.1
Total	1	22	81	8	18	2	1	0		2		.222	.241	.272	.513	72	-2	-2	101	0	6	.381	0			0	/3C	-0.1
■ **GEORGE KOPACZ** Kopacz, George Felix "Sonny" b: 2/26/41, Chicago, Ill. BL/TL, 6'1", 195 lbs. Deb: 9/18/66																												
1966	Atl-N	6	9	1	0	0	0	0	0	1	5	.000	.100	.000	.100	-70	-2	-2	99	0	0	.111	0	0	0	0	/1	-0.1
1970	Pit-N	10	16	1	3	0	0	0	0	0	5	.188	.188	.188	.375	1	-2	-2	97	0	1	.231	0	0	0	0	/1	-0.1
Total	2	16	25	2	3	0	0	0	0	1	10	.120	.154	.120	.274	-25	-4	-4	97	0	1	.182	0	0	0	0	/1	-0.2
■ **WALLY KOPF** Kopf, Walter Henry b: 7/10/1899, Stonington, Conn. d: 4/30/79, Hamilton Co., Ohio BB/TR, 5'11", 168 lbs. Deb: 10/01/21																												
1921	NY-N	2	3	0	1	0	0	0	0	1	1	.333	.500	.333	.833	128	0	0	98	0	1	1.000	0	0	0	0	/3	0.0
■ **LARRY KOPF** Kopf, William Lorenz (played under name of Fred Brady In 1913) b: 11/3/1890, Bristol, Conn. d: 10/15/86, Anderson Twp., O. BB/TR, 5'9", 160 lbs. Deb: 9/09/13																												
1913	Cle-A	5	9	1	2	0	0	0	1	0	0	.222	.222	.222	.444	28	-1	-1	106	178	0	.286	0			0	/23	0.0
1914	Phi-A	35	69	8	13	2	2	0	12	8	14	.188	.300	.275	.575	75	-2	-2	97	237	7	.643	6			1	S/32	0.2
1915	Phi-A	118	386	39	87	10	2	1	33	41	45	.225	.314	.269	.584	78	-11	-9	96	107	33	.516	5	9	-4	-8	S3/2	-1.2
1916	Cin-N	11	40	2	11	2	0	0	5	1	8	.275	.293	.325	.618	91	-1	-1	98	156	4	.517	1			-0	S	0.0
1917	Cin-N	148	573	81	146	19	8	2	26	28	48	.255	.297	.326	.623	98	-7	-2	92	50	59	.557	17			-12	*S	-1.4
1919	Cin-N	135	503	51	136	18	5	0	58	28	27	.270	.313	.326	.639	87	-5	-8	105	**146**	54	.580	18			-33	*S	-4.0
1920	Cin-N	126	458	56	112	15	6	0	59	35	24	.245	.305	.303	.609	84	-14	-8	90	174	43	.538	14	13	-4	-36	*S/23O	-4.5
1921	Cin-N	107	367	36	80	8	3	1	25	43	20	.218	.310	.264	.574	53	-23	-24	101	93	30	.495	3	14	-8	-19	S/23O	-4.0
1922	Bos-N	126	466	59	124	6	3	1	37	45	22	.266	.332	.298	.630	68	-24	-20	94	97	48	.550	8	9	-3	-8	2S3	-2.6
1923	Bos-N	39	138	15	38	3	1	0	10	13	6	.275	.338	.312	.649	72	-5	-5	100	83	15	.544	0	3	-2	1	S/2	-0.2
Total	10	850	3009	348	749	83	30	5	266	242	214	.249	.312	.301	.613	78	-92	-79	96	112	294	.543	72	48		-114	S/23O	-17.7
■ **MERLIN KOPP** Kopp, Merlin Henry "Manny" b: 1/2/1892, Toledo, Ohio d: 5/6/60, Sacramento, Cal. BB/TR, 5'8", 158 lbs. Deb: 8/02/15																												
1915	Was-A	16	32	2	8	0	0	0	0	5	7	.250	.351	.250	.601	79	-1	-1	101	0	3	.583	1			-1	/O	-0.1
1918	Phi-A	96	363	60	85	7	7	0	18	42	55	.234	.320	.292	.612	81	-6	-8	104	55	40	.626	22			3	O	-1.0
1919	Phi-A	75	235	34	53	2	4	1	12	42	43	.226	.348	.281	.629	73	-5	-7	106	64	27	.692	16			-2	O	-1.4
Total	3	187	630	96	146	9	11	1	30	89	105	.232	.332	.286	.618	78	-12	-15	105	56	70	.649	39			-1	O	-2.5
■ **JOE KOPPE** Koppe, Joseph b: 10/19/30, Detroit, Mich. BR/TR, 5'10", 165 lbs. Deb: 8/09/58																												
1958	Mil-N	16	9	3	4	0	0	0	0	1	1	.444	.500	.444	.944	171	1	1	89	0	2	1.000	0	0	0	0	/S	0.1
1959	Phi-N	126	422	68	110	18	7	7	28	41	80	.261	.329	.386	.715	90	-6	-6	99	63	54	.655	7	7	-2	-3	*S2	-0.5
1960	Phi-N	58	170	13	29	6	1	1	13	23	47	.171	.273	.235	.508	38	-14	-15	107	123	12	.462	3	2	-0	-7	S/3	-2.1
1961	Phi-N	6	3	1	0	0	0	0	0	0	0	.000	.000	.000	.000	-99	-1	-1	94	0	0	.000	0	0	0	0	/S	0.0
	LA-A	91	338	46	85	12	2	5	40	45	77	.251	.341	.343	.684	75	-7	-12	111	127	42	.635	3	3	-1	4	S/23	-0.1
1962	LA-A	128	375	47	85	16	0	4	40	73	84	.227	.356	.301	.657	77	-8	-10	102	127	45	.631	2	1	0	6	*S/23	0.4
1963	LA-A	76	143	11	30	4	1	1	12	9	30	.210	.261	.273	.534	55	-10	-8	91	120	10	.426	0	0	0	2	S32/O	-0.4
1964	LA-A	54	113	10	29	4	1	0	6	14	16	.257	.339	.310	.648	92	-2	-1	89	73	13	.570	0	0	0	3	S2/3	0.3
1965	Cal-A	23	33	3	7	1	0	1	2	3	10	.212	.278	.333	.611	74	-1	-1	98	59	3	.556	1	0	0	1	2/S3	0.1

YEAR	TM/L	G	AB	R	H	2B	3B	HR	RBI	BB	SO	AVG	OBP	SLG	PRO	/A	BR	/A	PF	CHI	RC	TA	SB	CS	SBR	FR	POS	TPR
Total	8	578	1606	202	379	61	12	19	141	209	345	.236	.327	.324	.651	75	-48	-53	102	103	181	.607	16	13	-3	6	S/23O	-2.2
■ **GEORGE KOPSHAW**	Kopshaw, George Karl b: 7/5/1895, Passaic, N.J. d: 12/26/34, Lynchburg, Va. BR/TR, 5'11.5", 176 lbs. Deb: 8/04/23																											
1923	StL-N	2	5	1	1	1	0	0	0	0	1	.200	.200	.400	.600	61	-0	-0	90	0	0	.500	0	0	0	0	/C	0.0
■ **STEVE KORCHECK**	Korcheck, Stephen Joseph "Hoss" b: 8/11/32, Mc Clellandtown, Pa. BR/TR, 6'1", 205 lbs. Deb: 9/06/54																											
1954	Was-A	2	7	0	1	0	0	0	0	0	2	.143	.143	.143	.286	-22	-1	-1	98	0	0	.167	0	0	0	0	/C	0.0
1955	Was-A	13	36	3	10	2	0	0	2	0	5	.278	.297	.333	.631	76	-2	-1	91	62	4	.500	0	0	0	0	C	0.0
1958	Was-A	21	51	6	4	2	1	0	1	1	16	.078	.096	.157	.253	-33	-9	-9	97	50	1	.191	0	0	0	0	C	-0.8
1959	Was-A	22	51	3	8	2	0	0	4	5	13	.157	.232	.196	.428	19	-6	-6	100	157	3	.349	0	0	0	-1	C	-0.5
Total	4	58	145	12	23	6	1	0	7	6	36	.159	.197	.214	.411	13	-18	-17	97	90	7	.311	0	0	0	-1	/C	-1.3
■ **ART KORES**	Kores, Arthur Emil "Dutch" b: 7/22/1886, Milwaukee, Wis. d: 3/26/74, Milwaukee, Wis. BR/TR, 5'9", 167 lbs. Deb: 7/24/15																											
1915	StL-F	60	201	18	47	9	2	1	22	21	13	.234	.306	.313	.620	80	-4	-5	105	122	24	.584	6			6	3	0.2
■ **ANDY KOSCO**	Kosco, Andrew John b: 10/5/41, Youngstown, Ohio BR/TR, 6'3", 205 lbs. Deb: 8/13/65																											
1965	Min-A	23	55	3	13	4	0	1	6	1	15	.236	.250	.364	.614	71	-2	-2	101	108	5	.500	0	0	0	1	O/1	-0.1
1966	Min-A	57	158	11	35	5	0	2	13	7	31	.222	.255	.291	.546	51	-9	-11	111	105	11	.414	0	1	-1	0	O/1	-1.3
1967	Min-A	9	28	4	4	1	0	0	4	2	4	.143	.200	.179	.379	12	-3	-3	107	334	1	.280	0	0	0	-0	/O	-0.3
1968	NY-A	131	466	47	112	19	1	15	59	16	71	.240	.270	.382	.652	95	-4	-5	101	116	45	.542	2	2	-1	-2	O1	-1.3
1969	LA-N	120	424	51	105	13	2	19	74	21	66	.248	.285	.422	.707	97	-5	-4	99	126	46	.600	0	1	-1	-7	*O/1	-1.7
1970	LA-N	74	224	21	51	12	0	8	27	1	40	.228	.231	.388	.620	70	-13	-10	90	94	17	.492	1	1	-0	-2	O/1	-1.4
1971	Mil-A	98	264	27	60	6	2	10	39	24	57	.227	.292	.379	.670	86	-5	-6	103	122	28	.587	1	3	-2	-1	O13	-1.2
1972	Cal-A	49	142	15	34	4	2	6	13	5	23	.239	.270	.423	.693	118	-0	2	88	70	15	.593	1	0	-0	-0	O	0.0
	Bos-A	17	47	5	10	2	1	3	6	2	9	.213	.260	.489	.749	114	1	0	105	78	4	.634	0	0	0	-0	O	0.0
	Yr	66	189	20	44	6	3	9	19	7	32	.233	.268	.439	.707	116	1	2	93	73	21	.624	1	0	0	-1		0.0
1973	Cin-N	47	118	17	33	7	0	9	21	13	26	.280	.351	.568	.919	162	7	8	93	90	22	.899	0	0	0	-5	O/1	0.2
1974	Cin-N	33	37	3	7	2	0	0	5	7	8	.189	.318	.243	.561	60	-2	-2	98	214	3	.516	0	0	0	-1	/3O	-0.2
Total	10	658	1963	204	464	75	8	73	267	99	350	.236	.275	.394	.669	91	-34	-32	99	115	197	.586	5	8	-3	-17	O/13	-7.3
■ **CLEM KOSHOREK**	Koshorek, Clement John "Scooter" b: 6/20/26, Royal Oak, Mich. BR/TR, 5'6", 165 lbs. Deb: 4/15/52																											
1952	Pit-N	98	322	27	84	17	0	0	15	26	39	.261	.320	.314	.634	77	-10	-10	100	58	33	.536	4	7	-3	4	S23	-0.6
1953	Pit-N	1	1	0	0	0	0	0	0	0	1	.000	.000	.000	.000	-98	-0	-0	102	0	0	.000	0	0	0	0	H	0.0
Total	2	99	323	27	84	17	0	0	15	26	40	.260	.319	.313	.632	76	-10	-10	100	58	33	.541	4	7	-3	4	/S23	-0.6
■ **MIKE KOSMAN**	Kosman, Michael Thomas b: 12/10/17, Hamtramck, Mich. BR/TR, 5'9", 160 lbs. Deb: 4/20/44																											
1944	Cin-N	1	0	0	0	0	0	0	0	0	0	—	—	—	—	—	0	0	95	—	—	—	0			0	R	0.0
■ **FRED KOSTER**	Koster, Frederick Charles "Fritz" b: 12/21/05, Louisville, Ky. d: 4/24/79, St.Matthews, Ky. BL/TL, 5'10.5", 165 lbs. Deb: 4/27/31																											
1931	Phi-N	76	151	21	34	2	2	0	8	14	21	.225	.291	.265	.556	47	-10	-11	106	71	13	.496	4			-3	O	-1.6
■ **FRANK KOSTRO**	Kostro, Frank Jerry b: 8/4/37, Windber, Pa. BR/TR, 6'2", 190 lbs. Deb: 9/02/62																											
1962	Det-A	16	41	5	11	3	0	0	3	1	6	.268	.286	.341	.627	61	-2	-2	111	85	4	.500	0	0	0	-1	3	-0.2
1963	Det-A	31	52	4	12	1	0	0	0	9	13	.231	.344	.250	.594	67	-2	-2	104	0	5	.524	0	0	0	-1	/31O	-0.2
	LA-A	43	99	6	22	2	1	2	10	6	17	.222	.267	.323	.590	70	-5	-4	91	110	8	.475	0	0	0	-1	3/1O	-0.4
	Yr	74	151	10	34	3	1	2	10	15	30	.225	.295	.298	.593	69	-6	-6	96	64	14	.500	0	0	0	-1		-0.6
1964	Min-A	59	103	10	28	5	0	3	12	4	21	.272	.306	.408	.713	96	-1	-1	101	100	12	.610	0	0	0	-1	3/2O1	0.0
1965	Min-A	20	31	2	5	2	0	0	1	4	5	.161	.257	.226	.483	38	-2	-3	101	59	2	.407	0	0	0	-1	/23O	-0.2
1967	Min-A	32	31	4	10	0	0	0	2	3	2	.323	.382	.323	.705	103	1	0	107	83	3	.565	0	0	0	-1	/O3	0.0
1968	Min-A	63	108	9	26	4	1	0	9	6	20	.241	.281	.296	.577	71	-3	-4	106	120	9	.452	0	0	0	-1	O/1	-0.7
1969	Min-A	2	2	0	0	0	0	0	0	0	1	.000	.000	.000	.000	-98	-1	-1	102	0	0	.000	0	0	0	0	H	0.0
Total	7	266	467	40	114	17	2	5	37	33	85	.244	.295	.321	.617	74	-15	-16	102	89	44	.521	0	0	0	-6	/3O21	-1.7
■ **ERNIE KOY**	Koy, Ernest Anyz "Chief" b: 9/17/09, Sealy, Tex. BR/TR, 6', 200 lbs. Deb: 4/19/38																											
1938	Bro-N	142	521	78	156	29	13	11	76	38	76	.299	.352	.468	.820	129	15	18	96	101	87	.801	15			6	*O/3	2.1
1939	Bro-N	125	425	57	118	37	5	8	67	39	64	.278	.338	.445	.783	102	4	0	107	115	63	.754	11			-2	*O	-0.3
1940	Bro-N	24	48	9	11	2	1	1	8	3	3	.229	.275	.375	.650	72	-2	-2	108	141	5	.595	1			-4	O	-0.6
	StL-N	93	348	44	108	19	5	8	52	28	59	.310	.368	.463	.831	125	13	12	102	106	60	.837	12			-3	O	0.5
	Yr	117	396	53	119	21	6	9	60	31	62	.301	.357	.452	.809	118	11	10	103	115	65	.805	13			-7		-0.1
1941	StL-N	13	40	5	8	1	0	2	4	1	8	.200	.220	.375	.595	59	-2	-3	110	69	3	.500	0			-2	O	-0.4
	Cin-N	67	204	24	51	11	2	2	27	14	22	.250	.301	.353	.654	85	-5	-5	99	125	22	.564	1			-2	O	-0.8
	Yr	80	244	29	59	12	2	4	31	15	30	.242	.288	.357	.645	80	-7	-7	101	117	25	.553	1			-4		-1.2
1942	Cin-N	3	2	0	0	0	0	0	0	0	0	.000	.000	.000	.000	-99	-0	-0	101	0	0	.000	0			0	H	0.0
	Phi-N	91	258	21	63	9	3	4	26	14	50	.244	.283	.349	.632	89	-6	-4	94	94	25	.523	0			-4	O	-1.1
	Yr	94	260	21	63	9	3	4	26	14	52	.242	.281	.346	.627	88	-7	-5	95	91	25	.517	0			-4		-1.1
Total	5	558	1846	238	515	108	29	36	260	137	284	.279	.332	.427	.759	109	18	16	100	107	266	.730	40			-11	O/3	-0.6
■ **AL KOZAR**	Kozar, Albert Kenneth b: 7/5/22, Mc Kees Rocks, Pa. BR/TR, 5'9.5", 173 lbs. Deb: 4/19/48																											
1948	Was-A	150	577	61	144	25	8	1	58	66	52	.250	.327	.326	.652	72	-22	-24	103	99	63	.570	4	2	0	-20	*2	-3.9
1949	Was-A	105	350	46	94	15	2	4	31	25	23	.269	.321	.357	.678	87	-12	-8	91	78	41	.583	2	1	0	-8	*2	-1.4
1950	Was-A	20	55	7	11	1	0	0	3	5	8	.200	.267	.218	.485	25	-6	-6	99	86	3	.370	0	0	0	0	2	-0.3
	Chi-A	10	10	4	3	0	0	1	2	0	3	.300	.300	.600	.900	130	0	0	97	77	1	.750	0	0	0	0	/23	0.0
	Yr	30	65	11	14	1	0	1	5	5	11	.215	.271	.277	.548	41	-6	-6	98	86	5	.442	0	0	0	0		-0.3
Total	3	285	992	118	252	41	10	6	94	96	86	.254	.321	.334	.655	74	-39	-37	99	90	108	.585	6	3	0	-28	2/3	-5.6
■ **JOE KRACHER**	Kracher, Joseph Peter "Jug" b: 11/4/15, Philadelphia, Pa. d: 12/24/81, San Angelo, Tex. BR/TR, 5'11", 185 lbs. Deb: 9/17/39																											
1939	Phi-N	5	5	1	1	0	0	0	0	2	1	.200	.429	.200	.629	79	-0	0	94	0	1	.750	0			0	/C	0.0
■ **CLARENCE KRAFT**	Kraft, Clarence Otto "Big Boy" b: 6/9/1887, Evansville, Ind. d: 3/26/58, Fort Worth, Tex. BR/TR, 6', 190 lbs. Deb: 5/01/14																											
1914	Bos-N	3	3	0	1	0	0	0	0	0	1	.333	.333	.333	.667	94	-0	-0	104	0	0	.500	0			0	/1	0.0
■ **ED KRANEPOOL**	Kranepool, Edward Emil b: 11/8/44, New York, N.Y. BL/TL, 6'3", 205 lbs. Deb: 9/22/62																											
1962	NY-N	3	6	0	1	1	0	0	0	0	1	.167	.167	.333	.500	29	-1	-1	104	0	0	.400	0	0	0	0	/1	0.0
1963	NY-N	86	273	22	57	12	2	2	14	18	50	.209	.258	.289	.547	58	-15	-15	99	69	19	.443	4	2	0	-1	O1	-2.0
1964	NY-N	119	420	47	108	19	4	10	45	32	50	.257	.313	.393	.706	102	-2	1	95	96	51	.618	0	1	-1	5	*1/O	0.1
1965	NY-N	153	525	44	133	24	4	10	53	39	71	.253	.307	.371	.679	90	-7	-7	100	100	57	.579	1	4	-2	-0	*1	-1.7
1966	NY-N	146	464	51	118	15	2	16	57	41	66	.254	.319	.399	.718	104	-1	2	94	103	60	.653	1	1	-0	4	*1O	0.0
1967	NY-N	141	469	37	126	17	1	10	54	37	51	.269	.323	.373	.697	100	-1	-0	99	111	53	.592	0	4	-2	4	*1	-0.4
1968	NY-N	127	373	29	86	13	1	3	20	19	39	.231	.272	.295	.566	69	-14	-15	102	71	29	.443	0	3	-2	2	*1/O	-2.2
1969	NY-N	112	353	36	84	9	2	11	49	37	32	.238	.310	.368	.679	89	-5	-5	100	120	39	.605	3	2	-0	-2	*1/O	-1.7
1970	NY-N	43	47	2	8	0	0	0	3	5	2	.170	.250	.170	.420	14	-6	-6	104	145	2	.333	0	0	0	0	/1	-0.6
1971	NY-N	122	421	61	118	20	4	14	58	38	33	.280	.341	.447	.788	126	11	13	96	105	63	.723	0	4	-2	-4	*1O	-0.1
1972	NY-N	122	327	28	88	15	1	8	34	34	35	.269	.340	.394	.734	113	4	5	95	91	42	.660	1	0	0	-2	*1/O	-0.3
1973	NY-N	100	284	28	68	12	2	1	35	30	28	.239	.312	.306	.618	72	-10	-11	101	156	28	.529	1	0	0	-4	1O	-1.8
1974	NY-N	94	217	20	65	11	1	4	24	18	14	.300	.353	.415	.768	115	4	4	99	91	32	.694	1	0	0	-5	O1	-0.3
1975	NY-N	106	325	42	105	16	0	4	43	27	21	.323	.375	.409	.784	124	8	10	95	115	47	.691	1	1	-0	2	1/O	0.7
1976	NY-N	123	415	47	121	17	1	10	49	35	38	.292	.347	.410	.756	124	7	11	92	94	58	.678	1	0	0	-3	1O	0.3
1977	NY-N	108	281	28	79	17	0	10	40	23	20	.281	.336	.448	.784	113	3	4	96	103	38	.694	1	4	-2	-5	O1	-0.6
1978	NY-N	66	81	7	17	2	0	3	19	8	12	.210	.289	.346	.635	78	-3	-2	98	204	7	.544	0	0	0	-3	O/1	-0.6
1979	NY-N	82	155	7	36	5	0	2	17	13	18	.232	.296	.303	.599	67	-8	-7	95	127	13	.484	0	1	-1	-0	1/O	-0.9
Total	18	1853	5436	536	1418	225	25	118	614	454	581	.261	.319	.377	.696	98	-36	-19	97	104	638	.625	15	27	-12	-11	*1O	-12.1

YEAR	TM/L	G	AB	R	H	2B	3B	HR	RBI	BB	SO	AVG	OBP	SLG	PRO	/A	BR	/A	PF	CHI	RC	TA	SB	CS	SBR	FR	POS	TPR
■ CHARLIE KRAUSE	Krause, Charles b: 10/2/1187, Detroit, Mich. d: 3/30/48, Eloise, Mich. TR , Deb: 7/27/01																											
1901	Cin-N	1	4	0	1	0	0	0	0	0		.250	.250	.250	.500	49	-0	-0	95	0	0	.333	0			0	/2	0.0
■ DANNY KRAVITZ	Kravitz, Daniel "Dusty" or "Beak" b: 12/21/30, Lopez, Pa. BL/TR, 5'11", 195 lbs. Deb: 4/17/56																											
1956	Pit-N	32	68	6	18	2	2	2	10	5	9	.265	.315	.441	.756	98	-0	-0	102	117	9	.679	1	1	-0	-1	C/3	0.0
1957	Pit-N	19	41	2	6	1	0	0	4	2	10	.146	.186	.171	.357	-4	-6	-6	94	237	1	.257	0	0	0	-1	C	-0.5
1958	Pit-N	45	100	9	24	3	2	1	5	11	10	.240	.315	.340	.655	77	-4	-3	95	56	10	.563	0	0	0	-1	C	-0.1
1959	Pit-N	52	162	18	41	9	1	3	21	5	14	.253	.275	.377	.652	69	-7	-8	103	121	16	.532	0	1	-1	-4	C	-0.9
1960	Pit-N	8	6	0	0	0	0	0	0	1	2	.000	.143	.000	.143	-57	-1	-1	99	0	0	.167	0	0	0	0	/C	0.0
	KC-A	59	175	17	41	7	2	4	14	11	19	.234	.280	.366	.645	74	-7	-7	99	72	16	.536	0	0	0	4	C	0.0
Total	5	215	552	52	130	22	7	10	54	35	64	.236	.281	.355	.636	69	-25	-25	99	100	53	.540	1	2	-1	-2	C/3	-1.5
■ MIKE KREEVICH	Kreevich, Michael Andreas b: 6/10/08, Mt.Olive, Ill. BR/TR, 5'7.5", 168 lbs. Deb: 9/07/31																											
1931	Chi-N	5	12	0	2	0	0	0	0	0	6	.167	.167	.167	.333	-11	-2	-2	96	0	0	.300	1			-0	/O	-0.1
1935	Chi-A	6	23	3	10	2	0	0	2	1	0	.435	.458	.522	.980	140	2	2	109	58	5	1.000	1	1	-0	-1	/3	0.0
1936	Chi-A	137	550	99	169	32	11	5	69	61	46	.307	.378	.433	.811	100	0	1	99	94	93	.806	10	5	0	7	*O	0.3
1937	Chi-A	144	583	94	176	29	**16**	12	73	43	45	.302	.350	.468	.818	102	2	-1	103	78	97	.799	10	1	2	5	*O	0.2
1938	Chi-A	129	489	73	145	26	12	6	73	55	23	.297	.371	.436	.807	104	1	3	98	113	82	.814	13	5	1	1	*O	0.4
1939	Chi-A	145	541	85	175	30	8	5	77	59	40	.323	.390	.436	.826	104	10	4	107	110	93	.815	23	10	1	12	*O/3	1.2
1940	Chi-A	144	582	86	154	27	10	8	55	34	49	.265	.305	.387	.692	75	-20	-23	104	77	66	.605	15	7	0	8	*O	-2.3
1941	Chi-A	121	436	44	101	16	8	0	37	35	26	.232	.289	.305	.594	61	-27	-23	94	101	40	.529	17	5	2	-3	*O	-3.0
1942	Phi-A	116	444	57	113	19	1	1	30	47	31	.255	.326	.309	.634	82	-12	-10	96	80	46	.549	7	9	-3	2	*O	-1.8
1943	StL-A	60	161	24	41	6	0	0	10	26	13	.255	.358	.292	.650	91	-1	-1	100	78	20	.626	4	1	1	7	O	0.6
1944	StL-A	105	402	55	121	15	6	5	44	27	24	.301	.348	.405	.754	113	7	6	102	94	56	.659	3	3	-1	-5	*O	-0.2
1945	StL-A	84	295	34	70	11	1	2	21	37	27	.237	.322	.302	.624	71	-6	-12	115	81	31	.558	4	1	1	1	O	-1.4
	Was-A	45	158	22	44	8	2	1	23	21	9	.278	.363	.373	.737	122	3	4	93	137	22	.713	7	5	-1	0	O	0.2
	Yr	129	453	56	114	19	3	3	44	58	36	.252	.337	.327	.663	86	-3	-7	107	101	56	.624	11	6	-0	1		-1.2
Total	12	1241	4676	676	1321	221	75	45	514	446	339	.283	.346	.391	.737	93	-43	-51	101	93	651	.702	115	53		35	*O/3	-5.9
■ CHARLIE KREHMEYER	Krehmeyer, Charles L. b: 7/5/1863, St.Louis, Mo. d: 2/10/26, St.Louis, Mo. BL , Deb: 7/08/1884																											
1884	StL-a	21	70	3	16	0	1	0		2		.229	.250	.257	.507	62	-2	-3	110	0	5	.370				0	O/C1	-0.2
1885	Lou-a	7	31	4	7	1	1	0		1		.226	.250	.323	.573	80	-1	-1	102	0	3	.458				0	/CO1	0.0
	StL-N	1	3	0	0	0	0	0	0	0	2	.000	.000	.000	.000	-99	-1	-1	92	0	0	.000				0	/C	0.0
Total	2	29	104	7	23	1	2	0	0	3	2	.221	.243	.269	.512	63	-4	-5	107	0	7	.383				0	/OC1	-0.2
■ MICKEY KREITNER	Kreitner, Albert Joseph b: 10/10/22, Nashville, Tenn. BR/TR, 6'3", 190 lbs. Deb: 9/28/43																											
1943	Chi-N	3	8	0	3	0	0	0	2	1	2	.375	.444	.375	.819	139	0	0	99	241	1	.800	0			-0	/C	0.0
1944	Chi-N	39	85	3	13	2	0	0	1	8	16	.153	.234	.176	.411	17	-9	-9	101	24	4	.329	0			-1	C	-0.8
Total	2	42	93	3	16	2	0	0	3	9	18	.172	.252	.194	.446	27	-9	-9	101	43	6	.359	0			-1	/C	-0.8
■ RALPH KREITZ	Kreitz, Ralph Wesley "Red" b: 11/13/1885, Plum Creek, Neb. d: 7/20/41, Portland, Ore. BR/TR, 5'9.5", 175 lbs. Deb: 8/01/11																											
1911	Chi-A	7	17	0	4	1	0	0	0	2		.235	.316	.294	.610	73	-1	-1	97	0	2	.538	0			-1	/C	0.0
■ WAYNE KRENCHICKI	Krenchicki, Wayne Richard b: 9/17/54, Trenton, N.J. BL/TR, 6'1", 180 lbs. Deb: 6/15/79																											
1979	Bal-A	16	21	1	4	1	0	0	0	0	0	.190	.190	.238	.429	15	-2	-2	97	0	1	.278	0	0	0	-0	/32	-0.1
1980	Bal-A	9	14	1	2	0	0	0	0	1	3	.143	.200	.143	.343	-4	-2	-2	101	0	0	.250	0	0	0	0	/S2D	-0.1
1981	Bal-A	33	56	7	12	4	0	0	6	4	9	.214	.267	.286	.552	60	-3	-3	99	147	4	.444	0	0	0	0	S/23D	0.0
1982	Cin-N	94	187	19	53	6	1	2	21	13	23	.283	.330	.358	.688	90	-2	-2	102	113	22	.607	5	3	-0	-3	3/2	-0.6
1983	Cin-N	51	77	6	21	2	0	0	11	8	4	.273	.349	.299	.648	79	-2	-2	103	189	8	.552	0	0	0	-1	3/2	-0.4
	Det-A	59	133	18	37	7	0	1	16	11	27	.278	.338	.353	.691	95	-1	-1	96	125	17	.608	0	0	0	-4	3/2S1	-0.3
1984	Cin-N	97	181	18	54	9	2	6	22	19	23	.298	.365	.470	.835	126	8	7	106	84	30	.788	0	1	-1	-2	3/12	0.4
1985	Cin-N	90	173	16	47	9	0	4	25	28	20	.272	.373	.393	.766	109	4	3	105	124	27	.744	0	0	0	-4	3/2	0.0
1986	Mon-N	101	221	21	53	6	2	2	23	22	32	.240	.309	.312	.621	73	-8	-8	98	122	22	.534	2	4	-2	0	13/2O	-1.1
Total	8	550	1063	107	283	44	5	15	124	106	141	.266	.334	.359	.693	92	-9	-10	101	117	131	.629	7	8	-3	-13	3/12SDO	-2.2
■ CHUCK KRESS	Kress, Charles Steven b: 12/9/21, Philadelphia, Pa. BL/TL, 6', 190 lbs. Deb: 4/16/47																											
1947	Cin-N	11	27	4	4	0	0	0	0	6	4	.148	.303	.148	.451	26	-3	-2	91	0	2	.435	0			-0	/1	-0.2
1949	Cin-N	27	29	3	6	3	0	0	3	3	5	.207	.281	.310	.592	61	-2	-2	96	126	2	.500	0			-0	1	-0.1
	Chi-A	97	353	45	98	17	6	1	44	39	44	.278	.349	.368	.718	92	-5	-4	98	116	47	.651	6	7	-2	0	1	-0.5
1950	Chi-A	3	8	0	0	0	0	0	0	0	2	.000	.000	.000	.000	-99	-2	-2	97	0	-0	.000	0	0	0	0	/1	-0.1
1954	Det-A	24	37	4	7	0	1	0	3	1	4	.189	.211	.243	.454	24	-4	-4	100	126	2	.323	0	1	-1	-0	/1O	-0.4
	Bro-N	13	12	1	1	0	0	0	2	0	0	.083	.083	.083	.167	-56	-3	-3	101	787	0	.091	0	0	0	0	/1	-0.2
Total	4	175	466	57	116	20	7	1	52	49	59	.249	.320	.328	.649	74	-19	-17	97	123	53	.581	6	8		-1	1/O	-1.5
■ RED KRESS	Kress, Ralph b: 1/2/07, Columbia, Cal. d: 11/29/62, Los Angeles, Cal. BR/TR, 5'11.5", 165 lbs. Deb: 9/24/27 C																											
1927	StL-A	7	23	3	7	2	1	1	3	3	3	.304	.385	.609	.993	146	2	1	106	60	5	1.063	0	0	0	0	/S	0.2
1928	StL-A	150	560	78	153	26	10	3	81	48	70	.273	.332	.371	.703	82	-13	-16	104	136	71	.637	5	4	-1	-18	*S	-1.9
1929	StL-A	147	557	82	170	38	4	9	107	52	54	.305	.366	.436	.802	106	4	5	100	**144**	88	.762	5	8	-3	0	*S	1.4
1930	StL-A	154	614	94	192	43	8	16	112	50	56	.313	.366	.487	.853	106	12	4	108	103	105	.816	3	12	-6	-1	*S3	1.0
1931	StL-A	150	605	87	188	46	8	16	114	46	48	.311	.360	.493	.853	119	17	15	102	115	101	.804	3	16	-9	0	3OS1	1.1
1932	StL-A	14	52	2	9	0	1	2	9	4	6	.173	.232	.327	.559	43	-5	-5	100	134	4	.500	1	1	-0	2	3	-0.1
	Chi-A	135	515	83	147	42	4	9	57	47	36	.285	.346	.435	.781	116	-0	10	87	81	79	.749	6	3	0	9	OS3/1	1.9
	Yr	149	567	85	156	42	5	11	66	51	42	.275	.336	.425	.761	108	-5	5	88	86	82	.723	7	4	-0	11		1.8
1933	Chi-A	129	467	47	116	20	5	10	78	37	40	.248	.304	.377	.680	79	-15	-16	101	126	54	.611	4	4	-1	-3	*1/O	-2.7
1934	Chi-A	8	14	3	4	0	0	0	1	3	3	.286	.412	.286	.697	83	-0	-0	99	83	2	.700	0	0	0	-0	/2	0.0
	Was-A	56	171	18	39	4	3	4	24	17	19	.228	.298	.357	.655	68	-9	-9	101	110	19	.614	3	0	1	-2	10/2S3	-1.3
	Yr	64	185	21	43	4	3	4	25	20	22	.232	.307	.351	.659	69	-9	-9	101	108	21	.620	3	0	1	-2		-1.3
1935	Was-A	84	252	32	75	13	4	2	42	25	16	.298	.361	.405	.766	107	-1	2	92	132	37	.722	3	3	-1	4	S/1PO2	0.8
1936	Was-A	109	391	51	111	20	6	8	51	39	25	.284	.349	.427	.776	93	-7	-5	98	88	60	.757	6	0	2	-1	S2/1	0.1
1938	StL-A	150	566	74	171	33	3	7	79	69	47	.302	.378	.408	.786	97	-2	-2	100	112	90	.764	5	4	-1	-14	*S	-0.6
1939	StL-A	13	43	5	12	1	0	0	8	6	2	.279	.367	.302	.670	73	-1	-1	100	208	4	.571	1	0	0	1	S	0.1
	Det-A	51	157	19	38	7	0	1	22	17	16	.242	.316	.306	.622	54	-9	-12	111	146	15	.528	2	1	0	-2	S2/3	-0.9
	Yr	64	200	24	50	8	0	1	30	23	18	.250	.327	.305	.632	57	-11	-14	109	161	20	.551	3	1	0	-1		-0.8
1940	Det-A	33	99	13	22	3	1	1	11	10	12	.222	.294	.303	.597	49	-7	-8	111	120	8	.476	0	0	0	0	3S	-0.5
1946	NY-N	1	1	0	0	0	0	0	0	1	0	.000	.500	.000	.500	47	0	0	102	0	0	1.000	0			1	/P	0.0
Total	14	1391	5087	691	1454	298	58	89	799	474	453	.286	.347	.420	.767	96	-32	-36	100	116	742	.722	47	56		-22	S31O/2P	-1.4
■ CHAD KREUTER	Kreuter, Chad Michael b: 8/26/64, Greenbrae, Cal. BB/TR, 6'2", 190 lbs. Deb: 9/14/88																											
1988	Tex-A	16	51	3	14	2	1	1	5	7	13	.275	.362	.412	.774	115	1	1	101	83	8	.737	0	0	0	-2	C	0.0
■ PAUL KRICHELL	Krichell, Paul Bernard b: 12/19/1882, New York, N.Y. d: 6/4/57, New York, N.Y. BR/TR, 5'7", 150 lbs. Deb: 5/12/11																											
1911	StL-A	28	82	6	19	3	0	0	8	4		.232	.276	.268	.544	55	-5	-5	95	123	7	.460	2			2	C	0.0
1912	StL-A	57	161	19	35	6	0	0	8	19		.217	.304	.255	.559	61	-8	-8	99	65	13	.500	2			1	C	0.0
Total	2	85	243	25	54	9	0	0	16	23		.222	.295	.259	.554	59	-13	-12	98	84	20	.487	4			3	/C	0.0
■ BILL KRIEG	Krieg, William Frederick b: 1/29/1859, Petersburg, Ill. d: 3/25/30, Chillicothe, Ill. BR/TR, 5'8", 180 lbs. Deb: 4/20/1884																											
1884	CP-U	71	279	35	69	15	4	0		11		.247	.276	.330	.606	105	1	1	99	0	26	.490	0			11	CO/S1	1.4
1885	Chi-N	1	3	0	0	0	0	0	0	0	2	.000	.000	.000	.000	-88	-1	-1	114	0	0	.000				0	/O	0.0
	Bro-a	17	60	7	9	4	0	1		2		.150	.177	.267	.444	39	-4	-4	104	0	3	.353				0	C/1	-0.3
1886	Was-N	27	98	11	25	6	3	1	15	3	12	.255	.277	.408	.685	113	0	1	94	116	12	.616	2			0	1	0.1

YEAR	TM/L	G	AB	R	H	2B	3B	HR	RBI	BB	SO	AVG	OBP	SLG	PRO	/A	BR	/A	PF	CHI	RC	TA	SB	CS	SBR	FR	POS	TPR
1887	Was-N	25	95	9	24	4	1	2	17	7	5	.253	.311	.379	.690	97	-1	-0	95	132	12	.648	2			0	1/O	0.0
Total	4	141	535	62	127	29	8	4	32	23	19	.237	.270	.344	.614	96	-4	-3	98	45	53	.520	4			11	/C1OS	1.2
■ JOHN KRONER	Kroner, John Harold b: 11/13/08, St.Louis, Mo. d: 8/26/68, St.Louis, Mo. BR/TR, 6', 185 lbs. Deb: 9/29/35																											
1935	Bos-A	2	4	1	1	0	0	0	0	1	1	.250	.400	.250	.650	66	-0	-0	108	0	1	.667	0	0	0	0	/3	0.0
1936	Bos-A	84	298	40	87	17	8	4	62	26	24	.292	.349	.443	.792	89	-4	-6	106	139	46	.748	2	3	-1	-7	23S/O	-0.8
1937	Cle-A	86	283	29	67	14	1	2	26	22	25	.237	.292	.314	.606	54	-21	-20	98	94	27	.516	1	1	-0	9	23	-0.4
1938	Cle-A	51	117	13	29	16	0	1	17	19	6	.248	.353	.410	.763	92	-2	-2	99	113	18	.753	0	1	-1	-1	2/13S	-0.1
Total	4	223	702	83	184	47	9	7	105	68	56	.262	.327	.385	.712	76	-26	-28	101	116	91	.652	3	5	-2	2	2/3S10	-1.3
■ MIKE KRSNICH	Krsnich, Michael b: 9/24/31, W.Allis, Wis. BR/TR, 6'1", 190 lbs. Deb: 4/23/60																											
1960	Mil-N	4	9	0	3	1	0	0	2	0	0	.333	.333	.444	.778	122	0	0	91	203	1	.571	0	0	0	-0	/O	0.0
1962	Mil-N	11	12	0	1	1	0	0	2	0	4	.083	.083	.167	.250	-35	-2	-2	99	394	0	.167	0	0	0	-1	/O13	-0.2
Total	2	15	21	0	4	2	0	0	4	0	4	.190	.190	.286	.476	28	-2	-2	95	312	1	.333	0	0	0	-1	/O31	-0.2
■ ROCKY KRSNICH	Krsnich, Rocco Peter b: 8/5/27, W.Allis, Wis. BR/TR, 6'1", 174 lbs. Deb: 9/13/49																											
1949	Chi-A	16	55	7	12	3	1	1	9	6	4	.218	.295	.364	.659	75	-2	-2	98	134	6	.578	0	1	-1	2	3	0.0
1952	Chi-A	40	91	11	21	7	2	1	15	12	9	.231	.327	.385	.712	98	-0	-0	100	147	11	.649	0	0	0	4	3	0.3
1953	Chi-A	64	129	9	26	8	0	1	14	12	11	.202	.270	.287	.556	47	-9	-10	106	130	10	.458	0	2	-1	-1	3	-1.4
Total	3	120	275	27	59	18	3	3	38	30	24	.215	.294	.335	.629	69	-12	-13	102	137	27	.557	0	3	-2	5	3	-1.1
■ OTTO KRUEGER	Krueger, Arthur William "Oom Paul" b: 9/17/1876, Chicago, Ill. d: 2/20/61, St.Louis, Mo. BR/TR, 5'7", 165 lbs. Deb: 9/16/1899																											
1899	Cle-N	13	44	4	10	1	0	0	2	8		.227	.358	.250	.608	79	-1	-0	89	59	4	.618	1			0	/3S2	0.0
1900	StL-N	12	35	8	14	3	2	1	3	10		.400	.533	.686	1.219	256	7	8	93	35	13	1.619	0			0	2	0.7
1901	StL-N	142	520	77	143	16	12	2	79	50		.275	.339	.363	.702	109	5	7	97	138	72	.684	19			-9	*3	0.7
1902	StL-N	128	467	55	124	7	8	0	46	29		.266	.308	.315	.623	99	-3	-1	95	111	51	.554	14			1	*S3	0.6
1903	Pit-N	80	256	42	63	6	8	1	28	21		.246	.303	.344	.647	82	-5	-7	105	99	29	.591	5			2	SO3/2	-0.3
1904	Pit-N	86	268	34	52	6	2	1	26	29		.194	.273	.243	.515	62	-11	-11	99	140	20	.472	8			-1	OS3	-1.3
1905	Phi-N	46	114	10	21	1	1	0	12	13		.184	.268	.211	.478	43	-7	-8	104	174	7	.409	1			-2	S/O3	-0.9
Total	7	507	1704	230	427	40	33	5	196	160		.251	.315	.322	.637	93	-16	-12	98	123	197	.593	48			-10	S3/O2	-0.5
■ ERNIE KRUEGER	Krueger, Ernest George b: 12/27/1890, Chicago, Ill. d: 4/22/76, Waukegan, Ill. BR/TR, 5'10.5", 185 lbs. Deb: 8/04/13																											
1913	Cle-A	5	6	0	0	0	0	0	0	0	2	.000	.000	.000	.000	-95	-1	-2	106	0	0	.000	0			0	/C	0.0
1915	NY-A	10	29	3	5	1	0	0	0	0	5	.172	.200	.207	.407	22	-3	-3	98	0	1	.280	0	1	-1	0	/C	-0.2
1917	NY-N	8	10	0	0	0	0	0	0	0	4	.000	.000	.000	.000	-99	-2	-2	97	0	0	.000	0			-0	/C	-0.2
	Bro-N	31	81	10	22	2	2	1	6	5	7	.272	.330	.383	.712	114	2	1	104	68	10	.661	1			-0	C	0.3
	Yr	39	91	10	22	2	2	1	6	5	11	.242	.296	.341	.637	93	-1	-1	102	54	9	.565	1			-0		0.1
1918	Bro-N	30	87	4	25	4	2	0	7	4	9	.287	.319	.379	.698	111	1	1	101	80	10	.629	2			3	C	0.7
1919	Bro-N	80	226	24	56	7	4	5	36	19	25	.248	.312	.381	.692	115	2	3	94	139	27	.653	4			1	C	0.9
1920	Bro-N	52	146	21	42	4	2	1	17	16	13	.288	.358	.363	.721	97	2	-0	111	117	20	.683	2	0	1	-4	C	0.0
1921	Bro-N	65	163	18	43	11	4	3	20	14	12	.264	.322	.436	.758	94	-1	-2	105	92	23	.713	2	2	-1	2	C	0.3
1925	Cin-N	37	88	7	27	4	0	1	7	6	8	.307	.351	.386	.737	91	-1	-1	97	67	11	.651	1	2	-1	-3	C	-0.3
Total	8	318	836	87	220	33	14	11	93	64	85	.263	.319	.376	.695	97	-3	-4	101	98	102	.636	12	5		-1	C	1.5
■ CHRIS KRUG	Krug, Everett Ben b: 12/25/39, Los Angeles, Cal. BR/TR, 6'4", 200 lbs. Deb: 5/30/65																											
1965	Chi-N	60	169	16	34	5	0	5	24	13	52	.201	.262	.320	.582	62	-8	-9	102	144	12	.472	0	1	-1	-2	C	-0.9
1966	Chi-N	11	28	1	6	1	0	0	1	1	8	.214	.241	.250	.491	37	-2	-2	100	60	2	.348	0	0	0	1	C	0.0
1969	SD-N	8	17	0	1	0	0	0	0	1	6	.059	.111	.059	.170	-53	-3	-3	97	0	0	.125	0	0	0	0	/C	-0.2
Total	3	79	214	17	41	6	0	5	25	15	66	.192	.248	.290	.538	50	-14	-15	101	122	14	.448	0	1	-1	-1	/C	-1.1
■ GENE KRUG	Krug, Gary Eugene b: 2/12/55, Garden City, Kan. BL/TL, 6'4", 225 lbs. Deb: 4/29/81																											
1981	Chi-N	7	5	0	2	0	0	0	0	1	1	.400	.500	.400	.900	152	0	0	104	0	1	1.000	0	0	0	0	/H	0.0
■ HENRY KRUG	Krug, Henry Charles b: 12/4/1876, San Francisco, Cal. d: 1/14/08, San Francisco, Cal TR , Deb: 7/26/02																											
1902	Phi-N	53	198	20	45	3	3	0	14	7		.227	.254	.273	.526	61	-8	-10	105	91	15	.412	2			-2	O2/S3	-1.2
■ MARTY KRUG	Krug, Martin John b: 9/10/1888, Coblenz, Germany d: 6/27/66, Glendale, Cal. BR/TR, 5'9", 165 lbs. Deb: 6/01/12																											
1912	Bos-A	20	39	6	12	2	1	0	7	5		.308	.386	.410	.797	120	1	1	107	146	7	.852	2			-1	/S2	0.1
1922	Chi-N	127	450	67	124	23	4	4	60	43	43	.276	.343	.371	.714	89	-10	-7	95	120	58	.657	7	9	-3	-2	*32/S	-0.3
Total	2	147	489	73	136	25	5	4	67	48	43	.278	.346	.374	.721	91	-9	-6	96	122	65	.671	9	9		-3	3/2S	-0.2
■ ART KRUGER	Kruger, Arthur T. b: 3/16/1881, San Antonio, Tex. d: 11/28/49, Hondo, Cal. BR/TR, 6', 185 lbs. Deb: 4/11/07																											
1907	Cin-N	100	317	25	74	10	9	0	28	18		.233	.275	.322	.596	93	-5	-3	95	104	32	.535	10			11	O	0.4
1910	Cle-A	62	223	19	38	6	3	0	14	20		.170	.251	.224	.475	49	-13	-13	100	110	16	.465	12			6	O	-1.0
	Bos-N	1	1	0	0	0	0	0	0	0	0	.000	.000	.000	.000	-88	-0	-0	114	0	0	.000	0			0	H	0.0
1914	KC-F	122	441	45	114	24	7	4	47	23	59	.259	.295	.372	.667	95	-7	-4	95	98	54	.606	11			-3	*O	-1.4
1915	KC-F	80	240	24	57	9	2	2	26	12	29	.237	.274	.317	.590	77	-8	-7	97	114	24	.508	5			-2	O	-1.2
Total	4	365	1222	113	283	49	21	6	115	73	88	.232	.277	.321	.598	82	-33	-28	96	105	126	.540	38			11	O	-3.2
■ JOHN KRUK	Kruk, John Martin b: 2/9/61, Charleston, W.Va. BL/TL, 5'10", 170 lbs. Deb: 4/07/86																											
1986	SD-N	122	278	33	86	16	2	4	38	45	58	.309	.406	.424	.830	136	13	15	95	117	47	.797	2	4	-2	-6	O/1	0.5
1987	SD-N	138	447	72	140	14	2	20	91	73	93	.313	.410	.488	.897	141	26	28	97	133	92	.957	18	10	-1	-0	*1O	2.0
1988	SD-N	120	378	54	91	17	1	9	44	80	68	.241	.373	.362	.736	115	9	11	97	109	56	.747	5	3	-0	-0	1O	0.6
Total	3	380	1103	159	317	47	5	33	173	198	219	.287	.396	.429	.825	131	48	53	97	121	195	.859	25	17	-3	-7	1O	3.1
■ DICK KRYHOSKI	Kryhoski, Richard David b: 3/24/25, Leonia, N.J. BL/TL, 6'2", 182 lbs. Deb: 4/19/49																											
1949	NY-A	54	177	18	52	10	3	1	27	9	17	.294	.335	.401	.736	94	-2	-2	100	125	22	.622	2	4	-2	-2	1	-0.5
1950	Det-A	53	169	20	37	10	0	4	19	8	11	.219	.258	.349	.608	56	-13	-12	97	92	15	.504	0	1	-1	1	1	-1.2
1951	Det-A	119	421	58	121	19	4	12	57	28	29	.287	.335	.437	.772	102	3	-1	106	93	60	.685	1	2	-1	6	*1	0.2
1952	StL-A	111	342	38	83	13	1	11	42	23	42	.243	.296	.383	.679	91	-7	-6	97	96	39	.596	2	0	1	-4	1	-1.4
1953	StL-A	104	338	35	94	18	4	16	50	26	33	.278	.333	.497	.830	114	8	5	107	86	52	.757	0	5	-3	-0	1	0.0
1954	Bal-A	100	300	32	78	13	2	1	34	19	24	.260	.308	.327	.635	78	-11	-9	95	128	29	.513	0	0	0	2	1	-0.9
1955	KC-A	28	47	2	10	2	0	0	2	6	7	.213	.302	.255	.557	50	-3	-3	101	62	4	.474	0	1	-1	1	1	-0.3
Total	7	569	1794	203	475	85	14	45	231	119	163	.265	.315	.403	.718	92	-25	-28	101	100	221	.645	5	13	-6	2	1	-4.1
■ TONY KUBEK	Kubek, Anthony Christopher b: 10/12/36, Milwaukee, Wis. BL/TR, 6'3", 190 lbs. Deb: 4/20/57																											
1957	NY-A	127	431	56	128	21	3	3	39	24	48	.297	.338	.381	.719	102	-3	1	94	89	56	.629	6	6	-2	3	OS3/2	0.3
1958	NY-A	138	559	66	148	21	1	2	48	25	57	.265	.297	.317	.614	67	-24	-26	103	111	52	.493	5	4	-1	20	*S/O12	1.3
1959	NY-A	132	512	67	143	25	7	6	51	24	46	.279	.314	.391	.705	100	-6	-2	93	98	60	.598	3	3	-1	2	SO3/2	0.1
1960	NY-A	147	568	77	155	25	3	14	62	31	42	.273	.314	.401	.715	98	-8	-4	94	95	70	.622	3	0	1	5	*SO	1.1
1961	NY-A	153	617	84	170	38	6	8	46	27	60	.276	.307	.395	.702	89	-14	-11	96	71	74	.597	1	3	-2	18	*S	1.5
1962	NY-A	45	169	28	53	6	1	4	17	12	17	.314	.359	.432	.791	119	3	4	94	81	26	.725	2	1	0	-2	S/O	0.4
1963	NY-A	135	557	72	143	21	3	7	44	28	68	.257	.295	.343	.638	78	-17	-17	101	84	57	.536	4	2	0	13	*S/O	0.2
1964	NY-A	106	415	46	95	16	3	8	31	26	55	.229	.276	.340	.616	68	-17	-19	103	84	39	.526	4	1	1	11	S	-0.6
1965	NY-A	109	339	26	74	5	3	5	35	20	48	.218	.262	.295	.557	57	-19	-19	101	126	25	.440	1	3	-2	2	S/O1	-1.5
Total	9	1092	4167	522	1109	178	30	57	373	217	441	.266	.305	.364	.669	85	-104	-92	98	93	459	.575	29	23	-5	70	SO/321	2.8
■ TED KUBIAK	Kubiak, Theodore Rodger b: 5/12/42, New Brunswick, N.J. BB/TR, 6', 175 lbs. Deb: 4/14/67																											
1967	KC-A	53	102	6	16	2	1	0	5	12	20	.157	.246	.196	.442	32	-8	-8	100	104	5	.364	0	0	0	-2	S2/3	-0.9
1968	Oak-A	48	120	10	30	5	2	0	8	8	18	.250	.308	.325	.633	93	-1	-1	98	88	12	.543	1	1	-0	1	2S	0.2
1969	Oak-A	92	305	38	76	9	1	2	27	25	35	.249	.308	.305	.613	78	-11	-8	92	109	29	.508	2	0	1	1	S2	-0.3

YEAR	TM/L	G	AB	R	H	2B	3B	HR	RBI	BB	SO	AVG	OBP	SLG	PRO	/A	BR	/A	PF	CHI	RC	TA	SB	CS	SBR	FR	POS	TPR
1970	Mil-A	158	540	63	136	9	6	4	41	72	51	.252	.340	.313	.653	83	-12	-11	98	94	56	.568	4	9	-4	-20	2S	-1.9
1971	Mil-A	89	260	26	59	6	5	3	17	41	31	.227	.332	.323	.655	84	-4	-5	103	75	28	.587	0	5	-3	-2	2S	-0.2
	StL-N	32	72	8	18	3	2	1	10	11	12	.250	.349	.389	.738	108	1	1	101	131	11	.741	1	0	0	2	S2	0.7
1972	Tex-A	46	116	5	26	3	0	0	7	12	12	.224	.302	.250	.552	70	-5	-4	94	101	8	.442	0	1	-1	-2	2S/3	-0.3
	Oak-A	51	94	14	17	4	1	0	8	9	11	.181	.252	.245	.497	50	-6	-6	97	145	6	.405	0	0	0	-2	2/3	-0.4
	Yr	97	210	19	43	7	1	0	15	21	23	.205	.280	.248	.528	61	-10	-10	96	125	16	.435	0	1	-1	-4		-0.7
1973	Oak-A	106	182	15	40	6	1	3	17	12	19	.220	.268	.313	.581	73	-9	-6	87	101	15	.483	1	1	-0	-2	2S/3	-0.1
1974	Oak-A	99	220	22	46	3	0	0	18	18	15	.209	.269	.223	.492	42	-16	-16	100	144	12	.368	1	1	-0	-2	2S3/D	-1.4
1975	Oak-A	20	28	2	7	1	0	0	4	2	2	.250	.300	.286	.586	71	-1	-1	93	192	2	.455	0	0	0	-1	/S32	0.0
	SD-N	87	196	13	44	5	0	0	14	24	18	.224	.309	.250	.559	57	-11	-11	100	110	16	.481	3	1	0	-2	32/1	-1.2
1976	SD-N	96	212	16	50	5	2	0	26	25	28	.236	.316	.278	.595	79	-8	-5	89	170	18	.483	0	3	-2	1	32/S1	-0.4
Total	10	977	2447	238	565	61	21	13	202	271	272	.231	.309	.289	.598	73	-91	-80	97	111	219	.520	13	22	-9	-30	2S3/1D	-6.2
■ JACK KUBISZYN	Kubiszyn, John Henry b: 12/19/36, Buffalo, N.Y. BR/TR, 5'11", 170 lbs. Deb: 4/23/61																											
1961	Cle-A	25	42	4	9	0	0	0	0	2	5	.214	.250	.214	.464	26	-4	-4	96	0	2	.324	0	0	0	-1	/3S2	-0.3
1962	Cle-A	25	59	3	10	2	0	1	2	5	7	.169	.234	.254	.489	32	-6	-6	98	44	4	.400	0	0	0	-1	S/3	-0.4
Total	2	50	101	7	19	2	0	1	2	7	12	.188	.241	.238	.478	30	-10	-10	97	26	6	.373	0	0	0	-1	/S32	-0.7
■ GIL KUBSKI	Kubski, Gilbert Thomas b: 10/12/54, Longview, Tex. BL/TR, 6'3", 185 lbs. Deb: 9/02/80																											
1980	Cal-A	22	63	11	16	3	0	0	6	6	10	.254	.319	.302	.620	74	-2	-2	96	123	6	.520	1	1	-0	-0	O	-0.2
■ STEVE KUCZEK	Kuczek, Stanislaw Leo b: 12/28/24, Amsterdam, N.Y. BR/TR, 6', 160 lbs. Deb: 9/29/49																											
1949	Bos-N	1	1	0	1	1	0	0	0	0	0	1.000	1.000	2.000	3.000	709	1	1	97	0	2	—	0			0	H	0.1
■ BILL KUEHNE	Kuehne, William J. (born William J. Knelme) b: 10/24/1858, Leipzig, Germany d: 10/27/21, Sulphur Springs, O BR/TR, 185 lbs. Deb: 5/01/1883																											
1883	Col-a	95	374	38	85	8	14	1		2		.227	.231	.332	.563	91	-9	-2	87	0	29	.436				-9	*32/SO	-0.8
1884	Col-a	110	415	48	98	13	16	5		9		.236	.254	.381	.635	110	3	4	97	0	41	.530				8	*3/O	1.2
1885	Pit-a	104	411	54	93	9	19	0		15		.226	.257	.341	.598	85	-5	-9	106	0	37	.494				-1	*3/S	-0.3
1886	Pit-a	117	481	73	98	16	17	1		19		.204	.237	.314	.551	79	-16	-10	93	0	43	.517	26			-4	O31	-1.2
1887	Pit-N	102	402	68	120	18	15	1	41	14	39	.299	.324	.425	.749	116	3	8	93	74	62	.720	17			-11	*S/31O	-0.4
1888	Pit-N	138	524	60	123	22	11	3	62	9	68	.235	.250	.336	.586	92	-8	-5	95	122	54	.551	34			-3	3S	-0.2
1889	Pit-N	97	390	43	96	20	5	5	57	9	36	.246	.263	.362	.625	84	-15	-8	89	111	42	.561	15			-3	3O/2S1	-0.5
1890	Pit-P	126	528	66	126	21	12	5	73	28	37	.239	.277	.352	.629	75	-25	-18	92	105	59	.585	21			5	*3	-0.2
1891	Col-a	68	261	32	56	9	0	2	22	10	22	.215	.244	.272	.516	55	-18	-13	89	84	23	.498	21			-5	3	-1.3
	Lou-a	41	159	28	44	3	1	1	18	8	13	.277	.315	.327	.643	96	-3	-1	90	96	20	.617	10			1	3	0.1
	Yr	109	420	60	100	12	1	3		18	35	.238	.271	.293	.564	71	-21	-14	90	89	43	.541	31			-4		-1.2
1892	Lou-N	76	287	22	48	4	5	0	36	13	36	.167	.203	.216	.419	30	-25	-22	92	182	14	.339	6			-5	3	-2.0
	StL-N	6	24	1	4	1	0	0	0	0	3	.167	.200	.208	.408	26	-2	-2	95	0	1	.350	1			0	/3S	-0.1
	Cin-N	6	24	3	5	1	0	1	4	1	5	.208	.240	.375	.615	84	-1	-1	103	108	2	.526	0			1	/32	0.0
	StL-N	1	4	0	0	0	0	0	0	0	1	.000	.000	.000	.000	-99	-1	-1	95	0	0	.000	0			1	/3	0.0
	Yr	89	339	26	57	6	5	1	40	14	45	.168	.203	.224	.428	33	-29	-25	93	166	17	.348	7			-3		-2.1
Total	10	1087	4284	536	996	145	115	25	313	137	260	.232	.258	.338	.595	84	-121	-79	94	67	428	.530	151			-24	3S/O21	-5.7
■ HARVEY KUENN	Kuenn, Harvey Edward b: 12/4/30, W.Allis, Wis. d: 2/28/88, Peoria, Ariz. BR/TR, 6'2", 187 lbs. Deb: 9/06/52 MC																											
1952	Det-A	19	80	2	26	2	2	0	8	2	1	.325	.349	.400	.749	109	1	1	99	82	10	.638	2	1	0	0	S	0.2
1953	Det-A	155	679	94	**209**	33	7	2	48	50	31	.308	.356	.386	.742	103	0	2	98	57	96	.658	6	5	-1	-21	*S	-0.7
1954	Det-A	155	656	81	**201**	28	6	5	48	29	13	.306	.337	.390	.727	99	-3	-3	100	59	80	.611	9	9	-3	5	*S	1.3
1955	Det-A	145	620	101	190	**38**	5	8	62	40	27	.306	.349	.423	.772	110	4	7	97	78	92	.707	8	3	1	-25	*S	-0.1
1956	Det-A	146	591	96	**196**	32	7	12	88	55	34	.332	.391	.470	.862	131	22	25	97	111	109	.839	9	5	-0	-10	*S/O	2.7
1957	Det-A	151	624	74	173	30	6	9	44	47	28	.277	.328	.388	.716	88	-5	-11	107	62	75	.620	5	8	-3	-35	*S3/1	-3.9
1958	Det-A	139	561	73	179	**39**	3	8	54	51	34	.319	.376	.442	.818	120	19	16	104	70	89	.751	5	10	-5	10	*O	1.3
1959	Det-A	139	561	99	**198**	**42**	7	9	71	48	37	**.353**	.405	.501	.906	133	36	28	111	87	117	.908	7	2	1	-2	*O	2.1
1960	Cle-A	126	474	65	146	24	0	9	54	55	25	.308	.381	.416	.797	118	11	13	98	100	77	.757	3	0	1	1	*O/3	1.0
1961	SF-N	131	471	60	125	22	4	5	46	47	34	.265	.333	.361	.694	86	-10	-9	98	102	55	.611	5	4	-1	1	O3/S	-1.5
1962	SF-N	130	487	73	148	23	5	10	68	49	37	.304	.369	.433	.802	113	10	10	101	118	77	.746	3	6	-3	-8	*O3	-0.5
1963	SF-N	120	417	61	121	13	2	6	31	44	38	.290	.361	.374	.735	117	8	10	96	76	57	.664	2	1	0	-12	O3	-0.5
1964	SF-N	111	351	42	92	16	2	4	22	35	32	.262	.331	.353	.684	93	-3	-3	100	66	42	.604	0	1	-1	-13	O1/3	-2.0
1965	SF-N	23	59	4	14	0	0	0	6	10	3	.237	.357	.237	.594	64	-2	-3	111	178	6	.596	3	1	0	-2	O/1	-0.5
	Chi-N	54	120	11	26	5	0	0	6	22	13	.217	.338	.258	.596	69	-4	-4	102	80	12	.551	1	0	0	-4	O/1	-0.8
	Yr	77	179	15	40	5	0	0	12	32	16	.223	.344	.251	.596	68	-5	-6	104	112	18	.569	4	1	1	-6		-1.3
1966	Chi-N	3	3	0	1	0	0	0	0	0	1	.333	.333	.333	.667	86	-0	-0	100	0	0	.500	0	0	0	-0	/O	0.0
	Phi-N	86	159	15	47	9	0	0	15	10	16	.296	.337	.352	.689	91	-2	-2	101	113	18	.564	0	0	0	-5	O1/3	-0.8
	Yr	89	162	15	48	9	0	0	15	10	17	.296	.337	.352	.689	91	-2	-2	101	109	19	.563	0	0	0	-6		-0.8
Total	15	1833	6913	951	2092	356	56	87	671	594	404	.303	.359	.408	.767	108	84	79	101	83	1013	.717	68	56	-13	-119	OS3/1	-2.7
■ JOE KUHEL	Kuhel, Joseph Anthony b: 6/25/06, Cleveland, Ohio d: 2/26/84, Kansas City, Kan. BL/TL, 6', 180 lbs. Deb: 7/31/30 M																											
1930	Was-A	18	63	9	18	3	3	0	17	5	6	.286	.348	.429	.776	94	-0	-1	101	209	10	.756	1	0	0	0	1	-0.1
1931	Was-A	139	524	70	141	34	8	8	85	47	45	.269	.335	.410	.745	94	-5	-5	101	120	73	.706	7	5	-1	-6	*1	-2.3
1932	Was-A	101	347	52	101	21	5	4	52	32	19	.291	.353	.415	.768	98	-1	-1	100	112	52	.734	5	2	0	-0	1	-0.8
1933	Was-A	153	602	89	194	34	10	11	107	59	48	.322	.385	.467	.851	130	21	25	96	120	110	.863	17	8	0	-7	*1	0.6
1934	Was-A	63	263	49	76	12	3	3	25	30	14	.289	.364	.392	.756	94	-2	-2	101	66	37	.701	2	7	-4	-1	1	-1.6
1935	Was-A	151	633	99	165	25	9	2	74	78	44	.261	.345	.338	.684	85	-20	-12	92	101	78	.638	5	4	-1	0	*1	-2.6
1936	Was-A	149	588	107	189	42	8	16	118	64	30	.321	.392	.502	.893	122	17	19	98	118	117	.931	15	7	0	-2	*1	-0.2
1937	Was-A	136	547	73	155	24	11	6	61	63	39	.283	.357	.400	.758	96	-8	-3	94	85	81	.729	6	3	0	2	*1	-1.5
1938	Chi-A	117	412	67	110	27	4	8	51	72	35	.267	.376	.410	.786	99	-1	1	98	91	67	.809	9	7	-2	-7	*1	-2.1
1939	Chi-A	139	546	107	164	24	9	15	56	64	51	.300	.376	.460	.836	106	10	5	107	61	99	.850	18	5	2	-4	*1	-0.8
1940	Chi-A	155	603	111	169	28	8	27	94	87	59	.280	.374	.488	.861	117	19	16	104	80	116	.880	12	5	1	-5	*1	0.4
1941	Chi-A	153	600	99	150	39	5	12	63	70	55	.250	.331	.392	.723	97	-9	-3	94	79	81	.695	20	5	3	-2	*1	-0.6
1942	Chi-A	115	413	60	103	14	4	4	52	60	22	.249	.347	.332	.679	92	-3	-3	99	130	54	.682	22	9	1	-7	*1	-0.9
1943	Chi-A	153	531	55	113	21	1	5	46	76	45	.213	.319	.284	.604	76	-13	-14	101	103	54	.571	14	8	-1	0	*1	-1.9
1944	Was-A	139	518	90	144	26	7	4	51	68	40	.278	.364	.378	.742	125	10	16	90	94	75	.707	11	6	-0	-3	*1	0.5
1945	Was-A	142	533	73	152	29	13	2	75	79	31	.285	.378	.400	.778	135	19	24	93	131	88	.771	10	5	0	-5	*1	1.5
1946	Was-A	14	20	2	3	0	0	0	2	5	2	.150	.320	.150	.470	37	-2	-1	92	254	1	.471	0	0	0	0	/1	-0.1
	Chi-A	64	238	24	65	9	3	4	20	21	24	.273	.335	.387	.721	104	0	1	97	75	30	.641	4	4	-1	-5	1	-0.8
	Yr	78	258	26	68	9	3	4	22	26	26	.264	.333	.368	.702	100	-1	-0	96	110	32	.627	4	4	-1	-5		-0.9
1947	Chi-A	3	3	0	0	0	0	0	0	0	3	.000	.000	.000	.000	-99	-1	-1	97	0	0	.000	0	0	0	0	H	0.0
Total	18	2104	7984	1236	2212	412	111	131	1049	980	612	.277	.359	.406	.765	105	33	61	97	100	1223	.757	178	90	-1	-50	*1	-13.3
■ KENNY KUHN	Kuhn, Kenneth Harold b: 3/20/37, Louisville, Ky. BL/TR, 5'10.5", 175 lbs. Deb: 7/07/55																											
1955	Cle-A	4	6	0	2	0	0	0	0	1	0	.333	.429	.333	.762	103	0	0	104	0	1	1.000	1	0	0	0	/S	0.1
1956	Cle-A	27	22	7	6	1	0	0	2	0	4	.273	.273	.318	.591	55	-1	-1	101	107	2	.412	0	1	-1	-1	S/2	0.0
1957	Cle-A	40	53	5	9	0	0	0	5	4	9	.170	.228	.170	.398	10	-6	-7	102	219	2	.289	0	0	0	-0	2/3S	-0.6
Total	3	71	81	12	17	1	0	0	7	5	13	.210	.256	.222	.478	30	-8	-8	102	173	5	.364	1	1	-0	-1	/S23	-0.5
■ WALT KUHN	Kuhn, Walter Charles "Red" b: 2/2/1884, Fresno, Cal. d: 6/14/35, Fresno, Cal. BR/TR, 5'7", 162 lbs. Deb: 4/18/12																											
1912	Chi-A	75	178	16	36	7	0	0	10	20		.202	.286	.242	.528	52	-11	-11	99	78	14	.486	5			-3	C	-0.5
1913	Chi-A	26	50	5	8	1	0	0	5	13	8	.160	.333	.180	.513	54	-2	-2	95	197	3	.548	1			0	C	0.0
1914	Chi-A	17	40	4	11	1	0	0	0	8	11	.275	.396	.300	.696	106	1	1	103	0	5	.688	2	3	-1	1	C	0.1

YEAR	TM/L	G	AB	R	H	2B	3B	HR	RBI	BB	SO	AVG	OBP	SLG	PRO	/A	BR	/A	PF	CHI	RC	TA	SB	CS	SBR	FR	POS	TPR
Total	3	118	268	25	55	9	0	0	15	41	19	.205	.313	.239	.552	61	-12	-12	99	90	22	.528	8	3		-2	C	-0.4
■ **CHARLIE KUHNS** Kuhns, Charles B. b: 10/27/1877, Freeport, Pa. d: 7/15/22, Pittsbugh, Pa. 5'9", 160 lbs. Deb: 6/04/1897																												
1897	Pit-N	1	3	0	0	0	0	0	0	1		.000	.250	.000	.250	-30	-1	-1	98	0	0	.333	0			0	/3	0.0
1899	Bos-N	7	18	2	5	0	0	0	3	2		.278	.350	.278	.628	72	-0	-1	105	184	2	.538	0			0	/S3	0.0
Total	2	8	21	2	5	0	0	0	3	3		.238	.333	.238	.571	57	-1	-1	104	153	2	.500	0			0	/3S	0.0
■ **DUANE KUIPER** Kuiper, Duane Eugene b: 6/19/50, Racine, Wis. BL/TR, 6', 175 lbs. Deb: 9/09/74																												
1974	Cle-A	10	22	7	11	2	0	0	4	2	2	.500	.542	.591	1.133	224	4	4	101	121	6	1.231	1	1	-0	1	/2	0.4
1975	Cle-A	90	346	42	101	11	1	0	25	30	26	.292	.362	.329	.691	97	-0	-0	100	89	39	.629	19	18	-5	-5	2/D	-0.6
1976	Cle-A	135	506	47	133	13	6	0	37	30	42	.263	.305	.312	.618	81	-12	-12	100	95	43	.494	10	17	-7	12	*2/1D	0.0
1977	Cle-A	148	610	62	169	15	8	1	50	37	55	.277	.326	.333	.658	82	-16	-14	98	85	66	.560	11	11	-3	2	*2	-0.3
1978	Cle-A	149	547	52	155	18	6	0	43	19	35	.283	.312	.338	.650	89	-13	-8	93	94	54	.515	4	9	-4	-19	*2	-2.4
1979	Cle-A	140	479	46	122	9	5	0	39	37	27	.255	.313	.294	.608	62	-23	-26	106	106	41	.489	4	9	-4	-7	*2	-3.0
1980	Cle-A	42	149	10	42	5	0	0	9	13	8	.282	.340	.315	.655	79	-4	-4	102	76	17	.550	0	1	-1	-4	2	-0.6
1981	Cle-A	72	206	15	53	6	0	0	14	8	13	.257	.285	.286	.571	70	-9	-8	93	93	17	.439	1	1	-0	-7	2	-1.3
1982	SF-N	107	218	26	61	9	1	0	17	32	24	.280	.377	.330	.707	106	1	3	94	93	28	.647	2	2	-1	-3	2	0.2
1983	SF-N	72	176	14	44	2	2	0	14	27	13	.250	.356	.284	.640	79	-4	-4	101	111	18	.564	0	1	-1	-10	2	-1.1
1984	SF-N	83	115	8	23	1	0	0	11	12	10	.200	.276	.209	.484	39	-9	-9	96	180	7	.379	0	1	-1	1	2/1	-0.7
1985	SF-N	9	5	0	3	0	0	0	0	1	0	.600	.667	.600	1.267	275	1	1	93	0	2	2.000	0	0	0	0	/H	0.1
Total	12	1057	3379	329	917	91	29	1	263	248	255	.271	.326	.316	.643	82	-83	-77	98	97	340	.552	52	71	-27	-39	2/1D	-9.3
■ **JEFF KUNKEL** Kunkel, Jeffrey William b: 3/25/62, W.Palm Beach, Fla. BR/TR, 6'2", 180 lbs. Deb: 7/23/84																												
1984	Tex-A	50	142	13	29	2	3	3	7	2	35	.204	.221	.324	.545	48	-10	-10	100	51	9	.449	4	3	-1	-4	S/D	-1.0
1985	Tex-A	2	4	1	1	0	0	0	0	0	3	.250	.250	.250	.500	35	-0	-0	108	0	0	.333	0	0	0	0	/S	0.0
1986	Tex-A	8	13	3	3	0	0	1	2	0	2	.231	.231	.462	.692	87	-0	-0	96	88	1	.600	0	0	0	0	/SD	0.0
1987	Tex-A	15	32	1	7	0	0	1	2	0	10	.219	.242	.313	.555	45	-2	-3	104	61	2	.423	0	1	-1	-1	2/3O1SD	-0.3
1988	Tex-A	55	154	14	35	9	3	2	15	4	35	.227	.252	.364	.615	69	-7	-7	101	96	12	.488	0	1	-1	-3	2S/3OPD	-0.7
Total	5	130	345	32	75	11	6	7	26	6	85	.217	.237	.345	.582	59	-20	-20	101	73	25	.471	4	5	-2	-8	/S23ODP1	-2.0
■ **RUSTY KUNTZ** Kuntz, Russell Jay b: 2/4/55, Orange, Cal. BR/TR, 6'3", 190 lbs. Deb: 9/01/79																												
1979	Chi-A	5	11	0	1	0	0	0	0	2	6	.091	.231	.091	.322	-9	-2	-2	102	0	0	.273	0	0	0	1	/O	0.0
1980	Chi-A	36	62	5	14	4	0	0	3	5	13	.226	.284	.290	.574	60	-4	-3	97	65	5	.480	1	0	0	-5	O	-0.8
1981	Chi-A	67	55	15	14	2	0	0	4	6	8	.255	.339	.291	.630	83	-1	-1	100	98	6	.571	1	0	0	-12	O/D	-1.4
1982	Chi-A	21	26	4	5	1	0	0	3	2	8	.192	.250	.231	.481	34	-2	-2	97	200	1	.364	0	0	0	-5	O	-0.8
1983	Chi-A	28	42	6	11	1	0	0	1	6	13	.262	.354	.286	.640	76	-1	-1	103	33	5	.594	1	0	0	-4	O/D	-0.5
	Min-A	31	100	13	19	3	0	3	5	12	28	.190	.277	.310	.587	58	-5	-6	105	49	8	.506	0	0	0	2	O	-0.4
	Yr	59	142	19	30	4	0	3	6	18	41	.211	.300	.303	.603	64	-6	-7	104	42	13	.534	1	0	0	-3		-0.9
1984	Det-A	84	140	32	40	12	0	2	22	25	28	.286	.398	.414	.812	130	6	7	96	137	25	.827	2	2	-1	-14	OD	-0.9
1985	Det-A	5	5	0	0	0	0	0	0	2	2	.000	.286	.000	.286	-13	-1	-1	106	0	0	.333	0	1	-1	0	/1D	0.0
Total	7	277	441	75	104	23	0	5	38	60	106	.236	.330	.322	.652	82	-10	-10	100	91	50	.615	5	3	-0	-38	O/D1	-4.8
■ **WHITEY KUROWSKI** Kurowski, George John b: 4/19/18, Reading, Pa. BR/TR, 5'11", 193 lbs. Deb: 9/23/41																												
1941	StL-N	5	9	1	3	2	0	0	2	0	2	.333	.400	.556	.956	152	1	1	110	144	2	1.000	0			0	/3	0.1
1942	StL-N	115	366	51	93	17	3	9	42	33	60	.254	.326	.391	.717	101	4	0	108	92	48	.677	7			4	*3/SO	0.4
1943	StL-N	139	522	69	150	24	8	13	70	31	54	.287	.330	.439	.768	116	11	9	105	96	74	.692	3			-1	*3/S	0.7
1944	StL-N	149	555	95	150	25	7	20	87	58	40	.270	.341	.449	.790	120	14	14	101	103	85	.746	2			2	*3/2S	2.5
1945	StL-N	133	511	84	165	27	3	21	102	45	45	.323	.383	.511	.894	147	31	31	100	112	100	.876	1			-4	*3/S	2.5
1946	StL-N	142	519	76	156	32	5	14	89	72	47	.301	.391	.462	.853	133	29	25	107	125	97	.855	2			1	*3	2.9
1947	StL-N	146	513	108	159	27	6	27	104	87	56	.310	.420	.544	.964	145	42	37	106	109	118	1.019	4			-7	*3	2.5
1948	StL-N	77	220	34	47	8	0	2	33	42	28	.214	.352	.277	.629	72	-7	-7	101	185	25	.614	0			-0	3	-0.8
1949	StL-N	10	14	0	2	0	0	0	0	1	0	.143	.200	.143	.343	-6	-2	-2	110	0	0	.231	0			0	/3	-0.1
Total	9	916	3229	518	925	162	32	106	529	369	332	.286	.366	.455	.821	124	123	107	104	112	551	.821	19			-6	3/S2O	10.7
■ **CRAIG KUSICK** Kusick, Craig Robert b: 9/30/48, Milwaukee, Wis. BR/TR, 6'3", 210 lbs. Deb: 9/08/73																												
1973	Min-A	15	48	4	12	2	0	0	4	7	9	.250	.357	.292	.649	81	-1	-1	104	112	6	.611	0	0	0	0	1/OD	0.0
1974	Min-A	76	201	36	48	7	1	8	26	35	36	.239	.354	.403	.757	116	5	5	101	97	30	.741	0	0	0	5	1	0.7
1975	Min-A	57	156	14	37	8	0	6	27	21	23	.237	.346	.404	.750	104	3	1	107	128	23	.730	0	0	0	2	1	0.0
1976	Min-A	109	266	33	69	13	0	11	36	35	44	.259	.348	.432	.780	130	9	10	98	93	43	.776	5	1	1	0	D1	1.0
1977	Min-A	115	268	34	68	12	0	12	45	49	60	.254	.375	.433	.808	116	9	8	103	117	43	.795	3	1	0	0	D1	0.7
1978	Min-A	77	191	23	33	3	2	4	20	37	38	.173	.310	.272	.582	69	-8	-6	94	123	17	.554	3	2	-0	-1	D1/O	-0.8
1979	Min-A	24	54	8	13	4	0	3	7	3	11	.241	.281	.481	.762	93	-0	-1	109	77	7	.690	0	0	0	0	D/1	0.0
	Tor-A	24	54	3	11	1	0	2	7	7	7	.204	.306	.333	.640	70	-2	-2	103	112	6	.578	0	0	0	-1	1/PD	-0.3
	Yr	48	108	11	24	5	0	5	14	10	18	.222	.294	.407	.702	82	-2	-3	106	96	13	.640	0	0	0	-0		-0.3
Total	7	497	1238	155	291	50	3	46	172	194	228	.235	.345	.392	.736	106	15	13	101	109	174	.738	11	4	1	7	1D/OP	1.3
■ **ART KUSNYER** Kusnyer, Arthur William b: 12/19/45, Akron, Ohio BR/TR, 6'2", 197 lbs. Deb: 9/21/70 C																												
1970	Chi-A	4	10	0	1	0	0	0	0	0	4	.100	.100	.100	.200	-42	-2	-2	106	0	0	.111	0	0	0	0	/C	-0.1
1971	Cal-A	6	13	0	2	0	0	0	0	0	3	.154	.154	.154	.308	-13	-2	-2	99	0	0	.182	0	0	0	-0	/C	-0.1
1972	Cal-A	64	179	13	37	2	1	2	13	16	33	.207	.276	.263	.538	69	-9	-6	88	102	14	.444	0	0	0	-10	C	-1.8
1973	Cal-A	41	64	5	8	2	0	0	3	2	12	.125	.152	.156	.308	-14	-10	-9	96	118	1	.211	0	1	-1	-9	C	-1.8
1976	Mil-A	15	34	2	4	1	0	0	3	1	5	.118	.167	.147	.314	-8	-5	-5	99	231	1	.267	1	0	0	1	C	-0.2
1978	KC-A	9	13	1	3	1	0	1	2	2	4	.231	.333	.538	.872	138	1	1	102	79	3	.900	0	0	0	0	/C	0.1
Total	6	139	313	21	55	6	1	3	21	21	61	.176	.232	.230	.462	38	-26	-23	93	111	19	.371	1	1	-0	-19	C	-3.9
■ **JUL KUSTUS** Kustus, Joseph J. "Joe" or "Kul" b: 9/5/1882, Detroit, Mich. d: 4/27/16, Eloise, Mich. BR/TR, 5'10", Deb: 09																												
1909	Bro-N	53	173	12	25	5	0	1	11	11		.145	.204	.191	.395	24	-15	-15	99	113	8	.372	9			0	O	-1.8
■ **RANDY KUTCHER** Kutcher, Randy Scott b: 4/20/60, Anchorage, Alaska BR/TR, 5'11", 170 lbs. Deb: 6/19/86																												
1986	SF-N	71	186	28	44	9	1	7	16	11	41	.237	.279	.409	.688	91	-4	-3	96	66	20	.620	6	5	-1	3	OS/32	-0.1
1987	SF-N	14	16	7	3	1	1	0	1	1	5	.188	.235	.375	.610	61	-1	-1	96	66	2	.615	1	0	0	-1	/O23S	0.0
1988	Bos-A	19	12	2	2	1	0	0	0	0	2	.167	.167	.250	.417	14	-1	-1	109	0	0	.273	0	1	-1	-1	/O3D	-0.2
Total	3	104	214	37	49	11	2	7	17	12	48	.229	.270	.397	.667	84	-6	-6	97	62	22	.608	7	6	-2	1	/OS3D2	-0.3
■ **JOE KUTINA** Kutina, Joseph Peter b: 1/16/1885, Chicago, Ill. d: 4/13/45, Chicago, Ill. BR/TR, 6'2", 205 lbs. Deb: 9/06/11																												
1911	StL-A	26	101	12	26	6	2	3	15	2		.257	.279	.446	.724	106	-1	-0	95	99	13	.667	2			-1	1	0.0
1912	StL-A	67	205	18	42	9	3	1	18	13		.205	.262	.293	.555	59	-12	-11	99	95	16	.466	0			0	1/O	-0.9
Total	2	93	306	30	68	15	5	4	33	15		.222	.268	.343	.611	75	-12	-12	98	97	28	.529	2			-1	/1O	-0.9
■ **AL KVASNAK** Kvasnak, Alexander b: 1/11/21, Sagamore, Pa. BR/TR, 6'1", 170 lbs. Deb: 4/15/42																												
1942	Was-A	5	11	3	2	0	0	0	0	2	1	.182	.308	.182	.490	41	-1	-1	96	0	1	.444	0	0	0	-0	/O	-0.1
■ **ANDY KYLE** Kyle, Andrew Ewing b: 10/29/1889, Toronto, Ont., Can. d: 9/6/71, Toronto, Ont., Can. BL/TL, 5'8", 160 lbs. Deb: 9/07/12																												
1912	Cin-N	9	21	3	7	1	0	0	4	4	2	.333	.440	.381	.821	136	1	1	92	168	4	.857	0			0	/O	0.1
■ **CHET LAABS** Laabs, Chester Peter b: 4/30/12, Milwaukee, Wis. d: 1/26/83, Warren, Mich. BR/TR, 5'8", 175 lbs. Deb: 5/05/37																												
1937	Det-A	72	242	31	58	13	5	8	37	24	66	.240	.308	.434	.742	78	-7	-10	109	98	33	.726	6	2	1	-5	O	-1.4
1938	Det-A	64	211	26	50	7	3	7	37	15	52	.237	.288	.398	.686	70	-11	-11	100	119	24	.626	3	2	-0	1	O	-0.8
1939	Det-A	5	16	1	5	1	1	0	2	2	0	.313	.389	.500	.889	113	1	0	111	84	3	.833	0	0	0	1	/O	0.1
	StL-A	95	317	52	95	20	5	10	62	33	62	.300	.368	.489	.856	117	7	7	100	113	57	.839	4	1	1	-4	O	0.1
	Yr	100	333	53	100	21	6	10	64	35	62	.300	.369	.489	.858	116	8	7	101	113	61	.842	4	1	1	-3		0.2

YEAR	TM/L	G	AB	R	H	2B	3B	HR	RBI	BB	SO	AVG	OBP	SLG	PRO	/A	BR	/A	PF	CHI	RC	TA	SB	CS	SBR	FR	POS	TPR
1940	StL-A	105	218	32	59	11	5	10	40	34	59	.271	.372	.505	.876	118	8	6	106	103	43	.902	3	3	-1	-4	O	-0.2
1941	StL-A	118	392	64	109	23	6	15	59	51	59	.278	.361	.482	.843	121	11	11	100	89	71	.833	5	2	0	-2	*O	0.3
1942	StL-A	144	520	90	143	21	7	27	99	88	88	.275	.380	.498	.878	140	32	29	104	105	103	.885	0	3	-2	-1	*O	1.6
1943	StL-A	151	580	83	145	27	7	17	85	73	105	.250	.338	.409	.747	117	12	12	100	104	82	.701	5	7	-3	7	*O	1.2
1944	StL-A	66	201	28	47	10	2	5	23	29	33	.234	.330	.378	.709	100	1	0	102	91	27	.684	3	1	0	-3	O	-0.4
1945	StL-A	35	109	15	26	4	3	1	8	16	17	.239	.352	.358	.709	92	1	-1	115	69	15	.682	0	0	0	-3	O	-0.5
1946	StL-A	80	264	40	69	13	0	16	52	20	50	.261	.316	.492	.808	126	6	7	98	111	38	.744	3	1	0	1	O	0.4
1947	Phi-A	15	32	5	7	1	0	1	5	4	4	.219	.306	.344	.649	80	-1	-1	100	131	4	.600	0	0	0	1	/O	0.0
Total	11	950	3102	467	813	151	44	117	509	389	595	.262	.346	.452	.798	113	60	50	103	102	501	.794	32	22	-4	-13	O	0.4
■ **COCO LABOY**	Laboy, Jose Alberto b: 7/3/39, Ponce, P.R. BR/TR, 5'10", 165 lbs. Deb: 4/08/69																											
1969	Mon-N	157	562	53	145	29	1	18	83	40	96	.258	.312	.409	.721	100	-1	-1	100	120	70	.634	0	2	-1	-1	*3	-0.3
1970	Mon-N	137	432	37	86	26	1	5	53	31	81	.199	.256	.299	.555	48	-33	-33	100	143	31	.450	0	2	-1	-13	*3/2	-5.0
1971	Mon-N	76	151	10	38	4	0	1	14	11	19	.252	.302	.298	.600	71	-6	-6	99	119	13	.479	0	1	-1	-3	3/2	-0.9
1972	Mon-N	28	69	6	18	2	0	3	14	10	16	.261	.354	.420	.775	116	2	2	102	151	11	.765	0	0	0	-0	3/2S	0.1
1973	Mon-N	22	33	2	4	1	0	1	2	5	8	.121	.237	.242	.479	32	-3	-3	104	73	2	.448	0	0	0	-0	3/2	-0.3
Total	5	420	1247	108	291	62	2	28	166	97	220	.233	.292	.354	.646	77	-41	-41	100	128	127	.566	0	5	-3	-18	3/2S	-6.4
■ **CANDY LaCHANCE**	LaChance, George Joseph b: 2/15/1870, Waterbury, Conn. d: 8/18/32, Waterville, Conn. BB/TR, 6'1", 183 lbs. Deb: 8/15/1893																											
1893	Bro-N	11	35	1	6	1	0	0	6	2	12	.171	.237	.200	.437	20	-4	-4	91	235	2	.345	0			0	/CO	-0.2
1894	Bro-N	68	257	48	83	13	8	5	52	16	32	.323	.365	.494	.859	114	2	5	94	103	55	.943	20			-5	1C/O	0.0
1895	Bro-N	127	536	99	167	22	8	8	108	29	48	.312	.356	.427	.783	110	2	7	94	115	97	.821	37			-6	*1/O	0.3
1896	Bro-N	89	348	60	99	10	13	7	58	23	32	.284	.331	.448	.779	121	1	9	87	100	59	.791	17			-3	*1	0.7
1897	Bro-N	126	520	86	160	28	16	4	90	15		.308	.333	.446	.779	105	3	1	102	114	88	.772	26			-5	*1	-0.3
1898	Bro-N	136	526	62	130	23	7	5	65	31		.247	.299	.346	.645	92	-10	-6	95	106	63	.616	23			-19	1SO	-2.0
1899	Bal-N	125	472	65	145	23	10	1	75	21		.307	.350	.405	.755	101	5	-0	108	126	80	.774	31			-8	*1	-0.5
1901	Cle-A	133	548	81	166	22	9	1	75	7		.303	.312	.381	.693	99	-6	-2	95	118	70	.594	11			-3	*1	-0.9
1902	Bos-A	138	541	60	151	13	4	6	56	18		.279	.302	.351	.654	83	-14	-13	99	94	61	.554	8			-11	*1	-2.1
1903	Bos-A	141	522	60	134	22	6	1	53	28		.257	.295	.328	.622	79	-7	-15	112	112	55	.544	12			-11	*1	-2.5
1904	Bos-A	157	573	55	130	19	5	1	47	23		.227	.257	.283	.539	69	-18	-21	105	108	44	.433	7			-13	*1	-3.4
1905	Bos-A	12	41	1	6	1	0	0	5	6		.146	.255	.171	.426	38	-3	-3	100	270	2	.371	0			-1	1	-0.4
Total	12	1263	4919	678	1377	197	86	39	690	219	124	.280	.315	.379	.694	94	-49	-40	100	112	676	.652	192			-86	*1/SOC	-11.3
■ **RENE LACHEMANN**	Lachemann, Rene George b: 5/4/45, Los Angeles, Cal. BR/TR, 6', 198 lbs. Deb: 5/04/65 MC																											
1965	KC-A	92	216	20	49	7	1	9	29	12	57	.227	.268	.394	.661	88	-5	-4	97	107	22	.567	0	0	0	5	C	0.6
1966	KC-A	7	5	0	1	1	0	0	0	0	1	.200	.200	.400	.600	72	-0	-0	94	0	0	.400	0	0	0	0	/C	0.0
1968	Oak-A	19	60	3	9	1	0	0	4	1	11	.150	.177	.167	.344	5	-7	-7	98	171	2	.235	0	0	0	-1	C	-0.8
Total	3	118	281	23	59	9	1	9	33	13	69	.210	.247	.345	.593	71	-12	-11	97	119	24	.500	0	0	0	3	/C	-0.2
■ **PETE LaCOCK**	LaCock, Ralph Pierre b: 1/17/52, Burbank, Cal. BL/TL, 6'2", 200 lbs. Deb: 9/06/72																											
1972	Chi-N	5	6	3	3	0	0	0	4	0	1	.500	.500	.500	1.000	162	1	1	114	548	2	1.333	1	0	0	-1	/O	0.0
1973	Chi-N	11	16	1	4	1	0	0	3	1	2	.250	.294	.313	.607	63	-1	-1	108	241	2	.500	0	0	0	-0	/O	0.0
1974	Chi-N	35	110	9	20	4	1	1	8	12	16	.182	.268	.264	.532	49	-7	-7	100	96	8	.457	0	0	0	0	O1	-0.8
1975	Chi-N	106	249	30	57	8	1	6	30	37	27	.229	.329	.341	.670	83	-4	-5	104	113	27	.598	0	2	-1	-2	1O	-1.2
1976	Chi-N	106	244	34	54	9	2	8	28	42	37	.221	.338	.373	.711	93	1	-2	109	94	31	.678	1	4	-2	-1	1O	-0.8
1977	KC-A	88	218	25	66	12	1	3	29	15	25	.303	.350	.408	.759	106	2	2	100	117	31	.682	2	1	0	-1	1DO	0.0
1978	KC-A	118	322	44	95	21	2	5	48	21	27	.295	.338	.419	.757	109	4	4	102	126	44	.668	1	0	0	-4	*1	-0.4
1979	KC-A	132	408	54	113	25	4	3	56	37	26	.277	.339	.380	.718	89	-3	-6	105	131	50	.625	2	1	0	-1	*1D	-1.2
1980	KC-A	114	156	14	32	6	0	1	18	17	10	.205	.287	.263	.550	53	-10	-10	98	160	11	.458	1	0	0	-6	1O	-2.0
Total	9	715	1729	214	444	86	11	27	224	182	171	.257	.329	.366	.695	89	-18	-26	104	123	206	.637	8	8	-2	-15	1O/D	-6.4
■ **LEON LACY**	Lacy, Leondaus b: 4/10/48, Longview, Tex. BR/TR, 6'1", 175 lbs. Deb: 6/30/72																											
1972	LA-N	60	243	34	63	7	3	0	12	19	37	.259	.313	.313	.626	83	-7	-5	94	62	24	.535	5	3	-0	-3	2	-0.4
1973	LA-N	57	135	14	28	2	0	0	8	15	34	.207	.287	.222	.509	43	-10	-10	100	107	9	.420	2	3	-1	-2	2	-1.2
1974	LA-N	48	78	13	22	6	0	0	8	2	14	.282	.300	.359	.659	90	-2	-1	93	110	9	.571	2	0	1	-2	2/3	0.0
1975	LA-N	101	306	44	96	11	5	7	40	22	29	.314	.360	.451	.811	131	9	11	95	97	44	.721	5	9	-4	0	2O/S	0.8
1976	Atl-N	50	180	25	49	4	2	3	20	6	12	.272	.299	.367	.666	79	-3	-6	111	105	18	.543	2	2	-1	-0	2/O3	-0.4
	LA-N	53	158	17	42	7	1	0	14	16	13	.266	.333	.323	.656	87	-2	-2	100	106	16	.544	1	2	-1	2	O/32	-0.2
	Yr	103	338	42	91	11	3	3	34	22	25	.269	.316	.346	.662	83	-6	-8	105	106	36	.554	3	4	-2	2		-0.6
1977	LA-N	75	169	28	45	7	0	6	21	10	21	.266	.307	.414	.721	91	-2	-2	100	95	22	.661	4	0	1	-7	O23	-0.8
1978	LA-N	103	245	29	64	16	4	13	40	27	30	.261	.337	.518	.855	137	11	11	99	96	42	.857	7	4	-0	-3	O2/3S	0.7
1979	Pit-N	84	182	17	45	9	3	5	15	22	36	.247	.332	.412	.744	96	0	-1	106	66	27	.748	6	1	1	-2	O/2	-0.2
1980	Pit-N	109	278	45	93	20	4	7	33	28	33	.335	.399	.511	.910	148	20	18	103	80	57	.964	18	9	0	2	O/3	1.7
1981	Pit-N	78	213	31	57	11	4	2	10	11	29	.268	.307	.385	.692	99	-2	-1	96	45	28	.738	24	3	5	0	O/3	0.3
1982	Pit-N	121	359	66	112	16	3	5	31	32	57	.312	.370	.415	.785	108	10	5	110	74	56	.825	40	15	3	-5	*O/3	0.2
1983	Pit-N	108	288	40	87	12	3	4	13	22	36	.302	.352	.406	.758	106	4	3	103	40	42	.787	31	13	2	-4	O	-0.1
1984	Pit-N	138	474	66	152	26	3	12	70	32	61	.321	.364	.464	.828	139	18	22	94	109	77	.796	21	11	-0	15	*O/2	3.2
1985	Bal-A	121	492	69	144	22	4	9	48	39	95	.293	.347	.409	.756	107	4	5	99	80	70	.698	10	3	1	-0	*O/D	0.4
1986	Bal-A	130	491	77	141	18	0	11	47	37	71	.287	.337	.391	.728	100	-1	-0	99	85	62	.633	4	6	-2	2	*O/D	-0.3
1987	Bal-A	87	258	35	63	13	3	7	28	32	49	.244	.328	.399	.727	94	-3	-2	98	90	34	.683	3	2	-0	1	O/D	-0.3
Total	16	1523	4549	650	1303	207	42	91	458	372	657	.286	.342	.410	.752	108	43	44	100	84	637	.729	185	86	4	-8	*O2/3DS	3.4
■ **GUY LACY**	Lacy, Osceola Guy b: 6/12/1897, Cleveland, Tenn. d: 11/19/53, Cleveland, Tenn. BR/TR, 5'11.5", 170 lbs. Deb: 5/17/26																											
1926	Cle-A	13	24	2	4	0	0	1	2	2	2	.167	.259	.292	.551	44	-2	-2	100	68	2	.500	0	0	0	-0	2/3	-0.1
■ **HI LADD**	Ladd, Arthur Clifford Hiram b: 2/9/1870, Willimantic, Conn. d: 5/7/48, Cranston, R.I. 6'4", 180 lbs. Deb: 7/12/1898																											
1898	Pit-N	1	1	0	0	0	0	0	0	0		.000	.000	.000	.000	-99	-0	-0	98	0	0	.000	0			0		0.0
	Bos-N	1	4	1	1	0	0	0	0	0		.250	.250	.250	.500	44	-0	-0	104	0	0	.333	0			0	/O	0.0
	Yr	2	5	1	1	0	0	0	0	0		.200	.200	.200	.400	16	-1	-1	101	0	0	.250	0			0		0.0
Total	1	2	5	1	1	0	0	0	0	0		.200	.200	.200	.400	16	-1	-1	102	0	0	.250	0			0	/O	0.0
■ **STEVE LADEW**	Ladew, Stephen b: St.Louis, Mo. Deb: 9/27/1889																											
1889	KC-a	2	4	0	0	0	0	0	0	0	3	.000	.000	.000	.000	-95	-1	-1	106	0	0	.000	0			0	/OP	0.0
■ **JOE LAFATA**	Lafata, Joseph Joseph b: 8/3/21, Detroit, Mich. BL/TL, 6', 163 lbs. Deb: 4/17/47																											
1947	NY-N	62	95	13	21	1	0	2	18	15	18	.221	.333	.295	.628	68	-4	-4	101	196	10	.584	1			0	O/1	-0.4
1948	NY-N	1	1	0	0	0	0	0	0	0	1	.000	.000	.000	.000	-99	-0	-0	100	0	0	.000	0			0	H	0.0
1949	NY-N	64	140	18	33	2	2	3	16	9	23	.236	.282	.343	.625	66	-7	-7	102	106	14	.537	1			-1	1	-0.7
Total	3	127	236	31	54	3	2	5	34	24	42	.229	.303	.322	.625	66	-11	-11	101	144	24	.563	2			-1	/1O	-1.1
■ **FLIP LAFFERTY**	Lafferty, Frank Bernard b: 5/4/1854, Scranton, Pa. d: 2/8/10, Wilmington, Del. TR , Deb: 9/15/1876																											
1876	Phi-N	1	3	0	0	0	0	0	0	0	0	.000	.000	.000	.000	-99	-1	-1	99	0	0	.000				0	/P	0.0
1877	Lou-N	4	17	2	1	1	0	0	0	0	4	.059	.059	.118	.176	-35	-3	-4	132	0	0	.125				0	/O	-0.2
Total	2	5	20	2	1	1	0	0	0	0	4	.050	.050	.100	.150	-42	-3	-4	127	0	0	.105				0	/OP	-0.2
■ **TY LaFOREST**	LaForest, Byron Joseph b: 4/18/17, Edmunston, N.B., Canada d: 5/5/47, Arlington, Mass. BR/TR, 5'9", 165 lbs. Deb: 8/04/45																											
1945	Bos-A	52	204	25	51	7	4	2	16	10	35	.250	.285	.353	.638	89	-5	-4	95	79	19	.524	4	4	-1	3	3/O	-0.1
■ **ROGER LaFRANCOIS**	LaFrancois, Roger Victor b: 8/2/54, Norwich, Conn. BL/TR, 6'2", 215 lbs. Deb: 5/27/82																											
1982	Bos-A	8	10	1	4	1	0	0	1	0	0	.400	.400	.500	.900	132	1	0	110	80	2	.833	0	0	0	0	/C	0.1

YEAR	TM/L	G	AB	R	H	2B	3B	HR	RBI	BB	SO	AVG	OBP	SLG	PRO	/A	BR	/A	PF	CHI	RC	TA	SB	CS	SBR	FR	POS	TPR
■ MIKE LAGA	Laga, Michael Russell b: 6/14/60, Ridgewood, N.J. BL/TL, 6'2", 210 lbs. Deb: 9/01/82																											
1982	Det-A	27	88	6	23	9	0	3	11	4	23	.261	.293	.466	.759	104	0	0	100	88	12	.697	1	0	0	0	1/D	0.0
1983	Det-A	12	21	2	4	0	0	0	2	1	9	.190	.227	.190	.418	17	-2	-2	96	195	1	.278	0	0	0	0	/1D	-0.1
1984	Det-A	9	11	1	6	0	0	0	1	1	2	.545	.583	.545	1.129	223	2	2	96	66	4	1.400	0	0	0	0	/1D	0.2
1985	Det-A	9	36	3	6	1	0	2	6	0	9	.167	.167	.361	.528	37	-3	-3	106	128	2	.419	0	0	0	0	/1D	-0.2
1986	Det-A	15	45	6	9	1	0	3	8	5	13	.200	.280	.422	.702	93	-1	-1	95	114	6	.667	0	0	0	1	1/D	0.0
	StL-N	18	46	7	10	4	0	3	8	5	18	.217	.308	.500	.808	115	1	1	103	100	7	.784	0	0	0	-0	1	0.0
1987	StL-N	17	29	4	4	1	0	1	4	2	7	.138	.194	.276	.469	23	-3	-3	99	145	1	.385	0	0	0	-0	1	-0.3
1988	StL-N	41	100	5	13	0	0	1	4	2	21	.130	.147	.160	.307	-11	-14	-15	104	84	2	.207	0	0	0	-0	1	-1.8
Total	7	148	376	34	75	16	0	13	44	20	102	.199	.242	.346	.588	60	-21	-21	101	105	35	.505	1	0	0	1	1/D	-2.2
■ JOE LAHOUD	Lahoud, Joseph Michael b: 4/14/47, Danbury, Conn. BL/TL, 6'1", 198 lbs. Deb: 4/10/68																											
1968	Bos-A	29	78	5	15	1	0	1	6	16	16	.192	.330	.244	.573	75	-2	-2	101	117	7	.530	0	2	-1	-4	O	-0.8
1969	Bos-A	101	218	32	41	5	0	9	21	40	43	.188	.317	.335	.651	79	-5	-6	105	84	26	.648	2	1	0	-6	O/1	-1.4
1970	Bos-A	17	49	6	12	1	0	2	5	7	6	.245	.339	.388	.727	90	0	-1	111	81	7	.684	0	0	0	2	O	0.1
1971	Bos-A	107	256	39	55	9	3	14	32	40	45	.215	.330	.438	.768	110	5	3	106	85	38	.763	2	2	-1	3	O	0.4
1972	Mil-A	111	316	35	75	9	3	12	34	45	54	.237	.332	.399	.731	123	7	9	95	88	41	.688	3	4	-2	-3	O	0.2
1973	Mil-A	96	225	29	46	9	0	5	26	27	36	.204	.304	.311	.615	77	-8	-6	96	120	20	.557	5	5	-2	1	DO	-0.8
1974	Cal-A	127	325	46	88	16	3	13	44	47	57	.271	.368	.458	.826	148	16	19	92	92	55	.819	4	5	-2	-8	*OD	0.7
1975	Cal-A	76	192	21	41	6	2	6	33	48	33	.214	.373	.359	.733	114	4	6	95	146	30	.784	2	1	0	-4	DO	0.1
1976	Cal-A	42	96	8	17	4	0	0	4	18	16	.177	.319	.219	.538	65	-4	-3	92	73	8	.500	0	0	0	-2	O/D	-0.5
	Tex-A	38	89	10	20	3	1	1	5	10	16	.225	.303	.315	.618	79	-2	-2	102	62	8	.542	1	0	0	-2	D/O	-0.3
	Yr	80	185	18	37	7	1	1	9	28	32	.200	.312	.265	.576	72	-6	-5	97	69	17	.530	1	0	0	-4		-0.8
1977	KC-A	34	65	8	17	5	0	2	8	11	16	.262	.368	.431	.799	117	2	2	100	93	11	.800	1	0	0	-2	O/D	0.0
1978	KC-A	13	16	0	2	0	0	0	0	0	1	.125	.125	.125	.250	-29	-3	-3	102	0	0	.143	0	0	0	-0	/OD	-0.2
Total	11	791	1925	239	429	68	12	65	218	309	339	.223	.335	.372	.707	104	11	16	98	96	252	.700	20	20	-6	-25	OD/1	-2.5
■ DICK LAJESKIE	Lajeskie, Richard Edward b: 1/8/26, Passaic, N.J. d: 8/15/76, Ramsey, N.J. BR/TR, 5'11", 175 lbs. Deb: 9/10/46																											
1946	NY-N	6	10	3	2	0	0	0	0	3	2	.200	.429	.200	.629	80	0	0	102	0	1	.750	0			0	/2	0.0
■ NAP LAJOIE	Lajoie, Napoleon "Larry" b: 9/5/1874, Woonsocket, R.I. d: 2/7/59, Daytona Beach, Fla. BR/TR, 6'1", 195 lbs. Deb: 8/12/1896 MH																											
1896	Phi-N	39	175	36	57	12	7	4	42	1	11	.326	.330	.543	.872	127	6	5	102	109	34	.873	7			-3	1	0.3
1897	Phi-N	127	545	107	197	40	23	9	127	15		.361	.391	**.569**	.959	161	38	42	96	106	132	1.023	20			-9	*1O/3	2.6
1898	Phi-N	147	608	113	197	**43**	11	6	**127**	21		.324	.353	.461	.813	143	24	29	95	124	110	.808	25			-4	*2/1	2.8
1899	Phi-N	77	312	70	118	19	9	6	70	12		.378	.414	.554	.968	173	27	28	97	119	79	1.057	13			21	2/O	4.6
1900	Phi-N	102	451	95	152	33	12	7	92	10		.337	.351	.510	.861	141	20	21	98	101	91	.876	22			27	*2/3	**4.8**
1901	Phi-A	131	544	**145**	**232**	**48**	14	**14**	**125**	24		**.426**	**.451**	**.643**	**1.094**	**203**	**72**	**71**	100	97	**174**	**1.285**	27			17	*2S	**7.4**
1902	Phi-A	1	4	0	1	0	0	0	1	0		.250	.250	.250	.500	37	-0	-0	108	336	1	.667	1			-0	/2	0.0
	Cle-A	86	348	81	132	35	5	7	64	19		.379	.411	.569	.980	178	32	33	97	102	92	1.093	19			11	2	4.4
	Yr	87	352	81	133	35	5	7	65	19		.378	.410	.565	.975	176	31	33	97	109	92	1.087	20			11		**4.4**
1903	Cle-A	125	485	90	167	41	11	7	93	24		**.344**	.375	**.518**	**.893**	**174**	**38**	**40**	96	131	105	**.931**	21			**37**	*2/13	**7.9**
1904	Cle-A	140	553	92	**208**	**49**	15	6	**102**	27		**.376**	**.405**	**.552**	**.957**	**201**	**62**	**61**	102	113	**139**	**1.046**	29			7	2S/1	**7.3**
1905	Cle-A	65	249	29	82	12	2	2	41	17		.329	.372	.418	.790	153	14	14	100	128	44	.790	11			1	2/1M	1.6
1906	Cle-A	152	602	88	**214**	**48**	9	0	91	30		.355	.386	.465	.851	163	45	42	103	125	119	.851	20			23	*23/SM	**6.8**
1907	Cle-A	137	509	53	152	30	6	2	63	30		.299	.338	.393	.731	145	18	22	93	105	78	.711	24			**39**	*2/1M	**6.5**
1908	Cle-A	157	581	77	168	32	6	2	74	47		.289	.342	.375	.718	128	22	19	106	119	77	.678	15			**47**	*2/1M	**6.8**
1909	Cle-A	128	469	56	152	33	7	1	47	35		.324	.378	.431	.809	152	29	28	102	85	79	.808	13			**23**	*2/1M	5.3
1910	Cle-A	159	591	92	**227**	**51**	7	4	76	60		**.384**	.445	.514	.960	201	**68**	**69**	100	85	147	1.088	27			24	*21	**8.9**
1911	Cle-A	90	315	36	115	20	1	2	60	26		.365	.420	.454	.874	140	19	18	103	139	65	.930	13			1	12	1.9
1912	Cle-A	117	448	66	165	34	4	0	90	28		.368	.414	.462	.876	149	29	28	101	140	93	.919	18			5	21	3.1
1913	Cle-A	137	465	66	156	25	2	1	68	33	17	.335	.398	.404	.802	127	21	18	106	129	79	.819	17			18	*2	3.4
1914	Cle-A	121	419	37	108	14	3	0	50	32	15	.258	.313	.305	.619	84	-7	-8	102	149	41	.540	14	15	-5	6	21	-0.8
1915	Phi-A	129	490	40	137	24	5	1	61	11	16	.280	.301	.355	.656	100	-5	-3	96	124	55	.554	10	6	-1	5	*2S/13	0.1
1916	Phi-A	113	426	33	105	14	4	2	35	14	26	.246	.272	.312	.584	77	-15	-14	98	95	42	.508	15			6	*2/1O	-0.5
Total	21	2480	9589	1502	3242	657	163	83	1599	516	85	.338	.376	.467	.843	151	555	562	100	115	1875	.854	381	21		300	*21/S03	85.2
■ EDDIE LAKE	Lake, Edward Erving "Sparky" b: 3/18/16, Antioch, Cal. BR/TR, 5'7", 159 lbs. Deb: 9/26/39																											
1939	StL-N	2	4	0	1	0	0	0	0	1	0	.250	.400	.250	.650	74	-0	-0	105	0	1	.667	0			0	/S	0.0
1940	StL-N	32	66	12	14	3	0	2	7	12	17	.212	.342	.348	.690	89	-1	-1	102	90	8	.685	1			-1	2/S	0.0
1941	StL-N	45	76	9	8	2	0	0	0	15	22	.105	.253	.132	.384	9	-9	-10	110	0	3	.400	3			2	S3/2	-0.5
1943	Bos-A	75	216	26	43	10	0	3	16	47	35	.199	.345	.287	.632	83	-2	-3	104	82	24	.617	3	6	-3	5	S	0.0
1944	Bos-A	57	126	21	26	5	0	0	8	23	22	.206	.329	.246	.575	67	-5	-4	98	93	13	.573	5	2	0	1	S/P23	0.0
1945	Bos-A	133	473	81	132	27	1	11	51	106	37	.279	**.412**	.410	.822	146	29	32	95	78	89	.868	9	7	-2	**27**	*S/2	**6.5**
1946	Det-A	155	587	105	149	24	1	8	31	103	69	.254	.369	.339	.708	91	3	-3	108	51	83	.705	15	9	-1	-15	*S	-1.7
1947	Det-A	158	602	96	127	19	6	12	46	120	54	.211	.343	.322	.665	82	-9	-12	104	65	74	.653	11	10	-3	-29	*S	-4.5
1948	Det-A	64	198	51	52	6	0	2	18	57	20	.263	.427	.323	.751	105	4	5	96	89	33	.810	3	3	-1	-3	23	0.1
1949	Det-A	94	240	38	47	9	1	1	15	61	33	.196	.359	.254	.613	59	-10	-13	108	80	26	.602	2	8	-4	-2	S23	-1.7
1950	Det-A	20	7	3	0	0	0	0	1	1	3	.000	.125	.000	.125	-68	-2	-2	97	0	0	.143	0	0	0	0	/S3	-0.1
Total	11	835	2595	442	599	105	9	39	193	546	312	.231	.366	.323	.689	91	-1	-11	103	69	354	.708	52	45		-15	S/23P	-1.9
■ FRED LAKE	Lake, Frederick Lovett b: 10/16/1866, Nova Scotia, Can. d: 11/24/31, Boston, Mass. Deb: 5/07/1891 M																											
1891	Bos-N	5	7	1	1	0	0	0	0	2	4	.143	.333	.143	.476	38	-0	-1	112	0	0	.500	0			0	/CO	0.0
1894	Lou-N	16	42	8	12	2	0	1	10	11	6	.286	.474	.405	.878	131	2	3	88	138	9	1.133	2			0	/2SC	0.3
1897	Bos-N	19	62	2	15	4	0	0	5	1		.242	.254	.306	.560	46	-5	-5	107	77	5	.468	2			0	C	-0.4
1898	Pit-N	5	13	1	1	0	0	0	1	2		.077	.200	.077	.277	-19	-2	-2	98	302	0	.250	0			0	/1	-0.1
1910	Bos-N	3	1	0	0	0	0	0	0	1	0	.000	.500	.000	.500	42	0	0	114	0	0	1.000	0			0	HM	0.0
Total	5	48	125	12	29	6	0	1	16	17	10	.232	.342	.304	.646	71	-5	-4	99	118	15	.656	4			0	/C2S10	-0.2
■ STEVE LAKE	Lake, Steven Michael b: 3/14/57, Inglewood, Cal. BR/TR, 6'1", 180 lbs. Deb: 4/09/83																											
1983	Chi-N	38	85	9	22	4	1	1	7	2	6	.259	.284	.365	.649	78	-3	-3	101	81	7	.507	0	0	0	0	C	-0.1
1984	Chi-N	25	54	4	12	4	0	2	7	0	7	.222	.236	.407	.644	71	-2	-3	110	98	5	.548	0	0	0	1	C	0.0
1985	Chi-N	58	119	5	18	2	0	1	11	3	21	.151	.179	.193	.372	3	-15	-17	116	169	4	.269	1	0	0	1	C	-1.4
1986	Chi-N	10	19	4	8	1	0	0	4	1	2	.421	.450	.474	.924	145	1	1	107	177	4	.833	0	0	0	1	C	0.2
	StL-N	26	49	4	12	1	0	2	10	2	5	.245	.275	.388	.662	78	-1	-2	103	159	5	.538	0	0	0	-1	C	-0.1
	Yr	36	68	8	20	2	0	2	14	3	7	.294	.324	.412	.736	98	-0	-0	104	169	9	.620	0	0	0	-0		0.1
1987	StL-N	74	179	19	45	7	2	2	19	10	18	.251	.291	.346	.637	69	-8	-8	99	111	18	.529	0	0	0	-3	C	-0.6
1988	StL-N	36	54	5	15	3	0	1	4	3	15	.278	.339	.389	.728	104	1	0	104	67	8	.667	0	0	0	0	C	0.2
Total	6	267	559	50	132	22	3	9	62	21	74	.236	.270	.335	.605	62	-28	-31	105	120	51	.501	1	0	0	-1	C	-1.8
■ AL LAKEMAN	Lakeman, Albert Wesley "Moose" b: 12/31/18, Cincinnati, Ohio d: 5/25/76, Spartanburg, S.C. BR/TR, 6'2", 195 lbs. Deb: 4/19/42 C																											
1942	Cin-N	20	38	0	6	1	0	0	2	3	10	.158	.238	.184	.422	24	-4	-4	101	106	2	.324	0			0	C	-0.3
1943	Cin-N	22	55	5	14	2	1	0	6	3	11	.255	.293	.327	.620	80	-2	-2	99	120	5	.488	0			1	C	0.0
1944	Cin-N	1	1	0	0	0	0	0	0	0	1	.000	.000	.000	.000	-99	-0	-0	95	0	0	.000	0			0	H	0.0
1945	Cin-N	76	258	22	66	9	4	8	31	17	45	.256	.304	.415	.719	105	-2	0	94	82	31	.628	0			2	C	0.4
1946	Cin-N	23	30	0	4	0	0	0	4	2	7	.133	.188	.133	.321	-8	-4	-4	104	373	1	.231	0			0	/C	-0.3
1947	Cin-N	2	2	0	0	0	0	0	0	0	1	.000	.000	.000	.000	-99	-1	-1	91	0	0	.000	0			0	H	0.0
	Phi-N	55	182	11	29	3	0	6	19	5	39	.159	.186	.275	.461	21	-21	-21	100	103	9	.361	0			-0	1C	-2.2
	Yr	57	184	11	29	3	0	6	19	5	40	.158	.184	.272	.456	20	-22	-22	100	100	9	.357	0			-0		-2.2

YEAR	TM/L	G	AB	R	H	2B	3B	HR	RBI	BB	SO	AVG	OBP	SLG	PRO	/A	BR	/A	PF	CHI	RC	TA	SB	CS	SBR	FR	POS	TPR
1948	Phi-N	32	68	2	11	2	0	1	4	5	22	.162	.219	.235	.454	24	-7	-7	94	79	4	.362	0			1	C/P	-0.3
1949	Bos-N	3	6	0	1	0	0	0	0	1	0	.167	.286	.167	.452	25	-1	-1	97	0	0	.333	0			1	/1	0.0
1954	Det-A	5	6	0	0	0	0	0	0	0	1	.000	.000	.000	.000	-99	-2	-2	100	0	0	.000	0	0	0	0	/C	0.0
Total	9	239	646	40	131	17	5	15	66	36	137	.203	.248	.314	.562	56	-43	-41	97	104	51	.470	0	0		4	C/1P	-2.7
■ DAN LALLY	Lally, Daniel J. b: 8/12/1867, Jersey City, N.J. d: 4/14/36, Milwaukee, Wis. BR/TR, 5'11.5", 210 lbs. Deb: 8/19/1891																											
1891	Pit-N	41	143	24	32	6	2	1	17	16	20	.224	.319	.315	.634	86	-2	-2	101	105	15	.586	0			-6	O	-0.9
1897	StL-N	87	355	56	99	15	5	2	42	9		.279	.310	.366	.676	86	-11	-7	93	96	45	.617	12			1	O/1	-1.0
Total	2	128	498	80	131	21	7	3	59	25	20	.263	.313	.351	.664	86	-13	-9	96	99	60	.608	12			-6	O/1	-1.9
■ RAY LAMANNO	Lamanno, Raymond Simond b: 11/17/19, Oakland, Cal. BR/TR, 6', 185 lbs. Deb: 9/11/41																											
1941	Cin-N	1	0	0	0	0	0	0	0	0	0	—	1.000	—	1.351	294	0	0	99	0	0	—	0			0	/C	0.0
1942	Cin-N	111	371	40	98	12	2	12	43	31	54	.264	.324	.404	.729	111	5	4	101	86	46	.638	0			0	*C	0.7
1946	Cin-N	85	239	18	58	12	0	1	30	11	26	.243	.285	.305	.590	65	-11	-12	104	147	20	.460	0			7	C	-0.2
1947	Cin-N	118	413	33	106	21	3	5	50	28	39	.257	.307	.358	.665	84	-15	-10	91	114	46	.569	0			11	*C	0.3
1948	Cin-N	127	385	31	93	12	0	0	27	48	32	.242	.329	.273	.601	62	-18	-19	103	96	35	.511	2			-6	*C	-1.5
Total	5	442	1408	122	355	57	5	18	150	118	151	.252	.314	.338	.653	81	-38	-36	99	107	147	.567	2			13	C	-0.7
■ BILL LAMAR	Lamar, William Harmong "Good Time Bill" b: 3/21/1897, Rockville, Md. d: 5/24/70, Rockport, Mass. BL/TR, 6'1", 185 lbs. Deb: 9/19/17																											
1917	NY-A	11	41	2	10	0	0	0	3	0	2	.244	.244	.244	.488	46	-3	-3	107	110	3	.355	1			0	O	-0.3
1918	NY-A	28	110	12	25	3	0	0	2	6	2	.227	.267	.255	.522	61	-6	-5	95	28	8	.424	2			-1	O	-0.7
1919	NY-A	11	16	1	3	1	0	0	0	2	1	.188	.278	.250	.528	46	-1	-1	106	0	1	.538	1			-1	/O1	-0.1
	Bos-A	48	148	18	43	5	1	0	14	5	9	.291	.314	.338	.652	91	-4	-2	91	102	16	.552	3			-1	O	-0.5
	Yr	59	164	19	46	6	1	0	14	7	10	.280	.310	.329	.639	84	-5	-4	94	83	18	.551	4			-1		-0.6
1920	Bro-N	24	44	5	12	4	0	0	4	0	1	.273	.273	.364	.636	73	-1	-2	111	97	4	.500	0	0	0	-3	O	-0.5
1921	Bro-N	3	3	2	1	0	0	0	0	0	0	.333	.333	.333	.667	74	-0	-0	105	0	0	.500	0	0	0	-0	/O	0.0
1924	Phi-A	87	367	68	121	22	5	7	48	18	21	.330	.361	.474	.835	115	6	6	99	70	60	.787	8	8	-2	4	O	0.1
1925	Phi-A	138	568	85	202	39	8	3	77	21	17	.356	.379	.468	.847	111	10	8	103	99	97	.777	2	6	-3	6	*O	0.0
1926	Phi-A	116	419	62	119	17	6	5	50	18	15	.284	.315	.389	.704	71	-12	-22	118	97	50	.610	4	5	-2	-5	*O	-3.5
1927	Phi-A	84	324	48	97	23	3	4	47	16	10	.299	.334	.426	.760	100	-3	-1	97	106	44	.700	4	0	1	-3	O	-0.8
Total	9	550	2040	303	633	114	23	19	245	86	78	.310	.339	.417	.755	95	-14	-23	103	90	284	.675	25	19		-2	O/1	-6.3
■ LYMAN LAMB	Lamb, Lyman Raymond b: 3/17/1895, Lincoln, Neb. d: 10/5/55, Fayetteville, Ark. BR/TR, 5'7", 150 lbs. Deb: 9/14/20																											
1920	StL-A	9	24	4	9	2	0	0	4	0	7	.375	.375	.458	.833	108	1	0	111	128	4	.867	2	0	1	-1	/O	0.0
1921	StL-A	45	134	18	34	9	2	1	17	4	12	.254	.281	.373	.654	65	-8	-8	101	110	14	.550	0	0	0	-4	3/2O	-0.9
Total	2	54	158	22	43	11	2	1	21	4	19	.272	.294	.386	.681	72	-7	-7	102	112	19	.591	2	0	1	-6	/3O2	-0.9
■ PETE LAMERE	Lamere, Pierre b: 1874, Hoboken, N.J. d: 10/24/31, Brooklyn, N.Y. TR , Deb: 9/10/02																											
1902	Chi-N	2	9	2	2	0	0	0	0	0		.222	.222	.222	.444	40	-1	-1	96	0	0	.286	0			0	/C	0.0
1907	Cin-N	1	2	0	0	0	0	0	0	0		.000	.000	.000	.000	-99	-0	-0	95	0	0	.000	0			0	/C	0.0
Total	2	3	11	2	2	0	0	0	0	0		.182	.182	.182	.364	14	-1	-1	96	0	0	.222	0			0	/C	0.0
■ GENE LAMONT	Lamont, Gene William b: 12/25/46, Rockford, Ill. BL/TR, 6'1", 195 lbs. Deb: 9/02/70 C																											
1970	Det-A	15	44	3	13	3	1	1	4	2	9	.295	.340	.477	.818	119	1	1	103	67	7	.774	0	0	0	0	C	0.2
1971	Det-A	7	15	2	1	0	0	0	1	0	5	.067	.067	.067	.133	-65	-3	-3	96	408	0	.071	0	0	0	-0	/C	-0.2
1972	Det-A	1	0	0	0	0	0	0	0	0	0	—	—	—	—	—	0	0	113	—	—	—	0	0	0	0	/C	0.0
1974	Det-A	60	92	9	20	4	0	3	8	7	19	.217	.273	.359	.631	76	-3	-3	106	75	9	.548	0	0	0	-4	C	-0.5
1975	Det-A	4	8	1	3	1	0	0	1	0	2	.375	.375	.500	.875	140	0	0	104	96	2	1.000	1	0	0	0	/C	0.1
Total	5	87	159	15	37	8	1	4	14	9	35	.233	.278	.371	.649	79	-4	-5	104	103	18	.574	1	0	0	-4	/C	-0.4
■ BOBBY LaMOTTE	LaMotte, Robert Eugene b: 2/15/1898, Savannah, Ga. d: 11/2/70, Chatham, Ga. BR/TR, 5'11", 160 lbs. Deb: 9/01/20																											
1920	Was-A	4	3	0	0	0	0	0	0	1	1	.000	.250	.000	.250	-31	-1	-1	95	0	0	.333	0	0	0	0	/S3	0.0
1921	Was-A	16	41	5	8	0	0	0	2	5	0	.195	.283	.195	.478	24	-5	-5	99	86	3	.394	0	0	0	-1	S	-0.2
1922	Was-A	68	214	22	54	10	2	1	23	15	21	.252	.307	.332	.639	72	-11	-8	92	111	23	.584	6	1	1	7	3/S	0.6
1925	StL-A	97	356	61	97	20	4	2	51	34	22	.272	.338	.368	.706	73	-12	-16	108	127	45	.648	5	5	-2	4	S/3	0.1
1926	StL-A	36	79	11	16	4	3	0	9	11	6	.203	.300	.329	.629	64	-4	-4	101	118	9	.587	0	0	0	0	S/3	-0.1
Total	5	221	693	99	175	34	9	3	85	66	50	.253	.320	.341	.661	69	-32	-33	101	118	80	.603	11	6	-0	11	S/3	0.4
■ KEITH LAMPARD	Lampard, Christopher Keith b: 12/20/45, Warrington, England BL/TR, 6'2", 197 lbs. Deb: 9/15/69																											
1969	Hou-N	9	12	2	3	0	0	1	2	0	3	.250	.250	.500	.750	104	-0	-0	102	89	2	.667	0	0	0	1	/O	0.1
1970	Hou-N	53	72	8	17	8	1	0	5	5	24	.236	.295	.375	.670	84	-2	-2	94	72	7	.569	0	0	0	-1	O/1	-0.2
Total	2	62	84	10	20	8	1	1	7	5	27	.238	.289	.393	.682	87	-2	-2	95	74	9	.582	0	0	0	1	/O1	-0.1
■ TOM LAMPKIN	Lampkin, Thomas Michael b: 3/4/64, Cincinnati, Ohio BL/TR, 5'11", 185 lbs. Deb: 9/10/88																											
1988	Cle-A	4	4	0	0	0	0	0	0	1	0	.000	.200	.000	.200	-38	-1	-1	102	0	0	.200	0	0	0	0	/C	0.0
■ RICK LANCELLOTTI	Lancellotti, Richard Anthony b: 7/5/56, Providence, R.I. BL/TL, 6'3", 195 lbs. Deb: 8/27/82																											
1982	SD-N	17	39	2	7	2	0	0	4	2	8	.179	.220	.231	.450	28	-4	-3	92	174	2	.344	0	0	0	-1	/1O	-0.4
1986	SF-N	15	18	2	4	0	0	2	6	0	7	.222	.222	.556	.778	112	-0	0	96	149	2	.714	0	0	0	1	/1O	0.1
Total	2	32	57	4	11	2	0	2	10	2	15	.193	.220	.333	.554	56	-4	-3	93	167	4	.457	0	0	0	-0	/1O	-0.3
■ GROVER LAND	Land, Grover Cleveland b: 9/22/1884, Frankfort, Ky. d: 7/22/58, Phoenix, Ariz. BR/TR, 6', 190 lbs. Deb: 9/02/08 C																											
1908	Cle-A	8	16	1	3	0	0	0	2	0		.188	.188	.188	.375	22	-1	-1	106	250	1	.231	0			-0	/C	0.0
1910	Cle-A	34	111	4	23	0	0	0	7	2		.207	.228	.207	.435	37	-8	-8	100	112	6	.307	1			-2	C	-0.7
1911	Cle-A	35	107	5	15	1	2	0	10	3		.140	.164	.187	.351	-2	-15	-15	103	169	3	.272	2			3	C/1	-0.7
1913	Cle-A	17	47	3	11	1	0	0	9	4	1	.234	.321	.255	.576	65	-2	-2	106	267	4	.528	1			1	C	0.0
1914	Bro-F	102	335	24	92	6	2	0	29	12	23	.275	.300	.304	.604	73	-12	-12	101	103	34	.498	7			-3	C	-1.0
1915	Bro-F	96	290	25	75	13	2	0	22	6	20	.259	.274	.317	.591	76	-10	-9	98	86	27	.470	3			-10	C	-1.7
Total	6	292	906	62	219	21	6	0	79	27	44	.242	.266	.278	.544	59	-48	-48	100	118	75	.431	14			-11	C/1	-4.1
■ DOC LAND	Land, William Gilbert (born Doc Burrell Land) b: 5/14/03, Bennsville, Miss. d: 4/14/86, Livingston, Ala. BL/TL, 5'11", 165 lbs. Deb: 10/06/29																											
1929	Was-A	1	3	0	0	0	0	0	0	1	0	.000	.250	.000	.250	-30	-1	-1	100	0	0	.333	0	0	0	-0	/O	0.0
■ KEN LANDENBERGER	Landenberger, Kenneth Henry "Red" b: 7/29/28, Lyndhurst, Ohio d: 7/28/60, Cleveland, Ohio BL/TL, 6'3", 200 lbs. Deb: 9/20/52																											
1952	Chi-A	2	5	0	1	0	0	0	0	0	2	.200	.200	.200	.400	12	-1	-1	100	0	0	.250	0	0	0	0	/1	0.0
■ RAFAEL LANDESTOY	Landestoy, Rafael Silvialdo (Santana) b: 5/28/53, Bani, D.R. BB/TR, 5'10", 165 lbs. Deb: 8/27/77																											
1977	LA-N	15	18	6	5	0	0	0	0	3	2	.278	.381	.278	.659	80	-0	-0	100	0	2	.714	2	0	1	0	/2S	0.2
1978	Hou-N	59	218	18	58	5	1	0	9	8	23	.266	.292	.298	.590	69	-10	-9	95	56	19	.482	7	4	-0	-9	S/O2	-1.5
1979	Hou-N	129	282	33	76	9	6	0	30	29	24	.270	.340	.344	.684	96	-4	-1	90	122	36	.664	13	4	2	2	*2/S	1.1
1980	Hou-N	149	393	42	97	13	8	1	27	31	37	.247	.307	.328	.635	79	-12	-11	98	81	41	.598	23	12	-0	-1	2S/3	0.1
1981	Hou-N	35	74	6	11	1	1	0	4	16	9	.149	.300	.189	.489	47	-5	-4	88	112	5	.500	4	1	1	-4	2	-0.5
	Cin-N	12	11	2	2	0	0	0	1	1	0	.182	.250	.182	.432	24	-1	-1	101	196	0	.364	1	0	0	0	/2	0.0
	Yr	47	85	8	13	1	1	0	5	17	9	.153	.294	.188	.482	43	-6	-5	92	136	6	.507	5	1	1	-4		-0.5
1982	Cin-N	73	111	11	21	3	0	1	9	8	14	.189	.250	.243	.493	38	-9	-9	102	118	6	.396	2	0	1	-1	32/OS	-0.9
1983	Cin-N	7	5	0	0	0	0	0	0	0	0	.000	.000	.000	.000	-97	-1	-1	103	0	0	.000	0	0	0	-1	/13O	-0.1
	LA-N	64	64	6	11	1	1	1	1	3	8	.172	.209	.266	.475	31	-6	-6	100	20	3	.357	0	2	-1	-3	23O/S	-1.0
	Yr	71	69	6	11	1	1	1	1	3	8	.159	.194	.246	.441	21	-7	-7	100	18	3	.328	0	2	-1	-4		-1.1
1984	LA-N	53	54	10	10	0	0	1	2	1	6	.185	.200	.241	.441	22	-6	-6	104	49	2	.348	2	1	0	-0	23/O	-0.5
Total	8	596	1230	134	291	32	17	4	83	100	123	.237	.297	.300	.597	69	-55	-49	96	87	115	.548	54	24	2	-16	2S/301	-3.1

YEAR	TM/L	G	AB	R	H	2B	3B	HR	RBI	BB	SO	AVG	OBP	SLG	PRO	/A	BR	/A	PF	CHI	RC	TA	SB	CS	SBR	FR	POS	TPR
■ JIM LANDIS — Landis, James Henry b: 3/9/34, Fresno, Cal. BR/TR, 6'1", 180 lbs. Deb: 4/16/57																												
1957	Chi-A	96	274	38	58	11	3	2	16	45	61	.212	.329	.296	.625	72	-9	-9	99	73	31	.641	14	4	2	6	O	-0.6
1958	Chi-A	142	523	72	145	23	7	15	64	52	80	.277	.352	.434	.786	117	11	12	98	100	82	.777	19	7	2	1	*O	0.5
1959	Chi-A	149	515	78	140	26	7	5	60	78	68	.272	.376	.379	.755	111	8	11	97	115	81	.774	20	9	1	9	*O	1.3
1960	Chi-A	148	494	89	125	25	6	10	49	80	84	.253	.367	.389	.756	103	5	5	101	88	78	.796	23	6	3	7	*O	0.9
1961	Chi-A	140	534	87	151	18	8	22	85	65	71	.283	.365	.470	.835	122	16	17	99	101	95	.852	19	5	3	12	*O	2.6
1962	Chi-A	149	534	82	122	21	6	15	61	80	105	.228	.339	.375	.713	97	-5	-1	95	105	73	.718	19	7	2	1	*O	-0.3
1963	Chi-A	133	396	56	89	6	6	13	45	47	75	.225	.316	.369	.685	87	-4	-6	104	102	48	.653	8	6	-1	-7	*O	-1.9
1964	Chi-A	106	298	30	62	8	4	1	18	36	64	.208	.306	.272	.578	65	-14	-13	96	91	28	.531	5	0	2	-10	*O	-2.6
1965	KC-A	118	364	46	87	15	1	3	36	57	84	.239	.347	.310	.657	91	-4	-2	97	122	42	.624	8	3	1	2	*O	-0.3
1966	Cle-A	85	158	23	35	5	1	3	14	20	25	.222	.317	.323	.639	83	-3	-3	101	98	17	.595	2	1	0	-6	O	-1.1
1967	Det-A	25	48	4	10	0	0	2	4	7	12	.208	.309	.333	.642	90	-1	-0	99	76	5	.575	0	2	-1	1	O	-0.1
	Bos-A	5	7	1	1	0	0	1	1	0	3	.143	.250	.571	.821	119	0	0	115	60	1	.833	0	0	0	-1	/O	0.0
	Yr	30	55	5	11	0	0	3	5	8	15	.200	.302	.364	.665	94	-0	-0	102	76	6	.609	0	2	-1	-1		-0.1
	Hou-N	50	143	19	36	11	1	1	14	20	35	.252	.348	.364	.711	111	1	2	94	105	20	.694	2	1	0	-1	O	0.0
Total	11	1346	4288	625	1061	169	50	93	467	588	767	.247	.346	.375	.721	100	3	12	98	100	602	.731	139	51	11	13	*O	-1.6
■ KEN LANDREAUX — Landreaux, Kenneth Francis b: 12/22/54, Los Angeles, Cal. BL/TR, 5'10", 165 lbs. Deb: 9/11/77																												
1977	Cal-A	23	76	6	19	5	1	0	5	5	15	.250	.296	.342	.638	78	-3	-2	95	76	8	.552	1	1	-0	7	O	0.4
1978	Cal-A	93	260	37	58	7	5	5	23	20	20	.223	.284	.346	.630	75	-9	-9	102	87	25	.567	7	3	0	-5	O/D	-1.5
1979	Min-A	151	564	81	172	27	5	15	83	37	57	.305	.352	.450	.802	106	11	4	109	109	88	.748	10	3	1	-20	*O	-1.9
1980	Min-A	129	484	56	136	23	11	7	62	39	42	.281	.337	.417	.754	97	3	-2	109	115	65	.684	8	6	-1	-5	*O/D	-1.0
1981	LA-N	99	390	48	98	16	4	7	41	25	42	.251	.298	.367	.665	90	-7	-6	98	104	44	.619	18	4	3	-9	O	-1.5
1982	LA-N	129	461	71	131	23	7	7	50	39	54	.284	.345	.410	.755	117	6	9	95	95	68	.758	31	10	3	-4	*O	0.8
1983	LA-N	141	481	63	135	25	3	17	66	34	52	.281	.331	.451	.782	115	8	8	100	98	70	.773	30	11	2	-9	*O	0.0
1984	LA-N	134	438	39	110	11	5	11	47	29	35	.251	.299	.374	.674	85	-8	-10	104	93	47	.593	10	9	-2	-7	*O	-2.5
1985	LA-N	147	482	70	129	26	2	12	50	33	37	.268	.316	.405	.720	108	-1	3	93	86	61	.665	15	5	2	-16	*O	-1.5
1986	LA-N	103	283	34	74	13	2	4	29	22	39	.261	.317	.364	.681	93	-5	-3	94	101	32	.621	10	5	0	-1	O	-0.5
1987	LA-N	115	182	17	37	4	0	6	23	16	28	.203	.271	.324	.596	62	-12	-10	92	119	16	.533	5	3	-0	-5	O	-1.7
Total	11	1264	4101	522	1099	180	45	91	479	299	421	.268	.321	.400	.721	98	-16	-18	100	100	524	.687	145	60	8	-73	*O/D	-10.9
■ HOBIE LANDRITH — Landrith, Hobert Neal b: 3/16/30, Decatur, Ill. BL/TR, 5'10", 170 lbs. Deb: 7/30/50																												
1950	Cin-N	4	14	1	3	0	0	0	1	2	1	.214	.313	.214	.527	40	-1	-1	105	131	1	.455	0			-0	/C	0.0
1951	Cin-N	4	13	3	5	1	0	0	0	1	1	.385	.429	.462	.890	139	1	1	101	0	3	.875	0	0	0	-0	/C	0.0
1952	Cin-N	15	50	1	13	4	0	0	4	0	4	.260	.260	.340	.600	65	-2	-2	100	92	4	.436	0	1	-1	0	C	-0.2
1953	Cin-N	52	154	15	37	3	1	3	16	12	8	.240	.299	.331	.631	65	-8	-8	99	104	16	.555	2	0	1	3	C	-0.1
1954	Cin-N	48	81	12	16	0	0	5	14	18	9	.198	.343	.383	.726	86	-1	-2	104	120	12	.758	1	0	0	0	C	0.0
1955	Cin-N	43	87	9	22	3	0	4	7	10	14	.253	.330	.425	.755	93	-0	-1	106	58	12	.691	0	1	-1	0	C	0.0
1956	Chi-N	111	312	22	69	10	3	4	32	39	38	.221	.310	.311	.621	69	-14	-13	99	124	32	.555	0	2	-1	4	C	-0.7
1957	StL-N	75	214	18	52	6	0	3	26	25	27	.243	.322	.313	.635	71	-8	-8	101	142	22	.554	1	2	-1	3	C	-0.1
1958	StL-N	70	144	9	31	4	0	3	13	26	21	.215	.335	.306	.641	67	-5	-7	106	101	16	.603	0	1	-1	0	C	-0.4
1959	SF-N	109	283	30	71	14	0	3	29	43	23	.251	.350	.332	.682	87	-6	-4	95	114	34	.617	0	4	-2	-11	*C	-1.0
1960	SF-N	71	190	18	46	10	0	1	20	23	11	.242	.324	.311	.634	83	-6	-4	90	131	20	.553	1	1	-0	-2	C	-0.1
1961	SF-N	43	71	11	17	4	0	2	10	12	7	.239	.349	.380	.730	95	-0	-0	98	122	9	.684	0	0	0	0	C	0.2
1962	NY-N	23	45	6	13	3	0	1	7	8	3	.289	.396	.422	.818	115	2	1	104	125	8	.844	0	0	0	-1	C	0.1
	Bal-A	60	167	18	37	4	1	4	17	19	9	.222	.305	.329	.634	75	-7	-6	95	101	17	.560	0	0	0	-4	C	-0.5
1963	Bal-A	2	1	0	0	0	0	0	0	0	0	.000	.000	.000	.000	-99	-0	-0	94	0	0	.000	0	0	0	0	/C	0.0
	Was-A	42	103	6	18	3	0	1	7	15	12	.175	.280	.233	.513	47	-7	-7	98	108	7	.443	0	0	0	-1	C	-0.7
	Yr	44	104	6	18	3	0	1	7	15	12	.173	.277	.231	.508	45	-7	-7	97	103	7	.438	0	0	0	-1		-0.7
Total	14	772	1929	179	450	69	5	34	203	253	188	.233	.323	.327	.650	76	-64	-60	98	114	213	.597	5	12		-7	C	-3.5
■ DON LANDRUM — Landrum, Donald Leroy b: 2/16/36, Santa Rosa, Cal. BL/TR, 6', 180 lbs. Deb: 9/28/57																												
1957	Phi-N	2	7	1	1	1	0	0	0	2	1	.143	.333	.286	.619	70	-0	-0	98	0	1	.667	0	0	0	1	/O	0.1
1960	StL-N	13	49	7	12	0	1	2	3	4	6	.245	.315	.408	.723	89	-0	-1	108	50	7	.757	3	0	1	2	O	0.2
1961	StL-N	28	66	5	11	2	0	1	3	5	14	.167	.225	.242	.468	21	-7	-8	113	64	4	.400	1	0	0	1	O/2	-0.8
1962	StL-N	32	35	11	11	0	0	0	3	4	2	.314	.385	.314	.699	83	-0	-1	109	107	5	.680	2	0	1	-6	O	-0.7
	Chi-N	83	238	29	67	5	2	1	15	30	31	.282	.369	.332	.701	85	-2	-4	106	72	33	.691	9	2	2	3	O	-0.1
	Yr	115	273	40	78	5	2	1	18	34	33	.286	.371	.330	.701	84	-2	-5	107	83	38	.693	11	2	2	-3		-0.8
1963	Chi-N	84	227	27	55	4	1	1	10	13	42	.242	.295	.282	.577	64	-9	-11	105	63	19	.489	6	3	0	-1	O	-1.5
1964	Chi-N	11	11	2	0	0	0	0	0	1	2	.000	.083	.000	.083	-70	-3	-3	105	0	0	.083	0	0	0	1	/O	-0.1
1965	Chi-N	131	425	60	96	20	4	6	34	36	84	.226	.301	.334	.636	77	-12	-13	102	88	45	.596	14	8	-1	-7	*O	-2.4
1966	SF-N	72	102	9	19	4	0	1	7	9	18	.186	.259	.255	.514	45	-8	-7	97	101	7	.430	1	1	-0	-6	O	-1.5
Total	8	456	1160	151	272	36	8	12	75	104	200	.234	.308	.310	.618	70	-41	-47	104	77	121	.574	36	14	2	-11	O/2	-6.8
■ JESSE LANDRUM — Landrum, Jesse Glenn b: 7/31/12, Crockett, Tex. d: 6/27/80, Beaumont, Tex. BR/TR, 5'11.5", 175 lbs. Deb: 4/26/38																												
1938	Chi-A	4	6	0	0	0	0	0	1	0	2	.000	.000	.000	.000	-99	-2	-2	98	0	0	.000	0	0	0	0	/2	-0.1
■ TITO LANDRUM — Landrum, Terry Lee b: 10/25/54, Joplin, Mo. BR/TR, 5'11", 175 lbs. Deb: 7/23/80																												
1980	StL-N	35	77	6	19	2	2	0	7	6	17	.247	.310	.325	.634	75	-2	-3	103	111	7	.556	3	2	-0	-4	O	-0.8
1981	StL-N	81	119	13	31	5	4	0	10	6	14	.261	.302	.370	.671	88	-2	-2	102	89	13	.598	4	2	0	-12	O	-1.7
1982	StL-N	79	72	12	20	3	0	2	14	8	18	.278	.358	.403	.761	109	1	1	103	157	11	.704	0	1	-1	-13	O	-1.3
1983	StL-N	6	5	0	1	0	1	0	0	1	2	.200	.333	.600	.933	157	0	0	98	0	1	1.250	1	0	0	-2	/O	-0.1
	Bal-A	26	42	8	13	2	0	1	4	1	11	.310	.326	.429	.754	105	0	0	100	74	5	.594	0	2	-1	-4	O	-0.5
1984	StL-N	105	173	21	47	9	1	3	26	10	27	.272	.311	.387	.699	97	-1	-1	99	134	18	.580	3	4	-2	-18	O	-2.5
1985	StL-N	85	161	21	45	8	2	4	21	19	30	.280	.356	.429	.784	124	4	5	96	103	24	.724	1	4	-2	-10	O	-0.9
1986	StL-N	96	205	24	43	7	1	2	17	20	41	.210	.283	.283	.566	55	-12	-13	103	106	17	.488	3	1	0	-2	O	-1.6
1987	StL-N	30	50	5	10	1	0	0	6	7	14	.200	.298	.220	.518	41	-4	-4	99	218	3	.452	1	1	-0	-0	O/1	-0.5
	LA-N	51	67	8	16	3	0	1	4	3	16	.239	.282	.328	.610	66	-4	-3	92	64	6	.519	1	1	-0	-5	O	-0.9
	Yr	81	117	13	26	4	0	1	10	10	30	.222	.289	.282	.571	55	-8	-7	94	123	10	.495	2	2	-1	-5		-1.4
1988	Bal-A	13	24	2	3	0	0	1	2	2	4	.125	.250	.208	.458	31	-2	-2	95	159	2	.429	0	0	0	-3	O/D	-0.4
Total	9	607	995	120	248	40	12	13	111	85	196	.249	.312	.353	.664	84	-22	-21	100	115	106	.599	17	18	-6	-74	O/D1	-11.2
■ CHAPPY LANE — Lane, George M. b: Pittsburgh, Pa. Deb: 5/16/1882																												
1882	Pit-a	57	214	26	38	8	2	3		5		.178	.196	.276	.472	59	-9	-8	97	0	12	.364				2	1O/C	-0.5
1884	Tol-a	57	215	26	49	9	5	1		2		.228	.242	.330	.572	84	-3	-4	104	0	18	.452				1	1/O3C	-0.4
Total	2	114	429	52	87	17	7	4		7		.203	.219	.303	.522	72	-12	-13	100	0	29	.406				3	/1OC3	-0.9
■ HUNTER LANE — Lane, James Hunter "Dodo" b: 7/20/1900, Pulaski, Tenn. BR/TR, 5'11", 165 lbs. Deb: 5/13/24																												
1924	Bos-N	7	15	0	1	0	0	0	0	1	1	.067	.125	.067	.192	-50	-3	-3	94	0	0	.143	0	0	0	-0	/32	-0.2
■ MARVIN LANE — Lane, Marvin b: 1/18/50, Sandersville, Ga. BR/TR, 5'11", 180 lbs. Deb: 9/04/71																												
1971	Det-A	8	14	0	2	0	0	0	1	1	3	.143	.200	.143	.343	-2	-2	-2	96	204	0	.250	0	0	0	-1	/O	-0.3
1972	Det-A	8	6	2	0	0	0	0	0	0	2	.000	.000	.000	.000	-88	-1	-2	113	0	0	.000	0	0	0	-1	/O	-0.2
1973	Det-A	6	8	2	2	0	0	1	2	2	2	.250	.400	.625	1.025	183	1	1	101	98	2	1.000	0	0	0	-0	/O	0.1
1974	Det-A	50	103	16	24	4	1	2	9	19	24	.233	.352	.350	.702	97	1	0	106	84	14	.704	2	0	1	-5	O/D	-0.4
1976	Det-A	18	48	3	9	1	0	0	5	6	11	.188	.278	.208	.486	42	-3	-3	104	192	3	.400	0	0	0	-2	O	-0.5
Total	5	90	179	23	37	5	1	3	17	28	42	.207	.314	.296	.610	74	-5	-6	104	119	19	.580	2	0	1	-8	/OD	-1.3

YEAR	TM/L	G	AB	R	H	2B	3B	HR	RBI	BB	SO	AVG	OBP	SLG	PRO	/A	BR	/A	PF	CHI	RC	TA	SB	CS	SBR	FR	POS	TPR
■ DICK LANE	Lane, Richard Harrison b: 6/28/27, Highland Park, Mich. BR/TR, 5'11", 178 lbs. Deb: 6/20/49																											
1949	Chi-A	12	42	4	5	0	0	0	4	5	3	.119	.213	.119	.332	-11	-7	-7	98	280	1	.256	0	1	-1	1	O	-0.5
■ DON LANG	Lang, Donald Charles b: 3/15/15, Selma, Cal. BR/TR, 6', 175 lbs. Deb: 7/04/38																											
1938	Cin-N	21	50	5	13	3	1	1	11	2	7	.260	.288	.420	.708	95	-1	-1	98	166	5	.575	0			0	3/2S	0.0
1948	StL-N	117	323	30	87	14	1	4	31	47	38	.269	.364	.356	.720	95	-1	-1	101	91	46	.690	2			-1	3/2	-0.2
Total	2	138	373	35	100	17	2	5	42	49	45	.268	.355	.365	.719	95	-1	-1	100	101	51	.681	2			-0	3/2S	-0.2
■ BILL LANGE	Lange, William Alexander "Little Eva" b: 6/6/1871, San Francisco, Cal d: 7/23/50, San Francisco, Cal. BR/TR, 6'1.5", 190 lbs. Deb: 4/27/1893																											
1893	Chi-N	117	469	92	132	8	7	8	88	52	20	.281	.358	.380	.738	95	-1	-4	104	126	83	.834	47			-5	2O/3SC	-0.8
1894	Chi-N	111	442	84	145	16	9	6	90	56	18	.328	.405	.446	.851	99	6	-1	108	122	109	1.074	65			9	*O/S3	0.0
1895	Chi-N	123	478	120	186	27	16	10	98	55	24	.389	.456	.575	1.032	162	48	45	103	95	160	1.373	67			9	*O	3.5
1896	Chi-N	122	469	114	153	21	16	4	92	65	24	.326	.414	.465	.879	123	24	17	108	111	128	1.177	84			8	*O/C	1.5
1897	Chi-N	118	479	119	163	24	14	5	83	48		.340	.406	.480	.886	136	25	25	100	88	126	1.127	**73**			1	*O	1.4
1898	Chi-N	113	442	79	141	16	10	6	69	36		.319	.377	.441	.818	133	20	18	103	104	84	.857	22			8	*O/1	1.8
1899	Chi-N	107	416	81	135	21	7	1	58	38		.325	.382	.416	.798	126	13	15	96	97	84	.900	41			16	O1	2.2
Total	7	811	3195	689	1055	133	79	40	578	350	86	.330	.401	.459	.859	125	136	117	103	106	773	1.047	399			46	O/21S3C	9.6
■ SAM LANGFORD	Langford, Elton J. b: 5/21/1900, Briggs, Tex. BL/TR, 6', 180 lbs. Deb: 4/13/26																											
1926	Bos-A	1	1	1	0	0	0	0	0	0	0	.000	.000	.000	.000	-99	-0	-0	101	0	0	.000	0	0	0	0	H	0.0
1927	Cle-A	20	67	10	18	5	0	1	7	5	7	.269	.347	.388	.735	93	-1	-1	97	82	9	.694	0	0	0	-1	O	-0.2
1928	Cle-A	110	427	50	118	17	8	4	50	21	35	.276	.312	.382	.694	77	-13	-16	106	104	49	.597	3	6	-3	1	*O	-2.2
Total	3	131	495	61	136	22	8	5	57	26	42	.275	.316	.382	.698	79	-14	-17	104	100	58	.608	3	6	-3	-1	O	-2.4
■ BOB LANGSFORD	Langsford, Robert William (born Robert Hugo Lankswert) b: 8/5/1865, Louisville, Ky. d: 1/10/07, Louisville, Ky. BR/TR, Deb: 6/18/1899																											
1899	Lou-N	1	4	0	0	0	0	0	0	0		.000	.000	.000	.000	-97	-1	-1	103	0	0	.000	0			0	/S	0.0
■ HAL LANIER	Lanier, Harold Clifton b: 7/4/42, Denton, N.C. BR/TR, 6'2", 180 lbs. Deb: 6/18/64 MC																											
1964	SF-N	98	383	40	105	16	3	2	28	5	44	.274	.284	.347	.631	76	-12	-12	100	84	34	.481	2	1	0	9	2/S	0.5
1965	SF-N	159	522	41	118	15	9	0	39	21	67	.226	.256	.289	.545	48	-33	-39	111	107	34	.408	2	1	0	-3	*2/S	-3.4
1966	SF-N	149	459	37	106	14	2	3	37	16	49	.231	.257	.290	.547	53	-30	-28	97	110	30	.402	1	0	0	9	*2S	-0.8
1967	SF-N	151	525	37	112	16	3	0	42	16	61	.213	.239	.255	.495	41	-40	-40	101	130	29	.356	2	2	-1	16	*S2	-0.6
1968	SF-N	151	486	37	100	14	1	0	27	12	57	.206	.225	.239	.464	40	-36	-35	98	98	23	.321	2	2	-1	7	*S	-1.1
1969	SF-N	150	495	37	113	9	1	0	35	25	68	.228	.265	.251	.516	45	-36	-37	101	113	31	.373	0	1	-1	20	*S	0.0
1970	SF-N	134	438	33	101	13	1	2	41	21	41	.231	.266	.279	.544	48	-34	-31	96	124	28	.401	1	2	-1	8	*S/21	-0.7
1971	SF-N	109	206	21	48	8	0	1	13	15	26	.233	.285	.286	.571	62	-10	-10	100	85	16	.451	0	0	0	-5	32/S1	-1.3
1972	NY-A	60	103	5	22	3	0	0	6	2	13	.214	.236	.243	.479	46	-7	-7	92	100	5	.337	1	2	-1	2	3/S2	-0.2
1973	NY-A	35	86	9	18	3	0	0	5	3	10	.209	.244	.244	.489	38	-7	-7	101	94	5	.352	0	0	0	1	S/23	-0.1
Total	10	1196	3703	297	843	111	20	8	273	136	436	.228	.256	.275	.531	50	-245	-246	100	108	236	.407	11	11	-3	64	S23/1	-7.7
■ RIMP LANIER	Lanier, Lorenzo b: 10/19/48, Tuskegee, Ala. BL/TR, 5'8", 150 lbs. Deb: 9/11/71																											
1971	Pit-N	6	4	0	0	0	0	0	0	0	1	.000	.200	.000	.200	-39	-1	-1	99	0	0	.250	0	0	0	0	H	0.0
■ RED LANNING	Lanning, Lester Alfred b: 5/13/1895, Harvard, Ill. d: 6/13/62, Bristol, Conn. BL/TL, 5'9", 165 lbs. Deb: 6/20/16																											
1916	Phi-A	19	33	5	6	2	0	0	1	10	9	.182	.372	.242	.615	87	0	0	98	45	3	.667	0			-2	/OP	-0.1
■ CARNEY LANSFORD	Lansford, Carney Ray b: 2/7/57, San Jose, Cal. BR/TR, 6'2", 195 lbs. Deb: 4/08/78																											
1978	Cal-A	121	453	63	133	23	2	8	52	31	67	.294	.344	.406	.750	109	6	5	102	101	65	.718	20	9	1	-25	*3/SD	-2.0
1979	Cal-A	157	654	114	188	30	5	19	79	39	115	.287	.330	.436	.766	113	3	10	93	85	91	.708	20	8	1	-24	*3	-1.0
1980	Cal-A	151	602	87	157	27	3	15	80	50	93	.261	.317	.390	.708	97	-7	-3	96	107	75	.647	14	5	1	-25	*3	-2.7
1981	Bos-A	102	399	61	134	23	3	4	52	34	28	**.336**	.391	.439	.829	131	20	17	106	115	68	.804	15	10	-2	1	3D	1.7
1982	Bos-A	128	482	65	145	28	4	11	63	46	48	.301	.364	.444	.808	109	14	7	110	108	76	.761	9	4	0	-0	*3D	0.5
1983	Oak-A	80	299	43	92	16	2	10	45	22	33	.308	.361	.475	.836	134	11	13	96	104	47	.762	3	8	-4	-6	3/S	0.2
1984	Oak-A	151	597	70	179	31	5	14	74	40	62	.300	.347	.439	.786	127	12	18	92	103	90	.725	9	3	1	-3	*3	1.8
1985	Oak-A	98	401	51	111	18	2	13	46	18	27	.277	.314	.429	.743	109	-0	3	93	83	53	.656	2	3	-1	-14	3	-1.4
1986	Oak-A	151	591	80	168	16	4	19	72	39	51	.284	.334	.421	.755	112	4	9	94	99	80	.693	16	7	1	-15	*31/2D	-1.2
1987	Oak-A	151	554	89	160	27	4	19	76	60	44	.289	.368	.455	.822	129	15	22	91	104	96	.847	27	8	3	0	*31/D	2.0
1988	Oak-A	150	556	80	155	20	2	7	57	35	35	.279	.329	.360	.689	98	-5	-2	95	105	65	.636	29	8	4	-12	*3/12D	-0.9
Total	11	1440	5588	803	1622	259	36	139	696	414	603	.290	.344	.424	.768	114	73	100	96	101	804	.737	164	73	5	-125	*3/1DS2	-3.0
■ JODY LANSFORD	Lansford, Joseph Dale b: 1/15/61, San Jose, Cal. BR/TR, 6'5", 225 lbs. Deb: 7/31/82																											
1982	SD-N	13	22	6	4	0	0	0	3	6	4	.182	.357	.182	.539	60	-1	-1	92	294	2	.526	0	1	-1	-0	/1	-0.1
1983	SD-N	12	8	1	2	0	0	1	2	0	3	.250	.250	.625	.875	136	0	0	99	99	1	.833	0	0	0	0	/1	0.0
Total	2	25	30	7	6	0	0	1	5	6	7	.200	.333	.300	.633	83	-1	-0	93	251	3	.600	0	1	-1	-0	/1	-0.1
■ PETE LAPAN	Lapan, Peter Nelson b: 6/25/1891, Easthampton, Mass d: 1/5/53, Norwalk, Cal. BR/TR, 5'7", 165 lbs. Deb: 9/16/22																											
1922	Was-A	11	34	7	11	1	0	1	6	3	4	.324	.378	.441	.820	123	1	1	92	119	6	.826	1	0	0	1	C	0.2
1923	Was-A	2	2	0	0	0	0	0	0	0	0	.000	.000	.000	.000	-99	-1	-1	95	0	0	.000	0	0	0	0	H	0.0
Total	2	13	36	7	11	1	0	1	6	3	4	.306	.359	.417	.776	111	0	0	92	113	6	.760	1	0	0	1	/C	0.2
■ RALPH LaPOINTE	LaPointe, Ralph Robert b: 1/8/22, Winooski, Vt. d: 9/13/67, Burlington, Vt. BR/TR, 5'11", 185 lbs. Deb: 4/15/47																											
1947	Phi-N	56	211	33	65	7	0	1	15	17	15	.308	.362	.355	.718	91	-2	-2	100	75	29	.692	8			-1	S	0.1
1948	StL-N	87	222	27	50	3	0	0	15	18	19	.225	.283	.239	.522	42	-17	-18	101	106	16	.416	1			3	2S/3	-0.7
Total	2	143	433	60	115	10	0	1	30	35	34	.266	.322	.296	.618	66	-20	-20	100	91	45	.542	9			2	/S23	-0.6
■ FRANK LaPORTE	LaPorte, Frank Breyfogle "Pot" b: 2/6/1880, Uhrichsville, Ohio d: 9/25/39, Newcomerstown, O. BR/TR, 5'8", 175 lbs. Deb: 9/29/05																											
1905	NY-A	11	40	4	16	1	0	1	12	1		.400	.415	.500	.915	189	4	4	102	190	9	.917	1			0	2	0.4
1906	NY-A	123	454	60	120	23	9	2	54	22		.264	.298	.368	.666	92	4	-6	120	120	54	.596	10			-6	*3/2O	-0.3
1907	NY-A	130	470	56	127	20	11	0	48	27		.270	.310	.360	.669	106	7	3	109	108	57	.601	10			3	3O/1	0.6
1908	Bos-A	62	156	14	37	1	3	0	15	12		.237	.292	.282	.574	90	-2	-1	98	128	13	.496	3			-3	23/O	-0.4
	NY-A	39	145	7	38	3	5	0	15	8		.262	.301	.352	.652	120	2	3	95	117	16	.579	3			-3	2O	0.0
	Yr	101	301	21	75	4	8	0	30	20		.249	.296	.316	.612	104	0	1	97	125	29	.535	6			-6		-0.4
1909	NY-A	89	309	35	92	19	3	0	21	18		.298	.340	.379	.719	128	9	9	99	71	40	.654	5			-21	2	-1.5
1910	NY-A	124	432	43	114	14	6	2	67	33		.264	.321	.338	.658	99	3	-1	107	166	52	.623	16			-2	2O3	-0.8
1911	StL-A	136	507	71	159	37	12	2	82	34		.314	.361	.446	.807	131	15	18	95	127	83	.770	4			-7	*2/3	1.0
1912	StL-A	80	266	32	83	11	4	1	38	20		.312	.367	.395	.762	119	6	6	99	120	40	.738	7			-1	2O	0.3
	Was-A	39	136	13	42	9	1	0	17	12		.309	.365	.390	.755	117	3	3	99	109	20	.723	3			-4	2	0.0
	Yr	119	402	45	125	20	5	1	55	32		.311	.366	.393	.759	118	9	9	99	117	60	.733	10			-5		0.3
1913	Was-A	79	242	25	61	5	4	0	18	17	16	.252	.309	.306	.615	76	-6	-8	106	86	24	.575	10			2	32O	-0.5
1914	Ind-F	133	505	86	157	27	12	4	**107**	36	36	.311	.357	.436	.792	114	16	9	111	**176**	88	.779	15			13	*2	2.4
1915	New-F	148	550	55	139	28	10	2	56	48	33	.253	.313	.351	.664	102	-3	1	94	107	68	.620	14			2	*2	0.4
Total	11	1193	4212	501	1185	198	80	14	550	288	85	.281	.330	.376	.706	108	56	39	104	124	565	.657	101			-26	23O/1	1.6
■ JACK LAPP	Lapp, John Walker b: 9/10/1884, Frazer, Pa. d: 2/6/20, Philadelphia, Pa. BL/TR, 5'8", Deb: 9/11/08																											
1908	Phi-A	13	35	4	5	0	1	0	1	5		.143	.250	.200	.450	45	-2	-2	108	54	2	.400	0			1	C	0.0
1909	Phi-A	21	56	8	19	3	1	0	10	3		.339	.373	.429	.801	150	3	3	102	161	9	.757	1			1	C	0.6
1910	Phi-A	71	192	18	45	4	3	0	17	20		.234	.310	.286	.596	85	-3	-3	102	114	17	.517	0			3	C	0.7
1911	Phi-A	68	167	35	59	10	3	1	26	24		.353	.435	.467	.902	163	12	14	93	108	36	.981	4			-5	C/1	1.6
1912	Phi-A	90	281	26	82	15	6	1	35	19		.292	.337	.399	.735	111	3	3	99	102	38	.673	3			-3	C	0.9
1913	Phi-A	82	238	23	54	4	4	1	20	37	26	.227	.336	.290	.626	86	-4	-3	97	99	23	.592	1			-3	C/1	0.0
1914	Phi-A	69	199	22	46	7	2	0	19	31	14	.231	.338	.286	.624	90	-2	-1	97	125	20	.573	1	4	-2	1	C	0.2

YEAR	TM/L	G	AB	R	H	2B	3B	HR	RBI	BB	SO	AVG	OBP	SLG	PRO	/A	BR	/A	PF	CHI	RC	TA	SB	CS	SBR	FR	POS	TPR
1915	Phi-A	112	312	26	85	16	5	2	31	30	29	.272	.340	.375	.715	119	5	6	96	86	43	.672	5	2	0	8	C1	2.2
1916	Chi-A	40	101	6	21	0	1	0	7	8	10	.208	.266	.228	.494	45	-6	-7	108	109	7	.400	1			3	C	-0.2
Total	9	566	1581	168	416	59	26	5	166	177	79	.263	.340	.343	.682	104	6	10	98	105	194	.633	16	6		8	C/1	6.0
■ NORM LARKER	Larker, Norman Howard John b: 12/27/30, Beaver Meadows, Pa. BL/TL, 6', 185 lbs. Deb: 4/15/58																											
1958	LA-N	99	253	32	70	16	5	4	29	29	21	.277	.358	.427	.785	102	3	1	105	100	38	.734	1	1	-0	-3	O1	-0.5
1959	LA-N	108	311	37	90	14	1	8	49	26	25	.289	.348	.418	.766	101	1	1	102	129	43	.675	0	1	-1	1	1O	-0.3
1960	LA-N	133	440	56	142	26	3	5	78	36	24	.323	.375	.430	.805	104	12	4	115	**155**	71	.739	1	0	0	4	*1/O	0.2
1961	LA-N	97	282	29	76	16	1	5	38	24	22	.270	.329	.387	.716	87	-4	-5	102	124	34	.618	0	0	0	0	1/O	-1.0
1962	Hou-N	147	506	58	133	19	5	9	63	70	47	.263	.360	.374	.734	105	0	5	93	117	71	.695	1	1	-0	2	*1/O	0.2
1963	Mil-N	64	147	15	26	6	0	1	14	24	24	.177	.301	.238	.539	57	-7	-8	101	155	12	.488	0	2	-1	-0	1	-1.0
	SF-N	19	14	0	1	0	0	0	0	2	2	.071	.188	.071	.259	-23	-2	-2	96	0	0	.214	0	0	0	0	1	-0.2
	Yr	83	161	15	27	6	0	1	14	26	26	.168	.291	.224	.515	51	-10	-9	100	121	12	.467	0	2	-1	-0		-1.2
Total	6	667	1953	227	538	97	15	32	271	211	165	.275	.351	.390	.741	97	3	-4	103	128	269	.697	3	5	-2	3	1/O	-2.6
■ BARRY LARKIN	Larkin, Barry Louis b: 4/28/64, Cincinnati, Ohio BR/TR, 6', 180 lbs. Deb: 8/13/86																											
1986	Cin-N	41	159	27	45	4	3	3	19	9	21	.283	.321	.403	.724	94	-1	-1	104	106	22	.698	8	0	2	-1	S/2	0.3
1987	Cin-N	125	439	64	107	16	2	12	43	36	52	.244	.308	.371	.680	76	-14	-16	104	88	52	.650	21	6	3	-12	*S	-1.0
1988	Cin-N	151	588	91	174	32	5	12	56	41	24	.296	.350	.429	.779	116	16	13	105	75	94	.797	40	7	8	14	*S	4.8
Total	3	317	1186	182	326	52	10	27	118	86	97	.275	.331	.404	.735	98	2	-4	105	84	167	.735	69	13	13	1	S/2	4.1
■ ED LARKIN	Larkin, Edward Francis b: 7/1/1885, Wyalusing, Pa. d: 3/28/34, Wyalusing, Pa. BR/TR, 5'8", Deb: 10/02/09																											
1909	Phi-A	2	6	0	1	0	0	0	1	1		.167	.286	.167	.452	43	-0	-0	102	393	0	.400	0			0	/C	0.0
■ GENE LARKIN	Larkin, Eugene Thomas b: 10/24/62, Flushing, N.Y. BB/TR, 6'3", 195 lbs. Deb: 5/21/87																											
1987	Min-A	85	233	23	62	11	2	4	28	25	31	.266	.342	.382	.724	97	-2	-1	96	111	30	.654	1	4	-2	-1	D1	-0.6
1988	Min-A	149	505	56	135	30	2	8	70	68	55	.267	.371	.382	.753	105	10	6	106	131	75	.727	3	2	-0	-3	D1	0.0
Total	2	234	738	79	197	41	4	12	98	93	86	.267	.362	.382	.744	102	8	6	103	125	105	.708	4	6	-2	-5	D/1	-0.6
■ HENRY LARKIN	Larkin, Henry E. "Ted" b: 1/12/1860, Reading, Pa. d: 1/31/42, Reading, Pa. BR/TR, 5'10", 175 lbs. Deb: 5/01/1884 M																											
1884	Phi-a	85	326	59	90	21	9	3		15		.276	.324	.423	.747	127	16	9	114	0	46	.682				-9	*O/2	0.0
1885	Phi-a	108	453	114	149	**37**	14	8		26		.329	.372	.525	.897	178	42	39	103	0	91	.885				9	*O	3.7
1886	Phi-a	139	565	133	180	**36**	16	2		59		.319	**.390**	.450	.839	165	43	43	100	0	114	.914	32			3	*O	3.5
1887	Phi-a	126	497	105	154	22	12	3		48		.310	.380	.421	.800	126	18	18	99	0	96	.880	37			-0	O12	1.2
1888	Phi-a	135	546	92	147	28	12	7	101	33		.269	.326	.403	.729	135	21	21	101	121	80	.717	20			-6	*12	0.6
1889	Phi-a	133	516	105	164	23	12	3	74	83	41	.318	.428	.426	.854	150	36	38	98	82	101	.938	11			-3	*1/32	2.0
1890	Cle-P	125	506	93	168	32	15	5	112	65	18	.332	.420	.484	.904	156	33	41	92	113	108	.967	5			-8	*1/OM	1.6
1891	Phi-a	133	526	94	147	27	14	10	93	66	56	.279	.376	.441	.817	133	25	22	103	91	90	.831	2			-5	*1O	1.0
1892	Was-N	119	464	76	130	13	7	8	96	39	21	.280	.346	.390	.736	119	13	10	105	152	72	.746	21			0	*1/O	0.1
1893	Was-N	81	319	54	101	20	3	4	73	50	5	.317	.422	.436	.857	145	16	22	90	140	61	.908	1			-8	1	1.1
Total	10	1184	4718	925	1430	259	114	53	549	484	141	.303	.380	.440	.820	143	262	264	100	70	858	.848	129			-27	1O/23	14.8
■ BOB LARMORE	Larmore, Robert Mc Kahan "Red" b: 12/6/1896, Anderson, Ind. d: 1/15/64, St.Louis, Mo. BR/TR, 5'10.5", 185 lbs. Deb: 5/14/18																											
1918	StL-N	4	7	0	2	0	0	0	1	0	2	.286	.286	.286	.571	80	-0	-0	93	189	1	.400	0			0	/S	0.0
■ SAM LaROQUE	LaRoque, Samuel H. J. b: 2/26/1864, St.Mathias, Que., Canada 5'11", 190 lbs. Deb: 1888																											
1888	Det-N	2	9	1	4	0	0	0	2	1	1	.444	.500	.444	.944	210	1	1	98	155	2	1.000	0			0	/2	0.1
1890	Pit-N	111	434	59	105	20	4	1	40	35	29	.242	.316	.313	.629	98	-7	1	88	84	53	.638	27			7	2S/1O	1.0
1891	Pit-N	1	4	0	0	0	0	0	0	0	1	.000	.000	.000	.000	-99	-1	-1	101	0	0	.000	0			0	/3	0.0
	Lou-a	10	35	6	11	2	1	1	8	5	8	.314	.429	.514	.943	192	3	4	90	117	8	1.083	1			0	2/1	0.3
Total	3	124	482	66	120	22	5	2	50	41	39	.249	.326	.328	.654	105	-4	5	88	87	63	.666	28			7	/2S130	1.4
■ VIC LaROSE	LaRose, Victor Raymond b: 12/23/44, Los Angeles, Cal. BR/TR, 5'11", 180 lbs. Deb: 9/13/68																											
1968	Chi-N	4	2	0	0	0	0	0	0	0	1	.000	.333	.000	.333	6	-0	-0	112	0	0	.500	0	0	0	0	/2S	0.0
■ HARRY LaROSS	LaRoss, Harry Raymond "Spike" b: 1/2/1888, Easton, Pa. d: 3/22/54, Chicago, Ill. 5'11.5", 170 lbs. Deb: 6/24/14																											
1914	Cin-N	22	48	7	11	1	0	0	5	2	10	.229	.260	.250	.510	50	-3	-3	105	151	4	.486	4			-6	O	-1.0
■ SWEDE LARSEN	Larsen, Erling Adeli b: 11/15/13, Jersey City, N.J. BR/TR, 5'11", 170 lbs. Deb: 6/17/36																											
1936	Bos-N	3	1	0	0	0	0	0	0	0	0	.000	.000	.000	.000	-99	-0	-0	95	0	0	.000	0			0	/2	0.0
■ TONY LaRUSSA	LaRussa, Anthony b: 10/4/44, Tampa, Fla. BR/TR, 6', 175 lbs. Deb: 5/10/63 MC																											
1963	KC-A	34	44	4	11	1	1	0	1	7	12	.250	.353	.318	.671	83	-0	-1	108	30	6	.636	0	0	0	0	S/2	0.0
1968	Oak-A	5	3	0	1	0	0	0	0	0	0	.333	.333	.333	.667	104	-0	0	98	0	0	.500	0	0	0	0	H	0.0
1969	Oak-A	8	8	0	0	0	0	0	0	0	1	.000	.000	.000	.000	-99	-2	-2	92	0	0	.000	0	0	0	0	H	-0.1
1970	Oak-A	52	106	6	21	4	1	0	6	15	19	.198	.303	.255	.558	57	-6	-6	97	90	9	.506	0	0	0	-1	2	-0.1
1971	Oak-A	23	8	3	0	0	0	0	0	0	4	.000	.000	.000	.000	-99	-2	-2	101	0	0	.000	0	0	0	0	/2S3	0.0
	Atl-N	9	7	1	2	0	0	0	0	1	1	.286	.375	.286	.661	81	-0	-0	110	0	0	.429	0	0	0	0	/2	0.1
1973	Chi-N	1	0	1	0	0	0	0	0	0	0	—	—	—	—	—	0	0	108	—	—	—	0	0	0	0	R	0.0
Total	6	132	176	15	35	5	2	0	7	23	37	.199	.295	.250	.545	53	-11	-11	100	62	16	.482	0	0	0	-0	/2S3	-0.1
■ LYN LARY	Lary, Lynford Hobart "Broadway" b: 1/28/06, Armona, Cal. d: 1/9/73, Downey, Cal. BR/TR, 6', 165 lbs. Deb: 5/11/29																											
1929	NY-A	80	236	48	73	9	2	5	26	24	15	.309	.380	.428	.808	109	3	4	99	77	40	.805	4	1	1	-2	3S/2	0.6
1930	NY-A	117	464	93	134	20	8	3	52	45	40	.289	.357	.386	.743	98	-7	0	90	97	68	.729	14	2	**3**	1	*S	1.4
1931	NY-A	155	610	100	171	35	9	10	107	88	54	.280	.376	.416	.793	110	9	11	98	132	99	.804	13	10	-2	9	*S	3.0
1932	NY-A	91	280	56	65	14	4	3	39	52	28	.232	.358	.343	.701	86	-6	-4	95	124	39	.734	9	3	1	-1	S/1230	0.1
1933	NY-A	52	127	25	28	3	3	0	13	28	17	.220	.361	.291	.653	82	-4	-2	91	117	16	.670	2	1	0	0	3S/1O	0.1
1934	NY-A	1	0	0	0	0	0	0	0	1	0	—	1.000	—	1.291	258	0	0	96	0	0	—	0	0	0	0	/1	0.0
	Bos-A	129	419	58	101	20	4	2	54	66	51	.241	.344	.322	.667	69	-16	-20	106	128	52	.659	12	5	1	-8	*S	-1.6
	Yr	130	419	58	101	20	4	2	54	67	51	.241	.346	.322	.668	69	-15	-19	106	127	52	.663	12	5	1	-8		-1.6
1935	Was-A	39	103	8	20	4	0	0	7	12	10	.194	.278	.233	.511	37	-10	-9	92	99	8	.470	3	0	1	2	S	-0.3
	StL-A	93	371	78	107	25	7	2	35	64	43	.288	.396	.410	.806	102	7	3	107	65	68	.907	25	4	5	8	S	1.9
	Yr	132	474	86	127	29	7	2	42	76	53	.268	.371	.371	.743	91	-3	-5	102	76	74	.803	28	4	**6**	10		1.6
1936	StL-A	155	619	112	179	30	6	2	52	117	54	.289	.404	.367	.771	89	-3	-6	103	62	105	.853	**37**	9	**6**	-4	*S	0.5
1937	Cle-A	156	644	110	187	46	7	8	77	88	64	.290	.378	.421	.799	104	2	5	98	77	107	.817	18	8	1	6	*S	1.8
1938	Cle-A	141	568	94	152	36	4	3	51	88	65	.268	.366	.361	.727	84	-13	-12	99	71	82	.749	23	6	3	-1	*S	0.0
1939	Cle-A	3	2	0	0	0	0	0	0	0	1	.000	.000	.000	.000	-99	-1	-1	98	0	0	.000	0	0	0	0	/S	0.0
	Bro-N	29	31	7	5	1	1	0	1	12	6	.161	.409	.258	.667	77	0	-0	107	46	5	.846	1			-1	S/3	0.0
	StL-N	34	75	11	14	3	0	0	9	16	15	.187	.330	.227	.556	49	-4	-5	105	194	6	.515	1			-1	S/3	-0.3
	Yr	63	106	18	19	4	1	0	10	28	21	.179	.356	.236	.591	58	-4	-5	106	126	11	.609	2			-2		-0.3
1940	StL-A	27	54	5	3	1	1	0	3	4	7	.056	.136	.111	.247	-33	-11	-11	106	181	1	.212	0	0	0	1	S/2	-0.8
Total	12	1302	4603	805	1239	247	56	38	526	705	470	.269	.369	.372	.741	90	-53	-46	99	95	696	.763	162	49		8	*S/3120	6.4
■ DON LASSETTER	Lassetter, Donald O'Neal b: 3/27/33, Newnan, Ga. BR/TR, 6'3", 200 lbs. Deb: 9/21/57																											
1957	StL-N	4	13	2	2	0	1	0	0	1	3	.154	.214	.308	.522	38	-1	-1	101	0	0	.385	0	0	0	0	/O	0.0
■ JUMBO LATHAM	Latham, George Warren b: 9/6/1852, Utica, N.Y. d: 5/26/14, Utica, N.Y. BR/TR, 240 lbs. Deb: 4/19/1875 M																											
1875	Bos-n	16	78	23	25							.321															1	
	NH-n	20	82	5	15							.183															1/S3M	
	Yr	36	160	28	40							.250																
1877	Lou-N	59	278	42	81	10	6	0	22	5	6	.291	.304	.371	.674	84	3	-10	132	63	32	.548				1	*1	-0.9

YEAR	TM/L	G	AB	R	H	2B	3B	HR	RBI	BB	SO	AVG	OBP	SLG	PRO	/A	BR	/A	PF	CHI	RC	TA	SB	CS	SBR	FR	POS	TPR
1882	Phi-a	74	323	47	92	10	2	0		10		.285	.306	.328	.634	102	4	-1	112	0	33	.502				0	*1M	-0.1
1883	Lou-a	88	368	60	92	7	6	0		12		.250	.274	.302	.575	90	-6	-3	94	0	31	.446				2	*12/S	-0.5
1884	Lou-a	77	308	31	52	3	3	0		8		.169	.197	.198	.396	35	-22	-17	89	0	12	.281				3	*1/3	-1.6
Total	4	298	1277	180	317	30	17	0	22	35	6	.248	.270	.298	.568	81	-20	-30	105	13	109	.436				6	1/2S3	-3.1
■ ARLIE LATHAM	Latham, Walter Arlington "The Freshest Man On Earth" b: 3/15/1860, W.Lebanon, N.H. d: 11/29/52, Garden City, N.Y. BR/TR, 5'8", 150 lbs. Deb: 7/05/1880 MC																											
1880	Buf-N	22	79	9	10	3	1	0	3	1	8	.127	.138	.190	.327	11	-7	-6	91	74	2	.232				0	SO/C	-0.5
1883	StL-a	98	406	86	96	12	7	0		18		.236	.269	.300	.569	77	-7	-12	108	0	34	.452				21	*3/C	0.8
1884	StL-a	110	474	115	130	17	12	1		19		.274	.311	.367	.678	112	12	5	110	0	55	.578				**37**	*3/C	3.8
1885	StL-a	110	485	84	100	15	3	1		18		.206	.242	.256	.498	64	-21	-16	93	0	31	.382				1	*3/C	-0.7
1886	StL-a	134	578	**152**	174	23	8	1		55		.301	.368	.374	.741	121	24	13	111	0	104	.834	60			-1	*3/2	1.6
1887	StL-a	136	627	163	198	35	10	2		45		.316	.366	.413	.779	109	16	5	110	0	146	1.021	129			2	*3/2C	0.2
1888	StL-a	133	570	119	151	19	5	2	31	43		.265	.325	.326	.652	101	9	-1	111	42	98	.826	**109**			2	*3/S	0.2
1889	StL-a	118	512	110	126	13	3	4	49	42	30	.246	.317	.307	.623	71	-13	-23	112	72	73	.723	69			11	*3/2	-0.9
1890	Chi-P	52	214	47	49	7	2	1	20	22	22	.229	.310	.294	.604	61	-11	-12	104	80	30	.727	32			3	3	-0.4
	Cin-N	41	164	35	41	6	2	0	15	23	18	.250	.346	.311	.657	87	-0	-3	108	78	25	.772	20			5	3	0.3
1891	Cin-N	135	533	119	145	20	10	7	53	74	35	.272	.372	.386	.759	135	18	26	91	59	112	.974	87			18	*3/C	**4.2**
1892	Cin-N	152	622	111	148	20	4	0	44	60	54	.238	.310	.283	.593	79	-13	-16	103	68	77	.648	66			-6	*3/2O	-1.1
1893	Cin-N	127	531	101	150	18	6	2	49	62	20	.282	.368	.350	.718	92	-3	-4	101	60	92	.827	57			-11	*3	-1.1
1894	Cin-N	129	524	129	164	23	6	4	60	60	24	.313	.393	.403	.796	94	-3	-3	100	71	109	.942	59			-12	*3/2	-1.2
1895	Cin-N	112	460	93	143	14	6	2	69	42	25	.311	.375	.380	.755	90	-1	-7	108	102	86	.852	48			-20	*3/12	-2.0
1896	StL-N	8	35	3	7	0	0	0	5	4	3	.200	.282	.200	.482	31	-3	-3	95	178	3	.464	2			0	/3M	-0.2
1899	Was-N	6	6	1	1	0	0	0	0	1		.167	.286	.167	.452	29	-1	-1	96	0	0	.400	0			0	/O2	0.0
1909	NY-N	4	2	1	0	0	0	0	0	0		.000	.000	.000	.000	-95	-0	-0	105	0	-0	.500	1			0	/2	0.0
Total	17	1627	6822	1478	1833	245	85	27	398	589	239	.269	.334	.341	.676	94	-5	-59	105	44	1076	.750	739			48	*3/2SOC1	3.0
■ CHICK LATHERS	Lathers, Charles Ten Eyck b: 10/22/1888, Detroit, Mich. d: 7/26/71, Petoskey, Mich. BL/TR, 6', 180 lbs. Deb: 5/01/10																											
1910	Det-A	41	82	4	19	2	0	0	3	8		.232	.300	.256	.556	73	-2	-2	102	53	6	.460	0			-1	3/2S	-0.2
1911	Det-A	29	45	5	10	1	0	0	4	5		.222	.314	.244	.558	52	-2	-3	108	123	4	.486	0			0	/23S1	-0.1
Total	2	70	127	9	29	3	0	0	7	13		.228	.305	.252	.557	65	-5	-5	104	78	10	.469	0			-0	/32S1	-0.3
■ TACKS LATIMER	Latimer, Clifford Wesley b: 11/30/1877, Loveland, Ohio d: 4/24/36, Loveland, Ohio TR, 6', 160 lbs. Deb: 10/01/1898																											
1898	NY-N	5	17	1	5	1	0	0	1	0		.294	.294	.353	.647	92	-0	-0	95	50	2	.500	0			0	/CO	0.0
1899	Lou-N	9	29	3	8	1	0	0	4	2		.276	.323	.310	.633	74	-1	-1	103	136	3	.571	1			0	/C1	0.0
1900	Pit-N	4	12	1	4	1	0	0	2	0		.333	.333	.417	.750	106	0	0	103	125	2	.625	0			0	/C	0.0
1901	Bal-A	1	4	0	1	0	0	0	0	0		.250	.250	.250	.500	38	-0	-0	107	0	0	.333	0			-0	/C	0.0
1902	Bro-N	8	24	0	1	0	0	0	0	0		.042	.042	.042	.083	-78	-5	-5	95	0	0	.043	0			-0	/C	-0.3
Total	5	27	86	5	19	3	0	0	7	2		.221	.239	.256	.494	43	-6	-6	99	75	7	.373	1			-0	/CO1	-0.3
■ CHARLIE LAU	Lau, Charles Richard b: 4/12/33, Romulus, Mich. d: 3/18/84, Key Colony Beach, Fla. BL/TR, 6', 190 lbs. Deb: 9/12/56 C																											
1956	Det-A	3	9	1	2	0	0	0	0	0	1	.222	.222	.222	.444	18	-1	-1	97	0	0	.286	0	0	0	0	/C	0.0
1958	Det-A	30	68	8	10	1	2	0	6	12	15	.147	.293	.221	.513	42	-5	-5	104	160	5	.483	0	0	0	-1	C	-0.5
1959	Det-A	2	6	0	1	0	0	0	0	0	2	.167	.167	.167	.333	-7	-1	-1	111	0	0	.200	0	0	0	0	/C	0.0
1960	Mil-N	21	53	4	10	2	0	0	2	6	10	.189	.271	.226	.498	42	-4	-4	91	68	4	.419	0	0	0	3	C	0.0
1961	Mil-N	28	82	3	17	5	0	0	5	14	11	.207	.330	.268	.598	66	-4	-3	92	92	8	.567	1	1	-0	4	C	0.2
	Bal-A	17	47	3	8	0	0	1	4	1	3	.170	.188	.234	.422	12	-6	-6	97	112	2	.300	0	0	0	-0	C	-0.6
1962	Bal-A	81	197	21	58	11	2	6	37	7	11	.294	.322	.462	.784	114	1	3	95	135	29	.704	0	0	0	-3	C	0.2
1963	Bal-A	29	48	4	9	2	0	0	6	1	5	.188	.204	.229	.433	23	-5	-5	94	228	2	.293	1	0	0	1	/C	-0.3
	KC-A	62	187	15	55	11	0	3	26	14	17	.294	.343	.401	.744	100	2	0	108	130	24	.647	1	0	0	3	C	0.4
	Yr	91	235	19	64	13	0	3	32	15	22	.272	.316	.366	.682	88	-3	-4	103	163	26	.573	1	0	0	4		0.1
1964	KC-A	43	118	11	32	7	1	2	9	10	18	.271	.328	.398	.726	97	0	-1	105	72	16	.655	0	0	0	-2	C	0.0
	Bal-A	62	158	16	41	15	1	1	14	17	27	.259	.335	.386	.721	95	0	-1	105	93	20	.648	0	0	0	-3	C	-0.1
	Yr	105	276	27	73	22	2	3	23	27	45	.264	.332	.391	.724	96	0	-1	105	85	36	.654	0	0	0	-4		-0.1
1965	Bal-A	68	132	15	39	5	2	2	18	17	18	.295	.376	.409	.785	123	4	4	100	124	20	.724	0	0	0	-0	C	0.7
1966	Bal-A	18	12	1	6	2	1	0	5	4	1	.500	.625	.833	1.458	312	4	4	101	210	7	2.333	0	0	0	0	H	0.4
1967	Bal-A	11	8	0	1	1	0	0	3	2	2	.125	.300	.250	.550	68	-0	-0	95	626	1	.571	0	0	0	0	H	0.0
	Atl-N	52	45	3	9	1	0	1	5	4	9	.200	.265	.289	.554	56	-2	-3	104	129	3	.459	0	0	0	0	H	-0.2
Total	11	527	1170	105	298	63	9	16	140	109	150	.255	.321	.365	.686	89	-17	-18	100	122	141	.622	3	1	0	1	C	0.2
■ BILLY LAUDER	Lauder, William b: 2/23/1874, New York, N.Y. d: 5/20/33, Norwalk, Conn. BR/TR, 5'10", 160 lbs. Deb: 6/25/1898 C																											
1898	Phi-N	97	361	42	95	14	7	2	67	19		.263	.300	.357	.657	96	-5	-3	95	153	42	.579	6			-19	3	-1.7
1899	Phi-N	151	583	74	156	17	6	3	90	34		.268	.310	.333	.643	81	-17	-15	97	139	66	.574	15			-16	*3	-2.8
1901	Phi-A	2	8	1	1	0	0	0	0	0		.125	.125	.125	.250	-30	-1	-1	100	0	0	.143	0			0	/3	0.0
1902	NY-N	125	482	41	114	20	1	1	44	10		.237	.252	.288	.540	68	-19	-19	100	114	41	.457	19			1	*3/O	-1.3
1903	NY-N	108	395	52	111	13	0	0	53	14		.281	.306	.314	.620	74	-11	-15	106	140	45	.553	19			-5	*3	-1.8
Total	5	483	1829	210	477	64	14	6	254	77		.261	.291	.321	.612	78	-54	-52	99	135	194	.536	59			-40	3/O	-7.6
■ TIM LAUDNER	Laudner, Timothy Jon b: 6/7/58, Mason City, Iowa BR/TR, 6'3", 212 lbs. Deb: 8/28/81																											
1981	Min-A	14	43	4	7	2	0	2	5	3	17	.163	.234	.349	.583	63	-2	-2	105	93	4	.528	0	0	0	1	C/D	0.0
1982	Min-A	93	306	37	78	19	1	7	33	34	74	.255	.329	.392	.722	97	-1	-1	100	94	39	.653	0	2	-1	3	C	0.5
1983	Min-A	62	168	20	31	9	0	6	18	15	49	.185	.251	.345	.597	59	-9	-10	105	93	15	.525	0	0	0	3	C/D	-0.4
1984	Min-A	87	262	31	54	16	1	10	35	18	78	.206	.260	.389	.649	73	-9	-11	106	106	26	.571	0	0	0	4	C/D	-0.2
1985	Min-A	72	164	16	39	5	0	7	19	12	45	.238	.294	.396	.690	84	-3	-4	103	88	19	.609	0	1	-1	-4	C/1	-0.4
1986	Min-A	76	193	21	47	10	0	10	29	24	56	.244	.336	.451	.787	104	4	1	108	99	30	.762	1	0	0	-4	C	0.2
1987	Min-A	113	288	30	55	7	1	16	43	23	80	.191	.253	.389	.642	71	-14	-13	96	107	29	.578	1	0	0	-9	*C/1D	-1.3
1988	Min-A	117	375	38	94	18	1	13	54	36	89	.251	.318	.408	.726	96	0	-3	106	112	46	.644	0	0	0	1	*C1/D	0.1
Total	8	634	1799	197	405	86	4	71	236	165	488	.225	.293	.396	.689	84	-35	-42	103	101	208	.629	2	3	-1	-6	C/1D	-1.5
■ CHUCK LAUER	Lauer, John Charles b: 1865, Pittsburgh, Pa. TR, Deb: 7/17/1884																											
1884	Pit-a	13	44	5	5	0	0	0		0		.114	.114	.114	.227	-25	-6	-5	97	0	1	.128				0	O/P1	-0.4
1889	Pit-N	4	16	2	3	0	0	0	1	0	5	.188	.188	.188	.375	6	-2	-2	89	101	1	.231	0			0	/CO	-0.1
1890	Chi-N	2	8	1	2	1	0	0	2	0	0	.250	.250	.375	.625	76	-0	-0	109	205	1	.500	0			0	/C	0.0
Total	3	19	68	8	10	1	0	0	3	0	5	.147	.147	.162	.309	-3	-8	-8	96	48	2	.190	0			0	/OCP1	-0.5
■ BEN LAUGHLIN	Laughlin, Benjamin Deb: 4/28/1873																											
1873	Res-n	12	54	3	12							.222															2/13	
■ BILL LAUTERBORN	Lauterborn, William Bernard b: 6/9/1879, Hornell, N.Y. d: 4/19/65, Andover, N.Y. BR/TR, 5'6", 140 lbs. Deb: 9/20/04																											
1904	Bos-N	20	69	7	19	2	0	0	2	1		.275	.286	.304	.590	87	-1	-1	97	36	6	.460	1			-0	2	0.0
1905	Bos-N	67	200	11	37	1	1	0	9	12		.185	.231	.200	.431	31	-17	-16	97	78	10	.325	1			-3	32/SO	-1.6
Total	2	87	269	18	56	3	1	0	11	13		.208	.245	.227	.471	45	-18	-17	97	68	16	.357	2			-3	/23SO	-1.6
■ COOKIE LAVAGETTO	Lavagetto, Harry Arthur b: 12/1/12, Oakland, Cal. BR/TR, 6', 170 lbs. Deb: 4/17/34 MC																											
1934	Pit-N	87	304	41	67	16	3	3	46	32	39	.220	.295	.322	.617	62	-15	-17	105	155	31	.567	6			-14	2	-2.1
1935	Pit-N	78	231	27	67	9	4	0	19	18	15	.290	.341	.364	.705	84	-3	-5	107	82	29	.609	1			-5	23	-0.5
1936	Pit-N	60	197	21	48	15	2	2	26	15	13	.244	.300	.371	.671	82	-6	-5	98	117	22	.582	0			-7	23/S	-0.7
1937	Bro-N	149	503	64	142	26	6	8	70	74	41	.282	.375	.406	.781	108	11	8	104	113	79	.772	13			-13	*23	0.1
1938	Bro-N	137	487	68	133	34	6	6	79	68	31	.273	.364	.405	.769	116	9	12	96	136	76	.770	15			-10	*3/2	-0.1
1939	Bro-N	153	587	93	176	28	5	10	87	78	30	.300	.387	.416	.802	108	15	10	107	112	95	.793	14			-5	*3	0.9

YEAR	TM/L	G	AB	R	H	2B	3B	HR	RBI	BB	SO	AVG	OBP	SLG	PRO	/A	BR	/A	PF	CHI	RC	TA	SB	CS	SBR	FR	POS	TPR
1940	Bro-N	118	448	56	115	21	3	4	43	70	32	.257	.361	.344	.705	88	-0	-5	108	102	59	.670	4			-9	*3	-1.4
1941	Bro-N	132	441	75	122	24	7	1	78	80	21	.277	.388	.370	.757	110	12	10	103	**173**	69	.769	7			-19	*3	-0.8
1946	Bro-N	88	242	36	57	9	1	3	27	38	17	.236	.339	.318	.657	85	-3	-4	103	117	28	.615	3			-1	3	-0.4
1947	Bro-N	41	69	6	18	1	0	3	11	12	5	.261	.370	.406	.776	101	1	0	105	110	11	.769	0			0	3/1	0.0
Total	10	1043	3509	487	945	183	37	40	486	485	244	.269	.360	.377	.737	98	20	2	104	124	500	.734	63			-82	32/1S	-5.0
■ **MIKE LaVALLIERE**	LaValliere, Michael Eugene b: 8/18/60, Charlotte, N.C. BL/TR, 5'10", 180 lbs. Deb: 9/09/84																											
1984	Phi-N	6	7	0	0	0	0	0	0	2	2	.000	.222	.000	.222	-32	-1	-1	102	0	0	.286	0	0	0	-0	/C	0.0
1985	StL-N	12	34	2	5	1	0	0	6	7	3	.147	.293	.176	.469	36	-3	-3	96	398	2	.419	0	0	0	-1	C	-0.3
1986	StL-N	110	303	18	71	10	2	3	30	36	37	.234	.318	.310	.628	72	-10	-11	103	116	31	.546	0	1	-1	-6	*C	-1.5
1987	Pit-N	121	340	33	102	19	0	1	36	43	32	.300	.380	.365	.745	95	1	-1	104	113	50	.694	0	0	0	-3	*C	0.5
1988	Pit-N	120	352	24	92	18	0	2	47	50	34	.261	.356	.330	.686	100	1	2	98	154	43	.633	3	2	-0	3	*C	1.1
Total	5	369	1036	77	270	48	2	6	119	138	108	.261	.350	.328	.678	87	-12	-14	101	137	126	.624	3	3	-1	-7	C	-0.2
■ **DOC LAVAN**	Lavan, John Leonard b: 10/28/1890, Grand Rapids, Mich d: 5/29/52, Detroit, Mich. BR/TR, 5'8.5", 151 lbs. Deb: 6/22/13																											
1913	StL-A	46	149	8	21	2	1	0	4	10	46	.141	.210	.168	.378	11	-17	-16	95	57	5	.320	3			-4	S	-1.7
	Phi-A	5	14	1	1	0	1	0	1	0	0	.071	.071	.214	.286	-18	-2	-2	97	118	0	.231	0			-0	/S	-0.1
	Yr	51	163	9	22	2	2	0	5	10	46	.135	.199	.172	.371	9	-19	-18	95	64	6	.312	3			-4		-1.8
1914	StL-A	74	239	21	63	7	4	1	21	17	39	.264	.318	.339	.657	100	-1	-1	98	96	24	.564	6	12	-5	-15	S	-1.5
1915	StL-A	157	514	44	112	17	7	1	48	42	83	.218	.281	.284	.565	72	-21	-18	96	112	42	.485	13	19	-8	4	*S	-0.7
1916	StL-A	110	343	32	81	13	1	0	19	32	38	.236	.305	.280	.585	80	-10	-8	95	71	32	.523	7			19	*S	2.1
1917	StL-A	118	355	19	85	8	5	0	30	19	34	.239	.284	.290	.574	79	-11	-9	95	105	30	.481	5			10	*S/2	0.6
1918	Was-A	117	464	44	129	17	2	0	45	14	21	.278	.302	.323	.625	85	-8	-10	104	116	47	.531	12			-8	*S/O	-1.1
1919	StL-N	100	356	25	86	12	2	1	25	11	30	.242	.264	.295	.559	72	-14	-12	94	92	28	.444	4			2	S	-0.7
1920	StL-N	142	516	52	149	21	10	1	63	19	38	.289	.318	.374	.692	100	-2	-1	98	127	58	.593	11	14	-5	11	*S	1.2
1921	StL-N	150	560	58	145	23	11	2	82	23	30	.259	.291	.350	.641	72	-26	-22	95	152	56	.540	7	7	-2	**18**	*S	0.8
1922	StL-N	89	264	24	60	8	1	0	27	13	10	.227	.271	.265	.537	38	-24	-24	101	135	20	.434	3	1	0	-5	S/3	-2.2
1923	StL-N	50	111	10	22	6	0	1	12	9	7	.198	.264	.279	.544	48	-9	-8	90	124	8	.446	0	3	-2	-2	S/312	-0.7
1924	StL-N	4	6	0	0	0	0	0	0	0	0	.000	.000	.000	.000	-98	-2	-2	103	0	0	.000	0	0	0	0	/2S	-0.1
Total	12	1162	3891	338	954	134	45	7	377	209	376	.245	.288	.308	.596	74	-147	-133	97	112	351	.502	71	56		31	*S/2310	-4.1
■ **ART LaVIGNE**	LaVigne, Arthur David b: 1/26/1885, Worcester, Mass. d: 7/18/50, Worcester, Mass. BR/TR, 5'10", 162 lbs. Deb: 4/24/14																											
1914	Buf-F	51	90	10	14	2	0	0	4	7	25	.156	.216	.178	.394	13	-10	-10	104	90	4	.303	0			0	C/1	-0.8
■ **JOHNNY LAVIN**	Lavin, John b: Bay City, Mich. 5'11", 175 lbs. Deb: 9/10/1884																											
1884	StL-a	16	52	9	11	2	0	0		3		.212	.268	.250	.518	66	-1	-2	110	0	4	.415				0	O	-0.1
■ **RUDY LAW**	Law, Rudy Karl b: 10/7/56, Waco, Tex. BL/TL, 6'1", 165 lbs. Deb: 9/12/78																											
1978	LA-N	11	12	2	3	0	0	0	1	1	2	.250	.308	.250	.558	58	-1	-1	99	132	1	.700	3	1	0	-2	/O	-0.2
1980	LA-N	128	388	55	101	5	4	1	23	23	27	.260	.307	.302	.608	73	-15	-14	97	76	39	.606	40	13	4	-7	*O	-2.1
1982	Chi-A	121	336	55	107	15	8	3	32	23	41	.318	.362	.438	.800	122	8	9	97	82	55	.844	36	10	5	-10	O/D	0.1
1983	Chi-A	141	501	95	142	20	7	3	34	42	36	.283	.341	.369	.711	93	-2	-4	103	70	74	.816	77	12	16	-9	*O/D	0.0
1984	Chi-A	136	487	68	122	14	7	6	37	39	42	.251	.310	.345	.655	73	-12	-19	111	81	50	.611	29	17	-2	-10	*O	-3.5
1985	Chi-A	125	390	62	101	21	6	4	36	27	40	.259	.312	.374	.686	87	-7	-7	100	90	49	.686	29	6	5	-1	*O/D	-0.3
1986	KC-A	87	307	42	80	26	5	1	36	29	22	.261	.328	.388	.716	95	-2	-2	100	120	40	.689	14	6	1	-5	O/D	-0.7
Total	7	749	2421	379	656	101	37	18	199	184	210	.271	.326	.366	.691	89	-31	-37	102	85	308	.714	228	65	29	-44	O/D	-6.7
■ **VANCE LAW**	Law, Vance Aaron b: 10/1/56, Boise, Idaho BR/TR, 6'2", 185 lbs. Deb: 6/01/80																											
1980	Pit-N	25	74	11	17	2	2	0	3	3	7	.230	.260	.311	.571	57	-4	-4	103	52	6	.475	2	0	1	1	2/S3	-0.1
1981	Pit-N	30	67	1	9	0	1	0	3	2	15	.134	.159	.164	.324	-8	-9	-9	96	107	1	.230	1	1	-0	-0	2/S3	-0.7
1982	Chi-A	114	359	40	101	20	1	5	54	26	46	.281	.332	.384	.716	99	-2	-1	97	141	45	.626	4	2	0	9	S32/O	1.5
1983	Chi-A	145	408	55	99	21	5	4	42	51	56	.243	.328	.348	.676	84	-7	-8	103	107	49	.621	3	1	0	10	*3/2SOD	0.2
1984	Chi-A	151	481	60	121	18	2	17	59	41	75	.252	.312	.403	.715	87	-3	-10	111	96	59	.642	4	1	1	-12	*32/OS	-1.7
1985	Mon-N	147	519	75	138	30	6	10	52	86	96	.266	.372	.405	.777	125	14	19	94	91	82	.766	6	5	-1	2	*213/O	2.1
1986	Mon-N	112	360	37	81	17	2	5	44	37	66	.225	.299	.325	.624	74	-14	-13	98	133	34	.539	3	5	-2	13	213/PO	0.0
1987	Mon-N	133	436	52	119	27	1	12	56	51	62	.273	.349	.422	.771	97	2	-1	106	102	65	.736	8	5	-1	-4	*231/P	-0.4
1988	Chi-N	151	556	73	163	29	2	11	78	55	79	.293	.360	.412	.772	116	16	13	104	121	80	.699	1	4	-2	-10	*3/O	0.1
Total	9	1008	3260	404	848	164	22	64	391	352	502	.260	.334	.383	.717	96	-7	-15	102	110	422	.670	32	24	-5	10	32S/1OPD	1.0
■ **GARLAND LAWING**	Lawing, Garland Frederick "Knobby" b: 8/29/19, Gastonia, N.C. BR/TR, 6'1", 180 lbs. Deb: 5/29/46																											
1946	Cin-N	2	3	0	0	0	0	0	0	0	2	.000	.000	.000	.000	-96	-1	-1	104	0	0	.000	0			-0	/O	0.0
	NY-N	8	12	2	2	0	0	0	0	0	3	.167	.167	.167	.333	-5	-2	-2	102	0	0	.200	0			-1	/O	-0.2
	Yr	10	15	2	2	0	0	0	0	0	5	.133	.133	.133	.267	-24	-2	-2	102	0	0	.154	0			-1		-0.2
Total	1	10	15	2	2	0	0	0	0	0	5	.133	.133	.133	.267	-24	-2	-2	102	0	0	.154	0			-1	/O	-0.2
■ **TOM LAWLESS**	Lawless, Thomas James b: 12/19/56, Erie, Pa. BR/TR, 5'11", 170 lbs. Deb: 7/15/82																											
1982	Cin-N	49	165	19	35	6	0	0	4	9	30	.212	.253	.248	.501	40	-13	-13	102	38	10	.471	16	5	2	3	2	-0.6
1984	Cin-N	43	80	10	20	2	0	1	2	8	12	.250	.318	.313	.631	74	-2	-3	106	28	8	.609	6	3	0	-2	2/3	-0.3
	Mon-N	11	17	1	3	1	0	0	0	0	4	.176	.176	.235	.412	16	-2	-2	91	0	0	.294	1	0	0	-1	/2	-0.1
	Yr	54	97	11	23	3	0	1	2	8	16	.237	.295	.299	.594	66	-4	-4	103	23	8	.550	7	3	0	-2		-0.4
1985	StL-N	47	58	8	12	3	1	0	8	5	4	.207	.270	.293	.563	60	-3	-3	96	187	5	.511	2	1	0	1	32	-0.1
1986	StL-N	46	39	5	11	1	0	0	3	2	8	.282	.317	.308	.625	71	-1	-2	103	100	5	.759	8	1	2	1	3/2O	0.1
1987	StL-N	19	25	5	2	1	0	0	0	3	5	.080	.179	.120	.299	-19	-4	-4	99	0	1	.333	2	0	1	-1	/23O	-0.3
1988	StL-N	54	65	9	10	2	1	1	3	7	9	.154	.236	.262	.498	41	-5	-5	104	60	5	.536	6	0	2	0	3/O21	-0.2
Total	6	269	449	57	93	16	2	2	20	34	72	.207	.263	.265	.528	47	-31	-32	102	61	34	.529	41	10	6	2	2/3O1	-1.5
■ **MIKE LAWLOR**	Lawlor, Michael H. b: 3/11/1854, Troy, N.Y. d: 8/3/18, Troy, N.Y. TR , Deb: 5/27/1880																											
1880	Tro-N	4	9	1	1	0	0	0	0	1	1	.111	.200	.111	.311	8	-1	-1	110	0	0	.250				0	/C	0.0
1884	Was-U	2	7	0	0	0	0	0		0		.000	.000	.000	.000	-99	-1	-1	97	0	0	.000	0			0	/C	0.0
Total	2	6	16	1	1	0	0	0	0	1	1	.063	.118	.063	.180	-36	-2	-2	105	0	0	.133	0			0	/C	0.0
■ **JIM LAWRENCE**	Lawrence, James Ross b: 2/12/39, Hamilton, Ont., Can. BL/TR, 6'1", 185 lbs. Deb: 5/30/63																											
1963	Cle-A	2	0	0	0	0	0	0	0	0	0	—	—	—	—	—	0	0	97	—	—	—	0	0	0	0	/C	0.0
■ **BILL LAWRENCE**	Lawrence, William Henry b: 3/11/06, San Mateo, Cal. BR/TR, 6'4", 194 lbs. Deb: 4/13/32																											
1932	Det-A	25	46	10	10	1	0	0	3	5	5	.217	.294	.239	.533	39	-4	-4	102	91	3	.421	0	2	-1	3	O	-0.2
■ **OTIS LAWRY**	Lawry, Otis Carroll "Rabbit" b: 11/1/1893, Fairfield, Me. d: 10/23/65, China, Maine BL/TR, 5'8", 133 lbs. Deb: 6/28/16																											
1916	Phi-A	41	123	10	25	0	0	0	4	9	21	.203	.263	.203	.466	41	-9	-8	98	57	8	.398	4			-0	2/O	-0.9
1917	Phi-A	30	55	7	9	1	0	0	1	2	9	.164	.193	.182	.375	15	-6	-5	94	36	2	.283	1			0	2/O	-0.4
Total	2	71	178	17	34	1	0	0	5	11	30	.191	.242	.197	.439	34	-14	-14	97	51	10	.361	5			-0	/2O	-1.3
■ **GENE LAYDEN**	Layden, Eugene Francis b: 3/14/1894, Pittsburgh, Pa. d: 12/12/84, Pittsburgh, Pa. BL/TL, 5'10", 160 lbs. Deb: 7/29/15																											
1915	NY-A	3	7	2	2	0	0	0	0	0	1	.286	.286	.286	.571	72	-0	-0	98	0	0	.333	0	1	-1	-0	/O	-0.1
■ **PETE LAYDON**	Laydon, Peter John b: 12/30/19, Dallas, Tex. d: 7/18/82, Edna, Tex. BR/TR, 5'11", 185 lbs. Deb: 4/28/48																											
1948	StL-A	41	104	11	26	2	1	0	4	6	10	.250	.297	.288	.586	53	-7	-7	106	45	9	.500	4	2	0	1	O	-0.7
■ **HERMAN LAYNE**	Layne, Herman b: 2/13/01, New Haven, W.Va. d: 8/27/73, Gallipolis, Ohio BR/TR, 5'11", 165 lbs. Deb: 4/16/27																											
1927	Pit-N	11	6	3	0	0	0	0	0	1	0	.000	.143	.000	.143	-58	-1	-1	102	0	0	.167	0			-1	/O	-0.2

YEAR	TM/L	G	AB	R	H	2B	3B	HR	RBI	BB	SO	AVG	OBP	SLG	PRO	/A	BR	/A	PF	CHI	RC	TA	SB	CS	SBR	FR	POS	TPR
■ **HILLIS LAYNE** Layne, Ivoria Hillis "Tony" b: 2/23/18, Whitwell, Tenn. BL/TR, 6', 170 lbs. Deb: 9/16/41																												
1941	Was-A	13	50	8	14	2	0	0	6	4	5	.280	.333	.320	.653	75	-2	-2	98	135	5	.538	1	1	-0	-1	3	-0.1
1944	Was-A	33	87	6	17	2	0	0	8	6	10	.195	.263	.218	.482	43	-7	-6	90	152	6	.403	2	0	1	0	3/2	-0.4
1945	Was-A	61	147	23	44	5	4	1	14	10	7	.299	.352	.408	.760	129	3	5	93	80	20	.649	0	1	-1	-1	3	0.4
Total	3	107	284	37	75	9	4	1	28	20	22	.264	.321	.335	.656	93	-5	-3	93	112	30	.560	3	2	-0	-2	/32	-0.1
■ **LES LAYTON** Layton, Lester Lee b: 11/18/21, Nardin, Okla. BR/TR, 6', 165 lbs. Deb: 4/24/48																												
1948	NY-N	63	91	14	21	4	4	2	12	6	21	.231	.286	.429	.714	91	-2	-2	100	100	11	.653	1			-2	O	-0.4
■ **JOHNNY LAZOR** Lazor, John Paul b: 9/9/12, Taylor, Wash. BL/TR, 5'9.5", 180 lbs. Deb: 4/22/43																												
1943	Bos-A	83	208	21	47	10	2	0	13	21	25	.226	.297	.293	.590	70	-7	-8	104	78	18	.512	5	6	-2	-2	O	-1.4
1944	Bos-A	16	24	0	2	1	0	0	0	1	0	.083	.120	.125	.245	-31	-4	-4	98	0	0	.182	0	0	0	0	/OC	-0.3
1945	Bos-A	101	335	35	104	19	2	5	45	18	17	.310	.346	.424	.769	130	8	10	95	104	50	.688	3	2	-0	-9	O	-0.2
1946	Bos-A	23	29	1	4	0	0	1	4	2	11	.138	.194	.241	.435	18	-3	-4	114	152	1	.333	0	0	0	-2	/O	-0.6
Total	4	223	596	57	157	30	4	6	62	42	53	.263	.312	.357	.669	95	-6	-6	99	93	70	.586	8	8	-2	-13	O/C	-2.5
■ **TONY LAZZERI** Lazzeri, Anthony Michael "Poosh 'Em Up Tony" b: 12/6/03, San Francisco, Cal. d: 8/6/48, San Francisco, Cal. BR/TR, 5'11.5", 170 lbs. Deb: 4/13/26 C																												
1926	NY-A	155	589	79	162	28	14	18	114	54	96	.275	.338	.462	.800	108	3	4	99	126	93	.793	16	7	1	-17	*2/S3	-0.5
1927	NY-A	153	570	92	176	29	8	18	102	69	82	.309	.383	.482	.866	124	19	19	100	105	104	.929	22	0	7	8	*2S/3	3.3
1928	NY-A	116	404	62	134	30	11	10	82	43	50	.332	.397	.535	.932	155	24	29	92	117	87	1.000	15	5	2	-1	*2	3.4
1929	NY-A	147	545	101	193	37	11	18	106	68	45	.354	.429	.561	.991	155	44	45	99	107	130	1.069	9	10	-3	-3	*2	3.9
1930	NY-A	143	571	109	173	34	15	9	121	60	62	.303	.372	.462	.835	123	9	19	90	**146**	100	.823	4	4	-1	-6	23/S1O	1.3
1931	NY-A	135	484	67	129	27	7	8	83	79	80	.267	.371	.401	.771	105	4	5	98	128	76	.802	18	9	0	2	23	1.3
1932	NY-A	142	510	79	153	28	16	15	113	82	64	.300	.399	.506	.905	139	26	30	95	127	104	.959	11	11	-3	1	*2/3	3.1
1933	NY-A	139	523	94	154	22	12	18	104	73	62	.294	.383	.486	.869	142	22	29	91	119	100	.915	15	7	0	-15	*2	1.1
1934	NY-A	123	438	59	117	24	6	14	67	71	64	.267	.369	.445	.815	114	6	9	96	96	77	.860	11	1	3	-15	23	0.0
1935	NY-A	130	477	72	130	18	6	13	83	63	75	.273	.361	.417	.778	108	1	6	93	121	75	.784	11	5	0	-27	*2/S	-1.4
1936	NY-A	150	537	82	154	29	6	14	109	97	65	.287	.397	.441	.838	113	8	13	95	129	100	.884	8	5	-1	-32	*2/S	-0.8
1937	NY-A	126	446	56	109	21	3	14	70	71	76	.244	.348	.399	.747	86	-8	-10	102	111	67	.757	7	1	2	-10	*2	-0.5
1938	Chi-N	54	120	21	32	5	0	5	23	22	30	.267	.380	.433	.814	117	4	4	105	124	20	.796	0			-0	S/32O	0.5
1939	Bro-N	14	39	6	11	2	0	3	6	10	7	.282	.451	.564	1.015	160	5	4	107	71	11	1.207	1			-1	2/3	0.3
	NY-N	13	44	7	13	0	0	1	8	7	6	.295	.392	.364	.756	105	1	1	99	157	6	.697	0			-1	3	0.0
	Yr	27	83	13	24	2	0	4	14	17	13	.289	.422	.458	.879	132	5	5	103	115	17	.951	1			-2		0.3
Total	14	1740	6297	986	1840	334	115	178	1191	869	864	.292	.380	.467	.846	122	166	205	96	120	1152	.879	148	65		-116	*23/S01	15.0
■ **FREDDY LEACH** Leach, Frederick b: 11/23/1897, Springfield, Mo. d: 12/10/81, Hagerman, Idaho BL/TR, 5'11", 183 lbs. Deb: 5/24/23																												
1923	Phi-N	52	104	5	27	4	0	1	16	3	14	.260	.280	.327	.607	53	-6	-8	114	152	9	.481	1	2	-1	-6	O	-1.5
1924	Phi-N	8	28	6	13	2	1	2	7	2	1	.464	.500	.821	1.321	231	6	5	108	90	11	1.667	0	0	0	-1	/O	0.4
1925	Phi-N	65	292	47	91	15	4	5	28	5	21	.312	.323	.442	.765	81	-4	-10	116	61	40	.665	1	2	-1	-4	O	-1.5
1926	Phi-N	129	492	73	162	29	7	11	71	16	33	.329	.352	.484	.835	119	13	11	103	93	79	.791	6			2	*O	0.9
1927	Phi-N	140	536	69	164	30	4	12	83	21	32	.306	.342	.444	.786	113	5	8	96	108	78	.723	2			11	*O	1.2
1928	Phi-N	145	588	83	179	36	11	13	96	30	30	.304	.342	.469	.812	106	6	3	104	115	91	.768	4			13	*O1	0.8
1929	NY-N	113	411	74	119	22	6	8	47	17	14	.290	.324	.431	.755	86	-11	-11	100	80	55	.712	10			-20	O	-3.5
1930	NY-N	126	544	90	178	19	13	13	71	22	25	.327	.361	.482	.843	104	0	2	98	78	91	.803	3			-7	*O	-1.1
1931	NY-N	129	515	75	159	30	5	6	61	29	9	.309	.348	.421	.769	110	4	6	97	98	76	.708	4			-9	*O	-0.8
1932	Bos-N	84	223	21	55	9	2	1	29	18	10	.247	.306	.318	.624	73	-10	-8	93	146	23	.542	1			-1	O	-1.1
Total	10	991	3733	543	1147	196	53	72	509	163	189	.307	.341	.446	.787	102	4	-1	101	98	553	.729	32	4		-21	O/1	-6.2
■ **RICK LEACH** Leach, Richard Max b: 5/4/57, Ann Arbor, Mich. BL/TL, 6'1", 180 lbs. Deb: 4/30/81																												
1981	Det-A	54	83	9	16	3	1	1	11	16	15	.193	.323	.289	.612	74	-2	-2	105	159	7	.548	0	1	-1	-4	1O/D	-0.8
1982	Det-A	82	218	23	52	7	2	3	12	21	29	.239	.305	.330	.636	74	-7	-8	100	59	24	.577	4	0	1	-1	1O/D	-0.9
1983	Det-A	99	242	22	60	17	0	3	26	19	21	.248	.305	.355	.661	85	-6	-5	96	107	25	.568	2	2	-1	2	1O/D	-0.6
1984	Tor-A	65	88	11	23	6	2	0	7	8	14	.261	.323	.375	.698	91	-1	-1	102	85	10	.603	0	0	0	-5	O1/PD	-0.7
1985	Tor-A	16	35	2	7	0	1	0	1	3	9	.200	.263	.257	.520	43	-3	-3	101	44	3	.429	0	0	0	-0	1/O	-0.3
1986	Tor-A	110	246	35	76	14	1	5	39	13	24	.309	.344	.435	.779	106	4	2	105	127	35	.682	0	0	0	-8	DO/1	-0.7
1987	Tor-A	98	195	26	55	13	1	3	25	25	25	.282	.372	.405	.777	106	3	3	101	113	30	.743	0	1	-1	-7	OD/1	-0.6
1988	Tor-A	87	199	21	55	13	1	0	23	18	27	.276	.336	.352	.688	93	-2	-1	100	131	22	.575	0	1	-1	-6	OD/1	-0.9
Total	8	611	1306	149	344	73	9	15	144	123	164	.263	.329	.368	.696	90	-14	-16	101	108	157	.629	6	5	-1	-31	1OD/P	-5.5
■ **TOMMY LEACH** Leach, Thomas William b: 11/4/1877, French Creek, N.Y. d: 9/29/69, Haines City, Fla. BR/TR, 5'6.5", 150 lbs. Deb: 9/28/1898																												
1898	Lou-N	3	10	0	1	0	0	0	0	0		.100	.100	.100	.200	-43	-2	-2	96	0	0	.111	0			0	/32	-0.1
1899	Lou-N	106	406	75	117	10	6	5	57	37		.288	.349	.379	.728	99	1	-1	103	110	62	.730	19			10	3S/2	0.9
1900	Pit-N	51	160	20	34	1	2	1	16	21		.213	.304	.262	.566	57	-8	-9	103	111	16	.563	8			0	3/S2O	-0.7
1901	Pit-N	98	374	64	114	12	13	2	44	20		.305	.340	.422	.763	122	10	9	101	92	61	.746	16			11	3/S	2.5
1902	Pit-N	135	514	97	143	14	**22**	**6**	85	45		.278	.336	.426	.762	130	21	17	105	132	84	.779	25			13	*3	3.8
1903	Pit-N	127	507	97	151	16	17	7	87	40		.298	.349	.438	.787	120	15	12	105	122	87	.798	22			7	*3	1.8
1904	Pit-N	146	579	92	149	15	12	2	56	45		.257	.311	.335	.646	102	1	1	99	91	69	.609	23			**32**	*3	4.1
1905	Pit-N	131	499	71	128	10	14	2	53	37		.257	.308	.345	.653	93	-3	-5	104	110	60	.609	17			9	O3/2S	0.3
1906	Pit-N	133	476	66	136	10	7	1	39	33		.286	.332	.342	.674	108	6	4	104	91	63	.638	21			-6	3O/S	-0.4
1907	Pit-N	149	547	102	166	19	12	4	43	40		.303	.351	.404	.755	132	23	20	105	74	95	.798	43			-10	*O3/S2	0.7
1908	Pit-N	152	583	93	151	24	16	5	41	54		.259	.322	.381	.703	133	16	20	95	59	77	.694	24			-6	*3/O	1.9
1909	Pit-N	151	587	**126**	153	29	8	6	43	66		.261	.337	.368	.705	115	14	10	105	59	80	.717	27			-12	*O3	-0.6
1910	Pit-N	135	529	83	143	24	5	4	52	38	62	.270	.319	.357	.677	87	-4	-11	112	87	66	.635	18			3	*O/S2	-1.2
1911	Pit-N	108	386	60	92	12	6	3	43	46	50	.238	.323	.324	.646	80	-10	-10	101	115	46	.653	19			10	OS/3	-0.1
1912	Pit-N	28	97	24	29	4	2	0	19	12	9	.299	.376	.381	.758	109	1	1	99	176	16	.809	6			5	O	0.5
	Chi-N	82	265	50	64	10	3	2	32	55	20	.242	.378	.325	.702	90	0	-1	104	119	38	.786	14			4	O/3	0.0
	Yr	110	362	74	93	14	5	2	51	67	29	.257	.377	.340	.717	95	1	-0	102	135	54	.792	20			9		0.5
1913	Chi-N	131	456	**99**	131	23	10	6	32	77	44	.287	.391	.421	.812	134	21	22	99	59	80	.895	21			-2	*O/3	1.8
1914	Chi-N	153	577	80	152	24	9	7	46	79	50	.263	.353	.373	.726	118	13	14	98	62	80	.732	16			1	*O3	1.2
1915	Cin-N	107	335	42	75	7	5	0	17	56	38	.224	.338	.275	.613	84	-3	-4	103	72	34	.620	20	14	-2	3	O	-0.6
1918	Pit-N	30	72	14	14	2	3	0	5	19	5	.194	.363	.306	.668	98	1	1	106	86	9	.741	2			-2	O/S	-0.1
Total	19	2156	7959	1355	2143	266	172	63	810	820	278	.269	.338	.370	.708	109	116	90	103	90	1120	.709	361	14		70	*O3/S2	15.7
■ **DAN LEAHY** Leahy, Daniel C. b: 8/8/1870, Knoxville, Tenn. d: 12/30/03, Knoxville, Tenn. Deb: 9/02/1896																												
1896	Phi-N	2	6	0	2	1	0	0	1	1	2	.333	.429	.500	.929	144	0	0	102	96	1	1.000	0			0	/S	0.0
■ **TOM LEAHY** Leahy, Thomas Joseph b: 6/2/1869, New Haven, Conn. d: 6/11/51, New Haven, Conn. TR , 168 lbs. Deb: 5/18/1897																												
1897	Pit-N	24	92	10	24	3	3	0	12	7		.261	.327	.359	.685	84	-2	-2	98	113	12	.662	3			0	O/C3	-0.1
	Was-N	19	52	12	20	2	1	0	7	9		.385	.529	.462	.991	164	7	6	101	85	16	1.438	6			0	O/32C	0.5
	Yr	43	144	22	44	5	4	0	19	16		.306	.408	.396	.804	116	4	4	100	103	28	.910	9			0		0.4
1898	Was-N	15	55	10	10	2	0	0	5	8		.182	.297	.218	.515	49	-3	-3	102	121	5	.600	6			0	3/2	-0.2
1901	Mil-A	33	99	18	24	6	2	0	10	11		.242	.318	.343	.662	90	-2	-1	95	93	12	.640	3			1	C/O2	0.2
	Phi-A	5	15	1	5	1	0	0	1	1		.333	.375	.400	.775	117	0	0	100	53	2	.700	0			0	/OCS	0.1
	Yr	38	114	19	29	7	2	0	11	12		.254	.325	.351	.676	93	-1	-1	96	90	14	.647	3			2		0.3
1905	StL-N	35	97	3	22	1	1	0	7	8		.227	.286	.299	.585	83	-3	-2	91	84	8	.493	0			-1	C	0.0
Total	4	131	410	54	105	15	9	0	42	44		.256	.343	.337	.679	94	-3	-1	97	96	57	.689	18			1	/CO32S	0.5
■ **FRED LEAR** Lear, Frederick Francis "King" b: 4/7/1894, New York, N.Y. d: 10/13/55, E.Orange, N.J. BR/TR, 6'0.5", 180 lbs. Deb: 6/07/15																												
1915	Phi-A	2	2	0	0	0	0	0	0	0	2	.000	.000	.000	.000	-99	-0	-0	96	0	0	.000	0			0	/3	0.0

YEAR	TM/L	G	AB	R	H	2B	3B	HR	RBI	BB	SO	AVG	OBP	SLG	PRO	/A	BR	/A	PF	CHI	RC	TA	SB	CS	SBR	FR	POS	TPR
1918	Chi-N	2	1	0	0	0	0	0	0	1	0	.000	.500	.000	.500	56	0	0	102	0	0	1.000	0			0	H	0.0
1919	Chi-N	40	76	8	17	3	1	1	11	8	11	.224	.306	.329	.635	90	-1	-1	100	153	8	.610	2			-1	/12S	0.0
1920	NY-N	31	87	12	22	0	1	1	7	8	15	.253	.323	.310	.633	83	-2	-2	100	90	9	.537	0	2	-1	1	3/2	0.0
Total	4	75	166	20	39	3	2	2	18	17	28	.235	.314	.313	.627	84	-3	-3	100	117	17	.566	2	2		0	/321S	0.0
■ BILL LEARD	Leard, William Wallace "Wild Bill" b: 10/14/1885, Oneida, N.Y. d: 1/15/70, San Francisco, Cal TR, 5'10", 155 lbs. Deb: 7/21/17																											
1917	Bro-N	3	3	0	0	0	0	0	0	0	1	.000	.000	.000	.000	-97	-1	-1	104	0	0	.000	0			0	/2	0.0
■ JACK LEARY	Leary, John J. b: 1858, New Haven, Conn. TL, 5'11", 186 lbs. Deb: 8/21/1880																											
1880	Bos-N	1	3	1	0	0	0	0	0	1	0	.000	.250	.000	.250	-8	-0	-0	92	0	0	.333				0	/OP	0.0
1881	Det-N	3	11	2	3	1	1	0	4	1	1	.273	.333	.545	.879	161	1	1	106	236	2	.875				0	/OP	0.0
1882	Pit-a	60	257	32	75	7	3	2		5		.292	.305	.366	.671	129	6	7	97	0	29	.544				-14	30/P12	-0.6
	Bal-a	4	18	3	4	1	0	0		0		.222	.222	.278	.500	73	-1	-0	92	0	1	.357				-0	/PO	0.0
	Yr	64	275	35	79	8	3	2		5		.287	.300	.360	.660	126	6	7	97	0	30	.531				-14		-0.6
1883	Lou-a	40	165	16	31	1	3	3		2		.188	.198	.285	.482	57	-8	-7	94	0	10	.366				-2	S	-0.8
	Bal-a	3	11	1	2	0	2	0		0		.182	.182	.545	.727	117	0	0	107	0	1	.667				0	/2	0.0
	Yr	43	176	17	33	1	5	3		2		.188	.197	.301	.498	61	-8	-7	95	0	11	.385				-2		-0.8
1884	Alt-U	8	33	1	3	0	0	0		1		.091	.118	.091	.209	-28	-4	-4	101	0	0	.133	0			0	/OP3	-0.3
	CP-U	10	40	0	7	1	0	0		0		.175	.175	.200	.375	27	-3	-3	99	0	1	.242	0			0	/23OP	-0.2
	Yr	18	73	1	10	1	0	0		1		.137	.149	.151	.299	1	-7	-7	100	0	2	.190	0			0		-0.5
Total	5	129	538	56	125	11	9	5	4	10	1	.232	.246	.314	.560	87	-9	-7	97	5	45	.433	0			-15	/SO3P21	-1.9
■ JOHN LEARY	Leary, John Louis "Jack" b: 5/2/1891, Waltham, Mass. d: 8/18/61, Waltham, Mass. BR/TR, 5'11.5", 180 lbs. Deb: 4/14/14																											
1914	StL-A	144	533	35	141	28	7	0	45	10	71	.265	.282	.343	.625	90	-11	-10	98	94	49	.504	9	15	-6	-5	*1C	-2.1
1915	StL-A	75	227	19	55	10	0	0	15	5	36	.242	.268	.286	.554	69	-10	-9	96	78	17	.426	2	4	-2	1	1C	-1.2
Total	2	219	760	54	196	38	7	0	60	15	107	.258	.278	.326	.604	84	-21	-19	97	89	66	.480	11	19	-8	-4	1/C	-3.3
■ HAL LEATHERS	Leathers, Harold Langford "Chuck" b: 12/2/1898, Selma, Cal. d: 4/12/77, Modesto, Cal. BL/TR, 5'8", 152 lbs. Deb: 9/13/20																											
1920	Chi-N	9	23	3	7	1	0	1	1	1	1	.304	.333	.478	.812	133	1	1	99	28	4	.813	1	0	0	1	/S2	0.2
■ EMIL LEBER	Leber, Emil Bohmiel b: 5/15/1881, Cleveland, Ohio d: 11/6/24, Cleveland, Ohio TR, 5'11", 170 lbs. Deb: 9/02/05																											
1905	Cle-A	2	6	1	0	0	0	0	0	1		.000	.143	.000	.143	-53	-1	-1	100	0	0	.167	0			0	/3	0.0
■ BEVO LeBOURVEAU	LeBourveau, De Witt Wiley b: 8/24/1894, Dana, Cal. d: 12/9/47, Nevada City, Cal. BL/TR, 5'11", 175 lbs. Deb: 9/09/19																											
1919	Phi-N	17	63	4	17	0	0	0	0	10	8	.270	.370	.270	.640	91	0	-0	104	0	7	.630	2			3	O	0.2
1920	Phi-N	84	261	29	67	7	2	3	12	11	36	.257	.295	.333	.628	74	-7	-10	109	48	26	.550	9	6	-1	2	O	-1.3
1921	Phi-N	93	281	42	83	12	5	6	35	29	51	.295	.361	.438	.799	109	4	4	102	91	44	.768	4	5	-2	-10	O	-1.1
1922	Phi-N	74	167	24	45	8	3	2	20	24	29	.269	.368	.389	.757	84	-1	-4	113	98	24	.728	0	3	-2	-4	O	-1.0
1929	Phi-A	12	16	1	5	0	1	0	2	5	1	.313	.476	.438	.914	126	1	1	109	98	3	1.000	0	1	-1	0	/O	0.0
Total	5	280	788	100	217	27	11	11	69	79	125	.275	.345	.379	.725	91	-2	-9	107	72	104	.679	15	15		-10	O	-3.2
■ MIKE LEDWITH	Ledwith, Michael b: Brooklyn, N.Y. d: 1/2/29, Bronx, N.Y. Deb: 8/19/1874																											
1874	Atl-n	1	4	0	1							.250															/C	
■ CLIFF LEE	Lee, Clifford Walker b: 8/4/1896, Lexington, Neb. d: 8/25/80, Denver, Colo. BR/TR, 6'1", 175 lbs. Deb: 5/15/19																											
1919	Pit-N	42	112	5	22	2	4	0	2	6	8	.196	.237	.286	.523	54	-6	-7	105	24	8	.444	2			-3	C/O	-0.8
1920	Pit-N	37	76	9	18	2	2	0	8	4	14	.237	.275	.316	.591	69	-3	-3	101	129	6	.475	0	1	-1	-0	C/O	-0.2
1921	Phi-N	88	286	31	88	14	4	4	29	13	34	.308	.338	.427	.764	99	-0	-1	102	79	41	.700	5	2	0	-4	1O/C	-0.6
1922	Phi-N	122	422	65	136	29	6	17	77	32	43	.322	.371	.540	.912	117	18	10	113	96	83	.910	2	3	-1	-5	O1/3	0.1
1923	Phi-N	107	355	54	114	20	4	11	47	20	39	.321	.357	.493	.850	108	10	3	114	80	61	.811	3	3	-1	-13	O1	-1.3
1924	Phi-N	21	56	4	14	3	2	1	7	2	5	.250	.276	.429	.704	80	-1	-2	108	95	6	.605	0	1	-1	-1	O/1	-0.3
	Cin-N	6	6	1	2	1	0	0	2	0	2	.333	.333	.500	.833	120	0	0	101	243	1	.750	0	0	0	-0	/O	0.0
	Yr	27	62	5	16	4	2	1	9	2	7	.258	.281	.435	.717	84	-1	-2	106	131	7	.617	0	1	-1	-2		-0.3
1925	Cle-A	77	230	43	74	15	6	4	42	21	33	.322	.378	.491	.870	112	6	4	106	112	43	.866	2	1	0	-6	O	-0.6
1926	Cle-A	21	40	4	7	1	0	1	2	6	8	.175	.283	.275	.558	46	-3	-3	100	49	3	.515	0	0	0	0	/OC	-0.3
Total	8	521	1583	216	475	87	28	38	216	104	186	.300	.344	.462	.806	102	20	2	108	88	252	.761	14	11		-32	O/1C3	-4.0
■ DUD LEE	Lee, Ernest Dudley (played under name of Ernest Dudley In 1920-21) b: 8/22/1899, Denver, Colo. d: 1/7/71, Denver, Colo. BL/TR, 5'9", 150 lbs. Deb: 10/03/20																											
1920	StL-A	1	2	2	2	0	0	0	1	0	0	1.000	1.000	1.000	2.000	387	1	1	111	176	2	—	1	0	0	0	/S	0.1
1921	StL-A	72	180	18	30	4	2	0	11	14	34	.167	.235	.211	.446	14	-23	-24	101	99	10	.364	1	1	-0	-5	S2/3	-2.2
1924	Bos-A	94	288	36	73	9	4	0	29	40	17	.253	.350	.313	.663	69	-11	-13	104	106	35	.644	8	4	0	-3	S	-0.5
1925	Bos-A	84	255	22	57	7	3	0	19	34	19	.224	.315	.275	.589	53	-19	-17	95	91	24	.527	2	3	-1	2	S	-0.3
1926	Bos-A	2	7	2	1	0	0	0	0	0	0	.143	.250	.143	.393	4	-1	-1	101	0	0	.333	0	0	0	0	/S	0.0
Total	5	253	732	80	163	20	9	0	60	88	70	.223	.311	.275	.586	51	-53	-53	100	98	71	.532	12	8	-1	-5	S/23	-2.9
■ HAL LEE	Lee, Harold Burnham "Sheriff" b: 2/15/05, Ludlow, Miss. BR/TR, 5'11", 180 lbs. Deb: 4/19/30																											
1930	Bro-N	22	37	5	6	0	0	1	4	4	5	.162	.244	.243	.487	18	-5	-5	101	115	2	.419	0			-3	O	-0.7
1931	Phi-N	44	131	13	29	10	0	2	12	10	18	.221	.282	.344	.625	63	-6	-7	106	84	13	.549	0			-2	O	-1.0
1932	Phi-N	149	595	76	180	42	10	18	85	36	45	.303	.343	.497	.841	110	17	8	112	92	102	.817	6			7	*O	0.4
1933	Phi-N	46	167	25	48	12	2	0	12	18	13	.287	.360	.383	.743	95	3	-0	118	72	24	.683	1			-0	O	-0.3
	Bos-N	88	312	32	69	15	9	1	28	18	26	.221	.266	.337	.602	74	-12	-11	96	99	29	.506	1			1	O	-1.5
	Yr	134	479	57	117	27	11	1	40	36	39	.244	.300	.353	.653	83	-9	-11	104	90	54	.571	2			1		-1.8
1934	Bos-N	139	521	70	152	23	6	8	79	47	43	.292	.353	.405	.758	119	2	12	86	124	76	.690	3			3	*O/2	0.9
1935	Bos-N	112	422	49	128	18	6	0	39	18	25	.303	.333	.374	.708	94	-6	-4	96	91	51	.577	0			3	*O	-0.4
1936	Bos-N	152	565	46	143	24	7	3	64	52	50	.253	.318	.336	.655	80	-18	-14	95	116	59	.557	4			-8	*O	-2.8
Total	7	752	2750	316	755	144	40	33	323	203	225	.275	.326	.392	.718	95	-25	-21	99	102	357	.647	15			1	O/2	-5.4
■ LEONIDAS LEE	Lee, Leonidas Pyrrhus (born Leonidas Pyrrhus Funkhouser) b: 12/13/1860, St.Louis, Mo. d: 6/11/12, Hendersonville, N.C. Deb: 7/17/1877																											
1877	StL-N	4	18	0	5	1	0	0	0	0	1	.278	.278	.333	.611	90	-0	-0	102	0	2	.462				0	/OS	0.0
■ LERON LEE	Lee, Le Ron b: 3/4/48, Bakersfield, Cal. BL/TR, 6', 196 lbs. Deb: 9/05/69																											
1969	StL-N	7	23	3	5	1	0	0	0	3	8	.217	.308	.261	.569	61	-1	-1	100	0	2	.500	0	0	0	-0	/O	-0.1
1970	StL-N	121	264	28	60	13	1	6	23	24	66	.227	.294	.352	.646	68	-11	-13	106	80	28	.589	5	1	1	-6	O	-2.1
1971	StL-N	25	28	3	5	1	0	1	2	4	12	.179	.281	.321	.603	70	-1	-1	101	68	2	.500	0	1	-1	-3	/O	-0.4
	SD-N	79	256	29	70	20	2	4	21	18	45	.273	.321	.414	.735	111	2	3	96	72	32	.656	4	5	-2	-7	O	-0.8
	Yr	104	284	32	75	21	2	5	23	22	57	.264	.317	.405	.722	106	1	1	97	72	35	.644	4	6	-2	-9		-1.2
1972	SD-N	101	370	50	111	23	7	12	47	29	58	.300	.356	.497	.853	159	18	23	88	89	62	.799	2	5	-2	2	O	2.0
1973	SD-N	118	333	36	79	7	2	3	30	33	61	.237	.308	.297	.605	73	-14	-11	94	112	31	.521	4	0	1	0	O	-1.4
1974	Cle-A	79	232	18	54	13	0	5	25	15	42	.233	.279	.353	.633	80	-6	-6	101	101	21	.532	3	2	-0	-0	O/D	-0.8
1975	Cle-A	13	23	3	3	1	0	0	0	2	5	.130	.231	.174	.405	16	-3	-3	100	0	1	.400	1	0	0	-1	/OD	-0.2
	LA-N	48	43	2	11	4	0	0	2	3	9	.256	.304	.349	.653	85	-1	-1	95	52	5	.563	0	0	0	-1	/O	-0.2
1976	LA-N	23	45	1	6	0	1	0	2	2	9	.133	.170	.178	.348	-1	-6	-6	100	96	1	.250	0	0	0	-2	O	-0.8
Total	8	614	1617	173	404	83	13	31	152	133	315	.250	.309	.375	.684	94	-23	-16	96	88	185	.622	19	14	-3	-18	O/D	-4.8
■ MANNY LEE	Lee, Manuel Lora (born b: 6/17/65, San Pedro De Macoris, D.R. BB/TR, 5'10", 145 lbs. Deb: 4/10/85																											
1985	Tor-A	64	40	9	8	0	0	0	0	2	9	.200	.238	.200	.438	21	-4	-4	101	0	1	.289	1	4	-2	-1	2/S3D	-0.4
1986	Tor-A	35	78	8	16	0	1	1	7	4	10	.205	.244	.269	.513	38	-6	-7	105	116	4	.368	0	1	-1	-1	2/S/3	-0.6
1987	Tor-A	56	121	14	31	2	3	1	11	6	13	.256	.291	.347	.638	69	-5	-5	101	98	13	.549	2	0	1	-1	2S/D	-0.1
1988	Tor-A	117	381	38	111	16	3	2	38	26	64	.291	.337	.365	.701	97	-2	-2	100	104	44	.587	3	3	-1	-3	2S/3	0.1
Total	4	272	620	69	166	18	7	4	56	38	96	.268	.310	.339	.649	78	-18	-18	101	98	62	.535	6	8	-3	-6	2/S3D	-1.0

YEAR	TM/L	G	AB	R	H	2B	3B	HR	RBI	BB	SO	AVG	OBP	SLG	PRO	/A	BR	/A	PF	CHI	RC	TA	SB	CS	SBR	FR	POS	TPR
■ **BILLY LEE**	Lee, William Joseph b: 1/9/1892, Bayonne, N.J. d: 1/6/84, West Hazelton, Pa. BR/TR, 5'9", 165 lbs. Deb: 4/15/15																											
1915	StL-A	18	59	2	11	1	0	0	4	6	5	.186	.262	.203	.465	41	-4	-4	96	116	3	.388	1	1	-0	3	O/3	-0.2
1916	StL-A	7	11	1	2	0	0	0	0	1	1	.182	.250	.182	.432	31	-1	-1	95	0	1	.333	0			-1	/O	-0.1
Total	2	25	70	3	13	1	0	0	4	7	6	.186	.260	.200	.460	39	-5	-5	96	98	4	.379	1	1		2	/O3	-0.3
■ **WATTY LEE**	Lee, Wyatt Arnold b: 8/12/1879, Lynch'S Station, Va. d: 3/6/36, Washington, D.C. TL, 5'10.5", 171 lbs. Deb: 4/30/01																											
1901	Was-A	43	129	15	33	6	3	0	12	7		.256	.294	.349	.643	80	-4	-3	99	84	14	.542	0			1	P/O	0.0
1902	Was-A	109	391	61	100	21	5	4	45	33		.256	.314	.366	.679	91	-6	-5	99	98	49	.632	8			7	OP	0.0
1903	Was-A	75	231	17	48	8	4	0	13	18		.208	.265	.277	.542	61	-10	-11	105	73	19	.475	5			-5	OP	-1.4
1904	Pit-N	8	12	1	4	0	1	0	0	0		.333	.333	.500	.833	159	1	1	99	0	2	.750	0			0	/P	0.0
Total	4	235	763	94	185	35	13	4	70	58		.242	.296	.338	.634	81	-18	-19	101	86	83	.569	13			3	O/P	-1.4
■ **GENE LEEK**	Leek, Eugene Harold b: 7/15/36, San Diego, Cal. BR/TR, 6', 185 lbs. Deb: 4/22/59																											
1959	Cle-A	13	36	7	8	3	0	1	5	2	7	.222	.263	.389	.652	79	-1	-1	97	116	4	.571	0	0	0	-0	3/S	-0.1
1961	LA-A	57	199	16	45	9	1	5	20	7	54	.226	.260	.357	.616	57	-11	-14	111	91	16	.491	0	1	-1	1	3/SO	-0.9
1962	LA-A	7	14	0	2	0	0	0	0	0	6	.143	.143	.143	.286	-22	-2	-2	102	0	0	.167	0	0	0	-0	/3	-0.2
Total	3	77	249	23	55	12	1	6	25	9	67	.221	.254	.349	.603	55	-15	-18	109	90	20	.503	0	1	-1	1	/3SO	-1.2
■ **DAVE LEEPER**	Leeper, David Dale b: 10/30/59, Santa Ana, Cal. BL/TL, 5'11", 170 lbs. Deb: 9/10/84																											
1984	KC-A	4	6	1	0	0	0	0	0	0	1	.000	.000	.000	.000	-99	-2	-2	99	0	0	.000	0	0	0	-0	/OD	-0.1
1985	KC-A	15	34	1	3	0	0	0	4	1	3	.088	.114	.088	.203	-43	-7	-7	102	529	0	.129	0	0	0	-1	/O	-0.7
Total	2	19	40	2	3	0	0	0	4	1	4	.075	.098	.075	.173	-51	-8	-8	101	451	0	.108	0	0	0	-1	/OD	-0.8
■ **GEORGE LEES**	Lees, George Edward b: 2/2/1895, Bethlehem, Pa. d: 1/2/80, Harrisburg, Pa. BR/TR, 5'9", 150 lbs. Deb: 5/07/21																											
1921	Chi-A	20	42	3	9	2	0	0	4	0	3	.214	.214	.262	.476	21	-5	-5	99	125	2	.324	0	1	-1	1	C	-0.3
■ **JIM LEFEBVRE**	Lefebvre, James Kenneth b: 1/7/43, Hawthorne, Cal. BB/TR, 6', 180 lbs. Deb: 4/12/65 C																											
1965	LA-N	157	544	57	136	21	4	12	69	71	92	.250	.339	.369	.708	109	1	7	91	123	71	.658	3	5	-2	-12	*2	0.1
1966	LA-N	152	544	69	149	23	3	24	74	48	72	.274	.336	.460	.796	122	13	15	97	99	84	.744	1	1	-0	3	*23	2.6
1967	LA-N	136	494	51	129	18	5	8	50	44	64	.261	.325	.366	.692	111	-1	6	88	103	57	.603	1	5	-3	1	32/1	0.0
1968	LA-N	84	286	23	69	12	1	5	31	26	55	.241	.307	.343	.649	105	-2	1	91	118	31	.568	0	0	0	-0	23/O1	0.4
1969	LA-N	95	275	29	65	15	2	4	44	48	37	.236	.352	.349	.701	98	0	1	99	163	35	.671	2	1	0	4	32/1	0.8
1970	LA-N	109	314	33	79	15	1	4	44	29	42	.252	.317	.344	.661	86	-10	-6	90	142	34	.572	1	1	-0	-5	23/1	-0.3
1971	LA-N	119	388	40	95	14	2	12	68	39	55	.245	.317	.384	.701	99	-1	-1	99	150	44	.613	0	2	-1	-11	*2/3	-0.8
1972	LA-N	70	169	11	34	8	0	5	24	17	30	.201	.274	.337	.611	78	-6	-5	94	137	16	.536	0	0	0	-1	23	-0.4
Total	8	922	3014	313	756	126	18	74	404	322	447	.251	.326	.378	.704	105	-7	18	93	125	372	.652	8	15	-7	-22	23/1O	2.4
■ **JOE LEFEBVRE**	Lefebvre, Joseph Henry b: 2/22/56, Concord, N.H. BL/TR, 5'10", 170 lbs. Deb: 5/22/80																											
1980	NY-A	74	150	26	34	1	1	8	21	27	30	.227	.345	.407	.751	106	1	2	99	96	21	.727	0	0	0	-15	O	-1.4
1981	SD-N	86	246	31	63	13	4	8	31	35	33	.256	.353	.439	.792	133	8	10	93	92	35	.759	6	4	-1	-0	O	0.7
1982	SD-N	102	239	25	57	9	0	4	21	18	50	.238	.295	.326	.621	80	-9	-6	92	91	24	.524	0	0	0	-3	3O/C	-1.0
1983	SD-N	18	20	1	5	0	0	0	1	2	3	.250	.318	.250	.568	60	-1	-1	99	79	2	.438	0	0	0	-1	/O3C	-0.2
	Phi-N	101	258	34	80	20	8	8	38	31	46	.310	.390	.543	.933	155	19	19	101	92	53	.947	5	3	-0	-7	O/3C	1.1
	Yr	119	278	35	85	20	8	8	39	33	49	.306	.385	.522	.907	148	18	18	101	90	54	.912	5	3	-0	-8		0.9
1984	Phi-N	52	160	22	40	9	0	3	18	23	37	.250	.351	.363	.714	99	1	0	102	105	20	.654	0	2	-1	0	O/3	-0.2
1986	Phi-N	14	18	0	2	0	0	0	0	3	5	.111	.238	.111	.349	-0	-2	-3	104	0	0	.263	0	0	0	-0	/O	-0.2
Total	6	447	1091	139	281	52	13	31	130	139	204	.258	.346	.414	.760	115	18	21	97	93	155	.742	11	9	-2	-27	O/3C	-1.2
■ **BILL LeFEBVRE**	LeFebvre, Wilfrid Henry "Lefty" b: 11/11/15, Natick, R.I. BL/TL, 5'11.5", 180 lbs. Deb: 6/10/38																											
1938	Bos-A	1	1	1	1	0	0	1	1	0	0	1.000	1.000	4.000	5.000	1071	1	1	102	48	4	—	0	0	0	-0	/P	0.0
1939	Bos-A	7	10	3	3	0	0	0	1	2	2	.300	.417	.300	.717	80	-0	-0	108	113	1	.714	0	0	0	-0	/P	0.0
1943	Was-A	7	14	0	4	3	0	0	1	1	0	.286	.333	.500	.833	137	1	1	104	52	2	.727	0	0	0	0	/P	0.0
1944	Was-A	60	62	4	16	2	2	0	8	12	9	.258	.378	.355	.733	123	1	2	90	131	9	.723	0	0	0	-0	P/1	0.6
Total	4	75	87	8	24	5	2	1	11	15	11	.276	.382	.414	.796	133	3	4	94	116	17	.797	0	0	0	-1	/P1	0.6
■ **AL LEFEVRE**	Lefevre, Alfredo Modesto b: 9/16/1898, New York, N.Y. d: 1/21/82, Glen Cove, N.Y. BR/TR, 5'10.5", 160 lbs. Deb: 6/28/20																											
1920	NY-N	17	27	5	4	0	1	0	0	0	13	.148	.148	.222	.370	5	-3	-3	100	0	1	.261	0	0	0	1	/S23	-0.1
■ **WADE LEFLER**	Lefler, Wade Hampton b: 6/5/1896, Cooleemee, N.C. d: 3/6/81, Hickory, N.C. BL, 5'11", 162 lbs. Deb: 4/16/24																											
1924	Bos-N	1	1	0	0	0	0	0	0	0	1	.000	.000	.000	.000	-99	-0	-0	94	0	0	.000	0	0	0	0	H	0.0
	Was-A	5	8	0	5	3	0	0	4	0	0	.625	.625	1.000	1.625	320	2	2	98	165	5	2.667	0	0	0	0	/O	0.2
Total	1	6	9	0	5	3	0	0	4	0	1	.556	.556	.889	1.444	276	2	2	98	147	5	2.000	0	0	0	0	/O	0.2
■ **RON LeFLORE**	LeFlore, Ronald b: 6/16/48, Detroit, Mich. BR/TR, 6', 200 lbs. Deb: 8/01/74																											
1974	Det-A	59	254	37	66	8	1	2	13	13	58	.260	.304	.323	.627	76	-7	-8	106	50	26	.605	23	9	2	10	O	0.2
1975	Det-A	136	550	66	142	13	6	8	37	33	139	.258	.303	.347	.650	80	-13	-15	104	58	57	.589	28	20	-4	-1	*O	-2.4
1976	Det-A	135	544	93	172	23	8	4	39	51	111	.316	.377	.410	.787	126	21	19	104	56	86	.827	58	20	5	9	*O/D	3.2
1977	Det-A	154	652	100	212	30	10	16	57	37	121	.325	.365	.475	.841	121	23	19	105	56	110	.830	39	19	0	-7	*O	0.7
1978	Det-A	155	666	**126**	198	30	3	12	62	65	104	.297	.363	.405	.769	108	15	8	108	69	105	.822	**68**	16	11	1	*O	1.7
1979	Det-A	148	600	110	180	22	10	9	57	52	95	.300	.356	.415	.771	111	6	9	96	70	94	.842	78	14	15	0	*OD	1.9
1980	Mon-N	139	521	95	134	21	11	4	39	62	99	.257	.337	.363	.700	96	-2	-2	99	81	76	.851	**97**	19	**18**	-2	*O	0.9
1981	Chi-A	82	337	46	83	10	4	0	24	28	70	.246	.306	.300	.606	75	-10	-10	100	82	32	.606	36	11	4	-1	O	-0.8
1982	Chi-A	91	334	58	96	15	4	4	25	22	91	.287	.331	.392	.724	100	-1	-0	97	71	42	.707	28	14	0	1	O/D	-0.1
Total	9	1099	4458	731	1283	172	57	59	353	363	888	.288	.344	.392	.735	103	33	20	102	66	628	.777	455	142	51	9	*O/D	5.3
■ **LOU LEGETT**	Legett, Louis Alfred "Doc" b: 6/1/01, New Orleans, La. d: 3/6/88, New Orleans, La. BR/TR, 5'10", 166 lbs. Deb: 5/08/29																											
1929	Bos-N	39	81	7	13	2	0	0	6	3	18	.160	.190	.185	.376	-7	-14	-13	94	137	3	.294	2			0	C	-0.8
1933	Bos-A	8	5	1	1	1	0	0	1	0	0	.200	.200	.400	.600	55	-0	-0	101	167	0	.500	0	0	0	0	/C	0.0
1934	Bos-A	19	38	4	11	0	0	0	1	2	4	.289	.325	.289	.614	56	-2	-3	106	30	4	.481	0	0	0	0	C	0.0
1935	Bos-A	2	0	1	0	0	0	0	0	0	0	—	—	—	—	—	0	0	108	—	—	—	0	0	0	0	R	0.0
Total	4	68	124	13	25	3	0	0	8	5	22	.202	.233	.226	.458	16	-16	-16	98	105	10	.354	2	0		1	/C	-0.8
■ **GREG LEGG**	Legg, Gregory Lynn b: 4/21/60, San Jose, Cal. BR/TR, 6'1", 185 lbs. Deb: 4/18/86																											
1986	Phi-N	11	20	2	9	1	0	0	1	0	3	.450	.450	.500	.950	155	2	2	104	40	5	.909	0	0	0	0	/2S	0.2
1987	Phi-N	3	2	1	0	0	0	0	0	0	0	.000	.000	.000	.000	-96	-1	-1	104	0	0	.000	0	0	0	0	/2S3	0.0
Total	2	14	22	3	9	1	0	0	1	0	3	.409	.409	.455	.864	131	1	1	104	36	5	.769	0	0	0	0	/2S3	0.2
■ **MIKE LEHANE**	Lehane, Michael Patrick b: Rhode Island BR, 6'1.5", 180 lbs. Deb: 4/26/1884																											
1884	Was-U	3	12	1	4	2	0	0		0		.333	.333	.500	.833	184	1	1	97	0	2	.750	0			0	/SO3	0.1
1890	Col-a	140	512	54	108	19	5	0		43		.211	.275	.268	.542	62	-24	-24	99	0	42	.483	13			7	*1	-1.9
1891	Col-a	137	511	59	110	12	7	1	52	34	77	.215	.268	.272	.540	64	-29	-20	89	108	43	.479	16			6	*1	-1.7
Total	3	280	1035	114	222	33	12	1	52	77	77	.214	.272	.272	.545	64	-52	-43	94	53	87	.483	29			13	1/S3O	-3.5
■ **PAUL LEHNER**	Lehner, Paul Eugene "Peanuts" or "Gulliver" b: 7/1/20, Dolomite, Ala. d: 12/27/67, Birmingham, Ala. BL/TL, 5'9", 160 lbs. Deb: 9/10/46																											
1946	StL-A	16	45	6	10	1	2	0	5	1	5	.222	.239	.333	.572	60	-3	-3	98	127	4	.457	0	0	0	-2	O	-0.5
1947	StL-A	135	483	59	120	25	9	7	48	28	29	.248	.294	.381	.675	85	-11	-12	102	88	50	.570	5	5	-2	-11	*O	-3.1
1948	StL-A	103	333	23	92	15	4	2	46	30	19	.276	.336	.363	.699	81	-7	-10	106	122	40	.599	0	2	-1	-10	O/1	-2.2
1949	StL-A	104	297	25	68	13	0	3	37	16	20	.229	.271	.303	.574	52	-22	-22	100	128	22	.440	0	2	-1	3	O1	-2.0
1950	Phi-A	114	427	48	132	17	5	9	52	32	33	.309	.357	.436	.793	114	0	6	90	86	66	.711	1	1	-0	7	*O	1.0
1951	Phi-A	9	28	1	4	1	0	0	1	1	1	.143	.172	.179	.351	-5	-4	-4	106	71	0	.222	0	0	0	1	/O	-0.3
	Chi-A	23	72	9	15	3	1	0	3	10	4	.208	.305	.278	.583	60	-4	-4	97	54	7	.526	0	0	0	2	O	-0.2

YEAR	TM/L	G	AB	R	H	2B	3B	HR	RBI	BB	SO	AVG	OBP	SLG	PRO	/A	BR	/A	PF	CHI	RC	TA	SB	CS	SBR	FR	POS	TPR
	StL-A	21	67	2	9	5	0	1	2	6	5	.134	.205	.254	.459	23	-8	-8	105	36	3	.377	0	1	-1	0	O	-0.8
	Cle-A	12	13	2	3	0	0	0	1	1	2	.231	.286	.231	.516	43	-1	-1	95	119	1	.400	0	0	0	-0	/O	0.0
	Yr	65	180	14	31	9	1	1	7	18	12	.172	.247	.250	.497	35	-17	-17	100	65	13	.420	0	1	-1	2		-1.3
1952	Bos-A	3	3	0	2	0	0	0	2	2	0	.667	.800	.667	1.467	291	1	1	107	374	2	4.000	0	0	0	-0	/O	0.1
Total	7	540	1768	175	455	80	21	22	197	127	118	.257	.309	.364	.672	80	-58	-56	99	99	196	.589	6	11	-5	-11	O/1	-8.0

■ **CLARENCE LEHR** Lehr, Clarence Emanuel "King" b: 5/16/1886, Escanaba, Mich. d: 1/31/48, Detroit, Mich. TR , 5'11", 165 lbs. Deb: 5/18/11

YEAR	TM/L	G	AB	R	H	2B	3B	HR	RBI	BB	SO	AVG	OBP	SLG	PRO	/A	BR	/A	PF	CHI	RC	TA	SB	CS	SBR	FR	POS	TPR
1911	Phi-N	23	27	2	4	0	0	0	2	0	7	.148	.148	.148	.296	-16	-4	-4	108	169	1	.174	0			-2	/O2S	-0.5

■ **HANK LEIBER** Leiber, Henry Edward b: 1/17/11, Phoenix, Ariz. BR/TR, 6'1.5", 205 lbs. Deb: 4/16/33

YEAR	TM/L	G	AB	R	H	2B	3B	HR	RBI	BB	SO	AVG	OBP	SLG	PRO	/A	BR	/A	PF	CHI	RC	TA	SB	CS	SBR	FR	POS	TPR
1933	NY-N	6	10	1	2	0	0	0	0	0	2	.200	.200	.200	.400	15	-1	-1	99	0	0	.222	0			1	/O	0.0
1934	NY-N	63	187	17	45	5	3	2	25	4	13	.241	.257	.332	.588	57	-12	-11	98	132	15	.459	1			-3	O	-1.6
1935	NY-N	154	613	110	203	37	4	22	107	48	29	.331	.389	.512	.901	145	34	37	96	108	121	.865	0			-17	*O	1.3
1936	NY-N	101	337	44	94	19	7	9	67	37	41	.279	.352	.457	.809	116	7	7	100	131	57	.778	1			-3	O/1	0.0
1937	NY-N	51	184	24	54	7	3	4	32	15	27	.293	.347	.429	.776	110	2	2	100	129	26	.683	1			-5	O	-0.4
1938	NY-N	98	360	50	97	18	4	12	65	31	45	.269	.327	.442	.769	106	4	2	103	123	54	.709	0			-12	O	-1.1
1939	Chi-N	112	365	65	113	16	1	24	88	59	42	.310	.411	.556	.967	156	30	30	101	120	83	1.004	1			-0	O	2.8
1940	Chi-N	117	440	68	133	24	2	17	86	45	68	.302	.371	.482	.853	134	20	20	100	129	80	.829	1			-5	*O1	1.0
1941	Chi-N	53	162	20	35	5	0	7	25	16	25	.216	.291	.377	.667	93	-3	-2	94	110	18	.600	0			-4	O1	-0.9
1942	NY-N	58	147	11	32	6	0	4	23	19	27	.218	.315	.340	.656	89	-1	-2	103	137	15	.573	0			1	O/P	-0.1
Total	10	813	2805	410	808	137	24	101	518	274	319	.288	.356	.462	.818	122	80	83	99	122	469	.796	5			-46	O/1P	1.0

■ **NEMO LEIBOLD** Leibold, Harry Loran b: 2/17/1892, Butler, Ind. d: 2/4/77, Detroit, Mich. BL/TR, 6'6.5", 157 lbs. Deb: 4/12/13

YEAR	TM/L	G	AB	R	H	2B	3B	HR	RBI	BB	SO	AVG	OBP	SLG	PRO	/A	BR	/A	PF	CHI	RC	TA	SB	CS	SBR	FR	POS	TPR
1913	Cle-A	93	286	37	74	11	6	0	12	21	43	.259	.309	.339	.649	85	-4	-6	106	44	33	.632	16			-3	O	-1.4
1914	Cle-A	114	402	46	106	13	3	0	32	54	56	.264	.354	.311	.665	98	2	1	102	102	45	.623	12	14	-5	15	*O	0.5
1915	Cle-A	57	207	28	53	5	4	0	4	24	16	.256	.339	.319	.658	94	-0	-1	104	22	24	.618	5	3	-0	8	O	0.4
	Chi-A	36	74	10	17	1	0	0	11	15	11	.230	.360	.243	.603	82	-1	-1	98	208	8	.567	1	3	-2	5	O	0.2
	Yr	93	281	38	70	6	4	0	15	39	27	.249	.345	.299	.644	91	-1	-2	101	94	31	.604	6	6	-2	13		0.6
1916	Chi-A	45	82	5	20	1	2	0	13	7	7	.244	.303	.305	.608	77	-2	-3	108	186	10	.629	7			-4	O	-0.8
1917	Chi-A	125	428	59	101	12	6	0	29	74	34	.236	.350	.292	.642	98	1	2	98	88	50	.694	27			-6	*O	-1.1
1918	Chi-A	116	440	57	110	14	6	1	31	63	32	.250	.344	.316	.660	99	1	1	101	77	51	.652	13			5	*O	0.1
1919	Chi-A	122	434	81	131	18	2	0	26	72	30	.302	.404	.353	.756	108	12	9	105	65	67	.805	17			3	*O	0.3
1920	Chi-A	108	413	61	91	16	3	1	28	55	30	.220	.316	.281	.597	62	-23	-21	96	88	37	.537	7	15	-7	3	*O	-3.3
1921	Bos-A	123	467	88	143	26	6	0	31	41	27	.306	.363	.388	.751	92	-5	-5	100	62	67	.713	13	7	-0	-0	*O	-1.4
1922	Bos-A	81	271	42	70	8	1	1	18	41	14	.258	.360	.306	.666	78	-8	-7	96	76	31	.614	1	6	-3	3	O	-1.1
1923	Bos-A	12	18	1	2	0	0	0	0	1	2	.111	.158	.111	.269	-28	-3	-3	102	0	0	.176	0	1	-1	-2	O	-0.6
	Was-A	95	315	68	96	13	4	1	22	53	16	.305	.408	.381	.789	115	7	9	95	62	53	.813	7	5	-1	-2	O	0.0
	Yr	107	333	69	98	13	4	1	22	54	18	.294	.396	.366	.762	106	3	6	95	55	52	.768	7	6	-2	-4		-0.6
1924	Was-A	84	246	41	72	6	4	0	20	42	10	.293	.398	.350	.748	95	-0	0	98	77	37	.754	6	5	-1	0	O	-0.5
1925	Was-A	56	84	14	23	1	1	0	7	8	7	.274	.337	.310	.646	66	-4	-4	98	90	9	.574	1	0	0	-5	O/3	-0.9
Total	13	1267	4167	638	1109	145	48	4	284	571	335	.266	.357	.327	.684	91	-30	-29	100	77	523	.668	133	59		20	*O/3	-9.6

■ **ELMER LEIFER** Leifer, Elmer Edwin b: 5/23/1893, Clarington, Ohio d: 9/26/48, Everett, Wash. BL/TR, 5'9.5", 170 lbs. Deb: 9/07/21

YEAR	TM/L	G	AB	R	H	2B	3B	HR	RBI	BB	SO	AVG	OBP	SLG	PRO	/A	BR	/A	PF	CHI	RC	TA	SB	CS	SBR	FR	POS	TPR
1921	Chi-A	9	10	0	3	0	0	0	1	0	4	.300	.300	.300	.600	54	-1	-1	99	114	1	.429	0	0	0	-1	/3O	0.0

■ **JOHN LEIGHTON** Leighton, John Atkinson b: 10/4/1861, Peabody, Mass. d: 10/31/56, Lynn, Mass. 5'11", 170 lbs. Deb: 7/12/1890

YEAR	TM/L	G	AB	R	H	2B	3B	HR	RBI	BB	SO	AVG	OBP	SLG	PRO	/A	BR	/A	PF	CHI	RC	TA	SB	CS	SBR	FR	POS	TPR
1890	Syr-a	7	27	6	8	2	0	0		3		.296	.367	.370	.737	133	1	1	90	0	5	.789	2			0	/O	0.1

■ **BILL LEINHAUSER** Leinhauser, William Charles b: 11/4/1893, Philadelphia, Pa. d: 4/14/78, Elkins Park, Pa. 5'10", 150 lbs. Deb: 5/18/12

YEAR	TM/L	G	AB	R	H	2B	3B	HR	RBI	BB	SO	AVG	OBP	SLG	PRO	/A	BR	/A	PF	CHI	RC	TA	SB	CS	SBR	FR	POS	TPR
1912	Det-A	1	4	0	0	0	0	0	0	0	0	.000	.000	.000	.000	-99	-1	-1	95	0	0	.000	0			0	/O	0.0

■ **ED LEIP** Leip, Edgar Ellsworth b: 11/29/10, Trenton, N.J. d: 11/24/83, Zephyrhills, Fla. BR/TR, 5'9", 160 lbs. Deb: 9/16/39

YEAR	TM/L	G	AB	R	H	2B	3B	HR	RBI	BB	SO	AVG	OBP	SLG	PRO	/A	BR	/A	PF	CHI	RC	TA	SB	CS	SBR	FR	POS	TPR
1939	Was-A	9	32	4	11	1	0	0	2	2	4	.344	.382	.375	.757	105	-0	0	90	56	4	.609	0	1	-1	0	/2	0.0
1940	Pit-N	3	5	2	1	0	0	0	0	0	0	.200	.200	.200	.400	11	-1	-1	95	0	0	.200	0			0	/2	0.0
1941	Pit-N	15	25	1	5	0	2	0	3	1	2	.200	.231	.360	.591	63	-1	-1	103	120	1	.500	1			0	/23	0.0
1942	Pit-N	3	0	0	0	0	0	0	0	0	0	—	—	—	—	—	0	0	101	—	—	—	0			0	R	0.0
Total	4	30	62	7	17	1	2	0	5	3	6	.274	.308	.355	.663	80	-2	-2	96	78	7	.565	1	1		0	/23	0.0

■ **FRANK LEJA** Leja, Frank John b: 2/7/36, Holyoke, Mass. BL/TL, 6'4", 205 lbs. Deb: 5/01/54

YEAR	TM/L	G	AB	R	H	2B	3B	HR	RBI	BB	SO	AVG	OBP	SLG	PRO	/A	BR	/A	PF	CHI	RC	TA	SB	CS	SBR	FR	POS	TPR
1954	NY-A	12	5	2	1	0	0	0	0	0	1	.200	.200	.200	.400	10	-1	-1	99	0	0	.250	0	0	0	0	/1	0.0
1955	NY-A	7	2	1	0	0	0	0	0	0	1	.000	.000	.000	.000	-99	-1	-1	98	0	0	.000	0	0	0	0	/1	0.0
1962	LA-A	7	16	0	0	0	0	0	0	1	6	.000	.059	.000	.059	-81	-4	-4	102	0	0	.059	0	0	0	-0	/1	-0.4
Total	3	26	23	3	1	0	0	0	0	1	8	.043	.083	.043	.127	-64	-5	-5	101	0	0	.087	0	0	0	-0	/1	-0.4

■ **LARRY LeJEUNE** LeJeune, Sheldon Aldenbert b: 7/22/1885, Chicago, Ill. d: 4/21/52, Eloise, Mich. 6', 185 lbs. Deb: 5/10/11

YEAR	TM/L	G	AB	R	H	2B	3B	HR	RBI	BB	SO	AVG	OBP	SLG	PRO	/A	BR	/A	PF	CHI	RC	TA	SB	CS	SBR	FR	POS	TPR
1911	Bro-N	6	19	2	3	0	0	0	2	2	8	.158	.238	.158	.396	12	-2	-2	97	225	1	.438	2			-2	/O	-0.3
1915	Pit-N	18	65	4	11	0	1	0	2	2	7	.169	.206	.200	.406	23	-6	-6	99	60	3	.351	4	3	-1	3	O	-0.3
Total	2	24	84	6	14	0	1	0	4	4	15	.167	.213	.190	.404	21	-8	-8	98	99	4	.370	6	3		2	/O	-0.6

■ **DON LeJOHN** LeJohn, Donald Everett b: 5/13/34, Daisytown, Pa. BR/TR, 5'10", 175 lbs. Deb: 6/30/65

YEAR	TM/L	G	AB	R	H	2B	3B	HR	RBI	BB	SO	AVG	OBP	SLG	PRO	/A	BR	/A	PF	CHI	RC	TA	SB	CS	SBR	FR	POS	TPR
1965	LA-N	34	78	2	20	2	0	0	7	5	13	.256	.301	.282	.583	72	-3	-3	91	132	6	.450	0	1	-1	1	3	-0.3

■ **JACK LELIVELT** Lelivelt, John Frank b: 11/14/1885, Chicago, Ill. d: 1/20/41, Seattle, Wash. BL/TL, 5'11", 175 lbs. Deb: 6/24/09

YEAR	TM/L	G	AB	R	H	2B	3B	HR	RBI	BB	SO	AVG	OBP	SLG	PRO	/A	BR	/A	PF	CHI	RC	TA	SB	CS	SBR	FR	POS	TPR
1909	Was-A	91	318	25	93	8	6	0	24	19		.292	.334	.355	.690	131	6	9	90	87	39	.627	8			5	O	1.2
1910	Was-A	110	347	40	92	10	3	0	33	40		.265	.343	.311	.654	104	3	3	101	115	45	.663	20			7	O/1	0.7
1911	Was-A	72	225	29	72	12	4	0	22	22		.320	.386	.409	.794	126	7	8	97	81	38	.804	7			2	O/1	0.6
1912	NY-A	36	149	12	54	6	7	2	23	4		.362	.383	.537	.920	160	11	10	101	94	32	.968	7			2	O	1.0
1913	NY-A	18	28	2	6	0	1	0	4	2	2	.214	.267	.286	.552	61	-1	-1	101	178	2	.500	1			1	/O	0.0
	Cle-A	23	23	0	9	2	0	0	7	0	3	.391	.391	.478	.870	146	1	1	106	226	4	.857	1			-0	/O	0.1
	Yr	41	51	2	15	2	1	0	11	2	5	.294	.321	.373	.693	99	-0	-0	104	209	6	.639	2			0		0.1
1914	Cle-A	32	64	6	21	5	1	0	13	2	10	.328	.348	.438	.786	133	2	2	102	174	9	.696	2	3	-1	-3	O/1	-0.2
Total	6	382	1154	114	347	43	22	2	126	89	15	.301	.353	.381	.735	125	29	32	97	105	170	.716	46	3		14	O/1	3.4

■ **JOHNNIE LeMASTER** LeMaster, Johnnie Lee b: 6/19/54, Portsmouth, Ohio BR/TR, 6'2", 165 lbs. Deb: 9/02/75

YEAR	TM/L	G	AB	R	H	2B	3B	HR	RBI	BB	SO	AVG	OBP	SLG	PRO	/A	BR	/A	PF	CHI	RC	TA	SB	CS	SBR	FR	POS	TPR
1975	SF-N	22	74	4	14	4	0	2	9	4	15	.189	.241	.324	.565	55	-5	-5	102	116	6	.508	2	1	0	0	S	-0.1
1976	SF-N	33	100	9	21	3	2	0	9	2	21	.210	.225	.280	.505	42	-8	-8	103	124	6	.395	2	0	1	1	S	-0.2
1977	SF-N	68	134	13	20	5	1	0	8	13	27	.149	.224	.201	.426	15	-16	-17	104	119	7	.365	2	1	0	2	S/3	-0.7
1978	SF-N	101	272	23	64	18	3	1	14	21	45	.235	.293	.335	.627	82	-9	-7	92	59	26	.546	6	6	-2	-8	S/2	-0.8
1979	SF-N	108	343	42	87	11	2	3	29	23	55	.254	.304	.324	.628	77	-13	-10	92	96	34	.543	9	5	-0	6	*S	0.0
1980	SF-N	135	405	33	87	16	6	3	31	25	57	.215	.260	.306	.567	60	-24	-21	96	92	32	.457	0	1	-1	-20	*S	-2.8
1981	SF-N	104	324	27	82	9	1	0	28	24	46	.253	.307	.287	.594	66	-13	-15	105	118	26	.469	3	7	-3	-7	*S	-1.4
1982	SF-N	130	436	34	94	14	1	2	30	31	78	.216	.268	.266	.534	53	-29	-26	94	96	30	.444	13	4	2	-2	*S	-1.6
1983	SF-N	141	534	81	128	16	1	6	30	60	96	.240	.319	.307	.626	74	-17	-18	101	69	57	.619	39	19	0	-14	*S	-1.9
1984	SF-N	132	451	46	98	13	2	4	32	31	97	.217	.268	.282	.549	57	-27	-25	96	90	36	.481	17	5	2	13	*S	0.3
1985	SF-N	12	16	1	0	0	0	0	0	1	5	.000	.059	.000	.059	-88	-4	-4	93	0	0	.063	0	0	0	-0	S	-0.2
	Cle-A	11	20	0	3	0	0	0	2	0	6	.150	.150	.150	.300	-19	-3	-3	94	264	0	.167	0	1	-1	-1	S	-0.3
	Pit-N	22	58	4	9	0	0	1	6	5	12	.155	.222	.207	.429	20	-6	-6	103	159	3	.360	1	0	0	3	S	0.0
1987	Oak-A	20	24	3	2	0	0	0	1	1	4	.083	.120	.083	.203	-49	-5	-5	91	200	0	.130	0	1	-1	0	/3S2D	-0.4
Total	12	1039	3191	320	709	109	19	22	229	241	564	.222	.278	.289	.567	60	-180	-170	97	94	263	.499	94	51	-2	-31	S/32D	-10.1

YEAR	TM/L	G	AB	R	H	2B	3B	HR	RBI	BB	SO	AVG	OBP	SLG	PRO	/A	BR	/A	PF	CHI	RC	TA	SB	CS	SBR	FR	POS	TPR
■ **STEVE LEMBO**	Lembo, Stephen Neal b: 11/13/26, Brooklyn, N.Y. BR/TR, 6'1", 185 lbs. Deb: 9/16/50																											
1950	Bro-N	5	6	0	1	0	0	0	0	1	0	.167	.286	.167	.452	21	-1	-1	107	0	0	.333	0			0	/C	0.0
1952	Bro-N	2	5	0	1	0	0	0	1	0	1	.200	.200	.200	.400	11	-1	-1	102	390	0	.250	0	0	0	0	/C	0.0
Total	2	7	11	0	2	0	0	0	1	1	1	.182	.250	.182	.432	17	-1	-1	104	163	0	.333	0	<u>0</u>		0	/C	0.0
■ **MARK LEMKE**	Lemke, Mark Alan b: 8/13/65, Utica, N.Y. BB/TR, 5'9", 165 lbs. Deb: 9/17/88																											
1988	Atl-N	16	58	8	13	4	0	0	2	4	5	.224	.274	.293	.567	60	-3	-3	104	48	4	.438	0	2	-1	1	2	-0.3
■ **CHET LEMON**	Lemon, Chester Earl b: 2/12/55, Jackson, Miss. BR/TR, 6', 190 lbs. Deb: 9/09/75																											
1975	Chi-A	9	35	2	9	2	0	0	1	2	6	.257	.297	.314	.612	71	-1	-1	103	37	4	.538	1	0	0	-0	/3OD	-0.1
1976	Chi-A	132	451	46	111	15	5	4	38	28	65	.246	.300	.328	.629	85	-9	-9	99	91	44	.551	13	7	-0	4	*O	-0.7
1977	Chi-A	150	553	99	151	38	4	19	67	52	88	.273	.347	.459	.807	118	13	14	99	87	89	.781	8	7	-2	27	*O	3.3
1978	Chi-A	105	357	51	107	24	6	13	55	39	46	.300	.381	.510	.891	147	23	23	101	100	65	.867	5	9	-4	8	OD	2.5
1979	Chi-A	148	556	79	177	**44**	2	17	86	56	68	.318	.394	.496	.890	135	31	29	102	107	104	.869	7	11	-5	3	*O	2.1
1980	Chi-A	146	514	76	150	32	6	11	51	71	56	.292	.390	.442	.832	132	22	24	97	81	90	.827	6	6	-2	-3	*O/2D	1.6
1981	Chi-A	94	328	50	99	23	6	9	50	33	48	.302	.388	.491	.879	152	22	23	100	106	60	.858	5	8	-3	-2	O	1.5
1982	Det-A	125	436	75	116	20	1	19	52	56	69	.266	.369	.447	.816	122	15	15	100	84	72	.792	1	4	-2	0	*O/D	0.9
1983	Det-A	145	491	78	125	21	5	24	69	54	70	.255	.352	.464	.817	128	16	19	96	92	79	.786	0	7	-4	4	*O	1.7
1984	Det-A	141	509	77	146	34	6	20	76	51	83	.287	.360	.495	.855	139	23	26	96	99	86	.820	5	5	-2	7	*O/D	2.6
1985	Det-A	145	517	69	137	28	4	18	68	45	93	.265	.336	.439	.775	104	7	3	106	98	78	.729	0	2	-1	4	*O	0.4
1986	Det-A	126	403	45	101	21	3	12	53	39	53	.251	.329	.407	.736	105	0	3	95	106	52	.670	2	1	0	-4	*O	-0.4
1987	Det-A	146	470	75	130	30	3	20	75	70	82	.277	.380	.481	.860	131	20	22	97	105	86	.852	0	0	0	-4	*O	1.3
1988	Det-A	144	512	67	135	29	4	17	64	59	65	.264	.348	.436	.783	125	13	16	94	95	75	.730	1	2	-1	1	*O	1.4
Total	14	1756	6132	889	1694	361	55	203	805	655	892	.276	.359	.452	.812	124	194	204	99	95	985	.800	54	69	-25	44	*O/D32	18.1
■ **JIM LEMON**	Lemon, James Robert b: 3/23/28, Covington, Va. BR/TR, 6'4", 200 lbs. Deb: 8/20/50 MC																											
1950	Cle-A	12	34	4	6	1	0	1	1	3	12	.176	.243	.294	.537	38	-3	-3	98	27	2	.433	0	0	0	-2	O	-0.4
1953	Cle-A	16	46	5	8	1	0	1	5	3	15	.174	.224	.261	.485	32	-5	-4	95	123	3	.395	0	0	0	-1	O/1	-0.5
1954	Was-A	37	128	12	30	2	3	2	13	9	34	.234	.285	.344	.628	73	-5	-5	98	99	12	.520	0	0	0	-5	O	-1.0
1955	Was-A	10	25	3	5	2	0	1	3	3	4	.200	.286	.400	.686	91	-1	-0	91	86	3	.650	0	0	0	-0	/O	0.0
1956	Was-A	146	538	77	146	21	**11**	27	96	65	138	.271	.352	.502	.854	121	16	14	102	104	94	.831	2	4	-2	7	*O	1.2
1957	Was-A	137	518	58	147	23	6	17	64	49	94	.284	.349	.450	.799	119	11	13	98	94	77	.731	1	7	-4	-8	*O/1	-0.7
1958	Was-A	142	501	65	123	15	9	26	75	50	120	.246	.315	.467	.782	116	7	9	97	98	71	.730	2	4	-2	-0	*O	-0.2
1959	Was-A	147	531	73	148	18	3	33	100	46	99	.279	.337	.510	.848	129	19	19	100	109	91	.820	5	2	0	-2	*O	1.0
1960	Was-A	148	528	81	142	10	1	38	100	67	114	.269	.359	.508	.866	129	22	21	102	105	99	.871	2	0	1	-4	*O	1.3
1961	Min-A	129	423	57	109	26	1	14	52	44	98	.258	.333	.423	.757	95	-0	-4	106	92	59	.699	1	1	-0	-11	*O	-1.9
1962	Min-A	12	17	1	3	0	0	1	5	3	4	.176	.300	.353	.653	72	-1	-1	105	221	2	.600	0	0	0	-1	/O	-0.1
1963	Min-A	7	17	0	2	0	0	0	1	1	5	.118	.167	.118	.284	-19	-3	-3	100	209	0	.200	0	0	0	-1	/O	-0.3
	Phi-N	31	59	6	16	2	0	2	6	8	18	.271	.358	.407	.765	117	2	1	103	84	9	.727	0	0	0	-2	O	0.0
	Chi-A	36	80	4	16	0	1	1	8	12	32	.200	.304	.262	.567	58	-4	-4	104	139	7	.516	0	0	0	-1	1	-0.6
Total	12	1010	3445	446	901	121	35	164	529	363	787	.262	.335	.460	.795	113	55	53	100	102	530	.772	13	18	-7	-31	O/1	-2.2
■ **BOB LEMON**	Lemon, Robert Granville b: 9/22/20, San Bernardino, Cal. BL/TR, 6', 180 lbs. Deb: 9/09/41 MCH																											
1941	Cle-A	5	4	0	1	0	0	0	0	0	1	.250	.250	.250	.500	32	-0	-0	101	0	0	.333	0	0	0	0	/3	0.0
1942	Cle-A	5	5	0	0	0	0	0	0	0	3	.000	.000	.000	.000	-99	-1	-1	92	0	0	.000	0	0	0	0	/3	0.0
1946	Cle-A	55	89	9	16	3	0	1	4	7	18	.180	.240	.247	.487	41	-8	-7	89	61	6	.392	0	1	-1	7	PO	0.0
1947	Cle-A	47	56	11	18	4	3	2	5	6	9	.321	.387	.607	.994	181	5	5	96	46	14	1.053	0	0	0	4	P/O	0.0
1948	Cle-A	52	119	20	34	9	0	5	21	8	23	.286	.331	.487	.818	118	2	2	99	97	20	.776	0	0	0	9	P	0.0
1949	Cle-A	46	108	17	29	6	2	7	19	10	20	.269	.331	.556	.886	135	4	4	98	80	21	.875	0	0	0	6	P	0.0
1950	Cle-A	72	136	21	37	9	1	6	26	13	25	.272	.340	.485	.825	112	1	1	98	107	24	.808	0	0	0	5	P	0.0
1951	Cle-A	56	102	11	21	4	1	3	13	9	22	.206	.270	.353	.623	71	-5	-4	95	103	10	.549	0	0	0	4	P	0.0
1952	Cle-A	54	124	14	28	5	0	2	9	4	21	.226	.250	.315	.565	62	-8	-6	91	75	10	.439	0	0	0	7	P	0.0
1953	Cle-A	51	112	12	26	9	1	2	17	7	20	.232	.277	.384	.661	81	-4	-3	95	128	13	.598	2	0	1	8	P	0.0
1954	Cle-A	40	98	11	21	4	1	2	10	6	24	.214	.260	.337	.596	59	-5	-6	106	97	9	.500	0	0	0	4	P	0.0
1955	Cle-A	49	78	11	19	0	0	1	9	13	16	.244	.352	.282	.634	69	-3	-3	104	134	9	.583	0	0	0	2	P	0.0
1956	Cle-A	43	93	8	18	0	0	5	12	9	21	.194	.272	.355	.627	63	-5	-5	101	93	10	.566	0	0	0	4	P	0.0
1957	Cle-A	25	46	2	3	1	0	1	1	0	14	.065	.065	.152	.217	-42	-9	-9	102	39	0	.159	0	0	0	3	P	0.0
1958	Cle-A	15	13	1	3	0	0	0	1	1	4	.231	.286	.231	.516	47	-1	-1	94	134	1	.400	0	0	0	1	P	0.0
Total	15	615	1183	148	274	54	9	37	147	93	241	.232	.289	.386	.675	83	-38	-34	97	93	147	.609	2	1	0	62	P/O3	0.0
■ **DON LENHARDT**	Lenhardt, Donald Eugene "Footsie" b: 10/4/22, Alton, Ill. BR/TR, 6'3", 190 lbs. Deb: 4/18/50 C																											
1950	StL-A	139	480	75	131	22	6	22	81	90	94	.273	.390	.481	.871	114	16	11	107	96	98	.911	3	2	-0	-9	1O3	-0.2
1951	StL-A	31	103	9	27	3	0	5	18	6	13	.262	.303	.437	.740	94	-1	-2	105	107	14	.675	1	0	0	-3	O/1	-0.4
	Chi-A	64	199	23	53	9	1	10	45	24	25	.266	.351	.472	.823	125	5	6	97	130	35	.807	1	1	-0	-2	O/1	0.1
	Yr	95	302	32	80	12	1	15	63	30	38	.265	.335	.460	.796	114	4	5	99	123	49	.765	2	1	0	-5		-0.3
1952	Bos-A	30	105	18	31	4	0	7	24	15	18	.295	.383	.533	.917	143	7	6	107	119	21	.910	0	1	-1	-3	O	0.3
	Det-A	45	144	18	27	2	1	3	13	28	18	.188	.320	.278	.598	68	-6	-6	99	101	14	.553	0	1	-1	2	O	-0.4
	StL-A	18	48	5	13	4	1	1	5	4	8	.271	.327	.458	.785	120	1	1	97	75	7	.722	0	0	0	-0	O/1	0.0
	Yr	93	297	41	71	10	2	11	42	47	44	.239	.343	.397	.740	104	2	2	101	104	45	.721	0	2	-1	-1		-0.1
1953	StL-A	97	303	37	96	15	0	10	35	41	41	.317	.400	.465	.865	125	15	12	107	76	58	.848	1	2	-1	-2	O/3	0.7
1954	Bal-A	13	33	2	5	1	0	0	1	3	9	.152	.222	.182	.404	12	-4	-4	95	63	1	.310	0	0	0	-1	/O1	-0.5
	Bos-A	44	66	5	18	4	0	3	17	3	9	.273	.314	.470	.784	112	1	1	100	161	9	.686	0	0	0	-3	O/3	-0.2
	Yr	57	99	7	23	5	0	3	18	6	18	.232	.283	.374	.657	79	-3	-3	99	140	10	.557	0	0	0	-5		-0.7
Total	5	481	1481	192	401	64	9	61	239	214	235	.271	.365	.450	.815	112	34	26	104	101	258	.818	6	7	-2	-20	O/13	-0.6
■ **BOB LENNON**	Lennon, Robert Albert "Arch" b: 9/15/28, Brooklyn, N.Y. BL/TL, 6', 200 lbs. Deb: 9/09/54																											
1954	NY-N	3	3	0	0	0	0	0	0	0	0	.000	.000	.000	.000	-95	-1	-1	105	0	0	.000	0	0	0	0	H	0.0
1956	NY-N	26	55	3	10	1	0	0	1	4	17	.182	.237	.200	.437	20	-6	-6	97	38	3	.333	0	0	0	-3	O	-1.0
1957	Chi-N	9	21	2	3	1	0	1	3	1	9	.143	.182	.333	.515	36	-2	-2	96	124	1	.444	0	0	0	-1	/O	-0.2
Total	3	38	79	5	13	2	0	1	4	5	26	.165	.214	.228	.442	19	-9	-9	97	59	4	.348	0	0	0	-4	/O	-1.2
■ **BILL LENNON**	Lennon, William F. b: 1848, Brooklyn, N.Y. 5'7", 145 lbs. Deb: 5/04/1871 M																											
1871	Kek-n	12	48	4	11							.229															CM	
1872	Nat-n	11	52	11	12							.231															C	
1873	Mar-n	4	15	1	3							.200															/1/C3	
Total	3 n	27	115	16	26							.226															/1/C3	
■ **ED LENNOX**	Lennox, James Edgar "Eggie" b: 11/3/1885, Camden, N.J. d: 10/26/39, Camden, N.J. BR/TR, 5'10", 174 lbs. Deb: 8/08/06																											
1906	Phi-A	6	17	1	1	0	0	0	0	1		.059	.111	.118	.229	-30	-2	-2	94	0	0	.188	0			0	/3	-0.1
1909	Bro-N	126	435	33	114	18	9	2	44	47		.262	.337	.359	.695	119	9	9	99	105	55	.673	11			-4	*3	0.8
1910	Bro-N	110	367	19	95	19	4	3	32	36	39	.259	.333	.357	.690	106	0	3	95	81	46	.658	7			-13	*3	-1.0
1912	Chi-N	27	81	13	19	4	1	1	16	12	10	.235	.347	.346	.693	87	-1	-1	104	174	11	.694	1			0	3	0.0
1914	Pit-F	124	430	71	134	25	10	11	84	71	38	.312	.409	.493	.902	167	34	37	94	131	98	1.020	19			-22	*3	1.8
1915	Pit-F	55	53	1	16	3	1	1	9	7	12	.302	.383	.453	.836	141	3	3	104	120	10	.838	0			0	/3	0.3
Total	6	448	1383	138	379	70	25	18	185	174	<u>99</u>	.274	.359	.400	.759	128	43	48	97	111	219	.771	38			-38	3	1.8
■ **JIM LENTINE**	Lentine, James Matthew b: 7/16/54, Los Angeles, Cal. BR/TR, 6', 175 lbs. Deb: 9/03/78																											
1978	StL-N	8	11	1	2	0	0	0	1	0	0	.182	.250	.182	.432	24	-1	-1	95	198	1	.444	1	0	0	-0	/O	0.0
1979	StL-N	11	23	2	9	1	0	0	1	3	6	.391	.462	.435	.896	139	2	2	105	40	5	.867	0	1	-1	0	/O	0.1

YEAR	TM/L	G	AB	R	H	2B	3B	HR	RBI	BB	SO	AVG	OBP	SLG	PRO	/A	BR	/A	PF	CHI	RC	TA	SB	CS	SBR	FR	POS	TPR
1980	StL-N	9	10	1	1	0	0	0	1	0	2	.100	.100	.100	.200	-43	-2	-2	103	396	0	.111	0	0	0	-2	/O	-0.3
	Det-A	67	161	19	42	8	1	1	17	28	30	.261	.377	.342	.719	93	1	-0	105	114	23	.707	2	1	0	-3	O/D	-0.3
Total	3	95	205	23	54	9	1	1	20	31	38	.263	.368	.332	.700	89	-0	-2	105	122	28	.673	3	2	-0	-5	/OD	-0.5
■ **LENTZ** Lentz Deb:5/07/1872																												
1872	Eck-n	4	12	2	1							.083															/C	
■ **EDDIE LEON** Leon, Eduardo Antonio b: 8/11/46, Tucson, Ariz. BR/TR, 6', 170 lbs. Deb: 9/09/68																												
1968	Cle-A	6	1	0	0	0	0	0	0	0	1	.000	.000	.000	.000	-99	-0	-0	101	0	0	.000	0	0	0	0	/S	0.0
1969	Cle-A	64	213	20	51	6	0	3	19	19	37	.239	.302	.310	.612	76	-8	-7	94	102	20	.521	2	2	-1	-1	S	-0.5
1970	Cle-A	152	549	58	136	20	4	10	56	47	89	.248	.309	.353	.663	72	-14	-24	115	107	61	.573	1	2	-1	12	*2S/3	0.4
1971	Cle-A	131	429	35	112	12	2	4	35	34	69	.261	.317	.326	.643	78	-10	-13	106	94	41	.527	3	5	-2	-3	*2S	-1.0
1972	Cle-A	89	225	14	45	2	1	4	16	20	47	.200	.268	.271	.539	57	-11	-13	107	92	15	.427	0	2	-1	0	2S	-0.8
1973	Chi-A	127	399	37	91	10	3	3	30	34	103	.228	.294	.291	.584	64	-18	-19	102	94	34	.477	1	5	-3	2	*S/2	-0.3
1974	Chi-A	31	46	1	5	1	0	0	3	2	12	.109	.146	.130	.276	-20	-7	-7	102	197	1	.178	0	0	0	1	S/23D	-0.4
1975	NY-A	1	0	0	0	0	0	0	0	0	0	—	—	—	—	—	0	0	99	—	—	—	0	0	0	0	/S	0.0
Total	8	601	1862	165	440	51	10	24	159	156	358	.236	.298	.313	.611	68	-68	-82	106	101	171	.524	7	16	-8	11	S2/3D	-2.6
■ **ANDY LEONARD** Leonard, Andrew Jackson b: 6/1/1846, County Cavan, Ireland d: 8/21/03, Roxbury, Mass. BR/TR, 5'7", 155 lbs. Deb: 5/05/1871																												
1871	Oly-n	31	151	34	43							.285															*2O/S	
1872	Bos-n	46	252	60	86							.341															*O/32	
1873	Bos-n	58	319	83	95							.298															*O2/S	
1874	Bos-n	71	350	71	119							.340															*OS/2	
1875	Bos-n	80	396	87	128							.323															*O/S32	
1876	Bos-N	64	303	53	85	10	2	0	27	4	6	.281	.290	.327	.617	111	1	4	95	80	29	.472				1	O2	0.4
1877	Bos-N	58	272	46	78	5	0	0	27	5	5	.287	.300	.305	.605	84	-3	-6	108	95	25	.454				-4	OS	-0.9
1878	Bos-N	60	262	41	68	8	5	0	16	3	19	.260	.268	.328	.596	88	-2	-4	108	56	24	.459				-8	*O	-1.5
1880	Cin-N	33	133	15	28	3	0	1	17	8	11	.211	.255	.256	.511	75	-3	-3	99	148	9	.400				-9	S3	-1.0
Total	5 n	286	1468	335	471							.321															S3	
Total	4	215	970	155	259	26	7	1	87	20	41	.267	.282	.311	.593	92	-6	-10	103	87	87	.453				-20	O/S23	-3.0
■ **JEFFERY LEONARD** Leonard, Jeffery b: 9/22/55, Philadelphia, Pa. BR/TR, 6'2", 200 lbs. Deb: 9/02/77																												
1977	LA-N	11	10	1	3	0	1	0	2	1	4	.300	.364	.500	.864	129	0	0	100	160	1	.750	0	0	0	-3	O	-0.2
1978	Hou-N	8	26	2	10	2	0	0	4	1	2	.385	.407	.462	.869	150	1	2	95	132	5	.765	0	1	-1	1	/O	0.2
1979	Hou-N	134	411	47	119	15	5	0	47	46	68	.290	.364	.350	.714	106	-1	4	90	129	53	.687	23	10	1	-4	*O	-0.1
1980	Hou-N	88	216	29	46	7	5	3	20	19	46	.213	.277	.333	.610	71	-9	-9	98	98	19	.531	4	1	1	-2	O1	-1.3
1981	Hou-N	7	18	1	3	1	1	0	3	0	4	.167	.167	.333	.500	44	-2	-1	88	196	1	.467	1	0	0	-0	/1O	-0.1
	SF-N	37	127	20	39	11	3	4	26	12	21	.307	.371	.535	.907	147	9	8	105	128	23	.895	4	2	0	5	O/1	1.3
	Yr	44	145	21	42	12	4	4	29	12	25	.290	.348	.510	.858	138	7	7	102	143	24	.836	5	2	0	5		1.2
1982	SF-N	80	278	32	72	16	1	9	49	19	65	.259	.311	.421	.732	110	0	2	94	133	34	.703	18	5	2	-4	O/1	0.0
1983	SF-N	139	516	74	144	17	7	21	87	35	116	.279	.326	.461	.787	115	9	8	101	117	77	.771	26	7	4	7	*O	1.7
1984	SF-N	136	514	76	155	27	2	21	86	47	123	.302	.360	.484	.845	141	23	25	96	110	87	.826	17	7	1	5	*O	2.7
1985	SF-N	133	507	49	122	20	3	17	62	21	107	.241	.272	.393	.665	90	-13	-9	93	101	47	.566	11	6	-0	-4	*O	-1.7
1986	SF-N	89	341	48	95	11	3	6	42	20	62	.279	.324	.381	.705	98	-3	-2	96	115	44	.668	16	3	3	0	O	0.0
1987	SF-N	131	503	70	141	29	4	19	63	21	68	.280	.312	.467	.779	107	0	3	96	88	66	.710	16	7	1	-8	*O	-0.9
1988	SF-N	44	160	12	41	8	1	2	20	9	24	.256	.296	.356	.652	92	-3	-2	94	129	15	.566	7	5	-1	-4	O	-0.8
	Mil-A	94	374	45	88	19	0	8	44	16	68	.235	.272	.350	.623	71	-14	-16	103	119	34	.533	10	4	1	-0	O	-1.7
Total	12	1131	4001	506	1078	183	36	110	555	267	778	.269	.318	.416	.733	105	-2	15	96	113	507	.701	153	58	11	-11	*O/1	-0.9
■ **JOE LEONARD** Leonard, Joseph Howard b: 11/15/1894, W.Chicago, Ill. d: 5/1/20, Washington, D.C. BL/TR, 5'7.5", 156 lbs. Deb: 5/07/14																												
1914	Pit-N	53	126	17	25	2	2	0	4	12	21	.198	.268	.246	.514	58	-7	-6	92	47	10	.465	4			-1	3/S	-0.5
1916	Cle-A	3	2	1	0	0	0	0	0	0	1	.000	.000	.000	.000	-99	-0	-0	100	0	0	.000	0			0	/2	0.0
	Was-A	42	168	20	46	7	0	0	14	22	23	.274	.358	.315	.673	102	1	1	100	81	20	.648	4			-7	3	-0.3
	Yr	45	170	21	46	7	0	0	14	22	24	.271	.354	.312	.666	100	1	1	100	76	20	.637	4			-7		-0.3
1917	Was-A	99	297	30	57	6	7	0	23	45	40	.192	.302	.259	.562	77	-9	-6	92	107	25	.542	6			-2	31/SO	-0.6
1919	Was-A	71	198	26	51	8	3	2	20	20	28	.258	.329	.359	.687	95	-2	-1	98	94	23	.646	3			-5	23/1O	-0.2
1920	Was-A	1	0	0	0	0	0	0	0	0	0	—	—	—	—	—	0	0	95	—	—	—	0	0	0	0	R	0.0
Total	5	269	791	94	179	23	12	2	61	99	113	.226	.315	.293	.608	84	-17	-13	95	89	101	.574	17	0		-14	3/21OS	-1.6
■ **JOHN LEOVICH** Leovich, John Joseph b: 5/5/18, Portland, Ore. BR/TR, 6'0.5", 200 lbs. Deb: 5/01/41																												
1941	Phi-A	1	2	0	1	1	0	0	0	0	0	.500	.500	1.000	1.500	286	0	0	101	0	0	1.000	0	0	0	0	/C	0.1
■ **TED LEPCIO** Lepcio, Thaddeus Stanley b: 7/28/30, Utica, N.Y. BR/TR, 5'10", 177 lbs. Deb: 4/15/52																												
1952	Bos-A	84	274	34	72	17	2	5	26	24	41	.263	.329	.394	.723	94	-0	-3	107	79	37	.660	3	3	-1	9	23/S	0.8
1953	Bos-A	66	161	17	38	4	2	4	11	17	24	.236	.313	.360	.673	75	-4	-6	109	58	18	.594	0	0	0	2	2S3	0.0
1954	Bos-A	116	398	42	102	19	4	8	45	42	62	.256	.332	.384	.716	95	-3	-3	100	96	51	.653	3	4	-2	13	23S	1.1
1955	Bos-A	51	134	19	31	9	0	6	15	12	36	.231	.313	.433	.746	80	-1	-5	124	74	18	.708	1	1	-0	2	3	-0.2
1956	Bos-A	83	284	34	74	10	0	15	51	30	77	.261	.338	.454	.792	105	2	1	103	109	44	.751	1	3	-2	2	23	0.6
1957	Bos-A	79	232	24	56	10	2	9	37	29	61	.241	.328	.418	.746	93	1	-2	110	118	32	.702	0	0	0	-1	2	0.0
1958	Bos-A	50	136	10	27	3	0	6	14	12	47	.199	.268	.353	.621	66	-6	-7	105	85	13	.545	0	1	-1	2	2	-0.2
1959	Bos-A	3	3	1	1	1	0	0	1	0	2	.333	.333	.667	1.000	158	0	0	106	197	1	1.000	0	0	0	0	/2	0.0
	Det-A	76	215	25	60	8	0	7	24	17	49	.279	.332	.414	.746	93	1	-2	111	86	28	.667	2	0	1	-1	S23	0.1
	Yr	79	218	26	61	9	0	7	25	17	51	.280	.332	.417	.749	94	1	-2	111	93	29	.671	2	0	1	-1		0.1
1960	Phi-N	69	141	16	32	7	0	2	8	17	41	.227	.319	.319	.638	70	-4	-6	107	64	14	.552	0	3	-2	-4	3S/2	-1.1
1961	Chi-A	5	2	0	0	0	0	0	0	1	0	.000	.333	.000	.333	-2	-0	-0	99	0	0	.333	0	0	0	0	/3	0.0
	Min-A	47	112	11	19	3	1	7	19	8	31	.170	.231	.402	.633	62	-6	-7	106	113	10	.579	1	0	0	-2	32/S	-0.3
	Yr	52	114	11	19	3	1	7	19	9	31	.167	.234	.395	.629	61	-7	-7	106	102	11	.577	1	0	0	-2		-0.3
Total	10	729	2092	233	512	91	11	69	251	209	471	.245	.319	.398	.717	88	-22	-40	107	91	266	.671	11	15	-6	21	23/S	0.8
■ **PETE LePINE** LePine, Louis Joseph b: 9/5/1876, Montreal, Que., Can d: 12/3/49, Woonsocket, R.I. BL/TL, Deb: 7/21/02																												
1902	Det-A	30	96	8	20	3	2	1	19	8		.208	.269	.313	.582	63	-5	-5	99	190	9	.513	1			0	O/1	-0.4
■ **DON LEPPERT** Leppert, Don Eugene "Tiger" b: 11/20/30, Memphis, Tenn. BL/TR, 5'8", 175 lbs. Deb: 4/11/55																												
1955	Bal-A	40	70	6	8	0	1	0	2	9	10	.114	.215	.143	.358	-3	-10	-9	90	75	2	.303	1	1	-0	-3	2	-1.0
■ **DON LEPPERT** Leppert, Donald George b: 10/19/31, Indianapolis, Ind. BR/TR, 6'2", 220 lbs. Deb: 6/18/61 C																												
1961	Pit-N	22	60	6	16	2	1	3	5	1	11	.267	.279	.483	.762	98	-1	-0	99	53	5	.600	0	0	0	-0	C	0.1
1962	Pit-N	45	139	14	37	6	1	3	18	12	21	.266	.329	.388	.717	90	-2	-2	102	113	16	.615	0	1	-1	2	C	0.0
1963	Was-A	73	211	20	50	11	0	6	24	20	29	.237	.306	.374	.680	92	-3	-2	98	104	23	.592	0	0	0	-2	C	-0.3
1964	Was-A	50	122	6	19	3	0	3	12	11	32	.156	.226	.254	.480	33	-11	-11	101	127	7	.396	0	0	0	0	C	-0.9
Total	4	190	532	46	122	22	2	15	59	44	93	.229	.291	.363	.653	79	-16	-16	100	106	51	.577	0	1	-1	-0	C	-1.1
■ **DUTCH LERCHEN** Lerchen, Bertram Roe b: 4/4/1889, Detroit, Mich. d: 1/7/62, Detroit, Mich. TR , 5'8", 160 lbs. Deb: 8/14/10																												
1910	Bos-A	6	15	1	0	0	0	0	0	1		.000	.063	.000	.063	-81	-3	-3	99	0	0	.067	0			-0	/S	-0.3
■ **GEORGE LERCHEN** Lerchen, George Edward b: 12/1/22, Detroit, Mich. BB/TR, 5'11", 175 lbs. Deb: 4/15/52																												
1952	Det-A	14	32	1	5	1	0	1	3	7	10	.156	.308	.281	.589	65	-1	-1	99	93	3	.607	1	0	0	-0	/O	-0.1
1953	Cin-N	22	17	2	5	1	0	0	2	5	6	.294	.455	.353	.807	115	1	1	99	130	3	.917	0	0	0	-0	/O	0.0
Total	2	36	49	3	10	2	0	1	5	12	16	.204	.361	.306	.667	84	-1	-1	99	107	7	.718	1	0	0	-0	/O	-0.1

YEAR	TM/L	G	AB	R	H	2B	3B	HR	RBI	BB	SO	AVG	OBP	SLG	PRO	/A	BR	/A	PF	CHI	RC	TA	SB	CS	SBR	FR	POS	TPR
■ **WALT LERIAN** Lerian, Walter Irvin "Peck" b: 2/10/03, Baltimore, Md. d: 10/22/29, Baltimore, Md. BR/TR, 5'11", 170 lbs. Deb: 4/16/28																												
1928	Phi-N	96	239	28	65	16	2	2	25	41	29	.272	.385	.381	.766	97	2	0	104	92	37	.782	1			8	C	1.2
1929	Phi-N	105	273	28	61	13	2	7	25	53	37	.223	.354	.363	.716	71	-9	-13	110	71	37	.726	0			-2	*C	-0.5
Total	2	201	512	56	126	29	4	9	50	94	66	.246	.368	.371	.739	82	-7	-13	107	81	74	.751	1			6	C	0.7
■ **ROY LESLIE** Leslie, Roy Reid b: 8/23/1894, Bailey, Tex. d: 4/9/72, Sherman, Tex. BR/TR, 6'1", 175 lbs. Deb: 9/06/17																												
1917	Chi-N	7	19	1	4	0	0	0	1	1	5	.211	.250	.211	.461	40	-1	-1	105	96	1	.400	1			0	/1	-0.1
1919	StL-N	12	24	2	5	1	0	0	4	4	3	.208	.321	.250	.571	77	-1	-0	94	259	2	.526	0			0	/1	0.0
1922	Phi-N	141	513	44	139	23	2	6	50	37	49	.271	.320	.359	.679	66	-20	-30	113	88	58	.588	3	7	-3	-5	*1	-3.6
Total	3	160	556	47	148	24	2	6	55	42	57	.266	.318	.349	.667	66	-21	-31	112	96	61	.578	4	7		-5	1	-3.7
■ **SAM LESLIE** Leslie, Samuel Andrew "Sambo" b: 7/26/05, Moss Point, Miss. d: 1/21/79, Pascagoula, Miss. BL/TL, 6', 192 lbs. Deb: 10/06/29																												
1929	NY-N	1	1	0	0	0	0	0	1	0	0	.000	.000	.000	.000	-99	-0	-0	100	0	0	.000	0			-0	/O	0.0
1930	NY-N	2	2	0	1	0	0	0	0	0	1	.500	.500	.500	1.000	146	0	0	98	0	0	1.000	0			0	H	0.0
1931	NY-N	53	53	11	16	4	0	3	5	1	2	.302	.315	.547	.862	132	2	2	97	47	9	.892	3			0	/1	0.1
1932	NY-N	77	75	5	22	4	0	1	15	2	5	.293	.329	.387	.716	93	-1	-1	99	174	10	.623	0			0	/1	0.0
1933	NY-N	40	137	21	44	12	3	3	27	12	9	.321	.380	.518	.898	157	9	10	99	127	27	.866	0			1	1	1.0
	Bro-N	96	364	41	104	11	4	5	46	23	14	.286	.340	.379	.719	109	3	4	97	120	45	.612	1			-4	1	-0.1
	Yr	136	501	62	148	23	7	8	73	35	23	.295	.351	.417	.768	122	12	14	97	123	73	.686	1			-3		0.9
1934	Bro-N	146	546	75	181	29	6	9	102	69	34	.332	.409	.456	.865	139	27	31	95	136	108	.869	5			6	*1	2.4
1935	Bro-N	142	520	72	160	30	7	5	93	55	19	.308	.379	.421	.800	122	12	17	94	**146**	87	.763	4			-3	*1	1.1
1936	NY-N	117	417	49	123	19	5	6	54	23	16	.295	.335	.408	.743	99	-1	-1	100	102	55	.631	0			3	1	-0.6
1937	NY-N	72	191	25	59	7	2	3	30	20	12	.309	.380	.414	.794	116	5	5	100	123	30	.729	1			2	1	0.4
1938	NY-N	76	154	12	39	7	1	1	16	11	6	.253	.307	.331	.638	73	-5	-6	103	107	16	.529	0			-1	1	-0.9
Total	10	822	2460	311	749	123	28	36	389	216	118	.304	.366	.421	.787	117	50	60	97	126	385	.752	14			3	1/O	3.4
■ **CHARLIE LETCHAS** Letchas, Charlie b: 10/3/15, Thomasville, Ga. BR/TR, 5'10", 150 lbs. Deb: 9/16/39																												
1939	Phi-N	12	44	2	10	2	0	1	3	1	2	.227	.244	.341	.585	59	-3	-3	94	62	3	.444	0			-1	2	-0.2
1941	Was-A	2	8	0	1	0	0	0	1	1	1	.125	.222	.125	.347	-6	-1	-1	98	340	0	.286	0	0	0	0	/2	0.0
1944	Phi-N	116	396	29	94	8	0	0	33	32	27	.237	.298	.258	.555	57	-22	-22	100	116	30	.433	0			3	23S	-0.9
1946	Phi-N	6	13	1	3	0	0	0	0	1	1	.231	.286	.231	.516	50	-1	-1	95	0	1	.400	0			-0	/2	0.0
Total	4	136	461	32	108	10	0	1	37	35	31	.234	.291	.262	.554	56	-27	-26	99	112	35	.448	0	0		2	/23S	-1.1
■ **TOM LETCHER** Letcher, Thomas F. b: 1868, Grand Rapids, Mich. Deb: 9/27/1891																												
1891	CM-a	6	21	3	4	1	0	0	2	0	1	.190	.190	.238	.429	22	-2	-2	112	116	1	.353	1			0	/O	-0.1
■ **JESSE LEVAN** Levan, Jesse Roy b: 7/15/26, Reading, Pa. BL/TR, 6', 172 lbs. Deb: 9/27/47																												
1947	Phi-N	2	9	3	4	0	0	0	1	0	0	.444	.444	.444	.889	137	0	0	100	82	2	.800	0			-1	/O	0.0
1954	Was-A	7	10	1	3	0	0	0	0	0	0	.300	.300	.300	.600	66	-0	-0	98	0	1	.429	0	0	0	0	/31	0.0
1955	Was-A	16	16	1	3	0	0	1	4	0	2	.188	.188	.375	.563	53	-1	-1	91	166	1	.429	0	0	0	0	H	0.0
Total	3	25	35	5	10	0	0	1	5	0	2	.286	.286	.371	.657	80	-1	-1	95	97	3	.500	0	0		-1	/3O1	0.0
■ **JIM LEVEY** Levey, James Julius b: 9/13/06, Pittsburgh, Pa. d: 3/14/70, Dallas, Tex. BB/TR, 5'10.5", 154 lbs. Deb: 9/17/30																												
1930	StL-A	8	37	7	9	2	0	0	3	3	2	.243	.300	.297	.597	48	-3	-3	108	78	3	.500	0	0	0	0	/S	-0.1
1931	StL-A	139	498	53	104	19	2	5	38	35	83	.209	.264	.285	.549	43	-41	-43	102	82	38	.478	13	8	-1	-15	*S	-4.2
1932	StL-A	152	568	59	159	30	8	4	63	21	48	.280	.310	.382	.692	78	-19	-19	100	94	66	.600	6	4	-1	-19	*S	-2.5
1933	StL-A	141	529	43	103	10	4	2	36	26	68	.195	.237	.240	.477	23	-56	-67	115	92	30	.370	4	6	-2	-6	*S	-6.1
Total	4	440	1632	162	375	61	14	11	140	85	201	.230	.272	.305	.576	48	-119	-132	106	89	138	.482	23	18	-4	-39	S	-12.9
■ **CHARLIE LEVIS** Levis, Charles H. b: 6/21/1860, St.Louis, Mo. d: 10/16/26, St.Louis, Mo. Deb: 4/17/1884																												
1884	Bal-U	87	373	59	85	11	4	6		3		.228	.234	.327	.561	80	-5	-11	110	0	29	.434	0			-0	*1	-1.0
	Was-U	1	3	0	0	0	0	0		0		.000	.000	.000	.000	-99	-1	-1	97	0	0	.000	0			0	/1	0.0
	Yr	88	376	59	85	11	4	6		3		.226	.232	.324	.557	78	-6	-12	110	0	29	.430	0			-0		-1.0
	Ind-a	3	10	0	2	0	0	0		0		.200	.200	.200	.400	34	-1	-1	96	0	0	.250				0	/1	0.0
1885	Bal-a	1	4	2	1	0	0	0		0		.250	.400	.250	.650	106	0	0	106	0	0	.667				0	/1	0.0
Total	2	92	390	61	88	11	4	6		3		.226	.234	.321	.554	78	-6	-12	110	0	30	.427				-0	/1	-1.0
■ **ED LEVY** Levy, Edward Clarence (born Edward Clarence Whitner) b: 10/28/16, Birmingham, Ala. BR/TR, 6'5.5", 190 lbs. Deb: 4/16/40																												
1940	Phi-N	1	1	0	0	0	0	0	0	0	0	.000	.000	.000	.000	-99	-0	-0	97	0	0	.000	0			0	H	0.0
1942	NY-A	13	41	5	5	0	0	0	3	4	5	.122	.200	.122	.322	-8	-6	-6	99	211	1	.263	1	0	0	1	1	-0.4
1944	NY-A	40	153	12	37	11	2	4	29	6	19	.242	.270	.418	.689	89	-2	-3	106	140	17	.597	1	1	-0	-2	O	-0.7
Total	3	54	195	17	42	11	2	4	32	10	24	.215	.254	.354	.608	69	-8	-9	105	155	18	.519	2	1		-2	/O1	-1.1
■ **ALLAN LEWIS** Lewis, Allan Sydney "The Panamanian Express" b: 12/12/41, Colon, Panama BB/TR, 6', 170 lbs. Deb: 4/11/67																												
1967	KC-A	34	6	7	1	0	0	0	0	0	3	.167	.167	.167	.333	-1	-1	-1	100	0	-6	1.500	14	5	1	0	R	0.1
1968	Oak-A	26	4	9	1	0	0	0	0	1	0	.250	.400	.250	.650	102	0	0	98	0	-2	1.429	8	4	0	-0	/O	0.0
1969	Oak-A	12	1	2	0	0	0	0	0	0	0	.000	.000	.000	.000	-99	-0	-0	92	0	0	.000	0	0	0	0	R	0.0
1970	Oak-A	25	8	8	2	0	0	1	1	0	0	.250	.250	.625	.875	138	0	0	97	51	1	1.714	7	1	2	-0	/O	0.1
1972	Oak-A	24	10	5	2	1	0	0	2	0	1	.200	.200	.300	.500	49	-1	-1	97	279	-1	1.000	8	3	1	-1	/O	0.0
1973	Oak-A	35	0	16	0	0	0	0	0	0	0	—	—	—	—	—	0	0	87	—	-1	1.750	7	4	-0	-0	/O	0.0
Total	6	156	29	47	6	1	0	1	3	1	4	.207	.233	.345	.578	68	-1	-1	97	106	-8	1.375	44	17	3	-2	/O	0.2
■ **FRED LEWIS** Lewis, Frederick Miller b: 10/13/1858, Buffalo, N.Y. d: 6/5/45, Utica, N.Y. BB/TR, 5'10.5", 194 lbs. Deb: 7/02/1881																												
1881	Bos-N	27	114	17	25	6	0	0	9	7	5	.219	.264	.272	.536	75	-4	-2	91	87	8	.427				-3	O	-0.5
1883	Phi-N	38	160	21	40	7	0	0	51	4	13	.250	.268	.294	.562	78	-5	-3	90	362	13	.425				-1	O	-0.2
	StL-a	49	209	37	63	8	4	1		1		.301	.305	.392	.697	114	5	2	108	0	26	.568				-2	O	0.1
1884	StL-a	73	300	59	97	25	3	0		16		.323	.366	.427	.792	146	20	15	110	0	48	.729				3	O	1.5
	StL-U	8	30	6	9	1	0	0		3		.300	.364	.333	.697	132	1	1	104	0	4	.619	0			0	/O	0.1
1885	StL-N	45	181	12	53	9	0	1	27	9	10	.293	.326	.359	.685	131	4	6	92	122	22	.578				5	O	0.9
1886	Cin-a	77	324	72	103	14	6	2		20		.318	.365	.417	.782	153	17	19	96	0	53	.756	8			-3	O/3	1.1
Total	5	317	1318	224	390	70	13	4	87	60	28	.296	.330	.378	.708	126	37	38	100	67	174	.619	8			-1	O/3	3.0
■ **DUFFY LEWIS** Lewis, George Edward b: 4/18/1888, San Francisco, Cal d: 6/17/79, Salem, N.H. BL/TL, 5'10.5", 165 lbs. Deb: 4/16/10 C																												
1910	Bos-A	151	541	64	153	29	7	8	68	32		.283	.328	.407	.734	131	16	17	99	105	76	.686	10			14	*O	2.5
1911	Bos-A	130	469	64	144	32	4	7	86	25		.307	.355	.437	.792	122	11	12	99	131	77	.772	11			7	*O	0.9
1912	Bos-A	154	581	85	165	36	9	6	109	52		.284	.346	.408	.754	108	10	4	107	**151**	86	.724	9			10	*O	0.5
1913	Bos-A	149	551	54	164	31	12	0	90	30	55	.298	.336	.397	.734	111	8	5	103	155	77	.680	12			11	*O/P3	0.9
1914	Bos-A	146	510	53	142	37	9	2	79	57	22	.278	.357	.398	.755	130	16	18	98	150	75	.767	41	31	-6	4	*O	0.7
1915	Bos-A	152	557	69	162	31	7	2	76	45	63	.291	.348	.382	.731	119	11	12	99	125	80	.687	14	7	0	-5	*O	-0.1
1916	Bos-A	152	563	56	151	29	5	1	56	33	56	.268	.313	.343	.656	104	-4	0	94	108	68	.597	16			1	*O	-0.8
1917	Bos-A	150	553	55	167	29	9	1	65	29	54	.302	.342	.392	.735	115	14	8	108	112	77	.671	8			7	*O	0.7
1919	NY-A	141	559	67	152	23	4	7	89	17	42	.272	.293	.365	.658	80	-14	-18	106	**152**	61	.563	8			-7	*O	-3.6
1920	NY-A	107	365	34	99	8	1	4	61	24	32	.271	.320	.332	.651	71	-14	-15	102	161	38	.544	2	8	-4	-0	O	-2.7
1921	Was-A	27	102	11	19	4	1	0	14	8	10	.186	.252	.245	.497	28	-11	-11	99	203	7	.417	1	1	-0	-2	O	-1.4
Total	11	1459	5351	612	1518	289	68	38	793	352	334	.284	.333	.384	.717	107	42	32	101	136	721	.665	132	47		39	*O/3P	-2.4
■ **JACK LEWIS** Lewis, John David b: 2/12/1884, Pittsburgh, Pa. d: 2/25/56, Steubenville, Ohio BR/TR, 5'8", 158 lbs. Deb: 9/16/11																												
1911	Bos-A	18	59	7	16	0	0	0	6	7		.271	.368	.271	.639	80	-1	-1	99	129	7	.628	2			1	2	0.0
1914	Pit-F	117	394	32	92	14	5	1	48	17	46	.234	.265	.302	.567	66	-20	-17	94	145	37	.480	9			-47	*2/S	-6.7
1915	Pit-F	82	231	24	61	6	5	0	26	8	31	.264	.289	.333	.622	81	-5	-6	104	122	26	.541	7			2	2S/O13	-0.3

YEAR	TM/L	G	AB	R	H	2B	3B	HR	RBI	BB	SO	AVG	OBP	SLG	PRO	/A	BR	/A	PF	CHI	RC	TA	SB	CS	SBR	FR	POS	TPR
Total	3	217	684	63	169	20	10	1	80	32	77	.247	.283	.310	.593	73	-26	-24	98	136	70	.513	18			-44	2/SO13	-7.0
■ BUDDY LEWIS Lewis, John Kelly b: 8/10/16, Gastonia, N.C. BL/TR, 6'1", 175 lbs. Deb: 9/16/35																												
1935	Was-A	8	28	0	3	0	0	0	2	0	5	.107	.107	.107	.214	-49	-6	-6	92	226	0	.120	0	0	0	1	/3	-0.4
1936	Was-A	143	601	100	175	21	13	6	67	47	46	.291	.347	.399	.746	86	-16	-14	98	81	83	.688	6	6	-2	8	*3	-0.5
1937	Was-A	156	668	107	210	32	6	10	79	52	44	.314	.367	.425	.792	105	-1	4	94	76	105	.756	11	5	0	-19	*3	-1.0
1938	Was-A	151	656	122	194	35	9	12	91	58	35	.296	.354	.431	.785	101	-6	-0	95	85	101	.762	17	9	-0	0	*3	0.4
1939	Was-A	140	536	87	171	23	**16**	10	75	72	27	.319	.402	.478	.879	137	20	29	90	85	106	.892	10	9	-2	10	*3	3.1
1940	Was-A	148	600	101	190	38	10	6	63	74	36	.317	.393	.443	.836	125	16	22	93	71	109	.828	15	10	-2	-0	*O3	1.4
1941	Was-A	149	569	97	169	29	11	9	72	82	30	.297	.386	.434	.820	119	15	17	98	99	99	.805	10	7	-1	7	O3	1.8
1945	Was-A	69	258	42	86	14	7	2	37	37	15	.333	.423	.465	.888	169	20	22	93	102	54	.899	1	2	-1	3	O	2.2
1946	Was-A	150	582	82	170	28	13	7	45	59	26	.292	.359	.421	.780	128	13	19	92	68	92	.732	5	3	-0	3	*O	1.5
1947	Was-A	140	506	67	132	15	4	6	48	51	27	.261	.330	.342	.672	90	-9	-7	97	98	56	.582	6	6	-2	-2	*O	-1.6
1949	Was-A	95	257	25	63	14	4	3	28	41	12	.245	.355	.366	.721	100	-3	0	91	93	36	.693	2	2	-1	-3	O	-0.5
Total	11	1349	5261	830	1563	249	93	71	607	573	303	.297	.368	.420	.789	112	44	87	94	85	841	.767	83	59	-11	8	3O	6.4
■ JOHNNY LEWIS Lewis, Johnny Joe b: 8/10/39, Greenville, Ala. BL/TR, 6'1", 189 lbs. Deb: 4/14/64 C																												
1964	StL-N	40	94	10	22	2	2	2	7	13	23	.234	.327	.362	.689	84	-1	-2	112	72	11	.653	2	2	-1	-1	O	-0.3
1965	NY-N	148	477	64	117	15	3	15	45	59	117	.245	.332	.384	.716	101	1	1	100	83	61	.664	4	7	-3	-8	*O	-1.4
1966	NY-N	65	166	21	32	6	1	5	20	21	43	.193	.283	.331	.615	75	-7	-5	94	120	17	.578	2	0	1	-2	O	-0.8
1967	NY-N	13	34	2	4	1	0	0	2	2	11	.118	.167	.147	.314	-10	-5	-5	99	166	1	.233	0	0	0	0	O	-0.5
Total	4	266	771	97	175	24	6	22	74	95	194	.227	.314	.359	.673	89	-11	-11	100	93	91	.633	8	9	-3	-11	O	-3.0
■ PHIL LEWIS Lewis, Philip b: 10/7/1883, Pittsburgh, Pa. d: 8/8/59, Port Wentworth, Ga. BR/TR, 6', 195 lbs. Deb: 4/14/05																												
1905	Bro-N	118	433	32	110	9	2	3	33	16		.254	.281	.305	.585	80	-13	-11	96	86	43	.508	16			-6	*S	-1.5
1906	Bro-N	136	452	40	110	8	4	0	37	43		.243	.309	.279	.588	99	-7	0	87	109	44	.535	14			-19	*S	-1.3
1907	Bro-N	136	475	52	118	11	1	0	30	23		.248	.283	.276	.559	82	-13	-10	94	89	43	.476	16			-24	*S	-3.2
1908	Bro-N	118	415	22	91	5	6	1	30	13		.219	.243	.267	.510	68	-17	-15	95	103	28	.410	9			-6	*S	-2.6
Total	4	508	1775	146	429	33	13	4	130	95		.242	.280	.282	.562	82	-49	-36	93	97	157	.483	55			-55	S	-8.6
■ BILL LEWIS Lewis, William Henry "Buddy" b: 10/15/04, Ripley, Tenn. d: 10/24/77, Memphis, Tenn. BR/TR, 5'9", 165 lbs. Deb: 6/03/33																												
1933	StL-N	15	35	8	14	1	0	1	8	2	3	.400	.432	.514	.947	166	3	3	102	143	8	.952	0			0	/C	0.3
1935	Bos-N	6	4	1	0	0	0	0	0	1	1	.000	.200	.000	.200	-43	-1	-1	96	0	0	.250	0			0	/C	0.0
1936	Bos-N	29	62	11	19	2	0	0	3	12	7	.306	.419	.339	.758	112	1	2	95	51	10	.767	0			1	C	0.4
Total	3	50	101	20	33	3	0	1	11	15	11	.327	.414	.386	.800	124	4	4	97	78	19	.794	0			1	/C	0.7
■ CARLOS LEZCANO Lezcano, Carlos Manuel (Rubio) b: 9/30/55, Arecibo, P.R. BR/TR, 6'2", 185 lbs. Deb: 4/10/80																												
1980	Chi-N	42	88	15	18	4	1	3	12	11	29	.205	.300	.375	.675	82	-2	-2	106	113	9	.613	1	2	-1	-1	O	-0.5
1981	Chi-N	7	14	1	1	0	0	0	2	0	4	.071	.071	.071	.143	-57	-3	-3	104	785	0	.077	0	0	0	-1	/O	-0.3
Total	2	49	102	16	19	4	1	3	14	11	33	.186	.272	.333	.605	65	-4	-5	106	196	9	.553	1	2	-1	-2	/O	-0.8
■ SIXTO LEZCANO Lezcano, Sixto Joaquin (Curras) b: 11/28/53, Arecibo, P.R. BR/TR, 5'10", 165 lbs. Deb: 9/10/74																												
1974	Mil-A	15	54	5	13	2	0	2	9	4	9	.241	.293	.389	.682	93	-1	-1	102	139	6	.591	1	1	-0	2	O	0.0
1975	Mil-A	134	429	55	106	19	3	11	43	46	93	.247	.326	.382	.708	99	-0	-0	100	84	51	.638	5	5	-2	-4	*O/D	-0.9
1976	Mil-A	145	513	53	146	19	5	7	56	51	112	.285	.352	.382	.734	116	10	11	99	101	70	.685	14	10	-2	8	*O/D	1.5
1977	Mil-A	109	400	50	109	21	4	21	49	52	78	.273	.359	.503	.862	139	17	20	95	78	72	.856	6	5	-1	8	*O	2.3
1978	Mil-A	132	442	62	129	21	4	15	61	64	83	.292	.383	.459	.842	128	22	19	106	99	81	.844	3	3	-1	8	*O/D	2.3
1979	Mil-A	138	473	84	152	29	3	28	101	77	74	.321	.420	.573	.992	165	45	45	100	112	115	1.060	4	3	-1	0	*O	3.7
1980	Mil-A	112	411	51	94	19	3	18	55	39	75	.229	.300	.421	.721	101	-4	-1	95	96	53	.667	1	1	-0	0	*O/D	-0.2
1981	StL-N	72	214	26	57	8	2	5	28	40	40	.266	.382	.393	.774	118	7	7	102	111	33	.747	0	1	-1	-7	O	-0.2
1982	SD-N	138	470	73	136	26	6	16	84	78	69	.289	.393	.472	.865	154	28	33	92	124	90	.879	2	1	0	12	*O	4.4
1983	SD-N	97	317	41	74	11	2	8	49	47	66	.233	.334	.356	.691	92	-3	-3	99	144	39	.641	0	0	0	1	O	-0.3
	Phi-N	18	39	8	11	1	0	0	7	5	9	.282	.364	.308	.671	87	-0	-0	101	231	5	.643	1	0	0	-1	O	0.0
	Yr	115	356	49	85	12	2	8	56	52	75	.239	.337	.351	.689	92	-3	-3	99	159	48	.661	1	0	0	0		-0.3
1984	Phi-N	109	256	36	71	6	2	14	40	38	43	.277	.371	.480	.851	135	13	12	102	95	44	.817	0	1	-1	-4	O	0.4
1985	Pit-N	72	116	16	24	2	0	3	9	35	17	.207	.395	.302	.696	95	2	1	103	81	16	.747	0	0	0	-3	O	-0.2
Total	12	1291	4134	560	1122	184	34	148	591	576	768	.271	.363	.440	.803	125	136	143	99	105	675	.804	37	31	-8	19	*O/D	12.8
■ STEVE LIBBY Libby, Stephen Augustus b: 12/8/1853, Scarborough, Me. 6'1.5", 168 lbs. Deb: 5/10/1879																												
1879	Buf-N	1	2	0	0	0	0	0	0	0	1	.000	.000	.000	.000	-88	-0	-0	114	0	0	.000				0	/1	0.0
■ AL LIBKE Libke, Albert Walter b: 9/12/18, Tacoma, Wash. BL/TR, 6'4", 215 lbs. Deb: 4/19/45																												
1945	Cin-N	130	449	41	127	23	5	4	53	34	62	.283	.336	.383	.719	106	-1	2	94	102	59	.650	6			2	*O/P1	0.0
1946	Cin-N	124	431	32	109	22	1	5	42	43	50	.253	.322	.343	.665	85	-7	-8	104	98	46	.568	0			-8	*O/P	-1.9
Total	2	254	880	73	236	45	6	9	95	77	112	.268	.329	.364	.693	95	-7	-6	99	100	105	.615	6			-6	O/P1	-1.9
■ FRANKIE LIBRAN Libran, Francisco (Rosas) b: 5/6/48, Mayaguez, P.R. BR/TR, 6', 168 lbs. Deb: 9/03/69																												
1969	SD-N	10	10	1	1	1	0	0	1	1	2	.100	.182	.200	.382	7	-1	-1	97	200	0	.333	0	0	0	-0	/S	0.0
■ JOHN LICKERT Lickert, John Wilbur b: 4/4/60, Pittsburgh, Pa. BR/TR, 5'11", 175 lbs. Deb: 9/19/81																												
1981	Bos-A	1	0	0	0	0	0	0	0	0	0	—	—	—	—	—	0	0	106	—	—	—	0	0	0	0	/C	0.0
■ FRED LIESE Liese, Frederick Richard b: 10/7/1885, Wisconsin d: 6/30/67, Los Angeles, Cal. TL , Deb: 4/14/10																												
1910	Bos-N	5	4	0	0	0	0	0	0	1	2	.000	.200	.000	.200	-36	-1	-1	114	0	0	.250	0			0	H	0.0
■ GENE LILLARD Lillard, Robert Eugene b: 11/12/13, Santa Barbara, Cal BR/TR, 5'10.5", 178 lbs. Deb: 5/08/36																												
1936	Chi-N	19	34	6	7	1	0	0	2	3	8	.206	.270	.235	.506	35	-3	-3	105	89	2	.367	0			0	/S3	-0.1
1939	Chi-N	23	10	3	1	0	0	0	0	6	3	.100	.438	.100	.538	51	-0	-0	101	0	1	.778	0			0	P	0.0
1940	StL-N	2	0	0	0	0	0	0	0	0	0	—	—	—	—	—	0	0	102	—	—	—	0			0	/P	0.0
Total	3	44	44	9	8	1	0	0	2	9	11	.182	.321	.205	.525	42	-3	-3	104	62	4	.500	0			0	/PS3	-0.1
■ BILL LILLARD Lillard, William Beverly b: 1/10/18, Goleta, Cal. BR/TR, 5'10", 170 lbs. Deb: 9/11/39																												
1939	Phi-A	7	19	4	6	1	0	0	1	3	1	.316	.409	.368	.778	103	0	0	97	48	3	.769	0	0	0	0	/S	0.1
1940	Phi-A	73	206	26	49	8	2	1	21	28	28	.238	.332	.311	.643	71	-9	-8	96	113	23	.578	0	1	-1	-9	S/2	-1.0
Total	2	80	225	30	55	9	2	1	22	31	29	.244	.339	.316	.654	74	-9	-8	96	108	27	.592	0	1	-1	-9	/S2	-0.9
■ JIM LILLIE Lillie, James J. "Grasshopper" b: 1862, New Haven, Conn. d: 11/9/1890, Kansas City, Mo. Deb: 5/17/1883																												
1883	Buf-N	50	201	25	47	7	3	1	29	1	31	.234	.238	.313	.551	66	-8	-8	100	155	15	.416				-5	O/PCS32	-1.0
1884	Buf-N	114	471	68	105	12	5	3	53	5	71	.223	.231	.289	.520	59	-20	-25	107	128	32	.385				12	*O/P	-1.2
1885	Buf-N	112	430	49	107	13	3	2	30	6	39	.249	.259	.307	.566	83	-9	-8	99	77	35	.427				-1	*O/S1	-1.1
1886	KC-N	114	416	37	73	9	0	0	22	11	80	.175	.197	.197	.394	19	-39	-43	107	89	19	.309	13			9	*O/P	-2.8
Total	4	390	1518	179	332	41	11	6	134	23	221	.219	.230	.272	.502	54	-77	-85	104	107	102	.379	13			15	O/PSC123	-6.1
■ BOB LILLIS Lillis, Robert Perry b: 6/2/30, Altadena, Cal. BR/TR, 5'11", 160 lbs. Deb: 8/30/58 MC																												
1958	LA-N	20	69	10	27	3	1	1	5	4	2	.391	.432	.507	.940	141	5	4	105	55	14	.911	1	2	-1	2	S	0.7
1959	LA-N	30	48	7	11	2	0	0	2	3	4	.229	.275	.271	.545	45	-4	-4	102	62	4	.432	0	0	0	1	S	-0.1
1960	LA-N	48	60	6	16	4	0	0	6	2	6	.267	.290	.333	.624	61	-3	-4	115	122	6	.522	2	0	1	4	S3/2	0.2
1961	LA-N	19	9	0	1	0	0	0	1	1	1	.111	.200	.111	.311	-14	-1	-2	102	403	0	.200	0	0	0	0	3/2S	-0.1
	StL-N	86	230	24	50	4	0	0	21	7	13	.217	.247	.235	.482	25	-23	-27	113	157	12	.349	3	3	-1	-1	S2	-2.0
	Yr	105	239	24	51	4	0	0	22	8	14	.213	.245	.230	.475	24	-25	-28	111	205	13	.345	3	3	-1	-1		-2.1
1962	Hou-N	129	457	38	114	12	4	1	30	28	23	.249	.293	.300	.593	64	-26	-22	93	84	40	.483	7	3	0	5	S2/3	-0.3
1963	Hou-N	147	469	31	93	13	1	1	19	15	35	.198	.230	.237	.466	37	-39	-35	92	70	24	.343	3	4	-2	-15	*S2/3	-4.2

YEAR	TM/L	G	AB	R	H	2B	3B	HR	RBI	BB	SO	AVG	OBP	SLG	PRO	/A	BR	/A	PF	CHI	RC	TA	SB	CS	SBR	FR	POS	TPR
1964	Hou-N	109	332	31	89	11	2	0	17	11	10	.268	.292	.313	.605	73	-13	-12	96	67	27	.458	4	9	-4	1	2S3	-0.8
1965	Hou-N	124	408	34	90	12	1	0	20	20	10	.221	.267	.255	.522	54	-28	-22	89	80	27	.400	2	2	-1	-15	*S/32	-2.8
1966	Hou-N	68	164	14	38	6	0	0	11	7	4	.232	.263	.268	.531	49	-11	-11	97	105	10	.380	1	1	-0	-7	2S/3	-1.5
1967	Hou-N	37	82	3	20	1	0	0	5	1	8	.244	.253	.256	.509	49	-6	-5	94	99	4	.328	0	1	-1	-0	S/23	-0.3
Total	10	817	2328	198	549	68	9	3	137	99	116	.236	.271	.277	.548	54	-149	-138	96	88	167	.431	23	25	-8	-25	S2/3	-11.2
■ **LOU LIMMER** Limmer, Louis b: 3/10/25, New York, N.Y. BL/TL, 6'2", 190 lbs. Deb: 4/22/51																												
1951	Phi-A	94	214	25	34	9	1	5	30	28	40	.159	.256	.280	.537	42	-17	-19	106	143	17	.484	1	0	0	5	1	-1.3
1954	Phi-A	115	316	41	73	10	3	14	32	35	37	.231	.308	.415	.722	98	-3	-2	98	70	40	.667	2	3	-1	2	1	-0.3
Total	2	209	530	66	107	19	4	19	62	63	77	.202	.287	.360	.647	74	-20	-21	101	100	57	.595	3	3	-1	7	1	-1.6
■ **RUFINO LINARES** Linares, Rufino (born Rufino De La Cruz (Linares)) b: 2/28/51, San Pedro De Macoris, D.R. BR/TR, 6', 170 lbs. Deb: 4/10/81																												
1981	Atl-N	78	253	27	67	9	2	5	25	9	28	.265	.290	.375	.666	88	-5	-5	100	89	23	.554	8	4	0	1	O	-0.5
1982	Atl-N	77	191	28	57	7	1	2	17	7	29	.298	.327	.377	.704	90	-1	-3	107	85	20	.582	5	2	0	-0	O	-0.3
1984	Atl-N	34	58	4	12	3	0	1	10	6	12	.207	.281	.310	.592	60	-3	-3	110	187	5	.511	0	0	0	0	O	-0.3
1985	Cal-A	18	43	7	11	2	0	3	11	2	5	.256	.289	.512	.801	113	1	1	101	141	6	.788	2	0	1	-1	D/O	0.0
Total	4	207	545	66	147	21	3	11	63	24	74	.270	.302	.380	.682	88	-8	-10	103	103	55	.610	15	6	1	0	O/D	-1.1
■ **CARL LIND** Lind, Henry Carl "Hooks" b: 9/19/03, New Orleans, La. d: 8/2/46, New York, N.Y. BR/TR, 6', 160 lbs. Deb: 9/14/27																												
1927	Cle-A	12	37	2	5	0	0	0	1	5	7	.135	.256	.135	.391	4	-5	-5	97	67	2	.375	1	0	0	-0	2/S	-0.4
1928	Cle-A	154	650	102	191	42	4	1	54	36	48	.294	.331	.375	.706	81	-15	-20	106	65	80	.618	8	7	-2	5	*2	-0.8
1929	Cle-A	66	225	19	54	8	1	0	13	13	17	.240	.282	.284	.566	46	-18	-18	100	69	18	.445	0	2	-1	8	2/3	-0.9
1930	Cle-A	24	69	8	17	3	0	0	6	3	7	.246	.278	.290	.568	42	-6	-6	105	100	5	.434	0	1	-1	2	S/2	-0.1
Total	4	256	981	131	267	53	5	1	74	57	79	.272	.313	.339	.652	67	-44	-49	104	68	106	.552	9	10	-3	14	2/S3	-2.2
■ **JACK LIND** Lind, Jackson Hugh b: 6/8/46, Denver, Col. BB/TR, 6', 170 lbs. Deb: 9/10/74																												
1974	Mil-A	9	17	4	4	2	0	0	1	3	2	.235	.350	.353	.703	100	0	0	102	65	2	.643	0	0	0	-1	/S2	0.0
1975	Mil-A	17	20	1	1	0	0	0	0	2	12	.050	.136	.050	.186	-46	-4	-4	100	0	0	.211	1	0	0	-0	/S31	-0.2
Total	2	26	37	5	5	2	0	0	1	5	14	.135	.238	.189	.427	23	-4	-4	101	31	2	.406	1	0	0	-1	/S321	-0.2
■ **JOSE LIND** Lind, Jose (Salgado) b: 5/1/64, Toabaja, P.R. BR/TR, 5'11", 155 lbs. Deb: 8/28/87																												
1987	Pit-N	35	143	21	46	8	4	0	11	8	12	.322	.358	.434	.791	104	2	1	104	68	21	.699	2	1	0	2	2	0.4
1988	Pit-N	154	611	82	160	24	4	2	49	42	75	.262	.309	.324	.633	84	-14	-12	98	102	63	.547	15	4	2	2	*2	-0.3
Total	2	189	754	103	206	32	8	2	60	50	87	.273	.318	.345	.663	88	-12	-12	99	95	84	.580	17	5	2	4	2	0.1
■ **EM LINDBECK** Lindbeck, Emerit Desmond b: 8/27/35, Kewanee, Ill. BL/TR, 6', 185 lbs. Deb: 4/22/60																												
1960	Det-A	2	1	0	0	0	0	0	0	1	0	.000	.500	.000	.500	47	0	0	102	0	0	1.000	0	0	0	0	H	0.0
■ **JOHNNY LINDELL** Lindell, John Harlan b: 8/30/16, Greeley, Colo. d: 8/27/85, Newport Beach, Cal. BR/TR, 6'4.5", 217 lbs. Deb: 4/18/41																												
1941	NY-A	1	1	0	0	0	0	0	0	0	0	.000	.000	.000	.000	-99	-0	-0	98	0	0	.000	0	0	0	0	H	0.0
1942	NY-A	27	24	1	6	1	0	0	4	0	5	.250	.250	.292	.542	52	-2	-2	99	201	2	.389	0	0	0	-0	P	0.0
1943	NY-A	122	441	53	108	17	**12**	4	51	51	55	.245	.329	.365	.694	107	1	3	96	110	53	.619	2	5	-2	0	*O	-0.2
1944	NY-A	149	594	91	178	33	**16**	18	103	44	56	.300	.351	.500	.851	133	29	24	106	112	102	.800	5	4	-1	5	*O	2.5
1945	NY-A	41	159	26	45	6	3	1	20	17	10	.283	.363	.377	.740	107	3	2	107	122	23	.689	2	1	0	2	O	0.2
1946	NY-A	102	332	41	86	10	5	10	40	32	47	.259	.328	.410	.738	105	1	1	100	92	44	.669	4	1	1	3	O1	0.0
1947	NY-A	127	476	66	131	18	7	11	67	32	70	.275	.322	.412	.734	107	-0	2	97	110	61	.635	1	2	-1	-5	*O	-0.9
1948	NY-A	88	309	58	98	17	2	13	55	35	50	.317	.387	.511	.898	137	15	15	100	96	62	.881	0	0	0	2	O	1.3
1949	NY-A	78	211	33	51	10	0	6	27	35	27	.242	.350	.374	.724	91	-3	-3	100	95	29	.692	3	0	1	-5	O	-0.7
1950	NY-A	7	21	2	4	0	0	0	2	4	2	.190	.320	.190	.510	33	-2	-2	99	173	1	.444	0	0	0	-2	/O	-0.3
	StL-N	36	113	16	21	5	2	5	16	15	24	.186	.287	.398	.685	76	-4	-5	103	103	12	.629	0			-2	O	-0.7
1953	Pit-N	58	91	11	26	6	1	4	15	16	15	.286	.404	.505	.909	133	5	5	102	101	18	.901	0	0	0	2	P/1	1.1
	Phi-N	11	18	3	7	1	0	0	2	6	2	.389	.542	.444	.986	163	2	2	99	97	5	1.273	0	0	0	-1	/PO	0.2
	Yr	69	109	14	33	7	1	4	17	22	17	.303	.429	.495	.924	138	7	7	101	102	26	1.026	0	0	0	2		1.3
1954	Phi-N	7	5	0	1	0	0	0	2	2	3	.200	.429	.200	.629	71	-0	-0	99	787	1	.750	0	0	0	0	H	0.0
Total	12	854	2795	401	762	124	48	72	404	289	366	.273	.344	.429	.773	113	47	44	101	108	412	.743	17	13		-2	O/P1	2.5
■ **JIM LINDEMAN** Lindeman, James William b: 1/10/62, Evanston, Ill. BR/TR, 6'1", 200 lbs. Deb: 9/03/86																												
1986	StL-N	19	55	7	14	1	0	1	6	2	10	.255	.281	.327	.608	65	-3	-3	103	114	4	.477	1	1	-0	-1	1/3O	-0.4
1987	StL-N	75	207	20	43	13	0	8	28	11	56	.208	.258	.386	.644	69	-10	-10	99	107	20	.574	3	1	0	-1	O1	-1.3
1988	StL-N	17	43	3	9	1	0	2	7	2	9	.209	.244	.372	.617	72	-2	-2	104	127	4	.514	0	0	0	-2	O/1	-0.4
Total	3	111	305	30	66	15	0	11	41	15	75	.216	.260	.374	.634	69	-14	-14	100	111	28	.562	4	2	0	-4	/O13	-2.1
■ **BOB LINDEMANN** Lindemann, John Frederick Mann b: 6/5/1881, Philadelphia, Pa. d: 12/19/51, Williamsport, Pa. BB/TR, 6', 175 lbs. Deb: 8/28/01																												
1901	Phi-A	3	9	0	1	0	0	0	0	0		.111	.111	.111	.222	-38	-2	-2	100	0	0	.125	0			0	/O	0.0
■ **WALT LINDEN** Linden, Walter Charles b: 3/27/24, Chicago, Ill. BR/TR, 6'1", 190 lbs. Deb: 4/30/50																												
1950	Bos-N	3	5	0	2	1	0	0	0	1	0	.400	.500	.600	1.100	218	1	1	86	0	2	1.333	0			0	/C	0.1
■ **CHRIS LINDSAY** Lindsay, Christian Haller "Pinky" or "The Crab" b: 7/24/1878, Baker'S Yard, Moon Township, Beaver County, Pa d: 1/25/41, Cleveland, Ohio BR/TR, Deb: 7/06/05																												
1905	Det-A	88	329	38	88	14	1	0	31	18		.267	.305	.316	.622	101	-0	0	98	113	36	.548	10			1	1	0.0
1906	Det-A	141	499	59	112	16	2	0	33	45		.224	.289	.265	.553	69	-13	-18	108	96	44	.504	18			-4	*12/3	-2.7
Total	2	229	828	97	200	30	3	0	64	63		.242	.295	.285	.580	81	-13	-17	104	103	80	.521	28			-3	1/23	-2.7
■ **BILL LINDSAY** Lindsay, William Gibbons b: 2/24/1881, Madison, N.C. d: 7/14/63, Greensboro, N.C. BL/TR, 5'10.5", 165 lbs. Deb: 6/21/11																												
1911	Cle-A	19	66	6	16	2	0	0	5	2		.242	.275	.273	.548	52	-4	-4	103	94	5	.460	2			1	3/2	-0.3
■ **BILL LINDSEY** Lindsey, William Donald b: 4/12/60, Staten Island, N.Y. BR/TR, 6'3", 195 lbs. Deb: 7/18/87																												
1987	Chi-A	9	16	2	3	0	0	0	1	0	3	.188	.188	.188	.375	0	-2	-2	109	133	0	.200	0	0	0	1	/C	0.0
■ **CHUCK LINDSTROM** Lindstrom, Charles William b: 9/7/36, Chicago, Ill. BR/TR, 5'11", 175 lbs. Deb: 9/28/58																												
1958	Chi-A	1	1	1	1	0	1	0	1	1	0	1.000	1.000	3.000	4.000	974	1	1	98	134	3	—	0	0	0	0	/C	0.1
■ **FREDDY LINDSTROM** Lindstrom, Frederick Charles (born Frederick Anthony Lindstrom) b: 11/21/05, Chicago, Ill. d: 10/4/81, Chicago, Ill. BR/TR, 5'11", 170 lbs. Deb: 4/15/24 H																												
1924	NY-N	52	79	19	20	3	1	0	4	6	10	.253	.314	.316	.630	76	-3	-2	91	58	8	.583	3	1	0	2	23	0.0
1925	NY-N	104	356	43	102	15	12	4	33	22	20	.287	.332	.430	.761	94	-5	-4	99	71	48	.692	5	9	-4	-3	3/2S	-0.3
1926	NY-N	140	543	90	164	19	9	9	76	39	21	.302	.351	.420	.771	109	4	6	98	99	78	.739	11			-2	*3/O	0.5
1927	NY-N	138	562	107	172	36	8	7	58	40	40	.306	.354	.436	.790	111	8	8	100	73	85	.762	10			-5	3O	0.5
1928	NY-N	153	646	99	**231**	39	9	14	107	25	21	.358	.383	.511	.894	129	28	26	102	98	120	.896	15			15	*3	4.1
1929	NY-N	130	549	99	175	23	6	15	91	30	28	.319	.354	.464	.819	101	-1	-0	100	100	87	.789	10			9	*3	1.7
1930	NY-N	148	609	127	231	39	7	22	106	48	33	.379	.425	.575	.999	142	38	40	98	93	143	1.093	15			6	*3	4.2
1931	NY-N	78	303	38	91	12	6	5	36	26	12	.300	.356	.429	.785	114	4	5	97	94	47	.759	5			-5	O/2	-0.2
1932	NY-N	144	595	83	161	26	5	15	92	27	28	.271	.303	.407	.710	90	-10	-9	99	126	74	.636	6			-2	*O3	-1.8
1933	Pit-N	138	538	70	167	39	10	5	55	33	22	.310	.350	.448	.798	133	17	21	95	86	86	.722	1			7	*O	2.1
1934	Pit-N	97	383	59	111	24	4	4	49	23	21	.290	.333	.405	.738	92	-2	-5	105	112	51	.642	1			-2	O	-1.0
1935	Chi-N	90	342	49	94	22	4	3	62	10	13	.275	.297	.389	.686	84	-9	-9	99	161	37	.560	1			6	O3	-0.3
1936	Bro-N	26	106	12	28	4	0	0	10	5	7	.264	.297	.302	.599	59	-6	-6	105	117	9	.463	1			1	O	-0.6
Total	13	1438	5611	895	1747	301	81	103	779	334	276	.311	.351	.449	.800	110	64	71	99	100	873	.761	84	10		27	3O/2S	8.9
■ **CARL LINHART** Linhart, Carl James b: 12/14/29, Zborov, Czech. BL/TR, 5'11", 184 lbs. Deb: 8/02/52																												
1952	Det-A	3	2	0	0	0	0	0	0	0	0	.000	.000	.000	.000	-99	-1	-1	99	0	0	.000	0	0	0	0	H	0.0
■ **LARRY LINTZ** Lintz, Larry b: 10/10/49, Martinez, Cal. BB/TR, 5'9", 150 lbs. Deb: 7/14/73																												
1973	Mon-N	52	116	20	29	1	0	0	3	17	18	.250	.351	.259	.609	69	-4	-4	104	40	14	.659	12	4	1	-1	2S	0.0

YEAR	TM/L	G	AB	R	H	2B	3B	HR	RBI	BB	SO	AVG	OBP	SLG	PRO	/A	BR	/A	PF	CHI	RC	TA	SB	CS	SBR	FR	POS	TPR
1974	Mon-N	113	319	60	76	10	1	0	20	44	50	.238	.334	.276	.610	69	-10	-12	104	88	40	.730	50	7	11	7	2S/3	1.2
1975	Mon-N	46	132	18	26	0	0	0	3	23	18	.197	.316	.197	.513	41	-9	-10	108	45	10	.559	17	9	-0	3	2/S	-0.5
	StL-N	27	18	6	5	1	0	0	1	3	2	.278	.381	.333	.714	96	0	0	103	64	3	1.000	4	0	1	-0	/2S	0.2
	Yr	73	150	24	31	1	0	0	4	26	20	.207	.324	.213	.537	48	-9	-10	106	52	14	.617	21	9	1	3		-0.3
1976	Oak-A	68	1	21	0	0	0	0	0	2	0	.000	.667	.000	.667	107	0	0	100	0	-39	2.750	31	11	3	-1	D/2O	0.2
1977	Oak-A	41	30	11	4	1	0	0	0	8	13	.133	.333	.167	.500	43	-2	-2	95	0	3	.871	13	5	1	-1	2/S3D	0.1
1978	Cle-A	3	0	1	0	0	0	0	0	0	0	—	—	—	—	—	0	0	93	—	3	.500	1	2	-1	0	R	0.0
Total	6	350	616	137	140	13	1	0	27	97	101	.227	.336	.252	.588	63	-24	-28	105	64	34	.747	128	38	16	6	2/SD03	1.2
■ PHIL LINZ	Linz, Philip Francis b: 6/4/39, Baltimore, Md. BR/TR, 6'1", 180 lbs. Deb: 4/13/62																											
1962	NY-A	71	129	28	37	8	0	1	14	6	17	.287	.319	.372	.691	91	-3	-2	94	109	15	.625	6	2	1	0	S/32O	0.1
1963	NY-A	72	186	22	50	9	0	2	12	15	18	.269	.330	.349	.680	90	-2	-2	101	71	19	.561	1	6	-3	1	S3O/2	-0.2
1964	NY-A	112	368	63	92	21	3	5	25	43	61	.250	.332	.364	.696	91	-3	-4	103	71	45	.632	3	4	-2	9	S3/2O	0.5
1965	NY-A	99	285	37	59	12	1	2	16	30	33	.207	.283	.277	.560	59	-15	-15	101	78	24	.481	2	1	0	4	S/3O2	-0.7
1966	Phi-N	40	70	4	14	3	0	0	6	2	14	.200	.222	.243	.465	29	-7	-7	101	148	3	.311	0	0	0	0	3/S2	-0.6
1967	Phi-N	23	18	4	4	2	0	1	5	2	1	.222	.300	.500	.800	120	0	0	104	173	2	.733	0	0	0	0	/S3	0.1
	NY-N	24	58	8	12	2	0	0	1	4	10	.207	.270	.241	.511	48	-4	-4	99	30	4	.396	0	0	0	0	2/S3O	-0.2
	Yr	47	76	12	16	4	0	1	6	6	11	.211	.277	.303	.580	65	-3	-4	102	103	6	.484	0	0	0	0		-0.1
1968	NY-N	78	258	19	54	7	0	0	17	10	41	.209	.244	.236	.481	44	-17	-18	102	117	14	.351	1	0	0	-4	2	-2.0
Total	7	519	1372	185	322	64	4	11	96	112	195	.235	.296	.311	.607	71	-49	-51	101	88	126	.522	13	13	-4	11	S2/3O	-3.0
■ JOHNNY LIPON	Lipon, John Joseph "Skids" b: 11/10/22, Martin's Ferry, O. BR/TR, 6', 175 lbs. Deb: 8/16/42 MC																											
1942	Det-A	34	131	5	25	2	0	0	9	7	7	.191	.232	.206	.438	21	-13	-15	113	124	6	.318	1	3	-2	-2	S	-1.7
1946	Det-A	14	20	4	6	0	0	0	1	5	3	.300	.440	.300	.740	101	1	0	108	63	3	.786	0	0	0	-1	/S3	0.0
1948	Det-A	121	458	65	133	18	8	5	52	68	22	.290	.384	.397	.782	112	7	9	96	94	75	.757	4	4	-1	-7	*S/23	0.1
1949	Det-A	127	439	57	110	14	6	3	59	75	24	.251	.362	.330	.693	78	-8	-13	108	134	55	.642	2	4	-2	0	*S	-1.2
1950	Det-A	147	601	104	176	27	6	2	63	81	26	.293	.378	.368	.745	95	-5	-2	97	83	87	.692	9	6	-1	9	*S	1.2
1951	Det-A	129	487	56	129	15	1	0	38	49	27	.265	.335	.300	.634	69	-18	-21	106	99	52	.550	7	6	-2	-5	*S	-1.9
1952	Det-A	39	136	17	30	4	2	0	12	16	6	.221	.303	.279	.582	63	-7	-7	99	120	12	.518	3	1	0	0	S	-0.3
	Bos-A	79	234	25	48	8	1	0	18	32	20	.205	.301	.248	.549	50	-14	-16	107	116	20	.476	1	1	-0	5	S/3	-0.7
	Yr	118	370	42	78	12	3	0	30	48	26	.211	.301	.259	.561	55	-21	-23	104	118	33	.497	4	2	0	5		-1.0
1953	Bos-A	60	145	18	31	7	0	0	13	14	16	.214	.283	.262	.545	44	-10	-12	109	127	11	.445	1	0	0	4	S	-0.3
	StL-A	7	9	0	2	0	0	0	1	0	1	.222	.222	.222	.444	19	-1	-1	107	185	0	.286	0	0	0	-0	/32	0.0
	Yr	67	154	18	33	7	0	0	14	14	17	.214	.280	.260	.540	43	-11	-13	108	135	13	.455	1	0	0	4		-0.3
1954	Cin-N	1	1	0	0	0	0	0	0	0	0	.000	.000	.000	.000	-96	-0	-0	104	0	0	.000	0	0	0	0	H	0.0
Total	9	758	2661	351	690	95	24	10	266	347	152	.259	.346	.324	.671	78	-69	-78	103	105	323	.624	28	25	-7	3	S/32	-4.8
■ NIG LIPSCOMB	Lipscomb, Gerard b: 2/24/11, Rutherfordton, N.C d: 2/27/78, Huntersville, N.C. BR/TR, 6', 175 lbs. Deb: 4/23/37																											
1937	StL-A	36	96	11	31	9	1	0	8	11	10	.323	.398	.438	.836	112	2	2	99	65	17	.831	0	0	0	-2	2/P3	0.2
■ BOB LIPSKI	Lipski, Robert Peter b: 7/7/38, Scranton, Pa. BL/TR, 6'1", 180 lbs. Deb: 4/28/63																											
1963	Cle-A	2	1	0	0	0	0	0	0	0	1	.000	.000	.000	.000	-99	-0	-0	97	0	0	.000	0	0	0	0	/C	0.0
■ NELSON LIRIANO	Liriano, Nelson Arturo (Bonilla) b: 6/3/64, Santo Domingo, D.R. BB/TR, 5'10", 165 lbs. Deb: 8/25/87																											
1987	Tor-A	37	158	29	38	6	2	2	10	16	22	.241	.310	.342	.652	73	-6	-6	101	57	18	.664	13	2	3	-3	2	-0.3
1988	Tor-A	103	276	36	73	6	2	3	23	11	40	.264	.298	.333	.631	77	-9	-9	100	90	27	.552	12	5	1	-2	2D/3	-0.5
Total	2	140	434	65	111	12	4	5	33	27	62	.256	.302	.336	.639	75	-15	-15	100	78	46	.599	25	7	3	-6	2/D3	-0.8
■ JOE LIS	Lis, Joseph Anthony b: 8/15/46, Somerville, N.J. BR/TR, 6', 175 lbs. Deb: 9/05/70																											
1970	Phi-N	13	37	1	7	2	0	1	4	5	11	.189	.286	.324	.610	66	-2	-2	96	103	4	.567	0	0	0	0	/O	-0.1
1971	Phi-N	59	123	16	26	6	0	6	10	16	43	.211	.312	.407	.719	99	0	-0	103	60	16	.687	0	1	-1	-5	O	-0.7
1972	Phi-N	62	140	13	34	6	0	6	18	30	34	.243	.380	.414	.794	130	6	6	97	97	24	.817	0	1	-1	0	1O	0.3
1973	Min-A	103	253	37	62	11	1	9	25	28	66	.245	.327	.403	.731	101	1	0	104	76	31	.649	0	1	-1	4	1/D	-0.1
1974	Min-A	24	41	5	8	0	0	0	3	5	12	.195	.298	.195	.493	44	-3	-3	101	147	3	.400	0	0	0	1	1	-0.1
	Cle-A	57	109	15	22	3	0	6	16	14	30	.202	.293	.394	.687	95	-1	-1	101	103	12	.630	1	0	0	-1	1/3OD	-0.2
	Yr	81	150	20	30	3	0	6	19	19	42	.200	.294	.340	.634	81	-3	-4	101	118	15	.576	1	0	0	-0		-0.3
1975	Cle-A	9	13	4	4	2	0	2	8	3	3	.308	.471	.923	1.394	287	3	3	100	171	6	1.778	0	0	0	0	/1D	0.3
1976	Cle-A	20	51	4	16	1	0	2	7	8	8	.314	.407	.451	.858	152	4	4	100	93	10	.886	0	0	0	0	1/D	0.3
1977	Sea-A	9	13	1	3	0	0	0	1	1	2	.231	.286	.231	.516	44	-1	-1	96	132	0	.308	0	0	0	0	/1C	0.0
Total	8	356	780	96	182	31	1	32	92	110	209	.233	.334	.399	.733	106	8	7	101	90	106	.712	1	3	-2	-1	1/OD3C	-0.3
■ RICK LISI	Lisi, Riccardo Patrick Emilio b: 3/17/56, Halifax, N.S., Can. BR/TR, 6', 175 lbs. Deb: 5/09/81																											
1981	Tex-A	9	16	6	5	0	0	0	1	4	0	.313	.450	.313	.762	135	1	1	91	78	2	.750	0	1	-1	-2	/O	-0.1
■ PETE LISTER	Lister, Morris Elmer b: 7/21/1881, Savanna, Ill. d: 3/27/47, St.Petersburg, Fla BR/TR, Deb: 9/14/07																											
1907	Cle-A	22	65	5	18	2	0	0	4	3		.277	.309	.308	.617	106	-0	0	93	71	7	.532	2			-0	1	0.0
■ HARRY LITTLE	Little, Harry A. b: St.Louis, Mo. TR , Deb: 7/16/1877																											
1877	StL-N	3	12	2	2	0	0	0	0	1	6	.167	.231	.167	.397	27	-1	-1	102	0	0	.300				0	/O	0.0
	Lou-N	1	3	0	0	0	0	0	0	1	1	.000	.250	.000	.250	-11	-0	-1	132	0	0	.333				0	/2	0.0
	Yr	4	15	2	2	0	0	0	0	2	7	.133	.235	.133	.369	17	-1	-2	109	0	0	.308				0		0.0
Total	1	4	15	2	2	0	0	0	0	2	7	.133	.235	.133	.369	17	-1	-2	109	0	0	.308				0	/O2	0.0
■ BRYAN LITTLE	Little, Richard Bryan "Twig" b: 10/8/59, Houston, Tex. BB/TR, 5'10", 160 lbs. Deb: 7/29/82																											
1982	Mon-N	29	42	6	9	0	0	0	3	4	6	.214	.283	.214	.497	39	-3	-3	105	131	3	.429	2	1	0	-1	2S	-0.2
1983	Mon-N	106	350	48	91	15	3	1	36	50	22	.260	.356	.329	.684	89	-3	-3	102	123	42	.624	4	5	-2	-13	S2	-1.0
1984	Mon-N	85	266	31	65	11	1	0	9	34	19	.244	.332	.293	.625	84	-7	-4	91	45	28	.556	2	3	-1	-11	2/S	-1.4
1985	Chi-A	73	188	35	47	9	1	2	27	26	21	.250	.350	.340	.691	90	-2	-2	100	153	24	.637	0	1	-1	2	2/3S	0.3
1986	Chi-A	20	35	3	6	1	0	0	2	4	4	.171	.256	.200	.456	27	-3	-3	101	114	2	.355	0	0	0	-0	2/S3	-0.2
	NY-A	14	41	3	8	1	0	0	0	2	7	.195	.233	.220	.452	24	-4	-4	103	0	2	.324	0	0	0	-0	2	-0.3
	Yr	34	76	6	14	2	0	0	2	6	11	.184	.244	.211	.454	25	-8	-8	102	70	4	.349	0	0	0	-1		-0.5
Total	5	327	922	126	226	37	5	3	77	120	79	.245	.336	.306	.642	80	-22	-20	99	102	100	.588	8	10	-4	-23	2/S3	-2.8
■ JACK LITTLE	Little, William Arthur b: 3/12/1891, Mart, Tex. d: 7/27/61, Dallas, Tex. BR/TR, 5'11", 175 lbs. Deb: 7/02/12																											
1912	NY-A	3	12	2	3	0	0	0	0	1		.250	.357	.250	.607	73	-0	-0	101	0	2	.778	2			1	/O	0.0
■ DENNIS LITTLEJOHN	Littlejohn, Dennis Gerald b: 10/4/54, Santa Monica, Cal. BR/TR, 6'2", 200 lbs. Deb: 7/09/78																											
1978	SF-N	2	0	0	0	0	0	0	0	0	0	—	—	—	—	—	0	0	92	—	—	—	0	0	0	0	/C	0.0
1979	SF-N	63	193	15	38	6	1	1	13	21	46	.197	.276	.254	.530	49	-14	-12	92	99	14	.440	0	0	0	-3	C	-1.4
1980	SF-N	13	29	2	7	1	0	0	2	7	7	.241	.389	.276	.665	93	-0	0	96	99	4	.652	0	0	0	0	C	0.1
Total	3	78	222	17	45	7	1	1	15	28	53	.203	.292	.257	.549	65	-14	-12	93	99	20	.478	0	0	0	-3	/C	-1.3
■ LARRY LITTLETON	Littleton, Larry Marvin b: 4/3/54, Charlotte, N.C. BR/TR, 6'1", 185 lbs. Deb: 4/12/81																											
1981	Cle-A	26	23	2	0	0	0	0	1	3	6	.000	.115	.000	.115	-69	-5	-5	93	0	0	.120	0	0	0	-9	O	-1.4
■ JACK LITTRELL	Littrell, Jack Napier b: 1/22/29, Louisville, Ky. BR/TR, 6', 179 lbs. Deb: 4/19/52																											
1952	Phi-A	4	2	0	0	0	0	0	0	1	2	.000	.333	.000	.333	-2	-0	-0	111	0	0	.500	0	0	0	0	/S3	0.0
1954	Phi-A	9	30	7	9	2	0	1	3	6	3	.300	.417	.467	.883	144	2	2	98	68	6	.913	1	0	0	-1	/S	0.2
1955	KC-A	37	70	7	14	0	1	0	1	4	12	.200	.243	.229	.472	27	-7	-7	101	23	4	.351	0	0	0	-1	S/12	-0.5
1957	Chi-N	61	153	8	29	4	2	1	13	9	43	.190	.235	.261	.496	34	-15	-14	96	125	10	.392	0	0	0	-5	S/23	-1.6
Total	4	111	255	22	52	6	3	2	17	20	60	.204	.262	.275	.536	45	-20	-19	98	89	20	.446	1	0	0	-7	/S213	-1.9

YEAR	TM/L	G	AB	R	H	2B	3B	HR	RBI	BB	SO	AVG	OBP	SLG	PRO	/A	BR	/A	PF	CHI	RC	TA	SB	CS	SBR	FR	POS	TPR
■ **DANNY LITWHILER** Litwhiler, Daniel Webster b: 8/31/16, Ringtown, Pa. BR/TR, 5'10.5", 198 lbs. Deb: 4/25/40 C																												
1940	Phi-N	36	142	10	49	2	2	5	17	3	13	.345	.363	.493	.856	138	6	6	97	79	25	.798	1			1	O	0.6
1941	Phi-N	151	590	72	180	29	6	18	66	39	43	.305	.350	.466	.816	132	20	22	97	77	93	.746	1			4	*O	2.0
1942	Phi-N	151	591	59	160	25	9	9	56	27	42	.271	.310	.389	.700	110	1	4	94	86	68	.595	2			0	*O	0.0
1943	Phi-N	36	139	23	36	6	0	5	17	11	14	.259	.313	.410	.723	116	1	2	94	90	18	.651	1			4	O	0.5
	StL-N	80	258	40	72	14	3	7	31	19	31	.279	.333	.438	.771	116	6	5	105	83	38	.714	1			0	O	0.2
	Yr	116	397	63	108	20	3	12	48	30	45	.272	.326	.428	.755	116	7	6	101	86	57	.699	2			4		0.7
1944	StL-N	140	492	53	130	25	5	15	82	37	56	.264	.328	.427	.755	111	6	6	101	118	69	.694	2			-3	*O	-0.7
1946	StL-N	6	5	0	0	0	0	0	0	1	1	.000	.167	.000	.167	-48	-1	-1	107	0	0	.200	0			0	H	0.0
	Bos-N	79	247	29	72	12	2	8	38	19	23	.291	.347	.453	.800	133	7	9	95	104	39	.749	1			-4	O/3	0.4
	Yr	85	252	29	72	12	2	8	38	20	24	.286	.343	.444	.788	129	6	8	95	97	39	.734	1			-4		0.4
1947	Bos-N	91	226	38	59	5	2	7	31	25	43	.261	.337	.394	.731	97	-2	-1	97	104	30	.671	1			-7	O	-1.0
1948	Bos-N	13	33	0	9	2	0	0	6	4	2	.273	.385	.333	.718	94	0	0	102	204	5	.708	0			2	/O	0.1
	Cin-N	106	338	51	93	19	2	14	44	48	41	.275	.365	.467	.833	120	11	10	103	82	56	.796	1			-3	O3	0.0
	Yr	119	371	51	102	21	2	14	50	52	43	.275	.367	.456	.823	118	11	10	103	97	61	.789	1			-1		0.1
1949	Cin-N	102	292	35	85	18	1	11	48	44	42	.291	.384	.473	.857	134	12	14	96	106	56	.863	0			-8	O/3	0.1
1950	Cin-N	54	112	15	29	4	0	6	12	20	21	.259	.371	.455	.827	111	3	2	105	67	19	.807	0			-4	O	-0.2
1951	Cin-N	12	29	3	8	1	0	2	3	2	5	.276	.323	.517	.840	121	1	1	101	55	5	.810	0	0	0	-1	/O	0.0
Total	11	1057	3494	428	982	162	32	107	451	299	377	.281	.342	.438	.780	119	71	78	98	93	521	.743	11	0		-20	O/3	2.0
■ **PADDY LIVINGSTON** Livingston, Patrick Joseph b: 1/14/1880, Cleveland, Ohio d: 9/19/77, Cleveland, Ohio BR/TR, 5'8", 197 lbs. Deb: 9/02/01																												
1901	Cle-A	1	2	0	0	0	0	0	0	0		.000	.000	.000	.000	-99	-1	-1	95	0	0	.000	0			0	/C	0.0
1906	Cin-N	50	139	8	22	1	4	0	8	12		.158	.225	.223	.448	36	-9	-12	115	94	7	.368	0			3	C	-0.4
1909	Phi-A	64	175	15	41	6	4	0	15	15		.234	.323	.314	.638	100	1	0	102	105	18	.612	4			4	C	1.0
1910	Phi-A	37	120	11	25	4	3	0	9	6		.208	.264	.292	.555	72	-4	-4	102	95	10	.484	2			2	C	0.2
1911	Phi-A	27	71	9	17	4	0	0	8	7		.239	.316	.296	.612	77	-3	-2	93	129	7	.556	1			-2	C	0.0
1912	Cle-A	19	47	5	11	2	1	0	3	1		.234	.280	.319	.599	70	-2	-2	101	67	4	.500	0			1	C	0.0
1917	StL-N	7	20	0	4	0	0	0	2	0	1	.200	.200	.200	.400	22	-2	-2	102	193	1	.375	2			0	/C	0.0
Total	7	205	574	48	120	17	12	0	45	41	1	.209	.278	.280	.559	69	-19	-22	104	103	48	.496	9			8	C	0.8
■ **MICKEY LIVINGSTON** Livingston, Thompson Orville b: 11/15/14, Newberry, S.C. d: 4/3/83, Newberry, S.C. BR/TR, 6'1.5", 185 lbs. Deb: 9/17/38																												
1938	Was-A	2	4	0	3	2	0	0	1	0	1	.750	.750	1.250	2.000	414	2	2	95	68	4	5.000	0	0	0	0	/C	0.2
1941	Phi-N	95	207	16	42	6	1	0	18	20	38	.203	.276	.242	.518	48	-14	-14	97	130	13	.417	2			4	C/1	-0.2
1942	Phi-N	89	239	20	49	6	1	2	22	25	20	.205	.283	.264	.547	64	-12	-10	94	118	19	.456	0			1	C/1	-0.8
1943	Phi-N	84	265	25	66	9	2	3	18	19	18	.249	.304	.332	.636	89	-6	-4	94	67	27	.539	1			5	C/1	0.5
	Chi-N	36	111	11	29	5	1	4	16	12	8	.261	.333	.432	.766	122	3	3	99	96	14	.685	1			-4	C/1	0.0
	Yr	120	376	36	95	14	3	7	34	31	26	.253	.313	.362	.675	99	-3	-1	95	76	43	.594	2			2		0.5
1945	Chi-N	71	224	19	57	4	2	2	23	19	6	.254	.324	.317	.641	79	-6	-6	99	104	23	.552	2			-7	C/1	-1.1
1946	Chi-N	66	176	14	45	14	0	2	20	20	19	.256	.338	.369	.708	107	0	1	94	105	23	.644	0			-5	C	-0.1
1947	Chi-N	19	33	2	7	2	0	0	3	1	5	.212	.235	.273	.508	34	-3	-3	101	123	2	.385	0			0	/C	-0.2
	NY-N	5	6	0	1	0	0	0	0	1	2	.167	.286	.167	.452	23	-1	-1	101	0	0	.400	0			0	/C	0.0
	Yr	24	39	2	8	2	0	0	3	2	7	.205	.244	.256	.500	33	-4	-4	101	103	3	.387	0			0		-0.2
1948	NY-N	45	99	9	21	4	1	2	12	21	11	.212	.350	.333	.683	86	-1	-1	100	115	13	.679	1			-2	C	0.0
1949	NY-N	19	57	6	17	2	0	4	12	2	8	.298	.333	.544	.877	129	2	2	102	105	10	.810	0			-0	C	0.2
	Bos-N	28	64	6	15	2	1	0	6	3	5	.234	.290	.297	.587	60	-4	-4	97	119	6	.490	0			0	C	-0.2
	Yr	47	121	12	32	4	1	4	18	5	13	.264	.310	.413	.723	94	-2	-2	99	116	16	.652	0			-0		0.0
1951	Bro-N	2	5	0	2	0	0	0	2	1	0	.400	.500	.400	.900	148	0	0	98	387	1	1.000	0	0	0	0	/C	0.0
Total	10	561	1490	128	354	56	9	19	153	144	141	.238	.310	.326	.636	82	-40	-34	96	105	154	.571	7	0		-8	C/1	-1.7
■ **ABEL LIZOTTE** Lizotte, Abel b: 4/13/1870, Lewiston, Me. d: 12/4/26, Wilkes-Barre, Pa. Deb: 9/17/1896																												
1896	Pit-N	7	29	3	3	0	0	0	3	2	2	.103	.161	.103	.265	-31	-5	-5	93	305	1	.231	1			0	/1	-0.3
■ **WINSTON LLENAS** Llenas, Winston Enriquillo (Davila) b: 9/23/43, Santiago, D.R. BR/TR, 5'10", 165 lbs. Deb: 8/15/68 C																												
1968	Cal-A	16	39	5	5	1	0	0	1	2	5	.128	.190	.154	.344	6	-4	-4	94	71	1	.257	0	0	0	0	/3	-0.4
1969	Cal-A	34	47	4	8	2	0	0	0	2	10	.170	.204	.213	.417	17	-5	-5	99	0	2	.300	0	0	0	0	/3	-0.4
1972	Cal-A	44	64	3	17	3	0	0	7	3	8	.266	.299	.313	.611	93	-1	-1	88	146	5	.451	0	0	0	-1	3/2O	0.0
1973	Cal-A	78	130	16	35	1	0	1	25	10	16	.269	.326	.300	.626	81	-4	-3	96	234	13	.505	0	0	0	-1	23/OD	-0.2
1974	Cal-A	72	138	16	36	6	0	2	17	11	19	.261	.315	.348	.663	98	-2	-0	92	124	15	.557	0	0	0	-6	O2D/3	-0.6
1975	Cal-A	56	113	6	21	4	0	0	11	10	11	.186	.252	.221	.473	37	-10	-9	95	169	6	.354	0	1	-1	2	2O/13D	-0.7
Total	6	300	531	50	122	17	0	3	61	38	69	.230	.284	.279	.562	66	-26	-22	94	149	42	.452	0	1	-1	-5	/2O3D1	-2.3
■ **MIKE LOAN** Loan, William Joseph b: 9/27/1894, Philadelphia, Pa. d: 11/21/66, Springfield, Pa. TR, 5'11", 185 lbs. Deb: 9/18/12																												
1912	Phi-N	1	2	1	1	0	0	0	0	0	0	.500	.500	.500	1.000	173	0	0	100	0	0	1.000	0			0	/C	0.0
■ **BOB LOANE** Loane, Robert Kenneth b: 8/6/14, Berkeley, Cal. BR/TR, 6', 190 lbs. Deb: 7/29/39																												
1939	Was-A	3	9	2	0	0	0	0	1	4	4	.000	.308	.000	.308	-17	-1	-1	90	0	0	.444	0	0	0	2	/O	0.0
1940	Bos-N	13	22	4	5	3	0	0	1	2	5	.227	.292	.364	.655	81	-1	-1	99	46	3	.706	2			1	O	0.0
Total	2	16	31	6	5	3	0	0	2	6	9	.161	.297	.258	.555	53	-2	-2	96	30	3	.615	2	0		3	/O	0.0
■ **FRANK LOBERT** Lobert, Frank John b: 11/26/1883, Williamsport, Pa. d: 5/29/32, Pittsburgh, Pa. TR, 6', 180 lbs. Deb: 6/06/14																												
1914	Bal-F	11	30	3	6	0	1	0	2	0	0	.200	.200	.267	.467	33	-3	-3	99	90	2	.333	0			0	/32	-0.2
■ **HANS LOBERT** Lobert, John Bernard "Honus" b: 10/18/1881, Wilmington, Del. d: 9/14/68, Philadelphia, Pa. BR/TR, 5'9", 170 lbs. Deb: 03 MC																												
1903	Pit-N	5	13	1	1	1	0	0	0	1		.077	.143	.154	.297	-14	-2	-2	105	0	0	.333	1			0	/32S	-0.1
1905	Chi-N	14	46	7	9	2	0	0	1	3		.196	.245	.239	.484	44	-3	-3	105	32	4	.486	4			-1	3/O	-0.2
1906	Cin-N	79	268	39	83	5	5	0	19	19		.310	.355	.366	.721	111	8	4	115	72	43	.741	20			-3	3S2/O	0.1
1907	Cin-N	148	537	61	132	9	12	1	41	37		.246	.294	.313	.607	97	-5	-3	95	96	60	.580	30			-21	*S/3	-1.9
1908	Cin-N	155	570	71	167	17	18	4	63	46		.293	.346	.407	.753	139	26	24	103	95	94	.806	47			-14	3SO	1.4
1909	Cin-N	122	425	50	90	13	5	4	52	48		.212	.304	.294	.598	92	-6	-3	94	146	45	.630	30			-12	*3	-1.4
1910	Cin-N	93	314	43	97	6	6	3	40	30	9	.309	.369	.395	.764	121	9	8	101	107	61	.899	41			2	3	1.1
1911	Phi-N	147	541	94	154	20	9	9	72	66	31	.285	.368	.405	.772	108	12	6	108	87	97	.853	40			-18	*3	-0.5
1912	Phi-N	65	257	37	84	12	5	2	33	19	13	.327	.373	.436	.809	120	7	7	100	90	46	.832	13			-3	3	0.4
1913	Phi-N	150	573	98	172	28	11	7	55	42	34	.300	.353	.424	.777	108	15	6	112	73	96	.825	41			-12	*3/S2	-0.7
1914	Phi-N	135	505	83	139	24	5	1	52	49	32	.275	.343	.349	.691	106	4	4	100	101	69	.708	31			-22	*3/S	-1.3
1915	NY-N	106	386	46	97	18	4	0	38	25	24	.251	.304	.319	.622	97	-6	-2	91	125	38	.546	14	15	-5	-4	*3	-0.6
1916	NY-N	48	76	6	17	3	2	0	11	5	8	.224	.272	.316	.587	84	-2	-2	96	182	8	.525	2			0	3	0.0
1917	NY-N	50	52	4	10	1	0	1	5	5	5	.192	.276	.269	.545	70	-2	-2	97	113	4	.524	2			1	3	0.0
Total	14	1317	4563	640	1252	159	82	32	482	395	156	.274	.336	.366	.702	108	55	43	102	100	666	.724	316	15		-106	3S/O2	-3.7
■ **HARRY LOCHHEAD** Lochhead, Robert Henry b: 3/29/1876, Stockton, Cal. d: 8/22/09, Stockton, Cal. TR, Deb: 4/16/1899																												
1899	Cle-N	148	541	52	129	7	1	1	43	21		.238	.277	.261	.538	56	-36	-28	89	93	47	.468	23			-5	*S/2P	-2.1
1901	Det-A	1	4	2	2	0	0	0	0	0		.500	.500	.500	1.000	164	0	0	110	0	1	1.000	0			0	/S	0.0
	Phi-A	9	34	3	3	0	0	0	2	3		.088	.162	.088	.250	-28	-6	-6	100	223	0	.194	0			0	/S	-0.4
	Yr	10	38	5	5	0	0	0	2	3		.132	.195	.132	.327	-7	-5	-5	101	200	1	.242	0			0		-0.4
Total	2	158	579	57	134	7	1	1	45	24		.231	.272	.252	.524	51	-41	-33	90	101	48	.452	23			-4	S/P2	-2.5
■ **DON LOCK** Lock, Don Wilson b: 7/27/36, Wichita, Kan. BR/TR, 6'2", 195 lbs. Deb: 7/17/62																												
1962	Was-A	71	225	30	57	6	2	12	37	30	63	.253	.341	.458	.799	112	4	4	101	106	33	.761	4	5	-2	2	O	0.1
1963	Was-A	149	531	71	134	20	1	27	82	70	151	.252	.342	.446	.788	122	14	15	98	114	83	.769	7	3	0	9	*O	2.0

YEAR	TM/L	G	AB	R	H	2B	3B	HR	RBI	BB	SO	AVG	OBP	SLG	PRO	/A	BR	/A	PF	CHI	RC	TA	SB	CS	SBR	FR	POS	TPR
1964	Was-A	152	512	73	127	17	4	28	80	79	137	.248	.350	.461	.811	122	17	16	101	108	84	.802	4	2	0	6	*O	1.7
1965	Was-A	143	418	52	90	15	1	16	39	57	115	.215	.317	.371	.687	95	-2	-2	100	80	48	.634	1	3	-2	-2	*O	-1.2
1966	Was-A	138	386	52	90	13	1	16	48	57	126	.233	.335	.396	.731	115	5	8	95	100	51	.688	2	6	-3	-1	*O	0.0
1967	Phi-N	112	313	46	79	13	1	14	51	43	98	.252	.352	.435	.786	119	10	9	104	119	50	.794	9	5	-0	3	O	0.7
1968	Phi-N	99	248	27	52	7	2	8	34	26	64	.210	.285	.351	.635	92	-3	-3	97	129	24	.563	3	4	-2	-1	O	-1.0
1969	Phi-N	4	4	0	0	0	0	0	0	0	1	.000	.000	.000	.000	-99	-1	-1	98	0	0	.000	0	0	0	-0	/O	-0.1
	Bos-A	53	58	8	13	1	0	1	2	11	21	.224	.348	.293	.641	77	-1	-1	105	40	6	.596	0	1	-1	-6	O/1	-0.9
Total	8	921	2695	359	642	92	12	122	373	373	776	.238	.334	.417	.751	112	42	44	99	105	379	.740	30	29	-8	9	O/1	1.3
■ **MARSHALL LOCKE**	Locke, Marshall b: Indianapolis, Ind. Deb: 7/29/1874																											
1874	Bal-n	1	5	0	0							.000															/S	
1884	Ind-a	7	29	5	7	0	1	0		0		.241	.241	.310	.552	84	-1	-0	96	0	2	.409				0	/O	0.0
■ **GENE LOCKLEAR**	Locklear, Gene b: 7/19/49, Lumberton, N.C. BL/TR, 5'10", 165 lbs. Deb: 4/05/73																											
1973	Cin-N	29	26	6	5	0	0	0	0	2	5	.192	.276	.192	.468	34	-2	-2	93	0	1	.333	0	0	0	-1	/O	-0.3
	SD-N	67	154	20	37	6	1	3	25	21	22	.240	.331	.351	.682	95	-2	-1	94	159	19	.683	9	4	0	1	O	-0.1
	Yr	96	180	26	42	6	1	3	25	23	27	.233	.324	.328	.651	86	-4	-3	94	111	21	.639	9	4	0	-1		-0.4
1974	SD-N	39	74	7	20	3	2	1	3	4	12	.270	.308	.405	.713	105	-0	0	93	35	9	.618	0	1	-1	0	O	0.0
1975	SD-N	100	237	31	76	11	1	5	27	22	26	.321	.381	.439	.820	127	9	9	100	88	40	.784	4	2	0	-2	O	0.5
1976	SD-N	43	67	9	15	3	0	0	8	4	15	.224	.268	.269	.536	59	-4	-3	89	171	5	.423	0	0	0	-1	O	-0.4
	NY-A	13	32	2	7	1	0	0	1	2	7	.219	.265	.250	.515	52	-2	-2	99	48	2	.400	0	0	0	-1	/OD	-0.2
1977	NY-A	1	5	1	3	0	0	0	2	0	0	.600	.600	.600	1.200	232	1	1	99	228	2	1.500	0	0	0	-0	/O	0.1
Total	5	292	595	76	163	24	4	9	66	55	87	.274	.337	.373	.711	102	-1	2	96	105	78	.665	13	7	-0	-4	O/D	-0.4
■ **STU LOCKLIN**	Locklin, Stuart Carlton b: 7/22/28, Appleton, Wis. BL/TL, 6'1.5", 190 lbs. Deb: 6/23/55																											
1955	Cle-A	16	18	4	3	1	0	0	0	3	4	.167	.286	.222	.508	37	-2	-2	104	0	1	.438	0	0	0	-2	/O	-0.4
1956	Cle-A	9	6	0	1	0	0	0	0	0	1	.167	.167	.167	.333	-12	-1	-1	101	0	0	.200	0	0	0	-0	/O	0.0
Total	2	25	24	4	4	1	0	0	0	3	5	.167	.259	.208	.468	26	-2	-3	103	0	1	.400	0	0	0	-2	/O	-0.4
■ **WHITEY LOCKMAN**	Lockman, Carroll Walter b: 7/25/26, Lowell, N.C. BL/TR, 6'1", 175 lbs. Deb: 7/05/45 MC																											
1945	NY-N	32	129	16	44	9	0	3	18	13	10	.341	.410	.481	.890	148	8	8	100	78	27	.907	1			-1	O	0.6
1947	NY-N	2	2	0	1	0	0	0	1	0	0	.500	.500	.500	1.000	165	0	0	101	370	1	1.000	0			0	H	0.0
1948	NY-N	146	584	117	167	24	10	18	59	68	63	.286	.361	.454	.815	120	15	16	100	61	101	.812	8			-2	*O	0.3
1949	NY-N	151	617	97	186	32	7	11	65	62	31	.301	.368	.429	.798	111	12	11	102	73	101	.779	12			2	*O	0.4
1950	NY-N	129	532	72	157	28	5	6	52	42	29	.295	.349	.400	.749	98	-3	-1	98	84	76	.677	1			12	*O	0.6
1951	NY-N	153	614	85	173	27	7	12	73	50	32	.282	.339	.407	.746	98	-1	-2	102	105	83	.663	4	5	-2	9	*1O	0.1
1952	NY-N	154	606	99	176	17	4	13	58	67	52	.290	.363	.396	.759	108	10	8	102	78	92	.704	2	4	-2	2	*1	0.2
1953	NY-N	150	607	85	179	22	4	9	61	52	36	.295	.351	.389	.739	94	-6	-4	98	87	87	.666	3	4	-2	5	*1O	-0.3
1954	NY-N	148	570	73	143	17	3	16	60	59	31	.251	.321	.375	.697	77	-16	-20	105	96	73	.637	2	2	-1	-9	*1/O	-3.4
1955	NY-N	147	576	76	157	19	0	15	49	39	34	.273	.322	.384	.706	88	-12	-10	99	79	72	.620	3	3	-1	-2	O1	-1.9
1956	NY-N	48	169	13	46	7	1	1	10	16	17	.272	.335	.343	.678	85	-4	-3	97	71	20	.587	0	2	-1	-1	O/1	-0.7
	StL-N	70	193	14	48	0	2	0	10	18	8	.249	.313	.269	.582	59	-11	-10	99	81	17	.483	2	2	-1	-4	O/1	-1.7
	Yr	118	362	27	94	7	3	1	20	34	25	.260	.323	.304	.627	71	-14	-14	98	77	37	.533	2	4	-2	-5		-2.4
1957	NY-N	133	456	51	113	9	4	7	30	39	19	.248	.310	.331	.641	71	-17	-19	102	72	48	.561	5	5	-2	-6	*1O	-3.7
1958	SF-N	92	122	15	29	5	0	2	7	13	8	.238	.311	.328	.639	69	-5	-5	100	63	14	.570	0	0	0	-8	O2/1	-1.3
1959	Bal-A	38	69	7	15	1	1	0	2	8	4	.217	.299	.261	.560	57	-4	-4	97	44	6	.473	0	0	0	-1	1/2O	-0.4
	Cin-N	52	84	10	22	5	1	0	7	4	6	.262	.295	.345	.641	68	-4	-4	103	98	9	.524	0	0	0	-1	1/23O	-0.5
1960	Cin-N	21	10	6	2	0	0	1	1	2	3	.200	.385	.500	.885	142	1	1	98	51	2	.889	0	0	0	0	/1	0.0
Total	15	1666	5940	836	1658	222	49	114	563	552	383	.279	.342	.391	.733	95	-36	-41	101	81	826	.681	43	27		-6	1O/23	-11.7
■ **DARIO LODIGIANI**	Lodigiani, Dario Antonio b: 6/6/16, San Francisco, Cal BR/TR, 5'8", 150 lbs. Deb: 4/18/38 C																											
1938	Phi-A	93	325	36	91	15	1	6	44	34	25	.280	.361	.388	.748	87	-6	-6	101	105	48	.726	3	0	1	-8	23	-0.8
1939	Phi-A	121	393	46	102	22	4	6	44	42	18	.260	.337	.382	.719	86	-10	-8	97	88	52	.660	2	0	1	-10	32	-1.6
1940	Phi-A	1	1	0	0	0	0	0	0	0	0	.000	.000	.000	.000	-99	-0	-0	96	0	0	.000	0	0	0	0	H	0.0
1941	Chi-A	87	322	39	77	19	2	4	40	31	19	.239	.316	.348	.663	81	-12	-9	94	121	34	.567	0	4	-2	6	3	0.0
1942	Chi-A	59	168	9	47	7	0	0	15	18	10	.280	.353	.321	.674	91	-2	-1	99	98	19	.589	3	4	-2	3	3/2	0.1
1946	Chi-A	44	155	12	38	8	0	0	13	16	14	.245	.324	.297	.620	77	-5	-4	97	110	17	.571	4	0	1	2	3	0.3
Total	6	405	1364	142	355	71	7	16	156	141	86	.260	.338	.358	.696	84	-34	-30	97	104	170	.648	12	8	-1	-7	32	-2.0
■ **GEORGE LOEPP**	Loepp, George Herbert b: 9/11/01, Detroit, Mich. d: 9/4/67, Los Angeles, Cal. BR/TR, 5'11", 170 lbs. Deb: 8/29/28																											
1928	Bos-A	15	51	6	9	3	1	0	3	5	12	.176	.250	.275	.525	38	-5	-5	98	75	4	.452	0	0	0	2	O	-0.3
1930	Was-A	50	134	23	37	7	1	0	14	20	9	.276	.382	.343	.725	84	-2	-2	101	101	18	.683	0	4	-2	-3	O	-0.8
Total	2	65	185	29	46	10	2	0	17	25	21	.249	.347	.324	.672	73	-7	-7	100	94	22	.615	0	4	-2	-1	/O	-1.1
■ **DICK LOFTUS**	Loftus, Richard Joseph b: 3/7/01, Concord, Mass. d: 1/21/72, Concord, Mass. BL/TR, 6', 155 lbs. Deb: 4/20/24																											
1924	Bro-N	46	81	18	22	6	0	0	8	7	2	.272	.330	.346	.675	82	-2	-2	99	104	10	.610	1	0	0	-3	O/1	-0.4
1925	Bro-N	51	131	16	31	6	0	0	13	5	5	.237	.275	.282	.558	46	-11	-10	94	125	11	.460	2	0	1	0	O	-0.9
Total	2	97	212	34	53	12	0	0	21	12	7	.250	.296	.307	.603	60	-13	-12	96	117	20	.516	3	0	1	-3	/O1	-1.3
■ **TOM LOFTUS**	Loftus, Thomas Joseph b: 11/15/1856, St.Louis, Mo. d: 4/16/10, Dubuque, Iowa 168 lbs. Deb: 8/17/1877 M																											
1877	StL-N	3	11	2	2	0	0	0	0	0	1	.182	.182	.182	.364	15	-1	-1	102	0	0	.222				0	/O	0.0
1883	StL-a	6	22	1	4	0	0	0		2		.182	.250	.182	.432	38	-1	-2	108	0	1	.333				0	/O	0.0
Total	2	9	33	3	6	0	0	0	0	2	1	.182	.229	.182	.410	31	-2	-3	106	0	1	.296				0	/O	0.0
■ **JOHNNY LOGAN**	Logan, John "Yatcha" b: 3/23/27, Endicott, N.Y. BR/TR, 5'11", 175 lbs. Deb: 4/17/51																											
1951	Bos-N	62	169	14	37	7	1	0	16	18	13	.219	.298	.272	.570	56	-11	-10	98	135	14	.471	0	0	0	0	S	-0.4
1952	Bos-N	117	456	56	129	21	3	4	42	31	33	.283	.334	.368	.702	100	-3	-1	95	96	57	.602	1	2	-1	6	*S	0.8
1953	Mil-N	150	611	100	167	27	8	11	73	41	33	.273	.326	.398	.724	93	-12	-7	94	91	80	.638	2	2	-1	**24**	*S	2.7
1954	Mil-N	154	560	66	154	17	7	8	66	51	51	.275	.342	.373	.715	92	-11	-6	93	114	73	.638	2	0	1	15	*S	1.9
1955	Mil-N	154	595	95	177	**37**	5	13	83	58	58	.297	.364	.442	.806	121	11	17	93	107	96	.758	3	3	-1	7	*S	2.7
1956	Mil-N	148	545	69	153	27	5	15	46	46	49	.281	.342	.431	.773	107	5	6	99	74	81	.714	3	0	1	11	*S	2.8
1957	Mil-N	129	494	59	135	19	7	10	49	31	49	.273	.321	.401	.722	102	-6	0	90	91	62	.638	5	0	2	22	*S	2.9
1958	Mil-N	145	530	54	120	20	0	11	53	40	57	.226	.287	.326	.613	69	-29	-22	89	108	51	.521	1	2	-1	14	*S	0.1
1959	Mil-N	138	470	59	137	17	0	13	50	57	45	.291	.372	.411	.782	114	7	10	95	89	71	.730	1	3	-2	-1	*S	1.3
1960	Mil-N	136	482	52	118	14	4	7	42	43	40	.245	.309	.334	.643	84	-16	-10	91	96	50	.552	1	1	-0	-2	*S	-0.7
1961	Mil-N	18	19	0	2	1	0	0	1	1	3	.105	.150	.158	.308	-20	-3	-3	92	134	0	.222	0	0	0	0	/S	-0.2
	Pit-N	27	52	5	12	4	0	0	5	4	8	.231	.286	.308	.593	58	-3	-3	99	126	4	.476	0	0	0	1	/3S	-0.1
	Yr	45	71	5	14	5	0	0	6	5	11	.197	.250	.268	.518	39	-6	-6	96	132	5	.407	0	0	0	1		-0.3
1962	Pit-N	44	80	7	24	3	0	1	12	7	6	.300	.356	.375	.731	94	-0	-0	102	143	10	.617	0	0	0	-1	3	0.0
1963	Pit-N	81	181	15	42	2	1	0	9	23	27	.232	.325	.254	.579	70	-6	-6	99	82	15	.490	0	0	0	4	S/3	0.2
Total	13	1503	5244	651	1407	216	41	93	547	451	472	.268	.331	.378	.710	95	-77	-34	94	98	665	.648	19	13	-2	101	*S/3	14.0
■ **PETE LOHMAN**	Lohman, George F. b: 10/21/1864, Lake Elmo, Minn. d: 11/21/28, Los Angeles, Cal. Deb: 5/11/1891																											
1891	Was-a	32	109	18	21	1	4	1	11	16	17	.193	.302	.303	.604	79	-3	-2	95	90	11	.580	1			0	C/O3S2	-0.1
■ **HOWARD LOHR**	Lohr, Howard Sylvester b: 6/3/1892, Philadelphia, Pa. d: 1/9/77, Philadelphia, Pa. BR/TR, 6', 165 lbs. Deb: 6/17/14																											
1914	Cin-N	18	47	6	10	1	1	0	7	0	8	.213	.213	.277	.489	43	-3	-4	105	195	3	.405	2			-2	O	-0.6
1916	Cle-A	3	7	0	1	0	0	0	1	0	1	.143	.143	.143	.286	-14	-1	-1	100	357	0	.333	1			-1	/O	-0.1
Total	2	21	54	6	11	1	1	0	8	0	9	.204	.204	.259	.463	36	-4	-5	104	216	3	.395	3			-3	/O	-0.7

YEAR	TM/L	G	AB	R	H	2B	3B	HR	RBI	BB	SO	AVG	OBP	SLG	PRO	/A	BR	/A	PF	CHI	RC	TA	SB	CS	SBR	FR	POS	TPR
■ **JACK LOHRKE**	Lohrke, Jack Wayne "Lucky" b: 2/25/24, Los Angeles, Cal. BR/TR, 6', 180 lbs. Deb: 4/18/47																											
1947	NY-N	112	329	44	79	12	4	11	35	46	29	.240	.337	.401	.738	95	-2	-3	101	79	45	.701	3			-5	*3	-1.0
1948	NY-N	97	280	35	70	15	1	5	31	30	30	.250	.323	.364	.687	86	-6	-6	100	99	33	.625	3			-2	32	-0.5
1949	NY-N	55	180	32	48	11	4	5	22	16	12	.267	.333	.456	.789	108	2	2	102	85	27	.752	3			-5	23S	0.0
1950	NY-N	30	43	4	8	0	0	0	4	4	8	.186	.255	.186	.441	19	-5	-5	98	193	2	.333	0			0	3/2	-0.4
1951	NY-N	23	40	3	8	0	0	1	3	10	2	.200	.360	.275	.635	72	-1	-1	102	83	4	.600	0	0	0	-1	3/S	-0.1
1952	Phi-N	25	29	4	6	0	0	0	1	4	3	.207	.303	.207	.510	43	-2	-2	101	65	2	.435	0	0	0	0	/S32	-0.1
1953	Phi-N	12	13	3	2	0	0	0	0	1	2	.154	.214	.154	.368	-2	-2	-2	99	0	0	.273	0	0	0	-0	/2S3	-0.1
Total	7	354	914	125	221	38	9	22	96	111	86	.242	.327	.375	.702	87	-16	-17	100	90	114	.674	9	0		-13	3/2S	-2.2
■ **ALBERTO LOIS**	Lois, Alberto b: 5/6/56, Hato Mayor, D.R. BR/TR, 5'9", 175 lbs. Deb: 9/08/78																											
1978	Pit-N	3	4	0	1	0	1	0	0	0	1	.250	.250	.750	1.000	161	0	0	105	0	1	1.000	0	0	0	0	/O	0.0
1979	Pit-N	11	0	6	0	0	0	0	0	0	0	—	—	—	—	—	0	0	106	—	1	1.000	1	1	-0	0	/R	0.0
Total	2	14	4	6	1	0	1	0	0	0	1	.250	.250	.750	1.000	161	0	0	105	0	2	1.000	1	1	-0	0	/O	0.0
■ **RON LOLICH**	Lolich, Ronald John b: 9/19/46, Portland, Ore. BR/TR, 6'1", 185 lbs. Deb: 7/18/71																											
1971	Chi-A	2	8	0	1	1	0	0	0	0	2	.125	.125	.250	.375	4	-1	-1	98	0	0	.286	0	0	0	-1	/O	-0.1
1972	Cle-A	24	80	4	15	1	0	2	8	4	20	.188	.226	.275	.501	45	-5	-6	107	119	5	.400	0	0	0	-1	O	-0.7
1973	Cle-A	61	140	16	32	7	0	2	15	7	27	.229	.265	.321	.587	66	-7	-6	97	116	11	.460	0	2	-1	-6	OD	-1.4
Total	3	87	228	20	48	9	0	4	23	11	49	.211	.247	.303	.549	57	-13	-13	101	113	16	.432	0	2	-1	-7	/OD	-2.2
■ **SHERM LOLLAR**	Lollar, John Sherman b: 8/23/24, Durham, Ark. d: 9/24/77, Springfield, Mo. BR/TR, 6'1", 185 lbs. Deb: 4/20/46 C																											
1946	Cle-A	28	62	7	15	6	0	1	9	5	9	.242	.299	.387	.686	102	-1	-0	89	127	7	.592	0	1	-1	-0	C	0.0
1947	NY-A	11	32	4	7	0	1	1	6	1	5	.219	.242	.375	.617	73	-2	-1	97	147	2	.448	0	1	-1	-1	/C	-0.1
1948	NY-A	22	38	0	8	0	0	0	4	1	6	.211	.231	.211	.441	18	-4	-4	100	169	1	.265	0	0	0	-0	C	-0.3
1949	StL-A	109	284	28	74	9	1	8	49	32	22	.261	.340	.384	.723	91	-4	-4	100	126	38	.653	0	1	-1	5	C	0.4
1950	StL-A	126	396	55	111	22	3	13	65	64	25	.280	.391	.449	.841	107	10	5	107	103	74	.848	2	0	1	5	*C	1.4
1951	StL-A	98	310	44	78	21	0	8	44	43	26	.252	.350	.397	.747	97	1	-1	105	107	41	.679	1	0	0	7	C/3	1.1
1952	Chi-A	132	375	35	90	15	0	13	50	54	34	.240	.354	.384	.738	105	4	4	100	102	53	.703	1	0	0	-18	*C	-0.7
1953	Chi-A	113	334	46	96	19	0	8	54	47	29	.287	.388	.416	.804	111	10	7	106	123	59	.796	1	0	0	-6	*C/1	0.5
1954	Chi-A	107	316	31	77	13	0	7	34	37	28	.244	.336	.351	.687	85	-5	-6	104	98	39	.633	0	1	-1	-2	C	-0.4
1955	Chi-A	138	426	67	111	13	1	16	61	68	34	.261	.375	.408	.783	110	8	7	101	103	68	.777	2	2	-1	-6	*C	0.5
1956	Chi-A	136	450	55	132	28	2	11	75	53	34	.293	.387	.438	.825	113	13	10	104	122	76	.795	2	0	1	-10	*C	0.2
1957	Chi-A	101	351	33	90	11	2	11	70	35	24	.256	.346	.393	.739	102	1	2	99	165	50	.701	2	0	1	-2	C	0.4
1958	Chi-A	127	421	53	115	16	0	20	84	57	37	.273	.370	.454	.824	128	16	17	98	137	72	.809	2	1	0	6	*C	2.4
1959	Chi-A	140	505	63	134	22	3	22	84	55	49	.265	.348	.451	.799	122	12	14	97	115	73	.738	4	3	-1	2	*C1	2.2
1960	Chi-A	129	421	43	106	23	0	7	46	42	39	.252	.331	.356	.688	85	-8	-8	101	105	47	.599	2	0	1	7	*C	0.6
1961	Chi-A	116	337	38	95	10	1	7	41	37	22	.282	.363	.380	.743	100	0	1	99	108	48	.692	0	0	0	-2	*C	-0.1
1962	Chi-A	84	220	17	59	12	0	2	26	32	23	.268	.369	.350	.719	100	-0	1	95	124	29	.681	1	0	0	-2	C	0.3
1963	Chi-A	35	73	4	17	4	0	0	6	8	7	.233	.317	.288	.605	68	-3	-3	104	120	7	.517	0	0	0	-3	C/1	-0.5
Total	18	1752	5351	623	1415	244	14	155	808	671	453	.264	.359	.402	.761	104	47	39	101	117	782	.749	20	10	0	-22	*C/13	7.9
■ **DOUG LOMAN**	Loman, Douglas Edward b: 5/9/58, Bakersfield, Cal. BL/TL, 5'11", 185 lbs. Deb: 9/03/84																											
1984	Mil-A	23	76	13	21	4	0	2	12	15	7	.276	.402	.408	.810	136	3	4	92	132	13	.825	0	2	-1	3	O	0.5
1985	Mil-A	24	66	10	14	3	2	0	7	1	12	.212	.224	.318	.542	44	-5	-5	105	132	5	.423	0	0	0	3	O	-0.2
Total	2	47	142	23	35	7	2	2	19	16	19	.246	.327	.366	.693	93	-2	-1	97	132	18	.633	0	2	-1	6	/O	0.3
■ **ERNIE LOMBARDI**	Lombardi, Ernesto Natali "Schnozz" or "Bocci" b: 4/6/08, Oakland, Cal. d: 9/26/77, Santa Cruz, Cal. BR/TR, 6'3", 230 lbs. Deb: 4/15/31 H																											
1931	Bro-N	73	182	20	54	7	1	4	23	12	12	.297	.340	.412	.752	100	0	-0	101	94	26	.688	1			-1	C	0.2
1932	Cin-N	118	413	43	125	22	9	11	68	41	19	.303	.371	.479	.851	132	16	18	96	112	76	.844	0			0	*C	2.2
1933	Cin-N	107	350	30	99	21	1	4	47	16	17	.283	.322	.383	.704	102	-0	0	99	121	36	.563	2			1	C	0.4
1934	Cin-N	132	417	42	127	19	4	9	62	16	22	.305	.335	.434	.769	103	2	1	101	107	53	.637	0			6	*C	1.1
1935	Cin-N	120	332	36	114	23	3	12	64	16	6	.343	.379	.539	.918	154	19	22	93	107	65	.865	0			2	C	2.3
1936	Cin-N	121	387	42	129	23	2	12	68	19	16	.333	.375	.496	.871	138	17	19	97	106	69	.802	1			1	*C	2.2
1937	Cin-N	120	368	41	123	22	1	9	59	14	17	.334	.362	.473	.835	137	12	16	91	106	60	.743	1			-0	C	1.8
1938	Cin-N	129	489	60	167	30	1	19	95	40	14	**.342**	.391	.524	.915	153	32	33	98	112	91	.841	0			-3	*C	3.5
1939	Cin-N	130	450	43	129	26	2	20	85	35	19	.287	.342	.487	.829	117	11	9	103	112	67	.745	0			-3	*C	1.0
1940	Cin-N	109	376	50	120	22	0	14	74	31	14	.319	.382	.489	.871	137	20	19	101	121	66	.810	0			-6	*C	1.8
1941	Cin-N	117	398	33	105	12	1	10	60	36	14	.264	.325	.374	.699	98	-2	-2	99	121	45	.596	1			-10	*C	0.0
1942	Bos-N	105	309	32	102	14	0	11	46	37	12	.330	.403	.482	.886	166	23	25	95	94	56	.839	1			-3	C	2.4
1943	NY-N	104	295	19	90	7	0	10	51	16	11	.305	.347	.431	.778	129	8	9	96	117	38	.659	1			-1	C	1.2
1944	NY-N	117	373	37	95	13	0	10	58	33	25	.255	.317	.370	.687	90	-4	-6	104	124	38	.571	0			-3	*C	-0.3
1945	NY-N	115	368	46	113	7	1	19	70	43	11	.307	.387	.486	.873	142	21	21	100	103	69	.850	0			2	C	2.5
1946	NY-N	88	238	19	69	4	1	12	39	18	24	.290	.347	.466	.814	128	8	8	102	99	37	.746	0			0	C	1.1
1947	NY-N	48	110	8	31	5	0	4	21	7	9	.282	.325	.436	.761	100	-0	-0	101	130	15	.663	0			0	C	0.0
Total	17	1853	5855	601	1792	277	27	190	990	430	262	.306	.358	.460	.818	126	180	192	98	111	907	.781	8			-15	*C	23.4
■ **PHIL LOMBARDI**	Lombardi, Phillip Andrew b: 2/20/63, Abilene, Tex. BR/TR, 6'2", 200 lbs. Deb: 4/26/86																											
1986	NY-A	20	36	6	10	3	0	2	6	4	7	.278	.366	.528	.894	137	2	2	103	96	6	.857	0	0	0	-1	/OC	0.1
1987	NY-A	5	8	0	1	0	0	0	0	0	2	.125	.125	.125	.250	-34	-1	-1	98	0	0	.143	0	0	0	-0	/C	0.0
Total	2	25	44	6	11	3	0	2	6	4	9	.250	.327	.455	.781	108	1	0	102	80	7	.758	0	0	0	-1	/OC	0.1
■ **STEVE LOMBARDOZZI**	Lombardozzi, Stephen Paul b: 4/26/60, Malden, Mass. BR/TR, 6', 175 lbs. Deb: 7/12/85																											
1985	Min-A	28	54	10	20	4	1	0	6	6	6	.370	.433	.481	.915	146	4	4	103	91	12	.972	3	2	-0	-2	2	0.2
1986	Min-A	156	453	53	103	20	5	8	33	52	76	.227	.308	.347	.655	73	-13	-18	108	73	50	.593	3	1	0	2	*2	-0.7
1987	Min-A	136	432	51	103	19	3	8	38	33	66	.238	.299	.352	.650	76	-17	-14	96	86	46	.571	5	1	1	-3	*2	-0.6
1988	Min-A	103	287	34	60	15	2	3	27	35	48	.209	.299	.307	.606	66	-11	-13	106	111	28	.543	2	5	-2	-8	2/S3	-1.8
Total	4	423	1226	148	286	58	11	19	104	126	196	.233	.308	.345	.653	75	-37	-42	103	87	136	.598	13	9	-2	-12	2/S3	-2.9
■ **WALTER LONERGAN**	Lonergan, Walter E. b: 9/22/1885, Boston, Mass. d: 1/23/58, Lexington, Mass. BR/TR, 5'7", 156 lbs. Deb: 8/17/11																											
1911	Bos-A	10	26	2	7	0	0	0	1	1		.269	.296	.269	.566	59	-1	-1	99	48	2	.474	1			0	/2S3	0.0
■ **DAN LONG**	Long, Daniel W. b: 8/27/1867, Boston, Mass. d: 4/30/29, Sausalito, Cal. Deb: 1888																											
1888	Lou-a	1	2	0	0	0	0	0	0	1		.000	.333	.000	.333	15	-0	-0	91	0	0	.500	0			0	/O	0.0
1890	BB-a	21	77	19	12	0	0	0		14		.156	.301	.156	.457	37	-5	-5	100	0	9	.677	16			0	O	-0.4
Total	2	22	79	19	12	0	0	0	0	15		.152	.302	.152	.454	37	-5	-5	100	0	9	.672	16			0	/O	-0.4
■ **HERMAN LONG**	Long, Herman C. "Germany" or "Flying Dutchman" b: 4/13/1866, Chicago, Ill. d: 9/17/09, Denver, Colo. BL/TR, 5'8.5", 160 lbs. Deb: 4/17/1889																											
1889	KC-a	136	574	137	158	32	6	3	60	64	63	.275	.358	.368	.726	103	8	2	106	67	110	.899	89			**45**	*S/2O	4.7
1890	Bos-N	101	431	95	108	15	3	8	52	40	34	.251	.320	.355	.675	89	-1	-8	111	78	66	.762	49			6	*S	-0.3
1891	Bos-N	139	577	129	163	21	11	9	74	80	51	.282	.377	.409	.786	117	25	14	112	71	115	.928	60			12	*S	2.8
1892	Bos-N	151	646	115	181	33	6	6	77	44	36	.280	.334	.378	.712	103	12	-0	113	80	103	.759	57			9	*SO/3	1.4
1893	Bos-N	128	552	**149**	159	22	6	6	58	73	32	.288	.376	.382	.758	101	5	2	103	60	96	.832	38			15	*S/2	1.7
1894	Bos-N	104	475	137	154	28	11	12	79	35	17	.324	.375	.505	.881	99	8	-5	113	70	102	.944	24			2	*S/O2	0.2
1895	Bos-N	124	535	109	169	23	10	9	75	31	12	.316	.357	.447	.803	105	5	2	103	76	100	.842	35			-11	*S/2	0.0
1896	Bos-N	120	501	105	172	26	8	6	100	26	16	.343	.382	.463	.845	115	16	10	108	122	105	.909	36			4	*S	1.2
1897	Bos-N	107	450	89	145	32	7	3	69	23		.322	.358	.444	.802	106	7	2	107	102	81	.810	22			-6	*S/O	0.0
1898	Bos-N	144	589	99	156	21	10	6	99	39		.265	.311	.365	.676	92	-5	-8	104	124	75	.633	20			-3	*S/2	-0.2
1899	Bos-N	145	578	91	153	30	8	6	100	45		.265	.321	.375	.697	89	-6	-11	105	125	78	.671	20			-15	*S/1	-1.5

YEAR	TM/L	G	AB	R	H	2B	3B	HR	RBI	BB	SO	AVG	OBP	SLG	PRO	/A	BR	/A	PF	CHI	RC	TA	SB	CS	SBR	FR	POS	TPR
1900	Bos-N	125	486	80	127	19	4	**12**	66	44		.261	.323	.391	.714	82	-2	-17	120	97	71	.724	26			-8	*S	-1.0
1901	Bos-N	138	518	54	112	14	6	3	68	25		.216	.252	.284	.536	51	-28	-36	112	155	43	.473	20			-5	*S	-3.3
1902	Bos-N	120	439	40	101	11	0	2	44	31		.230	.281	.269	.550	75	-14	-12	95	130	41	.512	24			18	*S2	1.2
1903	NY-A	22	80	6	15	3	0	0	8	2		.188	.207	.225	.432	31	-7	-7	100	163	4	.354	3			0	S	-0.5
	Det-A	69	239	21	53	12	0	0	23	10		.222	.253	.272	.525	61	-12	-11	97	130	20	.462	11			-3	S2	-1.1
	Yr	91	319	27	68	15	0	0	31	12		.213	.242	.260	.502	53	-18	-17	98	140	24	.434	14			-3		-1.6
1904	Phi-N	1	4	0	1	0	0	0	0	0		.250	.250	.250	.500	61	-0	-0	93	0	0	.333	0			0	/2	0.0
Total	16	1874	7674	1456	2127	342	96	91	1052	612	261	.277	.335	.383	.717	94	11	-82	108	97	1211	.745	534			60	*S/2013	5.3
■ **JIMMIE LONG**	Long, James Albert b: 6/29/1898, Ft.Dodge, Iowa d: 9/14/70, Ft.Dodge, Iowa BR/TR, 5'11", 160 lbs. Deb: 9/12/22																											
1922	Chi-A	3	3	0	0	0	0	0	0	1	0	.000	.250	.000	.250	-30	-1	-1	101	0	0	.333	0	0	0	0	/C	0.0
■ **JIM LONG**	Long, James M. b: 11/15/1862, Louisville, Ky. d: 12/12/32, Louisville, Ky. Deb: 8/09/1891																											
1891	Lou-a	6	25	5	6	0	0	0	4	3	6	.240	.367	.240	.607	85	-0	0	90	166	3	.632	1			0	/O	0.0
1893	Bal-N	55	226	31	48	8	1	2	25	16	27	.212	.276	.283	.560	47	-16	-19	107	103	25	.601	23			-2	O	-1.8
Total	2	61	251	36	54	8	1	2	29	19	33	.215	.286	.279	.565	51	-17	-19	105	110	27	.604	24			-2	/O	-1.8
■ **JEOFF LONG**	Long, Jeoffrey Keith b: 10/9/41, Covington, Ky. BR/TR, 6'1", 200 lbs. Deb: 7/31/63																											
1963	StL-N	5	5	0	1	0	0	0	0	0	1	.200	.200	.200	.400	14	-1	-1	107	0	0	.250	0	0	0	0	H	0.0
1964	StL-N	28	43	5	10	1	0	1	4	6	18	.233	.340	.326	.666	79	-0	-1	112	96	5	.618	0	0	0	-1	/O1	-0.1
	Chi-A	23	35	0	5	0	0	0	5	4	15	.143	.231	.143	.374	7	-4	-4	96	424	1	.290	0	0	0	-2	/1O	-0.6
Total	2	56	83	5	16	1	0	1	9	10	34	.193	.287	.241	.528	48	-5	-6	105	227	7	.456	0	0	0	-2	/O1	-0.7
■ **DALE LONG**	Long, Richard Dale b: 2/6/26, Springfield, Mo. BL/TL, 6'4", 205 lbs. Deb: 4/21/51																											
1951	Pit-N	10	12	1	2	0	0	1	1	0	3	.167	.167	.417	.583	48	-1	-1	107	48	1	.500	0	0	0	0	/1	0.0
	StL-A	34	105	11	25	5	1	2	11	10	22	.238	.310	.362	.672	78	-3	-4	105	89	13	.605	0	0	0	0	1/O	-0.3
1955	Pit-N	131	419	59	122	19	**13**	16	79	48	72	.291	.365	.513	.879	134	18	19	97	122	76	.846	0	1	-1	6	*1	1.6
1956	Pit-N	148	517	64	136	20	7	27	91	54	85	.263	.333	.485	.818	114	11	9	102	118	83	.783	1	0	0	-6	*1	-0.2
1957	Pit-N	7	22	0	4	1	0	0	5	4	10	.182	.308	.227	.535	50	-2	-1	94	423	2	.474	0	0	0	-0	/1	-0.1
	Chi-N	123	397	55	121	19	0	21	62	52	63	.305	.387	.511	.898	144	22	24	96	97	79	.899	1	1	-0	1	*1	1.6
	Yr	130	419	55	125	20	0	21	67	56	73	.298	.382	.496	.879	139	21	23	96	117	80	.875	1	1	-0	1		1.5
1958	Chi-N	142	480	68	130	26	4	20	75	66	64	.271	.361	.467	.828	116	12	12	101	111	80	.805	2	0	1	-2	*1/C	0.1
1959	Chi-N	110	296	34	70	10	3	14	37	31	53	.236	.309	.432	.741	96	-3	-2	98	88	39	.685	0	0	0	-1	1	-0.9
1960	SF-N	37	54	4	9	0	0	3	6	7	7	.167	.262	.333	.596	69	-3	-2	90	90	4	.521	0	0	0	-1	1	-0.3
	NY-A	26	41	6	15	3	1	3	10	5	6	.366	.435	.707	1.142	216	6	6	94	103	12	1.214	0	0	0	0	1	0.6
1961	Was-A	123	377	52	94	20	4	17	49	39	41	.249	.321	.459	.780	111	2	4	95	86	56	.734	0	0	0	-3	1	-0.7
1962	Was-A	67	191	17	46	8	0	4	24	18	22	.241	.310	.346	.655	75	-6	-7	101	122	20	.592	5	1	1	-0	1	-0.9
	NY-A	41	94	12	28	4	0	4	17	18	9	.298	.411	.468	.879	145	5	6	94	120	19	.926	1	0	0	-1	1	0.4
	Yr	108	285	29	74	12	0	8	41	36	31	.260	.345	.386	.731	98	-1	-0	98	123	41	.715	6	1	1	-1		-0.5
1963	NY-A	14	15	1	3	0	0	0	0	1	3	.200	.250	.200	.450	28	-1	-1	101	0	1	.333	0	0	0	0	/1	-0.1
Total	10	1013	3020	384	805	135	33	132	467	353	460	.267	.345	.464	.809	116	57	63	98	108	485	.799	10	3	1	-6	1/CO	0.8
■ **TOM LONG**	Long, Thomas Augustus b: 6/1/1890, Mitchum, Ala. d: 6/15/72, Mobile, Ala. BR/TR, 5'10.5", 165 lbs. Deb: 9/11/11																											
1911	Was-A	14	48	1	11	3	0	0	5	1		.229	.245	.292	.537	51	-3	-3	97	121	4	.514	4			-3	O	-0.6
1912	Was-A	1	1	0	0	0	0	0	0	0		.000	.000	.000	.000	-99	-0	-0	99	0	0	.000	0			0	H	0.0
1915	StL-N	140	507	61	149	21	**25**	2	61	31	50	.294	.339	.446	.785	136	20	20	100	102	77	.751	19	15	-3	-3	*O	1.1
1916	StL-N	119	403	37	118	11	10	1	33	10	43	.293	.312	.377	.689	115	4	5	97	85	48	.615	21	14	-2	-11	*O	-1.0
1917	StL-N	144	530	49	123	12	14	3	41	37	44	.232	.285	.325	.609	85	-9	-10	102	93	52	.570	21			-26	*O	-4.6
Total	5	418	1489	148	401	47	49	6	140	79	137	.269	.309	.379	.688	109	11	12	100	95	182	.640	65	29		-43	O	-5.1
■ **JOE LONNETT**	Lonnett, Joseph Paul b: 2/7/27, Beaver Falls, Pa. BR/TR, 5'10", 180 lbs. Deb: 4/22/56 C																											
1956	Phi-N	16	22	2	4	0	0	0	0	2	7	.182	.250	.182	.432	20	-2	-2	94	0	1	.316	0	0	0	0	/C	-0.1
1957	Phi-N	67	160	12	27	5	0	5	15	22	39	.169	.273	.294	.567	53	-11	-10	98	100	14	.515	0	0	0	0	C	-0.6
1958	Phi-N	17	50	0	7	2	0	0	2	2	11	.140	.173	.180	.353	-6	-8	-8	98	92	2	.250	0	0	0	0	C	-0.6
1959	Phi-N	43	93	8	16	1	0	1	10	14	17	.172	.287	.215	.502	36	-8	-8	99	176	6	.432	0	1	-1	-3	C	-0.9
Total	4	143	325	22	54	8	0	6	27	40	74	.166	.262	.246	.508	37	-29	-28	98	115	22	.444	0	1	-1	-3	C	-2.2
■ **BRUCE LOOK**	Look, Bruce Michael b: 6/9/43, Lansing, Mich. BL/TR, 5'11", 183 lbs. Deb: 4/17/68																											
1968	Min-A	59	118	7	29	4	0	0	9	20	24	.246	.355	.280	.635	89	0	-1	106	117	12	.558	0	1	-1	-2	C	0.0
■ **DEAN LOOK**	Look, Dean Zachary b: 7/23/37, Lansing, Mich. BR/TR, 5'11", 185 lbs. Deb: 9/22/61																											
1961	Chi-A	3	6	0	0	0	0	0	0	0	1	.000	.000	.000	.000	-99	-2	-2	99	0	0	.000	0	0	0	-0	/O	-0.1
■ **STAN LOPATA**	Lopata, Stanley Edward "Stash" b: 9/12/25, Delray, Mich. BR/TR, 6'2", 210 lbs. Deb: 9/19/48																											
1948	Phi-N	6	15	2	2	1	0	0	2	0	4	.133	.133	.200	.333	-12	-2	-2	94	250	0	.231	0			0	/C	-0.1
1949	Phi-N	83	240	31	65	9	2	8	27	21	44	.271	.330	.425	.755	100	-0	-0	101	81	33	.681	1			6	C	0.8
1950	Phi-N	58	129	10	27	2	2	1	11	22	25	.209	.325	.279	.604	62	-7	-6	97	109	12	.557	1			-1	C	-0.5
1951	Phi-N	3	5	0	0	0	0	0	0	0	0	.000	.000	.000	.000	-99	-1	-1	97	0	0	.000	0	0	0	0	/C	0.0
1952	Phi-N	57	179	25	49	9	1	4	27	36	33	.274	.395	.402	.798	120	7	6	101	128	31	.801	1	1	-0	2	C	1.0
1953	Phi-N	81	234	34	56	12	3	8	31	28	39	.239	.321	.419	.739	92	-3	-3	99	99	35	.721	3	1	0	-2	C	0.0
1954	Phi-N	86	259	42	75	14	5	14	42	33	37	.290	.372	.544	.916	137	13	13	99	90	50	.898	1	3	-2	2	C/1	1.5
1955	Phi-N	99	303	49	82	9	3	22	58	58	62	.271	.391	.538	.929	141	20	19	102	103	64	.974	4	1	1	10	C1	2.9
1956	Phi-N	146	535	96	143	33	7	32	95	75	93	.267	.358	.535	.893	144	27	31	94	111	100	.893	5	2	0	0	*C1	3.2
1957	Phi-N	116	388	50	92	18	2	18	67	56	81	.237	.335	.433	.768	106	3	3	98	128	56	.737	2	2	-1	0	*C	0.9
1958	Phi-N	86	258	36	64	9	0	9	33	60	63	.248	.394	.388	.781	110	6	6	98	107	39	.771	0	1	-1	1	C	1.1
1959	Mil-N	25	48	0	5	0	0	0	4	3	13	.104	.157	.104	.261	-30	-9	-8	95	323	1	.182	0	0	0	1	C/1	-0.6
1960	Mil-N	7	8	0	1	0	0	0	0	1	3	.125	.222	.125	.347	-2	-1	-1	91	0	0	.286	0	0	0	1	/C	0.0
Total	13	853	2601	375	661	116	25	116	397	393	497	.254	.354	.452	.805	115	50	56	98	111	422	.817	18	11		23	C/1	10.2
■ **DAVEY LOPES**	Lopes, David Earl b: 5/3/45, E.Providence, R.I. BR/TR, 5'9", 170 lbs. Deb: 9/22/72 C																											
1972	LA-N	11	42	6	9	4	0	0	1	7	6	.214	.327	.310	.636	87	-1	-1	94	28	5	.706	4	0	1	-1	2	0.1
1973	LA-N	142	535	77	147	13	5	6	37	62	77	.275	.355	.351	.707	96	-1	-1	100	76	69	.696	36	16	1	-12	*2/OS3	-0.6
1974	LA-N	145	530	95	141	26	3	10	35	66	71	.266	.352	.383	.735	114	5	10	93	59	77	.796	59	18	7	-14	*2	0.9
1975	LA-N	155	618	108	162	24	6	8	41	91	93	.262	.359	.359	.718	105	2	6	95	56	97	.831	**77**	12	**16**	-20	*2OS	0.9
1976	LA-N	117	427	72	103	17	7	4	20	56	49	.241	.335	.342	.677	93	-3	-3	100	52	58	.787	**63**	10	**13**	-6	*2O	0.9
1977	LA-N	134	502	85	142	19	5	11	53	73	69	.283	.376	.406	.782	110	9	9	100	95	87	.869	47	12	7	16	*2	4.0
1978	LA-N	151	587	93	163	25	4	17	58	71	70	.278	.356	.421	.776	117	13	14	99	74	97	.831	45	4	**11**	3	*2/O	3.9
1979	LA-N	153	582	109	154	20	6	28	73	97	88	.265	.373	.464	.837	127	23	24	100	72	113	.943	44	4	**11**	-30	*2	1.5
1980	LA-N	141	553	79	139	15	3	10	49	58	71	.251	.324	.344	.667	89	-9	-7	97	85	65	.634	23	7	3	-7	*2	-0.1
1981	LA-N	58	214	35	44	2	0	5	17	22	35	.206	.289	.285	.574	65	-10	-10	98	93	20	.592	20	2	5	1	2	0.0
1982	Oak-A	128	450	58	109	19	3	11	42	40	51	.242	.305	.371	.677	89	-10	-7	95	86	49	.643	28	12	1	-16	*2/O	-1.4
1983	Oak-A	147	494	64	137	13	4	17	67	51	61	.277	.347	.423	.770	116	8	11	96	103	76	.768	22	4	4	-28	*2D/O3	-0.8
1984	Oak-A	72	230	32	59	11	1	9	36	31	36	.257	.347	.430	.778	124	5	7	92	114	36	.799	12	0	4	-3	O2/3D	0.7
	Chi-N	16	17	5	4	1	0	0	0	6	5	.235	.435	.294	.729	98	1	0	110	0	4	1.077	3	0	1	-2	/O2	-0.1
1985	Chi-N	99	275	52	78	11	0	11	44	46	37	.284	.386	.444	.830	113	13	7	116	113	52	1.000	47	4	12	-8	O/32	0.9
1986	Chi-N	59	157	38	47	8	2	6	22	31	16	.299	.421	.490	.911	141	12	11	107	92	34	1.041	17	6	2	-4	3O	0.7
	Hou-N	37	98	11	23	2	1	1	13	12	9	.235	.318	.306	.624	71	-3	-4	103	157	10	.625	8	2	1	5	O/3	0.2
	Yr	96	255	49	70	10	3	7	35	43	25	.275	.383	.420	.803	115	9	7	105	118	46	.903	25	8	3	0		0.9
1987	Hou-N	47	43	4	10	2	0	1	6	13	8	.233	.411	.349	.760	112	1	1	93	133	7	.882	2	1	0	-1	/O	0.0

YEAR	TM/L	G	AB	R	H	2B	3B	HR	RBI	BB	SO	AVG	OBP	SLG	PRO	/A	BR	/A	PF	CHI	RC	TA	SB	CS	SBR	FR	POS	TPR
Total	16	1812	6354	1023	1671	232	50	155	614	833	852	.263	.351	.388	.740	106	54	68	98	80	955	.811	557	114	99	-126	*20/3DS	11.7

■ **AL LOPEZ** Lopez, Alfonso Ramon b: 8/20/08, Tampa, Fla. BR/TR, 5'11", 165 lbs. Deb: 9/27/28 MH

YEAR	TM/L	G	AB	R	H	2B	3B	HR	RBI	BB	SO	AVG	OBP	SLG	PRO	/A	BR	/A	PF	CHI	RC	TA	SB	CS	SBR	FR	POS	TPR
1928	Bro-N	3	12	0	0	0	0	0	0	0	0	.000	.000	.000	.000	-99	-3	-3	99	0	0	.000	0			0	/C	-0.2
1930	Bro-N	128	421	60	130	20	4	6	57	33	35	.309	.362	.418	.780	87	-8	-8	101	101	62	.735	3			-4	*C	-0.4
1931	Bro-N	111	360	38	97	13	4	0	40	28	33	.269	.324	.328	.652	75	-12	-12	101	121	40	.563	1			-1	*C	-0.8
1932	Bro-N	126	404	44	111	18	6	1	43	34	35	.275	.331	.356	.687	89	-8	-6	96	109	50	.618	3			-2	*C	-0.2
1933	Bro-N	126	372	39	112	11	4	3	41	21	39	.301	.338	.376	.715	107	2	3	97	103	47	.636	10			4	*C/2	1.2
1934	Bro-N	140	439	58	120	23	2	7	54	49	44	.273	.349	.383	.732	101	-2	2	95	103	60	.662	2			-7	*C/23	0.0
1935	Bro-N	128	379	50	95	12	4	3	39	35	36	.251	.316	.327	.643	78	-14	-11	94	106	41	.555	2			0	*C	-0.9
1936	Bos-N	128	426	46	103	12	5	7	50	41	41	.242	.311	.343	.654	80	-14	-11	95	106	45	.562	1			13	*C/1	0.5
1937	Bos-N	105	334	31	68	11	1	3	38	35	57	.204	.281	.269	.551	55	-23	-18	90	138	25	.459	3			11	*C	-0.3
1938	Bos-N	71	236	19	63	6	1	1	14	11	24	.267	.305	.314	.619	80	-9	-6	88	66	22	.505	5			5	C	0.1
1939	Bos-N	131	412	32	104	22	1	8	49	40	45	.252	.319	.369	.688	92	-9	-5	92	102	49	.607	1			5	*C	0.4
1940	Bos-N	36	119	20	35	3	1	2	17	6	8	.294	.328	.387	.715	98	-1	-1	99	121	15	.609	1			2	C	0.3
	Pit-N	59	174	15	45	6	2	1	24	13	13	.259	.310	.333	.643	81	-5	-4	95	146	17	.555	5			-1	C	-0.2
	Yr	95	293	35	80	9	3	3	41	19	21	.273	.317	.355	.672	88	-6	-5	97	138	32	.584	6			1		0.1
1941	Pit-N	114	317	33	84	9	1	5	43	31	23	.265	.330	.347	.677	89	-4	-5	103	124	36	.580	0			-3	*C	0.3
1942	Pit-N	103	289	17	74	8	2	1	26	34	17	.256	.338	.308	.646	89	-3	-3	101	105	31	.556	0			2	C	0.1
1943	Pit-N	118	372	40	98	9	4	1	39	44	25	.263	.341	.317	.659	87	-3	-5	104	116	43	.586	2			7	*C/3	0.7
1944	Pit-N	115	331	27	76	12	1	1	34	34	24	.230	.303	.281	.584	62	-15	-17	105	127	29	.504	4			-8	*C	-1.8
1945	Pit-N	91	243	22	53	8	0	0	18	35	12	.218	.317	.251	.568	57	-12	-13	103	102	21	.497	1			-5	C	-1.6
1946	Pit-N	56	150	13	46	2	0	1	12	23	14	.307	.399	.340	.739	107	3	3	103	83	21	.682	1			-0	C	0.4
1947	Cle-A	61	126	9	33	1	0	0	14	9	13	.262	.311	.270	.581	65	-6	-6	96	151	11	.463	1	1	-0	-2	C	-0.3
Total	19	1950	5916	613	1547	206	43	51	652	556	538	.261	.326	.337	.663	83	-147	-127	98	111	664	.597	46	1		16	*C/321	-2.7

■ **ART LOPEZ** Lopez, Arturo (Rodriguez) b: 6/8/37, Mayaguez, P.R. BL/TL, 5'9", 170 lbs. Deb: 4/12/65

YEAR	TM/L	G	AB	R	H	2B	3B	HR	RBI	BB	SO	AVG	OBP	SLG	PRO	/A	BR	/A	PF	CHI	RC	TA	SB	CS	SBR	FR	POS	TPR
1965	NY-A	38	49	5	7	0	0	0	0	1	6	.143	.160	.143	.303	-13	-7	-7	101	0	1	.190	0	0	0	-2	O	-0.9

■ **CARLOS LOPEZ** Lopez, Carlos Antonio (Morales) b: 9/27/50, Mazatlan, Mexico BR/TR, 6', 190 lbs. Deb: 9/17/76

YEAR	TM/L	G	AB	R	H	2B	3B	HR	RBI	BB	SO	AVG	OBP	SLG	PRO	/A	BR	/A	PF	CHI	RC	TA	SB	CS	SBR	FR	POS	TPR
1976	Cal-A	9	10	1	0	0	0	0	0	2	3	.000	.167	.000	.167	-53	-2	-2	92	0	0	.400	2	0	1	-1	/OD	-0.1
1977	Sea-A	99	297	39	84	18	1	8	34	14	61	.283	.322	.431	.753	107	1	2	96	89	44	.742	16	4	2	2	O/D	0.3
1978	Bal-A	129	193	21	46	6	0	4	20	9	34	.238	.276	.332	.607	77	-8	-6	91	104	15	.500	5	7	-3	-15	*O/D	-2.7
Total	3	237	500	61	130	24	1	12	54	25	98	.260	.301	.384	.685	93	-9	-6	94	92	59	.634	23	11	0	-14	O/D	-2.5

■ **HECTOR LOPEZ** Lopez, Hector Headley (Swainson) b: 7/9/29, Colon, Panama BR/TR, 5'11", 182 lbs. Deb: 5/12/55

YEAR	TM/L	G	AB	R	H	2B	3B	HR	RBI	BB	SO	AVG	OBP	SLG	PRO	/A	BR	/A	PF	CHI	RC	TA	SB	CS	SBR	FR	POS	TPR
1955	KC-A	128	483	50	140	15	2	15	68	33	58	.290	.339	.422	.761	102	1	0	101	104	65	.666	1	4	-2	9	32	1.1
1956	KC-A	151	561	91	153	27	3	18	69	63	73	.273	.349	.428	.777	103	3	2	101	93	83	.728	4	5	-2	10	*3O/2S	1.3
1957	KC-A	121	391	51	115	19	4	11	35	41	66	.294	.361	.448	.809	121	10	11	99	68	61	.748	1	6	-3	-0	*3/2O	1.0
1958	KC-A	151	564	84	147	28	4	17	73	49	61	.261	.322	.415	.737	96	-0	-4	106	109	70	.649	2	2	-1	1	23/SO	0.6
1959	KC-A	35	135	22	38	10	3	6	24	8	23	.281	.326	.533	.860	130	5	5	101	111	24	.837	1	0	0	1	2	0.7
	NY-A	112	406	60	115	16	2	16	69	28	54	.283	.339	.451	.789	124	7	11	93	120	61	.731	3	1	0	1	3O	1.0
	Yr	147	541	82	153	26	5	22	93	36	77	.283	.336	.471	.807	126	12	16	95	118	86	.759	4	1	1	1		1.7
1960	NY-A	131	408	66	116	14	6	9	42	46	64	.284	.362	.414	.777	116	6	9	94	84	63	.733	1	1	-0	1	*O/23	0.6
1961	NY-A	93	243	27	54	7	2	3	22	24	38	.222	.295	.305	.599	63	-14	-12	96	104	22	.508	1	0	0	-1	O	-1.5
1962	NY-A	106	335	45	92	19	1	6	48	33	53	.275	.340	.391	.731	103	-2	1	94	128	41	.628	0	1	-1	-6	O/23	-0.7
1963	NY-A	130	433	54	108	13	4	14	52	35	71	.249	.306	.395	.700	94	-4	-4	101	102	50	.611	1	2	-1	-7	*O/2	-1.6
1964	NY-A	127	285	34	74	9	3	10	34	24	54	.260	.319	.418	.737	100	1	-0	103	97	37	.659	1	1	-0	-14	*O/3	-1.9
1965	NY-A	111	283	25	74	12	2	7	39	26	61	.261	.326	.392	.718	102	1	1	101	123	34	.627	0	0	0	-8	O/1	-1.1
1966	NY-A	54	117	14	25	4	1	4	16	8	20	.214	.270	.368	.637	87	-3	-2	94	122	11	.542	0	0	0	-3	O	-0.6
Total	12	1450	4644	623	1251	193	37	136	591	418	696	.269	.333	.415	.747	104	12	17	99	102	622	.697	16	23	-9	-15	O32/S1	-1.1

■ **BRIS LORD** Lord, Bristol Robotham "The Human Eyeball" b: 9/21/1883, Upland, Pa. d: 11/13/64, Annapolis, Md. BR/TR, 5'9", 185 lbs. Deb: 4/21/05

YEAR	TM/L	G	AB	R	H	2B	3B	HR	RBI	BB	SO	AVG	OBP	SLG	PRO	/A	BR	/A	PF	CHI	RC	TA	SB	CS	SBR	FR	POS	TPR
1905	Phi-A	66	238	38	57	14	0	0	13	14		.239	.282	.298	.580	79	-4	-6	109	67	21	.486	3			2	O/3	-0.7
1906	Phi-A	118	434	50	101	13	7	1	44	27		.233	.278	.302	.580	89	-9	-5	94	127	41	.511	12			-0	*O	-1.1
1907	Phi-A	57	170	12	31	3	0	1	11	14		.182	.245	.218	.462	46	-9	-10	106	98	10	.381	2			-2	O/P	-1.6
1909	Cle-A	69	249	26	67	7	3	1	25	8		.269	.295	.333	.628	96	-1	-2	102	114	26	.560	10			4	O	0.0
1910	Cle-A	58	210	23	46	8	7	0	17	12		.219	.268	.324	.592	85	-4	-4	100	94	18	.524	4			3	O	-0.3
	Phi-A	70	279	55	78	13	11	1	20	23		.280	.337	.416	.752	133	10	10	102	60	40	.726	6			-4	O	0.3
	Yr	128	489	78	124	21	18	1	37	35		.254	.307	.376	.684	113	6	5	101	76	57	.636	10			-1		0.0
1911	Phi-A	134	574	92	178	36	11	3	55	35		.310	.355	.427	.782	127	12	17	93	63	91	.758	15			-11	*O	-0.4
1912	Phi-A	96	378	63	90	12	9	0	25	34		.238	.309	.317	.627	80	-10	-10	99	61	42	.604	15			-2	O	-1.7
1913	Bos-N	73	235	22	59	12	1	6	26	8	22	.251	.276	.387	.663	93	-5	-3	95	87	25	.602	7			-12	O	-1.6
Total	8	741	2767	381	707	118	49	13	236	175	22	.256	.303	.348	.651	97	-21	-15	99	84	315	.595	74			-22	O/P3	-7.1

■ **HARRY LORD** Lord, Harry Donald b: 3/8/1882, Porter, Me. d: 8/9/48, Westbrook, Maine BL/TR, 5'10.5", 165 lbs. Deb: 9/25/07 M

YEAR	TM/L	G	AB	R	H	2B	3B	HR	RBI	BB	SO	AVG	OBP	SLG	PRO	/A	BR	/A	PF	CHI	RC	TA	SB	CS	SBR	FR	POS	TPR
1907	Bos-A	10	38	4	6	1	0	0	3	1		.158	.179	.184	.364	17	-3	-4	101	162	1	.281	1			0	3	-0.2
1908	Bos-A	145	560	61	145	15	6	2	37	22		.259	.287	.318	.605	100	-2	-1	98	73	55	.537	23			-9	*3	0.0
1909	Bos-A	136	534	86	166	12	7	0	31	20		.311	.345	.360	.705	112	13	7	109	60	76	.696	36			-10	*3	0.3
1910	Bos-A	77	288	25	72	5	5	1	32	14		.250	.294	.313	.607	91	-4	-4	99	130	30	.579	17			-4	3/S	-0.4
	Chi-A	44	165	26	49	6	3	0	10	14		.297	.352	.370	.722	133	5	6	95	64	27	.793	17			-1	3	0.7
	Yr	121	453	51	121	11	8	1	42	28		.267	.315	.333	.649	106	1	2	98	107	56	.654	34			-5		0.3
1911	Chi-A	141	561	103	180	18	18	3	61	32		.321	.364	.433	.797	126	15	17	97	72	104	.850	43			-17	*3	0.0
1912	Chi-A	151	570	81	152	19	12	5	54	52		.267	.333	.368	.702	102	-0	1	99	77	80	.706	28			-19	*3O	-2.3
1913	Chi-A	150	547	62	144	18	12	1	42	45	39	.263	.327	.346	.673	102	-3	1	95	75	68	.658	24			-28	*3	-2.5
1914	Chi-A	21	69	8	13	1	1	1	3	5	3	.188	.243	.275	.519	54	-4	-4	103	52	5	.448	2	2	-1	-1	3/O	-0.5
1915	Buf-F	97	359	50	97	12	6	1	21	21	15	.270	.311	.345	.656	94	-3	-3	100	63	45	.611	15			-0	3/OM	0.0
Total	9	972	3691	506	1024	107	70	14	294	226	57	.277	.324	.356	.680	105	12	16	99	75	492	.665	206	2		-90	3/OS	-4.9

■ **CARLTON LORD** Lord, William Carlton b: 1/7/1900, Philadelphia, Pa. d: 8/15/47, Chester, Pa. BR/TR, 5'11", 170 lbs. Deb: 7/12/23

YEAR	TM/L	G	AB	R	H	2B	3B	HR	RBI	BB	SO	AVG	OBP	SLG	PRO	/A	BR	/A	PF	CHI	RC	TA	SB	CS	SBR	FR	POS	TPR
1923	Phi-N	17	47	3	11	2	0	0	2	2	3	.234	.265	.277	.542	38	-4	-5	114	54	3	.405	0	1	-1	-0	3	-0.4

■ **SCOTT LOUCKS** Loucks, Scott Gregory b: 11/11/56, Anchorage, Alaska BR/TR, 6', 178 lbs. Deb: 9/01/80

YEAR	TM/L	G	AB	R	H	2B	3B	HR	RBI	BB	SO	AVG	OBP	SLG	PRO	/A	BR	/A	PF	CHI	RC	TA	SB	CS	SBR	FR	POS	TPR
1980	Hou-N	8	3	4	1	0	0	0	0	0	2	.333	.333	.333	.667	89	-0	-0	98	0	0	.500	0	0	0	-1	/O	-0.1
1981	Hou-N	10	7	2	4	0	0	0	0	1	3	.571	.625	.571	1.196	273	1	2	88	0	3	2.000	1	0	0	-1	/O	0.1
1982	Hou-N	44	49	6	11	2	0	0	3	3	17	.224	.269	.265	.535	51	-3	-3	99	90	4	.500	4	1	1	-4	O	-0.7
1983	Hou-N	7	14	2	3	0	0	0	0	1	4	.214	.267	.214	.481	39	-1	-1	90	0	1	.462	2	2	-1	1	/O	0.0
1985	Pit-N	4	7	1	2	2	0	0	1	2	2	.286	.444	.571	1.016	177	1	1	103	100	2	1.200	0	0	0	-1	/O	0.0
Total	5	73	80	15	21	4	0	0	4	7	28	.262	.322	.313	.634	81	-2	-2	97	64	10	.629	7	3	0	-7	/O	-0.7

■ **BALDY LOUDEN** Louden, William b: 8/27/1885, Piedmont, W.Va. d: 12/8/35, Piedmont, W.Va. BR/TR, 5'11", 175 lbs. Deb: 9/13/07

YEAR	TM/L	G	AB	R	H	2B	3B	HR	RBI	BB	SO	AVG	OBP	SLG	PRO	/A	BR	/A	PF	CHI	RC	TA	SB	CS	SBR	FR	POS	TPR
1907	NY-A	4	9	4	1	0	0	0	0	2		.111	.273	.111	.384	23	-1	-1	109	0	1	.500	1			-0	/3	0.0
1912	Det-A	121	403	57	97	12	4	1	36	58		.241	.352	.298	.649	91	-5	-1	95	100	53	.709	28			14	23/S	1.1
1913	Det-A	76	191	28	46	4	5	0	23	24	22	.241	.344	.314	.658	94	-1	-1	99	136	23	.662	6			-1	23/SO	-0.1
1914	Buf-F	126	431	73	135	11	4	6	63	52	41	.313	.387	.399	.786	120	16	13	104	172	84	.875	35			-5	*S	1.6
1915	Buf-F	141	469	67	132	18	5	4	48	64	45	.281	.368	.367	.734	118	12	12	100	96	79	.789	30			11	2S3	2.8
1916	Cin-N	134	439	38	96	16	4	1	32	54	54	.219	.313	.280	.593	84	-7	-6	98	103	42	.569	12			15	*2S	1.5
Total	6	602	1942	267	507	61	22	12	202	254	162	.261	.353	.334	.687	103	15	17	99	108	282	.723	112			34	2S/3O	6.9

YEAR	TM/L	G	AB	R	H	2B	3B	HR	RBI	BB	SO	AVG	OBP	SLG	PRO	/A	BR	/A	PF	CHI	RC	TA	SB	CS	SBR	FR	POS	TPR
■ CHARLIE LOUDENSLAGER Loudenslager, Charles Edward b: 5/21/1881, Baltimore, Md. d: 10/31/33, Baltimore, Md. TR, 5'9", 186 lbs. Deb: 4/15/04																												
1904	Bro-N	1	2	0	0	0	0	0	0	0		.000	.000	.000	.000	-99	-0	-0	95	0	0	.000	0			0	/2	0.0
■ BILL LOUGHLIN Loughlin, William H. b: Baltimore, Md. Deb: 5/08/1883																												
1883	Bal-a	1	5	0	2	0	0	0		0		.400	.400	.400	.800	148	0	0	107	0	1	.667				0	/O	0.0
■ LOUGHRAN Loughran b:New York, N.Y. Deb: 6/06/1884																												
1884	NY-N	9	29	4	3	1	1	0	3	7	11	.103	.278	.207	.485	56	-1	-1	98	175	2	.500				0	/CO	0.0
■ TOM LOVELACE Lovelace, Thomas Rivers b: 10/19/1897, Wolfe City, Tex. d: 7/12/79, Dallas, Tex. BR/TR, 5'11", 170 lbs. Deb: 9/23/22																												
1922	Pit-N	1	1	0	0	0	0	0	0	0	0	.000	.000	.000	.000	-97	-0	-0	104	0	0	.000	0	0	0	0	H	0.0
■ LEN LOVETT Lovett, Leonard Walker b: 7/17/1852, Lancaster Co., Pa d: 11/18/22, Newark, Del. BR/TR, Deb: 8/04/1873																												
1873	Res-n	1	5	1	2							.400															/P	
1875	Cen-n	5	22	2	4							.182															/O	
Total	2 n	6	27	3	6							.222															/O	
■ MEM LOVETT Lovett, Merritt Marwood b: 6/15/12, Chicago, Ill. BR/TR, 5'9.5", 165 lbs. Deb: 9/04/33																												
1933	Chi-A	1	1	0	0	0	0	0	0	0	0	.000	.000	.000	.000	-99	-0	-0	101	0	0	.000	0	0	0	0	H	0.0
■ JAY LOVIGLIO Loviglio, John Paul b: 5/30/56, Freeport, N.Y. BR/TR, 5'9", 160 lbs. Deb: 9/02/80																												
1980	Phi-N	16	5	7	0	0	0	0	0	1	0	.000	.167	.000	.167	-46	-1	-1	107	0	-0	.286	1	2	-1	0	/2	-0.1
1981	Chi-A	14	15	5	4	0	0	0	2	1	1	.267	.313	.267	.579	69	-1	-1	100	196	0	.467	2	2	-1	1	/32D	0.0
1982	Chi-A	15	31	5	6	0	0	0	2	1	4	.194	.219	.194	.412	15	-4	-3	97	133	1	.346	2	1	0	2	2/D	0.0
1983	Chi-N	1	1	0	0	0	0	0	0	0	1	.000	.000	.000	.000	-99	-0	-0	101	0	0	.000	0	0	0	0	/H	0.0
Total	4	46	52	17	10	0	0	0	4	3	6	.192	.236	.192	.429	21	-5	-5	99	134	2	.383	5	5	-2	3	/2D3	-0.1
■ JOE LOVITTO Lovitto, Joseph b: 1/6/51, San Pedro, Cal. BB/TR, 6', 185 lbs. Deb: 4/15/72																												
1972	Tex-A	117	330	23	74	9	1	1	19	37	54	.224	.306	.267	.573	76	-11	-9	94	87	27	.509	13	11	-3	-1	*O	-1.6
1973	Tex-A	26	44	3	6	1	0	0	0	5	7	.136	.224	.159	.384	10	-5	-5	97	0	2	.342	1	0	0	-4	3/O	-0.9
1974	Tex-A	113	283	27	63	9	3	2	26	25	36	.223	.286	.297	.583	71	-12	-10	96	114	21	.483	6	8	-3	-1	*O/1	-1.7
1975	Tex-A	50	106	17	22	3	0	1	8	13	16	.208	.294	.264	.558	59	-6	-5	100	99	9	.489	2	2	-1	-2	O/1CD	-0.9
Total	4	306	763	70	165	22	4	4	53	80	113	.216	.292	.271	.564	67	-33	-29	96	93	59	.501	22	21	-6	-8	O/31DC	-5.1
■ TONY LOVULLO Lovullo, Salvatore Anthony b: 7/25/65, Santa Monica, Cal. BB/TR, 6', 185 lbs. Deb: 9/10/88																												
1988	Det-A	12	21	2	8	1	1	1	2	1	2	.381	.409	.667	1.076	208	3	3	94	47	5	1.071	0	0	0	-0	/23	0.3
■ FLETCHER LOW Low, Fletcher b: 4/7/1893, Essex, Mass. d: 6/6/73, Hanover, N.H. BR/TR, 5'10.5", 175 lbs. Deb: 10/07/15																												
1915	Bos-N	1	4	1	1	0	1	0	1	0	0	.250	.250	.750	1.000	201	0	0	98	130	1	1.000	0			0	/3	0.0
■ CHARLIE LOWE Lowe, Charles b: Baltimore, Md. Deb: 9/28/1872																												
1872	Atl-n	6	27	1	4							.148															/2	
■ DICK LOWE Lowe, Richard Alvern b: 1/28/1854, Evansville, Wis. d: 6/28/22, Janesville, Wis. Deb: 6/26/1884																												
1884	Det-N	1	3	0	1	0	0	0	0	0	1	.333	.333	.333	.667	118	0	0	94	0	0	.500				0	/C	0.0
■ BOBBY LOWE Lowe, Robert Lincoln "Link" b: 7/10/1868, Pittsburgh, Pa. d: 12/8/51, Detroit, Mich. BR/TR, 5'10", 150 lbs. Deb: 4/19/1890 M																												
1890	Bos-N	52	207	35	58	13	2	2	21	26	32	.280	.366	.391	.757	111	6	3	111	77	36	.832	15			0	SO3	0.3
1891	Bos-N	125	497	92	129	19	5	6	74	53	54	.260	.342	.354	.696	94	4	-5	112	118	77	.764	43			-0	*O2/S3P	-0.9
1892	Bos-N	124	475	79	115	16	7	3	57	37	46	.242	.308	.324	.632	82	-4	-13	113	110	60	.653	36			7	O3S2	-0.8
1893	Bos-N	126	526	130	157	19	5	14	89	55	29	.298	.369	.433	.803	112	10	8	103	87	95	.837	22			-1	*2/S	0.5
1894	Bos-N	133	613	158	212	34	11	17	115	50	25	.346	.401	.520	.921	108	21	5	113	74	140	.993	23			-9	*2/S3	0.3
1895	Bos-N	99	412	101	122	12	7	7	62	40	16	.296	.370	.410	.780	100	2	0	103	88	73	.831	24			14	*2	1.6
1896	Bos-N	73	305	59	98	11	4	2	48	20	11	.321	.371	.403	.774	98	3	-1	108	103	52	.783	15			23	2	2.0
1897	Bos-N	123	499	87	154	24	8	5	106	32		.309	.355	.419	.774	99	4	-2	107	147	82	.757	16			-8	*2	0.0
1898	Bos-N	147	559	65	152	11	7	4	94	29		.272	.311	.338	.649	85	-9	-12	104	144	64	.572	12			11	*2/S	0.5
1899	Bos-N	152	559	81	152	5	9	4	88	35		.272	.316	.335	.650	77	-15	-19	105	138	66	.590	17			-3	*2/S	-1.1
1900	Bos-N	127	474	65	132	11	5	3	71	26		.278	.316	.342	.658	70	-11	-25	120	132	57	.594	15			-11	*2	-2.6
1901	Bos-N	129	491	47	125	11	1	3	47	17		.255	.280	.299	.579	62	-19	-26	112	107	48	.508	22			-5	*32	-2.1
1902	Chi-N	119	472	41	116	13	3	0	31	11		.246	.263	.286	.549	74	-17	-15	96	84	41	.455	16			18	*2/3	1.2
1903	Chi-N	32	105	14	28	5	3	0	15	4		.267	.294	.371	.665	95	-2	-1	95	124	13	.623	5			-1	2/13	0.0
1904	Pit-N	1	1	0	0	0	0	0	0	0		.000	.000	.000	.000	-99	-0	-0	99	0	0	.000	0			0	H	0.0
	Det-A	140	506	47	105	14	6	0	40	17		.208	.233	.259	.492	60	-24	-22	96	116	35	.406	15			3	*2M	-2.0
1905	Det-A	58	181	17	35	7	2	0	9	13		.193	.247	.254	.502	62	-8	-7	98	70	12	.425	3			2	O3/2S1	-0.6
1906	Det-A	41	145	11	30	3	0	1	12	4		.207	.228	.248	.476	47	-8	-10	108	114	9	.374	3			1	S2/3	-0.9
1907	Det-A	17	37	2	9	2	0	0	5	4		.243	.317	.297	.614	97	0	-0	102	163	4	.536	0			-0	3/OS	0.0
Total	18	1818	7064	1131	1929	230	85	71	984	473	213	.273	.323	.360	.683	87	-66	-143	107	110	965	.656	302			40	*2O3/S1P	-4.6
■ JOHN LOWENSTEIN Lowenstein, John Lee b: 1/27/47, Wolf Point, Mont. BL/TR, 6', 175 lbs. Deb: 9/02/70																												
1970	Cle-A	17	43	5	11	3	1	1	6	1	9	.256	.273	.442	.715	82	-1	-1	115	110	5	.636	1	0	0	0	2/3OS	0.0
1971	Cle-A	58	140	15	26	5	0	4	9	16	28	.186	.269	.307	.576	60	-7	-8	106	67	11	.504	1	5	-3	-4	2O/S	-1.4
1972	Cle-A	68	151	16	32	8	1	6	21	20	43	.212	.304	.397	.701	100	1	0	107	112	18	.661	2	4	-2	-2	O/1	-0.6
1973	Cle-A	98	305	42	89	16	1	6	40	23	41	.292	.341	.410	.751	114	4	5	97	110	41	.671	5	3	-0	-2	O2/31D	0.2
1974	Cle-A	140	508	65	123	14	2	8	48	53	85	.242	.316	.325	.641	84	-9	-10	101	106	55	.627	36	17	1	-2	*O31/2	-1.3
1975	Cle-A	91	265	37	64	5	1	12	33	28	28	.242	.314	.404	.718	102	-0	0	100	89	32	.698	15	10	-2	-4	OD/32	-0.5
1976	Cle-A	93	229	33	47	8	2	2	14	25	35	.205	.283	.284	.567	67	-9	-9	100	76	18	.521	11	8	-2	-3	OD/1	-1.6
1977	Cle-A	81	149	24	36	6	1	4	12	21	29	.242	.335	.376	.711	96	-1	-1	98	70	16	.614	1	8	-5	-4	OD/1	-0.9
1978	Tex-A	77	176	28	39	8	3	5	21	37	29	.222	.363	.386	.749	115	4	5	96	100	29	.866	16	3	3	-9	3DO	-0.1
1979	Bal-A	97	197	33	50	8	2	11	34	30	37	.254	.355	.482	.837	127	7	7	97	102	36	.928	16	4	2	-5	O/13D	0.1
1980	Bal-A	104	196	38	61	8	0	4	27	32	29	.311	.408	.413	.821	125	8	8	101	113	36	.857	7	3	0	-14	O/D	-0.7
1981	Bal-A	83	189	19	47	7	0	6	20	22	32	.249	.330	.381	.711	106	1	1	99	87	22	.654	7	6	-2	-12	O/D	-1.3
1982	Bal-A	122	322	69	103	15	2	24	66	54	59	.320	.419	.602	1.022	177	35	35	100	99	81	1.108	7	6	-2	-11	*O	1.9
1983	Bal-A	122	310	52	87	13	2	15	60	49	55	.281	.381	.481	.861	135	16	16	100	121	61	.889	2	1	0	-13	*O/2D	0.1
1984	Bal-A	105	270	34	64	13	0	8	28	33	54	.237	.322	.374	.696	98	-3	-1	94	89	34	.645	1	0	0	-10	OD/1	-1.1
1985	Bal-A	12	26	0	2	0	0	0	2	2	3	.077	.143	.077	.220	-38	-5	-5	99	397	0	.167	0	0	0	-0	/OD	-0.4
Total	16	1368	3476	510	881	137	18	116	441	446	596	.253	.340	.403	.743	108	41	43	100	101	496	.743	128	78	-8	-93	OD/321S	-7.6
■ PEANUTS LOWREY Lowrey, Harry Lee b: 8/27/18, Culver City, Cal. d: 7/2/86, Inglewood, Cal. BR/TR, 5'8.5", 170 lbs. Deb: 4/14/42 C																												
1942	Chi-N	27	58	4	11	0	0	1	4	4	4	.190	.242	.241	.483	43	-4	-4	96	87	4	.383	0			1	O	-0.3
1943	Chi-N	130	480	59	140	25	12	1	63	35	24	.292	.340	.400	.740	115	7	8	99	119	64	.680	13			6	*OS/2	1.1
1945	Chi-N	143	523	72	148	22	7	7	89	48	27	.283	.343	.392	.735	105	2	3	99	139	73	.689	11			4	*O/S	0.1
1946	Chi-N	144	540	75	139	24	5	4	54	56	22	.257	.328	.343	.671	96	-7	-3	94	108	63	.612	10			2	*O3	-0.2
1947	Chi-N	115	448	56	126	17	5	5	37	38	26	.281	.339	.375	.714	88	-7	-7	101	79	58	.635	2			11	3O/2	0.1
1948	Chi-N	129	435	47	128	12	3	2	54	34	31	.294	.347	.349	.696	95	-6	-2	93	128	52	.594	2			5	*O/32S	-0.4
1949	Chi-N	38	111	18	30	5	0	2	10	9	8	.270	.325	.369	.694	91	-2	-1	94	80	13	.624	3			-4	O/3	-0.6
	Cin-N	89	309	48	85	16	2	2	25	37	11	.275	.354	.359	.714	96	-3	-1	96	82	39	.636	1			-1	O	-0.5
	Yr	127	420	66	115	21	2	4	35	46	19	.274	.347	.362	.709	95	-5	-2	95	82	53	.640	4			-4		-1.1
1950	Cin-N	91	264	34	60	14	0	1	11	36	7	.227	.320	.292	.612	59	-14	-15	105	53	25	.526	0			1	O/2	-1.6
	StL-N	17	56	10	15	0	0	1	4	6	1	.268	.349	.321	.671	75	-2	-2	103	73	7	.595	0			-0	/23O	-0.1
	Yr	108	320	44	75	14	0	2	15	42	8	.234	.325	.297	.622	62	-15	-17	104	57	35	.561	0			1		-1.7
1951	StL-N	114	370	52	112	19	5	5	40	35	12	.303	.366	.422	.788	110	6	6	101	90	57	.712	0	1	-1	-3	O3/2	0.0

YEAR	TM/L	G	AB	R	H	2B	3B	HR	RBI	BB	SO	AVG	OBP	SLG	PRO	/A	BR	/A	PF	CHI	RC	TA	SB	CS	SBR	FR	POS	TPR
1952	StL-N	132	374	48	107	18	2	1	48	34	13	.286	.352	.353	.705	98	-1	-0	98	139	48	.620	3	2	-0	-9	*O/3	-1.1
1953	StL-N	104	182	26	49	9	2	5	27	15	21	.269	.325	.423	.748	92	-2	-3	102	114	24	.660	1	0	0	-7	O2/3	-0.9
1954	StL-N	74	61	6	7	1	2	0	5	9	9	.115	.229	.197	.425	12	-8	-8	100	164	3	.375	0	0	0	-5	O	-1.2
1955	Phi-N	54	106	9	20	4	0	0	8	7	10	.189	.239	.226	.465	24	-11	-12	102	135	5	.351	2	0	1	-5	O/21	-1.6
Total	13	1401	4317	564	1177	186	45	37	479	403	226	.273	.336	.362	.699	93	-52	-42	98	108	533	.643	48	3		-3	O3/2S1	-7.2
■ **DWIGHT LOWRY**	Lowry, Dwight b: 10/23/57, Lumberton, N.C. BL/TR, 6'3", 210 lbs. Deb: 4/03/84																											
1984	Det-A	32	45	8	11	2	0	2	7	3	11	.244	.292	.422	.714	99	-0	-0	96	112	5	.595	0	0	0	-1	C	0.1
1986	Det-A	56	150	21	46	4	0	3	18	17	19	.307	.392	.393	.785	121	4	5	95	105	24	.741	0	0	0	5	C/1O	1.2
1987	Det-A	13	25	0	5	2	0	0	1	0	6	.200	.200	.280	.480	27	-3	-3	97	57	1	.350	0	0	0	0	C/1	-0.1
1988	Min-A	6	7	0	0	0	0	0	0	0	2	.000	.000	.000	.000	-94	-2	-2	106	0	0	.000	0	0	0	0	/CD	-0.1
Total	4	107	227	29	62	8	0	5	26	20	38	.273	.343	.374	.717	100	-1	0	96	99	30	.661	0	0	0	4	C/D1O	1.1
■ **JOHN LOWRY**	Lowry, John D. b: Baltimore, Md. Deb: 6/12/1875																											
1875	Nat-n	5	17	1	3							.176															/O	
■ **WILLIE LOZADO**	Lozado, William b: 5/12/59, New York, N.Y. BR/TR, 6', 166 lbs. Deb: 7/16/84																											
1984	Mil-A	43	107	15	29	8	2	1	20	12	23	.271	.345	.411	.756	118	1	2	92	170	15	.683	0	3	-2	2	3/S2D	0.4
■ **STEVE LUBRATICH**	Lubratich, Steven George b: 5/1/55, Oakland, Cal. BR/TR, 6', 170 lbs. Deb: 9/27/81																											
1981	Cal-A	7	21	2	3	1	0	0	1	0	2	.143	.143	.190	.333	-5	-3	-3	104	98	0	.263	1	0	0	-0	/3	-0.2
1983	Cal-A	57	156	12	34	9	0	0	7	4	17	.218	.237	.276	.513	43	-13	-12	96	64	10	.373	0	1	-1	10	S32	0.0
Total	2	64	177	14	37	10	0	0	8	4	19	.209	.227	.266	.492	37	-15	-15	97	68	10	.361	1	1	-0	9	/3S2	-0.2
■ **HAL LUBY**	Luby, Hugh Max b: 6/13/13, Blackfoot, Idaho d: 5/4/86, Eugene, Oregon BR/TR, 5'10", 185 lbs. Deb: 9/10/36																											
1936	Phi-A	9	38	3	7	1	0	0	3	0	7	.184	.205	.211	.416	3	-6	-6	101	129	2	.355	2	0	1	0	/2	-0.3
1944	NY-N	111	323	30	82	10	2	2	35	52	15	.254	.364	.316	.680	89	-1	-2	104	116	40	.640	2			9	32/1	1.4
Total	2	120	361	33	89	11	2	2	38	52	22	.247	.349	.305	.654	80	-7	-8	103	117	42	.609	4	0		9	/321	1.1
■ **JOHNNY LUCADELLO**	Lucadello, John b: 2/22/19, Thurber, Tex. BB/TR, 5'11", 160 lbs. Deb: 9/24/38																											
1938	StL-A	7	20	1	3	1	0	0	0	0	0	.150	.150	.200	.350	-13	-4	-4	100	0	1	.235	0	0	0	0	/3	-0.2
1939	StL-A	9	30	0	7	2	0	0	4	2	4	.233	.281	.300	.581	48	-2	-2	100	150	3	.478	0	0	0	0	/2	-0.1
1940	StL-A	17	63	15	20	4	2	2	10	6	4	.317	.394	.540	.934	132	4	3	106	92	15	1.000	1	0	0	2	2	0.6
1941	StL-A	107	351	58	98	22	4	2	31	48	23	.279	.366	.382	.748	98	-0	-0	100	78	54	.722	5	2	0	-3	2S/3O	0.4
1946	StL-A	87	210	21	52	7	1	1	15	36	20	.248	.358	.305	.662	88	-2	-2	98	85	26	.621	0	1	-1	0	32	0.2
1947	NY-A	12	12	0	1	0	0	0	0	1	5	.083	.154	.083	.237	-34	-2	-2	97	0	0	.167	0	0	0	0	/2	-0.1
Total	6	239	686	95	181	36	7	5	60	93	56	.264	.353	.359	.712	91	-7	-7	100	81	98	.682	6	3	0	-0	2/3SO	0.8
■ **RED LUCAS**	Lucas, Charles Frederick "The Nashville Narcissus" b: 4/28/02, Columbia, Tenn. d: 7/9/86, Nashville, Tenn. BL/TR, 5'9.5", 170 lbs. Deb: 4/19/23																											
1923	NY-N	3	2	0	0	0	0	0	0	0	1	.000	.000	.000	.000	-99	-1	-1	101	0	0	.000	0	0	0	1	/P	0.0
1924	Bos-N	33	33	5	11	1	0	0	5	1	4	.333	.353	.364	.717	98	-0	-0	94	152	4	.591	0	0	0	1	P/3	0.0
1925	Bos-N	6	20	1	3	0	0	0	2	2	4	.150	.227	.150	.377	-2	-3	-3	94	237	1	.294	0	0	0	-1	/2	-0.3
1926	Cin-N	66	76	15	23	4	4	0	14	10	13	.303	.384	.461	.844	133	3	3	95	138	13	.849	0			-1	P/2	0.0
1927	Cin-N	80	150	14	47	5	2	0	28	12	10	.313	.368	.373	.741	99	0	0	100	175	21	.670	0			-2	P/2SO	0.5
1928	Cin-N	39	73	8	23	2	1	0	7	4	6	.315	.351	.370	.721	92	-1	-1	96	92	9	.620	0			-0	P	0.0
1929	Cin-N	76	140	15	41	6	0	0	13	13	15	.293	.353	.336	.689	72	-6	-6	99	95	17	.616	1			0	P	0.1
1930	Cin-N	80	113	18	38	4	1	2	19	17	4	.336	.423	.442	.866	121	3	5	90	117	22	.893	0			-3	P	0.6
1931	Cin-N	97	153	15	43	4	0	0	17	12	9	.281	.333	.307	.641	77	-5	-4	95	129	17	.536	0			0	P	0.1
1932	Cin-N	76	150	13	43	11	2	0	19	10	9	.287	.335	.387	.722	97	-1	-1	96	122	20	.645	0			0	P	0.4
1933	Cin-N	75	122	14	35	6	1	1	15	12	6	.287	.356	.377	.733	111	2	2	99	115	17	.656	0			0	P	0.7
1934	Pit-N	68	105	11	23	5	1	0	8	6	16	.219	.261	.286	.547	44	-8	-9	105	96	8	.440	1			-3	P	-0.6
1935	Pit-N	47	66	6	21	6	0	0	10	7	11	.318	.392	.409	.801	108	2	1	107	134	11	.761	0			-1	P	0.3
1936	Pit-N	69	108	11	26	4	1	0	14	8	17	.241	.293	.296	.589	60	-6	-6	98	155	9	.460	0			-1	P	-0.2
1937	Pit-N	59	82	8	22	3	0	0	17	7	6	.268	.326	.305	.631	70	-3	-3	102	245	8	.516	0			-2	P	-0.1
1938	Pit-N	33	46	1	5	0	0	0	2	3	2	.109	.163	.109	.272	-24	-8	-8	100	145	1	.190	0			-1	P	-0.6
Total	16	907	1439	155	404	61	13	3	190	124	133	.281	.340	.347	.687	84	-33	-29	98	135	177	.608	2	0		-11	P/2S3O	0.9
■ **FRED LUCAS**	Lucas, Frederick Warrington "Fritz" b: 1/19/03, Vineland, N.J. d: 3/11/87, Cambridge, Md. BR/TR, 5'10", 165 lbs. Deb: 7/15/35																											
1935	Phi-N	20	34	1	9	0	0	0	2	3	6	.265	.324	.265	.589	53	-2	-2	114	80	3	.462	0			-2	O	-0.4
■ **JOHNNY LUCAS**	Lucas, John Charles "Buster" b: 2/10/03, Glen Carbon, Ill. d: 10/31/70, Maryville, Ill. BR/TL, 5'10", 186 lbs. Deb: 4/15/31																											
1931	Bos-A	3	2	0	0	0	0	0	0	0	1	.000	.000	.000	.000	-99	-1	-1	94	0	0	.000	0	0	0	-1	/O	-0.1
1932	Bos-A	1	1	0	0	0	0	0	0	0	0	.000	.000	.000	.000	-99	-0	-0	97	0	0	.000	0	0	0	0	H	0.0
Total	2	4	3	0	0	0	0	0	0	0	1	.000	.000	.000	.000	-99	-1	-1	95	0	0	.000	0	0	0	-1	/O	-0.1
■ **FRANK LUCE**	Luce, Frank Edward b: 12/6/1896, Spencer, Ohio d: 2/3/42, Milwaukee, Wis. BL/TR, 5'11", 180 lbs. Deb: 9/17/23																											
1923	Pit-N	9	12	2	6	0	0	0	3	2	2	.500	.571	.500	1.071	191	2	2	97	176	4	1.429	2	1	0	-2	/O	0.0
■ **FRED LUDERUS**	Luderus, Frederick William b: 9/12/1885, Milwaukee, Wis. d: 1/4/61, Milwaukee, Wis. BL/TR, 5'11.5", 185 lbs. Deb: 09																											
1909	Chi-N	11	37	8	11	1	1	1	9	3		.297	.366	.459	.825	157	2	2	101	167	6	.808	0			-0	1	0.2
1910	Chi-N	24	54	5	11	1	1	0	3	4	3	.204	.259	.259	.518	51	-3	-3	101	75	4	.419	0			-1	1	-0.4
	Phi-N	21	68	10	20	5	2	0	14	9	5	.294	.385	.426	.811	142	3	4	96	168	12	.854	2			-0	1	0.3
	Yr	45	122	15	31	6	3	0	17	13	8	.254	.331	.352	.683	101	-0	0	98	120	15	.648	2			-1		-0.1
1911	Phi-N	146	551	69	166	24	11	16	99	40	76	.301	.353	.472	.825	121	19	13	108	115	93	.805	6			-2	*1	0.6
1912	Phi-N	148	572	77	147	31	5	10	69	44	65	.257	.318	.381	.699	90	-9	-9	100	99	70	.652	8			8	*1	-0.6
1913	Phi-N	155	588	67	154	32	7	18	86	34	51	.262	.304	.432	.736	97	3	-5	112	107	75	.680	5			2	*1	-1.0
1914	Phi-N	121	443	55	110	16	5	12	55	33	31	.248	.308	.388	.696	106	2	2	100	98	51	.637	2			6	*1	0.5
1915	Phi-N	141	499	55	157	36	7	7	62	42	36	.315	.376	.457	.833	141	30	26	107	101	87	.819	9	7	-2	13	*1	3.3
1916	Phi-N	146	508	52	143	26	3	5	53	41	32	.281	.341	.374	.715	125	12	14	96	105	69	.668	8			-2	*1	0.7
1917	Phi-N	154	522	57	136	24	4	5	72	65	35	.261	.349	.351	.700	107	11	7	108	143	64	.671	5			4	*1	1.0
1918	Phi-N	125	468	54	135	23	2	5	67	42	33	.288	.351	.378	.729	112	13	8	109	140	61	.679	4			7	*1	1.3
1919	Phi-N	138	509	60	149	30	6	5	49	54	48	.293	.365	.405	.770	127	20	18	104	91	75	.750	6			10	*1	2.8
1920	Phi-N	16	32	1	5	2	0	0	4	3	6	.156	.229	.219	.447	27	-3	-3	109	221	2	.357	0	1	-1	0	/1	-0.3
Total	12	1346	4851	570	1344	251	54	84	642	414	421	.277	.340	.403	.743	113	100	73	105	113	669	.702	55	8		44	*1	8.4
■ **BILL LUDWIG**	Ludwig, William Lawrence b: 5/27/1882, Louisville, Ky. d: 9/5/47, Louisville, Ky. TR , Deb: 4/16/08																											
1908	StL-N	66	187	15	34	2	2	0	8	16		.182	.246	.214	.460	52	-10	-9	94	77	10	.386	3			2	C	-0.4
■ **ROY LUEBBE**	Luebbe, Roy John b: 9/17/1900, Parkersburg, Iowa d: 8/21/85, Papillion, Neb. BB/TR, 6', 175 lbs. Deb: 8/22/25																											
1925	NY-A	8	15	1	0	0	0	0	3	2	6	.000	.118	.000	.118	-71	-4	-4	96	0	0	.133	0	0	0	0	/C	-0.2
■ **HENRY LUFF**	Luff, Henry T. b: 9/14/1856, Philadelphia, Pa. d: 10/11/16, Philadelphia, Pa. Deb: 4/21/1875																											
1875	NH-n	38	172	15	45							.262															3/PO	
1882	Det-N	3	11	1	3	2	0	0	1	0	0	.273	.273	.455	.727	126	0	0	102	67	1	.625				0	/2O	0.0
	Cin-a	28	120	16	28	2	2	0		2		.233	.246	.283	.529	72	-3	-4	109	0	9	.391				-2	1/O	-0.5
1883	Lou-a	6	23	1	4	0	0	0		0		.174	.174	.174	.348	13	-2	-2	94	0	1	.211				0	/1O	-0.1
1884	Phi-U	26	111	9	30	4	2	0		4		.270	.296	.342	.638	124	2	3	93	0	12	.519	0			0	O/132	0.3
	KC-U	5	19	0	1	0	0	0		1		.053	.100	.053	.153	-54	-3	-2	87	0	0	.111	0			0	/3O	-0.1
	Yr	31	130	9	31	4	2	0		5		.238	.267	.300	.567	100	-1	1	92	0	11	.444	0			0		0.2
Total	3	68	284	27	66	8	4	0	1	7	0	.232	.251	.289	.540	81	-6	-5	99	3	22	.408	0			-2	/13OP2	-0.4

YEAR	TM/L	G	AB	R	H	2B	3B	HR	RBI	BB	SO	AVG	OBP	SLG	PRO	/A	BR	/A	PF	CHI	RC	TA	SB	CS	SBR	FR	POS	TPR
■ EDDIE LUKON	Lukon, Edward Paul "Mongoose" b: 8/5/20, Burgettstown, Pa. BL/TL, 5'10", 168 lbs. Deb: 8/06/41																											
1941	Cin-N	23	86	6	23	3	0	0	3	6	6	.267	.315	.302	.618	75	-3	-3	99	42	8	.516	1			1	O	-0.2
1945	Cin-N	2	8	1	1	0	0	0	0	0	1	.125	.125	.125	.250	-32	-1	-1	94	0	0	.143	0			0	/O	0.0
1946	Cin-N	102	312	31	78	8	8	12	34	26	29	.250	.310	.442	.752	108	3	2	104	73	43	.703	3			1	O	0.1
1947	Cin-N	86	200	26	41	6	1	11	33	28	36	.205	.306	.410	.716	97	-4	-2	91	106	26	.681	0			-1	O	-0.4
Total	4	213	606	64	143	17	9	23	70	60	72	.236	.307	.408	.714	98	-5	-4	99	79	77	.670	4			1	O	-0.5
■ MIKE LUM	Lum, Michael Ken-Wai b: 10/27/45, Honolulu, Hawaii BL/TL, 6', 180 lbs. Deb: 9/12/67 C																											
1967	Atl-N	9	26	1	6	0	0	0	1	1	4	.231	.259	.231	.490	40	-2	-2	104	69	1	.333	0	1	-1	1	/O	-0.1
1968	Atl-N	122	232	22	52	7	3	3	21	14	35	.224	.280	.319	.599	85	-6	-4	93	107	19	.497	3	5	-2	-11	O	-2.5
1969	Atl-N	121	168	20	45	8	0	1	22	16	18	.268	.332	.333	.665	84	-3	-3	104	149	18	.567	0	0	0	-9	O	-1.7
1970	Atl-N	123	291	25	74	17	2	7	28	17	43	.254	.307	.399	.705	84	-6	-8	104	79	36	.635	3	2	-0	-1	O	-1.3
1971	Atl-N	145	454	56	122	14	1	13	55	47	43	.269	.344	.390	.734	98	5	-0	110	104	61	.668	0	3	-2	10	*O/1	0.3
1972	Atl-N	123	369	40	84	14	2	9	38	50	52	.228	.325	.350	.674	87	-3	-5	105	100	43	.618	1	4	-2	4	*O/1	-0.8
1973	Atl-N	138	513	74	151	26	6	16	82	41	89	.294	.354	.462	.816	110	16	8	113	118	84	.773	2	5	-2	-1	1O	-0.1
1974	Atl-N	106	361	50	84	11	2	11	50	45	49	.233	.321	.366	.687	88	-4	-6	105	119	42	.622	0	2	-1	-3	1O	-1.5
1975	Atl-N	124	364	32	83	8	2	8	36	39	38	.228	.303	.327	.630	79	-13	-10	95	97	34	.541	2	4	-2	0	1O	-1.7
1976	Cin-N	84	136	15	31	5	1	3	20	22	24	.228	.340	.346	.685	92	-0	-1	103	138	17	.648	0	1	-1	-7	O	-1.0
1977	Cin-N	81	125	14	20	1	0	5	16	9	33	.160	.222	.288	.510	36	-12	-12	100	126	8	.449	2	0	1	-3	O/1	-1.5
1978	Cin-N	86	146	15	39	7	1	6	23	22	18	.267	.363	.452	.815	123	5	5	103	109	24	.793	0	0	0	1	O/1	0.4
1979	Atl-N	111	217	27	54	6	0	6	27	18	34	.249	.306	.359	.666	74	-6	-8	109	111	22	.558	0	2	-1	-1	1/O	-1.2
1980	Atl-N	93	83	7	17	3	0	0	5	18	19	.205	.347	.241	.587	66	-3	-3	101	99	8	.551	0	0	0	-5	O1	-0.8
1981	Atl-N	10	11	1	1	0	0	0	0	2	2	.091	.231	.091	.322	-6	-1	-1	100	0	0	.300	0	0	0	0	/O	0.0
	Chi-N	41	58	5	14	1	0	2	7	5	5	.241	.313	.362	.675	87	-1	-1	104	102	7	.600	0	0	0	-4	O/1	-0.5
	Yr	51	69	6	15	1	0	2	7	7	7	.217	.299	.319	.618	73	-2	-2	103	82	7	.545	0	0	0	-4		-0.5
Total	15	1517	3554	404	877	128	20	90	431	366	506	.247	.322	.370	.692	89	-34	-54	105	109	426	.636	13	29	-14	-28	O1	-14.0
■ HARRY LUMLEY	Lumley, Harry G "Judge" b: 9/29/1880, Forest City, Pa. d: 5/22/38, Binghamton, N.Y. BL/TL, 5'10", 183 lbs. Deb: 4/14/04 M																											
1904	Bro-N	150	577	79	161	23	**18**	**9**	78	41		.279	.327	.428	.755	141	21	24	95	92	93	.764	30			-3	*O	1.6
1905	Bro-N	130	505	50	148	19	10	7	47	36		.293	.340	.412	.752	131	15	17	96	63	80	.745	22			-9	*O	0.0
1906	Bro-N	133	484	72	157	23	12	9	61	48		.324	.385	**.477**	.863	**198**	38	**46**	87	83	105	.960	35			-4	*O	4.2
1907	Bro-N	127	454	47	121	23	11	9	66	31		.267	.313	.425	.739	141	15	17	94	120	68	.727	18			-22	*O	-0.9
1908	Bro-N	127	440	36	95	13	12	4	39	29		.216	.264	.327	.592	95	-6	-3	95	102	37	.513	4			-27	*O	-3.6
1909	Bro-N	55	172	13	43	8	3	0	14	16		.250	.314	.331	.645	103	0	0	99	89	18	.574	1			0	OM	-0.1
1910	Bro-N	8	21	3	3	0	0	0	0	3	6	.143	.280	.143	.423	25	-2	-2	95	0	1	.389	0			-1	/O	-0.2
Total	7	730	2653	300	728	109	66	38	305	204	6	.274	.326	.408	.735	138	82	100	94	90	401	.726	110			-65	O	1.0
■ JERRY LUMPE	Lumpe, Jerry Dean b: 6/2/33, Lincoln, Mo. BL/TR, 6'2", 185 lbs. Deb: 4/17/56 C																											
1956	NY-A	20	62	12	16	3	0	0	4	5	11	.258	.313	.306	.620	65	-3	-3	99	79	6	.521	1	1	-0	2	S/3	0.0
1957	NY-A	40	103	15	35	6	2	0	11	9	13	.340	.393	.437	.830	135	4	5	94	97	18	.789	2	2	-1	0	3/S	0.5
1958	NY-A	81	232	34	59	8	4	3	32	23	21	.254	.324	.362	.686	86	-3	-4	103	138	26	.599	1	2	-1	6	3/S	0.4
1959	NY-A	18	45	2	10	0	0	0	2	6	7	.222	.314	.222	.536	54	-3	-2	93	79	3	.432	0	0	0	0	3/S2	-0.1
	KC-A	108	403	47	98	11	5	3	28	41	32	.243	.313	.318	.631	73	-14	-15	101	85	41	.541	2	1	0	1	2S/3	-0.6
	Yr	126	448	49	108	11	5	3	30	47	39	.241	.313	.308	.621	71	-17	-17	100	85	44	.533	2	1	0	2		-0.7
1960	KC-A	146	574	69	156	19	3	8	53	48	49	.272	.328	.357	.685	86	-12	-11	99	87	67	.587	1	1	-0	-1	*2S	-0.1
1961	KC-A	148	569	81	167	29	9	3	54	48	39	.293	.351	.392	.742	96	-1	-3	102	97	79	.665	1	0	0	16	*2	3.1
1962	KC-A	156	641	89	193	34	10	10	83	44	38	.301	.346	.432	.778	108	6	6	100	103	94	.692	0	2	-1	-2	*2/S	1.4
1963	KC-A	157	595	75	161	26	7	5	59	58	44	.271	.335	.363	.698	89	-3	-8	108	113	74	.622	3	2	-0	3	*2	0.6
1964	Det-A	158	624	75	160	21	6	6	46	50	61	.256	.314	.338	.652	85	-15	-12	96	82	67	.556	2	1	0	-20	*2	-1.6
1965	Det-A	145	502	72	129	15	3	4	39	56	34	.257	.335	.323	.658	83	-7	-10	105	95	58	.594	7	0	2	-12	*2	-1.3
1966	Det-A	113	385	30	89	14	3	1	26	24	44	.231	.276	.291	.567	62	-18	-19	102	95	31	.450	0	3	-2	-4	2	-1.7
1967	Det-A	81	177	19	41	4	0	4	17	16	18	.232	.295	.322	.617	83	-4	-4	99	103	17	.525	0	0	0	0	2/3	-0.1
Total	12	1371	4912	620	1314	190	52	47	454	428	411	.268	.327	.356	.683	88	-73	-80	101	97	581	.610	20	15	-3	-11	*23S	0.5
■ DON LUND	Lund, Donald Andrew b: 5/18/23, Detroit, Mich. BR/TR, 6', 200 lbs. Deb: 7/03/45 C																											
1945	Bro-N	4	3	0	0	0	0	0	0	1	1	.000	.250	.000	.250	-28	-0	-0	96	0	0	.333	0			0	H	0.0
1947	Bro-N	11	20	5	6	2	0	2	5	3	7	.300	.391	.700	1.091	176	2	2	105	93	6	1.214	0			-0	/O	0.2
1948	Bro-N	27	69	9	13	4	0	1	5	5	16	.188	.243	.290	.533	42	-6	-6	104	81	5	.456	1			-2	O	-0.9
	StL-A	63	161	21	40	7	4	3	25	10	17	.248	.305	.398	.702	81	-4	-5	106	116	21	.631	0	0	0	-6	O	-1.2
1949	Det-A	2	2	0	0	0	0	0	0	0	1	.000	.000	.000	.000	-93	-1	-1	108	0	0	.000	0	0	0	0	H	0.0
1952	Det-A	8	23	1	7	0	0	0	1	3	3	.304	.385	.304	.689	94	-0	-0	99	53	3	.588	0	1	-1	-0	/O	0.0
1953	Det-A	131	421	51	108	21	4	9	47	39	65	.257	.323	.390	.712	94	-6	-5	98	91	53	.636	3	3	-1	8	*O	0.0
1954	Det-A	35	54	4	7	2	0	0	3	4	3	.130	.190	.167	.356	-2	-8	-8	100	126	2	.280	1	0	0	-8	O	-1.6
Total	7	281	753	91	181	36	8	15	86	65	113	.240	.305	.369	.674	81	-22	-23	100	96	89	.610	5	4		-9	O	-3.5
■ GORDY LUND	Lund, Gordon Thomas b: 2/23/41, Iron Mountain, Mich BR/TR, 5'11", 170 lbs. Deb: 8/01/67																											
1967	Cle-A	3	8	1	2	1	0	0	0	0	2	.250	.250	.375	.625	82	-0	-0	100	0	1	.500	0	0	0	0	/S	0.0
1969	Sea-A	20	38	4	10	0	0	0	1	5	7	.263	.349	.263	.612	75	-1	-1	98	40	4	.552	1	1	-0	-1	S/23	0.0
Total	2	23	46	5	12	1	0	0	1	5	9	.261	.333	.283	.616	76	-1	-1	99	34	5	.543	1	1	-0	-1	/S32	0.0
■ TOM LUNDSTEDT	Lundstedt, Thomas Robert b: 4/10/49, Davenport, Iowa BB/TR, 6'4", 195 lbs. Deb: 8/31/73																											
1973	Chi-N	4	5	0	0	0	0	0	0	0	1	.000	.000	.000	.000	-92	-1	-1	108	0	0	.000	0	0	0	0	/C	0.0
1974	Chi-N	22	32	1	3	0	0	0	0	5	7	.094	.216	.094	.310	-11	-5	-5	100	0	1	.276	0	0	0	-1	C	-0.4
1975	Min-A	18	28	2	3	0	0	0	1	4	5	.107	.219	.107	.326	-5	-4	-4	107	128	1	.269	0	0	0	-0	C/D	-0.3
Total	3	44	65	3	6	0	0	0	1	9	13	.092	.203	.092	.295	-14	-10	-10	104	55	2	.250	0	0	0	-2	/CD	-0.7
■ HARRY LUNTE	Lunte, Harry August b: 9/15/1892, St.Louis, Mo. d: 7/27/65, St.Louis, Mo. BR/TR, 5'11.5", 165 lbs. Deb: 5/19/19																											
1919	Cle-A	26	77	2	15	2	0	0	2	1	7	.195	.215	.221	.436	21	-8	-9	107	43	4	.306	0			0	S	-0.6
1920	Cle-A	23	71	6	14	0	0	0	7	5	6	.197	.250	.197	.447	19	-8	-8	104	176	3	.328	0	1	-1	2	S/2	-0.5
Total	2	49	148	8	29	2	0	0	9	6	13	.196	.232	.209	.442	20	-16	-17	105	108	7	.317	0	1		2	/S2	-1.1
■ TONY LUPIEN	Lupien, Ulysses John b: 4/23/17, Chelmsford, Mass. BL/TL, 5'10.5", 185 lbs. Deb: 9/12/40																											
1940	Bos-A	10	19	5	9	3	2	0	4	1	1	.474	.500	.842	1.342	239	4	4	101	90	8	1.700	0	0	0	0	/1	0.3
1942	Bos-A	128	463	63	130	25	7	3	70	50	20	.281	.351	.384	.735	103	4	2	104	**135**	65	.682	10	12	-4	-1	*1	-0.4
1943	Bos-A	154	608	65	155	21	9	4	47	54	23	.255	.317	.339	.656	89	-7	-9	104	83	70	.596	16	9	-1	4	*1	-1.0
1944	Phi-N	153	597	82	169	23	9	5	52	56	29	.283	.347	.377	.723	103	3	3	100	82	82	.697	18			0	*1	-0.9
1945	Phi-N	15	54	1	17	1	0	0	3	6	0	.315	.383	.333	.717	104	0	1	96	61	8	.703	2			0	1	0.0
1948	Chi-A	154	617	69	152	19	3	6	54	74	38	.246	.327	.316	.643	75	-25	-21	95	76	71	.589	11	7	-1	-4	*1	-1.7
Total	6	614	2358	285	632	92	30	18	230	241	111	.268	.337	.355	.692	93	-20	-21	100	91	304	.648	57	28	-1	-1	1	-3.7
■ AL LUPLOW	Luplow, Alvin David b: 3/13/39, Saginaw, Mich. BL/TR, 5'10", 175 lbs. Deb: 9/16/61																											
1961	Cle-A	5	18	0	1	0	0	0	0	2	6	.056	.150	.056	.206	-44	-4	-4	96	0	0	.176	0	0	0	2	/O	-0.1
1962	Cle-A	97	318	54	88	15	3	14	45	36	44	.277	.361	.475	.836	126	10	11	98	93	57	.833	1	0	0	-2	O	0.7
1963	Cle-A	100	295	34	69	6	2	7	27	33	62	.234	.317	.339	.656	87	-6	-5	97	93	32	.593	4	4	-1	2	O	-0.6
1964	Cle-A	19	18	1	2	0	0	0	1	1	8	.111	.158	.111	.269	-23	-3	-3	103	212	0	.158	0	0	0	-1	/O	-0.3
1965	Cle-A	53	45	3	6	2	0	1	4	3	14	.133	.188	.244	.432	22	-5	-5	98	119	2	.341	0	1	-1	-2	/O	-0.7
1966	NY-N	111	334	31	84	9	1	7	31	38	46	.251	.332	.347	.679	95	-4	-2	94	95	37	.594	2	6	-3	-7	*O	-1.4
1967	NY-N	41	112	11	23	1	0	3	9	8	19	.205	.264	.295	.559	60	-6	-6	99	89	9	.457	0	0	0	-1	O	-0.9
	Pit-N	55	103	13	19	1	0	1	8	6	14	.184	.236	.223	.460	32	-9	-9	100	127	6	.360	1	0	0	2	O	-0.7

YEAR	TM/L	G	AB	R	H	2B	3B	HR	RBI	BB	SO	AVG	OBP	SLG	PRO	/A	BR	/A	PF	CHI	RC	TA	SB	CS	SBR	FR	POS	TPR
	Yr	96	215	24	42	2	0	4	17	14	33	.195	.251	.260	.512	47	-15	-15	100	112	15	.417	1	0	0	1		-1.6
Total	7	481	1243	147	292	34	6	33	125	127	213	.235	.312	.352	.664	87	-26	-21	97	97	142	.607	8	11	-4	-6	O	-4.0
■ **SCOTT LUSADER**	Lusader, Scott Edward b: 9/30/64, Chicago, Ill. BL/TL, 5'10", 165 lbs. Deb: 9/01/87																											
1987	Det-A	23	47	8	15	3	1	1	8	5	7	.319	.385	.489	.874	135	2	2	97	123	9	.906	1	0	0	-4	O/D	-0.1
1988	Det-A	16	16	3	1	0	0	1	3	1	4	.063	.118	.250	.368	-0	-2	-2	94	170	0	.313	0	0	0	-0	/O	-0.2
Total	2	39	63	11	16	3	1	2	11	6	11	.254	.319	.429	.747	103	-0	0	96	134	10	.708	1	0	0	-4	/OD	-0.3
■ **ERNIE LUSH**	Lush, Ernest Benjamin b: 10/31/1884, Bridgeport, Conn. d: 2/26/37, Detroit, Mich. BR/TL, Deb: 4/20/10																											
1910	StL-N	1	4	0	0	0	0	0	0	1	1	.000	.200	.000	.200	-44	-1	-1	92	0	0	.250	0			-0	/O	0.0
■ **JOHNNY LUSH**	Lush, John Charles b: 10/8/1885, Williamsport, Pa. d: 11/18/46, Beverly Hills, Cal BL/TL, 5'9.5", 165 lbs. Deb: 4/22/04																											
1904	Phi-N	106	369	39	102	22	3	2	42	27		.276	.326	.369	.694	126	7	10	93	110	49	.655	12			0	1O/P	0.8
1905	Phi-N	6	16	3	5	0	0	0	1	1		.313	.353	.313	.665	97	0	-0	104	70	2	.545	0			0	/OP	0.0
1906	Phi-N	76	212	28	56	7	1	0	15	14		.264	.310	.307	.616	102	-2	0	92	84	23	.545	6			4	PO/1	1.2
1907	Phi-N	17	40	5	8	1	1	0	5	1		.200	.220	.275	.495	54	-2	-2	104	172	3	.406	1			1	/PO	0.0
	StL-N	27	82	6	23	2	3	0	5	5		.280	.322	.378	.700	127	2	2	96	61	12	.678	4			-1	P/O	0.0
	Yr	44	122	11	31	3	4	0	10	6		.254	.289	.344	.633	101	-0	-0	99	108	14	.582	5			-0		0.0
1908	StL-N	45	89	7	15	2	0	0	2	7		.169	.229	.191	.420	38	-6	-6	94	45	4	.338	1			0	P	0.0
1909	StL-N	45	92	11	22	5	0	0	14	6		.239	.293	.293	.586	86	-2	-2	96	189	8	.514	2			-1	P/1	0.0
1910	StL-N	47	93	8	21	1	3	0	10	8	11	.226	.287	.301	.588	78	-4	-3	92	125	8	.528	2			-2	P	0.0
Total	7	369	993	107	252	40	11	2	94	69	11	.254	.303	.322	.625	101	-7	0	94	105	108	.564	28			1	P/O1	2.0
■ **BILLY LUSH**	Lush, William Lucas b: 11/10/1873, Bridgeport, Conn. d: 8/28/51, Hawthorne, N.Y. BB/TR, 5'8", 165 lbs. Deb: 9/03/1895																											
1895	Was-N	5	18	2	6	0	0	0	2	2	1	.333	.400	.333	.733	90	-0	-0	103	95	2	.667	0			0	/O	0.0
1896	Was-N	97	352	74	87	9	11	4	45	66	49	.247	.369	.369	.738	102	0	4	95	97	60	.853	28			0	*O/2	-0.1
1897	Was-N	3	12	1	0	0	0	0	0	2		.000	.143	.000	.143	-59	-3	-3	101	0	0	.167	0			0	/O	-0.1
1901	Bos-N	7	27	2	5	1	1	0	3	3		.185	.267	.296	.563	58	-1	-2	112	111	2	.500	0			3	/O	0.1
1902	Bos-N	120	413	68	92	8	1	2	19	76		.223	.344	.262	.605	93	-1	2	95	61	49	.667	30			2	*O/3	-0.4
1903	Det-A	119	423	71	116	18	14	1	33	70		.274	.377	.390	.767	137	20	22	97	68	69	.811	14			2	*O3/2S	1.8
1904	Cle-A	138	477	76	123	13	8	1	50	72		.258	.355	.325	.680	117	13	13	102	125	61	.675	12			8	*O	1.4
Total	7	489	1722	294	429	49	35	8	152	291	50	.249	.358	.332	.690	110	29	35	98	88	243	.734	84			16	O/32S	2.7
■ **CHARLIE LUSKEY**	Luskey, Charles Melton b: 4/6/1876, Washington, D.C. d: 12/20/62, Bethesda, Md. 5'7", 165 lbs. Deb: 9/12/01																											
1901	Was-A	11	41	8	8	3	1	0	3	2		.195	.233	.317	.550	53	-3	-3	99	74	3	.455	0			0	/OC	-0.1
■ **LUKE LUTENBERG**	Lutenberg, Charles William b: 10/4/1864, Quincy, Ill. d: 12/24/38, Quincy, Ill. BR , 6'2", 225 lbs. Deb: 7/07/1894																											
1894	Lou-N	69	250	42	48	10	4	0	23	23	21	.192	.284	.264	.548	39	-27	-21	88	102	20	.505	4			1	1/2	-1.4
■ **LYLE LUTTRELL**	Luttrell, Lyle Kenneth b: 2/22/30, Bloomington, Ill. d: 7/11/84, Chattanooga, Tenn BR/TR, 6', 180 lbs. Deb: 5/15/56																											
1956	Was-A	38	122	17	23	5	3	2	9	8	19	.189	.256	.328	.584	52	-9	-9	102	73	9	.523	5	1	1	1	S	-0.3
1957	Was-A	19	45	4	9	4	0	0	5	3	8	.200	.250	.289	.539	48	-3	-3	98	152	3	.421	0	0	0	1	S	0.0
Total	2	57	167	21	32	9	3	2	14	11	27	.192	.254	.317	.572	51	-12	-12	101	94	12	.522	5	1	1	3	/S	-0.3
■ **RED LUTZ**	Lutz, Louis William b: 12/17/1898, Cincinnati, Ohio d: 2/22/84, Cincinnati, Ohio BR/TR, Deb: 5/31/22																											
1922	Cin-N	1	1	0	1	1	0	0	0	0	0	1.000	1.000	2.000	3.000	685	1	1	96	0	2	—	0	0	0	0	/C	0.1
■ **JOE LUTZ**	Lutz, Rollin Joseph b: 2/18/25, Keokuk, Iowa BL/TL, 6', 195 lbs. Deb: 4/17/51 C																											
1951	StL-A	14	36	7	6	0	1	0	2	6	9	.167	.286	.222	.508	37	-3	-3	105	89	3	.467	0	0	0	0	1	-0.2
■ **RUBE LUTZKE**	Lutzke, Walter John b: 11/17/1897, Milwaukee, Wis. d: 3/6/38, Granville, Wis. BR/TR, 5'11", 175 lbs. Deb: 4/18/23																											
1923	Cle-A	143	511	71	131	20	6	3	65	59	57	.256	.338	.337	.675	77	-16	-16	101	125	62	.635	10	6	-1	21	*3	2.1
1924	Cle-A	106	341	37	83	18	3	0	42	38	46	.243	.328	.314	.642	68	-17	-15	97	130	39	.597	4	0	1	15	*3/2	0.9
1925	Cle-A	81	238	31	52	9	0	1	16	26	29	.218	.295	.269	.564	41	-20	-23	106	80	20	.484	2	4	-2	1	32	-1.7
1926	Cle-A	142	475	42	124	28	6	0	59	34	35	.261	.313	.345	.658	72	-21	-20	100	122	53	.582	6	3	0	-1	*3	-0.7
1927	Cle-A	100	311	35	78	12	3	0	41	22	29	.251	.307	.309	.615	62	-18	-17	97	142	30	.528	2	0	1	4	3	-0.5
Total	5	572	1876	216	468	87	18	4	223	179	196	.249	.319	.321	.641	67	-92	-91	100	122	204	.577	24	13	-1	41	3/2	0.1
■ **GREG LUZINSKI**	Luzinski, Gregory Michael b: 11/22/50, Chicago, Ill. BR/TR, 6'1", 220 lbs. Deb: 9/09/70																											
1970	Phi-N	8	12	0	2	0	0	0	0	3	5	.167	.333	.167	.500	40	-1	-1	96	0	1	.417	0	1	-1	-0	/1	-0.1
1971	Phi-N	28	100	13	30	8	0	3	15	12	32	.300	.386	.470	.856	137	6	5	103	111	19	.863	2	0	1	1	1	0.5
1972	Phi-N	150	563	66	158	33	5	18	68	42	114	.281	.334	.453	.787	126	14	16	97	96	81	.709	0	4	-2	-2	*O/1	0.5
1973	Phi-N	161	610	76	174	26	4	29	97	51	135	.285	.347	.484	.831	119	21	15	108	108	101	.791	3	3	-1	-9	*O	-0.1
1974	Phi-N	85	302	29	82	14	1	7	48	29	76	.272	.335	.394	.729	100	1	-0	103	135	40	.662	3	0	1	3	O	0.0
1975	Phi-N	161	596	85	179	35	3	34	**120**	89	151	.300	.398	.540	.939	156	47	46	101	116	128	.970	3	6	-3	-10	*O	2.9
1976	Phi-N	149	533	74	162	28	1	21	95	50	107	.304	.375	.478	.854	131	28	24	107	117	96	.826	1	2	-1	-16	*O	0.1
1977	Phi-N	149	554	99	171	35	3	39	130	80	140	.309	.399	.594	.993	162	49	48	100	124	132	1.048	3	2	-0	-15	*O	2.8
1978	Phi-N	155	540	85	143	32	2	35	101	100	135	.265	.390	.526	.916	146	41	37	105	109	114	.973	8	7	-2	-15	*O	1.5
1979	Phi-N	137	452	47	114	23	1	18	81	56	103	.252	.347	.427	.774	114	7	9	97	133	68	.746	3	3	-1	-21	*O	-1.7
1980	Phi-N	106	368	44	84	19	1	19	56	60	100	.228	.346	.440	.786	110	9	6	107	103	60	.797	3	0	1	-18	*O	-1.6
1981	Chi-A	104	378	55	100	15	1	21	62	58	80	.265	.367	.476	.843	142	21	21	100	106	67	.837	0	0	0	0	*D	2.2
1982	Chi-A	159	583	87	170	37	1	18	102	89	120	.292	.391	.451	.842	134	27	29	97	136	103	.829	1	1	-0	0	*D	2.9
1983	Chi-A	144	502	73	128	26	1	32	95	70	117	.255	.358	.502	.860	130	24	21	103	113	93	.870	2	1	0	0	*D/1	2.1
1984	Chi-A	125	412	47	98	13	0	13	58	56	80	.238	.333	.364	.697	84	-3	-9	111	125	52	.656	5	1	1	0	*D	-0.7
Total	15	1821	6505	880	1795	344	24	307	1128	845	1495	.276	.366	.478	.844	129	291	269	103	116	1154	.857	37	31	-8	-103	*OD/1	11.3
■ **JERRY LYNCH**	Lynch, Gerald Thomas b: 7/17/30, Bay City, Mich. BL/TR, 6'1", 185 lbs. Deb: 4/15/54																											
1954	Pit-N	98	284	27	68	4	5	8	36	20	43	.239	.292	.373	.665	74	-12	-11	97	109	29	.568	2	2	-1	-4	O	-1.7
1955	Pit-N	88	282	43	80	18	6	5	28	22	33	.284	.336	.443	.779	108	1	3	97	81	40	.706	2	2	-1	-3	O/C	-0.2
1956	Pit-N	19	19	1	3	0	1	0	0	1	4	.158	.200	.263	.463	23	-2	-2	102	0	1	.375	0	0	0	0	/O	-0.1
1957	Cin-N	67	124	11	32	4	1	4	13	6	18	.258	.292	.403	.696	80	-3	-4	105	87	15	.602	0	0	0	-3	O/C	-0.7
1958	Cin-N	122	420	58	131	20	5	16	68	18	54	.312	.340	.498	.838	110	10	6	107	109	67	.760	1	4	-2	-9	*O	-0.8
1959	Cin-N	117	379	49	102	16	3	17	58	29	50	.269	.323	.462	.784	103	2	1	103	104	56	.729	2	0	1	-1	O	-0.1
1960	Cin-N	102	159	23	46	8	2	6	27	16	25	.289	.358	.478	.836	129	6	6	98	117	28	.809	0	0	0	-6	O	0.0
1961	Cin-N	96	181	33	57	13	2	13	50	27	25	.315	.407	.624	1.031	162	18	17	104	133	46	1.117	2	2	-1	-6	O	0.7
1962	Cin-N	114	288	41	81	15	4	12	57	24	38	.281	.339	.486	.825	116	7	6	102	128	46	.778	3	3	-1	-5	O	-0.3
1963	Cin-N	22	32	5	8	3	0	2	9	1	5	.250	.294	.531	.825	127	1	1	104	164	5	.792	0	0	0	-2	/O	0.0
	Pit-N	88	237	26	63	6	3	10	36	22	28	.266	.331	.443	.774	122	6	6	99	112	34	.711	0	1	-1	-10	O	-0.7
	Yr	110	269	31	71	9	3	12	45	23	33	.264	.327	.454	.780	122	7	7	100	124	39	.721	0	1	-1	-11		-0.7
1964	Pit-N	114	297	35	81	14	2	16	66	26	57	.273	.333	.495	.828	128	11	11	101	139	48	.784	0	1	-1	-17	O	-0.9
1965	Pit-N	73	121	7	34	1	0	5	16	8	26	.281	.331	.413	.744	108	1	1	100	102	14	.621	0	2	-1	-4	O	-0.5
1966	Pit-N	64	56	5	12	1	0	1	6	4	10	.214	.267	.286	.552	53	-3	-4	101	133	4	.444	0	0	0	-1	/O	-0.3
Total	13	1184	2879	364	798	123	34	115	470	224	416	.277	.331	.463	.795	110	42	36	101	112	434	.752	12	17	-7	-70	O/C	-5.6
■ **HENRY LYNCH**	Lynch, Henry W. b: 4/8/1866, Worcester, Mass. d: 11/23/25, Worcester, Mass. 5'7", 143 lbs. Deb: 9/21/1893																											
1893	Chi-N	4	14	0	3	2	0	0	2	1	1	.214	.267	.357	.624	64	-1	-1	104	109	1	.545	0			0	/O	0.0
■ **DANNY LYNCH**	Lynch, Matt Dan "Dummy" b: 2/7/27, Dallas, Tex. d: 6/30/78, Plano, Tex. BR/TR, 5'11", 174 lbs. Deb: 9/14/48																											
1948	Chi-N	7	7	3	2	0	0	1	1	1	1	.286	.375	.714	1.089	203	1	1	93	47	2	1.200	0			0	/2	0.1
■ **MIKE LYNCH**	Lynch, Michael Joseph b: 9/10/1875, St.Paul, Minn. d: 4/1/47, Jennings Lodge, Ore TR , 6'2", 170 lbs. Deb: 4/24/02																											
1902	Chi-N	7	28	4	4	0	0	0	0	2		.143	.200	.143	.343	8	-3	-3	96	0	1	.250	0			-1	/O	-0.4

YEAR	TM/L	G	AB	R	H	2B	3B	HR	RBI	BB	SO	AVG	OBP	SLG	PRO	/A	BR	/A	PF	CHI	RC	TA	SB	CS	SBR	FR	POS	TPR
■ TOM LYNCH	Lynch, Thomas James b: 4/3/1860, Bennington, Vt. d: 3/28/55, Cohoes, N.Y. BL/TR, 5'10.5", 170 lbs. Deb: 8/18/1884																											
1884	WiL-U	16	58	6	16	3	1	0		5		.276	.333	.362	.695	131	2	2	103	0	7	.619	0			0	/CO1	0.2
	Phi-N	13	48	7	15	4	2	0	3	4	5	.313	.365	.479	.845	177	3	4	92	46	9	.818				0	/CO	0.4
1885	Phi-N	13	53	7	10	3	0	0	1	10	3	.189	.317	.245	.563	81	-0	-1	104	23	4	.535				0	O	0.0
Total	2	42	159	20	41	10	3	0	4	19	8	.258	.337	.358	.696	127	5	5	100	21	20	.644				0	/OC1	0.6
■ WALT LYNCH	Lynch, Walter Edward "Jabber" b: 4/15/1897, Buffalo, N.Y. d: 12/21/76, Daytona Beach, Fla TR, 6', 176 lbs. Deb: 7/08/22																											
1922	Bos-A	3	2	1	1	0	0	0	0	0	0	.500	.500	.500	1.000	168	0	0	96	0	0	1.000	0	0	0	0	/C	0.0
■ BYRD LYNN	Lynn, Byrd "Birdie" b: 3/13/1889, Unionville, Ill. d: 2/5/40, Napa, Cal. BR/TR, 5'11", 165 lbs. Deb: 4/16/16																											
1916	Chi-A	31	40	4	9	1	0	0	3	4	7	.225	.311	.250	.561	64	-1	-2	108	107	4	.548	2			1	C	0.0
1917	Chi-A	35	72	7	16	2	0	0	5	7	11	.222	.300	.250	.550	70	-3	-2	98	100	6	.482	1			0	C	0.0
1918	Chi-A	5	8	0	2	0	0	0	0	2	1	.250	.400	.250	.650	96	0	0	101	0	1	.667	0			0	/C	0.0
1919	Chi-A	29	66	4	15	4	0	0	4	4	9	.227	.271	.288	.559	54	-4	-4	105	76	5	.451	0			-1	C	-0.3
1920	Chi-A	16	25	0	8	2	1	0	3	1	3	.320	.346	.480	.826	122	0	1	96	88	4	.765	0	0	0	0	C	0.2
Total	5	116	211	15	50	9	1	0	15	18	31	.237	.303	.289	.592	71	-7	-8	102	88	20	.522	3	0		1	/C	-0.1
■ FRED LYNN	Lynn, Fredric Michael b: 2/3/52, Chicago, Ill. BL/TL, 6'1", 185 lbs. Deb: 9/05/74																											
1974	Bos-A	15	43	5	18	2	2	2	10	6	6	.419	.500	.698	1.198	227	8	8	107	109	16	1.480	0	0	0	-0	O/D	0.7
1975	Bos-A	145	528	**103**	175	**47**	7	21	105	62	90	.331	.405	**.566**	**.971**	158	49	43	109	114	120	1.014	10	5	0	5	*O	4.4
1976	Bos-A	132	507	76	159	32	8	10	65	48	67	.314	.374	.467	.842	132	28	22	110	99	88	.820	14	9	-1	7	*O/D	2.7
1977	Bos-A	129	497	81	129	29	5	18	76	51	63	.260	.332	.447	.779	94	6	-6	117	116	72	.722	2	3	-1	1	*O/D	-0.9
1978	Bos-A	150	541	75	161	33	3	22	82	75	50	.298	.384	.492	.876	135	33	28	107	100	103	.873	3	6	-3	0	*O	2.2
1979	Bos-A	147	531	116	177	42	1	39	122	82	79	**.333**	.426	**.637**	**1.063**	**170**	**62**	**57**	107	109	**147**	**1.167**	2	2	-1	1	*O	4.9
1980	Bos-A	110	415	67	125	32	3	12	61	58	39	.301	.387	.480	.866	133	21	20	102	107	80	.897	12	0	4	5	*O	2.6
1981	Cal-A	76	256	28	56	8	1	5	31	38	42	.219	.327	.316	.643	83	-4	-5	104	129	27	.589	1	2	-1	-2	O	-0.9
1982	Cal-A	138	472	89	141	38	1	21	86	58	72	.299	.379	.517	.896	143	28	28	100	114	91	.897	7	8	-3	-9	*O	1.2
1983	Cal-A	117	437	56	119	20	3	22	74	55	83	.272	.356	.483	.839	134	17	20	96	111	76	.826	2	2	-1	-7	*O/D	1.1
1984	Cal-A	142	517	84	140	28	4	23	79	77	97	.271	.367	.474	.841	129	23	22	101	106	90	.830	2	2	-1	8	*O	2.5
1985	Bal-A	124	448	59	118	12	1	23	68	53	100	.263	.343	.449	.791	116	9	10	99	102	70	.771	7	3	0	-4	*O	0.4
1986	Bal-A	112	397	67	114	13	1	23	67	53	59	.287	.374	.499	.873	138	20	21	99	102	69	.836	2	2	-1	-10	*O/D	0.7
1987	Bal-A	111	396	49	100	24	0	23	60	39	72	.253	.321	.487	.808	114	5	7	98	93	58	.759	3	7	-3	-7	*O/D	-0.5
1988	Bal-A	87	301	37	76	13	1	18	37	28	66	.252	.316	.482	.798	126	7	9	95	75	44	.748	2	2	-1	-4	O/D	0.2
	Det-A	27	90	9	20	1	0	7	19	5	16	.222	.271	.467	.738	108	-0	0	94	120	11	.667	0	0	0	0	O/D	0.0
	Yr	114	391	46	96	14	1	25	56	33	82	.246	.306	.478	.784	122	7	9	95	87	58	.746	2	2	-1	-4		0.2
Total	15	1762	6376	1001	1828	374	41	289	1042	788	1001	.287	.368	.494	.862	131	314	283	104	106	1163	.877	69	53	-11	-17	*O/D	21.3
■ JERRY LYNN	Lynn, Jerome Edward b: 4/14/16, Scranton, Pa. d: 9/25/72, Scranton, Pa. BR/TR, 5'10", 164 lbs. Deb: 9/19/37																											
1937	Was-A	1	3	0	2	1	0	0	0	0	0	.667	.667	1.000	1.667	333	1	1	94	0	2	3.000	0	0	0	0	/2	0.1
■ RUSS LYON	Lyon, Russell Mayo b: 6/26/13, Ball Ground, Ga. BR/TR, 6'1", 230 lbs. Deb: 4/21/44																											
1944	Cle-A	7	11	1	2	0	0	0	0	1	1	.182	.250	.182	.432	24	-1	-1	100	0	0	.300	0	0	0	0	/C	0.0
■ BARRY LYONS	Lyons, Barry Stephen b: 6/3/60, Biloxi, Miss. BR/TR, 6'1", 205 lbs. Deb: 4/19/86																											
1986	NY-N	6	9	1	0	0	0	0	2	1	2	.000	.100	.000	.100	-73	-2	-2	96	0	0	.111	0	0	0	0	/C	-0.1
1987	NY-N	53	130	15	33	4	1	4	24	8	24	.254	.307	.392	.699	85	-3	-3	99	152	16	.622	0	0	0	1	C	0.2
1988	NY-N	50	91	5	21	7	1	0	11	3	12	.231	.255	.330	.585	74	-4	-3	90	147	7	.452	0	0	0	-2	C/1	-0.3
Total	3	109	230	21	54	11	2	4	37	12	38	.235	.279	.352	.631	75	-9	-8	95	144	23	.531	0	0	0	-1	/C1	-0.2
■ DENNY LYONS	Lyons, Dennis Patrick Aloysius b: 3/12/1866, Cincinnati, Ohio d: 1/3/29, W.Covington, Ky. BR/TR, 5'10", 185 lbs. Deb: 1885																											
1885	Pro-N	4	16	3	2	1	0	0	1	0	3	.125	.125	.188	.313	-0	-2	-2	91	123	0	.214				0	/3	0.0
1886	Phi-a	32	123	22	26	3	1	0		8		.211	.281	.252	.534	69	-4	-4	100	0	11	.515	7			0	3	-0.3
1887	Phi-a	137	570	128	209	43	14	6		47		.367	.421	.523	.943	166	48	49	99	0	160	1.175	73			-8	*3	2.9
1888	Phi-a	111	456	93	135	22	5	6	83	41		.296	.363	.406	.769	149	26	25	101	108	83	.847	39			-12	*3	1.2
1889	Phi-a	131	510	135	168	36	4	9	82	79	44	.329	.426	.469	.895	161	41	43	98	85	109	.980	10			7	*3/1	4.3
1890	Phi-a	88	339	79	120	29	5	7		57		.354	.458	.531	.989	200	42	44	97	0	94	1.215	21			10	3	4.5
1891	StL-a	120	451	124	142	24	3	11	84	88	58	.315	.445	.455	.900	141	41	29	114	108	98	1.036	9			-11	*3	1.9
1892	NY-N	108	389	71	100	16	7	8	51	59	36	.257	.359	.396	.755	133	15	17	98	93	61	.785	11			-8	*3	1.4
1893	Pit-N	131	490	103	150	19	16	3	105	97	29	.306	.430	.429	.858	123	26	20	106	139	101	.985	19			5	*3	2.2
1894	Pit-N	71	254	51	82	14	4	4	50	42	12	.323	.427	.457	.883	122	8	11	94	110	57	1.023	14			8	3	1.3
1895	StL-N	33	129	24	38	6	0	2	25	14	5	.295	.372	.388	.760	98	0	0	100	120	20	.758	3			-5	3	-0.2
1896	Pit-N	118	436	77	134	25	6	4	71	67	25	.307	.406	.420	.825	129	15	21	93	111	81	.887	13			-15	*3	0.9
1897	Pit-N	37	131	22	27	6	4	2	17	22		.206	.346	.359	.705	90	-2	-1	98	90	18	.769	5			0	1/3	0.0
Total	13	1121	4294	932	1333	244	69	62	569	621	212	.310	.407	.443	.850	141	256	252	101	83	894	.954	224			-30	*3/1	20.1
■ ED LYONS	Lyons, Edward Hoyte "Mouse" b: 5/12/23, Winston-Salem, N.C BR/TR, 5'9", 165 lbs. Deb: 9/15/47 C																											
1947	Was-A	7	26	2	4	0	0	0	0	2	2	.154	.214	.154	.368	3	-3	-3	97	0	1	.273	0	0	0	0	/2	-0.2
■ HARRY LYONS	Lyons, Harry P. b: 3/25/1866, Chester, Pa. d: 6/30/12, Mauricetown, N.J. BR/TR, 5'10.5", 157 lbs. Deb: 8/29/1887																											
1887	Phi-N	1	4	0	0	0	0	0	0	1	0	.000	.200	.000	.200	-40	-1	-1	97	0	0	.250	0			0	/O	0.0
	StL-a	2	8	2	1	0	0	0		0		.125	.125	.125	.250	-27	-1	-1	110	0	0	.429	2			0	/2O	0.0
1888	StL-a	123	499	66	97	10	5	4	63	20		.194	.230	.259	.488	53	-23	-30	111	142	39	.468	36			4	*O/3S2	-2.8
1889	NY-N	5	20	1	2	0	1	0	2	2	0	.100	.182	.200	.382	7	-3	-3	105	158	1	.333	0			0	/O	-0.1
1890	Roc-a	133	584	83	152	11	11	3		27		.260	.294	.332	.626	94	-12	-5	93	0	73	.623	47			12	*O/3CP	0.0
1892	NY-N	96	411	67	98	5	2	0	53	33	29	.238	.297	.260	.557	72	-14	-13	98	131	40	.530	25			0	O	-1.4
1893	NY-N	47	187	27	51	5	2	0	21	14	6	.273	.323	.321	.644	71	-7	-8	104	98	23	.618	10			2	O	-0.6
Total	6	407	1713	246	401	31	21	7	139	97	35	.234	.277	.289	.566	71	-60	-61	101	86	176	.546	120			18	O/32PCS	-4.9
■ PAT LYONS	Lyons, Patrick Jerry b: 1860, Canada d: 1/20/14, Springfield, Ohio TR, Deb: 7/21/1890																											
1890	Cle-N	11	38	2	2	1	0	0	1	4	4	.053	.143	.079	.222	-36	-6	-6	94	103	0	.194	0			0	2	-0.4
■ STEVE LYONS	Lyons, Stephen John b: 6/3/60, Tacoma, Wash. BL/TR, 6'3", 190 lbs. Deb: 4/15/85																											
1985	Bos-A	133	371	52	98	14	3	5	30	32	64	.264	.324	.358	.683	85	-6	-8	102	80	44	.627	12	9	-2	-13	*O/3SD	-2.3
1986	Bos-A	59	124	20	31	7	2	1	14	12	23	.250	.316	.363	.679	86	-2	-2	100	116	13	.596	2	3	-1	-1	O	-0.5
	Chi-A	42	123	10	25	2	1	0	6	7	24	.203	.252	.236	.488	34	-11	-11	101	82	7	.382	2	3	-1	0	O/31D	-1.2
	Yr	101	247	30	56	9	3	1	20	19	47	.227	.285	.300	.584	60	-13	-13	100	103	21	.495	4	6	-2	-1		-1.7
1987	Chi-A	76	193	26	54	11	1	1	19	12	37	.280	.322	.363	.685	76	-5	-7	109	104	22	.590	3	1	0	2	3O/2D	-0.5
1988	Chi-A	145	472	59	127	28	3	5	45	32	59	.269	.317	.373	.690	95	-5	-4	97	94	57	.595	1	2	-1	13	*3O/2C1	0.8
Total	4	455	1283	167	335	62	10	12	114	95	207	.261	.314	.353	.667	82	-30	-32	101	92	144	.587	20	18	-5	-0	O3/D2C1S	-3.7
■ TERRY LYONS	Lyons, Terence Hilbert b: 12/14/08, New Holland, Ohio d: 9/9/59, Dayton, Ohio BR/TR, 6'0.5", 165 lbs. Deb: 4/19/29																											
1929	Phi-N	1	0	0	0	0	0	0	0	0	0	—	—	—	—	—	0	0	110	—	—	—	0			0	/1	0.0
■ TED LYONS	Lyons, Theodore Amar b: 12/28/1900, Lake Charles, La. d: 7/25/86, Sulphur, La. BB/TR, 5'11", 200 lbs. Deb: 7/02/23 MCH																											
1923	Chi-A	9	5	0	1	0	0	0	1	1	3	.200	.333	.200	.533	43	-0	-0	98	342	0	.500	0	0	0	1	/P	0.0
1924	Chi-A	41	77	10	17	0	1	0	6	5	13	.221	.277	.247	.524	37	-7	-7	97	104	6	.417	0	0	0	-3	P	0.0
1925	Chi-A	43	97	6	18	3	0	0	7	3	13	.186	.218	.216	.434	11	-13	-13	96	112	5	.316	0	0	0	2	P	0.0
1926	Chi-A	41	104	7	22	1	1	0	3	1	10	.212	.219	.240	.459	22	-12	-11	92	41	6	.317	0	0	0	3	P	0.0
1927	Chi-A	41	110	16	28	6	2	1	9	6	17	.255	.293	.373	.666	70	-5	-5	102	68	12	.573	0	0	0	0	P	0.0
1928	Chi-A	49	91	10	23	2	0	0	8	1	9	.253	.261	.275	.536	41	-8	-8	99	110	7	.382	0	0	0	2	P	0.0
1929	Chi-A	40	91	7	20	4	0	0	11	9	13	.220	.290	.264	.554	46	-8	-7	95	157	8	.465	0	0	0	2	P/O	0.0

YEAR	TM/L	G	AB	R	H	2B	3B	HR	RBI	BB	SO	AVG	OBP	SLG	PRO	/A	BR	/A	PF	CHI	RC	TA	SB	CS	SBR	FR	POS	TPR
1930	Chi-A	57	122	20	38	6	3	1	15	2	18	.311	.323	.434	.757	88	-2	-3	103	89	17	.655	0	0	0	3	P	0.0
1931	Chi-A	42	33	6	5	0	0	0	3	2	1	.152	.200	.152	.352	-7	-5	-5	92	198	1	.250	0	0	0	-1	P	0.0
1932	Chi-A	49	73	11	19	2	1	1	10	4	10	.260	.308	.356	.664	82	-3	-2	87	115	8	.574	0	0	0	-1	P	0.0
1933	Chi-A	51	91	11	26	2	1	1	11	4	6	.286	.316	.363	.678	79	-3	-3	101	102	10	.561	0	1	-1	0	P	0.0
1934	Chi-A	50	97	9	20	4	0	1	16	3	19	.206	.245	.278	.523	35	-10	-10	99	178	7	.416	0	0	0	2	P	0.0
1935	Chi-A	29	82	5	18	4	0	0	6	3	4	.220	.256	.268	.524	33	-8	-9	109	93	6	.406	0	0	0	-1	P	0.0
1936	Chi-A	26	70	2	11	0	0	0	5	5	12	.157	.213	.157	.370	-7	-12	-12	99	147	3	.271	0	0	0	1	P	0.0
1937	Chi-A	23	57	6	12	0	0	0	3	9	14	.211	.318	.211	.529	35	-5	-6	103	86	5	.467	0	0	0	0	P	0.0
1938	Chi-A	24	72	9	14	2	0	0	4	2	9	.194	.216	.222	.438	10	-10	-10	98	84	4	.310	0	0	0	2	P	0.0
1939	Chi-A	21	61	5	18	3	0	0	8	5	7	.295	.348	.344	.693	73	-2	-3	107	129	8	.591	0	0	0	-1	P	0.0
1940	Chi-A	22	75	4	18	4	0	0	7	2	7	.240	.260	.293	.553	42	-6	-7	104	115	5	.393	0	0	0	-2	P	0.0
1941	Chi-A	22	74	8	20	2	0	0	6	2	6	.270	.289	.297	.587	59	-5	-4	94	97	6	.429	0	0	0	1	P	0.0
1942	Chi-A	20	67	10	16	4	0	0	10	3	7	.239	.282	.299	.580	64	-3	-3	99	176	6	.453	0	0	0	1	P	0.0
1946	Chi-A	5	14	0	0	0	0	0	0	1	3	.000	.067	.000	.067	-83	-3	-3	97	0	0	.071	0	0	0	0	/PM	0.0
Total	21	705	1563	162	364	49	9	5	149	73	201	.233	.270	.285	.556	44	-132	-129	99	111	128	.438	0	1	-1	10	P/O	0.0
■ BILL LYONS	Lyons, William Allen b: 4/26/58, Alton, Ill. BR/TR, 6'1", 175 lbs. Deb: 7/20/83																											
1983	StL-N	42	60	3	10	1	1	0	3	1	11	.167	.180	.217	.397	10	-7	-7	98	91	2	.321	3	2	-0	-1	2/3S	-0.7
1984	StL-N	46	73	13	16	3	0	0	3	9	13	.219	.305	.260	.565	61	-4	-4	99	62	7	.534	3	1	0	3	2S/3	0.1
Total	2	88	133	16	26	4	1	0	6	10	24	.195	.252	.241	.492	39	-11	-11	98	74	9	.436	6	3	0	2	/2S3	-0.6
■ DAD LYTLE	Lytle, Edward Benson "Pop" b: 3/10/1862, Racine, Wis. d: 12/21/50, Long Beach, Cal. 5'11", 160 lbs. Deb: 8/11/1890																											
1890	Chi-N	1	4	1	0	0	0	0	0	0	1	.000	.000	.000	.000	-92	-1	-1	109	0	0	.000	0			0	/O	0.0
	Pit-N	15	55	2	8	1	0	0	0	8	9	.145	.254	.164	.418	27	-5	-4	88	0	2	.362	0			0	/2O	-0.2
	Yr	16	59	3	8	1	0	0	0	8	10	.136	.239	.153	.391	18	-6	-5	89	0	2	.333	0			0		-0.2
Total	1	16	59	3	8	1	0	0	0	8	10	.136	.239	.153	.391	18	-6	-5	89	0	2	.333	0			0	/2O	-0.2
■ JIM LYTTLE	Lyttle, James Lawrence b: 5/20/46, Hamilton, Ohio BL/TR, 6', 180 lbs. Deb: 5/17/69																											
1969	NY-A	28	83	7	15	4	0	0	4	4	19	.181	.218	.229	.447	26	-8	-8	95	84	4	.343	1	2	-1	2	O	-0.7
1970	NY-A	87	126	20	39	7	1	3	14	10	26	.310	.360	.452	.813	133	4	5	92	86	18	.737	3	6	-3	-11	O	-1.2
1971	NY-A	49	86	7	17	5	0	1	7	8	18	.198	.274	.291	.564	62	-5	-4	97	102	6	.459	0	2	-1	-3	O	-0.9
1972	Chi-A	44	82	8	19	5	2	0	5	1	28	.232	.241	.341	.582	68	-3	-4	106	75	7	.453	0	1	-1	-1	O	-0.6
1973	Mon-N	49	116	12	30	5	1	4	19	9	14	.259	.312	.422	.734	98	-0	-1	104	125	14	.637	0	2	-1	2	O	-0.1
1974	Mon-N	25	9	1	3	0	0	0	2	1	3	.333	.400	.333	.733	102	0	0	104	257	1	.667	0	0	0	-5	O	-0.5
1975	Mon-N	44	55	7	15	4	0	0	6	13	6	.273	.412	.345	.757	103	2	1	108	122	9	.780	0	1	-1	-3	O	-0.2
1976	Mon-N	42	85	6	23	4	1	1	8	7	13	.271	.326	.376	.703	99	-0	-0	100	88	10	.609	0	0	0	-2	O	-0.2
	LA-N	23	68	3	15	3	0	0	5	8	12	.221	.303	.265	.567	62	-3	-3	100	107	6	.481	0	1	-1	6	O	0.2
	Yr	65	153	9	38	7	1	1	13	15	25	.248	.315	.327	.642	82	-3	-3	100	96	16	.560	0	1	-1	4		0.0
Total	8	391	710	71	176	37	5	9	70	61	139	.248	.308	.352	.660	86	-14	-14	100	101	75	.576	4	15	-8	-15	O	-4.2
■ HARVEY MacDONALD	MacDonald, Harvey Forsyth b: 5/18/1898, New York, N.Y. d: 10/4/65, Manoa, Pa. BL/TL, 5'11", 170 lbs. Deb: 6/12/28																											
1928	Phi-N	13	16	0	4	0	0	0	2	2	3	.250	.333	.250	.583	52	-1	-1	104	178	1	.500	0			-0	/O	-0.1
■ MACEY	Macey b:Columbus, Ohio Deb: 10/02/1890																											
1890	Phi-a	1	1	0	0	0	0	0		0		.000	.000	.000	.000	-99	-0	-0	97	0	0	.000	0			0	/C	0.0
■ MIKE MACFARLANE	Macfarlane, Michael Andrew b: 4/12/64, Stockton, Cal. BR/TR, 6', 195 lbs. Deb: 7/23/87																											
1987	KC-A	8	19	0	4	1	0	0	3	2	2	.211	.286	.263	.549	46	-1	-1	104	239	1	.438	0	0	0	0	/C	0.0
1988	KC-A	70	211	25	56	15	0	4	26	21	37	.265	.335	.393	.728	100	1	0	103	109	28	.656	0	0	0	-4	C	-0.1
Total	2	78	230	25	60	16	0	4	29	23	39	.261	.331	.383	.713	95	-0	-1	103	120	29	.640	0	0	0	-4	/C	-0.1
■ ED MacGAMWELL	MacGamwell, Edward M. b: 1/10/1879, Buffalo, N.Y. d: 5/26/24, Albany, N.Y. BL/TL, Deb: 4/14/05																											
1905	Bro-N	4	16	0	4	0	0	0	0	1		.250	.294	.250	.544	67	-1	-1	96	0	1	.417	0			0	/1	0.0
■ KEN MACHA	Macha, Kenneth Edward b: 9/29/50, Monroeville, Pa. BR/TR, 6'2", 215 lbs. Deb: 9/14/74 C																											
1974	Pit-N	5	5	1	3	1	0	0	1	0	0	.600	.600	.800	1.400	296	1	1	98	96	2	2.000	0	0	0	0	/C	0.1
1977	Pit-N	35	95	2	26	4	0	0	11	6	17	.274	.317	.316	.633	69	-4	-4	103	147	8	.487	1	1	-0	-2	31/O	-0.6
1978	Pit-N	29	52	5	11	1	1	0	5	12	10	.212	.359	.269	.629	74	-1	-1	105	142	6	.636	2	0	1	-0	3	0.0
1979	Mon-N	25	36	8	10	3	1	0	4	2	9	.278	.333	.417	.750	101	0	0	102	106	4	.621	0	0	0	-1	3/1OC	-0.1
1980	Mon-N	49	107	10	31	5	1	1	8	11	17	.290	.361	.383	.745	109	1	1	99	72	13	.639	0	2	-1	-2	3/1CO	-0.1
1981	Tor-A	37	85	4	17	2	0	0	6	8	15	.200	.269	.224	.492	39	-6	-7	111	124	5	.394	1	1	-0	-1	31/CD	-0.8
Total	6	180	380	30	98	16	3	1	35	39	68	.258	.330	.324	.654	79	-8	-10	104	115	39	.583	4	4	-1	-6	3/1OCD	-1.5
■ MIKE MACHA	Macha, Michael William b: 2/17/54, Victoria, Tex. BR/TR, 5'11", 180 lbs. Deb: 4/20/79																											
1979	Atl-N	6	13	2	2	0	0	0	1	1	5	.154	.214	.154	.368	2	-2	-2	109	198	0	.273	0	0	0	0	/3	-0.1
1980	Tor-A	5	8	0	0	0	0	0	0	0	1	.000	.000	.000	.000	-99	-2	-2	100	0	0	.000	0	0	0	-0	/3C	-0.1
Total	2	11	21	2	2	0	0	0	1	1	6	.095	.136	.095	.232	-34	-4	-4	106	126	0	.158	0	0	0	0	/3C	-0.2
■ DAVE MACHEMER	Machemer, David Ritchie b: 5/24/51, St.Joseph, Mo. BR/TR, 5'11.5", 180 lbs. Deb: 6/21/78																											
1978	Cal-A	10	22	6	6	1	0	1	2	2	1	.273	.333	.455	.788	118	1	0	102	61	3	.706	0	1	-1	-0	/23S	0.0
1979	Det-A	19	26	8	5	1	0	0	2	3	2	.192	.276	.231	.507	40	-2	-2	96	128	1	.375	0	3	-2	1	2/O	-0.2
Total	2	29	48	14	11	2	0	1	4	5	3	.229	.302	.333	.635	75	-2	-2	99	98	4	.512	0	4	-2	0	/23OS	-0.2
■ CONNIE MACK	Mack, Cornelius Alexander "The Tall Tactician" (born McGillicuddy) b: 12/22/1862, E.Brookfield, Mass d: 2/8/56, Germantown, Pa. BR/TR, 6'1", 150 lbs. Deb: 9/11/1886 MH																											
1886	Was-N	10	36	4	13	2	1	0	5	0	2	.361	.361	.472	.833	162	2	2	94	98	6	.739	0			0	C	0.2
1887	Was-N	82	314	35	63	6	1	0	20	8	17	.201	.228	.226	.454	29	-30	-27	95	89	23	.430	26			7	C/O2	-0.9
1888	Was-N	85	300	49	56	5	6	3	29	17	18	.187	.249	.273	.523	71	-10	-8	96	116	29	.566	31			14	C/OS1	0.8
1889	Was-N	98	386	51	113	16	1	0	42	15	12	.293	.333	.339	.672	98	-5	-0	92	98	54	.659	26			6	CO1	0.5
1890	Buf-P	123	503	95	134	15	12	0	53	47	13	.266	.353	.344	.697	96	-7	1	92	81	68	.694	16			12	*C/O1	1.4
1891	Pit-N	75	280	43	60	10	0	0	29	19	11	.214	.286	.250	.536	57	-14	-15	101	123	22	.464	4			2	C/1	-0.5
1892	Pit-N	97	346	39	84	9	4	1	31	21	22	.243	.298	.301	.598	88	-7	-4	94	91	35	.542	11			19	C/O1	1.8
1893	Pit-N	37	133	22	38	3	1	0	15	10	9	.286	.358	.323	.681	78	-3	-4	106	95	17	.653	4			2	C	0.1
1894	Pit-N	69	228	32	57	7	1	1	21	20	14	.250	.321	.303	.624	56	-17	-15	94	80	25	.591	8			5	CM	-0.1
1895	Pit-N	14	49	12	15	2	0	0	4	7	1	.306	.404	.347	.750	100	0	1	97	67	7	.765	1			0	C/1M	0.0
1896	Pit-N	33	120	9	26	4	1	0	16	5	8	.217	.248	.267	.515	40	-11	-10	93	144	8	.394	0			0	1/CM	-0.7
Total	11	723	2695	391	659	79	28	5	265	169	127	.245	.305	.300	.605	74	-102	-79	95	97	295	.574	127			68	C/1O2S	2.6
■ DENNY MACK	Mack, Dennis Joseph (born Dennis Joseph Mc Gee) b: 1851, Easton, Pa. d: 4/10/1888, Wilkes-Barre, Pa. BR/TR, 5'7", 164 lbs. Deb: 5/06/1871 M																											
1871	Rok-n	25	130	34	31							.238															*2/PS	
1872	Ath-n	46	227	66	56							.247															1S	
1873	Phi-n	46	218	54	61							.280															*1/O2S	
1874	Phi-n	56	261	47	53							.203															*1	
1876	StL-N	48	180	32	39	5	0	1	7	11	5	.217	.262	.261	.523	85	-4	-1	88	48	13	.411				-7	S/2O	-0.6
1880	Buf-N	17	59	5	12	0	0	0	3	5	7	.203	.266	.203	.469	68	-2	-1	91	93	3	.362				0	S/2	0.0
1882	Lou-a	72	264	41	48	3	1	0		16		.182	.229	.201	.429	49	-14	-12	94	0	12	.319				-13	S2/OM	-1.9
1883	Pit-a	60	224	26	44	5	3	0		13		.196	.241	.246	.486	61	-10	-8	94	0	14	.378				-1	S1/2	-1.1
Total	4 n	173	836	201	201							.240															S1/2	
Total	4	197	727	104	143	13	4	1	10	45	12	.197	.244	.230	.473	63	-31	-22	92	20	42	.363				-21	S1/2OP	-3.6
■ EARLE MACK	Mack, Earle Thaddeus (born Earle Thaddeus Mc Gillicuddy) b: 2/1/1890, Spencer, Mass. d: 2/4/67, Upper Darby Township, Pa. BL/TR, 5'8", 140 lbs. Deb: 10/05/10 MC																											
1910	Phi-A	1	4	0	2	0	1	0	0	0		.500	.500	1.000	1.500	361	1	1	102	0	2	2.000	0			0	/C	0.1

YEAR	TM/L	G	AB	R	H	2B	3B	HR	RBI	BB	SO	AVG	OBP	SLG	PRO	/A	BR	/A	PF	CHI	RC	TA	SB	CS	SBR	FR	POS	TPR
1911	Phi-A	2	4	0	0	0	0	0	0	0		.000	.000	.000	.000	-99	-1	-1	93	0	0	.000	0			0	/3	0.0
1914	Phi-A	2	8	0	0	0	0	0	1	0	0	.000	.000	.000	.000	-99	-2	-2	97	0	0	.125	1			0	/1	-0.1
Total	3	5	16	0	2	0	1	0	1	0	0	.125	.125	.250	.375	11	-2	-2	97	0	2	.357	1			0	/13C	0.0
■ REDDY MACK	Mack, Joseph (born Joseph Mc Namara) b: 5/2/1866, Ireland d: 12/30/16, Newport, Ky. Deb: 1885																											
1885	Lou-a	11	41	7	10	1	0	0		2		.244	.295	.268	.564	80	-1	-1	102	0	3	.452				0	2	0.0
1886	Lou-a	137	483	82	118	23	11	1		68		.244	.342	.344	.686	109	12	5	108	0	63	.688	13			6	*2	0.9
1887	Lou-a	128	478	117	147	23	8	1		83		.308	.415	.395	.811	121	23	17	107	0	90	.903	22			6	*2	1.9
1888	Lou-a	112	446	77	97	13	5	3	34	52		.217	.320	.289	.609	109	2	9	91	64	48	.613	18			6	*2	1.7
1889	Bal-a	136	519	84	125	24	7	1	87	60	69	.241	.329	.320	.649	87	-7	-7	100	142	64	.652	23			-12	*2/O	-1.3
1890	BB-a	26	95	14	27	3	5	0		10		.284	.370	.421	.791	136	4	4	100	0	18	.882	7			0	2	0.4
Total	6	550	2062	381	524	87	36	6	121	275	69	.254	.352	.340	.692	107	34	27	101	49	286	.712	83			6	2/O	3.6
■ JOE MACK	Mack, Joe John (born Joseph John Maciarz) b: 1/4/12, Chicago, Ill. BB/TL, 5'11.5", 185 lbs. Deb: 4/17/45																											
1945	Bos-N	66	260	30	60	13	1	3	44	34	39	.231	.320	.323	.643	70	-7	-11	112	158	29	.583	1			-1	1	-1.4
■ RAY MACK	Mack, Raymond James (born Raymond James Mlckovsky) b: 8/31/16, Cleveland, Ohio d: 5/7/69, Bucyrus, Ohio BR/TR, 6', 200 lbs. Deb: 9/09/38																											
1938	Cle-A	2	6	2	2	0	1	0	2	0	1	.333	.333	.667	1.000	146	0	0	99	169	1	1.000	0	0	0	0	/2	0.0
1939	Cle-A	36	112	12	17	4	1	1	6	12	19	.152	.240	.232	.472	22	-14	-13	98	70	6	.398	0	2	-1	-3	2/3	-1.4
1940	Cle-A	146	530	60	150	21	5	12	69	51	77	.283	.346	.409	.755	102	-4	1	93	101	76	.687	4	2	0	-9	*2	0.0
1941	Cle-A	145	500	54	114	22	4	9	44	54	69	.228	.303	.342	.645	70	-22	-23	101	80	55	.587	8	4	0	-6	*2	-1.4
1942	Cle-A	143	481	43	108	14	6	2	45	41	51	.225	.288	.291	.579	69	-24	-19	92	109	42	.497	9	3	1	-7	*2	-2.0
1943	Cle-A	153	545	56	120	25	2	7	62	47	61	.220	.285	.312	.596	83	-19	-12	90	121	49	.512	8	3	1	-3	*2	-0.8
1944	Cle-A	83	284	24	66	15	3	0	29	28	45	.232	.301	.306	.608	74	-10	-10	100	120	28	.527	4	1	1	2	2	-0.4
1946	Cle-A	61	171	13	35	6	2	1	9	23	27	.205	.299	.281	.580	71	-8	-6	89	67	16	.525	2	2	-1	-6	2	-0.7
1947	NY-A	1	0	0	0	0	0	0	0	0	0	—	—	—	—	—	0	0	97	—	—	—	0	0	0	0	R	0.0
	Chi-N	21	78	9	17	6	0	2	12	5	15	.218	.274	.372	.646	69	-4	-4	101	129	7	.547	0			1	2	0.0
Total	9	791	2707	273	629	113	24	34	278	261	365	.232	.301	.330	.631	77	-104	-85	94	102	297	.569	35	17		-30	2/3	-6.7
■ SHANE MACK	Mack, Shane Lee b: 12/7/63, Los Angeles, Cal. BR/TR, 6' ", 185 lbs. Deb: 5/25/87																											
1987	SD-N	105	238	28	57	11	3	4	25	18	47	.239	.301	.361	.663	77	-9	-8	97	102	22	.561	4	6	-2	-5	O	-1.9
1988	SD-N	56	119	13	29	3	0	0	12	14	21	.244	.338	.269	.607	78	-3	-3	97	150	13	.581	5	1	1	2	O	0.0
Total	2	161	357	41	86	14	3	4	37	32	68	.241	.314	.331	.644	78	-12	-10	97	118	35	.589	9	7	-2	-3	O	-1.9
■ PETE MACKANIN	Mackanin, Peter b: 8/1/51, Chicago, Ill. BR/TR, 6'2", 190 lbs. Deb: 7/03/73																											
1973	Tex-A	44	90	3	9	2	0	0	2	4	26	.100	.147	.122	.270	-24	-15	-14	97	71	2	.195	0	0	0	0	S3	-0.9
1974	Tex-A	2	6	0	1	0	1	0	0	0	2	.167	.167	.500	.667	89	-0	-0	96	0	1	.600	0	0	0	0	/S	0.0
1975	Mon-N	130	448	59	101	19	6	12	44	31	99	.225	.279	.375	.654	74	-14	-18	108	83	46	.589	11	5	0	10	*2/S3	-0.1
1976	Mon-N	114	380	36	85	15	2	8	33	15	66	.224	.257	.337	.594	67	-17	-18	100	84	31	.492	6	2	1	3	*2/3SO	-0.9
1977	Mon-N	55	85	9	19	2	2	1	6	4	17	.224	.258	.329	.588	57	-5	-5	98	77	7	.515	3	1	0	-2	/2S3O	-0.5
1978	Phi-N	5	8	0	2	0	0	0	1	0	4	.250	.250	.250	.500	38	-1	-1	105	198	1	.333	0	0	0	0	/13	0.0
1979	Phi-N	13	9	2	1	0	0	1	2	1	2	.111	.200	.444	.644	73	-0	-0	97	113	1	.625	0	0	0	0	/2S3	0.0
1980	Min-A	108	319	31	85	18	0	4	35	14	34	.266	.297	.361	.658	73	-10	-13	109	107	33	.556	6	2	1	6	2S/13D	0.0
1981	Min-A	77	225	21	52	7	1	4	18	7	40	.231	.258	.324	.582	64	-10	-11	105	83	18	.458	1	2	-1	-0	2S1/3D	-0.9
Total	9	548	1570	161	355	63	12	30	141	76	290	.226	.265	.339	.603	65	-72	-81	105	88	138	.521	27	12	1	17	2S/31DO	-3.3
■ ERIC MacKENZIE	MacKenzie, Eric Hugh b: 8/29/32, Glendon, Alt., Can. BL/TR, 6', 185 lbs. Deb: 4/23/55																											
1955	KC-A	1	1	0	0	0	0	0	0	0	0	.000	.000	.000	.000	-99	-0	-0	101	0	0	.000	0	0	0	0	/C	0.0
■ GORDON MacKENZIE	MacKenzie, Henry Gordon b: 7/9/37, St.Petersburg, Fla BR/TR, 5'11", 175 lbs. Deb: 8/13/61 C																											
1961	KC-A	11	24	1	3	0	0	0	1	1	6	.125	.160	.125	.285	-22	-4	-4	102	131	0	.182	0	0	0	0	/C	-0.3
■ FELIX MACKIEWICZ	Mackiewicz, Felix Thaddeus b: 11/20/17, Chicago, Ill. BR/TR, 6'2", 195 lbs. Deb: 9/07/41																											
1941	Phi-A	5	14	3	4	0	1	0	0	1	0	.286	.333	.429	.762	99	-0	-0	101	0	2	.700	0	0	0	-1	/O	0.0
1942	Phi-A	6	14	3	3	2	0	0	2	0	4	.214	.214	.357	.571	61	-1	-1	96	141	1	.455	0	0	0	1	/O	0.0
1943	Phi-A	9	16	1	1	0	0	0	0	2	8	.063	.167	.063	.229	-31	-3	-3	101	0	0	.200	0	0	0	0	/O	-0.2
1945	Cle-A	120	359	42	98	14	7	2	37	44	41	.273	.356	.368	.723	112	5	6	99	97	47	.656	5	5	-2	2	*O	0.2
1946	Cle-A	78	258	35	67	15	4	0	16	16	32	.260	.305	.349	.654	93	-7	-3	89	68	28	.566	5	1	1	2	O	-0.3
1947	Cle-A	2	5	0	0	0	0	0	0	0	2	.000	.000	.000	.000	-99	-1	-1	96	0	-0	.000	0	0	0	0	/O	-0.1
	Was-A	3	6	1	1	1	0	0	0	0	1	.167	.167	.333	.500	38	-1	-1	97	0	0	.400	0	0	0	-1	/O	-0.1
	Yr	5	11	1	1	1	0	0	0	0	3	.091	.091	.182	.273	-26	-2	-2	97	0	0	.200	0	0	0	-1		-0.2
Total	6	223	672	85	174	32	12	2	55	63	88	.259	.325	.351	.676	98	-7	-3	95	81	79	.619	10	6	-1	4	O	-0.5
■ STEVE MACKO	Macko, Steven Joseph b: 9/6/54, Burlington, Iowa d: 11/15/81, Arlington, Tex. BL/TR, 5'10", 160 lbs. Deb: 8/18/79																											
1979	Chi-N	19	40	2	9	1	0	0	3	4	8	.225	.295	.250	.545	45	-3	-3	112	119	3	.452	0	0	0	2	2/3	0.0
1980	Chi-N	6	20	2	6	2	0	0	2	0	3	.300	.300	.400	.700	88	-0	-0	106	99	2	.571	0	0	0	1	/S32	0.1
Total	2	25	60	4	15	3	0	0	5	4	11	.250	.297	.300	.597	58	-3	-4	110	113	6	.489	0	0	0	3	/23S	0.1
■ MAX MACON	Macon, Max Cullen b: 10/14/15, Pensacola, Fla. BL/TL, 6'3", 175 lbs. Deb: 4/21/38																											
1938	StL-N	46	36	5	11	0	0	0	3	2	4	.306	.342	.306	.648	71	-1	-1	111	99	4	.520	0			0	P/O	0.0
1940	Bro-N	2	1	0	1	0	0	0	0	0	0	1.000	1.000	1.000	2.000	420	0	0	108	0	1	—	0			0	/P	0.0
1942	Bro-N	26	43	4	12	2	1	0	1	2	4	.279	.311	.372	.683	98	-0	-0	102	23	5	.613	1			-0	P	0.0
1943	Bro-N	45	55	7	9	0	0	0	6	0	1	.164	.164	.164	.327	-5	-7	-7	100	241	1	.213	1			1	P/1	0.0
1944	Bos-N	106	366	38	100	15	3	3	36	12	23	.273	.296	.355	.651	88	-9	-7	95	93	38	.550	7			-2	1O/P	-1.6
1947	Bos-N	1	1	0	0	0	0	0	0	0	0	.000	.000	.000	.000	-99	-0	-0	97	0	0	.000	0			0	/P	0.0
Total	6	226	502	54	133	17	4	3	46	16	32	.265	.288	.333	.620	77	-18	-16	97	102	49	.520	9			-1	/P1O	-1.6
■ WADDY MacPHEE	MacPhee, Walter Scott b: 12/23/1899, Brooklyn, N.Y. d: 1/20/80, Charlotte, N.C. BR/TR, 5'8", 140 lbs. Deb: 9/27/22																											
1922	NY-N	2	7	2	2	0	1	0	0	1	0	.286	.375	.571	.946	136	0	0	104	0	2	1.000	0	0	0	0	/3	0.1
■ JIMMY MACULLAR	Macullar, James F. "Little Mac" b: 1/6/1855, Boston, Mass. d: 4/8/24, Baltimore, Md. BR/TL, Deb: 5/05/1879 M																											
1879	Syr-N	64	246	24	52	9	0	0	13	3	27	.211	.221	.248	.469	61	-12	-8	89	76	14	.330				-3	SO/23M	-0.7
1882	Cin-a	79	299	44	70	6	6	0		14		.234	.268	.294	.563	82	-3	-7	109	0	24	.445				-1	*O	-0.8
1883	Cin-a	14	48	4	8	2	0	0		4		.167	.231	.208	.439	41	-3	-3	103	0	2	.350				0	O/S	-0.2
1884	Bal-a	107	360	73	73	16	6	4		36		.203	.290	.314	.603	101	1	2	99	0	34	.547				1	*S	0.1
1885	Bal-a	100	320	52	61	7	6	3		49		.191	.306	.278	.584	83	-2	-5	106	0	28	.548				-1	*S/O	-0.3
1886	Bal-a	85	268	49	55	7	1	0		49		.205	.332	.239	.571	91	-3	2	91	0	30	.648	23			-12	S/O2P	-0.4
Total	6	449	1541	246	319	47	19	7	13	155	27	.207	.285	.276	.561	84	-21	-19	99	11	131	.505	23			-16	SO/2P3	-2.3
■ GENE MADDEN	Madden, Eugene b: 6/5/1890, Elm Grove, W.Va. d: 4/6/49, Utica, N.Y. BL/TR, 5'10", 155 lbs. Deb: 4/20/16																											
1916	Pit-N	1	1	0	0	0	0	0	0	0	0	.000	.000	.000	.000	-96	-0	-0	105	0	0	.000	0			0	H	0.0
■ FRANK MADDEN	Madden, Francis A. "Red" b: 10/17/1892, Pittsburgh, Pa. d: 4/30/52, Pittsburgh, Pa. Deb: 7/04/14																											
1914	Pit-F	2	2	0	1	0	0	0	1	0	0	.500	.500	.500	1.000	198	0	0	94	361	1	1.000	0			0	/C	0.0
■ BUNNY MADDEN	Madden, Thomas Francis b: 9/14/1882, Boston, Mass. d: 1/20/54, Cambridge, Mass. BR/TR, 5'10", 190 lbs. Deb: 6/03/09																											
1909	Bos-A	10	17	0	4	0	0	0	1	0		.235	.235	.235	.471	45	-1	-1	109	96	1	.308	0			0	/C	0.0
1910	Bos-A	14	35	4	13	3	0	0	4	3		.371	.436	.457	.893	181	3	3	99	92	7	.909	0			-1	C	0.4
1911	Bos-A	4	15	2	3	0	0	0	2	2		.200	.294	.200	.494	39	-1	-1	99	239	1	.417	0			0	/C	0.0
	Phi-N	28	76	4	21	1	1	0	4	0	13	.276	.276	.316	.592	61	-4	-4	108	56	6	.436	0			0	C	-0.2
Total	3	56	143	10	41	4	1	0	11	5	13	.287	.315	.329	.644	84	-3	-3	105	91	15	.520	0			-1	/C	0.2

YEAR	TM/L	G	AB	R	H	2B	3B	HR	RBI	BB	SO	AVG	OBP	SLG	PRO	/A	BR	/A	PF	CHI	RC	TA	SB	CS	SBR	FR	POS	TPR
■ TOMMY MADDEN	Madden, Thomas Joseph b: 7/31/1883, Philadelphia, Pa. d: 7/26/30, Philadelphia, Pa. BL/TL, 5'11", 160 lbs. Deb: 9/10/06																											
1906	Bos-N	4	15	1	4	0	0	0	0	0	1	.267	.313	.267	.579	83	-0	-0	100	0	1	.455	0			-0	/O	0.0
1910	NY-A	1	1	0	0	0	0	0	0	0	0	.000	.000	.000	.000	-93	-0	-0	107	0	0	.000	0			0	H	0.0
Total	2	5	16	1	4	0	0	0	0	0	1	.250	.294	.250	.544	71	-1	-1	101	0	1	.417	0			-0	/O	0.0
■ CLARENCE MADDERN	Maddern, Clarence James b: 9/26/21, Bisbee, Ariz. d: 8/9/86, Tucson, Ariz. BR/TR, 6'1", 185 lbs. Deb: 9/19/46																											
1946	Chi-N	3	3	0	0	0	0	0	0	0	0	.000	.250	.000	.250	-28	-0	-0	94	0	0	.333	0			-0	/O	0.0
1948	Chi-N	80	214	16	54	12	1	4	27	10	25	.252	.301	.374	.675	88	-6	-4	93	110	25	.586	0			-2	O	-0.9
1949	Chi-N	10	9	1	3	0	0	1	2	2	0	.333	.455	.667	1.121	209	1	1	94	84	3	1.333	0			0	/1	0.1
1951	Cle-A	11	12	0	2	0	0	0	0	0	1	.167	.167	.167	.333	-10	-2	-2	95	0	0	.200	0	0	0	-0	/O	-0.1
Total	4	104	238	17	59	12	1	5	29	12	26	.248	.301	.370	.671	86	-7	-5	93	102	28	.592	0	0		-2	/O1	-0.9
■ ELLIOTT MADDOX	Maddox, Elliott b: 12/21/47, East Orange, N.J. BR/TR, 5'11", 180 lbs. Deb: 4/07/70																											
1970	Det-A	109	258	30	64	13	4	3	24	30	42	.248	.333	.364	.698	89	-2	-3	103	94	31	.635	2	3	-1	-2	3OS/2	-0.6
1971	Was-A	128	258	38	56	8	2	1	18	51	42	.217	.346	.275	.621	84	-5	-3	92	99	28	.623	10	4	1	1	*O3	-0.5
1972	Tex-A	98	294	40	74	7	2	0	10	49	53	.252	.362	.289	.651	101	1	3	94	49	34	.658	20	10	0	8	O	0.9
1973	Tex-A	100	172	24	41	1	0	1	17	29	28	.238	.358	.262	.619	79	-4	-3	97	139	18	.594	5	4	-1	-3	O/3D	-0.9
1974	NY-A	137	466	75	141	26	2	3	45	69	48	.303	.397	.386	.783	132	19	22	96	96	74	.760	6	5	-1	1	*O/23	1.9
1975	NY-A	55	218	36	67	10	3	1	23	21	24	.307	.386	.394	.781	123	7	7	99	86	33	.755	9	3	1	6	O/2	1.2
1976	NY-A	18	46	4	10	2	0	0	3	4	3	.217	.280	.261	.541	59	-2	-2	99	96	3	.410	0	1	-1	-0	O/D	-0.3
1977	Bal-A	49	107	14	28	7	0	2	9	13	9	.262	.363	.383	.746	111	1	2	93	76	14	.698	2	2	-1	-1	O/3	0.0
1978	NY-N	119	389	43	100	18	2	2	39	71	38	.257	.374	.329	.704	100	2	3	98	118	50	.659	2	11	-6	0	O3/1	-0.5
1979	NY-N	86	224	21	60	13	0	1	12	20	27	.268	.336	.339	.675	89	-4	-3	95	60	26	.604	3	2	-0	1	O3	-0.4
1980	NY-N	130	411	35	101	16	1	4	34	52	44	.246	.339	.319	.658	88	-7	-5	96	94	44	.579	1	9	-5	-5	*3/O1	-1.6
Total	11	1029	2843	360	742	121	16	18	234	409	358	.261	.361	.334	.694	101	5	18	96	92	357	.671	60	54	-14	5	O3/S21D	-0.8
■ GARRY MADDOX	Maddox, Garry Lee b: 9/1/49, Cincinnati, Ohio BR/TR, 6'3", 175 lbs. Deb: 4/25/72																											
1972	SF-N	125	458	62	122	26	7	12	58	14	97	.266	.294	.432	.726	104	0	0	100	104	57	.660	13	6	0	-4	*O	-0.9
1973	SF-N	144	587	81	187	30	10	11	76	24	73	.319	.352	.460	.812	118	16	13	105	107	94	.779	24	10	1	3	*O	1.1
1974	SF-N	135	538	74	153	31	3	8	50	29	64	.284	.325	.398	.722	94	-1	-6	108	86	68	.663	21	9	1	-2	*O	-1.1
1975	SF-N	17	52	4	7	1	0	1	4	6	3	.135	.237	.212	.449	25	-5	-5	102	110	3	.413	1	1	-0	4	O	-0.1
	Phi-N	99	374	50	109	25	8	4	46	36	54	.291	.361	.433	.795	118	10	9	101	104	64	.838	24	3	5	15	O	2.7
	Yr	116	426	54	116	26	8	5	50	42	57	.272	.346	.406	.752	107	4	4	101	106	65	.776	25	4	5	19		2.6
1976	Phi-N	146	531	75	175	37	6	6	68	42	59	.330	.383	.456	.839	128	26	21	107	103	92	.839	29	12	2	17	*O	3.6
1977	Phi-N	139	571	85	167	27	10	14	74	24	58	.292	.326	.448	.774	105	2	2	100	105	84	.737	22	6	3	6	*O	0.6
1978	Phi-N	155	598	62	172	34	3	11	68	39	89	.288	.333	.410	.743	101	4	0	105	103	83	.722	33	7	6	13	*O	1.4
1979	Phi-N	148	548	70	154	28	6	13	61	17	71	.281	.308	.425	.733	101	-4	-2	97	91	68	.675	26	13	0	20	*O	1.5
1980	Phi-N	143	549	59	142	31	3	11	73	18	52	.259	.282	.386	.668	79	-13	-18	107	120	58	.603	25	5	5	5	*O	-1.4
1981	Phi-N	94	323	37	85	7	1	5	40	17	42	.263	.302	.337	.640	72	-8	-13	112	127	33	.548	9	4	0	4	O	-1.1
1982	Phi-N	119	412	39	117	27	2	8	61	12	32	.284	.304	.417	.722	107	-2	1	94	122	47	.612	7	5	-1	2	*O	0.1
1983	Phi-N	97	324	27	89	14	2	4	32	17	31	.275	.313	.367	.680	87	-6	-6	101	97	34	.576	7	6	-2	-5	O	-1.4
1984	Phi-N	77	241	29	68	11	0	5	19	13	29	.282	.319	.390	.709	96	-1	-2	102	68	30	.621	3	2	-0	-3	O	-0.7
1985	Phi-N	105	218	22	52	8	1	4	23	13	26	.239	.284	.339	.624	72	-8	-8	102	107	21	.535	4	2	0	-9	O	-2.0
1986	Phi-N	6	7	1	3	0	0	0	1	2	1	.429	.556	.429	.984	168	1	1	104	133	2	1.000	0	1	-1	-1	/O	0.0
Total	15	1749	6331	777	1802	337	62	117	754	323	781	.285	.323	.413	.736	100	12	-11	103	104	838	.697	248	92	19	66	*O	2.3
■ JERRY MADDOX	Maddox, Jerry Glenn b: 7/28/53, Whittier, Cal. BR/TR, 6'2", 200 lbs. Deb: 6/03/78																											
1978	Atl-N	7	14	1	3	0	0	0	1	1	2	.214	.267	.214	.481	32	-1	-1	112	132	1	.333	0	0	0	0	/3	0.0
■ ART MADISON	Madison, Arthur b: 1/14/1872, Clarksburg, Mass. d: 1/27/33, N.Adams, Mass. BR/TR, 5'9", 165 lbs. Deb: 9/09/1895																											
1895	Phi-N	11	34	6	12	3	0	0	8	1	1	.353	.371	.441	.813	112	0	1	99	149	7	.909	4			0	/S23	0.0
1899	Pit-N	42	118	20	32	2	4	0	19	11		.271	.338	.356	.694	94	-1	-1	99	139	15	.640	1			0	2S/3	0.0
Total	2	53	152	26	44	5	4	0	27	12	1	.289	.345	.375	.720	98	-1	-0	99	141	22	.694	5			0	/2S3	0.0
■ SCOTTI MADISON	Madison, Charles Scott b: 9/12/59, Pensacola, Fla. BB/TR, 5'11", 185 lbs. Deb: 7/06/85																											
1985	Det-A	6	11	0	0	0	0	0	1	2	0	.000	.154	.000	.154	-50	-2	-2	106	0	0	.182	0	0	0	0	/CD	-0.1
1986	Det-A	2	7	0	0	0	0	0	1	0	3	.000	.000	.000	.000	-99	-2	-2	95	0	0	.000	0	0	0	0	/3D	-0.1
1987	KC-A	7	15	4	4	3	0	0	0	1	5	.267	.313	.467	.779	100	0	-0	104	0	2	.727	0	0	0	0	/1C	0.0
1988	KC-A	16	35	4	6	2	0	0	2	4	5	.171	.256	.229	.485	36	-3	-3	103	99	2	.448	1	0	0	-1	/CO1D	-0.3
Total	4	31	68	8	10	5	0	0	4	7	13	.147	.227	.221	.447	23	-7	-7	103	52	5	.397	1	0	0	-1	/DC1O3	-0.5
■ ED MADJESKI	Madjeski, Edward William (born Edward William Majewski) b: 7/24/09, Far Rockaway, N.Y BR/TR, 5'11", 178 lbs. Deb: 5/02/32																											
1932	Phi-A	17	35	4	8	0	0	0	3	3	6	.229	.289	.229	.518	31	-3	-4	114	126	2	.407	0	0	0	1	/C	-0.2
1933	Phi-A	51	142	17	40	4	0	0	17	4	21	.282	.301	.310	.611	68	-8	-6	92	129	13	.471	0	0	0	0	C	-0.3
1934	Phi-A	8	8	1	3	1	0	0	2	0	1	.375	.375	.500	.875	128	0	0	97	167	1	.800	0	0	0	0	/C	0.0
	Chi-A	85	281	36	62	14	2	5	32	14	31	.221	.260	.338	.598	54	-21	-21	99	97	25	.511	2	0	1	8	C	-0.4
	Yr	93	289	37	65	15	2	5	34	14	32	.225	.263	.343	.606	56	-21	-20	99	105	26	.518	2	0	1	8		-0.4
1937	NY-N	5	15	0	3	0	0	0	2	0	2	.200	.200	.200	.400	9	-2	-2	100	240	1	.250	0			0	/C	-0.1
Total	4	166	481	58	116	19	2	5	56	21	61	.241	.274	.320	.595	55	-33	-32	98	114	43	.488	2	0		8	C	-1.0
■ BILL MADLOCK	Madlock, Bill b: 1/2/51, Memphis, Tenn. BR/TR, 5'11", 180 lbs. Deb: 9/07/73																											
1973	Tex-A	21	77	16	27	5	3	1	5	7	9	.351	.412	.532	.944	169	7	7	97	45	17	1.000	3	2	-0	-2	3	0.4
1974	Chi-N	128	453	65	142	21	5	9	54	42	39	.313	.378	.442	.820	129	17	17	100	94	72	.775	11	7	-1	-10	*3	0.5
1975	Chi-N	130	514	77	182	29	7	7	64	42	34	**.354**	.406	.479	.885	139	31	28	104	98	98	.857	9	7	-2	-5	*3	2.2
1976	Chi-N	142	514	68	174	36	1	15	84	56	27	**.339**	.415	.500	.915	145	41	35	109	113	100	.911	15	11	-2	-21	*3	1.1
1977	SF-N	140	533	70	161	28	1	12	46	43	33	.302	.361	.426	.787	106	8	5	104	74	73	.710	13	10	-2	-16	*3/2	-1.3
1978	SF-N	122	447	76	138	26	3	15	44	48	39	.309	.380	.481	.861	152	23	28	92	71	84	.881	16	5	2	-8	*2/1	2.9
1979	SF-N	69	249	37	65	9	2	7	41	18	19	.261	.311	.398	.708	99	-3	-1	92	138	31	.674	11	3	2	-3	2/1	0.1
	Pit-N	85	311	48	102	17	3	7	44	34	22	.328	.396	.469	.865	128	16	13	106	106	55	.874	21	8	2	-2	3	1.0
	Yr	154	560	85	167	26	5	14	85	52	41	.298	.359	.438	.796	116	12	13	100	121	87	.789	32	11	3	-5		1.1
1980	Pit-N	137	494	62	137	22	4	10	53	45	33	.277	.343	.399	.741	103	4	2	103	94	64	.686	16	10	-1	-11	*31	-1.0
1981	Pit-N	82	279	35	95	23	1	6	45	34	17	.341	.418	.495	.912	165	22	23	96	115	59	.990	18	6	2	-2	3	2.1
1982	Pit-N	154	568	92	181	33	3	19	95	48	39	.319	.376	.488	.863	127	29	22	110	114	103	.857	18	6	2	-2	*3/1	2.0
1983	Pit-N	130	473	68	153	21	0	12	68	49	24	**.323**	.389	.444	.833	127	20	19	103	112	78	.776	3	4	-2	-14	*3	0.0
1984	Pit-N	103	403	38	102	16	0	4	44	26	29	.253	.300	.323	.623	79	-14	-11	94	129	38	.511	3	1	0	-3	3/1	-1.4
1985	Pit-N	110	399	49	100	23	1	10	41	39	42	.251	.325	.388	.714	96	-1	-2	103	90	49	.643	3	3	-1	-10	31	-1.2
	LA-N	34	114	20	41	4	0	2	15	10	11	.360	.425	.447	.873	155	7	8	93	105	23	.922	7	1	2	8	3	1.8
	Yr	144	513	69	141	27	1	12	56	49	53	.275	.347	.402	.749	108	6	6	100	94	76	.720	10	4	1	-2		0.6
1986	LA-N	111	379	38	106	17	0	10	60	30	43	.280	.341	.404	.744	111	2	5	94	133	52	.675	3	3	-1	6	*3/1	0.7
1987	LA-N	21	61	5	11	1	0	3	7	6	5	.180	.265	.344	.609	65	-4	-3	92	93	5	.519	0	0	0	1	3/1	-0.2
	Det-A	87	326	56	91	17	0	14	50	28	45	.279	.354	.460	.815	118	7	9	97	110	52	.774	4	3	-1	1	D1/3	0.6
Total	15	1806	6594	920	2008	348	34	163	860	605	510	.305	.369	.442	.811	122	213	205	101	103	1053	.802	174	90	-2	-91	*32/D1	10.3
■ SAL MADRID	Madrid, Salvador b: 6/9/20, El Paso, Tex. d: 2/24/77, Ft.Wayne, Ind. BR/TR, 5'9", 165 lbs. Deb: 9/17/47																											
1947	Chi-N	8	24	0	3	1	0	0	1	1	6	.125	.160	.167	.327	-13	-4	-4	101	93	1	.238	0			1	/S	-0.2
■ DAVE MAGADAN	Magadan, David Joseph b: 9/30/62, Tampa, Fla. BL/TR, 6'3", 190 lbs. Deb: 9/07/86																											
1986	NY-N	10	18	3	8	0	0	0	3	3	1	.444	.524	.444	.968	177	2	2	96	149	4	1.000	0	0	0	1	/1	0.2
1987	NY-N	85	192	21	61	13	1	3	24	22	22	.318	.388	.443	.831	121	6	6	99	102	33	.787	0	0	0	-1	31	0.4

YEAR	TM/L	G	AB	R	H	2B	3B	HR	RBI	BB	SO	AVG	OBP	SLG	PRO	/A	BR	/A	PF	CHI	RC	TA	SB	CS	SBR	FR	POS	TPR
1988	NY-N	112	314	39	87	15	0	1	35	60	39	.277	.396	.334	.731	124	8	12	90	130	45	.705	0	1	-1	0	13/S	0.9
Total	3	207	524	63	156	28	1	4	62	85	62	.298	.398	.378	.776	125	16	20	93	120	82	.754	0	1	-1	0	/13S	1.5
■ **LEE MAGEE**	Magee, Leo Christopher (born Leopold Christopher Hoernschemeyer) b: 6/4/1889, Cincinnati, Ohio d: 3/14/66, Columbus, Ohio BB/TR, 5'11", 165 lbs. Deb: 7/04/11 M																											
1911	StL-N	26	69	9	18	1	1	0	8	8	8	.261	.338	.304	.642	79	-2	-2	101	129	8	.647	4			1	2/S	-0.1
1912	StL-N	128	458	60	133	13	8	0	40	39	29	.290	.347	.354	.701	92	-5	-4	100	85	63	.671	16			9	O2/1S	0.1
1913	StL-N	137	531	54	142	13	7	2	31	34	30	.267	.314	.330	.643	90	-11	-6	93	60	61	.602	23			5	*O2/1S	-0.3
1914	StL-N	142	529	59	150	23	4	2	40	42	24	.284	.337	.353	.691	102	3	1	104	66	74	.702	36			-4	*O1/2	-0.7
1915	Bro-F	121	452	87	146	19	10	4	49	22	19	.323	.354	.436	.790	136	17	18	98	90	86	.827	34			-18	*2/1M	0.2
1916	NY-A	131	510	57	131	18	4	3	45	50	31	.257	.324	.325	.650	94	-3	-4	101	81	56	.609	29	25	-6	-2	*O/2	-1.4
1917	NY-A	51	173	17	38	4	1	0	8	13	18	.220	.278	.254	.532	59	-8	-9	107	67	14	.452	3			-5	O	-1.8
	StL-A	36	112	11	19	1	0	0	4	6	6	.170	.212	.179	.390	20	-11	-10	95	72	5	.312	3			2	3/21O	-0.7
	Yr	87	285	28	57	5	1	0	12	19	24	.200	.252	.225	.477	45	-19	-19	102	69	19	.395	6			-3		-2.5
1918	Cin-N	119	459	61	133	22	13	0	28	28	19	.290	.331	.394	.725	124	10	12	97	56	65	.699	19			0	*2/3	-1.9
1919	Bro-N	45	181	16	43	7	2	0	7	5	8	.238	.262	.298	.560	73	-7	-6	94	44	16	.471	5			-1	2/3	-0.6
	Chi-N	79	267	36	78	12	4	1	17	18	16	.292	.339	.378	.717	115	5	5	100	65	38	.709	14			-1	OS3/2	0.3
	Yr	124	448	52	121	19	6	1	24	23	24	.270	.309	.346	.655	99	-2	-1	98	58	53	.609	19			-2		-0.3
Total	9	1015	3741	467	1031	133	54	12	277	265	208	.276	.325	.350	.675	99	-12	-7	99	71	486	.646	186	25		-14	O2/13S	-3.1
■ **SHERRY MAGEE**	Magee, Sherwood Robert b: 8/6/1884, Clarendon, Pa. d: 3/13/29, Philadelphia, Pa. BR/TR, 5'11", 179 lbs. Deb: 6/29/04																											
1904	Phi-N	95	364	51	101	15	12	3	57	14		.277	.304	.409	.714	131	7	10	93	140	50	.662	11			8	O/1	1.6
1905	Phi-N	155	603	100	180	24	17	5	98	44		.299	.346	.420	.766	125	21	17	104	122	107	.816	48			17	*O	2.4
1906	Phi-N	154	563	77	159	36	8	6	67	52		.282	.343	.407	.750	148	22	27	92	95	100	.832	55			3	*O	2.9
1907	Phi-N	140	503	75	165	28	12	4	**85**	53		.328	.392	.455	.847	162	39	36	104	128	111	.970	46			1	*O	3.6
1908	Phi-N	143	508	79	144	30	16	2	57	49		.283	.346	.417	.764	146	25	26	100	106	85	.827	40			-1	*O	2.6
1909	Phi-N	143	522	60	141	33	14	2	66	44		.270	.340	.398	.738	123	17	13	106	119	81	.790	38			-8	*O	0.1
1910	Phi-N	154	519	**110**	172	39	17	6	**123**	94	36	**.331**	**.445**	**.507**	**.952**	**185**	**55**	**58**	96	**162**	**139**	**1.205**	49			-7	*O	**4.7**
1911	Phi-N	121	445	79	128	32	5	15	94	49	33	.288	.366	.483	.849	127	20	16	108	130	86	.921	22			5	*O	1.7
1912	Phi-N	132	464	79	142	25	9	6	66	55	54	.306	.388	.438	.825	125	17	17	100	107	91	.916	30			-5	*O/1	0.7
1913	Phi-N	138	470	92	144	36	6	11	70	38	36	.306	.369	.479	.848	126	24	17	112	101	89	.905	23			-6	*O/1	0.9
1914	Phi-N	146	544	96	**171**	**39**	11	15	**103**	55	42	.314	.380	**.509**	.890	163	41	41	100	123	110	.965	25			-4	OS1/2	3.7
1915	Bos-N	156	571	72	160	34	12	2	87	54	39	.280	.350	.392	.742	127	17	18	98	153	82	.709	15	12	-3	8	*O1	2.0
1916	Bos-N	122	419	44	101	17	5	3	54	44	52	.241	.322	.327	.649	107	1	4	93	156	50	.619	10			-6	*O/1S	-0.6
1917	Bos-N	72	246	24	63	8	4	1	29	13	23	.256	.302	.333	.635	98	-2	-1	96	134	27	.574	7			2	O/1	0.0
	Cin-N	45	137	17	44	8	4	0	23	16	7	.321	.400	.438	.838	170	10	11	92	148	25	.882	4			2	O/1	1.3
	Yr	117	383	41	107	16	8	1	52	29	30	.279	.338	.371	.709	124	8	10	95	141	51	.678	11			5		1.3
1918	Cin-N	115	400	46	119	15	13	2	**76**	37	18	.298	.370	.415	.785	143	19	21	97	**170**	64	.804	14			-1	1O/2	1.8
1919	Cin-N	56	163	11	35	6	1	0	21	26	19	.215	.337	.264	.601	78	-2	-3	105	190	16	.602	4			-4	O/23	-0.9
Total	16	2087	7441	1112	2169	425	166	83	1176	737	359	.291	.362	.427	.788	137	330	327	100	130	1311	.839	441	12		5	*O1/S23	28.5
■ **HARL MAGGERT**	Maggert, Harl Vestin b: 2/13/1883, Cromwell, Ind. d: 1/7/63, Fresno, Cal. BL/TR, 5'8", 155 lbs. Deb: 9/04/07																											
1907	Pit-N	3	6	1	0	0	0	0	0	2		.000	.250	.000	.250	-19	-1	-1	105	0	0	.500	1			0	/O	0.0
1912	Phi-A	72	242	39	62	8	6	1	13	36		.256	.357	.351	.708	103	2	2	99	50	34	.739	10			-6	O	-0.7
Total	2	75	248	40	62	8	6	1	13	38		.250	.354	.343	.697	100	1	1	100	49	34	.731	11			-6	/O	-0.7
■ **HARL MAGGERT**	Maggert, Harl Warren b: 5/4/14, Los Angeles, Cal. d: 7/10/86, Citrus Heights, Cal. BR/TR, 6', 190 lbs. Deb: 4/19/38																											
1938	Bos-N	66	89	12	25	3	0	3	19	10	20	.281	.354	.416	.769	126	1	3	88	149	13	.701	0			-1	O/3	0.1
■ **STUBBY MAGNER**	Magner, Edmund Burke b: 2/20/1888, Kalamazoo, Mich. d: 9/6/56, Chillicother, Ohio BR/TR, 5'3", 135 lbs. Deb: 7/12/11																											
1911	NY-A	13	33	3	7	0	0	0	4	4		.212	.297	.212	.509	39	-2	-3	111	193	2	.462	1			-1	/S2	-0.2
■ **JOHN MAGNER**	Magner, John T. b: 1855, St.Louis, Mo. Deb: 7/14/1879																											
1879	Cin-N	1	4	0	0	0	0	0	1	0	1	.000	.000	.000	.000	-99	-1	-1	95	0	0	.000				0	/O	0.0
■ **GEORGE MAGOON**	Magoon, George Henry "Maggie" or "Topsy" b: 3/27/1875, St.Albans, Maine d: 12/6/43, Rochester, N.H. BR/TR, 5'10", 160 lbs. Deb: 6/29/1898																											
1898	Bro-N	93	343	35	77	7	0	1	39	30		.224	.293	.254	.546	63	-17	-14	95	139	28	.477	7			9	S	0.0
1899	Bal-N	62	207	26	53	8	3	0	31	26		.256	.353	.324	.677	82	-2	-5	108	145	27	.682	7			-0	S	0.0
	Chi-N	59	189	24	43	5	1	0	21	24		.228	.333	.265	.598	70	-7	-6	96	131	19	.582	5			3	S	0.1
	Yr	121	396	50	96	13	4	0	52	50		.242	.344	.295	.639	77	-9	-10	102	139	45	.633	12			3		0.1
1901	Cin-N	127	460	47	116	16	7	1	53	52		.252	.328	.324	.652	96	-3	-0	95	124	55	.628	15			-10	*S2	-0.3
1902	Cin-N	45	162	29	44	9	2	0	23	13		.272	.326	.352	.678	101	2	0	110	142	21	.653	7			-1	2/S	0.2
1903	Cin-N	42	139	6	30	6	0	0	9	19		.216	.310	.259	.569	59	-6	-8	109	82	12	.523	2			-4	2/3	-0.8
	Chi-A	94	334	32	76	11	3	0	25	30		.228	.291	.278	.570	80	-10	-7	92	99	29	.492	4			-23	2	-2.8
Total	5	522	1834	199	439	62	16	2	201	194		.239	.317	.294	.611	80	-43	-39	98	124	191	.569	47			-26	S2/3	-3.6
■ **FREDDIE MAGUIRE**	Maguire, Frederick Edward b: 5/10/1889, Roxbury, Mass. d: 11/3/61, Boston, Mass. BR/TR, 5'11", 155 lbs. Deb: 9/22/22																											
1922	NY-N	5	12	4	4	0	0	0	1	0	1	.333	.333	.333	.667	70	-0	-1	104	87	1	.625	1	0	0	0	/2	0.0
1923	NY-N	41	30	11	6	1	0	0	2	2	4	.200	.250	.233	.483	28	-3	-3	101	101	2	.417	1	0	0	0	2/3	-0.1
1928	Chi-N	140	574	67	160	24	7	1	41	25	38	.279	.312	.350	.662	77	-23	-19	95	63	62	.568	6			**48**	*2	3.0
1929	Bos-N	138	496	54	125	26	8	0	41	19	40	.252	.284	.337	.620	56	-37	-33	94	86	46	.531	8			-2	*2/S	-2.7
1930	Bos-N	146	516	54	138	21	5	0	52	20	22	.267	.297	.328	.625	53	-41	-38	97	108	49	.516	4			-5	*2	-2.3
1931	Bos-N	148	492	36	112	18	2	0	26	16	26	.228	.259	.272	.532	43	-39	-39	99	69	37	.416	3			5	*2	-2.6
Total	6	618	2120	226	545	90	22	1	163	82	131	.257	.289	.322	.611	57	-144	-132	96	81	197	.508	23	0		47	2/S3	-4.7
■ **JACK MAGUIRE**	Maguire, Jack b: 2/5/25, St.Louis, Mo. BR/TR, 5'11", 165 lbs. Deb: 4/18/50																											
1950	NY-N	29	40	3	7	2	0	0	3	3	13	.175	.233	.225	.458	21	-5	-5	98	129	2	.343	0			0	/O1	-0.4
1951	NY-N	16	20	6	8	1	1	1	4	2	2	.400	.455	.700	1.155	202	3	3	102	91	7	1.333	0	0	0	-1	/O	0.2
	Pit-N	8	5	1	0	0	0	0	0	1	0	.000	.167	.000	.167	-48	-1	-1	107	0	0	.200	0	0	0	0	/23	0.0
	Yr	24	25	7	8	1	1	1	4	3	2	.320	.393	.560	.953	148	2	2	103	64	6	1.000	0	0	0	-1		0.2
	StL-A	41	127	15	31	2	1	1	14	12	21	.244	.309	.299	.609	62	-6	-7	105	122	12	.505	1	0	0	1	O/32	-0.6
Total	2	94	192	25	46	5	2	2	21	18	36	.240	.305	.318	.622	65	-9	-10	103	117	20	.530	1	0		1	/O321	-0.8
■ **JIM MAHADY**	Mahady, James Bernard b: 4/22/01, Cortland, N.Y. d: 8/9/36, Cortland, N.Y. BR/TR, 5'11", 170 lbs. Deb: 10/02/21																											
1921	NY-N	1	0	0	0	0	0	0	0	0	0	—	—	—	—	—	0	0	98	—	—	—	0	0	0	0	/2	0.0
■ **ART MAHAN**	Mahan, Arthur Leo b: 6/8/13, Somerville, Mass. BL/TL, 5'11", 178 lbs. Deb: 4/30/40																											
1940	Phi-N	146	544	55	133	24	5	2	39	40	37	.244	.297	.318	.615	72	-22	-20	97	86	52	.518	4			2	*1/P	-3.1
■ **BILLY MAHARG**	Maharg, William Joseph b: 3/19/1881, Philadelphia, Pa. d: 11/20/53, Philadelphia, Pa. BR/TR, 5'4.5", Deb: 5/18/12																											
1912	Det-A	1	1	0	0	0	0	0	0	0		.000	.000	.000	.000	-99	-0	-0	95	0	0	.000	0			0	/3	0.0
1916	Phi-N	1	1	0	0	0	0	0	0	0	0	.000	.000	.000	.000	-99	-0	-0	96	0	0	.000	0			-0	/O	0.0
Total	2	2	2	0	0	0	0	0	0	0	0	.000	.000	.000	.000	-99	-0	-0	95	0	0	.000	0			-0	/O3	0.0
■ **FRANK MAHER**	Maher, Frank b: Philadelphia, Pa. TR , Deb: 8/29/02																											
1902	Phi-N	1	1	0	0	0	0	0	0	0		.000	.000	.000	.000	-95	-0	-0	105	0	0	.000	0			0	H	0.0
■ **TOM MAHER**	Maher, Thomas Francis b: 7/6/1870, Philadelphia, Pa. d: 8/5/ 25, 29 Philadelphia, Pa. Deb: 4/24/02																											
1902	Phi-N	1	0	0	0	0	0	0	0	0		—	—	—	—	—	0	0	105	—	—	—	0			0	R	0.0
■ **GREG MAHLBERG**	Mahlberg, Gregory John b: 8/8/52, Milwaukee, Wis. BR/TR, 5'10", 180 lbs. Deb: 9/24/78																											
1978	Tex-A	1	1	0	0	0	0	0	0	0	0	.000	.000	.000	.000	-99	-0	-0	96	0	0	.000	0	0	0	0	/C	0.0
1979	Tex-A	7	17	2	2	0	0	1	1	2	4	.118	.211	.294	.505	35	-2	-2	100	48	1	.412	0	0	0	0	/C	0.0

YEAR	TM/L	G	AB	R	H	2B	3B	HR	RBI	BB	SO	AVG	OBP	SLG	PRO	/A	BR	/A	PF	CHI	RC	TA	SB	CS	SBR	FR	POS	TPR
Total	2	8	18	2	2	0	0	1	1	2	4	.111	.200	.278	.478	28	-2	-2	100	46	1	.389	0	0	0	0	/C	0.0
■ **DANIEL MAHONEY** Mahoney, Daniel J. :Dan " b: 3/20/1864, Springfield, Mass. d: 2/1/04, Springfield, Mass. BR/TR, 5'9.5", 165 lbs. Deb: 8/20/1892																												
1892	Cin-N	5	21	1	4	0	1	0	1	1	4	.190	.227	.286	.513	54	-1	-1	103	49	1	.412	0			0	/C	0.0
1895	Was-N	6	12	2	2	0	0	0	1	0	0	.167	.167	.167	.333	-13	-2	-2	103	140	0	.200	0			0	/C1	-0.1
Total	2	11	33	3	6	0	1	0	2	1	4	.182	.206	.242	.448	28	-3	-3	103	81	2	.333	0			0	/C1	-0.1
■ **DANNY MAHONEY** Mahoney, Daniel Joseph b: 9/6/1888, Haverhill, Mass. d: 9/28/60, Utica, N.Y. 5'6.5", 145 lbs. Deb: 11																												
1911	Cin-N	1	0	0	0	0	0	0	0	0	0	—	—	—	—	—	0	0	92	—	—	—	0			0	R	0.0
■ **MIKE MAHONEY** Mahoney, George W. "Big Mike" b: 12/5/1873, Boston, Mass. d: 1/3/40, Boston, Mass. BR , 6'4", 220 lbs. Deb: 5/18/1897																												
1897	Bos-N	2	2	1	1	0	0	0	1	0		.500	.500	.500	1.000	156	0	0	107	293	1	1.000	0			0	/CP	0.0
1898	StL-N	2	7	0	0	0	0	0	0	0		.000	.000	.000	.000	-95	-2	-2	106	0	0	.000	0			0	/1	-0.1
Total	2	4	9	1	1	0	0	0	1	0		.111	.111	.111	.222	-35	-2	-2	106	65	1	.125	0			0	/1PC	-0.1
■ **JIM MAHONEY** Mahoney, James Thomas "Moe" b: 5/26/34, Englewood, N.J. BR/TR, 6', 175 lbs. Deb: 7/28/59 C																												
1959	Bos-A	31	23	10	3	0	0	1	4	3	7	.130	.231	.261	.492	33	-2	-2	106	175	2	.450	0	0	0	-1	S	0.0
1961	Was-A	43	108	10	26	0	1	0	6	5	23	.241	.274	.259	.534	46	-9	-8	95	84	7	.395	1	2	-1	1	S/2	-0.4
1962	Cle-A	41	74	12	18	4	0	3	5	3	14	.243	.273	.419	.692	85	-2	-2	98	50	8	.586	0	0	0	0	S/23	0.0
1965	Hou-N	5	5	0	1	0	0	0	0	0	3	.200	.200	.200	.400	15	-1	-1	89	0	0	.250	0	0	0	-0	/S	0.0
Total	4	120	210	32	48	4	1	4	15	11	47	.229	.267	.314	.581	57	-13	-13	97	81	17	.476	1	2	-1	0	/S23	-0.4
■ **BOB MAIER** Maier, Robert Phillip b: 9/5/15, Dunellen, N.J. BR/TR, 5'8", 180 lbs. Deb: 4/17/45																												
1945	Det-A	132	486	58	128	25	7	1	34	38	32	.263	.317	.350	.667	88	-5	-8	106	73	52	.567	7	11	-5	-12	*3/O	-2.3
■ **EMIL MAILHO** Mailho, Emil Pierre "Lefty" b: 12/16/09, Berkeley, Cal. BL/TL, 5'10", 165 lbs. Deb: 4/14/36																												
1936	Phi-A	21	18	5	1	0	0	0	0	5	3	.056	.261	.056	.316	-18	-3	-3	101	0	1	.353	0	0	0	0	/O	-0.2
■ **CHARLIE MAISEL** Maisel, Charles Louis b: 4/21/1894, Catonsville, Md. d: 8/25/53, Baltimore, Md. BR/TR, 6', Deb: 10/02/15																												
1915	Bal-F	1	4	0	0	0	0	0	0	0	0	.000	.000	.000	.000	-93	-1	-1	107	0	0	.000	0			0	/C	0.0
■ **FRITZ MAISEL** Maisel, Frederick Charles "Flash" b: 12/23/1889, Catonsville, Md. d: 4/22/67, Baltimore, Md. BR/TR, 5'7.5", 170 lbs. Deb: 8/11/13																												
1913	NY-A	51	187	33	48	4	3	0	12	34	20	.257	.371	.310	.681	99	2	1	101	65	29	.842	25			2	3	0.5
1914	NY-A	149	548	78	131	23	9	2	47	76	69	.239	.334	.325	.659	98	-0	0	100	92	74	.760	**74**	17	**12**	-18	*3	-0.2
1915	NY-A	135	530	77	149	16	6	4	46	48	35	.281	.342	.357	.699	111	5	6	98	69	76	.735	51	12	**8**	-8	*3	1.3
1916	NY-A	53	158	18	36	5	0	0	7	20	18	.228	.318	.259	.578	73	-4	-5	101	61	15	.541	4			-2	O3/2	-0.8
1917	NY-A	113	404	46	80	4	4	0	20	36	18	.198	.267	.228	.495	48	-23	-26	107	83	32	.491	29			-3	*2/3	-2.4
1918	StL-A	90	284	43	66	4	2	0	16	46	17	.232	.341	.261	.602	82	-4	-4	99	80	31	.606	11			-6	3/O	-1.0
Total	6	591	2111	295	510	56	24	6	148	260	177	.242	.327	.299	.626	87	-25	-28	101	78	258	.671	194	29		-35	32/O	-2.6
■ **GEORGE MAISEL** Maisel, George John b: 3/12/1892, Catonsville, Md. d: 11/20/68, Baltimore, Md. BR/TR, 5'10.5", 180 lbs. Deb: 5/01/13																												
1913	StL-A	11	18	2	3	2	0	0	1	1	7	.167	.211	.278	.488	45	-1	-1	95	71	1	.400	0			-2	/O	-0.2
1916	Det-A	8	5	2	0	0	0	0	0	0	2	.000	.000	.000	.000	-96	-1	-1	105	0	0	.000	0			0	/3	0.0
1921	Chi-N	111	393	54	122	7	2	0	43	11	13	.310	.334	.338	.673	74	-12	-15	107	121	45	.590	17	7	1	-4	*O	-2.2
1922	Chi-N	38	84	9	16	1	1	0	6	8	2	.190	.261	.226	.487	28	-9	-8	95	110	5	.394	1	3	-2	-2	O	-1.1
Total	4	168	500	67	141	10	3	0	50	20	24	.282	.314	.314	.628	64	-23	-26	104	116	51	.537	18	10		-7	O/3	-3.5
■ **HANK MAJESKI** Majeski, Henry "Heeney" b: 12/13/16, Staten Island, N.Y BR/TR, 5'9", 174 lbs. Deb: 5/17/39																												
1939	Bos-N	106	367	35	100	16	1	7	54	18	30	.272	.310	.379	.689	92	-9	-5	92	124	41	.581	2			13	3	1.1
1940	Bos-N	3	3	0	0	0	0	0	0	0	0	.000	.000	.000	.000	-99	-1	-1	99	0	0	.000	0			0	H	0.0
1941	Bos-N	19	55	5	8	5	0	0	3	1	13	.145	.161	.236	.397	12	-7	-6	93	83	2	.298	0			-0	3	-0.6
1946	NY-A	8	12	1	1	0	1	0	0	0	3	.083	.083	.250	.333	-9	-2	-2	100	0	0	.273	0	0	0	0	/3	-0.1
	Phi-A	78	264	25	66	14	3	1	25	26	13	.250	.320	.337	.657	80	-6	-7	104	105	29	.575	3	2	-0	4	3	0.3
	Yr	86	276	26	67	14	4	1	25	26	16	.243	.310	.333	.644	77	-8	-9	104	96	29	.560	3	2	-0	4		0.2
1947	Phi-A	141	479	54	134	26	5	8	72	53	31	.280	.358	.405	.763	111	8	7	100	124	70	.697	1	0	0	-2	*3/S2	0.9
1948	Phi-A	148	590	88	183	41	4	12	120	48	43	.310	.368	.454	.822	116	13	12	102	**141**	98	.759	2	1	0	2	*3/S	0.8
1949	Phi-A	114	448	62	124	26	5	9	67	29	23	.277	.326	.417	.744	97	-5	-5	99	114	58	.641	0	1	-1	-1	*3	-0.5
1950	Chi-A	122	414	47	128	18	2	6	46	42	34	.309	.377	.406	.783	103	1	2	97	87	62	.702	1	4	-2	9	*3	0.4
1951	Chi-A	12	35	4	9	4	0	0	6	1	0	.257	.278	.371	.649	77	-1	-1	97	165	3	.519	0	0	0	-0	/3	-0.1
	Phi-A	89	323	41	92	19	4	5	42	35	24	.285	.358	.415	.773	102	4	1	106	103	48	.711	1	2	-1	11	3	0.8
	Yr	101	358	45	101	23	4	5	48	36	24	.282	.351	.411	.762	100	2	-0	105	112	52	.694	1	2	-1	11		0.7
1952	Phi-A	34	117	14	30	2	2	2	20	19	10	.256	.365	.359	.724	92	1	-1	111	159	15	.653	0	1	-1	0	3	0.0
	Cle-A	36	54	7	16	2	0	0	9	7	7	.296	.377	.333	.710	109	0	1	91	187	6	.595	0	0	0	-1	3/2	0.0
	Yr	70	171	21	46	4	2	2	29	26	17	.269	.369	.351	.720	100	1	1	100	175	24	.669	0	1	-1	-1		0.0
1953	Cle-A	50	50	6	15	1	0	2	12	3	8	.300	.352	.440	.792	118	1	1	95	159	8	.722	0	0	0	0	2/3O	0.1
1954	Cle-A	57	121	10	34	4	0	3	17	7	14	.281	.320	.388	.709	88	-1	-2	106	115	14	.587	0	0	0	0	23	-0.1
1955	Cle-A	36	48	3	9	2	0	2	6	8	3	.188	.328	.354	.682	80	-1	-1	104	97	6	.659	0	0	0	0	/32	0.0
	Bal-A	16	41	2	7	1	0	0	2	2	4	.171	.209	.195	.404	10	-5	-5	90	93	2	.286	0	0	0	-1	/32	-0.4
	Yr	52	89	5	16	3	0	2	8	10	7	.180	.277	.281	.558	51	-6	-6	100	98	8	.500	0	0	0	-1		-0.4
Total	13	1069	3421	404	956	181	27	57	501	299	260	.279	.342	.398	.740	99	-12	-11	100	119	462	.686	10	11		34	3/2SO	2.6
■ **CHARLIE MALAY** Malay, Charles Francis b: 6/13/1879, Brooklyn, N.Y. d: 9/18/49, Brooklyn, N.Y. BB/TR, 5'11.5", 175 lbs. Deb: 4/24/05																												
1905	Bro-N	102	349	33	88	7	2	1	31	22		.252	.296	.292	.589	81	-9	-8	96	105	35	.525	13			-4	2O/S	-0.8
■ **JOE MALAY** Malay, Joseph Charles b: 10/25/05, Brooklyn, N.Y. BL/TL, 6', 175 lbs. Deb: 9/07/33																												
1933	NY-N	8	24	0	3	0	0	0	2	0	0	.125	.125	.125	.250	-29	-4	-4	99	251	0	.136	0			0	/1	-0.3
1935	NY-N	1	1	0	1	0	0	0	0	0	0	1.000	1.000	1.000	2.000	456	0	0	96	0	1	—	0			0	H	0.0
Total	2	9	25	0	4	0	0	0	2	0	0	.160	.160	.160	.320	-9	-3	-3	99	241	1	.190	0			0	/1	-0.3
■ **CANDY MALDONADO** Maldonado, Candido (Guadarrama) b: 9/5/60, Humacao, P.R. BR/TR, 6', 185 lbs. Deb: 9/07/81																												
1981	LA-N	11	12	0	1	0	0	0	0	0	5	.083	.083	.083	.167	-54	-2	-2	98	0	0	.091	0	0	0	-2	/O	-0.4
1982	LA-N	6	4	0	0	0	0	0	0	1	2	.000	.200	.000	.200	-42	-1	-1	95	0	0	.250	0	0	0	-0	/O	0.0
1983	LA-N	42	62	5	12	1	1	1	6	5	14	.194	.254	.290	.544	50	-4	-4	100	113	5	.451	0	0	0	-8	O	-1.3
1984	LA-N	116	254	25	68	14	0	5	28	19	29	.268	.321	.382	.703	93	-1	-2	104	98	30	.600	0	3	-2	-14	*O/3	-2.3
1985	LA-N	121	213	20	48	7	1	5	19	19	40	.225	.289	.338	.627	80	-7	-6	93	87	21	.544	1	1	-0	-16	*O	-2.6
1986	SF-N	133	405	49	102	31	3	18	85	20	77	.252	.292	.477	.769	113	2	4	96	137	51	.690	4	4	-1	-2	*O/3	0.0
1987	SF-N	118	442	69	129	28	4	20	85	34	78	.292	.351	.509	.860	129	14	17	96	121	75	.827	8	8	-2	-7	*O	0.2
1988	SF-N	142	499	53	127	23	1	12	68	37	89	.255	.315	.377	.692	104	-2	2	94	124	57	.610	6	5	-1	-8	*O	-1.1
Total	8	689	1891	221	487	104	10	61	291	135	334	.258	.313	.420	.733	105	-2	7	96	117	239	.671	19	21	-7	-58	O/3	-7.5
■ **JIM MALER** Maler, James Michael b: 8/16/58, New York, N.Y. BR/TR, 6'4", 230 lbs. Deb: 9/03/81																												
1981	Sea-A	12	23	1	8	1	0	0	2	2	1	.348	.423	.391	.814	136	1	1	100	87	4	.867	1	0	0	0	/1D	0.1
1982	Sea-A	64	221	18	50	8	3	4	26	12	35	.226	.275	.344	.619	63	-10	-12	109	118	21	.520	0	0	0	-0	1/D	-1.3
1983	Sea-A	26	66	5	12	1	0	1	3	5	11	.182	.260	.242	.503	40	-5	-5	100	62	3	.383	0	3	-2	1	1/D	-0.7
Total	3	102	310	24	70	10	3	5	31	19	47	.226	.284	.326	.609	63	-14	-16	106	103	28	.516	1	3	-2	1	/1D	-1.9
■ **TONY MALINOSKY** Malinosky, Anthony Francis b: 10/5/09, Collinsville, Ill. BR/TR, 5'10.5", 165 lbs. Deb: 4/26/37																												
1937	Bro-N	35	79	7	18	2	0	0	3	9	11	.228	.307	.253	.560	51	-5	-5	104	54	7	.468	0			-1	3S	-0.3
■ **BOBBY MALKMUS** Malkmus, Robert Edward b: 7/4/31, Newark, N.J. BR/TR, 5'9", 175 lbs. Deb: 6/01/57																												
1957	Mil-N	13	22	6	2	0	1	0	0	3	3	.091	.200	.182	.382	4	-3	-3	90	0	1	.350	0	0	0	1	/2	-0.1
1958	Was-A	41	70	5	13	2	1	0	3	4	15	.186	.230	.243	.473	31	-7	-6	97	71	3	.350	0	0	0	-0	2/3S	-0.4

YEAR	TM/L	G	AB	R	H	2B	3B	HR	RBI	BB	SO	AVG	OBP	SLG	PRO	/A	BR	/A	PF	CHI	RC	TA	SB	CS	SBR	FR	POS	TPR
1959	Was-A	6	0	0	0	0	0	0	0	0	0	—	—	—	—	—	0	0	100	—	—	—	0	0	0	0	R	0.0
1960	Phi-N	79	133	16	28	4	1	1	12	11	28	.211	.271	.278	.549	47	-9	-10	107	122	10	.459	2	2	-1	-2	S23	-0.9
1961	Phi-N	121	342	39	79	8	2	7	31	20	43	.231	.277	.327	.605	64	-20	-17	94	94	30	.495	1	3	-2	7	2S3	-0.2
1962	Phi-N	8	5	3	1	1	0	0	0	0	1	.200	.200	.400	.600	60	-0	-0	95	0	0	.500	0	0	0	0	/S	0.0
Total	6	268	572	69	123	15	5	8	46	38	90	.215	.266	.301	.567	53	-39	-37	97	93	48	.474	3	5	-2	5	2/S3	-1.6

■ **JERRY MALLETT** Mallett, Gerald Gordon b: 9/18/35, Bonne Terre, Mo. BR/TR, 6'5", 208 lbs. Deb: 9/19/59

YEAR	TM/L	G	AB	R	H	2B	3B	HR	RBI	BB	SO	AVG	OBP	SLG	PRO	/A	BR	/A	PF	CHI	RC	TA	SB	CS	SBR	FR	POS	TPR
1959	Bos-A	4	15	1	4	0	0	0	1	1	3	.267	.313	.267	.579	57	-1	-1	106	100	1	.417	0	0	0	4	/O	0.2

■ **LES MALLON** Mallon, Leslie Clyde b: 11/21/05, Sweetwater, Tex. Deceased BR/TR, 5'8", 160 lbs. Deb: 4/14/31

YEAR	TM/L	G	AB	R	H	2B	3B	HR	RBI	BB	SO	AVG	OBP	SLG	PRO	/A	BR	/A	PF	CHI	RC	TA	SB	CS	SBR	FR	POS	TPR
1931	Phi-N	122	375	41	116	19	2	1	45	29	40	.309	.359	.379	.738	93	-0	-3	106	111	53	.660	0			7	2/1S3	0.8
1932	Phi-N	103	347	44	90	16	0	5	31	28	28	.259	.318	.349	.667	71	-10	-15	112	85	40	.591	1			-17	2/3	-2.5
1934	Bos-N	42	166	23	49	6	1	0	18	15	12	.295	.354	.343	.697	102	-2	1	86	109	20	.585	0			-3	2	0.2
1935	Bos-N	116	412	48	113	24	2	2	25	28	37	.274	.322	.357	.679	86	-10	-8	96	60	47	.577	3			-8	23/O	-0.8
Total	4	383	1300	156	368	65	5	8	119	100	117	.283	.336	.359	.695	85	-23	-25	102	88	161	.609	4			-22	2/31SO	-2.3

■ **BEN MALLONEE** Mallonee, Howard Bennett "Lefty" b: 3/31/1894, Baltimore, Md. d: 2/19/78, Baltimore, Md. BL/TL, 5'6", 150 lbs. Deb: 9/14/21

YEAR	TM/L	G	AB	R	H	2B	3B	HR	RBI	BB	SO	AVG	OBP	SLG	PRO	/A	BR	/A	PF	CHI	RC	TA	SB	CS	SBR	FR	POS	TPR
1921	Phi-A	7	25	2	6	1	0	0	4	1	1	.240	.269	.280	.549	39	-2	-2	103	196	2	.474	1	0	0	1	/O	-0.1

■ **JULE MALLONEE** Mallonee, Julius Norris b: 4/4/1900, Charlotte, N.C. d: 12/26/34, Charlotte, N.C. BL/TR, 6'2", 180 lbs. Deb: 8/04/25

YEAR	TM/L	G	AB	R	H	2B	3B	HR	RBI	BB	SO	AVG	OBP	SLG	PRO	/A	BR	/A	PF	CHI	RC	TA	SB	CS	SBR	FR	POS	TPR
1925	Chi-A	2	3	1	0	0	0	0	0	1	0	.000	.250	.000	.250	-34	-1	-1	96	0	0	.333	0	0	0	-0	/O	0.0

■ **JIM MALLORY** Mallory, James Baugh "Sunny Jim" b: 9/1/18, Lawrenceville, Va. BR/TR, 6'1", 170 lbs. Deb: 9/08/40

YEAR	TM/L	G	AB	R	H	2B	3B	HR	RBI	BB	SO	AVG	OBP	SLG	PRO	/A	BR	/A	PF	CHI	RC	TA	SB	CS	SBR	FR	POS	TPR
1940	Was-A	4	12	2	2	0	0	0	0	1	1	.167	.231	.167	.397	5	-2	-2	93	0	1	.300	0	0	0	1	/O	0.0
1945	StL-N	13	43	3	10	2	0	0	5	0	2	.233	.233	.279	.512	42	-3	-3	100	145	3	.364	0			-1	O	-0.4
	NY-N	37	94	10	28	1	0	0	9	6	7	.298	.340	.309	.649	81	-2	-2	100	108	10	.537	1			0	O	-0.2
	Yr	50	137	13	38	3	0	0	14	6	9	.277	.308	.299	.607	69	-6	-6	100	120	13	.480	1			-1		-0.6
Total	2	54	149	15	40	3	0	0	14	7	10	.268	.301	.289	.590	64	-7	-7	99	109	14	.464	1	0		-0	/O	-0.6

■ **SHELDON MALLORY** Mallory, Sheldon b: 7/16/53, Argo, Ill. BL/TL, 6'2", 175 lbs. Deb: 4/10/77

YEAR	TM/L	G	AB	R	H	2B	3B	HR	RBI	BB	SO	AVG	OBP	SLG	PRO	/A	BR	/A	PF	CHI	RC	TA	SB	CS	SBR	FR	POS	TPR
1977	Oak-A	64	126	19	27	4	1	0	5	11	18	.214	.293	.262	.555	55	-8	-7	95	60	11	.557	12	5	1	-2	O/1D	-0.9

■ **HARRY MALMBERG** Malmberg, Harry William "Swede" b: 7/31/26, Fairfield, Ala. d: 10/29/76, San Francisco, Cal BR/TR, 6'1", 170 lbs. Deb: 4/12/55 C

YEAR	TM/L	G	AB	R	H	2B	3B	HR	RBI	BB	SO	AVG	OBP	SLG	PRO	/A	BR	/A	PF	CHI	RC	TA	SB	CS	SBR	FR	POS	TPR
1955	Det-A	67	208	25	45	5	2	0	19	29	19	.216	.312	.260	.572	57	-13	-12	97	131	17	.485	0	1	-1	2	2	-0.5

■ **EDDIE MALONE** Malone, Edward Russell b: 6/16/20, Chicago, Ill. BR/TR, 5'10", 175 lbs. Deb: 7/17/49

YEAR	TM/L	G	AB	R	H	2B	3B	HR	RBI	BB	SO	AVG	OBP	SLG	PRO	/A	BR	/A	PF	CHI	RC	TA	SB	CS	SBR	FR	POS	TPR
1949	Chi-A	55	170	17	46	7	2	1	16	29	19	.271	.377	.353	.730	96	-1	-0	98	87	25	.705	2	1	0	4	C	0.6
1950	Chi-A	31	71	2	16	2	0	0	10	10	8	.225	.321	.254	.575	50	-5	-5	97	192	5	.452	0	0	0	1	C	-0.2
Total	2	86	241	19	62	9	2	1	26	39	27	.257	.361	.324	.684	82	-6	-5	98	117	30	.636	2	1	0	5	/C	0.4

■ **FERGY MALONE** Malone, Ferguson G. b: 1842, Ireland d: 1/18/05, Seattle, Wash. BR/TL, 5'8", 156 lbs. Deb: 6/03/1871 M

YEAR	TM/L	G	AB	R	H	2B	3B	HR	RBI	BB	SO	AVG	OBP	SLG	PRO	/A	BR	/A	PF	CHI	RC	TA	SB	CS	SBR	FR	POS	TPR
1871	Ath-n	27	145	33	46							.317															*C	
1872	Ath-n	39	216	46	58							.269															C1	
1873	Phi-n	53	284	59	76							.268															*C/S	
1874	Chi-n	47	238	33	53							.223															*CM	
1875	Phi-n	27	114	15	26							.228															1/CO	
1876	Phi-N	22	96	14	22	2	0	0	6	0	1	.229	.229	.250	.479	60	-4	-4	99	89	6	.324				1	C/OS	-0.1
1884	Phi-U	1	4	0	1	0	0	0		0		.250	.250	.250	.500	75	-0	-0	93	0	0	.333	0			0	/CM	0.0
Total	5 n	193	997	186	259							.260															/CM	
Total	2	23	100	14	23	2	0	0	6	0	1	.230	.230	.250	.480	61	-4	-4	99	86	6	.325	0			1	C/1OS	-0.1

■ **LEW MALONE** Malone, Lewis Aloysius b: 3/13/1897, Baltimore, Md. d: 2/17/72, Brooklyn, N.Y. BR/TR, 5'11", 175 lbs. Deb: 5/31/15

YEAR	TM/L	G	AB	R	H	2B	3B	HR	RBI	BB	SO	AVG	OBP	SLG	PRO	/A	BR	/A	PF	CHI	RC	TA	SB	CS	SBR	FR	POS	TPR
1915	Phi-A	76	201	17	41	4	4	1	17	21	40	.204	.283	.279	.561	71	-8	-7	96	98	18	.528	7	1	2	2	23/OS	-0.3
1916	Phi-A	5	4	1	0	0	0	0	0	1	2	.000	.200	.000	.200	-40	-1	-1	98	0	0	.250	0			0	/S	0.0
1917	Bro-N	1	0	1	0	0	0	0	0	0	0	—	—	—	—	—	0	0	104	—	—	—	0			0	R	0.0
1919	Bro-N	51	162	9	33	7	3	0	11	6	18	.204	.232	.284	.516	58	-9	-8	94	93	11	.411	1			-6	3/2S	-1.5
Total	4	133	367	28	74	11	7	1	28	28	60	.202	.260	.278	.538	64	-18	-16	95	95	29	.473	8	1		-4	/32SO	-1.8

■ **JOHN MALONEY** Maloney, John d: 7/21/1890, Deb: 9/15/1876

YEAR	TM/L	G	AB	R	H	2B	3B	HR	RBI	BB	SO	AVG	OBP	SLG	PRO	/A	BR	/A	PF	CHI	RC	TA	SB	CS	SBR	FR	POS	TPR
1876	NY-N	2	7	1	2	0	1	0	2	0	1	.286	.286	.571	.857	206	1	1	87	169	1	.800				0	/O	0.1
1877	Har-N	1	4	0	1	0	0	0	0	0	0	.250	.250	.250	.500	65	-0	-0	89	0	0	.333				0	/O	0.0
Total	2	3	11	1	3	0	1	0	2	0	1	.273	.273	.455	.727	152	0	1	88	107	1	.625				0	/O	0.1

■ **PAT MALONEY** Maloney, Patrick William b: 1/19/1888, Grosvenordale, Conn. d: 6/27/79, Pawtucket, R.I. 6', 150 lbs. Deb: 6/19/12

YEAR	TM/L	G	AB	R	H	2B	3B	HR	RBI	BB	SO	AVG	OBP	SLG	PRO	/A	BR	/A	PF	CHI	RC	TA	SB	CS	SBR	FR	POS	TPR
1912	NY-A	22	79	9	17	1	0	0	4	6		.215	.279	.228	.507	45	-5	-6	101	78	6	.452	3			3	O	-0.2

■ **BILLY MALONEY** Maloney, William Alphonse b: 6/5/1878, Lewiston, Me. d: 9/2/60, Breckenridge, Tex. BL/TR, 5'10", 177 lbs. Deb: 5/02/01

YEAR	TM/L	G	AB	R	H	2B	3B	HR	RBI	BB	SO	AVG	OBP	SLG	PRO	/A	BR	/A	PF	CHI	RC	TA	SB	CS	SBR	FR	POS	TPR
1901	Mil-A	86	290	42	85	3	4	0	22	7		.293	.310	.331	.641	84	-8	-6	95	72	34	.556	11			5	C/O	0.5
1902	StL-A	30	112	8	23	3	0	0	11	6		.205	.246	.232	.478	33	-10	-10	102	142	7	.360	0			-0	O/C	-1.0
	Cin-N	27	89	13	22	4	0	1	7	2		.247	.264	.326	.590	76	-2	-3	110	76	10	.582	8			1	O/C	-0.2
1905	Chi-N	145	558	78	145	17	14	2	56	43		.260	.313	.351	.664	95	-1	-4	105	93	82	.722	**59**			-4	*O	-1.7
1906	Bro-N	151	566	71	125	15	7	0	32	49		.221	.283	.272	.555	87	-16	-7	87	67	56	.546	38			15	*O	0.5
1907	Bro-N	144	502	51	115	7	10	0	32	31		.229	.274	.283	.557	81	-14	-11	94	90	47	.512	25			3	*O	-1.4
1908	Bro-N	113	359	31	70	5	7	3	17	24		.195	.245	.273	.518	71	-13	-12	95	62	26	.471	14			-9	*O/C	-2.5
Total	6	696	2476	294	585	54	42	6	177	162		.236	.283	.299	.582	82	-64	-53	96	81	261	.559	155			11	O/C	-5.8

■ **FRANK MALZONE** Malzone, Frank James b: 2/28/30, Bronx, N.Y. BR/TR, 5'10", 180 lbs. Deb: 9/17/55

YEAR	TM/L	G	AB	R	H	2B	3B	HR	RBI	BB	SO	AVG	OBP	SLG	PRO	/A	BR	/A	PF	CHI	RC	TA	SB	CS	SBR	FR	POS	TPR
1955	Bos-A	6	20	2	7	1	0	0	1	1	3	.350	.381	.400	.781	89	0	-0	124	47	3	.692	0	0	0	0	/3	0.0
1956	Bos-A	27	103	15	17	3	1	2	11	9	8	.165	.232	.272	.504	32	-10	-11	103	123	6	.418	1	0	0	1	3	-0.8
1957	Bos-A	153	634	82	185	31	5	15	103	31	41	.292	.326	.427	.753	95	2	-6	110	136	85	.656	2	1	0	14	*3	1.2
1958	Bos-A	155	627	76	185	30	2	15	87	33	53	.295	.334	.421	.755	101	4	1	105	120	82	.648	1	3	-2	16	*3	2.2
1959	Bos-A	154	604	90	169	34	2	19	92	42	58	.280	.328	.437	.765	102	5	1	106	120	85	.696	6	0	2	8	*3	0.9
1960	Bos-A	152	595	60	161	30	2	14	79	36	42	.271	.317	.398	.715	89	-8	-10	103	117	70	.611	2	3	-1	6	*3	-0.2
1961	Bos-A	151	590	74	157	21	4	14	87	44	49	.266	.318	.386	.705	86	-11	-13	102	**134**	68	.602	1	3	-2	-0	*3	-0.4
1962	Bos-A	156	619	74	175	20	3	21	95	35	43	.283	.321	.426	.748	97	-2	-4	102	122	80	.647	0	1	-1	5	*3	0.3
1963	Bos-A	151	580	66	169	25	2	15	71	31	45	.291	.331	.419	.750	102	6	2	106	105	73	.634	0	2	-1	1	*3	0.3
1964	Bos-A	148	537	62	142	19	0	13	56	37	43	.264	.314	.372	.687	89	-7	-9	102	101	64	.595	0	0	0	0	*3	-0.6
1965	Bos-A	106	364	40	87	20	0	3	34	28	38	.239	.295	.319	.614	69	-12	-15	107	113	31	.493	1	1	-0	-3	3	-1.8
1966	Cal-A	82	155	6	32	5	0	2	12	10	11	.206	.255	.277	.532	53	-9	-9	99	103	10	.417	0	0	0	-1	3	-1.1
Total	12	1441	5428	647	1486	239	21	133	728	337	434	.274	.318	.399	.717	91	-44	-74	105	119	656	.640	14	14	-4	48	*3	-0.0

■ **GUS MANCUSO** Mancuso, August Rodney "Blackie" b: 12/5/05, Galveston, Tex. d: 10/26/84, Houston, Tex. BR/TR, 5'10", 185 lbs. Deb: 4/30/28 C

YEAR	TM/L	G	AB	R	H	2B	3B	HR	RBI	BB	SO	AVG	OBP	SLG	PRO	/A	BR	/A	PF	CHI	RC	TA	SB	CS	SBR	FR	POS	TPR
1928	StL-N	11	38	2	7	0	1	0	3	0	5	.184	.184	.237	.421	9	-5	-5	100	119	2	.290	0			0	C	-0.3
1930	StL-N	76	227	39	83	17	2	7	59	18	16	.366	.415	.551	.965	125	11	10	105	139	50	1.007	1			2	C	1.3
1931	StL-N	67	187	13	49	16	1	1	23	18	13	.262	.327	.374	.701	82	-3	-5	107	112	24	.652	2			1	C	0.0
1932	StL-N	103	310	25	88	23	1	5	43	30	15	.284	.347	.413	.760	103	2	2	100	112	46	.712	0			8	C	1.2
1933	NY-N	144	481	39	127	17	2	6	56	48	21	.264	.331	.345	.676	94	-3	-3	99	114	56	.580	0			-6	*C	-0.3
1934	NY-N	122	383	32	94	14	0	7	46	27	19	.245	.295	.337	.632	70	-17	-16	98	111	39	.523	0			-8	*C	-1.8
1935	NY-N	128	447	33	133	18	2	5	56	30	16	.298	.342	.380	.722	97	-4	-1	96	109	57	.609	1			-2	*C	-0.3
1936	NY-N	139	519	55	156	21	3	9	63	39	28	.301	.351	.405	.755	102	2	2	100	96	73	.660	0			4	*C	1.0
1937	NY-N	86	287	30	80	17	1	4	39	17	20	.279	.319	.387	.706	91	-4	-4	100	114	36	.611	1			0	C	0.0
1938	NY-N	52	158	19	55	8	0	2	15	17	13	.348	.411	.437	.848	129	8	7	103	72	29	.804	0			1	C	1.0

YEAR	TM/L	G	AB	R	H	2B	3B	HR	RBI	BB	SO	AVG	OBP	SLG	PRO	/A	BR	/A	PF	CHI	RC	TA	SB	CS	SBR	FR	POS	TPR
1939	Chi-N	80	251	17	58	10	0	2	17	24	19	.231	.298	.295	.593	59	-14	-14	101	78	23	.497	0			-0	C	-1.1
1940	Bro-N	60	144	16	33	8	0	0	16	13	7	.229	.293	.285	.578	56	-8	-9	108	145	12	.470	0			-3	C	-0.9
1941	StL-N	106	328	25	75	13	1	2	37	37	19	.229	.309	.293	.601	64	-12	-17	110	131	31	.511	0			1	*C	-0.5
1942	StL-N	5	13	0	1	0	0	0	1	0	0	.077	.077	.077	.154	-51	-3	-3	108	371	0	.083	0			0	/C	-0.2
	NY-N	39	109	4	21	1	1	0	8	14	7	.193	.285	.220	.505	47	-7	-7	103	124	7	.419	1			0	C	-0.5
	Yr	44	122	4	22	1	1	0	9	14	7	.180	.265	.205	.470	37	-9	-10	103	160	7	.381	1			1		-0.7
1943	NY-N	94	252	11	50	5	0	2	20	28	16	.198	.284	.242	.526	55	-15	-14	96	108	17	.423	0			-1	C	-1.1
1944	NY-N	78	195	15	49	4	1	1	25	30	20	.251	.351	.297	.649	81	-3	-4	104	147	22	.587	0			-2	C	-0.1
1945	Phi-N	70	176	11	35	5	0	0	16	28	10	.199	.309	.227	.536	52	-11	-10	96	139	13	.470	2			-1	C	-0.9
Total	17	1460	4505	386	1194	197	16	53	543	418	264	.265	.328	.351	.679	85	-85	-91	101	114	536	.607	8			-5	*C	-3.5
■ **FRANK MANCUSO** Mancuso, Frank Octavius b: 5/23/18, Houston, Tex. BR/TR, 6', 195 lbs. Deb: 4/18/44																												
1944	StL-A	88	244	19	50	11	0	1	24	20	32	.205	.271	.262	.533	52	-15	-16	102	129	17	.424	1	0	0	-12	C	-2.2
1945	StL-A	119	365	39	98	13	3	1	38	46	44	.268	.354	.329	.682	85	1	-6	115	112	43	.594	0	2	-1	-5	*C	-0.3
1946	StL-A	87	262	22	63	8	3	3	23	30	31	.240	.323	.328	.651	84	-6	-5	98	92	29	.578	1	0	0	-5	C	-0.5
1947	Was-A	43	131	5	30	5	1	0	13	5	11	.229	.257	.282	.540	52	-9	-9	97	129	8	.385	0	0	0	3	C	-0.2
Total	4	337	1002	85	241	37	7	5	98	101	118	.241	.314	.306	.620	73	-29	-35	105	113	96	.540	2	2	-1	-19	C	-3.2
■ **CARL MANDA** Manda, Carl Alan b: 11/16/1886, Little River, Kan. d: 3/9/83, Artesia, N.Mex. BR/TR, 5'10", 170 lbs. Deb: 9/11/14																												
1914	Chi-A	9	15	2	4	0	0	0	1	3	3	.267	.389	.267	.656	94	0	0	103	94	2	.727	1			0	/2	0.1
■ **JIM MANGAN** Mangan, James Daniel b: 9/24/29, San Francisco, Cal BR/TR, 5'10", 190 lbs. Deb: 4/16/52																												
1952	Pit-N	11	13	1	2	0	0	0	2	1	3	.154	.214	.154	.368	4	-2	-2	100	390	0	.273	0	0	0	0	/C	-0.1
1954	Pit-N	14	26	2	5	0	0	0	2	4	9	.192	.300	.192	.492	33	-3	-2	97	157	2	.429	0	0	0	1	/C	0.0
1956	NY-N	20	20	2	2	0	0	0	1	4	6	.100	.250	.100	.350	-1	-3	-3	97	211	1	.316	0	0	0	-1	C	-0.2
Total	3	45	59	5	9	0	0	0	5	9	18	.153	.265	.153	.417	15	-7	-7	97	224	3	.353	0	0	0	0	/C	-0.3
■ **ANGEL MANGUAL** Mangual, Angel Luis (Guilbe) b: 3/19/47, Juana Diaz, P.R. BR/TR, 5'10", 178 lbs. Deb: 9/15/69																												
1969	Pit-N	6	4	1	1	1	0	0	0	0	0	.250	.250	.500	.750	111	-0	0	95	0	1	.667	0	0	0	-1	/O	-0.1
1971	Oak-A	94	287	32	82	8	1	4	30	17	27	.286	.326	.362	.688	94	-2	-3	101	106	31	.562	1	4	-2	1	O	-0.6
1972	Oak-A	91	272	19	67	13	2	5	32	14	48	.246	.286	.364	.650	95	-3	-3	97	117	26	.533	0	1	-1	-3	O	-0.8
1973	Oak-A	74	192	20	43	4	1	3	13	8	34	.224	.259	.302	.561	66	-11	-8	87	76	15	.447	1	1	-0	-4	OD/12	-1.4
1974	Oak-A	115	365	37	85	14	4	9	43	17	59	.233	.267	.367	.634	81	-10	-10	100	105	36	.542	3	0	1	-3	OD/3	-1.4
1975	Oak-A	62	109	13	24	3	0	1	6	3	18	.220	.241	.275	.516	49	-8	-7	93	70	7	.375	0	1	-1	-8	OD	-1.7
1976	Oak-A	8	12	0	2	1	0	0	1	0	1	.167	.167	.250	.417	21	-1	-1	100	128	0	.273	0	1	-1	-2	/O	-0.3
Total	7	450	1241	122	304	44	8	22	125	59	187	.245	.280	.346	.627	82	-36	-32	97	100	116	.525	5	8	-3	-20	O/D132	-6.3
■ **PEPE MANGUAL** Mangual, Jose Manuel (Guilbe) b: 5/23/52, Ponce, P.R. BR/TR, 5'10", 157 lbs. Deb: 9/06/72																												
1972	Mon-N	8	11	2	3	0	0	0	0	1	5	.273	.333	.273	.606	72	-0	-0	102	0	1	.444	0	1	-1	-1	/O	-0.1
1973	Mon-N	33	62	9	11	2	1	3	7	6	18	.177	.250	.387	.637	71	-3	-3	104	85	5	.582	2	4	-2	-4	O	-0.9
1974	Mon-N	23	61	10	19	3	0	0	4	5	15	.311	.364	.361	.724	99	0	0	104	70	10	.762	5	0	2	-5	O	-0.3
1975	Mon-N	140	514	84	126	16	2	9	45	74	115	.245	.345	.337	.681	83	-5	-11	108	92	65	.693	33	11	3	-9	*O	-2.2
1976	Mon-N	66	215	34	56	9	1	3	16	50	49	.260	.404	.353	.758	116	8	8	100	77	37	.873	17	7	1	-3	O	0.3
	NY-N	41	102	15	19	5	2	1	9	10	32	.186	.259	.304	.563	65	-6	-5	92	102	9	.558	7	3	0	-1	O	-0.6
	Yr	107	317	49	75	14	3	4	25	60	81	.237	.361	.338	.699	102	2	3	97	87	46	.766	24	10	1	-4		-0.3
1977	NY-N	8	7	1	1	0	0	0	2	1	4	.143	.250	.143	.393	9	-1	-1	96	800	0	.333	0	0	0	-1	/O	-0.1
Total	6	319	972	155	235	35	6	16	83	147	238	.242	.345	.340	.684	88	-7	-12	104	92	127	.717	64	26	4	-23	O	-3.9
■ **GEORGE MANGUS** Mangus, George Graham b: 5/22/1890, Red Creek, N.Y. d: 8/10/33, Rutland, Mass. BL/TR, 5'11.5", 165 lbs. Deb: 8/20/12																												
1912	Phi-N	10	25	2	5	3	0	0	3	1	6	.200	.231	.320	.551	50	-2	-2	100	126	2	.450	0			-1	/O	-0.2
■ **CLYDE MANION** Manion, Clyde Jennings "Pete" b: 10/30/1896, Jefferson City, Mo d: 9/4/67, Detroit, Mich. BR/TR, 5'11", 175 lbs. Deb: 5/05/20																												
1920	Det-A	32	80	4	22	4	1	0	8	4	7	.275	.318	.350	.668	74	-3	-3	103	100	9	.569	0	0	0	-2	C	-0.1
1921	Det-A	12	10	0	2	0	0	0	2	2	2	.200	.385	.200	.585	55	-1	-0	96	343	1	.625	0	0	0	0	/C	0.0
1922	Det-A	42	69	9	19	4	1	0	12	4	6	.275	.315	.362	.677	78	-3	-2	98	172	8	.569	0	1	-1	-1	C/1	-0.2
1923	Det-A	23	22	0	3	0	0	0	2	2	2	.136	.208	.136	.345	-8	-3	-3	97	228	1	.263	0	0	0	0	/C1	-0.2
1924	Det-A	14	13	1	3	0	0	0	2	1	1	.231	.286	.231	.516	34	-1	-1	100	220	1	.400	0	0	0	0	/C1	0.0
1926	Det-A	75	176	15	35	4	0	0	14	24	16	.199	.295	.222	.517	37	-16	-15	97	122	13	.451	1	1	-0	-4	C	-1.3
1927	Det-A	1	0	0	0	0	0	0	0	1	0	—	1.000	—	1.222	214	0	0	108	0	0	—	0	0	0	0	H	0.0
1928	StL-A	76	243	25	55	5	1	2	31	15	18	.226	.274	.280	.554	44	-19	-20	104	144	20	.463	3	0	1	2	C	-1.2
1929	StL-A	35	111	16	27	2	0	0	11	15	3	.243	.333	.261	.595	55	-7	-7	100	130	11	.536	1	0	0	1	C	-0.2
1930	StL-A	57	148	12	32	1	0	1	11	24	17	.216	.326	.243	.569	43	-11	-13	108	94	13	.513	0	1	-1	3	C	-0.4
1932	Cin-N	49	135	7	28	4	0	0	12	14	16	.207	.282	.237	.519	43	-11	-10	96	140	10	.430	0			0	C	-0.7
1933	Cin-N	36	84	3	14	1	0	0	3	8	7	.167	.239	.179	.418	21	-8	-8	99	75	4	.319	0			0	C	-0.6
1934	Cin-N	25	54	4	10	0	0	0	4	4	7	.185	.241	.185	.427	16	-6	-6	101	144	3	.311	0			1	C	-0.4
Total	13	477	1145	96	250	25	3	3	112	118	102	.218	.293	.253	.546	45	-89	-91	101	130	94	.463	5	3		1	C/1	-5.3
■ **PHIL MANKOWSKI** Mankowski, Philip Anthony b: 1/9/53, Buffalo, N.Y. BL/TR, 6', 180 lbs. Deb: 8/30/76																												
1976	Det-A	24	85	9	23	2	1	1	4	4	8	.271	.303	.353	.656	89	-1	-1	104	47	8	.523	0	0	0	3	3	0.1
1977	Det-A	94	286	21	79	7	3	3	27	16	41	.276	.319	.353	.672	79	-7	-8	105	97	32	.563	1	2	-1	16	3/2	0.5
1978	Det-A	88	222	28	61	8	0	4	20	22	28	.275	.346	.365	.710	93	0	-2	108	85	26	.615	2	3	-1	0	3/D	-0.2
1979	Det-A	42	99	11	22	4	0	0	8	10	16	.222	.294	.263	.556	53	-7	-6	96	118	8	.450	0	0	0	2	3	-0.3
1980	NY-N	8	12	1	2	1	0	0	1	2	4	.167	.286	.250	.536	53	-1	-1	96	132	1	.500	0	0	0	0	/3	0.0
1982	NY-N	13	35	2	8	1	0	0	4	1	6	.229	.250	.257	.507	43	-3	-3	99	174	2	.333	0	1	-1	-0	3	-0.3
Total	6	269	739	72	195	23	4	8	64	55	103	.264	.318	.338	.657	79	-17	-21	104	95	76	.565	3	6	-3	21	3/D2	-0.2
■ **CHARLIE MANLOVE** Manlove, Charles Henry "Chick" b: 10/8/1862, Philadelphia, Pa. d: 2/12/52, Altoona, Pa. BR/TR, 5'9", 165 lbs. Deb: 5/31/1884																												
1884	Alt-U	2	7	1	3	0	0	0		0		.429	.429	.429	.857	188	1	1	101	0	1	.750	0			0	/CO	0.1
	NY-N	3	10	0	0	0	0	0	0	0	4	.000	.000	.000	.000	-99	-2	-2	98	0	0	.000				0	/CO	-0.1
Total	1	5	17	1	3	0	0	0	0	0	4	.176	.176	.176	.353	15	-2	-2	99	0	1	.214				0	/CO	0.0
■ **GARTH MANN** Mann, Ben Garth "Red" b: 11/16/15, Brandon, Tex. BR/TR, 6', 155 lbs. Deb: 5/14/44																												
1944	Chi-N	1	0	1	0	0	0	0	0	0	0	—	—	—	—	—	0	0	101	—	—	—	0			0	R	0.0
■ **FRED MANN** Mann, Fred J. b: 4/1/1858, Sutton, Vt. d: 4/6/16, Springfield, Mass. BL, 5'10.5", 178 lbs. Deb: 5/01/1882																												
1882	Wor-N	19	77	12	18	5	0	0	7	2	15	.234	.253	.299	.552	76	-2	-2	100	108	6	.424				0	3/1	-0.1
	Phi-a	29	121	13	28	7	4	0		4		.231	.256	.355	.611	93	0	-2	112	0	11	.505				-10	3	-1.1
1883	Col-a	96	394	61	98	18	13	1		18		.249	.282	.368	.650	123	3	11	87	0	42	.551				-1	*O/13S	0.9
1884	Col-a	99	366	70	101	12	18	7		25		.276	.341	.464	.805	168	26	27	97	0	59	.777				-6	*O/2	1.8
1885	Pit-a	99	391	60	99	17	6	0		31		.253	.318	.327	.645	101	4	0	106	0	42	.565				-9	*O/3	-1.2
1886	Pit-a	116	440	85	110	16	14	2		45		.250	.335	.364	.698	131	11	17	93	0	64	.733	26			-5	*O	0.7
1887	Cle-a	64	259	45	80	15	7	2		23		.309	.385	.444	.829	137	12	13	98	0	55	.961	25			2	O	1.0
	Phi-a	55	229	42	63	14	6	0		15		.275	.336	.389	.725	104	1	1	99	0	36	.759	16			-6	O	-0.4
	Yr	119	488	87	143	29	13	2		38		.293	.362	.418	.780	121	13	14	98	0	91	.864	41			-4		0.6
Total	6	577	2277	388	597	104	68	12	7	163	15	.262	.323	.383	.707	124	56	66	97	3	315	.682	67			-36	O/312S	1.6
■ **JOHNNY MANN** Mann, John Leo b: 2/4/1898, Fontanet, Ind. d: 3/31/77, Terre Haute, Ind. BR/TR, 5'11", 160 lbs. Deb: 4/18/28																												
1928	Chi-A	6	6	0	2	0	0	0	1	1	0	.333	.429	.333	.762	104	0	0	99	172	1	.750	0	0	0	0	/3	0.0
■ **LES MANN** Mann, Leslie "Major" b: 11/18/1893, Lincoln, Neb. d: 1/14/62, Pasadena, Cal. BR/TR, 5'9", 172 lbs. Deb: 4/30/13																												
1913	Bos-N	120	407	54	103	24	7	3	51	18	73	.253	.291	.369	.660	93	-8	-5	95	117	43	.589	7			-9	*O	-1.6

YEAR	TM/L	G	AB	R	H	2B	3B	HR	RBI	BB	SO	AVG	OBP	SLG	PRO	/A	BR	/A	PF	CHI	RC	TA	SB	CS	SBR	FR	POS	TPR
1914	Bos-N	126	389	44	96	16	11	4	40	24	50	.247	.292	.375	.668	94	-3	-5	104	92	43	.614	9			5	*O	-0.2
1915	Chi-F	135	470	74	144	12	**19**	4	58	36	40	.306	.356	.438	.794	138	19	20	97	98	83	.798	18			6	*O/S	2.1
1916	Chi-N	127	415	46	113	13	9	2	29	19	31	.272	.307	.361	.669	90	1	-6	117	74	48	.589	11	7	-1	-6	*O	-1.7
1917	Chi-N	117	444	63	121	19	10	1	44	27	46	.273	.316	.367	.683	104	4	2	105	108	54	.635	14			3	*O	0.1
1918	Chi-N	129	489	69	141	27	7	2	55	38	45	.288	.342	.384	.727	119	12	11	102	103	70	.716	21			-5	*O	0.0
1919	Chi-N	80	299	31	68	8	8	1	22	11	29	.227	.257	.318	.575	72	-11	-11	100	92	26	.515	12			-6	O	-2.2
	Bos-N	40	145	15	41	6	4	3	20	9	14	.283	.329	.441	.770	134	5	5	98	109	22	.779	7			2	O	0.6
	Yr	120	444	46	109	14	12	4	42	20	43	.245	.281	.358	.639	92	-6	-6	100	98	48	.597	19			-5		-1.6
1920	Bos-N	115	424	48	117	7	8	3	32	38	42	.276	.341	.351	.693	103	0	2	96	83	52	.631	7	7	-2	1	*O	-0.5
1921	StL-N	97	256	57	84	12	7	7	30	23	28	.328	.390	.512	.902	144	13	15	95	72	50	.915	5	5	-2	3	O	1.3
1922	StL-N	84	147	42	51	14	1	2	20	16	12	.347	.415	.497	.911	133	8	8	101	88	30	.928	0	1	-1	-9	O	-0.3
1923	StL-N	38	89	20	33	5	2	5	11	9	5	.371	.434	.640	1.075	200	10	11	90	54	25	1.196	0	0	0	-3	O	0.7
	Cin-N	8	1	1	0	0	0	0	0	0	0	.000	.000	.000	.000	-99	-0	-0	98	0	0	.000	0	0	0	0	H	0.0
	Yr	46	90	21	33	5	2	5	11	9	5	.367	.430	.633	1.063	194	10	11	91	46	25	1.175	0	0	0	-3		0.7
1924	Bos-N	32	102	13	28	7	4	0	10	8	10	.275	.333	.422	.755	108	-0	1	94	85	15	.716	1	0	0	1	O	0.1
1925	Bos-N	60	184	27	63	11	4	2	20	5	11	.342	.373	.478	.851	124	4	6	94	76	33	.844	6	1	1	-2	O	0.3
1926	Bos-N	50	129	23	39	8	2	1	20	9	9	.302	.348	.419	.766	122	1	3	86	121	18	.756	5			-4	O	-0.2
1927	Bos-N	29	66	8	17	3	1	0	6	8	3	.258	.338	.333	.671	86	-2	-1	93	95	8	.653	2			-2	O	-0.3
	NY-N	29	67	13	22	4	1	2	10	8	7	.328	.400	.507	.907	142	4	4	100	87	13	.978	2			-5	O	-0.1
	Yr	58	133	21	39	7	2	2	16	16	10	.293	.369	.421	.790	115	2	3	96	93	21	.809	4			-7		-0.4
1928	NY-N	82	193	29	51	7	1	2	25	18	9	.264	.330	.342	.672	74	-7	-7	102	124	22	.613	2			-14	O	-2.2
Total	16	1498	4716	677	1332	203	106	44	503	324	464	.282	.332	.398	.731	110	51	53	100	95	656	.693	129	21		-43	*O/S	-4.1

■ **JIM MANNING** Manning, James H. b: 1/31/1862, Fall River, Mass. d: 10/22/29, Edinburg, Tex. TR , 157 lbs. Deb: 5/16/1884 M

1884	Bos-N	89	345	52	83	8	6	2	35	19	47	.241	.280	.316	.596	89	-5	-4	98	107	31	.489				-2	O/S23	-0.4
1885	Bos-N	84	306	34	63	8	9	2	27	19	36	.206	.252	.310	.563	87	-6	-4	94	95	25	.469				6	*O/S	0.0
	Det-N	20	78	15	21	4	0	1	9	4	10	.269	.305	.359	.664	117	1	1	97	107	9	.561				0	S	0.1
	Yr	104	384	49	84	12	9	3	36	23	46	.219	.263	.320	.583	93	-5	-2	94	98	33	.487				6		0.1
1886	Det-N	26	97	14	18	2	3	0	7	6	10	.186	.233	.268	.501	48	-6	-7	109	89	8	.494	7			0	O/S	-0.5
1887	Det-N	13	52	5	10	1	0	0	3	5	4	.192	.276	.212	.487	38	-4	-4	102	89	4	.476	3			0	O/S	-0.3
1889	KC-a	132	506	68	103	16	7	3	68	54	61	.204	.297	.281	.577	63	-21	-26	106	136	61	.663	58			-10	O2/S3	-3.1
Total	5	364	1384	188	298	39	25	8	149	107	168	.215	.278	.297	.575	74	-41	-43	101	114	137	.552	68			-6	O/2S3	-4.2

■ **JACK MANNING** Manning, John E. b: 12/20/1853, Braintree, Mass. d: 8/15/29, Boston, Mass. BR/TR, 5'8.5", 158 lbs. Deb: 4/23/1873

1873	Bos-n	33	169	30	44							.260															1/O	
1874	Bal-n	42	184	35	55							.299															2P/S	
	Har-n	1	4	1	1							.250															/3	
	Yr	43	188	36	56							.298																
1875	Bos-n	77	351	71	100							.285															*OP13	
1876	Bos-N	70	288	52	76	13	0	2	25	7	5	.264	.281	.330	.611	109	1	3	95	85	27	.481				-4	*OP/S2	0.0
1877	Cin-N	57	252	47	80	16	7	0	36	5	6	.317	.331	.437	.767	171	11	18	82	98	37	.669				-12	S1OP/2	0.5
1878	Bos-N	60	248	41	63	10	1	0	23	10	16	.254	.283	.302	.585	86	-2	-4	108	100	22	.459				-16	*O/P	-2.3
1880	Cin-N	48	190	20	41	6	3	2	17	7	15	.216	.244	.311	.554	87	-3	-2	99	92	15	.443				-3	O/1	-0.5
1881	Buf-N	1	1	0	0	0	0	0	0	0	0	.000	.000	.000	.000	-99	-0	-0	101	0	0	.000				0	/O	0.0
1883	Phi-N	98	420	60	112	31	5	0	37	20	37	.267	.300	.364	.664	112	0	7	90	74	47	.562				7	*O	1.5
1884	Phi-N	104	424	71	115	29	4	5	52	40	67	.271	.334	.394	.728	139	14	20	92	87	57	.670				-5	*O	1.2
1885	Phi-N	107	445	61	114	24	4	3	40	37	27	.256	.313	.348	.662	110	7	5	104	73	50	.580				-8	*O	-0.5
1886	Bal-a	137	556	78	124	18	7	1		50		.223	.291	.286	.577	91	-10	-2	91	0	55	.546	24			-12	*O	-1.5
Total	3 n	153	708	137	200							.282															*O	
Total	9	682	2824	430	725	147	31	13	230	176	173	.257	.301	.345	.646	112	19	44	94	67	310	.560	24			-52	O/P1S23	-1.6

■ **RICK MANNING** Manning, Richard Eugene b: 9/2/54, Niagara Falls, N.Y. BL/TR, 6'1", 180 lbs. Deb: 5/23/75

1975	Cle-A	120	480	69	137	16	5	3	35	44	62	.285	.348	.358	.706	100	1	1	100	66	60	.653	19	11	-1	7	*O/D	0.4
1976	Cle-A	138	552	73	161	24	7	6	43	41	75	.292	.341	.393	.734	115	9	10	100	68	72	.665	16	10	-1	2	*O	0.8
1977	Cle-A	68	252	33	57	7	3	5	18	21	35	.226	.286	.337	.623	71	-11	-10	98	73	24	.564	9	5	-0	1	O	-1.1
1978	Cle-A	148	566	65	149	27	3	3	50	38	62	.263	.311	.337	.648	88	-13	-9	93	105	57	.551	12	12	-4	-2	*O	-1.8
1979	Cle-A	144	560	67	145	12	2	3	51	55	48	.259	.326	.304	.630	67	-21	-26	106	116	59	.587	30	8	4	10	*O	-1.6
1980	Cle-A	140	471	55	110	17	4	3	52	63	66	.234	.326	.306	.632	73	-15	-16	102	135	49	.583	12	6	0	2	*O	-1.6
1981	Cle-A	103	360	47	88	15	3	4	33	40	57	.244	.320	.336	.656	96	-4	-1	93	99	44	.667	25	3	6	9	*O	1.2
1982	Cle-A	152	562	71	152	18	2	8	44	54	60	.270	.334	.352	.687	89	-8	-8	100	81	66	.615	12	8	-1	-2	*O	-1.5
1983	Cle-A	50	194	20	54	6	0	1	10	12	22	.278	.320	.325	.645	74	-6	-7	105	63	20	.554	7	3	0	6	O	0.0
	Mil-A	108	375	40	86	14	4	3	33	26	40	.229	.281	.312	.593	69	-19	-15	92	102	33	.518	11	2	2	1	*O	-1.3
	Yr	158	569	60	140	20	4	4	43	38	62	.246	.294	.316	.611	71	-25	-22	96	90	55	.536	18	5	2	7		-1.3
1984	Mil-A	119	341	53	85	10	5	7	31	34	32	.249	.319	.370	.689	98	-5	-1	92	84	39	.615	5	7	-3	-5	*O/D	-1.1
1985	Mil-A	79	216	19	47	9	1	2	18	14	19	.218	.265	.296	.562	51	-14	-15	105	102	18	.462	1	0	0	-1	O/D	-1.6
1986	Mil-A	89	205	31	52	7	3	8	27	17	20	.254	.314	.434	.748	100	0	-0	102	95	27	.696	5	3	-0	-4	O/D	-0.6
1987	Mil-A	97	114	21	26	7	1	0	13	12	18	.228	.302	.307	.609	62	-6	-6	102	148	11	.560	4	0	1	-19	O/D	-2.5
Total	13	1555	5248	664	1349	189	43	56	458	471	616	.257	.319	.341	.661	85	-111	-104	99	94	580	.613	168	78	4	5	*O/D	-12.3

■ **TIM MANNING** Manning, Timothy Edward b: 12/3/1853, Henley-On-The- Thames, England d: 6/11/34, Oak Park, Ill. BR/TR, 5'10", 170 lbs. Deb: 5/01/1882

1882	Pro-N	21	76	7	8	0	0	0	8	5	13	.105	.160	.105	.266	-12	-9	-10	106	343	1	.191				0	S/C	-0.8
1883	Bal-a	35	121	23	26	5	0	0		14		.215	.296	.256	.552	74	-2	-4	107	0	9	.474				0	2	-0.2
1884	Bal-a	91	341	49	70	14	5	2		26		.205	.275	.293	.569	89	-3	-3	99	0	28	.491				-3	*2	-0.3
1885	Bal-a	43	157	17	32	8	1	0		10		.204	.265	.268	.532	67	-5	-6	106	0	11	.440				2	2/3	-0.2
	Pro-N	10	35	3	2	1	0	0	0	1	11	.057	.083	.086	.169	-50	-5	-5	91	0	0	.121				0	S	-0.4
Total	4	200	730	99	138	28	6	2	8	56	24	.189	.256	.252	.508	65	-25	-28	102	35	51	.422				-2	2/SC3	-1.9

■ **DON MANNO** Manno, Donald D. b: 5/15/15, Williamsport, Pa. BR/TR, 6'1", 190 lbs. Deb: 9/22/40

1940	Bos-N	3	7	1	2	0	0	1	4	0	2	.286	.286	.714	1.000	170	1	1	99	185	1	1.000	0			0	/O	0.0
1941	Bos-N	22	30	2	5	1	0	0	4	3	7	.167	.242	.200	.442	27	-3	-3	93	241	1	.333	0			-1	/O31	-0.3
Total	2	25	37	3	7	1	0	1	8	3	9	.189	.250	.297	.547	56	-2	-2	94	231	3	.438	0			-1	/O31	-0.3

■ **FRED MANRIQUE** Manrique, Fred Eloy (Reyes) b: 5/11/61, Edo Bolivar, Venez. BR/TR, 6'1", 175 lbs. Deb: 8/23/81

1981	Tor-A	14	28	1	4	0	0	0	1	0	12	.143	.172	.143	.315	-8	-4	-4	111	98	1	.200	0	1	-1	-1	S/3D	-0.4
1984	Tor-A	10	9	0	3	0	0	0	1	0	1	.333	.333	.333	.667	84	-0	-0	102	133	1	.429	0	0	0	0	/2D	0.0
1985	Mon-N	9	13	5	4	1	1	1	1	1	3	.308	.357	.769	1.126	221	2	2	94	31	4	1.222	0	0	0	0	/2S3	0.2
1986	StL-N	13	17	2	3	0	0	1	1	1	1	.176	.222	.353	.575	54	-1	-1	103	44	1	.533	1	0	0	0	/32	0.0
1987	Chi-A	115	298	30	77	13	3	4	29	19	69	.258	.305	.362	.667	71	-10	-13	109	96	33	.583	5	3	-0	-4	2S/D	-0.8
1988	Chi-A	140	345	43	81	10	6	5	37	21	54	.235	.285	.342	.627	77	-12	-11	97	111	33	.536	6	5	-1	2	*2S	0.0
Total	6	301	710	81	172	24	10	11	70	42	140	.242	.289	.351	.640	73	-25	-28	103	101	72	.556	12	9	-2	-2	2/SD3	-1.0

■ **JOHN MANSELL** Mansell, John b: 1861, Auburn, N.Y. d: 2/20/25, Willard, N.Y. BL , Deb: 5/09/1882

1882	Phi-a	31	126	17	30	3	1	0		4		.238	.262	.278	.539	73	-2	-4	112	0	9	.406				-4	O	-0.7

■ **MIKE MANSELL** Mansell, Michael R. b: 1/15/1858, Auburn, N.Y. d: 12/4/02, Auburn, N.Y. BL , Deb: 5/01/1879

1879	Syr-N	67	242	24	52	4	2	1	13	5	45	.215	.231	.260	.491	69	-10	-6	89	71	15	.358				15	*O	0.7
1880	Cin-N	53	187	22	36	6	2	2	12	4	37	.193	.209	.278	.487	64	-7	-7	99	77	11	.371				12	O	0.4
1882	Pit-a	79	347	59	96	**18**	**16**	2		7		.277	.291	.438	.729	147	14	16	97	0	45	.633				2	*O	1.5

YEAR	TM/L	G	AB	R	H	2B	3B	HR	RBI	BB	SO	AVG	OBP	SLG	PRO	/A	BR	/A	PF	CHI	RC	TA	SB	CS	SBR	FR	POS	TPR
1883	Pit-a	96	412	90	106	12	13	3		25		.257	.300	.371	.671	123	7	11	94	0	47	.582				3	*O	1.3
1884	Pit-a	27	100	15	14	0	3	1		7		.140	.204	.230	.434	45	-6	-5	97	0	5	.360				0	O	-0.4
	Phi-a	20	70	6	14	1	1	0		5		.200	.253	.243	.496	57	-2	-4	114	0	4	.393				-1	O	-0.4
	Ric-a	29	113	21	34	2	5	0		8		.301	.363	.407	.770	156	7	7	99	0	17	.722				-6	O	0.1
	Yr	76	283	42	62	3	9	1		20		.219	.280	.304	.584	91	-1	-2	102	0	25	.498				-7		-0.7
Total	5	371	1471	237	352	43	42	9	25	61	82	.239	.271	.344	.615	106	3	12	96	21	145	.510				26	O	3.2

■ **TOM MANSELL** Mansell, Thomas E. "Brick" b: 1/1/1855, Auburn, N.Y. d: 10/6/34, Auburn, N.Y. BL/TL, 5'8", 160 lbs. Deb: 5/01/1879

YEAR	TM/L	G	AB	R	H	2B	3B	HR	RBI	BB	SO	AVG	OBP	SLG	PRO	/A	BR	/A	PF	CHI	RC	TA	SB	CS	SBR	FR	POS	TPR
1879	Tro-N	40	177	29	43	6	0	0	11	3	9	.243	.256	.277	.532	81	-5	-3	93	68	13	.388				-6	O	-0.8
	Syr-N	1	4	0	1	0	0	0	0	0	0	.250	.250	.250	.500	74	-0	-0	89	0	0	.333				0	/O	0.0
	Yr	41	181	29	44	6	0	0	11	3	9	.243	.255	.276	.532	81	-5	-3	93	68	13	.387				-6		-0.8
1883	Det-N	34	131	22	29	4	1	0	10	8	13	.221	.266	.267	.533	69	-6	-4	91	101	10	.422				-3	O/P	-0.4
	StL-a	28	112	23	45	8	1	0		7		.402	.437	.491	.928	184	12	11	108	0	25	.925				-6	O	0.5
1884	Cin-a	65	266	49	66	4	6	0		15		.248	.301	.308	.609	96	1	-1	106	0	25	.510				-13	O	-1.3
	Col-a	23	77	9	15	1	3	0		6		.195	.262	.286	.548	83	-1	-1	97	0	6	.468				0	O	0.0
	Yr	88	343	58	81	5	9	0		21		.236	.292	.303	.595	94	-0	-2	104	0	31	.500				-13		-1.3
Total	3	191	767	132	199	23	11	0	21	39	22	.259	.300	.318	.619	101	2	2	100	32	78	.509				-27	O/P	-2.0

■ **FELIX MANTILLA** Mantilla, Felix (Lamela) b: 7/29/34, Isabela, P.R. BR/TR, 6', 160 lbs. Deb: 6/21/56

YEAR	TM/L	G	AB	R	H	2B	3B	HR	RBI	BB	SO	AVG	OBP	SLG	PRO	/A	BR	/A	PF	CHI	RC	TA	SB	CS	SBR	FR	POS	TPR
1956	Mil-N	35	53	9	15	1	1	0	3	1	8	.283	.309	.340	.649	75	-2	-2	99	70	5	.500	0	1	-1	1	S/3	0.0
1957	Mil-N	71	182	28	43	9	1	4	21	14	34	.236	.298	.363	.661	85	-6	-4	90	112	20	.592	2	0	1	5	S2/3O	0.5
1958	Mil-N	85	226	37	50	5	1	7	19	20	20	.221	.285	.345	.630	73	-11	-8	89	79	22	.549	2	0	1	-2	O2/S3	-0.8
1959	Mil-N	103	251	26	54	5	0	3	19	16	31	.215	.268	.271	.539	46	-20	-18	95	100	18	.447	6	1	1	-7	2S/3O	-1.8
1960	Mil-N	63	148	21	38	7	0	3	11	7	16	.257	.295	.365	.660	87	-4	-3	91	71	16	.580	3	1	0	-4	2S/O	-0.3
1961	Mil-N	45	93	13	20	3	0	1	5	10	16	.215	.298	.280	.578	59	-6	-5	92	70	8	.500	1	1	-0	-1	S2O/3	-0.3
1962	NY-N	141	466	54	128	17	4	11	59	37	51	.275	.335	.399	.734	92	-3	-5	104	106	62	.660	3	1	0	-1	3S2	0.0
1963	Bos-A	66	178	27	56	8	0	6	15	20	14	.315	.384	.461	.845	128	9	7	106	63	31	.813	2	1	0	-2	SO/2	0.7
1964	Bos-A	133	425	69	123	20	1	30	64	41	46	.289	.357	.553	.910	146	27	26	102	83	81	.889	0	1	-1	-7	O2/3S	2.2
1965	Bos-A	150	534	60	147	17	2	18	92	79	84	.275	.377	.416	.793	116	20	15	107	**147**	83	.763	7	3	0	-9	*2O/1	1.2
1966	Hou-N	77	151	16	33	5	0	6	22	11	32	.219	.280	.371	.651	81	-4	-4	97	125	15	.565	1	0	0	-1	13/2O	-0.4
Total	11	969	2707	360	707	97	10	89	330	256	352	.261	.331	.403	.734	100	-1	-1	100	103	361	.694	27	10	2	-27	2SO3/1	1.0

■ **MICKEY MANTLE** Mantle, Mickey Charles "The Commerce Comet" b: 10/20/31, Spavinaw, Okla. BB/TR, 5'11.5", 195 lbs. Deb: 4/17/51 H

YEAR	TM/L	G	AB	R	H	2B	3B	HR	RBI	BB	SO	AVG	OBP	SLG	PRO	/A	BR	/A	PF	CHI	RC	TA	SB	CS	SBR	FR	POS	TPR
1951	NY-A	96	341	61	91	11	5	13	65	43	74	.267	.349	.443	.792	123	5	9	92	125	55	.777	8	7	-2	-11	O	-0.6
1952	NY-A	142	549	94	171	37	7	23	87	75	111	.311	.394	.530	**.924**	159	**40**	42	98	96	**123**	.964	4	1	1	-6	*O/3	3.3
1953	NY-A	127	461	105	136	24	3	21	92	79	90	.295	.398	.497	.895	151	27	32	93	119	100	.955	8	4	0	-4	*O/S	2.4
1954	NY-A	146	543	**129**	163	17	12	27	102	102	107	.300	.411	.525	.936	157	43	44	99	102	127	1.018	5	2	0	-4	*O/S2	3.7
1955	NY-A	147	517	121	158	25	**11**	**37**	99	**113**	97	.306	**.433**	**.611**	**1.044**	**182**	59	**61**	98	92	**148**	**1.209**	8	1	2	3	*O/S	**5.7**
1956	NY-A	150	533	**132**	188	22	5	**52**	**130**	112	99	**.353**	.467	**.705**	**1.172**	**209**	**83**	**84**	99	97	**188**	**1.429**	10	1	2	1	*O	**7.6**
1957	NY-A	144	474	**121**	173	28	6	34	94	**146**	75	.365	.515	.665	1.179	**234**	89	**93**	94	94	**178**	1.544	16	3	3	-7	*O	**8.1**
1958	NY-A	150	519	**127**	158	21	1	**42**	97	**129**	120	.304	.445	.592	1.036	178	**64**	**62**	103	95	**147**	**1.216**	18	3	4	-5	*O	5.1
1959	NY-A	144	541	104	154	23	4	31	75	94	126	.285	.392	.514	.906	**158**	36	**42**	93	77	**118**	.995	21	3	5	2	*O	**4.1**
1960	NY-A	153	527	**119**	145	17	6	**40**	94	111	125	.275	.402	.558	**.960**	**166**	**44**	**48**	94	94	**125**	**1.061**	14	3	2	-8	*O	3.6
1961	NY-A	153	514	**132**	163	16	6	54	128	**126**	112	.317	.452	**.687**	1.138	207	76	79	96	103	174	1.387	12	1	3	-4	*O	7.0
1962	NY-A	123	377	96	121	15	1	30	89	**122**	78	.321	**.488**	**.605**	**1.093**	**205**	**57**	**61**	94	113	126	**1.385**	9	0	3	-4	*O	**5.4**
1963	NY-A	65	172	40	54	8	0	15	35	40	32	.314	.443	.622	1.065	194	23	23	101	96	49	1.202	2	1	0	-0	O	2.2
1964	NY-A	143	465	92	141	25	2	35	111	99	102	.303	**.426**	.591	**1.017**	**174**	**53**	**51**	103	126	121	**1.131**	6	3	0	-6	*O	4.1
1965	NY-A	122	361	44	92	12	1	19	46	73	76	.255	.380	.452	.832	134	19	18	101	87	64	.854	4	1	1	-7	*O	0.9
1966	NY-A	108	333	40	96	12	1	23	56	57	76	.288	.392	.538	.930	175	29	31	94	95	71	.960	1	1	-0	-1	O	2.7
1967	NY-A	144	440	63	108	17	0	22	55	107	113	.245	.394	.434	.828	153	29	32	94	91	82	.877	1	1	-0	3	*1	2.7
1968	NY-A	144	435	57	103	14	1	18	54	106	97	.237	.387	.398	.785	137	25	25	101	104	74	.834	6	2	1	-3	*1	1.8
Total	18	2401	8102	1677	2415	344	72	536	1509	1734	1710	.298	.423	.557	.979	173	803	838	97	100	2070	1.118	153	38	23	-60	*O1/S23	69.8

■ **CHUCK MANUEL** Manuel, Charles Fuqua b: 1/4/44, North Fork, W.Va. BL/TR, 6'4", 195 lbs. Deb: 4/08/69 C

YEAR	TM/L	G	AB	R	H	2B	3B	HR	RBI	BB	SO	AVG	OBP	SLG	PRO	/A	BR	/A	PF	CHI	RC	TA	SB	CS	SBR	FR	POS	TPR
1969	Min-A	83	164	14	34	6	0	2	24	28	33	.207	.323	.280	.603	69	-6	-6	102	185	16	.564	1	0	0	-7	O	-1.4
1970	Min-A	59	64	4	12	0	0	1	7	6	17	.188	.268	.234	.502	40	-5	-5	98	157	4	.415	0	0	0	-3	O	-0.8
1971	Min-A	18	16	1	2	1	0	0	1	1	8	.125	.176	.188	.364	3	-2	-2	104	136	1	.286	0	0	0	-0	/O	-0.2
1972	Min-A	63	122	6	25	5	0	1	8	4	16	.205	.236	.270	.507	47	-8	-8	107	93	8	.388	0	0	0	-1	O	-1.1
1974	LA-N	4	3	0	1	0	0	0	1	1	0	.333	.500	.333	.833	147	0	0	93	386	1	1.000	0	0	0	0	H	0.0
1975	LA-N	15	15	0	2	0	0	0	2	0	3	.133	.133	.133	.267	-27	-3	-2	95	387	0	.133	0	0	0	0	H	-0.2
Total	6	242	384	25	76	12	0	4	43	40	77	.198	.277	.260	.537	52	-23	-24	103	160	30	.461	1	0	0	-11	/O	-3.7

■ **JERRY MANUEL** Manuel, Jerry b: 12/23/53, Hahira, Ga. BB/TR, 6', 165 lbs. Deb: 9/18/75

YEAR	TM/L	G	AB	R	H	2B	3B	HR	RBI	BB	SO	AVG	OBP	SLG	PRO	/A	BR	/A	PF	CHI	RC	TA	SB	CS	SBR	FR	POS	TPR
1975	Det-A	6	18	0	1	0	0	0	0	0	4	.056	.056	.056	.111	-66	-4	-4	104	0	0	.056	0	0	0	0	/2	-0.3
1976	Det-A	54	43	4	6	1	0	0	2	3	9	.140	.213	.163	.376	11	-5	-5	104	110	2	.316	1	0	0	1	2/SD	0.0
1980	Mon-N	7	6	0	0	0	0	0	0	0	2	.000	.000	.000	.000	-99	-2	-2	99	0	0	.000	0	0	0	0	/S	0.0
1981	Mon-N	27	55	10	11	5	0	3	10	6	11	.200	.279	.455	.733	106	0	0	99	115	7	.689	0	0	0	-2	2/S	0.0
1982	SD-N	2	5	0	1	0	1	0	1	1	0	.200	.333	.600	.933	170	0	0	92	131	1	1.000	0	0	0	0	/2S3	0.0
Total	5	96	127	14	19	6	1	3	13	10	26	.150	.217	.283	.501	42	-10	-10	101	94	10	.444	1	0	0	-1	/2S3D	-0.3

■ **FRANK MANUSH** Manush, Frank Benjamin b: 9/18/1883, Tuscumbia, Ala. d: 1/5/65, Laguna Beach, Cal. BR/TR, 5'10.5", 175 lbs. Deb: 8/31/08

YEAR	TM/L	G	AB	R	H	2B	3B	HR	RBI	BB	SO	AVG	OBP	SLG	PRO	/A	BR	/A	PF	CHI	RC	TA	SB	CS	SBR	FR	POS	TPR
1908	Phi-A	23	77	6	12	2	1	0	0	2		.156	.177	.208	.385	24	-6	-7	108	0	3	.308	2			-2	3/2	-0.8

■ **HEINIE MANUSH** Manush, Henry Emmett b: 7/20/01, Tuscumbia, Ala. d: 5/12/71, Sarasota, Fla. BL/TL, 6'1", 200 lbs. Deb: 4/20/23 CH

YEAR	TM/L	G	AB	R	H	2B	3B	HR	RBI	BB	SO	AVG	OBP	SLG	PRO	/A	BR	/A	PF	CHI	RC	TA	SB	CS	SBR	FR	POS	TPR
1923	Det-A	109	308	59	103	20	5	4	54	20	21	.334	.406	.471	.877	135	14	15	97	118	59	.881	3	5	-2	-5	O	0.1
1924	Det-A	120	422	83	122	24	8	9	68	27	30	.289	.355	.448	.803	107	2	3	100	106	69	.807	14	5	1	-7	*O/1	-0.9
1925	Det-A	99	278	46	84	14	3	5	47	24	21	.302	.362	.428	.790	101	-1	-0	99	117	44	.777	8	3	1	-1	*O	-0.6
1926	Det-A	136	498	95	188	35	8	14	86	31	28	**.378**	.421	.564	.985	160	38	40	97	92	116	1.044	11	5	0	3	*O	3.3
1927	Det-A	151	593	102	177	31	18	6	90	47	29	.298	.354	.442	.796	98	3	-4	108	113	91	.781	12	0	4	-6	*O	-1.7
1928	StL-A	154	638	104	**241**	**47**	20	13	108	39	14	.378	.414	.575	.989	152	50	47	104	88	150	1.052	17	5	2	4	*O	4.2
1929	StL-A	142	574	85	204	**45**	10	6	81	43	24	.355	.401	.500	.901	131	26	26	100	87	113	.899	9	8	-2	-3	*O	1.4
1930	StL-A	49	198	26	65	16	4	2	29	5	7	.328	.345	.480	.825	99	1	-1	108	101	32	.769	3	1	0	0	O	-0.1
	Was-A	88	356	74	129	33	8	7	65	26	17	.362	.406	.559	.965	140	22	21	101	104	79	.996	4	3	-1	-3	O	1.3
	Yr	137	554	100	194	49	12	9	94	31	24	.350	.385	.531	.915	125	23	20	104	103	111	.912	7	4	-0	-3		1.2
1931	Was-A	146	616	110	189	41	11	6	70	36	27	.307	.351	.438	.789	106	4	4	101	77	94	.733	3	3	-1	-13	*O	-1.7
1932	Was-A	149	625	121	214	41	14	14	116	36	29	.342	.383	.520	.903	132	27	28	100	102	124	.903	7	2	1	-2	*O	1.9
1933	Was-A	153	658	115	**221**	32	**17**	5	95	36	18	.336	.372	.459	.831	124	17	20	96	100	111	.785	6	4	-1	-1	*O	1.2
1934	Was-A	137	556	88	194	42	11	11	89	36	23	.349	.392	.523	.915	133	26	25	101	97	113	.923	7	3	0	1	*O	2.2
1935	Was-A	119	479	68	131	26	9	4	56	35	17	.273	.328	.390	.719	93	-11	-6	92	98	62	.655	2	0	1	5	*O	-0.1
1936	Bos-A	82	313	43	91	15	5	0	45	17	11	.291	.329	.371	.700	68	-14	-17	106	128	37	.600	1	3	-2	-11	O	-2.7
1937	Bro-N	132	466	57	155	25	7	4	73	40	24	.333	.389	.442	.831	120	17	14	104	123	84	.802	6			-15	*O	-0.5
1938	Bro-N	17	51	9	12	3	1	0	6	5	4	.235	.304	.333	.637	78	-2	-1	96	128	5	.561	1			1	O	0.0
	Pit-N	15	13	2	4	1	1	0	4	2	0	.308	.400	.538	.938	156	1	1	100	207	3	.900	0			0	H	0.1
	Yr	32	64	11	16	4	2	0	10	7	4	.250	.324	.375	.699	94	-1	-1	98	169	8	.653	1			1		0.1
1939	Pit-N	10	12	0	0	0	0	0	1	1	1	.000	.077	.000	.077	-78	-3	-3	100	0	0	.077	0			-0	/O	-0.2
Total	17	2008	7654	1287	2524	491	160	110	1183	506	345	.330	.377	.479	.856	120	218	213	100	102	1387	.841	114	50		-54	*O/1	7.2

YEAR	TM/L	G	AB	R	H	2B	3B	HR	RBI	BB	SO	AVG	OBP	SLG	PRO	/A	BR	/A	PF	CHI	RC	TA	SB	CS	SBR	FR	POS	TPR
■ **KIRT MANWARING**	Manwaring, Kirt Dean b: 7/15/65, Elmira, N.Y. BR/TR, 6'1", 195 lbs. Deb: 9/15/87																											
1987	SF-N	6	7	0	1	0	0	0	0	0	1	.143	.250	.143	.393	8	-1	-1	96	0	0	.286	0	0	0	0	/C	0.0
1988	SF-N	40	116	12	29	7	0	1	15	2	21	.250	.281	.336	.617	81	-4	-3	94	143	11	.494	0	1	-1	-3	C	-0.4
Total	2	46	123	12	30	7	0	1	15	2	22	.244	.279	.325	.604	77	-5	-4	94	134	11	.484	0	1	-1	-3	/C	-0.4
■ **CLIFF MAPES**	Mapes, Clifford Franklin b: 3/13/22, Sutherland, Neb. BL/TR, 6'3", 205 lbs. Deb: 4/20/48																											
1948	NY-A	53	88	19	22	11	1	1	12	6	13	.250	.298	.432	.730	93	-2	-2	100	99	11	.662	1	1	-0	1	O	0.0
1949	NY-A	111	304	56	75	13	3	7	38	58	50	.247	.369	.378	.747	98	-0	-0	100	96	49	.773	6	0	**2**	5	*O	0.4
1950	NY-A	108	356	60	88	14	6	12	61	47	61	.247	.338	.421	.760	94	-5	-4	99	113	49	.694	1	6	-3	-8	*O	-1.5
1951	NY-A	45	51	6	11	3	1	2	8	4	14	.216	.273	.431	.704	96	-1	-1	92	102	6	.634	0	0	0	-11	O	-1.2
	StL-A	56	201	32	55	7	2	7	30	26	33	.274	.360	.433	.792	108	4	2	105	101	32	.745	0	1	-1	-0	O	0.0
	Yr	101	252	38	66	10	3	9	38	30	47	.262	.343	.433	.775	110	2	3	99	103	38	.725	0	1	-1	-11		-1.2
1952	Det-A	86	193	26	38	7	0	9	23	27	42	.197	.295	.373	.669	86	-4	-4	99	87	23	.627	0	1	-1	-9	O	-1.6
Total	5	459	1193	199	289	55	13	38	172	168	213	.242	.338	.406	.743	96	-8	-9	100	101	169	.726	8	9	-3	-22	O	-3.9
■ **HOWARD MAPLE**	Maple, Howard Albert "Mape" b: 7/20/03, Adrian, Mo. d: 11/9/70, Portland, Ore. BL/TR, 5'7", 175 lbs. Deb: 5/19/32																											
1932	Was-A	44	41	6	10	0	1	0	7	7	7	.244	.367	.293	.660	73	-1	-1	100	195	5	.645	0	0	0	-1	C	0.0
■ **GEORGE MAPPES**	Mappes, George Richard "Dick" b: 12/25/1865, St.Louis, Mo. d: 2/20/34, St.Louis, Mo. Deb: 1885																											
1885	Bal-a	6	19	2	4	0	1	0		1		.211	.250	.316	.566	76	-0	-1	106	0	2	.467				0	/2	0.0
1886	StL-N	6	14	1	2	0	0	0	0	1	5	.143	.200	.143	.343	6	-2	-1	95	0	0	.250	0			0	/C32	0.0
Total	2	12	33	3	6	0	1	0	0	2	5	.182	.229	.242	.471	47	-2	-2	101	0	2	.370	0			0	/2C3	0.0
■ **RABBIT MARANVILLE**	Maranville, Walter James Vincent b: 11/11/1891, Springfield, Mass. d: 1/5/54, New York, N.Y. BR/TR, 5'5", 155 lbs. Deb: 9/10/12 MH																											
1912	Bos-N	26	86	8	18	2	0	0	8	9	14	.209	.292	.233	.524	41	-6	-7	107	137	7	.456	1			-5	S	-0.9
1913	Bos-N	143	571	68	141	13	8	2	48	68	62	.247	.330	.308	.638	88	-11	-7	95	83	64	.633	25			14	*S	1.7
1914	Bos-N	156	586	74	144	23	6	4	78	45	56	.246	.306	.326	.632	84	-9	-12	104	148	66	.611	28			**50**	*S	**4.5**
1915	Bos-N	149	509	51	124	23	6	2	43	45	65	.244	.308	.324	.632	93	-5	-4	98	98	55	.579	18	12	-2	18	*S	1.7
1916	Bos-N	155	604	79	142	16	13	4	38	50	69	.235	.296	.325	.620	97	-7	-2	93	63	64	.587	32	15	1	20	*S	2.9
1917	Bos-N	142	561	69	146	19	13	3	43	40	47	.260	.312	.357	.668	109	2	5	96	76	67	.648	27			18	*S	2.7
1918	Bos-N	11	38	3	12	0	1	0	3	4	0	.316	.381	.368	.749	137	1	2	94	83	5	.692	0			1	S	0.3
1919	Bos-N	131	480	44	128	18	10	5	43	36	23	.267	.319	.377	.696	111	5	6	98	87	59	.653	12			**29**	*S	**4.3**
1920	Bos-N	134	493	48	131	19	15	1	43	28	24	.266	.305	.371	.676	97	-5	-3	96	91	54	.603	14	11	-2	15	*S	1.7
1921	Pit-N	153	612	90	180	25	12	1	70	47	38	.294	.347	.379	.727	89	-6	-9	103	105	82	.691	25	12	0	-10	*S	-0.3
1922	Pit-N	155	672	115	198	26	15	0	63	61	43	.295	.355	.378	.733	86	-10	-13	104	75	92	.700	24	13	-1	-2	*S2	-0.6
1923	Pit-N	141	581	78	161	19	9	1	41	42	34	.277	.327	.346	.673	80	-18	-16	97	68	66	.599	14	11	-2	4	*S	-0.1
1924	Pit-N	152	594	62	158	33	20	2	71	35	53	.266	.307	.399	.706	83	-12	-17	106	113	70	.644	18	14	-3	4	*2	-2.4
1925	Chi-N	75	266	37	62	10	3	0	23	29	20	.233	.308	.293	.602	56	-18	-17	97	107	25	.541	6	5	-1	-3	SM	-1.3
1926	Bro-N	78	234	32	55	8	5	0	24	26	24	.235	.312	.312	.624	69	-10	-10	99	114	23	.592	7			-1	S2	-0.5
1927	StL-N	9	29	0	7	1	0	0	0	2	2	.241	.290	.276	.566	49	-2	-2	107	0	2	.455	0			0	/S	0.0
1928	StL-N	112	366	40	88	14	10	1	34	36	27	.240	.310	.342	.652	70	-16	-16	100	95	39	.594	3			-8	*S/2	-0.7
1929	Bos-N	146	560	87	159	26	10	0	55	47	33	.284	.344	.366	.710	81	-21	-15	94	97	70	.671	13			19	*S/2	2.1
1930	Bos-N	142	558	85	157	26	8	2	43	48	23	.281	.344	.367	.711	74	-25	-22	97	68	70	.666	9			-16	*S/3	-2.2
1931	Bos-N	145	562	69	146	22	5	0	33	56	34	.260	.329	.317	.646	75	-19	-18	99	58	63	.589	9			-25	*S2	-3.1
1932	Bos-N	149	571	67	134	20	4	0	37	46	28	.235	.295	.284	.579	61	-34	-29	93	90	51	.492	4			5	*2	-1.2
1933	Bos-N	143	478	46	104	15	4	0	38	36	34	.218	.274	.266	.539	57	-28	-26	96	115	35	.425	2			-27	*2	-4.5
1935	Bos-N	23	67	3	10	2	0	0	5	3	3	.149	.186	.179	.365	-2	-10	-9	96	150	2	.246	0			-2	2	-0.8
Total	23	2670	10078	1255	2605	380	177	28	884	839	756	.258	.318	.340	.658	82	-263	-242	98	91	1132	.607	291	93		97	*S2/3	3.3
■ **JOHNNY MARCUM**	Marcum, John Alfred "Footsie" b: 9/9/09, Campbellsburg, Ky. d: 9/10/84, Louisville, Ky. BL/TR, 5'11", 197 lbs. Deb: 9/07/33																											
1933	Phi-A	5	12	2	2	0	0	0	0	2	1	.167	.286	.167	.452	24	-1	-1	92	0	1	.400	0	0	0	0	/P	0.0
1934	Phi-A	58	112	10	30	4	0	1	13	3	5	.268	.287	.330	.617	61	-7	-7	97	108	10	.482	0	1	-1	-0	P	0.0
1935	Phi-A	64	119	13	37	2	1	2	17	9	5	.311	.359	.395	.754	95	-1	-1	100	109	17	.683	0	0	0	-3	P	0.0
1936	Bos-A	48	88	6	18	3	0	2	7	3	5	.205	.231	.307	.538	30	-10	-11	106	69	6	.429	0	0	0	-0	P	0.0
1937	Bos-A	51	86	12	23	8	0	0	13	7	4	.267	.323	.360	.683	70	-4	-4	103	144	10	.603	0	0	0	1	P	0.0
1938	Bos-A	19	37	3	5	0	0	0	3	6	9	.135	.256	.135	.391	1	-6	-6	102	203	2	.344	0	0	0	-1	P	0.0
1939	StL-A	16	22	3	10	1	0	0	5	1	2	.455	.478	.500	.978	150	2	2	100	153	5	.923	0	0	0	-0	P	0.0
	Chi-A	38	57	7	16	0	0	0	12	5	1	.281	.339	.281	.619	56	-3	-4	107	253	6	.512	0	0	0	-1	P	0.0
	Yr	54	79	10	26	1	0	0	17	6	3	.329	.376	.342	.718	81	-1	-2	105	226	11	.623	0	0	0	-1		0.0
Total	7	299	533	56	141	18	1	5	70	36	32	.265	.311	.330	.641	62	-30	-31	102	130	57	.539	0	1	-1	-4	P	0.0
■ **RED MARION**	Marion, John Wyeth b: 3/14/14, Richburg, S.C. d: 3/13/75, San Jose, Cal. BR/TR, 6'2", 175 lbs. Deb: 9/16/35																											
1935	Was-A	4	11	1	2	1	0	1	1	0	2	.182	.182	.545	.727	89	-0	-0	92	38	1	.667	0	0	0	0	/O	0.0
1943	Was-A	14	17	2	3	0	0	0	1	3	1	.176	.300	.176	.476	39	-1	-1	104	122	1	.429	0	0	0	-1	/O	-0.1
Total	2	18	28	3	5	1	0	1	2	3	3	.179	.258	.321	.579	61	-2	-2	99	92	2	.522	0	0	0	-1	/O	-0.1
■ **MARTY MARION**	Marion, Martin Whitford "Slats" or "The Octopus" b: 12/1/17, Richburg, S.C. BR/TR, 6'2", 170 lbs. Deb: 4/16/40 MC																											
1940	StL-N	125	435	44	121	18	1	3	46	21	34	.278	.311	.345	.656	79	-12	-13	102	107	45	.552	9			-13	*S	-1.3
1941	StL-N	155	547	50	138	22	3	3	58	42	48	.252	.308	.320	.628	70	-17	-24	110	116	56	.542	8			7	*S	-0.2
1942	StL-N	147	485	66	134	**38**	5	0	54	48	50	.276	.343	.375	.718	102	6	1	108	110	64	.664	8			3	*S	1.5
1943	StL-N	129	418	38	117	15	3	1	52	32	37	.280	.334	.337	.671	90	-3	-5	105	130	49	.577	1			10	*S	1.8
1944	StL-N	144	506	50	135	26	2	6	63	43	50	.267	.324	.362	.686	92	-5	-5	101	115	61	.597	1			7	*S	2.0
1945	StL-N	123	430	63	119	27	5	1	59	39	39	.277	.340	.370	.709	97	-2	-2	100	127	56	.639	2			-8	*S	0.3
1946	StL-N	146	498	51	116	29	4	3	46	59	53	.233	.318	.325	.643	78	-11	-15	107	102	55	.575	1			**22**	*S	1.8
1947	StL-N	149	540	57	147	19	6	4	74	49	58	.272	.334	.352	.686	77	-13	-18	106	138	63	.594	3			**17**	*S	1.0
1948	StL-N	144	567	70	143	26	4	4	43	37	54	.252	.298	.333	.631	70	-24	-24	101	85	55	.519	1			12	*S	0.2
1949	StL-N	134	515	61	140	31	2	5	70	37	42	.272	.323	.369	.692	77	-11	-18	110	**136**	59	.584	0			11	*S	0.7
1950	StL-N	106	372	36	92	10	2	4	40	44	55	.247	.327	.317	.644	68	-15	-17	103	121	39	.562	1			9	*S	0.3
1952	StL-A	67	186	16	46	11	0	2	19	19	17	.247	.320	.339	.659	86	-4	-3	97	103	20	.561	0	2	-1	-6	SM	-0.7
1953	StL-A	3	7	0	0	0	0	0	0	0	0	.000	.000	.000	.000	-94	-2	-2	107	0	0	.000	0	0	0	0	/3M	-0.1
Total	13	1572	5506	602	1448	272	37	36	624	470	537	.263	.323	.345	.668	81	-113	-145	105	116	623	.596	35	2		70	*S/3	7.3
■ **ROGER MARIS**	Maris, Roger Eugene (born Roger Eugene Maras) b: 9/10/34, Hibbing, Minn. d: 12/14/85, Houston, Tex. BL/TR, 6', 197 lbs. Deb: 4/16/57																											
1957	Cle-A	116	358	61	84	9	5	14	51	60	79	.235	.346	.405	.751	103	3	2	102	108	53	.754	8	4	0	0	*O	-0.4
1958	Cle-A	51	182	26	41	5	1	9	27	17	33	.225	.291	.412	.704	97	-3	-1	94	108	23	.671	4	2	0	7	O	0.3
	KC-A	99	401	61	99	14	3	19	53	28	52	.247	.299	.439	.738	95	-1	-4	106	80	54	.678	0	0	0	3	O	-0.7
	Yr	150	583	87	140	19	4	28	80	45	85	.240	.297	.431	.727	96	-4	-5	102	91	77	.676	4	2	0	10		-0.4
1959	KC-A	122	433	69	118	21	7	16	72	58	53	.273	.362	.464	.827	124	15	15	101	116	76	.825	2	1	0	3	*O	1.2
1960	NY-A	136	499	98	141	18	7	39	**112**	70	65	.283	.374	**.581**	.955	164	36	40	94	114	111	.997	2	2	-1	2	*O	3.6
1961	NY-A	161	590	**132**	159	16	4	**61**	**142**	94	67	.269	.376	.620	.997	167	50	53	96	107	138	1.045	0	0	0	-10	*O	3.6
1962	NY-A	157	590	92	151	34	1	33	100	87	78	.256	.357	.485	.842	133	20	25	94	109	107	.852	1	0	0	1	*O	2.1
1963	NY-A	90	312	53	84	14	1	23	53	35	40	.269	.347	.542	.888	144	18	18	101	95	61	.900	1	0	0	1	O	1.7
1964	NY-A	141	513	86	144	12	2	26	71	62	78	.281	.365	.464	.829	125	21	19	103	97	91	.822	3	0	1	-18	*O	-0.4
1965	NY-A	46	155	22	37	7	0	8	27	29	29	.239	.359	.439	.797	124	6	5	101	124	25	.795	0	0	0	-3	O	0.1
1966	NY-A	119	348	37	81	9	2	13	43	36	60	.233	.310	.382	.692	104	-1	2	94	105	41	.625	0	0	0	-9	O	-1.1
1967	StL-N	125	410	64	107	18	7	9	55	52	61	.261	.350	.405	.755	114	9	8	101	118	59	.709	0	0	0	3	*O	0.6
1968	StL-N	100	310	25	79	18	2	5	45	24	38	.255	.310	.374	.685	110	1	3	95	145	37	.603	0	0	0	3	*O	0.2
Total	12	1463	5101	826	1325	195	42	275	851	652	733	.260	.348	.476	.824	128	174	184	98	109	878	.829	21	9	1	-17	*O	10.8

YEAR	TM/L	G	AB	R	H	2B	3B	HR	RBI	BB	SO	AVG	OBP	SLG	PRO	/A	BR	/A	PF	CHI	RC	TA	SB	CS	SBR	FR	POS	TPR
■ **GENE MARKLAND**	Markland, Cleneth Eugene "Mousey" b: 12/26/19, Detroit, Mich. BR/TR, 5'10", 160 lbs. Deb: 4/25/50																											
1950	Phi-A	5	8	2	1	0	0	0	0	3	0	.125	.364	.125	.489	33	-1	-1	90	0	1	.571	0	0	0	0	/2	0.0
■ **HAL MARNIE**	Marnie, Harry Sylvester b: 7/6/18, Philadelphia, Pa. BR/TR, 6'1", 178 lbs. Deb: 9/15/40																											
1940	Phi-N	11	34	4	6	0	0	0	4	4	2	.176	.263	.176	.440	24	-3	-3	97	247	2	.357	0			-1	2	-0.2
1941	Phi-N	61	158	12	38	3	3	0	11	13	25	.241	.298	.297	.596	70	-7	-6	97	84	13	.476	0			2	2S/3	0.0
1942	Phi-N	24	30	3	5	0	0	0	0	1	2	.167	.194	.167	.360	6	-4	-3	94	0	1	.269	1			1	2/S3	0.0
Total	3	96	222	19	49	3	3	0	15	18	29	.221	.279	.261	.540	55	-14	-13	97	99	16	.443	1			2	/2S3	-0.2
■ **FRED MAROLEWSKI**	Marolewski, Fred Daniel "Fritz" b: 10/6/28, Chicago, Ill. BR/TR, 6'2.5", 205 lbs. Deb: 9/19/53																											
1953	StL-N	1	0	0	0	0	0	0	0	0	0	—	—	—	—	—	0	0	102	—	—	—	0	0	0	0	/1	0.0
■ **OLLIE MARQUARDT**	Marquardt, Albert Ludwig b: 9/22/02, Toledo, Ohio d: 2/7/68, Fort Clinton, Ohio BR/TR, 5'9", 156 lbs. Deb: 4/14/31																											
1931	Bos-A	17	39	4	7	1	0	0	2	3	4	.179	.238	.205	.443	19	-5	-4	94	82	2	.333	0	1	-1	-0	2/S3	-0.3
■ **GONZALO MARQUEZ**	Marquez, Gonzalo Enrique (Moya) b: 3/31/46, Carupano, Venez. d: 12/20/84, Valencia, Venez. BL/TL, 5'11", 180 lbs. Deb: 8/11/72																											
1972	Oak-A	23	21	2	8	0	0	0	4	3	4	.381	.480	.381	.861	164	2	2	97	209	4	.929	1	1	-0	0	/1	0.2
1973	Oak-A	23	25	1	6	1	0	0	2	0	4	.240	.240	.280	.520	53	-2	-1	87	112	1	.350	0	0	0	-0	/21OD	-0.1
	Chi-N	19	58	5	13	2	0	1	4	3	4	.224	.274	.310	.585	57	-3	-4	108	76	5	.478	0	0	0	1	1	-0.2
1974	Chi-N	11	11	1	0	0	0	0	0	1	2	.000	.083	.000	.083	-75	-3	-3	100	0	0	.091	0	0	0	0	/1	-0.2
Total	3	76	115	9	27	3	0	1	10	7	14	.235	.290	.287	.577	63	-6	-6	101	103	11	.483	1	1	-0	1	/12DO	-0.3
■ **LUIS MARQUEZ**	Marquez, Luis Angel (Sanchez) "Canena" b: 10/28/25, Aguadilla, P.R. d: 3/1/88, Aguadilla, P.R. BR/TR, 5'10.5", 174 lbs. Deb: 4/18/51																											
1951	Bos-N	68	122	19	24	5	1	0	11	10	20	.197	.274	.254	.528	44	-10	-9	98	137	9	.462	4	4	-1	0	O	-1.1
1954	Chi-N	17	12	2	1	0	0	0	0	2	4	.083	.214	.083	.298	-19	-2	-2	101	0	1	.545	3	0	1	-3	O	-0.4
	Pit-N	14	9	3	1	0	0	0	0	4	0	.111	.385	.111	.496	38	-1	-1	97	0	1	.625	0	0	0	-1	/O	-0.1
	Yr	31	21	5	2	0	0	0	0	6	4	.095	.296	.095	.392	8	-3	-3	99	0	2	.579	3	0	1	-4		-0.5
Total	2	99	143	24	26	5	1	0	11	16	24	.182	.278	.231	.509	38	-12	-12	98	114	10	.488	7	4	-0	-4	/O	-1.6
■ **BOB MARQUIS**	Marquis, Robert Rudolph b: 12/23/24, Oklahoma City, Okla. BL/TL, 6'1", 170 lbs. Deb: 4/17/53																											
1953	Cin-N	40	44	9	12	1	1	2	3	4	11	.273	.333	.477	.811	109	0	0	99	43	8	.781	0	0	0	-1	O	0.0
■ **ROGER MARQUIS**	Marquis, Roger Julian "Noonie" b: 4/5/37, Holyoke, Mass. BL/TL, 6', 190 lbs. Deb: 9/25/55																											
1955	Bal-A	1	1	0	0	0	0	0	0	0	0	.000	.000	.000	.000	-99	-0	-0	90	0	0	.000	0	0	0	-0	/O	0.0
■ **LEFTY MARR**	Marr, Charles W. b: 9/19/1862, Cincinnati, Ohio d: 1/11/12, New Britain, Conn. BL/TL, Deb: 10/03/1886																											
1886	Cin-a	8	29	2	8	1	1	0		1		.276	.323	.379	.702	127	1	1	96	0	4	.667	1			0	/O	0.1
1889	Col-a	139	546	110	167	26	**15**	1	75	87	32	.306	.407	.414	.821	150	30	39	91	81	106	.918	29			10	3OS/1C	3.9
1890	Cin-N	130	527	91	158	17	12	1	73	46	29	.300	.363	.383	.746	111	13	7	108	103	91	.808	44			-13	O3/S	-0.4
1891	Cin-N	72	286	32	74	9	7	0	32	25	15	.259	.323	.339	.662	104	-2	2	91	92	37	.660	16			-10	O	-1.0
	CM-a	14	57	9	11	1	0	0	4	7	4	.193	.281	.211	.492	39	-4	-5	112	93	4	.457	2			0	O	-0.3
Total	4	363	1445	244	418	54	35	2	184	166	80	.289	.368	.379	.748	121	38	43	98	90	243	.799	92			-14	O3/SC1	2.3
■ **WILLIAM MARRIOTT**	Marriott, William Earl b: 4/18/1893, Pratt, Kan. d: 8/11/69, Berkeley, Cal. BL/TR, 6', 170 lbs. Deb: 9/06/17																											
1917	Chi-N	3	6	0	0	0	0	0	0	0	1	.000	.000	.000	.000	-96	-1	-1	105	0	0	.000	0			-0	/O	-0.1
1920	Chi-N	14	43	7	12	4	2	0	5	6	5	.279	.367	.465	.832	139	2	2	99	97	7	.844	1	1	-0	0	2	0.2
1921	Chi-N	30	38	3	12	1	1	0	7	4	1	.316	.381	.395	.776	99	0	0	107	171	6	.704	0	1	-1	1	/2S3O	0.0
1925	Bos-N	103	370	37	99	9	1	1	40	28	26	.268	.322	.305	.628	66	-21	-17	94	125	36	.523	3	8	-4	-5	3/O	-1.8
1926	Bro-N	109	360	39	96	13	9	3	42	17	20	.267	.303	.378	.681	83	-10	-9	99	100	40	.633	12			-4	*3	-1.2
1927	Bro-N	6	9	0	1	0	1	0	1	2	2	.111	.273	.333	.606	60	-1	-1	103	117	1	.625	0			0	/3	0.0
Total	6	265	826	86	220	27	14	4	95	57	55	.266	.317	.347	.664	77	-30	-26	97	114	90	.591	16	10		-9	3/2OS	-2.9
■ **ARMANDO MARSANS**	Marsans, Armando b: 10/3/1887, Matanzas, Cuba d: 9/3/60, Havana, Cuba BR/TR, 5'10", 157 lbs. Deb: 7/04/11																											
1911	Cin-N	58	138	17	36	2	2	0	11	15	11	.261	.346	.304	.651	90	-3	-1	92	89	18	.696	11			-4	O/13	-0.6
1912	Cin-N	110	416	59	132	19	7	1	38	20	17	.317	.353	.404	.757	116	3	7	92	79	70	.796	35			4	O/1	0.7
1913	Cin-N	118	435	49	129	7	6	0	38	17	25	.297	.327	.340	.668	89	-6	-6	102	95	57	.670	37			-2	O1/3S	-1.1
1914	Cin-N	36	124	16	37	3	0	0	22	14	6	.298	.374	.323	.697	103	2	1	105	211	19	.782	13			0	O	0.0
	StL-F	9	40	5	14	0	2	0	2	3	0	.350	.395	.450	.845	134	2	2	106	35	9	.962	4			0	/2S	0.2
1915	StL-F	36	124	16	22	3	0	0	6	14	5	.177	.261	.202	.462	36	-9	-10	105	88	9	.431	5			5	O	-0.6
1916	StL-A	151	528	51	134	12	1	1	60	57	41	.254	.333	.286	.619	91	-7	-4	95	142	58	.619	46	26	-2	0	*O	-1.3
1917	StL-A	75	257	31	59	12	0	0	20	20	6	.230	.285	.276	.561	75	-9	-7	95	103	23	.515	11			-7	O/32	-2.0
	NY-A	25	88	10	20	4	0	0	15	8	3	.227	.292	.273	.564	68	-3	-4	107	229	9	.559	6			5	O	0.0
	Yr	100	345	41	79	16	0	0	35	28	9	.229	.287	.275	.562	73	-12	-11	98	135	31	.526	17			-2		-2.0
1918	NY-A	37	123	13	29	5	1	0	9	5	3	.236	.266	.293	.558	72	-5	-4	95	91	10	.468	3			-5	O	-1.2
Total	8	655	2273	267	612	67	19	2	221	173	117	.269	.325	.318	.643	90	-35	-27	97	114	283	.642	171	26		-4	O/123S	-5.9
■ **FRED MARSH**	Marsh, Fred Francis b: 1/5/24, Valley Falls, Kan. BR/TR, 5'10", 180 lbs. Deb: 4/19/49																											
1949	Cle-A	1	0	0	0	0	0	0	0	0	0	—	—	—	—	—	0	0	98	—	—	—	0	0	0	0	R	0.0
1951	StL-A	130	445	44	108	21	4	4	43	36	56	.243	.299	.335	.634	68	-19	-21	105	96	45	.540	4	4	-1	-2	*3/S2	-2.7
1952	StL-A	11	24	3	5	1	0	0	1	5	4	.208	.345	.250	.595	69	-1	-1	97	62	2	.550	0	1	-1	-1	/2S	-0.1
	Was-A	9	24	1	1	0	0	0	1	1	4	.042	.080	.042	.122	-65	-5	-5	100	374	0	.080	0	0	0	-1	/2O	-0.6
	StL-A	76	223	25	64	8	1	2	26	22	29	.287	.351	.359	.710	101	-0	0	97	113	29	.636	3	2	-0	-3	S3	0.0
	Yr	96	271	29	70	9	1	2	28	28	37	.258	.328	.321	.649	83	-7	-6	97	136	30	.567	3	3	-1	-4		-0.7
1953	Chi-A	67	95	22	19	1	0	2	2	13	26	.200	.303	.274	.576	53	-6	-6	106	23	8	.494	0	3	-2	0	3S/12	-0.7
1954	Chi-A	62	98	21	30	5	2	0	4	9	16	.306	.364	.398	.762	105	1	1	104	39	14	.722	4	2	0	1	3/S1O	0.0
1955	Bal-A	89	303	30	66	7	1	2	19	35	33	.218	.301	.267	.568	60	-19	-15	90	83	25	.478	1	2	-1	-12	23S	-2.1
1956	Bal-A	20	24	2	3	0	0	0	0	4	3	.125	.250	.125	.375	2	-3	-3	94	0	1	.381	1	0	0	-1	/S32	-0.1
Total	7	465	1236	148	296	43	8	10	96	125	171	.239	.310	.311	.622	70	-52	-51	99	88	408	.550	13	14	-5	-18	3S/21O	-6.3
■ **CHARLIE MARSHALL**	Marshall, Charles Anthony (born Charles Anthony Marczlewicz) b: 8/28/19, Wilmington, Del. BR/TR, 5'10.5", 178 lbs. Deb: 6/14/41																											
1941	StL-N	1	0	0	0	0	0	0	0	0	0	—	—	—	—	—	0	0	110	—	—	—	0			0	/C	0.0
■ **DAVE MARSHALL**	Marshall, David Lewis b: 1/14/43, Artesia, Cal. BL/TR, 6'1", 182 lbs. Deb: 9/07/67																											
1967	SF-N	1	0	0	0	0	0	0	0	0	0	—	—	—	—	—	0	0	101	—	—	—	0	0	0	0	R	0.0
1968	SF-N	76	174	17	46	5	1	1	16	20	37	.264	.344	.322	.665	103	1	1	98	114	21	.612	2	1	0	-6	O	-0.7
1969	SF-N	110	267	32	62	7	1	2	33	40	68	.232	.343	.288	.631	78	-6	-6	101	159	28	.577	1	8	-5	-12	O	-2.8
1970	NY-N	92	189	21	46	10	1	6	29	17	43	.243	.306	.402	.708	85	-4	-5	104	120	23	.655	4	1	1	-1	O	-0.6
1971	NY-N	100	214	28	51	9	1	3	21	26	54	.238	.326	.332	.658	90	-3	-2	96	107	24	.600	3	1	0	-5	O	-0.9
1972	NY-N	72	156	21	39	5	0	4	11	22	28	.250	.346	.359	.705	106	1	2	95	66	19	.661	3	3	-1	-3	O	-0.4
1973	SD-N	39	49	4	14	5	0	0	4	8	9	.286	.397	.388	.784	125	2	2	94	85	7	.700	0	1	-1	-1	/O	0.0
Total	7	490	1049	123	258	41	4	16	114	133	239	.246	.336	.338	.675	92	-10	-8	99	117	531	.631	13	15	-5	-27	O	-5.4
■ **ED MARSHALL**	Marshall, Edward Herbert b: 6/4/06, New Albany, Miss. BR/TR, 5'11", 150 lbs. Deb: 9/28/29																											
1929	NY-N	5	15	6	6	2	0	0	2	1	0	.400	.438	.533	.971	140	1	1	100	86	3	1.000	0			0	/2	0.1
1930	NY-N	78	223	33	69	5	3	0	21	13	9	.309	.350	.359	.709	74	-10	-9	98	90	27	.610	0			2	S2/3	0.0
1931	NY-N	68	194	15	39	6	2	0	10	8	8	.201	.233	.253	.485	31	-19	-18	97	73	12	.374	1			-1	2S/3	-1.5
1932	NY-N	68	226	18	56	8	1	0	28	6	11	.248	.270	.292	.562	52	-15	-15	99	158	18	.435	1			-3	S	-1.2
Total	4	219	658	72	170	21	6	0	61	28	28	.258	.291	.309	.599	56	-43	-41	98	108	61	.482	2			-2	S/23	-2.6
■ **JOE MARSHALL**	Marshall, Joseph Hanley "Home Run Joe" b: 2/19/1876, Audubon, Minn. d: 9/11/31, Norwalk, Cal. BR/TR, Deb: 03																											
1903	Pit-N	10	23	2	6	1	2	0	2	0		.261	.261	.478	.739	106	0	-0	105	58	3	.647	0			0	/SO2	0.0
1906	StL-N	33	95	2	15	1	2	0	7	6		.158	.208	.211	.418	32	-7	-8	101	128	4	.325	0			1	O/1	-0.7

YEAR	TM/L	G	AB	R	H	2B	3B	HR	RBI	BB	SO	AVG	OBP	SLG	PRO	/A	BR	/A	PF	CHI	RC	TA	SB	CS	SBR	FR	POS	TPR
Total	2	43	118	4	21	2	4	0	9	6		.178	.218	.263	.480	48	-7	-8	101	115	7	.381	0			2	/O1S2	-0.7
■ KEITH MARSHALL	Marshall, Keith Alan b: 7/2/51, San Francisco, Cal. BR/TR, 6'2", 175 lbs. Deb: 4/07/73																											
1973	KC-A	8	9	0	2	1	0	0	3	1	4	.222	.300	.333	.633	72	-0	-0	109	393	1	.500	0	0	0	-2	/O	-0.2
■ MIKE MARSHALL	Marshall, Michael Allen b: 1/12/60, Libertyville, Ill. BR/TR, 6'5", 215 lbs. Deb: 9/07/81																											
1981	LA-N	14	25	2	5	3	0	0	1	1	4	.200	.259	.320	.579	65	-1	-1	98	49	2	.476	0	0	0	0	/13O	-0.1
1982	LA-N	49	95	10	23	3	0	5	9	13	23	.242	.339	.432	.771	121	2	3	95	63	15	.781	2	0	1	-3	O1	0.0
1983	LA-N	140	465	47	132	17	1	17	65	43	127	.284	.351	.434	.785	116	10	10	100	102	72	.747	7	3	0	-10	*O1	-0.3
1984	LA-N	134	495	69	127	27	0	21	65	40	93	.257	.316	.438	.754	106	5	3	104	96	66	.689	4	3	-1	-15	*O1	-1.8
1985	LA-N	135	518	72	152	27	2	28	95	37	137	.293	.344	.515	.860	148	23	28	93	114	87	.807	3	10	-5	-3	*O/1	1.7
1986	LA-N	103	330	47	77	11	0	19	53	27	90	.233	.299	.439	.739	107	-1	1	94	105	42	.687	4	4	-1	-4	O	-0.5
1987	LA-N	104	402	45	118	19	0	16	72	18	79	.294	.330	.460	.790	116	3	7	92	131	55	.685	0	5	-3	-8	*O	-0.7
1988	LA-N	144	542	63	150	27	2	20	82	24	93	.277	.316	.445	.761	109	9	6	106	111	71	.673	4	1	1	-4	O1	-0.3
Total	8	823	2872	355	784	134	5	126	442	203	646	.273	.327	.455	.782	117	50	56	99	107	409	.733	24	26	-8	-47	O1/3	-2.0
■ MAX MARSHALL	Marshall, Milo Max b: 9/18/13, Shenandoah, Iowa BL/TR, 6'1", 180 lbs. Deb: 5/10/42																											
1942	Cin-N	131	530	49	135	17	6	7	43	34	38	.255	.301	.349	.650	89	-8	-9	101	74	56	.556	4			-8	*O	-2.1
1943	Cin-N	132	508	55	120	11	8	4	39	34	52	.236	.287	.313	.600	74	-18	-18	99	87	47	.515	8			-6	*O	-3.0
1944	Cin-N	66	229	36	56	13	2	4	23	21	10	.245	.308	.371	.679	95	-3	-2	95	87	27	.623	3			-0	O	-0.6
Total	3	329	1267	140	311	41	16	15	105	89	100	.245	.297	.339	.635	84	-30	-29	99	82	131	.559	15			-14	O	-5.7
■ JIM MARSHALL	Marshall, Rufus James b: 5/25/31, Danville, Ill. BL/TL, 6'1", 190 lbs. Deb: 4/15/58 MC																											
1958	Bal-A	85	191	17	41	4	3	5	19	18	30	.215	.282	.346	.628	76	-8	-6	94	94	18	.558	3	2	-0	-4	1/O	-1.3
	Chi-N	26	81	12	22	2	0	5	11	12	13	.272	.372	.481	.854	123	3	3	101	84	16	.898	1	0	0	-3	1O	0.0
1959	Chi-N	108	294	39	74	10	1	11	40	33	39	.252	.327	.405	.732	95	-3	-2	98	106	39	.673	0	1	-1	-2	1/O	-0.9
1960	SF-N	75	118	19	28	2	2	2	13	17	24	.237	.333	.339	.672	94	-2	-1	90	115	13	.600	0	1	-1	-3	1/O	-0.5
1961	SF-N	44	36	5	8	0	0	1	7	3	8	.222	.282	.306	.588	57	-2	-2	98	202	3	.483	0	0	0	-1	/1O	-0.2
1962	NY-N	17	32	6	11	1	0	3	4	3	6	.344	.400	.656	1.056	171	3	3	104	53	9	1.143	0	0	0	0	/1O	0.3
	Pit-N	55	100	13	22	5	1	2	12	15	19	.220	.322	.350	.672	78	-3	-3	102	115	12	.646	1	0	0	0	1	-0.2
	Yr	72	132	19	33	6	1	5	16	18	25	.250	.340	.424	.764	101	1	0	103	101	20	.750	1	0	0	0		0.1
Total	5	410	852	111	206	24	7	29	106	101	139	.242	.323	.388	.711	93	-11	-8	97	106	111	.673	5	4	-1	-12	1/O	-2.8
■ WILLARD MARSHALL	Marshall, Willard Warren b: 2/8/21, Richmond, Va. BL/TR, 6'1", 205 lbs. Deb: 4/14/42																											
1942	NY-N	116	401	41	103	9	2	11	59	26	20	.257	.307	.372	.679	96	-2	-3	103	120	46	.587	1			-3	*O	-0.9
1946	NY-N	131	510	63	144	18	3	13	48	33	29	.282	.327	.406	.733	106	3	2	102	77	65	.640	3			3	*O	0.2
1947	NY-N	155	587	102	171	19	6	36	107	67	30	.291	.366	.528	.894	134	27	27	101	100	113	.888	3			8	*O	2.7
1948	NY-N	143	537	72	146	21	8	14	86	64	34	.272	.350	.419	.769	108	5	6	100	128	80	.726	2			-3	*O	-0.6
1949	NY-N	141	499	81	153	19	3	12	70	78	20	.307	.401	.429	.830	121	19	18	102	108	90	.834	4			0	*O	1.0
1950	Bos-N	105	298	38	70	10	2	5	40	36	5	.235	.319	.332	.652	83	-12	-6	86	135	32	.576	1			-2	O	-1.0
1951	Bos-N	136	469	65	132	24	7	11	62	48	18	.281	.351	.433	.784	112	6	7	98	104	69	.707	0	3	-2	-10	*O	-0.8
1952	Bos-N	21	66	5	15	4	1	2	11	4	4	.227	.271	.409	.681	91	-2	-1	95	130	7	.574	0	0	0	1	O	0.0
	Cin-N	107	397	52	106	23	1	8	46	37	21	.267	.333	.390	.723	100	-0	-0	100	106	53	.645	0	1	-1	1	*O	-0.1
	Yr	128	463	57	121	27	2	10	57	41	25	.261	.324	.393	.717	99	-2	-1	99	111	60	.639	0	1	-1	2		-0.1
1953	Cin-N	122	357	51	95	14	6	17	62	41	28	.266	.342	.482	.824	113	5	6	99	108	59	.783	0	0	0	3	O	0.5
1954	Chi-A	47	71	7	18	2	0	1	7	11	9	.254	.354	.324	.678	83	-1	-1	104	102	9	.618	0	0	0	-8	O	-1.0
1955	Chi-A	22	41	6	7	0	0	0	6	13	1	.171	.370	.171	.541	49	-2	-2	101	320	4	.588	0	0	0	-1	O	-0.3
Total	11	1246	4233	583	1160	163	39	130	604	458	219	.274	.347	.423	.770	109	46	51	99	111	625	.740	14	4		-12	*O	-0.3
■ BILL MARSHALL	Marshall, William Henry b: 2/14/11, Dorchester, Mass. d: 5/5/77, Sacramento, Cal. BR/TR, 5'8.5", 156 lbs. Deb: 6/20/31																											
1931	Bos-A	1	0	1	0	0	0	0	0	0	0	—	—	—	—	—	0	0	94	—	—	—	0	0	0	0	R	0.0
1934	Cin-N	6	8	0	1	0	0	0	0	0	2	.125	.125	.125	.250	-33	-1	-1	101	0	0	.143	0			0	/2	0.0
Total	2	7	8	1	1	0	0	0	0	0	2	.125	.125	.125	.250	-33	-1	-1	101	0	625	.143	0	0		0	/2	0.0
■ DOC MARSHALL	Marshall, William Riddle b: 9/22/1875, Butler, Pa. d: 12/11/59, Clinton, Ill. BR/TR, 6', 185 lbs. Deb: 4/15/04																											
1904	Phi-N	8	20	1	2	0	0	0	1	0		.100	.100	.100	.200	-41	-3	-3	93	183	0	.111	0			0	/C	-0.1
	NY-N	1	0	0	0	0	0	0	0	0		—	—	—	—	—	0	0	105	—	—	—	0			0	/C	0.0
	Bos-N	13	43	3	9	0	1	0	2	2		.209	.244	.256	.500	58	-2	-2	97	67	3	.441	2			1	C/O	0.0
	NY-N	10	17	3	6	1	0	0	2	1		.353	.389	.412	.801	142	1	1	105	105	3	.727	0			-0	/CO2	0.1
	Yr	32	80	7	17	1	1	0	5	3		.213	.241	.250	.491	54	-4	-4	98	113	5	.397	2			1		0.0
1906	NY-N	38	102	8	17	3	2	0	7	7		.167	.220	.235	.455	43	-7	-7	100	106	7	.447	7			-1	OC/1	-0.8
	StL-N	39	123	6	34	4	1	0	10	6		.276	.310	.325	.635	99	-0	-0	101	91	13	.528	1			-6	C	-0.3
	Yr	77	225	14	51	7	3	0	17	13		.227	.269	.284	.553	74	-7	-7	100	100	20	.489	8			-7		-1.1
1907	StL-N	84	268	19	54	8	2	2	18	12		.201	.236	.269	.504	62	-13	-12	96	87	18	.402	2			6	C	0.1
1908	StL-N	6	14	0	1	0	0	0	1	0		.071	.071	.071	.143	-58	-2	-2	94	384	0	.077	0			0	/C	-0.1
	Chi-N	12	20	4	6	0	1	0	3	0		.300	.300	.400	.700	118	0	0	106	144	2	.571	0			0	/CO	0.1
	Yr	18	34	4	7	0	1	0	4	0		.206	.206	.265	.471	50	-2	-2	102	245	2	.333	0			1		0.0
1909	Bro-N	50	149	7	30	7	1	0	10	6		.201	.232	.262	.494	55	-8	-8	99	93	9	.403	3			6	C/O	0.1
Total	5	261	756	51	159	23	8	2	54	34		.210	.244	.270	.514	63	-35	-33	98	100	56	.424	15			6	C/O12	-0.9
■ DOC MARTEL	Martel, Leon Alphonse "Marty" b: 1/29/1883, Weymouth, Mass. d: 10/11/47, Washington, D.C. TR , 6', 185 lbs. Deb: 09																											
1909	Phi-N	24	41	1	11	3	1	0	7	4		.268	.333	.390	.724	118	1	1	106	159	5	.667	0			0	C	0.2
1910	Bos-N	10	31	0	4	0	0	0	1	2	3	.129	.182	.129	.311	-8	-4	-5	114	87	1	.222	0			1	1	-0.4
Total	2	34	72	1	15	3	1	0	8	6	3	.208	.269	.278	.547	60	-3	-4	110	129	6	.456	0			1	/C1	-0.2
■ AL MARTIN	Martin, Albert Deb: 5/07/1872																											
1872	Eck-n	4	19	2	5							.263															/2	
1874	Atl-n	7	35	1	4							.114															/2O	
1875	Atl-n	6	26	1	3							.115															/O	
Total	3 n	17	80	4	12							.150															/O	
■ BILLY MARTIN	Martin, Alfred Manuel b: 5/16/28, Berkeley, Cal. BR/TR, 5'11.5", 165 lbs. Deb: 4/18/50 MC																											
1950	NY-A	34	36	10	9	1	0	1	8	3	3	.250	.308	.361	.669	71	-2	-2	99	173	4	.593	0	0	0	-1	2/3	0.0
1951	NY-A	51	58	10	15	1	2	0	2	4	9	.259	.328	.345	.673	90	-1	-1	92	36	5	.531	0	1	-1	-0	2/S3O	0.0
1952	NY-A	109	363	32	97	13	3	3	33	22	31	.267	.323	.344	.668	88	-7	-6	98	92	40	.564	3	6	-3	11	*2	0.7
1953	NY-A	149	587	72	151	24	6	15	75	43	56	.257	.314	.395	.710	98	-9	-4	93	106	70	.621	6	7	-2	3	*2S	0.6
1955	NY-A	20	70	8	21	2	0	1	9	7	9	.300	.364	.371	.735	100	-0	0	98	118	9	.642	1	2	-1	2	2/S	0.2
1956	NY-A	121	458	76	121	24	5	9	49	30	56	.264	.314	.397	.711	88	-10	-10	99	89	57	.638	7	3	0	5	*23	0.4
1957	NY-A	43	145	12	35	5	2	1	12	3	14	.241	.262	.324	.586	63	-8	-7	94	95	11	.453	2	1	0	1	23	-0.4
	KC-A	73	265	33	68	9	3	9	27	12	20	.257	.296	.415	.712	93	-4	-3	99	79	32	.644	7	1	2	-8	23/S	-0.6
	Yr	116	410	45	103	14	5	10	39	15	34	.251	.284	.383	.667	83	-12	-11	97	86	44	.585	9	2	2	-7		-1.0
1958	Det-A	131	498	56	127	19	1	7	42	16	62	.255	.282	.339	.622	68	-21	-23	104	94	44	.495	5	3	-0	-12	S3	-2.1
1959	Cle-A	73	242	37	63	7	0	9	24	7	18	.260	.290	.401	.691	91	-5	-4	97	76	26	.575	0	2	-1	-11	2/3	-1.4
1960	Cin-N	103	317	34	78	17	1	3	16	27	34	.246	.305	.334	.640	76	-11	-10	98	56	30	.530	0	1	-1	-8	2	-1.0
1961	Mil-N	6	6	1	0	0	0	0	0	0	1	.000	.000	.000	.000	-99	-2	-2	92	0	0	.000	0	0	0	0	H	-0.1
	Min-A	108	374	44	92	15	5	6	36	13	42	.246	.277	.361	.638	65	-17	-20	106	92	35	.526	3	2	-0	-8	*2/S	-1.5
Total	11	1021	3419	425	877	137	28	64	333	187	355	.257	.301	.369	.670	82	-99	-92	99	89	363	.587	34	29	-7	-26	2S/3O	-5.2
■ PHONNEY MARTIN	Martin, Alphonse Case b: 8/4/1845, New York, N.Y. d: 5/24/33, Hollis, N.Y. 5'7", 148 lbs. Deb: 4/26/1872																											
1872	Tro-n	25	122	27	35							.287															O/P	

YEAR	TM/L	G	AB	R	H	2B	3B	HR	RBI	BB	SO	AVG	OBP	SLG	PRO	/A	BR	/A	PF	CHI	RC	TA	SB	CS	SBR	FR	POS	TPR
	Eck-n	18	82	10	15							.183															P/O	
	Yr	43	204	37	50							.245																
1873	Mut-n	30	139	12	29							.209															O/P	
Total	2 n	73	343	49	79							.230															O/P	
■ BABE MARTIN	Martin, Boris Michael (born Boris Michael Martinovich) b: 3/28/20, Seattle, Wash. BR/TR, 5'11.5", 194 lbs. Deb: 9/25/44																											
1944	StL-A	2	4	0	3	1	0	0	1	0	0	.750	.750	1.000	1.750	390	1	1	102	90	3	4.000	0	0	0	-0	/O	0.1
1945	StL-A	54	185	13	37	5	2	2	16	11	24	.200	.245	.281	.526	46	-12	-15	115	100	12	.409	0	1	-1	5	O/1	-1.2
1946	StL-A	3	9	0	2	0	0	0	1	1	2	.222	.300	.222	.522	48	-1	-1	98	190	1	.429	0	0	0	-0	/C	0.0
1948	Bos-A	4	4	0	2	0	0	0	0	0	1	.500	.500	.500	1.000	166	0	0	100	0	1	1.000	0	0	0	0	/C	0.0
1949	Bos-A	2	2	0	0	0	0	0	0	0	0	.000	.000	.000	.000	-93	-1	-1	107	0	0	.000	0	0	0	0	/C	0.0
1953	StL-A	4	2	0	0	0	0	0	0	1	0	.000	.333	.000	.333	-3	-0	-0	107	0	0	.500	0	0	0	0	/C	0.0
Total	6	69	206	13	44	6	2	2	18	13	27	.214	.260	.291	.552	52	-11	-15	114	100	17	.448	0	1	-1	5	/O1C	-1.1
■ FRANK MARTIN	Martin, Frank b: 1877, Chicago, Ill. Deb: 6/30/1897																											
1897	Lou-N	2	8	1	2	0	0	0	0	0		.250	.250	.250	.500	35	-1	-1	95	0	1	.333	0			0	/2	0.0
1898	Chi-N	1	4	0	0	0	0	0	0	0		.000	.000	.000	.000	-97	-1	-1	103	0	0	.000	0			0	/2	0.0
1899	NY-N	17	54	5	14	2	0	0	1	2		.259	.298	.296	.595	67	-2	-2	97	19	5	.475	0			0	3	-0.1
Total	3	20	66	6	16	2	0	0	1	2		.242	.275	.273	.548	54	-4	-4	97	16	5	.420	0			0	/32	-0.1
■ HERSH MARTIN	Martin, Hershel Ray b: 9/19/09, Birmingham, Ala. d: 11/17/80, Cuba, Mo. BB/TR, 6'2", 190 lbs. Deb: 4/23/37																											
1937	Phi-N	141	579	102	164	35	7	8	49	69	66	.283	.362	.409	.771	101	8	2	108	58	92	.758	11			-1	*O	-0.5
1938	Phi-N	120	466	58	139	36	6	3	39	34	48	.298	.347	.421	.768	110	6	6	100	73	67	.701	8			-5	*O	0.0
1939	Phi-N	111	393	59	111	28	5	1	22	42	27	.282	.355	.387	.741	105	0	3	94	53	56	.697	4			6	O	0.8
1940	Phi-N	33	83	10	21	6	1	0	5	9	9	.253	.326	.349	.675	89	-1	-1	97	64	10	.629	1			1	O	-0.1
1944	NY-A	85	328	49	99	12	4	9	47	34	26	.302	.371	.445	.816	125	14	11	106	104	57	.796	5	2	0	4	O	1.4
1945	NY-A	117	408	53	109	18	6	7	53	65	31	.267	.368	.392	.760	113	12	8	107	108	66	.756	4	1	1	1	*O	0.7
Total	6	607	2257	331	643	135	29	28	215	253	207	.285	.359	.408	.766	108	38	29	103	76	350	.749	33	3		7	O	2.3
■ JERRY MARTIN	Martin, Jerry Lindsey b: 5/11/49, Columbia, S.C. BR/TR, 6'1", 195 lbs. Deb: 9/07/74																											
1974	Phi-N	13	14	2	3	1	0	0	1	1	5	.214	.267	.286	.552	53	-1	-1	103	96	1	.385	0	0	0	-3	O	-0.4
1975	Phi-N	57	113	15	24	7	1	2	11	11	16	.212	.288	.345	.633	74	-4	-4	101	95	11	.576	2	2	-1	-0	O	-0.6
1976	Phi-N	130	121	30	30	7	0	2	15	7	28	.248	.289	.355	.644	77	-3	-4	107	118	11	.541	3	2	-0	-32	*O/1	-4.3
1977	Phi-N	116	215	34	56	16	3	6	28	18	42	.260	.329	.447	.776	105	1	1	100	98	31	.747	6	4	-1	-18	*O/1	-2.0
1978	Phi-N	128	266	40	72	13	4	9	36	28	65	.271	.342	.451	.794	114	7	5	105	97	42	.782	9	5	-0	-11	*O	-1.1
1979	Chi-N	150	534	74	145	34	3	19	73	38	85	.272	.323	.453	.777	98	5	-3	112	99	74	.702	2	4	-2	-8	*O	-1.7
1980	Chi-N	141	494	57	112	22	2	23	73	38	107	.227	.285	.419	.704	89	-6	-10	106	107	57	.644	8	3	1	-13	*O	-2.9
1981	SF-N	72	241	23	58	5	3	4	25	21	52	.241	.309	.336	.646	79	-5	-7	105	105	24	.572	6	2	1	2	O	-0.6
1982	KC-A	147	519	52	138	22	1	15	65	38	138	.266	.318	.399	.717	95	-4	-4	100	105	66	.636	1	1	-0	1	*O/D	-0.6
1983	KC-A	13	44	4	14	2	0	2	13	1	7	.318	.333	.500	.833	124	1	1	101	182	8	.800	1	0	0	-2	O	0.0
1984	NY-N	51	91	6	14	1	0	3	5	6	29	.154	.206	.264	.470	31	-9	-9	100	59	4	.366	0	0	0	-2	O/1	-1.1
Total	11	1018	2652	337	666	130	17	85	345	207	574	.251	.309	.409	.718	92	-17	-33	105	102	329	.668	38	23	-2	-87	O/1D	-15.3
■ JACK MARTIN	Martin, John Christopher b: 4/19/1887, Plainfield, N.J. d: 7/4/80, Plainfield, N.J. BR/TR, 5'9", 159 lbs. Deb: 4/25/12																											
1912	NY-A	69	231	30	52	6	1	0	17	37		.225	.347	.260	.606	73	-6	-6	101	96	26	.654	14			-7	S/32	-0.6
1914	Bos-N	33	85	10	18	2	0	0	5	6	7	.212	.264	.235	.499	47	-5	-6	104	91	5	.388	0			1	3/12	-0.4
	Phi-N	83	292	26	74	5	3	0	21	27	29	.253	.319	.291	.610	82	-6	-6	100	91	29	.546	6			-7	S	-1.0
	Yr	116	377	36	92	7	3	0	26	33	36	.244	.307	.279	.585	73	-11	-12	101	92	34	.509	6			-6		-1.4
Total	2	185	608	66	144	13	4	0	43	70	36	.237	.323	.271	.594	74	-17	-18	101	93	61	.565	20			-13	S/321	-2.0
■ PEPPER MARTIN	Martin, John Leonard Roosevelt "The Wild Horse Of The Osage" b: 2/29/04, Temple, Okla. d: 3/5/65, Mc Alester, Okla. BR/TR, 5'8", 170 lbs. Deb: 4/16/28 C																											
1928	StL-N	39	13	11	4	0	0	0	0	1	2	.308	.400	.308	.708	87	-0	-0	100	0	2	.889	2			-2	/O	-0.1
1930	StL-N	6	1	5	0	0	0	0	0	0	0	.000	.000	.000	.000	-95	-0	-0	105	0	0	.000	0			0	H	0.0
1931	StL-N	123	413	68	124	32	8	7	75	30	40	.300	.351	.467	.818	111	9	6	107	125	69	.834	16			-4	*O	-0.3
1932	StL-N	85	323	47	77	19	6	4	34	30	31	.238	.305	.372	.677	81	-9	-9	100	101	38	.650	9			4	O3	-0.7
1933	StL-N	145	599	**122**	189	36	12	8	57	67	46	.316	.387	.456	.843	137	32	31	102	62	111	.881	**26**			-3	*3	3.3
1934	StL-N	110	454	74	131	25	11	5	49	32	41	.289	.337	.425	.762	90	1	-7	114	82	69	.769	**23**			-2	*3/P	0.0
1935	StL-N	135	539	121	161	41	6	9	54	33	58	.299	.341	.447	.789	106	7	4	104	77	84	.769	20			-8	*3O	0.0
1936	StL-N	143	572	121	177	36	11	11	76	58	66	.309	.373	.469	.842	133	20	24	94	95	103	.860	**23**			-5	*O3/P	1.5
1937	StL-N	98	339	60	103	27	8	5	38	33	50	.304	.366	.475	.841	126	12	12	101	79	62	.849	9			12	O/3	2.0
1938	StL-N	91	269	34	79	18	2	2	38	18	34	.294	.340	.398	.738	92	1	-3	111	122	38	.677	4			-2	O/3	-0.5
1939	StL-N	88	281	48	86	17	7	3	37	30	35	.306	.375	.448	.823	115	8	6	105	100	47	.807	6			-0	O3	0.6
1940	StL-N	86	228	28	72	15	4	3	39	22	24	.316	.378	.456	.835	127	9	9	102	128	41	.847	6			-4	O/3	0.2
1944	StL-N	40	86	15	24	4	0	2	4	15	11	.279	.386	.395	.781	120	3	3	101	36	14	.785	2			-4	O	-0.3
Total	13	1189	4117	754	1227	270	75	59	501	369	438	.298	.358	.443	.801	113	93	75	103	91	679	.813	146			-17	O3/P	5.7
■ J.C. MARTIN	Martin, Joseph Clifton b: 12/13/36, Axton, Va. BL/TR, 6'2", 188 lbs. Deb: 9/10/59 C																											
1959	Chi-A	3	4	0	1	0	0	0	1	0	1	.250	.250	.250	.500	39	-0	-0	97	394	0	.333	0	0	0	0	/3	0.0
1960	Chi-A	7	20	0	2	1	0	0	2	0	6	.100	.100	.150	.250	-33	-4	-4	101	261	0	.158	0	0	0	0	/31	-0.3
1961	Chi-A	110	274	26	63	8	3	5	32	21	31	.230	.290	.336	.625	67	-13	-13	99	117	27	.540	1	2	-1	1	13	-1.6
1962	Chi-A	18	26	0	2	0	0	0	2	0	3	.077	.077	.077	.154	-62	-6	-6	95	397	0	.080	0	0	0	0	/C13	-0.5
1963	Chi-A	105	259	25	53	11	1	5	28	26	35	.205	.280	.313	.592	63	-12	-13	104	122	24	.519	0	0	0	-13	C/13	-2.6
1964	Chi-A	122	294	23	58	10	1	4	22	16	30	.197	.244	.279	.523	47	-22	-20	96	99	20	.417	0	0	0	-20	*C	-3.8
1965	Chi-A	119	230	21	60	12	0	2	21	24	29	.261	.336	.339	.675	100	-2	0	92	104	28	.616	2	1	0	-17	*C/13	-0.8
1966	Chi-A	67	157	13	40	5	3	2	20	14	24	.255	.320	.363	.683	102	-1	0	94	133	18	.595	0	0	0	-5	C	-0.1
1967	Chi-A	101	252	22	59	12	1	4	22	30	41	.234	.318	.337	.655	100	-2	0	94	95	27	.597	4	4	-1	-7	C/1	-0.1
1968	NY-N	78	244	20	55	9	2	3	31	21	31	.225	.300	.316	.616	83	-4	-5	102	152	24	.534	0	0	0	6	C1	0.2
1969	NY-N	66	177	12	37	5	1	4	21	12	32	.209	.259	.316	.576	60	-10	-10	100	124	14	.466	0	0	0	1	C/1	-0.5
1970	Chi-N	40	77	11	12	1	0	1	4	20	11	.156	.337	.208	.545	41	-5	-7	120	82	6	.552	0	0	0	-1	C/1	-0.6
1971	Chi-N	47	125	13	33	5	0	2	17	12	16	.264	.338	.352	.690	87	-0	-2	110	138	15	.621	1	1	-0	-2	C/O	-0.2
1972	Chi-N	25	50	3	12	3	0	0	7	5	9	.240	.309	.300	.609	65	-2	-2	114	192	4	.512	1	0	0	-1	C	-0.1
Total	14	908	2189	189	487	82	12	32	230	201	299	.222	.293	.315	.608	72	-82	-81	100	123	207	.535	9	8	-2	-58	C/13O	-11.0
■ MIKE MARTIN	Martin, Joseph Michael b: 12/3/58, Portland, Ore. BL/TR, 6'2", 193 lbs. Deb: 8/15/86																											
1986	Chi-N	8	13	1	1	1	0	0	0	2	4	.077	.200	.154	.354	-1	-2	-2	107	0	0	.333	0	0	0	0	/C	0.0
■ JOE MARTIN	Martin, Joseph Samuel "Silent Joe" b: 1/1/1876, Hollidaysburg, Pa. d: 5/25/64, Altoona, Pa. BL/TR, 5'9.5", 155 lbs. Deb: 4/28/03																											
1903	Was-A	35	119	11	27	4	5	0	7	5		.227	.258	.345	.603	77	-3	-4	105	63	11	.522	2			-0	23/O	-0.4
	StL-A	44	173	18	37	6	4	0	7	6		.214	.240	.295	.535	64	-8	-7	95	47	13	.419	0			3	O/23	-0.6
	Yr	79	292	29	64	10	9	0	14	11		.219	.248	.315	.563	70	-11	-11	100	55	24	.461	2			2		-1.0
Total	1	79	292	29	64	10	9	0	14	11		.219	.248	.315	.563	70	-11	-11	99	54	24	.461	2			2	/O23	-1.0
■ JOE MARTIN	Martin, Stuart Mc Guire b: 11/17/13, Rich Square, N.C. BL/TR, 6', 155 lbs. Deb: 4/14/36																											
1936	StL-N	92	332	63	99	21	4	6	41	29	27	.298	.356	.440	.796	120	6	8	94	90	53	.801	17			-11	2/S	0.2
1937	StL-N	90	223	34	58	6	1	1	17	32	18	.260	.353	.309	.662	81	-5	-5	101	85	26	.605	3			-4	2/1S	-0.6
1938	StL-N	114	417	54	116	26	2	1	27	30	28	.278	.328	.357	.685	79	-7	-13	111	65	52	.603	4			-5	2	-1.0
1939	StL-N	120	425	60	114	26	7	3	30	33	40	.268	.325	.384	.709	85	-7	-9	105	64	54	.638	4			-5	*2/1	-1.0
1940	StL-N	112	369	45	88	12	6	4	32	33	35	.238	.301	.336	.637	74	-12	-13	102	87	39	.563	4			-10	32	-2.1
1941	Pit-N	88	233	37	71	13	2	0	19	10	17	.305	.341	.378	.719	100	0	-0	103	78	29	.609	2			-1	2/31	0.2

YEAR	TM/L	G	AB	R	H	2B	3B	HR	RBI	BB	SO	AVG	OBP	SLG	PRO	/A	BR	/A	PF	CHI	RC	TA	SB	CS	SBR	FR	POS	TPR
1942	Pit-N	42	120	16	27	4	2	1	12	8	10	.225	.273	.317	.590	72	-4	-5	101	108	11	.500	1			-5	2/1S	-0.7
1943	Chi-N	64	118	13	26	4	0	0	5	15	10	.220	.308	.254	.563	64	-5	-5	99	60	10	.489	1			2	2/31	-0.2
Total	8	722	2237	322	599	112	24	16	183	190	185	.268	.327	.361	.688	87	-33	-42	103	78	273	.635	36			-41	2/31S	-5.2

■ GENE MARTIN Martin, Thomas Eugene b: 1/12/47, Americus, Ga. BL/TR, 6'0.5", 190 lbs. Deb: 7/28/68

YEAR	TM/L	G	AB	R	H	2B	3B	HR	RBI	BB	SO	AVG	OBP	SLG	PRO	/A	BR	/A	PF	CHI	RC	TA	SB	CS	SBR	FR	POS	TPR
1968	Was-A	9	11	1	4	1	0	1	1	0	1	.364	.364	.727	1.091	245	1	2	91	39	2	1.000	0	0	0	-1	/O	0.1

■ BILLY MARTIN Martin, William Lloyd b: 2/13/1894, Washington, D.C. d: 9/14/49, Arlington, Va. BR/TR, 5'8.5", 170 lbs. Deb: 10/06/14

YEAR	TM/L	G	AB	R	H	2B	3B	HR	RBI	BB	SO	AVG	OBP	SLG	PRO	/A	BR	/A	PF	CHI	RC	TA	SB	CS	SBR	FR	POS	TPR
1914	Bos-N	1	3	0	0	0	0	0	0	0	0	.000	.000	.000	.000	-96	-1	-1	104	0	0	.000	0			0	/S	0.0

■ JOE MARTIN Martin, William Joseph "Smokey Joe" b: 8/28/11, Seymour, Mo. d: 9/28/60, Buffalo, N.Y. BR/TR, 5'11.5", 181 lbs. Deb: 5/05/36

YEAR	TM/L	G	AB	R	H	2B	3B	HR	RBI	BB	SO	AVG	OBP	SLG	PRO	/A	BR	/A	PF	CHI	RC	TA	SB	CS	SBR	FR	POS	TPR
1936	NY-N	7	15	0	4	1	0	0	2	0	4	.267	.313	.333	.646	74	-1	-1	100	142	1	.500	0			0	/3	0.0
1938	Chi-A	1	0	0	0	0	0	0	0	0	0	—	—	—	—	—	0	0	98	—	—	—	0	0	0	0	R	0.0
Total	2	8	15	0	4	1	0	0	2	0	4	.267	.313	.333	.646	74	-1	-1	100	142	3	.545	0	0		0	/3	0.0

■ CARLOS MARTINEZ Martinez, Carlos Alberto b: 8/11/64, La Guaira, Venez. BR/TR, 6'5", 175 lbs. Deb: 9/02/88

YEAR	TM/L	G	AB	R	H	2B	3B	HR	RBI	BB	SO	AVG	OBP	SLG	PRO	/A	BR	/A	PF	CHI	RC	TA	SB	CS	SBR	FR	POS	TPR
1988	Chi-A	17	55	5	9	1	0	0	0	0	12	.164	.164	.182	.345	-4	-7	-7	97	0	2	.234	1	0	0	1	3/D	-0.5

■ CARMELO MARTINEZ Martinez, Carmelo (Salgado) b: 7/28/60, Dorado, P.R. BR/TR, 6'1", 190 lbs. Deb: 8/22/83

YEAR	TM/L	G	AB	R	H	2B	3B	HR	RBI	BB	SO	AVG	OBP	SLG	PRO	/A	BR	/A	PF	CHI	RC	TA	SB	CS	SBR	FR	POS	TPR
1983	Chi-N	29	89	8	23	3	0	6	16	4	19	.258	.290	.494	.785	113	1	1	101	102	12	.696	0	0	0	3	1/3O	0.2
1984	SD-N	149	488	64	122	28	2	13	66	68	82	.250	.346	.395	.742	110	6	7	99	114	70	.707	1	3	-2	13	*O/1	1.4
1985	SD-N	150	514	64	130	28	1	21	72	87	82	.253	.364	.434	.798	120	17	16	102	102	84	.786	0	4	-2	4	*O/1	1.4
1986	SD-N	113	244	28	58	10	0	9	25	35	46	.238	.336	.389	.725	104	0	2	95	82	31	.673	1	1	-0	-4	O1/3	-0.4
1987	SD-N	139	447	59	122	21	2	15	70	70	82	.273	.375	.430	.805	116	10	12	97	118	73	.792	5	5	-2	-3	O1	0.0
1988	SD-N	121	365	48	86	12	0	18	65	35	57	.236	.303	.416	.719	107	1	2	97	126	44	.648	1	1	-0	0	O1	-0.1
Total	6	701	2147	271	541	102	5	82	314	299	368	.252	.346	.419	.765	113	35	40	98	110	314	.747	8	14	-6	12	O1/3	2.5

■ DAVE MARTINEZ Martinez, David b: 9/26/64, New York, N.Y. BL/TL, 5'10", 150 lbs. Deb: 6/15/86

YEAR	TM/L	G	AB	R	H	2B	3B	HR	RBI	BB	SO	AVG	OBP	SLG	PRO	/A	BR	/A	PF	CHI	RC	TA	SB	CS	SBR	FR	POS	TPR
1986	Chi-N	53	108	13	15	1	1	1	7	6	22	.139	.191	.194	.386	6	-14	-15	107	116	4	.333	4	2	0	-1	O	-1.7
1987	Chi-N	142	459	70	134	18	8	8	36	57	96	.292	.373	.418	.791	108	7	7	101	67	75	.792	16	8	0	-3	*O	-0.1
1988	Chi-N	75	256	27	65	10	1	4	34	21	46	.254	.315	.348	.663	86	-3	-4	104	135	29	.607	7	3	0	3	O	-0.3
	Mon-N	63	191	24	49	3	5	2	12	17	48	.257	.317	.356	.673	88	-2	-3	106	65	23	.678	16	6	1	0	O	-0.3
	Yr	138	447	51	114	13	6	6	46	38	94	.255	.316	.351	.667	87	-5	-7	105	104	53	.641	23	9	2	3		-0.6
Total	3	333	1014	134	263	32	15	15	89	101	212	.259	.329	.365	.694	88	-11	-15	103	88	131	.673	43	19	2	-2	O	-2.4

■ EDGAR MARTINEZ Martinez, Edgar b: 1/2/63, New York, N.Y. BR/TR, 6' ", 175 lbs. Deb: 9/12/87

YEAR	TM/L	G	AB	R	H	2B	3B	HR	RBI	BB	SO	AVG	OBP	SLG	PRO	/A	BR	/A	PF	CHI	RC	TA	SB	CS	SBR	FR	POS	TPR
1987	Sea-A	13	43	6	16	5	2	0	5	2	5	.372	.413	.581	.994	157	4	4	103	80	11	1.037	0	0	0	1	3/D	0.4
1988	Sea-A	14	32	0	9	4	0	0	5	4	7	.281	.361	.406	.767	106	1	0	108	153	5	.739	0	0	0	-1	3	0.0
Total	2	27	75	6	25	9	2	0	10	6	12	.333	.390	.507	.897	135	4	4	105	112	16	.900	0	0	0	1	/3D	0.4

■ TONY MARTINEZ Martinez, Gabriel Antonio (Diaz) b: 3/18/41, Perico, Cuba BR/TR, 5'10", 165 lbs. Deb: 4/09/63

YEAR	TM/L	G	AB	R	H	2B	3B	HR	RBI	BB	SO	AVG	OBP	SLG	PRO	/A	BR	/A	PF	CHI	RC	TA	SB	CS	SBR	FR	POS	TPR
1963	Cle-A	43	141	10	22	4	0	0	8	5	18	.156	.185	.184	.369	4	-18	-17	97	129	4	.258	1	1	-0	-7	S	-2.4
1964	Cle-A	9	14	1	3	1	0	0	2	0	2	.214	.214	.286	.500	37	-1	-1	103	212	0	.308	0	1	-1	0	/2S	0.0
1965	Cle-A	4	3	0	0	0	0	0	0	0	0	.000	.000	.000	.000	-99	-1	-1	98	0	0	.000	0	0	0	0	H	0.0
1966	Cle-A	17	17	2	5	0	0	0	0	1	6	.294	.333	.294	.627	81	-0	-0	101	0	2	.538	1	1	-0	0	/S2	0.0
Total	4	73	175	13	30	5	0	0	10	6	26	.171	.199	.200	.399	13	-20	-20	98	120	6	.291	2	3	-1	-7	/S2	-2.4

■ BUCK MARTINEZ Martinez, John Albert b: 11/7/48, Redding, Cal. BR/TR, 5'10", 190 lbs. Deb: 6/18/69

YEAR	TM/L	G	AB	R	H	2B	3B	HR	RBI	BB	SO	AVG	OBP	SLG	PRO	/A	BR	/A	PF	CHI	RC	TA	SB	CS	SBR	FR	POS	TPR
1969	KC-A	72	205	14	47	6	1	4	23	8	25	.229	.258	.327	.585	61	-11	-11	103	117	16	.463	0	0	0	-1	C/O	-0.9
1970	KC-A	6	9	1	1	0	0	0	0	2	1	.111	.273	.111	.384	10	-1	-1	98	0	0	.333	0	0	0	0	/C	0.0
1971	KC-A	22	46	3	7	2	0	0	1	5	9	.152	.235	.196	.431	23	-5	-5	99	45	2	.341	0	1	-1	0	C	-0.3
1973	KC-A	14	32	2	8	1	0	1	6	4	5	.250	.333	.375	.708	91	-0	-0	109	157	4	.615	0	0	0	-1	C	0.0
1974	KC-A	43	107	10	23	3	1	1	8	14	19	.215	.317	.290	.607	71	-3	-4	106	92	11	.547	0	1	-1	0	C	-0.2
1975	KC-A	80	226	15	51	9	2	3	23	21	28	.226	.294	.323	.617	73	-8	-8	102	108	22	.536	1	0	0	-1	C	-0.6
1976	KC-A	95	267	24	61	13	3	5	34	16	45	.228	.272	.356	.628	83	-7	-7	100	119	27	.534	0	0	0	-8	C	-1.1
1977	KC-A	29	80	3	18	4	0	1	9	3	12	.225	.253	.313	.566	53	-5	-5	100	127	6	.438	0	1	-1	-1	C	-0.5
1978	Mil-A	89	256	26	56	10	1	1	20	14	42	.219	.259	.277	.537	48	-17	-19	106	107	19	.420	1	1	-0	-4	C	-2.0
1979	Mil-A	69	196	17	53	8	0	4	26	8	25	.270	.299	.372	.671	80	-6	-6	100	118	21	.551	0	1	-1	3	C/P	0.0
1980	Mil-A	76	219	16	49	9	0	3	17	12	33	.224	.267	.306	.573	60	-13	-12	95	87	18	.468	1	0	0	1	C	-0.6
1981	Tor-A	45	128	13	29	8	1	4	21	11	16	.227	.293	.398	.691	88	-1	-2	111	130	14	.610	1	0	0	4	C	0.4
1982	Tor-A	96	260	26	63	17	0	10	37	24	34	.242	.306	.423	.729	90	-1	-4	109	106	31	.649	1	1	-0	-9	C	-0.7
1983	Tor-A	88	221	27	56	14	0	10	33	29	39	.253	.340	.452	.792	107	5	2	108	99	33	.746	0	1	-1	-7	C	0.0
1984	Tor-A	102	232	24	51	13	1	5	37	29	49	.220	.312	.349	.661	81	-5	-6	102	154	27	.602	0	3	-2	-11	C/D	-1.2
1985	Tor-A	42	99	11	16	3	0	4	14	10	12	.162	.245	.313	.559	51	-7	-7	101	129	8	.488	0	0	0	-2	C	-0.6
1986	Tor-A	81	160	13	29	8	0	2	12	20	25	.181	.272	.269	.541	46	-11	-12	105	98	12	.463	0	0	0	-10	C/D	-1.7
Total	17	1049	2743	245	618	128	10	58	321	230	419	.225	.287	.343	.630	73	-95	-107	103	112	272	.553	5	10	-5	-46	*C/DPO	-10.0

■ JOSE MARTINEZ Martinez, Jose (Azcuiz) b: 7/26/42, Cardenas, Cuba BR/TR, 5'10", 190 lbs. Deb: 6/18/69 C

YEAR	TM/L	G	AB	R	H	2B	3B	HR	RBI	BB	SO	AVG	OBP	SLG	PRO	/A	BR	/A	PF	CHI	RC	TA	SB	CS	SBR	FR	POS	TPR
1969	Pit-N	77	168	20	45	6	0	1	16	9	32	.268	.309	.321	.630	81	-5	-4	95	112	15	.500	1	3	-2	8	2S/3O	0.8
1970	Pit-N	19	20	1	1	0	0	0	0	1	5	.050	.095	.050	.145	-62	-5	-4	97	0	0	.100	0	0	0	1	/32S	-0.2
Total	2	96	188	21	46	6	0	1	16	10	37	.245	.286	.293	.579	65	-10	-9	95	101	16	.459	1	3	-2	9	/2S3O	0.6

■ MARTY MARTINEZ Martinez, Orlando (Oliva) b: 8/23/41, Havana, Cuba BB/TR, 6', 170 lbs. Deb: 5/02/62 MC

YEAR	TM/L	G	AB	R	H	2B	3B	HR	RBI	BB	SO	AVG	OBP	SLG	PRO	/A	BR	/A	PF	CHI	RC	TA	SB	CS	SBR	FR	POS	TPR
1962	Min-A	37	18	13	3	0	1	0	3	3	4	.167	.286	.278	.563	50	-1	-1	105	238	2	.533	0	0	0	1	S/3	0.0
1967	Atl-N	44	73	14	21	2	1	0	5	11	11	.288	.388	.342	.731	106	2	1	104	83	10	.673	0	1	-1	-2	S/2C31	0.2
1968	Atl-N	113	356	34	82	5	3	0	12	29	28	.230	.292	.261	.553	72	-14	-11	93	54	27	.451	6	6	-2	-6	S32C	-1.2
1969	Hou-N	78	198	14	61	5	4	0	15	10	21	.308	.341	.374	.715	99	-0	-0	102	81	24	.592	0	0	0	-4	OS3/CP2	-0.2
1970	Hou-N	75	150	12	33	3	0	0	12	9	22	.220	.264	.240	.504	39	-13	-12	94	129	9	.375	0	0	0	-2	S3/C2	-0.9
1971	Hou-N	32	62	4	16	3	1	0	4	3	6	.258	.292	.339	.631	85	-2	-1	93	78	5	.510	1	0	0	-0	/2S13	0.0
1972	StL-N	9	7	0	3	0	0	0	2	0	1	.429	.429	.429	.857	137	0	0	105	274	1	.750	0	0	0	0	/S23	0.1
	Oak-A	22	40	3	5	0	0	0	1	3	6	.125	.186	.125	.311	-6	-5	-5	97	84	1	.216	0	0	0	0	2/S3	-0.3
	Tex-A	26	41	3	6	1	1	0	3	2	8	.146	.186	.220	.406	22	-4	-4	94	139	1	.297	0	1	-1	-1	/S32	-0.4
	Yr	48	81	6	11	1	1	0	4	5	14	.136	.186	.173	.359	8	-9	-9	95	115	3	.264	0	1	-1	-1		-0.7
Total	7	436	945	97	230	19	11	0	57	70	107	.243	.298	.287	.584	71	-37	-34	96	85	82	.485	7	8	-3	-14	S/32CO1P	-2.7

■ HECTOR MARTINEZ Martinez, Rodolfo Hector (Santos) b: 5/11/39, Las Villas, Cuba BR/TR, 5'10", 160 lbs. Deb: 9/30/62

YEAR	TM/L	G	AB	R	H	2B	3B	HR	RBI	BB	SO	AVG	OBP	SLG	PRO	/A	BR	/A	PF	CHI	RC	TA	SB	CS	SBR	FR	POS	TPR
1962	KC-A	1	1	0	0	0	0	0	0	0	1	.000	.000	.000	.000	-99	-0	-0	100	0	0	.000	0	0	0	0	H	0.0
1963	KC-A	6	14	2	4	0	0	1	3	1	3	.286	.375	.500	.875	133	1	1	108	126	2	.818	0	1	-1	0	/O	0.0
Total	2	7	15	2	4	0	0	1	3	1	4	.267	.353	.467	.820	118	1	0	107	118	2	.750	0	1	-1	0	/O	0.0

■ TED MARTINEZ Martinez, Teodoro Noel (Encarnacion) b: 12/10/47, Central Barahona, D.R. BR/TR, 6', 165 lbs. Deb: 7/18/70

YEAR	TM/L	G	AB	R	H	2B	3B	HR	RBI	BB	SO	AVG	OBP	SLG	PRO	/A	BR	/A	PF	CHI	RC	TA	SB	CS	SBR	FR	POS	TPR
1970	NY-N	4	16	0	1	0	0	0	0	0	3	.063	.063	.063	.125	-64	-4	-4	104	0	0	.067	0	0	0	-1	/2S	-0.3
1971	NY-N	38	125	16	36	5	2	1	10	4	22	.288	.326	.384	.710	104	-0	0	96	80	17	.678	6	0	2	-1	S2/3O	0.5
1972	NY-N	103	330	22	74	5	5	1	19	12	49	.224	.254	.279	.532	54	-21	-20	95	82	21	.415	7	4	-0	-10	2SO/3	-2.3
1973	NY-N	92	263	34	67	11	0	1	14	13	38	.255	.295	.308	.603	67	-12	-12	101	67	22	.478	3	5	-2	-3	SO3/2	-1.1
1974	NY-N	116	334	32	73	15	7	2	43	14	40	.219	.250	.323	.573	60	-19	-19	99	146	23	.453	3	2	-0	12	S32O	0.0
1975	StL-N	16	21	1	4	2	0	0	2	0	2	.190	.190	.286	.476	30	-2	-2	103	129	1	.316	0	0	0	-1	/O2S3	-0.3
	Oak-A	86	87	7	15	0	0	0	3	2	9	.172	.200	.172	.372	6	-11	-10	93	77	3	.260	1	1	-0	-5	S23	-0.8
1977	LA-N	67	137	21	41	6	1	1	10	2	20	.299	.309	.380	.689	84	-3	-3	100	73	15	.564	3	4	-2	4	2S3	0.3
1978	LA-N	54	55	13	14	1	0	1	5	4	14	.255	.317	.327	.644	81	-1	-1	99	94	6	.605	3	2	-0	2	S32	0.2
1979	LA-N	81	112	19	30	5	1	0	2	4	16	.268	.293	.330	.623	70	-5	-5	100	21	10	.506	3	2	-0	-4	3S2	-0.6

YEAR	TM/L	G	AB	R	H	2B	3B	HR	RBI	BB	SO	AVG	OBP	SLG	PRO	/A	BR	/A	PF	CHI	RC	TA	SB	CS	SBR	FR	POS	TPR
Total	9	657	1480	165	355	50	16	7	108	55	213	.240	.271	.309	.580	63	-78	-75	98	88	118	.479	29	20	-3	-5	S2/3O	-4.4
■ **JOE MARTY**	Marty, Joseph Anton b: 9/1/13, Sacramento, Cal. d: 10/4/84, Sacramento, Cal. BR/TR, 6', 182 lbs. Deb: 4/22/37																											
1937	Chi-N	88	290	41	84	17	2	5	44	28	30	.290	.356	.414	.770	106	4	3	103	117	41	.692	3			3	O	0.1
1938	Chi-N	76	235	32	57	8	3	7	35	18	26	.243	.305	.391	.696	86	-4	-5	105	112	27	.604	0			0	O	-0.5
1939	Chi-N	23	76	6	10	1	0	2	10	4	13	.132	.175	.224	.399	6	-10	-10	101	159	2	.329	2			-2	O	-1.2
	Phi-N	91	299	32	76	12	6	9	44	24	27	.254	.310	.425	.734	102	-3	-1	94	105	38	.655	1			6	O/P	0.4
	Yr	114	375	38	86	13	6	11	54	28	40	.229	.283	.384	.667	81	-13	-11	95	117	40	.587	3			3		-0.8
1940	Phi-N	123	455	52	123	21	8	13	50	17	50	.270	.298	.437	.735	104	-2	-0	97	80	54	.631	2			0	*O	-0.4
1941	Phi-N	137	477	60	128	19	3	8	39	51	41	.268	.344	.371	.715	104	1	3	97	72	63	.665	6			-1	*O	-0.2
Total	5	538	1832	223	478	78	22	44	222	142	187	.261	.318	.400	.717	97	-14	-11	99	95	225	.659	14			6	O/P	-1.8
■ **BOB MARTYN**	Martyn, Robert Gordon b: 8/15/30, Weiser, Idaho BL/TR, 6', 176 lbs. Deb: 6/18/57																											
1957	KC-A	58	131	10	35	2	4	1	12	11	20	.267	.324	.366	.690	89	-2	-2	99	93	15	.594	1	3	-2	-4	O	-1.0
1958	KC-A	95	226	25	59	10	7	2	23	26	36	.261	.337	.394	.731	95	0	-1	106	97	30	.671	1	4	-2	-2	O	-0.8
1959	KC-A	1	1	0	0	0	0	0	0	0	0	.000	.000	.000	.000	-99	-0	-0	101	0	0	.000	0	0	0	0	R	0.0
Total	3	154	358	35	94	12	11	3	35	37	56	.263	.332	.383	.714	93	-2	-4	103	95	45	.649	2	7	-4	-5	O	-1.8
■ **GARY MARTZ**	Martz, Gary Arthur b: 1/10/51, Spokane, Wash. BR/TR, 6'4", 210 lbs. Deb: 7/08/75																											
1975	KC-A	1	1	0	0	0	0	0	0	0	0	.000	.000	.000	.000	-98	-0	-0	102	0	0	.000	0	0	0	-0	/O	0.0
■ **JOHN MARZANO**	Marzano, John Robert b: 2/14/63, Philadelphia, Pa. BR/TR, 5'11", 185 lbs. Deb: 7/31/87																											
1987	Bos-A	52	168	20	41	11	0	5	24	7	41	.244	.287	.399	.685	81	-5	-5	99	117	19	.588	0	1	-1	0	C	0.0
1988	Bos-A	10	29	3	4	1	0	0	1	1	3	.138	.167	.172	.339	-4	-4	-4	109	79	1	.231	0	0	0	-0	C	-0.3
Total	2	62	197	23	45	12	0	5	25	8	44	.228	.269	.365	.635	68	-9	-9	101	111	19	.539	0	1	-1	0	/C	-0.3
■ **CLYDE MASHORE**	Mashore, Clyde Wayne b: 5/29/45, Concord, Cal. BR/TR, 6', 182 lbs. Deb: 7/11/69																											
1969	Cin-N	2	1	1	0	0	0	0	0	0	0	.000	.000	.000	.000	-99	-0	-0	99	0	0	.000	0	0	0	0	H	0.0
1970	Mon-N	13	25	2	4	0	0	1	3	4	11	.160	.276	.280	.556	49	-2	-2	100	116	2	.524	0	0	0	-1	O	-0.3
1971	Mon-N	66	114	20	22	5	0	1	7	10	22	.193	.258	.263	.521	48	-8	-8	99	86	8	.436	1	0	0	-8	O/3	-1.8
1972	Mon-N	93	176	23	40	7	1	3	23	14	41	.227	.284	.330	.614	72	-6	-7	102	141	18	.557	6	1	1	-13	O	-2.3
1973	Mon-N	67	103	12	21	3	0	3	14	15	28	.204	.305	.320	.625	71	-4	-4	104	134	11	.598	4	3	-1	-3	O/2	-0.9
Total	5	241	419	58	87	15	1	8	47	43	102	.208	.281	.305	.587	64	-20	-21	102	123	38	.538	11	4	1	-25	O/23	-5.3
■ **PHIL MASI**	Masi, Philip Samuel b: 1/6/17, Chicago, Ill. BR/TR, 5'10", 177 lbs. Deb: 4/23/39																											
1939	Bos-N	46	114	14	29	7	2	1	14	9	15	.254	.315	.377	.692	93	-3	-1	92	112	13	.602	0			1	C	0.1
1940	Bos-N	63	138	11	27	4	1	1	14	14	14	.196	.270	.261	.531	47	-10	-10	99	133	9	.431	0			2	C	-0.4
1941	Bos-N	87	180	17	40	8	2	3	18	16	13	.222	.286	.339	.625	81	-6	-5	93	93	18	.566	4			-5	C	-0.1
1942	Bos-N	57	87	14	19	3	1	0	9	12	4	.218	.313	.276	.589	77	-3	-2	95	139	8	.551	2			-2	C/O	-0.3
1943	Bos-N	80	238	27	65	9	1	2	28	27	20	.273	.347	.345	.692	95	0	-1	106	115	28	.634	7			-0	C	0.2
1944	Bos-N	89	251	33	69	13	5	3	23	31	20	.275	.355	.402	.757	119	4	6	95	75	37	.731	4			2	C1/3	1.0
1945	Bos-N	114	371	55	101	25	4	7	46	42	32	.272	.348	.418	.766	100	6	-0	112	91	54	.739	9			14	C/1	1.5
1946	Bos-N	133	397	52	106	17	5	3	62	55	41	.267	.358	.358	.715	109	3	6	95	153	53	.674	5			-9	*C	0.0
1947	Bos-N	126	411	54	125	22	4	9	50	47	27	.304	.377	.443	.820	121	10	12	97	89	69	.795	7			-1	*C	1.4
1948	Bos-N	113	376	43	95	19	0	5	44	35	26	.253	.318	.343	.661	78	-11	-12	102	114	40	.564	2			5	*C	0.1
1949	Bos-N	37	105	13	22	2	0	0	6	14	10	.210	.303	.229	.531	46	-8	-7	97	94	7	.443	1			0	C	-0.5
	Pit-N	48	135	16	37	6	1	2	13	17	16	.274	.355	.378	.733	96	-0	-0	101	86	18	.670	1			-1	C/1	0.0
	Yr	85	240	29	59	8	1	2	19	31	26	.246	.332	.313	.645	75	-8	-8	99	91	26	.581	2			-1		-0.5
1950	Chi-A	122	377	38	105	17	2	7	55	49	36	.279	.366	.390	.756	96	-3	-1	97	113	54	.696	2	1	0	7	*C	0.9
1951	Chi-A	84	225	24	61	11	2	4	28	32	27	.271	.367	.391	.758	108	2	3	97	100	34	.719	1	0	0	-3	C	0.5
1952	Chi-A	30	63	9	16	1	1	0	7	10	10	.254	.356	.302	.658	84	-1	-1	100	138	8	.604	0	0	0	-3	C	-0.2
Total	14	1229	3468	420	917	164	31	47	417	410	311	.264	.344	.370	.714	96	-19	-14	99	108	450	.685	45	1		7	*C/1O3	4.2
■ **HARRY MASKREY**	Maskrey, Harry H. b: 12/21/1861, Mercer, Pa. d: 8/17/30, Mercer, Pa. Deb: 9/21/1882																											
1882	Lou-a	1	4	0	0	0	0	0		0		.000	.000	.000	.000	-99	-1	-1	94	0	0	.000				0	/O	0.0
■ **LEECH MASKREY**	Maskrey, Samuel Leech b: 2/11/1854, Mercer, Pa. d: 4/1/22, Mercer, Pa. BR/TR, 5'8", 150 lbs. Deb: 5/02/1882																											
1882	Lou-a	76	288	30	65	14	2	0		9		.226	.249	.288	.537	86	-6	-3	94	0	21	.413				-0	*O/2	-0.3
1883	Lou-a	96	361	50	73	13	8	1		10		.202	.224	.291	.515	68	-14	-11	94	0	24	.399				8	*O/S	0.0
1884	Lou-a	105	412	48	103	13	4	0		17		.250	.281	.301	.582	104	-3	4	89	0	36	.460				2	*O/3S	0.4
1885	Lou-a	109	423	54	97	8	11	1		19		.229	.269	.307	.576	82	-7	-9	102	0	36	.469				-3	*O/3	-1.5
1886	Lou-a	5	19	1	3	1	0	0		1		.158	.200	.211	.411	28	-2	-2	108	0	1	.313	0			0	/O	-0.1
	Cin-a	27	98	7	19	3	1	0		5		.194	.240	.245	.485	56	-5	-5	96	0	7	.430	4			0	O/3	-0.3
	Yr	32	117	8	22	4	1	0		6		.188	.234	.239	.473	51	-7	-6	98	0	8	.411	4			0		-0.4
Total	5	418	1601	190	360	52	26	2		61		.225	.256	.294	.550	83	-37	-25	95	0	125	.436	4			7	O/3S2	-1.8
■ **CHARLIE MASON**	Mason, Charles E. b: 6/25/1853, New Orleans, La. d: 10/21/36, Philadelphia, Pa. TR , Deb: 4/26/1875 M																											
1875	Cen-n	12	48	5	11							.229															/O1	
	Nat-n	7	30	1	3							.100															/O	
	Yr	19	78	6	14							.179																
1883	Phi-a	1	2	0	1	0	0	0		0		.500	.500	.500	1.000	217	0	0	103	0	1	1.000				0	/O	0.0
■ **DON MASON**	Mason, Donald Stetson b: 12/20/44, Boston, Mass. BL/TR, 5'11", 160 lbs. Deb: 4/14/66																											
1966	SF-N	42	25	8	3	0	0	1	1	0	2	.120	.120	.240	.360	-3	-3	-3	97	47	1	.261	0	1	-1	0	/2	-0.2
1967	SF-N	4	3	0	0	0	0	0	0	0	0	.000	.000	.000	.000	-99	-1	-1	101	0	0	.000	0	0	0	0	/2	0.0
1968	SF-N	10	19	3	3	0	0	0	1	1	4	.158	.200	.158	.358	9	-2	-2	98	140	1	.294	1	1	-0	-0	/2S3	-0.1
1969	SF-N	104	250	43	57	4	2	0	13	36	29	.228	.325	.260	.585	65	-10	-11	101	80	24	.515	1	5	-3	0	23/S	-0.7
1970	SF-N	46	36	4	5	0	0	0	1	5	7	.139	.244	.139	.383	6	-5	-5	96	78	1	.294	0	0	0	-1	2	-0.3
1971	SD-N	113	344	43	73	12	1	2	11	27	35	.212	.270	.270	.540	55	-21	-20	96	45	24	.441	6	4	-1	-4	2/3	-2.1
1972	SD-N	9	11	1	2	0	0	0	0	1	1	.182	.250	.182	.432	28	-1	-1	88	0	1	.333	0	0	0	0	/2	0.0
1973	SD-N	8	8	0	0	0	0	0	0	0	2	.000	.000	.000	.000	-99	-2	-2	94	0	0	.000	0	0	0	0	/2	-0.1
Total	8	336	696	102	143	16	3	3	27	70	80	.205	.278	.250	.528	51	-45	-44	98	61	50	.446	8	11	-4	-4	2/3S	-3.5
■ **JIM MASON**	Mason, James Percy b: 8/14/50, Mobile, Ala. BL/TR, 6'2", 185 lbs. Deb: 9/26/71																											
1971	Was-A	3	9	0	3	0	0	0	0	1	3	.333	.400	.333	.733	119	0	0	92	0	1	.667	0	0	0	0	/S	0.1
1972	Tex-A	46	147	10	29	3	0	0	10	9	39	.197	.248	.218	.466	42	-11	-10	94	131	8	.347	0	0	0	-4	S3	-1.2
1973	Tex-A	92	238	23	49	7	2	3	19	23	48	.206	.276	.290	.566	61	-13	-12	97	96	20	.477	0	1	-1	1	S2/3	0.0
1974	NY-A	152	440	41	110	18	6	5	37	35	87	.250	.305	.352	.658	93	-7	-5	96	86	48	.565	1	2	-1	1	*S	0.8
1975	NY-A	94	223	17	34	3	2	2	16	22	49	.152	.229	.211	.439	25	-22	-22	99	116	10	.343	0	2	-1	-7	S/2	-2.1
1976	NY-A	93	217	17	39	7	1	1	14	9	37	.180	.212	.235	.447	31	-19	-19	99	100	11	.330	0	0	0	-8	S	-2.2
1977	Tor-A	22	79	10	13	3	0	0	2	7	10	.165	.233	.203	.435	19	-9	-9	103	50	4	.353	1	1	-0	-2	S	-0.8
	Tex-A	36	55	9	12	3	0	1	7	6	10	.218	.295	.327	.622	66	-2	-3	105	132	6	.545	0	0	0	2	S/3D	0.3
	Yr	58	134	19	25	6	0	1	9	13	20	.187	.259	.254	.512	39	-11	-12	104	102	10	.432	1	1	-0	0		-0.5
1978	Tex-A	55	105	10	20	4	0	0	3	5	17	.190	.227	.229	.456	30	-10	-9	96	49	6	.333	0	0	0	1	S3/2D	-0.4
1979	Mon-N	40	71	3	13	5	1	0	6	7	16	.183	.256	.282	.538	46	-5	-6	102	119	4	.429	0	2	-1	-1	S/3	-0.4
Total	9	633	1584	140	322	53	12	12	114	124	316	.203	.262	.275	.536	54	-98	-93	98	96	117	.441	2	8	-4	-18	S/32D	-5.9
■ **GORDON MASSA**	Massa, Gordon Richard "Moose" or "Duke" b: 9/2/35, Cincinnati, Ohio BL/TR, 6'3", 210 lbs. Deb: 9/24/57																											
1957	Chi-N	6	15	2	7	1	0	0	3	4	3	.467	.579	.533	1.112	209	3	3	96	155	5	1.500	0	0	0	0	/C	0.3
1958	Chi-N	2	2	0	0	0	0	0	0	0	2	.000	.000	.000	.000	-99	-1	-1	101	0	0	.000	0	0	0	0	H	0.0

YEAR	TM/L	G	AB	R	H	2B	3B	HR	RBI	BB	SO	AVG	OBP	SLG	PRO	/A	BR	/A	PF	CHI	RC	TA	SB	CS	SBR	FR	POS	TPR
Total	2	8	17	2	7	1	0	0	3	4	5	.412	.524	.471	.994	175	2	2	97	141	5	1.200	0	0	0	0	/C	0.3
■ **RED MASSEY**	Massey, Roy Hardee "Roy" or "Red" b: 10/9/1890, Sevierville, Tenn. d: 6/23/54, Atlanta, Ga. BL/TR, 5'11", 170 lbs. Deb: 4/16/18																											
1918	Bos-N	66	203	20	59	6	2	0	18	23	20	.291	.363	.340	.703	122	4	6	94	99	25	.646	1			2	O/31S	0.6
■ **BILL MASSEY**	Massey, William Harry "Big Bill" b: 1/1871, Philadelphia, Pa. d: 10/9/40, Manila, Philippines BR , 5'11", 168 lbs. Deb: 9/18/1894																											
1894	Cin-N	13	53	7	15	3	0	0	5	3	2	.283	.321	.340	.661	61	-3	-3	100	81	6	.553	0			0	1/23	-0.2
■ **MIKE MASSEY**	Massey, William Herbert b: 9/28/1893, Galveston, Tex. d: 10/17/71, Shreveport, La. BB/TR, 6', 195 lbs. Deb: 4/12/17																											
1917	Bos-N	31	91	12	18	0	0	0	2	15	15	.198	.318	.198	.516	62	-3	-3	96	43	7	.493	2			-3	2	-0.4
■ **VICTOR MATA**	Mata, Victor Jose (Abreu) b: 6/17/61, Santiago, D.R. BR/TR, 6'1", 165 lbs. Deb: 7/22/84																											
1984	NY-A	30	70	8	23	5	0	1	6	0	12	.329	.338	.443	.781	121	1	2	94	70	10	.673	1	1	-0	-3	O	-0.2
1985	NY-A	6	7	1	1	0	0	0	0	0	0	.143	.143	.143	.286	-22	-1	-1	96	0	0	.167	0	0	0	-1	/O	-0.1
Total	2	36	77	9	24	5	0	1	6	0	12	.312	.321	.416	.736	108	-0	1	94	64	10	.630	1	1	-0	-4	/O	-0.3
■ **TOMMY MATCHICK**	Matchick, John Thomas b: 9/7/43, Hazleton, Pa. BL/TR, 6'1", 173 lbs. Deb: 9/02/67																											
1967	Det-A	8	6	1	1	0	0	0	0	0	2	.167	.167	.167	.333	-1	-1	-1	99	0	0	.200	0	0	0	0	/S	0.0
1968	Det-A	80	227	18	46	6	2	3	14	10	46	.203	.249	.286	.535	58	-11	-12	106	81	16	.425	0	2	-1	-4	S2/1	-1.4
1969	Det-A	94	298	25	72	11	2	0	32	15	51	.242	.278	.292	.570	58	-16	-18	103	148	23	.449	3	0	1	-1	23/S1	-1.5
1970	Bos-A	10	14	2	1	0	0	0	0	2	2	.071	.188	.071	.259	-23	-2	-3	111	0	0	.214	0	1	-1	0	/32S	-0.2
	KC-A	55	158	11	31	3	2	0	11	5	23	.196	.226	.241	.466	29	-15	-15	98	117	7	.326	0	0	0	1	S2/3	-0.9
	Yr	65	172	13	32	3	2	0	11	7	25	.186	.222	.227	.449	24	-18	-18	100	99	7	.315	0	1	-1	1		-1.1
1971	Mil-A	42	114	6	25	1	0	1	7	7	23	.219	.264	.254	.519	46	-8	-8	103	89	8	.424	3	2	-0	-5	3/2	-1.5
1972	Bal-A	3	9	0	2	0	0	0	0	0	1	.222	.222	.222	.444	33	-1	-1	98	0	0	.250	0	1	-1	0	/3	0.0
Total	6	292	826	63	178	21	6	4	64	39	148	.215	.255	.270	.525	49	-54	-57	103	110	54	.417	6	6	-2	-8	S/321	-5.5
■ **JOE MATHES**	Mathes, Joseph John b: 7/28/1891, Milwaukee, Wis. BB/TR, 6'0.5", 180 lbs. Deb: 9/19/12																											
1912	Phi-A	4	14	0	2	0	0	0	0	0		.143	.200	.143	.343	-1	-2	-2	99	0	0	.250	0			0	/3	-0.1
1914	StL-F	26	85	10	25	3	0	0	6	9	11	.294	.362	.329	.691	93	0	-0	106	77	11	.633	1			-7	2	-0.6
1916	Bos-N	2	0	0	0	0	0	0	0	0	0	—	—	—	—	—	0	0	93	—	—	—	0			0	/2	0.0
Total	3	32	99	10	27	3	0	0	6	9	11	.273	.339	.303	.642	81	-2	-2	105	67	22	.569	1			-7	/23	-0.7
■ **EDDIE MATHEWS**	Mathews, Edwin Lee b: 10/13/31, Texarkana, Tex. BL/TR, 6'1", 190 lbs. Deb: 4/15/52 MCH																											
1952	Bos-N	145	528	80	128	23	5	25	58	59	115	.242	.320	.447	.767	116	6	9	95	77	78	.731	6	4	-1	-9	*3	0.4
1953	Mil-N	157	579	110	175	31	8	**47**	135	99	83	.302	.406	.627	1.033	**174**	55	60	94	100	157	1.126	1	3	-2	3	*3	5.4
1954	Mil-N	138	476	96	138	21	4	40	103	113	61	.290	.428	.603	1.031	**177**	49	53	93	106	131	**1.177**	10	3	1	0	*3O	5.4
1955	Mil-N	141	499	108	144	23	5	41	101	**109**	98	.289	.417	.601	1.018	**179**	50	55	93	102	131	1.135	3	4	-2	-5	*3	4.6
1956	Mil-N	151	552	103	150	21	2	37	95	91	86	.272	.376	.518	.894	139	30	31	99	107	114	.946	6	0	2	-11	*3	2.1
1957	Mil-N	148	572	109	167	28	9	32	94	90	79	.292	.388	.540	.928	162	38	46	90	93	126	.976	3	1	0	0	*3	4.9
1958	Mil-N	149	546	97	137	18	1	31	77	85	85	.251	.354	.458	.812	126	11	19	89	89	94	.818	5	0	2	5	*3	2.5
1959	Mil-N	148	594	118	182	16	8	**46**	114	80	71	.306	.391	.593	.984	166	48	52	95	81	143	1.043	2	1	0	3	*3	5.0
1960	Mil-N	153	548	108	152	19	7	39	124	111	113	.277	.401	.551	.952	174	46	**53**	91	115	**128**	1.037	7	3	0	-13	*3	3.8
1961	Mil-N	152	572	103	175	23	6	32	91	**93**	95	.306	.405	.535	.940	159	40	47	92	88	128	.998	12	7	-1	-6	*3	3.3
1962	Mil-N	152	536	106	142	25	6	29	90	**101**	90	.265	.383	.496	.880	135	28	28	99	106	106	.916	4	2	0	7	*3/1	3.7
1963	Mil-N	158	547	82	144	27	4	23	84	**124**	119	.263	**.400**	.453	.854	144	37	37	101	118	106	.904	3	4	-2	11	*3O	4.7
1964	Mil-N	141	502	83	117	19	1	23	74	85	100	.233	.345	.412	.758	116	10	12	97	117	75	.747	2	2	-1	-0	*3/1	0.4
1965	Mil-N	156	546	77	137	23	0	32	95	73	110	.251	.342	.469	.811	121	19	16	104	114	89	.793	1	0	0	7	*3	1.8
1966	Atl-N	134	452	72	113	21	4	16	53	63	82	.250	.342	.420	.762	112	7	8	99	96	67	.734	1	1	-0	-2	*3	0.4
1967	Hou-N	101	328	39	78	13	2	10	38	48	65	.238	.337	.381	.718	112	3	6	94	102	43	.680	2	4	-2	-2	13	-0.3
	Det-A	36	108	14	25	3	0	6	19	15	23	.231	.336	.426	.762	125	3	3	99	124	17	.750	0	0	0	0	31	0.3
1968	Det-A	31	52	4	11	0	0	3	8	5	12	.212	.281	.385	.665	94	-0	-0	106	118	6	.610	0	0	0	0	/13	0.0
Total	17	2391	8537	1509	2315	354	72	512	1453	1444	1487	.271	.378	.509	.888	145	480	535	95	101	1738	.940	68	39	-3	-14	*31/O	48.4
■ **NELSON MATHEWS**	Mathews, Nelson Elmer b: 7/21/41, Columbia, Ill. BR/TR, 6'4", 195 lbs. Deb: 9/09/60																											
1960	Chi-N	3	8	1	2	0	0	0	0	0	2	.250	.250	.250	.500	38	-1	-1	98	0	1	.333	0	0	0	0	/O	0.0
1961	Chi-N	3	9	0	1	0	0	0	0	0	2	.111	.111	.111	.222	-41	-2	-2	100	0	0	.125	0	0	0	0	/O	-0.1
1962	Chi-N	15	49	5	15	2	0	2	13	5	4	.306	.393	.469	.862	123	2	2	106	180	8	.868	3	3	-1	-1	O	0.0
1963	Chi-N	61	155	12	24	3	2	4	10	16	48	.155	.234	.277	.511	44	-11	-12	105	76	9	.443	3	4	-2	1	O	-1.5
1964	KC-A	157	573	58	137	27	5	14	60	43	143	.239	.293	.377	.670	81	-13	-16	105	101	59	.573	2	3	-1	-0	*O	-2.4
1965	KC-A	67	184	17	39	7	7	2	15	24	49	.212	.303	.359	.662	90	-3	-2	97	86	20	.596	0	2	-1	-1	O	-0.6
Total	6	306	978	93	218	39	14	22	98	88	248	.223	.289	.359	.648	78	-27	-30	103	96	96	.580	8	12	-5	-1	O	-4.6
■ **JIMMY MATHISON**	Mathison, James I. b: 11/1878, Baltimore, Md. d: 7/4/11, Baltimore, Md. TR , Deb: 8/29/02																											
1902	Bal-A	29	91	12	24	2	1	0	7	9		.264	.330	.308	.638	78	-2	-3	102	82	10	.582	2			-6	3/S	-0.8
■ **JOHN MATIAS**	Matias, John Roy b: 8/15/44, Honolulu, Hawaii BL/TL, 5'11", 170 lbs. Deb: 4/07/70																											
1970	Chi-A	58	117	7	22	2	0	2	6	3	22	.188	.215	.256	.471	28	-11	-12	106	67	6	.361	1	0	0	-4	O1	-1.8
■ **GARY MATTHEWS**	Matthews, Gary Nathaniel b: 7/5/50, San Fernando, Cal. BR/TR, 6'2", 185 lbs. Deb: 9/06/72																											
1972	SF-N	20	62	11	18	1	1	4	14	7	13	.290	.362	.532	.895	152	4	4	100	128	11	.870	0	1	-1	-2	O	0.1
1973	SF-N	148	540	74	162	22	10	12	58	58	83	.300	.369	.444	.813	119	18	15	105	86	90	.800	17	5	2	-1	*O	1.0
1974	SF-N	154	561	87	161	27	6	16	82	70	69	.287	.369	.442	.811	117	20	14	108	113	90	.783	11	9	-2	-1	*O	0.6
1975	SF-N	116	425	67	119	22	3	12	58	65	53	.280	.378	.431	.809	122	15	14	102	108	71	.814	13	4	2	6	*O	1.8
1976	SF-N	156	587	79	164	28	4	20	84	75	94	.279	.362	.443	.805	124	21	19	103	107	98	.798	12	5	1	-12	*O	0.2
1977	Atl-N	148	555	89	157	25	5	17	64	67	90	.283	.362	.438	.800	101	11	2	113	92	89	.797	22	8	2	-1	*O	-0.2
1978	Atl-N	129	474	75	135	20	5	18	62	61	92	.285	.369	.462	.831	117	20	13	112	95	78	.801	8	7	-2	-1	*O	0.6
1979	Atl-N	156	631	97	192	34	5	27	90	60	75	.304	.365	.502	.867	123	28	21	109	79	118	.876	18	6	2	-17	*O	0.1
1980	Atl-N	155	571	79	159	17	3	19	75	42	93	.278	.328	.419	.746	106	4	3	101	102	76	.677	11	3	2	-9	*O	-1.0
1981	Phi-N	101	359	62	108	21	3	9	67	59	42	.301	.404	.451	.855	127	22	17	112	**147**	71	.916	15	2	3	-2	*O	1.6
1982	Phi-N	162	616	89	173	31	1	19	83	66	87	.281	.352	.427	.779	125	14	19	94	108	91	.749	21	4	4	-2	*O	2.0
1983	Phi-N	132	446	66	115	18	2	10	50	69	81	.258	.357	.374	.732	102	3	3	101	102	62	.716	13	9	-2	-5	*O	-0.5
1984	Chi-N	147	491	101	143	21	2	14	82	**103**	97	.291	**.417**	.428	.845	125	30	24	110	135	96	.910	17	8	0	-12	*O	0.7
1985	Chi-N	97	298	45	70	12	0	13	40	59	64	.235	.365	.406	.771	99	8	2	116	100	47	.780	2	0	1	-7	O	-0.6
1986	Chi-N	123	370	49	96	16	1	21	46	60	59	.259	.363	.478	.841	122	15	12	107	76	63	.825	3	2	-0	-12	*O	-0.1
1987	Chi-N	44	42	3	11	3	0	0	8	4	11	.262	.326	.333	.659	75	-1	-1	101	228	4	.563	0	0	0	-0	/O	-0.1
	Sea-A	45	119	10	28	1	0	3	15	15	22	.235	.321	.319	.640	70	-5	-5	103	127	11	.541	0	1	-1	0	D	-0.5
Total	16	2033	7147	1083	2011	319	51	234	978	940	1125	.281	.367	.439	.805	116	229	175	106	105	1167	.820	183	74	11	-77	*O/D	5.7
■ **BOB MATTHEWS**	Matthews, Robert b: Camden, N.J. Deb: 9/25/1891																											
1891	Phi-a	1	3	1	1	0	0	0	0	0	1	.333	.600	.333	.933	168	1	1	103	0	1	1.500	0			0	/O	0.0
■ **WID MATTHEWS**	Matthews, Wid Curry "Matty" b: 10/20/1896, Raleigh, Ill d: 10/5/65, Hollywood, Cal. BL/TL, 5'8.5", 155 lbs. Deb: 4/18/23																											
1923	Phi-A	129	485	52	133	11	6	1	25	50	27	.274	.343	.328	.671	77	-15	-15	100	56	54	.612	16	17	-5	-13	*O	-4.4
1924	Was-A	53	169	25	51	10	4	0	13	11	4	.302	.355	.408	.763	98	-1	-1	98	62	23	.683	3	8	-4	8	O	0.0
1925	Was-A	10	9	2	4	0	0	0	1	0	1	.444	.444	.444	.889	129	0	0	98	84	2	.800	0	0	0	-0	/O	0.0
Total	3	192	663	79	188	21	10	1	39	61	32	.284	.348	.350	.697	83	-16	-16	100	58	79	.632	19	25	-9	-6	O	-4.4
■ **STEVE MATTHIAS**	Matthias, Stephen J. b: 1860, Mitchellville, Md. 5'8", 160 lbs. Deb: 4/20/1884																											
1884	CP-U	37	142	24	39	7	1	0		5		.275	.299	.338	.637	116	2	2	99	0	15	.515	0			0	S/O	0.3

YEAR	TM/L	G	AB	R	H	2B	3B	HR	RBI	BB	SO	AVG	OBP	SLG	PRO	/A	BR	/A	PF	CHI	RC	TA	SB	CS	SBR	FR	POS	TPR
■ **BOBBY MATTICK**	Mattick, Robert James b: 12/5/15, Sioux City, Iowa BR/TR, 5'11", 178 lbs. Deb: 5/05/38 M																											
1938	Chi-N	1	1	0	1	0	0	0	1	0	0	1.000	1.000	1.000	2.000	430	0	0	105	362	1	—	0			0	/S	0.1
1939	Chi-N	51	178	16	51	12	1	0	23	6	19	.287	.314	.365	.679	81	-5	-5	101	130	20	.557	1			1	S	0.0
1940	Chi-N	128	441	30	96	15	0	0	33	19	33	.218	.250	.252	.502	39	-37	-36	100	110	27	.382	5			6	*S/3	-1.8
1941	Cin-N	20	60	8	11	3	0	0	7	8	7	.183	.279	.233	.513	46	-4	-4	99	181	4	.460	1			-0	S/32	-0.2
1942	Cin-N	6	10	0	2	1	0	0	0	0	1	.200	.200	.300	.500	45	-1	-1	101	0	1	.375	0			-0	/S	0.0
Total	5	206	690	54	161	31	1	0	64	33	60	.233	.269	.281	.550	51	-46	-46	100	121	53	.444	7			7	S/32	-1.9
■ **WALLY MATTICK**	Mattick, Walter Joseph "Chink" b: 3/12/1887, St.Louis, Mo. d: 11/5/68, Los Altos, Cal. BR/TR, 5'10", 180 lbs. Deb: 4/11/12																											
1912	Chi-A	88	285	45	74	7	9	1	35	27		.260	.334	.358	.692	99	-1	-0	99	113	40	.706	15			0	O	-0.4
1913	Chi-A	71	207	15	39	8	1	0	11	18	16	.188	.253	.237	.490	46	-15	-14	95	80	14	.417	3			5	O	-1.2
1918	StL-N	8	14	0	2	0	0	0	1	2	3	.143	.333	.143	.476	50	-1	-1	93	189	1	.500	0			0	/O	0.0
Total	3	167	506	60	115	15	10	1	47	47	19	.227	.302	.302	.604	77	-16	-14	97	102	54	.575	18			6	O	-1.6
■ **MIKE MATTIMORE**	Mattimore, Michael Joseph b: 1859, Renovo, Pa. d: 4/28/31, Butte, Mont. BL/TR, 5'8.5", 160 lbs. Deb: 5/03/1887																											
1887	NY-N	8	32	5	8	1	0	0	4	0	6	.250	.250	.281	.531	45	-2	-3	107	140	3	.417	1			0	/PO	0.0
1888	Phi-a	41	142	22	38	6	5	0	12	12		.268	.333	.380	.714	131	5	5	101	66	24	.808	16			0	PO	0.0
1889	Phi-a	23	73	10	17	1	2	1	8	9	7	.233	.333	.342	.676	97	-0	0	98	82	11	.750	6			0	O/1P	0.0
	KC-a	19	75	6	12	1	1	0	5	3	16	.160	.192	.200	.392	12	-8	-9	106	97	3	.286	0			0	O/P	-0.7
	Yr	42	148	16	29	2	3	1	13	12	23	.196	.265	.270	.536	54	-9	-9	101	91	13	.504	6			0		-0.7
1890	BB-a	33	129	14	17	1	1	0		16		.132	.238	.155	.393	18	-13	-13	100	0	8	.438	11			0	PO	0.0
Total	4	124	451	57	92	10	9	1	29	40	29	.204	.278	.273	.550	65	-18	-19	101	59	48	.565	34			0	/OP1	-0.7
■ **DON MATTINGLY**	Mattingly, Donald Arthur b: 4/20/61, Evansville, Ind. BL/TL, 6', 175 lbs. Deb: 9/08/82																											
1982	NY-A	7	12	0	2	0	0	0	1	0	1	.167	.167	.167	.333	-8	-2	-2	96	200	0	.167	0	0	0	0	/O1	-0.1
1983	NY-A	91	279	34	79	15	4	4	32	21	31	.283	.336	.409	.744	105	1	2	99	99	37	.654	0	0	0	-7	O1/2	-0.6
1984	NY-A	153	603	91	**207**	**44**	2	23	110	41	33	**.343**	.386	.537	.923	162	41	46	94	118	120	.891	1	1	-0	7	*1O	4.3
1985	NY-A	159	652	107	211	**48**	3	35	**145**	56	41	.324	.379	.567	.946	162	48	51	96	107	136	.939	2	2	-1	-12	*1	2.8
1986	NY-A	162	677	117	**238**	**53**	2	31	113	53	35	.352	.399	**.573**	**.973**	157	**57**	**54**	103	83	**150**	.969	0	0	0	-10	*1/3D	3.2
1987	NY-A	141	569	93	186	38	2	30	115	51	38	.327	.383	.559	.942	150	37	39	98	108	115	.921	1	4	-2	-3	*1/D	1.8
1988	NY-A	144	599	94	186	37	0	18	88	41	29	.311	.358	.462	.820	134	21	24	96	102	96	.756	1	0	0	-4	*1/OD	1.2
Total	7	857	3391	536	1109	235	13	141	604	263	208	.327	.377	.529	.906	149	204	215	97	103	655	.899	5	7	-3	-28	1/OD32	12.6
■ **RALPH MATTIS**	Mattis, Ralph "Matty" b: 8/24/1890, Roxborough, Pa. d: 9/13/60, Williamsport, Pa. BR/TR, 5'11", 172 lbs. Deb: 4/22/14																											
1914	Pit-F	36	85	14	21	4	1	0	8	9	11	.247	.319	.318	.637	88	-2	-1	94	107	10	.594	2			1	O	-0.1
■ **CLOY MATTOX**	Mattox, Cloy Mitchell "Monk" b: 11/24/02, Leesville, Va. d: 8/3/85, Danville, Va. BL/TR, 5'8", 168 lbs. Deb: 9/01/29																											
1929	Phi-A	3	6	0	1	0	0	0	0	1	1	.167	.286	.167	.452	18	-1	-1	109	0	0	.400	0	0	0	0	/C	0.0
■ **JIM MATTOX**	Mattox, James Powell b: 12/17/1896, Leesville, Va. d: 10/12/73, Myrtle Beach, S.C. BL/TR, 5'9.5", 168 lbs. Deb: 4/30/22																											
1922	Pit-N	29	51	11	15	1	1	0	3	1	3	.294	.308	.353	.661	68	-2	-3	104	58	5	.528	0	0	0	-0	C	-0.2
1923	Pit-N	22	32	4	6	1	1	0	1	0	5	.188	.235	.281	.517	37	-3	-3	97	39	2	.423	0	0	0	0	/C	-0.1
Total	2	51	83	15	21	2	2	0	4	1	8	.253	.279	.325	.604	56	-5	-5	101	51	8	.484	0	0	0	-0	/C	-0.3
■ **LEN MATUSZEK**	Matuszek, Leonard James b: 9/27/54, Toledo, Ohio BL/TR, 6'2", 190 lbs. Deb: 9/03/81																											
1981	Phi-N	13	11	1	3	1	0	0	1	3	1	.273	.429	.364	.792	113	1	0	112	98	2	.778	0	1	-1	1	/13	0.1
1982	Phi-N	25	39	1	3	1	0	0	3	1	10	.077	.122	.103	.225	-39	-7	-7	94	294	0	.150	0	1	-1	0	/31	-0.7
1983	Phi-N	28	80	12	22	6	1	4	16	4	14	.275	.310	.525	.835	126	2	2	101	117	12	.767	0	1	-1	0	1	0.1
1984	Phi-N	101	262	40	65	17	1	12	43	39	54	.248	.354	.458	.812	124	10	9	102	108	43	.807	4	3	-1	-0	1/O	0.6
1985	Tor-A	62	151	23	32	6	2	2	15	11	24	.212	.265	.318	.583	58	-9	-9	101	110	12	.488	2	1	0	0	D/1	-0.8
	LA-N	43	63	10	14	2	1	3	13	8	14	.222	.319	.429	.748	115	1	1	93	144	9	.720	0	1	-1	-2	O1/3	-0.1
1986	LA-N	91	199	26	52	7	0	9	28	21	47	.261	.335	.432	.767	117	2	4	94	99	29	.724	2	2	-1	-3	O1	-0.1
1987	LA-N	16	15	0	1	0	0	0	0	1	4	.067	.125	.067	.192	-52	-3	-3	92	0	0	.143	0	0	0	0	/1	-0.2
Total	7	379	820	113	192	40	5	30	119	88	168	.234	.314	.405	.719	99	-3	-2	99	116	107	.682	8	10	-4	-4	1/OD3	-1.1
■ **GENE MAUCH**	Mauch, Gene William "Skip" b: 11/18/25, Salina, Kan. BR/TR, 5'10", 165 lbs. Deb: 4/18/44 M																											
1944	Bro-N	5	15	2	2	1	0	0	2	2	3	.133	.235	.200	.435	24	-2	-2	99	239	1	.385	0			-1	/S	-0.1
1947	Pit-N	16	30	8	9	0	0	0	1	7	6	.300	.432	.300	.732	97	0	0	101	41	5	.762	0			-1	/2S	0.0
1948	Bro-N	12	13	1	2	0	0	0	0	1	4	.154	.214	.154	.368	1	-2	-2	104	0	1	.273	0			0	/2S	0.0
	Chi-N	53	138	18	28	3	2	1	7	26	10	.203	.329	.275	.605	70	-6	-5	93	64	15	.591	1			1	2S	0.0
	Yr	65	151	19	30	3	2	1	7	27	14	.199	.320	.265	.585	63	-8	-7	95	52	15	.562	1			1		0.0
1949	Chi-N	72	150	15	37	6	2	1	7	21	15	.247	.339	.333	.673	86	-4	-2	94	50	17	.617	3			5	2S/3	0.5
1950	Bos-N	48	121	17	28	5	0	1	15	14	9	.231	.316	.298	.614	73	-6	-4	86	148	11	.531	1			-4	2/3S	-0.6
1951	Bos-N	19	20	5	2	0	0	0	1	7	4	.100	.333	.100	.433	23	-2	-2	98	193	1	.500	0	0	0	0	S/32	0.0
1952	StL-N	7	3	0	0	0	0	0	0	1	2	.000	.250	.000	.250	-26	-0	-0	98	0	0	.333	0	0	0	0	/S	0.0
1956	Bos-A	7	25	4	8	0	0	0	1	3	3	.320	.393	.320	.713	88	-0	-0	103	47	3	.611	0	0	0	0	/2	0.0
1957	Bos-A	65	222	23	60	10	3	2	28	22	26	.270	.339	.369	.708	85	-2	-5	110	126	27	.620	1	0	0	-1	2	-0.1
Total	9	304	737	93	176	25	7	5	62	104	82	.239	.335	.312	.647	76	-23	-21	98	97	80	.600	6	0		-1	2/S3	-0.3
■ **AL MAUL**	Maul, Albert Joseph "Smiling Al" b: 10/9/1865, Philadelphia, Pa. d: 5/3/58, Philadelphia, Pa. BR/TR, 6', 175 lbs. Deb: 6/20/1884																											
1884	Phi-U	1	4	0	0	0	0	0		0		.000	.000	.000	.000	-99	-1	-1	93	0	0	.000	0			0	/P	0.0
1887	Phi-N	16	56	15	17	2	2	1	4	15	10	.304	.451	.464	.915	162	5	6	97	45	14	1.179	5			0	/OP1	0.5
1888	Pit-N	74	259	21	54	9	4	0	31	21	45	.208	.276	.274	.550	82	-6	-4	95	159	23	.507	9			-3	1O/P	-0.9
1889	Pit-N	68	257	37	71	6	6	4	44	29	41	.276	.356	.393	.749	125	4	9	89	123	43	.812	18			11	O/P	1.5
1890	Pit-P	45	162	31	42	6	2	0	21	22	12	.259	.348	.321	.669	88	-4	-1	92	113	20	.658	5			0	PO/S	0.0
1891	Pit-N	47	149	15	28	2	4	0	14	20	28	.188	.284	.255	.539	58	-7	-8	101	107	12	.512	4			-2	O/P	-1.0
1893	Was-N	44	134	10	34	8	4	0	12	33	14	.254	.405	.373	.778	122	3	6	90	66	21	.850	1			1	P/O	0.0
1894	Was-N	41	124	23	30	3	3	2	20	14	11	.242	.352	.363	.715	76	-5	-4	98	108	17	.713	1			2	PO	0.0
1895	Was-N	22	72	9	18	5	2	0	16	6	7	.250	.308	.375	.683	75	-3	-3	103	166	9	.611	0			0	P/O	0.0
1896	Was-N	8	28	6	8	1	1	0	5	3	2	.286	.355	.393	.748	104	-0	0	95	131	4	.700	0			0	/P	0.0
1897	Was-N	1	1	0	0	0	0	0	0	0		.000	.000	.000	.000	-99	-0	-0	101	0	0	.000	0			0	/P	0.0
	Bal-N	2	3	0	1	0	0	0	0	0		.333	.333	.333	.667	82	-0	-0	95	0	0	.500	0			0	/P	0.0
	Yr	3	4	0	1	0	0	0	0	0		.250	.250	.250	.500	35	-0	-0	97	0	0	.333	0			0		0.0
1898	Bal-N	29	93	21	19	3	2	0	10	16		.204	.333	.280	.613	76	-2	-2	103	119	9	.608	1			-4	P/O	0.0
1899	Bro-N	4	11	2	3	0	0	0	0	1		.273	.333	.273	.606	66	-0	-0	105	0	1	.500	0			0	/P	0.0
1900	Phi-N	5	15	2	3	0	0	0	1	2		.200	.294	.200	.494	40	-1	-1	98	104	1	.417	0			0	/P	0.0
1901	NY-N	3	8	1	3	0	0	0	1	0		.375	.375	.375	.750	132	0	0	91	112	1	.600	0			0	/P	0.0
Total	15	410	1376	193	331	45	30	7	179	182	170	.241	.336	.332	.668	93	-16	-4	95	116	176	.669	44			5	PO/1S	0.1
■ **MARK MAULDIN**	Mauldin, Marshall Reese b: 11/5/14, Atlanta, Ga. BR/TR, 5'11", 170 lbs. Deb: 9/10/34																											
1934	Chi-A	10	38	3	10	2	0	1	3	0	3	.263	.263	.395	.658	68	-2	-2	99	56	4	.536	0	0	0	0	3	-0.1
■ **CARMEN MAURO**	Mauro, Carmen Louis b: 11/10/26, St.Paul, Minn. BL/TR, 6', 167 lbs. Deb: 10/01/48																											
1948	Chi-N	3	5	2	1	0	0	1	1	2	0	.200	.429	.800	1.229	243	1	1	93	53	2	1.500	0			1	/O	0.1
1950	Chi-N	62	185	19	42	4	3	1	10	13	31	.227	.285	.297	.582	51	-13	-14	105	66	16	.497	3			-6	O	-2.0
1951	Chi-N	13	29	3	5	1	0	0	3	2	6	.172	.250	.207	.457	25	-3	-3	97	193	2	.375	0	0	0	1	/O	-0.1
1953	Bro-N	8	9	1	0	0	0	0	0	0	4	.000	.000	.000	.000	-96	-3	-3	104	0	0	.000	0	0	0	-0	/O	-0.2
	Was-A	17	23	1	4	0	1	0	2	1	3	.174	.208	.261	.469	28	-2	-2	94	123	1	.368	0	0	0	0	/O	-0.2
	Phi-A	64	165	14	44	4	4	0	17	19	21	.267	.342	.339	.682	83	-3	-4	102	112	18	.595	3	4	-2	3	O/3	-0.3
	Yr	81	188	15	48	4	5	0	19	20	24	.255	.327	.330	.657	77	-6	-6	101	116	20	.567	3	4	-2	3		-0.5

YEAR	TM/L	G	AB	R	H	2B	3B	HR	RBI	BB	SO	AVG	OBP	SLG	PRO	/A	BR	/A	PF	CHI	RC	TA	SB	CS	SBR	FR	POS	TPR
Total	4	167	416	40	96	9	8	2	33	37	65	.231	.298	.305	.604	60	-23	-24	102	95	39	.524	6	4		-1	O/3	-2.7

■ **BOB MAVIS** Mavis, Robert Henry b: 4/8/18, Milwaukee, Wis. BL/TR, 5'7", 160 lbs. Deb: 9/17/49

YEAR	TM/L	G	AB	R	H	2B	3B	HR	RBI	BB	SO	AVG	OBP	SLG	PRO	/A	BR	/A	PF	CHI	RC	TA	SB	CS	SBR	FR	POS	TPR
1949	Det-A	1	0	0	0	0	0	0	0	0	0	—	—	—	—	—	0	0	108	—	—	—	0	0	0	0	R	0.0

■ **DAL MAXVILL** Maxvill, Charles Dallan b: 2/18/39, Granite City, Ill. BR/TR, 5'11", 157 lbs. Deb: 6/10/62 C

YEAR	TM/L	G	AB	R	H	2B	3B	HR	RBI	BB	SO	AVG	OBP	SLG	PRO	/A	BR	/A	PF	CHI	RC	TA	SB	CS	SBR	FR	POS	TPR
1962	StL-N	79	189	20	42	3	1	1	18	17	39	.222	.290	.265	.554	46	-13	-15	109	134	15	.457	1	2	-1	1	S/3	-0.7
1963	StL-N	53	51	12	12	2	0	0	3	6	11	.235	.316	.275	.590	67	-2	-2	107	90	5	.500	0	0	0	-1	S/23	0.0
1964	StL-N	37	26	4	6	0	0	0	4	0	7	.231	.231	.231	.462	27	-2	-3	112	273	2	.350	1	0	0	-0	2S/3O	0.0
1965	StL-N	68	89	10	12	2	2	0	10	7	15	.135	.206	.202	.408	15	-10	-11	107	230	4	.329	0	0	0	-0	2S	-0.6
1966	StL-N	134	394	25	96	14	3	0	24	37	61	.244	.312	.294	.606	70	-15	-15	100	87	36	.511	3	0	1	8	*S/2O	0.5
1967	StL-N	152	476	37	108	14	4	1	41	48	66	.227	.299	.279	.578	66	-20	-20	101	125	39	.478	0	2	-1	-2	*S/2	-0.6
1968	StL-N	151	459	51	116	8	5	1	24	52	71	.253	.330	.298	.629	94	-4	-2	95	72	46	.538	0	2	-1	-5	*S	1.1
1969	StL-N	132	372	27	65	10	2	2	32	44	52	.175	.264	.228	.492	39	-30	-30	100	141	23	.409	1	1	-0	11	*S	-0.3
1970	StL-N	152	399	35	80	5	2	0	28	51	56	.201	.291	.223	.514	37	-33	-36	106	122	29	.428	0	0	0	**29**	*S2	1.2
1971	StL-N	142	356	31	80	10	1	0	24	43	45	.225	.310	.258	.568	62	-16	-17	101	106	28	.464	1	2	-1	**18**	*S	2.1
1972	StL-N	105	276	22	61	6	1	1	23	31	47	.221	.300	.261	.561	58	-14	-15	105	126	21	.452	0	1	-1	1	S2	-0.2
	Oak-A	27	36	2	9	1	0	0	1	1	11	.250	.270	.278	.548	65	-2	-2	97	42	3	.393	0	1	-1	-0	2/S	0.0
1973	Oak-A	29	19	0	4	0	0	0	1	1	3	.211	.250	.211	.461	35	-2	-1	87	98	1	.333	0	0	0	0	S2/3	0.2
	Pit-N	74	217	19	41	4	3	0	17	22	40	.189	.264	.235	.499	43	-18	-15	92	134	14	.399	0	0	0	4	S	0.0
1974	Pit-N	8	22	3	4	0	0	0	0	2	4	.182	.250	.182	.432	23	-2	-2	98	0	1	.316	0	0	0	-1	/S	-0.1
	Oak-A	60	52	3	10	0	0	0	2	8	10	.192	.300	.192	.492	44	-3	-3	100	79	4	.419	0	0	0	-1	2S/3	0.0
1975	Oak-A	20	10	1	2	0	0	0	0	0	0	.200	.200	.200	.400	14	-1	-1	93	0	0	.222	0	0	0	-1	S/2	0.0
Total	14	1423	3443	302	748	79	24	6	252	370	538	.217	.295	.259	.554	57	-186	-190	101	114	270	.472	7	11	-5	64	*S2/3O	2.6

■ **CHARLIE MAXWELL** Maxwell, Charles Richard "Smokey" b: 4/8/27, Lawton, Mich. BL/TL, 5'11", 185 lbs. Deb: 9/20/50

YEAR	TM/L	G	AB	R	H	2B	3B	HR	RBI	BB	SO	AVG	OBP	SLG	PRO	/A	BR	/A	PF	CHI	RC	TA	SB	CS	SBR	FR	POS	TPR
1950	Bos-A	3	8	1	0	0	0	0	0	1	3	.000	.111	.000	.111	-61	-2	-2	114	0	0	.125	0	0	0	0	/O	-0.1
1951	Bos-A	49	80	8	15	1	0	3	12	9	18	.188	.270	.313	.582	53	-5	-6	108	126	7	.507	0	1	-1	-2	O	-0.8
1952	Bos-A	8	15	0	1	1	0	0	0	3	11	.067	.222	.133	.356	0	-2	-2	107	0	1	.357	0	0	0	1	/1O	-0.1
1954	Bos-A	74	104	9	26	4	1	0	5	12	21	.250	.328	.308	.635	74	-3	-3	100	59	11	.573	3	0	1	-7	O	-1.0
1955	Bal-A	4	4	0	0	0	0	0	0	0	1	.000	.000	.000	.000	-99	-1	-1	90	0	0	.000	0	0	0	0	H	0.0
	Det-A	55	109	19	29	7	1	7	18	8	20	.266	.328	.541	.869	135	4	4	97	84	19	.841	0	0	0	1	O/1	0.4
	Yr	59	113	19	29	7	1	7	18	8	21	.257	.317	.522	.839	127	3	3	96	78	19	.802	0	0	0	1		0.4
1956	Det-A	141	500	96	163	14	3	28	87	79	74	.326	.420	.534	.954	156	38	40	97	94	118	1.017	1	1	-0	7	*O	3.8
1957	Det-A	138	492	75	136	23	3	24	82	76	84	.276	.379	.482	.860	124	24	19	107	107	94	.882	3	2	-0	9	*O	2.0
1958	Det-A	131	397	56	108	14	4	13	65	64	54	.272	.373	.426	.799	115	12	10	104	125	68	.810	6	1	1	-4	*O1	0.0
1959	Det-A	145	518	81	130	12	2	31	95	81	91	.251	.359	.461	.820	111	17	10	111	119	89	.817	0	2	-1	7	*O	0.8
1960	Det-A	134	482	70	114	16	5	24	81	58	75	.237	.326	.440	.766	104	2	1	102	114	73	.755	5	0	2	5	*O	0.3
1961	Det-A	79	131	11	30	4	2	5	18	20	24	.229	.336	.405	.740	101	-1	0	96	104	19	.725	0	0	0	1	O	0.0
1962	Det-A	30	67	5	13	2	0	1	9	8	10	.194	.280	.269	.549	44	-5	-6	111	170	5	.473	0	0	0	-1	O/1	-0.6
	Chi-A	69	206	30	61	8	3	9	43	34	32	.296	.396	.495	.891	145	12	13	95	132	42	.913	0	0	0	-1	O/1	0.9
	Yr	99	273	35	74	10	3	10	52	42	42	.271	.368	.440	.808	117	7	7	100	145	46	.798	0	0	0	-2		0.3
1963	Chi-A	71	130	17	30	4	2	3	17	31	27	.231	.379	.362	.740	104	3	2	104	127	20	.757	0	0	0	-3	O1	-0.1
1964	Chi-A	2	2	0	0	0	0	0	0	0	0	.000	.000	.000	.000	-99	-1	-1	96	0	0	.000	0	0	0	0	H	0.0
Total	14	1133	3245	478	856	110	26	148	532	484	545	.264	.363	.451	.814	116	92	79	103	111	566	.829	18	7	1	12	O/1	5.5

■ **CARLOS MAY** May, Carlos b: 5/17/48, Birmingham, Ala. BL/TR, 5'11", 200 lbs. Deb: 9/06/68

YEAR	TM/L	G	AB	R	H	2B	3B	HR	RBI	BB	SO	AVG	OBP	SLG	PRO	/A	BR	/A	PF	CHI	RC	TA	SB	CS	SBR	FR	POS	TPR
1968	Chi-A	17	67	4	12	1	0	0	1	3	15	.179	.214	.194	.408	24	-6	-6	101	35	3	.286	0	0	0	-2	O	-1.0
1969	Chi-A	100	367	62	103	18	2	18	62	58	66	.281	.387	.488	.875	132	22	18	108	103	69	.875	1	4	-2	-3	*O	1.1
1970	Chi-A	150	555	83	158	28	4	12	68	79	96	.285	.377	.414	.791	112	16	12	106	110	84	.759	12	5	1	-5	*O/1	0.0
1971	Chi-A	141	500	64	147	21	7	7	70	62	61	.294	.379	.406	.785	125	16	18	98	130	77	.763	16	7	1	-5	*1/O	0.7
1972	Chi-A	148	523	83	161	26	3	12	68	79	70	.308	.408	.438	.845	143	37	33	106	114	96	.881	23	14	-2	-5	*O/1	2.5
1973	Chi-A	149	553	62	148	20	0	20	96	53	73	.268	.337	.412	.749	108	7	5	102	139	75	.692	8	6	-1	-2	DO/1	0.0
1974	Chi-A	149	551	66	137	19	2	8	58	46	76	.249	.308	.334	.642	83	-11	-12	102	112	56	.553	8	9	-3	0	*OD	-1.8
1975	Chi-A	128	454	55	123	19	2	8	53	67	46	.271	.375	.374	.750	109	10	8	103	107	66	.737	12	7	-1	-3	1OD	0.0
1976	Chi-A	20	63	7	11	2	0	0	3	9	5	.175	.278	.206	.484	44	-4	-4	99	89	5	.500	4	0	1	-2	D/O	-0.4
	NY-A	87	288	38	80	11	2	3	40	34	32	.278	.364	.361	.725	113	6	6	99	136	39	.670	1	1	-0	0	D/O1	0.6
	Yr	107	351	45	91	13	2	3	43	43	37	.259	.348	.333	.682	101	2	2	99	128	44	.637	5	1	1	-1		0.2
1977	NY-A	65	181	21	41	7	1	2	16	17	24	.227	.296	.309	.606	66	-9	-8	99	102	16	.503	0	0	0	-1	D/O	-0.8
	Cal-A	11	18	0	6	0	0	0	1	5	1	.333	.478	.333	.812	133	1	1	95	66	3	.846	0	0	0	0	/1D	0.1
	Yr	76	199	21	47	7	1	2	17	22	25	.236	.315	.312	.627	73	-7	-7	98	98	21	.556	0	0	0	-1		-0.7
Total	10	1165	4120	545	1127	172	23	90	536	512	565	.274	.360	.392	.752	111	85	71	103	116	589	.741	85	53	-6	-28	OD1	1.0

■ **DAVE MAY** May, David La France b: 12/23/43, New Castle, Del. BL/TR, 5'10.5", 186 lbs. Deb: 7/28/67

YEAR	TM/L	G	AB	R	H	2B	3B	HR	RBI	BB	SO	AVG	OBP	SLG	PRO	/A	BR	/A	PF	CHI	RC	TA	SB	CS	SBR	FR	POS	TPR
1967	Bal-A	36	85	12	20	1	1	1	7	6	13	.235	.286	.306	.592	79	-3	-2	95	101	8	.492	0	0	0	-1	O	-0.3
1968	Bal-A	84	152	15	29	6	3	0	7	19	27	.191	.285	.270	.555	67	-5	-6	102	73	11	.492	3	3	-1	-10	O	-2.2
1969	Bal-A	78	120	8	29	6	0	3	10	9	23	.242	.305	.367	.672	84	-2	-3	104	76	12	.588	2	1	0	-5	O	-0.9
1970	Bal-A	25	31	6	6	0	1	1	6	4	4	.194	.286	.355	.641	78	-1	-1	97	173	2	.536	0	0	0	-3	/O	-0.3
	Mil-A	101	342	36	82	8	1	7	31	44	56	.240	.330	.330	.660	84	-7	-7	98	95	37	.607	8	6	-1	3	O	-0.9
	Yr	126	373	42	88	8	2	8	37	48	60	.236	.326	.332	.659	84	-8	-7	98	112	41	.607	8	6	-1	0		-1.2
1971	Mil-A	144	501	74	139	20	3	16	65	50	59	.277	.347	.425	.772	114	11	9	103	104	70	.722	15	9	-1	2	*O	0.6
1972	Mil-A	143	500	49	119	20	2	9	45	47	56	.238	.307	.340	.647	97	-5	-2	95	97	49	.569	11	13	-5	9	*O	-0.1
1973	Mil-A	156	624	96	189	23	4	25	93	44	78	.303	.354	.473	.826	137	24	27	96	105	100	.769	6	7	-2	-3	*O/D	1.7
1974	Mil-A	135	477	56	108	15	1	10	42	28	73	.226	.274	.325	.599	70	-18	-20	102	91	41	.497	4	3	-1	1	*O/D	-2.2
1975	Atl-N	82	203	28	56	8	0	12	40	25	27	.276	.361	.493	.853	142	9	10	95	114	36	.842	1	1	-0	-1	O	0.8
1976	Atl-N	105	214	27	46	5	3	3	23	26	31	.215	.303	.308	.611	66	-7	-10	111	118	21	.566	5	1	1	-3	O	-1.4
1977	Tex-A	120	340	46	82	14	1	7	42	32	43	.241	.314	.350	.664	77	-9	-11	105	119	38	.596	4	3	-1	-7	*O/D	-2.2
1978	Mil-A	39	77	9	15	4	0	2	11	9	10	.195	.295	.325	.620	70	-3	-3	106	140	7	.554	0	0	0	0	O/D	-0.2
	Pit-N	5	4	0	0	0	0	0	0	1	1	.000	.200	.000	.200	-38	-1	-1	105	0	0	.500	1	0	0	0	H	0.0
Total	12	1253	3670	462	920	130	20	96	422	344	501	.251	.320	.375	.695	97	-17	-18	100	102	435	.647	60	47	-10	-16	*O/D	-7.6

■ **JERRY MAY** May, Jerry Lee b: 12/14/43, Staunton, Va. BR/TR, 6'2", 190 lbs. Deb: 9/19/64

YEAR	TM/L	G	AB	R	H	2B	3B	HR	RBI	BB	SO	AVG	OBP	SLG	PRO	/A	BR	/A	PF	CHI	RC	TA	SB	CS	SBR	FR	POS	TPR
1964	Pit-N	11	31	1	8	0	0	0	3	3	9	.258	.324	.258	.582	65	-1	-1	101	154	3	.458	0	0	0	-1	C	-0.1
1965	Pit-N	4	2	0	1	0	0	0	1	0	0	.500	.500	.500	1.000	183	0	0	100	415	1	1.000	0	0	0	0	/C	0.0
1966	Pit-N	42	52	6	13	4	0	1	2	2	15	.250	.291	.385	.676	85	-1	-1	101	37	6	.575	0	1	-1	-3	C	-0.3
1967	Pit-N	110	325	23	88	13	2	3	22	36	55	.271	.349	.351	.700	101	1	1	100	74	37	.610	0	0	0	2	*C	1.1
1968	Pit-N	137	416	26	91	15	2	1	33	41	80	.219	.293	.272	.565	70	-14	-14	101	120	33	.469	0	0	0	-15	*C	-2.7
1969	Pit-N	62	190	21	44	8	0	7	23	9	53	.232	.274	.384	.658	87	-5	-4	95	98	20	.570	1	1	-0	3	C	0.2
1970	Pit-N	51	139	13	29	4	2	1	16	21	25	.209	.317	.288	.605	65	-7	-6	97	144	13	.549	0	0	0	5	C	0.1
1971	KC-A	71	218	16	55	13	2	1	24	27	37	.252	.335	.344	.679	94	-2	-1	99	126	25	.600	0	0	0	0	C	0.2
1972	KC-A	53	116	10	22	5	1	1	4	14	13	.190	.277	.276	.553	65	-5	-5	100	48	9	.469	0	0	0	0	C	-0.4
1973	KC-A	11	30	4	4	1	1	0	2	3	5	.133	.235	.233	.469	30	-3	-3	109	112	2	.407	0	0	0	-1	C	-0.3
	NY-N	4	8	0	2	0	0	0	0	1	1	.250	.333	.250	.583	64	-0	-0	101	0	1	.500	0	0	0	0	/C	0.0
Total	10	556	1527	120	357	63	10	15	130	157	293	.234	.310	.318	.627	81	-36	-35	99	103	148	.558	1	2	-1	-9	C	-2.2

■ **LEE MAY** May, Lee Andrew b: 3/23/43, Birmingham, Ala. BR/TR, 6'3", 195 lbs. Deb: 9/01/65 C

YEAR	TM/L	G	AB	R	H	2B	3B	HR	RBI	BB	SO	AVG	OBP	SLG	PRO	/A	BR	/A	PF	CHI	RC	TA	SB	CS	SBR	FR	POS	TPR
1965	Cin-N	5	4	1	0	0	0	0	0	0	1	.000	.000	.000	.000	-96	-1	-1	104	0	0	.000	0	0	0	0	H	0.0
1966	Cin-N	25	75	14	25	5	1	2	10	0	14	.333	.333	.507	.840	114	3	1	114	96	12	.731	0	1	-1	-1	1	0.0

YEAR	TM/L	G	AB	R	H	2B	3B	HR	RBI	BB	SO	AVG	OBP	SLG	PRO	/A	BR	/A	PF	CHI	RC	TA	SB	CS	SBR	FR	POS	TPR
1967	Cin-N	127	438	54	116	29	2	12	57	19	80	.265	.310	.422	.733	99	3	-1	109	109	53	.641	4	8	-4	0	1O	-1.0
1968	Cin-N	146	559	78	162	32	1	22	80	34	100	.290	.337	.469	.806	126	25	19	111	105	79	.722	4	7	-3	-1	*1O	0.9
1969	Cin-N	158	607	85	169	32	3	38	110	45	142	.278	.334	.529	.863	140	28	28	99	107	104	.830	5	4	-1	0	*1/O	1.5
1970	Cin-N	153	605	78	153	34	2	34	94	38	125	.253	.299	.484	.784	102	2	-2	104	98	81	.708	1	1	-0	-0	*1	-1.4
1971	Cin-N	147	553	85	154	17	3	39	98	42	135	.278	.334	.532	.866	147	27	29	96	103	96	.833	3	0	1	-8	*1	1.2
1972	Hou-N	148	592	87	168	31	2	29	98	52	145	.284	.344	.490	.834	127	25	20	106	113	97	.792	3	1	0	-2	*1	0.9
1973	Hou-N	148	545	65	147	24	3	28	105	34	122	.270	.315	.479	.794	123	10	13	95	125	78	.723	1	1	-0	-7	*1	0.0
1974	Hou-N	152	556	59	149	26	0	24	85	17	97	.268	.298	.444	.743	108	1	2	98	105	71	.649	1	0	0	-0	*1	-0.4
1975	Bal-A	146	580	67	152	28	3	20	99	36	91	.262	.311	.424	.735	117	2	9	91	132	68	.632	1	2	-1	3	*1/D	0.3
1976	Bal-A	148	530	61	137	17	4	25	**109**	41	104	.258	.315	.447	.763	125	12	14	98	137	73	.704	4	1	1	3	1D	1.3
1977	Bal-A	150	585	75	148	16	2	27	99	38	119	.253	.299	.426	.724	102	-6	-1	93	126	68	.630	2	2	-1	-6	*1D	-1.2
1978	Bal-A	148	556	56	137	16	1	25	80	31	110	.246	.287	.414	.701	105	-6	0	91	106	61	.608	5	2	0	0	*D/1	0.0
1979	Bal-A	124	456	59	116	15	0	19	69	28	100	.254	.299	.412	.711	92	-8	-6	97	110	50	.608	3	4	-2	0	*D/1	-0.7
1980	Bal-A	78	222	20	54	10	2	7	31	15	53	.243	.291	.401	.692	87	-4	-5	101	110	23	.592	2	0	1	-0	D/1	-0.4
1981	KC-A	26	55	3	16	3	0	0	8	3	14	.291	.328	.345	.673	95	-0	-0	99	165	5	.524	0	1	-1	-0	/1D	-0.1
1982	KC-A	42	91	12	28	5	2	3	12	14	18	.308	.400	.505	.905	147	6	6	100	87	20	.952	0	0	0	0	1/D	0.5
Total	18	2071	7609	959	2031	340	31	354	1244	487	1570	.267	.315	.459	.774	116	117	126	99	113	1039	.725	39	35	-9	-19	*1D/O	1.4

■ PINKY MAY May, Merrill Glend b: 1/18/11, Laconia, Ind. BR/TR, 5'11.5", 165 lbs. Deb: 4/21/39

YEAR	TM/L	G	AB	R	H	2B	3B	HR	RBI	BB	SO	AVG	OBP	SLG	PRO	/A	BR	/A	PF	CHI	RC	TA	SB	CS	SBR	FR	POS	TPR
1939	Phi-N	135	464	49	133	27	3	2	62	41	20	.287	.346	.371	.717	98	-4	-1	94	130	59	.628	4			6	*3	0.9
1940	Phi-N	136	501	59	147	24	2	1	48	58	33	.293	.371	.355	.727	104	3	5	97	104	69	.667	2			14	*3/S	1.8
1941	Phi-N	142	490	46	131	17	4	0	39	55	30	.267	.344	.318	.662	90	-7	-5	97	92	54	.570	2			**22**	*3	1.8
1942	Phi-N	115	345	25	82	15	0	0	18	51	17	.238	.338	.281	.619	87	-6	-3	94	69	36	.561	3			11	*3	0.8
1943	Phi-N	137	415	31	117	19	2	1	48	56	21	.282	.369	.345	.713	114	5	9	94	119	53	.639	2			2	*3	1.1
Total	5	665	2215	210	610	102	11	4	215	261	121	.275	.354	.337	.691	99	-8	5	95	104	270	.634	13			54	3/S	6.4

■ MILT MAY May, Milton Scott b: 8/1/50, Gary, Ind. BL/TR, 6', 190 lbs. Deb: 9/08/70 C

YEAR	TM/L	G	AB	R	H	2B	3B	HR	RBI	BB	SO	AVG	OBP	SLG	PRO	/A	BR	/A	PF	CHI	RC	TA	SB	CS	SBR	FR	POS	TPR
1970	Pit-N	5	4	1	2	1	0	0	2	0	0	.500	.600	.750	1.350	268	1	1	97	259	2	2.000	0	0	0	0	H	0.1
1971	Pit-N	49	126	15	35	1	0	6	25	9	16	.278	.326	.429	.754	113	2	2	99	141	16	.649	0	0	0	4	C	0.7
1972	Pit-N	57	139	12	39	10	0	0	14	10	13	.281	.329	.353	.681	91	-1	-2	103	117	16	.573	0	0	0	2	C	0.3
1973	Pit-N	101	283	29	76	8	1	7	31	34	26	.269	.351	.378	.729	111	1	4	92	97	36	.659	0	1	-1	1	C	1.0
1974	Hou-N	127	405	47	117	17	4	7	54	39	33	.289	.353	.402	.755	113	6	7	98	113	57	.681	0	1	-1	5	*C	1.6
1975	Hou-N	111	386	29	93	15	1	4	52	26	41	.241	.289	.316	.605	72	-17	-15	94	150	35	.493	1	2	-1	0	*C	-1.2
1976	Det-A	6	25	2	7	1	0	0	1	0	1	.280	.280	.320	.600	73	-1	-1	104	51	2	.444	0	0	0	0	/C	0.0
1977	Det-A	115	397	32	99	9	3	12	46	26	31	.249	.296	.378	.673	78	-11	-13	105	100	42	.564	0	0	0	16	*C	0.5
1978	Det-A	105	352	24	88	9	0	10	37	27	26	.250	.307	.361	.668	81	-6	-10	108	93	37	.563	0	0	0	6	C	0.0
1979	Det-A	6	11	1	3	2	0	0	3	1	1	.273	.333	.455	.788	114	0	0	96	231	1	.667	0	0	0	0	/C	0.1
	Chi-A	65	202	23	51	13	0	7	28	14	27	.252	.307	.421	.728	92	-2	-3	102	101	26	.656	0	0	0	-3	C	-0.2
	Yr	71	213	24	54	15	0	7	31	15	28	.254	.309	.423	.731	93	-2	-3	102	116	28	.660	0	0	0	-3		-0.1
1980	SF-N	111	358	27	93	16	2	6	50	25	40	.260	.310	.366	.676	92	-6	-4	96	133	38	.563	0	1	-1	2	*C	0.0
1981	SF-N	97	316	20	98	17	0	2	33	34	29	.310	.377	.383	.760	110	8	6	105	102	44	.681	1	4	-2	3	C	0.8
1982	SF-N	114	395	29	104	19	0	9	39	28	38	.263	.312	.380	.692	99	-5	-2	94	86	47	.601	0	1	-1	2	*C	0.1
1983	SF-N	66	186	18	46	6	0	6	20	21	23	.247	.324	.376	.700	93	-2	-2	101	90	21	.628	2	2	-1	2	C	0.2
	Pit-N	7	12	0	3	0	0	0	0	1	1	.250	.308	.250	.558	55	-1	-1	103	0	1	.444	0	0	0	0	/C	0.0
	Yr	73	198	18	49	6	0	6	20	22	24	.247	.323	.369	.691	90	-2	-3	101	82	25	.642	2	2	-1	3		0.2
1984	Pit-N	50	96	4	17	3	0	1	8	10	15	.177	.255	.240	.494	42	-8	-7	94	121	6	.398	0	1	-1	3	C	-0.3
Total	15	1192	3693	313	971	147	11	77	443	305	361	.263	.321	.371	.692	93	-41	-38	99	110	426	.617	4	13	-7	44	*C	3.7

■ JOHN MAYBERRY Mayberry, John Claiborn b: 2/18/49, Detroit, Mich. BL/TL, 6'3", 215 lbs. Deb: 9/10/68

YEAR	TM/L	G	AB	R	H	2B	3B	HR	RBI	BB	SO	AVG	OBP	SLG	PRO	/A	BR	/A	PF	CHI	RC	TA	SB	CS	SBR	FR	POS	TPR
1968	Hou-N	4	9	0	0	0	0	0	0	0	2	.000	.100	.000	.100	-69	-2	-2	99	0	0	.111	0	0	0	0	/1	-0.1
1969	Hou-N	5	4	0	0	0	0	0	0	1	1	.000	.200	.000	.200	-39	-1	-1	102	0	0	.250	0	0	0	0	H	0.0
1970	Hou-N	50	148	23	32	3	2	5	14	21	33	.216	.322	.365	.687	89	-3	-2	94	79	17	.634	1	1	-0	-1	1	-0.6
1971	Hou-N	46	137	16	25	0	1	7	14	13	32	.182	.263	.350	.614	78	-5	-4	93	83	13	.553	0	0	0	-2	1	-0.8
1972	KC-A	149	503	65	150	24	3	25	100	78	74	.298	.396	.507	.903	167	43	43	100	129	101	.916	0	2	-1	-2	*1	2.8
1973	KC-A	152	510	87	142	20	2	26	100	**122**	79	.278	**.420**	.478	.898	140	**41**	34	109	129	113	**.995**	3	0	1	-3	*1/D	2.4
1974	KC-A	126	427	63	100	13	1	22	69	77	72	.234	.359	.424	.783	117	15	12	106	112	70	.805	4	2	0	0	*1D	0.7
1975	KC-A	156	554	95	161	38	1	34	106	**119**	73	.291	.419	.547	.966	**168**	**56**	**55**	102	107	**135**	**1.067**	5	3	-0	5	*1D	5.1
1976	KC-A	161	594	76	138	22	2	13	95	82	73	.232	.327	.342	.669	96	-1	-1	100	**160**	70	.617	3	2	-0	-2	*1/D	-1.1
1977	KC-A	153	543	73	125	22	1	23	82	83	86	.230	.340	.401	.741	101	2	2	100	120	76	.712	1	3	-2	-5	*1/D	-1.2
1978	Tor-A	152	515	51	129	15	2	22	70	60	57	.250	.333	.416	.749	109	6	6	100	101	71	.696	1	2	-1	-14	*1/D	-1.4
1979	Tor-A	137	464	61	127	22	1	21	74	69	60	.274	.374	.461	.835	120	17	14	103	105	82	.830	1	1	-0	-4	*1	0.3
1980	Tor-A	149	501	62	124	19	2	30	82	77	80	.248	.351	.473	.824	124	16	17	100	100	86	.821	0	0	0	1	*1/D	0.9
1981	Tor-A	94	290	34	72	6	1	17	43	44	45	.248	.363	.452	.814	120	13	9	111	94	49	.814	1	1	-0	-4	1D	0.3
1982	Tor-A	17	33	7	9	0	0	2	3	7	5	.273	.415	.455	.869	128	2	2	109	57	7	.958	0	0	0	0	D/1	0.2
	NY-A	69	215	20	45	7	0	8	27	28	38	.209	.315	.353	.668	86	-5	-4	96	108	24	.616	0	0	0	-4	1/D	-0.8
	Yr	86	248	27	54	7	0	10	30	35	43	.218	.329	.367	.696	92	-3	-2	99	99	31	.657	0	0	0	-4		-0.6
Total	15	1620	5447	733	1379	211	19	255	879	881	810	.253	.363	.439	.802	122	195	180	102	114	913	.818	20	17	-4	-34	*1/D	6.7

■ LEE MAYE Maye, Arthur Lee b: 12/11/34, Tuscaloosa, Ala. BL/TR, 6'2", 190 lbs. Deb: 7/17/59

YEAR	TM/L	G	AB	R	H	2B	3B	HR	RBI	BB	SO	AVG	OBP	SLG	PRO	/A	BR	/A	PF	CHI	RC	TA	SB	CS	SBR	FR	POS	TPR
1959	Mil-N	51	140	17	42	5	1	4	16	7	26	.300	.338	.436	.774	110	1	2	95	89	20	.696	2	2	-1	0	O	0.0
1960	Mil-N	41	83	14	25	6	0	0	2	7	21	.301	.363	.373	.736	112	0	1	91	26	12	.746	5	0	2	-2	O	0.0
1961	Mil-N	110	373	68	101	11	5	14	41	36	50	.271	.340	.440	.779	114	2	6	92	80	60	.777	10	1	2	-4	O	0.0
1962	Mil-N	99	349	40	85	10	0	10	41	25	58	.244	.296	.358	.654	75	-13	-12	99	106	39	.595	9	3	1	-7	O	-2.3
1963	Mil-N	124	442	67	120	22	7	11	34	36	52	.271	.331	.428	.758	115	9	9	101	66	65	.733	14	2	3	-8	*O	-0.1
1964	Mil-N	153	588	96	179	**44**	5	10	74	34	54	.304	.347	.447	.794	126	16	18	97	106	86	.713	5	10	-5	5	*O/3	1.6
1965	Mil-N	15	53	8	16	2	0	2	7	2	6	.302	.339	.453	.792	116	1	1	104	99	8	.730	0	0	0	1	O	0.2
	Hou-N	108	415	38	104	17	7	3	36	20	37	.251	.287	.347	.634	87	-13	-7	89	99	40	.517	1	5	-3	-0	*O	-1.4
	Yr	123	468	46	120	19	7	5	43	22	43	.256	.293	.359	.652	91	-11	-6	91	100	48	.539	1	5	-3	1		-1.2
1966	Hou-N	115	358	38	103	12	4	9	36	20	26	.288	.325	.419	.744	108	2	3	97	85	47	.659	4	3	-1	-6	O	-0.6
1967	Cle-A	115	297	43	77	20	4	9	27	26	47	.259	.321	.444	.765	124	8	8	100	71	43	.720	3	3	-1	-7	O/2	-0.1
1968	Cle-A	109	299	20	84	13	2	4	26	15	24	.281	.317	.378	.695	109	3	3	101	89	36	.589	0	0	0	-2	O/1	-0.2
1969	Cle-A	43	108	9	27	5	0	1	15	8	15	.250	.308	.324	.632	81	-3	-3	94	158	11	.542	1	0	0	0	O	-0.2
	Was-A	71	238	41	69	9	3	9	26	20	25	.290	.345	.466	.811	129	7	8	97	76	35	.733	1	3	-2	-7	O	-0.1
	Yr	114	346	50	96	14	3	10	41	28	40	.277	.333	.422	.755	115	4	5	96	108	47	.678	2	3	-1	-7		-0.3
1970	Was-A	96	255	28	67	12	1	7	30	21	32	.263	.321	.400	.721	102	-1	-0	96	99	33	.663	4	2	0	-10	O/3	-1.2
	Chi-A	6	6	0	1	0	0	0	1	0	1	.167	.167	.167	.333	-7	-1	-1	106	405	0	.200	0	0	0	0	H	0.0
	Yr	102	261	28	68	12	1	7	31	21	33	.261	.318	.395	.713	99	-2	-1	97	118	34	.662	4	2	0	-10		-1.2
1971	Chi-A	32	44	6	9	2	0	1	7	5	7	.205	.286	.318	.604	73	-2	-2	98	168	4	.514	0	0	0	-1	O	-0.2
Total	13	1288	4048	533	1109	190	39	94	419	282	481	.274	.324	.410	.734	108	17	34	97	91	539	.679	59	34	-3	-45	*O/312	-4.6

■ ED MAYER Mayer, Edward H. b: 8/16/1866, Marshall, Ill. d: 5/18/13, Chicago, Ill. 5'8.5", 155 lbs. Deb: 4/19/1890

YEAR	TM/L	G	AB	R	H	2B	3B	HR	RBI	BB	SO	AVG	OBP	SLG	PRO	/A	BR	/A	PF	CHI	RC	TA	SB	CS	SBR	FR	POS	TPR
1890	Phi-N	117	484	49	117	25	5	1	70	22	36	.242	.286	.320	.606	73	-14	-20	108	142	51	.559	20			-8	*3	-2.0
1891	Phi-N	68	268	24	50	2	4	0	31	14	29	.187	.238	.224	.462	38	-21	-19	95	154	16	.390	7			0	3O/S2	-1.7
Total	2	185	752	73	167	27	9	1	101	36	65	.222	.269	.286	.555	61	-36	-40	103	146	68	.496	27			-8	3/OS2	-3.7

■ SAM MAYER Mayer, Samuel Frankel (born Samuel Frankel Erskine) b: 2/28/1893, Atlanta, Ga. d: 7/1/62, Atlanta, Ga. BR/TL, 5'10", 164 lbs. Deb: 9/14/15

YEAR	TM/L	G	AB	R	H	2B	3B	HR	RBI	BB	SO	AVG	OBP	SLG	PRO	/A	BR	/A	PF	CHI	RC	TA	SB	CS	SBR	FR	POS	TPR
1915	Was-A	11	29	5	7	0	0	1	4	4	2	.241	.333	.345	.678	102	0	0	101	105	3	.625	1	2	-1	-0	/OP1	-0.1

YEAR	TM/L	G	AB	R	H	2B	3B	HR	RBI	BB	SO	AVG	OBP	SLG	PRO	/A	BR	/A	PF	CHI	RC	TA	SB	CS	SBR	FR	POS	TPR
■ WALLY MAYER	Mayer, Walter A. b: 7/8/1890, Cincinnati, Ohio d: 11/18/51, Minneapolis, Minn. BR/TR, 5'11", 168 lbs. Deb: 9/28/11																											
1911	Chi-A	1	3	0	0	0	0	0	0	2		.000	.400	.000	.400	16	-0	-0	97	0	0	.667	0			-0	/C	0.0
1912	Chi-A	9	9	1	0	0	0	0	0	1		.000	.100	.000	.100	-71	-2	-2	99	0	0	.111	0			0	/C	-0.1
1914	Chi-A	39	85	7	14	3	1	0	5	14	23	.165	.290	.224	.514	53	-4	-5	103	99	6	.486	1	1	-0	1	C/3	0.0
1915	Chi-A	22	54	3	12	3	1	0	5	5	8	.222	.288	.315	.603	82	-1	-1	98	100	5	.500	0	2	-1	-1	C	-0.1
1917	Bos-A	4	12	2	2	0	0	0	0	5	2	.167	.412	.167	.578	71	0	-0	108	0	1	.700	0			-0	/C	0.0
1918	Bos-A	26	49	7	11	4	0	0	5	7	7	.224	.321	.306	.628	94	-1	-0	95	122	5	.579	0			-1	C	0.0
1919	StL-A	30	62	2	14	4	1	0	5	8	11	.226	.314	.323	.637	81	-2	-1	97	91	7	.583	0			0	C	0.0
Total	7	131	274	22	53	14	3	0	20	42	51	.193	.303	.266	.569	69	-10	-10	99	91	22	.522	1	3		-1	C/3	-0.2
■ PADDY MAYES	Mayes, Adair Bushyhead b: 3/17/1885, Locust Grove, Okla d: 5/28/62, Fayetteville, Ark. BL/TR, 5'11", 160 lbs. Deb: 6/11/11																											
1911	Phi-N	5	5	1	0	0	0	0	0	1	2	.000	.286	.000	.286	-16	-1	-1	108	0	0	.400	0			-1	/O	0.0
■ BUSTER MAYNARD	Maynard, James Walter b: 3/25/13, Henderson, S.C. d: 9/7/77, Durham, N.C. BR/TR, 5'11", 170 lbs. Deb: 9/17/40																											
1940	NY-N	7	29	6	8	2	2	1	2	2	6	.276	.323	.586	.909	146	2	2	100	36	6	.905	0			-1	/O	0.0
1942	NY-N	89	190	17	47	4	1	4	32	19	19	.247	.319	.342	.661	91	-2	-2	103	154	20	.587	3			0	O3/2	-0.3
1943	NY-N	121	393	43	81	8	2	9	32	24	27	.206	.252	.305	.557	63	-21	-19	96	79	30	.459	3			-1	O3	-2.5
1946	NY-N	7	4	2	0	0	0	0	0	1	1	.000	.200	.000	.200	-40	-1	-1	102	0	0	.250	0			-1	/O	-0.1
Total	4	224	616	68	136	14	5	14	66	46	53	.221	.276	.328	.604	76	-22	-21	98	100	56	.531	6			-3	O/32	-2.9
■ CHICK MAYNARD	Maynard, Le Roy Evans b: 11/2/1896, Turners Falls, Mass d: 1/31/57, Bangor, Maine TR, 5'9", 150 lbs. Deb: 6/27/22																											
1922	Bos-A	12	24	1	3	0	0	0	0	3	2	.125	.222	.125	.347	-8	-4	-4	96	0	1	.273	0	1	-1	-1	S	-0.3
■ EDDIE MAYO	Mayo, Edward Joseph "Hotshot" (born Edward Joseph Mayoski) b: 4/15/10, Holyoke, Mass. BL/TR, 5'11", 178 lbs. Deb: 5/29/36 C																											
1936	NY-N	46	141	11	28	4	1	1	8	11	12	.199	.257	.262	.519	40	-12	-12	100	71	10	.414	0			1	3	-0.7
1937	Bos-N	65	172	19	39	6	1	1	18	15	20	.227	.293	.291	.583	65	-10	-7	90	122	15	.479	1			-5	3	-1.0
1938	Bos-N	8	14	2	3	0	0	1	4	1	0	.214	.267	.429	.695	101	-0	-0	88	161	1	.583	0			-0	/3S	0.0
1943	Phi-A	128	471	49	103	10	1	0	28	34	32	.219	.278	.244	.523	53	-27	-28	101	94	36	.416	2	0	1	-3	*3	-3.1
1944	Det-A	154	607	76	151	18	3	5	63	57	23	.249	.317	.313	.630	76	-15	-19	105	98	62	.541	9	13	-5	**25**	*2S	0.6
1945	Det-A	134	501	71	143	24	3	10	54	47	29	.285	.347	.405	.752	111	10	7	106	89	72	.691	7	7	-2	20	*2	2.8
1946	Det-A	51	202	21	51	9	2	0	22	14	12	.252	.301	.317	.618	67	-8	-9	108	138	19	.525	6	2	1	0	2	-0.4
1947	Det-A	142	535	66	149	28	4	6	48	48	28	.279	.338	.379	.717	95	-1	-4	104	82	67	.621	3	7	-3	-10	*2	-1.0
1948	Det-A	106	370	35	92	20	1	2	42	30	19	.249	.310	.324	.634	71	-17	-15	96	115	35	.515	1	9	-5	-6	23	-2.3
Total	9	834	3013	350	759	119	16	26	287	257	175	.252	.313	.328	.641	79	-79	-88	102	98	316	.559	29	38		21	23/S	-5.1
■ JACKIE MAYO	Mayo, John Lewis b: 7/26/25, Litchfield, Ill. BL/TR, 6'1", 190 lbs. Deb: 9/19/48																											
1948	Phi-N	12	35	7	8	2	1	0	3	7	7	.229	.386	.343	.729	105	0	1	94	94	6	.815	1			1	O	0.1
1949	Phi-N	45	39	3	5	0	0	0	2	4	5	.128	.209	.128	.338	-7	-6	-6	101	151	1	.257	0			-8	O	-1.4
1950	Phi-N	18	36	1	8	3	0	0	3	2	5	.222	.263	.306	.569	50	-3	-3	97	105	3	.464	0			-3	O	-0.5
1951	Phi-N	9	7	1	1	0	0	0	0	0	0	.143	.143	.143	.286	-24	-1	-1	97	0	0	.167	0	0	0	-2	/O	-0.2
1952	Phi-N	50	119	13	29	5	0	1	4	12	17	.244	.313	.311	.624	73	-4	-4	101	39	11	.515	1	3	-2	0	O/1	-0.6
1953	Phi-N	5	4	0	0	0	0	0	0	0	1	.000	.000	.000	.000	-99	-1	-1	99	0	0	.000	0	0	0	-0	/O	-0.1
Total	6	139	240	25	51	10	1	1	12	25	35	.213	.292	.275	.567	56	-15	-14	99	74	21	.495	2	3		-12	/O1	-2.7
■ WILLIE MAYS	Mays, Willie Howard "Say Hey" b: 5/6/31, Westfield, Ala. BR/TR, 5'10.5", 170 lbs. Deb: 5/25/51 CH																											
1951	NY-N	121	464	59	127	22	5	20	68	57	60	.274	.356	.472	.828	119	13	12	102	100	80	.810	7	4	-0	5	*O	1.3
1952	NY-N	34	127	17	30	2	4	4	23	16	17	.236	.326	.409	.736	100	0	0	102	148	18	.730	4	1	1	11	O	1.1
1954	NY-N	151	565	119	195	33	**13**	41	110	66	57	**.345**	.415	**.667**	**1.083**	168	62	58	105	92	155	1.171	8	5	-1	12	*O	**6.2**
1955	NY-N	152	580	123	185	18	**13**	**51**	127	79	60	.319	.404	**.659**	**1.063**	179	**62**	**64**	99	92	**157**	**1.190**	24	4	**5**	15	*O	**7.8**
1956	NY-N	152	578	101	171	27	8	36	84	68	65	.296	.371	.557	.928	149	36	38	97	79	118	.995	**40**	10	**6**	9	*O	**4.7**
1957	NY-N	152	585	112	195	26	**20**	35	97	76	62	.333	.411	**.626**	1.037	170	**61**	**59**	102	82	**145**	**1.137**	**38**	19	0	5	*O	**5.9**
1958	SF-N	152	600	**121**	208	33	11	29	96	78	56	.347	.423	.583	**1.006**	**163**	**55**	**55**	100	87	**152**	**1.125**	**31**	6	**6**	9	*O	**6.4**
1959	SF-N	151	575	125	180	43	5	34	104	65	58	.313	.385	.583	.967	161	43	46	95	102	131	1.046	**27**	4	**6**	1	*O	4.9
1960	SF-N	153	595	107	**190**	29	12	29	103	61	70	.319	.386	.555	.941	172	44	51	90	96	124	.977	25	10	2	8	*O	**5.6**
1961	SF-N	154	572	**129**	176	32	3	40	123	81	77	.308	.395	.584	.979	158	46	47	98	116	130	1.038	18	9	0	3	*O	4.0
1962	SF-N	162	621	130	189	36	5	**49**	141	78	85	.304	.385	.615	1.001	162	54	53	101	101	146	1.064	18	2	4	7	*O	5.4
1963	SF-N	157	596	115	187	32	7	38	103	66	83	.314	.384	.582	.966	**182**	56	59	96	99	131	.991	8	3	1	4	*O/S	5.9
1964	SF-N	157	578	121	171	21	9	**47**	111	82	72	.296	.384	**.607**	**.992**	**174**	**57**	**56**	100	98	**136**	**1.071**	19	5	3	8	*O/1S3	**6.4**
1965	SF-N	157	558	118	177	21	3	**52**	112	76	71	.317	**.399**	**.645**	**1.044**	**171**	**65**	**57**	111	95	**143**	**1.124**	9	4	0	8	*O	**6.3**
1966	SF-N	152	552	99	159	29	4	37	103	70	81	.288	.370	.556	.926	157	39	41	97	110	113	.943	5	1	1	4	*O	4.3
1967	SF-N	141	486	83	128	22	2	22	70	51	92	.263	.336	.453	.788	123	14	14	101	103	74	.754	6	0	2	-6	*O	0.3
1968	SF-N	148	498	84	144	20	5	23	79	67	81	.289	.376	.488	.864	161	36	37	98	109	91	.869	12	6	0	-4	*O/1	2.9
1969	SF-N	117	403	64	114	17	3	13	58	49	71	.283	.365	.437	.802	122	13	13	101	108	66	.783	6	2	1	-2	*O/1	0.6
1970	SF-N	139	478	94	139	15	2	28	83	79	90	.291	.395	.506	.901	146	28	31	96	101	101	.951	5	0	2	-2	*O/1	2.3
1971	SF-N	136	417	82	113	24	5	18	61	**112**	123	.271	**.429**	.482	.911	158	38	38	100	99	98	1.076	23	3	5	-5	O1	3.2
1972	SF-N	19	49	8	9	2	0	0	3	17	5	.184	.394	.224	.618	80	-0	-0	100	112	6	.705	3	0	1	-0	O	0.0
	NY-N	69	195	27	52	9	1	8	19	43	43	.267	.402	.446	.848	148	12	13	95	70	35	.863	1	5	-3	4	O1	1.2
	Yr	88	244	35	61	11	1	8	22	60	48	.250	.400	.402	.802	133	12	13	96	80	42	.845	4	5	-2	4		1.2
1973	NY-N	66	209	24	44	10	0	6	25	27	47	.211	.304	.344	.648	79	-6	-6	101	112	22	.587	1	0	0	3	O1	-0.5
Total	22	2992	10881	2062	3283	523	140	660	1903	1464	1526	.302	.387	.557	.944	156	827	837	99	98	2372	1.026	338	103	40	96	*O/1S3	86.2
■ BILL MAZEROSKI	Mazeroski, William Stanley "Maz" b: 9/5/36, Wheeling, W.Va. BR/TR, 5'11.5", 183 lbs. Deb: 7/07/56 C																											
1956	Pit-N	81	255	30	62	8	1	3	14	18	24	.243	.293	.318	.611	63	-13	-13	102	66	24	.503	0	0	0	2	2	-0.5
1957	Pit-N	148	526	59	149	27	7	8	54	27	49	.283	.319	.407	.726	99	-6	-2	94	96	68	.635	3	3	-1	0	*2	1.0
1958	Pit-N	152	567	69	156	24	6	19	68	25	71	.275	.309	.439	.748	100	-6	-2	95	94	73	.651	1	1	-0	19	*2	2.5
1959	Pit-N	135	493	50	119	15	6	7	59	29	54	.241	.285	.339	.624	63	-25	-27	103	129	44	.504	1	3	-2	0	*2	-1.7
1960	Pit-N	151	538	58	147	21	5	11	64	40	50	.273	.325	.392	.717	96	-4	-3	99	109	68	.640	4	0	1	**26**	*2	3.7
1961	Pit-N	152	558	71	148	21	2	13	59	26	55	.265	.302	.380	.681	80	-17	-17	99	97	62	.579	2	1	0	**32**	*2	3.2
1962	Pit-N	159	572	55	155	24	9	14	81	37	47	.271	.318	.418	.735	93	-5	-7	102	116	71	.639	0	3	-2	**41**	*2	4.6
1963	Pit-N	142	534	43	131	22	3	8	52	32	46	.245	.288	.343	.631	82	-14	-13	99	108	50	.519	2	0	1	**47**	*2	4.6
1964	Pit-N	162	601	66	161	22	8	10	64	29	52	.268	.302	.381	.683	90	-8	-9	101	103	63	.561	1	1	-0	**34**	*2	3.9
1965	Pit-N	130	494	52	134	17	1	6	54	18	34	.271	.300	.346	.646	82	-13	-12	100	121	47	.512	2	1	0	**31**	*2	2.6
1966	Pit-N	162	621	56	163	22	7	16	82	31	62	.262	.299	.398	.696	91	-8	-9	101	119	69	.593	4	3	-1	**41**	*2	4.3
1967	Pit-N	163	639	62	167	25	3	9	77	30	55	.261	.294	.352	.647	84	-14	-14	100	134	62	.521	1	2	-1	17	*2	1.4
1968	Pit-N	143	506	36	127	18	2	3	42	38	38	.251	.306	.312	.618	85	-8	-9	101	108	45	.501	3	4	-2	**24**	*2	2.4
1969	Pit-N	67	227	13	52	7	1	3	25	22	16	.229	.303	.308	.611	76	-8	-7	95	127	21	.522	1	1	-0	15	2	1.3
1970	Pit-N	112	367	29	84	14	0	7	39	27	40	.229	.285	.324	.610	65	-20	-18	97	108	34	.519	2	0	1	19	*2	1.3
1971	Pit-N	70	193	17	49	3	1	1	16	15	8	.254	.308	.295	.603	72	-7	-7	99	109	18	.490	0	0	0	3	2/3	-0.1
1972	Pit-N	34	64	3	12	4	0	0	3	3	5	.188	.224	.250	.474	34	-6	-6	103	77	3	.352	0	0	0	3	2/3	-0.1
Total	17	2163	7755	769	2016	294	62	138	853	447	706	.260	.302	.367	.669	84	-180	-174	99	110	824	.580	27	23	-6	351	*2/3	34.4
■ MEL MAZZERA	Mazzera, Melvin Leonard "Mike" b: 1/31/14, Stockton, Cal. BL/TL, 5'11", 180 lbs. Deb: 9/09/35																											
1935	StL-A	12	30	4	7	2	0	1	2	4	9	.233	.324	.400	.724	81	-1	-1	107	45	4	.696	0	0	0	-1	O	-0.1
1937	StL-A	7	7	1	2	2	0	0	0	0	2	.286	.286	.571	.857	112	0	0	99	0	1	.800	0	0	0	0	H	0.0
1938	StL-A	86	204	33	57	8	2	6	29	12	25	.279	.329	.426	.755	88	-5	-5	100	93	29	.696	1	1	-0	-2	O	-0.5
1939	StL-A	33	110	21	33	5	2	3	0	0	0	.300	.300	.464	.764	92	-2	-2	100	0	15	.662	0	0	0	-1	O	-0.2
1940	Phi-N	69	156	16	37	5	4	0	13	19	15	.237	.320	.321	.641	79	-5	-4	97	96	16	.565	1			-3	O1	-0.9
Total	5	207	507	75	136	22	8	10	44	35	51	.268	.319	.402	.722	87	-12	-12	100	71	65	.647	2	1		-6	O/1	-1.7

YEAR	TM/L	G	AB	R	H	2B	3B	HR	RBI	BB	SO	AVG	OBP	SLG	PRO	/A	BR	/A	PF	CHI	RC	TA	SB	CS	SBR	FR	POS	TPR
■ LEE MAZZILLI Mazzilli, Lee Louis b: 3/25/55, New York, N.Y. BB/TR, 6'1", 180 lbs. Deb: 9/07/76																												
1976	NY-N	24	77	9	15	2	0	2	7	14	10	.195	.326	.299	.625	85	-2	-1	92	95	8	.652	5	4	-1	4	O	0.1
1977	NY-N	159	537	66	134	24	3	6	46	72	72	.250	.342	.339	.680	87	-11	-8	96	94	66	.661	22	15	-2	2	*O	-1.3
1978	NY-N	148	542	78	148	28	5	16	61	69	82	.273	.356	.432	.788	121	14	15	98	91	85	.783	20	13	-2	7	*O	1.6
1979	NY-N	158	597	78	181	34	4	15	79	93	74	.303	.397	.449	.846	137	28	32	95	96	115	.910	34	12	3	0	*O1	3.1
1980	NY-N	152	578	82	162	31	4	16	76	82	92	.280	.373	.431	.803	129	20	23	96	97	98	.854	41	15	3	0	1O	2.0
1981	NY-N	95	324	36	74	14	5	6	34	46	53	.228	.328	.358	.686	94	-2	-2	101	102	41	.691	17	7	1	2	O	-0.1
1982	Tex-A	58	195	23	47	8	0	4	17	28	26	.241	.339	.344	.683	95	-2	-1	93	88	24	.677	11	6	-0	-1	OD	-0.2
	NY-A	37	128	20	34	2	0	6	17	15	15	.266	.347	.422	.769	114	2	3	96	96	19	.727	2	3	-1	-2	1/OD	0.0
	Yr	95	323	43	81	10	0	10	34	43	41	.251	.342	.375	.717	103	-1	2	94	92	44	.708	13	9	-2	-3		-0.2
1983	Pit-N	109	246	37	59	9	0	5	24	49	43	.240	.370	.337	.708	95	1	0	103	97	34	.745	15	5	2	6	O/1	0.6
1984	Pit-N	111	266	37	63	11	1	4	21	40	42	.237	.339	.331	.670	94	-3	-1	94	82	33	.656	8	1	2	-11	O/1	-1.2
1985	Pit-N	92	117	20	33	8	0	1	9	29	17	.282	.425	.376	.801	123	6	5	103	76	21	.875	4	1	1	1	1/O	0.6
1986	Pit-N	61	93	18	21	2	1	1	8	26	25	.226	.395	.301	.696	95	1	1	100	103	13	.740	3	3	-1	-1	O/1	-0.1
	NY-N	39	58	10	16	3	0	2	7	12	11	.276	.417	.431	.848	140	3	4	96	90	11	.909	1	1	-0	0	O/1	0.3
	Yr	100	151	28	37	5	1	3	15	38	36	.245	.403	.351	.754	112	4	5	98	99	25	.815	4	4	-1	-1		0.2
1987	NY-N	88	124	26	38	8	1	3	24	21	14	.306	.407	.460	.867	131	6	6	99	145	24	.902	5	3	-0	-3	O1	0.1
1988	NY-N	68	116	9	17	2	0	0	12	12	16	.147	.233	.164	.396	17	-12	-11	90	253	5	.350	4	1	1	-1	O1	-1.3
Total	13	1399	3998	549	1042	186	24	87	442	608	592	.261	.361	.384	.745	110	49	66	97	100	595	.772	192	90	4	1	O1/D	4.2
■ JIMMY McALEER McAleer, James Robert "Loafer" b: 7/10/1864, Youngstown, Ohio d: 4/29/31, Youngstown, Ohio BR/TR, 6', 175 lbs. Deb: 4/24/1889 M																												
1889	Cle-N	110	447	66	105	6	6	1	35	30	49	.235	.289	.282	.571	59	-23	-25	103	78	48	.576	37			8	*O	-1.7
1890	Cle-P	86	341	58	91	8	7	1	42	37	33	.267	.340	.340	.681	91	-7	-2	92	98	48	.700	21			9	O	0.2
1891	Cle-N	136	565	97	134	16	11	1	61	49	47	.237	.304	.310	.613	77	-14	-18	105	106	70	.650	51			5	*O	-1.8
1892	Cle-N	150	576	92	136	26	7	4	70	63	54	.236	.316	.326	.642	93	-2	-5	103	114	74	.670	40			11	*O/S	0.1
1893	Cle-N	91	350	63	83	5	1	2	41	35	21	.237	.314	.274	.588	56	-20	-22	104	112	41	.625	32			2	*O	-1.9
1894	Cle-N	64	253	36	73	15	1	2	40	13	17	.289	.331	.379	.710	65	-12	-17	111	110	37	.700	14			2	O	-1.4
1895	Cle-N	131	528	84	143	17	2	0	68	38	37	.271	.327	.311	.638	69	-25	-22	97	123	66	.623	32			-1	*O	-2.7
1896	Cle-N	116	455	70	131	16	4	1	54	47	32	.288	.361	.347	.708	81	-5	-13	110	102	67	.722	24			6	*O	-1.2
1897	Cle-N	24	91	6	20	2	0	0	10	7		.220	.283	.242	.525	37	-7	-9	111	136	8	.479	4			0	O	-0.7
1898	Cle-N	106	366	47	87	3	0	0	48	46		.238	.331	.246	.577	72	-12	-10	96	164	33	.530	7			1	*O/2	-1.4
1901	Cle-A	3	7	0	1	0	0	0	0	0		.143	.143	.143	.286	-21	-1	-1	95	0	0	.167	0			0	/OP3M	0.0
1902	StL-A	2	3	0	2	0	0	0	0	0		.667	.667	.667	1.333	268	1	1	102	0	1	2.000	0			0	/OM	0.1
1907	StL-A	2	0	0	0	0	0	0	0	0		—	—	—	—	—	0	0	98	—	—	—	0			0	RM	0.0
Total	13	1021	3982	619	1006	114	39	12	469	365	290	.253	.321	.310	.631	74	-128	-143	102	112	495	.638	262			42	*O/23PS	-12.4
■ JACK McALEESE McAleese, John James b: 1877, Sharon, Pa. d: 11/15/50, New York, N.Y. TR , 5'8", Deb: 8/10/01																												
1901	Chi-A	1	1	0	0	0	0	0	0	0		.000	.000	.000	.000	-99	-0	-0	99	0	0	.000	0			0	/P	0.0
1909	StL-A	85	267	33	57	7	0	0	12	32		.213	.318	.240	.558	84	-5	-3	92	74	25	.586	18			7	O/3	0.1
Total	2	86	268	33	57	7	0	0	12	32		.213	.317	.239	.556	83	-6	-3	92	73	25	.583	18			7	/O3P	0.1
■ BILL McALLESTER McAllester, William Lusk b: 12/29/1889, Chattanooga, Tenn. d: 3/3/70, Chattanooga, Tenn. BR/TR, 5'11.5", 170 lbs. Deb: 5/02/13																												
1913	StL-A	49	85	3	13	4	0	0	6	11	12	.153	.250	.200	.450	34	-7	-7	95	125	4	.417	2			1	C	-0.2
■ SPORT McALLISTER McAllister, Lewis William b: 7/23/1874, Austin, Miss. d: 7/17/62, Wyandotte, Mich. BB/TR, 5'11", 180 lbs. Deb: 8/07/1896																												
1896	Cle-N	8	27	2	6	2	0	0	1	0	2	.222	.250	.296	.546	41	-2	-3	110	36	2	.476	1			0	/OCP	-0.1
1897	Cle-N	43	137	23	30	5	1	0	11	12		.219	.287	.270	.557	44	-10	-12	111	87	12	.495	3			0	O/SP1C2	-1.0
1898	Cle-N	17	57	8	13	3	1	0	9	5		.228	.290	.316	.606	79	-2	-1	96	151	5	.523	0			0	/PO	0.0
1899	Cle-N	113	418	29	99	6	8	1	31	19		.237	.273	.297	.570	65	-24	-17	89	76	36	.470	5			-6	OC/31SP2	-2.5
1901	Det-A	90	306	45	92	9	4	3	57	15		.301	.333	.386	.719	92	0	-5	110	142	46	.701	17			-5	C1O3/S	-0.6
1902	Det-A	21	67	8	14	1	0	1	8	2		.209	.232	.269	.501	40	-5	-5	99	126	4	.377	0			1	/1S2C3O	-0.3
	Bal-A	3	11	0	1	0	0	0	1	1		.091	.167	.091	.258	-26	-2	-2	102	349	0	.200	0			0	/21	-0.1
	Det-A	45	162	11	34	4	2	0	24	3		.210	.224	.259	.484	35	-14	-14	99	192	10	.359	1			1	1O/C3S	-1.1
	Yr	69	240	19	49	5	2	1	33	6		.204	.224	.254	.478	34	-21	-21	99	186	14	.356	1			2		-1.5
1903	Det-A	78	265	31	69	8	2	0	22	10		.260	.287	.306	.593	82	-6	-5	97	100	25	.490	5			-3	SC/O31	-0.4
Total	7	418	1450	157	358	38	18	5	164	67	2	.247	.282	.308	.590	67	-66	-65	99	115	141	.504	32			-13	O/C1S3P2	-6.1
■ JIM McANANY McAnany, James b: 9/4/36, Los Angeles, Cal. BR/TR, 5'10", 196 lbs. Deb: 9/19/58																												
1958	Chi-A	5	13	0	0	0	0	0	0	0	5	.000	.000	.000	.000	-99	-3	-3	98	0	0	.000	0	0	0	1	/O	-0.2
1959	Chi-A	67	210	22	58	9	3	0	27	19	26	.276	.339	.348	.687	92	-3	-2	97	146	26	.613	2	1	0	-2	O	-0.7
1960	Chi-A	3	2	0	0	0	0	0	0	0	2	.000	.000	.000	.000	-99	-1	-1	101	0	0	.000	0	0	0	0	H	0.0
1961	Chi-N	11	10	1	3	1	0	0	0	1	3	.300	.364	.400	.764	102	0	0	100	0	2	.714	0	0	0	-0	/O	0.0
1962	Chi-N	7	6	0	0	0	0	0	0	1	2	.000	.143	.000	.143	-55	-1	-1	106	0	0	.167	0	0	0	0	H	0.0
Total	5	93	241	23	61	10	3	0	27	21	38	.253	.316	.320	.635	77	-8	-7	97	127	27	.558	2	1	0	-2	/O	-0.9
■ BUB McATEE McAtee, Michael James "Butch" b: 3/1845, Troy, N.Y. d: 10/18/1876, Troy, N.Y. 5'9", 160 lbs. Deb: 5/08/1871																												
1871	Chi-n	26	141	34	39							.277															*1	
1872	Tro-n	25	129	31	27							.209															1	
Total	2 n	51	270	65	66							.244															1	
■ IKE McAULEY McAuley, James Earl b: 8/19/1891, Wichita, Kan. d: 4/6/28, Des Moines, Iowa BR/TR, 5'9.5", 150 lbs. Deb: 9/10/14																												
1914	Pit-N	15	24	3	3	0	0	0	0	0	8	.125	.125	.125	.250	-28	-4	-3	92	0	0	.143	0			0	/S32	-0.3
1915	Pit-N	5	15	0	2	1	0	0	0	0	6	.133	.133	.200	.333	0	-2	-2	99	0	0	.231	0			0	/S	-0.1
1916	Pit-N	4	8	1	2	0	0	0	1	0	1	.250	.250	.250	.500	51	-0	-0	105	199	1	.333	0			-0	/S	0.0
1917	StL-N	3	7	0	2	0	0	0	1	0	1	.286	.286	.286	.571	74	-0	-0	102	193	1	.400	0			0	/S	0.0
1925	Chi-N	37	125	10	35	7	2	0	11	11	12	.280	.343	.368	.711	84	-3	-3	97	87	17	.656	1	0	0	-2	S	0.0
Total	5	64	179	14	44	8	2	0	13	11	28	.246	.293	.313	.606	64	-9	-9	97	77	19	.511	1	0		-2	/S32	-0.4
■ GENE McAULIFFE McAuliffe, Eugene Leo b: 2/28/1872, Randolph, Mass. d: 4/29/53, Randolph, Mass. TR , 6'1", 180 lbs. Deb: 8/17/04																												
1904	Bos-N	1	2	0	1	0	0	0	0	0		.500	.500	.500	1.000	220	0	0	97	0	1	1.000	0			0	/C	0.0
■ DICK McAULIFFE McAuliffe, Richard John b: 11/29/39, Hartford, Conn. BL/TR, 5'11", 176 lbs. Deb: 9/17/60																												
1960	Det-A	8	27	2	7	0	1	0	1	2	6	.259	.310	.333	.644	73	-1	-1	102	43	3	.524	0	0	0	0	/S	0.0
1961	Det-A	80	285	36	73	12	4	6	33	24	39	.256	.323	.389	.712	93	-5	-3	96	102	36	.641	2	3	-1	-9	S3	-0.7
1962	Det-A	139	471	50	124	20	5	12	63	64	76	.263	.351	.403	.755	92	2	-5	111	113	68	.717	4	2	0	-29	23S	-2.7
1963	Det-A	150	568	77	149	18	6	13	61	64	75	.262	.337	.384	.721	98	2	-1	104	105	75	.672	11	5	0	-12	*S2	-0.4
1964	Det-A	162	557	85	134	18	7	24	66	77	96	.241	.336	.427	.763	116	8	11	96	92	81	.739	8	5	-1	-9	*S	0.2
1965	Det-A	113	404	61	105	13	6	15	54	49	62	.260	.343	.433	.776	113	10	8	105	104	60	.746	6	9	-4	-7	*S	0.2
1966	Det-A	124	430	83	118	16	8	23	56	66	80	.274	.375	.509	.884	148	29	28	102	83	83	.899	5	7	-3	1	*S3	3.4
1967	Det-A	153	557	92	133	16	7	22	65	105	118	.239	.366	.411	.777	130	24	24	99	88	93	.805	6	5	-1	1	*2S	3.5
1968	Det-A	151	570	**95**	142	24	10	16	56	82	99	.249	.346	.411	.756	121	21	17	106	82	87	.749	8	7	-2	-15	*2/S	0.6
1969	Det-A	74	271	49	71	10	5	11	33	47	41	.262	.371	.458	.829	126	12	11	103	81	48	.836	2	5	-2	0	2	1.1
1970	Det-A	146	530	73	124	21	1	12	50	101	62	.234	.360	.345	.705	92	-0	-2	103	89	74	.707	5	6	-2	-5	*2S3	0.5
1971	Det-A	128	477	67	99	16	6	18	57	53	67	.208	.293	.379	.673	93	-8	-5	96	105	55	.628	4	1	1	8	*2/S	1.0
1972	Det-A	122	408	47	98	16	3	8	30	59	59	.240	.339	.353	.692	94	4	-1	113	76	53	.657	0	0	0	-7	*2/S3	0.0
1973	Det-A	106	343	39	94	18	1	12	47	49	52	.274	.366	.437	.804	124	12	12	101	99	57	.784	0	4	-2	-6	*2/SD	0.8
1974	Bos-A	100	272	32	57	13	1	5	24	39	40	.210	.311	.320	.631	77	-6	-8	107	92	28	.581	2	0	1	-9	23/SD	-1.3
1975	Bos-A	7	15	0	2	0	0	0	1	1	2	.133	.188	.133	.321	-7	-2	-2	109	192	0	.214	0	0	0	-0	/3	-0.1
Total	16	1763	6185	888	1530	231	71	197	697	882	974	.247	.344	.403	.748	108	104	82	103	94	899	.736	63	59	-17	-98	2S3/D	6.1

YEAR	TM/L	G	AB	R	H	2B	3B	HR	RBI	BB	SO	AVG	OBP	SLG	PRO	/A	BR	/A	PF	CHI	RC	TA	SB	CS	SBR	FR	POS	TPR
■ GEORGE McAVOY McAvoy, George H. Deb: 7/17/14																												
1914	Phi-N	1	1	0	0	0	0	0	0	0	0	.000	.000	.000	.000	-99	-0	-0	100	0	0	.000	0			0	H	0.0
■ WICKEY McAVOY McAvoy, James Eugene b: 10/22/1894, Rochester, N.Y. d: 7/5/73, Rochester, N.Y. BR/TR, 5'11", 172 lbs. Deb: 9/29/13																												
1913	Phi-A	4	9	0	1	0	0	0	0	0	4	.111	.200	.111	.311	-9	-1	-1	97	0	0	.250	0			0	/C	0.0
1914	Phi-A	8	16	1	2	0	1	0	0	0	4	.125	.125	.250	.375	13	-2	-2	97	0	1	.286	0			0	/C	0.0
1915	Phi-A	68	184	12	35	7	2	0	6	11	32	.190	.236	.250	.486	47	-13	-12	96	44	11	.377	0	2	-1	5	C	-0.3
1917	Phi-A	10	24	1	6	1	0	1	4	0	3	.250	.250	.417	.667	110	-0	-0	94	110	2	.556	0			0	/C	0.1
1918	Phi-A	83	271	14	66	5	3	0	32	13	23	.244	.283	.284	.567	68	-10	-11	104	152	23	.473	5			14	C/P1O	1.1
1919	Phi-A	62	170	10	24	5	2	0	11	14	21	.141	.207	.194	.401	12	-20	-21	106	121	7	.329	1			6	C	-1.2
Total	6	235	674	38	134	18	8	1	53	38	87	.199	.245	.254	.498	46	-46	-48	102	107	43	.402	6	2		26	C/O1P	-0.3
■ ALGIE McBRIDE McBride, Algernon Griggs b: 5/23/1869, Washington, D.C. d: 1/10/56, Georgetown, Ohio BL/TL, 5'9", 152 lbs. Deb: 5/12/1896																												
1896	Chi-N	9	29	2	7	1	1	1	7	7	3	.241	.389	.448	.837	113	1	1	108	129	5	.909	0			0	/O	0.1
1898	Cin-N	120	486	94	147	14	12	2	43	51		.302	.376	.393	.769	114	16	10	108	57	80	.779	16			4	*O	0.6
1899	Cin-N	64	251	57	87	12	5	1	23	30		.347	.420	.446	.867	133	15	13	106	53	50	.909	5			-4	O	0.4
1900	Cin-N	112	436	59	120	15	8	4	59	25		.275	.315	.374	.688	100	-6	-0	92	112	56	.633	12			-3	*O	-1.1
1901	Cin-N	30	123	19	29	7	0	2	18	7		.236	.277	.341	.618	85	-3	-2	95	111	12	.521	0			1	O	-0.3
	NY-N	68	264	27	74	11	0	2	29	12		.280	.312	.345	.656	101	-3	0	91	106	30	.558	3			-3	O	-0.8
	Yr	98	387	46	103	18	0	4	47	19		.266	.300	.344	.644	96	-6	-2	92	108	42	.546	3			-2		-1.1
Total	5	403	1589	258	464	60	26	12	179	132	3	.292	.349	.385	.734	110	20	21	100	84	234	.700	36			-5	O	-1.1
■ BAKE McBRIDE McBride, Arnold Ray b: 2/3/49, Fulton, Mo. BL/TR, 6'2", 190 lbs. Deb: 7/26/73																												
1973	StL-N	40	63	8	19	3	0	0	5	4	10	.302	.362	.349	.712	108	0	1	91	91	8	.622	0	1	-1	1	O	0.0
1974	StL-N	150	559	81	173	19	5	6	56	43	57	.309	.372	.394	.766	110	12	9	104	93	85	.757	30	11	2	4	*O	1.1
1975	StL-N	116	413	70	124	10	9	5	36	34	52	.300	.355	.404	.759	107	5	4	103	78	62	.752	26	8	3	3	*O	0.7
1976	StL-N	72	272	40	91	13	4	3	24	18	28	.335	.389	.445	.833	131	13	12	104	75	48	.824	10	5	0	14	O	2.4
1977	StL-N	43	122	21	32	5	1	4	20	7	19	.262	.302	.418	.720	95	-2	-1	96	127	16	.713	9	3	1	-3	O	-0.3
	Phi-N	85	280	55	95	20	5	11	41	25	25	.339	.399	.564	.964	155	21	21	100	86	67	1.104	27	4	6	2	O	2.6
	Yr	128	402	76	127	25	6	15	61	32	44	.316	.371	.520	.891	138	20	20	99	101	82	.979	36	7	7	-1		2.3
1978	Phi-N	122	472	68	127	20	4	10	49	28	68	.269	.317	.392	.709	92	-3	-6	105	96	63	.699	28	3	7	2	*O	0.0
1979	Phi-N	151	582	82	163	16	12	12	60	41	77	.280	.332	.411	.742	105	0	3	97	92	79	.704	25	14	-1	15	*O	1.3
1980	Phi-N	137	554	68	171	33	10	9	87	26	58	.309	.345	.453	.798	113	14	9	107	131	79	.720	13	10	-2	1	*O	0.3
1981	Phi-N	58	221	26	60	17	1	2	21	11	25	.271	.306	.385	.691	85	-2	-5	112	92	25	.605	5	0	2	-7	O	-1.2
1982	Cle-A	27	85	8	31	3	3	0	13	2	12	.365	.379	.471	.850	132	3	3	100	130	14	.759	2	2	-1	-3	O	0.0
1983	Cle-A	70	230	21	67	8	1	1	18	9	26	.291	.321	.348	.669	80	-5	-7	105	85	24	.563	8	2	1	-2	OD	-0.7
Total	11	1071	3853	548	1153	167	55	63	430	248	457	.299	.348	.420	.768	109	57	43	103	96	570	.754	183	63	17	29	O/D	6.2
■ GEORGE McBRIDE McBride, George Florian b: 11/20/1880, Milwaukee, Wis. d: 7/2/73, Milwaukee, Wis. BR/TR, 5'11", 170 lbs. Deb: 9/12/01 MC																												
1901	Mil-A	3	12	0	2	0	0	0	0	1		.167	.231	.167	.397	13	-1	-1	95	0	0	.300	0			0	/S	0.0
1905	Pit-N	27	87	9	19	4	0	0	7	6		.218	.269	.264	.533	58	-4	-5	104	106	7	.456	2			1	3/S	-0.1
	StL-N	81	281	22	61	1	2	2	34	14		.217	.254	.256	.510	59	-16	-13	91	155	21	.436	10			-15	S/1	-2.7
	Yr	108	368	31	80	5	2	2	41	20		.217	.258	.258	.516	59	-20	-17	94	143	28	.441	12			-13		-2.8
1906	StL-N	90	313	24	53	8	2	0	13	17		.169	.212	.208	.420	32	-24	-25	101	74	15	.335	5			-1	S	-2.3
1908	Was-A	155	518	47	120	10	6	0	34	41		.232	.288	.274	.562	89	-8	-5	95	92	43	.490	12			32	*S	3.4
1909	Was-A	156	504	38	118	16	0	0	34	36		.234	.294	.266	.560	86	-12	-7	90	100	43	.503	17			11	*S	0.8
1910	Was-A	154	514	54	118	19	4	1	55	61		.230	.321	.288	.609	90	-4	-4	101	143	53	.576	11			23	*S	2.3
1911	Was-A	154	557	58	131	11	4	0	59	52		.235	.312	.269	.581	65	-26	-24	97	141	52	.533	15			25	*S	1.5
1912	Was-A	152	521	56	118	13	7	1	52	38		.226	.288	.284	.572	64	-25	-24	99	117	48	.521	17			**29**	*S	1.9
1913	Was-A	150	499	52	107	18	7	1	52	43	46	.214	.286	.285	.571	63	-21	-25	106	130	43	.520	12			10	*S	0.0
1914	Was-A	156	503	49	102	12	4	0	24	43	70	.203	.274	.243	.516	55	-27	-28	101	75	36	.441	12	14	-5	13	*S	-0.4
1915	Was-A	146	476	54	97	8	6	1	30	29	60	.204	.251	.252	.503	50	-30	-31	101	83	34	.417	10	5	0	3	*S	-1.5
1916	Was-A	139	466	36	106	15	4	1	36	23	58	.227	.271	.283	.555	67	-20	-20	100	97	41	.467	8			8	*S	-0.1
1917	Was-A	50	141	6	27	3	0	0	9	10	17	.191	.265	.213	.477	50	-9	-8	92	108	9	.395	1			-1	S/32	-0.7
1918	Was-A	18	53	2	7	0	0	0	1	0	11	.132	.132	.132	.264	-19	-8	-8	104	52	1	.174	1			-1	S/2	-0.8
1919	Was-A	15	40	3	8	1	1	0	4	3	6	.200	.256	.275	.531	50	-3	-3	98	132	3	.438	0			-1	S	-0.2
1920	Was-A	13	41	6	9	1	0	0	3	2	3	.220	.256	.244	.500	35	-4	-4	95	105	3	.375	0	0	0	-2	S	-0.4
Total	16	1659	5526	516	1203	140	47	7	447	419	271	.218	.280	.264	.543	65	-243	-233	98	109	452	.476	133	19		134	*S/321	0.7
■ JOHN McBRIDE McBride, John F. Deb: 10/12/1890																												
1890	Phi-a	1	2	0	0	0	0	0		0		.000	.000	.000	.000	-99	-0	-0	97	0	0	.000	0			0	/O	0.0
■ TOM McBRIDE McBride, Thomas Raymond b: 11/2/14, Bonham, Tex. BR/TR, 6'0.5", 188 lbs. Deb: 4/23/43																												
1943	Bos-A	26	96	11	23	3	1	0	7	7	3	.240	.291	.292	.583	68	-4	-4	104	93	7	.468	2	0	1	1	O	-0.2
1944	Bos-A	71	216	29	53	7	3	0	24	8	13	.245	.276	.306	.581	67	-10	-9	98	131	18	.465	4	0	1	0	O/1	-1.0
1945	Bos-A	100	344	38	105	11	7	1	47	26	17	.305	.354	.387	.741	121	6	8	95	125	47	.647	2	2	-1	5	O1	0.9
1946	Bos-A	61	153	21	46	5	2	0	19	9	6	.301	.340	.359	.699	83	-1	-4	114	131	18	.566	0	1	-1	-8	O	-1.4
1947	Bos-A	2	5	0	1	0	0	0	0	0	0	.200	.200	.200	.400	11	-1	-1	108	0	0	.200	0	0	0	1	/O	0.0
	Was-A	56	166	19	45	4	2	0	15	15	9	.271	.331	.319	.651	84	-4	-3	97	104	17	.546	3	1	0	-4	O/3	-0.9
	Yr	58	171	19	46	4	2	0	15	15	9	.269	.328	.316	.644	82	-5	-4	97	101	17	.537	3	1	0	-3		-0.9
1948	Was-A	92	206	22	53	9	1	1	29	28	15	.257	.346	.325	.671	77	-6	-7	103	140	23	.584	2	2	-1	-1	O	-0.9
Total	6	408	1186	140	326	39	16	2	141	93	63	.275	.328	.340	.668	88	-19	-20	100	124	130	.582	13	6	0	-6	O/13	-3.5
■ SWAT McCABE McCabe, James Arthur b: 11/20/1881, Towanda, Pa. d: 12/9/44, Bristol, Conn. BL/TR, 5'10", Deb: 09																												
1909	Cin-N	3	11	2	6	1	0	0	0	1		.545	.583	.636	1.220	299	2	2	94	0	5	1.800	1			0	/O	0.2
1910	Cin-N	13	35	3	9	1	0	0	5	1	2	.257	.297	.286	.583	69	-1	-1	101	174	3	.462	0			0	/O	-0.1
Total	2	16	46	5	15	2	0	0	5	2	2	.326	.367	.370	.737	119	1	1	99	132	7	.677	1			0	/O	0.1
■ JOE McCABE McCabe, Joseph Robert b: 8/27/38, Indianapolis, Ind. BR/TR, 6', 190 lbs. Deb: 4/18/64																												
1964	Min-A	14	19	1	3	0	0	0	2	0	8	.158	.158	.158	.316	-12	-3	-3	101	283	1	.188	0	0	0	-1	C	-0.3
1965	Was-A	14	27	1	5	0	0	1	5	4	13	.185	.290	.296	.587	67	-1	-1	100	189	3	.591	1	0	0	1	C	0.0
Total	2	28	46	2	8	0	0	1	7	4	21	.174	.240	.239	.479	35	-4	-4	100	224	3	.421	1	0	0	-0	/C	-0.3
■ BILL McCABE McCabe, William Francis b: 10/28/1892, Chicago, Ill. d: 9/2/66, Chicago, Ill. BB/TR, 5'9.5", 180 lbs. Deb: 4/16/18																												
1918	Chi-N	29	45	9	8	0	1	0	5	4	7	.178	.245	.222	.467	42	-3	-3	102	189	3	.432	2			-1	2/O	-0.3
1919	Chi-N	33	84	8	13	3	1	0	5	9	15	.155	.253	.214	.467	41	-6	-6	100	108	5	.451	3			-1	O/S3	-0.8
1920	Chi-N	3	2	1	1	0	0	0	0	0	0	.500	.500	.500	1.000	190	0	0	99	0	0	1.000	0	0	0	0	H	0.0
	Bro-N	41	68	10	10	0	0	0	3	2	6	.147	.171	.147	.318	-7	-9	-10	111	116	2	.217	1	2	-1	-2	S/O23	-1.3
	Yr	44	70	11	11	0	0	0	3	2	6	.157	.181	.157	.338	-2	-9	-10	110	108	2	.230	1	2	-1	-2		-1.3
Total	3	106	199	28	32	3	2	0	13	15	28	.161	.227	.196	.423	25	-18	-19	104	128	10	.367	6	2		-4	/OS23	-2.4
■ HARRY McCAFFERY McCaffery, Harry Charles b: 11/25/1858, St.Louis, Mo. d: 4/19/28, St.Louis, Mo. BR/TR, 5'10.5", 185 lbs. Deb: 6/15/1882																												
1882	Lou-a	1	4	1	1	0	0	0		0		.250	.250	.250	.500	74	-0	-0	94	0	0	.333				0	/2	0.0
	StL-a	38	153	23	42	8	6	0		3		.275	.288	.405	.694	132	5	5	100	0	18	.586				5	O/231	0.9
	Yr	39	157	24	43	8	6	0		3		.274	.287	.401	.689	130	5	5	100	0	19	.579				5		0.9
1883	StL-a	5	18	0	1	0	0	0		1		.056	.105	.056	.161	-43	-3	-3	108	0	0	.118				0	/O	-0.2
1885	Cin-a	1	5	0	0	0	0	0		0		.000	.000	.000	.000	-96	-1	-1	104	0	0	.000				0	/P	0.0
Total	3	45	180	24	44	8	6	0		4		.244	.261	.356	.616	104	1	0	101	0	19	.500				5	/O23P1	0.7

YEAR	TM/L	G	AB	R	H	2B	3B	HR	RBI	BB	SO	AVG	OBP	SLG	PRO	/A	BR	/A	PF	CHI	RC	TA	SB	CS	SBR	FR	POS	TPR
■ **SPARROW McCAFFREY**	McCaffrey, Charles P. b: Philadelphia, Pa. d: 4/29/1894, Philadelphia, Pa. 120 lbs. Deb: 8/13/1889																											
1889	Col-a	2	1	1	1	0	0	0	0	1	0	1.000	1.000	1.000	2.000	524	1	1	91	0	1	—	0			0	/C	0.1
■ **BRIAN McCALL**	McCall, Brian Allen "Bam" b: 1/25/43, Kentfield, Cal. BL/TL, 5'10", 170 lbs. Deb: 9/18/62																											
1962	Chi-A	4	8	2	3	0	0	2	3	0	2	.375	.375	1.125	1.500	301	2	2	95	79	3	1.800	0	0	0	0	/O	0.2
1963	Chi-A	3	7	1	0	0	0	0	0	1	2	.000	.125	.000	.125	-59	-2	-2	104	0	0	.143	0	0	0	-0	/O	-0.1
Total	2	7	15	3	3	0	0	2	3	1	4	.200	.250	.600	.850	125	0	0	100	40	3	.833	0	0	0	0	/O	0.1
■ **JACK McCANDLESS**	McCandless, Scott Cook b: 5/5/1891, Pittsburgh, Pa. d: 8/17/61, Pittsburgh, Pa. BL/TR, 6', 170 lbs. Deb: 9/10/14																											
1914	Bal-F	11	31	5	8	0	1	0	1	3	0	.258	.324	.323	.646	86	-1	-1	99	36	3	.565	0			0	/O	0.0
1915	Bal-F	117	406	47	87	6	7	5	34	41	99	.214	.286	.300	.587	69	-13	-17	107	91	39	.539	9			7	*O	-1.5
Total	2	128	437	52	95	6	8	5	35	44	99	.217	.289	.302	.591	70	-14	-17	106	87	43	.541	9			7	O	-1.5
■ **EMMETT McCANN**	McCann, Robert Emmett b: 3/4/02, Philadelphia, Pa. d: 4/15/37, Philadelphia, Pa. BR/TR, 5'11", 150 lbs. Deb: 4/19/20																											
1920	Phi-A	13	34	4	9	1	1	0	3	3	1	.265	.342	.353	.695	90	-1	-0	94	88	4	.615	0	1	-1	0	S	0.0
1921	Phi-A	52	157	15	35	5	0	0	15	4	6	.223	.242	.255	.497	26	-17	-18	103	128	10	.374	2	1	0	-6	S/321	-1.8
1926	Bos-A	6	3	0	0	0	0	0	0	1	1	.000	.250	.000	.250	-31	-1	-1	101	0	0	.333	0	0	0	0	/S3	0.0
Total	3	71	194	19	44	6	1	0	18	8	8	.227	.261	.268	.529	36	-19	-19	101	118	14	.414	2	2	-1	-6	/S321	-1.8
■ **ROGER McCARDELL**	McCardell, Roger Morton b: 8/29/32, Gorsuch Mills, Md. BR/TR, 6', 200 lbs. Deb: 5/08/59																											
1959	SF-N	4	4	0	0	0	0	0	0	0	0	.000	.000	.000	.000	-99	-1	-1	95	0	0	.000	0	0	0	0	/C	0.0
■ **BILL McCARREN**	McCarren, William Joseph b: 11/4/1895, Fortenia, Pa. d: 9/11/83, Denver, Colo. BR/TR, 5'11.5", 170 lbs. Deb: 5/04/23																											
1923	Bro-N	69	216	28	53	10	1	3	27	22	39	.245	.326	.343	.669	78	-7	-6	98	114	25	.610	0	1	-1	-0	3/O	-0.5
■ **ALEX McCARTHY**	McCarthy, Alexander George b: 5/12/1888, Chicago, Ill. d: 3/12/78, Salisbury, Md. BR/TR, 5'9", 150 lbs. Deb: 10/07/10																											
1910	Pit-N	3	12	1	1	0	1	0	0	0	2	.083	.083	.250	.333	-3	-2	-2	112	0	0	.273	0			0	/S	-0.1
1911	Pit-N	50	150	18	36	5	1	2	31	14	24	.240	.305	.327	.632	76	-5	-5	101	191	16	.588	4			-1	S2/3O	-0.4
1912	Pit-N	111	401	53	111	12	4	1	41	30	26	.277	.332	.334	.666	83	-10	-9	99	103	48	.603	8			-15	*2/3	-2.7
1913	Pit-N	31	74	7	15	5	0	0	10	7	7	.203	.298	.270	.568	65	-3	-3	96	182	7	.525	1			-1	S3/2	-0.3
1914	Pit-N	57	173	14	26	0	1	1	14	6	17	.150	.192	.179	.371	12	-19	-18	92	149	6	.286	2			-2	32/S	-1.9
1915	Pit-N	21	49	3	10	0	1	0	3	5	10	.204	.291	.245	.536	64	-2	-2	99	95	4	.463	1	2	-1	-2	/2S31	-0.4
	Chi-N	23	72	4	19	3	0	1	6	5	7	.264	.329	.347	.676	103	0	0	102	82	8	.607	2	3	-1	0	23/S	0.0
	Yr	44	121	7	29	3	1	1	9	10	17	.240	.313	.306	.619	87	-2	-2	100	90	12	.546	3	5	-2	-2		-0.4
1916	Chi-N	37	107	10	26	2	3	0	6	11	7	.243	.341	.318	.659	88	1	-1	117	70	12	.630	1			1	2/S	0.1
	Pit-N	50	146	11	29	3	0	0	3	15	10	.199	.282	.219	.501	53	-7	-8	105	37	11	.444	3			-5	S/23	-1.2
	Yr	87	253	21	55	5	3	0	9	26	17	.217	.308	.261	.569	69	-6	-9	110	52	24	.520	4			-5		-1.1
1917	Pit-N	49	151	15	33	4	0	0	8	11	13	.219	.276	.245	.521	61	-7	-7	100	83	11	.424	1			-5	32/S	-1.2
Total	8	432	1335	136	306	34	11	5	122	104	123	.229	.295	.282	.577	67	-53	-54	101	108	124	.507	23	5		-30	2S3/1O	-8.1
■ **JERRY McCARTHY**	McCarthy, Jerome Francis b: 5/23/23, Brooklyn, N.Y. d: 10/3/65, Oceanside, N.Y. BL/TL, 6'1", 205 lbs. Deb: 6/19/48																											
1948	StL-A	2	3	0	1	0	0	0	0	0	0	.333	.333	.333	.667	73	-0	-0	106	0	0	.500	0	0	0	0	/1	0.0
■ **JACK McCARTHY**	McCarthy, John Arthur b: 3/26/1869, Gilbertville, Mass d: 9/11/31, Chicago, Ill. BL/TL, 5'9", 155 lbs. Deb: 8/03/1893																											
1893	Cin-N	49	195	28	55	8	3	0	22	22	7	.282	.355	.354	.709	89	-2	-3	101	92	27	.693	6			-1	O/1	-0.3
1894	Cin-N	40	167	29	45	9	1	0	21	17	6	.269	.348	.335	.683	67	-9	-9	100	91	21	.648	3			0	O1	-0.6
1898	Pit-N	137	537	75	155	13	12	4	78	34		.289	.334	.380	.714	110	4	6	98	105	72	.649	7			1	*O	0.0
1899	Pit-N	138	560	108	171	22	17	3	67	39		.305	.355	.421	.776	117	11	12	99	81	96	.789	28			-8	*O	-0.4
1900	Chi-N	124	503	68	148	16	7	0	48	24		.294	.326	.354	.680	97	-7	-2	93	74	67	.631	22			-7	*O	-1.7
1901	Cle-A	86	343	60	110	14	7	0	32	30		.321	.375	.402	.778	125	9	12	95	70	57	.760	9			1	O	1.1
1902	Cle-A	95	359	45	102	31	5	0	41	24		.284	.329	.398	.727	106	1	2	97	96	52	.696	12			-4	O	-0.6
1903	Cle-A	108	415	47	110	20	8	0	43	19		.265	.297	.352	.649	99	-2	-1	96	112	49	.590	15			-14	*O	-2.2
	Chi-N	24	101	11	28	5	0	0	14	4		.277	.305	.327	.631	86	-3	-2	95	120	13	.616	8			2	O	0.0
1904	Chi-N	115	432	36	114	14	2	0	51	23		.264	.301	.306	.607	89	-5	-6	101	150	45	.531	14			-10	*O	-2.1
1905	Chi-N	59	170	16	47	4	3	0	14	10		.276	.317	.335	.652	92	-1	-2	105	85	21	.610	8			4	O/1	0.0
1906	Bro-N	91	322	23	98	13	1	0	35	20		.304	.345	.351	.696	138	7	11	87	120	43	.634	9			1	O	1.2
1907	Bro-N	25	91	4	20	2	0	0	8	2		.220	.237	.242	.478	54	-5	-5	94	146	6	.394	4			2	O	-0.3
Total	12	1091	4195	550	1203	171	66	7	474	268	13	.287	.331	.364	.695	103	-4	16	97	100	570	.652	145			-32	*O/1	-5.9
■ **JOHNNY McCARTHY**	McCarthy, John Joseph b: 1/7/10, Chicago, Ill. d: 9/13/73, Mundelein, Ill. BL/TL, 6'1.5", 185 lbs. Deb: 9/02/34																											
1934	Bro-N	17	39	7	7	2	0	1	5	2	2	.179	.220	.308	.527	42	-3	-3	95	120	3	.424	0			0	1	-0.3
1935	Bro-N	22	48	9	12	1	1	0	4	2	9	.250	.280	.313	.592	63	-3	-2	94	96	4	.500	1			-0	1	-0.2
1936	NY-N	4	16	1	7	0	0	1	2	0	1	.438	.438	.625	1.063	182	2	2	100	56	4	1.100	1			0	/1	0.1
1937	NY-N	114	420	53	117	19	3	10	65	24	37	.279	.322	.410	.732	97	-2	-2	100	118	56	.644	2			4	*1	-0.4
1938	NY-N	134	470	55	128	13	4	8	59	39	28	.272	.329	.368	.697	89	-5	-7	103	110	60	.621	3			-5	*1	-2.2
1939	NY-N	50	80	12	21	6	1	1	11	3	8	.262	.298	.400	.698	87	-2	-2	99	115	9	.590	0			-2	1/OP	-0.4
1940	NY-N	51	67	6	16	4	0	0	5	2	8	.239	.261	.299	.559	54	-4	-4	100	93	4	.407	0			0	/1	-0.4
1941	NY-N	14	40	1	13	3	0	0	12	3	0	.325	.372	.400	.772	114	1	1	103	271	6	.679	0			-0	/1O	0.0
1943	Bos-N	78	313	32	95	24	6	2	33	10	19	.304	.327	.438	.765	114	6	4	106	88	41	.651	1			1	1	0.2
1946	Bos-N	2	7	0	1	0	0	0	1	2	0	.143	.333	.143	.476	40	-0	-0	95	358	1	.500	0			0	/1	0.0
1948	NY-N	56	57	6	15	0	1	2	12	3	2	.263	.300	.404	.704	89	-1	-1	100	155	7	.605	0			0	/1	0.0
Total	11	542	1557	182	432	72	16	25	209	90	114	.277	.319	.392	.712	94	-13	-16	102	114	194	.635	8			-1	1/OP	-3.6
■ **JOE McCARTHY**	McCarthy, Joseph N. b: 12/25/1881, Syracuse, N.Y. d: 1/12/37, Syracuse, N.Y. TR , Deb: 9/27/05																											
1905	NY-A	1	2	0	0	0	0	0	0	0		.000	.000	.000	.000	-98	-0	-0	102	0	0	.000	0			0	/C	0.0
1906	StL-N	15	37	3	9	2	0	0	2	2		.243	.282	.297	.579	82	-1	-1	101	66	3	.464	0			-1	C	0.0
Total	2	16	39	3	9	2	0	0	2	2		.231	.268	.282	.550	73	-1	-1	101	63	3	.433	0			-1	/C	0.0
■ **TOMMY McCARTHY**	McCarthy, Thomas Francis Michael b: 7/24/1863, Boston, Mass. d: 8/5/22, Boston, Mass. BR/TR, 5'7", 170 lbs. Deb: 7/10/1884 M																											
1884	Bos-U	53	209	37	45	2	2	0		6		.215	.237	.244	.481	64	-8	-7	98	0	12	.348	0			-3	O/P	-0.9
1885	Bos-N	40	148	16	27	2	0	0	11	5	25	.182	.209	.196	.405	34	-11	-10	94	134	6	.281				2	O	-0.7
1886	Phi-N	8	27	6	5	2	1	0	3	2	3	.185	.241	.333	.575	75	-1	-1	98	111	2	.545	1			0	/OP	0.0
1887	Phi-N	18	70	7	13	4	0	0	6	2	5	.186	.219	.243	.462	30	-7	-6	97	111	7	.614	15			0	/O2S3	-0.4
1888	StL-a	131	511	107	140	20	3	1	68	38		.274	.328	.331	.659	103	9	1	111	125	88	.817	93			31	*O/P	2.4
1889	StL-a	140	604	136	176	24	7	2	63	46	26	.291	.348	.364	.712	93	4	-9	112	69	99	.769	57			15	*O/2P	0.1
1890	StL-a	133	548	137	192	28	9	6		66		.350	.430	.467	.898	145	**48**	33	116	0	**150**	**1.169**	**83**			3	*O3/2M	2.7
1891	StL-a	136	578	127	179	21	6	8	95	50	19	.310	.375	.408	.783	111	20	6	114	102	105	.835	37			3	*O2S/3P	0.4
1892	Bos-N	152	603	119	146	19	5	4	63	93	29	.242	.347	.310	.657	89	4	-8	113	86	85	.737	53			1	*O	-1.0
1893	Bos-N	116	462	107	160	28	6	5	111	64	10	.346	.429	.465	.894	136	28	26	103	140	115	1.086	46			3	*O/2S	2.0
1894	Bos-N	127	539	118	188	21	8	13	126	59	17	.349	.419	.490	.909	106	19	4	113	121	132	1.060	43			13	*O/S2P	0.7
1895	Bos-N	117	452	90	131	13	2	2	73	72	12	.290	.391	.341	.732	89	-2	-4	103	135	69	.769	18			-8	*O/2	-1.7
1896	Bro-N	104	377	62	94	8	4	3	47	34	17	.249	.316	.316	.632	78	-17	-8	87	108	46	.629	22			-1	*O	-1.4
Total	13	1275	5128	1069	1496	192	53	44	666	537	163	.292	.364	.376	.740	103	87	17	108	93	916	.821	468			60	*O/23SP	2.2
■ **BILL McCARTHY**	McCarthy, William John b: Boston, Mass. d: 2/4/28, Washington, D.C. TR , Deb: 6/05/05																											
1905	Bos-N	1	3	0	0	0	0	0	0	0		.000	.000	.000	.000	-99	-1	-1	97	0	0	.000	0			0	/C	0.0
1907	Cin-N	3	8	1	1	0	0	0	0	0		.125	.125	.125	.250	-22	-1	-1	95	0	0	.143	0			0	/C	0.0
Total	2	4	11	1	1	0	0	0	0	0		.091	.091	.091	.182	-45	-2	-2	96	0	0	.100	0			0	/C	0.0
■ **FRANK McCARTON**	McCarton, Francis b: 10/6/1854, Middleton, Conn. d: 6/17/07, New York, N.Y. Deb: 4/26/1872																											
1872	Man-n	19	85	17	23							.271															O	

YEAR	TM/L	G	AB	R	H	2B	3B	HR	RBI	BB	SO	AVG	OBP	SLG	PRO	/A	BR	/A	PF	CHI	RC	TA	SB	CS	SBR	FR	POS	TPR
■ **LEW McCARTY**	McCarty, George Lewis b: 11/17/1888, Milton, Pa. d: 6/9/30, Reading, Pa. BR/TR, 5'11.5", 192 lbs. Deb: 8/30/13																											
1913	Bro-N	9	26	1	6	0	0	0	2	2	2	.231	.286	.231	.516	46	-2	-2	104	121	2	.400	0			-2	/C	-0.3
1914	Bro-N	90	284	20	72	14	2	1	30	14	22	.254	.293	.327	.621	84	-6	-6	101	113	27	.519	1			9	C	0.5
1915	Bro-N	84	276	19	66	9	4	0	19	7	23	.239	.261	.301	.561	69	-11	-11	101	87	23	.458	7	4	-0	3	C	-0.3
1916	Bro-N	55	150	17	47	6	1	0	13	14	16	.313	.383	.367	.750	127	6	6	103	94	24	.738	4			1	C1	0.8
	NY-N	25	68	6	27	3	4	0	9	7	9	.397	.453	.559	1.012	219	9	9	96	94	18	1.098	0			-3	C	0.8
	Yr	80	218	23	74	9	5	0	22	21	25	.339	.405	.427	.832	154	15	15	101	95	41	.840	4			-2		1.6
1917	NY-N	56	162	15	40	3	2	2	19	14	6	.247	.311	.327	.638	99	-1	-0	97	124	16	.566	1			-12	C	-1.1
1918	NY-N	86	257	16	69	7	3	0	24	17	13	.268	.321	.319	.640	98	-1	-1	98	111	27	.559	3			-9	C	-0.3
1919	NY-N	85	210	17	59	5	4	2	21	18	15	.281	.341	.371	.712	114	4	4	100	97	27	.656	2			-7	C	0.1
1920	NY-N	36	38	2	5	0	0	0	0	4	2	.132	.214	.132	.346	1	-5	-5	100	0	1	.333	2	0	1	-0	/C	-0.3
	StL-N	5	7	0	2	0	0	0	0	5	0	.286	.583	.286	.869	158	1	1	98	0	2	1.400	0	0	0	0	/C	0.1
	Yr	41	45	2	7	0	0	0	0	9	2	.156	.296	.156	.452	32	-4	-3	99	0	3	.474	2	0	1	-0		-0.2
1921	StL-N	1	1	0	0	0	0	0	0	0	1	.000	.000	.000	.000	-99	-0	-0	95	0	0	.000	0	0	0	0	H	0.0
Total	9	532	1479	113	393	47	20	5	137	102	109	.266	.318	.335	.653	97	-6	-5	100	100	167	.576	20	4		-21	C/1	-0.0
■ **TIM McCARVER**	McCarver, James Timothy b: 10/16/41, Memphis, Tenn. BL/TR, 6', 183 lbs. Deb: 9/10/59																											
1959	StL-N	8	24	3	4	1	0	0	0	2	1	.167	.231	.208	.439	17	-3	-3	105	0	1	.350	0	0	0	-0	/C	-0.2
1960	StL-N	10	10	3	2	0	0	0	0	0	2	.200	.200	.200	.400	9	-1	-1	108	0	0	.222	0	0	0	-0	/C	0.0
1961	StL-N	22	67	5	16	2	1	1	6	0	5	.239	.239	.343	.582	46	-5	-6	113	93	5	.442	0	0	0	-2	C	-0.5
1963	StL-N	127	405	39	117	12	7	4	51	27	43	.289	.336	.383	.719	99	3	0	107	128	53	.643	5	2	0	-10	*C	-0.5
1964	StL-N	143	465	53	134	19	3	9	52	40	44	.288	.346	.400	.746	97	6	-1	112	100	64	.676	2	0	1	0	*C	0.4
1965	StL-N	113	409	48	113	17	2	11	48	31	26	.276	.329	.408	.737	100	3	-0	107	101	55	.673	5	1	1	12	*C	1.8
1966	StL-N	150	543	50	149	19	**13**	12	68	36	38	.274	.322	.424	.745	105	3	3	100	110	71	.676	9	6	-1	13	*C	2.0
1967	StL-N	138	471	68	139	26	3	14	69	54	32	.295	.374	.452	.826	134	22	22	101	114	78	.802	8	8	-2	16	*C	4.6
1968	StL-N	128	434	35	110	15	6	5	48	26	31	.253	.297	.350	.647	98	-4	-2	95	121	44	.550	4	3	-1	11	*C	1.4
1969	StL-N	138	515	46	134	27	3	7	51	49	26	.260	.327	.365	.692	94	-4	-4	100	104	60	.609	4	9	-4	14	*C	1.5
1970	Phi-N	44	164	16	47	11	1	4	14	14	10	.287	.346	.439	.785	113	2	3	96	66	24	.730	2	2	-1	-2	C	0.1
1971	Phi-N	134	474	51	132	20	5	8	46	43	26	.278	.340	.392	.732	104	4	3	103	91	62	.660	5	3	-0	7	*C	1.3
1972	Phi-N	45	152	14	36	8	0	2	14	17	15	.237	.322	.329	.651	88	-3	-2	97	105	17	.583	1	2	-1	-3	C	-0.3
	Mon-N	77	239	19	60	5	1	5	20	19	14	.251	.309	.343	.652	83	-5	-5	102	85	24	.558	4	4	-1	-4	CO/3	-0.9
	Yr	122	391	33	96	13	1	7	34	36	29	.246	.314	.338	.652	85	-7	-8	100	93	41	.571	5	6	-2	-8		-1.2
1973	StL-N	130	331	30	88	16	4	3	49	38	31	.266	.345	.366	.711	107	-1	3	91	151	44	.660	2	0	1	-0	1C	0.0
1974	StL-N	74	106	13	23	0	1	0	11	22	6	.217	.366	.236	.602	69	-3	-3	104	170	11	.581	0	1	-1	1	C/1	-0.1
	Bos-A	11	28	3	7	1	0	0	1	4	1	.250	.344	.286	.629	78	-0	-1	107	49	3	.619	1	0	0	0	/CD	0.0
1975	Bos-A	12	21	1	8	2	1	0	3	1	3	.381	.409	.571	.981	161	2	2	109	96	5	1.000	0	0	0	0	/C1	0.2
	Phi-N	47	59	6	15	2	0	1	7	14	7	.254	.397	.339	.736	104	1	1	101	118	9	.773	0	0	0	-1	C/1	0.1
1976	Phi-N	90	155	26	43	11	2	3	29	35	14	.277	.414	.432	.846	131	10	8	107	147	31	.921	2	1	0	-4	C/1	0.7
1977	Phi-N	93	169	28	54	13	2	6	30	28	11	.320	.422	.527	.949	152	14	13	100	112	37	.984	3	5	-2	-0	C/1	1.0
1978	Phi-N	90	146	18	36	9	1	1	14	28	24	.247	.375	.342	.717	96	2	1	105	105	20	.713	2	2	-1	-2	C1	-0.1
1979	Phi-N	79	137	13	33	5	1	1	12	19	12	.241	.338	.314	.651	81	-3	-3	97	103	14	.586	2	0	1	-1	C/O	-0.2
1980	Phi-N	6	5	2	1	1	0	0	2	1	0	.200	.333	.400	.733	97	0	-0	107	396	0	.600	0	0	0	0	/1	0.0
Total	21	1909	5529	590	1501	242	57	97	645	548	422	.271	.340	.388	.729	103	41	28	102	110	735	.683	61	49	-11	45	*C1/O3D	12.3
■ **AL McCAULEY**	McCauley, Allen A. b: 3/4/1863, Indianapolis, Ind. d: 8/24/17, Wayne Twnshp., Ind BL/TL, 6', 180 lbs. Deb: 6/21/1884																											
1884	Ind-a	17	53	7	10	0	1	0		12		.189	.358	.226	.585	102	1	1	96	0	4	.605				0	P/1O	0.0
1890	Phi-N	112	418	63	102	25	7	1	42	57	38	.244	.346	.344	.690	96	3	-2	108	91	54	.687	8			-6	*1	-1.3
1891	Was-a	59	206	36	58	5	8	1	31	30	13	.282	.378	.398	.776	131	7	9	95	107	35	.831	9			-2	1	0.4
Total	3	188	677	106	170	30	16	2	73	99	51	.251	.357	.352	.708	106	12	8	103	88	94	.722	17			-7	1/PO	-0.9
■ **JIM McCAULEY**	McCauley, James A. b: 3/24/1863, Stanley, N.Y. d: 9/14/30, Canandaiqua.N.Y. BL/TR, 6', 180 lbs. Deb: 9/17/1884																											
1884	StL-a	1	2	0	0	0	0	0		0		.000	.000	.000	.000	-91	-0	-0	110	0	0	.000				0	/C	0.0
1885	Buf-N	24	84	4	15	2	1	0	7	11	12	.179	.274	.226	.500	64	-3	-3	99	136	5	.435				0	C/O	-0.2
	Chi-N	3	6	1	1	0	0	0	0	2	3	.167	.375	.167	.542	70	0	-0	114	0	0	.600				0	/CO	0.0
	Yr	27	90	5	16	2	1	0	7	13	15	.178	.282	.222	.504	64	-3	-3	101	126	6	.446				0		-0.2
1886	Bro-a	11	30	5	7	1	0	0		11		.233	.439	.267	.706	125	2	2	100	0	5	.913	2			0	C	0.2
Total	3	39	122	10	23	3	1	0	7	24	15	.189	.322	.230	.551	79	-1	-2	100	88	10	.545	2			0	/CO	0.0
■ **PAT McCAULEY**	McCauley, Patrick M. b: 6/10/1870, Ware, Mass. d: 1/23/17, Newark, N.J. TR , Deb: 9/05/1893																											
1893	StL-N	5	16	0	1	0	0	0	0	0	1	.063	.063	.063	.125	-67	-4	-4	99	0	0	.067	0			0	/C	-0.2
1896	Was-N	26	84	14	21	3	0	2	11	7	8	.250	.315	.357	.672	83	-3	-2	95	88	11	.651	3			0	C/O	-0.1
1903	NY-A	6	19	0	1	0	0	0	1	0		.053	.053	.053	.105	-68	-4	-4	100	360	0	.056	0			-1	/C	-0.3
Total	3	37	119	14	23	3	0	2	12	7	9	.193	.244	.269	.513	41	-10	-9	96	118	11	.448	3			-1	/CO	-0.6
■ **BILL McCAULEY**	McCauley, William H. b: 12/20/1869, Washington, D.C. d: 1/27/26, Washington, D.C. Deb: 8/31/1895																											
1895	Was-N	1	2	0	0	0	0	0	0	0	0	.000	.000	.000	.000	-97	-1	-1	103	0	0	.000	0			0	/S	0.0
■ **HARRY McCHESNEY**	McChesney, Harry Vincent "Pud" b: 6/1/1880, Pittsburgh, Pa. d: 8/11/60, Pittsburgh, Pa. BR/TR, 5'9", 165 lbs. Deb: 9/17/04																											
1904	Chi-N	22	88	9	23	6	2	0	11	4		.261	.293	.375	.668	107	0	0	101	108	11	.600	2			-1	O	-0.1
■ **PETE McCLANAHAN**	McClanahan, Peter b: 10/24/06, Coldspring, Tex. BR/TR, 5'9", 170 lbs. Deb: 4/24/31																											
1931	Pit-N	7	4	2	2	0	0	0	0	2	0	.500	.667	.500	1.167	217	1	1	101	0	2	2.000	0			0	H	0.1
■ **HARVEY McCLELLAN**	McClellan, Harvey Mc Dowell "Little Mac" b: 12/22/1894, Cynthiana, Ky. d: 11/6/25, Cynthiana, Ky. BR/TR, 5'9.5", 143 lbs. Deb: 5/31/19																											
1919	Chi-A	7	12	2	4	0	0	0	1	1	1	.333	.385	.333	.718	98	0	0	105	91	1	.625	0			-0	/3S	0.0
1920	Chi-A	10	18	4	6	1	1	0	5	4	1	.333	.455	.500	.955	159	2	2	96	195	5	1.250	2	0	1	-0	/S3	0.2
1921	Chi-A	63	196	20	35	4	1	1	14	14	18	.179	.237	.224	.461	18	-24	-24	99	102	11	.372	2	3	-1	7	2SO/3	-1.5
1922	Chi-A	91	301	28	68	17	3	2	28	16	32	.226	.272	.322	.594	54	-21	-21	101	97	27	.506	3	2	-0	2	3/S2O	-1.0
1923	Chi-A	141	550	67	129	29	3	1	41	27	44	.235	.270	.304	.574	52	-40	-39	98	87	45	.481	14	11	-2	-17	*S/2	-4.3
1924	Chi-A	32	85	9	15	3	0	0	9	6	7	.176	.239	.212	.451	17	-11	-10	97	165	5	.386	2	0	1	-3	S/23O	-0.9
Total	6	344	1162	130	257	54	8	4	98	68	103	.221	.267	.292	.559	46	-95	-93	99	100	95	.472	23	16		-11	S/32O	-7.5
■ **BILL McCLELLAN**	McClellan, William Henry b: 3/22/1856, Chicago, Ill. d: 7/3/29, Chicago, Ill. BL/TL, 156 lbs. Deb: 5/20/1878																											
1878	Chi-N	48	205	26	46	6	1	0	29	2	13	.224	.232	.263	.495	58	-8	-10	108	**193**	13	.352				-10	*2/SO	-1.5
1881	Pro-N	68	259	30	43	3	1	0	16	15	21	.166	.212	.185	.397	28	-21	-19	93	118	10	.292				-8	SO/2	-2.1
1883	Phi-N	80	326	42	75	21	4	1	33	19	18	.230	.272	.328	.601	90	-7	-2	90	100	30	.502				4	*S/O3	0.5
1884	Phi-N	111	450	71	116	13	2	3	33	28	43	.258	.301	.316	.617	102	-3	3	92	72	44	.509				-12	*S/O	0.1
1885	Bro-a	112	464	85	124	22	7	0		28		.267	.317	.345	.662	108	7	4	104	0	52	.571				-6	32	0.3
1886	Bro-a	141	595	131	152	33	9	1		56		.255	.322	.346	.668	111	8	8	100	0	82	.693	43			-6	*2	0.1
1887	Bro-a	136	548	109	144	24	6	1		80		.263	.363	.334	.697	99	2	3	99	0	94	.839	70			-26	*2	-1.7
1888	Bro-a	74	278	33	57	7	3	0	21	40		.205	.307	.252	.559	79	-3	-5	105	86	26	.561	13			-9	2O	-1.1
	Cle-a	22	72	6	16	0	0	0	5	6		.222	.282	.222	.504	67	-2	-2	97	93	6	.500	6			-2	O/2S	-0.3
	Yr	96	350	39	73	7	3	0	26	46		.209	.302	.246	.548	77	-6	-7	103	89	33	.549	19			-11		-1.4
Total	8	792	3197	533	773	129	33	6	137	274	95	.242	.305	.308	.613	92	-28	-21	99	50	358	.580	132			-76	2S/3O	-5.7
■ **LLOYD McCLENDON**	McClendon, Lloyd Glenn b: 1/11/59, Gary, Ind. BR/TR, 5'10", 195 lbs. Deb: 4/06/87																											
1987	Cin-N	45	72	8	15	5	0	2	13	4	15	.208	.250	.361	.611	57	-4	-5	104	162	7	.534	1	0	0	-0	C/13O	-0.3
1988	Cin-N	72	137	9	30	4	0	3	14	15	22	.219	.305	.314	.619	74	-4	-5	105	108	13	.566	4	0	1	-3	CO1/3	-0.6
Total	2	117	209	17	45	9	0	5	27	19	37	.215	.287	.330	.617	68	-8	-9	105	126	20	.559	5	0	2	-3	/CO13	-0.9

YEAR	TM/L	G	AB	R	H	2B	3B	HR	RBI	BB	SO	AVG	OBP	SLG	PRO	/A	BR	/A	PF	CHI	RC	TA	SB	CS	SBR	FR	POS	TPR
■ **JEFF McCLESKEY** McCleskey, Jefferson Lamar b: 11/6/1891, Americus, Ga. d: 5/11/71, Americus, Ga. BL/TR, 5'11", 160 lbs. Deb: 9/08/13																												
1913	Bos-N	2	3	0	0	0	0	0	0	1	0	.000	.250	.000	.250	-27	-0	-0	95	0	0	.333	0			0	/3	0.0
■ **McCLOSKEY** McCloskey Deb: 5/25/1875																												
1875	Nat-n	10	38	1	5							.132															C	
■ **BILL McCLOSKEY** McCloskey, William George b: 5/1854 Pennsylvania 5'8", 155 lbs. Deb: 8/18/1884																												
1884	WiL-U	9	30	0	3	0	0	0		0		.100	.100	.100	.200	-31	-4	-4	103	0	0	.111	0			0	/OC	-0.3
■ **HALL McCLURE** McClure, Harold Murray "Mac" b: 8/8/1859, Lewisburg, Pa. d: 6/5/19, Wilkes-Barre, Pa. TR, 6', 165 lbs. Deb: 5/10/1882																												
1882	Bos-N	2	6	1	2	0	0	0	0	0	1	.333	.333	.333	.667	111	0	0	103	0	1	.500				0	/O	0.0
■ **LARRY McCLURE** McClure, Lawrence Ledwith b: 10/3/1885, Wayne, W.Va. d: 8/31/49, Huntington, W.Va. BR, 5'6.5", 130 lbs. Deb: 7/26/10																												
1910	NY-A	1	1	0	0	0	0	0	0	0		.000	.000	.000	.000	-93	-0	-0	107	0	0	.000	0			0	/O	0.0
■ **AMBY McCONNELL** McConnell, Ambrose Moses b: 4/29/1883, N.Pownal, Vt. d: 5/20/42, Utica, N.Y. BL/TR, 5'7", 150 lbs. Deb: 4/17/08																												
1908	Bos-A	140	502	77	140	10	6	2	43	38		.279	.330	.335	.664	120	10	11	98	98	63	.655	31			-10	*2/S	-0.1
1909	Bos-A	121	453	61	108	7	8	0	36	34		.238	.300	.289	.589	79	-7	-11	109	102	45	.571	26			8	*2	-0.6
1910	Bos-A	11	35	6	6	0	0	0	1	5		.171	.310	.171	.481	52	-2	-2	99	63	3	.586	4			-0	2	-0.2
	Chi-A	33	120	13	33	2	3	0	5	7		.275	.320	.342	.662	113	1	1	95	46	14	.609	4			-1	2	-0.1
	Yr	44	155	19	39	2	3	0	6	12		.252	.318	.303	.621	99	-1	-0	96	52	17	.603	8			-1		-0.3
1911	Chi-A	104	396	45	111	11	5	1	34	23		.280	.331	.341	.672	91	-7	-5	97	88	47	.604	7			2	*2	-0.3
Total	4	409	1506	202	398	30	22	3	119	107		.264	.320	.319	.639	97	-4	-5	101	92	173	.610	72			-1	2/S	-1.3
■ **SAM McCONNELL** McConnell, Samuel Faulkner b: 6/8/1895, Philadelphia, Pa. d: 6/27/81, Phoenixville, Pa. BL/TR, 5'6.5", 150 lbs. Deb: 4/19/15																												
1915	Phi-A	6	11	1	2	1	0	0	0	1	3	.182	.250	.273	.523	59	-1	-1	96	0	1	.444	0			0	/3	0.0
■ **DON McCORMACK** McCormack, Donald Ross b: 9/18/55, Omak, Wash. BR/TR, 6'3", 205 lbs. Deb: 9/30/80																												
1980	Phi-N	2	1	0	1	0	0	0	0	0	0	1.000	1.000	1.000	2.000	428	0	0	107	0	1	—	0	0	0	0	/C	0.1
1981	Phi-N	3	4	0	1	0	0	0	0	0	1	.250	.250	.250	.500	38	-0	-0	112	0	0	.250	0	0	0	0	/C	0.0
Total	2	5	5	0	2	0	0	0	0	0	1	.400	.400	.400	.800	114	0	0	111	0	1	.500	0	0	0	0	/C	0.1
■ **FRANK McCORMICK** McCormick, Frank Andrew "Buck" b: 6/9/11, New York, N.Y. d: 11/21/82, Manhassett, N.Y. BR/TR, 6'4", 205 lbs. Deb: 9/11/34 C																												
1934	Cin-N	12	16	1	5	2	1	0	5	0	1	.313	.313	.563	.875	128	1	1	101	200	2	.750	0			0	/1	0.0
1937	Cin-N	24	83	5	27	5	0	0	9	2	4	.325	.341	.386	.727	106	-0	0	91	101	9	.574	1			-1	1/2O	0.0
1938	Cin-N	151	640	89	**209**	40	4	5	106	18	17	.327	.348	.425	.773	114	8	10	98	128	93	.659	1			-3	*1	-0.5
1939	Cin-N	156	630	99	**209**	41	4	18	**128**	40	16	.332	.374	.495	.869	128	26	24	103	**136**	110	.800	1			1	*1	0.7
1940	Cin-N	155	618	93	**191**	**44**	3	19	127	52	26	.309	.367	.482	.850	131	26	26	101	141	104	.793	2			1	*1	1.3
1941	Cin-N	154	603	77	162	31	5	17	97	40	13	.269	.318	.421	.740	108	3	4	99	122	76	.648	2			0	*1	-1.8
1942	Cin-N	145	564	58	156	24	0	13	89	45	18	.277	.332	.388	.721	109	6	6	101	135	72	.633	1			5	*1	0.0
1943	Cin-N	126	472	56	143	28	0	8	56	29	15	.303	.345	.413	.758	119	10	10	99	94	67	.674	2			8	*1	1.3
1944	Cin-N	153	581	85	177	37	3	20	102	57	17	.305	.371	.482	.853	145	29	32	95	114	101	.823	7			12	*1	3.2
1945	Cin-N	152	580	68	160	33	0	10	81	56	22	.276	.345	.384	.729	109	2	6	94	118	75	.659	6			6	*1	0.6
1946	Phi-N	135	504	46	143	20	2	11	66	36	21	.284	.333	.397	.730	112	3	6	95	108	66	.642	2			3	*1	-0.2
1947	Phi-N	15	40	7	9	2	0	1	8	3	2	.225	.279	.350	.629	66	-2	-2	100	174	3	.515	0			-0	1	-0.2
	Bos-N	81	212	24	75	18	2	2	43	11	8	.354	.386	.486	.871	134	9	9	97	146	37	.800	2			-0	1	0.6
	Yr	96	252	31	84	20	2	3	51	14	10	.333	.368	.464	.833	123	6	7	97	152	41	.756	2			-0		0.4
1948	Bos-N	75	180	14	45	9	2	4	34	10	9	.250	.289	.389	.678	81	-5	-6	102	155	19	.571	0			1	1	-0.4
Total	13	1534	5723	722	1711	334	26	128	951	399	189	.299	.348	.434	.781	119	114	126	98	125	834	.730	27			33	*1/2O	4.6
■ **MOOSE McCORMICK** McCormick, Harry Elwood b: 2/28/1881, Philadelphia, Pa. d: 7/9/62, Lewisburg, Pa. TL, 5'11", 180 lbs. Deb: 4/14/04																												
1904	NY-N	59	203	28	54	9	5	1	26	13		.266	.310	.374	.685	107	3	1	105	123	28	.685	13			-2	O	-0.2
	Pit-N	66	238	25	69	10	6	2	23	13		.290	.327	.408	.734	129	7	7	99	83	34	.686	6			0	O	0.5
	Yr	125	441	53	123	19	11	3	49	26		.279	.319	.392	.711	119	10	9	102	103	63	.686	19			-2		0.3
1908	Phi-N	11	22	0	2	0	0	0	2	2		.091	.167	.091	.258	-16	-3	-3	100	384	0	.200	0			0	/O	-0.2
	NY-N	73	252	31	76	16	3	0	32	4		.302	.313	.389	.701	121	6	5	104	128	31	.614	6			-8	O	-0.3
	Yr	84	274	31	78	16	3	0	34	6		.285	.300	.365	.665	110	3	2	104	166	30	.571	6			-8		-0.5
1909	NY-N	110	413	68	120	21	8	3	27	49		.291	.373	.402	.775	135	21	18	105	54	62	.765	4			-8	*O	0.7
1912	NY-N	42	39	4	13	4	1	0	8	6	9	.333	.422	.487	.909	143	3	3	104	142	8	1.000	1			-3	/O1	0.0
1913	NY-N	57	80	9	22	2	3	0	15	5	13	.275	.318	.375	.693	95	-0	-1	103	182	9	.603	0			-3	O	-0.3
Total	5	418	1247	165	356	62	26	6	133	92	22	.285	.337	.391	.728	122	36	31	103	101	174	.690	30			-23	O/1	0.2
■ **JIM McCORMICK** McCormick, James Ambrose b: 11/2/1868, Spencer, Mass. d: 2/1/48, Saco, Maine BR/TR, 6'1", 160 lbs. Deb: 9/10/1892																												
1892	StL-N	3	11	0	0	0	0	0	0	1	5	.000	.083	.000	.083	-78	-2	-2	95	0	0	.091	0			0	/23	-0.1
■ **JERRY McCORMICK** McCormick, John b: Philadelphia, Pa. d: 9/19/05, Philadelphia, Pa. Deb: 5/01/1883																												
1883	Bal-a	93	389	40	102	16	6	0		2		.262	.266	.334	.600	86	-4	-8	107	0	35	.460				0	*3	-0.5
1884	Phi-U	67	295	41	84	12	2	0		4		.285	.294	.339	.633	123	4	7	93	0	30	.493	0			7	3/2OSP	1.3
	Was-U	42	157	23	34	8	2	0		1		.217	.222	.293	.515	75	-4	-4	97	0	10	.382	0			-9	3/S	-0.9
	Yr	109	452	64	118	20	4	0		5		.261	.269	.323	.592	106	-1	3	94	0	40	.452	0			-2		0.4
Total	2	202	841	104	220	36	10	0		7		.262	.268	.328	.596	96	-5	-5	100	0	76	.456	0			-2	3/SO2P	-0.1
■ **MIKE McCORMICK** McCormick, Michael J. "Kid" or "Dude" b: 1883, Jersey City, N.J. d: 11/18/53, Jersey City, N.J. BR/TR, 5'9", Deb: 4/14/04																												
1904	Bro-N	105	347	28	64	5	4	0	27	43		.184	.274	.222	.496	58	-16	-14	95	131	28	.502	22			-7	*3/2	-1.7
■ **MIKE McCORMICK** McCormick, Myron Winthrop b: 5/6/17, Angels Camp, Cal. d: 4/14/76, Ventura, Cal. BR/TR, 6', 195 lbs. Deb: 4/16/40																												
1940	Cin-N	110	417	48	125	20	0	1	30	13	36	.300	.326	.355	.681	87	-7	-8	101	75	48	.575	8			10	*O	-0.1
1941	Cin-N	110	369	52	106	17	3	4	31	30	24	.287	.341	.382	.723	105	1	2	99	75	48	.643	4			8	*O	0.6
1942	Cin-N	40	135	18	32	2	3	1	11	13	7	.237	.304	.319	.623	81	-3	-3	101	89	13	.528	0			2	O	-0.1
1943	Cin-N	4	15	0	2	0	0	0	0	2	0	.133	.235	.133	.369	8	-2	-2	99	0	1	.286	0			-0	/O	-0.1
1946	Cin-N	23	74	10	16	2	0	0	5	8	4	.216	.293	.243	.536	51	-4	-5	104	106	6	.433	0			2	O	-0.3
	Bos-N	59	164	23	43	6	2	1	16	11	7	.262	.309	.341	.650	89	-4	-3	95	101	18	.545	0			-1	O	-0.4
	Yr	82	238	33	59	8	2	1	21	19	11	.248	.304	.311	.614	77	-8	-7	97	104	24	.514	0			1		-0.7
1947	Bos-N	92	284	42	81	13	7	3	36	20	21	.285	.332	.412	.744	100	-2	-1	97	106	37	.648	1			-5	O	-0.8
1948	Bos-N	115	343	45	104	22	7	1	39	32	34	.303	.363	.417	.780	109	5	4	102	100	52	.715	1			-6	*O	-0.8
1949	Bro-N	55	139	17	29	5	1	2	14	14	12	.209	.281	.302	.583	56	-9	-9	102	110	12	.500	1			-6	O	-1.7
1950	NY-N	4	4	0	0	0	0	0	0	0	2	.000	.000	.000	.000	-99	-1	-1	98	0	0	.000	0			0	H	0.0
	Chi-A	55	138	16	32	4	3	0	10	16	6	.232	.312	.304	.616	60	-9	-8	97	82	12	.509	0	1	-1	2	O	-0.6
1951	Was-A	81	243	31	70	9	3	1	23	29	20	.288	.364	.362	.726	101	-0	1	95	90	30	.621	1	2	-1	1	O	-0.1
Total	10	748	2325	302	640	100	29	14	215	188	173	.275	.330	.361	.692	90	-35	-32	99	90	277	.615	16	3		7	O	-4.4
■ **BARRY McCORMICK** McCormick, William J. b: 12/25/1874, Maysville, Ky. d: 1/28/56, Cincinnati, Ohio TR, 5'9", Deb: 9/25/1895																												
1895	Lou-N	3	12	2	3	0	1	0	0	0	0	.250	.250	.417	.667	75	-1	-0	95	0	2	.667	1			0	/S2	0.0
1896	Chi-N	45	168	22	37	3	1	1	23	14	30	.220	.280	.268	.548	43	-13	-15	108	141	16	.519	9			-5	3/S2O	-1.5
1897	Chi-N	101	419	87	112	8	10	2	55	33		.267	.324	.348	.672	79	-12	-12	100	93	63	.733	44			-3	3S/2	-1.2
1898	Chi-N	137	530	76	131	15	9	2	78	47		.247	.313	.321	.634	82	-10	-13	103	142	59	.591	15			1	*3/S2	-0.7
1899	Chi-N	102	376	48	97	15	2	2	52	25		.258	.311	.324	.636	80	-12	-10	96	127	43	.591	14			2	2/S	0.0
1900	Chi-N	110	379	35	83	13	5	3	48	38		.219	.290	.303	.594	71	-17	-13	93	123	37	.544	8			-8	S3/2	-1.0
1901	Chi-N	115	427	45	100	15	6	2	32	31		.234	.286	.311	.598	75	-13	-13	100	82	43	.538	12			-9	*S/3	-1.5
1902	StL-A	139	504	55	124	14	4	3	51	37		.246	.298	.308	.605	68	-20	-22	102	105	50	.532	10			-13	*3/SO	-3.6
1903	StL-A	61	207	13	45	6	1	1	16	18		.217	.280	.271	.551	71	-8	-6	95	100	18	.488	5			-4	23/S	-0.9

YEAR	TM/L	G	AB	R	H	2B	3B	HR	RBI	BB	SO	AVG	OBP	SLG	PRO	/A	BR	/A	PF	CHI	RC	TA	SB	CS	SBR	FR	POS	TPR
	Was-A	63	219	14	47	10	2	0	23	10		.215	.249	.279	.527	56	-11	-12	105	139	16	.430	3			2	2	-0.8
	Yr	124	426	27	92	16	3	1	39	28		.216	.264	.275	.539	63	-18	-18	100	120	34	.458	8			-2		-1.7
1904	Was-A	113	404	36	88	11	1	0	39	27		.218	.267	.250	.517	71	-15	-11	93	153	30	.434	9			0	*2	-1.1
Total	10	989	3645	433	867	110	42	16	417	280	30	.238	.294	.304	.598	72	-131	-128	99	119	376	.550	130			-36	32S/O	-12.3
■ BARNEY McCOSKY McCosky, William Barney b: 4/11/18, Coal Run, Pa. BL/TR, 6'1", 184 lbs. Deb: 4/18/39																												
1939	Det-A	147	611	120	190	33	14	4	58	70	45	.311	.384	.430	.814	97	8	-2	111	63	108	.822	20	4	4	5	*O	0.1
1940	Det-A	143	589	123	**200**	39	**19**	4	57	67	41	.340	.408	.491	.899	118	29	19	111	66	123	.911	13	9	-2	-5	*O	0.3
1941	Det-A	127	494	80	160	25	8	3	55	61	33	.324	.401	.425	.827	112	15	11	106	94	92	.825	8	3	1	-0	*O	0.3
1942	Det-A	154	600	75	176	28	11	7	50	68	37	.293	.365	.412	.777	105	15	5	113	63	94	.739	11	5	0	5	*O	0.0
1946	Det-A	25	91	11	18	5	0	1	11	17	9	.198	.324	.286	.610	66	-3	-4	108	153	10	.573	0	0	0	1	O	-0.4
	Phi-A	92	308	33	109	17	4	1	34	43	13	.354	.433	.445	.878	139	21	19	104	94	63	.883	2	2	-1	3	O	1.8
	Yr	117	399	44	127	22	4	2	45	60	22	.318	.407	.409	.816	122	18	15	105	108	73	.806	2	2	-1	4		1.4
1947	Phi-A	137	546	77	179	22	7	1	52	57	29	.328	.395	.399	.795	121	17	17	100	76	92	.745	1	4	-2	9	*O	1.9
1948	Phi-A	135	515	95	168	21	5	0	46	68	22	.326	.405	.386	.791	109	11	10	102	75	86	.744	1	3	-2	-4	*O	0.0
1950	Phi-A	66	179	19	43	10	1	0	11	22	12	.240	.323	.307	.631	69	-10	-7	90	69	19	.550	0	0	0	-6	O	-1.3
1951	Phi-A	12	27	4	8	2	0	1	1	3	4	.296	.367	.481	.848	121	1	1	106	22	5	.842	0	0	0	-1	/O	0.0
	Cin-N	25	50	2	16	2	1	1	11	4	2	.320	.370	.460	.830	121	1	1	101	164	9	.794	0	0	0	-2	O	0.0
	Cle-A	31	61	8	13	3	0	0	2	8	5	.213	.304	.262	.567	57	-4	-3	95	45	5	.500	1	0	0	-2	O	-0.5
1952	Cle-A	54	80	14	17	4	1	1	6	8	5	.213	.284	.325	.609	76	-3	-3	91	77	7	.530	1	1	-0	-6	O	-0.9
1953	Cle-A	22	21	3	4	3	0	0	3	1	4	.190	.227	.333	.561	52	-2	-1	95	159	2	.471	0	0	0	0	H	0.0
Total	11	1170	4172	664	1301	214	71	24	397	497	261	.312	.386	.414	.801	108	96	62	106	76	715	.790	58	31	-1	-3	*O	1.3
■ WILLIE McCOVEY McCovey, Willie Lee "Stretch" b: 1/10/38, Mobile, Ala. BL/TL, 6'4", 198 lbs. Deb: 7/30/59 H																												
1959	SF-N	52	192	32	68	9	5	13	38	22	35	.354	.431	.656	1.087	194	23	24	95	99	53	1.176	2	0	1	-1	1	1.9
1960	SF-N	101	260	37	62	15	3	13	51	45	53	.238	.351	.469	.820	136	8	12	90	129	45	.832	1	1	-0	-6	1	0.2
1961	SF-N	106	328	59	89	12	3	18	50	37	60	.271	.354	.491	.845	123	10	11	98	94	56	.819	1	2	-1	-2	1	0.3
1962	SF-N	91	229	41	67	6	1	20	54	29	35	.293	.372	.590	.962	152	17	16	101	109	48	.977	3	3	-1	-5	O1	0.6
1963	SF-N	152	564	103	158	19	5	**44**	102	50	119	.280	.350	.566	.916	166	41	44	96	101	111	.914	1	1	-0	-5	*O1	3.3
1964	SF-N	130	364	55	80	14	1	18	54	61	73	.220	.340	.412	.752	110	6	6	100	109	53	.741	2	1	0	-9	O1	-0.6
1965	SF-N	160	540	93	149	17	4	39	92	88	118	.276	.383	.539	.922	142	42	35	111	95	115	.955	0	4	-2	-1	*1	2.4
1966	SF-N	150	502	85	148	26	6	36	96	76	100	.295	.394	.586	.979	172	47	49	97	102	119	1.041	2	1	0	-3	*1	3.9
1967	SF-N	135	456	73	126	17	4	31	91	71	110	.276	.381	.535	.916	158	36	36	101	114	94	.950	3	3	-1	-0	*1	3.1
1968	SF-N	148	523	81	153	16	4	**36**	**105**	72	71	.293	.383	**.545**	**.928**	**180**	**49**	**50**	98	119	110	**.958**	4	2	0	2	*1	5.1
1969	SF-N	149	491	101	157	26	2	**45**	**126**	121	66	.320	**.458**	**.656**	**1.114**	**206**	**76**	**75**	101	113	**151**	**1.296**	0	0	0	-5	*1	**5.9**
1970	SF-N	152	495	98	143	39	2	39	126	**137**	75	.289	.446	**.612**	**1.058**	**188**	**62**	**65**	96	119	140	**1.214**	0	0	0	10	*1	**6.1**
1971	SF-N	105	329	45	91	13	0	18	70	64	57	.277	.401	.480	.881	149	23	23	100	134	65	.919	0	2	-1	-3	1	1.2
1972	SF-N	81	263	30	56	8	0	14	35	38	45	.213	.317	.403	.720	103	1	1	100	97	35	.695	0	0	0	-3	1	-0.7
1973	SF-N	130	383	52	102	14	3	29	75	105	78	.266	.425	.546	.971	160	39	37	105	102	95	1.101	1	0	0	1	*1	3.3
1974	SD-N	128	344	53	87	19	1	22	63	96	76	.253	.417	.506	.923	169	30	33	93	101	79	1.026	1	0	0	-1	*1	2.9
1975	SD-N	122	413	43	104	17	0	23	68	57	80	.252	.347	.460	.807	123	12	12	100	103	66	.787	1	0	0	3	*1	0.9
1976	SD-N	71	202	20	41	9	0	7	36	21	39	.203	.281	.351	.633	89	-6	-3	89	151	20	.564	0	0	0	1	1	-0.4
	Oak-A	11	24	0	5	0	0	0	0	3	4	.208	.296	.208	.505	50	-1	-1	100	0	2	.421	0	0	0	0	/D	0.0
1977	SF-N	141	478	54	134	21	0	28	86	67	106	.280	.369	.500	.869	125	21	18	104	109	86	.858	3	0	1	-4	*1	0.7
1978	SF-N	108	351	32	80	19	2	12	64	36	57	.228	.300	.396	.696	102	-4	-1	92	145	40	.622	1	0	0	-5	1	-0.8
1979	SF-N	117	353	34	88	9	0	15	57	36	70	.249	.321	.402	.723	104	-2	1	92	121	45	.653	0	2	-1	-3	1	-0.6
1980	SF-N	48	113	8	23	8	0	1	16	13	23	.204	.291	.301	.592	69	-5	-4	96	171	10	.516	0	0	0	-1	1	-0.6
Total	22	2588	8197	1229	2211	353	46	521	1555	1345	1550	.270	.377	.515	.892	148	524	538	99	112	1638	.941	26	22	-5	-41	*1O/D	38.1
■ ART McCOY McCoy, Arthur Gray b: 1865, Danville, Pa. d: 3/22/04, Danville, Pa. 168 lbs. Deb: 7/08/1889																												
1889	Was-N	2	6	0	0	0	0	0	0	2	1	.000	.250	.000	.250	-29	-1	-1	92	0	0	.333	0			0	/2	0.0
■ BENNY McCOY McCoy, Benjamin Jenison b: 11/9/15, Jenison, Mich. BL/TR, 5'9", 170 lbs. Deb: 9/14/38																												
1938	Det-A	7	15	2	3	1	0	0	0	1	2	.200	.250	.267	.517	29	-2	-2	100	0	1	.417	0	0	0	0	/23	0.0
1939	Det-A	55	192	38	58	13	6	1	33	29	26	.302	.394	.448	.842	103	5	1	111	128	35	.849	3	1	0	0	2S	0.4
1940	Phi-A	134	490	56	126	26	5	7	62	65	44	.257	.345	.373	.719	90	-9	-6	96	112	65	.661	2	2	-1	-10	*2/3	-0.8
1941	Phi-A	141	517	86	140	12	7	8	61	95	50	.271	.384	.368	.751	99	3	3	101	107	80	.735	3	3	-1	-8	*2	0.6
Total	4	337	1214	182	327	52	18	16	156	190	122	.269	.369	.381	.750	96	-3	-4	100	111	182	.731	8	6	-1	-18	2/S3	0.2
■ TOMMY McCRAW McCraw, Tommy Lee b: 11/21/40, Malvern, Ark. BL/TL, 6', 183 lbs. Deb: 6/04/63 C																												
1963	Chi-A	102	280	38	71	11	3	6	33	21	46	.254	.313	.379	.691	89	-3	-4	104	111	34	.665	15	4	2	-5	1	-1.0
1964	Chi-A	125	368	47	96	11	5	6	36	32	65	.261	.327	.367	.694	97	-3	-1	96	100	46	.657	15	7	0	-6	1O	-1.1
1965	Chi-A	133	273	38	65	12	1	5	21	25	48	.238	.309	.344	.653	93	-5	-3	92	80	28	.601	12	7	-1	-8	1O	-1.7
1966	Chi-A	151	389	49	89	16	4	5	48	29	40	.229	.291	.329	.620	82	-11	-9	94	141	37	.576	20	11	-1	-2	*1O	-1.8
1967	Chi-A	125	453	55	107	18	3	11	45	33	55	.236	.290	.362	.652	97	-6	-3	94	97	46	.608	24	10	1	6	*1/O	-0.5
1968	Chi-A	136	477	51	112	16	12	9	44	36	58	.235	.295	.375	.671	101	0	-0	101	93	53	.633	20	5	3	1	*1	-0.1
1969	Chi-A	93	240	21	62	12	2	2	25	21	24	.258	.326	.350	.676	82	-3	-6	108	111	26	.586	1	3	-2	-7	1O	-1.9
1970	Chi-A	129	332	39	73	11	2	6	31	21	50	.220	.275	.319	.594	60	-17	-19	106	101	31	.544	12	3	2	-4	1O	-2.7
1971	Was-A	122	207	33	44	6	4	7	25	19	38	.213	.294	.382	.676	98	-3	-1	92	102	23	.624	3	3	-1	-8	O1	-1.3
1972	Cle-A	129	391	43	101	13	5	7	33	41	47	.258	.335	.371	.706	102	5	2	107	83	47	.650	12	10	-2	-3	O1	-0.9
1973	Cal-A	99	264	25	70	7	0	3	24	30	42	.265	.345	.326	.670	93	-3	-1	96	99	32	.611	3	2	-0	-2	O1/D	-0.5
1974	Cal-A	56	119	21	34	8	0	3	17	12	13	.286	.351	.429	.780	133	4	5	92	111	18	.730	2	1	0	0	1O/D	0.3
	Cle-A	45	112	17	34	8	0	3	17	5	11	.304	.339	.455	.794	126	3	3	101	111	16	.687	0	1	-1	-1	1/O	0.0
	Yr	101	231	38	68	16	0	6	34	17	24	.294	.345	.442	.787	130	7	8	96	112	35	.722	2	2	-1	-1		0.3
1975	Cle-A	23	51	7	14	1	1	2	5	7	7	.275	.362	.451	.813	129	2	2	100	66	9	.895	4	1	1	-1	1/O	0.0
Total	13	1468	3956	484	972	150	42	75	404	332	544	.246	.311	.362	.672	93	-41	-35	99	102	446	.638	143	68	2	-40	1O/D	-13.2
■ FRANK McCREA McCrea, Francis William b: 9/6/1896, Jersey City, N.J. d: 2/25/81, Dover, N.J. BR/TR, 5'9", 155 lbs. Deb: 9/26/25																												
1925	Cle-A	1	5	1	1	0	0	0	0	0	0	.200	.200	.200	.400	2	-1	-1	106	0	0	.250	0	0	0	0	/C	0.0
■ JUDGE McCREDIE McCredie, Walter Henry b: 11/29/1876, Manchester, Iowa d: 7/29/34, Portland, Ore. BL/TR, 6'2", 195 lbs. Deb: 4/20/03																												
1903	Bro-N	56	213	40	69	5	0	0	20	24		.324	.392	.347	.740	112	5	5	101	83	34	.750	10			1	O	0.3
■ TOM McCREERY McCreery, Thomas Livingston b: 10/19/1874, Beaver, Pa. d: 7/3/41, Beaver, Pa. BB, 5'11", 180 lbs. Deb: 6/08/1895																												
1895	Lou-N	31	108	18	35	3	1	0	10	8	15	.324	.376	.370	.746	100	-0	0	95	70	17	.712	3			0	O/PS31	0.0
1896	Lou-N	115	441	87	155	23	**21**	7	65	42	58	.351	.409	.546	.956	156	32	34	98	76	112	1.084	26			-1	*O/2P	2.1
1897	Lou-N	89	338	55	96	5	6	4	40	38		.284	.356	.370	.726	99	-2	1	95	82	50	.727	13			-5	*O	-0.9
	NY-N	49	177	36	53	8	5	1	28	22		.299	.380	.418	.798	115	4	4	98	108	35	.903	15			0	O/2	0.1
	Yr	138	515	91	149	13	11	5	68	60		.289	.365	.386	.751	104	2	5	96	92	85	.787	28			-4		-0.8
1898	NY-N	35	121	15	24	4	3	1	17	19		.198	.307	.306	.613	82	-3	-2	95	131	13	.608	3			-5	O	-0.8
	Pit-N	53	190	33	59	5	7	2	20	26		.311	.394	.442	.836	146	11	12	98	71	35	.863	3			-3	O	0.5
	Yr	88	311	48	83	9	10	3	37	45		.267	.360	.389	.749	122	8	9	96	96	47	.754	6			-7		-0.3
1899	Pit-N	118	455	76	147	21	9	2	64	47		.323	.389	.422	.811	127	16	17	99	105	81	.818	11			-3	O/S2	0.8
1900	Pit-N	43	132	20	29	4	3	1	13	16		.220	.304	.318	.622	72	-4	-5	103	90	14	.583	2			-0	O/P	-0.7
1901	Bro-N	91	335	47	97	11	14	3	53	32		.290	.351	.433	.784	122	12	9	106	117	57	.798	13			5	O/1S	0.6
1902	Bro-N	112	430	49	105	8	4	4	57	29		.244	.292	.309	.601	92	-6	-4	95	**144**	45	.548	16			-2	*1/O	-1.0
1903	Bro-N	40	141	13	37	5	2	0	10	20		.262	.354	.326	.680	95	0	-0	101	74	19	.683	5			1	O	0.0
	Bos-N	23	83	15	18	2	1	1	10	9		.217	.293	.301	.595	74	-3	-3	96	122	9	.615	6			1	O	-0.2

YEAR	TM/L	G	AB	R	H	2B	3B	HR	RBI	BB	SO	AVG	OBP	SLG	PRO	/A	BR	/A	PF	CHI	RC	TA	SB	CS	SBR	FR	POS	TPR
	Yr	63	224	28	55	7	3	1	20	29		.246	.332	.317	.649	88	-3	-3	99	92	28	.657	11			2		-0.2
Total	9	799	2951	464	855	99	76	26	387	308	73	.290	.358	.401	.759	115	55	63	98	101	485	.770	116			-11	O1/S2P3	0.5
■ FRANK McCUE McCue, Frank Aloysius b: 10/4/1898, Chicago, Ill. d: 7/5/53, Chicago, Ill. BB/TR, 5'9", 150 lbs. Deb: 9/15/22																												
1922	Phi-A	2	5	0	0	0	0	0	0	0	0	.000	.000	.000	.000	-96	-1	-1	104	0	0	.000	0	0	0	0	/3	0.0
■ CLYDE McCULLOUGH McCullough, Clyde Edward b: 3/4/17, Nashville, Tenn. d: 9/18/82, San Francisco, Cal. BR/TR, 5'11.5", 180 lbs. Deb: 4/28/40 C																												
1940	Chi-N	9	26	4	4	1	0	0	1	5	5	.154	.290	.192	.483	36	-2	-2	100	74	2	.435	0			0	/C	-0.1
1941	Chi-N	125	418	41	95	9	2	9	53	34	67	.227	.289	.323	.612	77	-16	-13	94	118	39	.527	5			6	*C	0.5
1942	Chi-N	109	337	39	95	22	1	5	31	25	47	.282	.331	.398	.729	117	4	6	96	77	43	.661	7			4	C	1.3
1943	Chi-N	87	266	20	63	5	2	2	23	24	33	.237	.302	.293	.596	73	-9	-9	99	99	24	.522	6			-9	C	-1.5
1946	Chi-N	95	307	38	88	18	5	4	34	22	39	.287	.338	.417	.755	121	4	6	94	91	42	.675	2			-8	C	0.1
1947	Chi-N	86	234	25	59	12	4	3	30	20	20	.252	.314	.376	.690	82	-6	-7	101	115	27	.604	1			3	C	-0.1
1948	Chi-N	69	172	10	36	4	2	1	7	15	25	.209	.273	.273	.546	52	-13	-11	93	52	12	.431	0			1	C	-0.5
1949	Pit-N	91	241	30	57	9	3	4	21	24	30	.237	.316	.349	.665	77	-7	-8	101	82	28	.604	1			-2	C	-0.6
1950	Pit-N	103	279	28	71	16	4	6	34	31	35	.254	.340	.405	.745	93	-2	-3	103	100	40	.714	3			-4	*C	-0.3
1951	Pit-N	92	259	26	77	9	2	8	39	27	31	.297	.366	.440	.806	109	6	4	107	109	40	.738	2	0	1	2	C	0.7
1952	Pit-N	66	172	10	40	5	1	1	15	10	18	.233	.283	.291	.573	59	-9	-9	100	110	14	.456	0	1	-1	2	C/1	-0.6
1953	Chi-N	77	229	21	59	3	2	6	23	15	23	.258	.303	.367	.670	72	-9	-10	103	88	24	.553	0	0	0	2	C	-0.3
1954	Chi-N	31	81	9	21	7	0	3	17	5	5	.259	.310	.457	.767	96	-1	-1	101	145	12	.705	0	0	0	-1	C/3	0.0
1955	Chi-N	44	81	7	16	0	0	0	10	8	15	.198	.278	.198	.475	29	-8	-8	100	253	5	.379	0	0	0	-1	C	-0.7
1956	Chi-N	14	19	0	4	1	0	0	1	0	5	.211	.211	.263	.474	27	-2	-2	99	84	1	.313	0	0	0	0	/C	-0.1
Total	15	1098	3121	308	785	121	28	52	339	265	398	.252	.314	.358	.672	85	-70	-66	99	101	352	.612	27	1		-5	C/31	-2.2
■ HARRY McCURDY McCurdy, Harry Henry "Hank" b: 9/15/1899, Stevens Point, Wis. d: 7/21/72, Houston, Tex. BL/TR, 5'11", 187 lbs. Deb: 7/04/22																												
1922	StL-N	13	27	3	8	2	2	0	5	1	1	.296	.321	.519	.840	112	0	0	101	125	4	.789	0	0	0	0	/C1	0.0
1923	StL-N	67	185	17	49	11	2	0	15	11	11	.265	.306	.346	.652	80	-8	-5	90	82	20	.569	3	1	0	-4	C	-0.5
1926	Chi-A	44	86	16	28	7	2	1	11	6	10	.326	.370	.488	.858	134	2	3	92	83	15	.814	0	1	-1	-2	C/1	0.2
1927	Chi-A	86	262	34	75	19	3	1	27	32	24	.286	.366	.393	.759	95	-1	-1	102	85	38	.759	6	0	2	1	C	0.2
1928	Chi-A	49	103	12	27	10	0	2	13	8	15	.262	.315	.417	.733	92	-2	-2	99	91	13	.658	1	3	-2	0	C	0.0
1930	Phi-N	80	148	23	49	6	2	1	25	15	12	.331	.393	.419	.812	91	-0	-2	106	133	24	.778	0			-0	C	0.0
1931	Phi-N	66	150	21	43	9	0	1	25	23	16	.287	.382	.367	.748	96	1	0	106	154	23	.748	2			1	C	0.3
1932	Phi-N	62	136	13	32	6	1	1	14	17	13	.235	.325	.316	.641	65	-5	-7	112	113	15	.587	0			-2	C	-0.7
1933	Phi-N	73	54	9	15	1	0	2	12	16	6	.278	.451	.407	.858	124	5	3	118	161	12	1.000	0			0	/C	0.4
1934	Cin-N	3	6	0	0	0	0	0	1	0	0	.000	.000	.000	.000	-99	-2	-2	101	0	0	.000	0			0	/1	-0.1
Total	10	543	1157	148	326	71	12	9	148	129	108	.282	.355	.387	.743	92	-8	-12	102	108	165	.708	12	5		-7	C/1	-0.2
■ RED McDERMOTT McDermott, Frank A. b: 11/12/1889, Philadelphia, Pa. d: 9/11/64, Philadelphia, Pa. BR/TR, 5'6", 150 lbs. Deb: 8/06/12																												
1912	Det-A	5	15	2	4	1	0	0	0	0		.267	.313	.333	.646	89	-0	-0	95	0	2	.636	1			-0	/O	0.0
■ MICKEY McDERMOTT McDermott, Maurice Joseph b: 8/29/28, Poughkeepsie, N.Y. BL/TL, 6'2", 170 lbs. Deb: 4/24/48																												
1948	Bos-A	7	8	2	3	1	0	0	0	0	0	.375	.375	.500	.875	131	0	0	100	0	2	.800	0	0	0	1	/P	0.0
1949	Bos-A	12	33	3	7	3	0	0	6	3	6	.212	.278	.303	.581	50	-2	-3	107	206	3	.500	0	0	0	-0	P	0.0
1950	Bos-A	39	44	11	16	5	0	0	12	9	3	.364	.472	.477	.949	125	3	2	114	197	11	1.034	0	0	0	1	P	0.0
1951	Bos-A	43	66	8	18	1	1	1	6	3	14	.273	.314	.364	.678	77	-2	-2	108	79	7	.538	0	1	-1	1	P	0.0
1952	Bos-A	36	62	10	14	1	1	1	7	4	11	.226	.273	.323	.595	61	-3	-4	107	114	6	.500	0	0	0	-0	P	0.0
1953	Bos-A	45	93	9	28	8	0	1	13	2	13	.301	.316	.419	.735	89	-1	-2	109	115	12	.603	0	1	-1	1	P	0.0
1954	Was-A	54	95	7	19	3	0	0	4	7	12	.200	.255	.232	.486	34	-9	-8	98	69	5	.363	0	0	0	0	P	0.0
1955	Was-A	70	95	10	25	4	0	1	10	6	16	.263	.314	.337	.651	82	-3	-2	91	107	11	.563	1	0	0	0	P	0.2
1956	NY-A	46	52	4	11	0	0	1	4	8	13	.212	.317	.269	.586	57	-3	-3	99	88	4	.489	0	0	0	-0	P	0.0
1957	KC-A	58	49	6	12	1	0	4	7	9	16	.245	.362	.510	.872	137	2	2	99	75	9	.872	0	0	0	1	P/1	0.8
1958	Det-A	4	3	0	1	0	0	0	1	0	2	.333	.333	.333	.667	81	-0	-0	104	401	0	.500	0	0	0	0	/P	0.0
1961	StL-N	22	14	1	1	1	0	0	3	0	4	.071	.071	.143	.214	-40	-3	-3	113	605	0	.154	0	0	0	-0	P	0.0
	KC-A	7	5	0	1	1	0	0	1	1	2	.200	.333	.400	.733	93	-0	-0	102	196	1	.750	0	0	0	-0	/P	0.0
Total	12	443	619	71	156	29	2	9	74	52	112	.252	.312	.349	.661	76	-20	-22	103	119	69	.583	1	2	-1	5	P/1	1.0
■ TERRY McDERMOTT McDermott, Terrence Michael b: 3/20/51, Rockville Cen., N.Y BR/TR, 6'3", 205 lbs. Deb: 9/12/72																												
1972	LA-N	9	23	2	3	0	0	0	0	2	8	.130	.200	.130	.330	-5	-3	-3	94	0	1	.238	0	0	0	0	/1	-0.3
■ SANDY McDERMOTT McDermott, Thomas Nathaniel b: 3/15/1856, Zanesville, Ohio d: 11/23/22, Mansfield, Ohio Deb: 1885																												
1885	Bal-a	1	0	0	0	0	0	0		0		—	—	—	—	—	0	0	106	—	—	—				0	/2	0.0
■ TEX McDONALD McDonald, Charles E. (born Charles C. Crabtree) b: 1/31/1891, Farmersville, Tex. d: 3/31/43, Houston, Tex. BL/TR, 5'10", 160 lbs. Deb: 4/11/12																												
1912	Cin-N	61	140	16	36	3	4	1	15	13	24	.257	.329	.357	.686	95	-2	-1	92	95	18	.673	5			-4	S	0.0
1913	Cin-N	11	10	1	3	0	0	0	2	0	1	.300	.300	.300	.600	70	-0	-0	102	242	1	.429	0			0	/S	0.0
	Bos-N	62	145	24	52	4	4	0	18	15	17	.359	.422	.441	.864	155	9	10	95	102	28	.903	4			-1	3/2O	0.9
	Yr	73	155	25	55	4	4	0	20	15	18	.355	.415	.432	.847	149	9	10	96	127	29	.870	4			-1		0.9
1914	Pit-F	67	223	27	71	16	7	3	29	13	0	.318	.356	.493	.849	150	11	12	94	88	43	.868	9			-1	O2/S	1.0
	Buf-F	69	250	32	74	13	6	3	32	20	0	.296	.348	.432	.780	118	7	5	104	101	42	.790	11			-3	O2	0.0
	Yr	136	473	59	145	29	13	6	61	33	0	.307	.352	.461	.813	132	18	18	99	95	86	.826	20			-5		1.0
1915	Buf-F	87	251	31	68	9	6	6	39	27	34	.271	.342	.426	.768	127	8	8	100	112	39	.760	5			-10	O	-0.5
Total	4	357	1019	131	304	45	27	13	135	88	76	.298	.356	.434	.790	128	32	35	98	102	172	.793	34			-20	O/S23	1.4
■ JACK McDONALD McDonald, Daniel b: 1847, Brooklyn, N.Y. d: 11/23/1880, Brooklyn, N.Y. Deb: 5/02/1872																												
1872	Atl-n	14	56	8	12							.214															O	
	Eck-n	1	5	0	0							.000															/S	
	Yr	15	61	8	12							.197																
■ DAVE McDONALD McDonald, David Bruce b: 5/20/43, New Albany, Ind. BL/TR, 6'3", 215 lbs. Deb: 9/15/69																												
1969	NY-A	9	23	0	5	1	0	0	2	2	5	.217	.280	.261	.541	55	-1	-1	95	134	2	.421	0	1	-1	-0	/1	-0.2
1971	Mon-N	24	39	3	4	2	0	1	4	4	14	.103	.186	.231	.417	18	-4	-4	99	136	1	.351	0	0	0	0	/1O	-0.4
Total	2	33	62	3	9	3	0	1	6	6	19	.145	.221	.242	.463	31	-6	-6	98	135	3	.375	0	1	-1	-0	/1O	-0.6
■ ED McDONALD McDonald, Edward C. b: 10/28/1886, Albany, N.Y. d: 3/11/46, Albany, N.Y. BR/TR, 6', 180 lbs. Deb: 8/05/11																												
1911	Bos-N	54	175	28	36	7	3	1	21	40	39	.206	.359	.297	.657	82	-2	-3	103	132	23	.755	11			-1	3/S	-0.1
1912	Bos-N	121	459	70	119	23	6	2	34	70	91	.259	.363	.349	.712	89	-1	-6	107	66	65	.756	22			2	*3	-0.2
1913	Chi-N	1	0	0	0	0	0	0	0	0	0	—	—	—	—	—	0	0	99	—	—	—	0			0	R	0.0
Total	3	176	634	98	155	30	9	3	55	110	130	.244	.362	.334	.697	87	-3	-9	106	85	153	.756	33			1	3/S	-0.3
■ JIM McDONALD McDonald, James b: Philadelphia, Pa. BR/TR, 6', 180 lbs. Deb: 6/02/02																												
1902	NY-N	2	9	0	3	0	0	0	1	0		.333	.333	.333	.667	108	0	0	100	100	1	.500	0			0	/O	0.0
■ JIM McDONALD McDonald, James A. b: 8/6/1860, San Francisco, Cal. d: 9/14/14, San Francisco, Cal. Deb: 10/02/1884																												
1884	Was-U	2	6	0	1	0	0	0		0		.167	.167	.167	.333	13	-1	-0	97	0	0	.200	0			0	/CO	0.0
	Pit-a	38	145	11	23	3	0	0		2		.159	.170	.179	.349	16	-13	-12	97	0	5	.230				0	3O/2	-1.0
1885	Buf-N	5	14	0	0	0	0	0	0	0	4	.000	.000	.000	.000	-99	-3	-3	99	0	0	.000				0	/SO	-0.2
Total	2	45	165	11	24	3	0	0	0	2	4	.145	.156	.164	.319	6	-16	-16	97	0	5	.206				0	/3OS2C	-1.2
■ JOE McDONALD McDonald, Malcolm Joseph b: 4/9/1888, Texas d: 5/30/63, Baytown, Tex. BR/TR, 5'11", 175 lbs. Deb: 9/06/10																												
1910	StL-A	10	32	4	5	0	0	0	1	1		.156	.182	.156	.338	6	-3	-3	94	74	1	.222	0			0	3	-0.2

YEAR	TM/L	G	AB	R	H	2B	3B	HR	RBI	BB	SO	AVG	OBP	SLG	PRO	/A	BR	/A	PF	CHI	RC	TA	SB	CS	SBR	FR	POS	TPR
■ **JIM McDONNELL**	McDonnell, James William "Mack" b: 8/15/22, Gagetown, Mich. BL/TR, 5'11", 165 lbs. Deb: 9/23/43																											
1943	Cle-A	2	1	1	0	0	0	0	0	2	1	.000	.667	.000	.667	113	0	0	90	0	0	2.000	0	0	0	0	/C	0.0
1944	Cle-A	20	43	5	10	0	0	0	4	4	3	.233	.298	.233	.530	53	-3	-3	100	144	3	.400	0	0	0	-0	C	-0.1
1945	Cle-A	28	51	3	10	2	0	0	8	2	4	.196	.226	.235	.462	35	-4	-4	99	241	3	.326	0	0	0	2	C	0.0
Total	3	50	95	9	20	2	0	0	12	8	8	.211	.272	.232	.503	46	-7	-6	99	190	6	.390	0	0	0	1	/C	-0.1
■ **ED McDONOUGH**	McDonough, Edward Sebastian b: 9/11/1886, Elgin, Ill. d: 9/2/26, Elgin, Ill. BR/TR, 6', 160 lbs. Deb: 09																											
1909	Phi-N	1	1	0	0	0	0	0	0	0		.000	.000	.000	.000	-94	-0	-0	106	0	0	.000	0			0	/C	0.0
1910	Phi-N	5	9	1	1	0	0	0	0	0	1	.111	.111	.111	.222	-37	-2	-1	96	0	0	.125	0			0	/C	0.0
Total	2	6	10	1	1	0	0	0	0	0	1	.100	.100	.100	.200	-43	-2	-2	97	0	0	.111	0			0	/C	0.0
■ **GIL McDOUGALD**	McDougald, Gilbert James b: 5/19/28, San Francisco, Cal BR/TR, 6', 175 lbs. Deb: 4/20/51																											
1951	NY-A	131	402	72	123	23	4	14	63	56	54	.306	.396	.488	.884	151	22	27	92	95	81	.912	14	5	1	-3	32	2.3
1952	NY-A	152	555	65	146	16	5	11	78	57	73	.263	.336	.369	.705	98	-3	-2	98	125	71	.636	6	5	-1	18	*32	1.7
1953	NY-A	141	541	82	154	27	7	10	83	60	65	.285	.361	.416	.777	118	7	13	93	128	85	.733	3	4	-2	14	*32	2.0
1954	NY-A	126	394	66	102	22	2	12	48	62	64	.259	.367	.416	.783	115	9	9	99	91	64	.777	3	4	-2	12	23	2.2
1955	NY-A	141	533	79	152	10	8	13	53	65	77	.285	.365	.407	.772	110	6	8	98	82	83	.742	6	4	-1	17	*23	3.1
1956	NY-A	120	438	79	136	13	3	13	56	68	59	.311	.407	.443	.850	126	17	18	99	95	82	.851	3	8	-4	11	S2/3	3.5
1957	NY-A	141	539	87	156	25	9	13	62	59	71	.289	.364	.442	.805	127	14	19	94	94	86	.757	2	5	-2	19	*S2/3	4.6
1958	NY-A	138	503	69	126	19	1	14	65	59	75	.250	.333	.376	.708	92	-3	-5	103	120	64	.652	6	2	1	1	*2S	0.7
1959	NY-A	127	434	44	109	16	8	4	34	35	40	.251	.311	.353	.664	88	-11	-7	93	81	46	.563	0	3	-2	5	2S3	0.2
1960	NY-A	119	337	54	87	16	4	8	34	38	45	.258	.339	.401	.739	105	-0	2	94	84	47	.690	2	4	-2	7	32	1.2
Total	10	1336	4676	697	1291	187	51	112	576	559	623	.276	.358	.410	.768	112	58	82	96	101	708	.745	45	44	-13	101	23S	21.5
■ **ODDIBE McDOWELL**	McDowell, Oddibe b: 8/25/62, Hollywood, Fla. BL/TL, 5'9", 165 lbs. Deb: 5/19/85																											
1985	Tex-A	111	406	63	97	14	5	18	42	36	85	.239	.306	.431	.737	91	-1	-6	108	77	55	.742	25	7	3	6	*O/D	0.1
1986	Tex-A	154	572	105	152	24	7	18	49	65	112	.266	.342	.427	.768	114	7	11	96	69	83	.767	33	15	1	12	*O/D	1.9
1987	Tex-A	128	407	65	98	26	4	14	52	51	99	.241	.325	.428	.753	95	-1	-3	104	96	61	.781	24	2	6	-7	*O	-0.6
1988	Tex-A	120	437	55	108	19	5	6	37	41	89	.247	.315	.355	.669	86	-7	-8	101	87	53	.675	33	10	4	-8	*O/D	-1.4
Total	4	513	1822	288	455	83	21	56	180	193	385	.250	.324	.411	.734	98	-3	-6	101	81	251	.756	115	34	14	3	O/D	0.0
■ **PRYOR McELVEEN**	McElveen, Pryor Mynatt "Humpty" b: 11/5/1883, Atlanta, Ga. d: 10/27/51, Pleasant Hill, Tenn. TR, 5'10", 168 lbs. Deb: 09																											
1909	Bro-N	81	258	22	51	8	1	3	25	14		.198	.242	.271	.513	61	-13	-12	99	115	17	.440	6			-2	3OS/12	-1.5
1910	Bro-N	74	213	19	48	8	3	1	26	22	47	.225	.307	.305	.612	83	-6	-4	95	133	22	.582	6			-7	3/S2C	-1.1
1911	Bro-N	16	31	1	6	0	0	0	5	0	3	.194	.194	.194	.387	9	-4	-4	97	282	1	.240	0			-0	/2S	-0.3
Total	3	171	502	42	105	16	4	4	56	36	50	.209	.268	.281	.548	67	-22	-21	97	133	41	.486	12			-9	/3S2O1C	-2.9
■ **LEE McELWEE**	McElwee, Leland Stanford b: 5/23/1894, La Mesa, Cal. d: 2/8/57, Union, Maine BR/TR, 5'10.5", 160 lbs. Deb: 7/03/16																											
1916	Phi-A	54	155	9	41	3	0	0	10	8	17	.265	.301	.284	.584	77	-5	-4	98	81	14	.456	0			0	3/O21S	-0.3
■ **FRANK McELYEA**	McElyea, Frank b: 8/4/18, Carmi, Ill. BR/TR, 6'6", 221 lbs. Deb: 9/10/42																											
1942	Bos-N	7	4	2	0	0	0	0	0	0	0	.000	.000	.000	.000	-99	-1	-1	95	0	0	.000	0			0	/O	0.0
■ **GUY McFADDEN**	McFadden, Guy G. b: 1873, Topeka, Kan. Deb: 8/24/1895																											
1895	StL-N	4	14	1	3	0	0	0	2	0	2	.214	.214	.214	.429	12	-2	-2	100	186	1	.273	0			0	/1	0.0
■ **LEON McFADDEN**	McFadden, Leon b: 4/26/44, Little Rock, Ark. BR/TR, 6'2", 195 lbs. Deb: 9/06/68																											
1968	Hou-N	16	47	2	13	1	0	0	1	6	10	.277	.358	.298	.656	100	0	0	99	30	6	.618	1	0	0	-0	S	0.2
1969	Hou-N	44	74	3	13	2	0	0	3	4	9	.176	.218	.203	.421	18	-8	-8	102	80	3	.308	1	2	-1	-3	O/S	-1.2
1970	Hou-N	2	0	0	0	0	0	0	0	0	0	—	—	—	—	—	0	0	94	—	—	—	0	0	0	0	R	0.0
Total	3	62	121	5	26	3	0	0	4	10	19	.215	.275	.240	.514	49	-8	-8	100	60	11	.423	2	2	-1	-4	/SO	-1.0
■ **ALEX McFARLAN**	McFarlan, Alexander Shepherd b: 11/11/1866, Kentucky d: 3/2/39, Peewee Valley, Ky. Deb: 6/19/1892																											
1892	Lou-N	14	42	2	7	0	0	0	1	8	11	.167	.300	.167	.467	47	-2	-2	92	44	2	.457	1			0	O/2	-0.1
■ **CHRIS McFARLAND**	McFarland, Christopher b: 8/17/1861, Fall River, Mass. d: 5/24/18, New Bedford, Mass. 5'9", 170 lbs. Deb: 4/19/1884																											
1884	Bal-U	3	14	2	3	1	0	0		0		.214	.214	.286	.500	61	-0	-1	110	0	1	.364	0			0	/OP	0.0
■ **ED McFARLAND**	McFarland, Edward William b: 8/3/1874, Cleveland, Ohio d: 11/28/59, Cleveland, Ohio BR/TR, 5'10", 180 lbs. Deb: 7/07/1893																											
1893	Cle-N	8	22	5	9	2	1	0	6	1	2	.409	.458	.591	1.049	174	2	2	104	126	6	1.154	0			0	/O3C	0.2
1896	StL-N	83	290	48	70	13	4	3	36	15	17	.241	.281	.345	.626	69	-15	-13	95	95	31	.559	7			18	C/O	1.1
1897	StL-N	31	107	14	35	5	2	1	17	8		.327	.374	.439	.813	125	2	4	93	99	19	.792	2			6	C/1O2	1.1
	Phi-N	38	130	18	29	3	5	1	16	14		.223	.308	.346	.654	78	-5	-4	96	97	15	.624	2			-1	C	0.0
	Yr	69	237	32	64	8	7	2	33	22		.270	.337	.388	.725	99	-2	-0	95	100	33	.694	4			5		1.1
1898	Phi-N	121	429	65	121	21	5	3	71	44		.282	.352	.375	.727	117	7	10	95	129	59	.685	4			2	*C	1.9
1899	Phi-N	96	324	59	108	22	10	1	57	36		.333	.403	.472	.876	147	19	21	97	112	67	.926	9			9	C	3.1
1900	Phi-N	94	344	50	105	14	8	0	38	29		.305	.359	.392	.752	112	5	6	98	90	53	.724	9			3	C/3	1.6
1901	Phi-N	74	295	33	84	14	2	1	32	18		.285	.326	.356	.682	97	-0	-1	103	105	39	.635	11			-2	C	0.6
1902	Chi-A	75	246	29	56	9	2	1	25	19		.228	.283	.293	.576	64	-13	-11	95	110	23	.521	8			1	C/O1	-0.4
1903	Chi-A	61	201	15	42	7	2	1	19	14		.209	.260	.279	.539	69	-9	-7	92	116	16	.459	3			-2	C/1	-0.1
1904	Chi-A	50	160	22	44	11	3	0	20	17		.275	.345	.381	.726	133	6	6	99	125	22	.690	2			-2	C	1.0
1905	Chi-A	80	250	24	70	13	4	0	31	23		.280	.341	.364	.705	130	7	8	97	122	34	.661	5			-2	C	1.4
1906	Chi-A	12	23	0	4	1	0	0	3	3		.174	.269	.217	.487	59	-1	-1	92	218	1	.421	0			-1	/C	0.0
1907	Chi-A	52	138	11	39	9	1	0	8	12		.283	.340	.362	.702	122	4	4	104	57	18	.657	3			-3	C	0.5
1908	Bos-A	19	48	5	10	2	1	0	4	1		.208	.224	.292	.516	70	-2	-2	98	107	3	.395	0			2	C	0.1
Total	14	894	3007	398	826	146	50	12	383	254	19	.275	.333	.368	.701	106	9	23	97	108	406	.658	65			28	C/O132	12.1
■ **HERM McFARLAND**	McFarland, Hermas Walter b: 3/11/1870, Des Moines, Iowa d: 9/21/35, Richmond, Va. BL/TR, 5'6", 150 lbs. Deb: 4/21/1896																											
1896	Lou-N	30	110	11	21	4	1	1	12	9	14	.191	.252	.273	.525	40	-10	-9	98	107	9	.483	4			0	O/C	-0.7
1898	Cin-N	19	64	10	18	1	3	0	11	7		.281	.361	.391	.752	110	2	1	108	136	10	.783	3			0	O	0.1
1901	Chi-A	132	473	83	130	21	9	4	59	75		.275	.374	.383	.757	113	11	11	99	102	82	.843	33			7	*O	1.4
1902	Chi-A	7	27	5	5	0	0	0	4	2		.185	.241	.185	.427	22	-3	-3	95	279	1	.364	1			-1	/O	-0.3
	Bal-A	61	242	54	78	19	6	3	36	36		.322	.410	.488	.898	147	17	16	102	81	54	1.000	10			-2	O	1.0
	Yr	68	269	59	83	19	6	3	40	38		.309	.394	.457	.851	136	14	14	101	105	54	.925	11			-3		0.7
1903	NY-A	103	362	41	88	16	9	5	45	46		.243	.328	.378	.707	113	7	7	100	113	50	.715	13			6	*O	0.7
Total	5	352	1278	204	340	61	28	13	167	175	14	.266	.355	.388	.743	112	24	24	100	107	207	.785	64			10	O/C	2.2
■ **HOWIE McFARLAND**	McFarland, Howard Alexander b: 3/7/11, El Reno, Okla. BR/TR, 6', 175 lbs. Deb: 7/16/45																											
1945	Was-A	6	11	0	1	0	0	0	2	0	3	.091	.091	.091	.182	-51	-2	-2	93	723	0	.091	0	0	0	-0	/O	-0.2
■ **ORLANDO McFARLANE**	McFarlane, Orlando Dejesus (Quesada) b: 6/28/38, Oriente, Cuba BR/TR, 6', 180 lbs. Deb: 4/23/62																											
1962	Pit-N	8	23	0	2	0	0	0	1	1	4	.087	.125	.087	.212	-41	-5	-5	102	197	0	.136	0	0	0	0	/C	-0.3
1964	Pit-N	37	78	5	19	5	0	0	1	4	27	.244	.280	.308	.588	65	-4	-4	101	17	7	.475	0	0	0	-2	C/O	-0.3
1966	Det-A	49	138	16	35	7	0	5	13	9	46	.254	.304	.413	.717	102	0	0	102	76	17	.638	0	0	0	5	C	0.7
1967	Cal-A	12	22	0	5	0	0	0	3	1	7	.227	.261	.227	.488	47	-1	-1	96	250	1	.300	0	0	0	0	/C	0.0
1968	Cal-A	18	31	1	9	0	0	0	2	5	9	.290	.389	.290	.679	115	1	1	94	95	4	.609	0	0	0	-0	/C	0.1
Total	5	124	292	22	70	12	0	5	20	20	93	.240	.291	.332	.623	78	-9	-9	100	85	29	.529	0	0	0	4	/CO	0.2
■ **PATSY McGAFFIGAN**	McGaffigan, Mark Andrew b: 9/12/1888, Carlyle, Ill. d: 12/22/40, Carlyle, Ill. BR/TR, 5'8", 140 lbs. Deb: 4/16/17																											
1917	Phi-N	19	60	5	10	1	0	0	6	0	7	.167	.167	.183	.350	7	-7	-7	108	210	2	.240	1			3	S/O	-0.4
1918	Phi-N	54	192	17	39	3	2	1	8	16	23	.203	.268	.255	.523	55	-9	-11	109	62	14	.451	3			-2	2/S	-1.0
Total	2	73	252	22	49	4	2	1	14	16	30	.194	.245	.238	.483	44	-16	-18	109	95	17	.399	4			1	/2SO	-1.4

YEAR	TM/L	G	AB	R	H	2B	3B	HR	RBI	BB	SO	AVG	OBP	SLG	PRO	/A	BR	/A	PF	CHI	RC	TA	SB	CS	SBR	FR	POS	TPR
■ EDDIE McGAH	McGah, Edward Joseph b: 9/30/21, Oakland, Cal. BR/TR, 6', 183 lbs. Deb: 4/26/46																											
1946	Bos-A	15	37	2	8	1	1	0	1	7	7	.216	.341	.297	.638	69	-1	-1	114	35	5	.621	0	0	0	-1	C	-0.1
1947	Bos-A	9	14	1	0	0	0	0	2	3	0	.000	.176	.000	.176	-45	-3	-3	108	0	0	.214	0	0	0	0	/C	-0.2
Total	2	24	51	3	8	1	1	0	3	10	7	.157	.295	.216	.511	39	-4	-4	113	25	5	.488	0	0	0	-1	/C	-0.3
■ DAN McGANN	McGann, Dennis Lawrence "Cap" b: 7/15/1871, Shelbyville, Ky. d: 12/13/10, Louisville, Ky. BB/TR, 6', 190 lbs. Deb: 5/02/1895																											
1895	Lou-N	20	73	9	21	5	2	0	9	8	6	.288	.358	.411	.769	105	-0	1	95	85	13	.846	6			0	/S3O	0.1
1896	Bos-N	43	171	25	55	6	7	2	30	12	10	.322	.383	.474	.857	118	6	4	108	105	33	.862	2			-16	2	-0.8
1898	Bal-N	145	535	99	161	18	8	5	106	53		.301	.403	.393	.795	127	26	23	103	151	100	.893	33			1	*1	2.3
1899	Bro-N	63	214	49	52	11	4	2	32	21		.243	.349	.360	.709	93	0	-2	105	121	33	.790	16			1	1	0.0
	Was-N	76	280	65	96	9	8	5	58	14		.343	.410	.486	.896	155	19	20	96	125	62	.973	11			1	1	2.1
	Yr	139	494	114	148	20	12	7	90	35		.300	.383	.431	.814	126	19	19	100	124	94	.887	27			2		2.1
1900	StL-N	121	444	79	132	10	9	4	58	32		.297	.345	.387	.732	112	2	7	93	101	70	.737	26			-2	*1/2	0.6
1901	StL-N	103	423	73	115	15	9	6	56	16		.272	.298	.392	.691	105	-1	1	97	108	56	.646	17			-1	*1	0.1
1902	Bal-A	68	250	40	79	10	8	0	42	19		.316	.364	.420	.784	116	6	6	102	134	46	.825	17			-1	1	0.5
	NY-N	61	227	25	68	5	7	0	21	12		.300	.335	.383	.718	124	6	6	100	88	34	.698	12			2	1	0.5
1903	NY-N	129	482	75	130	21	6	3	50	32		.270	.315	.357	.672	88	-5	-9	106	94	67	.682	36			-0	*1	-1.2
1904	NY-N	141	517	81	148	22	6	6	71	36		.286	.333	.387	.720	118	14	10	105	126	83	.753	42			3	*1	0.7
1905	NY-N	136	491	88	147	23	14	5	75	55		.299	.370	.434	.804	140	25	24	101	121	89	.843	22			3	*1	2.2
1906	NY-N	134	451	62	107	14	8	0	37	60		.237	.327	.304	.631	99	1	1	100	104	56	.660	30			4	*1	0.0
1907	NY-N	81	262	29	78	9	1	2	39	29		.298	.368	.363	.730	125	10	8	105	149	39	.723	9			0	1	0.7
1908	Bos-N	135	475	52	114	8	5	2	55	38		.240	.296	.291	.587	86	-5	-7	104	150	42	.512	9			8	*1/2	-0.2
Total	13	1456	5295	851	1503	186	102	42	739	437	16	.284	.347	.381	.728	114	104	94	101	121	822	.743	288			4	*1/2S3O	7.6
■ CHIPPY McGARR	McGarr, James B. b: 5/10/1863, Worcester, Mass. d: 6/6/04, Worcester, Mass. BR/TR, Deb: 7/11/1884																											
1884	CP-U	19	70	10	11	2	0	0		0		.157	.157	.186	.343	16	-6	-6	99	0	2	.220	0			0	2/O	-0.4
1886	Phi-a	71	267	41	71	9	3	2		9		.266	.295	.345	.640	102	-0	-0	100	0	33	.612	17			0	S	0.3
1887	Phi-a	137	536	93	158	23	6	1		23		.295	.326	.366	.692	95	-4	-4	99	0	94	.807	84			-2	*S	-0.5
1888	StL-a	34	132	17	31	1	0	0	13	6		.235	.268	.242	.511	60	-5	-7	111	124	16	.624	25			0	2/S	-0.5
1889	KC-a	25	108	22	31	3	0	0	16	6	11	.287	.330	.315	.645	81	-2	-3	106	119	16	.688	12			0	3/O2S	-0.1
	Bal-a	3	7	1	1	0	0	0	0	1	1	.143	.250	.143	.393	15	-1	-1	100	0	0	.333	0			0	/S	0.0
	Yr	28	115	23	32	3	0	0	16	7	12	.278	.325	.304	.630	78	-3	-4	105	110	16	.663	12			0		-0.1
1890	Bos-N	121	487	68	115	12	7	1	51	34	38	.236	.291	.296	.587	66	-17	-25	111	111	55	.594	39			-4	*3/SO	-2.0
1893	Cle-N	63	249	38	77	12	0	0	28	20	15	.309	.363	.357	.720	90	-2	-4	104	88	42	.779	24			-2	3	-0.3
1894	Cle-N	128	523	94	144	24	6	2	74	28	29	.275	.316	.356	.672	57	-32	-43	111	108	70	.654	31			-7	*3	-4.0
1895	Cle-N	112	419	85	111	14	2	2	59	34	33	.265	.322	.322	.644	70	-19	-17	97	119	51	.614	19			-9	*3/2	-1.9
1896	Cle-N	113	455	68	122	16	4	1	53	22	30	.268	.302	.327	.629	61	-22	-29	110	103	51	.562	16			-7	*3/C	-2.5
Total	10	826	3253	537	872	116	28	9	294	183	157	.268	.310	.329	.639	72	-109	-137	105	80	429	.645	267			-31	3S/2OC	-11.9
■ JIM McGARR	McGarr, James Vincent "Reds" b: 11/9/1888, Philadelphia, Pa. d: 7/21/81, Miami, Fla. 5'9.5", 170 lbs. Deb: 5/18/12																											
1912	Det-A	1	4	0	0	0	0	0	0	0	0	.000	.000	.000	.000	-99	-1	-1	95	0	0	.000	0			0	/2	0.0
■ DAN McGARVEY	McGarvey, Daniel Francis b: 12/2/1887, Philadelphia, Pa. d: 3/7/47, Philadelphia, Pa. Deb: 5/18/12																											
1912	Det-A	1	3	0	0	0	0	0	0	0	1	.000	.400	.000	.400	18	-0	-0	95	0	0	.667	0			0	/O	0.0
■ JACK McGEACHEY	McGeachey, John Charles b: 5/23/1864, Clinton, Mass. d: 4/5/30, Cambridge, Mass. BR, 5'8", 165 lbs. Deb: 6/17/1886																											
1886	Det-N	6	27	3	9	0	1	0	4	0	3	.333	.333	.407	.741	114	1	0	109	114	4	.722	2			-1	/O	0.0
	StL-N	59	226	31	46	12	3	2	24	1	37	.204	.207	.310	.517	58	-12	-11	95	109	17	.439	8			3	O/23	-0.5
	Yr	65	253	34	55	12	4	2	28	1	40	.217	.220	.320	.541	65	-12	-10	96	111	21	.465	10			3		-0.5
1887	Ind-N	99	405	49	109	17	3	1	56	5	16	.269	.280	.333	.613	74	-16	-13	96	133	46	.568	27			5	*O/3P	-0.5
1888	Ind-N	118	452	45	99	15	2	0	30	5	21	.219	.231	.261	.492	61	-21	-18	95	93	40	.493	49			3	*O/SP	-1.5
1889	Ind-N	131	532	83	142	32	1	2	63	9	39	.267	.282	.342	.624	69	-19	-26	109	102	63	.590	37			10	*O/P	-1.8
1890	Bro-P	104	443	84	108	24	4	1	65	19	12	.244	.278	.323	.601	58	-25	-30	106	129	47	.552	21			0	*O	-2.6
1891	Phi-a	50	201	24	46	4	3	2	13	6	12	.229	.255	.308	.563	61	-10	-11	103	56	19	.503	9			2	O	-0.9
	Bos-a	41	178	26	45	2	1	1	21	12	8	.253	.304	.292	.596	74	-6	-6	99	106	20	.571	11			-6	O	-1.1
	Yr	91	379	50	91	6	4	3		18	20	.240	.278	.301	.579	67	-16	-17	101	79	38	.535	20			-4		-2.0
Total	6	608	2464	345	604	106	18	9	276	57	148	.245	.265	.314	.579	66	-109	-115	101	108	255	.539	164			17	O/P32S	-8.9
■ MIKE McGEARY	McGeary, Michael Henry b: 1851, Philadelphia, Pa. BR/TR, 5'7", 138 lbs. Deb: 5/09/1871 M																											
1871	Tro-n	29	156	42	38							.244															*C/S	
1872	Ath-n	46	227	67	78							.344															CS/O	
1873	Ath-n	52	286	63	81							.283															*SC	
1874	Ath-n	54	276	61	100							.362															SC/O	
1875	Phi-n	69	313	71	92							.294															32S/OCM	
1876	StL-N	61	276	48	72	3	0	0	30	2	1	.261	.266	.272	.538	91	-6	-1	88	130	20	.377				4	*2/CO3	0.3
1877	StL-N	57	258	35	65	3	2	0	20	2	6	.252	.258	.279	.537	68	-9	-10	102	81	19	.383				8	23	0.1
1879	Pro-N	85	374	62	103	7	2	0	35	5	13	.275	.285	.305	.590	93	-2	-3	102	114	33	.439				6	*23	0.9
1880	Pro-N	18	59	5	8	0	0	0	1	0	6	.136	.136	.136	.271	-8	-6	-6	96	46	1	.157				-2	3/2SM	-0.7
	Cle-N	31	111	14	28	2	1	0	6	4	3	.252	.278	.288	.567	94	-1	-1	99	70	9	.434				-3	3/O	-0.3
	Yr	49	170	19	36	2	1	0	7	4	9	.212	.230	.235	.465	59	-7	-7	98	62	9	.328				-5		-1.0
1881	Cle-N	11	41	1	9	0	0	0	5	0	6	.220	.220	.220	.439	40	-3	-3	96	193	2	.281				0	3M	-0.1
1882	Det-N	34	133	14	19	4	1	0	2	2	20	.143	.156	.188	.344	9	-13	-13	102	27	4	.237				6	S/2	-0.3
Total	5 n	250	1258	304	389							.309															S/2	
Total	6	297	1252	179	304	19	6	0	99	15	55	.243	.252	.268	.519	71	-40	-36	98	97	89	.369				19	2S3/CO	-0.1
■ DAN McGEE	McGee, Daniel Aloysius b: 9/29/13, New York, N.Y. BR/TR, 5'8.5", 152 lbs. Deb: 7/14/34																											
1934	Bos-N	7	22	2	3	0	0	0	1	3	6	.136	.240	.136	.376	4	-3	-2	86	120	1	.316	0			-0	/S	-0.2
■ FRANK McGEE	McGee, Francis De Sales b: 4/28/1899, Columbus, Ohio d: 1/30/34, Columbus, Ohio BR/TR, 5'11.5", 175 lbs. Deb: 9/19/25																											
1925	Was-A	2	3	0	0	0	0	0	0	0	1	.000	.000	.000	.000	-99	-1	-1	98	0	0	.000	0	0	0	0	/1	0.0
■ PAT McGEE	McGee, Patrick d: 6/21/1889, New York, N.Y. Deb: 9/24/1874																											
1874	Atl-n	16	66	4	10							.152															O/S2	
1875	Mut-n	25	101	4	16							.158															O	
	Atl-n	18	67	3	9							.134															O/2	
	Yr	43	168	7	25							.149																
Total	2 n	59	234	11	35							.150															O/2	
■ WILLIE McGEE	McGee, Willie Dean b: 11/2/58, San Francisco, Cal. BB/TR, 6'1", 175 lbs. Deb: 5/10/82																											
1982	StL-N	123	422	43	125	12	8	4	56	12	58	.296	.319	.391	.710	94	-2	-4	103	124	49	.638	24	12	0	-16	*O	-2.2
1983	StL-N	147	601	75	172	22	8	5	75	26	98	.286	.316	.374	.690	92	-9	-7	98	131	73	.652	39	8	7	0	*O	-0.2
1984	StL-N	145	571	82	166	19	11	6	50	29	80	.291	.326	.394	.720	103	-0	1	99	85	74	.698	43	10	7	4	*O	0.7
1985	StL-N	152	612	114	**216**	26	**18**	10	82	34	86	**.353**	.387	.503	.890	154	37	40	96	102	123	.959	56	16	7	4	*O	4.9
1986	StL-N	124	497	65	127	22	7	7	48	37	82	.256	.308	.370	.679	84	-10	-12	103	90	53	.612	19	16	-4	9	*O	-0.9
1987	StL-N	153	620	76	177	37	11	11	105	24	90	.285	.314	.434	.748	97	-6	-4	99	147	77	.660	16	4	2	-1	*O/S	-0.9
1988	StL-N	137	562	73	164	24	6	3	50	32	84	.292	.331	.372	.703	98	1	-2	104	88	72	.684	41	6	9	3	*O	0.6
Total	7	981	3885	528	1147	162	69	46	466	194	578	.295	.330	.408	.738	104	11	11	100	110	522	.718	238	72	28	3	O/S	2.0
■ DAN McGEEHAN	McGeehan, Daniel De Sales b: 6/7/1885, Jeddo, Pa. d: 7/12/55, Hazleton, Pa. BR/TR, 5'6", 135 lbs. Deb: 4/22/11																											
1911	StL-N	3	9	0	2	0	0	0	1	0	1	.222	.222	.222	.444	24	-1	-1	101	169	0	.286	0			0	/2	0.0

YEAR	TM/L	G	AB	R	H	2B	3B	HR	RBI	BB	SO	AVG	OBP	SLG	PRO	/A	BR	/A	PF	CHI	RC	TA	SB	CS	SBR	FR	POS	TPR
■ **ED McGHEE**	McGhee, Warren Edward b: 9/29/24, Perry, Ark. d: 2/13/86, Memphis, Tenn. BR/TR, 5'11", 170 lbs. Deb: 9/20/50																											
1950	Chi-A	3	6	0	1	0	0	0	0	0	1	.167	.167	.500	.667	67	-0	-0	97	0	1	.600	0	0	0	-0	/O	0.0
1953	Phi-A	104	358	36	94	11	4	1	29	32	43	.263	.328	.324	.652	75	-11	-12	102	92	38	.556	4	3	-1	3	O	-1.2
1954	Phi-A	21	53	5	11	2	0	2	9	4	8	.208	.263	.358	.622	70	-3	-2	98	137	5	.535	0	1	-1	2	O	-0.1
	Chi-A	42	75	12	17	1	0	0	5	12	8	.227	.333	.240	.573	57	-4	-4	104	105	7	.565	5	0	2	-2	O	-0.5
	Yr	63	128	17	28	3	0	2	14	16	16	.219	.306	.289	.595	62	-6	-7	102	118	12	.552	5	1	1	-0		-0.6
1955	Chi-A	26	13	6	1	0	0	0	0	6	1	.077	.368	.077	.445	25	-1	-1	101	0	1	.600	2	1	0	-5	O	-0.6
Total	4	196	505	59	124	14	5	3	43	54	61	.246	.322	.311	.633	71	-19	-20	102	94	51	.580	11	5	0	-3	O	-2.4
■ **BILL McGHEE**	McGhee, William Mac "Fibber" b: 9/5/08, Shawmut, Ala. BL/TL, 5'10.5", 185 lbs. Deb: 7/05/44																											
1944	Phi-A	77	287	27	83	12	0	1	19	21	20	.289	.338	.341	.679	93	-2	-2	101	69	32	.563	2	1	0	1	1	-0.6
1945	Phi-A	93	250	24	63	6	1	0	19	24	16	.252	.320	.284	.604	81	-7	-5	94	97	24	.516	3	2	-0	-6	O/1	-1.4
Total	2	170	537	51	146	18	1	1	38	45	36	.272	.329	.315	.644	88	-9	-8	97	82	57	.554	5	3	-0	-5	/1O	-2.0
■ **BILL McGILVRAY**	McGilvray, William Alexander "Big Bill" b: 4/29/1883, Portland, Ore. d: 5/23/52, Denver, Colo. 6', 160 lbs. Deb: 4/17/08																											
1908	Cin-N	2	2	0	0	0	0	0	0	0		.000	.000	.000	.000	-98	-0	-0	103	0	0	.000	0			0	H	0.0
■ **TIM McGINLEY**	McGinley, Timothy S. b: Philadelphia, Pa. d: 11/2/1899, Oakland, Cal. 5'9.5", 155 lbs. Deb: 4/30/1875																											
1875	Cen-n	13	53	5	12							.226															C/O	
	NH-n	33	141	14	36							.255															C	
	Yr	46	194	19	48							.247																
1876	Bos-N	9	40	5	6	0	0	0	2	0	1	.150	.150	.150	.300	0	-4	-4	95	119	1	.176				0	/OC	-0.2
■ **FRANK McGINN**	McGinn, Frank J. b: Cincinnati, Ohio d: 11/19/1897, Cincinnati, Ohio Deb: 6/09/1890																											
1890	Pit-N	1	4	0	0	0	0	0	0	0	2	.000	.000	.000	.000	-99	-1	-1	88	0	0	.000	0			0	/O	0.0
■ **JOHN McGLONE**	McGlone, John T. b: 1864, Brooklyn, N.Y. d: 11/24/27, Brooklyn, N.Y. Deb: 10/07/1886																											
1886	Was-N	4	15	2	1	0	0	0	1	0	3	.067	.067	.067	.133	-63	-3	-3	94	332	0	.071	0			0	/3	-0.1
1887	Cle-a	21	79	14	20	2	1	0		7		.253	.337	.304	.641	84	-2	-1	98	0	13	.831	15			0	3	0.0
1888	Cle-a	55	203	22	37	1	3	1	22	16		.182	.249	.232	.480	58	-9	-8	97	139	19	.548	26			-6	3/O	-1.2
Total	3	80	297	38	58	3	4	1	23	23	3	.195	.265	.242	.507	60	-13	-12	97	110	32	.590	41			-6	/3O	-1.3
■ **ART McGOVERN**	McGovern, Arthur John b: 2/27/1882, St.John, N.B., Can. d: 11/14/15, Thornton, R.I. 160 lbs. Deb: 4/21/05																											
1905	Bos-A	15	44	1	5	1	0	0	1	4		.114	.188	.136	.324	5	-5	-5	100	59	1	.256	0			0	C	-0.3
■ **BEAUTY McGOWAN**	McGowan, Frank Bernard b: 11/8/01, Branford, Conn. d: 5/6/82, Hamden, Conn. BL/TR, 5'11", 190 lbs. Deb: 4/12/22																											
1922	Phi-A	99	300	36	69	10	5	1	20	40	46	.230	.323	.307	.629	62	-15	-17	104	75	32	.589	6	5	-1	4	O	-1.9
1923	Phi-A	95	287	41	73	9	1	1	19	36	25	.254	.340	.303	.643	70	-12	-12	100	72	32	.590	4	3	-1	-1	O	-2.0
1928	StL-A	47	168	35	61	13	4	2	18	16	15	.363	.425	.524	.949	143	12	11	104	70	38	1.000	2	1	0	-2	O	0.6
1929	StL-A	125	441	62	112	26	6	2	51	61	34	.254	.346	.354	.700	81	-12	-12	100	110	58	.674	5	2	0	6	*O	-0.9
1937	Bos-N	9	12	0	1	0	0	0	0	1	2	.083	.154	.083	.237	-38	-2	-2	90	0	0	.182	0			-1	/O	-0.2
Total	5	375	1208	174	316	58	16	6	108	154	122	.262	.347	.351	.698	81	-29	-31	101	86	160	.664	17	11		7	O	-4.4
■ **JOHN McGRAW**	McGraw, John Joseph "Mugsy" or "Little Napoleon" b: 4/7/1873, Truxton, N.Y. d: 2/25/34, New Rochelle, N.Y. BL/TR, 5'7", 155 lbs. Deb: 8/26/1891 MH																											
1891	Bal-a	33	115	17	31	3	5	0	14	12	17	.270	.359	.383	.741	114	2	2	101	94	18	.762	4			0	S/O2	0.2
1892	Bal-N	79	286	41	77	13	2	1	26	32	21	.269	.355	.339	.694	112	5	5	100	81	41	.718	15			0	O2/S3	0.5
1893	Bal-N	127	480	123	154	9	10	5	64	101	11	.321	.454	.412	.866	125	31	24	107	79	110	1.083	38			-24	*SO	0.3
1894	Bal-N	124	512	156	174	18	14	1	92	91	12	.340	.451	.436	.887	117	20	21	99	99	139	1.198	78			-2	*3/2	1.3
1895	Bal-N	96	388	110	143	13	6	2	48	60	9	.369	.459	.448	.908	128	26	20	107	64	111	1.224	61			9	*3/2	2.5
1896	Bal-N	23	77	20	25	2	2	0	14	11	4	.325	.422	.403	.825	118	3	3	102	130	19	1.096	13			0	3/1	0.2
1897	Bal-N	106	391	90	127	15	3	0	48	99		.325	**.471**	.379	.849	135	25	29	95	84	93	1.136	44			-16	*3	1.2
1898	Bal-N	143	515	**143**	176	8	10	0	53	**112**		.342	.474	.396	.871	149	**47**	44	103	69	120	1.112	43			-14	*3/O	3.1
1899	Bal-N	117	399	**140**	156	13	3	1	33	**124**		.391	**.547**	.446	.994	165	58	53	108	48	141	**1.601**	73			2	*3M	4.8
1900	StL-N	99	334	84	115	10	4	2	33	85		.344	.477	.416	.893	162	30	34	93	75	82	1.155	29			-14	*3	1.9
1901	Bal-A	73	232	71	81	14	9	0	28	61		.349	.485	.487	.972	162	27	25	107	83	68	1.311	24			-10	3M	1.1
1902	Bal-A	20	63	14	18	3	2	1	3	17		.286	.438	.444	.882	144	5	5	102	34	15	1.111	5			-3	3M	0.1
	NY-N	35	107	13	25	0	0	0	5	26		.234	.383	.234	.617	93	1	1	100	73	13	.707	7			-4	SM	-0.1
1903	NY-N	12	11	2	3	0	0	0	1	1		.273	.333	.273	.606	71	-0	-0	106	107	1	.625	1			0	/2OS3M	0.0
1904	NY-N	5	12	0	4	0	0	0	0	3		.333	.467	.333	.800	144	1	1	105	0	2	.875	0			1	/2SM	0.2
1905	NY-N	3	0	0	0	0	0	0	0	0		—	—	—	—	—	0	0	101	—	2	—	1			0	/OM	0.0
1906	NY-N	4	2	0	0	0	0	0	0	1		.000	.333	.000	.333	6	-0	-0	100	0	0	.500	0			0	/3M	0.0
Total	16	1099	3924	1024	1309	121	70	13	462	836	74	.334	.460	.410	.871	136	282	267	102	76	974	1.135	436			-76	3S/O21	17.3
■ **FRED McGRIFF**	McGriff, Frederick Stanley b: 10/31/63, Tampa, Fla. BL/TL, 6'3", 200 lbs. Deb: 5/17/86																											
1986	Tor-A	3	5	1	1	0	0	0	0	0	2	.200	.200	.200	.400	10	-1	-1	105	0	0	.250	0	0	0	0	/1D	0.0
1987	Tor-A	107	295	58	73	16	0	20	43	60	104	.247	.376	.505	.881	131	15	14	101	82	60	.938	3	2	-0	1	D1	1.2
1988	Tor-A	154	536	100	151	35	4	34	82	79	149	.282	.378	.552	.930	158	41	41	100	84	113	.960	6	1	1	-3	*1	3.1
Total	3	264	836	159	225	51	4	54	125	139	255	.269	.377	.533	.910	147	55	55	100	83	173	.952	9	3	1	-2	1/D	4.3
■ **TERRY McGRIFF**	McGriff, Terence Roy b: 9/23/63, Fort Pierce, Fla. BR/TR, 6'2", 190 lbs. Deb: 7/11/87																											
1987	Cin-N	34	89	6	20	3	0	2	11	8	17	.225	.289	.326	.615	60	-5	-5	104	125	8	.514	0	0	0	1	C	-0.1
1988	Cin-N	35	96	9	19	3	0	1	4	12	31	.198	.287	.260	.547	55	-5	-6	105	57	7	.475	1	0	0	-0	C	-0.3
Total	2	69	185	15	39	6	0	3	15	20	48	.211	.288	.292	.580	58	-10	-11	105	89	16	.503	1	0	0	1	/C	-0.4
■ **MARK McGRILLIS**	McGrillis, Mark A. b: 10/22/1872, Philadelphia, Pa. d: 5/16/35, Philadelphia, Pa. Deb: 9/17/1892																											
1892	StL-N	1	3	0	0	0	0	0	0	0	1	.000	.000	.000	.000	-99	-1	-1	95	0	0	.000	0			0	/3	0.0
■ **JOE McGUCKIN**	McGuckin, Joseph W. b: 1862, Paterson, N.J. d: 12/31/03, Yonkers, N.Y. Deb: 8/27/1890																											
1890	BB-a	11	37	2	4	0	0	0		6		.108	.250	.108	.358	8	-4	-4	100	0	2	.424	3			0	O	-0.3
■ **JOHN McGUINNESS**	McGuinness, John James b: 1857, Ireland d: 12/19/16, Binghamton, N.Y. Deb: 5/06/1876																											
1876	NY-N	1	4	0	0	0	0	0	0	0	0	.000	.000	.000	.000	-99	-1	-1	87	0	0	.000				0	/2C	0.0
1879	Syr-N	12	51	7	15	1	1	0	4	0	6	.294	.294	.353	.647	126	1	1	89	75	5	.500				0	1	0.1
1884	Phi-U	53	220	25	52	8	1	0		5		.236	.253	.282	.535	87	-4	-2	93	0	16	.399	0			-0	1/2S	-0.2
Total	3	66	275	32	67	9	2	0	4	5	6	.244	.257	.291	.548	91	-5	-1	92	14	22	.409	0			-0	/12SC	-0.1
■ **JIM McGUIRE**	McGuire, James A. b: 2/4/1875, Dunkirk, N.Y. d: 1/26/17, Buffalo, N.Y. TR , Deb: 9/10/01																											
1901	Cle-A	18	69	4	16	2	0	0	3	0		.232	.232	.261	.493	40	-6	-5	95	54	4	.340	0			-3	S	-0.6
■ **DEACON McGUIRE**	McGuire, James Thomas b: 11/2/1865, Youngstown, Ohio d: 10/31/36, Albion, Mich. BR/TL, 6'1", 185 lbs. Deb: 6/21/1884 M																											
1884	Tol-a	45	151	12	28	7	0	1		5		.185	.217	.252	.468	53	-7	-8	104	0	8	.358				-11	C/OS	-1.3
1885	Det-N	34	121	11	23	4	2	0	9	5	23	.190	.222	.256	.478	56	-6	-6	97	103	7	.367				18	C/O	1.4
1886	Phi-N	50	167	25	33	7	1	2	18	19	25	.198	.280	.287	.567	74	-5	-5	98	111	14	.515	2			-6	C/O	-0.6
1887	Phi-N	41	150	22	46	6	6	2	23	11	8	.307	.362	.467	.829	135	6	7	97	95	27	.827	3			-4	C	0.6
1888	Phi-N	12	51	7	17	4	2	0	11	4	9	.333	.382	.490	.872	158	4	4	114	136	10	.853	0			0	C/3	0.3
	Det-N	3	13	0	0	0	0	0	0	0	4	.000	.000	.000	.000	-99	-3	-3	98	0	0	.000	0			0	/C	-0.2
	Yr	15	64	7	17	4	2	0	11	4	13	.266	.309	.391	.699	112	2	1	111	118	8	.617	0			0		0.1
	Cle-a	26	94	15	24	1	3	1	13	7		.255	.333	.362	.695	130	3	3	97	111	12	.671	2			0	C/1O	0.3
1890	Roc-a	87	331	46	99	16	4	4		21		.299	.356	.408	.763	138	10	14	93	0	52	.741	8			12	C1/OP	2.9
1891	Was-a	114	413	55	125	22	10	3	66	43	34	.303	.382	.426	.808	141	18	22	95	105	73	.830	10			6	*CO/31	2.7
1892	Was-N	97	315	46	73	14	4	4	43	61	48	.232	.360	.340	.699	109	8	5	105	113	42	.731	7			-4	C/1O	0.6
1893	Was-N	63	237	29	62	14	3	1	26	26	12	.262	.342	.359	.701	98	-4	1	90	82	31	.669	3			-8	C1	-0.2

YEAR	TM/L	G	AB	R	H	2B	3B	HR	RBI	BB	SO	AVG	OBP	SLG	PRO	/A	BR	/A	PF	CHI	RC	TA	SB	CS	SBR	FR	POS	TPR
1894	Was-N	104	425	67	130	18	6	6	78	33	19	.306	.366	.419	.784	92	-7	-5	98	116	71	.776	11			5	*C	0.7
1895	Was-N	132	533	89	179	30	8	10	97	40	18	.336	.388	.478	.866	121	18	15	103	101	108	.893	16			23	*C/S	3.9
1896	Was-N	108	389	60	125	25	3	2	70	30	14	.321	.379	.416	.795	117	7	10	95	123	68	.795	12			1	*C/1	1.7
1897	Was-N	93	327	51	112	17	7	4	53	21		.343	.386	.474	.860	127	13	12	101	95	65	.870	9			7	C/1	2.5
1898	Was-N	131	489	59	131	18	3	1	57	24		.268	.310	.323	.633	82	-10	-12	102	109	53	.553	10			6	C1M	0.1
1899	Was-N	59	199	25	54	3	1	1	12	16		.271	.335	.312	.646	84	-5	-3	96	58	22	.579	3			2	C/1	0.2
	Bro-N	46	157	22	50	12	4	0	23	12		.318	.378	.446	.824	123	6	5	105	103	29	.832	4			-0	C	0.7
	Yr	105	356	47	104	15	5	1	35	28		.292	.354	.371	.725	102	1	1	100	78	50	.687	7			2		0.9
1900	Bro-N	71	241	20	69	15	2	0	34	19		.286	.338	.365	.704	90	-1	-4	108	121	31	.634	2			-5	C	-0.2
1901	Bro-N	85	301	28	89	16	4	0	40	18		.296	.335	.375	.711	102	3	1	106	118	40	.637	4			1	C/1	1.1
1902	Det-A	73	229	27	52	14	1	2	23	24		.227	.300	.323	.624	75	-8	-7	99	95	23	.554	0			-2	C	-0.2
1903	Det-A	72	248	15	62	12	1	0	21	19		.250	.303	.306	.610	88	-4	-3	97	101	25	.527	3			-3	C/1	0.3
1904	NY-A	101	322	17	67	12	2	0	20	27		.208	.269	.258	.527	62	-10	-15	112	90	23	.439	2			-1	C/1	-0.6
1905	NY-A	72	228	9	50	7	2	0	33	18		.219	.276	.268	.544	73	-6	-7	102	193	18	.461	3			-7	C	-0.6
1906	NY-A	51	144	11	43	5	0	0	14	12		.299	.353	.333	.686	98	3	-0	120	106	18	.624	3			-7	C/1	-0.2
1907	NY-A	1	1	0	0	0	0	0	0	0		.000	.000	.000	.000	-92	-0	-0	109	0	0	.000	0			0	/C	0.0
	Bos-A	6	4	1	3	0	0	1	1	0		.750	.750	1.500	2.250	614	2	2	101	40	5	6.000	0			0	HM	0.2
	Yr	7	5	1	3	0	0	1	1	0		.600	.600	1.200	1.800	466	2	2	102	34	4	3.000	0			0		0.2
1908	Bos-A	1	1	0	0	0	0	0	0	0		.000	.000	.000	.000	-99	-0	-0	98	0	0	.000	0			0	HM	0.0
	Cle-A	1	4	0	1	1	0	0	2	0		.250	.250	.500	.750	136	0	0	106	361	0	.667	0			0	/1	0.0
	Yr	2	5	0	1	1	0	0	2	0		.200	.200	.400	.600	94	-0	-0	102	180	0	.500	0			0		0.0
1910	Cle-A	1	3	0	1	0	0	0	0	0		.333	.500	.333	.833	162	0	0	100	0	0	1.000	0			0	/CM	0.0
1912	Det-A	1	2	1	1	0	0	0	0	0		.500	.500	.500	1.000	196	0	0	95	0	0	1.000	0			0	/C	0.0
Total	26	1781	6290	770	1749	300	79	45	787	515	214	.278	.339	.372	.711	102	26	24	101	100	877	.669	117			25	*C/103SP	16.1

■ **MICKEY McGUIRE** McGuire, M C Adolphus b: 1/18/41, Dayton, Ohio BR/TR, 5'10", 170 lbs. Deb: 9/07/62

YEAR	TM/L	G	AB	R	H	2B	3B	HR	RBI	BB	SO	AVG	OBP	SLG	PRO	/A	BR	/A	PF	CHI	RC	TA	SB	CS	SBR	FR	POS	TPR
1962	Bal-A	6	4	0	0	0	0	0	0	0	0	.000	.000	.000	.000	-99	-1	-1	95	0	0	.000	0	0	0	0	/S	0.0
1967	Bal-A	10	17	2	4	0	0	0	2	0	2	.235	.235	.235	.471	42	-1	-1	95	209	1	.286	0	0	0	0	/2	0.0
Total	2	16	21	2	4	0	0	0	2	0	2	.190	.190	.190	.381	11	-2	-2	95	169	1	.222	0	0	0	0	/S2	0.0

■ **BILL McGUIRE** McGuire, William Patrick b: 2/14/64, Omaha, Neb. BR/TR, 6'3", 195 lbs. Deb: 8/02/88

YEAR	TM/L	G	AB	R	H	2B	3B	HR	RBI	BB	SO	AVG	OBP	SLG	PRO	/A	BR	/A	PF	CHI	RC	TA	SB	CS	SBR	FR	POS	TPR
1988	Sea-A	9	16	1	3	0	0	0	2	3	2	.188	.316	.188	.503	41	-1	-1	108	265	1	.462	0	0	0	1	/C	0.0

■ **BILL McGUNNIGLE** McGunnigle, William Henry "Gunner" b: 1/1/1855, Boston, Mass. d: 3/9/1899, Brockton, Mass. BR/TR, 5'9", 155 lbs. Deb: 5/02/1879 M

YEAR	TM/L	G	AB	R	H	2B	3B	HR	RBI	BB	SO	AVG	OBP	SLG	PRO	/A	BR	/A	PF	CHI	RC	TA	SB	CS	SBR	FR	POS	TPR
1879	Buf-N	47	171	22	30	0	1	0	5	5	24	.175	.199	.187	.386	25	-13	-16	114	55	7	.262				-1	OP	-1.6
1880	Buf-N	7	22	0	4	0	0	0	1	0	4	.182	.182	.182	.364	26	-2	-1	91	91	1	.222				0	/PO	0.0
	Wor-N	1	4	0	0	0	0	0	0	0	2	.000	.000	.000	.000	-89	-1	-1	113	0	0	.000				0	/O	0.0
	Yr	8	26	0	4	0	0	0	1	0	6	.154	.154	.154	.308	5	-2	-2	93	91	1	.182				0		0.0
1882	Cle-N	1	5	2	1	0	0	0	0	0	1	.200	.200	.200	.400	32	-0	-0	90	0	0	.250				0	/O	0.0
Total	3	56	202	24	35	0	1	0	6	5	31	.173	.193	.183	.376	23	-16	-19	111	56	7	.251				-1	/OP	-1.6

■ **MARK McGWIRE** McGwire, Mark David b: 10/1/63, Pomona, Cal. BR/TR, 6'5", 215 lbs. Deb: 8/22/86

YEAR	TM/L	G	AB	R	H	2B	3B	HR	RBI	BB	SO	AVG	OBP	SLG	PRO	/A	BR	/A	PF	CHI	RC	TA	SB	CS	SBR	FR	POS	TPR
1986	Oak-A	18	53	10	10	1	0	3	9	4	18	.189	.259	.377	.636	76	-2	-2	94	124	5	.568	0	1	-1	-2	3	-0.4
1987	Oak-A	151	557	97	161	28	4	**49**	118	71	131	.289	.374	**.618**	.992	173	45	53	91	102	131	1.045	1	1	-0	-2	*1/3O	3.3
1988	Oak-A	155	550	87	143	22	1	32	99	76	117	.260	.354	.478	.832	138	23	26	95	112	93	.813	0	0	0	-8	*1/O	0.9
Total	3	324	1160	194	314	51	5	84	226	151	266	.271	.360	.541	.900	152	66	77	93	107	230	.914	1	2	-1	-12	1/3O	3.8

■ **JIM McHALE** McHale, James Bernard "J.B." b: 12/17/1875, Miners Mills, Pa. d: 6/17/59, Los Angeles, Cal. BR/TR, 5'11", 165 lbs. Deb: 4/14/08

YEAR	TM/L	G	AB	R	H	2B	3B	HR	RBI	BB	SO	AVG	OBP	SLG	PRO	/A	BR	/A	PF	CHI	RC	TA	SB	CS	SBR	FR	POS	TPR
1908	Bos-A	21	67	9	15	2	2	0	7	4		.224	.268	.313	.581	92	-1	-1	98	128	6	.558	4			0	O	-0.1

■ **JOHN McHALE** McHale, John Joseph b: 9/21/21, Detroit, Mich. BL/TR, 6', 200 lbs. Deb: 5/28/43

YEAR	TM/L	G	AB	R	H	2B	3B	HR	RBI	BB	SO	AVG	OBP	SLG	PRO	/A	BR	/A	PF	CHI	RC	TA	SB	CS	SBR	FR	POS	TPR
1943	Det-A	4	3	0	0	0	0	0	0	1	1	.000	.250	.000	.250	-23	-0	-0	106	0	0	.333	0	0	0	0	H	0.0
1944	Det-A	1	1	0	0	0	0	0	0	0	0	.000	.000	.000	.000	-95	-0	-0	105	0	0	.000	0	0	0	0	H	0.0
1945	Det-A	19	14	0	2	0	0	0	1	1	4	.143	.250	.143	.393	14	-1	-2	106	181	1	.333	0	0	0	0	/1	-0.1
1947	Det-A	39	95	10	20	1	0	3	11	7	24	.211	.265	.316	.580	59	-5	-6	104	104	8	.500	1	1	-0	2	1	-0.4
1948	Det-A	1	1	0	0	0	0	0	0	0	0	.000	.000	.000	.000	-99	-0	-0	96	0	0	.000	0	0	0	0	H	0.0
Total	5	64	114	10	22	1	0	3	12	9	29	.193	.258	.281	.539	49	-8	-8	104	109	9	.462	1	1	-0	2	/1	-0.5

■ **BOB McHALE** McHale, Robert Emmet "Rabbit" b: 2/25/1872, Michigan Bluff, Cal. d: 6/9/52, Sacramento, Cal. Deb: 5/09/1898

YEAR	TM/L	G	AB	R	H	2B	3B	HR	RBI	BB	SO	AVG	OBP	SLG	PRO	/A	BR	/A	PF	CHI	RC	TA	SB	CS	SBR	FR	POS	TPR
1898	Was-N	11	33	5	6	2	0	0	7	1		.182	.270	.242	.513	48	-2	-2	102	265	2	.481	1			0	/OS1	-0.1

■ **AUSTIN McHENRY** McHenry, Austin Bush "Mac" b: 9/22/1895, Wrightsville, O. d: 11/27/22, Jefferson, Ohio BR/TR, 5'11", 152 lbs. Deb: 6/22/18

YEAR	TM/L	G	AB	R	H	2B	3B	HR	RBI	BB	SO	AVG	OBP	SLG	PRO	/A	BR	/A	PF	CHI	RC	TA	SB	CS	SBR	FR	POS	TPR
1918	StL-N	80	272	32	71	12	6	1	29	21	24	.261	.319	.360	.679	114	2	4	93	111	33	.642	8			0	O	0.0
1919	StL-N	110	371	41	106	19	11	1	47	19	57	.286	.322	.404	.727	125	7	9	94	122	49	.668	7			4	*O	1.0
1920	StL-N	137	504	66	142	19	11	10	65	25	73	.282	.316	.423	.738	113	5	6	98	106	64	.660	8	11	-4	9	*O	0.4
1921	StL-N	152	574	92	201	37	8	17	102	38	48	.350	.393	.531	.924	150	33	37	95	107	111	.903	10	20	-9	-7	*O	1.3
1922	StL-N	64	238	31	72	18	3	5	43	14	27	.303	.344	.466	.810	106	2	1	101	122	37	.762	2	2	-1	6	O	0.4
Total	5	543	1959	262	592	105	39	34	286	117	229	.302	.343	.448	.791	126	49	58	96	112	294	.739	35	33		12	O	3.1

■ **VANCE McHENRY** McHenry, Vance Loren b: 7/10/56, Chico, Cal. BR/TR, 5'9", 165 lbs. Deb: 8/13/81

YEAR	TM/L	G	AB	R	H	2B	3B	HR	RBI	BB	SO	AVG	OBP	SLG	PRO	/A	BR	/A	PF	CHI	RC	TA	SB	CS	SBR	FR	POS	TPR
1981	Sea-A	15	18	3	4	0	0	0	2	1	1	.222	.263	.222	.485	41	-1	-1	100	196	1	.333	0	0	0	0	S/D	0.0
1982	Sea-A	3	1	0	0	0	0	0	0	0	0	.000	.000	.000	.000	-91	-0	-0	109	0	0	.000	0	0	0	0	/SD	0.0
Total	2	18	19	3	4	0	0	0	2	1	1	.211	.250	.211	.461	33	-2	-2	100	186	1	.333	0	0	0	0	/SD	0.0

■ **IRISH McILVEEN** McIlveen, Henry Cooke b: 7/27/1880, Belfast, Ireland d: 10/18/60, Lorain, Ohio TL, 5'11.5", 180 lbs. Deb: 7/10/06

YEAR	TM/L	G	AB	R	H	2B	3B	HR	RBI	BB	SO	AVG	OBP	SLG	PRO	/A	BR	/A	PF	CHI	RC	TA	SB	CS	SBR	FR	POS	TPR
1906	Pit-N	5	5	1	2	0	0	0	0	0		.400	.400	.400	.800	146	0	0	104	0	1	.667	0			0	/P	0.1
1908	NY-A	44	169	17	36	3	3	0	8	14		.213	.273	.266	.539	81	-4	-3	95	58	13	.489	6			-0	O	-0.5
1909	NY-A	4	3	0	0	0	0	0	0	1		.000	.250	.000	.250	-20	-0	-0	99	0	0	.333	0			0	H	0.0
Total	3	53	177	18	38	3	3	0	8	15		.215	.276	.266	.542	81	-4	-3	96	55	14	.489	6			-0	/OP	-0.4

■ **STUFFY McINNIS** McInnis, John Phalen "Jack" b: 9/19/1890, Gloucester, Mass. d: 2/16/60, Ipswich, Mass. BR/TR, 5'9.5", 162 lbs. Deb: 4/12/09 M

YEAR	TM/L	G	AB	R	H	2B	3B	HR	RBI	BB	SO	AVG	OBP	SLG	PRO	/A	BR	/A	PF	CHI	RC	TA	SB	CS	SBR	FR	POS	TPR
1909	Phi-A	19	46	4	11	0	0	1	4	2		.239	.286	.304	.590	85	-1	-1	102	91	4	.486	0			-3	S	-0.4
1910	Phi-A	38	73	10	22	2	4	0	12	7		.301	.363	.438	.801	147	4	4	102	139	12	.824	3			-1	S/23O	0.3
1911	Phi-A	126	468	76	150	20	10	3	77	25		.321	.361	.425	.787	128	11	15	93	128	80	.792	23			-6	1S	1.3
1912	Phi-A	153	568	83	186	25	13	3	101	49		.327	.384	.433	.817	134	24	24	99	140	105	.851	27			3	*1	3.0
1913	Phi-A	148	543	79	176	30	4	4	90	45	31	.324	.382	.416	.798	138	23	25	97	142	91	.798	16			-2	*1	2.4
1914	Phi-A	149	576	74	181	12	8	1	95	19	27	.314	.341	.368	.709	116	7	8	97	**176**	76	.628	25	19	-4	-0	*1	0.5
1915	Phi-A	119	456	44	143	14	4	0	49	14	17	.314	.337	.362	.699	114	3	5	96	107	57	.589	8	8	-2	2	*1	0.0
1916	Phi-A	140	512	42	151	25	3	1	60	25	19	.295	.331	.361	.693	110	3	4	98	121	67	.609	7			7	*1	0.9
1917	Phi-A	150	567	50	172	19	4	0	44	33	19	.303	.342	.351	.693	119	6	10	94	84	72	.633	18			2	*1	0.7
1918	Bos-A	117	423	40	115	11	5	0	56	19	10	.272	.306	.322	.628	94	-7	-5	95	**159**	46	.542	10			3	13	-0.7
1919	Bos-A	120	440	32	134	12	5	1	58	23	11	.305	.341	.361	.702	106	-2	2	91	132	57	.624	8			2	*1	-0.4
1920	Bos-A	148	559	50	166	21	3	2	71	18	19	.297	.321	.356	.677	83	-17	-14	96	129	62	.557	6	11	-5	-1	*1	-1.9
1921	Bos-A	152	584	72	179	31	10	0	76	21	9	.307	.335	.394	.729	86	-14	-14	100	120	76	.628	2	4	-2	5	*1	-1.1
1922	Cle-A	142	537	58	164	28	7	1	78	15	5	.305	.325	.389	.715	84	-13	-14	102	134	66	.598	1	5	-3	-4	*1	-3.0
1923	Bos-N	154	607	70	191	23	9	2	95	26	12	.315	.343	.392	.735	94	-6	-6	100	145	80	.639	7	8	-3	4	*1	-1.4
1924	Bos-N	146	581	57	169	23	7	1	59	15	6	.291	.311	.360	.671	84	-18	-13	94	108	65	.566	9	3	1	5	*1	-1.3
1925	Pit-N	59	155	19	57	10	4	0	24	17	1	.368	.437	.484	.921	133	9	9	102	114	33	.960	1	1	-0	-1	1	0.2
1926	Pit-N	47	127	12	38	6	1	0	13	7	3	.299	.336	.362	.698	78	-2	-4	112	98	15	.607	1			-1	1	-0.5
1927	Phi-N	1	0	0	0	0	0	0	0	0	0	—	—	—	—	—	0	0	96	—	—	—	0			0	/1M	0.0

YEAR	TM/L	G	AB	R	H	2B	3B	HR	RBI	BB	SO	AVG	OBP	SLG	PRO	/A	BR	/A	PF	CHI	RC	TA	SB	CS	SBR	FR	POS	TPR
Total	19	2128	7822	872	2405	312	101	20	1062	380	189	.307	.343	.381	.723	106	9	37	97	129	1080	.652	172	59		13	*1/S320	-1.4
■ MATTY McINTYRE McIntyre, Matthew W. b: 6/12/1880, Stonington, Conn. d: 4/2/20, Detroit, Mich. BL/TL, 5'11", 175 lbs. Deb: 7/03/01																												
1901	Phi-A	82	308	38	85	12	4	0	46	30		.276	.340	.341	.681	91	-3	-3	100	146	40	.655	11			-4	O	-0.6
1904	Det-A	152	578	74	146	11	10	2	46	44		.253	.305	.317	.622	104	0	3	96	87	61	.551	11			10	*O	0.4
1905	Det-A	131	495	59	130	21	5	0	30	48		.263	.328	.325	.653	112	6	7	98	59	57	.597	9			16	*O	1.8
1906	Det-A	133	493	63	128	19	11	0	39	56		.260	.335	.343	.678	106	9	5	108	74	68	.696	29			12	*O	1.3
1907	Det-A	20	81	6	23	1	1	0	9	7		.284	.341	.321	.662	112	1	1	102	107	10	.621	3			3	O	0.3
1908	Det-A	151	569	**105**	168	24	13	0	28	83		.295	**.385**	.383	.768	151	36	35	101	42	90	.800	20			13	*O	4.5
1909	Det-A	125	476	65	116	18	9	1	34	54		.244	.325	.326	.650	96	4	-1	110	72	53	.625	13			-5	*O	-1.2
1910	Det-A	83	305	40	72	15	5	0	25	39		.236	.323	.318	.641	99	1	0	102	101	32	.601	4			4	O	0.0
1911	Chi-A	146	569	102	184	19	11	1	52	64		.323	.397	.401	.797	127	19	22	97	73	96	.816	17			-3	*O	0.7
1912	Chi-A	45	84	10	14	0	0	0	10	14		.167	.300	.167	.467	35	-6	-6	99	238	5	.471	3			-2	O	-0.9
Total	10	1068	3958	562	1066	140	69	4	319	439		.269	.344	.343	.686	111	68	63	101	81	512	.666	120			44	*O	6.3
■ OTTO McIVOR McIvor, Edward Otto b: 7/26/1884, Greenville, Tex. d: 5/4/54, Dallas, Tex. BB/TL, 5'11.5", 175 lbs. Deb: 4/18/11																												
1911	StL-N	30	62	11	14	2	1	1	9	9	14	.226	.333	.339	.672	87	-1	-1	101	127	7	.646	0			-3	O	-0.4
■ DAVE McKAY McKay, David Lawrence b: 3/14/50, Vancouver, B.C., Can BB/TR, 6'1", 195 lbs. Deb: 8/22/75 C																												
1975	Min-A	33	125	8	32	4	1	2	16	6	14	.256	.295	.352	.647	77	-3	-4	107	125	12	.531	1	1	-0	4	3	0.0
1976	Min-A	45	138	8	28	2	0	0	8	9	27	.203	.272	.217	.489	45	-9	-9	98	102	8	.373	1	2	-1	0	3/SD	-0.9
1977	Tor-A	95	274	18	54	4	3	3	22	7	51	.197	.223	.266	.489	32	-26	-27	103	106	15	.365	2	1	0	-5	23S/D	-2.6
1978	Tor-A	145	504	59	120	20	8	7	45	20	91	.238	.269	.351	.620	73	-19	-19	100	90	43	.499	4	4	-1	2	*2/S3D	-1.1
1979	Tor-A	47	156	19	34	9	0	0	12	7	19	.218	.256	.276	.532	42	-12	-13	103	107	10	.406	1	1	-0	1	2/3	-0.9
1980	Oak-A	123	295	29	72	16	1	1	29	10	57	.244	.283	.315	.598	67	-15	-13	95	118	27	.482	1	1	-0	-21	23S	-3.0
1981	Oak-A	79	224	25	59	11	1	4	21	16	43	.263	.318	.375	.693	103	-0	1	96	86	27	.624	4	1	1	-13	32/S	-1.0
1982	Oak-A	78	212	25	42	4	1	4	17	11	35	.198	.238	.283	.521	44	-17	-16	95	94	16	.450	6	1	1	-6	23/S	-1.7
Total	8	645	1928	191	441	70	15	21	170	86	337	.229	.268	.313	.581	62	-102	-100	99	101	157	.485	20	12	-1	-37	23/SD	-11.2
■ ED McKEAN McKean, Edwin John "Mack" b: 6/6/1864, Grafton, Ohio d: 8/16/19, Cleveland, Ohio BR/TR, 5'9", 160 lbs. Deb: 4/16/1887																												
1887	Cle-a	132	539	97	154	16	13	2		60		.286	.358	.375	.733	110	6	9	98	0	102	.881	76			-9	*S/2O	-0.1
1888	Cle-a	131	548	94	164	21	15	6	68	28		.299	.340	.425	.765	152	28	30	97	72	99	.831	52			0	SO/23	2.9
1889	Cle-N	123	500	88	159	22	8	4	75	42	25	.318	.375	.418	.793	120	15	13	103	89	94	.850	35			4	*S/2	1.8
1890	Cle-N	136	530	95	157	15	14	7	61	87	25	.296	.401	.417	.818	150	31	36	94	66	100	.903	23			-23	*S/2	1.0
1891	Cle-N	141	603	115	170	13	12	6	69	64	19	.282	.352	.373	.725	108	11	6	105	73	86	.702	14			-15	*S	-0.1
1892	Cle-N	128	526	76	139	14	10	0	93	49	28	.264	.328	.329	.657	97	1	-2	103	**159**	65	.625	19			-46	*S	-3.7
1893	Cle-N	125	545	103	169	29	24	4	133	50	14	.310	.372	.473	.846	121	18	14	104	130	105	.872	16			-5	*S	1.0
1894	Cle-N	130	554	116	198	30	15	8	128	49	12	.357	.412	.509	.921	111	20	8	111	111	133	1.028	33			-23	*S	-0.6
1895	Cle-N	131	565	131	193	32	17	8	119	45	25	.342	.397	.501	.898	137	26	30	97	96	120	.933	12			-24	*S	1.3
1896	Cle-N	133	571	100	193	29	12	7	112	45	9	.338	.388	.468	.856	116	21	12	110	99	111	.865	13			-37	*S	-2.0
1897	Cle-N	125	523	83	143	21	14	2	78	40		.273	.330	.379	.708	80	-9	-18	111	99	72	.676	15			-26	*S	-3.5
1898	Cle-N	151	604	89	172	23	1	9	94	56		.285	.346	.371	.717	113	7	11	96	100	83	.676	11			-42	*S	-2.1
1899	StL-N	67	277	40	72	7	3	3	40	20		.260	.310	.339	.649	74	-8	-11	108	105	31	.576	4			-15	S12	-2.1
Total	13	1653	6885	1227	2083	272	158	66	1070	635	157	.303	.365	.417	.781	115	167	137	102	91	1202	.805	323			-261	*S/O213	-6.2
■ BILL McKECHNIE McKechnie, William Boyd "Deacon" b: 8/7/1886, Wilkinsburg, Pa. d: 10/29/65, Bradenton, Fla. BB/TR, 5'10", 160 lbs. Deb: 9/08/07 MCH																												
1907	Pit-N	3	8	0	1	0	0	0	0	0		.125	.125	.125	.250	-20	-1	-1	105	0	0	.143	0			0	/32	0.0
1910	Pit-N	71	212	23	46	1	2	0	12	11	23	.217	.256	.241	.496	40	-15	-18	112	82	14	.398	4			-4	2S/31	-2.1
1911	Pit-N	104	321	40	73	8	7	2	37	28	18	.227	.293	.315	.608	70	-13	-14	101	117	34	.565	9			-2	12S/3	-1.7
1912	Pit-N	24	73	8	18	0	1	0	4	4	5	.247	.286	.274	.560	54	-5	-5	99	67	6	.473	2			-2	3/S21	-0.5
1913	Bos-N	1	4	1	0	0	0	0	0	0	1	.000	.200	.000	.200	-42	-1	-1	95	0	0	.250	0			0	/O	0.0
	NY-A	45	112	7	15	0	0	0	8	8	17	.134	.198	.134	.332	-2	-14	-14	101	190	3	.268	2			0	2/S3	-1.5
1914	Ind-F	149	570	107	173	24	6	2	38	53	36	.304	.363	.377	.740	101	10	2	111	55	101	.793	47			22	*3	2.7
1915	New-F	127	451	49	113	22	5	1	43	41	31	.251	.313	.328	.641	95	-6	-2	94	109	59	.642	28			-8	*3/OM	-0.8
1916	NY-N	71	260	22	64	9	1	0	17	7	20	.246	.269	.288	.557	74	-9	-8	96	92	22	.459	7			1	3	-0.7
	Cin-N	37	130	4	36	3	0	0	10	3	12	.277	.293	.300	.593	84	-3	-3	98	104	13	.489	4			2	3M	0.0
	Yr	108	390	26	100	12	1	0	27	10	32	.256	.277	.292	.569	77	-12	-11	96	97	36	.469	11			3		-0.7
1917	Cin-N	48	134	11	34	3	1	0	15	7	7	.254	.296	.291	.587	87	-3	-2	92	148	12	.520	5			1	2S/3	0.1
1918	Pit-N	126	435	34	111	13	9	2	43	24	22	.255	.297	.340	.637	89	-4	-7	106	108	47	.574	12			0	*3	-0.4
1920	Pit-N	40	133	13	29	3	1	1	13	4	7	.218	.241	.278	.519	48	-9	-9	101	126	9	.444	7	4	-0	-3	3S/21	-1.0
Total	11	846	2843	319	713	86	33	8	240	190	199	.251	.300	.313	.612	78	-73	-82	102	99	322	.569	127	4		9	32/1SO	-5.9
■ FRANK McKEE McKee, Frank b: Philadelphia, Pa. Deb: 6/11/1884																												
1884	Was-U	4	17	2	3	0	0	0		1		.176	.222	.176	.399	38	-1	-1	97	0	1	.286	0			0	/O3C	0.0
■ RED McKEE McKee, Raymond Ellis b: 7/20/1890, Shawnee, Ohio d: 8/5/72, Saginaw, Mich. BL/TR, 5'11", 180 lbs. Deb: 4/19/13																												
1913	Det-A	68	187	18	53	3	4	1	20	21	21	.283	.359	.358	.717	111	3	3	99	102	27	.716	7			-2	C	0.6
1914	Det-A	32	64	7	12	1	1	0	8	14	16	.188	.342	.234	.576	72	-1	-1	102	200	5	.574	1	2	-1	-2	C	-0.2
1915	Det-A	55	106	10	29	5	0	1	17	13	16	.274	.353	.349	.702	102	1	0	108	145	14	.662	1			-4	C	0.0
1916	Det-A	32	76	3	16	1	2	0	4	6	11	.211	.268	.276	.545	61	-4	-4	105	68	6	.450	0			-3	C	-0.5
Total	4	187	433	38	110	10	7	2	49	54	64	.254	.339	.323	.663	94	-1	-2	103	122	52	.631	9	2		-11	C	-0.1
■ JIM McKEEVER McKeever, James b: 4/19/1861, Newfoundland, Can. d: 8/19/1897, Boston, Mass. Deb: 4/17/1884																												
1884	Bos-U	16	66	13	9	0	0	0		0		.136	.136	.136	.273	-8	-7	-7	98	0	1	.158	0			0	C/O	-0.5
■ JOHN McKELVEY McKelvey, John Wellington b: 8/27/1847, Rochester, N.Y. d: 5/31/44, Rochester, N.Y. 5'7.5", 175 lbs. Deb: 4/21/1875																												
1875	NH-n	43	202	26	42							.208															O/3	
■ RUSS McKELVY McKelvy, Russell Errett b: 9/8/1856, Meadville, Pa. d: 10/19/15, Omaha, Neb. TR , Deb: 5/01/1878																												
1878	Ind-N	63	253	33	57	4	3	2	36	5	38	.225	.240	.289	.529	84	-7	-2	87	164	18	.398				5	*O/P	-0.2
1882	Pit-a	1	4	0	0	0	0	0		0		.000	.000	.000	.000	-99	-1	-1	97	0	0	.000				0	/O	0.0
Total	2	64	257	33	57	4	3	2	36	5	38	.222	.237	.284	.521	81	-8	-3	87	161	18	.390				5	/OP	-0.2
■ ED McKENNA McKenna, Edward J. b: St.Louis, Mo. Deb: 7/29/1874																												
1874	Phi-n	1	4	0	0							.000															/1	
1877	StL-N	1	5	0	1	0	0	0	0	0	1	.200	.200	.200	.400	26	-0	-0	102	0	0	.250				0	/O	0.0
1884	Was-U	32	117	19	22	1	0	0		4		.188	.215	.197	.411	41	-7	-6	97	0	5	.284	0			0	CO/3	-0.5
Total	2	33	122	19	23	1	0	0	0	4	1	.189	.214	.197	.411	41	-7	-7	97	0	5	.283	0			0	/CO31	-0.5
■ DAVE McKEOUGH McKeough, David J. b: 12/1/1863, Utica, N.Y. d: 7/11/01, Utica, N.Y. 5'7", 158 lbs. Deb: 4/22/1890																												
1890	Roc-a	62	218	38	49	5	0	0		29		.225	.316	.248	.563	74	-7	-5	93	0	22	.574	14			-2	CS/23	-0.1
1891	Phi-a	15	54	4	14	1	1	0	3	8	6	.259	.355	.315	.670	92	-0	-0	103	52	6	.625	0			0	C/S	0.0
Total	2	77	272	42	63	6	1	0	3	37	6	.232	.324	.261	.585	78	-8	-5	95	10	28	.584	14			-2	/CS23	-0.1
■ RICH McKINNEY McKinney, Charles Richard b: 11/22/46, Piqua, Ohio BR/TR, 5'11", 185 lbs. Deb: 6/26/70																												
1970	Chi-A	43	119	12	20	5	0	4	17	11	25	.168	.244	.311	.555	49	-8	-9	106	140	8	.495	3	2	-0	2	3S	-0.5
1971	Chi-A	114	369	35	100	11	2	8	46	35	37	.271	.337	.377	.714	105	1	2	98	115	46	.624	0	0	0	-2	2O/3	0.2
1972	NY-A	37	121	10	26	2	0	1	7	7	13	.215	.258	.256	.514	58	-7	-6	92	86	7	.386	1	0	0	1	3	-0.3
1973	Oak-A	48	65	9	16	3	0	1	7	7	4	.246	.319	.338	.658	98	-1	-0	87	110	6	.547	0	0	0	-1	3/2OD	0.0
1974	Oak-A	5	7	0	1	0	0	0	0	0	0	.143	.143	.143	.286	-18	-1	-1	100	0	0	.167	0	0	0	0	/2	0.0
1975	Oak-A	8	7	0	1	0	0	0	2	1	2	.143	.250	.143	.393	14	-1	-1	93	768	0	.333	0	0	0	0	/1D	0.0

YEAR	TM/L	G	AB	R	H	2B	3B	HR	RBI	BB	SO	AVG	OBP	SLG	PRO	/A	BR	/A	PF	CHI	RC	TA	SB	CS	SBR	FR	POS	TPR
1977	Oak-A	86	198	13	35	7	0	6	21	16	43	.177	.238	.303	.541	49	-15	-14	95	107	12	.434	0	1	-1	-3	1D/3O2	-1.8
Total	7	341	886	79	199	28	2	20	100	77	124	.225	.289	.328	.617	76	-32	-29	97	117	80	.535	4	3	-1	-3	/321ODS	-2.4
■ BOB McKINNEY	McKinney, Robert Francis b: 10/4/1875, Mc Sherrystown, Pa. d: 8/19/46, Hanover, Pa. BR/TR, 5'7", 165 lbs. Deb: 7/23/01																											
1901	Phi-A	2	2	0	0	0	0	0	0	0		.000	.000	.000	.000	-99	-1	-1	100	0	0	.000	0			0	/23	0.0
■ ALEX McKINNON	McKinnon, Alexander J. b: 8/14/1856, Boston, Mass. d: 7/24/1887, Charlestown, Mass BR , 5'11.5", Deb: 5/01/1884 M																											
1884	NY-N	116	470	66	128	21	12	4	73	8	62	.272	.285	.394	.678	113	5	6	98	135	54	.564				-3	*1	-0.7
1885	StL-N	100	411	42	121	21	6	1	44	8	31	.294	.308	.382	.690	132	9	13	92	92	50	.569				-2	*1M	-0.5
1886	StL-N	122	491	75	148	24	7	8	72	21	23	.301	.330	.428	.758	136	16	19	95	89	74	.703	10			-5	*1/O	-0.6
1887	Pit-N	48	200	26	68	16	4	1	30	8	9	.340	.365	.475	.840	143	8	11	93	100	38	.826	6			3	1	0.5
Total	4	386	1572	209	465	82	29	14	219	45	125	.296	.315	.412	.727	129	37	49	95	105	216	.640	16			-7	1/O	-1.3
■ JIM McKNIGHT	McKnight, James Arthur b: 6/1/36, Bee Branch, Ark. BR/TR, 6'1", 185 lbs. Deb: 9/22/60																											
1960	Chi-N	3	6	0	2	0	0	0	1	0	1	.333	.333	.333	.667	85	-0	-0	98	203	1	.500	0	0	0	-0	/2O	0.0
1962	Chi-N	60	85	6	19	0	1	0	5	2	13	.224	.241	.247	.488	30	-8	-9	106	94	4	.324	0	0	0	1	/3O2	-0.7
Total	2	63	91	6	21	0	1	0	6	2	14	.231	.247	.253	.500	33	-8	-9	105	101	5	.333	0	0	0	1	/3O2	-0.7
■ ED McLANE	McLane, Edward Cameron b: 8/20/1881, Weston, Mass. Deb: 10/06/07																											
1907	Bro-N	1	2	0	0	0	0	0	0	0		.000	.000	.000	.000	-99	-0	-0	94	0	0	.000	0			0	/O	0.0
■ ART McLARNEY	McLarney, Arthur James b: 12/20/08, Ft.Worden, Wash. d: 12/20/84, Seattle, Wash. BB/TR, 6', 168 lbs. Deb: 8/23/32																											
1932	NY-N	9	23	2	3	1	0	0	3	1	3	.130	.167	.174	.341	-8	-3	-3	99	279	1	.250	0			-0	/S	-0.2
■ POLLY McLARRY	McLarry, Howard Zell b: 3/25/1891, Leonard, Tex. d: 11/4/71, Bonham, Tex. 6', 185 lbs. Deb: 9/02/12																											
1912	Chi-A	2	2	0	0	0	0	0	0	0		.000	.000	.000	.000	-99	-1	-1	99	0	0	.000	0			0	H	0.0
1915	Chi-N	68	127	16	25	3	0	1	12	14	20	.197	.277	.244	.521	57	-6	-6	102	135	9	.452	2	2	-1	-1	21	-0.9
Total	2	70	129	16	25	3	0	1	12	14	20	.194	.273	.240	.513	55	-7	-7	102	133	9	.443	2	2		-1	/21	-0.9
■ BARNEY McLAUGHLIN	McLaughlin, Bernard b: 1857, Ireland d: 2/13/21, Lowell, Mass. BR/TR, Deb: N/A.																											
1884	KC-U	42	162	15	37	7	3	0		9		.228	.269	.309	.578	109	-1	3	87	0	14	.472	0			0	O2/PS	0.2
1887	Phi-N	50	205	26	45	8	3	1	26	11	27	.220	.263	.302	.565	60	-12	-10	97	131	17	.475	2			-11	2	-1.5
1890	Syr-a	86	329	43	87	8	1	2		47		.264	.360	.313	.673	112	2	8	90	0	43	.682	13			-13	S	0.0
Total	3	178	696	84	169	23	7	3	26	67	27	.243	.312	.309	.621	95	-10	0	91	37	74	.569	15			-24	/S2OP	-1.3
■ FRANK McLAUGHLIN	McLaughlin, Francis Edward b: 6/19/1856, Lowell, Mass. d: 4/5/17, Lowell, Mass. BR/TR, 5'9", 160 lbs. Deb: 8/09/1882																											
1882	Wor-N	15	55	7	12	0	2	1	4	0	11	.218	.218	.345	.564	77	-1	-1	100	62	4	.442				0	S/O	0.0
1883	Pit-a	29	114	15	25	2	0	1		6		.219	.258	.263	.521	73	-4	-3	94	0	8	.404				-1	S/O2P	-0.3
1884	Cin-U	16	67	10	16	4	1	2		2		.239	.261	.418	.679	117	2	1	108	0	7	.588	0			0	S	0.1
	CP-U	15	67	11	16	4	1	0		1		.239	.250	.328	.578	95	-0	-0	99	0	6	.451	0			0	2/SO	0.0
	KC-U	32	123	17	28	11	0	1		9		.228	.280	.341	.622	126	1	4	87	0	12	.537	0			0	2O/3SP	0.3
	Yr	63	257	38	60	19	2	3		12		.233	.268	.358	.626	115	3	5	95	0	25	.528	0			0		0.4
Total	3	107	426	60	97	21	4	5	4	18	11	.228	.259	.331	.590	99	-3	0	96	8	37	.483	0			-1	/S2O3P	0.1
■ KID McLAUGHLIN	McLaughlin, James Anson "Sunshine" b: 4/12/1888, Randolph, N.Y. d: 11/13/34, Allegheny, N.Y. BL/TR, 5'8.5", 158 lbs. Deb: 6/30/14																											
1914	Cin-N	3	2	1	0	0	0	0	0	0	4	.000	.000	.000	.000	-96	-0	-0	105	0	0	.000	0			-1	/O	0.0
■ JIM McLAUGHLIN	McLaughlin, James C. b: 1860, Cleveland, Ohio d: 11/16/1895, Cleveland, Ohio TL , Deb: 5/03/1884																											
1884	Was-U	10	37	3	7	3	0	0		0		.189	.189	.270	.459	56	-2	-2	97	0	2	.333	0			0	/S3	0.0
	Bal-a	5	22	3	5	1	1	0		0		.227	.227	.364	.591	93	-0	-0	99	0	2	.471				0	/PO	0.0
Total	1	15	59	6	12	4	1	0		0		.203	.203	.305	.508	70	-2	-2	98	0	4	.383				0	/SOP3	0.0
■ JIM McLAUGHLIN	McLaughlin, James Robert b: 1/3/02, St. Louis, Mo. d: 12/18/68, Mount Vernon, Ill. BR/TR, 5'8.5", 168 lbs. Deb: 4/18/32																											
1932	StL-A	1	1	0	0	0	0	0	1	0	0	.000	.000	.000	.000	-99	-0	-0	100	0	0	.000	0	0	0	0	/3	0.0
■ TOM McLAUGHLIN	McLaughlin, Thomas b: 3/28/1860, Louisville, Ky. d: 7/21/21, Louisville, Ky. Deb: 7/17/1883																											
1883	Lou-a	42	146	16	28	1	2	0		5		.192	.219	.226	.445	46	-9	-8	94	0	7	.322				0	SO/132	-0.6
1884	Lou-a	98	335	41	67	11	5	1		22		.200	.262	.272	.533	86	-8	-2	89	0	24	.444				17	*S/32	1.2
1885	Lou-a	112	411	49	87	13	9	2		15		.212	.245	.302	.546	72	-12	-13	102	0	31	.438				-4	*2S	-1.1
1886	NY-a	74	250	27	34	3	1	0		26		.136	.220	.156	.376	19	-22	-23	104	0	12	.366	13			2	S2/O	-1.5
1891	Was-a	14	41	9	11	0	1	0	3	7	6	.268	.400	.317	.717	114	1	1	95	67	7	.833	3			0	S	0.1
Total	5	340	1183	142	227	28	18	3		75	6	.192	.247	.254	.501	63	-49	-45	98	3	81	.422	16			16	S2/O31	-1.9
■ RALPH McLAURIN	McLaurin, Ralph Edgar b: 5/23/1885, Kissimmee, Fla. d: 2/11/43, Mc Coll, S.C. Deb: 9/05/08																											
1908	StL-N	8	22	2	5	0	0	0	0	0		.227	.227	.227	.455	50	-1	-1	94	0	1	.294	0			-1	/O	-0.2
■ LARRY McLEAN	McLean, John Bannerman b: 7/18/1881, Cambridge, Mass. d: 3/24/21, Boston, Mass. BR/TR, 6'5", 228 lbs. Deb: 4/26/01																											
1901	Bos-A	9	19	4	4	1	0	0	2	0		.211	.211	.263	.474	33	-2	-2	97	126	1	.400	1			0	/1	-0.1
1903	Chi-N	1	4	0	0	0	0	0	1	1		.000	.200	.000	.200	-42	-1	-1	95	0	0	.250	0			0	/C	0.0
1904	StL-N	27	84	5	14	2	1	0	4	4		.167	.205	.214	.419	31	-7	-7	99	81	4	.329	1			-4	C	-0.8
1906	Cin-N	12	35	3	7	2	0	0	2	4		.200	.282	.257	.539	61	-1	-2	115	81	3	.464	0			1	C	0.0
1907	Cin-N	113	374	35	108	9	9	0	54	13		.289	.313	.361	.674	119	4	6	95	154	45	.571	4			4	C1	1.8
1908	Cin-N	99	309	24	67	9	4	1	28	15		.217	.253	.282	.535	71	-10	-11	103	119	21	.430	2			-1	C1	-0.9
1909	Cin-N	95	324	26	83	12	2	2	36	21		.256	.307	.324	.632	104	-2	1	94	120	31	.539	1			-8	C	0.0
1910	Cin-N	127	423	27	126	14	7	2	71	26	23	.298	.340	.378	.718	108	4	3	101	149	55	.643	4			-2	*C	0.7
1911	Cin-N	107	328	24	94	7	2	0	34	20	18	.287	.330	.320	.650	89	-8	-4	92	109	34	.543	1			-1	C	0.1
1912	Cin-N	102	333	17	81	15	1	1	27	18	15	.243	.284	.303	.587	66	-19	-15	92	87	28	.480	1			-0	C	-0.9
1913	StL-N	48	152	7	41	9	0	0	12	6	9	.270	.297	.329	.626	85	-4	-3	93	87	14	.505	0			4	C	0.3
	NY-N	30	75	3	24	4	0	0	9	4	4	.320	.354	.373	.728	105	1	0	103	117	10	.647	1			-2	C	0.0
	Yr	78	227	10	65	13	0	0	21	10	13	.286	.316	.344	.660	92	-4	-3	97	100	23	.549	1			1		0.3
1914	NY-N	79	154	8	40	6	0	0	14	4	9	.260	.283	.299	.582	76	-5	-5	96	110	13	.482	4			-8	C	-0.9
1915	NY-N	13	33	0	5	0	0	0	4	0	1	.152	.152	.152	.303	-9	-4	-4	91	306	1	.179	0			-1	C	-0.4
Total	13	862	2647	183	694	90	26	6	298	136	79	.262	.300	.323	.623	88	-54	-43	96	122	260	.521	20			-19	C/1	-1.1
■ MARK McLEMORE	McLemore, Mark Tremell b: 10/4/64, San Diego, Cal. BB/TR, 5'11", 175 lbs. Deb: 9/13/86																											
1986	Cal-A	5	4	0	0	0	0	0	0	1	2	.000	.200	.000	.200	-41	-1	-1	96	0	0	.200	0	1	-1	0	/2	0.0
1987	Cal-A	138	433	61	102	13	3	3	41	48	72	.236	.312	.300	.612	65	-21	-21	99	118	45	.587	25	8	3	-6	*2/SD	-1.3
1988	Cal-A	77	233	38	56	11	2	2	16	25	28	.240	.314	.330	.644	86	-6	-4	94	77	24	.605	13	7	-0	4	2/3D	0.4
Total	3	220	670	99	158	24	5	5	57	74	102	.236	.312	.309	.621	71	-28	-25	97	103	69	.597	38	16	2	-2	2/SD3	-0.9
■ RALPH McLEOD	McLeod, Ralph Alton b: 10/19/16, N.Quincy, Mass. BL/TL, 6', 170 lbs. Deb: 9/14/38																											
1938	Bos-N	6	7	1	2	1	0	0	0	0	2	.286	.286	.429	.714	107	-0	0	88	0	0	.500	0			-0	/O	0.0
■ JIM McLEOD	McLeod, Soule James b: 9/12/08, Jones, La. d: 8/3/81, Little Rock, Ark. BR/TR, 6', 187 lbs. Deb: 5/22/30																											
1930	Was-A	18	34	3	9	1	0	0	1	1	5	.265	.306	.294	.600	52	-2	-2	101	33	3	.500	1	1	-0	0	3/S	0.0
1932	Was-A	7	0	1	0	0	0	0	0	1	0	—	1.000	—	1.294	252	0	0	100	0	0	—	0	0	0	0	/S	0.0
1933	Phi-N	67	232	20	45	6	1	0	15	12	25	.194	.237	.228	.465	28	-20	-25	118	106	13	.351	1			4	3/S	-1.9
Total	3	92	266	24	54	7	1	0	16	14	30	.203	.248	.237	.485	32	-22	-27	116	97	16	.373	2	1		4	/3S	-1.9
■ JACK McMAHON	McMahon, John Henry b: 10/15/1869, Waterbury, Conn. d: 12/30/1894, Bridgeport, Conn. BR/TL, 5'10", 165 lbs. Deb: 8/08/1892																											
1892	NY-N	40	147	21	33	5	7	1	24	10	9	.224	.278	.374	.653	101	-1	-1	98	130	17	.605	3			0	1/C	0.0
1893	NY-N	11	30	5	10	2	1	0	4	2	0	.333	.375	.467	.842	121	1	1	104	78	5	.800	0			0	C	0.1
Total	2	51	177	26	43	7	8	1	28	12	9	.243	.295	.390	.685	105	-0	0	99	121	22	.634	3			0	/1C	0.1

■ **FRANK McMANUS** McManus, Francis E. b: 9/21/1875, Lawrence, Mass. d: 9/1/23, Syracuse, N.Y. TR, 5'10", Deb: 9/14/1899

YEAR	TM/L	G	AB	R	H	2B	3B	HR	RBI	BB	SO	AVG	OBP	SLG	PRO	/A	BR	/A	PF	CHI	RC	TA	SB	CS	SBR	FR	POS	TPR
1899	Was-N	7	21	3	8	1	0	0	2	2		.381	.435	.429	.863	147	1	1	96	68	5	1.077	3			0	/C	0.1
1903	Bro-N	2	7	0	0	0	0	0	0	0		.000	.000	.000	.000	-99	-2	-2	101	0	0	.000	0			-0	/C	-0.1
1904	Det-A	1	0	0	0	0	0	0	0	0		—	—	—	—	—	0	0	96	—	—	—	0			0	/C	0.0
	NY-A	4	7	0	0	0	0	0	0	0		.000	.000	.000	.000	-89	-2	-2	112	0	0	.000	0			0	/C	0.0
	Yr	5	7	0	0	0	0	0	0	0		.000	.000	.000	.000	-92	-2	-2	109	0	0	.000	0			0		0.0
Total	3	14	35	3	8	1	0	0	2	2		.229	.270	.257	.527	52	-2	-2	100	42	5	.519	3			-0	/C	0.0

■ **JIM McMANUS** McManus, James Michael b: 7/20/36, Brookline, Mass. BL/TL, 6'4", 215 lbs. Deb: 9/21/60

YEAR	TM/L	G	AB	R	H	2B	3B	HR	RBI	BB	SO	AVG	OBP	SLG	PRO	/A	BR	/A	PF	CHI	RC	TA	SB	CS	SBR	FR	POS	TPR
1960	KC-A	5	13	3	4	0	0	1	2	1	2	.308	.357	.538	.896	140	1	1	99	78	2	.800	0	0	0	0	/1	0.0

■ **MARTY McMANUS** McManus, Martin Joseph b: 3/14/1900, Chicago, Ill. d: 2/18/66, St.Louis, Mo. BR/TR, 5'10.5", 160 lbs. Deb: 9/26/20 M

YEAR	TM/L	G	AB	R	H	2B	3B	HR	RBI	BB	SO	AVG	OBP	SLG	PRO	/A	BR	/A	PF	CHI	RC	TA	SB	CS	SBR	FR	POS	TPR
1920	StL-A	1	3	0	1	0	1	0	1	0	0	.333	.333	1.000	1.333	219	1	0	111	119	1	1.500	0	0	0	0	/3	0.1
1921	StL-A	121	412	49	107	19	8	3	64	27	30	.260	.308	.367	.675	71	-19	-19	101	137	48	.601	5	3	-0	-14	23/1S	-2.7
1922	StL-A	154	606	88	189	34	11	11	109	38	41	.312	.358	.459	.817	106	9	4	106	133	99	.783	9	6	-1	1	*2/1	1.4
1923	StL-A	154	582	86	180	35	10	15	94	49	50	.309	.367	.481	.848	117	16	13	104	105	102	.842	14	10	-2	-6	*21	0.9
1924	StL-A	123	442	71	147	23	5	5	80	55	40	.333	.409	.441	.850	111	14	9	107	133	82	.872	13	9	-2	6	*2	1.6
1925	StL-A	154	587	108	169	**44**	8	13	90	73	69	.288	.371	.457	.828	101	7	0	108	104	99	.818	5	11	-5	3	*2/O	0.5
1926	StL-A	149	549	102	156	30	10	9	68	55	62	.284	.350	.424	.775	101	-0	-1	101	94	82	.735	5	7	-3	8	32/1	1.4
1927	Det-A	108	369	60	99	19	7	9	69	34	38	.268	.332	.431	.763	89	-3	-8	108	123	52	.748	8	0	2	5	S23/1	0.3
1928	Det-A	139	500	78	144	37	5	8	73	51	32	.288	.355	.430	.785	106	3	4	99	107	75	.753	11	13	-5	4	31/S	0.3
1929	Det-A	154	599	99	168	32	8	18	90	60	52	.280	.347	.451	.798	107	2	4	97	97	93	.785	16	11	-2	7	*3/S	1.8
1930	Det-A	132	484	74	155	40	4	9	89	59	28	.320	.396	.475	.872	114	16	12	105	122	95	.932	**23**	8	2	7	*3/S1	2.3
1931	Det-A	107	362	39	98	17	3	3	53	49	22	.271	.361	.359	.720	86	-4	-6	104	126	50	.704	7	3	0	4	32/1	0.4
	Bos-A	17	62	8	18	4	0	1	9	8	1	.290	.371	.403	.775	110	0	1	94	108	9	.756	1	1	-0	0	3/2	0.2
	Yr	124	424	47	116	21	3	4	62	57	23	.274	.362	.366	.728	90	-4	-5	102	124	59	.712	8	4	0	4		0.6
1932	Bos-A	93	302	39	71	19	4	5	24	36	30	.235	.317	.374	.691	81	-10	-9	97	63	37	.644	1	2	-1	-3	23/S1M	-0.7
1933	Bos-A	106	366	51	104	30	4	3	36	49	21	.284	.369	.413	.781	106	4	4	101	76	59	.775	3	0	1	-1	32/1M	0.8
1934	Bos-N	119	435	56	120	18	0	8	47	32	42	.276	.330	.372	.702	102	-7	1	86	93	53	.616	5			-6	23	0.5
Total	15	1831	6660	1008	1926	401	88	120	996	675	558	.289	.357	.430	.787	102	29	10	102	109	1036	.765	126	84		16	23/1SO	9.1

■ **JIMMY McMATH** McMath, Jimmy Lee b: 8/10/49, Tuscaloosa, Ala. BL/TL, 6'1.5", 195 lbs. Deb: 9/07/68

YEAR	TM/L	G	AB	R	H	2B	3B	HR	RBI	BB	SO	AVG	OBP	SLG	PRO	/A	BR	/A	PF	CHI	RC	TA	SB	CS	SBR	FR	POS	TPR
1968	Chi-N	6	14	0	2	0	0	0	2	0	6	.143	.143	.143	.286	-13	-2	-2	112	421	0	.167	0	0	0	0	/O	-0.2

■ **GEORGE McMILLAN** McMillan, George A. "Reddy" b: Evansville, Ind. 5'8", 175 lbs. Deb: 8/11/1890

YEAR	TM/L	G	AB	R	H	2B	3B	HR	RBI	BB	SO	AVG	OBP	SLG	PRO	/A	BR	/A	PF	CHI	RC	TA	SB	CS	SBR	FR	POS	TPR
1890	NY-N	10	35	4	5	0	0	0	1	7	4	.143	.286	.143	.429	29	-3	-3	95	64	2	.433	1			0	O	-0.1

■ **NORM McMILLAN** McMillan, Norman Alexis "Bub" b: 10/5/1895, Latta, S.C. d: 9/28/69, Marion, S.C. BR/TR, 6', 175 lbs. Deb: 4/12/22

YEAR	TM/L	G	AB	R	H	2B	3B	HR	RBI	BB	SO	AVG	OBP	SLG	PRO	/A	BR	/A	PF	CHI	RC	TA	SB	CS	SBR	FR	POS	TPR
1922	NY-A	33	78	7	20	1	2	0	11	6	10	.256	.310	.321	.630	63	-4	-4	102	157	8	.593	4	1	1	-7	O/3	-1.1
1923	Bos-A	131	459	37	116	24	5	0	42	28	44	.253	.299	.327	.625	63	-24	-25	102	98	46	.555	13	5	1	-8	32S	-1.9
1924	StL-A	76	201	25	56	12	2	0	27	12	17	.279	.332	.358	.690	73	-7	-9	107	124	24	.631	6	4	-1	1	23/S1	-0.4
1928	Chi-N	49	123	11	27	2	2	1	12	13	19	.220	.299	.293	.592	58	-8	-7	95	110	11	.521	0			4	23	-0.2
1929	Chi-N	124	495	77	134	35	5	5	55	36	43	.271	.324	.392	.716	76	-19	-20	101	95	62	.681	13			7	*3	-0.2
Total	5	413	1356	157	353	74	16	6	147	95	133	.260	.313	.352	.665	69	-62	-66	102	105	152	.610	36	10		-3	3/2SO1	-3.8

■ **ROY McMILLAN** McMillan, Roy David b: 7/17/30, Bonham, Tex. BR/TR, 5'11", 170 lbs. Deb: 4/17/51 MC

YEAR	TM/L	G	AB	R	H	2B	3B	HR	RBI	BB	SO	AVG	OBP	SLG	PRO	/A	BR	/A	PF	CHI	RC	TA	SB	CS	SBR	FR	POS	TPR
1951	Cin-N	85	199	21	42	4	0	1	8	17	26	.211	.273	.246	.519	41	-16	-17	101	59	15	.415	0	0	0	-2	S3/2	-1.3
1952	Cin-N	154	540	60	132	32	2	7	57	45	81	.244	.306	.350	.656	82	-14	-14	100	108	57	.566	4	5	-2	11	*S	0.0
1953	Cin-N	155	557	51	130	15	4	5	43	43	52	.233	.290	.302	.591	55	-37	-36	99	94	49	.484	2	4	-2	13	*S	-1.1
1954	Cin-N	154	588	86	147	21	2	4	42	47	54	.250	.311	.313	.624	61	-31	-34	104	89	61	.531	4	2	0	8	*S	-1.6
1955	Cin-N	151	470	50	126	21	2	1	37	66	33	.268	.366	.328	.694	82	-7	-10	106	95	60	.643	4	4	-1	**16**	*S	0.9
1956	Cin-N	150	479	51	126	16	7	3	62	76	54	.263	.370	.344	.714	86	-1	-7	108	**151**	64	.676	4	3	-1	**30**	*S	3.3
1957	Cin-N	151	448	50	122	25	5	1	55	66	44	.272	.373	.357	.730	92	1	-2	105	140	64	.701	5	1	1	-7	*S	-0.1
1958	Cin-N	145	393	48	90	18	3	1	25	47	33	.229	.313	.298	.611	58	-20	-24	107	86	38	.543	5	2	0	4	*S	-0.9
1959	Cin-N	79	246	38	65	14	2	9	24	27	27	.264	.347	.447	.794	106	3	2	103	71	35	.727	0	2	-1	3	S	0.7
1960	Cin-N	124	399	42	94	12	2	10	42	35	40	.236	.304	.351	.655	80	-12	-11	98	100	43	.575	2	0	1	-6	*S2	-1.1
1961	Mil-N	154	505	42	111	16	0	7	48	61	86	.220	.309	.293	.602	66	-27	-22	92	115	46	.519	2	4	-2	-2	*S	-0.9
1962	Mil-N	137	468	66	115	13	0	12	41	60	53	.246	.338	.350	.688	86	-9	-8	99	82	57	.626	2	2	-1	1	*S	0.4
1963	Mil-N	100	320	35	80	10	1	4	29	17	25	.250	.292	.325	.617	77	-9	-10	101	105	29	.498	1	5	-3	9	S	0.6
1964	Mil-N	8	13	1	4	0	0	0	2	0	2	.308	.308	.308	.615	76	-0	-0	97	205	1	.556	1	0	0	0	/S	0.1
	NY-N	113	379	30	80	8	2	1	25	14	16	.211	.247	.251	.498	43	-30	-27	95	105	20	.365	3	1	0	-5	*S	-2.5
	Yr	121	392	31	84	8	2	1	27	14	18	.214	.249	.253	.501	44	-30	-28	95	113	22	.370	4	1	1	-4		-2.4
1965	NY-N	157	528	44	128	19	2	1	42	24	60	.242	.281	.292	.572	61	-27	-27	100	113	44	.450	1	0	0	0	*S	-0.9
1966	NY-N	76	220	24	47	9	1	1	12	20	25	.214	.285	.277	.562	61	-12	-11	94	79	18	.472	1	1	-0	5	S	0.0
Total	16	2093	6752	739	1639	253	35	68	594	665	711	.243	.316	.321	.637	72	-249	-257	101	103	702	.568	41	36	-9	78	*S/32	-4.4

■ **TOM McMILLAN** McMillan, Thomas Erwin b: 9/13/51, Richmond, Va. BR/TR, 5'9", 165 lbs. Deb: 9/17/77

YEAR	TM/L	G	AB	R	H	2B	3B	HR	RBI	BB	SO	AVG	OBP	SLG	PRO	/A	BR	/A	PF	CHI	RC	TA	SB	CS	SBR	FR	POS	TPR
1977	Sea-A	2	5	0	0	0	0	0	0	0	0	.000	.000	.000	.000	-99	-1	-1	96	0	0	.000	0	0	0	0	/S	0.0

■ **TOMMY McMILLAN** McMillan, Thomas Law "Rebel" b: 4/18/1888, Pittston, Pa. d: 7/15/66, Orlando, Fla. BR/TR, 5'5", 130 lbs. Deb: 8/19/08

YEAR	TM/L	G	AB	R	H	2B	3B	HR	RBI	BB	SO	AVG	OBP	SLG	PRO	/A	BR	/A	PF	CHI	RC	TA	SB	CS	SBR	FR	POS	TPR
1908	Bro-N	43	147	9	35	3	0	0	3	9		.238	.282	.259	.541	79	-4	-3	95	31	12	.464	5			-3	SO	-0.7
1909	Bro-N	108	373	18	79	15	1	0	24	20		.212	.254	.257	.511	60	-18	-18	99	93	26	.435	11			-14	*S/23	-3.4
1910	Bro-N	23	74	2	13	1	0	0	2	6	10	.176	.237	.189	.427	26	-7	-7	95	50	4	.393	4			1	S	-0.4
	Cin-N	82	248	20	46	0	3	0	13	31	23	.185	.281	.210	.491	43	-17	-17	101	87	18	.455	7			-3	S	-1.7
	Yr	105	322	22	59	1	3	0	15	37	33	.183	.271	.205	.476	39	-24	-24	100	79	22	.441	11			-2		-2.1
1912	NY-A	41	149	24	34	2	0	0	12	15		.228	.303	.242	.545	56	-8	-8	101	118	17	.609	18			-4	S	-0.7
Total	4	297	991	73	207	21	4	0	54	81	33	.209	.271	.238	.510	55	-54	-53	99	83	76	.467	45			-22	S/O23	-6.9

■ **HUGH McMULLEN** McMullen, Hugh Raphael b: 12/16/01, La Cygne, Kan. d: 5/23/86, Whittier, Cal. BB/TR, 6'1", 180 lbs. Deb: 9/19/25

YEAR	TM/L	G	AB	R	H	2B	3B	HR	RBI	BB	SO	AVG	OBP	SLG	PRO	/A	BR	/A	PF	CHI	RC	TA	SB	CS	SBR	FR	POS	TPR
1925	NY-N	5	15	1	2	1	0	0	0	0	3	.133	.133	.200	.333	-16	-3	-3	99	0	0	.231	0	0	0	0	/C	-0.1
1926	NY-N	57	91	5	17	2	0	0	6	2	18	.187	.204	.209	.413	12	-11	-11	98	109	4	.297	1			-5	C	-1.3
1928	Was-A	1	1	0	0	0	0	0	0	0	1	.000	.000	.000	.000	-99	-0	-0	102	0	0	.000	0	0	0	0	H	0.0
1929	Cin-N	1	1	0	0	0	0	0	0	0	0	.000	.000	.000	.000	-99	-0	-0	99	0	0	.000	0			0	/C	0.0
Total	4	64	108	6	19	3	0	0	6	2	22	.176	.191	.204	.395	5	-15	-14	98	92	4	.281	1	0		-5	/C	-1.4

■ **KEN McMULLEN** McMullen, Kenneth Lee b: 6/1/42, Oxnard, Cal. BR/TR, 6'3", 190 lbs. Deb: 9/17/62

YEAR	TM/L	G	AB	R	H	2B	3B	HR	RBI	BB	SO	AVG	OBP	SLG	PRO	/A	BR	/A	PF	CHI	RC	TA	SB	CS	SBR	FR	POS	TPR
1962	LA-N	6	11	0	3	0	0	0	0	0	3	.273	.273	.273	.545	51	-1	-1	93	0	1	.375	0	0	0	-1	/O	0.0
1963	LA-N	79	233	16	55	9	0	5	28	20	46	.236	.299	.339	.638	88	-5	-4	95	125	22	.534	1	2	-1	3	3/2O	-0.1
1964	LA-N	24	67	3	14	0	0	1	2	3	7	.209	.243	.254	.497	44	-5	-5	92	41	3	.351	0	1	-1	-1	1/3O	-0.7
1965	Was-A	150	555	75	146	18	6	18	54	47	90	.263	.325	.414	.739	109	6	6	100	84	74	.671	2	0	1	5	*3/O1	1.2
1966	Was-A	147	524	48	122	19	4	13	54	44	89	.233	.292	.359	.651	91	-10	-7	95	102	53	.561	3	1	0	-2	*3/1O	-1.3
1967	Was-A	146	563	73	138	22	2	16	67	46	84	.245	.303	.377	.680	98	-1	-2	102	114	62	.596	5	3	-0	12	*3	1.3
1968	Was-A	151	557	66	138	11	2	20	62	63	66	.248	.327	.382	.710	125	10	15	91	103	70	.645	1	3	-2	7	*3S	2.9
1969	Was-A	158	562	83	153	25	2	19	87	70	103	.272	.354	.425	.779	121	13	15	97	120	86	.741	4	5	-2	16	*3	3.2
1970	Was-A	15	59	5	12	2	0	0	3	5	10	.203	.266	.237	.503	41	-5	-5	96	92	4	.388	0	0	0	4	3	0.0
	Cal-A	124	422	50	98	9	3	14	61	59	81	.232	.331	.367	.698	101	-4	1	92	128	52	.647	1	0	0	10	*3	1.1
	Yr	139	481	55	110	11	3	14	64	64	91	.229	.323	.351	.674	93	-9	-4	92	124	55	.617	1	0	0	13		1.1
1971	Cal-A	160	593	63	148	19	2	21	68	53	74	.250	.314	.395	.709	101	-1	-0	99	99	71	.627	1	1	-0	0	*3	-0.5
1972	Cal-A	137	472	36	127	18	1	9	34	48	59	.269	.337	.369	.705	124	6	12	88	72	58	.621	1	2	-1	-0	*3	1.7

YEAR	TM/L	G	AB	R	H	2B	3B	HR	RBI	BB	SO	AVG	OBP	SLG	PRO	/A	BR	/A	PF	CHI	RC	TA	SB	CS	SBR	FR	POS	TPR
1973	LA-N	42	85	6	21	5	0	5	18	6	13	.247	.297	.482	.779	112	1	1	100	129	12	.723	0	0	0	1	3	0.1
1974	LA-N	44	60	5	15	1	0	3	12	2	12	.250	.274	.417	.691	98	-1	-1	93	136	7	.587	0	0	0	-0	/32	0.0
1975	LA-N	39	46	4	11	1	1	2	14	7	12	.239	.340	.435	.774	120	1	1	95	208	7	.750	0	0	0	-0	3/1	0.1
1976	Oak-A	98	186	20	41	6	2	5	23	22	33	.220	.306	.355	.661	93	-2	-2	100	109	20	.600	1	1	-0	-2	31D/O2	-0.5
1977	Mil-A	63	136	15	31	7	1	5	19	15	33	.228	.305	.404	.709	96	-2	-1	95	108	16	.642	0	0	0	0	D1/3	0.0
Total	16	1583	5131	568	1273	172	26	156	606	510	815	.248	.318	.383	.701	105	-1	24	96	105	617	.647	20	19	-5	51	*3/1DOS2	8.5
■ **FRED McMULLIN** McMullin, Frederick William b: 10/13/1891, Scammon, Kan. d: 11/21/52, Los Angeles, Cal. BR/TR, 5'11", 170 lbs. Deb: 8/27/14																												
1914	Det-A	1	1	0	0	0	0	0	0	0	1	.000	.000	.000	.000	-98	-0	-0	102	0	0	.000	0			0	/S	0.0
1916	Chi-A	68	187	8	48	3	0	0	10	19	30	.257	.332	.273	.604	76	-4	-5	108	70	22	.583	9			0	3/S2	-0.2
1917	Chi-A	59	194	35	46	2	1	0	12	27	17	.237	.339	.258	.597	84	-3	-2	98	91	22	.601	9			-2	3/S	-0.1
1918	Chi-A	70	235	32	65	7	0	1	16	25	26	.277	.356	.319	.675	103	2	2	101	76	30	.653	7			-7	3/2	-0.5
1919	Chi-A	60	170	31	50	8	4	0	19	11	18	.294	.355	.388	.743	104	2	1	105	104	25	.717	4			-0	3/2	0.4
1920	Chi-A	46	127	14	25	1	4	0	13	9	13	.197	.255	.268	.523	40	-11	-11	96	134	9	.437	1	1	-0	-2	3/2S	-1.0
Total	6	304	914	120	234	21	9	1	70	91	105	.256	.333	.302	.635	85	-14	-16	102	91	108	.605	30	1		-11	3/2S	-1.4
■ **JOHN McMULLIN** McMullin, John F. "Lefty" b: 1848, Philadelphia, Pa. d: 4/11/1881, Philadelphia, Pa. BL/TL, 5'9", 160 lbs. Deb: 5/09/1871																												
1871	Tro-n	29	145	38	38							.262															*P	
1872	Mut-n	54	256	49	60							.234															*O/P	
1873	Ath-n	52	240	54	61							.254															*O/P	
1874	Ath-n	55	271	61	105							.387															*O/C	
1875	Phi-n	54	225	34	56							.249															*O/P	
Total	5 n	244	1137	236	320							.281															*O/P	
■ **CARL McNABB** McNabb, Carl Mac "Skinny" b: 1/25/17, Stevenson, Ala. BR/TR, 5'9", 155 lbs. Deb: 4/20/45																												
1945	Det-A	1	1	0	0	0	0	0	0	0	1	.000	.000	.000	.000	-94	-0	-0	106	0	0	.000	0	0	0	0	H	0.0
■ **ERIC McNAIR** McNair, Donald Eric "Boob" b: 4/12/09, Meridian, Miss. d: 3/11/49, Meridian, Miss. BR/TR, 5'8", 160 lbs. Deb: 9/20/29																												
1929	Phi-A	4	8	2	4	1	0	0	3	0	0	.500	.500	.625	1.125	173	1	1	109	205	3	1.500	1	0	0	-0	/S	0.1
1930	Phi-A	78	237	27	63	12	2	0	34	9	19	.266	.296	.333	.629	59	-15	-15	99	143	23	.534	5	2	0	-6	S3/2O	-1.4
1931	Phi-A	79	280	41	76	10	1	5	33	11	19	.271	.306	.368	.674	73	-10	-12	105	92	30	.567	1	4	-2	-0	32S	-0.8
1932	Phi-A	135	554	87	158	**47**	3	18	95	28	29	.285	.323	.478	.801	92	1	-10	114	102	84	.760	8	4	0	-14	*S	-1.2
1933	Phi-A	89	310	57	81	15	4	7	48	15	32	.261	.302	.403	.705	93	-8	-4	92	110	38	.630	2	1	0	-6	S2	-0.6
1934	Phi-A	151	599	80	168	20	4	17	82	35	42	.280	.321	.412	.734	91	-13	-11	97	97	77	.661	7	8	-3	3	*S	0.0
1935	Phi-A	137	526	55	142	22	2	4	57	35	33	.270	.319	.342	.661	71	-23	-23	100	103	57	.565	3	7	-3	-14	*S3/1	-3.1
1936	Bos-A	128	494	68	141	36	2	4	74	27	34	.285	.329	.391	.720	73	-19	-24	106	119	63	.640	3	3	-1	-10	S23	-2.2
1937	Bos-A	126	455	60	133	29	4	12	76	30	33	.292	.340	.453	.793	95	-3	-5	103	108	69	.757	10	7	-1	-3	*2/S31	0.1
1938	Bos-A	46	96	9	15	1	1	0	7	3	6	.156	.182	.188	.369	-7	-16	-16	102	131	3	.256	0	1	-1	1	S2/3	-1.3
1939	Chi-A	129	479	62	155	18	5	7	82	38	41	.324	.375	.426	.800	98	3	-1	107	126	74	.751	17	9	-0	-4	*32/S	-0.5
1940	Chi-A	66	251	26	57	13	1	7	31	12	26	.227	.265	.371	.636	61	-15	-16	104	100	21	.512	1	7	-4	-11	2/3	-2.6
1941	Det-A	23	59	5	11	1	0	0	3	4	4	.186	.250	.203	.453	20	-7	-7	106	89	2	.321	0	0	0	0	3/S	-0.5
1942	Det-A	26	68	5	11	2	0	1	4	3	5	.162	.197	.235	.432	19	-7	-8	113	74	2	.302	0	1	-1	-1	S	-0.8
	Phi-A	34	103	8	25	2	0	0	4	11	5	.243	.316	.262	.578	66	-5	-4	96	52	9	.488	1	0	0	-3	S/2	-0.5
	Yr	60	171	13	36	4	0	1	8	14	10	.211	.270	.251	.522	46	-12	-13	103	63	12	.420	1	1	-0	-4		-1.3
Total	14	1251	4519	592	1240	229	29	82	633	261	328	.274	.318	.392	.710	79	-135	-156	103	107	556	.635	59	54	-15	-69	S23/1O	-15.3
■ **MIKE McNALLY** McNally, Michael Joseph "Minooka Mike" b: 9/9/1892, Minooka, Pa. d: 5/29/65, Bethlehem, Pa. BR/TR, 5'11", 150 lbs. Deb: 4/21/15																												
1915	Bos-A	23	53	7	8	0	1	0	0	3	7	.151	.196	.189	.385	15	-6	-6	99	0	2	.277	0	2	-1	-1	3/2	-0.7
1916	Bos-A	87	135	28	23	0	0	0	9	10	19	.170	.228	.170	.398	21	-13	-12	94	140	8	.375	9			-1	23/SO	-1.2
1917	Bos-A	42	50	9	15	1	0	0	2	6	3	.300	.375	.320	.695	104	1	0	108	45	8	.714	3			-0	3/S2	0.2
1919	Bos-A	33	42	10	11	4	0	0	6	1	2	.262	.279	.357	.636	85	-1	-1	91	145	5	.645	4			1	S3/2	0.2
1920	Bos-A	93	312	42	80	5	1	0	23	31	24	.256	.326	.279	.604	64	-16	-15	96	95	30	.545	13	10	-2	4	2/S1	-0.9
1921	NY-A	71	215	36	56	4	2	1	24	14	15	.260	.306	.312	.617	56	-14	-15	103	117	20	.521	5	6	-2	9	32	-0.2
1922	NY-A	52	143	20	36	2	2	0	18	16	14	.252	.331	.294	.625	63	-7	-7	102	153	16	.570	2	0	1	-5	3/2S1	-0.6
1923	NY-A	30	38	5	8	0	0	0	1	3	4	.211	.268	.211	.479	26	-4	-4	104	43	3	.433	2	0	1	-0	S/32	-0.1
1924	NY-A	49	69	11	17	0	0	0	2	7	5	.246	.316	.246	.562	47	-5	-5	99	39	6	.472	1	1	-0	0	23/S	-0.2
1925	Was-A	12	21	1	3	0	0	0	0	1	4	.143	.182	.143	.325	-17	-4	-4	98	0	1	.222	0	0	0	0	/3S2	-0.2
Total	10	492	1078	169	257	16	6	1	85	92	97	.238	.299	.267	.567	54	-69	-68	99	100	98	.501	39	19		7	23/S1O	-3.7
■ **GEORGE McNAMARA** McNamara, George Francis b: 1/11/03, Chicago, Ill. BL/TR, 6', 175 lbs. Deb: 9/28/22																												
1922	Was-A	3	11	3	3	0	0	0	1	1	2	.273	.333	.273	.606	65	-1	-0	92	122	1	.500	0	0	0	-1	/O	-0.1
■ **DINNY McNAMARA** McNamara, John Raymond b: 9/16/05, Lexington, Mass. d: 12/20/63, Arlington, Mass. BL/TR, 5'9", 165 lbs. Deb: 7/02/27																												
1927	Bos-N	11	9	3	0	0	0	0	0	0	3	.000	.000	.000	.000	-99	-3	-2	93	0	0	.000	0			0	/O	-0.1
1928	Bos-N	9	4	2	1	0	0	0	0	0	1	.250	.250	.250	.500	32	-0	-0	97	0	0	.333	0			0	/O	0.0
Total	2	20	13	5	1	0	0	0	0	0	4	.077	.077	.077	.154	-62	-3	-3	94	0	0	.083	0			0	/O	-0.1
■ **BOB McNAMARA** McNamara, Robert Maxey b: 9/19/16, Denver, Colo. BR/TR, 5'10", 170 lbs. Deb: 5/27/39																												
1939	Phi-A	9	9	0	2	1	0	0	3	1	1	.222	.300	.333	.633	63	-1	-0	97	338	1	.571	0	0	0	-0	/3S12	0.0
■ **TOM McNAMARA** McNamara, Thomas Henry b: 11/5/1895, Roxbury, Mass. d: 5/5/74, Danvers, Mass. BR , 6'2", 200 lbs. Deb: 6/25/22																												
1922	Pit-N	1	1	0	0	0	0	0	0	0	0	.000	.000	.000	.000	-97	-0	-0	104	0	0	.000	0	0	0	0	H	0.0
■ **RUSTY McNEALY** McNealy, Robert Lee b: 8/12/58, Sacramento, Cal. BL/TL, 5'8", 160 lbs. Deb: 9/04/83																												
1983	Oak-A	15	4	5	0	0	0	0	0	0	0	.000	.000	.000	.000	-99	-1	-1	96	0	0	.000	0	1	-1	-1	/OD	-0.2
■ **EARL McNEELY** McNeely, George Earl b: 5/12/1898, Sacramento, Cal. d: 7/16/71, Sacramento, Cal. BR/TR, 5'9", 155 lbs. Deb: 8/09/24 C																												
1924	Was-A	43	179	31	59	5	6	0	15	5	21	.330	.355	.425	.779	102	-0	-0	98	63	27	.711	3	1	0	2	O	0.0
1925	Was-A	122	385	76	110	14	2	3	37	48	54	.286	.378	.356	.734	89	-6	-4	98	85	53	.715	14	16	-5	8	*O/1	-1.0
1926	Was-A	124	442	84	134	20	12	0	48	44	28	.303	.373	.403	.775	104	2	3	98	94	70	.780	18	6	2	3	*O	0.0
1927	Was-A	73	185	40	51	10	4	0	16	11	13	.276	.320	.373	.693	82	-6	-5	97	77	22	.687	11	0	3	-5	O/1	-1.2
1928	StL-A	127	496	66	117	27	7	0	44	37	39	.236	.299	.319	.618	60	-27	-30	104	101	49	.548	8	6	-1	5	*O	-3.1
1929	StL-A	69	230	27	56	8	1	1	18	7	13	.243	.272	.300	.572	47	-18	-18	100	86	19	.457	2	1	0	-10	O	-2.9
1930	StL-A	76	235	33	64	19	1	0	20	22	14	.272	.340	.362	.701	72	-8	-11	108	78	30	.672	8	3	1	-5	O1	-1.7
1931	StL-A	49	102	12	23	4	0	0	15	9	5	.225	.288	.265	.553	45	-8	-8	102	183	8	.482	4	4	-1	-4	O/1	-1.4
Total	8	683	2254	369	614	107	33	4	213	183	187	.272	.335	.354	.689	78	-71	-73	101	92	277	.643	68	37	-2	-6	O/1	-11.3
■ **NORM McNEIL** McNeil, Norman Francis b: 10/22/1892, Chicago, Ill. d: 4/11/42, Buffalo, N.Y. BR/TR, 5'11", 180 lbs. Deb: 6/21/19																												
1919	Bos-A	5	9	0	3	0	0	0	1	1	0	.333	.400	.333	.733	117	0	0	91	121	1	.667	0			0	/C	0.1
■ **JERRY McNERTNEY** McNertney, Gerald Edward b: 8/7/36, Boone, Iowa BR/TR, 6', 180 lbs. Deb: 4/16/64 C																												
1964	Chi-A	73	186	16	40	5	0	3	23	19	24	.215	.298	.290	.588	68	-9	-8	96	155	16	.500	0	0	0	-14	C	-1.9
1966	Chi-A	44	59	3	13	0	0	0	1	7	6	.220	.303	.220	.523	56	-3	-3	94	32	4	.420	1	1	-0	-2	C	-0.3
1967	Chi-A	56	123	8	28	6	0	3	13	6	14	.228	.275	.350	.624	89	-3	-2	94	104	11	.515	0	0	0	-4	C	-0.1
1968	Chi-A	74	169	18	37	4	1	3	18	18	29	.219	.302	.308	.609	84	-3	-3	101	126	17	.537	0	0	0	8	C/1	0.8
1969	Sea-A	128	410	39	99	18	1	8	55	29	63	.241	.292	.349	.640	80	-13	-12	98	132	40	.534	1	0	0	1	*C	-0.1
1970	Mil-A	111	296	27	72	11	1	6	22	22	33	.243	.304	.348	.652	81	-9	-8	98	74	27	.537	1	4	-2	-4	C1	-1.2
1971	StL-N	56	128	15	37	4	2	4	22	12	14	.289	.350	.445	.795	123	4	4	101	130	19	.719	0	0	0	1	C	0.5
1972	StL-N	39	48	3	10	3	1	0	9	6	16	.208	.296	.313	.609	70	-2	-2	105	246	5	.538	0	0	0	1	C	0.0
1973	Pit-N	9	4	0	1	0	0	0	0	0	0	.250	.250	.250	.500	42	-0	-0	92	0	0	.333	0	0	0	0	/C	0.0
Total	9	590	1423	129	337	51	6	27	163	119	199	.237	.301	.338	.639	82	-37	-34	98	119	140	.563	3	5	-2	-13	C/1	-2.3

YEAR	TM/L	G	AB	R	H	2B	3B	HR	RBI	BB	SO	AVG	OBP	SLG	PRO	/A	BR	/A	PF	CHI	RC	TA	SB	CS	SBR	FR	POS	TPR
■ **PAT McNULTY**	McNulty, Patrick Howard b: 2/27/1899, Cleveland, Ohio d: 5/4/63, Hollywood, Cal. BL/TR, 5'11", 160 lbs. Deb: 9/05/22																											
1922	Cle-A	22	59	10	16	2	1	0	5	9	5	.271	.368	.339	.707	84	-1	-1	102	89	8	.750	4	1	1	-3	O	-0.4
1924	Cle-A	101	291	46	78	13	5	0	26	33	22	.268	.347	.347	.694	82	-9	-7	97	85	36	.661	10	8	-2	-5	O	-1.8
1925	Cle-A	118	373	70	117	18	2	6	43	47	23	.314	.392	.421	.813	100	4	1	106	82	63	.806	7	7	-2	-2	*O	-1.2
1926	Cle-A	48	56	3	14	2	1	0	6	5	9	.250	.311	.321	.633	66	-3	-3	100	113	6	.535	0	1	-1	-2	/O	-0.5
1927	Cle-A	19	41	3	13	1	0	0	4	4	3	.317	.378	.341	.719	90	-1	-0	97	95	5	.679	1	0	0	0	O	0.0
Total	5	308	820	132	238	36	9	6	84	98	62	.290	.368	.378	.746	90	-9	-11	102	86	118	.723	22	17	-4	-12	O	-3.9
■ **BILL McNULTY**	McNulty, William Francis b: 8/29/46, Sacramento, Cal. BR/TR, 6'4", 205 lbs. Deb: 7/09/69																											
1969	Oak-A	5	17	0	0	0	0	0	0	0	10	.000	.000	.000	.000	-99	-4	-4	92	0	0	.000	0	0	0	1	/O	-0.2
1972	Oak-A	4	10	0	1	0	0	0	0	2	1	.100	.250	.100	.350	7	-1	-1	97	0	0	.333	0	0	0	0	/3	0.0
Total	2	9	27	0	1	0	0	0	0	2	11	.037	.103	.037	.140	-62	-6	-5	94	0	0	.115	0	0	0	1	/O3	-0.2
■ **BID McPHEE**	McPhee, John Alexander b: 11/1/1859, Massena, N.Y. d: 1/3/43, San Diego, Cal. BR/TR, 5'8", 152 lbs. Deb: 5/02/1882 M																											
1882	Cin-a	78	311	43	71	8	7	1		11		.228	.255	.309	.563	82	-3	-7	109	0	25	.446				-3	*2	-0.3
1883	Cin-a	96	367	61	90	10	10	2		18		.245	.281	.343	.624	97	0	-2	103	0	36	.520				0	*2	0.0
1884	Cin-a	112	450	107	125	8	7	5		27		.278	.327	.360	.687	120	14	10	106	0	54	.600				13	*2	2.3
1885	Cin-a	110	431	78	114	12	4	0		19		.265	.306	.311	.617	95	-0	-3	104	0	42	.505				4	*2	0.6
1886	Cin-a	140	560	139	149	23	12	**7**		59		.266	.341	.387	.729	136	20	24	96	0	90	.781	40			32	*2	**4.7**
1887	Cin-a	129	540	137	156	20	19	2		55		.289	.360	.407	.767	107	12	3	108	0	116	.977	95			25	*2	2.3
1888	Cin-a	111	458	88	110	12	10	4	51	43		.240	.312	.336	.648	110	6	6	101	79	67	.736	54			31	*2	3.7
1889	Cin-a	135	540	109	145	25	7	5	57	60	29	.269	.346	.369	.715	101	5	0	105	67	93	.825	63			38	*2/3	3.4
1890	Cin-N	132	528	125	135	16	22	3	39	82	26	.256	.362	.386	.748	112	15	9	108	48	96	.883	55			26	*2	3.4
1891	Cin-N	138	562	107	144	14	16	6	38	74	35	.256	.345	.370	.715	121	8	16	91	42	85	.758	33			22	*2	3.7
1892	Cin-N	144	573	111	157	19	12	4	60	84	48	.274	.373	.370	.743	123	22	19	103	71	98	.834	44			25	*2	4.1
1893	Cin-N	127	491	101	138	17	11	3	68	94	20	.281	.401	.379	.779	108	11	10	101	84	87	.875	25			**33**	*2	3.3
1894	Cin-N	126	474	107	144	21	9	5	88	90	23	.304	.420	.418	.838	104	7	8	100	110	99	.988	33			28	*2	3.3
1895	Cin-N	115	432	107	129	24	12	1	75	73	30	.299	.409	.417	.826	107	13	7	108	110	88	.960	30			13	*2	2.1
1896	Cin-N	117	433	81	132	18	7	1	87	51	18	.305	.391	.386	.776	102	7	3	105	156	86	.917	48			3	*2	0.8
1897	Cin-N	81	282	45	85	13	7	1	39	35		.301	.382	.408	.790	104	5	2	107	99	49	.817	9			6	2	1.3
1898	Cin-N	133	486	72	121	26	9	1	60	66		.249	.340	.346	.686	92	1	-5	108	112	66	.701	21			-13	*2/O	-1.1
1899	Cin-N	111	373	60	104	17	7	1	65	40		.279	.356	.372	.726	96	2	-1	106	144	57	.747	18			-7	*2/O3	-0.1
Total	18	2135	8291	1678	2249	303	188	52	727	981	229	.271	.354	.372	.726	108	145	96	103	62	1334	.780	568			276	*2/O3	37.5
■ **MART McQUAID**	McQuaid, Mortimer Martin b: 6/28/1861, Chicago, Ill. d: 3/5/28, Chicago, Ill. Deb: 8/15/1891																											
1891	StL-a	4	11	1	4	2	0	0	1	0	1	.364	.364	.545	.909	143	1	1	114	48	3	1.000	1			0	/2O	0.0
1898	Was-N	1	4	0	0	0	0	0	0	0		.000	.000	.000	.000	-98	-1	-1	102	0	0	.000	0			0	/O	0.0
Total	2	5	15	1	4	2	0	0	1	0	1	.267	.267	.400	.667	84	-0	-1	111	35	3	.636	1			0	/2O	0.0
■ **JERRY McQUAIG**	McQuaig, Gerald Joseph b: 1/31/12, Douglas, Ga. BR/TR, 5'11", 183 lbs. Deb: 8/25/34																											
1934	Phi-A	7	16	2	1	0	0	0	1	2	4	.063	.167	.063	.229	-40	-3	-3	97	334	0	.200	0	0	0	-1	/O	-0.4
■ **MOX McQUERY**	McQuery, William Thomas b: 6/28/1861, Garrard Co., Ky. d: 6/12/1900, Covington, Ky. 6'4", Deb: 8/20/1884																											
1884	Cin-U	35	132	31	37	5	0	2		8		.280	.321	.364	.685	122	4	3	108	0	16	.589	0			1	1	0.3
1885	Det-N	70	278	34	76	15	4	3	30	8	29	.273	.294	.388	.682	122	5	6	97	94	33	.574				3	1/O	-0.2
1886	KC-N	122	449	62	111	27	4	4	38	36	44	.247	.303	.352	.655	93	-1	-5	107	77	50	.586	4			1	*1	-2.4
1890	Syr-a	122	461	64	142	17	6	2		53		.308	.383	.384	.767	143	18	25	90	0	80	.812	26			8	*1	2.4
1891	Was-a	68	261	40	63	9	4	2	37	18	19	.241	.305	.330	.635	88	-6	-4	95	123	28	.571	3			1	1	-0.5
Total	5	417	1581	231	429	73	18	13	105	123	92	.271	.327	.365	.692	113	21	25	98	58	206	.644	33			13	1/O	-0.4
■ **GLENN McQUILLEN**	McQuillen, Glenn Richard "Red" b: 4/19/15, Strasburg, Va. BR/TR, 6', 198 lbs. Deb: 6/16/38																											
1938	StL-A	43	116	14	33	4	0	0	13	4	12	.284	.308	.319	.627	57	-8	-8	100	119	11	.488	0	1	-1	-2	O	-0.8
1941	StL-A	7	21	4	7	2	1	0	3	1	2	.333	.364	.524	.887	132	1	1	100	97	3	.750	0	1	-1	-0	/O	0.0
1942	StL-A	100	339	40	96	15	12	3	47	10	17	.283	.306	.425	.730	100	-0	-2	104	108	37	.589	1	1	-0	-5	O	-1.2
1946	StL-A	59	166	24	40	3	3	1	12	19	18	.241	.319	.313	.632	79	-5	-4	98	83	16	.530	0	2	-1	-2	O	-1.0
1947	StL-A	1	1	0	0	0	0	0	0	0	0	.000	.000	.000	.000	-98	-0	-0	102	0	0	.000	0	0	0	0	H	0.0
Total	5	210	643	82	176	24	16	4	75	34	49	.274	.311	.379	.691	87	-12	-13	102	103	67	.593	1	5	-3	-9	O	-3.0
■ **GEORGE McQUINN**	McQuinn, George Hartley b: 5/29/10, Arlington, Va. d: 12/24/78, Alexandria, Va. BL/TL, 5'11", 165 lbs. Deb: 4/14/36																											
1936	Cin-N	38	134	5	27	3	4	0	13	10	22	.201	.262	.284	.546	49	-10	-9	97	124	11	.454	0			1	1	-1.1
1938	StL-A	148	602	100	195	42	7	12	82	58	49	.324	.384	.477	.861	114	13	13	100	76	110	.850	4	5	-2	-1	*1	-0.8
1939	StL-A	154	617	101	195	37	13	20	94	65	42	.316	.383	.515	.898	127	24	24	100	81	122	.893	6	5	-1	10	*1	1.7
1940	StL-A	151	594	78	166	39	10	16	84	57	58	.279	.343	.460	.802	100	4	-1	106	100	95	.752	3	3	-1	9	*1	0.0
1941	StL-A	130	495	93	147	28	4	18	80	74	30	.297	.388	.479	.867	128	21	21	100	103	96	.873	5	4	-1	6	*1	2.1
1942	StL-A	145	554	86	145	32	5	12	78	60	77	.262	.335	.403	.737	103	4	1	104	112	78	.679	1	1	-0	2	*1	0.1
1943	StL-A	125	449	53	109	19	2	12	74	56	65	.243	.327	.374	.701	104	2	2	100	135	58	.650	4	3	-1	1	*1	0.0
1944	StL-A	146	516	83	129	26	3	11	72	85	74	.250	.357	.376	.733	107	8	7	102	121	79	.726	4	3	-1	-5	*1	-0.7
1945	StL-A	139	483	69	134	31	3	7	61	65	51	.277	.364	.398	.762	105	14	5	115	106	75	.723	1	1	-0	3	*1	0.3
1946	Phi-A	136	484	47	109	23	6	3	35	64	62	.225	.317	.316	.633	74	-14	-17	104	87	54	.580	4	2	0	3	*1	-2.1
1947	NY-A	144	517	84	157	24	3	13	80	78	66	.304	.395	.437	.832	136	23	26	97	118	97	.826	0	2	-1	-4	*1	1.7
1948	NY-A	94	302	33	75	11	4	11	41	40	38	.248	.336	.421	.757	100	-1	-1	100	87	45	.714	0	2	-1	-4	1	0.0
Total	12	1550	5747	832	1588	315	64	135	794	712	634	.276	.357	.424	.781	108	88	70	102	102	920	.760	32	31		22	*1	1.2
■ **HAL McRAE**	McRae, Harold Abraham b: 7/10/45, Avon Park, Fla. BR/TR, 5'11", 180 lbs. Deb: 7/11/68 C																											
1968	Cin-N	17	51	1	10	1	0	0	2	4	14	.196	.255	.216	.470	38	-3	-4	111	77	2	.364	1	1	-0	1	2	-0.2
1970	Cin-N	70	165	18	41	6	1	8	23	15	23	.248	.315	.442	.757	96	-0	-1	104	92	21	.674	0	2	-1	-7	O/32	-1.1
1971	Cin-N	99	337	39	89	24	2	9	34	11	35	.264	.291	.427	.719	105	-1	0	96	81	39	.620	3	2	-0	-3	O	-0.6
1972	Cin-N	61	97	9	27	4	0	5	26	2	10	.278	.307	.474	.781	128	2	3	93	175	12	.667	0	0	0	-3	O3	0.0
1973	KC-A	106	338	36	79	18	3	9	50	34	38	.234	.315	.385	.699	88	-2	-6	109	125	41	.642	2	2	-1	-5	OD/3	-1.3
1974	KC-A	148	539	71	167	36	4	15	88	54	68	.310	.378	.475	.853	135	30	26	106	117	95	.832	11	8	-2	0	DO/3	2.5
1975	KC-A	126	480	58	147	38	6	5	71	47	47	.306	.373	.442	.815	127	19	18	102	127	75	.763	11	8	-2	-4	*OD/3	1.0
1976	KC-A	149	527	75	175	34	5	8	73	64	43	.332	**.412**	.461	**.873**	**156**	39	39	100	107	101	.894	22	12	-1	-1	*DO	3.8
1977	KC-A	162	641	104	191	**54**	11	21	92	59	43	.298	.369	.515	.884	137	33	33	100	89	119	.882	18	14	-3	2	*DO	3.0
1978	KC-A	156	623	90	170	39	5	16	72	51	62	.273	.334	.429	.762	111	10	8	102	80	87	.716	17	8	0	0	*D/O	0.9
1979	KC-A	101	393	55	113	32	4	10	74	38	46	.288	.356	.466	.822	114	11	8	105	141	66	.793	5	4	-1	0	*D	0.7
1980	KC-A	124	489	73	145	39	5	14	83	29	56	.297	.346	.483	.829	126	15	16	98	123	79	.788	10	2	2	-1	*D/O	1.7
1981	KC-A	101	389	38	106	23	2	7	36	34	33	.272	.334	.396	.730	111	5	5	99	85	49	.648	3	4	-2	0	D/O	0.4
1982	KC-A	159	613	91	189	**46**	8	27	**133**	55	61	.308	.370	.542	.912	146	38	38	100	136	123	.908	4	4	-1	-0	*D/O	3.6
1983	KC-A	157	589	84	183	41	6	12	82	50	68	.311	.374	.462	.836	127	24	22	101	110	98	.782	2	3	-1	0	*D	2.1
1984	KC-A	106	317	30	96	13	4	3	42	34	47	.303	.372	.397	.770	114	7	7	99	124	45	.688	0	3	-2	0	D	0.5
1985	KC-A	112	320	41	83	19	0	14	70	44	45	.259	.351	.450	.801	115	8	7	102	149	49	.756	0	1	-1	0	*D	0.6
1986	KC-A	112	278	22	70	14	0	7	37	18	39	.252	.300	.378	.677	84	-6	-6	100	117	29	.571	0	0	0	0	D	-0.6
1987	KC-A	18	32	5	10	3	0	1	9	5	1	.313	.405	.500	.905	134	2	2	104	189	6	.913	0	0	0	0	/D	0.2
Total	19	2084	7218	940	2091	484	66	191	1097	648	779	.290	.355	.454	.809	122	227	213	101	113	1138	.791	109	78	-14	-21	*DO/32	17.2
■ **McREMER**	McRemer Deb: 6/20/1884																											
1884	Was-U	1	3	0	0	0	0	0		0		.000	.000	.000	.000	-99	-1	-1	97	0	0	.000	0			0	/O	0.0

YEAR	TM/L	G	AB	R	H	2B	3B	HR	RBI	BB	SO	AVG	OBP	SLG	PRO	/A	BR	/A	PF	CHI	RC	TA	SB	CS	SBR	FR	POS	TPR
■ KEVIN McREYNOLDS	McReynolds, Walter Kevin b: 10/16/59, Little Rock, Ark. BR/TR, 6', 205 lbs. Deb: 6/02/83																											
1983	SD-N	39	140	15	31	3	1	4	14	12	29	.221	.283	.343	.626	73	-5	-5	99	94	14	.559	2	1	0	5	O	0.0
1984	SD-N	147	525	68	146	26	6	20	75	34	69	.278	.322	.465	.787	121	11	12	99	99	72	.704	3	6	-3	11	*O	1.5
1985	SD-N	152	564	61	132	24	4	15	75	43	81	.234	.292	.371	.662	83	-13	-14	102	120	59	.577	4	0	1	15	*O	-0.1
1986	SD-N	158	560	89	161	31	6	26	96	66	83	.287	.364	.504	.867	144	27	30	95	108	103	.862	8	6	-1	-0	*O	2.7
1987	NY-N	151	590	86	163	32	5	29	95	39	70	.276	.322	.495	.817	114	8	9	99	102	93	.785	14	1	4	3	*O	0.9
1988	NY-N	147	552	82	159	30	2	27	99	38	56	.288	.338	.496	.835	152	24	30	90	114	97	.845	21	0	6	7	*O	4.2
Total	6	794	2931	401	792	146	24	121	454	232	388	.270	.326	.460	.786	119	51	62	97	108	438	.761	52	14	7	40	O	9.2
■ PETE McSHANNIC	McShannic, Peter Robert b: 3/20/1864, Pittsburgh, Pa. d: 11/30/46, Toledo, Ohio BB , 5'7", 190 lbs. Deb: 1888																											
1888	Pit-N	26	98	5	19	1	0	0	5	1	9	.194	.218	.204	.422	39	-7	-6	95	95	5	.329	3			0	3	-0.5
■ TRICK McSORLEY	McSorley, John Bernard b: 12/6/1858, St.Louis, Mo. d: 2/9/36, St.Louis, Mo. TR , 5'4", 142 lbs. Deb: 5/06/1875																											
1875	RS-n	14	51	4	9							.176															/3O	
1884	Tol-a	21	68	12	17	1	0	0		3		.250	.282	.265	.546	79	-1	-2	104	0	5	.412				0	1/O3P	0.0
1885	StL-N	2	6	2	3	1	0	0	1	2	1	.500	.625	.667	1.292	344	2	2	92	92	3	2.000				0	/3	0.2
1886	StL-a	5	20	1	3	3	0	0		0		.150	.150	.300	.450	36	-1	-2	111	0	1	.353	0			0	/S	-0.1
Total	3	28	94	15	23	5	0	0	1	5	1	.245	.283	.298	.581	86	-1	-2	104	7	9	.465	0			0	/1O3SP	0.1
■ PAUL McSWEENEY	McSweeney, Paul A. b: 4/3/1867, St.Louis, Mo. d: 8/12/51, St.Louis, Mo. Deb: 9/20/1891																											
1891	StL-a	3	12	2	3	1	0	0	2	0	0	.250	.308	.333	.641	75	-0	-1	114	147	2	.667	1			0	/23	0.0
■ JIM McTAMANY	McTamany, James Edward b: 7/1/1863, Philadelphia, Pa. d: 4/16/16, Lenni, Pa. BR/TR, 5'8", 190 lbs. Deb: 1885																											
1885	Bro-a	35	131	21	36	7	2	1		9		.275	.321	.382	.703	120	4	3	104	0	16	.621				-5	O	-0.3
1886	Bro-a	111	418	86	106	23	10	2		54		.254	.353	.371	.724	128	16	16	100	0	63	.760	18			12	*O	2.1
1887	Bro-a	134	520	123	134	22	10	1		76		.258	.365	.344	.709	102	4	6	99	0	92	.863	66			3	*O	0.3
1888	KC-a	130	516	94	127	12	10	4	41	67		.246	.345	.331	.677	114	15	10	106	58	80	.781	55			-2	*O	0.2
1889	Col-a	139	529	113	146	21	7	4	52	116	66	.276	.407	.365	.772	135	22	32	91	63	97	.914	40			-8	*O	1.6
1890	Col-a	125	466	**140**	120	27	7	1		**112**		.258	.405	.352	.757	127	22	23	99	0	86	.934	43			1	*O	1.5
1891	Col-a	81	304	59	76	17	9	3	35	58	48	.250	.374	.395	.768	138	11	16	89	69	54	.877	20			-4	O	0.8
	Phi-a	58	218	57	49	6	3	3	32	43	44	.225	.365	.321	.686	97	2	1	103	68	31	.775	13			-1	O	-0.1
	Yr	139	522	116	125	23	12	6		101	92	.239	.370	.364	.734	119	12	17	95	69	85	.834	33			-4		0.7
Total	7	813	3102	693	794	135	58	19	149	535	158	.256	.373	.355	.728	120	95	105	98	32	519	.839	255			-3	O	6.1
■ CAL McVEY	McVey, Calvin Alexander b: 8/30/1850, Montrose, Iowa d: 8/20/26, San Francisco, Cal BR/TR, 5'9", 170 lbs. Deb: 5/05/1871 M																											
1871	Bos-n	29	155	43	65							.419															*C/O	
1872	Bos-n	46	242	56	74							.306															*C/O	
1873	Bal-n	35	187	47	69							.369															C/OS123M	
1874	Bos-n	70	343	90	131							.382															*OC	
1875	Bos-n	82	392	90	138							.352															*1OC/P	
1876	Chi-N	63	308	62	107	15	0	1	53	2	4	.347	.352	.406	.757	121	16	4	125	134	45	.632				3	*1P/CO3	0.7
1877	Chi-N	60	266	58	98	9	7	0	36	8	11	.368	.387	.455	.842	167	19	20	98	89	48	.768				-18	*C3P/21	0.3
1878	Cin-N	61	271	43	83	10	4	2	28	5	10	.306	.319	.395	.714	140	9	11	95	74	35	.596				-11	*3/CM	0.3
1879	Cin-N	81	354	64	105	18	6	0	55	8	13	.297	.312	.381	.694	134	10	13	95	137	43	.574				-6	*1/OP3CM	0.1
Total	5 n	262	1319	326	477							.362															*1/OP3CM	
Total	4	265	1199	227	393	52	17	3	172	23	38	.328	.340	.407	.747	139	54	47	103	111	171	.634				-31	1CO/3PS2	1.4
■ GEORGE McVEY	McVey, George W. b: 1864, Port Jervis, N.Y. d: 5/3/1896, Quincy, Ill. 6'1", 185 lbs. Deb: 1885																											
1885	Bro-a	6	21	2	3	0	0	0		2		.143	.217	.143	.360	17	-2	-2	104	0	1	.278				0	/1C	-0.1
■ BILL McWILLIAMS	McWilliams, William Henry b: 11/28/10, Dubuque, Iowa BR/TR, 6', 185 lbs. Deb: 7/08/31																											
1931	Bos-A	2	2	0	0	0	0	0	0	0	1	.000	.000	.000	.000	-99	-1	-1	94	0	0	.000	0	0	0	0	H	0.0
■ BOB MEACHAM	Meacham, Robert Andrew b: 8/25/60, Los Angeles, Cal. BB/TR, 6'1", 175 lbs. Deb: 6/30/83																											
1983	NY-A	22	51	5	12	2	0	0	4	4	10	.235	.304	.275	.578	61	-3	-3	99	112	6	.692	8	0	2	1	S/3	0.2
1984	NY-A	99	360	62	91	13	4	2	25	32	70	.253	.319	.328	.647	85	-10	-7	94	82	41	.587	9	5	-0	1	S/2	0.2
1985	NY-A	156	481	70	105	16	2	1	47	54	102	.218	.304	.266	.570	60	-27	-24	96	142	45	.544	25	7	3	-17	*S	-2.5
1986	NY-A	56	161	19	36	7	1	0	10	17	39	.224	.309	.280	.589	61	-3	-8	103	88	13	.496	3	6	-3	2	S	-0.5
1987	NY-A	77	203	28	55	11	1	5	21	19	33	.271	.351	.409	.760	104	1	2	98	85	30	.735	6	5	-1	-2	S2/D	0.3
1988	NY-A	47	115	18	25	9	0	0	7	14	22	.217	.313	.296	.609	75	-4	-3	96	82	13	.620	7	1	2	1	2S/3	0.1
Total	6	457	1371	202	324	58	8	8	114	140	276	.236	.316	.308	.624	74	-50	-43	97	106	147	.597	58	24	3	-14	S/23D	-2.2
■ CHARLIE MEAD	Mead, Charles Richard b: 4/9/21, Vermilion, Alt., Canada BL/TR, 6'1.5", 185 lbs. Deb: 8/28/43																											
1943	NY-N	37	146	9	40	6	1	1	13	10	15	.274	.321	.349	.670	97	-1	-1	96	92	16	.587	3			0	O	-0.1
1944	NY-N	39	78	5	14	1	0	1	8	5	7	.179	.229	.231	.460	29	-7	-8	104	137	4	.348	0			2	O	-0.7
1945	NY-N	11	37	4	10	1	0	1	6	5	2	.270	.357	.378	.736	105	0	0	100	123	5	.704	0			1	O	0.1
Total	3	87	261	18	64	8	1	3	27	20	24	.245	.299	.318	.617	77	-8	-8	99	110	26	.538	3			3	/O	-0.7
■ LOUIE MEADOWS	Meadows, Michael Ray b: 4/29/61, Maysville, N.C. BL/TL, 5'11", 190 lbs. Deb: 7/03/86																											
1986	Hou-N	6	6	1	2	0	0	0	0	0	0	.333	.333	.333	.667	82	-0	-0	103	0	1	.750	1	0	0	-0	/O	0.0
1988	Hou-N	35	42	5	8	0	1	2	3	6	8	.190	.292	.381	.673	98	-0	-0	93	54	5	.703	4	2	0	0	O	0.0
Total	2	41	48	6	10	0	1	2	3	6	8	.208	.296	.375	.671	96	-1	-0	94	48	5	.707	5	2	0	0	/O	0.0
■ PAT MEANEY	Meaney, Patrick J. b: 1892, Philadelphia, Pa. d: 10/20/22, Philadelphia, Pa. TR , Deb: 5/18/12																											
1912	Det-A	1	2	0	0	0	0	0	0	1		.000	.500	.000	.500	49	0	0	95	0	0	1.000	0			0	/S	0.0
■ CHARLIE MEARA	Meara, Charles Edward "Goggy" b: 4/13/1891, New York, N.Y. d: 2/8/62, Bronx, N.Y. BL/TR, 5'10", 160 lbs. Deb: 6/01/14																											
1914	NY-A	4	7	2	2	0	0	0	1	2	2	.286	.444	.286	.730	120	0	0	100	188	1	.667	0	1	-1	-1	/O	0.0
■ RAY MEDEIROS	Medeiros, Ray Antone "Pep" b: 5/9/26, Oakland, Cal. BR/TR, 5'10", 163 lbs. Deb: 4/25/45																											
1945	Cin-N	1	0	0	0	0	0	0	0	0	0	—	—	—	—	—	0	0	94	—	—	—	0			0	R	0.0
■ LUIS MEDINA	Medina, Luis Main b: 3/26/63, Santa Monica, Cal. BR/TL, 6'3", 190 lbs. Deb: 9/02/88																											
1988	Cle-A	16	51	10	13	0	0	6	8	2	18	.255	.309	.608	.917	148	3	3	102	65	10	.921	0	0	0	0	1	0.2
■ JOE MEDWICK	Medwick, Joseph Michael "Ducky" or "Muscles" b: 11/24/11, Carteret, N.J. d: 3/21/75, St.Petersburg, Fla BR/TR, 5'10", 187 lbs. Deb: 9/02/32 H																											
1932	StL-N	26	106	13	37	12	1	2	12	2	10	.349	.367	.538	.905	140	5	5	100	75	21	.913	3			1	O	0.5
1933	StL-N	148	595	92	182	40	10	18	98	26	56	.306	.337	.497	.835	133	25	23	102	112	97	.769	5			6	*O	2.2
1934	StL-N	149	620	110	198	40	**18**	18	106	21	83	.319	.343	.529	.872	114	23	12	114	106	109	.808	3			-0	*O	0.4
1935	StL-N	154	634	132	224	46	13	23	126	30	59	.353	.386	.576	.962	149	46	43	104	111	139	.948	4			-1	*O	3.4
1936	StL-N	155	636	115	**223**	**64**	13	18	**138**	34	33	.351	.387	.577	.964	166	47	52	94	123	141	.956	3			13	*O	**5.5**
1937	StL-N	156	633	**111**	**237**	**56**	10	**31**	**154**	41	50	**.374**	.414	**.641**	**1.056**	**182**	**69**	**68**	101	107	**170**	1.113	4			1	*O	6.0
1938	StL-N	146	590	100	190	**47**	8	21	**122**	42	41	.322	.369	.536	.905	131	34	26	111	123	113	.855	0			11	*O	3.4
1939	StL-N	150	606	98	201	48	8	14	117	45	44	.332	.380	.507	.886	130	29	25	105	130	114	.857	6			1	*O	2.4
1940	StL-N	37	158	21	48	12	0	3	20	6	8	.304	.329	.437	.766	107	1	1	102	101	20	.636	0			-1	O	0.0
	Bro-N	106	423	62	127	18	12	14	66	26	28	.300	.345	.499	.844	121	16	11	108	102	70	.788	2			5	*O	1.2
	Yr	143	581	83	175	30	12	17	86	32	36	.301	.341	.482	.823	117	17	12	106	103	93	.760	2			4		1.2
1941	Bro-N	133	538	100	171	33	10	18	88	38	35	.318	.364	.517	.881	141	30	28	103	101	95	.824	2			1	*O	2.4
1942	Bro-N	142	553	69	166	37	4	4	96	32	25	.300	.338	.403	.742	114	10	9	102	**154**	72	.639	2			-1	*O	0.4
1943	Bro-N	48	173	13	47	10	0	0	25	10	8	.272	.315	.329	.645	87	-3	-3	100	158	18	.531	1			-7	O	-1.1
	NY-N	78	324	41	91	20	3	5	45	9	14	.281	.300	.407	.708	108	-1	1	96	117	35	.573	0			4	O/1	0.3
	Yr	126	497	54	138	30	3	5	70	19	22	.278	.306	.380	.686	100	-4	-2	97	134	55	.565	1			-2		-0.8

YEAR	TM/L	G	AB	R	H	2B	3B	HR	RBI	BB	SO	AVG	OBP	SLG	PRO	/A	BR	/A	PF	CHI	RC	TA	SB	CS	SBR	FR	POS	TPR
1944	NY-N	128	490	64	165	24	3	7	85	38	24	.337	.386	.441	.826	128	21	19	104	136	82	.763	2			-9	*O	0.0
1945	NY-N	26	92	14	28	4	0	3	11	2	2	.304	.319	.446	.765	112	1	1	100	76	12	.672	2			-2	O	-0.1
	Bos-N	66	218	17	62	13	0	0	26	12	12	.284	.325	.344	.669	76	-4	-8	112	120	23	.562	3			2	O1	-0.7
	Yr	92	310	31	90	17	0	3	37	14	14	.290	.323	.374	.697	86	-4	-7	109	109	37	.602	5			0		-0.8
1946	Bro-N	41	77	7	24	4	0	2	18	6	5	.312	.369	.442	.811	126	3	3	103	168	13	.759	0			-3	O/1	0.0
1947	StL-N	75	150	19	46	12	0	4	28	16	12	.307	.373	.467	.840	115	5	3	106	126	26	.804	0			-6	O	-0.3
1948	StL-N	20	19	0	4	0	0	0	2	1	2	.211	.250	.211	.461	26	-2	-2	101	187	1	.313	0			-0	/O	-0.2
Total	17	1984	7635	1198	2471	540	113	205	1383	437	551	.324	.362	.505	.867	132	353	317	104	119	1372	.844	42			15	*O/1	25.7

■ TOMMY MEE Mee, Thomas William "Judge" b: 3/18/1890, Chicago, Ill. d: 5/16/81, Chicago, Ill. BR/TR, 5'8", 165 lbs. Deb: 6/14/10

YEAR	TM/L	G	AB	R	H	2B	3B	HR	RBI	BB	SO	AVG	OBP	SLG	PRO	/A	BR	/A	PF	CHI	RC	TA	SB	CS	SBR	FR	POS	TPR
1910	StL-A	8	19	1	3	2	0	0	1	0		.158	.158	.263	.421	33	-2	-1	94	74	1	.313	0			0	/S23	0.0

■ DAD MEEK Meek, Frank J. b: St.Louis, Mo. d: 12/26/22, St.Louis, Mo. Deb: 5/10/1889

YEAR	TM/L	G	AB	R	H	2B	3B	HR	RBI	BB	SO	AVG	OBP	SLG	PRO	/A	BR	/A	PF	CHI	RC	TA	SB	CS	SBR	FR	POS	TPR
1889	StL-a	2	2	2	1	0	0	0	1	0	0	.500	.500	.500	1.000	168	0	0	112	286	1	2.000	1			0	/C	0.0
1890	StL-a	4	16	3	5	0	0	0		0		.313	.313	.313	.625	75	-0	-1	116	0	2	.545	1			0	/C	0.0
Total	2	6	18	5	6	0	0	0	1	0	0	.333	.333	.333	.667	85	-0	-1	115	32	3	.667	2			0	/C	0.0

■ SAMMY MEEKS Meeks, Samuel Mack b: 4/23/23, Anderson, S.C. BR/TR, 5'9", 160 lbs. Deb: 4/29/48

YEAR	TM/L	G	AB	R	H	2B	3B	HR	RBI	BB	SO	AVG	OBP	SLG	PRO	/A	BR	/A	PF	CHI	RC	TA	SB	CS	SBR	FR	POS	TPR
1948	Was-A	24	33	4	4	1	0	0	2	1	12	.121	.147	.152	.299	-20	-6	-6	103	135	1	.200	0	0	0	-1	S/2	-0.6
1949	Cin-N	16	36	10	11	2	0	2	6	2	6	.306	.342	.528	.870	136	1	1	96	90	6	.846	1			-1	/2S	0.2
1950	Cin-N	39	95	7	27	5	0	1	8	6	14	.284	.327	.368	.695	79	-2	-3	105	81	11	.600	1			-1	S/3	0.0
1951	Cin-N	23	35	4	8	0	0	0	2	0	4	.229	.229	.229	.457	23	-4	-4	101	97	1	.310	1	0	0	0	/3S	-0.2
Total	4	102	199	25	50	8	0	3	18	9	36	.251	.284	.337	.620	63	-11	-11	102	94	20	.523	3	0		-3	/S23	-0.6

■ DUTCH MEIER Meier, Arthur Ernst b: 3/30/1879, St.Louis, Mo. d: 3/23/48, Chicago, Ill. BR/TR, 5'10", 175 lbs. Deb: 5/12/06

YEAR	TM/L	G	AB	R	H	2B	3B	HR	RBI	BB	SO	AVG	OBP	SLG	PRO	/A	BR	/A	PF	CHI	RC	TA	SB	CS	SBR	FR	POS	TPR
1906	Pit-N	82	273	32	70	11	4	0	16	13		.256	.290	.326	.616	90	-3	-4	104	66	28	.522	4			4	OS	0.0

■ DAVE MEIER Meier, David Keith b: 8/8/59, Helena, Mont. BR/TR, 6', 185 lbs. Deb: 4/03/84

YEAR	TM/L	G	AB	R	H	2B	3B	HR	RBI	BB	SO	AVG	OBP	SLG	PRO	/A	BR	/A	PF	CHI	RC	TA	SB	CS	SBR	FR	POS	TPR
1984	Min-A	59	147	18	35	8	1	0	13	6	9	.238	.273	.306	.579	57	-8	-9	106	115	11	.441	0	1	-1	-5	O/3D	-1.6
1985	Min-A	71	104	15	27	6	0	1	8	18	12	.260	.374	.346	.720	96	1	0	103	81	13	.663	0	6	-4	-12	O/D	-1.6
1987	Tex-A	13	21	4	6	1	0	0	0	0	4	.286	.286	.333	.619	62	-1	-1	104	0	1	.412	0	0	0	-1	/O	-0.2
1988	Chi-N	2	5	0	2	0	0	0	1	0	1	.400	.400	.400	.800	125	0	0	104	200	1	.667	0	0	0	0	/3	0.0
Total	4	145	277	37	70	15	1	1	22	24	26	.253	.317	.325	.642	74	-8	-10	104	95	27	.542	0	7	-4	-19	O/D3	-3.4

■ WALT MEINERT Meinert, Walter Henry b: 12/11/1890, New York, N.Y. d: 11/9/58, Decatur, Ill. BL/TL, 5'7.5", 150 lbs. Deb: 9/06/13

YEAR	TM/L	G	AB	R	H	2B	3B	HR	RBI	BB	SO	AVG	OBP	SLG	PRO	/A	BR	/A	PF	CHI	RC	TA	SB	CS	SBR	FR	POS	TPR
1913	StL-A	4	8	1	3	0	0	0	0	1	3	.375	.444	.375	.819	147	0	1	95	0	2	1.000	1			-0	/O	0.0

■ FRANK MEINKE Meinke, Frank Louis b: 10/18/1863, Chicago, Ill. d: 11/8/31, Chicago, Ill. 5'10.5", 172 lbs. Deb: 5/01/1884

YEAR	TM/L	G	AB	R	H	2B	3B	HR	RBI	BB	SO	AVG	OBP	SLG	PRO	/A	BR	/A	PF	CHI	RC	TA	SB	CS	SBR	FR	POS	TPR
1884	Det-N	92	341	28	56	5	7	6	24	6	89	.164	.179	.273	.451	43	-23	-20	94	76	17	.347				-7	SP/O32	-1.4
1885	Det-N	1	3	0	0	0	0	0	0	0	1	.000	.000	.000	.000	-99	-1	-1	97	0	0	.000				0	/OP	0.0
Total	2	93	344	28	56	5	7	6	24	6	90	.163	.177	.270	.447	41	-24	-21	94	75	17	.344				-7	/SPO23	-1.4

■ BOB MEINKE Meinke, Robert Bernard b: 6/25/1887, Chicago, Ill. d: 12/29/52, Chicago, Ill. BR/TR, 5'10", 135 lbs. Deb: 8/22/10

YEAR	TM/L	G	AB	R	H	2B	3B	HR	RBI	BB	SO	AVG	OBP	SLG	PRO	/A	BR	/A	PF	CHI	RC	TA	SB	CS	SBR	FR	POS	TPR
1910	Cin-N	2	1	0	0	0	0	0	0	1	0	.000	.500	.000	.500	48	0	0	101	0	0	1.000	0			0	/S	0.0

■ GEORGE MEISTER Meister, George B. b: 1864, Germany d: 8/24/08, Pittsburgh, Pa. Deb: 8/15/1884

YEAR	TM/L	G	AB	R	H	2B	3B	HR	RBI	BB	SO	AVG	OBP	SLG	PRO	/A	BR	/A	PF	CHI	RC	TA	SB	CS	SBR	FR	POS	TPR
1884	Tol-a	34	119	9	23	6	0	0		3		.193	.244	.244	.488	60	-5	-5	104	0	7	.385				-11	3	-1.4

■ JOHN MEISTER Meister, John F. b: 5/10/1863, Allentown, Pa. d: 1/17/23, Philadelphia, Pa. Deb: 8/24/1886

YEAR	TM/L	G	AB	R	H	2B	3B	HR	RBI	BB	SO	AVG	OBP	SLG	PRO	/A	BR	/A	PF	CHI	RC	TA	SB	CS	SBR	FR	POS	TPR
1886	NY-a	45	186	35	44	7	3	2		4		.237	.253	.339	.591	83	-4	-5	104	0	17	.479	1			-8	2	-1.1
1887	NY-a	39	157	24	35	6	2	1		16		.223	.303	.306	.609	82	-6	-2	88	0	18	.615	9			0	O2/3S	-0.1
Total	2	84	343	59	79	13	5	3		20		.230	.277	.324	.600	83	-9	-7	96	0	34	.542	10			-8	/2O3S	-1.2

■ KARL MEISTER Meister, Karl Daniel "Dutch" b: 5/15/1891, Marietta, Ohio d: 8/15/67, Marietta, Ohio BR/TR, 6', 178 lbs. Deb: 8/10/13

YEAR	TM/L	G	AB	R	H	2B	3B	HR	RBI	BB	SO	AVG	OBP	SLG	PRO	/A	BR	/A	PF	CHI	RC	TA	SB	CS	SBR	FR	POS	TPR
1913	Cin-N	4	7	1	2	1	0	0	2	0	4	.286	.286	.429	.714	101	-0	-0	102	242	1	.600	0			-2	/O	-0.1

■ MOXIE MEIXELL Meixell, Merton Merrill b: 10/18/1887, Lake Crystal, Minn d: 8/17/82, Los Angeles, Cal. BL/TR, 5'10", 168 lbs. Deb: 7/07/12

YEAR	TM/L	G	AB	R	H	2B	3B	HR	RBI	BB	SO	AVG	OBP	SLG	PRO	/A	BR	/A	PF	CHI	RC	TA	SB	CS	SBR	FR	POS	TPR
1912	Cle-A	3	2	0	1	0	0	0	0	0	0	.500	.500	.500	1.000	184	0	0	101	0	0	1.000	0			0	H	0.0

■ ROMAN MEJIAS Mejias, Roman (Gomez) b: 8/9/30, Abreus, Las Villas, Cuba BR/TR, 6', 175 lbs. Deb: 4/13/55

YEAR	TM/L	G	AB	R	H	2B	3B	HR	RBI	BB	SO	AVG	OBP	SLG	PRO	/A	BR	/A	PF	CHI	RC	TA	SB	CS	SBR	FR	POS	TPR
1955	Pit-N	71	167	14	36	8	1	3	21	9	13	.216	.256	.329	.585	55	-11	-11	97	133	13	.474	1	3	-2	-1	O	-1.3
1957	Pit-N	58	142	12	39	7	4	2	15	6	13	.275	.309	.423	.731	100	-2	-0	94	94	17	.639	2	2	-1	-2	O	-0.5
1958	Pit-N	76	157	17	42	3	2	5	19	2	27	.268	.281	.408	.689	84	-5	-4	95	99	17	.580	2	0	1	-2	O	-0.7
1959	Pit-N	96	276	28	65	6	1	7	28	21	48	.236	.301	.341	.642	68	-12	-13	103	98	28	.558	1	2	-1	1	O	-1.3
1960	Pit-N	3	1	1	0	0	0	0	0	0	1	.000	.000	.000	.000	-99	-0	-0	99	0	0	.000	0	0	0	0	H	0.0
1961	Pit-N	4	1	1	0	0	0	0	0	0	1	.000	.000	.000	.000	-99	-0	-0	99	0	0	.000	0	0	0	-1	/O	0.0
1962	Hou-N	146	566	82	162	12	3	24	76	30	83	.286	.329	.445	.774	114	3	8	93	98	81	.713	12	4	1	-5	*O	-0.2
1963	Bos-A	111	357	43	81	18	0	11	39	14	36	.227	.262	.370	.632	71	-13	-15	106	99	32	.531	4	1	1	5	O	-1.3
1964	Bos-A	62	101	14	24	3	1	2	4	7	16	.238	.294	.347	.640	76	-3	-3	102	41	9	.531	0	0	0	-2	O	-0.7
Total	9	627	1768	212	449	57	12	54	202	89	238	.254	.296	.391	.688	85	-43	-39	98	98	197	.614	22	12	-1	-8	O	-5.9

■ SAM MEJIAS Mejias, Samuel Elias b: 5/9/52, Santiago, D.R. BR/TR, 6', 170 lbs. Deb: 9/06/76

YEAR	TM/L	G	AB	R	H	2B	3B	HR	RBI	BB	SO	AVG	OBP	SLG	PRO	/A	BR	/A	PF	CHI	RC	TA	SB	CS	SBR	FR	POS	TPR
1976	StL-N	18	21	1	3	1	0	0	0	2	2	.143	.217	.190	.408	16	-2	-2	104	0	1	.400	2	0	1	-3	O	-0.5
1977	Mon-N	74	101	14	23	4	1	3	8	2	17	.228	.243	.376	.619	64	-6	-5	98	68	9	.519	1	0	0	-11	O	-1.8
1978	Mon-N	67	56	9	13	1	0	0	6	2	5	.232	.259	.250	.509	45	-4	-4	96	170	3	.348	0	0	0	-14	O/P	-2.1
1979	Chi-N	31	11	4	2	0	0	0	0	2	5	.182	.308	.182	.490	33	-1	-1	112	0	1	.444	0	0	0	-9	O	-1.0
	Cin-N	7	2	1	1	0	0	0	0	0	0	.500	.500	.500	1.000	178	0	0	97	0	1	1.000	0	0	0	-2	/O	-0.1
	Yr	38	13	5	3	0	0	0	0	2	5	.231	.333	.231	.564	52	-1	-1	109	0	1	.500	0	0	0	-10		-1.1
1980	Cin-N	71	108	16	30	5	1	1	10	6	13	.278	.322	.370	.692	91	-1	-1	102	92	13	.630	4	2	0	-8	O	-1.2
1981	Cin-N	66	49	6	14	2	0	0	7	2	9	.286	.314	.327	.640	81	-1	-1	101	172	5	.528	1	0	0	-17	O	-2.1
Total	6	334	348	51	86	13	2	4	31	16	51	.247	.282	.330	.613	69	-15	-15	100	99	32	.528	8	2	1	-64	O/P	-8.8

■ DUTCH MELE Mele, Albert Ernest b: 1/11/15, New York, N.Y. d: 2/12/75, Hollywood, Fla. BL/TL, 5'0.5", 195 lbs. Deb: 9/14/37

YEAR	TM/L	G	AB	R	H	2B	3B	HR	RBI	BB	SO	AVG	OBP	SLG	PRO	/A	BR	/A	PF	CHI	RC	TA	SB	CS	SBR	FR	POS	TPR
1937	Cin-N	6	14	1	2	1	0	0	1	1	1	.143	.200	.214	.414	14	-2	-2	91	120	1	.333	0			-2	/O	-0.3

■ SAM MELE Mele, Sabath Anthony b: 1/21/23, Astoria, N.Y. BR/TR, 6'1", 183 lbs. Deb: 4/15/47 MC

YEAR	TM/L	G	AB	R	H	2B	3B	HR	RBI	BB	SO	AVG	OBP	SLG	PRO	/A	BR	/A	PF	CHI	RC	TA	SB	CS	SBR	FR	POS	TPR
1947	Bos-A	123	453	71	137	14	8	12	73	37	35	.302	.356	.448	.805	114	12	8	108	115	72	.730	0	3	-2	0	*O/1	0.2
1948	Bos-A	66	180	25	42	12	1	2	25	13	21	.233	.292	.344	.637	69	-9	-9	100	124	18	.542	1	1	-0	-8	O	-1.7
1949	Bos-A	18	46	1	9	1	1	0	7	7	14	.196	.302	.261	.563	46	-3	-4	107	200	4	.525	2	0	1	-1	O	-0.3
	Was-A	78	264	21	64	12	2	3	25	17	34	.242	.288	.337	.625	71	-15	-12	91	87	24	.512	2	1	0	-6	O1	-1.8
	Yr	96	310	22	73	13	3	3	32	24	48	.235	.290	.326	.616	67	-18	-15	94	111	29	.520	4	1	1	-6		-2.1
1950	Was-A	126	435	57	119	21	6	12	86	51	40	.274	.351	.432	.783	101	-1	-1	99	135	64	.718	2	0	1	-7	O1	-0.8
1951	Was-A	143	558	58	153	**36**	7	5	94	32	31	.274	.315	.391	.705	94	-10	-7	95	**147**	64	.588	2	3	-1	0	*O1	-1.2
1952	Was-A	9	28	2	12	3	0	2	10	1	2	.429	.448	.750	1.198	229	4	4	100	138	10	1.375	0	0	0	-1	/O	0.3
	Chi-A	123	423	46	105	18	2	14	59	48	40	.248	.328	.400	.727	102	0	0	100	104	53	.651	1	2	-1	-11	*O/1	-1.5
	Yr	132	451	48	117	21	2	16	69	49	42	.259	.335	.421	.756	110	5	5	100	108	62	.684	1	2	-1	-12		-1.2
1953	Chi-A	140	481	64	132	26	8	12	82	58	47	.274	.353	.437	.789	106	8	4	106	126	75	.745	3	1	0	-7	*O/1	-0.6
1954	Bal-A	72	230	17	55	9	4	5	32	18	26	.239	.294	.378	.673	87	-6	-5	95	119	23	.567	1	0	0	-6	O	-1.2
	Bos-A	42	132	22	42	6	0	7	23	12	12	.318	.384	.523	.906	146	8	8	100	97	25	.874	0	1	-1	1	1O	0.6
	Yr	114	362	39	97	15	4	12	55	30	38	.268	.327	.431	.758	110	2	3	97	112	52	.700	1	1	-0	-7		-0.6
1955	Bos-A	14	31	1	4	2	0	0	1	0	7	.129	.129	.194	.323	-11	-5	-6	124	62	1	.250	1	0	0	2	/O	-0.3
	Cin-N	35	62	4	13	1	0	2	7	5	13	.210	.279	.323	.602	56	-4	-4	106	109	4	.473	0	1	-1	-1	O/1	-0.6

YEAR	TM/L	G	AB	R	H	2B	3B	HR	RBI	BB	SO	AVG	OBP	SLG	PRO	/A	BR	/A	PF	CHI	RC	TA	SB	CS	SBR	FR	POS	TPR
1956	Cle-A	57	114	17	29	7	0	4	20	12	20	.254	.325	.421	.746	95	-1	-1	101	124	15	.667	0	1	-1	-1	O/1	-0.3
Total	10	1046	3437	406	916	168	39	80	544	311	342	.267	.329	.408	.737	97	-21	-23	100	122	451	.685	15	14	-4	-47	O/1	-9.2
■ **FRANCISCO MELENDEZ**	Melendez, Francisco Javier (Villegas) b: 1/25/64, Rio Piedras, P.R. BL/TL, 6', 190 lbs. Deb: 8/26/84																											
1984	Phi-N	21	23	0	3	0	0	0	2	1	5	.130	.167	.130	.297	-15	-3	-4	102	261	0	.190	0	0	0	0	1	-0.3
1986	Phi-N	9	8	0	2	0	0	0	0	0	2	.250	.250	.250	.500	37	-1	-1	104	0	1	.333	0	0	0	0	/1	0.0
1987	SF-N	12	16	2	5	0	0	1	1	0	3	.313	.313	.500	.813	116	0	0	96	36	3	.727	0	0	0	0	/1	0.0
1988	SF-N	23	26	1	5	0	0	0	3	3	2	.192	.276	.192	.468	39	-2	-2	94	240	1	.364	0	0	0	-0	/1O	-0.2
Total	4	65	73	3	15	0	0	1	6	4	12	.205	.247	.247	.493	39	-6	-6	98	179	5	.373	0	0	0	-0	/1O	-0.5
■ **LUIS MELENDEZ**	Melendez, Luis Antonio (Santana) b: 8/11/49, Aibonito, P.R. BR/TR, 6', 165 lbs. Deb: 9/07/70																											
1970	StL-N	21	70	11	21	1	0	0	8	2	12	.300	.319	.314	.634	66	-3	-3	106	141	7	.519	3	0	1	1	O	-0.2
1971	StL-N	88	173	25	39	3	1	0	11	24	29	.225	.320	.254	.574	64	-7	-7	101	102	15	.496	2	0	1	-8	O	-1.7
1972	StL-N	118	332	32	79	11	3	5	28	25	34	.238	.293	.334	.628	74	-10	-12	105	91	31	.536	5	4	-1	1	*O	-1.7
1973	StL-N	121	341	35	91	18	1	2	35	27	50	.267	.321	.343	.664	93	-7	-3	91	114	34	.545	2	7	-4	6	O	-0.5
1974	StL-N	83	124	15	27	4	3	0	8	11	9	.218	.287	.298	.585	62	-6	-7	104	83	11	.510	2	2	-1	-4	O/S	-1.2
1975	StL-N	110	291	33	77	8	5	2	27	16	25	.265	.303	.347	.650	78	-8	-9	103	98	28	.531	3	2	-0	-2	O	-1.5
1976	StL-N	20	24	0	3	0	0	0	0	0	3	.125	.125	.125	.250	-28	-4	-4	104	0	0	.125	0	0	0	-1	/O	-0.5
	SD-N	72	119	15	29	5	0	0	5	3	12	.244	.262	.286	.548	63	-7	-6	89	57	8	.404	1	1	-0	-10	O	-1.9
	Yr	92	143	15	32	5	0	0	5	3	15	.224	.240	.259	.498	45	-11	-10	92	44	8	.357	1	1	-0	-11		-2.4
1977	SD-N	8	3	1	0	0	0	0	0	1	1	.000	.250	.000	.250	-30	-1	-0	88	0	0	.333	0	0	0	-1	/O	0.0
Total	8	641	1477	167	366	50	13	9	122	109	175	.248	.300	.318	.618	73	-53	-52	99	96	135	.531	18	16	-4	-18	O/S	-9.2
■ **SKI MELILLO**	Melillo, Oscar Donald "Spinach" b: 8/4/1899, Chicago, Ill. d: 11/14/63, Chicago, Ill. BR/TR, 5'8", 150 lbs. Deb: 4/18/26 C																											
1926	StL-A	99	385	54	98	18	5	1	30	32	31	.255	.315	.335	.650	69	-18	-18	101	74	41	.575	6	7	-2	7	23	-0.7
1927	StL-A	107	356	45	80	18	2	0	26	25	28	.225	.276	.287	.562	43	-29	-32	106	85	29	.471	3	0	1	2	*2	-2.3
1928	StL-A	51	132	9	25	2	0	0	9	9	11	.189	.241	.205	.446	17	-16	-16	104	114	7	.352	2	1	0	-2	23	-1.5
1929	StL-A	141	494	57	146	17	10	5	67	29	30	.296	.337	.401	.738	89	-9	-9	100	108	67	.678	11	6	-0	18	*2	1.1
1930	StL-A	149	574	62	147	30	10	5	59	23	44	.256	.287	.369	.656	60	-32	-39	108	88	60	.578	15	9	-1	**27**	*2	-0.9
1931	StL-A	151	617	88	189	34	11	2	75	37	29	.306	.346	.407	.752	95	-3	-6	102	102	84	.672	7	11	-5	**34**	*2	3.0
1932	StL-A	154	612	71	148	19	11	3	66	36	42	.242	.286	.324	.610	58	-39	-39	100	113	57	.515	6	6	-2	12	*2	-2.0
1933	StL-A	132	496	50	145	23	6	3	79	29	18	.292	.333	.381	.714	77	-9	-19	115	136	61	.640	12	10	-2	16	*2	-0.6
1934	StL-A	144	552	54	133	19	3	2	55	28	27	.241	.279	.297	.576	47	-43	-46	104	110	45	.464	4	6	-2	11	*2	-2.8
1935	StL-A	19	62	8	13	3	0	0	5	8	4	.210	.300	.258	.558	43	-5	-6	107	106	5	.490	0	0	0	-1	2	-0.4
	Bos-A	106	400	45	104	13	2	1	39	38	22	.260	.327	.310	.637	61	-20	-24	108	106	42	.560	3	2	-0	6	*2	-1.3
	Yr	125	462	53	117	16	2	1	44	46	26	.253	.324	.303	.627	58	-25	-30	108	107	48	.550	3	2	-0	6		-1.7
1936	Bos-A	98	327	39	74	12	4	0	32	28	16	.226	.287	.287	.575	40	-30	-33	106	110	29	.482	0	0	0	-11	2	-3.3
1937	Bos-A	26	56	8	14	2	0	0	6	5	4	.250	.311	.286	.597	50	-4	-4	103	128	5	.488	0	1	-1	-0	2/S3	-0.2
Total	12	1377	5063	590	1316	210	64	22	548	327	306	.260	.306	.340	.646	64	-255	-291	105	105	532	.559	69	59	-15	119	*2/3S	-11.9
■ **JOE MELLANA**	Mellana, Joseph Peter b: 3/11/05, Oakland, Cal. d: 11/1/69, Larkspur, Cal. BR/TR, 5'10", 180 lbs. Deb: 9/21/27																											
1927	Phi-A	4	7	1	2	0	0	0	2	0	1	.286	.286	.286	.571	50	-1	-0	97	333	1	.400	0	0	0	0	/3	0.0
■ **BILL MELLOR**	Mellor, William Harpin b: 6/6/1874, Camden, N.J. d: 11/5/40, Bridgeton, R.I. BR/TR, 6', 190 lbs. Deb: 7/28/02																											
1902	Bal-A	10	36	4	13	3	0	0	5	3		.361	.410	.444	.855	136	2	2	102	105	7	.870	1			0	1	0.2
■ **PAUL MELOAN**	Meloan, Paul B. "Molly" b: 8/23/1888, Paynesville, Mo. d: 2/11/50, Taft, Cal. BR/TL, 5'10.5", 175 lbs. Deb: 8/02/10																											
1910	Chi-A	65	222	23	54	6	6	0	23	17		.243	.314	.324	.639	105	0	1	95	120	24	.589	4			0	O	-0.1
1911	Chi-A	1	3	0	1	0	0	0	0	1		.333	.333	.333	.667	89	-0	-0	97	338	0	.500	0			-1	/O	0.0
	StL-A	64	206	30	54	11	2	3	14	15		.262	.318	.379	.697	99	-2	-1	95	54	26	.671	7			-9	O	-1.4
	Yr	65	209	30	55	11	2	3	15	15		.263	.319	.378	.697	99	-2	-1	95	64	26	.669	7			-10		-1.4
Total	2	130	431	53	109	17	8	3	38	32		.253	.316	.350	.667	102	-2	0	95	90	50	.627	11			-10	O	-1.5
■ **DAVE MELTON**	Melton, David Olin b: 10/3/28, Pampa, Tex. BR/TR, 6', 185 lbs. Deb: 4/17/56																											
1956	KC-A	3	3	0	1	0	0	0	0	0	0	.333	.333	.333	.667	76	-0	-0	101	0	0	.500	0	0	0	-1	/O	0.0
1958	KC-A	9	6	0	0	0	0	0	0	0	5	.000	.000	.000	.000	-95	-2	-2	106	0	0	.000	0	0	0	-0	/O	-0.1
Total	2	12	9	0	1	0	0	0	0	0	5	.111	.111	.111	.222	-38	-2	-2	104	0	0	.125	0	0	0	-1	/O	-0.1
■ **BILL MELTON**	Melton, William Edwin b: 7/7/45, Gulfport, Miss. BR/TR, 6'2", 200 lbs. Deb: 5/04/68																											
1968	Chi-A	34	109	5	29	8	0	2	16	10	32	.266	.328	.394	.722	117	2	2	101	140	14	.651	1	1	-0	1	3	0.4
1969	Chi-A	157	556	67	142	26	2	23	87	56	106	.255	.329	.433	.762	103	7	2	108	115	79	.708	1	2	-1	4	*3O	0.7
1970	Chi-A	141	514	74	135	15	1	33	96	56	107	.263	.345	.488	.834	121	18	14	106	118	88	.815	2	4	-2	2	O3	1.2
1971	Chi-A	150	543	72	146	18	2	**33**	86	61	87	.269	.354	.492	.846	141	26	27	98	102	96	.838	3	3	-1	24	*3	4.8
1972	Chi-A	57	208	22	51	5	0	7	30	23	31	.245	.320	.370	.691	99	1	-0	106	135	26	.631	1	1	-0	6	3	0.8
1973	Chi-A	152	560	83	155	29	1	20	87	75	66	.277	.364	.439	.803	123	20	18	102	118	87	.762	4	4	-1	13	*3/D	2.8
1974	Chi-A	136	495	63	120	17	0	21	63	59	60	.242	.329	.404	.733	108	6	5	102	100	65	.679	3	2	-0	-3	*3D	0.4
1975	Chi-A	149	512	62	123	16	0	15	70	78	106	.240	.349	.359	.709	97	3	0	103	120	67	.677	5	4	-1	1	*3D	0.2
1976	Cal-A	118	341	31	71	17	3	6	42	44	53	.208	.302	.328	.631	92	-6	-3	92	124	36	.582	2	0	1	2	D13	-0.1
1977	Cle-A	50	133	17	32	11	0	0	14	17	21	.241	.336	.323	.659	83	-3	-3	98	129	13	.558	1	3	-2	0	1D3	-0.4
Total	10	1144	3971	496	1004	162	9	160	591	479	669	.253	.340	.419	.759	112	74	63	102	116	571	.737	23	24	-8	50	3/DO1	10.8
■ **BOB MELVIN**	Melvin, Robert Paul b: 10/28/61, Palo Alto, Cal. BR/TR, 6'4", 205 lbs. Deb: 5/25/85																											
1985	Det-A	41	82	10	18	4	1	0	4	3	21	.220	.247	.293	.540	44	-6	-7	106	66	6	.415	0	0	0	-1	C	-0.5
1986	SF-N	89	268	24	60	14	2	5	25	15	69	.224	.265	.347	.612	70	-13	-11	96	92	23	.512	3	2	-0	-5	C/3	-1.5
1987	SF-N	84	246	31	49	8	0	11	31	17	44	.199	.251	.366	.617	63	-15	-13	96	101	20	.514	0	4	-2	1	C/1	-0.8
1988	SF-N	92	273	23	64	13	1	8	27	13	46	.234	.269	.377	.647	89	-7	-5	94	85	26	.537	0	2	-1	-8	C/1	-1.0
Total	4	306	869	88	191	39	4	24	87	48	180	.220	.261	.357	.617	71	-40	-36	96	90	75	.522	3	8	-4	-14	C/13	-3.8
■ **MINNIE MENDOZA**	Mendoza, Cristobal Rigoberto (Carreras) b: 11/16/33, Ceiba Del Agua, Cuba BR/TR, 6', 180 lbs. Deb: 4/09/70																											
1970	Min-A	16	16	2	3	0	0	0	2	0	1	.188	.188	.188	.375	4	-2	-2	98	270	1	.231	0	0	0	-0	/32	-0.1
■ **MARIO MENDOZA**	Mendoza, Mario (Aizpuru) b: 12/26/50, Chihuahua, Mex. BR/TR, 5'11", 170 lbs. Deb: 4/26/74 C																											
1974	Pit-N	91	163	10	36	1	2	0	15	8	35	.221	.262	.252	.513	45	-12	-12	98	141	10	.381	1	1	-0	-4	S	-0.5
1975	Pit-N	56	50	8	9	1	0	0	2	3	17	.180	.226	.200	.426	19	-5	-5	99	77	2	.310	0	0	0	-0	S/3	0.0
1976	Pit-N	50	92	6	17	5	0	0	12	4	15	.185	.219	.239	.458	30	-9	-9	100	210	4	.329	0	1	-1	1	S/32	-0.3
1977	Pit-N	70	81	5	16	3	0	0	4	3	10	.198	.226	.235	.461	23	-9	-9	103	84	4	.333	0	0	0	-2	S3/P	-0.3
1978	Pit-N	57	55	5	12	1	0	1	3	2	9	.218	.283	.291	.574	58	-3	-3	105	63	5	.545	3	1	0	-1	23S	-0.1
1979	Sea-A	148	373	26	74	10	3	1	29	9	62	.198	.219	.249	.469	26	-39	-39	100	116	19	.341	3	0	1	5	*S	-1.4
1980	Sea-A	114	277	27	68	6	3	2	14	16	42	.245	.287	.310	.597	62	-14	-15	103	59	24	.482	3	4	-2	6	*S	0.0
1981	Tex-A	88	229	18	53	6	1	0	22	7	25	.231	.257	.266	.524	56	-14	-12	91	141	15	.382	2	1	0	3	S	-0.2
1982	Tex-A	12	17	1	2	0	0	0	0	0	4	.118	.118	.118	.235	-38	-3	-3	93	0	0	.125	0	0	0	0	S/D	-0.1
Total	9	686	1337	106	287	33	9	4	101	52	219	.215	.247	.262	.509	41	-108	-107	99	111	84	.397	12	8	-1	9	S/32DP	-2.9
■ **MIKE MENDOZA**	Mendoza, Michael Joseph b: 11/26/55, Inglewood, Cal. BR/TR, 6'5", 215 lbs. Deb: 9/07/79																											
1979	Hou-N	2	0	0	0	0	0	0	0	0	0	—	—	—	—	—	0	0	90	—	—	—	0	0	0	0	/P	0.0
■ **DENIS MENKE**	Menke, Denis John b: 7/21/40, Algona, Iowa BR/TR, 6', 185 lbs. Deb: 4/14/62 C																											
1962	Mil-N	50	146	12	28	3	1	2	16	16	38	.192	.280	.267	.548	48	-11	-10	99	140	11	.467	0	1	-1	-1	23/S10	-0.8
1963	Mil-N	146	518	58	121	16	4	11	50	37	106	.234	.292	.344	.636	82	-12	-12	101	102	51	.551	6	7	-2	14	S32/10	1.0
1964	Mil-N	151	505	79	143	29	5	20	65	68	77	.283	.373	.479	.852	142	26	29	97	90	91	.848	4	2	0	14	*S2/3	5.4
1965	Mil-N	71	181	16	44	13	1	4	18	18	28	.243	.315	.392	.707	94	-1	-1	104	90	22	.636	1	3	-2	1	S/13	0.3

YEAR	TM/L	G	AB	R	H	2B	3B	HR	RBI	BB	SO	AVG	OBP	SLG	PRO	/A	BR	/A	PF	CHI	RC	TA	SB	CS	SBR	FR	POS	TPR
1966	Atl-N	138	454	55	114	20	4	15	60	71	87	.251	.360	.412	.772	116	10	11	99	111	68	.742	0	7	-4	-16	*S3/1	-0.1
1967	Atl-N	129	418	37	95	14	3	7	39	65	62	.227	.335	.325	.661	86	-4	-6	104	105	48	.620	5	7	-3	-11	*S/3	-0.5
1968	Hou-N	150	542	56	135	23	6	6	56	64	81	.249	.335	.347	.682	106	5	5	99	121	65	.625	5	8	-3	-7	*2S/13	0.6
1969	Hou-N	154	553	72	149	25	5	10	90	87	87	.269	.373	.387	.760	111	12	11	102	**157**	81	.724	2	7	-4	-13	*S2/13	1.2
1970	Hou-N	154	562	82	171	26	6	13	92	82	80	.304	.398	.441	.839	133	22	27	94	132	103	.844	6	5	-1	-16	*S2/130	2.8
1971	Hou-N	146	475	57	117	26	3	1	43	59	68	.246	.332	.320	.652	92	-8	-3	93	115	51	.576	4	5	-2	-5	*13S/2	-1.6
1972	Cin-N	140	447	41	104	19	2	9	50	58	76	.233	.327	.345	.672	98	-4	-0	93	114	53	.616	0	1	-1	-5	*31	-0.8
1973	Cin-N	139	241	38	46	10	0	3	26	69	53	.191	.375	.270	.645	87	-2	0	93	141	29	.672	1	1	-0	2	*3/S21	0.0
1974	Hou-N	30	29	2	3	1	0	0	1	4	10	.103	.212	.138	.350	-1	-4	-4	98	96	1	.296	0	0	0	0	1/32S	-0.3
Total	13	1598	5071	605	1270	225	40	101	606	698	853	.250	.346	.370	.717	104	32	46	98	118	675	.689	34	54	-22	-43	S321/0	7.2
■ MIKE MENOSKY	Menosky, Michael William "Leaping Mike" b: 10/16/1894, Glen Campbell, Pa. d: 4/11/83, Detroit, Mich. BL/TR, 5'10", 163 lbs. Deb: 4/18/14																											
1914	Pit-F	68	140	26	37	4	1	2	9	16	30	.264	.340	.350	.690	104	-0	1	94	59	19	.680	5			-5	O	-0.6
1915	Pit-F	17	21	3	2	0	0	0	1	2	0	.095	.174	.095	.269	-19	-3	-3	104	180	1	.316	2			0	/O	-0.2
1916	Was-A	11	37	5	6	1	1	0	3	1	10	.162	.184	.243	.427	28	-3	-3	100	119	2	.355	1			2	/O	-0.1
1917	Was-A	114	322	46	83	12	10	1	34	45	55	.258	.359	.366	.726	132	9	12	92	101	48	.799	22			9	O	1.7
1919	Was-A	116	342	62	98	15	3	6	39	44	46	.287	.379	.401	.780	121	10	11	98	91	54	.824	13			0	*O	0.4
1920	Bos-A	141	532	80	158	24	9	3	64	65	52	.297	.383	.393	.776	110	7	10	96	99	82	.779	23	19	-5	0	*O	-0.6
1921	Bos-A	133	477	77	143	18	5	3	45	60	45	.300	.388	.377	.766	96	-0	-0	100	86	75	.768	12	6	0	-1	*O	-1.1
1922	Bos-A	126	406	61	115	16	5	3	32	40	33	.283	.355	.369	.724	92	-6	-4	96	72	55	.689	9	5	-0	8	*O	-0.2
1923	Bos-A	84	188	22	43	8	4	0	25	22	19	.229	.310	.314	.623	63	-10	-10	102	145	18	.556	3	6	-3	3	O	-1.3
Total	9	810	2465	382	685	98	38	18	252	295	290	.278	.363	.370	.734	102	3	13	97	93	355	.735	90	36		17	O	-2.0
■ ED MENSOR	Mensor, Edward "The Midget" b: 11/7/1886, Woodville, Ore. d: 4/20/70, Salem, Ore. BB , 5'6", 145 lbs. Deb: 7/15/12																											
1912	Pit-N	39	99	19	26	3	2	0	1	23	12	.263	.402	.333	.735	103	2	2	99	10	17	.904	10			-3	O	-0.1
1913	Pit-N	44	56	9	10	1	0	0	1	8	13	.179	.292	.196	.489	43	-4	-4	96	33	4	.478	2			1	O/2S	-0.2
1914	Pit-N	44	89	15	18	2	1	1	6	22	13	.202	.372	.281	.653	103	1	2	92	78	11	.718	2			1	O	0.3
Total	3	127	244	43	54	6	3	1	8	53	38	.221	.367	.283	.649	90	-2	-0	96	40	31	.732	14			-1	/OS2	0.0
■ TED MENZE	Menze, Theodore Charles b: 11/4/1897, St.Louis, Mo. d: 12/23/69, St.Louis, Mo. BR/TR, 5'9", 172 lbs. Deb: 4/23/18																											
1918	StL-N	1	3	0	0	0	0	0	0	0	2	.000	.000	.000	.000	-99	-1	-1	93	0	0	.000	0			-0	/O	0.0
■ RUDY MEOLI	Meoli, Rudolph Bartholomew b: 5/1/51, Troy, N.Y. BL/TR, 5'9", 165 lbs. Deb: 9/09/71																											
1971	Cal-A	7	3	0	0	0	0	0	0	0	1	.000	.000	.000	.000	-99	-1	-1	99	0	0	.000	0	0	0	0	H	0.0
1973	Cal-A	120	305	36	68	12	1	2	23	31	38	.223	.295	.289	.583	67	-14	-12	96	96	26	.492	2	4	-2	-4	S3/2	-0.5
1974	Cal-A	36	90	9	22	2	0	0	3	8	10	.244	.306	.267	.573	71	-4	-3	92	49	6	.453	2	4	-2	-1	3/S12	-0.4
1975	Cal-A	70	126	12	27	2	1	0	6	15	20	.214	.298	.246	.544	58	-7	-6	95	74	10	.485	3	0	1	-1	S32/D	-0.2
1978	Chi-N	47	29	10	3	0	1	0	2	6	4	.103	.257	.172	.430	20	-3	-3	110	159	2	.462	1	0	0	1	/23	-0.1
1979	Phi-N	30	73	2	13	4	1	0	6	9	15	.178	.268	.260	.529	46	-6	-5	97	125	6	.484	2	0	1	-1	S2/3	-0.2
Total	6	310	626	69	133	20	4	2	40	69	88	.212	.291	.267	.557	60	-34	-31	96	91	51	.489	10	8	-2	-6	S/32D1	-1.4
■ ORLANDO MERCADO	Mercado, Orlando (Rodriguez) b: 11/7/61, Arecibo, P.R. BR/TR, 6', 180 lbs. Deb: 9/13/82																											
1982	Sea-A	9	17	1	2	0	0	1	6	0	5	.118	.118	.294	.412	8	-2	-2	109	300	1	.333	0	0	0	-1	/C	-0.2
1983	Sea-A	66	178	10	35	11	2	1	16	14	27	.197	.259	.298	.557	53	-12	-11	100	112	14	.473	2	2	-1	-1	C	-1.0
1984	Sea-A	30	78	5	17	3	1	0	5	4	12	.218	.265	.282	.547	50	-5	-5	102	91	6	.452	1	0	0	0	C	-0.2
1986	Tex-A	46	102	7	24	1	1	1	7	6	13	.235	.284	.294	.579	62	-6	-5	96	84	7	.440	0	1	-1	-4	C	-0.6
1987	Det-A	10	22	2	3	0	0	0	1	2	0	.136	.208	.136	.345	-5	-3	-3	97	133	1	.263	0	0	0	0	C	-0.1
	LA-N	7	5	1	3	1	0	0	1	1	1	.600	.667	.800	1.467	312	1	2	92	100	3	2.500	0	0	0	0	/C	0.2
1988	Oak-A	16	24	3	3	0	0	1	1	3	8	.125	.222	.250	.472	34	-2	-2	95	44	2	.429	0	0	0	-1	C	-0.1
Total	6	184	426	29	87	16	4	4	37	30	66	.204	.261	.289	.550	52	-29	-28	99	105	33	.465	3	3	-1	-6	C	-2.0
■ WIN MERCER	Mercer, George Barclay b: 6/20/1874, Chester, W.Va. d: 1/12/03, San Francisco, Cal TR , 5'7", 140 lbs. Deb: 4/21/1894																											
1894	Was-N	52	162	27	46	5	2	2	29	9	20	.284	.322	.377	.698	71	-8	-8	98	119	23	.681	9			2	P/O	0.0
1895	Was-N	63	196	26	50	9	1	1	26	12	32	.255	.308	.327	.635	63	-10	-11	103	108	22	.589	7			-1	P/SO32	0.0
1896	Was-N	49	156	23	38	1	1	1	14	9	18	.244	.302	.282	.584	59	-10	-8	95	86	16	.559	9			1	P/O	0.0
1897	Was-N	48	135	22	43	2	5	0	19	6		.319	.357	.407	.764	102	1	0	101	101	23	.761	7			0	P	0.0
1898	Was-N	80	249	38	80	3	5	2	25	18		.321	.369	.398	.767	120	7	6	102	72	43	.781	14			0	PSO/32	0.6
1899	Was-N	108	375	73	112	6	7	1	35	32		.299	.360	.360	.720	105	1	4	96	79	56	.711	16			-21	3PO/S1	-1.5
1900	NY-N	75	248	32	73	4	0	0	27	26		.294	.361	.310	.672	91	-2	-1	97	112	34	.674	15			2	P3O/S2	0.7
1901	Was-A	51	140	26	42	7	2	0	16	23		.300	.399	.379	.777	120	5	5	99	95	26	.878	10			0	PO/1S3	0.8
1902	Det-A	35	100	8	18	2	0	0	6	6		.180	.226	.200	.426	20	-11	-10	99	99	5	.329	1			3	P	0.0
Total	9	561	1761	275	502	39	23	7	197	141	70	.285	.343	.345	.688	89	-28	-24	99	94	248	.676	88			-14	P/3OS12D	0.6
■ JOHN MERCER	Mercer, John Locke b: 1/22/1892, Taylortown, La. d: 12/22/82, Shreveport, La. 5'10.5", 155 lbs. Deb: 6/25/12																											
1912	StL-N	1	1	0	0	0	0	0	0	0	0	.000	.000	.000	.000	-99	-0	-0	100	0	0	.000	0			0	/1	0.0
■ ANDY MERCHANT	Merchant, James Anderson b: 8/30/50, Mobile, Ala. BL/TR, 5'11", 185 lbs. Deb: 9/28/75																											
1975	Bos-A	1	4	1	2	0	0	0	0	1	0	.500	.600	.500	1.100	196	1	1	109	0	1	1.500	0	0	0	0	/C	0.1
1976	Bos-A	2	2	0	0	0	0	0	0	0	2	.000	.000	.000	.000	-91	-0	-1	110	0	0	.000	0	0	0	0	/C	0.0
Total	2	3	6	1	2	0	0	0	0	1	2	.333	.429	.333	.762	110	0	0	109	0	1	.750	0	0	0	0	/C	0.1
■ ART MEREWETHER	Merewether, Arthur Francis "Merry" b: 7/1/02, E.Providence, R.I. BR/TR, 5'9.5", 155 lbs. Deb: 7/10/22																											
1922	Pit-N	1	1	0	0	0	0	0	0	0	0	.000	.000	.000	.000	-97	-0	-0	104	0	0	.000	0	0	0	0	H	0.0
■ FRED MERKLE	Merkle, Frederick Charles b: 12/20/1888, Watertown, Wis. d: 3/2/56, Daytona Beach, Fla. BR/TR, 6'1", 190 lbs. Deb: 9/21/07 C																											
1907	NY-N	15	47	0	12	1	0	0	5	1		.255	.271	.277	.547	70	-2	-2	105	146	4	.400	0			0	1	-0.1
1908	NY-N	38	41	6	11	2	1	1	7	4		.268	.333	.439	.772	142	2	2	104	128	6	.733	0			0	1/O23	0.2
1909	NY-N	79	236	15	45	9	1	0	20	16		.191	.245	.237	.482	48	-14	-15	105	130	15	.424	8			2	1/2	-1.6
1910	NY-N	144	506	75	148	35	14	4	70	44	59	.292	.353	.441	.793	138	18	21	95	106	86	.818	23			2	*1	2.2
1911	NY-N	149	541	80	153	24	10	12	84	43	60	.283	.342	.431	.773	113	9	7	102	108	95	.853	49			13	*1	1.5
1912	NY-N	129	479	82	148	22	6	11	84	42	70	.309	.374	.449	.823	120	15	13	104	121	93	.912	37			-3	*1	0.5
1913	NY-N	153	563	78	147	30	12	3	69	41	60	.261	.315	.373	.688	93	-4	-6	103	117	72	.695	35			-3	*1	-1.7
1914	NY-N	146	512	71	132	25	7	7	63	52	80	.258	.327	.375	.702	114	5	8	96	109	66	.705	23			5	*1	1.0
1915	NY-N	140	505	52	151	25	3	4	62	36	39	.299	.348	.384	.732	133	13	17	91	122	70	.683	20	15	-3	5	*1O	1.4
1916	NY-N	112	401	45	95	19	3	7	44	33	46	.237	.308	.352	.659	107	1	3	96	114	49	.650	17			-1	*1	-0.2
	Bro-N	23	69	6	16	1	0	0	2	7	4	.232	.312	.246	.558	70	-2	-2	103	47	6	.509	2			0	1/O	-0.2
	Yr	135	470	51	111	20	3	7	46	40	50	.236	.308	.336	.644	101	-1	1	97	103	55	.630	19			-1		-0.4
1917	Bro-N	2	8	1	1	1	0	0	0	0	1	.125	.125	.250	.375	13	-1	-1	104	0	0	.286	0			0	/1	0.0
	Chi-N	146	549	65	146	30	9	3	57	42	60	.266	.323	.370	.692	107	7	5	105	110	67	.650	13			-1	*1/O	0.2
	Yr	148	557	66	147	31	9	3	57	42	61	.264	.320	.368	.688	106	7	4	104	108	67	.644	13			-1		0.2
1918	Chi-N	129	482	55	143	25	5	3	65	35	36	.297	.349	.388	.737	122	14	13	102	133	71	.729	21			2	*1	1.2
1919	Chi-N	133	498	52	133	20	6	3	62	33	35	.267	.315	.349	.665	99	-1	-1	100	140	58	.627	20			-10	*1/2	-1.3
1920	Chi-N	92	330	33	94	20	4	3	38	24	32	.285	.335	.397	.732	111	4	4	99	107	43	.660	3	5	-2	-3	1/O	-0.1
1925	NY-A	7	13	4	5	1	0	0	1	1	1	.385	.429	.462	.890	131	1	1	96	56	3	1.000	1	0	0	0	/1	0.1
1926	NY-A	1	2	0	0	0	0	0	0	0	0	.000	.000	.000	.000	-99	-1	-1	99	0	0	.000	0	0	0	0	/1	0.0
Total	16	1638	5782	720	1580	290	81	61	733	454	583	.273	.331	.383	.714	110	65	66	100	117	804	.707	272	20		8	*1/O23	3.1
■ ED MERRILL	Merrill, Edward Mason b: 1860, Chicago, Ill. d: 8/18/24, Chicago, Ill. 5'11", 176 lbs. Deb: 6/20/1882																											
1882	Wor-N	2	8	0	1	0	0	0	4	0	1	.125	.125	.125	.250	-19	-1	-1	100	0	0	.143				0	/3	0.0
1884	Ind-a	55	196	14	35	3	1	0		6		.179	.207	.204	.411	38	-13	-12	96	0	8	.292				-6	2	-1.5

YEAR	TM/L	G	AB	R	H	2B	3B	HR	RBI	BB	SO	AVG	OBP	SLG	PRO	/A	BR	/A	PF	CHI	RC	TA	SB	CS	SBR	FR	POS	TPR
Total	2	57	204	14	36	3	1	0	4	6	1	.176	.204	.201	.405	36	-14	-13	97	0	9	.286				-6	/23	-1.5
■ **LLOYD MERRIMAN**	Merriman, Lloyd Archer "Citation" b: 8/2/24, Clovis, Cal. BL/TL, 6', 190 lbs. Deb: 4/24/49																											
1949	Cin-N	103	287	35	66	12	5	4	26	21	36	.230	.285	.348	.633	72	-13	-12	96	87	28	.549	2			4	O	-1.2
1950	Cin-N	92	298	44	77	15	3	2	31	30	23	.258	.330	.349	.679	75	-9	-11	105	109	36	.634	6			-7	O	-1.9
1951	Cin-N	114	359	34	87	23	2	5	36	31	34	.242	.303	.359	.662	77	-12	-12	101	97	41	.600	8	4	0	4	*O	-1.1
1954	Cin-N	73	112	12	30	8	1	0	16	23	10	.268	.406	.357	.763	97	1	1	104	157	19	.831	3	0	1	-2	O	0.0
1955	Chi-A	1	1	0	0	0	0	0	0	0	0	.000	.000	.000	.000	-99	-0	-0	101	0	0	.000	0	0	0	0	H	0.0
	Chi-N	72	145	15	31	6	1	1	8	21	21	.214	.313	.290	.603	61	-8	-8	100	72	15	.561	1	0	0	-3	O	-1.1
Total	5	455	1202	140	291	64	12	12	117	126	124	.242	.317	.345	.662	76	-40	-42	101	101	140	.620	20	4		-5	O	-5.3
■ **GEORGE MERRITT**	Merritt, George Washington b: 4/14/1880, Paterson, N.J. d: 2/21/38, Memphis, Tenn. TR , 6', 160 lbs. Deb: 9/06/01																											
1901	Pit-N	4	11	2	3	0	1	0	0	0		.273	.273	.455	.727	110	0	0	101	0	1	.625	0			-0	/P	0.0
1902	Pit-N	2	9	2	3	1	0	0	2	0		.333	.333	.444	.778	134	0	0	105	149	1	.667	0			-1	/O	0.0
1903	Pit-N	9	27	4	4	0	1	0	3	2		.148	.207	.222	.429	22	-3	-3	105	161	1	.391	1			-17	/OP	-2.1
Total	3	15	47	8	10	1	2	0	5	2		.213	.245	.319	.564	62	-2	-2	104	123	4	.486	1			-18	/OP	-2.1
■ **HERM MERRITT**	Merritt, Herman G. b: 11/12/1900, Independence, Kan. d: 5/26/27, Kansas City, Mo. BR/TR, Deb: 8/25/21																											
1921	Det-A	20	46	3	17	1	2	0	6	1	5	.370	.396	.478	.874	127	1	2	96	93	9	.862	1	0	0	-1	S	0.3
■ **JOHN MERRITT**	Merritt, John Howard b: 10/12/1894, Tupelo, Miss. d: 11/3/55, Tupelo, Miss. 5'11", 170 lbs. Deb: 9/27/13																											
1913	NY-N	1	0	0	0	0	0	0	0	0	0	—	—	—	—	—	0	0	103	—	—	—	0			-0	/O	0.0
■ **BILL MERRITT**	Merritt, William Henry b: 7/30/1870, Lowell, Mass. d: 11/17/37, Lowell, Mass. 5'7", 160 lbs. Deb: 8/08/1891																											
1891	Chi-N	11	42	4	9	1	0	0	4	2	2	.214	.250	.238	.488	41	-3	-3	106	119	3	.364	0			0	C/1	-0.2
1892	Lou-N	46	168	22	33	4	2	1	13	11	15	.196	.246	.262	.508	60	-9	-7	92	87	12	.430	3			-1	C	-0.4
1893	Bos-N	39	141	30	49	6	3	3	26	13	13	.348	.403	.496	.899	137	8	7	103	90	30	.935	3			-5	C/O	0.5
1894	Bos-N	10	26	3	6	1	0	0	6	8	0	.231	.412	.269	.681	61	-1	-2	113	236	3	.750	0			0	/CO	0.0
	Pit-N	36	109	18	30	1	2	1	18	15	7	.275	.363	.349	.712	78	-4	-3	94	121	15	.696	2			0	C/1O	-0.1
	Cin-N	29	113	17	37	6	1	1	21	9	3	.327	.387	.425	.812	97	-0	-0	100	116	21	.829	4			0	C/31O	0.0
	Yr	75	248	38	73	8	3	2	45	32	10	.294	.379	.375	.754	85	-5	-5	99	139	39	.760	6			0		-0.1
1895	Cin-N	22	79	9	14	2	0	0	12	6	5	.177	.235	.203	.438	14	-10	-11	108	210	4	.369	2			2	C/2	-0.5
	Pit-N	67	239	32	68	5	1	0	27	18	16	.285	.340	.314	.654	74	-10	-8	97	103	27	.567	2			-2	C/1	-0.3
	Yr	89	318	41	82	7	1	0	39	24	21	.258	.314	.286	.600	58	-19	-19	99	131	31	.513	4			-0		-0.8
1896	Pit-N	77	282	26	82	8	2	1	42	18	10	.291	.336	.344	.680	87	-7	-4	93	121	34	.595	3			4	C/321S	0.5
1897	Pit-N	62	209	21	55	6	1	1	26	9		.263	.297	.316	.613	65	-11	-10	98	110	21	.506	2			-4	C/1	-0.5
1899	Bos-N	1	2	0	0	0	0	0	0	0		.000	.333	.000	.333	-3	-0	-0	105	0	0	.500	0			0	/C	0.0
Total	8	400	1410	182	383	40	12	8	195	109	71	.272	.327	.334	.661	78	-48	-42	98	116	169	.592	21			-5	C/1O2S	-1.0
■ **JACK MERSON**	Merson, John Warren b: 1/17/22, Elk Ridge, Md. BR/TR, 5'11", 175 lbs. Deb: 9/14/51																											
1951	Pit-N	13	50	6	18	2	2	1	14	1	7	.360	.373	.540	.913	134	3	2	107	184	10	.875	0	0	0	0	2	0.3
1952	Pit-N	111	398	41	98	20	2	5	38	22	38	.246	.287	.344	.632	75	-15	-14	100	99	38	.516	1	1	-0	2	23	-0.8
1953	Bos-A	1	4	0	0	0	0	0	0	0	0	.000	.000	.000	.000	-92	-1	-1	109	0	0	.000	0	0	0	0	/2	0.0
Total	3	125	452	47	116	22	4	6	52	23	45	.257	.294	.363	.657	80	-13	-13	101	108	49	.561	1	1	-0	2	/23	-0.5
■ **SAM MERTES**	Mertes, Samuel Blair "Sandow" b: 8/6/1872, San Francisco, Cal. d: 3/11/45, San Francisco, Cal BR/TR, 5'10", 185 lbs. Deb: 6/30/1896																											
1896	Phi-N	37	143	20	34	4	4	0	14	8	10	.238	.288	.322	.609	61	-8	-8	102	89	19	.688	19			-1	O/S2	-0.9
1898	Chi-N	83	269	45	80	4	8	1	47	34		.297	.388	.383	.771	120	10	9	103	134	52	.899	27			3	OS/21	0.8
1899	Chi-N	117	426	83	127	13	16	9	81	33		.298	.349	.467	.816	130	13	15	96	112	87	.926	45			-6	*O/1S	0.2
1900	Chi-N	127	481	72	142	25	4	7	60	42		.295	.352	.407	.759	121	7	13	93	83	84	.814	38			-3	O1/S	0.2
1901	Chi-A	137	545	94	151	16	17	5	98	52		.277	.340	.396	.736	106	4	5	99	129	91	.797	46			-7	*2/O	-0.6
1902	Chi-A	129	497	60	140	23	7	1	79	37		.282	.331	.362	.694	98	-4	-1	95	151	77	.737	46			7	*O/SCP123	0.0
1903	NY-N	138	517	100	145	**32**	14	7	**104**	61		.280	.356	.437	.794	120	18	13	106	130	99	.892	45			12	*O/C1	1.7
1904	NY-N	148	532	83	147	28	11	4	78	54		.276	.343	.393	.736	123	18	15	105	137	90	.805	47			5	*O/S	1.5
1905	NY-N	150	551	81	154	27	17	5	108	56		.279	.346	.417	.763	128	19	18	101	**162**	100	.851	52			-7	*O	0.1
1906	NY-N	71	253	37	60	9	6	1	33	29		.237	.316	.332	.648	104	1	1	100	146	34	.694	21			-8	O	-0.8
	StL-N	53	191	20	47	7	4	0	19	16		.246	.304	.325	.629	97	-1	-1	101	118	22	.611	10			-3	O	-0.4
	Yr	124	444	57	107	16	10	1	52	45		.241	.311	.329	.640	101	1	1	100	136	56	.659	31			-10		-1.2
Total	10	1190	4405	695	1227	188	108	40	721	422	10	.279	.343	.398	.740	114	79	80	100	130	756	.811	396			-6	O2/1SC3P	1.8
■ **LENNIE MERULLO**	Merullo, Leonard Richard b: 5/5/17, Boston, Mass. BR/TR, 5'11.5", 166 lbs. Deb: 9/12/41																											
1941	Chi-N	7	17	3	6	1	0	0	1	2	0	.353	.421	.412	.833	144	1	1	94	52	3	.909	1			-0	/S	0.1
1942	Chi-N	143	515	53	132	23	3	2	37	35	45	.256	.310	.324	.634	89	-10	-7	96	81	52	.557	14			6	*S	1.0
1943	Chi-N	129	453	37	115	18	3	1	25	26	42	.254	.297	.313	.611	77	-14	-14	99	62	42	.509	7			-5	*S	-0.6
1944	Chi-N	66	193	20	41	8	1	1	16	16	18	.212	.276	.280	.556	56	-11	-11	101	101	16	.481	3			2	S/1	-0.2
1945	Chi-N	121	394	40	94	18	0	2	37	31	30	.239	.297	.299	.597	67	-18	-17	99	104	34	.502	7			-3	*S	-0.7
1946	Chi-N	65	126	14	19	8	0	0	7	11	13	.151	.219	.214	.433	25	-13	-12	94	97	6	.360	2			0	S	-0.8
1947	Chi-N	108	373	24	90	16	1	0	29	15	26	.241	.274	.290	.564	49	-27	-27	101	99	28	.439	4			9	*S	-0.9
Total	7	639	2071	191	497	92	8	6	152	136	174	.240	.291	.301	.591	68	-92	-88	98	87	180	.510	38			10	S/1	-2.1
■ **STEVE MESNER**	Mesner, Stephan Mathias b: 1/13/18, Los Angeles, Cal. d: 4/6/81, San Diego, Cal. BR/TR, 5'9", 178 lbs. Deb: 9/23/38																											
1938	Chi-N	2	4	2	1	0	0	0	0	1	1	.250	.400	.250	.650	78	-0	-0	105	0	1	.667	0			0	/S	0.0
1939	Chi-N	17	43	7	12	4	0	0	6	3	4	.279	.340	.372	.713	91	-0	-1	101	137	5	.625	0			0	S/23	0.0
1941	StL-N	24	69	8	10	1	0	0	10	5	6	.145	.203	.159	.362	3	-9	-10	110	328	2	.267	0			2	3	-0.7
1943	Cin-N	137	504	53	137	26	1	0	52	26	20	.272	.309	.327	.636	84	-11	-11	99	116	50	.520	6			3	*3	-0.9
1944	Cin-N	121	414	31	100	17	4	1	47	34	20	.242	.301	.309	.610	75	-15	-13	95	131	38	.506	1			-7	*3	-1.4
1945	Cin-N	150	540	52	137	19	1	1	52	52	18	.254	.322	.298	.620	77	-19	-15	94	117	52	.521	4			9	*3/2	-0.7
Total	6	451	1574	153	397	67	6	2	167	121	69	.252	.308	.306	.614	76	-55	-49	97	130	149	.518	11			6	3/S2	-3.7
■ **BOBBY MESSENGER**	Messenger, Charles Walter b: 3/19/1884, Bangor, Me. d: 7/10/51, Bath, Maine BB/TR, 5'10.5", 165 lbs. Deb: 8/30/09																											
1909	Chi-A	31	112	18	19	1	1	0	0	13		.170	.268	.196	.464	48	-6	-6	97	0	7	.473	7			2	O	-0.5
1910	Chi-A	9	26	7	6	0	1	0	4	4		.231	.375	.308	.683	120	1	1	95	185	4	.850	3			-0	/O	0.0
1911	Chi-A	13	17	4	2	0	1	0	0	3		.118	.250	.235	.485	37	-1	-1	97	0	1	.467	0			-1	/O	-0.1
1914	StL-A	1	2	0	0	0	0	0	0	0	0	.000	.000	.000	.000	-99	-0	-0	98	0	0	.000	0			-0	/O	0.0
Total	4	54	157	29	27	1	3	0	4	20	0	.172	.282	.217	.498	57	-7	-7	97	33	12	.523	10			1	/O	-0.6
■ **TOM MESSITT**	Messitt, Thomas John b: 7/27/1874, Frankfort, Pa. d: 9/22/34, Chicago, Ill. 5'9", 177 lbs. Deb: 9/14/1899																											
1899	Lou-N	3	11	0	1	0	0	0	0	0		.091	.091	.091	.182	-48	-2	-2	103	0	0	.100	0			0	/C	-0.1
■ **BOB METCALF**	Metcalf, Robert b: Brooklyn, N.Y. Deb: 5/27/1875																											
1875	Mut-n	7	31	1	6							.194															/3OS	
■ **SCAT METHA**	Metha, Frank Joseph b: 12/13/13, Los Angeles, Cal. d: 3/2/75, Fountain Valley, Cal. BR/TR, 5'11", 165 lbs. Deb: 4/22/40																											
1940	Det-A	26	37	6	9	0	1	0	3	2	8	.243	.282	.297	.579	45	-3	-3	111	99	3	.448	0	1	-1	-0	2/3	-0.2
■ **BUD METHENY**	Metheny, Arthur Beauregard b: 6/1/15, St.Louis, Mo. BL/TL, 5'11", 190 lbs. Deb: 4/27/43																											
1943	NY-A	103	360	51	94	18	2	9	36	39	34	.261	.333	.397	.731	118	5	7	96	79	49	.669	2	3	-1	-15	O	-1.3
1944	NY-A	137	518	72	124	16	1	14	67	56	57	.239	.316	.355	.671	86	-6	-10	106	113	59	.600	5	5	-2	-11	*O	-2.7
1945	NY-A	133	509	64	126	18	2	8	53	54	31	.248	.325	.338	.662	86	-5	-9	107	104	60	.596	5	2	0	-9	*O	-2.4
1946	NY-A	3	3	0	0	0	0	0	0	0	0	.000	.000	.000	.000	-99	-1	-1	100	0	0	.000	0	0	0	0	H	0.0
Total	4	376	1390	187	344	52	5	31	156	149	122	.247	.323	.359	.682	93	-6	-13	104	101	169	.631	12	10	-2	-35	O	-6.4

■ CATFISH METKOVICH Metkovich, George Michael b: 10/8/21, Angel's Camp, Cal. BL/TL, 6'1", 185 lbs. Deb: 7/16/43

YEAR	TM/L	G	AB	R	H	2B	3B	HR	RBI	BB	SO	AVG	OBP	SLG	PRO	/A	BR	/A	PF	CHI	RC	TA	SB	CS	SBR	FR	POS	TPR
1943	Bos-A	78	321	34	79	14	4	5	27	19	38	.246	.294	.361	.656	88	-5	-6	104	72	34	.554	1	3	-2	1	O/1	-0.8
1944	Bos-A	134	549	94	152	28	8	9	59	31	57	.277	.319	.406	.725	109	2	4	98	90	73	.662	13	4	2	-1	O1	0.0
1945	Bos-A	138	539	65	140	26	3	5	62	51	70	.260	.331	.347	.677	102	-2	1	95	118	67	.640	19	6	2	-1	1O	-0.2
1946	Bos-A	86	281	42	69	15	2	4	25	36	39	.246	.333	.356	.689	81	-2	-7	114	85	37	.668	8	3	1	-12	O	-2.3
1947	Cle-A	126	473	68	120	22	7	5	40	32	51	.254	.302	.362	.664	88	-12	-9	96	81	52	.573	5	3	-0	-3	*O/1	-1.8
1949	Chi-A	93	338	50	80	9	4	5	45	41	24	.237	.321	.331	.652	74	-14	-13	98	124	34	.568	5	4	-1	-9	O	-2.4
1951	Pit-N	120	423	51	124	21	3	3	40	28	23	.293	.338	.378	.717	87	-5	-8	107	92	54	.615	3	2	-0	-6	O1	-1.6
1952	Pit-N	125	373	41	101	18	3	7	41	32	29	.271	.335	.391	.726	101	0	0	100	96	50	.661	5	2	0	-1	1O	-0.3
1953	Pit-N	26	41	5	6	0	1	1	7	6	3	.146	.255	.268	.524	36	-4	-4	102	195	3	.486	0	0	0	0	/1O	-0.3
	Chi-N	61	124	19	29	9	0	2	12	16	10	.234	.326	.355	.681	75	-4	-4	103	94	14	.618	2	1	0	-3	O/1	-0.9
	Yr	87	165	24	35	9	1	3	19	22	13	.212	.309	.333	.642	66	-8	-8	103	126	17	.584	2	1	0	-3		-1.2
1954	Mil-N	68	123	7	34	5	1	1	15	15	15	.276	.360	.358	.717	94	-2	-1	93	126	15	.632	0	0	0	-2	1O	-0.3
Total	10	1055	3585	476	934	167	36	47	373	307	359	.261	.323	.367	.689	91	-47	-48	100	98	434	.635	61	28	2	-35	O1	-10.9

■ CHARLIE METRO Metro, Charles (born Charles Moreskonich) b: 4/28/19, Nanty-Glo, Pa. BR/TR, 5'11.5", 178 lbs. Deb: 5/04/43 MC

YEAR	TM/L	G	AB	R	H	2B	3B	HR	RBI	BB	SO	AVG	OBP	SLG	PRO	/A	BR	/A	PF	CHI	RC	TA	SB	CS	SBR	FR	POS	TPR
1943	Det-A	44	40	12	8	0	0	0	2	3	6	.200	.256	.200	.456	32	-3	-4	106	91	2	.353	1	1	-0	-2	O	-0.5
1944	Det-A	38	78	8	15	0	1	0	5	3	10	.192	.222	.218	.440	25	-8	-8	105	106	4	.323	1	0	0	-0	O	-0.8
	Phi-A	24	40	4	4	0	0	0	1	7	6	.100	.234	.100	.334	-3	-5	-5	101	90	1	.289	0	0	0	-2	O/32	-0.7
	Yr	62	118	12	19	0	1	0	6	10	16	.161	.227	.178	.405	16	-13	-13	103	102	5	.317	1	0	0	-2		-1.5
1945	Phi-A	65	200	18	42	10	1	3	15	23	33	.210	.291	.315	.606	81	-6	-5	94	75	20	.540	1	1	-0	-6	O	-1.3
Total	3	171	358	42	69	10	2	3	23	36	55	.193	.266	.257	.523	53	-22	-22	98	85	27	.447	3	2	-0	-9	O/32	-3.3

■ LENNY METZ Metz, Leonard Raymond b: 7/6/1899, Louisville, Colo. d: 2/24/53, Denver, Colo. BR/TR, 5'10.5", 170 lbs. Deb: 9/11/23

YEAR	TM/L	G	AB	R	H	2B	3B	HR	RBI	BB	SO	AVG	OBP	SLG	PRO	/A	BR	/A	PF	CHI	RC	TA	SB	CS	SBR	FR	POS	TPR
1923	Phi-N	12	37	4	8	0	0	0	3	4	3	.216	.310	.216	.526	36	-3	-4	114	132	3	.448	0	0	0	1	/2S	-0.1
1924	Phi-N	7	7	1	2	0	0	0	1	1	0	.286	.375	.286	.661	74	-0	-0	108	182	1	.600	0	0	0	0	/S	0.0
1925	Phi-N	11	14	1	0	0	0	0	0	0	2	.000	.000	.000	.000	-87	-4	-4	116	0	0	.000	0	0	0	-0	/S2	-0.3
Total	3	30	58	6	10	0	0	0	4	5	5	.172	.250	.172	.422	11	-7	-8	113	109	4	.333	0	0	0	1	/S2	-0.4

■ ROGER METZGER Metzger, Roger Henry b: 10/10/47, Fredericksburg, Tex BB/TR, 6', 165 lbs. Deb: 6/16/70

YEAR	TM/L	G	AB	R	H	2B	3B	HR	RBI	BB	SO	AVG	OBP	SLG	PRO	/A	BR	/A	PF	CHI	RC	TA	SB	CS	SBR	FR	POS	TPR
1970	Chi-N	1	2	0	0	0	0	0	0	0	0	.000	.000	.000	.000	-83	-1	-1	120	0	0	.000	0	0	0	0	/S	0.0
1971	Hou-N	150	562	64	132	14	**11**	0	26	44	50	.235	.295	.299	.594	74	-23	-18	93	67	52	.524	15	6	1	-6	*S	-0.3
1972	Hou-N	153	641	84	142	12	3	2	38	60	71	.222	.289	.259	.548	53	-35	-40	106	78	52	.485	23	9	2	5	*S	-1.6
1973	Hou-N	154	580	67	145	11	**14**	1	35	39	70	.250	.301	.322	.623	77	-22	-18	95	78	57	.532	10	4	1	-11	*S	-0.7
1974	Hou-N	143	572	66	145	18	10	0	30	37	73	.253	.299	.320	.619	75	-21	-20	98	56	54	.512	9	7	-2	-4	*S	-0.9
1975	Hou-N	127	450	54	102	7	9	2	26	41	39	.227	.291	.296	.587	67	-22	-19	94	74	40	.496	4	5	-2	10	*S	0.4
1976	Hou-N	152	481	37	101	13	8	0	29	52	63	.210	.287	.270	.557	68	-25	-17	86	86	38	.467	1	1	-0	-5	*S/2	-0.9
1977	Hou-N	97	269	24	50	9	6	0	16	32	24	.186	.272	.264	.536	48	-21	-18	93	90	20	.465	2	0	1	-18	S/2	-2.2
1978	Hou-N	45	123	11	27	4	1	0	6	12	9	.220	.289	.268	.557	60	-7	-6	95	72	8	.433	0	0	0	-8	S/2	-1.1
	SF-N	75	235	17	61	6	1	0	17	12	17	.260	.296	.294	.589	71	-11	-9	92	98	21	.497	8	1	2	-7	S	-0.7
	Yr	120	358	28	88	10	2	0	23	24	26	.246	.293	.285	.578	67	-18	-15	93	89	32	.487	8	1	2	-15		-1.8
1979	SF-N	94	259	24	65	7	8	0	31	23	31	.251	.312	.340	.652	84	-8	-5	92	140	28	.601	11	3	2	-0	S2/3	0.4
1980	SF-N	28	27	5	2	0	0	0	0	3	2	.074	.167	.074	.241	-32	-5	-5	96	0	0	.185	0	0	0	-1	S/2	-0.4
Total	11	1219	4201	453	972	101	71	5	254	355	449	.231	.293	.293	.585	67	-200	-176	95	79	372	.513	83	36	3	-45	*S/23	-8.0

■ WILLIAM METZIG Metzig, William Andrew b: 12/4/18, Ft.Dodge, Iowa BR/TR, 6'1", 180 lbs. Deb: 9/19/44

YEAR	TM/L	G	AB	R	H	2B	3B	HR	RBI	BB	SO	AVG	OBP	SLG	PRO	/A	BR	/A	PF	CHI	RC	TA	SB	CS	SBR	FR	POS	TPR
1944	Chi-A	5	16	1	2	0	0	0	1	1	4	.125	.176	.125	.301	-13	-2	-2	100	180	0	.200	0	0	0	-0	/2	-0.2

■ ALEX METZLER Metzler, Alexander b: 1/4/03, Fresno, Cal. d: 11/30/73, Fresno, Cal. BL/TR, 5'9", 167 lbs. Deb: 9/16/25

YEAR	TM/L	G	AB	R	H	2B	3B	HR	RBI	BB	SO	AVG	OBP	SLG	PRO	/A	BR	/A	PF	CHI	RC	TA	SB	CS	SBR	FR	POS	TPR
1925	Chi-N	9	38	2	7	2	0	0	2	3	7	.184	.244	.237	.481	24	-4	-4	97	68	2	.387	0	0	0	3	/O	-0.1
1926	Phi-A	20	67	8	16	3	0	0	12	7	5	.239	.311	.284	.594	47	-4	-6	118	215	6	.529	1	0	0	1	O	-0.4
1927	Chi-A	134	543	87	173	29	11	3	61	61	39	.319	.396	.429	.826	112	13	11	102	72	93	.859	15	0	5	14	*O	1.6
1928	Chi-A	139	464	71	141	18	14	3	55	77	30	.304	.410	.422	.832	120	16	17	99	94	86	.891	16	8	0	2	*O	1.1
1929	Chi-A	146	568	80	156	23	13	2	49	80	45	.275	.367	.371	.739	96	-6	-1	95	68	83	.733	11	4	1	2	*O	-0.4
1930	Chi-A	56	79	12	14	4	0	0	5	11	6	.177	.278	.228	.506	29	-8	-9	103	92	5	.433	0	2	-1	-6	O	-1.5
	StL-A	56	209	30	54	6	3	1	23	21	12	.258	.326	.330	.656	62	-10	-13	108	112	24	.609	5	1	1	-3	O	-1.5
	Yr	112	288	42	68	10	3	1	28	32	18	.236	.313	.302	.615	54	-19	-21	105	103	29	.556	5	3	-0	-10		-3.0
Total	6	560	1968	290	561	85	41	9	207	260	144	.285	.374	.384	.757	96	-4	-5	100	86	300	.760	48	15	5	13	O	-1.2

■ IRISH MEUSEL Meusel, Emil Frederick b: 6/9/1893, Oakland, Cal. d: 3/1/63, Long Beach, Cal. BR/TR, 5'11.5", 178 lbs. Deb: 10/01/14 C

YEAR	TM/L	G	AB	R	H	2B	3B	HR	RBI	BB	SO	AVG	OBP	SLG	PRO	/A	BR	/A	PF	CHI	RC	TA	SB	CS	SBR	FR	POS	TPR
1914	Was-A	1	2	0	0	0	0	0	0	0	0	.000	.000	.000	.000	-99	-0	-0	101	0	0	.000	0			-0	/O	0.0
1918	Phi-N	124	473	48	132	25	6	4	62	30	21	.279	.323	.383	.706	105	7	3	109	129	61	.674	18			9	*O/2	0.6
1919	Phi-N	135	521	65	159	26	7	5	59	15	13	.305	.327	.411	.738	117	11	9	104	102	74	.704	24			-1	*O	0.3
1920	Phi-N	138	518	75	160	27	8	14	69	32	27	.309	.349	.473	.822	124	21	16	109	99	83	.797	17	11	-2	1	*O/1	0.8
1921	Phi-N	84	343	59	121	21	7	12	51	18	17	.353	.385	.560	.945	144	22	21	102	79	72	.965	8	4	0	1	O	1.7
	NY-N	62	243	37	80	12	6	2	36	15	12	.329	.373	.453	.826	120	6	7	98	121	38	.767	5	9	-4	-1	O	0.0
	Yr	146	586	96	201	33	13	14	87	33	29	.343	.380	.515	.895	135	28	28	100	97	110	.879	13	13	-4	-0		1.7
1922	NY-N	154	617	100	204	28	17	16	132	35	33	.331	.369	.509	.877	120	20	17	104	135	112	.858	12	10	-2	-12	*O	-0.2
1923	NY-N	146	595	102	177	22	14	19	**125**	38	16	.297	.341	.477	.818	112	9	8	101	137	94	.777	8	8	-2	-12	*O	-1.0
1924	NY-N	139	549	75	170	26	9	6	102	33	18	.310	.351	.423	.774	117	4	11	91	158	81	.720	11	7	-1	-8	*O	0.0
1925	NY-N	135	516	82	169	35	8	21	111	26	19	.328	.363	.548	.912	131	20	21	99	116	100	.903	5	4	-1	-7	*O	0.9
1926	NY-N	129	449	51	131	25	10	6	65	16	18	.292	.322	.432	.754	104	-1	0	98	108	60	.689	5			-11	*O	-1.4
1927	Bro-N	42	74	7	18	3	1	1	7	11	5	.243	.341	.351	.693	83	-1	-2	103	84	9	.661	0			-1	O	-0.2
Total	11	1289	4900	701	1521	250	93	106	819	269	199	.310	.348	.464	.813	118	118	110	102	120	783	.779	113	53		-42	*O/21	1.5

■ BOB MEUSEL Meusel, Robert William "Long Bob" b: 7/19/1896, San Jose, Cal. d: 11/28/77, Downey, Cal. BR/TR, 6'3", 190 lbs. Deb: 4/14/20

YEAR	TM/L	G	AB	R	H	2B	3B	HR	RBI	BB	SO	AVG	OBP	SLG	PRO	/A	BR	/A	PF	CHI	RC	TA	SB	CS	SBR	FR	POS	TPR
1920	NY-A	119	460	75	151	40	7	11	83	20	72	.328	.359	.517	.876	127	17	15	102	110	83	.843	4	4	-1	0	O3/1	1.1
1921	NY-A	149	598	104	190	40	16	24	135	34	88	.318	.356	.559	.915	127	23	20	103	121	117	.935	17	6	2	-0	*O	0.8
1922	NY-A	121	473	61	151	26	11	16	84	40	58	.319	.376	.522	.898	130	20	19	102	108	91	.915	13	9	-2	-2	*O	0.7
1923	NY-A	132	460	59	144	29	10	9	91	31	52	.313	.359	.478	.837	114	10	8	104	126	74	.804	13	15	-5	-8	*O	-1.5
1924	NY-A	143	579	93	188	40	11	12	120	32	43	.325	.365	.494	.859	121	14	15	99	130	102	.862	26	14	-1	-8	*O/3	-0.3
1925	NY-A	156	624	101	181	34	12	**33**	**138**	54	55	.290	.348	.542	.889	128	16	20	96	102	112	.882	10	14	-5	-4	*O3	0.0
1926	NY-A	108	413	73	130	22	3	12	81	37	32	.315	.373	.470	.842	119	10	11	99	127	68	.827	16	17	-5	-8	*O	-1.0
1927	NY-A	135	516	75	174	47	9	8	103	45	58	.337	.393	.510	.902	133	24	24	100	122	100	.977	24	0	7	-5	*O	1.0
1928	NY-A	131	518	77	154	45	5	11	113	39	56	.297	.349	.467	.816	122	8	14	92	**149**	82	.775	6	9	-4	4	*O	0.7
1929	NY-A	100	391	46	102	15	3	10	57	17	42	.261	.292	.391	.683	75	-16	-16	99	109	43	.582	1	5	-3	1	O	-2.0
1930	Cin-N	113	443	62	128	30	8	10	62	26	63	.289	.330	.460	.790	98	-10	-3	90	97	65	.762	9			-3	*O	-1.2
Total	11	1407	5475	826	1693	368	95	156	1067	375	619	.309	.356	.497	.852	119	116	127	99	118	937	.840	139	93		-33	*O/31	-1.7

■ BENNY MEYER Meyer, Bernhard "Earache" b: 1/1/1888, Hematite, Mo. d: 2/6/74, Festus, Mo. BR/TR, 5'9", 170 lbs. Deb: 4/09/13 C

YEAR	TM/L	G	AB	R	H	2B	3B	HR	RBI	BB	SO	AVG	OBP	SLG	PRO	/A	BR	/A	PF	CHI	RC	TA	SB	CS	SBR	FR	POS	TPR
1913	Bro-N	38	87	12	17	0	1	1	10	10	14	.195	.278	.253	.531	50	-5	-6	104	145	8	.571	8			-2	O/C	-0.7
1914	Bal-F	143	500	76	152	18	10	5	40	71	53	.304	.391	.410	.801	131	21	22	99	70	94	.859	23			-12	*O/S	0.3
1915	Bal-F	35	120	20	29	2	0	0	5	37	0	.242	.420	.258	.679	96	4	2	107	50	16	.813	6			-3	O	-0.1
	Buf-F	93	333	37	77	8	6	1	29	40	0	.231	.314	.300	.614	82	-7	-7	100	107	35	.582	9			-7	O	-1.9
	Yr	128	453	57	106	10	6	1	34	77	0	.234	.345	.289	.634	87	-3	-4	102	92	52	.643	15			-10		-2.0
1925	Phi-N	1	1	1	1	1	0	0	0	0	0	1.000	1.000	2.000	3.000	559	1	1	116	0	2	—	0	0	0	0	/2	0.1
Total	4	310	1041	146	276	29	17	7	84	158	67	.265	.362	.346	.708	105	14	13	101	85	155	.737	46	0		-23	O/S2C	-2.3

YEAR	TM/L	G	AB	R	H	2B	3B	HR	RBI	BB	SO	AVG	OBP	SLG	PRO	/A	BR	/A	PF	CHI	RC	TA	SB	CS	SBR	FR	POS	TPR
■ DAN MEYER Meyer, Daniel Thomas b: 8/3/52, Hamilton, Ohio BL/TR, 5'11", 180 lbs. Deb: 9/14/74																												
1974	Det-A	13	50	5	10	1	1	3	7	1	1	.200	.231	.440	.671	84	-1	-1	106	90	4	.595	1	0	0	0	O	0.0
1975	Det-A	122	470	56	111	17	3	8	47	26	25	.236	.279	.336	.615	71	-18	-20	104	105	41	.513	8	3	1	-7	O1	-3.1
1976	Det-A	105	294	37	74	8	4	2	16	17	22	.252	.293	.327	.619	78	-7	-9	104	60	28	.535	10	0	3	-4	O1/D	-1.1
1977	Sea-A	159	582	75	159	24	4	22	90	43	51	.273	.324	.442	.766	111	4	7	96	113	77	.693	11	8	-2	1	*1	-0.2
1978	Sea-A	123	444	38	101	18	1	8	56	24	39	.227	.267	.327	.594	65	-21	-22	102	133	38	.499	7	3	0	2	*1/OD	-2.5
1979	Sea-A	144	525	72	146	21	7	20	74	29	35	.278	.321	.459	.780	107	4	4	100	96	72	.714	11	7	-1	-7	*3O1	-0.3
1980	Sea-A	146	531	56	146	25	6	11	71	31	42	.275	.316	.407	.723	94	-4	-6	103	113	66	.640	8	4	0	-13	*O/31D	-2.1
1981	Sea-A	83	252	26	66	10	1	3	22	10	16	.262	.293	.345	.638	84	-6	-6	100	90	24	.523	4	3	-1	-1	3O/1D	-0.7
1982	Oak-A	120	383	28	92	17	3	8	59	18	33	.240	.274	.363	.637	77	-15	-12	95	145	37	.530	1	1	-0	-3	1DO	-1.7
1983	Oak-A	69	169	15	32	9	0	1	13	19	11	.189	.271	.260	.532	49	-12	-11	96	108	11	.434	0	0	0	-6	1DO/3	-1.8
1984	Oak-A	20	22	1	7	3	1	0	4	0	2	.318	.318	.545	.864	146	1	1	92	133	3	.706	0	0	0	-0	/1D	0.1
1985	Oak-A	14	12	2	0	0	0	0	0	1	0	.000	.077	.000	.077	-83	-3	-3	93	0	0	.077	0	0	0	-0	/3OD	-0.2
Total	12	1118	3734	411	944	153	31	86	459	219	277	.253	.296	.379	.675	86	-78	-78	100	109	402	.605	61	29	1	-38	1O3/D	-13.6
■ GEORGE MEYER Meyer, George Francis b: 8/3/09, Chicago, Ill. BR/TR, 5'9", 160 lbs. Deb: 9/03/38																												
1938	Chi-A	24	81	10	24	2	2	0	9	11	17	.296	.387	.370	.757	93	-1	-0	98	103	13	.776	3	1	0	-2	2	0.0
■ DUTCH MEYER Meyer, Lambert Dalton b: 10/6/15, Waco, Tex. BR/TR, 5'10.5", 181 lbs. Deb: 6/23/37																												
1937	Chi-N	1	0	0	0	0	0	0	0	0	0	—	—	—	—	—	0	0	103	—	—	—	0			0	R	0.0
1940	Det-A	23	58	12	15	3	0	0	6	4	10	.259	.317	.310	.628	57	-3	-4	111	120	7	.581	2	0	1	-1	2	-0.3
1941	Det-A	46	153	12	29	9	1	1	14	8	13	.190	.230	.281	.511	32	-15	-16	106	108	10	.406	1	1	-0	1	2	-1.1
1942	Det-A	14	52	5	17	3	0	2	9	4	4	.327	.386	.500	.886	131	3	2	113	101	9	.816	0	1	-1	1	2	0.4
1945	Cle-A	130	524	71	153	29	8	7	48	40	32	.292	.342	.418	.760	122	12	12	99	70	74	.674	2	4	-2	-26	*2	-1.4
1946	Cle-A	72	207	13	48	5	3	0	16	26	16	.232	.321	.285	.606	79	-8	-5	89	103	20	.518	0	1	-1	-6	2	-0.5
Total	6	286	994	113	262	49	12	10	93	82	75	.264	.322	.367	.689	94	-11	-10	99	87	132	.611	5	7		-31	2	-2.9
■ LEE MEYER Meyer, Lee TR , Deb: 09																												
1909	Bro-N	7	23	1	3	0	0	0	0	2		.130	.200	.130	.330	3	-3	-2	99	0	1	.250	0			-2	/S	-0.4
■ SCOTT MEYER Meyer, Scott William b: 8/19/57, Evergreen Park, Ill BR/TR, 6'1", 195 lbs. Deb: 9/10/78																												
1978	Oak-A	8	9	1	1	1	0	0	0	0	4	.111	.111	.222	.333	-8	-1	-1	101	0	0	.250	0	0	0	-0	/C	0.0
■ JOEY MEYER Meyer, Tanner Joe b: 5/10/62, Honolulu, Hawaii BR/TR, 6'3", 250 lbs. Deb: 4/04/88																												
1988	Mil-A	103	327	22	86	18	0	11	45	23	88	.263	.313	.419	.732	100	1	-1	103	105	41	.641	0	1	-1	2	D1	0.0
■ BILLY MEYER Meyer, William Adam b: 1/14/1892, Knoxville, Tenn. d: 3/31/57, Knoxville, Tenn. BR/TR, 5'9.5", 170 lbs. Deb: 9/06/13 M																												
1913	Chi-A	1	1	0	1	0	0	0	0	0	0	1.000	1.000	1.000	2.000	511	0	0	95	0	1	—	0			0	/C	0.1
1916	Phi-A	50	138	6	32	2	2	1	12	8	11	.232	.274	.297	.571	73	-5	-5	98	97	13	.491	3			10	C	0.8
1917	Phi-A	62	162	9	38	5	1	0	9	7	14	.235	.271	.278	.548	72	-7	-6	94	72	12	.427	0			1	C	0.0
Total	3	113	301	15	71	7	3	1	21	15	25	.236	.274	.289	.563	74	-11	-10	96	83	25	.461	3			11	C	0.9
■ LEVI MEYERLE Meyerle, Levi Samuel "Long Levi" b: 7/1845, Philadelphia, Pa. d: 11/4/21, Philadelphia, Pa. BR/TR, 6'1", 177 lbs. Deb: 5/20/1871																												
1871	Ath-n	26	132	45	65							.492															*3	
1872	Ath-n	27	154	30	49							.318															O/S3	
1873	Phi-n	48	248	52	82							.331															*3	
1874	Chi-n	52	263	63	97							.369															23/OS	
1875	Phi-n	68	296	55	93							.314															231	
1876	Phi-N	55	256	46	87	12	8	0	34	3	2	.340	.347	.449	.797	165	16	17	99	88	41	.698				-2	*3/O2P	1.2
1877	Cin-N	27	107	11	35	7	2	0	15	0	4	.327	.327	.430	.757	167	4	7	82	113	15	.639				-4	S2/O	0.3
1884	Phi-U	3	11	0	1	1	0	0		0		.091	.091	.182	.273	-11	-1	-1	93	0	0	.200	0			0	/1O	0.0
Total	5 n	221	1093	245	386							.353															/1O	
Total	3	85	374	57	123	20	10	0	49	3	6	.329	.334	.436	.770	160	19	23	94	93	57	.661	0			-5	3/2OS1P	1.5
■ HENRY MEYERS Meyers, Henry L. b: 1860, Philadelphia, Pa. d: 6/28/1898, Harrisburg, Pa. Deb: 8/30/1890																												
1890	Phi-a	5	19	2	3	0	0	0		1		.158	.238	.158	.396	19	-2	-2	97	0	1	.438	2			0	/3	-0.1
■ CHIEF MEYERS Meyers, John Tortes b: 7/29/1880, Riverside, Cal. d: 7/25/71, San Bernardino, Cal. BR/TR, 5'11", 194 lbs. Deb: 09																												
1909	NY-N	90	220	15	61	10	5	1	30	22		.277	.359	.382	.741	125	8	7	105	125	30	.723	3			-1	C	1.1
1910	NY-N	127	365	25	104	18	0	1	62	40	18	.285	.362	.342	.704	111	4	6	95	169	48	.667	5			-15	*C	-0.3
1911	NY-N	133	391	48	130	18	9	1	61	25	33	.332	.392	.432	.824	127	16	15	102	120	69	.820	7			-34	*C	-1.0
1912	NY-N	126	371	60	133	16	5	6	54	47	20	.358	.441	.477	.918	146	28	26	104	93	82	1.008	8			-31	*C	0.2
1913	NY-N	120	378	37	118	18	5	3	47	37	22	.312	.387	.410	.797	124	15	13	103	104	60	.800	7			-14	*C	0.7
1914	NY-N	134	381	33	109	13	5	1	55	34	25	.286	.357	.354	.711	117	6	8	96	144	48	.665	4			-17	*C	-0.4
1915	NY-N	110	289	24	67	10	5	1	26	26	18	.232	.311	.311	.622	97	-4	-1	91	107	28	.562	4	4	-1	-11	C	-0.7
1916	Bro-N	80	239	21	59	10	3	0	21	26	15	.247	.336	.314	.650	97	1	0	103	111	26	.606	2			2	C	0.7
1917	Bro-N	47	132	8	28	3	0	0	3	13	7	.212	.283	.235	.518	57	-6	-6	104	37	10	.462	4			-0	C	-0.4
	Bos-N	25	68	5	17	4	4	0	4	4	4	.250	.311	.426	.737	130	2	2	96	53	9	.686	0			1	C	0.5
	Yr	72	200	13	45	7	4	0	7	17	11	.225	.292	.300	.592	81	-4	-4	101	43	18	.535	4			1		0.1
Total	9	992	2834	276	826	120	41	14	363	274	162	.291	.367	.378	.744	118	70	70	100	117	409	.721	44	4		-120	C	0.4
■ LOU MEYERS Meyers, Lewis Henry "Crazy Horse" b: 12/9/1859, Cincinnati, Ohio d: 11/30/20, Cincinnati, Ohio BR/TR, 5'11", 165 lbs. Deb: 5/10/1884																												
1884	Cin-U	2	3	1	0	0	0	0		1		.000	.250	.000	.250	-8	-0	-0	108	0	0	.333	0			0	/CO	0.0
■ MICKEY MICELOTTA Micelotta, Robert Peter b: 10/20/28, Corona, N.Y. BR/TR, 5'11", 185 lbs. Deb: 4/20/54																												
1954	Phi-N	13	3	2	0	0	0	0	0	1	1	.000	.250	.000	.250	-29	-1	-1	99	0	0	.333	0	0	0	0	/S	0.0
1955	Phi-N	4	4	0	0	0	0	0	0	0	0	.000	.000	.000	.000	-98	-1	-1	102	0	0	.000	0	0	0	-0	/S	0.0
Total	2	17	7	2	0	0	0	0	0	1	1	.000	.125	.000	.125	-63	-2	-2	100	0	0	.143	0	0	0	-0	/S	0.0
■ GENE MICHAEL Michael, Eugene Richard "Stick" b: 6/2/38, Kent, Ohio BB/TR, 6'2", 183 lbs. Deb: 7/15/66 MC																												
1966	Pit-N	30	33	9	5	2	1	0	2	0	7	.152	.152	.273	.424	15	-4	-4	101	93	1	.310	0	0	0	1	/S23	-0.1
1967	LA-N	98	223	20	45	3	1	0	7	11	30	.202	.246	.224	.470	40	-18	-15	88	58	12	.346	1	3	-2	1	S	-0.6
1968	NY-A	61	116	8	23	3	0	1	8	2	23	.198	.218	.250	.468	41	-8	-8	101	107	6	.361	3	2	-0	2	S/P	-0.4
1969	NY-A	119	412	41	112	24	4	2	31	43	56	.272	.342	.364	.706	102	-1	1	95	81	52	.642	7	4	-0	-1	*S	0.6
1970	NY-A	134	435	42	93	10	1	2	38	50	93	.214	.295	.255	.550	57	-27	-23	92	131	35	.467	3	1	0	3	*S/32	-0.8
1971	NY-A	139	456	36	102	15	0	3	35	48	64	.224	.302	.276	.578	67	-20	-19	97	106	37	.481	3	3	-1	22	*S	1.8
1972	NY-A	126	391	29	91	7	4	1	32	32	45	.233	.292	.279	.571	76	-14	-11	92	119	31	.466	4	2	0	23	*S	2.8
1973	NY-A	129	418	30	94	11	1	3	47	26	51	.225	.270	.278	.548	54	-25	-26	101	148	29	.422	1	3	-2	5	*S	-0.4
1974	NY-A	81	177	19	46	9	0	0	13	14	24	.260	.314	.311	.625	84	-4	-3	96	93	17	.504	0	0	0	-1	2S/3	0.0
1975	Det-A	56	145	15	31	2	0	3	13	8	28	.214	.255	.290	.545	52	-9	-10	104	98	11	.427	0	0	0	-2	S/23	-0.6
Total	10	973	2806	249	642	86	12	15	226	234	421	.229	.290	.284	.574	67	-131	-117	96	109	231	.486	22	18	-4	53	S/23P	2.3
■ CASS MICHAELS Michaels, Casimir Eugene (a.k.a. real name of Kwietniewski) b: 3/4/26, Detroit, Mich. d: 11/12/82, Grosse Pointe, Mich. BR/TR, 5'11", 175 lbs. Deb: 8/19/43																												
1943	Chi-A	2	7	0	0	0	0	0	0	0	0	.000	.000	.000	.000	-99	-2	-2	101	0	0	.000	0	0	0	0	/3	-0.1
1944	Chi-A	27	68	4	12	4	1	0	5	2	5	.176	.200	.265	.465	32	-6	-6	100	100	4	.351	0	0	0	-0	S/3	-0.5
1945	Chi-A	129	445	47	109	8	5	2	54	37	28	.245	.307	.299	.606	80	-13	-11	95	143	41	.508	8	7	-2	8	*S/2	0.0
1946	Chi-A	91	291	37	75	8	0	1	22	29	36	.258	.333	.296	.629	79	-8	-7	97	94	32	.571	9	3	1	3	23/S	0.3
1947	Chi-A	110	355	31	97	15	4	3	34	39	28	.273	.350	.363	.714	102	-0	1	97	91	45	.653	10	5	0	12	23/S	1.8
1948	Chi-A	145	484	47	120	12	6	5	56	69	42	.248	.344	.329	.673	83	-13	-10	95	111	60	.631	8	2	1	9	S2/O	0.2
1949	Chi-A	154	561	73	173	27	9	6	83	101	50	.308	.417	.421	.837	125	21	23	98	119	102	.831	5	7	-3	11	*2	3.2
1950	Chi-A	36	138	21	43	6	3	4	19	13	8	.312	.375	.486	.861	122	3	4	97	80	25	.810	0	0	0	-1	2	0.5

YEAR	TM/L	G	AB	R	H	2B	3B	HR	RBI	BB	SO	AVG	OBP	SLG	PRO	/A	BR	/A	PF	CHI	RC	TA	SB	CS	SBR	FR	POS	TPR
	Was-A	106	388	48	97	8	4	4	47	55	39	.250	.345	.322	.667	72	-16	-15	99	125	45	.600	2	3	-1	4	*2	-0.4
	Yr	142	526	69	140	14	7	8	66	68	47	.266	.352	.365	.717	85	-12	-11	99	114	72	.660	2	3	-1	3		0.1
1951	Was-A	138	485	59	125	20	4	4	45	61	41	.258	.342	.340	.682	89	-9	-6	95	93	58	.606	1	1	-0	-19	*2	-1.9
1952	Was-A	22	86	10	20	4	1	1	7	7	15	.233	.290	.337	.628	74	-3	-3	100	86	7	.507	0	0	0	-1	2	-0.3
	StL-A	55	166	21	44	8	2	3	25	23	16	.265	.354	.392	.746	111	2	2	97	126	25	.712	1	0	0	3	3/2	0.6
	Phi-A	55	200	22	50	4	5	1	18	23	11	.250	.330	.335	.665	77	-4	-6	111	98	24	.606	3	0	1	-8	2	-1.0
	Yr	132	452	53	114	16	8	5	50	53	42	.252	.332	.356	.688	89	-5	-7	103	109	59	.638	4	0	1	-6		-0.7
1953	Phi-A	117	411	53	103	10	0	12	42	51	56	.251	.335	.363	.697	86	-6	-8	102	86	55	.662	7	0	**2**	-9	*2	-0.8
1954	Chi-A	101	282	35	74	13	2	7	44	56	31	.262	.392	.397	.789	112	9	7	104	125	50	.850	10	4	1	2	3/2	0.5
Total	12	1288	4367	508	1142	147	46	53	501	566	406	.262	.349	.353	.702	92	-46	-37	98	109	572	.673	64	32	0	13	2S3/O	2.1
■ **RALPH MICHAELS**	Michaels, Ralph Joseph b: 5/3/02, Etna, Pa. BR/TR, 5'10.5", 178 lbs. Deb: 4/16/24																											
1924	Chi-N	8	11	0	4	0	0	0	2	0	1	.364	.364	.364	.727	94	-0	-0	101	182	1	.571	0	0	0	0	/S	0.0
1925	Chi-N	22	50	10	14	1	0	0	6	6	9	.280	.357	.300	.657	72	-2	-2	97	142	6	.611	1	0	0	0	3/12S	0.0
1926	Chi-N	2	0	1	0	0	0	0	0	0	0	—	—	—	—	—	0	0	106	—	—	—	0			0	H	0.0
Total	3	32	61	11	18	1	0	0	8	6	10	.295	.358	.311	.670	76	-2	-2	98	149	13	.605	1	0		0	/3S21	0.0
■ **ED MICKELSON**	Mickelson, Edward Allen b: 9/9/26, Ottawa, Ill. BR/TR, 6'3", 205 lbs. Deb: 9/18/50																											
1950	StL-N	5	10	1	1	0	0	0	0	2	3	.100	.250	.100	.350	-4	-1	-2	103	0	0	.300	0			0	/1	-0.1
1953	StL-A	7	15	1	2	1	0	0	2	2	6	.133	.235	.200	.435	17	-2	-2	107	247	1	.357	0	0	0	0	/1	-0.1
1957	Chi-N	6	12	0	0	0	0	0	1	0	4	.000	.000	.000	.000	-99	-3	-3	96	0	0	.000	0	0	0	0	/1	-0.3
Total	3	18	37	2	3	1	0	0	3	4	13	.081	.171	.108	.279	-23	-7	-7	103	102	1	.235	0	0		0	/1	-0.5
■ **EZRA MIDKIFF**	Midkiff, Ezra Millington Ezr " b: 11/13/1882, Salt Rock, W.Va. d: 3/20/57, Huntington, W.Va. BL/TR, 5'10", 180 lbs. Deb: 09																											
1909	Cin-N	1	2	0	0	0	0	0	0	0		.000	.000	.000	.000	-99	-0	-0	94	0	0	.000	0			0	/3	0.0
1912	NY-A	21	86	9	21	1	0	0	9	7		.244	.301	.256	.557	59	-4	-5	101	118	8	.508	4			-1	3	-0.5
1913	NY-A	83	284	22	56	9	1	0	14	12	33	.197	.232	.236	.468	37	-23	-23	101	76	17	.390	9			3	3/S2	-1.9
Total	3	105	372	31	77	10	1	0	23	19	33	.207	.247	.239	.487	41	-28	-28	101	85	25	.414	13			2	/3S2	-2.4
■ **ED MIERKOWICZ**	Mierkowicz, Edward Frank "Butch" or "Mouse" b: 3/6/24, Wyandotte, Mich. BR/TR, 6'4", 205 lbs. Deb: 8/31/45																											
1945	Det-A	10	15	0	2	2	0	0	2	1	3	.133	.188	.267	.454	29	-1	-1	106	181	1	.385	0	0	0	-1	/O	-0.2
1947	Det-A	21	42	6	8	1	0	1	1	1	12	.190	.209	.286	.495	35	-4	-4	104	24	2	.389	1	0	0	-2	O	-0.5
1948	Det-A	3	5	0	1	0	0	0	1	2	2	.200	.429	.200	.629	73	-0	-0	96	338	0	.600	0	0	0	0	/O	0.0
1950	StL-N	1	1	0	0	0	0	0	0	0	1	.000	.000	.000	.000	-97	-0	-0	103	0	0	.000	0			0	H	0.0
Total	4	35	63	6	11	3	0	1	4	4	18	.175	.224	.270	.494	36	-5	-6	104	94	3	.423	1	0		-3	/O	-0.7
■ **LARRY MIGGINS**	Miggins, Lawrence Edward "Irish" b: 8/20/25, Bronx, N.Y. BR/TR, 6'4", 198 lbs. Deb: 10/03/48																											
1948	StL-N	1	1	1	0	0	0	0	0	0	0	.000	.000	.000	.000	-99	-0	-0	101	0	0	.000	0			0	H	0.0
1952	StL-N	42	96	7	22	5	1	2	10	3	19	.229	.253	.365	.617	71	-4	-4	98	95	9	.507	0	1	-1	-6	O/1	-1.1
Total	2	43	97	8	22	5	1	2	10	3	19	.227	.250	.361	.611	69	-5	-4	98	94	9	.500	0	1		-6	/O1	-1.1
■ **JOHN MIHALIC**	Mihalic, John Michael b: 11/13/11, Cleveland, Ohio d: 4/24/87, Ft.Oglethorpe, Ga. BR/TR, 5'11", 172 lbs. Deb: 9/18/35																											
1935	Was-A	6	22	4	5	3	0	0	6	2	3	.227	.292	.364	.655	75	-1	-1	92	255	3	.647	1	0	0	0	/S	0.0
1936	Was-A	25	88	15	21	2	1	0	8	14	14	.239	.343	.284	.627	58	-6	-5	98	106	10	.603	2	1	0	1	2	-0.2
1937	Was-A	38	107	13	27	5	2	0	8	17	9	.252	.355	.336	.691	80	-4	-3	94	76	14	.679	2	1	0	-2	2/S	-0.1
Total	3	69	217	32	53	10	3	0	22	33	26	.244	.344	.318	.662	70	-10	-9	95	105	26	.645	5	2	0	-1	/2S	-0.3
■ **EDDIE MIKSIS**	Miksis, Edward Thomas b: 9/11/26, Burlington, N.J. BR/TR, 6'0.5", 185 lbs. Deb: 6/17/44																											
1944	Bro-N	26	91	12	20	2	0	0	11	6	11	.220	.268	.242	.510	45	-7	-7	99	179	6	.444	4			-5	3S	-0.9
1946	Bro-N	23	48	3	7	0	0	0	5	3	3	.146	.212	.146	.357	2	-6	-6	103	267	1	.256	0			-0	3/2	-0.6
1947	Bro-N	45	86	18	23	1	0	4	10	9	8	.267	.337	.419	.755	95	-0	-1	105	77	12	.692	0			1	2O/3S	0.1
1948	Bro-N	86	221	28	47	7	1	2	16	19	27	.213	.278	.281	.559	49	-15	-16	104	88	19	.497	5			-0	23/S	-1.2
1949	Bro-N	50	113	17	25	5	0	1	6	7	8	.221	.267	.292	.559	49	-8	-8	102	63	8	.467	3			1	3/S21	-0.5
1950	Bro-N	51	76	13	19	2	1	2	10	5	10	.250	.296	.382	.678	72	-3	-3	107	110	8	.627	3			2	2S/3	0.0
1951	Bro-N	19	10	6	2	1	0	0	0	1	2	.200	.333	.300	.633	73	-0	-0	98	0	1	.625	0	0	0	0	/32	0.0
	Chi-N	102	421	48	112	13	3	4	35	33	36	.266	.319	.340	.659	80	-13	-12	97	77	46	.577	11	5	0	1	*2	-0.6
	Yr	121	431	54	114	14	3	4	35	34	38	.265	.320	.339	.658	79	-14	-12	97	65	48	.578	11	5	0	1		-0.6
1952	Chi-N	93	383	44	89	20	1	2	19	20	32	.232	.272	.305	.578	58	-21	-23	103	58	31	.466	4	4	-1	-13	2S	-3.5
1953	Chi-N	142	577	61	145	17	6	8	39	33	59	.251	.293	.343	.636	63	-30	-32	103	66	57	.540	13	4	2	-19	2S	-4.0
1954	Chi-N	38	99	9	20	3	0	2	3	3	9	.202	.225	.293	.518	34	-10	-10	101	34	6	.407	1	0	0	-0	2/3O	-0.8
1955	Chi-N	131	481	52	113	14	2	9	41	32	55	.235	.283	.328	.611	62	-27	-27	100	92	42	.501	3	6	-3	-6	*O3	-3.7
1956	Chi-N	114	356	54	85	10	3	9	27	32	40	.239	.303	.360	.663	78	-11	-11	99	74	38	.583	4	2	0	-7	3O2/S	-1.7
1957	StL-N	49	38	3	8	0	0	1	2	7	7	.211	.333	.289	.623	69	-1	-1	101	59	4	.563	0	0	0	-11	O	-1.3
	Bal-A	1	1	0	0	0	0	0	0	0	0	.000	.000	.000	.000	-99	-0	-0	93	0	0	.000	0	0	0	0	H	0.0
1958	Bal-A	3	2	0	0	0	0	0	0	0	1	.000	.000	.000	.000	-99	-1	-1	94	0	0	.000	0	0	0	0	/S	0.0
	Cin-N	69	50	15	7	0	0	0	4	5	5	.140	.218	.140	.358	-2	-7	-8	107	236	2	.283	1	1	-0	-10	O3/2S1	-1.8
Total	14	1042	3053	383	722	95	17	44	228	215	313	.236	.288	.322	.610	62	-161	-166	101	82	283	.533	52	22		-68	2O3S/1	-20.5
■ **HORACE MILAN**	Milan, Horace Robert b: 4/7/1894, Linden, Tenn. d: 6/29/55, Texarkana, Ark. BR/TR, 5'9", 175 lbs. Deb: 8/29/15																											
1915	Was-A	11	27	6	11	1	1	0	7	8	7	.407	.543	.519	1.061	215	5	5	101	170	9	1.500	2			-2	O	0.2
1917	Was-A	31	73	8	21	3	1	0	9	4	9	.288	.342	.356	.698	122	1	2	92	124	10	.692	4			-4	O	-0.3
Total	2	42	100	14	32	4	2	0	16	12	16	.320	.404	.400	.804	152	6	6	95	138	18	.882	6			-6	/O	-0.1
■ **CLYDE MILAN**	Milan, Jesse Clyde "Deerfoot" b: 3/25/1887, Linden, Tenn. d: 3/3/53, Orlando, Fla. BL/TR, 5'9", 168 lbs. Deb: 8/19/07 MC																											
1907	Was-A	48	183	22	51	3	3	0	9	8		.279	.309	.328	.637	117	1	3	90	57	22	.576	8			1	O	0.2
1908	Was-A	130	485	55	116	10	12	1	32	38		.239	.294	.315	.610	105	0	3	95	74	51	.596	29			-12	*O	-1.6
1909	Was-A	130	400	36	80	12	4	1	15	31		.200	.268	.257	.525	73	-15	-11	90	55	29	.469	10			2	*O	-1.4
1910	Was-A	142	531	89	148	17	6	0	16	71		.279	.379	.333	.713	122	18	18	101	29	83	.802	44			4	*O	1.6
1911	Was-A	154	616	109	194	24	8	3	35	74		.315	.395	.394	.789	125	19	22	97	41	117	.905	58			5	*O	1.5
1912	Was-A	154	601	105	184	19	11	1	79	63		.306	.377	.379	.756	117	14	15	99	101	117	.921	**88**			3	*O	0.8
1913	Was-A	154	579	92	174	18	9	3	54	58	25	.301	.367	.378	.745	112	14	9	106	74	101	.874	**74**			-9	*O	-0.7
1914	Was-A	115	437	63	129	19	11	1	39	32	26	.295	.346	.396	.742	122	11	10	101	88	63	.745	38	21	-1	-8	*O	-0.6
1915	Was-A	153	573	83	165	13	7	2	66	53	32	.288	.353	.346	.699	108	7	6	101	106	77	.693	40	19	1	-3	*O	-0.4
1916	Was-A	150	565	58	154	14	3	1	45	56	31	.273	.343	.313	.657	97	-1	-1	100	86	66	.630	34	21	-2	12	*O	0.3
1917	Was-A	155	579	60	170	15	4	0	48	58	26	.294	.364	.333	.697	122	10	16	92	86	76	.677	20			-8	*O	-0.1
1918	Was-A	128	503	56	146	18	5	0	56	36	14	.290	.344	.346	.690	104	4	2	104	124	65	.675	26			-2	*O	-0.6
1919	Was-A	88	321	43	92	12	6	0	37	40	16	.287	.371	.361	.732	108	4	5	98	122	46	.742	11			-6	O	-0.7
1920	Was-A	126	506	70	163	22	5	3	41	28	12	.322	.364	.403	.767	108	2	5	95	65	72	.696	10	12	-4	10	*O	0.0
1921	Was-A	113	406	55	117	19	11	1	40	37	13	.288	.351	.397	.747	91	-6	-5	99	85	57	.694	4	5	-2	2	O	-1.1
1922	Was-A	42	74	8	17	5	0	0	5	2	2	.230	.250	.297	.547	46	-6	-6	92	81	5	.421	0	0	0	0	OM	-0.5
Total	16	1982	7359	1004	2100	240	105	17	617	685	197	.285	.352	.353	.705	109	76	91	98	79	1048	.721	494	78		-9	*O	-3.3
■ **LARRY MILBOURNE**	Milbourne, Lawrence William b: 2/14/51, Port Norris, N.J. BB/TR, 6', 161 lbs. Deb: 4/06/74																											
1974	Hou-N	112	136	31	38	2	1	0	9	10	14	.279	.329	.309	.638	81	-4	-3	98	83	15	.574	6	2	1	0	2/SO	0.3
1975	Hou-N	73	151	17	32	1	2	1	9	6	14	.212	.247	.265	.512	45	-12	-11	94	81	9	.384	1	2	-1	3	2S	-0.4
1976	Hou-N	59	145	22	36	4	0	0	7	14	10	.248	.319	.276	.595	81	-5	-3	86	67	14	.540	6	1	1	3	2	0.3
1977	Sea-A	86	242	24	53	10	0	2	21	6	20	.219	.244	.285	.529	45	-19	-18	96	111	17	.412	3	1	0	5	2S/3D	-0.3
1978	Sea-A	93	234	31	53	6	2	2	20	9	6	.226	.255	.295	.550	53	-14	-15	102	105	15	.426	5	7	-3	2	3S2D	-1.3
1979	Sea-A	123	356	40	99	13	4	2	26	19	20	.278	.315	.354	.669	80	-10	-10	100	76	38	.562	5	3	-0	6	S23	0.5

YEAR	TM/L	G	AB	R	H	2B	3B	HR	RBI	BB	SO	AVG	OBP	SLG	PRO	/A	BR	/A	PF	CHI	RC	TA	SB	CS	SBR	FR	POS	TPR
1980	Sea-A	106	258	31	68	6	6	0	26	19	13	.264	.317	.333	.650	76	-8	-9	103	118	26	.554	7	6	-2	3	2S/3D	-0.1
1981	NY-A	61	163	24	51	7	2	1	12	9	14	.313	.353	.399	.751	116	3	3	100	69	23	.670	2	0	1	-1	S2/3D	0.6
1982	NY-A	14	27	2	4	1	0	0	0	1	4	.148	.179	.185	.364	0	-4	-4	96	0	1	.250	0	1	-1	0	/S23	-0.2
	Min-A	29	98	9	23	1	1	0	1	7	8	.235	.286	.265	.551	52	-6	-6	100	15	7	.420	1	1	-0	-3	2	-0.7
	Cle-A	82	291	29	80	11	4	2	25	12	20	.275	.308	.361	.669	83	-7	-7	100	90	29	.535	2	5	-2	-1	2S/3D	-0.4
	Yr	125	416	40	107	13	5	2	26	20	32	.257	.295	.327	.621	71	-17	-17	100	63	37	.494	3	7	-3	-4		-1.3
1983	Phi-N	41	66	3	16	0	1	0	4	4	7	.242	.286	.273	.558	55	-4	-4	101	88	5	.444	2	1	0	2	2/S3	0.0
	NY-A	31	70	5	14	4	0	0	2	5	10	.200	.263	.257	.520	44	-5	-5	99	43	5	.439	1	1	-0	1	2/S3	-0.3
1984	Sea-A	79	211	22	56	5	1	1	22	12	16	.265	.305	.313	.618	70	-8	-9	102	127	19	.476	0	2	-1	-2	32/SD	-1.0
Total	11	989	2448	290	623	71	24	11	184	133	176	.254	.295	.317	.612	70	-103	-100	99	88	222	.514	41	33	-8	18	2S3/DO	-3.0
■ **DON MILES** Miles, Donald Ray b: 3/13/36, Indianapolis, Ind. BL/TR, 6'1", 210 lbs. Deb: 9/09/58																												
1958	LA-N	8	22	2	4	0	0	0	0	0	6	.182	.217	.182	.399	7	-3	-3	105	0	1	.278	0	0	0	1	/O	-0.1
■ **DEE MILES** Miles, Wilson Daniel b: 2/15/09, Kellerman, Ala. d: 11/2/76, Birmingham, Ala. BL/TR, 6', 175 lbs. Deb: 7/07/35																												
1935	Was-A	60	215	28	57	5	2	0	29	7	13	.265	.291	.307	.598	60	-14	-12	92	149	19	.494	6	4	-1	-1	O	-1.2
1936	Was-A	25	59	8	14	1	2	0	7	1	5	.237	.250	.322	.572	41	-6	-6	98	119	4	.435	0	1	-1	0	O	-0.5
1939	Phi-A	106	320	49	96	17	6	1	37	15	17	.300	.331	.400	.731	88	-7	-6	97	95	42	.632	3	4	-2	-8	O	-1.6
1940	Phi-A	88	236	26	71	9	6	1	23	8	18	.301	.327	.403	.729	92	-5	-3	96	85	32	.625	1	1	-0	-1	O	-0.7
1941	Phi-A	80	170	14	53	7	1	0	15	4	8	.312	.331	.365	.696	83	-4	-4	101	86	20	.549	0	1	-1	-1	O	-0.7
1942	Phi-A	99	346	41	94	12	5	0	22	12	10	.272	.300	.335	.635	81	-11	-9	96	67	36	.523	5	3	-0	-1	O	-1.6
1943	Bos-A	45	121	9	26	2	2	0	10	3	3	.215	.234	.264	.498	44	-9	-9	104	114	7	.357	0	2	-1	1	O	-1.0
Total	7	503	1467	175	411	53	24	2	143	50	74	.280	.306	.353	.659	77	-56	-49	97	96	159	.548	15	16	-5	-10	O	-7.3
■ **MIKE MILEY** Miley, Michael Wilfred b: 3/30/53, Yazoo City, Miss. d: 1/6/77, Baton Rouge, La. BB/TR, 6'1", 185 lbs. Deb: 7/06/75																												
1975	Cal-A	70	224	17	39	3	2	4	26	16	54	.174	.232	.259	.491	41	-18	-17	95	143	13	.391	0	1	-1	-7	S	-1.7
1976	Cal-A	14	38	4	7	2	0	0	4	4	8	.184	.262	.237	.499	51	-2	-2	92	171	3	.438	1	0	0	-1	S	-0.1
Total	2	84	262	21	46	5	2	4	30	20	62	.176	.237	.256	.492	42	-21	-19	94	147	16	.408	1	1	-0	-8	/S	-1.8
■ **FELIX MILLAN** Millan, Felix Bernardo (Martinez) b: 8/21/43, Yabucoa, P.R. BR/TR, 5'11", 172 lbs. Deb: 6/02/66																												
1966	Atl-N	37	91	20	25	6	0	0	5	2	6	.275	.290	.341	.631	76	-3	-3	99	68	8	.514	3	1	0	-2	2/S3	-0.3
1967	Atl-N	41	136	13	32	3	3	2	6	4	10	.235	.268	.346	.613	71	-5	-5	104	47	11	.482	0	3	-2	2	2	-0.2
1968	Atl-N	149	570	49	165	22	2	1	33	22	26	.289	.323	.340	.663	107	-1	3	93	75	58	.533	6	6	-2	1	*2	1.2
1969	Atl-N	162	652	98	174	23	5	6	57	34	35	.267	.311	.345	.656	81	-15	-17	104	90	69	.564	14	3	2	-16	*2	-1.9
1970	Atl-N	142	590	100	183	25	5	2	37	35	23	.310	.354	.380	.734	93	-2	-6	104	55	79	.656	16	5	2	-17	*2	-0.4
1971	Atl-N	143	577	65	167	20	8	2	45	37	22	.289	.335	.362	.698	89	-2	-8	110	82	69	.606	11	7	-1	10	*2	0.8
1972	Atl-N	125	498	46	128	19	3	1	38	23	28	.257	.294	.313	.607	69	-18	-21	105	104	46	.493	6	4	-1	-7	*2	-2.1
1973	NY-N	153	638	82	185	23	4	3	37	35	22	.290	.333	.353	.686	90	-8	-9	101	56	72	.564	2	2	-1	-4	*2	-0.7
1974	NY-N	136	518	50	139	15	2	1	33	31	14	.268	.320	.311	.630	77	-16	-15	99	82	53	.523	5	1	1	-13	*2	-2.1
1975	NY-N	162	676	81	191	37	2	1	56	36	28	.283	.330	.348	.678	93	-11	-7	95	80	75	.559	1	6	-3	-25	*2	-2.9
1976	NY-N	139	531	55	150	25	2	1	35	41	19	.282	.342	.343	.685	103	-3	2	92	77	60	.580	2	4	-2	-22	*2	-1.5
1977	NY-N	91	314	40	78	11	2	2	21	18	9	.248	.296	.315	.611	67	-16	-14	96	82	28	.494	1	1	-0	-12	2	-2.1
Total	12	1480	5791	699	1617	229	38	22	403	318	242	.279	.324	.343	.667	87	-100	-101	100	77	628	.577	67	43	-6	-104	*2/3S	-12.2
■ **FRANK MILLARD** Millard, Frank E. b: 7/4/1865, E.St.Louis, Ill. d: 7/4/1892, Galveston, Tex. Deb: 5/04/1890																												
1890	StL-a	1	1	0	0	0	0	0		1		.000	.500	.000	.500	45	0	0	116	0	0	1.000	0			0	/2	0.0
■ **DUSTY MILLER** Miller, Charles Bradley b: 9/10/1868, Oil City, Pa. d: 9/3/45, Memphis, Tenn. BL/TR, 5'11.5", 170 lbs. Deb: 9/23/1889																												
1889	Bal-a	11	40	4	6	1	1	0	6	2	11	.150	.209	.225	.434	25	-4	-4	100	194	3	.441	3			0	/SO	-0.2
1890	StL-a	26	96	17	21	5	3	1		8		.219	.279	.365	.643	79	-1	-4	116	0	11	.627	4			0	O/S	-0.2
1895	Cin-N	132	529	103	177	31	17	10	112	33	34	.335	.378	.514	.892	121	22	14	108	110	122	1.000	43			11	*O	1.1
1896	Cin-N	125	504	91	162	38	12	4	93	33	30	.321	.368	.468	.836	116	14	10	105	104	118	1.020	76			-3	*O	-0.1
1897	Cin-N	119	440	83	139	27	1	4	70	48		.316	.391	.409	.800	106	10	5	107	113	84	.874	29			2	*O	-0.1
1898	Cin-N	152	586	99	175	24	12	3	90	38		.299	.348	.396	.744	107	11	4	108	120	94	.749	32			7	*O	0.2
1899	Cin-N	80	323	44	81	12	5	0	37	9		.251	.273	.319	.592	61	-16	-19	106	117	34	.541	18			6	O	-1.5
	StL-N	10	39	3	8	1	0	0	3	3		.205	.279	.231	.510	39	-3	-3	108	98	3	.452	1			-1	O	-0.3
	Yr	90	362	47	89	13	5	0	40	12		.246	.274	.309	.583	58	-19	-22	106	116	37	.531	19			6		-1.8
Total	7	655	2557	444	769	139	51	22	411	174	75	.301	.351	.421	.772	103	32	3	107	109	468	.827	206			22	O/S	-1.1
■ **BRUCE MILLER** Miller, Charles Bruce b: 3/4/47, Fort Wayne, Ind. BR/TR, 6'1", 185 lbs. Deb: 8/04/73																												
1973	SF-N	12	21	1	3	0	0	0	2	2	3	.143	.217	.143	.360	2	-3	-3	105	268	1	.278	0	0	0	-0	/32S	-0.2
1974	SF-N	73	198	19	55	7	1	0	16	11	15	.278	.319	.323	.642	74	-5	-7	108	96	19	.510	1	1	-0	1	3S/2	-0.5
1975	SF-N	99	309	22	74	6	3	1	31	15	26	.239	.277	.288	.565	56	-18	-19	102	130	21	.418	0	1	-1	3	32/S	-1.5
1976	SF-N	12	25	1	4	1	0	0	2	2	5	.160	.222	.200	.422	20	-3	-3	103	154	1	.333	0	0	0	0	/23	-0.1
Total	4	196	553	43	136	14	4	1	51	30	49	.246	.287	.291	.578	59	-29	-32	104	125	42	.463	1	2	-1	4	3/2S	-2.3
■ **CHARLIE MILLER** Miller, Charles Elmer b: 1/4/1892, Warrensburg, Mo. d: 4/23/72, Warrensburg, Mo. TR , Deb: 9/18/12																												
1912	StL-A	1	2	0	0	0	0	0	0	0		.000	.000	.000	.000	-99	-1	-1	99	0	0	.000	0			0	/S	0.0
■ **CHARLIE MILLER** Miller, Charles Hess b: 12/30/1877, Contestoga Center Pa. d: 1/13/51, Millersville, Pa. BR/TR, 6', 190 lbs. Deb: 10/02/15																												
1915	Bal-F	1	1	0	0	0	0	0	0	0	0	.000	.000	.000	.000	-93	-0	-0	107	0	0	.000	0			0	H	0.0
■ **CHUCK MILLER** Miller, Charles Marion b: 9/18/1889, Woodville, Ohio d: 6/16/61, Houston, Tex. BL/TL, 5'8.5", 155 lbs. Deb: 9/19/13																												
1913	StL-N	4	12	0	2	0	0	0	1	0	2	.167	.167	.167	.333	-5	-2	-2	93	182	0	.200	0			-1	/O	-0.1
1914	StL-N	36	36	4	7	1	0	0	2	3	9	.194	.256	.222	.479	41	-3	-3	104	91	2	.448	2			-4	O	-0.6
Total	2	40	48	4	9	1	0	0	3	3	11	.188	.235	.208	.444	31	-4	-4	101	112	3	.385	2			-4	/O	-0.7
■ **DUSTY MILLER** Miller, Dakin Evans b: 9/2/1877, Malvern, Iowa d: 4/20/50, Stockton, Cal. 5'10", 175 lbs. Deb: 4/17/02																												
1902	Chi-N	51	187	17	46	4	1	0	13	7		.246	.273	.278	.551	75	-6	-5	96	88	17	.489	10			6	O	-0.3
■ **DARRELL MILLER** Miller, Darrell Keith b: 2/26/58, Washington, D.C. BR/TR, 6'2", 200 lbs. Deb: 8/14/84																												
1984	Cal-A	17	41	5	7	0	0	0	1	4	9	.171	.244	.171	.415	17	-5	-5	101	57	2	.324	0	0	0	-1	1/O	-0.6
1985	Cal-A	51	48	8	18	2	1	2	7	1	10	.375	.400	.583	.983	164	4	4	101	82	11	.968	0	1	-1	-12	O/C3D	-0.8
1986	Cal-A	33	57	6	13	2	1	0	4	4	8	.228	.279	.298	.577	60	-3	-3	96	94	4	.447	0	0	0	-8	OC/D	-1.0
1987	Cal-A	53	108	14	26	5	0	4	16	9	13	.241	.311	.398	.709	88	-2	-2	99	116	13	.632	1	0	0	-4	CO/3D	-0.2
1988	Cal-A	70	140	21	31	4	1	2	7	9	29	.221	.292	.307	.599	72	-6	-5	94	57	13	.532	2	1	0	-5	C/OD	-0.7
Total	5	224	394	54	95	13	3	8	35	27	69	.241	.303	.350	.653	81	-12	-10	97	81	43	.583	3	2	-0	-30	/CO1D3	-3.3
■ **BING MILLER** Miller, Edmund John b: 8/30/1894, Vinton, Iowa d: 5/7/66, Philadelphia, Pa. BR/TR, 6', 185 lbs. Deb: 4/16/21 C																												
1921	Was-A	114	420	57	121	28	8	9	71	25	50	.288	.334	.457	.791	102	-2	-1	99	113	63	.739	3	4	-2	4	*O	-0.7
1922	Phi-A	143	535	90	179	29	12	21	90	24	42	.335	.371	.551	.922	132	26	23	104	92	104	.918	10	10	-3	10	*O	1.9
1923	Phi-A	123	458	68	137	25	4	12	64	27	34	.299	.344	.450	.793	107	3	3	100	92	71	.759	9	3	1	-2	*O	-0.8
1924	Phi-A	113	398	62	136	22	4	6	62	12	24	.342	.376	.462	.839	116	8	8	99	103	69	.813	11	5	0	-4	O/1	-0.2
1925	Phi-A	124	474	78	151	29	10	10	81	19	14	.319	.355	.485	.841	108	6	4	103	106	80	.815	11	6	-0	-14	*O1	-1.8
1926	Phi-A	38	110	13	32	6	2	2	13	11	6	.291	.355	.436	.792	90	1	-2	118	82	18	.797	4	1	1	-5	O/1	-0.8
	StL-A	94	353	60	117	27	5	4	50	22	12	.331	.382	.470	.852	121	10	10	101	101	60	.818	7	11	-5	-5	O	-0.6
	Yr	132	463	73	149	33	7	6	63	33	18	.322	.376	.462	.838	112	11	7	105	96	78	.813	11	12	-4	-10		-1.4
1927	StL-A	143	492	83	160	32	7	5	75	30	26	.325	.375	.449	.824	107	9	5	106	108	81	.810	9	0	3	-2	*O	-0.5
1928	Phi-A	139	510	76	168	34	7	8	85	27	24	.329	.372	.471	.843	117	14	12	103	113	88	.819	10	6	-1	-15	*O	-1.0
1929	Phi-A	147	556	84	186	32	16	8	93	40	25	.335	.383	.493	.876	114	19	12	109	109	105	.902	24	9	2	0	*O	0.7
1930	Phi-A	154	585	89	177	38	7	9	100	47	22	.303	.357	.438	.795	101	0	1	99	120	90	.758	13	13	-4	4	*O	-0.4

YEAR	TM/L	G	AB	R	H	2B	3B	HR	RBI	BB	SO	AVG	OBP	SLG	PRO	/A	BR	/A	PF	CHI	RC	TA	SB	CS	SBR	FR	POS	TPR
1931	Phi-A	137	534	75	150	43	5	8	77	36	16	.281	.338	.425	.763	95	-2	-5	105	107	77	.718	5	3	-0	4	*O	-0.9
1932	Phi-A	95	305	40	90	17	4	7	58	20	11	.295	.343	.446	.788	90	0	-6	114	124	47	.757	7	3	0	-3	O	-1.0
1933	Phi-A	67	120	22	33	7	1	2	17	12	7	.275	.346	.400	.746	106	-1	1	92	105	17	.730	4	2	0	-6	O/1	-0.5
1934	Phi-A	81	177	22	43	10	2	1	22	16	14	.243	.309	.339	.648	69	-9	-8	97	117	19	.582	1	0	0	-5	O	-1.2
1935	Bos-A	78	138	18	42	8	1	3	26	10	8	.304	.356	.442	.798	97	1	-1	108	126	22	.742	0	1	-1	-4	O	-0.4
1936	Bos-A	30	47	9	14	2	1	1	6	5	5	.298	.377	.447	.824	97	0	-0	106	81	8	.818	0	0	0	-2	O	-0.2
Total	16	1820	6212	946	1936	389	96	116	990	383	340	.312	.359	.461	.821	107	83	53	103	107	1020	.794	128	77	-8	-45	*O/1	-8.4
■ **EDDIE MILLER**	Miller, Edward Lee b: 6/29/57, San Pablo, Cal. BB/TR, 5'9", 175 lbs. Deb: 9/05/77																											
1977	Tex-A	17	6	7	2	0	0	0	1	1	1	.333	.429	.333	.762	106	0	0	105	198	1	1.200	3	1	0	0	/OD	0.0
1978	Atl-N	6	21	5	3	1	0	0	2	2	4	.143	.250	.190	.440	22	-2	-2	112	202	2	.556	3	0	1	-1	/O	-0.2
1979	Atl-N	27	113	12	35	1	0	0	5	5	24	.310	.350	.319	.669	77	-2	-4	109	47	15	.716	15	2	3	5	O	0.4
1980	Atl-N	11	19	3	3	0	0	0	0	0	5	.158	.158	.158	.316	-12	-3	-3	101	0	0	.222	1	2	-1	-3	/O	-0.7
1981	Atl-N	50	134	29	31	3	1	0	7	7	29	.231	.285	.269	.553	58	-7	-7	100	76	12	.633	23	5	4	-2	O	-0.6
1982	Det-A	14	25	3	1	0	0	0	0	4	4	.040	.250	.040	.290	-14	-4	-4	100	0	1	.296	0	3	-2	-0	/OD	-0.5
1984	SD-N	13	14	4	4	0	1	1	2	0	4	.286	.286	.643	.929	157	1	1	99	65	3	1.300	4	0	1	-1	/O	0.1
Total	7	138	332	63	79	5	2	1	17	19	71	.238	.297	.274	.571	58	-17	-19	104	66	34	.632	49	13	7	-2	/OD	-1.5
■ **EDDIE MILLER**	Miller, Edward Robert "Eppie" b: 11/26/16, Pittsburgh, Pa. BR/TR, 5'9", 180 lbs. Deb: 9/09/36																											
1936	Cin-N	5	10	0	1	0	0	0	0	1	1	.100	.182	.100	.282	-23	-2	-2	97	0	0	.222	0			0	/S2	0.0
1937	Cin-N	36	60	3	9	3	1	0	5	3	8	.150	.190	.233	.424	16	-7	-7	91	129	2	.304	0			1	S/3	-0.2
1939	Bos-N	77	296	32	79	12	2	4	31	16	21	.267	.315	.361	.677	89	-8	-5	92	101	33	.587	4			6	S	0.5
1940	Bos-N	151	569	78	157	33	3	14	79	41	43	.276	.330	.418	.748	106	3	4	99	107	76	.682	8			15	*S	3.3
1941	Bos-N	154	585	54	140	27	3	6	68	35	72	.239	.288	.326	.614	78	-22	-17	93	120	54	.523	8			12	*S	0.8
1942	Bos-N	142	534	47	130	28	2	6	47	22	42	.243	.279	.337	.616	84	-16	-13	95	90	47	.517	11			4	*S	0.1
1943	Cin-N	154	576	49	129	26	4	2	71	33	43	.224	.271	.293	.564	63	-28	-28	99	149	47	.468	8			**25**	*S	1.3
1944	Cin-N	155	536	48	112	21	5	4	55	41	41	.209	.269	.289	.558	60	-31	-28	95	121	43	.479	9			13	*S	0.5
1945	Cin-N	115	421	46	100	27	2	13	49	18	38	.238	.275	.404	.679	93	-10	-7	94	83	44	.589	4			-0	*S	0.5
1946	Cin-N	91	299	30	58	10	0	6	36	25	34	.194	.258	.288	.546	53	-18	-20	104	129	22	.474	5			6	*S	-0.7
1947	Cin-N	151	545	69	146	**38**	4	19	87	49	40	.268	.333	.457	.790	119	4	11	91	107	81	.742	5			-3	*S	1.9
1948	Phi-N	130	468	45	115	20	1	14	61	19	40	.246	.281	.382	.664	83	-16	-13	94	106	47	.555	1			-16	*S	-1.5
1949	Phi-N	85	266	21	55	10	1	6	29	29	21	.207	.294	.320	.614	64	-13	-14	101	106	26	.548	1			-8	2/S	-1.7
1950	StL-N	64	172	17	39	8	0	3	22	19	21	.227	.307	.326	.633	65	-8	-9	103	131	18	.555	0			4	S/2	0.0
Total	14	1510	5337	539	1270	263	28	97	640	351	465	.238	.290	.352	.643	81	-174	-147	96	112	540	.575	64			57	*S/23	4.8
■ **ED MILLER**	Miller, Edwin J. "Big Ed" b: 11/24/1888, Annville, Pa. d: 4/17/80, S.Lebanon Twsp, Pa BR/TR, 6', 180 lbs. Deb: 6/29/12																											
1912	StL-A	13	46	4	9	1	0	0	5	2		.196	.245	.217	.462	33	-4	-4	99	170	3	.378	1			-0	/1S	-0.3
1914	StL-A	35	58	8	8	0	1	0	4	4	13	.138	.219	.172	.391	18	-6	-6	98	150	2	.321	1	3	-2	-2	/12O3	-0.9
1918	Cle-A	32	96	9	22	4	3	0	3	12	10	.229	.321	.333	.654	90	-0	-1	108	34	11	.635	2			-1	1/O	-0.3
Total	3	80	200	21	39	5	4	0	12	18	23	.195	.275	.260	.535	58	-10	-11	103	98	15	.476	4	3		-3	/1O2S3	-1.5
■ **ELMER MILLER**	Miller, Elmer b: 7/28/1890, Sandusky, Ohio d: 11/28/44, Beloit, Wis. BR/TR, 6', 175 lbs. Deb: 4/27/12																											
1912	StL-N	12	37	5	7	1	0	0	3	4	9	.189	.268	.216	.485	33	-3	-3	100	126	2	.433	1			0	O	-0.2
1915	NY-A	26	83	4	12	1	0	0	3	4	14	.145	.193	.157	.350	5	-10	-10	98	78	3	.254	0			-4	O	-1.5
1916	NY-A	43	152	12	34	3	2	1	18	11	18	.224	.280	.289	.570	70	-6	-6	101	139	15	.542	8			5	O	-0.3
1917	NY-A	114	379	43	95	11	3	3	35	40	44	.251	.336	.319	.656	94	1	-2	107	99	45	.637	11			-2	*O	-1.1
1918	NY-A	67	202	18	49	9	2	1	22	19	17	.243	.317	.322	.639	98	-2	-1	95	118	22	.582	2			1	O	-0.3
1921	NY-A	56	242	41	72	9	8	4	36	19	16	.298	.356	.450	.806	102	1	0	103	88	39	.773	2	2	-1	1	O	-0.3
1922	NY-A	51	172	31	46	7	2	3	18	11	12	.267	.311	.384	.695	79	-5	-6	102	86	20	.612	2	3	-1	-1	O	-1.0
	Bos-A	44	147	16	28	2	3	4	16	5	10	.190	.222	.327	.549	43	-13	-13	96	95	11	.475	3	1	0	1	O	-1.3
	Yr	95	319	47	74	9	5	7	34	16	22	.232	.271	.357	.628	63	-19	-18	99	91	30	.546	5	4	-1	1		-2.3
Total	7	413	1414	170	343	43	20	16	151	113	140	.243	.307	.335	.642	80	-37	-40	101	102	157	.589	29	6		2	O	-6.0
■ **ELMER MILLER**	Miller, Elmer Joseph "Lefty" b: 4/17/03, Detroit, Mich. BL/TL, 5'11", 189 lbs. Deb: 6/21/29																											
1929	Phi-N	31	38	3	9	1	0	1	4	1	5	.237	.256	.342	.599	43	-3	-4	110	86	3	.483	0			2	/PO	0.0
■ **KOHLY MILLER**	Miller, Frank A. b: Philadelphia, Pa. TR , Deb: 10/03/1892																											
1892	Was-N	1	3	0	0	0	0	0	0	0	1	.000	.000	.000	.000	-96	-1	-1	105	0	0	.000	0			0	/S	0.0
	StL-N	1	4	0	0	0	0	0	0	0	0	.000	.000	.000	.000	-99	-1	-1	95	0	0	.000	0			0	/3	0.0
	Yr	2	7	0	0	0	0	0	0	0	1	.000	.000	.000	.000	-99	-2	-2	100	0	0	.000	0			0		0.0
1897	Phi-N	3	11	2	2	0	0	0	1	2		.182	.308	.182	.490	34	-1	-1	96	155	1	.444	0			0	/2	0.0
Total	2	5	18	2	2	0	0	0	1	2	1	.111	.200	.111	.311	-12	-3	-3	97	101	1	.250	0			0	/23S	0.0
■ **GEORGE MILLER**	Miller, George C. b: 2/19/1853, Newport, Ky. d: 7/24/29, Norwood, Ohio BR/TR, 5'5", 160 lbs. Deb: 9/06/1877																											
1877	Cin-N	11	37	4	6	1	0	0	3	5	2	.162	.262	.189	.451	54	-2	-1	82	148	2	.387				0	C	0.0
1884	Cin-a	6	20	6	5	1	1	0		1		.250	.318	.400	.718	128	1	1	106	0	3	.667				0	/C	0.1
Total	2	17	57	10	11	2	1	0	3	6	2	.193	.281	.263	.544	84	-1	-0	90	97	4	.478				0	/C	0.1
■ **DOGGIE MILLER**	Miller, George Frederick "Foghorn" or "Calliope" b: 8/15/1864, Brooklyn, N.Y. d: 4/6/09, Brooklyn, N.Y. BR/TR, 5'6", Deb: 5/01/1884 M																											
1884	Pit-a	89	347	46	78	10	2	0		13		.225	.257	.265	.522	75	-10	-8	97	0	24	.398				1	OC/32	-0.4
1885	Pit-a	42	166	19	27	3	1	0		4		.163	.182	.193	.375	19	-14	-16	106	0	6	.259				-4	C/OS3	-1.3
1886	Pit-a	83	317	70	80	15	1	2		43		.252	.343	.325	.668	121	6	10	93	0	49	.768	35			-25	CO/2	-0.9
1887	Pit-N	87	342	58	83	17	4	1	34	35	13	.243	.317	.325	.641	86	-8	-4	93	88	47	.699	33			-20	CO/3	-1.3
1888	Pit-N	103	404	50	112	17	5	0	36	18	16	.277	.319	.344	.663	120	6	9	95	89	54	.654	27			-15	CO/3	-0.2
1889	Pit-N	104	422	77	113	25	3	6	56	31	11	.268	.321	.384	.705	110	-2	5	89	98	59	.683	16			-4	CO/3	0.2
1890	Pit-N	138	549	85	150	24	3	4	66	68	11	.273	.357	.350	.707	124	8	19	88	86	82	.742	32			9	3OSC/2	2.7
1891	Pit-N	135	548	80	156	19	6	4	57	59	26	.285	.357	.363	.721	111	9	8	101	70	86	.755	35			-10	CS3O/1	0.3
1892	Pit-N	149	623	103	158	15	12	2	59	69	14	.254	.335	.326	.661	109	3	9	94	75	79	.660	28			-10	OCS/3	0.0
1893	Pit-N	41	154	23	28	6	1	0	17	17	8	.182	.284	.234	.518	37	-13	-15	106	132	11	.484	3			-1	C	-0.9
1894	StL-N	127	481	93	163	9	11	8	86	58	9	.339	.414	.453	.868	110	10	9	101	104	100	.934	17			-10	3C21/OSM	0.1
1895	StL-N	121	490	81	143	15	4	5	74	25	12	.292	.334	.369	.703	83	-13	-12	100	112	68	.663	18			-24	3CO/S1	-2.5
1896	Lou-N	98	324	54	89	17	4	1	33	27	9	.275	.334	.361	.695	87	-7	-6	98	79	46	.689	16			-4	C2/O31S	-0.4
Total	13	1317	5167	839	1380	192	57	33	518	467	129	.267	.333	.345	.679	99	-24	8	96	76	710	.675	260			-116	CO3/S21	-4.6
■ **HUGHIE MILLER**	Miller, Hugh Stanley "Cotton" b: 12/28/1887, St.Louis, Mo. d: 12/24/45, Jefferson Barracks, Mo. BR/TR, 6'1.5", 175 lbs. Deb: 6/18/11																											
1911	Phi-N	1	0	0	0	0	0	0	0	0	0	—	—	—	—	—	0	0	108	—	—	—	0			0	R	0.0
1914	StL-F	132	490	51	109	20	5	0	46	27	57	.222	.263	.284	.547	54	-28	-31	106	122	40	.446	4			-2	*1	-3.1
1915	StL-F	7	6	0	3	1	0	0	3	0	0	.500	.500	.667	1.167	233	1	1	105	270	2	1.333	0			0	/1	0.1
Total	3	140	496	51	112	21	5	0	49	27	57	.226	.266	.288	.554	56	-27	-31	106	124	753	.453	4			-2	1	-3.0
■ **JAKE MILLER**	Miller, Jacob George (born Jacob George Munzing) b: 12/1/1895, Baltimore, Md. d: 8/24/74, Towson, Md. BR/TR, 5'10", 170 lbs. Deb: 7/16/22																											
1922	Pit-N	3	11	0	1	0	0	0	0	2	0	.091	.231	.091	.322	-14	-2	-2	104	0	0	.400	1	0	0	0	/O	-0.1
■ **JIM MILLER**	Miller, James Mc Curdy "Rabbit" b: 10/2/1880, Pittsburgh, Pa. d: 2/7/37, Pittsburgh, Pa. BR/TR, 5'8", 165 lbs. Deb: 9/09/01																											
1901	NY-N	18	58	3	8	0	0	0	3	6		.138	.219	.138	.357	7	-7	-6	91	125	2	.300	1			-8	2	-1.2
■ **HACK MILLER**	Miller, James Eldridge b: 2/13/13, Celeste, Tex. d: 11/21/66, Dallas, Tex. BR/TR, 5'11.5", 215 lbs. Deb: 4/18/44																											
1944	Det-A	5	5	1	1	0	0	1	3	1	1	.200	.333	.800	1.133	208	1	1	105	155	1	1.250	0	0	0	0	/C	0.1
1945	Det-A	2	4	0	3	0	0	0	1	0	0	.750	.750	.750	1.500	317	1	1	106	121	1	1.500	0	0	0	0	/C	0.1
Total	2	7	9	1	4	0	0	1	4	1	1	.444	.500	.778	1.278	251	2	2	105	141	3	1.333	0	0	0	0	/C	0.2

YEAR	TM/L	G	AB	R	H	2B	3B	HR	RBI	BB	SO	AVG	OBP	SLG	PRO	/A	BR	/A	PF	CHI	RC	TA	SB	CS	SBR	FR	POS	TPR
■ **JOHN MILLER** Miller, John Allen b: 3/14/44, Alhambra, Cal. BR/TR, 5'11", 195 lbs. Deb: 9/11/66																												
1966	NY-A	6	23	1	2	0	0	1	2	0	9	.087	.087	.217	.304	-17	-3	-3	94	107	0	.238	0	0	0	-0	/1O	-0.3
1969	LA-N	26	38	3	8	1	0	1	1	2	9	.211	.250	.316	.566	58	-2	-2	99	27	3	.467	0	0	0	-2	/O132	-0.4
Total	2	32	61	4	10	1	0	2	3	2	18	.164	.190	.279	.469	32	-6	-5	97	56	4	.373	0	0	0	-2	/O132	-0.7
■ **DOTS MILLER** Miller, John Barney b: 9/9/1886, Kearny, N.J. d: 9/5/23, Saranac Lake, N.Y. BR/TR, 5'11.5", 170 lbs. Deb: 09																												
1909	Pit-N	151	560	71	156	31	13	3	87	39		.279	.329	.396	.725	121	15	12	105	140	75	.688	14			-13	*2	-0.2
1910	Pit-N	120	444	45	101	13	10	1	48	33	41	.227	.284	.309	.592	65	-17	-23	112	127	43	.534	11			-10	*2/1S	-3.2
1911	Pit-N	137	470	82	126	17	8	6	78	51	48	.268	.348	.377	.725	102	2	1	101	138	69	.733	17			3	*2	0.1
1912	Pit-N	148	567	74	156	33	12	4	87	37	45	.275	.324	.397	.721	98	-5	-4	99	131	78	.691	18			-1	*1	-0.9
1913	Pit-N	154	580	75	158	24	20	7	90	37	52	.272	.317	.419	.736	114	4	7	96	131	81	.713	20			-3	*1/S	-0.2
1914	StL-N	155	573	67	166	27	10	4	88	34	52	.290	.339	.393	.732	113	11	8	104	143	79	.698	16			-7	1S/2	0.2
1915	StL-N	150	553	73	146	17	10	2	72	43	48	.264	.324	.342	.666	101	1	1	100	149	65	.622	27	19	-3	0	12/3S	-0.6
1916	StL-N	143	505	47	120	22	7	1	46	40	49	.238	.300	.315	.615	92	-6	-5	97	119	54	.577	18			4	12S/3	-0.2
1917	StL-N	148	544	61	135	15	9	2	45	33	52	.248	.295	.320	.615	87	-8	-9	102	102	54	.548	14			19	21S	1.7
1919	StL-N	101	346	38	80	10	4	1	24	13	23	.231	.265	.292	.557	71	-14	-12	94	91	28	.462	6			3	12	-0.9
1920	Phi-N	98	343	41	87	12	2	1	27	16	17	.254	.289	.309	.598	66	-13	-16	109	98	31	.519	13	6	0	-3	23S/10	-1.6
1921	Phi-N	84	320	37	95	11	3	0	23	15	27	.297	.330	.350	.680	79	-9	-10	102	80	36	.570	3	5	-2	2	31/2	-0.9
Total	12	1589	5805	711	1526	232	108	32	715	391	454	.263	.314	.357	.671	95	-38	-48	101	124	693	.623	177	30		-4	12S/30	-6.7
■ **JOE MILLER** Miller, Joseph A. b: 2/17/1861, Baltimore, Md. d: 4/23/28, Wheeling, W.V.A 5'9.5", 165 lbs. Deb: 5/01/1884																												
1884	Tol-a	105	423	46	101	12	8	1		26		.239	.284	.312	.597	94	-1	-3	104	0	38	.494				2	*S	-0.2
1885	Lou-a	98	339	44	62	9	5	0		28		.183	.249	.239	.488	56	-15	-17	102	0	21	.401				-1	*S3/2	-1.4
Total	2	203	762	90	163	21	13	1		54		.214	.269	.280	.548	77	-16	-20	103	0	59	.451				1	S/32	-1.6
■ **JOE MILLER** Miller, Joseph Wick b: 7/24/1850, Germany d: 8/30/1891, White Bear Lake, Minn. 5'10.5", 169 lbs. Deb: 6/26/1872 M																												
1872	Nat-n	1	4	0	1							.250															/1M	
1875	Wes-n	13	54	4	6							.111															2	
	Chi-n	16	65	2	9							.138															2/O	
	Yr	29	119	6	15							.126																
Total	2 n	30	123	6	16							.130															2/O	
■ **KEITH MILLER** Miller, Keith Alan b: 6/12/63, Midland, Mich. BR/TR, 5'11", 175 lbs. Deb: 6/16/87																												
1987	NY-N	25	51	14	19	2	2	0	1	2	6	.373	.407	.490	.898	139	3	3	99	16	11	1.059	8	1	2	-1	2	0.4
1988	NY-N	40	70	9	15	1	1	1	5	6	10	.214	.276	.300	.576	72	-3	-2	90	83	5	.443	0	5	-3	-1	2/S3O	-0.5
Total	2	65	121	23	34	3	3	1	6	8	16	.281	.331	.380	.711	103	-0	0	94	55	16	.670	8	6	-1	-2	/23SO	-0.1
■ **ED MILLER** Miller, L. Edward b: Tecumseh, Mich. Deb: 7/18/1884																												
1884	Tol-a	8	24	2	6	0	0	0		1		.250	.280	.250	.530	74	-1	-1	104	0	2	.389				0	/O	0.0
■ **HACK MILLER** Miller, Lawrence H. b: 1/1/1894, New York, N.Y. d: 9/17/71, Oakland, Cal. BR/TR, 5'9", 195 lbs. Deb: 9/22/16																												
1916	Bro-N	3	3	0	1	0	1	0	1	1	1	.333	.500	1.000	1.500	344	1	1	103	132	2	2.000	0			-1	/O	0.0
1918	Bos-A	12	29	2	8	2	0	0	4	0	4	.276	.276	.345	.621	92	-1	-1	95	146	3	.476	0			-3	O	-0.4
1922	Chi-N	122	466	61	164	28	5	12	78	26	39	.352	.389	.511	.899	137	20	23	95	102	91	.882	3	3	-1	-4	*O	1.3
1923	Chi-N	135	485	74	146	24	2	20	88	27	39	.301	.343	.482	.825	111	9	6	104	108	79	.788	6	5	-1	2	*O	0.2
1924	Chi-N	53	131	17	44	8	1	4	25	8	11	.336	.379	.504	.882	133	6	6	101	117	25	.874	1	0	0	-5	O	0.0
1925	Chi-N	24	86	10	24	3	2	2	9	2	9	.279	.303	.430	.734	87	-2	-2	97	74	11	.635	0	1	-1	-4	O	-0.6
Total	6	349	1200	164	387	65	11	38	205	64	103	.322	.361	.490	.851	122	33	33	100	105	209	.815	10	9		-15	O	0.5
■ **LEMMIE MILLER** Miller, Lemmie Earl b: 6/2/60, Dallas, Tex. BR/TR, 6'1", 190 lbs. Deb: 5/22/84																												
1984	LA-N	8	12	1	2	0	0	0	0	1	2	.167	.231	.167	.397	13	-1	-1	104	0	1	.300	0	0	0	-1	/O	-0.2
■ **OTTO MILLER** Miller, Lowell Otto "Moonie" b: 6/1/1889, Minden, Neb. d: 3/29/62, Brooklyn, N.Y. BR/TR, 6', 196 lbs. Deb: 7/16/10 C																												
1910	Bro-N	31	66	5	11	3	0	0	2	2	19	.167	.203	.212	.415	22	-7	-6	95	50	3	.327	1			3	C	-0.1
1911	Bro-N	25	62	7	13	2	2	0	8	0	4	.210	.210	.306	.516	45	-5	-5	97	142	4	.429	2			1	C	-0.1
1912	Bro-N	98	316	35	88	18	1	1	31	18	50	.278	.325	.351	.677	89	-7	-5	95	92	39	.632	11			12	C	1.2
1913	Bro-N	104	320	26	87	11	7	0	26	10	31	.272	.294	.350	.644	80	-8	-10	104	84	34	.554	7			-26	*C/1	-3.0
1914	Bro-N	54	169	17	39	6	1	0	9	7	20	.231	.261	.278	.539	60	-9	-9	101	69	12	.415	0			5	C	-0.1
1915	Bro-N	84	254	20	57	4	6	0	25	6	28	.224	.245	.287	.533	60	-13	-13	101	131	20	.421	3			4	C	-0.3
1916	Bro-N	73	216	16	55	9	2	1	17	7	29	.255	.281	.329	.610	84	-4	-5	103	91	22	.528	6			2	C	0.1
1917	Bro-N	92	274	19	63	5	4	1	17	14	29	.230	.272	.288	.561	69	-9	-10	104	80	23	.474	5			-1	C	-0.6
1918	Bro-N	75	228	8	44	6	1	0	8	9	20	.193	.230	.228	.458	39	-16	-17	101	58	11	.348	1			9	C/1	-0.2
1919	Bro-N	51	164	18	37	5	0	0	5	7	14	.226	.257	.256	.513	58	-9	-8	94	46	11	.402	2			1	C	-0.3
1920	Bro-N	90	301	16	87	9	2	0	33	9	18	.289	.312	.332	.644	76	-6	-10	111	128	30	.502	0	5	-3	-10	C	-1.7
1921	Bro-N	91	286	22	67	8	6	1	27	9	26	.234	.260	.315	.575	49	-20	-22	105	106	24	.464	2	1	0	3	C	-1.2
1922	Bro-N	59	180	20	47	11	1	1	23	6	13	.261	.285	.350	.635	66	-10	-9	95	122	18	.519	0	0	0	-1	C	-0.8
Total	13	927	2836	229	695	97	33	5	231	104	301	.245	.275	.308	.583	66	-123	-128	102	94	250	.480	40	6		2	C/1	-7.1
■ **KEITH MILLER** Miller, Neal Keith b: 3/7/63, Dallas, Tex. BB/TR, 5'11", 175 lbs. Deb: 4/23/88																												
1988	Phi-N	47	48	4	8	3	0	0	6	5	13	.167	.245	.229	.474	36	-4	-4	101	218	3	.400	0	0	0	-1	/O3S	-0.5
■ **NORM MILLER** Miller, Norman Calvin b: 2/5/46, Los Angeles, Cal. BL/TR, 5'10", 185 lbs. Deb: 9/11/65																												
1965	Hou-N	11	15	2	3	0	1	0	1	1	7	.200	.250	.333	.583	71	-1	-1	89	83	1	.462	0	0	0	-0	/O	0.0
1966	Hou-N	11	34	1	5	0	0	1	3	2	8	.147	.194	.235	.430	19	-4	-4	97	115	2	.345	0	0	0	-1	/O3	-0.4
1967	Hou-N	64	190	15	39	9	3	1	14	19	42	.205	.278	.300	.578	70	-9	-7	94	97	14	.484	2	0	1	-1	O	-1.0
1968	Hou-N	79	257	35	61	18	2	6	28	22	48	.237	.310	.393	.703	111	3	3	99	101	31	.654	6	5	-1	-2	O	-0.3
1969	Hou-N	119	409	58	108	21	4	4	50	47	77	.264	.350	.364	.714	99	1	1	102	127	54	.666	4	4	-1	1	*O	-0.6
1970	Hou-N	90	226	29	54	9	0	4	29	41	33	.239	.358	.332	.690	92	-3	-1	94	129	29	.674	3	1	0	-4	O/C	-0.7
1971	Hou-N	45	74	5	19	5	0	2	10	5	13	.257	.313	.405	.718	110	0	1	93	113	9	.621	0	0	0	-4	O/C	-0.3
1972	Hou-N	67	107	18	26	4	0	4	13	13	23	.243	.331	.393	.723	99	1	-0	106	99	14	.671	1	0	0	-4	O	-0.4
1973	Hou-N	3	3	0	0	0	0	0	0	0	2	.000	.000	.000	.000	-99	-1	-1	95	0	0	.000	0	0	0	-0	/O	0.0
	Atl-N	9	8	2	3	1	0	1	6	3	3	.375	.545	.875	1.420	254	2	2	113	241	4	2.000	0	0	0	-0	/O	0.2
	Yr	12	11	2	3	1	0	1	6	3	5	.273	.429	.636	1.065	176	1	1	108	181	3	1.250	0	0	0	-0		0.2
1974	Atl-N	42	41	1	7	1	0	1	5	7	9	.171	.292	.268	.560	55	-2	-3	105	138	4	.529	0	0	0	-0	/O	-0.2
Total	10	540	1364	166	325	68	10	24	159	160	265	.238	.325	.356	.680	94	-12	-9	98	116	162	.644	16	10	-1	-15	O/C3	-3.7
■ **OTTO MILLER** Miller, Otis Louis b: 2/2/01, Belleville, Ill. d: 7/26/59, Belleville, Ill. BR/TR, 5'10.5", 168 lbs. Deb: 4/17/27																												
1927	StL-A	51	76	8	17	5	0	0	8	8	5	.224	.306	.289	.595	52	-5	-6	106	121	7	.525	0	0	0	1	S3	0.0
1930	Bos-A	112	370	49	106	22	5	0	40	26	21	.286	.333	.373	.706	85	-12	-8	93	96	46	.619	2	4	-2	-2	32	-0.6
1931	Bos-A	107	389	38	106	12	1	0	43	15	20	.272	.301	.308	.610	65	-22	-19	94	121	36	.482	1	1	-0	2	32	-1.0
1932	Bos-A	2	2	0	0	0	0	0	0	0	0	.000	.000	.000	.000	-99	-1	-1	97	0	0	.000	0	0	0	0	H	0.0
Total	4	272	837	95	229	39	6	0	91	49	46	.274	.315	.335	.650	72	-40	-33	95	109	89	.545	3	5	-2	1	3/2S	-1.6
■ **RALPH MILLER** Miller, Ralph Joseph b: 2/29/1896, Ft.Wayne, Ind. d: 3/18/39, Ft.Wayne, Ind. BR/TR, 6', 190 lbs. Deb: 4/14/20																												
1920	Phi-N	97	338	28	74	14	1	0	28	11	32	.219	.246	.266	.512	43	-23	-27	109	120	22	.392	3	4	-2	5	3/1SO	-2.0
1921	Phi-N	57	204	19	62	10	0	3	26	6	10	.304	.327	.397	.724	89	-3	-3	102	108	25	.619	3	5	-2	0	S3	0.0
1924	Was-A	9	15	1	2	0	0	0	0	1	1	.133	.188	.133	.321	-17	-3	-3	98	0	0	.231	0	0	0	-0	/2	-0.2
Total	3	163	557	48	138	24	1	3	54	18	43	.248	.274	.311	.584	59	-29	-33	106	112	47	.465	6	9	-4	5	3/S210	-2.2
■ **RAY MILLER** Miller, Raymond Peter b: 2/12/1888, Pittsburgh, Pa. d: 4/7/27, Pittsburgh, Pa. 5'10", 168 lbs. Deb: 4/14/17																												
1917	Cle-A	19	21	1	4	1	0	0	2	8	3	.190	.414	.238	.652	87	1	0	114	144	2	.765	0			0	/1	0.0

YEAR	TM/L	G	AB	R	H	2B	3B	HR	RBI	BB	SO	AVG	OBP	SLG	PRO	/A	BR	/A	PF	CHI	RC	TA	SB	CS	SBR	FR	POS	TPR
	Pit-N	6	27	1	4	1	0	0	0	2	3	.148	.207	.185	.392	21	-3	-2	100	0	1	.304	0			0	/1	-0.2
Total	1	25	48	2	8	2	0	0	2	10	6	.167	.310	.208	.519	55	-2	-2	107	72	3	.500	0			0	/1	-0.2
■ **RICK MILLER** Miller, Richard Alan b: 4/19/48, Grand Rapids, Mich. BL/TL, 6', 175 lbs. Deb: 9/04/71																												
1971	Bos-A	15	33	9	11	5	0	1	7	8	8	.333	.463	.576	1.039	183	4	4	106	130	9	1.125	0	2	-1	1	O	0.3
1972	Bos-A	89	98	13	21	4	1	3	15	11	27	.214	.294	.367	.661	91	-1	-1	105	139	10	.587	0	2	-1	-10	O	-1.5
1973	Bos-A	143	441	65	115	17	7	6	43	51	59	.261	.341	.372	.713	95	1	-2	106	93	58	.678	12	7	-1	5	*O	-0.1
1974	Bos-A	114	280	41	73	8	1	5	22	37	47	.261	.347	.350	.697	95	1	-1	107	77	38	.695	13	2	3	9	*O	0.9
1975	Bos-A	77	108	21	21	2	1	0	15	21	20	.194	.326	.231	.557	55	-5	-6	109	230	9	.533	3	2	-0	-9	O	-1.6
1976	Bos-A	105	269	40	76	15	3	0	27	34	47	.283	.363	.361	.724	102	5	2	110	107	36	.686	11	10	-3	7	O/D	0.5
1977	Bos-A	86	189	34	48	9	3	0	24	22	30	.254	.341	.333	.674	72	-3	-8	117	151	23	.669	11	5	0	-6	O/D	-1.6
1978	Cal-A	132	475	66	125	25	4	1	37	54	70	.263	.343	.339	.682	91	-3	-4	102	91	53	.589	3	13	-7	6	*O	-0.8
1979	Cal-A	120	427	60	125	15	5	2	28	50	69	.293	.368	.365	.734	107	1	5	93	68	60	.677	5	4	-1	6	*O	0.5
1980	Cal-A	129	412	52	113	14	3	2	38	48	71	.274	.351	.337	.689	94	-4	-2	96	102	53	.639	7	3	0	-0	*O	-0.4
1981	Bos-A	97	316	38	92	17	2	2	33	28	36	.291	.351	.377	.727	103	4	2	106	103	41	.640	3	5	-2	2	O	0.0
1982	Bos-A	135	409	50	104	13	2	4	38	40	41	.254	.324	.325	.649	72	-11	-17	110	105	43	.566	5	6	-2	-12	*O	-3.4
1983	Bos-A	104	262	41	75	10	2	2	21	28	30	.286	.357	.363	.720	98	0	-0	101	81	34	.648	3	3	-1	1	O/1D	0.0
1984	Bos-A	95	123	17	32	5	1	0	12	17	22	.260	.350	.317	.667	78	-2	-3	110	123	14	.600	1	1	-0	-6	O/1	-1.0
1985	Bos-A	41	45	5	15	2	0	0	9	5	6	.333	.400	.378	.778	112	1	1	102	210	7	.742	1	0	0	-2	/OD	0.0
Total	15	1482	3887	552	1046	161	35	28	369	454	583	.269	.348	.350	.698	92	-11	-31	104	103	488	.657	78	65	-16	-8	*O/D1	-8.2
■ **ROD MILLER** Miller, Rodney Carter b: 1/16/40, Portland, Ore. BL/TR, 5'10", 160 lbs. Deb: 9/28/57																												
1957	Bro-N	1	1	0	0	0	0	0	0	0	1	.000	.000	.000	.000	-86	-0	-0	116	0	0	.000	0	0	0	0	H	0.0
■ **DOC MILLER** Miller, Roy Oscar b: 1883, Chatham, Ont., Canada d: 7/31/38, Jersey City, N.J. BL/TL, 5'10.5", 170 lbs. Deb: 5/04/10																												
1910	Chi-N	1	1	0	0	0	0	0	0	0	0	.000	.000	.000	.000	-99	-0	-0	101	0	0	.000	0			0	H	0.0
	Bos-N	130	482	48	138	27	4	3	55	33	52	.286	.333	.378	.711	94	3	-5	114	106	66	.677	17			-13	*O	-2.4
	Yr	131	483	48	138	27	4	3	55	33	52	.286	.333	.377	.710	94	3	-6	114	105	66	.675	17			-13		-2.4
1911	Bos-N	146	577	69	**192**	36	3	7	91	43	43	.333	.379	.442	.821	125	21	18	103	118	107	.857	32			-2	*O	1.2
1912	Bos-N	51	201	26	47	8	1	2	24	14	17	.234	.287	.313	.600	60	-10	-12	107	124	20	.545	6			0	O	-1.3
	Phi-N	67	177	24	51	12	5	0	21	9	13	.288	.323	.412	.735	100	-1	-1	100	97	24	.675	3			-1	O	-0.2
	Yr	118	378	50	98	20	6	2	45	23	30	.259	.303	.360	.663	78	-11	-13	103	110	44	.604	9			-1		-1.5
1913	Phi-N	69	87	9	30	6	0	0	11	6	6	.345	.400	.414	.814	118	4	3	112	111	14	.807	2			-5	O	-0.1
1914	Cin-N	93	192	8	49	7	2	0	33	16	18	.255	.313	.313	.625	82	-3	-4	105	199	19	.559	4			-4	O	-1.0
Total	5	557	1717	184	507	96	15	12	235	121	149	.295	.343	.390	.733	101	13	-2	107	122	251	.709	64			-25	O	-3.8
■ **RUDY MILLER** Miller, Rudel Charles b: 7/12/1900, Kalamazoo, Mich. BR/TR, 6'1", 180 lbs. Deb: 9/19/29																												
1929	Phi-A	2	4	1	1	0	0	0	1	3	0	.250	.571	.250	.821	109	1	0	109	342	1	1.333	0	0	0	0	/3	0.0
■ **TOM MILLER** Miller, Thomas P. "Reddy" b: Philadelphia, Pa. d: 5/29/1876, Philadelphia, Pa. Deb: N/A.																												
1875	StL-n	52	211	17	35							.166															*C/3	
■ **TOM MILLER** Miller, Thomas Royall b: 7/5/1897, Powhatan Court House, Va. d: 8/13/80, Richmond, Va. BL/TR, 5'11", 180 lbs. Deb: 7/29/18																												
1918	Bos-N	2	2	0	0	0	0	0	0	0	0	.000	.000	.000	.000	-99	-0	-0	94	0	-0	.500	1			0	H	0.0
1919	Bos-N	7	6	2	2	0	0	0	0	0	1	.333	.333	.333	.667	103	-0	0	98	0	1	.500	0			0	H	0.0
Total	2	9	8	2	2	0	0	0	0	0	1	.250	.250	.250	.500	53	-0	-0	97	0	1	.500	1			0		0.0
■ **WARD MILLER** Miller, Ward Taylor "Windy" or "Grump" b: 7/5/1884, Mt.Carroll, Ill. d: 9/4/58, Dixon, Ill. BL/TR, 5'11", 177 lbs. Deb: 09																												
1909	Pit-N	15	56	2	8	0	1	0	4	4		.143	.213	.179	.392	21	-5	-5	105	154	2	.354	2			-1	O	-0.7
	Cin-N	43	113	17	35	3	1	0	4	6		.310	.345	.354	.699	126	2	3	94	36	16	.705	9			-0	O	0.2
	Yr	58	169	19	43	3	2	0	8	10		.254	.300	.296	.596	89	-3	-2	97	69	18	.571	11			-1		-0.5
1910	Cin-N	81	126	21	30	6	0	0	10	22	13	.238	.356	.286	.641	87	-1	-1	101	97	17	.719	10			1	O	0.0
1912	Chi-N	86	241	45	74	11	4	0	22	26	18	.307	.377	.386	.763	105	3	2	104	80	39	.784	11			-7	O	-0.6
1913	Chi-N	80	203	23	48	5	7	1	16	34	33	.236	.349	.345	.694	100	1	1	99	80	27	.761	13			6	O	0.5
1914	StL-F	121	402	49	118	17	7	4	50	59	36	.294	.384	.400	.784	118	15	12	106	106	72	.838	18			3	*O	0.9
1915	StL-F	154	536	80	164	19	9	1	63	79	39	.306	.395	.381	.776	124	23	20	105	116	99	.849	33			-10	*O	0.3
1916	StL-A	146	485	72	129	17	5	1	50	72	76	.266	.371	.328	.699	116	9	12	95	112	65	.703	25	21	-5	-18	*O/2	-1.4
1917	StL-A	43	82	13	17	1	1	1	2	16	15	.207	.350	.280	.630	98	0	1	95	28	10	.738	7			-5	O	-0.5
Total	8	769	2244	322	623	79	35	8	221	318	230	.278	.371	.355	.726	112	48	44	101	99	349	.766	128	21		-31	O/2	-1.3
■ **WARREN MILLER** Miller, Warren Lemuel "Gitz" b: 7/14/1885, Philadelphia, Pa. d: 8/12/56, Philadelphia, Pa. BL/TL, 5'10", 160 lbs. Deb: 7/29/09																												
1909	Was-A	26	51	5	11	0	0	0	1	4		.216	.273	.216	.488	61	-3	-2	90	35	3	.375	0			0	O	-0.2
1911	Was-A	21	34	3	5	0	0	0	0	0		.147	.147	.147	.294	-18	-5	-5	97	0	1	.172	0			-2	/O	-0.7
Total	2	47	85	8	16	0	0	0	1	4		.188	.225	.188	.413	26	-8	-7	92	22	4	.290	0			-2	/O	-0.9
■ **BILL MILLER** Miller, William b: Cleveland, Ohio Deb: 8/23/02																												
1902	Pit-N	1	5	0	1	0	0	0	2	0		.200	.200	.200	.400	23	-0	-0	105	597	0	.250	0			0	/O	0.0
■ **WALLY MILLIES** Millies, Walter Louis b: 10/18/06, Chicago, Ill. BR/TR, 5'10.5", 170 lbs. Deb: 9/23/34																												
1934	Bro-N	2	7	0	0	0	0	0	0	0	0	.000	.000	.000	.000	-99	-2	-2	95	0	0	.000	0			0	/C	-0.1
1936	Was-A	74	215	26	67	10	2	0	25	11	8	.312	.345	.377	.722	80	-7	-7	98	100	28	.628	1	0	0	-2	C	-0.1
1937	Was-A	59	179	21	40	7	1	0	28	9	15	.223	.261	.274	.534	37	-18	-17	94	196	13	.424	1	0	0	-0	C	-1.1
1939	Phi-N	84	205	12	48	3	0	0	12	9	5	.234	.270	.249	.519	43	-17	-16	94	86	13	.372	0			-2	C	-1.4
1940	Phi-N	26	43	1	3	0	0	0	0	4	4	.070	.149	.070	.219	-39	-8	-8	97	0	0	.167	0			1	C	-0.5
1941	Phi-N	1	2	0	0	0	0	0	0	0	0	.000	.000	.000	.000	-99	-1	-1	97	0	0	.000	0			0	/C	0.0
Total	6	246	651	60	158	20	3	0	65	33	32	.243	.280	.283	.563	47	-53	-49	95	114	55	.446	2	0		-3	C	-3.2
■ **JOCKO MILLIGAN** Milligan, John b: 8/8/1861, Philadelphia, Pa. d: 8/29/23, Philadelphia, Pa. BR/TR, 6', 192 lbs. Deb: 5/01/1884																												
1884	Phi-a	66	268	39	77	20	3	3		8		.287	.308	.418	.726	120	10	5	114	0	35	.628				13	C/O	2.0
1885	Phi-a	67	265	35	71	15	4	2		7		.268	.289	.377	.667	108	3	2	103	0	30	.557				12	C/1O	2.0
1886	Phi-a	75	301	52	76	17	3	5		21		.252	.301	.379	.680	114	4	4	100	0	41	.680	18			3	C1/O3	0.8
1887	Phi-a	95	377	54	114	27	4	2		21		.302	.344	.411	.755	113	5	6	99	0	57	.711	8			4	1C/O	1.4
1888	StL-a	63	219	19	55	6	2	5	37	17		.251	.311	.365	.676	108	5	1	111	116	26	.622	3			2	C/1	0.9
1889	StL-a	72	273	53	100	30	2	12	76	16	19	.366	.408	.623	1.030	173	31	25	112	108	72	1.104	2			5	C/1	3.0
1890	Phi-P	62	234	38	69	9	3	3	57	19	19	.295	.363	.397	.760	103	2	1	102	156	35	.727	2			4	C/1	0.5
1891	Phi-a	118	455	75	138	**35**	12	11	106	56	51	.303	.397	.505	.903	157	36	33	103	112	94	.956	2			13	C1	4.2
1892	Was-N	88	323	40	89	20	9	4	43	26	24	.276	.335	.430	.766	127	12	9	105	89	48	.726	2			5	C1	1.6
1893	Bal-N	24	102	19	25	5	2	1	19	5	7	.245	.294	.363	.656	71	-4	-5	107	138	12	.597	2			-1	1/C	-0.4
	NY-N	42	147	16	34	5	6	1	25	14	13	.231	.302	.367	.670	76	-5	-6	104	120	17	.628	2			10	C	0.6
	Yr	66	249	35	59	10	8	2	44	19	20	.237	.299	.365	.664	74	-9	-11	105	128	29	.616	4			9		0.2
Total	10	772	2964	440	848	189	50	49	363	210	133	.286	.341	.433	.774	123	98	75	105	70	469	.742	41			70	C1/O3	16.6
■ **RANDY MILLIGAN** Milligan, Randy Andre b: 11/27/61, San Diego, Cal. BR/TR, 6'2", 200 lbs. Deb: 9/12/87																												
1987	NY-N	3	1	0	0	0	0	0	0	1	1	.000	.500	.000	.500	47	0	0	99	0	0	1.000	0	0	0	0	/H	0.0
1988	Pit-N	40	82	10	18	5	0	3	8	20	24	.220	.379	.390	.769	124	3	3	98	78	13	.794	1	2	-1	2	1/O	0.3
Total	2	43	83	10	18	5	0	3	8	21	25	.217	.381	.386	.766	123	3	3	98	77	13	.797	1	2	-1	2	/1O	0.3
■ **JACK MILLS** Mills, Abbott Paige b: 10/23/1889, S.Williamstown, Mass. d: 6/3/73, Washington, D.C. BL/TR, 6', 165 lbs. Deb: 7/01/11																												
1911	Cle-A	13	17	5	5	0	0	0	1	1		.294	.368	.294	.663	83	-0	-0	103	68	2	.667	1			0	/3	0.0

YEAR	TM/L	G	AB	R	H	2B	3B	HR	RBI	BB	SO	AVG	OBP	SLG	PRO	/A	BR	/A	PF	CHI	RC	TA	SB	CS	SBR	FR	POS	TPR
■ CHARLIE MILLS	Mills, Charles b: Brooklyn, N.Y. d: 4/10/1874, Brooklyn, N.Y. 6', Deb: 5/18/1871																											
1871	Mut-n	32	149	27	37							.248															*C/O2	
1872	Mut-n	6	30	6	4							.133															/OC	
Total	2 n	38	179	33	41							.229															/OC	
■ BUSTER MILLS	Mills, Colonel Buster "Bus" b: 9/16/08, Ranger, Tex. BR/TR, 5'11.5", 195 lbs. Deb: 4/18/34 MC																											
1934	StL-N	29	72	7	17	4	1	1	8	4	11	.236	.295	.361	.656	66	-3	-4	114	99	8	.561	0			0	O	-0.3
1935	Bro-N	17	56	12	12	2	1	1	7	5	11	.214	.323	.339	.662	83	-2	-1	94	115	6	.583	0			-2	O	-0.3
1937	Bos-A	123	505	85	149	25	8	7	58	46	41	.295	.361	.418	.779	93	-3	-6	103	82	77	.753	11	8	-2	-4	*O	-1.4
1938	StL-A	123	466	66	133	24	4	3	46	43	46	.285	.350	.373	.723	81	-13	-13	100	90	61	.666	7	8	-3	3	*O	-1.1
1940	NY-A	34	63	10	25	3	3	1	15	7	5	.397	.457	.587	1.044	171	7	7	99	135	15	1.000	0	0	0	-3	O	0.3
1942	Cle-A	80	195	19	54	4	2	1	26	23	18	.277	.353	.333	.687	102	-1	1	92	135	23	.612	5	4	-1	4	O	0.1
1946	Cle-A	9	22	1	6	0	0	0	3	3	5	.273	.360	.273	.633	89	-0	-0	89	190	2	.500	0	1	-1	-1	/O	-0.1
Total	7	415	1379	200	396	62	19	14	163	131	137	.287	.355	.390	.746	92	-16	-17	100	99	191	.703	23	21		-1	O	-2.8
■ EVERETT MILLS	Mills, Everett b: 1845, Newark, N.J. d: 6/22/08, Newark, N.J. 6'1", 174 lbs. Deb: 5/05/1871 M																											
1871	Oly-n	32	161	38	44							.273															*1	
1872	Bal-n	53	259	52	71							.274															*1M	
1873	Bal-n	53	262	62	83							.317															*1/O	
1874	Har-n	53	242	40	69							.285															*1	
1875	Har-n	78	353	58	92							.261															*1	
1876	Har-N	63	254	28	66	8	1	0	23	1	3	.260	.263	.299	.562	80	-4	-7	108	104	20	.410				-2	*1	-0.6
Total	5 n	269	1277	250	359							.281															*1	
■ FRANK MILLS	Mills, Frank Le Moyne b: 5/13/1895, Knoxville, Ohio d: 8/31/83, Youngstown, Ohio BL/TR, 6', 180 lbs. Deb: 9/22/14																											
1914	Cle-A	4	8	0	1	0	0	0	0	1	2	.125	.222	.125	.347	5	-1	-1	102	0	0	.286	0			0	/C	0.0
■ BRAD MILLS	Mills, James Bradley b: 1/19/57, Exter, Cal. BL/TR, 6', 195 lbs. Deb: 6/08/80																											
1980	Mon-N	21	60	1	18	1	0	0	8	5	6	.300	.354	.317	.671	89	-1	-1	99	167	7	.558	0	1	-1	-2	3	-0.2
1981	Mon-N	17	21	3	5	1	0	0	1	2	1	.238	.304	.286	.590	69	-1	-1	99	65	2	.471	0	0	0	-1	/32	-0.1
1982	Mon-N	54	67	6	15	3	0	1	2	5	11	.224	.278	.313	.591	62	-3	-4	105	33	5	.473	0	0	0	-0	3	-0.3
1983	Mon-N	14	20	1	5	0	0	0	1	2	3	.250	.318	.250	.568	58	-1	-1	102	79	2	.467	0	0	0	0	/31	0.0
Total	4	106	168	11	43	5	0	1	12	14	21	.256	.313	.304	.617	72	-6	-6	102	90	16	.516	0	1	-1	-3	/321	-0.6
■ RUPERT MILLS	Mills, Rupert Frank b: 10/12/1892, Newark, N.J. d: 7/20/29, Lake Hopatcong, N.J. BR/TR, 6'2", 185 lbs. Deb: 6/23/15																											
1915	New-F	41	134	12	27	5	1	0	16	6	21	.201	.236	.254	.489	48	-9	-8	94	170	10	.430	6			-1	1	-0.9
■ BILL MILLS	Mills, William Henry b: 11/2/20, Boston, Mass. BR/TR, 5'10", 175 lbs. Deb: 5/19/44																											
1944	Phi-A	5	4	0	1	0	0	0	0	1	1	.250	.400	.250	.650	87	0	0	101	0	0	.500	0	0	0	0	/C	0.0
■ PETE MILNE	Milne, William James b: 4/10/25, Mobile, Ala. BL/TR, 6'1", 180 lbs. Deb: 9/15/48																											
1948	NY-N	12	27	0	6	0	1	0	2	1	6	.222	.250	.296	.546	47	-2	-2	100	94	2	.429	0			-2	/O	-0.4
1949	NY-N	31	29	5	7	1	0	1	6	3	6	.241	.313	.379	.692	83	-1	-1	102	162	3	.609	0			0	/O	0.0
1950	NY-N	4	4	1	1	0	1	0	1	0	1	.250	.250	.750	1.000	154	0	0	98	129	1	1.000	0			0	H	0.0
Total	3	47	60	6	14	1	2	1	9	4	13	.233	.281	.367	.648	73	-2	-3	101	130	6	.565	0			-2	/O	-0.4
■ BRIAN MILNER	Milner, Brian Tate b: 11/17/59, Fort Worth, Tex. BR/TR, 6'2", 200 lbs. Deb: 6/23/78																											
1978	Tor-A	2	9	3	4	0	1	0	2	0	1	.444	.444	.667	1.111	208	1	1	100	114	3	1.200	0	0	0	0	/C	0.1
■ EDDIE MILNER	Milner, Eddie James b: 5/21/55, Columbus, Ohio BL/TL, 5'11", 173 lbs. Deb: 9/02/80																											
1980	Cin-N	6	3	1	0	0	0	0	0	0	0	.000	.000	.000	.000	-98	-1	-1	102	0	0	.000	0	0	0	0	/H	0.0
1981	Cin-N	8	5	0	1	1	0	0	1	1	1	.200	.333	.400	.733	106	0	0	101	196	1	.750	0	0	0	-1	/O	0.0
1982	Cin-N	113	407	61	109	23	5	4	31	41	40	.268	.338	.378	.716	98	0	-1	102	75	52	.678	18	12	-2	6	*O	0.2
1983	Cin-N	146	502	77	131	23	6	9	33	68	60	.261	.350	.384	.735	101	3	2	103	61	72	.769	41	12	5	12	*O	1.7
1984	Cin-N	117	336	44	78	8	4	7	29	51	50	.232	.337	.342	.679	86	-3	-5	106	84	42	.692	21	13	-2	5	*O	-0.5
1985	Cin-N	145	453	82	115	19	7	3	33	61	31	.254	.344	.347	.690	89	-2	-5	105	79	60	.718	35	13	3	8	*O	0.2
1986	Cin-N	145	424	70	110	22	6	15	47	36	56	.259	.317	.446	.763	104	3	1	104	80	59	.741	18	11	-1	0	*O	-0.2
1987	SF-N	101	214	38	54	14	0	4	19	24	33	.252	.328	.374	.702	89	-4	-3	96	82	26	.667	10	9	-2	-6	O	-1.5
1988	Cin-N	23	51	3	9	1	0	0	2	4	9	.176	.236	.196	.432	24	-5	-5	105	80	2	.364	2	2	-1	0	O	-0.6
Total	9	804	2395	376	607	111	28	42	195	286	280	.253	.335	.376	.710	94	-8	-18	103	76	314	.719	145	72	0	24	O	-0.7
■ JOHN MILNER	Milner, John David "The Hammer" b: 12/28/49, Atlanta, Ga. BL/TL, 6', 185 lbs. Deb: 9/15/71																											
1971	NY-N	9	18	1	3	1	0	0	1	0	3	.167	.167	.222	.389	10	-2	-2	96	102	1	.267	0	0	0	1	/O	0.0
1972	NY-N	117	362	52	86	12	2	17	38	51	74	.238	.340	.423	.762	121	8	10	95	76	54	.740	2	1	0	0	O1	0.5
1973	NY-N	129	451	69	108	12	3	23	72	62	84	.239	.333	.432	.765	110	6	6	101	112	64	.721	1	1	-0	-6	1O	-0.6
1974	NY-N	137	507	70	128	19	0	20	63	66	77	.252	.339	.408	.747	109	5	6	99	97	69	.709	10	2	2	-4	*1	-0.2
1975	NY-N	91	220	24	42	11	0	7	29	33	22	.191	.302	.336	.638	81	-7	-6	95	118	23	.598	1	1	-0	2	O1	-0.6
1976	NY-N	127	443	56	120	25	4	15	78	65	53	.271	.364	.447	.811	141	17	22	92	126	70	.769	0	7	-4	-1	*O1	1.2
1977	NY-N	131	388	43	99	20	3	12	57	61	55	.255	.356	.415	.771	111	4	6	96	116	59	.760	6	2	1	-1	1O	0.1
1978	Pit-N	108	295	39	80	17	0	6	38	34	25	.271	.347	.390	.736	100	2	1	105	113	41	.697	5	0	2	-5	O1	-0.6
1979	Pit-N	128	326	52	90	9	4	16	60	53	38	.276	.379	.475	.854	125	15	13	106	117	60	.862	3	5	-2	-6	O1	0.0
1980	Pit-N	114	238	31	58	6	0	8	34	52	29	.244	.379	.370	.749	106	5	4	103	120	36	.759	2	2	-1	-6	1O	-0.6
1981	Pit-N	34	59	6	14	1	0	2	9	5	3	.237	.297	.356	.653	88	-1	-1	96	131	6	.553	0	0	0	-2	/1O	-0.2
	Mon-N	31	76	6	18	5	0	3	9	12	6	.237	.341	.421	.762	117	2	2	99	86	11	.733	0	1	-1	-1	1	0.0
	Yr	65	135	12	32	6	0	5	18	17	9	.237	.322	.393	.715	105	0	1	97	111	18	.667	0	1	-1	-2		-0.2
1982	Mon-N	26	28	1	3	0	0	0	2	4	2	.107	.219	.107	.326	-6	-4	-4	105	261	1	.269	0	0	0	-0	/1	-0.4
	Pit-N	33	25	5	6	2	0	2	8	6	3	.240	.406	.560	.966	152	2	2	110	157	7	1.158	1	0	0	0	/1	0.2
	Yr	59	53	6	9	2	0	2	10	10	5	.170	.313	.321	.633	72	-1	-2	108	207	6	.659	1	0	0	-0		-0.2
Total	12	1215	3436	455	855	140	16	131	498	504	474	.249	.347	.413	.760	112	53	58	99	111	501	.755	31	22	-4	-28	1O	-1.2
■ MIKE MILOSEVICH	Milosevich, Michael "Mollie" b: 1/13/15, Zeigler, Ill. d: 2/3/66, E.Chicago, Ind. BR/TR, 5'10.5", 172 lbs. Deb: 4/30/44																											
1944	NY-A	94	312	27	77	11	4	0	32	30	37	.247	.313	.308	.621	73	-9	-11	106	120	29	.510	1	2	-1	-1	S	-0.8
1945	NY-A	30	69	5	15	2	0	0	7	6	6	.217	.289	.246	.536	52	-4	-4	107	149	5	.421	0	0	0	-1	S/2	-0.4
Total	2	124	381	32	92	13	4	0	39	36	43	.241	.309	.297	.605	69	-13	-15	106	125	34	.514	1	2	-1	-2	S/2	-1.2
■ DON MINCHER	Mincher, Donald Ray b: 6/24/38, Huntsville, Ala. BL/TR, 6'3", 205 lbs. Deb: 4/18/60																											
1960	Was-A	27	79	10	19	4	1	2	5	11	11	.241	.333	.392	.726	94	-0	-1	102	53	9	.636	0	1	-1	-2	1	-0.3
1961	Min-A	35	101	18	19	5	1	5	11	22	11	.188	.333	.406	.739	91	-0	-1	106	77	13	.716	0	1	-1	-2	1	-0.5
1962	Min-A	86	121	20	29	1	1	9	29	34	24	.240	.406	.488	.894	133	8	7	105	134	26	.969	0	0	0	2	1	0.7
1963	Min-A	82	225	41	58	8	0	17	42	30	51	.258	.353	.520	.873	140	12	12	100	105	44	.898	0	0	0	-1	1	1.0
1964	Min-A	120	287	45	68	12	4	23	56	27	51	.237	.303	.547	.850	129	10	10	101	105	45	.811	0	0	0	-0	1	0.7
1965	Min-A	128	346	43	87	17	3	22	65	49	73	.251	.348	.509	.856	139	18	17	101	111	62	.860	1	3	-2	-6	1/O	0.5
1966	Min-A	139	431	53	108	30	0	14	62	58	68	.251	.342	.418	.760	105	10	4	111	117	61	.719	3	2	-0	-2	*1	-0.2
1967	Cal-A	147	487	81	133	23	3	25	76	69	69	.273	.368	.487	.855	157	31	34	96	104	87	.842	0	3	-2	-2	*1/O	2.0
1968	Cal-A	120	399	35	94	12	1	13	48	43	65	.236	.316	.368	.685	114	3	6	94	113	47	.616	0	2	-1	2	*1	0.2
1969	Sea-A	140	427	53	105	14	0	25	78	78	69	.246	.369	.454	.823	131	18	19	98	116	72	.842	10	11	-4	6	*1	1.4
1970	Oak-A	140	463	62	114	18	0	27	74	56	71	.246	.331	.460	.791	120	9	11	97	104	70	.765	5	4	-1	-1	*1	0.3
1971	Oak-A	28	92	9	22	6	1	2	8	20	14	.239	.375	.391	.766	117	3	3	101	79	14	.781	1	1	-0	1	1	0.2
	Was-A	100	323	35	94	15	1	10	45	53	52	.291	.394	.437	.831	146	17	20	92	110	58	.835	2	1	0	5	1	2.1
	Yr	128	415	44	116	21	2	12	53	73	66	.280	.390	.427	.816	139	19	22	94	103	73	.828	3	2	-0	6		2.3

YEAR	TM/L	G	AB	R	H	2B	3B	HR	RBI	BB	SO	AVG	OBP	SLG	PRO	/A	BR	/A	PF	CHI	RC	TA	SB	CS	SBR	FR	POS	TPR
1972	Tex-A	61	191	23	45	10	0	6	39	46	23	.236	.389	.382	.771	138	9	11	94	183	33	.826	2	1	0	2	1	0.8
	Oak-A	47	54	2	8	1	0	0	5	10	16	.148	.281	.167	.448	37	-4	-4	97	232	2	.365	0	2	-1	0	1	-0.6
	Yr	108	245	25	53	11	0	6	44	56	39	.216	.366	.335	.701	115	6	7	95	206	34	.714	2	3	-1	2		0.2
Total	13	1400	4026	530	1003	176	16	200	643	606	668	.249	.351	.450	.801	128	144	148	99	113	644	.807	24	32	-12	3	*1/O	8.3

■ ED MINCHER Mincher, Edward John b: Baltimore, Md. Deb: 5/04/1871

YEAR	TM/L	G	AB	R	H	2B	3B	HR	RBI	BB	SO	AVG	OBP	SLG	PRO	/A	BR	/A	PF	CHI	RC	TA	SB	CS	SBR	FR	POS	TPR
1871	Kek-n	9	36	4	8							.222															/O	
1872	Nat-n	11	51	5	6							.118															O	
Total	2 n	20	87	9	14							.161															O	

■ DAN MINNEHAN Minnehan, Daniel Joseph b: 11/28/1865, Troy, N.Y. d: 8/8/29, Troy, N.Y. BR/TR, 5'10", 145 lbs. Deb: 9/20/1895

YEAR	TM/L	G	AB	R	H	2B	3B	HR	RBI	BB	SO	AVG	OBP	SLG	PRO	/A	BR	/A	PF	CHI	RC	TA	SB	CS	SBR	FR	POS	TPR
1895	Lou-N	8	34	6	13	0	0	0	6	1	1	.382	.400	.382	.782	110	0	1	95	137	5	.667	0			0	/3O	0.0

■ MINNIE MINOSO Minoso, Saturnino Orestes Armas (Arrieta) b: 11/29/22, Havana, Cuba BR/TR, 5'10", 175 lbs. Deb: 4/19/49 C

YEAR	TM/L	G	AB	R	H	2B	3B	HR	RBI	BB	SO	AVG	OBP	SLG	PRO	/A	BR	/A	PF	CHI	RC	TA	SB	CS	SBR	FR	POS	TPR
1949	Cle-A	9	16	2	3	0	0	1	1	2	2	.188	.350	.375	.725	94	-0	-0	98	38	1	.625	0	1	-1	-1	/O	-0.1
1951	Cle-A	8	14	3	6	2	0	0	2	1	1	.429	.529	.571	1.101	209	2	2	95	89	5	1.375	0	0	0	-0	/1	0.2
	Chi-A	138	516	109	167	32	14	10	74	71	41	.324	.419	.498	.917	152	36	38	97	98	115	1.005	31	10	3	-12	O3/S	2.3
	Yr	146	530	112	173	34	**14**	10	76	72	42	.326	.422	.500	.922	154	38	41	97	98	120	1.013	**31**	10	3	-13		2.5
1952	Chi-A	147	569	96	160	24	9	13	61	71	46	.281	.375	.424	.798	122	18	18	100	72	92	.791	**22**	16	-3	10	*O/3S	2.2
1953	Chi-A	151	556	104	174	24	8	15	104	74	43	.313	.410	.466	.875	128	31	26	106	134	106	.891	**25**	16	-2	2	*O3	2.1
1954	Chi-A	153	568	119	182	29	**18**	19	116	77	46	.320	.416	.535	.951	154	47	45	104	117	125	.995	18	11	-1	13	*O/3	5.3
1955	Chi-A	139	517	79	149	26	7	10	70	76	43	.288	.390	.424	.813	118	16	15	101	101	87	.822	19	8	1	12	*O/3	2.0
1956	Chi-A	151	545	106	172	29	**11**	21	88	86	40	.316	.430	.525	.954	145	43	40	104	100	130	1.046	12	6	0	-2	*O/31	2.9
1957	Chi-A	153	568	96	176	**36**	5	12	103	79	54	.310	.413	.454	.867	138	33	33	99	**147**	106	.883	18	15	-4	-1	*O/3	2.0
1958	Cle-A	149	556	94	168	25	2	24	80	59	53	.302	.384	.484	.868	145	29	33	94	100	101	.860	14	14	-4	7	*O/3	2.7
1959	Cle-A	148	570	92	172	32	0	21	92	54	46	.302	.379	.468	.848	136	25	28	97	106	100	.826	8	10	-4	12	*O	2.9
1960	Chi-A	154	591	89	**184**	32	4	20	105	52	63	.311	.380	.481	.860	129	26	25	101	127	104	.839	17	13	-3	3	*O	1.9
1961	Chi-A	152	540	91	151	28	3	14	82	67	46	.280	.376	.420	.796	113	11	12	99	126	89	.790	9	4	0	-4	*O	0.3
1962	StL-N	39	97	14	19	5	0	1	10	7	17	.196	.271	.278	.549	44	-7	-8	109	131	8	.519	4	0	1	-3	O	-1.0
1963	Was-A	109	315	38	72	12	2	4	30	33	38	.229	.317	.317	.635	81	-8	-7	98	112	30	.567	8	6	-1	-9	O/3	-2.1
1964	Chi-A	30	31	4	7	0	0	1	5	5	3	.226	.351	.323	.674	93	-0	-0	96	163	4	.667	0	0	0	-0	/O	0.0
1976	Chi-A	3	8	0	1	0	0	0	0	0	2	.125	.125	.125	.250	-27	-1	-1	99	0	0	.143	0	0	0	0	/D	0.0
1980	Chi-A	2	2	0	0	0	0	0	0	0	0	.000	.000	.000	.000	-99	-1	-1	97	0	0	.000	0	0	0	0	/H	0.0
Total	17	1835	6579	1136	1963	336	83	186	1023	814	584	.298	.391	.459	.851	130	299	298	100	112	1204	.892	205	130	-16	25	*O3/1DS	23.6

■ WILLIE MIRANDA Miranda, Guillermo (Perez) b: 5/24/26, Velasco, Cuba BB/TR, 5'9.5", 150 lbs. Deb: 5/06/51

YEAR	TM/L	G	AB	R	H	2B	3B	HR	RBI	BB	SO	AVG	OBP	SLG	PRO	/A	BR	/A	PF	CHI	RC	TA	SB	CS	SBR	FR	POS	TPR
1951	Was-A	7	9	2	4	0	0	0	0	0	0	.444	.444	.444	.889	148	0	1	95	0	2	.800	0	0	0	-0	/S1	0.0
1952	Chi-A	12	8	1	2	1	0	0	0	3	0	.250	.455	.375	.830	133	1	1	100	0	2	1.000	0	0	0	0	/S32	0.1
	StL-A	7	11	2	1	0	1	0	1	3	1	.091	.286	.273	.558	58	-1	-1	97	124	1	.600	0	0	0	-0	/S	0.0
	Chi-A	58	142	13	31	3	1	0	7	10	14	.218	.275	.254	.528	48	-10	-10	100	73	11	.425	1	0	0	-1	S/23	-0.8
	Yr	77	161	16	34	4	2	0	8	16	15	.211	.287	.261	.547	53	-10	-10	100	68	14	.465	1	0	0	-2		-0.7
1953	StL-A	17	6	2	1	0	0	0	0	1	1	.167	.286	.167	.452	23	-1	-1	107	0	0	.500	1	1	-0	0	/S3	0.0
	NY-A	48	58	12	13	0	0	1	5	5	10	.224	.286	.276	.562	56	-4	-3	93	97	4	.440	1	1	-0	2	S	0.2
	Yr	65	64	14	14	0	0	1	5	6	11	.219	.286	.266	.551	51	-4	-4	96	72	4	.446	2	2	-1	3		0.2
1954	NY-A	92	116	12	29	4	2	1	12	10	10	.250	.310	.345	.654	80	-4	-3	99	106	12	.543	0	3	-2	4	S/23	0.6
1955	Bal-A	153	487	42	124	12	6	1	38	42	58	.255	.315	.310	.625	76	-21	-15	90	92	48	.528	4	3	-1	19	*S/2	2.0
1956	Bal-A	148	461	38	100	16	4	2	34	46	73	.217	.288	.282	.570	54	-33	-29	94	93	38	.477	3	6	-3	-1	*S	-1.8
1957	Bal-A	115	314	29	61	3	0	0	20	24	42	.194	.251	.204	.455	28	-32	-29	93	123	17	.347	2	1	0	-1	*S	-2.1
1958	Bal-A	102	214	15	43	6	0	1	8	14	25	.201	.250	.243	.493	39	-19	-17	94	58	13	.385	1	1	-0	-11	*S	-1.4
1959	Bal-A	65	88	8	14	5	0	0	7	7	16	.159	.221	.216	.437	21	-10	-9	97	145	4	.342	0	0	0	0	S3/2	-0.4
Total	9	824	1914	176	423	50	14	6	132	165	250	.221	.284	.271	.555	54	-131	-116	94	95	152	.463	13	16	-6	11	S/321	-3.6

■ JOHN MISSE Misse, John Beverly b: 5/30/1885, Highland, Kan. d: 3/18/70, St.Joseph, Mo. BR/TR, 5'8", 150 lbs. Deb: 5/26/14

YEAR	TM/L	G	AB	R	H	2B	3B	HR	RBI	BB	SO	AVG	OBP	SLG	PRO	/A	BR	/A	PF	CHI	RC	TA	SB	CS	SBR	FR	POS	TPR
1914	StL-F	99	306	28	60	8	1	0	22	36	52	.196	.281	.229	.509	44	-20	-22	106	113	24	.443	3			-18	2S/3	-3.7

■ CLARENCE MITCHELL Mitchell, Clarence Elmer b: 2/22/1891, Franklin, Neb. d: 11/6/63, Grand Island, Neb. BL/TL, 5'11.5", 190 lbs. Deb: 6/02/11

YEAR	TM/L	G	AB	R	H	2B	3B	HR	RBI	BB	SO	AVG	OBP	SLG	PRO	/A	BR	/A	PF	CHI	RC	TA	SB	CS	SBR	FR	POS	TPR
1911	Det-A	5	4	2	2	0	0	0	0	1		.500	.600	.500	1.100	193	1	1	108	0	1	1.500	0			0	/P	0.0
1916	Cin-N	56	117	11	28	2	1	0	11	4	6	.239	.264	.274	.538	67	-5	-5	98	136	9	.416	1			-0	P/1O	0.0
1917	Cin-N	47	90	13	25	3	0	0	5	5	5	.278	.316	.311	.627	100	-1	-0	92	69	9	.508	0			-0	P/1O	0.0
1918	Bro-N	10	24	2	6	1	1	0	2	0	3	.250	.250	.375	.625	88	-0	-0	101	84	2	.500	0			-2	/O1P	-0.3
1919	Bro-N	34	49	7	18	1	0	1	2	4	4	.367	.415	.449	.864	170	4	4	94	31	9	.839	0			1	P	0.0
1920	Bro-N	55	107	9	25	2	2	0	11	8	9	.234	.287	.290	.577	59	-5	-6	111	137	9	.488	1	0	0	2	P1/O	-0.1
1921	Bro-N	46	91	11	24	5	0	0	12	5	7	.264	.316	.319	.635	66	-4	-5	105	152	10	.574	3	1	0	3	P	0.0
1922	Bro-N	56	155	21	45	6	3	3	28	19	6	.290	.371	.426	.797	110	1	3	95	130	25	.782	0	0	0	2	1/P	0.5
1923	Phi-N	53	78	10	21	3	2	1	9	4	11	.269	.305	.397	.702	74	-2	-3	114	93	9	.614	0	0	0	-3	P	0.0
1924	Phi-N	69	102	7	26	3	0	0	13	2	7	.255	.276	.284	.561	47	-7	-8	108	163	8	.434	1	0	0	3	P	0.0
1925	Phi-N	52	92	7	18	2	0	0	13	5	9	.196	.237	.217	.455	15	-11	-14	116	231	5	.365	2	0	1	4	P/1	0.0
1926	Phi-N	39	78	8	19	4	0	0	6	5	5	.244	.289	.295	.584	56	-5	-5	103	90	7	.475	0			4	P/1	0.0
1927	Phi-N	18	42	5	10	2	0	1	6	2	1	.238	.273	.357	.630	70	-2	-2	96	117	4	.531	0			0	P	0.0
1928	Phi-N	5	4	0	1	0	0	0	0	0	0	.250	.250	.250	.500	30	-0	-0	104	0	0	.333	0			0	/P	0.0
	StL-N	19	56	0	7	1	0	0	1	0	3	.125	.125	.143	.268	-30	-11	-11	100	44	1	.163	0			3	P	0.0
	Yr	24	60	0	8	1	0	0	1	0	3	.133	.133	.150	.283	-26	-11	-11	101	35	1	.173	0			3		0.0
1929	StL-N	26	66	9	18	3	1	0	9	4	6	.273	.314	.348	.663	65	-4	-4	98	134	7	.583	1			-1	P	0.0
1930	StL-N	1	2	0	1	0	0	0	0	0	0	.500	.500	.500	1.000	136	0	0	105	0	0	1.000	0			0	/P	0.0
	NY-N	24	47	9	12	1	0	0	1	1	5	.255	.271	.277	.547	34	-5	-5	98	26	3	.400	0			2	P	0.0
	Yr	25	49	9	13	1	0	0	1	1	5	.265	.280	.286	.566	38	-5	-5	98	25	4	.417	0			2		0.0
1931	NY-N	27	73	5	16	2	0	1	4	2	4	.219	.240	.288	.528	43	-6	-6	97	59	5	.404	0			-2	P	0.0
1932	NY-N	8	10	2	2	0	0	0	0	1	1	.200	.273	.200	.473	30	-1	-1	99	0	1	.375	0			-1	/P	0.0
Total	18	650	1287	138	324	41	10	7	133	72	92	.252	.293	.315	.609	64	-63	-67	102	116	125	.509	9	1		15	P/1O	0.1

■ FRED MITCHELL Mitchell, Frederick Francis (born Frederick Francis Yapp) b: 6/5/1878, Cambridge, Mass. d: 10/13/70, Newton, Mass. BR/TR, 5'9.5", 185 lbs. Deb: 4/27/01 M

YEAR	TM/L	G	AB	R	H	2B	3B	HR	RBI	BB	SO	AVG	OBP	SLG	PRO	/A	BR	/A	PF	CHI	RC	TA	SB	CS	SBR	FR	POS	TPR
1901	Bos-A	20	44	5	7	0	2	0	4	2		.159	.196	.250	.446	25	-5	-4	97	115	2	.351	0			0	P/2S	0.0
1902	Bos-A	1	1	0	0	0	0	0	0	0		.000	.000	.000	.000	-99	-0	-0	99	0	0	.000	0			0	/P	0.0
	Phi-A	19	48	7	9	1	1	0	3	1		.188	.204	.250	.454	24	-5	-5	108	82	3	.359	1			2	P/O	0.0
	Yr	20	49	7	9	1	1	0	3	1		.184	.200	.245	.445	22	-5	-6	108	78	3	.350	1			3		0.0
1903	Phi-N	29	95	11	19	4	0	0	10	0		.200	.200	.242	.442	29	-9	-8	92	140	5	.303	0			-3	P	0.0
1904	Phi-N	25	82	9	17	3	1	0	3	5		.207	.253	.268	.521	67	-4	-3	93	50	6	.431	1			2	P/13O	0.0
	Bro-N	8	24	3	7	1	1	0	6	1		.292	.320	.417	.737	135	1	1	95	220	3	.647	0			1	/P	0.0
	Yr	33	106	12	24	4	2	0	9	6		.226	.268	.302	.570	83	-3	-2	93	92	9	.476	1			3		0.0
1905	Bro-N	27	79	4	15	0	0	0	8	4		.190	.229	.190	.419	28	-7	-6	96	185	4	.297	0			1	P/13SO	-0.2
1910	NY-A	68	196	16	45	7	2	0	18	9		.230	.274	.286	.560	70	-6	-8	107	119	16	.490	6			-5	C	-0.5
1913	Bos-N	4	3	0	1	0	0	0	0	0	2	.333	.333	.333	.667	96	-0	-0	95	0	0	.500	0			0	H	0.0
Total	7	201	572	55	120	16	7	0	52	22	2	.210	.243	.262	.505	52	-34	-34	100	121	39	.405	8			-1	/PC13OS2	-0.7

■ JOHNNY MITCHELL Mitchell, John Franklin b: 8/9/1894, Detroit, Mich. d: 11/4/65, Birmingham, Mich. BB/TR, 5'8", 155 lbs. Deb: 5/21/21

YEAR	TM/L	G	AB	R	H	2B	3B	HR	RBI	BB	SO	AVG	OBP	SLG	PRO	/A	BR	/A	PF	CHI	RC	TA	SB	CS	SBR	FR	POS	TPR
1921	NY-A	13	42	4	11	1	0	0	2	4	4	.262	.326	.286	.612	56	-3	-3	103	57	4	.548	1	0	0	0	/S2	0.0
1922	NY-A	4	4	1	0	0	0	0	0	0	1	.000	.000	.000	.000	-99	-1	-1	102	0	0	.000	0	0	0	0	/S	0.0
	Bos-A	59	203	20	51	4	1	1	8	16	17	.251	.318	.296	.614	63	-11	-10	96	46	20	.526	1	2	-1	-7	S	-1.0

YEAR	TM/L	G	AB	R	H	2B	3B	HR	RBI	BB	SO	AVG	OBP	SLG	PRO	/A	BR	/A	PF	CHI	RC	TA	SB	CS	SBR	FR	POS	TPR
	Yr	63	207	21	51	4	1	1	8	16	18	.246	.313	.290	.603	60	-12	-11	97	43	20	.513	1	2	-1	-7		-1.0
1923	Bos-A	92	347	40	78	15	4	0	19	34	18	.225	.296	.291	.587	54	-23	-24	102	68	29	.511	7	11	-5	2	S/2	-1.6
1924	Bro-N	64	243	42	64	10	0	1	16	37	22	.263	.361	.317	.678	84	-4	-4	99	64	31	.650	3	1	0	-3	S	0.0
1925	Bro-N	97	336	45	84	8	3	0	18	28	19	.250	.308	.292	.599	58	-23	-20	94	65	32	.508	2	0	1	0	S	-1.0
Total	5	329	1175	152	288	38	8	2	63	119	81	.245	.317	.296	.613	62	-65	-61	98	62	117	.539	14	14	-4	-7	S/2	-3.6
■ **KEVIN MITCHELL** Mitchell, Kevin Darnell b: 1/13/62, San Diego, Cal. BR/TR, 5'10", 186 lbs. Deb: 9/04/84																												
1984	NY-N	7	14	0	3	0	0	0	1	0	3	.214	.214	.214	.429	21	-1	-1	100	131	0	.250	0	1	-1	-0	/3	-0.1
1986	NY-N	108	328	51	91	22	2	12	43	33	61	.277	.345	.466	.812	127	9	11	96	91	52	.772	3	3	-1	-1	OS/31	1.0
1987	SD-N	62	196	19	48	7	1	7	26	20	38	.245	.315	.398	.713	90	-4	-3	97	105	24	.641	0	0	0	-1	3/O	-0.3
	SF-N	69	268	49	82	13	1	15	44	28	50	.306	.376	.530	.906	142	14	15	96	99	52	.919	9	6	-1	0	3/OS	1.3
	Yr	131	464	68	130	20	2	22	70	48	88	.280	.350	.474	.824	120	10	12	96	103	78	.809	9	6	-1	-1		1.0
1988	SF-N	148	505	60	127	25	7	19	80	48	85	.251	.323	.442	.764	125	10	14	94	117	71	.717	5	5	-2	3	*3O	1.5
Total	4	394	1311	179	351	67	11	53	194	129	237	.268	.337	.457	.794	123	28	36	95	105	200	.765	17	15	-4	2	3O/S1	3.4
■ **DALE MITCHELL** Mitchell, Loren Dale b: 8/23/21, Colony, Okla. d: 1/5/87, Tulsa, Okla. BL/TL, 6'1", 195 lbs. Deb: 9/15/46																												
1946	Cle-A	11	44	7	19	3	0	0	5	1	2	.432	.444	.500	.944	185	4	4	89	92	10	.923	1	0	0	1	O	0.4
1947	Cle-A	123	493	69	156	16	10	1	34	23	14	.316	.347	.396	.742	111	3	5	96	67	69	.640	2	5	-2	1	*O	0.0
1948	Cle-A	141	608	82	204	30	8	4	56	45	17	.336	.383	.431	.814	118	13	15	99	61	98	.747	13	18	-7	3	*O	0.5
1949	Cle-A	149	640	81	**203**	16	**23**	3	56	43	11	.317	.360	.428	.788	111	5	7	98	60	102	.730	10	3	1	2	*O	0.6
1950	Cle-A	130	506	81	156	27	5	3	49	67	21	.308	.390	.399	.789	105	4	5	98	85	83	.750	3	7	-3	-12	*O	-1.1
1951	Cle-A	134	510	83	148	21	7	11	62	53	16	.290	.358	.424	.782	117	7	11	95	94	79	.735	7	7	-2	-4	*O	0.0
1952	Cle-A	134	511	61	165	26	3	5	58	52	9	.323	.387	.415	.801	136	17	22	91	101	82	.740	6	6	-2	-5	*O	1.2
1953	Cle-A	134	500	76	150	26	4	13	60	42	20	.300	.354	.446	.800	121	9	12	95	87	80	.740	3	1	0	-11	*O	-0.1
1954	Cle-A	53	60	6	17	1	0	1	6	9	1	.283	.377	.350	.727	94	0	-0	106	95	8	.682	0	0	0	-1	/O1	0.0
1955	Cle-A	61	58	4	15	2	1	0	10	4	3	.259	.306	.328	.634	68	-2	-3	104	196	5	.511	0	0	0	-1	/1O	-0.3
1956	Cle-A	38	30	2	4	0	0	0	6	7	2	.133	.297	.133	.431	17	-3	-3	101	560	2	.423	0	0	0	-0	/O	-0.3
	Bro-N	19	24	3	7	1	0	0	1	0	3	.292	.292	.333	.625	66	-1	-1	103	53	2	.421	0	0	0	-0	/O	-0.1
Total	11	1127	3984	555	1244	169	61	41	403	346	119	.312	.368	.416	.784	115	54	73	96	84	622	.736	45	47	-15	-28	O/1	0.8
■ **MIKE MITCHELL** Mitchell, Michael Francis b: 12/12/1879, Springfield, Ohio d: 7/16/61, Phoenix, Ariz. BR/TR, 6'1", 185 lbs. Deb: 4/11/07																												
1907	Cin-N	148	558	64	163	17	12	3	47	37		.292	.336	.382	.718	133	16	18	95	77	79	.676	17			16	*O/1	3.2
1908	Cin-N	119	406	41	90	9	6	1	37	46		.222	.301	.281	.582	86	-4	-5	103	129	38	.563	18			0	*O/1	-0.6
1909	Cin-N	145	523	83	162	17	**17**	4	86	57		.310	.378	.430	.808	162	31	35	94	140	97	.884	37			1	*O/1	3.3
1910	Cin-N	156	583	79	167	16	**18**	5	88	59	56	.286	.356	.401	.757	119	14	14	101	131	96	.798	35			-4	*O/1	0.4
1911	Cin-N	142	529	74	154	22	22	2	84	44	34	.291	.348	.427	.775	127	10	15	92	130	90	.819	35			8	*O	1.8
1912	Cin-N	147	552	60	156	14	13	4	78	41	43	.283	.333	.377	.710	102	-6	0	92	127	76	.689	23			-7	*O	-1.1
1913	Chi-N	82	279	37	73	11	6	4	35	32	33	.262	.340	.387	.727	109	3	3	99	108	41	.757	15			6	O	0.8
	Pit-N	54	199	25	54	8	2	1	16	14	15	.271	.319	.347	.666	94	-3	-2	96	82	23	.628	8			4	O	0.1
	Yr	136	478	62	127	19	8	5	51	46	48	.266	.331	.370	.702	103	-0	1	98	99	63	.704	23			10		0.9
1914	Pit-N	76	273	31	64	11	5	2	23	16	16	.234	.279	.333	.613	89	-7	-5	92	88	26	.541	5			8	O	0.2
	Was-A	55	193	20	55	5	3	1	20	22	19	.285	.361	.358	.719	115	4	4	101	110	27	.697	9	7	-2	4	O	0.4
Total	8	1124	4095	514	1138	130	104	27	514	368	216	.278	.339	.380	.719	117	58	78	96	116	592	.721	202	7		36	*O/1	8.5
■ **BOBBY MITCHELL** Mitchell, Robert Van b: 4/7/55, Salt Lake City, Utah BL/TL, 5'10", 170 lbs. Deb: 9/01/80																												
1980	LA-N	9	3	1	1	0	0	0	0	1	0	.333	.500	.333	.833	141	0	0	97	0	1	1.000	0	0	0	-2	/O	-0.2
1981	LA-N	10	8	0	1	0	0	0	0	1	4	.125	.222	.125	.347	1	-1	-1	98	0	0	.286	0	0	0	-2	/O	-0.2
1982	Min-A	124	454	48	113	11	6	2	28	54	53	.249	.331	.313	.644	78	-12	-12	100	80	48	.579	8	9	-3	10	*O	-0.9
1983	Min-A	59	152	26	35	4	2	1	15	28	21	.230	.354	.303	.656	79	-2	-4	105	120	18	.628	1	1	-0	0	O	-0.3
Total	4	202	617	75	150	15	8	3	43	84	78	.243	.337	.308	.645	78	-15	-17	101	89	67	.596	9	10	-3	6	O	-1.6
■ **BOBBY MITCHELL** Mitchell, Robert Vance b: 10/22/43, Norristown, Pa. BR/TR, 6'3", 185 lbs. Deb: 7/05/70																												
1970	NY-A	10	22	1	5	2	0	0	4	2	3	.227	.320	.318	.638	83	-1	-0	92	231	2	.526	0	2	-1	1	/O	0.0
1971	Mil-A	35	55	7	10	1	1	2	6	6	18	.182	.262	.345	.608	69	-2	-2	103	98	5	.532	0	2	-1	1	O	-0.3
1973	Mil-A	47	130	12	29	6	0	5	20	5	32	.223	.252	.385	.636	80	-5	-4	96	121	13	.578	4	1	1	-5	OD	-0.8
1974	Mil-A	88	173	27	42	6	2	5	20	18	46	.243	.318	.387	.705	100	0	-0	102	96	20	.664	7	6	-2	-6	DO	-0.8
1975	Mil-A	93	229	39	57	14	3	9	41	25	69	.249	.323	.454	.777	118	5	5	100	120	32	.729	3	4	-2	-6	OD	-0.4
Total	5	273	609	86	143	29	6	21	91	56	168	.235	.301	.406	.707	99	-3	-3	100	115	72	.656	14	15	-5	-15	O/D	-2.3
■ **RALPH MITTERLING** Mitterling, Ralph "Sarge" b: 4/19/1890, Freeburg, Pa. d: 1/22/56, Pittsburgh, Pa. 5'10", 165 lbs. Deb: 7/07/16																												
1916	Phi-A	13	39	1	6	0	0	0	2	3	6	.154	.214	.154	.368	11	-4	-4	98	119	1	.273	0			-1	O	-0.6
■ **GEORGE MITTERWALD** Mitterwald, George Eugene b: 6/7/45, Berkeley, Cal. BR/TR, 6'2", 195 lbs. Deb: 9/15/66 C																												
1966	Min-A	3	5	1	1	0	0	0	0	0	0	.200	.200	.200	.400	14	-1	-1	111	0	0	.250	0	0	0	-0	/C	0.0
1968	Min-A	11	34	1	7	1	0	0	1	3	8	.206	.270	.235	.506	51	-2	-2	106	54	2	.393	0	0	0	-1	C	-0.2
1969	Min-A	69	187	18	48	8	0	5	13	17	47	.257	.329	.380	.708	96	-1	-1	102	61	23	.623	0	1	-1	-5	C/O	-0.2
1970	Min-A	117	369	36	82	12	2	15	46	34	84	.222	.291	.388	.679	87	-8	-8	98	99	39	.601	3	5	-2	-8	*C	-1.6
1971	Min-A	125	388	38	97	13	1	13	44	39	104	.250	.319	.389	.708	96	-1	-3	104	95	47	.637	3	3	-1	-3	*C	-0.1
1972	Min-A	64	163	12	30	4	1	1	8	9	37	.184	.227	.239	.466	36	-12	-14	107	80	8	.345	0	1	-1	-9	C	-2.6
1973	Min-A	125	432	50	112	15	0	16	64	39	111	.259	.328	.405	.733	102	3	1	104	113	57	.671	3	1	0	1	*C/D	0.5
1974	Chi-N	78	215	17	54	7	0	7	28	18	42	.251	.315	.381	.696	94	-2	-2	100	105	25	.613	1	3	-2	-7	C	-0.7
1975	Chi-N	84	200	19	44	4	3	5	26	19	42	.220	.288	.345	.633	72	-7	-8	104	120	20	.553	0	0	0	-5	C1	-1.2
1976	Chi-N	101	303	19	65	7	0	5	28	16	63	.215	.254	.287	.541	49	-19	-22	109	106	20	.418	1	2	-1	0	C1	-2.1
1977	Chi-N	110	349	40	83	22	0	9	43	28	69	.238	.296	.378	.675	70	-11	-17	114	108	34	.575	3	1	0	-2	*C/1	-2.0
Total	11	887	2645	251	623	93	7	76	301	222	607	.236	.298	.362	.660	80	-61	-77	105	100	275	.587	14	17	-6	-39	C/1DO	-10.2
■ **JOHNNY MIZE** Mize, John Robert "The Big Cat" b: 1/7/13, Demorest, Ga. BL/TR, 6'2", 215 lbs. Deb: 4/16/36 H																												
1936	StL-N	126	414	76	136	30	8	19	93	50	32	.329	.402	.577	.979	170	35	38	94	111	102	1.032	1			-1	1/O	2.7
1937	StL-N	145	560	103	204	40	7	25	113	56	57	.364	.427	.595	1.021	174	57	57	101	106	150	1.097	2			-13	*1	3.5
1938	StL-N	149	531	85	179	34	**16**	27	102	74	47	.337	.422	**.614**	**1.036**	163	59	51	111	92	141	1.104	0			-2	*1	3.7
1939	StL-N	153	564	104	197	44	14	**28**	108	92	49	**.349**	.444	**.626**	**1.070**	176	**69**	**65**	105	96	**162**	**1.194**	0			-4	*1	**4.2**
1940	StL-N	155	579	111	182	31	13	**43**	**137**	82	49	.314	.404	**.636**	**1.039**	**179**	**64**	**62**	102	108	**152**	**1.135**	7			-7	*1	4.2
1941	StL-N	126	473	67	150	**39**	8	16	100	70	45	.317	.406	.535	.941	149	40	34	110	127	106	.991	4			1	*1	1.9
1942	NY-N	142	541	97	165	25	7	26	**110**	60	39	.305	.380	**.521**	.901	158	41	39	103	120	110	.911	3			-2	*1	2.7
1946	NY-N	101	377	70	127	18	3	22	70	62	26	.337	.437	.576	1.013	183	44	43	102	89	100	1.125	3			1	*1	3.6
1947	NY-N	154	586	**137**	177	26	2	**51**	**138**	74	42	.302	.384	.614	.998	160	48	48	101	106	143	1.060	2			8	*1	4.5
1948	NY-N	152	560	110	162	26	4	**40**	125	94	37	.289	.395	.564	.959	157	45	45	100	114	131	1.032	4			3	*1	4.6
1949	NY-N	106	388	59	102	15	0	18	62	50	19	.263	.351	.441	.792	109	6	5	102	110	63	.773	1			-2	*1	0.3
	NY-A	13	23	4	6	1	0	1	2	4	2	.261	.393	.435	.828	118	1	1	100	53	5	.882	0	0	0	-0	/1	0.0
1950	NY-A	90	274	43	76	12	0	25	72	29	24	.277	.351	.595	.946	139	13	13	99	104	59	.956	0	1	-1	-3	1	0.5
1951	NY-A	113	332	37	86	14	1	10	49	36	24	.259	.339	.398	.736	108	-1	3	92	108	47	.684	1	0	0	-0	1	0.1
1952	NY-A	78	137	9	36	9	0	4	29	11	15	.263	.327	.416	.743	108	1	1	98	157	18	.654	0	0	0	-0	1	0.0
1953	NY-A	81	104	6	26	3	0	4	27	12	17	.250	.339	.394	.733	105	-0	1	93	189	15	.696	0	0	0	-0	1	0.0
Total	15	1884	6443	1118	2011	367	83	359	1337	856	524	.312	.397	.562	.959	157	520	505	102	109	1502	1.028	28	1		-21	*1/O	36.5
■ **JOHN MIZEROCK** Mizerock, John Joseph b: 12/8/60, Punxsutawney, Pa. BL/TR, 5'11", 190 lbs. Deb: 4/12/83																												
1983	Hou-N	33	85	8	13	4	1	1	10	12	15	.153	.265	.259	.524	51	-6	-5	90	158	6	.473	0	0	0	-2	C	-0.5
1985	Hou-N	15	38	6	9	4	0	0	6	2	8	.237	.293	.342	.635	80	-1	-1	96	184	3	.485	0	0	0	0	C	0.0
1986	Hou-N	44	81	9	15	1	1	1	6	24	16	.185	.377	.259	.637	77	-1	-1	103	100	9	.657	0	0	0	-6	C	-0.6

YEAR	TM/L	G	AB	R	H	2B	3B	HR	RBI	BB	SO	AVG	OBP	SLG	PRO	/A	BR	/A	PF	CHI	RC	TA	SB	CS	SBR	FR	POS	TPR
Total	3	92	204	23	37	9	2	2	22	38	39	.181	.318	.275	.593	68	-8	-7	96	137	18	.567	0	0	0	-8	/C	-1.1
■ **BILL MIZEUR**	Mizeur, William Francis "Bad Bill" b: 6/22/1897, Nokomis, Ill. d: 8/27/76, Decatur, Ill. BL/TR, 6', 180 lbs. Deb: 9/30/23																											
1923	StL-A	1	1	0	0	0	0	0	0	0	0	.000	.000	.000	.000	-96	-0	-0	104	0	0	.000	0	0	0	0	H	0.0
1924	StL-A	1	1	0	0	0	0	0	0	0	0	.000	.000	.000	.000	-93	-0	-0	107	0	0	.000	0	0	0	0	H	0.0
Total	2	2	2	0	0	0	0	0	0	0	0	.000	.000	.000	.000	-95	-1	-1	106	0	0	.000	0	0	0	0		0.0
■ **DAVE MOATES**	Moates, David Allan b: 1/30/48, Great Lakes, Ill. BL/TL, 5'9", 163 lbs. Deb: 9/21/74																											
1974	Tex-A	1	0	0	0	0	0	0	0	0	0	—	—	—	—	—	0	0	96	—	—	—	0	0	0	0	R	0.0
1975	Tex-A	54	175	21	48	9	0	3	14	13	15	.274	.324	.377	.702	98	-1	-1	100	72	20	.638	9	2	2	4	O/D	0.4
1976	Tex-A	85	137	21	33	7	1	0	13	11	18	.241	.297	.307	.604	75	-4	-4	102	119	13	.551	6	3	0	-7	O/D	-1.2
Total	3	140	312	42	81	16	1	3	27	24	33	.260	.313	.346	.659	88	-5	-5	101	92	33	.623	15	5	2	-3	O/D	-0.8
■ **DANNY MOELLER**	Moeller, Daniel Edward b: 3/23/1885, De Witt, Iowa d: 4/14/51, Florence, Ala. BB/TR, 5'11", 165 lbs. Deb: 9/24/07																											
1907	Pit-N	11	42	4	12	1	1	0	3	4		.286	.348	.357	.705	117	1	1	105	65	6	.700	2			1	O	0.1
1908	Pit-N	36	109	14	21	3	1	0	9	9		.193	.254	.239	.493	62	-5	-4	95	133	7	.443	4			1	O	-0.3
1912	Was-A	132	519	90	143	26	10	6	46	52		.276	.346	.399	.745	114	8	8	99	60	81	.779	30			8	*O	0.8
1913	Was-A	153	589	88	139	15	10	5	42	72	103	.236	.322	.321	.643	83	-8	-12	106	63	75	.724	62			0	*O	-2.1
1914	Was-A	151	571	83	143	19	10	1	45	71	89	.250	.341	.324	.665	99	1	1	101	79	65	.638	26	25	-7	-8	*O	-2.5
1915	Was-A	118	438	65	99	11	10	2	23	59	63	.226	.319	.311	.630	88	-6	-6	101	49	51	.653	32	10	4	-6	*O	-1.5
1916	Was-A	78	240	30	59	8	1	1	23	30	35	.246	.335	.300	.635	91	-2	-2	100	110	29	.646	13			-1	O	-0.6
	Cle-A	25	30	5	2	0	0	0	1	5	6	.067	.200	.067	.267	-20	-4	-4	100	179	1	.321	2			-2	/O2	-0.7
	Yr	103	270	35	61	8	1	1	24	35	41	.226	.319	.274	.593	78	-6	-6	100	127	29	.603	15			-3		-1.3
Total	7	704	2538	379	618	83	43	15	192	302	296	.243	.328	.328	.656	93	-15	-19	101	72	314	.676	171	35		-8	O/2	-6.8
■ **JOE MOFFETT**	Moffett, Joseph W. b: 6/1859, Wheeling, W.Va. 6', Deb: 5/06/1884																											
1884	Tol-a	56	204	17	41	5	3	0		2		.201	.209	.255	.464	51	-10	-11	104	0	11	.331				-3	13/O2	-1.4
■ **SAM MOFFETT**	Moffett, Samuel R. b: 3/14/1857, Wheeling, W.Va. d: 5/5/07, Butte, Mont. TR , Deb: 5/15/1884																											
1884	Cle-N	67	256	26	47	12	2	0	15	8	56	.184	.208	.246	.454	41	-17	-18	102	87	13	.340				-4	OP/132	-1.9
1887	Ind-N	11	41	6	5	1	0	0	1	1	6	.122	.143	.146	.289	-20	-6	-6	96	52	1	.250	2			0	/PO	0.0
1888	Ind-N	10	35	6	4	0	0	0	0	5	4	.114	.225	.114	.339	13	-3	-3	95	0	1	.290	0			0	/PO	0.0
Total	3	88	332	38	56	13	2	0	16	14	66	.169	.202	.220	.422	31	-26	-27	101	72	16	.322	2			-4	/OP123	-1.9
■ **JOHN MOHARDT**	Mohardt, John Henry b: 1/21/1898, Pittsburgh, Pa. d: 11/24/61, La Jolla, Cal. 5'10", 165 lbs. Deb: 4/15/22																											
1922	Det-A	5	1	2	1	0	0	0	0	1	0	1.000	1.000	1.000	2.000	432	1	1	98	0	1	2.000	0	1	-1	-1	/O	0.0
■ **KID MOHLER**	Mohler, Ernest Follette b: 12/13/1874, Oneida, Ill. d: 11/4/61, San Francisco, Cal. 5'4.5", 145 lbs. Deb: 9/29/1894																											
1894	Was-N	3	9	0	1	0	0	0	0	2	4	.111	.273	.111	.384	-3	-1	-1	98	0	0	.375	0			0	/2	0.0
■ **JOHNNY MOKAN**	Mokan, John Leo b: 9/23/1895, Buffalo, N.Y. d: 2/10/85, Buffalo, N.Y. BR/TR, 5'7", 165 lbs. Deb: 4/15/21																											
1921	Pit-N	19	52	7	14	3	2	0	9	5	3	.269	.333	.404	.737	91	-0	-1	103	157	7	.684	0	0	0	-1	O	-0.2
1922	Pit-N	31	89	9	23	3	1	0	8	9	3	.258	.327	.315	.641	64	-4	-5	104	100	9	.552	0	1	-1	-4	O	-0.9
	Phi-N	47	151	20	38	7	1	3	27	16	25	.252	.327	.371	.698	70	-5	-8	113	145	19	.655	1	0	0	-4	O/3	-1.1
	Yr	78	240	29	61	10	2	3	35	25	28	.254	.327	.350	.677	68	-9	-12	109	128	29	.617	1	1	-0	-8		-2.0
1923	Phi-N	113	400	76	125	23	3	10	48	53	31	.313	.401	.460	.861	111	17	9	114	80	73	.871	6	11	-5	6	*O/3	0.7
1924	Phi-N	96	366	50	95	15	1	7	44	30	27	.260	.321	.363	.684	77	-9	-13	108	110	43	.627	7	5	-1	0	O	-1.4
1925	Phi-N	75	209	30	69	11	2	6	42	27	9	.330	.417	.488	.905	113	10	5	116	124	43	.938	3	5	-2	-12	O	-0.9
1926	Phi-N	127	456	68	138	23	5	6	62	41	31	.303	.365	.414	.780	106	6	4	103	106	69	.748	4			-6	*O	-0.6
1927	Phi-N	74	213	22	61	13	2	0	33	25	21	.286	.361	.366	.728	99	-1	0	96	148	29	.711	5			-11	O	-1.2
Total	7	582	1936	282	563	98	17	32	273	206	150	.291	.364	.409	.773	97	15	-7	108	112	292	.746	26	22		-31	O/3	-5.6
■ **FENTON MOLE**	Mole, Fenton Le Roy "Muscles" b: 6/14/25, San Leandro, Cal. BL/TL, 6'1.5", 200 lbs. Deb: 9/01/49																											
1949	NY-A	10	27	2	5	2	1	0	2	3	5	.185	.267	.333	.600	58	-2	-2	100	76	2	.500	0	0	0	-0	/1	-0.1
■ **BOB MOLINARO**	Molinaro, Robert Joseph b: 5/21/50, Newark, N.J. BL/TR, 6', 190 lbs. Deb: 9/18/75																											
1975	Det-A	6	19	2	5	0	1	0	1	1	0	.263	.300	.368	.668	85	-0	-0	104	55	2	.571	0	0	0	-0	/O	0.0
1977	Det-A	4	4	0	1	1	0	0	0	0	2	.250	.250	.500	.750	94	-0	-0	105	0	1	.667	0	0	0	0	H	0.0
	Chi-A	1	2	0	1	0	0	0	0	0	1	.500	.500	.500	1.000	175	0	0	99	0	1	2.000	1	0	0	-0	/O	0.0
	Yr	5	6	0	2	1	0	0	0	0	3	.333	.333	.500	.833	119	0	0	104	0	1	1.000	1	0	0	-0		0.0
1978	Chi-A	105	286	39	75	5	5	6	27	19	12	.262	.315	.378	.693	93	-3	-3	101	85	35	.685	22	6	3	-9	OD	-1.0
1979	Bal-A	8	6	0	0	0	0	0	0	1	3	.000	.143	.000	.143	-59	-1	-1	97	0	0	.286	1	0	0	-1	/O	-0.1
1980	Chi-A	119	344	48	100	16	4	5	36	26	29	.291	.353	.404	.757	111	4	5	97	91	50	.745	18	7	1	-4	OD	0.1
1981	Chi-A	47	42	7	11	1	1	1	9	8	1	.262	.392	.405	.797	130	2	2	100	176	7	.844	1	0	0	-0	/OD	0.2
1982	Chi-N	65	66	6	13	1	0	1	12	6	5	.197	.264	.258	.521	45	-5	-5	103	235	5	.444	1	1	-0	-1	/O	-0.6
	Phi-N	19	14	0	4	0	0	0	2	3	1	.286	.412	.286	.697	105	0	0	94	196	2	.800	1	0	0	0	H	0.1
	Yr	84	80	6	17	1	0	1	14	9	6	.213	.292	.262	.555	56	-5	-5	101	229	7	.500	2	1	0	-1		-0.5
1983	Phi-N	19	18	1	2	1	0	1	3	0	2	.111	.111	.333	.444	19	-2	-2	101	132	1	.375	0	0	0	0	H	-0.1
	Det-A	8	2	3	0	0	0	0	0	1	1	.000	.333	.000	.333	1	-0	-0	96	0	0	.667	1	1	-0	0	/D	0.0
Total	8	401	803	106	212	25	11	14	90	65	57	.264	.328	.375	.702	96	-5	-4	99	106	104	.698	46	15	5	-15	O/D	-1.4
■ **PAUL MOLITOR**	Molitor, Paul Leo b: 8/22/56, St.Paul, Minn. BR/TR, 6', 185 lbs. Deb: 4/07/78																											
1978	Mil-A	125	521	73	142	26	4	6	45	19	54	.273	.303	.372	.676	84	-9	-12	106	81	59	.622	30	12	2	0	2S/3D	-0.2
1979	Mil-A	140	584	88	188	27	16	9	62	48	48	.322	.375	.469	.845	126	21	21	100	70	103	.854	33	13	2	3	*2S/D	3.2
1980	Mil-A	111	450	81	137	29	2	9	37	48	48	.304	.375	.438	.813	129	14	18	95	57	78	.857	34	7	6	-2	2S/3D	2.7
1981	Mil-A	64	251	45	67	11	0	2	19	25	29	.267	.341	.335	.675	99	-1	0	96	79	30	.632	10	6	-1	-0	OD	-0.1
1982	Mil-A	160	666	**136**	201	26	8	19	71	69	93	.302	.368	.450	.819	131	22	27	94	69	117	.851	41	9	7	3	*3/SD	3.4
1983	Mil-A	152	608	95	164	28	6	15	47	59	74	.270	.336	.410	.746	114	3	10	92	60	88	.756	41	8	8	5	*3/D	2.2
1984	Mil-A	13	46	3	10	1	0	0	6	2	8	.217	.250	.239	.489	39	-4	-3	92	222	3	.389	1	0	0	1	/3D	-0.1
1985	Mil-A	140	576	93	171	28	3	10	48	54	80	.297	.358	.408	.766	104	8	5	105	62	85	.733	21	7	2	-4	*3/D	-0.1
1986	Mil-A	105	437	62	123	24	6	9	55	40	81	.281	.342	.426	.767	106	5	4	102	89	65	.750	20	5	3	-1	3D/O	0.3
1987	Mil-A	118	465	**114**	164	**41**	5	16	75	69	67	.353	.438	.566	1.004	161	46	44	102	85	125	1.203	45	10	8	-4	D32	4.5
1988	Mil-A	154	609	115	190	34	6	13	60	71	54	.312	.386	.452	.837	129	29	26	103	67	112	.886	41	10	6	-4	*3D/2	2.9
Total	11	1282	5213	905	1557	275	56	108	525	504	636	.299	.363	.435	.798	119	135	140	99	72	865	.828	317	87	43	-3	32D/SO	18.7
■ **FRED MOLLENKAMP**	Mollenkamp, Frederick Henry b: 3/15/1890, Cincinnati, Ohio d: 11/1/48, Cincinnati, Ohio Deb: 8/29/14																											
1914	Phi-N	3	8	0	1	0	0	0	0	2	0	.125	.300	.125	.425	28	-1	-1	100	0	0	.429	0			0	/1	0.0
■ **FRITZ MOLLWITZ**	Mollwitz, Frederick August b: 6/16/1890, Coburg, Germany d: 10/3/67, Bradenton, Fla. BR/TR, 6'2", 170 lbs. Deb: 9/26/13																											
1913	Chi-N	2	7	1	3	0	0	0	0	0	0	.429	.429	.429	.857	147	0	0	99	0	1	.750	0			0	/1	0.0
1914	Chi-N	13	20	0	3	0	0	0	1	0	3	.150	.150	.150	.300	-11	-3	-3	98	121	1	.235	1			-1	/1O	-0.3
	Cin-N	32	111	12	18	2	0	0	5	3	9	.162	.198	.180	.378	12	-12	-13	105	92	4	.290	2			-1	1	-1.5
	Yr	45	131	12	21	2	0	0	6	3	12	.160	.191	.176	.367	9	-15	-15	103	103	5	.282	3			-2		-1.8
1915	Cin-N	153	525	36	136	21	3	1	51	15	49	.259	.281	.316	.597	78	-14	-15	103	118	50	.503	19	11	-1	1	*1	-2.4
1916	Cin-N	65	183	12	41	4	4	0	16	5	12	.224	.245	.290	.534	65	-8	-8	98	120	15	.451	6			-2	1	-1.3
	Chi-N	33	71	1	19	2	0	0	11	7	6	.268	.333	.296	.629	80	-0	-2	117	208	8	.615	4			-1	1/O	-0.4
	Yr	98	254	13	60	6	4	0	27	12	18	.236	.271	.291	.562	69	-9	-10	104	151	24	.495	10			-3		-1.7
1917	Pit-N	36	140	15	36	4	1	0	12	8	8	.257	.297	.300	.597	84	-3	-3	100	97	14	.519	4			-1	1/2	-0.3
1918	Pit-N	119	432	43	116	12	7	0	45	23	24	.269	.305	.329	.634	88	-4	-7	106	127	50	.595	23			-2	*1	-1.2
1919	Pit-N	56	168	11	29	2	4	0	12	15	18	.173	.249	.232	.481	43	-11	-12	105	120	11	.468	9			-2	1/O	-1.6
	StL-N	25	83	7	19	3	0	0	5	7	3	.229	.289	.265	.554	71	-3	-3	94	90	7	.484	2			0	1	-0.2

YEAR	TM/L	G	AB	R	H	2B	3B	HR	RBI	BB	SO	AVG	OBP	SLG	PRO	/A	BR	/A	PF	CHI	RC	TA	SB	CS	SBR	FR	POS	TPR
	Yr	81	251	18	48	5	4	0	17	22	21	.191	.262	.243	.505	51	-14	-15	102	112	18	.473	11			-2		-1.8
Total	7	534	1740	138	420	50	19	1	158	83	132	.241	.278	.294	.572	71	-57	-64	103	119	162	.503	70	11		-8	1/O2	-9.2

■ **BLAS MONACO** Monaco, Blas b: 11/16/15, San Antonio, Tex. BB/TR, 5'11", 170 lbs. Deb: 8/18/37

YEAR	TM/L	G	AB	R	H	2B	3B	HR	RBI	BB	SO	AVG	OBP	SLG	PRO	/A	BR	/A	PF	CHI	RC	TA	SB	CS	SBR	FR	POS	TPR
1937	Cle-A	5	7	0	2	0	1	0	2	0	2	.286	.375	.571	.946	139	0	0	98	171	2	1.000	0	0	0	0	/2	0.1
1946	Cle-A	12	6	2	0	0	0	0	0	1	1	.000	.143	.000	.143	-65	-1	-1	89	0	0	.167	0	0	0	0	H	0.0
Total	2	17	13	2	2	0	1	0	2	1	3	.154	.267	.308	.574	55	-1	-1	93	91	2	.545	0	0	0	0	/2	0.1

■ **FREDDIE MONCEWICZ** Moncewicz, Frederick Alfred b: 9/1/03, Brockton, Mass. d: 4/23/69, Brockton, Mass. BR/TR, 5'8.5", 175 lbs. Deb: 6/19/28

YEAR	TM/L	G	AB	R	H	2B	3B	HR	RBI	BB	SO	AVG	OBP	SLG	PRO	/A	BR	/A	PF	CHI	RC	TA	SB	CS	SBR	FR	POS	TPR
1928	Bos-A	3	1	0	0	0	0	0	0	0	1	.000	.000	.000	.000	-99	-0	-0	98	0	0	.000	0	0	0	0	/S	0.0

■ **ALEX MONCHAK** Monchak, Alex b: 12/22/19, Bayonne, N.J. BR/TR, 6', 180 lbs. Deb: 6/22/40 C

YEAR	TM/L	G	AB	R	H	2B	3B	HR	RBI	BB	SO	AVG	OBP	SLG	PRO	/A	BR	/A	PF	CHI	RC	TA	SB	CS	SBR	FR	POS	TPR
1940	Phi-N	19	14	1	2	0	0	0	0	0	6	.143	.143	.143	.286	-22	-2	-2	97	0	0	.250	1			0	/S2	0.0

■ **RICK MONDAY** Monday, Robert James b: 11/20/45, Batesville, Ark. BL/TL, 6'3", 193 lbs. Deb: 9/03/66

YEAR	TM/L	G	AB	R	H	2B	3B	HR	RBI	BB	SO	AVG	OBP	SLG	PRO	/A	BR	/A	PF	CHI	RC	TA	SB	CS	SBR	FR	POS	TPR
1966	KC-A	17	41	4	4	1	1	0	2	6	16	.098	.213	.171	.383	12	-5	-4	94	120	2	.368	1	1	-0	-0	O	-0.5
1967	KC-A	124	406	52	102	14	6	14	58	42	107	.251	.324	.419	.743	119	9	9	100	116	55	.689	3	6	-3	12	*O	1.6
1968	Oak-A	148	482	56	132	24	7	8	49	72	143	.274	.373	.402	.775	137	22	23	98	98	78	.787	14	6	1	-5	*O	1.5
1969	Oak-A	122	399	57	108	17	4	12	54	72	100	.271	.389	.424	.812	138	17	21	92	106	71	.860	12	3	2	-8	*O	1.2
1970	Oak-A	112	376	63	109	19	7	10	37	58	99	.290	.388	.457	.845	137	18	19	97	76	68	.871	17	11	-2	-5	*O	0.8
1971	Oak-A	116	355	53	87	9	3	18	56	49	93	.245	.337	.439	.776	118	8	8	101	109	52	.748	6	9	-4	-5	*O	-0.4
1972	Chi-N	138	434	68	108	22	5	11	42	78	102	.249	.365	.399	.763	102	12	4	114	84	67	.779	12	9	-2	-12	*O	-1.7
1973	Chi-N	149	554	93	148	24	5	26	56	92	124	.267	.372	.469	.842	122	25	19	108	64	100	.850	5	12	-6	-4	*O	0.3
1974	Chi-N	142	538	84	158	19	7	20	58	70	94	.294	.377	.467	.844	135	25	25	100	76	97	.840	7	9	-3	-6	*O	1.1
1975	Chi-N	136	491	89	131	29	4	17	60	83	95	.267	.374	.446	.820	122	19	16	104	91	86	.838	8	3	1	-3	*O	0.9
1976	Chi-N	137	534	107	145	20	5	32	77	60	125	.272	.347	.507	.855	128	26	20	109	78	92	.835	5	9	-4	2	*O1	1.4
1977	LA-N	118	392	47	90	13	1	15	48	60	109	.230	.332	.383	.715	91	-4	-4	100	98	52	.681	1	4	-2	-19	*O/1	-2.9
1978	LA-N	119	342	54	87	14	1	19	57	49	100	.254	.349	.468	.817	128	12	12	99	104	56	.806	2	4	-2	0	*O/1	0.7
1979	LA-N	12	33	2	10	0	0	0	2	5	6	.303	.395	.303	.698	93	0	0	100	79	4	.625	0	0	0	1	O	0.1
1980	LA-N	96	194	35	52	7	1	10	25	28	49	.268	.363	.469	.832	135	8	9	97	82	35	.841	2	2	-1	-3	O	0.3
1981	LA-N	66	130	24	41	1	2	11	25	24	42	.315	.426	.608	1.033	195	16	16	98	88	35	1.154	1	2	-1	-7	O	0.7
1982	LA-N	104	210	37	54	6	4	11	42	39	51	.257	.376	.481	.857	146	11	13	95	123	40	.894	2	1	0	-9	O/1	0.3
1983	LA-N	99	178	21	44	7	1	6	20	29	42	.247	.353	.399	.752	108	2	2	100	89	26	.730	0	0	0	-5	O/1	-0.3
1984	LA-N	31	47	4	9	2	0	1	7	8	16	.191	.309	.298	.607	69	-2	-2	104	161	5	.579	0	0	0	0	1/O	-0.1
Total	19	1986	6136	950	1619	248	64	241	775	924	1513	.264	.362	.443	.805	124	220	208	102	91	1020	.817	98	91	-25	-77	*O/1	5.0

■ **DON MONEY** Money, Donald Wayne "Brooks" b: 6/7/47, Washington, D.C. BR/TR, 6'1", 170 lbs. Deb: 4/10/68

YEAR	TM/L	G	AB	R	H	2B	3B	HR	RBI	BB	SO	AVG	OBP	SLG	PRO	/A	BR	/A	PF	CHI	RC	TA	SB	CS	SBR	FR	POS	TPR
1968	Phi-N	4	13	1	3	2	0	0	2	2	4	.231	.333	.385	.718	118	0	0	97	172	1	.636	0	1	-1	0	/S	0.0
1969	Phi-N	127	450	41	103	22	2	6	42	43	83	.229	.298	.327	.624	76	-15	-14	98	104	41	.525	1	3	-2	17	*S	1.7
1970	Phi-N	120	447	66	132	25	4	14	66	43	68	.295	.366	.463	.829	125	13	15	96	109	75	.793	4	7	-3	10	*3/S	1.9
1971	Phi-N	121	439	40	98	22	8	7	38	31	80	.223	.279	.358	.637	77	-13	-15	103	89	44	.560	4	1	1	7	3O2	-0.7
1972	Phi-N	152	536	54	119	16	2	15	52	41	92	.222	.280	.343	.623	79	-18	-16	97	95	50	.537	5	7	-3	21	*3/S	0.2
1973	Mil-A	145	556	75	158	28	2	11	61	53	53	.284	.350	.401	.751	116	8	11	96	99	80	.725	22	5	4	-21	*3S	-0.4
1974	Mil-A	159	629	85	178	32	3	15	65	62	80	.283	.349	.415	.764	116	15	13	102	74	93	.735	19	6	2	-7	*3/2D	1.1
1975	Mil-A	109	405	58	112	16	1	15	43	31	51	.277	.333	.432	.765	115	7	7	100	79	58	.713	7	9	-3	-15	3/S	-0.8
1976	Mil-A	117	439	51	117	18	4	12	62	47	50	.267	.337	.408	.745	119	9	10	99	117	59	.686	6	5	-1	-9	*3D/S	0.0
1977	Mil-A	152	570	86	159	28	3	25	83	57	70	.279	.352	.470	.822	128	17	20	95	102	92	.785	8	5	-1	10	*2O3/D	3.7
1978	Mil-A	137	518	88	152	30	2	14	54	48	70	.293	.361	.440	.801	118	17	13	106	84	84	.761	3	0	1	1	123D/S	1.5
1979	Mil-A	92	350	52	83	20	1	6	38	40	47	.237	.319	.351	.670	81	-9	-9	100	110	40	.599	1	0	0	-2	D312	-0.9
1980	Mil-A	86	289	39	74	17	1	17	46	40	36	.256	.348	.498	.847	137	11	13	95	94	52	.845	0	0	0	-0	31D/2	1.2
1981	Mil-A	60	185	17	40	7	0	2	14	19	27	.216	.293	.286	.579	70	-7	-6	96	93	17	.500	0	0	0	-3	3/1D	-1.0
1982	Mil-A	96	275	40	78	14	3	16	55	32	38	.284	.360	.531	.891	150	15	17	94	113	53	.882	0	2	-1	0	D31/2	1.6
1983	Mil-A	43	114	5	17	5	0	1	8	11	17	.149	.224	.219	.443	25	-12	-11	92	112	6	.360	0	0	0	1	D3/1	-0.9
Total	16	1720	6215	798	1623	302	36	176	729	600	866	.261	.330	.406	.736	107	38	50	99	97	847	.698	80	51	-7	10	*32DS1/O	8.2

■ **FRANK MONROE** Monroe, Frank W. b: Hamilton, Ohio Deb: 7/18/1884

YEAR	TM/L	G	AB	R	H	2B	3B	HR	RBI	BB	SO	AVG	OBP	SLG	PRO	/A	BR	/A	PF	CHI	RC	TA	SB	CS	SBR	FR	POS	TPR
1884	Ind-a	2	8	1	0	0	0	0		0		.000	.000	.000	.000	-99	-2	-2	96	0	0	.000				0	/OC	-0.1

■ **JOHN MONROE** Monroe, John Allen b: 8/24/1898, Farmersville, Tex. d: 6/19/56, Conroe, Tex. BL/TR, 5'10", 160 lbs. Deb: 4/16/21

YEAR	TM/L	G	AB	R	H	2B	3B	HR	RBI	BB	SO	AVG	OBP	SLG	PRO	/A	BR	/A	PF	CHI	RC	TA	SB	CS	SBR	FR	POS	TPR
1921	NY-N	19	21	4	3	0	0	1	3	3	6	.143	.280	.286	.566	51	-2	-1	98	122	2	.556	0	0	0	0	/2S	0.0
	Phi-N	41	133	13	38	4	2	1	8	11	9	.286	.345	.368	.713	87	-2	-2	102	56	17	.649	2	2	-1	4	2/3	0.1
	Yr	60	154	17	41	4	2	2	11	14	15	.266	.335	.357	.692	83	-3	-4	100	79	19	.635	2	2	-1	4		0.1
Total	1	60	154	17	41	4	2	2	11	14	15	.266	.335	.357	.692	82	-3	-4	101	66	19	.635	2	2	-1	4	/23S	0.1

■ **ED MONTAGUE** Montague, Edward Francis b: 7/24/05, San Francisco, Cal. d: 6/17/88, Daly City, Cal. BR/TR, 5'10", 165 lbs. Deb: 5/14/28

YEAR	TM/L	G	AB	R	H	2B	3B	HR	RBI	BB	SO	AVG	OBP	SLG	PRO	/A	BR	/A	PF	CHI	RC	TA	SB	CS	SBR	FR	POS	TPR
1928	Cle-A	32	51	12	12	0	1	0	3	6	7	.235	.339	.275	.613	59	-2	-3	106	74	5	.564	0	0	0	3	S/3	0.1
1930	Cle-A	58	179	37	47	5	2	1	16	37	38	.263	.392	.330	.721	81	-2	-4	105	86	25	.715	1	5	-3	4	S3	0.2
1931	Cle-A	64	193	27	55	8	3	1	26	21	22	.285	.358	.373	.731	87	-2	-4	106	114	26	.683	3	4	-2	6	S	0.6
1932	Cle-A	66	192	29	47	5	1	0	24	21	24	.245	.326	.281	.607	54	-11	-14	108	149	19	.541	3	3	-1	-9	S3	-1.7
Total	4	220	615	105	161	18	7	2	69	85	91	.262	.357	.324	.681	73	-18	-24	106	113	76	.637	7	12	-5	3	S/3	-0.8

■ **WILLIE MONTANEZ** Montanez, Guillermo (Naranjo) b: 4/1/48, Catano, P.R. BL/TL, 6', 170 lbs. Deb: 4/12/66

YEAR	TM/L	G	AB	R	H	2B	3B	HR	RBI	BB	SO	AVG	OBP	SLG	PRO	/A	BR	/A	PF	CHI	RC	TA	SB	CS	SBR	FR	POS	TPR
1966	Cal-A	8	2	2	0	0	0	0	0	0	2	.000	.000	.000	.000	-99	-1	-1	99	0	0	.500	1	0	0	0	/1	0.0
1970	Phi-N	18	25	3	6	0	0	0	3	1	4	.240	.269	.240	.509	39	-2	-2	96	194	2	.368	0	0	0	-1	O/1	-0.3
1971	Phi-N	158	599	78	153	27	6	30	99	67	105	.255	.333	.471	.804	122	19	17	103	115	89	.756	4	7	-3	-1	*O/1	0.6
1972	Phi-N	147	531	60	131	**39**	3	13	64	58	108	.247	.322	.405	.727	109	3	5	97	106	70	.674	1	3	-2	8	*O1	0.5
1973	Phi-N	146	552	69	145	16	5	11	65	46	80	.263	.326	.370	.696	86	-6	-11	108	117	65	.608	2	6	-3	-1	1O	-2.2
1974	Phi-N	143	527	55	160	33	1	7	79	32	57	.304	.347	.410	.757	108	7	5	103	131	72	.665	3	6	-3	-2	*1/O	-0.6
1975	Phi-N	21	84	9	24	8	0	2	16	4	12	.286	.318	.452	.771	110	1	1	101	149	11	.683	1	0	0	1	1	0.0
	SF-N	135	518	52	158	26	2	8	85	45	50	.305	.365	.409	.774	113	10	9	102	148	72	.689	5	3	-0	0	*1	0.2
	Yr	156	602	61	182	34	2	10	101	49	62	.302	.359	.415	.774	113	11	10	102	**149**	85	.693	6	3	0	1		0.2
1976	SF-N	60	230	22	71	15	2	2	20	15	15	.309	.354	.417	.771	115	5	4	103	80	31	.671	2	1	0	3	1	0.5
	Atl-N	103	420	52	135	14	0	9	64	21	32	.321	.354	.419	.773	107	9	4	111	129	56	.646	0	4	-2	-4	*1	-0.6
	Yr	163	650	74	206	29	2	11	84	36	47	.317	.354	.418	.772	109	14	8	108	111	91	.669	2	5	-2	-0		-0.1
1977	Atl-N	136	544	70	156	31	1	20	68	35	60	.287	.330	.458	.788	96	5	-3	113	93	77	.700	1	1	-0	-3	*1	-1.3
1978	NY-N	159	609	66	156	32	0	17	96	60	92	.256	.324	.392	.716	101	-1	0	98	139	76	.657	9	4	0	4	*1	-0.1
1979	NY-N	109	410	36	96	19	0	5	47	25	48	.234	.280	.317	.597	66	-22	-19	95	131	33	.473	0	1	-1	3	*1	-2.2
	Tex-A	38	144	19	46	6	0	8	24	8	14	.319	.359	.528	.887	136	7	7	100	94	26	.825	0	1	-1	0	1D	0.5
1980	SD-N	128	481	39	132	12	4	6	63	36	52	.274	.329	.353	.682	97	-6	-2	93	135	55	.586	3	4	-2	0	*1	-0.9
	Mon-N	14	19	1	4	0	0	0	1	3	3	.211	.318	.211	.529	51	-1	-1	99	99	1	.438	0	1	-1	0	/1	-0.1
	Yr	142	500	40	136	12	4	6	64	39	55	.272	.328	.348	.676	95	-7	-3	94	133	60	.593	3	5	-2	0		-1.0
1981	Mon-N	26	62	6	11	0	1	0	5	4	9	.177	.227	.210	.437	25	-6	-6	99	151	2	.304	0	0	0	-0	1	-0.7
	Pit-N	29	38	2	10	0	0	1	1	1	2	.263	.282	.342	.624	80	-1	-1	96	24	3	.483	0	0	0	-0	1	-0.1
	Yr	55	100	8	21	0	1	1	6	5	11	.210	.248	.260	.508	45	-7	-7	97	87	7	.387	0	0	0	-1		-0.8
1982	Pit-N	36	32	4	9	1	0	0	1	3	3	.281	.343	.313	.655	77	-1	-1	110	39	3	.520	0	0	0	-1	/1O	-0.1
	Phi-N	18	16	0	1	0	0	0	1	1	3	.063	.118	.063	.180	-52	-3	-3	94	392	0	.133	0	0	0	0	/1	-0.3
	Yr	54	48	4	10	1	0	0	2	4	6	.208	.269	.229	.498	39	-4	-4	105	158	3	.395	0	0	0	-1		-0.4
Total	14	1632	5843	645	1604	279	25	139	802	465	751	.275	.331	.402	.733	101	16	1	102	122	744	.671	32	42	-16	5	*1O/D	-7.2

YEAR	TM/L	G	AB	R	H	2B	3B	HR	RBI	BB	SO	AVG	OBP	SLG	PRO	/A	BR	/A	PF	CHI	RC	TA	SB	CS	SBR	FR	POS	TPR
■ **RENE MONTEAGUDO** Monteagudo, Rene (Miranda) b: 3/12/16, Havana, Cuba d: 9/14/73, Hialeah, Fla. BL/TL, 5'7", 165 lbs. Deb: 9/06/38																												
1938	Was-A	5	6	0	3	0	0	0	1	0	0	.500	.500	.500	1.000	159	0	1	95	113	1	1.000	0	0	0	-1	/P	0.0
1940	Was-A	27	33	4	6	1	1	0	1	1	4	.182	.206	.273	.479	25	-4	-4	93	40	2	.370	0	0	0	-1	P	0.0
1944	Was-A	10	38	2	11	2	0	0	4	0	1	.289	.289	.342	.632	89	-1	-1	90	111	4	.481	0	0	0	-2	/O	-0.2
1945	Phi-N	114	193	26	58	6	0	0	15	28	7	.301	.389	.332	.721	105	2	3	96	81	26	.667	2			-2	OP	0.1
Total	4	156	270	32	78	9	1	0	21	29	12	.289	.358	.330	.687	95	-3	-1	95	81	33	.606	2	0		-5	/PO	-0.1
■ **FELIPE MONTEMAYOR** Montemayor, Felipe Angel "Monty" b: 2/7/30, Monterrey, Mexico BL/TL, 6'2", 185 lbs. Deb: 4/14/53																												
1953	Pit-N	28	55	5	6	4	0	0	2	4	13	.109	.210	.182	.391	3	-8	-8	102	78	2	.340	0	0	0	2	O	-0.6
1955	Pit-N	36	95	10	20	1	3	2	8	18	24	.211	.342	.347	.689	86	-2	-1	97	83	12	.688	1	0	0	-5	O	-0.5
Total	2	64	150	15	26	5	3	2	10	22	37	.173	.295	.287	.582	55	-10	-10	99	81	15	.556	1	0	0	-3	/O	-1.1
■ **AL MONTGOMERY** Montgomery, Alvin Atlas b: 7/3/20, Loving, N.Mex. d: 4/26/42, Waverly, Va. BR/TR, 5'10.5", 185 lbs. Deb: 6/20/41																												
1941	Bos-N	42	52	4	10	1	0	0	4	9	8	.192	.323	.212	.534	56	-3	-2	93	131	4	.477	0			-1	C	0.0
■ **BOB MONTGOMERY** Montgomery, Robert Edward b: 4/16/44, Nashville, Tenn. BR/TR, 6'1", 195 lbs. Deb: 9/06/70																												
1970	Bos-A	22	78	8	14	2	0	1	4	6	20	.179	.247	.244	.491	32	-7	-8	111	75	4	.382	0	0	0	2	C	-0.5
1971	Bos-A	67	205	19	49	11	2	2	24	16	43	.239	.304	.341	.645	78	-5	-6	106	129	21	.556	1	0	0	0	C	-0.2
1972	Bos-A	24	77	7	22	1	0	2	7	3	17	.286	.313	.377	.689	99	0	-0	105	84	9	.571	0	0	0	3	C	0.3
1973	Bos-A	34	128	18	41	6	2	7	25	7	36	.320	.356	.563	.918	146	8	7	106	108	23	.859	0	0	0	4	C	1.2
1974	Bos-A	88	254	26	64	10	0	4	38	13	50	.252	.291	.339	.630	76	-7	-9	107	152	24	.518	3	0	1	1	C/D	-0.3
1975	Bos-A	62	195	16	44	10	1	2	26	4	37	.226	.245	.318	.563	53	-11	-13	109	147	15	.439	1	1	-0	0	C/1D	-1.2
1976	Bos-A	31	93	10	23	3	1	3	13	5	20	.247	.286	.398	.684	89	-1	-2	110	109	10	.583	0	1	-1	3	C/D	0.2
1977	Bos-A	17	40	6	12	2	0	2	7	4	9	.300	.378	.500	.878	117	2	1	117	107	8	.862	0	0	0	1	C	0.2
1978	Bos-A	10	29	2	7	1	1	0	5	2	12	.241	.290	.345	.635	73	-1	-1	107	198	3	.522	0	0	0	1	C	0.0
1979	Bos-A	32	86	13	30	4	1	0	7	4	24	.349	.378	.419	.796	107	2	1	107	75	13	.695	1	0	0	-7	C	-0.3
Total	10	387	1185	125	306	50	8	23	156	64	268	.258	.300	.372	.672	83	-19	-30	108	123	129	.586	6	2	1	8	C/D1	-0.6
■ **AL MONTREUIL** Montreuil, Allan Arthur b: 8/23/43, New Orleans, La. BR/TR, 5'5", 158 lbs. Deb: 9/01/72																												
1972	Chi-N	5	11	0	1	0	0	0	0	1	4	.091	.167	.091	.258	-22	-2	-2	114	0	0	.182	0	0	0	1	/2	0.0
■ **DAN MONZON** Monzon, Daniel Francisco b: 5/17/46, Bronx, N.Y. BR/TR, 5'10", 182 lbs. Deb: 4/25/72																												
1972	Min-A	55	55	13	15	1	0	0	5	8	12	.273	.365	.291	.656	90	0	-0	107	131	7	.610	1	0	0	-1	2/3SO	0.1
1973	Min-A	39	76	10	17	1	1	0	4	11	9	.224	.330	.263	.593	66	-3	-3	104	79	8	.559	1	0	0	0	23/O	-0.1
Total	2	94	131	23	32	2	1	0	9	19	21	.244	.344	.275	.619	76	-3	-3	105	100	15	.586	2	0	1	-0	/23SO	0.0
■ **JOE MOOCK** Moock, Joseph Geoffrey b: 3/12/44, Plaquemine, La. BL/TR, 6'1", 180 lbs. Deb: 9/01/67																												
1967	NY-N	13	40	2	9	2	0	0	5	0	7	.225	.225	.275	.500	43	-3	-3	99	188	2	.344	0	0	0	1	3	-0.2
■ **GEORGE MOOLIC** Moolic, George Henry "Prunes" b: 3/12/1865, Lawrence, Mass. d: 2/19/15, Lawrence, Mass. 5'7", 145 lbs. Deb: 5/01/1886																												
1886	Chi-N	16	56	9	8	3	0	0	2	2	17	.143	.172	.196	.369	10	-6	-7	116	59	2	.271	0			0	C/O	-0.6
■ **WALLY MOON** Moon, Wallace Wade b: 4/3/30, Bay, Ark. BL/TR, 6', 169 lbs. Deb: 4/13/54 C																												
1954	StL-N	151	635	106	193	29	9	12	76	71	73	.304	.375	.435	.809	110	10	10	100	85	106	.792	18	10	-1	-3	*O	0.1
1955	StL-N	152	593	86	175	24	8	19	76	47	65	.295	.350	.459	.809	112	10	10	101	99	91	.757	11	11	-3	-1	*O1	0.0
1956	StL-N	149	540	86	161	22	11	16	68	80	50	.298	.390	.469	.858	131	24	25	99	101	99	.863	12	9	-2	1	O1	1.8
1957	StL-N	142	516	86	152	28	5	24	73	62	57	.295	.371	.508	.879	132	24	24	101	92	94	.859	5	6	-2	-4	*O	1.4
1958	StL-N	108	290	36	69	10	3	7	38	47	30	.238	.344	.366	.710	83	-4	-7	106	124	37	.665	2	3	-1	-6	O	-1.6
1959	LA-N	145	543	93	164	26	**11**	19	74	81	64	.302	.396	.495	.891	133	29	28	102	97	111	.934	15	6	1	-1	*O/1	2.6
1960	LA-N	138	469	74	140	21	6	13	69	67	53	.299	.387	.452	.839	112	20	11	115	114	77	.794	6	10	-4	1	*O	0.4
1961	LA-N	134	463	79	152	25	3	17	88	89	79	.328	**.438**	.505	.943	146	37	36	102	**132**	107	1.018	7	5	-1	-9	*O	1.7
1962	LA-N	95	244	36	59	9	1	4	31	30	33	.242	.327	.336	.663	85	-7	-5	93	130	28	.611	5	2	0	-4	O1	-1.1
1963	LA-N	122	343	41	90	13	2	8	48	45	43	.262	.350	.382	.732	116	6	8	95	130	45	.674	5	5	-2	-10	O	-0.9
1964	LA-N	68	118	8	26	2	1	2	9	12	22	.220	.292	.305	.597	74	-5	-4	92	88	10	.505	1	1	-0	-2	O	-0.6
1965	LA-N	53	89	6	18	3	0	1	11	13	22	.202	.304	.270	.574	69	-4	-3	91	169	8	.527	2	0	1	-3	O	-0.5
Total	12	1457	4843	737	1399	212	60	142	661	644	591	.289	.374	.445	.819	117	142	133	101	108	810	.826	89	68	-14	-41	*O1	3.3
■ **AL MOORE** Moore, Albert James b: 8/4/02, Brooklyn, N.Y. d: 11/29/74, At Sea N.Y.To P.R BR/TR, 5'10", 174 lbs. Deb: 9/27/25																												
1925	NY-N	2	8	0	1	0	0	0	0	1	2	.125	.222	.125	.347	-9	-1	-1	99	0	0	.250	0	1	-1	-0	/O	-0.1
1926	NY-N	28	81	12	18	4	0	0	10	5	7	.222	.267	.272	.539	46	-6	-6	98	157	6	.460	2			4	O	-0.2
Total	2	30	89	12	19	4	0	0	10	6	9	.213	.263	.258	.522	41	-8	-7	98	142	6	.437	2	1		4	/O	-0.3
■ **JUNIOR MOORE** Moore, Alvin Earl b: 1/25/53, Waskom, Tex. BR/TR, 5'11", 185 lbs. Deb: 8/02/76																												
1976	Atl-N	20	26	1	7	1	0	0	2	4	4	.269	.387	.308	.695	89	0	-0	111	96	4	.684	0	0	0	0	/32O	0.0
1977	Atl-N	112	361	41	94	9	3	5	34	33	29	.260	.324	.343	.668	70	-10	-16	113	98	38	.568	4	5	-2	-2	*3/2	-2.0
1978	Chi-A	24	65	8	19	0	1	0	4	6	7	.292	.352	.323	.675	90	-1	-1	101	75	7	.549	1	1	-0	1	D/3O	0.0
1979	Chi-A	88	201	24	53	6	2	1	23	12	20	.264	.305	.328	.634	69	-8	-9	102	128	18	.494	0	2	-1	-10	OD/2	-2.1
1980	Chi-A	45	121	9	31	4	1	1	10	7	11	.256	.297	.331	.627	74	-5	-4	97	91	10	.485	0	2	-1	1	3/O1D	-0.4
Total	5	289	774	83	204	20	7	7	73	62	71	.264	.320	.335	.654	73	-23	-30	107	102	77	.561	5	10	-5	-10	3/OD21	-4.5
■ **ANSE MOORE** Moore, Anselm Winn b: 9/22/17, Delhi, La. BL/TR, 6'1", 190 lbs. Deb: 4/17/46																												
1946	Det-A	51	134	16	28	4	0	1	8	12	9	.209	.279	.261	.540	48	-9	-10	108	80	11	.454	1	1	-0	-0	O	-1.2
■ **ARCHIE MOORE** Moore, Archie Francis b: 8/30/41, Upper Darby, Pa. BL/TL, 6'2", 190 lbs. Deb: 4/20/64																												
1964	NY-A	31	23	4	4	2	0	0	1	2	9	.174	.240	.261	.501	38	-2	-2	103	71	2	.421	0	0	0	-2	/O1	-0.4
1965	NY-A	9	17	1	7	2	0	1	4	4	4	.412	.524	.706	1.230	243	4	3	101	111	6	1.455	0	0	0	0	/O	0.4
Total	2	40	40	5	11	4	0	1	5	6	13	.275	.370	.450	.820	126	2	2	102	89	8	.800	0	0	0	-2	/O1	0.0
■ **CHARLEY MOORE** Moore, Charles Wesley b: 12/1/1884, Jackson Co., Ind. d: 7/29/70, Portland, Ore. 5'10", 160 lbs. Deb: 4/16/12																												
1912	Chi-N	5	9	2	2	0	1	0	2	0	1	.222	.222	.444	.667	77	-0	-0	104	168	1	.571	0			0	/S23	0.0
■ **CHARLIE MOORE** Moore, Charles William b: 6/21/53, Birmingham, Ala. BR/TR, 5'11", 180 lbs. Deb: 9/08/73																												
1973	Mil-A	8	27	0	5	0	1	0	3	2	4	.185	.241	.259	.501	43	-2	-2	96	168	2	.409	0	0	0	1	/C	0.0
1974	Mil-A	72	204	17	50	10	4	0	19	21	34	.245	.316	.333	.649	85	-3	-4	102	110	21	.568	3	4	-2	6	C/D	0.3
1975	Mil-A	73	241	26	70	20	1	1	29	17	31	.290	.337	.394	.731	106	2	2	100	114	30	.621	1	5	-3	6	CO/D	0.5
1976	Mil-A	87	241	33	46	7	4	3	16	43	45	.191	.316	.290	.606	79	-5	-5	99	78	24	.572	1	2	-1	-0	CO/3D	-0.4
1977	Mil-A	138	375	42	93	15	6	5	45	31	39	.248	.307	.360	.667	85	-10	-7	95	119	38	.556	1	7	-4	1	*C	-0.6
1978	Mil-A	96	268	30	72	7	1	5	31	12	24	.269	.300	.358	.658	80	-6	-8	106	110	28	.554	4	2	0	-3	C	-0.8
1979	Mil-A	111	337	45	101	16	2	5	38	29	32	.300	.357	.404	.761	105	3	3	100	97	46	.690	8	5	-1	6	*C	1.2
1980	Mil-A	111	320	42	93	13	2	2	30	24	28	.291	.340	.363	.703	98	-3	-1	95	96	39	.628	10	5	0	1	*C	0.5
1981	Mil-A	48	156	16	47	8	3	1	9	12	13	.301	.351	.410	.761	124	4	4	96	53	21	.658	1	4	-2	0	C/OD	0.4
1982	Mil-A	133	456	53	116	22	4	6	45	29	49	.254	.300	.360	.660	85	-13	-9	94	99	45	.543	2	10	-5	4	*OC/2	-1.2
1983	Mil-A	151	529	65	150	27	6	2	49	55	42	.284	.355	.369	.724	109	1	7	92	97	71	.668	11	4	1	-7	*O/CD	0.0
1984	Mil-A	70	188	13	44	7	1	2	17	10	26	.234	.276	.314	.590	69	-10	-8	92	104	14	.455	0	4	-2	-3	O/C	-1.4
1985	Mil-A	105	349	35	81	13	4	0	31	27	53	.232	.289	.292	.581	57	-19	-21	105	121	29	.479	4	0	1	10	*C/O	-0.5
1986	Mil-A	80	235	24	61	12	3	3	39	21	38	.260	.320	.374	.695	87	-3	-4	102	160	27	.616	5	5	-2	14	C/O2D	1.2
1987	Tor-A	51	107	15	23	10	1	1	7	13	12	.215	.306	.355	.661	75	-4	-4	101	68	12	.605	0	0	0	-2	C/O	-0.1
Total	15	1334	4033	456	1052	187	43	36	408	346	470	.261	.321	.355	.676	89	-69	-57	98	104	447	.606	51	57	-19	32	CO/D23	-0.9
■ **DEE MOORE** Moore, D C b: 4/6/14, Hedley, Tex. BR/TR, 5'11", 190 lbs. Deb: 9/12/36																												
1936	Cin-N	6	10	4	4	2	1	0	1	0	3	.400	.400	.800	1.200	224	1	2	97	44	3	1.333	0			0	/PC	0.2
1937	Cin-N	7	13	2	1	0	0	0	0	1	2	.077	.200	.077	.277	-24	-2	-2	91	0	0	.250	0			0	/C	-0.1

YEAR	TM/L	G	AB	R	H	2B	3B	HR	RBI	BB	SO	AVG	OBP	SLG	PRO	/A	BR	/A	PF	CHI	RC	TA	SB	CS	SBR	FR	POS	TPR
1943	Bro-N	37	79	8	20	3	0	0	12	11	8	.253	.344	.291	.636	85	-1	-1	100	188	9	.583	1			0	C/3	0.0
	Phi-N	37	113	13	27	4	1	1	8	15	8	.239	.328	.319	.647	93	-2	-1	94	74	12	.567	0			1	C/O31	0.1
	Yr	74	192	21	47	7	1	1	20	26	16	.245	.335	.307	.642	89	-3	-2	97	134	21	.577	1			1		0.1
1946	Phi-N	11	13	2	1	0	0	0	1	7	3	.077	.400	.077	.477	41	-0	-0	95	373	1	.667	0			1	/C1	0.0
Total	4	98	228	29	53	9	2	1	22	34	24	.232	.335	.303	.637	87	-4	-3	96	131	25	.600	1			2	/C301P	0.2
■ GENE MOORE	Moore, Eugene Jr. "Rowdy" b: 8/26/09, Lancaster, Tex. d: 3/12/78, Jackson, Miss. BL/TL, 5'11", 175 lbs. Deb: 9/20/31																											
1931	Cin-N	4	14	2	2	1	0	0	1	0	0	.143	.143	.214	.357	-6	-2	-2	95	119	0	.250	0			0	/O	-0.1
1933	StL-N	11	38	6	15	3	2	0	8	4	10	.395	.452	.579	1.031	189	5	5	102	137	10	1.125	1			1	O	0.5
1934	StL-N	9	18	2	5	1	0	0	1	2	2	.278	.350	.333	.683	74	-0	-1	114	60	2	.615	0			1	/O	0.0
1935	StL-N	3	3	0	0	0	0	0	0	0	1	.000	.000	.000	.000	-96	-1	-1	104	0	0	.000	0			0	H	0.0
1936	Bos-N	151	637	91	185	38	12	13	67	40	80	.290	.335	.449	.784	115	6	11	95	65	100	.733	6			13	*O	1.6
1937	Bos-N	148	561	88	159	29	10	16	70	61	73	.283	.358	.456	.814	132	15	22	90	88	96	.808	11			11	*O	2.6
1938	Bos-N	54	180	27	49	8	3	3	19	16	20	.272	.338	.400	.738	116	1	3	88	85	25	.679	1			-2	O	0.1
1939	Bro-N	107	306	45	69	13	6	3	39	40	50	.225	.315	.337	.652	70	-11	-13	107	128	35	.610	4			-6	O/1	-2.1
1940	Bro-N	10	26	3	7	2	0	0	2	1	3	.269	.296	.346	.642	71	-1	-1	108	82	3	.526	0			-1	/O	-0.2
	Bos-N	103	363	46	106	24	1	5	39	25	32	.292	.338	.405	.743	105	2	2	99	91	48	.652	2			3	O	0.2
	Yr	113	389	49	113	26	1	5	41	26	35	.290	.335	.401	.736	103	1	1	100	91	51	.643	2			2		0.0
1941	Bos-N	129	397	42	108	17	8	5	43	45	37	.272	.349	.393	.742	117	5	8	93	91	57	.705	5			3	*O	0.6
1942	Was-A	1	2	0	0	0	0	0	0	0	1	.000	.000	.000	.000	-99	-1	-1	96	0	0	.000	0	0	0	-0	/O	0.0
1943	Was-A	92	254	41	68	14	3	2	39	19	29	.268	.321	.370	.691	98	-0	-1	104	142	29	.582	0	2	-1	-1	O/1	-0.5
1944	StL-A	110	390	56	93	13	6	6	58	24	37	.238	.284	.349	.633	79	-11	-12	102	136	37	.521	0	5	-3	-1	O/1	-1.9
1945	StL-A	110	354	48	92	16	2	5	50	40	26	.260	.337	.359	.695	88	1	-5	115	127	46	.631	1	3	-2	-6	*O	-1.7
Total	14	1042	3543	497	958	179	53	58	436	317	401	.270	.333	.400	.733	104	7	14	99	101	489	.685	31	10		15	O/1	-0.9
■ FERDIE MOORE	Moore, Ferdinand Depage b: 2/21/1896, Camden, N.J. d: 5/6/47, Atlantic City, N.J. Deb: 10/02/14																											
1914	Phi-A	2	4	1	2	0	0	0	1	0	2	.500	.500	.500	1.000	206	0	0	97	188	1	1.000	0			0	/1	0.1
■ GARY MOORE	Moore, Gary Douglas b: 2/24/45, Tulsa, Okla. BR/TL, 5'10", 175 lbs. Deb: 5/03/70																											
1970	LA-N	7	16	2	3	0	2	0	0	0	1	.188	.188	.438	.625	69	-1	-1	90	0	0	.533	1	0	0	-1	/O1	-0.1
■ EDDIE MOORE	Moore, Graham Edward b: 1/18/1899, Barlow, Ky. d: 2/10/76, Ft.Myers, Fla. BR/TR, 5'7", 165 lbs. Deb: 9/25/23																											
1923	Pit-N	6	26	6	7	1	0	0	1	2	3	.269	.321	.308	.629	69	-1	-1	97	38	3	.579	1	0	0	0	/S	0.0
1924	Pit-N	72	209	47	75	8	4	2	13	27	12	.359	.437	.464	.901	133	14	12	106	46	42	.936	6	7	-2	3	O3/2	1.2
1925	Pit-N	142	547	106	163	29	8	6	77	73	26	.298	.383	.413	.796	101	5	3	102	108	92	.818	19	7	2	-3	*2O/3	0.0
1926	Pit-N	43	132	19	30	8	1	0	19	12	6	.227	.292	.303	.595	54	-7	-10	112	164	12	.539	3			0	2/3S	-0.7
	Bos-N	54	184	17	49	3	2	0	15	16	12	.266	.325	.304	.629	81	-7	-4	86	94	19	.578	6			-8	2S/3	-0.8
	Yr	97	316	36	79	11	3	0	34	28	18	.250	.311	.304	.615	67	-15	-14	98	127	31	.561	9			-8		-1.5
1927	Bos-N	112	411	53	124	14	4	1	32	39	17	.302	.364	.363	.726	102	-2	2	93	75	54	.676	5			-10	32O/S	-0.5
1928	Bos-N	68	215	27	51	9	0	2	18	19	12	.237	.299	.307	.606	60	-13	-12	97	89	20	.561	7			4	O/2	-0.9
1929	Bro-N	111	402	48	119	18	6	0	48	44	16	.296	.370	.371	.740	89	-9	-5	94	112	56	.703	3			-11	2S/O3	-0.7
1930	Bro-N	76	196	24	55	13	1	1	20	21	7	.281	.356	.372	.729	76	-7	-7	101	91	26	.688	1			-2	2OS/3	-0.5
1932	NY-N	37	87	9	23	3	0	1	6	9	6	.264	.340	.333	.674	83	-2	-2	99	70	10	.625	1			-1	S/32	0.0
1934	Cle-A	27	65	4	10	2	0	0	8	10	4	.154	.267	.185	.451	18	-8	-8	101	223	4	.400	0	0	0	3	2/3S	-0.3
Total	10	748	2474	360	706	108	26	13	257	272	121	.285	.359	.366	.725	89	-37	-31	98	98	338	.696	52	14		-24	2O/S3	-3.2
■ HARRY MOORE	Moore, Henry S. Deb: 4/17/1884																											
1884	Was-U	111	461	77	155	23	5	1		19		.336	.363	.414	.777	168	29	31	97	0	71	.686	0			-4	*O/S	2.2
■ JACKIE MOORE	Moore, Jackie Spencer b: 2/19/39, Jay, Fla. BR/TR, 6', 180 lbs. Deb: 4/18/65 MC																											
1965	Det-A	21	53	2	5	0	0	0	2	6	12	.094	.186	.094	.281	-17	-8	-8	105	166	1	.216	0	0	0	2	C	-0.4
■ JIMMY MOORE	Moore, James William b: 4/24/03, Paris, Tenn. d: 3/7/86, Memphis, Tenn. BR/TR, 6'0.5", 187 lbs. Deb: 8/31/30																											
1930	Chi-A	16	39	4	8	2	0	0	2	6	3	.205	.326	.256	.582	49	-3	-3	103	66	4	.548	0	0	0	0	O	-0.2
	Phi-A	15	50	10	19	3	0	2	12	2	4	.380	.404	.560	.964	142	3	3	99	117	11	.969	1	1	-0	-1	O	0.1
	Yr	31	89	14	27	5	0	2	14	8	7	.303	.367	.427	.794	100	0	0	101	93	14	.762	1	1	-0	-1		-0.1
1931	Phi-A	49	143	18	32	5	1	2	21	11	13	.224	.284	.315	.599	54	-9	-10	105	136	13	.509	0	1	-1	-0	O	-1.2
Total	2	80	232	32	59	10	1	4	35	19	20	.254	.316	.358	.674	72	-9	-10	103	119	27	.600	1	2	-1	-1	/O	-1.3
■ JERRIE MOORE	Moore, Jeremiah S. b: Detroit, Mich. d: 9/26/1890, Wayne, Mich. BL , Deb: 4/17/1884																											
1884	Alt-U	20	80	10	25	3	1	1		0		.313	.313	.412	.725	141	3	3	101	0	11	.600	0			0	C/O	0.3
	Cle-N	9	30	1	6	0	0	0	10	0	5	.200	.200	.200	.400	26	-2	-3	102	573	1	.250				0	/C	-0.1
1885	Det-N	6	23	2	4	1	0	0	0	1	3	.174	.208	.217	.426	39	-2	-1	97	0	1	.316				0	/C	0.0
Total	2	35	133	13	35	4	1	1	10	1	8	.263	.269	.331	.599	96	-1	-1	101	128	13	.459				0	/CO	0.2
■ JOHNNY MOORE	Moore, John Francis b: 3/23/02, Waterville, Conn. BL/TR, 5'10.5", 175 lbs. Deb: 9/15/28																											
1928	Chi-N	4	4	0	0	0	0	0	0	0	0	.000	.000	.000	.000	-99	-1	-1	95	0	0	.000	0			0	H	0.0
1929	Chi-N	37	63	13	18	1	0	2	8	4	6	.286	.338	.397	.735	80	-2	-2	101	88	8	.667	0			-1	O	-0.3
1931	Chi-N	39	104	19	25	3	1	2	16	7	5	.240	.288	.346	.634	73	-5	-4	96	136	11	.557	1			1	O	-0.3
1932	Chi-N	119	443	59	135	24	5	13	64	22	38	.305	.342	.470	.811	111	9	6	104	98	71	.769	4			-5	*O	-0.6
1933	Cin-N	135	514	60	135	19	5	1	44	29	16	.263	.306	.325	.631	81	-13	-12	99	103	52	.522	4			7	*O	-1.3
1934	Cin-N	16	42	5	8	1	1	0	5	3	2	.190	.244	.262	.506	35	-4	-4	101	164	3	.412	0			-0	O	-0.4
	Phi-N	116	458	68	157	34	6	11	93	40	18	.343	.397	.515	.912	131	27	22	108	132	97	.922	7			7	*O	2.2
	Yr	132	500	73	165	35	7	11	98	43	20	.330	.384	.494	.878	124	23	18	107	137	98	.871	7			7		1.8
1935	Phi-N	153	600	84	194	33	3	19	93	45	50	.323	.375	.483	.859	113	24	13	114	102	114	.835	4			-12	*O	-0.4
1936	Phi-N	124	472	85	155	24	3	16	68	26	22	.328	.365	.494	.858	119	18	13	108	87	83	.791	1			-9	*O	0.0
1937	Phi-N	96	307	46	98	16	2	9	59	18	18	.319	.357	.472	.829	114	9	6	108	124	52	.771	2			-3	O	0.0
1945	Chi-N	7	6	0	1	0	0	0	2	1	1	.167	.286	.167	.452	28	-1	-1	99	694	0	.400	0			0	H	0.0
Total	10	846	3013	439	926	155	26	73	452	195	176	.307	.352	.449	.801	109	62	36	106	109	492	.759	23			-15	O	-1.1
■ JO-JO MOORE	Moore, Joseph Gregg "The Gause Ghost" b: 12/25/08, Gause, Tex. BL/TR, 5'11", 155 lbs. Deb: 9/17/30																											
1930	NY-N	3	5	1	1	0	0	0	0	0	1	.200	.200	.200	.400	-3	-1	-1	98	0	0	.250	0			0	/O	0.0
1931	NY-N	4	8	0	2	1	0	0	3	0	1	.250	.250	.375	.625	68	-0	-0	97	356	1	.667	1			0	/O	0.0
1932	NY-N	86	361	53	110	15	2	2	27	20	18	.305	.341	.374	.715	94	-4	-3	99	68	47	.633	4			-7	O	-1.5
1933	NY-N	132	524	56	153	16	5	0	42	21	27	.292	.323	.342	.665	91	-7	-6	99	93	59	.549	4			4	*O	-1.0
1934	NY-N	139	580	106	192	37	4	15	61	31	23	.331	.370	.486	.856	130	21	23	98	65	109	.824	5			-12	*O	0.4
1935	NY-N	155	681	108	201	28	9	15	71	53	24	.295	.353	.429	.782	113	9	12	96	66	110	.740	5			-1	*O	0.4
1936	NY-N	152	649	110	205	29	9	7	63	37	27	.316	.358	.421	.779	109	8	7	100	73	103	.711	2			6	*O	0.7
1937	NY-N	142	580	89	180	37	10	6	57	46	37	.310	.364	.440	.804	117	14	14	100	72	96	.760	7			-10	*O	-0.2
1938	NY-N	125	506	76	153	23	6	11	56	22	27	.302	.335	.437	.772	107	6	4	103	84	77	.699	2			-3	*O	-0.1
1939	NY-N	138	562	80	151	23	2	10	47	45	17	.269	.324	.370	.694	87	-11	-11	99	70	69	.620	5			-0	*O	-1.2
1940	NY-N	138	543	83	150	33	4	6	46	43	30	.276	.337	.385	.722	99	-1	-1	100	80	72	.663	7			-2	*O	-0.7
1941	NY-N	121	428	47	117	16	2	7	40	30	15	.273	.322	.369	.692	92	-4	-5	103	82	52	.611	4			-4	*O	-1.4
Total	12	1335	5427	809	1615	258	53	79	513	348	247	.298	.344	.408	.752	105	29	32	100	75	795	.693	46			-29	*O	-4.6
■ KELVIN MOORE	Moore, Kelvin Orlando b: 9/26/57, Le Roy, Ala. BR/TL, 6'1", 195 lbs. Deb: 8/28/81																											
1981	Oak-A	14	47	5	12	0	1	1	3	5	15	.255	.327	.362	.689	102	-0	0	96	59	6	.639	1	0	0	-0	1	0.0
1982	Oak-A	21	67	6	15	1	1	2	6	3	23	.224	.257	.358	.615	70	-3	-3	95	80	5	.491	0	1	-1	-0	1	-0.3
1983	Oak-A	41	124	12	26	4	0	5	16	10	39	.210	.274	.363	.637	77	-5	-4	96	104	11	.552	2	4	-2	-3	1	-1.0
Total	3	76	238	23	53	5	2	8	25	18	77	.223	.280	.361	.642	80	-8	-7	96	88	22	.560	3	5	-2	-3	/1	-1.3

YEAR	TM/L	G	AB	R	H	2B	3B	HR	RBI	BB	SO	AVG	OBP	SLG	PRO	/A	BR	/A	PF	CHI	RC	TA	SB	CS	SBR	FR	POS	TPR
■ MOLLY MOORE	Moore, Maurice d: 2/24/1881, New York, N.Y. Deb: 6/30/1875																											
1875	Atl-n	23	90	6	20							.222															S/13	
■ RANDY MOORE	Moore, Randolph Edward b: 6/21/05, Naples, Tex. BL/TR, 6', 185 lbs. Deb: 4/12/27																											
1927	Chi-A	6	15	0	0	0	0	0	0	0	2	.000	.000	.000	.000	-98	-4	-4	102	0	0	.000	0	0	0	0	/O	-0.3
1928	Chi-A	24	61	6	13	4	1	0	5	3	5	.213	.250	.311	.561	47	-5	-5	99	90	5	.449	0	1	-1	-1	O	-0.6
1930	Bos-N	83	191	24	55	9	0	2	34	10	13	.288	.323	.366	.690	68	-10	-9	97	154	22	.610	3			-2	O3	-1.1
1931	Bos-N	83	192	19	50	8	1	3	34	13	3	.260	.311	.359	.670	80	-6	-5	99	155	22	.592	1			-1	O3/2	-0.5
1932	Bos-N	107	351	41	103	21	2	3	43	15	11	.293	.322	.390	.713	97	-5	-2	93	110	44	.617	1			-7	O31/C	-0.9
1933	Bos-N	135	497	64	150	23	7	8	70	40	16	.302	.356	.425	.781	127	14	16	96	119	74	.705	3			0	*O1	0.9
1934	Bos-N	123	422	55	120	21	2	7	64	40	16	.284	.346	.393	.740	114	-1	7	86	123	59	.667	2			-1	O1	0.0
1935	Bos-N	125	407	42	112	20	4	4	42	26	16	.275	.319	.373	.692	89	-9	-6	96	92	48	.587	1			-0	O1	-0.9
1936	Bro-N	42	88	4	21	3	0	0	14	8	1	.239	.302	.273	.575	53	-5	-6	105	207	7	.457	0			-5	O	-1.1
1937	Bro-N	13	22	3	3	1	0	0	2	3	2	.136	.240	.182	.422	15	-3	-3	104	180	1	.350	0			-0	C	-0.2
	StL-N	8	7	0	0	0	0	0	0	0	0	.000	.000	.000	.000	-99	-2	-2	101	0	0	.000	0			-0	/O	-0.1
	Yr	21	29	3	3	1	0	0	2	3	2	.103	.188	.138	.325	-10	-4	-5	103	120	1	.259	0			-1		-0.3
Total	10	749	2253	258	627	110	17	27	308	158	85	.278	.326	.378	.705	94	-35	-19	95	122	283	.629	11	1		-17	O/13C2	-4.8
■ TERRY MOORE	Moore, Terry Bluford b: 5/27/12, Vernon, Ala. BR/TR, 5'11", 195 lbs. Deb: 4/16/35 MC																											
1935	StL-N	119	456	63	131	34	3	6	53	15	40	.287	.314	.414	.729	91	-5	-7	104	94	60	.665	13			12	*O	0.0
1936	StL-N	143	590	85	156	39	4	5	47	37	52	.264	.309	.369	.678	87	-16	-12	94	76	70	.602	9			17	*O	0.0
1937	StL-N	115	461	76	123	17	3	5	43	32	41	.267	.317	.349	.666	80	-12	-13	101	85	53	.601	13			10	*O	-0.7
1938	StL-N	94	312	49	85	21	3	4	21	46	19	.272	.366	.397	.763	99	5	0	111	57	49	.768	9			4	O/3	0.2
1939	StL-N	130	417	65	123	25	2	17	77	43	38	.295	.362	.487	.849	120	15	12	105	111	73	.830	6			6	*O/P	1.6
1940	StL-N	136	537	92	163	33	4	17	64	42	44	.304	.356	.475	.831	125	19	17	102	82	92	.834	18			15	*O	2.8
1941	StL-N	122	493	86	145	26	4	6	68	52	31	.294	.364	.400	.763	105	10	4	110	110	74	.713	3			3	*O	0.2
1942	StL-N	130	489	80	141	26	3	6	49	56	26	.288	.364	.391	.754	112	13	9	108	92	72	.723	10			5	*O/3	1.1
1946	StL-N	91	278	32	73	14	1	3	28	18	26	.263	.312	.353	.665	83	-5	-7	107	98	32	.573	0			-2	O	-1.0
1947	StL-N	127	460	61	130	17	1	7	45	38	39	.283	.339	.370	.708	83	-8	-12	106	89	58	.618	1			-4	*O	-1.9
1948	StL-N	91	207	30	48	11	0	4	18	27	12	.232	.321	.343	.664	79	-6	-6	101	81	24	.601	0			-6	O	-1.6
Total	11	1298	4700	719	1318	263	28	80	513	406	368	.280	.340	.399	.739	98	11	-14	104	89	656	.703	82			61	*O/3P	0.7
■ SCRAPPY MOORE	Moore, William Allen b: 12/16/1892, St.Louis, Mo. d: 10/13/64, Little Rock, Ark. BR/TR, 5'8", 153 lbs. Deb: 6/21/17																											
1917	StL-A	4	8	1	1	0	0	0	0	1	0	.125	.222	.125	.347	6	-1	-1	95	0	0	.286	0			0	/3	0.0
■ BILL MOORE	Moore, William Henry "Willie" b: 12/12/01, Kansas City, Mo. d: 5/24/72, Kansas City, Mo. BL/TR, 5'11", 170 lbs. Deb: 9/07/26																											
1926	Bos-A	5	18	2	3	0	0	0	0	0	2	.167	.167	.167	.333	-13	-3	-3	101	0	0	.200	0	0	0	0	/C	-0.2
1927	Bos-A	44	69	7	15	2	0	0	4	13	8	.217	.341	.246	.588	58	-4	-4	95	78	7	.556	0	0	0	-2	C	-0.3
Total	2	49	87	9	18	2	0	0	4	13	10	.207	.310	.230	.540	44	-7	-7	96	64	7	.478	0	0	0	-2	/C	-0.5
■ BILL MOORE	Moore, William Ross b: 8/10/60, Los Angeles, Cal. BR/TL, 6'1", 185 lbs. Deb: 7/19/86																											
1986	Mon-N	6	12	0	2	0	0	0	0	0	4	.167	.167	.167	.333	-8	-2	-2	98	0	0	.200	0	0	0	-0	/1O	-0.2
■ ANDRES MORA	Mora, Andres (Ibarra) b: 5/25/55, Rio Bravo, Mex. BR/TR, 6', 180 lbs. Deb: 4/13/76																											
1976	Bal-A	73	220	18	48	11	0	6	25	13	49	.218	.262	.350	.612	80	-7	-6	98	101	20	.517	1	0	0	-2	DO	-0.9
1977	Bal-A	77	233	32	57	8	2	13	44	5	53	.245	.264	.464	.727	101	-3	-1	93	119	27	.633	0	0	0	-11	O/3D	-1.3
1978	Bal-A	76	229	21	49	8	0	8	14	13	47	.214	.259	.354	.613	78	-10	-7	91	53	20	.511	0	1	-1	-3	O/D	-1.2
1980	Cle-A	9	18	0	2	0	0	0	0	0	0	.111	.111	.111	.222	-38	-3	-3	102	0	0	.125	0	0	0	0	/O	-0.3
Total	4	235	700	71	156	27	2	27	83	31	149	.223	.258	.383	.641	83	-23	-18	94	88	67	.554	1	1	-0	-16	O/D3	-3.7
■ JOSE MORALES	Morales, Jose Manuel (Hernandez) b: 12/30/44, Frederiksted, V.I. BR/TR, 5'11", 187 lbs. Deb: 8/13/73 C																											
1973	Oak-A	6	14	0	4	1	0	0	1	1	5	.286	.333	.357	.690	108	-0	0	87	79	1	.545	0	1	-1	0	/D	0.0
	Mon-N	5	5	0	2	0	0	0	0	0	0	.400	.400	.400	.800	118	0	0	104	0	1	.667	0	0	0	0	H	0.0
1974	Mon-N	25	26	3	7	4	0	1	5	1	7	.269	.296	.538	.835	124	1	1	104	114	3	.714	0	0	0	0	/C	0.1
1975	Mon-N	93	163	18	49	6	1	2	24	14	21	.301	.356	.387	.742	98	1	-0	108	134	20	.631	0	2	-1	1	1/OC	-0.1
1976	Mon-N	104	158	12	50	11	0	4	37	3	20	.316	.337	.462	.799	125	4	4	100	168	23	.690	0	0	0	2	1C	0.6
1977	Mon-N	65	74	3	15	4	1	1	9	5	12	.203	.253	.324	.577	55	-5	-5	98	133	5	.460	0	0	0	1	/C1	-0.4
1978	Min-A	101	242	22	76	13	1	2	38	20	35	.314	.369	.401	.770	123	6	7	94	146	34	.667	0	1	-1	-0	D/C1O	0.6
1979	Min-A	92	191	21	51	5	1	2	27	14	27	.267	.324	.335	.659	72	-6	-8	109	148	19	.533	0	0	0	0	D/1	-0.7
1980	Min-A	97	241	36	73	17	2	8	36	22	19	.303	.364	.490	.853	121	10	7	109	99	40	.788	0	0	0	0	D/C1	0.7
1981	Bal-A	38	86	6	21	3	0	2	14	3	13	.244	.270	.349	.619	78	-3	-3	99	152	6	.465	0	0	0	0	D/1	-0.2
1982	Bal-A	3	3	0	0	0	0	0	0	0	2	.000	.000	.000	.000	-99	-1	-1	100	0	0	.000	0	0	0	0	/H	0.0
	LA-N	35	30	1	9	1	0	1	8	4	8	.300	.382	.433	.816	135	1	1	95	196	5	.773	0	0	0	0	H	0.1
1983	LA-N	47	53	4	15	3	0	3	8	1	11	.283	.296	.509	.806	119	1	1	100	88	7	.700	0	0	0	0	/1	0.1
1984	LA-N	22	19	0	3	0	0	0	0	1	2	.158	.200	.158	.358	2	-2	-3	104	0	1	.250	0	0	0	0	H	-0.2
Total	12	733	1305	126	375	68	6	26	207	89	182	.287	.336	.408	.744	103	8	3	103	133	164	.672	0	4	-2	3	D/1CO	0.6
■ JERRY MORALES	Morales, Julio Ruben (Torres) b: 2/18/49, Yabucao, P.R. BR/TR, 5'10", 155 lbs. Deb: 9/05/69																											
1969	SD-N	19	41	5	8	2	0	1	6	5	7	.195	.283	.317	.600	70	-2	-2	97	150	3	.500	0	2	-1	0	O	-0.3
1970	SD-N	28	58	6	9	0	1	1	4	3	11	.155	.197	.241	.438	18	-7	-7	95	91	2	.333	0	0	0	-5	O	-1.3
1971	SD-N	12	17	1	2	0	0	0	1	2	2	.118	.211	.118	.328	-5	-2	-2	96	204	0	.313	1	0	0	-1	/O	-0.3
1972	SD-N	115	347	38	83	15	7	4	18	35	54	.239	.309	.357	.666	101	-5	-0	88	54	38	.593	4	6	-2	10	O/3	0.3
1973	SD-N	122	388	47	109	23	2	9	34	27	55	.281	.328	.420	.748	112	2	5	94	72	49	.658	6	5	-1	4	*O	0.3
1974	Chi-N	151	534	70	146	21	7	15	82	46	63	.273	.333	.423	.757	111	6	6	100	119	69	.665	2	12	-7	-2	*O	-0.8
1975	Chi-N	153	578	62	156	21	0	12	91	50	65	.270	.333	.369	.702	91	-4	-7	104	144	69	.612	3	7	-3	-0	*O	-1.6
1976	Chi-N	140	537	66	147	17	0	16	67	41	49	.274	.325	.395	.720	95	1	-4	109	105	62	.612	3	8	-4	6	*O	-0.7
1977	Chi-N	136	490	56	142	34	5	11	69	43	75	.290	.350	.447	.796	98	8	-1	114	112	75	.731	0	3	-2	-12	*O	-1.9
1978	StL-N	130	457	44	109	19	8	4	46	33	44	.239	.291	.341	.633	80	-15	-13	95	111	43	.532	4	4	-1	-1	*O	-2.0
1979	Det-A	129	440	50	93	23	1	14	56	30	56	.211	.265	.364	.628	70	-21	-19	96	107	39	.552	10	4	1	-6	*O/D	-2.8
1980	NY-N	94	193	19	49	7	1	3	30	13	31	.254	.304	.347	.651	85	-5	-4	96	156	20	.557	2	3	-1	-3	O	-1.1
1981	Chi-N	84	245	27	70	6	2	1	25	22	29	.286	.347	.339	.686	92	-1	-2	104	114	29	.588	1	1	-0	-2	O	-0.7
1982	Chi-N	65	116	14	33	2	2	4	30	9	7	.284	.336	.440	.776	112	2	2	103	187	15	.678	1	2	-1	1	O	0.2
1983	Chi-N	63	87	11	17	9	0	0	11	7	19	.195	.255	.299	.554	53	-6	-6	101	167	7	.465	0	0	0	-5	O	-1.1
Total	15	1441	4528	516	1173	199	36	95	570	366	567	.259	.316	.382	.698	92	-49	-54	101	113	520	.629	37	57	-23	-17	*O/D3	-13.8
■ RICH MORALES	Morales, Richard Angelo b: 9/20/43, San Francisco, Cal. BR/TR, 5'11", 170 lbs. Deb: 8/08/67 C																											
1967	Chi-A	8	10	0	0	0	0	0	0	0	2	.000	.000	.000	.000	-99	-2	-2	94	0	0	.000	0	0	0	0	/S	-0.1
1968	Chi-A	10	29	2	5	0	0	0	0	2	5	.172	.226	.172	.398	22	-3	-3	101	0	1	.280	0	0	0	1	/S2	0.0
1969	Chi-A	55	121	12	26	0	1	0	6	7	18	.215	.269	.231	.501	38	-9	-11	108	86	8	.388	1	0	0	6	2S/3	-0.1
1970	Chi-A	62	112	6	18	2	0	1	2	9	16	.161	.230	.205	.435	20	-12	-13	106	31	6	.354	1	0	0	4	S32	-0.5
1971	Chi-A	84	185	19	45	8	0	2	14	22	26	.243	.336	.319	.655	89	-3	-2	98	88	20	.596	2	3	-1	3	S3/2O	0.6
1972	Chi-A	110	287	24	59	7	1	2	20	19	49	.206	.262	.258	.520	52	-16	-18	106	104	17	.405	2	3	-1	-3	S23	-1.2
1973	Chi-A	7	4	1	0	0	0	0	1	1	1	.000	.200	.000	.200	-39	-1	-1	102	0	0	.200	0	0	0	0	/32	0.0
	SD-N	90	244	9	40	6	1	0	16	27	36	.164	.247	.197	.444	26	-25	-23	94	134	13	.361	0	1	-1	1	2S	-1.8
1974	SD-N	54	61	8	12	3	0	1	5	8	6	.197	.290	.295	.585	68	-3	-2	93	92	6	.529	1	0	0	-2	S2/31	0.0
Total	8	480	1053	81	205	26	3	6	64	95	159	.195	.268	.242	.510	46	-73	-74	101	94	70	.428	7	7	-2	11	S2/31O	-3.1
■ CHARLIE MORAN	Moran, Charles Barthell "Uncle Charlie" b: 2/22/1878, Nashville, Tenn. d: 6/14/49, Horse Cave, Ky. BR/TR, 5'8", 180 lbs. Deb: 03																											
1903	StL-N	4	14	2	6	0	0	0	1	0		.429	.429	.429	.857	153	1	1	96	54	3	.875	1			-1	/PS	0.0

YEAR	TM/L	G	AB	R	H	2B	3B	HR	RBI	BB	SO	AVG	OBP	SLG	PRO	/A	BR	/A	PF	CHI	RC	TA	SB	CS	SBR	FR	POS	TPR
1908	StL-N	21	63	2	11	1	2	0	2	0		.175	.175	.254	.429	40	-5	-4	94	48	3	.308	0			0	C	-0.2
Total	2	25	77	4	17	1	2	0	3	0		.221	.221	.286	.506	63	-4	-3	94	49	6	.383	1			-0	/CPS	-0.2
■ **CHARLES MORAN**	Moran, Charles Vincent b: 3/26/1879, Washington, D.C. d: 4/11/34, Washington, D.C. TR , Deb: 4/29/03																											
1903	Was-A	98	373	41	84	14	5	1	24	33		.225	.288	.298	.586	74	-9	-12	105	67	35	.526	8			2	S/2	-0.5
1904	Was-A	62	243	27	54	10	0	0	7	23		.222	.289	.263	.553	84	-5	-3	93	35	21	.497	7			-2	S/3	-0.4
	StL-A	82	272	15	47	3	1	0	14	25		.173	.242	.191	.434	42	-17	-16	95	102	13	.351	2			-8	3/O	-2.3
	Yr	144	515	42	101	13	1	0	21	48		.196	.265	.225	.490	62	-23	-19	94	74	34	.418	9			-9		-2.7
1905	StL-A	27	82	6	16	1	0	0	5	10		.195	.283	.207	.490	64	-3	-3	91	105	6	.455	3			-2	2/3	-0.4
Total	3	269	970	89	201	28	6	1	50	91		.207	.275	.252	.527	67	-35	-33	98	72	75	.462	20			-10	S/32O	-3.6
■ **HERBIE MORAN**	Moran, John Herbert b: 2/16/1884, Costello, Pa. d: 9/21/54, Clarkson, N.Y. BL/TR, 5'5", 150 lbs. Deb: 4/16/08																											
1908	Phi-A	19	59	4	9	0	0	0	4	6		.153	.231	.153	.383	25	-4	-5	108	170	2	.320	1			-1	O	-0.6
	Bos-N	8	29	3	8	0	0	0	2	2		.276	.323	.276	.598	90	-0	-0	104	102	3	.524	1			0	/O	0.0
1909	Bos-N	8	31	8	7	1	0	0	0	5		.226	.333	.258	.591	88	-0	-0	96	0	3	.542	0			0	/O	0.0
1910	Bos-N	20	67	11	8	0	0	0	3	13	14	.119	.280	.119	.400	15	-6	-8	114	138	4	.492	6			4	O	-0.3
1912	Bro-N	130	508	77	140	18	10	1	40	69	38	.276	.368	.356	.724	103	1	4	95	65	76	.769	28			9	*O	0.9
1913	Bro-N	132	515	71	137	15	5	0	26	45	29	.266	.333	.315	.648	82	-8	-11	104	56	58	.622	21			-3	*O	-1.6
1914	Cin-N	107	395	43	93	10	5	1	35	41	29	.235	.312	.294	.606	77	-9	-11	105	102	42	.616	26			-6	*O	-2.1
	Bos-N	41	154	24	41	3	1	0	4	17	11	.266	.347	.299	.646	89	-1	-2	104	30	17	.611	4			-5	O	-0.7
	Yr	148	549	67	134	13	6	1	39	58	40	.244	.322	.295	.617	80	-10	-13	105	83	59	.614	30			-11		-2.8
1915	Bos-N	130	419	59	84	13	5	0	21	66	41	.200	.320	.255	.576	77	-10	-9	98	76	38	.571	16	10	-1	-7	*O	-2.2
Total	7	595	2177	300	527	60	26	2	135	264	162	.242	.331	.296	.628	82	-38	-41	101	74	243	.626	103	10		-8	O	-6.6
■ **PAT MORAN**	Moran, Patrick Joseph b: 2/7/1876, Fitchburg, Mass. d: 3/7/24, Orlando, Fla. TR , 5'10", 180 lbs. Deb: 5/15/01 M																											
1901	Bos-N	52	180	12	38	5	1	2	18	3		.211	.224	.283	.507	43	-12	-15	112	106	12	.401	3			2	C1/3S02	-0.8
1902	Bos-N	80	251	22	60	5	5	1	24	17		.239	.287	.311	.598	90	-4	-3	95	103	25	.529	6			3	C/1O	0.8
1903	Bos-N	109	389	40	102	25	5	7	54	29		.262	.313	.406	.720	111	2	4	96	99	53	.679	8			9	*C/1	2.0
1904	Bos-N	113	398	26	90	11	3	4	34	18		.226	.260	.299	.559	77	-13	-11	97	97	34	.477	10			10	C3/1	0.7
1905	Bos-N	85	267	22	64	11	5	2	22	8		.240	.262	.341	.603	83	-7	-6	97	79	25	.502	3			7	C	0.9
1906	Chi-N	70	226	22	57	13	1	0	35	7		.252	.275	.319	.593	81	-4	-6	107	177	22	.503	6			0	C	0.0
1907	Chi-N	65	198	8	45	5	1	1	19	10		.227	.264	.278	.542	67	-7	-8	106	124	16	.458	5			-2	C	-0.5
1908	Chi-N	50	150	12	39	5	1	0	12	13		.260	.319	.307	.626	96	1	-0	106	100	16	.586	6			1	C	0.3
1909	Chi-N	77	246	18	54	11	1	1	23	16		.220	.278	.285	.563	75	-7	-7	101	115	19	.479	2			-5	C	-0.7
1910	Phi-N	68	199	13	47	7	1	0	11	17	16	.236	.306	.281	.587	75	-7	-6	96	68	19	.539	6			2	C	-0.1
1911	Phi-N	34	103	2	19	3	0	0	8	3	13	.184	.208	.214	.421	17	-11	-12	108	123	5	.298	0			1	C	-0.9
1912	Phi-N	13	26	1	3	1	0	0	1	1	7	.115	.148	.154	.302	-17	-4	-4	100	84	1	.217	0			0	C	-0.2
1913	Phi-N	1	1	0	0	0	0	0	0	0	0	.000	.000	.000	.000	-89	-0	-0	112	0	0	.000	0			0	H	0.0
1914	Phi-N	1	0	0	0	0	0	0	1	0	0	—	—	—	—	—	0	0	100	—	—	—	0			0	/C	0.0
Total	14	818	2634	198	618	102	24	18	262	142	36	.235	.276	.312	.588	78	-75	-75	100	106	247	.509	55			26	C/31OS2	1.5
■ **AL MORAN**	Moran, Richard Alan b: 12/5/38, Detroit, Mich. BR/TR, 6'1.5", 190 lbs. Deb: 4/09/63																											
1963	NY-N	119	331	26	64	5	2	1	23	36	60	.193	.274	.230	.504	47	-22	-22	99	122	21	.414	3	7	-3	0	*S/3	-1.4
1964	NY-N	16	22	2	5	0	0	0	4	2	2	.227	.292	.227	.519	51	-1	-1	95	328	1	.389	0	0	0	-0	S/3	0.0
Total	2	135	353	28	69	5	2	1	27	38	62	.195	.276	.229	.505	47	-23	-23	99	135	22	.421	3	7	-3	-0	S/3	-1.4
■ **ROY MORAN**	Moran, Roy Ellis "Deedle" b: 9/17/1884, Vincennes, Ind. d: 7/18/66, Atlanta, Ga. BR/TR, 5'8", 155 lbs. Deb: 9/03/12																											
1912	Was-A	7	13	1	2	0	0	0	0	8		.154	.476	.154	.630	83	1	1	99	0	2	1.182	3			-1	/O	0.0
■ **BILL MORAN**	Moran, William L. b: 10/10/1869, Joliet, Ill. d: 4/8/16, Joliet, Ill. 175 lbs. Deb: 5/07/1892																											
1892	StL-N	24	81	2	11	1	0	0	5	2	12	.136	.157	.148	.305	-7	-10	-10	95	128	2	.200	0			0	C/O	-0.8
1895	Chi-N	15	55	8	9	2	1	1	9	3	2	.164	.220	.291	.511	31	-6	-6	103	135	4	.478	2			0	C	-0.4
Total	2	39	136	10	20	3	1	1	14	5	14	.147	.183	.206	.389	11	-16	-16	98	131	6	.310	2			0	/CO	-1.2
■ **BILLY MORAN**	Moran, William Nelson b: 11/27/33, Montgomery, Ala. BR/TR, 5'11", 185 lbs. Deb: 4/15/58																											
1958	Cle-A	115	257	26	58	11	0	1	18	13	23	.226	.263	.280	.543	52	-18	-16	94	96	18	.423	3	2	-0	-4	2S	-1.0
1959	Cle-A	11	17	1	5	0	0	0	2	0	1	.294	.294	.294	.588	64	-1	-1	97	157	1	.417	0	0	0	-1	/2S	0.0
1961	LA-A	54	173	17	45	7	1	2	22	17	16	.260	.330	.347	.677	73	-4	-7	111	131	20	.586	0	0	0	6	2/S	0.5
1962	LA-A	160	659	90	186	25	3	17	74	39	80	.282	.326	.407	.733	94	-5	-7	102	89	89	.656	5	1	1	22	*2	2.8
1963	LA-A	153	597	67	164	29	5	7	65	31	57	.275	.314	.375	.689	101	-7	-1	91	118	68	.578	1	1	-0	18	*2	2.8
1964	LA-A	50	198	26	53	10	1	0	11	13	20	.268	.316	.328	.644	90	-5	-3	89	63	18	.510	1	3	-2	-3	3/2S	-0.5
	Cle-A	69	151	14	31	6	0	1	10	18	16	.205	.294	.265	.559	55	-8	-9	103	99	12	.468	0	1	-1	-0	32/1	-0.7
	Yr	119	349	40	84	16	1	1	21	31	36	.241	.306	.301	.607	72	-14	-12	97	84	33	.507	1	4	-2	-3		-1.2
1965	Cle-A	22	24	1	3	0	0	0	0	2	5	.125	.222	.125	.347	1	-3	-3	98	0	1	.286	0	0	0	0	/2S	-0.2
Total	7	634	2076	242	545	88	10	28	202	133	218	.263	.310	.355	.665	84	-51	-46	98	99	227	.579	10	8	-2	38	2/3S1	3.7
■ **RAY MOREHART**	Morehart, Raymond Anderson b: 12/2/1899, Near Abner, Tex. BL/TR, 5'9", 157 lbs. Deb: 8/09/24																											
1924	Chi-A	31	100	10	20	4	2	0	8	17	7	.200	.316	.280	.596	56	-7	-6	97	94	10	.593	3	1	0	-3	S/2	-0.5
1926	Chi-A	73	192	27	61	10	3	0	21	11	15	.318	.358	.401	.759	107	-1	1	92	93	24	.648	3	11	-6	-3	2	-0.4
1927	NY-A	73	195	45	50	7	2	1	20	29	18	.256	.353	.328	.681	78	-6	-6	100	99	24	.669	4	0	1	3	2	0.0
Total	3	177	487	82	131	21	7	1	49	57	40	.269	.347	.347	.694	84	-13	-10	96	96	58	.644	10	12	-4	-3	2/S	-0.9
■ **DANNY MOREJON**	Morejon, Daniel (Torres) b: 7/21/30, Havana, Cuba BR/TR, 6'1", 175 lbs. Deb: 7/11/58																											
1958	Cin-N	12	26	4	5	0	0	0	1	9	2	.192	.400	.192	.592	59	-1	-1	107	83	3	.682	1	0	0	-2	O	-0.2
■ **KEITH MORELAND**	Moreland, Bobby Keith b: 5/2/54, Dallas, Tex. BR/TR, 6', 190 lbs. Deb: 10/01/78																											
1978	Phi-N	1	2	0	0	0	0	0	0	0	0	.000	.000	.000	.000	-95	-1	-1	105	0	0	.000	0	0	0	0	/C	0.0
1979	Phi-N	14	48	3	18	3	2	0	8	3	5	.375	.412	.521	.933	158	3	4	97	127	10	.903	0	0	0	-0	C	0.4
1980	Phi-N	62	159	13	50	8	0	4	29	8	14	.314	.347	.440	.788	110	4	2	107	140	22	.698	3	1	0	2	C/3O	0.5
1981	Phi-N	61	196	16	50	7	0	6	37	15	13	.255	.311	.383	.694	86	-1	-4	112	156	20	.582	1	2	-1	-3	C/31O	-0.7
1982	Chi-N	138	476	50	124	17	2	15	68	46	71	.261	.330	.399	.729	100	2	-0	103	116	61	.651	0	6	-4	8	OC/3	0.3
1983	Chi-N	154	533	76	161	30	3	16	70	68	73	.302	.384	.460	.844	132	25	24	101	96	93	.808	0	3	-2	-12	*O/C	0.8
1984	Chi-N	140	495	59	138	17	3	16	80	34	71	.279	.329	.422	.751	100	5	-1	110	124	64	.655	1	4	-2	-8	*O1/3C	-1.6
1985	Chi-N	161	587	74	180	30	3	14	106	68	58	.307	.380	.440	.819	111	23	12	116	149	100	.800	12	3	2	-10	*O13/C	0.0
1986	Chi-N	156	586	72	159	30	0	12	79	53	48	.271	.332	.384	.716	91	-3	-7	107	128	72	.627	3	6	-3	-4	*O3C1	-1.7
1987	Chi-N	153	563	63	150	29	1	27	88	39	66	.266	.314	.465	.779	102	0	-0	101	104	78	.705	3	3	-1	0	*3/1	-0.1
1988	SD-N	143	511	40	131	23	0	5	64	40	51	.256	.310	.331	.641	86	-10	-9	97	**142**	50	.527	2	3	-1	-5	1O/3	-2.1
Total	11	1183	4156	466	1161	194	14	115	629	374	470	.279	.340	.416	.756	103	47	20	106	125	568	.703	25	31	-11	-30	O3C1	-4.2
■ **HARRY MORELOCK**	Morelock, A. Harry b: Philadelphia, Pa. Deb: 8/21/1891																											
1891	Phi-N	4	14	1	1	0	0	0	0	3	3	.071	.235	.071	.307	-8	-2	-2	95	0	0	.308	0			0	/S	-0.1
1892	Phi-N	1	3	0	0	0	0	0	0	1	0	.000	.250	.000	.250	-21	-0	-0	104	0	0	.333	0			0	/3	0.0
Total	2	5	17	1	1	0	0	0	0	4	3	.059	.238	.059	.297	-10	-2	-2	97	0	0	.313	0			0	/S3	-0.1
■ **JOSE MORENO**	Moreno, Jose De Los Santos (born De Los Santos Mauricio (Moreno)) b: 11/1/57, Santo Domingo, D.R. BB/TR, 6', 175 lbs. Deb: 5/24/80																											
1980	NY-N	37	46	6	9	2	1	2	9	3	12	.196	.245	.413	.658	84	-1	-1	96	142	4	.605	1	0	0	-0	/23	0.0
1981	SD-N	34	48	5	11	2	0	0	6	1	8	.229	.245	.271	.516	49	-3	-3	93	181	3	.450	4	1	1	-1	/O2	-0.3
1982	Cal-A	11	3	3	0	0	0	0	0	2	0	.000	.400	.000	.400	21	-0	-0	100	0	0	.400	0	2	-1	0	/2D	0.0
Total	3	82	97	14	20	4	1	2	15	6	20	.206	.252	.330	.582	66	-5	-5	95	154	7	.538	5	3	-0	-1	/O23D	-0.3

YEAR	TM/L	G	AB	R	H	2B	3B	HR	RBI	BB	SO	AVG	OBP	SLG	PRO	/A	BR	/A	PF	CHI	RC	TA	SB	CS	SBR	FR	POS	TPR
■ OMAR MORENO	Moreno, Omar Renan (Quintero) b: 10/24/52, Puerto Armuelles, Panama BL/TL, 6'2", 180 lbs. Deb: 9/06/75																											
1975	Pit-N	6	6	1	1	0	0	0	0	1	1	.167	.286	.167	.452	28	-1	-1	99	0	1	.600	1	0	0	-1	/O	0.0
1976	Pit-N	48	122	24	33	4	1	2	12	16	24	.270	.360	.369	.729	107	2	2	100	91	19	.819	15	5	2	2	O	0.3
1977	Pit-N	150	492	69	118	19	9	7	34	38	102	.240	.296	.358	.653	72	-18	-20	103	69	55	.680	53	16	6	0	*O	-1.8
1978	Pit-N	155	515	95	121	15	7	2	33	81	104	.235	.342	.303	.645	77	-10	-13	105	82	65	.739	**71**	22	8	10	*O	-0.1
1979	Pit-N	162	695	110	196	21	12	8	69	51	104	.282	.334	.381	.715	90	-5	-10	106	82	94	.751	**77**	21	11	15	*O	1.1
1980	Pit-N	162	676	87	168	20	**13**	2	36	57	101	.249	.309	.325	.634	75	-20	-23	103	54	71	.682	96	33	9	18	*O	-0.2
1981	Pit-N	103	434	62	120	18	8	1	35	26	76	.276	.322	.362	.684	98	-4	-2	96	76	53	.684	39	14	3	4	*O	0.3
1982	Pit-N	158	645	82	158	18	9	3	44	44	121	.245	.294	.315	.609	64	-26	-34	110	78	61	.593	60	26	2	5	*O	-2.9
1983	Hou-N	97	405	48	98	12	11	0	25	22	72	.242	.283	.326	.609	76	-18	-13	90	72	38	.575	30	13	1	4	O	-0.9
	NY-A	48	152	17	38	9	1	1	17	8	31	.250	.287	.342	.630	73	-6	-6	99	121	14	.554	7	3	0	3	O	-0.2
1984	NY-A	117	355	37	92	12	6	4	38	18	48	.259	.297	.361	.657	86	-10	-7	94	108	37	.603	20	11	-1	-4	*O/D	-1.4
1985	NY-A	34	66	12	13	4	1	1	4	1	16	.197	.209	.333	.542	48	-5	-5	96	63	4	.436	1	1	-0	1	O/D	-0.3
	KC-A	24	70	9	17	1	3	2	12	3	8	.243	.284	.429	.712	90	-1	-1	102	132	8	.618	0	1	-1	-2	O	-0.4
	Yr	58	136	21	30	5	4	3	16	4	24	.221	.248	.382	.631	71	-6	-6	98	93	12	.532	1	2	-1	-1		-0.7
1986	Atl-N	118	359	46	84	18	6	4	27	21	77	.234	.276	.351	.627	70	-15	-15	102	78	32	.560	17	16	-5	-3	O	-2.5
Total	12	1382	4992	699	1257	171	87	37	386	387	885	.252	.308	.343	.651	78	-137	-148	102	78	553	.664	487	182	37	52	*O/D	-9.0
■ CHARLIE MORGAN	Morgan, Charles H. Deb: N/A.																											
1882	Pit-a	17	66	10	17	2	1	0		4		.258	.300	.318	.618	112	1	1	97	0	6	.510				0	O/C	0.1
1883	Pit-a	32	114	12	18	2	1	0		7		.158	.207	.193	.400	31	-9	-7	94	0	5	.302				0	S/OC2	-0.6
Total	2	49	180	22	35	4	2	0		11		.194	.241	.239	.480	61	-8	-6	95	0	11	.372				0	/SOC2	-0.5
■ CHET MORGAN	Morgan, Chester Collins "Chick" b: 6/6/10, Cleveland, Miss. BL/TR, 5'9", 160 lbs. Deb: 4/19/35																											
1935	Det-A	14	23	2	4	1	0	0	1	5	0	.174	.321	.217	.539	43	-2	-2	97	68	2	.526	0	0	0	-0	/O	-0.1
1938	Det-A	74	306	50	87	6	1	0	27	20	12	.284	.330	.310	.641	61	-18	-18	100	92	31	.538	5	6	-2	-2	O	-2.0
Total	2	88	329	52	91	7	1	0	28	25	12	.277	.330	.304	.634	60	-20	-20	100	90	33	.537	5	6	-2	-2	/O	-2.1
■ DAN MORGAN	Morgan, Daniel b: 5/1855 Missouri Deb: 5/04/1875																											
1875	RS-n	18	73	11	15							.205															/O3P	
1878	Mil-N	14	56	2	11	0	0	0	5	3	9	.196	.237	.196	.434	41	-3	-4	107	163	3	.311				0	O/32	-0.3
■ ED MORGAN	Morgan, Edward Carre b: 5/22/04, Cairo, Ill. d: 4/9/80, New Orleans, La. BR/TR, 6'0.5", 180 lbs. Deb: 4/11/28																											
1928	Cle-A	76	265	42	83	24	6	4	54	21	17	.313	.366	.494	.860	117	8	6	106	132	47	.845	5	5	-2	1	1O3	0.2
1929	Cle-A	93	318	60	101	19	10	3	37	37	24	.318	.392	.469	.861	120	10	10	100	82	59	.873	4	3	-1	-17	O	-0.9
1930	Cle-A	150	584	122	204	47	11	26	136	62	66	.349	.413	.601	1.014	146	46	42	105	111	144	1.099	8	4	0	-1	*1O	2.2
1931	Cle-A	131	462	87	162	33	4	11	86	83	46	.351	.451	.511	.961	143	39	34	106	108	110	1.062	4	5	-2	3	*1/3	2.3
1932	Cle-A	144	532	96	156	32	7	4	68	94	44	.293	.402	.402	.804	101	11	4	108	107	92	.832	7	6	-2	-6	*1/3	-1.7
1933	Cle-A	39	121	10	32	3	3	1	13	7	9	.264	.305	.364	.668	73	-4	-5	105	92	13	.578	1	1	-0	1	1/O	-0.5
1934	Bos-A	138	528	95	141	28	4	3	79	81	46	.267	.367	.352	.719	81	-9	-13	106	143	74	.711	7	1	2	-6	*1	-3.9
Total	7	771	2810	512	879	186	45	52	473	385	252	.313	.398	.467	.864	116	102	78	106	114	540	.891	36	25	-4	-25	1O/3	-2.3
■ EDDIE MORGAN	Morgan, Edwin Willis "Pepper" b: 11/19/14, Brady Lake, Ohio d: 6/27/82, Lakewood, Ohio BL/TL, 5'10", 160 lbs. Deb: 4/14/36																											
1936	StL-N	8	18	4	5	0	0	1	3	2	4	.278	.350	.444	.794	119	0	0	94	97	3	.769	0			-1	/O	0.0
1937	Bro-N	31	48	4	9	3	0	0	5	9	7	.188	.316	.250	.566	53	-3	-3	104	150	5	.538	0			-1	/1O	-0.4
Total	2	39	66	8	14	3	0	1	8	11	11	.212	.325	.303	.628	70	-2	-3	102	136	8	.596	0			-2	/O1	-0.4
■ BILL MORGAN	Morgan, Henry William b: 10/1857, Washington, D.C. Deb: N/A.																											
1884	Was-a	45	162	8	28	1	1	0		8		.173	.216	.191	.408	41	-11	-8	88	0	7	.299				-5	OC/2S	-1.2
	Ric-a	11	36	2	6	0	1	0		2		.167	.211	.222	.433	44	-2	-2	99	0	2	.333				0	/PCO2	-0.1
	Yr	56	198	10	34	1	2	0		10		.172	.215	.197	.412	41	-13	-10	90	0	9	.305				-5		-1.3
	Bal-U	2	9	1	2	0	0	0		1		.222	.300	.222	.522	72	-0	-0	110	0	1	.429	0			0	/C2O	0.0
Total	1	58	207	11	36	1	2	0		11		.174	.219	.198	.417	43	-13	-10	91	0	9	.310	0			-5	/OCP2S	-1.3
■ RED MORGAN	Morgan, James Edward b: 10/6/1883, Neola, Iowa Deceased TR , Deb: 6/20/06																											
1906	Bos-A	88	307	20	66	6	3	1	21	16		.215	.254	.264	.518	65	-13	-12	98	93	23	.432	7			-5	3	-1.1
■ JOE MORGAN	Morgan, Joe Leonard b: 9/19/43, Bonham, Tex. BL/TR, 5'7", 160 lbs. Deb: 9/21/63																											
1963	Hou-N	8	25	5	6	0	1	0	3	5	5	.240	.367	.320	.687	108	0	0	92	161	4	.737	1	0	0	-1	/2	0.0
1964	Hou-N	10	37	4	7	0	0	0	0	6	7	.189	.302	.189	.492	44	-3	-2	96	0	2	.419	0	1	-1	0	2	-0.1
1965	Hou-N	157	601	100	163	22	12	14	40	**97**	77	.271	.375	.418	.793	138	21	30	89	50	103	.823	20	9	1	-1	*2	3.9
1966	Hou-N	122	425	60	121	14	8	5	42	89	43	.285	.412	.391	.803	128	19	21	97	94	77	.857	11	8	-2	-23	*2	0.4
1967	Hou-N	133	494	73	136	27	11	6	42	81	51	.275	.380	.411	.790	135	20	23	94	76	88	.863	29	5	**6**	-8	*2/O	3.1
1968	Hou-N	10	20	6	5	0	1	0	0	7	4	.250	.444	.350	.794	142	2	2	99	0	5	1.133	3	0	1	-0	/2O	0.3
1969	Hou-N	147	535	94	126	18	5	15	43	110	74	.236	.367	.372	.739	106	9	8	102	68	86	.839	49	14	6	3	*2O	2.7
1970	Hou-N	144	548	102	147	28	9	8	52	102	55	.268	.384	.396	.780	117	11	16	94	74	92	.852	42	13	5	15	*2	5.0
1971	Hou-N	160	583	87	149	27	**11**	13	56	88	52	.256	.354	.407	.761	124	13	18	93	79	95	.821	40	8	7	-2	*2	3.3
1972	Cin-N	149	552	**122**	161	23	4	16	73	**115**	44	.292	**.419**	.435	.854	153	37	42	93	92	117	1.015	58	17	7	-4	*2	5.8
1973	Cin-N	157	576	116	167	35	2	26	82	111	61	.290	.408	.493	.901	160	42	47	93	88	128	1.069	67	15	**11**	-3	*2	**6.2**
1974	Cin-N	149	512	107	150	31	3	22	67	120	69	.293	**.430**	.494	.924	161	45	**47**	98	86	125	**1.139**	58	12	10	-5	*2	5.9
1975	Cin-N	146	498	107	163	27	6	17	94	**132**	52	.327	**.471**	.508	**.979**	**164**	**57**	**54**	104	127	**145**	**1.307**	67	10	14	5	*2	**8.0**
1976	Cin-N	141	472	113	151	30	5	27	111	114	41	.320	**.453**	**.576**	**1.029**	**185**	**61**	**60**	103	124	**144**	**1.346**	60	9	13	-23	*2	5.8
1977	Cin-N	153	521	113	150	21	6	22	78	117	58	.288	.420	.478	.898	140	35	35	100	105	121	1.080	49	10	9	-8	*2	4.4
1978	Cin-N	132	441	68	104	27	0	13	75	79	40	.236	.354	.385	.740	104	6	4	103	**145**	67	.776	19	5	3	-13	*2	0.2
1979	Cin-N	127	436	70	109	26	1	9	32	93	45	.250	.383	.376	.759	111	9	10	97	70	72	.839	28	6	5	-11	*2	1.2
1980	Hou-N	141	461	66	112	17	5	11	49	**93**	47	.243	.370	.373	.743	110	8	10	98	97	73	.805	24	6	4	-9	*2	1.3
1981	SF-N	90	308	47	74	16	1	8	31	66	37	.240	.374	.377	.751	108	8	6	105	92	49	.810	14	5	1	-5	2	0.9
1982	SF-N	134	463	68	134	19	4	14	61	85	60	.289	.402	.438	.840	144	25	29	94	100	92	.935	24	4	5	-8	*2/3	3.2
1983	Phi-N	123	404	72	93	20	1	16	59	89	54	.230	.374	.403	.778	114	11	11	101	113	68	.840	18	2	4	11	*2	3.2
1984	Oak-A	116	365	50	89	21	0	6	43	66	39	.244	.361	.351	.712	107	1	6	92	117	51	.712	8	3	1	-20	*2/D	-0.8
Total	22	2649	9277	1650	2517	449	96	268	1133	1865	1015	.271	.395	.427	.823	133	438	476	97	93	1804	.946	689	162	110	-110	*2/OD3	63.9
■ JOE MORGAN	Morgan, Joseph Michael b: 11/19/30, Walpole, Mass. BL/TR, 5'10", 170 lbs. Deb: 4/14/59 MC																											
1959	Mil-N	13	23	2	5	1	0	0	1	2	4	.217	.280	.261	.541	48	-2	-2	95	67	2	.421	0	0	0	-0	/2	-0.1
	KC-A	20	21	2	4	0	1	0	3	3	7	.190	.292	.286	.577	58	-1	-1	101	197	2	.500	0	0	0	0	/3	0.0
1960	Phi-N	26	83	5	11	2	2	0	2	6	11	.133	.191	.205	.396	8	-11	-11	107	48	3	.307	0	0	0	-2	3	-1.4
	Cle-A	22	47	6	14	2	0	2	4	6	4	.298	.377	.468	.845	130	2	2	98	56	8	.824	0	0	0	-2	3/O	0.0
1961	Cle-A	4	10	0	2	0	0	0	0	1	3	.200	.273	.200	.473	30	-1	-1	96	0	1	.375	0	0	0	0	/O	0.0
1964	StL-N	3	3	0	0	0	0	0	0	0	2	.000	.000	.000	.000	-89	-1	-1	112	0	0	.000	0	0	0	0	H	0.0
Total	4	88	187	15	36	5	3	2	10	18	31	.193	.263	.283	.547	48	-13	-14	102	66	15	.470	0	0	0	-4	/32O	-1.5
■ RAY MORGAN	Morgan, Raymond Caryll b: 6/14/1889, Baltimore, Md. d: 2/15/40, Baltimore, Md. BR/TR, 5'8.5", 155 lbs. Deb: 8/07/11																											
1911	Was-A	25	89	11	19	2	0	0	5	4		.213	.247	.236	.483	36	-8	-7	97	82	6	.386	2			2	3	-0.4
1912	Was-A	80	273	40	65	10	7	1	30	29		.238	.318	.337	.655	88	-5	-4	99	107	33	.649	11			-9	2/S3	-1.3
1913	Was-A	138	481	58	131	19	8	0	57	68	63	.272	.369	.345	.714	103	8	4	106	129	66	.740	19			-5	*2/S	-0.3
1914	Was-A	147	491	50	126	22	8	1	49	62	34	.257	.352	.340	.692	107	6	6	101	110	63	.688	24	17	-3	-12	*2	-1.0
1915	Was-A	62	193	21	45	5	4	0	21	30	15	.233	.342	.301	.643	91	-1	-1	101	126	22	.627	6	5	-1	-4	2/S3	-0.6
1916	Was-A	99	315	41	84	12	4	1	29	59	29	.267	.398	.340	.738	122	12	12	100	100	50	.823	14			-5	2/S13	1.1
1917	Was-A	101	338	32	90	9	1	1	33	40	29	.266	.346	.308	.653	108	1	4	92	113	38	.613	7			-8	2/3	0.2

YEAR	TM/L	G	AB	R	H	2B	3B	HR	RBI	BB	SO	AVG	OBP	SLG	PRO	/A	BR	/A	PF	CHI	RC	TA	SB	CS	SBR	FR	POS	TPR
1918	Was-A	88	300	25	70	11	1	0	30	28	14	.233	.311	.277	.588	74	-8	-9	104	134	27	.526	4			-5	2/O	-1.1
Total	8	740	2480	278	630	90	33	4	254	320	184	.254	.348	.322	.670	99	7	5	101	116	304	.664	87	22		-46	2/3S10	-3.4
■ **BOBBY MORGAN**	Morgan, Robert Morris b: 6/29/26, Oklahoma City, Okla. BR/TR, 5'9", 175 lbs. Deb: 4/18/50																											
1950	Bro-N	67	199	38	45	10	3	7	21	32	43	.226	.342	.412	.754	91	-1	-3	107	79	29	.727	0			5	3S	0.3
1952	Bro-N	67	191	36	45	8	0	7	16	46	35	.236	.392	.387	.779	115	6	6	102	66	33	.817	2	2	-1	-1	3/2S	0.7
1953	Bro-N	69	196	35	51	6	2	7	33	33	47	.260	.370	.418	.788	101	2	1	104	125	31	.766	2	2	-1	-0	3S	0.0
1954	Phi-N	135	455	58	119	25	2	14	50	70	68	.262	.360	.418	.778	103	2	3	99	87	70	.747	3	1	0	-22	*S/32	-0.9
1955	Phi-N	136	483	61	112	20	2	10	49	73	72	.232	.333	.344	.676	78	-13	-14	102	107	57	.631	6	4	-1	-28	2S/31	-3.4
1956	Phi-N	8	25	1	5	0	0	0	1	6	4	.200	.355	.200	.555	58	-1	-1	94	86	2	.524	0	0	0	-1	/32	-0.1
	StL-N	61	113	14	22	7	0	3	20	15	24	.195	.289	.336	.625	68	-5	-5	99	180	10	.546	0	2	-1	2	23/S	-0.2
	Yr	69	138	15	27	7	0	3	21	21	28	.196	.302	.312	.613	66	-7	-6	98	170	13	.547	0	2	-1	1		-0.3
1957	Phi-N	2	0	0	0	0	0	0	0	0	0	—	—	—	—	—	0	0	98	—	—	—	0	0	0	0	/2	0.0
	Chi-N	125	425	43	88	20	2	5	27	52	87	.207	.295	.299	.594	62	-23	-21	96	80	41	.538	5	0	2	5	*23	-0.5
	Yr	127	425	43	88	20	2	5	27	52	87	.207	.295	.299	.594	62	-23	-21	96	79	41	.538	5	0	2	5		-0.5
1958	Chi-N	1	1	0	0	0	0	0	0	0	1	.000	.000	.000	.000	-99	-0	-0	101	0	0	.000	0	0	0	0	H	0.0
Total	8	671	2088	286	487	96	11	53	217	327	381	.233	.339	.366	.705	87	-33	-34	100	96	285	.693	18	11		-41	2S3/1	-4.1
■ **VERN MORGAN**	Morgan, Vernon Thomas b: 8/8/28, Emporia, Va. d: 11/8/75, Minneapolis, Minn. BL/TR, 6'1", 190 lbs. Deb: 8/10/54 C																											
1954	Chi-N	24	64	3	15	2	0	0	2	1	10	.234	.246	.266	.512	33	-6	-6	101	46	4	.353	0	0	0	-0	3	-0.6
1955	Chi-N	7	7	1	1	0	0	0	1	3	4	.143	.400	.143	.543	52	-0	-0	100	405	1	.667	0	0	0	0	/3	0.0
Total	2	31	71	4	16	2	0	0	3	4	14	.225	.267	.254	.520	37	-7	-7	100	94	5	.400	0	0	0	-0	/3	-0.6
■ **MOE MORHARDT**	Morhardt, Meredith Goodwin b: 1/16/37, Manchester, Conn. BL/TL, 6'1", 185 lbs. Deb: 9/07/61																											
1961	Chi-N	7	18	3	5	0	0	0	1	3	5	.278	.381	.278	.659	78	-0	-0	100	81	2	.615	0	0	0	-0	/1	0.0
1962	Chi-N	18	16	1	2	0	0	0	2	2	8	.125	.222	.125	.347	-4	-2	-2	106	394	1	.286	0	0	0	0	H	-0.1
Total	2	25	34	4	7	0	0	0	3	5	13	.206	.308	.206	.514	39	-3	-3	103	225	3	.444	0	0	0	-0	/1	-0.1
■ **ED MORIARTY**	Moriarty, Edward Jerome b: 10/12/12, Holyoke, Mass. BR/TR, 5'10.5", 180 lbs. Deb: 6/21/35																											
1935	Bos-N	8	34	4	11	2	1	1	1	0	6	.324	.324	.529	.853	131	1	1	96	18	6	.783	0			-1	/2	0.1
1936	Bos-N	6	6	1	1	0	0	0	0	0	1	.167	.167	.167	.333	-11	-1	-1	95	0	0	.200	0			0	H	0.0
Total	2	14	40	5	12	2	1	1	1	0	7	.300	.300	.475	.775	110	0	0	95	15	6	.679	0			-1	/2	0.1
■ **GENE MORIARITY**	Moriarity, Eugene John b: Holyoke, Mass. BL/TL, 5'8", 190 lbs. Deb: 6/18/1884																											
1884	Bos-N	4	16	1	1	0	0	0	0	0	8	.063	.063	.063	.125	-62	-3	-3	98	0	0	.067				0	/O	-0.2
	Ind-a	10	37	4	8	0	2	0		0		.216	.216	.324	.541	79	-1	-1	96	0	3	.414				0	/OP3	0.0
1885	Det-N	11	39	1	1	1	0	0	0	0	10	.026	.026	.051	.077	-78	-7	-7	97	0	0	.053				0	/O3SP	-0.6
1892	StL-N	47	177	20	31	4	1	3	19	4	37	.175	.207	.260	.466	44	-13	-12	95	108	11	.411	7			1	O	-1.1
Total	3	72	269	26	41	5	3	3	19	4	55	.152	.174	.227	.401	25	-24	-22	96	72	14	.329	7			1	/O3PS	-1.9
■ **GEORGE MORIARTY**	Moriarty, George Joseph b: 7/7/1884, Chicago, Ill. d: 4/8/64, Miami, Fla. TR , 6', 185 lbs. Deb: 03 MU																											
1903	Chi-N	1	5	1	0	0	0	0	0	0		.000	.000	.000	.000	-99	-1	-1	95	0	0	.000	0			-0	/3	-0.1
1904	Chi-N	4	13	0	0	0	0	0	0	1		.000	.071	.000	.071	-77	-3	-3	101	0	0	.077	0			-0	/3O	-0.2
1906	NY-A	65	197	22	46	7	7	0	23	17		.234	.294	.340	.634	83	-0	-4	120	125	23	.609	8			-3	3O2/1	-0.5
1907	NY-A	126	437	51	121	16	5	0	43	25		.277	.316	.336	.652	101	4	0	109	107	57	.633	28			-5	31/O2S	0.0
1908	NY-A	101	348	25	82	12	1	0	27	11		.236	.259	.276	.535	79	-10	-8	95	108	29	.485	22			3	13O/2	-0.4
1909	Det-A	133	473	43	129	20	4	1	39	24		.273	.309	.338	.648	95	1	-4	110	94	58	.637	34			0	*31	0.1
1910	Det-A	136	490	53	123	24	3	2	60	33		.251	.308	.324	.632	96	-2	-3	102	137	58	.632	33			4	*3	0.7
1911	Det-A	130	478	51	116	20	4	1	60	27		.243	.287	.308	.595	61	-23	-28	108	138	51	.566	28			-5	*3/1	-3.1
1912	Det-A	105	375	38	93	23	1	0	54	26		.248	.316	.315	.630	85	-10	-7	95	156	46	.645	27			-4	13	-1.0
1913	Det-A	105	347	29	83	5	2	0	30	24	25	.239	.302	.265	.567	67	-14	-14	99	118	36	.591	33			3	3	-0.8
1914	Det-A	130	465	56	118	19	5	1	40	39	27	.254	.318	.323	.641	91	-5	-6	102	104	55	.630	34	15	1	15	*3/1	1.5
1915	Det-A	31	38	2	8	1	0	0	0	5	7	.211	.318	.237	.555	61	-1	-2	108	0	3	.516	1	1	-0	0	3/12O	0.0
1916	Chi-A	7	5	1	1	0	0	0	0	2	0	.200	.429	.200	.629	83	0	0	108	0	0	.750	0			0	/13	0.0
Total	13	1074	3671	372	920	147	32	5	376	234	59	.251	.302	.312	.614	84	-62	-79	104	118	417	.601	248	16		8	31/O2S	-3.8
■ **BILL MORIARTY**	Moriarty, William Joseph b: 1883, Chicago, Ill. d: 12/25/16, Elgin, Ill. BR/TR, 6'2", 180 lbs. Deb: 09																											
1909	Cin-N	6	20	1	4	1	0	0	1	0		.200	.200	.250	.450	43	-1	-1	94	73	1	.438	2			-0	/S	-0.1
■ **BILL MORLEY**	Morley, William M. (born William Morley Jennings) b: 1/23/1890, Holland, Mich. d: 5/14/85, Lubbock, Tex. BR/TR, 5'11", 170 lbs. Deb: 9/08/13																											
1913	Was-A	2	3	0	0	0	0	0	0	0	0	.000	.000	.000	.000	-95	-1	-1	106	0	0	.000	0			0	/2	0.0
■ **RUSS MORMAN**	Morman, Russell Lee b: 4/28/62, Independence, Mo. BR/TR, 6'4", 215 lbs. Deb: 8/03/86																											
1986	Chi-A	49	159	18	40	5	0	4	17	16	36	.252	.328	.358	.686	87	-2	-3	101	98	19	.613	1	0	0	-2	1	-0.6
1988	Chi-A	40	75	8	18	2	0	0	3	3	17	.240	.269	.267	.536	52	-5	-5	97	60	4	.371	0	0	0	-3	1O/D	-0.8
Total	2	89	234	26	58	7	0	4	20	19	53	.248	.310	.329	.639	76	-7	-7	100	86	23	.547	1	0	0	-5	/1OD	-1.4
■ **JEFF MORONKO**	Moronko, Jeffrey Robert b: 8/17/59, Houston, Tex. BR/TR, 6'2", 190 lbs. Deb: 9/01/84																											
1984	Cle-A	7	19	1	3	1	0	0	3	3	5	.158	.273	.211	.483	34	-2	-2	106	299	1	.438	0	0	0	-2	/3D	-0.3
1987	NY-A	7	11	0	1	0	0	0	0	0	2	.091	.167	.091	.258	-29	-2	-2	98	0	0	.200	0	0	0	-1	/3SO	-0.2
Total	2	14	30	1	4	1	0	0	3	3	7	.133	.235	.167	.402	12	-4	-4	103	193	2	.346	0	0	0	-3	/3OSD	-0.5
■ **JOHN MORRILL**	Morrill, John Francis "Honest John" b: 2/19/1855, Boston, Mass. d: 4/2/32, Boston, Mass. BR/TR, 5'10.5", 155 lbs. Deb: 4/24/1876 M																											
1876	Bos-N	66	278	38	73	5	2	0	26	3	5	.263	.270	.295	.565	93	-3	-1	95	109	23	.415				8	2C/O1	0.7
1877	Bos-N	61	242	47	73	5	1	0	28	6	15	.302	.319	.331	.649	97	1	-2	108	121	26	.509				-7	31O/2	-0.5
1878	Bos-N	60	233	26	56	5	1	0	23	5	16	.240	.256	.270	.527	68	-7	-9	108	126	17	.384				3	*1/O3	-0.3
1879	Bos-N	84	348	56	98	18	5	0	49	14	32	.282	.309	.362	.671	112	8	4	107	145	40	.560				3	31	0.5
1880	Bos-N	86	342	51	81	16	8	2	44	11	37	.237	.261	.348	.609	114	1	5	92	136	32	.498				-1	13/P	0.2
1881	Bos-N	81	311	47	90	19	3	1	39	12	30	.289	.316	.379	.695	128	6	10	91	119	38	.588				6	*1/2P3	0.5
1882	Bos-N	83	349	73	101	19	11	2	54	18	29	.289	.324	.424	.748	134	14	13	103	113	49	.669				-1	*1/S2O3PM	0.0
1883	Bos-N	97	404	83	129	33	16	6	68	15	68	.319	.344	.525	.868	150	28	24	106	109	75	.825				0	*1/O3S2PM	1.1
1884	Bos-N	111	438	80	114	19	7	3	61	30	87	.260	.308	.356	.664	110	4	6	98	135	49	.574				4	*12/P3OM	0.0
1885	Bos-N	111	394	74	89	20	7	4	44	64	78	.226	.334	.343	.677	127	11	15	94	110	46	.652				0	*12/3M	0.0
1886	Bos-N	117	430	86	106	25	6	7	69	56	81	.247	.333	.381	.715	120	10	12	97	129	59	.707	9			1	S12/PM	0.3
1887	Bos-N	127	504	79	141	32	6	12	81	37	86	.280	.330	.438	.769	116	8	10	98	103	81	.766	19			4	*1M	-0.5
1888	Bos-N	135	486	60	96	18	7	4	39	55	68	.198	.282	.288	.570	79	-7	-11	106	94	46	.559	21			8	*1/2M	-1.4
1889	Was-N	44	146	20	27	5	0	2	16	30	23	.185	.328	.260	.588	73	-5	-3	92	111	17	.681	12			1	1/32PM	-0.4
1890	Bos-P	2	7	1	1	0	0	0	2	2	1	.143	.333	.143	.476	29	-1	-1	107	579	0	.500	0			0	/S1	0.0
Total	15	1265	4912	821	1275	239	80	43	643	358	656	.260	.310	.367	.677	112	69	72	100	118	599	.612	61			28	132/SOCP	0.2
■ **DOYT MORRIS**	Morris, Doyt Theodore b: 7/15/16, Stanley, N.C. d: 7/4/84, Gastonia, N.C. BR/TR, 6'4", 195 lbs. Deb: 6/06/37																											
1937	Phi-A	6	13	0	2	0	0	0	0	0	3	.154	.154	.154	.308	-24	-2	-2	94	0	0	.182	0	0	0	0	/O	-0.1
■ **JOHN MORRIS**	Morris, John Daniel b: 2/23/61, Freeport, N.Y. BL/TL, 6'1", 185 lbs. Deb: 8/05/86																											
1986	StL-N	39	100	8	24	0	1	1	14	7	15	.240	.290	.290	.580	59	-5	-6	103	174	8	.525	6	2	1	0	O	-0.5
1987	StL-N	101	157	22	41	6	4	3	23	11	22	.261	.314	.408	.721	91	-3	-2	99	126	20	.675	5	2	0	-14	O	-1.8
1988	StL-N	20	38	3	11	2	1	0	3	1	7	.289	.308	.395	.702	96	-0	-0	104	80	5	.593	0	0	0	-5	O	-0.5
Total	3	160	295	33	76	8	6	4	40	19	44	.258	.305	.366	.671	80	-8	-8	101	137	33	.623	11	4	1	-18	O	-2.8
■ **WALTER MORRIS**	Morris, John Walter b: 1/31/1880, Rockwall, Tex. d: 8/2/61, Dallas, Tex. BR/TR, 5'11", Deb: 8/31/08																											
1908	StL-N	23	73	1	13	1	1	0	2	0		.178	.178	.219	.397	30	-6	-5	94	48	3	.283	1			-4	S	-1.1

YEAR	TM/L	G	AB	R	H	2B	3B	HR	RBI	BB	SO	AVG	OBP	SLG	PRO	/A	BR	/A	PF	CHI	RC	TA	SB	CS	SBR	FR	POS	TPR
■ **P. MORRIS**	Morris, P. b: Rockford, Ill. Deb: 5/14/1884																											
1884	Was-U	1	3	0	0	0	0	0		0		.000	.000	.000	.000	-99	-1	-1	97	0	0	.000	0			0	/S	0.0
■ **HAL MORRIS**	Morris, William Harold b: 4/9/65, Fort Rucker, Ala. BL/TL, 6'4", 200 lbs. Deb: 7/29/88																											
1988	NY-A	15	20	1	2	0	0	0	0	0	9	.100	.100	.100	.200	-46	-4	-4	96	0	0	.111	0	0	0	-0	/OD	-0.3
■ **JIM MORRISON**	Morrison, James Forrest b: 9/23/52, Pensacola, Fla. BR/TR, 5'11", 175 lbs. Deb: 9/18/77																											
1977	Phi-N	5	7	3	3	0	0	0	1	1	1	.429	.500	.429	.929	151	1	1	100	133	2	1.000	0	0	0	0	/3	0.1
1978	Phi-N	53	108	12	17	1	1	3	10	10	21	.157	.235	.269	.504	38	-9	-10	105	104	7	.436	1	1	-0	4	2/3O	-0.3
1979	Chi-A	67	240	38	66	14	0	14	35	15	48	.275	.328	.508	.837	119	6	5	102	84	41	.849	11	3	2	-5	23	0.4
1980	Chi-A	162	604	66	171	40	0	15	57	36	74	.283	.332	.424	.756	109	4	6	97	78	80	.675	9	6	-1	-1	*2/SD	1.3
1981	Chi-A	90	290	27	68	8	1	10	34	10	29	.234	.265	.372	.637	82	-8	-8	100	96	26	.528	3	2	-0	8	3/2D	0.0
1982	Chi-A	51	166	17	37	7	3	7	19	13	15	.223	.279	.428	.707	93	-3	-2	97	83	18	.622	0	1	-1	-1	3/D	-0.3
	Pit-N	44	86	10	24	4	1	4	15	5	14	.279	.319	.488	.807	111	2	1	110	109	12	.742	2	0	1	-1	3/O2S	0.0
1983	Pit-N	66	158	16	48	7	2	6	25	9	25	.304	.349	.487	.836	126	6	5	103	104	24	.756	2	6	-3	0	23/S	0.3
1984	Pit-N	100	304	38	87	14	2	11	45	20	52	.286	.332	.454	.786	126	7	9	94	103	43	.700	0	1	-1	-2	32/S1	0.6
1985	Pit-N	92	244	17	62	10	0	4	22	8	44	.254	.281	.344	.625	72	-9	-10	103	91	23	.516	3	0	1	-10	32/O	-1.9
1986	Pit-N	154	537	58	147	35	4	23	88	47	88	.274	.337	.482	.819	123	15	15	100	109	86	.790	9	8	-2	-14	*3/2S	-0.3
1987	Pit-N	96	348	41	92	22	1	9	46	27	57	.264	.319	.411	.730	88	-5	-7	104	110	44	.663	8	5	-1	-6	3S/2	-1.1
	Det-A	34	117	15	24	1	1	4	19	2	26	.205	.225	.333	.558	47	-9	-9	97	149	9	.463	2	1	0	-0	3/2SO1D	-0.8
1988	Det-A	24	74	7	16	5	0	0	6	0	14	.216	.216	.284	.500	41	-6	-6	94	114	3	.339	0	2	-1	0	D/13OS	-0.6
	Atl-N	51	92	6	14	2	0	2	13	10	13	.152	.235	.239	.474	35	-8	-8	104	186	5	.395	0	1	-1	-0	3/OP	-0.9
Total	12	1089	3375	371	876	170	16	112	435	213	521	.260	.308	.419	.727	99	-16	-16	100	101	424	.671	50	37	-7	-27	32/SD01P	-3.5
■ **JON MORRISON**	Morrison, Jonathan W. b: 1859, Port Huron, Mich. Deb: 8/01/1884																											
1884	Ind-a	44	182	26	48	6	8	1		7		.264	.306	.401	.707	137	6	7	96	0	23	.627				3	O	0.9
1887	NY-a	9	34	7	4	0	0	0		6		.118	.268	.118	.386	13	-4	-3	88	0	1	.367	0			0	/O	-0.1
Total	2	53	216	33	52	6	8	1		13		.241	.299	.356	.656	116	2	4	95	0	24	.579	0			3	/O	0.8
■ **TOM MORRISON**	Morrison, Thomas J. b: 1875, St.Louis, Mo. 5'3", 145 lbs. Deb: 9/18/1895																											
1895	Lou-N	6	22	3	6	0	2	0	4	1	1	.273	.304	.455	.759	101	-0	-0	95	112	3	.688	0			0	/S3	0.0
1896	Lou-N	8	27	3	4	1	0	0	0	4	4	.148	.258	.185	.443	20	-3	-3	98	0	1	.391	0			0	/3OS	-0.2
Total	2	14	49	6	10	1	2	0	4	5	5	.204	.278	.306	.584	56	-3	-3	97	48	4	.513	0			0	/3SO	-0.2
■ **JACK MORRISSEY**	Morrissey, John Albert "King" b: 5/2/1876, Lansing, Mich. d: 10/30/36, Lansing, Mich. BB/TR, 5'10", 160 lbs. Deb: 9/18/02																											
1902	Cin-N	12	39	5	11	1	1	0	3	4		.282	.349	.359	.708	110	1	1	110	74	5	.643	0			-0	2/O	0.1
1903	Cin-N	29	89	14	22	1	0	0	9	14		.247	.350	.258	.608	70	-2	-3	109	126	9	.597	3			-1	2/OS	-0.2
Total	2	41	128	19	33	2	1	0	12	18		.258	.349	.289	.638	81	-1	-3	109	111	14	.611	3			-1	/2OS	-0.1
■ **JOHN MORRISSEY**	Morrissey, John H. b: 1856, Janesville, Wis. d: 4/29/1884, Janesville, Wis. Deb: 5/02/1881																											
1881	Buf-N	12	47	3	10	2	0	0	3	0	3	.213	.213	.255	.468	46	-3	-3	101	88	3	.324				0	3	-0.2
1882	Det-N	2	7	1	2	0	0	0	0	0	2	.286	.286	.286	.571	83	-0	-0	102	0	1	.400				0	/3	0.0
Total	2	14	54	4	12	2	0	0	3	0	5	.222	.222	.259	.481	50	-3	-3	101	77	3	.333				0	/3	-0.2
■ **JO-JO MORRISSEY**	Morrissey, Joseph Anselm b: 1/16/04, Warren, R.I. d: 5/2/50, Worcester, Mass. BR/TR, 6'1.5", 178 lbs. Deb: 4/12/32																											
1932	Cin-N	89	269	15	65	10	1	0	13	14	15	.242	.282	.286	.568	55	-17	-16	96	63	22	.461	2			-9	S23/O	-1.6
1933	Cin-N	148	534	43	123	20	0	0	26	20	22	.230	.261	.268	.529	52	-34	-33	99	70	35	.394	5			-8	2S3	-3.1
1936	Chi-A	17	38	3	7	1	0	0	6	2	3	.184	.225	.211	.436	8	-6	-6	99	243	2	.323	0	0	0	0	/3S2	-0.3
Total	3	254	841	61	195	31	1	0	45	36	40	.232	.266	.271	.537	51	-57	-54	98	75	59	.424	7	0		-16	2S/3O	-5.0
■ **TOM MORRISSEY**	Morrissey, Thomas J. b: 1861, Janesville, Wis. d: 9/23/41, Janesville, Wis. Deb: 9/27/1884																											
1884	Mil-U	12	47	3	8	2	0	0		0		.170	.170	.213	.383	29	-3	-3	100	0	2	.256	0			0	3	-0.2
■ **BUD MORSE**	Morse, Newell Obediah b: 9/4/04, Berkeley, Cal. d: 4/6/87, Sparks, Nev. BL/TR, 5'9", 150 lbs. Deb: 9/14/29																											
1929	Phi-A	8	27	1	2	0	0	0	0	0	2	.074	.074	.074	.148	-57	-6	-7	109	0	0	.080	0	0	0	-1	/2	-0.6
■ **HAP MORSE**	Morse, Peter Raymond "Pete" b: 12/6/1886, St.Paul, Minn. d: 6/19/74, St.Paul, Minn. BR/TR, 5'8", 160 lbs. Deb: 4/18/11																											
1911	StL-N	4	8	0	0	0	0	0	0	1	2	.000	.111	.000	.111	-67	-2	-2	101	0	0	.125	0			-0	/SO	-0.1
■ **CHARLIE MORTON**	Morton, Charles Hazen b: 10/12/1854, Kingsville, Ohio d: 12/9/21, Massillon, Ohio TR , Deb: 5/02/1882 M																											
1882	Pit-a	25	103	12	29	0	3	0		5		.282	.315	.340	.655	124	2	3	97	0	11	.541				0	O/3S	0.2
	StL-a	9	32	2	2	0	1	0		2		.063	.118	.125	.243	-18	-4	-4	100	0	0	.200				0	/2O	-0.3
	Yr	34	135	14	31	0	4	0		7		.230	.268	.289	.556	90	-2	-1	98	0	11	.442				0		-0.1
1884	Tol-a	32	111	11	18	6	2	0		7		.162	.212	.252	.464	51	-5	-6	104	0	6	.376				0	3O/P2M	-0.5
1885	Det-N	22	79	9	14	1	2	0	3	5	10	.177	.226	.241	.467	52	-4	-4	97	56	4	.369				0	3/SM	-0.3
Total	3	88	325	34	63	7	8	0	3	19	10	.194	.238	.265	.503	67	-11	-11	100	14	22	.401				0	/O32SP	-0.9
■ **MOOSE MORTON**	Morton, Guy Jr. b: 11/4/30, Tuscaloosa, Ala. BR/TR, 6'2", 200 lbs. Deb: 9/17/54																											
1954	Bos-A	1	1	0	0	0	0	0	0	0	1	.000	.000	.000	.000	-99	-0	-0	100	0	0	.000	0	0	0	0	H	0.0
■ **BUBBA MORTON**	Morton, Wycliffe Nathaniel b: 12/13/31, Washington, D.C. BR/TR, 5'10", 175 lbs. Deb: 4/19/61																											
1961	Det-A	77	108	26	31	5	1	2	19	9	25	.287	.347	.407	.755	105	0	1	96	149	16	.722	3	1	0	-4	O	-0.3
1962	Det-A	90	195	30	51	6	3	4	17	32	32	.262	.366	.385	.750	92	1	-2	111	78	28	.720	1	1	-0	0	O/1	-0.3
1963	Det-A	6	11	2	1	0	0	0	2	2	1	.091	.231	.091	.322	-5	-2	-2	104	837	0	.300	0	0	0	0	/O	-0.1
	Mil-N	15	28	1	5	0	0	0	4	2	3	.179	.258	.179	.437	28	-2	-3	101	336	1	.320	0	0	0	-1	/O	-0.3
1966	Cal-A	15	50	4	11	1	0	0	4	2	6	.220	.250	.240	.490	42	-4	-4	99	140	3	.366	1	1	-0	0	O	-0.4
1967	Cal-A	80	201	23	63	9	3	0	32	22	29	.313	.387	.388	.775	135	8	9	96	171	29	.685	0	3	-2	-6	O	0.0
1968	Cal-A	81	163	13	44	6	0	1	18	14	18	.270	.343	.325	.668	110	1	2	94	138	18	.579	2	1	0	-6	O/3	-0.6
1969	Cal-A	87	172	18	42	10	1	7	32	28	29	.244	.360	.436	.796	122	5	5	99	134	28	.791	0	0	0	-1	O/1	0.3
Total	7	451	928	117	248	37	8	14	128	111	143	.267	.352	.370	.722	105	8	8	100	147	124	.683	7	7	-2	-18	O/13	-1.7
■ **WALT MORYN**	Moryn, Walter Joseph "Moose" b: 4/12/26, St.Paul, Minn. BL/TR, 6'2", 205 lbs. Deb: 6/29/54																											
1954	Bro-N	48	91	16	25	4	2	2	14	7	11	.275	.333	.429	.762	96	-1	-1	101	122	13	.681	0	0	0	-1	O	-0.1
1955	Bro-N	11	19	3	5	1	0	1	3	5	4	.263	.417	.474	.890	130	1	1	104	101	4	1.000	0	0	0	-2	/O	0.0
1956	Chi-N	147	529	69	151	27	3	23	67	50	67	.285	.351	.478	.829	122	14	15	99	90	89	.797	4	2	0	8	*O	1.8
1957	Chi-N	149	568	76	164	33	0	19	88	50	90	.289	.349	.447	.797	116	10	12	96	124	88	.736	0	2	-1	3	*O	1.0
1958	Chi-N	143	512	77	135	26	7	26	77	62	83	.264	.352	.494	.846	120	15	15	101	98	91	.839	1	2	-1	-3	*O	0.7
1959	Chi-N	117	381	41	89	14	1	14	48	44	66	.234	.318	.386	.704	88	-8	-7	98	103	46	.636	0	0	0	-2	*O	-0.9
1960	Chi-N	38	109	12	32	4	0	2	11	13	19	.294	.369	.385	.754	109	1	2	98	93	16	.712	2	1	0	-1	O	0.0
	StL-N	75	200	24	49	4	3	11	35	17	38	.245	.304	.460	.764	98	1	-1	108	114	26	.694	0	0	0	-3	O	-0.5
	Yr	113	309	36	81	8	3	13	46	30	57	.262	.327	.434	.761	101	2	0	105	107	44	.706	2	1	0	-3		-0.5
1961	StL-N	17	32	0	4	2	0	0	2	1	5	.125	.152	.188	.339	-9	-5	-6	113	134	1	.241	0	0	0	-1	/O	-0.7
	Pit-N	40	65	6	13	1	0	3	9	2	10	.200	.235	.354	.589	54	-5	-4	99	113	4	.456	0	0	0	1	O	-0.3
	Yr	57	97	6	17	3	0	3	11	3	15	.175	.208	.299	.507	31	-10	-10	103	122	5	.388	0	0	0	-1		-1.0
Total	8	785	2506	324	667	116	16	101	354	251	393	.266	.338	.446	.784	108	25	26	99	106	377	.754	7	7	-2	-0	O	1.0
■ **ROSS MOSCHITTO**	Moschitto, Rosaire Allen b: 2/15/45, Fresno, Cal. BR/TR, 6'2", 175 lbs. Deb: 4/15/65																											
1965	NY-A	96	27	12	5	0	0	1	3	0	12	.185	.185	.296	.481	34	-2	-2	101	113	2	.364	0	0	0	-25	O	-3.2
1967	NY-A	14	9	1	1	0	0	0	0	1	2	.111	.200	.111	.311	-6	-1	-1	94	0	0	.250	0	0	0	-2	/O	-0.3
Total	2	110	36	13	6	0	0	1	3	1	14	.167	.189	.250	.439	25	-4	-3	99	83	2	.333	0	0	0	-27	/O	-3.5

YEAR	TM/L	G	AB	R	H	2B	3B	HR	RBI	BB	SO	AVG	OBP	SLG	PRO	/A	BR	/A	PF	CHI	RC	TA	SB	CS	SBR	FR	POS	TPR
■ LLOYD MOSEBY	Moseby, Lloyd Anthony b: 11/5/59, Portland, Ark. BL/TR, 6'3", 200 lbs. Deb: 5/24/80																											
1980	Tor-A	114	389	44	89	24	1	9	46	25	85	.229	.282	.365	.647	76	-14	-14	100	106	37	.552	4	6	-2	1	*O/D	-1.6
1981	Tor-A	100	378	36	88	16	2	9	43	24	86	.233	.280	.357	.638	75	-9	-14	111	110	37	.566	11	8	-2	-4	*O	-2.2
1982	Tor-A	147	487	51	115	20	9	9	52	33	106	.236	.295	.370	.665	75	-13	-18	109	101	52	.596	11	7	-1	-8	*O	-3.1
1983	Tor-A	151	539	104	170	31	7	18	81	51	85	.315	.380	.499	.879	129	29	23	108	100	104	.910	27	8	3	3	*O	2.8
1984	Tor-A	158	592	97	166	28	**15**	18	92	78	122	.280	.372	.470	.841	129	26	25	102	117	110	.910	39	9	6	7	*O	3.3
1985	Tor-A	152	584	92	151	30	7	18	70	76	91	.259	.348	.426	.774	110	9	9	101	88	89	.796	37	15	2	-7	*O	0.2
1986	Tor-A	152	589	89	149	24	5	21	86	64	122	.253	.332	.418	.750	99	3	-1	105	117	86	.760	32	11	3	-5	*O/D	-0.6
1987	Tor-A	155	592	106	167	27	4	26	96	70	124	.282	.360	.473	.833	118	17	16	101	113	106	.883	39	7	8	-1	*O/D	1.7
1988	Tor-A	128	472	77	113	17	7	10	42	70	93	.239	.345	.369	.714	100	2	2	100	87	66	.749	31	8	5	-8	*O/D	-0.3
Total	9	1257	4622	696	1208	217	57	138	608	491	914	.261	.338	.423	.761	104	51	28	104	105	686	.777	231	79	22	-22	*O/D	0.2
■ ARNIE MOSER	Moser, Arnold Robert b: 8/9/15, Houston, Tex. BR/TR, 5'11", 165 lbs. Deb: 6/20/37																											
1937	Cin-N	5	5	0	0	0	0	0	0	0	2	.000	.000	.000	.000	-99	-1	-1	91	0	0	.000	0			0	H	0.0
■ JERRY MOSES	Moses, Gerald Braheen b: 8/9/46, Yazoo City, Miss. BR/TR, 6'3", 210 lbs. Deb: 5/09/65																											
1965	Bos-A	4	4	1	1	0	0	1	1	0	2	.250	.250	1.000	1.250	222	1	1	107	59	1	1.333	0	0	0	0	H	0.1
1968	Bos-A	6	18	2	6	0	0	2	4	1	4	.333	.368	.667	1.035	207	2	2	101	95	3	.929	0	1	-1	-0	/C	0.2
1969	Bos-A	53	135	13	41	9	1	4	17	5	23	.304	.333	.474	.807	118	4	3	105	90	21	.729	0	1	-1	-0	C	0.4
1970	Bos-A	92	315	26	83	18	1	6	35	21	45	.263	.314	.384	.698	83	-4	-8	111	102	37	.607	1	1	-0	7	C/O	0.0
1971	Cal-A	69	181	12	41	8	2	4	15	10	34	.227	.267	.359	.626	77	-6	-6	99	79	15	.503	0	0	0	-9	C/O	-1.2
1972	Cle-A	52	141	9	31	3	0	4	14	11	29	.220	.290	.326	.617	78	-3	-4	107	101	14	.536	0	0	0	4	C/1	0.0
1973	NY-A	21	59	5	15	2	0	0	3	2	6	.254	.279	.288	.567	59	-3	-3	101	69	4	.413	0	0	0	3	C/D	0.0
1974	Det-A	74	198	19	47	6	3	4	19	11	38	.237	.284	.359	.643	79	-5	-6	106	90	19	.535	0	1	-1	-8	C	-1.2
1975	SD-N	13	19	1	3	2	0	0	1	2	3	.158	.238	.263	.501	39	-2	-2	100	77	1	.412	0	0	0	0	/C	0.0
	Chi-A	2	2	1	1	0	1	0	0	0	0	.500	.500	1.500	2.000	433	1	1	103	0	2	3.000	0	0	0	0	/1D	0.1
Total	9	386	1072	89	269	48	8	25	109	63	184	.251	.297	.381	.678	86	-16	-23	106	92	116	.595	1	4	-2	-3	C/1DO	-1.6
■ JOHN MOSES	Moses, John William b: 8/9/57, Los Angeles, Cal. BB/TL, 5'10", 165 lbs. Deb: 8/23/82																											
1982	Sea-A	22	44	7	14	5	1	1	3	4	5	.318	.375	.545	.920	136	3	2	109	44	10	1.065	5	1	1	-4	O	0.0
1983	Sea-A	93	130	19	27	4	1	0	6	12	20	.208	.280	.254	.534	48	-9	-9	100	71	9	.509	11	5	0	-7	OD	-1.6
1984	Sea-A	19	35	3	12	1	1	0	2	2	5	.343	.395	.429	.823	125	1	1	102	53	6	.826	1	0	0	-2	O/D	0.0
1985	Sea-A	33	62	4	12	0	0	0	3	2	8	.194	.219	.194	.412	15	-7	-7	95	99	2	.345	5	2	0	-5	O	-1.1
1986	Sea-A	103	399	56	102	16	3	3	34	34	65	.256	.314	.333	.647	74	-12	-15	105	101	40	.596	25	18	-3	8	O/1D	-1.2
1987	Sea-A	116	390	58	96	16	4	3	38	29	49	.246	.303	.331	.634	67	-17	-18	103	110	38	.584	23	15	-2	-6	*O/1D	-2.8
1988	Min-A	105	206	33	65	10	3	2	12	15	21	.316	.368	.422	.790	114	6	4	106	51	31	.762	11	6	-0	-11	O/D	-0.8
Total	7	491	1266	180	328	52	13	9	98	98	173	.259	.316	.342	.658	77	-35	-41	103	89	137	.626	81	47	-4	-27	O/1D	-7.5
■ WALLY MOSES	Moses, Wallace b: 10/8/10, Uvalda, Ga. BL/TL, 5'10", 160 lbs. Deb: 4/17/35 C																											
1935	Phi-A	85	345	60	112	21	3	5	35	25	18	.325	.375	.446	.822	112	6	6	100	74	57	.781	3	4	-2	-2	O	0.1
1936	Phi-A	146	585	98	202	35	11	7	66	62	32	.345	.410	.479	.888	118	18	18	101	68	117	.915	12	6	0	-2	*O	1.0
1937	Phi-A	154	649	113	208	48	13	25	86	54	38	.320	.374	.550	.925	139	27	32	94	59	132	.942	9	7	-2	2	*O	2.5
1938	Phi-A	142	589	86	181	29	8	8	49	58	31	.307	.369	.424	.794	97	-2	-2	101	53	95	.782	15	5	2	5	*O	0.3
1939	Phi-A	115	437	68	134	28	7	3	33	44	23	.307	.370	.423	.793	105	2	4	97	61	71	.759	7	4	-0	-2	*O	-0.1
1940	Phi-A	142	537	91	166	41	9	9	50	75	44	.309	.396	.469	.865	129	20	24	96	69	108	.884	6	4	-1	2	*O	1.4
1941	Phi-A	116	438	78	132	31	4	4	35	62	27	.301	.388	.418	.806	112	10	9	101	67	76	.787	3	3	-1	7	*O	0.8
1942	Chi-A	146	577	73	156	28	4	7	49	74	27	.270	.353	.369	.722	104	3	4	99	65	81	.695	16	10	-1	7	*O	0.0
1943	Chi-A	150	599	82	147	22	**12**	3	48	55	47	.245	.310	.337	.647	88	-9	-9	101	80	69	.661	56	14	8	7	*O	0.1
1944	Chi-A	136	535	82	150	26	9	3	34	52	22	.280	.345	.379	.725	107	5	5	100	56	77	.705	21	7	2	-6	*O	-0.2
1945	Chi-A	140	569	79	168	**35**	15	2	50	69	33	.295	.373	.420	.793	136	22	25	95	64	97	.783	11	5	0	5	*O	2.6
1946	Chi-A	56	168	20	46	9	1	4	16	17	20	.274	.344	.411	.755	114	2	3	97	75	24	.701	2	2	-1	0	O	0.0
	Bos-A	48	175	23	36	11	3	2	17	14	15	.206	.268	.337	.606	60	-8	-11	114	101	16	.528	2	4	-2	-1	O	-1.6
	Yr	104	343	43	82	20	4	6	33	31	35	.239	.306	.373	.679	85	-6	-8	105	88	41	.616	4	6	-2	-0		-1.6
1947	Bos-A	90	255	32	70	18	2	2	27	27	16	.275	.344	.384	.728	95	1	-2	108	96	35	.670	3	0	1	-6	O	-0.9
1948	Bos-A	78	189	26	49	12	1	2	29	21	19	.259	.340	.365	.705	87	-4	-4	100	131	27	.688	5	0	2	-1	O	-0.4
1949	Phi-A	110	308	49	85	19	3	1	25	51	19	.276	.381	.367	.747	99	1	1	99	74	48	.725	1	3	-2	-6	O	-0.8
1950	Phi-A	88	265	47	70	16	5	2	21	40	17	.264	.365	.385	.750	103	-3	1	90	67	40	.713	0	1	-1	3	O	0.3
1951	Phi-A	70	136	17	26	6	0	0	9	21	9	.191	.304	.235	.539	44	-10	-11	106	100	10	.479	2	2	-1	0	O	-1.1
Total	17	2012	7356	1124	2138	435	110	89	679	821	457	.291	.364	.416	.779	109	81	93	99	70	1179	.768	174	81	4	10	*O	4.0
■ DOC MOSKIMAN	Moskiman, William Bankhead b: 12/20/1879, Oakland, Cal. d: 1/11/53, San Leandro, Cal. BR/TR, 6', 170 lbs. Deb: 8/23/10																											
1910	Bos-A	5	9	0	1	0	0	0	1	2		.111	.273	.111	.384	21	-1	-1	99	370	0	.375	0			0	/1O	0.0
■ JIM MOSOLF	Mosolf, James Frederick b: 8/21/05, Puyallup, Wash. d: 12/28/79, Dallasyore. BL/TR, 5'10", 186 lbs. Deb: 9/09/29																											
1929	Pit-N	8	13	3	6	1	1	0	2	1	1	.462	.500	.692	1.192	186	2	2	103	76	4	1.429	0			-0	/O	0.1
1930	Pit-N	40	51	16	17	2	1	0	9	8	7	.333	.424	.412	.835	106	1	1	97	148	9	.853	0			-4	O/P	-0.2
1931	Pit-N	39	44	7	11	1	0	1	8	8	5	.250	.365	.341	.706	90	-0	-0	101	158	6	.697	0			-1	/O	-0.1
1933	Chi-N	31	82	13	22	5	1	1	9	5	8	.268	.326	.390	.716	107	0	1	97	97	11	.639	0			0	O	0.0
Total	4	118	190	39	56	9	3	2	28	22	21	.295	.374	.405	.779	109	3	3	98	124	31	.748	0			-5	/OP	-0.2
■ CHARLIE MOSS	Moss, Charles Crosby b: 3/20/11, Meridian, Miss. BR/TR, 5'10", 160 lbs. Deb: 5/19/34																											
1934	Phi-A	10	10	3	2	0	0	0	1	0	0	.200	.200	.200	.400	4	-1	-1	97	167	0	.250	0	0	0	0	/C	0.0
1935	Phi-A	4	3	1	1	0	0	0	1	1	0	.333	.500	.333	.833	119	0	0	100	340	1	1.000	0	0	0	0	/C	0.0
1936	Phi-A	33	44	2	11	1	1	0	10	6	5	.250	.340	.318	.658	63	-2	-2	101	231	5	.636	1	0	0	-0	C	0.0
Total	3	47	57	6	14	1	1	0	12	7	5	.246	.328	.298	.626	57	-4	-4	100	228	6	.581	1	0	0	-0	/C	0.0
■ HOWIE MOSS	Moss, Howard Glenn b: 10/17/19, Gastonia, N.C. BR/TR, 5'11.5", 185 lbs. Deb: 4/14/42																											
1942	NY-N	7	14	0	0	0	0	0	0	0	4	.000	.000	.000	.000	-97	-3	-4	103	0	0	.000	0			0	/O	-0.3
1946	Cin-N	7	26	1	5	0	0	0	1	0	4	.192	.222	.192	.415	17	-3	-3	104	76	1	.286	0			0	/O	-0.2
	Cle-A	8	32	2	2	0	0	0	0	3	9	.063	.143	.063	.205	-47	-6	-6	89	0	0	.152	0	1	-1	-1	/3	-0.6
Total	2	22	72	3	7	0	0	0	1	3	17	.097	.145	.097	.242	-32	-12	-12	97	27	1	.162	0	1		-1	/O3	-1.1
■ LES MOSS	Moss, John Lester b: 5/14/25, Tulsa, Okla. BR/TR, 5'11", 205 lbs. Deb: 9/10/46 MC																											
1946	StL-A	12	35	4	13	3	0	0	5	3	5	.371	.436	.457	.893	153	2	3	98	119	8	.955	1	0	0	-1	C	0.3
1947	StL-A	96	274	17	43	5	2	6	27	35	48	.157	.255	.255	.510	41	-22	-23	102	113	20	.451	0	0	0	-1	C	-1.5
1948	StL-A	107	335	35	86	12	1	14	46	39	50	.257	.334	.424	.758	95	-1	-4	106	84	46	.683	0	0	0	0	*C	0.3
1949	StL-A	97	278	28	81	11	0	10	39	49	32	.291	.399	.439	.838	122	10	10	100	88	51	.827	0	1	-1	5	C	1.7
1950	StL-A	84	222	24	59	6	0	8	34	26	32	.266	.343	.401	.744	84	-4	-6	107	104	30	.673	0	1	-1	3	C	-0.1
1951	StL-A	16	47	5	8	2	0	1	7	6	8	.170	.264	.277	.541	44	-4	-4	105	156	3	.452	0	0	0	1	C	-0.1
	Bos-A	71	202	18	40	6	0	3	26	25	34	.198	.289	.272	.562	49	-13	-16	108	145	16	.474	0	0	0	-6	C	-1.6
	Yr	87	249	23	48	8	0	4	33	31	42	.193	.285	.273	.558	48	-17	-19	107	149	20	.476	0	0	0	-5		-1.7
1952	StL-A	52	118	11	29	3	0	3	12	15	13	.246	.331	.347	.678	91	-2	-1	97	90	13	.583	0	1	-1	2	C	0.2
1953	StL-A	78	239	21	66	14	1	2	28	18	31	.276	.329	.368	.698	83	-4	-6	107	110	27	.582	0	1	-1	-2	C	-0.5
1954	Bal-A	50	126	7	31	3	0	0	5	14	16	.246	.321	.270	.591	66	-6	-5	95	56	11	.490	0	0	0	1	C	-0.2
1955	Bal-A	29	56	5	19	1	0	2	6	7	4	.339	.413	.464	.877	151	3	4	90	70	10	.846	0	1	-1	-0	C	0.4
	Chi-A	32	59	5	15	2	0	2	7	6	10	.254	.333	.390	.723	93	-1	-1	101	90	8	.682	0	0	0	-1	C	0.0
	Yr	61	115	10	34	3	0	4	13	13	14	.296	.372	.426	.798	119	2	3	96	82	19	.768	0	1	-1	-1		0.4
1956	Chi-A	56	127	20	31	4	0	10	22	18	15	.244	.338	.512	.850	117	3	2	104	86	20	.806	0	0	0	-2	C	0.1
1957	Chi-A	42	115	10	31	3	0	2	12	20	18	.270	.378	.348	.726	100	1	1	99	103	16	.682	0	0	0	-1	C	0.2

YEAR	TM/L	G	AB	R	H	2B	3B	HR	RBI	BB	SO	AVG	OBP	SLG	PRO	/A	BR	/A	PF	CHI	RC	TA	SB	CS	SBR	FR	POS	TPR
1958	Chi-A	2	1	0	0	0	0	0	0	1	0	.000	.500	.000	.500	51	0	0	98	0	0	1.000	0	0	0	0	H	0.0
Total	13	824	2234	210	552	75	4	63	276	282	316	.247	.333	.369	.702	86	-37	-46	103	100	280	.660	1	5	-3	-3	C	-0.8
■ **JOHNNY MOSTIL**	Mostil, John Anthony "Bananas" b: 6/1/1896, Chicago, Ill. d: 12/10/70, Midlothian, Ill. BR/TR, 5'8.5", 168 lbs. Deb: 6/20/18																											
1918	Chi-A	10	33	4	9	2	2	0	4	1	6	.273	.294	.455	.749	125	1	1	101	97	4	.708	1			-0	/2	0.1
1921	Chi-A	100	326	43	98	21	7	3	42	28	35	.301	.379	.436	.814	108	4	4	99	95	53	.804	10	12	-4	-4	O/2	-1.0
1922	Chi-A	132	458	74	139	28	14	7	70	38	39	.303	.375	.472	.846	118	12	12	101	108	81	.857	14	10	-2	0	*O	0.1
1923	Chi-A	153	546	91	159	37	15	3	64	62	51	.291	.376	.430	.806	114	10	11	98	91	92	.866	41	17	**2**	17	*O/3S	1.7
1924	Chi-A	118	385	75	125	22	5	4	49	45	41	.325	.401	.439	.840	120	10	12	97	89	67	.830	7	11	-5	4	*O	0.4
1925	Chi-A	153	605	**135**	181	36	16	2	50	**90**	52	.299	.400	.421	.822	114	11	15	96	57	108	.899	**43**	21	0	-0	*O	0.1
1926	Chi-A	148	600	120	197	41	15	4	42	79	55	.328	.415	.467	.882	142	28	36	92	42	122	.969	**35**	14	**2**	12	*O	3.7
1927	Chi-A	13	16	3	2	0	0	0	1	0	1	.125	.176	.125	.301	-20	-3	-3	102	166	0	.286	1	0	0	-1	/O	-0.4
1928	Chi-A	133	503	69	136	19	8	0	51	66	54	.270	.360	.340	.699	85	-9	-8	99	98	63	.680	23	21	-6	10	*O	-1.0
1929	Chi-A	12	35	4	8	3	0	0	3	6	2	.229	.341	.314	.656	74	-1	-1	95	93	4	.667	1	0	0	0	O	0.0
Total	10	972	3507	618	1054	209	82	23	376	415	336	.301	.386	.427	.812	114	63	79	97	80	596	.843	176	106		37	O/23S	3.7
■ **MANNY MOTA**	Mota, Manuel Rafael (Geronimo) b: 2/18/38, Santo Domingo, D.R. BR/TR, 5'10", 160 lbs. Deb: 4/16/62 C																											
1962	SF-N	47	74	9	13	1	0	0	9	7	8	.176	.256	.189	.445	21	-8	-8	101	253	4	.379	3	2	-0	-4	O/32	-1.2
1963	Pit-N	59	126	20	34	2	3	0	7	7	18	.270	.313	.333	.647	88	-2	-2	99	70	12	.515	0	2	-1	-6	O/2	-1.1
1964	Pit-N	115	271	43	75	8	3	5	32	10	31	.277	.310	.384	.694	93	-2	-3	101	110	32	.599	4	1	1	-9	O/C2	-1.3
1965	Pit-N	121	294	47	82	7	6	4	29	22	32	.279	.333	.384	.718	102	1	1	100	96	37	.632	2	2	-1	-8	O	-1.0
1966	Pit-N	116	322	54	107	16	7	5	46	25	28	.332	.387	.472	.860	137	17	16	101	116	57	.821	7	7	-2	-6	O/3	0.6
1967	Pit-N	120	349	53	112	14	8	4	56	14	46	.321	.351	.441	.792	125	10	11	100	140	52	.700	3	2	-0	-1	O/3	0.5
1968	Pit-N	111	331	35	93	10	2	1	33	20	19	.281	.324	.332	.656	96	-1	-1	101	123	36	.547	4	2	0	-4	O/23	-1.1
1969	Mon-N	31	89	6	28	1	1	0	0	6	11	.315	.358	.348	.706	98	-0	-0	100	0	10	.567	1	3	-2	-1	O	-0.3
	LA-N	85	294	35	95	6	4	3	30	26	25	.323	.380	.401	.781	121	8	9	99	97	45	.718	5	4	-1	-1	O	0.3
	Yr	116	383	41	123	7	5	3	30	32	36	.321	.375	.389	.764	115	8	8	99	71	56	.689	6	7	-2	-2		0.0
1970	LA-N	124	417	63	127	12	6	3	37	47	37	.305	.379	.384	.763	117	4	10	90	85	61	.715	11	6	-0	-5	*O/3	0.0
1971	LA-N	91	269	24	84	13	5	0	34	20	20	.312	.362	.398	.760	116	5	6	99	129	37	.670	4	3	-1	-10	O	-0.7
1972	LA-N	118	371	57	120	16	5	5	48	27	15	.323	.377	.434	.811	138	15	17	94	112	58	.743	4	4	-1	-11	O	0.1
1973	LA-N	89	293	33	92	11	2	0	23	25	12	.314	.370	.365	.735	104	2	2	100	86	37	.623	1	3	-2	-10	O	-1.2
1974	LA-N	66	57	5	16	2	0	0	16	5	4	.281	.349	.316	.665	94	-1	-0	93	343	7	.585	0	0	0	-1	/O	0.0
1975	LA-N	52	49	3	13	1	0	0	10	5	1	.265	.357	.286	.643	84	-1	-1	95	276	5	.538	0	0	0	-0	/O	0.0
1976	LA-N	50	52	1	15	3	0	0	13	7	5	.288	.373	.346	.719	105	1	1	100	278	7	.658	0	0	0	0	/O	0.1
1977	LA-N	49	38	5	15	1	0	1	4	10	0	.395	.521	.500	1.021	175	5	5	100	73	10	1.200	1	1	-0	-0	/O	0.4
1978	LA-N	37	33	2	10	1	0	0	6	3	4	.303	.361	.333	.694	96	-0	-0	99	216	4	.609	0	0	0	0	H	0.0
1979	LA-N	47	42	1	15	0	0	0	3	3	4	.357	.400	.357	.757	109	1	1	100	79	6	.621	0	0	0	-0	/O	0.0
1980	LA-N	7	7	0	3	0	0	0	2	0	0	.429	.429	.429	.857	145	0	0	97	264	1	.600	0	0	0	0	/H	0.0
1982	LA-N	1	1	0	0	0	0	0	0	0	0	.000	.000	.000	.000	-99	-0	-0	95	0	0	.000	0	0	0	0	/H	0.0
Total	20	1536	3779	496	1149	125	52	31	438	289	320	.304	.358	.389	.747	112	53	63	98	117	517	.688	50	42	-10	-74	*O/32C	-5.9
■ **DARRYL MOTLEY**	Motley, Darryl De Wayne b: 1/21/60, Muskogee, Okla. BR/TR, 5'9", 196 lbs. Deb: 8/10/81																											
1981	KC-A	42	125	15	29	4	0	2	8	7	15	.232	.278	.312	.590	71	-5	-5	99	70	10	.475	1	3	-2	1	O	-0.5
1983	KC-A	19	68	9	16	1	2	3	11	2	8	.235	.268	.441	.709	90	-1	-1	101	112	7	.625	2	1	0	1	O/D	0.0
1984	KC-A	146	522	64	148	25	6	15	70	28	73	.284	.321	.441	.762	109	5	5	99	104	63	.659	10	11	-4	1	*O	-0.1
1985	KC-A	123	383	45	85	20	1	17	49	18	57	.222	.261	.413	.673	79	-12	-12	102	93	35	.577	6	4	-1	-11	*O/D	-2.5
1986	KC-A	72	217	22	44	9	1	7	20	11	31	.203	.241	.350	.591	59	-13	-13	100	82	16	.475	0	2	-1	-10	O/D	-2.4
	Atl-N	5	10	1	2	1	0	0	0	1	1	.200	.273	.300	.573	57	-1	-1	102	0	1	.500	0	0	0	-0	/O	0.0
1987	Atl-N	6	8	0	0	0	0	0	1	0	1	.000	.000	.000	.000	-92	-2	-2	108	0	0	.000	0	0	0	-0	/O	-0.2
Total	6	413	1333	156	324	60	10	44	159	67	186	.243	.282	.402	.684	86	-29	-29	100	93	131	.609	19	21	-7	-18	O/D	-5.7
■ **BITSY MOTT**	Mott, Elisha Matthew b: 6/12/18, Arcadia, Fla. BR/TR, 5'8", 155 lbs. Deb: 4/17/45																											
1945	Phi-N	90	289	21	64	8	0	0	22	27	25	.221	.290	.249	.539	53	-19	-17	96	106	22	.440	2			6	S2/3	-0.2
■ **CURT MOTTON**	Motton, Curtell Howard b: 9/24/40, Darnell, La. BR/TR, 5'8", 164 lbs. Deb: 7/05/67																											
1967	Bal-A	27	65	5	13	2	0	2	9	5	14	.200	.278	.323	.601	82	-2	-1	95	139	6	.509	0	1	-1	0	O	-0.2
1968	Bal-A	83	217	27	43	7	0	8	25	31	43	.198	.301	.341	.642	92	-1	-2	102	109	22	.582	1	3	-2	-1	O	-0.6
1969	Bal-A	56	89	15	27	6	0	6	21	13	10	.303	.398	.573	.971	163	8	8	104	122	22	1.079	3	1	0	-3	O	0.5
1970	Bal-A	52	84	16	19	3	1	3	19	18	20	.226	.369	.393	.762	114	2	2	97	183	14	.791	1	2	-1	-1	O	0.0
1971	Bal-A	38	53	13	10	1	0	4	8	10	12	.189	.317	.434	.751	108	1	1	103	93	8	.750	0	0	0	-2	O	-0.1
1972	Mil-A	6	6	1	1	0	0	1	2	1	2	.167	.286	.667	.952	186	1	1	95	119	1	1.000	0	0	0	-1	/O	0.0
	Cal-A	42	39	6	6	1	0	0	1	5	12	.154	.250	.179	.429	33	-3	-3	88	60	2	.353	0	0	0	-1	/O	-0.3
	Yr	48	45	7	7	1	0	1	3	6	14	.156	.255	.244	.499	55	-3	-2	89	70	3	.436	0	0	0	-2		-0.3
1973	Bal-A	5	6	2	2	0	0	1	4	1	1	.333	.429	.833	1.262	231	1	1	107	196	2	1.500	0	0	0	-0	/OD	0.1
1974	Bal-A	7	8	0	0	0	0	0	0	2	2	.000	.200	.000	.200	-42	-1	-1	93	0	0	.250	0	0	0	-0	/OD	-0.1
Total	8	316	567	85	121	20	1	25	89	86	116	.213	.322	.384	.707	105	4	5	100	121	76	.693	5	7	-3	-9	O/D	-0.7
■ **FRANK MOTZ**	Motz, Frank H. b: 10/1/1868, Freeburg, Pa. d: 3/18/44, Akron, Ohio 6', 160 lbs. Deb: 8/27/1890																											
1890	Phi-N	1	2	1	0	0	0	0	3	1	1	.000	.333	.000	.333	1	-0	-0	108	0	0	1.000	1			0	/1	0.0
1893	Cin-N	43	156	16	40	7	1	2	25	19	10	.256	.352	.353	.705	88	-2	-2	101	114	21	.698	3			6	1	0.3
1894	Cin-N	18	69	8	14	4	0	0	12	9	1	.203	.304	.261	.565	39	-7	-7	100	195	6	.545	2			0	1	-0.4
Total	3	62	227	25	54	11	1	2	40	29	12	.238	.337	.322	.659	71	-9	-9	101	137	27	.653	6			6	/1	-0.1
■ **ALLIE MOULTON**	Moulton, Albert Theodore b: 1/16/1886, Medway, Mass. d: 9/10/68, Peabody, Mass. BR/TR, 5'6", 155 lbs. Deb: 9/25/11																											
1911	StL-A	4	15	4	1	0	0	0	1	4		.067	.263	.067	.330	-6	-2	-2	95	292	0	.357	0			0	/2	-0.1
■ **RAY MOWE**	Mowe, Raymond Benjamin b: 7/12/1889, Rochester, Ind. d: 8/14/68, Sarasota, Fla. BL/TR, 5'7.5", 160 lbs. Deb: 9/25/13																											
1913	Bro-N	5	9	0	1	0	0	0	0	0	1	.111	.200	.111	.311	-9	-1	-1	104	0	0	.250	0			-0	/S	-0.1
■ **MIKE MOWREY**	Mowrey, Harry Harlan b: 4/20/1884, Browns Mill, Pa. d: 3/20/47, Chambersburg, Pa. BR/TR, 5'10", 180 lbs. Deb: 9/24/05																											
1905	Cin-N	7	30	4	8	1	0	0	6	1		.267	.290	.300	.590	75	-1	-1	103	200	3	.455	0			0	/3	0.0
1906	Cin-N	21	53	3	17	3	0	0	6	5		.321	.379	.377	.757	120	2	2	115	109	9	.750	2			-1	3/2S	0.0
1907	Cin-N	138	448	43	113	16	6	1	44	35		.252	.306	.321	.628	104	-1	1	95	116	48	.564	10			-16	*3S	-1.6
1908	Cin-N	77	227	17	50	9	1	0	23	12		.220	.259	.269	.528	69	-8	-8	103	145	16	.441	5			-4	3/SO2	-1.2
1909	Cin-N	38	115	10	22	5	0	0	5	20		.191	.311	.235	.546	75	-3	-2	94	69	9	.527	2			-2	3S	-0.3
	StL-N	12	29	3	7	1	0	0	4	4		.241	.333	.276	.609	94	-0	-0	96	182	3	.591	1			-1	/23	0.0
	Yr	50	144	13	29	6	0	0	9	24		.201	.315	.243	.559	79	-3	-2	94	97	12	.539	3			-3		-0.3
1910	StL-N	143	489	69	138	24	6	2	70	67	38	.282	.375	.368	.744	128	12	18	92	134	76	.781	21			14	*3	3.3
1911	StL-N	137	471	59	126	29	7	0	61	59	46	.268	.355	.359	.714	99	1	0	101	125	66	.719	15			6	*3/S	1.2
1912	StL-N	114	408	59	104	13	8	2	50	46	29	.255	.335	.341	.675	85	-8	-8	100	123	54	.681	19			1	*3	-0.5
1913	StL-N	132	450	61	117	18	4	0	33	53	40	.260	.342	.318	.660	96	-5	-0	93	86	55	.661	21			**32**	*3	3.1
1914	Pit-N	79	284	24	72	7	5	1	25	22	20	.254	.316	.324	.640	98	-3	-1	92	101	31	.594	8			-2	3	0.0
1915	Pit-F	151	521	56	146	26	6	1	49	66	39	.280	.361	.359	.720	109	10	8	104	99	87	.781	40			-15	*3	-0.3
1916	Bro-N	144	495	57	121	22	6	0	60	50	60	.244	.320	.313	.633	92	-2	-4	103	**157**	59	.604	16			-2	*3	-0.3
1917	Bro-N	83	271	20	58	9	5	0	25	29	25	.214	.292	.284	.576	74	-7	-8	104	128	24	.535	7			-0	3/2	-1.0
Total	13	1276	4291	485	1099	183	54	7	461	469	297	.256	.333	.329	.662	98	-11	-3	99	120	539	.650	167			11	*3/S2O	2.4
■ **JOE MOWRY**	Mowry, Joseph Aloysius b: 4/6/08, St.Louis, Mo. BB/TR, 6', 198 lbs. Deb: 5/13/33																											
1933	Bos-N	86	249	25	55	8	5	0	20	15	22	.221	.273	.293	.567	64	-12	-11	96	103	21	.465	1			-0	O	-1.6

YEAR	TM/L	G	AB	R	H	2B	3B	HR	RBI	BB	SO	AVG	OBP	SLG	PRO	/A	BR	/A	PF	CHI	RC	TA	SB	CS	SBR	FR	POS	TPR
1934	Bos-N	25	79	9	17	3	0	1	4	3	13	.215	.244	.291	.535	50	-6	-5	86	55	6	.419	0			-1	O/2	-0.6
1935	Bos-N	81	136	17	36	8	1	1	13	11	13	.265	.324	.360	.685	88	-3	-2	96	90	17	.598	0			-9	O	-1.2
Total	3	192	464	51	108	19	6	2	37	29	48	.233	.284	.313	.596	69	-22	-18	94	91	44	.500	1			-10	O/2	-3.4
■ **MIKE MOYNAHAN** Moynahan, Michael b: 1856, Chicago, Ill. d: 4/9/1899, Chicago, Ill. BL/TR, Deb: 8/20/1880																												
1880	Buf-N	27	100	12	33	5	1	0	14	6	9	.330	.368	.400	.768	177	6	8	91	135	15	.687				-8	S	0.1
1881	Cle-N	33	135	12	31	5	1	0	8	3	14	.230	.246	.281	.528	68	-5	-5	96	77	10	.394				-2	O/3	-0.6
	Det-N	1	4	1	1	0	0	0	0	0	1	.250	.250	.250	.500	54	-0	-0	106	0	0	.333				0	/3	0.0
	Yr	34	139	13	32	5	1	0	8	3	15	.230	.246	.281	.527	68	-6	-5	96	77	10	.393				-2		-0.6
1883	Phi-a	95	400	90	123	18	10	1		30		.308	.356	.410	.766	142	21	19	103	0	60	.700				-1	*S	1.3
1884	Phi-a	1	4	0	0	0	0	0		0		.000	.000	.000	.000	-87	-1	-1	114	0	0	.000				0	/O	0.0
	Cle-N	12	45	9	13	2	1	0	6	7	11	.289	.385	.378	.762	138	2	2	102	107	7	.750				0	/2SO	0.2
Total	4	169	688	124	201	30	13	1	28	46	35	.292	.337	.378	.714	130	23	23	100	42	91	.628				-10	S/O23	1.0
■ **HEINIE MUELLER** Mueller, Clarence Francis b: 9/16/1899, Creve Coeur, Mo. d: 1/23/75, De Soto, Mo. BL/TL, 5'8", 158 lbs. Deb: 9/25/20																												
1920	StL-N	4	22	0	7	1	0	0	1	2	4	.318	.375	.364	.739	115	0	0	98	42	3	.733	1	0	0	0	/O	0.1
1921	StL-N	55	176	25	62	10	6	1	34	11	22	.352	.397	.494	.891	142	9	10	95	139	33	.864	2	4	-2	-0	O	0.5
1922	StL-N	61	159	20	43	7	2	3	26	14	18	.270	.329	.396	.726	85	-3	-4	101	126	21	.675	2	1	0	-1	O	-0.5
1923	StL-N	78	265	39	91	16	9	5	41	18	16	.343	.392	.528	.920	156	15	18	90	93	54	.932	4	3	-1	7	O	2.1
1924	StL-N	92	296	39	78	12	6	2	37	19	16	.264	.312	.365	.677	79	-8	-9	103	118	33	.609	8	7	-2	-1	O1	-1.3
1925	StL-N	78	243	33	76	16	4	1	26	17	11	.313	.365	.424	.789	99	0	-0	102	87	37	.724	0	3	-2	0	O	-0.3
1926	StL-N	52	191	36	51	7	5	3	28	11	6	.267	.330	.403	.733	94	-1	-2	102	115	25	.736	8			0	O	-0.3
	NY-N	85	305	36	76	6	2	4	29	21	17	.249	.300	.321	.621	69	-14	-13	98	93	29	.555	7			6	O	-0.9
	Yr	137	496	72	127	13	7	7	57	32	23	.256	.312	.353	.664	79	-15	-15	100	102	54	.623	15			6		-1.2
1927	NY-N	84	190	33	55	6	1	3	19	25	12	.289	.384	.379	.763	105	2	2	100	82	29	.763	2			-9	O/1	-0.8
1928	Bos-N	42	151	25	34	3	1	0	19	17	9	.225	.316	.258	.574	53	-10	-9	97	184	14	.513	1			9	O	-0.1
1929	Bos-N	46	93	10	19	2	1	0	11	12	12	.204	.302	.247	.549	40	-9	-8	94	164	8	.514	2			-3	O	-1.1
1935	StL-A	16	27	0	5	1	0	0	1	1	4	.185	.214	.222	.437	12	-4	-4	107	57	1	.318	0	0	0	-1	/1O	-0.4
Total	11	693	2118	296	597	87	37	22	272	168	147	.282	.342	.389	.731	94	-23	-18	98	112	287	.686	37	18		9	O/1	-3.0
■ **DON MUELLER** Mueller, Donald Frederick "Mandrake The Magician" b: 4/14/27, St.Louis, Mo. BL/TR, 6', 185 lbs. Deb: 8/02/48																												
1948	NY-N	36	81	12	29	4	1	1	9	0	3	.358	.358	.469	.827	123	2	2	100	82	12	.691	0			-2	O	0.0
1949	NY-N	51	56	5	13	4	0	0	1	5	6	.232	.295	.304	.599	60	-3	-3	102	22	3	.440	0			-1	/O	-0.4
1950	NY-N	132	525	60	153	15	6	7	84	10	26	.291	.309	.383	.691	82	-16	-15	98	149	60	.564	1			-9	*O	-2.7
1951	NY-N	122	469	58	130	10	7	16	69	19	13	.277	.307	.431	.737	95	-4	-5	102	109	63	.648	1	1	-0	-4	*O	-1.3
1952	NY-N	126	456	61	128	14	7	12	49	34	24	.281	.333	.421	.754	105	4	3	102	86	65	.682	2	1	0	-2	*O	-0.1
1953	NY-N	131	480	56	160	12	2	6	60	19	13	.333	.360	.404	.764	101	-1	1	98	113	71	.661	2	0	1	-8	*O	-1.1
1954	NY-N	153	619	90	**212**	35	8	4	71	22	17	.342	.367	.444	.811	105	8	5	105	103	94	.702	2	3	-1	-3	*O	-0.4
1955	NY-N	147	605	67	185	21	4	8	83	19	12	.306	.330	.393	.724	92	-8	-7	99	136	75	.600	1	2	-1	-14	*O	-2.4
1956	NY-N	138	453	38	122	12	1	5	41	15	7	.269	.293	.333	.626	70	-21	-19	97	104	39	.474	0	1	-1	-10	*O	-3.4
1957	NY-N	135	450	45	116	7	1	6	37	13	16	.258	.280	.318	.598	59	-25	-26	102	95	39	.466	2	0	1	-4	*O	-3.4
1958	Chi-A	70	166	7	42	5	0	0	16	11	9	.253	.299	.283	.583	62	-9	-8	98	136	14	.460	0	0	0	-5	O	-1.5
1959	Chi-A	4	4	0	2	0	0	0	0	0	0	.500	.500	.500	1.000	181	0	0	97	0	1	1.000	0	0	0	0	H	0.0
Total	12	1245	4364	499	1292	139	37	65	520	167	146	.296	.324	.390	.713	89	-72	-74	100	112	538	.614	11	8		-61	*O	-16.7
■ **HEINIE MUELLER** Mueller, Emmett Jerome b: 7/20/12, St.Louis, Mo. d: 10/3/86, Orlando, Fla. BB/TR, 5'6", 167 lbs. Deb: 4/19/38																												
1938	Phi-N	136	444	53	111	12	4	4	34	64	43	.250	.346	.322	.668	84	-7	-7	100	81	55	.619	2			-17	*23	-1.7
1939	Phi-N	115	341	46	95	19	4	9	43	33	34	.279	.342	.437	.779	115	3	6	94	90	49	.721	4			-8	23O/S	0.0
1940	Phi-N	97	263	24	65	13	2	3	28	37	23	.247	.344	.346	.690	94	-2	-1	97	104	33	.647	2			-3	2O3/1	-0.2
1941	Phi-N	93	233	21	53	11	1	1	22	22	24	.227	.302	.296	.598	71	-9	-8	97	110	21	.519	2			-2	2O3	-0.9
Total	4	441	1281	144	324	55	11	17	127	156	124	.253	.337	.353	.690	92	-16	-11	97	93	159	.649	10			-29	2/3O1S	-2.8
■ **RAY MUELLER** Mueller, Ray Coleman "Iron Man" b: 3/8/12, Pittsburg, Kan. BR/TR, 5'9", 175 lbs. Deb: 5/11/35 C																												
1935	Bos-N	42	97	10	22	5	0	3	11	3	11	.227	.250	.371	.621	68	-5	-5	96	88	9	.513	0			-0	C	-0.4
1936	Bos-N	24	71	5	14	4	0	0	5	5	17	.197	.250	.254	.504	38	-6	-6	95	98	5	.404	0			2	C	-0.2
1937	Bos-N	64	187	21	47	9	2	2	26	18	36	.251	.317	.353	.670	90	-5	-2	90	130	21	.578	1			5	C	0.5
1938	Bos-N	83	274	23	65	8	6	4	35	16	28	.237	.282	.354	.636	84	-10	-6	88	116	27	.544	3			5	C	0.1
1939	Pit-N	86	180	14	42	8	1	2	18	14	22	.233	.289	.322	.611	64	-9	-9	100	103	18	.514	0			0	C	-0.6
1940	Pit-N	4	3	1	1	0	0	0	1	2	0	.333	.600	.333	.933	172	1	1	95	371	1	1.500	0			0	/C	0.1
1943	Cin-N	141	427	50	111	19	4	8	52	56	42	.260	.347	.379	.726	110	6	6	99	101	59	.677	1			8	*C	2.1
1944	Cin-N	155	555	54	159	24	4	10	73	53	47	.286	.353	.398	.751	117	8	12	95	106	79	.691	4			-4	*C	1.6
1946	Cin-N	114	378	35	96	18	4	8	48	27	37	.254	.309	.386	.695	93	-3	-5	104	105	45	.605	0			13	*C	1.2
1947	Cin-N	71	192	17	48	11	0	6	33	16	25	.250	.311	.401	.712	97	-4	-2	91	129	22	.625	1			4	C	0.4
1948	Cin-N	14	34	2	7	1	0	0	2	4	3	.206	.289	.235	.525	42	-3	-3	103	94	2	.429	0			-1	C	-0.2
1949	Cin-N	32	106	7	29	4	0	1	13	5	13	.274	.319	.340	.658	80	-4	-3	96	126	12	.564	1			0	C	-0.1
	NY-N	56	170	17	38	2	2	5	23	13	14	.224	.279	.347	.626	66	-8	-9	102	117	15	.521	1			-1	C	-0.7
	Yr	88	276	24	67	6	2	6	36	18	27	.243	.294	.344	.638	71	-12	-12	99	122	27	.539	2			-1		-0.8
1950	NY-N	4	11	0	1	1	0	0	0	0	2	.091	.091	.182	.273	-31	-2	-2	98	0	0	.182	0			0	/C	-0.1
	Pit-N	67	156	17	42	7	0	6	24	11	14	.269	.321	.429	.751	93	-1	-2	103	109	19	.659	2			-2	C	-0.1
	Yr	71	167	17	43	8	0	6	24	11	16	.257	.307	.413	.720	86	-4	-4	102	103	19	.624	2			-2		-0.2
1951	Bos-N	28	70	8	11	2	0	1	9	7	11	.157	.234	.229	.462	25	-7	-7	98	183	4	.371	0	0	0	1	C	-0.5
Total	14	985	2911	281	733	123	23	56	373	250	322	.252	.314	.368	.681	90	-54	-42	97	111	337	.618	14	0		31	C	3.1
■ **WALTER MUELLER** Mueller, Walter John b: 12/6/1894, Central, Mo. d: 8/16/71, St.Louis, Mo. BR/TR, 5'8", 160 lbs. Deb: 5/08/22																												
1922	Pit-N	32	122	21	33	5	1	2	18	5	7	.270	.305	.377	.682	72	-5	-5	104	123	14	.596	1	0	0	5	O	0.0
1923	Pit-N	40	111	11	34	4	4	0	20	4	6	.306	.336	.414	.751	100	-1	-0	97	153	15	.671	2	2	-1	0	O	-0.1
1924	Pit-N	30	50	6	13	1	1	0	8	4	4	.260	.327	.320	.647	70	-2	-2	106	182	6	.595	1	0	0	-1	O	-0.2
1926	Pit-N	19	62	8	15	0	1	0	3	0	2	.242	.242	.274	.516	34	-5	-6	112	61	4	.362	0			-0	O	-0.6
Total	4	121	345	46	95	10	7	2	49	13	19	.275	.307	.362	.670	73	-13	-14	103	131	39	.575	4	2		5	/O	-0.9
■ **BILL MUELLER** Mueller, William Lawrence "Hawk" b: 11/9/20, Bay City, Mich. BR/TR, 6'1.5", 180 lbs. Deb: 8/29/42																												
1942	Chi-A	26	85	5	14	1	0	0	5	12	9	.165	.276	.176	.452	29	-8	-8	99	120	4	.390	2	1	0	9	O	0.0
1945	Chi-A	13	9	3	0	0	0	0	0	2	1	.000	.182	.000	.182	-48	-2	-2	95	0	0	.333	1	0	0	-2	/O	-0.3
Total	2	39	94	8	14	1	0	0	5	14	10	.149	.266	.160	.426	22	-9	-9	98	108	4	.407	3	1	0	6	/O	-0.3
■ **MIKE MULDOON** Muldoon, Michael D. b: 1860, Hartford, Conn. 5'8", 165 lbs. Deb: 5/01/1882																												
1882	Cle-N	84	341	50	84	17	5	6	45	10	28	.246	.268	.378	.646	116	1	7	90	109	35	.541				-1	*3O	0.6
1883	Cle-N	98	378	54	86	22	3	0	29	10	39	.228	.247	.302	.549	63	-15	-18	105	94	29	.425				-14	*3/O	-2.7
1884	Cle-N	110	422	46	101	16	6	2	38	18	67	.239	.270	.320	.590	83	-7	-9	102	98	37	.477				-6	*3/O2	-1.8
1885	Bal-a	102	410	47	103	20	6	2		20		.251	.293	.344	.637	97	1	-2	106	0	42	.537				-3	*3/2	0.0
1886	Bal-a	101	381	57	76	13	8	0		34		.199	.269	.276	.544	80	-12	-6	91	0	32	.502	12			3	23	0.0
Total	5	495	1932	254	450	88	28	10	112	92	134	.233	.270	.323	.593	87	-31	-28	99	58	176	.495	12			-22	3/2O	-3.9
■ **TONY MULLANE** Mullane, Anthony John "Count" or "The Apollo Of The Box" b: 1/20/1859, Cork, Ireland d: 4/25/44, Chicago, Ill. BB/TB, 5'10.5", 165 lbs. Deb: 8/27/1881																												
1881	Det-N	5	19	0	5	0	0	0	1	0	0	.263	.263	.263	.526	62	-1	-1	106	71	1	.357				0	/P	0.0
1882	Lou-a	77	303	46	78	13	1	0		13		.257	.288	.307	.595	108	0	3	94	0	27	.471				10	*P1O/2	0.0
1883	StL-a	83	307	38	69	11	6	0		13		.225	.256	.300	.556	73	-7	-11	108	0	24	.441				2	PO/21	0.0
1884	Tol-a	95	352	49	97	19	3	3		33		.276	.339	.372	.712	131	14	12	104	0	46	.647				8	PO/13S2D	0.0
1886	Cin-a	91	324	59	73	12	5	0		25		.225	.283	.293	.576	86	-6	-4	96	0	33	.562	20			3	PO/13S2D	0.0

YEAR	TM/L	G	AB	R	H	2B	3B	HR	RBI	BB	SO	AVG	OBP	SLG	PRO	/A	BR	/A	PF	CHI	RC	TA	SB	CS	SBR	FR	POS	TPR
1887	Cin-a	56	199	35	44	6	3	3		16		.221	.292	.327	.619	68	-7	-10	108	0	25	.677	20			-2	P/O	0.0
1888	Cin-a	51	175	27	44	4	4	1	16	8		.251	.296	.337	.633	105	1	1	101	77	22	.626	12			1	P/1O2	0.0
1889	Cin-a	63	196	53	58	16	4	0	29	27	21	.296	.387	.418	.805	125	9	7	105	101	42	.978	24			0	P3O/1	0.0
1890	Cin-N	81	286	41	79	9	8	0	34	39	30	.276	.375	.364	.738	109	8	4	108	101	47	.812	19			0	OP3S/1	0.4
1891	Cin-N	64	209	16	31	1	2	0	10	18	33	.148	.229	.172	.402	21	-21	-18	91	81	9	.348	4			3	PO/3	0.0
1892	Cin-N	39	118	14	20	3	1	0	9	9	8	.169	.246	.212	.458	39	-8	-9	103	111	7	.418	4			0	P/1	0.0
1893	Cin-N	16	52	11	15	0	0	1	6	5	3	.288	.383	.346	.729	95	0	-0	101	78	7	.730	1			0	P/3	0.0
	Bal-N	38	114	15	26	2	1	0	14	5	14	.228	.261	.263	.524	38	-10	-11	107	128	9	.455	5			3	P/O1	0.0
	Yr	54	166	26	41	2	1	1	20	10	17	.247	.302	.289	.591	56	-10	-11	105	114	17	.536	6			3		0.0
1894	Bal-N	21	53	3	21	3	0	0	9	6	3	.396	.475	.453	.928	128	3	3	99	103	13	1.063	2			0	P	0.0
	Cle-N	4	13	0	1	0	0	0	0	4	2	.077	.294	.077	.371	-5	-2	-3	111	0	1	.500	1			0	/P	0.0
	Yr	25	66	3	22	3	0	0	9	10	5	.333	.436	.379	.815	99	1	1	101	91	13	.909	3			0		0.0
Total	13	784	2720	407	661	99	38	8	128	221	114	.243	.307	.316	.623	89	-27	-36	102	44	315	.593	112			28	PO/31S2D	0.4
■ **GREG MULLEAVY** Mulleavy, Gregory Thomas "Moe" b: 9/25/05, Detroit, Mich. d: 2/1/80, Arcadia, Cal. BR/TR, 5'9", 167 lbs. Deb: 7/04/30 C																												
1930	Chi-A	77	289	27	76	14	5	0	28	20	23	.263	.311	.346	.657	64	-15	-16	103	95	32	.581	5	2	0	-11	S	-1.6
1932	Chi-A	1	3	0	0	0	0	0	0	0	0	.000	.000	.000	.000	-99	-1	-1	87	0	0	.000	0	0	0	0	/2	0.0
1933	Bos-A	1	0	1	0	0	0	0	0	0	0	—	—	—	—	—	0	0	101	—	—	—	0	0	0	0	R	0.0
Total	3	79	292	28	76	14	5	0	28	20	23	.260	.308	.342	.650	63	-16	-17	103	94	32	.573	5	2	0	-11	/S2	-1.6
■ **MULLEN** Mullen Deb:8/17/1872																												
1872	Cle-n	1	6	1	4							.667															/O	
■ **CHARLIE MULLEN** Mullen, Charles George b: 3/15/1889, Seattle, Wash. d: 6/6/63, Seattle, Wash. BR/TR, 5'10.5", 155 lbs. Deb: 5/18/10																												
1910	Chi-A	41	123	15	24	2	1	0	13	4		.195	.220	.228	.448	43	-9	-8	95	172	8	.364	4			2	1/O	-0.4
1911	Chi-A	20	59	7	12	2	1	0	5	5		.203	.266	.271	.537	52	-4	-4	97	106	5	.468	1			1	1	-0.1
1914	NY-A	93	323	33	84	8	0	0	44	33	55	.260	.332	.285	.617	86	-5	-5	100	190	32	.539	11	17	-7	-3	1	-1.5
1915	NY-A	40	90	11	24	1	0	0	7	10	12	.267	.340	.278	.618	86	-1	-1	98	95	10	.588	5	2	0	0	1	-0.1
1916	NY-A	59	146	11	39	9	1	0	18	9	13	.267	.310	.342	.652	95	-1	-1	101	129	18	.617	7			-1	21/O	-0.2
Total	5	253	741	77	183	22	3	0	87	61	80	.247	.306	.285	.591	78	-20	-19	99	157	72	.523	28	19		-1	1/2O	-2.3
■ **MOON MULLEN** Mullen, Ford Parker b: 2/9/17, Olympia, Wash. BL/TR, 5'9", 165 lbs. Deb: 4/18/44																												
1944	Phi-N	118	464	51	124	9	4	0	31	28	32	.267	.315	.304	.618	74	-15	-15	100	84	46	.516	4			0	*2/3	-0.3
■ **JOHN MULLEN** Mullen, John b: Philadelphia, Pa. BL/TL, Deb: N/A.																												
1874	Ath-n	4	16	1	8							.500															C	
1876	Phi-N	1	3	0	0	0	0	0	0	0	0	.000	.000	.000	.000	-99	-1	-1	99	0	0	.000				0	/C	0.0
■ **BILLY MULLEN** Mullen, William John b: 1/23/1896, St.Louis, Mo. d: 5/4/71, St.Louis, Mo. BR/TR, 5'8", 160 lbs. Deb: 10/02/20																												
1920	StL-A	2	4	0	0	0	0	0	0	0	0	.000	.000	.000	.000	-90	-1	-1	111	0	0	.000	0	0	0	0	/2	0.0
1921	StL-A	4	4	0	0	0	0	0	0	2	1	.000	.333	.000	.333	-9	-1	-1	101	0	0	.500	0	0	0	0	/3	0.0
1923	Bro-N	4	11	1	3	0	0	0	0	0	0	.273	.273	.273	.545	45	-1	-1	98	0	1	.375	0	0	0	0	/3	0.0
1926	Det-A	11	13	2	1	0	0	0	0	5	1	.077	.333	.077	.410	11	-1	-1	97	0	1	.583	1	0	0	0	/3	0.0
1928	StL-A	15	18	2	7	1	0	0	2	3	4	.389	.476	.444	.921	138	1	1	104	86	4	1.000	0	0	0	-0	/3	0.1
Total	5	36	50	5	11	1	0	0	2	10	6	.220	.350	.240	.590	56	-3	-3	101	30	6	.590	1	0	0	-0	/32	0.1
■ **FREDDIE MULLER** Muller, Frederick William b: 12/21/07, Newark, Cal. d: 10/20/76, Davis, Cal. BR/TR, 5'10", 170 lbs. Deb: 7/08/33																												
1933	Bos-A	15	48	6	9	1	1	0	3	5	5	.188	.264	.250	.514	36	-4	-4	101	83	4	.462	1	0	0	-0	2	-0.3
1934	Bos-A	2	1	1	0	0	0	0	0	1	0	.000	.500	.000	.500	36	0	-0	106	0	0	1.000	0	0	0	0	/23	0.0
Total	2	17	49	7	9	1	1	0	3	6	5	.184	.273	.245	.518	37	-4	-4	101	80	4	.475	1	0	0	-0	/23	-0.3
■ **MULLIGAN** Mulligan Deb:6/14/1884																												
1884	Was-U	1	4	2	1	0	0	0		0		.250	.250	.250	.500	72	-0	-0	97	0	0	.333	0			0	/3	0.0
■ **JOE MULLIGAN** Mulligan, Edward Joseph "Big Joe" b: 8/27/1894, St.Louis, Mo. d: 3/15/82, San Rafael, Cal. BR/TR, 5'9", 152 lbs. Deb: 9/23/15																												
1915	Chi-N	11	22	5	8	1	0	0	2	5	1	.364	.481	.409	.891	167	2	2	102	85	5	1.000	2	2	-1	-1	S/3	0.1
1916	Chi-N	58	189	13	29	3	4	0	9	8	30	.153	.200	.212	.412	23	-16	-20	117	89	9	.325	1			-7	S	-2.7
1921	Chi-A	151	609	82	153	21	12	1	45	32	53	.251	.293	.330	.623	59	-39	-38	99	73	57	.527	13	18	-7	-12	*3/S	-4.2
1922	Chi-A	103	372	39	87	14	8	0	31	22	32	.234	.278	.315	.593	54	-26	-26	101	97	33	.503	7	7	-2	3	3/S	-1.4
1928	Pit-N	27	43	4	10	2	0	0	1	3	4	.233	.283	.279	.562	44	-3	-4	107	30	4	.455	0			-0	/32	-0.3
Total	5	350	1235	143	287	41	24	1	88	70	120	.232	.278	.307	.585	53	-82	-86	103	81	107	.492	23	27		-17	3/S2	-8.5
■ **GEORGE MULLIN** Mullin, George Joseph "Wabash George" b: 7/4/1880, Toledo, Ohio d: 1/7/44, Wabash, Ind. BR/TR, 5'11", 188 lbs. Deb: 5/04/02																												
1902	Det-A	40	120	20	39	4	3	0	11	8		.325	.367	.408	.776	118	3	3	99	74	19	.716	1			1	P/O	0.0
1903	Det-A	46	126	11	35	9	1	1	12	2		.278	.289	.389	.678	107	0	1	97	83	15	.571	1			5	P/O	0.0
1904	Det-A	53	155	14	45	10	2	0	8	10		.290	.333	.381	.714	134	5	6	96	51	21	.636	1			8	P/O	0.0
1905	Det-A	47	135	15	35	4	0	0	12	12		.259	.320	.289	.609	97	-0	-0	98	110	14	.550	4			6	P/O	0.0
1906	Det-A	50	142	13	32	6	4	0	6	4		.225	.247	.324	.571	74	-4	-5	108	47	12	.473	2			3	P/2O	0.0
1907	Det-A	70	157	16	34	5	3	0	13	12		.217	.272	.287	.559	79	-3	-4	102	103	13	.480	2			4	P/1	0.0
1908	Det-A	55	125	13	32	2	2	1	8	7		.256	.295	.328	.623	104	0	0	101	68	12	.538	2			3	P	0.0
1909	Det-A	53	126	13	27	7	0	0	17	13		.214	.288	.270	.558	69	-3	-5	110	193	10	.495	2			1	P/O	0.0
1910	Det-A	50	129	15	33	6	2	1	11	8		.256	.299	.357	.656	103	0	0	102	83	14	.573	1			-0	P/O	0.0
1911	Det-A	40	98	4	28	7	2	0	5	10		.286	.352	.398	.750	101	1	-0	108	43	14	.714	1			-2	P	0.0
1912	Det-A	38	90	13	25	5	1	0	12	17		.278	.393	.356	.748	121	2	3	95	125	13	.754	0			0	P	0.0
1913	Det-A	12	20	1	7	0	0	0	1	4	1	.350	.458	.350	.808	139	1	1	99	51	3	.846	0			1	/P	0.0
	Was-A	11	21	4	4	0	0	0	0	2	5	.190	.292	.190	.482	39	-1	-2	106	0	1	.471	1			1	P	0.0
	Yr	23	41	5	11	0	0	0	1	6	6	.268	.375	.268	.643	87	-0	-0	102	29	4	.633	1			1		0.0
1914	Ind-F	43	77	11	24	5	3	0	21	11	15	.312	.398	.455	.852	130	5	3	111	217	15	.868	0			-2	P	0.0
1915	New-F	6	10	0	1	0	0	0	0	2	0	.100	.250	.100	.350	6	-1	-1	94	0	0	.333	0			0	/P	0.0
Total	14	614	1531	163	401	70	23	3	137	122	21	.262	.317	.344	.660	101	5	1	102	93	175	.590	18			26	P/O12	0.0
■ **HENRY MULLIN** Mullin, Henry b: Boston, Mass. BR , Deb: 6/04/1884																												
1884	Was-a	34	120	13	17	3	1	0		8		.142	.195	.183	.379	29	-9	-7	88	0	4	.291				-1	O/3	-0.6
	Bos-U	2	8	1	0	0	0	0		0		.000	.000	.000	.000	-99	-2	-2	98	0	0	.000	0			0	/O	0.0
Total	1	36	128	14	17	3	1	0		8		.133	.184	.172	.356	21	-11	-9	89	0	4	.270	0			-1	/O3	-0.6
■ **JIM MULLIN** Mullin, James Henry b: 10/16/1883, New York, N.Y. d: 1/24/25, Philadelphia, Pa. TR , 5'10", 173 lbs. Deb: 6/01/04																												
1904	Phi-A	22	52	5	14	1	0	1	5	3		.269	.309	.346	.655	107	1	0	102	89	6	.605	2			-0	/12SO	0.0
	Was-A	27	102	10	19	2	2	0	4	4		.186	.217	.245	.462	52	-6	-5	93	63	6	.386	3			0	2	-0.5
	Phi-A	19	58	4	10	0	0	0	4	2		.172	.200	.172	.372	20	-5	-5	102	149	2	.292	2			-0	1	-0.5
	Yr	68	212	19	43	3	2	1	13	9		.203	.235	.250	.485	56	-10	-10	98	98	14	.408	7			-0		-1.0
1905	Was-A	50	163	18	31	7	6	0	13	5		.190	.214	.307	.521	63	-7	-7	104	93	12	.455	5			1	2/1	-0.7
Total	2	118	375	37	74	10	8	1	26	14		.197	.226	.275	.501	60	-17	-17	100	93	27	.429	12			0	/21SO	-1.7
■ **PAT MULLIN** Mullin, Patrick Joseph b: 11/1/17, Trotter, Pa. BL/TR, 6'2", 190 lbs. Deb: 9/18/40 C																												
1940	Det-A	4	4	0	0	0	0	0	0	0	0	.000	.000	.000	.000	-90	-1	-1	111	0	0	.000	0	0	0	-0	/O	-0.1
1941	Det-A	54	220	42	76	11	5	5	23	18	18	.345	.400	.509	.909	131	12	10	106	68	48	.932	5	1	1	-1	O	0.6
1946	Det-A	93	276	34	68	13	4	3	35	25	36	.246	.311	.355	.666	79	-6	-8	108	124	31	.585	3	5	-2	-5	O	-2.0
1947	Det-A	116	398	62	102	28	6	15	62	63	66	.256	.359	.470	.829	124	15	13	104	100	69	.819	3	8	-4	5	*O	1.0
1948	Det-A	138	496	91	143	16	11	23	80	77	57	.288	.385	.504	.889	140	24	27	96	86	103	.914	1	2	-1	-3	*O	1.7
1949	Det-A	104	310	55	83	8	6	12	59	42	29	.268	.357	.448	.805	104	4	1	108	116	52	.782	1	2	-1	-2	O	-0.3

YEAR	TM/L	G	AB	R	H	2B	3B	HR	RBI	BB	SO	AVG	OBP	SLG	PRO	/A	BR	/A	PF	CHI	RC	TA	SB	CS	SBR	FR	POS	TPR
1950	Det-A	69	142	16	31	5	0	6	23	20	23	.218	.315	.380	.695	80	-5	-5	97	110	18	.652	1	4	-2	-1	O	-0.7
1951	Det-A	110	295	41	83	11	6	12	51	40	38	.281	.367	.481	.849	121	11	9	106	102	55	.848	2	2	-1	-9	O	-0.3
1952	Det-A	97	255	29	64	13	5	7	35	31	30	.251	.332	.424	.756	110	3	3	99	101	36	.708	4	2	0	3	O	0.4
1953	Det-A	79	97	11	26	1	0	4	17	14	15	.268	.360	.402	.762	108	1	1	98	123	14	.707	0	1	-1	-3	O	-0.2
Total	10	864	2493	381	676	106	43	87	385	330	312	.271	.358	.453	.811	115	58	49	103	101	426	.804	20	27	-10	-16	O	0.1

■ RANCE MULLINIKS Mulliniks, Steven Rance b: 1/15/56, Tulare, Cal. BL/TR, 5'11", 162 lbs. Deb: 6/18/77

YEAR	TM/L	G	AB	R	H	2B	3B	HR	RBI	BB	SO	AVG	OBP	SLG	PRO	/A	BR	/A	PF	CHI	RC	TA	SB	CS	SBR	FR	POS	TPR
1977	Cal-A	78	271	36	73	13	2	3	21	23	36	.269	.329	.365	.694	94	-4	-2	95	79	34	.617	1	1	-0	-0	S	0.6
1978	Cal-A	50	119	6	22	3	1	1	6	8	23	.185	.242	.252	.494	39	-10	-10	102	72	7	.410	2	0	1	-3	S/D	-0.8
1979	Cal-A	22	68	7	10	0	0	1	8	4	14	.147	.205	.191	.397	8	-9	-8	93	192	3	.300	0	0	0	0	S	-0.5
1980	KC-A	36	54	8	14	3	0	0	6	7	10	.259	.344	.315	.659	83	-1	-1	98	138	6	.571	0	0	0	-2	S2	0.0
1981	KC-A	24	44	6	10	3	0	0	5	2	7	.227	.261	.295	.556	61	-2	-2	99	151	3	.405	0	1	-1	-2	2/S3	-0.4
1982	Tor-A	112	311	32	76	25	0	4	35	37	49	.244	.327	.363	.690	82	-4	-8	109	112	36	.623	3	2	-0	-10	*3S	-1.8
1983	Tor-A	129	364	54	100	34	3	10	49	57	43	.275	.374	.467	.841	120	16	12	108	96	62	.817	0	2	-1	-16	*3S/2	-0.3
1984	Tor-A	125	343	41	111	21	5	3	42	33	44	.324	.385	.440	.825	126	13	13	102	105	58	.779	2	3	-1	-4	*3/S2	0.9
1985	Tor-A	129	366	55	108	26	1	10	57	55	54	.295	.387	.454	.841	128	16	16	101	115	66	.832	2	0	1	-7	*3	0.5
1986	Tor-A	117	348	50	90	22	0	11	45	43	60	.259	.342	.417	.759	101	3	1	105	101	48	.701	1	1	-0	2	*3/2D	0.0
1987	Tor-A	124	332	37	103	28	1	11	44	34	55	.310	.374	.500	.874	129	14	14	101	88	60	.837	1	1	-0	0	3D/S	1.1
1988	Tor-A	119	337	49	101	21	1	12	48	56	57	.300	.399	.475	.874	144	21	22	100	97	65	.882	1	0	0	1	*D/3	2.3
Total	12	1065	2957	381	818	199	14	66	366	359	452	.277	.356	.420	.777	110	55	46	102	102	450	.751	13	11	-3	-42	3SD/2	1.6

■ FRAN MULLINS Mullins, Francis Joseph b: 5/14/57, Oakland, Cal. BR/TR, 6', 180 lbs. Deb: 9/01/80

YEAR	TM/L	G	AB	R	H	2B	3B	HR	RBI	BB	SO	AVG	OBP	SLG	PRO	/A	BR	/A	PF	CHI	RC	TA	SB	CS	SBR	FR	POS	TPR
1980	Chi-A	21	62	9	12	4	0	0	3	9	8	.194	.296	.258	.554	55	-4	-4	97	73	4	.463	0	1	-1	1	3	-0.2
1984	SF-N	57	110	8	24	8	0	2	10	9	29	.218	.277	.345	.623	77	-4	-4	96	89	10	.556	3	1	0	1	S3/2	0.0
1986	Cle-A	28	40	3	7	4	0	0	5	2	11	.175	.214	.275	.489	34	-4	-4	98	181	3	.394	0	0	0	0	2S/1D	-0.1
Total	3	106	212	20	43	16	0	2	18	20	48	.203	.272	.307	.578	62	-12	-11	97	101	17	.515	3	2	-0	2	/3S2D1	-0.3

■ JOE MULVEY Mulvey, Joseph H. b: 10/27/1858, Providence, R.I. d: 8/21/28, Philadelphia, Pa. BR/TR, 5'11.5", 178 lbs. Deb: 5/31/1883

YEAR	TM/L	G	AB	R	H	2B	3B	HR	RBI	BB	SO	AVG	OBP	SLG	PRO	/A	BR	/A	PF	CHI	RC	TA	SB	CS	SBR	FR	POS	TPR
1883	Pro-N	4	16	1	2	1	0	0	2	0	1	.125	.125	.188	.313	-7	-2	-2	101	236	0	.214				0	/S	-0.1
	Phi-N	3	12	2	6	1	0	0	3	0	1	.500	.500	.583	1.083	253	2	2	90	152	4	1.167				0	/3	0.2
	Yr	7	28	3	8	2	0	0	5	0	2	.286	.286	.357	.643	98	-0	-0	96	233	3	.500				0		0.1
1884	Phi-N	100	401	47	92	11	2	2	32	4	49	.229	.237	.282	.519	68	-17	-13	92	98	27	.379				10	*3	-0.6
1885	Phi-N	107	443	74	119	25	6	6	64	3	18	.269	.274	.393	.666	110	5	3	104	102	49	.546				-7	*3	-0.2
1886	Phi-N	107	430	71	115	16	10	2	53	15	31	.267	.292	.365	.657	101	-1	-0	98	112	55	.632	27			-19	*3/O	-1.3
1887	Phi-N	111	474	93	136	21	6	2	78	21	14	.287	.321	.369	.690	96	-5	-2	97	141	72	.716	43			-18	*3	-1.6
1888	Phi-N	100	398	37	86	12	3	0	39	9	33	.216	.235	.261	.497	53	-18	-25	114	142	29	.423	18			-19	*3	-3.9
1889	Phi-N	129	544	77	157	21	9	6	77	23	25	.289	.319	.393	.712	96	-2	-6	104	105	77	.674	23			-1	*3	0.2
1890	Phi-P	120	519	96	149	26	15	6	87	27	36	.287	.326	.430	.756	100	-1	-3	102	105	81	.738	20			-18	*3	-0.9
1891	Phi-a	113	453	62	115	9	13	5	66	17	32	.254	.287	.364	.651	86	-9	-11	103	108	52	.583	11			0	*3	-0.6
1892	Phi-N	25	98	9	14	1	1	0	4	6	9	.143	.200	.173	.373	14	-10	-11	104	76	4	.310	2			0	3	-0.9
1893	Was-N	55	226	21	53	9	4	0	19	7	8	.235	.264	.310	.574	60	-16	-12	90	76	19	.468	2			4	3	-0.5
1895	Bro-N	13	49	8	15	4	1	0	8	2	0	.306	.333	.429	.762	104	-0	0	94	109	8	.706	1			0	3	0.0
Total	12	987	4063	598	1059	157	70	29	532	134	257	.261	.287	.355	.642	87	-74	-79	101	111	478	.579	147			-69	3/SO	-10.2

■ JERRY MUMPHREY Mumphrey, Jerry Wayne b: 9/9/52, Tyler, Tex. BB/TR, 6'2", 185 lbs. Deb: 9/10/74

YEAR	TM/L	G	AB	R	H	2B	3B	HR	RBI	BB	SO	AVG	OBP	SLG	PRO	/A	BR	/A	PF	CHI	RC	TA	SB	CS	SBR	FR	POS	TPR
1974	StL-N	5	2	2	0	0	0	0	0	0	0	.000	.000	.000	.000	-97	-1	-1	104	0	0	.000	0	0	0	-0	/O	0.0
1975	StL-N	11	16	2	6	2	0	0	1	4	3	.375	.500	.500	1.000	173	2	2	103	48	5	1.200	0	0	0	1	/O	0.2
1976	StL-N	112	384	51	99	15	5	1	26	37	53	.258	.325	.331	.655	83	-6	-8	104	78	46	.638	22	6	3	4	O	-0.4
1977	StL-N	145	463	73	133	20	10	2	38	47	70	.287	.354	.387	.741	103	-0	2	96	82	64	.713	22	15	-2	5	*O	0.0
1978	StL-N	125	367	41	96	13	4	2	37	30	40	.262	.319	.335	.654	87	-8	-6	95	114	37	.577	14	10	-2	-6	*O	-1.9
1979	StL-N	124	339	53	100	10	3	3	32	26	39	.295	.345	.369	.714	91	-2	-4	105	95	41	.621	8	11	-4	-13	*O	-2.5
1980	SD-N	160	564	61	168	24	3	4	59	49	90	.298	.354	.372	.726	110	3	8	93	107	79	.742	52	5	13	-2	*O	1.3
1981	NY-A	80	319	44	98	11	5	6	32	24	27	.307	.356	.429	.785	125	10	10	100	71	47	.738	14	9	-1	4	O	1.1
1982	NY-A	123	477	76	143	24	10	9	68	50	66	.300	.366	.449	.815	127	15	17	96	120	76	.777	11	3	2	3	*O	1.8
1983	NY-A	83	267	41	70	11	4	7	36	28	33	.262	.332	.412	.744	105	1	2	99	107	34	.664	2	3	-1	4	O	0.3
	Hou-N	44	143	17	48	10	2	1	17	22	23	.336	.428	.455	.882	161	10	12	90	101	31	.969	5	0	2	3	O	1.6
1984	Hou-N	151	524	66	152	20	3	9	83	56	79	.290	.359	.391	.750	120	8	13	93	**143**	74	.706	15	7	0	-6	*O	0.2
1985	Hou-N	130	444	52	123	25	2	8	61	37	57	.277	.333	.396	.729	107	1	4	96	121	56	.650	6	7	-2	0	*O	-0.1
1986	Chi-N	111	309	37	94	11	2	5	32	26	45	.304	.358	.401	.760	102	4	2	107	92	45	.688	2	3	-1	-3	O	-0.4
1987	Chi-N	118	309	41	103	19	2	13	44	35	47	.333	.401	.534	.935	144	20	20	101	86	66	.948	1	1	-0	-5	O	1.1
1988	Chi-N	63	66	3	9	2	0	0	9	7	16	.136	.219	.167	.386	12	-7	-8	104	327	2	.300	0	0	0	-1	/O	-0.8
Total	15	1585	4993	660	1442	217	55	70	575	478	688	.289	.351	.396	.748	109	50	64	98	106	702	.725	174	80	4	-13	*O	1.5

■ BIG JOHN MUNCE Munce, John Lewis "John" or "Big John" b: 11/18/1857, Philadelphia, Pa. d: 3/15/17, Philadelphia, Pa. 6', Deb: 8/19/1884

YEAR	TM/L	G	AB	R	H	2B	3B	HR	RBI	BB	SO	AVG	OBP	SLG	PRO	/A	BR	/A	PF	CHI	RC	TA	SB	CS	SBR	FR	POS	TPR
1884	WiL-U	7	21	1	4	0	0	0		1		.190	.227	.190	.418	41	-1	-1	103	0	1	.294	0			0	/O	0.0

■ JAKE MUNCH Munch, Jacob Ferdinand b: 11/16/1890, Morton, Pa. d: 6/8/66, Lansdowne, Pa. BL/TL, 6'2.5", 170 lbs. Deb: 5/27/18

YEAR	TM/L	G	AB	R	H	2B	3B	HR	RBI	BB	SO	AVG	OBP	SLG	PRO	/A	BR	/A	PF	CHI	RC	TA	SB	CS	SBR	FR	POS	TPR
1918	Phi-A	22	30	3	8	0	1	0	0	0	5	.267	.267	.333	.600	78	-1	-1	104	0	2	.455	0			-1	/O1	-0.2

■ GEORGE MUNDINGER Mundinger, George b: 11/20/1854, New Orleans, La. d: 10/12/10, Covington, La. BR/TR, 6'2", 200 lbs. Deb: 5/09/1884

YEAR	TM/L	G	AB	R	H	2B	3B	HR	RBI	BB	SO	AVG	OBP	SLG	PRO	/A	BR	/A	PF	CHI	RC	TA	SB	CS	SBR	FR	POS	TPR
1884	Ind-a	3	8	1	2	0	0	0		0		.250	.250	.250	.500	68	-0	-0	96	0	1	.333				0	/C	0.0

■ BILL MUNDY Mundy, William Edward b: 6/28/1889, Salineville, Ohio d: 9/23/58, Kalamazoo, Mich. BL/TL, 5'10", 154 lbs. Deb: 8/17/13

YEAR	TM/L	G	AB	R	H	2B	3B	HR	RBI	BB	SO	AVG	OBP	SLG	PRO	/A	BR	/A	PF	CHI	RC	TA	SB	CS	SBR	FR	POS	TPR
1913	Bos-A	16	47	4	12	0	0	0	4	4	12	.255	.314	.255	.569	65	-2	-2	103	118	4	.457	0			-1	1	-0.2

■ MUNN Munn Deb:9/06/1875

YEAR	TM/L	G	AB	R	H	2B	3B	HR	RBI	BB	SO	AVG	OBP	SLG	PRO	/A	BR	/A	PF	CHI	RC	TA	SB	CS	SBR	FR	POS	TPR
1875	Atl-n	1	4	0	0							.000															/2	

■ RED MUNSON Munson, Clarence Hanford b: 7/31/1883, Cincinnati, Ohio d: 2/19/57, Mishawaka, Ind. TR , Deb: 8/28/05

YEAR	TM/L	G	AB	R	H	2B	3B	HR	RBI	BB	SO	AVG	OBP	SLG	PRO	/A	BR	/A	PF	CHI	RC	TA	SB	CS	SBR	FR	POS	TPR
1905	Phi-N	9	26	1	3	1	0	0	2	0		.115	.115	.154	.269	-19	-4	-4	104	174	0	.174	0			0	/C	-0.2

■ JOE MUNSON Munson, Joseph Martin Napoleon (born Joseph Martin Napoleon Carlson) b: 11/6/1899, Renovo, Pa. BL/TR, 5'9", 184 lbs. Deb: 9/18/25

YEAR	TM/L	G	AB	R	H	2B	3B	HR	RBI	BB	SO	AVG	OBP	SLG	PRO	/A	BR	/A	PF	CHI	RC	TA	SB	CS	SBR	FR	POS	TPR
1925	Chi-N	9	35	5	13	3	1	0	3	3	1	.371	.436	.514	.950	146	2	2	97	57	8	1.000	1	1	-0	0	/O	0.2
1926	Chi-N	33	101	17	26	2	2	3	15	8	4	.257	.318	.406	.724	88	-1	-2	106	104	13	.667	0			-3	O	-0.5
Total	2	42	136	22	39	5	3	3	18	11	5	.287	.349	.434	.783	103	1	0	104	91	21	.745	1	1		-3	/O	-0.3

■ THURMAN MUNSON Munson, Thurman Lee b: 6/7/47, Akron, Ohio d: 8/2/79, Canton, Ohio BR/TR, 5'11", 190 lbs. Deb: 8/08/69

YEAR	TM/L	G	AB	R	H	2B	3B	HR	RBI	BB	SO	AVG	OBP	SLG	PRO	/A	BR	/A	PF	CHI	RC	TA	SB	CS	SBR	FR	POS	TPR
1969	NY-A	26	86	6	22	1	2	1	9	10	10	.256	.333	.349	.682	95	-1	-0	95	112	9	.571	0	1	-1	3	C	0.4
1970	NY-A	132	453	59	137	25	4	6	53	57	56	.302	.389	.415	.804	132	15	20	92	106	72	.765	5	7	-3	17	*C	3.7
1971	NY-A	125	451	71	113	15	4	10	42	52	65	.251	.337	.368	.705	103	0	2	97	93	57	.654	6	5	-1	9	*C/O	1.6
1972	NY-A	140	511	54	143	16	3	7	46	47	58	.280	.344	.364	.708	120	7	11	92	98	62	.624	6	7	-2	18	*C	3.2
1973	NY-A	147	519	80	156	29	4	20	74	48	64	.301	.364	.487	.852	137	25	25	101	95	89	.811	4	6	-2	21	*C/D	4.6
1974	NY-A	144	517	64	135	19	2	13	60	44	66	.261	.320	.381	.701	106	0	3	96	102	61	.616	2	0	1	18	*C/D	2.7
1975	NY-A	157	597	83	190	24	3	12	102	45	52	.318	.372	.429	.801	127	20	21	99	**142**	90	.718	3	2	-0	23	*CD/103	4.7
1976	NY-A	152	616	79	186	27	1	17	105	29	38	.302	.343	.432	.774	126	18	18	99	135	85	.694	14	11	-2	4	*CDO	2.5
1977	NY-A	149	595	85	183	28	5	18	100	39	55	.308	.352	.462	.814	122	15	17	99	128	90	.736	5	6	-2	1	*CD	1.9
1978	NY-A	154	617	73	183	27	1	6	71	35	70	.297	.337	.373	.710	101	-1	0	99	120	73	.591	2	3	-1	-3	*CDO	0.0
1979	NY-A	97	382	42	110	18	3	3	39	32	37	.288	.343	.374	.717	98	-3	-1	96	104	46	.609	1	2	-1	-5	C/1D	-0.2
Total	11	1423	5344	696	1558	229	32	113	701	438	571	.292	.350	.410	.760	117	97	116	97	114	735	.706	48	50	-16	106	*C/DO13	25.1

YEAR	TM/L	G	AB	R	H	2B	3B	HR	RBI	BB	SO	AVG	OBP	SLG	PRO	/A	BR	/A	PF	CHI	RC	TA	SB	CS	SBR	FR	POS	TPR
■ **JOHN MUNYAN**	Munyan, John B. b: 11/14/1860, Chester, Pa. d: 2/18/45, Endicott, N.Y. Deb: 7/12/1887																											
1887	Cle-a	16	58	9	14	1	1	0		3		.241	.279	.293	.572	63	-3	-3	98	0	6	.545	4			0	O/C3	-0.1
1890	Col-a	2	7	1	1	0	0	0		0		.143	.250	.143	.393	18	-1	-1	99	0	0	.333	0			0	/O	0.0
	StL-a	96	342	61	91	15	7	4		32		.266	.341	.386	.727	101	7	-2	116	0	50	.725	11			-11	C/O23S	-0.3
	Yr	98	349	62	92	15	7	4	0	32		.264	.339	.381	.720	99	6	-3	116	0	50	.716	11			-11	C/O23S	-0.3
1891	StL-a	62	182	44	42	4	3	0	20	43	39	.231	.389	.286	.674	85	2	-3	114	111	26	.800	13			-18	CO/S3	-1.6
Total	3	176	589	115	148	20	11	4	20	78	39	.251	.351	.343	.693	92	5	-8	113	37	82	.726	28			-29	C/O3S2	-2.0
■ **BOBBY MURCER**	Murcer, Bobby Ray b: 5/20/46, Oklahoma City, Okla BL/TR, 5'11", 160 lbs. Deb: 9/08/65																											
1965	NY-A	11	37	2	9	0	1	1	4	5	12	.243	.333	.378	.712	101	0	0	101	100	5	.679	0	0	0	1	S	0.1
1966	NY-A	21	69	3	12	1	1	0	5	4	5	.174	.219	.217	.437	28	-7	-6	94	140	3	.356	2	2	-1	-1	S	-0.6
1969	NY-A	152	564	82	146	24	4	26	82	50	103	.259	.323	.454	.776	121	9	12	95	104	82	.733	7	5	-1	-1	*O3	0.8
1970	NY-A	159	581	95	146	23	3	23	78	87	100	.251	.351	.420	.771	121	10	16	92	107	89	.770	15	10	-2	1	*O	0.9
1971	NY-A	146	529	94	175	25	6	25	94	91	60	.331	**.429**	.543	**.972**	**179**	**54**	**56**	97	112	**126**	**1.057**	14	8	-1	-7	*O	4.5
1972	NY-A	153	585	**102**	171	30	7	33	96	63	67	.292	.363	.537	.900	179	45	50	92	93	114	.909	11	9	-2	3	*O	5.1
1973	NY-A	160	616	83	187	29	2	22	95	50	67	.304	.359	.464	.823	129	23	23	101	112	100	.772	6	7	-2	-5	*O	1.1
1974	NY-A	156	606	69	166	25	4	10	88	57	59	.274	.338	.378	.716	110	5	8	96	128	79	.662	14	5	1	7	*O	1.2
1975	SF-N	147	526	80	157	29	4	11	91	91	45	.298	.404	.432	.835	130	26	25	102	143	97	.855	9	5	-0	-11	*O	0.9
1976	SF-N	147	533	73	138	20	2	23	90	84	78	.259	.364	.433	.797	122	19	17	103	122	86	.801	12	7	-1	-2	*O	0.9
1977	Chi-N	154	554	90	147	18	3	27	89	80	77	.265	.361	.455	.816	103	14	4	114	113	95	.836	16	7	1	-7	*O/2S	-0.6
1978	Chi-N	146	499	66	140	22	6	9	64	80	57	.281	.380	.403	.783	108	15	9	110	114	79	.785	14	5	1	-11	*O	-0.6
1979	Chi-N	58	190	22	49	4	1	7	22	36	20	.258	.379	.400	.779	100	5	1	112	92	31	.782	2	3	-1	2	O	0.1
	NY-A	74	264	42	72	12	0	8	33	25	32	.273	.340	.409	.749	106	0	2	96	98	35	.670	1	1	-0	-4	O	-0.4
1980	NY-A	100	297	41	80	9	1	13	57	34	28	.269	.348	.438	.786	115	6	6	99	132	45	.743	2	0	1	-10	OD	-0.3
1981	NY-A	50	117	14	31	6	0	6	24	12	15	.265	.333	.470	.803	129	4	4	100	129	18	.753	0	0	0	0	D	0.4
1982	NY-A	65	141	12	32	6	0	7	30	12	15	.227	.292	.418	.711	96	-2	-1	96	150	16	.649	2	1	0	0	D	0.0
1983	NY-A	9	22	2	4	2	0	1	1	1	1	.182	.217	.409	.626	69	-1	-1	99	33	1	.476	0	0	0	0	/D	0.0
Total	17	1908	6730	972	1862	285	45	252	1043	862	841	.277	.361	.445	.806	125	226	224	100	115	1103	.811	127	75	-7	-46	*OD/3S2	13.5
■ **SIMMY MURCH**	Murch, Simeon Augustus b: 11/21/1880, Castine, Me. d: 6/6/39, Exeter, N.H. TR, 6'4", 220 lbs. Deb: 9/20/04																											
1904	StL-N	13	51	3	7	1	0	0	1	1		.137	.154	.157	.311	-3	-6	-6	99	48	1	.205	0			0	/23S	-0.5
1905	StL-N	4	9	0	1	0	0	0	0	0		.111	.111	.111	.222	-36	-1	-1	91	0	0	.125	0			-0	/2S	-0.1
1908	Bro-N	6	11	1	2	1	0	0	0	1		.182	.250	.273	.523	72	-0	-0	95	0	1	.444	0			-0	/1	0.0
Total	3	23	71	4	10	2	0	0	1	2		.141	.164	.169	.333	4	-8	-8	97	34	2	.230	0			-1	/231S	-0.6
■ **WILBUR MURDOCH**	Murdoch, Wilbur Edwin b: 3/14/1875, Avon, N.Y. d: 10/29/41, Los Angeles, Cal. Deb: 8/29/08																											
1908	StL-N	27	62	5	16	3	0	0	5	3		.258	.292	.306	.599	100	-1	-0	94	101	6	.565	4			-1	O	-0.1
■ **TIM MURNANE**	Murnane, Timothy Hayes b: 6/4/1852, Naugatuck, Conn. d: 2/7/17, Boston, Mass. BL/TR, 5'9.5", 172 lbs. Deb: 4/26/1872 M																											
1872	Man-n	24	115	29	34							.296															1	
1873	Ath-n	42	201	54	43							.214															O/12	
1874	Ath-n	19	84	9	21							.250															O/21	
1875	Phi-n	69	316	71	90							.285															1O2	
1876	Bos-N	69	308	60	87	4	3	2	34	8	12	.282	.301	.334	.635	117	4	6	95	101	32	.502				-5	*1/O2	0.2
1877	Bos-N	35	140	23	39	7	1	1	15	6	7	.279	.308	.364	.673	102	2	0	108	96	16	.564				-3	O/1	-0.3
1878	Pro-N	49	188	35	45	6	1	0	14	8	12	.239	.270	.282	.552	84	-3	-3	98	91	15	.427				1	*1/O	0.0
1884	Bos-U	76	311	55	73	5	2	0		22		.235	.285	.264	.549	88	-3	-3	98	0	24	.437	0			-4	1OM	-0.6
Total	4 n	154	716	163	188							.263															1OM	
Total	4	229	947	173	244	22	7	3	63	44	31	.258	.291	.305	.596	99	-1	1	99	65	87	.474	0			-11	1O/2	-0.7
■ **CLARENCE MURPHY**	Murphy, Clarence Deb: 6/17/1886																											
1886	Lou-a	1	3	0	0	0	0	0		0		.000	.000	.000	.000	-93	-1	-1	108	0	0	.000	0			0	/O	0.0
■ **CONNIE MURPHY**	Murphy, Cornelius David "Stone Face" b: 11/1/1870, Northfield, Mass. d: 12/14/45, New Bedford, Mass. BL/TR, 5'8", 155 lbs. Deb: 9/17/1893																											
1893	Cin-N	6	17	3	3	1	0	0	2	1	2	.176	.222	.235	.458	22	-2	-2	101	137	1	.357	0			0	/C	-0.1
1894	Cin-N	1	4	0	0	0	0	0	0	1	1	.000	.200	.000	.200	-47	-1	-1	100	0	0	.250	0			0	/C	0.0
Total	2	7	21	3	3	1	0	0	2	2	3	.143	.217	.190	.408	8	-3	-3	101	107	1	.333	0			0	/C	-0.1
■ **DALE MURPHY**	Murphy, Dale Bryan b: 3/12/56, Portland, Ore. BR/TR, 6'4", 210 lbs. Deb: 9/13/76																											
1976	Atl-N	19	65	3	17	6	0	0	9	7	9	.262	.333	.354	.687	85	-0	-1	111	154	8	.625	0	0	0	0	C	0.0
1977	Atl-N	18	76	5	24	8	1	2	14	0	8	.316	.316	.526	.842	108	2	1	113	129	11	.714	0	1	-1	1	C	0.1
1978	Atl-N	151	530	66	120	14	3	23	79	42	145	.226	.287	.394	.681	79	-10	-17	112	115	56	.613	11	7	-1	5	*1C	-1.7
1979	Atl-N	104	384	53	106	7	2	21	57	38	67	.276	.344	.469	.813	110	10	5	109	98	60	.777	6	1	1	-3	1C	0.1
1980	Atl-N	156	569	98	160	27	2	33	89	59	133	.281	.350	.510	.859	136	26	26	101	96	101	.849	9	6	-1	-1	*O/1	1.9
1981	Atl-N	104	369	43	91	12	1	13	50	44	72	.247	.327	.390	.717	103	1	1	100	109	47	.689	14	5	1	-1	*O/1	-0.1
1982	Atl-N	162	598	113	168	23	2	36	**109**	93	134	.281	.380	.507	.887	136	38	32	107	110	118	.936	23	11	0	-2	*O	3.0
1983	Atl-N	162	589	131	178	24	4	36	**121**	90	110	.302	.396	**.540**	**.936**	149	**46**	42	106	119	**131**	**1.023**	30	4	7	-4	*O	4.3
1984	Atl-N	162	607	94	176	32	8	**36**	100	79	134	.290	.374	**.547**	.920	142	**44**	37	110	94	123	.958	19	7	2	-7	*O	2.6
1985	Atl-N	162	616	**118**	185	32	2	**37**	111	**90**	141	.300	.390	.539	.929	148	48	43	106	96	**131**	.967	10	3	1	-13	*O	2.8
1986	Atl-N	160	614	89	163	29	7	29	83	75	141	.265	.347	.477	.825	123	20	18	102	84	102	.806	7	7	-2	-11	*O	0.2
1987	Atl-N	159	566	115	167	27	1	44	105	115	136	.295	.420	.580	1.000	149	53	47	108	97	**143**	1.120	16	6	1	9	*O	4.9
1988	Atl-N	156	592	77	134	35	4	24	77	74	125	.226	.314	.421	.735	105	6	3	104	92	72	.674	3	5	-2	12	*O	1.0
Total	13	1675	6175	1005	1689	276	37	334	1004	806	1355	.274	.360	.492	.852	127	284	237	106	101	1103	.879	148	63	7	-13	*O1/C	19.1
■ **DANNY MURPHY**	Murphy, Daniel Francis b: 8/11/1876, Philadelphia, Pa. d: 11/22/55, Jersey City, N.J. BR/TR, 5'9", 175 lbs. Deb: 9/17/00 C																											
1900	NY-N	22	74	11	20	1	0	0	6	8		.270	.341	.284	.625	78	-2	-2	97	91	9	.611	4			0	2	-0.1
1901	NY-N	5	20	0	4	0	0	0	0	1		.200	.238	.200	.438	32	-2	-2	91	0	1	.313	0			-2	/2	-0.2
1902	Phi-A	76	291	48	91	11	8	1	48	13		.313	.342	.416	.758	102	4	0	108	130	47	.730	12			-17	2	-1.2
1903	Phi-A	133	513	66	140	31	11	1	60	13		.273	.291	.382	.673	99	0	-2	104	115	64	.606	17			-16	*2	-1.5
1904	Phi-A	150	557	78	160	30	17	7	77	22		.287	.314	.440	.754	137	22	21	102	114	86	.728	22			11	*2	3.6
1905	Phi-A	150	533	71	148	34	4	6	71	42		.278	.330	.390	.721	119	18	12	109	114	78	.709	23			-21	*2	-1.0
1906	Phi-A	119	448	48	135	24	7	2	60	21		.301	.333	.400	.732	140	14	17	94	125	67	.693	17			-12	*2	0.2
1907	Phi-A	124	469	51	127	23	3	2	57	30		.271	.315	.345	.660	106	6	3	106	129	56	.594	11			3	*2	0.5
1908	Phi-A	142	525	51	139	28	7	4	66	32		.265	.307	.368	.675	113	11	7	108	128	62	.624	16			6	O2/1	0.8
1909	Phi-A	149	541	61	152	28	14	5	69	35		.281	.332	.412	.744	132	19	18	102	118	78	.728	19			5	*O	2.0
1910	Phi-A	151	560	70	168	28	18	4	64	31		.300	.338	.436	.774	139	24	22	102	94	88	.750	18			-6	*O	1.0
1911	Phi-A	141	508	104	167	27	11	6	66	50		.329	.398	.461	.858	150	27	32	93	90	102	.921	22			-2	*O/2	1.9
1912	Phi-A	36	130	27	42	6	2	2	20	16		.323	.401	.446	.848	143	7	7	99	110	26	.943	8			-8	O	-0.2
1913	Phi-A	40	59	3	19	5	1	0	6	4	8	.322	.365	.441	.806	140	2	3	97	82	9	.750	0			-3	/O	0.0
1914	Bro-F	52	161	16	49	9	0	4	32	17	16	.304	.371	.435	.806	129	6	6	101	141	29	.813	4			-1	O	0.3
1915	Bro-F	5	6	0	1	0	0	0	0	0	0	.167	.167	.167	.333	-1	-1	-1	98	0	0	.200	0			0	/2O	0.0
Total	16	1495	5395	705	1562	285	103	44	702	335	24	.290	.333	.405	.738	124	156	143	102	114	801	.712	193			-61	2O/1	6.1
■ **DANNY MURPHY**	Murphy, Daniel Joseph "Handsome Dan" b: 9/10/1864, Brooklyn, N.Y. d: 12/14/15, Brooklyn, N.Y. Deb: 4/26/1892																											
1892	NY-N	8	26	2	3	0	0	0	0	5	4	.115	.258	.115	.373	16	-2	-2	98	0	1	.348	0			0	/C	-0.1
■ **DAVE MURPHY**	Murphy, David Francis "Dirty Dave" b: 5/4/1876, Adams, Mass. d: 4/8/40, Adams, Mass. TR, Deb: 8/28/05																											
1905	Bos-N	3	11	0	2	0	0	0	1	0		.182	.182	.182	.364	10	-1	-1	97	177	0	.222	0			0	/S3	0.0

YEAR	TM/L	G	AB	R	H	2B	3B	HR	RBI	BB	SO	AVG	OBP	SLG	PRO	/A	BR	/A	PF	CHI	RC	TA	SB	CS	SBR	FR	POS	TPR
■ DWAYNE MURPHY	Murphy, Dwayne Keith b: 3/18/55, Merced, Cal. BL/TR, 6'1", 185 lbs. Deb: 4/08/78																											
1978	Oak-A	60	52	15	10	2	0	0	5	7	14	.192	.288	.231	.519	47	-3	-4	101	165	4	.442	0	1	-1	-9	O/D	-1.4
1979	Oak-A	121	388	57	99	10	4	11	40	84	80	.255	.389	.387	.776	124	9	16	89	89	62	.806	15	11	-2	4	*O	1.2
1980	Oak-A	159	573	86	157	18	2	13	68	102	96	.274	.386	.380	.766	117	13	17	95	99	90	.786	26	15	-1	17	*O	2.9
1981	Oak-A	107	390	58	98	10	3	15	60	73	91	.251	.372	.408	.780	130	15	17	96	102	64	.808	10	4	1	7	*O/D	2.3
1982	Oak-A	151	543	84	129	15	1	27	94	94	122	.238	.353	.418	.771	116	10	14	95	117	88	.814	26	8	3	15	*O/SD	2.6
1983	Oak-A	130	471	55	107	17	2	17	75	62	105	.227	.317	.380	.697	95	-6	-3	96	135	55	.644	7	5	-1	3	*O/D	-0.1
1984	Oak-A	153	559	93	143	18	2	33	88	74	111	.256	.346	.472	.818	135	18	24	92	102	90	.791	4	5	-2	11	*O	2.9
1985	Oak-A	152	523	77	122	21	3	20	59	84	123	.233	.343	.400	.742	110	3	8	93	89	73	.714	4	5	-2	1	*O	0.5
1986	Oak-A	98	329	50	83	11	3	9	39	56	80	.252	.368	.386	.754	114	5	8	94	103	51	.757	3	1	0	7	O/D	1.2
1987	Oak-A	82	219	39	51	7	0	8	35	58	61	.233	.394	.374	.768	117	5	8	91	132	36	.814	4	4	-1	4	O/12	0.8
1988	Det-A	49	144	14	36	5	0	4	19	24	26	.250	.361	.368	.729	111	2	3	94	116	21	.725	1	1	-0	6	O/D	0.8
Total	11	1262	4191	628	1035	134	20	157	582	718	909	.247	.360	.401	.760	117	70	109	93	107	635	.783	100	60	-6	65	*O/D21S	13.7
■ ED MURPHY	Murphy, Edward Joseph b: 8/23/18, Joliet, Ill. BR/TR, 5'11", 190 lbs. Deb: 9/10/42																											
1942	Phi-N	13	28	2	7	2	0	0	4	2	4	.250	.300	.321	.621	87	-1	-1	94	165	3	.500	0			0	/1	0.0
■ TONY MURPHY	Murphy, Frank J. b: Brooklyn, N.Y. Deb: 10/15/1884																											
1884	NY-a	1	3	1	1	0	0	0		0		.333	.333	.333	.667	121	0	0	100	0	0	.500				0	/C	0.0
■ FRANK MURPHY	Murphy, Frank Morton b: 1880, Hackensack, N.J. d: 11/2/12, New York, N.Y. Deb: 7/02/01																											
1901	Bos-N	45	176	13	46	5	3	1	18	4		.261	.278	.341	.619	72	-5	-7	112	101	19	.538	6			5	O	-0.6
	NY-N	35	130	10	21	3	0	0	8	6		.162	.199	.185	.383	14	-14	-13	91	114	5	.284	1			0	2O	-1.2
	Yr	80	306	23	67	8	3	1	26	10		.219	.244	.275	.518	50	-19	-20	103	108	23	.423	7			5		-1.8
Total	1	80	306	23	67	8	3	1	26	10		.219	.244	.275	.518	50	-19	-20	103	107	24	.423	7			5	/O2	-1.8
■ DUMMY MURPHY	Murphy, Herbert Courtland b: 12/18/1886, Olney, Ill. d: 8/10/62, Tallahassee, Fla. BR/TR, 5'10", 165 lbs. Deb: 4/14/14																											
1914	Phi-N	9	26	1	4	1	0	0	3	0	4	.154	.185	.192	.377	12	-3	-3	100	218	1	.273	0			-1	/S	-0.3
■ HOWARD MURPHY	Murphy, Howard b: 1/1/1882, Birmingham, Ala. d: 10/5/26, Fort Worth, Tex. 5'8.5", 150 lbs. Deb: 09																											
1909	StL-N	25	60	3	12	0	0	0	3	4		.200	.250	.200	.450	42	-4	-4	96	91	3	.354	1			-0	O	-0.5
■ JERRY MURPHY	Murphy, Jeremiah Francis b: 1871, Pawtucket, R.I. d: 6/1/14, Baker, Oregon Deb: 03																											
1903	Det-A	5	22	1	4	1	0	0	1	0		.182	.182	.227	.409	24	-2	-2	97	62	1	.278	0			-0	/S	-0.1
■ EDDIE MURPHY	Murphy, John Edward b: 10/2/1891, Hancock, N.Y. d: 2/21/69, Dunmore, Pa. BL/TR, 5'9", 155 lbs. Deb: 8/26/12																											
1912	Phi-A	33	142	24	45	4	1	0	6	11		.317	.370	.359	.729	109	2	2	99	34	21	.722	7			-2	O	-0.1
1913	Phi-A	137	508	105	150	14	7	1	30	70	44	.295	.391	.356	.747	123	16	18	97	56	76	.788	21			-19	*O	-0.9
1914	Phi-A	148	573	101	156	12	9	3	43	87	46	.272	.379	.340	.720	120	16	18	97	68	77	.735	36	32	-8	-13	*O	-1.3
1915	Phi-A	68	260	37	60	3	4	0	17	29	15	.231	.315	.273	.588	79	-7	-6	96	78	25	.571	13	3	2	-11	O/3	-1.8
	Chi-A	70	273	51	86	11	5	0	26	39	12	.315	.410	.392	.802	143	15	16	98	71	47	.859	20	12	-1	-4	O	0.7
	Yr	138	533	88	146	14	9	0	43	68	27	.274	.365	.334	.698	113	8	10	97	75	71	.714	33	15	1	-16		-1.1
1916	Chi-A	51	105	14	22	5	1	0	4	9	5	.210	.284	.276	.561	63	-4	-5	108	49	9	.518	3			-4	O/3	-1.1
1917	Chi-A	53	51	9	16	2	1	0	16	5	1	.314	.386	.392	.778	141	2	3	98	287	9	.857	4			-4	/O	-0.2
1918	Chi-A	91	286	36	85	9	3	0	23	22	18	.297	.350	.350	.699	110	4	3	101	84	37	.642	6			-9	O/2	-0.8
1919	Chi-A	30	35	8	17	4	0	0	5	7	0	.486	.571	.600	1.171	218	7	6	105	86	12	1.556	0			-0	/O	0.6
1920	Chi-A	58	118	22	40	2	1	0	19	12	4	.339	.405	.373	.777	111	2	3	96	152	18	.716	1	3	-2	0	O/3	0.0
1921	Chi-A	6	5	1	1	0	0	0	0	0	0	.200	.200	.200	.400	2	-1	-1	99	0	0	.250	0	0	0	0	H	0.0
1926	Pit-N	16	17	3	2	0	0	0	6	3	0	.118	.250	.118	.368	1	-2	-3	112	0	1	.333	0			-0	/O	-0.2
Total	11	761	2373	411	680	66	32	4	195	294	145	.287	.374	.346	.720	115	49	54	98	74	331	.725	111	50		-66	O/32	-5.1
■ JOHN MURPHY	Murphy, John P. "Soldier Boy" b: 1879, New Haven, Conn. d: 6/1/14, Baker, Ore. Deb: 9/10/02																											
1902	StL-N	1	3	1	2	1	0	0	1	1		.667	.750	1.000	1.750	467	1	1	95	122	2	4.000	0			0	/3	0.1
■ LARRY MURPHY	Murphy, Lawrence Patrick BL , Deb: 5/30/1891																											
1891	Was-a	101	400	73	106	15	3	1	35	63	27	.265	.372	.325	.697	108	4	7	95	66	61	.772	29			-4	*O	0.0
■ LEO MURPHY	Murphy, Leo Joseph "Red" b: 1/7/1889, Terre Haute, Ind. d: 8/12/60, Racine, Wis. BR/TR, 6'1", 179 lbs. Deb: 5/02/15																											
1915	Pit-N	31	41	4	4	0	0	0	4	4	12	.098	.178	.098	.275	-16	-6	-6	99	382	1	.216	0			0	C	-0.4
■ MIKE MURPHY	Murphy, Michael Jerome b: 8/19/1888, Forestville, Pa. d: 10/26/52, Johnson City, N.Y. BR/TR, 5'9", 170 lbs. Deb: 5/17/12																											
1912	StL-N	1	1	0	0	0	0	0	0	0	0	.000	.000	.000	.000	-99	-0	-0	100	0	0	.000	0			0	/C	0.0
1916	Phi-A	14	27	0	3	0	0	0	1	1	3	.111	.143	.111	.254	-24	-4	-4	98	119	1	.167	0			1	C	-0.1
Total	2	15	28	0	3	0	0	0	1	1	3	.107	.138	.107	.245	-27	-4	-4	98	115	1	.160	0			1	/C	-0.1
■ MORGAN MURPHY	Murphy, Morgan Edward b: 2/14/1867, E.Providence, R.I. d: 10/3/38, Providence, R.I. BR/TR, 5'8", 160 lbs. Deb: 4/22/1890																											
1890	Bos-P	68	246	38	56	10	2	2	32	24	31	.228	.301	.309	.610	61	-12	-15	107	107	28	.621	16			-6	C/SO3	-1.4
1891	Bos-a	106	402	60	87	11	4	4	54	36	58	.216	.289	.294	.582	70	-16	-15	99	123	40	.559	17			11	*C/O	0.0
1892	Cin-N	74	234	29	46	8	2	2	24	25	57	.197	.277	.274	.550	66	-9	-10	103	105	19	.500	4			-5	C	-0.9
1893	Cin-N	57	200	25	47	5	1	1	19	14	35	.235	.295	.285	.580	55	-13	-13	101	87	18	.490	1			-12	C/1	-1.6
1894	Cin-N	75	255	42	70	9	0	1	37	26	34	.275	.344	.322	.666	63	-15	-15	100	120	31	.622	6			-7	C/S3	-1.1
1895	Cin-N	25	82	15	22	2	0	0	16	11	8	.268	.355	.293	.648	65	-3	-4	108	186	11	.683	6			0	C	-0.3
1896	StL-N	49	175	12	45	5	2	0	11	8	14	.257	.290	.309	.598	62	-10	-9	95	60	16	.485	1			4	C	0.0
1897	StL-N	62	207	13	35	2	0	0	12	6		.169	.196	.179	.375	1	-29	-27	93	95	8	.262	1			2	C/1	-1.5
1898	Pit-N	5	16	0	2	0	0	0	2	1		.125	.176	.125	.301	-12	-2	-2	98	302	0	.214	0			0	/C	-0.1
	Phi-N	25	86	6	17	3	0	0	11	6		.198	.258	.233	.491	45	-6	-5	95	166	5	.391	0			0	C	-0.4
	Yr	30	102	6	19	3	0	0	13	7		.186	.245	.216	.461	36	-8	-8	95	199	6	.361	0			0		-0.5
1900	Phi-N	11	36	2	10	0	1	0	3	0		.278	.278	.333	.611	72	-2	-1	98	78	3	.462	0			0	C	0.0
1901	Phi-A	9	28	5	6	1	0	0	6	0		.214	.214	.250	.464	30	-3	-3	100	271	2	.364	1			0	/C1	-0.1
Total	11	566	1967	247	443	56	12	10	227	157	237	.225	.287	.281	.568	56	-120	-120	100	114	182	.510	53			-14	C/1OS3	-7.4
■ PAT MURPHY	Murphy, Patrick J. b: 1/2/1857, Auburn, Mass. d: 5/16/27, Worcester, Mass. 5'10", 160 lbs. Deb: 9/02/1887																											
1887	NY-N	17	56	4	12	2	0	0	4	2	4	.214	.241	.250	.491	35	-5	-5	107	88	4	.386	1			0	C	-0.3
1888	NY-N	28	106	11	18	1	0	0	4	6	11	.170	.214	.179	.394	30	-8	-7	93	80	5	.318	3			0	C	-0.6
1889	NY-N	9	28	5	10	1	1	1	4	2	0	.357	.400	.571	.971	164	2	2	105	63	7	1.000	0			0	/C	0.2
1890	NY-N	32	119	14	28	5	1	0	9	14	13	.235	.321	.294	.615	86	-2	-1	95	79	12	.582	3			0	C/OS	0.0
Total	4	86	309	34	68	9	2	1	21	24	28	.220	.278	.272	.550	67	-13	-12	97	79	28	.481	7			0	/COS	-0.7
■ DICK MURPHY	Murphy, Richard Lee b: 10/25/31, Cincinnati, Ohio BL/TL, 5'11", 170 lbs. Deb: 6/13/54																											
1954	Cin-N	6	1	1	0	0	0	0	0	0	1	.000	.000	.000	.000	-96	-0	-0	104	0	0	.000	0	0	0	0	H	0.0
■ BUZZ MURPHY	Murphy, Robert R. b: 4/26/1895, Denver, Colo. d: 5/11/38, Denver, Colo. BL/TL, 5'8.5", 155 lbs. Deb: 7/14/18																											
1918	Bos-N	9	32	6	12	2	3	1	9	3	5	.375	.429	.719	1.147	264	5	6	94	133	10	1.300	0			-2	/O	0.3
1919	Was-A	79	252	19	66	7	4	0	28	19	32	.262	.326	.321	.648	84	-6	-5	98	125	28	.591	5			5	O	-0.4
Total	2	88	284	25	78	9	7	1	37	22	37	.275	.338	.366	.704	102	-0	0	98	126	38	.660	5			3	/O	-0.1
■ BILLY MURPHY	Murphy, William Eugene b: 5/7/44, Pineville, La. BR/TR, 6'1", 190 lbs. Deb: 4/15/66																											
1966	NY-N	84	135	15	31	4	1	3	13	7	34	.230	.273	.341	.613	74	-6	-5	94	99	12	.505	1	2	-1	-7	O	-1.4
■ YALE MURPHY	Murphy, William Henry "Tot" or "Midget" b: 11/11/1869, Southville, Mass. d: 2/14/06, Southville, Mass. BL/TR, 5'3", 125 lbs. Deb: 4/19/1894																											
1894	NY-N	74	280	64	76	6	2	0	28	51	23	.271	.384	.307	.691	70	-11	-11	100	86	45	.809	28			-11	SO/321	-1.4
1895	NY-N	51	184	35	37	6	2	0	16	27	13	.201	.303	.255	.559	49	-14	-12	95	97	17	.551	7			-1	O/S32	-1.2
1897	NY-N	5	8	1	0	0	0	0	0	1	2	.000	.200	.000	.200	-44	-2	-2	98	0	0	.250	0			0	/S2	0.0

YEAR	TM/L	G	AB	R	H	2B	3B	HR	RBI	BB	SO	AVG	OBP	SLG	PRO	/A	BR	/A	PF	CHI	RC	TA	SB	CS	SBR	FR	POS	TPR
Total	3	130	472	100	113	12	4	0	45	80	36	.239	.350	.282	.631	61	-27	-25	98	89	62	.691	35			-12	/SO321	-2.6
■ **WILLIE MURPHY**	Murphy, William N. "Gentle Willie" b: 1865, Boston, Mass. 5'11", 198 lbs. Deb: 5/01/1884																											
1884	Cle-N	42	168	18	38	3	3	1	9	1	23	.226	.231	.298	.528	63	-7	-7	102	62	12	.392				2	O	-0.4
	Was-a	5	21	3	10	0	0	0		1		.476	.542	.476	1.018	271	3	4	88	0	6	1.182				0	/O	0.3
	Bos-U	1	3	0	0	0	0	0		1		.000	.250	.000	.250	-9	-0	-0	98	0	0	.333	0			0	/CO	0.0
Total	1	48	192	21	48	3	3	1	9	3	23	.250	.269	.313	.582	83	-4	-4	100	53	17	.451	0			2	/OC	-0.1
■ **TONY MURRAY**	Murray, Anthony Joseph b: 4/30/04, Chicago, Ill. d: 3/19/74, Chicago, Ill. BR/TR, 5'10.5", 154 lbs. Deb: 10/06/23																											
1923	Chi-N	2	4	0	1	0	0	0	0	0	0	.250	.400	.250	.650	72	-0	-0	104	0	0	.667	0	0	0	-1	/O	0.0
■ **EDDIE MURRAY**	Murray, Eddie Clarence b: 2/24/56, Los Angeles, Cal. BB/TR, 6'2", 190 lbs. Deb: 4/07/77																											
1977	Bal-A	160	611	81	173	29	2	27	88	48	104	.283	.336	.470	.806	126	13	18	93	100	90	.729	0	1	-1	-2	*D1/O	1.3
1978	Bal-A	161	610	85	174	32	3	27	95	70	97	.285	.360	.480	.840	148	27	34	91	106	104	.811	6	5	-1	1	*1/3D	2.8
1979	Bal-A	159	606	90	179	30	2	25	99	72	78	.295	.372	.475	.847	130	23	25	97	111	107	.836	10	2	2	-2	*1	1.6
1980	Bal-A	158	621	100	186	36	2	32	116	54	71	.300	.357	.519	.876	136	30	29	101	115	111	.846	7	2	1	-8	*1/D	1.2
1981	Bal-A	99	378	57	111	21	2	**22**	**78**	40	43	.294	.363	.534	.897	157	26	26	99	121	70	.875	2	3	-1	9	1	3.2
1982	Bal-A	151	550	87	174	30	1	32	110	70	82	.316	.395	.549	.944	156	42	43	100	113	116	.962	7	2	1	1	*1/D	4.0
1983	Bal-A	156	582	115	178	30	3	33	111	86	90	.306	.398	.538	.936	154	45	45	100	112	**133**	1.002	5	1	1	2	*1/D	4.0
1984	Bal-A	162	588	97	180	26	3	29	110	**107**	87	.306	**.415**	.509	.923	**163**	**47**	**51**	94	120	130	.998	10	2	2	7	*1/D	5.0
1985	Bal-A	156	583	111	173	37	1	31	124	84	68	.297	.387	.523	.910	148	38	39	99	131	122	.943	5	2	0	12	*1/D	4.1
1986	Bal-A	137	495	61	151	25	1	17	84	78	49	.305	.400	.463	.862	137	27	27	99	127	92	.859	3	0	1	-2	*1D	1.8
1987	Bal-A	160	618	89	171	28	3	30	91	73	80	.277	.353	.477	.830	121	17	18	98	100	103	.795	1	2	-1	10	*1/D	1.1
1988	Bal-A	161	603	75	171	27	2	28	84	75	78	.284	.363	.474	.837	139	26	30	95	96	101	.806	5	2	0	12	*1D	3.6
Total	12	1820	6845	1048	2021	351	25	333	1190	857	927	.295	.375	.500	.875	142	361	388	97	112	1279	.894	61	24	4	40	*1D/3O	33.7
■ **ED MURRAY**	Murray, Edward Francis b: 5/8/1895, Mystic, Conn. d: 11/8/70, Cheyenne, Wyoming BR/TR, 5'6", 145 lbs. Deb: 6/24/17																											
1917	StL-A	1	1	0	0	0	0	0	0	0	1	.000	.000	.000	.000	-99	-0	-0	95	0	0	.000	0			0	/S	0.0
■ **JIM MURRAY**	Murray, James Oscar b: 1/16/1878, Galveston, Tex. d: 4/25/45, Galveston, Tex. BR/TL, 5'10", 180 lbs. Deb: 9/02/02																											
1902	Chi-N	12	47	3	8	0	0	0	1	2		.170	.204	.170	.374	18	-4	-4	96	46	2	.256	0			1	O	-0.3
1911	StL-A	31	102	8	19	5	0	3	11	5		.186	.224	.324	.548	55	-7	-7	95	88	7	.458	0			-2	O	-0.9
1914	Bos-N	39	112	10	26	4	2	0	12	6	24	.232	.277	.304	.581	70	-4	-5	104	128	10	.500	2			-8	O	-1.4
Total	3	82	261	21	53	9	2	3	24	13	24	.203	.244	.287	.531	55	-16	-15	99	98	18	.438	2			-9	/O	-2.6
■ **MIAH MURRAY**	Murray, Jeremiah J. b: 1/1/1865, Boston, Mass. d: 1/11/22, Boston, Mass. BR/TR, 5'11.5", 170 lbs. Deb: 5/17/1884																											
1884	Pro-N	8	27	1	5	0	0	0	1	1	8	.185	.214	.185	.399	26	-2	-2	102	69	1	.273				0	/CO1	-0.1
1885	Lou-a	12	43	4	8	0	0	0		2		.186	.239	.186	.425	37	-3	-3	102	0	2	.314				0	C/1	-0.2
1888	Was-N	12	42	1	4	1	0	0	3	1	7	.095	.116	.119	.235	-25	-6	-5	96	219	1	.158	0			0	C/1	-0.4
1891	Was-a	2	8	0	0	0	0	0	0	0	1	.000	.000	.000	.000	-99	-2	-2	95	0	0	.000	0			0	/C	-0.1
Total	4	34	120	6	17	1	0	0	4	4	16	.142	.176	.150	.326	4	-13	-13	100	91	4	.223	0			0	/C1O	-0.8
■ **RED MURRAY**	Murray, John Joseph b: 3/4/1884, Arnot, Pa. d: 12/4/58, Sayre, Pa. BR/TR, 5'10.5", 190 lbs. Deb: 6/16/06																											
1906	StL-N	46	144	18	37	9	7	1	16	9		.257	.301	.438	.738	131	4	4	101	88	21	.720	5			2	O/C	0.6
1907	StL-N	132	485	46	127	10	10	7	46	24		.262	.297	.367	.664	115	3	5	96	93	61	.628	23			10	*O	1.2
1908	StL-N	154	593	64	167	19	15	7	62	37		.282	.324	.400	.723	142	20	24	94	81	89	.756	48			20	*O	4.7
1909	NY-N	149	570	74	150	15	12	**7**	91	45		.263	.319	.368	.688	110	8	5	105	**152**	80	.726	48			2	*O	0.1
1910	NY-N	149	553	78	153	27	8	4	87	52	51	.277	.345	.376	.721	116	7	10	95	146	91	.808	57			2	*O	0.7
1911	NY-N	140	488	70	142	27	15	3	78	43	37	.291	.354	.426	.781	115	10	9	102	124	89	.879	48			-11	*O	-0.5
1912	NY-N	143	549	83	152	26	20	3	92	27	45	.277	.320	.413	.734	96	-3	-6	104	**139**	83	.756	38			-2	*O	-1.1
1913	NY-N	147	520	70	139	21	3	2	59	34	28	.267	.320	.331	.650	83	-10	-11	103	123	63	.648	35			5	*O	-0.8
1914	NY-N	86	139	19	31	6	3	0	23	9	7	.223	.270	.309	.580	76	-5	-4	96	194	14	.583	11			-10	O	-1.6
1915	NY-N	45	127	12	28	1	2	3	11	7	15	.220	.261	.331	.592	86	-4	-3	91	82	10	.500	2	3	-1	1	O	-0.4
	Chi-N	51	144	20	43	6	1	0	11	8	8	.299	.340	.354	.694	108	2	1	102	82	18	.623	6	5	-1	1	O/2	0.0
	Yr	96	271	32	71	7	3	3	22	15	23	.262	.303	.343	.646	98	-2	-1	97	83	28	.563	8	8	-2	2		-0.4
1917	NY-N	22	22	1	1	1	0	0	3	4	3	.045	.192	.091	.283	-12	-3	-3	97	579	0	.286	0			-3	O/C	-0.6
Total	11	1264	4334	555	1170	168	96	37	579	299	194	.270	.321	.379	.700	109	30	31	99	124	621	.722	321	8		16	*O/C2	2.3
■ **LARRY MURRAY**	Murray, Larry b: 4/1/53, Chicago, Ill. BB/TR, 5'11", 179 lbs. Deb: 9/07/74																											
1974	NY-A	6	1	1	0	0	0	0	0	0	0	.000	.000	.000	.000	-99	-0	-0	96	0	0	.000	0	1	-1	-1	/O	-0.1
1975	NY-A	6	1	1	0	0	0	0	0	0	0	.000	.000	.000	.000	-99	-0	-0	99	0	0	.000	0	0	0	-2	/O	-0.1
1976	NY-A	8	10	2	1	0	0	0	2	1	2	.100	.182	.100	.282	-16	-1	-1	99	769	0	.444	2	0	1	-1	/O	-0.1
1977	Oak-A	90	162	19	29	5	2	1	9	17	36	.179	.257	.253	.510	42	-13	-12	95	81	12	.511	12	3	2	-8	O/SD	-2.1
1978	Oak-A	11	12	1	1	0	0	0	0	3	2	.083	.267	.083	.350	3	-1	-1	101	0	0	.364	0	0	0	-1	/O	-0.2
1979	Oak-A	105	226	25	42	11	2	2	20	28	34	.186	.276	.279	.554	56	-16	-12	89	111	18	.505	6	6	-2	-2	O/2	-1.8
Total	6	226	412	49	73	16	4	3	31	49	74	.177	.265	.257	.522	46	-33	-28	92	111	31	.499	20	10	0	-15	O/2DS	-4.4
■ **RAY MURRAY**	Murray, Raymond Lee "Deacon" b: 10/12/17, Spring Hope, N.C. BR/TR, 6'3", 204 lbs. Deb: 4/25/48																											
1948	Cle-A	4	4	0	0	0	0	0	0	0	3	.000	.000	.000	.000	-99	-1	-1	99	0	0	.000	0	0	0	0	H	0.0
1950	Cle-A	55	139	16	38	8	2	1	13	12	13	.273	.331	.381	.712	84	-4	-4	98	80	16	.600	1	0	0	2	C	0.0
1951	Cle-A	1	1	0	1	0	0	0	1	0	0	1.000	1.000	1.000	2.000	467	0	0	95	357	1	—	0	0	0	0	/C	0.1
	Phi-A	40	122	10	26	6	0	0	13	14	8	.213	.294	.262	.556	48	-8	-9	106	145	10	.455	0	0	0	3	C	-0.3
	Yr	41	123	10	27	6	0	0	14	14	8	.220	.299	.268	.568	51	-8	-9	106	159	10	.465	0	0	0	3		-0.2
1952	Phi-A	44	136	14	28	5	0	1	10	9	13	.206	.255	.265	.520	40	-10	-12	111	96	9	.405	0	0	0	4	C	-0.5
1953	Phi-A	84	268	25	76	14	3	6	41	18	25	.284	.331	.425	.756	101	0	-1	102	115	38	.672	0	0	0	14	C	1.6
1954	Bal-A	22	61	4	15	4	1	0	2	2	5	.246	.270	.344	.614	71	-3	-3	95	36	6	.489	0	0	0	0	C	0.0
Total	6	250	731	69	184	37	6	8	80	55	67	.252	.305	.352	.657	74	-26	-29	103	103	79	.573	1	0	0	23	C	0.9
■ **RICH MURRAY**	Murray, Richard Dale b: 7/6/57, Los Angeles, Cal. BR/TR, 6'4", 195 lbs. Deb: 6/07/80																											
1980	SF-N	53	194	19	42	8	2	4	24	11	48	.216	.259	.340	.599	69	-9	-8	96	124	15	.491	2	1	0	-2	1	-1.3
1983	SF-N	4	10	0	2	0	0	0	1	0	3	.200	.200	.200	.400	11	-1	-1	101	198	0	.222	0	0	0	0	/1	0.0
Total	2	57	204	19	44	8	2	4	25	11	51	.216	.256	.333	.589	66	-11	-10	96	128	15	.500	2	1	0	-2	/1	-1.3
■ **BOBBY MURRAY**	Murray, Robert Hayes b: 7/4/1894, St.Albans, Vt. d: 1/4/79, Nashua, N.H. TR , 5'7", 155 lbs. Deb: 9/24/23																											
1923	Was-A	10	37	2	7	1	0	0	2	1	4	.189	.211	.216	.427	13	-5	-4	95	87	2	.333	1	0	0	0	3	-0.2
■ **TOM MURRAY**	Murray, Thomas W. b: 1866, Savannah, Ga. Deb: 6/20/1894																											
1894	Phi-N	1	2	0	0	0	0	0	0	0	2	.000	.000	.000	.000	-99	-1	-1	95	0	0	.000	0			0	/S	0.0
■ **BILL MURRAY**	Murray, William Allenwood "Dasher" b: 9/6/1893, Vinalhaven, Me. d: 9/14/43, Boston, Mass. BB/TR, 5'11", 165 lbs. Deb: 6/27/17																											
1917	Was-A	8	21	2	3	0	1	0	4	2	2	.143	.217	.238	.455	42	-2	-1	92	287	1	.444	1			-0	/2S	-0.1
■ **IVAN MURRELL**	Murrell, Ivan Augustus (Peters) b: 4/24/45, Almirante, Panama BR/TR, 6'2", 195 lbs. Deb: 9/28/63																											
1963	Hou-N	2	5	1	1	0	0	0	0	0	2	.200	.200	.200	.400	17	-1	-0	92	0	0	.250	0	0	0	-0	/O	0.0
1964	Hou-N	10	14	1	2	1	0	0	1	0	6	.143	.143	.214	.357	-1	-2	-2	96	137	0	.250	0	0	0	-1	/O	-0.3
1967	Hou-N	10	29	2	9	0	0	0	1	1	9	.310	.333	.310	.644	91	-1	-0	94	46	3	.550	1	0	0	-0	/O	0.0
1968	Hou-N	32	59	3	6	1	1	0	3	1	17	.102	.117	.153	.269	-20	-9	-8	99	140	1	.182	0	0	0	2	O	-0.8
1969	SD-N	111	247	19	63	10	6	3	25	11	65	.255	.292	.381	.673	90	-5	-4	97	97	26	.573	3	4	-2	0	O/1	-0.9
1970	SD-N	125	347	43	85	9	3	12	35	17	93	.245	.288	.392	.680	84	-11	-9	95	79	36	.601	9	7	-2	1	*O/1	-1.3
1971	SD-N	103	255	23	60	6	3	7	24	7	60	.235	.264	.365	.629	79	-9	-8	96	86	22	.527	5	2	0	-2	O	-1.2
1972	SD-N	5	7	0	1	0	0	0	1	0	3	.143	.143	.143	.286	-21	-1	-1	88	411	0	.167	0	0	0	0	/O	0.0

YEAR	TM/L	G	AB	R	H	2B	3B	HR	RBI	BB	SO	AVG	OBP	SLG	PRO	/A	BR	/A	PF	CHI	RC	TA	SB	CS	SBR	FR	POS	TPR
1973	SD-N	93	210	23	48	13	1	9	21	2	52	.229	.236	.429	.664	85	-7	-5	94	72	20	.566	2	0	1	-0	O1	-0.7
1974	Atl-N	73	133	11	33	1	1	2	12	5	35	.248	.275	.316	.591	62	-7	-7	105	96	11	.461	0	0	0	-1	O1	-0.9
Total	10	564	1306	126	308	41	15	33	123	44	342	.236	.266	.366	.632	76	-51	-45	97	88	120	.544	20	13	-2	-1	O/1	-6.1
■ **DANNY MURTAUGH** Murtaugh, Daniel Edward b: 10/8/17, Chester, Pa. d: 12/2/76, Chester, Pa. BR/TR, 5'9", 165 lbs. Deb: 7/06/41 MC																												
1941	Phi-N	85	347	34	76	8	1	0	11	26	31	.219	.275	.248	.523	49	-24	-22	97	41	25	.478	**18**			5	2/S	-1.1
1942	Phi-N	144	506	48	122	16	4	0	27	49	39	.241	.311	.289	.599	80	-15	-11	94	73	47	.529	13			14	S32	1.0
1943	Phi-N	113	451	65	123	17	4	1	35	57	23	.273	.357	.335	.692	107	2	5	94	71	57	.635	4			-3	*2	0.5
1946	Phi-N	6	19	1	4	1	0	1	3	2	2	.211	.286	.421	.707	105	-0	-0	95	102	2	.667	0			-0	/2	0.0
1947	Bos-N	3	8	0	1	0	0	0	0	1	2	.125	.222	.125	.347	-6	-1	-1	97	0	0	.286	0			0	/23	0.0
1948	Pit-N	146	514	56	149	21	5	1	71	60	40	.290	.365	.356	.721	92	-1	-4	104	**146**	70	.681	10			6	*2	1.2
1949	Pit-N	75	236	16	48	7	2	2	24	29	17	.203	.291	.275	.566	52	-16	-16	101	127	21	.505	2			-2	2	-1.4
1950	Pit-N	118	367	34	108	20	5	2	37	47	42	.294	.376	.392	.768	100	3	1	103	95	56	.727	2			1	*2	0.5
1951	Pit-N	77	151	9	30	7	0	1	11	16	19	.199	.284	.265	.549	46	-11	-12	107	99	11	.457	0	0	0	1	2/3	-0.8
Total	9	767	2599	263	661	97	21	8	219	287	215	.254	.331	.317	.648	81	-63	-60	99	92	290	.601	49	0		21	2/S3	-0.1
■ **TONY MUSER** Muser, Anthony Joseph b: 8/1/47, Van Nuys, Cal. BL/TL, 6'2", 180 lbs. Deb: 9/14/69 C																												
1969	Bos-A	2	9	0	1	0	0	0	1	1	1	.111	.200	.111	.311	-11	-1	-1	105	346	0	.250	0	0	0	0	/1	-0.1
1971	Chi-A	11	16	2	5	0	1	0	0	1	1	.313	.353	.438	.790	126	0	0	98	0	2	.615	0	0	0	0	/1	0.0
1972	Chi-A	44	61	6	17	2	2	1	9	2	6	.279	.302	.426	.728	108	1	0	106	130	7	.630	1	1	-0	-1	1/O	-0.3
1973	Chi-A	109	309	38	88	14	3	4	30	33	36	.285	.354	.388	.742	106	4	3	102	89	43	.694	8	4	0	-1	1D/O	-0.2
1974	Chi-A	103	206	16	60	5	1	1	18	6	22	.291	.315	.340	.654	87	-3	-4	102	97	20	.500	1	4	-2	-4	1D	-1.3
1975	Chi-A	43	111	11	27	3	0	0	6	7	8	.243	.288	.270	.558	57	-6	-6	103	77	8	.429	2	1	0	-0	1	-0.9
	Bal-A	80	82	11	26	3	0	0	11	8	9	.317	.378	.354	.731	119	1	2	91	146	11	.627	0	0	0	1	1	0.0
	Yr	123	193	22	53	6	0	0	17	15	17	.275	.327	.306	.633	84	-5	-4	95	122	20	.528	2	1	0	0		-0.9
1976	Bal-A	136	326	25	74	7	1	1	30	21	34	.227	.274	.264	.538	59	-17	-16	98	129	23	.412	1	1	-0	-1	*1OD	-2.4
1977	Bal-A	120	118	14	27	6	0	0	7	13	16	.229	.305	.280	.585	65	-6	-5	93	84	9	.485	1	2	-1	-2	1O/D	-1.2
1978	Mil-A	15	30	0	4	1	1	0	5	3	5	.133	.212	.233	.445	24	-3	-3	106	282	1	.370	0	0	0	0	1	-0.3
Total	9	663	1268	123	329	41	9	7	117	95	138	.259	.312	.323	.634	81	-31	-30	100	110	124	.545	14	13	-4	-9	1/DO	-6.7
■ **STAN MUSIAL** Musial, Stanley Frank "Stan The Man" b: 11/21/20, Donora, Pa. BL/TL, 6', 175 lbs. Deb: 9/17/41 H																												
1941	StL-N	12	47	8	20	4	0	1	7	2	1	.426	.449	.574	1.023	170	5	5	110	86	12	1.111	1			-0	O	0.4
1942	StL-N	140	467	87	147	32	10	10	72	62	25	.315	.397	.490	.888	147	35	30	108	103	96	.926	6			-10	*O	1.8
1943	StL-N	157	617	108	**220**	**48**	**20**	13	81	72	18	**.357**	**.425**	**.562**	**.988**	**176**	**65**	**62**	105	73	**147**	**1.039**	9			-4	*O	**5.5**
1944	StL-N	146	568	112	**197**	**51**	14	12	94	90	28	.347	**.440**	**.549**	**.990**	**176**	**61**	**60**	101	93	**145**	**1.095**	7			-5	*O	**4.4**
1946	StL-N	156	624	**124**	**228**	**50**	**20**	16	103	73	31	**.365**	.434	**.587**	**1.021**	**177**	**71**	**66**	107	89	**164**	**1.114**	7			0	*1O	**5.8**
1947	StL-N	149	587	113	183	30	13	19	95	80	24	.312	.398	.504	.902	130	33	28	106	96	118	.910	4			-6	*1	1.2
1948	StL-N	155	611	**135**	**230**	**46**	**18**	39	**131**	79	34	**.376**	**.450**	**.702**	**1.152**	**207**	**90**	**90**	101	86	**191**	**1.298**	7			5	*O/1	**8.1**
1949	StL-N	157	612	128	**207**	**41**	**13**	36	123	107	38	.338	**.438**	.624	1.062	165	**72**	63	110	84	**173**	1.185	3			-3	*O/1	5.0
1950	StL-N	146	555	105	192	41	7	28	109	87	36	**.346**	.437	**.596**	**1.034**	164	**57**	**55**	103	97	**149**	**1.139**	5			-9	O1	3.9
1951	StL-N	152	578	**124**	205	30	**12**	32	108	98	40	**.355**	.449	.614	1.063	**182**	70	**69**	101	89	**169**	1.193	4	5	-2	8	O1	7.0
1952	StL-N	154	578	**105**	**194**	**42**	6	21	91	96	29	**.336**	.432	**.538**	**.970**	**171**	**56**	**57**	98	91	**141**	**1.035**	7	7	-2	-7	*O1/P	4.5
1953	StL-N	157	593	127	200	**53**	9	30	113	**105**	32	.337	**.437**	.609	1.046	167	**63**	**61**	102	94	**166**	**1.152**	3	4	-2	-2	*O	4.8
1954	StL-N	153	591	**120**	195	**41**	9	35	126	103	39	.330	.433	.607	1.040	167	61	60	100	103	153	1.104	1	7	-4	-1	*O1	4.8
1955	StL-N	154	562	97	179	30	5	33	108	80	39	.319	.411	.566	.977	155	46	46	101	111	131	1.030	5	4	-1	-2	*1O	3.3
1956	StL-N	156	594	87	184	33	6	27	**109**	75	39	.310	.390	.522	.912	144	36	37	99	125	119	.909	2	0	1	3	*1O	3.4
1957	StL-N	134	502	82	176	38	3	29	102	66	34	**.351**	**.428**	.612	**1.040**	174	54	54	101	114	129	1.106	1	1	-0	-0	*1	4.1
1958	StL-N	135	472	64	159	35	2	17	62	72	26	.337	.426	.528	.953	141	37	33	106	87	102	.970	0	0	0	5	*1	2.9
1959	StL-N	115	341	37	87	13	2	14	44	60	25	.255	.367	.428	.795	106	7	4	105	95	53	.769	0	2	-1	0	1/O	-0.3
1960	StL-N	116	331	49	91	17	1	17	63	41	34	.275	.358	.486	.845	119	13	10	108	121	59	.833	1	1	-0	-4	O1	0.2
1961	StL-N	123	372	46	107	22	4	15	70	52	35	.288	.376	.489	.866	113	15	8	113	124	69	.864	0	0	0	-5	*O	-0.1
1962	StL-N	135	433	57	143	18	1	19	82	64	46	.330	.420	.508	.928	136	31	26	109	117	94	.957	3	0	1	-10	*O	1.0
1963	StL-N	124	337	34	86	10	2	12	58	35	43	.255	.329	.404	.732	102	4	1	107	142	47	.689	2	0	1	-12	O	-1.6
Total	22	3026	10972	1949	3630	725	177	475	1951	1599	696	.331	.418	.559	.977	157	983	927	104	99	2625	1.066	78	31		-59	*O1/P	70.1
■ **DANNY MUSSER** Musser, William Daniel b: 9/5/05, Zion, Pa. BL/TR, 5'9.5", 160 lbs. Deb: 9/18/32																												
1932	Was-A	1	2	0	1	0	0	0	0	0	0	.500	.500	.500	1.000	160	0	0	100	0	0	1.000	0	0	0	0	/3	0.0
■ **GEORGE MYATT** Myatt, George Edward "Mercury', "Stud" or "Foghorn" b: 6/14/14, Denver, Colo. BL/TR, 5'11", 167 lbs. Deb: 8/16/38 MC																												
1938	NY-N	43	170	27	52	2	1	3	10	14	13	.306	.362	.382	.745	101	1	1	103	47	24	.732	10			5	S3	0.7
1939	NY-N	22	53	7	10	2	0	0	3	6	6	.189	.271	.226	.498	35	-5	-5	99	92	4	.455	2			-1	3	-0.4
1943	Was-A	42	53	11	13	3	0	0	3	13	7	.245	.394	.302	.696	101	1	1	104	68	9	.800	3	0	1	0	2/S3	0.2
1944	Was-A	140	538	86	153	19	6	0	40	54	44	.284	.357	.342	.699	112	2	9	90	75	72	.669	26	10	2	-16	*2S/O	0.0
1945	Was-A	133	490	81	145	17	7	1	39	63	43	.296	.378	.365	.744	125	12	16	93	82	77	.763	30	11	2	-14	2O/3S	0.5
1946	Was-A	15	34	7	8	1	0	0	4	2	3	.235	.297	.265	.562	63	-2	-2	92	169	3	.481	1	1	-0	-0	/32	-0.1
1947	Was-A	12	7	1	0	0	0	0	0	4	4	.000	.364	.000	.364	6	-1	-1	97	0	0	.571	0	0	0	0	/2	0.0
Total	7	407	1345	220	381	44	14	4	99	156	120	.283	.362	.346	.708	109	9	20	94	76	188	.714	72	22		-26	2/3SO	0.9
■ **GLENN MYATT** Myatt, Glenn Calvin b: 7/9/1897, Argenta, Ark. d: 8/9/69, Houston, Tex. BL/TR, 5'11", 165 lbs. Deb: 4/15/20																												
1920	Phi-A	70	196	14	49	8	3	0	18	12	22	.250	.293	.321	.615	67	-11	-9	94	100	18	.507	1	3	-2	-3	OC	-1.4
1921	Phi-A	44	69	6	14	2	0	0	5	6	7	.203	.267	.232	.499	27	-7	-8	103	107	5	.400	0	0	0	1	C	-0.5
1923	Cle-A	92	220	36	63	7	6	3	40	16	18	.286	.338	.414	.751	96	-2	-2	101	137	30	.679	0	2	-1	-8	C	-0.5
1924	Cle-A	105	342	55	117	22	7	8	73	33	12	.342	.402	.518	.919	141	17	19	97	120	72	.960	6	1	1	0	C	2.4
1925	Cle-A	106	358	51	97	15	9	11	54	29	24	.271	.329	.455	.784	92	-4	-7	106	92	54	.748	2	1	0	-1	C/O	-0.1
1926	Cle-A	56	117	14	29	5	2	0	13	13	13	.248	.323	.325	.648	70	-5	-5	100	116	13	.591	1	0	0	0	C	-0.1
1927	Cle-A	55	94	15	23	6	0	2	8	12	7	.245	.336	.372	.709	86	-2	-2	97	65	12	.690	1	0	0	2	C	0.1
1928	Cle-A	58	125	9	36	7	2	1	15	13	13	.288	.355	.400	.755	93	-0	-1	106	97	17	.692	0	2	-1	2	C	0.2
1929	Cle-A	59	129	14	30	4	1	1	17	7	5	.233	.277	.302	.580	49	-10	-10	100	138	11	.470	0	1	-1	-1	C	-0.6
1930	Cle-A	86	265	30	78	23	2	2	37	18	17	.294	.342	.419	.760	87	-4	-6	105	105	37	.695	2	3	-1	3	C	0.2
1931	Cle-A	65	195	21	48	14	2	1	29	21	13	.246	.319	.354	.673	72	-7	-8	106	133	23	.622	2	1	0	-1	C	-0.5
1932	Cle-A	82	252	45	62	12	1	8	46	27	21	.246	.326	.397	.723	80	-5	-9	108	124	34	.688	2	2	-1	0	C	-0.5
1933	Cle-A	40	77	10	18	4	0	0	7	15	8	.234	.372	.286	.658	73	-2	-2	105	106	9	.650	0	1	-1	1	C	0.0
1934	Cle-A	36	107	18	34	6	1	0	12	13	5	.318	.392	.393	.784	102	1	1	101	95	17	.767	1	0	0	-1	C	0.3
1935	Cle-A	10	36	1	3	1	0	0	2	4	3	.083	.175	.111	.286	-25	-7	-7	99	173	1	.242	0	0	0	-2	C	-0.7
	NY-N	13	18	2	4	0	1	1	6	0	3	.222	.222	.500	.722	91	-0	-0	96	180	2	.643	0			0	/C	0.0
1936	Det-A	27	78	5	17	1	0	0	5	9	4	.218	.299	.231	.530	34	-8	-8	95	90	6	.443	0	0	0	-2	C	-0.6
Total	16	1004	2678	346	722	137	37	38	387	248	195	.270	.334	.391	.725	85	-56	-64	102	112	362	.672	18	17		-9	C/O	-2.3
■ **BUDDY MYER** Myer, Charles Solomon b: 3/16/04, Ellisville, Miss. d: 10/31/74, Baton Rouge, La. BL/TR, 5'10.5", 163 lbs. Deb: 9/26/25																												
1925	Was-A	4	8	1	2	0	0	0	0	0	1	.250	.250	.250	.500	28	-1	-1	98	0	0	.333	0	0	0	0	/S	0.0
1926	Was-A	132	434	66	132	18	6	1	62	45	19	.304	.370	.380	.750	98	-2	-1	98	125	61	.703	10	11	-4	-12	*S/3	-0.5
1927	Was-A	15	51	7	11	1	0	0	7	8	3	.216	.322	.235	.557	48	-4	-4	97	198	4	.575	3	0	1	-1	S	-0.2
	Bos-A	133	469	59	135	22	11	2	47	48	15	.288	.359	.394	.753	101	-3	1	95	84	67	.737	9	0	3	6	*S3O/2	1.5
	Yr	148	520	66	146	23	11	2	54	56	18	.281	.355	.379	.734	95	-7	-3	95	96	71	.719	12	0	4	5		1.3
1928	Bos-A	147	536	78	168	26	6	1	44	53	28	.313	.379	.390	.769	104	4	5	98	76	82	.771	**30**	16	-1	-1	*3	0.5
1929	Was-A	141	563	80	169	29	10	3	82	63	33	.300	.373	.403	.776	100	1	1	100	114	88	.773	18	7	1	-3	23	0.4
1930	Was-A	138	541	97	164	18	8	2	61	58	31	.303	.373	.377	.750	90	-6	-7	101	102	78	.716	14	11	-2	-9	*2/O	-1.5
1931	Was-A	139	591	114	173	33	11	4	56	58	42	.293	.360	.406	.766	100	1	1	101	63	85	.725	11	14	-5	-17	*2	-1.2

YEAR	TM/L	G	AB	R	H	2B	3B	HR	RBI	BB	SO	AVG	OBP	SLG	PRO	/A	BR	/A	PF	CHI	RC	TA	SB	CS	SBR	FR	POS	TPR
1932	Was-A	143	577	120	161	38	16	5	52	69	33	.279	.360	.426	.786	103	3	3	100	64	91	.783	12	7	-1	-16	*2	-0.6
1933	Was-A	131	530	95	160	29	15	4	61	60	29	.302	.374	.436	.810	119	11	14	96	89	87	.788	6	8	-3	2	*2	1.0
1934	Was-A	139	524	103	160	33	8	3	57	102	32	.305	.419	.416	.835	115	17	16	101	81	98	.884	6	6	-2	-7	*2	1.2
1935	Was-A	151	616	115	215	36	11	5	100	96	40	**.349**	.440	.468	.907	147	37	45	92	99	132	.971	7	6	-2	8	*2	5.2
1936	Was-A	51	156	31	42	5	2	0	15	42	11	.269	.427	.327	.754	91	-0	1	98	95	27	.871	7	2	1	1	2	0.5
1937	Was-A	125	430	54	126	16	10	1	65	78	41	.293	.407	.384	.791	107	4	8	94	135	72	.806	2	6	-3	-10	*2/O	0.6
1938	Was-A	127	437	79	147	22	8	6	71	93	32	.336	.454	.465	.918	138	26	30	95	111	99	1.037	9	5	-0	2	*2	3.2
1939	Was-A	83	258	33	78	10	3	1	32	40	18	.302	.396	.376	.772	109	1	5	90	108	42	.766	4	1	1	5	2	1.2
1940	Was-A	71	210	28	61	14	4	0	29	34	10	.290	.389	.395	.785	112	2	5	93	126	34	.778	6	3	0	4	2	1.1
1941	Was-A	53	107	14	27	3	1	0	9	18	10	.252	.360	.299	.659	78	-3	-3	98	100	13	.627	2	0	1	3	2	0.3
Total	17	1923	7038	1174	2131	353	130	38	850	965	428	.303	.389	.406	.795	109	89	120	97	96	1160	.800	156	103	-15	-47	*2S3/O	12.7
■ GEORGE MYERS	Myers, George D. b: 11/13/1860, Buffalo, N.Y. d: 12/14/26, Buffalo, N.Y. BR , Deb: 5/02/1884																											
1884	Buf-N	78	325	34	59	9	2	2	32	13	33	.182	.213	.240	.453	40	-21	-24	107	139	17	.342				-20	CO	-3.6
1885	Buf-N	89	326	40	67	7	2	0	19	23	40	.206	.258	.239	.497	62	-13	-13	99	86	21	.390				3	CO	-0.3
1886	StL-N	79	295	26	56	7	3	0	27	18	42	.190	.236	.234	.470	46	-20	-17	95	135	18	.389	6			-5	C/O3	-1.5
1887	Ind-N	69	235	25	51	8	1	1	20	22	7	.217	.298	.272	.570	64	-12	-10	96	94	27	.636	26			-6	CO/13	-0.7
1888	Ind-N	66	248	36	59	9	0	2	16	16	14	.238	.292	.298	.591	95	-2	-1	95	76	31	.640	28			-1	C3O/1	0.0
1889	Ind-N	43	149	22	29	3	0	0	12	17	13	.195	.294	.215	.509	41	-10	-12	109	114	13	.542	12			0	OC/1	-1.0
Total	6	424	1578	183	321	43	8	5	126	109	149	.203	.260	.250	.510	57	-78	-77	100	108	127	.468	72			-29	CO/31	-7.1
■ GREG MYERS	Myers, Gregory Richard b: 4/14/66, Riverside, Cal. BL/TR, 6'1", 200 lbs. Deb: 9/12/87																											
1987	Tor-A	7	9	1	1	0	0	0	0	0	3	.111	.111	.111	.222	-40	-2	-2	101	0	-0	.100	0	0	0	0	/C	0.0
■ HENRY MYERS	Myers, Henry C. b: 5/1858, Philadelphia, Pa. d: 4/18/1895, Philadelphia, Pa. BR/TR, 5'9", 159 lbs. Deb: 8/20/1881 M																											
1881	Pro-N	1	4	0	0	0	0	0	0	0	2	.000	.000	.000	.000	-99	-1	-1	93	0	0	.000				0	/S	0.0
1882	Bal-a	69	294	43	53	3	0	0		12		.180	.212	.190	.403	40	-19	-15	92	0	12	.282				-6	*S/PM	-1.8
1884	WiL-U	6	24	3	3	0	0	0		0		.125	.125	.125	.250	-15	-3	-3	103	0	0	.143	0			0	/S2	-0.2
Total	3	76	322	46	56	3	0	0	0	12	2	.174	.204	.183	.387	33	-22	-19	93	0	13	.267	0			-6	/SP2	-2.0
■ HI MYERS	Myers, Henry Harrison b: 4/27/1889, E.Liverpool, Ohio d: 5/1/65, Minerva, Ohio BR/TR, 5'9.5", 175 lbs. Deb: 09																											
1909	Bro-N	6	22	1	5	1	0	0	6	2		.227	.292	.273	.564	77	-1	-1	99	350	2	.529	1			0	/O	0.0
1911	Bro-N	13	43	2	7	1	0	0	0	2	3	.163	.200	.186	.386	9	-5	-5	97	0	2	.306	1			-1	O	-0.6
1914	Bro-N	70	227	35	65	3	9	0	17	7	24	.286	.316	.379	.695	105	1	1	101	72	27	.605	2			-5	O	-0.6
1915	Bro-N	153	605	69	150	21	7	2	46	17	51	.248	.275	.316	.591	78	-17	-18	101	86	52	.488	19	22	-8	18	*O	-1.3
1916	Bro-N	113	412	54	108	12	14	3	36	21	35	.262	.308	.381	.689	107	4	3	103	88	55	.661	17			-3	*O	-0.3
1917	Bro-N	120	471	37	126	15	10	1	41	18	25	.268	.294	.348	.643	93	-3	-5	104	100	49	.542	5			5	O123	-0.1
1918	Bro-N	107	407	36	104	9	8	4	40	20	26	.256	.292	.346	.638	93	-4	-5	101	105	44	.591	17			10	*O	0.0
1919	Bro-N	133	512	62	157	23	**14**	5	**73**	23	34	.307	.339	**.436**	.774	141	18	21	94	126	78	.735	13			5	*O	2.3
1920	Bro-N	154	582	83	177	36	**22**	4	80	35	54	.304	.345	.462	.807	117	20	13	111	117	88	.751	9	13	-5	1	*O/3	0.0
1921	Bro-N	144	549	51	158	14	4	4	68	22	51	.288	.318	.350	.667	73	-19	-22	105	130	61	.564	8	6	-1	2	*O2/3	-2.5
1922	Bro-N	153	618	82	196	20	9	6	89	13	26	.317	.331	.408	.739	94	-11	-7	95	122	79	.634	9	10	-3	0	*O/2	-1.4
1923	StL-N	96	330	29	99	18	2	2	48	12	19	.300	.330	.385	.715	98	-6	-2	90	127	42	.628	5	3	-0	4	O	0.0
1924	StL-N	43	124	12	26	5	1	1	15	3	10	.210	.228	.290	.519	37	-11	-11	103	140	8	.400	1	2	-1	-0	O3/2	-1.1
1925	StL-N	1	1	0	0	0	0	0	0	0	0	.000	.000	.000	.000	-98	-0	-0	102	0	0	.000	0	0	0	0	H	0.0
	Cin-N	3	6	1	1	1	0	0	0	0	0	.167	.167	.333	.500	25	-1	-1	97	0	0	.400	0	0	0	-1	/O	0.0
	StL-N	1	1	1	1	0	0	0	0	0	0	1.000	1.000	1.000	2.000	405	0	0	102	0	1	—	0	0	0	0	H	0.0
	Yr	5	8	2	2	1	0	0	0	0	0	.250	.250	.375	.625	58	-1	-1	99	0	1	.500	0	0	0	-1		0.0
Total	14	1310	4910	555	1380	179	100	32	559	195	358	.281	.312	.378	.690	96	-34	-38	101	110	587	.608	107	56		34	*O/231	-5.6
■ BERT MYERS	Myers, James Albert b: 4/8/1874, Frederick, Md. d: 10/12/15, Washington, D.C. BR/TR, 5'10", Deb: 4/25/1896																											
1896	StL-N	122	454	47	116	12	8	0	37	40	32	.256	.320	.317	.637	74	-19	-15	95	79	50	.577	8			-8	*3/S	-1.4
1898	Was-N	31	110	14	29	1	4	0	13	13		.264	.341	.345	.687	98	0	-0	102	105	14	.654	2			0	3	0.0
1900	Phi-N	7	28	5	5	1	0	0	2	3		.179	.258	.214	.472	33	-2	-2	98	100	2	.435	1			0	/3	-0.1
Total	3	160	592	66	150	14	12	0	52	56	32	.253	.321	.318	.639	76	-21	-18	96	85	66	.584	11			-8	3/S	-1.5
■ AL MYERS	Myers, James Albert "Cod" b: 10/22/1863, Danville, Ill. d: 12/24/27, Marshall, Ill. 5'8.5", 165 lbs. Deb: 9/27/1884																											
1884	Mil-U	12	46	6	15	6	0	0		0		.326	.326	.457	.783	162	3	3	100	0	7	.677	0			0	2	0.2
1885	Phi-N	93	357	25	73	13	2	1	28	11	41	.204	.228	.261	.489	56	-17	-18	104	107	22	.366				-20	*2	-2.6
1886	KC-N	118	473	69	131	22	9	4	51	22	42	.277	.309	.387	.696	104	5	0	107	82	59	.608	3			-2	*2	0.3
1887	Was-N	105	362	45	84	9	5	2	36	40	26	.232	.312	.301	.613	76	-12	-9	95	98	41	.608	18			-6	2S	-0.8
1888	Was-N	132	502	46	104	12	7	2	46	37	46	.207	.270	.271	.541	78	-13	-10	96	112	43	.500	20			-28	*2	-3.3
1889	Was-N	46	176	24	46	3	0	0	20	22	7	.261	.347	.278	.625	84	-4	-2	92	129	21	.631	10			2	2	0.3
	Phi-N	75	305	52	82	14	2	0	28	36	9	.269	.354	.328	.681	89	-2	-4	104	80	39	.664	8			-11	2	-0.7
	Yr	121	481	76	128	17	2	0	48	58	16	.266	.351	.310	.661	87	-6	-6	100	100	60	.652	18			-9		-0.4
1890	Phi-N	117	487	95	135	29	7	2	81	57	46	.277	.365	.378	.742	110	13	6	108	114	85	.838	44			10	*2	1.8
1891	Phi-N	135	514	67	118	27	2	2	69	69	46	.230	.331	.302	.633	91	-6	-2	95	132	55	.609	8			-11	*2	-0.7
Total	8	833	3222	429	788	135	34	13	359	294	263	.245	.314	.320	.634	89	-33	-36	101	106	372	.603	111			-66	2/S	-5.5
■ LYNN MYERS	Myers, Lynnwood Lincoln b: 2/23/14, Enola, Pa. BR/TR, 5'6.5", 145 lbs. Deb: 7/13/38																											
1938	StL-N	70	227	18	55	10	2	1	19	9	25	.242	.271	.317	.588	55	-12	-15	111	92	20	.517	9			-6	S	-1.6
1939	StL-N	74	117	24	28	6	1	0	10	12	23	.239	.310	.308	.618	63	-5	-6	105	102	12	.544	1			-1	S3/2	-0.4
Total	2	144	344	42	83	16	3	1	29	21	48	.241	.285	.314	.599	58	-18	-22	109	95	32	.531	10			-8	S/32	-2.0
■ HAP MYERS	Myers, Ralph Edward b: 4/8/1888, San Francisco, Cal. d: 6/30/67, San Francisco, Cal BR/TR, 6'3", 175 lbs. Deb: 4/16/10																											
1910	Bos-A	3	6	0	2	0	0	0	0	0		.333	.333	.333	.667	110	0	0	99	0	1	.500	0			0	/O	0.0
1911	StL-A	11	37	4	11	1	0	0	1	1		.297	.316	.324	.640	83	-1	-1	95	28	4	.500	0			-1	1	0.0
	Bos-A	13	38	3	14	2	0	0	0	4		.368	.429	.421	.850	139	2	2	99	0	5	.714	0	4	-2	-0	1	0.2
	Yr	24	75	7	25	3	0	0	1	5		.333	.375	.373	.748	112	1	1	97	14	9	.611	0	4	-2	-1		0.2
1913	Bos-N	140	524	74	143	20	1	2	50	38	48	.273	.333	.326	.659	94	-7	-3	95	109	73	.722	57			5	*1	-0.5
1914	Bro-F	92	305	61	67	10	5	1	29	44	43	.220	.318	.295	.613	76	-8	-9	101	115	44	.744	43			1	1	-0.5
1915	Bro-F	118	341	61	98	9	1	1	36	32	39	.287	.349	.328	.677	103	1	2	98	113	53	.708	28			-2	*1	0.2
Total	5	377	1251	203	335	42	7	4	116	119	130	.268	.336	.322	.658	93	-13	-8	97	105	180	.716	128	4		4	1/O	-0.6
■ RICHIE MYERS	Myers, Richard b: 4/7/30, Sacramento, Cal. BR , 5'6", 150 lbs. Deb: 4/21/56																											
1956	Chi-N	4	1	1	0	0	0	0	0	0	0	.000	.000	.000	.000	-99	-0	-0	99	0	0	.000	0	0	0	0	H	0.0
■ BILLY MYERS	Myers, William Harrison b: 8/14/10, Enola, Pa. BR/TR, 5'8", 168 lbs. Deb: 4/16/35																											
1935	Cin-N	117	445	60	119	15	10	5	36	29	81	.267	.315	.380	.695	92	-9	-5	93	75	55	.633	10			-5	*S	-0.4
1936	Cin-N	98	323	45	87	9	6	6	27	28	56	.269	.328	.390	.718	96	-4	-2	97	66	43	.664	6			-1	S	0.3
1937	Cin-N	124	335	35	84	13	3	7	43	44	57	.251	.339	.370	.710	102	-3	1	91	107	46	.660	0			6	*S/2	1.6
1938	Cin-N	134	442	57	112	18	6	12	47	41	80	.253	.317	.403	.719	99	-3	-2	98	79	58	.652	2			0	*S2	0.8
1939	Cin-N	151	509	79	143	18	6	9	56	71	90	.281	.369	.393	.762	102	5	3	103	92	81	.745	4			4	*S	1.6
1940	Cin-N	90	282	33	57	14	2	5	30	30	56	.202	.283	.319	.603	65	-13	-14	101	106	27	.533	0			-4	S	-0.8
1941	Chi-N	24	63	10	14	1	0	1	4	7	25	.222	.310	.286	.596	73	-2	-2	94	69	6	.540	1			-0	S/2	0.0
Total	7	738	2399	319	616	88	33	45	243	250	445	.257	.328	.377	.706	94	-29	-20	97	86	316	.664	23			1	S/2	3.1
■ BILL NAGEL	Nagel, William Taylor b: 8/19/15, Memphis, Tenn. d: 10/8/81, Freehold, N.J. BR/TR, 6'1", 190 lbs. Deb: 4/20/39																											
1939	Phi-A	105	341	39	86	19	4	12	39	25	86	.252	.307	.437	.744	91	-8	-7	97	71	42	.657	2	1	0	-13	23/P	-1.6
1941	Phi-N	17	56	2	8	1	1	0	6	3	14	.143	.186	.196	.383	8	-7	-7	97	197	2	.286	0			1	2/O3	-0.4

YEAR	TM/L	G	AB	R	H	2B	3B	HR	RBI	BB	SO	AVG	OBP	SLG	PRO	/A	BR	/A	PF	CHI	RC	TA	SB	CS	SBR	FR	POS	TPR
1945	Chi-A	67	220	21	46	10	3	3	27	15	41	.209	.263	.323	.585	73	-9	-8	95	122	18	.492	3	1	0	-1	1/3	-1.1
Total	3	189	617	62	140	30	8	15	72	43	141	.227	.281	.374	.655	78	-24	-22	97	100	61	.579	5	2		-13	/2130P	-3.1
■ LOU NAGELSEN	Nagelsen, Louis Marcellus (born Louis Marcellus Nageleisen) b: 6/29/1887, Piqua, Ohio d: 10/22/65, Fort Wayne, Ind. BR/TR, 6'2", 180 lbs. Deb: 9/10/12																											
1912	Cle-A	2	3	0	0	0	0	0	0	0	0	.000	.000	.000	.000	-99	-1	-1	101	0	0	.000	0			0	/C	0.0
■ RUSS NAGELSON	Nagelson, Russell Charles b: 9/19/44, Cincinnati, Ohio BL/TR, 6', 205 lbs. Deb: 9/11/68																											
1968	Cle-A	5	3	0	1	0	0	0	0	2	2	.333	.600	.333	.933	187	1	1	101	0	1	1.500	0	0	0	0	H	0.1
1969	Cle-A	12	17	1	6	0	0	0	0	3	3	.353	.450	.353	.803	135	1	1	94	0	3	.818	0	0	0	-1	/O1	0.0
1970	Cle-A	17	24	3	3	1	0	1	2	3	9	.125	.222	.292	.514	35	-2	-2	115	81	2	.476	0	0	0	-0	/O	-0.2
	Det-A	28	32	5	6	0	0	0	2	5	6	.188	.297	.188	.485	35	-3	-3	103	135	2	.423	0	0	0	-1	/O1	-0.3
	Yr	45	56	8	9	1	0	1	4	8	15	.161	.266	.232	.498	36	-5	-5	107	116	4	.447	0	0	0	-1		-0.5
Total	3	62	76	9	16	1	0	1	4	13	20	.211	.326	.263	.589	63	-3	-4	105	81	8	.550	0	0	0	-2	/O1	-0.4
■ TOM NAGLE	Nagle, Thomas Edward b: 10/30/1865, Milwaukee, Wis. d: 3/9/46, Milwaukee, Wis. BR/TR, 5'10", 150 lbs. Deb: 4/22/1890																											
1890	Chi-N	38	144	21	39	5	1	1	11	7	24	.271	.318	.340	.658	86	-1	-3	109	65	17	.600	4			0	C/O	-0.2
1891	Chi-N	8	25	3	3	0	0	0	1	1	3	.120	.154	.120	.274	-18	-4	-4	106	97	0	.182	0			0	/CO	-0.3
Total	2	46	169	24	42	5	1	1	12	8	27	.249	.294	.308	.602	71	-5	-7	109	70	18	.528	4			0	/CO	-0.5
■ BILL NAHORODNY	Nahorodny, William Gerard b: 8/31/53, Hamtramck, Mich. BR/TR, 6'2", 200 lbs. Deb: 9/27/76																											
1976	Phi-N	3	5	0	1	1	0	0	0	0	0	.200	.200	.400	.600	63	-0	-0	107	0	0	.500	0	0	0	0	/C	0.0
1977	Chi-A	7	23	3	6	1	0	1	4	2	3	.261	.320	.435	.755	104	0	0	99	122	3	.667	0	0	0	1	/C	0.1
1978	Chi-A	107	347	29	82	11	2	8	35	23	52	.236	.288	.349	.636	77	-11	-11	101	95	35	.544	1	0	0	1	*C/1D	-0.6
1979	Chi-A	65	179	20	46	10	0	6	29	18	23	.257	.325	.413	.738	95	-1	-1	102	121	23	.662	0	1	-1	-2	C/D	-0.1
1980	Atl-N	59	157	14	38	12	0	5	18	8	21	.242	.287	.414	.701	93	-2	-2	101	89	17	.595	0	2	-1	0	C/1	-0.1
1981	Atl-N	14	13	0	3	1	0	0	2	1	3	.231	.286	.308	.593	69	-1	-1	100	196	1	.500	0	0	0	0	/C1	0.0
1982	Cle-A	39	94	6	21	5	1	4	18	2	9	.223	.240	.426	.665	78	-3	-3	100	138	8	.553	0	0	0	-3	C	-0.3
1983	Det-A	2	1	0	0	0	0	0	0	1	0	.000	.500	.000	.500	54	0	0	96	0	0	1.000	0	0	0	0	/H	0.0
1984	Sea-A	12	25	2	6	0	0	1	3	1	7	.240	.321	.360	.681	86	-0	-0	102	100	3	.600	0	1	-1	0	C/1	0.0
Total	9	308	844	74	203	41	3	25	109	56	118	.241	.292	.385	.678	85	-18	-19	101	106	91	.602	1	4	-2	-3	C/1D	-1.0
■ FRANK NALEWAY	Naleway, Frank "Chick" b: 7/5/02, Chicago, Ill. d: 1/28/49, Chicago, Ill. BR/TR, 5'9.5", 165 lbs. Deb: 9/16/24																											
1924	Chi-A	1	2	0	0	0	0	0	0	1	0	.000	.333	.000	.333	-10	-0	-0	97	0	0	.500	0	0	0	0	/S	0.0
■ DOC NANCE	Nance, William G. "Kid" (born Willie G. Cooper) b: 8/2/1876, Ft.Worth, Tex. d: 5/28/58, Fort Worth, Tex. BR/TR, Deb: 8/19/1897																											
1897	Lou-N	35	120	25	29	5	3	3	17	20		.242	.355	.408	.763	108	1	2	95	91	19	.802	3			5	O	0.4
1898	Lou-N	22	76	13	24	5	0	1	16	12		.316	.416	.421	.837	148	5	5	96	146	14	.904	2			0	O	0.5
1901	Det-A	132	461	72	129	24	5	3	66	51		.280	.352	.373	.725	94	3	-4	110	117	65	.699	9			4	*O	-0.1
Total	3	189	657	110	182	34	8	7	99	83		.277	.360	.385	.745	102	9	3	106	116	99	.741	14			9	O	0.8
■ AL NAPLES	Naples, Aloysius Francis b: 8/29/27, St.George, S.I., N.Y. BR/TR, 5'9", 168 lbs. Deb: 6/25/49																											
1949	StL-A	2	7	0	1	1	0	0	0	0	1	.143	.143	.286	.429	12	-1	-1	100	0	0	.333	0	0	0	0	/S	0.0
■ DANNY NAPOLEON	Napoleon, Daniel b: 1/11/42, Claysburg, Pa. BR/TR, 5'11", 190 lbs. Deb: 4/14/65																											
1965	NY-N	68	97	5	14	1	1	0	7	8	23	.144	.224	.175	.400	14	-11	-11	100	171	4	.310	0	0	0	0	O/3	-1.1
1966	NY-N	12	33	2	7	2	0	0	0	1	10	.212	.235	.273	.508	43	-3	-2	94	0	2	.357	0	1	-1	-1	O	-0.4
Total	2	80	130	7	21	3	1	0	7	9	33	.162	.227	.200	.427	21	-14	-13	99	129	5	.333	0	1	-1	-1	/O3	-1.5
■ HAL NARAGON	Naragon, Harold Richard b: 10/1/28, Zanesville, Ohio BL/TR, 6', 160 lbs. Deb: 9/23/51 C																											
1951	Cle-A	3	8	0	2	0	0	0	0	1	0	.250	.400	.250	.650	83	-0	-0	95	0	1	.667	0	0	0	0	/C	0.0
1954	Cle-A	46	101	10	24	2	2	0	12	9	12	.238	.300	.297	.597	60	-5	-6	106	152	10	.506	0	0	0	-2	C	-0.5
1955	Cle-A	57	127	12	41	9	2	1	14	15	8	.323	.394	.449	.843	122	5	4	104	87	23	.820	1	0	0	-5	C	0.1
1956	Cle-A	53	122	11	35	3	1	3	18	13	9	.287	.360	.402	.762	100	0	0	101	116	18	.700	0	0	0	-6	C	-0.4
1957	Cle-A	57	121	12	31	1	1	0	8	12	9	.256	.328	.281	.609	67	-5	-5	102	93	11	.495	0	0	0	-2	C	-0.5
1958	Cle-A	9	9	2	3	0	1	0	0	0	0	.333	.333	.556	.889	148	0	0	94	0	2	.833	0	0	0	0	H	0.0
1959	Cle-A	14	36	6	10	4	1	0	5	3	2	.278	.350	.444	.794	121	1	1	97	123	6	.769	0	0	0	-0	C	0.1
	Was-A	71	195	12	47	3	2	0	11	8	9	.241	.275	.277	.551	52	-13	-13	100	80	14	.412	0	1	-1	-4	C	-1.3
	Yr	85	231	18	57	7	3	0	16	11	11	.247	.287	.303	.590	62	-12	-12	99	89	20	.464	0	1	-1	-4		-1.2
1960	Was-A	33	92	7	19	2	0	0	5	8	4	.207	.277	.228	.505	38	-8	-8	102	93	6	.400	0	0	0	2	C	-0.4
1961	Min-A	57	139	10	42	2	1	2	11	4	8	.302	.326	.374	.700	82	-3	-4	106	74	16	.559	0	0	0	2	C	-0.1
1962	Min-A	24	35	1	8	1	0	0	3	3	1	.229	.289	.257	.547	46	-2	-3	105	132	3	.429	0	0	0	-0	/C	-0.1
Total	10	424	985	83	262	27	11	6	87	76	62	.266	.323	.334	.657	76	-30	-33	102	97	109	.570	1	1	-0	-15	C	-3.1
■ BILL NARLESKI	Narleski, William Edward "Cap" b: 6/9/1899, Perth Amboy, N.J. d: 7/22/64, Laurel Springs, N.J. BR/TR, 5'9", 160 lbs. Deb: 4/18/29																											
1929	Bos-A	96	260	30	72	16	1	0	25	21	22	.277	.333	.346	.679	74	-9	-10	102	95	30	.604	4	4	-1	-5	S2/3	-0.9
1930	Bos-A	39	98	11	23	9	0	0	7	7	5	.235	.306	.327	.632	65	-6	-5	93	73	10	.560	0	0	0	-1	S3/2	-0.2
Total	2	135	358	41	95	25	1	0	32	28	27	.265	.326	.341	.666	72	-15	-15	99	89	41	.592	4	4	-1	-6	/S23	-1.1
■ JERRY NARRON	Narron, Jerry Austin b: 1/15/56, Goldsboro, N.C. BL/TR, 6'3", 205 lbs. Deb: 4/13/79																											
1979	NY-A	61	123	17	21	3	1	4	18	9	26	.171	.227	.309	.536	45	-10	-9	96	138	9	.452	0	0	0	-2	C	-0.8
1980	Sea-A	48	107	7	21	3	0	4	18	13	18	.196	.283	.336	.620	67	-5	-5	103	146	11	.557	0	0	0	-3	C/D	-0.6
1981	Sea-A	76	203	13	45	5	0	3	17	16	35	.222	.285	.291	.576	66	-9	-9	100	98	17	.478	0	0	0	-12	C	-1.8
1983	Cal-A	10	22	1	3	0	0	1	4	1	3	.136	.174	.273	.447	22	-2	-2	96	174	1	.368	0	0	0	0	/CD	-0.1
1984	Cal-A	69	150	9	37	5	0	3	17	8	12	.247	.289	.340	.629	72	-6	-6	101	113	13	.500	0	0	0	2	C/1	-0.1
1985	Cal-A	67	132	12	29	4	0	5	14	11	17	.220	.280	.364	.643	74	-5	-5	101	88	13	.562	0	0	0	1	C/1D	-0.1
1986	Cal-A	57	95	5	21	3	1	1	8	9	14	.221	.295	.305	.601	67	-4	-4	96	100	8	.494	0	0	0	-1	C/D	-0.1
1987	Sea-A	4	8	0	0	0	0	0	0	0	2	.000	.000	.000	.000	-97	-2	-2	103	0	0	.000	0	0	0	0	/C	-0.1
Total	8	392	840	64	177	23	2	21	96	67	127	.211	.272	.318	.590	63	-43	-42	100	112	72	.510	0	0	0	-14	C/D1	-3.7
■ SAM NARRON	Narron, Samuel b: 8/25/13, Middlesex, N.C. BR/TR, 5'10", 180 lbs. Deb: 9/15/35 C																											
1935	StL-N	4	7	0	3	0	0	0	0	0	0	.429	.429	.429	.857	126	0	0	104	0	1	.750	0			0	/C	0.0
1942	StL-N	10	10	0	4	0	0	0	1	0	0	.400	.400	.400	.800	124	0	0	108	93	2	.667	0			0	/C	0.0
1943	StL-N	10	11	0	1	0	0	0	0	1	2	.091	.167	.091	.258	-24	-2	-2	105	0	0	.200	0			0	/C	-0.1
Total	3	24	28	0	8	0	0	0	1	1	2	.286	.310	.286	.596	67	-1	-1	106	32	3	.450	0			0	/C	-0.1
■ COTTON NASH	Nash, Charles Francis b: 7/24/42, Jersey City, N.J. BR/TR, 6'6", 220 lbs. Deb: 9/01/67																											
1967	Chi-A	3	3	1	0	0	0	0	0	1	0	.000	.250	.000	.250	-22	-0	-0	94	0	0	.333	0	0	0	0	/1	0.0
1969	Min-A	6	9	0	2	0	0	0	0	1	2	.222	.300	.222	.522	47	-1	-1	102	0	1	.429	0	0	0	-0	/1O	-0.1
1970	Min-A	4	4	1	1	0	0	0	2	1	1	.250	.400	.250	.650	85	-0	-0	98	810	0	.500	0	1	-1	0	/1	0.0
Total	3	13	16	2	3	0	0	0	2	3	3	.188	.316	.188	.503	45	-1	-1	99	213	1	.429	0	1	-1	-0	/1O	-0.1
■ KEN NASH	Nash, Kenneth Leland (Played One Game In 1912 Under Name Of Costello) b: 7/14/1888, S.Weymouth, Mass. d: 2/16/77, Epsom, N.H. BB/TR, 5'8", 140 lbs. Deb: 7/04/12																											
1912	Cle-A	11	23	2	4	0	0	0	0	3		.174	.269	.174	.443	27	-2	-2	101	0	1	.368	0			-0	/S	-0.1
1914	StL-N	24	51	4	14	3	1	0	6	6	10	.275	.351	.373	.723	111	1	1	104	114	6	.676	0			-0	3/2S	0.1
Total	2	35	74	6	18	3	1	0	6	9	10	.243	.325	.311	.636	85	-1	-1	103	79	8	.571	0			-0	/S32	0.0
■ BILLY NASH	Nash, William Mitchell b: 6/24/1865, Richmond, Va. d: 11/15/29, E.Orange, N.J. BR/TR, 5'8.5", 167 lbs. Deb: 8/05/1884 M																											
1884	Ric-a	45	166	31	33	8	8	1		12		.199	.281	.361	.643	112	2	3	99	0	17	.594				7	3	0.9
1885	Bos-N	26	94	9	24	4	0	0	11	2	9	.255	.271	.298	.569	90	-2	-1	94	139	8	.429				0	3/2	0.0
1886	Bos-N	109	417	61	117	11	8	1	45	24	28	.281	.320	.353	.672	107	2	4	97	100	53	.623	16			-1	*3S	0.6
1887	Bos-N	121	475	100	140	24	12	6	94	60	30	.295	.376	.434	.810	129	18	20	98	124	96	.928	43			4	*3/O	2.1
1888	Bos-N	135	526	71	149	18	15	4	75	50	46	.283	.350	.397	.747	133	25	21	106	117	82	.751	20			15	*32	3.8

YEAR	TM/L	G	AB	R	H	2B	3B	HR	RBI	BB	SO	AVG	OBP	SLG	PRO	/A	BR	/A	PF	CHI	RC	TA	SB	CS	SBR	FR	POS	TPR
1889	Bos-N	128	481	84	132	20	2	3	76	79	44	.274	.379	.343	.722	102	6	5	102	138	74	.779	26			10	*3/P	2.0
1890	Bos-P	129	488	103	130	28	6	5	90	88	43	.266	.383	.379	.762	99	7	0	107	**130**	83	.846	26			16	*3/P	2.1
1891	Bos-N	140	537	92	148	24	9	5	95	74	50	.276	.369	.382	.750	108	16	6	112	133	88	.802	28			-14	*3	-0.2
1892	Bos-N	135	526	94	137	25	5	4	95	59	41	.260	.338	.350	.688	97	7	-3	113	158	75	.712	31			22	*3/O	2.6
1893	Bos-N	128	485	115	141	27	6	10	123	85	29	.291	.399	.433	.832	120	18	15	103	149	98	.951	30			6	*3	1.9
1894	Bos-N	132	512	132	148	23	6	8	87	91	23	.289	.399	.404	.804	85	-0	-15	113	110	93	.882	20			7	*3	-0.7
1895	Bos-N	132	508	97	147	23	6	10	108	74	19	.289	.383	.417	.800	105	8	5	103	132	90	.850	18			-9	*3	-0.1
1896	Phi-N	65	227	29	56	9	1	3	30	34	21	.247	.355	.335	.690	83	-4	-5	102	104	29	.684	3			6	3M	0.3
1897	Phi-N	104	337	45	87	20	2	0	39	60		.258	.373	.329	.703	93	-3	-0	96	103	44	.708	4			-2	3S/2	-0.1
1898	Phi-N	20	70	9	17	2	1	0	9	11		.243	.346	.300	.646	93	-1	-0	95	132	7	.604	0			0	3	0.0
Total	15	1549	5849	1072	1606	266	87	60	977	803	383	.275	.366	.381	.747	105	100	55	104	124	938	.786	265			67	*3/2SOP	15.2
■ **PETE NATON**	Naton, Peter Alphonsus b: 9/9/31, Flushing, N.Y. BR/TR, 6'1", 200 lbs. Deb: 6/16/53																											
1953	Pit-N	6	12	2	2	0	0	0	1	2	1	.167	.286	.167	.452	21	-1	-1	102	195	1	.400	0	0	0	0	/C	0.0
■ **SANDY NAVA**	Nava, Vincent P. (born Irwin Sandy) b: 4/12/1850, San Francisco, Cal d: 6/15/06, Baltimore, Md. 5'6", 155 lbs. Deb: 5/05/1882																											
1882	Pro-N	28	97	15	20	2	0	0	7	1	13	.206	.214	.227	.441	39	-6	-7	106	107	5	.299				-9	C/O	-1.2
1883	Pro-N	29	100	18	24	4	2	0	16	3	17	.240	.262	.320	.582	75	-3	-3	101	173	9	.461				-6	C/O	-0.6
1884	Pro-N	34	116	10	11	0	0	0	6	11	35	.095	.173	.095	.268	-13	-15	-15	102	188	2	.210				-2	C/S2	-1.2
1885	Bal-a	8	27	2	5	1	0	0		1		.185	.214	.222	.437	38	-2	-2	106	0	1	.318				0	/C	-0.1
1886	Bal-a	2	5	0	1	0	0	0		0		.200	.200	.200	.400	29	-0	-0	91	0	0	.500	1			0	/SC	0.0
Total	5	101	345	45	61	7	2	0	29	16	65	.177	.213	.209	.422	32	-26	-27	103	144	17	.313	1			-17	/CSO2	-3.1
■ **EARL NAYLOR**	Naylor, Earl Eugene b: 5/19/19, Kansas City, Mo. BR/TR, 6', 190 lbs. Deb: 4/15/42																											
1942	Phi-N	76	168	9	33	4	1	0	14	11	18	.196	.246	.232	.478	43	-13	-12	94	133	9	.359	1			-4	OP	-1.4
1943	Phi-N	33	120	12	21	2	0	3	14	12	16	.175	.256	.267	.522	54	-8	-7	94	126	7	.430	1			8	O	0.0
1946	Bro-N	3	2	1	0	0	0	0	0	0	1	.000	.000	.000	.000	-97	-1	-1	103	0	0	.000	0			0	H	0.0
Total	3	112	290	22	54	6	1	3	28	23	35	.186	.248	.245	.493	46	-21	-19	94	129	16	.409	2			4	/OP	-1.4
■ **CHARLIE NEAL**	Neal, Charles Lenard b: 1/30/31, Longview, Tex. BR/TR, 5'10", 165 lbs. Deb: 4/17/56																											
1956	Bro-N	62	136	22	39	5	1	2	14	14	19	.287	.353	.382	.736	95	-0	-1	103	102	18	.673	2	2	-1	3	2/S	0.6
1957	Bro-N	128	448	62	121	13	7	12	62	53	83	.270	.358	.411	.768	91	5	-5	116	119	69	.757	11	4	1	2	*S3/2	0.2
1958	LA-N	140	473	87	120	9	6	22	65	61	91	.254	.345	.438	.783	101	4	1	105	100	71	.757	7	6	-2	9	*2/S	1.7
1959	LA-N	151	616	103	177	30	**11**	19	83	43	86	.287	.338	.464	.802	109	8	7	102	86	91	.749	17	6	2	19	*2/S	3.8
1960	LA-N	139	477	60	122	23	2	8	40	48	75	.256	.325	.363	.688	76	-8	-17	115	84	54	.601	5	5	-2	-18	*2/S	-2.5
1961	LA-N	108	341	40	80	6	1	10	48	30	49	.235	.298	.346	.644	69	-15	-16	102	131	35	.563	3	2	-0	2	*2	-0.1
1962	NY-N	136	508	59	132	14	9	11	58	56	90	.260	.333	.388	.721	89	-5	-8	104	105	62	.636	2	8	-4	1	2S3	0.0
1963	NY-N	72	253	26	57	12	1	3	18	27	49	.225	.302	.316	.619	79	-7	-6	99	87	25	.548	1	2	-1	2	3/S	-0.4
	Cin-N	34	64	2	10	1	0	0	3	5	15	.156	.217	.172	.389	13	-7	-7	104	115	3	.291	0	1	-1	-1	3/2S	-0.9
	Yr	106	317	28	67	13	1	3	21	32	64	.211	.286	.287	.573	65	-14	-14	101	96	28	.494	1	3	-2	1		-1.3
Total	8	970	3316	461	858	113	38	87	391	337	557	.259	.331	.394	.725	89	-24	-51	106	101	429	.687	48	36	-7	18	2S3	2.4
■ **OFFA NEAL**	Neal, Theophilus Fountain b: 6/5/1876, Logan, Ill. d: 4/12/50, Mt.Vernon, Ill. BL/TR, 6', 185 lbs. Deb: 9/30/05																											
1905	NY-N	4	13	0	0	0	0	0	0	0		.000	.000	.000	.000	-99	-3	-3	101	0	0	.000	0			0	/32	-0.2
■ **GREASY NEALE**	Neale, Alfred Earle b: 11/5/1891, Parkersburg, W.Va. d: 11/2/73, Lake Worth, Fla. BL/TR, 6', 170 lbs. Deb: 4/12/16 C																											
1916	Cin-N	138	530	53	139	13	5	0	20	19	79	.262	.295	.306	.601	86	-10	-9	98	52	54	.522	17			17	*O	0.4
1917	Cin-N	121	385	40	113	14	9	3	33	24	36	.294	.343	.400	.743	138	12	15	92	78	58	.765	25			-3	*O	0.9
1918	Cin-N	107	371	57	100	11	11	1	32	24	38	.270	.324	.367	.691	114	4	5	97	89	50	.697	23			9	*O	1.0
1919	Cin-N	139	500	57	121	10	12	1	54	47	51	.242	.316	.316	.632	86	-5	-8	105	138	59	.633	28			0	*O	-1.4
1920	Cin-N	150	530	55	135	10	7	3	46	45	48	.255	.322	.317	.639	94	-10	-3	90	103	58	.614	29	12	2	14	*O	0.3
1921	Phi-N	22	57	7	12	1	0	0	1	14	9	.211	.366	.228	.594	60	-2	-3	102	28	5	.612	3	4	-2	-6	O	-1.0
	Cin-N	63	241	39	58	10	5	0	12	22	16	.241	.307	.324	.630	66	-11	-12	101	60	24	.582	9	6	-1	0	O	-1.4
	Yr	85	298	46	70	11	5	0	13	36	25	.235	.319	.305	.625	65	-14	-14	101	52	30	.588	12	10	-2	-6		-2.4
1922	Cin-N	25	43	11	10	2	1	0	2	6	3	.233	.353	.326	.679	79	-1	-1	96	50	6	.771	5	2	0	-5	O	-0.5
1924	Cin-N	3	4	0	0	0	0	0	0	0	1	.000	.000	.000	.000	-99	-1	-1	101	0	0	.000	0	0	0	-0	/O	-0.1
Total	8	768	2661	319	688	71	50	8	200	201	281	.259	.319	.332	.651	95	-25	-16	97	87	314	.630	139	24		26	O	-1.8
■ **JIM NEALON**	Nealon, James Joseph b: 12/15/1884, Sacramento, Cal. d: 4/2/10, San Francisco, Cal. 6'1.5", Deb: 4/12/06																											
1906	Pit-N	154	556	82	142	21	12	3	**83**	53		.255	.320	.353	.673	107	7	4	104	156	69	.638	15			1	*1	0.0
1907	Pit-N	105	381	29	98	10	8	0	47	23		.257	.300	.325	.625	93	-2	-4	105	152	41	.558	11			-1	*1	-0.8
Total	2	259	937	111	240	31	20	3	130	76		.256	.312	.342	.653	101	5	1	105	155	111	.605	26			-0	1	-0.8
■ **TOM NEEDHAM**	Needham, Thomas J. "Deerfoot" b: 4/7/1879, Ireland d: 12/13/26, Steubenville, Ohio BR/TR, 5'10", 180 lbs. Deb: 5/12/04																											
1904	Bos-N	84	269	18	70	12	3	4	19	11		.260	.289	.372	.661	109	1	2	97	62	31	.573	3			8	C/O	1.8
1905	Bos-N	83	271	21	59	6	1	2	17	24		.218	.281	.269	.551	68	-11	-10	97	76	22	.472	3			5	C/O1	0.3
1906	Bos-N	83	285	11	54	8	2	1	12	13		.189	.225	.242	.467	47	-18	-18	100	62	17	.368	3			11	C/2130	0.0
1907	Bos-N	86	260	19	51	6	2	1	19	18		.196	.248	.246	.494	59	-13	-12	95	107	17	.411	4			2	C/1	-0.3
1908	NY-N	54	91	8	19	3	0	0	11	12		.209	.301	.242	.543	73	-2	-2	104	192	6	.472	0			-6	C	-0.7
1909	Chi-N	13	28	3	4	0	0	0	0	0		.143	.143	.143	.286	-11	-4	-4	101	0	1	.167	0			-1	/C	-0.3
1910	Chi-N	31	76	9	14	3	1	0	10	10	10	.184	.287	.250	.537	57	-4	-4	101	184	6	.500	1			1	C/1	-0.1
1911	Chi-N	27	62	4	12	2	0	0	5	9	14	.194	.315	.226	.541	54	-4	-3	97	121	5	.540	2			1	C	0.0
1912	Chi-N	33	90	12	16	5	0	0	10	7	13	.178	.260	.233	.493	34	-8	-8	104	160	6	.459	3			-1	C	-0.6
1913	Chi-N	20	42	5	10	4	1	0	11	4	8	.238	.304	.381	.685	96	-0	-0	99	250	5	.625	0			1	C/1	0.1
1914	Chi-N	9	17	3	2	1	0	0	3	1	4	.118	.167	.176	.343	2	-2	-2	98	363	1	.333	1			0	/C	-0.1
Total	11	523	1491	113	311	50	10	8	117	109	49	.209	.265	.272	.537	65	-64	-61	98	104	116	.458	20			21	C/1203	0.1
■ **CAL NEEMAN**	Neeman, Calvin Amandus b: 2/18/29, Valmeyer, Ill. BR/TR, 6'1", 192 lbs. Deb: 4/16/57																											
1957	Chi-N	122	415	37	107	17	1	10	39	22	87	.258	.300	.376	.676	83	-12	-10	96	87	46	.573	0	0	0	4	*C	0.0
1958	Chi-N	76	201	30	52	7	0	12	29	21	41	.259	.338	.473	.810	111	3	3	101	91	32	.773	0	0	0	-5	C	0.1
1959	Chi-N	44	105	7	17	2	0	3	9	11	23	.162	.241	.267	.508	36	-10	-10	98	98	7	.438	0	0	0	-1	C	-0.8
1960	Chi-N	9	13	0	2	1	0	0	0	0	5	.154	.154	.231	.385	4	-2	-2	98	0	0	.273	0	0	0	-1	/C	-0.2
	Phi-N	59	160	13	29	6	2	4	13	16	42	.181	.264	.319	.583	55	-9	-11	107	84	13	.507	0	0	0	6	C	-0.1
	Yr	68	173	13	31	7	2	4	13	16	47	.179	.257	.312	.569	52	-11	-12	106	73	13	.490	0	0	0	5		-0.3
1961	Phi-N	19	31	0	7	1	0	0	2	4	8	.226	.314	.258	.572	58	-2	-2	94	101	2	.500	1	0	0	0	C	0.0
1962	Pit-N	24	50	5	9	1	1	1	5	3	10	.180	.226	.300	.526	39	-4	-5	102	109	3	.419	0	0	0	1	C	-0.2
1963	Cle-A	9	9	0	0	0	0	0	0	1	5	.000	.100	.000	.100	-71	-2	-2	97	0	0	.111	0	0	0	0	/C	-0.1
	Was-A	14	18	1	1	0	0	0	0	1	0	.056	.105	.056	.161	-55	-4	-4	98	0	0	.118	0	0	0	-0	C	-0.3
	Yr	23	27	1	1	0	0	0	0	2	5	.037	.103	.037	.140	-60	-6	-6	97	0	0	.115	0	0	0	-0		-0.4
Total	7	376	1002	93	224	35	4	30	97	79	221	.224	.286	.356	.642	72	-42	-41	99	87	104	.572	1	0	0	5	C	-1.6
■ **DOUG NEFF**	Neff, Douglas Williams b: 10/8/1891, Harrisonburg, Va. d: 5/23/32, Cape Charles, Va. BR/TR, 5'9", 141 lbs. Deb: 6/26/14																											
1914	Was-A	3	2	0	0	0	0	0	0	0	0	.000	.000	.000	.000	-99	-0	-0	101	0	0	.000	0			0	/S	0.0
1915	Was-A	30	60	1	10	1	0	0	4	4	6	.167	.219	.183	.402	20	-6	-6	101	124	3	.308	1	2	-1	-0	32/S	-0.5
Total	2	33	62	1	10	1	0	0	4	4	6	.161	.212	.177	.390	16	-6	-6	101	120	3	.296	1	2		0	/32S	-0.5
■ **CY NEIGHBORS**	Neighbors, Cecil F. b: 9/23/1880, Missouri d: 5/20/64, Tacoma, Wash. BR , Deb: 4/29/08																											
1908	Pit-N	1	0	0	0	0	0	0	0	0		—	—	—	—	—	0	0	95	—	—	—	0			0	/O	0.0

YEAR	TM/L	G	AB	R	H	2B	3B	HR	RBI	BB	SO	AVG	OBP	SLG	PRO	/A	BR	/A	PF	CHI	RC	TA	SB	CS	SBR	FR	POS	TPR
■ **BOB NEIGHBORS**	Neighbors, Robert Otis b: 11/9/17, Talahina, Okla. d: 8/52, North Korea (Mia) BR/TR, 5'11", 165 lbs. Deb: 9/16/39																											
1939	StL-A	7	11	3	2	0	0	1	1	0	1	.182	.182	.455	.636	57	-1	-1	100	42	1	.556	0	0	0	0	/S	0.0
■ **TOMMY NEILL**	Neill, Thomas White b: 11/7/19, Hartselle, Ala. BL/TR, 6'2", 200 lbs. Deb: 9/10/46																											
1946	Bos-N	13	45	8	12	2	0	0	7	2	1	.267	.298	.311	.609	77	-2	-1	95	187	4	.457	0			-2	O	-0.3
1947	Bos-N	7	10	1	2	0	1	0	0	1	2	.200	.333	.400	.733	97	-0	-0	97	0	1	.667	0			-1	/O	0.0
Total	2	20	55	9	14	2	1	0	7	3	3	.255	.305	.327	.632	81	-2	-1	95	149	5	.524	0			-2	/O	-0.3
■ **BERNIE NEIS**	Neis, Bernard Edmund b: 9/26/1895, Bloomington, Ill. d: 11/29/72, Inverness, Fla. BB/TR, 5'7", 160 lbs. Deb: 4/14/20																											
1920	Bro-N	95	249	38	63	11	2	2	22	26	35	.253	.329	.337	.666	82	-2	-6	111	95	28	.621	9	9	-3	-2	O	-1.5
1921	Bro-N	102	230	34	59	5	4	4	34	25	41	.257	.332	.365	.697	81	-5	-6	105	130	28	.669	9	7	-2	-5	O/2	-1.6
1922	Bro-N	61	70	15	16	4	1	1	9	13	8	.229	.349	.357	.707	87	-2	-1	95	112	9	.732	3	2	-0	-6	O	-0.7
1923	Bro-N	126	445	78	122	17	4	5	37	36	38	.274	.330	.364	.694	85	-11	-10	98	74	53	.625	8	8	-2	14	*O	-0.1
1924	Bro-N	80	211	43	64	8	3	4	26	27	17	.303	.385	.427	.811	118	6	6	99	93	36	.819	4	2	0	-4	O	0.1
1925	Bos-N	106	355	47	101	20	2	5	45	38	19	.285	.354	.394	.748	97	-4	-1	94	103	49	.705	8	10	-4	7	O	0.0
1926	Bos-N	30	93	16	20	5	2	0	8	8	10	.215	.277	.312	.589	68	-6	-4	86	95	8	.562	4			1	O	-0.3
1927	Cle-A	32	96	17	29	9	0	4	18	18	9	.302	.412	.521	.933	145	6	7	97	98	21	1.015	0	0	0	6	O	1.0
	Chi-A	45	76	9	22	5	0	0	11	10	9	.289	.372	.355	.727	88	-1	-1	102	136	10	.704	1	0	0	-2	O	-0.3
	Yr	77	172	26	51	14	0	4	29	28	18	.297	.395	.448	.843	118	5	5	100	121	31	.876	1	0	0	4		0.7
Total	8	677	1825	297	496	84	18	25	210	201	186	.272	.346	.379	.724	93	-19	-16	99	98	243	.690	46	38		10	O/2	-3.4
■ **ERNIE NEITZKE**	Neitzke, Ernest Fredrich b: 11/13/1894, Toledo, Ohio d: 4/27/77, Sylvania, Ohio BR/TR, 5'10", 180 lbs. Deb: 6/02/21																											
1921	Bos-A	11	25	3	6	0	0	0	2	4	4	.240	.345	.240	.585	52	-2	-2	100	114	2	.526	0	0	0	-1	/OP	-0.2
■ **DAVE NELSON**	Nelson, David Earl b: 6/20/44, Fort Sill, Okla. BR/TR, 5'10", 160 lbs. Deb: 4/11/68 C																											
1968	Cle-A	88	189	26	44	4	5	0	19	17	35	.233	.300	.307	.606	83	-4	-4	101	140	20	.647	23	7	3	-6	2S	-0.4
1969	Cle-A	52	123	11	25	0	0	0	6	9	26	.203	.263	.203	.466	34	-11	-10	94	96	7	.379	4	3	-1	-1	2/O	-1.0
1970	Was-A	47	107	5	17	1	0	0	4	7	24	.159	.211	.168	.379	6	-14	-13	96	90	4	.290	2	1	0	4	2	-0.6
1971	Was-A	85	329	47	92	11	3	5	33	23	29	.280	.329	.377	.706	108	-1	2	92	103	39	.650	17	8	0	-5	3/2	-0.5
1972	Tex-A	145	499	68	113	16	3	2	28	67	81	.226	.324	.283	.607	86	-9	-6	94	84	54	.649	51	17	5	-11	*3O	-0.9
1973	Tex-A	142	576	71	165	24	4	7	48	34	78	.286	.326	.378	.705	101	-2	-0	97	76	70	.674	43	16	3	-7	*2	0.2
1974	Tex-A	121	474	71	112	13	1	3	42	34	72	.236	.293	.287	.580	70	-20	-17	96	109	38	.508	25	13	-0	10	*2/D	-0.2
1975	Tex-A	28	80	9	17	1	0	2	10	8	10	.213	.292	.300	.592	68	-3	-3	100	128	8	.591	6	0	2	2	2/D	0.1
1976	KC-A	78	153	24	36	4	2	1	17	14	26	.235	.299	.307	.607	78	-4	-4	100	131	16	.618	15	5	2	1	2D/1	0.1
1977	KC-A	27	48	8	9	3	1	0	4	7	11	.188	.291	.292	.583	59	-3	-3	100	113	4	.512	1	3	-2	0	2/D	-0.2
Total	10	813	2578	340	630	77	19	20	211	220	392	.244	.307	.312	.619	82	-70	-58	96	99	259	.606	187	73	12	-13	23/DOS1	-3.4
■ **ROCKY NELSON**	Nelson, Glenn Richard b: 11/18/24, Portsmouth, Ohio BL/TL, 5'10.5", 175 lbs. Deb: 4/27/49																											
1949	StL-N	82	244	28	54	8	4	4	32	11	12	.221	.258	.336	.594	53	-15	-18	110	128	20	.487	1			-4	1	-2.2
1950	StL-N	76	235	27	58	10	4	1	20	26	9	.247	.324	.336	.661	72	-9	-10	103	94	27	.611	4			-0	1	-1.2
1951	StL-N	9	18	3	4	1	0	0	1	1	0	.222	.263	.278	.541	45	-1	-1	101	77	1	.400	0	0	0	-1	/1O	-0.1
	Pit-N	71	195	29	52	7	4	1	14	10	7	.267	.302	.359	.661	72	-7	-8	107	74	21	.544	1	1	-0	-1	1O	-1.0
	Yr	80	213	32	56	8	4	1	15	11	7	.263	.299	.352	.651	70	-8	-10	106	75	22	.534	1	1	-0	-2		-1.1
	Chi-A	6	5	0	0	0	0	0	0	1	0	.000	.167	.000	.167	-54	-1	-1	97	0	0	.200	0	0	0	0	H	0.0
1952	Bro-N	37	39	6	10	1	0	0	3	7	4	.256	.370	.282	.652	82	-1	-1	102	106	5	.621	0	0	0	0	/1	0.0
1954	Cle-A	4	4	0	0	0	0	0	0	0	1	.000	.000	.000	.000	-94	-1	-1	106	0	0	.000	0	0	0	0	/1	0.0
1956	Bro-N	31	96	7	20	2	0	4	15	4	10	.208	.240	.354	.594	55	-6	-6	103	138	8	.487	0	0	0	1	1	-0.6
	StL-N	38	56	6	13	5	0	3	8	6	6	.232	.306	.482	.789	109	0	0	99	94	8	.733	0	0	0	-1	1/O	-0.1
	Yr	69	152	13	33	7	0	7	23	10	16	.217	.265	.401	.667	75	-6	-6	101	116	16	.587	0	0	0	0		-0.7
1959	Pit-N	98	175	31	51	11	0	6	32	23	19	.291	.383	.457	.840	119	6	5	103	132	32	.841	0	0	0	-1	1/O	0.0
1960	Pit-N	93	200	34	60	11	1	7	35	24	15	.300	.389	.470	.859	135	10	10	99	123	38	.861	1	2	-1	0	1	0.6
1961	Pit-N	75	127	15	25	5	1	5	13	17	11	.197	.301	.370	.671	77	-4	-4	99	85	14	.629	0	0	0	-0	1	-0.6
Total	9	620	1394	186	347	61	14	31	173	130	94	.249	.318	.379	.698	83	-28	-35	104	108	174	.644	7	3		-8	1/O	-5.2
■ **CANDY NELSON**	Nelson, John W b: 3/12/1854, Portland, Maine d: 9/4/10, Brooklyn, N.Y. BL/TR, 5'6", 145 lbs. Deb: 6/11/1872																											
1872	Tro-n	4	19	4	7							.368															/OS	
	Eck-n	18	81	10	19							.235															/2O3	
	Yr	22	100	14	26							.260																
1873	Mut-n	36	177	27	54							.305															2/O3	
1874	Mut-n	65	313	57	69							.220															*2S	
1875	Mut-n	70	300	28	56							.187															23/O	
1878	Ind-N	19	84	12	11	1	0	0	5	5	11	.131	.180	.143	.323	8	-8	-6	87	122	2	.233				-6	S	-1.0
1879	Tro-N	28	106	17	28	7	1	0	10	8	4	.264	.316	.349	.665	127	2	3	93	100	12	.577				3	S/O	0.8
1881	Wor-N	24	103	13	29	1	0	1	15	5	6	.282	.315	.320	.635	95	0	-1	105	139	11	.514				3	S	0.4
1883	NY-a	97	417	75	127	19	6	0		31		.305	.353	.379	.732	126	17	12	108	0	57	.652				-7	*S	0.1
1884	NY-a	111	432	114	110	15	3	1		**74**		.255	.375	.310	.685	129	19	18	100	0	51	.674				-16	*S/2	0.1
1885	NY-a	107	420	98	107	12	4	1		**61**		.255	.353	.310	.663	136	10	21	84	0	47	.620				11	*S/3	3.0
1886	NY-a	109	413	89	93	7	2	0		64		.225	.332	.252	.584	83	-3	-6	104	0	40	.575	14			-9	SO	-1.0
1887	NY-a	68	257	61	63	5	1	0		48		.245	.380	.272	.653	98	-1	5	88	0	39	.799	29			8	OS/2	1.0
	NY-N	1	2	0	0	0	0	0	0	0	1	.000	.000	.000	.000	-93	-1	-1	107	0	0	.000	0			0	/3	0.0
1890	BB-a	60	223	44	56	3	2	0		35		.251	.365	.283	.648	94	0	0	100	0	28	.689	12			-12	S/O	-0.6
Total	4 n	193	890	126	205							.230															S/O	
Total	9	624	2457	523	624	70	19	3	30	331	22	.254	.349	.302	.650	109	35	47	97	13	287	.630	55			-24	S2O/3	2.8
■ **JAMIE NELSON**	Nelson, James Victor b: 9/5/59, Clinton Okla. BR/TR, 5'11", 180 lbs. Deb: 7/21/83																											
1983	Sea-A	40	96	9	21	3	0	1	5	13	12	.219	.312	.281	.593	65	-4	-4	100	65	9	.557	4	2	0	-1	C	-0.2
■ **LYNN NELSON**	Nelson, Lynn Bernard "Line Drive" b: 2/24/05, Sheldon, N.Dak. d: 2/15/55, Kansas City, Mo. BL/TR, 5'10.5", 170 lbs. Deb: 4/18/30																											
1930	Chi-N	37	18	0	4	1	1	0	2	0	1	.222	.222	.389	.611	42	-2	-2	105	98	1	.500	0			1	P	0.0
1933	Chi-N	29	21	5	5	1	1	0	1	1	3	.238	.273	.381	.654	87	-0	-0	97	47	2	.563	0			0	P	0.0
1934	Chi-N	2	0	0	0	0	0	0	0	0	0	—	—	—	—	—	0	0	98	—	—	—	0			0	/P	0.0
1937	Phi-A	74	113	18	40	6	2	4	29	6	13	.354	.387	.549	.935	142	5	6	94	134	24	.945	1	0	0	-1	P/O	1.0
1938	Phi-A	67	112	12	31	0	0	0	15	7	12	.277	.319	.277	.596	50	-8	-8	101	164	10	.469	0	0	0	-1	P	-0.1
1939	Phi-A	40	80	3	15	2	0	0	5	2	13	.188	.217	.213	.429	10	-11	-11	97	99	3	.299	0	1	-1	-1	P	0.0
1940	Det-A	19	23	4	8	0	0	1	3	0	6	.348	.348	.478	.826	100	0	-0	111	77	4	.733	0	0	0	0	/P	0.1
Total	7	268	367	42	103	10	4	5	55	16	48	.281	.313	.371	.683	74	-16	-15	99	126	47	.581	1	1		-0	P/O	1.0
■ **RAY NELSON**	Nelson, Raymond "Kell" (born Raymond Nelson Kellogg) b: 8/4/1875, Holyoke, Mass. d: 1/8/61, Mt.Vernon, N.Y. BR/TR, 5'9", 150 lbs. Deb: 5/06/01																											
1901	NY-N	39	130	12	26	2	0	0	7	10		.200	.257	.215	.473	43	-10	-8	91	84	8	.394	3			-14	2	-1.8
■ **RICKY NELSON**	Nelson, Ricky Lee b: 5/8/59, Eloy, Ariz. BL/TR, 6', 200 lbs. Deb: 5/17/83																											
1983	Sea-A	98	291	32	74	13	3	5	36	17	50	.254	.295	.371	.667	83	-8	-7	100	114	31	.587	7	4	-0	-8	O/D	-1.6
1984	Sea-A	9	15	2	3	0	0	1	2	2	4	.200	.294	.400	.694	88	-0	-0	102	89	2	.667	0	0	0	-0	/OD	0.0
1985	Sea-A	6	2	2	0	0	0	0	0	0	1	.000	.000	.000	.000	-99	-1	-1	95	0	0	.000	0	0	0	-1	/O	-0.1
1986	Sea-A	10	12	2	2	0	0	0	1	0	4	.167	.167	.167	.333	-8	-2	-2	105	199	0	.300	1	0	0	-0	/OD	-0.1
Total	4	123	320	38	79	13	3	6	39	19	59	.247	.289	.363	.652	78	-10	-10	100	115	34	.584	8	4	0	-10	/OD	-1.8
■ **ROB NELSON**	Nelson, Robert Augustus b: 5/17/64, Pasadena, Cal. BL/TL, 6'4", 215 lbs. Deb: 9/09/86																											
1986	Oak-A	5	9	1	2	1	0	0	0	1	4	.222	.300	.333	.633	78	-0	-0	94	0	1	.571	0	0	0	0	/1D	0.0
1987	Oak-A	7	24	1	4	1	0	0	0	0	12	.167	.167	.208	.375	-1	-3	-3	91	0	1	.250	0	0	0	0	/1	-0.3

YEAR	TM/L	G	AB	R	H	2B	3B	HR	RBI	BB	SO	AVG	OBP	SLG	PRO	/A	BR	/A	PF	CHI	RC	TA	SB	CS	SBR	FR	POS	TPR
	SD-N	10	11	0	1	0	0	0	1	1	8	.091	.167	.091	.258	-30	-2	-2	97	399	0	.200	0	0	0	0	/1	-0.1
1988	SD-N	7	21	4	4	0	0	1	3	2	9	.190	.261	.333	.594	71	-1	-1	97	120	2	.529	0	0	0	0	/1	0.0
Total	3	29	65	6	11	2	0	1	4	4	33	.169	.217	.246	.464	28	-7	-6	95	109	4	.370	0	0	0	0	/1D	-0.4
■ **TEX NELSON**	Nelson, Robert Sidney "Babe" b: 8/7/36, Dallas, Tex. BL/TL, 6'3", 205 lbs. Deb: 6/22/55																											
1955	Bal-A	25	31	4	6	0	0	0	1	7	13	.194	.342	.194	.536	52	-2	-2	90	62	3	.520	0	0	0	0	/O1	-0.1
1956	Bal-A	39	68	5	14	2	0	0	5	7	22	.206	.280	.235	.515	40	-6	-6	94	117	5	.411	0	0	0	-3	O	-0.9
1957	Bal-A	15	23	2	5	0	2	0	5	1	5	.217	.280	.391	.671	87	-1	-0	93	219	3	.611	0	0	0	-2	/O	-0.2
Total	3	79	122	11	25	2	2	0	11	15	40	.205	.297	.254	.551	52	-9	-8	93	120	10	.485	0	0	0	-5	/O1	-1.2
■ **TOMMY NELSON**	Nelson, Tom Cousineau b: 5/1/17, Chicago, Ill. d: 9/24/73, San Diego, Cal. BR/TR, 5'11.5", 180 lbs. Deb: 4/17/45																											
1945	Bos-N	40	121	6	20	2	0	0	6	4	13	.165	.192	.182	.374	4	-16	-17	112	95	3	.252	1			-2	32	-1.9
■ **DICK NEN**	Nen, Richard Le Roy b: 9/24/39, South Gate, Cal. BL/TL, 6'2", 200 lbs. Deb: 9/18/63																											
1963	LA-N	7	8	2	1	0	0	1	1	3	3	.125	.364	.500	.864	154	1	1	95	60	1	.875	0	0	0	0	/1	0.0
1965	Was-A	69	246	18	64	7	1	6	31	19	47	.260	.316	.370	.686	94	-2	-2	100	120	29	.599	1	2	-1	0	1	-0.5
1966	Was-A	94	235	20	50	8	0	6	30	28	46	.213	.297	.323	.620	82	-6	-5	95	134	21	.531	0	2	-1	-3	1	-1.2
1967	Was-A	110	238	21	52	7	1	6	29	21	39	.218	.282	.332	.614	79	-6	-6	102	125	21	.518	0	1	-1	-0	1/O	-1.3
1968	Chi-N	81	94	8	17	1	1	2	16	6	17	.181	.230	.277	.507	46	-6	-7	112	211	6	.416	0	0	0	-0	1	-1.0
1970	Was-A	6	5	1	1	0	0	0	0	0	0	.200	.200	.200	.400	11	-1	-1	96	0	0	.250	0	0	0	0	/1	0.0
Total	6	367	826	70	185	23	3	21	107	77	152	.224	.291	.335	.626	81	-20	-20	100	134	79	.551	1	5	-3	-3	1/O	-4.0
■ **JACK NESS**	Ness, John Charles b: 11/11/1885, Chicago, Ill. d: 12/3/57, De Land, Fla. BR/TR, 6'2", 165 lbs. Deb: 5/09/11																											
1911	Det-A	12	39	6	6	0	0	0	2	2		.154	.195	.154	.349	-2	-5	-6	108	113	1	.242	0			-1	1	-0.6
1916	Chi-A	75	258	32	69	7	5	1	34	9	32	.267	.310	.345	.655	90	-2	-4	108	135	30	.577	4			-2	1	-0.8
Total	2	87	297	38	75	7	5	1	36	11	32	.253	.295	.320	.615	77	-7	-10	108	132	31	.527	4			-3	/1	-1.4
■ **GRAIG NETTLES**	Nettles, Graig b: 8/20/44, San Diego, Cal. BL/TR, 6', 180 lbs. Deb: 9/06/67																											
1967	Min-A	3	3	0	1	1	0	0	0	0	0	.333	.333	.667	1.000	177	0	0	107	0	1	1.000	0	0	0	0	H	0.0
1968	Min-A	22	76	13	17	2	1	5	8	7	20	.224	.298	.474	.771	123	2	2	106	68	10	.721	0	0	0	1	O/31	0.3
1969	Min-A	96	225	27	50	9	2	7	26	32	47	.222	.322	.373	.695	92	-2	-2	102	99	27	.645	1	2	-1	-7	O3	-1.1
1970	Cle-A	157	549	81	129	13	1	26	62	81	77	.235	.336	.404	.741	90	3	-7	115	85	77	.714	3	1	0	25	*3/O	1.8
1971	Cle-A	158	598	78	156	18	1	28	86	82	56	.261	.353	.435	.788	116	18	14	106	98	93	.764	7	4	-0	**40**	*3	**5.0**
1972	Cle-A	150	557	65	141	28	0	17	70	57	50	.253	.327	.395	.722	106	9	5	107	114	73	.661	2	3	-1	7	*3	1.7
1973	NY-A	160	552	65	129	18	0	22	81	78	76	.234	.336	.386	.722	102	3	3	101	116	73	.680	0	0	0	26	*3/D	2.7
1974	NY-A	155	566	74	139	21	1	22	75	59	75	.246	.320	.403	.723	112	4	7	96	102	75	.667	1	0	0	17	*3/S	2.8
1975	NY-A	157	581	71	155	24	4	21	91	51	88	.267	.328	.430	.758	114	8	9	99	118	82	.696	1	3	-2	13	*3	2.3
1976	NY-A	158	583	88	148	29	2	**32**	93	62	94	.254	.330	.475	.805	135	23	23	99	98	92	.788	11	6	-0	17	*3/S	**4.1**
1977	NY-A	158	589	99	150	23	4	37	107	68	79	.255	.335	.496	.831	125	17	19	99	111	98	.808	2	5	-2	1	*3/D	1.3
1978	NY-A	159	587	81	162	23	2	27	93	59	69	.276	.348	.460	.808	127	19	20	99	111	91	.753	1	1	-0	-4	*3/S	1.5
1979	NY-A	145	521	71	132	15	1	20	73	59	53	.253	.329	.401	.730	100	-3	0	96	106	68	.664	1	2	-1	12	*3	1.3
1980	NY-A	89	324	52	79	14	0	16	45	42	42	.244	.332	.435	.768	109	4	4	99	95	47	.727	0	0	0	-4	3/S	0.0
1981	NY-A	103	349	46	85	7	1	15	46	47	49	.244	.335	.398	.733	110	5	5	100	100	48	.690	0	2	-1	10	3/D	1.4
1982	NY-A	122	405	47	94	11	2	18	55	51	49	.232	.319	.402	.722	100	-2	0	96	101	50	.661	1	5	-3	6	*3/D	0.1
1983	NY-A	129	462	56	123	17	3	20	75	51	65	.266	.343	.446	.789	117	10	10	99	112	71	.745	0	1	-1	0	*3/D	1.0
1984	SD-N	124	395	56	90	11	1	20	65	58	55	.228	.334	.413	.747	110	5	6	99	114	55	.713	0	0	0	-3	*3	0.2
1985	SD-N	137	440	66	115	23	1	15	61	72	59	.261	.365	.420	.786	117	13	12	102	106	70	.767	0	0	0	-8	*3	0.4
1986	SD-N	126	354	36	77	9	0	16	55	41	62	.218	.302	.379	.681	91	-7	-5	95	120	41	.623	0	1	-1	-2	*3	-1.0
1987	Atl-N	112	177	16	37	8	1	5	33	22	25	.209	.296	.350	.647	65	-8	-10	108	171	18	.582	1	0	0	-1	3/1	-1.0
1988	Mon-N	80	93	5	16	4	0	1	14	9	19	.172	.245	.247	.492	40	-7	-8	106	215	5	.395	0	0	0	0	3/1	-0.7
Total	22	2700	8986	1193	2225	328	28	390	1314	1088	1209	.248	.332	.421	.753	109	115	107	101	108	1264	.728	32	36	-12	143	*3/O1DS	24.1
■ **JIM NETTLES**	Nettles, James William b: 3/2/47, San Diego, Cal. BL/TL, 6', 186 lbs. Deb: 9/07/70																											
1970	Min-A	13	20	3	5	0	0	0	0	1	5	.250	.286	.250	.536	50	-1	-1	98	0	1	.375	0	1	-1	-3	O	-0.4
1971	Min-A	70	168	17	42	5	1	6	24	19	24	.250	.326	.399	.725	100	1	0	104	115	22	.685	3	2	-0	5	O	0.2
1972	Min-A	102	235	28	48	5	2	4	15	32	52	.204	.302	.294	.596	73	-6	-8	107	77	21	.544	4	3	-1	2	O/1	-0.9
1974	Det-A	43	141	20	32	5	1	6	17	15	26	.227	.306	.404	.710	97	0	-1	106	89	17	.667	3	4	-2	-2	O	-0.4
1979	KC-A	11	23	0	2	0	0	0	1	3	2	.087	.192	.087	.279	-21	-4	-4	105	192	1	.238	0	0	0	0	/O1	-0.3
1981	Oak-A	1	0	0	0	0	0	0	0	0	0	—	—	—	—	—	0	0	96	—	0	—	0	0	0	-0	/O	0.0
Total	6	240	587	68	129	15	4	16	57	70	109	.220	.305	.341	.646	82	-10	-14	106	93	63	.603	10	10	-3	1	O/1	-1.8
■ **MORRIS NETTLES**	Nettles, Morris b: 1/26/52, Los Angeles, Cal. BL/TL, 6'1", 170 lbs. Deb: 4/26/74																											
1974	Cal-A	56	175	27	48	4	0	0	8	16	38	.274	.335	.297	.632	90	-3	-2	92	60	18	.624	20	11	-1	-3	O	-0.7
1975	Cal-A	112	294	50	68	11	0	0	23	26	57	.231	.296	.269	.565	64	-15	-13	95	112	24	.527	22	15	-2	1	O/D	-1.6
Total	2	168	469	77	116	15	0	0	31	42	95	.247	.311	.279	.590	73	-18	-15	94	93	41	.567	42	26	-3	-3	O/D	-2.3
■ **MILO NETZEL**	Netzel, Miles A. b: 5/12/1886, Eldred, Pa. d: 3/18/38, Oxnard, Cal. TL , Deb: 9/16/09																											
1909	Cle-A	10	37	2	7	1	0	0	3	3		.189	.250	.216	.466	46	-2	-2	102	139	2	.400	1			0	/3O	-0.1
■ **OTTO NEU**	Neu, Otto Adam b: 9/24/1894, Springfield, Ohio d: 9/19/32, Kenton, Ohio BR/TR, 5'11", 170 lbs. Deb: 7/10/17																											
1917	StL-A	1	0	0	0	0	0	0	0	0	0	—	—	—	—	—	0	0	95	—	—	—	0			0	/S	0.0
■ **JOHNNY NEUN**	Neun, John Henry b: 10/28/1900, Baltimore, Md. BB/TL, 5'10.5", 175 lbs. Deb: 4/14/25 MC																											
1925	Det-A	60	75	15	20	3	3	0	4	9	12	.267	.345	.387	.732	86	-2	-2	99	46	10	.690	2	3	-1	0	1	-0.2
1926	Det-A	97	242	47	72	14	4	0	15	27	26	.298	.370	.388	.759	101	-0	1	97	54	34	.712	4	7	-3	-2	1	-0.5
1927	Det-A	79	204	38	66	9	4	0	27	35	13	.324	.427	.407	.834	109	7	5	108	108	37	1.029	22	0	7	-1	1	0.1
1928	Det-A	36	108	15	23	3	1	0	5	7	10	.213	.261	.259	.520	37	-10	-10	99	61	7	.425	2	2	-1	1	1	-1.0
1930	Bos-N	81	212	39	69	12	2	2	23	21	18	.325	.389	.429	.818	101	-0	1	97	82	35	.853	9			2	1	0.0
1931	Bos-N	79	104	17	23	1	3	0	11	11	14	.221	.302	.288	.590	60	-6	-6	99	131	10	.543	2			-0	1	-0.8
Total	6	432	945	171	273	42	17	2	85	110	93	.289	.366	.376	.742	90	-11	-11	100	81	133	.747	41	12		-1	1	-2.4
■ **NEVINS**	Nevins Deb:6/17/1873																											
1873	Res-n	13	56	7	11							.196															3/2O	
■ **DON NEWCOMBE**	Newcombe, Donald "Newk" b: 6/14/26, Madison, N.J. BL/TR, 6'4", 220 lbs. Deb: 5/20/49																											
1949	Bro-N	39	96	8	22	4	0	0	10	5	16	.229	.267	.271	.538	44	-8	-8	102	145	6	.397	0			1	P	0.0
1950	Bro-N	40	97	8	24	3	1	1	8	10	19	.247	.318	.330	.648	66	-4	-5	107	88	10	.553	0			-0	P	0.0
1951	Bro-N	40	103	11	23	3	1	0	8	8	9	.223	.286	.272	.558	52	-7	-7	98	110	9	.463	0	0	0	1	P	0.0
1954	Bro-N	31	47	6	15	1	0	0	4	4	6	.319	.373	.340	.713	86	-1	-1	101	98	7	.625	0	0	0	-1	P	0.0
1955	Bro-N	57	117	18	42	9	1	7	23	6	18	.359	.395	.632	1.028	160	11	10	104	98	30	1.079	1	0	0	-2	P	0.0
1956	Bro-N	52	111	13	26	6	0	2	16	12	18	.234	.315	.342	.657	74	-4	-4	103	154	12	.584	1	0	0	0	P	0.0
1957	Bro-N	34	74	8	17	2	0	1	7	11	11	.230	.329	.297	.627	60	-3	-4	116	116	7	.532	0	1	-1	1	P	0.0
1958	LA-N	11	12	2	5	0	0	0	0	2	2	.417	.500	.417	.917	140	1	1	105	0	3	1.000	0	0	0	0	P	0.0
	Cin-N	39	60	9	21	1	0	1	9	8	10	.350	.426	.417	.843	116	3	2	107	133	12	.846	0	0	0	-2	P	0.0
	Yr	50	72	11	26	1	0	1	9	10	12	.361	.439	.417	.856	120	4	3	107	104	14	.870	0	0	0	-2		0.0
1959	Cin-N	61	105	10	32	2	0	3	21	17	23	.305	.402	.410	.811	113	3	3	103	163	19	.811	0	0	0	-1	P	0.6
1960	Cin-N	24	36	0	5	1	0	0	1	3	8	.139	.205	.167	.372	3	-5	-5	98	68	2	.290	0	0	0	-1	P	0.0
	Cle-A	24	20	1	6	1	0	0	1	1	7	.300	.333	.350	.683	87	-0	-0	98	56	2	.571	0	0	0	-1	P	0.0
Total	10	452	878	94	238	33	3	15	108	87	147	.271	.339	.367	.706	85	-13	-18	104	119	117	.646	2	1		-5	P	0.6

YEAR	TM/L	G	AB	R	H	2B	3B	HR	RBI	BB	SO	AVG	OBP	SLG	PRO	/A	BR	/A	PF	CHI	RC	TA	SB	CS	SBR	FR	POS	TPR
■ **JOHN NEWELL** Newell, John A. b: 1/14/1868, Wilmington, Del. d: 1/28/19, Wilmington, Del. BR/TL, Deb: 7/22/1891																												
1891	Pit-N	5	18	1	2	0	0	0	2	0	0	.111	.158	.111	.269	-20	-3	-3	101	292	0	.188	0			0	/3	-0.1
■ **T. E. NEWELL** Newell, T. E. b: St.Louis, Mo. Deb: 8/08/1877																												
1877	StL-N	1	3	0	0	0	0	0	0	0	0	.000	.000	.000	.000	-98	-1	-1	102	0	0	.000				0	/S	0.0
■ **AL NEWMAN** Newman, Albert Dwayne b: 6/30/60, Kansas City, Mo. BB/TR, 5'9", 175 lbs. Deb: 6/14/85																												
1985	Mon-N	25	29	7	5	1	0	0	1	3	4	.172	.250	.207	.457	31	-3	-2	94	66	2	.440	2	1	0	-0	2/S	-0.2
1986	Mon-N	95	185	23	37	3	0	1	8	21	20	.200	.282	.232	.514	44	-14	-13	98	69	12	.460	11	11	-3	3	2S	-1.0
1987	Min-A	110	307	44	68	15	5	0	29	34	27	.221	.299	.303	.602	64	-17	-15	96	124	28	.557	15	11	-2	2	S23/OD	-0.8
1988	Min-A	105	260	35	58	7	0	0	19	29	34	.223	.301	.250	.551	53	-14	-17	106	116	22	.507	12	3	2	-5	32S/D	-1.7
Total	4	335	781	109	168	26	5	1	57	87	85	.215	.294	.265	.559	54	-48	-47	100	106	63	.519	40	26	-4	-1	2S/3DO	-3.7
■ **CHARLIE NEWMAN** Newman, Charles "Decker" b: 11/5/1868, Juda, Wis. d: 11/23/47, San Diego, Cal. BR/TR, Deb: N/A.																												
1892	NY-N	3	12	1	4	0	0	0	1	2	0	.333	.429	.333	.762	136	1	1	98	66	3	1.125	3			0	/O	0.1
	Chi-N	16	61	4	10	0	0	0	2	1	6	.164	.177	.164	.341	5	-7	-6	92	63	2	.255	2			0	O	-0.5
	Yr	19	73	5	14	0	0	0	3	3	6	.192	.224	.192	.415	29	-6	-6	93	67	4	.373	5			0		-0.4
Total	1	19	73	5	14	0	0	0	3	3	6	.192	.224	.192	.415	29	-6	-6	93	63	5	.373	5			0	/O	-0.4
■ **JEFF NEWMAN** Newman, Jeffrey Lynn b: 9/11/48, Fort Worth, Tex. BR/TR, 6'2", 215 lbs. Deb: 6/30/76 MC																												
1976	Oak-A	43	77	5	15	4	0	0	4	4	12	.195	.235	.247	.481	41	-6	-6	100	81	5	.371	0	0	0	-7	C	-1.1
1977	Oak-A	94	162	17	36	9	0	4	15	4	24	.222	.246	.352	.597	64	-9	-8	95	86	14	.500	2	0	1	-10	C/P	-1.5
1978	Oak-A	105	268	25	64	7	1	9	32	18	40	.239	.289	.373	.662	84	-6	-6	101	100	28	.564	0	3	-2	-5	C1/D	-1.2
1979	Oak-A	143	516	53	119	17	2	22	71	27	88	.231	.270	.399	.669	88	-18	-10	89	102	51	.569	2	1	0	15	C1/3D	0.5
1980	Oak-A	127	438	37	102	19	1	15	56	25	81	.233	.276	.384	.659	83	-14	-11	95	103	43	.563	3	4	-2	7	1C/32D	-0.6
1981	Oak-A	68	216	17	50	12	0	3	15	9	28	.231	.262	.329	.591	72	-9	-8	96	73	16	.457	0	2	-1	4	C1	-0.3
1982	Oak-A	72	251	19	50	11	0	6	30	14	49	.199	.242	.315	.556	54	-17	-16	95	124	18	.445	0	1	-1	8	C/13D	-0.4
1983	Bos-A	59	132	11	25	4	0	3	7	10	31	.189	.257	.288	.545	49	-9	-9	101	58	9	.446	0	1	-1	-1	C/D	-0.8
1984	Bos-A	24	63	5	14	2	0	1	3	5	16	.222	.279	.302	.581	55	-3	-4	110	54	6	.480	0	0	0	-0	C	-0.2
Total	9	735	2123	189	475	85	4	63	233	116	369	.224	.266	.357	.622	74	-92	-78	95	95	190	.533	7	12	-5	11	C1/D32P	-5.6
■ **PATRICK NEWNAM** Newnam, Patrick Henry b: 12/10/1880, Hempstead, Tex. d: 6/20/38, San Antonio, Tex. BR/TR, 6', 180 lbs. Deb: 5/29/10																												
1910	StL-A	103	384	45	83	3	8	2	26	29		.216	.275	.281	.556	79	-12	-9	94	81	33	.515	16			-2	*1	-0.8
1911	StL-A	20	62	11	12	4	0	0	5	12		.194	.351	.258	.609	74	-2	-1	95	108	7	.700	4			-1	1	-0.1
Total	2	123	446	56	95	7	8	2	31	41		.213	.287	.278	.565	78	-14	-11	94	85	40	.541	20			-3	1	-0.9
■ **SKEETER NEWSOME** Newsome, Lamar Ashby b: 10/18/10, Phenix City, Ala. BR/TR, 5'9", 155 lbs. Deb: 4/19/35																												
1935	Phi-A	59	145	18	30	7	1	1	10	5	9	.207	.233	.290	.523	35	-14	-14	100	75	10	.422	2	1	0	-3	S2/3O	-1.4
1936	Phi-A	127	471	41	106	15	2	0	46	25	27	.225	.266	.265	.531	31	-51	-52	101	122	35	.444	13	4	2	8	*S/23O	-3.0
1937	Phi-A	122	438	53	111	22	1	1	30	37	22	.253	.312	.315	.627	62	-28	-24	94	74	45	.560	11	5	0	4	*S	-1.1
1938	Phi-A	17	48	7	13	4	0	0	7	1	4	.271	.286	.354	.640	59	-3	-3	101	139	5	.528	1	1	-0	-2	S	-0.4
1939	Phi-A	99	248	22	55	9	1	0	17	19	12	.222	.277	.266	.543	41	-23	-22	97	87	17	.433	5	7	-3	-2	S/2	-1.5
1941	Bos-A	93	227	28	51	6	0	2	17	22	11	.225	.296	.278	.574	51	-15	-16	103	87	20	.519	10	4	1	2	S2	-0.8
1942	Bos-A	29	95	7	26	6	0	0	9	9	5	.274	.337	.337	.673	86	-1	-2	104	99	11	.597	2	1	0	1	32/S	0.0
1943	Bos-A	114	449	48	119	21	2	1	22	21	21	.265	.301	.327	.628	81	-10	-12	104	57	43	.506	5	6	-2	8	S3	-0.4
1944	Bos-A	136	472	41	114	26	3	0	41	33	21	.242	.291	.309	.600	73	-18	-17	98	101	43	.492	4	3	-1	3	*S/23	-0.6
1945	Bos-A	125	438	45	127	30	1	1	48	20	15	.290	.322	.370	.692	106	-1	1	95	105	51	.578	6	3	0	7	2S3	1.2
1946	Phi-N	112	375	35	87	10	2	1	23	30	23	.232	.289	.277	.566	64	-19	-17	95	82	33	.474	4			-11	*S/23	-2.1
1947	Phi-N	95	310	36	71	8	2	2	22	24	24	.229	.284	.287	.572	52	-21	-21	100	86	26	.480	4			-2	S/23	-1.5
Total	12	1128	3716	381	910	164	15	9	292	246	194	.245	.293	.304	.597	62	-206	-198	98	90	338	.509	67	35		12	S2/3O	-11.6
■ **GUS NIARHOS** Niarhos, Constantine Gregory b: 12/6/20, Birmingham, Ala. BR/TR, 6', 160 lbs. Deb: 6/09/46 C																												
1946	NY-A	37	40	11	9	1	1	0	2	11	2	.225	.392	.300	.692	95	0	0	100	63	6	.727	1	0	0	0	C	0.2
1948	NY-A	83	228	41	61	12	2	0	19	52	15	.268	.404	.338	.741	98	2	2	100	83	36	.751	1	3	-2	-2	C	0.4
1949	NY-A	32	43	7	12	2	1	0	6	13	8	.279	.456	.372	.828	120	2	2	100	129	9	.938	0	0	0	-0	C	0.3
1950	NY-A	1	0	0	0	0	0	0	0	0	0	—	—	—	—	—	0	0	99	—	—	—	0	0	0	0	R	0.0
	Chi-A	41	105	17	34	4	0	0	16	14	6	.324	.408	.362	.770	101	1	1	97	145	16	.716	0	0	0	3	C	0.5
	Yr	42	105	17	34	4	0	0	16	14	6	.324	.408	.362	.770	101	1	1	97	142	16	.716	0	0	0	3		0.5
1951	Chi-A	66	168	27	43	6	0	1	10	47	9	.256	.419	.310	.728	102	3	4	97	65	26	.774	4	3	-1	-3	C	0.5
1952	Bos-A	29	58	4	6	0	0	0	4	12	9	.103	.268	.103	.371	6	-7	-8	107	249	3	.358	0	0	0	1	C	-0.5
1953	Bos-A	16	35	6	7	1	1	0	2	4	4	.200	.300	.286	.586	54	-2	-2	109	74	3	.517	0	1	-1	0	C	-0.1
1954	Phi-N	3	5	0	1	0	0	0	0	0	1	.200	.200	.200	.400	5	-1	-1	99	0	0	.250	0	0	0	0	/C	0.0
1955	Phi-N	7	9	1	1	0	0	0	0	0	2	.111	.111	.111	.222	-40	-2	-2	102	0	0	.111	0	0	0	0	/C	0.0
Total	9	315	691	114	174	26	5	1	59	153	56	.252	.390	.308	.699	88	-3	-3	100	101	107	.716	6	7	-2	-1	C	1.3
■ **SAM NICHOL** Nichol, Samuel Anderson b: 4/20/1869, Ireland d: 4/19/37, Steubenville, Ohio BR/TR, 5'10", 178 lbs. Deb: 1888																												
1888	Pit-N	8	22	3	1	0	0	0	0	2	2	.045	.125	.045	.170	-45	-3	-3	95	0	0	.143	0			0	/O	-0.2
1890	Col-a	14	56	7	9	0	0	0		2		.161	.190	.161	.350	5	-7	-6	99	0	2	.298	3			0	O	-0.5
Total	2	22	78	10	10	0	0	0	0	4	2	.128	.171	.128	.299	-9	-10	-10	98	0	2	.250	3			0	/O	-0.7
■ **DON NICHOLAS** Nicholas, Donald Leigh b: 10/30/30, Phoenix, Ariz. BL/TR, 5'7", 150 lbs. Deb: 4/16/52																												
1952	Chi-A	3	2	0	0	0	0	0	0	0	0	.000	.000	.000	.000	-99	-1	-1	100	0	0	.000	0	0	0	0	H	0.0
1954	Chi-A	7	0	3	0	0	0	0	0	1	0	—	1.000	—	1.000	184	0	0	104	0	0	1.000	0	1	-1	0	H	0.0
Total	2	10	2	3	0	0	0	0	0	1	0	.000	.333	.000	.333	-2	-0	-0	101	0	0	.333	0	1	-1	0		0.0
■ **SIMON NICHOLLS** Nicholls, Simon Burdette b: 7/18/1882, Germantown, Md. d: 3/12/11, Baltimore, Md. BL/TR, Deb: 03																												
1903	Det-A	2	8	0	3	0	0	0	0	0		.375	.375	.375	.750	132	0	0	97	0	1	.600	0			0	/S	0.0
1906	Phi-A	12	44	1	8	1	0	0	1	3		.182	.234	.205	.439	42	-3	-3	94	43	2	.333	0			0	S	-0.2
1907	Phi-A	124	460	75	139	12	2	0	23	24		.302	.337	.337	.674	110	8	5	106	56	58	.598	13			5	S23	1.4
1908	Phi-A	150	550	58	119	17	3	4	31	35		.216	.263	.280	.543	73	-13	-17	108	74	42	.471	14			-25	*S2/3	-4.4
1909	Phi-A	21	71	10	15	2	1	0	3	3		.211	.243	.268	.511	60	-3	-3	102	62	4	.393	0			-3	S/31	-0.5
1910	Cle-A	3	0	0	0	0	0	0	0	0		—	—	—	—	—	0	0	100	—	—	—	0			0	/S	0.0
Total	6	312	1133	144	284	32	6	4	58	65		.251	.291	.300	.591	87	-11	-18	106	64	112	.509	27			-22	S/231	-3.7
■ **AL NICHOLS** Nichols, Alfred H. b: Brooklyn, N.Y. 5'11", 180 lbs. Deb: 4/24/1875																												
1875	Atl-n	32	132	4	21							.159															3	
1876	NY-N	57	212	20	38	4	0	0	9	2	3	.179	.187	.198	.385	33	-15	-11	87	72	8	.253				6	*3	-0.5
1877	Lou-N	6	19	1	4	0	1	0	0	0	2	.211	.211	.316	.526	48	-1	-2	132	0	1	.400				0	/2S31	-0.1
Total	2	63	231	21	42	4	1	0	9	2	5	.182	.189	.208	.397	35	-16	-13	91	66	9	.265				6	/321S	-0.6
■ **ART NICHOLS** Nichols, Arthur Francis (born Arthur Francis Meikle) b: 7/14/1871, Manchester, N.H. d: 8/9/45, Willimantic, Conn. 5'10", 175 lbs. Deb: 9/16/1898																												
1898	Chi-N	14	42	7	12	1	0	0	6	4		.286	.388	.310	.697	100	1	0	103	140	8	.867	6			0	C	0.0
1899	Chi-N	17	47	5	12	2	0	1	11	0		.255	.286	.362	.647	82	-1	-1	96	169	6	.629	3			0	C	0.0
1900	Chi-N	8	25	1	5	0	0	0	0	3		.200	.286	.200	.486	40	-2	-2	93	0	2	.450	1			0	/C	-0.1
1901	StL-N	93	308	50	75	11	3	1	33	10		.244	.267	.308	.576	71	-13	-11	97	113	30	.511	14			4	CO	-0.5
1902	StL-N	73	251	36	67	12	0	1	31	21		.267	.324	.327	.650	108	1	2	95	129	33	.658	18			-3	1C/O	-0.1
1903	StL-N	36	120	13	23	2	0	0	9	12		.192	.265	.208	.473	38	-9	-9	96	118	9	.474	9			-3	1/OC	-1.1
Total	6	241	793	112	194	28	3	3	90	50		.245	.294	.299	.592	79	-24	-20	96	120	87	.573	51			-2	/C1O	-1.8
■ **CARL NICHOLS** Nichols, Carl Edward b: 10/14/62, Los Angeles, Cal. BR/TR, 6', 184 lbs. Deb: 9/14/86																												
1986	Bal-A	5	5	0	0	0	0	0	0	1	4	.000	.167	.000	.167	-50	-1	-1	99	0	0	.200	0	0	0	0	/C	0.0

YEAR	TM/L	G	AB	R	H	2B	3B	HR	RBI	BB	SO	AVG	OBP	SLG	PRO	/A	BR	/A	PF	CHI	RC	TA	SB	CS	SBR	FR	POS	TPR
1987	Bal-A	13	21	4	8	1	0	0	3	1	4	.381	.409	.429	.838	127	1	1	98	133	4	.769	0	0	0	1	C	0.3
1988	Bal-A	18	47	2	9	1	0	0	1	3	10	.191	.240	.213	.453	29	-4	-4	95	40	2	.317	0	0	0	2	C/O	-0.1
Total	3	36	73	6	17	2	0	0	4	5	18	.233	.282	.260	.542	53	-5	-4	96	63	6	.407	0	0	0	3	/CO	0.2
■ ROY NICHOLS	Nichols, Roy b: 3/3/21, Little Rock, Ark. BR/TR, 5'11", 155 lbs. Deb: 5/06/44																											
1944	NY-N	11	9	3	2	1	0	0	0	2	2	.222	.364	.333	.697	94	0	0	104	0	1	.714	0			0	/23	0.0
■ REID NICHOLS	Nichols, Thomas Reid b: 8/5/58, Ocala, Fla. BR/TR, 5'11", 165 lbs. Deb: 9/16/80																											
1980	Bos-A	12	36	5	8	0	1	0	3	3	8	.222	.282	.278	.560	53	-2	-2	102	117	3	.448	0	1	-1	1	/OD	-0.1
1981	Bos-A	39	48	13	9	0	1	0	3	2	6	.188	.220	.229	.449	28	-4	-5	106	107	3	.325	0	1	-1	-3	O/3D	-0.8
1982	Bos-A	92	245	35	74	16	1	7	33	14	28	.302	.342	.461	.804	107	6	2	110	98	38	.751	5	3	-0	4	O/D	0.4
1983	Bos-A	100	274	35	78	22	1	6	22	26	36	.285	.353	.438	.791	115	6	6	101	62	42	.757	7	5	-1	3	OD/S	0.7
1984	Bos-A	74	124	14	28	5	1	1	14	12	18	.226	.309	.306	.616	64	-5	-6	110	136	13	.567	2	1	0	-4	O/D	-1.1
1985	Bos-A	21	32	3	6	1	0	1	3	2	4	.188	.257	.313	.570	54	-2	-2	102	91	3	.519	1	0	0	-2	O/2D	-0.3
	Chi-A	51	118	20	35	7	1	1	15	15	13	.297	.376	.398	.774	112	2	2	100	119	18	.753	5	5	-2	-6	O/D	-0.5
	Yr	72	150	23	41	8	1	2	18	17	17	.273	.351	.380	.731	100	0	0	101	112	21	.704	6	5	-1	-8		-0.8
1986	Chi-A	74	136	9	31	4	0	2	18	11	23	.228	.286	.301	.587	60	-7	-7	101	153	12	.514	5	4	-1	-3	O/2D	-1.2
1987	Mon-N	77	147	22	39	8	2	4	20	14	13	.265	.333	.429	.762	94	-0	-1	106	106	21	.708	2	1	0	-1	O/3	-0.3
Total	8	540	1160	156	308	63	8	22	131	99	149	.266	.328	.391	.719	92	-6	-13	105	104	151	.670	27	21	-5	-9	O/D23S	-3.2
■ DAVE NICHOLSON	Nicholson, David Lawrence b: 8/29/39, St.Louis, Mo. BR/TR, 6'2", 215 lbs. Deb: 5/24/60																											
1960	Bal-A	54	113	17	21	1	1	5	11	20	55	.186	.308	.345	.653	75	-4	-4	102	80	12	.615	0	2	-1	-5	O	-1.2
1962	Bal-A	97	173	25	30	4	1	9	15	27	76	.173	.289	.364	.653	79	-7	-5	95	66	19	.631	3	4	-2	-7	O	-1.7
1963	Chi-A	126	449	53	103	11	4	22	70	63	175	.229	.324	.419	.743	102	4	1	104	118	65	.723	2	1	0	-2	*O	-0.4
1964	Chi-A	97	294	40	60	6	1	13	39	52	126	.204	.330	.364	.693	97	-2	-0	96	113	38	.672	0	2	-1	-7	O	-1.2
1965	Chi-A	54	85	11	13	2	1	2	12	9	40	.153	.234	.271	.505	47	-6	-6	92	172	6	.438	0	0	0	-8	O	-1.6
1966	Hou-N	100	280	36	69	8	4	10	31	46	92	.246	.359	.411	.769	116	6	7	97	90	45	.778	1	1	-0	1	O	0.6
1967	Atl-N	10	25	2	5	0	0	0	1	2	9	.200	.259	.200	.459	32	-2	-2	104	83	2	.350	0	0	0	0	/O	-0.2
Total	7	538	1419	184	301	32	12	61	179	219	573	.212	.320	.381	.701	95	-11	-9	99	104	186	.684	6	10	-4	-28	O	-5.7
■ FRED NICHOLSON	Nicholson, Fred "Shoemaker" b: 9/1/1894, Honey Grove, Tex. d: 1/23/72, Kilgore, Tex. BR/TR, 5'10.5", 173 lbs. Deb: 4/11/17																											
1917	Det-A	13	14	4	4	1	0	0	1	1	2	.286	.333	.357	.690	113	0	0	98	72	2	.600	0			-1	/O	0.0
1919	Pit-N	30	66	8	18	2	2	1	6	6	11	.273	.333	.409	.742	117	2	1	105	78	9	.729	2			-1	O/1	0.0
1920	Pit-N	99	247	33	89	16	7	4	30	18	31	.360	.404	.530	.934	165	20	20	101	81	51	.963	9	6	-1	2	O	1.9
1921	Bos-N	83	245	36	80	11	7	5	41	17	29	.327	.370	.490	.860	135	9	11	93	111	43	.840	5	4	-1	-6	O/12	0.1
1922	Bos-N	78	222	31	56	4	5	2	29	23	24	.252	.336	.342	.678	80	-8	-6	94	124	26	.630	5	7	-3	-6	O	-1.5
Total	5	303	794	112	247	34	21	12	107	65	97	.311	.367	.452	.819	126	23	27	97	102	131	.798	21	17		-12	O/12	0.5
■ OVID NICHOLSON	Nicholson, Ovid Edward b: 12/30/1888, Salem, Ind. d: 3/24/68, Salem, Ind. BL/TR, 5'9.5", 155 lbs. Deb: 9/17/12																											
1912	Pit-N	6	11	2	5	0	0	0	3	1	2	.455	.500	.455	.955	164	1	1	99	202	3	1.000	0			-0	/O	0.0
■ PARSON NICHOLSON	Nicholson, Thomas C. "Deacon" b: 4/14/1863, Blaine, Ohio d: 2/28/17, Bellaire, Ohio 6'6", 190 lbs. Deb: 1888																											
1888	Det-N	24	85	11	22	2	3	1	9	2	7	.259	.284	.388	.672	116	1	1	98	90	11	.667	6			0	2	0.1
1890	Tol-a	134	523	78	140	16	11	4		42		.268	.328	.363	.691	103	3	1	103	0	79	.739	46			-14	*2/C	-0.6
1895	Was-N	10	38	7	7	2	1	0	5	7	4	.184	.311	.289	.601	55	-2	-3	103	122	5	.774	6			0	S	-0.1
Total	3	168	646	96	169	20	15	5	14	51	11	.262	.321	.362	.684	102	2	-0	102	19	96	.732	58			-14	2/SC	-0.6
■ BILL NICHOLSON	Nicholson, William Beck "Swish" b: 12/11/14, Chestertown, Md. BL/TR, 6', 205 lbs. Deb: 6/13/36																											
1936	Phi-A	11	12	2	0	0	0	0	0	0	5	.000	.000	.000	.000	-99	-4	-4	101	0	0	.000	0	0	0	-0	/O	-0.3
1939	Chi-N	58	220	37	65	12	5	5	38	20	29	.295	.354	.464	.818	117	5	5	101	126	38	.782	0			0	O	0.4
1940	Chi-N	135	491	78	146	27	7	25	98	50	67	.297	.366	.534	.899	146	29	29	100	110	97	.901	2			-4	*O	2.0
1941	Chi-N	147	532	74	135	26	1	26	98	82	91	.254	.357	.453	.810	136	19	24	94	118	90	.807	1			-0	*O	1.7
1942	Chi-N	152	588	83	173	22	11	21	78	76	80	.294	.382	.476	.859	157	38	40	96	81	112	.882	8			10	*O	**4.9**
1943	Chi-N	154	608	95	188	30	9	**29**	**128**	71	86	.309	.386	.531	.917	166	48	49	99	108	129	.944	4			4	*O	4.9
1944	Chi-N	156	582	**116**	167	35	8	**33**	**122**	93	71	.287	.391	.545	.935	160	47	47	101	111	132	1.002	3			0	*O	3.5
1945	Chi-N	151	559	82	136	28	4	13	88	92	73	.243	.356	.377	.734	105	5	6	99	129	81	.725	4			-1	*O	-0.1
1946	Chi-N	105	296	36	65	13	2	8	41	44	44	.220	.325	.358	.683	99	-2	-0	94	118	37	.651	1			0	O	-0.1
1947	Chi-N	148	487	69	119	28	1	26	75	87	83	.244	.364	.466	.831	118	14	13	101	93	90	.860	1			-6	*O	0.2
1948	Chi-N	143	494	68	129	24	5	19	67	81	60	.261	.371	.445	.816	129	15	20	93	92	88	.832	2			-9	*O	0.1
1949	Phi-N	98	299	42	70	8	3	11	40	45	53	.234	.344	.391	.735	96	-1	-1	101	101	44	.730	1			-1	O	-0.7
1950	Phi-N	41	58	3	13	2	1	3	10	8	16	.224	.318	.448	.766	102	-0	-0	97	110	8	.723	0			-3	O	-0.3
1951	Phi-N	85	170	23	41	9	2	8	30	25	24	.241	.342	.459	.801	117	3	4	97	114	29	.794	0	1	-1	-5	O	-0.2
1952	Phi-N	55	88	17	24	3	0	6	19	14	26	.273	.390	.511	.902	147	6	6	101	118	20	.969	0	0	0	-2	O	0.3
1953	Phi-N	38	62	12	13	5	1	2	16	12	20	.210	.338	.419	.757	97	-0	-0	99	195	9	.745	0	0	0	-3	O	-0.3
Total	16	1677	5546	837	1484	272	60	235	948	800	828	.268	.365	.465	.830	132	221	236	98	108	1005	.851	27	1		-21	*O	16.0
■ GEORGE NICOL	Nicol, George Edward b: 10/17/1870, Barry, Ill. d: 8/10/24, Milwaukee, Wis. TL , 5'7", 155 lbs. Deb: 9/23/1890																											
1890	StL-a	3	7	4	2	1	0	0		4		.286	.545	.429	.974	165	1	1	116	0	2	1.400	0			0	/P	0.0
1891	Chi-N	3	6	0	2	0	1	0	3	0	1	.333	.333	.667	1.000	179	1	1	106	219	1	1.000	0			0	/P	0.0
1894	Pit-N	8	20	8	9	1	0	0	3	0	1	.450	.450	.500	.950	139	1	1	94	83	5	.909	0			0	/P	0.0
	Lou-N	27	108	12	38	6	4	0	19	2	3	.352	.375	.481	.856	121	1	3	88	107	22	.857	4			0	O/P	0.3
	Yr	35	128	20	47	7	4	0	22	2	4	.367	.386	.484	.871	123	2	4	89	103	26	.864	4			0		0.3
Total	3	41	141	24	51	8	5	0	25	6	5	.362	.396	.489	.885	129	4	6	92	100	29	.900	4			0	/OP	0.3
■ HUGH NICOL	Nicol, Hugh b: 1/1/1858, Campsie, Scotland d: 6/27/21, Lafayette, Ind. BR/TR, 5'4", 145 lbs. Deb: 5/03/1881 M																											
1881	Chi-N	26	108	13	22	2	0	0	7	4	12	.204	.232	.222	.454	40	-7	-8	108	107	6	.326				4	O/S	-0.3
1882	Chi-N	47	186	19	37	9	1	1	16	7	29	.199	.228	.274	.502	60	-8	-8	101	102	12	.389				8	O/S	0.0
1883	StL-a	94	368	73	106	13	3	0		18		.288	.321	.340	.661	105	5	1	108	0	41	.546				11	*O2	1.1
1884	StL-a	110	442	79	115	14	5	0		22		.260	.300	.314	.614	94	2	-5	110	0	43	.502				19	*O2/S3	1.2
1885	StL-a	112	425	59	88	11	1	0		34		.207	.271	.238	.508	69	-16	-11	93	0	28	.409				9	*O/3	-0.7
1886	StL-a	67	253	44	52	6	3	0		26		.206	.280	.253	.533	62	-8	-13	111	0	29	.637	38			-0	O/S2	-1.2
1887	Cin-a	125	475	122	102	18	2	1		86		.215	.341	.267	.608	67	-13	-21	108	0	93	.954	**138**			-4	*O	-2.3
1888	Cin-a	135	548	112	131	10	2	1	35	67		.239	.330	.270	.600	96	1	1	101	60	85	.779	103			-1	*O2/S	-0.4
1889	Cin-a	122	474	82	121	7	8	2	58	54	35	.255	.338	.316	.654	85	-5	-9	105	102	80	.819	80			0	*O/23	-1.1
1890	Cin-N	50	186	28	39	1	4	0	19	19	12	.210	.283	.258	.541	55	-9	-11	108	122	21	.619	24			-1	O/S2	-1.1
Total	10	888	3465	631	813	91	29	5	135	337	88	.235	.307	.282	.589	79	-57	-86	105	39	437	.649	383			45	O/2S3	-4.8
■ STEVE NICOSIA	Nicosia, Steven Richard b: 8/6/55, Paterson, N.J. BR/TR, 5'10", 185 lbs. Deb: 7/08/78																											
1978	Pit-N	3	5	0	0	0	0	0	0	1	0	.000	.167	.000	.167	-47	-1	-1	105	0	0	.200	0	0	0	0	/C	0.0
1979	Pit-N	70	191	22	55	16	0	4	13	23	17	.288	.364	.435	.799	111	5	3	106	54	29	.741	0	2	-1	-3	C	0.1
1980	Pit-N	60	176	16	38	8	0	1	22	19	16	.216	.296	.278	.574	59	-9	-10	103	167	14	.476	0	1	-1	2	C	-0.7
1981	Pit-N	54	169	21	39	10	1	2	18	13	10	.231	.286	.337	.623	79	-6	-5	96	112	15	.529	3	1	0	4	C	0.0
1982	Pit-N	39	100	6	28	3	0	1	7	11	13	.280	.351	.340	.691	85	-0	-2	110	74	12	.608	0	1	-1	0	C/O	-0.1
1983	Pit-N	21	46	4	6	2	0	1	1	1	7	.130	.149	.239	.388	6	-6	-6	103	28	1	.267	0	0	0	1	C	-0.4
	SF-N	15	33	4	11	0	0	0	6	3	2	.333	.389	.333	.722	101	0	0	101	216	4	.583	0	0	0	0	/C	0.1
	Yr	36	79	8	17	2	0	1	7	4	9	.215	.253	.278	.531	46	-6	-6	102	107	5	.406	0	0	0	1		-0.3
1984	SF-N	48	132	9	40	11	2	2	19	8	14	.303	.343	.462	.805	129	4	4	96	111	20	.729	1	1	-0	-1	C	0.5
1985	Mon-N	42	71	4	12	2	0	0	1	7	11	.169	.244	.197	.441	26	-7	-7	94	28	4	.361	1	0	0	-3	C/1	-0.8
	Tor-A	6	15	0	4	0	0	0	1	0	0	.267	.267	.267	.533	46	-1	-1	101	99	1	.364	0	0	0	-0	/C	0.0

YEAR	TM/L	G	AB	R	H	2B	3B	HR	RBI	BB	SO	AVG	OBP	SLG	PRO	/A	BR	/A	PF	CHI	RC	TA	SB	CS	SBR	FR	POS	TPR
Total	8	358	938	86	233	52	3	11	88	86	90	.248	.312	.345	.658	82	-21	-23	101	99	99	.585	5	6	-2	-0	C/O1	-1.3
■ **CHARLIE NIEBERGALL** Niebergall, Charles Arthur "Nig" b: 5/23/1899, New York, N.Y. d: 8/29/82, Holiday, Fla. BR/TR, 5'10", 160 lbs. Deb: 6/17/21																												
1921	StL-N	5	6	1	1	0	0	0	0	0	0	.167	.167	.167	.333	-12	-1	-1	95	0	0	.200	0	0	0	0	/C	0.0
1923	StL-N	9	28	2	3	1	0	0	1	2	2	.107	.167	.143	.310	-20	-5	-4	90	88	1	.240	0	0	0	-1	/C	-0.4
1924	StL-N	40	58	6	17	6	0	0	7	3	9	.293	.339	.397	.735	94	-0	-1	103	111	8	.659	0	0	0	-1	C	0.0
Total	3	54	92	9	21	7	0	0	8	5	11	.228	.276	.304	.580	55	-6	-6	98	97	9	.479	0	0	0	-2	/C	-0.4
■ **AL NIEHAUS** Niehaus, Albert Bernard b: 6/1/1899, Cincinnati, Ohio d: 10/14/31, Cincinnati, Ohio BR/TR, 5'11", 175 lbs. Deb: 4/22/25																												
1925	Pit-N	17	64	7	14	8	0	0	7	1	5	.219	.242	.344	.586	47	-5	-5	102	115	5	.480	0	0	0	-0	1	-0.6
	Cin-N	51	147	16	44	10	2	0	14	13	10	.299	.360	.395	.755	95	-1	-1	97	86	20	.682	1	4	-2	0	1	-0.6
	Yr	68	211	23	58	18	2	0	21	14	15	.275	.326	.379	.705	81	-7	-6	99	95	25	.618	1	4	-2	-0		-1.2
Total	1	68	211	23	58	18	2	0	21	14	15	.275	.326	.379	.705	81	-7	-6	99	94	25	.618	1	4	-2	-0	/1	-1.2
■ **BERT NIEHOFF** Niehoff, John Albert b: 5/13/1884, Louisville, Colo. d: 12/8/74, Inglewood, Cal. BR/TR, 5'10.5", 170 lbs. Deb: 10/04/13 C																												
1913	Cin-N	2	8	0	0	0	0	0	0	0	2	.000	.000	.000	.000	-98	-2	-2	102	0	0	.000	0			0	/3	-0.1
1914	Cin-N	142	484	46	117	16	9	4	49	38	77	.242	.298	.337	.635	85	-8	-10	105	104	52	.605	20			6	*3/2	0.1
1915	Phi-N	148	529	61	126	27	2	2	49	30	63	.238	.280	.308	.588	73	-15	-19	107	113	50	.519	21	11	-0	-4	*2	-2.4
1916	Phi-N	146	548	65	133	**42**	4	4	61	37	57	.243	.292	.356	.648	103	-2	0	96	113	60	.590	20	14	-2	2	*2/3	0.6
1917	Phi-N	114	361	30	92	17	4	2	42	23	29	.255	.303	.341	.644	90	-2	-5	108	126	39	.580	8			6	2/13	0.7
1918	StL-N	22	84	5	15	2	0	0	5	3	10	.179	.207	.202	.409	27	-8	-7	93	118	4	.319	2			4	2	-0.1
	NY-N	7	23	3	6	0	0	0	1	0	4	.261	.261	.261	.522	61	-1	-1	98	63	1	.353	0			-1	/2	-0.1
	Yr	29	107	8	21	2	0	0	6	3	14	.196	.218	.215	.433	34	-9	-8	94	109	5	.326	2			3		-0.2
Total	6	581	2037	210	489	104	19	12	207	131	242	.240	.288	.327	.615	84	-37	-44	103	112	206	.556	71	25		13	23/1	-1.3
■ **MILT NIELSEN** Nielsen, Milton Robert b: 2/8/25, Tyler, Minn. BL/TL, 5'11", 190 lbs. Deb: 9/27/49																												
1949	Cle-A	3	9	1	1	0	0	0	0	2	4	.111	.273	.111	.384	4	-1	-1	98	0	0	.375	0	0	0	-0	/O	-0.1
1951	Cle-A	16	6	1	0	0	0	0	0	1	1	.000	.143	.000	.143	-62	-1	-1	95	0	0	.167	0	0	0	0	H	0.0
Total	2	19	15	2	1	0	0	0	0	3	5	.067	.222	.067	.289	-22	-3	-2	96	0	0	.286	0	0	0	-0	/O	-0.1
■ **BUTCH NIEMAN** Nieman, Elmer Le Roy b: 2/8/18, Herkimer, Kan. BL/TL, 6'2", 195 lbs. Deb: 5/02/43																												
1943	Bos-N	101	335	39	84	15	8	7	46	39	39	.251	.331	.406	.737	106	5	2	106	106	47	.709	4			-0	O	0.0
1944	Bos-N	134	468	65	124	16	6	16	65	47	47	.265	.332	.427	.759	119	7	10	95	96	69	.724	5			-1	*O	0.0
1945	Bos-N	97	247	43	61	15	0	14	56	43	33	.247	.361	.478	.839	117	10	6	112	121	44	.906	11			-1	O	0.3
Total	3	332	1050	147	269	46	14	37	167	129	119	.256	.339	.432	.771	114	22	19	102	105	161	.770	20			-2	O	0.3
■ **BOB NIEMAN** Nieman, Robert Charles b: 1/26/27, Cincinnati, Ohio d: 3/10/85, Corona, Cal. BR/TR, 5'11", 195 lbs. Deb: 9/14/51																												
1951	StL-A	12	43	6	16	3	1	2	8	3	5	.372	.413	.628	1.041	171	4	4	105	88	11	1.071	0	0	0	0	O	0.4
1952	StL-A	131	478	66	138	22	2	18	74	46	73	.289	.352	.456	.808	127	14	15	97	104	75	.740	0	4	-2	-3	*O	0.7
1953	Det-A	142	508	72	143	32	5	15	69	57	57	.281	.354	.453	.807	119	11	12	98	95	82	.753	0	3	-2	0	*O	0.7
1954	Det-A	91	251	24	66	14	1	8	35	22	32	.263	.322	.422	.745	103	-0	0	100	102	31	.650	0	2	-1	-5	O	-0.7
1955	Chi-A	99	272	36	77	11	2	11	53	36	37	.283	.371	.460	.831	121	8	8	101	125	46	.804	1	0	0	-8	O	-0.3
1956	Chi-A	14	40	3	12	1	0	2	4	4	4	.300	.364	.475	.839	115	1	1	104	60	5	.697	0	1	-1	0	O	0.0
	Bal-A	114	388	60	125	20	6	12	64	86	59	.322	.445	.497	.943	158	31	35	94	111	89	1.007	1	5	-3	2	*O	2.7
	Yr	128	428	63	137	21	6	14	68	90	63	.320	.438	.495	.934	153	32	35	95	105	96	.987	1	6	-3	2		2.7
1957	Bal-A	129	445	61	123	17	6	13	70	63	86	.276	.369	.429	.798	126	12	16	93	123	70	.765	4	4	-1	-0	*O	0.7
1958	Bal-A	105	366	56	119	20	2	16	60	44	57	.325	.398	.522	.919	160	26	28	94	103	71	.888	2	8	-4	-12	*O	0.6
1959	Bal-A	118	360	49	105	18	2	21	60	42	55	.292	.369	.528	.897	148	21	22	97	93	67	.874	1	2	-1	-3	O	1.3
1960	StL-N	81	188	19	54	13	5	4	31	24	31	.287	.374	.473	.847	120	8	6	108	125	33	.821	0	1	-1	-11	O	-0.6
1961	StL-N	6	17	0	8	1	0	0	2	0	2	.471	.471	.529	1.000	146	2	1	113	90	4	1.000	0	0	0	-1	/O	0.0
	Cle-A	39	65	2	23	6	0	2	10	7	4	.354	.417	.538	.955	159	5	5	96	95	16	1.024	1	0	0	0	O	0.5
1962	Cle-A	2	1	0	0	0	0	0	1	0	1	.000	.000	.000	.000	-99	-0	-0	98	0	0	.000	0	0	0	0	H	0.0
	SF-N	30	30	1	9	2	0	1	3	1	9	.300	.300	.467	.789	108	0	0	101	70	5	.714	0	0	0	-1	/O	0.0
Total	12	1113	3452	455	1018	180	32	125	544	435	512	.295	.375	.474	.849	133	142	154	97	106	605	.849	10	30	-15	-41	O	6.0
■ **AL NIEMIEC** Niemiec, Alfred Joseph b: 5/18/11, Meriden, Conn. BR/TR, 5'11", 158 lbs. Deb: 9/19/34																												
1934	Bos-A	9	32	2	7	0	0	0	3	3	4	.219	.286	.219	.504	30	-3	-3	106	146	2	.400	0	0	0	0	/2	-0.2
1936	Phi-A	69	203	22	40	3	2	1	20	26	16	.197	.291	.246	.538	34	-21	-21	101	122	16	.479	2	2	-1	4	2/S	-1.2
Total	2	78	235	24	47	3	2	1	23	29	20	.200	.291	.243	.533	33	-24	-25	101	125	18	.468	2	2	-1	4	/2S	-1.4
■ **TOM NIETO** Nieto, Thomas Andrew b: 10/27/60, Downey, Cal. BR/TR, 6'1", 193 lbs. Deb: 5/10/84																												
1984	StL-N	33	86	7	24	4	0	3	12	5	18	.279	.319	.430	.749	110	1	1	99	102	11	.646	0	0	0	1	C	0.2
1985	StL-N	95	253	15	57	10	2	0	34	26	37	.225	.305	.281	.586	68	-11	-10	96	191	21	.483	0	2	-1	-10	C	-1.8
1986	Mon-N	30	65	5	13	3	1	1	7	6	21	.200	.278	.323	.601	67	-3	-3	98	116	5	.500	0	1	-1	-3	C	-0.5
1987	Min-A	41	105	7	21	7	1	1	12	8	24	.200	.276	.314	.590	59	-6	-6	96	133	10	.518	0	0	0	-4	C/D	-0.5
1988	Min-A	24	60	1	4	0	0	0	0	1	17	.067	.097	.067	.163	-50	-12	-13	106	0	0	.103	0	0	0	0	C	-1.1
Total	5	223	569	35	119	24	4	5	65	46	117	.209	.278	.292	.569	59	-32	-31	97	139	47	.484	0	3	-2	-16	C/D	-3.7
■ **TOM NILAND** Niland, Thomas James "Honest Tom" b: 4/14/1870, Brookfield, Mass. d: 4/30/50, Lynn, Mass. BR/TR, 5'11", 160 lbs. Deb: 4/19/1896																												
1896	StL-N	18	68	3	12	0	1	0	3	5	4	.176	.243	.206	.449	21	-8	-7	95	65	3	.357	0			0	O/S	-0.5
■ **HARRY NILES** Niles, Herbert Clyde b: 9/10/1880, Buchanan, Mich. d: 4/18/53, Sturgis, Mich. BR/TR, 5'8", 175 lbs. Deb: 4/24/06																												
1906	StL-A	142	541	71	124	14	4	2	31	46		.229	.290	.281	.571	82	-11	-10	98	63	54	.547	30			-0	*O3	-1.2
1907	StL-A	120	492	65	142	9	5	2	35	28		.289	.327	.339	.666	117	8	9	98	64	62	.611	19			-2	*2/O	0.7
1908	NY-A	96	362	43	90	14	6	4	24	25		.249	.297	.354	.651	119	5	6	95	62	42	.629	18			-9	2/O	-0.4
	Bos-A	17	32	4	8	0	0	1	3	6		.250	.368	.344	.712	137	2	2	98	80	5	.833	3			-1	/2S	0.1
	Yr	113	394	47	98	14	6	5	27	31		.249	.304	.353	.656	120	6	8	96	65	47	.645	21			-9		-0.3
1909	Bos-A	145	546	64	134	12	5	1	39	39		.245	.311	.291	.602	83	-5	-11	109	89	56	.578	27			9	*O3/S2	-0.5
1910	Bos-A	18	57	6	12	3	0	1	3	4		.211	.262	.316	.578	82	-1	-1	99	53	5	.511	1			-1	O	-0.2
	Cle-A	70	240	25	51	6	4	1	18	15		.213	.267	.283	.551	73	-8	-8	100	96	20	.503	9			-2	O/S3	-1.3
	Yr	88	297	31	63	9	4	2	21	19		.212	.266	.290	.556	74	-9	-9	99	87	24	.504	10			-3		-1.5
Total	5	608	2270	278	561	58	24	12	153	163		.247	.302	.310	.612	95	-12	-13	100	73	243	.579	107			-5	O2/3S	-2.8
■ **BILL NILES** Niles, William A. b: 1/1874 Vermont d: 7/3/36, Springfield, Ohio 160 lbs. Deb: 5/13/1895																												
1895	Pit-N	11	37	2	8	0	0	0	0	5	2	.216	.310	.216	.526	40	-3	-3	97	0	3	.517	2			0	3/2	-0.1
■ **RABBIT NILL** Nill, George Charles b: 7/14/1881, Ft.Wayne, Ind. d: 5/24/62, Fort Wayne, Ind. BR/TR, 5'7", 160 lbs. Deb: 9/27/04																												
1904	Was-A	15	48	4	8	0	1	0	3	5		.167	.245	.208	.454	50	-3	-2	93	114	3	.375	0			0	2	-0.2
1905	Was-A	103	319	46	58	7	3	3	31	33		.182	.259	.251	.509	61	-12	-14	104	127	24	.479	12			1	32/S	-1.2
1906	Was-A	89	315	37	74	8	2	0	15	47		.235	.334	.273	.607	102	-0	3	91	61	35	.618	16			-4	S23O	0.0
1907	Was-A	66	215	21	47	7	3	0	25	15		.219	.270	.279	.549	85	-6	-3	90	149	18	.482	6			-12	2O/3	-1.8
	Cle-A	12	43	5	12	1	0	0	2	3		.279	.326	.302	.628	110	0	1	93	58	5	.581	2			0	/3S	0.1
	Yr	78	258	26	59	8	3	0	27	18		.229	.279	.283	.562	89	-5	-3	90	137	23	.497	8			-12		-1.7
1908	Cle-A	11	23	3	5	0	0	0	1	0		.217	.217	.217	.435	41	-1	-2	106	75	1	.278	0			-1	/SO2	-0.2
Total	5	296	963	116	204	23	9	3	77	103		.212	.288	.264	.552	80	-22	-17	96	104	86	.518	36			-16	2/3SO	-3.3
■ **AL NIXON** Nixon, Albert Richard "Humpty Dumpty" b: 4/11/1886, Atlantic City, N.J d: 11/9/60, Opelousas, La. BR/TL, 5'7.5", 164 lbs. Deb: 9/04/15																												
1915	Bro-N	14	26	3	6	1	0	0	2	2	4	.231	.286	.269	.555	67	-1	-1	101	109	2	.476	1	1	-0	-3	O	-0.5
1916	Bro-N	1	2	0	2	0	0	0	0	0	0	1.000	1.000	1.000	2.000	499	1	1	103	0	2	—	0			-0	/O	0.0
1918	Bro-N	6	11	1	5	0	0	0	0	0	0	.455	.455	.455	.909	175	1	1	101	0	2	.833	0			-1	/O	0.0
1921	Bos-N	55	138	25	33	6	3	1	9	7	11	.239	.281	.348	.629	70	-7	-6	93	65	13	.551	3	2	-0	-1	O	-0.8

YEAR	TM/L	G	AB	R	H	2B	3B	HR	RBI	BB	SO	AVG	OBP	SLG	PRO	/A	BR	/A	PF	CHI	RC	TA	SB	CS	SBR	FR	POS	TPR
1922	Bos-N	86	318	35	84	14	4	2	22	9	19	.264	.284	.352	.637	67	-18	-15	94	66	30	.529	6	6	-2	2	O	-1.7
1923	Bos-N	88	321	53	88	12	4	0	19	24	14	.274	.334	.336	.671	78	-10	-10	100	63	37	.589	2	3	-1	13	O	0.0
1926	Phi-N	93	311	38	91	18	2	4	41	13	20	.293	.323	.402	.725	91	-3	-5	103	104	39	.655	5			2	O	-0.5
1927	Phi-N	54	154	18	48	7	0	0	18	5	5	.312	.333	.357	.690	88	-3	-3	96	114	18	.575	1			3	O	-0.1
1928	Phi-N	25	64	7	15	2	0	0	7	6	4	.234	.300	.266	.566	47	-5	-5	104	147	5	.490	1			-1	O	-0.6
Total	9	422	1345	180	372	60	13	7	118	66	77	.277	.314	.356	.670	78	-46	-43	98	83	148	.580	19	12		13	O	-4.2
■ **OTIS NIXON**	Nixon, Otis Junior b: 1/9/59, Columbus Co., N.C. BB/TR, 6'2", 180 lbs. Deb: 9/09/83																											
1983	NY-A	13	14	2	2	0	0	0	0	1	5	.143	.200	.143	.343	-4	-2	-2	99	0	1	.417	2	0	1	-1	/O	-0.1
1984	Cle-A	49	91	16	14	0	0	0	1	8	11	.154	.222	.154	.376	6	-11	-12	106	28	3	.400	12	6	0	-3	O	-1.6
1985	Cle-A	104	162	34	38	4	0	3	9	8	27	.235	.271	.315	.585	63	-9	-8	94	59	12	.577	20	11	-1	-8	OD	-1.6
1986	Cle-A	105	95	33	25	4	1	0	8	13	12	.263	.352	.326	.678	89	-1	-1	98	103	13	.870	23	6	3	-24	O/D	-2.3
1987	Cle-A	19	17	2	1	0	0	0	1	3	4	.059	.200	.059	.259	-25	-3	-3	103	399	0	.316	2	3	-1	-3	O/D	-0.7
1988	Mon-N	90	271	47	66	8	2	0	15	28	42	.244	.314	.288	.602	70	-8	-10	106	77	30	.697	46	13	6	2	O	-0.4
Total	6	380	650	134	146	16	3	3	34	61	101	.225	.291	.272	.563	58	-35	-36	101	77	60	.632	105	39	8	-37	O/D	-6.7
■ **DONELL NIXON**	Nixon, Robert Donell b: 12/31/61, Evergreen, N.C. BR/TR, 6'1", 185 lbs. Deb: 4/07/87																											
1987	Sea-A	46	132	17	33	4	0	3	12	13	28	.250	.327	.348	.675	78	-3	-4	103	87	16	.752	21	7	2	2	O/D	0.0
1988	SF-N	59	78	15	27	3	0	0	6	10	12	.346	.420	.385	.805	141	4	4	94	80	12	.850	11	8	-2	-8	O	-0.6
Total	2	105	210	32	60	7	0	3	18	23	40	.286	.362	.362	.724	100	0	0	99	84	28	.801	32	15	1	-6	/OD	-0.6
■ **RUSS NIXON**	Nixon, Russell Eugene b: 2/19/35, Cleves, Ohio BL/TR, 6'1", 195 lbs. Deb: 4/20/57 MC																											
1957	Cle-A	62	185	15	52	7	1	2	18	12	12	.281	.325	.362	.687	86	-3	-4	102	97	20	.564	0	1	-1	-3	C	-0.5
1958	Cle-A	113	376	42	113	17	4	9	46	13	38	.301	.324	.439	.763	114	3	5	94	96	47	.633	0	3	-2	-11	*C	-0.6
1959	Cle-A	82	258	23	62	10	3	1	29	15	28	.240	.282	.314	.596	66	-13	-12	97	136	21	.468	0	0	0	-3	C	-1.0
1960	Cle-A	25	82	6	20	5	0	1	6	6	6	.244	.311	.341	.653	78	-3	-2	98	76	8	.545	0	1	-1	0	C	-0.1
	Bos-A	80	272	24	81	17	3	5	33	13	23	.298	.330	.438	.767	102	1	0	103	96	36	.653	0	1	-1	-7	C	-0.2
	Yr	105	354	30	101	22	3	6	39	19	29	.285	.325	.415	.741	97	-1	-2	102	92	45	.634	0	2	-1	-6		-0.3
1961	Bos-A	87	242	24	70	12	2	1	19	13	19	.289	.331	.368	.699	85	-5	-5	102	81	29	.584	0	1	-1	-1	C	-0.6
1962	Bos-A	65	151	11	42	7	2	1	19	8	14	.278	.314	.371	.685	82	-4	-4	102	128	17	.566	0	0	0	-1	C	-0.2
1963	Bos-A	98	287	27	77	18	1	5	30	22	32	.268	.329	.390	.719	95	0	-2	106	99	36	.633	0	0	0	4	C	0.3
1964	Bos-A	81	163	10	38	7	0	1	20	14	29	.233	.302	.294	.596	66	-7	-7	102	166	14	.485	0	0	0	2	C	-0.3
1965	Bos-A	59	137	11	37	5	1	0	11	6	23	.270	.301	.321	.622	71	-4	-5	107	104	11	.463	0	0	0	4	C	0.1
1966	Min-A	51	96	5	25	2	1	0	7	7	13	.260	.317	.302	.619	71	-2	-4	111	101	9	.507	0	0	0	-2	C	-0.4
1967	Min-A	74	170	16	40	6	1	1	22	18	29	.235	.309	.300	.609	75	-4	-5	107	170	16	.515	0	0	0	-15	C	-1.6
1968	Bos-A	29	85	1	13	2	0	0	6	7	13	.153	.217	.176	.394	20	-8	-8	101	171	3	.297	0	0	0	-1	C	-0.8
Total	12	906	2504	215	670	115	19	27	266	154	279	.268	.313	.361	.674	85	-49	-53	102	113	266	.580	0	7	-4	-34	C	-5.9
■ **RAY NOBLE**	Noble, Rafael Miguel (Magee) b: 3/15/19, Central Hatillo, Cuba BR/TR, 5'11", 210 lbs. Deb: 4/18/51																											
1951	NY-N	55	141	16	33	6	0	5	26	6	26	.234	.265	.383	.648	71	-6	-6	102	146	13	.526	0	0	0	-2	C	-0.7
1952	NY-N	6	5	0	0	0	0	0	0	0	1	.000	.000	.000	.000	-98	-1	-1	102	0	0	.000	0	0	0	0	/C	0.0
1953	NY-N	46	97	15	20	0	1	4	14	19	14	.206	.353	.351	.703	86	-2	-1	98	119	14	.722	1	0	0	-4	C	-0.1
Total	3	107	243	31	53	6	1	9	40	25	41	.218	.299	.362	.661	75	-9	-9	100	131	27	.609	1	0	0	-5	/C	-0.8
■ **JUNIOR NOBOA**	Noboa, Miliciades Arturo (Diaz) b: 11/10/64, Azua, D.R. BR/TR, 5'10", 155 lbs. Deb: 8/22/84																											
1984	Cle-A	23	11	3	4	0	0	0	0	0	2	.364	.364	.364	.727	96	0	-0	106	0	1	.625	1	0	0	0	2/D	0.1
1987	Cle-A	39	80	7	18	2	1	0	7	3	6	.225	.253	.275	.528	40	-7	-7	103	127	6	.413	1	0	0	-2	2/S3D	-0.6
1988	Cal-A	21	16	4	1	0	0	0	0	0	1	.063	.063	.063	.125	-69	-3	-3	94	0	-0	.059	0	0	0	0	/2S3	-0.1
Total	3	83	107	14	23	2	1	0	7	3	9	.215	.236	.252	.489	31	-10	-10	102	96	7	.372	2	0	1	-1	/2S3D	-0.6
■ **PAUL NOCE**	Noce, Paul David b: 12/16/59, San Francisco, Cal. BR/TR, 5'10", 175 lbs. Deb: 6/01/87																											
1987	Chi-N	70	180	17	41	9	2	3	14	6	49	.228	.261	.350	.611	60	-11	-11	101	78	16	.528	5	3	-0	4	2S/3	-0.2
■ **GEORGE NOFTSKER**	Noftsker, George Washington b: 8/24/1859, Shippensburg, Pa. d: 5/8/31, Shippensburg, Pa. BR/TR, 5'8", 135 lbs. Deb: 4/17/1884																											
1884	Alt-U	7	25	0	1	0	0	0		0		.040	.040	.040	.080	-72	-4	-4	101	0	0	.042	0			0	/OC	-0.3
■ **MATT NOKES**	Nokes, Matthew Dodge b: 10/31/63, San Diego, Cal. BL/TR, 6'1", 185 lbs. Deb: 9/03/85																											
1985	SF-N	19	53	3	11	2	0	2	5	1	9	.208	.236	.358	.595	69	-3	-2	93	80	4	.477	0	0	0	1	C	0.0
1986	Det-A	7	24	2	8	1	0	1	2	1	1	.333	.360	.500	.860	139	1	1	95	53	4	.765	0	0	0	1	/C	0.2
1987	Det-A	135	461	69	133	14	2	32	87	35	70	.289	.347	.536	.882	134	19	21	97	101	82	.848	2	1	0	-2	*CD/O3	2.6
1988	Det-A	122	382	53	96	18	0	16	53	34	58	.251	.314	.424	.738	111	2	4	94	100	49	.661	0	1	-1	1	*C/D	0.9
Total	4	283	920	127	248	35	2	51	147	71	138	.270	.327	.478	.806	122	19	24	96	98	139	.761	2	2	-1	1	C/DO3	3.7
■ **JOE NOLAN**	Nolan, Joseph William b: 5/12/51, St.Louis, Mo. BL/TR, 5'11", 175 lbs. Deb: 9/21/72																											
1972	NY-N	4	10	0	0	0	0	0	0	1	3	.000	.091	.000	.091	-76	-2	-2	95	0	0	.100	0	0	0	0	/C	-0.1
1975	Atl-N	4	4	0	1	0	0	0	0	1	0	.250	.400	.250	.650	88	-0	0	95	0	1	.667	0	0	0	0	/C	0.0
1977	Atl-N	62	82	13	23	3	0	3	9	13	12	.280	.379	.427	.806	103	2	1	113	82	14	.803	1	0	0	1	C	0.2
1978	Atl-N	95	213	22	49	7	3	4	22	34	28	.230	.339	.347	.686	82	-2	-5	112	101	27	.663	3	2	-0	2	C	0.0
1979	Atl-N	89	230	28	57	9	3	4	21	27	28	.248	.335	.365	.700	83	-3	-5	109	87	28	.635	1	3	-2	-3	C	-0.7
1980	Atl-N	17	22	2	6	1	0	0	2	2	4	.273	.333	.318	.652	82	-0	-0	101	113	2	.529	0	0	0	0	/C	0.0
	Cin-N	53	154	14	48	7	0	3	24	13	8	.312	.365	.416	.781	115	4	3	102	130	24	.706	0	0	0	-4	C	0.1
	Yr	70	176	16	54	8	0	3	26	15	12	.307	.361	.403	.765	111	3	3	102	128	26	.688	0	0	0	-4		0.1
1981	Cin-N	81	236	25	73	18	1	1	26	24	19	.309	.375	.407	.782	121	7	7	101	103	35	.709	1	2	-1	-16	C	-0.9
1982	Bal-A	77	219	24	51	7	1	6	35	16	35	.233	.285	.356	.641	75	-8	-8	100	146	22	.546	1	1	-0	-3	C	-0.7
1983	Bal-A	73	184	25	51	11	1	5	24	16	31	.277	.342	.429	.771	110	3	3	100	100	26	.703	0	0	0	-1	C	0.4
1984	Bal-A	35	62	2	18	1	1	1	9	12	10	.290	.405	.387	.793	128	2	3	94	133	11	.818	0	0	0	0	D/C	0.4
1985	Bal-A	31	38	1	5	2	0	0	6	5	5	.132	.233	.184	.417	16	-4	-4	99	340	2	.353	0	0	0	0	/CD	-0.3
Total	11	621	1454	156	382	66	10	27	178	164	183	.263	.340	.378	.718	95	-1	-8	104	114	190	.673	7	8	-3	-24	C/D	-1.6
■ **RED NONNENKAMP**	Nonnenkamp, Leo William b: 7/7/11, St.Louis, Mo. BL/TL, 5'11", 165 lbs. Deb: 9/06/33																											
1933	Pit-N	1	1	0	0	0	0	0	0	0	1	.000	.000	.000	.000	-99	-0	-0	95	0	0	.000	0			0	H	0.0
1938	Bos-A	87	180	37	51	4	1	0	18	21	13	.283	.358	.317	.675	69	-7	-8	102	107	22	.646	6	1	1	1	O/1	-0.5
1939	Bos-A	58	75	12	18	2	1	0	5	12	6	.240	.345	.293	.638	60	-4	-5	108	77	8	.567	0	1	-1	-3	O	-0.7
1940	Bos-A	9	7	0	0	0	0	0	1	0	4	.000	.125	.000	.125	-64	-2	-2	101	0	0	.143	0	0	0	0	H	-0.1
Total	4	155	263	49	69	6	2	0	24	33	24	.262	.347	.300	.647	62	-13	-15	104	95	30	.607	6	2		-2	/O1	-1.3
■ **PETE NOONAN**	Noonan, Peter John b: 11/24/1881, W.Stockbridge, Mass. d: 2/11/65, Great Barrington, Mass. BR/TR, 6', 180 lbs. Deb: 6/20/04																											
1904	Phi-A	39	114	13	23	3	1	2	13	1		.202	.209	.298	.507	60	-5	-5	102	121	7	.396	1			-1	C1	-0.4
1906	Chi-N	5	3	0	1	0	0	0	0	0		.333	.333	.333	.667	103	0	0	107	0	0	.500	0			0	/1	0.0
	StL-N	44	125	8	21	1	3	1	9	11		.168	.235	.248	.483	52	-7	-7	101	97	8	.413	1			-4	C1	-1.0
	Yr	49	128	8	22	1	3	1	9	11		.172	.237	.250	.487	53	-7	-7	101	87	8	.415	1			-4		-1.0
1907	StL-N	74	237	19	53	7	3	1	19	9		.224	.252	.291	.543	75	-8	-7	96	100	19	.440	3			6	C	0.4
Total	3	162	479	40	98	11	7	4	41	21		.205	.238	.282	.520	65	-20	-20	99	103	34	.423	5			0	C/1	-1.0
■ **TIM NORDBROOK**	Nordbrook, Timothy Charles b: 7/7/49, Baltimore, Md. BR/TR, 6'1", 180 lbs. Deb: 9/13/74																											
1974	Bal-A	6	15	4	4	0	0	0	1	2	2	.267	.353	.267	.620	87	-0	-0	93	98	2	.636	1	0	0	0	/S2	0.1
1975	Bal-A	40	34	6	4	1	0	0	0	7	7	.118	.268	.147	.415	22	-3	-3	91	0	2	.400	0	0	0	2	S/2	0.3
1976	Bal-A	27	22	4	5	0	0	0	0	3	5	.227	.320	.227	.547	64	-1	-1	98	0	2	.444	0	0	0	1	2S	0.1
	Cal-A	5	8	1	0	0	0	0	0	1	3	.000	.111	.000	.111	-71	-2	-2	92	0	0	.250	1	0	0	-0	/S2D	0.0
	Yr	32	30	5	5	0	0	0	0	4	8	.167	.265	.167	.431	29	-3	-2	97	0	2	.400	1	0	0	1		0.1

YEAR	TM/L	G	AB	R	H	2B	3B	HR	RBI	BB	SO	AVG	OBP	SLG	PRO	/A	BR	/A	PF	CHI	RC	TA	SB	CS	SBR	FR	POS	TPR
1977	Chi-A	15	20	2	5	0	0	0	1	7	4	.250	.444	.250	.694	96	0	0	99	79	3	.867	1	0	0	-2	S/3D	0.0
	Tor-A	24	63	9	11	0	1	0	1	4	11	.175	.224	.206	.430	18	-7	-7	103	30	3	.327	1	0	0	-2	S	-0.5
	Yr	39	83	11	16	0	1	0	2	11	15	.193	.287	.217	.504	39	-7	-7	101	51	6	.443	2	0	1	-4		-0.5
1978	Tor-A	7	0	1	0	0	0	0	0	0	0	—	1.000	—	1.217	260	0	0	100	0	0	—	0	0	0	0	/S	0.1
	Mil-A	2	5	0	0	0	0	0	0	1	1	.000	.167	.000	.167	-47	-1	-1	106	0	0	.200	0	0	0	0	/S	0.0
	Yr	9	5	1	0	0	0	0	0	1	1	.000	.286	.000	.286	-13	-1	-1	101	0	0	.400	0	0	0	0		0.1
1979	Mil-A	2	2	0	1	0	0	0	0	0	0	.500	.500	.500	1.000	171	0	0	100	0	1	1.000	0	0	0	0	/S	0.0
Total	6	128	169	27	30	1	1	0	3	25	33	.178	.287	.195	.482	38	-13	-13	98	30	12	.453	4	0	1	-1	S/2D3	0.1

■ **WAYNE NORDHAGEN** Nordhagen, Wayne Oren b: 7/4/48, Thief River Falls, Minn. BR/TR, 6'2", 205 lbs. Deb: 7/16/76

YEAR	TM/L	G	AB	R	H	2B	3B	HR	RBI	BB	SO	AVG	OBP	SLG	PRO	/A	BR	/A	PF	CHI	RC	TA	SB	CS	SBR	FR	POS	TPR
1976	Chi-A	22	53	6	10	2	0	0	5	4	12	.189	.246	.226	.472	39	-4	-4	99	160	3	.364	0	0	0	0	O/CD	-0.3
1977	Chi-A	52	124	16	39	7	3	4	22	2	12	.315	.325	.516	.842	126	4	4	99	115	20	.761	1	0	0	-10	O/CD	-0.6
1978	Chi-A	68	206	28	62	16	0	5	35	5	18	.301	.318	.451	.769	113	3	3	101	128	27	.649	0	1	-1	-6	ODC	-0.3
1979	Chi-A	78	193	20	54	15	0	7	25	13	22	.280	.325	.466	.792	108	2	2	102	87	26	.696	0	0	0	1	DO/CP	0.3
1980	Chi-A	123	415	45	115	22	4	15	59	10	45	.277	.296	.458	.754	107	-0	2	97	98	51	.640	0	1	-1	-6	OD	-0.6
1981	Chi-A	65	208	19	64	8	1	6	33	10	25	.308	.342	.442	.785	125	6	6	100	117	29	.673	0	1	-1	-7	O	-0.3
1982	Tor-A	44	115	8	32	3	0	1	14	9	13	.278	.331	.330	.661	76	-3	-4	109	136	11	.528	0	2	-1	-0	DO	-0.5
	Pit-N	1	4	0	2	0	0	0	2	0	1	.500	.500	.500	1.000	164	0	0	110	400	1	1.000	0	0	0	0	/O	0.0
	Tor-A	28	70	4	18	3	0	0	6	1	9	.257	.268	.300	.568	51	-4	-5	109	114	5	.407	0	0	0	0	D	-0.4
1983	Chi-N	21	35	1	5	1	0	1	4	0	5	.143	.167	.257	.424	16	-4	-4	101	132	1	.313	0	0	0	-1	/O	-0.5
Total	8	502	1423	147	401	77	8	39	205	54	162	.282	.309	.429	.739	102	-0	-1	101	113	174	.650	1	5	-3	-29	OD/CP	-3.2

■ **LOU NORDYKE** Nordyke, Louis Ellis b: 8/7/1876, Brighton, Iowa d: 9/27/45, Los Angeles, Cal. TR , 6', 185 lbs. Deb: 4/18/06

YEAR	TM/L	G	AB	R	H	2B	3B	HR	RBI	BB	SO	AVG	OBP	SLG	PRO	/A	BR	/A	PF	CHI	RC	TA	SB	CS	SBR	FR	POS	TPR
1906	StL-A	25	53	4	13	1	0	0	7	10		.245	.365	.264	.629	102	1	1	98	182	6	.675	3			1	1	0.1

■ **IRV NOREN** Noren, Irving Arnold b: 11/29/24, Jamestown, N.Y. BL/TL, 6', 190 lbs. Deb: 4/18/50 C

YEAR	TM/L	G	AB	R	H	2B	3B	HR	RBI	BB	SO	AVG	OBP	SLG	PRO	/A	BR	/A	PF	CHI	RC	TA	SB	CS	SBR	FR	POS	TPR
1950	Was-A	138	542	80	160	27	10	14	98	67	77	.295	.375	.459	.834	114	10	10	99	112	98	.820	5	2	0	14	*O1	2.0
1951	Was-A	129	509	82	142	33	5	8	86	51	35	.279	.345	.411	.755	109	2	5	95	140	72	.696	10	7	-1	16	*O	1.4
1952	Was-A	12	49	4	12	3	1	0	2	6	3	.245	.327	.347	.674	88	-1	-1	100	38	6	.632	1	0	0	4	O	0.3
	NY-A	93	272	36	64	13	2	5	21	26	34	.235	.316	.353	.669	88	-5	-5	98	71	33	.626	4	2	0	-7	O1	-1.4
	Yr	105	321	40	76	16	3	5	23	32	37	.237	.318	.352	.670	88	-6	-5	98	67	40	.629	5	2	0	-2		-1.1
1953	NY-A	109	345	55	92	12	6	6	46	42	39	.267	.350	.388	.738	107	-0	3	93	112	50	.693	3	3	-1	4	O	0.3
1954	NY-A	125	426	70	136	21	6	12	66	43	38	.319	.383	.481	.864	137	20	21	99	104	79	.843	4	6	-2	2	*O/1	1.8
1955	NY-A	132	371	49	94	19	1	8	59	43	33	.253	.336	.375	.710	93	-5	-4	98	135	48	.667	5	2	0	-1	*O	-1.0
1956	NY-A	29	37	4	8	1	0	0	6	12	7	.216	.408	.243	.651	77	-1	-0	99	249	4	.700	0	0	0	-3	O/1	-0.3
1957	KC-A	81	160	8	34	8	0	2	16	11	19	.213	.267	.300	.567	55	-10	-10	99	117	12	.455	0	0	0	2	1/O	-0.8
	StL-N	17	30	3	11	4	1	1	10	4	6	.367	.441	.667	1.108	191	4	4	101	180	8	1.143	0	1	-1	-2	/O	0.1
1958	StL-N	117	178	24	47	9	1	4	22	13	21	.264	.328	.393	.721	84	-3	-4	106	111	23	.644	0	1	-1	-17	O	-2.4
1959	StL-N	8	8	0	1	1	0	0	0	0	2	.125	.125	.250	.375	-3	-1	-1	105	0	0	.250	0	0	0	-1	/O1	-0.1
	Chi-N	65	156	27	50	6	2	4	19	13	24	.321	.384	.462	.845	126	6	6	98	91	29	.841	2	0	1	3	O/1	0.9
	Yr	73	164	27	51	7	2	4	19	13	26	.311	.372	.451	.823	119	4	5	99	81	29	.807	2	0	1	2		0.8
1960	Chi-N	12	11	0	1	0	0	0	1	3	4	.091	.286	.091	.377	9	-1	-1	98	406	0	.364	0	0	0	-0	/1O	-0.1
	LA-N	26	25	1	5	0	0	1	1	1	8	.200	.231	.320	.551	42	-2	-2	115	37	2	.429	0	0	0	0	H	-0.1
	Yr	38	36	1	6	0	0	1	2	4	12	.167	.250	.250	.500	34	-3	-4	110	164	2	.419	0	0	0	-0		-0.2
Total	11	1093	3119	443	857	157	35	65	453	335	350	.275	.349	.410	.759	105	12	20	98	115	464	.730	34	24	-4	14	O/1	0.6

■ **DAN NORMAN** Norman, Daniel Edmund b: 1/11/55, Los Angeles, Cal. BR/TR, 6'2", 195 lbs. Deb: 9/27/77

YEAR	TM/L	G	AB	R	H	2B	3B	HR	RBI	BB	SO	AVG	OBP	SLG	PRO	/A	BR	/A	PF	CHI	RC	TA	SB	CS	SBR	FR	POS	TPR
1977	NY-N	7	16	2	4	1	0	0	0	4	2	.250	.400	.313	.712	98	0	0	96	0	2	.692	0	0	0	-1	/O	0.0
1978	NY-N	19	64	7	17	0	1	4	10	2	14	.266	.288	.484	.772	114	1	1	98	92	9	.723	1	0	0	-0	O	0.0
1979	NY-N	44	110	9	27	3	1	3	11	10	26	.245	.314	.373	.687	91	-2	-1	95	87	14	.643	2	0	1	-1	O	-0.2
1980	NY-N	69	92	5	17	1	1	2	9	6	14	.185	.235	.283	.517	46	-7	-7	96	111	7	.487	5	0	2	-3	O	-0.9
1982	Mon-N	53	66	6	14	3	0	2	7	7	20	.212	.288	.348	.636	73	-2	-3	105	95	7	.566	0	1	-1	-6	O	-0.9
Total	5	192	348	29	79	8	3	11	37	29	76	.227	.288	.362	.650	81	-11	-10	98	91	39	.607	8	1	2	-11	O	-2.0

■ **BILL NORMAN** Norman, Henry Willis Patrick b: 7/16/10, St.Louis, Mo. d: 4/21/62, Milwaukee, Wis. BR/TR, 6'2", 190 lbs. Deb: 8/08/31 MC

YEAR	TM/L	G	AB	R	H	2B	3B	HR	RBI	BB	SO	AVG	OBP	SLG	PRO	/A	BR	/A	PF	CHI	RC	TA	SB	CS	SBR	FR	POS	TPR
1931	Chi-A	24	55	7	10	2	0	0	6	4	10	.182	.237	.218	.455	22	-6	-6	92	165	3	.348	0	1	-1	0	O	-0.6
1932	Chi-A	13	48	6	11	3	1	0	2	2	3	.229	.260	.333	.593	60	-4	-3	87	43	4	.486	0	0	0	-1	O	-0.3
Total	2	37	103	13	21	5	1	0	8	6	13	.204	.248	.272	.520	39	-10	-8	90	109	7	.410	0	1	-1	-1	/O	-0.9

■ **NELSON NORMAN** Norman, Nelson Augusto b: 5/23/58, San Pedro De Macoris, D.R. BR/TR, 6'2", 160 lbs. Deb: 5/20/78

YEAR	TM/L	G	AB	R	H	2B	3B	HR	RBI	BB	SO	AVG	OBP	SLG	PRO	/A	BR	/A	PF	CHI	RC	TA	SB	CS	SBR	FR	POS	TPR
1978	Tex-A	23	34	1	9	2	0	0	1	0	5	.265	.265	.324	.588	67	-2	-2	96	36	3	.423	0	0	0	1	S/3	0.0
1979	Tex-A	147	343	36	76	9	3	0	21	19	41	.222	.262	.265	.528	43	-27	-27	100	89	25	.418	4	1	1	-22	*S/2	-3.0
1980	Tex-A	17	32	4	7	0	0	0	1	1	1	.219	.242	.219	.461	27	-3	-3	100	56	1	.286	0	1	-1	-0	S	-0.2
1981	Tex-A	7	13	1	3	1	0	0	2	1	2	.231	.286	.308	.593	78	-0	-0	91	196	1	.500	0	0	0	0	/S	0.0
1982	Pit-N	3	3	0	0	0	0	0	0	0	0	.000	.000	.000	.000	-91	-1	-1	110	0	0	.000	0	0	0	0	/2S	0.0
1987	Mon-N	1	4	0	0	0	0	0	0	0	1	.000	.000	.000	.000	-94	-1	-1	106	0	0	.000	0	0	0	0	/S	0.0
Total	6	198	429	42	95	12	3	0	25	21	50	.221	.258	.263	.521	42	-35	-34	99	84	30	.411	4	2	0	-21	S/32	-3.2

■ **JIM NORRIS** Norris, James Francis b: 12/20/48, Brooklyn, N.Y. BL/TL, 5'10", 175 lbs. Deb: 4/07/77

YEAR	TM/L	G	AB	R	H	2B	3B	HR	RBI	BB	SO	AVG	OBP	SLG	PRO	/A	BR	/A	PF	CHI	RC	TA	SB	CS	SBR	FR	POS	TPR
1977	Cle-A	133	440	59	119	23	6	2	37	64	57	.270	.363	.364	.727	101	1	3	98	90	59	.718	26	17	-2	16	*O/1	1.2
1978	Cle-A	113	315	41	89	14	5	2	27	42	20	.283	.367	.378	.745	118	5	8	93	85	45	.724	12	7	-1	1	OD/1	0.6
1979	Cle-A	124	353	50	87	15	6	3	30	44	35	.246	.330	.348	.678	79	-8	-11	106	87	39	.632	15	10	-2	2	OD	-1.2
1980	Tex-A	119	174	23	43	5	0	0	16	23	16	.247	.335	.276	.611	69	-6	-7	100	130	15	.531	6	3	0	-19	O1/D	-2.8
Total	4	489	1282	173	338	57	17	7	110	173	128	.264	.351	.351	.702	94	-7	-6	99	94	159	.688	59	37	-5	-0	O/D1	-2.2

■ **LEO NORRIS** Norris, Leo John b: 5/17/08, Bay St.Louis, Miss BR/TR, 5'11", 165 lbs. Deb: 4/14/36

YEAR	TM/L	G	AB	R	H	2B	3B	HR	RBI	BB	SO	AVG	OBP	SLG	PRO	/A	BR	/A	PF	CHI	RC	TA	SB	CS	SBR	FR	POS	TPR
1936	Phi-N	154	581	64	154	27	4	11	76	39	79	.265	.315	.382	.697	80	-12	-18	108	108	69	.602	4			-1	*S2	-0.9
1937	Phi-N	116	381	45	98	24	3	9	36	21	53	.257	.296	.407	.703	82	-7	-11	108	71	48	.626	3			2	23S	-0.2
Total	2	270	962	109	252	51	7	20	112	60	132	.262	.307	.392	.699	81	-19	-29	108	93	117	.627	7			1	S2/3	-1.1

■ **BILL NORTH** North, William Alex b: 5/15/48, Seattle, Wash. BB/TR, 5'11", 185 lbs. Deb: 9/03/71

YEAR	TM/L	G	AB	R	H	2B	3B	HR	RBI	BB	SO	AVG	OBP	SLG	PRO	/A	BR	/A	PF	CHI	RC	TA	SB	CS	SBR	FR	POS	TPR
1971	Chi-N	8	16	3	6	0	0	0	0	4	6	.375	.524	.375	.899	144	2	2	110	0	4	1.091	1	1	-0	-2	/O	0.0
1972	Chi-N	66	127	22	23	2	3	0	4	13	33	.181	.262	.244	.507	39	-9	-11	114	53	9	.481	6	0	2	-6	O	-1.8
1973	Oak-A	146	554	98	158	10	5	5	34	78	89	.285	.376	.348	.725	121	7	17	87	68	81	.773	53	20	4	18	*O/D	3.5
1974	Oak-A	149	543	79	141	20	5	4	33	69	86	.260	.348	.337	.685	97	1	0	100	71	68	.712	**54**	26	1	12	*O/D	0.9
1975	Oak-A	140	524	74	143	17	5	1	43	81	80	.273	.374	.330	.705	108	4	9	93	90	73	.718	30	12	2	11	*O/D	1.9
1976	Oak-A	154	590	91	163	20	5	2	31	73	95	.276	.358	.337	.695	105	6	6	100	56	78	.752	**75**	29	5	-2	*O/D	0.6
1977	Oak-A	56	184	32	48	3	3	1	9	32	25	.261	.376	.326	.702	98	-0	1	95	58	24	.740	17	13	-3	-0	O/D	-0.2
1978	Oak-A	24	52	5	11	4	0	0	5	9	13	.212	.349	.288	.638	80	-1	-1	101	132	6	.659	3	2	-0	-1	O	-0.1
	LA-N	110	304	54	71	10	0	0	10	65	48	.234	.372	.266	.638	82	-4	-4	99	49	38	.714	27	8	3	-7	*O	-1.1
1979	SF-N	142	460	87	119	15	4	5	30	96	84	.259	.388	.341	.729	109	5	10	92	71	71	.843	58	24	3	-4	*O	0.6
1980	SF-N	128	415	73	104	12	1	1	19	81	78	.251	.374	.292	.666	92	-2	0	96	62	54	.743	45	19	2	3	*O	0.0
1981	SF-N	46	131	22	29	7	0	1	12	26	28	.221	.354	.298	.652	82	-1	-2	105	112	18	.829	26	8	3	1	O	0.1
Total	11	1169	3900	640	1016	120	31	20	230	627	665	.261	.366	.323	.689	100	7	27	96	69	524	.756	395	162	21	24	*O/D	4.4

■ **HUB NORTHEN** Northen, Hubbard Elwin b: 8/16/1885, Atlanta, Tex. d: 10/1/47, Shreveport, La. BL/TL, 5'8", 175 lbs. Deb: 9/10/10

YEAR	TM/L	G	AB	R	H	2B	3B	HR	RBI	BB	SO	AVG	OBP	SLG	PRO	/A	BR	/A	PF	CHI	RC	TA	SB	CS	SBR	FR	POS	TPR
1910	StL-A	26	96	6	19	1	0	0	16	5		.198	.238	.208	.446	42	-7	-6	94	313	5	.351	2			-1	O	-0.8
1911	Cin-N	1	0	0	0	0	0	0	0	0	0	—	—	—	—	—	0	0	92	—	—	—	0			0	H	0.0
	Bro-N	19	76	16	24	2	2	0	1	14	9	.316	.429	.395	.823	135	4	4	97	10	14	.942	4			3	O	0.6

YEAR	TM/L	G	AB	R	H	2B	3B	HR	RBI	BB	SO	AVG	OBP	SLG	PRO	/A	BR	/A	PF	CHI	RC	TA	SB	CS	SBR	FR	POS	TPR
	Yr	20	76	16	24	2	2	0	1	14	9	.316	.429	.395	.823	135	4	4	97	9	14	.942	4			3		0.6
1912	Bro-N	118	412	54	116	26	6	3	46	41	46	.282	.352	.396	.748	109	2	5	95	92	60	.730	8			-7	*O	-0.4
Total	3	164	584	76	159	29	8	3	63	60	55	.272	.345	.365	.710	104	-0	3	95	115	85	.687	14			-5	O	-0.6
■ **RON NORTHEY**	Northey, Ronald James b: 4/26/20, Mahanoy City, Pa. d: 4/16/71, Pittsburgh, Pa. BL/TR, 5'10", 195 lbs. Deb: 4/14/42 C																											
1942	Phi-N	127	402	31	101	13	2	5	31	28	33	.251	.300	.331	.631	90	-9	-6	94	78	41	.533	2			-0	*O	-0.9
1943	Phi-N	147	586	72	163	31	5	16	68	51	52	.278	.339	.430	.769	130	14	18	94	79	88	.718	2			2	*O	1.7
1944	Phi-N	152	570	72	164	35	9	22	104	67	51	.288	.367	.496	.863	141	30	30	100	113	107	.860	1			3	*O	2.1
1946	Phi-N	128	438	55	109	24	6	16	62	39	59	.249	.313	.441	.754	119	5	7	95	98	61	.701	1			-9	*O	-0.4
1947	Phi-N	13	47	7	12	3	0	0	3	6	3	.255	.340	.319	.659	76	-1	-1	100	78	6	.629	1			-1	O	-0.2
	StL-N	110	311	52	91	19	3	15	63	48	29	.293	.391	.518	.908	131	18	15	106	113	65	.930	0			-15	O/3	-0.3
	Yr	123	358	59	103	22	3	15	66	54	32	.288	.384	.492	.876	124	16	13	106	110	70	.889	1			-16		-0.5
1948	StL-N	96	246	40	79	10	1	13	64	38	25	.321	.420	.528	.949	154	20	20	101	142	55	.983	0			-13	O	0.2
1949	StL-N	90	265	28	69	18	2	7	50	31	15	.260	.338	.423	.760	93	1	-3	110	142	37	.698	0			-14	O	-2.0
1950	Cin-N	27	77	11	20	5	0	5	9	15	6	.260	.380	.519	.900	128	4	3	105	63	16	.932	0			-7	O	-0.3
	Chi-N	53	114	11	32	9	0	4	20	10	9	.281	.339	.465	.804	104	1	0	105	119	18	.741	0			-2	O	-0.2
	Yr	80	191	22	52	14	0	9	29	25	15	.272	.356	.487	.843	114	5	4	105	101	34	.831	0			-9		-0.5
1952	Chi-N	1	1	0	0	0	0	0	0	0	0	.000	.000	.000	.000	-97	-0	-0	103	0	0	.000	0	0	0	0	H	0.0
1955	Chi-A	14	14	1	5	2	0	1	4	3	3	.357	.471	.714	1.185	213	2	2	101	115	4	1.300	0	0	0	-1	/O	0.1
1956	Chi-A	53	48	4	17	2	0	3	23	8	1	.354	.446	.583	1.030	163	5	5	104	232	12	1.091	0	0	0	-0	/O	0.4
1957	Chi-A	40	27	0	5	1	0	0	7	11	5	.185	.421	.222	.643	81	0	0	99	461	4	.739	0	0	0	0	H	0.0
	Phi-N	33	26	1	7	0	0	1	5	6	6	.269	.406	.385	.791	116	1	1	98	159	5	.842	0	0	0	0	H	0.1
Total	12	1084	3172	385	874	172	28	108	513	361	297	.276	.352	.450	.802	123	90	92	99	110	517	.787	7	0		-57	O/3	0.3
■ **SCOTT NORTHEY**	Northey, Scott Richard b: 10/15/46, Philadelphia, Pa. BR/TR, 6', 175 lbs. Deb: 9/02/69																											
1969	KC-A	20	61	11	16	2	2	1	7	7	19	.262	.338	.410	.748	105	1	0	103	100	9	.792	6	3	0	0	O	0.0
■ **JIM NORTHRUP**	Northrup, James Thomas b: 11/24/39, Breckenridge, Mich. BL/TR, 6'3", 190 lbs. Deb: 9/30/64																											
1964	Det-A	5	12	1	1	1	0	0	0	0	3	.083	.083	.167	.250	-34	-2	-2	96	0	0	.273	1	0	0	0	/O	-0.1
1965	Det-A	80	219	20	45	12	3	2	16	12	50	.205	.253	.315	.568	57	-12	-13	105	88	16	.464	1	1	-0	-4	O	-2.0
1966	Det-A	123	419	53	111	24	6	16	58	33	52	.265	.325	.465	.790	121	12	11	102	100	56	.711	4	7	-3	-1	*O	0.2
1967	Det-A	144	495	63	134	18	6	10	61	43	83	.271	.333	.392	.725	114	8	8	99	114	63	.655	7	1	2	-10	*O	-0.4
1968	Det-A	154	580	76	153	29	7	21	90	50	87	.264	.326	.447	.773	124	21	17	106	127	82	.711	4	5	-2	13	*O	2.5
1969	Det-A	148	543	79	160	31	5	25	66	52	83	.295	.360	.508	.868	136	27	25	103	77	100	.852	4	2	0	2	*O	2.4
1970	Det-A	139	504	71	132	21	3	24	80	58	68	.262	.346	.458	.805	116	13	11	103	113	78	.767	3	6	-3	9	*O	1.2
1971	Det-A	136	459	72	124	27	2	16	71	60	43	.270	.357	.442	.799	131	15	18	96	118	71	.771	7	4	-0	-1	*O1	1.2
1972	Det-A	134	426	40	111	15	2	8	42	38	47	.261	.324	.362	.686	92	2	-4	113	99	45	.586	4	7	-3	-1	*O/1	-1.3
1973	Det-A	119	404	55	124	14	7	12	44	38	41	.307	.368	.465	.833	132	17	17	101	77	68	.791	4	4	-1	-2	*O	1.1
1974	Det-A	97	376	41	89	12	1	11	42	36	46	.237	.303	.362	.665	86	-5	-8	106	103	42	.585	0	0	0	2	O	-0.7
	Mon-N	21	54	3	13	1	0	2	8	5	9	.241	.305	.370	.675	85	-1	-1	104	119	5	.568	0	0	0	-3	O	-0.4
	Bal-A	8	7	2	4	0	0	1	3	2	1	.571	.667	1.000	1.667	404	3	3	93	118	5	3.000	0	0	0	-1	/OD	0.1
1975	Bal-A	84	194	27	53	13	0	5	29	22	22	.273	.353	.418	.771	129	4	7	91	116	27	.700	0	1	-1	-8	O/D	-0.3
Total	12	1392	4692	603	1254	218	42	153	610	449	635	.267	.335	.429	.765	115	104	89	103	104	659	.727	39	38	-11	-4	*O/1D	3.5
■ **PETE NORTON**	Norton, Peter J. b: 6/19/1850, Watertown, Wis. d: 2/8/23, Oak Park, Ill. Deb: 5/05/1871																											
1871	Oly-n	1	0	0	0							.000															/O	
■ **WILLIE NORWOOD**	Norwood, Willie b: 11/7/50, Green County, Ala. BR/TR, 6', 185 lbs. Deb: 4/21/77																											
1977	Min-A	39	83	15	19	3	0	3	9	6	17	.229	.281	.373	.654	74	-3	-3	103	89	9	.652	6	1	1	-1	O/D	-0.3
1978	Min-A	125	428	56	109	22	3	8	46	28	64	.255	.305	.376	.681	96	-6	-3	94	98	46	.631	25	10	2	-5	*O/D	-0.9
1979	Min-A	96	270	32	67	13	3	6	30	20	51	.248	.300	.385	.685	77	-7	-10	109	94	29	.616	9	5	-0	-1	OD	-1.3
1980	Min-A	34	73	6	12	2	0	1	8	3	13	.164	.197	.233	.430	16	-8	-9	109	156	3	.323	1	1	-0	1	O/D	-0.8
Total	4	294	854	109	207	40	6	18	93	57	145	.242	.292	.367	.659	80	-24	-25	101	101	87	.621	41	17	2	-7	O/D	-3.3
■ **JOE NOSSEK**	Nossek, Joseph Rudolph b: 11/8/40, Cleveland, Ohio BR/TR, 6', 178 lbs. Deb: 4/18/64 C																											
1964	Min-A	7	1	1	0	0	0	0	0	0	0	.000	.000	.000	.000	-99	-0	-0	101	0	0	.000	0	0	0	-1	/O	0.0
1965	Min-A	87	170	19	37	9	0	2	16	7	22	.218	.253	.306	.559	57	-10	-10	101	114	13	.449	2	0	1	-5	O/3	-1.6
1966	Min-A	4	0	0	0	0	0	0	0	0	0	—	—	—	—	—	0	0	111	—	—	—	0	0	0	-1	/O	0.0
	KC-A	87	230	13	60	10	3	1	27	8	21	.261	.286	.343	.629	85	-6	-5	94	138	21	.508	4	2	0	-2	O/3	-0.9
	Yr	91	230	13	60	10	3	1	27	8	21	.261	.286	.343	.629	84	-6	-5	95	132	21	.508	4	2	0	-2		-0.9
1967	KC-A	87	166	12	34	6	1	0	10	4	26	.205	.224	.253	.477	41	-12	-12	100	99	9	.358	2	0	1	-1	O	-1.6
1969	Oak-A	13	6	0	0	0	0	0	0	0	0	.000	.000	.000	.000	-99	-2	-2	92	0	0	.000	0	0	0	-4	O	-0.5
	StL-N	9	5	2	1	0	0	0	0	0	3	.200	.200	.200	.400	12	-1	-1	100	0	0	.250	0	0	0	0	/O	0.0
1970	StL-N	1	1	0	0	0	0	0	0	0	0	.000	.000	.000	.000	-94	-0	-0	106	0	0	.000	0	0	0	0	H	0.0
Total	6	295	579	47	132	25	4	3	53	19	72	.228	.254	.301	.554	61	-31	-30	98	117	55	.450	8	2	1	-13	O/3	-4.6
■ **LOU NOVIKOFF**	Novikoff, Louis Alexander "The Mad Russian" b: 10/12/15, Glendale, Ariz. d: 9/30/70, South Gate, Cal. BR/TR, 5'10", 185 lbs. Deb: 4/15/41																											
1941	Chi-N	62	203	22	49	8	0	5	24	11	15	.241	.284	.355	.638	84	-6	-5	94	100	19	.522	0			-4	O	-1.1
1942	Chi-N	128	483	48	145	25	5	7	64	24	28	.300	.337	.416	.753	125	10	12	96	109	64	.654	3			-1	*O	0.8
1943	Chi-N	78	233	22	65	7	3	0	28	18	15	.279	.333	.335	.668	94	-2	-2	99	130	24	.545	0			-10	O	-1.4
1944	Chi-N	71	139	15	39	4	2	3	19	10	11	.281	.329	.403	.732	104	1	1	101	105	19	.657	1			-6	O	-0.7
1946	Phi-N	17	23	0	7	1	0	0	3	1	2	.304	.333	.348	.681	98	-0	-0	95	140	2	.529	0			0	/O	0.0
Total	5	356	1081	107	305	45	10	15	138	64	71	.282	.325	.384	.709	107	2	6	97	112	129	.628	4			-21	O	-2.4
■ **RUBE NOVOTNEY**	Novotney, Ralph Joseph b: 8/5/24, Streator, Ill. BR/TR, 6', 187 lbs. Deb: 4/29/49																											
1949	Chi-N	22	67	4	18	2	1	0	6	3	11	.269	.300	.328	.628	73	-3	-3	94	103	6	.481	0			0	C	-0.1
■ **LES NUNAMAKER**	Nunamaker, Leslie Grant b: 1/25/1889, Malcolm, Neb. d: 11/14/38, Hastings, Neb. BR/TR, 6'2", 190 lbs. Deb: 4/28/11																											
1911	Bos-A	62	183	18	47	4	3	0	19	12		.257	.303	.311	.614	72	-7	-7	99	113	18	.515	1			0	C	0.0
1912	Bos-A	35	103	15	26	5	2	0	6	6		.252	.313	.340	.652	81	-2	-3	107	57	12	.597	2			-3	C	-0.1
1913	Bos-A	29	65	9	14	5	2	0	9	8	8	.215	.311	.354	.665	91	-1	-1	103	139	8	.667	2			0	C	0.1
1914	Bos-A	4	5	0	1	0	0	0	0	1	0	.200	.333	.200	.533	62	-0	-0	98	0	0	.500	0			0	/C1	0.0
	NY-A	87	257	19	68	10	3	2	29	22	34	.265	.327	.350	.678	104	1	1	100	113	30	.631	11	9	-2	9	C/1	1.4
	Yr	91	262	19	69	10	3	2	29	23	34	.263	.328	.347	.675	103	1	1	100	108	30	.629	11	9	-2	9		1.4
1915	NY-A	87	249	24	56	6	3	0	17	23	24	.225	.293	.273	.566	71	-9	-9	98	85	21	.487	3	2	-0	4	C/1	0.0
1916	NY-A	91	260	25	77	14	7	0	28	34	21	.296	.380	.404	.784	133	12	11	101	95	41	.787	4			10	C	2.7
1917	NY-A	104	310	22	81	9	2	0	33	21	25	.261	.310	.303	.613	82	-5	-7	107	126	30	.528	5			3	C	0.3
1918	StL-A	85	274	22	71	9	2	0	22	28	16	.259	.339	.307	.645	95	-1	-1	99	95	30	.606	6			0	C/1O	0.7
1919	Cle-A	26	56	6	14	1	1	0	7	2	6	.250	.276	.304	.579	59	-3	-3	107	149	5	.452	0			-1	C	-0.3
1920	Cle-A	34	54	10	18	3	3	0	14	4	5	.333	.379	.500	.879	127	2	2	104	182	10	.889	1	0	0	-1	C/1	0.3
1921	Cle-A	46	131	16	47	7	2	0	25	11	8	.359	.408	.443	.851	118	4	4	99	148	24	.824	1	1	-0	-4	C	0.1
1922	Cle-A	25	43	8	13	2	0	0	7	4	3	.302	.362	.349	.711	84	-1	-1	102	167	6	.633	0	0	0	-1	C	-0.1
Total	12	715	1990	194	533	75	30	2	216	176	150	.268	.332	.339	.670	94	-11	-14	102	110	234	.613	36	12		16	C/1O	5.1
■ **EMORY NUSZ**	Nusz, Emory Moberly b: 4/2/1866, d: 8/3/1893, Point Of Rocks, Md. Deb: 4/26/1884																											
1884	Was-U	1	4	1	0	0	0	0		0		.000	.000	.000	.000	-99	-1	-1	97	0	0	.000	0			0	/O	0.0
■ **DIZZY NUTTER**	Nutter, Everett Clarence b: 8/27/1893, Roseville, Ohio d: 7/25/58, Battle Creek, Mich. BL/TR, 5'9", 160 lbs. Deb: 9/07/19																											
1919	Bos-N	18	52	4	11	0	0	0	3	4	5	.212	.268	.212	.479	46	-3	-3	98	106	3	.390	1			2	O	0.0

YEAR	TM/L	G	AB	R	H	2B	3B	HR	RBI	BB	SO	AVG	OBP	SLG	PRO	/A	BR	/A	PF	CHI	RC	TA	SB	CS	SBR	FR	POS	TPR
■ CHARLIE NYCE	Nyce, Charles Reiff (born Charles Reiff Nice) b: 7/1/1870, Philadelphia, Pa. d: 5/9/08, Philadelphia, Pa. 5'8", 160 lbs. Deb: 5/28/1895																											
1895	Bos-N	9	35	7	8	5	0	2	9	4	2	.229	.325	.543	.868	120	1	1	103	107	6	.889	0			0	/S	0.1
■ CHRIS NYMAN	Nyman, Christopher Curtis b: 6/6/55, Pomona, Cal. BR/TR, 6'4", 200 lbs. Deb: 7/28/82																											
1982	Chi-A	28	65	6	16	1	0	0	2	3	9	.246	.279	.262	.541	51	-4	-4	97	47	4	.426	3	2	-0	0	1/O	-0.4
1983	Chi-A	21	28	12	8	0	0	2	4	4	7	.286	.394	.500	.894	140	2	2	103	78	5	.955	2	2	-1	0	1D	0.1
Total	2	49	93	18	24	1	0	2	6	7	16	.258	.317	.333	.650	79	-3	-2	99	57	10	.603	5	4	-1	0	/1DO	-0.3
■ NYLS NYMAN	Nyman, Nyls Wallace Rex b: 3/7/54, Detroit, Mich. BL/TR, 6', 170 lbs. Deb: 9/06/74																											
1974	Chi-A	5	14	5	9	2	1	0	4	0	1	.643	.667	.929	1.595	349	5	4	102	121	8	2.500	1	0	0	1	/O	0.6
1975	Chi-A	106	327	36	74	6	3	2	28	11	34	.226	.256	.281	.537	50	-21	-22	103	110	23	.439	10	4	1	-4	O/D	-2.8
1976	Chi-A	8	15	2	2	1	0	0	1	0	3	.133	.133	.200	.333	-3	-2	-2	99	128	0	.308	1	0	0	-1	/O	-0.2
1977	Chi-A	1	1	0	0	0	0	0	0	0	0	.000	.000	.000	.000	-99	-0	-0	99	0	0	.000	0	0	0	0	H	0.0
Total	4	120	357	43	85	9	4	2	33	11	38	.238	.267	.303	.569	59	-19	-20	103	111	32	.486	12	4	1	-3	O/D	-2.4
■ REBEL OAKES	Oakes, Ennis Telfair b: 12/17/1886, Homer, La. d: 2/29/48, Rocky Springs, Lisbon, La. BL/TR, 5'8", 170 lbs. Deb: 09 M																											
1909	Cin-N	120	415	55	112	10	5	3	31	40		.270	.341	.340	.681	120	7	9	94	77	54	.690	23			3	*O	0.9
1910	StL-N	131	468	50	118	14	6	0	43	38	38	.252	.315	.308	.623	89	-11	-6	92	106	51	.586	18			-13	*O	-2.4
1911	StL-N	154	551	69	145	13	6	2	59	41	35	.263	.320	.319	.639	78	-16	-16	101	112	64	.608	25			6	*O	-1.4
1912	StL-N	136	495	57	139	19	5	3	58	31	24	.281	.328	.358	.686	88	-9	-9	100	107	66	.669	26			-5	*O	-1.7
1913	StL-N	147	539	60	158	14	5	0	49	43	32	.293	.350	.338	.687	104	-1	4	93	104	71	.659	22			7	*O	0.8
1914	Pit-F	145	571	82	178	18	10	7	75	35	22	.312	.351	.415	.767	126	13	17	94	101	97	.763	28			12	*OM	2.1
1915	Pit-F	153	580	55	161	24	5	0	82	37	19	.278	.321	.336	.657	91	-4	-7	104	**146**	74	.604	21			-6	*OM	-2.1
Total	7	986	3619	428	1011	112	42	15	397	265	170	.279	.332	.346	.678	99	-22	-8	97	109	478	.653	163			4	O	-3.8
■ PRINCE OANA	Oana, Henry Kauhane b: 1/22/08, Waipahu, Hawaii d: 6/19/76, Austin, Tex. BR/TR, 6'2", 193 lbs. Deb: 4/22/34																											
1934	Phi-N	6	21	3	5	1	0	0	3	0	1	.238	.238	.286	.524	37	-2	-2	108	180	1	.353	0			1	/O	0.0
1943	Det-A	20	26	5	10	2	1	1	7	1	2	.385	.407	.654	1.061	197	3	3	106	128	6	1.000	0	0	0	-0	P	0.4
1945	Det-A	4	5	0	1	0	0	0	0	0	0	.200	.200	.200	.400	15	-1	-1	106	0	0	.250	0	0	0	-0	/P	0.0
Total	3	30	52	8	16	3	1	1	10	1	3	.308	.321	.462	.782	111	1	0	107	136	7	.694	0	0		0	/PO	0.4
■ JOHNNY OATES	Oates, Johnny Lane b: 1/21/46, Sylva, N.C. BL/TR, 5'11", 188 lbs. Deb: 9/17/70 C																											
1970	Bal-A	5	18	2	5	0	1	0	2	2	0	.278	.350	.389	.739	107	0	0	97	118	3	.692	0	0	0	-0	/C	0.0
1972	Bal-A	85	253	20	66	12	1	4	21	28	31	.261	.335	.364	.698	110	3	3	98	84	29	.628	5	7	-3	-3	C	-0.1
1973	Atl-N	93	322	27	80	6	0	4	27	22	31	.248	.299	.304	.603	60	-14	-19	113	99	28	.480	1	4	-2	-3	C	-1.9
1974	Atl-N	100	291	22	65	10	0	1	21	23	24	.223	.280	.268	.548	51	-18	-20	105	100	22	.442	2	3	-1	5	C	-1.2
1975	Atl-N	8	18	0	4	1	0	0	0	1	4	.222	.263	.278	.541	53	-1	-1	95	0	1	.429	0	0	0	0	/C	0.0
	Phi-N	90	269	28	77	14	0	1	25	33	29	.286	.364	.349	.714	97	1	0	101	100	35	.646	1	0	0	-4	C	0.0
	Yr	98	287	28	81	15	0	1	25	34	33	.282	.358	.345	.703	95	-1	-1	101	91	36	.632	1	0	0	-4		0.0
1976	Phi-N	37	99	10	25	2	0	0	8	8	12	.253	.308	.273	.581	61	-4	-5	107	114	7	.438	0	1	-1	-2	C	-0.6
1977	LA-N	60	156	18	42	4	0	3	11	11	11	.269	.317	.353	.670	79	-5	-5	100	69	17	.573	1	0	0	0	C	-0.4
1978	LA-N	40	75	5	23	1	0	0	6	5	3	.307	.350	.320	.670	89	-1	-1	99	99	8	.547	0	1	-1	-1	C	-0.1
1979	LA-N	26	46	4	6	2	0	0	2	4	1	.130	.200	.174	.374	3	-6	-6	100	99	2	.293	0	1	-1	0	C	-0.5
1980	NY-A	39	64	6	12	3	0	1	3	2	3	.188	.224	.281	.505	38	-6	-6	99	56	3	.400	1	2	-1	-0	C	-0.4
1981	NY-A	10	26	4	5	1	0	0	0	2	0	.192	.250	.231	.481	39	-2	-2	100	0	2	.381	0	0	0	0	C	-0.1
Total	11	593	1637	146	410	56	2	14	126	141	149	.250	.311	.313	.623	73	-53	-60	103	91	158	.535	11	19	-8	-8	C	-5.3
■ HENRY OBERBECK	Oberbeck, Henry A. b: 5/17/1858, Missouri d: 8/26/21, St.Louis, Mo. Deb: 5/07/1883																											
1883	Pit-a	2	9	1	2	1	0	0		0		.222	.222	.333	.556	82	-0	-0	94	0	1	.429				0	/1	0.0
	StL-a	4	14	0	0	0	0	0		0		.000	.000	.000	.000	-93	-3	-3	108	0	0	.000				0	/O	-0.2
	Yr	6	23	1	2	1	0	0		0		.087	.087	.130	.217	-30	-3	-3	103	0	0	.143				0		-0.2
1884	Bal-U	33	125	19	23	4	0	0		3		.184	.203	.216	.419	38	-7	-9	110	0	6	.294	0			3	O/3P	-0.5
	KC-U	27	90	7	17	3	0	0		7		.189	.247	.222	.470	69	-3	-2	87	0	5	.370	0			0	3/OP1	0.0
	Yr	60	215	26	40	7	0	0		10		.186	.222	.219	.441	50	-11	-11	100	0	11	.326	0			3		-0.5
Total	2	66	238	27	42	8	0	0		10		.176	.210	.210	.420	41	-14	-14	101	0	11	.306	0			3	/O3P1	-0.7
■ KEN OBERKFELL	Oberkfell, Kenneth Ray b: 5/4/56, Highland, Ill. BL/TR, 6', 175 lbs. Deb: 8/22/77																											
1977	StL-N	9	9	0	1	0	0	0	1	0	3	.111	.111	.111	.222	-42	-2	-2	96	400	0	.125	0	0	0	0	/2	0.0
1978	StL-N	24	50	7	6	1	0	0	0	3	1	.120	.170	.140	.310	-13	-8	-7	95	0	1	.222	0	0	0	0	2/3	-0.5
1979	StL-N	135	369	53	111	19	5	1	35	57	35	.301	.400	.388	.788	111	11	9	105	95	60	.776	4	1	1	5	*23/S	2.2
1980	StL-N	116	422	58	128	27	6	3	46	51	23	.303	.380	.417	.797	119	14	12	103	104	66	.751	4	4	-1	-5	*23	1.4
1981	StL-N	102	376	43	110	12	6	2	45	37	28	.293	.356	.372	.728	105	4	3	102	123	49	.674	13	5	1	11	*3/S	1.1
1982	StL-N	137	470	55	136	22	5	2	34	40	31	.289	.346	.370	.717	97	1	-1	103	74	58	.638	11	9	-2	7	*3/2	0.1
1983	StL-N	151	488	62	143	26	5	3	38	61	27	.293	.373	.385	.758	113	9	10	98	76	71	.722	12	6	0	1	*32/S	0.8
1984	StL-N	50	152	17	47	11	1	0	11	16	10	.309	.379	.395	.773	119	4	4	99	72	22	.709	1	2	-1	5	3/2S	0.9
	Atl-N	50	172	21	40	8	1	1	10	15	17	.233	.294	.308	.602	63	-7	-9	110	71	15	.496	1	3	-2	-0	3/2	-1.1
	Yr	100	324	38	87	19	2	1	21	31	27	.269	.334	.349	.683	88	-3	-5	104	72	38	.598	2	5	-2	5		-0.2
1985	Atl-N	134	412	30	112	19	4	3	35	51	38	.272	.360	.359	.720	96	3	-0	106	89	54	.660	1	2	-1	-4	*32	-0.4
1986	Atl-N	151	503	62	136	24	3	5	48	83	40	.270	.376	.360	.736	102	6	5	102	100	72	.715	7	4	-0	15	*32	1.7
1987	Atl-N	135	508	59	142	29	2	3	48	48	29	.280	.344	.362	.706	81	-8	-14	108	105	63	.620	3	3	-1	-4	*32	-1.9
1988	Atl-N	120	422	42	117	20	4	3	40	32	28	.277	.331	.365	.696	95	-0	-2	104	100	51	.608	4	5	-2	-6	*3/2	-1.0
	Pit-N	20	54	7	12	2	0	0	2	5	6	.222	.288	.259	.547	60	-3	-3	98	57	4	.432	0	0	0	0	2/S31	-0.1
	Yr	140	476	49	129	22	4	3	42	37	34	.271	.326	.353	.679	92	-3	-5	103	95	57	.596	4	5	-2	-6		-1.1
Total	12	1334	4407	516	1241	220	42	26	393	499	316	.282	.357	.368	.726	98	23	5	103	93	588	.686	61	44	-8	26	32/S1	3.2
■ MIKE O'BERRY	O'Berry, Preston Michael b: 4/20/54, Birmingham, Ala. BR/TR, 6'2", 190 lbs. Deb: 4/08/79																											
1979	Bos-A	43	59	8	10	1	0	1	4	5	16	.169	.246	.237	.483	29	-6	-6	107	90	3	.385	0	0	0	-6	C	-0.9
1980	Chi-N	19	48	7	10	1	0	0	5	5	13	.208	.283	.229	.512	42	-3	-4	106	180	4	.421	0	0	0	3	C	0.0
1981	Cin-N	55	111	6	20	3	1	1	5	14	19	.180	.272	.252	.524	49	-7	-7	101	63	8	.447	0	0	0	-9	C	-1.6
1982	Cin-N	21	45	5	10	2	0	0	3	10	13	.222	.364	.267	.630	77	-1	-1	102	98	5	.611	0	0	0	-1	C	0.0
1983	Cal-A	26	60	7	10	1	0	1	5	3	11	.167	.206	.233	.440	22	-7	-6	96	115	3	.333	0	0	0	2	C	-0.2
1984	NY-A	13	32	3	8	2	0	0	5	2	2	.250	.294	.313	.607	72	-1	-1	94	199	3	.500	0	0	0	0	C/3	0.0
1985	Mon-N	20	21	2	4	0	0	0	0	4	3	.190	.320	.190	.510	49	-1	-1	94	0	2	.529	1	0	0	-2	C	-0.1
Total	7	197	376	38	72	10	1	3	27	43	77	.191	.276	.247	.524	46	-26	-27	101	102	28	.454	1	0	0	-12	C/3	-2.8
■ JIM OBRADOVICH	Obradovich, James Thomas b: 9/13/49, Fort Campbell, Ky. BL/TL, 6'2", 200 lbs. Deb: 9/12/78																											
1978	Hou-N	10	17	3	3	0	1	0	2	1	3	.176	.222	.294	.516	46	-1	-1	95	159	1	.429	0	0	0	0	/1	0.0
■ CHARLIE O'BRIEN	O'Brien, Charles Hugh b: 5/1/60, Tulsa, Okla. BR/TR, 6'2", 195 lbs. Deb: 6/02/85																											
1985	Oak-A	16	11	3	3	1	0	0	1	3	3	.273	.429	.364	.792	129	0	1	93	99	2	.875	0	0	0	-0	C	0.1
1987	Mil-A	10	35	2	7	3	1	0	0	4	4	.200	.282	.343	.625	64	-2	-2	102	0	3	.552	0	1	-1	2	C	0.0
1988	Mil-A	40	118	12	26	6	0	2	9	5	16	.220	.252	.322	.574	58	-7	-7	103	81	9	.448	0	1	-1	4	C	-0.1
Total	3	66	164	17	36	10	1	2	10	12	23	.220	.273	.329	.602	64	-8	-8	102	65	14	.496	0	2	-1	6	/C	0.0
■ EDDIE O'BRIEN	O'Brien, Edward Joseph b: 12/11/30, S.Amboy, N.J. BR/TR, 5'9", 165 lbs. Deb: 4/25/53 C																											
1953	Pit-N	89	261	21	62	5	3	0	14	17	30	.238	.289	.280	.569	48	-19	-20	102	75	23	.480	6	1	1	-6	S	-1.6
1955	Pit-N	75	236	26	55	3	1	0	8	18	13	.233	.290	.254	.544	48	-18	-17	97	54	18	.441	4	5	-2	1	O/3S	-1.8
1956	Pit-N	63	53	17	14	2	0	0	3	2	2	.264	.291	.302	.593	58	-3	-3	102	79	5	.475	1	1	-0	-1	S/O32P	-0.2
1957	Pit-N	3	4	0	0	0	0	0	0	0	0	.000	.000	.000	.000	-99	-1	-1	94	0	0	.000	1	0	0	0	/P	0.0
1958	Pit-N	1	0	0	0	0	0	0	0	0	0	—	—	—	—	—	0	0	95	—	—	—	0	0	0	0	/P	0.0

YEAR	TM/L	G	AB	R	H	2B	3B	HR	RBI	BB	SO	AVG	OBP	SLG	PRO	/A	BR	/A	PF	CHI	RC	TA	SB	CS	SBR	FR	POS	TPR
Total	5	231	554	64	131	10	4	0	25	37	45	.236	.288	.269	.557	48	-41	-41	100	66	45	.465	11	7	-1	-6	S/O3P2	-3.6
■ MICKEY O'BRIEN	O'Brien, Frank Aloysius b: 9/13/1894, San Francisco, Cal. d: 11/4/71, Monterey Park, Cal. BR/TR, 5'8", 160 lbs. Deb: 4/26/23																											
1923	Phi-N	15	21	3	7	2	0	0	0	2	1	.333	.391	.429	.820	102	1	0	114	0	4	.786	0	0	0	0	/C	0.0
■ GEORGE O'BRIEN	O'Brien, George Joseph b: 11/4/1889, Cleveland, Ohio d: 3/24/66, Columbus, Ohio BR/TR, 6', 185 lbs. Deb: 8/16/15																											
1915	StL-A	3	9	1	2	0	0	0	0	1	2	.222	.300	.222	.522	59	-0	-0	96	0	1	.429	0			0	/C	0.0
■ JERRY O'BRIEN	O'Brien, Jeremiah b: 2/2/1864, New York d: 7/4/11, Binghamton, N.Y. Deb: 7/30/1887																											
1887	Was-N	1	4	0	0	0	0	0	0	0	2	.000	.000	.000	.000	-99	-1	-1	95	0	0	.000	0			0	/2	0.0
■ JOHN O'BRIEN	O'Brien, John E. b: 10/22/1851, Columbus, Ohio d: 12/31/14, Fall River, Mass. TR, 5'11.5", 187 lbs. Deb: 4/19/1884																											
1884	Bal-U	18	77	7	19	1	1	0		2		.247	.266	.286	.552	78	-1	-2	110	0	6	.414	0			0	O	-0.1
■ JOHN O'BRIEN	O'Brien, John J. "Chewing Gum" b: 7/14/1870, St.John, N.B., Can d: 5/13/13, Lewiston, Maine BL/TR, 175 lbs. Deb: 4/22/1891																											
1891	Bro-N	43	167	22	41	4	2	0	26	12	17	.246	.308	.293	.601	79	-5	-4	97	164	17	.540	4			-26	2	-2.5
1893	Chi-N	4	14	3	5	0	1	0	1	2	2	.357	.471	.500	.971	155	1	1	104	40	3	1.111	0			0	/2	0.1
1895	Lou-N	128	539	82	138	10	4	1	50	45	20	.256	.325	.295	.620	65	-28	-24	95	74	58	.571	15			2	*2/1	-1.1
1896	Lou-N	49	186	24	63	9	1	2	24	13	7	.339	.385	.430	.815	119	4	5	98	85	33	.797	4			-2	2	0.4
	Was-N	73	270	38	72	6	3	4	33	27	12	.267	.344	.356	.700	91	-5	-2	95	90	35	.667	4			2	2	0.2
	Yr	122	456	62	135	15	4	6	57	40	19	.296	.361	.386	.747	103	-0	3	96	89	68	.717	8			0		0.6
1897	Was-N	86	320	37	78	12	2	3	45	19		.244	.307	.322	.628	67	-15	-15	101	120	34	.570	6			3	2	-0.4
1899	Bal-N	39	135	14	26	4	0	1	17	15		.193	.283	.244	.527	44	-9	-11	108	148	11	.495	4			6	2	-0.1
	Pit-N	79	279	26	63	2	4	1	33	21		.226	.282	.272	.555	55	-17	-16	99	131	24	.491	8			-2	2	-1.2
	Yr	118	414	40	89	6	4	2	50	36		.215	.283	.263	.546	51	-26	-27	102	137	35	.492	12			4		-1.3
Total	6	501	1910	246	486	47	17	12	229	154	58	.254	.321	.316	.637	73	-73	-66	98	106	216	.586	45			-17	2/1	-4.6
■ JACK O'BRIEN	O'Brien, John Joseph b: 2/5/1873, Watervliet, N.Y. d: 6/10/33, Watervliet, N.Y. 6'1", 165 lbs. Deb: 4/14/1899																											
1899	Was-N	127	468	68	132	11	5	6	51	31		.282	.329	.365	.695	97	-5	-2	96	84	63	.658	17			3	*O/3	-0.5
1901	Was-A	11	45	5	8	0	0	0	5	3		.178	.229	.178	.407	15	-5	-5	99	190	2	.351	2			-0	O	-0.4
	Cle-A	92	375	54	106	14	5	0	39	22		.283	.322	.347	.669	92	-6	-3	95	91	47	.613	13			-11	O/3	-1.3
	Yr	103	420	59	114	14	5	0	44	25		.271	.312	.329	.641	84	-11	-8	95	103	49	.582	15			-11		-1.7
1903	Bos-A	96	338	44	71	14	4	3	38	21		.210	.256	.302	.558	61	-13	-18	112	126	29	.498	10			-3	O3/2S	-2.5
Total	3	326	1226	171	317	39	14	9	133	77		.259	.303	.335	.639	82	-29	-27	100	102	142	.585	42			-11	O/32S	-4.7
■ JACK O'BRIEN	O'Brien, John K. (born John K. Bryne) b: 6/12/1860, Philadelphia, Pa. d: 11/2/10, Philadelphia, Pa. BR/TR, 5'10", 184 lbs. Deb: 5/02/1882																											
1882	Phi-a	62	241	44	73	13	3	3		13		.303	.339	.419	.758	138	13	9	112	0	35	.679				4	CO/31	1.2
1883	Phi-a	94	390	74	113	14	10	0		25		.290	.333	.377	.709	125	12	11	103	0	50	.621				-7	CO3/S	0.8
1884	Phi-a	36	138	25	39	6	1	1		9		.283	.340	.362	.702	116	5	2	114	0	17	.626				-4	C/O1	0.0
1885	Phi-a	62	225	35	60	9	1	2		20		.267	.340	.342	.682	115	6	4	103	0	27	.618				-15	C/S1O3	-0.3
1886	Phi-a	105	423	65	107	25	7	0		38		.253	.325	.345	.670	112	6	6	100	0	56	.677	23			-5	C31S/2O	0.3
1887	Bro-a	30	123	18	28	4	1	1		6		.228	.264	.301	.564	60	-7	-7	99	0	12	.537	8			0	C/O2	-0.4
1888	Bal-a	57	196	25	44	11	5	0	18	17		.224	.300	.332	.631	110	1	3	96	84	24	.658	14			-4	CO/1	0.2
1890	Phi-a	109	433	80	113	24	14	4		52		.261	.354	.409	.762	131	15	17	97	0	75	.844	31			2	*1/OC	1.3
Total	8	555	2169	366	577	106	42	11	18	180		.266	.331	.369	.699	118	52	45	102	8	297	.682	76			-29	C1/O3S2	3.1
■ JOHNNY O'BRIEN	O'Brien, John Thomas b: 12/11/30, S.Amboy, N.J. BR/TR, 5'9", 170 lbs. Deb: 4/19/53																											
1953	Pit-N	89	279	28	69	13	2	2	22	21	36	.247	.309	.330	.639	66	-13	-14	102	88	28	.536	1	1	-0	1	2/S	-0.8
1955	Pit-N	84	278	22	83	15	2	1	25	20	19	.299	.348	.378	.726	95	-3	-2	97	94	36	.626	1	1	-0	3	2	0.8
1956	Pit-N	73	104	13	18	1	0	0	3	5	7	.173	.211	.183	.394	7	-13	-14	102	67	4	.273	0	0	0	-0	2/PS	-0.8
1957	Pit-N	34	35	7	11	2	1	0	1	1	4	.314	.368	.429	.797	121	1	1	94	28	5	.720	0	0	0	-1	P/S2	0.3
1958	Pit-N	3	1	1	0	0	0	0	0	0	1	.000	.000	.000	.000	-99	-0	-0	95	0	0	.000	0	0	0	0	H	0.0
	StL-N	12	2	3	0	0	0	0	0	1	0	.000	.333	.000	.333	-2	-0	-0	106	0	0	.500	0	0	0	-0	/SP2	0.0
	Yr	15	3	4	0	0	0	0	0	1	1	.000	.250	.000	.250	-25	-1	-1	104	0	0	.333	0	0	0	-0		0.0
1959	Mil-N	44	116	16	23	4	0	1	8	11	15	.198	.273	.259	.532	45	-9	-9	95	98	9	.438	0	0	0	-4	2	-0.9
Total	6	339	815	90	204	35	5	4	59	59	82	.250	.307	.320	.628	67	-39	-38	99	86	82	.536	2	2	-1	0	2/PS	-1.4
■ PETE O'BRIEN	O'Brien, Peter J. b: 6/17/1877, Binghamton, N.Y. d: 1/31/17, Jersey City, N.J. BL/TR, 5'7", 170 lbs. Deb: 9/21/01																											
1901	Cin-N	16	54	1	11	1	0	1	3	2		.204	.232	.278	.510	52	-4	-3	95	56	4	.395	0			1	2	0.0
1906	StL-A	151	524	44	122	9	4	2	57	42		.233	.290	.277	.566	81	-11	-10	98	140	50	.527	25			-36	*23S	-5.3
1907	Cle-A	43	145	9	33	5	2	0	6	7		.228	.263	.290	.553	84	-4	-3	93	52	12	.446	1			3	23/S	0.1
	Was-A	39	134	6	25	3	1	0	12	12		.187	.253	.224	.477	60	-7	-5	90	146	9	.422	4			1	3S/2	-0.1
	Yr	82	279	15	58	8	3	0	18	19		.208	.258	.258	.516	72	-10	-8	92	97	20	.434	5			4		0.0
Total	3	249	857	60	191	18	7	3	78	63		.223	.276	.271	.547	76	-25	-21	96	121	74	.488	30			-31	2/3S	-5.3
■ PETE O'BRIEN	O'Brien, Peter James b: 6/16/1867, Chicago, Ill. d: 6/30/37, York Township, Du Page County, Ill. BR/TR, 5'9.5", 165 lbs. Deb: 4/29/1890																											
1890	Chi-N	27	106	15	30	7	0	3	16	5	10	.283	.315	.434	.749	110	2	0	109	90	16	.724	4			0	2	0.0
■ PETE O'BRIEN	O'Brien, Peter Michael b: 2/9/58, Santa Monica, Cal. BR/TR, 6'1", 185 lbs. Deb: 9/03/82																											
1982	Tex-A	20	67	13	16	4	1	4	13	6	8	.239	.301	.507	.809	126	1	2	93	115	11	.804	1	0	0	-1	O/1D	0.1
1983	Tex-A	154	524	53	124	24	5	8	53	58	62	.237	.314	.347	.661	81	-13	-13	101	103	57	.591	5	4	-1	9	*1O/D	-1.0
1984	Tex-A	142	520	57	149	26	2	18	80	53	50	.287	.353	.448	.801	120	14	14	100	113	80	.747	3	5	-2	-0	*1/O	0.2
1985	Tex-A	159	573	69	153	34	3	22	92	69	53	.267	.347	.452	.799	108	13	7	108	119	85	.746	5	10	-5	-6	*1	-1.3
1986	Tex-A	156	551	86	160	23	3	23	90	87	66	.290	.387	.468	.855	139	27	31	96	116	98	.843	4	4	-1	2	*1	2.0
1987	Tex-A	159	569	84	163	26	1	23	88	59	61	.286	.354	.457	.810	110	11	9	104	109	91	.761	0	4	-2	17	*1/OD	0.6
1988	Tex-A	156	547	57	149	24	1	16	71	72	73	.272	.357	.408	.765	112	11	10	101	106	80	.715	1	4	-2	14	*1/D	1.3
Total	7	946	3351	419	914	161	16	114	487	404	373	.273	.351	.432	.784	112	66	59	102	111	503	.756	19	31	-13	35	1/OD	1.9
■ RAY O'BRIEN	O'Brien, Raymond Joseph b: 10/31/1892, St.Louis, Mo. d: 3/31/42, St.Louis, Mo. BL/TL, 5'9", 175 lbs. Deb: 6/27/16																											
1916	Pit-N	16	57	5	12	3	2	0	3	1	14	.211	.224	.333	.557	67	-2	-3	105	64	5	.444	0			-1	O	-0.4
■ SYD O'BRIEN	O'Brien, Sydney Lloyd b: 12/18/44, Compton, Cal. BR/TR, 6'1", 185 lbs. Deb: 4/15/69																											
1969	Bos-A	100	263	47	64	10	5	9	29	15	37	.243	.287	.422	.709	92	-3	-4	105	84	31	.629	2	3	-1	-1	3S2	-0.4
1970	Chi-A	121	441	48	109	13	2	8	44	22	62	.247	.286	.340	.626	68	-18	-21	106	104	41	.513	3	3	-1	10	32/S	-0.6
1971	Cal-A	90	251	25	50	8	1	5	21	15	33	.199	.247	.299	.546	55	-16	-15	99	95	16	.427	0	2	-1	-3	S/231O	-1.4
1972	Cal-A	36	39	10	7	2	0	1	1	6	10	.179	.289	.308	.597	88	-1	-1	88	28	4	.545	0	0	0	0	/3S21	0.0
	Mil-A	31	58	5	12	2	0	1	5	2	13	.207	.233	.293	.526	59	-3	-3	95	104	3	.388	0	1	-1	-1	/32	-0.4
	Yr	67	97	15	19	4	0	2	6	8	23	.196	.257	.299	.556	71	-4	-3	92	64	7	.457	0	1	-1	-1		-0.4
Total	4	378	1052	135	242	35	8	24	100	60	155	.230	.274	.347	.621	71	-40	-44	102	94	95	.529	5	9	-4	6	3/S21O	-2.8
■ TOMMY O'BRIEN	O'Brien, Thomas Edward "Obie" b: 12/19/18, Anniston, La. BR/TR, 5'11", 195 lbs. Deb: 4/24/43																											
1943	Pit-N	89	232	35	72	12	7	2	26	15	24	.310	.352	.448	.801	125	8	7	104	85	35	.708	0			-8	O/3	-0.2
1944	Pit-N	85	156	27	39	6	2	3	20	21	12	.250	.343	.372	.714	96	1	-0	105	107	19	.653	1			-11	O/3	-1.5
1945	Pit-N	58	161	23	54	6	5	0	18	9	13	.335	.374	.435	.809	120	5	4	103	89	27	.741	0			-7	O	-0.4
1949	Bos-A	49	125	24	28	5	0	3	10	21	12	.224	.336	.336	.672	73	-4	-5	107	67	15	.634	1	0	0	-3	O	-0.7
1950	Bos-A	9	31	0	4	1	0	0	3	3	5	.129	.206	.161	.367	-4	-5	-6	114	207	1	.276	0	0	0	-1	/O	-0.6
	Was-A	3	9	1	1	0	0	0	1	1	0	.111	.200	.111	.311	-19	-2	-2	99	345	0	.222	0	0	0	1	/O	0.0
	Yr	12	40	1	5	1	0	0	4	4	5	.125	.205	.150	.355	-7	-7	-7	111	259	1	.278	0	0	0	-0		-0.6
Total	5	293	714	110	198	30	14	8	78	70	66	.277	.344	.392	.736	99	3	-2	105	96	97	.685	2	0		-29	O/3	-3.4
■ TOM O'BRIEN	O'Brien, Thomas H. b: 6/22/1860, Salem, Mass. d: 4/21/21, Worcester, Mass. Deb: 6/14/1882																											
1882	Wor-N	22	89	9	18	1	1	0	7	1	10	.202	.211	.236	.447	43	-6	-5	100	119	5	.310				0	O/23	-0.4

YEAR	TM/L	G	AB	R	H	2B	3B	HR	RBI	BB	SO	AVG	OBP	SLG	PRO	/A	BR	/A	PF	CHI	RC	TA	SB	CS	SBR	FR	POS	TPR
1883	Bal-a	33	138	16	37	6	4	0		5		.268	.294	.370	.663	105	2	0	107	0	15	.554				-3	2/O	-0.1
1884	Bos-U	103	449	80	118	31	8	4		12		.263	.282	.394	.676	128	12	13	98	0	51	.571	0			0	*2/O1C	0.7
1885	Bal-a	8	33	4	7	3	0	0		2		.212	.257	.303	.560	74	-1	-1	106	0	3	.462				0	/12	0.0
1887	NY-a	31	129	13	25	3	2	0		2		.194	.212	.248	.460	34	-12	-9	88	0	9	.433	10			0	1/O32P	-0.7
1890	Roc-a	73	273	36	52	6	5	0		30		.190	.273	.249	.522	60	-15	-11	93	0	21	.475	6			-5	1/2	-1.6
Total	6	270	1111	158	257	50	20	4	7	52	10	.231	.267	.323	.590	88	-20	-14	97	9	104	.502	16			-8	2/1O3PC	-2.1
■ TOM O'BRIEN	O'Brien, Thomas J. b: 2/20/1873, Verona, Pa. d: 2/4/01, Phoenix, Arizona Deb: 5/10/1897																											
1897	Bal-N	50	147	25	37	6	0	0	32	20		.252	.349	.293	.642	76	-5	-4	95	218	18	.655	7			0	1O	-0.2
1898	Bal-N	18	60	9	13	0	0	0	14	10		.217	.338	.217	.555	61	-2	-3	103	332	5	.511	0			1	O	-0.1
	Pit-N	107	413	53	107	10	8	1	45	25		.259	.318	.329	.648	90	-6	-5	98	94	49	.605	13			3	O1/32S	-0.5
	Yr	125	473	62	120	10	8	1	59	35		.254	.321	.315	.636	86	-8	-7	98	131	53	.592	13			3	O1/32S	-0.6
1899	NY-N	150	573	100	170	21	10	6	77	44		.297	.350	.400	.750	111	6	8	97	101	90	.742	23			-2	*O3/S21	-0.1
1900	Pit-N	102	376	61	109	22	6	3	61	21		.290	.327	.404	.732	101	1	-1	103	121	55	.693	12			-7	1O/2S	-0.6
Total	4	427	1569	248	436	59	24	10	229	120		.278	.336	.365	.701	98	-7	-3	99	125	216	.675	55			-6	O1/32S	-1.5
■ DARBY O'BRIEN	O'Brien, William D. b: 9/1/1863, Peoria, Ill. d: 6/15/1893, Peoria, Ill. BR/TR, 6'1", 186 lbs. Deb: 4/16/1887																											
1887	NY-a	127	522	97	157	30	13	5		40		.301	.355	.437	.792	140	15	26	88	0	101	.879	49			4	*O1/S3P	2.1
1888	Bro-a	136	532	105	149	27	6	2	65	30		.280	.327	.365	.692	119	14	11	105	103	83	.747	55			-2	*O	0.3
1889	Bro-a	136	567	146	170	30	11	5	80	61	76	.300	.384	.418	.802	136	24	28	96	78	129	1.020	91			-8	*O	1.2
1890	Bro-N	85	350	78	110	28	6	2	63	32	43	.314	.378	.446	.824	142	18	18	100	104	75	.958	38			1	O	1.5
1891	Bro-N	103	395	79	100	18	6	5	57	39	53	.253	.331	.367	.698	108	3	4	97	110	60	.753	31			1	*O	0.0
1892	Bro-N	122	490	72	119	14	5	1	56	29	52	.243	.289	.298	.587	78	-13	-14	101	122	60	.633	57			2	*O	-1.4
Total	6	709	2856	577	805	147	47	20	321	231	224	.282	.344	.387	.732	120	61	74	98	84	508	.828	321			-3	O/1SP3	3.7
■ BILLY O'BRIEN	O'Brien, William Smith b: 3/14/1860, Albany, N.Y. d: 5/26/11, Kansas City, Mo. BR , 6', 185 lbs. Deb: 9/27/1884																											
1884	StP-U	8	30	1	7	3	0	0		0		.233	.233	.333	.567	90	-0	-0	100	0	2	.435	0			0	/3P	0.0
	KC-U	4	17	2	4	0	0	0		0		.235	.235	.235	.471	68	-1	-0	87	0	1	.308	0			0	/31	0.0
	Yr	12	47	3	11	3	0	0		0		.234	.234	.298	.532	82	-1	-1	96	0	3	.389	0			0		0.0
1887	Was-N	113	453	71	126	16	12	**19**	73	21	17	.278	.317	.492	.810	129	12	16	95	85	76	.795	11			-5	*1/O32	-0.5
1888	Was-N	133	528	42	119	15	2	9	66	9	70	.225	.238	.313	.551	79	-15	-12	96	130	43	.450	10			-5	*1/3	-2.9
1889	Was-N	2	8	1	0	0	0	0	0	1	1	.000	.111	.000	.111	-73	-2	-2	92	0	0	.125	0			0	/1	0.0
1890	BB-a	96	388	47	108	25	8	4		28		.278	.332	.415	.747	122	9	9	100	0	56	.704	5			-5	*1	0.0
Total	5	356	1424	164	364	59	22	32	139	59	88	.256	.289	.395	.684	108	4	10	97	74	179	.619	26			-15	1/3O2P	-3.4
■ WHITEY OCK	Ock, Harold David b: 3/17/12, Brooklyn, N.Y. d: 3/18/75, Mt.Kisco, N.Y. BR/TR, 5'11", 180 lbs. Deb: 9/29/35																											
1935	Bro-N	1	3	0	0	0	0	0	0	1	2	.000	.250	.000	.250	-28	-1	-0	94	0	0	.333	0			0	/C	0.0
■ DANNY O'CONNELL	O'Connell, Daniel Francis b: 1/21/27, Paterson, N.J. d: 10/2/69, Clifton, N.J. BR/TR, 5'11", 168 lbs. Deb: 7/14/50 C																											
1950	Pit-N	79	315	39	92	16	1	8	32	24	33	.292	.342	.425	.768	98	-0	-1	103	83	45	.714	7			-4	S3	0.1
1953	Pit-N	149	588	88	173	26	8	7	55	57	42	.294	.361	.401	.762	97	-0	-2	102	80	87	.694	3	4	-2	8	*32	0.4
1954	Mil-N	146	541	61	151	28	4	2	37	38	46	.279	.329	.357	.685	84	-17	-12	93	75	64	.583	2	2	-1	4	*23/1S	-0.2
1955	Mil-N	124	453	47	102	15	4	6	40	28	43	.225	.278	.316	.593	61	-28	-24	93	103	40	.494	2	2	-1	14	*2/3S	0.0
1956	Mil-N	139	498	71	119	17	9	2	42	76	42	.239	.344	.321	.666	81	-11	-11	99	113	61	.626	3	3	-1	-2	*2/3S	-0.2
1957	Mil-N	48	183	29	43	9	1	1	8	19	20	.235	.314	.311	.625	76	-8	-5	90	58	20	.560	1	0	0	6	2	0.4
	NY-N	95	364	57	97	18	3	7	28	33	30	.266	.331	.390	.721	91	-4	-5	102	75	47	.661	8	3	1	6	23	0.8
	Yr	143	547	86	140	27	4	8	36	52	50	.256	.325	.364	.689	86	-11	-10	98	70	67	.629	9	3	1	12		1.2
1958	SF-N	107	306	44	71	12	2	3	23	51	35	.232	.342	.314	.655	75	-10	-10	100	90	36	.613	2	1	0	-3	*2/3	-0.6
1959	SF-N	34	58	6	11	3	0	0	0	5	15	.190	.254	.241	.495	34	-6	-5	95	0	4	.396	0	1	-1	0	3/2	-0.5
1961	Was-A	138	493	61	128	30	1	1	37	77	62	.260	.363	.331	.694	91	-6	-3	95	92	67	.686	15	5	2	8	32	1.8
1962	Was-A	84	236	24	62	7	2	2	18	23	28	.263	.328	.335	.663	78	-7	-7	101	84	27	.591	5	1	1	3	32	0.0
Total	10	1143	4035	527	1049	181	35	39	320	431	396	.260	.335	.351	.686	84	-96	-84	98	86	496	.636	48	22		40	23/S1	2.0
■ JIMMY O'CONNELL	O'Connell, James Joseph b: 2/11/01, Sacramento, Cal. d: 11/11/76, Bakersfield, Cal. BL/TR, 5'10.5", 175 lbs. Deb: 4/17/23																											
1923	NY-N	87	252	42	63	9	2	6	39	34	32	.250	.351	.373	.724	90	-3	-3	101	123	35	.729	7	3	0	-9	O/1	-1.3
1924	NY-N	52	104	24	33	4	2	2	18	11	16	.317	.388	.452	.840	136	4	5	91	124	19	.847	2	1	0	-6	O/2	0.0
Total	2	139	356	66	96	13	4	8	57	45	48	.270	.361	.396	.757	102	1	2	99	123	54	.761	9	4	0	-15	/O12	-1.3
■ JOHN O'CONNELL	O'Connell, John Charles b: 6/13/04, Pittsburgh, Pa. BR/TR, 6', 170 lbs. Deb: 8/16/28																											
1928	Pit-N	1	1	0	0	0	0	0	0	0	0	.000	.000	.000	.000	-94	-0	-0	107	0	0	.000	0			0	/C	0.0
1929	Pit-N	2	7	1	1	1	0	0	0	1	1	.143	.250	.286	.536	31	-1	-1	103	0	1	.500	0			0	/C	0.0
Total	2	3	8	1	1	1	0	0	0	1	1	.125	.222	.250	.472	17	-1	-1	104	0	1	.429	0			0	/C	0.0
■ JOHN O'CONNELL	O'Connell, John Joseph b: 5/16/1872, Lawrence, Mass. d: 5/14/08, Derry, N.H. Deb: 8/22/1891																											
1891	Bal-a	8	29	2	5	1	0	0	7	3	6	.172	.250	.207	.457	33	-2	-3	101	344	2	.458	2			0	/S2O	-0.1
1902	Det-A	8	22	1	4	0	0	0	0	3		.182	.280	.182	.462	32	-2	-2	99	0	1	.389	0			0	/21	0.0
Total	2	16	51	3	9	1	0	0	7	6	6	.176	.263	.196	.459	32	-4	-4	100	193	3	.429	2			0	/2S1O	-0.1
■ PAT O'CONNELL	O'Connell, Patrick H. b: 6/10/1861, Bangor, Me. d: 1/24/43, Lewiston, Maine BR/TR, 5'10", 175 lbs. Deb: 7/22/1886																											
1886	Bal-a	42	166	20	30	3	2	0		11		.181	.236	.223	.459	50	-10	-8	91	0	11	.434	10			-5	O/1P	-1.1
1890	BB-a	11	40	7	9	2	1	0		7		.225	.340	.325	.665	99	0	0	100	0	6	.742	3			0	3/1	0.0
Total	2	53	206	27	39	5	3	0	0	18		.189	.258	.243	.500	61	-10	-7	93	0	17	.491	13			-5	/O31P	-1.1
■ DAN O'CONNOR	O'Connor, Daniel Cornelius b: 8/1868, Guelph, Ont., Canada d: 3/3/42, Guelph, Ont., Canada 6'2", 185 lbs. Deb: 6/03/1890																											
1890	Lou-a	6	26	3	12	1	1	0		1		.462	.481	.577	1.058	201	3	3	107	0	10	1.500	5			0	/1	0.3
■ JOHNNY O'CONNOR	O'Connor, John Charles "Bucky" b: 12/1/1891, Cahersiveen, Ire. d: 5/30/82, Bonner Springs, Kan. BR/TR, 5'9", Deb: 9/16/16																											
1916	Chi-N	1	0	0	0	0	0	0	0	0	0	—	—	—	—	—	0	0	117	—	—	—	0			0	/C	0.0
■ JACK O'CONNOR	O'Connor, John Joseph "Rowdy Jack" or "Peach Pie" b: 6/2/1869, St.Louis, Mo. d: 11/14/37, St.Louis, Mo. BR/TR, 5'10", 170 lbs. Deb: 4/20/1887 M																											
1887	Cin-a	12	40	4	4	0	0	0		2		.100	.143	.100	.243	-28	-7	-7	108	0	1	.250	3			0	/OC	-0.5
1888	Cin-a	36	137	14	28	3	1	1	17	6		.204	.243	.263	.506	64	-5	-5	101	133	12	.505	12			0	O/C	-0.4
1889	Col-a	107	398	69	107	17	7	4	60	33	37	.269	.331	.377	.708	114	1	8	91	108	60	.732	26			0	CO/21	1.4
1890	Col-a	121	457	89	148	14	10	2		38		.324	.377	.411	.788	136	19	20	99	0	84	.828	29			-5	*C/OS23	2.3
1891	Col-a	56	229	28	61	12	3	0	37	11	14	.266	.300	.345	.645	97	-5	-1	89	143	27	.595	10			0	OC	-0.1
1892	Cle-N	140	572	71	142	22	5	1	58	25	48	.248	.282	.309	.592	78	-15	-17	103	105	56	.514	17			3	*OC	-1.6
1893	Cle-N	96	384	72	110	23	1	4	75	29	12	.286	.341	.383	.724	90	-4	-7	104	132	62	.759	29			-8	CO	-0.9
1894	Cle-N	86	330	67	104	23	7	2	51	15	7	.315	.345	.445	.790	82	-6	-13	111	92	57	.783	15			1	CO/1	-0.7
1895	Cle-N	89	340	51	99	14	10	0	58	30	22	.291	.354	.391	.745	97	-3	-1	97	124	52	.734	11			-7	C1/3	-0.2
1896	Cle-N	68	256	41	76	11	1	1	43	15	12	.297	.343	.359	.702	79	-5	-9	110	133	38	.694	15			-7	C1O	-0.9
1897	Cle-N	103	397	49	115	21	4	2	69	26		.290	.338	.378	.716	82	-5	-12	111	132	59	.706	20			-13	O1C	-2.5
1898	Cle-N	131	478	50	119	17	4	1	56	26		.249	.292	.308	.599	77	-16	-13	96	115	46	.513	8			1	1CO	-0.7
1899	StL-N	84	289	33	73	5	6	0	43	15		.253	.299	.311	.610	65	-12	-15	108	147	30	.537	7			-4	C1	-1.3
1900	StL-N	10	32	4	7	0	0	0	6	2		.219	.265	.219	.483	39	-3	-2	93	268	2	.360	0			-1	C	-0.1
	Pit-N	43	147	15	35	4	1	0	19	3		.238	.253	.279	.532	47	-10	-11	103	145	12	.438	5			-14	C/1	-1.9
	Yr	53	179	19	42	4	1	0	25	5		.235	.255	.268	.524	46	-13	-13	101	173	14	.423	5			-15		-2.0
1901	Pit-N	61	202	16	39	7	3	0	22	10		.193	.231	.257	.489	43	-14	-15	101	142	13	.393	2			-8	C	-1.4
1902	Pit-N	49	170	13	50	1	2	1	28	3		.294	.306	.341	.648	96	-0	-1	105	159	19	.525	2			-5	C/1O	-0.1
1903	NY-A	64	212	13	43	4	1	0	12	8		.203	.232	.231	.463	41	-15	-15	100	88	13	.361	4			-8	C/1	-1.5
1904	StL-A	14	47	4	10	1	0	0	2	2		.213	.245	.234	.479	57	-2	-2	95	68	3	.351	0			0	C	0.0

YEAR	TM/L	G	AB	R	H	2B	3B	HR	RBI	BB	SO	AVG	OBP	SLG	PRO	/A	BR	/A	PF	CHI	RC	TA	SB	CS	SBR	FR	POS	TPR
1906	StL-A	55	174	8	33	0	0	0	11	2		.190	.199	.190	.389	24	-15	-15	98	121	8	.284	5			-0	C	-1.1
1907	StL-A	25	89	2	14	2	0	0	4	0		.157	.157	.180	.337	9	-9	-9	98	89	3	.213	0			0	C	-0.6
1910	StL-A	1	0	0	0	0	0	0	0	0		—	—	—	—	—	0	0	94	—	—	—	0			0	/CM	0.0
Total	21	1451	5380	713	1417	201	66	19	671	301	152	.263	.306	.336	.642	81	-131	-143	101	111	657	.594	220			-74	CO1/S23	-12.8
■ PADDY O'CONNOR	O'Connor, Patrick Francis b: 8/4/1879, County Kerry, Ireland d: 8/17/50, Springfield, Mass. BR/TR, 5'8", 168 lbs. Deb: 4/17/08																											
1908	Pit-N	12	16	1	3	0	0	0	2	0		.188	.188	.188	.375	22	-1	-1	95	256	1	.231	0			0	/C	0.0
1909	Pit-N	9	16	1	5	1	0	0	3	0		.313	.313	.375	.688	110	0	0	105	182	2	.545	0			-0	/C3	0.0
1910	Pit-N	6	4	0	1	0	0	0	0	1	1	.250	.400	.250	.650	81	0	-0	112	0	0	.667	0			0	/C	0.0
1914	StL-N	10	9	0	0	0	0	0	0	2	2	.000	.250	.000	.250	-23	-1	-1	104	0	0	.333	0			0	/C	0.0
1915	Pit-F	70	219	15	50	10	1	0	16	14	30	.228	.275	.283	.558	63	-10	-11	104	93	19	.473	4			4	C	-0.4
1918	NY-A	1	3	0	1	0	0	0	0	0	1	.333	.333	.333	.667	107	-0	0	95	0	0	.500	0			0	/C	0.0
Total	6	108	267	17	60	11	1	0	21	17	34	.225	.274	.273	.547	61	-12	-13	103	101	22	.459	4			4	/C3	-0.4
■ KEN O'DEA	O'Dea, James Kenneth b: 3/16/13, Lima, N.Y. d: 12/17/85, Lima, N.Y. BL/TR, 6', 180 lbs. Deb: 4/21/35																											
1935	Chi-N	76	202	30	52	13	2	6	38	26	18	.257	.345	.431	.776	108	2	2	99	131	31	.731	0			0	C	0.2
1936	Chi-N	80	189	36	58	10	3	2	38	38	18	.307	.423	.423	.846	122	10	8	105	157	37	.861	0			1	C	1.0
1937	Chi-N	83	219	31	66	7	5	4	32	24	26	.301	.370	.434	.804	115	6	5	103	108	38	.779	1			-4	C	0.3
1938	Chi-N	86	247	22	65	12	1	3	33	12	18	.263	.297	.356	.654	75	-8	-9	105	123	25	.529	1			-2	C	-0.8
1939	NY-N	52	97	7	17	1	0	3	11	10	16	.175	.252	.278	.531	43	-8	-8	99	112	7	.451	0			3	C	-0.3
1940	NY-N	48	96	9	23	4	1	0	12	16	15	.240	.348	.302	.650	81	-2	-2	100	153	11	.600	0			3	C	0.2
1941	NY-N	59	89	13	19	5	1	3	17	8	20	.213	.278	.393	.672	85	-2	-2	103	140	10	.597	0			2	C	0.2
1942	StL-N	58	192	22	45	7	1	5	32	17	23	.234	.297	.359	.656	85	-3	-4	108	141	20	.566	0			1	C	-0.1
1943	StL-N	71	203	15	57	11	2	3	25	19	25	.281	.345	.399	.744	110	4	2	105	100	29	.682	0			-2	C	0.3
1944	StL-N	85	265	35	66	11	2	6	37	37	29	.249	.343	.374	.717	101	1	1	101	113	37	.687	1			2	C	0.6
1945	StL-N	100	307	36	78	18	2	4	43	50	31	.254	.359	.365	.723	101	2	2	100	120	43	.686	0			5	C	0.8
1946	StL-N	22	57	2	7	2	0	1	3	8	8	.123	.231	.211	.441	24	-6	-6	107	75	3	.370	0			-2	C	-0.7
	Bos-N	12	32	4	7	0	0	0	2	8	4	.219	.375	.219	.594	75	-1	-0	95	107	3	.556	0			-1	C	0.0
	Yr	34	89	6	14	2	0	1	5	16	12	.157	.286	.213	.499	42	-6	-7	102	88	6	.455	0			-3		-0.7
Total	12	832	2195	262	560	101	20	40	323	273	251	.255	.338	.374	.712	95	-5	-12	102	123	292	.672	3			6	C	1.7
■ PAUL O'DEA	O'Dea, Paul "Lefty" b: 7/3/20, Cleveland, Ohio d: 12/11/78, Cleveland, Ohio BL/TL, 6', 200 lbs. Deb: 4/19/44																											
1944	Cle-A	76	173	25	55	9	0	0	13	23	21	.318	.401	.370	.771	121	6	6	100	73	24	.687	2	2	-1	-6	O/P1	-0.1
1945	Cle-A	87	221	21	52	2	2	1	21	20	26	.235	.299	.276	.575	68	-9	-9	99	119	18	.469	3	0	1	1	O/P	-0.9
Total	2	163	394	46	107	11	2	1	34	43	47	.272	.345	.317	.662	92	-3	-3	99	98	43	.582	5	2	0	-5	/OP1	-1.0
■ HEINIE ODOM	Odom, Herman Boyd b: 10/13/1900, Rusk, Tex. d: 8/31/70, Rusk, Tex. BB/TR, 6', 170 lbs. Deb: 4/22/25																											
1925	NY-A	1	1	0	1	0	0	0	0	0	0	1.000	1.000	1.000	2.000	425	0	0	96	0	1	—	0	0	0	0	/3	0.0
■ BLUE MOON ODOM	Odom, Johnny Lee b: 5/29/45, Macon, Ga. BR/TR, 6', 178 lbs. Deb: 9/05/64																											
1964	KC-A	5	5	1	0	0	0	0	0	1	4	.000	.167	.000	.167	-47	-1	-1	105	0	0	.200	0	0	0	0	/P	0.0
1965	KC-A	1	0	0	0	0	0	0	0	0	0	—	—	—	—	—	0	0	97	—	—	—	0	0	0	0	/P	0.0
1966	KC-A	17	31	1	3	0	0	0	2	3	16	.097	.176	.097	.273	-20	-5	-5	94	280	1	.214	0	0	0	2	P	0.0
1967	KC-A	33	28	4	8	1	0	0	0	1	14	.286	.310	.321	.632	87	-0	-0	100	0	3	.476	0	1	-1	0	P	0.0
1968	Oak-A	42	78	14	17	2	0	1	2	6	29	.218	.282	.282	.564	73	-3	-2	98	34	7	.475	0	0	0	1	P	0.0
1969	Oak-A	43	79	15	21	2	1	5	16	2	24	.266	.293	.506	.799	130	1	2	92	117	12	.741	0	0	0	1	P	0.0
1970	Oak-A	37	54	8	13	2	0	3	7	3	18	.241	.281	.444	.725	100	-1	-0	97	86	7	.667	1	0	0	2	P	0.0
1971	Oak-A	37	50	8	8	0	1	1	1	2	24	.160	.192	.260	.452	27	-5	-5	101	25	2	.349	0	0	0	-1	P	0.0
1972	Oak-A	59	66	16	8	1	0	2	2	1	29	.121	.134	.227	.362	6	-8	-8	97	40	2	.333	4	2	0	0	P	0.0
1973	Oak-A	51	1	5	0	0	0	0	0	0	0	.000	.000	.000	.000	-99	-0	-0	87	0	-1	.333	1	2	-1	-1	P	0.0
1974	Oak-A	43	0	3	0	0	0	0	0	0	0	—	—	—	—	—	0	0	100	—	—	—	0	0	0	1	P	0.0
1975	Oak-A	8	0	1	0	0	0	0	0	0	0	—	—	—	—	—	0	0	93	—	—	—	0	0	0	0	/P	0.0
	Cle-A	3	0	0	0	0	0	0	0	0	0	—	—	—	—	—	0	0	100	—	—	—	0	0	0	-0	/P	0.0
	Yr	11	0	1	0	0	0	0	0	0	0	—	—	—	—	—	0	0	95	—	—	—	0	0	0	-0		0.0
	Atl-N	15	13	0	1	1	0	0	1	0	5	.077	.077	.154	.231	-39	-2	-2	95	193	0	.167	0	0	0	0	P	0.0
1976	Chi-A	8	0	0	0	0	0	0	0	0	0	—	—	—	—	—	0	0	99	—	—	—	0	0	0	-1	/P	0.0
Total	13	402	405	76	79	9	2	12	31	19	163	.195	.235	.316	.551	60	-23	-22	97	78	30	.468	6	5	-1	6	P	0.0
■ O'DONNELL	O'Donnell b:Littlestown, Pa. Deb: 7/16/1884																											
1884	Phi-U	1	4	0	1	0	0	0		0		.250	.250	.250	.500	75	-0	-0	93	0	0	.333	0			0	/C	0.0
■ HARRY O'DONNELL	O'Donnell, Harry Herman "Butch" b: 4/2/1894, Philadelphia, Pa. d: 1/31/58, Philadelphia, Pa. BR/TR, 5'8", 175 lbs. Deb: 4/30/27																											
1927	Phi-N	16	16	1	1	0	0	0	2	2	2	.063	.167	.063	.229	-38	-3	-3	96	700	0	.200	0			-0	C	-0.1
■ LEFTY O'DOUL	O'Doul, Francis Joseph b: 3/4/1897, San Francisco, Cal. d: 12/7/69, San Francisco, Cal. BL/TL, 6', 180 lbs. Deb: 4/29/19																											
1919	NY-A	19	16	2	4	0	0	0	1	1	2	.250	.294	.250	.544	51	-1	-1	106	91	1	.500	1			-1	/PO	0.0
1920	NY-A	13	12	2	2	1	0	0	1	1	1	.167	.231	.250	.481	27	-1	-1	102	117	1	.400	0	0	0	-1	/PO	-0.1
1922	NY-A	8	9	0	3	1	0	0	4	0	2	.333	.333	.444	.778	100	-0	-0	102	358	1	.667	0	0	0	0	/P	0.0
1923	Bos-A	36	35	2	5	0	0	0	4	2	3	.143	.189	.143	.332	-12	-6	-6	102	273	1	.233	0	0	0	1	P/O	0.0
1928	NY-N	114	354	67	113	19	4	8	46	30	8	.319	.372	.463	.836	115	8	8	102	87	60	.842	9			-14	O	-0.9
1929	Phi-N	154	638	152	**254**	35	6	32	122	76	19	**.398**	**.465**	.622	1.087	152	68	59	110	75	180	1.247	2			-1	*O	3.9
1930	Phi-N	140	528	122	202	37	7	22	97	63	21	.383	.453	.604	1.057	144	47	42	106	89	141	1.196	3			-10	*O	1.9
1931	Bro-N	134	512	85	172	32	11	7	75	48	16	.336	.396	.482	.879	133	26	25	101	106	100	.891	5			-7	*O	1.1
1932	Bro-N	148	595	120	219	32	8	21	90	50	20	**.368**	.423	.555	.978	167	51	54	96	82	142	1.059	11			-11	*O	3.2
1933	Bro-N	43	159	14	40	5	1	5	21	15	6	.252	.320	.390	.710	105	0	1	97	109	21	.656	2			-4	O	-0.4
	NY-N	78	229	31	70	9	1	9	35	29	17	.306	.388	.472	.860	147	14	14	99	97	43	.843	1			-7	O	0.3
	Yr	121	388	45	110	14	2	14	56	44	23	.284	.361	.438	.799	130	14	15	98	102	64	.772	3			-11		-0.1
1934	NY-N	83	177	27	56	4	3	9	46	18	7	.316	.383	.525	.908	143	10	10	98	138	38	.942	2			-6	O	0.2
Total	11	970	3264	624	1140	175	41	113	542	333	122	.349	.413	.532	.945	141	217	205	102	94	730	1.002	36	0		-60	O/P	9.2
■ FRED ODWELL	Odwell, Frederick William "Fritz" b: 9/25/1872, Downsville, N.Y. d: 8/19/48, Downsville, N.Y. BL/TR, 5'9.5", 160 lbs. Deb: 4/16/04																											
1904	Cin-N	129	468	75	133	22	10	1	58	26		.284	.322	.380	.702	104	9	1	114	120	69	.699	30			19	*O/2	1.6
1905	Cin-N	130	468	79	113	10	9	**9**	65	26		.241	.281	.359	.640	89	-6	-8	103	118	55	.606	21			12	*O	-0.3
1906	Cin-N	58	202	20	45	5	4	0	21	15		.223	.276	.287	.564	67	-5	-9	115	135	20	.535	11			-3	O	-1.4
1907	Cin-N	94	274	24	74	5	7	0	24	22		.270	.324	.339	.664	115	3	4	95	98	34	.625	10			-1	O/2	0.0
Total	4	411	1412	198	365	42	30	10	168	89		.258	.302	.352	.654	96	1	-11	107	117	177	.628	72			27	O/2	-0.1
■ CHUCK OERTEL	Oertel, Charles Frank "Ducky" or "Snuffy" b: 3/12/31, Coffeyville, Kan. BL/TR, 5'8", 165 lbs. Deb: 9/01/58																											
1958	Bal-A	14	12	4	2	0	0	1	1	1	1	.167	.231	.417	.647	79	-1	-0	94	50	1	.600	0	0	0	-1	/O	0.0
■ RON OESTER	Oester, Ronald John b: 5/5/56, Cincinnati, Ohio BB/TR, 6'2", 185 lbs. Deb: 9/10/78																											
1978	Cin-N	6	8	1	3	0	0	0	1	0	2	.375	.375	.375	.750	107	0	0	103	132	1	.600	0	0	0	0	/S	0.1
1979	Cin-N	6	3	0	0	0	0	0	0	0	1	.000	.000	.000	.000	-99	-1	-1	97	0	0	.000	0	0	0	0	/S	0.0
1980	Cin-N	100	303	40	84	16	2	2	20	26	44	.277	.336	.363	.699	94	-2	-2	102	68	37	.627	6	2	1	-6	2S/3	0.0
1981	Cin-N	105	354	45	96	16	7	5	42	42	49	.271	.348	.398	.747	110	6	5	101	108	48	.683	2	5	-2	5	*2/S	1.7
1982	Cin-N	151	549	63	143	19	4	9	47	35	82	.260	.305	.359	.664	83	-12	-13	102	84	56	.554	5	6	-2	10	*2S3	0.1
1983	Cin-N	157	549	63	145	23	5	11	58	49	106	.264	.326	.384	.710	93	-3	-5	103	96	66	.622	2	2	-1	-24	*2	-2.4
1984	Cin-N	150	553	54	134	26	3	3	38	41	97	.242	.296	.316	.612	68	-21	-24	106	83	50	.513	7	2	1	-12	*2/S	-3.3
1985	Cin-N	152	526	59	155	26	3	1	34	51	65	.295	.357	.361	.718	96	2	-1	105	72	68	.641	5	0	2	4	*2	0.6
1986	Cin-N	153	523	52	135	23	2	8	44	52	84	.258	.326	.356	.682	84	-8	-11	104	84	59	.608	9	2	2	15	*2	0.8

YEAR	TM/L	G	AB	R	H	2B	3B	HR	RBI	BB	SO	AVG	OBP	SLG	PRO	/A	BR	/A	PF	CHI	RC	TA	SB	CS	SBR	FR	POS	TPR
1987	Cin-N	69	237	28	60	9	6	2	23	22	51	.253	.317	.367	.684	78	-7	-8	104	99	26	.590	2	3	-1	-2	2	-0.8
1988	Cin-N	54	150	20	42	7	0	0	10	9	24	.280	.321	.327	.647	82	-3	-4	105	82	15	.518	0	2	-1	0	2/S	-0.2
Total	11	1103	3755	425	997	165	32	41	317	327	605	.266	.325	.359	.684	87	-48	-64	104	86	425	.617	38	24	-3	-9	*2/S3	-3.4

■ BOB O'FARRELL O'Farrell, Robert Arthur b: 10/19/1896, Waukegan, Ill. d: 2/20/88, Waukegan, Ill. BR/TR, 5'9.5", 180 lbs. Deb: 9/05/15 M

YEAR	TM/L	G	AB	R	H	2B	3B	HR	RBI	BB	SO	AVG	OBP	SLG	PRO	/A	BR	/A	PF	CHI	RC	TA	SB	CS	SBR	FR	POS	TPR
1915	Chi-N	2	3	0	1	0	0	0	0	0	0	.333	.333	.333	.667	100	-0	-0	102	0	0	.500	0			0	/C	0.0
1916	Chi-N	1	0	0	0	0	0	0	0	0	0	—	—	—	—	—	0	0	117	—	—	—	0			0	/C	0.0
1917	Chi-N	3	8	1	3	2	0	0	1	1	0	.375	.444	.625	1.069	216	1	1	105	77	2	1.400	1			0	/C	0.1
1918	Chi-N	52	113	9	32	7	3	1	14	10	15	.283	.347	.425	.772	132	4	4	102	104	16	.728	0			-2	C	0.6
1919	Chi-N	49	125	11	27	4	2	0	9	7	10	.216	.258	.280	.538	61	-6	-6	100	100	9	.449	2			0	C	-0.3
1920	Chi-N	94	270	29	67	11	4	3	19	34	23	.248	.332	.352	.684	98	-1	-0	99	71	34	.640	1	0	0	4	C	1.0
1921	Chi-N	96	260	32	65	12	7	4	32	18	14	.250	.299	.396	.695	77	-7	-10	107	102	31	.631	2	0	1	2	C	0.0
1922	Chi-N	128	392	68	127	18	8	4	60	79	34	.324	.439	.441	.880	134	21	24	95	113	82	.963	5	3	-0	14	*C	3.6
1923	Chi-N	131	452	73	144	25	4	12	84	67	38	.319	.408	.471	.879	126	22	19	104	121	91	.936	10	3	1	6	*C	3.2
1924	Chi-N	71	183	25	44	6	2	3	28	30	13	.240	.347	.344	.692	85	-3	-3	101	142	24	.683	2	0	1	1	C	0.0
1925	Chi-N	17	22	2	4	0	1	0	3	2	5	.182	.250	.273	.523	34	-2	-2	97	178	2	.444	0	0	0	0	/C	-0.1
	StL-N	94	317	37	88	13	2	3	32	46	26	.278	.373	.360	.732	86	-4	-5	102	94	45	.704	0	1	-1	4	C	0.2
	Yr	111	339	39	92	13	3	3	35	48	31	.271	.365	.354	.719	83	-6	-7	101	109	46	.685	0	1	-1	4		0.1
1926	StL-N	147	492	63	144	30	9	7	68	61	44	.293	.371	.433	.804	113	11	10	102	101	79	.790	1			11	*C	2.5
1927	StL-N	61	178	19	47	10	1	0	18	23	22	.264	.348	.331	.680	77	-4	-5	107	107	21	.649	3			-1	CM	-0.1
1928	StL-N	16	52	6	11	1	0	0	4	13	9	.212	.369	.231	.600	60	-2	-2	100	121	5	.659	2			0	C	0.0
	NY-N	75	133	23	26	6	0	2	20	34	16	.195	.359	.286	.645	69	-4	-5	102	162	16	.692	2			-5	C	-0.5
	Yr	91	185	29	37	7	0	2	24	47	25	.200	.362	.270	.632	66	-7	-7	102	156	21	.682	4			-5		-0.5
1929	NY-N	91	248	35	76	14	3	4	42	28	30	.306	.384	.435	.819	103	1	2	100	120	41	.826	3			-8	C	0.1
1930	NY-N	94	249	37	75	16	4	4	54	31	21	.301	.381	.446	.827	101	0	1	98	151	42	.828	1			0	C	0.4
1931	NY-N	85	174	11	39	8	3	1	19	21	23	.224	.311	.322	.633	73	-7	-6	97	115	19	.578	0			-7	C	-0.9
1932	NY-N	50	67	7	16	3	0	0	8	11	10	.239	.354	.284	.638	75	-2	-2	99	157	8	.608	0			-1	C	0.0
1933	StL-N	55	163	16	39	4	2	2	20	15	25	.239	.303	.325	.629	78	-4	-5	102	127	16	.531	0			0	C	-0.2
1934	Cin-N	44	123	10	30	8	3	1	9	11	19	.244	.306	.382	.688	82	-3	-3	101	65	14	.592	0			2	CM	0.0
	Chi-N	22	67	3	15	3	0	0	5	3	11	.224	.257	.269	.526	42	-6	-5	98	100	5	.396	0			1	C	-0.3
	Yr	66	190	13	45	11	3	1	14	14	30	.237	.289	.342	.631	68	-9	-9	100	78	20	.541	0			3		-0.3
1935	StL-N	14	10	0	0	0	0	0	0	2	0	.000	.167	.000	.167	-49	-2	-2	104	0	0	.182	0			-0	/C	-0.1
Total	21	1492	4101	517	1120	201	58	51	549	547	408	.273	.360	.388	.748	98	4	-1	101	112	604	.730	35	7		22	*C	9.2

■ ROWLAND OFFICE Office, Rowland Johnie b: 10/25/52, Sacramento, Cal. BL/TL, 6', 170 lbs. Deb: 8/05/72

YEAR	TM/L	G	AB	R	H	2B	3B	HR	RBI	BB	SO	AVG	OBP	SLG	PRO	/A	BR	/A	PF	CHI	RC	TA	SB	CS	SBR	FR	POS	TPR
1972	Atl-N	2	5	1	2	0	0	0	0	1	2	.400	.500	.400	.900	151	0	0	105	0	1	1.000	0	0	0	0	/O	0.1
1974	Atl-N	131	248	20	61	16	1	3	31	16	30	.246	.292	.355	.647	77	-7	-9	105	123	23	.548	5	3	-0	-17	*O	-3.1
1975	Atl-N	126	355	30	103	14	1	3	30	23	41	.290	.339	.361	.699	99	-3	-1	95	85	42	.591	2	2	-1	-10	*O	-1.6
1976	Atl-N	99	359	51	101	17	1	4	34	37	49	.281	.352	.368	.719	94	3	-2	111	96	46	.641	2	8	-4	-7	O	-1.7
1977	Atl-N	124	428	42	103	13	1	5	39	23	58	.241	.284	.311	.595	53	-25	-31	113	105	36	.476	2	4	-2	2	*O/1	-3.5
1978	Atl-N	146	404	40	101	13	1	9	40	22	52	.250	.299	.354	.653	73	-11	-16	112	93	41	.565	8	6	-1	-9	*O	-3.3
1979	Atl-N	124	277	35	69	14	2	2	37	27	33	.249	.320	.336	.656	72	-8	-11	109	148	30	.585	5	4	-1	-6	O	-2.1
1980	Mon-N	116	292	36	78	13	4	6	30	36	39	.267	.348	.401	.748	109	4	4	99	88	42	.703	3	3	-1	-10	O	-1.1
1981	Mon-N	26	40	4	7	0	0	0	0	4	6	.175	.250	.175	.425	22	-4	-4	99	0	2	.314	0	0	0	-4	O	-0.8
1982	Mon-N	3	3	0	1	1	0	0	0	0	1	.333	.333	.667	1.000	165	0	0	105	0	1	1.000	0	0	0	0	/O	0.0
1983	NY-A	2	2	0	0	0	0	0	1	0	0	.000	.000	.000	.000	-99	-1	-1	99	0	0	.000	0	0	0	-0	/O	0.0
Total	11	899	2413	259	626	101	11	32	242	189	311	.259	.317	.350	.668	79	-50	-70	107	101	264	.593	27	30	-10	-61	O/1	-17.1

■ JIM OGLESBY Oglesby, James Dorn b: 8/10/05, Schofield, Mo. d: 9/1/55, Tulsa, Okla. BL/TL, 6', 190 lbs. Deb: 4/14/36

YEAR	TM/L	G	AB	R	H	2B	3B	HR	RBI	BB	SO	AVG	OBP	SLG	PRO	/A	BR	/A	PF	CHI	RC	TA	SB	CS	SBR	FR	POS	TPR
1936	Phi-A	3	11	0	2	0	0	0	2	2	0	.182	.308	.182	.490	24	-1	-1	101	343	1	.444	0	0	0	0	/1	-0.1

■ BEN OGLIVIE Oglivie, Benjamin Ambrosio (Palmer) b: 2/11/49, Colon, Panama BL/TL, 6'2", 160 lbs. Deb: 9/04/71

YEAR	TM/L	G	AB	R	H	2B	3B	HR	RBI	BB	SO	AVG	OBP	SLG	PRO	/A	BR	/A	PF	CHI	RC	TA	SB	CS	SBR	FR	POS	TPR
1971	Bos-A	14	38	2	10	3	0	0	4	0	5	.263	.263	.342	.605	67	-2	-2	106	126	3	.464	0	0	0	1	O	-0.1
1972	Bos-A	94	253	27	61	10	2	8	30	18	61	.241	.294	.391	.685	98	0	-1	105	102	29	.604	1	1	-0	-3	O	-0.6
1973	Bos-A	58	147	16	32	9	1	2	9	9	32	.218	.272	.333	.605	66	-6	-7	106	64	13	.508	1	1	-0	-1	OD	-0.9
1974	Det-A	92	252	28	68	11	3	4	29	34	38	.270	.357	.385	.742	107	5	3	106	105	36	.745	12	3	2	-10	O1/D	-0.6
1975	Det-A	100	332	45	95	14	1	9	36	16	62	.286	.323	.416	.739	104	2	1	104	84	40	.655	11	8	-2	3	O/1D	0.0
1976	Det-A	115	305	36	87	12	3	15	47	11	44	.285	.317	.492	.808	130	11	10	104	93	43	.742	9	4	0	2	O/1D	1.1
1977	Det-A	132	450	63	118	24	2	21	61	40	80	.262	.327	.464	.791	108	7	4	105	89	64	.741	9	9	-3	2	*O/D	0.0
1978	Mil-A	128	469	71	142	29	4	18	72	52	69	.303	.372	.497	.869	135	26	23	106	101	85	.860	11	7	-1	-1	OD1	1.8
1979	Mil-A	139	514	88	145	30	4	29	81	48	56	.282	.346	.525	.871	131	21	21	100	89	91	.862	12	5	1	-2	*OD/1	1.3
1980	Mil-A	156	592	94	180	26	2	**41**	118	54	71	.304	.367	.563	.930	160	39	44	95	107	121	.946	11	9	-2	16	*O/D	5.3
1981	Mil-A	107	400	53	97	15	2	14	72	37	49	.243	.316	.395	.711	108	2	4	96	149	49	.646	2	2	-1	-5	*O/D	-0.3
1982	Mil-A	159	602	92	147	22	1	34	102	70	81	.244	.327	.453	.780	119	9	14	94	115	90	.751	3	5	-2	7	*O	1.4
1983	Mil-A	125	411	49	115	19	3	13	66	60	64	.280	.377	.436	.812	134	14	19	92	121	67	.794	4	6	-2	3	*O/D	1.8
1984	Mil-A	131	461	49	121	16	2	12	60	44	56	.262	.328	.384	.712	105	-2	3	92	115	55	.620	0	6	-4	-3	*O/D	-0.7
1985	Mil-A	101	341	40	99	17	2	10	61	37	51	.290	.363	.440	.803	113	9	7	105	137	54	.750	0	2	-1	-3	O/D	0.2
1986	Mil-A	103	346	31	98	20	1	5	53	30	33	.283	.340	.390	.731	97	-0	-1	102	141	45	.646	1	2	-1	3	OD	0.0
Total	16	1754	5913	784	1615	277	33	235	901	560	852	.273	.340	.450	.790	119	135	139	100	109	886	.765	87	70	-16	10	*OD/1	9.7

■ BRUCE OGRODOWSKI Ogrodowski, Ambrose Francis "Brusie" b: 2/17/12, Hoytville, Pa. d: 3/5/56, San Francisco, Cal. BR/TR, 5'11", 175 lbs. Deb: 4/14/36

YEAR	TM/L	G	AB	R	H	2B	3B	HR	RBI	BB	SO	AVG	OBP	SLG	PRO	/A	BR	/A	PF	CHI	RC	TA	SB	CS	SBR	FR	POS	TPR
1936	StL-N	94	237	28	54	15	1	1	20	10	20	.228	.259	.312	.571	56	-16	-14	94	92	18	.438	0			-3	C	-1.4
1937	StL-N	90	279	37	65	10	3	3	31	11	17	.233	.267	.323	.590	59	-16	-16	101	113	22	.465	2			-0	C	-1.3
Total	2	184	516	65	119	25	4	4	51	21	37	.231	.263	.318	.581	58	-32	-31	98	103	39	.462	2			-4	C	-2.7

■ HAL O'HAGEN O'Hagen, Harry P. b: 9/30/1873, Washington, D.C. d: 1/14/13, Newark, N.J. 6', 173 lbs. Deb: 9/24/1892

YEAR	TM/L	G	AB	R	H	2B	3B	HR	RBI	BB	SO	AVG	OBP	SLG	PRO	/A	BR	/A	PF	CHI	RC	TA	SB	CS	SBR	FR	POS	TPR
1892	Was-N	1	4	1	1	0	0	0	0	0	2	.250	.250	.250	.500	50	-0	-0	105	0	0	.333	0			0	/C	0.0
1902	Chi-N	31	108	10	21	1	3	0	10	11		.194	.269	.259	.528	67	-4	-4	96	126	10	.540	8			-1	1	-0.5
	NY-N	4	11	0	1	0	0	0	0	0		.091	.091	.091	.182	-43	-2	-2	100	0	0	.100	0			2	/O	0.0
	Yr	35	119	10	22	1	3	0	10	11		.185	.254	.244	.498	57	-6	-5	96	115	10	.495	8			1		-0.5
	Cle-A	3	13	2	5	2	0	0	1	0		.385	.385	.538	.923	161	1	1	97	45	4	1.125	2			-0	/1	0.1
	NY-N	22	73	5	11	2	1	0	8	2		.151	.173	.205	.379	18	-7	-7	100	185	3	.323	3			2	1/O	-0.5
Total	2	61	209	18	39	5	4	0	19	13	2	.187	.234	.249	.483	51	-12	-12	98	133	17	.459	13			3	/1OC	-0.9

■ KID O'HARA O'Hara, James Francis b: 12/19/1875, Wilkes-Barre, Pa. d: 12/1/54, Canton, Ohio BB/TR, 5'7.5", 152 lbs. Deb: 9/15/04

YEAR	TM/L	G	AB	R	H	2B	3B	HR	RBI	BB	SO	AVG	OBP	SLG	PRO	/A	BR	/A	PF	CHI	RC	TA	SB	CS	SBR	FR	POS	TPR
1904	Bos-N	8	29	3	6	0	0	0	0	4		.207	.303	.207	.510	62	-1	-1	97	0	2	.478	1			0	/O	0.0

■ TOM O'HARA O'Hara, Thomas F. b: 7/13/1885, Waverly, N.Y. d: 6/8/54, Denver, Colo. Deb: 9/19/06

YEAR	TM/L	G	AB	R	H	2B	3B	HR	RBI	BB	SO	AVG	OBP	SLG	PRO	/A	BR	/A	PF	CHI	RC	TA	SB	CS	SBR	FR	POS	TPR
1906	StL-N	14	53	8	16	1	0	0	0	3		.302	.339	.321	.660	107	0	0	101	0	7	.622	3			-1	O	0.0
1907	StL-N	48	173	11	41	2	1	0	5	12		.237	.286	.260	.547	76	-5	-4	96	45	14	.439	1			3	O	-0.2
Total	2	62	226	19	57	3	1	0	5	15		.252	.299	.274	.573	84	-5	-4	97	34	20	.479	4			3	/O	-0.2

■ BILL O'HARA O'Hara, William Alexander b: 8/14/1883, Toronto, Ont., Can. d: 6/15/31, Jersey City, N.J. BL/TR, 5'10", Deb: 09

YEAR	TM/L	G	AB	R	H	2B	3B	HR	RBI	BB	SO	AVG	OBP	SLG	PRO	/A	BR	/A	PF	CHI	RC	TA	SB	CS	SBR	FR	POS	TPR
1909	NY-N	115	360	48	85	9	3	1	30	41		.236	.318	.286	.604	85	-4	-6	105	103	41	.644	31			3	*O	-0.6
1910	StL-N	9	20	1	3	0	0	0	2	1	3	.150	.190	.150	.340	-1	-3	-2	92	232	1	.235	0			0	/OP1	-0.1
Total	2	124	380	49	88	9	3	1	32	42	3	.232	.311	.279	.590	80	-6	-8	104	109	42	.620	31			4	O/1P	-0.7

■ LEN OKRIE Okrie, Leonard Joseph b: 7/16/23, Detroit, Mich. BR/TR, 6', 185 lbs. Deb: 6/16/48 C

YEAR	TM/L	G	AB	R	H	2B	3B	HR	RBI	BB	SO	AVG	OBP	SLG	PRO	/A	BR	/A	PF	CHI	RC	TA	SB	CS	SBR	FR	POS	TPR
1948	Was-A	19	42	1	10	0	1	0	1	1	7	.238	.256	.286	.542	43	-3	-4	103	28	2	.371	0	0	0	0	C	-0.1

YEAR	TM/L	G	AB	R	H	2B	3B	HR	RBI	BB	SO	AVG	OBP	SLG	PRO	/A	BR	/A	PF	CHI	RC	TA	SB	CS	SBR	FR	POS	TPR
1950	Was-A	17	27	1	6	0	0	0	2	6	7	.222	.382	.222	.605	58	-1	-1	99	115	3	.619	0	0	0	-0	C	0.0
1951	Was-A	5	8	1	1	1	0	0	0	2	1	.125	.300	.250	.550	52	-1	-0	95	0	1	.571	0	0	0	-0	/C	0.0
1952	Bos-A	1	1	0	0	0	0	0	0	0	1	.000	.000	.000	.000	-94	-0	-0	107	0	0	.000	0	0	0	0	/C	0.0
Total	4	42	78	3	17	1	1	0	3	9	16	.218	.307	.256	.563	49	-6	-6	101	58	6	.492	0	0	0	-0	/C	-0.1
■ **DAVE OLDFIELD** Oldfield, David b: 12/18/1864, Philadelphia, Pa. d: 8/28/39, Philadelphia, Pa. BB/TL, 5'7", 175 lbs. Deb: 1883																												
1883	Bal-a	1	4	0	0	0	0	0		0		.000	.000	.000	.000	-94	-1	-1	107	0	0	.000				0	/C	0.0
1885	Bro-a	10	25	2	8	1	0	0		3		.320	.414	.360	.774	144	2	1	104	0	4	.765				0	/CO	0.1
1886	Bro-a	14	55	7	13	1	0	0		2		.236	.263	.255	.518	64	-2	-2	100	0	4	.405	1			0	C/SO	-0.1
	Was-N	21	71	2	10	2	0	0	2	5	15	.141	.197	.169	.366	13	-7	-7	94	55	2	.279	0			0	C/O	-0.5
Total	3	46	155	11	31	4	0	0	2	10	15	.200	.253	.226	.479	51	-9	-8	98	25	10	.379	1			0	/COS	-0.5
■ **JOHN OLDHAM** Oldham, John Hardin b: 11/6/32, Salinas, Cal. BL, 6'3", 198 lbs. Deb: 9/02/56																												
1956	Cin-N	1	0	0	0	0	0	0	0	0	0	—	—	—	—	—	0	0	108	—	—	—	0	0	0	0	R	0.0
■ **BOB OLDIS** Oldis, Robert Carl b: 1/5/28, Preston, Iowa BR/TR, 6'1", 185 lbs. Deb: 4/28/53 C																												
1953	Was-A	7	16	0	4	0	0	0	3	1	2	.250	.294	.250	.544	51	-1	-1	94	278	1	.385	0	0	0	0	/C	0.0
1954	Was-A	11	24	1	8	1	0	0	0	1	3	.333	.360	.375	.735	103	0	0	98	0	3	.625	0	0	0	-0	/C3	0.0
1955	Was-A	6	6	1	0	0	0	0	0	1	0	.000	.143	.000	.143	-65	-1	-1	91	0	0	.143	0	0	0	0	/C	0.0
1960	Pit-N	22	20	1	4	1	0	0	1	1	2	.200	.238	.250	.488	34	-2	-2	99	81	1	.375	0	0	0	0	C	0.0
1961	Pit-N	4	5	0	0	0	0	0	0	0	0	.000	.000	.000	.000	-99	-1	-1	99	0	0	.000	0	0	0	0	/C	0.0
1962	Phi-N	38	80	9	21	1	0	1	10	13	10	.262	.366	.313	.678	89	-1	-1	95	141	10	.613	0	1	-1	1	C	0.0
1963	Phi-N	47	85	8	19	3	0	0	8	3	5	.224	.250	.259	.509	46	-6	-6	103	153	5	.368	0	0	0	-3	C	-0.8
Total	7	135	236	20	56	6	0	1	22	20	22	.237	.297	.275	.572	60	-13	-12	98	129	21	.464	0	1	-1	-2	C/3	-0.8
■ **RUBE OLDRING** Oldring, Reuben Henry b: 5/30/1884, New York, N.Y. d: 9/9/61, Bridgeton, N.J. BR/TR, 5'10", 186 lbs. Deb: 10/02/05																												
1905	NY-A	8	30	2	9	0	1	1	6	2		.300	.344	.467	.810	156	2	2	102	121	6	.952	4			0	/S	0.3
1906	Phi-A	59	174	15	42	10	1	0	19	2		.241	.250	.310	.560	82	-5	-4	94	128	16	.477	7			2	3/S21	0.1
1907	Phi-A	117	441	48	126	27	8	1	40	7		.286	.297	.390	.687	114	8	5	106	83	61	.660	29			-4	*O	-0.6
1908	Phi-A	116	434	38	96	14	2	1	39	18		.221	.252	.270	.522	66	-14	-17	108	129	31	.438	13			-4	*O	-3.0
1909	Phi-A	90	326	39	75	14	7	1	28	20		.230	.287	.325	.612	91	-3	-4	102	105	34	.594	17			-18	O/1	-2.8
1910	Phi-A	134	546	79	168	27	14	4	57	23		.308	.340	.430	.771	138	22	21	102	75	85	.738	17			9	*O	2.6
1911	Phi-A	121	495	84	147	11	14	3	59	21		.297	.332	.394	.726	110	-0	4	93	94	72	.695	21			1	*O	-0.3
1912	Phi-A	98	395	61	119	14	5	1	24	10		.301	.324	.370	.693	99	-3	-2	99	57	53	.638	17			5	O	-0.3
1913	Phi-A	137	538	101	152	27	9	5	71	34	37	.283	.328	.394	.722	115	5	7	97	118	78	.746	40			-5	*O/S	-0.5
1914	Phi-A	119	466	68	129	21	7	3	49	18	35	.277	.308	.371	.679	107	-0	1	97	107	53	.589	14	16	-5	-0	*O	-1.2
1915	Phi-A	107	408	49	101	23	3	6	42	22	21	.248	.293	.363	.655	100	-5	-3	96	91	45	.591	11	6	-0	-2	O/3	-0.9
1916	Phi-A	40	146	10	36	8	3	0	14	9	9	.247	.290	.342	.633	92	-2	-2	98	102	15	.545	1			-2	O	-0.6
	NY-A	43	158	17	37	8	0	1	12	12	13	.234	.288	.304	.592	77	-5	-5	101	86	16	.545	6			-6	O	-1.4
	Yr	83	304	27	73	16	3	1	26	21	22	.240	.289	.322	.612	84	-7	-7	100	95	31	.545	7			-8		-2.0
1918	Phi-A	49	133	5	31	2	1	0	11	8	10	.233	.282	.263	.545	62	-6	-6	104	115	10	.431	0			-7	O/23	-1.6
Total	13	1238	4690	616	1268	206	75	27	471	206	125	.270	.305	.364	.669	103	-6	-3	100	97	574	.620	197	22		-31	*O/3S21	-10.2
■ **CHARLEY O'LEARY** O'Leary, Charles Timothy b: 10/15/1882, Chicago, Ill. d: 1/6/41, Chicago, Ill. BR/TR, 5'7", 165 lbs. Deb: 4/14/04 C																												
1904	Det-A	135	456	39	97	10	3	1	16	21		.213	.247	.254	.502	64	-20	-18	96	51	32	.407	9			3	*S	-1.4
1905	Det-A	148	512	47	109	13	1	0	33	29		.213	.255	.242	.497	61	-23	-22	98	97	36	.412	13			-8	*S	-2.7
1906	Det-A	128	443	34	97	13	2	2	34	17		.219	.248	.271	.519	59	-19	-23	108	100	33	.419	8			-4	*S	-2.7
1907	Det-A	139	465	61	112	19	1	0	34	32		.241	.290	.286	.576	84	-7	-8	102	93	43	.499	11			-3	*S	-0.8
1908	Det-A	65	211	21	53	9	3	0	17	9		.251	.282	.322	.604	97	-1	-1	101	94	19	.513	4			-3	S/2	-0.2
1909	Det-A	76	261	29	53	10	0	0	13	6		.203	.224	.241	.465	43	-16	-19	110	81	15	.380	9			1	32/SO	-1.8
1910	Det-A	65	211	23	51	7	1	0	9	9		.242	.276	.284	.560	74	-6	-7	102	55	19	.481	7			-3	2S/3	-1.3
1911	Det-A	74	256	29	68	8	2	0	25	21		.266	.336	.313	.648	75	-6	-9	108	108	32	.622	10			4	2/3	-0.4
1912	Det-A	3	10	1	2	0	0	0	1	0		.200	.200	.200	.400	15	-1	-1	95	167	0	.250	0			0	/2	0.0
1913	StL-N	121	406	32	88	15	5	0	31	20	34	.217	.260	.278	.539	58	-25	-21	93	102	30	.440	3			-9	*S2	-2.4
1934	StL-A	1	1	1	1	0	0	0	0	0	0	1.000	1.000	1.000	2.000	401	0	0	104	0	1	—	0	0	0	0	H	0.0
Total	11	955	3232	317	731	104	18	3	213	164	34	.226	.266	.272	.538	67	-123	-127	101	88	259	.452	74	0		-23	S2/3O	-13.7
■ **DAN O'LEARY** O'Leary, Daniel "Hustling Dan" b: 10/22/1856, Detroit, Mich. d: 6/24/22, Chicago, Ill. BL, Deb: 9/03/1879 M																												
1879	Pro-N	2	7	1	3	0	0	0	2	0	0	.429	.429	.429	.857	181	1	1	102	234	1	.750				0	/O	0.1
1880	Bos-N	3	12	1	3	2	0	0	1	0	3	.250	.250	.417	.667	132	0	0	92	74	1	.556				0	/O	0.0
1881	Det-N	2	8	0	0	0	0	0	0	0	2	.000	.000	.000	.000	-94	-2	-2	106	0	0	.000				0	/O	-0.1
1882	Wor-N	6	22	2	4	1	0	0	2	5	5	.182	.333	.227	.561	84	-0	-0	100	116	2	.556				0	/O	0.0
1884	Cin-U	32	132	14	34	0	2	1		5		.258	.285	.311	.595	94	0	-1	108	0	12	.469	0			1	OM	0.0
Total	5	45	181	18	44	3	2	1	5	10	10	.243	.283	.298	.581	90	-1	-2	105	30	16	.467	0			1	/O	0.0
■ **FRANK OLIN** Olin, Franklin Walter b: 1/9/1860, Woodford, Vt. d: 5/21/51, St.Louis, Mo. BL, Deb: 7/04/1884																												
1884	Was-a	21	83	12	32	4	1	0		8		.386	.440	.458	.897	223	9	10	88	0	17	.902				0	2O	0.9
	Was-U	1	4	0	0	0	0	0		0		.000	.000	.000	.000	-99	-1	-1	97	0	0	.000	0			0	/O	0.0
	Tol-a	26	86	16	22	0	1	1		5		.256	.304	.314	.618	101	1	0	104	0	8	.516				-0	O	0.0
1885	Det-N	1	4	1	2	0	0	0	0	0	0	.500	.500	.500	1.000	230	1	1	97	0	1	1.000				0	/1	0.0
Total	2	49	177	29	56	4	2	1	0	13	0	.316	.366	.379	.745	153	9	10	96	0	27	.669				-0	/O2	0.9
■ **TONY OLIVA** Oliva, Pedro (Lopez) b: 7/20/40, Pinar Del Rio, Cuba BL/TR, 6'1", 175 lbs. Deb: 9/09/62 C																												
1962	Min-A	9	9	3	4	1	0	0	3	3	2	.444	.583	.556	1.139	199	2	2	105	238	3	1.600	0	0	0	-0	/O	0.1
1963	Min-A	7	7	0	3	0	0	0	1	0	2	.429	.429	.429	.857	141	0	0	100	139	1	.750	0	0	0	0	H	0.0
1964	Min-A	161	672	**109**	**217**	**43**	9	32	94	34	68	**.323**	.361	.557	.918	150	43	42	101	81	**132**	.906	12	6	0	7	*O	4.4
1965	Min-A	149	576	107	**185**	40	5	16	98	55	64	**.321**	.384	.491	.876	145	35	35	101	130	109	.885	19	9	0	7	*O	3.8
1966	Min-A	159	622	99	**191**	32	7	25	87	42	72	.307	.356	.502	.857	129	33	25	111	91	106	.819	13	7	-0	15	*O	3.5
1967	Min-A	146	557	76	161	**34**	6	17	83	44	61	.289	.350	.463	.813	130	26	21	107	119	91	.787	11	3	2	9	*O	3.0
1968	Min-A	128	470	54	136	24	5	18	68	45	61	.289	.360	.477	.837	143	29	26	106	111	77	.810	10	9	-2	4	*O	2.5
1969	Min-A	153	637	97	**197**	**39**	4	24	101	45	66	.309	.358	.496	.854	134	29	27	102	100	107	.808	10	13	-5	-5	*O	1.3
1970	Min-A	157	628	96	**204**	**36**	7	23	107	38	67	.325	.366	.514	.881	143	32	33	98	117	112	.831	5	4	-1	19	*O	4.5
1971	Min-A	126	487	73	164	30	3	22	81	25	44	**.337**	.372	**.546**	.918	151	34	31	104	106	90	.861	4	1	1	-1	*O	2.9
1972	Min-A	10	28	1	9	1	0	0	1	2	5	.321	.367	.357	.724	108	1	0	107	42	4	.600	0	0	0	-3	/O	-0.2
1973	Min-A	146	571	63	166	20	0	16	92	45	44	.291	.347	.410	.757	108	9	6	104	136	79	.680	2	1	0	0	*D	0.6
1974	Min-A	127	459	43	131	16	2	13	57	27	31	.285	.328	.414	.742	111	6	6	101	100	58	.638	0	1	-1	0	*D	0.5
1975	Min-A	131	455	46	123	10	0	13	58	41	45	.270	.348	.378	.726	98	4	-0	107	108	60	.659	0	1	-1	0	*D	0.0
1976	Min-A	67	123	3	26	3	0	1	16	2	13	.211	.236	.260	.496	46	-9	-8	98	176	7	.364	0	0	0	0	D	-0.8
Total	15	1676	6301	870	1917	329	48	220	947	448	645	.304	.356	.476	.832	130	272	246	104	110	1036	.810	86	55	-7	51	*OD	26.1
■ **ED OLIVARES** Olivares, Edward (Balzac) b: 11/5/38, Mayaguez, P.R. BR/TR, 5'11", 180 lbs. Deb: 9/16/60																												
1960	StL-N	3	5	0	0	0	0	0	0	0	3	.000	.000	.000	.000	-93	-1	-1	108	0	0	.000	0	0	0	0	/3	0.0
1961	StL-N	21	30	2	5	0	0	0	1	0	4	.167	.167	.167	.333	-10	-5	-5	113	81	1	.231	1	0	0	-2	O	-0.7
Total	2	24	35	2	5	0	0	0	1	0	7	.143	.143	.143	.286	-21	-6	-7	112	69	1	.194	1	0	0	-2	/O3	-0.7
■ **AL OLIVER** Oliver, Albert b: 10/14/46, Portsmouth, Ohio BL/TL, 6', 195 lbs. Deb: 9/23/68																												
1968	Pit-N	4	8	1	1	0	0	0	0	0	4	.125	.125	.125	.250	-25	-1	-1	101	0	0	.143	0	0	0	0	/O	0.0
1969	Pit-N	129	463	55	132	19	2	17	70	21	38	.285	.334	.445	.779	123	9	12	95	111	62	.701	8	5	-1	-1	*1O	0.0
1970	Pit-N	151	551	63	149	33	5	12	83	35	35	.270	.330	.414	.744	101	-2	-0	97	124	75	.673	1	1	-0	2	O1	-0.8

YEAR	TM/L	G	AB	R	H	2B	3B	HR	RBI	BB	SO	AVG	OBP	SLG	PRO	/A	BR	/A	PF	CHI	RC	TA	SB	CS	SBR	FR	POS	TPR
1971	Pit-N	143	529	69	149	31	7	14	64	27	72	.282	.323	.446	.769	117	9	9	99	96	72	.685	4	3	-1	5	*O1	0.9
1972	Pit-N	140	565	88	176	27	4	12	89	34	44	.312	.356	.437	.793	121	17	15	103	137	85	.709	2	4	-2	-6	*O/1	0.1
1973	Pit-N	158	654	90	191	38	7	20	99	22	52	.292	.320	.463	.783	125	10	16	92	105	92	.699	6	0	2	-4	*O1	0.7
1974	Pit-N	147	617	96	198	38	12	11	85	33	58	.321	.360	.475	.835	135	24	26	98	97	101	.775	10	1	2	1	O1	2.4
1975	Pit-N	155	628	90	176	39	8	18	84	25	73	.280	.313	.454	.767	112	5	6	99	102	83	.674	4	2	0	-3	*O/1	-0.2
1976	Pit-N	121	443	62	143	22	5	12	61	26	29	.323	.367	.476	.843	138	21	20	100	97	74	.787	6	2	1	2	*O/1	2.0
1977	Pit-N	154	568	75	175	29	6	19	82	40	38	.308	.358	.481	.838	119	17	15	103	101	91	.786	13	16	-6	0	*O	0.5
1978	Tex-A	133	525	65	170	35	5	14	89	31	41	.324	.364	.490	.853	143	25	27	96	125	90	.803	8	9	-3	1	*OD	2.3
1979	Tex-A	136	492	69	159	28	4	12	76	34	34	.323	.372	.470	.841	125	17	17	100	112	81	.776	4	5	-2	-10	*OD	0.1
1980	Tex-A	163	656	96	209	43	3	19	117	39	47	.319	.361	.480	.842	128	24	24	100	130	108	.778	5	7	-3	-1	*O/1D	1.7
1981	Tex-A	102	421	53	130	29	1	4	55	24	28	.309	.349	.411	.760	130	9	14	91	112	56	.656	3	0	1	0	*D/1	1.5
1982	Mon-N	160	617	90	**204**	**43**	2	22	**109**	61	59	**.331**	.394	.514	.908	145	43	39	105	118	**125**	.908	5	2	0	-9	*1	2.3
1983	Mon-N	157	614	70	184	**38**	3	8	84	44	44	.300	.348	.410	.759	108	7	6	102	128	81	.659	1	3	-2	1	*1/O	-0.1
1984	SF-N	91	339	27	101	19	2	0	34	20	27	.298	.339	.366	.705	102	-1	1	96	110	36	.568	2	2	-1	-1	1	-0.3
	Phi-N	28	93	9	29	7	0	0	14	7	9	.312	.360	.387	.747	108	1	1	102	152	11	.629	1	2	-1	-0	1/O	0.0
	Yr	119	432	36	130	26	2	0	48	27	36	.301	.343	.370	.714	103	0	2	97	120	55	.616	3	4	-2	-1		-0.3
1985	LA-N	35	79	1	20	5	0	0	8	5	11	.253	.298	.316	.614	77	-3	-2	93	127	7	.500	1	0	0	-3	O	-0.5
	Tor-A	61	187	20	47	6	1	5	23	7	13	.251	.282	.374	.656	77	-6	-6	101	107	17	.527	0	0	0	0	D/1	-0.5
Total	18	2368	9049	1189	2743	529	77	219	1326	535	756	.303	.348	.451	.799	122	224	238	99	113	1348	.750	84	64	-13	-24	*O1D	12.1

■ **DAVE OLIVER** Oliver, David Jacob b: 4/7/51, Stockton, Cal. BL/TR, 5'11", 175 lbs. Deb: 9/25/77 C

YEAR	TM/L	G	AB	R	H	2B	3B	HR	RBI	BB	SO	AVG	OBP	SLG	PRO	/A	BR	/A	PF	CHI	RC	TA	SB	CS	SBR	FR	POS	TPR
1977	Cle-A	7	22	2	7	0	1	0	3	4	0	.318	.444	.409	.854	138	1	1	98	135	5	.933	0	0	0	0	/2	0.2

■ **GENE OLIVER** Oliver, Eugene George b: 3/22/35, Moline, Ill. BR/TR, 6'2", 225 lbs. Deb: 6/06/59

YEAR	TM/L	G	AB	R	H	2B	3B	HR	RBI	BB	SO	AVG	OBP	SLG	PRO	/A	BR	/A	PF	CHI	RC	TA	SB	CS	SBR	FR	POS	TPR
1959	StL-N	68	172	14	42	9	0	6	28	7	41	.244	.274	.401	.675	73	-6	-7	105	130	17	.581	3	2	-0	-5	O/C1	-1.2
1961	StL-N	22	52	8	14	2	0	4	9	6	10	.269	.367	.538	.905	121	3	2	113	91	10	.900	0	0	0	-2	C/O	0.1
1962	StL-N	122	345	42	89	19	1	14	45	50	59	.258	.354	.441	.794	103	6	2	109	91	54	.779	5	2	0	-29	C/O1	-2.5
1963	StL-N	39	102	10	23	4	0	6	18	13	19	.225	.313	.441	.754	107	2	1	107	120	13	.699	0	0	0	-3	C	0.0
	Mil-N	95	296	34	74	12	2	11	47	27	59	.250	.323	.416	.739	110	4	4	101	127	38	.679	4	4	-1	-8	1O/C	-0.8
	Yr	134	398	44	97	16	2	17	65	40	78	.244	.321	.422	.743	109	6	5	103	126	53	.693	4	4	-1	-11		-0.8
1964	Mil-N	93	279	45	77	15	1	13	49	17	41	.276	.320	.477	.797	125	7	8	97	117	37	.706	3	7	-3	-2	1/C	0.0
1965	Mil-N	122	392	56	106	20	0	21	58	36	61	.270	.336	.482	.819	123	14	12	104	95	60	.769	5	4	-1	7	C1/O	1.8
1966	Atl-N	76	191	19	37	9	1	8	24	16	43	.194	.256	.377	.633	74	-7	-7	99	105	19	.573	2	0	1	5	C/1O	0.0
1967	Atl-N	17	51	8	10	2	0	3	6	6	8	.196	.281	.412	.692	92	-0	-1	104	83	5	.614	0	0	0	1	C	0.1
	Phi-N	85	263	29	59	16	0	7	34	29	56	.224	.304	.365	.669	87	-3	-5	104	120	29	.607	2	2	-1	-2	C/1	-0.2
	Yr	102	314	37	69	18	0	10	40	35	64	.220	.300	.373	.673	88	-4	-5	104	115	36	.615	2	2	-1	-1		-0.1
1968	Bos-A	16	35	2	5	0	0	0	1	4	12	.143	.250	.143	.393	21	-3	-3	101	86	2	.333	0	0	0	-1	C/O	-0.3
	Chi-N	8	11	1	4	0	0	0	1	3	2	.364	.500	.364	.864	145	1	1	112	105	2	.875	0	0	0	-0	/1CO	0.1
1969	Chi-N	23	27	0	6	3	0	0	0	1	9	.222	.276	.333	.609	66	-1	-1	107	0	2	.500	0	0	0	0	/C	0.0
Total	10	786	2216	268	546	111	5	93	320	215	420	.246	.317	.427	.744	102	15	5	103	107	289	.709	24	21	-5	-37	C1/O	-2.9

■ **NATE OLIVER** Oliver, Nathaniel "Peewee" b: 12/13/40, St.Petersburg, Fla. BR/TR, 5'10", 160 lbs. Deb: 4/09/63

YEAR	TM/L	G	AB	R	H	2B	3B	HR	RBI	BB	SO	AVG	OBP	SLG	PRO	/A	BR	/A	PF	CHI	RC	TA	SB	CS	SBR	FR	POS	TPR
1963	LA-N	65	163	23	39	2	3	1	9	13	25	.239	.299	.307	.606	79	-5	-4	95	71	14	.511	3	4	-2	-1	2/S	-0.3
1964	LA-N	99	321	28	78	9	0	0	21	31	57	.243	.310	.271	.581	71	-14	-11	92	99	26	.484	7	4	-0	-15	2/S	-1.8
1965	LA-N	8	1	3	1	0	0	0	0	0	0	1.000	1.000	1.000	2.000	509	0	0	91	0	1	—	1	0	0	0	/2	0.1
1966	LA-N	80	119	17	23	2	0	0	3	13	17	.193	.278	.210	.488	39	-10	-9	97	50	7	.408	3	3	-1	2	2/S3	-0.3
1967	LA-N	77	232	18	55	6	2	0	7	13	50	.237	.283	.280	.564	70	-11	-8	88	45	18	.446	3	2	-0	0	2S/O	-0.1
1968	SF-N	36	73	3	13	2	0	0	1	1	13	.178	.189	.205	.395	19	-7	-7	98	28	3	.262	0	1	-1	-1	2S/3	-0.6
1969	NY-A	1	1	0	0	0	0	0	0	0	0	.000	.000	.000	.000	-99	-0	-0	95	0	0	.000	0	0	0	0	H	0.0
	Chi-N	44	44	15	7	3	0	1	4	1	10	.159	.196	.295	.491	34	-4	-4	107	100	2	.385	0	1	-1	1	2	-0.2
Total	7	410	954	107	216	24	5	2	45	72	172	.226	.284	.268	.553	62	-51	-43	93	70	71	.464	17	15	-4	-14	2/S3O	-3.2

■ **BOB OLIVER** Oliver, Robert Lee b: 2/8/43, Shreveport, La. BR/TR, 6'3", 205 lbs. Deb: 9/10/65

YEAR	TM/L	G	AB	R	H	2B	3B	HR	RBI	BB	SO	AVG	OBP	SLG	PRO	/A	BR	/A	PF	CHI	RC	TA	SB	CS	SBR	FR	POS	TPR
1965	Pit-N	3	2	1	0	0	0	0	0	0	0	.000	.000	.000	.000	-99	-1	-1	100	0	0	.000	0	0	0	-1	/O	0.0
1969	KC-A	118	394	43	100	8	4	13	43	21	74	.254	.295	.393	.688	89	-6	-7	103	89	39	.577	5	5	-2	9	O1/3	-0.2
1970	KC-A	160	612	83	159	24	6	27	99	42	126	.260	.311	.451	.761	109	4	5	98	119	82	.688	3	3	-1	-11	*13	-1.3
1971	KC-A	128	373	35	91	12	2	8	52	14	88	.244	.281	.351	.632	79	-12	-11	99	137	34	.508	0	0	0	1	1O/3	-1.6
1972	KC-A	16	63	7	17	2	1	1	6	2	12	.270	.292	.381	.673	99	-0	-0	100	95	7	.563	1	0	0	3	O	0.3
	Cal-A	134	509	47	137	20	4	19	70	27	97	.269	.310	.436	.746	136	10	16	88	111	64	.656	4	3	-1	-5	*1/O	-0.1
	Yr	150	572	54	154	22	5	20	76	29	109	.269	.308	.430	.738	132	10	16	90	110	71	.649	5	3	-0	-2		0.2
1973	Cal-A	151	544	51	144	24	1	18	89	33	100	.265	.313	.412	.724	107	0	3	96	128	66	.632	1	1	-0	-1	3O1D	-0.1
1974	Cal-A	110	359	22	89	9	1	8	55	16	51	.248	.282	.345	.627	86	-10	-7	92	146	29	.490	2	1	0	-5	13/OD	-1.4
	Bal-A	9	20	1	3	2	0	0	4	0	5	.150	.150	.250	.400	14	-2	-2	93	315	1	.333	1	1	-0	0	/1D	-0.2
	Yr	119	379	23	92	11	1	8	59	16	56	.243	.275	.340	.616	82	-12	-9	92	160	37	.516	3	2	-0	-5		-1.6
1975	NY-A	18	38	3	5	1	0	0	1	1	9	.132	.154	.158	.312	-12	-6	-6	99	64	1	.200	0	0	0	0	/13D	-0.5
Total	8	847	2914	293	745	102	19	94	419	156	562	.256	.298	.400	.698	101	-23	-10	96	121	322	.622	17	14	-3	-9	1O3/D	-5.1

■ **TOM OLIVER** Oliver, Thomas Noble "Rebel" b: 1/15/03, Montgomery, Ala. d: 2/26/88, Montgomery, Ala. BR/TR, 6', 168 lbs. Deb: 4/14/30 C

YEAR	TM/L	G	AB	R	H	2B	3B	HR	RBI	BB	SO	AVG	OBP	SLG	PRO	/A	BR	/A	PF	CHI	RC	TA	SB	CS	SBR	FR	POS	TPR
1930	Bos-A	154	646	86	189	34	2	0	46	42	25	.293	.339	.351	.690	81	-23	-16	93	58	77	.600	6	6	-2	7	*O	-1.5
1931	Bos-A	148	586	52	162	35	5	0	70	25	17	.276	.307	.353	.660	78	-24	-19	94	118	62	.551	4	6	-2	6	*O	-2.2
1932	Bos-A	122	455	39	120	23	3	0	37	25	12	.264	.305	.327	.632	66	-24	-22	97	85	45	.519	1	6	-3	3	*O	-2.5
1933	Bos-A	90	244	25	63	9	1	0	23	13	7	.258	.296	.303	.599	58	-14	-15	101	104	22	.484	1	1	-0	5	O	-1.2
Total	4	514	1931	202	534	101	11	0	176	105	61	.277	.316	.340	.656	73	-86	-72	95	88	206	.551	12	19	-8	21	O	-7.4

■ **LUIS OLMO** Olmo, Luis Francisco (Rodriguez) (born Luis Francisco Rodriquez (Olmo)) b: 8/11/19, Arecibo, P.R. BR/TR, 5'11.5", 185 lbs. Deb: 7/23/43

YEAR	TM/L	G	AB	R	H	2B	3B	HR	RBI	BB	SO	AVG	OBP	SLG	PRO	/A	BR	/A	PF	CHI	RC	TA	SB	CS	SBR	FR	POS	TPR
1943	Bro-N	57	238	39	72	6	4	4	37	8	20	.303	.325	.412	.737	113	2	3	100	129	29	.619	3			2	O	0.3
1944	Bro-N	136	520	65	134	20	5	9	85	17	37	.258	.284	.367	.651	83	-14	-14	99	143	53	.557	10			-1	O23	-1.4
1945	Bro-N	141	556	62	174	27	**13**	10	110	36	33	.313	.356	.462	.818	132	17	20	96	136	90	.786	15			-4	*O3/2	1.1
1949	Bro-N	38	105	15	32	4	1	1	14	5	11	.305	.336	.390	.727	93	-1	-1	102	120	12	.608	2			-4	O	-0.6
1950	Bos-N	69	154	23	35	7	1	5	22	18	23	.227	.308	.383	.691	94	-5	-2	86	115	17	.635	3			-10	O/3	-1.3
1951	Bos-N	21	56	4	11	1	1	0	4	4	4	.196	.250	.250	.500	36	-5	-5	98	110	4	.391	0	1	-1	-2	O	-0.7
Total	6	462	1629	208	458	65	25	29	272	88	128	.281	.319	.405	.724	104	-5	1	97	133	204	.669	33	1		-19	O/32	-2.6

■ **BARNEY OLSEN** Olsen, Bernard Charles b: 9/11/19, Everett, Mass. d: 3/30/77, Everett, Mass. BR/TR, 5'11", 179 lbs. Deb: 4/17/41

YEAR	TM/L	G	AB	R	H	2B	3B	HR	RBI	BB	SO	AVG	OBP	SLG	PRO	/A	BR	/A	PF	CHI	RC	TA	SB	CS	SBR	FR	POS	TPR
1941	Chi-N	24	73	13	21	6	1	1	4	4	11	.288	.325	.438	.763	121	1	2	94	41	10	.679	0			2	O	0.2

■ **IVY OLSON** Olson, Ivan Massie b: 10/14/1885, Kansas City, Mo. d: 9/1/65, Inglewood, Cal. BR/TR, 5'10.5", 175 lbs. Deb: 4/12/11 C

YEAR	TM/L	G	AB	R	H	2B	3B	HR	RBI	BB	SO	AVG	OBP	SLG	PRO	/A	BR	/A	PF	CHI	RC	TA	SB	CS	SBR	FR	POS	TPR
1911	Cle-A	140	545	89	142	20	8	1	50	34		.261	.311	.332	.643	77	-16	-18	103	88	63	.598	20			-13	*S/3	-1.7
1912	Cle-A	123	467	68	118	13	1	0	33	21		.253	.291	.285	.575	64	-22	-23	101	88	45	.499	16			-4	S32/O	-2.2
1913	Cle-A	104	370	47	92	13	3	0	32	22	28	.249	.296	.300	.596	70	-12	-15	106	104	35	.514	7			6	31/2	-0.7
1914	Cle-A	89	310	22	75	6	2	1	20	13	24	.242	.275	.284	.559	66	-13	-14	102	84	26	.480	15	9	-1	4	S23/O1	-0.8
1915	Cin-N	63	207	18	48	5	4	0	14	12	13	.232	.274	.295	.569	70	-7	-8	103	88	18	.503	10	6	-1	5	23/1	-0.2
	Bro-N	18	26	2	2	0	1	0	3	1	0	.077	.111	.154	.265	-20	-4	-4	101	286	1	.208	0			-2	/S23O	-0.6
	Yr	81	233	20	50	5	5	0	17	13	13	.215	.256	.279	.535	60	-11	-12	102	133	18	.466	10	6	-1	3		-0.8
1916	Bro-N	108	351	29	89	13	4	1	38	21	27	.254	.298	.322	.620	87	-4	-6	103	130	40	.569	14			-11	*S/21	-1.2
1917	Bro-N	139	580	64	156	18	5	2	38	14	34	.269	.291	.328	.619	86	-9	-11	104	66	55	.505	6			-5	*S/3	-1.6
1918	Bro-N	126	506	63	121	16	4	1	17	27	18	.239	.286	.292	.578	75	-14	-15	101	37	46	.525	21			-25	*S	-4.2
1919	Bro-N	140	590	73	**164**	14	9	1	38	30	12	.278	.316	.337	.654	103	-3	1	94	63	67	.606	26			-1	*S	0.5

YEAR	TM/L	G	AB	R	H	2B	3B	HR	RBI	BB	SO	AVG	OBP	SLG	PRO	/A	BR	/A	PF	CHI	RC	TA	SB	CS	SBR	FR	POS	TPR
1920	Bro-N	143	637	71	162	13	11	1	46	20	19	.254	.278	.314	.592	63	-26	-34	111	76	54	.467	4	7	-3	-10	*S2	-4.2
1921	Bro-N	151	652	88	174	22	10	3	35	28	26	.267	.301	.345	.646	68	-28	-32	105	47	66	.536	4	9	-4	10	*S2	-1.2
1922	Bro-N	136	551	63	150	26	6	1	47	25	10	.272	.306	.347	.653	72	-27	-23	95	90	58	.557	8	5	-1	-4	2S	-2.3
1923	Bro-N	82	292	33	76	11	1	1	35	14	10	.260	.296	.315	.611	63	-16	-15	98	130	29	.519	5	0	2	3	2/31S	-0.9
1924	Bro-N	10	27	0	6	1	0	0	0	3	1	.222	.300	.259	.559	52	-2	-2	99	0	2	.476	0	0	0	-0	/S2	-0.1
Total	14	1572	6111	730	1575	191	69	13	446	285	222	.258	.295	.318	.613	74	-203	-217	102	79	605	.529	156	36		-47	*S23/10	-21.4
■ **KARL OLSON**	Olson, Karl Arthur "Ole" b: 7/6/30, Ross, Cal. BR/TR, 6'3", 205 lbs. Deb: 6/30/51																											
1951	Bos-A	5	10	0	1	0	0	0	0	0	3	.100	.100	.100	.200	-43	-2	-2	108	0	0	.100	0	0	0	-1	/O	-0.2
1953	Bos-A	25	57	5	7	2	0	1	6	1	9	.123	.138	.211	.348	-6	-9	-9	109	148	1	.241	0	0	0	-5	O	-1.4
1954	Bos-A	101	227	25	59	12	2	1	20	12	23	.260	.297	.344	.641	75	-8	-8	100	94	21	.511	2	1	0	-5	O	-1.5
1955	Bos-A	26	48	7	12	1	2	0	1	1	10	.250	.265	.354	.619	53	-3	-4	124	22	4	.462	0	0	0	-3	O	-0.8
1956	Was-A	106	313	34	77	10	2	4	22	28	41	.246	.310	.329	.639	67	-14	-15	102	71	30	.532	1	1	-0	-4	*O	-2.3
1957	Was-A	8	12	2	2	0	0	0	0	1	2	.167	.231	.167	.397	11	-1	-1	98	0	1	.300	0	0	0	-1	/O	-0.1
	Det-A	8	14	1	2	0	0	0	1	0	6	.143	.143	.143	.286	-20	-2	-2	107	198	0	.167	0	0	0	-1	/O	-0.3
	Yr	16	26	3	4	0	0	0	1	1	8	.154	.185	.154	.339	-6	-4	-4	103	99	1	.227	0	0	0	-1		-0.4
Total	6	279	681	74	160	25	6	6	50	43	94	.235	.281	.316	.597	58	-40	-43	103	82	56	.501	3	2	-0	-19	O	-6.6
■ **MARV OLSON**	Olson, Marvin Clement "Sparky" b: 5/28/07, Gayville, S.Dak. BR/TR, 5'7", 160 lbs. Deb: 9/13/31																											
1931	Bos-A	15	53	8	10	1	0	0	5	9	3	.189	.306	.208	.514	40	-5	-4	94	159	4	.465	0	0	0	-1	2	-0.3
1932	Bos-A	115	403	58	100	14	6	0	25	61	26	.248	.347	.313	.660	74	-15	-13	97	70	47	.610	1	5	-3	-5	*2/3	-1.4
1933	Bos-A	3	1	1	0	0	0	0	0	0	1	.000	.000	.000	.000	-99	-0	-0	101	0	0	.000	0	0	0	0	/2	0.0
Total	3	133	457	67	110	15	6	0	30	70	30	.241	.342	.300	.641	70	-20	-17	97	81	51	.591	1	5	-3	-6	2/3	-1.7
■ **TOM O'MALLEY**	O'Malley, Thomas Patrick b: 12/25/60, Orange, N.J. BL/TR, 6', 180 lbs. Deb: 5/08/82																											
1982	SF-N	92	291	26	80	12	4	2	27	33	39	.275	.351	.364	.715	107	1	3	94	95	35	.622	0	3	-2	-3	3/2S	-0.2
1983	SF-N	135	410	40	106	16	1	5	45	52	47	.259	.348	.339	.687	90	-3	-4	101	116	49	.616	2	4	-2	-1	*3	-1.0
1984	SF-N	13	25	2	3	0	0	0	0	2	2	.120	.185	.120	.305	-13	-4	-4	96	0	1	.227	0	0	0	-1	/3	-0.4
	Chi-A	12	16	0	2	0	0	0	3	0	5	.125	.125	.125	.250	-28	-3	-3	111	598	0	.133	0	0	0	-0	/3	-0.2
1985	Bal-A	8	14	1	1	0	0	1	2	0	2	.071	.071	.286	.357	-8	-2	-2	99	113	0	.286	0	0	0	0	/3	-0.1
1986	Bal-A	56	181	19	46	9	0	1	18	17	21	.254	.318	.320	.639	76	-6	-6	99	118	18	.536	0	1	-1	1	3	-0.6
1987	Tex-A	45	117	10	32	8	0	1	12	15	9	.274	.356	.368	.724	90	-1	-1	104	104	14	.630	0	0	0	-2	3/2	-0.3
1988	Mon-N	14	27	3	7	0	0	0	2	3	4	.259	.333	.259	.593	68	-1	-1	106	114	3	.500	0	0	0	0	/3	0.0
Total	7	375	1081	101	277	45	5	10	109	122	129	.256	.334	.335	.669	86	-18	-17	99	113	119	.605	2	8	-4	-6	3/2S	-2.8
■ **OLLIE O'MARA**	O'Mara, Oliver Edward b: 3/8/1891, St.Louis, Mo. TR , 5'9", 155 lbs. Deb: 9/08/12																											
1912	Det-A	1	4	0	0	0	0	0	0	0		.000	.000	.000	.000	-99	-1	-1	95	0	0	.000	0			0	/S	0.0
1914	Bro-N	67	247	41	65	10	2	1	7	16	26	.263	.316	.332	.648	92	-2	-3	101	32	29	.632	14			-9	S	-1.0
1915	Bro-N	149	577	77	141	26	3	0	31	51	40	.244	.308	.300	.608	83	-10	-11	101	60	56	.529	11	12	-4	-32	*S	-4.9
1916	Bro-N	72	193	18	39	5	2	0	15	12	20	.202	.249	.249	.497	51	-11	-11	103	124	15	.455	10			-5	S	-1.5
1918	Bro-N	121	450	29	96	8	1	1	24	7	18	.213	.242	.242	.484	47	-28	-29	101	86	29	.387	11			-1	*3	-3.1
1919	Bro-N	2	7	1	0	0	0	0	0	0	0	.000	.000	.000	.000	-99	-2	-2	94	0	-0	.000	0			-0	/3	-0.1
Total	6	412	1478	166	341	49	8	2	77	86	104	.231	.280	.279	.559	68	-54	-57	101	71	129	.487	46	12		-48	S3	-10.6
■ **TOM O'MEARA**	O'Meara, Thomas Edward b: 12/12/1872, Chicago, Ill. d: 2/16/02, Fort Wayne, Ind. Deb: 9/29/1895																											
1895	Cle-N	1	1	1	0	0	0	0	0	1	0	.000	.500	.000	.500	40	0	0	97	0	0	1.000	0			0	/C	0.0
1896	Cle-N	12	33	5	5	0	0	0	0	5	7	.152	.263	.152	.415	11	-4	-5	110	0	1	.357	0			0	/C1	-0.3
Total	2	13	34	6	5	0	0	0	0	6	7	.147	.275	.147	.422	13	-4	-5	109	0	1	.379	0			0	/C1	-0.3
■ **O'NEAL**	O'Neal Deb:10/23/1874																											
1874	Har-n	1	3	0	0							.000															/O	
■ **DENNY O'NEIL**	O'Neil, Dennis b: 11/22/1866, Holyoke, Mass. d: 11/15/22, Rushville, Ind. BL/TL, 6'2.5", 200 lbs. Deb: 6/18/1893																											
1893	StL-N	7	25	3	3	0	0	0	2	4	0	.120	.241	.120	.361	-2	-4	-3	99	186	1	.455	3			0	/1	-0.2
■ **MICKEY O'NEIL**	O'Neil, George Michael b: 4/12/1900, St.Louis, Mo. d: 4/8/64, St.Louis, Mo. BR/TR, 5'10", 185 lbs. Deb: 9/12/19																											
1919	Bos-N	11	28	3	6	0	0	0	1	1	7	.214	.241	.214	.456	38	-2	-2	98	65	2	.318	0			1	C	0.0
1920	Bos-N	112	304	19	86	5	4	0	28	21	20	.283	.339	.326	.665	95	-3	-1	96	109	35	.581	4	4	-1	15	*C/2	2.1
1921	Bos-N	98	277	26	69	9	4	2	29	23	21	.249	.307	.332	.639	74	-12	-9	93	109	29	.557	2	2	-1	5	C	0.0
1922	Bos-N	83	251	18	56	5	2	0	26	14	11	.223	.267	.259	.526	38	-24	-22	94	140	18	.415	1	0	0	3	C	-1.6
1923	Bos-N	96	306	29	65	7	4	0	20	17	14	.212	.258	.261	.520	38	-28	-28	100	88	21	.420	3	2	-0	5	C	-1.6
1924	Bos-N	106	362	32	89	4	1	0	22	14	27	.246	.276	.262	.538	48	-28	-25	94	84	26	.413	4	3	-1	13	*C	-1.0
1925	Bos-N	70	222	29	57	6	5	2	30	21	16	.257	.327	.356	.682	79	-8	-6	94	125	26	.617	1	2	-1	-1	C	-0.4
1926	Bro-N	75	201	19	42	5	3	0	20	23	8	.209	.293	.264	.557	51	-14	-13	99	131	17	.503	3			2	C	-0.8
1927	Was-A	5	6	0	0	0	0	0	0	0	1	.000	.000	.000	.000	-99	-2	-2	97	0	0	.000	0	0	0	0	/C	-0.1
	NY-N	16	38	2	5	0	0	0	3	5	2	.132	.233	.132	.364	-0	-5	-5	100	210	1	.303	0			-2	C	-0.5
Total	9	672	1995	177	475	41	23	4	179	139	127	.238	.292	.288	.579	58	-125	-113	96	111	175	.485	18	13		40	C/2	-3.9
■ **JOHN O'NEIL**	O'Neil, John Francis b: 4/19/20, Shelbiana, Ky. BR/TR, 5'9", 155 lbs. Deb: 4/16/46																											
1946	Phi-N	46	94	12	25	3	0	0	9	5	12	.266	.303	.298	.601	75	-4	-3	95	120	9	.478	0			-3	S	-0.3
■ **FRED O'NEILL**	O'Neill, Frederick James "Tip" b: 1865, London, Ontario, Canada d: 3/7/1892, London, Ont., Can. 5'7", 142 lbs. Deb: 5/03/1887																											
1887	NY-a	6	26	4	8	1	1	0		1		.308	.357	.423	.780	136	1	1	88	0	5	.889	3			0	/O	0.1
■ **HARRY O'NEILL**	O'Neill, Harry Mink b: 5/8/17, Philadelphia, Pa. d: 3/6/45, Iwo Jima, Marianas Islands BR/TR, 6'3", 205 lbs. Deb: 7/23/39																											
1939	Phi-A	1	0	0	0	0	0	0	0	0	0	—	—	—	—	—	0	0	97	—	—	—	0	0	0	0	/C	0.0
■ **TIP O'NEILL**	O'Neill, James Edward b: 5/25/1858, Woodstock, Ont., Canada d: 12/31/15, Woodstock, Ont., Canada. BR/TR, 6'1.5", 167 lbs. Deb: 5/05/1883																											
1883	NY-N	23	76	8	15	3	0	0	5	3	15	.197	.228	.237	.465	42	-5	-5	100	96	4	.344				0	P/O	0.0
1884	StL-a	78	297	49	82	13	11	3		12		.276	.309	.424	.733	127	12	8	110	0	40	.651				-7	OP/1	0.0
1885	StL-a	52	206	44	72	7	4	3		13		.350	.399	.466	.865	189	18	20	93	0	39	.843				-1	O	1.4
1886	StL-a	138	579	106	190	28	14	3		47		.328	.385	.440	.826	144	40	29	111	0	104	.817	9			6	*O	2.7
1887	StL-a	124	517	**167**	**225**	**52**	19	**14**		50		**.435**	**.490**	**.691**	**1.180**	**210**	**88**	**79**	110	0	**194**	**1.514**	30			-9	*O	**5.2**
1888	StL-a	130	529	96	**177**	24	10	5	98	44		**.335**	.390	.446	.836	155	42	33	111	112	105	.881	26			-4	*O	2.2
1889	StL-a	134	534	123	179	33	8	9	110	72	37	.335	.419	.478	.897	140	42	30	112	99	122	1.014	28			-4	*O	1.7
1890	Chi-P	137	577	112	174	20	16	3	75	65	36	.302	.377	.407	.784	107	10	6	104	74	102	.829	29			-13	*O	-1.0
1891	StL-a	129	521	112	167	28	4	10	95	62	33	.321	.402	.447	.849	128	32	19	114	111	106	.929	25			-18	*O	-0.3
1892	Cin-N	109	419	63	105	14	6	2	52	53	25	.251	.339	.327	.666	100	3	1	103	107	52	.659	14			-5	*O	-0.6
Total	10	1054	4255	880	1386	222	92	52	435	421	146	.326	.392	.458	.850	141	281	220	109	63	869	.897	161			-55	*O/P1	11.3
■ **JIM O'NEILL**	O'Neill, James Leo b: 2/23/1893, Minooka, Pa. d: 9/5/76, Chambersburg, Pa. BR/TR, 5'10.5", 165 lbs. Deb: 4/15/20																											
1920	Was-A	86	294	27	85	17	7	1	40	13	30	.289	.324	.405	.728	97	-4	-2	95	115	38	.665	7	3	0	-12	S/2	-0.6
1923	Was-A	23	33	6	9	1	0	0	3	1	3	.273	.294	.303	.597	61	-2	-2	95	103	3	.458	0	0	0	0	/23SO	0.0
Total	2	109	327	33	94	18	7	1	43	14	33	.287	.321	.394	.715	93	-6	-4	95	114	41	.644	7	3	0	-12	/S23O	-0.6
■ **JOHN O'NEILL**	O'Neill, John J. b: New York, N.Y. TR , Deb: 9/06/1899																											
1899	NY-N	2	7	0	0	0	0	0	0	0		.000	.000	.000	.000	-99	-2	-2	97	0	0	.000	0			0	/C	-0.1
1902	NY-N	2	8	0	0	0	0	0	0	0		.000	.000	.000	.000	-99	-2	-2	100	0	0	.000	0			0	/C	-0.1
Total	2	4	15	0	0	0	0	0	0	0		.000	.000	.000	.000	-99	-4	-4	99	0	0	.000	0			0	/C	-0.2
■ **JACK O'NEILL**	O'Neill, John Joseph b: 1/10/1873, Galway, Ireland d: 6/29/35, Scranton, Pa. TR , 5'10", 165 lbs. Deb: 4/21/02																											
1902	StL-N	63	192	13	27	1	1	0	12	13		.141	.195	.156	.351	10	-20	-19	95	138	6	.273	2			1	C	-1.2

YEAR	TM/L	G	AB	R	H	2B	3B	HR	RBI	BB	SO	AVG	OBP	SLG	PRO	/A	BR	/A	PF	CHI	RC	TA	SB	CS	SBR	FR	POS	TPR
1903	StL-N	75	246	23	58	9	1	0	27	13		.236	.274	.280	.555	62	-13	-12	96	126	22	.495	11			12	C	0.6
1904	Chi-N	51	168	8	36	5	0	1	19	6		.214	.241	.262	.503	57	-9	-9	101	148	11	.386	1			-2	C	-0.5
1905	Chi-N	53	172	16	34	4	2	0	12	8		.198	.233	.244	.478	42	-12	-13	105	99	11	.406	6			-1	C	-0.8
1906	Bos-N	61	167	14	30	5	1	0	4	12		.180	.235	.222	.456	44	-11	-11	100	39	9	.358	0			9	C/1O	0.3
Total	5	303	945	74	185	24	5	1	74	52		.196	.238	.235	.473	44	-64	-62	99	112	60	.387	20			20	C/1O	-1.6
■ PAUL O'NEILL	O'Neill, Paul Andrew b: 2/25/63, Columbus, Ohio BL/TL, 6'4", 200 lbs. Deb: 9/03/85																											
1985	Cin-N	5	12	1	4	1	0	0	1	0	2	.333	.333	.417	.750	103	0	0	105	80	2	.625	0	0	0	1	/O	0.1
1986	Cin-N	3	2	0	0	0	0	0	0	1	1	.000	.333	.000	.333	-0	-0	-0	104	0	0	.500	0	0	0	0	/H	0.0
1987	Cin-N	84	160	24	41	14	1	7	28	18	29	.256	.331	.488	.819	110	3	2	104	113	26	.797	2	1	0	-2	O/1P	-0.1
1988	Cin-N	145	485	58	122	25	3	16	73	38	65	.252	.309	.414	.723	100	2	-0	105	117	61	.662	8	6	-1	-1	*O1	-0.7
Total	4	237	659	83	167	40	4	23	102	57	97	.253	.315	.431	.746	102	5	1	105	115	89	.698	10	7	-1	-2	O/1P	-0.7
■ PEACHES O'NEILL	O'Neill, Philip Bernard b: 8/30/1879, Anderson, Ind. d: 8/2/55, Anderson, Ind. TR , 5'11", 165 lbs. Deb: 4/16/04																											
1904	Cin-N	8	15	0	4	0	0	0	1	1		.267	.313	.267	.579	71	-0	-1	114	91	1	.455	0			0	/C1	0.0
■ STEVE O'NEILL	O'Neill, Stephen Francis b: 7/6/1891, Minooka, Pa. d: 1/26/62, Cleveland, Ohio BR/TR, 5'10", 165 lbs. Deb: 9/18/11 MC																											
1911	Cle-A	9	27	1	4	1	0	0	1	4		.148	.281	.185	.466	30	-2	-2	103	68	2	.522	2			1	/C	0.0
1912	Cle-A	68	215	17	49	4	0	0	14	12		.228	.272	.247	.518	48	-14	-15	101	88	15	.410	2			5	C	-0.2
1913	Cle-A	80	234	19	69	13	3	0	29	10	24	.295	.329	.376	.705	100	1	-1	106	117	30	.636	5			2	C	0.8
1914	Cle-A	86	269	28	68	12	2	0	20	15	35	.253	.292	.312	.605	80	-7	-7	102	89	24	.490	1	3	-2	7	C/1	0.4
1915	Cle-A	121	386	32	91	14	2	2	34	26	41	.236	.293	.298	.590	74	-12	-14	104	96	35	.497	2	3	-1	17	*C	1.2
1916	Cle-A	130	378	30	89	23	0	0	29	24	33	.235	.288	.296	.584	76	-12	-12	100	92	35	.491	2			1	*C	-0.5
1917	Cle-A	129	370	21	68	10	2	0	29	41	55	.184	.272	.222	.494	44	-21	-27	114	127	24	.427	2			-1	*C	-2.0
1918	Cle-A	114	359	34	87	8	7	1	35	48	22	.242	.343	.312	.655	90	0	-3	108	111	39	.632	5			-2	*C	0.6
1919	Cle-A	125	398	46	115	35	7	2	47	48	21	.289	.373	.427	.800	117	13	10	107	97	63	.802	4			-18	*C	-0.1
1920	Cle-A	149	489	63	157	39	5	3	66	69	39	.321	.408	.440	.848	120	20	17	104	104	91	.861	3	5	-2	-11	*C	1.6
1921	Cle-A	106	335	39	108	22	1	1	50	57	22	.322	.424	.403	.827	113	9	10	99	124	61	.851	0	1	-1	-10	*C	0.2
1922	Cle-A	133	392	33	122	27	4	2	65	73	25	.311	.423	.416	.839	117	15	14	102	138	74	.886	2	2	-1	-17	*C	0.0
1923	Cle-A	113	330	31	82	12	0	0	50	64	34	.248	.374	.285	.659	74	-9	-9	101	182	39	.635	0	4	-2	-15	*C	-1.8
1924	Bos-A	106	307	29	73	15	1	0	38	63	23	.238	.371	.293	.664	70	-10	-12	104	140	38	.657	0	2	-1	2	C	-0.4
1925	NY-A	35	91	7	26	5	0	1	13	10	3	.286	.363	.374	.736	91	-2	-1	96	118	13	.692	0	0	0	1	C	0.2
1927	StL-A	74	191	14	44	7	0	1	22	20	6	.230	.303	.283	.586	50	-13	-15	106	128	17	.503	0	0	0	4	C	-0.7
1928	StL-A	10	24	4	7	1	0	0	6	8	0	.292	.485	.333	.818	114	2	1	104	257	5	1.000	0	0	0	0	C	0.2
Total	17	1588	4795	448	1259	248	34	13	548	592	383	.263	.349	.337	.685	88	-42	-66	104	118	605	.641	30	20		-32	*C/1	-0.5
■ BILL O'NEILL	O'Neill, William John b: 1/22/1880, St.John, N.B., Can. d: 7/27/20, St.John, N.B., Can BB , 5'11", 175 lbs. Deb: 5/07/04																											
1904	Bos-A	17	51	7	10	1	0	0	5	2		.196	.226	.216	.442	40	-3	-3	105	170	3	.317	0			-2	/OS	-0.6
	Was-A	95	365	33	89	10	1	1	16	22		.244	.287	.285	.572	90	-6	-4	93	49	37	.536	22			-4	O/2	-1.5
	Yr	112	416	40	99	11	1	1	21	24		.238	.280	.276	.556	83	-10	-7	94	69	39	.508	22			-6		-2.1
1906	Chi-A	94	330	37	82	4	1	1	21	22		.248	.295	.276	.571	88	-7	-4	92	83	33	.532	19			10	O	0.3
Total	2	206	746	77	181	15	2	2	42	46		.243	.287	.276	.563	85	-16	-11	93	72	73	.519	41			4	O/2S	-1.8
■ RALPH ONIS	Onis, Manuel Dominguez "Curly" b: 10/24/08, Tampa, Fla. BR/TR, 5'9", 180 lbs. Deb: 4/27/35																											
1935	Bro-N	1	1	0	1	0	0	0	0	0	0	1.000	1.000	1.000	2.000	468	0	0	94	0	1	—	0			0	/C	0.0
■ EDDIE ONSLOW	Onslow, Edward Joseph b: 2/17/1893, Meadville, Pa. d: 5/8/81, Dennison, Ohio BL/TL, 6', 170 lbs. Deb: 8/07/12																											
1912	Det-A	35	128	11	29	1	2	1	13	3		.227	.250	.289	.539	57	-8	-7	95	111	10	.444	3			-3	1	-0.9
1913	Det-A	17	55	7	14	1	0	0	8	5	9	.255	.328	.273	.601	77	-1	-1	99	190	5	.537	1			-1	1	-0.1
1918	Cle-A	2	6	0	1	0	0	0	0	0	1	.167	.167	.167	.333	1	-1	-1	108	0	0	.200	0			-1	/O	-0.1
1927	Was-A	9	18	1	4	1	0	0	1	1	0	.222	.263	.278	.541	42	-2	-2	97	67	1	.429	0	0	0	0	/1	-0.1
Total	4	63	207	19	48	3	2	1	22	9	10	.232	.271	.280	.551	59	-12	-11	96	126	16	.459	4	0		-4	/1O	-1.2
■ JACK ONSLOW	Onslow, John James b: 10/13/1888, Scottdale, Pa. d: 12/22/60, Concord, Mass. BR/TR, 5'11", 180 lbs. Deb: 5/02/12 MC																											
1912	Det-A	31	69	7	11	1	0	0	4	10		.159	.284	.174	.458	34	-6	-5	95	111	4	.431	1			-3	C	-0.4
1917	NY-N	9	8	1	2	1	0	0	0	0	1	.250	.333	.375	.708	121	0	0	97	0	1	.667	0			-1	/C	0.0
Total	2	40	77	8	13	2	0	0	4	10	1	.169	.289	.195	.484	42	-6	-5	95	100	5	.453	1			-3	/C	-0.4
■ STEVE ONTIVEROS	Ontiveros, Steven Robert b: 10/26/51, Bakersfield, Cal. BB/TR, 6', 185 lbs. Deb: 8/05/73																											
1973	SF-N	24	33	3	8	0	0	1	5	4	7	.242	.324	.333	.658	79	-1	-1	105	143	4	.600	0	0	0	-0	/1O	0.0
1974	SF-N	120	343	45	91	15	1	4	33	57	41	.265	.375	.350	.725	96	4	1	108	96	46	.682	0	0	0	-0	31/O	-0.1
1975	SF-N	108	325	21	94	16	0	3	31	55	44	.289	.395	.366	.761	110	8	7	102	94	50	.742	2	0	1	1	3/O1	0.8
1976	SF-N	59	74	8	13	3	0	0	5	6	11	.176	.247	.216	.463	31	-7	-7	103	120	4	.365	0	0	0	-2	/3O1	-0.9
1977	Chi-N	156	546	54	163	32	3	10	68	81	69	.299	.392	.423	.815	104	17	7	114	106	92	.793	3	3	-1	-3	*3	0.2
1978	Chi-N	82	276	34	67	14	4	1	22	34	33	.243	.326	.333	.659	77	-5	-9	110	94	31	.586	0	2	-1	7	3/1	-0.3
1979	Chi-N	152	519	58	148	28	2	4	57	58	68	.285	.365	.370	.735	90	3	-6	112	113	69	.657	0	1	-1	2	*3/1	-1.0
1980	Chi-N	31	77	7	16	3	0	1	3	14	17	.208	.330	.286	.615	69	-2	-3	106	47	8	.581	0	0	0	0	3	-0.2
Total	8	732	2193	230	600	111	10	24	224	309	290	.274	.367	.366	.734	93	17	-10	109	102	305	.708	5	6	-2	4	3/1O	-1.5
■ JOSE OQUENDO	Oquendo, Jose Manuel (Contreras) b: 7/4/63, Rio Piedras, P.R. BB/TR, 5'10", 160 lbs. Deb: 5/02/83																											
1983	NY-N	120	328	29	70	7	0	1	17	19	60	.213	.261	.244	.505	41	-26	-26	99	81	19	.394	8	9	-3	-1	*S	-1.9
1984	NY-N	81	189	23	42	5	0	0	10	15	26	.222	.286	.249	.535	52	-12	-12	100	83	16	.493	10	1	2	-3	S	-0.4
1986	StL-N	76	138	20	41	4	1	0	13	15	20	.297	.366	.341	.707	93	-0	-1	103	110	17	.621	2	3	-1	-3	S2/3O	-0.1
1987	StL-N	116	248	43	71	9	0	1	24	54	29	.286	.414	.335	.749	103	4	4	99	111	38	.754	4	4	-1	-2	O2S/31P	0.2
1988	StL-N	148	451	36	125	10	1	7	46	52	40	.277	.352	.350	.702	98	3	1	104	103	57	.629	4	6	-2	5	231OS/PC	0.5
Total	5	541	1354	151	349	35	2	9	110	155	175	.258	.336	.306	.642	79	-32	-33	101	98	145	.581	28	23	-5	-4	S2/O31PC	-1.7
■ TOM ORAN	Oran, Thomas b: 1845, d: 9/22/1886, St.Louis, Mo. Deb: 5/04/1875																											
1875	RS-n	18	79	8	14							.177															O	
■ ERNIE ORAVETZ	Oravetz, Ernest Eugene b: 1/24/32, Johnstown, Pa. BB/TL, 5'4", 145 lbs. Deb: 4/11/55																											
1955	Was-A	100	263	24	71	5	1	0	25	26	19	.270	.338	.297	.635	79	-10	-7	91	120	27	.533	1	2	-1	-3	O	-1.2
1956	Was-A	88	137	20	34	3	2	0	11	27	20	.248	.372	.299	.671	78	-3	-3	102	100	18	.663	1	0	0	-3	O	-0.6
Total	2	188	400	44	105	8	3	0	36	53	39	.262	.350	.298	.648	78	-13	-10	95	112	45	.587	2	2	-1	-5	/O	-1.8
■ TONY ORDENANA	Ordenana, Antonio (Rodriguez) "Mosquito" b: 10/30/18, Guanabacoa, Havana, Cuba d: 9/29/88, Miami, Fla. BR/TR, 5'9", 158 lbs. Deb: 10/03/43																											
1943	Pit-N	1	4	0	2	0	0	0	3	0	0	.500	.500	.500	1.000	181	0	0	104	552	1	1.000	0			0	/S	0.1
■ JOE ORENGO	Orengo, Joseph Charles b: 11/29/14, San Francisco, Cal d: 7/14/88, San Francisco, Cal. BR/TR, 6', 185 lbs. Deb: 4/18/39																											
1939	StL-N	7	3	0	0	0	0	0	0	0	1	.000	.000	.000	.000	-95	-1	-1	105	0	0	.000	0			0	/S	0.0
1940	StL-N	129	415	58	119	23	4	7	56	65	90	.287	.383	.412	.795	117	13	12	102	108	72	.819	9			-14	23S	0.4
1941	NY-N	77	252	23	54	11	2	4	25	28	49	.214	.298	.321	.619	72	-9	-10	103	97	24	.546	1			3	3/S2	-0.4
1943	NY-N	83	266	28	58	8	2	6	29	36	46	.218	.311	.331	.642	89	-5	-3	96	99	28	.579	1			-1	1	-0.7
	Bro-N	7	15	1	3	2	0	0	1	4	2	.200	.368	.333	.702	104	0	0	100	72	2	.692	0			-0	/3	0.0
	Yr	90	281	29	61	10	2	6	30	40	48	.217	.315	.331	.646	90	-5	-3	96	98	33	.606	1			-1		-0.7
1944	Det-A	46	154	14	31	10	0	0	10	20	29	.201	.297	.266	.563	59	-7	-8	105	90	13	.492	1	1	-0	3	S3/12	-0.3
1945	Chi-A	17	15	5	1	0	0	0	1	3	2	.067	.222	.067	.289	-15	-2	-2	95	362	0	.286	0	0	0	0	/32	-0.1
Total	6	366	1120	129	266	54	8	17	122	156	219	.237	.332	.346	.678	90	-10	-12	101	104	139	.653	12	1		-9	3/12S	-1.1
■ GEORGE ORME	Orme, George William b: 9/16/1891, Lebanon, Ind. d: 3/16/62, Indianapolis, Ind. BR/TR, 5'10", 160 lbs. Deb: 9/14/20																											
1920	Bos-A	4	6	4	2	0	0	0	1	3	0	.333	.556	.333	.889	145	1	1	96	176	1	1.250	0	0	0	0	/O	0.1

YEAR	TM/L	G	AB	R	H	2B	3B	HR	RBI	BB	SO	AVG	OBP	SLG	PRO	/A	BR	/A	PF	CHI	RC	TA	SB	CS	SBR	FR	POS	TPR
■ JESS ORNDORFF	Orndorff, Jesse Walworth Thayer b: 1/15/1881, Chicago, Ill. d: 9/28/60, Cardiff-By-The- Sea, Cal. BB/TR, 6', 168 lbs. Deb: 4/18/07																											
1907	Bos-N	5	17	0	2	0	0	0	0	0		.118	.118	.118	.235	-27	-2	-2	95	0	0	.133	0			0	/C	-0.1
■ FRANK O'ROURKE	O'Rourke, James Francis "Blackie" b: 11/28/1894, Hamilton, Ont., Can d: 5/14/86, Chatham, N.J. BR/TR, 5'10.5", 165 lbs. Deb: 6/12/12																											
1912	Bos-N	61	196	11	24	3	1	0	16	11	50	.122	.177	.148	.325	-10	-30	-32	107	186	6	.250	1			-10	S	-3.6
1917	Bro-N	64	198	18	47	7	1	0	15	14	25	.237	.294	.283	.577	75	-5	-6	104	103	19	.550	11			-0	3	-0.7
1918	Bro-N	4	12	0	2	0	0	0	2	1	3	.167	.231	.167	.397	22	-1	-1	101	378	0	.300	0			1	/2O	0.0
1920	Was-A	14	54	8	16	1	0	0	5	2	5	.296	.321	.315	.636	73	-2	-2	95	105	6	.538	2	1	0	-3	S/3	-0.3
1921	Was-A	123	444	51	104	17	8	3	54	26	56	.234	.287	.329	.616	58	-30	-29	99	122	42	.533	6	7	-2	-8	*S	-2.2
1922	Bos-A	67	216	28	57	14	3	1	17	20	28	.264	.335	.370	.705	87	-5	-4	96	73	27	.661	6	6	-2	-6	S3	-0.4
1924	Det-A	47	181	28	50	11	2	0	19	12	19	.276	.332	.359	.691	78	-6	-6	100	102	22	.644	7	4	-0	3	2/S	-0.1
1925	Det-A	124	482	88	141	40	7	5	57	32	37	.293	.350	.436	.786	99	-3	-2	99	90	73	.739	5	8	-3	15	*2/3	1.4
1926	Det-A	111	363	43	88	16	1	1	41	35	33	.242	.321	.300	.621	65	-19	-18	97	124	37	.566	8	6	-1	1	32S	-0.9
1927	StL-A	140	538	85	144	25	3	1	39	64	43	.268	.358	.331	.689	75	-14	-19	106	63	66	.693	19	0	6	4	*32/1	-0.4
1928	StL-A	99	391	54	103	24	3	1	62	21	19	.263	.303	.348	.650	68	-17	-19	104	162	43	.579	10	2	2	-10	3/S	-2.5
1929	StL-A	154	585	81	147	23	9	2	62	41	28	.251	.306	.332	.637	64	-32	-32	100	112	62	.571	14	7	0	-20	*3/2S	-3.9
1930	StL-A	115	400	52	107	15	4	1	41	35	30	.268	.326	.333	.659	63	-19	-24	108	102	44	.593	11	9	-2	-1	3S/1	-1.9
1931	StL-A	8	9	0	2	0	0	0	0	0	1	.222	.222	.222	.444	17	-1	-1	102	0	0	.375	1	1	-0	0	/S1	0.0
Total	14	1131	4069	547	1032	196	42	15	430	314	377	.254	.315	.333	.649	68	-185	-195	102	110	447	.591	101	51		-35	3S2/1O	-15.5
■ JIM O'ROURKE	O'Rourke, James Henry "Orator Jim" b: 8/24/1852, Bridgeport, Conn. d: 1/8/19, Bridgeport, Conn. BR/TR, 5'8", 185 lbs. Deb: 4/26/1872 MH																											
1872	Man-n	23	101	23	29							.287															S/DD	
1873	Bos-n	57	300	79	99							.330															1O/C	
1874	Bos-n	70	334	80	115							.344															*1	
1875	Bos-n	75	374	96	108							.289															O3/1	
1876	Bos-N	70	312	61	102	17	3	2	43	15	17	.327	.358	.420	.778	167	19	22	95	94	48	.695				-4	*O/1C	1.5
1877	Bos-N	61	265	**68**	96	14	4	0	23	**20**	9	.362	**.407**	.445	.852	155	21	18	108	58	49	.817				-2	*O/1	1.2
1878	Bos-N	60	255	44	71	17	7	1	29	5	21	.278	.292	.412	.704	120	7	5	108	87	31	.598				4	*O/1C	0.3
1879	Pro-N	81	362	69	126	19	9	1	46	13	10	.348	**.371**	.459	.829	169	27	26	102	101	63	.758				-10	*O1/C3	1.4
1880	Bos-N	86	363	71	100	20	11	**6**	45	21	8	.275	.315	.441	.756	167	20	24	92	80	52	.688				2	O1S3/C	2.3
1881	Buf-N	83	348	71	105	21	7	0	30	27	18	.302	.352	.402	.754	135	15	14	101	66	51	.687				-17	*3O/CS1M	0.2
1882	Buf-N	84	370	62	104	15	6	2	37	13	13	.281	.305	.370	.676	111	6	4	104	77	43	.564				-2	*O/SC3M	0.0
1883	Buf-N	94	436	102	143	29	8	1	38	15	13	.328	.350	.438	.788	138	19	19	100	59	69	.703				-12	OC/3SPM	0.9
1884	Buf-N	108	467	119	**162**	33	7	5	63	35	17	.347	.392	.480	.872	162	39	34	107	78	90	.849				-7	*O1C/P3M	2.3
1885	NY-N	112	477	119	143	21	**16**	5	42	40	21	.300	.354	.442	.796	143	30	23	109	56	77	.751				-17	*O/C	0.2
1886	NY-N	105	440	106	136	26	6	1	34	39	21	.309	.365	.402	.768	151	18	26	89	53	72	.757	14			2	OC/1	2.9
1887	NY-N	103	397	73	113	15	13	3	88	36	11	.285	.352	.411	.762	105	7	2	107	**167**	75	.880	46			-22	C3O/2	-1.1
1888	NY-N	107	409	50	112	16	6	4	50	24	30	.274	.319	.372	.690	132	10	14	93	116	58	.687	25			3	OC/13	1.6
1889	NY-N	128	502	89	161	36	7	3	81	40	34	.321	.372	.438	.810	122	18	14	105	108	96	.862	33			-10	*O/C	0.0
1890	NY-P	111	478	112	172	37	5	9	115	33	20	.360	.410	.515	.925	136	31	24	109	122	113	1.013	23			2	*O	1.6
1891	NY-N	136	555	92	164	28	7	5	95	26	29	.295	.334	.398	.732	123	8	14	94	124	82	.696	19			-4	*OC	0.2
1892	NY-N	115	448	62	136	28	5	0	56	30	30	.304	.354	.388	.742	129	14	15	98	105	69	.721	16			-12	*O/C1	0.0
1893	Was-N	129	547	75	157	22	5	2	95	49	26	.287	.354	.356	.711	102	-6	4	90	124	76	.685	15			1	O1/CM	0.1
1904	NY-N	1	4	1	1	0	0	0	0	0		.250	.250	.250	.500	53	-0	-0	105	0	0	.333	0			0	/C	0.0
Total	4 n	225	1109	278	351							.317															/C	
Total	19	1774	7435	1446	2304	414	132	50	1010	481	348	.310	.355	.421	.776	134	303	300	100	95	1214	.748	191			-104	*OC13/SDP	15.6
■ CHARLIE O'ROURKE	O'Rourke, James Patrick b: 6/22/37, Walla Walla, Wash BR/TR, 6'2", 195 lbs. Deb: 6/16/59																											
1959	StL-N	2	2	0	0	0	0	0	0	0	0	.000	.000	.000	.000	-96	-1	-1	105	0	0	.000	0	0	0	0	H	0.0
■ QUEENIE O'ROURKE	O'Rourke, James Stephen b: 12/26/1883, Bridgeport, Conn. d: 12/22/55, Sparrows Point, Md BR/TR, 5'7", 150 lbs. Deb: 8/15/08																											
1908	NY-A	34	108	5	25	1	0	0	3	4		.231	.259	.241	.500	68	-4	-4	95	43	7	.410	4			-1	OS/23	-0.4
■ JOHN O'ROURKE	O'Rourke, John b: 1853, Bridgeport, Conn. d: 6/23/11, Boston, Mass. BL , 6', 190 lbs. Deb: 5/01/1879																											
1879	Bos-N	72	317	69	108	17	11	6	**62**	8	32	.341	.357	**.521**	**.877**	173	28	25	107	114	60	.828				1	*O	2.1
1880	Bos-N	81	313	30	86	22	8	3	36	18	32	.275	.314	.425	.739	161	16	19	92	98	43	.665				2	*O	1.8
1883	NY-a	77	315	49	85	19	5	2		21		.270	.315	.381	.696	115	8	4	108	0	39	.613				-5	*O/1	0.0
Total	3	230	945	148	279	58	24	11	98	47	64	.295	.329	.442	.771	149	52	48	102	70	142	.698				-2	O/1	3.9
■ JOE O'ROURKE	O'Rourke, Joseph Leo Jr. b: 10/28/04, Philadelphia, Pa. BL/TR, 5'7", 145 lbs. Deb: 4/19/29																											
1929	Phi-N	3	3	0	0	0	0	0	0	0	1	.000	.000	.000	.000	-91	-1	-1	110	0	0	.000	0			0	H	0.0
■ PATSY O'ROURKE	O'Rourke, Joseph Leo Sr. b: 4/13/1881, Philadelphia, Pa. d: 4/18/56, Philadelphia, Pa. TR , 5'7", 160 lbs. Deb: 4/16/08																											
1908	StL-N	53	164	8	32	4	2	0	16	14		.195	.258	.244	.502	67	-7	-6	94	157	10	.424	2			-7	S	-1.5
■ TOM O'ROURKE	O'Rourke, Thomas Joseph b: 1862, New York, N.Y. d: 7/19/29, New York, N.Y. TR , 5'9", 158 lbs. Deb: 5/11/1887																											
1887	Bos-N	22	78	12	12	3	0	0	10	7	6	.154	.233	.192	.425	21	-8	-8	98	210	5	.409	4			0	C/O3	-0.6
1888	Bos-N	20	74	3	13	0	0	0	4	1	9	.176	.187	.176	.362	16	-7	-7	106	112	3	.262	2			0	C/O	-0.6
1890	NY-N	2	7	1	0	0	0	0	0	1	0	.000	.125	.000	.125	-65	-1	-1	95	0	0	.143	0			0	/C	0.0
	Syr-a	41	153	16	33	8	0	0		12		.216	.273	.268	.541	68	-7	-5	90	0	12	.458	2			-5	C/1	-0.4
Total	3	85	312	32	58	11	0	0	14	21	15	.186	.240	.221	.461	39	-24	-21	96	79	19	.390	8			-5	/CO13	-1.6
■ TIM O'ROURKE	O'Rourke, Timothy Patrick "Voiceless Tim" b: 5/18/1864, Chicago, Ill. d: 4/20/38, Seattle, Wash. BL/TR, 5'10", 170 lbs. Deb: 5/27/1890																											
1890	Syr-a	87	332	48	94	13	6	1		36		.283	.362	.367	.729	130	8	13	90	0	53	.777	22			-14	3	-0.1
1891	Col-a	34	136	22	38	1	3	0	12	15	7	.279	.359	.331	.690	113	1	3	89	68	20	.724	9			0	3	0.3
1892	Bal-N	63	239	40	74	8	4	0	35	24	19	.310	.373	.377	.749	129	9	9	100	126	39	.764	12			-11	S/O3	0.0
1893	Bal-N	31	135	22	49	4	1	0	19	12	4	.363	.423	.407	.830	115	5	3	107	83	26	.860	5			-1	O/3S	0.2
	Lou-N	92	352	80	99	8	4	0	53	77	15	.281	.421	.327	.748	106	7	9	96	111	59	.877	22			-15	SO/3	-0.2
	Yr	123	487	102	148	12	5	0	72	89	19	.304	.422	.349	.771	109	12	13	99	105	85	.873	27			-16		0.0
1894	Lou-N	55	220	46	61	3	3	0	27	23	9	.277	.351	.318	.669	72	-12	-7	88	94	28	.654	9			0	1O/S32	-0.4
	StL-N	18	71	10	20	4	1	0	10	8	3	.282	.354	.366	.721	75	-3	-3	101	102	10	.706	2			0	3	-0.1
	Was-N	7	25	4	5	2	1	0	2	2	1	.200	.259	.360	.619	50	-2	-2	98	61	2	.550	0			0	/2S	-0.1
	Yr	80	316	60	86	9	5	0	39	33	13	.272	.345	.332	.677	71	-17	-12	92	95	41	.657	11			0		-0.6
Total	5	387	1510	272	440	43	23	1	158	197	58	.291	.380	.352	.732	108	12	26	95	80	238	.775	81			-41	3S/O12	-0.4
■ DAVE ORR	Orr, David L. b: 9/29/1859, New York, N.Y. d: 6/3/15, Brooklyn, N.Y. BL/TR, 5'11", 250 lbs. Deb: 1883 M																											
1883	NY-a	1	4	1	1	1	0	0		0		.250	.250	.500	.750	126	0	0	108	0	1	.667				0	/1	0.0
	NY-N	1	3	0	0	0	0	0	0	0	1	.000	.000	.000	.000	-99	-1	-1	100	0	0	.000				0	/O	0.0
	NY-a	12	46	5	15	3	3	2		0		.326	.326	.652	.978	193	5	5	108	0	10	.968				0	1	0.4
1884	NY-a	110	458	82	**162**	32	13	9		5		**.354**	.362	.539	.901	**193**	43	**43**	100	0	92	.855				-5	*1/O	3.0
1885	NY-a	107	444	76	152	29	**21**	6		8		.342	.358	**.543**	.901	**220**	40	**50**	84	0	88	.863				-3	*1/P	3.4
1886	NY-a	136	571	93	**193**	25	**31**	**7**		17		.338	.363	**.527**	**.890**	**174**	**47**	44	104	0	**118**	.897	16			0	*1	3.2
1887	NY-a	84	345	63	127	25	10	2		22		.368	.408	.516	.924	181	26	34	88	0	81	1.000	17			-1	1/OM	2.5
1888	Bro-a	99	394	57	120	20	5	1	59	7		.305	.330	.388	.718	127	13	11	105	120	55	.653	11			3	*1	0.7
1889	Col-a	134	560	70	183	31	12	4	87	9	38	.327	.340	.446	.786	138	15	23	91	101	91	.724	12			9	*1	1.7
1890	Bro-P	107	464	89	173	32	13	6	124	30	11	.373	.416	.537	.952	147	34	29	106	122	110	1.007	10			-5	*1	1.1
Total	8	791	3289	536	1126	198	108	37	270	98	50	.342	.366	.502	.868	166	223	238	97	49	647	.850	66			-0	1/OP	16.0
■ BILLY ORR	Orr, William John b: 4/22/1891, San Francisco, Cal d: 3/10/67, Santarium, Cal. BR/TR, 5'11", 168 lbs. Deb: 5/03/13																											
1913	Phi-A	30	67	6	13	1	1	0	7	4	10	.194	.239	.239	.478	41	-5	-5	97	155	4	.389	1			-1	S/132	-0.4

YEAR	TM/L	G	AB	R	H	2B	3B	HR	RBI	BB	SO	AVG	OBP	SLG	PRO	/A	BR	/A	PF	CHI	RC	TA	SB	CS	SBR	FR	POS	TPR
1914	Phi-A	10	24	3	4	1	1	0	1	2	5	.167	.231	.292	.522	59	-1	-1	97	54	2	.476	1	1	-0	0	/S3	0.0
Total	2	40	91	9	17	2	2	0	8	6	15	.187	.237	.253	.490	46	-7	-6	97	128	5	.413	2	1		-1	/S312	-0.4

■ **ERNIE ORSATTI** Orsatti, Ernest Ralph b: 9/8/02, Los Angeles, Cal. d: 9/4/68, Canoga Park, Cal. BL/TL, 5'7.5", 154 lbs. Deb: 9/04/27

YEAR	TM/L	G	AB	R	H	2B	3B	HR	RBI	BB	SO	AVG	OBP	SLG	PRO	/A	BR	/A	PF	CHI	RC	TA	SB	CS	SBR	FR	POS	TPR
1927	StL-N	27	92	15	29	7	3	0	12	11	12	.315	.388	.457	.845	117	3	3	107	102	16	.873	2			-1	O	0.1
1928	StL-N	27	69	10	21	6	0	3	15	10	11	.304	.400	.522	.922	139	4	4	100	119	14	.979	0			-2	O/1	0.1
1929	StL-N	113	346	64	115	21	7	3	39	33	43	.332	.394	.460	.853	112	6	7	98	79	62	.870	7			8	O1	0.7
1930	StL-N	48	131	24	42	8	4	1	15	12	18	.321	.382	.466	.848	99	1	-0	105	81	23	.843	1			1	1O	0.0
1931	StL-N	70	158	27	46	16	6	0	19	14	16	.291	.349	.468	.817	110	4	2	107	91	26	.795	1			-7	O/1	-0.6
1932	StL-N	101	375	44	126	27	6	2	44	18	29	.336	.368	.456	.824	120	10	10	100	94	63	.783	5			-6	O/1	-0.2
1933	StL-N	120	436	55	130	21	6	0	38	33	33	.298	.348	.374	.721	104	4	3	102	89	58	.665	14			-0	*O/1	-0.3
1934	StL-N	105	337	39	101	14	4	0	31	27	31	.300	.353	.365	.718	82	-3	-9	114	91	45	.646	6			-4	O	-1.6
1935	StL-N	90	221	28	53	9	3	1	24	18	25	.240	.297	.321	.618	64	-10	-12	104	117	21	.563	10			-4	O	-1.7
Total	9	701	2165	306	663	129	39	10	237	176	218	.306	.360	.416	.776	102	19	8	104	93	328	.747	46			-14	O/1	-3.5

■ **JOHN ORSINO** Orsino, John Joseph "Horse" b: 4/22/38, Teaneck, N.J. BR/TR, 6'3", 215 lbs. Deb: 7/14/61

YEAR	TM/L	G	AB	R	H	2B	3B	HR	RBI	BB	SO	AVG	OBP	SLG	PRO	/A	BR	/A	PF	CHI	RC	TA	SB	CS	SBR	FR	POS	TPR
1961	SF-N	25	83	5	23	3	2	4	12	3	13	.277	.310	.506	.816	114	1	1	98	90	13	.767	0	0	0	0	C	0.3
1962	SF-N	18	48	4	13	2	0	0	4	5	11	.271	.340	.313	.652	76	-1	-2	101	105	5	.541	0	0	0	0	C	0.0
1963	Bal-A	116	379	53	103	18	1	19	56	38	53	.272	.352	.475	.827	138	15	18	94	99	63	.801	2	3	-1	7	*C/1	2.6
1964	Bal-A	81	248	21	55	10	0	8	23	23	55	.222	.293	.359	.652	76	-7	-8	105	86	26	.573	0	0	0	-4	C/1	-1.0
1965	Bal-A	77	232	30	54	10	2	9	28	23	51	.233	.315	.409	.725	104	1	1	100	95	26	.642	1	0	0	-0	C/1	0.5
1966	Was-A	14	23	1	4	1	0	0	0	0	7	.174	.174	.217	.391	12	-3	-2	95	0	1	.263	0	0	0	0	/1C	-0.2
1967	Was-A	1	1	0	0	0	0	0	0	0	1	.000	.000	.000	.000	-98	-0	-0	102	0	0	.000	0	0	0	0	H	0.0
Total	7	332	1014	114	252	44	5	40	123	92	191	.249	.321	.420	.742	106	6	8	99	92	135	.703	3	3	-1	4	C/1	2.2

■ **JOE ORSULAK** Orsulak, Joseph Michael b: 5/31/62, Parispanny, N, J. BL/TL, 6'1", 185 lbs. Deb: 9/01/83

YEAR	TM/L	G	AB	R	H	2B	3B	HR	RBI	BB	SO	AVG	OBP	SLG	PRO	/A	BR	/A	PF	CHI	RC	TA	SB	CS	SBR	FR	POS	TPR
1983	Pit-N	7	11	0	2	0	0	0	1	0	2	.182	.182	.182	.364	1	-1	-1	103	198	0	.200	0	1	-1	0	/O	-0.1
1984	Pit-N	32	67	12	17	1	2	0	3	1	7	.254	.275	.328	.604	73	-3	-2	94	53	6	.529	3	1	0	-1	O	-0.4
1985	Pit-N	121	397	54	119	14	6	0	21	26	27	.300	.344	.365	.710	96	-1	-2	103	58	51	.667	24	11	1	5	*O	0.1
1986	Pit-N	138	401	60	100	19	6	2	19	28	38	.249	.300	.342	.642	77	-13	-13	100	53	42	.601	24	11	1	-3	*O	-1.8
1988	Bal-A	125	379	48	109	21	3	8	27	23	30	.288	.333	.422	.755	116	4	7	95	58	51	.684	9	8	-2	-4	*O	0.0
Total	5	423	1255	174	347	55	17	10	71	78	104	.276	.322	.371	.693	93	-14	-12	99	57	150	.644	60	32	-1	-2	O	-2.2

■ **JORGE ORTA** Orta, Jorge (Nunez) b: 11/26/50, Mazatlan, Mexico BL/TR, 5'10", 170 lbs. Deb: 4/15/72

YEAR	TM/L	G	AB	R	H	2B	3B	HR	RBI	BB	SO	AVG	OBP	SLG	PRO	/A	BR	/A	PF	CHI	RC	TA	SB	CS	SBR	FR	POS	TPR
1972	Chi-A	51	124	20	25	3	1	3	11	6	37	.202	.244	.315	.559	62	-6	-6	106	96	9	.471	3	3	-1	-1	S2/3	-0.5
1973	Chi-A	128	425	46	113	9	10	6	40	37	87	.266	.326	.376	.703	95	-2	-3	102	88	51	.630	8	8	-2	-17	*2/S	-1.7
1974	Chi-A	139	525	73	166	31	2	10	67	40	88	.316	.368	.440	.808	129	21	20	102	107	85	.761	9	5	-0	-2	*2D/S	2.4
1975	Chi-A	140	542	64	165	26	10	11	83	48	67	.304	.365	.450	.816	125	20	18	103	122	85	.774	16	9	-1	-7	*2/D	1.5
1976	Chi-A	158	636	74	174	29	8	14	72	38	77	.274	.320	.410	.730	114	8	9	99	97	81	.676	24	8	2	2	O3D	1.2
1977	Chi-A	144	564	71	159	27	8	11	84	46	49	.282	.338	.417	.755	105	3	4	99	132	78	.682	4	4	-1	-40	*2	-2.6
1978	Chi-A	117	420	45	115	19	2	13	53	42	39	.274	.345	.421	.767	114	8	8	101	103	61	.709	1	2	-1	-24	*2/D	-1.0
1979	Chi-A	113	325	49	85	18	3	11	46	44	33	.262	.351	.437	.788	109	5	4	102	101	50	.749	1	5	-3	-5	D2	-0.1
1980	Cle-A	129	481	78	140	18	3	10	64	71	44	.291	.384	.403	.788	113	13	12	102	118	78	.771	6	5	-1	7	*O/D	1.5
1981	Cle-A	88	338	50	92	14	3	5	34	21	43	.272	.317	.376	.692	106	-1	2	93	99	38	.588	4	3	-1	0	O	0.0
1982	LA-N	86	115	13	25	5	0	2	8	12	13	.217	.297	.313	.610	75	-4	-4	95	75	11	.533	0	1	-1	1	O	-0.3
1983	Tor-A	103	245	30	58	6	3	10	38	19	29	.237	.292	.408	.700	83	-4	-7	108	114	28	.615	1	2	-1	-3	DO	-1.0
1984	KC-A	122	403	50	120	23	7	9	50	28	39	.298	.346	.457	.803	121	10	11	99	94	63	.738	0	1	-1	-3	DO/2	0.6
1985	KC-A	110	300	32	80	21	1	4	45	22	28	.267	.321	.383	.704	90	-3	-4	102	141	36	.616	2	1	0	0	D	-0.3
1986	KC-A	106	336	35	93	14	2	9	46	23	34	.277	.323	.411	.734	99	-1	-1	100	111	42	.631	0	3	-2	0	D	-0.2
1987	KC-A	21	50	3	9	4	0	2	4	3	8	.180	.226	.380	.606	55	-3	-3	104	64	4	.537	0	0	0	0	D	-0.2
Total	16	1755	5829	733	1619	267	63	130	745	500	715	.278	.338	.412	.750	108	66	58	101	108	800	.705	79	60	-12	-93	2DO/3S	-0.7

■ **FRANK ORTENZIO** Ortenzio, Frank Joseph b: 2/24/51, Fresno, Cal. BR/TR, 6'2", 215 lbs. Deb: 9/09/73

YEAR	TM/L	G	AB	R	H	2B	3B	HR	RBI	BB	SO	AVG	OBP	SLG	PRO	/A	BR	/A	PF	CHI	RC	TA	SB	CS	SBR	FR	POS	TPR
1973	KC-A	9	25	1	7	2	0	1	6	2	6	.280	.333	.480	.813	116	1	0	109	157	4	.778	0	0	0	0	/1D	0.0

■ **AL ORTH** Orth, Albert Lewis "Smiling Al" or "The Curveless Wonder" b: 9/5/1872, Tipton, Ind. d: 10/8/48, Lynchburg, Va. BL/TR, 6', 200 lbs. Deb: 8/15/1895 U

YEAR	TM/L	G	AB	R	H	2B	3B	HR	RBI	BB	SO	AVG	OBP	SLG	PRO	/A	BR	/A	PF	CHI	RC	TA	SB	CS	SBR	FR	POS	TPR
1895	Phi-N	11	45	8	16	4	0	1	13	1	6	.356	.370	.511	.881	129	2	2	99	140	9	.828	0			0	P	0.0
1896	Phi-N	25	82	12	21	3	3	1	13	3	11	.256	.282	.402	.685	79	-3	-3	102	104	10	.623	2			0	P	0.0
1897	Phi-N	53	152	26	50	7	4	1	17	3		.329	.342	.447	.789	114	1	2	96	70	26	.745	5			2	P/O	0.0
1898	Phi-N	39	123	17	36	6	4	1	14	3		.293	.310	.431	.740	121	1	2	95	76	17	.655	1			0	P/O	0.0
1899	Phi-N	22	62	5	13	3	1	1	5	1		.210	.222	.339	.561	56	-4	-4	97	64	5	.490	2			0	P/O	0.0
1900	Phi-N	39	129	6	40	4	1	1	21	2		.310	.321	.380	.700	97	-1	-1	98	126	17	.596	2			2	P/O	0.0
1901	Phi-N	41	128	14	36	6	0	1	15	3		.281	.298	.352	.649	87	-2	-2	103	105	15	.554	3			3	P/O	0.0
1902	Was-A	56	175	20	38	3	2	2	10	9		.217	.255	.291	.547	53	-11	-11	99	58	14	.453	2			0	P/O1S	0.0
1903	Was-A	55	162	19	49	9	7	0	11	4		.302	.319	.444	.764	123	5	4	105	55	25	.699	3			-1	P/SO1	0.0
1904	Was-A	31	102	7	22	3	1	0	11	1		.216	.223	.265	.488	60	-5	-4	93	152	7	.375	2			0	OP	-0.3
	NY-A	24	64	6	19	1	1	0	7	0		.297	.297	.344	.641	93	0	-1	112	119	7	.533	2			1	P/O	0.0
	Yr	55	166	13	41	4	2	0	18	1		.247	.251	.295	.547	74	-5	-5	101	140	14	.432	4			1		-0.3
1905	NY-A	55	131	13	24	3	1	1	8	4		.183	.207	.244	.452	44	-8	-8	102	82	7	.355	2			-1	P/1O	0.0
1906	NY-A	47	135	12	37	2	2	1	17	6		.274	.305	.341	.646	86	0	-3	120	126	15	.551	2			-1	P/O	0.0
1907	NY-A	44	105	11	34	6	0	1	13	4		.324	.349	.410	.758	132	5	4	109	101	16	.676	1			2	P/O	0.0
1908	NY-A	38	69	4	20	1	2	0	4	2		.290	.310	.362	.672	126	1	2	95	60	7	.551	0			-1	P	0.0
1909	NY-A	22	34	3	9	9	1	**9**	5	5		.265	.359	.324	.683	117	1	1	99	51	4	.680	1			-2	/2P	0.0
Total	15	602	1698	183	464	70	30	21	184	51	17	.273	.294	.366	.660	92	-18	-21	102	91	200	.569	30			3	P/OS21	-0.3

■ **JUNIOR ORTIZ** Ortiz, Adalberto Colon b: 10/24/59, Humacao, P.R. BR/TR, 5'11", 174 lbs. Deb: 9/20/82

YEAR	TM/L	G	AB	R	H	2B	3B	HR	RBI	BB	SO	AVG	OBP	SLG	PRO	/A	BR	/A	PF	CHI	RC	TA	SB	CS	SBR	FR	POS	TPR
1982	Pit-N	7	15	1	3	1	0	0	0	1	3	.200	.250	.267	.517	40	-1	-1	110	0	1	.385	0	0	0	0	/C	0.0
1983	Pit-N	5	8	1	1	0	0	0	0	1	0	.125	.222	.125	.347	-1	-1	-1	103	0	0	.286	0	0	0	0	/C	0.0
	NY-N	68	185	10	47	5	0	0	12	3	34	.254	.270	.281	.551	54	-12	-12	99	91	14	.410	1	0	0	-2	C	-1.1
	Yr	73	193	11	48	5	0	0	12	4	34	.249	.268	.275	.542	51	-13	-13	99	85	15	.404	1	0	0	-2		-1.1
1984	NY-N	40	91	6	18	3	0	0	11	5	15	.198	.240	.231	.470	33	-8	-8	100	205	5	.360	1	0	0	-0	C	-0.7
1985	Pit-N	23	72	4	21	2	0	1	5	3	17	.292	.320	.361	.681	88	-1	-1	103	69	8	.577	1	0	0	4	C	0.4
1986	Pit-N	49	110	11	37	6	0	0	14	9	13	.336	.387	.391	.777	115	2	2	100	130	16	.667	0	1	-1	4	C	0.7
1987	Pit-N	75	192	16	52	8	1	1	22	15	23	.271	.324	.339	.662	73	-6	-8	104	129	20	.541	0	2	-1	-1	C	-0.3
1988	Pit-N	49	118	8	33	6	0	2	18	9	9	.280	.341	.381	.722	110	1	1	98	141	13	.600	1	4	-2	1	C	0.2
Total	7	316	791	57	212	31	1	4	82	46	114	.268	.311	.325	.636	75	-26	-27	101	122	77	.524	4	7	-3	6	C	-0.8

■ **JOSE ORTIZ** Ortiz, Jose Luis (Irizarry) b: 6/25/47, Ponce, P.R. BR/TR, 5'9.5", 155 lbs. Deb: 9/04/69

YEAR	TM/L	G	AB	R	H	2B	3B	HR	RBI	BB	SO	AVG	OBP	SLG	PRO	/A	BR	/A	PF	CHI	RC	TA	SB	CS	SBR	FR	POS	TPR
1969	Chi-A	16	11	0	3	1	0	0	2	1	0	.273	.333	.364	.697	87	-0	-0	108	201	1	.625	0	0	0	-2	/O	-0.1
1970	Chi-A	15	24	4	8	1	0	0	1	2	2	.333	.407	.375	.782	111	1	1	106	45	4	.813	1	0	0	1	/O	0.2
1971	Chi-N	36	88	10	26	7	1	0	3	4	10	.295	.347	.398	.745	101	1	0	110	35	12	.688	2	2	-1	-0	/O	-0.1
Total	3	67	123	14	37	9	1	0	6	7	12	.301	.358	.390	.748	102	2	1	109	52	18	.705	3	2	-0	-1	/O	0.0

■ **ROBERTO ORTIZ** Ortiz, Roberto Gonzalo (Nunez) b: 6/30/15, Camaguey, Cuba d: 9/15/71, Miami, Fla. BR/TR, 6'4", 200 lbs. Deb: 9/06/41

YEAR	TM/L	G	AB	R	H	2B	3B	HR	RBI	BB	SO	AVG	OBP	SLG	PRO	/A	BR	/A	PF	CHI	RC	TA	SB	CS	SBR	FR	POS	TPR
1941	Was-A	22	79	10	26	1	2	1	17	3	10	.329	.354	.430	.784	109	1	1	98	163	11	.661	0	1	-1	-3	O	-0.3
1942	Was-A	20	42	4	7	1	3	1	4	5	11	.167	.271	.405	.676	93	-1	-1	96	70	5	.657	0	0	0	-1	/O	-0.1
1943	Was-A	1	4	0	1	0	0	0	0	0	0	.250	.250	.250	.500	45	-0	-0	104	0	0	.250	0	1	-1	0	/O	0.0
1944	Was-A	85	316	36	80	11	4	5	35	19	47	.253	.312	.361	.673	103	-4	0	90	100	38	.607	4	1	1	-8	O	-1.0
1949	Was-A	40	129	12	36	3	0	1	11	9	12	.279	.326	.326	.652	80	-5	-4	91	84	13	.526	0	0	0	-3	O	-0.6

YEAR	TM/L	G	AB	R	H	2B	3B	HR	RBI	BB	SO	AVG	OBP	SLG	PRO	/A	BR	/A	PF	CHI	RC	TA	SB	CS	SBR	FR	POS	TPR
1950	Was-A	39	75	4	17	2	1	0	8	7	12	.227	.301	.280	.581	50	-6	-6	99	132	7	.483	0	0	0	-3	O	-0.8
	Phi-A	6	14	1	1	0	0	0	3	0	3	.071	.071	.071	.143	-71	-3	-3	90	0	0	.071	0	0	0	-1	/O	-0.3
	Yr	45	89	5	18	2	1	0	11	7	15	.202	.268	.247	.515	33	-9	-9	98	117	6	.417	0	0	0	-4		-1.1
Total	6	213	659	67	168	18	10	8	78	43	95	.255	.310	.349	.659	87	-19	-13	92	103	75	.580	4	3	-1	-18	O	-3.1
■ **OSSIE ORWOLL**	Orwoll, Oswald Christian b: 11/17/1900, Portland, Ore. d: 5/8/67, Decorah, Iowa BL/TL, 6', 174 lbs. Deb: 4/13/28																											
1928	Phi-A	64	170	28	52	13	2	0	22	16	24	.306	.366	.406	.771	100	1	0	103	109	26	.739	3	1	0	-3	1P	0.0
1929	Phi-A	30	51	6	13	2	1	0	6	2	11	.255	.283	.333	.616	53	-3	-4	109	121	5	.500	0	0	0	-1	P/O	-0.2
Total	2	94	221	34	65	15	3	0	28	18	35	.294	.347	.389	.736	89	-3	-4	104	112	31	.682	3	1	0	-4	/P1O	-0.2
■ **FRED OSBORN**	Osborn, Wilfred Pearl "Ossie" b: 11/28/1883, Nevada, Ohio d: 9/2/54, Upper Sandusky, O. BL/TR, 5'9", 178 lbs. Deb: 6/08/07																											
1907	Phi-N	56	163	22	45	2	3	0	9	3		.276	.289	.325	.614	91	-2	-2	104	64	17	.508	4			2	O/1	-0.2
1908	Phi-N	152	555	62	148	19	12	2	44	30		.267	.304	.355	.659	113	6	6	100	88	62	.597	16			11	*O	1.8
1909	Phi-N	58	189	14	35	4	1	0	19	12		.185	.238	.217	.455	40	-13	-14	106	169	11	.390	6			2	O	-1.5
Total	3	266	907	98	228	25	16	2	72	45		.251	.288	.321	.608	92	-8	-10	102	101	90	.535	26			14	O/1	0.1
■ **FRED OSBORNE**	Osborne, Frederick W. b: Hampton, Iowa Deb: 7/14/1890																											
1890	Pit-N	41	168	24	40	8	3	1	14	6	18	.238	.269	.339	.608	90	-5	-2	88	75	16	.500	0			0	O/P	-0.1
■ **BOBO OSBORNE**	Osborne, Lawrence Sidney b: 10/12/35, Chattahoochee, Ga. BL/TR, 6'1", 205 lbs. Deb: 6/27/57																											
1957	Det-A	11	27	4	4	1	0	0	1	3	7	.148	.233	.185	.419	15	-3	-3	107	79	1	.348	0	0	0	-1	/O1	-0.4
1958	Det-A	2	2	0	0	0	0	0	0	0	0	.000	.000	.000	.000	-96	-1	-1	104	0	0	.000	0	0	0	0	H	0.0
1959	Det-A	86	209	27	40	7	1	3	21	16	41	.191	.256	.278	.533	42	-16	-18	111	123	15	.448	1	0	0	-1	1/O	-1.8
1961	Det-A	71	93	8	20	7	0	2	13	20	15	.215	.354	.355	.709	94	-1	-0	96	131	13	.730	1	0	0	-2	/31	-0.1
1962	Det-A	64	74	12	17	1	0	0	7	16	25	.230	.374	.243	.617	63	-2	-3	111	154	8	.614	0	0	0	-1	3/1C	-0.4
1963	Was-A	125	358	42	76	14	1	12	44	49	83	.212	.312	.358	.670	89	-6	-5	98	112	42	.627	0	0	0	1	13	-0.5
Total	6	359	763	93	157	30	2	17	86	104	171	.206	.306	.317	.623	70	-28	-31	103	120	81	.579	2	0	1	-3	1/3OC	-3.2
■ **HARRY OSTDIEK**	Ostdiek, Henry Girard b: 4/12/1881, Ottumwa, Iowa d: 5/6/56, Minneapolis, Minn. BR/TR, 5'11", 185 lbs. Deb: 9/10/04																											
1904	Cle-A	7	18	1	3	0	1	0	3	3		.167	.286	.278	.563	80	-0	-0	102	224	2	.600	1			-0	/C	0.0
1908	Bos-A	1	3	0	0	0	0	0	0	0		.000	.000	.000	.000	-99	-1	-1	98	0	0	.000	0			0	/C	0.0
Total	2	8	21	1	3	0	1	0	3	3		.143	.250	.238	.488	57	-1	-1	101	196	2	.500	1			0	/C	0.0
■ **CHAMP OSTEEN**	Osteen, James Champlin b: 2/24/1877, Hendersonville, N.C. d: 12/14/62, Greenville, S.C. BL/TR, 5'8", 150 lbs. Deb: 03																											
1903	Was-A	10	40	4	8	0	2	0	4	2		.200	.238	.300	.538	59	-2	-2	105	104	3	.438	0			0	S	0.0
1904	NY-A	28	107	15	21	1	4	2	9	1		.196	.204	.336	.540	63	-4	-5	112	85	8	.430	0			1	3/S1	-0.3
1908	StL-N	29	112	2	22	4	0	0	11	0		.196	.196	.232	.429	41	-8	-7	94	172	5	.289	0			-2	S3	-1.0
1909	StL-N	16	45	6	9	1	0	0	7	7		.200	.308	.222	.530	68	-1	-1	96	255	3	.500	1			-1	S	-0.1
Total	4	83	304	27	60	6	6	2	31	10		.197	.223	.276	.499	57	-15	-16	102	146	18	.389	1			-1	/S31	-1.4
■ **RED OSTERGARD**	Ostergard, Roy Lund b: 5/16/1896, Denmark, Wis. d: 1/13/77, Hemet, Cal. BR/TR, 5'10.5", 175 lbs. Deb: 6/14/21																											
1921	Chi-A	12	11	2	4	0	0	0	0	0	2	.364	.364	.364	.727	87	-0	-0	99	0	1	.571	0	0	0	0	H	0.0
■ **CHARLIE OSTERHOUT**	Osterhout, Charles H. b: 1856, Syracuse, N.Y. d: 5/21/33, Syracuse, N.Y. TR , Deb: 6/23/1879																											
1879	Syr-N	2	8	0	0	0	0	0	0	0	0	.000	.000	.000	.000	-99	-2	-2	89	0	0	.000				0	/OC	0.0
■ **BRIAN OSTROSSER**	Ostrosser, Brian Leonard b: 6/17/49, Hamilton, Ont., Can BL/TR, 6', 175 lbs. Deb: 8/05/73																											
1973	NY-N	4	5	0	0	0	0	0	0	0	2	.000	.000	.000	.000	-99	-1	-1	101	0	0	.000	0	0	0	0	/S	0.0
■ **JOHNNY OSTROWSKI**	Ostrowski, John Thaddeus b: 10/17/17, Chicago, Ill. BR/TR, 5'10.5", 170 lbs. Deb: 9/24/43																											
1943	Chi-N	10	29	2	6	0	1	0	3	3	8	.207	.303	.276	.579	68	-1	-1	99	135	2	.480	0			-1	/O3	-0.1
1944	Chi-N	8	13	2	2	1	0	0	2	1	4	.154	.214	.231	.445	25	-1	-1	101	239	1	.364	0			-1	/O	-0.2
1945	Chi-N	7	10	4	3	2	0	0	1	0	0	.300	.300	.500	.800	122	0	0	99	69	2	.714	0			0	/3	0.0
1946	Chi-N	64	160	20	34	4	2	3	12	20	31	.213	.300	.319	.619	80	-5	-4	94	75	16	.563	1			-0	3/2	-0.3
1948	Bos-A	1	1	0	0	0	0	0	0	0	1	.000	.000	.000	.000	-99	-0	-0	100	0	0	.000	0	0	0	0	H	0.0
1949	Chi-A	49	158	19	42	9	4	5	31	15	41	.266	.333	.468	.802	113	1	2	98	119	24	.764	4	3	-1	-3	O/3	-0.2
1950	Chi-A	21	45	9	10	1	1	2	2	9	8	.222	.364	.422	.786	104	0	0	97	28	8	.806	0	0	0	-1	O	0.0
	Was-A	55	141	16	32	2	1	4	23	20	31	.227	.327	.340	.668	72	-6	-6	99	132	17	.628	2	0	1	-1	O	-0.6
	Chi-A	1	4	1	2	1	0	0	0	0	1	.500	.500	.750	1.250	223	1	1	97	0	2	1.500	0	0	0	-0	/O	0.0
	Yr	77	190	26	44	4	2	6	25	29	40	.232	.339	.368	.708	82	-5	-5	99	104	28	.705	2	0	1	-2		-0.6
Total	7	216	561	73	131	20	9	14	74	68	125	.234	.321	.376	.697	89	-12	-10	97	104	71	.670	7	3		-6	O/32	-1.4
■ **REGGIE OTERO**	Otero, Regino Jose (Gomez) b: 9/7/15, Havana, Cuba BL/TR, 6', 165 lbs. Deb: 9/02/45 C																											
1945	Chi-N	14	23	1	9	0	0	0	5	2	2	.391	.440	.391	.831	134	1	1	99	193	4	.786	0			0	/1	0.1
■ **AMOS OTIS**	Otis, Amos Joseph b: 4/26/47, Mobile, Ala. BR/TR, 5'11.5", 165 lbs. Deb: 9/06/67 C																											
1967	NY-N	19	59	6	13	2	0	0	1	5	13	.220	.292	.254	.547	58	-3	-3	99	28	4	.420	0	4	-2	0	O/3	-0.6
1969	NY-N	48	93	6	14	3	1	0	4	6	27	.151	.202	.204	.406	14	-11	-11	100	84	4	.329	1	0	0	-2	O/3	-1.4
1970	KC-A	159	620	91	176	**36**	9	11	58	68	67	.284	.356	.424	.780	116	12	13	98	76	102	.804	33	2	**9**	6	*O	2.1
1971	KC-A	147	555	80	167	26	4	15	79	40	74	.301	.350	.443	.793	125	16	17	99	117	87	.821	**52**	8	**11**	14	*O	3.9
1972	KC-A	143	540	75	158	28	2	11	54	50	59	.293	.356	.413	.769	128	19	18	100	93	82	.760	28	12	1	4	*O	2.2
1973	KC-A	148	583	89	175	21	4	26	93	63	47	.300	.369	.484	.853	127	29	22	109	108	103	.841	13	9	-2	-2	*OD	1.5
1974	KC-A	146	552	87	157	31	9	12	73	58	67	.284	.355	.438	.793	119	19	15	106	109	86	.769	18	5	2	2	*O/D	1.6
1975	KC-A	132	470	87	116	26	6	9	46	66	48	.247	.344	.385	.730	104	5	3	102	87	68	.777	39	11	5	-5	*O	0.1
1976	KC-A	153	592	93	165	**40**	2	18	86	55	100	.279	.345	.444	.789	130	21	21	100	110	92	.781	26	7	4	-12	*O	1.0
1977	KC-A	142	478	85	120	20	8	17	78	71	88	.251	.348	.433	.781	111	8	8	100	122	74	.796	23	7	3	-7	*O	0.0
1978	KC-A	141	486	74	145	30	7	22	96	66	54	.298	.387	.525	.911	151	35	34	102	121	102	**.994**	32	8	5	2	*O/D	3.8
1979	KC-A	151	577	100	170	28	2	18	90	68	92	.295	.372	.444	.816	113	16	12	105	118	100	.842	30	5	6	-0	*O/D	1.1
1980	KC-A	107	394	56	99	16	3	10	53	39	70	.251	.323	.383	.707	94	-4	-3	98	116	52	.685	16	1	4	15	*O	1.4
1981	KC-A	99	372	49	100	22	3	9	57	31	59	.269	.328	.417	.745	115	6	6	99	130	51	.713	16	7	1	7	O/D	1.2
1982	KC-A	125	475	73	136	25	3	11	88	37	65	.286	.340	.421	.762	108	5	5	100	**160**	64	.687	9	5	-0	6	*O	0.7
1983	KC-A	98	356	35	93	16	3	4	41	27	63	.261	.313	.357	.670	83	-8	-8	101	118	39	.585	5	2	0	5	O/D	-0.4
1984	Pit-N	40	97	6	16	4	0	0	10	7	15	.165	.221	.206	.427	22	-10	-10	94	196	4	.318	0	0	0	0	O	-1.0
Total	17	1998	7299	1092	2020	374	66	193	1007	757	1008	.277	.347	.425	.773	114	155	140	102	112	1114	.788	341	93	47	32	*O/D3	17.2
■ **BILL OTIS**	Otis, Paul Franklin b: 12/24/1889, Scituate, Mass. 5'10.5", 150 lbs. Deb: 7/04/12																											
1912	NY-A	4	20	1	1	0	0	0	2	3		.050	.174	.050	.224	-35	-3	-4	101	576	0	.211	0			1	/O	-0.2
■ **MEL OTT**	Ott, Melvin Thomas "Master Melvin" b: 3/2/09, Gretna, La. d: 11/21/58, New Orleans, La. BL/TR, 5'9", 170 lbs. Deb: 4/27/26 MH																											
1926	NY-N	35	60	7	23	2	0	0	4	1	9	.383	.393	.417	.810	121	1	2	98	55	9	.730	1			1	O	0.2
1927	NY-N	82	163	23	46	7	3	1	19	13	9	.282	.335	.380	.716	91	-2	-2	100	102	20	.658	2			-5	O	-0.7
1928	NY-N	124	435	69	140	26	4	18	77	52	36	.322	.397	.524	.921	136	24	23	102	99	89	.966	3			-2	*O/23	1.7
1929	NY-N	150	545	138	179	37	2	42	151	**113**	38	.328	.449	.635	1.084	166	58	59	100	116	157	1.287	6			16	*O/2	5.4
1930	NY-N	148	521	122	182	34	5	25	119	103	35	.349	**.458**	.578	1.036	152	45	48	98	116	139	1.224	9			-5	*O	2.8
1931	NY-N	138	497	104	145	23	8	29	115	**80**	44	.292	.392	.545	.937	**155**	35	37	97	121	111	1.031	10			-2	*O	2.8
1932	NY-N	154	566	119	180	30	8	**38**	123	**100**	39	.318	**.424**	.601	1.025	**174**	60	**61**	99	107	151	1.166	6			1	*O	4.9
1933	NY-N	152	580	98	164	36	1	23	103	**75**	48	.283	.367	.467	.834	139	28	29	99	109	105	.819	1			-9	*O	1.2
1934	NY-N	153	582	119	190	29	10	**35**	**135**	85	43	.326	.415	.591	1.006	**169**	**55**	**57**	98	115	**150**	**1.075**	0			-10	*O	3.8
1935	NY-N	152	593	113	191	33	6	31	114	82	58	.322	.407	.555	.962	162	48	51	96	103	144	1.037	7			4	*O3	4.7
1936	NY-N	150	534	120	175	28	6	**33**	135	111	41	.328	.448	**.588**	**1.036**	**176**	**62**	**62**	100	123	**153**	**1.188**	6			-5	*O	4.8
1937	NY-N	151	545	99	160	28	2	**31**	95	**102**	69	.294	.408	.523	.931	151	41	41	100	96	128	1.021	7			1	3O	3.9

YEAR	TM/L	G	AB	R	H	2B	3B	HR	RBI	BB	SO	AVG	OBP	SLG	PRO	/A	BR	/A	PF	CHI	RC	TA	SB	CS	SBR	FR	POS	TPR
1938	NY-N	150	527	**116**	164	23	6	**36**	116	118	47	.311	**.442**	.583	1.024	**174**	**62**	**59**	103	107	**149**	**1.164**	2			-1	*3O	5.4
1939	NY-N	125	396	85	122	23	2	27	80	100	50	.308	**.449**	.581	1.030	**177**	46	47	99	96	112	1.194	2			-5	O3	3.9
1940	NY-N	151	536	89	155	27	3	19	79	100	50	.289	.407	.457	.864	138	32	32	100	103	107	.915	6			-2	*O3	2.5
1941	NY-N	148	525	89	150	29	0	27	90	100	68	.286	.403	.495	.898	147	39	36	103	101	115	.976	5			-2	*O	2.9
1942	NY-N	152	549	**118**	162	21	0	**30**	93	**109**	61	.295	.415	.497	**.912**	**162**	49	**47**	103	91	122	**.990**	6			-2	*OM	4.4
1943	NY-N	125	380	65	89	12	2	18	47	95	48	.234	.391	.418	.810	139	20	22	96	81	71	.895	7			-1	*O/3M	1.9
1944	NY-N	120	399	91	115	16	4	26	82	90	47	.288	.423	.544	.967	165	40	38	104	102	101	1.087	2			-6	*O/3M	2.5
1945	NY-N	135	451	73	139	23	0	21	79	71	41	.308	.411	.499	.910	153	33	34	100	97	98	.959	1			-5	*OM	2.3
1946	NY-N	31	68	2	5	1	0	1	4	8	15	.074	.171	.132	.303	-13	-10	-10	102	124	2	.266	0			-1	OM	-1.2
1947	NY-N	4	4	0	0	0	0	0	0	0	0	.000	.000	.000	.000	-99	-1	-1	101	0	0	.000	0			0	HM	0.0
Total	22	2730	9456	1859	2876	488	72	511	1860	1708	896	.304	.414	.533	.947	155	767	772	100	105	2235	1.049	89			-39	*O3/2	60.1
■ **ED OTT**	Ott, Nathan Edward b: 7/11/51, Muncy, Pa. BL/TR, 5'10", 190 lbs. Deb: 6/10/74																											
1974	Pit-N	7	5	1	0	0	0	0	0	0	1	.000	.000	.000	.000	-99	-1	-1	98	0	0	.000	0	0	0	-1	/O	-0.1
1975	Pit-N	5	5	0	1	0	0	0	0	0	0	.200	.200	.200	.400	11	-1	-1	99	0	0	.250	0	0	0	0	/C	0.0
1976	Pit-N	27	39	2	12	2	0	0	5	3	5	.308	.357	.359	.716	103	0	0	100	138	5	.630	0	0	0	0	/C	0.1
1977	Pit-N	104	311	40	82	14	3	7	38	32	41	.264	.336	.395	.732	93	-2	-3	103	106	41	.683	7	7	-2	0	C	-0.5
1978	Pit-N	112	379	49	102	18	4	9	38	27	56	.269	.318	.409	.727	97	-0	-2	105	83	49	.653	4	1	1	8	C/O	0.9
1979	Pit-N	117	403	49	110	20	2	7	51	26	62	.273	.317	.385	.702	86	-6	-9	106	115	48	.599	0	1	-1	-5	*C	-1.1
1980	Pit-N	120	392	35	102	14	0	8	41	33	47	.260	.318	.357	.675	85	-6	-8	103	99	42	.570	1	6	-3	2	*C/O	-0.6
1981	Cal-A	75	258	20	56	8	1	2	22	17	42	.217	.268	.279	.547	56	-14	-15	104	110	19	.438	2	1	0	6	C	-0.6
Total	8	567	1792	196	465	76	10	33	195	138	254	.259	.314	.368	.682	85	-30	-39	104	102	203	.604	14	16	-5	11	C/O	-1.9
■ **BILLY OTT**	Ott, William Joseph b: 11/23/40, New York, N.Y. BB/TR, 6'1", 180 lbs. Deb: 9/04/62																											
1962	Chi-N	12	28	3	4	0	0	1	2	2	10	.143	.200	.250	.450	19	-3	-3	106	79	1	.360	0	0	0	-0	/O	-0.3
1964	Chi-N	20	39	4	7	3	0	0	1	3	10	.179	.238	.256	.495	37	-3	-3	105	41	2	.394	0	1	-1	-1	O	-0.5
Total	2	32	67	7	11	3	0	1	3	5	20	.164	.222	.254	.476	29	-6	-7	106	57	4	.386	0	1	-1	-2	/O	-0.8
■ **JOE OTTEN**	Otten, Joseph G. b: Murphysboro, Ill. TR , Deb: 7/05/1895																											
1895	StL-N	26	87	8	21	0	0	0	8	5	8	.241	.283	.241	.524	38	-8	-8	100	106	7	.424	2			0	C/O	-0.5
■ **BILLY OTTERSON**	Otterson, William John b: 5/4/1862, Pittsburgh, Pa. d: 9/21/40, Pittsburgh, Pa. BR/TR, 5'7", 124 lbs. Deb: 9/04/1887																											
1887	Bro-a	30	100	16	20	4	1	2		8		.200	.259	.320	.579	64	-5	-5	99	0	11	.600	8			0	S	-0.3
■ **PHIL OUELLETTE**	Ouellette, Philip Roland b: 11/10/61, Salem, Ore. BB/TR, 6', 190 lbs. Deb: 9/10/86																											
1986	SF-N	10	23	1	4	0	0	0	0	3	3	.174	.269	.174	.443	26	-2	-2	96	0	1	.318	0	0	0	-0	/C	-0.2
■ **JOHNNY OULLIBER**	Oulliber, John Andrew b: 2/24/11, New Orleans, La. d: 12/26/80, New Orleans, La. BR/TR, 5'11", 165 lbs. Deb: 7/25/33																											
1933	Cle-A	22	75	9	20	1	0	0	3	4	5	.267	.313	.280	.592	55	-4	-5	105	48	7	.473	0	0	0	-4	O	-0.8
■ **CHINK OUTEN**	Outen, William Austin b: 6/17/05, Mt.Holly, N.C. d: 9/11/61, Durham, N.C. BL/TR, 6', 200 lbs. Deb: 4/16/33																											
1933	Bro-N	93	153	20	38	10	0	4	17	20	15	.248	.335	.392	.727	111	2	2	97	89	22	.692	1			1	C	0.5
■ **JIMMY OUTLAW**	Outlaw, James Paulus b: 1/20/13, Orme, Tenn. BR/TR, 5'8", 165 lbs. Deb: 4/20/37																											
1937	Cin-N	49	165	18	45	7	3	0	11	3	31	.273	.290	.352	.641	81	-6	-5	91	68	17	.529	2			6	3	0.3
1938	Cin-N	4	0	1	0	0	0	0	0	0	0	—	—	—	—	—	0	0	98	—	—	—	0			0	R	0.0
1939	Bos-N	65	133	15	35	2	0	0	5	10	14	.263	.315	.278	.593	66	-7	-6	92	49	13	.490	1			-2	O/3	-0.8
1943	Det-A	20	67	8	18	1	0	1	6	8	4	.269	.347	.328	.675	93	-0	-0	106	88	8	.600	0	0	0	0	O	0.0
1944	Det-A	139	535	69	146	20	6	3	57	41	40	.273	.327	.350	.677	89	-5	-8	105	111	60	.578	7	8	-3	-3	*O	-1.8
1945	Det-A	132	446	56	121	16	5	0	34	45	33	.271	.338	.330	.668	89	-3	-6	106	84	52	.588	6	7	-2	-3	*O3	-1.6
1946	Det-A	92	299	36	78	14	2	2	31	29	24	.261	.328	.341	.669	81	-5	-8	108	109	33	.583	5	4	-1	-2	O3	-1.0
1947	Det-A	70	127	20	29	7	1	0	15	21	14	.228	.338	.299	.637	75	-3	-4	104	145	15	.614	3	1	0	-6	O/3	-1.0
1948	Det-A	74	198	33	56	12	0	0	25	31	15	.283	.383	.343	.726	97	-0	1	96	124	27	.662	0	1	-1	-4	3O	-0.5
1949	Det-A	5	4	1	1	0	0	0	0	0	1	.250	.250	.250	.500	30	-0	-0	108	0	0	.250	0	0	0	0	H	0.0
Total	10	650	1974	257	529	79	17	6	184	188	176	.268	.333	.334	.668	85	-30	-37	103	100	243	.598	24	21		-13	O3	-6.4
■ **MICKEY OWEN**	Owen, Arnold Malcolm b: 4/4/16, Nixa, Mo. BR/TR, 5'10", 190 lbs. Deb: 5/02/37 C																											
1937	StL-N	80	234	17	54	4	2	0	20	15	13	.231	.277	.265	.542	48	-17	-17	101	116	17	.415	1			-0	C	-1.4
1938	StL-N	122	397	45	106	25	2	4	36	32	14	.267	.325	.370	.695	82	-5	-11	111	82	46	.598	2			2	*C	-0.3
1939	StL-N	131	344	32	89	18	2	3	35	43	28	.259	.344	.349	.693	82	-6	-8	105	99	42	.643	6			-12	*C	-1.5
1940	StL-N	117	307	27	81	16	2	0	27	34	13	.264	.341	.329	.670	84	-5	-6	102	99	35	.597	4			-8	*C	-0.9
1941	Bro-N	128	386	32	89	15	2	1	44	34	14	.231	.296	.288	.584	63	-18	-19	103	139	33	.477	1			-2	*C	-0.8
1942	Bro-N	133	421	53	109	16	3	0	44	44	17	.259	.330	.311	.642	87	-5	-6	102	125	43	.567	10			-6	*C	-0.9
1943	Bro-N	106	365	31	95	11	2	0	54	25	15	.260	.309	.301	.611	77	-11	-11	100	177	34	.502	4			-1	*C/3S	-0.7
1944	Bro-N	130	461	43	126	20	3	1	42	36	17	.273	.326	.336	.662	87	-8	-7	99	97	48	.552	4			10	*C/2	0.9
1945	Bro-N	24	84	5	24	9	0	0	11	10	2	.286	.368	.393	.761	117	2	2	96	118	11	.677	0			-2	C	0.1
1949	Chi-N	62	198	15	54	9	3	2	18	12	13	.273	.318	.379	.696	91	-4	-3	94	84	24	.610	1			1	C	0.0
1950	Chi-N	86	259	22	63	11	0	2	21	13	16	.243	.282	.309	.591	53	-17	-19	105	94	21	.471	2			2	C	-1.3
1951	Chi-N	58	125	10	23	6	0	0	15	19	13	.184	.292	.232	.524	44	-10	-9	97	200	9	.462	1	0	0	-1	C	-0.8
1954	Bos-A	32	68	6	16	3	0	1	11	9	6	.235	.325	.324	.648	78	-2	-2	100	167	7	.554	0	1	-1	-0	C	-0.1
Total	13	1209	3649	338	929	163	21	14	378	326	181	.255	.318	.322	.640	76	-106	-116	102	117	371	.569	36	1		-16	*C/32S	-7.7
■ **DAVE OWEN**	Owen, Dave b: 4/25/58, Cleburne, Tex. BB/TR, 6'2", 170 lbs. Deb: 9/06/83																											
1983	Chi-N	16	22	1	2	0	1	0	2	2	7	.091	.167	.182	.348	-3	-3	-3	101	198	1	.350	1	0	0	1	S/3	0.0
1984	Chi-N	47	93	8	18	2	2	1	10	8	15	.194	.272	.290	.562	53	-5	-6	110	131	8	.494	1	2	-1	0	S/32	-0.2
1985	Chi-N	22	19	6	7	0	0	0	4	1	5	.368	.400	.368	.768	100	0	0	116	228	3	.692	1	1	-0	0	/S32	0.0
1988	KC-A	8	5	0	0	0	0	0	0	0	3	.000	.000	.000	.000	-97	-1	-1	103	0	0	.000	0	0	0	-0	/SC	0.0
Total	4	93	139	15	27	2	3	1	16	11	30	.194	.263	.273	.537	46	-9	-11	109	150	11	.470	3	3	-1	1	/S32C	-0.2
■ **LARRY OWEN**	Owen, Lawrence Thomas b: 5/31/55, Cleveland, Ohio BR/TR, 5'11", 185 lbs. Deb: 8/14/81																											
1981	Atl-N	13	16	0	0	0	0	0	0	1	4	.000	.059	.000	.059	-83	-4	-4	100	0	0	.063	0	0	0	1	C	-0.2
1982	Atl-N	2	3	1	1	1	0	0	0	0	1	.333	.333	.667	1.000	162	0	0	107	0	1	1.000	0	0	0	0	/C	0.0
1983	Atl-N	17	17	0	2	0	0	0	1	0	2	.118	.118	.118	.235	-33	-3	-3	106	198	0	.125	0	1	-1	0	C	-0.2
1985	Atl-N	26	71	7	17	3	0	2	12	8	17	.239	.316	.366	.683	85	-1	-1	106	149	8	.607	0	0	0	1	C	0.1
1987	KC-A	76	164	17	31	6	0	5	14	16	51	.189	.261	.317	.578	51	-11	-12	104	83	13	.493	0	0	0	-0	C	-0.5
1988	KC-A	40	81	5	17	1	0	1	3	9	23	.210	.304	.259	.564	58	-4	-4	103	50	7	.500	0	0	0	-2	C	-0.4
Total	6	174	352	30	68	11	0	8	30	34	98	.193	.268	.293	.561	51	-23	-25	104	89	30	.488	0	1	-1	-1	C	-1.2
■ **MARV OWEN**	Owen, Marvin James "Freck" b: 3/22/06, Agnew, Cal. BR/TR, 6'1", 175 lbs. Deb: 4/16/31																											
1931	Det-A	105	377	35	84	11	6	3	39	29	38	.223	.282	.308	.590	53	-25	-27	104	105	34	.505	2	2	-1	-2	S31/2	-2.4
1933	Det-A	138	550	77	144	24	9	2	65	44	56	.262	.321	.349	.670	73	-18	-23	107	116	63	.593	2	2	-1	-8	*3	-1.9
1934	Det-A	154	565	79	179	34	9	8	96	59	37	.317	.385	.451	.837	118	13	15	98	117	100	.825	3	3	-1	-6	*3	0.8
1935	Det-A	134	483	52	127	24	5	2	71	43	37	.263	.326	.346	.672	76	-19	-16	97	139	56	.592	1	4	-2	-9	*3	-2.4
1936	Det-A	154	583	72	172	20	4	9	105	53	41	.295	.361	.389	.750	89	-13	-9	95	137	84	.710	9	6	-1	-3	*3/1	-0.9
1937	Det-A	107	396	48	114	22	5	1	45	41	24	.288	.358	.376	.734	78	-8	-14	109	103	54	.682	3	4	-2	-8	*3	-1.8
1938	Chi-A	141	577	84	162	23	6	6	55	45	31	.281	.337	.373	.710	79	-20	-18	98	77	74	.644	6	4	-1	-1	*3	-1.4
1939	Chi-A	58	194	22	46	9	0	0	15	16	15	.237	.302	.284	.585	47	-14	-16	107	92	17	.494	4	5	-2	-3	3	-2.0
1940	Bos-A	20	57	4	12	0	0	0	6	8	4	.211	.308	.211	.518	37	-5	-5	101	181	4	.417	0	0	0	1	/31	-0.3
Total	9	1011	3782	473	1040	167	44	31	497	338	283	.275	.339	.367	.706	80	-110	-114	101	114	485	.643	30	30	-9	-39	3/1S2	-12.3

YEAR	TM/L	G	AB	R	H	2B	3B	HR	RBI	BB	SO	AVG	OBP	SLG	PRO	/A	BR	/A	PF	CHI	RC	TA	SB	CS	SBR	FR	POS	TPR
■ SPIKE OWEN	Owen, Spike Dee b: 4/19/61, Cleburne, Tex. BB/TR, 5'9", 165 lbs. Deb: 6/25/83																											
1983	Sea-A	80	306	36	60	11	3	2	21	24	44	.196	.259	.271	.530	46	-22	-22	100	89	23	.469	10	6	-1	13	S	-0.4
1984	Sea-A	152	530	67	130	18	8	3	43	46	63	.245	.309	.326	.636	74	-17	-18	102	96	56	.576	16	8	0	17	*S	1.0
1985	Sea-A	118	352	41	91	10	6	6	37	34	27	.259	.324	.372	.696	95	-5	-2	95	98	44	.649	11	5	0	15	*S	2.2
1986	Sea-A	112	402	46	99	22	6	0	35	34	42	.246	.307	.331	.637	71	-14	-16	105	107	40	.533	1	3	-2	29	*S	1.7
	Bos-A	42	126	21	23	2	1	1	10	17	9	.183	.285	.238	.523	45	-9	-9	100	121	10	.481	3	1	0	-5	S	-1.1
	Yr	154	528	67	122	24	7	1	45	51	51	.231	.301	.309	.610	65	-23	-26	104	111	53	.534	4	4	-1	24		0.6
1987	Bos-A	132	437	50	113	17	7	2	48	53	43	.259	.340	.343	.683	84	-9	-9	99	123	52	.630	11	8	-2	-10	*S	-1.3
1988	Bos-A	89	257	40	64	14	1	5	18	27	27	.249	.325	.370	.695	86	-2	-5	109	65	31	.617	0	1	-1	-1	S/D	-0.2
Total	6	725	2410	301	580	94	32	19	212	235	255	.241	.311	.330	.641	75	-78	-82	101	100	255	.584	52	32	-4	58	S/D	1.9
■ FRANK OWENS	Owens, Frank Walter "Yip" b: 1/26/1886, Toronto, Ont., Can. d: 7/2/58, Minneapolis, Minn. BR/TR, 6', 170 lbs. Deb: 9/11/05																											
1905	Bos-A	1	2	0	0	0	0	0	0	0		.000	.000	.000	.000	-99	-0	-0	100	0	0	.000	0			0	/C	0.0
1909	Chi-A	64	174	12	35	4	1	0	17	8		.201	.245	.236	.480	53	-10	-9	97	160	10	.388	3			-3	C	-0.8
1914	Bro-F	58	184	15	51	7	3	2	20	9	16	.277	.311	.380	.691	97	-1	-1	101	95	23	.609	2			-1	C	0.0
1915	Bal-F	99	334	32	84	14	7	3	28	17	34	.251	.288	.362	.650	86	-5	-7	107	78	38	.568	4			1	C	-0.4
Total	4	222	694	59	170	25	11	5	65	34	50	.245	.282	.334	.616	81	-16	-18	103	103	71	.529	9			-3	C	-1.2
■ JACK OWENS	Owens, Furman Lee b: 5/6/08, Converse, S.C. d: 11/14/58, Greenville, S.C. BR/TR, 6'1", 186 lbs. Deb: 9/21/35																											
1935	Phi-A	2	8	0	2	0	0	0	1	0	1	.250	.250	.250	.500	30	-1	-1	100	173	0	.333	0	0	0	0	/C	0.0
■ RED OWENS	Owens, Thomas Llewellyn b: 11/1/1874, Pottsville, Pa. d: 8/20/52, Harrisburg, Pa. BR/TR, Deb: 7/28/1899																											
1899	Phi-N	8	21	0	1	0	0	0	1	2		.048	.130	.048	.178	-51	-4	-4	97	307	0	.150	0			0	/2	-0.3
1905	Bro-N	43	168	14	36	6	2	1	20	6		.214	.241	.292	.533	63	-8	-8	96	128	12	.424	1			-1	2	-0.5
Total	2	51	189	14	37	6	2	1	21	8		.196	.228	.265	.493	49	-13	-12	96	149	13	.388	1			-1	/2	-0.8
■ HENRY OXLEY	Oxley, Henry Havelock b: 1/4/1858, Covehead, P.E.I., Canada. d: 10/12/45, Somerville, Mass. Deb: 7/30/1884																											
1884	NY-N	3	4	0	0	0	0	0	0	1	2	.000	.200	.000	.200	-32	-1	-1	98	0	0	.250				0	/C	0.0
	NY-a	1	3	0	0	0	0	0		0		.000	.000	.000	.000	-99	-1	-1	100	0	0	.000				0	/C	0.0
Total	1	4	7	0	0	0	0	0	0	1	2	.000	.125	.000	.125	-57	-1	-1	99	0	0	.143				0	/C	0.0
■ ANDY OYLER	Oyler, Andrew Paul "Pepper" b: 5/5/1880, Newville, Pa. d: 10/24/70, E.Pennsboro Twp., Cumberland County, Pa. BR/TR, 5'6.5", 138 lbs. Deb: 5/08/02																											
1902	Bal-A	27	77	9	17	1	0	1	6	8		.221	.294	.273	.567	58	-4	-4	102	82	7	.533	3			-4	3/OS2	-0.7
■ RAY OYLER	Oyler, Raymond Francis b: 8/4/38, Indianapolis, Ind. d: 1/26/81, Seattle, Wash. BR/TR, 5'11", 165 lbs. Deb: 4/18/65																											
1965	Det-A	82	194	22	36	6	0	5	13	21	61	.186	.265	.294	.559	56	-11	-12	105	75	14	.473	1	0	0	-4	S2/13	-1.2
1966	Det-A	71	210	16	36	8	3	1	9	23	62	.171	.263	.252	.515	48	-14	-14	102	67	14	.439	0	0	0	2	S	-0.8
1967	Det-A	148	367	33	76	14	2	1	29	37	91	.207	.283	.264	.548	63	-16	-16	99	121	28	.449	0	2	-1	5	*S	-0.1
1968	Det-A	111	215	13	29	6	1	1	12	20	59	.135	.215	.186	.401	21	-20	-21	106	120	8	.316	0	2	-1	-7	*S	-2.4
1969	Sea-A	106	255	24	42	5	0	7	22	31	80	.165	.260	.267	.527	48	-18	-18	98	99	17	.455	1	2	-1	-7	*S	-2.1
1970	Cal-A	24	24	2	2	0	0	0	1	3	6	.083	.185	.083	.269	-26	-4	-4	92	202	1	.227	0	0	0	0	S/3	-0.2
Total	6	542	1265	110	221	39	6	15	86	135	359	.175	.259	.251	.510	48	-83	-85	102	102	83	.441	2	6	-3	-10	S/231	-6.8
■ CHARLIE PABOR	Pabor, Charles Henry b: 9/24/1849, New York, N.Y. d: 4/22/13, New Haven, Conn. TL, 5'8", 155 lbs. Deb: 5/04/1871 M																											
1871	Cle-n	29	142	24	44							.310															*O/PM	
1872	Cle-n	20	93	12	25							.269															O/P	
1873	Atl-n	55	237	36	82							.346															*O	
1874	Phi-n	17	83	11	18							.217															/O	
1875	Atl-n	42	157	15	36							.229															O/PM	
	NH-n	6	25	4	8							.320															OM	
	Yr	48	182	19	44							.242																
Total	5 n	169	737	102	213							.289															OM	
■ ED PABST	Pabst, Edward D. A. b: 1868, St.Louis, Mo. d: 6/19/40, St.Louis, Mo. 5'11", 170 lbs. Deb: 9/26/1890																											
1890	Phi-a	8	25	7	10	2	0	0		5		.400	.500	.480	.980	198	3	3	97	0	8	1.333	3			0	/O	0.3
	StL-a	4	14	1	2	0	1	0		0		.143	.143	.286	.429	23	-1	-2	116	0	1	.333	0			0	/O	-0.1
	Yr	12	39	8	12	2	1	0	0	5		.308	.386	.410	.797	133	2	2	103	0	8	.889	3			0		0.2
Total	1	12	39	8	12	2	1	0	0	5		.308	.386	.410	.797	133	2	2	103	0	8	.889	3			0	/O	0.2
■ JIM PACIOREK	Paciorek, James Joseph b: 6/7/60, Detroit, Mich. BB/TR, 6'3", 203 lbs. Deb: 4/09/87																											
1987	Mil-A	48	101	16	23	5	0	2	10	12	20	.228	.310	.337	.646	71	-4	-4	102	100	11	.580	1	0	0	-2	13/OD	-0.7
■ JOHN PACIOREK	Paciorek, John Francis b: 2/11/45, Detroit, Mich. BR/TR, 6'2", 200 lbs. Deb: 9/29/63																											
1963	Hou-N	1	3	4	3	0	0	0	3	2	0	1.000	1.000	1.000	2.000	518	2	2	92	363	4	—	0	0	0	0	/O	0.2
■ TOM PACIOREK	Paciorek, Thomas Marian b: 11/2/46, Detroit, Mich. BR/TR, 6'4", 215 lbs. Deb: 9/12/70																											
1970	LA-N	8	9	2	2	1	0	0	0	0	3	.222	.300	.333	.633	77	-0	-0	90	0	1	.571	0	0	0	-1	/O	0.0
1971	LA-N	2	2	0	1	0	0	0	1	0	0	.500	.500	.500	1.000	186	0	0	99	407	1	1.000	0	0	0	-0	/O	0.0
1972	LA-N	11	47	4	12	4	0	1	6	1	7	.255	.271	.404	.675	95	-1	-1	94	108	5	.583	1	0	0	1	/1O	0.0
1973	LA-N	96	195	26	51	8	0	5	18	11	35	.262	.304	.379	.684	88	-3	-4	100	81	20	.574	3	3	-1	-13	O/1	-2.2
1974	LA-N	85	175	23	42	8	6	1	24	10	32	.240	.285	.371	.656	89	-5	-3	93	136	17	.554	1	3	-2	-15	O/1	-2.3
1975	LA-N	62	145	14	28	8	0	1	5	11	29	.193	.250	.269	.519	46	-11	-10	95	46	9	.439	4	3	-1	-10	O	-2.3
1976	Atl-N	111	324	39	94	10	4	4	36	19	57	.290	.335	.383	.718	93	1	-3	111	102	40	.614	2	3	-1	-12	O1/3	-2.0
1977	Atl-N	72	155	20	37	8	0	3	15	6	46	.239	.267	.348	.615	56	-8	-11	113	95	15	.513	1	0	0	-2	1/O3	-1.4
1978	Atl-N	5	9	2	3	0	0	0	0	0	1	.333	.333	.333	.667	78	-0	-0	112	0	1	.500	0	0	0	0	/1	0.0
	Sea-A	70	251	32	75	20	3	4	30	15	39	.299	.338	.450	.789	118	6	5	102	97	36	.707	2	2	-1	-4	OD/1	0.0
1979	Sea-A	103	310	38	89	23	4	6	42	28	62	.287	.356	.445	.801	114	6	6	100	103	49	.766	6	4	-1	-5	O1	-0.2
1980	Sea-A	126	418	44	114	19	1	15	59	17	67	.273	.303	.431	.733	96	-2	-4	103	102	50	.630	3	2	-0	-4	O1D	-1.0
1981	Sea-A	104	405	50	132	28	2	14	66	35	50	.326	.385	.509	.894	156	28	29	100	110	76	.881	13	10	-2	8	*O	3.3
1982	Chi-A	104	382	49	119	27	4	11	55	24	53	.312	.366	.490	.856	136	17	18	97	102	68	.820	3	3	-1	2	*1/O	1.6
1983	Chi-A	115	420	65	129	32	3	9	63	25	58	.307	.350	.462	.812	118	12	10	103	114	67	.757	6	1	1	-10	1O/D	-0.1
1984	Chi-A	111	363	35	93	21	2	4	29	25	69	.256	.311	.358	.669	77	-8	-12	111	81	42	.600	6	0	2	-9	1O	-2.5
1985	Chi-A	46	122	14	30	2	0	0	9	8	22	.246	.298	.262	.560	55	-7	-7	100	112	10	.453	2	0	1	-3	OD/1	-1.0
	NY-N	46	116	14	33	3	1	1	11	6	14	.284	.325	.353	.679	92	-2	-1	97	100	13	.576	1	0	0	-4	O/1	-0.5
1986	Tex-A	88	213	17	61	7	0	4	22	3	41	.286	.306	.376	.682	89	-5	-3	96	95	22	.544	1	3	-2	-2	O13/SD	-0.9
1987	Tex-A	27	60	6	17	3	0	3	12	1	19	.283	.306	.483	.790	102	0	0	104	126	7	.660	0	1	-1	-0	1O/D	-0.1
Total	18	1392	4121	494	1162	232	30	86	503	245	704	.282	.328	.415	.744	103	18	8	102	100	548	.683	55	38	-6	-82	O1/D3S	-11.6
■ FRANKIE PACK	Pack, Frank b: 4/10/28, Morristown, Tenn. BL/TR, 6', 190 lbs. Deb: 6/05/49																											
1949	StL-A	1	1	0	0	0	0	0	0	0	1	.000	.000	.000	.000	-99	-0	-0	100	0	0	.000	0	0	0	0	H	0.0
■ DICK PADDEN	Padden, Richard Joseph "Brains" b: 9/17/1870, Martins Ferry, O. d: 10/31/22, Martins Ferry, O. BR/TR, 5'10", 165 lbs. Deb: 7/15/1896																											
1896	Pit-N	61	219	33	53	4	8	2	24	14	9	.242	.294	.361	.654	79	-9	-6	93	81	26	.620	8			-13	2	-1.4
1897	Pit-N	134	517	84	146	16	10	2	58	38		.282	.348	.364	.712	92	-7	-5	98	84	73	.695	18			-1	*2	0.4
1898	Pit-N	128	463	61	119	7	6	2	43	35		.257	.328	.311	.639	88	-7	-5	98	92	52	.593	11			-5	*2	-0.4
1899	Was-N	134	451	66	125	20	7	2	61	24		.277	.333	.366	.699	98	-4	-1	96	112	66	.706	27			-5	S2	0.1
1901	StL-N	123	489	71	125	17	7	2	62	31		.256	.300	.331	.631	88	-9	-7	97	131	58	.602	26			3	*2/S	0.4
1902	StL-A	117	413	54	109	26	3	1	40	30		.264	.314	.349	.662	83	-8	-10	102	92	50	.609	11			10	*2	0.4
1903	StL-A	29	94	7	19	3	0	0	6	9		.202	.272	.234	.506	57	-5	-4	95	100	8	.480	5			-6	2	-0.9
1904	StL-A	132	453	42	108	19	4	0	36	40		.238	.300	.298	.598	97	-3	-1	95	102	49	.574	23			-12	*2	-1.3
1905	StL-A	16	58	5	10	1	1	0	4	3		.172	.213	.224	.437	44	-4	-3	91	112	3	.396	3			-1	2	-0.4

YEAR	TM/L	G	AB	R	H	2B	3B	HR	RBI	BB	SO	AVG	OBP	SLG	PRO	/A	BR	/A	PF	CHI	RC	TA	SB	CS	SBR	FR	POS	TPR
Total	9	874	3157	423	814	113	46	11	334	224	9	.258	.316	.333	.649	88	-56	-43	97	101	385	.620	132			-30	2/S	-3.1
■ **TOM PADDEN**	Padden, Thomas Francis b: 10/6/08, Manchester, N.H. d: 6/10/73, Manchester, N.H. BR/TR, 5'11.5", 170 lbs. Deb: 5/29/32																											
1932	Pit-N	47	118	13	31	6	1	0	10	9	7	.263	.315	.331	.645	74	-4	-4	99	95	13	.552	0			0	C	-0.1
1933	Pit-N	30	90	5	19	2	0	0	8	2	6	.211	.237	.233	.470	36	-8	-7	95	143	5	.329	0			1	C	-0.5
1934	Pit-N	82	237	27	76	12	2	0	22	30	23	.321	.399	.388	.787	106	5	4	105	86	37	.733	3			-3	C	0.3
1935	Pit-N	97	302	35	82	9	1	1	30	48	26	.272	.371	.318	.689	81	-3	-6	107	109	39	.639	1			8	C	0.1
1936	Pit-N	88	281	22	70	9	2	1	31	22	41	.249	.304	.306	.610	66	-14	-13	98	123	27	.495	0			5	C	-0.4
1937	Pit-N	35	98	14	28	2	0	0	8	13	11	.286	.369	.306	.675	83	-1	-2	102	96	12	.611	1			2	C	0.1
1943	Phi-N	17	41	5	12	0	0	0	1	2	6	.293	.341	.293	.634	89	-1	-0	94	30	4	.484	0			1	C	0.1
	Was-A	3	3	1	0	0	0	0	0	1	1	.000	.250	.000	.250	-23	-0	-0	104	0	0	.333	0	0	0	0	/C	0.0
Total	7	399	1170	122	318	40	6	2	110	127	121	.272	.345	.321	.666	80	-26	-29	102	105	136	.600	5	0		13	C	-0.4
■ **DEL PADDOCK**	Paddock, Delmar Harold b: 6/8/1887, Volga, S.Dak. d: 2/6/52, Remer, Minn BL/TR, 5'9", 165 lbs. Deb: 4/14/12																											
1912	Chi-A	1	1	0	0	0	0	0	0	0		.000	.000	.000	.000	-99	-0	-0	99	0	0	.000	0			0	H	0.0
	NY-A	45	156	26	45	5	3	1	14	23		.288	.393	.378	.772	119	5	5	101	80	27	.856	9			-3	3/2O	0.1
	Yr	46	157	26	45	5	3	1	14	23		.287	.391	.376	.767	118	5	5	101	78	26	.848	9			-3	3/2O	0.1
Total	1	46	157	26	45	5	3	1	14	23		.287	.391	.376	.767	118	5	5	101	79	27	.848	9			-3	/32O	0.1
■ **DON PADGETT**	Padgett, Don Wilson b: 12/5/11, Caroleen, N.C. d: 12/9/80, High Point, N.C. BL/TR, 6', 190 lbs. Deb: 4/23/37																											
1937	StL-N	123	446	62	140	22	6	10	74	30	43	.314	.357	.457	.815	119	11	11	101	116	75	.765	4			2	*O	0.7
1938	StL-N	110	388	59	105	26	5	8	65	18	28	.271	.303	.425	.728	88	-3	-8	111	124	48	.620	0			5	O1/C	-0.5
1939	StL-N	92	233	38	93	15	3	5	53	18	11	.399	.444	.554	.998	159	22	20	105	135	54	.987	1			-7	C/1	1.5
1940	StL-N	93	240	24	58	15	1	6	41	26	14	.242	.321	.387	.708	93	-2	-3	102	137	30	.649	1			-5	C/1	-0.4
1941	StL-N	107	324	39	80	18	0	5	44	21	16	.247	.293	.349	.642	73	-9	-13	110	124	32	.532	0			-6	OC/1	-2.0
1946	Bro-N	19	30	2	5	1	0	1	9	4	4	.167	.265	.300	.565	58	-2	-2	103	280	2	.500	0			0	C	-0.1
	Bos-N	44	98	6	25	3	0	2	21	5	7	.255	.291	.347	.638	85	-3	-2	95	196	10	.534	0			-1	C	-0.2
	Yr	63	128	8	30	4	0	3	30	9	11	.234	.285	.336	.621	78	-4	-4	97	226	13	.531	0			-1		-0.3
1947	Phi-N	75	158	14	50	8	1	0	24	16	5	.316	.383	.380	.763	103	1	1	100	148	22	.675	0			0	C	0.2
1948	Phi-N	36	74	3	17	3	0	0	7	3	2	.230	.260	.270	.530	46	-6	-5	94	131	5	.397	0			1	C	-0.2
Total	8	699	1991	247	573	111	16	37	338	141	130	.288	.336	.415	.752	101	10	-0	104	133	279	.689	6			-12	CO/1	-1.0
■ **ERNIE PADGETT**	Padgett, Ernest Kitchen "Red" b: 3/1/1899, Philadelphia, Pa. d: 4/15/57, E.Orange, N.J. BR/TR, 5'8", 155 lbs. Deb: 10/03/23																											
1923	Bos-N	4	11	3	2	0	0	0	0	2	0	.182	.308	.182	.490	32	-1	-1	100	0	1	.444	0	0	0	0	/S2	0.0
1924	Bos-N	138	502	42	128	25	9	1	46	37	56	.255	.310	.347	.657	81	-17	-13	94	97	53	.569	4	9	-4	-6	*32	-1.6
1925	Bos-N	86	256	31	78	9	7	0	29	14	14	.305	.341	.395	.735	93	-5	-3	94	102	33	.645	3	5	-2	-7	2S/3	-0.9
1926	Cle-A	36	62	7	13	0	1	0	6	8	3	.210	.300	.242	.542	43	-5	-5	100	136	5	.490	1	0	0	0	3/S	-0.1
1927	Cle-A	7	7	1	2	0	0	0	0	0	2	.286	.286	.286	.571	50	-1	-0	97	0	1	.400	0	0	0	0	/2	0.0
Total	5	271	838	84	223	34	17	1	81	61	75	.266	.318	.351	.669	81	-29	-22	94	99	92	.582	8	14	-6	-13	3/2S	-2.6
■ **DENNIS PAEPKE**	Paepke, Dennis Ray b: 4/17/45, Long Beach, Cal. BR/TR, 6', 202 lbs. Deb: 6/02/69																											
1969	KC-A	12	27	2	3	1	0	0	0	2	3	.111	.172	.148	.321	-9	-4	-4	103	0	1	.240	0	0	0	-0	/C	-0.3
1971	KC-A	60	152	11	31	6	0	2	14	8	29	.204	.244	.283	.527	49	-10	-10	99	117	9	.402	0	0	0	-3	CO	-1.3
1972	KC-A	2	6	0	0	0	0	0	0	1	2	.000	.143	.000	.143	-55	-1	-1	100	0	0	.167	0	0	0	0	/C	0.0
1974	KC-A	6	12	0	2	0	0	0	0	1	2	.167	.231	.167	.397	15	-1	-1	106	0	0	.250	0	1	-1	-0	/CO	-0.1
Total	4	80	197	13	36	7	0	2	14	12	36	.183	.230	.249	.478	36	-17	-17	100	89	10	.374	0	1	-1	-4	/CO	-1.7
■ **ANDY PAFKO**	Pafko, Andrew "Handy Andy" or "Pruschka" b: 2/25/21, Boyceville, Wis. BR/TR, 6', 190 lbs. Deb: 9/24/43 C																											
1943	Chi-N	13	58	7	22	3	0	0	10	2	5	.379	.400	.431	.831	142	3	3	99	127	9	.737	1			-2	O	0.1
1944	Chi-N	128	469	47	126	16	2	6	62	28	23	.269	.315	.350	.665	86	-9	-9	101	125	50	.555	2			12	*O	-0.6
1945	Chi-N	144	534	64	159	24	12	12	110	45	36	.298	.361	.455	.816	128	17	18	99	145	92	.794	5			-2	*O	1.0
1946	Chi-N	65	234	18	66	6	4	3	39	27	15	.282	.366	.380	.746	119	4	6	94	151	33	.701	4			14	O	1.9
1947	Chi-N	129	513	68	155	25	7	13	66	31	39	.302	.346	.454	.800	110	6	6	101	95	75	.719	4			2	*O	0.3
1948	Chi-N	142	548	82	171	30	2	26	101	50	50	.312	.375	.516	.891	149	28	33	93	111	105	.874	3			8	*3	3.8
1949	Chi-N	144	519	79	146	29	2	18	69	63	33	.281	.369	.449	.818	125	14	18	94	96	86	.792	4			-1	O3	1.2
1950	Chi-N	146	514	95	156	24	8	36	92	69	32	.304	.397	.591	.989	149	41	38	105	91	124	1.057	4			-6	*O	2.6
1951	Chi-N	49	178	26	47	5	3	12	35	17	10	.264	.342	.528	.870	134	7	7	97	106	31	.841	1	1	-0	6	O	1.1
	Bro-N	84	277	42	69	11	0	18	58	35	27	.249	.350	.484	.834	125	8	9	98	119	47	.809	1	4	-2	-0	O	0.4
	Yr	133	455	68	116	16	3	30	93	52	37	.255	.347	.501	.848	128	15	16	98	115	81	.835	2	5	-2	5		1.5
1952	Bro-N	150	551	76	158	17	5	19	85	64	48	.287	.366	.439	.805	121	17	16	102	113	91	.768	4	3	-1	-0	*O3	1.2
1953	Mil-N	140	516	70	153	23	4	17	72	37	33	.297	.347	.455	.803	114	5	9	94	100	81	.733	2	1	0	-8	*O	-0.4
1954	Mil-N	138	510	61	146	22	4	14	69	37	36	.286	.339	.427	.767	105	-2	3	93	107	72	.684	1	2	-1	-5	*O	-0.7
1955	Mil-N	86	252	29	67	3	5	5	34	7	23	.266	.297	.377	.674	83	-9	-6	93	125	26	.549	1	2	-1	-8	O3	-1.5
1956	Mil-N	45	93	15	24	5	0	2	9	10	13	.258	.330	.376	.706	90	-1	-1	99	93	12	.652	0	0	0	-7	O	-0.9
1957	Mil-N	83	220	31	61	6	1	8	27	10	22	.277	.312	.423	.734	105	-2	1	90	96	28	.636	1	0	0	-9	O	-1.0
1958	Mil-N	95	164	17	39	7	1	3	23	15	17	.238	.309	.348	.657	82	-6	-4	89	144	18	.578	0	0	0	-17	O	-2.3
1959	Mil-N	71	142	17	31	8	2	1	15	14	15	.218	.293	.324	.617	68	-7	-6	95	124	13	.530	0	0	0	-9	O	-1.6
Total	17	1852	6292	844	1796	264	62	213	976	561	477	.285	.351	.449	.800	117	115	140	97	112	992	.775	38	13		-33	*O3	4.6
■ **JOSE PAGAN**	Pagan, Jose Antonio (Rodriguez) b: 5/5/35, Barceloneta, P.R. BR/TR, 5'9", 160 lbs. Deb: 8/04/59 C																											
1959	SF-N	31	46	7	8	1	0	0	1	2	8	.174	.208	.196	.404	9	-6	-6	95	45	2	.316	1	0	0	0	3/S2	-0.5
1960	SF-N	18	49	8	14	2	2	0	2	1	6	.286	.300	.408	.708	102	-1	-0	90	41	5	.590	2	2	-1	-0	S/3	0.0
1961	SF-N	134	434	38	110	15	2	5	46	31	45	.253	.306	.332	.638	70	-19	-18	98	117	42	.541	8	5	-1	-21	*S/O	-2.6
1962	SF-N	164	580	73	150	25	6	7	57	47	77	.259	.315	.359	.674	80	-16	-17	101	100	63	.593	13	9	-2	-25	*S	-2.7
1963	SF-N	148	483	46	113	12	1	6	39	26	67	.234	.279	.300	.579	70	-21	-18	96	101	40	.483	10	7	-1	-16	*S/2O	-2.3
1964	SF-N	134	367	33	82	10	1	1	28	35	66	.223	.293	.264	.557	58	-19	-19	100	115	29	.466	5	4	-1	-23	*S/O	-3.6
1965	SF-N	26	83	10	17	4	0	0	5	8	9	.205	.275	.253	.528	45	-5	-6	111	99	6	.435	1	0	0	-4	S	-0.7
	Pit-N	42	38	6	9	1	0	0	1	1	7	.237	.275	.263	.538	53	-2	-2	100	41	3	.419	1	0	0	1	3/S	0.0
	Yr	68	121	16	26	5	0	0	6	9	16	.215	.275	.256	.531	49	-8	-8	104	65	9	.443	2	0	1	-3		-0.7
1966	Pit-N	109	368	44	97	15	6	4	54	13	38	.264	.296	.370	.666	83	-8	-9	101	153	38	.543	0	2	-1	3	3S/2O	-0.6
1967	Pit-N	81	211	17	61	6	2	1	19	10	28	.289	.330	.351	.681	95	-1	-1	100	102	24	.568	1	1	-0	3	3OS/2C	0.1
1968	Pit-N	80	163	24	36	7	1	4	21	11	32	.221	.282	.350	.632	88	-2	-3	101	128	15	.549	2	3	-1	-5	3O/S21	-0.9
1969	Pit-N	108	274	29	78	11	4	9	42	17	46	.285	.329	.453	.781	123	5	7	95	111	41	.719	1	0	0	-2	3O/2	0.4
1970	Pit-N	95	230	21	61	14	1	7	29	20	24	.265	.324	.426	.750	103	-1	0	97	95	31	.676	1	1	-0	-1	3/O12	-0.2
1971	Pit-N	57	158	16	38	1	0	5	15	16	25	.241	.314	.342	.656	86	-3	-3	99	88	17	.573	0	0	0	-3	3/O1	-0.5
1972	Pit-N	53	127	11	32	9	0	3	8	5	17	.252	.286	.394	.679	89	-2	-2	103	56	14	.583	0	0	0	-6	3/O	-0.9
1973	Phi-N	46	78	4	16	5	0	0	5	1	15	.205	.215	.269	.484	31	-7	-8	108	96	3	.333	0	1	-1	1	3/1O2	-0.7
Total	15	1326	3689	387	922	138	26	52	372	244	510	.250	.300	.344	.644	79	-109	-106	99	106	373	.563	46	35	-7	-97	S3/O21C	-15.7
■ **MIKE PAGE**	Page, Michael Randy b: 7/12/40, Woodruff, S.C. BL/TR, 6'2.5", 210 lbs. Deb: 6/30/68																											
1968	Atl-N	20	28	1	5	0	0	0	1	1	9	.179	.207	.179	.385	18	-3	-3	93	84	1	.250	0	0	0	-1	/O	-0.4
■ **MITCHELL PAGE**	Page, Mitchell Otis b: 10/15/51, Los Angeles, Cal. BL/TR, 6'2", 205 lbs. Deb: 4/09/77																											
1977	Oak-A	145	501	85	154	28	8	21	75	78	95	.307	.407	.521	.928	159	37	41	95	97	117	1.078	42	5	**10**	3	*O/D	4.8
1978	Oak-A	147	516	62	147	25	7	17	70	53	95	.285	.356	.459	.815	127	19	18	101	98	82	.803	23	19	-5	-7	*OD	0.4
1979	Oak-A	133	478	51	118	11	2	9	42	52	93	.247	.325	.335	.659	88	-14	-6	89	91	51	.603	17	16	-5	-1	*D/O	-1.0
1980	Oak-A	110	348	58	85	10	4	17	51	35	87	.244	.315	.443	.758	111	2	4	95	97	47	.731	14	7	0	0	*D	0.4
1981	Oak-A	34	92	9	13	1	0	4	13	7	29	.141	.202	.283	.485	40	-8	-7	96	134	5	.432	2	1	0	0	D	-0.7
1982	Oak-A	31	78	14	20	5	0	4	7	7	24	.256	.333	.474	.808	125	2	2	95	57	10	.754	3	4	-2	0	D	0.1

YEAR	TM/L	G	AB	R	H	2B	3B	HR	RBI	BB	SO	AVG	OBP	SLG	PRO	/A	BR	/A	PF	CHI	RC	TA	SB	CS	SBR	FR	POS	TPR
1983	Oak-A	57	79	16	19	3	0	0	1	10	22	.241	.341	.278	.619	76	-2	-2	96	18	8	.569	3	3	-1	-2	DO	-0.4
1984	Pit-N	16	12	2	4	1	0	0	0	3	4	.333	.467	.417	.883	159	1	1	94	0	3	1.000	0	0	0	0	H	0.1
Total	8	673	2104	297	560	84	21	72	259	245	449	.266	.348	.429	.776	118	37	51	95	92	322	.794	104	55	-2	-7	DO	3.7
■ KARL PAGEL	Pagel, Karl Douglas b: 3/29/55, Madison, Wis. BL/TL, 6'2", 188 lbs. Deb: 9/21/78																											
1978	Chi-N	2	2	0	0	0	0	0	0	0	2	.000	.000	.000	.000	-91	-1	-1	110	0	0	.000	0	0	0	0	H	0.0
1979	Chi-N	1	1	0	0	0	0	0	0	0	1	.000	.000	.000	.000	-89	-0	-0	112	0	0	.000	0	0	0	0	/H	0.0
1981	Cle-A	14	15	3	4	0	2	1	4	4	1	.267	.421	.733	1.154	244	3	3	93	112	5	1.364	0	0	0	0	/1D	0.3
1982	Cle-A	23	18	3	3	0	0	0	2	7	11	.167	.400	.167	.567	62	-0	-0	100	267	2	.667	0	0	0	0	1/D	0.0
1983	Cle-A	8	20	1	6	0	0	0	1	0	5	.300	.300	.300	.600	62	-1	-1	105	65	2	.429	0	0	0	-1	/OD	-0.1
Total	5	48	56	7	13	0	2	1	7	11	20	.232	.358	.357	.715	100	0	0	100	151	9	.721	0	0	0	-0	/1DO	0.2
■ JIM PAGLIARONI	Pagliaroni, James Vincent "Pag" b: 12/8/37, Dearborn, Mich. BR/TR, 6'4", 210 lbs. Deb: 8/13/55																											
1955	Bos-A	1	0	0	0	0	0	0	1	0	0	—	—	—	—	—	0	-0	124	—	0	—	0	0	0	0	/C	0.0
1960	Bos-A	28	62	7	19	5	2	2	9	13	11	.306	.434	.548	.983	159	6	6	103	88	16	1.116	0	0	0	-2	C	0.5
1961	Bos-A	120	376	50	91	17	0	16	58	55	74	.242	.345	.415	.760	100	1	1	102	111	56	.735	1	1	-0	-1	*C	-0.1
1962	Bos-A	90	260	39	67	14	0	11	37	36	55	.258	.359	.438	.797	111	5	5	102	100	43	.789	2	1	0	-2	C	0.6
1963	Pit-N	92	252	27	58	5	0	11	26	36	57	.230	.331	.381	.712	106	2	2	99	85	31	.657	0	0	0	-3	C	0.2
1964	Pit-N	97	302	33	89	12	3	10	36	41	56	.295	.383	.454	.836	133	15	15	101	88	52	.808	1	0	0	-7	C	1.2
1965	Pit-N	134	403	42	108	15	0	17	65	41	84	.268	.340	.432	.772	116	8	9	100	120	57	.708	0	0	0	-15	*C	-0.1
1966	Pit-N	123	374	37	88	20	0	11	49	50	71	.235	.332	.377	.709	96	-1	-1	101	118	47	.659	0	5	-3	-19	*C	-2.0
1967	Pit-N	44	100	4	20	1	1	0	9	16	26	.200	.316	.230	.546	59	-5	-5	100	162	7	.476	0	0	0	1	C	-0.1
1968	Oak-A	66	199	19	49	4	0	6	20	24	42	.246	.333	.357	.690	111	3	3	98	96	25	.630	0	0	0	-7	C	0.0
1969	Oak-A	14	27	1	4	1	0	1	2	5	2	.148	.303	.296	.599	74	-1	-1	92	73	3	.609	0	0	0	-2	/C	-0.2
	Sea-A	40	110	10	29	4	1	5	14	13	16	.264	.341	.455	.796	123	3	3	98	86	18	.768	0	0	0	0	C/1O	0.5
	Yr	54	137	11	33	5	1	6	16	18	18	.241	.333	.423	.757	114	2	2	97	84	21	.733	0	0	0	-2		0.3
Total	11	849	2465	269	622	98	7	90	326	330	494	.252	.346	.407	.754	109	37	36	100	106	355	.736	4	7	-3	-57	C/1O	0.5
■ MIKE PAGLIARULO	Pagliarulo, Michael Timothy b: 3/15/60, Medford, Mass. BR/TR, 6'1", 205 lbs. Deb: 7/07/84																											
1984	NY-A	67	201	24	48	15	3	7	34	15	46	.239	.292	.448	.739	108	-0	1	94	122	25	.665	0	0	0	5	3	0.7
1985	NY-A	138	380	55	91	16	2	19	62	45	86	.239	.326	.442	.768	113	4	6	96	109	56	.736	0	0	0	-12	*3	-0.9
1986	NY-A	149	504	71	120	24	3	28	71	54	120	.238	.317	.464	.781	107	6	4	103	89	74	.749	4	1	1	8	*3/S	0.9
1987	NY-A	150	522	76	122	26	3	32	87	53	111	.234	.307	.479	.786	108	2	4	98	102	75	.743	1	3	-2	6	*3/1	0.5
1988	NY-A	125	444	46	96	20	1	15	67	37	104	.216	.280	.367	.647	83	-13	-11	96	131	46	.575	1	0	0	2	*3	-0.7
Total	5	629	2051	272	477	101	12	101	321	204	467	.233	.306	.441	.747	103	-1	5	98	108	277	.712	6	4	-1	9	3/S1	0.5
■ TOM PAGNOZZI	Pagnozzi, Thomas Alan b: 7/30/62, Tucson, Ariz. BR/TR, 6', 190 lbs. Deb: 4/12/87																											
1987	StL-N	27	48	8	9	1	0	2	9	4	13	.188	.250	.333	.583	54	-3	-3	99	163	4	.538	1	0	0	-1	C/1	-0.1
1988	StL-N	81	195	17	55	9	0	0	15	11	32	.282	.320	.328	.649	83	-3	-4	104	94	20	.517	0	0	0	1	C1/3	-0.3
Total	2	108	243	25	64	10	0	2	24	15	45	.263	.306	.329	.635	77	-7	-8	103	108	24	.522	1	0	0	0	/C13	-0.4
■ REY PALACIOS	Palacios, Robert Rey b: 11/8/62, Brooklyn, N.Y. BR/TR, 5'10", 190 lbs. Deb: 9/08/88																											
1988	KC-A	5	11	2	1	0	0	0	0	0	4	.091	.091	.091	.182	-47	-2	-2	103	0	0	.091	0	0	0	0	/3	-0.1
■ RAFAEL PALMEIRO	Palmeiro, Rafael (Corrales) b: 9/24/64, Havana, Cuba BL/TL, 6', 175 lbs. Deb: 9/08/86																											
1986	Chi-N	22	73	9	18	4	0	3	12	4	6	.247	.295	.425	.720	90	-1	-1	107	120	8	.617	1	1	-0	0	O	-0.1
1987	Chi-N	84	221	32	61	15	1	14	30	20	26	.276	.339	.543	.882	128	8	8	101	74	40	.861	2	2	-1	-4	O1	0.0
1988	Chi-N	152	580	75	178	41	5	8	53	38	34	.307	.353	.436	.789	120	18	15	104	81	89	.737	12	2	2	-0	*O/1	1.4
Total	3	258	874	116	257	60	6	25	95	62	66	.294	.344	.462	.807	119	26	22	104	82	136	.768	15	5	2	-4	O/1	1.3
■ EDDIE PALMER	Palmer, Edwin Henry "Baldy" b: 6/1/1893, Petty, Tex. d: 1/9/83, Marlow, Okla. BR/TR, 5'9.5", 175 lbs. Deb: 9/06/17																											
1917	Phi-A	16	52	7	11	1	0	0	5	7	7	.212	.305	.231	.536	68	-2	-2	94	150	4	.488	1			1	3/S	0.0
■ JOE PALMISANO	Palmisano, Joseph b: 11/19/02, West Point, Ga. d: 11/5/71, Albuquerque, N.Mex. BR/TR, 5'8", 160 lbs. Deb: 5/31/31																											
1931	Phi-A	19	44	5	10	2	0	0	4	6	3	.227	.320	.273	.593	54	-3	-3	105	110	4	.529	0	0	0	-0	C/2	-0.1
■ STAN PALYS	Palys, Stanley Francis b: 5/1/30, Blakely, Pa. BR/TR, 6'2", 190 lbs. Deb: 9/20/53																											
1953	Phi-N	2	2	0	0	0	0	0	0	1	0	.000	.333	.000	.333	-4	-0	-0	99	0	0	.500	0	0	0	-0	/O	0.0
1954	Phi-N	2	4	0	1	0	0	0	0	1	1	.250	.400	.250	.650	75	-0	-0	99	0	1	.667	0	0	0	0	/O	0.0
1955	Phi-N	15	52	8	15	3	0	1	8	6	5	.288	.362	.404	.766	101	0	0	102	138	8	.737	1	0	0	-0	O	0.0
	Cin-N	79	222	29	51	14	0	7	30	12	35	.230	.272	.387	.660	69	-9	-11	106	113	23	.568	1	1	-0	0	O/1	-1.1
	Yr	94	274	37	66	17	0	8	38	18	40	.241	.290	.391	.681	75	-9	-11	105	119	31	.601	2	1	0	0		-1.1
1956	Cin-N	40	53	5	12	0	0	2	5	6	13	.226	.305	.340	.645	67	-2	-3	108	88	6	.585	0	0	0	-2	O	-0.4
Total	4	138	333	42	79	17	0	10	43	26	54	.237	.294	.378	.673	73	-11	-14	105	111	37	.608	2	1	0	-2	/O1	-1.5
■ JIM PANKOVITS	Pankovits, James Franklin b: 8/6/55, Pennington Gap, Va. BR/TR, 5'10", 195 lbs. Deb: 5/27/84																											
1984	Hou-N	53	81	6	23	7	0	1	14	2	20	.284	.301	.407	.709	105	-1	0	93	152	10	.617	2	1	0	0	2/S/O	0.1
1985	Hou-N	75	172	24	42	3	0	4	14	17	29	.244	.316	.331	.647	85	-4	-3	96	81	19	.571	1	0	0	0	O2/S3	-0.3
1986	Hou-N	70	113	12	32	6	1	1	7	11	25	.283	.347	.381	.727	98	0	-0	103	61	14	.640	1	1	-0	-5	2/OC	-0.5
1987	Hou-N	50	61	7	14	2	0	1	8	6	13	.230	.299	.311	.610	67	-3	-3	93	145	6	.551	2	0	1	2	/2O3	0.0
1988	Hou-N	68	140	13	31	7	1	2	12	8	28	.221	.273	.329	.602	77	-5	-4	93	92	13	.523	2	1	0	-0	23/1	-0.3
Total	5	316	567	62	142	25	2	9	55	44	115	.250	.308	.349	.657	87	-13	-10	96	96	61	.590	8	3	1	-3	2/O3S1C	-1.0
■ KEN PAPE	Pape, Kenneth Wayne b: 10/1/51, San Antonio, Tex. BR/TR, 5'11", 195 lbs. Deb: 5/17/76																											
1976	Tex-A	21	23	7	5	1	0	1	4	3	2	.217	.357	.391	.748	117	1	1	102	128	3	.700	0	1	-1	0	/S32D	0.1
■ STAN PAPI	Papi, Stanley Gerard b: 2/4/51, Fresno, Cal. BR/TR, 6', 170 lbs. Deb: 4/11/74																											
1974	StL-N	8	4	0	1	0	0	0	0	0	0	.250	.250	.250	.500	39	-0	-0	104	386	0	.333	0	0	0	0	/S2	0.0
1977	Mon-N	13	43	5	10	2	1	0	4	1	9	.233	.250	.326	.576	54	-3	-3	98	114	3	.471	1	0	0	-1	3/S2	-0.2
1978	Mon-N	67	152	15	35	11	0	0	11	10	28	.230	.287	.303	.589	68	-7	-6	96	95	12	.468	0	0	0	-1	S3/2	-0.5
1979	Bos-A	50	117	9	22	8	0	1	6	5	20	.188	.221	.282	.503	32	-11	-12	107	64	8	.400	0	0	0	2	2S	-0.5
1980	Bos-A	1	0	0	0	0	0	0	0	0	0	—	—	—	—	—	0	0	102	—	—	—	0	0	0	0	/3	0.0
	Det-A	46	114	12	27	3	4	3	17	5	24	.237	.269	.412	.681	79	-3	-4	105	118	12	.578	0	0	0	-1	23/S/1	-0.1
	Yr	47	114	12	27	3	4	3	17	5	24	.237	.269	.412	.681	80	-3	-4	105	116	12	.578	0	0	0	-1		-0.1
1981	Det-A	40	93	8	19	2	1	3	12	3	18	.204	.229	.344	.573	60	-5	-5	105	115	7	.474	1	0	0	-1	3/12OD	-0.5
Total	6	225	523	49	114	26	6	7	51	24	99	.218	.255	.331	.586	59	-29	-31	102	100	50	.489	2	0	1	-1	/32SD1O	-1.8
■ AL PARDO	Pardo, Alberto Judas b: 9/8/62, Oviedo, Spain BB/TR, 6'2", 187 lbs. Deb: 7/03/85																											
1985	Bal-A	34	75	3	10	1	0	0	1	3	15	.133	.167	.147	.313	-13	-12	-11	99	36	2	.215	0	0	0	-1	C	-1.0
1986	Bal-A	16	51	3	7	1	0	1	3	0	14	.137	.137	.216	.353	-5	-7	-7	99	85	1	.239	0	0	0	-1	C/D	-0.6
1988	Phi-N	2	2	0	0	0	0	0	0	0	2	.000	.000	.000	.000	-99	-1	-1	101	0	0	.000	0	0	0	0	/C	0.0
Total	3	52	128	6	17	2	0	1	4	3	31	.133	.153	.172	.325	-11	-19	-19	99	55	3	.225	0	0	0	-1	/CD	-1.6
■ JOHNNY PAREDES	Paredes, Johnny Alfonso (Isambert) b: 9/2/62, Maracaibo, Venez. BR/TR, 5'11", 165 lbs. Deb: 4/29/88																											
1988	Mon-N	35	91	6	17	2	0	1	10	9	17	.187	.282	.242	.523	49	-5	-6	106	160	7	.506	5	2	0	2	2/O	-0.3
■ FREDDY PARENT	Parent, Frederick Alfred b: 11/25/1875, Biddeford, Me. d: 11/2/72, Sanford, Maine BR/TR, 5'7", 154 lbs. Deb: 7/14/1899																											
1899	StL-N	2	8	0	1	0	0	0	1	0		.125	.125	.125	.250	-28	-1	-1	108	313	0	.143	0			0	/2	0.0
1901	Bos-A	138	517	87	158	23	9	4	59	41		.306	.357	.408	.765	117	10	12	97	85	83	.747	16			-1	*S	1.7
1902	Bos-A	138	567	91	156	31	8	3	62	24		.275	.305	.374	.678	89	-10	-9	99	89	71	.613	16			5	*S	0.7
1903	Bos-A	139	560	83	170	31	17	4	80	13		.304	.319	.441	.760	115	17	9	112	118	89	.728	24			9	*S	2.5
1904	Bos-A	155	591	85	172	22	9	6	77	28		.291	.323	.389	.712	121	17	14	105	123	83	.663	20			-11	*S	0.4

YEAR	TM/L	G	AB	R	H	2B	3B	HR	RBI	BB	SO	AVG	OBP	SLG	PRO	/A	BR	/A	PF	CHI	RC	TA	SB	CS	SBR	FR	POS	TPR
1905	Bos-A	153	602	55	141	16	5	0	33	47		.234	.290	.277	.567	82	-11	-11	100	62	57	.518	25			-5	*S	-1.2
1906	Bos-A	149	600	67	141	14	10	1	49	31		.235	.273	.297	.569	81	-14	-13	98	87	54	.490	16			-2	*S/2	-1.4
1907	Bos-A	114	409	51	113	19	5	1	26	22		.276	.313	.355	.668	114	6	5	101	64	50	.605	12			3	OS/32	0.8
1908	Chi-A	119	391	28	81	7	5	0	35	50		.207	.297	.251	.548	85	-6	-4	94	137	31	.506	9			0	*S	0.0
1909	Chi-A	136	472	61	123	10	5	0	30	46		.261	.335	.303	.638	105	2	4	97	86	57	.653	32			14	SO/2	2.1
1910	Chi-A	81	258	23	46	6	1	1	16	29		.178	.266	.221	.487	56	-13	-12	95	100	19	.481	14			-3	O2/S3	-1.9
1911	Chi-A	3	9	2	4	1	0	0	3	2		.444	.545	.556	1.101	215	1	2	97	203	3	1.400	0			0	/2	0.1
Total	12	1327	4984	633	1306	180	74	20	471	333		.262	.309	.340	.649	99	-3	-5	100	95	597	.604	184			9	*SO/23	3.8
■ MARK PARENT	Parent, Mark Allen b: 9/16/61, Ashland, Ore. BR/TR, 6'5", 215 lbs. Deb: 9/20/86																											
1986	SD-N	8	14	1	2	0	0	0	0	1	3	.143	.200	.143	.343	-4	-2	-2	95	0	0	.231	0	0	0	0	/C	-0.1
1987	SD-N	12	25	0	2	0	0	0	2	0	9	.080	.080	.080	.160	-59	-6	-5	97	399	0	.087	0	0	0	0	C	-0.3
1988	SD-N	41	118	9	23	3	0	6	15	6	23	.195	.234	.373	.607	74	-5	-5	97	97	10	.521	0	0	0	4	C	0.2
Total	3	61	157	10	27	3	0	6	17	7	35	.172	.207	.306	.513	44	-12	-12	97	134	11	.420	0	0	0	5	/C	-0.2
■ KELLY PARIS	Paris, Kelly Jay b: 10/17/57, Encino, Cal. BB/TR, 6', 175 lbs. Deb: 9/01/82																											
1982	StL-N	12	29	1	3	0	0	0	1	0	7	.103	.103	.103	.207	-41	-5	-6	103	131	0	.111	0	0	0	1	/3S	-0.4
1983	Cin-N	56	120	13	30	6	0	0	7	15	22	.250	.338	.300	.638	76	-3	-3	103	77	13	.632	8	2	1	-4	32/S1	-0.5
1985	Bal-A	5	9	0	0	0	0	0	0	0	1	.000	.000	.000	.000	-99	-2	-2	99	0	0	.000	0	0	0	-0	/2D	-0.2
1986	Bal-A	5	10	0	2	0	0	0	0	0	3	.200	.200	.200	.400	10	-1	-1	99	0	0	.200	0	1	-1	0	/3D	-0.1
1988	Chi-A	14	44	6	11	0	0	3	6	0	6	.250	.250	.455	.705	95	-1	-1	97	82	5	.588	0	0	0	-0	/13	-0.1
Total	5	92	212	20	46	6	0	3	14	15	39	.217	.272	.288	.560	55	-13	-13	101	78	18	.500	8	3	1	-3	/312SD	-1.3
■ TONY PARISSE	Parisse, Louis Peter b: 6/25/11, Philadelphia, Pa. d: 6/2/56, Philadelphia, Pa. BR/TR, 5'10", 165 lbs. Deb: 9/22/43																											
1943	Phi-A	6	17	0	3	0	0	0	1	2	2	.176	.263	.176	.440	29	-1	-1	101	122	1	.333	0	0	0	0	/C	0.0
1944	Phi-A	4	4	0	0	0	0	0	0	0	1	.000	.000	.000	.000	-99	-1	-1	101	0	0	.000	0	0	0	0	/C	0.0
Total	2	10	21	0	3	0	0	0	1	2	3	.143	.217	.143	.360	6	-2	-3	101	100	1	.278	0	0	0	0	/C	0.0
■ ACE PARKER	Parker, Clarence Mc Kay b: 5/17/12, Portsmouth, Va. BR/TR, 6', 180 lbs. Deb: 4/24/37																											
1937	Phi-A	38	94	8	11	0	1	2	13	4	17	.117	.153	.202	.355	-12	-16	-16	94	178	3	.277	0	0	0	-1	S/2O	-1.3
1938	Phi-A	56	113	12	26	5	0	0	12	10	16	.230	.293	.274	.567	42	-10	-10	101	131	9	.472	1	2	-1	-4	S/23	-1.1
Total	2	94	207	20	37	5	1	2	25	14	33	.179	.231	.242	.472	19	-26	-26	98	152	12	.378	1	2	-1	-4	/S23O	-2.4
■ PAT PARKER	Parker, Clarence Perkins b: 5/22/1893, Somerville, Mass. d: 3/21/67, Claremont, N.H. 5'7", 160 lbs. Deb: 8/10/15																											
1915	StL-A	3	6	0	1	0	0	0	1	0	3	.167	.167	.167	.333	-0	-1	-1	96	340	0	.167	0	1	-1	-0	/O	-0.1
■ DAVE PARKER	Parker, David Gene b: 6/9/51, Calhoun, Miss. BL/TR, 6'5", 230 lbs. Deb: 7/12/73																											
1973	Pit-N	54	139	17	40	9	1	4	14	2	27	.288	.308	.453	.761	118	1	2	92	75	18	.667	1	1	-0	1	O	0.1
1974	Pit-N	73	220	27	62	10	3	4	29	10	53	.282	.322	.409	.731	106	0	1	98	110	28	.646	3	3	-1	2	O/1	0.0
1975	Pit-N	148	558	75	172	35	10	25	101	38	89	.308	.358	**.541**	.899	148	32	32	99	106	101	.861	8	6	-1	7	*O	3.3
1976	Pit-N	138	537	82	168	28	10	13	90	30	80	.313	.351	.475	.826	132	21	21	100	125	85	.781	19	7	2	5	*O	2.4
1977	Pit-N	159	637	107	**215**	**44**	8	21	88	58	107	**.338**	.399	.531	.929	143	42	40	103	84	130	.938	17	19	-6	30	*O/2	5.8
1978	Pit-N	148	581	102	194	32	12	30	117	57	92	**.334**	.395	**.585**	**.981**	162	**53**	**49**	105	104	**134**	1.042	20	7	2	5	*O	**5.2**
1979	Pit-N	158	622	109	193	45	7	25	94	67	101	.310	.385	.526	.911	138	39	35	106	89	131	.961	20	4	4	9	*O	4.4
1980	Pit-N	139	518	71	153	31	1	17	79	25	69	.295	.330	.458	.788	114	10	8	103	111	75	.721	10	7	-1	-2	*O	0.0
1981	Pit-N	67	240	29	62	14	3	9	48	9	25	.258	.291	.454	.745	114	1	2	96	139	30	.681	6	2	1	-6	O	-0.4
1982	Pit-N	73	244	41	66	19	3	6	29	22	45	.270	.333	.447	.780	106	5	2	110	90	34	.732	7	5	-1	-3	O	-0.2
1983	Pit-N	144	552	68	154	29	4	12	69	28	89	.279	.314	.411	.725	97	-2	-4	103	106	67	.639	12	9	-2	1	*O	-0.7
1984	Cin-N	156	607	73	173	28	0	16	94	41	89	.285	.331	.410	.741	102	5	1	106	131	80	.668	11	10	-3	0	*O	-0.7
1985	Cin-N	160	635	88	198	**42**	4	34	**125**	52	80	.312	.367	.551	.918	146	43	39	105	106	112	.861	5	13	-6	7	*O	3.7
1986	Cin-N	162	637	89	174	31	3	31	116	56	126	.273	.333	.477	.810	116	16	12	104	123	94	.743	1	6	-3	-6	*O	0.0
1987	Cin-N	153	589	77	149	28	0	26	97	44	104	.253	.314	.433	.747	92	-5	-8	104	123	77	.687	7	3	0	6	*O/1	-0.7
1988	Oak-A	101	377	43	97	18	1	12	55	32	70	.257	.315	.406	.721	106	-0	2	95	118	49	.651	0	1	-1	-2	DO/1	0.0
Total	16	2033	7693	1098	2270	443	70	285	1245	571	1246	.295	.348	.482	.830	124	259	234	103	109	1245	.809	147	103	-18	55	*O/D12	22.2
■ DIXIE PARKER	Parker, Douglas Woolley b: 4/24/1895, Forest Home, Ala. d: 5/15/72, Tuscaloosa, Ala. BL/TR, 5'11", 160 lbs. Deb: 7/28/23																											
1923	Phi-N	4	5	0	1	0	0	0	1	0	1	.200	.200	.200	.400	5	-1	-1	114	352	0	.250	0	0	0	0	/C	0.0
■ SALTY PARKER	Parker, Francis James b: 7/8/13, E.St.Louis, Ill. BR/TR, 6', 173 lbs. Deb: 8/13/36 MC																											
1936	Det-A	11	25	6	7	2	0	0	4	2	3	.280	.333	.360	.693	75	-1	-1	95	144	2	.550	0	2	-1	0	/S1	-0.1
■ WES PARKER	Parker, Maurice Wesley b: 11/13/39, Evanston, Ill. BB/TL, 6'1", 180 lbs. Deb: 4/19/64																											
1964	LA-N	124	214	29	55	7	1	3	10	14	45	.257	.306	.341	.647	89	-5	-3	92	50	23	.564	5	4	-1	-11	O1	-1.8
1965	LA-N	154	542	80	129	24	7	8	51	75	95	.238	.336	.352	.688	103	-2	4	91	104	70	.667	13	7	-0	-1	*1/O	-0.5
1966	LA-N	156	475	67	120	17	5	12	51	69	83	.253	.353	.385	.739	109	5	7	97	98	67	.714	7	3	0	3	*1O	0.3
1967	LA-N	139	413	56	102	16	5	5	31	65	83	.247	.359	.346	.705	117	4	10	88	81	55	.690	10	5	0	6	*1O	1.1
1968	LA-N	135	468	42	112	22	2	3	27	49	87	.239	.314	.314	.628	98	-5	-0	91	74	49	.553	4	6	-2	-3	*1O	-1.4
1969	LA-N	132	471	76	131	23	4	13	68	56	46	.278	.357	.427	.784	121	12	13	99	116	73	.749	4	1	1	4	*1/O	0.7
1970	LA-N	161	614	84	196	**47**	4	10	111	79	70	.319	.397	.458	.854	143	26	35	90	**147**	113	.848	8	2	1	5	*1	2.6
1971	LA-N	157	533	69	146	24	1	6	62	63	63	.274	.352	.356	.708	102	2	3	99	124	69	.648	6	1	1	0	*1O	-0.7
1972	LA-N	130	427	45	119	14	3	4	59	62	43	.279	.371	.354	.725	114	6	10	94	**152**	57	.666	3	5	-2	1	*1/O	0.0
Total	9	1288	4157	548	1110	194	32	64	470	532	615	.267	.353	.375	.729	113	44	78	93	110	575	.703	60	34	-2	3	*1O	0.3
■ BILLY PARKER	Parker, William David b: 1/14/47, Hayneville, Ala. BR/TR, 5'8", 168 lbs. Deb: 9/09/71																											
1971	Cal-A	20	70	4	16	0	1	1	6	2	20	.229	.250	.300	.550	56	-4	-4	99	102	5	.421	1	1	-0	2	2	-0.1
1972	Cal-A	36	80	11	17	2	0	2	8	9	17	.213	.292	.313	.605	90	-2	-1	88	108	7	.500	0	2	-1	-0	3/2OS	-0.1
1973	Cal-A	38	102	14	23	2	1	0	7	8	23	.225	.288	.265	.553	59	-6	-5	96	102	8	.439	0	1	-1	-1	2/SD	-0.5
Total	3	94	252	29	56	4	2	3	21	19	60	.222	.279	.290	.569	67	-12	-10	94	104	19	.465	1	4	-2	0	/23OSD	-0.7
■ FRANK PARKINSON	Parkinson, Frank Joseph "Parky" b: 3/23/1895, Dickson City, Pa. d: 7/4/60, Trenton, N.J. BR/TR, 5'11", 175 lbs. Deb: 4/13/21																											
1921	Phi-N	108	391	36	99	20	2	5	32	13	81	.253	.277	.353	.630	64	-20	-21	102	78	37	.520	3	4	-2	-1	*S/3	-1.3
1922	Phi-N	141	545	86	150	18	6	15	70	55	93	.275	.344	.413	.757	83	-5	-16	113	96	79	.714	3	4	-2	**28**	*2	0.9
1923	Phi-N	67	219	21	53	12	0	3	28	13	31	.242	.288	.338	.625	57	-12	-16	114	119	20	.518	0	4	-2	5	2S3	-1.0
1924	Phi-N	62	156	14	33	7	0	1	19	14	28	.212	.281	.276	.556	46	-11	-13	108	151	13	.492	3	1	0	0	3S2	-0.8
Total	4	378	1311	157	335	57	8	24	149	95	233	.256	.308	.366	.674	69	-48	-65	109	101	149	.595	9	13	-5	32	2S/3	-2.2
■ ART PARKS	Parks, Artie William b: 11/1/11, Paris, Ark. BL/TR, 5'9", 170 lbs. Deb: 9/25/37																											
1937	Bro-N	7	16	2	5	2	0	0	0	2	2	.313	.389	.438	.826	119	1	0	104	0	3	.818	0			0	/O	0.0
1939	Bro-N	71	239	27	65	13	2	1	19	28	14	.272	.348	.356	.704	83	-3	-5	107	79	30	.635	2			-5	O	-1.1
Total	2	78	255	29	70	15	2	1	19	30	16	.275	.351	.361	.712	86	-2	-5	107	74	33	.646	2			-5	/O	-1.1
■ BILL PARKS	Parks, William Robert b: 6/4/1849, Easton, Pa. d: 10/10/11, Easton, Pa. 5'8", 150 lbs. Deb: 4/26/1875																											
1875	Nat-n	26	115	12	21							.183															OP	
	Phi-n	2	8	0	1							.125															O	
	Yr	28	123	12	22							.179																
1876	Bos-N	1	4	0	0	0	0	0	0	0	0	.000	.000	.000	.000	-99	-1	-1	95	0	0	.000				0	/O	0.0
■ SAM PARRILLA	Parrilla, Samuel b: 6/12/43, Santurce, P.R. BR/TR, 5'11", 185 lbs. Deb: 4/11/70																											
1970	Phi-N	11	16	0	2	1	0	0	0	1	4	.125	.176	.188	.364	-3	-2	-2	96	0	1	.286	0	0	0	0	/O	-0.2
■ LANCE PARRISH	Parrish, Lance Michael b: 6/15/56, Clairton, Pa. BR/TR, 6'3", 210 lbs. Deb: 9/05/77																											
1977	Det-A	12	46	10	9	2	0	3	7	5	12	.196	.275	.435	.709	86	-1	-1	105	101	5	.641	0	0	0	2	C	0.1

YEAR	TM/L	G	AB	R	H	2B	3B	HR	RBI	BB	SO	AVG	OBP	SLG	PRO	/A	BR	/A	PF	CHI	RC	TA	SB	CS	SBR	FR	POS	TPR
1978	Det-A	85	288	37	63	11	3	14	41	11	71	.219	.255	.424	.679	81	-6	-9	108	99	29	.584	0	0	0	5	C	0.0
1979	Det-A	143	493	65	136	26	3	19	65	49	105	.276	.344	.456	.800	118	9	11	96	90	73	.744	6	7	-2	5	*C	1.9
1980	Det-A	144	553	79	158	34	6	24	82	31	109	.286	.327	.499	.826	117	15	11	105	94	80	.747	6	4	-1	8	*CD/1O	2.3
1981	Det-A	96	348	39	85	18	2	10	46	34	52	.244	.312	.394	.705	97	0	-2	105	110	38	.613	2	3	-1	1	C/D	0.2
1982	Det-A	133	486	75	138	19	2	32	87	40	99	.284	.340	.529	.868	134	21	21	100	101	86	.843	3	4	-2	10	*C/O	3.6
1983	Det-A	155	605	80	163	42	3	27	114	44	106	.269	.320	.483	.803	123	12	16	96	127	86	.725	1	3	-2	2	*CD	2.2
1984	Det-A	147	578	75	137	16	2	33	98	41	120	.237	.290	.443	.733	103	-3	0	96	117	71	.660	2	3	-1	-5	*CD	0.2
1985	Det-A	140	549	64	150	27	1	28	98	41	90	.273	.326	.479	.805	110	11	7	106	119	82	.742	2	6	-3	-4	*CD	0.5
1986	Det-A	91	327	53	84	6	1	22	62	38	83	.257	.343	.483	.826	129	10	12	95	112	57	.817	0	0	0	9	C/D	2.5
1987	Phi-N	130	466	42	114	21	0	17	67	47	104	.245	.315	.399	.714	84	-9	-11	104	115	53	.622	0	1	-1	13	*C	1.1
1988	Phi-N	123	424	44	91	17	2	15	60	47	93	.215	.296	.370	.666	89	-6	-6	101	121	46	.599	0	0	0	13	*C/1	1.3
Total	12	1399	5163	663	1328	239	25	244	827	428	1044	.257	.317	.455	.772	109	55	49	101	110	706	.728	22	31	-12	59	*C/DO1	15.9

■ **LARRY PARRISH** Parrish, Larry Alton b: 11/10/53, Winter Haven, Fla. BR/TR, 6'3", 190 lbs. Deb: 9/06/74

YEAR	TM/L	G	AB	R	H	2B	3B	HR	RBI	BB	SO	AVG	OBP	SLG	PRO	/A	BR	/A	PF	CHI	RC	TA	SB	CS	SBR	FR	POS	TPR
1974	Mon-N	25	69	9	14	5	0	0	4	6	19	.203	.286	.275	.561	55	-4	-4	104	81	6	.482	0	0	0	-3	3	-0.7
1975	Mon-N	145	532	50	146	32	5	10	65	28	74	.274	.316	.410	.725	93	-2	-7	108	103	64	.627	4	5	-2	1	*3/2S	-0.8
1976	Mon-N	154	543	65	126	28	5	11	61	41	91	.232	.288	.363	.651	84	-13	-13	100	104	54	.555	2	6	-3	4	*3	-1.4
1977	Mon-N	123	402	50	99	19	2	11	46	37	71	.246	.316	.386	.702	89	-8	-7	98	98	47	.623	2	4	-2	-6	*3	-1.5
1978	Mon-N	144	520	68	144	39	4	15	70	32	103	.277	.321	.454	.775	119	8	10	96	101	69	.683	2	3	-1	-5	*3	0.3
1979	Mon-N	153	544	83	167	39	2	30	82	41	101	.307	.358	.551	.909	141	31	29	102	85	106	.902	5	1	1	-5	*3	1.9
1980	Mon-N	126	452	55	115	27	3	15	72	36	80	.254	.315	.427	.742	106	2	2	99	122	57	.662	2	6	-3	-10	*3	-1.1
1981	Mon-N	97	349	41	85	19	3	8	44	28	73	.244	.300	.384	.684	94	-4	-4	99	112	39	.591	0	0	0	-16	3	-2.6
1982	Tex-A	128	440	59	116	15	0	17	62	30	84	.264	.316	.414	.730	106	-2	3	93	108	56	.654	5	2	0	-11	*O/3D	-1.1
1983	Tex-A	145	555	76	151	26	4	26	88	46	91	.272	.331	.474	.805	117	13	12	101	107	82	.736	0	0	0	-12	*OD	-0.1
1984	Tex-A	156	613	72	175	42	1	22	101	42	116	.285	.337	.465	.802	119	15	15	100	122	89	.725	2	4	-2	1	OD3	1.1
1985	Tex-A	94	346	44	86	11	1	17	51	33	77	.249	.316	.434	.749	95	1	-3	108	107	44	.669	0	2	-1	-5	OD/3	-0.9
1986	Tex-A	129	464	67	128	22	1	28	94	52	114	.276	.351	.509	.860	138	20	23	96	119	80	.830	3	1	0	1	D3	2.2
1987	Tex-A	152	557	79	149	22	1	32	100	49	154	.268	.330	.483	.813	109	9	7	104	112	88	.773	3	1	0	-2	*D3/O	0.3
1988	Tex-A	68	248	22	47	9	1	7	26	20	79	.190	.256	.319	.574	59	-14	-14	101	105	20	.493	0	0	0	0	D	-1.3
	Bos-A	52	158	10	41	5	0	7	26	8	32	.259	.299	.424	.723	92	-0	-2	109	117	19	.623	0	1	-1	-0	D1/O	-0.2
	Yr	120	406	32	88	14	1	14	52	28	111	.217	.272	.360	.632	72	-14	-17	105	111	40	.548	0	1	-1	-0		-1.5
Total	15	1891	6792	850	1789	360	33	256	992	529	1359	.263	.321	.439	.760	107	51	46	101	107	919	.711	30	36	-13	-69	*3DO/1S2	-5.9

■ **TOM PARROTT** Parrott, Thomas William "Tacky Tom" b: 4/10/1868, Portland, Ore. d: 1/1/32, Dundee, Ore. BR/TR, 5'10.5", 170 lbs. Deb: 6/18/1893

YEAR	TM/L	G	AB	R	H	2B	3B	HR	RBI	BB	SO	AVG	OBP	SLG	PRO	/A	BR	/A	PF	CHI	RC	TA	SB	CS	SBR	FR	POS	TPR
1893	Chi-N	7	27	4	7	1	0	0	3	1	2	.259	.286	.296	.582	54	-2	-2	104	103	2	.450	0			0	/P32	0.0
	Cin-N	24	68	5	13	1	1	1	9	1	9	.191	.203	.279	.482	28	-7	-7	101	112	4	.364	0			0	P/O	0.0
	Yr	31	95	9	20	2	1	1	12	2	11	.211	.227	.284	.511	36	-9	-9	102	113	6	.387	0			0		0.0
1894	Cin-N	68	229	51	74	12	6	4	40	17	10	.323	.372	.480	.853	106	2	2	100	90	44	.852	4			4	PO1/S32D	0.0
1895	Cin-N	64	201	35	69	13	7	3	41	11	8	.343	.377	.522	.900	123	9	6	108	100	44	.955	10			3	P1/O	0.0
1896	StL-N	118	474	62	138	13	12	7	70	11	24	.291	.307	.414	.721	95	-9	-5	95	99	65	.652	12			10	*O/P1	-0.1
Total	4	281	999	157	301	40	26	15	163	41	53	.301	.329	.438	.768	99	-8	-7	99	98	160	.725	26			16	OP/132DS	-0.1

■ **JIGGS PARROTT** Parrott, Walter Edward b: 7/14/1871, Portland, Ore. d: 4/16/1898, Phoenix, Ariz. 5'11", 160 lbs. Deb: 7/11/1892

YEAR	TM/L	G	AB	R	H	2B	3B	HR	RBI	BB	SO	AVG	OBP	SLG	PRO	/A	BR	/A	PF	CHI	RC	TA	SB	CS	SBR	FR	POS	TPR
1892	Chi-N	78	333	38	67	8	5	2	22	8	30	.201	.222	.273	.495	55	-21	-17	92	67	22	.402	7			-3	3	-1.3
1893	Chi-N	110	455	54	111	10	9	1	65	13	25	.244	.267	.312	.579	53	-31	-33	104	125	46	.526	25			11	*3/2O	-1.7
1894	Chi-N	124	517	82	128	17	9	3	64	16	35	.248	.274	.333	.607	44	-46	-53	108	99	57	.568	30			-10	*2/3	-4.2
1895	Chi-N	3	4	0	1	0	0	0	0	0	0	.250	.250	.250	.500	30	-0	-0	103	0	0	.333	0			0	/OS1	0.0
Total	4	315	1309	174	307	35	23	6	151	37	90	.235	.258	.310	.568	49	-97	-104	102	100	125	.509	62			-2	32/O1S	-7.2

■ **CASEY PARSONS** Parsons, Casey Robert b: 4/14/54, Wenatchee, Wash. BL/TR, 6'1", 180 lbs. Deb: 5/31/81

YEAR	TM/L	G	AB	R	H	2B	3B	HR	RBI	BB	SO	AVG	OBP	SLG	PRO	/A	BR	/A	PF	CHI	RC	TA	SB	CS	SBR	FR	POS	TPR
1981	Sea-A	36	22	6	5	1	0	1	5	1	4	.227	.320	.409	.729	109	0	0	100	163	3	.706	0	0	0	-5	O/1	-0.5
1983	Chi-A	8	5	1	1	0	0	0	0	2	1	.200	.429	.200	.629	77	0	-0	103	0	1	.750	0	0	0	-1	/OD	0.0
1984	Chi-A	1	1	0	0	0	0	0	0	0	1	.000	.000	.000	.000	-90	-0	-0	111	0	0	.000	0	0	0	0	/H	0.0
1987	Cle-A	18	25	2	4	0	0	1	5	0	5	.160	.160	.280	.440	14	-3	-3	103	200	1	.304	0	0	0	-1	/O1D	-0.3
Total	4	63	53	9	10	1	0	2	10	3	11	.189	.259	.321	.579	58	-3	-3	102	156	4	.489	0	0	0	-7	/OD1	-0.8

■ **DIXIE PARSONS** Parsons, Edward Dixon b: 5/12/16, Talladega, Ala. BR/TR, 6'2", 180 lbs. Deb: 8/16/39

YEAR	TM/L	G	AB	R	H	2B	3B	HR	RBI	BB	SO	AVG	OBP	SLG	PRO	/A	BR	/A	PF	CHI	RC	TA	SB	CS	SBR	FR	POS	TPR
1939	Det-A	5	1	0	0	0	0	0	0	1	1	.000	.500	.000	.500	34	0	-0	111	0	0	1.000	0	0	0	0	/C	0.0
1942	Det-A	63	188	8	37	4	0	2	11	13	22	.197	.249	.250	.499	36	-15	-18	113	73	12	.391	1	0	0	1	C	-0.8
1943	Det-A	40	106	2	15	3	0	0	4	6	16	.142	.188	.170	.357	5	-13	-13	106	81	3	.250	0	0	0	2	C	-1.0
Total	3	108	295	10	52	7	0	2	15	20	39	.176	.229	.220	.449	26	-28	-31	110	75	15	.347	1	0	0	3	C	-1.8

■ **JOHN PARSONS** Parsons, John S. b: Napoleon, Ohio Deb: 10/15/1884

YEAR	TM/L	G	AB	R	H	2B	3B	HR	RBI	BB	SO	AVG	OBP	SLG	PRO	/A	BR	/A	PF	CHI	RC	TA	SB	CS	SBR	FR	POS	TPR
1884	Cin-a	1	3	0	0	0	0	0		0		.000	.000	.000	.000	-95	-1	-1	106	0	0	.000				0	/O	0.0

■ **ROY PARTEE** Partee, Roy Robert b: 9/7/17, Los Angeles, Cal. BR/TR, 5'10", 180 lbs. Deb: 4/23/43

YEAR	TM/L	G	AB	R	H	2B	3B	HR	RBI	BB	SO	AVG	OBP	SLG	PRO	/A	BR	/A	PF	CHI	RC	TA	SB	CS	SBR	FR	POS	TPR
1943	Bos-A	96	299	30	84	14	2	0	31	39	33	.281	.368	.341	.709	104	4	3	104	111	40	.638	0	0	0	-1	C	0.7
1944	Bos-A	89	280	18	68	12	0	2	41	37	29	.243	.333	.307	.640	85	-5	-4	98	161	30	.556	0	1	-1	2	C	0.3
1946	Bos-A	40	111	13	35	5	2	0	9	13	14	.315	.387	.396	.783	104	3	1	114	78	17	.704	0	0	0	-2	C	0.1
1947	Bos-A	60	169	14	39	2	0	0	16	18	23	.231	.305	.243	.547	49	-10	-12	108	144	14	.440	0	0	0	-1	C	-0.8
1948	StL-A	82	231	14	47	8	1	0	17	25	21	.203	.284	.247	.531	40	-19	-21	106	101	16	.440	2	2	-1	0	C	-1.5
Total	5	367	1090	89	273	41	5	2	114	132	120	.250	.334	.303	.636	76	-27	-33	104	123	116	.566	2	3	-1	-2	C	-1.2

■ **STEVE PARTENHEIMER** Partenheimer, Harold Philip b: 8/30/1891, Greenfield, Mass. d: 6/16/71, Mansfield, Ohio TR, 5'8.5", 145 lbs. Deb: 6/18/13

YEAR	TM/L	G	AB	R	H	2B	3B	HR	RBI	BB	SO	AVG	OBP	SLG	PRO	/A	BR	/A	PF	CHI	RC	TA	SB	CS	SBR	FR	POS	TPR
1913	Det-A	1	2	0	0	0	0	0	0	0	0	.000	.333	.000	.333	-1	-0	-0	99	0	0	.500	0			0	/3	0.0

■ **JAY PARTRIDGE** Partridge, James Bugg b: 11/15/02, Mountville, Ga. d: 1/14/74, Nashville, Tenn. BL/TR, 5'11", 160 lbs. Deb: 4/12/27

YEAR	TM/L	G	AB	R	H	2B	3B	HR	RBI	BB	SO	AVG	OBP	SLG	PRO	/A	BR	/A	PF	CHI	RC	TA	SB	CS	SBR	FR	POS	TPR
1927	Bro-N	146	572	72	149	17	6	7	40	20	36	.260	.289	.348	.637	68	-26	-27	103	67	56	.546	9			-13	*2	-4.2
1928	Bro-N	37	73	18	18	0	1	0	12	13	6	.247	.368	.274	.642	71	-2	-2	99	214	8	.655	2			-1	2/3	-0.2
Total	2	183	645	90	167	17	7	7	52	33	42	.259	.299	.340	.639	69	-28	-30	102	86	64	.559	11			-14	2/3	-4.4

■ **BEN PASCHAL** Paschal, Benjamin Edwin b: 10/13/1895, Enterprise, Ala. d: 11/10/74, Charlotte, N.C. BR/TR, 5'11", 185 lbs. Deb: 8/16/15

YEAR	TM/L	G	AB	R	H	2B	3B	HR	RBI	BB	SO	AVG	OBP	SLG	PRO	/A	BR	/A	PF	CHI	RC	TA	SB	CS	SBR	FR	POS	TPR
1915	Cle-A	9	9	0	1	0	0	0	0	0	3	.111	.111	.111	.222	-32	-1	-2	104	0	0	.125	0			0	H	-0.1
1920	Bos-A	9	28	5	10	0	0	0	5	5	2	.357	.455	.357	.812	122	1	1	96	176	5	.889	1	0	0	-1	/O	0.0
1924	NY-A	4	12	2	3	1	0	0	3	1	0	.250	.308	.333	.641	66	-1	-1	99	248	1	.556	0	0	0	0	/O	0.0
1925	NY-A	89	247	49	89	16	5	12	56	22	29	.360	.417	.611	1.028	165	20	22	96	100	60	1.132	14	9	-1	-6	O	0.8
1926	NY-A	96	258	46	74	12	3	7	33	26	35	.287	.354	.438	.792	107	2	2	99	84	40	.774	7	6	-2	-4	O	-0.8
1927	NY-A	50	82	16	26	9	2	2	16	4	10	.317	.349	.549	.898	130	3	3	100	104	15	.875	0	0	0	-5	O	-0.3
1928	NY-A	65	79	12	25	6	1	1	15	8	11	.316	.379	.456	.835	129	2	3	92	132	14	.833	1	0	0	-6	O	-0.3
1929	NY-A	42	72	13	15	3	0	2	11	6	3	.208	.269	.333	.603	55	-5	-5	99	125	7	.534	1	1	-0	-1	O	-0.6
Total	8	364	787	143	243	47	11	24	139	72	93	.309	.369	.488	.857	123	21	24	97	105	142	.863	24	16		-23	O	-1.3

■ **JOHNNY PASEK** Pasek, John Paul b: 6/25/05, Niagara Falls, N.Y. d: 3/13/76, Niagara Falls, N.Y BR/TR, 5'10", 175 lbs. Deb: 7/28/33

YEAR	TM/L	G	AB	R	H	2B	3B	HR	RBI	BB	SO	AVG	OBP	SLG	PRO	/A	BR	/A	PF	CHI	RC	TA	SB	CS	SBR	FR	POS	TPR
1933	Det-A	28	61	6	15	4	0	0	4	7	7	.246	.324	.311	.635	65	-3	-3	107	70	7	.609	2	0	1	-2	C	-0.2
1934	Chi-A	4	9	1	3	0	0	0	0	1	1	.333	.400	.333	.733	91	-0	-0	99	0	1	.667	0	0	0	0	/C	0.1
Total	2	32	70	7	18	4	0	0	4	8	8	.257	.333	.314	.648	68	-3	-3	106	61	8	.615	2	0	1	-2	/C	-0.1

■ **DODE PASKERT** Paskert, George Henry b: 8/28/1881, Cleveland, Ohio d: 2/12/59, Cleveland, Ohio BR/TR, 5'11", 165 lbs. Deb: 9/21/07

YEAR	TM/L	G	AB	R	H	2B	3B	HR	RBI	BB	SO	AVG	OBP	SLG	PRO	/A	BR	/A	PF	CHI	RC	TA	SB	CS	SBR	FR	POS	TPR
1907	Cin-N	16	50	10	14	4	0	1	8	2		.280	.308	.420	.728	136	1	2	95	126	7	.694	2			2	O	0.3
1908	Cin-N	118	395	40	96	14	4	1	36	27		.243	.291	.306	.598	91	-3	-4	103	114	41	.579	25			9	*O	0.5

YEAR	TM/L	G	AB	R	H	2B	3B	HR	RBI	BB	SO	AVG	OBP	SLG	PRO	/A	BR	/A	PF	CHI	RC	TA	SB	CS	SBR	FR	POS	TPR
1909	Cin-N	104	322	49	81	7	4	0	33	34		.252	.327	.298	.625	101	-1	1	94	125	38	.643	23			3	O/1	0.1
1910	Cin-N	144	506	63	152	21	5	2	46	70	60	.300	.389	.374	.762	121	17	16	101	87	93	.884	51			8	*O/1	2.0
1911	Phi-N	153	560	96	153	18	5	4	47	70	70	.273	.358	.345	.703	90	-1	-7	108	75	81	.725	28			3	*O	-0.8
1912	Phi-N	145	540	102	170	37	5	2	43	91	67	.315	.420	.413	.833	128	26	25	100	56	108	.965	36			2	*O/23	2.2
1913	Phi-N	124	454	83	119	21	9	4	29	65	69	.262	.358	.374	.733	98	7	-0	112	56	65	.746	12			12	*O	1.0
1914	Phi-N	132	451	59	119	25	6	3	44	56	68	.264	.349	.366	.715	112	8	8	100	94	64	.744	23			5	*O/S	1.0
1915	Phi-N	109	328	51	80	17	4	3	39	35	38	.244	.319	.348	.666	95	1	-2	107	121	41	.626	9	6	-1	4	O/1	-0.1
1916	Phi-N	149	555	82	155	30	7	8	46	54	76	.279	.346	.402	.748	135	19	22	96	71	77	.717	22	21	-6	-4	*O/S	1.4
1917	Phi-N	141	546	78	137	27	11	4	43	62	63	.251	.331	.363	.693	105	9	4	108	70	68	.689	19			-5	*O	-0.5
1918	Chi-N	127	461	69	132	24	4	2	59	53	49	.286	.362	.369	.731	120	14	13	102	134	68	.745	20			-7	*O/3	0.0
1919	Chi-N	88	270	21	53	11	3	2	29	28	33	.196	.274	.281	.556	67	-10	-11	100	137	22	.516	7			-0	O	-1.5
1920	Chi-N	139	487	57	136	22	10	5	71	64	58	.279	.366	.396	.763	120	14	14	99	140	72	.756	16	14	-4	-3	*O	0.0
1921	Cin-N	27	92	8	16	1	1	0	4	4	8	.174	.208	.207	.415	10	-12	-12	101	77	4	.295	0	2	-1	2	O	-1.2
Total	15	1716	6017	868	1613	279	78	41	577	715	659	.268	.349	.361	.710	107	88	69	102	94	850	.723	293	43		30	*O/13S2	4.4

■ KEVIN PASLEY Pasley, Kevin Patrick b: 7/22/53, Bronx, N.Y. BR/TR, 6', 185 lbs. Deb: 10/02/74

YEAR	TM/L	G	AB	R	H	2B	3B	HR	RBI	BB	SO	AVG	OBP	SLG	PRO	/A	BR	/A	PF	CHI	RC	TA	SB	CS	SBR	FR	POS	TPR
1974	LA-N	1	0	0	0	0	0	0	0	0	0	—	—	—	—	—	0	0	93	—	—	—	0	0	0	0	/C	0.0
1976	LA-N	23	52	4	12	2	0	0	2	3	7	.231	.273	.269	.542	54	-3	-3	100	55	4	.425	0	0	0	1	C	0.0
1977	LA-N	2	3	0	1	0	0	0	0	0	0	.333	.333	.333	.667	79	-0	-0	100	0	0	.500	0	0	0	0	/C	0.0
	Sea-A	4	13	1	5	0	0	0	2	1	2	.385	.429	.385	.813	129	0	1	96	162	2	.750	0	0	0	0	/C	0.1
1978	Sea-A	25	54	3	13	5	0	1	5	2	4	.241	.268	.389	.657	81	-1	-2	102	82	5	.535	0	0	0	-2	C	-0.2
Total	4	55	122	8	31	7	0	1	9	6	13	.254	.289	.336	.625	75	-4	-4	100	77	862	.505	0	0	0	-1	/C	-0.1

■ DAN PASQUA Pasqua, Daniel Anthony b: 10/17/61, Yonkers, N.Y. BL/TL, 6', 203 lbs. Deb: 5/30/85

YEAR	TM/L	G	AB	R	H	2B	3B	HR	RBI	BB	SO	AVG	OBP	SLG	PRO	/A	BR	/A	PF	CHI	RC	TA	SB	CS	SBR	FR	POS	TPR
1985	NY-A	60	148	17	31	3	1	9	25	16	38	.209	.291	.426	.717	97	-2	-1	96	110	19	.678	0	0	0	-0	OD	-0.1
1986	NY-A	102	280	44	82	17	0	16	45	47	78	.293	.400	.525	.925	146	21	20	103	92	62	.985	2	0	1	-4	O/1D	1.3
1987	NY-A	113	318	42	74	7	1	17	42	40	99	.233	.320	.421	.742	98	-2	-1	98	91	43	.692	0	2	-1	-5	OD1	-0.9
1988	Chi-A	129	422	48	96	16	2	20	50	46	100	.227	.308	.417	.725	104	-0	1	97	84	54	.673	1	0	0	4	*O/1D	0.3
Total	4	404	1168	151	283	43	4	62	162	149	315	.242	.332	.445	.777	112	17	19	99	91	178	.758	3	2	-0	-5	O/D1	0.6

■ MIKE PASQUARIELLO Pasquariello, Michael John "Toney" b: 11/7/1898, Philadelphia, Pa. d: 4/5/65, Bridgeport, Conn. BR/TR, 5'11", 167 lbs. Deb: 7/09/19

YEAR	TM/L	G	AB	R	H	2B	3B	HR	RBI	BB	SO	AVG	OBP	SLG	PRO	/A	BR	/A	PF	CHI	RC	TA	SB	CS	SBR	FR	POS	TPR
1919	Phi-N	1	1	1	1	0	0	0	0	0	0	1.000	1.000	1.000	2.000	484	0	0	104	0	1	—	0			0	/1	0.0
	StL-N	1	1	0	0	0	0	0	0	0	1	.000	.000	.000	.000	-99	-0	-0	94	0	0	.000	0			0	H	0.0
	Yr	2	2	1	1	0	0	0	0	0	1	.500	.500	.500	1.000	203	0	0	99	0	0	1.000	0			0		0.0
Total	1	2	2	1	1	0	0	0	0	0	1	.500	.500	.500	1.000	203	0	0	99	0	1	1.000	0			0	/1	0.0

■ CLIFF PASTORNICKY Pastornicky, Clifford Scott b: 11/18/58, Seattle, Was. BR/TR, 5'10", 170 lbs. Deb: 6/14/83

YEAR	TM/L	G	AB	R	H	2B	3B	HR	RBI	BB	SO	AVG	OBP	SLG	PRO	/A	BR	/A	PF	CHI	RC	TA	SB	CS	SBR	FR	POS	TPR
1983	KC-A	10	32	4	4	0	0	2	5	0	3	.125	.125	.313	.438	16	-4	-4	101	122	0	.313	0	0	0	-0	3	-0.3

■ BOB PATE Pate, Robert Wayne b: 12/3/53, Los Angeles, Cal. BR/TR, 6'3", 200 lbs. Deb: 6/02/80

YEAR	TM/L	G	AB	R	H	2B	3B	HR	RBI	BB	SO	AVG	OBP	SLG	PRO	/A	BR	/A	PF	CHI	RC	TA	SB	CS	SBR	FR	POS	TPR
1980	Mon-N	23	39	3	10	2	0	0	5	3	6	.256	.310	.308	.617	73	-1	-1	99	165	4	.500	0	1	-1	-4	O	-0.6
1981	Mon-N	8	6	0	2	0	0	0	0	1	0	.333	.429	.333	.762	120	0	0	99	0	1	.750	0	0	0	-2	/O	-0.1
Total	2	31	45	3	12	2	0	0	5	4	6	.267	.327	.311	.638	80	-1	-1	99	141	5	.529	0	1	-1	-6	/O	-0.7

■ FREDDIE PATEK Patek, Frederick Joseph "The Flea" b: 10/9/44, Seguin, Tex. BR/TR, 5'5", 148 lbs. Deb: 6/03/68

YEAR	TM/L	G	AB	R	H	2B	3B	HR	RBI	BB	SO	AVG	OBP	SLG	PRO	/A	BR	/A	PF	CHI	RC	TA	SB	CS	SBR	FR	POS	TPR
1968	Pit-N	61	208	31	53	4	2	2	18	12	37	.255	.302	.322	.624	86	-3	-3	101	106	22	.611	18	7	1	7	S/O3	1.2
1969	Pit-N	147	460	48	110	9	1	5	32	53	86	.239	.319	.296	.615	77	-15	-12	95	85	43	.551	15	8	-0	-4	*S	0.0
1970	Pit-N	84	237	42	58	10	5	1	19	29	46	.245	.327	.342	.669	82	-7	-5	97	88	29	.645	8	2	1	16	S	1.9
1971	KC-A	147	591	86	158	21	**11**	6	36	44	80	.267	.323	.371	.694	97	-4	-3	99	55	75	.700	49	14	6	16	*S	3.7
1972	KC-A	136	518	59	110	25	4	0	32	47	64	.212	.282	.276	.558	66	-21	-21	100	99	44	.533	33	7	6	**28**	*S	2.9
1973	KC-A	135	501	82	117	19	5	5	45	54	63	.234	.312	.321	.633	72	-14	-20	109	106	53	.624	36	14	2	**35**	*S	3.6
1974	KC-A	149	537	72	121	18	6	3	38	77	69	.225	.326	.298	.624	76	-11	-16	106	94	58	.623	33	15	1	14	*S	1.1
1975	KC-A	136	483	58	110	14	5	5	45	42	65	.228	.292	.308	.601	69	-19	-20	102	108	47	.578	32	7	5	1	*S/D	0.0
1976	KC-A	144	432	58	104	19	3	1	43	50	63	.241	.322	.306	.628	85	-7	-7	100	122	48	.673	51	15	6	-1	*S/D	0.7
1977	KC-A	154	497	72	130	26	6	5	60	41	84	.262	.324	.368	.692	88	-8	-8	100	120	65	.731	**53**	13	8	-13	*S	0.5
1978	KC-A	138	440	54	109	23	1	2	46	42	56	.248	.315	.318	.633	77	-12	-13	102	124	48	.635	38	11	5	-27	*S	-2.4
1979	KC-A	106	306	30	77	17	0	1	37	16	42	.252	.295	.317	.612	62	-15	-17	105	142	26	.514	11	12	-4	-17	*S	-2.5
1980	Cal-A	86	273	41	72	10	5	5	34	15	26	.264	.304	.392	.696	93	-5	-3	96	109	28	.596	7	6	-2	-15	S	-1.3
1981	Cal-A	27	47	3	11	1	1	0	5	1	6	.234	.250	.298	.548	55	-3	-3	104	140	3	.432	1	0	0	1	2/3S	0.0
Total	14	1650	5530	736	1340	216	55	41	490	523	787	.242	.311	.324	.635	79	-143	-152	101	103	592	.631	385	131	37	39	*S/23OD	9.4

■ BOB PATRICK Patrick, Robert Lee b: 10/27/17, Ft.Smith, Ark. BR/TR, 6'2", 190 lbs. Deb: 9/20/41

YEAR	TM/L	G	AB	R	H	2B	3B	HR	RBI	BB	SO	AVG	OBP	SLG	PRO	/A	BR	/A	PF	CHI	RC	TA	SB	CS	SBR	FR	POS	TPR
1941	Det-A	5	7	2	2	0	0	0	0	0	1	.286	.286	.286	.571	48	-0	-1	106	0	1	.400	0	0	0	-1	/O	-0.1
1942	Det-A	4	8	1	2	1	0	1	3	1	0	.250	.333	.750	1.083	177	1	1	113	117	2	1.167	0	0	0	-0	/O	0.0
Total	2	9	15	3	4	1	0	1	3	1	1	.267	.313	.533	.846	117	0	0	110	66	3	.818	0	0	0	-1	/O	-0.1

■ HARRY PATTEE Pattee, Harry Ernest b: 1/17/1882, Charlestown, Mass. d: 7/17/71, Lynchburg, Va. BL/TR, 5'8", 149 lbs. Deb: 4/14/08

YEAR	TM/L	G	AB	R	H	2B	3B	HR	RBI	BB	SO	AVG	OBP	SLG	PRO	/A	BR	/A	PF	CHI	RC	TA	SB	CS	SBR	FR	POS	TPR
1908	Bro-N	80	264	19	57	5	2	0	9	25		.216	.284	.250	.534	76	-7	-6	95	53	24	.556	24			6	2	0.0

■ DAN PATTERSON Patterson, Daniel Thomas b: 1846, New York, N.Y. 5'9", 143 lbs. Deb: 5/18/1871

YEAR	TM/L	G	AB	R	H	2B	3B	HR	RBI	BB	SO	AVG	OBP	SLG	PRO	/A	BR	/A	PF	CHI	RC	TA	SB	CS	SBR	FR	POS	TPR
1871	Mut-n	32	151	31	31							.205															*O/2	
1872	Eck-n	12	50	5	8							.160															O/1	
1874	Mut-n	1	5	1	2							.400															/1O	
1875	Atl-n	10	38	3	8							.211															/2O	
Total	4 n	55	244	40	49							.201															/2O	

■ HAM PATTERSON Patterson, Hamilton b: 10/13/1877, Belleville, Ill. d: 11/25/45, E.St.Louis, Ill. TR, 6'2", 185 lbs. Deb: 5/18/09

YEAR	TM/L	G	AB	R	H	2B	3B	HR	RBI	BB	SO	AVG	OBP	SLG	PRO	/A	BR	/A	PF	CHI	RC	TA	SB	CS	SBR	FR	POS	TPR
1909	StL-A	17	49	2	10	1	0	0	5	0		.204	.204	.224	.429	39	-4	-3	92	175	2	.308	1			-0	/1O	-0.4
	Chi-A	1	3	2	0	0	0	0	0	1		.000	.250	.000	.250	-21	-0	-0	97	0	0	.333	0			-0	/1	0.0
	Yr	18	52	4	10	1	0	0	5	1		.192	.208	.212	.419	35	-4	-4	92	175	2	.310	1			-0		-0.4
Total	1	18	52	4	10	1	0	0	5	1		.192	.208	.212	.419	35	-4	-4	92	162	2	.310	1			-0	/1O	-0.4

■ HANK PATTERSON Patterson, Henry Joseph Colquit b: 7/17/07, San Francisco, Cal. d: 9/30/70, Panorama City, Cal. BR/TR, 5'11.5", 170 lbs. Deb: 9/05/32

YEAR	TM/L	G	AB	R	H	2B	3B	HR	RBI	BB	SO	AVG	OBP	SLG	PRO	/A	BR	/A	PF	CHI	RC	TA	SB	CS	SBR	FR	POS	TPR
1932	Bos-A	1	1	0	0	0	0	0	0	0	0	.000	.000	.000	.000	-99	-0	-0	97	0	0	.000	0	0	0	0	/C	0.0

■ CLAIRE PATTERSON Patterson, Lorenzo Claire b: 10/5/1887, Arkansas City, Kan. d: 3/28/13, Mojave, Cal. BL/TR, 6' ", 180 lbs. Deb: 09

YEAR	TM/L	G	AB	R	H	2B	3B	HR	RBI	BB	SO	AVG	OBP	SLG	PRO	/A	BR	/A	PF	CHI	RC	TA	SB	CS	SBR	FR	POS	TPR
1909	Cin-N	4	8	0	1	0	0	0	1	0		.125	.125	.125	.250	-23	-1	-1	94	364	0	.143	0			0	/O	0.0

■ MIKE PATTERSON Patterson, Michael Lee b: 1/26/58, Santa Monica, Cal. BL/TR, 5'10", 170 lbs. Deb: 4/15/81

YEAR	TM/L	G	AB	R	H	2B	3B	HR	RBI	BB	SO	AVG	OBP	SLG	PRO	/A	BR	/A	PF	CHI	RC	TA	SB	CS	SBR	FR	POS	TPR
1981	Oak-A	12	23	4	8	1	1	0	1	2	5	.348	.400	.478	.878	159	2	2	96	36	4	.813	0	1	-1	-1	/OD	0.0
	NY-A	4	9	2	2	0	2	0	0	0	0	.222	.222	.667	.889	147	0	0	100	0	1	.857	0	0	0	-0	/O	0.0
	Yr	16	32	6	10	1	3	0	1	2	5	.313	.353	.531	.884	156	2	2	97	29	6	.826	0	1	-1	-1		0.0
1982	NY-A	11	16	3	3	1	0	1	1	2	6	.188	.278	.438	.715	96	-0	-0	96	40	2	.769	1	0	0	-3	/OD	-0.2
Total	2	27	48	9	13	2	3	1	2	4	11	.271	.327	.500	.827	135	2	2	97	31	8	.806	1	1	-0	-4	/OD	-0.2

■ PAT PATTERSON Patterson, William Jennings Bryan b: 1/29/01, Belleville, Ill. d: 10/1/77, St.Louis, Mo. BR/TR, 6', 175 lbs. Deb: 4/14/21

YEAR	TM/L	G	AB	R	H	2B	3B	HR	RBI	BB	SO	AVG	OBP	SLG	PRO	/A	BR	/A	PF	CHI	RC	TA	SB	CS	SBR	FR	POS	TPR
1921	NY-N	23	35	5	14	0	0	1	5	2	5	.400	.432	.486	.918	146	2	2	98	92	7	.864	0	1	-1	1	3/S	0.3

■ GEORGE PATTISON Pattison, George Deb: 4/24/1884

YEAR	TM/L	G	AB	R	H	2B	3B	HR	RBI	BB	SO	AVG	OBP	SLG	PRO	/A	BR	/A	PF	CHI	RC	TA	SB	CS	SBR	FR	POS	TPR
1884	Phi-U	2	7	0	1	0	0	0		0		.143	.143	.143	.286	-3	-1	-1	93	0	0	.167	0			0	/O	0.0

YEAR	TM/L	G	AB	R	H	2B	3B	HR	RBI	BB	SO	AVG	OBP	SLG	PRO	/A	BR	/A	PF	CHI	RC	TA	SB	CS	SBR	FR	POS	TPR
■ GENE PATTON Patton, Gene Tunney b: 7/8/26, Coatesville, Pa. BL/TR, 5'10", 165 lbs. Deb: 6/17/44																												
1944	Bos-N	1	0	0	0	0	0	0	0	0	0	—	—	—	—	—	0	0	95	—	—	—	0			0	R	0.0
■ BILL PATTON Patton, George William b: 10/7/12, Cornwall, Pa. d: 3/15/86, Philadelphia, Pa. BR/TR, 6'2", 180 lbs. Deb: 6/29/35																												
1935	Phi-A	9	10	1	3	1	0	0	2	2	3	.300	.417	.400	.817	112	0	0	100	170	2	.857	0	0	0	0	/C	0.0
■ TOM PATTON Patton, Thomas Allen b: 9/5/35, Honey Brook, Pa. BR/TR, 5'9.5", 185 lbs. Deb: 4/30/57																												
1957	Bal-A	1	2	0	0	0	0	0	0	0	2	.000	.000	.000	.000	-99	-1	-1	93	0	0	.000	0	0	0	0	/C	0.0
■ LOU PAUL Paul, Louis BR/TR, Deb: 9/05/1876																												
1876	Phi-N	3	12	2	2	1	0	0	0	0	0	.167	.167	.250	.417	37	-1	-1	99	0	1	.300				0	/C	0.0
■ CARLOS PAULA Paula, Carlos (Conill) b: 11/28/27, Havana, Cuba d: 4/25/83, Miami, Fla. BR/TR, 6'3", 195 lbs. Deb: 9/06/54																												
1954	Was-A	9	24	2	4	1	0	0	2	2	4	.167	.231	.208	.439	21	-3	-3	98	152	1	.350	0	0	0	1	/O	-0.1
1955	Was-A	115	351	34	105	20	7	6	45	17	43	.299	.335	.447	.782	120	3	7	91	96	49	.690	2	3	-1	-4	O	-0.2
1956	Was-A	33	82	8	15	2	1	3	13	8	15	.183	.256	.341	.597	55	-6	-6	102	131	5	.486	0	2	-1	-2	O	-0.9
Total	3	157	457	44	124	23	8	9	60	27	62	.271	.315	.416	.731	101	-6	-2	93	105	56	.644	2	5	-2	-5	O	-1.2
■ GENE PAULETTE Paulette, Eugene Edward b: 5/26/1891, Centralia, Ill. d: 2/8/66, Little Rock, Ark. BR/TR, 6', 150 lbs. Deb: 6/16/11																												
1911	NY-N	10	12	1	2	0	0	0	1	0	1	.167	.167	.167	.333	-6	-2	-2	102	169	0	.200	0			0	/1S3	-0.1
1916	StL-A	5	4	1	2	0	0	0	0	1	1	.500	.600	.500	1.100	242	1	1	95	0	1	1.500	0			0	H	0.1
1917	StL-A	12	22	3	4	0	0	0	0	3	3	.182	.280	.182	.462	43	-1	-1	95	0	1	.389	0			0	/123	0.0
	StL-N	95	332	32	88	21	7	0	34	16	16	.265	.303	.370	.673	104	1	1	102	109	38	.615	9			0	1	0.0
1918	StL-N	125	461	33	126	15	3	0	52	27	16	.273	.316	.319	.635	100	-4	-0	93	142	49	.558	11			-0	1S/2O3PC	-0.2
1919	StL-N	43	144	11	31	6	0	0	11	9	6	.215	.261	.257	.518	59	-8	-7	94	116	10	.442	4			0	1/S	-0.7
	Phi-N	67	243	20	63	8	3	1	31	19	10	.259	.316	.329	.645	91	-2	-3	104	148	27	.611	10			-1	2O/1	-0.2
	Yr	110	387	31	94	14	3	1	42	28	16	.243	.296	.302	.598	80	-9	-9	100	136	36	.546	14			-1		-0.9
1920	Phi-N	143	562	59	162	16	6	1	36	33	16	.288	.332	.343	.676	87	-4	-10	109	75	64	.586	9	8	-2	5	*1/S	-0.7
Total	6	500	1780	160	478	66	19	2	165	108	69	.269	.314	.330	.644	91	-18	-20	101	111	191	.571	43	8		5	1/2SO3CP	-1.8
■ SI PAUXTIS Pauxtis, Simon Francis b: 7/20/1885, Pittston, Pa. d: 3/13/61, Philadelphia, Pa. BR/TR, 6' ", 175 lbs. Deb: 09																												
1909	Cin-N	4	8	0	1	0	0	0	1	0		.125	.125	.125	.250	-23	-1	-1	94	364	0	.143	0			0	/C	0.0
■ DON PAVLETICH Pavletich, Donald Stephen b: 7/13/38, Milwaukee, Wis. BR/TR, 5'11", 190 lbs. Deb: 4/20/57																												
1957	Cin-N	1	1	0	0	0	0	0	0	0	0	.000	.000	.000	.000	-95	-0	-0	105	0	0	.000	0	0	0	0	H	0.0
1959	Cin-N	1	0	1	0	0	0	0	0	0	0	—	—	—	—	—	0	0	103	—	—	—	0	0	0	0	R	0.0
1962	Cin-N	34	63	7	14	3	0	1	7	8	18	.222	.310	.317	.627	68	-3	-3	102	120	7	.571	0	0	0	0	1/C	-0.2
1963	Cin-N	71	183	18	38	11	0	5	18	17	12	.208	.275	.350	.625	76	-5	-6	104	96	18	.547	0	0	0	1	1C	-0.5
1964	Cin-N	34	91	12	22	4	0	5	11	10	17	.242	.317	.451	.767	110	1	1	103	81	13	.729	0	0	0	2	C/1	0.4
1965	Cin-N	68	191	25	61	11	1	8	32	23	27	.319	.395	.513	.908	148	14	13	104	109	38	.904	1	1	-0	5	C/1	2.0
1966	Cin-N	83	235	29	69	13	2	12	38	18	37	.294	.346	.519	.866	120	11	7	114	101	41	.830	1	0	0	-1	C1	0.7
1967	Cin-N	74	231	25	55	14	3	6	34	21	38	.238	.313	.403	.715	95	1	-2	109	127	26	.632	2	1	0	-4	C/13	-0.1
1968	Cin-N	46	98	11	28	3	1	2	11	8	23	.286	.352	.398	.750	112	3	2	111	103	12	.636	0	0	0	0	1/C	0.1
1969	Chi-A	78	188	26	46	12	0	6	33	28	45	.245	.343	.404	.747	100	2	0	108	141	28	.722	0	0	0	-4	C1	0.0
1970	Bos-A	32	65	4	9	1	1	0	6	10	15	.138	.253	.185	.438	20	-7	-8	111	202	3	.397	1	0	0	1	1C	-0.7
1971	Bos-A	14	27	5	7	1	0	1	3	5	5	.259	.375	.407	.782	115	1	1	106	87	5	.800	0	0	0	0	/C	0.1
Total	12	536	1373	163	349	73	8	46	193	148	237	.254	.330	.420	.750	102	18	6	108	116	190	.718	5	2	0	1	C1/3	1.8
■ TED PAWELEK Pawelek, Theodore John "Porky" b: 8/15/19, Chicago Heights, Ill. d: 2/12/64, Chicago Heights, Ill. BL/TR, 5'10.5", 202 lbs. Deb: 9/13/46																												
1946	Chi-N	4	4	0	1	1	0	0	0	0	0	.250	.250	.500	.750	117	0	0	94	0	1	.667	0			0	/C	0.0
■ STAN PAWLOSKI Pawloski, Stanley Walter b: 9/6/31, Wanamie, Pa. BR/TR, 6'1", 175 lbs. Deb: 9/24/55																												
1955	Cle-A	2	8	0	1	0	0	0	0	0	2	.125	.125	.125	.250	-31	-1	-2	104	0	0	.143	0	0	0	0	/2	0.0
■ FRED PAYNE Payne, Frederick Thomas b: 9/2/1880, Camden, N.Y. d: 1/16/54, Camden, N.Y. BR/TR, 5'10", 162 lbs. Deb: 4/21/06																												
1906	Det-A	72	222	23	60	5	5	0	20	13		.270	.311	.338	.648	97	1	-1	108	97	25	.568	4			7	CO	1.0
1907	Det-A	53	169	17	28	2	2	0	14	7		.166	.199	.201	.400	28	-13	-14	102	147	8	.319	4			3	C/O	-0.7
1908	Det-A	20	45	3	3	0	0	0	2	3		.067	.125	.067	.192	-36	-6	-7	101	250	0	.167	1			1	C/O	-0.4
1909	Chi-A	32	82	8	20	2	0	0	12	5		.244	.295	.268	.564	80	-2	-2	97	210	6	.452	0			-1	C/O	0.0
1910	Chi-A	91	252	17	56	5	4	0	19	11		.222	.260	.274	.534	71	-10	-9	95	102	20	.449	6			2	C/O	0.2
1911	Chi-A	66	133	14	27	2	1	1	19	8		.203	.259	.256	.514	45	-10	-10	97	174	10	.472	6			-7	C	-0.9
Total	6	334	903	82	194	16	12	1	86	47		.215	.258	.262	.520	62	-41	-41	100	137	70	.437	21			5	C/O	-0.8
■ GEORGE PAYNTER Paynter, George Washington (born George Washington Paner) b: 7/6/1871, Cincinnati, Ohio d: 10/1/50, Cincinnati, Ohio 5'9", 125 lbs. Deb: 8/12/1894																												
1894	StL-N	1	4	0	0	0	0	0	0	1	0	.000	.200	.000	.200	-47	-1	-1	101	0	0	.500	1			0	/O	0.0
■ JOHNNY PEACOCK Peacock, John Gaston b: 1/10/10, Fremont, N.C. d: 10/17/81, Wilson, N.C. BL/TR, 5'11", 165 lbs. Deb: 9/23/37																												
1937	Bos-A	9	32	3	10	2	1	0	6	1	0	.313	.333	.438	.771	90	-0	-1	103	147	5	.682	0	0	0	0	/C	0.0
1938	Bos-A	72	195	29	59	7	1	1	39	17	4	.303	.358	.364	.723	79	-5	-6	102	178	26	.672	4	1	1	-3	C/1O	-0.6
1939	Bos-A	92	274	33	76	11	4	0	36	29	11	.277	.347	.347	.693	72	-9	-12	108	128	35	.616	1	1	-0	1	C	-0.5
1940	Bos-A	63	131	20	37	4	1	0	13	23	10	.282	.390	.328	.718	88	-1	-1	101	109	17	.657	1	0	0	-4	C	0.0
1941	Bos-A	79	261	28	74	20	1	0	27	21	3	.284	.339	.368	.707	84	-5	-6	103	100	34	.625	2	1	0	1	C	0.0
1942	Bos-A	88	286	17	76	7	3	0	25	21	11	.266	.316	.311	.627	74	-9	-10	104	99	29	.514	1	1	-0	-1	C	-0.1
1943	Bos-A	48	114	7	23	3	1	0	7	10	9	.202	.266	.246	.512	48	-7	-8	104	91	8	.411	1	1	-0	-0	C	-0.6
1944	Bos-A	4	4	0	0	0	0	0	0	0	0	.000	.000	.000	.000	-99	-1	-1	98	0	0	.000	0	0	0	0	/C	0.0
	Phi-N	83	253	21	57	9	3	0	21	31	15	.225	.310	.285	.594	68	-10	-10	100	105	23	.515	1			3	C/2	-0.3
1945	Phi-N	33	74	6	15	6	0	0	6	6	0	.203	.262	.284	.546	54	-5	-5	96	99	5	.459	1			-0	C	-0.4
	Bro-N	48	110	11	28	5	1	0	14	24	10	.255	.388	.318	.706	102	1	2	96	139	16	.735	2			-3	C	0.0
	Yr	81	184	17	43	11	1	0	20	30	10	.234	.341	.304	.645	83	-4	-3	96	124	21	.627	3			-3		-0.4
Total	9	619	1734	175	455	74	16	1	194	183	73	.262	.333	.325	.658	76	-52	-58	103	117	197	.593	14	5		-6	C/2O1	-2.5
■ ELIAS PEAK Peak, Elias b: 5/23/1859, Philadelphia, Pa. d: 12/17/16, Philadelphia, Pa. Deb: 4/19/1884																												
1884	Bos-U	1	3	2	2	0	0	0		1		.667	.750	.667	1.417	389	1	1	98	0	2	3.000	0			0	/O	0.1
	Phi-U	54	215	35	42	6	4	0		7		.195	.221	.260	.481	67	-8	-6	93	0	13	.364	0			-5	2/OS	-1.0
	Yr	55	218	37	44	6	4	0		8		.202	.230	.266	.496	73	-7	-5	93	0	14	.379	0			-5		-0.9
Total	1	55	218	37	44	6	4	0		8		.202	.230	.266	.496	73	-7	-5	93	0	14	.379	0			-5	/2OS	-0.9
■ HARRY PEARCE Pearce, Harry James b: 7/12/1889, Philadelphia, Pa. d: 1/8/42, Philadelphia, Pa. BR/TR, 5'9", 158 lbs. Deb: 10/02/17																												
1917	Phi-N	7	16	2	4	3	0	0	2	0	4	.250	.294	.438	.732	114	0	0	108	110	2	.667	0			1	/S	0.1
1918	Phi-N	60	164	16	40	3	2	0	18	9	31	.244	.295	.287	.582	71	-4	-6	109	145	15	.516	5			-2	2/S13	-0.5
1919	Phi-N	68	244	24	44	3	3	0	9	8	27	.180	.209	.217	.427	27	-21	-22	104	67	12	.340	6			2	2S/3	-1.9
Total	3	135	424	42	88	9	5	0	29	17	62	.208	.247	.252	.499	48	-25	-28	106	99	29	.417	11			1	/2S31	-2.3
■ DICKEY PEARCE Pearce, Richard J. b: 1/2/1836, Brooklyn, N.Y. d: 10/12/08, Onset, Mass. BR/TR, 5'3.5", 161 lbs. Deb: 5/18/1871 M																												
1871	Mut-n	33	165	31	44							.267															*S	
1872	Mut-n	43	208	28	39							.188															*S/OM	
1873	Atl-n	55	279	42	72							.258															*S	
1874	Atl-n	56	262	49	76							.290															*S/3	
1875	StL-n	70	293	49	75							.256															*SM	
1876	StL-N	25	102	12	21	1	0	0	10	3	5	.206	.229	.216	.444	56	-5	-3	88	157	5	.309				6	S/O2	0.2
1877	StL-N	8	29	1	5	0	0	0	4	1	4	.172	.200	.172	.372	18	-3	-3	102	277	1	.250				0	/S	-0.1
Total	5 n	257	1207	199	306							.254															/S	

YEAR	TM/L	G	AB	R	H	2B	3B	HR	RBI	BB	SO	AVG	OBP	SLG	PRO	/A	BR	/A	PF	CHI	RC	TA	SB	CS	SBR	FR	POS	TPR
Total	2	33	131	13	26	1	0	0	14	4	9	.198	.222	.206	.428	46	-8	-6	91	183	6	.295				6	S/3O2	0.1
■ **DUCKY PEARCE**	Pearce, William C. b: 3/17/1885, Corning, Ohio d: 5/22/33, Brownstown, Ind. BR/TR, 6'1", 185 lbs. Deb: 7/01/08																											
1908	Cin-N	2	2	0	0	0	0	0	0	0		.000	.000	.000	.000	-98	-0	-0	103	0	0	.000	0			0	/C	0.0
1909	Cin-N	2	2	0	0	0	0	0	0	0		.000	.000	.000	.000	-99	-0	-0	94	0	0	.000	0			0	/C	0.0
Total	2	4	4	0	0	0	0	0	0	0		.000	.000	.000	.000	-99	-1	-1	98	0	0	.000	0			0	/C	0.0
■ **ALBIE PEARSON**	Pearson, Albert Gregory b: 9/12/34, Alhambra, Cal. BL/TL, 5'5", 140 lbs. Deb: 4/14/58																											
1958	Was-A	146	530	63	146	25	5	3	33	64	31	.275	.356	.358	.714	101	-0	2	97	70	69	.653	7	8	-3	1	*O	-0.8
1959	Was-A	25	80	9	15	1	0	0	2	14	3	.188	.309	.200	.509	43	-6	-6	100	50	6	.470	1	1	-0	-2	O	-0.8
	Bal-A	80	138	22	32	4	2	0	6	13	5	.232	.298	.290	.588	64	-7	-6	97	59	12	.518	4	0	1	-5	O	-1.2
	Yr	105	218	31	47	5	2	0	8	27	8	.216	.302	.257	.559	56	-13	-12	98	57	19	.500	5	1	1	-7		-2.0
1960	Bal-A	48	82	17	20	2	0	1	6	17	3	.244	.374	.305	.679	84	-1	-1	102	84	11	.708	4	0	1	-5	O	-0.5
1961	LA-A	144	427	92	123	21	3	7	41	96	40	.288	.422	.400	.823	109	18	11	111	84	84	.906	11	3	2	-6	*O	0.3
1962	LA-A	160	614	**115**	160	29	6	5	42	95	36	.261	.361	.352	.712	91	-3	-5	102	69	85	.700	15	6	1	-2	*O	-1.1
1963	LA-A	154	578	92	176	26	5	6	47	92	37	.304	.403	.398	.801	137	24	30	91	76	100	.820	17	10	-1	-0	*O	2.5
1964	LA-A	107	265	34	59	5	1	2	16	35	22	.223	.316	.272	.587	74	-11	-8	89	87	25	.533	6	4	-1	-7	O	-1.8
1965	Cal-A	122	360	41	100	17	2	4	21	51	17	.278	.370	.369	.740	113	7	8	98	60	55	.742	12	1	3	-2	*O	0.5
1966	Cal-A	2	3	0	0	0	0	0	0	0	1	.000	.000	.000	.000	-99	-1	-1	99	0	0	.000	0	0	0	-0	/O	0.0
Total	9	988	3077	485	831	130	24	28	214	477	195	.270	.370	.355	.725	102	20	24	99	73	447	.728	77	33	3	-28	O	-2.9
■ **CHARLIE PECHOUS**	Pechous, Charles Edward b: 10/5/1896, Chicago, Ill. d: 9/13/80, Kenosha, Wis. BR/TR, 6', 170 lbs. Deb: 9/14/15																											
1915	Chi-F	18	51	4	9	3	0	0	4	4	15	.176	.236	.235	.472	41	-4	-4	97	120	4	.405	1			0	3	-0.2
1916	Chi-N	22	69	5	10	1	1	0	4	3	21	.145	.181	.188	.369	11	-7	-8	117	122	3	.288	1			3	3	-0.5
1917	Chi-N	13	41	2	10	0	0	0	1	2	9	.244	.295	.244	.539	63	-2	-2	105	39	3	.452	1			-1	/3S	-0.2
Total	3	53	161	11	29	4	1	0	9	9	45	.180	.228	.217	.445	33	-12	-14	107	100	9	.364	3			2	/3S	-0.9
■ **HAL PECK**	Peck, Harold Arthur b: 4/20/17, Big Bend, Wis. BL/TL, 5'11", 175 lbs. Deb: 5/13/43																											
1943	Bro-N	1	1	0	0	0	0	0	0	0	0	.000	.000	.000	.000	-99	-0	-0	100	0	0	.000	0			0	H	0.0
1944	Phi-A	2	8	0	2	0	0	0	1	0	2	.250	.250	.250	.500	43	-1	-1	101	184	0	.250	0	2	-1	-0	/O	-0.2
1945	Phi-A	112	449	51	124	22	9	5	39	37	28	.276	.331	.399	.730	119	5	8	94	70	61	.662	5	3	-0	-11	*O	-0.7
1946	Phi-A	48	150	14	37	8	2	2	11	16	14	.247	.319	.367	.686	87	-2	-3	104	69	18	.615	1	2	-1	-4	O	-0.9
1947	Cle-A	114	392	58	115	18	2	8	44	27	31	.293	.342	.411	.753	113	3	5	96	87	56	.675	3	3	-1	-12	O	-1.1
1948	Cle-A	45	63	12	18	3	0	0	8	4	8	.286	.328	.333	.662	77	-2	-2	99	129	8	.578	1	0	0	-2	/O	-0.3
1949	Cle-A	33	29	1	9	1	0	0	9	3	3	.310	.375	.345	.720	93	-0	-0	98	309	4	.650	0	0	0	-1	/O	0.0
Total	7	355	1092	136	305	52	13	15	112	87	86	.279	.334	.392	.726	108	3	8	96	86	147	.661	10	10		-29	O	-3.2
■ **ROGER PECKINPAUGH**	Peckinpaugh, Roger Thorpe b: 2/5/1891, Wooster, Ohio d: 11/17/77, Cleveland, Ohio BR/TR, 5'10.5", 165 lbs. Deb: 9/15/10 M																											
1910	Cle-A	15	45	1	9	0	0	0	6	1		.200	.234	.200	.434	36	-3	-3	100	246	3	.389	3			-0	S	-0.3
1912	Cle-A	69	236	18	50	4	1	1	22	16		.212	.262	.250	.512	46	-17	-17	101	121	18	.462	11			-6	S	-1.6
1913	Cle-A	1	0	1	0	0	0	0	0	0	0	—	—	—	—	—	0	0	106	—	—	—	0			0	H	0.0
	NY-A	95	340	35	91	10	7	1	32	24	47	.268	.316	.347	.663	93	-4	-4	101	96	41	.647	19			-10	S	-0.6
	Yr	96	340	36	91	10	7	1	32	24	47	.268	.316	.347	.663	93	-4	-4	101	95	41	.647	19			-10		-0.6
1914	NY-A	157	570	55	127	14	6	3	51	51	73	.223	.288	.284	.572	72	-20	-20	100	119	52	.548	38	17	1	4	*SM	0.0
1915	NY-A	142	540	67	119	18	7	5	44	49	72	.220	.289	.307	.596	80	-16	-15	98	73	53	.547	19	12	-2	2	*S	-0.1
1916	NY-A	145	552	65	141	22	8	4	58	62	50	.255	.332	.346	.678	102	2	1	101	98	72	.662	18			1	*S	1.5
1917	NY-A	148	543	63	141	24	7	0	41	64	46	.260	.340	.330	.670	98	4	-1	107	87	66	.652	17			8	*S	1.4
1918	NY-A	122	446	59	103	15	3	0	43	43	41	.231	.303	.278	.581	80	-13	-10	95	134	42	.531	12			**27**	*S	2.7
1919	NY-A	122	453	89	138	20	2	7	33	59	37	.305	.390	.404	.794	116	16	12	106	56	75	.813	10			26	*S	4.9
1920	NY-A	139	534	109	144	26	6	8	54	72	47	.270	.356	.386	.742	94	-2	-4	102	79	75	.711	8	12	-5	8	*S	1.1
1921	NY-A	149	577	128	166	25	7	8	71	84	44	.288	.380	.397	.777	96	1	-2	103	85	93	.768	2	2	-1	-5	*S	1.0
1922	Was-A	147	520	62	132	14	4	2	48	55	36	.254	.329	.308	.636	73	-24	-18	92	106	57	.581	11	6	-0	16	*S	1.4
1923	Was-A	154	568	73	150	18	4	2	62	64	30	.264	.340	.320	.660	79	-20	-15	95	119	66	.603	10	8	-2	**23**	*S	2.0
1924	Was-A	155	523	72	142	20	5	2	73	72	45	.272	.360	.340	.700	82	-13	-12	98	134	69	.673	11	7	-1	9	*S	1.1
1925	Was-A	126	422	67	124	16	4	4	64	49	23	.294	.367	.379	.746	92	-6	-4	98	125	63	.735	13	4	2	-14	*S/1	0.1
1926	Was-A	57	147	19	35	4	1	1	14	28	12	.238	.360	.299	.659	75	-5	-4	98	101	18	.670	3	0	1	-4	S/1	-0.3
1927	Chi-A	68	217	23	64	6	3	0	23	21	6	.295	.360	.350	.710	83	-4	-5	102	101	28	.654	2	0	1	-5	S	-0.3
Total	17	2011	7233	1006	1876	256	75	48	739	814	609	.259	.336	.335	.672	87	-124	-120	100	102	908	.639	207	68		78	*S/1	14.0
■ **BILL PECOTA**	Pecota, William Joseph b: 2/16/60, Redwood City, Cal. BR/TR, 6'2", 195 lbs. Deb: 9/19/86																											
1986	KC-A	12	29	3	6	2	0	0	2	3	3	.207	.303	.276	.579	60	-2	-2	100	100	2	.462	0	2	-1	1	3/SD	-0.1
1987	KC-A	66	156	22	43	5	1	3	14	15	25	.276	.343	.378	.721	89	-1	-2	104	82	21	.690	5	0	2	6	S32/D	0.7
1988	KC-A	90	178	25	37	3	3	1	15	18	34	.208	.288	.275	.563	57	-10	-10	103	115	16	.528	7	2	1	-3	S31/O2C	-1.0
Total	3	168	363	50	86	10	4	4	31	36	62	.237	.313	.320	.632	71	-13	-14	103	99	40	.596	12	4	1	3	/S321ODC	-0.4
■ **LES PEDEN**	Peden, Leslie Earl "Gooch" b: 9/17/23, Azle, Tex. BR/TR, 6'1.5", 212 lbs. Deb: 4/17/53																											
1953	Was-A	9	28	4	7	1	0	1	1	4	3	.250	.344	.393	.737	104	-0	0	94	26	4	.714	0	0	0	0	/C	0.1
■ **STU PEDERSON**	Pederson, Stuart Russell b: 1/28/60, Palo Alto, Cal. BL/TL, 6', 185 lbs. Deb: 9/08/85																											
1985	LA-N	8	4	1	0	0	0	0	1	0	2	.000	.000	.000	.000	-99	-1	-1	93	0	0	.000	0	0	0	-2	/O	-0.2
■ **AL PEDRIQUE**	Pedrique, Alfredo Jose (Garcia) b: 8/11/60, Aragua, Venez. BR/TR, 6' ", 155 lbs. Deb: 4/14/87																											
1987	NY-N	5	6	1	0	0	0	0	0	1	2	.000	.143	.000	.143	-59	-1	-1	99	0	0	.167	0	0	0	0	/S2	0.0
	Pit-N	88	246	23	74	10	1	1	27	18	27	.301	.356	.362	.718	87	-3	-4	104	117	31	.628	5	4	-1	-4	S/32	0.0
	Yr	93	252	24	74	10	1	1	27	19	29	.294	.350	.353	.704	84	-4	-5	104	111	30	.614	5	4	-1	-4		0.0
1988	Pit-N	50	128	7	23	5	0	0	4	8	17	.180	.234	.219	.452	31	-11	-11	98	57	6	.339	0	0	0	-4	S/3	-1.2
Total	2	143	380	31	97	15	1	1	31	27	46	.255	.311	.308	.619	68	-16	-17	102	95	37	.526	5	4	-1	-8	S/32	-1.2
■ **CHICK PEDROES**	Pedroes, Charles P. b: 10/27/1869, Chicago, Ill. d: 8/6/27, Chicago, Ill. Deb: 8/21/02																											
1902	Chi-N	2	6	0	0	0	0	0	0	0		.000	.000	.000	.000	-99	-1	-1	96	0	0	.000	0			0	/O	-0.1
■ **HOMER PEEL**	Peel, Homer Hefner b: 10/10/02, Port Sullivan, Tex BR/TR, 5'9.5", 170 lbs. Deb: 9/13/27																											
1927	StL-N	2	2	0	0	0	0	0	0	0	1	.000	.000	.000	.000	-93	-1	-1	107	0	0	.000	0			-0	/O	0.0
1929	Phi-N	53	156	16	42	12	1	0	19	12	7	.269	.329	.359	.688	64	-7	-10	110	116	18	.623	1			0	O/1	-1.1
1930	StL-N	26	73	9	12	2	0	0	10	3	4	.164	.197	.197	.389	-5	-13	-13	105	246	3	.279	0			-4	O	-1.6
1933	NY-N	84	148	16	38	1	1	1	12	14	10	.257	.325	.297	.622	80	-4	-3	99	96	15	.513	0			-13	O	-1.9
1934	NY-N	21	41	7	8	0	0	1	3	1	2	.195	.214	.268	.483	29	-4	-4	98	77	2	.343	0			-3	O	-0.6
Total	5	186	420	48	100	15	2	2	44	30	24	.238	.294	.298	.591	53	-28	-31	104	127	38	.494	1			-20	O/1	-5.2
■ **JACK PEERSON**	Peerson, Jack Chiles b: 8/28/10, Brunswick, Ga. d: 10/23/66, Ft.Walton Beach, Fla. BR/TR, 5'11", 175 lbs. Deb: 9/07/35																											
1935	Phi-A	10	19	3	6	1	0	0	1	1	1	.316	.350	.368	.718	86	-0	-0	100	48	2	.615	0	0	0	-0	/S	0.0
1936	Phi-A	8	34	7	11	1	1	0	5	0	3	.324	.324	.412	.735	80	-1	-1	101	122	4	.583	0	1	-1	1	/S2	0.0
Total	2	18	53	10	17	2	1	0	6	1	4	.321	.333	.396	.730	82	-2	-2	100	95	6	.595	0	1	-1	0	/S2	0.0
■ **CHARLIE PEETE**	Peete, Charles "Mule" b: 2/22/29, Franklin, Va. d: 11/27/56, Caracas, Venez. BL/TR, 5'9.5", 190 lbs. Deb: 7/17/56																											
1956	StL-N	23	52	3	10	2	2	0	6	6	10	.192	.288	.308	.596	61	-3	-3	99	158	3	.460	0	2	-1	1	O	-0.3
■ **MONTE PEFFER**	Peffer, Monte (born Montague Pfeiffer) b: 10/8/1891, New York, N.Y. d: 9/27/41, New York, N.Y. BR/TR, 5'4.5", 147 lbs. Deb: 9/29/13																											
1913	Phi-A	1	3	0	0	0	0	0	0	0	1	.000	.250	.000	.250	-27	-0	-0	97	0	0	.333	0			0	/S	0.0
■ **HEINIE PEITZ**	Peitz, Henry Clement b: 11/28/1870, St.Louis, Mo. d: 10/23/43, Cincinnati, Ohio BR/TR, 5'11", 165 lbs. Deb: 10/15/1892 C																											
1892	StL-N	1	3	0	0	0	0	0	0	0	0	.000	.000	.000	.000	-99	-1	-1	95	0	0	.000	0			0	/C	0.0

YEAR	TM/L	G	AB	R	H	2B	3B	HR	RBI	BB	SO	AVG	OBP	SLG	PRO	/A	BR	/A	PF	CHI	RC	TA	SB	CS	SBR	FR	POS	TPR
1893	StL-N	96	362	53	92	12	9	1	45	54	20	.254	.353	.345	.698	88	-5	-5	99	98	50	.711	12			7	CSO/1	0.7
1894	StL-N	99	338	52	89	19	9	3	49	43	21	.263	.348	.399	.748	80	-11	-11	101	96	53	.775	14			-3	3C1/P	-0.8
1895	StL-N	90	334	44	95	14	12	2	65	29	20	.284	.345	.416	.761	98	-2	-2	100	128	52	.749	9			13	C13	1.4
1896	Cin-N	68	211	33	63	12	5	2	34	30	15	.299	.386	.431	.817	112	6	4	105	101	39	.865	7			-7	C	0.3
1897	Cin-N	77	266	35	78	11	7	1	44	18		.293	.340	.398	.739	90	-2	-5	107	120	38	.681	3			6	C/P	0.9
1898	Cin-N	105	330	49	90	15	5	1	43	35		.273	.344	.358	.702	96	2	-2	108	107	45	.679	9			-9	*C	-0.2
1899	Cin-N	93	290	45	79	13	2	1	43	45		.272	.374	.341	.715	94	2	-1	106	129	42	.744	11			-4	C/P	0.1
1900	Cin-N	91	294	34	75	14	1	2	34	20		.255	.303	.330	.632	83	-9	-6	92	103	32	.557	5			9	C/1	1.0
1901	Cin-N	82	269	24	82	13	5	1	24	23		.305	.360	.401	.761	129	8	10	95	72	41	.717	3			5	C2/31	2.2
1902	Cin-N	112	387	54	122	22	5	1	60	24		.315	.355	.406	.761	125	16	11	110	132	60	.709	7			3	2C/13	2.4
1903	Cin-N	105	358	45	93	15	3	0	42	37		.260	.329	.318	.648	79	-5	-10	109	121	41	.596	7			-4	C1/32	-0.6
1904	Cin-N	84	272	32	66	13	2	1	30	14		.243	.280	.316	.596	75	-5	-9	114	123	25	.490	1			2	C1/3	-0.2
1905	Pit-N	88	278	18	62	10	0	0	27	24		.223	.285	.259	.544	62	-12	-13	104	130	22	.454	2			-5	C/2	-0.8
1906	Pit-N	40	125	13	30	8	0	0	20	13		.240	.312	.304	.616	90	-1	-1	104	192	12	.547	1			-3	C	-0.1
1913	StL-N	3	4	1	1	0	1	0	0	0	0	.250	.250	.750	1.000	194	0	0	93	0	1	1.000	0			-0	/CO	0.0
Total	16	1234	4121	532	1117	191	66	16	560	409	76	.271	.338	.361	.699	93	-18	-40	104	115	552	.664	91			10	C/312OSP	6.3

■ **JOE PEITZ** Peitz, Joseph b: 11/8/1869, St.Louis, Mo. d: 12/4/19, St.Louis, Mo. Deb: 7/05/1894

YEAR	TM/L	G	AB	R	H	2B	3B	HR	RBI	BB	SO	AVG	OBP	SLG	PRO	/A	BR	/A	PF	CHI	RC	TA	SB	CS	SBR	FR	POS	TPR
1894	StL-N	7	26	10	11	2	3	0	3	6	1	.423	.531	.731	1.262	202	5	5	101	38	11	1.800	2			0	/O	0.3

■ **EDDIE PELLAGRINI** Pellagrini, Edward Charles b: 3/13/18, Boston, Mass. BR/TR, 5'9", 160 lbs. Deb: 4/22/46

YEAR	TM/L	G	AB	R	H	2B	3B	HR	RBI	BB	SO	AVG	OBP	SLG	PRO	/A	BR	/A	PF	CHI	RC	TA	SB	CS	SBR	FR	POS	TPR
1946	Bos-A	22	71	7	15	3	1	2	4	3	18	.211	.253	.366	.620	63	-3	-4	114	48	6	.525	1	0	0	0	3/S	-0.2
1947	Bos-A	74	231	29	47	8	1	4	19	23	35	.203	.281	.299	.580	57	-12	-15	108	86	21	.508	2	2	-1	-2	3S	-1.7
1948	StL-A	105	290	31	69	8	3	2	27	34	40	.238	.320	.307	.627	63	-13	-16	106	96	30	.548	1	2	-1	11	S	-0.4
1949	StL-A	79	235	26	56	8	1	2	15	14	24	.238	.284	.306	.590	56	-16	-16	100	66	21	.478	2	1	0	-6	S	-2.0
1951	Phi-N	86	197	31	46	4	5	5	30	23	25	.234	.326	.381	.707	92	-3	-2	97	129	26	.682	5	1	1	-7	2/S3	-0.5
1952	Cin-N	46	100	15	17	2	0	1	3	8	18	.170	.231	.220	.451	26	-10	-10	100	47	5	.365	1	0	0	-1	2/1S3	-1.0
1953	Pit-N	78	174	16	44	3	2	4	19	14	20	.253	.309	.362	.671	73	-7	-7	102	99	21	.591	1	1	-0	1	23/S	-0.4
1954	Pit-N	73	125	12	27	6	0	0	16	9	21	.216	.290	.264	.554	47	-10	-9	97	191	11	.465	0	0	0	-0	3/2S	-0.8
Total	8	563	1423	167	321	42	13	20	133	128	201	.226	.295	.316	.611	62	-74	-79	103	97	140	.543	13	7	-0	-6	S23/1	-7.0

■ **BILL PELOUZE** Pelouze, William Nelson b: 9/12/1865, Washington, D.C. d: 6/20/43, Lake Geneva, Wis. TR, 5'8", 170 lbs. Deb: 7/22/1886

YEAR	TM/L	G	AB	R	H	2B	3B	HR	RBI	BB	SO	AVG	OBP	SLG	PRO	/A	BR	/A	PF	CHI	RC	TA	SB	CS	SBR	FR	POS	TPR
1886	StL-N	1	3	0	0	0	0	0	0	0	2	.000	.000	.000	.000	-99	-1	-1	95	0	0	.000	0			0	/O	0.0

■ **JOHN PELTZ** Peltz, John b: 4/23/1861, New Orleans, La. d: 2/27/06, New Orleans, La. BR/TR, Deb: 5/01/1884

YEAR	TM/L	G	AB	R	H	2B	3B	HR	RBI	BB	SO	AVG	OBP	SLG	PRO	/A	BR	/A	PF	CHI	RC	TA	SB	CS	SBR	FR	POS	TPR
1884	Ind-a	106	393	40	86	13	17	3		7		.219	.236	.361	.598	98	-3	-1	96	0	34	.492				1	*O	0.0
1888	Bal-a	1	4	1	1	0	0	0	0	0		.250	.250	.250	.500	66	-0	-0	96	0	1	.667	1			0	/O	0.0
1890	BB-a	98	384	55	87	9	6	1		32		.227	.289	.289	.579	73	-13	-13	100	0	36	.522	10			2	*O	-1.3
	Syr-a	5	17	2	3	1	1	0		3		.176	.300	.353	.653	105	-0	0	90	0	2	.643	0			0	/O	0.0
	Tol-a	20	73	8	18	2	2	0		3		.247	.276	.329	.605	78	-2	-2	103	0	9	.618	7			0	O	-0.1
	Yr	123	474	65	108	12	9	1	0	38		.228	.288	.297	.585	75	-15	-15	100	0	47	.541	17			2		-1.4
Total	3	230	871	106	195	25	26	4	0	45		.224	.265	.326	.591	85	-18	-16	98	0	81	.519	18			4	O	-1.4

■ **BROCK PEMBERTON** Pemberton, Brock b: 11/6/53, Tulsa, Okla. BB/TL, 6'3", 190 lbs. Deb: 9/10/74

YEAR	TM/L	G	AB	R	H	2B	3B	HR	RBI	BB	SO	AVG	OBP	SLG	PRO	/A	BR	/A	PF	CHI	RC	TA	SB	CS	SBR	FR	POS	TPR
1974	NY-N	11	22	0	4	0	0	0	1	0	3	.182	.182	.182	.364	2	-3	-3	99	96	1	.211	0	1	-1	0	/1	-0.3
1975	NY-N	2	2	0	0	0	0	0	0	0	1	.000	.000	.000	.000	-99	-1	-1	95	0	0	.000	0	0	0	0	H	0.0
Total	2	13	24	0	4	0	0	0	1	0	4	.167	.167	.167	.333	-7	-3	-3	99	88	1	.190	0	1	-1	0	/1	-0.3

■ **BERT PENA** Pena, Adalberto (Rivera) b: 7/11/59, Santurce, P.R. BB/TR, 5'11", 165 lbs. Deb: 9/14/81

YEAR	TM/L	G	AB	R	H	2B	3B	HR	RBI	BB	SO	AVG	OBP	SLG	PRO	/A	BR	/A	PF	CHI	RC	TA	SB	CS	SBR	FR	POS	TPR
1981	Hou-N	4	2	0	1	0	0	0	0	0	0	.500	.500	.500	1.000	209	0	0	88	0	1	1.000	0	0	0	0	/S	0.1
1983	Hou-N	4	8	0	1	0	0	0	0	2	2	.125	.300	.125	.425	24	-1	-1	90	0	0	.429	0	0	0	0	/S	0.0
1984	Hou-N	24	39	3	8	1	0	1	4	3	8	.205	.262	.308	.570	64	-2	-2	93	104	2	.441	0	0	0	2	S	0.3
1985	Hou-N	20	29	7	8	2	0	0	4	1	6	.276	.300	.345	.645	83	-1	-1	96	159	3	.500	0	0	0	0	/3S2	0.0
1986	Hou-N	15	29	3	6	1	0	0	2	5	5	.207	.324	.241	.565	57	-1	-2	103	114	2	.500	1	0	0	-1	S/32	0.0
1987	Hou-N	21	46	5	7	0	0	0	0	2	7	.152	.204	.152	.356	-4	-7	-6	93	0	1	.238	0	0	0	-2	S/3	-0.5
Total	6	88	153	18	31	4	0	1	10	13	28	.203	.269	.248	.518	45	-12	-11	95	78	9	.424	1	0	0	-0	/S32	-0.1

■ **TONY PENA** Pena, Antonio Francisco (Padilla) b: 6/4/57, Monte Cristi, D.R. BR/TR, 6', 175 lbs. Deb: 9/01/80

YEAR	TM/L	G	AB	R	H	2B	3B	HR	RBI	BB	SO	AVG	OBP	SLG	PRO	/A	BR	/A	PF	CHI	RC	TA	SB	CS	SBR	FR	POS	TPR
1980	Pit-N	8	21	1	9	1	1	0	1	0	4	.429	.429	.571	1.000	171	2	2	103	33	4	.857	0	1	-1	0	/C	0.2
1981	Pit-N	66	210	16	63	9	1	2	17	8	23	.300	.329	.381	.710	105	-0	1	96	78	25	.588	1	2	-1	4	C	0.5
1982	Pit-N	138	497	53	147	28	4	11	63	17	57	.296	.324	.435	.759	100	5	-1	110	99	63	.642	2	5	-2	4	*C	0.2
1983	Pit-N	151	542	51	163	22	3	15	70	31	73	.301	.339	.435	.774	110	8	6	103	101	75	.684	6	7	-2	10	*C	1.9
1984	Pit-N	147	546	77	156	27	2	15	78	36	79	.286	.334	.425	.759	119	8	11	94	113	74	.689	12	8	-1	19	*C	3.4
1985	Pit-N	147	546	53	136	27	2	10	59	29	67	.249	.287	.361	.648	78	-16	-17	103	106	51	.545	12	8	-1	33	*C/1	2.1
1986	Pit-N	144	510	56	147	26	2	10	52	53	69	.288	.356	.406	.762	110	7	7	100	89	68	.685	9	10	-3	20	*C/1	2.7
1987	StL-N	116	384	40	82	13	4	5	44	36	54	.214	.283	.307	.590	57	-24	-24	99	132	30	.500	6	1	1	-9	*C/1O	-2.1
1988	StL-N	149	505	55	133	23	1	10	51	33	60	.263	.310	.372	.682	91	-4	-6	104	94	56	.591	6	2	1	5	*C1	0.6
Total	9	1066	3761	402	1036	176	20	78	435	243	486	.275	.321	.395	.717	97	-14	-21	101	102	445	.645	54	44	-10	86	*C/1O	9.5

■ **ROBERTO PENA** Pena, Roberto Cesar "Baby" (born Roberto Cesar Zapata (Pena)) b: 4/17/37, Santo Domingo, D.R. d: 7/23/82, Santiago, D.R. BR/TR, 5'8", 170 lbs. Deb: 4/12/65

YEAR	TM/L	G	AB	R	H	2B	3B	HR	RBI	BB	SO	AVG	OBP	SLG	PRO	/A	BR	/A	PF	CHI	RC	TA	SB	CS	SBR	FR	POS	TPR
1965	Chi-N	51	170	17	37	5	1	2	12	16	19	.218	.293	.294	.587	65	-7	-8	102	91	14	.496	1	2	-1	0	S	-0.2
1966	Chi-N	6	17	0	3	2	0	0	1	0	4	.176	.176	.294	.471	28	-2	-2	100	84	1	.357	0	0	0	-0	/S	-0.1
1968	Phi-N	138	500	56	130	13	2	1	38	34	63	.260	.310	.300	.610	86	-9	-8	97	107	45	.490	3	5	-2	6	*S	1.3
1969	SD-N	139	472	44	118	16	3	4	30	21	63	.250	.286	.322	.608	73	-19	-18	97	75	41	.480	0	3	-2	-6	S231	-1.6
1970	Oak-A	19	58	4	15	1	0	0	3	3	4	.259	.295	.276	.571	60	-3	-3	97	76	4	.435	1	1	-0	-1	S/3	-0.3
	Mil-A	121	416	36	99	19	1	3	42	25	45	.238	.284	.310	.595	65	-21	-20	98	123	34	.475	3	5	-2	-12	S2/1	-2.5
	Yr	140	474	40	114	20	1	3	45	28	49	.241	.286	.306	.592	64	-24	-23	98	117	39	.472	4	6	-2	-13		-2.8
1971	Mil-A	113	274	17	65	9	3	3	28	15	37	.237	.279	.325	.604	68	-11	-12	103	117	24	.493	2	1	0	-2	13S/2	-1.6
Total	6	587	1907	174	467	65	10	13	154	114	235	.245	.291	.310	.601	72	-73	-70	99	101	164	.495	10	17	-7	-16	S/132	-5.0

■ **ELMER PENCE** Pence, Elmer Clair b: 8/17/1900, Valley Springs, Cal. d: 9/17/68, San Francisco, Cal. BR/TR, 6', 185 lbs. Deb: 8/23/22

YEAR	TM/L	G	AB	R	H	2B	3B	HR	RBI	BB	SO	AVG	OBP	SLG	PRO	/A	BR	/A	PF	CHI	RC	TA	SB	CS	SBR	FR	POS	TPR
1922	Chi-A	1	0	0	0	0	0	0	0	0	0	—	—	—	—	—	0	0	101	—	—	—	0	0	0	-0	/O	0.0

■ **JIM PENDLETON** Pendleton, James Edward b: 1/7/24, St.Charles, Mo. BR/TR, 6', 185 lbs. Deb: 4/17/53

YEAR	TM/L	G	AB	R	H	2B	3B	HR	RBI	BB	SO	AVG	OBP	SLG	PRO	/A	BR	/A	PF	CHI	RC	TA	SB	CS	SBR	FR	POS	TPR
1953	Mil-N	120	251	48	75	12	4	7	27	7	36	.299	.323	.462	.785	108	-0	2	94	77	35	.704	6	5	-1	-14	*O/S	-1.6
1954	Mil-N	71	173	20	38	3	1	1	16	4	21	.220	.237	.266	.503	33	-18	-16	93	129	11	.377	2	1	0	-3	O	-2.0
1955	Mil-N	8	10	0	0	0	0	0	0	0	2	.000	.000	.000	.000	-99	-3	-3	93	0	0	.000	0	0	0	0	/S3O	-0.2
1956	Mil-N	14	11	0	0	0	0	0	0	1	3	.000	.083	.000	.083	-76	-3	-3	99	0	0	.083	0	0	0	0	/S312	-0.2
1957	Pit-N	46	59	9	18	1	1	0	9	9	14	.305	.406	.356	.762	114	1	2	94	178	9	.721	0	0	0	-2	/O3S	0.0
1958	Pit-N	3	3	0	1	0	0	0	0	0	0	.333	.333	.333	.667	81	-0	-0	95	0	0	.500	0	0	0	0	H	0.0
1959	Cin-N	65	113	13	29	2	0	3	9	8	18	.257	.311	.354	.665	74	-4	-4	103	74	12	.591	3	0	1	-3	O3/S	-0.6
1962	Hou-N	117	321	30	79	12	2	8	36	14	57	.246	.282	.371	.653	79	-13	-10	93	99	33	.544	0	0	0	-6	O/13S	-2.0
Total	8	444	941	120	240	30	8	19	97	43	151	.255	.292	.365	.656	76	-39	-32	95	98	100	.565	11	6	-0	-28	O/3S12	-6.6

■ **TERRY PENDLETON** Pendleton, Terry Lee b: 7/16/60, Los Angeles, Cal. BB/TR, 5'9", 178 lbs. Deb: 7/18/84

YEAR	TM/L	G	AB	R	H	2B	3B	HR	RBI	BB	SO	AVG	OBP	SLG	PRO	/A	BR	/A	PF	CHI	RC	TA	SB	CS	SBR	FR	POS	TPR
1984	StL-N	67	262	37	85	16	3	1	33	16	32	.324	.363	.420	.783	121	6	7	99	121	40	.772	20	5	3	11	3	2.1
1985	StL-N	149	559	56	134	16	3	5	69	37	75	.240	.287	.306	.593	69	-26	-23	96	151	45	.495	17	12	-2	26	*3	0.2
1986	StL-N	159	578	56	138	26	5	1	59	34	59	.239	.282	.306	.588	60	-30	-32	103	133	50	.515	24	6	4	24	*3/O	-0.8
1987	StL-N	159	583	82	167	29	4	12	96	70	74	.286	.365	.412	.777	107	6	7	99	142	86	.742	19	12	-2	16	*3	2.0
1988	StL-N	110	391	44	99	20	2	6	53	21	51	.253	.295	.361	.655	84	-7	-9	104	136	39	.549	3	3	-1	9	*3	0.0

YEAR	TM/L	G	AB	R	H	2B	3B	HR	RBI	BB	SO	AVG	OBP	SLG	PRO	/A	BR	/A	PF	CHI	RC	TA	SB	CS	SBR	FR	POS	TPR
Total	5	644	2373	275	623	107	17	25	310	178	291	.263	.315	.354	.669	85	-51	-50	100	139	260	.615	83	38	2	86	3/O	3.5
■ **JIMMY PEOPLES**	Peoples, James Elsworth b: 10/8/1863, Big Beaver, Mich. d: 8/29/20, Detroit, Mich. TR, 5'8", 200 lbs. Deb: 5/29/1884																											
1884	Cin-a	69	267	28	45	2	3	0		6		.169	.187	.199	.385	26	-20	-22	106	0	10	.266				-8	SCO/31	-2.9
1885	Cin-a	7	22	1	4	0	0	0		1		.182	.217	.182	.399	28	-2	-2	104	0	1	.278				-3	/CPO	-0.3
	Bro-a	41	151	21	30	4	1	1		5		.199	.229	.258	.488	54	-7	-8	104	0	9	.372				-4	C/S1O	-0.5
	Yr	48	173	22	34	4	1	1		6		.197	.228	.249	.476	51	-9	-10	104	0	10	.360				-7		-0.8
1886	Bro-a	93	340	43	74	7	3	3		20		.218	.261	.282	.543	72	-11	-11	100	0	31	.511	20			5	CS/O3	-0.1
1887	Bro-a	73	268	36	68	14	2	1		16		.254	.306	.332	.638	81	-7	-7	99	0	35	.655	22			-3	C/OS12	0.0
1888	Bro-a	32	103	15	20	5	3	0	17	8		.194	.259	.301	.560	78	-2	-3	105	164	11	.602	10			0	C/SO	-0.2
1889	Col-a	29	100	13	23	6	2	1	16	6	8	.230	.274	.360	.634	90	-3	-1	91	117	11	.584	3			0	C/O2S	0.0
Total	6	344	1251	157	264	38	14	6	33	62	8	.211	.252	.278	.530	63	-52	-54	101	23	108	.477	55			-14	C/SO123P	-4.0
■ **JOE PEPITONE**	Pepitone, Joseph Anthony "Pepi" b: 10/9/40, Brooklyn, N.Y. BL/TL, 6'2", 185 lbs. Deb: 4/10/62 C																											
1962	NY-A	63	138	14	33	3	2	7	17	3	21	.239	.255	.442	.697	89	-4	-3	94	82	13	.586	1	1	-0	-8	O1	-1.3
1963	NY-A	157	580	79	157	16	3	27	89	23	63	.271	.307	.448	.755	108	5	4	101	111	76	.669	3	5	-2	-1	*1O	-0.3
1964	NY-A	160	613	71	154	12	3	28	100	24	63	.251	.283	.418	.700	89	-9	-11	103	127	67	.597	2	1	0	-1	*1O	-1.8
1965	NY-A	143	531	51	131	18	3	18	62	43	59	.247	.306	.394	.699	96	-3	-4	101	100	62	.623	4	2	0	1	*1O	-1.0
1966	NY-A	152	585	85	149	21	4	31	83	29	58	.255	.292	.463	.755	121	8	12	94	101	74	.675	4	3	-1	6	*1O	1.1
1967	NY-A	133	501	45	126	18	3	13	64	34	62	.251	.303	.377	.680	106	-1	2	94	124	53	.576	1	3	-2	-0	*O/1	-0.3
1968	NY-A	108	380	41	93	9	3	15	56	37	45	.245	.313	.403	.716	114	7	6	101	124	48	.672	8	2	1	-9	O1	-0.6
1969	NY-A	135	513	49	124	16	3	27	70	30	42	.242	.285	.442	.727	106	-3	0	95	97	59	.652	8	6	-1	-5	*1	-1.6
1970	Hou-N	75	279	44	70	9	5	14	35	18	28	.251	.299	.470	.768	110	-1	2	94	80	37	.711	5	2	0	-1	1O	-0.4
	Chi-N	56	213	38	57	9	2	12	44	15	15	.268	.316	.498	.813	95	3	-2	120	127	33	.756	0	2	-1	4	O1	-0.3
	Yr	131	492	82	127	18	7	26	79	33	43	.258	.306	.482	.788	103	2	-1	105	101	73	.744	5	4	-1	3		-0.7
1971	Chi-N	115	427	50	131	19	4	16	61	24	41	.307	.349	.482	.832	122	17	12	110	100	67	.753	1	2	-1	0	1O	0.4
1972	Chi-N	66	214	23	56	5	0	8	21	13	22	.262	.313	.397	.710	88	-0	-4	114	79	26	.622	1	2	-1	3	1	-0.5
1973	Chi-N	31	112	16	30	3	0	3	18	8	6	.268	.322	.375	.697	85	-1	-2	108	145	14	.643	3	1	0	2	1	0.0
	Atl-N	3	11	0	4	0	0	0	1	1	1	.364	.417	.364	.780	104	0	0	113	102	1	.556	0	0	0	0	/1	0.0
	Yr	34	123	16	34	3	0	3	19	9	7	.276	.331	.374	.705	87	-1	-2	109	145	16	.641	3	1	0	2		0.0
Total	12	1397	5097	606	1315	158	35	219	721	302	526	.258	.303	.432	.735	105	18	13	101	108	629	.674	41	32	-7	-9	1O	-6.6
■ **HENRY PEPLOSKI**	Peploski, Henry Stephen "Pep" b: 9/15/05, Garlin, Poland d: 1/28/82, Dover, N.J. BL/TR, 5'9", 155 lbs. Deb: 9/19/29																											
1929	Bos-N	6	10	1	2	0	0	0	1	1	3	.200	.273	.200	.473	20	-1	-1	94	171	1	.375	0			-0	/3	0.0
■ **PEPPER PEPLOSKI**	Peploski, Joseph Aloysius b: 9/12/1891, Brooklyn, N.Y. Deceased BR/TR, 5'8", 155 lbs. Deb: 6/24/13																											
1913	Det-A	2	4	1	2	0	0	0	0	0	0	.500	.500	.500	1.000	195	0	0	99	0	1	1.000	0			0	/3	0.1
■ **DON PEPPER**	Pepper, Donald Hoyte b: 10/8/43, Saratoga Sprgs., N.Y BL/TR, 6'4.5", 215 lbs. Deb: 9/10/66																											
1966	Det-A	4	3	0	0	0	0	0	0	0	1	.000	.000	.000	.000	-98	-1	-1	102	0	0	.000	0	0	0	0	/1	0.0
■ **ROY PEPPER**	Pepper, Raymond Watson b: 8/5/05, Decatur, Ala. BR/TR, 6'2", 195 lbs. Deb: 4/15/32																											
1932	StL-N	21	57	3	14	2	1	0	7	5	13	.246	.306	.316	.622	68	-3	-3	100	145	6	.558	1			-1	O	-0.4
1933	StL-N	3	9	2	2	0	0	1	2	0	1	.222	.222	.556	.778	114	0	0	102	94	1	.625	0			-0	/O	0.0
1934	StL-A	148	564	71	168	24	6	7	101	29	67	.298	.333	.399	.732	85	-11	-14	104	140	73	.640	1	4	-2	10	*O	-0.7
1935	StL-A	92	261	20	66	15	3	4	37	20	32	.253	.306	.379	.685	72	-10	-12	107	113	30	.604	0	2	-1	-4	O	-1.6
1936	StL-A	75	124	13	35	5	0	2	23	5	23	.282	.310	.371	.681	65	-7	-7	103	143	13	.560	0	2	-1	-2	O	-0.9
Total	5	339	1015	109	285	46	10	14	170	59	136	.281	.321	.387	.708	78	-30	-36	104	133	123	.617	2	8		2	O	-3.6
■ **JACK PERCONTE**	Perconte, John Patrick b: 8/31/54, Joliet, Ill. BL/TR, 5'10", 160 lbs. Deb: 9/13/80																											
1980	LA-N	14	17	2	4	0	0	0	2	2	1	.235	.316	.235	.551	58	-1	-1	97	198	2	.643	3	0	1	-0	/2	0.0
1981	LA-N	8	9	2	2	0	1	0	1	2	2	.222	.364	.444	.808	131	0	0	98	98	1	.875	1	1	-0	0	/2	0.0
1982	Cle-A	93	219	27	52	4	4	0	15	22	25	.237	.307	.292	.599	65	-10	-10	100	94	22	.556	9	3	1	-1	2/D	-0.4
1983	Cle-A	14	26	1	7	1	0	0	0	5	2	.269	.387	.308	.695	89	0	-0	105	0	4	.800	3	1	0	1	2	0.2
1984	Sea-A	155	612	93	180	24	4	0	31	57	47	.294	.359	.346	.705	94	-1	-3	102	56	84	.684	29	6	5	5	*2	1.5
1985	Sea-A	125	485	60	128	17	7	2	23	50	36	.264	.336	.340	.677	91	-8	-5	95	57	62	.677	31	2	8	14	*2	2.2
1986	Chi-A	24	73	6	16	1	0	0	4	11	10	.219	.321	.233	.554	55	-4	-4	101	94	6	.508	2	0	1	-1	2	-0.2
Total	7	433	1441	191	389	47	16	2	76	149	123	.270	.342	.329	.671	86	-24	-22	99	65	181	.664	78	13	16	19	2/D	3.3
■ **TONY PEREZ**	Perez, Atanacio (Rigal) b: 5/14/42, Camaguey, Cuba BR/TR, 6'2", 175 lbs. Deb: 7/26/64 C																											
1964	Cin-N	12	25	1	2	1	0	0	1	3	9	.080	.179	.120	.299	-14	-4	-4	103	137	1	.261	0	0	0	0	/1	-0.3
1965	Cin-N	104	281	40	73	14	4	12	47	21	67	.260	.316	.466	.782	113	6	4	104	117	38	.700	0	2	-1	-1	1	-0.2
1966	Cin-N	99	257	25	68	10	4	4	39	14	44	.265	.308	.381	.689	79	-4	-8	114	149	27	.572	1	0	0	-4	1	-1.6
1967	Cin-N	156	600	78	174	28	7	26	102	33	102	.290	.331	.490	.821	121	22	16	109	120	91	.745	0	3	-2	-23	*31/2	-1.7
1968	Cin-N	160	625	93	176	25	7	18	92	51	92	.282	.342	.430	.772	117	23	15	111	127	88	.700	3	2	-0	5	*3	2.3
1969	Cin-N	160	629	103	185	31	2	37	122	63	131	.294	.360	.526	.886	147	36	37	99	117	114	.858	4	2	0	0	*3	3.9
1970	Cin-N	158	587	107	186	28	6	40	129	83	134	.317	.405	.589	.994	156	52	49	104	114	140	1.053	8	3	1	-4	*3/1	3.9
1971	Cin-N	158	609	72	164	22	3	25	91	51	120	.269	.327	.438	.765	119	10	13	96	115	86	.704	4	1	1	12	*31	2.3
1972	Cin-N	136	515	64	146	33	7	21	90	55	121	.283	.353	.497	.850	149	25	29	93	123	90	.829	4	2	0	-7	*1	1.4
1973	Cin-N	151	564	73	177	33	3	27	101	74	117	.314	.396	.527	.923	165	41	46	93	114	118	.940	3	1	0	-5	*1	3.5
1974	Cin-N	158	596	81	158	28	2	28	101	61	112	.265	.335	.460	.795	123	14	16	98	111	88	.738	1	3	-2	-3	*1	0.4
1975	Cin-N	137	511	74	144	28	3	20	109	54	101	.282	.354	.466	.820	121	17	14	104	144	83	.777	1	2	-1	-5	*1	0.1
1976	Cin-N	139	527	77	137	32	6	19	91	50	88	.260	.330	.452	.782	117	12	10	103	121	78	.748	10	5	0	-4	*1	0.0
1977	Mon-N	154	559	71	158	32	6	19	91	63	111	.283	.357	.463	.821	120	14	15	98	118	91	.785	4	3	-1	8	*1	1.5
1978	Mon-N	148	544	63	158	38	3	14	78	38	104	.290	.339	.449	.788	124	12	12	96	110	82	.722	2	0	1	-2	*1	0.8
1979	Mon-N	132	489	58	132	29	4	13	73	38	82	.270	.326	.425	.752	101	1	-0	102	119	65	.675	2	1	0	-4	*1	-1.0
1980	Bos-A	151	585	73	161	31	3	25	105	41	93	.275	.324	.467	.790	112	9	8	102	125	80	.704	1	0	0	1	*1D	0.0
1981	Bos-A	84	306	35	77	11	3	9	39	27	66	.252	.312	.395	.708	97	1	-2	106	105	37	.622	0	0	0	0	1D	-0.3
1982	Bos-A	69	196	18	51	14	2	6	31	19	48	.260	.326	.444	.769	99	2	-1	110	118	27	.697	0	1	-1	0	D/1	0.0
1983	Phi-N	91	253	18	61	11	2	6	43	28	57	.241	.319	.372	.691	90	-3	-3	101	152	29	.617	1	0	0	1	1	-0.5
1984	Cin-N	71	137	9	33	6	1	2	15	11	21	.241	.297	.343	.640	75	-4	-5	106	111	12	.518	0	0	0	-2	1	-0.7
1985	Cin-N	72	183	25	60	8	0	6	33	22	22	.328	.400	.470	.870	135	11	10	105	126	35	.850	0	2	-1	-0	1	0.7
1986	Cin-N	77	200	14	51	12	1	2	29	25	25	.255	.338	.355	.693	87	-2	-3	104	150	24	.619	0	0	0	-2	1	-0.7
Total	23	2777	9778	1272	2732	505	79	379	1652	925	1867	.279	.344	.463	.808	122	292	272	102	121	1523	.783	49	33	-5	-41	*13/D2	13.8
■ **MARTY PEREZ**	Perez, Martin Roman b: 2/28/47, Visalia, Cal. BR/TR, 5'11", 160 lbs. Deb: 9/09/69																											
1969	Cal-A	13	13	3	3	0	0	0	0	2	1	.231	.333	.231	.564	61	-1	-1	99	0	1	.455	0	0	0	-0	/S23	0.0
1970	Cal-A	3	3	0	0	0	0	0	1	0	0	.000	.000	.000	.000	-99	-1	-1	92	0	0	.000	0	0	0	0	/S	0.0
1971	Atl-N	130	410	28	93	15	3	4	32	25	44	.227	.273	.307	.580	58	-20	-24	110	94	32	.459	1	2	-1	-18	*S/2	-2.8
1972	Atl-N	141	479	33	109	13	1	1	28	30	55	.228	.277	.265	.542	52	-28	-31	105	89	32	.406	0	3	-2	-31	*S	-5.1
1973	Atl-N	141	501	66	125	15	5	8	57	49	66	.250	.319	.347	.666	75	-10	-18	113	118	54	.572	2	3	-1	-12	*S	-1.2
1974	Atl-N	127	447	51	116	20	5	2	34	35	51	.260	.315	.340	.655	79	-10	-13	105	85	47	.552	2	0	1	-2	*2S/3	-0.8
1975	Atl-N	120	461	50	127	14	2	2	34	37	44	.275	.329	.328	.657	87	-10	-8	95	89	48	.540	2	2	-1	-3	*2/S	-0.4
1976	Atl-N	31	96	12	24	4	0	1	6	8	9	.250	.308	.323	.631	71	-3	-4	111	68	9	.500	0	0	0	-0	2S/3	-0.1
	SF-N	93	332	37	86	13	1	2	26	30	28	.259	.320	.322	.643	80	-7	-8	103	90	36	.556	3	4	-2	9	2/S	0.4
	Yr	124	428	49	110	17	1	3	32	38	37	.257	.318	.322	.640	78	-10	-12	105	85	47	.552	3	4	-2	9		0.3
1977	NY-A	1	4	0	2	0	0	0	0	0	1	.500	.500	.500	1.000	176	0	0	99	0	1	.667	0	0	0	0	/3	0.0
	Oak-A	115	373	32	86	14	5	2	23	29	65	.231	.291	.311	.602	68	-18	-16	95	75	33	.500	1	3	-2	-5	*23/S	-1.3
	Yr	116	377	32	88	14	5	2	23	29	66	.233	.293	.313	.606	69	-18	-15	95	74	34	.503	1	3	-2	-5		-1.3

YEAR	TM/L	G	AB	R	H	2B	3B	HR	RBI	BB	SO	AVG	OBP	SLG	PRO	/A	BR	/A	PF	CHI	RC	TA	SB	CS	SBR	FR	POS	TPR
1978	Oak-A	16	12	1	0	0	0	0	0	0	5	.000	.000	.000	.000	-99	-3	-3	101	0	0	.000	0	0	0	-0	3/S2	-0.3
Total	10	931	3131	313	771	108	22	22	241	245	369	.246	.303	.316	.619	70	-111	-126	104	91	291	.528	11	17	-7	-63	S2/3	-11.6
■ **TONY PEREZCHIA** Perezchia, Antonio Llamas b: 4/20/66, Mexicali, Mex. BR/TR, 5'11", 165 lbs. Deb: 9/07/88																												
1988	SF-N	7	8	1	1	0	0	0	1	2	1	.125	.300	.125	.425	28	-1	-1	94	400	1	.429	0	0	0	0	/2	0.0
■ **BRODERICK PERKINS** Perkins, Broderick Phillip b: 11/23/54, Pittsburg, Cal. BL/TL, 5'10", 180 lbs. Deb: 7/07/78																												
1978	SD-N	62	217	14	52	14	1	2	33	5	29	.240	.257	.341	.598	71	-11	-9	93	164	18	.488	4	0	1	-1	1	-1.0
1979	SD-N	57	87	8	23	0	0	0	8	8	12	.264	.326	.264	.591	65	-4	-4	96	138	7	.463	0	0	0	0	1	-0.4
1980	SD-N	43	100	18	37	9	0	2	14	11	10	.370	.432	.520	.952	177	9	10	93	96	24	1.016	2	1	0	-3	1O	0.6
1981	SD-N	92	254	27	71	18	3	2	40	14	16	.280	.317	.398	.715	109	-0	2	93	147	29	.596	0	4	-2	-2	1/O	-0.5
1982	SD-N	125	347	32	94	10	4	2	34	26	20	.271	.327	.340	.667	95	-6	-2	92	108	39	.573	2	1	0	-5	1O	-1.3
1983	Cle-A	79	184	23	50	10	0	0	24	9	19	.272	.306	.326	.632	70	-6	-8	105	156	17	.493	1	5	-3	2	1OD	-0.8
1984	Cle-A	58	66	5	13	1	0	0	4	7	10	.197	.284	.212	.496	37	-5	-6	106	114	4	.393	0	0	0	0	D/1	-0.5
Total	7	516	1255	127	340	62	8	8	157	80	116	.271	.317	.352	.669	91	-23	-17	95	133	138	.576	9	11	-4	-8	1/OD	-3.9
■ **CY PERKINS** Perkins, Ralph Foster b: 2/27/1896, Gloucester, Mass. d: 10/2/63, Philadelphia, Pa. BR/TR, 5'10.5", 158 lbs. Deb: 9/25/15 MC																												
1915	Phi-A	7	20	2	4	1	0	0	0	3	3	.200	.304	.250	.554	69	-1	-1	96	0	2	.500	0			1	/C	0.1
1917	Phi-A	6	18	1	3	0	0	0	2	2	1	.167	.250	.167	.417	29	-2	-1	94	239	1	.333	0			0	/C	0.0
1918	Phi-A	68	218	9	41	4	1	1	14	8	15	.188	.217	.229	.446	33	-18	-19	104	96	11	.333	1			13	C	0.0
1919	Phi-A	101	305	22	77	12	7	2	29	27	22	.252	.313	.357	.671	83	-5	-8	106	91	33	.605	2			11	C/S	0.9
1920	Phi-A	148	492	40	128	24	6	5	52	28	35	.260	.303	.364	.667	81	-18	-14	94	94	53	.578	5	6	-2	14	*C/2	0.9
1921	Phi-A	141	538	58	155	31	4	12	73	32	32	.288	.329	.428	.757	89	-9	-11	103	96	73	.684	5	9	-4	8	*C	-0.2
1922	Phi-A	148	505	58	135	20	6	6	69	40	30	.267	.322	.366	.689	76	-16	-19	104	124	59	.602	1	7	-4	2	*C	-1.6
1923	Phi-A	143	500	53	135	34	5	2	65	65	30	.270	.356	.370	.726	91	-5	-6	100	119	69	.688	1	3	-2	-5	*C	-0.1
1924	Phi-A	128	392	31	95	19	4	0	32	31	20	.242	.304	.311	.616	59	-24	-24	99	87	38	.532	3	4	-2	-8	*C	-2.4
1925	Phi-A	65	140	21	43	10	0	1	18	26	6	.307	.426	.400	.826	107	4	3	103	102	26	.876	0	0	0	-7	C/3	0.0
1926	Phi-A	63	148	14	43	6	0	0	19	18	7	.291	.371	.331	.702	72	-3	-7	118	132	19	.636	0	2	-1	-1	C	-0.4
1927	Phi-A	59	137	11	35	7	2	1	15	12	8	.255	.315	.358	.673	77	-5	-5	97	96	15	.598	0	0	0	-1	C/1	-0.3
1928	Phi-A	19	29	1	5	0	0	0	1	1	1	.172	.200	.172	.372	-1	-4	-4	103	69	1	.240	0	1	-1	0	C	-0.2
1929	Phi-A	38	76	4	16	4	0	0	9	5	4	.211	.259	.263	.522	32	-7	-8	109	154	5	.417	0	0	0	-1	C	-0.4
1930	Phi-A	20	38	1	6	2	0	0	4	2	3	.158	.200	.211	.411	4	-6	-6	99	166	2	.313	0	0	0	-0	C/1	-0.3
1931	NY-A	16	47	3	12	1	0	0	7	1	4	.255	.286	.277	.562	49	-3	-3	98	178	4	.429	0	0	0	-0	C	-0.2
1934	Det-A	1	1	0	0	0	0	0	0	0	0	.000	.000	.000	.000	-99	-0	-0	98	0	0	.000	0	0	0	0	H	0.0
Total	17	1171	3604	329	933	175	35	30	409	301	221	.259	.319	.352	.670	75	-124	-133	102	106	411	.593	18	32		24	*C/S132	-4.2
■ **SAM PERLOZZO** Perlozzo, Samuel Benedict b: 3/4/51, Cumberland, Md. BR/TR, 5'9", 170 lbs. Deb: 9/13/77 C																												
1977	Min-A	10	24	6	7	0	2	0	0	2	3	.292	.346	.458	.804	114	1	0	103	0	4	.765	0	0	0	0	2/3	0.2
1979	SD-N	2	2	0	0	0	0	0	0	1	0	.000	.333	.000	.333	-1	-0	-0	96	0	0	.500	0	0	0	0	/2	0.0
Total	2	12	26	6	7	0	2	0	0	3	3	.269	.345	.423	.768	106	0	0	102	0	4	.737	0	0	0	0	/23	0.2
■ **JOHN PERRIN** Perrin, John Stephenson b: 2/4/1898, Escanaba, Mich. d: 6/24/69, Detroit, Mich. BL/TR, 5'9", 160 lbs. Deb: 7/11/21																												
1921	Bos-A	4	13	3	3	0	0	0	1	0	3	.231	.231	.231	.462	18	-2	-2	100	114	1	.300	0	0	0	-2	/O	-0.3
■ **NIG PERRINE** Perrine, John Grover b: 1/14/1885, Clinton, Wis. d: 8/13/48, Kansas City, Mo. TR, 5'9", 160 lbs. Deb: 4/11/07																												
1907	Was-A	44	146	13	25	4	1	0	15	13		.171	.239	.212	.451	51	-9	-7	90	176	10	.446	10			-7	2S/3	-1.5
■ **GEORGE PERRING** Perring, George Wilson b: 8/13/1884, Sharon, Wis. d: 8/20/60, Beloit, Wis. BR/TR, 6', 190 lbs. Deb: 4/30/08																												
1908	Cle-A	89	310	23	67	8	5	0	19	16		.216	.255	.274	.529	70	-9	-11	106	86	21	.416	0			-13	S3	-2.3
1909	Cle-A	88	283	26	63	10	9	0	20	19		.223	.283	.322	.605	89	-3	-4	102	86	26	.550	6			-3	3S/2	-0.4
1910	Cle-A	39	122	14	27	6	3	0	8	3		.221	.240	.320	.560	75	-4	-4	100	76	10	.474	3			1	3/1	-0.1
1914	KC-F	144	496	68	138	28	10	2	69	59	39	.278	.355	.387	.742	118	9	12	95	128	74	.721	7			9	*31/PS	2.4
1915	KC-F	153	553	67	143	23	7	7	67	57	30	.259	.328	.363	.691	108	3	5	97	105	73	.654	10			12	*312/S	2.1
Total	5	513	1764	198	438	75	34	9	183	154	69	.248	.310	.345	.655	99	-5	-2	99	103	204	.598	26			5	3/1S2P	1.7
■ **BOYD PERRY** Perry, Boyd Glenn b: 3/21/14, Snow Camp, N.C. BR/TR, 5'10", 158 lbs. Deb: 5/23/41																												
1941	Det-A	36	83	9	15	5	0	0	11	10	9	.181	.269	.241	.510	34	-8	-8	106	195	6	.437	1	0	0	-0	S2	-0.5
■ **CLAY PERRY** Perry, Clayton Shields b: 12/18/1881, Rice Lake, Wis. d: 1/16/54, Rice Lake, Wis. TR, 5'10.5", 175 lbs. Deb: 9/02/08																												
1908	Det-A	7	17	0	2	0	0	0	0	0		.118	.118	.118	.235	-22	-2	-2	101	0	0	.133	0			-0	/3	-0.2
■ **GERALD PERRY** Perry, Gerald June b: 10/30/60, Savannah, Ga. BL/TR, 5'11", 180 lbs. Deb: 8/11/83																												
1983	Atl-N	27	39	5	14	2	0	1	6	5	4	.359	.432	.487	.919	146	3	3	106	108	8	.889	0	1	-1	-0	/1O	0.1
1984	Atl-N	122	347	52	92	12	2	7	47	61	38	.265	.378	.372	.750	102	8	3	110	123	50	.750	15	12	-3	-7	1O	-1.0
1985	Atl-N	110	238	22	51	5	0	3	13	23	28	.214	.284	.273	.557	53	-14	-15	106	70	18	.487	9	5	-0	-0	1/O	-1.8
1986	Atl-N	29	70	6	19	2	0	2	11	8	4	.271	.346	.386	.732	100	0	0	102	133	8	.625	0	1	-1	-5	O/1	-0.6
1987	Atl-N	142	533	77	144	35	2	12	74	48	63	.270	.332	.411	.742	88	-4	-10	108	118	69	.733	42	16	3	-5	*1/O	-1.9
1988	Atl-N	141	547	61	164	29	1	8	74	36	49	.300	.344	.400	.745	108	9	6	104	129	70	.687	29	14	0	2	*1	0.1
Total	6	571	1774	223	484	85	5	33	225	181	186	.273	.342	.382	.724	94	2	-13	107	116	224	.706	95	49	-1	-16	1/O	-5.1
■ **BOB PERRY** Perry, Melvin Gray b: 9/14/34, New Bern, N.C. BR/TR, 6'2", 180 lbs. Deb: 5/17/63																												
1963	LA-A	61	166	16	42	9	0	3	14	9	31	.253	.303	.361	.665	93	-3	-2	91	85	18	.566	1	1	-0	-7	O	-1.0
1964	LA-A	70	221	19	61	8	1	3	16	14	52	.276	.319	.362	.681	100	-3	-0	89	76	25	.576	1	1	-0	0	O	-0.3
Total	2	131	387	35	103	17	1	6	30	23	83	.266	.312	.362	.674	97	-7	-2	90	80	43	.579	2	2	-1	-7	O	-1.3
■ **HANK PERRY** Perry, William Henry "Socks" b: 7/28/1886, Howell, Mich. d: 7/18/56, Pontiac, Mich. BL/TR, 5'11", 190 lbs. Deb: 4/12/12																												
1912	Det-A	13	36	3	6	1	0	0	0	3		.167	.231	.194	.425	23	-4	-3	95	0	2	.333	0			2	/O	-0.1
■ **JOHNNY PESKY** Pesky, John Michael (born John Michael Paveskovich) b: 9/27/19, Portland, Ore. BL/TR, 5'9", 168 lbs. Deb: 4/14/42 MC																												
1942	Bos-A	147	620	105	**205**	29	9	2	51	42	36	.331	.375	.416	.791	118	18	15	104	60	100	.730	12	7	-1	19	*S	4.0
1946	Bos-A	153	621	115	**208**	43	4	2	55	65	29	.335	.401	.427	.827	115	27	17	114	68	111	.797	9	8	-2	12	*S	2.9
1947	Bos-A	155	638	106	**207**	27	8	0	39	72	22	.324	.393	.392	.785	110	18	12	108	51	103	.742	12	9	-2	-12	*S3	-0.1
1948	Bos-A	143	565	124	159	26	6	3	55	99	32	.281	.394	.365	.759	102	6	6	100	76	90	.746	3	5	-2	10	*3	0.8
1949	Bos-A	148	604	111	185	27	7	2	69	100	19	.306	.408	.384	.792	103	13	7	107	86	104	.791	8	4	0	20	*3	2.6
1950	Bos-A	127	490	112	153	22	6	1	49	104	31	.312	.437	.388	.825	98	16	5	114	84	93	.858	2	1	0	14	*3/S	1.4
1951	Bos-A	131	480	93	150	20	6	3	41	84	15	.313	.417	.398	.815	112	18	13	108	78	87	.816	2	2	-1	11	*S3/2	2.9
1952	Bos-A	25	67	10	10	2	0	0	2	15	5	.149	.313	.179	.492	37	-5	-6	107	62	4	.459	0	3	-2	-0	3/S	-0.7
	Det-A	69	177	26	45	4	0	1	9	41	11	.254	.394	.294	.688	94	1	1	99	61	25	.691	1	2	-1	-0	S2/3	0.3
	Yr	94	244	36	55	6	0	1	11	56	16	.225	.372	.262	.634	78	-4	-4	101	62	29	.622	1	5	-3	-1		-0.4
1953	Det-A	103	308	43	90	22	1	2	24	27	10	.292	.353	.390	.743	103	0	1	98	70	43	.664	3	7	-3	-3	2	0.0
1954	Det-A	20	17	5	3	0	0	0	1	3	1	.176	.300	.353	.653	78	-1	-1	100	42	1	.563	0	0	0	0	H	0.0
	Was-A	49	158	17	40	4	3	0	9	10	7	.253	.298	.316	.614	69	-7	-7	98	68	15	.504	1	1	-0	-1	2/S	-0.6
	Yr	69	175	22	43	4	3	1	10	13	8	.246	.298	.320	.618	70	-8	-7	99	61	17	.519	1	1	-0	-1		-0.6
Total	10	1270	4745	867	1455	226	50	17	404	662	218	.307	.394	.386	.780	105	105	64	106	71	777	.770	53	49	-14	69	S32	13.5
■ **BILL PETERMAN** Peterman, William David b: 3/20/21, Philadelphia, Pa. BR/TR, 6'2", 185 lbs. Deb: 4/26/42																												
1942	Phi-N	1	1	0	1	0	0	0	0	0	0	1.000	1.000	1.000	2.000	515	0	0	94	0	1	—	0			0	/C	0.1
■ **JOHN PETERS** Peters, John Paul b: 4/8/1850, Louisiana, Mo. d: 1/4/24, St.Louis, Mo. BR/TR, 180 lbs. Deb: 5/23/1874																												
1874	Chi-n	54	248	39	69							.278															S2/3	
1875	Chi-n	70	314	40	87							.277															*S/2	
1876	Chi-N	66	316	70	111	14	2	1	47	3	2	.351	.357	.418	.775	126	18	6	125	125	48	.659				-1	*S/P	0.4

YEAR	TM/L	G	AB	R	H	2B	3B	HR	RBI	BB	SO	AVG	OBP	SLG	PRO	/A	BR	/A	PF	CHI	RC	TA	SB	CS	SBR	FR	POS	TPR
1877	Chi-N	60	265	45	84	10	3	0	41	1	7	.317	.320	.377	.697	121	5	6	98	134	33	.558				**21**	*S	**2.4**
1878	Mil-N	55	246	33	76	6	1	0	22	5	8	.309	.323	.341	.664	111	5	2	107	77	28	.524				5	2S	1.0
1879	Chi-N	83	379	45	93	13	2	1	31	1	19	.245	.247	.298	.546	75	-9	-11	105	83	29	.399				-9	*S	-1.3
1880	Pro-N	86	359	30	82	5	0	0	24	5	15	.228	.239	.242	.481	66	-13	-11	96	107	21	.332				-2	*S	-0.8
1881	Buf-N	54	229	21	49	8	1	0	25	3	12	.214	.224	.258	.482	50	-13	-13	101	156	14	.344				5	S/O	-0.3
1882	Pit-a	78	333	46	96	10	1	0		4		.288	.297	.324	.621	113	3	4	97	0	33	.473				6	*S/2	1.1
1883	Pit-a	8	28	3	3	0	0	0		0		.107	.107	.107	.214	-33	-4	-4	94	0	0	.120				0	/S	-0.2
1884	Pit-a	1	4	0	0	0	0	0		0		.000	.000	.000	.000	-99	-1	-1	97	0	0	.000				0	/S	0.0
Total	2 n	124	562	79	156							.278															/S	
Total	9	491	2159	293	594	66	10	2	190	22	63	.275	.282	.318	.600	93	-9	-22	104	92	206	.452				24	S/2OP3	2.3
■ **JOHN PETERS** Peters, John William "Big Pete" or "Shotgun" b: 7/14/1893, Kansas City, Kan. d: 2/21/32, Kansas City, Mo. BR/TR, 6', 192 lbs. Deb: 5/01/15																												
1915	Det-A	1	3	0	0	0	0	0	0	0	1	.000	.000	.000	.000	-92	-1	-1	108	0	0	.000	0			-0	/C	0.0
1918	Cle-A	1	1	0	0	0	0	0	0	1	1	.000	.500	.000	.500	47	0	0	108	0	0	1.000	0			0	/C	0.0
1921	Phi-N	55	155	7	45	4	0	3	23	6	13	.290	.329	.374	.703	84	-3	-4	102	126	19	.618	1	0	0	1	C	0.0
1922	Phi-N	55	143	15	35	9	1	4	24	9	18	.245	.308	.406	.713	73	-4	-7	113	120	18	.651	0	1	-1	1	C	-0.5
Total	4	112	302	22	80	13	1	7	47	16	33	.265	.317	.384	.701	77	-8	-11	107	121	37	.628	1	1		1	/C	-0.5
■ **RICK PETERS** Peters, Richard Devin b: 11/21/55, Lynwood, Cal. BB/TR, 5'9", 170 lbs. Deb: 9/08/79																												
1979	Det-A	12	19	3	5	0	0	0	2	5	3	.263	.417	.263	.680	91	0	0	96	154	3	.714	0	0	0	0	/32OD	0.0
1980	Det-A	133	477	79	139	19	7	2	42	54	48	.291	.371	.373	.744	99	5	1	105	91	66	.693	13	7	-0	-6	*OD	-0.6
1981	Det-A	63	207	26	53	7	3	0	15	29	28	.256	.353	.319	.672	90	-0	-2	105	91	22	.583	1	6	-3	6	OD	0.0
1983	Oak-A	55	178	20	51	7	0	0	20	12	21	.287	.335	.326	.661	87	-4	-3	96	135	18	.543	4	9	-4	8	O/D	0.0
1986	Oak-A	44	38	7	7	1	0	0	1	7	7	.184	.311	.211	.522	50	-3	-2	94	50	2	.486	2	2	-1	-6	O/2	-0.9
Total	5	307	919	135	255	34	10	2	80	107	107	.277	.358	.343	.701	93	-2	-5	103	99	111	.654	20	24	-8	2	O/D23	-1.5
■ **RUSTY PETERS** Peters, Russell Dixon b: 12/14/14, Roanoke, Va. BR/TR, 5'11", 170 lbs. Deb: 4/14/36																												
1936	Phi-A	45	119	12	26	3	2	3	16	4	28	.218	.244	.353	.597	45	-11	-11	101	102	10	.500	1	1	-0	-0	S3/O2	-0.8
1937	Phi-A	116	339	39	88	17	6	3	43	41	59	.260	.339	.372	.711	84	-11	-8	94	109	44	.671	4	4	-1	-3	23S	-0.3
1938	Phi-A	2	7	0	0	0	0	0	0	0	1	.000	.000	.000	.000	-99	-2	-2	101	0	0	.000	0	0	0	-0	/S	-0.1
1940	Cle-A	30	71	5	17	3	2	0	7	4	14	.239	.280	.338	.618	64	-4	-4	93	105	7	.518	1	0	0	-1	/2S31	-0.2
1941	Cle-A	29	63	6	13	2	0	0	2	7	10	.206	.286	.238	.524	40	-5	-5	101	47	4	.423	0	1	-1	2	S/32	-0.2
1942	Cle-A	34	58	6	13	5	1	0	2	2	14	.224	.250	.345	.595	72	-3	-2	92	35	4	.458	0	0	0	0	S/23	0.0
1943	Cle-A	79	215	22	47	6	2	1	19	18	29	.219	.282	.279	.561	71	-10	-7	90	110	18	.460	1	1	-0	2	3S/2O	-0.4
1944	Cle-A	88	282	23	63	13	3	1	24	15	35	.223	.268	.301	.569	62	-14	-14	100	98	23	.460	2	1	0	3	2S/3	-0.8
1946	Cle-A	9	21	0	6	0	0	0	2	1	1	.286	.318	.286	.604	79	-1	-1	89	127	2	.438	0	1	-1	1	/S	0.0
1947	StL-A	39	47	10	16	4	0	0	2	6	8	.340	.415	.426	.841	131	2	2	102	37	9	.813	0	0	0	0	2/S	0.3
Total	10	471	1222	123	289	53	16	8	117	98	199	.236	.295	.326	.620	70	-59	-52	96	96	120	.539	9	9	-3	4	2S3/O1	-2.5
■ **BUDDY PETERSON** Peterson, Carl Francis b: 4/23/25, Portland, Ore. BR/TR, 5'9.5", 170 lbs. Deb: 9/14/55																												
1955	Chi-A	6	21	7	6	1	0	0	2	3	1	.286	.400	.333	.733	98	0	0	101	109	3	.733	0	0	0	0	/S	0.1
1957	Bal-A	7	17	1	3	2	0	0	0	2	2	.176	.263	.294	.557	56	-1	-1	93	0	1	.467	0	0	0	0	/S	0.0
Total	2	13	38	8	9	3	0	0	2	5	3	.237	.341	.316	.657	81	-1	-1	97	62	4	.600	0	0	0	0	/S	0.1
■ **CAP PETERSON** Peterson, Charles Andrew b: 8/15/42, Tacoma, Wash. d: 5/16/80, Tacoma, Wash. BR/TR, 6'2", 195 lbs. Deb: 9/12/62																												
1962	SF-N	4	6	1	1	0	0	0	0	1	4	.167	.286	.167	.452	25	-1	-1	101	0	0	.400	0	0	0	0	/S	0.0
1963	SF-N	22	54	7	14	2	0	1	2	2	13	.259	.286	.352	.638	86	-1	-1	96	38	6	.525	0	0	0	-2	/23OS	-0.2
1964	SF-N	66	74	8	15	1	1	1	8	3	20	.203	.234	.284	.518	45	-5	-5	100	137	5	.407	0	0	0	-2	O/123	-0.7
1965	SF-N	63	105	14	26	7	0	3	15	10	16	.248	.313	.400	.713	90	-0	-2	111	122	12	.627	0	0	0	-5	O	-0.7
1966	SF-N	89	190	13	45	6	1	2	19	11	32	.237	.282	.311	.593	66	-9	-8	97	123	15	.474	2	0	1	-6	O/1	-1.5
1967	Was-A	122	405	35	97	17	2	8	46	32	61	.240	.300	.351	.651	90	-5	-5	102	116	41	.551	0	3	-2	0	*O	-1.0
1968	Was-A	94	226	20	46	8	1	3	18	18	31	.204	.265	.288	.553	74	-9	-7	91	104	18	.467	2	1	0	-3	O	-1.3
1969	Cle-A	76	110	8	25	3	0	1	14	24	18	.227	.370	.282	.652	90	-1	-0	94	165	12	.622	0	0	0	-2	O/3	-0.2
Total	8	536	1170	106	269	44	5	19	122	101	195	.230	.294	.325	.619	80	-31	-30	99	118	109	.540	4	4	-1	-18	O/321S	-5.6
■ **HARDY PETERSON** Peterson, Harding William b: 10/17/29, Perth Amboy, N.J. BR/TR, 6', 205 lbs. Deb: 5/05/55																												
1955	Pit-N	32	81	7	20	6	0	1	10	7	7	.247	.315	.358	.673	80	-3	-2	97	126	9	.578	0	0	0	1	C	0.0
1957	Pit-N	30	73	10	22	2	1	2	11	9	10	.301	.378	.438	.816	126	2	3	94	120	10	.719	0	1	-1	-3	C	0.1
1958	Pit-N	2	6	0	2	0	0	0	0	1	0	.333	.429	.333	.762	111	0	0	95	0	1	.750	0	0	0	0	/C	0.0
1959	Pit-N	2	1	0	0	0	0	0	0	0	0	.000	.000	.000	.000	-97	-0	-0	103	0	0	.000	0	0	0	0	/C	0.0
Total	4	66	161	17	44	8	1	3	21	17	17	.273	.346	.391	.738	101	-1	0	96	118	20	.686	0	1	-1	-1	/C	0.1
■ **BOB PETERSON** Peterson, Robert A. b: 7/16/1884, Philadelphia, Pa. d: 11/27/62, Eveshan Township, N.J. TR , 6'1", 160 lbs. Deb: 4/18/06																												
1906	Bos-A	39	118	10	24	1	1	1	9	11		.203	.271	.254	.526	68	-4	-4	98	99	9	.447	1			3	C/21O	0.1
1907	Bos-A	4	13	1	1	0	0	0	0	0		.077	.077	.077	.154	-50	-2	-2	101	0	0	.083	0			1	/C	0.0
Total	2	43	131	11	25	1	1	1	9	11		.191	.254	.237	.490	56	-6	-6	98	90	9	.406	1			4	/C21O	0.1
■ **TED PETOSKEY** Petoskey, Frederick Lee b: 1/5/11, St.Charles, Mich. BR/TR, 5'11.5", 183 lbs. Deb: 9/09/34																												
1934	Cin-N	6	7	0	0	0	0	0	1	0	5	.000	.000	.000	.000	-99	-2	-2	101	0	0	.000	0			1	/O	0.0
1935	Cin-N	4	5	0	2	0	0	0	0	0	1	.400	.400	.400	.800	124	0	0	93	0	1	1.000	1			-1	/O	0.0
Total	2	10	12	0	2	0	0	0	1	0	6	.167	.167	.167	.333	-11	-2	-2	98	0	1	.300	1			1	/O	0.0
■ **GENE PETRALLI** Petralli, Eugene James b: 9/25/59, Sacramento, Cal. BB/TR, 6'1", 180 lbs. Deb: 9/04/82																												
1982	Tor-A	16	44	3	16	2	0	0	1	4	6	.364	.417	.409	.826	118	2	1	109	22	8	.759	0	0	0	-1	C/3	0.0
1983	Tor-A	6	4	0	0	0	0	0	0	1	1	.000	.200	.000	.200	-36	-1	-1	108	0	0	.250	0	0	0	0	/CD	0.0
1984	Tor-A	3	3	0	0	0	0	0	0	0	0	.000	.000	.000	.000	-99	-1	-1	102	0	0	.000	0	0	0	0	/CD	0.0
1985	Tex-A	42	100	7	27	2	0	0	11	8	12	.270	.330	.290	.620	66	-4	-5	108	150	10	.506	1	0	0	-2	C	-0.3
1986	Tex-A	69	137	17	35	9	3	2	18	5	14	.255	.282	.409	.690	90	-3	-2	96	116	14	.587	3	0	1	-2	C3/2D	0.0
1987	Tex-A	101	202	28	61	11	2	7	31	27	29	.302	.390	.480	.870	126	9	8	104	105	38	.857	0	2	-1	-15	C3/12OD	-0.2
1988	Tex-A	129	351	35	99	14	2	7	36	41	52	.282	.360	.393	.754	110	6	5	101	90	49	.683	0	1	-1	-10	CD/312	0.0
Total	7	366	841	90	238	38	7	16	97	86	114	.283	.353	.402	.755	104	9	7	102	100	118	.701	4	3	-1	-30	C/3D12O	-0.5
■ **RICO PETROCELLI** Petrocelli, Americo Peter b: 6/27/43, Brooklyn, N.Y. BR/TR, 6', 175 lbs. Deb: 9/21/63																												
1963	Bos-A	1	4	0	1	1	0	0	1	0	1	.250	.250	.500	.750	98	-0	-0	106	213	1	.667	0	0	0	0	/S	0.0
1965	Bos-A	103	323	38	75	15	2	13	33	36	71	.232	.311	.412	.723	96	1	-2	107	80	41	.664	0	2	-1	3	S	0.4
1966	Bos-A	139	522	58	124	20	1	18	59	41	99	.238	.297	.383	.680	86	-5	-10	109	99	60	.602	1	1	-0	4	*S/3	0.0
1967	Bos-A	142	491	53	127	24	2	17	66	49	93	.259	.332	.420	.752	105	12	4	115	109	70	.704	2	4	-2	-2	*S	1.1
1968	Bos-A	123	406	41	95	17	2	12	46	31	73	.234	.295	.374	.669	101	0	-0	101	105	45	.586	0	1	-1	0	*S/1	0.8
1969	Bos-A	154	535	92	159	32	2	40	97	98	68	.297	.407	.589	.996	168	55	51	105	91	129	1.061	3	5	-2	3	*S/3	6.1
1970	Bos-A	157	583	82	152	31	3	29	103	67	82	.261	.339	.473	.812	110	16	8	111	122	92	.772	1	1	-0	-6	*S3	1.4
1971	Bos-A	158	553	82	139	24	4	28	89	91	108	.251	.359	.461	.820	124	23	19	106	114	92	.806	2	0	1	-0	*3	1.5
1972	Bos-A	147	521	62	125	15	2	15	75	78	91	.240	.341	.363	.704	104	8	5	105	142	68	.664	0	1	-1	-5	*3	0.5
1973	Bos-A	100	356	44	87	13	1	13	45	47	64	.244	.334	.396	.730	99	3	-0	106	100	47	.677	0	0	0	5	3	0.4
1974	Bos-A	129	454	53	121	23	1	15	76	48	74	.267	.339	.421	.760	110	10	6	107	129	65	.703	1	0	0	-10	*3/D	-0.1
1975	Bos-A	115	402	31	96	15	1	7	59	41	66	.239	.314	.333	.647	76	-9	-13	109	149	40	.549	0	2	-1	-8	*3/D	-2.0
1976	Bos-A	85	240	17	51	7	1	3	24	34	36	.213	.310	.287	.598	69	-7	-10	110	118	20	.507	0	5	-3	-6	3/21SD	-1.8
Total	13	1553	5390	653	1352	237	22	210	773	661	926	.251	.336	.420	.755	108	107	59	107	114	769	.727	10	22	-10	-22	S3/D21	8.3
■ **PAT PETTEE** Pettee, Patrick E. b: 1/10/1863, Natick, Mass. d: 10/9/34, Natick, Mass. BR/TR, 5'10", 170 lbs. Deb: 4/08/1891																												
1891	Lou-a	2	5	1	0	0	0	0	0	3	1	.000	.375	.000	.375	13	-0	-0	90	0	0	.800	1			0	/2	0.0

YEAR	TM/L	G	AB	R	H	2B	3B	HR	RBI	BB	SO	AVG	OBP	SLG	PRO	/A	BR	/A	PF	CHI	RC	TA	SB	CS	SBR	FR	POS	TPR
■ **NED PETTIGREW**	Pettigrew, Jim Ned b: 8/25/1881, Honey Grove, Tex. d: 8/20/52, Duncan, Okla. 5'11", 175 lbs. Deb: 4/23/14																											
1914	Buf-F	2	2	0	0	0	0	0	0	0	0	.000	.000	.000	.000	-96	-1	-1	104	0	0	.000	0			0	H	0.0
■ **JOE PETTINI**	Pettini, Joseph Paul b: 1/26/55, Wheeling, W.Va. BR/TR, 5'9", 165 lbs. Deb: 7/10/80																											
1980	SF-N	63	190	19	44	3	1	1	9	17	33	.232	.295	.274	.568	62	-10	-9	96	65	17	.490	5	2	0	-3	S3/2	-0.7
1981	SF-N	35	29	3	2	1	0	0	2	4	5	.069	.182	.103	.285	-17	-4	-5	105	262	1	.296	1	0	0	-0	2S/3	-0.2
1982	SF-N	29	39	5	8	1	0	0	2	3	4	.205	.262	.231	.493	42	-3	-3	94	87	2	.364	0	1	-1	-0	S/3	-0.1
1983	SF-N	61	86	11	16	0	1	0	7	9	11	.186	.263	.209	.472	32	-8	-8	101	154	5	.419	4	1	1	-3	S23	-0.7
Total	4	188	344	38	70	5	2	1	20	33	53	.203	.273	.238	.512	45	-25	-24	98	107	25	.445	10	4	1	-7	S/32	-1.7
■ **GARY PETTIS**	Pettis, Gary George b: 4/3/58, Oakland, Cal. BB/TR, 6'1", 165 lbs. Deb: 9/13/82																											
1982	Cal-A	10	5	5	1	0	0	1	1	0	2	.200	.200	.800	1.000	159	0	0	100	57	1	1.000	0	0	0	-2	/O	-0.1
1983	Cal-A	22	85	19	25	2	3	3	6	7	15	.294	.348	.494	.842	134	3	4	96	49	15	.891	8	3	1	4	O	0.8
1984	Cal-A	140	397	63	90	11	6	2	29	60	115	.227	.333	.300	.632	75	-11	-12	101	92	46	.701	48	17	4	-7	*O	-1.8
1985	Cal-A	125	443	67	114	10	8	1	32	62	125	.257	.349	.323	.671	85	-7	-7	101	89	61	.761	56	9	11	12	*O	1.4
1986	Cal-A	154	539	93	139	23	4	5	58	69	132	.258	.342	.343	.685	92	-7	-4	96	118	71	.724	50	13	7	13	*O/D	1.1
1987	Cal-A	133	394	49	82	13	2	1	17	52	124	.208	.302	.259	.561	52	-26	-26	99	65	35	.551	24	5	4	12	*O	-1.1
1988	Det-A	129	458	65	96	14	4	3	36	47	85	.210	.285	.277	.562	62	-25	-22	94	107	42	.584	44	10	7	5	*O/D	-1.1
Total	7	713	2321	361	547	73	27	16	179	297	598	.236	.324	.311	.635	77	-72	-66	98	94	271	.684	230	57	35	36	O/D	-0.8
■ **BOB PETTIT**	Pettit, Robert Henry b: 7/19/1861, Williamstown, Mass. d: 11/1/10, Derby, Conn. BL/TR, 5'9", 160 lbs. Deb: 9/03/1887																											
1887	Chi-N	32	138	29	36	3	3	2	12	8	15	.261	.301	.370	.671	75	-3	-6	116	56	21	.735	16			-2	O/CP	-0.6
1888	Chi-N	43	169	23	43	1	4	4	23	7	9	.254	.288	.379	.667	106	2	1	107	115	21	.627	7			-3	O	-0.2
1891	CM-a	21	80	10	14	4	0	1	5	7	7	.175	.267	.262	.529	48	-5	-6	112	64	6	.500	2			0	/2O3	-0.5
Total	3	96	387	62	93	8	7	7	40	22	31	.240	.288	.351	.640	81	-5	-12	111	83	48	.636	25			-5	/O23PC	-1.3
■ **LARRY PEZOLD**	Pezold, Lorenz Johannes b: 6/22/1893, New Orleans, La. d: 10/22/57, Baton Rouge, La. BR/TR, 5'9.5", 175 lbs. Deb: 7/28/14																											
1914	Cle-A	23	71	4	16	0	1	0	5	9	6	.225	.313	.254	.566	69	-2	-3	102	104	6	.500	2	3	-1	1	3/O	-0.1
■ **FRED PFEFFER**	Pfeffer, Nathaniel Frederick "Fritz" or "Dandelion" b: 3/17/1860, Louisville, Ky. d: 4/10/32, Chicago, Ill. BR/TR, 5'10.5", 184 lbs. Deb: 5/01/1882 M																											
1882	Tro-N	85	330	26	72	7	4	1	43	1	24	.218	.221	.273	.493	60	-16	-13	95	159	20	.353				7	*S/2	0.2
1883	Chi-N	96	371	41	87	22	7	1	45	8	50	.235	.251	.340	.590	71	-10	-15	109	123	32	.472				6	*2S/31	-1.1
1884	Chi-N	112	467	105	135	10	10	25	101	25	47	.289	.325	.514	.839	148	30	25	108	117	80	.798				**40**	*2/P	**5.8**
1885	Chi-N	112	469	90	113	12	7	5	73	26	47	.241	.281	.328	.609	85	-2	-11	114	159	44	.506				20	*2/PO	1.9
1886	Chi-N	118	474	88	125	17	8	7	95	36	46	.264	.316	.378	.693	95	6	-6	116	**164**	68	.702	30			5	*2/1	0.3
1887	Chi-N	123	479	95	133	21	6	16	89	34	20	.278	.327	.447	.774	99	8	-5	116	111	91	.884	57			21	*2/O	1.9
1888	Chi-N	135	517	90	129	22	10	8	57	32	38	.250	.297	.377	.674	108	9	4	107	99	79	.758	64			**37**	*2	4.5
1889	Chi-N	134	531	85	121	15	7	7	77	53	51	.228	.302	.322	.624	76	-17	-16	99	127	67	.663	45			18	*2	1.0
1890	Chi-P	124	499	86	128	21	8	5	80	44	23	.257	.319	.361	.680	80	-13	-16	104	119	68	.682	27			**22**	*2	0.9
1891	Chi-N	137	498	93	123	12	9	7	77	79	60	.247	.353	.349	.703	101	7	2	106	117	78	.789	40			23	*2	2.5
1892	Lou-N	124	470	78	121	14	9	2	76	67	36	.257	.353	.338	.691	121	8	14	92	136	67	.731	27			12	*21/OPM	2.5
1893	Lou-N	125	508	85	129	29	12	3	75	51	18	.254	.322	.376	.698	90	-11	-7	96	109	74	.723	32			5	*2	-0.2
1894	Lou-N	104	409	68	126	12	14	5	59	30	14	.308	.357	.443	.799	106	-5	4	88	88	78	.859	31			10	*2S/P	1.5
1895	Lou-N	11	45	8	13	1	0	0	5	5	3	.289	.360	.311	.671	80	-1	-1	95	88	6	.656	2			0	/S21	0.0
1896	NY-N	4	14	1	2	0	0	0	4	1	1	.143	.250	.143	.393	6	-2	-2	99	588	1	.333	0			0	/2	-0.1
	Chi-N	94	360	45	88	16	7	2	52	23	20	.244	.294	.344	.638	64	-17	-22	108	118	44	.629	22			8	*2	-0.8
	Yr	98	374	46	90	16	7	2	56	24	21	.241	.292	.337	.629	62	-18	-23	108	143	44	.616	22			8		-0.9
1897	Chi-N	32	114	10	26	0	1	0	11	12		.228	.318	.246	.563	52	-7	-7	100	117	11	.545	5			0	2	-0.5
Total	16	1670	6555	1094	1671	231	119	94	1019	527	498	.255	.312	.369	.682	93	-32	-74	104	125	906	.686	382			234	*2S/1PO3	20.3
■ **BOBBY PFEIL**	Pfeil, Robert Raymond b: 11/13/43, Passaic, N.J. BR/TR, 6'1", 180 lbs. Deb: 6/26/69																											
1969	NY-N	62	211	20	49	9	0	0	10	7	27	.232	.260	.275	.535	50	-14	-14	100	69	14	.393	0	1	-1	-4	32/O	-1.8
1971	Phi-N	44	70	5	19	3	0	2	9	6	9	.271	.329	.400	.729	103	0	0	103	108	8	.636	1	1	-0	-1	3/CO12S	0.0
Total	2	106	281	25	68	12	0	2	19	13	36	.242	.278	.306	.584	63	-14	-14	101	79	22	.463	1	2	-1	-4	/32OCS1	-1.8
■ **GEORGE PFISTER**	Pfister, George Edward b: 9/4/18, Bound Brook, N.J. BR/TR, 6', 200 lbs. Deb: 9/27/41																											
1941	Bro-N	1	2	0	0	0	0	0	0	0	0	.000	.000	.000	.000	-97	-1	-1	103	0	0	.000	0			0	/C	0.0
■ **MONTE PFYL**	Pfyl, Meinhard Charles b: 5/11/1884, St.Louis, Mo. d: 10/18/45, San Francisco, Cal BL/TL, 6'3", 190 lbs. Deb: 7/30/07																											
1907	NY-N	1	0	0	0	0	0	0	0	0		—	—	—	—	—	0	0	105	—	—	—	0			0	/1	0.0
■ **ART PHELAN**	Phelan, Arthur Thomas "Dugan" b: 8/14/1887, Niantic, Ill. d: 12/27/64, Ft.Worth, Tex. BR/TR, 5'8", 160 lbs. Deb: 6/25/10																											
1910	Cin-N	23	42	7	9	0	0	0	4	7	6	.214	.327	.214	.541	58	-2	-2	101	155	5	.636	5			-1	/32OS	-0.2
1912	Cin-N	130	461	56	112	9	11	3	54	46	37	.243	.314	.330	.644	83	-15	-10	92	120	56	.645	25			-0	*3/2	-0.9
1913	Chi-N	91	261	41	65	11	6	2	35	29	26	.249	.331	.360	.691	99	-1	-0	99	127	33	.684	8			4	23/S	0.2
1914	Chi-N	25	46	5	13	2	1	0	3	4	3	.283	.340	.370	.710	113	1	1	98	64	6	.636	0			-1	/32S	0.0
1915	Chi-N	133	448	41	98	16	7	3	35	55	42	.219	.307	.306	.613	84	-7	-8	102	93	45	.574	12	9	-2	1	*32	-0.3
Total	5	402	1258	150	297	38	25	8	131	141	114	.236	.317	.325	.642	87	-24	-20	98	111	144	.626	50	9		3	3/2SO	-1.2
■ **DAN PHELAN**	Phelan, Daniel B. b: Waterbury, Conn. Deb: 4/18/1890																											
1890	Lou-a	8	32	4	8	1	1	0		0		.250	.250	.344	.594	72	-1	-1	107	0	3	.500	1			0	/1	0.0
■ **DICK PHELAN**	Phelan, James Dickson b: 12/10/1854, Towanda, Pa. d: 2/13/31, San Antonio, Tex. Deb: 4/17/1884																											
1884	Bal-U	101	402	63	99	13	3	3		12		.246	.268	.316	.584	88	-1	-8	110	0	35	.459	0			-15	*2/3O	-2.3
1885	Buf-N	4	16	2	2	0	0	1	3	0	3	.125	.125	.313	.438	38	-1	-1	99	138	1	.357				0	/2	0.0
	StL-N	2	4	1	1	1	0	0	1	0	2	.250	.250	.500	.750	149	0	0	92	174	1	.667				0	/3	0.0
	Yr	6	20	3	3	1	0	1	4	0	5	.150	.150	.350	.500	60	-1	-1	97	173	1	.412				0		0.0
Total	2	107	422	66	102	14	3	4	4	12	5	.242	.263	.318	.580	86	-2	-9	110	7	36	.456				-15	2/3O	-2.3
■ **NEAL PHELPS**	Phelps, Cornelius Carman b: 11/19/1840, New York, N.Y. d: 2/12/1885, New York, N.Y. Deb: 7/01/1871																											
1871	Kek-n	1	4	0	0							.000															/1	
1873	Mut-n	1	6	0	0							.000															/O	
1874	Mut-n	6	23	5	3							.130															/O	
1875	Mut-n	2	6	1	2							.333															/O	
1876	NY-N	1	3	0	0	0	0	0	0	0	1	.000	.000	.000	.000	-99	-1	-1	87	0	0	.000				0	/O	0.0
	Phi-N	1	4	0	0	0	0	0	0	0	0	.000	.000	.000	.000	-99	-1	-1	99	0	0	.000				0	/C	0.0
	Yr	2	7	0	0	0	0	0	0	0	1	.000	.000	.000	.000	-99	-1	-1	93	0	0	.000				0		0.0
Total	4 n	10	39	6	5							.128															/C	
■ **ED PHELPS**	Phelps, Edward Jaykill "Yaller" b: 3/3/1879, Albany, N.Y. d: 1/31/42, E.Greenbush, N.Y. BR/TR, 5'11", 185 lbs. Deb: 9/03/02																											
1902	Pit-N	18	61	5	13	1	0	0	6	4		.213	.262	.230	.491	51	-3	-4	105	148	4	.417	2			-1	C/1	-0.3
1903	Pit-N	81	273	32	77	7	3	2	31	17		.282	.324	.352	.676	90	-2	-4	105	98	33	.587	2			-7	C/1	-0.4
1904	Pit-N	94	302	29	73	5	3	0	28	15		.242	.278	.278	.556	74	-9	-9	99	122	24	.441	2			-5	C/1	-0.5
1905	Cin-N	44	156	18	36	5	3	0	18	12		.231	.286	.301	.587	74	-4	-5	103	136	15	.525	4			3	C	0.3
1906	Cin-N	12	40	3	11	0	2	1	5	3		.275	.326	.450	.776	125	2	1	115	89	7	.793	2			1	C	0.3
	Pit-N	43	118	9	28	3	1	0	12	9		.237	.291	.280	.571	77	-3	-3	104	133	10	.478	1			-3	C	-0.3
	Yr	55	158	12	39	3	3	1	17	12		.247	.300	.323	.623	90	-1	-2	107	125	17	.555	3			-2		0.0
1907	Pit-N	43	113	11	24	1	0	0	12	9		.212	.270	.221	.492	53	-5	-6	105	182	7	.393	1			-2	C/1	-0.5
1908	Pit-N	34	64	3	15	2	2	0	11	2		.234	.258	.328	.586	93	-1	-1	95	201	5	.469	0			-2	C	0.0
1909	StL-N	104	306	43	76	13	1	0	22	39		.248	.350	.297	.648	106	3	4	96	88	33	.635	7			-1	C	1.0
1910	StL-N	93	270	25	71	4	2	0	37	36	29	.263	.356	.293	.649	98	-2	1	92	163	32	.638	9			-5	C	0.0

YEAR	TM/L	G	AB	R	H	2B	3B	HR	RBI	BB	SO	AVG	OBP	SLG	PRO	/A	BR	/A	PF	CHI	RC	TA	SB	CS	SBR	FR	POS	TPR
1912	Bro-N	52	111	8	32	4	3	0	23	16	15	.288	.388	.378	.766	115	2	3	95	184	17	.772	1			4	C	0.8
1913	Bro-N	15	18	0	4	0	0	0	0	1	2	.222	.263	.222	.485	38	-1	-1	104	0	1	.357	0			-0	/C	-0.1
Total	11	633	1832	186	460	45	20	3	205	163	46	.251	.317	.302	.619	88	-25	-24	100	130	189	.555	31			-19	C/1	0.3

■ **BABE PHELPS** Phelps, Ernest Gordon "Blimp" b: 4/19/08, Odenton, Md. BL/TR, 6'2", 225 lbs. Deb: 9/17/31

YEAR	TM/L	G	AB	R	H	2B	3B	HR	RBI	BB	SO	AVG	OBP	SLG	PRO	/A	BR	/A	PF	CHI	RC	TA	SB	CS	SBR	FR	POS	TPR
1931	Was-A	3	3	0	1	0	0	0	0	0	0	.333	.333	.333	.667	75	-0	-0	101	0	0	.500	0	0	0	0	H	0.0
1933	Chi-N	3	7	0	2	0	0	0	2	0	1	.286	.286	.286	.571	65	-0	-0	97	376	1	.400	0			0	/C	0.0
1934	Chi-N	44	70	7	20	5	2	2	12	1	8	.286	.296	.500	.796	111	0	1	98	105	10	.706	0			0	C	0.2
1935	Bro-N	47	121	17	44	7	2	5	22	9	10	.364	.408	.579	.986	172	10	11	94	93	28	.988	0			0	C	1.1
1936	Bro-N	115	319	36	117	23	2	5	57	27	18	.367	.421	.498	.920	140	21	19	105	116	69	.913	1			-12	C/O	1.0
1937	Bro-N	121	409	42	128	37	3	7	58	25	28	.313	.357	.469	.826	118	12	10	104	98	67	.758	2			-6	*C	0.7
1938	Bro-N	66	208	33	64	12	2	5	46	23	15	.308	.379	.457	.836	135	8	10	96	151	35	.791	2			-3	C	0.9
1939	Bro-N	98	323	33	92	21	2	6	42	24	24	.285	.336	.418	.754	95	0	-3	107	101	43	.658	0			2	C	0.2
1940	Bro-N	118	370	47	109	24	5	13	61	30	27	.295	.349	.492	.841	120	14	10	108	102	59	.776	2			-6	C/1	0.8
1941	Bro-N	16	30	3	7	3	0	2	4	1	2	.233	.258	.533	.791	115	0	0	103	66	4	.739	0			0	C	0.1
1942	Pit-N	95	257	21	73	11	1	9	41	20	24	.284	.345	.440	.785	128	9	8	101	109	39	.735	2			2	C	1.2
Total	11	726	2117	239	657	143	19	54	345	160	157	.310	.362	.472	.835	123	74	65	103	109	356	.807	9	0		-22	C/1O	6.2

■ **KEN PHELPS** Phelps, Kenneth Allen b: 8/6/54, Seattle, Wash. BL/TL, 6'1", 209 lbs. Deb: 9/20/80

YEAR	TM/L	G	AB	R	H	2B	3B	HR	RBI	BB	SO	AVG	OBP	SLG	PRO	/A	BR	/A	PF	CHI	RC	TA	SB	CS	SBR	FR	POS	TPR
1980	KC-A	3	4	0	0	0	0	0	0	0	2	.000	.000	.000	.000	-99	-1	-1	98	0	0	.000	0	0	0	0	/1	0.0
1981	KC-A	21	22	1	3	0	1	0	1	1	13	.136	.174	.227	.401	15	-2	-2	99	78	1	.316	0	0	0	0	/1D	-0.2
1982	Mon-N	10	8	0	2	0	0	0	0	0	3	.250	.333	.250	.583	62	-0	-0	105	0	1	.500	0	0	0	0	H	0.0
1983	Sea-A	50	127	10	30	4	1	7	16	13	25	.236	.307	.449	.756	106	1	1	100	80	19	.722	0	0	0	1	1D	0.0
1984	Sea-A	101	290	52	70	9	0	24	51	61	73	.241	.382	.521	.903	144	20	19	102	91	63	.982	3	3	-1	-0	D/1	1.7
1985	Sea-A	61	116	18	24	3	0	9	24	24	33	.207	.343	.466	.808	126	3	4	95	117	20	.860	2	0	1	0	D/1	0.4
1986	Sea-A	125	344	69	85	16	4	24	64	88	96	.247	.409	.526	.935	146	29	26	105	101	81	1.041	2	3	-1	-1	1D	1.9
1987	Sea-A	120	332	68	86	13	1	27	68	80	75	.259	.414	.548	.962	150	29	27	103	103	81	1.067	1	1	-0	0	*D/1	2.5
1988	Sea-A	72	190	37	54	8	0	14	32	51	35	.284	.438	.547	.985	162	21	19	108	87	50	1.129	1	0	0	0	D/1	1.9
	NY-A	45	107	17	24	5	0	10	22	19	26	.224	.341	.551	.893	152	6	7	96	98	20	.907	0	0	0	0	D/1	0.7
	Yr	117	297	54	78	13	0	24	54	70	61	.263	.405	.549	.954	160	28	26	103	92	72	1.059	1	0	0	0		2.6
Total	9	608	1540	272	378	58	7	115	278	337	381	.245	.388	.516	.904	142	105	100	102	96	335	.991	9	7	-2	-1	D1	8.9

■ **DAVE PHILLEY** Philley, David Earl b: 5/16/20, Paris, Tex. BB/TR, 6', 188 lbs. Deb: 9/06/41

YEAR	TM/L	G	AB	R	H	2B	3B	HR	RBI	BB	SO	AVG	OBP	SLG	PRO	/A	BR	/A	PF	CHI	RC	TA	SB	CS	SBR	FR	POS	TPR
1941	Chi-A	7	9	4	2	1	0	0	0	3	3	.222	.417	.333	.750	107	0	0	94	0	2	.857	0	0	0	-1	/O	0.0
1946	Chi-A	17	68	10	24	2	3	0	17	4	4	.353	.389	.471	.859	144	3	4	97	214	14	.911	5	0	2	5	O	0.9
1947	Chi-A	143	551	55	142	25	11	2	45	35	39	.258	.303	.354	.657	85	-15	-13	97	87	56	.574	21	16	-3	-7	*O/3	-2.9
1948	Chi-A	137	488	51	140	28	3	5	42	50	33	.287	.353	.387	.740	101	-3	0	95	71	67	.669	8	10	-4	11	*O	0.3
1949	Chi-A	146	598	84	171	20	8	0	44	54	51	.286	.347	.346	.693	86	-14	-12	98	70	76	.623	13	4	2	-4	*O	-1.7
1950	Chi-A	156	619	69	150	21	5	14	80	52	57	.242	.302	.360	.662	71	-31	-29	97	100	67	.577	6	3	0	-3	*O	-3.1
1951	Chi-A	7	25	0	6	2	0	0	2	2	3	.240	.296	.320	.616	69	-1	-1	97	89	2	.500	0	0	0	-0	/O	-0.1
	Phi-A	125	468	71	123	18	7	7	59	63	38	.263	.354	.376	.730	92	-1	-5	106	113	68	.707	9	6	-1	-3	*O/3	-1.2
	Yr	132	493	71	129	20	7	7	61	65	41	.262	.351	.373	.724	91	-2	-6	105	113	71	.698	9	6	-1	-3		-1.3
1952	Phi-A	151	586	80	154	25	4	7	71	59	35	.263	.334	.355	.689	83	-6	-14	111	111	67	.606	11	4	1	5	*O/3	-1.2
1953	Phi-A	157	620	80	188	30	9	9	59	51	35	.303	.358	.424	.782	108	8	7	102	80	92	.717	13	5	1	-0	*O/3	0.3
1954	Cle-A	133	452	48	102	13	3	12	60	57	48	.226	.312	.347	.660	76	-12	-16	106	120	48	.584	2	4	-2	-9	*O	-3.0
1955	Cle-A	43	104	15	31	4	2	2	9	12	10	.298	.371	.433	.803	111	2	2	104	66	15	.712	0	2	-1	-3	O	-0.4
	Bal-A	83	311	50	93	13	3	6	41	34	38	.299	.368	.418	.786	124	5	9	90	109	47	.721	1	2	-1	-2	O/3	0.2
	Yr	126	415	65	124	17	5	8	50	46	48	.299	.369	.422	.790	119	7	10	95	95	64	.730	1	4	-2	-5		-0.2
1956	Bal-A	32	117	13	24	4	2	1	17	18	13	.205	.311	.299	.610	66	-6	-5	94	177	10	.554	3	1	0	-1	O/3	-0.6
	Chi-A	86	279	44	74	14	2	4	47	28	27	.265	.334	.373	.707	83	-6	-7	104	151	33	.618	1	3	-2	-4	1O	-1.5
	Yr	118	396	57	98	18	4	5	64	46	40	.247	.327	.351	.678	78	-12	-13	101	160	46	.611	4	4	-1	-4		-2.1
1957	Chi-A	22	71	9	23	4	0	0	9	4	10	.324	.360	.380	.740	103	0	0	99	132	10	.640	1	1	-0	0	O/1	0.0
	Det-A	65	173	15	49	8	1	2	16	7	16	.283	.311	.376	.687	81	-4	-5	107	89	19	.581	3	1	0	-3	1O/3	-0.8
	Yr	87	244	24	72	12	1	2	25	11	26	.295	.325	.377	.703	87	-3	-5	105	101	29	.601	4	2	0	-3		-0.8
1958	Phi-N	91	207	30	64	11	4	3	31	15	20	.309	.359	.444	.803	113	3	4	98	127	31	.717	1	1	-0	-4	O1	-0.2
1959	Phi-N	99	254	32	74	18	2	7	37	18	27	.291	.341	.461	.801	112	3	4	99	108	40	.743	0	0	0	2	O1	0.3
1960	Phi-N	14	15	2	5	2	0	0	4	3	2	.333	.444	.467	.911	139	1	1	107	232	3	.909	0	0	0	-1	/O1	0.0
	SF-N	39	61	5	10	0	0	1	7	6	14	.164	.239	.213	.452	28	-6	-5	90	178	3	.358	0	0	0	-1	O/3	-0.6
	Yr	53	76	7	15	2	0	1	11	9	16	.197	.282	.263	.546	53	-5	-5	94	196	6	.460	0	0	0	-2		-0.6
	Bal-A	14	34	6	9	2	1	1	5	4	5	.265	.342	.471	.813	115	1	1	102	103	6	.840	1	0	0	-0	/O3	0.0
1961	Bal-A	99	144	13	36	9	2	1	23	10	20	.250	.299	.361	.660	77	-5	-5	97	164	13	.547	2	0	1	-6	O/1	-1.1
1962	Bos-A	38	42	3	6	2	0	0	4	5	3	.143	.250	.190	.440	20	-5	-5	102	198	1	.341	0	0	0	-0	/O	-0.4
Total	18	1904	6296	789	1700	276	72	84	729	594	551	.270	.335	.377	.711	90	-87	-91	101	105	790	.661	101	63	-8	-29	*O1/3	-16.8

■ **ADOLFO PHILLIPS** Phillips, Adolfo Emilio (Lopez) b: 12/16/41, Bethania, Panama BR/TR, 6'1", 175 lbs. Deb: 9/02/64

YEAR	TM/L	G	AB	R	H	2B	3B	HR	RBI	BB	SO	AVG	OBP	SLG	PRO	/A	BR	/A	PF	CHI	RC	TA	SB	CS	SBR	FR	POS	TPR
1964	Phi-N	13	13	4	3	0	0	0	0	3	3	.231	.375	.231	.606	76	-0	-0	99	0	2	.600	0	0	0	0	/O	0.0
1965	Phi-N	41	87	14	20	4	0	3	5	5	34	.230	.272	.379	.651	86	-2	-2	95	49	9	.586	3	3	-1	-3	O	-0.6
1966	Phi-N	2	3	1	0	0	0	0	0	0	0	.000	.000	.000	.000	-99	-1	-1	101	0	0	.000	0	0	0	0	/O	0.0
	Chi-N	116	416	68	109	29	1	16	36	43	135	.262	.348	.452	.800	120	12	12	100	65	66	.838	32	15	1	7	*O	1.6
	Yr	118	419	69	109	29	1	16	36	43	135	.260	.346	.449	.795	119	11	11	100	64	66	.831	32	15	1	7		1.6
1967	Chi-N	144	448	66	120	20	7	17	70	80	93	.268	.386	.458	.843	138	26	25	102	113	82	.908	24	10	1	10	*O	3.2
1968	Chi-N	143	439	49	106	20	5	13	33	47	90	.241	.322	.399	.720	103	8	3	112	65	55	.678	9	7	-2	2	*O	-0.4
1969	Chi-N	28	49	5	11	3	1	0	1	16	15	.224	.424	.327	.751	106	2	2	107	25	7	.791	1	3	-2	-1	O	-0.2
	Mon-N	58	199	25	43	4	4	4	7	19	62	.216	.288	.337	.624	74	-7	-7	100	36	19	.571	6	5	-1	-3	O	-1.5
	Yr	86	248	30	54	7	5	4	8	35	77	.218	.319	.335	.654	81	-5	-6	102	33	27	.623	7	8	-3	-4		-1.7
1970	Mon-N	92	214	36	51	6	3	6	21	36	51	.238	.353	.379	.732	96	-0	-0	100	82	31	.746	7	1	2	-4	O	-0.5
1972	Cle-A	12	7	2	0	0	0	0	0	2	2	.000	.222	.000	.222	-28	-1	-1	107	0	0	.286	0	0	0	-3	O	-0.4
Total	8	649	1875	270	463	86	21	59	173	251	485	.247	.344	.410	.754	110	36	30	103	73	270	.775	82	44	-2	5	O	1.2

■ **DAMON PHILLIPS** Phillips, Damon Roswell "Dee" b: 6/8/19, Corsicana, Tex. BR/TR, 6', 176 lbs. Deb: 7/19/42

YEAR	TM/L	G	AB	R	H	2B	3B	HR	RBI	BB	SO	AVG	OBP	SLG	PRO	/A	BR	/A	PF	CHI	RC	TA	SB	CS	SBR	FR	POS	TPR
1942	Cin-N	28	84	4	17	2	0	0	6	7	5	.202	.264	.226	.490	44	-6	-6	101	117	5	.377	0			-1	S	-0.5
1944	Bos-N	140	489	35	126	30	1	1	53	28	34	.258	.301	.329	.630	82	-15	-12	95	118	49	.519	0			0	3S	0.0
1946	Bos-N	2	2	0	1	0	0	0	0	0	0	.500	.500	.500	1.000	195	0	0	95	0	1	1.000	1			0	H	0.0
Total	3	170	575	39	144	32	1	1	59	35	39	.250	.296	.315	.611	76	-21	-18	95	118	55	.508	1			-1	/3S	-0.5

■ **EDDIE PHILLIPS** Phillips, Edward David b: 2/17/01, Worcester, Mass. d: 1/26/68, Buffalo, N.Y. BR/TR, 6', 178 lbs. Deb: 5/04/24

YEAR	TM/L	G	AB	R	H	2B	3B	HR	RBI	BB	SO	AVG	OBP	SLG	PRO	/A	BR	/A	PF	CHI	RC	TA	SB	CS	SBR	FR	POS	TPR
1924	Bos-N	3	3	0	0	0	0	0	0	0	2	.000	.000	.000	.000	-99	-1	-1	94	0	0	.000	0	0	0	0	/C	0.0
1929	Det-A	68	221	24	52	13	1	2	21	20	16	.235	.302	.330	.632	64	-13	-12	97	91	23	.553	0	1	-1	2	C	-0.4
1931	Pit-N	106	353	30	82	18	3	7	44	41	49	.232	.317	.360	.677	81	-9	-9	101	106	43	.635	1			1	*C	-0.3
1932	NY-A	9	31	4	9	1	0	2	4	2	3	.290	.333	.516	.849	122	1	1	95	61	5	.864	1	0	0	-0	/C	0.1
1934	Was-A	56	169	6	33	6	1	2	16	26	24	.195	.306	.278	.584	51	-12	-12	101	101	16	.551	1	0	0	-4	C	-0.9
1935	Cle-A	70	220	18	60	16	1	1	41	15	21	.273	.319	.368	.687	78	-8	-8	99	166	26	.600	0	0	0	-9	C	-1.3
Total	6	312	997	82	236	54	6	14	126	104	115	.237	.312	.345	.657	72	-42	-41	100	113	113	.598	3	1		-11	C	-2.8

■ **EDDIE PHILLIPS** Phillips, Howard Edward b: 7/8/31, St.Louis, Mo. BB/TR, 6'1", 180 lbs. Deb: 9/10/53

YEAR	TM/L	G	AB	R	H	2B	3B	HR	RBI	BB	SO	AVG	OBP	SLG	PRO	/A	BR	/A	PF	CHI	RC	TA	SB	CS	SBR	FR	POS	TPR
1953	StL-N	9	0	4	0	0	0	0	0	0	0	—	—	—	—	—	0	0	102	—	—	—	0	0	0	0	R	0.0

YEAR	TM/L	G	AB	R	H	2B	3B	HR	RBI	BB	SO	AVG	OBP	SLG	PRO	/A	BR	/A	PF	CHI	RC	TA	SB	CS	SBR	FR	POS	TPR
■ **JACK PHILLIPS** Phillips, Jack Dorn "Stretch" b: 9/6/21, Clarence, N.Y. BR/TR, 6'4", 193 lbs. Deb: 8/22/47																												
1947	NY-A	16	36	5	10	0	1	1	2	3	5	.278	.333	.417	.750	112	0	0	97	41	5	.692	0	0	0	-0	1	0.0
1948	NY-A	1	2	0	0	0	0	0	0	0	1	.000	.000	.000	.000	-99	-1	-1	100	0	0	.000	0	0	0	0	/1	0.0
1949	NY-A	45	91	16	28	4	1	1	10	12	9	.308	.388	.407	.795	110	2	1	100	86	15	.758	1	0	0	-1	1	0.1
	Pit-N	18	56	6	13	3	1	0	3	4	6	.232	.283	.321	.605	61	-3	-3	101	63	5	.523	1			1	1/3	-0.1
1950	Pit-N	69	208	25	61	7	6	5	34	20	17	.293	.355	.457	.812	109	3	3	103	119	35	.779	1			0	1/3P	0.0
1951	Pit-N	70	156	12	37	7	3	0	12	15	17	.237	.304	.321	.625	64	-7	-8	107	93	15	.524	1	2	-1	-1	1/3	-1.0
1952	Pit-N	1	1	0	0	0	0	0	0	0	0	.000	.000	.000	.000	-99	-0	-0	100	0	0	.000	0	0	0	0	/1	0.0
1955	Det-A	55	117	15	37	8	2	1	20	10	12	.316	.370	.444	.815	122	3	3	97	136	19	.747	0	0	0	-0	1/3	0.1
1956	Det-A	67	224	31	66	13	2	1	20	21	19	.295	.355	.384	.739	98	-1	-0	97	84	28	.635	1	1	-0	-2	1/2O	-0.4
1957	Det-A	1	1	1	0	0	0	0	0	0	0	.000	.000	.000	.000	-93	-0	-0	107	0	0	.000	0	0	0	0	H	0.0
Total	9	343	892	111	252	42	16	9	101	85	86	.283	.345	.396	.741	96	-5	-5	100	97	122	.689	5	3		-4	1/3O2P	-1.3
■ **BUBBA PHILLIPS** Phillips, John Melvin b: 2/24/30, West Point, Miss. BR/TR, 5'9", 180 lbs. Deb: 4/30/55																												
1955	Det-A	95	184	18	43	4	0	3	23	14	20	.234	.295	.304	.599	63	-10	-9	97	132	17	.510	2	1	0	-3	O/3	-1.5
1956	Chi-A	67	99	16	27	6	0	2	11	6	12	.273	.321	.394	.715	84	-2	-3	104	91	13	.635	1	2	-1	-2	O/3	-0.6
1957	Chi-A	121	393	38	106	13	3	7	42	28	32	.270	.323	.372	.695	90	-6	-6	99	99	48	.617	5	3	-0	17	3O	1.2
1958	Chi-A	84	260	26	71	10	0	5	30	15	14	.273	.315	.369	.684	89	-5	-4	98	108	29	.578	3	0	1	-1	3O	-0.4
1959	Chi-A	117	379	43	100	27	1	5	40	27	28	.264	.320	.380	.699	94	-5	-3	97	99	45	.611	1	1	-0	1	*3O	-0.4
1960	Cle-A	113	304	34	63	14	1	4	33	14	37	.207	.252	.299	.551	49	-23	-22	98	125	23	.445	1	0	0	-15	3O/S	-3.7
1961	Cle-A	143	546	64	144	23	1	18	72	29	61	.264	.307	.408	.715	93	-10	-7	96	104	66	.620	1	0	0	-17	*3	-1.4
1962	Cle-A	148	562	53	145	26	0	10	54	20	55	.258	.292	.358	.650	75	-22	-20	98	95	56	.535	4	0	1	-17	*3/O2	-3.4
1963	Det-A	128	464	42	114	11	2	5	45	19	42	.246	.281	.310	.592	63	-21	-23	104	121	38	.470	6	2	1	3	*3/O	-1.9
1964	Det-A	46	87	14	22	1	0	3	6	10	13	.253	.330	.368	.698	98	-1	-0	96	62	10	.623	1	2	-1	-0	3/O	0.0
Total	10	1062	3278	348	835	135	8	62	356	182	314	.255	.300	.358	.658	79	-104	-97	98	106	343	.574	25	11	1	-35	3O/2S	-12.1
■ **JACK PHILLIPS** Phillips, John Stephen b: 5/24/19, St.Louis, Mo. d: 6/16/58, St.Louis, Mo. BR/TR, 6'1", 185 lbs. Deb: 7/13/45																												
1945	NY-N	2	2	1	1	0	0	0	0	0	0	.500	.500	.500	1.000	179	0	0	100	0	1	1.000	0			0	/P	0.0
■ **TONY PHILLIPS** Phillips, Keith Anthony b: 4/25/59, Atlanta, Ga. BB/TR, 5'10", 160 lbs. Deb: 5/10/82																												
1982	Oak-A	40	81	11	17	2	2	0	8	12	26	.210	.326	.284	.610	73	-3	-2	95	139	8	.582	2	3	-1	-5	S	-0.4
1983	Oak-A	148	412	54	102	12	3	4	35	48	70	.248	.329	.320	.649	83	-10	-8	96	95	48	.619	16	5	2	-17	*S2/3D	-1.4
1984	Oak-A	154	451	62	120	24	3	4	37	42	86	.266	.329	.359	.688	99	-6	-1	92	85	55	.626	10	6	-1	-21	S2/O	-1.0
1985	Oak-A	42	161	23	45	12	2	4	17	13	34	.280	.333	.453	.787	122	3	4	93	84	25	.748	3	2	-0	-8	32	-0.3
1986	Oak-A	118	441	76	113	14	5	5	52	76	82	.256	.369	.345	.714	104	1	5	94	110	63	.724	15	10	-2	1	23/OSD	0.9
1987	Oak-A	111	379	48	91	20	0	10	46	57	76	.240	.339	.372	.711	98	-5	0	91	109	49	.677	7	6	-2	-2	23/SOD	0.3
1988	Oak-A	79	212	32	43	8	4	2	17	36	50	.203	.321	.307	.628	81	-6	-4	95	95	22	.576	0	2	-1	-8	O23/S1	-1.1
Total	7	692	2137	306	531	92	19	29	212	284	424	.248	.339	.350	.689	96	-25	-5	93	100	270	.664	53	34	-5	-59	2S3/OD1	-3.0
■ **MARR PHILLIPS** Phillips, Marr B. b: 6/16/1857, Pittsburgh, Pa. d: 4/1/28, Pittsburgh, Pa. Deb: 5/01/1884																												
1884	Ind-a	97	413	41	111	18	8	0		5		.269	.279	.351	.630	111	2	5	96	0	42	.500				13	*S	1.4
1885	Det-N	33	139	13	29	5	0	0	17	0	13	.209	.209	.245	.453	47	-8	-8	97	184	7	.309				2	S	-0.3
	Pit-a	4	15	1	4	0	0	0		2		.267	.353	.267	.620	95	0	-0	106	0	1	.545				0	/S	0.0
1890	Roc-a	64	257	18	53	8	0	0		16		.206	.261	.237	.498	53	-16	-13	93	0	19	.441	10			3	S	-0.5
Total	3	198	824	73	197	31	8	0	17	23	13	.239	.263	.296	.559	81	-22	-16	95	30	69	.448	10			18	S	0.6
■ **MIKE PHILLIPS** Phillips, Michael Dwaine b: 8/19/50, Beaumont, Tex. BL/TR, 6', 170 lbs. Deb: 4/15/73																												
1973	SF-N	63	104	18	25	3	4	1	9	6	17	.240	.288	.375	.663	79	-3	-3	105	86	10	.541	0	3	-2	-2	3S/2	-0.4
1974	SF-N	100	283	19	62	6	1	2	20	14	37	.219	.258	.269	.527	44	-20	-23	108	94	19	.413	4	5	-2	0	32S	-2.1
1975	SF-N	10	31	3	6	0	0	0	1	6	4	.194	.324	.194	.518	46	-2	-2	102	64	2	.500	1	0	0	0	/23	0.0
	NY-N	116	383	31	98	10	7	1	28	25	47	.256	.303	.326	.630	79	-13	-11	95	85	38	.526	3	0	1	-6	*S/2	-0.2
	Yr	126	414	34	104	10	7	1	29	31	51	.251	.305	.316	.621	76	-15	-13	96	83	41	.525	4	0	1	-6		-0.2
1976	NY-N	87	262	30	67	4	6	4	29	25	29	.256	.321	.363	.683	102	-2	0	92	104	31	.613	2	2	-1	-6	S23	0.0
1977	NY-N	38	86	5	18	2	1	1	3	2	15	.209	.244	.291	.535	45	-7	-7	96	43	6	.414	0	1	-1	-2	S/32	-0.5
	StL-N	48	87	17	21	3	2	0	9	9	13	.241	.320	.322	.641	76	-3	-3	96	129	10	.582	1	0	0	3	2/S3	0.3
	Yr	86	173	22	39	5	3	1	12	11	28	.225	.283	.306	.590	61	-10	-9	96	91	16	.500	1	1	-0	1		-0.2
1978	StL-N	76	164	14	44	8	1	1	28	13	25	.268	.330	.348	.677	94	-2	-1	95	185	19	.581	0	0	0	2	2S/3	0.6
1979	StL-N	44	97	10	22	3	1	1	6	10	9	.227	.306	.309	.615	65	-4	-5	105	72	9	.512	0	0	0	4	S2/3	0.2
1980	StL-N	63	128	13	30	5	0	0	7	9	17	.234	.285	.273	.558	55	-7	-8	103	79	9	.419	0	0	0	7	S/23	0.4
1981	SD-N	14	29	1	6	0	1	0	0	0	3	.207	.207	.276	.483	39	-2	-2	93	0	1	.346	1	0	0	-1	/2S	-0.1
	Mon-N	34	55	5	12	2	0	0	4	5	15	.218	.283	.255	.538	54	-3	-3	99	112	4	.413	0	1	-1	-2	S/2	-0.2
	Yr	48	84	6	18	2	1	0	4	5	18	.214	.258	.262	.520	49	-6	-5	97	79	5	.406	1	1	-0	-3		-0.3
1982	Mon-N	14	8	0	1	0	0	0	1	0	3	.125	.125	.125	.250	-28	-1	-1	105	392	0	.143	0	0	0	-0	2/S	0.0
1983	Mon-N	5	2	0	0	0	0	0	0	0	0	.000	.000	.000	.000	-98	-1	-1	102	0	0	.000	0	0	0	0	/S3	0.0
Total	11	712	1719	166	412	46	24	11	145	124	234	.240	.294	.314	.608	70	-72	-69	99	98	156	.519	12	12	-4	-2	S23	-2.0
■ **DICK PHILLIPS** Phillips, Richard Eugene b: 11/24/31, Racine, Wis. BL/TR, 6', 180 lbs. Deb: 4/15/62																												
1962	SF-N	5	3	1	0	0	0	0	1	1	1	.000	.250	.000	.250	-26	-1	-1	101	0	0	.333	0	0	0	0	/1	0.0
1963	Was-A	124	321	33	76	8	0	10	32	29	35	.237	.304	.355	.659	86	-7	-6	98	93	36	.586	1	0	0	1	1/23	-0.6
1964	Was-A	109	234	17	54	6	1	2	23	27	22	.231	.313	.291	.604	69	-9	-9	101	132	23	.524	1	2	-1	-1	1/3	-1.3
1966	Was-A	25	37	3	6	0	0	0	4	2	5	.162	.225	.162	.387	14	-4	-4	95	280	1	.273	0	0	0	-0	/1	-0.4
Total	4	263	595	54	136	14	1	12	60	59	63	.229	.302	.316	.618	74	-21	-20	99	119	60	.546	2	2	-1	0	1/32	-2.3
■ **BILL PHILLIPS** Phillips, William B. b: 1857, St.John, N.B., Canada d: 10/7/1900, Chicago, Ill. BR/TR, 202 lbs. Deb: 5/01/1879																												
1879	Cle-N	81	365	58	99	15	4	0	29	2	20	.271	.275	.334	.609	100	-0	-0	99	72	34	.466				2	*1C/O	-0.3
1880	Cle-N	85	334	41	85	14	10	1	36	6	29	.254	.268	.365	.633	114	4	4	99	111	33	.514				2	*1	0.2
1881	Cle-N	85	357	51	97	18	10	1	44	5	19	.272	.282	.387	.668	112	2	4	96	115	40	.550				-1	*1	-0.7
1882	Cle-N	78	335	40	87	17	7	4	47	7	18	.260	.275	.388	.663	122	3	8	90	98	37	.552				3	*1/C	-0.1
1883	Cle-N	97	382	42	94	29	8	2	40	8	49	.246	.262	.380	.641	88	-4	-7	105	97	39	.531				-2	*1	-1.8
1884	Cle-N	111	464	58	128	25	12	3	46	18	80	.276	.303	.401	.704	117	9	8	102	72	58	.607				-2	*1	-0.5
1885	Bro-a	99	391	65	118	16	11	3		27		.302	.364	.422	.786	145	23	21	104	0	62	.744				0	*1	1.1
1886	Bro-a	141	585	68	160	26	15	0		33		.274	.313	.369	.683	115	9	9	100	0	74	.619	13			-2	*1	0.0
1887	Bro-a	132	533	82	142	34	11	2		45		.266	.330	.383	.713	102	0	2	99	0	75	.693	16			3	*1	0.2
1888	KC-a	129	509	57	120	20	10	1	56	27		.236	.284	.320	.604	91	-2	-7	106	107	50	.532	10			3	*1	-1.1
Total	10	1038	4255	562	1130	214	98	17	298	178	215	.266	.299	.374	.673	110	45	42	100	61	501	.587	39			4	*1/CO	-3.0
■ **ROB PICCIOLO** Picciolo, Robert Michael b: 2/4/53, Santa Monica, Cal. BR/TR, 6'2", 185 lbs. Deb: 4/09/77																												
1977	Oak-A	148	419	35	84	12	3	2	22	9	55	.200	.219	.258	.477	31	-41	-38	95	76	22	.343	1	4	-2	-6	*S	-2.8
1978	Oak-A	78	93	16	21	1	0	2	7	2	13	.226	.242	.301	.543	51	-6	-6	101	81	6	.413	1	1	-0	-7	S23	-0.9
1979	Oak-A	115	348	37	88	16	2	2	27	3	45	.253	.261	.328	.589	65	-21	-16	89	86	27	.444	2	1	0	-13	*S/23O	-1.5
1980	Oak-A	95	271	32	65	9	2	5	18	2	63	.240	.245	.343	.589	63	-16	-14	95	65	21	.451	1	1	-0	-24	S2/O	-3.1
1981	Oak-A	82	179	23	48	5	3	4	13	5	22	.268	.292	.397	.689	101	-1	-1	96	61	19	.558	0	1	-1	-16	S	-1.1
1982	Oak-A	18	49	3	11	1	0	0	3	1	10	.224	.240	.245	.485	35	-4	-4	95	100	3	.368	1	0	0	-4	S	-0.5
	Mil-A	22	21	7	6	1	0	0	1	1	4	.286	.318	.333	.652	84	-1	-0	94	57	2	.533	0	0	0	0	2/SD	0.1
	Yr	40	70	10	17	2	0	0	4	2	14	.243	.264	.271	.535	50	-5	-5	95	79	6	.415	1	0	0	-4		-0.4
1983	Mil-A	14	27	2	6	3	0	0	1	0	4	.222	.222	.333	.556	55	-2	-2	92	43	2	.429	0	0	0	-0	/S231D	0.0
1984	Cal-A	87	119	18	24	6	0	1	9	0	21	.202	.202	.277	.479	31	-11	-11	101	100	6	.337	0	1	-1	2	S3/2O	-0.4
1985	Oak-A	71	102	19	28	2	0	1	8	2	17	.275	.288	.324	.612	73	-5	-4	93	88	9	.494	3	2	-0	-5	321D/SO	-0.8

YEAR	TM/L	G	AB	R	H	2B	3B	HR	RBI	BB	SO	AVG	OBP	SLG	PRO	/A	BR	/A	PF	CHI	RC	TA	SB	CS	SBR	FR	POS	TPR
Total	9	730	1628	192	381	56	10	17	109	25	254	.234	.247	.312	.559	56	-108	-96	94	78	118	.433	9	11	-4	-73	S2/31DO	-11.0
■ NICK PICCIUTO	Picciuto, Nicholas Thomas b: 8/27/21, Newark, N.J. BR/TR, 5'8.5", 165 lbs. Deb: 5/11/45																											
1945	Phi-N	36	89	7	12	6	0	0	6	6	17	.135	.189	.202	.392	9	-11	-11	96	116	4	.308	0			-1	3/2	-1.1
■ VAL PICINICH	Picinich, Valentine John b: 9/8/1896, New York, N.Y. d: 12/5/42, Nobleboro, Maine BR/TR, 5'9", 165 lbs. Deb: 7/25/16 C																											
1916	Phi-A	40	118	8	23	3	1	0	5	6	33	.195	.234	.237	.471	42	-9	-8	98	64	7	.368	1			8	C	0.2
1917	Phi-A	2	6	0	2	0	0	0	0	1	2	.333	.429	.333	.762	142	0	0	94	0	1	.750	0			0	/C	0.1
1918	Was-A	47	148	13	34	3	2	1	12	9	25	.230	.274	.297	.571	69	-5	-6	104	93	12	.465	0			-0	C	-0.2
1919	Was-A	80	212	18	58	12	3	3	22	17	43	.274	.330	.401	.731	107	1	1	98	85	30	.708	6			5	C	1.0
1920	Was-A	48	133	14	27	6	2	3	14	9	33	.203	.259	.346	.605	62	-8	-8	95	89	12	.528	0	0	0	5	C	0.1
1921	Was-A	45	141	10	39	9	0	0	12	16	21	.277	.354	.340	.695	79	-4	-4	99	86	17	.619	0	3	-2	2	C	-0.1
1922	Was-A	76	210	16	48	12	2	0	19	23	33	.229	.311	.305	.615	66	-12	-9	92	106	22	.556	1	0	0	4	C	-0.2
1923	Bos-A	87	268	33	74	21	1	2	31	46	32	.276	.386	.384	.770	102	3	2	102	99	42	.774	3	5	-2	5	C	1.0
1924	Bos-A	69	161	25	44	6	3	1	24	29	19	.273	.394	.366	.760	93	0	-0	104	128	26	.814	5	1	1	1	C	0.4
1925	Bos-A	90	251	31	64	21	0	1	25	33	21	.255	.344	.351	.694	81	-9	-7	95	92	33	.663	2	0	1	6	C/1	0.4
1926	Cin-N	89	240	33	63	16	1	2	31	29	22	.262	.342	.363	.705	94	-3	-1	95	115	30	.678	4			-8	C	-0.5
1927	Cin-N	65	173	16	44	8	3	0	12	24	15	.254	.345	.335	.680	83	-4	-4	100	72	21	.659	3			-2	C	-0.1
1928	Cin-N	96	324	29	98	15	1	7	35	20	25	.302	.343	.420	.763	102	-1	0	96	79	45	.695	1			2	C	0.8
1929	Bro-N	93	273	28	71	16	6	4	31	34	24	.260	.342	.407	.749	90	-7	-4	94	86	38	.733	3			5	C	0.7
1930	Bro-N	23	46	4	10	3	0	0	3	5	6	.217	.294	.283	.577	40	-4	-4	101	80	4	.528	1			-0	C	-0.2
1931	Bro-N	24	45	5	12	4	0	1	4	4	9	.267	.327	.422	.749	99	-0	-0	101	65	6	.727	1			0	C	0.0
1932	Bro-N	41	70	8	18	6	0	1	11	4	8	.257	.297	.386	.683	86	-2	-2	96	136	8	.596	0			-0	C	0.0
1933	Bro-N	6	6	1	1	1	0	0	0	0	1	.167	.167	.333	.500	41	-0	-0	97	0	0	.400	0			0	/C	0.0
	Pit-N	16	52	6	13	4	0	1	7	5	10	.250	.316	.385	.700	105	-0	0	95	114	7	.625	0			0	C	0.1
	Yr	22	58	7	14	5	0	1	7	5	11	.241	.302	.379	.681	98	-1	-0	95	83	7	.600	0			0		0.1
Total	18	1037	2877	298	743	166	25	27	298	314	382	.258	.334	.361	.695	86	-65	-54	97	93	362	.651	31	9		32	C/1	3.5
■ CHARLIE PICK	Pick, Charles Thomas b: 4/10/1888, Brookneal, Va. d: 6/26/54, Lynchburg, Va. BL/TR, 5'10", 160 lbs. Deb: 9/20/14																											
1914	Was-A	10	23	0	9	0	0	0	1	4	4	.391	.481	.391	.873	161	2	2	101	42	4	.875	1	2	-1	-0	/O	0.1
1915	Was-A	3	2	0	0	0	0	0	0	0	0	.000	.000	.000	.000	-99	-0	-0	101	0	0	.000	0			0	H	0.0
1916	Phi-A	121	398	29	96	10	3	0	20	40	24	.241	.315	.281	.597	81	-9	-8	98	65	39	.566	25	16	-2	-2	*3/O	-0.6
1918	Chi-N	29	89	13	29	4	1	0	12	14	4	.326	.417	.393	.811	144	6	6	102	132	17	.933	7			-1	2/3	0.6
1919	Chi-N	75	269	27	65	8	6	0	18	14	12	.242	.292	.316	.608	82	-6	-6	100	87	29	.593	17			-0	2/3	-0.3
	Bos-N	34	114	12	29	1	1	1	7	7	5	.254	.325	.307	.632	93	-1	-1	98	73	12	.600	4			-3	2/3O1	-0.3
	Yr	109	383	39	94	9	7	1	25	21	17	.245	.302	.313	.615	85	-7	-7	100	83	41	.595	21			-3		-0.6
1920	Bos-N	95	383	34	105	16	6	2	28	23	11	.274	.320	.363	.683	99	-2	-1	96	66	41	.595	10	16	-7	6	2	0.1
Total	6	367	1278	115	333	39	17	3	86	102	60	.261	.323	.325	.648	94	-11	-9	98	75	142	.610	64	34		-0	23/O1	-0.4
■ EDDIE PICK	Pick, Edgar Everett b: 5/7/1899, Attleboro, Mass. d: 5/13/67, Santa Monica, Cal. BB/TR, 6', 185 lbs. Deb: 9/13/23																											
1923	Cin-N	9	8	2	3	0	0	0	2	3	3	.375	.545	.375	.920	150	1	1	98	235	2	1.200	0	0	0	-2	/O	0.0
1924	Cin-N	3	2	0	0	0	0	0	0	0	1	.000	.000	.000	.000	-99	-1	-1	101	0	0	.000	0	0	0	-0	/O	0.0
1927	Chi-N	54	181	23	31	5	2	2	15	20	26	.171	.254	.254	.508	36	-16	-17	100	101	12	.440	0			1	3/2O	-1.2
Total	3	66	191	25	34	5	2	2	17	23	30	.178	.266	.257	.523	40	-16	-16	100	107	15	.459	0	0		-1	/3O2	-1.2
■ OLLIE PICKERING	Pickering, Oliver Daniel b: 4/9/1870, Olney, Ill. d: 1/20/52, Vincennes, Ind. BL/TR, 5'11", 170 lbs. Deb: 8/09/1896																											
1896	Lou-N	45	165	28	50	6	4	1	22	12	11	.303	.350	.406	.756	103	0	1	98	92	29	.800	13			4	O	0.1
1897	Lou-N	63	246	34	62	5	2	1	20	25		.252	.326	.301	.627	71	-10	-9	95	67	31	.658	20			4	O	-0.7
	Cle-N	46	182	33	64	5	2	1	22	11		.352	.392	.418	.809	105	4	1	111	86	38	.898	18			0	O/2	-0.1
	Yr	109	428	67	126	10	4	2	42	36		.294	.353	.350	.704	87	-6	-7	102	76	68	.752	38			5		-0.8
1901	Cle-A	137	547	102	169	25	6	0	40	58		.309	.375	.377	.752	117	10	15	95	54	93	.794	36			21	*O	3.0
1902	Cle-A	69	293	46	75	5	2	3	26	19		.256	.301	.317	.619	76	-10	-9	97	72	36	.615	22			6	O/1	-0.6
1903	Phi-A	137	512	93	144	18	6	1	36	53		.281	.349	.346	.694	107	9	6	104	69	78	.734	40			0	*O	-0.2
1904	Phi-A	124	455	56	103	10	3	0	30	45		.226	.296	.262	.558	78	-9	-10	102	90	41	.514	17			2	*O	-1.6
1907	StL-A	151	576	63	159	15	10	0	60	35		.276	.318	.337	.654	113	6	8	98	117	68	.585	15			-10	*O	-1.0
1908	Was-A	113	373	45	84	7	4	2	30	28		.225	.279	.282	.561	88	-6	-4	95	103	32	.505	13			8	O	0.0
Total	8	885	3349	500	910	96	39	9	286	286	11	.272	.330	.332	.661	98	-6	-1	99	84	445	.654	194			36	O/12	-1.1
■ URBANE PICKERING	Pickering, Urbane Henry "Pick" b: 6/3/1899, Hoxie, Kan. d: 5/13/70, Modesto, Cal. BR/TR, 5'10", 180 lbs. Deb: 4/18/31																											
1931	Bos-A	103	341	48	86	13	4	9	52	33	53	.252	.318	.393	.711	92	-8	-5	94	107	43	.656	3	4	-2	3	32	0.2
1932	Bos-A	132	457	47	119	28	5	2	40	39	71	.260	.320	.357	.677	77	-17	-15	97	81	53	.602	3	4	-2	-6	*3/C	-1.2
Total	2	235	798	95	205	41	9	11	92	72	124	.257	.319	.372	.691	83	-25	-20	96	92	95	.626	6	8	-3	-3	3/2C	-1.0
■ DAVE PICKETT	Pickett, David T. b: 5/26/1874, Brookline, Mass. 5'7.5", 170 lbs. Deb: 6/21/1898																											
1898	Bos-N	14	43	3	12	1	0	0	3	6		.279	.380	.302	.682	95	0	0	104	70	6	.710	2			0	O	0.0
■ JOHN PICKETT	Pickett, John Thomas b: 2/20/1866, Chicago, Ill. d: 7/4/22, Chicago, Ill. BR/TR, Deb: 6/06/1889																											
1889	KC-a	53	201	20	45	7	0	0	12	11	21	.224	.271	.259	.530	50	-12	-14	106	67	16	.462	7			0	O32	-1.1
1890	Phi-P	100	407	82	114	7	9	4	64	40	17	.280	.347	.371	.718	92	-3	-5	102	114	58	.700	12			-23	*2	-1.7
1892	Bal-N	36	141	13	30	2	3	1	12	7	10	.213	.260	.291	.551	68	-6	-6	100	85	11	.468	2			0	2	-0.4
Total	3	189	749	115	189	16	12	5	88	58	48	.252	.311	.326	.637	77	-21	-25	103	96	86	.587	21			-23	2/O3	-3.2
■ TY PICKUP	Pickup, Clarence William b: 10/29/1897, Philadelphia, Pa. d: 8/2/74, Philadelphia, Pa. 6', 180 lbs. Deb: 4/30/18																											
1918	Phi-N	1	1	0	1	0	0	0	0	0	0	1.000	1.000	1.000	2.000	468	0	0	109	0	1	—	0			-0	/O	0.0
■ GRACIE PIERCE	Pierce, Grayson S. b: New York, N.Y. d: 8/28/1894, New York, N.Y. BR/TR, Deb: N/A.																											
1882	Lou-a	9	33	3	10	1	0	0		1		.303	.324	.333	.657	130	1	1	94	0	4	.522				-0	/2	0.1
	Bal-a	41	151	8	30	2	1	0		3		.199	.214	.225	.439	52	-8	-6	92	0	7	.306				-11	2/OS	-1.2
	Yr	50	184	11	40	3	1	0		4		.217	.234	.245	.479	66	-7	-5	93	0	11	.340				-11		-1.1
1883	Col-a	11	41	5	7	0	0	0		0		.171	.171	.171	.341	12	-4	-3	87	0	1	.206				0	/2O	-0.2
	NY-N	18	62	3	5	0	1	0	2	1	9	.081	.095	.113	.208	-37	-10	-10	100	99	1	.140				0	O/2	-0.8
1884	NY-a	5	20	2	5	1	0	0		0		.250	.250	.300	.550	81	-0	-0	100	0	2	.400				0	/O2	0.0
Total	3	84	307	21	57	4	2	0	2	5	9	.186	.199	.212	.410	37	-21	-19	94	20	15	.280				-11	/2OS	-2.1
■ JACK PIERCE	Pierce, Lavern Jack b: 6/2/48, Laurel, Miss. BL/TR, 6', 210 lbs. Deb: 4/27/73																											
1973	Atl-N	11	20	0	1	0	0	0	0	1	8	.050	.095	.050	.145	-52	-4	-5	113	0	0	.105	0	0	0	0	/1	-0.4
1974	Atl-N	6	9	1	1	0	0	0	0	1	0	.111	.200	.111	.311	-11	-1	-1	105	0	0	.250	0	0	0	0	/1	-0.1
1975	Det-A	53	170	19	40	6	1	8	22	20	40	.235	.323	.424	.746	106	2	1	104	90	24	.712	0	0	0	-2	1	-0.3
Total	3	70	199	20	42	6	1	8	22	22	48	.211	.296	.372	.668	83	-4	-5	105	77	25	.616	0	0	0	-2	/1	-0.8
■ MAURY PIERCE	Pierce, Maurice b: Baltimore, Md. Deb: 4/23/1884																											
1884	Was-U	2	7	0	1	0	0	0		0		.143	.143	.143	.286	-3	-1	-1	97	0	0	.167	0			0	/3	0.0
■ ANDY PIERCY	Piercy, Andrew J. b: 8/1856, San Jose, Cal. d: 12/27/32, San Jose, Cal. TR, Deb: 5/12/1881																											
1881	Chi-N	2	8	1	2	0	0	0	0	0	1	.250	.250	.250	.500	53	-0	-0	108	0	1	.333				0	/32	0.0
■ DICK PIERRE	Pierre, Richard J. b: Grand Haven, Mich. Deb: 9/25/1883																											
1883	Phi-N	5	19	1	3	0	0	0	0	0	2	.158	.158	.158	.316	-4	-2	-2	90	0	0	.188				0	/S	-0.1
■ JIM PIERSALL	Piersall, James Anthony b: 11/14/29, Waterbury, Conn. BR/TR, 6', 175 lbs. Deb: 9/07/50 C																											
1950	Bos-A	6	7	4	2	0	0	0	0	4	0	.286	.545	.286	.831	103	1	0	114	0	2	1.200	0	0	0	1	/O	0.1
1952	Bos-A	56	161	28	43	8	0	1	16	28	26	.267	.379	.335	.714	93	1	-0	107	105	23	.699	3	3	-1	2	SO/3	0.1

YEAR	TM/L	G	AB	R	H	2B	3B	HR	RBI	BB	SO	AVG	OBP	SLG	PRO	/A	BR	/A	PF	CHI	RC	TA	SB	CS	SBR	FR	POS	TPR
1953	Bos-A	151	585	76	159	21	9	3	52	41	52	.272	.329	.354	.683	78	-13	-20	109	94	69	.598	11	10	-3	16	*O	-1.0
1954	Bos-A	133	474	77	135	24	2	8	38	36	42	.285	.339	.395	.734	100	-0	-1	100	68	63	.654	5	1	1	-0	*O	-0.2
1955	Bos-A	149	515	68	146	25	5	13	62	67	52	.283	.368	.427	.795	91	10	-7	124	91	82	.764	6	1	1	7	*O	-0.5
1956	Bos-A	155	601	91	176	**40**	6	14	87	58	48	.293	.356	.449	.805	109	9	6	103	110	92	.745	7	7	-2	9	*O	0.6
1957	Bos-A	151	609	103	159	27	5	19	63	62	54	.261	.333	.415	.749	94	2	-6	110	71	83	.704	14	6	1	5	*O	-0.8
1958	Bos-A	130	417	55	99	13	5	8	48	42	43	.237	.307	.350	.657	77	-11	-14	105	113	46	.604	12	2	2	5	*O	-1.4
1959	Cle-A	100	317	42	78	13	2	4	30	24	31	.246	.303	.338	.641	78	-11	-9	97	99	34	.570	6	3	0	-4	O/3	-1.7
1960	Cle-A	138	486	70	137	12	4	18	66	24	38	.282	.316	.434	.750	103	-1	-0	98	98	62	.682	18	5	2	5	*O	0.2
1961	Cle-A	121	484	81	156	26	7	6	40	43	46	.322	.380	.442	.822	123	13	16	96	65	79	.767	8	2	1	10	*O	2.2
1962	Was-A	135	471	38	115	20	4	4	31	39	53	.244	.302	.329	.631	69	-20	-20	101	75	45	.549	12	7	-1	-2	*O	-2.7
1963	Was-A	29	94	9	23	1	0	1	5	6	11	.245	.290	.287	.577	64	-5	-4	98	70	8	.507	4	0	1	2	O	-0.1
	NY-N	40	124	13	24	4	1	1	10	10	14	.194	.254	.266	.520	50	-8	-8	99	117	8	.419	1	2	-1	1	O	-1.0
	LA-A	20	52	4	16	1	0	0	4	5	5	.308	.368	.327	.695	106	-0	1	91	98	6	.579	0	1	-1	-2	O	-0.2
1964	LA-A	87	255	28	80	11	0	2	13	16	32	.314	.354	.380	.735	118	2	5	89	53	34	.645	5	3	-0	-3	O	0.0
1965	Cal-A	53	112	10	30	5	2	2	12	5	15	.268	.305	.402	.707	101	-0	-0	98	98	13	.609	2	2	-1	-4	O	-0.6
1966	Cal-A	75	123	14	26	5	0	0	14	13	19	.211	.287	.252	.539	57	-7	-7	99	190	8	.421	1	2	-1	-10	O	-2.1
1967	Cal-A	5	3	0	0	0	0	0	0	0	2	.000	.000	.000	.000	-99	-1	-1	96	0	0	.000	0	0	0	-0	/O	0.0
Total	17	1734	5890	811	1604	256	52	104	591	523	583	.272	.334	.386	.721	92	-39	-68	104	90	756	.677	115	57	0	38	*O/S3	-9.1
■ DAVE PIERSON	Pierson, David P. b: 8/20/1855, Wilkes-Barre, Pa. d: 11/11/22, Trenton, N.J. BR/TR, 5'7", 142 lbs. Deb: 4/25/1876																											
1876	Cin-N	57	233	33	55	4	1	0	13	1	9	.236	.239	.262	.501	75	-8	-4	90	76	15	.348				2	CO/S32P	0.0
■ DICK PIERSON	Pierson, Edmund Dana b: 10/24/1857, Wilkes-Barre, Pa. d: 7/20/22, Newark, N.J. TR , Deb: 1885																											
1885	NY-a	3	9	1	1	0	0	0		2		.111	.273	.111	.384	32	-1	-0	84	0	0	.375				0	/2	0.0
■ TONY PIET	Piet, Anthony Francis (born Anthony Francis Pietruszka) b: 12/7/06, Berwick, Pa. d: 12/1/81, Hinsdale, Ill. BR/TR, 6', 175 lbs. Deb: 8/15/31																											
1931	Pit-N	44	167	22	50	12	4	0	24	13	24	.299	.354	.419	.773	106	2	1	101	125	25	.803	10			-5	2/S	-0.1
1932	Pit-N	154	574	66	162	25	8	7	85	46	56	.282	.343	.390	.733	97	-2	-2	99	132	80	.718	19			-28	*2	-1.7
1933	Pit-N	107	362	45	117	21	5	1	42	19	28	.323	.367	.417	.784	130	11	13	95	102	57	.749	12			-10	2	1.1
1934	Cin-N	106	421	58	109	20	5	1	38	23	44	.259	.307	.337	.644	72	-16	-17	101	100	43	.548	6			-3	32	-0.9
1935	Cin-N	6	5	2	1	1	0	0	2	0	0	.200	.200	.400	.600	61	-0	-0	93	361	0	.500	0			-0	/O	0.0
	Chi-A	77	292	47	87	17	5	3	27	33	27	.298	.375	.421	.796	97	3	-1	109	74	48	.782	2	1	0	-3	23	0.0
1936	Chi-A	109	352	69	96	15	2	7	42	66	48	.273	.400	.386	.787	96	0	0	99	87	61	.866	15	5	2	7	23	1.2
1937	Chi-A	100	332	34	78	15	1	4	38	32	36	.235	.314	.322	.636	59	-20	-22	103	109	36	.612	14	6	1	-1	32	-1.7
1938	Det-A	41	80	9	17	6	0	0	14	15	11	.213	.351	.287	.638	61	-4	-4	100	206	8	.627	2	4	-2	1	3/2	-0.3
Total	8	744	2585	352	717	132	30	23	312	247	274	.277	.350	.378	.728	91	-28	-30	101	109	359	.714	80	16		-41	23/OS	-2.4
■ SANDY PIEZ	Piez, Charles William b: 10/13/1888, New York, N.Y. d: 12/29/30, Atlantic City, N.J BR/TR, 5'10", 170 lbs. Deb: 4/17/14																											
1914	NY-N	35	8	9	3	0	1	0	3	0	1	.375	.375	.625	1.000	205	1	1	96	218	3	1.800	4			-0	/O	0.1
■ JOE PIGNATANO	Pignatano, Joseph Benjamin b: 8/4/29, Brooklyn, N.Y. BR/TR, 5'10", 180 lbs. Deb: 4/28/57 C																											
1957	Bro-N	8	14	0	3	1	0	0	1	0	5	.214	.214	.286	.500	28	-1	-2	116	104	1	.333	0	0	0	0	/C	0.0
1958	LA-N	63	142	18	31	4	0	9	17	16	26	.218	.306	.437	.743	90	-2	-3	105	79	19	.730	4	1	1	-2	C	-0.1
1959	LA-N	52	139	17	33	4	1	1	11	21	15	.237	.346	.302	.648	73	-4	-5	102	99	16	.611	1	0	0	5	C	0.4
1960	LA-N	58	90	11	21	4	0	2	9	15	17	.233	.343	.344	.687	77	-1	-3	115	99	12	.671	1	1	-0	1	C	0.0
1961	KC-A	92	243	31	59	10	3	4	22	36	42	.243	.350	.358	.708	88	-3	-3	102	87	34	.694	2	2	-1	2	C/3	-0.2
1962	SF-N	7	5	2	1	0	0	0	0	4	0	.200	.556	.200	.756	111	1	1	101	0	1	1.250	0	0	0	0	/C	0.1
	NY-N	27	56	2	13	2	0	0	2	2	11	.232	.259	.268	.526	40	-5	-5	104	53	3	.370	0	0	0	-1	C	-0.4
	Yr	34	61	4	14	2	0	0	2	6	11	.230	.299	.262	.561	50	-4	-4	103	42	4	.440	0	0	0	-1		-0.3
Total	6	307	689	81	161	25	4	16	62	94	116	.234	.332	.351	.684	79	-15	-19	105	86	86	.658	8	4	0	6	C/3	-0.2
■ JAY PIKE	Pike, Jacob Emanuel b: Brooklyn, N.Y. BL/TL, Deb: 8/27/1877																											
1877	Har-N	1	4	0	1	0	0	0	0	0	0	.250	.250	.250	.500	65	-0	-0	89	0	0	.333				0	/O	0.0
■ JESS PIKE	Pike, Jess Willard b: 7/31/15, Dustin, Okla. d: 3/28/84, San Diego, Cal. BL/TR, 6'3", 175 lbs. Deb: 4/18/46																											
1946	NY-N	16	41	4	7	1	1	1	6	6	9	.171	.277	.317	.594	67	-2	-2	102	140	4	.559	0			-2	O	-0.4
■ LIP PIKE	Pike, Lipman Emanuel b: 5/25/1845, New York, N.Y. d: 10/10/1893, Brooklyn, N.Y. BL/TL, 5'8", 158 lbs. Deb: 5/09/1871 M																											
1871	Tro-n	28	134	42	47							.351															O/21M	
1872	Bal-n	54	278	69	80							.288															O2/3	
1873	Bal-n	56	301	73	89							.296															*O/2	
1874	Har-n	52	228	58	79							.346															OS/2M	
1875	StL-n	70	313	61	107							.342															*O/2	
1876	StL-N	63	282	55	91	19	10	1	50	8	9	.323	.341	.472	.813	192	20	25	88	119	47	.738				-5	*O/2	1.7
1877	Cin-N	58	262	45	78	12	4	**4**	23	9	7	.298	.321	.420	.741	161	9	16	82	55	36	.647				-8	O2/SM	0.7
1878	Cin-N	31	145	28	47	5	1	0	11	4	9	.324	.342	.372	.715	141	5	6	95	60	19	.592				-5	O	0.0
	Pro-N	5	22	4	5	0	1	0	4	1	1	.227	.261	.318	.579	92	-0	-0	98	167	2	.471				0	/2	0.0
	Yr	36	167	32	52	5	2	0	15	5	10	.311	.331	.365	.697	135	5	6	96	76	21	.574				-5		0.0
1881	Wor-N	5	18	1	2	0	0	0	0	4	3	.111	.273	.111	.384	24	-1	-1	105	0	1	.375				0	/O	0.0
1887	NY-a	1	4	0	0	0	0	0		0		.000	.000	.000	.000	-99	-1	-1	88	0	0	.000	0			0	/O	0.0
Total	5 n	260	1254	303	402							.321															/O	
Total	5	163	733	133	223	36	16	5	88	26	29	.304	.328	.417	.746	160	31	45	88	82	104	.651	0			-17	O/2S31	2.4
■ AL PILARCIK	Pilarcik, Alfred James b: 7/3/30, Whiting, Ind. BL/TL, 5'10", 180 lbs. Deb: 7/13/56																											
1956	KC-A	69	239	28	60	10	1	4	22	30	32	.251	.335	.351	.686	81	-6	-7	101	87	31	.672	9	2	2	-1	O	-0.8
1957	Bal-A	142	407	52	113	16	3	9	49	53	28	.278	.366	.398	.764	117	6	10	93	103	62	.756	14	7	0	5	*O	0.8
1958	Bal-A	141	379	40	92	21	0	1	24	42	37	.243	.322	.306	.628	78	-13	-10	94	81	39	.562	7	3	0	-4	*O	-2.1
1959	Bal-A	130	273	37	77	12	1	3	16	30	25	.282	.355	.366	.722	102	0	1	97	58	37	.680	9	3	1	-17	*O	-2.0
1960	Bal-A	104	194	30	48	5	1	4	17	15	16	.247	.315	.345	.660	77	-6	-6	102	84	21	.566	0	2	-1	-13	O	-2.3
1961	KC-A	35	60	9	12	1	1	0	9	6	7	.200	.273	.250	.523	40	-5	-5	102	235	4	.431	1	0	0	-1	O	-0.6
	Chi-A	47	62	9	11	1	0	1	6	9	5	.177	.282	.242	.524	42	-5	-5	99	131	4	.463	1	1	-0	0	O	-0.5
	Yr	82	122	18	23	2	1	1	15	15	12	.189	.277	.246	.523	41	-10	-10	100	178	9	.461	2	1	0	-1		-1.1
Total	6	668	1614	205	413	66	7	22	143	185	150	.256	.336	.346	.683	89	-29	-22	97	91	198	.652	41	18	2	-30	O	-7.5
■ ANDY PILNEY	Pilney, Antone James b: 1/19/13, Frontenac, Kan. BR/TR, 5'11", 174 lbs. Deb: 6/12/36																											
1936	Bos-N	3	2	0	0	0	0	0	0	0	1	.000	.000	.000	.000	-99	-1	-1	95	0	0	.000	0			0	H	0.0
■ BABE PINELLI	Pinelli, Ralph Arthur (born Rinaldo Angelo Paolinelli) b: 10/18/1895, San Francisco, Cal d: 10/2/ 22, 84 Daly City, Cal. BR/TR, 5'9", 165 lbs. Deb: 8/03/18 U																											
1918	Chi-A	24	78	7	18	1	1	1	7	7	8	.231	.302	.308	.610	84	-2	-2	101	95	8	.583	3			-3	3	-0.4
1920	Det-A	102	284	33	65	9	3	0	21	25	16	.229	.296	.282	.578	52	-19	-20	103	92	24	.498	6	8	-3	6	3S/2	-0.9
1922	Cin-N	156	547	77	167	19	7	1	72	48	37	.305	.368	.371	.739	95	-6	-2	96	125	73	.682	17	22	-8	21	*3	2.1
1923	Cin-N	117	423	44	117	14	5	0	51	27	29	.277	.320	.333	.653	74	-17	-15	98	130	43	.556	10	14	-5	9	*3	-0.8
1924	Cin-N	144	510	61	156	16	7	0	70	32	32	.306	.353	.365	.718	92	-4	-5	101	140	65	.663	23	17	-3	26	*3	2.7
1925	Cin-N	130	492	68	139	33	6	2	49	22	28	.283	.316	.386	.702	80	-17	-15	97	94	55	.597	8	19	-9	19	*3S	0.3
1926	Cin-N	71	207	26	46	7	4	0	24	15	5	.222	.284	.295	.579	59	-13	-11	95	136	18	.503	2			6	3S/2	-0.2
1927	Cin-N	30	76	11	15	2	0	1	4	6	7	.197	.265	.263	.528	42	-6	-6	100	61	5	.475	2			1	3/S2	-0.3
Total	8	774	2617	327	723	101	33	5	298	182	162	.276	.328	.346	.674	79	-83	-76	98	117	292	.597	71	80		84	3/S2	2.5
■ LOU PINIELLA	Piniella, Louis Victor b: 8/28/43, Tampa, Fla. BR/TR, 6', 182 lbs. Deb: 9/04/64 MC																											
1964	Bal-A	4	1	0	0	0	0	0	0	0	0	.000	.000	.000	.000	-95	-0	-0	105	0	0	.000	0	0	0	0	H	0.0

YEAR	TM/L	G	AB	R	H	2B	3B	HR	RBI	BB	SO	AVG	OBP	SLG	PRO	/A	BR	/A	PF	CHI	RC	TA	SB	CS	SBR	FR	POS	TPR
1968	Cle-A	6	5	1	0	0	0	0	1	0	0	.000	.000	.000	.000	-99	-1	-1	101	0	0	.000	0	0	0	-0	/O	-0.1
1969	KC-A	135	493	43	139	21	6	11	68	33	56	.282	.331	.416	.747	105	4	2	103	117	65	.657	2	4	-2	12	*O	1.0
1970	KC-A	144	542	54	163	24	5	11	88	35	42	.301	.345	.424	.770	113	7	8	98	**138**	74	.675	3	6	-3	-0	*O/1	0.0
1971	KC-A	126	448	43	125	21	5	3	51	21	43	.279	.314	.368	.683	94	-5	-5	99	122	49	.571	5	3	-0	-3	*O	-1.2
1972	KC-A	151	574	65	179	**33**	4	11	72	34	59	.312	.359	.441	.800	137	25	25	100	111	84	.716	7	2	1	-2	*O	2.2
1973	KC-A	144	513	53	128	28	1	9	69	30	65	.250	.294	.361	.654	76	-12	-18	109	128	47	.536	5	7	-3	-8	*O/D	-3.2
1974	NY-A	140	518	71	158	26	0	9	70	32	58	.305	.348	.407	.755	122	10	13	96	118	66	.637	1	8	-5	8	*O/1D	1.3
1975	NY-A	74	199	7	39	4	1	0	22	16	22	.196	.266	.226	.492	41	-15	-15	99	188	10	.370	0	0	0	-4	OD	-2.0
1976	NY-A	100	327	36	92	16	6	3	38	18	34	.281	.323	.394	.717	110	3	3	99	106	41	.621	0	1	-1	-0	OD	0.1
1977	NY-A	103	339	47	112	19	3	12	45	20	31	.330	.369	.510	.880	139	16	17	99	85	59	.813	2	2	-1	-6	OD/1	0.8
1978	NY-A	130	472	67	148	34	5	6	69	34	36	.314	.362	.445	.807	127	16	16	99	122	74	.739	3	1	0	-2	*OD	1.3
1979	NY-A	130	461	49	137	22	2	11	69	17	31	.297	.325	.425	.750	105	-1	2	96	118	58	.636	3	2	-0	-0	*OD	-0.2
1980	NY-A	116	321	39	92	18	0	2	27	29	20	.287	.346	.361	.707	95	-2	-2	99	86	36	.585	0	2	-1	-10	*O/D	-1.4
1981	NY-A	60	159	16	44	9	0	5	18	13	9	.277	.331	.428	.759	117	3	3	100	85	20	.659	0	1	-1	0	OD	0.2
1982	NY-A	102	261	33	80	17	1	6	37	18	18	.307	.354	.448	.802	123	6	8	96	110	37	.701	0	1	-1	-2	DO	0.3
1983	NY-A	53	148	19	43	9	1	2	16	11	12	.291	.344	.405	.749	107	1	1	99	95	20	.664	1	1	-0	-3	O/D	-0.1
1984	NY-A	29	86	8	26	4	1	1	6	7	5	.302	.355	.407	.762	117	1	2	94	63	10	.627	0	0	0	-0	O/D	0.1
Total	18	1747	5867	651	1705	305	41	102	766	368	541	.291	.336	.409	.745	109	56	60	99	116	750	.672	32	41	-15	-21	*OD/1	-0.9

■ **ED PINKHAM** Pinkham, Edward b: 1849, Brooklyn, N.Y. TL , 5'7", 142 lbs. Deb: 5/08/1871

YEAR	TM/L	G	AB	R	H	2B	3B	HR	RBI	BB	SO	AVG	OBP	SLG	PRO	/A	BR	/A	PF	CHI	RC	TA	SB	CS	SBR	FR	POS	TPR
1871	Chi-n	24	110	27	25							.227															3/OP	

■ **GEORGE PINKNEY** Pinkney, George Burton b: 1/11/1862, Orange Prairie, Ill. d: 11/10/26, Peoria, Ill. BR/TR, 5'7", 160 lbs. Deb: 8/16/1884

YEAR	TM/L	G	AB	R	H	2B	3B	HR	RBI	BB	SO	AVG	OBP	SLG	PRO	/A	BR	/A	PF	CHI	RC	TA	SB	CS	SBR	FR	POS	TPR
1884	Cle-N	36	144	18	45	9	0	0	16	10	7	.313	.357	.375	.732	128	5	5	102	90	20	.646				0	2S	0.4
1885	Bro-a	110	447	77	124	16	5	0		27		.277	.328	.336	.664	109	7	5	104	0	51	.570				-14	23/S	-0.3
1886	Bro-a	141	597	119	156	22	7	0		**70**		.261	.339	.322	.660	109	8	8	100	0	78	.667	32			-17	*3/P	-0.2
1887	Bro-a	138	580	133	155	26	6	3		61		.267	.343	.348	.691	97	-2	-1	99	0	92	.772	59			10	*3/S	0.4
1888	Bro-a	143	575	**134**	156	18	8	4	52	66		.271	.358	.351	.710	126	23	19	105	63	93	.790	51			-26	*3	-0.6
1889	Bro-a	138	545	103	134	25	7	4	82	59	43	.246	.327	.339	.667	96	-5	-1	96	114	78	.725	47			-7	*3	-0.5
1890	Bro-N	126	485	115	150	20	9	7	83	80	19	.309	.411	.431	.842	148	32	32	100	96	108	1.015	47			-16	*3	1.9
1891	Bro-N	135	501	80	137	19	6	2	71	66	32	.273	.366	.347	.713	113	9	11	97	122	82	.799	44			-21	*3/S	-0.4
1892	StL-N	78	290	31	50	3	2	0	25	36	26	.172	.268	.197	.465	45	-19	-17	95	143	17	.412	4			-9	3	-1.8
1893	Lou-N	118	446	64	105	12	6	1	62	50	8	.235	.323	.296	.619	69	-20	-17	96	128	48	.592	12			-2	*3	-1.4
Total	10	1163	4610	874	1212	170	56	21	391	525	135	.263	.345	.338	.683	105	39	44	99	70	665	.715	296			-102	*3/2SP	-2.5

■ **VADA PINSON** Pinson, Vada Edward b: 8/11/36, Memphis, Tenn. BL/TL, 5'11", 170 lbs. Deb: 4/15/58 C

YEAR	TM/L	G	AB	R	H	2B	3B	HR	RBI	BB	SO	AVG	OBP	SLG	PRO	/A	BR	/A	PF	CHI	RC	TA	SB	CS	SBR	FR	POS	TPR
1958	Cin-N	27	96	20	26	7	0	1	8	11	18	.271	.352	.375	.727	86	-1	-2	107	86	13	.694	2	1	0	2	O	0.0
1959	Cin-N	154	648	**131**	205	**47**	9	20	84	55	98	.316	.371	.509	.880	127	28	26	103	77	124	.889	21	6	3	13	*O	3.8
1960	Cin-N	154	652	107	187	**37**	12	20	61	47	96	.287	.339	.472	.812	122	16	17	98	59	104	.803	32	12	2	3	*O	1.8
1961	Cin-N	154	607	101	**208**	34	8	16	87	39	63	.343	.383	.504	.887	128	28	25	104	105	116	.883	23	10	1	12	*O	2.8
1962	Cin-N	155	619	107	181	31	7	23	100	45	68	.292	.344	.477	.821	116	14	12	102	115	101	.808	26	8	3	1	*O	0.8
1963	Cin-N	162	652	96	**204**	37	**14**	22	106	36	80	.313	.350	.514	.864	140	35	33	104	107	113	.845	27	8	3	-1	*O	2.8
1964	Cin-N	156	625	99	166	23	11	23	84	42	99	.266	.317	.448	.765	109	9	7	103	95	89	.713	8	2	1	-3	*O	0.1
1965	Cin-N	159	669	97	204	34	10	22	94	43	81	.305	.353	.484	.838	129	28	25	104	96	112	.811	21	8	2	5	*O	2.8
1966	Cin-N	156	618	70	178	35	6	16	76	33	83	.288	.329	.442	.771	98	9	-1	114	105	87	.715	18	10	-1	0	*O	-0.6
1967	Cin-N	158	650	90	187	28	**13**	18	66	26	86	.288	.318	.454	.772	109	13	7	109	75	94	.734	26	8	3	-1	*O	0.2
1968	Cin-N	130	499	60	135	29	6	5	48	32	59	.271	.315	.383	.697	97	4	-1	111	100	59	.632	17	11	-2	-5	*O	-1.5
1969	StL-N	132	495	58	126	22	6	10	70	35	63	.255	.308	.384	.692	93	-6	-6	100	135	56	.603	4	4	-1	1	*O	-1.2
1970	Cle-A	148	574	74	164	28	6	24	82	28	69	.286	.322	.481	.803	103	11	2	115	101	84	.734	7	6	-2	-12	*O/1	-1.8
1971	Cle-A	146	566	60	149	23	4	11	35	21	58	.263	.297	.376	.673	85	-10	-13	106	62	63	.613	25	6	4	-2	*O/1	-1.7
1972	Cal-A	136	484	56	133	24	2	7	49	30	54	.275	.324	.376	.700	122	4	10	88	103	59	.643	17	6	2	-2	*O/1	0.6
1973	Cal-A	124	466	56	121	14	6	8	57	20	55	.260	.290	.367	.657	87	-11	-9	96	117	46	.543	5	5	-2	2	*O	-1.2
1974	KC-A	115	406	46	112	18	2	6	41	21	45	.276	.315	.374	.689	92	-2	-5	106	95	49	.643	21	5	3	-6	*O/1D	-1.0
1975	KC-A	103	319	38	71	14	5	4	22	10	21	.223	.251	.335	.586	63	-16	-17	102	71	24	.479	5	6	-2	-4	O/1D	-2.5
Total	18	2469	9645	1366	2757	485	127	256	1170	574	1196	.286	.330	.442	.772	109	155	109	104	95	1394	.741	305	122	18	3	*O/1D	4.2

■ **WALLY PIPP** Pipp, Walter Clement b: 2/17/1893, Chicago, Ill. d: 1/11/65, Grand Rapids, Mich BL/TL, 6'1", 180 lbs. Deb: 6/29/13

YEAR	TM/L	G	AB	R	H	2B	3B	HR	RBI	BB	SO	AVG	OBP	SLG	PRO	/A	BR	/A	PF	CHI	RC	TA	SB	CS	SBR	FR	POS	TPR
1913	Det-A	12	31	3	5	0	3	0	5	2	6	.161	.235	.355	.590	73	-1	-1	99	162	2	.538	0			-0	1	-0.1
1915	NY-A	136	479	59	118	20	13	4	60	66	81	.246	.339	.367	.706	113	6	7	98	115	65	.709	18	7	1	3	*1	0.6
1916	NY-A	151	545	70	143	20	14	**12**	93	54	82	.262	.331	.417	.748	123	14	13	101	129	82	.744	16			5	*1	1.7
1917	NY-A	155	587	82	143	29	12	**9**	70	60	66	.244	.320	.380	.700	106	8	3	107	106	72	.676	11			4	*1	0.2
1918	NY-A	91	349	48	106	15	9	2	44	22	34	.304	.345	.415	.760	137	10	13	95	112	52	.733	11			-1	1	0.6
1919	NY-A	138	523	74	144	23	10	7	50	39	42	.275	.330	.398	.728	98	1	-2	106	84	71	.686	9			0	*1	-1.2
1920	NY-A	153	610	109	171	30	14	11	76	48	54	.280	.339	.430	.768	100	0	-2	102	80	87	.713	4	10	-5	-0	*1	-0.6
1921	NY-A	153	588	96	174	35	9	8	97	45	28	.296	.347	.427	.774	94	-4	-7	103	128	87	.741	17	10	-1	-4	*1	-1.1
1922	NY-A	152	577	96	190	32	10	9	90	56	32	.329	.392	.466	.859	121	20	18	102	115	104	.842	7	12	-5	-6	*1	-0.4
1923	NY-A	144	569	79	173	19	8	6	108	36	28	.304	.352	.397	.749	93	-3	-7	104	**160**	77	.670	6	13	-6	-5	*1	-2.2
1924	NY-A	153	589	88	174	30	**19**	9	113	51	36	.295	.352	.457	.808	108	4	5	99	134	95	.789	12	6	0	2	*1	0.0
1925	NY-A	62	178	19	41	6	3	3	24	13	12	.230	.286	.348	.635	63	-12	-10	96	113	18	.564	3	3	-1	-1	1	-1.2
1926	Cin-N	155	574	72	167	22	15	6	99	49	26	.291	.352	.413	.765	111	4	8	95	**142**	83	.735	8			2	*1	0.4
1927	Cin-N	122	443	49	115	19	6	2	41	32	11	.260	.309	.343	.653	75	-16	-16	100	93	47	.567	2			1	*1	-2.1
1928	Cin-N	95	272	30	77	11	3	2	26	23	13	.283	.341	.368	.709	89	-6	-4	96	87	34	.641	1			4	1	-0.7
Total	15	1872	6914	974	1941	311	148	90	996	596	551	.281	.341	.408	.749	103	25	17	101	116	976	.711	125	61		5	*1	-6.1

■ **JIM PISONI** Pisoni, James Pete b: 8/14/29, St.Louis, Mo. BR/TR, 5'10", 169 lbs. Deb: 9/25/53

YEAR	TM/L	G	AB	R	H	2B	3B	HR	RBI	BB	SO	AVG	OBP	SLG	PRO	/A	BR	/A	PF	CHI	RC	TA	SB	CS	SBR	FR	POS	TPR
1953	StL-A	3	12	1	1	0	0	1	1	0	5	.083	.083	.333	.417	8	-2	-2	107	54	0	.364	0	0	0	0	/O	-0.1
1956	KC-A	10	30	4	8	0	0	2	5	2	8	.267	.313	.467	.779	102	-0	-0	101	93	4	.667	0	0	0	4	/O	0.3
1957	KC-A	44	97	14	23	2	2	3	12	10	17	.237	.321	.392	.713	95	-1	-1	99	101	13	.676	0	0	0	1	O	-0.1
1959	Mil-N	9	24	4	4	1	0	0	0	2	6	.167	.231	.208	.439	19	-3	-3	95	0	1	.333	0	0	0	-0	/O	-0.2
	NY-A	17	17	2	3	0	1	0	1	1	9	.176	.222	.294	.516	44	-1	-1	93	79	1	.429	0	0	0	-3	O	-0.4
1960	NY-A	20	9	1	1	0	0	0	1	1	2	.111	.200	.111	.311	-14	-1	-1	94	392	0	.250	0	0	0	-5	O	-0.6
Total	5	103	189	26	40	3	3	6	20	16	47	.212	.280	.354	.635	72	-8	-8	98	96	20	.570	0	0	0	-2	/O	-1.1

■ **ALEX PITKO** Pitko, Alexander "Spunk" b: 11/22/14, Burlington, N.J. BR/TR, 5'10", 180 lbs. Deb: 9/11/38

YEAR	TM/L	G	AB	R	H	2B	3B	HR	RBI	BB	SO	AVG	OBP	SLG	PRO	/A	BR	/A	PF	CHI	RC	TA	SB	CS	SBR	FR	POS	TPR
1938	Phi-N	7	19	2	6	1	0	0	2	3	3	.316	.409	.368	.778	115	1	1	100	103	3	.786	1			-2	/O	-0.1
1939	Was-A	4	8	0	1	0	0	0	1	1	3	.125	.222	.125	.347	-10	-1	-1	90	338	0	.250	0	0	0	-1	/O	-0.1
Total	2	11	27	2	7	1	0	0	3	4	6	.259	.355	.296	.651	79	-1	-1	97	171	3	.619	1	0		-3	/O	-0.2

■ **JAKE PITLER** Pitler, Jacob Albert b: 4/22/1894, New York, N.Y. d: 2/3/68, Binghamton, N.Y. BR/TR, 5'8", 150 lbs. Deb: 5/30/17 C

YEAR	TM/L	G	AB	R	H	2B	3B	HR	RBI	BB	SO	AVG	OBP	SLG	PRO	/A	BR	/A	PF	CHI	RC	TA	SB	CS	SBR	FR	POS	TPR
1917	Pit-N	109	382	39	89	8	5	0	23	30	24	.233	.297	.280	.577	78	-9	-9	100	88	34	.505	6			-16	*2/O	-2.0
1918	Pit-N	2	1	1	0	0	0	0	0	1	0	.000	.500	.000	.500	54	0	0	106	0	1	3.000	2			0	/2	0.0
Total	2	111	383	40	89	8	5	0	23	31	24	.232	.298	.279	.578	78	-9	-9	100	87	35	.514	8			-16	2/O	-2.0

■ **CHRIS PITTARO** Pittaro, Christopher Francis b: 9/16/61, Trenton, N.J. BB/TR, 5'11", 170 lbs. Deb: 4/08/85

YEAR	TM/L	G	AB	R	H	2B	3B	HR	RBI	BB	SO	AVG	OBP	SLG	PRO	/A	BR	/A	PF	CHI	RC	TA	SB	CS	SBR	FR	POS	TPR
1985	Det-A	28	62	10	15	3	1	0	7	5	13	.242	.299	.323	.621	66	-3	-3	106	139	6	.542	1	1	-0	-0	3/2D	-0.3
1986	Min-A	11	21	0	2	0	0	0	0	0	8	.095	.095	.095	.190	-44	-4	-4	108	0	0	.105	0	0	0	0	/2S	-0.3
1987	Min-A	14	12	6	4	0	0	0	0	1	0	.333	.385	.333	.718	98	-0	0	96	0	2	.750	1	0	0	0	/2D	0.1
Total	3	53	95	16	21	3	1	0	7	6	21	.221	.267	.274	.541	46	-7	-7	105	92	8	.453	2	1	0	-0	/32SD	-0.5

YEAR	TM/L	G	AB	R	H	2B	3B	HR	RBI	BB	SO	AVG	OBP	SLG	PRO	/A	BR	/A	PF	CHI	RC	TA	SB	CS	SBR	FR	POS	TPR
■ **PINKY PITTINGER** Pittinger, Clarke Alonzo b: 2/24/1899, Hudson, Mich. d: 11/4/77, Ft.Lauderdale, Fla. BR/TR, 5'10", 160 lbs. Deb: 4/15/21																												
1921	Bos-A	40	91	6	18	1	0	0	5	4	13	.198	.232	.209	.440	13	-12	-12	100	90	5	.347	3	2	-0	2	O/3S2	-1.1
1922	Bos-A	66	186	16	48	3	0	0	7	9	10	.258	.299	.274	.574	52	-13	-12	96	49	15	.448	2	5	-2	-5	3S	-1.2
1923	Bos-A	60	177	15	38	5	0	0	15	5	10	.215	.236	.243	.479	26	-19	-19	102	119	10	.364	3	1	0	-5	2S/3	-2.0
1925	Chi-N	59	173	21	54	7	2	0	15	12	7	.312	.364	.376	.739	92	-2	-2	97	82	24	.683	5	4	-1	-0	S3	0.0
1927	Cin-N	31	84	17	23	5	0	1	10	2	5	.274	.291	.369	.660	76	-3	-3	100	103	9	.607	4			-1	2/S3	-0.2
1928	Cin-N	40	38	12	9	0	1	0	4	0	1	.237	.237	.289	.526	38	-4	-3	96	129	2	.448	2			0	S/23	0.0
1929	Cin-N	77	210	31	62	11	0	0	27	5	4	.295	.318	.348	.666	65	-12	-11	99	127	22	.595	8			-0	S/32	-0.3
Total	7	373	959	118	252	32	3	1	83	37	50	.263	.294	.306	.600	55	-65	-63	99	96	87	.505	27	12		-10	S/32O	-4.8
■ **JOE PITTMAN** Pittman, Joseph W. b: 1/1/54, Houston, Tex. BR/TR, 6'1", 180 lbs. Deb: 4/25/81																												
1981	Hou-N	52	135	11	38	4	2	0	7	11	16	.281	.336	.341	.676	104	-1	1	88	60	15	.587	4	4	-1	-4	2/3	-0.2
1982	Hou-N	15	10	0	2	1	0	0	0	0	2	.200	.200	.300	.500	38	-1	-1	99	0	1	.375	0	0	0	0	/3O	0.0
	SD-N	55	118	16	30	2	0	0	7	9	13	.254	.307	.271	.578	69	-6	-4	92	86	10	.521	8	3	1	-5	2S	-0.6
	Yr	70	128	16	32	3	0	0	7	9	15	.250	.299	.273	.573	66	-6	-5	93	67	11	.510	8	3	1	-5		-0.6
1984	SF-N	17	22	2	5	0	0	0	2	0	6	.227	.227	.227	.455	29	-2	-2	96	157	1	.316	1	1	-0	0	/S23	0.0
Total	3	139	285	29	75	7	2	0	16	20	37	.263	.311	.302	.613	81	-10	-7	91	76	26	.543	13	8	-1	-9	/2S3O	-0.8
■ **GAYLEN PITTS** Pitts, Gaylen Richard b: 6/6/46, Wichita, Kan. BR/TR, 6'1", 175 lbs. Deb: 5/12/74																												
1974	Oak-A	18	41	4	10	3	0	0	3	5	4	.244	.326	.317	.643	85	-1	-1	100	91	4	.563	0	0	0	-1	3/21	0.0
1975	Oak-A	10	3	1	1	1	0	0	1	0	0	.333	.333	.667	1.000	190	0	0	93	192	0	.667	0	0	0	-0	/3S2	0.0
Total	2	28	44	5	11	4	0	0	4	5	4	.250	.327	.341	.667	92	-0	-0	100	97	4	.588	0	0	0	-1	/32S1	0.0
■ **HERMAN PITZ** Pitz, Herman b: 7/18/1865, Brooklyn, N.Y. d: 9/3/24, Far Rockaway, N.Y. 5'6", 140 lbs. Deb: 4/18/1890																												
1890	BB-a	61	189	26	26	0	0	0		45		.138	.312	.138	.450	35	-12	-12	100	0	16	.607	25			0	C3/OS2	-1.0
	Syr-a	29	95	17	21	0	0	0		13		.221	.321	.221	.542	69	-4	-2	90	0	12	.662	14			0	C/SO	-0.1
	Yr	90	284	43	47	0	0	0	0	58		.165	.315	.165	.481	46	-16	-15	97	0	28	.624	39			0		-1.1
Total	1	90	284	43	47	0	0	0	0	58		.165	.315	.165	.481	45	-16	-15	97	0	28	.624	39			0	/C3OS2	-1.1
■ **DON PLARSKI** Plarski, Donald Joseph b: 11/9/29, Chicago, Ill. d: 12/29/81, St.Louis, Mo. BR/TR, 5'6", 160 lbs. Deb: 7/20/55																												
1955	KC-A	8	11	0	1	0	0	0	0	0	2	.091	.091	.091	.182	-50	-2	-2	101	0	0	.200	1	0	0	-1	/O	-0.3
■ **ELMO PLASKETT** Plaskett, Elmo Alexander b: 6/27/38, Frederiksted, V.I. BR/TR, 5'10", 195 lbs. Deb: 9/08/62																												
1962	Pit-N	7	14	2	4	0	0	1	3	1	3	.286	.333	.500	.833	118	0	0	102	118	2	.800	0	0	0	0	/C	0.0
1963	Pit-N	10	21	1	3	0	0	0	2	0	5	.143	.143	.143	.286	-18	-3	-3	99	280	0	.167	0	0	0	0	/C3	-0.2
Total	2	17	35	3	7	0	0	1	5	1	8	.200	.222	.286	.508	41	-3	-3	100	213	3	.393	0	0	0	0	/C3	-0.2
■ **WHITEY PLATT** Platt, Mizell George b: 8/21/20, W.Palm Beach, Fla. d: 7/27/70, W.Palm Beach, Fla BR/TR, 6'1.5", 190 lbs. Deb: 9/16/42																												
1942	Chi-N	4	16	1	1	0	0	0	2	0	3	.063	.063	.063	.125	-66	-3	-3	96	756	-0	.059	0			0	/O	-0.2
1943	Chi-N	20	41	2	7	3	0	0	2	1	7	.171	.190	.244	.434	25	-4	-4	99	72	2	.314	0			-3	O	-0.8
1946	Chi-A	84	247	28	62	8	5	3	32	17	34	.251	.307	.360	.667	89	-5	-4	97	124	24	.547	1	7	-4	-2	O	-1.3
1948	StL-A	123	454	57	123	22	10	7	82	39	51	.271	.331	.410	.741	91	-4	-8	106	136	60	.653	1	4	-2	-8	*O	-2.0
1949	StL-A	102	244	29	63	8	2	3	29	24	27	.258	.325	.344	.669	77	-9	-9	100	107	27	.568	0	1	-1	-1	O/1	-1.0
Total	5	333	1002	117	256	41	17	13	147	81	122	.255	.314	.369	.684	83	-25	-28	102	133	112	.598	2	12		-13	O/1	-5.3
■ **AL PLATTE** Platte, Alfred Frederick Joseph b: 4/13/1890, Grand Rapids, Mich d: 8/29/76, Grand Rapids, Mich BL/TL, 5'7", 160 lbs. Deb: 9/01/13																												
1913	Det-A	9	18	1	2	1	0	0	0	1	1	.111	.158	.167	.325	-5	-2	-2	99	0	0	.250	0			-1	/O	-0.3
■ **RANCE PLESS** Pless, Rance b: 12/6/25, Greeneville, Tenn. BR/TR, 6', 145 lbs. Deb: 4/21/56																												
1956	KC-A	48	85	4	23	3	1	0	9	10	13	.271	.354	.329	.684	81	-2	-2	101	120	9	.574	0	1	-1	0	1/3	-0.2
■ **HERB PLEWS** Plews, Herbert Eugene b: 6/14/28, Helena, Mont. BL/TR, 5'11", 160 lbs. Deb: 4/18/56																												
1956	Was-A	91	256	24	69	10	7	1	25	26	40	.270	.339	.375	.714	87	-4	-5	102	94	32	.636	1	2	-1	1	2/S3	0.0
1957	Was-A	104	329	51	89	19	4	1	26	28	39	.271	.331	.362	.693	91	-5	-4	98	84	38	.589	0	3	-2	-0	23/S	0.0
1958	Was-A	111	380	46	98	12	6	2	29	17	45	.258	.291	.337	.628	75	-15	-13	97	87	36	.507	2	3	-1	-4	23	-1.2
1959	Was-A	27	40	4	9	0	0	0	2	3	5	.225	.279	.225	.504	40	-3	-3	100	87	2	.353	0	1	-1	-0	/2	-0.3
	Bos-A	13	12	0	1	1	0	0	0	0	4	.083	.083	.167	.250	-31	-2	-2	106	0	0	.167	0	0	0	0	/2	-0.1
	Yr	40	52	4	10	1	0	0	2	3	9	.192	.236	.212	.448	24	-5	-5	102	61	2	.318	0	1	-1	-0		-0.4
Total	4	346	1017	125	266	42	17	4	82	74	133	.262	.314	.348	.662	81	-29	-28	99	87	107	.572	3	9	-5	-4	2/3S	-1.6
■ **WALTER PLOCK** Plock, Walter S. b: 7/2/1869, Philadelphia, Pa. d: 4/28/1900, Richmond, Va. 6'3", Deb: 8/21/1891																												
1891	Phi-N	2	5	2	2	0	0	0	0	0	1	.400	.500	.400	.900	175	1	1	95	0	1	1.000	0			0	/O	0.0
■ **BILL PLUMMER** Plummer, William Francis b: 3/21/47, Oakland, Cal. BR/TR, 6'1", 190 lbs. Deb: 4/19/68 C																												
1968	Chi-N	2	2	0	0	0	0	0	0	0	1	.000	.000	.000	.000	-89	-0	-0	112	0	0	.000	0	0	0	0	/C	0.0
1970	Cin-N	4	8	0	1	0	0	0	0	0	2	.125	.222	.125	.347	-4	-1	-1	104	0	0	.286	0	0	0	0	/C	0.0
1971	Cin-N	10	19	0	0	0	0	0	0	0	4	.000	.000	.000	.000	-99	-5	-5	96	0	0	.000	0	0	0	0	/C3	-0.4
1972	Cin-N	38	102	8	19	4	0	2	9	4	20	.186	.217	.284	.501	44	-8	-7	93	106	6	.384	0	0	0	1	C/13	-0.4
1973	Cin-N	50	119	8	18	3	0	2	11	18	26	.151	.268	.227	.495	41	-10	-9	93	134	8	.456	1	0	0	0	C/3	-0.5
1974	Cin-N	50	120	7	27	7	0	2	10	6	21	.225	.262	.333	.595	67	-6	-6	98	84	10	.485	1	0	0	-1	C/3	-0.3
1975	Cin-N	65	159	17	29	7	0	1	19	24	28	.182	.297	.245	.543	50	-10	-11	104	175	14	.508	1	0	0	0	C	-0.7
1976	Cin-N	56	153	16	38	6	1	4	19	14	36	.248	.311	.379	.690	92	-1	-2	103	104	16	.581	0	2	-1	2	C	0.1
1977	Cin-N	51	117	10	16	5	0	1	7	17	34	.137	.246	.205	.451	23	-13	-13	100	104	7	.408	1	1	-0	-2	C	-1.6
1978	Sea-A	41	93	6	20	5	0	2	7	12	19	.215	.305	.333	.638	78	-2	-3	102	75	9	.566	0	0	0	-2	C	-0.3
Total	10	367	892	72	168	37	1	14	82	95	191	.188	.269	.279	.549	53	-57	-56	100	113	70	.482	4	3	-1	-2	C/31	-4.1
■ **BIFF POCOROBA** Pocoroba, Biff b: 7/25/53, Burbank, Cal. BB/TR, 5'10", 175 lbs. Deb: 4/25/75																												
1975	Atl-N	67	188	15	48	7	1	1	22	20	11	.255	.327	.319	.646	84	-5	-4	95	135	20	.552	0	0	0	2	C	0.1
1976	Atl-N	54	174	16	42	7	0	0	14	19	12	.241	.316	.282	.598	63	-6	-9	111	110	15	.493	1	0	0	1	C	-0.4
1977	Atl-N	113	321	46	93	24	1	8	44	57	27	.290	.398	.445	.844	112	14	8	113	105	57	.846	3	4	-2	6	*C	1.1
1978	Atl-N	92	289	21	70	8	0	6	34	29	14	.242	.316	.332	.648	73	-7	-11	112	118	27	.536	0	3	-2	4	C	-0.7
1979	Atl-N	28	38	6	12	4	0	0	4	7	0	.316	.422	.421	.843	120	2	2	109	99	6	.828	1	1	-0	-0	/C	0.1
1980	Atl-N	70	83	7	22	4	0	2	8	11	11	.265	.351	.386	.737	104	1	1	101	83	12	.698	1	0	0	0	C	0.1
1981	Atl-N	57	122	4	22	4	0	0	8	12	15	.180	.265	.213	.478	37	-10	-10	100	121	7	.381	0	0	0	-2	3/C	-1.3
1982	Atl-N	56	120	5	33	7	0	2	22	13	12	.275	.351	.383	.734	98	1	0	107	166	16	.674	0	0	0	-0	C/3	0.0
1983	Atl-N	55	120	11	32	6	0	2	16	12	7	.267	.333	.367	.700	89	-1	-2	106	127	14	.615	0	0	0	1	C	0.0
1984	Atl-N	4	2	1	0	0	0	0	0	2	0	.000	.500	.000	.500	47	0	0	110	0	0	1.000	0	0	0	0	/H	0.0
Total	10	596	1457	132	374	71	2	21	172	182	109	.257	.342	.351	.693	86	-11	-25	107	118	175	.647	6	8	-3	12	C/3	-1.0
■ **MIKE POEPPING** Poepping, Michael Harold b: 8/7/50, Little Falls, Minn. BR/TR, 6'6", 230 lbs. Deb: 9/06/75																												
1975	Min-A	14	37	0	5	1	0	0	1	5	7	.135	.238	.162	.400	14	-4	-4	107	64	1	.324	0	0	0	-2	O	-0.6
■ **JIMMY POFAHL** Pofahl, James Willard b: 6/18/17, Faribault, Minn. d: 9/14/84, Owatonna, Minn. BR/TR, 5'11", 185 lbs. Deb: 4/16/40																												
1940	Was-A	119	406	34	95	23	5	2	36	37	55	.234	.298	.330	.628	67	-23	-19	93	93	41	.537	2	0	1	-3	*S/2	-1.0
1941	Was-A	22	75	9	14	3	2	0	6	10	11	.187	.282	.280	.562	50	-6	-5	98	101	7	.516	1	0	0	-0	S	-0.4
1942	Was-A	84	283	22	59	7	2	0	28	29	30	.208	.282	.247	.529	52	-19	-17	96	141	20	.435	4	3	-1	-6	S23	-2.0
Total	3	225	764	65	168	33	9	2	70	76	96	.220	.290	.295	.585	60	-47	-41	94	112	67	.506	7	3	0	-10	S/23	-3.4
■ **JOHN POFF** Poff, John William b: 10/23/52, Chillicothe, Ohio BL/TL, 6'2", 190 lbs. Deb: 9/08/79																												
1979	Phi-N	12	19	2	2	1	0	0	1	1	4	.105	.150	.158	.308	-16	-3	-3	97	132	0	.222	0	0	0	-1	/O1	-0.3
1980	Mil-A	19	68	7	17	1	2	1	7	3	7	.250	.282	.368	.649	81	-2	-2	95	97	7	.538	0	0	0	-0	/O1D	-0.2
Total	2	31	87	9	19	2	2	1	8	4	11	.218	.253	.322	.575	59	-5	-5	95	105	7	.464	0	0	0	-1	/OD1	-0.5

YEAR	TM/L	G	AB	R	H	2B	3B	HR	RBI	BB	SO	AVG	OBP	SLG	PRO	/A	BR	/A	PF	CHI	RC	TA	SB	CS	SBR	FR	POS	TPR
■ **AARON POINTER**	Pointer, Aaron Elton "Hawk" b: 4/19/42, Little Rock, Ark. BR/TR, 6'2", 185 lbs. Deb: 9/22/63																											
1963	Hou-N	2	5	0	1	0	0	0	0	0	1	.200	.200	.200	.400	17	-1	-0	92	0	0	.250	0	0	0	-0	/O	0.0
1966	Hou-N	11	26	5	9	1	0	1	5	5	6	.346	.469	.500	.969	174	3	3	97	131	7	1.111	1	1	-0	1	O	0.4
1967	Hou-N	27	70	6	11	4	0	1	10	13	26	.157	.298	.257	.555	64	-3	-3	94	197	6	.550	1	0	0	0	O	-0.2
Total	3	40	101	11	21	5	0	2	15	18	33	.208	.339	.317	.656	93	-1	-0	94	172	13	.659	2	1	0	2	/O	0.2
■ **HUGH POLAND**	Poland, Hugh Reid b: 1/19/13, Tompkinsville, Ky. d: 3/30/84, Guthrie, Ky. BL/TR, 5'11.5", 185 lbs. Deb: 4/22/43																											
1943	NY-N	4	12	1	1	0	1	0	2	1	0	.083	.154	.250	.404	16	-1	-1	96	241	1	.364	0			0	/C	0.0
	Bos-N	44	141	5	27	7	0	0	13	4	11	.191	.214	.241	.455	30	-13	-14	106	138	7	.325	0			-0	C	-1.2
	Yr	48	153	6	28	7	1	0	15	5	11	.183	.209	.242	.451	29	-14	-15	105	151	7	.328	0			-0		-1.2
1944	Bos-N	8	23	1	3	1	0	0	2	0	1	.130	.130	.174	.304	-16	-3	-3	95	179	0	.190	0			0	/C	-0.2
1946	Bos-N	4	6	0	1	1	0	0	0	0	0	.167	.167	.333	.500	42	-1	-0	95	0	0	.400	0			0	/C	0.0
1947	Phi-N	4	8	0	0	0	0	0	0	0	0	.000	.000	.000	.000	-99	-2	-2	100	0	0	.000	0			0	/C	-0.1
	Cin-N	16	18	1	6	1	0	0	2	1	4	.333	.368	.389	.757	111	0	0	91	106	3	.667	0			0	/C	0.0
	Yr	20	26	1	6	1	0	0	2	1	4	.231	.259	.269	.528	44	-2	-2	93	85	2	.400	0			0		-0.1
1948	Cin-N	3	3	0	1	0	0	0	0	0	0	.333	.333	.333	.667	78	-0	-0	103	0	0	.500	0			0	H	0.0
Total	5	83	211	8	39	10	1	0	19	6	16	.185	.207	.242	.449	27	-20	-21	102	135	11	.331	0			0	/C	-1.5
■ **MARK POLHEMUS**	Polhemus, Mark S. "Humpty Dumpty" b: 10/4/1862, Brooklyn, N.Y. d: 11/12/23, Lynn, Mass. 5'6.5", 185 lbs. Deb: 7/13/1887																											
1887	Ind-N	20	75	6	18	1	0	0	8	2	9	.240	.260	.253	.513	46	-5	-5	96	132	6	.439	4			0	O	-0.3
■ **GUS POLIDOR**	Polidor, Gustavo Adolfo (Gonzalez) b: 10/26/61, Caracas, Venezuela BR/TR, 6', 170 lbs. Deb: 9/07/85																											
1985	Cal-A	2	1	1	1	0	0	0	0	0	0	1.000	1.000	1.000	2.000	446	0	0	101	0	1	—	0	0	0	-0	/SO	0.0
1986	Cal-A	6	19	1	5	1	0	0	1	1	0	.263	.300	.316	.616	71	-1	-1	96	66	1	.438	0	0	0	0	/2S3	0.0
1987	Cal-A	63	137	12	36	3	0	2	15	2	15	.263	.279	.328	.607	62	-8	-7	99	117	12	.462	0	0	0	-4	S3/2	-0.8
1988	Cal-A	54	81	4	12	3	0	0	4	3	11	.148	.179	.185	.364	2	-11	-10	94	106	3	.254	0	0	0	1	S3/21	-0.7
Total	4	125	238	18	54	7	0	2	20	6	26	.227	.249	.282	.530	45	-18	-18	97	109	17	.398	0	0	0	-4	/S3210	-1.5
■ **NICK POLLY**	Polly, Nicholas (born Nicholas Joseph Polachanin) b: 4/18/17, Chicago, Ill. BR/TR, 5'11", 190 lbs. Deb: 9/11/37																											
1937	Bro-N	10	18	2	4	0	0	0	2	0	1	.222	.222	.222	.444	20	-2	-2	104	180	1	.286	0			0	/3	-0.1
1945	Bos-A	4	7	0	1	0	0	0	1	0	0	.143	.143	.143	.286	-18	-1	-1	95	362	0	.167	0	0	0	0	/3	0.0
Total	2	14	25	2	5	0	0	0	3	0	1	.200	.200	.200	.400	11	-3	-3	102	231	1	.250	0	0		0	/3	-0.1
■ **LUIS POLONIA**	Polonia, Luis Andrew (Almonte) b: 12/10/64, Santiago, D.R. BB/TL, 5'8", 155 lbs. Deb: 4/24/87																											
1987	Oak-A	125	435	78	125	16	10	4	49	32	64	.287	.336	.398	.734	104	-3	2	91	106	61	.729	29	7	5	-6	*OD	-0.1
1988	Oak-A	84	288	51	84	11	4	2	27	21	40	.292	.340	.378	.718	106	0	2	95	93	38	.713	24	9	2	-1	O/D	0.2
Total	2	209	723	129	209	27	14	6	76	53	104	.289	.338	.390	.728	105	-3	4	93	101	100	.728	53	16	6	-6	O/D	0.1
■ **CARLOS PONCE**	Ponce, Carlos Antonio (Diaz) b: 2/7/59, Rio Piedras, P.R. BR/TR, 5'10", 170 lbs. Deb: 8/14/85																											
1985	Mil-A	21	62	4	10	2	0	1	5	1	9	.161	.175	.242	.417	12	-7	-8	105	110	2	.286	0	0	0	-0	1/OD	-0.8
■ **RALPH POND**	Pond, Ralph Benjamin b: 5/4/1888, Eau Claire, Wis. d: 9/8/47, Cleveland, Ohio Deb: 6/08/10																											
1910	Bos-A	1	4	0	1	0	0	0	0	0		.250	.250	.250	.500	57	-0	-0	99	0	0	.667	1			-1	/O	0.0
■ **HARLIN POOL**	Pool, Harlin Welty "Samson" b: 3/12/08, Lakeport, Cal. d: 2/15/63, Rodeo, Cal. BL/TR, 5'10", 195 lbs. Deb: 5/30/34																											
1934	Cin-N	99	358	38	117	22	5	2	50	17	18	.327	.369	.433	.802	113	7	7	101	114	58	.734	3			-3	O	0.0
1935	Cin-N	28	68	8	12	6	2	0	11	2	2	.176	.200	.324	.524	41	-6	-6	93	180	4	.421	0			-4	O	-0.9
Total	2	127	426	46	129	28	7	2	61	19	20	.303	.343	.415	.758	102	1	1	100	124	62	.691	3			-6	O	-0.9
■ **JIM POOLE**	Poole, James Robert "Easy" b: 5/12/1895, Taylorsville, N.C. d: 1/2/75, Hickory, N.C. BL/TR, 6', 175 lbs. Deb: 4/14/25																											
1925	Phi-A	133	480	65	143	29	8	5	67	27	37	.298	.338	.423	.761	89	-8	-10	103	103	68	.695	5	4	-1	-6	*1	-1.7
1926	Phi-A	112	361	49	106	23	5	8	63	23	25	.294	.339	.452	.791	89	1	-8	118	114	55	.744	4	3	-1	0	*1/O	-1.1
1927	Phi-A	38	99	4	22	2	0	0	10	9	6	.222	.287	.242	.529	40	-9	-8	97	139	7	.429	0	0	0	-0	1	-0.9
Total	3	283	940	118	271	54	13	13	140	59	68	.288	.333	.415	.748	85	-16	-26	108	111	130	.683	9	7	-2	-6	1/O	-3.7
■ **RAY POOLE**	Poole, Raymond Herman b: 1/16/20, Salisbury, N.C. BL/TR, 6', 180 lbs. Deb: 9/09/41																											
1941	Phi-A	2	2	0	0	0	0	0	0	0	1	.000	.000	.000	.000	-99	-1	-1	101	0	0	.000	0	0	0	0	H	0.0
1947	Phi-A	13	13	1	3	0	0	0	1	1	4	.231	.286	.231	.516	44	-1	-1	100	123	1	.364	0	0	0	0	H	0.0
Total	2	15	15	1	3	0	0	0	1	1	5	.200	.250	.200	.450	25	-2	-2	100	107	1	.308	0	0	0	0		0.0
■ **TOM POORMAN**	Poorman, Thomas Iverson b: 10/14/1857, Lock Haven, Pa. d: 2/18/05, Lock Haven, Pa. BL/TR, 5'10.5", 170 lbs. Deb: 5/05/1880																											
1880	Buf-N	19	70	5	11	1	0	0	1	0	13	.157	.157	.171	.329	12	-6	-5	91	31	2	.203				0	PO	0.0
	Chi-N	7	25	3	5	1	2	0	0	0	2	.200	.200	.400	.600	93	-0	-0	105	0	2	.500				0	/OP	0.0
	Yr	26	95	8	16	2	2	0	1	0	15	.168	.168	.232	.400	36	-6	-6	95	24	4	.278				0		0.0
1884	Tol-a	94	382	56	89	8	7	0		10		.233	.254	.291	.545	77	-8	-10	104	0	29	.416				1	*O/P	-0.8
1885	Bos-N	56	227	44	54	5	3	3	25	7	32	.238	.261	.326	.587	95	-3	-1	94	111	20	.468				-3	O	-0.5
1886	Bos-N	88	371	72	97	16	6	3	41	19	52	.261	.297	.361	.659	102	-1	1	97	83	50	.672	31			3	*O	0.5
1887	Phi-a	135	585	140	155	18	19	4		35		.265	.317	.381	.699	97	-4	-3	99	0	101	.828	88			2	*O/2P	-0.4
1888	Phi-a	97	383	76	87	16	6	2	44	31		.227	.294	.316	.609	98	-0	-1	101	110	50	.686	46			-12	*O	-1.4
Total	6	496	2043	396	498	65	43	12	111	102	99	.244	.285	.335	.620	92	-22	-20	99	49	254	.627	165			-9	O/P2	-2.6
■ **DAVE POPE**	Pope, David b: 6/17/25, Talladega, Ala. BL/TR, 5'10.5", 170 lbs. Deb: 7/01/52																											
1952	Cle-A	12	34	9	10	1	1	1	4	1	7	.294	.314	.471	.785	128	0	1	91	79	5	.708	0	0	0	-2	O	-0.1
1954	Cle-A	60	102	21	30	2	1	4	13	10	22	.294	.357	.451	.808	113	3	2	106	85	16	.773	2	1	0	-4	O	-0.2
1955	Cle-A	35	104	17	31	5	0	6	22	12	31	.298	.376	.519	.895	134	5	5	104	114	21	.905	0	0	0	-2	O	0.2
	Bal-A	86	222	21	55	8	4	1	30	16	34	.248	.304	.333	.638	79	-9	-6	90	145	22	.554	5	2	0	-1	O	-1.0
	Yr	121	326	38	86	13	4	7	52	28	65	.264	.328	.393	.720	99	-4	-1	94	137	42	.661	5	2	0	-3		-0.8
1956	Bal-A	12	19	1	3	0	0	0	1	0	7	.158	.200	.158	.358	-5	-3	-3	94	124	1	.250	0	0	0	-1	/O	-0.3
	Cle-A	25	70	6	17	3	1	0	3	1	12	.243	.254	.314	.568	49	-5	-5	101	51	6	.434	0	0	0	0	O	-0.5
	Yr	37	89	7	20	3	1	0	4	1	19	.225	.242	.281	.523	38	-8	-8	99	78	6	.391	0	0	0	-1		-0.8
Total	4	230	551	75	146	19	7	12	73	40	113	.265	.319	.390	.710	93	-9	-7	97	112	71	.652	7	3	0	-10	O	-1.9
■ **PAUL POPOVICH**	Popovich, Paul Edward b: 8/18/40, Flemington, W.Va. BB/TR, 6', 175 lbs. Deb: 4/19/64																											
1964	Chi-N	1	1	0	1	0	0	0	0	0	0	1.000	1.000	1.000	2.000	442	0	0	105	0	1	—	0	0	0	0	H	0.0
1966	Chi-N	2	6	0	0	0	0	0	0	0	2	.000	.000	.000	.000	-99	-2	-2	100	0	0	.000	0	0	0	-0	/2	-0.1
1967	Chi-N	49	159	18	34	4	0	0	2	9	12	.214	.265	.239	.504	45	-11	-11	102	22	9	.371	0	1	-1	-1	S2/3	-0.8
1968	LA-N	134	418	35	97	8	1	2	25	29	37	.232	.283	.270	.554	74	-16	-12	91	88	32	.435	1	3	-2	1	2S/3	-0.2
1969	LA-N	28	50	5	10	0	0	0	4	1	4	.200	.216	.200	.416	17	-5	-5	99	160	2	.268	0	0	0	-0	2/S	-0.3
	Chi-N	60	154	26	48	6	0	1	14	18	14	.312	.387	.370	.757	106	3	2	107	93	24	.704	0	1	-1	2	2/S3O	0.7
	Yr	88	204	31	58	6	0	1	18	19	18	.284	.348	.328	.677	87	-2	-3	104	117	25	.588	0	1	-1	2		0.4
1970	Chi-N	78	186	22	47	5	1	4	20	18	18	.253	.325	.355	.680	68	-5	-10	120	99	22	.601	0	1	-1	3	2S3	-0.2
1971	Chi-N	89	226	24	49	7	1	4	28	14	17	.217	.262	.310	.572	56	-12	-14	110	139	17	.454	0	1	-1	0	23/S	-1.3
1972	Chi-N	58	129	8	25	3	2	1	11	12	8	.194	.262	.271	.534	46	-8	-10	114	119	9	.431	0	1	-1	6	2/S3	-0.1
1973	Chi-N	99	280	24	66	6	3	2	24	18	27	.236	.284	.300	.584	57	-14	-17	108	107	23	.473	3	2	-0	7	2/S3	-0.5
1974	Pit-N	59	83	9	18	2	1	0	5	5	10	.217	.261	.265	.526	49	-6	-6	98	88	6	.415	0	0	0	0	2S	-0.3
1975	Pit-N	25	40	5	8	1	0	0	1	3	2	.200	.273	.225	.498	39	-3	-3	99	43	3	.406	0	0	0	1	/2S	0.0
Total	11	682	1732	176	403	42	9	14	134	127	151	.233	.288	.292	.580	62	-79	-88	104	96	147	.481	4	10	-5	19	2S/3O	-3.1
■ **TOM POQUETTE**	Poquette, Thomas Arthur b: 10/30/51, Eau Claire, Wis. BL/TR, 5'10", 175 lbs. Deb: 9/01/73																											
1973	KC-A	21	28	4	6	1	0	0	3	1	4	.214	.267	.250	.517	42	-2	-2	109	168	2	.435	1	1	-0	-5	O	-0.7
1976	KC-A	104	344	43	104	18	10	2	34	29	31	.302	.363	.430	.794	132	14	14	100	85	52	.736	6	5	-1	-10	O/D	0.0

YEAR	TM/L	G	AB	R	H	2B	3B	HR	RBI	BB	SO	AVG	OBP	SLG	PRO	/A	BR	/A	PF	CHI	RC	TA	SB	CS	SBR	FR	POS	TPR
1977	KC-A	106	342	43	100	23	6	2	33	19	21	.292	.339	.412	.751	103	1	1	100	89	47	.664	1	4	-2	-3	O	-0.6
1978	KC-A	80	204	16	44	9	2	4	30	14	9	.216	.266	.338	.604	67	-9	-9	102	146	18	.512	2	0	1	2	O/D	-0.8
1979	KC-A	21	26	1	5	0	0	0	3	1	4	.192	.222	.192	.415	12	-3	-3	105	231	1	.286	0	0	0	-2	O	-0.5
	Bos-A	63	154	14	51	9	0	2	23	8	7	.331	.376	.429	.804	109	4	2	107	123	25	.738	2	2	-1	-4	O/D	-0.3
	Yr	84	180	15	56	9	0	2	26	9	11	.311	.354	.394	.749	95	0	-1	107	152	25	.664	2	2	-1	-6		-0.8
1981	Bos-A	3	2	0	0	0	0	0	0	0	0	.000	.000	.000	.000	-94	-1	-1	106	0	0	.000	0	0	0	-1	/O	-0.1
	Tex-A	30	64	2	10	1	0	0	7	5	1	.156	.229	.172	.400	18	-7	-6	91	249	2	.293	0	1	-1	-3	O	-1.0
	Yr	33	66	2	10	1	0	0	7	5	1	.152	.222	.167	.389	15	-7	-7	92	226	2	.283	0	1	-1	-4		-1.1
1982	KC-A	24	62	4	9	1	0	0	3	4	5	.145	.209	.161	.370	3	-8	-8	100	120	3	.302	1	0	0	-2	O	-1.0
Total	7	452	1226	127	329	62	18	10	136	81	82	.268	.321	.373	.694	93	-11	-13	101	116	149	.622	13	13	-4	-28	O/D	-5.0
■ **DAN PORTER**	Porter, Daniel Edward b: 10/17/31, Decatur, Ill. BL/TL, 6', 164 lbs. Deb: 8/16/51																											
1951	Was-A	13	19	2	4	0	0	0	0	2	4	.211	.286	.211	.496	37	-2	-2	95	0	1	.400	0	0	0	-1	/O	-0.1
■ **DARRELL PORTER**	Porter, Darrell Ray b: 1/17/52, Joplin, Mo. BL/TR, 6', 193 lbs. Deb: 9/02/71																											
1971	Mil-A	22	70	4	15	2	0	2	9	9	20	.214	.304	.329	.632	77	-2	-2	103	129	7	.596	2	2	-1	1	C	0.0
1972	Mil-A	18	56	2	7	1	0	1	2	5	21	.125	.210	.196	.406	22	-5	-5	95	60	2	.340	0	0	0	0	C	-0.4
1973	Mil-A	117	350	50	89	19	2	16	67	57	85	.254	.365	.457	.822	136	15	17	96	127	61	.840	5	2	0	8	CD	2.7
1974	Mil-A	131	432	59	104	15	4	12	56	50	88	.241	.326	.377	.704	100	1	0	102	113	54	.663	8	7	-2	13	*C/D	1.5
1975	Mil-A	130	409	66	95	12	5	18	60	89	77	.232	.376	.418	.794	124	16	16	100	105	68	.817	2	5	-2	18	*C/D	3.5
1976	Mil-A	119	389	43	81	14	1	5	32	51	61	.208	.302	.288	.590	74	-12	-12	99	99	37	.532	2	0	1	8	*C/D	0.1
1977	KC-A	130	425	61	117	21	3	16	60	53	70	.275	.357	.452	.809	118	11	11	100	99	71	.787	1	0	0	-3	*C/D	1.1
1978	KC-A	150	520	77	138	27	6	18	78	75	75	.265	.360	.444	.804	122	18	17	102	110	82	.770	0	5	-3	-1	*C/D	1.7
1979	KC-A	157	533	101	155	23	10	20	112	**121**	65	.291	**.429**	.484	.913	138	41	36	105	**143**	119	.992	3	4	-2	10	*CD	4.9
1980	KC-A	118	418	51	104	14	2	7	51	69	50	.249	.358	.342	.700	94	-2	-1	98	124	54	.662	1	1	-0	7	CD	1.0
1981	StL-N	61	174	22	39	10	2	6	31	39	32	.224	.369	.408	.777	118	6	5	102	137	28	.800	1	2	-1	-4	C	0.2
1982	StL-N	120	373	46	86	18	5	12	48	66	66	.231	.349	.402	.751	106	6	4	103	101	55	.740	1	1	-0	-5	*C	0.0
1983	StL-N	145	443	57	116	24	3	15	66	68	94	.262	.365	.431	.796	122	13	14	98	111	71	.781	1	3	-2	-4	*C	1.3
1984	StL-N	127	422	56	98	16	3	11	68	60	79	.232	.335	.363	.697	97	-1	-1	99	146	52	.662	5	3	-0	2	*C	0.6
1985	StL-N	84	240	30	53	12	2	10	36	41	48	.221	.337	.412	.749	113	3	4	96	111	36	.770	6	1	1	-10	C	0.0
1986	Tex-A	68	155	21	41	6	0	12	29	22	51	.265	.360	.535	.895	148	9	10	96	97	30	.907	1	1	-0	-2	CD	0.8
1987	Tex-A	85	130	19	31	3	0	7	21	30	43	.238	.389	.423	.812	113	4	4	104	110	24	.861	0	0	0	-0	D/C1	0.3
Total	17	1782	5539	765	1369	237	48	188	826	905	1025	.247	.357	.409	.766	113	121	118	100	116	853	.773	39	37	-11	38	*CD/1	19.3
■ **IRV PORTER**	Porter, Irving Marble b: 5/17/1888, Lynn, Mass. d: 2/20/71, Lynn, Mass. BB/TR, 5'9", 155 lbs. Deb: 8/20/14																											
1914	Chi-A	1	4	1	1	0	0	0	0	0	1	.250	.250	.250	.500	49	-0	-0	103	0	0	.333	0			-0	/O	0.0
■ **JAY PORTER**	Porter, J W "J W" b: 1/17/33, Shawnee, Okla. BR/TR, 6'2", 180 lbs. Deb: 7/30/52																											
1952	StL-A	33	104	12	26	4	1	0	7	10	10	.250	.316	.308	.623	76	-4	-3	97	82	11	.561	4	0	1	2	O/3	0.0
1955	Det-A	24	55	6	13	2	0	0	3	8	15	.236	.333	.273	.606	66	-3	-2	97	75	5	.535	0	0	0	-1	/1CO	-0.3
1956	Det-A	14	21	0	2	0	0	0	3	0	8	.095	.095	.095	.190	-51	-4	-4	97	560	0	.100	0	0	0	-1	/CO	-0.4
1957	Det-A	58	140	14	35	8	0	2	18	14	20	.250	.323	.350	.673	78	-3	-4	107	129	17	.604	0	0	0	-3	OC/1	-0.7
1958	Cle-A	40	85	13	17	1	0	4	19	9	23	.200	.284	.353	.637	79	-3	-3	94	181	8	.563	0	0	0	-2	C/13	-0.4
1959	Was-A	37	106	8	24	4	0	1	10	11	16	.226	.305	.292	.598	65	-5	-5	100	116	10	.506	0	0	0	-2	C/1	-0.4
	StL-N	23	33	5	7	3	0	1	2	1	4	.212	.257	.394	.651	67	-2	-2	105	50	3	.577	0	0	0	-1	C/1	-0.1
Total	6	229	544	58	124	22	1	8	62	53	96	.228	.301	.316	.617	69	-23	-23	100	130	54	.555	4	0	1	-6	/CO13	-2.3
■ **MATTHEW PORTER**	Porter, Matthew S. b: Kansas City, Mo. Deb: 6/27/1884 M																											
1884	KC-U	3	12	1	1	1	0	0		0		.083	.083	.167	.250	-20	-1	-1	87	0	0	.182	0			0	/OM	0.0
■ **DICK PORTER**	Porter, Richard Twilley "Wiggles" or "Twitches" b: 12/30/01, Princess Anne, Md. d: 9/24/74, Philadelphia, Pa. BL/TR, 5'10", 170 lbs. Deb: 4/16/29																											
1929	Cle-A	71	192	26	63	16	5	1	24	17	14	.328	.386	.479	.865	121	6	6	100	86	34	.843	3	5	-2	-0	O2	0.2
1930	Cle-A	119	480	100	168	43	8	4	57	55	31	.350	.420	.498	.918	126	25	21	105	72	102	.952	3	3	-1	-6	*O	0.8
1931	Cle-A	114	414	82	129	24	3	1	38	56	36	.312	.395	.391	.786	101	7	3	106	78	65	.765	6	9	-4	-8	*O/2	-1.4
1932	Cle-A	146	621	106	191	42	8	4	60	64	43	.308	.373	.420	.793	97	6	-2	108	64	99	.756	2	4	-2	-16	*O	-2.3
1933	Cle-A	132	499	73	133	19	6	0	41	51	42	.267	.335	.329	.663	73	-16	-19	105	88	57	.592	4	4	-1	-4	*O	-2.7
1934	Cle-A	13	44	9	10	2	1	1	6	4	5	.227	.292	.386	.678	73	-2	-2	101	100	5	.618	0	0	0	-2	O	-0.3
	Bos-A	80	265	30	80	13	6	0	56	21	15	.302	.355	.396	.752	88	-3	-5	106	178	38	.706	5	2	0	-9	O	-1.3
	Yr	93	309	39	90	15	7	1	62	25	20	.291	.346	.395	.741	86	-5	-7	105	168	43	.692	5	2	0	-11		-1.6
Total	6	675	2515	426	774	159	37	11	282	268	186	.308	.376	.414	.790	99	22	1	106	87	400	.757	23	27	-9	-45	O/2	-7.0
■ **BOB PORTER**	Porter, Robert Lee b: 7/22/59, Yuma, Ariz. BL/TL, 5'10", 180 lbs. Deb: 5/13/81																											
1981	Atl-N	17	14	2	4	1	0	0	4	2	1	.286	.375	.357	.732	109	0	0	100	314	2	.700	0	0	0	0	/H	0.0
1982	Atl-N	24	27	1	3	0	0	0	0	1	9	.111	.143	.111	.254	-26	-5	-5	107	0	1	.167	0	0	0	-1	/O1	-0.5
Total	2	41	41	3	7	1	0	0	4	3	10	.171	.227	.195	.422	19	-4	-5	104	114	3	.324	0	0	0	-1	/O1	-0.5
■ **LEO POSADA**	Posada, Leopoldo Jesus (Hernandez) b: 4/15/36, Havana, Cuba BR/TR, 5'11", 175 lbs. Deb: 9/21/60																											
1960	KC-A	10	36	8	13	0	2	1	2	3	7	.361	.410	.556	.966	161	3	3	99	35	8	1.000	1	0	0	-1	/O	0.2
1961	KC-A	116	344	37	87	10	4	7	53	36	84	.253	.331	.366	.697	85	-7	-7	102	141	43	.626	0	0	0	1	*O	-0.9
1962	KC-A	29	46	6	9	1	1	0	3	7	14	.196	.302	.261	.563	53	-3	-3	100	99	4	.500	0	0	0	-0	O	-0.3
Total	3	155	426	51	109	11	7	8	58	46	105	.256	.334	.371	.705	87	-7	-7	101	128	55	.657	1	0	0	0	O	-1.0
■ **LEW POST**	Post, Lewis G. b: 4/12/1875, Hastings, Mich. d: 8/1/44, Chicago, Ill. Deb: 9/21/02																											
1902	Det-A	3	12	2	1	0	0	0	2	0		.083	.083	.083	.167	-54	-2	-2	99	698	0	.091	0			-1	/O	-0.2
■ **SAM POST**	Post, Samuel Gilbert b: 11/17/1896, Richmond, Va. d: 3/31/71, Portsmouth, Va. BL/TL, 6'1.5", 170 lbs. Deb: 4/22/22																											
1922	Bro-N	9	25	3	7	0	0	0	4	1	4	.280	.308	.280	.588	55	-2	-2	95	200	2	.500	1	0	0	0	/1	0.0
■ **WALLY POST**	Post, Walter Charles b: 7/9/29, St.Wendelin, Ohio d: 1/6/82, St.Henry, Ohio BR/TR, 6'1", 190 lbs. Deb: 9/18/49																											
1949	Cin-N	6	8	1	2	0	0	0	1	0	3	.250	.250	.250	.500	36	-1	-1	96	188	0	.286	0			-1	/O	-0.1
1951	Cin-N	15	41	6	9	3	0	1	7	3	4	.220	.273	.366	.639	70	-2	-2	101	150	4	.529	0	0	0	1	/O	0.0
1952	Cin-N	19	58	5	9	1	0	2	7	4	20	.155	.222	.276	.498	38	-5	-5	100	124	4	.420	0	0	0	1	O	-0.4
1953	Cin-N	11	33	3	8	1	0	1	4	4	6	.242	.324	.364	.688	80	-1	-1	99	104	4	.630	1	0	0	1	O	0.0
1954	Cin-N	130	451	46	115	21	3	18	83	26	70	.255	.300	.435	.735	85	-9	-12	104	131	56	.652	2	2	-1	3	*O	-1.2
1955	Cin-N	154	601	116	186	33	3	40	109	60	102	.309	.374	.574	.948	139	39	34	106	101	125	.954	7	4	-0	-1	*O	3.0
1956	Cin-N	143	539	94	134	25	3	36	83	37	124	.249	.302	.506	.808	104	7	1	108	94	81	.771	6	0	2	10	*O	0.8
1957	Cin-N	134	467	68	114	26	2	20	74	33	84	.244	.294	.437	.731	88	-6	-9	105	116	57	.651	2	2	-1	6	*O	-0.6
1958	Phi-N	110	379	51	107	21	3	12	62	32	74	.282	.343	.449	.792	109	4	5	98	124	59	.740	0	2	-1	6	O	0.6
1959	Phi-N	132	468	62	119	17	6	22	94	36	101	.254	.312	.457	.769	102	-0	-0	99	138	67	.711	0	0	0	6	*O	0.4
1960	Phi-N	34	84	11	24	6	1	2	12	9	24	.286	.355	.452	.807	111	2	1	107	111	14	.770	0	0	0	-0	O	0.1
	Cin-N	77	249	36	70	14	0	17	38	28	51	.281	.354	.542	.896	144	13	14	98	83	43	.849	0	2	-1	1	O	1.2
	Yr	111	333	47	94	20	1	19	50	37	75	.282	.354	.520	.874	134	16	15	101	92	58	.833	0	2	-1	1		1.3
1961	Cin-N	99	282	44	83	16	3	20	57	22	61	.294	.348	.585	.933	136	15	14	104	102	55	.908	0	1	-1	-1	O	0.8
1962	Cin-N	109	285	43	75	10	3	17	62	32	67	.263	.342	.498	.840	120	8	8	102	127	48	.812	1	0	0	-11	O	-0.7
1963	Cin-N	5	7	1	0	0	0	0	0	0	1	.000	.125	.000	.125	-58	-1	-1	104	0	-0	.111	0	0	0	0	/O	0.0
	Min-A	21	47	6	9	0	1	2	6	2	17	.191	.224	.362	.586	61	-3	-3	100	109	4	.487	0	0	0	-2	O	-0.5
1964	Cle-A	5	8	1	0	0	0	0	0	3	4	.000	.273	.000	.273	-16	-1	-1	103	0	0	.375	0	0	0	-0	/O	-0.1
Total	15	1204	4007	594	1064	194	28	210	699	331	813	.266	.325	.485	.810	109	59	42	103	113	620	.783	19	13		19	*O	3.3

YEAR	TM/L	G	AB	R	H	2B	3B	HR	RBI	BB	SO	AVG	OBP	SLG	PRO	/A	BR	/A	PF	CHI	RC	TA	SB	CS	SBR	FR	POS	TPR
■ MIKE POTTER	Potter, Michael Gary b: 5/16/51, Montebello, Cal. BR/TR, 6'1", 195 lbs. Deb: 9/06/76																											
1976	StL-N	9	16	0	0	0	0	0	0	1	6	.000	.059	.000	.059	-79	-4	-4	104	0	0	.063	0	0	0	0	/O	-0.3
1977	StL-N	5	7	0	0	0	0	0	0	0	2	.000	.000	.000	.000	-99	-2	-2	96	0	0	.000	0	0	0	-0	/O	-0.1
Total	2	14	23	0	0	0	0	0	0	1	8	.000	.042	.000	.042	-86	-6	-6	102	0	0	.043	0	0	0	-0	/O	-0.4
■ DAN POTTS	Potts, Daniel b: Kent, Ohio Deb: 10/03/1892																											
1892	Was-N	1	4	0	1	0	0	0	0	0	1	.250	.250	.250	.500	50	-0	-0	105	0	0	.333	0			0	/C	0.0
■ JOHN POTTS	Potts, John Frederick "Fred" b: 2/6/1887, Tipp City, Ohio d: 9/5/62, Cleveland, Ohio BL/TR, 5'7", 165 lbs. Deb: 4/18/14																											
1914	KC-F	41	102	14	27	4	0	1	9	25	13	.265	.409	.333	.743	120	4	4	95	88	18	.880	7			-5	O	-0.2
■ KEN POULSEN	Poulsen, Ken Sterling b: 8/4/47, Van Nuys, Cal. BL/TR, 6'1", 190 lbs. Deb: 7/03/67																											
1967	Bos-A	5	5	0	1	1	0	0	0	0	2	.200	.200	.400	.600	64	-0	-0	115	0	0	.500	0	0	0	0	/3S	0.0
■ ALONZO POWELL	Powell, Alonzo Sidney b: 12/12/64, San Francisco, Cal. BR/TR, 6'2", 190 lbs. Deb: 4/06/87																											
1987	Mon-N	14	41	3	8	3	0	0	4	5	17	.195	.283	.268	.551	44	-3	-3	106	145	3	.485	0	0	0	-2	O	-0.5
■ JAKE POWELL	Powell, Alvin Jacob b: 7/15/08, Silver Spring, Md d: 11/4/48, Washington, D.C. BR/TR, 5'11.5", 180 lbs. Deb: 8/03/30																											
1930	Was-A	3	4	1	0	0	0	0	0	0	1	.000	.000	.000	.000	-99	-1	-1	101	0	0	.000	0	0	0	-0	/O	-0.1
1934	Was-A	9	35	6	10	2	0	0	1	4	2	.286	.359	.343	.702	81	-1	-1	101	29	4	.654	1	1	-0	1	/O	0.0
1935	Was-A	139	551	88	172	26	10	6	98	37	37	.312	.360	.428	.788	113	2	8	92	134	85	.756	15	7	0	-3	*O/2	0.4
1936	Was-A	53	210	40	62	11	5	1	30	19	21	.295	.357	.410	.766	91	-4	-3	98	116	31	.763	10	4	1	-3	O	-0.5
	NY-A	87	328	62	99	13	3	7	48	33	30	.302	.366	.424	.789	100	-3	-0	95	99	52	.797	16	7	1	4	O	0.1
	Yr	140	538	102	161	24	8	8	78	52	51	.299	.362	.418	.780	96	-7	-3	96	106	83	.784	26	11	1	1		-0.4
1937	NY-A	97	365	54	96	22	3	3	45	25	36	.263	.314	.364	.678	69	-17	-18	102	111	42	.609	7	5	-1	0	O	-2.0
1938	NY-A	45	164	27	42	12	1	2	20	15	20	.256	.326	.378	.704	72	-6	-8	105	101	21	.667	3	1	0	-4	O	-0.9
1939	NY-A	31	86	12	21	4	1	1	9	3	8	.244	.270	.349	.619	62	-6	-5	91	92	7	.500	1	2	-1	0	O	-0.5
1940	NY-A	12	27	3	5	0	0	0	2	1	4	.185	.214	.185	.399	5	-4	-4	99	145	1	.261	0	0	0	0	/O	-0.3
1943	Was-A	37	132	14	35	10	2	0	20	5	13	.265	.297	.371	.668	91	-1	-2	104	149	13	.558	3	5	-2	2	O	-0.2
1944	Was-A	96	367	29	88	9	1	1	37	16	26	.240	.272	.278	.549	64	-21	-16	90	130	29	.439	7	2	1	-1	O/3	-2.0
1945	Was-A	31	98	4	19	2	0	0	3	8	8	.194	.255	.214	.469	39	-8	-7	93	52	6	.370	1	1	-0	-2	O	-1.0
	Phi-N	48	173	13	40	5	0	1	14	8	13	.231	.265	.277	.543	53	-12	-11	96	97	11	.401	1			-4	O	-1.7
Total	11	688	2540	353	689	116	26	22	327	174	219	.271	.320	.363	.684	82	-82	-68	96	114	303	.618	65	<u>35</u>		-10	O/23	-8.7
■ ABNER POWELL	Powell, Charles Abner "Ab" b: 12/15/1860, Shenandoah, Pa. d: 8/7/53, New Orleans, La. BR/TR, 5'7", 160 lbs. Deb: 8/04/1884																											
1884	Was-U	48	191	36	54	10	5	0		3		.283	.294	.387	.681	133	5	6	97	0	22	.562	0			-2	OP/3S2	0.3
1886	Bal-a	11	39	4	7	2	1	0		1		.179	.200	.282	.482	57	-2	-2	91	0	3	.500	4			0	/PO	0.0
	Cin-a	19	74	13	17	1	1	0		4		.230	.269	.270	.540	74	-2	-2	96	0	6	.421	0			0	O/SP	-0.1
	Yr	30	113	17	24	3	2	0		5		.212	.246	.274	.520	68	-5	-4	94	0	9	.449	4			0		-0.1
Total	2	78	304	53	78	13	7	0		8		.257	.276	.345	.621	108	1	3	96	0	31	.518	4			-2	/OPS32	0.2
■ HOSKEN POWELL	Powell, Hosken b: 5/14/55, Selma, Ala. BL/TL, 6'1", 175 lbs. Deb: 4/05/78																											
1978	Min-A	121	381	55	94	20	2	3	31	45	31	.247	.326	.333	.660	91	-6	-4	94	90	44	.616	11	5	0	-3	*O	-0.9
1979	Min-A	104	338	49	99	17	3	2	36	33	25	.293	.361	.379	.740	92	1	-3	109	103	47	.679	5	1	1	-4	O/D	-0.9
1980	Min-A	137	485	58	127	17	5	6	35	32	46	.262	.312	.355	.666	76	-12	-17	109	73	53	.589	14	3	2	-0	*O	-1.7
1981	Min-A	80	264	30	63	11	3	2	25	17	31	.239	.287	.326	.613	73	-8	-10	105	106	24	.526	7	4	-0	-1	O/D	-1.2
1982	Tor-A	112	265	43	73	13	4	3	26	12	23	.275	.307	.389	.696	83	-4	-7	109	93	30	.595	4	4	-1	-11	OD	-2.1
1983	Tor-A	40	83	6	14	0	0	1	7	5	8	.169	.216	.205	.421	15	-9	-10	108	137	4	.343	2	0	1	-5	O/1D	-1.4
Total	6	594	1816	241	470	78	17	17	160	144	164	.259	.316	.349	.664	80	-40	-51	105	93	202	.606	43	17	3	-25	O/D1	-8.2
■ JIM POWELL	Powell, James E. b: 1859, Richmond, Va. Deb: N/A.																											
1884	Ric-a	41	151	23	37	8	4	0		7		.245	.296	.351	.647	115	2	3	99	0	16	.561				1	1	0.1
■ BOOG POWELL	Powell, John Wesley b: 8/17/41, Lakeland, Fla. BL/TR, 6'4.5", 230 lbs. Deb: 9/26/61																											
1961	Bal-A	4	13	0	1	0	0	0	1	0	2	.077	.077	.077	.154	-60	-3	-3	97	392	0	.083	0	0	0	-1	/O	-0.3
1962	Bal-A	124	400	44	97	13	2	15	53	38	79	.243	.311	.398	.709	94	-7	-4	95	103	47	.629	1	1	-0	-10	*O/1	-1.7
1963	Bal-A	140	491	67	130	22	2	25	82	49	87	.265	.331	.470	.802	130	13	17	94	114	74	.749	1	2	-1	-10	*O1	0.1
1964	Bal-A	134	424	74	123	17	0	39	99	76	91	.290	.400	**.606**	1.007	167	44	41	105	114	105	1.081	0	0	0	-2	*O/1	3.6
1965	Bal-A	144	472	54	117	20	2	17	72	71	93	.248	.351	.407	.758	115	10	10	100	125	71	.738	1	1	-0	-2	1O	0.1
1966	Bal-A	140	491	78	141	18	0	34	109	67	125	.287	.374	.532	.905	155	36	36	101	129	97	.909	0	4	-2	-6	*1	2.4
1967	Bal-A	125	415	53	97	14	1	13	55	55	94	.234	.326	.366	.693	110	3	6	95	122	51	.642	1	3	-2	1	*1	-0.4
1968	Bal-A	154	550	60	137	21	1	22	85	73	97	.249	.340	.411	.751	124	18	17	102	132	79	.725	7	1	2	-5	*1	0.7
1969	Bal-A	152	533	83	162	25	0	37	121	72	76	.304	.388	.559	.947	156	43	41	104	121	112	.954	1	1	-0	-3	*1	2.9
1970	Bal-A	154	526	82	156	28	0	35	114	104	80	.297	.417	.549	.967	170	49	51	97	119	123	1.036	1	1	-0	-4	*1	4.0
1971	Bal-A	128	418	59	107	19	0	22	92	82	64	.256	.383	.459	.842	134	23	21	103	149	77	.869	1	0	0	-5	*1	1.1
1972	Bal-A	140	465	53	117	20	1	21	81	65	92	.252	.348	.434	.783	135	19	20	98	130	71	.762	4	0	1	-1	*1	0.7
1973	Bal-A	114	370	52	98	13	1	11	54	85	64	.265	.402	.395	.797	117	17	13	107	121	62	.811	0	2	-1	0	*1	0.5
1974	Bal-A	110	344	37	91	13	1	12	45	52	58	.265	.361	.413	.774	132	11	14	93	99	49	.721	0	1	-1	-1	*1/D	0.8
1975	Cle-A	134	435	64	129	18	0	27	86	59	72	.297	.382	.524	.906	155	31	31	100	107	89	.920	1	3	-2	-3	*1/D	2.0
1976	Cle-A	95	293	29	63	9	0	9	33	41	43	.215	.311	.338	.649	90	-3	-3	100	101	31	.585	1	1	-0	-1	1	-0.8
1977	LA-N	50	41	0	10	0	0	0	5	12	9	.244	.415	.244	.659	82	-0	-0	100	200	5	.710	0	0	0	0	/1	0.0
Total	17	2042	6681	889	1776	270	11	339	1187	1001	1226	.266	.364	.462	.826	134	305	309	100	121	1145	.839	20	21	-7	-53	*1O/D	15.7
■ MARTIN POWELL	Powell, Martin J. b: 3/25/1856, Fitchburg, Mass. d: 2/5/1888, Fitchburg, Mass. BL/TL, 6'4.5", Deb: 6/18/1881																											
1881	Det-N	55	219	47	74	9	4	1	38	15	9	.338	.380	.429	.810	144	14	12	106	131	37	.752				-2	1/C	0.2
1882	Det-N	80	338	44	81	13	0	0	29	19	27	.240	.280	.278	.558	79	-7	-8	102	92	27	.440				-5	*1	-2.4
1883	Det-N	101	421	76	115	17	5	1	48	28	23	.273	.318	.344	.663	111	1	7	91	108	47	.565				-3	*1	-0.7
1884	Cin-U	43	185	46	59	4	2	1		13		.319	.364	.378	.742	140	10	8	108	0	26	.659	0			-2	1	0.4
1885	Phi-a	19	75	5	12	0	3	0		1		.160	.192	.240	.432	36	-5	-6	103	0	4	.333				0	1	-0.4
Total	5	298	1238	218	341	43	14	3	<u>115</u>	76	<u>59</u>	.275	.318	.340	.658	108	13	13	100	85	141	.556				-12	1/C	-2.9
■ PAUL POWELL	Powell, Paul Ray b: 3/19/48, San Angelo, Tex. BR/TR, 5'11", 185 lbs. Deb: 4/07/71																											
1971	Min-A	20	31	7	5	0	0	1	2	3	12	.161	.235	.258	.493	38	-3	-3	104	74	2	.407	0	0	0	-1	O	-0.4
1973	LA-N	2	1	0	0	0	0	0	0	0	1	.000	.000	.000	.000	-99	-0	-0	100	0	0	.000	0	0	0	-0	/O	0.0
1975	LA-N	8	10	2	2	1	0	0	0	1	2	.200	.273	.300	.573	62	-1	-1	95	0	1	.444	0	0	0	-0	/CO	0.0
Total	3	30	42	9	7	1	0	1	2	4	15	.167	.239	.262	.501	40	-3	-3	102	55	2	.417	0	0	0	-2	/OC	-0.4
■ RAY POWELL	Powell, Raymond Reath "Rabbit" b: 11/20/1888, Siloam Springs, Ark. d: 10/16/62, Chillicothe, Mo. BL/TR, 5'9", 160 lbs. Deb: 4/16/13																											
1913	Det-A	2	0	0	0	0	0	0	0	0	0	—	—	—	—	—	0	0	99	—	—	—	0			-0	/O	0.0
1917	Bos-N	88	357	42	97	10	4	4	30	24	54	.272	.318	.356	.673	111	2	4	96	73	42	.627	12			6	O	0.8
1918	Bos-N	53	188	31	40	7	5	0	20	29	30	.213	.321	.303	.624	97	-1	0	94	140	19	.601	2			-2	O	-0.5
1919	Bos-N	123	470	51	111	12	12	2	33	41	79	.236	.303	.326	.628	91	-6	-5	98	85	49	.596	16			-1	*O	-1.2
1920	Bos-N	147	609	69	137	12	12	6	29	44	83	.225	.282	.314	.595	73	-23	-21	96	47	51	.508	10	18	-8	2	*O	-3.7
1921	Bos-N	149	624	114	191	25	**18**	12	74	58	85	.306	.369	.462	.830	127	16	23	93	72	102	.791	6	17	-8	-3	*O	0.4
1922	Bos-N	142	550	82	163	22	11	6	37	59	66	.296	.369	.409	.778	107	1	6	94	51	82	.729	3	12	-6	6	*O	0.1
1923	Bos-N	97	338	57	102	20	4	4	38	45	36	.302	.385	.420	.806	113	7	7	100	89	55	.781	1	6	-3	-6	O	-0.4
1924	Bos-N	74	188	21	49	9	1	1	15	21	28	.261	.338	.335	.673	86	-5	-3	94	83	22	.606	1	3	-2	7	O	0.1
Total	9	875	3324	467	890	117	67	35	276	321	461	.268	.336	.375	.711	102	-8	12	96	73	424	.657	51	<u>56</u>		9	O	-4.4
■ LEROY POWELL	Powell, Robert Leroy b: 10/17/33, Flint, Mich. BR/TR, 6'1", 190 lbs. Deb: 9/16/55																											
1955	Chi-A	1	0	0	0	0	0	0	0	0	0	—	—	—	—	—	0	0	101	—	—	—	0	0	0	0	R	0.0

YEAR	TM/L	G	AB	R	H	2B	3B	HR	RBI	BB	SO	AVG	OBP	SLG	PRO	/A	BR	/A	PF	CHI	RC	TA	SB	CS	SBR	FR	POS	TPR
1957	Chi-A	1	0	1	0	0	0	0	0	0	0	—	—	—	—	—	0	0	99	—	—	—	0	0	0	0	R	0.0
Total	2	2	0	1	0	0	0	0	0	0	0	—	—	—	—	—	0	0	99	—	847	—	0	0	0	0		0.0
■ **TOM POWER**	Power, Thomas E. b: San Francisco, Cal. d: 2/25/1898, San Francisco, Cal 5'11", 164 lbs. Deb: 8/27/1890																											
1890	BB-a	38	125	11	26	3	1	0		13		.208	.288	.248	.536	60	-6	-6	100	0	11	.515	6			0	12	-0.4
■ **VIC POWER**	Power, Victor Pellot (born b: 11/1/31, Arecibo, P.R. BR/TR, 6', 186 lbs. Deb: 4/13/54																											
1954	Phi-A	127	462	36	118	17	5	8	38	19	19	.255	.288	.366	.654	79	-16	-15	98	76	44	.532	2	1	0	**15**	*O1/S3	-0.2
1955	KC-A	147	596	91	190	34	10	19	76	35	27	.319	.357	.505	.862	128	21	20	101	84	103	.800	0	2	-1	14	*1	2.5
1956	KC-A	127	530	77	164	21	5	14	63	24	16	.309	.341	.447	.788	105	3	2	101	81	80	.708	2	2	-1	2	12/O	0.3
1957	KC-A	129	467	48	121	15	1	14	42	19	21	.259	.292	.385	.678	85	-12	-11	99	76	50	.573	3	2	-0	9	*1/O2	-0.3
1958	KC-A	52	205	35	62	13	4	4	27	7	3	.302	.325	.463	.789	108	3	2	106	107	28	.678	1	1	-0	0	1/2	0.0
	Cle-A	93	385	63	122	24	6	12	53	13	11	.317	.341	.504	.845	137	13	16	94	89	65	.781	2	1	0	1	312/SO	1.9
	Yr	145	590	98	184	37	**10**	16	80	20	14	.312	.336	.490	.825	126	17	18	98	96	96	.758	3	2	-0	1		1.9
1959	Cle-A	147	595	102	172	31	6	10	60	40	22	.289	.336	.412	.748	108	3	5	97	83	75	.651	9	13	-5	8	*12/3	0.8
1960	Cle-A	147	580	69	167	26	3	10	84	24	20	.288	.316	.395	.711	93	-9	-7	98	135	69	.609	9	5	-0	21	*1/S3	0.4
1961	Cle-A	147	563	64	151	34	4	5	63	38	16	.268	.316	.369	.685	86	-15	-12	96	117	62	.578	4	3	-1	9	*1/2	-1.5
1962	Min-A	144	611	80	177	28	2	16	63	22	35	.290	.318	.421	.738	92	-4	-8	105	79	79	.644	7	1	2	10	*1/2	-0.6
1963	Min-A	138	541	65	146	28	2	10	52	22	24	.270	.298	.384	.683	89	-8	-9	100	93	59	.567	3	1	0	-6	*12/3	-1.7
1964	Min-A	19	45	6	10	2	0	0	1	1	3	.222	.239	.267	.506	40	-4	-4	101	35	3	.371	0	0	0	0	1/2	-0.3
	LA-A	68	221	17	55	6	0	3	13	8	14	.249	.278	.317	.595	73	-11	-8	89	70	18	.460	1	1	-0	-1	13/2	-0.9
	Yr	87	266	23	65	8	0	3	14	9	17	.244	.272	.308	.580	67	-14	-11	91	62	21	.445	1	1	-0	-1		-1.2
	Phi-N	18	48	1	10	4	0	0	3	2	3	.208	.240	.292	.532	49	-3	-3	99	88	3	.421	0	0	0	-1	1	-0.4
1965	Cal-A	124	197	11	51	7	1	1	20	5	13	.259	.281	.320	.601	72	-8	-7	98	126	17	.470	2	2	-1	0	*1/23	-1.3
Total	12	1627	6046	765	1716	290	49	126	658	279	247	.284	.317	.411	.728	98	-46	-38	99	92	755	.646	45	35	-7	81	*120/3S	-1.3
■ **MIKE POWERS**	Powers, Ellis Foree b: 3/2/06, Crestwood, Ky. d: 12/2/83, Louisville, Ky. BL/TL, 6'1", 185 lbs. Deb: 8/19/32																											
1932	Cle-A	14	33	4	6	4	0	0	5	2	2	.182	.229	.303	.532	34	-3	-4	108	167	2	.444	0	0	0	-2	/O	-0.5
1933	Cle-A	24	47	6	13	2	1	0	2	6	6	.277	.358	.362	.720	87	-0	-1	105	39	6	.714	2	1	0	-2	O	-0.2
Total	2	38	80	10	19	6	1	0	7	8	8	.237	.307	.338	.644	65	-4	-4	106	90	9	.597	2	1	0	-3	/O	-0.7
■ **JOHN POWERS**	Powers, John Calvin b: 7/8/29, Birmingham, Ala. BL/TR, 6'1", 185 lbs. Deb: 9/24/55																											
1955	Pit-N	2	4	0	1	0	0	0	0	0	0	.250	.250	.250	.500	34	-0	-0	97	0	0	.333	0	0	0	0	/O	0.0
1956	Pit-N	11	21	0	1	0	0	0	0	1	4	.048	.091	.048	.139	-60	-5	-5	102	0	0	.091	0	0	0	-0	/O	-0.5
1957	Pit-N	20	35	7	10	3	0	2	8	5	9	.286	.419	.543	.961	166	3	3	94	133	9	1.080	0	0	0	-0	/O	0.3
1958	Pit-N	57	82	6	15	1	0	2	2	8	19	.183	.256	.268	.524	41	-7	-7	95	29	5	.429	0	0	0	0	O	-0.6
1959	Cin-N	43	43	8	11	2	1	2	4	3	13	.256	.319	.488	.808	108	1	0	103	60	7	.781	0	0	0	-1	/O	0.0
1960	Bal-A	10	18	3	2	0	0	0	0	3	1	.111	.238	.111	.349	-2	-3	-3	102	0	1	.313	0	0	0	-1	/O	-0.3
	Cle-A	8	12	2	2	1	1	0	0	2	2	.167	.286	.417	.702	89	-0	-0	98	0	1	.636	0	0	0	-0	/O	0.0
	Yr	18	30	5	4	1	1	0	0	5	3	.133	.257	.233	.490	34	-3	-3	100	0	2	.444	0	0	0	-1		-0.3
Total	6	151	215	26	42	7	2	6	14	22	48	.195	.282	.330	.612	64	-12	-11	98	46	23	.557	0	0	0	-3	/O	-1.1
■ **LES POWERS**	Powers, Leslie Edwin b: 11/5/09, Ballard, Wash. d: 11/13/78, Santa Monica, Cal. BL/TL, 6', 175 lbs. Deb: 9/17/38																											
1938	NY-N	2	3	0	0	0	0	0	0	0	1	.000	.000	.000	.000	-97	-1	-1	103	0	0	.000	0			0	H	0.0
1939	Phi-N	19	52	7	18	1	1	0	2	4	6	.346	.393	.404	.797	122	1	2	94	35	9	.735	0			-0	1	0.0
Total	2	21	55	7	18	1	1	0	2	4	7	.327	.373	.382	.755	109	0	1	94	33	9	.676	0			0	/1	0.0
■ **MIKE POWERS**	Powers, Michael Riley "Doc" b: 9/22/1870, Pittsfield, Mass. d: 4/26/09, Philadelphia, Pa. BR/TR, Deb: 6/12/1898																											
1898	Lou-N	34	99	13	27	4	3	1	19	5		.273	.308	.404	.712	110	0	1	96	134	13	.639	1			0	C/1O	0.1
1899	Lou-N	49	169	15	35	8	2	0	22	6		.207	.239	.278	.517	42	-13	-14	103	144	12	.410	1			-7	C/1	-1.6
	Was-N	14	38	3	10	2	0	0	3	1		.263	.282	.316	.598	69	-2	-2	96	77	3	.464	0			-2	C/1	-0.1
	Yr	63	207	18	45	10	2	0	25	7		.217	.247	.285	.532	47	-15	-16	102	131	15	.420	1			-9		-1.7
1901	Phi-A	116	431	53	108	26	5	1	47	18		.251	.281	.341	.622	73	-16	-16	100	101	45	.542	10			1	*C/1	-0.4
1902	Phi-A	71	246	35	65	7	1	2	39	14		.264	.304	.325	.629	70	-8	-11	108	150	26	.536	3			8	C/1	0.3
1903	Phi-A	75	247	19	56	11	1	0	23	5		.227	.242	.279	.521	55	-13	-14	104	120	17	.393	1			5	C/1	0.0
1904	Phi-A	57	184	11	35	3	0	0	11	6		.190	.216	.207	.422	35	-13	-13	102	108	9	.315	3			-8	C/O	-1.7
1905	Phi-A	21	60	4	10	0	0	0	5	1		.167	.180	.167	.347	11	-6	-6	109	178	2	.260	2			-1	C	-0.6
	NY-A	11	33	3	6	1	0	0	2	1		.182	.206	.212	.418	33	-2	-2	102	102	1	.296	0			-1	/1C	-0.2
	Phi-A	19	61	4	8	0	0	0	5	2		.131	.159	.131	.290	-6	-7	-8	109	223	2	.226	2			-1	C	-0.7
	Yr	51	154	11	24	1	0	0	12	4		.156	.177	.162	.340	8	-15	-17	108	184	5	.254	4			-3		-1.5
1906	Phi-A	58	185	5	29	1	0	0	7	1		.157	.161	.162	.323	2	-20	-19	94	85	5	.212	2			5	C/1	-1.0
1907	Phi-A	59	159	9	29	3	0	0	9	7		.182	.217	.201	.418	33	-11	-12	106	101	7	.308	1			6	C	0.0
1908	Phi-A	62	172	8	31	6	1	0	7	5		.180	.203	.227	.430	38	-11	-12	108	67	8	.319	1			5	C/1	-0.1
1909	Phi-A	1	4	1	1	0	0	0	0	0		.250	.250	.250	.500	57	-0	-0	102	0	0	.333	0			0	/C	0.0
Total	11	647	2088	183	450	72	13	4	199	72		.216	.242	.268	.510	51	-123	-129	103	116	151	.403	27			11	C/1O	-6.0
■ **PHIL POWERS**	Powers, Phillip B. "Grandmother" b: 7/26/1854, New York, N.Y. d: 12/22/14, New York, N.Y. BR/TR, 5'7", 166 lbs. Deb: 8/31/1878																											
1878	Chi-N	8	31	2	5	1	1	0	2	1	5	.161	.188	.258	.446	42	-2	-2	108	86	2	.346				0	/C	-0.1
1880	Bos-N	37	126	11	18	5	0	0	10	5	15	.143	.176	.183	.358	23	-10	-8	92	159	4	.259				-3	C/O	-0.7
1881	Cle-N	5	15	1	1	0	0	0	0	1	2	.067	.125	.067	.192	-40	-2	-2	96	0	0	.143				0	/C3	-0.1
1882	Cin-a	16	60	4	13	1	1	0		3		.217	.254	.267	.521	70	-1	-2	109	0	4	.404				0	C/1O	-0.1
1883	Cin-a	30	114	16	28	1	4	0		3		.246	.265	.325	.590	86	-1	-2	103	0	10	.465				0	CO	-0.1
1884	Cin-a	34	130	10	18	1	0	0		5		.138	.170	.146	.317	6	-13	-14	106	0	3	.214				4	C/O1	-0.6
1885	Cin-a	15	60	6	16	2	0	0		0		.267	.267	.300	.567	78	-1	-2	104	0	5	.409				0	C	-0.1
	Bal-a	9	34	6	4	1	0	0		1		.118	.143	.147	.290	-7	-4	-4	106	0	1	.200				0	/CO	-0.3
	Yr	24	94	12	20	3	0	0		1		.213	.221	.245	.466	47	-5	-6	105	0	5	.324				0		-0.4
Total	7	154	570	56	103	12	6	0	12	19	22	.181	.207	.223	.430	41	-35	-37	102	40	29	.313				1	C/O13	-2.1
■ **CARL POWIS**	Powis, Carl Edgar "Jug" b: 1/11/28, Philadelphia, Pa. BR/TR, 6', 185 lbs. Deb: 4/15/57																											
1957	Bal-A	15	41	4	8	3	1	0	2	7	9	.195	.327	.317	.644	82	-1	-1	93	61	5	.676	2	0	1	-1	O	-0.1
■ **JOHNNY PRAMESA**	Pramesa, John Steven b: 8/28/25, Barton, Ohio BR/TR, 6'2", 210 lbs. Deb: 4/24/49																											
1949	Cin-N	17	25	2	6	1	0	1	2	3	5	.240	.321	.400	.721	96	-0	-0	96	58	3	.684	0			0	C	0.0
1950	Cin-N	74	228	14	70	10	1	5	30	19	15	.307	.363	.425	.788	102	2	1	105	103	34	.705	0			-5	C	-0.1
1951	Cin-N	72	227	12	52	5	2	6	22	5	17	.229	.246	.348	.594	58	-14	-14	101	88	18	.462	0	0	0	-4	C	-1.7
1952	Chi-N	22	46	1	13	1	0	1	5	4	4	.283	.340	.370	.710	94	-0	-0	103	98	6	.618	0	0	0	-0	C	0.0
Total	4	185	526	29	141	17	3	13	59	31	41	.268	.310	.386	.696	83	-12	-14	102	94	61	.609	0	0		-8	C	-1.8
■ **DEL PRATT**	Pratt, Derrill Burnham b: 1/10/1888, Walhalla, S.C. d: 9/30/77, Texas City, Tex. BR/TR, 5'11", 175 lbs. Deb: 4/11/12																											
1912	StL-A	151	570	76	172	26	15	5	69	36		.302	.348	.426	.774	122	13	14	99	95	91	.771	24			5	*2S/O3	1.9
1913	StL-A	155	592	60	175	31	13	2	87	40	57	.296	.341	.402	.743	123	10	14	95	122	89	.758	37			1	*2/1	1.2
1914	StL-A	158	584	85	165	34	13	5	64	50	45	.283	.341	.411	.752	129	16	18	98	91	83	.736	37	28	-6	1	*2	1.3
1915	StL-A	159	602	61	175	31	11	3	78	26	43	.291	.323	.394	.717	120	7	10	96	104	80	.662	32	23	-4	11	*2	1.6
1916	StL-A	158	596	64	159	35	12	5	**103**	54	56	.267	.331	.391	.722	123	10	13	95	**157**	80	.696	26	17	-2	23	*2	4.4
1917	StL-A	123	450	40	111	22	8	1	53	33	36	.247	.301	.338	.639	100	-4	-1	95	130	49	.605	18			15	*2/1	2.3
1918	NY-A	126	477	65	131	19	7	2	55	35	26	.275	.327	.356	.683	112	2	5	95	121	59	.633	12			13	*2	2.6
1919	NY-A	140	527	69	154	27	7	4	56	36	24	.292	.342	.393	.735	100	3	-0	106	98	75	.721	22			**27**	*2	4.1
1920	NY-A	154	574	84	180	37	8	4	97	50	24	.314	.372	.427	.798	109	9	7	102	140	91	.767	12	10	-2	12	*2	1.9
1921	Bos-A	135	521	80	169	36	10	5	102	44	10	.324	.378	.461	.839	113	10	10	100	145	89	.809	8	10	-4	-6	*2	0.4

YEAR	TM/L	G	AB	R	H	2B	3B	HR	RBI	BB	SO	AVG	OBP	SLG	PRO	/A	BR	/A	PF	CHI	RC	TA	SB	CS	SBR	FR	POS	TPR
1922	Bos-A	154	607	73	183	44	7	6	86	53	20	.301	.361	.427	.788	109	4	7	96	107	93	.744	7	10	-4	-13	*2	0.1
1923	Det-A	101	297	43	92	18	3	0	40	25	9	.310	.375	.391	.766	105	1	3	97	118	46	.738	5	1	1	-2	213	0.4
1924	Det-A	121	429	56	130	32	3	1	77	31	10	.303	.353	.399	.751	94	-5	-4	100	146	59	.682	6	9	-4	3	21/3O	-0.5
Total	13	1835	6826	856	1996	392	117	43	967	513	360	.292	.345	.403	.748	113	76	94	98	120	984	.718	246	108		89	*2/1S3O	21.7
■ **FRANK PRATT** Pratt, Francis Bruce "Truckhorse" b: 8/24/1897, Blocton, Ala. d: 3/8/74, Centreville, Ala. TR, 5'9.5", 155 lbs. Deb: 5/13/21																												
1921	Chi-A	1	1	0	0	0	0	0	0	0	0	.000	.000	.000	.000	-99	-0	-0	99	0	0	.000	0	0	0	0	H	0.0
■ **LARRY PRATT** Pratt, Lester John b: 10/8/1886, Gibson City, Ill. d: 1/8/69, Peoria, Ill. BR/TR, 6' ", 183 lbs. Deb: 9/19/14																												
1914	Bos-A	5	4	0	0	0	0	0	0	0	4	.000	.000	.000	.000	-99	-1	-1	98	0	0	.000	0			-0	/C	0.0
1915	Bro-F	20	49	5	9	1	0	1	2	2	0	.184	.216	.265	.481	43	-4	-4	98	45	3	.425	2			0	C	-0.3
	New-F	5	4	2	2	2	0	0	0	3	0	.500	.714	1.000	1.714	429	2	2	94	0	4	4.500	2			0	/C	0.2
	Yr	25	53	7	11	3	0	1	2	5	0	.208	.276	.321	.597	79	-2	-1	97	38	6	.619	4			0		-0.1
Total	2	30	57	7	11	3	0	1	2	5	4	.193	.258	.298	.556	66	-3	-2	97	37	8	.565	4			-0	/C	-0.1
■ **TOM PRATT** Pratt, Thomas J. b: 1844, Chelsea, Mass. d: 9/28/08, Philadelphia, Pa. TL, 5'7.5", 150 lbs. Deb: 10/18/1871																												
1871	Ath-n	1	6	2	2							.333															/1	
■ **MEL PREIBISCH** Preibisch, Melvin Adolphus "Primo" b: 11/23/14, Sealy, Tex. BR/TR, 5'11", 185 lbs. Deb: 9/17/40																												
1940	Bos-N	11	40	3	9	2	0	0	5	2	4	.225	.262	.275	.537	49	-3	-3	99	172	3	.419	0			1	O	-0.1
1941	Bos-N	5	4	0	0	0	0	0	0	1	2	.000	.200	.000	.200	-44	-1	-1	93	0	0	.250	0			-1	/O	-0.1
Total	2	16	44	3	9	2	0	0	5	3	6	.205	.255	.250	.505	41	-4	-3	98	154	3	.400	0			1	/O	-0.2
■ **BOBBY PRESCOTT** Prescott, George Bertrand b: 3/27/31, Colon, Panama BR/TR, 5'11", 180 lbs. Deb: 6/17/61																												
1961	KC-A	10	12	0	1	0	0	0	0	2	5	.083	.214	.083	.298	-17	-2	-2	102	0	0	.250	0	0	0	-1	/O	-0.2
■ **JIM PRESLEY** Presley, James Arthur b: 10/23/61, Pensacola, Fla. BR/TR, 6'1", 200 lbs. Deb: 6/24/84																												
1984	Sea-A	70	251	27	57	12	1	10	36	6	63	.227	.248	.402	.650	75	-9	-10	102	110	24	.548	1	1	-0	-7	3/D	-1.5
1985	Sea-A	155	570	71	157	33	1	28	84	44	100	.275	.328	.484	.813	126	13	17	95	94	80	.727	2	2	-1	6	*3	1.7
1986	Sea-A	155	616	83	163	33	4	27	107	32	172	.265	.305	.463	.768	101	4	-1	105	123	80	.676	0	4	-2	8	*3	0.1
1987	Sea-A	152	575	78	142	23	6	24	88	38	157	.247	.298	.433	.731	89	-8	-10	103	112	72	.654	2	0	1	10	*3/SD	-0.1
1988	Sea-A	150	544	50	125	26	0	14	62	36	114	.230	.283	.355	.637	72	-17	-22	108	107	52	.539	3	5	-2	-13	*3/D	-3.7
Total	5	682	2556	309	644	127	12	103	377	156	606	.252	.299	.432	.731	95	-18	-25	102	109	306	.662	8	12	-5	4	3/DS	-3.5
■ **WALT PRESTON** Preston, Walter B. b: 1870, Richmond, Va. BL/TR, 6', 175 lbs. Deb: 4/18/1895																												
1895	Lou-N	50	197	42	55	6	4	1	24	17	17	.279	.366	.365	.732	96	-2	-0	95	86	31	.775	11			0	O3	0.0
■ **JIM PRICE** Price, Jimmie William b: 10/13/41, Harrisburg, Pa. BR/TR, 6', 192 lbs. Deb: 4/11/67																												
1967	Det-A	44	92	9	24	4	0	0	8	4	10	.261	.292	.304	.596	77	-3	-3	99	119	7	.444	0	0	0	1	C	0.0
1968	Det-A	64	132	12	23	4	0	3	13	13	14	.174	.253	.273	.526	56	-6	-7	106	124	8	.435	0	0	0	2	C	-0.3
1969	Det-A	72	192	21	45	8	0	9	28	18	20	.234	.300	.417	.717	95	-1	-2	103	105	24	.649	0	0	0	7	C	0.9
1970	Det-A	52	132	12	24	4	0	5	15	21	23	.182	.294	.326	.620	69	-5	-6	103	105	13	.561	0	0	0	1	C	-0.3
1971	Det-A	29	54	4	13	2	0	1	7	6	3	.241	.328	.333	.661	92	-1	-0	96	136	6	.568	0	0	0	-1	C	0.0
Total	5	261	602	58	129	22	0	18	71	62	70	.214	.290	.341	.630	78	-16	-18	103	114	58	.565	0	0	0	10	C	0.3
■ **JACKIE PRICE** Price, John Thomas Reid "Johnny" b: 11/13/12, Windborn, Miss. d: 10/2/67, San Francisco, Cal. BL/TR, 5'10.5", 150 lbs. Deb: 8/18/46																												
1946	Cle-A	7	13	1	3	0	0	0	0	0	0	.231	.231	.231	.462	33	-1	-1	89	0	1	.273	0	0	0	0	/S	0.0
■ **JOE PRICE** Price, Joseph Preston "Lumber" b: 4/10/1897, Milligan College, Tenn. d: 1/15/61, Washington, D.C. BR/TR, 6'1.5", 187 lbs. Deb: 9/05/28																												
1928	NY-N	1	1	0	0	0	0	0	0	0	1	.000	.000	.000	.000	-98	-0	-0	102	0	0	.000	0			-0	/O	0.0
■ **BOB PRICHARD** Prichard, Robert Alexander b: 10/21/17, Paris, Tex. BL/TL, 6'1", 195 lbs. Deb: 6/14/39																												
1939	Was-A	26	85	8	20	5	0	0	8	19	16	.235	.375	.294	.669	81	-3	-1	90	110	11	.657	0	2	-1	-1	1	-0.5
■ **JERRY PRIDDY** Priddy, Gerald Edward b: 11/9/19, Los Angeles, Cal. d: 3/3/80, N.Hollywood, Cal. BR/TR, 5'11.5", 180 lbs. Deb: 4/17/41																												
1941	NY-A	56	174	18	37	7	0	1	26	18	16	.213	.290	.270	.560	50	-13	-12	98	184	14	.483	4	2	0	2	231	-0.6
1942	NY-A	59	189	23	53	9	2	2	28	31	27	.280	.385	.381	.766	116	5	5	99	127	31	.748	0	1	-1	1	31/2S	0.6
1943	Was-A	149	560	68	152	31	3	4	62	67	76	.271	.350	.359	.709	104	6	4	104	113	72	.637	5	5	-2	3	*2S/3	1.1
1946	Was-A	138	511	54	130	22	8	6	58	57	73	.254	.332	.364	.696	102	-4	1	92	115	64	.640	9	3	1	4	*2	1.7
1947	Was-A	147	505	42	108	20	3	3	49	62	79	.214	.301	.283	.584	65	-25	-23	97	121	44	.508	7	6	-2	2	*2	-1.5
1948	StL-A	151	560	96	166	40	9	8	79	86	71	.296	.391	.443	.834	115	18	13	106	104	101	.824	6	5	-1	**23**	*2	3.7
1949	StL-A	145	544	83	158	26	4	11	63	80	81	.290	.382	.414	.796	111	9	9	100	81	89	.766	5	3	-0	-1	*2	1.0
1950	Det-A	157	618	104	171	26	6	13	75	95	95	.277	.376	.401	.777	103	0	4	97	80	95	.731	2	7	-4	**33**	*2	**4.0**
1951	Det-A	154	584	73	152	22	6	8	57	69	73	.260	.338	.360	.698	84	-9	-13	106	92	73	.625	4	3	-1	12	*2/S	0.4
1952	Det-A	75	279	37	79	23	3	4	20	42	29	.283	.379	.430	.809	126	10	10	99	60	46	.774	1	8	-5	-3	2	0.6
1953	Det-A	65	196	14	46	6	2	1	24	17	19	.235	.299	.301	.600	64	-10	-10	98	143	18	.497	1	1	-0	-1	21/3	-0.8
Total	11	1296	4720	612	1252	232	46	61	541	624	639	.265	.353	.373	.725	97	-12	-11	100	103	646	.694	44	44	-13	74	*2/31S	10.2
■ **JOHNNY PRIEST** Priest, John Gooding b: 6/23/1886, St.Joseph, Mo. d: 11/4/79, Washington, D.C. BR/TR, 5'11", 170 lbs. Deb: 5/30/11																												
1911	NY-A	8	21	2	3	0	0	0	2	2		.143	.250	.143	.393	10	-2	-3	111	225	1	.500	3			0	/23	-0.2
1912	NY-A	2	2	1	1	0	0	0	1	0		.500	.500	.500	1.000	184	0	0	101	334	0	1.000	0			0	H	0.0
Total	2	10	23	3	4	0	0	0	3	2		.174	.269	.174	.443	23	-2	-3	110	234	2	.526	3			0	/23	-0.2
■ **TOM PRINCE** Prince, Thomas Albert b: 8/13/64, Kankakee, Ill. BR/TR, 5'11", 185 lbs. Deb: 9/22/87																												
1987	Pit-N	4	9	1	2	1	0	1	2	0	2	.222	.222	.667	.889	119	0	0	104	89	1	.857	0	0	0	0	/C	0.0
1988	Pit-N	29	74	3	13	2	0	0	6	4	15	.176	.218	.203	.421	22	-7	-7	98	160	3	.288	0	0	0	1	C	-0.5
Total	2	33	83	4	15	3	0	1	8	4	17	.181	.218	.253	.471	34	-7	-7	98	153	4	.342	0	0	0	1	/C	-0.5
■ **WALTER PRINCE** Prince, Walter Farr b: 5/9/1861, Amherst, N.H. d: 3/2/38, Bristol, N.H. BL/TR, 5'9", 150 lbs. Deb: 1883																												
1883	Lou-a	4	11	1	2	0	0	0		0		.182	.182	.182	.364	19	-1	-1	94	0	0	.222				0	/O1S	0.0
1884	Det-N	7	21	0	3	0	0	0	1	3	4	.143	.250	.143	.393	29	-2	-1	94	115	1	.333				0	/O	0.0
	Was-a	43	166	22	36	3	2	0		13		.217	.286	.259	.545	92	-3	0	88	0	13	.454				-5	1	-0.6
	Was-U	1	4	0	1	0	0	0		0		.250	.250	.250	.500	72	-0	-0	97	0	0	.333	0			0	/1	0.0
Total	2	55	202	23	42	3	2	0	1	16	4	.208	.276	.243	.519	81	-5	-2	89	12	14	.425	0			-5	/1OS	-0.6
■ **BUDDY PRITCHARD** Pritchard, Harold William b: 1/25/36, South Gate, Cal. BR/TR, 6'1", 195 lbs. Deb: 4/21/57																												
1957	Pit-N	23	11	1	1	0	0	0	0	0	4	.091	.091	.091	.182	-54	-2	-2	94	0	0	.100	0	0	0	-1	S/O	-0.2
■ **GEORGE PROESER** Proeser, George "Yatz" b: 5/30/1864, Cincinnati, Ohio d: 10/13/41, New Burlington, O. BL/TL, 5'10", 190 lbs. Deb: 1888																												
1888	Cle-a	7	23	5	7	2	0	0	1	1		.304	.333	.391	.725	139	1	1	97	33	3	.625	0			0	/P	0.0
1890	Syr-a	13	53	11	13	1	1	1		10		.245	.365	.358	.724	128	1	2	90	0	7	.750	1			0	O	0.2
Total	2	20	76	16	20	3	1	1	1	11		.263	.356	.368	.725	132	2	3	92	9	11	.714	1			0	/OP	0.2
■ **JAKE PROPST** Propst, William Jacob b: 3/10/1895, Kennedy, Ala. d: 2/24/67, Columbus, Miss. 5'10", 165 lbs. Deb: 8/07/23																												
1923	Was-A	1	1	0	0	0	0	0	0	0	0	.000	.000	.000	.000	-99	-0	-0	95	0	0	.000	0	0	0	0	H	0.0
■ **DOC PROTHRO** Prothro, James Thompson b: 7/16/1893, Memphis, Tenn. d: 10/14/71, Memphis, Tenn. BR/TR, 5'10.5", 170 lbs. Deb: 9/26/20 M																												
1920	Was-A	6	13	2	5	0	0	0	2	0	4	.385	.385	.385	.769	110	0	0	95	140	2	.625	0	0	0	-0	/S3	0.0
1923	Was-A	6	8	2	2	0	1	0	3	1	3	.250	.333	.500	.833	124	0	0	95	256	1	.833	0	0	0	0	/3	0.1
1924	Was-A	46	159	17	53	11	5	0	24	15	11	.333	.394	.465	.860	123	5	5	98	109	29	.855	4	4	-1	-5	3	0.2
1925	Bos-A	119	415	44	130	23	3	0	51	52	21	.313	.390	.383	.773	102	-0	3	95	109	62	.743	9	11	-4	-5	*3/S	0.0
1926	Cin-N	3	5	1	1	0	1	0	1	1	1	.200	.333	.600	.933	155	0	0	95	115	1	1.000	0			0	/3	0.0
Total	5	180	600	66	191	34	10	0	81	69	40	.318	.390	.408	.798	108	5	9	96	112	95	.774	13	15		-11	3/S	0.3

YEAR	TM/L	G	AB	R	H	2B	3B	HR	RBI	BB	SO	AVG	OBP	SLG	PRO	/A	BR	/A	PF	CHI	RC	TA	SB	CS	SBR	FR	POS	TPR
■ EARL PRUESS	Pruess, Earl Henry "Gibby" b: 4/2/1895, Chicago, Ill. d: 8/28/79, Branson, Mo. BR/TR, 5'10.5", 170 lbs. Deb: 9/15/20																											
1920	StL-A	1	0	1	0	0	0	0	0	1	0	—	1.000	—	1.408	254	0	0	111	0	1	—	1	0	0	0	/O	0.0
■ JIM PRUETT	Pruett, James Calvin b: 12/16/17, Nashville, Tenn. BR/TR, 5'10", 178 lbs. Deb: 9/26/44																											
1944	Phi-A	3	4	1	1	0	0	0	0	1	0	.250	.500	.250	.750	117	0	0	101	0	1	.750	0	0	0	0	/C	0.0
1945	Phi-A	6	9	1	2	0	0	0	0	1	2	.222	.300	.222	.522	56	-1	-0	94	0	0	.375	0	1	-1	0	/C	0.0
Total	2	9	13	2	3	0	0	0	0	2	2	.231	.375	.231	.606	80	-0	-0	96	0	1	.545	0	1	-1	0	/C	0.0
■ RON PRUITT	Pruitt, Ronald Ralph b: 10/21/51, Flint, Mich. BR/TR, 6', 185 lbs. Deb: 6/25/75																											
1975	Tex-A	14	17	2	3	0	0	0	0	1	3	.176	.222	.176	.399	14	-2	-2	100	0	1	.267	0	0	0	-0	C/O	-0.1
1976	Cle-A	47	86	7	23	1	1	0	5	16	8	.267	.382	.302	.685	103	1	1	100	74	11	.657	2	3	-1	-0	O/C31D	0.0
1977	Cle-A	78	219	29	63	10	2	2	32	28	22	.288	.373	.379	.752	108	3	3	98	142	30	.680	2	3	-1	-8	O/C3D	-0.7
1978	Cle-A	71	187	17	44	6	1	6	17	16	20	.235	.296	.374	.670	94	-4	-2	93	76	21	.599	2	1	0	-4	CO/3D	-0.4
1979	Cle-A	64	166	23	47	7	0	2	21	19	21	.283	.357	.361	.718	89	-1	-2	106	122	22	.653	2	0	1	-5	ODC/3	-0.6
1980	Cle-A	23	36	1	11	1	0	0	4	4	6	.306	.375	.333	.708	94	-0	-0	102	130	5	.615	0	0	0	0	/O3D	0.0
	Chi-A	33	70	8	21	2	0	2	11	8	7	.300	.372	.414	.786	119	2	2	97	123	10	.698	0	0	0	-1	O/C31D	0.1
	Yr	56	106	9	32	3	0	2	15	12	13	.302	.373	.387	.760	110	2	2	99	128	15	.679	0	0	0	-1		0.1
1981	Cle-A	5	9	0	0	0	0	0	0	1	2	.000	.100	.000	.100	-74	-2	-2	93	0	0	.100	0	0	0	-1	/OCD	-0.2
1982	SF-N	5	4	1	2	1	0	0	2	1	1	.500	.600	.750	1.350	294	1	1	94	261	2	2.000	0	0	0	-0	/CO	0.1
1983	SF-N	1	1	0	0	0	0	0	0	0	0	.000	.000	.000	.000	-99	-0	-0	101	0	0	.000	0	0	0	0	/H	0.0
Total	9	341	795	88	214	28	4	12	92	94	90	.269	.348	.360	.708	97	-2	-1	99	109	100	.663	8	7	-2	-19	O/CD31	-1.8
■ GREG PRYOR	Pryor, Gregory Russell b: 10/2/49, Marietta, Ohio BR/TR, 6', 180 lbs. Deb: 6/04/76																											
1976	Tex-A	5	8	2	3	0	0	0	1	0	1	.375	.375	.375	.750	118	0	0	102	128	1	.600	0	0	0	0	/2S3	0.0
1978	Chi-A	82	222	27	58	11	0	2	15	11	18	.261	.299	.338	.637	78	-6	-7	101	73	22	.533	3	1	0	-5	2S3	-0.7
1979	Chi-A	143	476	60	131	23	3	3	34	35	41	.275	.327	.355	.683	82	-10	-12	102	73	52	.573	3	4	-2	-4	*S23	-0.1
1980	Chi-A	122	338	32	81	18	4	1	29	12	35	.240	.270	.325	.595	64	-18	-16	97	100	28	.468	2	2	-1	10	S3/2D	0.0
1981	Chi-A	47	76	4	17	1	0	0	6	6	8	.224	.298	.237	.534	56	-4	-4	100	130	6	.426	0	0	0	2	3S/2	0.0
1982	KC-A	73	152	23	41	10	1	2	12	10	20	.270	.315	.388	.703	92	-2	-2	100	74	18	.612	2	0	1	-1	321/S	-0.1
1983	KC-A	68	115	9	25	4	0	1	14	7	8	.217	.262	.278	.541	48	-8	-8	101	156	8	.419	0	0	0	-2	3/12	-1.0
1984	KC-A	123	270	32	71	11	1	4	25	12	28	.263	.302	.356	.657	82	-7	-7	99	92	26	.526	0	3	-2	6	*32/S1D	0.0
1985	KC-A	63	114	8	25	3	0	1	3	8	12	.219	.270	.272	.542	48	-8	-8	102	35	7	.406	0	1	-1	3	32S/1D	-0.4
1986	KC-A	63	112	7	19	4	0	0	7	3	14	.170	.191	.205	.397	9	-14	-14	100	121	3	.273	1	1	-0	1	3S2/1	-1.1
Total	10	789	1883	204	471	85	9	14	146	104	185	.250	.293	.327	.620	70	-77	-78	100	89	172	.519	11	12	-4	8	3S2/1D	-3.4
■ GEORGE PUCCINELLI	Puccinelli, George Lawrence "Pooch" or "Count" b: 6/22/07, San Francisco, Cal. d: 4/16/56, San Francisco, Cal BR/TR, 6'0.5", 190 lbs. Deb: 7/17/30																											
1930	StL-N	11	16	5	9	1	0	3	8	0	1	.563	.563	1.188	1.750	294	5	5	105	98	10	2.714	0			-1	/O	0.3
1932	StL-N	31	108	17	30	8	0	3	11	12	13	.278	.350	.435	.785	110	2	2	100	74	17	.769	1			1	O	0.1
1934	StL-A	10	26	4	6	1	0	2	5	1	8	.231	.286	.500	.786	96	-0	-0	104	88	4	.750	0	0	0	1	/O	0.0
1936	Phi-A	135	457	83	127	30	3	11	78	65	70	.278	.369	.429	.798	96	-3	-3	101	113	75	.793	2	3	-1	-2	*O	-0.8
Total	4	187	607	109	172	40	3	19	102	78	92	.283	.367	.453	.820	104	4	3	101	105	105	.817	3	3		-1	O	-0.4
■ KIRBY PUCKETT	Puckett, Kirby b: 3/14/61, Chicago, Ill. BR/TR, 5'8", 178 lbs. Deb: 5/08/84																											
1984	Min-A	128	557	63	165	12	5	0	31	16	69	.296	.321	.336	.656	78	-14	-17	106	57	58	.539	14	7	0	22	*O	0.1
1985	Min-A	161	691	80	199	29	13	4	74	41	87	.288	.332	.385	.716	93	-4	-7	103	91	88	.647	21	12	-1	14	*O	0.4
1986	Min-A	161	680	119	223	37	6	31	96	34	99	.328	.366	.537	.903	132	38	31	108	74	127	.882	20	12	-1	3	*O	2.7
1987	Min-A	157	624	96	**207**	32	5	28	99	32	91	.332	.370	.534	.904	143	32	35	96	100	116	.870	12	7	-1	-1	*O/D	2.7
1988	Min-A	158	657	109	**234**	42	5	24	121	23	83	.356	.380	.545	.925	147	46	41	106	108	126	.870	6	7	-2	13	*O	4.8
Total	5	765	3209	467	1028	152	34	87	421	146	429	.320	.354	.470	.825	119	97	82	104	87	516	.781	73	45	-5	51	O/D	10.7
■ JOHN PUHL	Puhl, John G. b: 1875, Bayonne, N.J. d: 8/24/1900, Bayonne, N.J. Deb: 10/13/1898																											
1898	NY-N	2	9	1	2	0	0	0	1	0		.222	.222	.222	.444	31	-1	-1	95	130	0	.286	0			0	/3	0.0
1899	NY-N	1	2	0	0	0	0	0	0	0		.000	.333	.000	.333	-3	-0	-0	97	0	0	.500	0			0	/3	0.0
Total	2	3	11	1	2	0	0	0	1	0		.182	.250	.182	.432	26	-1	-1	95	98	0	.333	0			0	/3	0.0
■ TERRY PUHL	Puhl, Terry Stephen b: 7/8/56, Melville, Sask., Can BL/TR, 6'2", 195 lbs. Deb: 7/12/77																											
1977	Hou-N	60	229	40	69	13	5	0	10	30	31	.301	.385	.402	.786	120	5	7	93	42	39	.811	10	1	2	0	O	0.8
1978	Hou-N	149	585	87	169	25	6	3	35	48	46	.289	.347	.368	.714	105	0	4	95	60	75	.678	32	14	1	20	*O	2.0
1979	Hou-N	157	600	87	172	22	4	8	49	58	46	.287	.353	.377	.730	110	1	8	90	75	80	.696	30	22	-4	-6	*O	-0.6
1980	Hou-N	141	535	75	151	24	5	13	55	60	52	.282	.359	.419	.778	119	12	14	98	88	85	.791	27	11	2	14	*O	2.5
1981	Hou-N	96	350	43	88	19	4	3	28	31	49	.251	.319	.354	.674	103	-4	1	88	88	44	.673	22	4	4	3	O	0.5
1982	Hou-N	145	507	64	133	17	9	8	50	51	49	.262	.332	.379	.711	99	-1	-0	99	93	66	.674	17	9	-0	-2	*O	-0.3
1983	Hou-N	137	465	66	136	25	7	8	44	36	48	.292	.346	.428	.774	126	8	13	90	78	70	.759	24	11	1	-5	*O	0.6
1984	Hou-N	132	449	66	135	19	7	9	55	59	45	.301	.383	.434	.817	140	19	23	93	99	77	.820	13	8	-1	-3	*O	1.5
1985	Hou-N	57	194	34	55	14	3	2	23	18	23	.284	.347	.418	.765	118	3	4	96	107	30	.752	6	2	1	-0	O	0.3
1986	Hou-N	81	172	17	42	10	0	3	14	15	24	.244	.305	.355	.659	79	-5	-5	103	80	18	.572	3	2	-0	-4	O	-1.0
1987	Hou-N	90	122	9	28	5	0	2	15	11	16	.230	.293	.320	.613	67	-7	-5	93	133	11	.520	1	1	-0	-6	O	-1.2
1988	Hou-N	113	234	42	71	7	2	3	19	35	30	.303	.396	.389	.785	135	10	11	93	76	42	.892	22	4	4	-8	O	0.6
Total	12	1358	4442	630	1249	200	52	62	397	452	459	.281	.351	.391	.742	113	41	75	94	82	637	.738	207	89	9	3	*O	5.7
■ RICH PUIG	Puig, Richard Gerald b: 3/16/53, Tampa, Fla. BL/TR, 5'10", 165 lbs. Deb: 9/13/74																											
1974	NY-N	4	10	0	0	0	0	0	0	1	2	.000	.091	.000	.091	-73	-2	-2	99	0	0	.100	0	0	0	0	/23	-0.1
■ LUIS PUJOLS	Pujols, Luis Bienvenido (Toribio) b: 11/18/55, Santiago, D.R. BR/TR, 6'2", 175 lbs. Deb: 9/22/77																											
1977	Hou-N	6	15	0	1	0	0	0	0	0	5	.067	.067	.067	.133	-69	-3	-3	93	0	0	.071	0	0	0	0	/C	-0.2
1978	Hou-N	56	153	11	20	8	1	1	11	12	45	.131	.199	.216	.414	17	-18	-17	95	121	6	.331	0	0	0	-1	C/1	-1.7
1979	Hou-N	26	75	7	17	2	1	0	8	2	14	.227	.247	.280	.527	48	-6	-5	90	151	5	.377	0	0	0	-2	C	-0.6
1980	Hou-N	78	221	15	44	6	1	0	20	13	29	.199	.247	.235	.482	36	-19	-18	98	152	13	.363	0	0	0	-7	C/3	-2.5
1981	Hou-N	40	117	5	28	3	1	1	14	10	17	.239	.299	.308	.607	82	-4	-3	88	141	10	.505	1	0	0	1	C	0.0
1982	Hou-N	65	176	8	35	6	2	4	15	10	40	.199	.242	.324	.566	58	-11	-10	99	85	12	.453	0	3	-2	-0	C	-1.2
1983	Hou-N	40	87	4	17	2	0	0	12	5	14	.195	.239	.218	.458	31	-8	-7	90	250	4	.324	0	0	0	-2	C	-0.8
1984	KC-A	4	5	0	1	0	0	0	1	0	0	.200	.200	.200	.400	11	-1	-1	99	399	0	.250	0	0	0	0	/C	0.0
1985	Tex-A	1	1	0	1	0	0	0	0	0	0	1.000	1.000	1.000	2.000	415	0	0	108	0	1	—	0	0	0	0	/C	0.0
Total	9	316	850	50	164	27	6	6	81	52	164	.193	.241	.260	.501	42	-69	-64	95	140	51	.401	1	3	-2	-11	C/31	-7.0
■ BLONDIE PURCELL	Purcell, William Aloysius b: Paterson, N.J. 5'9.5", 159 lbs. Deb: 5/01/1879 M																											
1879	Syr-N	63	277	32	72	6	3	0	25	3	13	.260	.268	.303	.571	99	-4	1	89	92	23	.424				-12	OP/C	-1.1
	Cin-N	12	50	10	11	0	0	0	4	0	3	.220	.220	.220	.440	48	-3	-2	95	130	2	.282				0	O/P	-0.2
	Yr	75	327	42	83	6	3	0	29	3	16	.254	.261	.291	.551	91	-6	-2	90	99	25	.402				-12		-1.3
1880	Cin-N	77	325	48	95	13	6	1	24	5	13	.292	.303	.378	.681	131	9	10	99	61	38	.557				-3	OP/S	0.5
1881	Cle-N	20	80	3	14	2	1	0	4	5	8	.175	.224	.225	.449	43	-5	-5	96	82	4	.348				-3	O	-0.6
	Buf-N	30	113	15	33	7	2	0	17	8	8	.292	.339	.389	.728	127	4	4	101	137	15	.650				-7	O/P	-0.2
	Yr	50	193	18	47	9	3	0	21	13	16	.244	.291	.321	.613	93	-1	-1	99	116	19	.514				-9		-0.8
1882	Buf-N	84	380	79	105	18	6	2	40	14	27	.276	.302	.371	.673	110	6	4	104	79	44	.564				-8	*O/P	-0.4
1883	Phi-N	97	425	70	114	20	5	1	32	13	26	.268	.290	.346	.636	102	-4	3	90	64	44	.514				5	3OPM	0.8
1884	Phi-N	103	428	67	108	11	7	1	31	29	30	.252	.300	.318	.618	102	-2	3	92	68	42	.516				0	*O/P	0.2
1885	Phi-a	66	304	71	90	15	5	0		16		.296	.337	.378	.716	125	10	8	103	0	40	.626				-1	O/P	0.3
	Bos-N	21	87	9	19	1	1	0	3	3	15	.218	.244	.253	.497	65	-4	-3	94	46	6	.368				0	O	-0.2
1886	Bal-a	26	85	17	19	0	1	0		17		.224	.365	.247	.612	105	1	2	91	0	13	.803	13			0	O/SP	0.2

YEAR	TM/L	G	AB	R	H	2B	3B	HR	RBI	BB	SO	AVG	OBP	SLG	PRO	/A	BR	/A	PF	CHI	RC	TA	SB	CS	SBR	FR	POS	TPR
1887	Bal-a	140	567	101	142	25	8	4		46		.250	.318	.344	.662	90	-10	-6	96	0	92	.798	88			-6	*O/P	-1.2
1888	Bal-a	101	406	53	96	9	4	2	39	27		.236	.289	.293	.582	93	-4	-2	96	82	40	.532	16			-6	*O/S1	-1.0
	Phi-a	18	66	10	11	3	1	0	6	5		.167	.236	.242	.479	55	-3	-3	101	114	6	.582	10			0	O/3	-0.2
	Yr	119	472	63	107	12	5	2	45	32		.227	.281	.286	.568	88	-7	-5	97	88	46	.540	26			-6		-1.2
1889	Phi-a	129	507	72	160	19	7	0	85	50	27	.316	.383	.381	.763	123	15	17	98	133	84	.778	22			-12	*O	0.0
1890	Phi-a	110	463	110	128	28	3	2		43		.276	.343	.363	.706	114	6	8	97	0	76	.785	48			1	*O	0.3
Total	12	1097	4563	767	1217	177	60	13	310	284	170	.267	.314	.340	.654	105	11	37	96	59	569	.616	197			-49	O/P3S1C	-2.8
■ **PID PURDY**	Purdy, Everett Virgil b: 6/15/04, Beatrice, Neb. d: 1/16/51, Beatrice, Neb. BL/TR, 5'6", 150 lbs. Deb: 9/07/26																											
1926	Chi-A	11	33	5	6	2	1	0	6	2	1	.182	.229	.303	.532	41	-3	-3	92	204	2	.429	0	1	-1	-0	/O	-0.3
1927	Cin-N	18	62	15	22	2	4	1	12	4	3	.355	.412	.565	.976	159	5	5	100	113	14	1.025	0			-2	O	0.2
1928	Cin-N	70	223	32	69	11	1	0	25	23	13	.309	.377	.368	.744	99	-1	1	96	109	31	.695	1			-2	O	-0.3
1929	Cin-N	82	181	22	49	7	5	1	16	19	8	.271	.350	.381	.731	81	-5	-5	99	76	24	.705	2			-4	O	-1.0
Total	4	181	499	74	146	22	11	2	59	48	25	.293	.362	.393	.754	96	-4	-2	97	103	72	.715	3	1		-8	O	-1.4
■ **JESSE PURNELL**	Purnell, Jesse Rhoades b: 5/11/1881, Glenside, Pa. d: 7/4/66, Philadelphia, Pa. 5'5.5", 140 lbs. Deb: 10/01/04																											
1904	Phi-N	7	19	2	2	0	0	0	1	4		.105	.261	.105	.366	17	-2	-1	93	183	1	.412	1			-0	/3	-0.1
■ **BILLY PURTELL**	Purtell, William Patrick b: 1/6/1886, Columbus, Ohio d: 3/17/62, Bradenton, Fla. BR/TR, 5'9", 170 lbs. Deb: 4/16/08																											
1908	Chi-A	26	69	3	9	2	0	0	3	2		.130	.155	.159	.314	4	-7	-7	94	102	2	.250	2			3	3	-0.2
1909	Chi-A	103	361	34	93	9	3	0	40	19		.258	.302	.299	.601	93	-4	-3	97	146	35	.541	14			-3	32	-0.4
1910	Chi-A	102	368	21	82	5	3	1	36	21		.223	.272	.261	.533	71	-14	-12	95	137	26	.441	5			-3	*3	-1.2
	Bos-A	49	168	15	35	1	2	1	15	18		.208	.289	.256	.545	71	-5	-5	99	123	12	.481	2			-2	3/S	-0.5
	Yr	151	536	36	117	6	5	2	51	39		.218	.278	.259	.537	71	-19	-17	96	133	39	.453	7			-5		-1.7
1911	Bos-A	27	82	5	23	5	3	0	7	1		.280	.298	.415	.712	99	-1	-1	99	70	10	.627	1			0	3/2SO	0.0
1914	Det-A	26	76	4	13	4	0	0	3	2	7	.171	.203	.224	.426	28	-7	-7	102	66	3	.308	0	2	-1	2	3/2S	-0.5
Total	5	333	1124	82	255	26	11	2	104	63	7	.227	.275	.275	.550	73	-39	-35	97	126	89	.467	24	2		-4	3/2SO	-2.8
■ **ED PUTMAN**	Putman, Eddy William b: 9/25/53, Los Angeles, Cal. BR/TR, 6'1", 190 lbs. Deb: 9/07/76																											
1976	Chi-N	5	7	0	3	0	0	0	0	0	0	.429	.429	.429	.857	132	0	0	109	0	0	.500	0	0	0	0	/C1	0.0
1978	Chi-N	17	25	2	5	0	0	0	3	4	6	.200	.310	.200	.510	41	-2	-2	110	238	2	.450	0	0	0	1	/31C	0.0
1979	Det-A	21	39	4	9	3	0	2	4	4	12	.231	.302	.462	.764	106	-0	0	96	64	5	.688	0	1	-1	0	C/1	0.0
Total	3	43	71	6	17	3	0	2	7	8	18	.239	.316	.366	.683	85	-1	-2	103	122	7	.607	0	1	-1	1	/C13	0.0
■ **PAT PUTNAM**	Putnam, Patrick Edward b: 12/3/53, Bethel, Vt. BL/TR, 6', 205 lbs. Deb: 9/02/77																											
1977	Tex-A	11	26	3	8	4	0	0	3	1	4	.308	.333	.462	.795	109	0	0	105	99	3	.650	0	1	-1	0	/1D	0.0
1978	Tex-A	20	46	4	7	1	0	1	2	2	5	.152	.188	.239	.427	20	-5	-5	96	56	2	.333	0	0	0	0	D/1	-0.4
1979	Tex-A	139	426	57	118	19	2	18	64	23	50	.277	.323	.458	.781	108	3	3	100	99	57	.690	1	6	-3	1	1D	-0.3
1980	Tex-A	147	410	42	108	16	2	13	55	36	49	.263	.323	.407	.730	98	-1	-1	100	104	51	.640	0	2	-1	-1	*1/3D	-1.2
1981	Tex-A	95	297	33	79	17	2	8	35	17	38	.266	.306	.418	.723	117	1	5	91	93	37	.647	4	2	0	1	1/O	0.3
1982	Tex-A	43	122	14	28	8	0	2	9	10	18	.230	.293	.344	.637	80	-4	-3	93	75	11	.535	0	2	-1	-2	1/3O	-0.7
1983	Sea-A	144	469	58	126	23	2	19	67	39	57	.269	.329	.448	.777	112	6	7	100	98	67	.713	2	1	0	4	*1D	0.5
1984	Sea-A	64	155	11	31	6	0	2	16	12	27	.200	.257	.277	.535	47	-11	-11	102	130	11	.450	3	0	1	-3	DO/1	-1.4
	Min-A	14	38	1	3	1	0	0	4	4	12	.079	.167	.105	.272	-22	-6	-7	106	399	1	.229	0	0	0	0	D	-0.6
	Yr	78	193	12	34	7	0	2	20	16	39	.176	.239	.244	.483	33	-17	-18	103	180	13	.415	3	0	1	-3		-2.0
Total	8	677	1989	223	508	95	8	63	255	144	260	.255	.309	.406	.715	97	-16	-12	98	105	241	.650	10	14	-5	0	1D/O3	-3.8
■ **JIM PYBURN**	Pyburn, James Edward b: 11/1/32, Fairfield, Ala. BR/TR, 6', 190 lbs. Deb: 4/17/55																											
1955	Bal-A	39	98	5	20	2	2	0	7	8	24	.204	.271	.265	.536	50	-8	-6	90	100	7	.439	1	1	-0	-3	3/O	-0.9
1956	Bal-A	84	156	23	27	3	3	2	11	17	26	.173	.254	.269	.524	41	-14	-13	94	86	11	.470	4	1	1	-6	O	-2.2
1957	Bal-A	35	40	8	9	0	0	1	2	9	6	.225	.367	.300	.667	91	-0	-0	93	53	5	.667	1	0	0	-1	O/C	-0.2
Total	3	158	294	36	56	5	5	3	20	34	56	.190	.277	.272	.549	51	-22	-20	93	85	23	.500	6	2	1	-11	O/3C	-3.3
■ **FRANKIE PYTLAK**	Pytlak, Frank Anthony b: 7/30/08, Buffalo, N.Y. d: 5/8/77, Buffalo, N.Y. BR/TR, 5'7.5", 160 lbs. Deb: 4/22/32																											
1932	Cle-A	12	29	5	7	1	1	0	4	3	2	.241	.333	.345	.678	70	-1	-1	108	134	4	.636	0	0	0	0	C	0.0
1933	Cle-A	80	248	36	77	10	6	2	33	17	10	.310	.355	.423	.778	101	2	-0	105	99	36	.714	3	4	-2	3	C	0.5
1934	Cle-A	91	289	46	75	12	4	0	35	36	11	.260	.352	.329	.680	76	-9	-9	101	123	37	.681	11	2	2	-3	C	-0.1
1935	Cle-A	55	149	14	44	6	1	1	12	11	4	.295	.348	.369	.717	86	-3	-3	99	70	19	.654	3	2	-0	-7	C	-0.7
1936	Cle-A	75	224	35	72	15	4	0	31	24	11	.321	.394	.424	.819	97	1	-1	106	106	39	.825	5	2	0	2	C	0.5
1937	Cle-A	125	397	60	125	15	6	1	44	52	15	.315	.404	.390	.794	104	3	5	98	95	68	.830	16	5	2	2	*C	1.6
1938	Cle-A	113	364	46	112	14	7	1	43	36	15	.308	.376	.393	.769	94	-3	-2	99	100	55	.747	9	5	-0	6	C	0.4
1939	Cle-A	63	183	20	49	2	5	0	14	20	5	.268	.343	.333	.676	75	-7	-6	98	77	22	.619	4	1	1	0	C	-0.1
1940	Cle-A	62	149	16	21	2	1	0	16	17	5	.141	.234	.168	.401	6	-21	-19	93	231	7	.326	0	1	-1	1	C/O	-1.4
1941	Bos-A	106	336	36	91	23	1	2	39	28	19	.271	.329	.363	.692	80	-9	-10	103	108	40	.605	5	7	-3	2	C	-0.4
1945	Bos-A	9	17	1	2	0	0	0	0	3	0	.118	.250	.118	.368	8	-2	-2	95	0	1	.333	0	0	0	-0	/C	-0.1
1946	Bos-A	4	14	1	2	0	0	0	1	0	0	.143	.143	.143	.286	-18	-2	-2	114	190	0	.167	0	0	0	-0	/C	-0.2
Total	12	795	2399	316	677	100	36	7	272	247	97	.282	.355	.363	.718	84	-51	-52	100	108	328	.684	56	29	-1	6	C/O	0.0
■ **TIM PYZNARSKI**	Pyznarski, Timothy Matthew b: 2/4/60, Chicago, Ill. BR/TR, 6'2", 195 lbs. Deb: 9/14/86																											
1986	SD-N	15	42	3	10	1	0	0	0	4	11	.238	.319	.262	.581	65	-2	-2	95	0	4	.529	2	0	1	-2	1	-0.2
■ **JIM QUALLS**	Qualls, James Robert b: 10/9/46, Exeter, Cal. BB/TR, 5'10", 158 lbs. Deb: 4/10/69																											
1969	Chi-N	43	120	12	30	5	3	0	9	2	14	.250	.268	.342	.610	65	-5	-6	107	88	11	.505	2	1	0	-1	O/2	-0.8
1970	Mon-N	9	9	1	1	0	0	0	1	0	0	.111	.111	.111	.222	-40	-2	-2	100	388	0	.125	0	0	0	-1	/2O	-0.1
1972	Chi-A	11	10	0	0	0	0	0	0	0	2	.000	.000	.000	.000	-94	-2	-2	106	0	0	.000	0	0	0	0	/O	-0.2
Total	3	63	139	13	31	5	3	0	10	2	16	.223	.239	.302	.542	48	-9	-10	106	101	11	.431	2	1	0	-2	/O2	-1.1
■ **MEL QUEEN**	Queen, Melvin Douglas b: 3/26/42, Johnson City, N.Y. BL/TR, 6'1", 189 lbs. Deb: 4/13/64 C																											
1964	Cin-N	48	95	7	19	2	0	2	12	4	19	.200	.232	.284	.517	43	-7	-7	103	149	5	.383	0	1	-1	1	O	-0.7
1965	Cin-N	5	3	0	0	0	0	0	0	0	1	.000	.000	.000	.000	-96	-1	-1	104	0	0	.000	0	0	0	-0	/O	0.0
1966	Cin-N	56	55	4	7	1	0	0	5	10	12	.127	.262	.145	.407	15	-6	-7	114	263	3	.367	0	0	0	-4	O/P	-1.1
1967	Cin-N	49	81	6	17	4	0	0	5	4	10	.210	.247	.259	.506	41	-6	-7	109	99	5	.403	2	0	1	-2	P	0.0
1968	Cin-N	10	8	2	1	0	0	0	0	1	3	.125	.222	.125	.347	6	-1	-1	111	0	0	.286	0	0	0	0	/P	0.0
1969	Cin-N	2	6	0	1	0	0	0	1	0	2	.167	.167	.167	.333	-6	-1	-1	99	401	0	.200	0	0	0	-0	/P	0.0
1970	Cal-A	37	16	1	4	0	0	0	1	0	2	.250	.250	.250	.500	42	-1	-1	92	101	1	.333	0	0	0	-1	P	0.0
1971	Cal-A	45	8	0	0	0	0	0	1	1	0	.000	.111	.000	.111	-67	-2	-2	99	0	0	.125	0	0	0	-1	P	0.0
1972	Cal-A	17	2	0	0	0	0	0	0	1	1	.000	.333	.000	.333	6	-0	-0	88	0	0	.500	0	0	0	-0	P	0.0
Total	9	269	274	20	49	7	0	2	25	21	50	.179	.237	.226	.464	30	-25	-27	106	150	15	.376	2	1	0	-7	P/O	-1.8
■ **BILLY QUEEN**	Queen, William Eddleman "Doc" b: 11/28/28, Gastonia, N.C. BR/TR, 6'1", 185 lbs. Deb: 4/13/54																											
1954	Mil-N	3	2	0	0	0	0	0	0	0	2	.000	.000	.000	.000	-99	-1	-1	93	0	0	.000	0	0	0	-0	/O	0.0
■ **GEORGE QUELLICH**	Quellich, George William b: 2/10/06, Johnsville, Cal. d: 8/31/58, Johnsville, Cal. BR/TR, 6'1", 180 lbs. Deb: 8/01/31																											
1931	Det-A	13	54	6	12	5	0	1	11	3	4	.222	.263	.370	.634	63	-3	-3	104	167	5	.571	1	0	0	1	O	-0.2
■ **JOE QUEST**	Quest, Joseph L. b: 1852, New Castle, Pa. BR/TR, 5'6", 150 lbs. Deb: 8/30/1871																											
1871	Cle-n	3	16	1	3							.188															/2S	
1878	Ind-N	62	278	45	57	3	2	0	13	12	24	.205	.238	.230	.468	63	-13	-8	87	59	16	.344				-1	*2	-0.3
1879	Chi-N	83	334	38	69	16	1	0	22	9	33	.207	.227	.260	.488	58	-14	-16	105	91	20	.362				27	*2	1.7
1880	Chi-N	82	300	37	71	12	1	0	27	8	16	.237	.256	.283	.540	79	-5	-7	105	118	22	.406				1	*2/S3	-0.2
1881	Chi-N	78	293	35	72	6	0	1	26	2	29	.246	.251	.276	.527	60	-12	-15	108	108	21	.376				3	*2/S	-0.8

YEAR	TM/L	G	AB	R	H	2B	3B	HR	RBI	BB	SO	AVG	OBP	SLG	PRO	/A	BR	/A	PF	CHI	RC	TA	SB	CS	SBR	FR	POS	TPR
1882	Chi-N	42	159	24	32	5	2	0	15	8	16	.201	.240	.258	.497	59	-7	-7	101	123	10	.386				-5	2/S	-0.9
1883	Det-N	37	137	22	32	8	2	0	25	10	18	.234	.286	.321	.607	92	-2	-0	91	201	13	.514				-2	2	-0.3
	StL-a	19	78	12	20	3	1	0		1		.256	.266	.321	.586	81	-1	-2	108	0	7	.448				0	2	-0.1
1884	StL-a	81	310	46	64	9	5	0		19		.206	.257	.268	.525	67	-8	-13	110	0	22	.423				-11	*2	-1.9
	Pit-a	12	43	2	9	3	0	0		0		.209	.227	.279	.506	69	-2	-1	97	0	3	.382				1	/2S	0.0
	Yr	93	353	48	73	12	5	0		19		.207	.253	.269	.522	67	-10	-14	108	0	25	.418				-10		-1.9
1885	Det-N	55	200	24	39	8	2	0	21	14	25	.195	.248	.255	.503	64	-8	-7	97	146	13	.404				-1	2S/O	-0.3
1886	Phi-a	42	150	14	31	4	1	0		20		.207	.300	.247	.547	74	-4	-4	100	0	13	.521	5			1	S/2	0.0
Total	9	593	2282	299	496	77	17	1	149	103	161	.217	.252	.267	.519	68	-75	-80	102	83	159	.404	5			13	2/SO3	-3.1

■ **HAL QUICK** Quick, James Harold "Blondie" b: 10/4/17, Rome, Ga. d: 3/9/74, Swansea, Ill. BR/TR, 5'10.5", 163 lbs. Deb: 9/07/39

YEAR	TM/L	G	AB	R	H	2B	3B	HR	RBI	BB	SO	AVG	OBP	SLG	PRO	/A	BR	/A	PF	CHI	RC	TA	SB	CS	SBR	FR	POS	TPR
1939	Was-A	12	41	3	10	1	0	0	2	1	1	.244	.279	.268	.547	45	-4	-3	90	61	3	.424	1	0	0	-0	S	-0.1

■ **FRANK QUILICI** Quilici, Francis Ralph "Guido" b: 5/11/39, Chicago, Ill. BR/TR, 6'1", 170 lbs. Deb: 7/18/65 MC

YEAR	TM/L	G	AB	R	H	2B	3B	HR	RBI	BB	SO	AVG	OBP	SLG	PRO	/A	BR	/A	PF	CHI	RC	TA	SB	CS	SBR	FR	POS	TPR
1965	Min-A	56	149	16	31	5	1	0	7	15	33	.208	.280	.255	.536	53	-9	-9	101	76	11	.439	1	1	-0	-1	2/S	-0.7
1967	Min-A	23	19	2	2	1	0	0	0	3	4	.105	.227	.158	.385	15	-2	-2	107	0	1	.333	0	0	0	-0	2/3S	-0.1
1968	Min-A	97	229	22	56	11	4	1	22	21	45	.245	.311	.341	.651	92	-1	-2	106	116	25	.562	0	0	0	2	23/S1	0.3
1969	Min-A	118	144	19	25	3	1	2	12	12	22	.174	.237	.250	.487	36	-12	-13	102	115	9	.413	2	0	1	-0	32/S	-0.9
1970	Min-A	111	141	19	32	3	0	2	12	15	16	.227	.301	.291	.592	65	-7	-6	98	103	11	.479	0	2	-1	-5	23/S	-0.5
Total	5	405	682	78	146	23	6	5	53	66	120	.214	.284	.287	.572	63	-31	-33	103	101	57	.488	3	3	-1	-5	23/S1	-1.9

■ **LEE QUILLEN** Quillen, Leon Abner b: 5/5/1882, North Branch, Minn. d: 5/14/65, St.Paul, Minn. TR , 5'10", 165 lbs. Deb: 9/30/06

YEAR	TM/L	G	AB	R	H	2B	3B	HR	RBI	BB	SO	AVG	OBP	SLG	PRO	/A	BR	/A	PF	CHI	RC	TA	SB	CS	SBR	FR	POS	TPR
1906	Chi-A	4	9	1	3	0	0	0	0	0		.333	.333	.333	.667	121	0	0	92	0	1	.667	1			0	/S	0.0
1907	Chi-A	49	151	17	29	5	0	0	14	10		.192	.242	.225	.467	49	-8	-9	104	147	10	.426	8			2	3	-0.4
Total	2	53	160	18	32	5	0	0	14	10		.200	.247	.231	.478	52	-8	-9	103	139	12	.438	9			2	/3S	-0.4

■ **QUINLAN** Quinlan Deb:9/07/1874

YEAR	TM/L	G	AB	R	H	2B	3B	HR	RBI	BB	SO	AVG	OBP	SLG	PRO	/A	BR	/A	PF	CHI	RC	TA	SB	CS	SBR	FR	POS	TPR
1874	Phi-n	1	4	0	0							.000															S	

■ **FRANK QUINLAN** Quinlan, Francis Patrick b: 3/9/1869, Marlboro, Mass. d: 5/4/04, Brockton, Mass. Deb: 10/05/1891

YEAR	TM/L	G	AB	R	H	2B	3B	HR	RBI	BB	SO	AVG	OBP	SLG	PRO	/A	BR	/A	PF	CHI	RC	TA	SB	CS	SBR	FR	POS	TPR
1891	Bos-a	2	5	0	0	0	0	0	0	0	2	.000	.000	.000	.000	-99	-1	-1	99	0	0	.000	0			0	/CO	0.0

■ **FINNERS QUINLAN** Quinlan, Thomas Finners b: 10/21/1887, Scranton, Pa. d: 2/17/66, Scranton, Pa. BL/TL, 5'8", 154 lbs. Deb: 9/06/13

YEAR	TM/L	G	AB	R	H	2B	3B	HR	RBI	BB	SO	AVG	OBP	SLG	PRO	/A	BR	/A	PF	CHI	RC	TA	SB	CS	SBR	FR	POS	TPR
1913	StL-N	13	50	1	8	0	0	0	1	1	9	.160	.176	.160	.336	-4	-7	-6	93	46	1	.214	0			1	O	-0.5
1915	Chi-A	42	114	11	22	3	0	0	7	4	11	.193	.270	.219	.489	48	-7	-7	98	95	7	.417	3	4	-2	-1	O	-1.2
Total	2	55	164	12	30	3	0	0	8	5	20	.183	.243	.201	.444	32	-14	-13	96	81	9	.355	3	4		-0	/O	-1.7

■ **FRANK QUINN** Quinn, Frank J. b: 1876, Grand Rapids, Mich. d: 2/17/20, Camden, Ind. 5'8", Deb: 8/09/1899

YEAR	TM/L	G	AB	R	H	2B	3B	HR	RBI	BB	SO	AVG	OBP	SLG	PRO	/A	BR	/A	PF	CHI	RC	TA	SB	CS	SBR	FR	POS	TPR
1899	Chi-N	12	34	6	6	0	1	0	1	6		.176	.300	.235	.535	52	-2	-2	96	38	3	.536	1			0	O/2	-0.1

■ **JOHN QUINN** Quinn, John Edward "Pick" b: 9/12/1885, Framingham, Mass. d: 4/9/56, Marlboro, Mass. BR/TR, 5'11", 150 lbs. Deb: 10/09/11

YEAR	TM/L	G	AB	R	H	2B	3B	HR	RBI	BB	SO	AVG	OBP	SLG	PRO	/A	BR	/A	PF	CHI	RC	TA	SB	CS	SBR	FR	POS	TPR
1911	Phi-N	1	2	0	0	0	0	0	0	0	0	.000	.000	.000	.000	-93	-1	-1	108	0	0	.000	0			0	/C	0.0

■ **JOE QUINN** Quinn, Joseph C. b: 1851, Chicago, Ill. d: 1/2/09, Chicago, Ill. 5'8.5", 148 lbs. Deb: 7/26/1871

YEAR	TM/L	G	AB	R	H	2B	3B	HR	RBI	BB	SO	AVG	OBP	SLG	PRO	/A	BR	/A	PF	CHI	RC	TA	SB	CS	SBR	FR	POS	TPR
1871	Kek-n	5	21	8	4							.190															/C	
1875	Wes-n	11	47	6	14							.298															/CO	
	Har-n	3	10	0	1							.100															/CO	
	Chi-n	17	67	10	13							.194															C/O	
	Yr	31	124	16	28							.226																
1881	Bos-N	1	4	0	0	0	0	0	0	0	0	.000	.000	.000	.000	-99	-1	-1	91	0	0	.000				0	/1	0.0
	Wor-N	2	7	0	1	0	0	0	1	1	2	.143	.250	.143	.393	25	-1	-1	105	354	0	.333				0	/C	0.0
	Yr	3	11	0	1	0	0	0	1	1	2	.091	.167	.091	.258	-17	-1	-1	100	236	0	.200				0		0.0
Total	2 n	36	145	24	32							.221															/C	

■ **JOE QUINN** Quinn, Joseph J. b: 12/25/1864, Sydney, Australia d: 11/12/40, St.Louis, Mo. BR/TR, 5'7", 158 lbs. Deb: 4/26/1884 M

YEAR	TM/L	G	AB	R	H	2B	3B	HR	RBI	BB	SO	AVG	OBP	SLG	PRO	/A	BR	/A	PF	CHI	RC	TA	SB	CS	SBR	FR	POS	TPR
1884	StL-U	103	429	74	116	21	1	0		9		.270	.285	.324	.609	102	2	-0	104	0	41	.473	0			-0	*1/OS	-0.1
1885	StL-N	97	343	27	73	8	2	0	15	9	38	.213	.233	.248	.481	60	-17	-13	92	63	20	.348				-12	O31	-2.4
1886	StL-N	75	271	33	63	11	3	1	21	8	31	.232	.254	.306	.561	74	-10	-8	95	81	25	.495	12			5	O2/13S	-0.1
1888	Bos-N	38	156	19	47	8	3	4	29	2	5	.301	.310	.468	.778	139	7	6	106	129	27	.798	12			-6	2	0.2
1889	Bos-N	112	444	57	116	13	5	2	69	25	21	.261	.308	.327	.635	77	-13	-14	102	**144**	53	.607	24			-31	S2/3	-3.3
1890	Bos-P	130	509	87	153	19	8	7	82	44	24	.301	.359	.411	.769	100	4	-2	107	100	87	.798	29			13	*2	1.4
1891	Bos-N	124	508	70	122	8	10	3	63	28	28	.240	.288	.313	.601	69	-16	-25	112	116	54	.562	24			-24	*2	-4.0
1892	Bos-N	143	532	63	116	14	1	1	59	35	40	.218	.275	.254	.529	55	-24	-34	113	134	43	.466	17			1	*2	-2.9
1893	StL-N	135	547	68	126	18	6	0	71	33	7	.230	.279	.285	.564	52	-38	-37	99	127	51	.515	24			-32	*2	-5.8
1894	StL-N	106	405	59	116	18	1	4	61	24	8	.286	.328	.365	.693	68	-21	-22	101	107	58	.685	25			21	*2	0.4
1895	StL-N	134	543	84	169	19	9	2	74	36	6	.311	.356	.390	.747	95	-4	-4	100	101	85	.727	22			-5	*2M	0.0
1896	StL-N	48	191	19	40	6	1	1	17	9	5	.209	.252	.267	.519	40	-17	-15	95	96	15	.464	8			1	2	-1.0
	Bal-N	24	82	22	27	1	1	0	5	6	1	.329	.375	.366	.741	96	-0	-0	102	48	14	.764	6			-2	/2O3S	-0.1
	Yr	72	273	41	67	7	2	1	22	15	6	.245	.290	.297	.586	58	-17	-16	97	81	28	.544	14			-1		-1.1
1897	Bal-N	75	285	33	74	11	4	1	45	13		.260	.299	.337	.636	73	-13	-10	95	136	33	.588	12			3	3S2/O1	-0.6
1898	Bal-N	12	32	5	8	1	0	0	5	1		.250	.273	.281	.554	59	-2	-2	103	168	3	.417	0			0	/32O	-0.1
	StL-N	103	375	35	94	10	5	0	36	24		.251	.301	.304	.605	72	-12	-15	106	97	39	.548	13			-7	2S/O	-1.5
	Yr	115	407	40	102	11	5	0	41	25		.251	.299	.302	.601	71	-13	-16	105	106	42	.538	13			-7		-1.6
1899	Cle-N	147	615	73	176	24	6	0	72	21		.286	.312	.345	.657	92	-16	-6	89	92	75	.585	22			-3	*2M	0.0
1900	StL-N	22	80	12	21	2	0	1	11	10		.262	.344	.325	.669	94	-1	-0	93	125	11	.678	4			-6	2/S3	-0.4
	Cin-N	74	266	18	73	5	2	0	25	16		.274	.316	.308	.624	81	-9	-6	92	97	29	.544	7			-23	2	-2.2
	Yr	96	346	30	94	7	2	1	36	26		.272	.323	.312	.635	84	-10	-6	92	105	39	.575	11			-28		-2.6
1901	Was-A	66	266	33	67	11	2	2	34	11		.252	.282	.331	.612	72	-11	-10	99	121	27	.533	7			-3	2	-1.4
Total	17	1768	6879	891	1797	228	70	29	794	364	214	.261	.302	.327	.629	77	-208	-217	101	103	791	.575	268			-109	*2SO1/3	-23.9

■ **PADDY QUINN** Quinn, Patrick b: Boston, Mass. d: 3/18/ 1893 Deb: 9/09/1875

YEAR	TM/L	G	AB	R	H	2B	3B	HR	RBI	BB	SO	AVG	OBP	SLG	PRO	/A	BR	/A	PF	CHI	RC	TA	SB	CS	SBR	FR	POS	TPR
1875	Atl-n	2	8	2	1							.125															/O	
1877	Chi-N	4	14	1	1	0	0	0	0	1	0	.071	.133	.071	.205	-34	-2	-2	98	0	0	.154				0	/O	-0.1

■ **TOM QUINN** Quinn, Thomas Oscar b: 4/25/1864, Annapolis, Md. d: 7/24/32, Pittsburgh, Pa. BR/TR, 5'8", 180 lbs. Deb: 9/02/1886

YEAR	TM/L	G	AB	R	H	2B	3B	HR	RBI	BB	SO	AVG	OBP	SLG	PRO	/A	BR	/A	PF	CHI	RC	TA	SB	CS	SBR	FR	POS	TPR
1886	Pit-a	3	11	1	0	0	0	0		0		.000	.000	.000	.000	-99	-2	-2	93	0	0	.091	1			0	/C	-0.1
1889	Bal-a	55	194	18	34	2	1	1	15	19	22	.175	.252	.211	.464	34	-16	-16	100	99	12	.419	6			5	C	-0.4
1890	Pit-P	55	207	23	44	4	3	1	15	17	8	.213	.282	.275	.557	55	-14	-11	92	70	17	.479	1			-4	C	-0.9
Total	3	113	412	42	78	6	4	2	30	36	30	.189	.261	.238	.499	42	-33	-30	96	82	29	.437	8			2	C	-1.4

■ **LUIS QUINONES** Quinones, Luis Raul b: 4/28/62, Ponce, P.R. BB/TR, 5'11", 165 lbs. Deb: 5/27/83

YEAR	TM/L	G	AB	R	H	2B	3B	HR	RBI	BB	SO	AVG	OBP	SLG	PRO	/A	BR	/A	PF	CHI	RC	TA	SB	CS	SBR	FR	POS	TPR
1983	Oak-A	19	42	5	8	2	1	0	4	1	4	.190	.209	.286	.495	36	-4	-4	96	130	2	.400	1	1	-0	-3	/23OSD	-0.5
1986	SF-N	71	106	13	19	1	3	0	11	3	17	.179	.209	.245	.454	26	-11	-10	96	169	6	.371	3	1	0	-1	S3/2	-0.8
1987	Chi-N	49	101	12	22	6	0	0	8	10	16	.218	.288	.277	.566	50	-7	-7	101	114	9	.481	0	0	0	1	S/23	-0.2
1988	Cin-N	23	52	4	12	3	0	1	11	2	11	.231	.259	.346	.605	69	-2	-2	105	209	5	.512	1	1	-0	1	/S23	0.0
Total	4	162	301	34	61	12	4	1	34	16	48	.203	.245	.279	.524	44	-24	-23	99	151	22	.436	5	3	-0	-1	/S32DO	-1.5

■ **REY QUINONES** Quinones, Rey Francisco (Santiago) b: 11/11/63, Rio Pedras, P.R. BR/TR, 5'11", 160 lbs. Deb: 5/17/86

YEAR	TM/L	G	AB	R	H	2B	3B	HR	RBI	BB	SO	AVG	OBP	SLG	PRO	/A	BR	/A	PF	CHI	RC	TA	SB	CS	SBR	FR	POS	TPR
1986	Bos-A	62	190	26	45	12	1	2	15	19	26	.237	.316	.342	.658	81	-5	-5	100	84	20	.584	3	2	-0	-6	S	-0.7
	Sea-A	36	122	6	23	4	0	0	7	5	31	.189	.220	.221	.442	20	-13	-14	105	103	6	.330	1	1	-0	8	S	-0.3
	Yr	98	312	32	68	16	1	2	22	24	57	.218	.280	.295	.575	57	-18	-19	102	92	28	.498	4	3	-1	2		-1.0

YEAR	TM/L	G	AB	R	H	2B	3B	HR	RBI	BB	SO	AVG	OBP	SLG	PRO	/A	BR	/A	PF	CHI	RC	TA	SB	CS	SBR	FR	POS	TPR
1987	Sea-A	135	478	55	132	18	2	12	56	26	71	.276	.319	.397	.716	87	-7	-9	103	101	57	.609	1	3	-2	-0	*S	-0.4
1988	Sea-A	140	499	63	124	30	3	12	52	23	71	.248	.286	.393	.678	82	-9	-14	108	91	52	.569	0	3	-2	-0	*S/D	-0.9
Total	3	373	1289	150	324	64	6	26	130	73	199	.251	.297	.371	.667	78	-35	-42	104	95	135	.574	5	9	-4	1	S/D	-2.3
■ **CARLOS QUINTANA**	Quintana, Carlos Narcis b: 8/26/65, Estado Miranda, Ven BR/TR, 6', 175 lbs. Deb: 9/16/88																											
1988	Bos-A	5	6	1	2	0	0	0	2	2	3	.333	.500	.333	.833	127	1	0	109	398	1	1.000	0	0	0	-0	/OD	0.0
■ **MARSHALL QUINTON**	Quinton, Marshall J. b: Philadelphia, Pa. 5'11", 190 lbs. Deb: 8/07/1884																											
1884	Ric-a	26	94	12	22	5	0	0		0		.234	.242	.287	.529	75	-3	-2	99	0	7	.389				0	CO/S	-0.1
1885	Phi-a	7	29	6	6	1	0	0		1		.207	.258	.241	.499	59	-1	-1	103	0	2	.391				0	/C	0.0
Total	2	33	123	18	28	6	0	0		1		.228	.246	.276	.522	71	-4	-4	100	0	9	.389				0	/COS	-0.1
■ **JAMIE QUIRK**	Quirk, James Patrick b: 10/22/54, Whittier, Cal. BL/TR, 6'4", 190 lbs. Deb: 9/04/75 C																											
1975	KC-A	14	39	2	10	0	0	1	5	2	7	.256	.293	.333	.626	75	-1	-1	102	120	4	.500	0	0	0	-0	O/3D	-0.1
1976	KC-A	64	114	11	28	6	0	1	15	2	22	.246	.259	.325	.583	70	-5	-5	100	144	8	.429	0	0	0	0	DS3/1	-0.3
1977	Mil-A	93	221	16	48	14	1	3	13	8	47	.217	.251	.330	.581	60	-14	-12	95	63	17	.466	0	1	-1	0	DO/3	-1.2
1978	KC-A	17	29	3	6	2	0	0	2	5	4	.207	.324	.276	.599	69	-1	-1	102	99	3	.565	0	0	0	0	3/SD	0.0
1979	KC-A	51	79	8	24	6	1	1	11	5	13	.304	.353	.443	.796	107	1	1	105	111	13	.745	0	0	0	0	/CS3D	0.2
1980	KC-A	62	163	13	45	5	0	5	21	7	24	.276	.310	.399	.709	94	-2	-2	98	102	18	.598	3	2	-0	-1	3C/O1D	-0.1
1981	KC-A	46	100	8	25	7	0	0	10	6	17	.250	.299	.320	.619	79	-3	-3	99	122	8	.476	0	2	-1	-2	C/32O	-0.4
1982	KC-A	36	78	8	18	3	0	1	5	3	15	.231	.259	.308	.567	55	-5	-5	100	74	6	.435	0	0	0	-2	C/13O	-0.5
1983	StL-N	48	86	3	18	2	1	2	11	6	27	.209	.269	.326	.594	65	-4	-4	98	128	7	.500	0	0	0	-0	C/3S	-0.3
1984	Chi-A	3	2	0	0	0	0	0	1	0	2	.000	.000	.000	.000	-90	-1	-1	111	0	0	.000	0	0	0	-0	/3	0.0
	Cle-A	1	1	1	1	0	0	1	1	0	0	1.000	1.000	4.000	5.000	1142	1	1	106	57	4	—	0	0	0	0	/C	0.1
	Yr	4	3	1	1	0	0	1	2	0	2	.333	.333	1.333	1.667	308	1	1	109	14	1	2.000	0	0	0	-0		0.1
1985	KC-A	19	57	3	16	3	1	0	4	2	9	.281	.305	.368	.674	82	-1	-1	102	76	6	.548	0	0	0	1	C/1	0.0
1986	KC-A	80	219	24	47	10	0	8	26	17	41	.215	.274	.370	.644	74	-8	-8	100	99	22	.559	0	1	-1	5	C3/1O	-0.2
1987	KC-A	109	296	24	70	17	0	5	33	28	56	.236	.311	.345	.656	72	-10	-12	104	113	32	.577	1	0	0	-1	*C/S	-0.3
1988	KC-A	84	196	22	47	7	1	8	25	28	41	.240	.338	.408	.746	105	2	2	103	96	27	.705	1	5	-3	-6	C/13	-0.3
Total	14	727	1680	146	403	82	5	36	183	119	325	.240	.295	.359	.654	79	-50	-51	101	101	175	.573	5	11	-5	-5	C3/DOS12	-3.4
■ **JOHN RABB**	Rabb, John Andrew b: 6/23/60, Los Angeles, Cal. BR/TR, 6'1", 180 lbs. Deb: 9/04/82																											
1982	SF-N	2	2	0	1	0	1	0	0	0	1	.500	.500	1.500	2.000	470	1	1	94	0	2	3.000	0	0	0	-0	/O	0.1
1983	SF-N	40	104	10	24	9	0	1	14	9	17	.231	.292	.346	.638	76	-3	-4	101	142	10	.548	1	0	0	2	C/O	0.0
1984	SF-N	54	82	10	16	1	0	3	9	10	33	.195	.283	.317	.600	71	-3	-3	96	101	8	.552	1	1	-0	-1	1/OC	-0.4
1985	Atl-N	3	2	0	0	0	0	0	0	0	1	.000	.000	.000	.000	-94	-1	-1	106	0	0	.000	0	0	0	-0	/O	0.0
1988	Sea-A	9	14	2	5	2	0	0	4	0	1	.357	.357	.500	.857	128	1	0	108	227	3	.778	0	0	0	0	/O1D	0.1
Total	5	108	204	22	46	12	1	4	27	19	53	.225	.291	.353	.644	79	-6	-6	99	128	22	.585	2	1	0	1	/C1OD	-0.2
■ **JOE RABBITT**	Rabbitt, Joseph Patrick b: 1/16/1900, Frontenac, Kan. d: 12/5/69, Norwalk, Conn. BL/TR, 5'10", 165 lbs. Deb: 9/15/22																											
1922	Cle-A	2	3	1	1	0	0	0	0	0	0	.333	.333	.333	.667	73	-0	-0	102	0	0	.500	0	0	0	-0	/O	0.0
■ **MARV RACKLEY**	Rackley, Marvin Eugene b: 7/25/21, Seneca, S.C. BL/TL, 5'10", 170 lbs. Deb: 4/15/47																											
1947	Bro-N	18	9	2	2	0	0	0	2	1	0	.222	.300	.222	.522	39	-1	-1	105	370	1	.429	0			0	/O	0.0
1948	Bro-N	88	281	55	92	13	5	0	15	19	25	.327	.370	.409	.779	106	4	3	104	49	44	.747	8			-2	O	-0.4
1949	Bro-N	9	9	2	4	1	0	0	1	1	0	.444	.500	.556	1.056	180	1	1	102	75	3	1.200	0			-1	/O	0.0
	Pit-N	11	35	5	11	2	0	0	2	2	3	.314	.351	.371	.723	93	-0	-0	101	58	5	.667	1			1	/O	0.0
	Bro-N	54	141	23	41	4	1	1	14	13	8	.291	.351	.355	.705	88	-2	-2	102	100	18	.627	1			-7	O	-1.0
	Yr	74	185	30	56	7	1	1	17	16	11	.303	.358	.368	.726	94	-1	-1	101	92	25	.656	2			-7		-1.0
1950	Cin-N	5	2	0	1	0	0	0	1	0	0	.500	.500	.500	1.000	157	0	0	105	386	1	1.000	0			0	H	0.0
Total	4	185	477	87	151	20	6	1	35	36	36	.317	.365	.390	.754	100	3	1	103	73	71	.712	10			-9	O	-1.4
■ **CHARLEY RADBOURN**	Radbourn, Charles Gardner "Old Hoss" b: 12/11/1854, Rochester, N.Y. d: 2/5/1897, Bloomington, Ill. BR/TR, 5'9", 168 lbs. Deb: 5/05/1880 H																											
1880	Buf-N	6	21	1	3	0	0	0	1	0	1	.143	.143	.143	.286	-3	-2	-2	91	122	0	.167				0	/O2	-0.1
1881	Pro-N	72	270	27	59	9	0	0	28	10	15	.219	.246	.252	.498	61	-13	-10	93	146	17	.370				-3	POS	0.0
1882	Pro-N	83	326	30	78	11	0	1	32	12	22	.239	.266	.282	.548	72	-8	-11	106	116	25	.419				-1	PO/S	0.0
1883	Pro-N	89	381	59	108	11	3	3	48	14	16	.283	.309	.352	.661	100	0	-0	101	123	42	.542				6	*PO/1	0.0
1884	Pro-N	87	361	48	83	7	1	1	37	26	42	.230	.282	.263	.545	71	-11	-11	102	125	27	.435				-3	*P/O1S2	0.0
1885	Pro-N	66	249	34	58	9	2	0	22	36	27	.233	.330	.285	.615	110	2	5	91	95	24	.560				3	PO/2	0.0
1886	Bos-N	66	253	30	60	5	1	2	22	17	36	.237	.285	.289	.574	77	-7	-6	97	96	23	.492	5			2	P	0.0
1887	Bos-N	51	175	25	40	2	2	1	24	18	21	.229	.308	.280	.588	68	-7	-7	98	142	17	.556	6			-4	P/O	0.0
1888	Bos-N	24	79	6	17	1	0	0	6	3	14	.215	.262	.228	.490	56	-3	-4	106	119	6	.435	4			0	P	0.0
1889	Bos-N	35	122	17	23	1	0	1	13	9	19	.189	.256	.221	.477	34	-10	-11	102	129	8	.414	3			0	P/O3	0.0
1890	Bos-P	45	154	20	39	6	0	0	16	9	20	.253	.299	.292	.591	56	-9	-11	107	97	16	.539	7			4	P/O1	0.0
1891	Cin-N	29	96	11	17	2	2	0	10	4	11	.177	.225	.240	.465	40	-8	-6	91	127	6	.380	1			0	P/O3	0.0
Total	12	653	2487	308	585	64	11	9	259	158	244	.235	.283	.281	.564	73	-77	-75	99	119	212	.468	26			4	PO/S123D	-0.1
■ **JOHN RADCLIFF**	Radcliff, John J. b: 1846, Camden, N.J. d: 7/26/11, Ocean City, N.J. 5'6", 140 lbs. Deb: 5/20/1871																											
1871	Ath-n	28	153	47	40							.261															*S	
1872	Bal-n	54	293	71	83							.283															*S/32	
1873	Bal-n	44	246	57	69							.280															S3	
1874	Phi-n	23	102	19	21							.206															O/2S13	
1875	Cen-n	5	25	2	4							.160															/S	
Total	5 n	154	819	196	217							.265															/S	
■ **RIP RADCLIFF**	Radcliff, Raymond Allen b: 1/19/06, Kiowa, Okla. d: 5/23/62, Enid, Okla. BL/TL, 5'10", 170 lbs. Deb: 9/17/34																											
1934	Chi-A	14	56	7	15	2	1	0	5	0	2	.268	.268	.339	.607	56	-4	-4	99	90	5	.488	1	0	0	0	O	-0.3
1935	Chi-A	146	623	95	178	28	8	10	68	53	21	.286	.346	.404	.750	86	-7	-15	109	72	88	.697	4	4	-1	-16	*O	-3.1
1936	Chi-A	138	618	120	207	31	7	8	82	44	12	.335	.381	.447	.828	104	3	4	99	78	105	.792	6	3	0	-21	*O	-1.7
1937	Chi-A	144	584	105	190	38	10	4	79	53	25	.325	.383	.445	.829	105	8	5	103	96	102	.813	6	1	1	-4	*O	-0.2
1938	Chi-A	129	503	64	166	23	6	5	81	36	17	.330	.376	.429	.805	104	1	3	98	126	80	.750	5	7	-3	0	O1	-0.2
1939	Chi-A	113	397	49	105	25	2	2	53	26	21	.264	.313	.353	.666	66	-19	-22	107	123	44	.578	6	4	-1	-14	O1	-3.8
1940	StL-A	150	584	83	**200**	33	9	7	81	47	20	.342	.392	.466	.858	115	19	14	106	106	109	.817	6	4	-1	-6	*O/1	-0.2
1941	StL-A	19	71	12	20	2	2	2	14	10	1	.282	.370	.451	.821	116	2	2	100	133	12	.811	1	1	-0	-2	O/1	-0.1
	Det-A	96	379	47	120	14	5	3	40	19	13	.317	.351	.404	.755	93	-1	-4	106	89	53	.656	4	4	-1	-6	O	-1.5
	Yr	115	450	59	140	16	7	5	54	29	14	.311	.354	.411	.765	97	1	-2	105	98	66	.683	5	5	-2	-8		-1.6
1942	Det-A	62	144	13	36	5	0	1	20	9	6	.250	.294	.306	.600	61	-6	-8	113	150	13	.473	0	1	-1	-2	O/1	-1.2
1943	Det-A	70	115	3	30	4	0	0	10	13	3	.261	.341	.296	.637	82	-1	-2	106	107	12	.551	1	1	-0	-1	O/1	-0.3
Total	10	1081	4074	598	1267	205	50	42	533	310	141	.311	.362	.417	.779	96	-5	-28	104	99	623	.726	40	30	-6	-72	O/1	-12.6
■ **DAVE RADER**	Rader, David Martin b: 12/26/48, Claremore, Okla. BL/TR, 5'11", 165 lbs. Deb: 9/05/71																											
1971	SF-N	3	4	0	0	0	0	0	0	0	0	.000	.000	.000	.000	-99	-1	-1	100	0	0	.000	0	0	0	0	/C	0.0
1972	SF-N	133	459	44	119	14	1	6	41	29	31	.259	.308	.333	.641	82	-11	-11	100	99	45	.525	1	2	-1	-0	*C	-0.4
1973	SF-N	148	462	59	106	15	4	9	41	63	22	.229	.330	.338	.667	81	-8	-11	105	90	51	.603	0	0	0	-12	*C	-1.4
1974	SF-N	113	323	26	94	16	2	1	26	31	21	.291	.353	.362	.715	93	1	-3	108	84	41	.626	1	0	0	-7	*C	-0.4
1975	SF-N	98	292	39	85	15	0	5	31	32	30	.291	.363	.394	.757	108	4	4	102	92	41	.690	1	0	0	-4	C	0.3
1976	SF-N	88	255	25	67	15	0	1	22	27	21	.263	.333	.333	.667	87	-3	-4	103	96	27	.570	2	0	1	-8	C	-0.7
1977	StL-N	66	114	15	30	7	1	1	16	9	10	.263	.317	.368	.685	87	-3	-2	96	142	15	.619	1	0	0	0	C	-0.1
1978	Chi-N	116	305	29	62	13	3	3	36	34	26	.203	.285	.295	.580	57	-15	-19	110	144	24	.490	1	1	-0	-16	*C	-3.4

YEAR	TM/L	G	AB	R	H	2B	3B	HR	RBI	BB	SO	AVG	OBP	SLG	PRO	/A	BR	/A	PF	CHI	RC	TA	SB	CS	SBR	FR	POS	TPR
1979	Phi-N	31	54	3	11	1	1	1	5	6	7	.204	.283	.315	.598	65	-3	-3	97	99	4	.500	0	0	0	-0	C	-0.1
1980	Bos-A	50	137	14	45	11	0	3	17	14	12	.328	.391	.474	.865	133	7	7	102	90	25	.825	1	1	-0	3	C/D	1.1
Total	10	846	2405	254	619	107	12	30	235	245	180	.257	.329	.349	.678	86	-32	-43	104	101	272	.615	8	4	0	-44	C/D	-5.1
■ **DON RADER**	Rader, Donald Russell b: 9/5/1893, Wolcott, Ind. d: 6/26/83, Walla Walla, Wash BL/TR, 5'10", 164 lbs. Deb: 7/25/13																											
1913	Chi-A	4	3	1	1	0	0	0	0	0	0	.333	.333	.667	1.000	201	0	0	95	0	1	1.000	0			0	/3O	0.0
1921	Phi-N	9	32	4	9	2	0	0	3	3	5	.281	.343	.344	.687	81	-1	-1	102	102	4	.609	0	0	0	0	/S	0.0
Total	2	13	35	5	10	2	0	0	3	3	5	.286	.342	.371	.714	89	-0	-1	101	94	5	.640	0	0		0	/SO3	0.0
■ **DOUG RADER**	Rader, Douglas Lee "Rojo" or "The Red Rooster" b: 7/30/44, Chicago, Ill. BR/TR, 6'2", 208 lbs. Deb: 7/31/67 MC																											
1967	Hou-N	47	162	24	54	10	4	2	26	7	31	.333	.368	.481	.850	151	8	9	94	128	27	.763	0	3	-2	-1	1/3	0.5
1968	Hou-N	98	333	42	89	16	4	6	43	31	51	.267	.332	.393	.725	118	7	7	99	124	43	.650	2	2	-1	1	3/1	0.8
1969	Hou-N	155	569	62	140	25	3	11	83	62	103	.246	.327	.359	.685	90	-6	-7	102	143	65	.605	1	5	-3	13	*3/1	0.5
1970	Hou-N	156	576	90	145	25	3	25	87	57	102	.252	.323	.436	.759	108	-0	5	94	106	76	.691	3	2	-0	22	*3/1	2.1
1971	Hou-N	135	484	51	118	21	4	12	56	40	112	.244	.306	.378	.684	100	-5	-1	93	106	56	.613	5	1	1	-1	*3	-0.1
1972	Hou-N	152	553	70	131	24	7	22	90	57	120	.237	.314	.425	.739	102	5	1	106	125	70	.679	5	5	-2	18	*3	1.7
1973	Hou-N	154	574	79	146	26	0	21	89	46	97	.254	.313	.409	.722	104	-2	1	95	122	73	.653	4	3	-1	-1	*3	-0.3
1974	Hou-N	152	533	61	137	27	3	17	78	60	131	.257	.337	.415	.751	112	6	7	98	113	74	.709	7	2	1	9	*3	1.5
1975	Hou-N	129	448	41	100	23	2	12	48	42	101	.223	.297	.364	.661	88	-12	-8	94	95	47	.592	5	4	-1	4	*3/S	-0.6
1976	SD-N	139	471	45	121	22	4	9	55	55	102	.257	.338	.378	.716	116	2	9	89	105	60	.653	3	4	-2	9	*3	1.5
1977	SD-N	52	170	19	46	8	3	5	27	33	40	.271	.392	.441	.833	140	7	10	88	122	30	.838	0	1	-1	-0	3	0.8
	Tor-A	96	313	47	75	18	2	13	40	38	65	.240	.328	.435	.762	103	2	1	103	92	44	.716	2	1	0	1	3D/1O	0.0
Total	11	1465	5186	631	1302	245	39	155	722	528	1055	.251	.325	.403	.728	106	11	33	97	115	665	.686	37	33	-9	73	*3/1DSO	8.4
■ **PAUL RADFORD**	Radford, Paul Revere "Shorty" b: 10/14/1861, Roxbury, Mass. d: 2/21/45, Boston, Mass. BR/TR, 5'6", 148 lbs. Deb: 5/01/1883																											
1883	Bos-N	72	258	46	53	6	3	0	14	9	26	.205	.232	.252	.484	44	-16	-18	106	75	15	.361				-5	*O	-1.8
1884	Pro-N	97	355	56	70	11	2	1	29	25	43	.197	.250	.248	.498	56	-17	-18	102	112	23	.396				2	*O/P	-1.4
1885	Pro-N	105	371	55	90	12	5	0	32	33	43	.243	.304	.302	.606	106	-1	4	91	101	35	.516				6	*OS/P2	0.7
1886	KC-N	122	493	78	113	17	5	0	20	58	48	.229	.310	.284	.594	77	-9	-14	107	40	57	.624	39			2	*OS/2	-0.9
1887	NY-a	128	486	127	129	15	5	4		**106**		.265	.403	.342	.745	127	14	27	88	0	99	.983	73			-1	SO2/P	1.8
1888	Bro-a	90	308	48	67	9	3	2	29	35		.218	.305	.286	.591	89	-1	-3	105	94	38	.664	33			6	O/2	0.0
1889	Cle-N	136	487	94	116	21	5	1	46	91	37	.238	.365	.308	.673	88	-2	-4	103	95	67	.747	30			2	*O/3	-0.6
1890	Cle-P	122	466	98	136	24	12	2	62	82	28	.292	.406	.408	.814	131	17	24	92	92	90	.924	25			3	OS/32P	2.0
1891	Bos-a	133	456	102	118	11	5	0	65	96	36	.259	.393	.305	.698	105	8	9	99	138	78	.873	55			14	*S/OP	2.5
1892	Was-N	137	510	93	130	19	4	1	37	86	47	.255	.366	.314	.679	103	9	5	105	67	73	.747	35			1	O3S	0.7
1893	Was-N	124	464	87	106	18	3	2	34	105	42	.228	.380	.293	.673	91	-6	3	90	69	65	.785	32			6	*O/2P	0.3
1894	Was-N	95	325	61	78	13	5	0	49	65	23	.240	.378	.311	.689	71	-14	-12	98	136	48	.798	24			6	S2O	-0.2
Total	12	1361	4979	945	1206	176	57	13	417	791	373	.242	.351	.308	.660	94	-17	4	98	82	688	.721	346			39	OS/32P	3.1
■ **JACK RADTKE**	Radtke, Jack William b: 4/14/13, Denver, Colo. BB/TR, 5'7", 160 lbs. Deb: 8/01/36																											
1936	Bro-N	33	31	8	3	0	0	0	2	4	9	.097	.200	.097	.297	-17	-5	-5	105	236	1	.357	3			-1	2/3S	-0.4
■ **JACK RAFTER**	Rafter, John Cornelius b: 2/20/1875, Troy, N.Y. d: 1/5/43, Troy, N.Y. TR , 5'8", 165 lbs. Deb: 9/24/04																											
1904	Pit-N	1	3	0	0	0	0	0	0	0		.000	.000	.000	.000	-99	-1	-1	99	0	0	.000	0			0	/C	0.0
■ **TOM RAFTERY**	Raftery, Thomas Francis b: 10/5/1881, Boston, Mass. d: 12/31/54, Boston, Mass. 5'10.5", 175 lbs. Deb: 4/18/09																											
1909	Cle-A	8	32	6	7	2	1	0	0	4		.219	.306	.344	.649	103	0	0	102	0	4	.640	1			0	/O	0.0
■ **TOM RAGLAND**	Ragland, Thomas b: 6/16/46, Talladega, Ala. BR/TR, 5'10", 155 lbs. Deb: 4/05/71																											
1971	Was-A	10	23	1	4	0	0	0	0	0	5	.174	.208	.174	.382	10	-3	-3	92	0	0	.227	0	0	0	1	2	-0.1
1972	Tex-A	25	58	3	10	2	0	0	2	5	11	.172	.238	.207	.445	35	-5	-4	94	70	3	.340	0	1	-1	-1	2/3S	-0.4
1973	Cle-A	67	183	16	47	7	1	0	12	8	31	.257	.292	.306	.598	70	-8	-7	97	84	16	.472	2	3	-1	8	2/S	0.3
Total	3	102	264	20	61	9	1	0	14	13	47	.231	.272	.273	.545	58	-15	-14	96	74	19	.424	2	4	-2	8	/2S3	-0.2
■ **LARRY RAINES**	Raines, Lawrence Glenn Hope b: 3/9/30, St.Albans, W.Va. d: 1/28/78, Lansing, Mich. BR/TR, 5'10", 165 lbs. Deb: 4/16/57																											
1957	Cle-A	96	244	39	64	14	0	2	16	19	40	.262	.318	.344	.662	80	-6	-7	102	70	27	.589	5	2	0	-3	3S2/O	-0.7
1958	Cle-A	7	9	1	0	0	0	0	0	0	5	.000	.000	.000	.000	-99	-2	-2	94	0	0	.000	0	1	-1	0	/2	-0.2
Total	2	103	253	40	64	14	0	2	16	19	45	.253	.308	.332	.640	74	-9	-9	101	68	27	.568	5	3	-0	-3	/3S2O	-0.9
■ **TIM RAINES**	Raines, Timothy b: 9/16/59, Sanford, Fla. BB/TR, 5'8", 160 lbs. Deb: 9/11/79																											
1979	Mon-N	6	0	3	0	0	0	0	0	0	0	—	—	—	—	—	0	0	102	—	27	—	2	0	1	0	/R	0.1
1980	Mon-N	15	20	5	1	0	0	0	0	6	3	.050	.269	.050	.319	-6	-3	-3	99	0	1	.632	5	0	2	-0	/2O	0.0
1981	Mon-N	88	313	61	95	13	7	5	37	45	31	.304	.394	.438	.832	137	16	17	99	101	64	1.081	**71**	11	**15**	-1	O/2	2.9
1982	Mon-N	156	647	90	179	32	8	4	43	75	83	.277	.354	.369	.723	97	4	-0	105	58	96	.804	**78**	16	**14**	0	*O2	1.4
1983	Mon-N	156	615	**133**	183	32	8	11	71	97	70	.298	.395	.429	.824	126	27	26	102	84	120	.989	**90**	14	**19**	13	*O/2	5.6
1984	Mon-N	160	622	106	192	**38**	9	8	60	87	69	.309	.395	.437	.833	146	30	37	91	70	124	**.975**	**75**	10	**17**	2	*O/2	5.1
1985	Mon-N	150	575	115	184	30	13	11	41	81	60	.320	.407	.475	.881	156	38	42	94	47	124	1.044	70	9	16	2	*O	5.7
1986	Mon-N	151	580	91	194	35	10	9	62	78	60	**.334**	**.415**	.476	.891	149	38	40	98	78	**130**	**1.062**	70	9	16	3	*O	**5.7**
1987	Mon-N	139	530	**123**	175	34	8	18	68	90	52	.330	.431	.526	.958	143	43	39	106	72	132	1.146	50	5	12	-2	*O	4.2
1988	Mon-N	109	429	66	116	19	7	12	48	53	44	.270	.353	.431	.785	118	14	11	106	77	69	.832	33	7	6	-7	*O	0.8
Total	10	1130	4331	793	1319	233	70	78	430	612	472	.305	.393	.445	.838	133	207	208	100	71	887	1.000	544	81	115	11	*O/2	31.5
■ **JOHN RAINEY**	Rainey, John Paul b: 7/26/1864, Birmingham, Mich. d: 11/11/12, Detroit, Mich. BL/TR, 6'1.5", 164 lbs. Deb: 8/25/1887																											
1887	NY-N	17	58	6	17	3	0	0	12	5	6	.293	.349	.345	.694	89	-0	-1	107	185	7	.610	0			0	3	0.0
1890	Buf-P	42	166	29	39	5	1	1	20	24	15	.235	.349	.295	.644	81	-5	-2	92	101	22	.709	12			0	O/S32	-0.1
Total	2	59	224	35	56	8	1	1	32	29	21	.250	.349	.308	.657	84	-5	-3	95	121	29	.685	12			0	/O3S2	-0.1
■ **GARY RAJSICH**	Rajsich, Gary Louis b: 10/28/54, Youngstown, Ohio BL/TL, 6'2", 210 lbs. Deb: 4/09/82																											
1982	NY-N	80	162	17	42	8	3	2	12	17	40	.259	.333	.383	.716	101	0	0	99	69	20	.648	1	3	-2	-3	O/1	-0.4
1983	NY-N	11	36	5	12	3	0	1	3	3	1	.333	.400	.500	.900	150	2	2	99	56	7	.880	0	0	0	1	0.2	
1984	StL-N	7	7	1	1	0	0	0	2	2	1	.143	.333	.143	.476	39	-0	-0	99	784	1	.500	0	0	0	0	/1	0.0
1985	SF-N	51	91	5	15	6	0	0	10	17	22	.165	.296	.231	.527	53	-6	-5	93	190	7	.494	0	1	-1	-1	1	-0.6
Total	4	149	296	28	70	17	3	3	27	39	64	.236	.329	.345	.674	91	-4	-3	97	125	35	.626	1	4	-2	-3	/1O	-0.8
■ **DOC RALSTON**	Ralston, Samuel Beryl b: 8/3/1885, Pierpont, Ohio d: 8/29/50, Lancaster, Pa. BR/TR, 6', 185 lbs. Deb: 9/08/10																											
1910	Was-A	21	73	4	15	1	0	0	3	3		.205	.256	.219	.476	49	-4	-4	101	71	5	.397	2			1	O	-0.3
■ **BOB RAMAZZOTTI**	Ramazzotti, Robert Louis b: 1/16/17, Elanora, Pa. BR/TR, 5'8.5", 175 lbs. Deb: 4/20/46																											
1946	Bro-N	62	120	10	25	4	0	0	7	9	13	.208	.264	.242	.505	43	-9	-9	103	90	8	.396	0			-1	32	-0.9
1948	Bro-N	4	3	0	0	0	0	0	0	0	1	.000	.000	.000	.000	-96	-1	-1	104	0	0	.000	0			0	/32	0.0
1949	Bro-N	5	13	1	2	0	0	1	3	0	3	.154	.154	.385	.538	39	-1	-1	102	141	1	.455	0			0	/3	0.0
	Chi-N	65	190	14	34	3	1	0	6	5	33	.179	.200	.205	.405	9	-24	-23	94	58	6	.319	9			0	3S/2	-2.0
	Yr	70	203	15	36	3	1	1	9	5	36	.177	.197	.217	.414	11	-26	-24	95	66	7	.328	9			0		-2.0
1950	Chi-N	61	145	19	38	3	3	1	6	4	16	.262	.287	.345	.631	62	-8	-8	105	44	14	.537	3			-0	23/S	-0.7
1951	Chi-N	73	158	13	39	5	2	1	15	10	23	.247	.292	.323	.614	67	-8	-7	97	107	15	.496	0	0	0	-1	S/23	-0.3
1952	Chi-N	50	183	26	52	5	3	1	12	14	14	.284	.338	.361	.699	91	-1	-2	103	69	22	.604	3	1	0	-3	2	-0.2
1953	Chi-N	26	39	3	6	2	0	0	4	3	4	.154	.214	.205	.419	10	-5	-5	103	195	2	.324	0	0	0	-2	2	-0.5
Total	7	346	851	86	196	22	9	4	53	45	107	.230	.271	.291	.562	52	-57	-58	100	79	68	.472	15	1		-7	2/3S	-4.6
■ **MARIO RAMIREZ**	Ramirez, Mario (Torres) b: 9/12/57, Yauco, P.R. BR/TR, 5'9", 155 lbs. Deb: 4/25/80																											
1980	NY-N	18	24	2	5	0	0	0	0	1	7	.208	.240	.208	.448	27	-2	-2	96	0	1	.300	0	0	0	-1	/S/23	-0.1

YEAR	TM/L	G	AB	R	H	2B	3B	HR	RBI	BB	SO	AVG	OBP	SLG	PRO	/A	BR	/A	PF	CHI	RC	TA	SB	CS	SBR	FR	POS	TPR
1981	SD-N	13	13	1	1	0	0	0	1	2	5	.077	.200	.077	.277	-20	-2	-2	93	393	0	.250	0	0	0	0	/S3	-0.1
1982	SD-N	13	23	1	4	1	0	0	1	2	4	.174	.240	.217	.457	31	-2	-2	92	78	1	.368	0	0	0	-1	/S23	-0.1
1983	SD-N	55	107	11	21	6	3	0	12	20	23	.196	.328	.308	.637	78	-3	-3	99	144	12	.614	0	0	0	-3	S/3	-0.2
1984	SD-N	48	59	12	7	1	0	2	9	13	14	.119	.278	.237	.515	47	-4	-4	99	176	4	.500	0	0	0	-3	S/32	-0.3
1985	SD-N	37	60	6	17	0	0	2	5	3	11	.283	.317	.383	.701	93	-1	-1	102	69	8	.605	0	0	0	-1	S/2	0.1
Total	6	184	286	33	55	8	3	4	28	41	64	.192	.296	.283	.579	63	-14	-13	98	132	27	.532	0	0	0	-9	S/23	-0.7
■ MILT RAMIREZ	Ramirez, Milton (Barboza) b: 4/2/50, Mayaguez, P.R. BR/TR, 5'9", 150 lbs. Deb: 4/11/70																											
1970	StL-N	62	79	8	15	2	1	0	3	8	9	.190	.264	.241	.505	34	-7	-8	106	61	4	.391	0	1	-1	8	S/3	0.7
1971	StL-N	4	11	2	3	0	0	0	0	2	1	.273	.385	.273	.657	88	-0	-0	101	0	1	.625	0	0	0	1	/S	0.2
1979	Oak-A	28	62	4	10	1	1	0	3	3	8	.161	.200	.210	.410	12	-8	-7	89	89	3	.302	0	0	0	-2	32/S	-0.6
Total	3	94	152	14	28	3	2	0	6	13	18	.184	.248	.230	.479	30	-15	-15	99	67	8	.381	0	1	-1	7	/S32	0.3
■ ORLANDO RAMIREZ	Ramirez, Orlando (Leal) b: 12/18/51, Cartagena, Colombia BR/TR, 5'10", 175 lbs. Deb: 7/06/74																											
1974	Cal-A	31	86	4	14	0	0	0	7	6	23	.163	.217	.163	.380	12	-10	-9	92	197	4	.297	2	1	0	0	S	-0.6
1975	Cal-A	44	100	10	24	4	1	0	4	11	22	.240	.315	.300	.615	79	-3	-2	95	51	9	.595	9	6	-1	-4	S	-0.3
1976	Cal-A	30	70	3	14	1	0	0	5	6	11	.200	.263	.214	.477	44	-5	-4	92	128	4	.400	3	2	-0	-1	S	-0.3
1977	Cal-A	25	13	6	1	0	0	0	0	0	3	.077	.077	.077	.154	-61	-3	-3	95	0	0	.167	1	0	0	0	/2SD	-0.1
1979	Cal-A	13	12	1	0	0	0	0	0	1	6	.000	.143	.000	.143	-62	-3	-3	93	0	0	.250	1	0	0	0	S	0.0
Total	5	143	281	24	53	5	1	0	16	24	65	.189	.255	.214	.468	37	-23	-21	93	109	17	.426	16	9	-1	-5	S/2D	-1.3
■ RAFAEL RAMIREZ	Ramirez, Rafael Emilio (Peguero) b: 2/18/59, San Pedro De Macoris, D.R. BR/TR, 6', 170 lbs. Deb: 8/04/80																											
1980	Atl-N	50	165	17	44	6	1	2	11	2	33	.267	.292	.352	.644	78	-5	-5	101	68	17	.532	2	1	0	-0	S	0.0
1981	Atl-N	95	307	30	67	16	2	2	20	24	47	.218	.277	.303	.580	65	-15	-14	100	79	27	.508	7	3	0	-5	S	-0.9
1982	Atl-N	157	609	74	169	24	4	10	52	36	49	.278	.321	.379	.700	89	-5	-10	107	83	73	.640	27	14	-0	19	*S	2.1
1983	Atl-N	152	622	82	185	13	5	7	58	36	48	.297	.338	.368	.706	90	-4	-8	106	88	76	.619	16	12	-2	7	*S	1.1
1984	Atl-N	145	591	51	157	22	4	2	48	26	70	.266	.298	.327	.624	69	-20	-26	110	91	53	.509	14	17	-6	1	*S	-1.5
1985	Atl-N	138	568	54	141	25	4	5	58	20	63	.248	.274	.333	.607	65	-25	-29	106	120	45	.465	2	6	-3	12	*S	-0.9
1986	Atl-N	134	496	57	119	21	1	8	33	21	60	.240	.275	.335	.610	66	-23	-24	102	71	42	.521	19	8	1	21	S3/O	0.4
1987	Atl-N	56	179	22	47	12	0	1	21	8	16	.263	.302	.346	.648	66	-8	-9	108	129	18	.565	6	3	0	3	S3	-0.1
1988	Hou-N	155	566	51	156	30	5	6	59	18	61	.276	.302	.378	.680	101	-6	-2	93	104	60	.556	3	2	-0	-12	*S	-0.2
Total	9	1082	4103	438	1085	169	26	43	360	191	447	.264	.300	.350	.650	78	-109	-128	104	92	411	.562	96	66	-11	46	*S/3O	-0.0
■ DOMINGO RAMOS	Ramos, Domingo Antonio (De Ramos) b: 3/29/58, Santiago, D.R. BR/TR, 5'10", 154 lbs. Deb: 9/08/78																											
1978	NY-A	1	0	0	0	0	0	0	0	0	0	—	—	—	—	—	0	0	99	—	—	—	0	0	0	0	/S	0.0
1980	Tor-A	5	16	0	2	0	0	0	0	2	5	.125	.222	.125	.347	-2	-2	-2	100	0	1	.286	0	0	0	0	/2SD	-0.1
1982	Sea-A	8	26	3	4	2	0	0	1	3	2	.154	.241	.231	.472	28	-2	-3	109	67	2	.409	0	0	0	1	/S	-0.1
1983	Sea-A	53	127	14	36	4	0	2	10	7	12	.283	.326	.362	.688	90	-2	-2	100	75	14	.594	3	1	0	4	S/23D	0.4
1984	Sea-A	59	81	6	15	2	0	0	2	5	12	.185	.233	.210	.442	23	-8	-9	102	47	3	.333	2	2	-1	-2	3S/12	-0.9
1985	Sea-A	75	168	19	33	6	0	1	15	17	23	.196	.270	.250	.520	46	-13	-12	95	132	12	.421	0	1	-1	5	S21/3	-0.4
1986	Sea-A	49	99	8	18	2	0	0	5	8	13	.182	.250	.202	.452	24	-10	-11	105	100	4	.326	0	1	-1	7	S2/3D	-0.2
1987	Sea-A	42	103	9	32	6	0	2	11	3	12	.311	.336	.427	.764	99	0	-0	103	88	14	.658	0	1	-1	1	S/32D	0.2
1988	Cle-A	22	46	7	12	1	0	0	5	3	7	.261	.320	.283	.603	69	-2	-2	102	153	5	.500	0	0	0	-0	2/1S3	0.0
	Cal-A	10	15	3	2	0	0	0	0	0	0	.133	.133	.133	.267	-27	-2	-2	94	0	0	.133	0	0	0	-1	/3O	-0.2
	Yr	32	61	10	14	1	0	0	5	3	7	.230	.277	.246	.523	48	-4	-4	99	110	4	.388	0	0	0	-1		-0.2
Total	9	324	681	69	154	23	0	5	49	48	86	.226	.281	.282	.563	55	-42	-42	100	93	466	.465	5	6	-2	15	S/321DO	-1.3
■ CHUCHO RAMOS	Ramos, Jesus Manuel (Garcia) b: 4/12/18, Maturin, Venez. BR/TL, 5'10.5", 167 lbs. Deb: 5/07/44																											
1944	Cin-N	4	10	1	5	1	0	0	0	0	0	.500	.500	.600	1.100	219	1	1	95	0	3	1.200	0			-1	/O	0.1
■ PEDRO RAMOS	Ramos, Pedro (Guerra) "Pete" b: 4/28/35, Pinar Del Rio, Cuba BB/TR, 6', 175 lbs. Deb: 4/11/55																											
1955	Was-A	59	38	6	3	0	0	0	0	2	18	.079	.125	.079	.204	-49	-8	-7	91	0	0	.139	0	1	-1	-1	P	0.0
1956	Was-A	56	44	9	9	0	2	0	2	2	16	.205	.239	.295	.535	40	-4	-4	102	57	3	.405	0	1	-1	-0	P	0.0
1957	Was-A	56	76	6	13	0	0	1	10	2	27	.171	.192	.211	.403	10	-9	-9	98	208	3	.286	0	0	0	-0	P	0.0
1958	Was-A	53	88	9	21	1	0	0	10	0	33	.239	.239	.250	.489	36	-8	-7	97	182	6	.328	0	0	0	-1	P	0.0
1959	Was-A	45	75	7	11	1	1	1	2	4	38	.147	.190	.227	.417	14	-9	-9	100	39	4	.338	1	0	0	-1	P	0.0
1960	Was-A	53	86	6	10	3	0	2	4	1	36	.116	.126	.221	.347	-8	-13	-13	102	63	3	.263	0	0	0	0	P	0.0
1961	Min-A	53	93	8	16	1	0	3	11	3	42	.172	.206	.280	.486	27	-10	-10	106	123	5	.385	0	0	0	-3	P	0.0
1962	Cle-A	39	68	6	10	3	0	3	8	1	29	.147	.171	.324	.495	30	-7	-7	98	102	3	.400	0	0	0	0	P	0.0
1963	Cle-A	54	55	13	6	0	0	3	7	3	32	.109	.155	.273	.428	18	-6	-6	97	122	3	.367	0	0	0	-1	P	0.0
1964	Cle-A	44	39	6	7	0	0	2	2	2	22	.179	.220	.333	.553	50	-3	-3	103	45	3	.469	0	0	0	-1	P	0.0
	NY-A	13	5	0	0	0	0	0	0	0	2	.000	.000	.000	.000	-97	-1	-1	103	0	0	.000	0	0	0	-1	P	0.0
	Yr	57	44	6	7	0	0	2	2	2	24	.159	.196	.295	.491	33	-4	-4	103	35	3	.405	0	0	0	-1		0.0
1965	NY-A	65	12	0	1	0	0	0	0	0	8	.083	.083	.083	.167	-52	-2	-2	101	0	0	.182	1	0	0	-1	P	0.0
1966	NY-A	52	13	0	2	0	0	0	0	0	8	.154	.154	.154	.308	-12	-2	-2	94	0	0	.182	0	0	0	-0	P	0.0
1967	Phi-N	6	1	0	0	0	0	0	0	0	0	.000	.000	.000	.000	-96	-0	-0	104	0	0	.000	0	0	0	1	/P	0.0
1969	Pit-N	5	1	0	0	0	0	0	0	0	1	.000	.000	.000	.000	-99	-0	-0	95	0	0	.000	0	0	0	0	/P	0.0
	Cin-N	38	8	0	0	0	0	0	0	1	4	.000	.111	.000	.111	-67	-2	-2	99	0	0	.125	0	0	0	0	P	0.0
	Yr	43	9	0	0	0	0	0	0	1	5	.000	.100	.000	.100	-71	-2	-2	98	0	0	.111	0	0	0	0		0.0
1970	Was-A	5	1	0	0	0	0	0	0	1	0	.000	.500	.000	.500	51	0	0	96	0	0	1.000	0	0	0	0	/P	0.0
Total	15	696	703	76	109	9	3	15	56	22	316	.155	.183	.240	.423	14	-84	-84	100	98	34	.327	2	2	-1	-8	P	0.0
■ BOBBY RAMOS	Ramos, Roberto b: 11/5/55, Havana, Cuba BR/TR, 5'11", 190 lbs. Deb: 9/26/78																											
1978	Mon-N	2	4	0	0	0	0	0	0	0	1	.000	.000	.000	.000	-99	-1	-1	96	0	0	.000	0	0	0	0	/C	0.0
1980	Mon-N	13	32	5	5	2	0	0	2	5	5	.156	.270	.219	.489	38	-3	-3	99	113	2	.429	0	0	0	1	C	0.0
1981	Mon-N	26	41	4	8	1	0	1	3	3	5	.195	.250	.293	.543	54	-3	-3	99	78	3	.429	0	0	0	1	C	0.0
1982	NY-A	4	11	1	1	0	0	1	2	0	3	.091	.091	.364	.455	19	-1	-1	96	114	0	.400	0	0	0	0	/C	0.0
1983	Mon-N	27	61	2	14	3	1	0	5	8	11	.230	.329	.311	.640	77	-2	-2	102	104	7	.596	0	0	0	4	C	0.3
1984	Mon-N	31	83	8	16	1	0	2	5	6	13	.193	.247	.277	.524	51	-6	-5	91	68	5	.403	0	0	0	2	C	-0.2
Total	6	103	232	20	44	7	1	4	17	22	38	.190	.263	.280	.543	54	-15	-14	97	87	17	.456	0	0	0	8	/C	0.1
■ MIKE RAMSEY	Ramsey, Michael James b: 7/8/60, Thomson, Ga. BB/TL, 6' ", 170 lbs. Deb: 4/06/87																											
1987	LA-N	48	125	18	29	4	2	0	12	10	32	.232	.289	.296	.585	60	-8	-7	92	129	10	.476	2	4	-2	-2	O	-1.1
■ MIKE RAMSEY	Ramsey, Michael Jeffrey b: 3/29/54, Roanoke, Va. BB/TR, 6'1", 170 lbs. Deb: 9/04/78																											
1978	StL-N	12	5	4	1	0	0	0	0	0	1	.200	.200	.200	.400	13	-1	-1	95	0	0	.250	0	0	0	0	/S	0.0
1980	StL-N	59	126	11	33	8	1	0	8	3	17	.262	.279	.341	.620	70	-5	-5	103	74	11	.484	0	0	0	3	2S/3	0.1
1981	StL-N	47	124	19	32	3	0	0	9	8	16	.258	.303	.282	.585	66	-5	-6	102	101	10	.480	4	0	1	4	S/32O	0.4
1982	StL-N	112	256	18	59	8	2	1	21	22	34	.230	.294	.289	.583	62	-12	-13	103	107	21	.493	6	5	-1	6	23S/O	-0.5
1983	StL-N	97	175	25	46	4	3	1	16	12	23	.263	.314	.337	.651	82	-5	-4	98	102	18	.563	4	2	0	-3	2S/3O	-0.2
1984	StL-N	21	15	1	1	1	0	0	0	1	3	.067	.125	.133	.258	-28	-3	-3	99	0	0	.214	0	0	0	1	/2S3	0.0
	Mon-N	37	70	2	15	1	0	0	3	0	13	.214	.214	.229	.443	27	-7	-6	91	73	3	.281	0	0	0	-4	S2	-0.7
	Yr	58	85	3	16	2	0	0	3	1	16	.188	.198	.212	.409	16	-10	-9	94	47	3	.268	0	0	0	-4		-0.7
1985	LA-N	9	15	1	2	1	0	0	0	2	4	.133	.235	.200	.435	25	-2	-1	93	0	1	.385	0	0	0	0	/S2	0.0
Total	7	394	786	81	189	26	6	2	57	48	111	.240	.286	.296	.582	63	-39	-39	100	92	65	.492	14	7	0	7	2S/3O	-0.9
■ BILL RAMSEY	Ramsey, William Thrace "Square Jaw" b: 2/20/21, Osceola, Ark. BR/TR, 6'1", 190 lbs. Deb: 4/19/45																											
1945	Bos-N	78	137	16	40	8	0	1	12	4	22	.292	.326	.372	.699	84	-1	-4	112	77	16	.590	1			-7	O	-1.2

YEAR	TM/L	G	AB	R	H	2B	3B	HR	RBI	BB	SO	AVG	OBP	SLG	PRO	/A	BR	/A	PF	CHI	RC	TA	SB	CS	SBR	FR	POS	TPR
■ DICK RAND	Rand, Richard Hilton b: 3/7/31, South Gate, Cal. BR/TR, 6'2", 185 lbs. Deb: 9/16/53																											
1953	StL-N	9	31	3	9	1	0	0	1	2	6	.290	.333	.323	.656	71	-1	-1	102	39	4	.545	0	0	0	-1	/C	-0.1
1955	StL-N	3	10	1	3	0	0	1	3	1	1	.300	.364	.600	.964	149	1	1	101	135	2	.875	0	1	-1	0	/C	0.0
1957	Pit-N	60	105	7	23	2	1	1	9	11	24	.219	.293	.286	.579	60	-6	-5	94	113	10	.500	0	0	0	-4	C	-0.6
Total	3	72	146	11	35	3	1	2	13	14	31	.240	.306	.315	.621	69	-7	-6	96	99	15	.536	0	1	-1	-5	/C	-0.7
■ SAP RANDALL	Randall, James Odell b: 8/19/60, Mobile, Ala. BB/TR, 5'11", 195 lbs. Deb: 8/02/88																											
1988	Chi-A	4	12	1	0	0	0	0	1	2	3	.000	.143	.000	.143	-58	-3	-2	97	0	0	.167	0	0	0	-0	/1OD	-0.2
■ NEWT RANDALL	Randall, Newton J. b: 2/3/1880, New Lowell, Ont., Canada d: 5/3/55, Duluth, Minn. 5'10", Deb: 4/18/07																											
1907	Chi-N	22	78	6	16	4	2	0	4	8		.205	.279	.308	.587	81	-1	-2	106	67	7	.548	2			3	O	0.0
	Bos-N	75	258	16	55	6	3	0	15	19		.213	.267	.260	.527	70	-10	-8	95	86	19	.443	4			-4	O	-1.6
	Yr	97	336	22	71	10	5	0	19	27		.211	.270	.271	.541	73	-11	-10	98	83	27	.468	6			-1		-1.6
Total	1	97	336	22	71	10	5	0	19	27		.211	.270	.271	.541	73	-11	-10	98	82	27	.468	6			-1	/O	-1.6
■ BOB RANDALL	Randall, Robert Lee b: 6/10/48, Norton, Kan. BR/TR, 6'2", 175 lbs. Deb: 4/13/76 C																											
1976	Min-A	153	475	55	127	18	4	1	34	28	38	.267	.311	.328	.639	89	-8	-7	98	82	49	.526	3	5	-2	-2	*2	-0.2
1977	Min-A	103	306	36	73	13	2	0	22	15	25	.239	.290	.294	.584	58	-17	-18	103	97	27	.471	1	4	-2	7	*2/13D	-0.4
1978	Min-A	119	330	36	89	11	3	0	21	24	22	.270	.331	.321	.652	89	-6	-4	94	78	36	.562	5	3	-0	9	*2/3D	1.1
1979	Min-A	80	199	25	49	7	0	0	14	15	17	.246	.299	.281	.580	53	-12	-14	109	96	18	.474	2	2	-1	9	2/3SO	-0.2
1980	Min-A	5	15	2	3	1	0	0	0	1	0	.200	.250	.267	.517	38	-1	-1	109	0	1	.385	0	0	0	0	/32	0.0
Total	5	460	1325	154	341	50	9	1	91	83	102	.257	.309	.311	.619	75	-44	-44	100	86	130	.522	11	14	-5	22	2/3DOS1	0.3
■ LEN RANDLE	Randle, Leonard Shenoff b: 2/12/49, Long Beach, Cal. BB/TR, 5'10", 169 lbs. Deb: 6/16/71																											
1971	Was-A	75	215	27	47	11	0	2	13	24	56	.219	.300	.298	.598	75	-8	-6	92	76	21	.523	1	1	-0	5	2	0.2
1972	Tex-A	74	249	23	48	13	0	2	21	13	51	.193	.236	.269	.505	53	-16	-14	94	120	14	.397	4	5	-2	-2	2/SO	-1.5
1973	Tex-A	10	29	3	6	1	1	1	1	0	2	.207	.207	.414	.621	73	-1	-1	97	26	2	.480	0	2	-1	-1	/2O	-0.3
1974	Tex-A	151	520	65	157	17	4	1	49	29	43	.302	.341	.356	.697	105	0	3	96	105	61	.621	26	17	-2	-0	32O/SD	0.3
1975	Tex-A	156	601	85	166	24	7	4	57	57	80	.276	.343	.359	.702	99	-0	0	100	102	73	.634	16	19	-7	9	2O3/CSD	0.3
1976	Tex-A	142	539	53	121	11	6	1	51	46	63	.224	.288	.273	.561	63	-23	-25	102	138	45	.515	30	15	0	-7	*2O/3D	-2.7
1977	NY-N	136	513	78	156	22	7	5	27	65	70	.304	.384	.404	.788	116	11	13	96	47	78	.781	33	21	-3	3	*32/OS	1.4
1978	NY-N	132	437	53	102	16	8	2	35	64	57	.233	.333	.320	.653	85	-8	-7	98	97	49	.620	14	11	-2	-7	*3/2	-1.7
1979	NY-A	20	39	2	7	0	0	0	3	3	2	.179	.238	.179	.418	15	-5	-4	96	165	2	.303	0	0	0	0	O	-0.3
1980	Chi-N	130	489	67	135	19	6	5	39	50	55	.276	.344	.370	.715	94	0	-3	106	83	61	.661	19	13	-2	2	*32/O	-0.2
1981	Sea-A	82	273	22	63	9	1	4	25	17	22	.231	.278	.315	.593	71	-11	-10	100	100	24	.528	11	6	-0	2	32/OS	-0.7
1982	Sea-A	30	46	10	8	2	0	0	1	4	4	.174	.240	.217	.457	24	-5	-5	109	40	2	.390	2	2	-1	-1	D/32	-0.5
Total	12	1138	3950	488	1016	145	40	27	322	372	505	.257	.323	.335	.658	87	-65	-60	99	96	430	.612	156	112	-20	4	32O/DSC	-5.7
■ WILLIE RANDOLPH	Randolph, Willie Larry b: 7/6/54, Holly Hill, S.C. BR/TR, 5'11", 165 lbs. Deb: 7/29/75																											
1975	Pit-N	30	61	9	10	1	0	0	3	7	6	.164	.250	.180	.430	21	-6	-6	99	105	3	.352	1	0	0	1	2/3	-0.3
1976	NY-A	125	430	59	115	15	4	1	40	58	39	.267	.358	.328	.686	102	3	4	99	109	55	.709	37	12	4	10	*2	2.5
1977	NY-A	147	551	91	151	28	11	4	40	64	53	.274	.351	.387	.737	102	2	3	99	75	77	.698	13	6	0	8	*2	2.2
1978	NY-A	134	499	87	139	18	6	3	42	82	51	.279	.385	.357	.741	111	10	11	99	85	78	.792	36	7	7	4	*2	2.9
1979	NY-A	153	574	98	155	15	13	5	61	95	39	.270	.376	.368	.744	106	5	9	96	92	82	.753	33	12	3	12	*2	2.9
1980	NY-A	138	513	99	151	23	7	7	46	**119**	45	.294	.429	.407	.836	132	29	29	99	69	105	.965	30	5	6	-3	*2	3.9
1981	NY-A	93	357	59	83	14	3	2	24	57	24	.232	.338	.305	.643	86	-4	-4	100	71	40	.623	14	5	1	-1	2	-0.1
1982	NY-A	144	553	85	155	21	4	3	36	75	35	.280	.369	.349	.718	102	2	5	96	69	75	.683	16	9	-1	3	*2/D	1.5
1983	NY-A	104	420	73	117	21	1	2	38	53	32	.279	.361	.348	.708	97	-0	0	99	86	55	.667	12	4	1	5	*2	0.9
1984	NY-A	142	564	86	162	24	2	2	31	86	42	.287	.382	.348	.729	110	6	11	94	54	79	.690	10	6	-1	13	*2	3.0
1985	NY-A	143	497	75	137	21	2	5	40	85	39	.276	.386	.356	.742	109	7	10	96	84	69	.718	16	9	-1	5	*2	1.9
1986	NY-A	141	492	76	136	15	2	5	50	94	49	.276	.396	.346	.741	102	9	6	103	114	77	.764	15	2	3	-5	*2/D	1.2
1987	NY-A	120	449	96	137	24	2	7	67	82	25	.305	.415	.414	.829	125	18	20	98	114	82	.857	11	1	3	2	*2/D	3.1
1988	NY-A	110	404	43	93	20	1	2	34	55	39	.230	.325	.300	.625	80	-11	-9	96	113	42	.572	8	4	0	11	*2	0.9
Total	14	1724	6364	1036	1741	260	58	48	552	1012	518	.274	.376	.355	.731	105	70	89	98	86	918	.754	252	82	26	63	*2/D3	26.5
■ MERRITT RANEW	Ranew, Merritt Thomas b: 5/10/38, Albany, Ga. BL/TR, 5'11", 170 lbs. Deb: 4/13/62																											
1962	Hou-N	71	218	26	51	6	8	4	24	14	43	.234	.289	.390	.679	87	-7	-5	93	97	24	.608	2	2	-1	7	C	0.3
1963	Chi-N	78	154	18	52	8	1	3	15	9	32	.338	.382	.461	.843	135	8	7	105	79	27	.790	1	0	0	1	C/1	1.0
1964	Chi-N	16	33	0	3	0	0	0	1	2	6	.091	.167	.091	.258	-24	-5	-6	105	137	1	.194	0	0	0	-0	/C	-0.5
	Mil-N	9	17	1	2	0	0	0	0	0	3	.118	.118	.118	.235	-35	-3	-3	97	0	0	.125	0	1	-1	0	/C	-0.3
	Yr	25	50	1	5	0	0	0	1	2	9	.100	.151	.100	.251	-27	-8	-8	102	93	1	.174	0	1	-1	-0		-0.8
1965	Cal-A	41	91	12	19	4	0	1	10	7	22	.209	.265	.286	.551	58	-5	-5	98	143	7	.440	0	0	0	1	C	-0.1
1969	Sea-A	54	81	11	20	2	0	0	4	10	14	.247	.330	.272	.601	71	-3	-3	98	73	7	.492	0	0	0	-1	C/O3	-0.2
Total	5	269	594	68	147	20	9	8	54	42	120	.247	.304	.352	.656	83	-15	-14	98	96	66	.573	3	3	-1	9	C/1O3	0.2
■ JEFF RANSOM	Ransom, Jeffrey Dean b: 11/11/60, Fresno, Cal. BB/TR, 5'11", 185 lbs. Deb: 9/05/81																											
1981	SF-N	5	15	2	4	1	0	0	0	1	1	.267	.313	.333	.646	79	-0	-0	105	0	1	.500	0	0	0	0	/C	0.0
1982	SF-N	15	44	5	7	0	0	0	3	6	7	.159	.260	.159	.419	21	-5	-4	94	168	2	.325	0	0	0	0	C	-0.3
1983	SF-N	6	20	3	4	0	0	1	3	4	7	.200	.333	.350	.683	89	-0	-0	101	121	2	.647	0	0	0	0	/C	0.0
Total	3	26	79	10	15	1	0	1	6	11	15	.190	.289	.241	.529	51	-5	-5	98	126	5	.462	0	0	0	1	/C	-0.3
■ EARL RAPP	Rapp, Earl Wellington b: 5/20/21, Corunna, Mich. BL/TR, 6'2", 185 lbs. Deb: 4/28/49																											
1949	Det-A	1	0	0	0	0	0	0	0	1	0	—	1.000	—	1.241	220	0	0	108	0	0	—	0	0	0	0	H	0.0
	Chi-A	19	54	3	14	1	1	0	11	5	6	.259	.322	.315	.637	70	-2	-2	98	222	6	.548	1	1	-0	2	O	0.0
	Yr	20	54	3	14	1	1	0	11	6	6	.259	.333	.315	.648	73	-2	-2	98	211	6	.571	1	1	-0	2		0.0
1951	NY-N	13	11	0	1	0	0	0	1	2	3	.091	.231	.091	.322	-10	-2	-2	102	387	0	.273	0	0	0	0	H	-0.1
	StL-A	26	98	14	32	5	3	2	14	11	11	.327	.394	.500	.894	134	5	5	105	96	21	.910	1	0	0	-2	O	0.2
1952	StL-A	30	49	3	7	4	0	0	4	0	8	.143	.143	.224	.367	1	-7	-6	97	136	1	.250	0	0	0	-1	/O	-0.7
	Was-A	46	67	7	19	6	0	0	9	6	13	.284	.351	.373	.724	102	0	0	100	134	10	.667	0	0	0	-3	O	-0.2
	Yr	76	116	10	26	10	0	0	13	6	21	.224	.268	.310	.579	61	-6	-6	99	137	10	.478	0	0	0	-4		-0.9
Total	3	135	279	27	73	16	4	2	39	25	41	.262	.325	.369	.694	88	-5	-5	101	148	38	.633	2	1	0	-3	/O	-0.8
■ GOLDIE RAPP	Rapp, Joseph Aloysius b: 2/6/1892, Cincinnati, Ohio d: 7/1/66, La Mesa, Cal. BB/TR, 5'10", 165 lbs. Deb: 4/13/21																											
1921	NY-N	58	181	21	39	9	1	0	15	15	13	.215	.276	.276	.552	48	-14	-13	98	110	12	.444	3	11	-6	7	3	-1.1
	Phi-N	52	202	28	56	7	1	1	10	14	8	.277	.324	.337	.661	74	-7	-7	102	55	21	.575	6	7	-2	2	3/2	-0.6
	Yr	110	383	49	95	16	2	1	25	29	21	.248	.301	.308	.609	62	-21	-21	99	85	33	.510	9	18	-8	9		-1.7
1922	Phi-N	119	502	58	127	26	3	0	38	32	29	.253	.299	.317	.616	52	-31	-40	113	74	46	.512	6	12	-5	5	*3/S	-2.9
1923	Phi-N	47	179	27	47	5	0	1	10	14	14	.263	.320	.307	.627	58	-8	-12	114	62	18	.534	1	1	-0	-2	3	-1.2
Total	3	276	1064	134	269	47	5	2	73	75	64	.253	.303	.312	.615	56	-60	-73	108	74	97	.515	16	31	-14	12	3/S2	-5.8
■ BILL RARIDEN	Rariden, William Angel "Bedford Bill" b: 2/4/1888, Bedford, Ind. d: 8/28/42, Bedford, Ind. BR/TR, 5'10", 168 lbs. Deb: 09																											
1909	Bos-N	13	42	1	6	1	0	0	1	4		.143	.217	.167	.384	21	-4	-4	96	53	2	.333	1			1	C	-0.1
1910	Bos-N	49	137	15	31	5	1	1	14	12	22	.226	.293	.299	.593	64	-5	-7	114	111	13	.519	1			-0	C	-0.5
1911	Bos-N	70	246	22	56	9	0	0	21	21	18	.228	.288	.264	.553	53	-15	-16	103	111	19	.468	3			11	C/32	0.0
1912	Bos-N	79	247	27	55	3	1	1	14	18	35	.223	.281	.255	.536	44	-18	-20	107	71	19	.448	3			7	C	-0.8
1913	Bos-N	95	246	31	58	9	2	3	30	30	21	.236	.324	.325	.649	90	-4	-2	95	122	27	.622	5			3	C	0.5
1914	Ind-F	131	396	44	93	15	5	0	47	61	43	.235	.337	.298	.635	75	-7	-12	111	144	47	.630	12			11	*C	0.4
1915	New-F	142	444	49	120	30	7	0	40	60	29	.270	.357	.369	.727	122	10	13	94	88	64	.716	8			**24**	*C	4.2
1916	NY-N	120	351	23	78	9	3	1	29	55	32	.222	.333	.274	.606	91	-3	-1	96	116	34	.579	4			-15	*C	-1.0

YEAR	TM/L	G	AB	R	H	2B	3B	HR	RBI	BB	SO	AVG	OBP	SLG	PRO	/A	BR	/A	PF	CHI	RC	TA	SB	CS	SBR	FR	POS	TPR
1917	NY-N	101	266	20	72	10	1	0	25	42	17	.271	.372	.316	.688	115	6	7	97	115	32	.670	3			-19	*C	-0.7
1918	NY-N	69	183	15	41	5	1	0	17	15	15	.224	.283	.262	.545	68	-7	-7	98	134	14	.451	1			-6	C	-0.7
1919	Cin-N	74	218	16	47	6	3	1	24	17	19	.216	.275	.284	.560	65	-8	-10	105	144	18	.491	4			1	C	-0.3
1920	Cin-N	39	101	9	25	3	0	0	10	5	0	.248	.283	.277	.560	68	-5	-4	90	138	8	.461	2	0	1	-1	C	-0.1
Total	12	982	2877	272	682	105	24	7	272	340	251	.237	.320	.298	.617	81	-59	-63	101	115	296	.571	47	0		15	C/32	0.9
■ **MORRIE RATH** Rath, Maurice Charles b: 12/25/1886, Mobeetie, Tex. d: 11/18/45, Upper Darby, Pa. BL/TR, 5'8.5", 160 lbs. Deb: 9/28/09																												
1909	Phi-A	7	26	4	7	1	0	0	3	2		.269	.387	.308	.695	118	1	1	102	125	3	.737	1			-2	/S3	0.0
1910	Phi-A	18	26	3	4	0	0	0	1	5		.154	.290	.154	.444	39	-2	-2	102	92	1	.409	0			0	3/2	0.0
	Cle-A	24	67	5	13	3	0	0	0	10		.194	.299	.239	.538	69	-2	-2	100	0	5	.519	2			0	3/S	0.0
	Yr	42	93	8	17	3	0	0	1	15		.183	.296	.215	.511	60	-4	-4	101	42	6	.487	2			0		0.0
1912	Chi-A	157	591	104	161	10	2	1	19	95		.272	.380	.301	.681	96	2	3	99	30	80	.721	30			18	*2	1.8
1913	Chi-A	92	295	37	59	2	0	0	12	46	22	.200	.310	.207	.517	54	-16	-14	95	74	26	.551	22			1	2	-1.6
1919	Cin-N	138	537	77	142	13	1	1	29	64	24	.264	.343	.298	.641	89	-2	-5	105	60	61	.610	17			13	*2	1.4
1920	Cin-N	129	506	61	135	7	4	2	28	36	24	.267	.319	.308	.628	90	-12	-5	90	59	51	.537	10	11	-4	-2	*2/3O	-0.8
Total	6	565	2048	291	521	36	7	4	92	258	70	.254	.342	.285	.626	86	-30	-24	98	52	227	.609	82	11		29	2/3SO	0.8
■ **GENE RATLIFF** Ratliff, Kelly Eugene b: 9/28/45, Macon, Ga. BR/TR, 6'5", 185 lbs. Deb: 5/15/65																												
1965	Hou-N	4	4	0	0	0	0	0	0	0	4	.000	.000	.000	.000	-99	-1	-1	89	0	0	.000	0	0	0	0	H	0.0
■ **PAUL RATLIFF** Ratliff, Paul Hawthorne b: 1/23/44, San Diego, Cal. BL/TR, 6'2", 190 lbs. Deb: 4/14/63																												
1963	Min-A	10	21	2	4	1	0	1	3	2	7	.190	.292	.381	.673	86	-0	-0	100	114	3	.647	0	0	0	-0	/C	0.0
1970	Min-A	69	149	19	40	7	2	5	22	15	51	.268	.363	.443	.806	123	4	5	98	110	25	.800	0	0	0	-2	C	0.4
1971	Min-A	21	44	3	7	1	0	2	6	4	17	.159	.229	.318	.547	52	-3	-3	104	122	3	.486	0	0	0	-0	C	-0.2
	Mil-A	23	41	3	7	1	0	3	7	5	21	.171	.277	.415	.691	91	-1	-1	103	110	5	.676	0	0	0	0	C	0.0
	Yr	44	85	6	14	2	0	5	13	9	38	.165	.253	.365	.617	71	-3	-4	104	119	8	.577	0	0	0	0		-0.2
1972	Mil-A	22	42	1	3	0	0	1	4	2	23	.071	.114	.143	.256	-25	-6	-6	95	186	1	.200	0	0	0	0	C	-0.6
Total	4	145	297	28	61	10	2	12	42	28	119	.205	.293	.374	.667	87	-6	-6	100	122	37	.624	0	0	0	-2	C	-0.4
■ **TOMMY RAUB** Raub, Thomas Jefferson b: 12/1/1870, Raubsville, Pa. d: 2/16/49, Phillipsburg, N.J. BR/TR, 5'10", 155 lbs. Deb: 03																												
1903	Chi-N	36	84	6	19	3	2	0	7	5		.226	.270	.310	.579	70	-4	-3	95	87	8	.523	3			-1	C/1O3	-0.3
1906	StL-N	24	78	9	22	2	4	0	2	4		.282	.317	.410	.727	128	2	2	101	23	11	.679	2			-3	C	0.1
Total	2	60	162	15	41	5	6	0	9	9		.253	.292	.358	.650	97	-2	-1	98	56	19	.595	5			-3	/C1O3	-0.2
■ **BOB RAUDMAN** Raudman, Robert Joyce "Shorty" b: 3/14/42, Erie, Pa. BL/TL, 5'9.5", 185 lbs. Deb: 9/13/66																												
1966	Chi-N	8	29	1	7	2	0	0	2	1	4	.241	.267	.310	.577	60	-2	-2	100	93	2	.435	0	0	0	0	/O	-0.1
1967	Chi-N	8	26	0	4	0	0	0	1	1	4	.154	.185	.154	.339	-2	-3	-3	102	104	0	.208	0	0	0	0	/O	-0.3
Total	2	16	55	1	11	2	0	0	3	2	8	.200	.228	.236	.464	31	-5	-5	101	98	3	.326	0	0	0	0	/O	-0.4
■ **JOHNNY RAWLINGS** Rawlings, John William "Red" b: 8/17/1892, Bloomfield, Iowa d: 10/16/72, Inglewood, Cal. BR/TR, 5'8", 158 lbs. Deb: 4/14/14																												
1914	Cin-N	33	60	9	13	1	0	0	8	6	8	.217	.288	.233	.521	53	-3	-3	105	207	5	.447	1			1	3/2S	-0.1
	KC-F	61	193	19	41	3	0	0	15	22	25	.212	.293	.228	.521	53	-12	-10	95	123	16	.474	6			-12	S	-1.9
1915	KC-F	120	399	40	86	9	2	2	24	27	40	.216	.265	.263	.528	59	-22	-20	97	79	36	.476	17			-1	*S	-1.2
1917	Bos-N	122	371	37	95	9	4	2	31	38	32	.256	.337	.318	.655	105	2	4	96	96	43	.634	12			-10	2S/3O	0.0
1918	Bos-N	111	410	32	85	7	3	0	21	30	31	.207	.265	.239	.504	58	-22	-19	94	86	29	.431	10			8	S2O	-1.0
1919	Bos-N	77	275	30	70	8	2	1	16	16	20	.255	.298	.309	.607	85	-6	-5	98	72	28	.546	10			-8	2O/S	-1.2
1920	Bos-N	5	3	0	0	0	0	0	2	0	1	.000	.000	.000	.000	-99	-1	-1	96	0	0	.000	0	0	0	0	/2	0.0
	Phi-N	98	384	39	90	19	2	3	30	22	25	.234	.278	.318	.595	65	-15	-19	109	85	34	.513	9	6	-1	-8	2	-2.7
	Yr	103	387	39	90	19	2	3	32	22	26	.233	.276	.315	.591	64	-16	-19	108	81	34	.508	9	6	-1	-8		-2.7
1921	Phi-N	60	254	20	74	14	2	1	16	8	12	.291	.318	.374	.692	81	-7	-7	102	53	29	.589	4	5	-2	10	2	0.1
	NY-N	86	307	40	82	8	1	1	30	18	19	.267	.316	.309	.626	68	-14	-13	98	114	31	.528	4	4	-1	3	2/S	-1.0
	Yr	146	561	60	156	22	3	2	46	26	31	.278	.317	.339	.656	74	-21	-20	99	89	60	.556	8	9	-3	13		-0.9
1922	NY-N	88	308	46	87	13	8	1	30	23	15	.282	.342	.386	.729	85	-6	-7	104	88	41	.678	7	6	-2	2	2/3	-0.6
1923	Pit-N	119	461	53	131	18	4	1	45	25	29	.284	.322	.347	.669	79	-16	-13	97	103	54	.591	9	0	3	-12	*2	-2.0
1924	Pit-N	3	3	0	1	0	0	0	2	0	0	.333	.333	.333	.667	74	-0	-0	106	730	0	.500	0	0	0	0	H	0.0
1925	Pit-N	36	110	17	31	7	0	2	13	8	8	.282	.336	.400	.736	86	-2	-2	102	92	15	.663	0	1	-1	-1	2	-0.3
1926	Pit-N	61	181	27	42	6	0	0	20	14	10	.232	.287	.265	.552	44	-13	-16	112	144	15	.468	3			-0	2	-1.2
Total	12	1080	3719	409	928	122	28	14	303	257	275	.250	.302	.309	.611	72	-135	-134	100	95	375	.541	92	22		-29	2S/O3	-13.1
■ **IRV RAY** Ray, Irving Burton "Stubby" b: 1/22/1864, Harrington, Me. d: 2/21/48, Harrington, Me. TL, 5'6", Deb: 1888																												
1888	Bos-N	50	206	26	51	2	3	2	26	6	11	.248	.272	.316	.588	84	-3	-4	106	139	20	.510	7			-10	S/2	-1.2
1889	Bos-N	9	33	8	10	1	0	0	2	4	0	.303	.378	.333	.712	100	0	0	102	55	5	.696	1			0	/S3	0.0
	Bal-a	26	106	20	36	4	1	0	17	7	6	.340	.397	.396	.793	129	4	4	100	102	22	.914	12			0	S/O	0.4
1890	BB-a	38	139	28	50	6	2	1		15		.360	.433	.453	.886	164	12	12	100	0	33	1.034	11			-18	S	-0.3
1891	Bal-a	103	418	72	116	17	5	0	58	54	18	.278	.366	.342	.708	105	5	4	101	104	64	.758	28			-16	OS	-1.1
Total	4	226	902	154	263	30	11	3	103	86	35	.292	.360	.359	.720	112	18	16	102	93	144	.751	59			-45	S/O32	-2.2
■ **JOHNNY RAY** Ray, John Cornelius b: 3/1/57, Chouteau, Okla. BB/TR, 5'11", 170 lbs. Deb: 9/02/81																												
1981	Pit-N	31	102	10	25	11	0	0	6	6	9	.245	.287	.353	.640	84	-3	-2	96	65	10	.525	0	0	0	0	2	0.0
1982	Pit-N	162	647	79	182	30	7	7	63	36	34	.281	.320	.382	.702	87	-5	-13	110	98	80	.625	16	7	1	8	*2	0.3
1983	Pit-N	151	576	68	163	**38**	7	5	53	35	26	.283	.324	.399	.723	97	-2	-4	103	91	73	.654	18	9	0	20	*2/3	2.2
1984	Pit-N	155	555	75	173	**38**	6	6	67	37	31	.312	.358	.434	.792	129	15	19	94	103	83	.723	11	6	-0	-7	*2	1.6
1985	Pit-N	154	594	67	163	33	3	7	70	46	24	.274	.328	.375	.703	94	-3	-5	103	121	71	.627	13	9	-2	-11	*2	-1.7
1986	Pit-N	155	579	67	174	33	0	7	78	58	47	.301	.367	.394	.761	110	9	9	100	132	79	.678	6	9	-4	9	*2	1.7
1987	Pit-N	123	472	48	129	19	3	5	54	41	36	.273	.331	.358	.689	79	-11	-14	104	124	53	.590	4	2	0	11	*2	0.0
	Cal-A	30	127	16	44	11	0	0	15	3	10	.346	.362	.433	.795	112	2	2	99	115	19	.667	0	0	0	-1	2/D	0.3
1988	Cal-A	153	602	75	184	42	7	6	83	36	38	.306	.349	.429	.777	124	12	17	94	127	90	.704	4	1	1	3	*2O/D	2.7
Total	8	1114	4254	505	1237	255	33	43	489	298	255	.291	.339	.397	.736	102	15	9	101	112	556	.674	72	43	-4	32	*2/OD3	7.1
■ **LARRY RAY** Ray, Larry Dale b: 3/11/58, Madison, Ind. BL/TR, 6'1", 195 lbs. Deb: 9/10/82																												
1982	Hou-N	5	6	0	1	0	0	0	1	0	4	.167	.167	.167	.333	-7	-1	-1	99	392	0	.200	0	0	0	-0	/O	0.0
■ **FLOYD RAYFORD** Rayford, Floyd Kinnard b: 7/27/57, Memphis, Tenn. BR/TR, 5'10", 190 lbs. Deb: 4/17/80																												
1980	Bal-A	8	18	1	4	0	0	0	1	0	5	.222	.222	.222	.444	22	-2	-2	101	97	1	.267	0	0	0	0	/32D	0.0
1982	Bal-A	34	53	7	7	0	0	3	5	6	14	.132	.220	.302	.522	42	-4	-4	100	80	4	.468	0	1	-1	0	3/CD	-0.4
1983	StL-N	56	104	5	22	4	0	3	14	10	27	.212	.281	.337	.617	72	-4	-4	98	126	10	.541	1	0	0	1	3	-0.4
1984	Bal-A	86	250	24	64	14	0	4	27	12	51	.256	.298	.360	.658	86	-7	-5	94	106	25	.541	0	3	-2	6	C3/1	0.3
1985	Bal-A	105	359	55	110	21	1	18	48	10	69	.306	.325	.521	.846	129	12	12	99	79	56	.769	3	1	0	-1	3C/D	1.0
1986	Bal-A	81	210	15	37	4	0	8	19	15	50	.176	.231	.310	.541	47	-16	-16	99	85	14	.444	0	0	0	-1	3C/D	-1.6
1987	Bal-A	20	50	5	11	0	0	2	3	2	9	.220	.250	.340	.590	56	-3	-3	98	52	4	.463	0	0	0	2	C/3D	0.0
Total	7	390	1044	112	255	43	1	38	117	55	225	.244	.284	.397	.681	86	-25	-22	98	90	113	.598	4	5	-2	9	3C/D12	-1.1
■ **FRED RAYMER** Raymer, Frederick Charles b: 11/12/1875, Leavenworth, Kan. d: 6/11/57, Los Angeles, Cal. TR, 5'11", 185 lbs. Deb: 4/24/01																												
1901	Chi-N	120	463	41	108	14	2	0	43	11		.233	.251	.272	.523	53	-27	-27	100	117	37	.437	18			-7	3S/12	-2.6
1904	Bos-N	114	419	28	88	12	3	1	27	13		.210	.234	.260	.494	56	-23	-21	97	90	30	.420	17			-2	*2	-2.1
1905	Bos-N	137	498	26	105	14	2	0	31	8		.211	.223	.247	.470	43	-36	-34	97	89	32	.372	15			-15	*2/1O	-4.3
Total	3	371	1380	95	301	40	7	1	101	32		.218	.236	.259	.495	50	-86	-82	98	99	99	.408	50			-24	2/3S1O	-9.0
■ **HARRY RAYMOND** Raymond, Harry H. "Jack" b: 2/20/1862, Utica, N.Y. d: 3/21/25, San Diego, Cal. 5'9", 179 lbs. Deb: 1888																												
1888	Lou-a	32	123	8	26	2	0	0	13	1		.211	.218	.228	.445	50	-7	-6	91	142	8	.371	7			0	3/O	-0.4

YEAR	TM/L	G	AB	R	H	2B	3B	HR	RBI	BB	SO	AVG	OBP	SLG	PRO	/A	BR	/A	PF	CHI	RC	TA	SB	CS	SBR	FR	POS	TPR
1889	Lou-a	130	515	58	123	12	9	0	47	19	45	.239	.270	.297	.567	66	-25	-22	96	93	48	.495	19			-3	*3/OP	-1.9
1890	Lou-a	123	521	91	135	7	4	2		22		.259	.293	.299	.592	72	-16	-22	107	0	52	.516	18			-11	*3/S	-3.0
1891	Lou-a	14	59	4	12	2	0	0	2	5	6	.203	.288	.237	.525	58	-3	-2	90	36	5	.511	3			0	S	-0.1
1892	Pit-N	12	49	4	4	0	1	0	2	4	8	.082	.151	.122	.273	-17	-7	-6	94	98	1	.244	1			0	3	-0.5
	Was-N	4	15	2	1	0	0	0	0	3	2	.067	.222	.067	.289	-10	-2	-2	105	0	0	.357	1			0	/3	-0.1
	Yr	16	64	6	5	0	1	0	2	7	10	.078	.169	.109	.278	-15	-9	-8	96	80	2	.271	2			0		-0.6
Total	5	315	1282	167	301	23	14	2	64	54	61	.235	.270	.279	.549	63	-61	-60	100	56	114	.478	49			-14	3/SOP	-6.0
■ **LOU RAYMOND**	Raymond, Louis Anthony (born Louis Anthony Raymondjack) b: 12/11/1894, Buffalo, N.Y. d: 5/2/79, Rochester, N.Y. 5'10.5", 187 lbs. Deb: 5/02/19																											
1919	Phi-N	1	2	0	1	0	0	0	0	0	0	.500	.500	.500	1.000	194	0	0	104	0	0	1.000	0			0	/2	0.0
■ **AL REACH**	Reach, Alfred James b: 5/25/1840, London, England d: 1/14/28, Atlantic City, N.J TL , 5'6", 155 lbs. Deb: 5/20/1871 M																											
1871	Ath-n	26	135	43	47							.348															*2	
1872	Ath-n	23	115	21	22							.191															O/1	
1873	Ath-n	13	64	13	15							.234															/O2	
1874	Ath-n	14	53	8	9							.170															O	
1875	Ath-n	5	22	4	5							.227															/O2	
Total	5 n	81	389	89	98							.252															/O2	
■ **BOB REACH**	Reach, Robert b: 8/28/1843, Williamsburg, N.Y. d: 5/19/22, Springfield, Mass. 5'5", 155 lbs. Deb: 4/23/1872																											
1872	Oly-n	1	5	1	1							.200															/S	
1873	Nat-n	1	5	1	1							.200															/S	
Total	2 n	2	10	2	2							.200															/S	
■ **RANDY READY**	Ready, Randy Max b: 1/8/60, Fremont, Cal. BR/TR, 5'11", 180 lbs. Deb: 9/04/83																											
1983	Mil-A	12	37	8	15	3	2	1	6	6	3	.405	.488	.676	1.164	236	6	7	92	84	12	1.348	0	1	-1	0	/3D	0.6
1984	Mil-A	37	123	13	23	6	1	3	13	14	18	.187	.270	.325	.595	70	-6	-5	92	108	11	.529	0	0	0	3	3	-0.1
1985	Mil-A	48	181	29	48	9	5	1	21	14	23	.265	.321	.387	.708	89	-2	-3	105	121	22	.612	0	0	0	4	O/32D	0.1
1986	Mil-A	23	79	8	15	4	0	1	4	9	9	.190	.273	.278	.551	50	-5	-5	102	65	6	.493	2	0	1	-2	O/23D	-0.6
	SD-N	1	3	0	0	0	0	0	0	0	1	.000	.000	.000	.000	-99	-1	-1	95	0	0	.000	0	0	0	0	/3	0.0
1987	SD-N	124	350	69	108	26	6	12	54	67	44	.309	.424	.520	.944	154	27	29	97	99	81	1.028	7	3	0	1	32O	2.9
1988	SD-N	114	331	43	88	16	2	7	39	39	38	.266	.349	.390	.738	115	6	7	97	104	48	.714	6	2	1	-2	32O	0.6
Total	6	359	1104	170	297	64	16	25	137	149	136	.269	.360	.424	.783	117	25	28	98	102	181	.783	15	6	1	4	3/2OD	3.5
■ **LEROY REAMS**	Reams, Leroy b: 8/11/43, Pine Bluff, Ark. BL/TR, 6'2", 175 lbs. Deb: 5/07/69																											
1969	Phi-N	1	1	0	0	0	0	0	0	0	1	.000	.000	.000	.000	-99	-0	-0	98	0	0	.000	0	0	0	0	H	0.0
■ **PHIL REARDON**	Reardon, Philip Michael b: 10/3/1883, Brooklyn, N.Y. d: 9/28/20, Brooklyn, N.Y. BR/TR, Deb: 9/19/06																											
1906	Bro-N	5	14	0	1	0	0	0	0	0		.071	.071	.071	.143	-64	-2	-2	87	0	0	.077	0			-0	/O	-0.2
■ **ART REBEL**	Rebel, Arthur Anthony b: 3/4/15, Cincinnati, Ohio BL/TL, 5'8", 180 lbs. Deb: 4/19/38																											
1938	Phi-N	7	9	2	2	0	0	0	1	1	1	.222	.300	.222	.522	45	-1	-1	100	181	0	.375	0			-1	/O	-0.1
1945	StL-N	26	72	12	25	4	0	0	5	6	4	.347	.397	.403	.800	123	2	2	100	60	11	.720	1			1	O	0.3
Total	2	33	81	14	27	4	0	0	6	7	5	.333	.386	.383	.769	114	2	2	100	74	11	.684	1			0	/O	0.2
■ **JOHN RECCIUS**	Reccius, John b: 6/7/1862, Louisville, Ky. d: 9/1/30, Louisville, Ky. 5'6.5", Deb: 5/02/1882																											
1882	Lou-a	74	266	46	63	12	3	1		23		.237	.298	.316	.613	114	3	5	94	0	26	.527				-2	*OP	0.2
1883	Lou-a	18	63	10	9	2	0	0		7		.143	.229	.175	.403	34	-4	-4	94	0	3	.333				0	O/P	-0.2
Total	2	92	329	56	72	14	3	1		30		.219	.284	.289	.573	98	-2	1	94	0	28	.486				-2	/OP	0.0
■ **PHIL RECCIUS**	Reccius, Phillip b: 6/7/1862, Louisville, Ky. d: 2/15/03, Louisville, Ky. 5'9", 163 lbs. Deb: 9/25/1882																											
1882	Lou-a	4	15	0	2	0	0	0		0		.133	.133	.133	.267	-11	-2	-2	94	0	0	.154				0	/O	0.0
1883	Lou-a	1	3	1	1	1	0	0		0		.333	.333	.667	1.000	228	0	0	94	0	1	1.000				0	/O	0.0
1884	Lou-a	73	263	23	63	9	2	3		5		.240	.267	.323	.591	106	-2	3	89	0	23	.475				-7	3PS	-0.3
1885	Lou-a	102	402	57	97	8	10	1		13		.241	.267	.318	.585	85	-6	-8	102	0	35	.466				-2	*3/P	-0.3
1886	Lou-a	5	13	4	4	1	1	0		3		.308	.471	.538	1.009	202	2	2	108	0	3	1.222	0			0	/OP	0.2
1887	Lou-a	11	37	9	9	2	0	0		8		.243	.391	.297	.689	90	0	-0	107	0	6	.821	3			0	O/S	0.0
	Cle-a	62	229	23	47	6	3	0		24		.205	.295	.258	.552	58	-12	-11	98	0	21	.533	9			7	3/P	-0.4
	Yr	73	266	32	56	8	3	0		32		.211	.309	.263	.572	63	-12	-12	99	0	26	.571	12			7		-0.4
1888	Lou-a	2	9	0	2	1	0	0	4	1		.222	.300	.333	.633	117	0	0	91	344	1	.571	0			0	/3	0.0
1890	Roc-a	1	4	0	0	0	0	0		0		.000	.000	.000	.000	-99	-1	-1	93	0	0	.000	0			0	/O	0.0
Total	8	261	975	117	225	28	16	4	4	54		.231	.280	.305	.585	84	-20	-17	98	3	90	.501	12			-2	3/POS	-0.8
■ **JOHNNY REDER**	Reder, John Anthony b: 9/24/09, Lublin, Poland BR/TR, 6', 184 lbs. Deb: 4/16/32																											
1932	Bos-A	17	37	4	5	1	0	0	3	6	6	.135	.256	.162	.418	11	-5	-5	97	167	2	.375	0	0	0	0	1/3	-0.4
■ **BUCK REDFERN**	Redfern, George Howard b: 4/7/02, Asheville, N.C. d: 9/8/64, Asheville, N.C. BR/TR, 5'11", 165 lbs. Deb: 4/11/28																											
1928	Chi-A	86	261	22	61	6	3	0	35	12	19	.234	.267	.280	.547	44	-21	-21	99	165	21	.460	8	2	1	-3	2S/3	-1.6
1929	Chi-A	21	46	0	6	0	0	0	3	3	3	.130	.184	.130	.314	-19	-8	-8	95	171	1	.244	1	1	-0	1	2/3S	-0.5
Total	2	107	307	22	67	6	3	0	38	15	22	.218	.255	.257	.512	35	-29	-29	98	165	22	.424	9	3	1	-3	/2S3	-2.1
■ **JOE REDFIELD**	Redfield, Joseph Randall b: 1/14/61, Doylestown, Pa. BR/TR, 6'2", 185 lbs. Deb: 6/04/88																											
1988	Cal-A	1	2	0	0	0	0	0	0	0	0	.000	.000	.000	.000	-99	-1	-1	94	0	0	.000	0	0	0	0	/3	0.0
■ **GLENN REDMON**	Redmon, Glenn Vincent b: 1/11/48, Detroit, Mich. BR/TR, 5'11", 180 lbs. Deb: 9/08/74																											
1974	SF-N	7	17	0	4	3	0	0	4	1	3	.235	.278	.412	.690	84	-0	-0	108	221	2	.615	0	0	0	-0	/2	0.0
■ **HARRY REDMOND**	Redmond, Harry John b: 9/13/1887, Cleveland, Ohio d: 7/10/60, Cleveland, Ohio TR , Deb: 09																											
1909	Bro-N	6	19	3	0	0	0	0	1	0		.000	.000	.000	.000	-99	-4	-4	99	0	0	.000	0			1	/2	-0.3
■ **WAYNE REDMOND**	Redmond, Howard Wayne b: 11/25/45, Athens, Ala. BR/TR, 5'10", 165 lbs. Deb: 9/07/65																											
1965	Det-A	4	4	1	0	0	0	0	0	1	1	.000	.200	.000	.200	-36	-1	-1	105	0	0	.250	0	0	0	0	/O	0.0
1969	Det-A	5	3	0	0	0	0	0	0	0	2	.000	.000	.000	.000	-97	-1	-1	103	0	0	.000	0	0	0	0	H	0.0
Total	2	9	7	1	0	0	0	0	0	1	3	.000	.125	.000	.125	-59	-2	-2	105	0	0	.143	0	0	0	0	/O	0.0
■ **JACK REDMOND**	Redmond, John Mc Kittrick "Red" b: 9/3/10, Florence, Ariz. d: 7/27/68, Garland, Tex. BL/TR, 5'11", 185 lbs. Deb: 4/22/35																											
1935	Was-A	22	34	8	6	1	0	1	7	3	1	.176	.243	.294	.537	42	-3	-3	92	183	3	.464	0	0	0	-1	C	-0.2
■ **BILLY REDMOND**	Redmond, William T. b: Brooklyn, N.Y. BL/TL, Deb: 5/04/1875																											
1875	RS-n	18	80	10	14							.175															S/3	
1877	Cin-N	3	12	1	3	1	0	0	3	1	1	.250	.308	.333	.641	125	0	0	82	269	1	.556				0	/S	0.0
1878	Mil-N	48	187	16	43	8	0	0	21	8	13	.230	.262	.273	.534	71	-5	-6	107	148	14	.410				-17	S/O3C	-1.9
Total	2	51	199	17	46	9	0	0	24	9	14	.231	.264	.276	.541	74	-5	-6	105	155	15	.418				-17	/SO3C	-1.9
■ **GARY REDUS**	Redus, Gary Eugene b: 11/1/56, Athens, Ala. BR/TR, 6'1", 180 lbs. Deb: 9/07/82																											
1982	Cin-N	20	83	12	18	3	2	1	7	5	21	.217	.261	.337	.599	65	-4	-4	102	78	8	.657	11	2	2	0	O	-0.1
1983	Cin-N	125	453	90	112	20	9	17	51	71	111	.247	.353	.444	.797	116	12	11	103	85	76	.870	39	14	3	5	*O	1.8
1984	Cin-N	123	394	69	100	21	3	7	22	52	71	.254	.342	.376	.718	96	2	-1	106	51	58	.806	48	11	8	-3	*O	0.0
1985	Cin-N	101	246	51	62	14	4	6	28	44	52	.252	.368	.415	.782	113	7	6	105	93	45	.995	48	12	7	-6	O	0.5
1986	Phi-N	90	340	62	84	22	4	11	33	47	78	.247	.344	.432	.776	108	6	4	104	77	55	.838	25	7	3	5	O	1.1
1987	Chi-A	130	475	78	112	26	6	12	48	69	90	.236	.333	.392	.724	85	-4	-11	109	91	69	.806	52	11	9	7	*O/D	0.2
1988	Chi-A	77	262	42	69	10	4	6	34	33	52	.263	.350	.401	.751	113	4	5	97	112	42	.830	26	2	7	2	O/D	1.2
	Pit-N	30	71	12	14	2	0	2	4	15	19	.197	.345	.310	.655	91	-0	-0	98	57	9	.717	5	2	0	1	O	0.1

YEAR	TM/L	G	AB	R	H	2B	3B	HR	RBI	BB	SO	AVG	OBP	SLG	PRO	/A	BR	/A	PF	CHI	RC	TA	SB	CS	SBR	FR	POS	TPR
Total	7	696	2324	416	571	118	32	62	227	336	494	.246	.344	.404	.748	102	22	9	104	82	362	.848	254	61	40	12	O/D	4.8
■ BOB REECE	Reece, Robert Scott b: 1/5/51, Sacramento, Cal. BR/TR, 6'1", 190 lbs. Deb: 4/22/78																											
1978	Mon-N	9	11	2	2	1	0	0	3	0	4	.182	.182	.273	.455	27	-1	-1	96	397	1	.333	0	0	0	1	/C	0.0
■ HUGH REED	Reed, Hugh b: 1837, Chicago, Ill. d: 11/3/1883, Chicago, Ill. Deb: 8/26/1874																											
1874	Bal-n	1	4	0	0							.000															/O	
■ JEFF REED	Reed, Jeffrey Scott b: 11/12/62, Joliet, Ill. BL/TR, 6'2", 185 lbs. Deb: 4/05/84																											
1984	Min-A	18	21	3	3	3	0	0	1	2	6	.143	.217	.286	.503	36	-2	-2	106	66	1	.444	0	0	0	0	C	0.0
1985	Min-A	7	10	2	2	0	0	0	0	0	3	.200	.200	.200	.400	10	-1	-1	103	0	0	.250	0	0	0	0	/C	0.0
1986	Min-A	68	165	13	39	6	1	2	9	16	19	.236	.308	.321	.629	67	-6	-8	108	61	17	.555	1	0	0	-4	C	-0.7
1987	Mon-N	75	207	15	44	11	0	1	21	12	20	.213	.259	.280	.539	40	-17	-19	106	137	14	.413	0	1	-1	-9	C	-2.2
1988	Mon-N	43	123	10	27	3	2	0	9	13	22	.220	.294	.276	.571	61	-5	-6	106	106	10	.485	1	0	0	2	C	-0.1
	Cin-N	49	142	10	33	6	0	1	7	15	19	.232	.306	.296	.602	70	-5	-5	105	62	13	.514	0	0	0	-0	C	-0.3
	Yr	92	265	20	60	9	2	1	16	28	41	.226	.300	.287	.587	66	-10	-12	105	84	25	.507	1	0	0	2		-0.4
Total	5	260	668	53	148	29	3	4	47	58	89	.222	.286	.292	.578	56	-36	-41	106	92	57	.491	2	1	0	-11	C	-3.3
■ JODY REED	Reed, Jody Eric b: 7/26/62, Tampa, Fla. BR/TR, 5'9", 170 lbs. Deb: 9/12/87																											
1987	Bos-A	9	30	4	9	1	1	0	8	4	0	.300	.382	.400	.782	110	1	1	99	266	5	.773	1	1	-0	0	/S23	0.0
1988	Bos-A	109	338	60	99	23	1	1	28	45	21	.293	.382	.376	.758	104	8	4	109	86	51	.717	1	3	-2	-1	S2/3	0.6
Total	2	118	368	64	108	24	2	1	36	49	21	.293	.382	.378	.760	104	8	4	108	100	56	.721	2	4	-2	-1	/S23	0.6
■ JACK REED	Reed, John Burwell b: 2/2/33, Silver City, Miss. BR/TR, 6', 185 lbs. Deb: 4/23/61																											
1961	NY-A	28	13	4	2	0	0	0	1	1	1	.154	.214	.154	.368	0	-2	-2	96	196	0	.273	0	0	0	-9	O	-1.1
1962	NY-A	88	43	17	13	2	1	1	4	4	7	.302	.362	.465	.827	129	1	2	94	69	7	.813	2	1	0	-22	O	-2.3
1963	NY-A	106	73	18	15	3	1	0	1	9	14	.205	.293	.274	.567	60	-4	-4	101	21	7	.567	5	1	1	-20	O	-2.7
Total	3	222	129	39	30	5	2	1	6	14	22	.233	.308	.326	.633	76	-4	-4	98	54	14	.618	7	2	1	-51	O	-6.1
■ MILT REED	Reed, Milton D. b: 7/4/1890, Atlanta, Ga. d: 7/27/38, Atlanta, Ga. BL/TR, 5'9.5", 150 lbs. Deb: 9/09/11																											
1911	StL-N	1	1	0	0	0	0	0	0	0	0	.000	.000	.000	.000	-99	-0	-0	101	0	0	.000	0			0	H	0.0
1913	Phi-N	13	24	4	6	1	0	0	0	1	5	.250	.280	.292	.572	57	-1	-2	112	0	2	.500	1			0	/S2	0.0
1914	Phi-N	44	107	10	22	2	1	0	2	10	13	.206	.280	.243	.523	56	-6	-6	100	28	8	.482	4			-1	S2/3	-0.5
1915	Bro-F	10	31	2	9	1	1	0	8	2	0	.290	.333	.387	.720	116	0	1	98	240	5	.727	2			0	S	0.1
Total	4	68	163	16	37	4	2	0	10	13	18	.227	.288	.276	.564	66	-7	-7	101	63	15	.524	7			-0	/S23	-0.4
■ TED REED	Reed, Ralph Edwin b: 10/18/1890, Beaver, Pa. d: 2/16/59, Beaver, Pa. BR/TR, 5'11", 190 lbs. Deb: 9/10/15																											
1915	New-F	20	77	5	20	1	2	0	4	2	7	.260	.278	.325	.603	83	-2	-2	94	51	8	.491	1			-2	3	-0.2
■ BILLY REED	Reed, William Joseph b: 11/12/22, Shawano, Wis. BL/TR, 5'10.5", 175 lbs. Deb: 4/15/52																											
1952	Bos-N	15	52	4	13	0	0	0	0	0	5	.250	.264	.250	.514	46	-4	-4	95	0	3	.341	0	0	0	-0	2	-0.3
■ ICICLE REEDER	Reeder, James Edward b: 1865, Cincinnati, Ohio Deb: 6/24/1884																											
1884	Cin-a	3	14	0	2	0	0	0		0		.143	.143	.143	.286	-5	-2	-2	106	0	0	.167				0	/O	-0.1
	Was-U	3	12	0	2	0	0	0		0		.167	.167	.167	.333	13	-1	-1	97	0	0	.200	0			0	/O	0.0
Total	1	6	26	0	4	0	0	0		0		.154	.154	.154	.308	3	-3	-3	102	0	1	.182	0			0	/O	-0.1
■ NICK REEDER	Reeder, Nicholas (born Nicholas Herchenroeder) b: 3/22/1867, Louisville, Ky. d: 9/26/1894, Louisville, Ky. BR/TR, 5'9", 189 lbs. Deb: 4/11/1891																											
1891	Lou-a	1	2	0	0	0	0	0	0	0	1	.000	.000	.000	.000	-99	-1	-0	90	0	0	.000	0			0	/3	0.0
■ RANDY REESE	Reese, Andrew Jackson b: 2/7/04, Tupelo, Miss. d: 1/10/66, Tupelo, Miss. BR/TR, 5'11", 180 lbs. Deb: 4/15/27																											
1927	NY-N	97	355	43	94	14	2	4	21	13	52	.265	.298	.349	.648	73	-14	-14	100	55	36	.559	5			1	3O/1	-0.9
1928	NY-N	109	406	61	125	18	4	6	44	13	24	.308	.331	.416	.747	92	-5	-6	102	85	53	.676	7			-9	O2/1S3	-1.5
1929	NY-N	58	209	36	55	11	3	0	21	15	19	.263	.316	.344	.660	64	-12	-12	100	100	23	.623	8			2	2/O3	-0.8
1930	NY-N	67	172	26	47	4	2	4	25	10	12	.273	.313	.390	.703	70	-9	-8	98	109	20	.624	1			-2	O3/1	-1.1
Total	4	331	1142	166	321	47	11	14	111	51	107	.281	.315	.378	.694	78	-40	-40	100	82	132	.621	21			-8	O/321S	-4.3
■ PEE WEE REESE	Reese, Harold Henry b: 7/23/18, Ekron, Ky. BR/TR, 5'10", 160 lbs. Deb: 4/23/40 CH																											
1940	Bro-N	84	312	58	85	8	4	5	28	45	42	.272	.366	.372	.738	96	3	-0	108	84	47	.776	15			-9	S	0.0
1941	Bro-N	152	595	76	136	23	5	2	46	68	56	.229	.311	.294	.605	69	-22	-24	103	97	59	.551	10			8	*S	-0.2
1942	Bro-N	151	564	87	144	24	5	3	53	82	55	.255	.350	.332	.681	98	2	1	102	106	71	.664	15			**18**	*S	3.1
1946	Bro-N	152	542	79	154	16	10	5	60	87	71	.284	.384	.378	.762	114	15	13	103	108	85	.761	10			0	*S	2.5
1947	Bro-N	142	476	81	135	24	4	12	73	**104**	67	.284	.414	.426	.841	118	21	18	105	115	93	.908	7			3	*S	3.1
1948	Bro-N	151	566	96	155	31	4	9	75	79	63	.274	.363	.390	.753	100	4	1	104	120	82	.761	25			11	*S	2.8
1949	Bro-N	155	617	**132**	172	27	3	16	73	116	59	.279	.396	.410	.806	115	19	18	102	79	111	.887	26			3	*S	3.6
1950	Bro-N	141	531	97	138	21	5	11	52	91	62	.260	.369	.380	.750	92	1	-4	107	82	81	.777	17			1	*S/3	1.0
1951	Bro-N	154	616	94	176	20	8	10	84	81	57	.286	.371	.393	.763	108	7	9	98	105	91	.729	20	14	-2	-5	*S	1.3
1952	Bro-N	149	559	94	152	18	8	6	58	86	59	.272	.369	.365	.734	103	6	5	102	108	84	.748	**30**	5	**6**	-12	*S	0.3
1953	Bro-N	140	524	108	142	25	7	13	61	82	61	.271	.374	.420	.794	103	7	4	104	97	88	.814	22	6	**3**	0	*S	1.7
1954	Bro-N	141	554	98	171	35	8	10	69	90	62	.309	.408	.455	.863	123	23	22	101	85	104	.865	8	5	-1	-3	*S	2.7
1955	Bro-N	145	553	99	156	29	4	10	61	78	60	.282	.374	.403	.777	102	7	4	104	94	82	.732	8	7	-2	-12	*S	-0.5
1956	Bro-N	147	572	85	147	19	2	9	46	56	69	.257	.324	.344	.669	78	-15	-17	103	83	66	.603	13	4	2	-1	*S3	-0.6
1957	Bro-N	103	330	33	74	3	1	1	29	39	32	.224	.308	.248	.557	45	-21	-28	116	141	27	.479	5	2	0	4	3S	-2.1
1958	LA-N	59	147	21	33	7	2	4	17	26	15	.224	.341	.381	.722	87	-2	-3	105	103	20	.697	1	2	-1	5	S3	0.3
Total	16	2166	8058	1338	2170	330	80	126	885	1210	890	.269	.366	.377	.743	98	56	17	103	100	1191	.759	232	45		11	*S3	19.0
■ JIMMIE REESE	Reese, James Herman (born James Herman Soloman) b: 10/1/05, Los Angeles, Cal. BL/TR, 5'11.5", 165 lbs. Deb: 4/19/30 C																											
1930	NY-A	77	188	44	65	14	2	3	18	11	8	.346	.382	.489	.871	133	5	8	90	59	35	.839	1	1	-0	-2	2/3	0.6
1931	NY-A	65	245	41	59	10	2	3	26	17	10	.241	.293	.335	.627	66	-13	-12	98	94	24	.540	2	3	-1	2	2	-0.6
1932	StL-N	90	309	38	82	15	0	2	26	20	19	.265	.314	.333	.648	74	-11	-11	100	89	33	.568	4			15	2	1.0
Total	3	232	742	123	206	39	4	8	70	48	37	.278	.324	.373	.697	85	-19	-15	97	83	92	.620	7	4		16	2/3	1.0
■ RICH REESE	Reese, Richard Benjamin b: 9/29/41, Leipsic, Ohio BL/TL, 6'3", 185 lbs. Deb: 9/04/64																											
1964	Min-A	10	7	0	0	0	0	0	0	0	1	.000	.000	.000	.000	-99	-2	-2	101	0	0	.000	0	0	0	0	/1	-0.1
1965	Min-A	14	7	0	2	1	0	0	0	2	2	.286	.444	.429	.873	148	1	1	101	0	1	1.000	0	0	0	-0	/1O	0.0
1966	Min-A	3	2	0	0	0	0	0	0	1	2	.000	.333	.000	.333	5	-0	-0	111	0	0	.500	0	0	0	0	H	0.0
1967	Min-A	95	101	13	25	5	0	4	20	8	17	.248	.303	.416	.719	103	1	0	107	154	13	.649	0	0	0	-1	1O	-0.3
1968	Min-A	126	332	40	86	15	2	4	28	18	36	.259	.303	.352	.656	92	-1	-3	106	93	35	.557	3	1	0	0	1O	-0.8
1969	Min-A	132	419	52	135	24	4	16	69	23	57	.322	.365	.513	.878	140	22	21	102	105	76	.827	1	5	-3	-4	*1/O	0.7
1970	Min-A	153	501	63	131	15	5	10	56	48	70	.261	.335	.371	.706	96	-4	-2	98	105	64	.646	5	4	-1	-5	*1	-1.5
1971	Min-A	120	329	40	72	8	3	10	39	20	35	.219	.274	.353	.627	73	-11	-13	104	109	30	.548	7	4	-0	-2	1/O	-2.0
1972	Min-A	132	197	23	43	3	2	5	26	25	27	.218	.306	.330	.636	83	-2	-4	107	136	20	.566	0	1	-1	4	1O	-1.2
1973	Det-A	59	102	10	14	1	0	2	4	7	17	.137	.193	.206	.399	12	-12	-12	101	58	4	.311	0	0	0	-3	1O	-1.8
	Min-A	22	23	7	4	1	1	1	3	6	6	.174	.345	.435	.780	114	1	1	104	91	4	.842	0	0	0	0	1	0.0
	Yr	81	125	17	18	2	1	3	7	13	23	.144	.225	.248	.473	32	-11	-12	102	68	8	.411	0	0	0	-3		-1.8
Total	10	866	2020	248	512	73	17	52	245	158	270	.253	.314	.384	.698	96	-8	-14	103	106	247	.636	16	15	-4	-10	1/O	-7.0
■ BOBBY REEVES	Reeves, Robert Edwin "Gunner" b: 6/24/04, Hill City, Tenn. BR/TR, 5'11", 170 lbs. Deb: 6/09/26																											
1926	Was-A	20	49	4	11	0	1	0	7	6	9	.224	.321	.265	.587	55	-3	-3	98	183	4	.538	1	1	-0	-2	3/2S	-0.3
1927	Was-A	112	380	37	97	11	5	1	39	21	53	.255	.296	.318	.614	61	-23	-21	97	105	36	.516	3	0	1	-8	S3/2	-1.9
1928	Was-A	102	353	44	107	16	8	3	42	24	47	.303	.351	.419	.770	100	0	-0	102	92	50	.701	4	8	-4	3	S2/3O	0.6
1929	Bos-A	140	460	66	114	19	2	2	28	60	57	.248	.343	.311	.654	68	-19	-20	102	66	52	.613	7	8	-3	7	*3/2S1	-0.7

YEAR	TM/L	G	AB	R	H	2B	3B	HR	RBI	BB	SO	AVG	OBP	SLG	PRO	/A	BR	/A	PF	CHI	RC	TA	SB	CS	SBR	FR	POS	TPR
1930	Bos-A	92	272	41	59	7	4	2	18	50	36	.217	.345	.294	.639	69	-14	-10	93	69	32	.647	6	2	1	-2	3S2	-0.6
1931	Bos-A	36	84	11	14	2	2	0	1	14	16	.167	.293	.238	.531	44	-7	-6	94	16	7	.493	0	1	-1	-1	2/P	-0.5
Total	6	502	1598	203	402	55	22	8	135	175	218	.252	.331	.329	.660	72	-66	-62	98	82	181	.605	21	20	-6	-4	3S/2P1O	-3.4

■ **RUDY REGALADO** Regalado, Rudolph Valentino b: 5/21/30, Los Angeles, Cal. BR/TR, 6'1", 185 lbs. Deb: 4/13/54

YEAR	TM/L	G	AB	R	H	2B	3B	HR	RBI	BB	SO	AVG	OBP	SLG	PRO	/A	BR	/A	PF	CHI	RC	TA	SB	CS	SBR	FR	POS	TPR
1954	Cle-A	65	180	21	45	5	0	2	24	19	16	.250	.335	.311	.646	73	-5	-6	106	147	19	.556	0	2	-1	-9	3/2	-1.9
1955	Cle-A	10	26	2	7	2	0	0	5	2	4	.269	.321	.346	.668	76	-1	-1	104	207	3	.579	0	0	0	-0	/32	0.0
1956	Cle-A	16	47	4	11	1	0	0	2	4	1	.234	.308	.255	.563	49	-3	-3	101	62	4	.459	0	0	0	-1	3/1	-0.3
Total	3	91	253	27	63	8	0	2	31	25	21	.249	.329	.304	.633	69	-9	-11	105	137	26	.554	0	2	-1	-10	/321	-2.2

■ **JOE REGAN** Regan, Joseph Charles b: 7/12/1872, Seymour, Conn. d: 11/18/48, Hartford, Conn. BR/TR, 6'1", Deb: 9/21/1898

YEAR	TM/L	G	AB	R	H	2B	3B	HR	RBI	BB	SO	AVG	OBP	SLG	PRO	/A	BR	/A	PF	CHI	RC	TA	SB	CS	SBR	FR	POS	TPR
1898	NY-N	2	5	1	1	0	0	0	2	0		.200	.200	.200	.400	17	-1	-0	95	605	0	.250	0			0	/O	0.0

■ **BILL REGAN** Regan, William Wright b: 1/23/1899, Pittsburgh, Pa. d: 6/11/68, Pittsburgh, Pa. BR/TR, 5'10", 155 lbs. Deb: 6/02/26

YEAR	TM/L	G	AB	R	H	2B	3B	HR	RBI	BB	SO	AVG	OBP	SLG	PRO	/A	BR	/A	PF	CHI	RC	TA	SB	CS	SBR	FR	POS	TPR
1926	Bos-A	108	403	40	106	21	3	4	34	23	37	.263	.309	.360	.669	73	-16	-17	101	75	45	.593	6	3	0	13	*2	0.1
1927	Bos-A	129	468	43	128	37	10	2	66	26	51	.274	.315	.408	.723	91	-11	-8	95	114	58	.674	10	0	3	1	*2	0.0
1928	Bos-A	138	511	53	135	30	6	7	75	21	40	.264	.296	.387	.683	80	-18	-17	98	120	58	.602	9	6	-1	8	*2/O	-0.2
1929	Bos-A	104	371	38	107	27	7	1	54	22	38	.288	.328	.407	.735	87	-7	-8	102	122	49	.669	7	5	-1	-12	23/1	-1.7
1930	Bos-A	134	507	54	135	35	10	3	53	25	60	.266	.303	.393	.696	81	-21	-15	93	86	60	.615	4	2	0	-7	*2/3	-1.9
1931	Pit-N	28	104	8	21	8	0	1	10	5	19	.202	.239	.308	.546	46	-8	-8	101	104	8	.470	2			-3	2	-1.0
Total	6	641	2364	236	632	158	36	18	292	122	245	.267	.306	.387	.694	81	-82	-73	97	103	278	.621	38	16		-0	2/31O	-4.7

■ **TONY REGO** Rego, Antone (born Antone Do Rego) b: 10/31/1897, Wailuku, Hawaii d: 1/6/78, Tulsa, Okla. BR/TR, 5'4", 165 lbs. Deb: 6/21/24

YEAR	TM/L	G	AB	R	H	2B	3B	HR	RBI	BB	SO	AVG	OBP	SLG	PRO	/A	BR	/A	PF	CHI	RC	TA	SB	CS	SBR	FR	POS	TPR
1924	StL-A	24	59	5	13	1	0	0	5	1	3	.220	.233	.237	.471	20	-7	-8	107	118	3	.326	0	0	0	0	C	-0.5
1925	StL-A	20	32	5	13	2	1	0	3	3	2	.406	.472	.531	1.003	143	3	2	108	59	8	1.105	0	0	0	0	C	0.4
Total	2	44	91	10	26	3	1	0	8	4	5	.286	.323	.341	.664	65	-4	-5	107	96	11	.554	0	0	0	0	/C	-0.1

■ **WALLY REHG** Rehg, Walter Phillip b: 8/31/1888, Summerfield, Ill. d: 4/5/46, Burbank, Cal. BR/TR, 5'8", 160 lbs. Deb: 4/15/12

YEAR	TM/L	G	AB	R	H	2B	3B	HR	RBI	BB	SO	AVG	OBP	SLG	PRO	/A	BR	/A	PF	CHI	RC	TA	SB	CS	SBR	FR	POS	TPR
1912	Pit-N	8	9	1	0	0	0	0	0	0	1	.000	.000	.000	.000	-99	-2	-2	99	0	0	.000	0			-1	/O	-0.2
1913	Bos-A	30	101	13	28	3	2	0	9	2	7	.277	.291	.347	.638	84	-2	-3	103	91	11	.562	4			-4	O	-0.8
1914	Bos-A	84	151	14	33	4	2	0	11	18	11	.219	.306	.272	.577	76	-5	-4	98	101	12	.516	5	8	-3	-6	O	-1.7
1915	Bos-A	5	5	2	1	0	0	0	0	0	1	.200	.200	.200	.400	20	-1	-0	99	0	0	.500	1			-0	/O	0.0
1917	Bos-N	87	341	48	92	12	6	1	31	24	32	.270	.320	.349	.669	109	2	3	96	94	41	.631	13			-10	O	-1.0
1918	Bos-N	40	133	6	32	5	1	1	12	5	14	.241	.268	.316	.584	83	-4	-3	94	101	11	.495	3			1	O	-0.4
1919	Cin-N	5	12	1	2	0	0	0	3	1	0	.167	.231	.167	.397	19	-1	-1	105	583	1	.300	0			-0	/O	-0.1
Total	7	259	752	85	188	24	11	2	66	50	66	.250	.299	.319	.618	89	-13	-11	97	103	76	.556	26	8		-20	O	-4.2

■ **FRANK REIBER** Reiber, Frank Bernard "Tubby" b: 9/19/09, Huntington, W.Va. BR/TR, 5'8.5", 169 lbs. Deb: 4/13/33

YEAR	TM/L	G	AB	R	H	2B	3B	HR	RBI	BB	SO	AVG	OBP	SLG	PRO	/A	BR	/A	PF	CHI	RC	TA	SB	CS	SBR	FR	POS	TPR
1933	Det-A	13	18	3	5	0	1	1	3	2	3	.278	.350	.556	.906	128	1	1	107	77	4	.923	0	0	0	-0	/C	0.1
1934	Det-A	3	1	0	0	0	0	0	0	2	0	.000	.667	.000	.667	86	0	0	98	0	0	2.000	0	0	0	0	H	0.0
1935	Det-A	8	11	3	3	0	0	0	1	3	3	.273	.429	.273	.701	88	-0	0	97	113	2	.750	0	0	0	0	/C	0.0
1936	Det-A	20	55	7	15	2	0	1	5	5	7	.273	.333	.364	.697	75	-2	-2	95	70	7	.610	0	1	-1	-2	C/O	-0.2
Total	4	44	85	13	23	2	1	2	9	12	13	.271	.361	.388	.749	91	-1	-1	98	76	12	.714	0	1	-1	-2	/CO	-0.1

■ **HERMAN REICH** Reich, Herman Charles b: 11/23/17, Bell, Cal. BR/TL, 6'2", 200 lbs. Deb: 5/03/49

YEAR	TM/L	G	AB	R	H	2B	3B	HR	RBI	BB	SO	AVG	OBP	SLG	PRO	/A	BR	/A	PF	CHI	RC	TA	SB	CS	SBR	FR	POS	TPR
1949	Was-A	2	2	0	0	0	0	0	0	0	1	.000	.000	.000	.000	-99	-1	-1	91	0	0	.000	0	0	0	0	H	0.0
	Cle-A	1	2	0	1	0	0	0	0	1	0	.500	.667	.500	1.167	216	0	1	98	0	1	2.000	0	0	0	-0	/O	0.0
	Yr	3	4	0	1	0	0	0	0	1	1	.250	.400	.250	.650	79	-0	-0	93	0	1	.667	0	0	0	-0		0.0
	Chi-N	108	386	43	108	18	2	3	34	13	32	.280	.305	.360	.665	82	-13	-10	94	88	41	.547	4			12	1O	0.1
Total	1	111	390	43	109	18	2	3	34	14	33	.279	.306	.359	.665	82	-13	-10	94	87	41	.548	4	0		12	/1O	0.1

■ **RICK REICHARDT** Reichardt, Frederic Carl b: 3/16/43, Madison, Wis. BR/TR, 6'3", 210 lbs. Deb: 9/01/64

YEAR	TM/L	G	AB	R	H	2B	3B	HR	RBI	BB	SO	AVG	OBP	SLG	PRO	/A	BR	/A	PF	CHI	RC	TA	SB	CS	SBR	FR	POS	TPR
1964	LA-A	11	37	0	6	0	0	0	0	1	12	.162	.184	.162	.346	-3	-5	-5	89	0	1	.250	1	0	0	1	O	-0.3
1965	Cal-A	20	75	8	20	4	0	1	6	5	12	.267	.321	.360	.681	95	-1	-0	98	88	9	.638	4	1	1	1	O	0.0
1966	Cal-A	89	319	48	92	5	4	16	44	27	61	.288	.368	.480	.847	143	17	18	99	97	57	.848	8	4	0	2	O	1.7
1967	Cal-A	146	498	56	132	14	2	17	69	35	90	.265	.322	.404	.726	118	7	10	96	117	61	.644	5	3	-0	5	*O	1.1
1968	Cal-A	151	534	62	136	20	3	21	73	42	118	.255	.330	.421	.751	134	17	20	94	115	72	.699	8	7	-2	4	*O	1.8
1969	Cal-A	137	493	60	125	11	4	13	68	43	100	.254	.324	.371	.695	94	-4	-4	99	130	56	.608	3	6	-3	5	*O/1	-0.5
1970	Cal-A	9	6	1	1	0	0	0	1	3	0	.167	.444	.167	.611	82	0	0	92	405	1	.800	0	0	0	-0	/O	0.0
	Was-A	107	277	42	70	14	2	15	46	23	69	.253	.330	.480	.810	125	7	8	96	105	39	.746	2	4	-2	-6	O/3	-0.2
	Yr	116	283	43	71	14	2	15	47	26	69	.251	.333	.473	.807	125	7	8	96	131	40	.747	2	4	-2	-6		-0.2
1971	Chi-A	138	496	53	138	14	2	19	62	37	90	.278	.336	.429	.765	118	9	10	98	96	68	.690	5	10	-5	-9	*O/1	-0.7
1972	Chi-A	101	291	31	73	14	4	8	43	28	63	.251	.323	.409	.732	110	6	4	106	126	39	.676	2	2	-1	-13	O	-1.3
1973	Chi-A	46	153	15	42	8	1	3	16	8	29	.275	.315	.399	.714	98	-0	-1	102	90	18	.615	2	3	-1	-3	O/D	-0.5
	KC-A	41	127	15	28	5	2	3	17	11	28	.220	.283	.362	.645	74	-4	-5	109	121	12	.548	0	1	-1	-1	D/O	-0.6
	Yr	87	280	30	70	13	3	6	33	19	57	.250	.300	.382	.682	86	-4	-6	106	106	31	.592	2	4	-2	-4		-1.1
1974	KC-A	1	1	0	1	0	0	0	0	0	0	1.000	1.000	1.000	2.000	448	0	0	106	0	1	—	0	0	0	0	H	0.0
Total	11	997	3307	391	864	109	24	116	445	263	672	.261	.328	.414	.742	115	49	55	98	111	434	.700	40	41	-13	-13	O/D13	0.5

■ **DICK REICHLE** Reichle, Richard Wendell b: 11/23/1896, Lincoln, Ill. d: 6/13/67, St.Louis, Mo. BL/TR, 6', 185 lbs. Deb: 9/19/22

YEAR	TM/L	G	AB	R	H	2B	3B	HR	RBI	BB	SO	AVG	OBP	SLG	PRO	/A	BR	/A	PF	CHI	RC	TA	SB	CS	SBR	FR	POS	TPR
1922	Bos-A	6	24	3	6	1	0	0	0	0	2	.250	.280	.292	.572	51	-2	-2	96	0	2	.444	0	0	0	0	/O	-0.1
1923	Bos-A	122	361	40	93	17	3	1	39	22	34	.258	.315	.330	.644	69	-16	-17	102	109	37	.555	3	6	-3	-2	O/1	-2.9
Total	2	128	385	43	99	18	3	1	39	22	36	.257	.313	.327	.640	68	-18	-19	101	103	39	.548	3	6	-3	-2	/O1	-3.0

■ **JESSIE REID** Reid, Jessie Thomas b: 6/1/62, Honolulu, Hawaii BL/TL, 6'1", 200 lbs. Deb: 9/09/87

YEAR	TM/L	G	AB	R	H	2B	3B	HR	RBI	BB	SO	AVG	OBP	SLG	PRO	/A	BR	/A	PF	CHI	RC	TA	SB	CS	SBR	FR	POS	TPR
1987	SF-N	6	8	1	1	0	0	1	1	1	5	.125	.222	.500	.722	88	-0	-0	96	57	1	.714	0	0	0	-1	/O	0.0
1988	SF-N	2	2	0	0	0	0	0	0	0	1	.000	.000	.000	.000	-99	-1	-0	94	0	0	.000	0	0	0	0	H	0.0
Total	2	8	10	1	1	0	0	1	1	1	6	.100	.182	.400	.582	54	-1	-1	96	47	1	.556	0	0	0	-1	/O	0.0

■ **SCOTT REID** Reid, Scott Donald b: 1/7/47, Chicago, Ill. BL/TR, 6'1", 195 lbs. Deb: 9/10/69

YEAR	TM/L	G	AB	R	H	2B	3B	HR	RBI	BB	SO	AVG	OBP	SLG	PRO	/A	BR	/A	PF	CHI	RC	TA	SB	CS	SBR	FR	POS	TPR
1969	Phi-N	13	19	5	4	0	0	0	0	7	5	.211	.423	.211	.634	84	0	0	98	0	2	.647	0	1	-1	-0	/O	0.0
1970	Phi-N	25	49	5	6	1	0	0	1	11	22	.122	.283	.143	.426	19	-5	-5	96	55	3	.409	0	0	0	4	O	-0.1
Total	2	38	68	10	10	1	0	0	1	18	27	.147	.326	.162	.487	38	-5	-5	97	39	5	.483	0	1	-1	4	/O	-0.1

■ **BILLY REID** Reid, William Alexander b: 5/17/1857, London, Ont., Can. d: 6/26/40, London, Ont., Can. BR/TR, 6', 170 lbs. Deb: 5/01/1883

YEAR	TM/L	G	AB	R	H	2B	3B	HR	RBI	BB	SO	AVG	OBP	SLG	PRO	/A	BR	/A	PF	CHI	RC	TA	SB	CS	SBR	FR	POS	TPR
1883	Bal-a	24	97	14	27	3	0	0		4		.278	.307	.309	.616	93	-0	-1	107	0	9	.486				0	2/S	0.0
1884	Pit-a	19	70	11	17	2	0	0		4		.243	.293	.271	.565	91	-1	-0	97	0	6	.453				0	O/321	0.0
Total	2	43	167	25	44	5	0	0		8		.263	.301	.293	.595	92	-1	-2	103	0	15	.472				0	/2O13S	0.0

■ **DUKE REILLEY** Reilley, Alexander Aloysius "Midget" b: 8/25/1884, Chicago, Ill. d: 3/4/68, Indianapolis, Ind. BB/TR, 5'4.5", 148 lbs. Deb: 8/28/09

YEAR	TM/L	G	AB	R	H	2B	3B	HR	RBI	BB	SO	AVG	OBP	SLG	PRO	/A	BR	/A	PF	CHI	RC	TA	SB	CS	SBR	FR	POS	TPR
1909	Cle-A	20	62	10	13	0	0	0	0	4		.210	.258	.210	.467	47	-4	-4	102	0	4	.449	5			9	O	0.5

■ **CHARLIE REILLEY** Reilley, Charles E. b: 1856, Hartford, Conn. d: 1888, BR/TR, 5'10", 165 lbs. Deb: 5/01/1879

YEAR	TM/L	G	AB	R	H	2B	3B	HR	RBI	BB	SO	AVG	OBP	SLG	PRO	/A	BR	/A	PF	CHI	RC	TA	SB	CS	SBR	FR	POS	TPR
1879	Tro-N	62	236	17	54	5	1	0	19	1	20	.229	.232	.258	.491	66	-10	-7	93	111	15	.341				-13	C1/O	-1.9
1880	Cin-N	30	103	8	21	1	0	0	9	0	5	.204	.204	.214	.417	42	-6	-6	99	149	5	.268				0	OC/3	-0.5
1881	Det-N	19	70	8	12	2	0	0	3	0	10	.171	.171	.200	.371	15	-7	-7	106	74	2	.241				0	C/OS31	-0.6
	Wor-N	2	8	2	3	0	0	0	1	0	1	.375	.375	.375	.750	130	0	0	105	118	1	.600				0	/C	0.0
	Yr	21	78	10	15	2	0	0	4	0	11	.192	.192	.218	.410	27	-6	-7	106	82	3	.270				0		-0.6
1882	Pro-N	3	11	0	2	0	0	0	2	1	2	.182	.250	.182	.432	39	-1	-1	106	343	1	.333				0	/C	0.0
Total	4	116	428	35	92	8	1	0	34	2	38	.215	.219	.238	.457	51	-23	-21	97	121	23	.310				-13	/CO13S	-3.0

YEAR	TM/L	G	AB	R	H	2B	3B	HR	RBI	BB	SO	AVG	OBP	SLG	PRO	/A	BR	/A	PF	CHI	RC	TA	SB	CS	SBR	FR	POS	TPR
■ **ARCH REILLY**	Reilly, Archer Edwin b: 8/17/1891, Alton, Ill. d: 11/29/63, Columbus, Ohio BR/TR, 5'10", 163 lbs. Deb: 6/01/17																											
1917	Pit-N	1	0	0	0	0	0	0	0	0	0	—	—	—	—	—	0	0	100	—	—	—	0			0	/3	0.0
■ **BARNEY REILLY**	Reilly, Bernard Eugene b: 2/7/1885, Brockton, Mass. d: 11/15/34, St.Joseph, Mo. BR/TR, 6' ", 175 lbs. Deb: 7/02/09																											
1909	Chi-A	12	25	3	5	0	0	0	3	3		.200	.286	.200	.486	55	-1	-1	97	231	2	.500	2			-0	2/O	-0.1
■ **JOSH REILLY**	Reilly, Charles b: 1868, San Francisco, Cal. d: 6/13/38, San Francisco, Cal. Deb: 5/02/1896																											
1896	Chi-N	9	42	6	9	1	0	0	2	1	1	.214	.233	.238	.471	23	-4	-5	108	50	3	.394	2			0	/2S	-0.3
■ **CHARLIE REILLY**	Reilly, Charles Thomas "Princeton Charlie" b: 6/24/1855, Princeton, N.J. d: 12/16/37, Los Angeles, Cal. BB/TR, 5'11", 190 lbs. Deb: 10/09/1889																											
1889	Col-a	6	23	5	11	1	0	3	6	2	2	.478	.538	.913	1.452	345	6	7	91	61	17	2.750	9			0	/3	0.5
1890	Col-a	137	530	75	141	23	3	4		35		.266	.319	.343	.662	98	-3	-2	99	0	74	.684	43			25	*3/2	1.8
1891	Pit-N	114	415	43	91	8	5	3	44	29	58	.219	.277	.284	.561	64	-18	-19	101	103	39	.528	20			-3	*3S/O	-1.6
1892	Phi-N	91	331	42	65	7	3	1	24	18	43	.196	.242	.245	.487	47	-21	-23	104	89	23	.429	13			7	3O/2	-1.0
1893	Phi-N	104	416	64	102	16	7	4	56	33	36	.245	.314	.346	.661	77	-14	-14	100	100	51	.634	13			-2	*3	-1.1
1894	Phi-N	39	135	21	40	1	2	0	19	16	10	.296	.383	.333	.716	80	-4	-3	95	116	21	.768	9			0	3/O2S1	-0.1
1895	Phi-N	49	179	28	48	6	1	0	25	13	12	.268	.335	.313	.648	70	-8	-7	99	125	22	.618	7			0	S3/2O	-0.5
1897	Was-N	101	351	64	97	18	3	2	60	34		.276	.359	.362	.720	91	-3	-3	101	135	53	.748	18			16	*3	1.1
Total	8	641	2380	342	595	80	24	17	234	180	161	.250	.314	.325	.639	79	-64	-65	100	85	299	.631	132			43	3/SO21	-0.9
■ **HAL REILLY**	Reilly, Harold J. Deb: 7/19/19																											
1919	Chi-N	1	3	0	0	0	0	0	0	0	1	.000	.000	.000	.000	-99	-1	-1	100	0	0	.000	0			-0	/O	-0.1
■ **JOHN REILLY**	Reilly, John Good "Long John" b: 10/5/1858, Cincinnati, Ohio d: 5/31/37, Cincinnati, Ohio BR/TR, 6'3", 178 lbs. Deb: 5/18/1880																											
1880	Cin-N	73	272	21	56	8	4	0	16	3	36	.206	.215	.265	.479	62	-11	-10	99	83	16	.347				-3	*1/O	-1.6
1883	Cin-a	98	437	103	136	21	14	9		9		.311	.325	.485	.810	152	26	24	103	0	71	.734				-1	*1/O	1.2
1884	Cin-a	105	448	114	152	24	19	**11**		5		.339	.366	**.551**	**.918**	188	46	42	106	0	**93**	.899				-0	*1/OS	3.3
1885	Cin-a	111	482	92	143	18	11	5		11		.297	.322	.411	.733	128	17	14	104	0	65	.637				-3	*1/O	0.2
1886	Cin-a	115	441	92	117	12	11	4		31		.265	.321	.370	.690	123	9	11	96	0	60	.673	19			0	*1/O	0.5
1887	Cin-a	134	551	106	170	35	14	10		22		.309	.352	.477	.829	122	21	13	108	0	113	.919	50			-2	*1/O	0.6
1888	Cin-a	127	527	112	169	28	14	**13**	**103**	17		.321	.363	**.501**	**.864**	178	**44**	**43**	101	98	**129**	**1.064**	82			-1	*1O	3.1
1889	Cin-a	111	427	84	111	24	13	5	66	34	37	.260	.340	.412	.752	110	8	5	105	105	76	.858	43			-1	*1/O	-0.4
1890	Cin-N	133	553	114	166	25	**26**	6	86	16	41	.300	.328	.472	.800	125	19	13	108	99	98	.809	29			-3	*1/O	0.1
1891	Cin-N	135	546	60	132	20	13	4	64	9	42	.242	.267	.348	.615	88	-16	-9	91	98	58	.558	22			-7	*1O	-1.8
Total	10	1142	4684	898	1352	215	139	67	335	157	156	.289	.325	.437	.762	130	164	146	102	49	778	.763	245			-22	*1/OS	5.2
■ **JOE REILLY**	Reilly, Joseph J. b: 1861, New York, N.Y. 5'10", 140 lbs. Deb: 4/23/1884																											
1884	Bos-U	3	11	1	0	0	0	0		1		.000	.083	.000	.083	-71	-2	-2	98	0	0	.091	0			0	/O3	-0.1
1885	NY-a	10	40	6	7	3	0	0		2		.175	.214	.250	.464	57	-2	-1	84	0	2	.364				0	/23	0.0
Total	2	13	51	7	7	3	0	0		3		.137	.185	.196	.381	27	-4	-3	87	0	2	.295				0	/23O	-0.1
■ **TOM REILLY**	Reilly, Thomas Henry b: 8/3/1884, St.Louis, Mo. d: 10/18/18, New Orleans, La. BR/TR, 5'10". Deb: 7/27/08																											
1908	StL-N	29	81	5	14	1	0	1	3	2		.173	.193	.222	.415	36	-6	-6	94	55	4	.358	4			-3	S	-1.0
1909	StL-N	5	7	0	2	0	1	0	2	0		.286	.286	.571	.857	174	0	0	96	182	1	.800	0			0	/S	0.0
1914	Cle-A	1	1	0	0	0	0	0	0	0	0	.000	.000	.000	.000	-98	-0	-0	102	0	0	.000	0			0	H	0.0
Total	3	35	89	5	16	1	1	1	5	2	0	.180	.198	.247	.445	46	-6	-5	94	64	5	.384	4			-3	/S	-1.0
■ **KEVIN REIMER**	Reimer, Kevin Michael b: 6/28/64, Macon, Ga. BL/TR, 6'2", 215 lbs. Deb: 9/13/88																											
1988	Tex-A	12	25	2	3	0	0	1	2	0	6	.120	.120	.240	.360	-2	-3	-3	101	88	1	.273	0	0	0	-0	/OD	-0.3
■ **MIKE REINBACH**	Reinbach, Michael Wayne b: 8/6/49, San Diego, Cal. BL/TR, 6'2", 195 lbs. Deb: 4/07/74																											
1974	Bal-A	12	20	2	5	1	0	0	2	2	5	.250	.318	.300	.618	85	-1	-0	93	131	2	.533	0	0	0	-1	/OD	0.0
■ **ART REINHOLZ**	Reinholz, Arthur August b: 1/27/03, Detroit, Mich. d: 12/29/80, Newport Richey, Fla. BR/TR, 5'10.5", 175 lbs. Deb: 9/25/28																											
1928	Cle-A	2	3	0	1	0	0	0	0	1	0	.333	.500	.333	.833	116	0	0	106	0	1	1.000	0	0	0	0	/3	0.0
■ **WALLY REINECKER**	Reinecker, Walter (born Walter Joseph Smith) b: 4/21/1890, Pittsburgh, Pa. d: 4/18/57, Pittsburgh, Pa. BR/TR, 5'6", 150 lbs. Deb: 9/17/15																											
1915	Bal-F	3	8	0	1	0	0	0	0	0	0	.125	.125	.125	.250	-24	-1	-1	107	0	0	.143	0			0	/3	0.0
■ **CHARLIE REIPSCHLAGER**	Reipschlager, Charles W. b: 2/1854, New York, N.Y. Deceased BR/TR, 5'6.5", 160 lbs. Deb: 5/02/1883																											
1883	NY-a	37	145	8	27	4	2	0		4		.186	.208	.241	.449	41	-9	-10	108	0	7	.331				5	C/O	-0.2
1884	NY-a	59	233	21	56	13	2	0		1		.240	.250	.313	.563	85	-4	-4	100	0	19	.429				15	C/O	1.3
1885	NY-a	72	268	29	65	11	1	0		9		.243	.270	.291	.561	95	-6	0	84	0	22	.433				1	C/O3S2	0.9
1886	NY-a	65	232	21	49	4	6	0		9		.211	.244	.280	.524	63	-9	-11	104	0	17	.421	2			-3	C/O	-0.8
1887	Cle-a	63	231	20	49	8	3	0		11		.212	.251	.273	.524	49	-16	-15	98	0	18	.451	7			6	C1	0.0
Total	5	296	1109	99	246	40	14	0		34		.222	.248	.283	.531	68	-44	-40	97	0	82	.419	9			24	C/O132S	1.2
■ **BOBBY REIS**	Reis, Robert Joseph Thomas b: 1/2/09, Woodside, N.Y. d: 5/1/73, St.Paul, Minn. BR/TR, 6'1", 175 lbs. Deb: 9/19/31																											
1931	Bro-N	6	17	3	5	0	0	0	2	2	0	.294	.368	.294	.663	79	-0	-0	101	143	2	.583	0			0	/3	0.0
1932	Bro-N	1	4	0	1	0	0	0	0	0	1	.250	.250	.250	.500	36	-0	-0	96	0	0	.333	0			0	/3	0.0
1935	Bro-N	52	85	10	21	3	2	0	4	6	13	.247	.297	.329	.626	72	-4	-3	94	51	8	.545	2			1	OP/213	0.0
1936	Bos-N	37	60	3	13	2	0	0	5	3	6	.217	.254	.250	.504	38	-5	-5	95	118	4	.383	0			3	P/O	0.0
1937	Bos-N	45	86	10	21	5	0	0	6	13	12	.244	.343	.302	.646	85	-2	-1	90	83	10	.612	2			-2	O/P1	-0.3
1938	Bos-N	34	49	6	9	0	0	0	4	1	3	.184	.200	.184	.384	7	-6	-5	88	161	2	.268	1			-2	PO/SC2	-0.4
Total	6	175	301	32	70	10	2	0	21	25	35	.233	.291	.279	.570	60	-18	-15	93	95	26	.491	5			-0	/PO312SC	-0.7
■ **PETE REISER**	Reiser, Harold Patrick b: 3/17/19, St.Louis, Mo. d: 10/25/81, Palm Springs, Cal. BL/TR, 5'11", 185 lbs. Deb: 7/23/40 C																											
1940	Bro-N	58	225	34	66	11	4	3	20	15	33	.293	.338	.418	.755	99	2	-0	108	73	31	.681	2			-7	3O/S	-0.7
1941	Bro-N	137	536	**117**	184	**39**	**17**	14	76	46	71	**.343**	.406	**.558**	**.964**	**164**	48	46	103	85	124	1.006	4			7	*O	**4.7**
1942	Bro-N	125	480	89	149	33	5	10	64	48	45	.310	.375	.463	.838	142	26	25	102	100	88	.882	**20**			-6	*O	1.7
1946	Bro-N	122	423	75	117	21	5	11	73	55	58	.277	.361	.428	.789	120	13	12	103	130	70	.877	**34**			5	O3	1.6
1947	Bro-N	110	388	68	120	23	2	5	46	68	41	.309	.415	.418	.832	116	15	13	105	98	74	.908	14			-2	*O	0.6
1948	Bro-N	64	127	17	30	8	2	1	19	29	21	.236	.382	.354	.736	96	1	1	104	148	20	.798	4			-4	O/3	-0.4
1949	Bos-N	84	221	32	60	8	3	8	40	33	42	.271	.369	.443	.812	121	6	7	97	124	38	.818	3			-1	O/3	0.4
1950	Bos-N	53	78	12	16	2	0	1	10	18	22	.205	.367	.269	.637	82	-2	-1	86	161	9	.667	1			-2	O/3	-0.3
1951	Pit-N	74	140	22	38	9	3	2	13	27	20	.271	.389	.421	.811	111	4	3	107	77	25	.849	4	2	0	-2	O/3	0.0
1952	Cle-A	34	44	7	6	1	0	3	7	4	16	.136	.208	.364	.572	63	-3	-2	91	105	3	.525	1	1	-0	-1	O	-0.3
Total	10	861	2662	473	786	155	41	58	368	343	369	.295	.380	.450	.829	127	110	102	102	105	483	.876	87	3		-10	O/3S	7.3
■ **CHARLIE REISING**	Reising, Charles "Pop" b: 8/28/1861, Indiana d: 7/26/15, Louisville, Ky. Deb: 7/19/1884																											
1884	Ind-a	2	8	0	0	0	0	0		1		.000	.111	.000	.111	-62	-1	-1	96	0	0	.125				0	/O	0.0
■ **AL REISS**	Reiss, Albert Allen b: 1/8/09, Elizabeth, N.J. BB/TR, 5'10.5", 165 lbs. Deb: 6/22/32																											
1932	Phi-A	9	5	0	1	0	0	0	1	1	1	.200	.333	.200	.533	36	-0	-1	114	335	0	.500	0	0	0	0	/S	0.0
■ **HEINIE REITZ**	Reitz, Henry P. b: 6/29/1867, Chicago, Ill. d: 11/10/14, San Francisco, Cal BL/TR, 5'7", 158 lbs. Deb: 4/27/1893																											
1893	Bal-N	130	490	90	140	17	13	1	76	65	32	.286	.377	.360	.757	97	4	-2	107	112	81	.806	24			-2	*2	-0.3
1894	Bal-N	108	446	86	135	22	**31**	2	105	42	24	.303	.372	.504	.876	112	6	7	99	133	93	.939	18			18	*23	2.4
1895	Bal-N	71	245	45	72	15	5	0	29	18	11	.294	.350	.396	.746	88	-2	-6	107	84	40	.769	15			-6	23/S	-0.6
1896	Bal-N	120	464	76	133	15	6	4	106	49	32	.287	.357	.371	.728	92	-3	-5	102	**176**	73	.758	28			-19	*2/S	-1.6
1897	Bal-N	128	477	76	138	15	6	2	84	50		.289	.370	.358	.728	100	-1	3	95	142	74	.752	23			15	*2	2.4
1898	Was-N	132	489	62	148	20	2	2	47	32		.303	.357	.364	.721	107	6	5	102	82	69	.674	11			4	*2	1.3
1899	Pit-N	34	130	11	34	4	2	0	15	10		.262	.314	.323	.637	78	-4	-4	99	112	14	.573	3			0	2	-0.2

YEAR	TM/L	G	AB	R	H	2B	3B	HR	RBI	BB	SO	AVG	OBP	SLG	PRO	/A	BR	/A	PF	CHI	RC	TA	SB	CS	SBR	FR	POS	TPR
Total	7	723	2741	446	800	108	65	11	462	266	99	.292	.363	.391	.754	99	6	-1	101	124	444	.772	122			11	2/3S	3.4
■ KEN REITZ	Reitz, Kenneth John b: 6/24/51, San Francisco, Cal BR/TR, 6', 180 lbs. Deb: 9/05/72																											
1972	StL-N	21	78	5	28	4	0	0	10	2	4	.359	.375	.410	.785	117	2	2	105	131	10	.618	0	1	-1	-3	3	-0.1
1973	StL-N	147	426	40	100	20	2	6	42	9	25	.235	.257	.333	.591	69	-23	-18	91	105	31	.449	0	1	-1	-13	*3/S	-3.5
1974	StL-N	154	579	48	157	28	2	7	54	23	63	.271	.301	.363	.664	82	-13	-16	104	92	56	.526	0	0	0	-19	*3/S2	-3.8
1975	StL-N	161	592	43	159	25	1	5	63	22	54	.269	.300	.340	.640	75	-19	-21	103	115	56	.507	1	1	-0	-22	*3	-4.6
1976	SF-N	155	577	40	154	21	1	5	66	24	48	.267	.297	.333	.630	76	-17	-19	103	125	51	.492	5	4	-1	-1	*3/S	-2.3
1977	StL-N	157	587	58	153	36	1	17	79	19	74	.261	.292	.412	.704	90	-13	-10	96	110	64	.591	2	6	-3	-5	*3	-1.9
1978	StL-N	150	540	41	133	26	2	10	75	23	61	.246	.283	.357	.641	82	-17	-14	95	136	52	.529	1	0	0	-1	*3	-1.7
1979	StL-N	159	605	42	162	41	2	8	73	25	85	.268	.301	.382	.683	81	-14	-17	105	116	67	.572	1	0	0	-12	*3	-3.6
1980	StL-N	151	523	39	141	33	0	8	58	22	44	.270	.303	.379	.682	87	-9	-10	103	103	56	.559	0	1	-1	-9	*3	-2.1
1981	Chi-N	82	260	10	56	9	1	2	28	15	56	.215	.266	.281	.547	53	-15	-17	104	139	18	.427	0	0	0	-0	3	-2.2
1982	Pit-N	7	10	0	0	0	0	0	0	0	4	.000	.091	.000	.091	-66	-2	-2	110	0	0	.100	0	0	0	0	/3	-0.2
Total	11	1344	4777	366	1243	243	12	68	548	184	518	.260	.293	.359	.651	79	-141	-143	100	115	461	.548	10	14	-5	-84	*3/S2	-26.0
■ BUTCH REMENTER	Rementer, Willis J. H. b: 3/14/1878, Philadelphia, Pa. d: 9/23/22, Philadelphia, Pa. TR , Deb: 10/08/04																											
1904	Phi-N	1	2	0	0	0	0	0	0	0		.000	.000	.000	.000	-99	-0	-0	93	0	0	.000	0			0	/C	0.0
■ JACK REMSEN	Remsen, John J. b: 4/1850, Brooklyn, N.Y. BR , 5'11", 189 lbs. Deb: 5/02/1872																											
1872	Atl-n	35	166	22	34							.205															*O	
1873	Atl-n	51	215	29	63							.293															*O	
1874	Mut-n	64	286	51	64							.224															*O/1	
1875	Har-n	85	371	71	95							.256															*O	
1876	Har-N	69	324	62	89	12	5	1	30	1	15	.275	.277	.352	.629	100	2	-2	108	75	32	.489				7	*O	0.4
1877	StL-N	33	123	14	32	3	4	0	13	4	3	.260	.283	.350	.633	97	-0	-1	102	104	12	.516				1	O	0.0
1878	Chi-N	56	224	32	52	11	1	1	19	**17**	33	.232	.286	.304	.590	87	-1	-3	108	96	20	.494				6	*O	-0.1
1879	Chi-N	42	152	14	33	4	2	0	8	2	23	.217	.227	.270	.497	60	-6	-7	105	68	10	.361				-2	O1	-0.9
1881	Cle-N	48	172	14	30	4	3	0	13	9	31	.174	.215	.233	.448	42	-11	-10	96	113	9	.345				-2	O	-1.1
1884	Phi-N	12	43	9	9	2	0	0	3	6	9	.209	.306	.256	.562	85	-1	-0	92	99	3	.500				0	O	0.0
	Bro-a	81	301	45	67	6	6	3		23		.223	.278	.312	.590	97	-1	0	98	0	27	.500				2	*O	0.1
Total	4 n	235	1038	173	256							.247															*O	
Total	6	341	1339	190	312	42	21	5	86	62	114	.233	.267	.307	.574	85	-18	-23	103	69	113	.461				12	O/1	-1.6
■ JERRY REMY	Remy, Gerald Peter b: 11/8/52, Fall River, Mass. BL/TR, 5'9", 165 lbs. Deb: 4/07/75																											
1975	Cal-A	147	569	82	147	17	5	1	46	45	55	.258	.313	.311	.624	81	-17	-13	95	104	53	.559	34	21	-2	13	*2	0.2
1976	Cal-A	143	502	64	132	14	3	0	28	38	43	.263	.315	.303	.618	89	-11	-6	92	72	50	.575	35	16	1	13	*2/D	1.5
1977	Cal-A	154	575	74	145	19	10	4	44	59	59	.252	.324	.341	.665	86	-14	-10	95	89	67	.654	41	17	2	-7	*2/3	-0.1
1978	Bos-A	148	583	87	162	24	6	2	44	40	55	.278	.324	.350	.674	83	-8	-13	107	88	66	.613	30	13	1	6	*2/SD	0.1
1979	Bos-A	80	306	49	91	11	2	0	29	26	25	.297	.352	.346	.699	83	-4	-7	107	111	39	.646	14	9	-1	-1	2	-0.5
1980	Bos-A	63	230	24	72	7	2	0	9	10	14	.313	.342	.361	.703	91	-2	-3	102	43	27	.629	14	6	1	4	2/O	0.5
1981	Bos-A	88	358	55	110	9	1	0	31	36	30	.307	.371	.338	.709	99	4	1	106	89	48	.648	9	2	2	-7	2	-0.1
1982	Bos-A	155	636	89	178	22	3	0	47	55	77	.280	.339	.324	.663	75	-13	-22	110	81	71	.580	16	9	-1	-10	*2	-2.3
1983	Bos-A	146	592	73	163	16	5	0	43	40	35	.275	.321	.319	.640	76	-18	-19	101	86	62	.541	11	3	2	-24	*2	-3.6
1984	Bos-A	30	104	8	26	1	1	0	8	7	11	.250	.297	.279	.576	55	-5	-7	110	110	9	.488	4	3	-1	-0	2	-0.6
Total	10	1154	4455	605	1226	140	38	7	329	356	404	.275	.329	.328	.658	83	-89	-98	102	87	492	.610	208	99	3	-14	*2/DOS3	-4.9
■ RICK RENICK	Renick, Warren Richard b: 3/16/44, London, Ohio BR/TR, 6', 188 lbs. Deb: 7/11/68 C																											
1968	Min-A	42	97	16	21	5	2	3	13	9	42	.216	.283	.402	.685	100	0	-0	106	116	11	.615	0	0	0	-2	S	0.1
1969	Min-A	71	139	21	34	3	0	5	17	12	32	.245	.309	.374	.683	89	-2	-2	102	102	15	.591	0	1	-1	-5	3O/S	-0.7
1970	Min-A	81	179	20	41	8	0	7	25	22	29	.229	.317	.391	.708	96	-2	-1	98	111	21	.637	0	2	-1	-7	3O/S	-0.9
1971	Min-A	27	45	4	10	2	0	1	8	5	14	.222	.314	.333	.647	80	-1	-1	104	181	5	.583	0	0	0	-2	/3O	-0.3
1972	Min-A	55	93	10	16	2	0	4	8	15	25	.172	.287	.323	.610	76	-2	-3	107	80	8	.542	0	1	-1	-3	O/13S	-0.8
Total	5	276	553	71	122	20	2	20	71	63	142	.221	.304	.373	.676	90	-6	-8	103	110	60	.618	0	4	-2	-18	/3OS1	-2.6
■ BILL RENNA	Renna, William Beneditto "Big Bill" b: 10/14/24, Hanford, Cal. BR/TR, 6'3", 218 lbs. Deb: 4/14/53																											
1953	NY-A	61	121	19	38	6	3	2	13	13	31	.314	.385	.463	.848	138	5	6	93	78	22	.814	0	1	-1	-8	O	-0.3
1954	Phi-A	123	422	52	98	15	4	13	53	41	60	.232	.305	.379	.684	88	-9	-8	98	103	49	.614	1	3	-2	3	*O	-0.9
1955	KC-A	100	249	33	53	7	3	7	28	31	42	.213	.305	.349	.654	75	-9	-9	101	97	27	.591	0	3	-2	-9	O	-2.4
1956	KC-A	33	48	12	13	3	0	2	5	3	10	.271	.314	.458	.772	101	-0	-0	101	67	7	.722	1	0	0	-7	O	-0.7
1958	Bos-A	39	56	5	15	5	0	4	18	6	14	.268	.339	.571	.910	139	3	3	105	164	11	.905	0	0	0	-1	O	0.1
1959	Bos-A	14	22	2	2	0	0	0	2	5	9	.091	.259	.091	.350	0	-3	-3	106	394	1	.350	0	0	0	-2	/O	-0.5
Total	6	370	918	123	219	36	10	28	119	99	166	.239	.317	.391	.708	92	-13	-12	99	107	117	.660	2	7	-4	-24	O	-4.7
■ TONY RENSA	Rensa, George Anthony "Pug" b: 9/29/01, Parsons, Pa. d: 1/4/87, Wilkes-Barre, Pa. BR/TR, 5'10", 180 lbs. Deb: 5/05/30																											
1930	Det-A	20	37	6	10	2	1	1	3	6	7	.270	.386	.459	.846	108	1	1	105	50	7	.926	1	0	0	-1	C	0.2
	Phi-N	54	172	31	49	11	2	3	31	10	18	.285	.328	.424	.752	76	-6	-7	106	130	23	.683	0			-1	C	-0.4
1931	Phi-N	19	29	2	3	1	0	0	2	6	2	.103	.257	.138	.395	8	-4	-4	106	178	1	.385	0			0	C	-0.2
1933	NY-A	8	29	4	9	2	1	0	3	1	3	.310	.333	.448	.782	116	0	0	91	77	4	.667	0	1	-1	1	/C	0.1
1937	Chi-A	26	57	10	17	5	1	0	5	8	6	.298	.385	.421	.806	100	0	0	103	71	10	.875	3	0	1	1	C	0.3
1938	Chi-A	59	165	15	41	5	0	3	19	25	16	.248	.351	.333	.684	74	-7	-6	98	100	21	.656	1	1	-0	2	C	-0.2
1939	Chi-A	14	25	3	5	0	0	0	2	1	2	.200	.231	.200	.431	10	-3	-4	107	135	1	.261	0	0	0	-0	C	-0.2
Total	6	200	514	71	134	26	5	7	65	57	54	.261	.338	.372	.710	76	-18	-20	102	108	67	.665	5	2		2	C	-0.4
■ RICH RENTERIA	Renteria, Richard Avina b: 12/25/61, Harbor City, Cal. BR/TR, 5'9", 172 lbs. Deb: 9/14/86																											
1986	Pit-N	10	12	2	3	1	0	0	1	0	4	.250	.250	.333	.583	59	-1	-1	100	100	1	.444	0	0	0	-0	/3	0.0
1987	Sea-A	12	10	2	1	1	0	0	0	1	2	.100	.182	.200	.382	2	-1	-1	103	0	0	.400	1	0	0	0	/2SD	0.0
1988	Sea-A	31	88	6	18	9	0	0	6	2	8	.205	.222	.307	.529	43	-6	-7	108	88	4	.395	1	3	-2	-1	SD/32	-0.8
Total	3	53	110	10	22	11	0	0	7	3	14	.200	.221	.300	.521	41	-9	-9	106	81	6	.404	2	3	-1	-1	/DS23	-0.8
■ BOB REPASS	Repass, Robert Willis b: 11/6/17, W.Pittston, Pa. BR/TR, 6'1", 185 lbs. Deb: 9/18/39																											
1939	StL-N	3	6	0	2	1	0	0	1	0	2	.333	.333	.500	.833	115	0	0	105	122	1	.600	0			0	/2	0.0
1942	Was-A	81	259	30	62	11	1	2	23	33	30	.239	.328	.313	.640	84	-6	-5	96	93	29	.593	6	1	1	-5	23S	-0.6
Total	2	84	265	30	64	12	1	2	24	33	32	.242	.328	.317	.645	85	-6	-5	96	94	29	.596	6	1		-5	/23S	-0.6
■ ROGER REPOZ	Repoz, Roger Allen b: 8/3/40, Bellingham, Wash. BL/TL, 6'3", 190 lbs. Deb: 9/11/64																											
1964	NY-A	11	1	1	0	0	0	0	0	1	1	.000	.500	.000	.500	52	0	0	103	0	0	1.000	0	0	0	-3	/O	-0.3
1965	NY-A	79	218	34	48	7	4	12	28	25	57	.220	.300	.454	.755	110	2	2	101	86	30	.723	1	1	-0	-4	O	-0.4
1966	NY-A	37	43	4	15	4	1	0	9	4	8	.349	.404	.488	.893	166	3	3	94	180	9	.893	0	0	0	-8	O	-0.5
	KC-A	101	319	40	69	10	3	11	34	44	80	.216	.315	.370	.685	102	-1	1	94	96	38	.645	3	3	-1	1	O1	-0.2
	Yr	138	362	44	84	14	4	11	43	48	88	.232	.325	.384	.709	110	2	5	94	120	47	.669	3	3	-1	-7		-0.7
1967	KC-A	40	87	9	21	6	1	2	8	12	20	.241	.340	.402	.742	119	2	2	100	81	12	.754	4	2	0	1	O	0.3
	Cal-A	74	176	25	44	9	1	5	20	19	37	.250	.323	.398	.721	117	3	3	96	98	24	.679	2	2	-1	0	O	0.1
	Yr	114	263	34	65	15	2	7	28	31	57	.247	.329	.399	.728	118	5	6	97	93	37	.708	6	4	-1	1		0.4
1968	Cal-A	133	375	30	90	8	1	13	54	38	83	.240	.315	.371	.686	114	3	6	94	130	46	.644	8	7	-2	4	*O	0.4
1969	Cal-A	103	219	25	36	1	1	8	19	32	52	.164	.271	.288	.559	57	-13	-13	99	88	19	.516	1	3	-2	-5	O1	-2.3
1970	Cal-A	137	407	50	97	17	6	18	47	45	90	.238	.319	.442	.761	118	3	7	92	81	60	.739	4	2	0	3	*O1	0.5
1971	Cal-A	113	297	39	59	11	1	13	41	60	69	.199	.335	.374	.709	102	1	2	99	112	40	.711	3	5	-2	-1	O1	-0.4
1972	Cal-A	3	3	0	1	0	0	0	0	0	2	.333	.333	.333	.667	112	-0	0	88	0	0	.500	0	0	0	0	H	0.0

YEAR	TM/L	G	AB	R	H	2B	3B	HR	RBI	BB	SO	AVG	OBP	SLG	PRO	/A	BR	/A	PF	CHI	RC	TA	SB	CS	SBR	FR	POS	TPR
Total	9	831	2145	257	480	73	19	82	260	280	499	.224	.316	.390	.706	106	4	15	96	100	279	.682	26	25	-7	-12	O1	-2.8
■ **RIP REPULSKI** Repulski, Eldon John b: 10/4/27, Sauk Rapids, Minn. BR/TR, 6', 195 lbs. Deb: 4/14/53																												
1953	StL-N	153	567	75	156	25	4	15	66	33	71	.275	.325	.413	.738	89	-8	-10	102	94	74	.647	3	6	-3	-12	*O	-2.9
1954	StL-N	152	619	99	175	39	5	19	79	43	75	.283	.333	.454	.787	102	1	1	100	97	88	.715	8	10	-4	-5	*O	-1.2
1955	StL-N	147	512	64	138	28	2	23	73	49	66	.270	.338	.467	.805	110	7	7	101	98	75	.746	5	7	-3	-7	*O	-0.5
1956	StL-N	112	376	44	104	18	3	11	55	24	46	.277	.332	.428	.760	103	1	1	99	120	50	.674	2	2	-1	-4	*O	-0.6
1957	Phi-N	134	516	65	134	23	4	20	68	19	74	.260	.293	.436	.729	94	-7	-6	98	101	64	.651	7	1	2	2	*O	-0.5
1958	Phi-N	85	238	33	58	9	4	13	40	15	47	.244	.300	.479	.779	104	-0	0	98	108	31	.704	0	0	0	-5	O	-0.6
1959	LA-N	53	94	11	24	4	0	2	14	13	23	.255	.346	.362	.707	87	-1	-1	102	141	11	.635	0	1	-1	-6	O	-0.8
1960	LA-N	4	5	0	1	0	0	0	0	0	1	.200	.200	.200	.400	9	-1	-1	115	0	0	.200	0	0	0	-1	/O	0.0
	Bos-A	73	136	14	33	6	1	3	20	10	25	.243	.295	.368	.662	76	-4	-5	103	133	13	.550	0	0	0	-2	O	-0.8
1961	Bos-A	15	25	2	7	1	0	0	1	1	5	.280	.308	.320	.628	67	-1	-1	102	49	2	.450	0	2	-1	-1	/O	-0.2
Total	9	928	3088	407	830	153	23	106	416	207	433	.269	.322	.436	.758	98	-15	-15	100	103	409	.705	25	29	-10	-40	O	-8.1
■ **LARRY RESSLER** Ressler, Lawrence P. b: 8/10/1848, France d: 6/12/18, Reading, Pa. Deb: 4/26/1875																												
1875	Nat-n	26	106	15	20							.189															O/2	
■ **DINO RESTELLI** Restelli, Dino Paul "Dingo" b: 9/23/24, St.Louis, Mo. BR/TR, 6'1.5", 191 lbs. Deb: 6/14/49																												
1949	Pit-N	72	232	41	58	11	0	12	40	35	26	.250	.358	.453	.811	115	5	5	101	109	38	.808	3			0	O/1	0.2
1951	Pit-N	21	38	1	7	1	0	1	3	2	4	.184	.225	.289	.514	35	-3	-4	107	83	3	.419	0	0	0	-0	O	-0.3
Total	2	93	270	42	65	12	0	13	43	37	30	.241	.341	.430	.770	104	2	1	102	106	41	.780	3	0		-0	/O1	-0.1
■ **MERV RETTENMUND** Rettenmund, Mervin Weldon b: 6/6/43, Flint, Mich. BR/TR, 5'10", 190 lbs. Deb: 4/14/68 C																												
1968	Bal-A	31	64	10	19	5	0	2	7	18	20	.297	.458	.469	.927	177	8	7	102	83	16	1.087	1	1	-0	-2	O	0.5
1969	Bal-A	95	190	27	47	10	3	4	25	28	28	.247	.344	.395	.739	102	2	1	104	115	27	.727	6	1	1	-8	O	-0.8
1970	Bal-A	106	338	60	109	17	2	18	58	38	59	.322	.396	.544	.940	162	26	27	97	99	72	.975	13	7	-0	7	O	3.0
1971	Bal-A	141	491	81	156	23	4	11	75	87	60	.318	.424	.448	.872	143	35	33	103	123	99	.921	15	6	1	8	*O	3.9
1972	Bal-A	102	301	40	70	10	2	6	21	41	37	.233	.325	.339	.663	100	-0	1	98	73	33	.608	6	4	-1	-1	O	-0.3
1973	Bal-A	95	321	59	84	17	2	9	44	57	38	.262	.380	.411	.791	114	12	8	107	111	56	.840	11	2	2	1	O	0.9
1974	Cin-N	80	208	30	45	6	0	6	28	37	39	.216	.340	.332	.672	90	-2	-2	98	124	25	.661	5	1	1	-6	O	-0.9
1975	Cin-N	93	188	24	45	6	1	2	19	35	22	.239	.359	.314	.673	84	-2	-3	104	113	23	.664	5	0	2	-7	O/3	-1.0
1976	SD-N	86	140	16	32	7	0	2	11	29	23	.229	.361	.321	.682	107	0	2	89	83	19	.696	4	1	1	1	O	0.3
1977	SD-N	107	126	23	36	6	1	4	17	33	28	.286	.438	.444	.882	156	9	11	88	100	27	.968	1	2	-1	-5	O/3	0.4
1978	Cal-A	50	108	16	29	5	1	1	14	30	13	.269	.436	.361	.797	124	6	6	102	132	19	.835	0	3	-2	-4	OD	0.0
1979	Cal-A	35	76	7	20	2	0	1	10	11	14	.263	.364	.329	.693	96	-1	0	93	137	9	.644	1	0	0	-3	D/O	-0.2
1980	Cal-A	2	4	0	1	0	0	0	0	1	1	.250	.400	.250	.650	86	-0	-0	96	0	1	.667	0	0	0	0	/D	0.0
Total	13	1023	2555	393	693	114	16	66	329	445	382	.271	.383	.406	.789	123	92	92	100	108	425	.830	68	28	4	-19	O/D3	5.8
■ **KEN RETZER** Retzer, Kenneth Leo b: 4/30/34, Wood River, Ill. BL/TR, 6', 185 lbs. Deb: 9/09/61																												
1961	Was-A	16	53	7	18	4	0	1	3	4	5	.340	.386	.472	.858	134	2	2	95	42	10	.833	1	0	0	0	C	0.2
1962	Was-A	109	340	36	97	11	2	8	37	26	21	.285	.336	.400	.736	96	-2	-2	101	92	45	.653	2	0	1	-4	C	0.0
1963	Was-A	95	265	21	64	10	0	5	31	17	20	.242	.292	.336	.628	77	-9	-8	98	125	26	.537	2	0	1	-3	C	-0.9
1964	Was-A	17	32	1	3	0	0	0	1	5	4	.094	.237	.094	.331	-4	-4	-4	101	141	1	.300	0	0	0	0	C	-0.3
Total	4	237	690	65	182	25	2	14	72	52	50	.264	.318	.367	.685	88	-13	-12	99	103	82	.615	5	0	2	-6	C	-1.0
■ **REVELS** Revels Deb:10/14/1874																												
1874	Bal-n	1	4	0	0							.000															/O	
■ **DAVE REVERING** Revering, David Alvin b: 2/12/53, Roseville, Cal. BL/TR, 6'4", 210 lbs. Deb: 4/08/78																												
1978	Oak-A	152	521	49	141	21	3	16	46	26	55	.271	.305	.415	.720	100	-1	-2	101	70	63	.616	0	1	-1	5	*1/D	-0.3
1979	Oak-A	125	472	63	136	25	5	19	77	34	65	.288	.337	.483	.820	133	11	18	89	110	75	.763	1	4	-2	2	*1D	1.1
1980	Oak-A	106	376	48	109	21	5	15	62	32	37	.290	.346	.492	.838	134	13	15	95	107	64	.799	1	0	0	2	1/D	1.1
1981	Oak-A	31	87	12	20	1	1	2	10	11	12	.230	.323	.333	.657	93	-1	-1	96	112	9	.586	0	1	-1	-1	1/D	-0.2
	NY-A	45	119	8	28	4	1	2	7	11	20	.235	.300	.336	.636	83	-3	-3	100	60	12	.543	0	1	-1	2	1	-0.2
	Yr	76	206	20	48	5	2	4	17	22	32	.233	.310	.335	.645	87	-4	-3	99	82	22	.568	0	2	-1	1		-0.4
1982	NY-A	14	40	2	6	2	0	0	2	3	4	.150	.209	.200	.409	14	-5	-5	96	100	1	.297	0	0	0	-1	1/D	-0.5
	Tor-A	55	135	15	29	6	0	5	18	22	30	.215	.325	.370	.695	83	-2	-3	109	111	16	.649	0	3	-2	0	D/1	-0.4
	Sea-A	29	82	8	17	3	1	3	12	9	17	.207	.286	.378	.664	74	-2	-3	109	120	8	.588	0	0	0	0	1	-0.3
	Yr	98	257	25	52	11	1	8	32	34	51	.202	.296	.346	.642	71	-9	-11	107	114	27	.583	0	3	-2	-1		-1.2
Total	5	557	1832	205	486	83	16	62	234	148	240	.265	.321	.430	.750	109	10	17	97	95	248	.691	2	10	-5	8	1/D	0.3
■ **REXTER** Rexter Deb:9/25/1875																												
1875	Atl-n	1	5	0	0							.000															/O	
■ **GIL REYES** Reyes, Gilberto R. (Polanco) b: 12/10/63, Santo Domingo, D.R. BR/TR, 6'2", 200 lbs. Deb: 6/11/83																												
1983	LA-N	19	31	1	5	2	0	0	0	0	5	.161	.188	.226	.413	14	-4	-4	100	0	1	.276	0	0	0	-1	C	-0.3
1984	LA-N	4	5	0	0	0	0	0	0	0	3	.000	.000	.000	.000	-96	-1	-1	104	0	0	.000	0	0	0	0	/C	0.0
1985	LA-N	6	1	0	0	0	0	0	0	1	1	.000	.667	.000	.667	110	0	0	93	0	0	2.000	0	0	0	0	/C	0.1
1987	LA-N	1	0	0	0	0	0	0	0	0	0	—	—	—	—	—	0	0	92	—	—	—	0	0	0	0	/C	0.0
1988	LA-N	5	9	1	1	0	0	0	0	0	3	.111	.111	.111	.222	-34	-2	-2	106	0	0	.125	0	0	0	-0	/C	-0.1
Total	5	35	46	2	6	2	0	0	0	1	12	.130	.184	.174	.358	0	-6	-6	101	0	1	.275	0	0	0	-1	/C	-0.3
■ **NAP REYES** Reyes, Napoleon Aguilera b: 11/24/19, Santiago De Cuba, Cuba BR/TR, 6'1", 205 lbs. Deb: 5/19/43																												
1943	NY-N	40	125	13	32	4	2	0	13	4	12	.256	.290	.320	.610	79	-4	-4	96	117	12	.511	2			-0	1/3	-0.5
1944	NY-N	116	374	38	108	16	5	8	53	15	24	.289	.325	.422	.747	105	3	2	104	104	49	.650	2			2	13/O	0.0
1945	NY-N	122	431	39	124	15	4	5	44	25	26	.288	.338	.376	.714	99	-1	-1	100	86	53	.609	1			2	*3/1	-0.1
1950	NY-N	1	1	0	0	0	0	0	0	0	0	.000	.000	.000	.000	-99	-0	-0	98	0	0	.000	0			0	/1	0.0
Total	4	279	931	90	264	35	11	13	110	44	62	.284	.326	.387	.713	99	-3	-4	101	97	113	.636	5			4	31/O	-0.6
■ **CARL REYNOLDS** Reynolds, Carl Nettles b: 2/1/03, La Rue, Tex. d: 5/29/78, Houston, Tex. BR/TR, 6', 194 lbs. Deb: 9/01/27																												
1927	Chi-A	14	42	5	9	3	0	1	7	5	7	.214	.313	.357	.670	72	-2	-2	102	129	5	.667	1	0	0	2	O	0.0
1928	Chi-A	84	291	51	94	21	11	2	36	17	13	.323	.371	.491	.862	126	10	10	99	85	54	.900	15	3	3	-5	O	0.3
1929	Chi-A	131	517	81	164	24	12	11	67	20	37	.317	.348	.474	.821	115	5	9	95	87	83	.796	19	9	0	-3	*O	0.0
1930	Chi-A	138	563	103	202	25	18	22	104	20	39	.359	.388	.584	.973	139	34	31	103	93	126	1.019	16	4	2	-4	*O	2.2
1931	Chi-A	118	462	71	134	24	14	6	77	24	26	.290	.333	.442	.775	111	-0	5	92	117	68	.751	17	6	2	2	*O	0.1
1932	Was-A	102	406	53	124	28	7	9	63	14	19	.305	.332	.475	.807	107	2	2	100	98	62	.759	8	4	0	1	O	0.0
1933	StL-A	135	475	81	136	26	14	8	71	50	25	.286	.357	.451	.807	98	8	-2	115	102	77	.790	5	4	-1	0	*O	-0.6
1934	Bos-A	113	413	61	125	26	9	4	86	27	28	.303	.350	.438	.788	97	0	-3	106	152	63	.742	5	3	-0	-2	*O	-0.5
1935	Bos-A	78	244	33	66	13	4	6	35	24	20	.270	.336	.430	.766	90	-2	-5	108	97	36	.743	4	1	1	2	O	-0.2
1936	Was-A	89	293	41	81	18	2	4	41	21	22	.276	.329	.392	.722	79	-11	-10	98	104	38	.676	8	4	0	-1	O	-1.1
1937	Chi-N	7	11	0	3	1	0	0	1	2	2	.273	.385	.364	.748	102	0	0	103	90	1	.667	0			-0	/O	0.0
1938	Chi-N	125	497	59	150	28	10	3	67	22	32	.302	.335	.416	.752	101	3	-0	105	119	69	.675	9			0	*O	-0.2
1939	Chi-N	88	281	33	69	10	6	4	44	16	38	.246	.298	.367	.665	77	-9	-10	101	140	30	.586	5			3	O	-0.7
Total	13	1222	4495	672	1357	247	107	80	699	262	308	.302	.346	.458	.804	106	37	25	102	108	714	.776	112	38		-6	*O	-0.7
■ **CHARLIE REYNOLDS** Reynolds, Charles Lawrence b: 5/1/1865, Williamsburg, Ind. d: 7/3/44, Denver, Colo. 5'9", 175 lbs. Deb: 5/08/1889																												
1889	KC-a	1	4	1	1	0	0	0	1	0	1	.250	.250	.250	.500	42	-0	-0	106	292	0	.333	0			0	/C	0.0
	Bro-a	12	42	5	9	1	1	0	3	1	6	.214	.233	.286	.518	51	-3	-3	96	71	3	.455	2			0	C	-0.1
	Yr	13	46	6	10	1	1	0	4	1	7	.217	.234	.283	.517	50	-3	-3	97	111	4	.444	2			0		-0.1

YEAR	TM/L	G	AB	R	H	2B	3B	HR	RBI	BB	SO	AVG	OBP	SLG	PRO	/A	BR	/A	PF	CHI	RC	TA	SB	CS	SBR	FR	POS	TPR
Total	1	13	46	6	10	1	1	0	4	1	7	.217	.234	.283	.517	50	-3	-3	97	90	4	.444	2			0	/C	-0.1
■ **DANNY REYNOLDS**	Reynolds, Daniel Vance "Squirrel" b: 11/27/19, Stony Point, N.C. BR/TR, 5'11", 158 lbs. Deb: 5/26/45																											
1945	Chi-A	29	72	6	12	2	1	0	4	3	8	.167	.200	.222	.422	24	-7	-7	95	90	2	.303	1	2	-1	1	S2	-0.6
■ **DON REYNOLDS**	Reynolds, Donald Edward b: 4/16/53, Arkadelphia, Ark. BR/TR, 5'8", 178 lbs. Deb: 4/07/78																											
1978	SD-N	57	87	8	22	2	0	0	10	15	14	.253	.363	.276	.639	87	-1	-1	93	165	10	.615	1	0	0	-5	O	-0.6
1979	SD-N	30	45	6	10	1	2	0	6	7	6	.222	.327	.333	.660	84	-1	-1	96	158	4	.564	0	1	-1	-1	O	-0.2
Total	2	87	132	14	32	3	2	0	16	22	20	.242	.351	.295	.646	86	-3	-2	94	163	14	.596	1	1	-0	-6	/O	-0.8
■ **CRAIG REYNOLDS**	Reynolds, Gordon Craig b: 12/27/52, Houston, Tex. BL/TR, 6'1", 175 lbs. Deb: 8/01/75																											
1975	Pit-N	31	76	8	17	3	0	0	4	3	5	.224	.253	.263	.516	44	-6	-6	99	77	5	.377	0	1	-1	-1	S	-0.3
1976	Pit-N	7	4	1	1	0	0	1	1	0	0	.250	.250	1.000	1.250	242	1	1	100	55	1	1.333	0	0	0	0	/S2	0.1
1977	Sea-A	135	420	41	104	12	3	4	28	15	23	.248	.279	.319	.598	65	-22	-20	96	76	36	.479	6	6	-2	4	*S	-0.1
1978	Sea-A	148	548	57	160	16	7	5	44	36	41	.292	.339	.374	.713	99	0	-1	102	84	71	.636	9	6	-1	8	*S	1.9
1979	Hou-N	146	555	63	147	20	9	0	39	21	49	.265	.294	.333	.627	78	-23	-16	90	88	57	.529	12	6	0	-7	*S	-0.8
1980	Hou-N	137	381	34	86	9	6	3	28	20	39	.226	.264	.304	.569	60	-22	-21	98	89	32	.460	2	1	0	5	*S	0.0
1981	Hou-N	87	323	43	84	10	**12**	4	31	12	31	.260	.287	.402	.689	106	-4	0	88	87	35	.585	3	3	-1	-1	S	0.8
1982	Hou-N	54	118	16	30	2	3	1	7	11	9	.254	.323	.347	.671	88	-2	-2	99	62	14	.622	3	1	0	2	S/3	0.4
1983	Hou-N	65	98	10	21	3	0	1	6	6	10	.214	.260	.276	.535	54	-7	-6	90	79	7	.423	0	1	-1	1	23/SO	-0.4
1984	Hou-N	146	527	61	137	15	11	6	60	22	53	.260	.290	.364	.654	89	-13	-9	93	114	57	.559	7	1	2	16	*S/3	2.5
1985	Hou-N	107	379	43	103	18	8	4	32	12	30	.272	.294	.393	.687	94	-6	-4	96	79	42	.581	4	4	-1	9	*S/2	1.2
1986	Hou-N	114	313	32	78	7	3	6	41	12	31	.249	.277	.348	.625	69	-13	-14	103	129	28	.508	3	1	0	-5	S/13OP	-0.9
1987	Hou-N	135	374	35	95	17	3	4	28	30	44	.254	.309	.348	.657	79	-14	-11	93	79	42	.581	5	1	1	-18	*S/3	-1.2
1988	Hou-N	78	161	20	41	7	0	1	14	8	23	.255	.290	.317	.607	79	-5	-4	93	104	15	.512	3	0	1	-1	S321	-0.3
Total	14	1390	4277	464	1104	139	65	40	363	208	388	.258	.294	.349	.643	81	-137	-112	95	90	443	.551	57	32	-2	13	*S/321OP	2.9
■ **HAROLD REYNOLDS**	Reynolds, Harold Craig b: 11/26/60, Eugene, Ore. BB/TR, 5'11", 165 lbs. Deb: 9/02/83																											
1983	Sea-A	20	59	8	12	4	1	0	1	2	9	.203	.230	.305	.535	46	-4	-4	100	22	3	.400	0	2	-1	1	2	-0.3
1984	Sea-A	10	10	3	3	0	0	0	0	0	1	.300	.364	.300	.664	84	-0	-0	102	0	1	.625	1	1	-0	0	/2	0.0
1985	Sea-A	67	104	15	15	3	1	0	6	17	14	.144	.264	.192	.457	29	-10	-9	95	119	7	.440	3	2	-0	4	2	-0.2
1986	Sea-A	126	445	46	99	19	4	1	24	29	42	.222	.275	.290	.565	52	-27	-30	105	74	37	.525	30	12	2	**29**	*2	0.7
1987	Sea-A	160	530	73	146	31	8	1	35	39	34	.275	.327	.370	.697	83	-10	-12	103	70	67	.723	**60**	20	6	20	*2	2.3
1988	Sea-A	158	598	61	169	26	**11**	4	41	51	51	.283	.341	.383	.724	95	2	-3	108	72	74	.679	35	29	-7	8	*2	0.8
Total	6	541	1746	206	444	83	25	6	107	138	151	.254	.312	.341	.653	75	-50	-60	104	73	189	.632	129	66	-1	61	2	3.3
■ **R. J. REYNOLDS**	Reynolds, Robert James b: 4/19/59, Sacramento, Cal. BB/TR, 6', 190 lbs. Deb: 9/01/83																											
1983	LA-N	24	55	5	13	0	0	2	11	3	11	.236	.276	.345	.621	71	-2	-2	100	174	6	.628	5	0	2	-1	O	-0.1
1984	LA-N	73	240	23	62	12	2	2	24	14	38	.258	.302	.350	.652	80	-6	-7	104	104	24	.561	7	5	-1	-1	O	-1.1
1985	LA-N	73	207	22	55	10	4	0	25	13	31	.266	.312	.353	.665	92	-4	-2	93	136	23	.589	6	3	0	-1	O	-0.4
	Pit-N	31	130	22	40	5	3	3	17	9	18	.308	.357	.462	.819	124	4	4	103	85	22	.863	12	2	2	3	O	0.8
	Yr	104	337	44	95	15	7	3	42	22	49	.282	.330	.395	.724	106	0	2	96	122	46	.700	18	5	2	2		0.4
1986	Pit-N	118	402	63	108	30	2	9	48	40	78	.269	.336	.420	.757	107	4	4	100	100	55	.722	16	9	-1	-9	*O	-0.8
1987	Pit-N	117	335	47	87	24	1	7	51	34	80	.260	.328	.400	.728	88	-4	-6	104	131	46	.717	14	1	4	-8	O	-1.3
1988	Pit-N	130	323	35	80	14	2	6	51	20	62	.248	.292	.359	.651	88	-6	-6	98	152	35	.604	15	2	3	-8	O	-1.3
Total	6	566	1692	217	445	95	14	29	227	133	318	.263	.318	.387	.705	94	-15	-15	100	122	211	.681	75	22	9	-25	O	-4.2
■ **RONN REYNOLDS**	Reynolds, Ronn Dwayne b: 8/28/58, Wichita, Kan. BR/TR, 6', 200 lbs. Deb: 9/29/82																											
1982	NY-N	2	4	0	0	0	0	0	0	1	1	.000	.200	.000	.200	-40	-1	-1	99	0	0	.250	0	0	0	0	/C	0.0
1983	NY-N	24	66	4	13	1	0	0	2	8	12	.197	.284	.212	.496	40	-5	-5	99	56	4	.400	0	0	0	-1	C	-0.4
1985	NY-N	28	43	4	9	2	0	0	1	0	18	.209	.227	.256	.483	36	-4	-4	97	36	2	.343	0	0	0	1	C	-0.1
1986	Phi-N	43	126	8	27	4	0	3	10	5	30	.214	.244	.317	.562	52	-8	-9	104	81	9	.437	0	0	0	2	C	-0.5
1987	Hou-N	38	102	5	17	4	0	1	7	3	29	.167	.190	.235	.426	13	-13	-12	93	103	4	.303	0	1	-1	-4	C	-1.3
Total	5	135	341	21	66	11	0	4	20	17	90	.194	.234	.261	.495	35	-31	-30	99	76	19	.384	0	1	-1	-2	C	-2.3
■ **TOMMIE REYNOLDS**	Reynolds, Tommie D b: 8/15/41, Arizona, La. BB/TR, 6'2", 190 lbs. Deb: 9/05/63																											
1963	KC-A	8	19	1	1	1	0	0	0	1	7	.053	.143	.105	.248	-27	-3	-3	108	0	0	.211	0	0	0	-1	/O	-0.4
1964	KC-A	31	94	11	19	1	0	2	9	10	22	.202	.292	.277	.569	57	-5	-5	105	119	7	.481	0	0	0	-0	O/3	-0.6
1965	KC-A	90	270	34	64	11	3	1	22	36	41	.237	.327	.311	.638	85	-5	-4	97	105	28	.592	9	2	2	6	O/3	0.0
1967	NY-N	101	136	16	28	1	0	2	9	11	26	.206	.280	.257	.537	55	-8	-8	99	91	10	.446	1	1	-0	-12	O/3C	-2.5
1969	Oak-A	107	315	51	81	10	0	2	20	34	29	.257	.345	.308	.652	91	-6	-2	92	78	34	.571	1	3	-2	4	O	-0.2
1970	Cal-A	59	120	11	30	3	1	1	6	6	10	.250	.291	.317	.608	74	-5	-4	92	59	10	.479	1	1	-0	-0	O/3	-0.5
1971	Cal-A	45	86	4	16	3	0	2	8	9	6	.186	.286	.291	.576	65	-4	-4	99	105	6	.481	0	1	-1	-1	O/3	-0.6
1972	Mil-A	72	130	13	26	5	1	2	13	10	25	.200	.262	.300	.562	70	-5	-5	95	121	10	.463	0	0	0	-2	O/13	-0.9
Total	8	513	1170	141	265	35	5	12	87	117	166	.226	.307	.296	.603	74	-42	-36	96	93	106	.539	12	8	-1	-8	O/31C	-5.7
■ **BILL REYNOLDS**	Reynolds, William Dee b: 8/14/1884, Eastland, Tex. d: 6/5/24, Carnegie, Okla. BR/TR, 6', 185 lbs. Deb: 9/15/13																											
1913	NY-A	5	5	0	0	0	0	0	0	0	1	.000	.000	.000	.000	-99	-1	-1	101	0	0	.000	0			0	/C	0.0
1914	NY-A	4	5	0	2	0	0	0	0	0	3	.400	.400	.400	.800	141	0	0	100	0	1	.667	0			0	/C	0.0
Total	2	9	10	0	2	0	0	0	0	0	4	.200	.200	.200	.400	19	-1	-1	100	0	1	.250	0			0	/C	0.0
■ **ROCKY RHAWN**	Rhawn, Robert John b: 2/13/19, Catawissa, Pa. d: 6/9/84, Danville, Pa. BR/TR, 5'8", 180 lbs. Deb: 9/17/47																											
1947	NY-N	13	45	7	14	3	0	1	3	8	1	.311	.415	.444	.860	127	2	2	101	51	9	.875	0			0	/23	0.3
1948	NY-N	36	44	11	12	2	1	1	8	8	6	.273	.385	.432	.816	121	1	1	100	136	7	.882	3			-0	S/3	0.3
1949	NY-N	14	29	8	5	0	0	0	2	7	2	.172	.333	.172	.506	39	-2	-2	102	151	2	.542	1			-0	/2	-0.1
	Pit-N	3	7	0	1	0	0	0	0	0	0	.143	.143	.143	.286	-23	-1	-1	101	0	0	.143	0			0	/3	0.0
	Yr	17	36	8	6	0	0	0	2	7	2	.167	.302	.167	.469	29	-3	-3	101	133	2	.452	1			-0		-0.1
	Chi-A	24	73	12	15	4	1	0	5	12	8	.205	.318	.288	.605	62	-4	-4	98	82	7	.550	0	1	-1	3	3/S	0.0
Total	3	90	198	38	47	9	2	2	18	35	17	.237	.352	.333	.685	84	-4	-4	100	95	26	.686	4	1		3	/3S2	0.5
■ **CY RHEAM**	Rheam, Kenneth Johnston b: 9/28/1893, Pittsburgh, Pa. d: 10/23/47, Pittsburgh, Pa. BR/TR, 6' ", 175 lbs. Deb: 5/20/14																											
1914	Pit-F	73	214	15	45	5	3	0	20	9	33	.210	.242	.262	.504	47	-16	-14	94	129	16	.420	6			-1	132/O	-1.4
1915	Pit-F	34	69	10	12	0	0	1	5	1	7	.174	.186	.217	.403	18	-7	-7	104	100	4	.351	4			-0	O/1	-0.9
Total	2	107	283	25	57	5	3	1	25	10	40	.201	.229	.251	.480	40	-23	-21	97	122	20	.403	10			-1	/1O32	-2.3
■ **BILLY RHIEL**	Rhiel, William Joseph b: 8/16/1900, Youngstown, Ohio d: 8/16/46, Youngstown, Ohio BR/TR, 5'11", 175 lbs. Deb: 4/20/29																											
1929	Bro-N	76	205	27	57	9	4	4	25	19	25	.278	.339	.420	.759	92	-5	-3	94	87	29	.709	0			-6	2/3S	-0.6
1930	Bos-N	20	47	3	8	4	0	0	4	2	5	.170	.204	.255	.459	10	-7	-7	97	115	2	.359	0			-1	3/2	-0.5
1932	Det-A	85	250	30	70	13	3	3	38	17	23	.280	.328	.392	.720	84	-6	-6	102	119	33	.656	2	0	1	2	31/O2	-0.2
1933	Det-A	19	17	1	3	0	1	0	1	5	4	.176	.364	.294	.658	71	-0	-1	107	67	2	.714	0	0	0	0	/O	0.0
Total	4	200	519	61	138	26	8	7	68	43	57	.266	.323	.387	.711	80	-18	-16	99	104	66	.648	2	0		-5	/321OS	-1.3
■ **DUSTY RHODES**	Rhodes, James Lamar b: 5/13/27, Mathews, Ala. BL/TR, 6', 178 lbs. Deb: 7/15/52																											
1952	NY-N	67	176	34	44	8	1	10	36	23	33	.250	.340	.477	.817	121	5	5	102	123	29	.796	1	0	0	-6	O	-0.1
1953	NY-N	76	163	18	38	7	0	11	30	10	28	.233	.277	.479	.756	94	-3	-2	98	105	21	.682	0	1	-1	-1	O	-0.5
1954	NY-N	82	164	31	56	7	3	15	50	18	25	.341	.410	.695	1.105	173	19	18	105	124	47	1.218	1	0	0	-4	O	1.2
1955	NY-N	94	187	22	57	5	2	6	32	27	26	.305	.393	.449	.842	125	7	7	99	127	35	.855	1	1	-0	-6	O	0.0
1956	NY-N	111	244	20	53	10	3	8	33	30	41	.217	.303	.381	.684	85	-6	-5	97	119	27	.615	0	0	0	-9	O	-1.6
1957	NY-N	92	190	20	39	5	1	4	19	18	34	.205	.278	.305	.583	55	-12	-12	102	113	15	.487	0	0	0	-8	O	-2.1
1959	SF-N	54	48	1	9	2	0	0	7	5	9	.188	.264	.229	.493	34	-5	-4	95	257	3	.400	0	0	0	0	H	-0.3

YEAR	TM/L	G	AB	R	H	2B	3B	HR	RBI	BB	SO	AVG	OBP	SLG	PRO	/A	BR	/A	PF	CHI	RC	TA	SB	CS	SBR	FR	POS	TPR
Total	7	576	1172	146	296	44	10	54	207	131	196	.253	.329	.445	.775	104	6	6	100	124	178	.750	3	2	-0	-33	O	-3.4
■ **KEVIN RHOMBERG** Rhomberg, Kevin Jay b: 11/22/55, Dubuque, Iowa BR/TR, 6', 175 lbs. Deb: 9/01/82																												
1982	Cle-A	16	18	3	6	0	0	1	1	2	4	.333	.400	.500	.900	145	1	1	100	33	3	.786	0	2	-1	-1	/O3D	0.0
1983	Cle-A	12	21	2	10	0	0	0	2	2	4	.476	.522	.476	.998	168	2	2	105	78	5	1.083	1	1	-0	-2	/OD	0.0
1984	Cle-A	13	8	0	2	0	0	0	0	0	3	.250	.250	.250	.500	37	-1	-1	106	0	1	.333	0	0	0	-2	/O12D	-0.2
Total	3	41	47	5	18	0	0	1	3	4	11	.383	.431	.447	.878	138	3	3	103	48	9	.813	1	3	-2	-5	/OD213	-0.2
■ **HAL RHYNE** Rhyne, Harold J. b: 3/30/1899, Paso Robles, Cal. d: 1/7/71, Orangeville, Cal. BR/TR, 5'8.5", 163 lbs. Deb: 4/18/26																												
1926	Pit-N	109	366	46	92	14	3	2	39	35	21	.251	.327	.322	.649	67	-12	-18	112	111	40	.584	1			-3	2S/3	-1.4
1927	Pit-N	62	168	21	46	5	0	0	17	14	9	.274	.330	.304	.633	69	-7	-7	102	117	17	.533	0			-7	23/S	-1.3
1929	Bos-A	120	346	41	87	24	5	0	38	25	14	.251	.309	.350	.659	68	-16	-17	102	107	39	.592	4	1	1	-5	*S/3O	-0.9
1930	Bos-A	107	296	34	60	8	5	0	23	25	19	.203	.269	.264	.533	38	-29	-26	93	98	22	.442	1	4	-2	-3	*S	-1.7
1931	Bos-A	147	565	75	154	34	3	0	51	57	41	.273	.341	.343	.685	86	-15	-10	94	92	68	.618	3	3	-1	15	*S	1.7
1932	Bos-A	71	207	26	47	12	5	0	14	23	14	.227	.310	.333	.644	69	-10	-9	97	68	22	.599	3	2	-0	7	S/32	0.2
1933	Chi-A	39	83	9	22	1	1	0	10	5	9	.265	.315	.301	.616	63	-4	-4	101	133	8	.516	1	1	-0	2	23/S	-0.1
Total	7	655	2031	252	508	98	22	2	192	184	127	.250	.318	.323	.641	68	-93	-92	100	100	217	.567	13	11		6	S2/3O	-3.5
■ **DEL RICE** Rice, Delbert b: 10/27/22, Portsmouth, Ohio d: 1/26/83, Buena Park, Cal. BR/TR, 6'2", 190 lbs. Deb: 5/02/45 MC																												
1945	StL-N	83	253	27	56	17	3	1	28	16	33	.261	.313	.364	.676	87	-5	-5	100	102	28	.569	0			4	C	0.1
1946	StL-N	55	139	10	38	8	1	1	12	8	16	.273	.313	.367	.680	87	-2	-3	107	83	15	.557	0			-4	C	-0.5
1947	StL-N	97	261	28	57	7	3	12	44	36	40	.218	.315	.406	.722	85	-4	-7	106	115	35	.689	1			-13	C	-1.7
1948	StL-N	100	290	24	57	10	1	4	34	37	46	.197	.298	.279	.578	57	-17	-17	101	137	26	.519	1			-1	C	-1.0
1949	StL-N	92	284	25	67	16	1	4	29	30	40	.236	.320	.342	.661	70	-9	-13	110	100	32	.592	0			-7	C	-1.6
1950	StL-N	130	414	39	101	20	3	9	54	43	65	.244	.323	.372	.694	80	-11	-13	103	115	50	.623	0			1	*C	-0.7
1951	StL-N	122	374	34	94	13	1	9	47	34	26	.251	.319	.364	.682	82	-9	-9	101	112	44	.595	0	0	0	-2	*C	-0.9
1952	StL-N	147	495	43	128	27	2	11	65	33	38	.259	.313	.388	.701	95	-6	-4	98	113	60	.608	0	1	-1	-8	*C	-1.0
1953	StL-N	135	419	32	99	22	1	6	37	48	49	.236	.323	.337	.660	71	-16	-17	102	91	47	.586	0	0	0	-9	*C	-1.7
1954	StL-N	56	147	13	37	10	1	2	16	16	21	.252	.325	.374	.699	81	-4	-4	100	103	18	.623	0	1	-1	-4	C	-0.7
1955	StL-N	20	59	6	12	3	0	1	7	7	6	.203	.288	.305	.593	57	-4	-4	101	135	5	.510	0	0	0	-0	C	-0.2
	Mil-N	27	71	5	14	0	1	2	7	6	12	.197	.260	.310	.570	54	-5	-4	93	101	6	.483	0	0	0	1	C	-0.2
	Yr	47	130	11	26	3	1	3	14	13	18	.200	.273	.308	.580	56	-9	-8	96	118	12	.505	0	0	0	1		-0.4
1956	Mil-N	71	188	15	40	9	1	3	17	18	34	.213	.282	.319	.601	62	-10	-10	99	104	16	.510	0	0	0	-1	C	-0.9
1957	Mil-N	54	144	15	33	1	1	9	20	17	37	.229	.311	.438	.748	109	-1	1	90	92	18	.690	0	0	0	5	C	0.9
1958	Mil-N	43	121	10	27	7	0	1	8	8	30	.223	.271	.306	.577	59	-8	-7	89	83	10	.464	0	0	0	3	C	-0.1
1959	Mil-N	13	29	3	6	0	0	0	1	2	3	.207	.258	.207	.465	27	-3	-3	95	67	1	.320	0	0	0	1	/C	0.0
1960	Chi-N	18	52	2	12	3	0	0	4	2	7	.231	.259	.288	.548	51	-4	-3	98	108	3	.395	0	0	0	-3	C	-0.5
	StL-N	1	2	0	0	0	0	0	0	1	0	.000	.333	.000	.333	1	-0	-0	108	0	0	.333	0	0	0	0	/C	0.0
	Yr	19	54	2	12	3	0	0	4	3	7	.222	.263	.278	.541	49	-4	-4	98	108	4	.419	0	0	0	-3		-0.5
	Bal-A	1	1	0	0	0	0	0	0	0	0	.000	.000	.000	.000	-98	-0	-0	102	0	0	.000	0	0	0	0	/C	0.0
1961	LA-A	44	83	11	20	4	0	4	11	20	19	.241	.388	.434	.822	107	3	1	111	90	15	.862	0	1	-1	-1	C	0.0
Total	17	1309	3826	342	908	177	20	79	441	382	522	.237	.312	.356	.668	78	-115	-121	101	106	430	.609	2	3		-38	*C	-10.7
■ **SAM RICE** Rice, Edgar Charles b: 2/20/1890, Morocco, Ind. d: 10/13/74, Rossmor, Md. BL/TR, 5'9", 150 lbs. Deb: 8/07/15 H																												
1915	Was-A	4	8	0	3	0	0	0	0	0	1	.375	.375	.375	.750	123	0	0	101	0	1	.600	0			0	/P	0.0
1916	Was-A	58	197	26	59	8	3	1	17	15	13	.299	.352	.386	.738	122	5	5	100	78	28	.696	4			-1	O/P	0.2
1917	Was-A	155	586	77	177	25	7	0	69	50	41	.302	.360	.369	.729	133	15	20	92	121	86	.743	35			-0	*O	1.1
1918	Was-A	7	23	3	8	1	0	0	3	2	0	.348	.400	.391	.791	133	1	1	104	122	4	.800	1			3	/O	0.4
1919	Was-A	141	557	80	179	23	9	3	71	42	26	.321	.376	.411	.787	123	16	17	98	104	91	.804	26			3	*O	1.0
1920	Was-A	153	624	83	211	29	9	3	80	39	23	.338	.381	.428	.809	120	12	17	95	98	100	.842	**63**	30	1	**16**	*O	1.9
1921	Was-A	143	561	83	185	39	13	4	79	38	10	.330	.382	.467	.849	117	13	14	99	105	100	.861	25	12	0	4	*O	0.5
1922	Was-A	154	633	91	187	37	13	6	69	48	13	.295	.347	.423	.770	109	-1	6	92	76	93	.743	20	9	1	3	*O	-0.1
1923	Was-A	148	595	117	188	35	**18**	3	75	57	12	.316	.381	.450	.832	125	15	20	95	89	105	.846	20	8	1	5	*O	1.2
1924	Was-A	154	646	106	**216**	39	14	1	76	46	24	.334	.382	.443	.825	114	11	12	98	77	109	.813	24	13	-1	3	*O	0.3
1925	Was-A	152	649	111	227	31	13	1	87	37	10	.350	.388	.442	.831	113	10	12	98	89	112	.818	26	11	1	10	*O	0.9
1926	Was-A	152	641	98	**216**	32	14	3	76	42	20	.337	.380	.445	.824	117	13	14	98	78	103	.790	25	23	-6	12	*O	0.8
1927	Was-A	142	603	98	179	33	14	2	65	36	11	.297	.336	.408	.744	95	-8	-6	97	76	80	.710	19	0	6	-6	*O	-1.9
1928	Was-A	148	616	95	202	32	15	2	55	49	15	.328	.379	.438	.818	112	13	12	102	60	105	.808	16	3	**3**	-12	*O	-0.4
1929	Was-A	150	616	119	199	39	10	1	62	55	9	.323	.382	.424	.806	108	8	8	100	71	102	.791	16	8	0	-1	*O	0.1
1930	Was-A	147	593	121	207	35	13	1	73	55	14	.349	.407	.457	.864	117	19	17	101	85	111	.868	13	8	-1	4	*O	1.4
1931	Was-A	120	413	81	128	21	8	0	42	35	11	.310	.365	.400	.765	100	1	1	101	84	61	.714	6	5	-1	1	*O	-0.4
1932	Was-A	106	288	58	93	16	7	1	34	32	6	.323	.391	.438	.828	115	7	7	100	88	50	.829	7	4	-0	-3	O	0.1
1933	Was-A	73	85	19	25	4	3	1	12	3	7	.294	.326	.447	.773	107	-0	0	96	98	11	.677	0	2	-1	-7	O	-0.8
1934	Cle-A	97	335	48	98	19	1	1	33	28	9	.293	.351	.364	.715	84	-7	-8	101	88	44	.660	5	1	1	-9	O	-1.5
Total	20	2404	9269	1514	2987	498	184	34	1078	709	275	.322	.374	.427	.801	113	140	170	98	86	1497	.790	351	137		27	*O/P	4.8
■ **HAL RICE** Rice, Harold Housten "Hoot" b: 2/11/24, Morganette, W.Va. BL/TR, 6'1", 195 lbs. Deb: 4/29/48																												
1948	StL-N	8	31	3	10	1	2	0	3	2	4	.323	.364	.484	.848	127	1	1	101	76	6	.810	0			-1	/O	0.0
1949	StL-N	40	46	3	9	2	1	1	9	3	7	.196	.245	.348	.593	52	-3	-4	110	179	4	.514	0			-2	O	-0.6
1950	StL-N	44	128	12	27	3	1	2	11	10	10	.211	.268	.297	.565	47	-10	-10	103	96	11	.471	0			-2	O	-1.2
1951	StL-N	69	236	20	60	12	1	4	38	24	22	.254	.323	.364	.687	84	-5	-5	101	150	27	.595	0	1	-1	-5	O	-1.2
1952	StL-N	98	295	37	85	14	5	7	45	16	26	.288	.325	.441	.765	113	3	4	98	116	39	.662	1	3	-2	-7	O	-0.6
1953	StL-N	8	8	0	2	0	0	0	0	0	3	.250	.250	.250	.500	30	-1	-1	102	0	1	.333	0	0	0	0	H	0.0
	Pit-N	78	286	39	89	16	1	4	42	17	22	.311	.350	.416	.766	97	-1	-1	102	127	42	.670	0	1	-1	11	O	0.6
	Yr	86	294	39	91	16	1	4	42	17	25	.310	.347	.412	.759	95	-1	-2	102	116	42	.660	0	1	-1	11		0.6
1954	Pit-N	28	81	10	14	4	1	1	9	14	24	.173	.295	.284	.579	53	-6	-5	97	136	7	.521	0	2	-1	3	O	-0.4
	Chi-N	51	72	5	11	0	0	0	5	8	15	.153	.237	.153	.390	4	-10	-10	101	179	3	.306	0	0	0	-6	O	-1.6
	Yr	79	153	15	25	4	1	1	14	22	39	.163	.269	.222	.491	30	-16	-16	99	165	10	.427	0	2	-1	-3		-2.0
Total	7	424	1183	129	307	52	12	19	162	94	133	.260	.314	.372	.686	82	-31	-32	101	130	139	.605	1	7		-8	O	-5.0
■ **HARRY RICE** Rice, Harry Francis b: 11/22/01, Ware Station, Ill. d: 1/1/71, Portland, Ore. BL/TR, 5'9", 185 lbs. Deb: 4/18/23																												
1923	StL-A	4	3	0	0	0	0	0	0	0	0	.000	.000	.000	.000	-96	-1	-1	104	0	0	.000	0	0	0	0	H	0.0
1924	StL-A	54	93	19	26	7	0	0	15	7	5	.280	.350	.355	.704	76	-2	-3	107	150	11	.629	1	3	-2	-0	3/21SO	-0.3
1925	StL-A	103	354	87	127	25	8	11	47	54	15	.359	.450	.568	1.018	146	32	28	108	69	92	1.145	8	7	-2	3	O/1C23	2.0
1926	StL-A	148	578	86	181	27	10	9	59	63	40	.313	.384	.441	.826	114	13	12	101	68	98	.814	10	11	-4	11	*O/32S	1.0
1927	StL-A	137	520	90	149	26	9	7	68	50	21	.287	.351	.412	.763	92	-3	-7	106	102	75	.733	6	0	2	12	*O/3	-0.2
1928	Det-A	131	510	87	154	21	12	6	81	44	27	.302	.360	.425	.785	106	4	4	99	125	78	.767	20	13	-2	-6	*O/3	-1.0
1929	Det-A	130	536	97	163	33	7	6	69	61	23	.304	.379	.425	.805	110	7	9	97	85	87	.781	6	10	-4	3	*O/3	0.2
1930	Det-A	37	128	16	39	6	0	2	24	19	8	.305	.403	.398	.801	99	2	1	105	142	21	.783	0	3	-2	-2	O	-0.3
	NY-A	100	346	62	103	17	5	7	74	31	21	.298	.361	.436	.797	113	0	6	90	143	55	.764	3	3	-1	3	O/13	0.3
	Yr	137	474	78	142	23	5	9	98	50	29	.300	.372	.426	.799	109	2	7	94	144	76	.769	3	6	-3	1		0.0
1931	Was-A	47	162	32	43	5	6	0	15	12	10	.265	.320	.370	.690	80	-5	-5	101	82	20	.625	2	1	0	-1	O	-0.7
1933	Cin-N	143	510	44	133	19	6	0	54	35	24	.261	.316	.322	.637	84	-11	-10	99	126	53	.535	4			2	*O/3	-1.6
Total	10	1034	3740	620	1118	186	63	48	506	376	194	.299	.368	.421	.789	106	36	34	100	103	588	.760	60	51		26	O/312SC	-0.6
■ **JIM RICE** Rice, James Edward b: 3/8/53, Anderson, S.C. BR/TR, 6'2", 200 lbs. Deb: 8/19/74																												
1974	Bos-A	24	67	6	18	2	1	1	13	4	12	.269	.319	.373	.693	93	-0	-1	107	183	8	.588	0	0	0	-1	D/O	-0.1
1975	Bos-A	144	564	92	174	29	4	22	102	36	122	.309	.354	.491	.845	126	25	19	109	121	92	.790	10	5	0	-4	OD	1.3

YEAR	TM/L	G	AB	R	H	2B	3B	HR	RBI	BB	SO	AVG	OBP	SLG	PRO	/A	BR	/A	PF	CHI	RC	TA	SB	CS	SBR	FR	POS	TPR
1976	Bos-A	153	581	75	164	25	8	25	85	28	123	.282	.320	.482	.802	120	20	13	110	94	83	.727	8	5	-1	-3	OD	0.8
1977	Bos-A	160	644	104	206	29	15	**39**	114	53	120	.320	.379	**.593**	.972	136	51	36	117	87	136	.968	5	4	-1	0	*DO	3.4
1978	Bos-A	163	677	121	**213**	25	**15**	**46**	**139**	58	126	.315	.373	**.600**	**.973**	158	**59**	**52**	107	89	**147**	.983	7	5	-1	6	*OD	**5.5**
1979	Bos-A	158	619	117	201	39	6	39	130	57	97	.325	.385	.596	.981	149	50	44	107	109	138	1.002	9	4	0	-3	*OD	3.5
1980	Bos-A	124	504	81	148	22	6	24	86	30	87	.294	.338	.504	.842	125	17	16	102	109	81	.789	8	3	1	3	*OD	1.7
1981	Bos-A	108	451	51	128	18	1	17	62	34	76	.284	.338	.441	.779	116	12	9	106	93	64	.702	2	2	-1	3	*O	0.9
1982	Bos-A	145	573	86	177	24	5	24	97	55	98	.309	.376	.494	.870	124	29	21	110	116	98	.810	0	1	-1	-5	*O	1.1
1983	Bos-A	155	626	90	191	34	1	**39**	**126**	52	102	.305	.364	.550	.914	146	39	38	101	103	113	.859	0	2	-1	14	*O/D	4.8
1984	Bos-A	159	657	98	184	25	7	28	122	44	102	.280	.326	.467	.793	106	13	4	110	120	88	.699	4	0	1	8	*O/D	0.8
1985	Bos-A	140	546	85	159	20	3	27	103	51	75	.291	.354	.487	.841	125	20	18	102	125	83	.761	2	0	1	-6	*O/D	1.0
1986	Bos-A	157	618	98	200	39	2	20	110	62	78	.324	.389	.490	.879	139	34	34	100	128	115	.842	0	1	-1	-8	*O/D	2.0
1987	Bos-A	108	404	66	112	14	0	13	62	45	77	.277	.360	.408	.768	105	4	4	99	124	55	.692	1	1	-0	1	OD	0.2
1988	Bos-A	135	485	57	128	18	3	15	72	48	89	.264	.334	.406	.740	97	4	-2	109	121	63	.662	1	1	-0	-2	*DO	-0.4
Total	15	2033	8016	1227	2403	363	77	379	1423	657	1384	.300	.357	.506	.864	128	376	307	107	110	1362	.853	57	34	-3	2	*OD	26.5

■ **LEN RICE** Rice, Leonard Oliver b: 9/2/18, Lead, S.Dak. BR/TR, 6′, 175 lbs. Deb: 4/26/44

1944	Cin-N	10	4	1	0	0	0	0	0	0	0	.000	.000	.000	.000	-99	-1	-1	95	0	0	.000	0			0	/C	0.0
1945	Chi-N	32	99	10	23	3	0	0	7	5	8	.232	.269	.263	.532	49	-7	-7	99	93	6	.412	2			-3	C	-0.9
Total	2	42	103	11	23	3	0	0	7	5	8	.223	.259	.252	.512	43	-8	-8	99	90	6	.393	2			-3	/C	-0.9

■ **BOB RICE** Rice, Robert Turnbull b: 5/28/1899, Philadelphia, Pa. d: 2/20/86, Elizabethtown, Pa BR/TR, 5′10″, 170 lbs. Deb: 9/01/26

1926	Phi-N	19	54	3	8	0	1	0	10	3	4	.148	.193	.185	.378	2	-7	-8	103	346	2	.283	0			1	3/2S	-0.5

■ **LEE RICHARD** Richard, Lee Edward "Bee Bee" b: 9/18/48, Lafayette, La. BR/TR, 5′11″, 165 lbs. Deb: 4/07/71

1971	Chi-A	87	260	38	60	7	3	2	17	20	46	.231	.288	.304	.592	70	-11	-10	98	82	21	.505	8	9	-3	3	SO	-0.3
1972	Chi-A	11	29	5	7	0	0	0	1	0	7	.241	.241	.241	.483	41	-2	-2	106	60	2	.348	1	0	0	0	/OS	-0.1
1974	Chi-A	32	67	5	11	1	0	0	1	5	8	.164	.222	.179	.401	16	-7	-7	102	33	3	.304	0	0	0	0	3/S2OD	-0.6
1975	Chi-A	43	45	11	9	0	1	0	5	4	7	.200	.265	.244	.510	43	-3	-3	103	175	3	.436	2	3	-1	1	3/S2D	-0.2
1976	StL-N	66	91	12	16	4	2	0	5	4	9	.176	.211	.264	.474	33	-8	-8	104	80	4	.367	1	0	0	-0	2S/3	-0.6
Total	5	239	492	71	103	12	6	2	29	33	77	.209	.260	.270	.531	51	-32	-32	100	82	33	.442	12	12	-4	4	/S23OD	-1.8

■ **GENE RICHARDS** Richards, Eugene b: 9/29/53, Monticello, S.C. BL/TL, 6′, 175 lbs. Deb: 4/06/77

1977	SD-N	146	525	79	152	16	11	5	32	60	80	.290	.365	.390	.755	117	3	12	88	59	81	.820	56	12	10	0	*O1	1.6
1978	SD-N	154	555	90	171	26	12	4	45	64	80	.308	.384	.420	.803	134	20	25	93	77	92	.824	37	17	1	-8	*O1	1.2
1979	SD-N	150	545	77	152	17	9	4	41	47	62	.279	.345	.365	.710	97	-4	-1	96	79	72	.681	24	8	2	-6	*O	-0.8
1980	SD-N	158	642	91	193	26	8	4	41	61	73	.301	.363	.385	.748	117	9	14	93	55	96	.783	61	16	9	7	*O	2.4
1981	SD-N	104	393	47	113	14	**12**	3	42	53	44	.288	.374	.407	.781	130	12	15	93	94	63	.796	20	8	1	-1	*O	1.3
1982	SD-N	132	521	63	149	13	8	3	28	36	52	.286	.335	.359	.693	102	-4	1	92	59	62	.642	30	20	-3	-0	*O/1	-0.4
1983	SD-N	95	233	37	64	11	3	3	22	17	17	.275	.327	.386	.713	98	-1	-1	99	88	28	.670	14	5	1	-2	O	-0.2
1984	SF-N	87	135	18	34	4	0	0	4	18	28	.252	.340	.281	.621	79	-4	-3	96	41	13	.570	5	3	-0	-2	O	-0.5
Total	8	1026	3549	502	1028	127	63	26	255	356	436	.290	.358	.383	.741	113	32	62	93	69	508	.759	247	89	21	-13	O/1	4.6

■ **FRED RICHARDS** Richards, Fred Charles "Fuzzy" b: 11/3/27, Warren, Ohio BL/TL, 6′1.5″, 185 lbs. Deb: 9/15/51

1951	Chi-N	10	27	1	8	2	0	0	4	2	3	.296	.345	.370	.715	95	-0	-0	97	155	4	.632	0	0	0	0	/1	0.0

■ **PAUL RICHARDS** Richards, Paul Rapier b: 11/21/08, Waxahachie, Tex. d: 5/4/86, Waxahachie, Tex. BR/TR, 6′1.5″, 180 lbs. Deb: 4/17/32 M

1932	Bro-N	3	8	0	0	0	0	0	0	0	2	.000	.000	.000	.000	-99	-2	-2	96	0	0	.000	0			0	/C	-0.1
1933	NY-N	51	87	4	17	3	0	0	10	3	12	.195	.222	.230	.452	30	-8	-8	99	188	4	.307	0			-1	C	-0.7
1934	NY-N	42	75	10	12	1	0	0	3	13	8	.160	.284	.173	.457	26	-8	-7	98	83	4	.400	0			-1	C	-0.6
1935	NY-N	7	4	0	1	0	0	0	0	2	1	.250	.500	.250	.750	112	0	0	96	0	1	1.000	0			0	/C	0.0
	Phi-A	85	257	31	63	10	1	4	29	24	12	.245	.310	.339	.648	68	-13	-13	100	99	28	.572	0	0	0	3	C	-0.6
1943	Det-A	100	313	32	69	7	1	5	33	38	35	.220	.307	.297	.604	73	-9	-11	106	112	31	.530	1	0	0	6	*C	0.1
1944	Det-A	95	300	24	71	13	0	3	37	35	30	.237	.318	.310	.628	76	-7	-9	105	131	30	.559	8	3	1	6	C	0.4
1945	Det-A	83	234	26	60	12	1	3	32	19	31	.256	.315	.355	.670	89	-2	-4	106	126	29	.611	4	0	1	1	C	0.5
1946	Det-A	57	139	13	28	5	2	0	11	23	18	.201	.315	.266	.581	59	-6	-8	108	113	13	.525	2	0	1	-3	C	-0.8
Total	8	523	1417	140	321	51	5	15	155	157	149	.227	.305	.301	.606	68	-55	-61	104	118	139	.544	15	3		11	C	-1.8

■ **HARDY RICHARDSON** Richardson, Abram Harding "Old True Blue" b: 4/21/1855, Clarksboro, N.J. d: 1/14/31, Utica, N.Y. BR/TR, 5′9.5″, 170 lbs. Deb: 5/01/1879

1879	Buf-N	79	336	54	95	18	10	0	37	16	30	.283	.315	.396	.711	116	12	5	114	86	43	.618				-6	*3/C	0.1
1880	Buf-N	83	343	48	89	18	8	0	17	14	37	.259	.289	.359	.647	130	6	11	91	45	36	.539				-6	*3/C	0.4
1881	Buf-N	83	344	62	100	18	9	2	53	12	27	.291	.315	.413	.727	125	10	9	101	132	46	.631				24	*O/2S3	**3.0**
1882	Buf-N	83	354	61	96	20	8	2	57	11	33	.271	.293	.390	.683	112	6	4	104	141	41	.578				14	*2	1.8
1883	Buf-N	92	399	73	124	34	7	1	56	22	20	.311	.347	.439	.785	137	17	17	100	105	62	.716				20	*2	2.9
1884	Buf-N	102	439	85	132	27	9	6	60	22	41	.301	.334	.444	.778	134	21	16	107	93	67	.707				3	2O/31	1.8
1885	Buf-N	96	426	90	136	19	11	6	44	20	22	.319	.350	.458	.808	161	27	27	99	62	70	.741				9	2O/SP	3.7
1886	Det-N	125	538	125	**189**	27	11	**11**	61	46	27	.351	.402	.504	.906	160	47	40	109	56	129	1.029	42			2	O2/PS3	4.0
1887	Det-N	120	543	131	178	25	18	8	94	31	40	.328	.366	.484	.851	134	25	24	102	87	110	.890	29			13	2O	3.4
1888	Det-N	58	266	60	77	18	2	6	32	17	23	.289	.335	.440	.774	150	14	14	98	73	45	.783	13			3	2	1.9
1889	Bos-N	132	536	122	163	33	10	6	79	48	44	.304	.367	.437	.803	124	18	16	102	90	106	.895	47			11	2O	2.8
1890	Bos-P	130	555	126	181	26	14	11	**143**	52	46	.326	.384	.483	.867	124	24	17	107	125	122	.968	42			-2	*O/S1	0.8
1891	Bos-a	74	278	45	71	9	4	7	51	40	26	.255	.351	.392	.743	117	6	6	99	116	45	.802	16			-4	O/3S1	0.0
1892	Was-N	10	37	2	4	0	0	0	0	5	3	.108	.214	.108	.322	-1	-4	-5	105	0	1	.333	2			0	/O32	-0.3
	NY-N	64	248	36	53	11	5	2	34	21	26	.214	.278	.323	.600	85	-6	-5	98	129	27	.595	14			0	2O/1S	-0.4
	Yr	74	285	38	57	11	5	2	34	26	29	.200	.269	.295	.564	73	-10	-9	99	111	28	.557	16			0		-0.7
Total	14	1331	5642	1120	1688	303	126	68	818	377	445	.299	.344	.434	.778	130	223	198	103	93	949	.769	205			81	2O3/S1CP	25.9

■ **ART RICHARDSON** Richardson, Arthur L. b: 1862, Hamilton, Ont., Can. d: 25, Deb: 7/10/1884

1884	CP-U	1	4	0	0	0	0	0		0		.000	.000	.000	.000	-99	-1	-1	99	0	0	.000	0			0	/2	0.0

■ **NOLEN RICHARDSON** Richardson, Clifford Nolen b: 1/18/03, Chattanooga, Tenn. d: 9/25/51, Athens, Ga. BR/TR, 6′1.5″, 170 lbs. Deb: 4/16/29

1929	Det-A	13	21	2	4	0	0	0	2	2	1	.190	.261	.190	.451	18	-3	-2	97	171	1	.389	1	1	-0	-1	S	-0.2
1931	Det-A	38	148	13	40	9	2	0	16	6	3	.270	.299	.358	.657	69	-6	-7	104	102	16	.560	2	1	0	2	3	-0.2
1932	Det-A	69	155	13	34	5	2	0	12	9	13	.219	.262	.277	.540	39	-14	-14	102	93	12	.463	5	2	0	2	3/S	-0.6
1935	NY-A	12	46	3	10	1	1	0	5	3	1	.217	.265	.283	.548	45	-4	-4	93	133	4	.444	0	0	0	-2	S	-0.4
1938	Cin-N	35	100	8	29	4	0	0	10	3	4	.290	.311	.330	.641	78	-3	-3	98	110	10	.493	0			0	S	0.0
1939	Cin-N	1	3	0	0	0	0	0	0	0	0	.000	.000	.000	.000	-97	-1	-1	103	0	0	.000	0			0	/S	0.0
Total	6	168	473	39	117	19	5	0	45	23	22	.247	.282	.309	.591	55	-31	-31	100	106	42	.492	8	4		1	3/S	-1.4

■ **DANNY RICHARDSON** Richardson, Daniel b: 1/25/1863, Elmira, N.Y. d: 9/12/26, New York, N.Y. BR/TR, 5′8″, 165 lbs. Deb: 5/22/1884 M

1884	NY-N	74	277	36	70	8	1	1	27	16	17	.253	.294	.300	.593	89	-4	-3	98	110	25	.478				5	OS	0.1
1885	NY-N	49	198	26	52	9	3	0	25	10	14	.263	.298	.338	.636	96	1	-2	109	137	20	.527				0	O3/P	0.0
1886	NY-N	68	237	43	55	9	1	1	27	17	21	.232	.283	.291	.575	85	-7	-3	89	125	24	.538	12			-6	O/PS32	-0.6
1887	NY-N	122	450	79	125	19	10	3	62	36	25	.278	.337	.384	.721	95	1	-4	107	107	74	.782	41			12	*23/P	1.2
1888	NY-N	135	561	82	127	16	7	8	61	15	35	.226	.248	.323	.570	89	-11	-6	93	102	55	.535	35			10	*2	0.8
1889	NY-N	125	497	88	139	22	8	7	100	46	37	.280	.342	.398	.740	103	5	1	105	144	81	.774	32			3	*2	1.2
1890	NY-P	123	528	102	135	12	9	4	80	37	19	.256	.307	.335	.642	67	-21	-29	109	123	67	.644	37			16	S2	-0.4
1891	NY-N	123	516	85	139	18	5	4	51	33	27	.269	.313	.347	.660	100	-5	0	94	75	66	.637	28			**44**	*2/S	4.1
1892	Was-N	142	551	48	132	13	4	3	58	25	45	.240	.274	.294	.568	70	-19	-22	105	106	52	.508	25			**49**	S2/3M	2.9
1893	Bro-N	54	206	36	46	6	2	0	27	13	18	.223	.279	.272	.551	53	-15	-12	91	135	18	.494	7			-18	2/3S	-2.5

YEAR	TM/L	G	AB	R	H	2B	3B	HR	RBI	BB	SO	AVG	OBP	SLG	PRO	/A	BR	/A	PF	CHI	RC	TA	SB	CS	SBR	FR	POS	TPR
1894	Lou-N	116	430	51	109	17	2	1	40	35	31	.253	.317	.309	.626	60	-32	-22	88	83	46	.564	8			3	*S2	-1.0
Total	11	1131	4451	676	1129	149	52	32	558	283	289	.254	.301	.332	.633	83	-107	-102	99	110	528	.603	225			118	2SO/3P	5.8
■ **KEN RICHARDSON** Richardson, Kenneth Franklin b: 5/2/15, Orleans, Ind. BR/TR, 5'10.5", 187 lbs. Deb: 4/14/42																												
1942	Phi-A	6	15	1	1	0	0	0	0	2	0	.067	.176	.067	.243	-31	-3	-3	96	0	0	.214	0	0	0	0	/O13	-0.2
1946	Phi-N	6	20	1	3	1	0	0	2	0	2	.150	.150	.200	.350	-1	-3	-3	95	187	0	.222	0			-0	/2	-0.2
Total	2	12	35	2	4	1	0	0	2	2	2	.114	.162	.143	.305	-14	-5	-5	96	101	1	.219	0	0		-0	/2O31	-0.4
■ **BOBBY RICHARDSON** Richardson, Robert Clinton b: 8/19/35, Sumter, S.C. BR/TR, 5'9", 170 lbs. Deb: 8/05/55																												
1955	NY-A	11	26	2	4	0	0	0	3	2	0	.154	.214	.154	.368	0	-4	-4	98	280	1	.292	1	1	-0	1	/2S	-0.2
1956	NY-A	5	7	1	1	0	0	0	0	0	1	.143	.143	.143	.286	-25	-1	-1	99	0	0	.167	0	0	0	0	/2	0.0
1957	NY-A	97	305	36	78	11	1	0	19	9	26	.256	.277	.298	.575	61	-18	-16	94	82	23	.423	1	3	-2	2	2	-1.0
1958	NY-A	73	182	18	45	6	2	0	14	8	5	.247	.279	.302	.581	58	-10	-11	103	102	15	.454	1	3	-2	0	23/S	-0.7
1959	NY-A	134	469	53	141	18	6	2	33	26	20	.301	.337	.377	.715	104	-3	1	93	71	60	.619	5	5	-2	6	*2S3	1.0
1960	NY-A	150	460	45	116	12	3	1	26	35	19	.252	.305	.298	.603	68	-23	-20	94	73	42	.499	6	6	-2	-5	*23	-1.6
1961	NY-A	162	662	80	173	17	5	3	49	30	23	.261	.295	.316	.611	66	-35	-31	96	93	59	.489	9	7	-2	-7	*2	-2.0
1962	NY-A	161	692	99	**209**	38	5	8	59	37	24	.302	.338	.406	.744	106	-1	4	94	68	92	.653	11	9	-2	-3	*2	1.0
1963	NY-A	151	630	72	167	20	6	3	48	25	22	.265	.295	.330	.625	75	-21	-22	101	82	63	.530	15	1	4	4	*2	-0.2
1964	NY-A	159	679	90	181	25	4	4	50	28	36	.267	.296	.333	.628	72	-24	-26	103	79	66	.515	11	2	2	-14	*2/S	-2.3
1965	NY-A	160	664	76	164	28	2	6	47	37	39	.247	.288	.322	.610	72	-24	-25	101	74	61	.502	7	5	-1	-2	*2	-2.0
1966	NY-A	149	610	71	153	21	3	7	42	25	28	.251	.281	.330	.611	80	-20	-16	94	70	52	.485	6	6	-2	1	*2/3	-0.4
Total	12	1412	5386	643	1432	196	37	34	390	262	243	.266	.301	.335	.636	77	-184	-165	97	79	534	.534	73	48	-7	-18	*2/3S	-8.4
■ **TOM RICHARDSON** Richardson, Thomas Mitchell b: 8/7/1883, Louisville, Ill. d: 11/15/39, Onawa, Iowa BR/TR, 6', 190 lbs. Deb: 8/02/17																												
1917	StL-A	1	1	0	0	0	0	0	0	0	0	.000	.000	.000	.000	-99	-0	-0	95	0	0	.000	0			0	H	0.0
■ **BILL RICHARDSON** Richardson, William Hezekiah b: 10/8/1877, Decatur County, Ind d: 4/11/54, Batesville, Ind. Deb: 9/20/01																												
1901	StL-N	15	52	7	11	2	0	2	7	6		.212	.293	.365	.658	95	-1	-0	97	96	6	.634	1			0	1	0.0
■ **MIKE RICHARDT** Richardt, Michael Anthony b: 5/24/58, Los Angeles, Cal. BR/TR, 6', 170 lbs. Deb: 8/30/80																												
1980	Tex-A	22	71	2	16	2	0	0	8	1	7	.225	.236	.254	.490	34	-6	-6	100	173	4	.339	0	0	0	2	2/D	-0.3
1982	Tex-A	119	402	34	97	10	0	3	43	23	42	.241	.284	.289	.573	62	-23	-19	93	138	32	.467	9	1	2	4	2D/O	-0.7
1983	Tex-A	22	83	9	13	2	1	1	7	2	11	.157	.176	.241	.417	13	-10	-10	101	121	3	.329	2	1	0	-0	2	-0.9
1984	Tex-A	6	9	0	1	0	0	0	0	1	1	.111	.200	.111	.311	-11	-1	-1	100	0	0	.222	0	1	-1	-0	/2	-0.1
	Hou-N	16	15	1	4	1	0	0	2	0	1	.267	.267	.333	.600	73	-1	-1	93	157	1	.455	0	0	0	0	H	0.0
Total	4	185	580	46	131	15	1	4	60	27	62	.226	.262	.276	.537	50	-41	-38	95	138	41	.440	11	3	2	6	2/DO	-2.0
■ **LANCE RICHBOURG** Richbourg, Lance Clayton b: 12/18/1897, De Funiak Springs Fla. d: 9/10/75, Crestview, Fla. BL/TR, 5'10.5", 160 lbs. Deb: 7/04/21																												
1921	Phi-N	10	5	2	1	1	0	0	0	0	3	.200	.200	.400	.600	54	-0	-0	102	0	0	.600	1	1	-0	0	/2	0.0
1924	Was-A	15	32	3	9	2	1	0	1	2	0	.281	.324	.406	.730	89	-1	-1	98	25	4	.652	0	0	0	1	/O	0.0
1927	Bos-N	115	450	57	139	12	9	2	34	22	30	.309	.342	.389	.731	102	-3	1	93	70	58	.714	24			-5	*O	-0.8
1928	Bos-N	148	612	105	206	26	12	2	52	62	39	.337	.399	.428	.828	120	17	19	97	60	104	.830	11			6	*O	1.9
1929	Bos-N	139	557	76	170	24	13	3	56	42	26	.305	.355	.411	.766	95	-9	-4	94	77	80	.721	7			8	*O	-0.7
1930	Bos-N	130	529	81	161	23	8	3	54	19	31	.304	.331	.395	.726	77	-22	-19	97	90	66	.660	13			5	*O	-2.1
1931	Bos-N	97	286	32	82	11	6	2	29	19	14	.287	.331	.388	.719	94	-3	-3	99	88	38	.681	9			-4	O	-1.0
1932	Chi-N	44	148	22	38	2	2	1	21	8	4	.257	.295	.318	.612	62	-7	-8	104	156	14	.500	0			-2	O	-1.1
Total	8	698	2619	378	806	101	51	13	247	174	147	.308	.352	.400	.752	96	-30	-16	96	79	364	.713	65	1		9	O/2	-3.8
■ **DON RICHMOND** Richmond, Donald Lester b: 10/27/19, Gillett, Pa. d: 5/24/81, Elmira, N.Y. BL/TR, 6'1", 175 lbs. Deb: 9/16/41																												
1941	Phi-A	9	35	3	7	1	1	0	5	0	1	.200	.200	.286	.486	27	-4	-4	101	181	1	.323	0	2	-1	-0	/3	-0.4
1946	Phi-A	16	62	3	18	3	0	1	9	0	10	.290	.290	.387	.677	84	-1	-2	104	129	7	.568	1	0	0	1	3	0.1
1947	Phi-A	19	21	2	4	1	1	0	4	3	3	.190	.292	.333	.625	73	-1	-1	100	210	2	.556	0	0	0	0	/32	0.0
1951	StL-N	12	34	3	3	1	0	1	4	3	3	.088	.162	.206	.368	-2	-5	-5	101	155	1	.303	0	1	-1	1	3	-0.3
Total	4	56	152	11	32	6	2	2	22	6	17	.211	.241	.316	.556	50	-11	-11	102	159	11	.444	1	3	-2	2	/32	-0.6
■ **JOHN RICHMOND** Richmond, John H. b: 1854, Pennsylvania TR , Deb: 4/22/1875																												
1875	Ath-n	29	122	30	26							.213															2O/C	
1879	Syr-N	62	254	31	54	8	4	1	23	4	24	.213	.225	.287	.512	76	-9	-5	89	113	17	.385				-8	OS/C	-1.0
1880	Bos-N	32	129	12	32	3	1	0	9	2	18	.248	.260	.287	.546	93	-2	-1	92	94	10	.402				-11	S/O	-0.9
1881	Bos-N	27	98	13	27	2	2	1	12	6	7	.276	.317	.367	.685	125	2	3	91	109	12	.592				1	O/S	0.3
1882	Cle-N	41	140	12	24	6	2	0	11	11	27	.171	.232	.243	.475	59	-7	-5	90	109	8	.388				1	O	-0.3
	Phi-a	18	65	8	12	2	2	0		11		.185	.303	.277	.580	86	0	-1	112	0	6	.547				0	O	0.0
1883	Col-a	92	385	63	109	7	8	0		25		.283	.327	.343	.670	133	7	15	87	0	44	.569				23	*S/O	3.0
1884	Col-a	105	398	57	100	13	7	3		35		.251	.317	.342	.658	121	9	10	97	0	44	.584				-10	*S	0.0
1885	Pit-a	34	131	14	27	2	2	0		8		.206	.262	.252	.514	61	-5	-6	106	0	9	.413				0	SO	-0.5
Total	7	411	1600	210	385	43	28	5	55	102	76	.241	.288	.312	.600	103	-5	11	94	40	149	.499				-5	SO/2C	0.6
■ **AL RICHTER** Richter, Allen Gordon b: 2/7/27, Norfolk, Va. BR/TR, 6', 175 lbs. Deb: 9/23/51																												
1951	Bos-A	5	11	1	1	0	0	0	0	3	0	.091	.286	.091	.377	5	-1	-2	108	0	0	.308	0	0	0	0	/S	0.0
1953	Bos-A	1	0	0	0	0	0	0	0	0	0	—	—	—	—	—	0	0	109	—	—	—	0	0	0	0	/S	0.0
Total	2	6	11	1	1	0	0	0	0	3	0	.091	.286	.091	.377	5	-1	-2	108	0	0	.400	0	0	0	0	/S	0.0
■ **JOHN RICHTER** Richter, John M. b: 2/8/1873, Louisville, Ky. d: 10/4/27, Louisville, Ky. Deb: 10/06/1898																												
1898	Lou-N	3	13	1	2	0	0	0	0	0		.154	.154	.154	.308	-11	-2	-2	96	0	0	.182	0			0	/3	-0.1
■ **JOE RICKERT** Rickert, Joseph Francis "Diamond Joe" b: 12/12/1876, London, Ohio d: 10/15/43, Springfield, Ohio 5'10.5", 165 lbs. Deb: 10/12/1898																												
1898	Pit-N	2	6	0	1	0	0	0	0	0		.167	.167	.167	.333	-3	-1	-1	98	0	0	.200	0			0	/O	0.0
1901	Bos-N	13	60	6	10	1	2	0	1	3		.167	.206	.250	.456	30	-5	-6	112	19	3	.380	1			2	O	-0.5
Total	2	15	66	6	11	1	2	0	1	3		.167	.203	.242	.445	27	-6	-7	110	18	4	.364	1			2	/O	-0.5
■ **MARV RICKERT** Rickert, Marvin August "Twitch" b: 1/8/21, Long Branch, Wash. d: 6/3/78, Oakville, Wash. BL/TR, 6'2", 195 lbs. Deb: 9/10/42																												
1942	Chi-N	8	26	5	7	0	0	0	1	1	5	.269	.296	.269	.566	69	-1	-1	96	53	2	.400	0			2	/O	0.0
1946	Chi-N	111	392	44	103	18	3	7	47	28	54	.263	.314	.378	.691	101	-4	-1	94	104	46	.604	3			-7	*O	-1.0
1947	Chi-N	71	137	7	20	0	0	2	15	15	17	.146	.230	.190	.420	13	-17	-17	101	174	6	.336	0			-2	O/1	-2.0
1948	Cin-N	8	6	0	1	0	0	0	0	0	0	.167	.167	.167	.333	-9	-1	-1	103	0	0	.200	0			0	H	0.0
	Bos-N	3	13	1	3	0	1	0	2	0	1	.231	.286	.385	.670	79	-0	-0	102	132	2	.600	0			1	/O	0.0
	Yr	11	19	1	4	0	1	0	2	0	1	.211	.250	.316	.566	51	-1	-1	103	36	2	.467	0			1		0.0
1949	Bos-N	100	277	44	81	18	3	6	49	23	38	.292	.347	.444	.791	114	4	5	97	131	42	.724	1			0	O1	0.0
1950	Pit-N	17	20	0	3	0	0	0	4	0	4	.150	.150	.150	.300	-20	-3	-4	103	514	0	.167	0			-1	/O	-0.4
	Chi-A	84	278	38	66	9	2	4	27	21	42	.237	.291	.327	.618	60	-18	-17	97	90	25	.500	0	1	-1	-6	O/1	-2.3
Total	6	402	1149	139	284	45	9	19	145	88	161	.247	.302	.352	.653	79	-41	-37	97	121	122	.568	4	1		-13	O/1	-5.7
■ **DAVE RICKETTS** Ricketts, David William b: 7/12/35, Pottstown, Pa. BB/TR, 6', 190 lbs. Deb: 9/25/63 C																												
1963	StL-N	3	8	0	2	0	0	0	0	0	2	.250	.250	.250	.500	41	-1	-1	107	0	1	.333	0	0	0	-0	/C	0.0
1965	StL-N	11	29	1	7	0	0	0	0	1	3	.241	.267	.241	.508	42	-2	-2	107	0	2	.364	0	0	0	1	C	0.0
1967	StL-N	52	99	11	27	8	0	1	14	4	7	.273	.301	.384	.685	94	-1	-1	101	141	11	.560	0	0	0	2	C	0.3
1968	StL-N	20	22	1	3	0	0	0	1	0	3	.136	.136	.136	.273	-19	-3	-3	95	140	0	.158	0	0	0	0	/C	-0.2
1969	StL-N	30	44	2	12	1	0	0	5	4	5	.273	.333	.295	.629	78	-1	-1	100	154	5	.515	0	0	0	1	/C	0.0
1970	Pit-N	14	11	0	2	0	0	0	0	1	3	.182	.250	.182	.432	18	-1	-1	97	0	1	.333	0	0	0	0	/C	0.0
Total	6	130	213	15	53	9	0	1	20	10	23	.249	.283	.305	.588	67	-9	-9	101	112	19	.469	0	0	0	4	/C	0.1

YEAR	TM/L	G	AB	R	H	2B	3B	HR	RBI	BB	SO	AVG	OBP	SLG	PRO	/A	BR	/A	PF	CHI	RC	TA	SB	CS	SBR	FR	POS	TPR
■ **BRANCH RICKEY** Rickey, Wesley Branch "The Mahatma" b: 12/20/1881, Lucasville, Ohio d: 12/9/65, Columbia, Mo. BL/TR, 5'9", 175 lbs. Deb: 6/16/05 MH																												
1905	StL-A	1	3	0	0	0	0	0	0	0		.000	.000	.000	.000	-99	-1	-1	91	0	0	.000	0			0	/C	0.0
1906	StL-A	65	201	22	57	7	3	3	24	16		.284	.336	.393	.729	133	7	7	98	99	29	.688	4			-0	C/O	1.2
1907	NY-A	52	137	16	25	1	3	0	15	11		.182	.243	.234	.477	49	-7	-8	109	168	9	.420	4			2	OC/1	-0.6
1914	StL-A	2	2	0	0	0	0	0	0	0	1	.000	.000	.000	.000	-99	-0	-0	98	0	0	.000	0			0	HM	0.0
Total	4	120	343	38	82	8	6	3	39	27	1	.239	.295	.324	.618	95	-1	-2	102	125	38	.559	8			2	/CO1	0.6
■ **CHRIS RICKLEY** Rickley, Christian b: 10/7/1859, Philadelphia, Pa. d: 10/25/11, Philadelphia, Pa. 5'8", 160 lbs. Deb: 6/09/1884																												
1884	Phi-U	6	25	5	5	2	0	0		2		.200	.259	.280	.539	89	-0	-0	93	0	2	.450	0			0	/S	0.0
■ **JOHN RICKS** Ricks, John Deb: 9/21/1891																												
1891	StL-a	5	18	3	3	0	0	0	0	0	2	.167	.167	.167	.333	-3	-2	-3	114	0	1	.200	0			0	/3	-0.1
1894	StL-N	1	1	0	0	0	0	0	0	0	0	.000	.000	.000	.000	-99	-0	-0	101	0	0	.000	0			0	/3	0.0
Total	2	6	19	3	3	0	0	0	0	0	2	.158	.158	.158	.316	-8	-3	-3	113	0	1	.188	0			0	/3	-0.1
■ **FRED RICO** Rico, Alfredo (Cruz) b: 7/4/44, Jerome, Ariz. BR/TR, 5'10", 180 lbs. Deb: 9/01/69																												
1969	KC-A	12	26	2	6	2	0	0	2	9	10	.231	.429	.308	.736	106	1	1	103	100	4	.773	0	1	-1	3	/O3	0.3
■ **ART RICO** Rico, Arthur Raymond b: 7/23/1896, Roxbury, Mass. d: 1/3/19, Boston, Mass. BR/TR, 5'9.5", 185 lbs. Deb: 7/31/16																												
1916	Bos-N	4	4	0	0	0	0	0	0	0	0	.000	.000	.000	.000	-99	-1	-1	93	0	0	.000	0			0	/C	0.0
1917	Bos-N	13	14	1	4	1	0	0	2	0	2	.286	.286	.357	.643	100	-0	-0	96	154	1	.500	0			-1	C/O	0.0
Total	2	17	18	1	4	1	0	0	2	0	2	.222	.222	.278	.500	55	-1	-1	95	120	1	.357	0			-1	/CO	0.0
■ **HARRY RICONDA** Riconda, Henry Paul b: 3/17/1897, New York, N.Y. d: 11/15/58, Mahopac, N.Y. BR/TR, 5'10", 175 lbs. Deb: 4/19/23																												
1923	Phi-A	55	175	23	46	11	4	0	12	12	18	.263	.317	.371	.689	81	-5	-5	100	63	21	.634	4	2	0	-5	3/S	-0.4
1924	Phi-A	83	281	34	71	16	3	1	21	27	43	.253	.323	.342	.664	72	-12	-12	99	71	32	.598	3	4	-2	-2	3/S	-0.8
1926	Bos-N	4	12	1	2	0	0	0	0	2	2	.167	.286	.167	.452	28	-1	-1	86	0	1	.400	0			0	/3	0.0
1928	Bro-N	92	281	22	63	15	4	3	35	20	28	.224	.285	.338	.623	63	-16	-16	99	120	27	.573	6			-3	23S	-1.4
1929	Pit-N	8	15	3	7	2	0	0	2	0	0	.467	.467	.600	1.067	157	1	1	103	76	4	1.125	0			-1	/S	0.1
1930	Cin-N	1	1	0	0	0	0	0	0	0	0	.000	.000	.000	.000	-99	-0	-0	90	0	0	.000	0			0	H	0.0
Total	6	243	765	83	189	44	11	4	70	61	91	.247	.309	.349	.658	72	-34	-33	99	86	84	.600	13	6		-11	3/2S	-2.5
■ **JOHN RIDDLE** Riddle, John H. b: 2/1864 Pennsylvania BR , Deb: 9/18/1889																												
1889	Was-N	11	37	3	8	3	0	0	3	2	8	.216	.256	.297	.554	61	-2	-2	92	81	3	.448	0			0	/CO	-0.1
1890	Phi-a	27	85	7	7	0	1	0		17		.082	.243	.106	.349	5	-9	-9	97	0	3	.397	4			0	CO/23	-0.7
Total	2	38	122	10	15	3	1	0	3	19	8	.123	.246	.164	.410	22	-12	-11	96	22	6	.411	4			0	/CO23	-0.8
■ **JOHNNY RIDDLE** Riddle, John Ludy "Mutt" b: 10/3/05, Clinton, S.C. BR/TR, 5'11", 190 lbs. Deb: 4/17/30 C																												
1930	Chi-A	25	58	7	14	3	1	0	4	3	6	.241	.290	.328	.618	55	-4	-4	103	70	6	.523	0	0	0	0	C	-0.1
1937	Was-A	8	26	2	7	0	0	0	3	0	2	.269	.296	.269	.566	46	-2	-2	94	147	2	.421	0	0	0	0	/C	0.0
	Bos-N	2	3	0	0	0	0	0	0	1	0	.000	.250	.000	.250	-30	-1	-0	90	0	0	.333	0			0	/C	0.0
1938	Bos-N	19	57	6	16	1	0	0	2	4	2	.281	.328	.298	.626	83	-2	-1	88	42	6	.512	0			1	C	0.1
1941	Cin-N	10	10	2	3	0	0	0	0	0	1	.300	.300	.300	.600	70	-0	-0	99	0	1	.429	0			-0	C	0.0
1944	Cin-N	1	0	0	0	0	0	0	0	0	0	—	—	—	—	—	0	0	95	—	—	—	0			0	/C	0.0
1945	Cin-N	23	45	0	8	0	0	0	2	4	6	.178	.245	.178	.423	20	-5	-5	94	87	2	.324	0			1	C	-0.3
1948	Pit-N	10	15	1	3	0	0	0	0	1	2	.200	.250	.200	.450	22	-2	-2	104	0	1	.308	0			-0	C	0.0
Total	7	98	214	18	51	4	1	0	11	13	19	.238	.288	.266	.555	51	-15	-14	96	66	19	.439	0	0		1	/C	-0.3
■ **HANK RIEBE** Riebe, Harvey Donald b: 10/10/21, Cleveland, Ohio BR/TR, 5'9.5", 175 lbs. Deb: 8/26/42																												
1942	Det-A	11	35	1	11	2	0	0	2	0	6	.314	.314	.371	.686	82	-1	-1	113	54	4	.520	0	0	0	0	C	0.1
1947	Det-A	8	7	0	0	0	0	0	2	0	2	.000	.000	.000	.000	-96	-2	-2	104	0	0	.000	0	0	0	0	/C	-0.1
1948	Det-A	25	62	0	12	0	0	0	5	3	5	.194	.231	.194	.424	14	-8	-7	96	141	2	.278	0	1	-1	-3	C	-0.8
1949	Det-A	17	33	1	6	2	0	0	2	0	5	.182	.182	.242	.424	11	-4	-5	108	86	1	.310	1	0	0	-0	C	-0.3
Total	4	61	137	2	29	4	0	0	11	3	18	.212	.229	.241	.469	26	-14	-15	103	99	7	.333	1	1	-0	-3	/C	-1.1
■ **JOE RIGGERT** Riggert, Joseph Aloysius b: 12/11/1886, Janesville, Wis. d: 12/10/73, Kansas City, Mo. BR/TR, 5'9.5", 170 lbs. Deb: 5/12/11																												
1911	Bos-A	50	146	19	31	4	4	2	13	12		.212	.290	.336	.626	75	-5	-5	99	80	16	.609	5			-4	O	-1.2
1914	Bro-N	27	83	6	16	1	3	2	6	4	20	.193	.230	.349	.579	71	-3	-4	101	62	7	.522	2			-0	O	-0.4
	StL-N	34	89	9	19	5	2	0	8	5	14	.213	.255	.315	.570	67	-4	-4	104	104	8	.529	4			-3	O	-0.8
	Yr	61	172	15	35	6	5	2	14	9	34	.203	.243	.331	.574	68	-7	-8	103	86	15	.526	6			-3		-1.2
1919	Bos-N	63	240	34	68	8	5	4	17	25	30	.283	.356	.408	.764	132	9	9	98	64	36	.779	9			-0	O	0.7
Total	3	174	558	68	134	18	14	8	44	46	64	.240	.305	.366	.671	97	-4	-3	99	74	66	.651	20			-8	O	-1.7
■ **LEW RIGGS** Riggs, Lewis Sidney b: 4/22/10, Mebane, N.C. d: 8/12/75, Durham, N.C. BL/TR, 6', 175 lbs. Deb: 4/28/34																												
1934	StL-N	2	1	0	0	0	0	0	0	0	1	.000	.000	.000	.000	-88	-0	-0	114	0	0	.000	0			0	H	0.0
1935	Cin-N	142	532	73	148	26	8	5	46	43	32	.278	.334	.385	.720	99	-5	-0	93	80	72	.660	8			8	*3	1.2
1936	Cin-N	141	538	69	138	20	12	6	57	38	33	.257	.314	.372	.686	87	-13	-10	97	98	63	.605	5			14	*3	1.4
1937	Cin-N	122	384	43	93	17	5	6	45	24	17	.242	.289	.359	.648	82	-14	-10	91	104	40	.560	4			17	*3/2S	1.1
1938	Cin-N	142	531	53	134	21	13	2	55	40	28	.252	.311	.352	.663	84	-13	-12	98	105	60	.577	3			2	*3	-1.3
1939	Cin-N	22	38	5	6	1	0	0	1	5	4	.158	.256	.184	.440	19	-4	-4	103	52	2	.394	1			0	3	-0.3
1940	Cin-N	41	72	8	21	7	1	1	9	2	4	.292	.311	.458	.769	109	1	0	101	93	10	.673	0			1	3	0.1
1941	Bro-N	77	197	27	60	13	4	5	36	16	12	.305	.357	.487	.844	132	9	8	103	117	35	.813	1			-8	3/12	0.0
1942	Bro-N	70	180	20	50	5	0	3	22	13	9	.278	.333	.356	.689	100	0	-0	102	112	22	.594	0			-4	3/1	-0.4
1946	Bro-N	1	4	0	0	0	0	0	0	0	0	.000	.000	.000	.000	-97	-1	-1	103	0	0	.000	0			0	/3	0.0
Total	10	760	2477	298	650	110	43	28	271	181	140	.262	.317	.375	.692	92	-42	-30	96	98	304	.629	22			29	3/21S	1.8
■ **TOPPER RIGNEY** Rigney, Emory Elmo b: 1/7/1897, Groveton, Tex. d: 6/6/72, San Antonio, Tex. BR/TR, 5'9", 150 lbs. Deb: 4/12/22																												
1922	Det-A	155	536	68	161	17	7	2	63	68	44	.300	.380	.369	.750	98	-1	1	98	113	81	.747	19	8	1	-12	*S	0.7
1923	Det-A	129	470	63	148	24	11	1	74	55	35	.315	.389	.419	.808	117	10	12	97	134	80	.798	7	5	-1	-8	*S	1.5
1924	Det-A	147	499	81	144	29	9	4	93	102	39	.289	.410	.407	.817	112	12	13	100	146	90	.866	11	11	-3	8	*S	3.0
1925	Det-A	62	146	21	36	5	2	2	18	21	15	.247	.341	.349	.691	76	-5	-5	99	106	18	.661	2	2	-1	-1	S/3	0.1
1926	Bos-A	148	525	71	142	32	6	4	53	108	31	.270	.395	.377	.772	101	6	5	101	76	85	.798	6	8	-3	**18**	*S	3.0
1927	Bos-A	8	18	0	2	1	0	0	0	1	2	.111	.158	.167	.325	-17	-3	-3	95	0	1	.250	0	0	0	0	/3S	-0.1
	Was-A	45	132	20	36	5	4	0	13	22	10	.273	.381	.371	.752	99	-0	1	97	88	20	.760	1	0	0	-3	S/3	0.1
	Yr	53	150	20	38	6	4	0	13	23	12	.253	.356	.347	.703	86	-3	-2	97	75	19	.688	1	0	0	-2		0.0
Total	6	694	2326	324	669	113	39	13	314	377	176	.288	.388	.387	.775	103	19	23	99	113	375	.785	46	34	-7	3	S/3	8.3
■ **BILL RIGNEY** Rigney, William Joseph "Specs" or "The Cricket" b: 1/29/18, Alameda, Cal. BR/TR, 6'1", 178 lbs. Deb: 4/16/46 M																												
1946	NY-N	110	360	38	85	9	1	3	31	36	29	.236	.307	.292	.599	69	-14	-14	102	101	34	.535	9			2	3S	-0.9
1947	NY-N	130	531	84	142	24	3	17	59	51	54	.267	.337	.420	.757	99	-1	-1	101	69	76	.717	7			6	23S	1.3
1948	NY-N	113	424	72	112	17	3	10	43	47	54	.264	.342	.389	.731	98	-1	-1	100	88	58	.682	4			1	*2/S	0.7
1949	NY-N	122	389	53	108	19	6	6	47	47	38	.278	.356	.404	.759	102	2	1	102	101	56	.711	3			-8	S23	0.3
1950	NY-N	56	83	8	15	2	0	0	8	8	13	.181	.253	.205	.458	22	-9	-9	98	182	4	.352	0			1	23	-0.6
1951	NY-N	44	69	9	16	2	0	4	9	8	7	.232	.321	.435	.755	100	-0	-0	102	83	10	.722	0	1	-1	-1	3/2	-0.1
1952	NY-N	60	90	15	27	5	1	1	14	11	6	.300	.388	.411	.799	119	3	3	102	137	14	.765	2	3	-1	-0	3/2S1	0.2
1953	NY-N	19	20	2	5	0	0	0	1	0	5	.250	.250	.250	.500	31	-2	-2	98	78	1	.333	0	0	0	0	/32	-0.1
Total	8	654	1966	281	510	78	14	41	212	208	206	.259	.334	.376	.710	91	-22	-24	101	94	254	.674	25	4		0	23S/1	0.8
■ **CULLEY RIKARD** Rikard, Culley b: 5/9/14, Oxford, Miss. BL/TR, 5'11", 183 lbs. Deb: 9/20/41																												
1941	Pit-N	6	20	1	4	1	0	0	0	1	1	.200	.238	.250	.488	37	-2	-2	103	0	1	.375	0			1	/O	0.0
1942	Pit-N	38	52	6	10	2	1	0	5	7	8	.192	.288	.269	.557	63	-2	-2	101	132	4	.488	0			-3	O	-0.6

YEAR	TM/L	G	AB	R	H	2B	3B	HR	RBI	BB	SO	AVG	OBP	SLG	PRO	/A	BR	/A	PF	CHI	RC	TA	SB	CS	SBR	FR	POS	TPR
1947	Pit-N	109	324	57	93	16	4	4	32	50	39	.287	.384	.398	.782	107	5	5	101	84	51	.754	1			-2	O	0.0
Total	3	153	396	64	107	19	5	4	37	58	48	.270	.365	.374	.739	98	1	1	101	86	57	.698	1			-4	O	-0.6
■ **ERNIE RILES**	Riles, Ernest b: 10/2/60, Cairo, Ga. BL/TR, 6'1", 180 lbs. Deb: 5/14/85																											
1985	Mil-A	116	448	54	128	12	7	5	45	36	54	.286	.342	.377	.719	92	-2	-4	105	103	55	.618	2	2	-1	-10	*S/D	-0.6
1986	Mil-A	145	524	69	132	24	2	9	47	54	80	.252	.323	.357	.680	84	-10	-11	102	89	59	.603	7	7	-2	-25	*S	-3.0
1987	Mil-A	83	276	38	72	11	1	4	38	30	47	.261	.336	.351	.687	82	-6	-7	102	139	33	.612	3	4	-2	-7	3S	-1.4
1988	Mil-A	41	127	7	32	6	1	1	9	7	26	.252	.291	.339	.630	73	-4	-5	103	78	12	.520	2	2	-1	-2	3/SD	-0.6
	SF-N	79	187	26	55	7	2	3	28	10	33	.294	.330	.401	.731	116	2	3	94	133	23	.619	1	2	-1	1	32S	0.5
Total	4	464	1562	194	419	60	13	22	167	137	240	.268	.329	.366	.694	88	-19	-24	102	106	182	.624	15	17	-6	-43	S3/2D	-5.1
■ **JIM RILEY**	Riley, James Joseph b: 11/10/1886, Buffalo, N.Y. d: 3/25/49, Buffalo, N.Y. BR/TR, 6', 165 lbs. Deb: 8/02/10																											
1910	Bos-N	1	1	0	0	0	0	0	0	1	1	.000	.500	.000	.500	42	0	0	114	0	0	1.000	0			-0	/O	0.0
■ **JIM RILEY**	Riley, James Norman b: 5/25/1895, Bayfield, N.B., Can d: 5/25/69, Seguin, Tex. BL/TR, 5'10.5", 185 lbs. Deb: 7/03/21																											
1921	StL-A	4	11	0	0	0	0	0	0	1	3	.000	.083	.000	.083	-77	-3	-3	101	0	0	.091	0	0	0	-0	/2	-0.2
1923	Was-A	2	3	1	0	0	0	0	0	2	0	.000	.400	.000	.400	12	-0	-0	95	0	0	.667	0	0	0	0	/1	0.0
Total	2	6	14	1	0	0	0	0	0	3	3	.000	.176	.000	.176	-52	-3	-3	99	0	0	.214	0	0	0	-0	/21	-0.2
■ **LEE RILEY**	Riley, Leon Francis b: 8/20/06, Princeton, Neb. d: 9/13/70, Schenectady, N.Y. BL/TR, 6'1", 185 lbs. Deb: 4/19/44																											
1944	Phi-N	4	12	1	1	1	0	0	1	0	0	.083	.083	.167	.250	-31	-2	-2	100	179	0	.182	0			-1	/O	-0.3
■ **BILLY RILEY**	Riley, William James "Pigtail Billy" b: 1857, Cincinnati, Ohio d: 11/9/1887, Cincinnati, Ohio 5'10", 160 lbs. Deb: 5/05/1875																											
1875	Wes-n	8	34	4	5							.147															/O	
1879	Cle-N	44	165	14	24	2	0	0	9	2	26	.145	.156	.158	.313	4	-16	-16	99	124	4	.199				5	O/1C	-1.1
■ **FRANK RINGO**	Ringo, Frank C. b: 10/12/1860, Parkville, Mo. d: 4/12/1889, Kansas City, Mo. 5'11", 175 lbs. Deb: 5/01/1883																											
1883	Phi-N	60	221	24	42	10	1	0	12	6	34	.190	.211	.244	.456	42	-16	-13	90	79	12	.335				9	CO/S32	0.0
1884	Phi-N	26	91	4	12	2	0	0	6	3	19	.132	.160	.154	.313	-1	-10	-9	92	147	2	.215				0	C	-0.7
	Phi-a	2	6	0	0	0	0	0		0		.000	.000	.000	.000	-87	-1	-1	114	0	0	.000				0	/C	0.0
1885	Det-N	17	65	12	16	3	0	0	2	0	7	.246	.246	.292	.538	76	-2	-2	97	37	5	.388				0	/C3O	-0.1
	Pit-a	3	11	0	2	0	0	0		0		.182	.182	.182	.364	16	-1	-1	106	0	0	.222				0	/C	0.0
1886	Pit-a	15	56	3	12	2	2	0		1		.214	.228	.321	.549	79	-2	-1	93	0	4	.432	0			0	/1C	0.0
	KC-N	16	56	6	13	7	0	0	7	5	10	.232	.295	.357	.652	92	-0	-1	107	116	6	.581	0			0	C/O3	0.0
Total	4	139	506	49	97	24	3	0	27	15	70	.192	.215	.251	.466	47	-33	-28	94	79	29	.347	0			9	/C3O1S2	-0.8
■ **BOB RINKER**	Rinker, Robert John b: 4/21/21, Audenried, Pa. BR/TR, 6', 190 lbs. Deb: 9/06/50																											
1950	Phi-A	3	3	0	1	0	0	0	0	0	0	.333	.333	.333	.667	79	-0	-0	90	0	0	.500	0	0	0	0	/C	0.0
■ **JUAN RIOS**	Rios, Juan Onofre Velez (born Juan Onofre Velez (Rios)) b: 6/14/42, Mayaguez, P.R. BR/TR, 6'3", 185 lbs. Deb: 4/09/69																											
1969	KC-A	87	196	20	44	5	1	1	5	7	19	.224	.262	.276	.538	49	-13	-14	103	35	12	.404	1	3	-2	-11	2S/3	-2.3
■ **CAL RIPKEN**	Ripken, Calvin Edwin Jr. b: 8/24/60, Havre De Grace, Md. BR/TR, 6'4", 200 lbs. Deb: 8/10/81																											
1981	Bal-A	23	39	1	5	0	0	0	0	1	8	.128	.150	.128	.278	-19	-6	-6	99	0	0	.158	0	0	0	0	S/3	-0.4
1982	Bal-A	160	598	90	158	32	5	28	93	46	95	.264	.320	.475	.795	115	10	10	100	103	87	.732	3	3	-1	-7	S3	0.9
1983	Bal-A	162	663	**121**	**211**	**47**	2	27	102	58	97	.318	.373	.517	.890	142	37	37	100	90	120	.835	0	4	-2	16	*S	**5.8**
1984	Bal-A	162	641	103	195	37	7	27	86	71	89	.304	.375	.510	.885	151	37	41	94	81	122	.868	2	1	0	**39**	*S	**9.0**
1985	Bal-A	161	642	116	181	32	5	26	110	67	68	.282	.351	.469	.820	123	19	20	99	111	96	.748	2	3	-1	7	*S	3.7
1986	Bal-A	162	627	98	177	35	1	25	81	70	60	.282	.358	.461	.819	123	20	21	99	94	102	.779	4	2	0	10	*S	3.8
1987	Bal-A	162	624	97	157	28	3	27	98	81	77	.252	.339	.436	.774	107	4	6	98	107	90	.727	3	5	-2	-3	*S	0.7
1988	Bal-A	161	575	87	152	25	1	23	81	102	69	.264	.377	.431	.808	132	23	27	95	98	99	.814	2	2	-1	-1	*S	3.2
Total	8	1153	4409	713	1236	236	24	183	651	496	563	.280	.355	.469	.824	127	144	156	98	97	716	.810	16	20	-7	60	*S/3	26.7
■ **BILLY RIPKEN**	Ripken, William Oliver b: 12/16/64, Havre De Grace, Md. BR/TR, 6'1", 180 lbs. Deb: 7/11/87																											
1987	Bal-A	58	234	27	72	9	0	2	20	21	23	.308	.365	.372	.737	99	-0	0	98	82	33	.675	4	1	1	-3	2	0.2
1988	Bal-A	150	512	52	106	18	1	2	34	33	63	.207	.262	.258	.520	48	-37	-33	95	100	35	.422	8	2	1	-0	*2/3	-2.3
Total	2	208	746	79	178	27	1	4	54	54	86	.239	.294	.294	.588	65	-37	-33	96	94	68	.496	12	3	2	-3	2/3	-2.1
■ **JIMMY RIPPLE**	Ripple, James Albert b: 10/14/09, Export, Pa. d: 7/16/59, Greensburg, Pa. BL/TR, 5'10", 170 lbs. Deb: 4/20/36																											
1936	NY-N	96	311	42	95	17	2	7	47	28	15	.305	.365	.441	.805	115	7	7	100	105	51	.752	1			-4	O	0.0
1937	NY-N	121	426	70	135	23	3	5	66	29	20	.317	.362	.420	.782	112	7	7	100	125	65	.704	3			-18	*O	-1.5
1938	NY-N	134	501	68	131	21	3	10	60	49	21	.261	.333	.375	.709	91	-4	-6	103	105	62	.627	2			-2	*O	-1.0
1939	NY-N	66	123	10	28	4	0	1	12	8	7	.228	.286	.285	.570	54	-8	-8	99	116	10	.455	0			-2	O	-0.9
	Bro-N	28	106	18	35	8	4	0	22	11	8	.330	.398	.481	.879	126	5	4	107	167	19	.829	0			-2	O	0.1
	Yr	94	229	28	63	12	4	1	34	19	15	.275	.339	.376	.714	90	-3	-3	101	132	29	.632	0			-4		-0.8
1940	Bro-N	7	13	0	3	0	0	0	0	2	2	.231	.333	.231	.564	54	-1	-1	108	0	1	.500	0			1	/O	0.0
	Cin-N	32	101	15	31	10	0	4	20	13	5	.307	.397	.525	.921	151	7	7	101	114	22	.972	1			-5	O	0.1
	Yr	39	114	15	34	10	0	4	20	15	7	.298	.389	.491	.881	138	7	6	102	94	23	.914	1			-5		0.1
1941	Cin-N	38	102	10	22	6	1	1	9	9	4	.216	.279	.324	.603	70	-4	-4	99	90	10	.525	0			-3	O	-0.8
1943	Phi-A	32	126	8	30	3	1	0	15	7	7	.238	.284	.278	.561	64	-6	-6	101	150	11	.443	0	0	0	-5	O	-1.2
Total	7	554	1809	241	510	92	14	28	251	156	89	.282	.343	.395	.738	100	4	1	101	116	252	.685	7	0		-40	O	-5.2
■ **SWEDE RISBERG**	Risberg, Charles August b: 10/13/1894, San Francisco, Cal d: 10/13/75, Red Bluff, Cal. BR/TR, 6', 175 lbs. Deb: 4/11/17																											
1917	Chi-A	149	474	59	96	20	8	1	45	59	65	.203	.297	.285	.582	80	-12	-11	98	119	45	.569	16			-35	*S	-4.5
1918	Chi-A	82	273	36	70	12	3	1	27	23	32	.256	.321	.333	.654	97	-1	-1	101	105	30	.601	5			-5	S32/1O	-0.4
1919	Chi-A	119	414	48	106	19	6	2	38	35	38	.256	.317	.345	.662	82	-8	-11	105	94	49	.646	19			-7	S1	-1.1
1920	Chi-A	126	458	53	122	21	10	2	65	31	45	.266	.316	.369	.685	84	-14	-11	96	133	53	.618	12	10	-2	-6	*S	-0.7
Total	4	476	1619	196	394	72	27	6	175	148	180	.243	.311	.332	.644	84	-35	-34	99	114	177	.607	52	10		-53	S/132O	-6.7
■ **POP RISING**	Rising, Percival Sumner b: 1/1877, Industry, Pa. d: 1/28/38, Rochester, Pa. Deb: 8/10/05																											
1905	Bos-A	11	29	2	3	1	1	0	2	2		.103	.161	.207	.368	18	-3	-3	100	119	1	.308	0			0	/O3	-0.2
■ **CLAUDE RITCHEY**	Ritchey, Claude Cassius "Little All Right" b: 10/5/1873, Emlenton, Pa. d: 11/8/51, Emlenton, Pa. BB/TR, 5'6.5", 167 lbs. Deb: 4/22/1897																											
1897	Cin-N	101	337	58	95	12	4	0	41	42		.282	.368	.341	.709	84	-3	-7	107	106	48	.711	11			-21	SO/2	-2.2
1898	Lou-N	151	551	65	140	10	4	5	51	46		.254	.320	.314	.634	87	-10	-7	96	87	63	.596	19			-20	S2	-1.8
1899	Lou-N	147	536	65	161	15	7	4	71	49		.300	.370	.377	.747	104	7	4	103	104	85	.752	21			-9	*2S	0.3
1900	Pit-N	123	476	62	139	17	8	1	67	29		.292	.333	.368	.700	93	-3	-5	103	125	66	.659	18			7	*2	0.7
1901	Pit-N	140	540	66	160	20	4	1	74	47		.296	.353	.354	.706	107	6	6	101	135	74	.666	15			7	*2/S	2.1
1902	Pit-N	115	405	54	112	13	1	2	55	53		.277	.360	.328	.689	109	9	7	105	140	53	.669	10			4	*2/O	1.8
1903	Pit-N	138	506	66	145	28	10	0	59	55		.287	.357	.381	.738	107	9	5	105	100	76	.729	15			16	*2	2.7
1904	Pit-N	156	544	79	143	22	12	0	51	59		.263	.335	.347	.682	114	9	10	99	105	69	.648	12			-2	*2/S	1.2
1905	Pit-N	153	533	54	136	29	6	0	52	51		.255	.320	.332	.652	93	-2	-4	104	104	62	.605	12			-6	*2/S	-0.1
1906	Pit-N	152	484	46	130	21	5	1	62	68		.269	.359	.339	.698	115	13	11	104	138	63	.672	6			-2	*2	1.0
1907	Bos-N	144	499	45	127	17	4	2	51	50		.255	.322	.317	.639	107	2	5	95	120	55	.581	8			14	*2	2.3
1908	Bos-N	121	421	44	115	10	3	2	36	50		.273	.350	.325	.676	114	10	9	104	102	49	.634	7			8	*2	1.8
1909	Bos-N	30	87	4	15	1	0	0	3	8		.172	.242	.184	.426	34	-7	-6	96	68	4	.347	1			0	2	-0.6
Total	13	1671	5919	708	1618	215	68	18	673	607		.273	.343	.342	.685	102	42	26	102	113	765	.652	155			-5	*2S/O	9.2
■ **RITTER**	Ritter Deb:1885																											
1885	Buf-N	2	6	0	1	0	0	0	0	0	2	.167	.167	.167	.333	8	-1	-1	99	0	0	.200				0	/2	0.0

YEAR	TM/L	G	AB	R	H	2B	3B	HR	RBI	BB	SO	AVG	OBP	SLG	PRO	/A	BR	/A	PF	CHI	RC	TA	SB	CS	SBR	FR	POS	TPR
■ **FLOYD RITTER**	Ritter, Floyd Alexander b: 6/1/1870, Dorset, Ohio d: 2/7/43, Stevenson, Wash. BR/TR, 5'8", 155 lbs. Deb: 6/04/1890																											
1890	Tol-a	1	3	0	0	0	0	0		0		.000	.000	.000	.000	-97	-1	-1	103	0	0	.000	0			0	/C	0.0
■ **LEW RITTER**	Ritter, Lewis Elmer "Old Dog" b: 9/7/1875, Liverpool, Pa. d: 5/27/52, Harrisburg, Pa. BR/TR, 5'9", 150 lbs. Deb: 9/10/02																											
1902	Bro-N	16	57	5	12	1	0	0	2	0		.211	.211	.228	.439	39	-4	-4	95	53	3	.311	1			-1	C	-0.2
1903	Bro-N	78	259	26	61	9	6	0	37	19		.236	.288	.317	.604	73	-9	-9	101	145	27	.556	9			-7	C/O	-0.9
1904	Bro-N	72	214	23	53	4	1	0	19	20		.248	.312	.276	.588	88	-3	-2	95	118	24	.596	17			7	C/23	1.1
1905	Bro-N	92	311	32	68	10	5	1	28	15		.219	.255	.293	.547	67	-14	-12	96	106	28	.502	16			6	C/O3	0.2
1906	Bro-N	73	226	22	47	1	3	0	15	16		.208	.260	.239	.499	66	-11	-8	87	101	16	.425	6			4	C/O13	0.0
1907	Bro-N	93	271	15	55	6	1	0	17	18		.203	.253	.232	.485	57	-14	-13	94	102	18	.398	5			-4	C	-1.0
1908	Bro-N	38	99	6	19	2	1	0	2	7		.192	.245	.232	.478	57	-5	-4	95	33	5	.375	0			4	C	0.1
Total	7	462	1437	129	315	33	17	1	120	95		.219	.268	.268	.536	68	-60	-52	95	106	121	.476	54			9	C/O321	-0.7
■ **WHITEY RITTERSON**	Ritterson, Edward West b: 4/26/1855, Philadelphia, Pa. d: 7/28/17, Sellersville, Pa. BR/TR, 5'8", Deb: 5/03/1876																											
1876	Phi-N	16	52	8	13	3	0	0	4	0	2	.250	.250	.308	.558	86	-1	-1	99	84	4	.410				0	C/O3	0.0
■ **JIM RITZ**	Ritz, James L. b: 1874, Pittsburgh, Pa. d: 11/10/1896, Pittsburgh, Pa. Deb: 7/20/1894																											
1894	Pit-N	1	4	1	0	0	0	0	0	0	0	.000	.200	.000	.200	-50	-1	-1	94	0	0	.500	1			0	/3	0.0
■ **GERMAN RIVERA**	Rivera, German (Diaz) b: 7/6/60, Santurce, P.R. BR/TR, 6'2", 195 lbs. Deb: 9/02/83																											
1983	LA-N	13	17	1	6	1	0	0	0	2	2	.353	.421	.412	.833	132	1	1	100	0	3	.750	0	1	-1	0	/3	0.0
1984	LA-N	94	227	20	59	12	2	2	17	21	30	.260	.325	.357	.682	88	-2	-3	104	77	23	.568	1	0	0	7	3	0.3
1985	Hou-N	13	36	3	7	2	1	0	2	4	8	.194	.275	.306	.581	65	-2	-2	96	72	3	.484	0	0	0	-0	3	-0.1
Total	3	120	280	24	72	15	3	2	19	27	40	.257	.325	.354	.678	88	-3	-4	102	71	28	.607	1	1	-0	7	3	0.2
■ **BOMBO RIVERA**	Rivera, Jesus Manuel (Torres) b: 8/2/52, Ponce, Pr. BR/TR, 5'10", 187 lbs. Deb: 4/17/75																											
1975	Mon-N	5	9	1	1	0	0	0	0	2	3	.111	.273	.111	.384	9	-1	-1	108	0	0	.333	0	0	0	-1	/O	-0.1
1976	Mon-N	68	185	22	51	11	4	2	19	13	32	.276	.323	.411	.734	107	1	1	100	89	24	.647	1	0	0	-1	O	-0.1
1978	Min-A	101	251	35	68	8	2	3	23	35	47	.271	.365	.355	.719	109	2	4	94	93	35	.693	5	3	-0	-8	O/D	-0.6
1979	Min-A	112	263	37	74	13	5	2	31	17	40	.281	.325	.392	.717	85	-3	-6	109	109	32	.625	5	5	-2	-5	*O	-1.5
1980	Min-A	44	113	13	25	7	0	3	10	4	20	.221	.248	.363	.611	60	-6	-7	109	78	9	.489	0	0	0	-5	O/D	-1.2
1982	KC-A	5	10	1	1	0	0	0	0	0	2	.100	.100	.100	.200	-45	-2	-2	100	0	0	.111	0	0	0	-1	/O	-0.2
Total	6	335	831	109	220	39	11	10	83	71	144	.265	.324	.374	.698	91	-8	-11	102	93	100	.638	11	8	-2	-20	O/D	-3.7
■ **LUIS RIVERA**	Rivera, Luis Antonio (Pedraza) b: 1/3/64, Cidra, P.R. BR/TR, 5'11", 165 lbs. Deb: 8/03/86																											
1986	Mon-N	55	166	20	34	11	1	0	13	17	33	.205	.286	.283	.570	59	-9	-9	98	110	15	.500	1	1	-0	-8	S	-1.2
1987	Mon-N	18	32	0	5	2	0	0	1	1	8	.156	.182	.219	.401	5	-4	-5	106	57	1	.296	0	0	0	-1	S	-0.3
1988	Mon-N	123	371	35	83	17	3	4	30	24	69	.224	.273	.318	.591	65	-15	-17	106	92	30	.485	3	4	-2	-9	*S	-2.0
Total	3	196	569	55	122	30	4	4	44	42	110	.214	.272	.302	.574	60	-29	-31	103	96	46	.479	4	5	-2	-18	S	-3.5
■ **JIM RIVERA**	Rivera, Manuel Joseph "Jungle Jim" b: 7/22/22, New York, N.Y. BL/TL, 6', 196 lbs. Deb: 4/15/52																											
1952	StL-A	97	336	45	86	13	6	4	30	29	59	.256	.319	.366	.685	93	-5	-4	97	83	40	.623	8	7	-2	3	O	-0.4
	Chi-A	53	201	27	50	7	3	3	18	21	27	.249	.320	.358	.678	89	-3	-3	100	88	26	.688	13	2	3	1	O	0.0
	Yr	150	537	72	136	20	9	7	48	50	86	.253	.319	.363	.682	91	-8	-7	98	85	68	.652	21	9	1	4		-0.4
1953	Chi-A	156	567	79	147	26	**16**	11	78	53	70	.259	.329	.420	.749	95	-1	-5	106	109	76	.709	22	15	-2	-7	*O	-1.8
1954	Chi-A	145	490	62	140	16	8	13	61	49	68	.286	.358	.431	.788	111	10	8	104	93	77	.774	18	10	-1	-12	*O	-0.8
1955	Chi-A	147	454	71	120	24	4	10	52	62	59	.264	.354	.401	.755	102	2	1	101	92	66	.761	**25**	16	-2	14	*O	0.6
1956	Chi-A	139	491	76	125	23	5	12	66	49	75	.255	.326	.395	.721	86	-8	-11	104	109	66	.704	20	9	1	2	*O	-1.4
1957	Chi-A	125	402	51	103	21	6	14	52	40	80	.256	.328	.443	.771	110	4	4	99	93	59	.766	18	2	**4**	-6	O1	-0.3
1958	Chi-A	116	276	37	62	8	4	9	35	24	49	.225	.289	.380	.669	84	-7	-7	98	106	31	.674	21	3	5	-5	O	-1.3
1959	Chi-A	80	177	18	39	9	4	4	19	11	19	.220	.270	.384	.654	80	-6	-5	97	93	18	.599	5	3	-0	-10	O	-1.9
1960	Chi-A	48	17	17	5	0	0	1	1	3	3	.294	.400	.471	.871	133	1	1	101	36	4	1.250	4	0	1	-7	O	-0.5
1961	Chi-A	1	0	0	0	0	0	0	0	0	0	—	—	—	—	—	0	0	99	—	4	.000	0	1	-1	0	H	0.0
	KC-A	64	141	20	34	8	0	2	10	24	14	.241	.352	.340	.692	84	-2	-3	102	72	18	.696	6	2	1	-9	O	-1.1
	Yr	65	141	20	34	8	0	2	10	24	14	.241	.352	.340	.692	84	-2	-3	102	71	18	.690	6	3	0	-9		-1.1
Total	10	1171	3552	503	911	155	56	83	422	365	523	.256	.330	.402	.731	96	-17	-24	101	96	488	.728	160	70	6	-36	*O/1	-8.9
■ **MICKEY RIVERS**	Rivers, John Milton b: 10/31/48, Miami, Fla. BL/TL, 5'10", 165 lbs. Deb: 8/04/70																											
1970	Cal-A	17	25	6	8	2	0	0	3	3	5	.320	.414	.400	.814	137	1	1	92	121	5	.882	1	0	0	0	/O	0.1
1971	Cal-A	78	268	31	71	12	2	1	12	19	38	.265	.316	.336	.652	86	-5	-5	99	54	32	.621	13	1	3	4	O	0.0
1972	Cal-A	58	159	18	34	6	2	0	7	8	26	.214	.256	.277	.533	66	-8	-6	88	66	11	.435	4	3	-1	2	O	-0.7
1973	Cal-A	30	129	26	45	6	4	0	16	8	11	.349	.391	.457	.849	144	6	7	96	92	24	.864	8	3	1	-1	O	0.6
1974	Cal-A	118	466	69	133	19	**11**	3	31	39	47	.285	.342	.393	.735	120	6	11	92	56	64	.719	30	13	1	5	*O	1.4
1975	Cal-A	155	616	70	175	17	**13**	1	53	43	42	.284	.333	.359	.692	101	-4	0	95	96	81	.729	**70**	14	**13**	1	*O/D	1.0
1976	NY-A	137	590	95	184	31	8	8	67	13	51	.312	.330	.432	.762	123	13	14	99	89	88	.755	43	7	9	2	*O	2.3
1977	NY-A	138	565	79	184	18	5	12	69	18	45	.326	.351	.439	.790	115	10	11	99	102	86	.736	22	14	-2	5	*O/D	0.9
1978	NY-A	141	559	78	148	25	8	11	48	29	51	.265	.305	.397	.702	97	-5	-4	99	79	69	.658	25	5	5	3	*O	0.0
1979	NY-A	74	286	37	82	18	5	3	25	13	21	.287	.320	.416	.736	101	-2	-0	96	79	36	.636	3	7	-3	-0	O	-0.5
	Tex-A	58	247	35	74	9	3	6	25	9	18	.300	.327	.433	.760	103	0	0	100	68	35	.701	7	2	1	8	O	0.6
	Yr	132	533	72	156	27	8	9	50	22	39	.293	.323	.424	.747	102	-2	0	97	75	72	.670	10	9	-2	7		0.1
1980	Tex-A	147	630	96	210	32	6	7	60	20	34	.333	.355	.437	.791	115	12	12	100	76	98	.729	18	7	1	5	*O/D	1.5
1981	Tex-A	99	399	62	114	21	2	3	26	24	31	.286	.328	.371	.699	111	0	4	91	62	49	.621	9	5	-0	0	O	0.2
1982	Tex-A	19	68	6	16	1	1	1	4	0	7	.235	.235	.324	.559	56	-5	-4	93	64	5	.415	0	0	0	0	D	-0.3
1983	Tex-A	96	309	37	88	17	0	1	20	11	21	.285	.312	.350	.661	81	-8	-8	101	70	35	.571	9	4	0	-1	DO	-0.8
1984	Tex-A	102	313	40	94	13	1	4	33	9	23	.300	.320	.387	.706	94	-3	-3	100	99	38	.600	5	5	-2	-1	DO	-0.5
Total	15	1467	5629	785	1660	247	71	61	499	266	471	.295	.329	.397	.726	106	10	30	97	80	756	.686	267	90	26	31	*OD	5.8
■ **JOHNNY RIZZO**	Rizzo, John Costa b: 7/30/12, Houston, Tex. d: 12/4/77, Houston, Tex. BR/TR, 6', 190 lbs. Deb: 4/19/38																											
1938	Pit-N	143	555	97	167	31	9	23	111	54	61	.301	.368	.514	.882	140	29	29	100	120	105	.854	1			-6	*O	2.0
1939	Pit-N	94	330	49	86	23	3	6	55	42	27	.261	.349	.403	.752	102	1	1	100	136	46	.690	0			-3	O	-0.2
1940	Pit-N	9	28	1	5	1	0	0	2	5	5	.179	.324	.214	.538	54	-2	-1	95	124	2	.500	0			-2	/O	-0.3
	Cin-N	31	110	17	31	6	0	4	17	14	14	.282	.363	.445	.808	121	3	3	101	105	19	.800	1			4	O	0.7
	Phi-N	103	367	53	107	12	2	20	53	37	31	.292	.358	.499	.857	138	16	17	97	82	67	.845	2			5	O/3	1.9
	Yr	143	505	71	143	19	2	24	72	56	50	.283	.357	.471	.828	130	18	19	98	92	89	.817	3			7		2.3
1941	Phi-N	99	235	20	51	9	2	4	24	24	34	.217	.295	.323	.618	76	-8	-7	97	98	22	.536	1			1	O/3	-0.9
1942	Bro-N	78	217	31	50	8	0	4	27	24	25	.230	.307	.323	.630	83	-4	-5	102	122	21	.552	2			-3	O	-1.0
Total	5	557	1842	268	497	90	16	61	289	200	197	.270	.345	.435	.781	116	35	37	99	112	282	.755	7			-4	O/3	2.2
■ **PHIL RIZZUTO**	Rizzuto, Philip Francis "Scooter" b: 9/25/17, Brooklyn, N.Y. BR/TR, 5'6", 150 lbs. Deb: 4/15/41																											
1941	NY-A	133	515	65	158	20	9	3	46	27	36	.307	.343	.398	.741	97	-4	-3	98	78	70	.659	14	5	1	17	*S	1.8
1942	NY-A	144	553	79	157	24	7	4	68	44	40	.284	.343	.374	.718	102	1	1	99	116	74	.672	22	6	3	**29**	*S	4.0
1946	NY-A	126	471	53	121	17	1	2	38	34	39	.257	.315	.310	.625	75	-15	-16	100	97	48	.545	14	7	0	13	*S	0.0
1947	NY-A	153	549	78	150	26	9	2	60	57	31	.273	.350	.364	.714	102	-0	2	97	109	76	.672	11	6	-0	14	*S	1.6
1948	NY-A	128	464	65	117	13	2	6	50	60	24	.252	.340	.328	.668	78	-14	-14	100	101	57	.615	6	5	-1	-15	*S	-2.8
1949	NY-A	153	614	110	169	22	7	5	65	72	34	.275	.352	.358	.711	88	-10	-11	100	84	82	.663	18	6	**2**	4	*S	-0.2
1950	NY-A	155	617	125	200	36	7	7	66	92	39	.324	.418	.439	.857	120	22	22	99	69	124	.886	12	8	-1	9	*S	3.4
1951	NY-A	144	540	87	148	21	6	2	43	58	27	.274	.350	.346	.696	97	-7	-1	92	84	73	.662	18	3	**4**	10	*S	2.1
1952	NY-A	152	578	89	147	24	10	2	43	67	42	.254	.337	.341	.678	91	-8	-6	98	84	73	.641	17	6	2	**20**	*S	2.4
1953	NY-A	134	413	54	112	21	3	2	54	71	39	.271	.383	.351	.734	107	3	7	93	132	63	.723	4	3	-1	9	*S	2.5

YEAR	TM/L	G	AB	R	H	2B	3B	HR	RBI	BB	SO	AVG	OBP	SLG	PRO	/A	BR	/A	PF	CHI	RC	TA	SB	CS	SBR	FR	POS	TPR
1954	NY-A	127	307	47	60	11	0	2	15	41	23	.195	.292	.251	.543	50	-21	-20	99	69	25	.477	3	2	-0	8	*S/2	-0.1
1955	NY-A	81	143	19	37	4	1	1	9	22	18	.259	.369	.322	.691	89	-2	-1	98	68	20	.716	7	1	2	-4	S/2	0.5
1956	NY-A	31	52	6	12	0	0	0	6	6	6	.231	.310	.231	.541	45	-4	-4	99	187	5	.512	3	0	1	2	S	0.2
Total	13	1661	5816	877	1588	239	62	38	563	651	398	.273	.351	.355	.706	93	-60	-43	98	93	789	.680	149	58	10	114	*S/2	15.4
■ **MIKE ROACH** Roach, James Michael b: 1876, New York, N.Y. d: 11/12/16, Binghamton, N.Y. Deb: 8/10/1899																												
1899	Was-N	24	78	7	17	1	0	0	7	3		.218	.265	.231	.496	40	-6	-6	96	119	6	.426	3			0	C/1	-0.4
■ **MEL ROACH** Roach, Melvin Earl b: 1/25/33, Richmond, Va. BR/TR, 6'1", 190 lbs. Deb: 7/31/53																												
1953	Mil-N	5	2	1	0	0	0	0	0	0	1	.000	.000	.000	.000	-99	-1	-1	94	0	0	.000	0	0	0	0	/2	0.0
1954	Mil-N	3	4	0	0	0	0	0	0	0	1	.000	.000	.000	.000	-99	-1	-1	93	0	0	.000	0	0	0	0	/1	0.0
1957	Mil-N	7	6	1	1	0	0	0	0	0	3	.167	.167	.167	.333	-11	-1	-1	90	0	0	.200	0	0	0	0	/2	0.0
1958	Mil-N	44	136	14	42	7	0	3	10	6	15	.309	.338	.426	.764	113	-0	2	89	62	20	.674	0	0	0	-1	2/O1	0.2
1959	Mil-N	19	31	1	3	0	0	0	0	2	4	.097	.152	.097	.248	-34	-6	-6	95	0	1	.179	0	0	0	0	/2O3	-0.4
1960	Mil-N	48	140	12	42	12	0	3	18	6	19	.300	.333	.450	.783	123	2	4	91	101	17	.648	0	0	0	-3	O2/13	0.2
1961	Mil-N	13	36	3	6	0	0	1	6	2	4	.167	.250	.250	.500	36	-3	-3	92	202	3	.433	0	0	0	-2	/O1	-0.4
	Chi-N	23	39	1	5	2	0	0	1	3	9	.128	.190	.179	.370	-1	-6	-6	100	58	1	.297	1	0	0	0	/12	-0.4
	Yr	36	75	4	11	2	0	1	7	5	13	.147	.220	.213	.433	16	-9	-9	97	115	3	.358	1	0	0	-2		-0.8
1962	Phi-N	65	105	9	20	4	0	0	8	5	19	.190	.227	.229	.456	24	-11	-11	95	131	5	.333	0	0	0	-2	3/21O	-1.0
Total	8	227	499	42	119	25	0	7	43	24	75	.238	.278	.331	.608	67	-27	-22	92	92	47	.505	1	0	0	-7	/2O31	-1.8
■ **ROXEY ROACH** Roach, Wilbur Charles b: 11/28/1882, Anita, Pa. d: 12/26/47, Bay City, Mich. BR/TR, 5'11", 160 lbs. Deb: 5/02/10																												
1910	NY-A	70	220	27	47	9	2	0	20	29		.214	.313	.273	.586	78	-3	-5	107	126	24	.618	15			-5	S/O	-0.9
1911	NY-A	13	40	4	10	2	1	0	2	6		.250	.348	.350	.698	86	-0	-1	111	48	5	.667	0			-1	/S2	0.0
1912	Was-A	2	2	1	1	0	0	1	1	0		.500	.500	2.000	2.500	610	1	1	99	48	2	4.000	0			0	/S	0.1
1915	Buf-F	92	346	35	93	20	3	2	31	17	34	.269	.303	.361	.664	96	-3	-3	100	90	43	.605	11			16	S	2.2
Total	4	177	608	67	151	31	6	3	54	52	34	.248	.311	.334	.645	91	-5	-7	103	101	73	.621	26			11	S/O2	1.4
■ **MIKE ROARKE** Roarke, Michael Thomas b: 11/8/30, West Warwick, R.I. BR/TR, 6'2", 195 lbs. Deb: 4/19/61 C																												
1961	Det-A	86	229	21	51	6	1	2	22	20	31	.223	.285	.284	.569	55	-15	-14	96	121	18	.462	0	0	0	-9	C	-2.3
1962	Det-A	56	136	11	29	4	1	4	14	13	17	.213	.287	.346	.632	62	-6	-8	111	94	13	.550	0	0	0	-0	C	-0.5
1963	Det-A	23	44	5	14	0	0	0	1	2	3	.318	.362	.318	.680	89	-0	-0	104	30	5	.548	0	0	0	0	C	0.0
1964	Det-A	29	82	4	19	1	0	0	7	10	10	.232	.315	.244	.559	61	-4	-4	96	148	7	.469	0	0	0	4	C	0.1
Total	4	194	491	41	113	11	2	6	44	45	61	.230	.297	.297	.595	61	-26	-26	101	110	43	.509	0	0	0	-5	C	-2.7
■ **FRED ROAT** Roat, Frederick R. b: 11/10/1867, Oregon, Ill. d: 9/24/13, Oregon, Ill. TR , Deb: 5/10/1890																												
1890	Pit-N	57	215	18	48	2	0	2	17	16	22	.223	.286	.260	.547	70	-10	-6	88	88	18	.491	7			3	3/1O	0.0
1892	Chi-N	8	31	4	6	0	1	0	2	2	3	.194	.242	.258	.500	57	-2	-1	92	81	2	.480	2			0	/2	0.0
Total	2	65	246	22	54	2	1	2	19	18	25	.220	.281	.260	.541	68	-12	-7	88	87	21	.490	9			3	/312O	0.0
■ **TOMMY ROBELLO** Robello, Thomas Vardasco "Tony" b: 2/9/13, San Leandro, Cal. BR/TR, 5'10.5", 175 lbs. Deb: 8/13/33																												
1933	Cin-N	14	30	1	7	3	0	0	3	1	5	.233	.258	.333	.591	69	-1	-1	99	113	3	.478	0			0	2/3	0.0
1934	Cin-N	2	2	0	0	0	0	0	0	0	1	.000	.000	.000	.000	-99	-1	-1	101	0	0	.000	0			0	H	0.0
Total	2	16	32	1	7	3	0	0	3	1	6	.219	.242	.313	.555	58	-2	-2	99	106	3	.440	0			0	/23	0.0
■ **SKIPPY ROBERGE** Roberge, Joseph Albert Armand b: 5/19/17, Lowell, Mass. BR/TR, 5'11", 185 lbs. Deb: 7/18/41																												
1941	Bos-N	55	167	12	36	6	0	0	15	9	18	.216	.256	.251	.507	46	-13	-11	93	129	12	.389	0			-1	2/3S	-0.9
1942	Bos-N	74	172	10	37	7	0	1	12	9	19	.215	.258	.273	.531	58	-10	-9	95	89	13	.423	1			-0	23/S	-0.7
1946	Bos-N	48	169	13	39	6	2	2	20	7	12	.231	.270	.325	.595	72	-8	-7	95	122	15	.489	1			1	3	-0.5
Total	3	177	508	35	112	19	2	3	47	25	49	.220	.261	.283	.545	59	-30	-27	94	113	39	.436	2			-1	/32S	-2.1
■ **RED ROBERTS** Roberts, Charles Emory b: 8/8/18, Carrollton, Ga. BR/TR, 6', 170 lbs. Deb: 9/03/43																												
1943	Was-A	9	23	1	6	1	0	1	3	4	2	.261	.370	.435	.805	130	1	1	104	84	4	.824	0	0	0	0	/S3	0.1
■ **SKIPPER ROBERTS** Roberts, Clarence Ashley b: 1/11/1888, Wardner, Idaho d: 12/24/63, Long Beach, Cal. BL/TR, 5'10.5", 175 lbs. Deb: 6/12/13																												
1913	StL-N	26	41	4	6	2	0	0	3	3	13	.146	.205	.195	.400	16	-5	-4	93	136	2	.343	1			1	C	-0.1
1914	Pit-F	33	55	7	12	2	1	0	4	1	0	.218	.232	.291	.523	52	-4	-3	94	90	4	.442	2			0	C	-0.3
	Chi-F	4	3	0	1	0	0	0	1	1	0	.333	.500	.333	.833	155	0	0	91	361	1	1.000	0			0	H	0.0
	Pit-F	19	39	5	10	2	1	1	2	1	0	.256	.275	.436	.711	108	-0	0	94	36	5	.655	1			0	/CO	0.0
	Yr	56	97	12	23	4	2	1	7	3	0	.237	.260	.351	.611	79	-4	-3	94	99	10	.541	3			0		-0.3
Total	2	82	138	16	29	6	2	1	10	6	13	.210	.243	.304	.547	60	-8	-7	94	97	12	.477	4			1	/CO	-0.4
■ **CURT ROBERTS** Roberts, Curtis Benjamin b: 8/16/29, Pineland, Tex. d: 11/14/69, Oakland, Cal. BR/TR, 5'8", 165 lbs. Deb: 4/13/54																												
1954	Pit-N	134	496	47	115	18	7	1	36	55	49	.232	.311	.302	.613	63	-28	-26	97	98	50	.546	6	3	0	0	*2	-1.6
1955	Pit-N	6	17	1	2	1	0	0	0	2	1	.118	.211	.176	.387	4	-2	-2	97	0	1	.333	0	0	0	0	/2	-0.1
1956	Pit-N	31	62	6	11	5	2	0	4	5	12	.177	.239	.323	.561	48	-5	-5	102	84	5	.500	1	0	0	0	2	-0.1
Total	3	171	575	54	128	24	9	1	40	62	62	.223	.300	.301	.601	60	-35	-33	97	94	56	.541	7	3	0	1	2	-1.8
■ **DAVE ROBERTS** Roberts, David Leonard b: 6/30/33, Panama City, Pan. BL/TL, 6', 172 lbs. Deb: 9/05/62																												
1962	Hou-N	16	53	3	13	3	0	1	10	8	8	.245	.355	.358	.713	99	-0	0	93	183	8	.700	0	0	0	-1	O/1	-0.1
1964	Hou-N	61	125	9	23	4	1	1	7	14	28	.184	.271	.256	.527	51	-8	-8	96	82	9	.448	0	1	-1	-0	1/O	-0.9
1966	Pit-N	14	16	3	2	1	0	0	0	0	7	.125	.125	.188	.313	-14	-2	-2	101	0	0	.200	0	0	0	0	/1	-0.2
Total	3	91	194	15	38	8	1	2	17	22	43	.196	.284	.278	.563	59	-11	-10	96	105	17	.494	0	1	-1	-1	/1O	-1.2
■ **DAVE ROBERTS** Roberts, David Wayne b: 2/17/51, Lebanon, Ore. BR/TR, 6'3", 215 lbs. Deb: 6/07/72																												
1972	SD-N	100	418	38	102	17	0	5	33	18	64	.244	.275	.321	.596	78	-18	-12	88	80	37	.492	7	2	1	-5	32/SC	-1.6
1973	SD-N	127	479	56	137	20	3	21	64	17	83	.286	.312	.472	.784	121	7	10	94	91	70	.729	11	2	2	4	*32	1.4
1974	SD-N	113	318	26	53	10	1	5	18	32	69	.167	.247	.252	.499	43	-26	-23	93	73	20	.423	2	0	1	-5	*3/SO	-3.0
1975	SD-N	33	113	7	32	2	0	2	12	13	19	.283	.367	.354	.721	101	1	1	100	103	16	.699	3	1	0	-1	3/2	0.0
1977	SD-N	82	186	15	41	14	1	1	23	11	32	.220	.268	.323	.590	66	-11	-9	88	146	16	.493	2	1	0	-5	C/23S	-1.3
1978	SD-N	54	97	7	21	4	1	1	7	12	25	.216	.309	.309	.618	79	-3	-2	93	84	9	.551	0	0	0	-3	C/1O	-0.4
1979	Tex-A	44	84	12	22	2	1	3	14	7	17	.262	.319	.417	.735	97	-1	-1	100	122	11	.662	1	0	0	-1	CO/213	0.0
1980	Tex-A	101	235	27	56	4	0	10	30	13	38	.238	.281	.383	.664	80	-7	-7	100	97	24	.562	0	1	-1	2	3SC/O12	-0.2
1981	Hou-N	27	54	4	13	3	0	1	5	3	6	.241	.281	.352	.633	89	-2	-1	88	89	5	.548	1	0	0	0	1/32C	0.0
1982	Phi-N	28	33	2	6	1	0	0	2	2	8	.182	.229	.212	.441	26	-3	-3	94	112	2	.321	0	1	-1	0	3C/2	-0.2
Total	10	709	2017	194	483	77	7	49	208	128	361	.239	.288	.357	.645	84	-64	-48	93	94	210	.573	27	8	3	-13	3C/2S1O	-5.3
■ **BIP ROBERTS** Roberts, Leon Joseph b: 10/27/63, Berkeley, Cal. BB/TR, 5'7", 150 lbs. Deb: 4/07/86																												
1986	SD-N	101	241	34	61	5	2	1	12	14	29	.253	.294	.303	.597	68	-11	-10	95	63	20	.521	14	12	-3	-1	2	-1.3
1988	SD-N	5	9	1	3	0	0	0	0	1	2	.333	.400	.333	.733	116	0	0	97	0	1	.500	0	2	-1	0	/32	0.0
Total	2	106	250	35	64	5	2	1	12	15	31	.256	.298	.304	.602	70	-11	-10	95	61	21	.525	14	14	-4	-1	/23	-1.3
■ **LEON ROBERTS** Roberts, Leon Kauffman b: 1/22/51, Vicksburg, Mich. BR/TR, 6'3", 200 lbs. Deb: 9/03/74																												
1974	Det-A	17	63	5	17	3	2	0	7	3	10	.270	.303	.381	.684	90	-1	-1	106	117	6	.529	0	2	-1	-3	O	-0.5
1975	Det-A	129	447	51	115	17	5	10	38	36	94	.257	.318	.385	.703	94	-2	-4	104	74	53	.618	3	7	-3	6	*O/D	-0.4
1976	Hou-N	87	235	31	68	11	2	7	33	19	43	.289	.350	.443	.793	144	7	11	86	102	38	.751	1	0	0	-6	O	0.3
1977	Hou-N	19	27	1	2	0	0	0	2	1	8	.074	.107	.074	.181	-54	-6	-5	93	400	0	.115	0	0	0	-2	/O	-0.7
1978	Sea-A	134	472	78	142	21	7	22	92	41	52	.301	.367	.515	.881	143	27	26	102	120	90	.876	6	3	0	8	*O/D	3.1
1979	Sea-A	140	450	61	122	24	6	15	54	56	64	.271	.354	.451	.805	115	10	10	100	84	73	.779	3	3	-1	0	*O	0.4
1980	Sea-A	119	374	48	94	18	3	10	33	43	59	.251	.330	.396	.726	95	-1	-3	103	72	48	.676	8	4	0	-10	*O/D	-1.3
1981	Tex-A	72	233	26	65	17	2	4	31	25	38	.279	.351	.421	.772	134	7	9	91	110	33	.706	3	4	-2	-6	O	0.0

YEAR	TM/L	G	AB	R	H	2B	3B	HR	RBI	BB	SO	AVG	OBP	SLG	PRO	/A	BR	/A	PF	CHI	RC	TA	SB	CS	SBR	FR	POS	TPR
1982	Tex-A	31	73	7	17	3	0	1	6	4	14	.233	.282	.315	.597	69	-4	-3	93	92	6	.467	0	0	0	-5	O/D	-0.8
	Tor-A	40	105	6	24	4	0	1	5	7	16	.229	.277	.295	.572	53	-6	-7	109	59	8	.459	1	1	-0	-3	DO	-1.0
	Yr	71	178	13	41	7	0	2	11	11	30	.230	.279	.303	.582	59	-10	-10	102	75	15	.475	1	1	-0	-7		-1.8
1983	KC-A	84	213	24	55	7	0	8	24	17	27	.258	.316	.404	.720	95	-1	-2	101	85	26	.633	1	1	-0	-7	O/D	-0.9
1984	KC-A	29	45	4	10	1	1	0	3	4	3	.222	.300	.289	.589	64	-2	-2	99	92	4	.500	0	0	0	-3	O/PD	-0.5
Total	11	901	2737	342	731	126	28	78	328	256	428	.267	.335	.419	.754	109	28	29	100	94	383	.714	26	25	-7	-29	O/DP	-2.3
■ **TOM ROBERTS**	Roberts, Thomas b: Baltimore, Md. Deb: 5/13/1874																											
1874	Atl-n	1	4	0	0							.000															/O	
■ **JIM ROBERTSON**	Robertson, Alfred James b: 1/29/28, Chicago, Ill. BR/TR, 5'9", 183 lbs. Deb: 4/15/54																											
1954	Phi-A	63	147	9	27	8	0	0	8	23	25	.184	.298	.238	.536	49	-10	-10	98	87	12	.484	0	0	0	2	C	-0.4
1955	KC-A	6	8	1	2	0	0	0	0	1	2	.250	.333	.250	.583	58	-0	-0	101	0	1	.500	0	0	0	0	/C	0.0
Total	2	69	155	10	29	8	0	0	8	24	27	.187	.300	.239	.539	49	-10	-10	99	82	13	.492	0	0	0	3	/C	-0.4
■ **ANDRE ROBERTSON**	Robertson, Andre Levett b: 10/2/57, Orange, Tex. BR/TR, 5'10", 155 lbs. Deb: 9/03/81																											
1981	NY-A	10	19	1	5	1	0	0	0	0	3	.263	.263	.316	.579	66	-1	-1	100	0	1	.467	1	1	-0	-0	/S2	0.0
1982	NY-A	44	118	16	26	5	0	2	9	8	19	.220	.270	.314	.583	62	-7	-6	96	84	9	.469	0	0	0	1	S2/3	-0.1
1983	NY-A	98	322	37	80	16	3	1	22	8	54	.248	.273	.326	.599	65	-16	-15	99	80	28	.472	2	4	-2	6	S2	-0.5
1984	NY-A	52	140	10	30	5	1	0	6	4	20	.214	.236	.264	.500	41	-12	-11	94	65	6	.336	0	1	-1	1	S/2	-0.6
1985	NY-A	50	125	16	41	5	0	2	17	6	24	.328	.364	.416	.780	118	2	3	96	116	18	.674	1	2	-1	-3	3S/2	0.0
Total	5	254	724	80	182	32	4	5	54	26	120	.251	.281	.327	.609	69	-33	-30	97	82	62	.490	4	8	-4	5	S/23	-1.2
■ **DARYL ROBERTSON**	Robertson, Daryl Berdene b: 1/5/36, Cripple Creek, Colo BR/TR, 6', 184 lbs. Deb: 5/04/62																											
1962	Chi-N	9	19	0	2	0	0	0	2	2	10	.105	.190	.105	.296	-17	-3	-3	106	394	1	.235	0	0	0	0	/S3	-0.1
■ **DAVE ROBERTSON**	Robertson, Davis Aydelotte b: 9/25/1889, Portsmouth, Va. d: 11/5/70, Virginia Beach, Va. BL/TL, 6', 186 lbs. Deb: 6/05/12																											
1912	NY-N	3	2	0	1	0	0	0	1	0	1	.500	.500	.500	1.000	168	0	0	104	337	1	2.000	1			-0	/1O	0.0
1914	NY-N	82	256	25	68	12	3	2	32	10	26	.266	.299	.359	.658	100	-3	-1	96	118	29	.601	9			-3	O	-0.6
1915	NY-N	141	544	72	160	17	10	3	58	22	52	.294	.326	.379	.705	124	7	12	91	109	71	.645	22	10	1	-6	*O	0.3
1916	NY-N	150	587	88	180	18	8	**12**	69	14	56	.307	.326	.426	.752	136	18	20	96	102	82	.679	21	17	-4	-2	*O	1.5
1917	NY-N	142	532	64	138	16	9	**12**	54	10	47	.259	.276	.391	.667	107	-1	1	97	87	59	.602	17			-7	*O	-1.1
1919	NY-N	1	0	0	0	0	0	0	0	0	0	—	—	—	—	—	0	0	100	—	—	—	0			0	R	0.0
	Chi-N	27	96	8	20	2	0	1	10	1	10	.208	.224	.260	.485	45	-6	-6	100	142	6	.395	3			-1	O	-0.9
	Yr	28	96	8	20	2	0	1	10	1	10	.208	.224	.260	.485	45	-6	-6	100	136	6	.395	3			-1		-0.9
1920	Chi-N	134	500	68	150	29	11	10	75	40	44	.300	.353	.462	.815	134	20	20	99	118	75	.775	17	23	-9	-10	*O	-0.6
1921	Chi-N	22	36	7	8	3	0	0	14	1	3	.222	.243	.306	.549	42	-3	-3	107	467	2	.400	0	2	-1	-2	/O	-0.6
	Pit-N	60	230	29	74	18	3	6	48	12	16	.322	.361	.504	.865	122	8	7	103	139	40	.832	4	5	-2	-6	O	-0.3
	Yr	82	266	36	82	21	3	6	62	13	19	.308	.345	.477	.823	111	5	4	104	233	41	.764	4	7	-3	-8		-0.9
1922	NY-N	42	47	5	13	2	0	1	3	3	7	.277	.320	.383	.703	78	-1	-2	104	50	6	.618	0	0	0	-1	/O	-0.2
Total	9	804	2830	366	812	117	44	47	364	113	262	.287	.318	.409	.727	118	38	48	97	113	428	.665	94	57		-38	O/1	-2.5
■ **DON ROBERTSON**	Robertson, Donald Alexander b: 10/15/30, Harvey, Ill. BL/TL, 5'10", 180 lbs. Deb: 4/13/54																											
1954	Chi-N	14	6	2	0	0	0	0	0	0	2	.000	.000	.000	.000	-99	-2	-2	101	0	0	.000	0	0	0	-3	/O	-0.4
■ **GENE ROBERTSON**	Robertson, Eugene Edward b: 12/25/1899, St.Louis, Mo. d: 10/21/81, Fallon, Nev. BL/TR, 5'7", 152 lbs. Deb: 7/04/19																											
1919	StL-A	5	7	1	1	0	0	0	0	1	2	.143	.250	.143	.393	12	-1	-1	97	0	0	.333	0			0	/S	0.0
1922	StL-A	18	27	2	8	2	1	0	1	1	1	.296	.321	.444	.766	93	-0	-0	106	30	4	.737	1	0	0	0	/32S	0.1
1923	StL-A	78	251	36	62	10	1	0	17	21	7	.247	.310	.295	.605	57	-14	-16	104	78	25	.529	4	2	0	-5	3/2	-1.1
1924	StL-A	121	439	70	140	25	4	4	52	36	14	.319	.373	.421	.795	98	3	-2	107	89	69	.743	3	5	-2	-6	*3/2	0.0
1925	StL-A	154	582	97	158	26	5	14	76	81	30	.271	.364	.405	.770	88	-4	-11	108	97	90	.768	10	7	-1	-2	*3/S	-0.4
1926	StL-A	78	247	23	62	12	6	1	19	17	10	.251	.302	.360	.662	72	-11	-11	101	70	28	.602	5	1	1	1	3S/2	-0.2
1928	NY-A	83	251	29	73	9	0	1	36	14	6	.291	.328	.339	.667	82	-9	-6	92	140	28	.555	2	4	-2	-12	3/2	-1.7
1929	NY-A	90	309	45	92	15	6	0	35	28	6	.298	.358	.385	.743	92	-4	-3	99	101	43	.686	3	3	-1	-8	3	-0.6
	Bos-N	8	28	1	8	0	0	0	6	1	0	.286	.310	.286	.596	52	-2	-2	94	262	2	.500	1			-1	/3S	-0.1
1930	Bos-N	21	59	7	11	1	0	0	7	5	3	.186	.250	.203	.453	12	-8	-8	97	201	3	.354	0			-1	3	-0.7
Total	9	656	2200	311	615	100	23	20	249	205	79	.280	.344	.373	.717	82	-51	-60	103	99	292	.663	29	22		-34	3/2S	-4.7
■ **BOB ROBERTSON**	Robertson, Robert Eugene b: 10/2/46, Frostburg, Md. BR/TR, 6'1", 195 lbs. Deb: 9/18/67																											
1967	Pit-N	9	35	4	6	0	0	2	4	3	12	.171	.237	.343	.580	64	-2	-2	100	97	3	.517	0	0	0	0	/1	-0.1
1969	Pit-N	32	96	7	20	4	1	1	9	8	30	.208	.269	.302	.571	63	-5	-5	95	113	7	.469	1	0	0	-1	1	-0.7
1970	Pit-N	117	390	69	112	19	4	27	82	51	98	.287	.372	.564	.937	152	25	27	97	108	83	.965	4	1	1	2	1/3O	2.0
1971	Pit-N	131	469	65	127	18	2	26	72	60	101	.271	.358	.484	.842	138	22	23	99	98	83	.832	1	2	-1	10	*1	2.4
1972	Pit-N	115	306	25	59	11	0	12	41	41	84	.193	.294	.346	.641	79	-8	-9	103	119	33	.599	1	1	-0	-3	1O3	-1.9
1973	Pit-N	119	397	43	95	16	0	14	40	55	77	.239	.333	.385	.719	107	-0	4	98	84	50	.657	0	4	-2	4	*1	0.0
1974	Pit-N	91	236	25	54	11	0	16	48	33	48	.229	.323	.479	.802	125	6	7	98	115	36	.768	0	0	0	-2	1	0.2
1975	Pit-N	75	124	17	34	4	0	6	18	23	25	.274	.396	.452	.848	136	7	7	99	94	25	.900	0	0	0	-1	1	0.4
1976	Pit-N	61	129	10	28	5	1	2	25	16	23	.217	.303	.318	.621	76	-4	-4	100	205	13	.553	0	1	-1	-2	1	-0.7
1978	Sea-A	64	174	17	40	5	2	8	28	24	39	.230	.327	.420	.746	106	2	1	102	114	24	.700	0	0	0	0	D1	0.1
1979	Tor-A	15	29	1	3	0	0	1	1	3	9	.103	.188	.207	.394	6	-4	-4	103	43	1	.346	0	0	0	-0	/1	-0.4
Total	11	829	2385	283	578	93	10	115	368	317	546	.242	.334	.434	.769	115	39	45	98	108	357	.756	7	9	-3	8	1/DO3	1.3
■ **SHERRY ROBERTSON**	Robertson, Sherrard Alexander b: 1/1/19, Montreal, Que., Can. d: 10/23/70, Houghton, S.Dak. BL/TR, 6', 180 lbs. Deb: 9/08/40 C																											
1940	Was-A	10	33	4	7	0	1	0	0	5	6	.212	.316	.273	.589	58	-2	-2	93	0	3	.538	0	0	0	-0	S	0.0
1941	Was-A	1	3	0	0	0	0	0	0	0	3	.000	.000	.000	.000	-99	-1	-1	98	0	0	.000	0	0	0	0	/3	0.0
1943	Was-A	59	120	22	26	4	1	3	14	17	19	.217	.319	.342	.661	90	-1	-1	104	102	14	.608	0	2	-1	-1	3/S	-0.3
1946	Was-A	74	230	30	46	6	3	6	19	30	42	.200	.292	.330	.623	80	-8	-6	92	77	25	.602	6	2	1	-2	32S/O	-0.3
1947	Was-A	95	266	25	62	9	3	1	23	32	52	.233	.318	.301	.618	75	-9	-8	97	102	27	.552	4	5	-2	-0	O3/2	-1.2
1948	Was-A	71	187	19	46	11	3	2	22	24	26	.246	.335	.369	.704	84	-4	-4	103	99	27	.713	8	0	**2**	-4	O	-0.7
1949	Was-A	110	374	59	94	17	3	11	42	42	35	.251	.329	.401	.730	101	-6	-1	91	79	52	.702	10	3	1	-8	23O	-0.6
1950	Was-A	71	123	19	32	3	3	2	16	22	18	.260	.372	.382	.755	94	-1	-1	99	104	19	.745	1	1	-0	-2	O2/3	-0.2
1951	Was-A	62	111	14	21	2	1	1	10	9	22	.189	.256	.252	.508	40	-10	-9	95	115	8	.435	2	1	0	1	O	-0.8
1952	Was-A	1	0	0	0	0	0	0	0	0	0	—	—	—	—	—	0	0	100	—	—	—	0	0	0	0	R	0.0
	Phi-A	43	60	8	12	3	0	0	5	21	15	.200	.407	.250	.657	77	0	-1	111	124	8	.725	1	2	-1	-1	/2O3	-0.2
	Yr	44	60	8	12	3	0	0	5	21	15	.200	.407	.250	.657	78	0	-1	110	122	8	.725	1	2	-1	-1		-0.2
Total	10	597	1507	200	346	55	18	26	151	202	238	.230	.323	.342	.664	83	-41	-35	97	92	191	.640	32	16	0	-18	O2/3S	-4.3
■ **BILLY ROBIDOUX**	Robidoux, William Joseph b: 1/13/64, Ware, Mass. BL/TR, 6'1", 200 lbs. Deb: 9/11/85																											
1985	Mil-A	18	51	5	9	2	0	3	8	12	16	.176	.333	.392	.725	94	0	-0	105	109	7	.744	0	0	0	-1	O/1D	-0.1
1986	Mil-A	56	181	15	41	8	0	1	21	33	36	.227	.346	.287	.633	74	-5	-5	102	155	19	.574	0	0	0	-2	1D	-1.0
1987	Mil-A	23	62	9	12	0	0	0	4	8	17	.194	.286	.194	.479	31	-6	-6	102	133	4	.392	0	1	-1	0	1D	-0.6
1988	Mil-A	33	91	9	23	5	0	0	5	8	14	.253	.313	.308	.621	72	-3	-3	103	71	8	.514	1	1	-0	2	1/D	-0.2
Total	4	130	385	38	85	15	0	4	38	61	83	.221	.327	.291	.618	69	-14	-15	103	126	38	.570	1	2	-1	-1	/1DO	-1.9
■ **AARON ROBINSON**	Robinson, Aaron Andrew b: 6/23/15, Lancaster, S.C. d: 3/9/66, Lancaster, S.C. BL/TR, 6'2", 205 lbs. Deb: 5/06/43																											
1943	NY-A	1	1	0	0	0	0	0	0	0	1	.000	.000	.000	.000	-99	-0	-0	96	0	0	.000	0	0	0	0	H	0.0
1945	NY-A	50	160	19	45	6	1	8	24	21	23	.281	.368	.481	.849	136	9	8	107	86	30	.839	0	0	0	-1	C	1.1
1946	NY-A	100	330	32	98	17	2	16	64	48	39	.297	.388	.506	.894	148	21	21	100	115	69	.911	0	1	-1	-1	C	2.5
1947	NY-A	82	252	23	68	11	5	5	36	40	26	.270	.370	.413	.783	121	6	8	97	111	41	.758	0	1	-1	-4	C	0.9
1948	Chi-A	98	326	47	82	14	2	8	39	46	30	.252	.344	.380	.724	97	-4	-2	95	91	45	.672	0	1	-1	6	C	0.9

YEAR	TM/L	G	AB	R	H	2B	3B	HR	RBI	BB	SO	AVG	OBP	SLG	PRO	/A	BR	/A	PF	CHI	RC	TA	SB	CS	SBR	FR	POS	TPR
1949	Det-A	110	331	38	89	12	0	13	56	73	21	.269	.402	.423	.825	110	11	7	108	107	60	.833	0	2	-1	-11	*C	0.0
1950	Det-A	107	283	37	64	7	0	9	37	75	35	.226	.388	.346	.735	92	-2	-0	97	102	45	.772	0	1	-1	-13	*C	-0.9
1951	Det-A	36	82	3	17	6	0	0	9	17	9	.207	.343	.280	.624	66	-3	-4	106	140	8	.580	0	0	0	-2	C	-0.2
	Bos-A	26	74	9	15	1	1	2	7	17	10	.203	.352	.324	.676	78	-1	-2	108	83	10	.683	0	0	0	-2	C	-0.2
	Yr	62	156	12	32	7	1	2	16	34	19	.205	.347	.301	.649	72	-4	-6	106	118	20	.648	0	0	0	-4		-0.4
Total	8	610	1839	208	478	74	11	61	272	337	194	.260	.375	.412	.787	112	38	36	101	104	307	.802	0	6	-4	-28	C	4.1
■ **AL ROBINSON** Robinson, Alfred V. Deb: 5/01/1872																												
1872	Oly-n	7	32	6	6							.188															/O	
■ **BROOKS ROBINSON** Robinson, Brooks Calbert b: 5/18/37, Little Rock, Ark. BR/TR, 6'1", 180 lbs. Deb: 9/17/55 CH																												
1955	Bal-A	6	22	0	2	0	0	0	1	0	10	.091	.091	.091	.182	-57	-5	-4	90	187	0	.100	0	0	0	-0	/3	-0.4
1956	Bal-A	15	44	5	10	4	0	1	1	1	5	.227	.244	.386	.631	68	-3	-2	94	19	4	.529	0	0	0	-0	3/2	-0.1
1957	Bal-A	50	117	13	28	6	1	2	14	7	10	.239	.288	.359	.647	81	-4	-3	93	115	11	.548	1	0	0	-1	3	-0.2
1958	Bal-A	145	463	31	110	16	3	3	32	31	51	.238	.293	.305	.597	69	-22	-19	94	86	38	.476	1	2	-1	5	*32	-0.7
1959	Bal-A	88	313	29	89	15	2	4	24	17	37	.284	.325	.383	.709	97	-3	-2	97	73	38	.610	2	2	-1	4	3/2	0.1
1960	Bal-A	152	595	74	175	27	9	14	88	35	49	.294	.333	.440	.774	105	4	3	102	120	78	.663	2	2	-1	13	*3/2	1.8
1961	Bal-A	163	668	89	192	38	7	7	61	47	57	.287	.338	.397	.735	98	-5	-2	97	74	85	.634	1	3	-2	-5	*3/2S	0.1
1962	Bal-A	162	634	77	192	29	9	23	86	42	70	.303	.347	.486	.833	128	17	22	95	96	102	.768	3	1	0	6	*3/S2	3.0
1963	Bal-A	161	589	67	148	26	4	11	67	46	84	.251	.307	.365	.672	93	-10	-6	94	115	66	.584	2	3	-1	9	*3/S	0.3
1964	Bal-A	163	612	82	194	35	3	28	**118**	51	64	.317	.373	.521	.895	139	37	33	105	131	115	.862	1	0	0	-2	*3	3.5
1965	Bal-A	144	559	81	166	25	2	18	80	47	47	.297	.354	.445	.799	126	18	18	100	116	86	.738	3	0	1	-7	*3	1.4
1966	Bal-A	157	620	91	167	35	2	23	100	56	36	.269	.335	.444	.778	120	17	16	101	129	88	.713	2	3	-1	4	*3	1.6
1967	Bal-A	158	610	88	164	25	5	22	77	54	54	.269	.332	.434	.767	132	18	22	95	103	83	.689	1	3	-2	**30**	*3	5.7
1968	Bal-A	162	608	65	154	36	6	17	75	44	55	.253	.308	.416	.724	115	11	10	102	112	76	.647	1	1	-0	16	*3	3.4
1969	Bal-A	156	598	73	140	21	3	23	84	56	55	.234	.303	.395	.698	90	-7	-9	104	117	69	.621	2	1	0	19	*3	1.2
1970	Bal-A	158	608	84	168	31	4	18	94	53	53	.276	.338	.429	.768	114	7	10	97	123	85	.695	1	1	-0	-3	*3	0.7
1971	Bal-A	156	589	67	160	21	1	20	92	63	50	.272	.345	.413	.758	110	11	8	103	131	83	.696	0	0	0	7	*3	1.0
1972	Bal-A	153	556	48	139	23	2	8	64	43	45	.250	.306	.342	.648	95	-6	-4	98	132	58	.550	1	0	0	5	*3	0.7
1973	Bal-A	155	549	53	141	17	2	9	72	55	50	.257	.328	.344	.672	83	-7	-12	107	134	61	.583	2	0	1	8	*3	-0.5
1974	Bal-A	153	553	46	159	27	0	7	59	56	47	.288	.356	.374	.731	119	8	13	93	104	74	.657	2	0	1	**23**	*3	4.0
1975	Bal-A	144	482	50	97	15	1	6	53	44	33	.201	.269	.274	.543	59	-29	-24	91	136	37	.453	0	0	0	4	*3	-1.7
1976	Bal-A	71	218	16	46	8	2	3	11	8	24	.211	.242	.307	.550	62	-12	-11	98	56	16	.429	0	0	0	-2	3	-1.3
1977	Bal-A	24	47	3	7	2	0	1	4	4	4	.149	.216	.255	.471	30	-5	-4	93	106	2	.381	0	0	0	1	3	-0.3
Total	23	2896	10654	1232	2848	482	68	268	1357	860	990	.267	.325	.401	.726	105	32	52	99	112	1358	.666	28	22	-5	134	*3/2S	23.3
■ **BRUCE ROBINSON** Robinson, Bruce Philip b: 4/16/54, La Jolla, Cal. BL/TR, 6'1", 185 lbs. Deb: 8/19/78																												
1978	Oak-A	28	84	5	21	3	1	0	8	3	8	.250	.276	.310	.585	64	-4	-4	101	122	7	.446	0	0	0	-4	C	-0.6
1979	NY-A	6	12	0	2	0	0	0	2	1	0	.167	.231	.167	.397	10	-2	-1	96	384	1	.300	0	0	0	-0	/C	-0.1
1980	NY-A	4	5	0	0	0	0	0	0	0	4	.000	.000	.000	.000	-99	-1	-1	99	0	0	.000	0	0	0	0	/C	0.0
Total	3	38	101	5	23	3	1	0	10	4	12	.228	.257	.277	.534	49	-7	-7	100	148	7	.410	0	0	0	-4	/C	-0.7
■ **CHARLIE ROBINSON** Robinson, Charles Henry b: 7/27/1856, Westerly, R.I. d: 5/18/13, Deb: 8/02/1884																												
1884	Ind-a	20	80	11	23	2	0	0		3		.287	.313	.313	.626	112	1	1	96	0	8	.491				0	C/SO	0.1
1885	Bro-a	11	40	5	6	2	1	0		3		.150	.209	.250	.459	45	-2	-3	104	0	2	.382				0	C	-0.1
Total	2	31	120	16	29	4	1	0		6		.242	.278	.292	.569	87	-2	-2	99	0	10	.451				0	/CSO	0.0
■ **RABBIT ROBINSON** Robinson, Clyde b: 3/5/1882, Wellsburg, W.Va. d: 4/9/15, Waterbury, Conn. BR/TR, 5'6", 148 lbs. Deb: 4/22/03																												
1903	Was-A	103	373	41	79	10	8	1	20	33		.212	.276	.290	.565	68	-12	-15	105	69	35	.534	16			2	2OS/3	-1.2
1904	Det-A	101	320	30	77	13	6	0	37	29		.241	.304	.319	.622	104	0	2	96	138	36	.597	14			1	S3O2	0.3
1910	Cin-N	2	7	0	0	0	0	0	1	1	0	.000	.125	.000	.125	-62	-1	-1	101	0	0	.143	0			0	/3	-0.1
Total	3	206	700	71	156	23	14	1	58	63	0	.223	.287	.300	.587	82	-13	-14	101	100	71	.557	30			3	/2SO3	-1.0
■ **CRAIG ROBINSON** Robinson, Craig George b: 8/21/48, Abington, Pa. BR/TR, 5'10", 165 lbs. Deb: 9/09/72																												
1972	Phi-N	5	15	0	3	1	0	0	0	1	2	.200	.250	.267	.517	48	-1	-1	97	0	1	.417	0	0	0	0	/S	0.0
1973	Phi-N	46	146	11	33	7	0	0	7	0	25	.226	.226	.274	.500	35	-12	-14	108	70	8	.353	1	1	-0	0	S/2	-0.7
1974	Atl-N	145	452	52	104	4	6	0	29	30	57	.230	.282	.265	.548	51	-28	-30	105	93	34	.448	11	2	2	-16	*S	-2.9
1975	Atl-N	10	17	1	1	0	0	0	0	0	5	.059	.059	.059	.118	-71	-4	-4	95	0	0	.059	0	0	0	-1	/S	-0.3
	SF-N	29	29	4	2	1	0	0	0	2	6	.069	.129	.103	.232	-34	-5	-5	102	0	0	.179	0	0	0	0	S/2	-0.3
	Yr	39	46	5	3	1	0	0	0	2	11	.065	.104	.087	.191	-47	-9	-9	100	0	0	.136	0	0	0	-1		-0.6
1976	SF-N	15	13	4	4	1	0	0	2	3	4	.308	.438	.385	.822	131	1	1	103	154	2	.800	0	1	-1	0	/23S	0.1
	Atl-N	15	17	4	4	0	0	0	3	5	2	.235	.409	.235	.644	78	0	-0	111	289	2	.692	0	0	0	0	/2S3	0.0
	Yr	30	30	8	8	1	0	0	5	8	6	.267	.421	.300	.721	100	1	1	107	227	5	.739	0	1	-1	0		0.1
1977	Atl-N	27	29	4	6	1	0	0	1	1	6	.207	.233	.241	.475	24	-3	-3	113	57	2	.348	0	0	0	-2	S	-0.1
Total	6	292	718	80	157	15	6	0	42	42	107	.219	.265	.256	.521	43	-52	-57	105	87	50	.427	12	4	1	-18	S/23	-4.2
■ **DAVE ROBINSON** Robinson, David Tanner b: 5/22/46, Minneapolis, Minn. BB/TL, 6'1", 186 lbs. Deb: 9/10/70																												
1970	SD-N	15	38	5	12	2	0	2	6	5	4	.316	.395	.526	.922	152	2	3	95	90	8	.964	2	0	1	1	O	0.3
1971	SD-N	7	6	0	0	0	0	0	0	1	3	.000	.143	.000	.143	-59	-1	-1	96	0	0	.167	0	0	0	0	H	0.0
Total	2	22	44	5	12	2	0	2	6	6	7	.273	.360	.455	.815	124	1	1	95	77	8	.875	2	0	1	1	/O	0.3
■ **EARL ROBINSON** Robinson, Earl John b: 11/3/36, New Orleans, La. BR/TR, 6'1", 190 lbs. Deb: 9/10/58																												
1958	LA-N	8	15	3	3	0	0	0	0	1	4	.200	.250	.200	.450	20	-2	-2	105	0	0	.286	0	0	0	1	/3	0.0
1961	Bal-A	96	222	37	59	12	3	8	30	31	54	.266	.356	.455	.811	118	5	6	97	94	36	.795	4	3	-1	-2	O	0.0
1962	Bal-A	29	63	12	18	3	1	1	4	8	10	.286	.366	.413	.779	115	1	1	95	55	10	.783	2	0	1	0	O	0.1
1964	Bal-A	37	121	11	33	5	1	3	10	7	24	.273	.313	.405	.717	93	-1	-1	105	73	15	.620	1	2	-1	2	O	0.0
Total	4	170	421	63	113	20	5	12	44	47	92	.268	.342	.425	.767	107	3	4	99	79	61	.740	7	5	-1	1	O/3	0.1
■ **FLOYD ROBINSON** Robinson, Floyd Andrew b: 5/9/36, Prescott, Ark. BL/TR, 5'9", 175 lbs. Deb: 8/10/60																												
1960	Chi-A	22	46	7	13	0	0	0	1	11	8	.283	.431	.283	.714	96	1	1	101	30	7	.750	2	3	-1	-3	O	-0.3
1961	Chi-A	132	432	69	134	20	7	11	59	52	32	.310	.389	.465	.855	128	18	18	99	99	82	.863	7	4	-0	2	*O	1.6
1962	Chi-A	156	600	89	187	**45**	10	11	109	72	47	.312	.387	.475	.862	138	27	31	95	**144**	113	.854	4	2	0	1	*O	2.6
1963	Chi-A	146	527	71	149	21	6	13	71	62	43	.283	.363	.419	.782	113	14	11	104	117	81	.742	4	3	-1	-2	*O	0.4
1964	Chi-A	141	525	83	158	17	3	11	59	70	41	.301	.388	.408	.796	127	18	21	96	107	87	.784	9	5	-0	-5	*O	1.1
1965	Chi-A	156	577	70	153	15	6	14	66	76	51	.265	.356	.385	.740	120	10	15	92	110	83	.706	4	1	1	-5	*O	0.5
1966	Chi-A	127	342	44	81	11	2	5	35	44	32	.237	.332	.325	.657	95	-3	-1	94	117	41	.634	8	2	1	-14	*O	-1.9
1967	Cin-N	55	130	19	31	6	2	1	10	14	14	.238	.313	.338	.651	79	-2	-4	109	88	14	.598	3	1	0	-4	O	-0.9
1968	Oak-A	53	81	5	20	5	0	1	14	4	10	.247	.282	.346	.628	91	-1	-1	98	193	8	.525	0	0	0	-2	O	-0.4
	Bos-A	24	24	1	3	0	0	0	2	3	4	.125	.250	.125	.375	16	-2	-2	101	286	1	.364	1	0	0	-3	O	-0.6
	Yr	77	105	6	23	5	0	1	16	7	14	.219	.274	.295	.570	73	-4	-3	99	225	9	.482	1	0	0	-6		-1.0
Total	9	1012	3284	458	929	140	36	67	426	408	282	.283	.367	.409	.775	119	78	90	97	117	517	.765	42	21	0	-36	O	2.1
■ **FRANK ROBINSON** Robinson, Frank b: 8/31/35, Beaumont, Tex. BR/TR, 6'1", 183 lbs. Deb: 4/17/56 MCH																												
1956	Cin-N	152	572	**122**	166	27	6	38	83	64	95	.290	.381	.558	.939	137	39	33	108	86	121	.969	8	4	0	1	*O	2.8
1957	Cin-N	150	611	97	197	29	5	29	75	44	92	.322	.379	.529	.908	133	34	30	105	80	122	.907	10	2	2	17	*O1	4.3
1958	Cin-N	148	554	90	149	25	6	31	83	62	80	.269	.350	.504	.854	114	17	12	107	98	99	.854	10	1	2	-11	*O3	0.0
1959	Cin-N	146	540	106	168	31	4	36	125	69	93	.311	.397	.583	.980	152	44	42	103	127	122	1.035	18	8	1	-6	*1O	2.6
1960	Cin-N	139	464	86	138	33	6	31	83	82	67	.297	.413	**.595**	**1.007**	**175**	**48**	49	98	93	113	**1.086**	13	6	0	8	1O/3	5.2
1961	Cin-N	153	545	117	176	32	7	37	124	71	64	.323	.411	**.611**	**1.022**	160	**52**	49	104	119	**137**	**1.127**	22	3	**5**	9	*O/3	**5.3**

YEAR	TM/L	G	AB	R	H	2B	3B	HR	RBI	BB	SO	AVG	OBP	SLG	PRO	/A	BR	/A	PF	CHI	RC	TA	SB	CS	SBR	FR	POS	TPR
1962	Cin-N	162	609	**134**	208	**51**	2	39	136	76	62	.342	**.424**	**.624**	**1.048**	**174**	**67**	**65**	102	114	**160**	**1.147**	18	9	0	8	*O	**6.3**
1963	Cin-N	140	482	79	125	19	3	21	91	81	69	.259	.381	.442	.823	131	26	23	104	**147**	87	.893	26	10	2	7	*O/1	2.7
1964	Cin-N	156	568	103	174	38	6	29	96	79	67	.306	.399	.548	.947	159	50	47	103	105	127	1.024	23	5	4	5	*O	5.4
1965	Cin-N	156	582	109	172	33	5	33	113	70	100	.296	.388	.540	.928	153	46	43	104	120	120	.958	13	9	-2	4	*O	4.3
1966	Bal-A	155	576	**122**	182	34	2	**49**	**122**	87	90	**.316**	**.415**	**.637**	**1.052**	**196**	**74**	**73**	101	106	**146**	**1.116**	8	5	-1	-4	*O/1	**6.5**
1967	Bal-A	129	479	83	149	23	7	30	94	71	84	.311	.408	.576	.984	**199**	53	56	95	114	113	1.038	2	3	-1	-4	*O/1	5.1
1968	Bal-A	130	421	69	113	27	1	15	52	73	84	.268	.391	.444	.835	149	30	29	102	98	77	.871	11	2	2	-6	*O/1	2.3
1969	Bal-A	148	539	111	166	19	5	32	100	88	62	.308	.417	.540	.957	160	50	47	104	110	126	1.034	9	3	1	-3	*O1	4.1
1970	Bal-A	132	471	88	144	24	1	25	78	69	70	.306	.402	.520	.922	157	35	37	97	101	99	.947	2	1	0	4	*O/1	3.6
1971	Bal-A	133	455	82	128	16	2	28	99	72	62	.281	.390	.510	.900	149	33	31	103	130	88	.905	3	0	1	-4	O1	2.5
1972	LA-N	103	342	41	86	6	1	19	59	55	76	.251	.358	.442	.800	134	12	15	94	119	55	.784	2	3	-1	-2	O	0.8
1973	Cal-A	147	534	85	142	29	0	30	97	82	93	.266	.374	.489	.863	147	30	33	96	115	99	.872	1	1	-0	3	*DO	3.6
1974	Cal-A	129	427	75	107	26	2	20	63	75	85	.251	.375	.461	.836	151	24	28	92	98	77	.867	5	1	1	-0	*D/O	2.9
	Cle-A	15	50	6	10	1	1	2	5	10	10	.200	.333	.380	.713	104	0	0	101	83	7	.690	0	1	-1	0	D/1	0.0
	Yr	144	477	81	117	27	3	22	68	85	95	.245	.371	.453	.823	146	24	29	93	97	89	.871	5	2	0	-0		2.9
1975	Cle-A	49	118	19	28	5	0	9	24	29	15	.237	.388	.508	.896	152	9	9	100	106	25	.967	0	0	0	0	DM	0.9
1976	Cle-A	36	67	5	15	0	0	3	10	11	12	.224	.333	.358	.692	103	0	0	100	116	8	.636	0	0	0	-0	D/1OM	0.0
Total	21	2808	10006	1829	2943	528	72	586	1812	1420	1532	.294	.392	.537	.929	154	773	754	101	109	2126	1.007	204	77	15	25	*OD1/3	71.2

■ **FRED ROBINSON** Robinson, Frederic Henry b: 7/6/1856, South Acton, Mass. d: 12/18/33, Hudson, Mass. BR/TR, Deb: 4/17/1884

YEAR	TM/L	G	AB	R	H	2B	3B	HR	RBI	BB	SO	AVG	OBP	SLG	PRO	/A	BR	/A	PF	CHI	RC	TA	SB	CS	SBR	FR	POS	TPR
1884	Cin-U	3	13	1	3	0	0	0		0		.231	.231	.231	.462	52	-1	-1	108	0	1	.300	0			0	/2	0.0

■ **JACKIE ROBINSON** Robinson, Jack Roosevelt b: 1/31/19, Cairo, Ga. d: 10/24/72, Stamford, Conn. BR/TR, 5'11.5", 195 lbs. Deb: 4/15/47 H

YEAR	TM/L	G	AB	R	H	2B	3B	HR	RBI	BB	SO	AVG	OBP	SLG	PRO	/A	BR	/A	PF	CHI	RC	TA	SB	CS	SBR	FR	POS	TPR
1947	Bro-N	151	590	125	175	31	5	12	48	74	36	.297	.383	.427	.810	110	14	10	105	55	104	.867	**29**			-2	*1	0.0
1948	Bro-N	147	574	108	170	38	8	12	85	57	37	.296	.367	.453	.820	116	16	13	104	114	99	.842	22			2	*21/3	2.2
1949	Bro-N	156	593	122	203	38	12	16	124	86	27	**.342**	.432	.528	.960	154	50	49	102	124	135	1.078	**37**			-1	*2	5.1
1950	Bro-N	144	518	99	170	39	4	14	81	80	24	.328	.423	.500	.923	133	34	29	107	110	114	.992	12			13	*2	4.4
1951	Bro-N	153	548	106	185	33	7	19	88	79	27	.338	.429	.527	.957	159	46	47	98	100	133	1.055	25	8	3	21	*2	**7.5**
1952	Bro-N	149	510	104	157	17	3	19	75	106	40	.308	**.440**	.465	.904	149	42	41	102	105	116	1.013	24	7	3	10	*2	**6.1**
1953	Bro-N	136	484	109	159	34	7	12	95	74	30	.329	.425	.502	.927	135	32	29	104	135	111	1.000	17	4	3	3	O3/21S	2.9
1954	Bro-N	124	386	62	120	22	4	15	59	63	20	.311	.417	.505	.922	137	24	23	101	97	83	.965	7	3	0	-8	O3/2	1.3
1955	Bro-N	105	317	51	81	6	2	8	36	61	18	.256	.381	.363	.743	94	2	-0	104	105	49	.773	12	3	2	11	3O/12	1.2
1956	Bro-N	117	357	61	98	15	2	10	43	60	32	.275	.383	.412	.795	111	9	8	103	103	60	.813	12	5	1	16	32/1O	2.6
Total	10	1382	4877	947	1518	273	54	137	734	740	291	.311	.410	.474	.883	131	269	250	103	105	1002	.977	197	30		65	231O/S	33.3

■ **JACK ROBINSON** Robinson, John W. "Bridgeport" b: 7/15/1880, Portland, Maine d: 7/22/21, Macon, Ga. TR , Deb: 9/06/02

YEAR	TM/L	G	AB	R	H	2B	3B	HR	RBI	BB	SO	AVG	OBP	SLG	PRO	/A	BR	/A	PF	CHI	RC	TA	SB	CS	SBR	FR	POS	TPR
1902	NY-N	4	9	0	0	0	0	0	0	0		.000	.000	.000	.000	-99	-2	-2	100	0	0	.000	0			0	/C	-0.1

■ **WILBERT ROBINSON** Robinson, Wilbert "Uncle Robby" b: 6/29/1863, Bolton, Mass. d: 8/8/34, Atlanta, Ga. BR/TR, 5'8.5", 215 lbs. Deb: 4/19/1886 MCH

YEAR	TM/L	G	AB	R	H	2B	3B	HR	RBI	BB	SO	AVG	OBP	SLG	PRO	/A	BR	/A	PF	CHI	RC	TA	SB	CS	SBR	FR	POS	TPR
1886	Phi-a	87	342	57	69	11	3	1		21		.202	.254	.260	.514	63	-14	-14	100	0	32	.535	33			-5	C1/O	-1.3
1887	Phi-a	68	264	28	60	6	2	1		14		.227	.269	.277	.545	54	-16	-16	99	0	24	.505	15			-1	C/1O	-0.3
1888	Phi-a	66	254	32	62	7	2	1	31	9		.244	.270	.299	.569	84	-4	-5	101	120	24	.500	11			25	C/1	2.5
1889	Phi-a	69	264	31	61	13	2	0	28	6	34	.231	.251	.295	.546	58	-15	-14	98	103	22	.463	9			0	C	-0.5
1890	Phi-a	82	329	32	78	13	4	4		16		.237	.279	.337	.616	86	-8	-7	97	0	37	.598	20			8	C	0.9
	BB-a	14	48	7	13	1	0	0		3		.271	.314	.292	.605	81	-1	-1	100	0	5	.514	1			7	C/1	0.6
	Yr	96	377	39	91	14	4	4	0	19		.241	.283	.332	.615	85	-9	-8	98	0	42	.587	21			15		1.5
1891	Bal-a	93	334	25	72	8	5	2	46	16	37	.216	.251	.287	.539	56	-20	-20	101	130	29	.496	18			3	C/O	-1.1
1892	Bal-N	90	330	36	88	14	4	2	57	15	35	.267	.303	.352	.654	100	-1	-1	100	146	38	.570	5			-11	C/1O	-0.6
1893	Bal-N	95	359	49	120	21	3	3	57	26	22	.334	.382	.435	.817	111	9	5	107	96	68	.841	17			-6	*C/1	0.6
1894	Bal-N	109	414	69	146	21	4	1	98	46	18	.353	.421	.430	.851	108	7	8	99	**152**	82	.892	12			-8	*C	0.7
1895	Bal-N	77	282	38	74	19	1	0	48	12	19	.262	.295	.337	.632	60	-15	-19	107	141	32	.572	11			3	C	-0.7
1896	Bal-N	67	245	43	85	9	6	2	38	14	13	.347	.385	.457	.842	121	8	7	102	93	48	.850	9			-2	C	0.9
1897	Bal-N	48	181	25	57	9	0	0	23	8		.315	.347	.365	.712	95	-2	-1	95	102	23	.605	0			-6	C	0.0
1898	Bal-N	79	289	29	80	12	2	0	38	16		.277	.317	.332	.649	86	-4	-6	103	122	32	.555	3			-7	C	-0.6
1899	Bal-N	108	356	40	101	15	2	0	47	31		.284	.344	.337	.682	83	-4	-8	108	120	44	.620	5			-26	*C	-2.5
1900	StL-N	60	210	26	52	5	1	0	28	11		.248	.285	.281	.566	63	-12	-9	93	148	19	.487	7			3	C	-0.1
1901	Bal-A	68	239	32	72	12	3	0	26	10		.301	.329	.377	.706	91	-1	-3	107	93	33	.653	9			-9	C	-0.5
1902	Bal-A	91	335	38	98	16	7	1	57	12		.293	.317	.391	.708	95	-2	-3	102	143	46	.650	11			-7	CM	-0.2
Total	17	1371	5075	637	1388	212	51	18	622	286	178	.273	.315	.346	.661	85	-98	-109	101	100	640	.613	196			-41	*C/1O	-2.2

■ **EDDIE ROBINSON** Robinson, William Edward b: 12/15/20, Paris, Tex. BL/TR, 6'2.5", 210 lbs. Deb: 9/09/42 C

YEAR	TM/L	G	AB	R	H	2B	3B	HR	RBI	BB	SO	AVG	OBP	SLG	PRO	/A	BR	/A	PF	CHI	RC	TA	SB	CS	SBR	FR	POS	TPR
1942	Cle-A	8	8	1	1	0	0	0	2	1	0	.125	.222	.125	.347	-1	-1	-1	92	705	0	.286	0	0	0	0	/1	0.0
1946	Cle-A	8	30	6	12	1	0	3	4	2	4	.400	.438	.733	1.171	252	5	5	89	52	10	1.333	0	0	0	0	/1	0.5
1947	Cle-A	95	318	52	78	10	1	14	52	30	18	.245	.314	.415	.729	106	-1	1	96	110	41	.660	1	0	0	1	1	0.0
1948	Cle-A	134	493	53	125	18	5	16	83	36	42	.254	.307	.408	.715	90	-11	-10	99	115	61	.630	1	0	0	-0	*1	-0.2
1949	Was-A	143	527	66	155	27	3	18	78	67	30	.294	.381	.459	.840	133	16	22	91	96	93	.812	3	4	-2	-1	*1	2.0
1950	Was-A	36	129	21	30	4	2	1	13	25	4	.233	.365	.318	.683	77	-4	-4	99	108	17	.667	0	0	0	1	1	-0.3
	Chi-A	119	424	62	133	11	2	20	73	60	28	.314	.405	.491	.895	132	19	20	97	100	90	.916	0	0	0	-0	*1	1.3
	Yr	155	553	83	163	15	4	21	86	85	32	.295	.395	.450	.846	119	15	17	98	102	107	.859	0	0	0	1		1.0
1951	Chi-A	151	564	85	159	23	5	29	117	77	54	.282	.371	.495	.866	137	24	27	97	121	107	.857	2	5	-2	-5	*1	1.7
1952	Chi-A	155	594	79	176	33	1	22	104	70	49	.296	.382	.466	.848	135	28	28	100	120	113	.847	2	0	1	-7	*1	1.2
1953	Phi-A	156	615	64	152	28	4	22	102	63	56	.247	.322	.413	.735	95	-4	-6	102	113	84	.676	1	2	-1	-13	*1	-2.3
1954	NY-A	85	142	11	37	9	0	3	27	19	21	.261	.348	.387	.735	102	0	1	99	160	21	.698	0	0	0	0	1	0.0
1955	NY-A	88	173	25	36	1	0	16	42	36	26	.208	.360	.491	.851	130	7	7	98	118	31	.875	0	0	0	0	1	0.5
1956	NY-A	26	54	7	12	1	0	5	11	5	3	.222	.323	.519	.841	120	1	1	99	96	9	.837	0	1	-1	1	1	0.1
	KC-A	75	172	13	34	5	1	2	12	26	20	.198	.310	.273	.583	55	-11	-11	101	85	15	.517	0	0	0	0	1	-1.2
	Yr	101	226	20	46	6	1	7	23	31	23	.204	.313	.332	.645	70	-10	-10	100	88	24	.590	0	1	-1	1		-1.1
1957	Det-A	13	9	0	0	0	0	0	0	3	0	.000	.308	.000	.308	-8	-1	-1	107	0	0	.400	0	0	0	0	/1	0.0
	Cle-A	19	27	1	6	1	0	1	3	0	3	.222	.250	.370	.620	66	-1	-1	102	91	2	.478	0	0	0	0	/1	-0.1
	Bal-A	4	3	0	0	0	0	0	0	1	1	.000	.250	.000	.250	-28	-1	-0	93	0	0	.333	0	0	0	0	H	0.0
	Yr	36	39	1	6	1	0	1	3	4	4	.154	.267	.256	.523	42	-3	-3	103	51	3	.485	0	0	0	0		-0.1
Total	13	1315	4282	546	1146	172	24	172	723	521	359	.268	.354	.440	.793	115	65	78	98	112	694	.782	10	12	-4	-23	*1	3.2

■ **YANK ROBINSON** Robinson, William H. b: 9/19/1859, Philadelphia, Pa. d: 8/25/1894, St.Louis, Mo. BR/TR, 5'6.5", 170 lbs. Deb: 8/24/1882

YEAR	TM/L	G	AB	R	H	2B	3B	HR	RBI	BB	SO	AVG	OBP	SLG	PRO	/A	BR	/A	PF	CHI	RC	TA	SB	CS	SBR	FR	POS	TPR
1882	Det-N	11	39	1	7	1	0	0	2	1	13	.179	.200	.205	.405	30	-3	-3	102	84	2	.281				0	S/OP	-0.2
1884	Bal-U	102	415	101	111	24	4	2		**37**		.267	.327	.359	.686	120	15	8	110	0	50	.612	0			14	3SCP/2	2.0
1885	StL-a	78	287	63	75	8	8	0		29		.261	.344	.345	.689	130	8	11	93	0	35	.637				-1	O2/C31	0.6
1886	StL-a	133	481	89	132	26	9	3		64		.274	.377	.385	.761	127	26	16	111	0	91	.903	51			-2	*2/3OSP	1.1
1887	StL-a	125	430	102	131	32	4	1		92		.305	.445	.405	.850	128	31	22	110	0	114	1.197	75			-14	*2/3OSCP	0.7
1888	StL-a	134	455	111	105	17	6	3	53	**116**		.231	**.400**	.314	.714	121	27	18	111	100	82	.934	56			-39	*2S	-1.6
1889	StL-a	132	452	97	94	17	3	5	70	**118**	55	.208	.378	.292	.671	84	4	-7	112	144	66	.824	39			-34	*2	-3.2
1890	Pit-P	98	306	59	70	10	3	0	38	101	33	.229	.434	.281	.715	104	7	12	92	123	46	.907	17			-22	*2	-0.3
1891	CM-a	97	342	48	61	9	4	1	37	68	51	.178	.328	.237	.565	58	-12	-20	112	135	35	.641	23			-11	*2	-2.0
	StL-a	1	3	0	0	0	0	0	0	0	0	.000	.000	.000	.000	-88	-1	-1	114	0	0	.000	0			-1	/2	-0.1
	Yr	98	345	48	61	9	4	1		68	51	.177	.325	.235	.560	57	-13	-21	112	135	35	.634	23			-12		-2.1
1892	Was-N	67	218	26	39	4	3	0	19	38	28	.179	.301	.225	.526	58	-9	-10	105	121	18	.547	11			-5	3/S2	-0.9
Total	10	978	3428	697	825	148	44	15	219	664	180	.241	.375	.323	.698	105	92	46	107	68	538	.813	272			-115	23/SOCP1	-3.9

YEAR	TM/L	G	AB	R	H	2B	3B	HR	RBI	BB	SO	AVG	OBP	SLG	PRO	/A	BR	/A	PF	CHI	RC	TA	SB	CS	SBR	FR	POS	TPR
■ BILL ROBINSON	Robinson, William Henry b: 6/26/43, Mc Keesport, Pa. BR/TR, 6'2", 189 lbs. Deb: 9/20/66 C																											
1966	Atl-N	6	11	1	3	0	1	0	3	0	1	.273	.273	.455	.727	99	-0	-0	99	252	1	.625	0	0	0	-1	/O	-0.1
1967	NY-A	116	342	31	67	6	1	7	29	28	56	.196	.261	.281	.541	64	-17	-15	94	103	24	.443	2	2	-1	0	*O	-2.0
1968	NY-A	107	342	34	82	16	7	6	40	26	54	.240	.297	.380	.677	103	1	1	101	116	36	.596	7	6	-2	3	O	-0.2
1969	NY-A	87	222	23	38	11	2	3	21	16	39	.171	.227	.279	.506	43	-18	-17	95	119	13	.424	3	1	0	-2	O/1	-2.1
1972	Phi-N	82	188	19	45	9	1	8	21	5	30	.239	.259	.426	.685	94	-3	-3	97	83	16	.561	2	3	-1	-6	O	-1.3
1973	Phi-N	124	452	62	130	32	1	25	65	27	91	.288	.329	.529	.858	124	18	14	108	85	74	.805	5	4	-1	4	*O3	1.1
1974	Phi-N	100	280	32	66	14	1	5	29	17	61	.236	.282	.346	.628	73	-10	-11	103	100	24	.522	5	3	-0	3	O	-1.2
1975	Pit-N	92	200	26	56	12	2	6	33	11	36	.280	.318	.450	.768	112	2	2	99	118	27	.689	3	1	0	-1	O	0.0
1976	Pit-N	122	393	55	119	22	3	21	64	16	73	.303	.332	.534	.866	142	19	19	100	90	62	.784	2	4	-2	-5	O3/1	0.9
1977	Pit-N	137	507	74	154	32	1	26	104	25	92	.304	.340	.525	.865	125	18	16	103	123	88	.834	12	6	0	-12	1O3	-0.1
1978	Pit-N	136	499	70	123	36	2	14	80	35	105	.246	.302	.411	.713	93	-3	-6	105	136	60	.657	14	11	-2	-2	*O3/1	-1.6
1979	Pit-N	148	421	59	111	17	6	24	75	24	80	.264	.305	.504	.808	110	7	4	106	105	60	.769	13	2	3	-19	*O1/3	-1.7
1980	Pit-N	100	272	28	78	10	1	12	36	15	45	.287	.324	.463	.787	114	5	4	103	88	36	.686	1	4	-2	-9	1O	-1.1
1981	Pit-N	39	88	8	19	3	0	2	8	5	18	.216	.258	.318	.576	65	-5	-4	96	92	7	.479	1	0	0	-1	1/O3	-0.6
1982	Pit-N	31	71	8	17	3	0	4	12	5	19	.239	.289	.451	.740	94	0	-1	110	107	8	.638	0	1	-1	-1	O	-0.2
	Phi-N	35	69	6	18	6	0	3	19	7	15	.261	.329	.478	.807	132	2	2	94	177	10	.759	1	1	-0	-1	O/1	0.1
	Yr	66	140	14	35	9	0	7	31	12	34	.250	.309	.464	.773	112	2	2	101	146	19	.716	1	2	-1	-2		-0.1
1983	Phi-N	10	7	0	1	0	0	0	2	1	4	.143	.250	.143	.393	11	-1	-1	101	791	0	.286	0	0	0	-0	/13O	-0.1
Total	16	1472	4364	536	1127	229	29	166	641	263	819	.258	.303	.438	.741	104	14	4	102	109	545	.688	71	49	-8	-51	*O13	-10.2
■ RAFAEL ROBLES	Robles, Rafael Orlando (Natera) b: 10/20/47, San Pedro De Macoris, D.R. BR/TR, 6', 170 lbs. Deb: 4/08/69																											
1969	SD-N	6	20	1	2	0	0	0	0	1	3	.100	.143	.100	.243	-32	-3	-3	97	0	0	.200	1	1	-0	-0	/S	-0.3
1970	SD-N	23	89	5	19	1	0	0	3	5	11	.213	.263	.225	.488	34	-8	-8	95	62	6	.408	3	0	1	1	S	-0.2
1972	SD-N	18	24	1	4	0	0	0	0	0	3	.167	.167	.167	.333	-6	-3	-3	88	0	1	.190	0	0	0	-0	S/3	-0.1
Total	3	47	133	7	25	1	0	0	3	6	17	.188	.229	.195	.424	18	-15	-14	94	42	7	.336	4	1	1	1	/S3	-0.6
■ SERGIO ROBLES	Robles, Sergio (Valenzuela) b: 4/16/46, Magdalena, Mexico BR/TR, 6'2", 190 lbs. Deb: 8/27/72																											
1972	Bal-A	2	5	0	1	0	0	0	0	0	0	.200	.200	.200	.400	20	-0	-0	98	0	0	.250	0	0	0	0	/C	0.0
1973	Bal-A	8	13	0	1	0	0	0	0	3	1	.077	.250	.077	.327	-4	-2	-2	107	0	0	.333	0	0	0	-0	/C	-0.1
1976	LA-N	6	3	0	0	0	0	0	0	0	2	.000	.000	.000	.000	-99	-1	-1	100	0	0	.000	0	0	0	0	/C	0.0
Total	3	16	21	0	2	0	0	0	0	3	3	.095	.208	.095	.304	-11	-3	-3	104	0	1	.263	0	0	0	-0	/C	-0.1
■ TOM ROBSON	Robson, Thomas James b: 1/15/46, Rochester, N.Y. BR/TR, 6'3", 215 lbs. Deb: 9/14/74 C																											
1974	Tex-A	6	13	2	3	1	0	0	2	4	3	.231	.412	.308	.719	114	0	1	96	197	2	.727	0	0	0	0	/1D	0.1
1975	Tex-A	17	35	3	7	0	0	0	2	1	3	.200	.222	.200	.422	20	-4	-4	100	110	1	.267	0	0	0	0	/1D	-0.3
Total	2	23	48	5	10	1	0	0	4	5	6	.208	.283	.229	.512	48	-3	-3	98	138	3	.400	0	0	0	0	/D1	-0.2
■ ADAM ROCAP	Rocap, Adam b: 1854, Philadelphia, Pa. d: 3/29/1892, Philadelphia, Pa. 5'9", 170 lbs. Deb: 5/05/1875																											
1875	Ath-n	13	70	13	12							.171															O/2	
■ MIKE ROCCO	Rocco, Michael Dominick b: 3/2/16, St.Paul, Minn. BL/TL, 5'11", 188 lbs. Deb: 6/05/43																											
1943	Cle-A	108	405	43	97	14	4	5	46	51	40	.240	.328	.331	.658	103	-3	2	90	119	47	.593	1	2	-1	-6	*1	-0.8
1944	Cle-A	155	653	87	174	29	7	13	70	56	51	.266	.325	.392	.717	104	2	2	100	76	84	.637	4	8	-4	17	*1	0.6
1945	Cle-A	143	565	81	149	28	6	10	56	52	40	.264	.326	.388	.713	108	3	4	99	78	72	.627	0	4	-2	5	*1	0.2
1946	Cle-A	34	98	8	24	2	0	2	14	15	15	.245	.345	.327	.672	100	-1	0	89	140	12	.623	1	1	-0	1	1	0.0
Total	4	440	1721	219	444	73	17	30	186	174	146	.258	.327	.372	.700	105	1	8	96	91	215	.637	6	15	-7	16	1	0.0
■ JACK ROCHE	Roche, John Joseph "Red" b: 11/22/1890, Los Angeles, Cal. d: 3/30/83, Peoria, Ariz. BR/TR, 6'1", 178 lbs. Deb: 5/24/14																											
1914	StL-N	12	9	1	6	2	1	0	3	0	1	.667	.700	1.111	1.811	419	4	4	104	109	7	4.000	1			0	/C	0.4
1915	StL-N	46	39	2	8	0	1	0	6	4	8	.205	.295	.256	.552	67	-1	-1	100	229	3	.516	1			0	/C	0.0
1917	StL-N	1	1	0	0	0	0	0	0	0	0	.000	.000	.000	.000	-98	-0	-0	102	0	0	.000	0			0	/C	0.0
Total	3	59	49	3	14	2	2	0	9	4	9	.286	.364	.408	.772	131	2	2	101	203	11	.800	2			0	/C	0.4
■ BEN ROCHEFORT	Rochefort, Bennett Harold (born Bennett Harold Rochefort Gilbert) b: 8/15/1896, Camden, N.J. d: 4/2/81, Red Bank, N.J. BL/TR, 6'2", 185 lbs. Deb: 10/03/14																											
1914	Phi-A	1	2	0	1	0	0	0	0	0	1	.500	.500	.500	1.000	206	0	0	97	0	1	1.000	0			0	/1	0.0
■ LOU ROCHELLI	Rochelli, Louis Joseph b: 1/11/19, Williamson, Ill. BR/TR, 6'1", 175 lbs. Deb: 8/25/44																											
1944	Bro-N	5	17	0	3	0	1	0	2	2	6	.176	.263	.294	.557	57	-1	-1	99	143	1	.500	0			-1	/2	0.0
■ LES ROCK	Rock, Lester Henry (born Lester Henry Schwarzrock) b: 8/19/12, Springfield, Minn. BL/TR, 6'2", 184 lbs. Deb: 9/11/36																											
1936	Chi-A	2	1	0	0	0	0	0	0	1	0	.000	.000	.000	.000	-99	-0	-0	99	0	0	.000	0	0	0	0	/1	0.0
■ IKE ROCKENFIELD	Rockenfield, Isaac Broc b: 11/3/1876, Omaha, Neb. d: 2/21/27, San Diego, Cal. BR/TR, 5'7", 150 lbs. Deb: 5/05/05																											
1905	StL-A	95	322	40	70	12	0	0	16	46		.217	.315	.255	.570	91	-4	-1	91	74	30	.552	11			-7	2	-0.8
1906	StL-A	27	89	3	21	4	0	0	8	1		.236	.244	.281	.525	67	-4	-3	98	116	6	.382	0			-9	2	-1.4
Total	2	122	411	43	91	16	0	0	24	47		.221	.301	.260	.562	87	-7	-4	93	82	36	.516	11			-16	2	-2.2
■ PAT ROCKETT	Rockett, Patrick Edward b: 1/9/55, San Antonio, Tex. BR/TR, 5'11", 170 lbs. Deb: 9/17/76																											
1976	Atl-N	4	5	0	1	0	0	0	0	0	1	.200	.200	.200	.400	12	-1	-1	111	0	0	.250	0	0	0	0	/S	0.0
1977	Atl-N	93	264	27	67	10	0	1	24	27	32	.254	.330	.303	.633	63	-10	-14	113	116	26	.539	1	2	-1	-10	S	-1.3
1978	Atl-N	55	142	6	20	2	0	0	4	13	12	.141	.213	.155	.368	4	-18	-20	112	72	4	.277	1	2	-1	-5	S	-2.3
Total	3	152	411	33	88	12	0	1	28	40	45	.214	.289	.251	.539	43	-29	-35	112	99	31	.444	2	4	-2	-15	S	-3.6
■ ANDRE RODGERS	Rodgers, Kenneth Andre Ian "Andy" b: 12/2/34, Nassau, Bahamas BR/TR, 6'3", 200 lbs. Deb: 4/16/57																											
1957	NY-N	32	86	8	21	2	1	3	9	9	21	.244	.323	.395	.718	90	-1	-1	102	87	12	.677	0	0	0	2	S/3	0.2
1958	SF-N	22	63	7	13	3	1	2	11	4	14	.206	.254	.381	.635	65	-3	-3	100	151	6	.538	0	0	0	-0	S	-0.2
1959	SF-N	71	228	32	57	12	1	6	24	32	50	.250	.345	.390	.735	100	-1	0	95	91	32	.701	2	1	0	-6	S	-0.2
1960	SF-N	81	217	22	53	8	5	2	22	24	44	.244	.328	.355	.683	97	-4	-1	90	108	25	.610	1	1	-0	-0	S3/1O	0.0
1961	Chi-N	73	214	27	57	17	0	6	23	25	54	.266	.346	.430	.776	104	1	1	100	84	31	.726	1	1	-0	1	1S/O2	0.2
1962	Chi-N	138	461	40	128	20	8	5	44	44	93	.278	.344	.388	.733	91	-2	-6	106	89	60	.658	5	6	-2	5	*S/1	1.0
1963	Chi-N	150	516	51	118	17	4	5	33	65	90	.229	.325	.306	.632	79	-9	-12	105	85	52	.564	5	7	-3	-5	*S	-0.6
1964	Chi-N	129	448	50	107	17	3	12	46	53	88	.239	.319	.371	.690	89	-3	-6	105	95	55	.638	5	1	1	8	*S	1.2
1965	Pit-N	75	178	17	51	12	0	2	25	18	28	.287	.352	.388	.740	108	2	2	100	138	24	.664	2	1	0	3	S3/12	0.8
1966	Pit-N	36	49	6	9	1	0	0	4	8	7	.184	.298	.204	.502	43	-4	-4	101	168	3	.409	0	1	-1	0	/S3O1	-0.3
1967	Pit-N	47	61	8	14	3	0	2	4	8	18	.230	.319	.377	.696	99	-0	-0	100	57	7	.640	1	1	-0	1	/13S2	0.0
Total	11	854	2521	268	628	112	23	45	245	290	507	.249	.331	.365	.696	90	-23	-29	102	96	305	.653	22	20	-5	9	S/13O2	2.1
■ BOB RODGERS	Rodgers, Robert Leroy b: 8/16/38, Delaware, Ohio BB/TR, 6'2", 190 lbs. Deb: 9/08/61 MC																											
1961	LA-A	16	56	8	18	2	0	2	13	1	6	.321	.333	.464	.798	99	1	-0	111	159	7	.659	0	0	0	-1	C	0.0
1962	LA-A	155	565	65	146	34	6	6	61	45	68	.258	.313	.372	.685	82	-14	-15	102	108	61	.578	1	8	-5	9	*C	-0.2
1963	LA-A	100	300	24	70	6	0	4	23	29	35	.233	.305	.293	.598	75	-12	-9	91	96	28	.508	2	2	-1	-1	C	-0.9
1964	LA-A	148	514	38	125	18	3	4	54	40	71	.243	.303	.313	.616	81	-19	-12	89	**135**	47	.514	4	3	-1	20	*C	1.4
1965	Cal-A	132	411	33	86	14	3	1	32	35	61	.209	.276	.265	.541	56	-24	-23	98	119	28	.438	4	5	-2	10	*C	-0.5
1966	Cal-A	133	454	45	107	20	3	7	48	29	57	.236	.285	.339	.624	79	-13	-13	99	115	41	.519	3	4	-2	7	*C	0.0
1967	Cal-A	139	429	29	94	13	3	6	41	34	55	.219	.280	.305	.585	76	-15	-13	96	115	35	.479	1	4	-2	5	*C/O	-0.1
1968	Cal-A	91	258	13	49	6	0	1	14	16	48	.190	.245	.225	.470	46	-17	-16	94	98	15	.369	2	1	0	-3	C	-1.7
1969	Cal-A	18	46	4	9	1	0	0	2	5	8	.196	.288	.217	.506	43	-3	-3	99	80	3	.432	0	0	0	1	C	0.0
Total	9	932	3033	259	704	114	18	31	288	234	409	.232	.291	.312	.603	73	-117	-103	96	114	265	.516	17	27	-11	46	C/O	-2.0

YEAR	TM/L	G	AB	R	H	2B	3B	HR	RBI	BB	SO	AVG	OBP	SLG	PRO	/A	BR	/A	PF	CHI	RC	TA	SB	CS	SBR	FR	POS	TPR
■ **BILL RODGERS**	Rodgers, Wilbur Kincaid "Rawmeat Bill" b: 4/18/1887, Pleasant Ridge, O. d: 12/24/78, Goliad, Tex. BL/TR, 5'9.5", 170 lbs. Deb: 4/15/15																											
1915	Cle-A	16	45	8	14	2	0	0	7	8	7	.311	.415	.356	.771	126	2	2	104	149	7	.794	3	3	-1	-1	2	0.0
	Bos-A	11	6	2	0	0	0	0	0	3	2	.000	.333	.000	.333	-0	-1	-1	99	0	0	.500	0			0	/2	0.0
	Yr	27	51	10	14	2	0	0	7	11	9	.275	.403	.314	.717	113	2	1	102	94	7	.750	3	3	-1	-1		0.0
	Cin-N	72	213	20	51	13	4	0	12	11	29	.239	.299	.338	.637	90	-2	-3	103	64	22	.587	8	5	-1	5	2/S3O	0.2
1916	Cin-N	3	4	0	0	0	0	0	0	0	2	.000	.000	.000	.000	-99	-1	-1	98	0	0	.000	0			0	/S	0.0
Total	2	102	268	30	65	15	4	0	19	22	40	.243	.316	.328	.645	92	-1	-2	103	76	29	.607	11	8		4	/2SO3	0.2
■ **BILL RODGERS**	Rodgers, William Sherman b: 12/5/22, Harrisburg, Pa. BL/TL, 6', 162 lbs. Deb: 9/27/44																											
1944	Pit-N	2	4	1	1	0	0	0	0	0	1	.250	.250	.250	.500	39	-0	-0	105	0	0	.333	0			-0	/O	0.0
1945	Pit-N	1	1	0	1	0	0	0	0	0	0	1.000	1.000	1.000	2.000	442	0	0	103	0	1	—	0			0	H	0.0
Total	2	3	5	1	2	0	0	0	0	0	1	.400	.400	.400	.800	119	0	0	105	0	1	.667	0			-0	/O	0.0
■ **ERIC RODIN**	Rodin, Eric Chapman b: 2/5/30, Orange, N.J. BR/TR, 6'2", 215 lbs. Deb: 9/07/54																											
1954	NY-N	5	6	0	0	0	0	0	0	0	2	.000	.000	.000	.000	-95	-2	-2	105	0	0	.000	0	0	0	-1	/O	-0.2
■ **AURELIO RODRIGUEZ**	Rodriguez, Aurelio (Ituarte) b: 12/28/47, Cananea, Sonora, Mex BR/TR, 5'10", 180 lbs. Deb: 9/01/67																											
1967	Cal-A	29	130	14	31	3	1	1	8	2	21	.238	.250	.300	.550	65	-6	-6	96	69	10	.420	1	0	0	0	3	-0.5
1968	Cal-A	76	223	14	54	10	1	1	16	17	36	.242	.299	.309	.608	90	-4	-3	94	95	19	.492	0	2	-1	0	3/2	-0.1
1969	Cal-A	159	561	47	130	17	2	7	49	32	88	.232	.276	.307	.582	63	-29	-28	99	104	45	.472	5	3	-0	6	*3	-2.0
1970	Cal-A	17	63	6	17	2	2	0	7	3	6	.270	.313	.365	.679	94	-1	-1	92	126	6	.551	0	1	-1	1	3	0.0
	Was-A	142	547	64	135	31	5	19	76	37	81	.247	.303	.426	.729	103	-3	-0	96	112	67	.673	15	5	2	15	*3/S	1.7
	Yr	159	610	70	152	33	7	19	83	40	87	.249	.304	.420	.724	102	-4	-1	96	115	74	.663	15	6	1	17		1.7
1971	Det-A	154	604	68	153	30	7	15	39	27	93	.253	.289	.401	.689	98	-8	-5	96	59	65	.586	4	6	-2	11	*3/S	0.0
1972	Det-A	153	601	65	142	23	5	13	56	28	104	.236	.273	.356	.629	76	-12	-20	113	98	55	.517	2	3	-1	24	*3/S	0.9
1973	Det-A	160	555	46	123	27	3	9	58	31	85	.222	.267	.330	.596	66	-25	-26	101	109	48	.497	3	1	0	8	*3/S	-2.0
1974	Det-A	159	571	54	127	23	5	5	49	26	70	.222	.258	.306	.564	58	-29	-33	106	103	43	.443	2	0	1	22	*3	-0.8
1975	Det-A	151	507	47	124	20	6	13	60	30	63	.245	.287	.385	.671	85	-10	-12	104	99	55	.577	1	1	-0	18	*3	0.8
1976	Det-A	128	480	40	115	13	2	8	50	19	61	.240	.270	.325	.595	71	-17	-19	104	109	37	.454	0	4	-2	16	*3	-0.5
1977	Det-A	96	306	30	67	14	1	10	32	16	36	.219	.258	.369	.627	66	-14	-16	105	89	27	.524	1	1	-0	14	3/S	-0.4
1978	Det-A	134	385	40	102	25	2	7	43	19	37	.265	.305	.395	.699	88	-3	-7	108	98	44	.594	0	1	-1	1	*3	-0.7
1979	Det-A	106	343	27	87	18	0	5	36	11	40	.254	.279	.350	.629	71	-16	-14	96	102	31	.494	0	2	-1	6	*3/1	-0.7
1980	SD-N	89	175	7	35	7	2	2	13	6	26	.200	.227	.297	.524	48	-13	-12	93	89	11	.404	1	1	-0	1	3/S	-1.1
	NY-A	52	164	14	36	6	1	3	14	7	35	.220	.251	.323	.575	57	-10	-10	99	88	12	.444	0	0	0	-2	3/2	-1.1
1981	NY-A	27	52	4	18	2	0	2	8	2	10	.346	.370	.500	.870	148	3	3	100	98	9	.800	0	0	0	2	3/21D	0.5
1982	Chi-A	118	257	24	62	15	1	3	31	11	35	.241	.275	.342	.618	70	-11	-11	97	128	23	.495	0	0	0	-2	*3/2S	-1.4
1983	Bal-A	45	67	0	8	0	0	0	2	0	13	.119	.132	.119	.252	-30	-12	-12	100	98	1	.153	0	0	0	-1	3	-1.2
	Chi-A	22	20	1	4	1	0	1	1	0	3	.200	.200	.400	.600	59	-1	-1	103	36	1	.471	0	0	0	0	3	0.0
	Yr	67	87	1	12	1	0	1	3	0	16	.138	.148	.184	.332	-9	-13	-13	101	79	2	.224	0	0	0	-0		-1.2
Total	17	2017	6611	612	1570	287	46	124	648	324	943	.237	.276	.351	.627	75	-223	-233	101	98	610	.534	35	31	-8	140	*3/S2D1	-8.6
■ **EDWIN RODRIGUEZ**	Rodriguez, Edwin (Morales) b: 8/14/60, Ponce, P.R. BR/TR, 5'11", 175 lbs. Deb: 9/28/82																											
1982	NY-A	3	9	2	3	0	0	0	1	1	1	.333	.400	.333	.733	108	0	0	96	133	1	.667	0	0	0	0	/2	0.0
1983	SD-N	7	12	1	2	1	0	0	0	1	3	.167	.231	.250	.481	33	-1	-1	99	0	1	.400	0	0	0	0	/2S3	0.0
1985	SD-N	1	1	0	0	0	0	0	0	0	0	.000	.000	.000	.000	-98	-0	-0	102	0	0	.000	0	0	0	0	/H	0.0
Total	3	11	22	3	5	1	0	0	1	2	4	.227	.292	.273	.564	58	-1	-1	98	56	2	.471	0	0	0	0	/2S3	0.0
■ **ELLIE RODRIGUEZ**	Rodriguez, Eliseo (Delgado) b: 5/24/46, Fajardo, P.R. BR/TR, 5'11", 185 lbs. Deb: 5/26/68																											
1968	NY-A	9	24	1	5	0	0	0	1	3	3	.208	.296	.208	.505	54	-1	-1	101	86	2	.421	0	0	0	1	/C	0.0
1969	KC-A	95	267	27	63	10	0	2	20	31	26	.236	.333	.296	.629	75	-7	-8	103	94	27	.565	3	2	-0	-4	C	-0.6
1970	KC-A	80	231	25	52	8	2	1	15	27	35	.225	.317	.290	.607	70	-9	-9	98	87	21	.524	2	1	0	4	C	-0.3
1971	Mil-A	115	319	28	67	10	1	1	30	41	51	.210	.315	.257	.572	62	-14	-15	103	144	27	.498	1	1	-0	3	*C	-0.6
1972	Mil-A	116	355	31	101	14	2	2	35	52	43	.285	.386	.352	.739	127	12	14	95	112	51	.698	1	4	-2	2	*C	1.6
1973	Mil-A	94	290	30	78	8	1	0	30	41	28	.269	.378	.303	.682	98	0	2	96	134	36	.641	4	3	-1	7	CD	1.0
1974	Cal-A	140	395	48	100	20	0	7	36	69	56	.253	.376	.357	.733	121	9	13	92	87	56	.719	4	5	-2	6	*C/D	2.2
1975	Cal-A	90	226	20	53	6	0	3	27	49	37	.235	.384	.301	.685	101	2	4	95	135	30	.687	2	2	-1	-13	C	-0.7
1976	LA-N	36	66	10	14	0	0	0	9	19	12	.212	.409	.212	.621	80	-0	0	100	248	8	.679	0	0	0	1	C	0.3
Total	9	775	2173	220	533	76	6	16	203	332	291	.245	.359	.308	.667	94	-8	-0	97	117	258	.647	17	18	-6	7	C/D	2.9
■ **HECTOR RODRIGUEZ**	Rodriguez, Hector Antonio (Ordenana) b: 6/13/20, Alquizar, Cuba BR/TR, 5'8", 165 lbs. Deb: 4/15/52																											
1952	Chi-A	124	407	55	108	14	0	1	40	47	22	.265	.346	.307	.653	83	-8	-8	100	117	45	.578	7	6	-2	12	*3	0.2
■ **JOSE RODRIGUEZ**	Rodriguez, Jose "El Hombre Goma" b: 2/23/1894, Havana, Cuba d: 1/21/53, Havana, Cuba BR/TR, 5'8", 150 lbs. Deb: 10/05/16																											
1916	NY-N	1	0	0	0	0	0	0	0	0	0	—	—	—	—	—	0	0	96	—	—	—	0			0	R	0.0
1917	NY-N	7	20	2	4	0	1	0	2	2	1	.200	.273	.300	.573	78	-1	-1	97	129	2	.625	2			-0	/1	0.0
1918	NY-N	50	125	15	20	0	2	0	15	12	3	.160	.239	.192	.431	33	-10	-10	98	236	7	.410	6			-5	2/13	-1.4
Total	3	58	145	17	24	0	3	0	17	14	4	.166	.244	.207	.451	39	-10	-10	98	221	54	.438	8			-5	/213	-1.4
■ **RUBEN RODRIGUEZ**	Rodriguez, Ruben Dario (Martinez) b: 8/4/64, Cabrera, D.R. BR/TR, 6'3", 190 lbs. Deb: 9/17/86																											
1986	Pit-N	2	3	0	0	0	0	0	0	0	1	.000	.000	.000	.000	-99	-1	-1	100	0	0	.000	0	0	0	0	/C	0.0
1988	Pit-N	2	5	1	1	0	1	0	1	0	2	.200	.200	.600	.800	124	0	0	98	133	1	.750	0	0	0	0	/C	0.0
Total	2	4	8	1	1	0	1	0	1	0	3	.125	.125	.375	.500	37	-1	-1	99	83	1	.429	0	0	0	0	/C	0.0
■ **VIC RODRIGUEZ**	Rodriguez, Victor Manuel (Rivera) b: 7/14/61, New York, N.Y. BR/TR, 5'11", 173 lbs. Deb: 9/05/84																											
1984	Bal-A	11	17	4	7	3	0	0	2	0	2	.412	.412	.588	1.000	183	2	2	94	80	4	1.000	0	0	0	-0	/2D	0.2
■ **GARY ROENICKE**	Roenicke, Gary Steven b: 12/5/54, Covina, Cal. BR/TR, 6'3", 205 lbs. Deb: 6/08/76																											
1976	Mon-N	29	90	9	20	3	1	2	5	4	18	.222	.263	.344	.608	71	-4	-4	100	52	8	.507	0	0	0	-1	O	-0.5
1978	Bal-A	27	58	5	15	3	0	3	15	8	3	.259	.358	.466	.824	143	2	3	91	165	9	.766	0	1	-1	-4	O	-0.1
1979	Bal-A	133	376	60	98	16	1	25	64	61	74	.261	.381	.508	.889	141	21	22	97	92	73	.908	1	3	-2	-2	*O	1.3
1980	Bal-A	118	297	40	71	13	0	10	28	41	49	.239	.343	.384	.727	98	0	0	101	76	40	.691	2	0	1	-6	*O	-0.7
1981	Bal-A	85	219	31	59	16	0	3	20	23	29	.269	.344	.384	.728	111	3	3	99	84	26	.632	1	2	-1	-2	O	-0.1
1982	Bal-A	137	393	58	106	25	1	21	74	70	73	.270	.392	.499	.891	143	25	25	100	114	79	.934	6	7	-2	3	*O1	2.1
1983	Bal-A	115	323	45	84	13	0	19	64	30	35	.260	.331	.477	.807	119	8	8	100	119	49	.760	2	2	-1	-10	*O/13D	-0.4
1984	Bal-A	121	326	36	73	19	1	10	44	58	43	.224	.348	.380	.728	108	2	5	94	114	45	.706	1	2	-1	-12	*O	-1.1
1985	Bal-A	114	225	36	49	9	0	15	43	44	36	.218	.346	.458	.804	119	6	6	99	115	37	.814	2	2	-1	-9	OD	-0.4
1986	NY-A	69	136	11	36	5	0	3	18	27	30	.265	.390	.368	.758	106	3	2	103	122	22	.775	1	1	-0	-6	OD/31	-0.5
1987	Atl-N	67	151	25	33	8	0	9	28	32	23	.219	.359	.450	.809	104	3	3	100	118	26	.828	0	0	0	-6	O/1	-0.6
1988	Atl-N	49	114	11	26	5	0	1	7	8	15	.228	.279	.298	.577	63	-5	-6	104	76	9	.457	0	0	0	-5	O/1	-1.2
Total	12	1064	2708	367	670	135	4	121	410	406	428	.247	.354	.434	.788	116	65	67	99	103	424	.795	16	20	-7	-61	O/D13	-2.2
■ **RON ROENICKE**	Roenicke, Ronald Jon b: 8/19/56, Covina, Cal. BB/TL, 6', 180 lbs. Deb: 9/02/81																											
1981	LA-N	22	47	6	11	0	0	0	0	6	8	.234	.321	.234	.555	61	-2	-2	98	0	4	.486	1	1	-0	0	O	-0.2
1982	LA-N	109	143	18	37	8	0	1	12	21	32	.259	.361	.336	.697	102	0	1	95	92	20	.704	5	0	2	-18	O	-1.6
1983	LA-N	81	145	12	32	4	0	2	12	14	26	.221	.289	.290	.579	61	-8	-8	100	99	12	.492	3	2	-0	-9	O	-1.9
	Sea-A	59	198	23	50	12	0	4	23	33	22	.253	.365	.374	.739	104	2	2	100	111	30	.757	6	2	1	6	O/1D	0.8
1984	SD-N	12	20	4	6	1	0	1	2	2	5	.300	.364	.500	.864	143	1	1	99	60	4	.857	0	0	0	-2	O	-0.1
1985	SF-N	65	133	23	34	9	1	3	13	35	27	.256	.411	.406	.817	138	7	8	93	82	26	.931	6	2	1	-1	O	0.7
1986	Phi-N	102	275	42	68	13	1	5	42	61	52	.247	.384	.356	.740	101	5	3	104	148	42	.756	2	2	-1	4	O	0.6
1987	Phi-N	63	78	9	13	3	1	1	4	14	15	.167	.293	.269	.563	48	-5	-6	104	66	7	.537	1	0	0	-5	O	-1.1

YEAR	TM/L	G	AB	R	H	2B	3B	HR	RBI	BB	SO	AVG	OBP	SLG	PRO	/A	BR	/A	PF	CHI	RC	TA	SB	CS	SBR	FR	POS	TPR
1988	Cin-N	14	37	4	5	1	0	0	5	4	8	.135	.238	.162	.400	16	-4	-4	105	333	2	.333	0	0	0	-2	O	-0.7
Total	8	527	1076	141	256	51	3	17	113	190	195	.238	.355	.338	.693	93	-4	-4	100	112	146	.702	24	9	2	-27	O/1D	-3.5
■ **OSCAR ROETTGER** Roettger, Oscar Frederick Louis "Okkie" b: 2/19/1900, St.Louis, Mo. d: 7/4/86, St.Louis, Mo. BR/TR, 6', 170 lbs. Deb: 7/07/23																												
1923	NY-A	5	2	0	0	0	0	0	0	0	0	.000	.000	.000	.000	-96	-1	-1	104	0	0	.000	0	0	0	0	/P	0.0
1924	NY-A	1	0	0	0	0	0	0	0	0	0	—	—	—	—	—	0	0	99	—	—	—	0	0	0	0	/P	0.0
1927	Bro-N	5	4	0	0	0	0	0	0	1	1	.000	.333	.000	.333	-4	-0	-1	103	0	0	.500	0			-0	/O	0.0
1932	Phi-A	26	60	7	14	1	0	0	6	5	4	.233	.292	.250	.542	37	-5	-6	114	134	5	.435	0	0	0	-0	1	-0.7
Total	4	37	66	7	14	1	0	0	6	6	5	.212	.288	.227	.515	31	-6	-7	113	119	5	.423	0	0		-0	/1PO	-0.7
■ **WALLY ROETTGER** Roettger, Walter Henry b: 8/28/02, St.Louis, Mo. d: 9/14/51, Champaign, Ill. BR/TR, 6'1.5", 190 lbs. Deb: 5/01/27																												
1927	StL-N	5	1	0	0	0	0	0	0	1	0	.000	.500	.000	.500	41	0	0	107	0	0	1.000	0			-2	/O	-0.1
1928	StL-N	68	261	27	89	17	4	6	44	10	22	.341	.372	.506	.878	128	9	9	100	106	47	.855	2			-3	O	0.4
1929	StL-N	79	269	27	68	11	3	3	42	13	27	.253	.287	.349	.637	58	-19	-18	98	140	26	.532	0			-5	O	-2.7
1930	NY-N	121	420	51	119	15	5	5	51	25	29	.283	.330	.379	.708	72	-20	-18	98	101	51	.628	1			1	*O	-2.2
1931	Cin-N	44	185	25	65	11	4	1	20	7	9	.351	.378	.470	.849	133	7	8	95	70	33	.800	1			-2	O	0.3
	StL-N	45	151	16	43	12	2	0	17	9	14	.285	.337	.391	.728	89	-1	-2	107	103	21	.657	0			-6	O	-1.0
	Yr	89	336	41	108	23	6	1	37	16	23	.321	.360	.435	.794	111	6	5	101	87	53	.732	1			-8		-0.7
1932	Cin-N	106	347	26	96	18	3	3	43	23	24	.277	.323	.372	.695	90	-7	-5	96	116	43	.610	0			-6	O	-1.6
1933	Cin-N	84	209	13	50	7	1	1	17	8	10	.239	.267	.297	.564	62	-11	-10	99	98	15	.414	0			-1	O	-1.4
1934	Pit-N	47	106	7	26	5	1	0	11	3	8	.245	.266	.311	.577	51	-7	-8	105	120	8	.434	0			-0	O	-0.8
Total	8	599	1949	192	556	96	23	19	245	99	143	.285	.324	.387	.711	85	-48	-45	99	107	244	.623	4			-24	O	-9.1
■ **ED ROETZ** Roetz, Edward Bernard b: 8/6/05, Philadelphia, Pa. d: 3/16/65, Philadelphia, Pa. BR/TR, 5'10", 160 lbs. Deb: 5/26/29																												
1929	StL-A	16	45	7	11	4	1	0	5	4	6	.244	.306	.378	.684	75	-2	-2	100	101	5	.618	0	0	0	0	/S123	0.0
■ **BILLY ROGELL** Rogell, William George b: 11/24/04, Springfield, Ill. BB/TR, 5'10.5", 163 lbs. Deb: 4/14/25																												
1925	Bos-A	58	169	12	33	5	1	0	17	11	17	.195	.244	.237	.481	24	-20	-19	95	142	10	.367	0	3	-2	2	2/S	-1.3
1927	Bos-A	82	207	35	55	14	6	2	28	24	28	.266	.342	.420	.762	103	-1	0	95	100	30	.750	3	0	1	-1	3/2O	0.3
1928	Bos-A	102	296	33	69	10	4	0	29	22	47	.233	.295	.294	.589	56	-19	-18	98	114	26	.494	2	6	-3	5	S2/O3	-0.8
1930	Det-A	54	144	20	24	4	2	0	9	15	23	.167	.250	.222	.472	20	-17	-19	105	93	9	.402	1	2	-1	-1	S3/O	-1.4
1931	Det-A	48	185	21	56	12	3	2	24	24	17	.303	.383	.432	.815	110	4	3	104	97	30	.818	8	8	-2	-3	S	0.2
1932	Det-A	144	554	88	150	29	6	9	61	50	38	.271	.332	.394	.726	86	-11	-13	102	88	74	.690	14	6	1	12	*S/3	1.0
1933	Det-A	155	587	67	173	42	11	0	57	79	33	.295	.381	.404	.785	101	9	3	107	85	93	.768	6	9	-4	**19**	*S	2.9
1934	Det-A	154	592	114	175	32	8	3	100	74	36	.296	.374	.392	.766	100	-1	2	98	147	92	.760	13	3	2	9	*S	2.2
1935	Det-A	150	560	88	154	23	11	6	71	80	29	.275	.367	.387	.754	98	-3	0	97	105	83	.731	3	6	-3	11	*S	1.5
1936	Det-A	146	585	85	160	27	5	6	68	73	41	.274	.357	.368	.725	83	-18	-14	95	100	80	.701	14	10	-2	1	*S/3	-0.4
1937	Det-A	146	536	85	148	30	7	8	64	83	48	.276	.376	.403	.779	88	-1	-9	109	93	86	.781	5	5	-2	2	*S	0.0
1938	Det-A	136	501	76	130	22	8	3	55	86	37	.259	.373	.353	.727	83	-11	-11	100	106	73	.743	9	2	2	7	*S	0.5
1939	Det-A	74	174	24	40	6	3	2	23	26	14	.230	.330	.333	.663	63	-8	-11	111	121	21	.635	3	1	0	-3	S3/2	-0.8
1940	Chi-N	33	59	7	8	0	0	1	3	2	8	.136	.164	.186	.350	-4	-8	-8	100	79	2	.275	1			1	S/32	-0.5
Total	14	1482	5149	755	1375	256	75	42	609	649	416	.267	.351	.370	.722	85	-106	-112	101	105	707	.693	82	61		62	*S3/2O	3.4
■ **EMMETT ROGERS** Rogers, Emmett b: 1865, Rome, N.Y. BB , 5'10", 165 lbs. Deb: 4/19/1890																												
1890	Tol-a	35	110	18	19	3	3	0		14		.173	.266	.255	.521	54	-6	-6	103	0	8	.484	2			0	C/O	-0.5
■ **FRALEY ROGERS** Rogers, Fraley W. b: 1850, Brooklyn, N.Y. d: 5/10/1881, New York, N.Y. Deb: 4/30/1872																												
1872	Bos-n	46	201	40	59							.294															O/1	
■ **JIM ROGERS** Rogers, James F. b: 4/9/1872, Hartford, Conn. 5'7.5", 180 lbs. Deb: 4/17/1896 M																												
1896	Was-N	38	154	21	43	6	4	1	30	10	9	.279	.323	.390	.713	94	-3	-2	95	145	21	.658	3			0	3/2O	0.0
	Lou-N	72	290	39	75	8	6	0	38	15	14	.259	.297	.328	.625	68	-14	-13	98	122	33	.577	13			1	1S	-0.8
	Yr	110	444	60	118	14	10	1	68	25	23	.266	.306	.349	.655	76	-17	-15	97	131	54	.604	16			1		-0.8
1897	Lou-N	41	150	22	22	3	2	2	22	22		.147	.260	.233	.493	34	-14	-13	95	166	10	.484	4			-4	2/1M	-1.1
Total	2	151	594	82	140	17	12	3	90	47	23	.236	.294	.320	.614	66	-32	-28	97	140	64	.570	20			-3	/123SO	-1.9
■ **JAY ROGERS** Rogers, Jay Lewis b: 8/3/1888, Sandusky, N.Y. d: 7/1/64, Carlisle, N.Y. BR/TR, 5'11.5", 178 lbs. Deb: 5/22/14																												
1914	NY-A	5	8	0	0	0	0	0	0	0	4	.000	.000	.000	.000	-99	-2	-2	100	0	0	.000	0			0	/C	-0.1
■ **PACKY ROGERS** Rogers, Stanley Frank (born Stanley Frank Hazinski) b: 4/26/13, Swoyersville, Pa. BR/TR, 5'8", 175 lbs. Deb: 7/12/38																												
1938	Bro-N	23	37	3	7	1	1	0	5	6	6	.189	.302	.270	.573	61	-2	-2	96	181	3	.485	0			-2	/S32O	-0.2
■ **MIKE ROGODZINSKI** Rogodzinski, Michael George b: 2/22/48, Evanston, Ill. BL/TR, 6', 185 lbs. Deb: 5/04/73																												
1973	Phi-N	66	80	13	19	3	0	2	7	12	19	.237	.337	.350	.687	84	-1	-2	108	83	10	.635	0	0	0	-2	O	-0.4
1974	Phi-N	17	15	1	1	0	0	0	1	2	3	.067	.176	.067	.243	-29	-3	-3	103	386	0	.214	0	0	0	-0	/O	-0.2
1975	Phi-N	16	19	3	5	1	0	0	4	3	2	.263	.364	.316	.679	89	-0	-0	101	258	2	.600	0	1	-1	-1	/O	-0.1
Total	3	99	114	17	25	4	0	2	12	17	24	.219	.321	.307	.628	71	-4	-4	106	151	12	.578	0	1	-1	-3	/O	-0.7
■ **GEORGE ROHE** Rohe, George Anthony "Whitey" b: 9/15/1875, Cincinnati, Ohio d: 6/10/57, Cincinnati, Ohio BR/TR, 5'9", 165 lbs. Deb: 5/07/01																												
1901	Bal-A	14	36	7	10	2	0	0	4	5		.278	.366	.333	.699	91	0	-0	107	105	5	.692	1			-1	/13	-0.1
1905	Chi-A	34	113	14	24	1	0	1	12	12		.212	.288	.248	.536	75	-3	-3	97	141	9	.472	2			3	23	0.1
1906	Chi-A	77	225	14	58	5	1	0	25	16		.258	.307	.289	.596	97	-3	-0	92	140	23	.533	8			12	3/2O	1.7
1907	Chi-A	144	494	46	105	11	2	2	51	39		.213	.270	.255	.525	67	-16	-18	104	141	39	.465	16			5	32S	-0.9
Total	4	269	868	81	197	19	3	3	92	72		.227	.286	.266	.552	76	-22	-22	100	139	76	.492	27			19	3/2S1O	0.8
■ **DAN ROHN** Rohn, Daniel Jay b: 1/10/56, Alpena, Mich. BL/TR, 5'7", 165 lbs. Deb: 9/02/83																												
1983	Chi-N	23	31	3	12	3	2	0	6	2	2	.387	.424	.613	1.037	182	3	3	101	125	8	1.158	1	0	0	2	/2S	0.6
1984	Chi-N	25	31	1	4	0	0	1	3	1	6	.129	.156	.226	.382	6	-4	-4	110	118	1	.286	0	0	0	0	/32S	-0.3
1986	Cle-A	6	10	1	2	0	0	0	2	1	1	.200	.273	.200	.473	33	-1	-1	98	398	1	.375	0	0	0	0	/23S	0.0
Total	3	54	72	5	18	3	2	1	11	4	9	.250	.289	.389	.678	83	-1	-2	104	161	10	.611	1	0	0	2	/23S	0.3
■ **RAY ROHWER** Rohwer, Ray b: 6/5/1895, Dixon, Cal. d: 1/24/88, Davis, Cal. BL/TL, 5'10", 155 lbs. Deb: 4/13/21																												
1921	Pit-N	30	40	6	10	3	2	0	6	4	8	.250	.318	.425	.743	92	-0	-1	103	129	5	.677	0	1	-1	-1	O	-0.2
1922	Pit-N	53	129	19	38	6	3	3	22	10	17	.295	.350	.457	.807	103	1	0	104	113	21	.780	1	0	0	-0	O	0.0
Total	2	83	169	25	48	9	5	3	28	14	25	.284	.342	.450	.792	100	1	-0	103	117	26	.754	1	1	-0	-2	/O	-0.2
■ **TONY ROIG** Roig, Anton Ambrose b: 12/23/27, New Orleans, La. BR/TR, 6'1", 180 lbs. Deb: 9/13/53																												
1953	Was-A	3	8	0	1	1	0	0	0	0	1	.125	.125	.250	.375	-1	-1	-1	94	0	0	.286	0	0	0	0	/2	0.0
1955	Was-A	29	57	3	13	1	1	0	4	2	15	.228	.254	.281	.535	48	-5	-4	91	93	4	.391	0	0	0	1	S/32	0.0
1956	Was-A	44	119	11	25	5	2	0	7	20	29	.210	.324	.286	.609	61	-6	-6	102	77	11	.560	2	0	1	1	2S	-0.1
Total	3	76	184	14	39	7	3	0	11	22	45	.212	.296	.283	.579	55	-12	-12	98	79	15	.503	2	0	1	2	/S23	-0.1
■ **COOKIE ROJAS** Rojas, Octavio Victor (Rivas) b: 3/6/39, Havana, Cuba BR/TR, 5'10", 160 lbs. Deb: 4/10/62 MC																												
1962	Cin-N	39	86	9	19	2	0	0	6	9	4	.221	.302	.244	.546	48	-6	-6	102	113	6	.451	1	1	-0	-2	2/3	-0.4
1963	Phi-N	64	77	18	17	0	1	1	2	3	8	.221	.259	.286	.545	55	-4	-5	103	34	5	.469	4	1	1	1	2/O	-0.1
1964	Phi-N	109	340	58	99	19	5	2	31	22	17	.291	.338	.394	.732	107	2	3	99	91	42	.621	1	3	-2	-2	O2S/C3	0.1
1965	Phi-N	142	521	78	158	25	3	3	42	42	33	.303	.359	.380	.739	114	7	10	95	86	71	.658	5	5	-2	-2	2OS/C1	1.1
1966	Phi-N	156	626	77	168	18	1	6	55	35	46	.268	.311	.329	.640	77	-18	-19	101	109	63	.523	4	6	-2	-4	*2O/S	-2.0
1967	Phi-N	147	528	60	137	21	2	4	45	30	58	.259	.299	.330	.629	76	-14	-17	104	102	50	.518	8	4	0	-10	*2/OCSP3	-1.8
1968	Phi-N	152	621	53	144	19	0	9	48	16	55	.232	.251	.306	.557	68	-26	-25	97	90	43	.422	4	8	-4	10	*2/C	-1.1
1969	Phi-N	110	391	35	89	11	1	4	30	23	28	.228	.272	.292	.564	59	-22	-21	98	97	28	.434	1	6	-3	-4	2/O	-2.2
1970	StL-N	23	47	2	5	0	0	0	2	3	4	.106	.176	.106	.283	-21	-8	-9	106	155	1	.209	0	0	0	0	2/OS	-0.6

YEAR	TM/L	G	AB	R	H	2B	3B	HR	RBI	BB	SO	AVG	OBP	SLG	PRO	/A	BR	/A	PF	CHI	RC	TA	SB	CS	SBR	FR	POS	TPR
	KC-A	98	384	36	100	13	3	2	28	20	29	.260	.297	.326	.623	73	-15	-14	98	92	34	.495	3	7	-3	2		-1.0
1971	KC-A	115	414	56	124	22	2	6	59	39	35	.300	.363	.406	.768	119	10	10	99	137	60	.711	8	3	1	-6	*2/SO	1.0
1972	KC-A	137	487	49	127	25	0	3	53	41	35	.261	.319	.331	.650	93	-4	-4	100	133	47	.532	2	8	-4	3	*2/3S	0.3
1973	KC-A	139	551	78	152	29	3	6	69	37	38	.276	.323	.372	.695	87	-4	-10	109	129	65	.623	18	4	3	10	*2	0.9
1974	KC-A	144	542	52	147	17	1	6	60	30	43	.271	.313	.339	.653	82	-9	-13	106	119	52	.532	8	4	0	-10	*2	-1.7
1975	KC-A	120	406	34	103	18	2	2	37	30	24	.254	.305	.323	.628	76	-12	-13	102	104	37	.511	4	5	-2	-2	*2/D	-1.3
1976	KC-A	63	132	11	32	6	0	0	16	8	15	.242	.286	.288	.574	68	-5	-5	100	162	11	.457	2	0	1	1	2/31D	-0.1
1977	KC-A	64	156	8	39	9	1	0	10	8	17	.250	.287	.321	.607	65	-8	-8	100	79	12	.472	1	3	-2	4	32/D	-0.4
Total	16	1822	6309	714	1660	254	25	54	593	396	489	.263	.309	.337	.646	83	-137	-145	101	108	630	.554	74	68	-19	-14	*2O/3SDC1	-9.3
■ **STAN ROJEK**	Rojek, Stanley Andrew b: 4/21/19, N.Tonawanda, N.Y. BR/TR, 5'10", 170 lbs. Deb: 9/22/42																											
1942	Bro-N	1	0	1	0	0	0	0	0	0	0	—	—	—	—	—	0	0	102	—	—	—	0			0	R	0.0
1946	Bro-N	45	47	11	13	2	1	0	2	4	1	.277	.333	.362	.695	95	-0	-0	103	44	5	.595	1			0	S/23	0.1
1947	Bro-N	32	80	7	21	0	1	0	7	7	3	.262	.322	.287	.609	60	-4	-5	105	113	7	.500	1			1	S/32	-0.1
1948	Pit-N	156	641	85	186	27	5	4	51	61	41	.290	.355	.367	.721	91	-3	-7	104	67	87	.698	24			-6	*S	0.4
1949	Pit-N	144	557	72	136	19	2	0	31	50	31	.244	.309	.285	.594	60	-30	-31	101	78	52	.499	4			-3	*S	-1.7
1950	Pit-N	76	230	28	59	12	1	0	17	18	13	.257	.313	.317	.631	65	-11	-12	103	90	23	.537	2			-3	S/2	-0.7
1951	Pit-N	8	16	0	3	0	0	0	0	0	1	.188	.188	.188	.375	1	-2	-2	107	0	1	.231	0	0	0	0	/S	-0.1
	StL-N	51	186	21	51	7	3	0	14	10	10	.274	.318	.344	.662	77	-6	-6	101	86	19	.524	0	3	-2	6	S	0.2
	Yr	59	202	21	54	7	3	0	14	10	11	.267	.308	.332	.640	71	-8	-8	102	75	19	.500	0	3	-2	6		0.1
1952	StL-A	9	7	0	1	0	0	0	0	2	0	.143	.333	.143	.476	37	-1	-0	97	0	0	.429	0	0	0	-0	/S2	0.0
Total	8	522	1764	225	470	67	13	4	122	152	100	.266	.327	.326	.653	74	-57	-63	103	76	823	.591	32	3		-6	S/23	-1.9
■ **RED ROLFE**	Rolfe, Robert Abial b: 10/17/08, Penacook, N.H. d: 7/8/69, Guilford, N.H. BL/TR, 5'11.5", 170 lbs. Deb: 6/29/31 MC																											
1931	NY-A	1	0	0	0	0	0	0	0	0	0	—	—	—	—	—	0	0	98	—	—	—	0	0	0	0	/S	0.0
1934	NY-A	89	279	54	80	13	2	0	18	26	16	.287	.348	.348	.695	83	-8	-6	96	62	34	.619	2	3	-1	-5	S3	-0.8
1935	NY-A	149	639	108	192	33	9	5	67	57	39	.300	.361	.404	.764	105	-2	4	93	74	95	.722	7	3	0	-6	*3S	0.0
1936	NY-A	135	568	116	181	39	**15**	10	70	68	38	.319	.392	.493	.884	123	15	20	95	70	113	.907	3	0	1	5	*3	2.3
1937	NY-A	154	648	143	179	34	10	4	62	90	53	.276	.365	.378	.743	86	-11	-12	102	71	94	.722	4	2	0	5	*3	-0.3
1938	NY-A	151	631	132	196	36	8	10	80	74	44	.311	.386	.441	.826	101	7	2	105	78	113	.844	13	1	3	-8	*3	0.2
1939	NY-A	152	648	**139**	**213**	**46**	10	14	80	81	41	.329	.404	.495	.899	141	29	37	91	66	134	.917	7	6	-2	-15	*3	1.6
1940	NY-A	139	588	102	147	26	6	10	53	50	48	.250	.311	.366	.677	76	-23	-21	99	69	71	.606	4	2	0	-3	*3	-1.4
1941	NY-A	136	561	106	148	22	5	8	42	57	38	.264	.332	.364	.695	85	-13	-12	98	63	73	.632	3	2	-0	-3	*3	-0.7
1942	NY-A	69	265	42	58	8	2	8	25	23	18	.219	.281	.355	.636	79	-9	-9	99	76	28	.565	1	1	-0	-1	3	-0.8
Total	10	1175	4827	942	1394	257	67	69	497	526	335	.289	.360	.413	.773	100	-15	3	98	70	1579	.745	44	20	1	-30	*3/S	0.1
■ **RAY ROLLING**	Rolling, Raymond Copeland b: 9/8/1886, Martinsburg, Mo. d: 8/25/66, St.Paul, Minn. BR/TR, 5'10.5", 160 lbs. Deb: 9/06/12																											
1912	StL-N	5	15	0	3	0	0	0	0	0	5	.200	.200	.200	.400	10	-2	-2	100	0	1	.250	0			0	/2	-0.1
■ **RED ROLLINGS**	Rollings, William Russell b: 3/21/04, Mobile, Ala. d: 12/31/64, Mobile, Ala. BL/TR, 5'11", 167 lbs. Deb: 4/17/27																											
1927	Bos-A	82	184	19	49	4	1	0	9	12	10	.266	.325	.299	.624	66	-10	-8	95	54	18	.548	3	0	1	0	31/2	-0.4
1928	Bos-A	50	48	7	11	3	1	0	9	6	8	.229	.315	.333	.648	72	-2	-2	98	193	5	.595	0	0	0	-1	/12O3	-0.2
1930	Bos-N	52	123	10	29	6	0	0	10	9	5	.236	.288	.285	.572	40	-12	-11	97	98	10	.489	2			-2	32	-1.0
Total	3	184	355	36	89	13	2	0	28	27	23	.251	.311	.299	.609	58	-24	-22	96	89	34	.534	5	0		-3	/321O	-1.6
■ **RICH ROLLINS**	Rollins, Richard John "Red" b: 4/16/38, Mount Pleasant, Pa. BR/TR, 5'10", 185 lbs. Deb: 6/16/61																											
1961	Min-A	13	17	3	5	1	0	0	3	2	2	.294	.400	.353	.753	97	0	0	106	196	3	.750	0	0	0	-0	/23	0.1
1962	Min-A	159	624	96	186	23	5	16	96	75	61	.298	.379	.428	.807	111	16	12	105	116	104	.777	3	1	0	-1	*3/S	1.4
1963	Min-A	136	531	75	163	23	1	16	61	36	59	.307	.360	.444	.804	124	17	17	100	95	84	.740	2	0	1	-5	*3/2	1.4
1964	Min-A	148	596	87	161	25	**10**	12	68	53	80	.270	.335	.406	.741	104	4	3	101	100	80	.668	2	5	-2	-1	*3	0.3
1965	Min-A	140	469	59	117	22	1	5	32	37	54	.249	.310	.333	.642	82	-11	-11	101	78	48	.551	4	0	1	0	*32	-0.8
1966	Min-A	90	269	30	66	7	1	10	40	13	34	.245	.290	.390	.681	84	-3	-6	111	124	28	.570	0	2	-1	-5	3/2O	-1.4
1967	Min-A	109	339	31	83	11	2	6	39	27	58	.245	.306	.342	.648	86	-4	-6	107	121	34	.551	1	1	-0	-9	3	-1.4
1968	Min-A	93	203	14	49	5	0	6	30	10	34	.241	.287	.355	.642	88	-2	-3	106	143	20	.547	3	1	0	3	3	0.2
1969	Sea-A	58	187	15	42	7	0	4	21	7	19	.225	.271	.326	.598	68	-9	-8	98	115	16	.503	2	0	1	2	3/S	-0.4
1970	Mil-A	14	25	3	5	1	0	0	5	3	4	.200	.286	.240	.526	47	-2	-2	98	337	2	.450	0	0	0	0	/3	-0.1
	Cle-A	42	43	6	10	0	0	2	4	3	5	.233	.283	.372	.655	69	-1	-2	115	74	5	.576	0	0	0	0	/3	-0.1
	Yr	56	68	9	15	1	0	2	9	6	9	.221	.284	.324	.607	61	-3	-4	111	145	7	.528	0	0	0	0		-0.2
Total	10	1002	3303	419	887	125	20	77	399	266	410	.269	.330	.388	.719	98	6	-7	103	109	424	.662	17	10	-1	-14	3/2SO	-0.8
■ **ROLLINSON**	Rollinson Deb:6/17/1884																											
1884	Was-U	1	3	0	0	0	0	0		0		.000	.000	.000	.000	-99	-1	-1	97	0	0	.000	0			0	/C	0.0
■ **BILL ROMAN**	Roman, William Anthony b: 10/11/38, Detroit, Mich. BL/TL, 6'4", 190 lbs. Deb: 9/30/64																											
1964	Det-A	3	8	2	3	0	0	1	1	0	2	.375	.375	.750	1.125	213	1	1	96	47	2	1.200	0	0	0	0	/1	0.1
1965	Det-A	21	27	0	2	0	0	0	0	2	7	.074	.138	.074	.212	-36	-5	-5	105	0	0	.154	0	0	0	0	/1	-0.5
Total	2	24	35	2	5	0	0	1	1	2	9	.143	.189	.229	.418	17	-4	-4	103	10	3	.323	0	0	0	0	/1	-0.4
■ **JOHN ROMANO**	Romano, John Anthony "Honey" b: 8/23/34, Hoboken, N.J. BR/TR, 5'11", 205 lbs. Deb: 9/12/58																											
1958	Chi-A	4	7	1	2	0	0	0	1	1	0	.286	.375	.286	.661	86	-0	-0	98	200	1	.600	0	0	0	0	/C	0.0
1959	Chi-A	53	126	20	37	5	1	5	25	23	18	.294	.407	.468	.875	144	8	8	97	133	25	.892	0	1	-1	1	C	1.0
1960	Cle-A	108	316	40	86	12	2	16	52	37	50	.272	.354	.475	.829	125	9	10	98	103	53	.802	0	0	0	1	C	1.6
1961	Cle-A	142	509	76	152	29	1	21	80	61	60	.299	.379	.483	.862	134	21	24	96	103	95	.850	0	0	0	15	*C	3.6
1962	Cle-A	135	459	71	120	19	3	25	81	73	64	.261	.369	.479	.848	129	18	19	98	111	82	.842	0	1	-1	14	*C	3.9
1963	Cle-A	89	255	28	55	5	2	10	34	38	49	.216	.322	.369	.691	96	-2	-1	97	115	32	.670	4	3	-1	-1	C/O	0.0
1964	Cle-A	106	352	46	85	18	1	19	47	51	83	.241	.349	.460	.809	120	11	10	103	93	54	.782	2	2	-1	10	C/1	2.4
1965	Chi-A	122	356	39	86	11	0	18	48	59	74	.242	.357	.424	.781	132	11	15	92	97	54	.754	0	2	-1	-27	*C/O1	-0.5
1966	Chi-A	122	329	33	76	12	0	15	47	58	72	.231	.348	.404	.752	122	8	10	94	111	50	.750	0	0	0	-12	*C	0.3
1967	StL-N	24	58	1	7	1	0	0	2	13	15	.121	.282	.138	.420	23	-5	-5	101	104	3	.423	1	0	0	2	C	-0.1
Total	10	905	2767	355	706	112	10	129	417	414	485	.255	.358	.443	.801	123	79	90	97	106	450	.809	7	9	-3	4	C/O1	12.2
■ **TOM ROMANO**	Romano, Thomas Michael b: 10/25/58, Syracuse, N.Y. BR/TR, 5'10", 170 lbs. Deb: 9/01/87																											
1987	Mon-N	7	3	1	0	0	0	0	0	0	1	.000	.000	.000	.000	-94	-1	-1	106	0	0	.000	0	0	0	-1	/O	-0.1
■ **ED ROMERO**	Romero, Edgardo Ralph (Rivera) b: 12/9/57, Santurce, P.R. BR/TR, 5'11", 160 lbs. Deb: 7/16/77																											
1977	Mil-A	10	25	4	7	1	0	0	2	4	3	.280	.379	.320	.699	98	-0	0	95	99	3	.632	0	0	0	-0	S	0.1
1980	Mil-A	42	104	20	27	7	0	1	10	9	11	.260	.319	.356	.674	89	-2	-1	95	97	12	.600	2	0	1	0	S2/3	0.2
1981	Mil-A	44	91	6	18	3	0	1	10	4	9	.198	.232	.264	.495	44	-7	-6	96	145	4	.354	0	2	-1	8	S2/3	0.2
1982	Mil-A	52	144	18	36	8	0	1	7	8	16	.250	.289	.326	.616	73	-6	-5	94	56	13	.491	0	0	0	1	2S/3O	0.0
1983	Mil-A	59	145	17	46	7	0	1	18	8	8	.317	.353	.386	.739	113	1	2	92	119	20	.644	1	0	0	-2	SO/32D	0.1
1984	Mil-A	116	357	36	90	12	0	1	31	29	25	.252	.310	.294	.604	74	-15	-11	92	114	31	.489	3	3	-1	5	3S2/1OD	-0.1
1985	Mil-A	88	251	24	63	11	1	0	21	26	20	.251	.321	.303	.624	69	-9	-11	105	110	26	.536	1	1	-0	-2	S2O/3	-0.8
1986	Bos-A	100	233	41	49	11	0	2	23	18	16	.210	.273	.283	.556	53	-15	-15	100	127	19	.466	2	0	1	-8	S3/2O	-1.7
1987	Bos-A	88	235	23	64	5	0	0	14	18	22	.272	.324	.294	.618	67	-11	-10	99	81	21	.478	0	2	-1	6	2S3/1	-0.3
1988	Bos-A	31	75	3	18	3	0	0	5	3	8	.240	.278	.280	.558	52	-4	-5	109	95	5	.410	0	0	0	-0	3/S/21D	-0.4
Total	10	630	1660	192	418	68	1	7	141	127	138	.252	.307	.307	.613	71	-68	-62	97	106	155	.518	9	8	-2	7	S23/O1D	-2.7
■ **KEVIN ROMINE**	Romine, Kevin Andrew b: 5/23/61, Exeter, N.H. BR/TR, 5'11", 185 lbs. Deb: 9/05/85																											
1985	Bos-A	24	28	3	6	2	0	0	1	1	4	.214	.241	.286	.527	43	-2	-2	102	50	2	.435	1	0	0	-5	O/D	-0.7
1986	Bos-A	35	35	6	9	2	0	0	2	3	9	.257	.316	.314	.630	74	-1	-1	100	72	4	.593	2	0	1	-4	O	-0.4

YEAR	TM/L	G	AB	R	H	2B	3B	HR	RBI	BB	SO	AVG	OBP	SLG	PRO	/A	BR	/A	PF	CHI	RC	TA	SB	CS	SBR	FR	POS	TPR
1987	Bos-A	9	24	5	7	2	0	0	2	2	6	.292	.346	.375	.721	93	-0	-0	99	89	3	.647	0	0	0	0	/OD	0.0
1988	Bos-A	57	78	17	15	2	1	1	6	7	15	.192	.259	.282	.541	47	-5	-6	109	95	6	.470	2	0	1	-10	O/D	-1.6
Total	4	125	165	31	37	8	1	1	11	13	34	.224	.281	.303	.584	58	-9	-10	105	82	15	.519	5	0	2	-19	O/D	-2.7
■ **HENRI RONDEAU**	Rondeau, Henri Joseph b: 5/5/1887, Danielson, Conn. d: 5/28/43, Woonsocket, R.I. BR/TR, 5'10.5", 175 lbs. Deb: 4/11/13																											
1913	Det-A	35	70	5	13	2	0	0	5	14	16	.186	.321	.214	.536	58	-3	-3	99	118	5	.526	1			-0	C/1	-0.2
1915	Was-A	14	40	3	7	0	0	0	4	4	3	.175	.250	.175	.425	27	-3	-4	101	194	2	.343	1	2	-1	2	O	-0.2
1916	Was-A	50	162	20	36	5	3	1	28	18	18	.222	.311	.309	.620	86	-3	-3	100	192	18	.619	7			2	O	-0.3
Total	3	99	272	28	56	7	3	1	37	36	37	.206	.305	.265	.570	70	-9	-9	100	173	25	.550	9	2		4	/OC1	-0.7
■ **GENE ROOF**	Roof, Eugene Lawrence b: 1/13/58, Paducah, Ky. BB/TR, 6'2", 180 lbs. Deb: 9/03/81																											
1981	StL-N	23	60	11	18	6	0	0	3	12	16	.300	.417	.400	.817	130	3	3	102	49	11	.932	5	1	1	-2	O	0.1
1982	StL-N	11	15	3	4	0	0	0	2	1	4	.267	.313	.267	.579	61	-1	-1	103	196	1	.583	2	0	1	-1	/O	0.0
1983	StL-N	6	3	1	0	0	0	0	0	0	0	.000	.000	.000	.000	-99	-1	-1	98	0	0	.000	0	0	0	-0	/O	0.0
	Mon-N	8	12	2	2	2	0	0	1	1	3	.167	.231	.333	.564	54	-1	-1	102	99	1	.500	0	0	0	-1	/O	-0.2
	Yr	14	15	3	2	2	0	0	1	1	3	.133	.188	.267	.454	24	-2	-2	100	56	1	.385	0	0	0	-2		-0.2
Total	3	48	90	17	24	8	0	0	6	14	23	.267	.365	.356	.721	102	1	1	102	76	14	.791	7	1	2	-5	/O	-0.1
■ **PHIL ROOF**	Roof, Phillip Anthony b: 3/5/41, Paducah, Ky. BR/TR, 6'2", 190 lbs. Deb: 4/29/61 C																											
1961	Mil-N	1	0	0	0	0	0	0	0	0	0	—	—	—	—	—	0	0	92	—	—	—	0	0	0	0	/C	0.0
1964	Mil-N	1	2	0	0	0	0	0	0	0	1	.000	.000	.000	.000	-99	-1	-1	97	0	0	.000	0	0	0	0	/C	0.0
1965	Cal-A	9	22	1	3	0	0	0	0	0	6	.136	.136	.136	.273	-23	-3	-3	98	0	0	.150	0	0	0	1	/C	-0.1
	Cle-A	43	52	3	9	1	0	0	3	5	13	.173	.259	.192	.451	31	-5	-5	98	124	3	.364	0	0	0	-2	C	-0.3
	Yr	52	74	4	12	1	0	0	3	5	19	.162	.225	.176	.401	16	-8	-8	98	103	3	.302	0	0	0	-1		-0.4
1966	KC-A	127	369	33	77	14	3	7	44	37	95	.209	.286	.320	.606	78	-12	-10	94	133	31	.513	2	5	-2	-1	*C/1	-0.7
1967	KC-A	114	327	23	67	14	5	6	24	23	85	.205	.268	.333	.601	77	-10	-10	100	79	30	.534	4	1	1	-9	*C	-1.2
1968	Oak-A	34	64	5	12	0	0	1	2	2	15	.188	.212	.234	.446	36	-5	-5	98	48	3	.333	1	0	0	-2	C	-0.5
1969	Oak-A	106	247	19	58	6	1	2	19	33	55	.235	.337	.291	.628	84	-6	-4	92	98	25	.561	1	0	0	-26	*C	-2.4
1970	Mil-A	110	321	39	73	7	1	13	37	32	72	.227	.307	.377	.684	89	-6	-5	98	94	36	.619	3	2	-0	-7	*C/1	-1.0
1971	Mil-A	41	114	6	22	2	1	1	10	8	28	.193	.252	.254	.506	42	-8	-9	103	128	7	.392	0	0	1	1	C	-0.6
	Min-A	31	87	6	21	4	0	0	6	8	18	.241	.305	.287	.593	66	-3	-4	104	98	6	.452	0	1	-1	-1	C	-0.3
	Yr	72	201	12	43	6	1	1	16	16	46	.214	.275	.269	.544	53	-12	-13	103	117	14	.430	0	1	-1	0		-0.9
1972	Min-A	61	146	16	30	11	1	3	12	6	27	.205	.237	.356	.593	70	-5	-6	107	82	12	.492	0	1	-1	-9	C	-1.7
1973	Min-A	47	117	10	23	4	1	1	15	13	27	.197	.277	.274	.550	53	-7	-7	104	168	9	.459	0	0	0	0	C	-0.5
1974	Min-A	44	97	10	19	1	0	2	13	6	24	.196	.257	.268	.525	51	-6	-6	101	160	6	.400	0	0	0	-2	C	-0.6
1975	Min-A	63	126	18	38	2	0	7	21	9	28	.302	.353	.484	.837	126	5	4	107	98	22	.789	0	0	0	-3	C	0.3
1976	Min-A	18	46	1	10	3	0	0	4	2	6	.217	.250	.283	.533	57	-3	-3	98	118	3	.405	0	0	0	1	C/D	0.0
	Chi-A	4	9	0	1	0	0	0	0	0	3	.111	.111	.111	.222	-35	-2	-1	99	0	0	.111	0	0	0	0	/C	-0.1
	Yr	22	55	1	11	3	0	0	4	2	9	.200	.228	.255	.483	42	-4	-4	98	102	3	.356	0	0	0	1		-0.1
1977	Tor-A	3	5	0	0	0	0	0	0	0	1	.000	.000	.000	.000	-97	-1	-1	103	0	0	.000	0	0	0	0	/C	0.0
Total	15	857	2151	190	463	69	13	43	210	184	504	.215	.284	.319	.604	73	-79	-76	99	106	206	.533	11	10	-3	-58	C/1D	-9.7
■ **GEORGE ROOKS**	Rooks, George Brinton Mc Clellan (born George Brinton Mc Clellan Ruckser) b: 10/21/1863, Chicago, Ill. d: 3/11/35, Chicago, Ill. BR/TR, 5'11", 170 lbs. Deb: 5/12/1891																											
1891	Bos-N	5	16	1	2	0	0	0	0	4	1	.125	.300	.125	.425	24	-1	-2	112	0	1	.429	0			0	/O	0.0
■ **ROLANDO ROOMES**	Roomes, Rolando Audley b: 2/15/62, Kingston, Jamaica BR/TR, 6'3", 180 lbs. Deb: 4/12/88																											
1988	Chi-N	17	16	3	3	0	0	0	0	0	4	.188	.188	.188	.375	8	-2	-2	104	0	0	.214	0	1	-1	-1	/O	-0.3
■ **FRANK ROONEY**	Rooney, Frank (born Frank Rovny) b: 10/12/1884, Podebrady, Bohemia (Austria-Hungary) d: 4/6/77, Bessemer, Mich. Deb: 4/18/14																											
1914	Ind-F	12	35	1	7	0	1	1	8	1	0	.200	.222	.343	.565	55	-2	-2	111	192	3	.536	2			0	/1	-0.2
■ **PAT ROONEY**	Rooney, Patrick Eugene b: 11/28/57, Chicago, Ill. BR/TR, 6'1", 190 lbs. Deb: 9/09/81																											
1981	Mon-N	4	5	0	0	0	0	0	0	0	3	.000	.000	.000	.000	-99	-1	-1	99	0	0	.000	0	0	0	-1	/O	-0.1
■ **JORGE ROQUE**	Roque, Jorge (Vargas) b: 4/28/50, Ponce, P.R. BR/TR, 5'10", 158 lbs. Deb: 9/04/70																											
1970	StL-N	5	1	2	0	0	0	0	0	0	1	.000	.500	.000	.500	43	0	0	106	0	0	1.000	0	0	0	-0	/O	0.0
1971	StL-N	3	10	2	3	0	0	0	1	0	3	.300	.300	.300	.600	70	-0	-0	101	136	1	.571	1	0	0	0	/O	0.0
1972	StL-N	32	67	3	7	2	1	1	5	6	19	.104	.178	.209	.387	9	-8	-8	105	121	2	.328	1	1	-0	-0	O	-1.0
1973	Mon-N	25	61	7	9	2	0	1	6	4	17	.148	.212	.230	.442	21	-7	-7	104	142	2	.375	2	2	-1	-2	O	-1.0
Total	4	65	139	14	19	4	1	2	12	10	40	.137	.205	.223	.428	19	-15	-16	104	129	6	.376	4	3	-1	-2	/O	-2.0
■ **LUIS ROSADO**	Rosado, Luis (Robles) b: 12/6/55, Santurce, P.R. BR/TR, 6', 180 lbs. Deb: 9/08/77																											
1977	NY-N	9	24	1	5	1	0	0	3	1	3	.208	.269	.250	.519	42	-2	-2	96	200	2	.400	0	0	0	0	/1C	-0.1
1980	NY-N	2	4	0	0	0	0	0	0	0	1	.000	.000	.000	.000	-99	-1	-1	96	0	0	.000	0	0	0	0	/1	0.0
Total	2	11	28	1	5	1	0	0	3	1	4	.179	.233	.214	.448	23	-3	-3	96	173	2	.333	0	0	0	0	/1C	-0.1
■ **BUDDY ROSAR**	Rosar, Warren Vincent b: 7/3/14, Buffalo, N.Y. BR/TR, 5'9", 190 lbs. Deb: 4/29/39																											
1939	NY-A	43	105	18	29	5	1	0	12	13	10	.276	.356	.343	.699	87	-3	-2	91	113	14	.671	4	0	1	0	C	0.2
1940	NY-A	73	228	34	68	11	3	4	37	19	11	.298	.357	.425	.783	104	1	1	99	123	36	.749	7	1	2	2	C	0.9
1941	NY-A	67	209	25	60	17	2	1	36	22	10	.287	.355	.402	.757	102	-0	1	98	147	29	.675	0	0	0	-3	C	0.1
1942	NY-A	69	209	18	48	10	0	2	34	17	20	.230	.288	.306	.594	67	-9	-9	99	171	17	.477	1	2	-1	1	C	-0.2
1943	Cle-A	115	382	53	108	17	1	1	41	33	12	.283	.340	.340	.680	110	-0	4	90	113	44	.566	0	4	-2	-0	*C	0.7
1944	Cle-A	99	331	29	87	9	3	0	30	34	17	.263	.339	.308	.647	85	-5	-5	100	106	37	.557	1	2	-1	-5	C	-0.4
1945	Phi-A	92	300	23	63	12	1	1	25	20	16	.210	.262	.267	.528	57	-18	-16	94	109	20	.414	2	1	0	-0	C	-1.0
1946	Phi-A	121	424	34	120	22	2	2	47	36	17	.283	.339	.358	.698	91	-3	-5	104	115	48	.578	1	3	-2	14	*C	1.3
1947	Phi-A	102	359	40	93	20	2	1	33	40	13	.259	.335	.334	.669	86	-6	-6	100	101	41	.579	1	3	-2	15	*C	1.6
1948	Phi-A	90	302	30	77	13	0	4	41	39	12	.255	.344	.338	.682	80	-7	-8	102	121	38	.622	0	2	-1	6	C	0.3
1949	Phi-A	32	95	7	19	2	0	0	6	16	5	.200	.315	.221	.536	44	-7	-7	99	98	8	.468	0	0	0	1	C	-0.3
1950	Bos-A	27	84	13	25	2	0	1	12	7	4	.298	.352	.357	.709	71	-2	-4	114	126	10	.597	0	0	0	-0	C	-0.2
1951	Bos-A	58	170	11	39	7	0	1	13	19	14	.229	.307	.288	.595	57	-9	-11	108	89	16	.507	0	0	0	-5	C	-1.1
Total	13	988	3198	335	836	147	15	18	367	315	161	.261	.330	.334	.663	84	-70	-68	99	117	358	.591	17	18	-6	25	C	1.9
■ **JIMMY ROSARIO**	Rosario, Angel Ramon b: 5/5/45, Bayamon, P.R. BB/TR, 5'11", 170 lbs. Deb: 4/08/71																											
1971	SF-N	92	192	26	43	6	1	0	13	33	35	.224	.341	.266	.606	74	-5	-5	100	104	20	.590	7	4	-0	3	O	-0.4
1972	SF-N	7	2	1	0	0	0	0	0	0	0	.000	.000	.000	.000	-99	-1	-1	100	0	0	.000	0	1	-1	-0	/O	-0.1
1976	Mil-A	15	37	4	7	0	0	1	5	3	8	.189	.250	.270	.520	53	-2	-2	99	148	2	.424	1	3	-2	-2	O/D	-0.5
Total	3	114	231	31	50	6	1	1	18	36	43	.216	.325	.264	.589	70	-8	-8	100	109	22	.561	8	8	-2	1	/OD	-1.0
■ **SANTIAGO ROSARIO**	Rosario, Santiago b: 7/25/39, Guayanilla, P.R. BL/TL, 5'11", 165 lbs. Deb: 6/23/65																											
1965	KC-A	81	85	8	20	3	0	2	8	6	16	.235	.293	.341	.635	82	-2	-2	97	95	8	.537	0	0	0	-1	1/O	-0.5
■ **PETE ROSE**	Rose, Peter Edward "Charlie Hustle" b: 4/14/41, Cincinnati, Ohio BB/TR, 5'11", 192 lbs. Deb: 4/08/63 M																											
1963	Cin-N	157	623	101	170	25	9	6	41	55	72	.273	.337	.371	.708	100	4	1	104	61	77	.639	13	15	-5	-21	*2/O	-1.6
1964	Cin-N	136	516	64	139	13	2	4	34	36	51	.269	.319	.326	.645	80	-12	-13	103	82	53	.534	4	10	-5	-8	*2	-1.6
1965	Cin-N	162	670	117	**209**	35	11	11	81	69	76	.312	.383	.446	.829	128	31	27	104	89	118	.810	8	3	1	-18	*2	1.9
1966	Cin-N	156	654	97	205	38	5	16	70	37	61	.313	.351	.460	.811	108	20	9	114	74	100	.730	4	9	-4	-12	*23	0.2
1967	Cin-N	148	585	86	176	32	8	12	76	56	66	.301	.365	.444	.809	120	23	17	109	94	95	.778	11	6	-0	-1	*O2	1.4
1968	Cin-N	149	626	94	**210**	42	6	10	49	56	76	**.335**	**.394**	.470	.863	142	45	37	111	55	**113**	.823	3	7	-3	10	*O/21	4.2
1969	Cin-N	156	627	**120**	218	33	11	16	82	88	65	**.348**	.432	.512	.944	165	56	57	99	77	138	.975	7	10	-4	8	*O/2	5.4
1970	Cin-N	159	649	120	**205**	37	9	15	52	73	64	.316	.387	.470	.857	123	27	23	104	51	121	.856	12	7	-1	3	*O	1.8
1971	Cin-N	160	632	86	192	27	4	13	44	68	50	.304	.374	.421	.795	130	22	24	96	52	100	.764	13	9	-2	2	*O	2.0

YEAR	TM/L	G	AB	R	H	2B	3B	HR	RBI	BB	SO	AVG	OBP	SLG	PRO	/A	BR	/A	PF	CHI	RC	TA	SB	CS	SBR	FR	POS	TPR
1972	Cin-N	154	645	107	**198**	31	11	6	57	73	46	.307	.383	.417	.801	137	25	30	93	70	109	.786	10	3	1	12	*O	3.8
1973	Cin-N	160	680	115	**230**	36	8	5	64	65	42	**.338**	.401	.437	.838	142	31	37	93	71	119	.803	10	7	-1	9	*O	3.8
1974	Cin-N	163	652	**110**	185	**45**	7	3	51	106	54	.284	.388	.388	.776	120	19	21	98	65	104	.762	2	4	-2	12	*O	2.6
1975	Cin-N	162	662	**112**	210	**47**	4	7	74	89	50	.317	.407	.432	.839	127	33	29	104	82	120	.828	0	1	-1	-25	*3O	0.2
1976	Cin-N	162	665	**130**	**215**	**42**	6	10	63	86	54	.323	.406	.450	.855	138	40	37	103	71	123	.847	9	5	-0	-12	*3/O	2.4
1977	Cin-N	162	655	95	204	38	7	9	64	66	42	.311	.379	.432	.811	117	17	17	100	79	111	.797	16	4	2	-17	*3	0.1
1978	Cin-N	159	655	103	198	**51**	3	7	52	62	30	.302	.365	.421	.787	116	17	15	103	61	102	.747	13	9	-2	-18	*3/O1	-0.5
1979	Phi-N	163	628	90	208	40	5	4	59	95	32	.331	.421	.430	.851	137	33	35	97	73	116	.862	20	11	-1	-3	*1/32	2.5
1980	Phi-N	162	655	95	185	**42**	1	1	64	66	33	.282	.354	.354	.708	91	0	-6	107	95	83	.644	12	8	-1	12	*1	-0.1
1981	Phi-N	107	431	73	**140**	18	5	0	33	46	26	**.325**	.394	.390	.784	110	15	9	112	68	67	.729	4	4	-1	9	*1	1.4
1982	Phi-N	162	634	80	172	25	4	3	54	66	32	.271	.347	.338	.684	98	-5	0	94	84	75	.612	8	8	-2	6	*1	-0.4
1983	Phi-N	151	493	52	121	14	3	0	45	52	28	.245	.320	.286	.606	68	-19	-20	101	126	46	.518	7	7	-2	-4	*1O	-3.3
1984	Mon-N	95	278	34	72	6	2	0	23	31	20	.259	.335	.295	.630	86	-7	-4	91	110	27	.530	1	1	-0	2	1O	-0.4
	Cin-N	26	96	9	35	9	0	0	11	9	7	.365	.430	.458	.888	142	7	6	106	100	20	.887	0	0	0	-2	1/M	0.4
	Yr	121	374	43	107	15	2	0	34	40	27	.286	.360	.337	.697	102	-0	2	94	109	49	.632	1	1	-0	-0		0.0
1985	Cin-N	119	405	60	107	12	2	2	46	86	35	.264	.398	.319	.716	98	7	4	105	144	59	.735	8	1	2	-1	*1/M	0.1
1986	Cin-N	72	237	15	52	8	2	0	25	30	31	.219	.317	.270	.587	61	-11	-12	104	156	23	.540	3	0	1	-3	1/M	-1.6
Total	24	3562	14053	2165	4256	746	135	160	1314	1566	1143	.303	.377	.409	.786	118	416	382	102	79	2220	.766	198	149	-30	-59	*O132	24.7
■ **JOHN ROSEBORO** Roseboro, John Junior b: 5/13/33, Ashland, Ohio BL/TR, 5'11.5", 190 lbs. Deb: 6/14/57 C																												
1957	Bro-N	35	69	6	10	2	0	2	6	10	20	.145	.253	.261	.514	33	-6	-8	116	104	5	.475	0	0	0	1	C/1	-0.5
1958	LA-N	114	384	52	104	11	9	14	43	36	56	.271	.336	.456	.792	102	3	1	105	83	58	.765	11	8	-2	-6	*C/O	-0.1
1959	LA-N	118	397	39	92	14	7	10	38	52	69	.232	.325	.378	.703	85	-7	-8	102	87	50	.669	7	5	-1	14	*C	1.2
1960	LA-N	103	287	22	61	15	3	8	42	44	53	.213	.325	.369	.695	78	-4	-9	115	131	37	.691	7	6	-2	3	C/13	-0.3
1961	LA-N	128	394	59	99	16	6	18	59	56	62	.251	.350	.459	.810	110	7	6	102	101	67	.823	6	4	-1	2	*C	1.7
1962	LA-N	128	389	45	97	16	7	7	55	50	60	.249	.345	.380	.726	102	-2	2	93	128	54	.716	12	3	2	-6	*C	0.0
1963	LA-N	135	470	50	111	13	7	9	49	36	50	.236	.295	.351	.646	90	-9	-7	95	109	48	.564	7	6	-2	2	*C	-0.1
1964	LA-N	134	414	42	119	24	1	3	45	44	61	.287	.361	.372	.733	116	5	9	92	113	57	.672	3	3	-1	-15	*C	-0.1
1965	LA-N	136	437	42	102	10	0	8	57	34	51	.233	.292	.311	.603	76	-17	-13	91	148	39	.500	1	6	-3	-4	*C/3	-1.5
1966	LA-N	142	445	47	123	23	2	9	53	44	51	.276	.346	.398	.743	109	4	6	97	109	60	.678	3	2	-0	3	*C	1.2
1967	LA-N	116	334	37	91	18	2	4	24	38	33	.272	.350	.374	.725	122	4	9	88	73	43	.655	2	4	-2	-8	*C	0.6
1968	Min-A	135	380	31	82	12	0	8	39	46	57	.216	.304	.311	.614	81	-6	-8	106	118	37	.545	2	3	-1	-6	*C	-1.1
1969	Min-A	115	361	33	95	12	0	3	32	39	44	.263	.335	.321	.656	83	-7	-8	102	103	39	.578	5	5	-2	-8	*C	-1.0
1970	Was-A	46	86	7	20	4	0	1	6	18	10	.233	.365	.314	.679	93	-1	-0	96	81	11	.676	1	1	-0	-3	C	-0.2
Total	14	1585	4847	512	1206	190	44	104	548	547	677	.249	.329	.371	.700	95	-34	-27	99	108	604	.661	67	56	-14	-30	*C/1O3	-0.2
■ **BOB ROSELLI** Roselli, Robert Edward b: 12/10/31, San Francisco, Cal BR/TR, 5'11", 185 lbs. Deb: 8/16/55																												
1955	Mil-N	6	9	1	2	1	0	0	0	1	4	.222	.364	.333	.697	93	-0	-0	93	0	1	.714	0	0	0	0	/C	0.0
1956	Mil-N	4	2	1	1	0	0	1	1	0	1	.500	.500	2.000	2.500	536	1	1	99	60	2	4.000	0	0	0	0	/C	0.1
1958	Mil-N	1	1	0	0	0	0	0	0	0	0	.000	.000	.000	.000	-99	-0	-0	89	0	0	.000	0	0	0	0	H	0.0
1961	Chi-A	22	38	2	10	3	0	0	4	0	11	.263	.263	.342	.605	61	-2	-2	99	120	3	.448	0	0	0	0	C	-0.1
1962	Chi-A	35	64	4	12	3	1	1	5	11	15	.188	.316	.313	.628	74	-3	-2	95	86	7	.623	1	0	0	-1	C	0.0
Total	5	68	114	8	25	7	1	2	10	12	31	.219	.305	.351	.656	78	-4	-3	96	88	13	.611	1	0	0	-0	/C	0.0
■ **DAVE ROSELLO** Rosello, David (Rodriguez) b: 6/26/50, Mayaguez, P.R. BR/TR, 5'11", 160 lbs. Deb: 9/10/72																												
1972	Chi-N	5	12	2	3	0	0	1	3	3	2	.250	.400	.500	.900	135	1	1	114	137	3	1.000	0	0	0	1	/S	0.2
1973	Chi-N	16	38	4	10	2	0	0	2	2	4	.263	.300	.316	.616	65	-2	-2	108	67	2	.485	2	2	-1	1	2/S	0.0
1974	Chi-N	62	148	9	30	7	0	0	10	10	28	.203	.253	.250	.503	41	-12	-12	100	104	10	.403	1	1	-0	-3	2S	-1.1
1975	Chi-N	19	58	7	15	2	0	1	8	9	8	.259	.358	.345	.703	92	-0	-0	104	134	7	.644	0	1	-1	0	S	0.2
1976	Chi-N	91	227	27	55	5	1	1	11	41	33	.242	.361	.286	.647	78	-2	-5	109	62	25	.607	1	2	-1	0	S/2	0.2
1977	Chi-N	56	82	18	18	2	1	1	9	12	12	.220	.319	.305	.624	60	-3	-5	114	129	9	.569	0	0	0	0	3S/2	-0.2
1979	Cle-A	59	107	20	26	6	1	3	14	15	27	.243	.336	.402	.738	93	-0	-1	106	103	16	.711	1	0	0	-1	23S	0.1
1980	Cle-A	71	117	16	29	3	0	2	12	9	19	.248	.302	.325	.626	70	-5	-5	102	106	12	.522	0	0	0	-3	23/SD	-0.5
1981	Cle-A	43	84	11	20	4	0	1	7	7	12	.238	.297	.321	.618	84	-2	-2	93	91	8	.507	0	1	-1	-3	2/3SD	-0.4
Total	9	422	873	114	206	31	3	10	76	108	145	.236	.321	.313	.633	73	-25	-31	105	95	92	.572	5	7	-3	-8	2S/3D	-1.5
■ **CHIEF ROSEMAN** Roseman, James John b: 1856, New York, N.Y. d: 7/4/38, Brooklyn, N.Y. BR/TR, 5'7", 167 lbs. Deb: 5/01/1882 M																												
1882	Tro-N	82	331	41	78	21	6	1	29	3	41	.236	.243	.344	.587	90	-5	-3	95	88	28	.462				-6	*O	-0.8
1883	NY-a	93	398	48	100	13	6	0		11		.251	.271	.314	.585	82	-5	-10	108	0	35	.456				-7	*O/1	-1.3
1884	NY-a	107	436	97	130	16	11	4		21		.298	.339	.413	.752	147	22	22	100	0	63	.676				-3	*O	1.6
1885	NY-a	101	410	72	114	13	15	3		25		.278	.335	.405	.740	162	17	27	84	0	57	.679				-8	*O/P	1.2
1886	NY-a	134	559	90	127	19	10	5		24		.227	.269	.324	.593	84	-9	-12	104	0	52	.507	6			-3	*O/P	-1.7
1887	Phi-a	21	73	16	16	2	1	0		10		.219	.352	.274	.626	79	-1	-1	99	0	8	.667	3			0	O	0.0
	NY-a	60	241	30	55	10	1	0		9		.228	.265	.278	.543	61	-15	-10	88	0	19	.441	3			-3	O/1P	-1.2
	Bro-a	1	3	2	1	0	0	0		0		.333	.500	.333	.833	140	0	0	99	0	1	1.000	0			0	/O	0.0
	Yr	82	317	48	72	12	2	0		19		.227	.290	.278	.567	67	-16	-11	91	0	28	.498	6			-3		-1.2
1890	StL-a	80	302	47	103	26	0	2		30		.341	.447	.447	.894	144	28	20	116	0	65	1.005	7			-10	O1M	0.6
	Lou-a	2	8	0	2	0	0	0		0		.250	.250	.250	.500	46	-1	-1	107	0	1	.333	0			0	/1	0.0
	Yr	82	310	47	105	26	0	2	0	30		.339	.443	.442	.885	142	28	19	116	0	65	.985	7			-10		0.6
Total	7	681	2761	443	726	120	50	15	29	133	41	.263	.311	.359	.670	110	30	32	100	10	328	.592	19			-40	O/1P	-1.6
■ **AL ROSEN** Rosen, Albert Leonard "Flip" b: 2/29/24, Spartanburg, S.C. BR/TR, 5'10.5", 180 lbs. Deb: 9/10/47																												
1947	Cle-A	7	9	1	1	0	0	0	0	0	3	.111	.111	.111	.222	-40	-2	-2	96	0	0	.125	0	0	0	1	/3O	0.0
1948	Cle-A	5	5	0	1	0	0	0	0	0	2	.200	.200	.200	.400	7	-1	-1	99	0	0	.200	0	0	0	0	/3	0.0
1949	Cle-A	23	44	3	7	2	0	0	5	7	4	.159	.275	.205	.479	28	-5	-4	98	190	3	.410	0	1	-1	-0	3	-0.4
1950	Cle-A	155	554	100	159	23	4	**37**	116	100	72	.287	.405	.543	.948	144	34	36	98	103	120	.970	5	7	-3	0	*3	2.5
1951	Cle-A	154	573	82	152	30	1	24	102	85	71	.265	.362	.447	.809	125	14	18	95	118	96	.795	7	5	-1	-15	*3	-0.2
1952	Cle-A	148	567	101	171	32	5	28	**105**	75	54	.302	.387	.524	.911	167	39	**45**	91	109	115	.914	8	6	-1	-19	*3/1S	2.6
1953	Cle-A	155	599	**115**	201	27	5	**43**	**145**	85	48	.336	.422	**.613**	**1.034**	**185**	**63**	**67**	95	104	**155**	**1.094**	8	7	-2	0	*3/1S	**5.7**
1954	Cle-A	137	466	76	140	20	2	24	102	85	43	.300	.412	.506	.918	142	34	30	106	128	100	.965	6	2	1	-13	31/2S	1.2
1955	Cle-A	139	492	61	120	13	1	21	81	92	44	.244	.367	.402	.770	103	7	4	104	123	76	.768	4	2	0	-4	*31	0.0
1956	Cle-A	121	416	64	111	18	2	15	61	58	44	.267	.357	.428	.784	105	4	3	101	104	62	.738	1	3	-2	-13	*3	-0.7
Total	10	1044	3725	603	1063	165	20	192	717	587	385	.285	.386	.495	.882	138	188	197	98	113	729	.922	39	33	-8	-62	3/1S2O	10.7
■ **GOODY ROSEN** Rosen, Goodwin George b: 8/28/12, Toronto, Ont., Can. BL/TL, 5'10", 155 lbs. Deb: 9/14/37																												
1937	Bro-N	22	77	10	24	5	1	0	6	6	6	.312	.361	.403	.764	103	1	0	104	70	12	.736	2			1	O	0.1
1938	Bro-N	138	473	75	133	17	11	4	51	65	43	.281	.368	.389	.757	113	7	10	96	96	74	.722	0			2	*O	0.9
1939	Bro-N	54	183	22	46	6	4	1	12	23	21	.251	.335	.344	.679	77	-4	-6	107	68	23	.652	4			-1	O	-0.7
1944	Bro-N	89	264	38	69	8	3	0	23	26	27	.261	.330	.314	.644	83	-6	-5	99	99	29	.558	0			10	O	0.0
1945	Bro-N	145	606	126	197	24	11	12	75	50	36	.325	.379	.460	.840	139	26	29	96	79	110	.814	4			-3	*O	2.0
1946	Bro-N	3	3	0	1	0	0	0	0	0	1	.333	.333	.333	.667	87	-0	-0	103	0	0	.500	0			-0	/O	0.0
	NY-N	100	310	39	87	11	4	5	30	48	32	.281	.377	.390	.767	116	9	8	102	82	47	.734	2			-5	O	0.1
	Yr	103	313	39	88	11	4	5	30	48	33	.281	.377	.390	.767	116	8	8	102	80	47	.732	2			-5		0.1
Total	6	551	1916	310	557	71	34	22	197	218	166	.291	.364	.398	.762	113	32	36	99	85	295	.728	12			3	O	2.4
■ **HARRY ROSENBERG** Rosenberg, Harry b: 6/22/09, San Francisco, Cal. BR/TR, 5'10", 180 lbs. Deb: 7/15/30																												
1930	NY-N	9	5	1	0	0	0	0	0	1	4	.000	.167	.000	.167	-56	-1	-1	98	0	0	.200	0			-1	/O	-0.1

YEAR	TM/L	G	AB	R	H	2B	3B	HR	RBI	BB	SO	AVG	OBP	SLG	PRO	/A	BR	/A	PF	CHI	RC	TA	SB	CS	SBR	FR	POS	TPR
■ **LOU ROSENBERG** Rosenberg, Louis C. b: 3/5/03, San Francisco, Cal. BR/TR, 5'7", 155 lbs. Deb: 5/22/23																												
1923	Chi-A	3	4	0	1	0	0	0	0	0	1	.250	.250	.250	.500	32	-0	-0	98	0	0	.250	0	1	-1	0	/2	0.0
■ **MAX ROSENFELD** Rosenfeld, Max b: 12/23/02, New York, N.Y. d: 3/10/69, Miami, Fla. BR/TR, 5'8", 175 lbs. Deb: 4/21/31																												
1931	Bro-N	3	9	0	2	1	0	0	0	1	1	.222	.300	.333	.633	69	-0	-0	101	0	1	.571	0			-0	/O	0.0
1932	Bro-N	34	39	8	14	3	0	2	7	0	10	.359	.359	.590	.949	156	2	3	96	90	8	1.000	2			-9	O	-0.7
1933	Bro-N	5	9	0	1	0	0	0	0	1	1	.111	.200	.111	.311	-10	-1	-1	97	0	0	.222	0			0	/O	0.0
Total	3	42	57	8	17	4	0	2	7	2	12	.298	.322	.474	.796	116	1	1	97	59	9	.756	2			-8	/O	-0.7
■ **LARRY ROSENTHAL** Rosenthal, Lawrence John b: 5/21/12, St.Paul, Minn. BL/TL, 6'0.5", 190 lbs. Deb: 6/20/36																												
1936	Chi-A	85	317	71	89	15	8	3	46	59	37	.281	.394	.407	.801	99	1	1	99	114	55	.833	2	0	1	3	O	0.2
1937	Chi-A	58	97	20	28	5	3	0	9	9	20	.289	.355	.402	.757	88	-1	-2	103	79	14	.725	1	0	0	-1	O	-0.2
1938	Chi-A	61	105	14	30	5	1	1	12	12	13	.286	.359	.381	.740	87	-2	-2	98	94	15	.684	0	1	-1	-0	O	-0.1
1939	Chi-A	107	324	50	86	21	5	10	51	53	46	.265	.369	.454	.822	102	5	1	107	97	58	.841	6	4	-1	-3	O	-0.4
1940	Chi-A	107	276	46	83	14	5	6	42	64	32	.301	.432	.453	.885	125	15	14	104	106	61	.960	2	3	-1	-3	O	0.3
1941	Chi-A	20	59	9	14	4	0	0	1	12	5	.237	.366	.305	.671	85	-1	-1	94	20	7	.625	0	0	0	-2	O	-0.3
	Cle-A	45	75	10	14	3	1	1	8	9	10	.187	.274	.293	.567	50	-6	-6	101	113	7	.516	1	0	0	1	O/1	-0.4
	Yr	65	134	19	28	7	1	1	9	21	15	.209	.316	.299	.615	64	-7	-7	98	85	15	.579	1	0	0	-1		-0.7
1944	NY-A	36	101	9	20	3	0	0	9	19	15	.198	.325	.228	.553	56	-5	-5	106	141	9	.524	1	0	0	2	O	-0.3
	Phi-A	32	54	5	11	2	0	1	6	5	9	.204	.271	.296	.567	61	-3	-3	101	114	5	.488	0	0	0	-5	O	-0.8
	Yr	68	155	14	31	5	0	1	15	24	24	.200	.307	.252	.559	58	-7	-8	104	130	15	.516	1	0	0	-3		-1.1
1945	Phi-A	28	75	6	15	3	2	0	5	9	8	.200	.286	.293	.579	73	-3	-2	94	82	7	.508	0	1	-1	-3	O	-0.6
Total	8	579	1483	240	390	75	25	22	189	251	195	.263	.370	.392	.762	95	-0	-5	102	102	237	.768	13	9	-2	-10	O/1	-2.6
■ **SI ROSENTHAL** Rosenthal, Simon b: 11/13/03, Boston, Mass. d: 4/7/69, Boston, Mass. BL/TL, 5'9", 165 lbs. Deb: 9/08/25																												
1925	Bos-A	19	72	6	19	5	2	0	8	7	3	.264	.329	.389	.718	86	-2	-2	95	97	10	.679	1	0	0	-1	O	-0.2
1926	Bos-A	104	285	34	76	12	3	4	34	19	18	.267	.317	.372	.689	78	-9	-10	101	98	34	.624	4	1	1	-15	O	-2.8
Total	2	123	357	40	95	17	5	4	42	26	21	.266	.319	.375	.695	80	-12	-12	100	98	44	.635	5	1	1	-16	/O	-3.0
■ **BUNNY ROSER** Roser, John William Joseph "Jack" b: 11/15/01, St.Louis, Mo. d: 5/6/79, Rocky Hill, Conn. BL/TL, 5'11", 175 lbs. Deb: 8/24/22																												
1922	Bos-N	32	113	13	27	3	4	0	16	10	19	.239	.306	.336	.643	70	-6	-5	94	156	12	.586	2	1	0	-3	O	-0.8
■ **CHET ROSS** Ross, Chester James b: 4/1/17, Buffalo, N.Y. BR/TR, 6'1", 195 lbs. Deb: 9/15/39																												
1939	Bos-N	11	31	4	10	1	1	0	0	2	10	.323	.364	.419	.783	120	0	1	92	0	5	.714	0			1	/O	0.2
1940	Bos-N	149	569	84	160	23	14	17	89	59	127	.281	.352	.460	.812	124	17	17	99	112	96	.792	4			6	*O	1.8
1941	Bos-N	29	50	1	6	1	0	0	4	9	17	.120	.254	.140	.394	14	-6	-5	93	206	2	.348	0			-1	O	-0.6
1942	Bos-N	76	220	20	43	7	2	5	19	16	37	.195	.250	.314	.564	67	-11	-10	95	84	17	.470	0			-0	O	-1.1
1943	Bos-N	94	285	27	62	12	2	7	32	26	67	.218	.285	.347	.633	78	-7	-9	106	96	28	.552	1			0	O	-1.1
1944	Bos-N	54	154	20	35	9	2	5	26	12	23	.227	.287	.409	.697	100	-2	-1	95	120	18	.631	1			3	O	0.0
Total	6	413	1309	156	316	53	21	34	170	124	281	.241	.309	.392	.701	98	-8	-6	99	106	166	.651	6			9	O	-0.8
■ **DON ROSS** Ross, Donald Raymond b: 7/16/14, Pasadena, Cal. BR/TR, 6'1", 185 lbs. Deb: 4/19/38																												
1938	Det-A	77	265	22	69	7	1	1	30	29	11	.260	.333	.306	.639	61	-15	-15	100	121	29	.566	1	0	0	6	3	-0.5
1940	Bro-N	10	38	4	11	2	0	1	8	3	3	.289	.341	.421	.763	101	0	0	108	159	6	.741	1			-1	3	0.0
1942	Det-A	87	226	29	62	10	2	3	30	36	16	.274	.379	.376	.755	100	5	1	113	112	34	.727	2	1	0	-2	O3	-0.2
1943	Det-A	89	247	19	66	13	0	0	18	20	3	.267	.325	.320	.644	84	-3	-5	106	83	27	.545	2	0	1	-5	OS/23	-1.0
1944	Det-A	66	167	14	35	5	0	2	15	14	9	.210	.275	.275	.550	55	-9	-10	105	104	13	.457	2	1	0	-4	O/S1	-1.5
1945	Det-A	8	29	3	11	4	0	0	4	5	1	.379	.471	.517	.988	176	3	3	106	102	8	1.158	2	0	1	-0	/3	0.4
	Cle-A	106	363	26	95	15	1	2	43	42	15	.262	.340	.325	.665	95	-2	-2	99	128	41	.571	0	4	-2	-13	*3	-1.5
	Yr	114	392	29	106	19	1	2	47	47	16	.270	.350	.339	.689	101	1	2	99	127	48	.610	2	4	-2	-13		-1.1
1946	Cle-A	55	153	12	41	7	0	3	14	17	12	.268	.341	.373	.714	112	-0	2	89	81	20	.643	4	0	0	-3	3/O	0.2
Total	7	498	1488	129	390	63	4	12	162	166	70	.262	.338	.334	.672	86	-22	-26	102	110	177	.612	10	6		-22	3O/S21	-4.1
■ **JOE ROSSI** Rossi, Joseph Anthony b: 3/13/23, Oakland, Cal. BR/TR, 6'1", 205 lbs. Deb: 4/20/52																												
1952	Cin-N	55	145	14	32	0	1	1	6	20	20	.221	.319	.255	.574	61	-7	-7	100	58	13	.509	1	0	0	1	C	-0.4
■ **CLAUDE ROSSMAN** Rossman, Claude R. b: 6/17/1881, Philmont, N.Y. d: 1/16/28, Poughkeepsie, N.Y. BL/TL, 6', Deb: 9/16/04																												
1904	Cle-A	18	62	5	13	5	0	0	6	0		.210	.210	.290	.500	58	-3	-3	102	124	4	.367	0			1	O	-0.3
1906	Cle-A	118	396	49	122	13	2	1	53	17		.308	.337	.359	.695	116	8	7	103	133	53	.620	11			-4	*1/O	0.0
1907	Det-A	153	571	60	158	21	8	0	69	33		.277	.316	.342	.658	110	7	6	102	134	70	.600	20			-13	*1	-0.9
1908	Det-A	138	524	45	154	33	13	2	71	27		.294	.328	.418	.746	143	23	23	101	126	72	.686	8			5	*1	2.7
1909	Det-A	82	287	16	75	8	3	0	39	13		.261	.293	.310	.603	82	-4	-7	110	172	28	.528	10			-2	1	-1.0
	StL-A	2	8	0	1	0	0	0	0	0		.125	.125	.125	.250	-23	-1	-1	92	0	0	.143	0			0	/O	0.0
	Yr	84	295	16	76	8	3	0	39	13		.258	.289	.305	.594	80	-5	-8	110	170	28	.516	10			-2		-1.0
Total	5	511	1848	175	523	80	26	3	238	90		.283	.316	.359	.676	113	30	24	103	136	226	.606	49			-13	1/O	0.5
■ **FRANK ROTH** Roth, Francis Charles b: 10/11/1878, Chicago, Ill. d: 3/27/55, Burlington, Wis. BR/TR, 5'10", 160 lbs. Deb: 4/18/03 C																												
1903	Phi-N	68	220	27	60	11	4	0	22	9		.273	.301	.359	.660	97	-4	-1	92	90	25	.569	3			3	C/3	0.6
1904	Phi-N	81	229	28	59	8	1	1	20	12		.258	.295	.314	.609	97	-3	-1	93	98	24	.541	8			2	C/12	0.7
1905	StL-A	35	107	9	25	3	0	0	7	6		.234	.274	.262	.536	79	-3	-2	91	89	8	.427	1			2	C	0.3
1906	Chi-A	16	51	4	10	1	1	0	7	3		.196	.241	.255	.496	62	-3	-2	92	196	3	.415	1			-2	C	-0.2
1909	Cin-N	56	147	12	35	7	2	0	16	6		.238	.287	.313	.600	93	-3	-2	94	127	14	.545	5			-4	C	-0.1
1910	Cin-N	26	29	3	7	2	0	0	3	0	2	.241	.267	.310	.577	67	-1	-1	101	116	3	.500	1			0	/C1	0.0
Total	6	282	783	83	196	32	8	1	75	36	2	.250	.288	.315	.603	91	-16	-9	93	107	78	.523	19			2	C/123	1.3
■ **BRAGGO ROTH** Roth, Robert Frank b: 8/28/1892, Burlington, Wis. d: 9/11/36, Chicago, Ill. BR/TR, 5'7.5", 170 lbs. Deb: 9/01/14																												
1914	Chi-A	34	126	14	37	4	6	1	10	8	25	.294	.355	.444	.800	136	6	5	103	67	20	.772	3	3	-1	0	O	0.3
1915	Chi-A	70	240	44	60	6	10	3	35	29	50	.250	.338	.396	.734	122	5	6	98	117	34	.747	12	6	0	-6	3O	0.0
	Cle-A	39	144	23	43	4	7	4	20	22	22	.299	.399	.507	.906	165	12	12	104	71	32	1.057	14	4	2	-3	O	0.8
	Yr	109	384	67	103	10	17	**7**	55	51	72	.268	.361	.438	.799	139	18	18	100	101	66	.859	26	10	2	-9		0.8
1916	Cle-A	125	409	50	117	19	7	4	72	38	48	.286	.350	.396	.746	124	11	11	100	151	62	.755	29	14	0	-5	*O	0.0
1917	Cle-A	145	495	69	141	30	9	1	72	52	73	.285	.355	.388	.743	111	15	7	114	135	82	.839	51			-8	*O	-0.8
1918	Cle-A	106	375	53	106	21	12	1	59	53	41	.283	.383	.411	.794	129	19	15	108	145	69	.929	35			-9	*O	0.1
1919	Phi-A	48	195	33	63	13	8	5	29	15	21	.323	.377	.549	.926	150	14	12	106	76	42	1.023	11			-7	O	0.2
	Bos-A	63	227	32	58	9	4	0	23	24	32	.256	.337	.330	.668	96	-3	-1	91	118	27	.663	9			-6	O	-1.0
	Yr	111	422	65	121	22	12	5	52	39	53	.287	.355	.431	.787	123	11	12	98	100	68	.821	20			-13		-0.8
1920	Was-A	138	468	80	136	23	8	9	92	75	57	.291	.395	.432	.827	125	15	19	95	144	85	.892	24	12	0	-15	*O	-0.7
1921	NY-A	43	152	29	43	9	2	2	10	19	20	.283	.370	.408	.778	96	-0	-1	103	51	24	.757	1	2	-1	-4	O	-0.7
Total	8	811	2831	427	804	138	73	30	422	335	389	.284	.367	.416	.783	123	94	86	103	122	477	.840	189	41		-61	O/3	-1.8
■ **BOB ROTHEL** Rothel, Robert Burton b: 9/17/23, Columbia Station Ohio d: 3/21/84, Huron, Ohio BR/TR, 5'10.5", 170 lbs. Deb: 4/22/45																												
1945	Cle-A	4	10	0	2	0	0	0	0	3	1	.200	.385	.200	.585	73	-0	-0	99	0	1	.556	0	0	0	-0	/3	0.0
■ **BOBBY ROTHERMEL** Rothermel, Edward Hill b: 12/18/1870, Fleetwood, Pa. d: 2/11/27, Detroit, Mich. Deb: 6/18/1899																												
1899	Bal-N	10	21	1	2	0	0	0	3	1		.095	.136	.095	.232	-33	-4	-4	108	460	0	.158	0			0	/23S	-0.3
■ **JACK ROTHFUSS** Rothfuss, John Albert b: 4/18/1872, Newark, N.J. d: 4/20/47, Basking Ridge, N.J 5'11.5", 195 lbs. Deb: 8/02/1897																												
1897	Pit-N	35	115	20	36	3	1	2	18	5		.313	.352	.409	.761	105	0	1	98	99	18	.722	3			0	1	0.1
■ **CLAUDE ROTHGEB** Rothgeb, Claude James b: 1/1/1880, Milford, Ill. d: 7/6/44, Manitowoc, Wis. BB, 6'0.5", 200 lbs. Deb: 6/17/05																												
1905	Was-A	7	16	2	2	0	0	0	0	0		.125	.125	.125	.250	-19	-2	-2	104	0	0	.214	1			0	/O	-0.1

YEAR	TM/L	G	AB	R	H	2B	3B	HR	RBI	BB	SO	AVG	OBP	SLG	PRO	/A	BR	/A	PF	CHI	RC	TA	SB	CS	SBR	FR	POS	TPR
■ **JACK ROTHROCK** Rothrock, John Houston b: 3/14/05, Long Beach, Cal. d: 2/2/80, San Bernardino, Cal BB/TR, 5'11.5", 165 lbs. Deb: 7/28/25																												
1925	Bos-A	22	55	6	19	3	3	0	7	3	7	.345	.379	.509	.888	130	2	2	95	84	10	.861	0	0	0	0	S	0.5
1926	Bos-A	15	17	3	5	1	0	0	2	3	1	.294	.400	.353	.753	97	0	0	101	113	3	.750	0	0	0	0	/S	0.0
1927	Bos-A	117	428	61	111	24	8	1	36	24	46	.259	.302	.360	.662	75	-19	-16	95	78	45	.584	5	0	2	3	S231	-0.6
1928	Bos-A	117	344	52	92	9	4	3	22	33	40	.267	.333	.343	.676	79	-11	-10	98	59	41	.636	12	6	0	-6	O31S/2PC	-1.7
1929	Bos-A	143	473	70	142	19	7	6	59	43	47	.300	.361	.408	.769	96	-1	-3	102	98	70	.759	23	13	-1	-2	*O	-0.9
1930	Bos-A	45	65	4	18	3	1	0	4	2	9	.277	.299	.354	.652	70	-4	-3	93	58	6	.510	0	2	-1	0	/O3	-0.3
1931	Bos-A	133	475	81	132	32	3	4	42	47	48	.278	.343	.383	.726	97	-6	-2	94	73	64	.691	13	7	-0	-1	O2/13S	-0.6
1932	Bos-A	12	48	3	10	1	0	0	0	5	5	.208	.283	.229	.512	35	-5	-4	97	0	4	.500	3	0	1	2	O	-0.1
	Chi-A	39	64	8	12	2	1	0	6	5	9	.188	.246	.250	.496	33	-7	-6	87	126	4	.423	1	0	0	-8	O/31	-1.2
	Yr	51	112	11	22	3	1	0	6	10	14	.196	.262	.241	.503	35	-11	-10	90	96	8	.456	4	0	1	-7		-1.3
1934	StL-N	154	647	106	184	35	3	11	72	49	56	.284	.336	.399	.734	84	-4	-16	114	79	91	.678	10			4	*O/2	-1.8
1935	StL-N	129	502	76	137	18	5	3	56	57	29	.273	.347	.347	.694	84	-8	-10	104	106	66	.642	7			-2	*O	-1.7
1937	Phi-A	88	232	28	62	15	0	0	21	28	15	.267	.346	.332	.678	76	-9	-7	94	93	28	.624	1	0	0	-2	O/2	-0.9
Total	11	1014	3350	498	924	162	35	28	327	299	312	.276	.336	.370	.706	84	-72	-75	101	83	433	.660	75	28		-12	O/S231CP	-9.3
■ **EDD ROUSH** Roush, Edd J b: 5/8/1893, Oakland City, Ind. d: 3/21/88, Bradenton, Fla. BL/TL, 5'11", 170 lbs. Deb: 8/20/13 CH																												
1913	Chi-A	9	10	2	1	0	0	0	0	0	2	.100	.100	.100	.200	-44	-2	-2	95	0	0	.111	0			-0	/O	-0.1
1914	Ind-F	74	166	26	54	8	4	1	30	6	20	.325	.349	.440	.789	113	5	2	111	142	32	.813	12			2	O/1	0.2
1915	New-F	145	551	73	164	20	11	3	60	38	25	.298	.343	.390	.733	124	10	14	94	102	88	.726	28			2	*O	1.0
1916	NY-N	39	69	4	13	0	1	0	5	1	4	.188	.200	.217	.417	29	-6	-6	96	132	4	.357	4			-1	O	-0.8
	Cin-N	69	272	34	78	7	14	0	15	13	19	.287	.336	.415	.751	133	9	10	98	51	43	.763	15			3	O	1.2
	Yr	108	341	38	91	7	15	0	20	14	23	.267	.309	.375	.685	113	3	4	97	81	46	.672	19			2		0.4
1917	Cin-N	136	522	82	178	19	14	4	67	27	24	**.341**	.379	.454	.833	**168**	32	37	92	100	94	.843	21			-2	*O	3.4
1918	Cin-N	113	435	61	145	18	10	5	62	22	10	.333	.368	**.455**	**.823**	**155**	24	26	97	97	80	**.848**	24			4	*O	2.6
1919	Cin-N	133	504	73	162	19	13	3	71	42	19	**.321**	.380	.429	.809	136	27	24	105	118	87	.830	20			5	*O	2.6
1920	Cin-N	149	579	81	196	22	16	4	90	42	22	.339	.386	.453	.839	156	30	37	90	122	98	.843	36	24	-4	12	*O1/2	3.9
1921	Cin-N	112	418	68	147	27	12	4	71	31	8	.352	.403	.502	.905	137	23	23	101	124	80	.920	19	17	-5	-2	*O	1.1
1922	Cin-N	49	165	29	58	7	4	1	24	19	5	.352	.428	.461	.888	135	8	9	96	108	33	.936	5	3	-0	3	O	0.9
1923	Cin-N	138	527	88	185	**41**	18	6	88	46	16	.351	.406	.531	.938	149	34	36	98	110	109	.950	10	15	-6	-7	*O	1.7
1924	Cin-N	121	483	67	168	23	**21**	3	72	22	11	.348	.376	.501	.877	132	21	21	101	111	86	.857	17	13	-3	-7	*O	0.9
1925	Cin-N	134	540	91	183	28	16	8	83	35	14	.339	.383	.494	.878	126	18	20	97	98	97	.870	22	20	-5	-2	*O	0.8
1926	Cin-N	144	563	95	182	37	10	7	79	38	17	.323	.366	.462	.828	128	16	20	95	103	92	.803	8			-6	*O/1	0.8
1927	NY-N	140	570	83	173	27	4	7	58	26	15	.304	.335	.402	.737	97	-4	-4	100	86	74	.690	18			-8	*O	-1.7
1928	NY-N	46	163	20	41	5	3	2	13	14	8	.252	.315	.356	.670	73	-6	-7	102	72	18	.607	1			5	O	-0.2
1929	NY-N	115	450	76	146	19	7	8	52	45	16	.324	.390	.451	.841	108	6	6	100	83	78	.845	6			-4	*O	-0.6
1931	Cin-N	101	376	46	102	12	5	1	41	17	5	.271	.308	.338	.646	77	-14	-12	95	115	40	.544	2			-2	O	-1.7
Total	18	1967	7363	1099	2376	339	183	67	981	484	260	.323	.368	.446	.814	127	231	254	98	103	1233	.803	268	92		-5	*O/12	16.0
■ **PHIL ROUTCLIFFE** Routcliffe, Philip John "Chicken" b: 10/24/1870, Oswego, N.Y. d: 10/4/18, Oswego, N.Y. 6', 175 lbs. Deb: 4/21/1890																												
1890	Pit-N	1	4	1	1	0	0	0	1	0	0	.250	.400	.250	.650	106	0	0	88	261	1	1.000	1			0	/O	0.0
■ **DAVE ROWAN** Rowan, David (born David Drohan) b: 12/6/1882, Elora, Ont., Canada d: 7/30/55, Toronto, Ont., Can BL/TL, 5'11", 175 lbs. Deb: 5/27/11																												
1911	StL-A	18	65	7	25	1	1	0	11	4		.385	.420	.431	.851	145	3	4	95	135	12	.800	0			-1	1	0.3
■ **WADE ROWDON** Rowdon, Wade Lee b: 9/7/60, Riverhead, N.Y. BR/TR, 6'2", 170 lbs. Deb: 9/08/84																												
1984	Cin-N	4	7	0	2	0	0	0	0	0	1	.286	.286	.286	.571	58	-0	-0	106	0	1	.400	0	0	0	-0	/S3	0.0
1985	Cin-N	5	9	2	2	0	0	0	2	2	1	.222	.364	.222	.586	64	-0	-0	105	398	1	.571	0	0	0	0	/3	0.0
1986	Cin-N	38	80	9	20	5	1	0	10	9	17	.250	.333	.338	.671	82	-1	-2	104	148	10	.650	2	0	1	-2	/3SO2	-0.2
1987	Chi-N	11	31	2	7	1	1	1	4	3	10	.226	.294	.419	.713	86	-1	-1	101	100	3	.593	0	2	-1	0	/3	-0.1
1988	Bal-A	20	30	1	3	0	0	0	0	0	6	.100	.100	.100	.200	-46	-6	-5	95	0	-0	.129	1	1	-0	-1	/3OD	-0.6
Total	5	78	157	14	34	6	2	1	16	14	35	.217	.285	.299	.584	59	-8	-9	102	122	15	.504	3	3	-1	-3	/3OSD2	-0.9
■ **DAVE ROWE** Rowe, David E. b: 2/1856, Jacksonville, Ill. BR , 5'9", 180 lbs. Deb: 5/30/1877 M																												
1877	Chi-N	2	7	0	2	0	0	0	0	0	3	.286	.286	.286	.571	82	-0	-0	98	0	1	.400				0	/OP	0.0
1882	Cle-N	24	97	13	25	4	3	1	17	4	9	.258	.287	.392	.679	128	2	3	90	148	11	.583				-3	O/P	0.0
1883	Bal-a	59	256	40	80	11	6	0		2		.313	.318	.402	.720	122	8	5	107	0	34	.597				-9	O/S1P	-0.2
1884	StL-U	109	485	95	142	32	11	3		10		.293	.307	.423	.730	140	21	18	104	0	65	.627	0			3	*OS/21P	1.7
1885	StL-N	16	62	8	10	3	0	0	3	5	8	.161	.224	.210	.434	44	-4	-3	92	77	3	.346				0	O	-0.2
1886	KC-N	105	429	53	103	24	8	3	57	15	43	.240	.266	.354	.620	82	-8	-12	107	111	42	.518	2			-9	*OS/2M	-1.7
1888	KC-a	32	122	14	21	3	4	0	13	6		.172	.217	.262	.479	52	-6	-7	106	124	8	.406	2			0	OM	-0.6
Total	7	347	1458	223	383	77	32	7	90	42	63	.263	.284	.374	.658	106	13	5	104	57	162	.551	4			-19	O/S21P	-1.0
■ **HARLAND ROWE** Rowe, Harland Stimson "Hypie" b: 4/20/1896, Springvale, Me. d: 5/26/69, Springvale, Maine BL/TR, 6'1", 170 lbs. Deb: 6/23/16																												
1916	Phi-A	17	36	2	5	1	0	0	3	2	8	.139	.184	.167	.351	6	-4	-4	98	179	1	.258	0			-0	/3O	-0.4
■ **JACK ROWE** Rowe, John Charles b: 12/8/1856, Harrisburg, Pa. d: 4/25/11, St.Louis, Mo. BL/TR, 5'8", 170 lbs. Deb: 9/06/1879 M																												
1879	Buf-N	8	34	8	12	1	0	0	8	0	1	.353	.353	.382	.735	125	1	1	114	229	5	.591				0	/CO	0.1
1880	Buf-N	79	326	43	82	10	6	1	36	6	17	.252	.265	.328	.593	110	-0	4	91	115	29	.463				-22	*CO/3	-1.3
1881	Buf-N	64	246	30	82	11	**11**	1	43	1	12	.333	.336	.480	.816	152	14	13	101	126	41	.726				-12	C/S3O	0.1
1882	Buf-N	75	308	43	82	14	5	1	42	12	0	.266	.294	.354	.648	102	2	0	104	134	33	.535				-10	CS/3O	-0.2
1883	Buf-N	87	374	65	104	18	7	1	38	15	14	.278	.306	.372	.678	105	2	2	100	98	44	.570				-10	COS/3	-0.3
1884	Buf-N	93	400	85	126	14	14	4	61	23	14	.315	.352	.450	.802	141	23	18	107	96	65	.741				-12	CO/S	1.0
1885	Buf-N	98	421	62	122	28	8	2	51	13	19	.290	.311	.409	.720	132	13	14	99	86	55	.619				-18	SCO	0.0
1886	Det-N	111	468	97	142	21	9	6	87	26	27	.303	.340	.425	.765	121	17	11	109	126	74	.727	12			-22	*S/C	-1.1
1887	Det-N	124	537	135	171	30	10	6	96	39	11	.318	.368	.445	.813	125	19	18	102	102	98	.828	22			-33	*S	-1.5
1888	Det-N	105	451	62	125	19	8	2	74	19	28	.277	.311	.368	.679	120	9	9	98	148	56	.607	10			-8	*S	0.4
1889	Pit-N	75	317	57	82	14	3	2	32	22	16	.259	.313	.341	.654	94	-7	-1	89	74	36	.587	5			-6	S	-0.3
1890	Buf-P	125	504	77	126	22	7	2	76	48	18	.250	.324	.333	.657	84	-16	-8	92	127	59	.616	10			-8	*SM	-0.6
Total	12	1044	4386	764	1256	202	88	28	644	224	177	.286	.323	.392	.715	116	77	81	99	113	594	.644	59			-160	SCO/3	-3.7
■ **SCHOOLBOY ROWE** Rowe, Lynwood Thomas b: 1/11/10, Waco, Tex. d: 1/8/61, El Dorado, Ark. BR/TR, 6'4.5", 210 lbs. Deb: 4/15/33 C																												
1933	Det-A	21	50	6	11	1	0	0	6	1	4	.220	.235	.240	.475	25	-5	-6	107	167	3	.333	0	0	0	2	P	0.0
1934	Det-A	51	109	15	33	8	1	2	22	6	20	.303	.339	.450	.789	105	-0	0	98	134	17	.724	0	0	0	-0	P	0.0
1935	Det-A	45	109	19	34	3	2	3	28	12	12	.312	.380	.459	.839	120	3	3	97	161	19	.827	0	0	0	-2	P	0.0
1936	Det-A	45	90	16	23	2	1	1	12	13	15	.256	.356	.333	.689	74	-4	-3	95	118	12	.657	0	0	0	2	P	0.0
1937	Det-A	10	10	2	2	0	0	0	1	1	4	.200	.273	.200	.473	19	-1	-1	109	171	1	.375	0	0	0	0	P	0.0
1938	Det-A	4	6	1	1	1	0	0	0	0	1	.167	.167	.333	.500	22	-1	-1	100	0	0	.400	0	0	0	1	/P	0.0
1939	Det-A	31	61	7	15	0	1	1	12	5	7	.246	.303	.328	.631	55	-4	-5	111	176	5	.520	1	1	-0	0	P	0.0
1940	Det-A	27	67	7	18	6	1	1	18	5	13	.269	.319	.433	.752	84	-1	-2	111	203	9	.673	1	1	-0	-0	P	0.0
1941	Det-A	32	55	10	15	0	3	1	12	5	8	.273	.333	.436	.770	96	-0	-0	106	157	8	.707	0	0	0	1	P	0.0
1942	Det-A	2	4	0	0	0	0	0	0	0	0	.000	.000	.000	.000	-89	-1	-1	113	0	0	.000	0	0	0	0	/P	0.0
	Bro-N	14	19	2	4	0	0	0	2	1	4	.211	.250	.211	.461	35	-2	-2	102	185	1	.333	0			0	/P	0.0
1943	Phi-N	82	120	14	36	7	0	4	18	15	21	.300	.382	.458	.841	152	7	7	94	97	20	.798	0			0	P	1.2
1946	Phi-N	30	61	4	11	5	0	1	6	3	16	.180	.219	.311	.530	52	-4	-4	95	102	4	.440	0			-2	P	0.0
1947	Phi-N	43	79	9	22	2	0	2	11	13	18	.278	.380	.380	.760	102	1	1	100	113	12	.741	0			-1	P	0.0
1948	Phi-N	31	52	3	10	0	0	1	4	4	10	.192	.250	.250	.500	38	-5	-4	94	94	4	.429	1			1	P	0.0
1949	Phi-N	23	17	1	4	1	0	1	1	2	4	.235	.316	.471	.786	108	0	0	101	34	3	.769	0			1	P	0.0

YEAR	TM/L	G	AB	R	H	2B	3B	HR	RBI	BB	SO	AVG	OBP	SLG	PRO	/A	BR	/A	PF	CHI	RC	TA	SB	CS	SBR	FR	POS	TPR
Total	15	491	909	116	239	36	9	18	153	86	157	.263	.328	.382	.710	88	-18	-17	100	133	119	.652	3	2		1	P	1.2
■ **BAMA ROWELL**	Rowell, Carvel William b: 1/13/16, Citronelle, Ala. BL/TR, 5'11", 185 lbs. Deb: 9/04/39																											
1939	Bos-N	21	59	5	11	2	2	0	6	1	4	.186	.200	.288	.488	32	-6	-5	92	129	3	.360	0			-1	O	-0.6
1940	Bos-N	130	486	46	148	19	8	3	58	18	22	.305	.331	.395	.726	101	-1	-1	99	109	64	.652	12			0	*2/O	0.7
1941	Bos-N	138	483	49	129	23	6	7	60	39	36	.267	.322	.383	.705	105	-2	2	93	105	61	.653	11			-3	*2O/3	0.5
1946	Bos-N	95	293	37	82	12	6	3	31	29	15	.280	.345	.392	.737	115	3	5	95	93	41	.690	5			-1	O	0.3
1947	Bos-N	113	384	48	106	23	2	5	40	18	14	.276	.310	.385	.696	86	-10	-8	97	91	47	.619	7			-8	*O/23	-1.9
1948	Phi-N	77	196	15	47	16	2	1	22	8	14	.240	.270	.357	.627	73	-9	-8	94	113	18	.526	2			-3	3O2	-1.0
Total	6	574	1901	200	523	95	26	19	217	113	105	.275	.316	.382	.699	96	-26	-16	96	103	233	.636	37			-16	2O/3	-2.0
■ **ED ROWEN**	Rowen, W. Edward b: 10/22/1857, Bridgeport, Conn. d: 2/22/1892, Bridgeport, Conn. 6'1", 170 lbs. Deb: 5/01/1882																											
1882	Bos-N	83	327	36	81	7	4	1	43	19	18	.248	.289	.303	.592	87	-3	-5	103	150	29	.480				-10	OC/S3	-1.1
1883	Phi-a	49	196	28	43	10	1	0		10		.219	.257	.281	.538	71	-6	-6	103	0	15	.425				-2	C/O32	-0.4
1884	Phi-a	4	15	4	6	1	0	0		1		.400	.471	.467	.937	185	2	2	114	0	3	1.000				0	/C	0.1
Total	3	136	538	68	130	18	5	1	43	30	18	.242	.283	.299	.582	85	-7	-10	103	91	47	.471				-13	/COS32	-1.4
■ **CHUCK ROWLAND**	Rowland, Charles Leland b: 7/23/1899, Warrenton, N.C. BR/TR, 6'1", 185 lbs. Deb: 5/11/23																											
1923	Phi-A	5	6	0	0	0	0	0	0	0	2	.000	.000	.000	.000	-99	-2	-2	100	0	0	.000	0	0	0	0	/C	0.0
■ **JIM ROXBURGH**	Roxburgh, James A. b: 1/17/1858, San Francisco, Cal d: 2/21/34, San Francisco, Csl BR/TR, Deb: 5/30/1884																											
1884	Bal-a	2	4	1	2	0	0	0		1		.500	.667	.500	1.167	295	1	1	99	0	1	2.000				0	/C	0.1
1887	Phi-a	2	8	0	1	0	0	0		0		.125	.125	.125	.250	-30	-1	-1	99	0	0	.143	0			0	/C2	0.0
Total	2	4	12	1	3	0	0	0		1		.250	.357	.250	.607	85	-0	-0	99	0	1	.556	0			0	/C2	0.1
■ **JERRY ROYSTER**	Royster, Jeron Kennis b: 10/18/52, Sacramento, Cal. BR/TR, 6', 165 lbs. Deb: 8/14/73																											
1973	LA-N	10	19	1	4	0	0	0	2	0	5	.211	.211	.211	.421	17	-2	-2	100	201	1	.333	1	0	0	0	/32	-0.1
1974	LA-N	6	0	2	0	0	0	0	0	0	0	—	—	—	—	—	0	0	93	—	—	—	0	0	0	0	/23O	0.0
1975	LA-N	13	36	2	9	2	1	0	1	1	3	.250	.270	.361	.631	78	-1	-1	95	30	3	.536	1	0	0	-2	/O23S	-0.2
1976	Atl-N	149	533	65	132	13	1	5	45	52	53	.248	.316	.304	.620	69	-16	-23	111	100	52	.562	24	13	-1	15	*3/S	-1.0
1977	Atl-N	140	445	64	96	10	2	6	28	38	67	.216	.279	.288	.567	46	-30	-37	113	77	36	.527	28	10	2	-5	3S2/O	-3.1
1978	Atl-N	140	529	67	137	17	8	2	35	56	49	.259	.333	.333	.666	77	-8	-16	112	73	60	.627	27	17	-2	-11	2S/3	-2.0
1979	Atl-N	154	601	103	164	25	6	3	51	62	59	.273	.341	.349	.690	81	-8	-15	109	89	78	.678	35	8	6	8	32	0.1
1980	Atl-N	123	392	42	95	17	5	1	20	37	48	.242	.309	.319	.628	75	-12	-13	101	62	39	.585	22	13	-1	1	23O	-1.2
1981	Atl-N	64	93	13	19	4	1	0	9	7	14	.204	.260	.269	.529	50	-6	-6	100	141	6	.481	7	5	-1	-3	32	-1.0
1982	Atl-N	108	261	43	77	13	2	2	25	22	36	.295	.354	.383	.738	99	2	0	107	92	37	.715	14	6	1	-4	3O2S	-0.2
1983	Atl-N	91	268	32	63	10	3	3	30	28	35	.235	.307	.328	.636	72	-9	-10	106	122	25	.567	11	7	-1	1	32OS	-1.0
1984	Atl-N	81	227	22	47	13	2	1	21	15	41	.207	.259	.295	.554	51	-14	-16	110	118	16	.464	6	4	-1	4	23SO	-1.1
1985	SD-N	90	249	31	70	13	2	5	31	32	31	.281	.365	.410	.775	114	6	6	102	106	37	.742	6	5	-1	-7	23/SO	-0.1
1986	SD-N	118	257	31	66	12	0	5	26	32	45	.257	.339	.362	.701	98	-2	-0	95	96	31	.634	3	5	-2	-5	3S2/O	-0.6
1987	Chi-A	55	154	25	37	11	0	7	23	19	28	.240	.328	.448	.776	96	1	-1	109	102	23	.758	2	1	0	-1	3O/2D	-0.2
	NY-A	18	42	1	15	2	0	0	4	4	4	.357	.413	.405	.818	122	1	2	98	94	6	.742	2	1	0	-0	3/2SO	0.1
	Yr	73	196	26	52	13	0	7	27	23	32	.265	.345	.439	.784	101	2	0	106	101	31	.765	4	2	0	-1		-0.1
1988	Atl-N	68	102	8	18	3	0	0	1	6	16	.176	.222	.206	.428	23	-10	-10	104	19	5	.314	0	0	0	-1	O3/2S	-1.2
Total	16	1428	4208	552	1049	165	33	40	352	411	534	.249	.318	.333	.650	75	-107	-145	107	90	457	.618	189	95	-0	-11	32SO/D	-12.8
■ **WILLIE ROYSTER**	Royster, Willie Arthur b: 4/11/54, Clarksville, Va. BR/TR, 5'11", 180 lbs. Deb: 9/03/81																											
1981	Bal-A	4	4	0	0	0	0	0	0	0	2	.000	.000	.000	.000	-99	-1	-1	99	0	0	.000	0	0	0	0	/C	0.0
■ **VIC ROZNOVSKY**	Roznovsky, Victor Joseph b: 10/19/38, Shiner, Tex. BL/TR, 6', 170 lbs. Deb: 6/28/64																											
1964	Chi-N	35	76	2	15	1	0	0	2	5	18	.197	.247	.211	.457	29	-7	-7	105	51	4	.339	0	1	-1	-0	C	-0.7
1965	Chi-N	71	172	9	38	4	1	3	15	16	30	.221	.298	.308	.607	70	-6	-7	102	100	17	.533	1	0	0	-2	C	-0.6
1966	Bal-A	41	97	4	23	5	0	1	10	9	11	.237	.308	.320	.628	80	-2	-2	101	123	10	.539	0	0	0	1	C	0.0
1967	Bal-A	45	97	7	20	5	0	0	10	1	20	.206	.214	.258	.472	41	-7	-7	95	167	4	.321	0	0	0	0	C	-0.5
1969	Phi-N	13	13	0	3	0	0	0	1	1	4	.231	.286	.231	.516	47	-1	-1	98	134	1	.400	0	0	0	0	/C	0.0
Total	5	205	455	22	99	15	1	4	38	32	83	.218	.275	.281	.556	59	-24	-24	101	111	36	.462	1	1	-0	-2	C	-1.8
■ **AL RUBELING**	Rubeling, Albert William b: 5/10/13, Baltimore, Md. d: 1/28/88, Baltimore, Md. BR/TR, 6', 185 lbs. Deb: 4/16/40																											
1940	Phi-A	108	376	49	92	16	6	4	38	48	58	.245	.330	.351	.681	80	-13	-10	96	97	45	.622	4	5	-2	-9	32	-1.3
1941	Phi-A	6	19	0	5	0	0	0	2	2	1	.263	.333	.263	.596	59	-1	-1	101	142	2	.500	0	0	0	-0	/3	0.0
1943	Pit-N	47	168	23	44	8	4	0	9	8	17	.262	.295	.357	.653	84	-3	-4	104	55	17	.527	0			-3	2/3	-0.5
1944	Pit-N	92	184	22	45	7	2	4	30	19	19	.245	.322	.370	.692	90	-1	-3	105	134	23	.655	4			-1	O23	-0.2
Total	4	253	747	94	186	31	12	8	79	77	95	.249	.321	.355	.676	83	-18	-18	100	99	87	.619	8	5		-13	3/2O	-2.0
■ **SONNY RUBERTO**	Ruberto, John Edward b: 1/2/46, Staten Island, N.Y. BR/TR, 5'11", 175 lbs. Deb: 5/25/69 C																											
1969	SD-N	19	21	3	3	0	0	0	0	1	7	.143	.182	.143	.325	-8	-3	-3	97	0	1	.222	0	0	0	0	C	-0.1
1972	Cin-N	2	3	0	0	0	0	0	0	0	1	.000	.250	.000	.250	-25	-0	-0	93	0	0	.333	0	0	0	0	/C	0.0
Total	2	21	24	3	3	0	0	0	0	1	8	.125	.192	.125	.317	-10	-3	-3	96	0	1	.238	0	0	0	0	/C	-0.1
■ **ART RUBLE**	Ruble, William Arthur "Speedy" b: 3/11/03, Knoxville, Tenn. d: 11/1/83, Maryville, Tenn. BL/TR, 5'10.5", 168 lbs. Deb: 4/18/27																											
1927	Det-A	56	91	16	15	4	2	0	11	14	15	.165	.283	.253	.536	37	-8	-9	108	159	7	.526	2	0	1	-6	O	-1.7
1934	Phi-N	19	54	7	15	4	0	0	8	7	3	.278	.361	.352	.713	84	-0	-1	108	152	7	.619	0			-1	O	-0.2
Total	2	75	145	23	30	8	2	0	19	21	18	.207	.311	.290	.601	54	-9	-10	108	156	14	.559	2	0		-7	/O	-1.9
■ **JOHNNY RUCKER**	Rucker, John Joel b: 1/15/17, Crabapple, Ga. d: 8/7/85, Moultrie, Ga. BL/TR, 6'2", 175 lbs. Deb: 4/16/40																											
1940	NY-N	86	277	38	82	7	5	4	23	7	32	.296	.313	.401	.714	95	-2	-3	100	69	34	.616	4			-1	O	-0.5
1941	NY-N	143	622	95	179	38	9	1	42	29	61	.288	.320	.383	.702	94	-4	-6	103	56	76	.611	8			0	*O	-1.2
1943	NY-N	132	505	56	138	19	4	2	46	22	44	.273	.304	.339	.642	89	-11	-8	96	96	53	.532	4			-2	*O	-1.5
1944	NY-N	144	587	79	143	14	8	6	39	24	48	.244	.275	.325	.600	66	-26	-28	104	71	54	.502	8			7	*O	-3.3
1945	NY-N	105	429	58	117	19	11	7	51	20	36	.273	.305	.417	.722	100	-3	-2	100	94	55	.654	7			-4	O	-1.0
1946	NY-N	95	197	28	52	8	2	1	13	7	27	.264	.300	.340	.640	80	-5	-6	102	69	20	.551	4			-7	O	-1.4
Total	6	705	2617	354	711	105	39	21	214	109	248	.272	.302	.366	.668	87	-51	-54	101	75	293	.579	35			-8	O	-8.9
■ **JOHN RUDDERHAM**	Rudderham, John Edmund b: 8/30/1863, Quincy, Mass. d: 4/3/42, Randolph, Mass. BR/TR, 5'8", 170 lbs. Deb: 9/18/1884																											
1884	Bos-U	1	4	0	1	0	0	0		0		.250	.250	.250	.500	71	-0	-0	98	0	0	.333	0			0	/O	0.0
■ **JOE RUDI**	Rudi, Joseph Oden b: 9/7/46, Modesto, Cal. BR/TR, 6'2", 200 lbs. Deb: 4/11/67 C																											
1967	KC-A	19	43	4	8	2	0	0	1	3	7	.186	.239	.233	.472	40	-3	-3	100	42	2	.361	0	0	0	-0	/1O	-0.4
1968	Oak-A	68	181	10	32	5	1	1	12	12	32	.177	.236	.232	.468	43	-13	-12	98	114	10	.373	1	1	-0	-6	O	-2.3
1969	Oak-A	35	122	10	23	3	1	2	6	5	16	.189	.220	.279	.499	42	-10	-9	92	60	7	.388	1	1	-0	2	O1	-0.8
1970	Oak-A	106	350	40	108	23	2	11	42	16	61	.309	.342	.480	.822	129	10	11	97	85	54	.744	3	1	0	-0	O1	0.7
1971	Oak-A	127	513	62	137	23	4	10	52	28	62	.267	.306	.386	.692	94	-5	-5	101	99	57	.585	3	2	-0	5	*O/1	-0.4
1972	Oak-A	147	593	94	**181**	32	**9**	19	75	37	62	.305	.348	.486	.834	151	31	33	97	80	95	.766	3	4	-2	-6	*O/3	2.4
1973	Oak-A	120	437	53	118	25	1	12	66	30	72	.270	.320	.414	.734	121	2	9	87	122	55	.642	0	0	0	1	*O/1D	0.7
1974	Oak-A	158	593	73	174	**39**	4	22	99	34	92	.293	.337	.484	.821	133	23	23	100	117	94	.759	2	3	-1	-12	*O1/D	0.5
1975	Oak-A	126	468	66	130	26	6	21	75	40	56	.278	.339	.494	.832	143	18	22	93	100	76	.789	2	1	0	-11	1O/D	0.5
1976	Oak-A	130	500	54	135	32	3	13	94	41	71	.270	.329	.424	.753	120	11	11	100	152	68	.689	6	1	1	-4	*O/1D	0.6
1977	Cal-A	64	242	48	64	13	2	13	53	22	48	.264	.336	.496	.832	130	7	9	95	140	42	.817	1	0	0	3	O/D	1.0
1978	Cal-A	133	497	58	127	27	1	17	79	28	82	.256	.298	.416	.714	97	-3	-3	102	123	60	.627	2	1	0	1	*OD1	-0.5
1979	Cal-A	90	330	35	80	11	3	11	61	24	61	.242	.296	.394	.690	91	-8	-5	93	147	38	.603	0	0	0	3	O/1D	-0.4
1980	Cal-A	104	372	42	88	17	1	16	53	17	84	.237	.279	.417	.696	92	-8	-6	96	104	41	.605	1	0	0	6	O/1D	-0.1

YEAR	TM/L	G	AB	R	H	2B	3B	HR	RBI	BB	SO	AVG	OBP	SLG	PRO	/A	BR	/A	PF	CHI	RC	TA	SB	CS	SBR	FR	POS	TPR
1981	Bos-A	49	122	14	22	3	0	6	24	8	29	.180	.242	.352	.595	66	-5	-6	106	154	10	.520	0	0	0	-0	D/1O	-0.6
1982	Oak-A	71	193	21	41	6	1	5	18	24	35	.212	.303	.332	.634	78	-7	-5	95	91	21	.578	0	0	0	-5	1O/D	-1.1
Total	16	1547	5556	684	1468	287	39	179	810	369	870	.264	.314	.427	.741	112	41	63	97	112	730	.682	25	15	-1	-23	*O1/D3	-0.2

■ **DUTCH RUDOLPH** Rudolph, John Herman b: 7/10/1882, Natrona, Pa. d: 4/17/67, Natrona, Pa. 5'10", 160 lbs. Deb: 03

YEAR	TM/L	G	AB	R	H	2B	3B	HR	RBI	BB	SO	AVG	OBP	SLG	PRO	/A	BR	/A	PF	CHI	RC	TA	SB	CS	SBR	FR	POS	TPR
1903	Phi-N	1	1	0	0	0	0	0	0	0		.000	.000	.000	.000	-99	-0	-0	92	0	0	.000	0			0	H	0.0
1904	Chi-N	2	3	0	1	0	0	0	0	0		.333	.333	.333	.667	108	0	0	101	0	0	.500	0			0	/O	0.0
Total	2	3	4	0	1	0	0	0	0	0		.250	.250	.250	.500	54	-0	-0	98	0	0	.333	0			0	/O	0.0

■ **KEN RUDOLPH** Rudolph, Kenneth Victor b: 12/29/46, Rockford, Ill. BR/TR, 6'1", 180 lbs. Deb: 4/20/69

YEAR	TM/L	G	AB	R	H	2B	3B	HR	RBI	BB	SO	AVG	OBP	SLG	PRO	/A	BR	/A	PF	CHI	RC	TA	SB	CS	SBR	FR	POS	TPR
1969	Chi-N	27	34	7	7	1	0	1	6	6	11	.206	.325	.324	.649	77	-1	-1	107	172	4	.607	0	0	0	-0	C/O	0.0
1970	Chi-N	20	40	1	4	1	0	0	2	1	12	.100	.122	.125	.247	-28	-8	-9	120	155	1	.162	0	0	0	-1	C	-0.8
1971	Chi-N	25	76	5	15	3	0	0	7	6	20	.197	.265	.237	.502	39	-6	-6	110	158	5	.391	0	0	0	-1	C	-0.6
1972	Chi-N	42	106	10	25	1	1	2	9	6	14	.236	.283	.321	.604	63	-4	-6	114	92	8	.483	1	2	-1	-2	C	-0.6
1973	Chi-N	64	170	12	35	8	1	2	17	7	25	.206	.242	.300	.542	45	-12	-14	108	120	10	.414	1	4	-2	-3	C	-1.5
1974	SF-N	57	158	11	41	3	0	0	10	21	15	.259	.350	.278	.628	72	-4	-5	108	88	15	.537	0	0	0	-4	C	-0.6
1975	StL-N	44	80	5	16	2	0	1	6	3	10	.200	.229	.262	.491	35	-7	-7	103	97	4	.353	0	0	0	-1	C	-0.6
1976	StL-N	27	50	1	8	3	0	0	5	1	7	.160	.176	.220	.396	12	-6	-6	104	175	2	.273	0	0	0	1	C	-0.4
1977	SF-N	11	15	1	3	0	0	0	0	1	3	.200	.250	.200	.450	21	-2	-2	104	0	1	.333	0	0	0	-0	C	-0.1
	Bal-A	11	14	2	4	1	0	0	2	0	4	.286	.286	.357	.643	79	-1	-0	93	159	1	.500	0	0	0	0	C	0.0
Total	9	328	743	55	158	23	2	6	64	52	121	.213	.268	.273	.541	47	-49	-56	108	116	51	.442	2	6	-3	-10	C/O	-5.2

■ **MUDDY RUEL** Ruel, Herold Dominic b: 2/20/1896, St.Louis, Mo. d: 11/13/63, Palo Alto, Cal. BR/TR, 5'9", 150 lbs. Deb: 5/29/15 MC

YEAR	TM/L	G	AB	R	H	2B	3B	HR	RBI	BB	SO	AVG	OBP	SLG	PRO	/A	BR	/A	PF	CHI	RC	TA	SB	CS	SBR	FR	POS	TPR
1915	StL-A	10	14	0	0	0	0	0	1	5	5	.000	.263	.000	.263	-22	-2	-2	96	0	0	.357	0			0	/C	-0.1
1917	NY-A	6	17	1	2	0	0	0	1	2	2	.118	.211	.118	.328	0	-2	-2	107	179	1	.333	1			0	/C	-0.1
1918	NY-A	3	6	0	2	0	0	0	0	2	1	.333	.500	.333	.833	160	1	1	95	0	1	1.250	1			0	/C	0.1
1919	NY-A	79	233	18	56	6	0	0	31	34	26	.240	.340	.266	.606	67	-7	-9	106	181	22	.571	4			-4	C	-0.9
1920	NY-A	82	261	30	70	14	1	1	15	15	18	.268	.310	.341	.651	71	-11	-11	102	57	28	.565	4	2	0	-9	C	-1.2
1921	Bos-A	113	358	41	99	21	1	1	45	41	15	.277	.352	.349	.702	80	-10	-10	100	120	45	.635	2	7	-4	5	*C	-0.4
1922	Bos-A	116	361	34	92	15	1	0	28	41	26	.255	.333	.302	.634	69	-17	-15	96	92	39	.572	4	2	0	6	*C	-0.5
1923	Was-A	136	449	63	142	24	3	0	54	55	21	.316	.394	.383	.778	111	6	9	95	107	70	.748	4	6	-2	20	*C	3.4
1924	Was-A	149	501	50	142	20	2	0	57	62	20	.283	.370	.331	.702	83	-11	-10	98	116	65	.654	7	11	-5	3	*C	-0.2
1925	Was-A	127	393	55	122	9	2	0	54	63	16	.310	.411	.344	.754	95	-0	1	98	134	60	.746	4	5	-2	7	*C/1	1.3
1926	Was-A	117	368	42	110	22	4	1	53	61	14	.299	.401	.389	.790	109	6	7	98	123	61	.807	7	6	-2	3	*C	1.6
1927	Was-A	131	428	61	132	16	5	1	52	63	18	.308	.403	.376	.779	106	5	7	97	106	67	.804	9	0	3	1	*C	1.2
1928	Was-A	108	350	31	90	18	2	0	55	44	14	.257	.342	.320	.662	74	-12	-12	102	169	40	.626	12	10	-2	9	*C/1	0.0
1929	Was-A	69	188	16	46	4	2	0	20	31	7	.245	.352	.287	.639	67	-8	-8	100	127	20	.582	0	4	-2	2	C	-0.2
1930	Was-A	66	198	18	50	3	4	0	26	24	13	.253	.342	.308	.650	65	-9	-10	101	141	23	.601	1	0	0	2	C	-0.1
1931	Bos-A	33	83	6	25	5	0	0	6	9	6	.301	.370	.361	.731	99	-1	0	94	66	12	.672	0	0	0	0	C	0.3
	Det-A	14	50	1	6	1	0	0	3	5	1	.120	.200	.140	.340	-9	-8	-8	104	144	2	.273	0	0	0	1	C	-0.5
	Yr	47	133	7	31	6	0	0	9	14	7	.233	.306	.278	.584	56	-9	-8	97	91	12	.500	0	0	0	1		-0.2
1932	Det-A	51	136	10	32	4	2	0	18	17	6	.235	.320	.294	.614	59	-8	-8	102	151	14	.558	1	0	0	-1	C	-0.5
1933	StL-A	36	63	13	12	2	0	0	8	24	4	.190	.414	.222	.636	63	-1	-2	115	191	8	.745	0	0	0	2	C	0.1
1934	Chi-A	22	57	4	12	3	0	0	7	8	5	.211	.308	.263	.571	49	-4	-4	99	156	5	.511	0	0	0	2	C	0.0
Total	19	1468	4514	494	1242	187	29	4	534	606	238	.275	.365	.332	.697	83	-93	-86	99	122	583	.660	61	53		48	*C/1	3.3

■ **DUTCH RUETHER** Ruether, Walter Henry b: 9/13/1893, Alameda, Cal. d: 5/16/70, Phoenix, Ariz. BL/TL, 6'1.5", 180 lbs. Deb: 4/13/17

YEAR	TM/L	G	AB	R	H	2B	3B	HR	RBI	BB	SO	AVG	OBP	SLG	PRO	/A	BR	/A	PF	CHI	RC	TA	SB	CS	SBR	FR	POS	TPR
1917	Chi-N	31	44	3	12	1	3	0	11	8	11	.273	.385	.432	.816	144	3	3	105	223	7	.844	0			0	P/1	0.5
	Cin-N	19	24	1	5	2	0	0	1	3	6	.208	.296	.292	.588	87	-0	-0	92	55	2	.579	1			-0	/P	0.0
	Yr	50	68	4	17	3	3	0	12	11	17	.250	.354	.382	.737	126	2	2	100	164	9	.745	1			0		0.5
1918	Cin-N	2	3	0	0	0	0	0	0	0	2	.000	.000	.000	.000	-99	-1	-1	97	0	0	.000	0			0	/P	0.0
1919	Cin-N	42	92	8	24	2	3	0	6	4	18	.261	.292	.348	.639	87	-1	-2	105	73	9	.544	1			-2	P	0.0
1920	Cin-N	45	104	3	20	4	0	0	10	5	24	.192	.229	.231	.460	36	-9	-8	90	161	6	.345	0	0	0	0	P	0.0
1921	Bro-N	49	97	12	34	5	2	2	13	4	9	.351	.376	.505	.881	125	4	3	105	87	18	.857	1	0	0	-0	P	0.0
1922	Bro-N	67	125	12	26	6	1	2	20	12	11	.208	.283	.320	.603	58	-9	-8	95	152	12	.535	0	0	0	-0	P	0.0
1923	Bro-N	49	117	6	32	1	0	0	10	12	12	.274	.341	.282	.623	68	-5	-5	98	107	12	.529	0	0	0	-2	P/1	0.0
1924	Bro-N	34	62	5	15	1	1	0	4	5	2	.242	.299	.290	.589	59	-4	-3	99	81	6	.489	0	0	0	1	P	0.0
1925	Was-A	55	108	18	36	3	2	1	15	10	8	.333	.390	.426	.816	109	1	2	98	102	18	.767	0	1	-1	-2	P/1	0.0
1926	Was-A	47	92	6	23	2	0	1	11	6	10	.250	.296	.304	.600	58	-6	-6	98	121	9	.493	0	0	0	-2	P	-0.2
	NY-A	13	21	2	2	0	0	0	0	0	1	.095	.136	.095	.232	-39	-4	-4	99	0	0	.158	0	0	0	-1	/P	-0.3
	Yr	60	113	8	25	2	0	1	11	6	11	.221	.267	.265	.532	40	-10	-10	98	96	8	.420	0	0	0	-3		-0.5
1927	NY-A	35	80	7	21	3	0	1	10	8	15	.262	.330	.338	.667	73	-3	-3	100	111	9	.593	0	0	0	0	P	0.0
Total	11	488	969	83	250	30	12	7	111	77	129	.258	.314	.335	.649	76	-34	-32	98	115	108	.565	3	1		-8	P/1	0.0

■ **RUDY RUFER** Rufer, Rudolph Joseph b: 10/28/26, Ridgewood, N.Y. BR/TR, 6'0.5", 165 lbs. Deb: 9/22/49

YEAR	TM/L	G	AB	R	H	2B	3B	HR	RBI	BB	SO	AVG	OBP	SLG	PRO	/A	BR	/A	PF	CHI	RC	TA	SB	CS	SBR	FR	POS	TPR
1949	NY-N	7	15	1	1	0	0	0	2	2	0	.067	.176	.067	.243	-32	-3	-3	102	754	0	.214	0			-0	/S	-0.1
1950	NY-N	15	11	1	1	0	0	0	0	0	1	.091	.091	.091	.182	-53	-2	-2	98	0	0	.200	1			0	/S	-0.1
Total	2	22	26	2	2	0	0	0	2	2	1	.077	.143	.077	.220	-40	-5	-5	100	458	0	.208	1			-0	/S	-0.2

■ **RED RUFFING** Ruffing, Charles Herbert b: 5/3/04, Granville, Ill. d: 2/17/86, Mayfield Hts., O. BR/TR, 6'1.5", 205 lbs. Deb: 5/31/24 CH

YEAR	TM/L	G	AB	R	H	2B	3B	HR	RBI	BB	SO	AVG	OBP	SLG	PRO	/A	BR	/A	PF	CHI	RC	TA	SB	CS	SBR	FR	POS	TPR
1924	Bos-A	8	7	0	1	0	1	0	0	0	1	.143	.143	.429	.571	42	-1	-1	104	0	0	.500	0	0	0	-0	/P	0.0
1925	Bos-A	37	79	6	17	4	2	0	11	1	22	.215	.235	.316	.551	41	-8	-7	95	147	6	.435	0	0	0	-1	P	0.0
1926	Bos-A	37	51	8	10	1	0	1	5	2	12	.196	.226	.275	.501	30	-5	-5	101	100	3	.381	0	1	-1	-1	P	0.0
1927	Bos-A	29	55	5	14	3	1	0	4	0	6	.255	.268	.345	.613	62	-4	-3	95	70	5	.488	0	0	0	0	P	0.0
1928	Bos-A	60	121	12	38	13	1	2	19	3	12	.314	.331	.488	.818	114	1	2	98	100	19	.747	0	0	0	-3	P	0.0
1929	Bos-A	60	114	9	35	9	0	2	17	2	13	.307	.325	.439	.763	93	-1	-2	102	104	16	.671	0	0	0	-2	P/O	0.0
1930	Bos-A	6	11	2	3	2	0	0	1	0	1	.273	.273	.455	.727	87	-0	-0	93	66	1	.625	0	0	0	-1	/P	0.0
	NY-A	52	99	15	37	6	2	4	21	7	7	.374	.415	.596	1.011	171	8	9	90	98	24	1.065	0	0	0	-3	P	0.0
	Yr	58	110	17	40	8	2	4	22	7	8	.364	.402	.582	.984	162	7	9	90	96	25	1.014	0	0	0	-3		0.0
1931	NY-A	48	109	14	36	8	1	3	12	1	13	.330	.336	.505	.841	121	2	2	98	62	18	.767	0	0	0	-3	P/O	0.0
1932	NY-A	55	124	20	38	6	1	3	19	6	10	.306	.338	.444	.782	106	-0	1	95	99	18	.709	0	0	0	-2	P	0.0
1933	NY-A	55	115	10	29	3	1	2	13	7	15	.252	.295	.348	.643	77	-5	-4	91	94	12	.547	0	0	0	-0	P	0.0
1934	NY-A	45	113	11	28	3	0	2	13	3	17	.248	.274	.327	.601	57	-8	-7	96	101	10	.482	0	0	0	-3	P	0.0
1935	NY-A	50	109	13	37	10	0	2	18	3	9	.339	.363	.486	.849	127	2	3	93	104	19	.792	0	0	0	-2	P	0.0
1936	NY-A	53	127	14	37	5	0	5	22	11	12	.291	.348	.449	.797	101	-1	-0	95	99	20	.756	0	0	0	2	P	0.0
1937	NY-A	54	129	11	26	3	0	1	10	13	24	.202	.275	.248	.523	32	-13	-14	102	98	9	.437	0	0	0	-4	P	0.0
1938	NY-A	45	107	12	24	4	1	3	17	17	21	.224	.331	.364	.695	70	-4	-5	105	120	14	.675	0	0	0	-2	P	0.0
1939	NY-A	44	114	12	35	1	0	1	20	7	18	.307	.347	.342	.689	84	-4	-2	91	161	14	.587	1	0	0	-2	P	0.0
1940	NY-A	33	89	8	11	4	0	1	7	3	9	.124	.152	.202	.354	-9	-15	-14	99	120	2	.250	0	0	0	-3	P	0.0
1941	NY-A	38	89	10	27	8	1	2	22	4	12	.303	.333	.483	.816	116	1	1	98	159	14	.734	0	0	0	-3	P	0.0
1942	NY-A	30	80	8	20	4	0	1	13	5	13	.250	.302	.338	.640	80	-2	-2	99	153	8	.532	0	0	0	-2	P	0.0
1945	NY-A	21	46	4	10	0	1	1	5	0	8	.217	.217	.326	.543	53	-3	-3	107	100	3	.417	0	0	0	-2	P	0.0
1946	NY-A	8	25	1	3	1	0	0	1	1	8	.120	.154	.160	.314	-12	-4	-4	100	95	1	.217	0	0	0	-1	/P	0.0
1947	Chi-A	14	24	2	5	0	0	0	3	1	3	.208	.240	.208	.448	26	-2	-2	97	221	1	.300	0	0	0	-0	/P	0.0
Total	22	882	1937	207	521	98	13	36	273	97	266	.269	.306	.389	.695	81	-67	-58	97	110	238	.604	1	1	-0	-35	P/O	0.0

■ **CHICO RUIZ** Ruiz, Hiraldo (Sablon) b: 12/5/38, Santo Domingo, Cuba d: 2/9/72, San Diego, Cal. BB/TR, 6', 169 lbs. Deb: 4/13/64

YEAR	TM/L	G	AB	R	H	2B	3B	HR	RBI	BB	SO	AVG	OBP	SLG	PRO	/A	BR	/A	PF	CHI	RC	TA	SB	CS	SBR	FR	POS	TPR
1964	Cin-N	77	311	33	76	13	2	2	16	7	41	.244	.270	.318	.589	63	-15	-16	103	60	28	.504	11	3	2	-3	32	-1.8

YEAR	TM/L	G	AB	R	H	2B	3B	HR	RBI	BB	SO	AVG	OBP	SLG	PRO	/A	BR	/A	PF	CHI	RC	TA	SB	CS	SBR	FR	POS	TPR
1965	Cin-N	29	18	7	2	1	0	0	1	0	5	.111	.111	.167	.278	-22	-3	-3	104	138	-0	.211	1	2	-1	-0	/3S	-0.3
1966	Cin-N	82	110	13	28	2	1	0	5	5	14	.255	.287	.291	.578	54	-6	-7	114	66	9	.452	1	2	-1	-4	3/OS	-1.2
1967	Cin-N	105	250	32	55	12	4	0	13	11	35	.220	.259	.300	.559	54	-13	-16	109	72	18	.469	9	4	0	-4	23S/O	-1.6
1968	Cin-N	85	139	15	36	2	1	0	9	12	18	.259	.318	.288	.606	74	-3	-4	111	95	13	.514	4	3	-1	2	21/3S	-0.1
1969	Cin-N	88	196	19	48	4	1	0	13	14	28	.245	.295	.276	.571	61	-10	-10	99	96	17	.477	4	2	0	-4	2S/310	-0.7
1970	Cal-A	68	107	10	26	3	1	0	12	7	16	.243	.296	.290	.585	68	-5	-4	92	157	9	.494	3	0	1	2	3/2S1C	0.0
1971	Cal-A	31	19	4	5	0	0	0	0	2	7	.263	.333	.263	.596	72	-1	-1	99	0	2	.571	1	0	0	0	/32	0.0
Total	8	565	1150	133	276	37	10	2	69	58	164	.240	.281	.295	.575	61	-55	-61	104	83	96	.492	34	16	1	-11	23/S10C	-5.7
■ **CHICO RUIZ** Ruiz, Manuel (Cruz) b: 11/1/51, Santurce, P.R. BR/TR, 5'11.5", 170 lbs. Deb: 7/29/78																												
1978	Atl-N	18	46	3	13	3	0	0	2	2	4	.283	.313	.348	.660	75	-1	-2	112	50	5	.529	0	0	0	-1	2/3	0.0
1980	Atl-N	25	26	3	8	2	1	0	2	3	7	.308	.379	.462	.841	132	1	1	101	66	4	.789	0	1	-1	1	3/S2	0.2
Total	2	43	72	6	21	5	1	0	4	5	11	.292	.338	.389	.727	95	0	-0	108	56	9	.635	0	1	-1	0	/32S	0.2
■ **JOE RULLO** Rullo, Joseph Vincent b: 6/16/16, New York, N.Y. d: 10/28/69, Philadelphia, Pa. BR/TR, 5'11", 168 lbs. Deb: 9/22/43																												
1943	Phi-A	16	55	2	16	3	0	0	6	8	7	.291	.381	.345	.726	112	1	1	101	118	8	.675	0	0	0	-1	2	0.1
1944	Phi-A	35	96	5	16	0	0	0	5	6	19	.167	.223	.167	.390	12	-11	-11	101	113	4	.286	1	0	0	-2	2/1	-1.2
Total	2	51	151	7	32	3	0	0	11	14	26	.212	.283	.232	.515	49	-10	-10	101	115	12	.415	1	0	0	-3	/21	-1.1
■ **WILLIAM RUMLER** Rumler, William George b: 3/27/1891, Milford, Neb. d: 5/26/66, Lincoln, Neb. BR/TR, 6'1", 190 lbs. Deb: 5/04/14																												
1914	StL-A	33	46	2	8	1	0	0	6	3	12	.174	.240	.196	.436	32	-4	-4	98	250	2	.375	2	2	-1	-3	/CO	-0.7
1916	StL-A	27	37	6	12	3	0	0	10	3	7	.324	.375	.405	.780	141	1	2	95	238	6	.720	0			-0	/C	0.2
1917	StL-A	78	88	7	23	3	4	1	16	8	9	.261	.323	.420	.743	134	2	3	95	144	12	.723	2			-1	/O	0.2
Total	3	138	171	15	43	7	4	1	32	14	28	.251	.312	.357	.669	107	-0	1	96	193	20	.615	4	2		-3	/CO	-0.3
■ **PAUL RUNGE** Runge, Paul William b: 5/21/58, Kingston, N.Y. BR/TR, 6', 165 lbs. Deb: 9/25/81																												
1981	Atl-N	10	27	2	7	1	0	0	2	4	4	.259	.355	.296	.651	87	-0	-0	100	98	3	.571	0	0	0	-0	S	0.0
1982	Atl-N	4	2	0	0	0	0	0	0	0	0	.000	.000	.000	.000	-93	-1	-1	107	0	0	.000	0	0	0	0	/H	0.0
1983	Atl-N	5	8	0	2	0	0	0	1	1	4	.250	.333	.250	.583	60	-0	-0	106	198	1	.500	0	0	0	0	/2	0.0
1984	Atl-N	28	90	5	24	3	1	0	3	10	14	.267	.340	.322	.662	79	-1	-2	110	41	10	.620	5	3	-0	4	2/S3	0.3
1985	Atl-N	50	87	15	19	3	0	1	5	18	18	.218	.352	.287	.640	76	-1	-2	106	71	10	.597	0	1	-1	-1	3/S2	-0.2
1986	Atl-N	7	8	1	2	0	0	0	0	2	4	.250	.400	.250	.650	82	-0	-0	102	0	1	.571	0	0	0	1	/2	0.1
1987	Atl-N	27	47	9	10	1	0	3	8	5	10	.213	.288	.426	.714	80	-1	-2	108	110	5	.641	0	1	-1	-0	3/S2	-0.1
1988	Atl-N	52	76	11	16	5	0	0	7	14	21	.211	.333	.276	.610	74	-2	-2	104	133	7	.547	0	0	0	-1	3/2S	-0.2
Total	8	183	345	43	80	13	1	4	26	54	75	.232	.336	.310	.646	77	-7	-10	106	85	37	.606	5	5	-2	3	/32S	-0.1
■ **TOM RUNNELLS** Runnells, Thomas William b: 4/17/55, Greeley, Colo. BB/TR, 6', 175 lbs. Deb: 8/09/85																												
1985	Cin-N	28	35	3	7	1	0	0	0	3	4	.200	.263	.229	.492	37	-3	-3	105	0	2	.379	0	0	0	-1	S/2	-0.2
1986	Cin-N	12	11	1	1	1	0	0	0	0	2	.091	.091	.182	.273	-26	-2	-2	104	0	0	.182	0	0	0	0	/23	-0.1
Total	2	40	46	4	8	2	0	0	0	3	6	.174	.224	.217	.442	23	-5	-5	105	0	2	.333	0	0	0	-1	/S23	-0.3
■ **PETE RUNNELS** Runnels, James Edward (born James Edward Runnells) b: 1/28/28, Lufkin, Tex. BL/TR, 6', 170 lbs. Deb: 7/01/51 MC																												
1951	Was-A	78	273	31	76	12	2	0	25	31	24	.278	.354	.337	.691	92	-4	-2	95	99	34	.605	0	3	-2	-9	S	-0.7
1952	Was-A	152	555	70	158	18	3	1	64	72	55	.285	.368	.333	.701	96	-0	-0	100	**130**	69	.613	0	10	-6	-14	*S/2	-1.2
1953	Was-A	137	486	64	125	15	5	2	50	64	36	.257	.347	.321	.668	86	-11	-7	94	117	55	.590	3	4	-2	-14	*S2	-1.2
1954	Was-A	139	488	75	131	17	15	3	56	78	60	.268	.369	.383	.752	108	6	7	98	111	72	.722	2	3	-1	-6	*S2/O	1.0
1955	Was-A	134	503	66	143	16	4	2	49	55	51	.284	.356	.344	.700	98	-7	-1	91	108	60	.606	3	9	-5	3	*2/S	0.5
1956	Was-A	147	578	72	179	29	9	8	76	58	64	.310	.375	.433	.807	110	11	9	102	110	91	.746	5	5	-2	1	12/S	1.1
1957	Was-A	134	473	53	109	18	4	2	35	55	51	.230	.313	.298	.611	69	-20	-19	98	96	46	.535	2	3	-1	-4	132	-2.3
1958	Bos-A	147	568	103	183	32	5	8	59	87	49	.322	.418	.438	.856	129	32	28	105	77	107	.853	1	2	-1	5	*21	3.9
1959	Bos-A	147	560	95	176	33	6	6	57	95	48	.314	.415	.427	.841	124	29	24	106	84	102	.840	6	5	-1	8	*21/S	3.5
1960	Bos-A	143	528	80	169	29	2	2	35	71	51	**.320**	.403	.394	.797	113	15	13	103	68	86	.759	5	2	0	7	*21/3	2.6
1961	Bos-A	143	360	49	114	20	3	3	38	46	32	.317	.399	.414	.812	116	11	10	102	94	60	.784	5	1	1	1	*13/2S	0.2
1962	Bos-A	152	562	80	183	33	5	10	60	79	57	**.326**	.411	.456	.867	130	29	27	102	88	110	.879	3	4	-2	-2	*1	1.4
1963	Hou-N	124	388	35	98	9	1	2	23	45	42	.253	.335	.296	.631	90	-7	-3	92	80	38	.532	2	0	1	-8	12/3	-0.9
1964	Hou-N	22	51	3	10	1	0	0	3	8	7	.196	.305	.216	.521	51	-3	-3	96	112	3	.432	0	0	0	-0	1	-0.3
Total	14	1799	6373	876	1854	282	64	49	630	844	627	.291	.376	.378	.755	106	81	84	100	97	934	.726	37	51	-20	-31	12S/30	7.6
■ **REB RUSSELL** Russell, Ewell Albert b: 4/12/1889, Jackson, Miss. d: 9/30/73, Indianapolis, Ind BL/TL, 5'11", 185 lbs. Deb: 4/18/13																												
1913	Chi-A	52	106	9	20	5	3	0	7	1	29	.189	.204	.292	.496	47	-8	-7	95	122	6	.384	0			1	P	-0.4
1914	Chi-A	44	62	6	17	1	1	0	7	1	14	.274	.286	.323	.608	80	-2	-2	103	131	6	.467	0			0	P	0.0
1915	Chi-A	45	86	11	21	2	3	0	7	4	14	.244	.293	.337	.631	91	-2	-1	98	82	9	.554	1			-2	P	0.0
1916	Chi-A	56	91	9	13	2	0	0	6	0	18	.143	.152	.165	.317	-4	-12	-13	108	143	3	.218	1			-1	P	0.0
1917	Chi-A	39	68	5	19	3	3	0	9	2	10	.279	.300	.412	.712	120	1	1	98	115	8	.612	0			-1	P/O	0.0
1918	Chi-A	27	50	2	7	3	0	0	3	0	6	.140	.157	.200	.357	8	-6	-6	101	109	2	.256	0			-1	P/O	0.0
1919	Chi-A	1	0	0	0	0	0	0	0	0	0	—	—	—	—	—	0	0	105	—	—	—	0			0	/P	0.0
1922	Pit-N	60	220	51	81	14	8	12	75	14	18	.368	.423	.668	1.091	171	24	23	104	146	61	1.220	4	2	0	-3	O	1.6
1923	Pit-N	94	291	49	84	18	7	9	58	20	21	.289	.341	.491	.832	121	6	7	97	120	49	.813	3	1	0	-5	O	0.0
Total	9	418	974	142	262	48	25	21	172	42	130	.269	.309	.434	.744	105	2	2	100	125	145	.684	9	3		-12	PO	1.2
■ **RIP RUSSELL** Russell, Glen David b: 1/26/15, Los Angeles, Cal. d: 9/26/76, Los Alamitos, Cal BR/TR, 6'1", 180 lbs. Deb: 5/05/39																												
1939	Chi-N	143	542	55	148	24	5	9	79	36	56	.273	.318	.386	.704	88	-10	-10	101	125	66	.608	2			-5	*1	-3.2
1940	Chi-N	68	215	15	53	7	2	5	33	8	23	.247	.277	.367	.644	77	-8	-7	100	130	20	.527	1			0	1/3	-1.1
1941	Chi-N	6	17	1	5	1	0	0	1	1	5	.294	.333	.353	.686	100	-0	-0	94	60	2	.583	0			-0	/1	0.0
1942	Chi-N	102	302	32	73	9	0	8	41	17	21	.242	.282	.351	.633	88	-7	-6	96	117	29	.523	0			-0	123/O	-0.6
1946	Bos-A	80	274	22	57	10	1	6	35	13	30	.208	.247	.318	.564	50	-17	-21	114	127	19	.445	1	1	-0	-1	3/2	-1.7
1947	Bos-A	26	52	8	8	1	0	1	3	8	7	.154	.267	.231	.497	36	-4	-5	108	74	3	.417	0	0	0	-0	3	-0.4
Total	6	425	1402	133	344	52	8	29	192	83	142	.245	.289	.356	.644	76	-46	-50	102	122	140	.553	4	1		-6	1/32O	-7.0
■ **HARVEY RUSSELL** Russell, Harvey Holmes b: 1/10/1887, Marshall, Va. d: 1/8/80, Alexnadria, Va. BL/TR, 5'9.5", 163 lbs. Deb: 4/17/14																												
1914	Bal-F	81	168	18	39	3	2	0	13	18	17	.232	.306	.274	.580	68	-7	-7	99	102	16	.512	2			-6	C/SO	-1.0
1915	Bal-F	53	73	5	19	1	2	0	11	14	5	.260	.379	.329	.708	103	2	1	107	165	11	.722	1			0	C	0.2
Total	2	134	241	23	58	4	4	0	24	32	22	.241	.330	.290	.620	79	-5	-6	102	122	26	.574	3			-6	/COS	-0.8
■ **JIM RUSSELL** Russell, James William b: 10/1/18, Fayette City, Pa. d: 11/24/87, Pittsburgh, Pa. BB/TR, 6'1", 181 lbs. Deb: 9/12/42																												
1942	Pit-N	5	14	2	1	0	0	0	0	1	4	.071	.133	.071	.205	-39	-2	-2	101	0	0	.154	0			1	/O	-0.1
1943	Pit-N	146	533	79	138	19	11	4	44	77	67	.259	.354	.358	.712	101	6	3	104	83	70	.689	12			3	*O/1	0.1
1944	Pit-N	152	580	109	181	34	14	8	66	79	63	.312	.399	.460	.859	135	34	30	105	86	112	.877	6			12	*O	3.1
1945	Pit-N	146	510	88	145	24	8	12	77	71	40	.284	.377	.433	.810	121	18	16	103	106	88	.839	15			0	*O	1.0
1946	Pit-N	146	516	68	143	29	6	8	50	67	54	.277	.362	.403	.765	113	12	10	103	82	78	.750	11			-0	*O/1	0.7
1947	Pit-N	128	478	68	121	21	8	8	51	63	58	.253	.343	.381	.723	91	-5	-6	101	97	64	.688	7			6	*O	-0.3
1948	Bos-N	89	322	44	85	18	1	9	54	46	31	.264	.361	.410	.771	107	4	4	102	130	49	.755	4			2	O	0.0
1949	Bos-N	130	415	57	96	22	1	8	54	64	68	.231	.337	.347	.684	87	-9	-7	97	121	52	.649	3			-15	*O	-2.8
1950	Bro-N	77	214	37	49	8	2	10	32	31	36	.229	.329	.425	.755	91	-1	-3	107	102	30	.725	1			4	O	-0.1
1951	Bro-N	16	13	2	0	0	0	0	0	4	6	.000	.278	.000	.278	-19	-2	-2	98	0	0	.333	0	0	0	-1	/O	-0.3
Total	10	1035	3595	554	959	175	51	67	428	503	427	.267	.360	.400	.760	107	54	42	103	98	544	.766	59	0		11	O/1	1.3
■ **JOHN RUSSELL** Russell, John William b: 1/5/61, Oklahoma City, Okla. BR/TR, 6', 200 lbs. Deb: 6/22/84																												
1984	Phi-N	39	99	11	28	8	1	2	11	12	33	.283	.360	.444	.805	123	3	3	102	86	16	.757	0	1	-1	-1	O/C	0.0
1985	Phi-N	81	216	22	47	12	0	9	23	18	72	.218	.278	.398	.676	85	-5	-5	102	81	24	.609	2	0	1	-5	O1	-1.1

YEAR	TM/L	G	AB	R	H	2B	3B	HR	RBI	BB	SO	AVG	OBP	SLG	PRO	/A	BR	/A	PF	CHI	RC	TA	SB	CS	SBR	FR	POS	TPR
1986	Phi-N	93	315	35	76	21	2	13	60	25	103	.241	.303	.444	.748	99	0	-1	104	134	42	.683	0	1	-1	4	C	0.5
1987	Phi-N	24	62	5	9	1	0	3	8	3	17	.145	.185	.306	.491	26	-7	-7	104	114	2	.379	0	1	-1	1	O/C	-0.6
1988	Phi-N	22	49	5	12	1	0	2	4	3	15	.245	.302	.388	.690	95	-0	-0	101	64	5	.590	0	0	0	2	C	0.2
Total	5	259	741	78	172	43	3	29	106	61	240	.232	.294	.416	.710	92	-8	-11	103	106	88	.653	2	3	-1	1	C/O1	-1.0

■ **LLOYD RUSSELL** Russell, Lloyd Opal b: 4/10/13, Atoka, Okla. d: 5/24/68, Waco, Tex. BR/TR, 5'11", 166 lbs. Deb: 4/26/38

YEAR	TM/L	G	AB	R	H	2B	3B	HR	RBI	BB	SO	AVG	OBP	SLG	PRO	/A	BR	/A	PF	CHI	RC	TA	SB	CS	SBR	FR	POS	TPR
1938	Cle-A	2	0	0	0	0	0	0	0	0	0	—	—	—	—	—	0	0	99	—	—	—	0	0	0	0	R	0.0

■ **PAUL RUSSELL** Russell, Paul A. b: 1870, Reading, Pa. d: Pottstown, Pa. Deb: 7/29/1894

YEAR	TM/L	G	AB	R	H	2B	3B	HR	RBI	BB	SO	AVG	OBP	SLG	PRO	/A	BR	/A	PF	CHI	RC	TA	SB	CS	SBR	FR	POS	TPR
1894	StL-N	3	10	1	1	0	0	0	0	0	2	.100	.100	.100	.200	-51	-2	-2	101	0	0	.111	0			0	/O32	-0.1

■ **BILL RUSSELL** Russell, William Ellis b: 10/21/48, Pittsburg, Kan. BR/TR, 6', 175 lbs. Deb: 4/07/69 C

YEAR	TM/L	G	AB	R	H	2B	3B	HR	RBI	BB	SO	AVG	OBP	SLG	PRO	/A	BR	/A	PF	CHI	RC	TA	SB	CS	SBR	FR	POS	TPR
1969	LA-N	98	212	35	48	6	2	5	15	22	45	.226	.302	.344	.646	82	-6	-5	99	68	23	.595	4	1	1	-3	O	-1.3
1970	LA-N	81	278	30	72	11	9	0	28	16	28	.259	.306	.363	.670	88	-9	-5	90	108	32	.608	9	1	2	7	O/S	0.0
1971	LA-N	91	211	29	48	7	4	2	15	11	39	.227	.266	.327	.593	68	-10	-9	99	81	18	.512	6	3	0	-10	2O/S	-1.8
1972	LA-N	129	434	47	118	19	5	4	34	34	64	.272	.328	.366	.694	103	-2	1	94	82	53	.639	14	7	0	7	*S/O	2.4
1973	LA-N	162	615	55	163	26	3	4	56	34	63	.265	.305	.337	.641	77	-19	-19	100	105	62	.549	15	7	0	8	*S	1.2
1974	LA-N	160	553	61	149	18	6	5	65	53	53	.269	.338	.351	.689	100	-5	0	93	122	64	.621	14	5	1	-18	*S/O	0.1
1975	LA-N	84	252	24	52	9	2	0	14	23	28	.206	.278	.258	.536	52	-17	-15	95	83	19	.461	5	0	2	-15	S	-1.9
1976	LA-N	149	554	53	152	17	3	5	65	21	46	.274	.304	.343	.647	84	-13	-13	100	125	55	.544	15	5	2	-3	*S	0.0
1977	LA-N	153	634	84	176	28	6	4	51	24	43	.278	.306	.360	.666	78	-20	-20	100	90	64	.553	16	7	1	9	*S	1.1
1978	LA-N	155	625	72	179	32	4	3	46	30	34	.286	.321	.365	.686	92	-8	-7	99	82	69	.576	10	6	-1	16	*S	2.1
1979	LA-N	153	627	72	170	26	4	7	56	24	43	.271	.299	.359	.658	79	-19	-19	100	87	60	.527	6	9	-4	-26	*S	-3.4
1980	LA-N	130	466	38	123	23	2	3	34	18	44	.264	.296	.341	.637	80	-15	-13	97	82	48	.550	13	2	3	-13	*S	-0.8
1981	LA-N	82	262	20	61	9	2	0	22	19	20	.233	.287	.282	.570	63	-13	-12	98	117	19	.447	2	1	0	-1	S	-0.4
1982	LA-N	153	497	64	136	20	2	3	46	63	30	.274	.360	.340	.700	102	0	4	95	101	63	.653	10	2	2	4	*S	2.2
1983	LA-N	131	451	47	111	13	1	1	30	33	31	.246	.303	.286	.589	64	-21	-21	100	92	40	.506	13	9	-2	5	*S	-0.6
1984	LA-N	89	262	25	70	12	1	0	19	25	24	.267	.331	.321	.652	81	-5	-6	104	89	28	.557	4	4	-1	7	SO/2	0.6
1985	LA-N	76	169	19	44	6	1	0	13	18	9	.260	.335	.308	.643	87	-4	-2	93	100	19	.591	4	0	1	-4	SO/23	-0.3
1986	LA-N	105	216	21	54	11	0	0	18	15	23	.250	.305	.301	.606	72	-9	-8	94	110	21	.530	7	0	2	-8	OS/23	-1.1
Total	18	2181	7318	796	1926	293	57	46	627	483	667	.263	.312	.338	.650	83	-195	-172	97	96	759	.577	167	69	9	-36	*SO/23	-1.9

■ **HANK RUSZKOWSKI** Ruszkowski, Henry Alexander b: 11/10/25, Cleveland, Ohio BR/TR, 6', 190 lbs. Deb: 9/26/44

YEAR	TM/L	G	AB	R	H	2B	3B	HR	RBI	BB	SO	AVG	OBP	SLG	PRO	/A	BR	/A	PF	CHI	RC	TA	SB	CS	SBR	FR	POS	TPR
1944	Cle-A	3	8	1	3	0	0	0	1	0	1	.375	.375	.375	.750	114	0	0	100	120	1	.500	0	0	0	0	/C	0.0
1945	Cle-A	14	49	2	10	0	0	0	5	4	9	.204	.264	.204	.468	37	-4	-4	99	184	3	.341	0	0	0	1	C	-0.1
1947	Cle-A	23	27	5	7	2	0	3	4	2	6	.259	.310	.667	.977	174	2	2	96	54	6	1.000	0	0	0	-0	C	0.3
Total	3	40	84	8	20	2	0	3	10	6	16	.238	.289	.369	.658	89	-2	-2	98	137	9	.578	0	0	0	1	/C	0.2

■ **BABE RUTH** Ruth, George Herman "The Bambino" or "The Sultan Of Swat" b: 2/6/1895, Baltimore, Md. d: 8/16/48, New York, N.Y. BL/TL, 6'2", 215 lbs. Deb: 7/11/14 CH

YEAR	TM/L	G	AB	R	H	2B	3B	HR	RBI	BB	SO	AVG	OBP	SLG	PRO	/A	BR	/A	PF	CHI	RC	TA	SB	CS	SBR	FR	POS	TPR
1914	Bos-A	5	10	1	2	1	0	0	2	0	4	.200	.200	.300	.500	51	-1	-1	98	250	1	.375	0			-0	/P	0.0
1915	Bos-A	42	92	16	29	10	1	4	21	9	23	.315	.376	.576	.952	186	9	9	99	110	20	.984	0			1	P	0.0
1916	Bos-A	67	136	18	37	5	3	3	15	10	23	.272	.322	.419	.741	131	3	4	94	81	19	.677	0			1	P	0.0
1917	Bos-A	52	123	14	40	6	3	2	12	12	18	.325	.385	.472	.857	149	9	7	108	67	22	.843	0			2	P	0.0
1918	Bos-A	95	317	50	95	26	11	**11**	66	57	58	.300	.410	.555	.965	200	35	37	95	122	72	1.086	6			-0	OP1	3.8
1919	Bos-A	130	432	**103**	139	34	12	**29**	**114**	101	58	.322	**.456**	**.657**	**1.114**	**231**	**66**	**72**	91	118	**128**	**1.358**	7			4	*OP/1	**7.1**
1920	NY-A	142	458	**158**	172	36	9	**54**	**137**	**148**	80	.376	**.530**	**.847**	**1.378**	**255**	**113**	**111**	102	93	**211**	**1.843**	14	14	-4	-1	*O/1P	**8.8**
1921	NY-A	152	540	**177**	204	44	16	**59**	**171**	**144**	81	.378	**.512**	**.846**	**1.358**	**235**	**119**	**117**	103	89	**238**	**1.782**	17	13	-3	8	*O/P1	**9.9**
1922	NY-A	110	406	94	128	24	8	35	96	84	80	.315	.434	**.672**	**1.106**	**182**	51	50	102	87	120	1.268	2	6	-3	2	*O/1	3.9
1923	NY-A	152	522	**151**	205	45	13	**41**	**130**	**170**	93	.393	**.545**	**.764**	**1.309**	**232**	**119**	**115**	104	82	**223**	**1.746**	17	21	-8	3	*O/1	**9.0**
1924	NY-A	153	529	**143**	200	39	7	**46**	121	**142**	81	**.378**	**.513**	**.739**	**1.252**	**222**	**101**	**102**	99	73	**205**	**1.596**	9	13	-5	6	*O	**8.3**
1925	NY-A	98	359	61	104	12	2	25	66	59	68	.290	.393	.543	.936	141	19	21	96	87	78	.996	2	4	-2	6	*O	1.5
1926	NY-A	152	495	**139**	184	30	5	**47**	**146**	**144**	76	.372	**.516**	**.737**	**1.253**	**226**	**97**	**98**	99	104	**196**	**1.634**	11	9	-2	-1	*O/1	**7.8**
1927	NY-A	151	540	**158**	192	29	8	**60**	164	**138**	89	.356	**.487**	**.772**	**1.259**	**223**	101	101	100	88	204	**1.615**	7	0	2	1	*O	**8.5**
1928	NY-A	154	536	**163**	173	29	8	**54**	**142**	**135**	87	.323	.461	**.709**	**1.170**	**221**	**84**	**91**	92	95	**182**	**1.418**	4	5	-2	-6	*O	**7.0**
1929	NY-A	135	499	121	172	26	6	**46**	154	72	60	.345	.430	**.697**	**1.128**	**188**	62	**63**	99	115	150	**1.297**	5	3	-0	-13	*O	4.1
1930	NY-A	145	518	150	186	28	9	**49**	153	**136**	61	.359	**.493**	**.732**	**1.225**	**230**	**90**	**99**	90	93	191	**1.538**	10	10	-3	-3	*O/P	**7.7**
1931	NY-A	145	534	149	199	31	3	**46**	163	**128**	51	.373	**.495**	**.700**	**1.195**	**215**	**92**	**93**	98	111	**192**	**1.499**	5	4	-1	-13	*O/1	**6.4**
1932	NY-A	133	457	120	156	13	5	41	137	**130**	62	.341	**.489**	.661	1.150	**204**	71	75	95	114	157	1.439	2	2	-1	-8	*O/1	5.5
1933	NY-A	137	459	97	138	21	3	34	103	**114**	90	.301	.442	.582	1.023	186	50	56	91	95	124	1.187	4	5	-2	-8	*O/P1	3.9
1934	NY-A	125	365	78	105	17	4	22	84	103	63	.288	.447	.537	.984	160	33	36	96	107	95	1.148	1	3	-2	-9	*O	2.2
1935	Bos-N	28	72	13	13	0	0	6	12	20	24	.181	.359	.431	.789	116	2	2	96	88	12	.836	0			-5	O	-0.3
Total	22	2503	8399	2174	2873	506	136	714	2209	2056	1330	.342	.474	.690	1.163	209	1322	1357	97	97	2841	1.421	123	112		-33	*OP/1	105.1

■ **JIM RUTHERFORD** Rutherford, James Hollis b: 9/26/1886, Stillwater, Minn. d: 9/18/56, Cleveland, Ohio 6'1", 180 lbs. Deb: 7/12/10

YEAR	TM/L	G	AB	R	H	2B	3B	HR	RBI	BB	SO	AVG	OBP	SLG	PRO	/A	BR	/A	PF	CHI	RC	TA	SB	CS	SBR	FR	POS	TPR
1910	Cle-A	1	2	0	1	0	0	0	0	0		.500	.500	.500	1.000	214	0	0	100	0	0	1.000	0			-0	/O	0.0

■ **MICKEY RUTNER** Rutner, Milton b: 3/18/20, Hempstead, N.Y. BR/TR, 5'11.5", 185 lbs. Deb: 9/11/47

YEAR	TM/L	G	AB	R	H	2B	3B	HR	RBI	BB	SO	AVG	OBP	SLG	PRO	/A	BR	/A	PF	CHI	RC	TA	SB	CS	SBR	FR	POS	TPR
1947	Phi-A	12	48	4	12	1	0	1	4	3	2	.250	.294	.333	.627	74	-2	-2	100	82	4	.475	0	0	0	0	3	-0.1

■ **MARK RYAL** Ryal, Mark Dwayne b: 4/28/60, Henryetta, Okla. BL/TL, 6'1", 185 lbs. Deb: 9/07/82

YEAR	TM/L	G	AB	R	H	2B	3B	HR	RBI	BB	SO	AVG	OBP	SLG	PRO	/A	BR	/A	PF	CHI	RC	TA	SB	CS	SBR	FR	POS	TPR
1982	KC-A	6	13	0	1	0	0	0	0	1	3	.077	.143	.077	.220	-38	-2	-2	100	0	0	.167	0	0	0	-1	/O	-0.2
1985	Chi-A	12	33	4	5	3	0	0	3	3	3	.152	.222	.242	.465	27	-3	-3	100	149	2	.367	0	0	0	-1	O	-0.4
1986	Cal-A	13	32	6	12	0	0	2	5	2	4	.375	.412	.563	.974	170	3	3	96	83	7	1.000	1	0	0	-1	/O1D	0.2
1987	Cal-A	58	100	7	20	6	0	5	18	3	15	.200	.223	.410	.633	64	-6	-5	99	128	8	.524	0	0	0	-5	O/1D	-1.0
Total	4	89	178	17	38	9	0	7	26	9	25	.213	.251	.382	.633	68	-9	-8	99	114	17	.542	1	0	0	-8	/O1D	-1.4

■ **CONNIE RYAN** Ryan, Cornelius Joseph b: 2/27/20, New Orleans, La. BR/TR, 5'11", 175 lbs. Deb: 4/14/42 MC

YEAR	TM/L	G	AB	R	H	2B	3B	HR	RBI	BB	SO	AVG	OBP	SLG	PRO	/A	BR	/A	PF	CHI	RC	TA	SB	CS	SBR	FR	POS	TPR
1942	NY-N	11	27	4	5	0	0	0	2	4	3	.185	.290	.185	.476	40	-2	-2	103	148	2	.455	1			0	2	0.0
1943	Bos-N	132	457	52	97	10	2	1	24	58	56	.212	.301	.249	.550	57	-22	-25	106	76	38	.488	7			-13	*23	-3.8
1944	Bos-N	88	332	56	98	18	5	4	25	36	40	.295	.364	.416	.780	126	9	11	95	57	50	.763	13			11	23	3.1
1946	Bos-N	143	502	55	121	28	8	1	48	55	63	.241	.317	.335	.652	90	-10	-7	95	107	56	.592	7			-12	*23	-1.5
1947	Bos-N	150	544	60	144	33	5	5	69	71	60	.265	.351	.371	.722	95	-5	-3	97	120	74	.677	5			-7	*2/S	0.7
1948	Bos-N	51	122	14	26	3	0	0	10	21	16	.213	.333	.238	.571	56	-6	-7	102	129	11	.520	0			1	2/3	-0.2
1949	Bos-N	85	208	28	52	13	1	6	20	21	30	.250	.319	.409	.727	97	-2	-1	97	73	27	.669	1			0	3S2/1	0.2
1950	Bos-N	20	72	12	14	2	0	3	6	12	9	.194	.326	.347	.673	89	-2	-1	86	72	8	.639	0			-3	2	-0.2
	Cin-N	106	367	45	95	18	5	3	43	52	46	.259	.352	.360	.712	84	-5	-8	105	120	48	.670	4			3	*2	-0.1
	Yr	126	439	57	109	20	5	6	49	64	55	.248	.348	.358	.705	85	-8	-9	102	113	58	.671	4			0		-0.3
1951	Cin-N	136	473	75	112	17	4	16	53	79	72	.237	.350	.391	.741	98	1	0	101	93	69	.732	11	6	-0	-8	*2/31O	-0.3
1952	Phi-N	154	577	81	139	24	6	12	49	69	72	.241	.327	.366	.693	91	-6	-7	101	82	73	.654	13	5	1	-5	*2	-0.3
1953	Phi-N	90	247	47	73	14	6	5	26	30	35	.296	.372	.462	.833	117	6	6	99	79	45	.832	5	1	1	0	2/1	1.0
	Chi-A	17	54	6	12	1	0	0	6	9	12	.222	.333	.241	.574	54	-3	-3	106	171	5	.522	2	0	1	-0	3	-0.3
1954	Cin-N	1	0	0	0	0	0	0	0	1	0	—	1.000	—	1.241	235	0	0	104	0	0	—	0	0	0	0	H	0.0
Total	12	1184	3982	535	988	181	42	56	381	518	514	.248	.337	.357	.694	90	-49	-45	99	95	506	.673	69	12		-33	23/S1O	-1.7

■ **CYCLONE RYAN** Ryan, Daniel R. b: 1866, Capperwhite, Ireland d: 1/30/17, Medfield, Mass. TR , 6', Deb: 8/08/1887

YEAR	TM/L	G	AB	R	H	2B	3B	HR	RBI	BB	SO	AVG	OBP	SLG	PRO	/A	BR	/A	PF	CHI	RC	TA	SB	CS	SBR	FR	POS	TPR
1887	NY-a	8	32	4	7	1	0	0		3		.219	.286	.250	.536	59	-2	-1	88	0	3	.480	1			0	/1P	0.0
1891	Bos-N	1	1	0	0	0	0	0	0	0	0	.000	.000	.000	.000	-90	-0	-0	112	0	0	.000	0			0	/P	0.0
Total	2	9	33	4	7	1	0	0	0	3	0	.212	.278	.242	.520	54	-2	-1	88	0	3	.462	1			0	/1P	0.0

YEAR	TM/L	G	AB	R	H	2B	3B	HR	RBI	BB	SO	AVG	OBP	SLG	PRO	/A	BR	/A	PF	CHI	RC	TA	SB	CS	SBR	FR	POS	TPR
■ **MIKE RYAN**	Ryan, J. b: St.Louis, Mo. Deb: 7/25/1895																											
1895	StL-N	2	2	0	0	0	0	0	0	0	0	.000	.000	.000	.000	-99	-1	-1	100	0	0	.000	0			0	/3	0.0
■ **JIMMY RYAN**	Ryan, James Edward "Pony" b: 2/11/1863, Clinton, Mass. d: 10/26/23, Chicago, Ill. BR/TL, 5'9", 162 lbs. Deb: 1885																											
1885	Chi-N	3	13	2	6	1	0	0	2	1	1	.462	.500	.538	1.038	207	2	2	114	88	4	1.143				0	/SO	0.2
1886	Chi-N	84	327	58	100	17	6	4	53	12	28	.306	.330	.431	.762	112	11	3	116	115	51	.718	10			-2	O/S32P	0.2
1887	Chi-N	126	508	117	145	23	10	11	74	53	19	.285	.360	.435	.795	105	16	1	116	79	100	.909	50			-8	*O/P2	-0.4
1888	Chi-N	129	549	115	**182**	**33**	10	**16**	64	35	50	.332	.377	**.515**	.892	173	**51**	46	107	60	**133**	**1.044**	60			2	*O/P	**4.5**
1889	Chi-N	135	576	140	177	31	14	17	72	70	62	.307	.388	.498	.886	150	37	38	99	55	**132**	1.023	45			13	*OS	4.0
1890	Chi-P	118	486	99	165	32	5	6	89	60	36	.340	.416	.463	.879	132	27	23	104	88	109	.994	30			-1	*O	1.4
1891	Chi-N	118	505	110	140	22	15	9	66	53	38	.277	.355	.434	.789	124	19	14	106	68	90	.841	27			-1	*O/SP	0.6
1892	Chi-N	128	505	105	148	21	11	10	65	61	41	.293	.375	.438	.812	160	29	35	92	70	95	.880	27			5	*O/S	3.3
1893	Chi-N	83	341	82	102	21	7	3	30	59	25	.299	.407	.428	.835	120	14	11	104	46	64	.904	8			0	OS/P	0.7
1894	Chi-N	108	474	132	171	37	7	3	62	50	23	.361	.425	.487	.912	113	18	10	108	62	105	.974	11			9	*O	0.9
1895	Chi-N	108	438	83	139	22	8	6	49	48	22	.317	.392	.445	.837	114	12	10	103	57	86	.893	18			1	*O	0.1
1896	Chi-N	128	489	83	149	24	10	3	86	46	16	.305	.369	.413	.782	100	6	-1	108	125	87	.826	29			-3	*O	-1.0
1897	Chi-N	136	520	103	156	33	17	5	85	50		.300	.369	.458	.827	120	14	14	100	104	100	.885	27			8	*O	1.0
1898	Chi-N	144	572	122	185	32	13	4	79	73		.323	.405	.446	.850	142	36	33	103	79	118	.935	29			-10	*O	1.3
1899	Chi-N	125	525	91	158	20	10	3	68	43		.301	.356	.394	.750	113	6	9	96	83	79	.711	9			-3	*O	-0.1
1900	Chi-N	105	415	66	115	25	4	5	59	29		.277	.324	.393	.717	108	-1	4	93	91	61	.703	19			2	*O	-0.2
1902	Was-A	120	484	92	155	32	6	6	44	43		.320	.376	.448	.824	131	19	20	99	55	87	.821	10			-10	*O	0.3
1903	Was-A	114	437	42	109	25	4	7	46	17		.249	.278	.373	.651	91	-3	-6	105	87	49	.576	9			2	*O	-1.0
Total	18	2012	8164	1642	2502	451	157	118	1093	803	361	.306	.373	.444	.817	125	311	265	103	77	1549	.866	418			5	*O/SP23	15.8
■ **JOHN RYAN**	Ryan, John A. (Played 1 Game Under Real Name Of Daniel Sheehan) b: Birmingham, Mich. Deb: 5/27/1884																											
1884	Was-U	7	28	2	4	0	1	0		1		.143	.172	.214	.387	31	-2	-2	97	0	1	.292	0			0	/O3	-0.1
	WiL-U	2	6	0	1	0	0	0		1		.167	.286	.167	.452	55	-0	-0	103	0	0	.400	0			0	/O	0.0
	Yr	9	34	2	5	0	1	0		2		.147	.194	.206	.400	36	-2	-2	98	0	1	.310	0			0		-0.1
Total	1	9	34	2	5	0	1	0		2		.147	.194	.206	.400	36	-2	-2	98	0	1	.310	0			0	/O3	-0.1
■ **JACK RYAN**	Ryan, John Bernard b: 11/12/1868, Haverhill, Mass. d: 8/21/52, Boston, Mass. BR/TR, 5'10.5", 165 lbs. Deb: 9/02/1889 C																											
1889	Lou-a	21	79	8	14	1	0	0	2	3	17	.177	.207	.190	.397	15	-9	-8	96	39	4	.308	2			0	C/O3	-0.6
1890	Lou-a	93	337	43	73	16	4	0		12		.217	.244	.288	.531	54	-19	-22	107	0	26	.436	6			-6	C/OS1	-1.5
1891	Lou-a	75	253	24	57	5	4	2	25	15	40	.225	.271	.300	.572	73	-12	-8	90	88	22	.485	3			1	C1/3O2	-0.3
1894	Bos-N	53	201	39	54	12	7	1	29	13	16	.269	.316	.413	.729	67	-9	-14	113	93	28	.680	3			-3	C/1	-0.8
1895	Bos-N	49	189	22	55	7	0	0	18	6	6	.291	.313	.328	.641	65	-9	-10	103	81	21	.530	3			2	C/2O	-0.3
1896	Bos-N	8	32	2	3	1	0	0	0	0	1	.094	.094	.125	.219	-39	-6	-7	108	0	0	.138	0			0	/C	-0.5
1898	Bro-N	87	301	39	57	11	4	0	24	15		.189	.233	.252	.485	43	-23	-21	95	95	19	.402	5			4	C/31	-0.9
1899	Bal-N	2	4	0	2	1	0	0	1	0		.500	.500	.750	1.250	227	1	1	108	102	2	2.000	1			0	/C	0.1
1901	StL-N	83	300	27	59	6	5	0	31	7		.197	.215	.250	.465	37	-24	-23	97	138	18	.361	5			-1	C/21O	-1.5
1902	StL-N	76	267	23	48	4	4	0	14	4		.180	.192	.225	.417	31	-22	-21	95	82	12	.301	2			1	C/132S	-1.3
1903	StL-N	67	227	18	54	5	1	1	10	10		.238	.270	.282	.552	61	-12	-11	96	49	18	.439	2			4	C1/S	-0.2
1912	Was-A	1	1	0	0	0	0	0	0	0		.000	.000	.000	.000	-99	-0	-0	99	0	0	.000	0			0	/3	0.0
1913	Was-A	1	1	0	0	0	0	0	0	0	0	.000	.000	.000	.000	-95	-0	-0	106	0	0	.000	0			0	/C	0.0
Total	13	616	2192	245	476	69	29	4	154	85	80	.217	.248	.281	.528	51	-145	-144	99	74	170	.429	32			3	C/123OS	-7.8
■ **BUDDY RYAN**	Ryan, John Budd b: 10/6/1885, Denver, Colo. d: 7/9/56, Sacramento, Cal. BL/TR, 5'9.5", 172 lbs. Deb: 4/11/12																											
1912	Cle-A	93	328	53	89	12	9	1	31	30		.271	.343	.372	.715	103	2	1	101	84	46	.711	12			5	O	0.0
1913	Cle-A	73	243	26	72	6	1	0	32	11	13	.296	.332	.329	.661	88	-2	-4	106	145	29	.596	9			2	O/1	-0.5
Total	2	166	571	79	161	18	10	1	63	41	13	.282	.339	.354	.692	97	-0	-3	103	109	75	.663	21			7	O/1	-0.5
■ **BLONDY RYAN**	Ryan, John Collins b: 1/4/06, Lynn, Mass d: 11/28/59, Swampscott, Mass. BR/TR, 6'1", 178 lbs. Deb: 7/13/30																											
1930	Chi-A	28	87	9	18	0	4	1	10	6	13	.207	.258	.333	.591	47	-7	-7	103	104	8	.536	2	0	1	2	3/S2	-0.2
1933	NY-N	146	525	47	125	10	5	3	48	15	62	.238	.259	.293	.553	58	-29	-28	99	111	38	.407	0			17	*S	-0.1
1934	NY-N	110	385	35	93	19	0	2	41	19	68	.242	.277	.306	.584	57	-24	-23	98	119	31	.458	3			13	3S2	-0.1
1935	Phi-N	39	129	13	34	3	0	1	10	7	20	.264	.312	.310	.622	59	-6	-8	114	84	12	.495	1			-1	S/23	-0.6
	NY-A	30	105	12	25	1	3	0	11	3	10	.238	.259	.305	.564	49	-9	-8	93	117	8	.438	0	0	0	-5	S	-0.9
1937	NY-N	21	75	10	18	3	1	1	13	6	8	.240	.296	.347	.643	74	-3	-3	100	165	7	.533	0			5	S/23	0.4
1938	NY-N	12	24	1	5	0	0	0	0	1	3	.208	.240	.208	.448	23	-2	-3	103	0	1	.273	0			0	/23S	-0.1
Total	6	386	1330	127	318	36	13	8	133	57	184	.239	.271	.304	.575	57	-80	-80	100	112	105	.462	6	0		33	S/32	-1.6
■ **JACK RYAN**	Ryan, John Francis b: 5/5/05, Mineral, Minn. d: 9/2/67, Rochester, Minn. BR/TR, 6', 185 lbs. Deb: 6/18/29																											
1929	Bos-A	2	3	0	0	0	0	0	0	0	0	.000	.000	.000	.000	-98	-1	-1	102	0	0	.000	0	0	0	-1	/O	-0.1
■ **JOHNNY RYAN**	Ryan, John Joseph b: Philadelphia, Pa. d: 3/22/02, Philadelphia, Pa. 5'7.5", 150 lbs. Deb: 8/19/1873																											
1873	Phi-n	2	9	1	2							.222															/1O	
1874	Bal-n	47	196	28	35							.179															*O	
1875	NH-n	37	153	17	23							.150															O/PS3	
1876	Lou-N	64	241	32	61	5	1	1	18	6	23	.253	.271	.295	.566	85	-3	-4	104	84	20	.428				-6	*O/P	-0.9
1877	Cin-N	6	26	2	4	0	1	0	2	1	5	.154	.185	.231	.416	37	-2	-1	82	100	1	.318				0	/O	0.0
Total	3 n	86	358	46	60							.168															/O	
Total	2	70	267	34	65	5	2	1	20	7	28	.243	.263	.288	.551	81	-5	-5	102	85	21	.416				-6	O/P3S1	-0.9
■ **MIKE RYAN**	Ryan, Michael James b: 11/25/41, Haverhill, Mass. BR/TR, 6'2", 205 lbs. Deb: 10/03/64 C																											
1964	Bos-A	1	3	0	1	0	0	0	2	1	0	.333	.500	.333	.833	135	0	0	102	864	1	1.000	0	0	0	0	/C	0.0
1965	Bos-A	33	107	7	17	0	1	3	9	5	19	.159	.196	.262	.458	27	-10	-11	107	101	4	.344	0	0	0	4	C	-0.5
1966	Bos-A	116	369	27	79	15	3	2	32	29	68	.214	.271	.287	.559	56	-19	-22	109	120	28	.453	1	0	0	1	*C	-1.6
1967	Bos-A	79	226	21	45	4	2	2	27	26	42	.199	.285	.261	.546	54	-10	-14	115	173	17	.466	2	0	1	-4	C	-1.3
1968	Phi-N	96	296	12	53	6	1	1	15	15	59	.179	.219	.216	.435	32	-25	-24	97	94	12	.306	0	3	-2	-2	C	-2.8
1969	Phi-N	133	446	41	91	17	2	12	44	30	66	.204	.257	.332	.589	65	-23	-22	98	96	36	.492	1	1	-0	1	*C	-1.2
1970	Phi-N	46	134	14	24	8	0	2	11	16	24	.179	.267	.284	.550	49	-10	-9	96	97	9	.458	0	0	0	-2	C	-0.8
1971	Phi-N	43	134	9	22	5	1	3	6	10	32	.164	.222	.284	.506	41	-10	-11	103	52	8	.421	0	0	0	2	C	-0.7
1972	Phi-N	46	106	6	19	4	0	2	10	10	25	.179	.256	.274	.530	52	-7	-7	97	117	7	.435	0	0	0	-3	C	-0.6
1973	Phi-N	28	69	7	16	1	2	1	5	6	19	.232	.293	.348	.641	71	-2	-3	108	74	6	.526	0	0	0	2	C	0.1
1974	Pit-N	15	30	2	3	0	0	0	0	4	16	.100	.206	.100	.306	-13	-4	-4	98	0	1	.241	0	0	0	0	C	-0.3
Total	11	636	1920	146	370	60	12	28	161	152	370	.193	.253	.280	.534	51	-120	-127	103	107	128	.449	4	4	-1	-0	C	-9.7
■ **TOM RYDER**	Ryder, Thomas Deb: 7/22/1884																											
1884	StL-U	8	28	4	7	1	0	0		2		.250	.300	.286	.586	96	0	-0	104	0	2	.476	0			0	/O	0.0
■ **GENE RYE**	Rye, Eugene Rudolph "Half-Pint" (born Eugene Rudolph Mercantelli) b: 11/15/06, Chicago, Ill. d: 1/21/80, Park Ridge, Ill. BL/TR, 5'6", 165 lbs. Deb: 4/22/31																											
1931	Bos-A	17	39	3	7	0	0	0	1	2	5	.179	.220	.179	.399	6	-5	-5	94	47	2	.281	0	0	0	-2	O	-0.6
■ **ALEX SABO**	Sabo, Alexander "Giz" (born Alexander Szabo) b: 2/14/10, New Brunswick, N.J BR/TR, 6', 192 lbs. Deb: 8/01/36																											
1936	Was-A	4	8	1	3	0	0	0	1	0	2	.375	.375	.375	.750	88	-0	-0	98	108	1	.600	0	0	0	0	/C	0.0
1937	Was-A	1	0	0	0	0	0	0	0	0	0	—	—	—	—	—	0	0	94	—	—	—	0	0	0	0	/C	0.0
Total	2	5	8	1	3	0	0	0	1	0	2	.375	.375	.375	.750	88	-0	-0	98	108	2	.600	0	0	0	0	/C	0.0
■ **CHRIS SABO**	Sabo, Christopher Andrew b: 1/19/62, Detroit, Mich. BR/TR, 6', 185 lbs. Deb: 4/04/88																											
1988	Cin-N	137	538	74	146	40	2	11	44	29	52	.271	.316	.414	.730	103	4	1	105	73	69	.727	46	14	5	16	*3/S	2.3

YEAR	TM/L	G	AB	R	H	2B	3B	HR	RBI	BB	SO	AVG	OBP	SLG	PRO	/A	BR	/A	PF	CHI	RC	TA	SB	CS	SBR	FR	POS	TPR
■ **FRANK SACKA**	Sacka, Frank b: 8/30/24, Romulus, Mich. BR/TR, 6', 195 lbs. Deb: 4/29/51																											
1951	Was-A	7	16	1	4	0	0	0	3	0	5	.250	.250	.250	.500	37	-1	-1	95	268	1	.333	0	0	0	-0	/C	0.0
1953	Was-A	7	18	2	5	0	0	0	3	3	1	.278	.381	.278	.659	85	-0	-0	94	222	2	.571	0	0	0	0	/C	0.0
Total	2	14	34	3	9	0	0	0	6	3	6	.265	.324	.265	.589	64	-2	-2	95	242	3	.462	0	0	0	0	/C	0.0
■ **MIKE SADEK**	Sadek, Michael George b: 5/30/46, Minneapolis, Minn. BR/TR, 5'9", 165 lbs. Deb: 4/13/73																											
1973	SF-N	39	66	6	11	1	1	0	4	11	8	.167	.286	.212	.498	38	-5	-6	105	115	5	.464	1	0	0	-2	C	-0.5
1975	SF-N	42	106	14	25	5	2	0	9	14	14	.236	.325	.321	.646	78	-3	-3	102	102	10	.563	1	0	0	-2	C	-0.2
1976	SF-N	55	93	8	19	2	0	0	7	11	10	.204	.295	.226	.521	48	-6	-6	103	128	7	.434	0	0	0	-4	C	-0.8
1977	SF-N	61	126	12	29	7	0	1	15	12	5	.230	.297	.310	.607	60	-7	-7	104	143	12	.530	2	1	0	-3	C	-1.1
1978	SF-N	40	109	15	26	3	0	2	9	10	11	.239	.303	.321	.624	81	-4	-3	92	87	11	.541	1	0	0	1	C	0.0
1979	SF-N	63	126	14	30	5	0	1	11	15	24	.238	.324	.302	.626	78	-5	-3	92	106	12	.539	1	0	0	-2	C/O	-0.3
1980	SF-N	64	151	14	38	4	1	1	16	27	18	.252	.365	.311	.676	95	-1	0	96	127	19	.638	0	0	0	1	C	0.3
1981	SF-N	19	36	5	6	3	0	0	3	8	7	.167	.318	.250	.568	60	-2	-2	105	131	4	.567	0	0	0	0	C	0.0
Total	8	383	813	88	184	30	4	5	74	108	97	.226	.319	.292	.610	71	-31	-29	99	117	80	.560	6	1	1	-11	C/O	-2.6
■ **ED SADOWSKI**	Sadowski, Edward Roman b: 1/19/32, Pittsburgh, Pa. BR/TR, 5'11", 175 lbs. Deb: 4/20/60																											
1960	Bos-A	38	93	10	20	2	0	3	8	8	13	.215	.284	.333	.618	64	-5	-5	103	78	8	.513	0	0	0	-3	C	-0.5
1961	LA-A	69	164	16	38	13	0	4	12	11	33	.232	.280	.384	.664	68	-6	-9	111	63	16	.576	2	3	-1	-3	C	-1.2
1962	LA-A	27	55	4	11	4	0	1	3	2	14	.200	.228	.327	.555	46	-4	-4	102	57	4	.467	1	0	0	1	C	-0.1
1963	LA-A	80	174	24	30	1	1	4	15	17	33	.172	.246	.259	.505	46	-14	-12	91	110	11	.430	2	1	0	-1	C	-1.2
1966	Atl-N	3	9	1	1	0	0	0	1	1	1	.111	.200	.111	.311	-11	-1	-1	99	420	0	.250	0	0	0	0	/C	0.0
Total	5	217	495	55	100	20	1	12	39	39	94	.202	.262	.319	.581	57	-30	-31	101	89	39	.509	5	4	-1	-6	C	-3.0
■ **BOB SADOWSKI**	Sadowski, Robert Frank "Sid" b: 1/15/37, St.Louis, Mo. BL/TR, 6', 175 lbs. Deb: 9/16/60																											
1960	StL-N	1	1	0	0	0	0	0	0	1	0	.000	.500	.000	.500	47	0	0	108	0	0	1.000	0	0	0	0	/2	0.0
1961	Phi-N	16	54	4	7	0	0	0	0	4	7	.130	.203	.130	.333	-10	-8	-8	94	0	1	.265	1	0	0	0	3	-0.7
1962	Chi-A	79	130	22	30	3	3	6	24	13	22	.231	.301	.438	.739	101	-1	-0	95	127	17	.680	0	0	0	-1	32	0.0
1963	LA-A	88	144	12	36	6	0	1	22	15	34	.250	.321	.313	.633	86	-4	-2	91	192	15	.564	2	1	0	-2	O/32	-0.4
Total	4	184	329	38	73	9	3	7	46	33	63	.222	.295	.331	.626	76	-13	-11	93	134	34	.566	3	1	0	-3	/3O2	-1.1
■ **TOM SAFFELL**	Saffell, Thomas Judson b: 7/26/21, Etowah, Tenn. BL/TR, 5'11", 170 lbs. Deb: 7/02/49																											
1949	Pit-N	73	205	36	66	7	1	2	25	21	27	.322	.385	.395	.780	109	3	3	101	108	32	.754	5			0	O	0.1
1950	Pit-N	67	182	18	37	7	0	2	6	14	34	.203	.264	.275	.539	41	-15	-16	103	41	14	.452	1			9	O	-0.7
1951	Pit-N	49	65	11	13	0	0	1	5	5	18	.200	.257	.246	.503	34	-6	-6	107	102	4	.407	1	1	-0	-3	O	-0.9
1955	Pit-N	73	113	21	19	1	0	1	3	15	22	.168	.266	.204	.469	28	-12	-11	97	47	7	.411	1	0	0	-5	O	-1.6
	KC-A	9	37	5	8	0	0	0	1	4	7	.216	.293	.216	.509	38	-3	-3	101	41	3	.433	1	0	0	1	/O	-0.2
Total	4	271	602	91	143	15	1	6	40	59	108	.238	.307	.296	.602	60	-33	-34	101	72	61	.536	9	1		2	O	-3.3
■ **HARRY SAGE**	Sage, Harry "Doc" b: 3/16/1864, Rock Island, Ill. d: 5/27/47, Rock Island, Ill. BR/TR, 5'10", 185 lbs. Deb: 4/17/1890																											
1890	Tol-a	81	275	40	41	8	4	2		29		.149	.235	.229	.464	38	-21	-22	103	0	18	.444	10			5	C/O	-0.7
■ **PONY SAGER**	Sager, Samuel B. b: 1847, Marshalltown, Iowa 140 lbs. Deb: 5/06/1871																											
1871	Rok-n	8	40	9	12							.300															/SO	
■ **VIC SAIER**	Saier, Victor Sylvester b: 5/4/1891, Lansing, Mich. d: 5/14/67, E.Lansing, Mich. BL/TR, 5'11", 185 lbs. Deb: 5/03/11																											
1911	Chi-N	86	259	42	67	15	1	1	37	25	37	.259	.340	.336	.676	93	-3	-2	97	139	34	.677	11			-3	1	-0.7
1912	Chi-N	122	451	74	130	25	14	2	61	34	65	.288	.340	.419	.759	103	3	0	104	107	67	.732	11			-6	*1	-0.9
1913	Chi-N	149	519	94	150	15	**21**	14	92	62	62	.289	.370	.480	.850	143	28	28	99	117	97	.927	26			-6	*1	1.5
1914	Chi-N	153	537	87	129	24	8	18	72	94	61	.240	.357	.415	.773	132	21	22	98	91	85	.833	19			-11	*1	0.9
1915	Chi-N	144	497	74	131	35	11	11	64	64	62	.264	.350	.445	.795	137	24	22	102	98	83	.843	29	9	3	-6	*1	1.4
1916	Chi-N	147	498	60	126	25	3	7	50	79	68	.253	.356	.357	.714	102	14	5	117	106	66	.715	20	17	-4	-0	*1	-0.1
1917	Chi-N	6	21	5	5	1	0	0	2	2	1	.238	.304	.286	.590	78	-0	-1	105	131	2	.500	0			0	/1	0.0
1919	Pit-N	58	166	19	37	3	3	2	17	18	13	.223	.306	.313	.620	82	-2	-3	105	114	17	.597	5			-2	1	-0.6
Total	8	865	2948	455	775	143	61	55	395	378	369	.263	.351	.409	.760	118	83	72	103	107	450	.785	121	26		-34	1	1.5
■ **EBBA ST.CLAIRE**	St.Claire, Edward Joseph b: 8/5/21, Whitehall, N.Y. d: 8/22/82, Whitehill, N.Y. BB/TR, 6'1", 219 lbs. Deb: 4/17/51																											
1951	Bos-N	72	220	22	62	17	2	1	25	12	24	.282	.322	.391	.713	93	-3	-3	98	109	29	.631	2	0	1	3	C	0.2
1952	Bos-N	39	108	5	23	2	0	2	4	8	12	.213	.267	.287	.554	57	-7	-6	95	42	8	.438	0	1	-1	0	C	-0.5
1953	Mil-N	33	80	7	16	3	0	2	5	3	9	.200	.229	.313	.541	42	-7	-7	94	63	6	.438	0	0	0	1	C	-0.3
1954	NY-N	20	42	5	11	1	0	2	6	12	7	.262	.436	.429	.865	120	2	2	105	98	9	.969	0	0	0	-2	C	0.0
Total	4	164	450	39	112	23	2	7	40	35	52	.249	.306	.356	.662	79	-15	-13	97	84	52	.585	2	1	0	2	C	-0.6
■ **LENN SAKATA**	Sakata, Lenn Haruki b: 6/8/54, Honolulu, Hawaii BR/TR, 5'9", 160 lbs. Deb: 7/21/77																											
1977	Mil-A	53	154	13	25	2	0	2	12	9	22	.162	.209	.214	.423	16	-18	-17	95	122	7	.323	1	3	-2	4	2	-0.9
1978	Mil-A	30	78	8	15	4	0	0	3	8	11	.192	.267	.244	.511	42	-6	-6	106	62	5	.424	1	0	0	-1	2	-0.5
1979	Mil-A	4	14	1	7	2	0	0	1	0	1	.500	.500	.643	1.143	206	2	2	100	43	5	1.286	0	0	0	0	/2	0.2
1980	Bal-A	43	83	12	16	3	2	1	9	6	10	.193	.247	.313	.560	52	-6	-6	101	121	6	.479	2	1	0	1	2/SD	-0.2
1981	Bal-A	61	150	19	34	4	0	5	15	11	18	.227	.284	.353	.637	84	-4	-3	99	86	15	.570	4	0	1	0	S2	0.2
1982	Bal-A	136	343	40	89	18	1	6	31	30	39	.259	.326	.370	.697	91	-4	-4	100	85	42	.634	7	4	-0	-16	2S	-1.0
1983	Bal-A	66	134	23	34	7	0	3	12	16	17	.254	.338	.373	.711	95	-1	-1	100	79	17	.694	8	4	0	-6	2/CD	-0.3
1984	Bal-A	81	157	23	30	1	0	3	11	6	15	.191	.221	.255	.476	33	-15	-14	94	89	8	.379	4	1	1	-3	2/O	-1.2
1985	Bal-A	55	97	15	22	3	0	3	6	6	15	.227	.279	.351	.629	72	-4	-4	99	55	9	.550	3	2	-0	-4	2/D	-0.5
1986	Oak-A	17	34	4	12	2	0	0	5	3	6	.353	.405	.412	.817	133	1	2	94	142	5	.708	0	1	-1	1	2/D	0.2
1987	NY-A	19	45	5	12	0	1	2	4	2	4	.267	.313	.444	.757	101	-0	-0	98	61	5	.639	0	1	-1	0	3/2	0.0
Total	11	565	1289	163	296	46	4	25	109	97	158	.230	.288	.330	.617	71	-53	-51	99	88	123	.553	30	17	-1	-24	2S/3DOC	-4.0
■ **MARK SALAS**	Salas, Mark Bruce b: 3/8/61, Montebello, Cal. BL/TR, 6', 180 lbs. Deb: 6/19/84																											
1984	StL-N	14	20	1	2	1	0	0	1	0	3	.100	.100	.150	.250	-31	-3	-3	99	131	0	.167	0	0	0	-1	/CO	-0.4
1985	Min-A	120	360	51	108	20	5	9	41	18	37	.300	.335	.458	.793	111	6	5	103	85	53	.708	0	1	-1	-8	*C/D	0.1
1986	Min-A	91	258	28	60	7	4	8	33	18	32	.233	.285	.384	.669	75	-7	-10	108	107	27	.585	3	1	0	-4	C/D	-0.9
1987	Min-A	22	45	8	17	2	0	3	9	5	6	.378	.440	.622	1.062	186	5	5	96	97	12	1.138	0	1	-1	-1	C	0.4
	NY-A	50	115	13	23	4	0	3	12	10	17	.200	.281	.313	.594	60	-7	-6	98	106	11	.521	0	0	0	-4	C/OD	-0.7
	Yr	72	160	21	40	6	0	6	21	15	23	.250	.326	.400	.726	95	-2	-1	97	105	21	.667	0	1	-1	-6		-0.3
1988	Chi-A	75	196	17	49	7	0	3	9	12	17	.250	.303	.332	.635	80	-6	-5	97	48	20	.533	0	0	0	3	C/D	0.0
Total	5	372	994	118	259	41	9	26	105	63	112	.261	.310	.398	.708	90	-12	-15	102	87	123	.634	3	3	-1	-16	C/DO	-1.5
■ **ANGEL SALAZAR**	Salazar, Argenis Antonio (Yepez) b: 11/4/61, El Tigre, Venez. BR/TR, 6', 170 lbs. Deb: 8/10/83																											
1983	Mon-N	36	37	5	8	1	1	0	1	1	8	.216	.237	.297	.534	46	-3	-3	102	36	2	.400	0	0	0	-3	S	-0.2
1984	Mon-N	80	174	12	27	4	2	0	12	4	38	.155	.179	.201	.380	7	-22	-20	91	134	6	.273	1	1	-0	-12	S	-2.4
1986	KC-A	117	298	24	73	20	2	0	24	7	47	.245	.267	.326	.593	61	-16	-16	100	99	26	.467	1	1	-0	-3	*S/2	-1.3
1987	KC-A	116	317	24	65	7	0	2	21	6	46	.205	.220	.246	.466	23	-34	-36	104	100	16	.336	4	4	-1	15	*S	-1.5
1988	Chi-N	34	60	4	15	1	1	0	1	1	11	.250	.262	.300	.562	58	-3	-3	104	22	5	.413	0	0	0	1	S/23	0.0
Total	5	383	886	69	188	33	6	2	59	19	150	.212	.231	.270	.501	36	-78	-78	100	98	55	.379	6	6	-2	-2	S/23	-5.4
■ **LUIS SALAZAR**	Salazar, Luis Ernesto (Garcia) b: 5/19/56, Barcelona, Venez. BR/TR, 6', 185 lbs. Deb: 8/15/80																											
1980	SD-N	44	169	28	57	4	7	1	25	9	25	.337	.374	.462	.836	142	7	8	93	129	29	.839	11	2	2	1	3/O	1.2
1981	SD-N	109	400	37	121	19	6	3	38	16	72	.303	.331	.403	.733	115	3	6	93	90	51	.643	11	8	-2	1	3O	0.0
1982	SD-N	145	524	55	127	15	5	8	62	23	80	.242	.277	.336	.613	77	-22	-16	92	124	48	.560	32	9	4	11	*3S/O	-0.2
1983	SD-N	134	481	52	124	16	2	14	45	17	80	.258	.286	.387	.673	85	-12	-11	99	80	53	.621	24	9	2	16	*3S	0.4

YEAR	TM/L	G	AB	R	H	2B	3B	HR	RBI	BB	SO	AVG	OBP	SLG	PRO	/A	BR	/A	PF	CHI	RC	TA	SB	CS	SBR	FR	POS	TPR
1984	SD-N	93	228	20	55	7	2	3	17	6	38	.241	.261	.329	.590	66	-11	-11	99	79	17	.497	11	7	-1	-2	3O/S	-1.4
1985	Chi-A	122	327	39	80	18	2	10	45	12	60	.245	.271	.404	.675	82	-9	-9	100	110	35	.617	14	4	2	-9	O3/1D	-1.8
1986	Chi-A	4	7	1	1	0	0	0	0	1	3	.143	.250	.143	.393	11	-1	-1	101	0	0	.333	0	0	0	0	/D	0.0
1987	SD-N	84	189	13	48	5	0	3	17	14	30	.254	.305	.328	.633	70	-9	-8	97	96	19	.541	3	3	-1	-2	3SO/P1	-0.8
1988	Det-A	130	452	61	122	14	1	12	62	21	70	.270	.307	.385	.692	98	-5	-2	94	117	52	.595	6	0	2	-5	OS3/21	-0.4
Total	9	865	2777	306	735	98	25	54	311	119	458	.265	.297	.376	.673	90	-59	-44	96	103	304	.613	112	42	8	11	3O/S1D2P	-3.0

■ ED SALES Sales, Edward A. b: 1861, Harrisburg, Pa. d: 8/10/12, New Haven, Conn. TR , Deb: 7/15/1890

YEAR	TM/L	G	AB	R	H	2B	3B	HR	RBI	BB	SO	AVG	OBP	SLG	PRO	/A	BR	/A	PF	CHI	RC	TA	SB	CS	SBR	FR	POS	TPR
1890	Pit-N	51	189	19	43	7	3	1	23	16	15	.228	.298	.312	.610	91	-5	-1	88	114	19	.555	3			-16	S	-1.5

■ BILL SALKELD Salkeld, William Franklin b: 3/8/17, Pocatello, Idaho d: 4/22/67, Los Angeles, Cal. BL/TR, 5'10", 190 lbs. Deb: 4/18/45

YEAR	TM/L	G	AB	R	H	2B	3B	HR	RBI	BB	SO	AVG	OBP	SLG	PRO	/A	BR	/A	PF	CHI	RC	TA	SB	CS	SBR	FR	POS	TPR
1945	Pit-N	95	267	45	83	16	1	15	52	50	16	.311	.420	.547	.966	162	25	24	103	94	63	1.031	2			-4	C	2.1
1946	Pit-N	69	160	18	47	8	0	3	19	39	16	.294	.432	.400	.832	133	10	9	103	97	32	.921	2			-0	C	1.1
1947	Pit-N	47	61	5	13	2	0	0	8	6	8	.213	.284	.246	.529	41	-5	-5	101	198	4	.420	0			0	C	-0.4
1948	Bos-N	78	198	26	48	8	1	8	28	42	37	.242	.378	.414	.792	112	5	5	102	99	34	.824	1			3	C	1.2
1949	Bos-N	66	161	17	41	5	0	5	25	44	24	.255	.417	.379	.796	119	6	7	97	124	29	.856	1			-0	C	0.8
1950	Chi-A	1	3	0	0	0	0	0	0	1	0	.000	.250	.000	.250	-33	-1	-1	97	0	0	.333	0	0	0	0	/C	0.0
Total	6	356	850	111	232	39	2	31	132	182	101	.273	.402	.433	.835	127	41	39	101	108	162	.903	6	0		-2	C	4.8

■ CHICO SALMON Salmon, Ruthford Eduardo b: 12/3/40, Colon, Panama BR/TR, 5'10", 160 lbs. Deb: 6/28/64

YEAR	TM/L	G	AB	R	H	2B	3B	HR	RBI	BB	SO	AVG	OBP	SLG	PRO	/A	BR	/A	PF	CHI	RC	TA	SB	CS	SBR	FR	POS	TPR
1964	Cle-A	86	283	43	87	17	2	4	25	13	37	.307	.342	.424	.766	109	4	3	103	80	41	.711	10	6	-1	-3	O21	0.1
1965	Cle-A	79	120	20	29	8	0	3	12	5	19	.242	.283	.383	.667	89	-2	-2	98	90	12	.619	7	4	-0	-4	1O/23	-0.8
1966	Cle-A	126	422	46	108	13	2	7	40	21	41	.256	.291	.346	.637	81	-10	-11	101	101	44	.555	10	1	2	-10	S21O/3	-1.4
1967	Cle-A	90	203	19	46	13	1	2	19	17	29	.227	.290	.330	.620	82	-4	-5	100	109	20	.576	10	4	1	-3	O12S/3	-0.8
1968	Cle-A	103	276	24	59	8	1	3	12	12	30	.214	.254	.283	.537	62	-13	-13	101	59	19	.437	7	7	-2	-10	23SO1	-2.6
1969	Bal-A	52	91	18	27	5	0	3	12	10	22	.297	.379	.451	.829	127	4	3	104	96	16	.815	0	0	0	-1	1/2S3O	0.2
1970	Bal-A	63	172	19	43	4	0	7	22	8	30	.250	.287	.395	.683	89	-4	-3	97	100	19	.590	2	2	-1	-1	S23/1	0.0
1971	Bal-A	42	84	11	15	1	0	2	7	3	21	.179	.207	.262	.469	31	-8	-8	103	102	4	.347	0	0	0	-0	/123S	-0.8
1972	Bal-A	17	16	2	1	1	0	0	0	0	4	.063	.063	.125	.188	-46	-3	-3	98	0	0	.125	0	0	0	0	/13	-0.2
Total	9	658	1667	202	415	70	6	31	149	89	233	.249	.291	.354	.645	84	-36	-38	101	89	174	.576	46	24	-1	-31	2S1O/3	-6.3

■ JACK SALTZGAVER Saltzgaver, Otto Hamlin b: 1/23/03, Croton, Iowa d: 2/1/78, Keokuk, Iowa BL/TR, 5'11", 165 lbs. Deb: 4/12/32

YEAR	TM/L	G	AB	R	H	2B	3B	HR	RBI	BB	SO	AVG	OBP	SLG	PRO	/A	BR	/A	PF	CHI	RC	TA	SB	CS	SBR	FR	POS	TPR
1932	NY-A	20	47	10	6	2	1	0	5	10	10	.128	.281	.213	.493	31	-5	-4	95	167	4	.500	1	1	-0	0	2	-0.3
1934	NY-A	94	350	64	95	8	1	6	36	48	28	.271	.359	.351	.711	88	-7	-5	96	87	48	.699	8	1	2	-6	3/1	-0.8
1935	NY-A	61	149	17	39	6	0	3	18	23	12	.262	.368	.362	.730	96	-2	-0	93	97	21	.705	0	2	-1	-4	23/1	-0.3
1936	NY-A	34	90	14	19	5	0	1	13	13	18	.211	.311	.300	.611	54	-7	-6	95	140	9	.563	0	0	0	-1	3/21	-0.5
1937	NY-A	17	11	6	2	0	0	0	0	3	4	.182	.357	.182	.539	39	-1	-1	102	0	1	.556	0	0	0	0	/1	0.0
1945	Pit-N	52	117	20	38	5	3	0	10	8	8	.325	.368	.419	.787	114	3	2	103	71	18	.712	0			3	2/3	0.7
Total	6	278	764	131	199	26	5	10	82	105	80	.260	.351	.347	.698	85	-19	-14	96	97	101	.668	9	4		-8	3/21	-1.2

■ ED SAMCOFF Samcoff, Edward William b: 9/1/24, Sacramento, Cal. BR/TR, 5'10", 165 lbs. Deb: 4/21/51

YEAR	TM/L	G	AB	R	H	2B	3B	HR	RBI	BB	SO	AVG	OBP	SLG	PRO	/A	BR	/A	PF	CHI	RC	TA	SB	CS	SBR	FR	POS	TPR
1951	Phi-A	4	11	0	0	0	0	0	0	1	2	.000	.083	.000	.083	-72	-3	-3	106	0	0	.091	0	0	0	0	/2	-0.2

■ RON SAMFORD Samford, Ronald Edward b: 2/28/30, Dallas, Tex. BR/TR, 5'11", 156 lbs. Deb: 4/15/54

YEAR	TM/L	G	AB	R	H	2B	3B	HR	RBI	BB	SO	AVG	OBP	SLG	PRO	/A	BR	/A	PF	CHI	RC	TA	SB	CS	SBR	FR	POS	TPR
1954	NY-N	12	5	2	0	0	0	0	0	0	1	.000	.000	.000	.000	-95	-1	-1	105	0	0	.000	0	1	-1	0	/2	-0.1
1955	Det-A	1	1	0	0	0	0	0	0	0	1	.000	.000	.000	.000	-99	-0	-0	97	0	0	.000	0	0	0	0	/S	0.0
1957	Det-A	54	91	6	20	1	2	0	5	6	15	.220	.276	.275	.550	47	-6	-7	107	79	7	.458	1	0	0	-5	S2/3	-0.8
1959	Was-A	91	237	23	53	13	0	5	22	11	29	.224	.264	.342	.606	65	-12	-12	100	90	19	.490	1	0	0	3	S2	-0.2
Total	4	158	334	31	73	14	2	5	27	17	46	.219	.263	.317	.580	57	-20	-21	102	86	27	.471	2	1	0	-2	S/23	-1.1

■ BILL SAMPLE Sample, William Amos b: 4/2/55, Roanoke, Va. BR/TR, 5'9", 175 lbs. Deb: 9/02/78

YEAR	TM/L	G	AB	R	H	2B	3B	HR	RBI	BB	SO	AVG	OBP	SLG	PRO	/A	BR	/A	PF	CHI	RC	TA	SB	CS	SBR	FR	POS	TPR
1978	Tex-A	8	15	2	7	2	0	0	3	0	3	.467	.467	.600	1.067	206	2	2	96	132	4	1.125	0	0	0	-1	/OD	0.1
1979	Tex-A	128	325	60	95	21	2	5	35	37	28	.292	.368	.415	.784	111	6	6	100	90	50	.752	8	6	-1	-5	*O/D	-0.4
1980	Tex-A	99	204	29	53	10	0	4	19	18	15	.260	.338	.368	.705	93	-2	-2	100	85	26	.669	8	5	-1	-10	O/D	-1.3
1981	Tex-A	66	230	36	65	16	0	3	25	17	21	.283	.350	.391	.742	125	4	7	91	101	33	.698	4	1	1	-0	O	0.6
1982	Tex-A	97	360	56	94	14	2	10	29	27	35	.261	.318	.394	.712	102	-3	0	93	71	47	.669	10	2	2	0	O/D	0.0
1983	Tex-A	147	554	80	152	28	3	12	57	44	46	.274	.333	.401	.734	100	1	-0	101	92	79	.754	44	8	8	3	*O	0.9
1984	Tex-A	130	489	67	121	20	2	5	33	29	46	.247	.290	.327	.617	70	-20	-20	100	77	46	.540	18	6	2	4	*O/D	-1.7
1985	NY-A	59	139	18	40	5	0	1	15	9	10	.288	.340	.345	.685	92	-2	-1	96	117	17	.598	2	1	0	-6	O	-0.7
1986	Atl-N	92	200	23	57	11	0	6	14	14	26	.285	.341	.430	.771	109	3	2	102	54	31	.738	4	2	0	-7	O/2	-0.5
Total	9	826	2516	371	684	127	9	46	230	195	230	.272	.331	.384	.715	98	-11	-6	98	84	334	.691	98	31	11	-22	O/D2	-3.0

■ AMADO SAMUEL Samuel, Amado Ruperto b: 12/6/38, San Pedro De Macoris, D.R. BR/TR, 6'1", 170 lbs. Deb: 4/10/62

YEAR	TM/L	G	AB	R	H	2B	3B	HR	RBI	BB	SO	AVG	OBP	SLG	PRO	/A	BR	/A	PF	CHI	RC	TA	SB	CS	SBR	FR	POS	TPR
1962	Mil-N	76	209	16	43	10	0	3	20	12	54	.206	.249	.297	.546	46	-16	-16	99	111	15	.433	0	2	-1	-1	S2/3	-1.2
1963	Mil-N	15	17	0	3	1	0	0	0	0	4	.176	.176	.235	.412	17	-2	-2	101	0	1	.267	0	1	-1	0	/S2	0.0
1964	NY-N	53	142	7	33	7	0	0	5	4	24	.232	.264	.282	.545	56	-9	-8	95	51	10	.411	0	1	-1	-0	S3/2	-0.7
Total	3	144	368	23	79	18	0	3	25	16	82	.215	.251	.288	.539	49	-27	-26	98	83	26	.420	0	4	-2	-1	/S23	-1.9

■ JUAN SAMUEL Samuel, Juan Milton b: 12/9/60, San Pedro De Macoris, , D.R. BR/TR, 5'11", 170 lbs. Deb: 8/24/83

YEAR	TM/L	G	AB	R	H	2B	3B	HR	RBI	BB	SO	AVG	OBP	SLG	PRO	/A	BR	/A	PF	CHI	RC	TA	SB	CS	SBR	FR	POS	TPR
1983	Phi-N	18	65	14	18	1	2	2	5	4	16	.277	.329	.446	.775	112	1	1	101	58	9	.740	3	2	-0	2	2	0.3
1984	Phi-N	160	701	105	191	36	**19**	15	69	28	168	.272	.307	.442	.749	106	5	3	102	67	99	.785	72	15	13	-16	*2	0.4
1985	Phi-N	161	663	101	175	31	13	19	74	33	141	.264	.305	.436	.741	103	2	0	102	82	87	.740	53	19	5	1	*2	0.6
1986	Phi-N	145	591	90	157	36	12	16	78	26	142	.266	.306	.448	.754	101	2	-1	104	105	80	.748	42	14	4	-8	*2	-0.2
1987	Phi-N	160	655	113	178	37	**15**	28	100	60	162	.272	.338	.502	.840	114	16	12	104	85	109	.851	35	15	2	-17	*2	0.0
1988	Phi-N	157	629	68	153	32	9	12	67	39	151	.243	.300	.380	.680	93	-6	-7	101	94	73	.654	33	10	4	-22	*2/O3	-2.1
Total	6	801	3304	491	872	173	70	92	393	190	780	.264	.312	.442	.754	104	18	8	103	85	457	.767	238	75	26	-60	2/O3	-1.0

■ IKE SAMUELS Samuels, Samuel Earl b: 2/20/1876, Chicago, Ill. BR/TR, Deb: 8/03/1895

YEAR	TM/L	G	AB	R	H	2B	3B	HR	RBI	BB	SO	AVG	OBP	SLG	PRO	/A	BR	/A	PF	CHI	RC	TA	SB	CS	SBR	FR	POS	TPR
1895	StL-N	24	74	5	17	2	0	0	5	5	7	.230	.278	.257	.535	40	-6	-6	100	74	7	.509	5			0	3/S	-0.4

■ GUS SANBERG Sanberg, Gustave E. b: 2/23/1896, Long Island City, N.Y. d: 2/3/30, Los Angeles, Cal. BR/TR, 6'1", 189 lbs. Deb: 5/11/23

YEAR	TM/L	G	AB	R	H	2B	3B	HR	RBI	BB	SO	AVG	OBP	SLG	PRO	/A	BR	/A	PF	CHI	RC	TA	SB	CS	SBR	FR	POS	TPR
1923	Cin-N	7	17	1	3	1	0	0	1	1	1	.176	.222	.235	.458	21	-2	-2	98	88	1	.357	0	0	0	0	/C	-0.1
1924	Cin-N	24	52	1	9	0	0	0	3	2	7	.173	.204	.173	.377	2	-7	-7	101	122	2	.256	0	0	0	-1	C	-0.7
Total	2	31	69	2	12	1	0	0	4	3	8	.174	.208	.188	.397	7	-9	-9	100	113	3	.281	0	0	0	-1	/C	-0.8

■ ALEJANDRO SANCHEZ Sanchez, Alejandro (Pimentel) b: 2/14/59, San Pedro, D.R. BR/TR, 6', 185 lbs. Deb: 9/06/82

YEAR	TM/L	G	AB	R	H	2B	3B	HR	RBI	BB	SO	AVG	OBP	SLG	PRO	/A	BR	/A	PF	CHI	RC	TA	SB	CS	SBR	FR	POS	TPR
1982	Phi-N	7	14	3	4	1	0	2	4	0	4	.286	.286	.786	1.071	203	1	2	94	92	3	1.100	0	0	0	-0	/O	0.1
1983	Phi-N	8	7	2	2	0	0	0	2	0	2	.286	.286	.286	.571	58	-0	-0	101	396	0	.333	0	0	0	-1	/O	0.0
1984	SF-N	13	41	3	8	0	1	0	2	0	12	.195	.195	.244	.439	24	-4	-4	96	78	1	.333	2	3	-1	0	O	-0.5
1985	Det-A	71	133	19	33	6	2	6	12	0	39	.248	.248	.459	.707	83	-3	-4	106	60	13	.594	2	2	-1	-7	OD	-1.0
1986	Min-A	8	16	1	2	0	0	0	1	1	8	.125	.176	.125	.301	-14	-3	-3	108	199	0	.188	0	0	0	-0	/OD	-0.2
1987	Oak-A	2	3	0	0	0	0	0	0	0	1	.000	.000	.000	.000	-99	-1	-1	91	0	0	.000	0	0	0	-0	/OD	0.0
Total	6	109	214	28	49	7	3	8	21	1	66	.229	.233	.402	.634	69	-9	-10	103	87	18	.535	4	5	-2	-8	/OD	-1.6

■ CELERINO SANCHEZ Sanchez, Celerino (Perez) b: 2/3/44, Veracruz, Mexico BR/TR, 5'11", 160 lbs. Deb: 6/13/72

YEAR	TM/L	G	AB	R	H	2B	3B	HR	RBI	BB	SO	AVG	OBP	SLG	PRO	/A	BR	/A	PF	CHI	RC	TA	SB	CS	SBR	FR	POS	TPR
1972	NY-A	71	250	18	62	8	3	0	22	12	30	.248	.293	.304	.597	84	-7	-5	92	123	21	.467	0	0	0	2	3	0.0
1973	NY-A	34	64	12	14	3	0	1	9	2	12	.219	.242	.313	.555	55	-4	-4	101	154	5	.451	1	1	-0	0	3D/SO	-0.3
Total	2	105	314	30	76	11	3	1	31	14	42	.242	.283	.306	.589	78	-11	-9	94	129	26	.481	1	1	-0	3	/3DOS	-0.3

■ ORLANDO SANCHEZ Sanchez, Orlando b: 9/7/56, Canovanas, P.R. BL/TR, 6', 185 lbs. Deb: 5/06/81

YEAR	TM/L	G	AB	R	H	2B	3B	HR	RBI	BB	SO	AVG	OBP	SLG	PRO	/A	BR	/A	PF	CHI	RC	TA	SB	CS	SBR	FR	POS	TPR
1981	StL-N	27	49	5	14	2	1	0	6	2	6	.286	.314	.367	.681	91	-1	-1	102	131	5	.568	1	0	0	-1	C	0.0

YEAR	TM/L	G	AB	R	H	2B	3B	HR	RBI	BB	SO	AVG	OBP	SLG	PRO	/A	BR	/A	PF	CHI	RC	TA	SB	CS	SBR	FR	POS	TPR
1982	StL-N	26	37	6	7	0	1	0	3	5	5	.189	.286	.243	.529	48	-2	-3	103	131	3	.467	0	0	0	-0	C	-0.2
1983	StL-N	6	6	0	0	0	0	0	0	0	4	.000	.000	.000	.000	-99	-2	-2	98	0	0	.000	0	0	0	0	/C	-0.1
1984	KC-A	10	10	0	1	1	0	0	2	0	2	.100	.100	.200	.300	-19	-2	-2	99	399	0	.200	0	0	0	0	/C	-0.1
	Bal-A	4	8	0	2	0	0	0	1	0	2	.250	.250	.250	.500	41	-1	-1	94	199	1	.333	0	0	0	0	/C	0.0
	Yr	14	18	0	3	1	0	0	3	0	4	.167	.167	.222	.389	7	-2	-2	98	370	1	.267	0	0	0	0		-0.1
Total	4	73	110	11	24	3	2	0	12	7	19	.218	.265	.282	.547	53	-7	-7	101	152	9	.453	1	0	0	-1	/C	-0.4
■ HEINIE SAND Sand, John Henry b: 7/3/1897, San Francisco, Cal d: 11/3/58, San Francisco, Cal. BR/TR, 5'8", 160 lbs. Deb: 4/17/23																												
1923	Phi-N	132	470	85	107	16	5	4	32	82	56	.228	.347	.309	.656	65	-15	-25	114	76	57	.650	7	3	0	0	*S3	-1.2
1924	Phi-N	137	539	79	132	21	6	6	40	52	57	.245	.316	.340	.655	70	-18	-24	108	70	60	.594	5	4	-1	7	*S	-0.5
1925	Phi-N	148	496	69	138	30	7	3	55	64	65	.278	.364	.385	.749	79	-5	-17	116	98	73	.721	1	1	-0	-8	*S	-1.1
1926	Phi-N	149	567	99	154	30	5	4	37	66	56	.272	.350	.363	.713	89	-5	-8	103	62	73	.668	2			-3	*S	0.0
1927	Phi-N	141	535	87	160	22	8	1	49	58	59	.299	.369	.376	.744	103	1	4	96	81	75	.707	5			6	S3	2.1
1928	Phi-N	141	426	38	90	26	1	0	38	60	47	.211	.310	.277	.587	52	-27	-30	104	115	40	.536	1			-3	*S	-1.3
Total	6	848	3033	457	781	145	32	18	251	382	340	.258	.343	.344	.688	77	-69	-98	107	82	378	.647	21	8		0	S/3	-2.0
■ RYNE SANDBERG Sandberg, Ryne Dee b: 9/18/59, Spokane, Wash. BR/TR, 6'1", 175 lbs. Deb: 9/02/81																												
1981	Phi-N	13	6	2	1	0	0	0	0	0	1	.167	.167	.167	.333	-5	-1	-1	112	0	0	.200	0	0	0	-0	/S2	0.0
1982	Chi-N	156	635	103	172	33	5	7	54	36	90	.271	.314	.372	.686	88	-8	-11	103	79	75	.639	32	12	2	-4	*32	-1.4
1983	Chi-N	158	633	94	165	25	4	8	48	51	79	.261	.319	.351	.669	85	-13	-13	101	74	75	.643	37	11	5	**41**	*2/S	3.9
1984	Chi-N	156	636	**114**	200	36	**19**	19	84	52	101	.314	.369	.520	.889	134	38	30	110	75	**126**	.929	32	7	5	23	*2	**6.5**
1985	Chi-N	153	609	113	186	31	6	26	83	57	97	.305	.366	.504	.870	121	32	20	116	83	117	.944	54	11	10	8	*2/S	4.0
1986	Chi-N	154	627	68	178	28	5	14	76	46	79	.284	.333	.411	.744	98	2	-2	107	97	86	.718	34	11	4	8	*2	1.1
1987	Chi-N	132	523	81	154	25	2	16	59	59	79	.294	.368	.442	.810	113	11	10	101	81	89	.819	21	2	5	12	*2	2.9
1988	Chi-N	155	618	77	163	23	8	19	69	54	91	.264	.324	.419	.743	107	8	5	104	84	82	.708	25	10	2	10	*2	2.3
Total	8	1077	4287	652	1219	201	49	109	473	355	617	.284	.341	.430	.771	107	70	39	106	82	650	.778	235	64	32	96	23/S	19.3
■ JOHN SANDERS Sanders, John Frank b: 11/20/45, Grand Island, Neb. BR/TR, 6'2", 200 lbs. Deb: 4/13/65																												
1965	KC-A	1	0	0	0	0	0	0	0	0	0	—	—	—	—	—	0	0	97	—	—	—	0	0	0	0	R	0.0
■ RAY SANDERS Sanders, Raymond Floyd b: 12/4/16, Bonne Terre, Mo. d: 10/28/83, Washington, Mo. BL/TR, 6'2", 185 lbs. Deb: 4/14/42																												
1942	StL-N	95	282	37	71	17	2	5	39	42	31	.252	.351	.379	.730	105	6	3	108	118	39	.697	2			-3	1	-0.6
1943	StL-N	144	478	69	134	21	5	11	73	77	33	.280	.381	.414	.796	124	20	17	105	116	80	.782	1			-5	*1	0.7
1944	StL-N	154	601	87	177	34	9	12	102	71	50	.295	.371	.441	.812	127	23	22	101	129	101	.780	2			-12	*1	-0.1
1945	StL-N	143	537	85	148	29	3	8	78	83	55	.276	.375	.385	.760	111	11	11	100	124	84	.747	3			-4	*1	0.0
1946	Bos-N	80	259	43	63	12	0	6	35	50	38	.243	.368	.359	.727	113	4	6	95	120	38	.724	0			-1	1	-0.1
1948	Bos-N	5	4	0	1	0	0	0	0	2	1	.250	.400	.250	.650	78	-0	-0	102	750	0	.500	0			0	H	0.0
1949	Bos-N	9	21	0	3	1	0	0	0	4	9	.143	.280	.190	.470	29	-2	-2	97	0	1	.444	0			0	/1	-0.1
Total	7	630	2182	321	597	114	19	42	329	328	216	.274	.370	.401	.771	117	61	56	102	122	344	.768	8			-25	1	-0.2
■ REGGIE SANDERS Sanders, Reginald Jerome b: 9/9/49, Birmingham, Ala. BR/TR, 6'2", 205 lbs. Deb: 9/01/74																												
1974	Det-A	26	99	12	27	7	0	3	10	5	20	.273	.308	.434	.742	105	1	0	106	77	13	.662	1	0	0	0	1/D	0.0
■ MIKE SANDLOCK Sandlock, Michael Joseph b: 10/17/15, Old Greenwich, Conn. BB/TR, 6'1", 180 lbs. Deb: 9/19/42																												
1942	Bos-N	2	1	1	1	0	0	0	0	0	0	1.000	1.000	1.000	2.000	509	0	0	95	0	1	—	0			0	/S	0.1
1944	Bos-N	30	30	1	3	0	0	0	2	5	3	.100	.250	.100	.350	1	-4	-4	95	239	1	.321	0			0	3/S	0.0
1945	Bro-N	80	195	21	55	14	2	2	17	18	19	.282	.346	.405	.751	113	2	3	96	69	28	.699	2			-5	CS/23	0.1
1946	Bro-N	19	34	1	5	0	0	0	0	3	4	.147	.216	.147	.363	4	-4	-4	103	0	1	.276	0			-0	C/3	-0.3
1953	Pit-N	64	186	10	43	5	0	0	12	12	19	.231	.281	.258	.539	41	-16	-16	102	97	14	.418	0	0	0	1	C	-1.0
Total	5	195	446	34	107	19	2	2	31	38	45	.240	.304	.305	.609	66	-21	-20	99	88	46	.523	2	0		-4	C/S32	-1.1
■ CHARLIE SANDS Sands, Charles Duane b: 12/17/47, Newport News, Va. BL/TR, 6'2", 200 lbs. Deb: 6/21/67																												
1967	NY-A	1	1	0	0	0	0	0	0	0	1	.000	.000	.000	.000	-99	-0	-0	94	0	0	.000	0	0	0	0	H	0.0
1971	Pit-N	28	25	4	5	2	0	1	5	7	6	.200	.375	.400	.775	121	1	1	99	157	4	.810	0	0	0	0	/C	0.1
1972	Pit-N	1	1	0	0	0	0	0	0	0	0	.000	.000	.000	.000	-97	-0	-0	103	0	0	.000	0	0	0	0	H	0.0
1973	Cal-A	17	33	5	9	2	1	1	5	5	10	.273	.368	.485	.853	144	2	2	96	103	6	.875	0	0	0	-2	C	0.0
1974	Cal-A	43	83	6	16	2	0	4	13	23	17	.193	.374	.361	.735	121	2	3	92	122	12	.771	0	0	0	0	D/C	0.4
1975	Oak-A	3	2	0	1	0	0	0	0	1	1	.500	.667	.500	1.167	251	1	1	93	0	1	2.000	0	0	0	0	/D	0.1
Total	6	93	145	15	31	6	1	6	23	36	35	.214	.374	.393	.767	126	5	6	94	121	24	.825	0	0	0	-2	/DC	0.6
■ TOMMY SANDT Sandt, Thomas James b: 12/22/50, Brooklyn, N.Y. BR/TR, 5'11", 175 lbs. Deb: 6/29/75 C																												
1975	Oak-A	1	0	0	0	0	0	0	0	0	0	—	—	—	—	—	0	0	93	—	—	—	0	0	0	0	/2	0.0
1976	Oak-A	41	67	6	14	1	0	0	3	7	9	.209	.284	.224	.508	50	-4	-4	100	77	5	.407	0	0	0	-1	S/23	-0.2
Total	2	42	67	6	14	1	0	0	3	7	9	.209	.284	.224	.508	50	-4	-4	100	77	28	.407	0	0	0	-1	/S23	-0.2
■ JACK SANFORD Sanford, John Doward b: 6/23/17, Chatham, Va. BR/TR, 6'3", 195 lbs. Deb: 8/24/40																												
1940	Was-A	34	122	5	24	4	2	0	10	6	17	.197	.234	.262	.497	31	-13	-12	93	113	8	.384	0	0	0	-1	1	-1.3
1941	Was-A	3	5	1	2	0	1	0	0	0	1	.400	.500	.800	1.300	245	1	1	98	0	2	1.667	0	0	0	0	/1	0.1
1946	Was-A	10	26	7	6	0	1	0	1	2	6	.231	.286	.308	.593	71	-1	-1	92	48	2	.500	0	0	0	0	/1	-0.1
Total	3	47	153	13	32	4	4	0	11	9	24	.209	.253	.288	.541	45	-13	-12	93	97	12	.438	0	0	0	-1	/1	-1.3
■ MANNY SANGUILLEN Sanguillen, Manuel De Jesus (Magan) b: 3/21/44, Colon, Panama BR/TR, 6', 193 lbs. Deb: 7/23/67																												
1967	Pit-N	30	96	6	26	4	0	0	8	4	12	.271	.300	.313	.613	76	-3	-3	100	110	8	.466	0	1	-1	1	C	-0.1
1969	Pit-N	129	459	62	139	21	6	5	57	12	48	.303	.325	.407	.732	110	1	4	95	113	56	.623	8	4	0	7	*C	1.8
1970	Pit-N	128	486	63	158	19	9	7	61	17	45	.325	.348	.444	.792	114	6	8	97	102	69	.679	2	3	-1	14	*C	2.6
1971	Pit-N	138	533	60	170	26	5	7	81	19	32	.319	.346	.426	.772	119	11	11	99	136	70	.657	6	4	-1	18	*C	3.3
1972	Pit-N	136	520	55	155	18	8	7	71	21	38	.298	.325	.404	.729	103	3	1	103	129	65	.615	1	2	-1	9	*C/O	1.7
1973	Pit-N	149	589	64	166	26	7	12	65	17	29	.282	.305	.411	.716	105	-5	1	92	100	67	.593	2	5	-2	8	CO	0.9
1974	Pit-N	151	596	77	171	21	4	7	68	21	27	.287	.317	.371	.688	94	-8	-6	98	111	65	.560	2	2	-1	6	*C	0.5
1975	Pit-N	133	481	60	158	24	4	9	58	48	31	.328	.393	.451	.844	134	22	23	99	94	83	.805	5	4	-1	6	*C	3.3
1976	Pit-N	114	389	52	113	16	6	2	36	28	18	.290	.341	.378	.719	104	2	2	100	91	46	.609	2	4	-2	5	*C	1.1
1977	Oak-A	152	571	42	157	17	5	6	58	22	35	.275	.304	.354	.658	83	-17	-14	95	107	57	.528	2	5	-2	-14	CD/O1	-2.8
1978	Pit-N	85	220	15	58	5	1	3	16	9	10	.264	.299	.336	.635	73	-7	-8	105	76	21	.515	2	2	-1	0	1C	-0.9
1979	Pit-N	56	74	8	17	5	2	0	4	2	5	.230	.250	.351	.601	59	-4	-5	106	61	6	.467	0	0	0	-0	/C1	-0.4
1980	Pit-N	47	48	2	12	3	0	0	2	3	1	.250	.294	.313	.607	67	-2	-2	103	53	4	.538	3	2	-0	-0	/1	-0.2
Total	13	1448	5062	566	1500	205	57	65	585	223	331	.296	.329	.398	.727	103	-2	11	98	107	616	.637	35	38	-12	59	*C/OD1	10.8
■ ED SANICKI Sanicki, Edward Robert "Butch" b: 7/7/23, Wallington, N.J. BR/TR, 5'9", 175 lbs. Deb: 9/14/49																												
1949	Phi-N	7	13	4	3	0	0	3	7	1	4	.231	.286	.923	1.209	210	2	2	101	126	3	1.300	0			-1	/O	0.1
1951	Phi-N	13	4	1	2	1	0	0	1	1	1	.500	.600	.750	1.350	269	1	1	97	129	2	2.500	1	0	0	-5	O	-0.3
Total	2	20	17	5	5	1	0	3	8	2	5	.294	.368	.882	1.251	226	3	3	100	126	6	1.500	1	0		-5	/O	-0.2
■ BEN SANKEY Sankey, Benjamin Turner b: 9/2/07, Nauvoo, Ala. BR/TR, 5'10", 155 lbs. Deb: 10/05/29																												
1929	Pit-N	2	7	1	1	0	0	0	0	0	1	.143	.143	.143	.286	-28	-1	-1	103	0	0	.167	0			-0	/S	0.0
1930	Pit-N	13	30	6	5	0	0	0	0	2	3	.167	.219	.167	.385	-5	-5	-5	97	0	1	.280	0			-0	/S2	-0.3
1931	Pit-N	57	132	14	30	2	5	0	14	14	10	.227	.301	.318	.620	66	-6	-6	101	119	14	.549	0			-0	S/23	-0.1
Total	3	72	169	21	36	2	5	0	14	16	14	.213	.281	.284	.565	49	-13	-13	100	94	15	.481	0			-1	/S23	-0.4
■ RAFAEL SANTANA Santana, Rafael Francisco (De La Cruz) b: 1/31/58, La Romana, D.R. BR/TR, 6'1", 165 lbs. Deb: 4/05/83																												
1983	StL-N	30	14	1	3	0	0	0	2	2	2	.214	.353	.214	.567	62	-1	-1	98	264	1	.500	0	1	-1	0	/2S3	0.0
1984	NY-N	51	152	14	42	11	1	1	12	9	17	.276	.317	.382	.698	95	-1	-1	100	77	17	.578	0	3	-2	-3	S	0.0

YEAR	TM/L	G	AB	R	H	2B	3B	HR	RBI	BB	SO	AVG	OBP	SLG	PRO	/A	BR	/A	PF	CHI	RC	TA	SB	CS	SBR	FR	POS	TPR
1985	NY-N	154	529	41	136	19	1	1	29	29	54	.257	.296	.302	.598	70	-23	-21	97	71	45	.467	1	0	0	-12	*S	-2.1
1986	NY-N	139	394	38	86	11	0	1	28	36	43	.218	.287	.254	.541	53	-26	-24	96	108	27	.427	0	0	0	10	*S/2	0.0
1987	NY-N	139	439	41	112	21	2	5	44	29	57	.255	.303	.346	.649	72	-18	-17	99	105	44	.540	1	1	-0	7	*S	0.5
1988	NY-A	148	480	50	115	12	1	4	38	33	61	.240	.290	.294	.584	67	-23	-20	96	99	38	.458	1	2	-1	-14	*S	-2.7
Total	6	661	2008	185	494	74	5	12	153	138	234	.246	.296	.306	.602	68	-92	-84	97	95	172	.494	3	7	-3	-12	S/23	-4.3
■ **BENITO SANTIAGO** Santiago, Benito (Rivera) b: 3/9/65, Ponce, P.R. BR/TR, 6'1", 180 lbs. Deb: 9/14/86																												
1986	SD-N	17	62	10	18	2	0	3	6	2	12	.290	.313	.468	.780	118	1	1	95	64	9	.689	0	1	-1	0	C	0.1
1987	SD-N	146	546	64	164	33	2	18	79	16	112	.300	.326	.467	.793	111	4	6	97	104	77	.732	21	12	-1	8	*C	2.4
1988	SD-N	139	492	49	122	22	2	10	46	24	82	.248	.284	.362	.646	87	-11	-10	97	90	46	.552	15	7	0	15	*C	1.4
Total	3	302	1100	123	304	57	4	31	131	42	206	.276	.307	.420	.727	101	-7	-3	97	96	131	.655	36	20	-1	23	C	3.9
■ **RON SANTO** Santo, Ronald Edward b: 2/25/40, Seattle, Wash. BR/TR, 6', 190 lbs. Deb: 6/26/60																												
1960	Chi-N	95	347	44	87	24	2	9	44	31	44	.251	.312	.409	.721	98	-3	-2	98	108	42	.636	0	3	-2	-17	3	-2.2
1961	Chi-N	154	578	84	164	32	6	23	83	73	77	.284	.364	.479	.843	121	18	18	100	103	95	.796	2	3	-1	4	*3	1.4
1962	Chi-N	162	604	44	137	20	4	17	83	65	94	.227	.304	.358	.662	73	-20	-25	106	130	65	.592	4	1	1	13	*3/S	-0.6
1963	Chi-N	162	630	79	187	29	6	25	99	42	92	.297	.345	.481	.826	128	27	23	105	106	99	.765	6	4	-1	13	*3	3.8
1964	Chi-N	161	592	94	185	33	**13**	30	114	**86**	96	.313	**.401**	.564	.966	160	55	51	105	117	135	1.007	3	4	-2	17	*3	5.9
1965	Chi-N	164	608	88	173	30	4	33	101	88	109	.285	.379	.510	.889	145	40	38	102	108	121	.906	3	1	0	19	*3	5.2
1966	Chi-N	155	561	93	175	21	8	30	94	**95**	78	.312	**.417**	.538	.955	163	51	51	100	107	127	1.000	4	5	-2	27	*3/S	**7.6**
1967	Chi-N	161	586	107	176	23	4	31	98	**96**	103	.300	.401	.512	.913	157	48	47	102	99	120	.926	1	5	-3	**31**	*3	**7.0**
1968	Chi-N	162	577	86	142	17	3	26	98	**96**	106	.246	.357	.421	.778	118	25	18	112	136	87	.755	3	4	-2	17	*3	3.7
1969	Chi-N	160	575	97	166	18	4	29	123	96	97	.289	.392	.485	.877	136	36	31	107	143	108	.873	1	3	-2	6	*3	3.8
1970	Chi-N	154	555	83	148	30	4	26	114	92	108	.267	.372	.476	.848	104	21	5	120	137	100	.847	2	0	1	9	*3/O	1.0
1971	Chi-N	154	555	77	148	22	1	21	88	79	95	.267	.358	.423	.781	110	16	10	110	127	84	.745	4	0	1	-2	*3/O	0.9
1972	Chi-N	133	464	68	140	25	5	17	74	69	75	.302	.397	.487	.884	132	32	24	114	112	89	.880	1	4	-2	7	*3/2SO	3.0
1973	Chi-N	149	536	65	143	29	2	20	77	63	97	.267	.348	.440	.789	108	12	7	108	107	76	.720	1	2	-1	-13	*3	-0.9
1974	Chi-A	117	375	29	83	12	1	5	41	37	72	.221	.295	.299	.593	70	-14	-14	102	127	31	.487	0	2	-1	-2	D23/1S	-1.5
Total	15	2243	8143	1138	2254	365	67	342	1331	1108	1343	.277	.366	.464	.830	123	345	282	106	118	1379	.834	35	41	-14	129	*3/D2SO1	38.1
■ **RAFAEL SANTO DOMINGO** Santo Domingo, Rafael (Molina) b: 11/24/55, Orocovis, P.R. BB/TR, 6', 160 lbs. Deb: 9/07/79																												
1979	Cin-N	7	6	0	1	0	0	0	0	1	3	.167	.286	.167	.452	27	-1	-1	97	0	0	.400	0	0	0	0	/H	0.0
■ **NELSON SANTOVENIA** Santovenia, Nelson Gil (Mayol) b: 7/27/61, Pinar Del Rio, Cuba BR/TR, 6'3", 195 lbs. Deb: 9/16/87																												
1987	Mon-N	2	1	0	0	0	0	0	0	0	0	.000	.000	.000	.000	-94	-0	-0	106	0	0	.000	0	0	0	0	/C	0.0
1988	Mon-N	92	309	26	73	20	2	8	41	24	77	.236	.298	.392	.689	91	-2	-4	106	113	36	.617	2	3	-1	4	C/1	0.4
Total	2	94	310	26	73	20	2	8	41	24	77	.235	.297	.390	.687	91	-2	-4	106	113	36	.615	2	3	-1	4	/C1	0.4
■ **EDWARD SANTRY** Santry, Edward b: Chicago, Ill. d: 3/6/1899, Chicago, Ill. Deb: 8/07/1884																												
1884	Det-N	6	22	1	4	0	0	0	0	1	2	.182	.217	.182	.399	29	-2	-2	94	0	1	.278				0	/S2	0.0
■ **JOE SARGENT** Sargent, Joseph Alexander "Horse Belly" b: 9/24/1893, Rochester, N.Y. d: 7/5/50, Rochester, N.Y. BR/TR, 5'10", 165 lbs. Deb: 4/27/21																												
1921	Det-A	66	178	21	45	8	5	2	22	24	26	.253	.342	.388	.729	89	-4	-3	96	100	24	.699	2	3	-1	-3	23S	-0.1
■ **BILL SARNI** Sarni, William Florine b: 9/19/27, Los Angeles, Cal. d: 4/15/83, Creve Coeur, Mo. BR/TR, 5'11", 180 lbs. Deb: 5/09/51																												
1951	StL-N	36	86	7	15	1	0	0	2	9	13	.174	.253	.186	.439	20	-10	-10	101	48	4	.347	1	0	0	-0	C	-0.9
1952	StL-N	3	5	0	1	0	0	0	0	0	1	.200	.200	.200	.400	11	-1	-1	98	0	0	.250	0	0	0	-0	/C	0.0
1954	StL-N	123	380	40	114	18	4	9	70	25	42	.300	.343	.439	.783	102	1	0	100	142	55	.699	3	3	-1	-8	*C	-0.5
1955	StL-N	107	325	32	83	15	2	3	34	27	33	.255	.314	.342	.656	74	-12	-12	101	115	33	.547	1	1	-0	-2	C	-1.1
1956	StL-N	43	148	12	43	7	2	5	22	8	15	.291	.331	.466	.797	112	2	2	99	111	22	.725	1	0	0	2	C	0.6
	NY-N	78	238	16	55	9	3	5	23	20	31	.231	.293	.357	.651	76	-9	-8	97	97	25	.564	0	1	-1	-8	C	-1.5
	Yr	121	386	28	98	16	5	10	45	28	46	.254	.308	.399	.707	90	-7	-6	98	103	48	.631	1	1	-0	-6		-0.9
Total	5	390	1182	107	311	50	11	22	151	89	135	.263	.316	.380	.696	84	-28	-28	100	114	139	.622	6	5	-1	-17	C	-3.4
■ **MACKEY SASSER** Sasser, Mack Daniel b: 8/3/62, Fort Gaines, Ga. BL/TR, 6'1", 190 lbs. Deb: 7/17/87																												
1987	SF-N	2	4	0	0	0	0	0	0	0	0	.000	.000	.000	.000	-99	-1	-1	96	0	0	.000	0	0	0	0	/C	0.0
	Pit-N	12	23	2	5	0	0	0	2	0	2	.217	.217	.217	.435	15	-3	-3	104	160	1	.263	0	0	0	0	/C	-0.2
	Yr	14	27	2	5	0	0	0	2	0	2	.185	.185	.185	.370	-1	-4	-4	103	137	1	.217	0	0	0	0		-0.2
1988	NY-N	60	123	9	35	10	1	1	17	6	9	.285	.318	.407	.724	118	1	2	90	128	15	.609	0	0	0	-4	C/3O	0.1
Total	2	74	150	11	40	10	1	1	19	6	11	.267	.295	.367	.662	93	-3	-2	92	130	15	.535	0	0	0	-4	/CO3	-0.1
■ **TOM SATRIANO** Satriano, Thomas Victor Nicholas b: 8/28/40, Pittsburgh, Pa. BL/TR, 6'1", 185 lbs. Deb: 7/23/61																												
1961	LA-A	35	96	15	19	5	1	1	8	12	16	.198	.294	.302	.596	53	-5	-7	111	98	10	.564	2	0	1	1	32/S	-0.2
1962	LA-A	10	19	4	8	2	0	2	6	0	1	.421	.421	.842	1.263	225	3	3	102	108	6	1.333	0	0	0	0	/3	0.3
1963	LA-A	23	50	1	9	1	0	0	2	9	10	.180	.305	.200	.505	49	-3	-3	91	84	4	.463	0	0	0	0	3/C1	-0.2
1964	LA-A	108	255	18	51	9	0	1	17	30	37	.200	.284	.247	.531	56	-17	-13	89	109	17	.427	0	2	-1	2	31C/2	-1.1
1965	Cal-A	47	79	8	13	2	0	1	4	10	10	.165	.258	.228	.486	40	-6	-6	98	79	5	.420	1	1	-0	1	3C2/1	-0.3
1966	Cal-A	103	226	16	54	5	3	0	24	27	32	.239	.320	.288	.608	77	-6	-6	99	155	21	.528	3	3	-1	1	C13/2	-0.4
1967	Cal-A	90	201	13	45	7	0	4	21	28	25	.224	.319	.318	.637	93	-2	-1	96	115	21	.578	1	0	0	1	3C2/1	0.2
1968	Cal-A	111	297	20	75	9	0	8	35	37	44	.253	.337	.364	.701	120	5	7	94	114	37	.638	0	0	0	-3	C23/1	1.0
1969	Cal-A	41	108	5	28	2	0	1	16	18	15	.259	.370	.306	.676	91	-0	-0	99	178	13	.612	0	2	-1	3	C/12	0.4
	Bos-A	47	127	9	24	2	0	0	11	22	12	.189	.318	.205	.523	47	-8	-9	105	170	9	.459	0	0	0	-0	C	-0.5
	Yr	88	235	14	52	4	0	1	27	40	27	.221	.342	.251	.593	66	-8	-9	102	176	22	.534	0	2	-1	3		-0.1
1970	Bos-A	59	165	21	39	9	1	3	13	21	23	.236	.326	.358	.684	80	-2	-5	111	77	19	.609	0	0	0	4	C	0.0
Total	10	674	1623	130	365	53	5	21	157	214	225	.225	.317	.303	.620	79	-43	-40	98	121	160	.564	7	8	-3	11	C3/12S	-0.8
■ **FRANK SAUCIER** Saucier, Francis Field b: 5/28/26, Leslie, Mo. BL/TR, 6'1", 180 lbs. Deb: 7/21/51																												
1951	StL-A	18	14	4	1	1	0	0	1	3	4	.071	.278	.143	.421	15	-2	-2	105	179	1	.429	0	0	0	-1	/O	-0.2
■ **EDDIE SAUER** Sauer, Edward "Horn" b: 1/3/20, Pittsburgh, Pa. d: 7/1/88, Thousand Oaks, Cal BR/TR, 6'1", 188 lbs. Deb: 9/17/43																												
1943	Chi-N	14	55	3	15	3	0	0	9	3	6	.273	.322	.327	.649	89	-1	-1	99	191	6	.548	1			2	O	0.0
1944	Chi-N	23	50	3	11	4	0	0	5	2	6	.220	.250	.300	.550	54	-3	-3	101	120	4	.425	0			-1	O	-0.4
1945	Chi-N	49	93	8	24	4	1	2	11	8	23	.258	.317	.387	.704	96	-1	-1	99	91	12	.657	2			-3	O	-0.4
1949	StL-N	24	45	5	10	2	1	0	1	3	8	.222	.271	.311	.582	50	-3	-3	110	27	4	.472	0			-2	O	-0.5
	Bos-N	79	214	26	57	12	0	3	31	17	34	.266	.323	.364	.688	87	-5	-4	97	134	25	.593	0			-6	O	-1.3
	Yr	103	259	31	67	14	1	3	32	20	42	.259	.314	.355	.669	79	-8	-8	100	110	29	.574	0			-8		-1.8
Total	4	189	457	45	117	25	2	5	57	33	77	.256	.309	.352	.661	81	-13	-12	99	120	50	.577	3			-10	O	-2.6
■ **HANK SAUER** Sauer, Henry John b: 3/17/17, Pittsburgh, Pa. BR/TR, 6'3", 198 lbs. Deb: 9/09/41																												
1941	Cin-N	9	33	4	10	4	0	0	5	1	4	.303	.324	.424	.748	111	0	0	99	131	4	.625	0			2	/O	0.1
1942	Cin-N	7	20	4	5	0	0	2	4	2	2	.250	.318	.550	.868	150	1	1	101	87	4	.867	0			0	/1	0.1
1945	Cin-N	31	116	18	34	1	0	5	20	6	16	.293	.328	.431	.759	117	1	2	94	109	17	.707	2			-1	O/1	0.0
1948	Cin-N	145	530	78	138	22	1	35	97	60	85	.260	.340	.504	.844	122	17	14	103	104	92	.828	2			4	*O1	0.9
1949	Cin-N	42	152	22	36	6	0	4	16	18	19	.237	.318	.355	.673	84	-4	-3	96	93	16	.581	0			5	O/1	0.0
	Chi-N	96	357	59	104	17	1	27	83	37	47	.291	.363	.571	.934	156	22	24	94	116	75	.946	0			0	O	1.9
	Yr	138	509	81	140	23	1	31	99	55	66	.275	.349	.507	.856	134	17	21	95	110	93	.845	0			5		1.9
1950	Chi-N	145	540	85	148	32	2	32	103	60	67	.274	.350	.519	.868	119	18	14	105	112	96	.845	1			0	*O1	0.9
1951	Chi-N	141	525	77	138	19	4	30	89	45	77	.263	.325	.486	.810	118	9	10	97	102	84	.766	2	1	0	9	*O	1.5
1952	Chi-N	151	567	89	153	31	3	**37**	**121**	77	92	.270	.361	.531	.892	140	33	30	103	110	111	.891	1	2	-1	12	*O	3.8
1953	Chi-N	108	395	61	104	16	5	19	60	50	56	.263	.349	.473	.822	109	7	5	103	102	66	.789	0	0	0	1	*O	0.1

YEAR	TM/L	G	AB	R	H	2B	3B	HR	RBI	BB	SO	AVG	OBP	SLG	PRO	/A	BR	/A	PF	CHI	RC	TA	SB	CS	SBR	FR	POS	TPR
1954	Chi-N	142	520	98	150	18	1	41	103	70	68	.288	.379	.563	.943	141	31	31	101	103	114	.979	2	1	0	-1	*O	2.4
1955	Chi-N	79	261	29	55	8	1	12	28	26	47	.211	.287	.387	.674	77	-9	-9	100	83	28	.603	0	0	0	-4	O	-1.3
1956	StL-N	75	151	11	45	4	0	5	24	25	31	.298	.408	.424	.832	125	6	7	99	128	27	.829	0	0	0	-4	O	0.2
1957	NY-N	127	378	46	98	14	1	26	76	49	59	.259	.344	.508	.852	122	13	12	102	117	67	.843	1	0	0	-15	O	-0.5
1958	SF-N	88	236	27	59	8	0	12	46	35	37	.250	.356	.436	.793	108	3	3	100	137	39	.785	0	0	0	-9	O	-0.6
1959	SF-N	13	15	1	1	0	0	1	1	0	7	.067	.067	.267	.333	-17	-3	-2	95	58	0	.286	0	0	0	-0	/O	-0.2
Total	15	1399	4796	709	1278	200	19	288	876	561	714	.266	.347	.496	.844	122	144	139	101	108	840	.848	11	4		-1	*O/1	9.3

■ **RUSTY SAUNDERS** Saunders, Russell Collier b: 3/12/06, Trenton, N.J. d: 11/24/67, Trenton, N.J. BR/TR, 6'2", 205 lbs. Deb: 9/24/27

1927	Phi-A	5	15	2	2	1	0	0	2	3	2	.133	.278	.200	.478	26	-2	-2	97	222	1	.462	0	0	0	0	/O	-0.1

■ **AL SAUTERS** Sauters, Al b: Philadelphia, Pa. Deb: 9/08/1890

1890	Phi-a	14	41	1	4	0	0	0		11		.098	.288	.098	.386	17	-4	-3	97	0	1	.405	0			0	3/O2	-0.2

■ **DON SAVAGE** Savage, Donald Anthony b: 3/5/19, Bloomfield, N.J. d: 12/25/61, Montclair, N.J. BR/TR, 6', 180 lbs. Deb: 4/18/44

1944	NY-A	71	239	31	63	7	5	4	24	20	41	.264	.323	.385	.708	96	0	-2	106	83	29	.616	1	1	-0	-8	3	-1.0
1945	NY-A	34	58	5	13	1	0	0	3	3	14	.224	.262	.241	.504	43	-4	-4	107	77	4	.383	1	0	0	0	3/O	-0.3
Total	2	105	297	36	76	8	5	4	27	23	55	.256	.312	.357	.668	86	-4	-6	106	82	33	.589	2	1	0	-8	/3O	-1.3

■ **JIMMIE SAVAGE** Savage, James Harold b: 8/29/1883, Southington, Conn. d: 6/26/40, New Castle, Pa. BB/TR, 5'5", 150 lbs. Deb: 9/03/12

1912	Phi-N	2	3	1	0	0	0	0	0	1	0	.000	.250	.000	.250	-29	-1	-1	100	0	0	.333	0			0	/2	0.0
1914	Pit-F	132	479	81	136	9	9	1	26	67	32	.284	.372	.347	.718	113	7	10	94	59	71	.729	17			-6	O3S/2	0.0
1915	Pit-F	14	21	0	3	0	0	0	0	1	0	.143	.182	.143	.325	-3	-3	-3	104	0	1	.222	0			0	/O3	-0.2
Total	3	148	503	82	139	9	9	1	26	69	32	.276	.364	.336	.700	107	4	7	95	56	72	.701	17			-6	/O3S2	-0.2

■ **TED SAVAGE** Savage, Theodore Edmund (born Ephesian Savage) b: 2/21/36, Venice, Ill. BR/TR, 6'1", 185 lbs. Deb:4/09/62

1962	Phi-N	127	335	54	89	11	2	7	39	40	66	.266	.347	.373	.721	99	-2	0	95	105	46	.712	16	5	2	-4	*O	-0.7
1963	Pit-N	85	149	22	29	2	1	5	14	14	31	.195	.268	.322	.590	70	-6	-6	99	93	11	.515	4	3	-1	-6	O	-1.6
1965	StL-N	30	63	7	10	3	0	1	4	6	9	.159	.232	.254	.486	34	-5	-6	107	87	3	.411	1	1	-0	-1	O	-0.8
1966	StL-N	16	29	4	5	2	1	0	3	4	7	.172	.273	.310	.583	62	-1	-1	100	140	3	.680	4	0	1	-1	/O	-0.1
1967	StL-N	9	8	1	1	0	0	0	0	1	3	.125	.222	.125	.347	2	-1	-1	101	0	0	.286	0	0	0	0	H	0.0
	Chi-N	96	225	40	49	10	1	5	33	40	54	.218	.348	.338	.686	96	1	0	102	150	27	.677	7	6	-2	-3	O/3	-0.8
	Yr	105	233	41	50	10	1	5	33	41	57	.215	.344	.330	.675	93	-0	-1	101	137	27	.663	7	6	-2	-3		-0.8
1968	Chi-N	3	8	0	2	0	0	0	0	0	1	.250	.250	.250	.500	45	-0	-1	112	0	0	.286	0	1	-1	-0	/O	-0.1
	LA-N	61	126	7	26	6	1	2	7	10	20	.206	.270	.317	.588	84	-4	-3	91	64	9	.477	1	2	-1	0	O	-0.5
	Yr	64	134	7	28	6	1	2	7	10	21	.209	.269	.313	.582	81	-4	-3	92	61	9	.466	1	3	-2	0		-0.6
1969	Cin-N	68	110	20	25	7	0	2	11	20	27	.227	.346	.345	.692	95	-0	-0	99	100	15	.701	3	0	1	4	O/2	0.4
1970	Mil-A	114	276	43	77	10	5	12	50	57	44	.279	.406	.482	.888	146	18	19	98	120	57	.957	10	6	-1	-8	O/1	0.8
1971	Mil-A	14	17	2	3	0	0	0	1	5	4	.176	.364	.176	.540	55	-1	-1	103	136	2	.643	1	0	0	-2	/O	-0.2
	KC-A	19	29	2	5	0	0	0	1	3	6	.172	.250	.172	.422	22	-3	-3	99	82	1	.385	2	0	1	-1	/O	-0.3
	Yr	33	46	4	8	0	0	0	2	8	10	.174	.296	.174	.470	36	-4	-4	101	109	3	.475	3	0	1	-3		-0.5
Total	9	642	1375	202	321	51	11	34	163	200	272	.233	.335	.361	.696	97	-5	-1	98	109	175	.700	49	24	0	-21	O/123	-3.9

■ **BOB SAVERINE** Saverine, Robert Paul "Rabbit" b: 6/2/41, Norwalk, Conn. BB/TR, 5'10", 160 lbs. Deb: 9/12/59

1959	Bal-A	1	0	1	0	0	0	0	0	0	0	—	—	—	—	—	0	0	97	—	—	—	0	0	0	0	R	0.0
1962	Bal-A	8	21	2	5	2	0	0	3	1	3	.238	.273	.333	.606	66	-1	-1	95	170	1	.421	0	2	-1	0	/2	-0.1
1963	Bal-A	115	167	21	39	1	2	1	12	25	44	.234	.333	.281	.615	79	-5	-3	94	100	17	.593	8	3	1	-16	O2S	-1.9
1964	Bal-A	46	34	14	5	1	0	0	0	3	6	.147	.216	.176	.393	10	-4	-4	105	0	1	.375	3	1	0	-0	S/O	-0.4
1966	Was-A	120	406	54	102	10	4	5	24	27	62	.251	.301	.333	.634	86	-10	-7	95	68	41	.535	4	3	-1	-4	23S/O	-0.6
1967	Was-A	89	233	22	55	13	0	0	8	17	34	.236	.288	.292	.580	70	-8	-9	102	49	20	.505	8	0	2	2	2S/3O	-0.1
Total	6	379	861	114	206	27	6	6	47	73	149	.239	.300	.305	.606	77	-28	-24	97	69	256	.539	23	9	2	-18	2/OS3	-3.1

■ **CARL SAWATSKI** Sawatski, Carl Ernest "Swats" b: 11/4/27, Shickshinny, Pa. BL/TR, 5'10", 210 lbs. Deb: 9/29/48

1948	Chi-N	2	2	0	0	0	0	0	0	0	0	.000	.000	.000	.000	-99	-1	-1	93	0	0	.000	0			0	H	0.0
1950	Chi-N	38	103	4	18	1	0	1	7	11	19	.175	.254	.214	.468	23	-11	-12	105	108	6	.379	0			1	C	-0.9
1953	Chi-N	43	59	5	13	3	0	1	5	7	7	.220	.303	.322	.625	61	-3	-3	103	89	6	.542	0	0	0	0	C	-0.1
1954	Chi-A	43	109	6	20	3	3	1	12	15	20	.183	.282	.294	.576	56	-6	-7	104	130	9	.511	0	0	0	-1	C	-0.5
1957	Mil-N	58	105	13	25	4	0	6	17	10	15	.238	.316	.448	.764	113	0	1	90	108	15	.720	0	0	0	3	C	0.6
1958	Mil-N	10	10	1	1	0	0	0	1	2	5	.100	.250	.100	.350	-3	-1	-1	89	413	0	.300	0	0	0	0	/C	0.0
	Phi-N	60	183	12	42	4	1	5	12	16	42	.230	.302	.344	.646	72	-8	-7	98	64	19	.569	0	0	0	1	C	-0.3
	Yr	70	193	13	43	4	1	5	13	18	47	.223	.299	.332	.631	69	-9	-8	97	119	20	.556	0	0	0	1		-0.3
1959	Phi-N	74	198	15	58	10	0	9	43	32	36	.293	.394	.480	.874	132	10	10	99	142	38	.883	0	0	0	-6	C	0.8
1960	StL-N	78	179	16	41	4	0	6	27	22	24	.229	.313	.352	.665	76	-4	-6	108	135	19	.590	0	0	0	-7	C	-0.9
1961	StL-N	86	174	23	52	8	0	10	33	25	17	.299	.387	.517	.904	121	10	6	113	111	35	.913	0	0	0	-5	C/O	0.6
1962	StL-N	85	222	26	56	9	1	13	42	36	38	.252	.357	.477	.834	112	7	4	109	114	39	.840	0	0	0	-19	C	-1.3
1963	StL-N	56	105	12	25	0	0	6	14	15	28	.238	.333	.410	.743	105	2	1	107	96	15	.750	2	0	1	-2	C	0.1
Total	11	633	1449	133	351	46	5	58	213	191	251	.242	.333	.401	.734	92	-7	-15	104	114	202	.710	2	0		-34	C/O	-1.9

■ **CARL SAWYER** Sawyer, Carl Everett "Huck" b: 10/19/1890, Seattle, Wash. d: 1/17/57, Los Angeles, Cal. BR/TR, 5'11", 160 lbs. Deb: 9/11/15

1915	Was-A	10	32	8	8	1	0	0	3	4	5	.250	.351	.281	.633	88	-0	-0	101	116	4	.667	2			-0	/2S	0.0
1916	Was-A	16	31	3	6	1	0	0	2	4	4	.194	.306	.226	.531	60	-1	-1	100	102	3	.600	3			0	/2S3	0.0
Total	2	26	63	11	14	2	0	0	5	8	9	.222	.329	.254	.583	74	-2	-2	100	109	7	.633	5			-0	/2S3	0.0

■ **DAVE SAX** Sax, David John b: 9/22/58, Sacramento, Cal. BR/TR, 6', 185 lbs. Deb: 9/01/82

1982	LA-N	2	2	0	0	0	0	0	0	0	0	.000	.000	.000	.000	-99	-1	-1	95	0	0	.000	0	0	0	-0	/O	0.0
1983	LA-N	7	8	0	0	0	0	0	1	0	0	.000	.000	.000	.000	-99	-2	-2	100	0	0	.000	0	0	0	-0	/C	-0.1
1985	Bos-A	22	36	2	11	3	0	0	6	3	3	.306	.359	.389	.748	102	0	0	102	170	5	.654	0	1	-1	-1	C/O	0.0
1986	Bos-A	4	11	1	5	1	0	1	1	0	1	.455	.455	.818	1.273	240	2	2	100	33	4	1.500	0	0	0	0	/C1	0.2
1987	Bos-A	2	3	0	0	0	0	0	0	0	1	.000	.000	.000	.000	-99	-1	-1	99	0	0	.000	0	0	0	0	/C	0.0
Total	5	37	60	3	16	4	0	1	8	3	5	.267	.302	.383	.685	85	-1	-1	101	111	9	.578	0	1	-1	-1	/CO1	0.1

■ **OLLIE SAX** Sax, Erik Oliver b: 11/5/04, Branford, Conn. d: 3/21/82, Newark, N.J. BR/TR, 5'8", 164 lbs. Deb: 4/13/28

1928	StL-A	16	17	4	3	0	0	0	0	5	3	.176	.364	.176	.540	44	-1	-1	104	0	2	.571	0	0	0	-0	/3	0.0

■ **STEVE SAX** Sax, Stephen Louis b: 1/29/60, Sacramento, Cal. BR/TR, 5'11", 185 lbs. Deb: 8/18/81

1981	LA-N	31	119	15	33	2	0	2	9	7	14	.277	.317	.345	.662	90	-2	-2	98	77	12	.570	5	7	-3	1	2	-0.1
1982	LA-N	150	638	88	180	23	7	4	47	49	53	.282	.335	.359	.694	100	-5	-0	95	68	79	.676	49	19	3	-6	*2	0.4
1983	LA-N	155	623	94	175	18	5	5	41	58	73	.281	.343	.350	.693	92	-5	-5	100	61	76	.685	56	30	-1	-24	*2	-2.6
1984	LA-N	145	569	70	138	24	4	1	35	47	53	.243	.301	.304	.606	68	-22	-24	104	75	51	.552	34	19	-1	13	*2	-0.8
1985	LA-N	136	488	62	136	8	4	1	42	54	43	.279	.354	.318	.672	96	-5	-1	93	108	56	.632	27	11	2	-10	*2/3	-0.8
1986	LA-N	157	633	91	210	43	4	6	56	59	58	.332	.391	.441	.832	137	26	30	94	66	110	.843	40	17	2	-4	*2	3.1
1987	LA-N	157	610	84	171	22	7	6	46	44	61	.280	.332	.369	.701	93	-13	-6	92	80	76	.667	37	11	5	5	*2/3O	0.6
1988	LA-N	160	632	70	175	19	4	5	57	45	51	.277	.326	.343	.669	87	-6	-10	106	94	73	.635	42	12	5	-17	*2	-1.8
Total	8	1091	4312	574	1218	159	35	30	333	363	406	.282	.340	.356	.697	96	-31	-18	98	78	532	.682	290	126	11	-43	*2/3O	-2.0

■ **JIMMY SAY** Say, James I. b: 1862, Baltimore, Md. d: 6/23/1894, Baltimore, Md. Deb: 7/22/1882

1882	Lou-a	1	4	1	1	0	0	0		0		.250	.250	.250	.500	74	-0	-0	94	0	0	.333				0	/3	0.0
	Phi-a	22	82	12	17	2	0	0		1		.207	.217	.232	.449	46	-4	-5	112	0	4	.308				1	S	-0.3
	Yr	23	86	13	18	2	0	0		1		.209	.218	.233	.451	47	-4	-6	111	0	4	.309				1		-0.3
1884	WiL-U	16	59	3	13	1	2	0		1		.220	.233	.305	.538	79	-1	-1	103	0	4	.413	0			0	3	0.0

YEAR	TM/L	G	AB	R	H	2B	3B	HR	RBI	BB	SO	AVG	OBP	SLG	PRO	/A	BR	/A	PF	CHI	RC	TA	SB	CS	SBR	FR	POS	TPR
	KC-U	2	8	0	2	0	0	0		0		.250	.250	.250	.500	80	-0	-0	87	0	1	.333	0			0	/3	0.0
	Yr	18	67	3	15	1	2	0		1		.224	.235	.299	.534	79	-1	-2	101	0	5	.404	0			0		0.0
1887	Cle-a	16	64	9	24	5	3	0		1		.375	.385	.547	.931	165	5	5	98	0	14	.900	0			0	3	0.4
Total	3	57	217	25	57	8	5	0		3		.263	.273	.346	.618	93	-1	-2	104	0	23	.488	0			1	/3S	0.1
■ **LOU SAY** Say, Louis I. b: 2/4/1854, Baltimore, Md. d: 6/5/30, Fallston, Md. BR/TR, 5'7", 145 lbs. Deb: 4/14/1873																												
1873	Mar-n	3	12	1	2							.167															/SO	
1874	Bal-n	18	71	3	12							.169															S	
1875	Nat-n	9	38	4	9							.237															/S2O	
1880	Cin-N	48	191	14	38	8	1	0	15	4	31	.199	.215	.251	.467	58	-8	-8	99	121	11	.340				1	S	-0.3
1882	Phi-a	49	199	35	45	4	3	1		8		.226	.256	.291	.547	75	-3	-7	112	0	15	.429				6	S	0.1
1883	Bal-a	74	324	52	83	13	2	1		10		.256	.278	.318	.596	86	-3	-6	107	0	29	.469				6	*S	-0.2
1884	Bal-U	78	339	65	81	14	2	2		11		.239	.263	.310	.573	84	-2	-8	110	0	28	.450	0			-2	*S	-0.6
	KC-U	17	70	6	14	2	0	1		2		.200	.222	.271	.494	76	-2	-1	87	0	4	.375	0			0	S/2	0.0
	Yr	95	409	71	95	16	2	3		13		.232	.256	.303	.559	83	-5	-9	106	0	33	.436	0			-2		-0.6
Total	3 n	30	121	8	23							.190															S/2	
Total	4	266	1123	172	261	41	8	5	15	35	31	.232	.256	.297	.552	79	-19	-30	106	20	88	.427	0			11	S/2O	-1.0
■ **JERRY SCALA** Scala, Gerard Daniel b: 9/27/26, Bayonne, N.J. BL/TR, 5'11", 178 lbs. Deb: 4/22/48																												
1948	Chi-A	3	6	1	0	0	0	0	0	0	3	.000	.000	.000	.000	-99	-2	-2	95	0	0	.000	0	0	0	0	/O	-0.1
1949	Chi-A	37	120	17	30	7	1	1	13	17	19	.250	.348	.350	.698	87	-3	-2	98	99	16	.677	3	3	-1	-1	O	-0.4
1950	Chi-A	40	67	8	13	2	1	0	6	10	10	.194	.299	.254	.552	44	-6	-5	97	122	5	.482	0	0	0	-2	O	-0.7
Total	3	80	193	26	43	9	2	1	19	27	32	.223	.321	.306	.627	66	-10	-9	97	104	22	.581	3	3	-1	-4	/O	-1.2
■ **SKEETER SCALZI** Scalzi, Frank John b: 6/16/13, Lafferty, Ohio d: 8/25/84, Pittsburgh, Pa. BR/TR, 5'6", 160 lbs. Deb: 7/21/39																												
1939	NY-N	11	18	3	6	0	0	0	0	3	2	.333	.429	.333	.762	108	0	0	99	0	2	.714	1			1	/S3	0.1
■ **JOHNNY SCALZI** Scalzi, John Anthony b: 3/22/07, Stamford, Conn. d: 9/27/62, Port Chester, N.Y BR/TR, 5'7", 170 lbs. Deb: 6/19/31																												
1931	Bos-N	2	1	0	0	0	0	0	0	0	1	.000	.000	.000	.000	-99	-0	-0	99	0	0	.000	0			0	H	0.0
■ **MORT SCANLAN** Scanlan, Mortimer J. b: 3/18/1861, Chicago, Ill. d: 12/29/28, Chicago, Ill. 6'1", 186 lbs. Deb: 4/21/1890																												
1890	NY-N	3	10	0	0	0	0	0	0	2	5	.000	.167	.000	.167	-52	-2	-2	95	0	0	.300	1			0	/1	-0.1
■ **PAT SCANLON** Scanlon, James Patrick b: 9/23/52, Minneapolis, Minn. BL/TR, 6', 180 lbs. Deb: 9/27/74																												
1974	Mon-N	2	4	1	1	0	0	0	0	0	1	.250	.250	.250	.500	38	-0	-0	104	0	0	.333	0	0	0	0	/3	0.0
1975	Mon-N	60	109	5	20	3	1	2	15	17	25	.183	.294	.284	.578	56	-6	-7	108	157	9	.522	0	1	-1	0	3/1	-0.7
1976	Mon-N	11	27	2	5	1	0	1	2	2	5	.185	.241	.333	.575	62	-1	-1	100	64	2	.478	0	0	0	0	/31	-0.1
1977	SD-N	47	79	9	15	3	0	1	11	12	20	.190	.297	.266	.563	60	-5	-4	88	183	6	.478	0	0	0	-2	23/O	-0.5
Total	4	120	219	17	41	7	1	4	28	31	51	.187	.288	.283	.571	58	-13	-12	100	153	17	.505	0	1	-1	-2	/321O	-1.3
■ **JOHN SCANNELL** Scannell, John J. (born P. Scanlan) Deb: 7/04/1884																												
1884	Bos-U	6	24	2	7	1	0	0		0		.292	.292	.333	.625	113	0	0	98	0	2	.471	0			0	/O	0.0
■ **RUSS SCARRITT** Scarritt, Russell Mallory b: 1/14/03, Pensacola, Fla. BL/TR, 5'10.5", 165 lbs. Deb: 4/18/29																												
1929	Bos-A	151	540	69	159	26	17	1	71	34	38	.294	.337	.411	.749	90	-8	-9	102	110	73	.689	13	11	-3	0	*O	-1.6
1930	Bos-A	113	447	48	129	17	8	2	48	12	49	.289	.312	.376	.688	79	-19	-14	93	97	50	.575	4	7	-3	2	*O	-1.6
1931	Bos-A	10	39	2	6	1	0	0	1	2	2	.154	.195	.179	.375	-1	-6	-5	94	48	1	.273	0	0	0	0	/O	-0.4
1932	Phi-N	11	11	0	2	0	0	0	0	1	2	.182	.250	.182	.432	16	-1	-1	112	0	1	.333	0			0	/O	-0.1
Total	4	285	1037	119	296	44	25	3	120	49	91	.285	.320	.385	.705	81	-33	-30	98	101	125	.618	17	18		3	O	-3.7
■ **LES SCARSELLA** Scarsella, Leslie George b: 11/23/13, Santa Cruz, Cal. d: 12/17/58, San Francisco, Cal BL/TL, 5'11", 185 lbs. Deb: 9/15/35																												
1935	Cin-N	6	10	4	2	1	0	0	0	3	1	.200	.385	.300	.685	93	-0	0	93	0	1	.750	0			0	/1	0.0
1936	Cin-N	115	485	63	152	21	9	3	65	14	36	.313	.335	.412	.748	104	-1	1	97	117	66	.647	6			2	*1	-0.6
1937	Cin-N	110	329	35	81	11	4	3	34	17	26	.246	.285	.331	.617	73	-15	-12	91	104	30	.512	5			-3	1O	-1.9
1939	Cin-N	16	14	0	2	0	0	0	2	0	2	.143	.143	.143	.286	-22	-2	-2	103	367	0	.154	0			0	H	-0.1
1940	Bos-N	18	60	7	18	1	3	0	8	3	5	.300	.344	.417	.760	110	1	1	99	119	9	.738	2			1	1	0.0
Total	5	265	898	109	255	34	16	6	109	37	70	.284	.315	.378	.693	91	-18	-12	95	114	107	.611	13			-1	1/O	-2.6
■ **PAUL SCHAAL** Schaal, Paul b: 3/3/43, Pittsburgh, Pa. BR/TR, 5'11", 165 lbs. Deb: 9/03/64																												
1964	LA-A	17	32	3	4	0	0	0	0	2	5	.125	.176	.125	.301	-16	-5	-4	89	0	1	.200	0	1	-1	0	/23	-0.3
1965	Cal-A	155	483	48	108	12	2	9	45	61	88	.224	.312	.313	.625	80	-13	-12	98	105	50	.567	6	3	0	-10	*3/2	-2.1
1966	Cal-A	138	386	59	94	15	7	6	24	68	56	.244	.364	.365	.729	111	8	8	99	63	55	.721	6	4	-1	-3	*3	0.2
1967	Cal-A	99	272	31	51	9	1	6	20	38	39	.188	.289	.294	.584	76	-9	-7	96	85	25	.535	2	2	-1	0	3/S2	-0.6
1968	Cal-A	60	219	22	46	7	1	2	16	29	25	.210	.308	.279	.587	84	-5	-3	94	98	19	.530	5	7	-3	-0	3	-0.4
1969	KC-A	61	205	22	54	6	0	1	13	25	27	.263	.349	.307	.656	83	-3	-4	103	81	24	.597	2	1	0	-6	3/2S	-0.8
1970	KC-A	124	380	50	102	12	3	5	35	43	39	.268	.344	.355	.700	95	-3	-2	98	94	47	.637	7	4	-0	-11	3S/2	-1.2
1971	KC-A	161	548	80	150	31	6	11	63	103	51	.274	.391	.412	.803	129	24	25	99	105	95	.820	7	5	-1	-13	*3	0.5
1972	KC-A	127	435	47	99	19	3	6	41	61	59	.228	.325	.326	.652	94	-2	-2	100	109	46	.584	1	3	-2	-13	*3/S	-1.3
1973	KC-A	121	396	61	114	14	3	8	42	63	45	.288	.392	.399	.791	113	15	10	109	92	63	.767	5	6	-2	-12	*3	-0.5
1974	KC-A	12	34	3	6	2	0	1	4	5	5	.176	.300	.324	.624	75	-1	-1	106	112	3	.548	0	0	0	-1	3	-0.1
	Cal-A	53	165	10	41	5	0	2	20	18	27	.248	.322	.315	.638	91	-3	-2	92	136	16	.550	2	2	-1	-4	3	-0.5
	Yr	65	199	13	47	7	0	3	24	23	32	.236	.318	.317	.635	87	-4	-3	95	133	20	.560	2	2	-1	-5		-0.6
Total	11	1128	3555	436	869	132	26	57	323	516	466	.244	.344	.344	.688	98	4	6	99	96	444	.661	43	38	-10	-73	*3/2S	-7.1
■ **GERMANY SCHAEFER** Schaefer, Herman A. b: 2/4/1877, Chicago, Ill. d: 5/16/19, Saranac Lake, N.Y. BR/TR, 5'9", 175 lbs. Deb: 10/05/01																												
1901	Chi-N	2	5	0	3	1	0	0	0	2		.600	.714	.800	1.514	343	2	2	100	0	3	3.000	0			0	/23	0.2
1902	Chi-N	81	291	32	57	2	3	0	14	19		.196	.245	.223	.469	48	-18	-16	96	76	19	.410	12			-12	3/1OS	-2.6
1905	Det-A	153	554	64	135	17	9	2	47	45		.244	.301	.318	.618	100	-1	0	98	98	60	.573	19			5	*2/S	0.5
1906	Det-A	124	446	48	106	14	3	2	42	32		.238	.289	.296	.585	78	-7	-12	108	117	48	.574	31			8	*2/S	-0.6
1907	Det-A	109	372	45	96	12	3	1	32	30		.258	.313	.315	.628	101	1	1	102	97	44	.609	21			-19	2S3/O	-1.8
1908	Det-A	153	584	96	151	20	10	3	52	37		.259	.303	.342	.645	111	7	6	101	90	70	.640	40			-11	S23	-0.3
1909	Det-A	87	280	26	70	12	0	0	22	14		.250	.286	.293	.579	75	-6	-9	110	103	26	.514	12			3	2/O	-0.9
	Was-A	37	128	13	31	5	1	1	4	6		.242	.281	.320	.602	100	-2	-0	90	36	12	.515	2			0	2/3	0.0
	Yr	124	408	39	101	17	1	1	26	20		.248	.284	.301	.586	82	-8	-9	104	84	37	.515	14			3		-0.9
1910	Was-A	74	229	27	63	6	5	0	14	25		.275	.352	.345	.697	117	5	5	101	67	34	.741	17			-4	2O/3	-0.2
1911	Was-A	125	440	74	147	14	7	0	45	57		.334	.412	.398	.809	131	18	20	97	92	82	.870	22			4	*1/O	2.5
1912	Was-A	60	166	21	41	7	3	0	19	23		.247	.342	.325	.667	92	-1	-1	99	117	22	.712	11			-5	O12/P	-0.6
1913	Was-A	54	100	17	32	1	1	0	7	15	12	.320	.419	.350	.769	118	4	4	106	71	17	.853	6			0	2/13PO	0.4
1914	Was-A	25	29	6	7	1	0	0	2	3	5	.241	.313	.276	.588	76	-1	-1	101	94	3	.652	4	1	1	0	/2O	0.0
1915	New-F	59	154	26	33	5	3	0	8	25	11	.214	.324	.286	.610	86	-3	-2	94	66	16	.595	3			-3	O1/32	-0.5
1916	NY-A	1	1	0	0	0	0	0	0	0	0	.000	.000	.000	.000	-99	-0	-0	101	0	0	.000	0			-0	/O	0.0
1918	Cle-A	1	5	2	0	0	0	0	0	0	0	.000	.000	.000	.000	-93	-1	-1	108	0	-0	.200	1			0	/2	0.0
Total	15	1145	3784	497	972	117	48	9	308	333	28	.257	.318	.320	.638	98	-3	-5	101	91	456	.623	201	1		-34	213/SOP	-3.9
■ **HARRY SCHAFER** Schafer, Harry C. "Silk Stocking" b: 8/14/1846, Philadelphia, Pa. d: 2/28/35, Philadelphia, Pa. BR/TR, 5'9.5", 143 lbs. Deb: 5/05/1871																												
1871	Bos-n	31	151	38	41							.272															*3/2	
1872	Bos-n	48	225	50	59							.262															*3/O	
1873	Bos-n	60	301	64	79							.262															*3O	
1874	Bos-n	71	324	71	86							.265															*3	
1875	Bos-n	51	224	50	66							.295															*3/O	

YEAR	TM/L	G	AB	R	H	2B	3B	HR	RBI	BB	SO	AVG	OBP	SLG	PRO	/A	BR	/A	PF	CHI	RC	TA	SB	CS	SBR	FR	POS	TPR
1876	Bos-N	70	286	47	72	11	0	0	35	4	11	.252	.262	.290	.552	88	-5	-2	95	145	22	.407				3	*3	0.0
1877	Bos-N	33	141	20	39	5	2	0	13	0	7	.277	.277	.340	.617	86	-1	-3	108	94	14	.471				-6	O/3S	-0.8
1878	Bos-N	2	8	0	1	0	0	0	0	0	1	.125	.125	.125	.250	-16	-1	-1	108	0	0	.143				0	/O	0.0
Total	5 n	261	1225	273	331							.270															/O	
Total	3	105	435	67	112	16	2	0	48	4	19	.257	.264	.303	.568	86	-7	-6	99	126	36	.421				-3	3/OS2	-0.8

■ **JIMMIE SCHAFFER** Schaffer, Jimmie Ronald b: 4/5/36, Limeport, Pa. BR/TR, 5'9", 170 lbs. Deb: 5/20/61 C

YEAR	TM/L	G	AB	R	H	2B	3B	HR	RBI	BB	SO	AVG	OBP	SLG	PRO	/A	BR	/A	PF	CHI	RC	TA	SB	CS	SBR	FR	POS	TPR
1961	StL-N	68	153	15	39	7	0	1	16	9	29	.255	.301	.320	.621	57	-8	-10	113	124	14	.496	0	0	0	-5	C	-0.9
1962	StL-N	70	66	7	16	2	1	0	6	6	16	.242	.306	.303	.609	59	-3	-4	109	118	6	.519	1	0	0	-7	C	-0.9
1963	Chi-N	57	142	17	34	7	0	7	19	11	35	.239	.294	.437	.731	102	1	0	105	96	16	.640	0	0	0	2	C	0.4
1964	Chi-N	54	122	9	25	6	1	2	9	17	17	.205	.307	.320	.627	73	-3	-4	105	82	10	.551	2	4	-2	-1	C	-0.5
1965	Chi-A	17	31	2	6	3	1	0	1	3	4	.194	.265	.355	.620	81	-1	-1	92	38	2	.500	0	0	0	-2	C	-0.1
	NY-N	24	37	0	5	2	0	0	0	1	15	.135	.158	.189	.347	-3	-5	-5	100	0	1	.235	0	0	0	-2	C	-0.5
1966	Phi-N	8	15	2	2	1	0	1	4	1	7	.133	.188	.400	.587	57	-1	-1	101	187	1	.538	0	0	0	0	/C	0.0
1967	Phi-N	2	2	1	0	0	0	0	0	1	1	.000	.333	.000	.333	3	-0	-0	104	0	0	.500	0	0	0	0	/C	0.0
1968	Cin-N	4	6	0	1	0	0	0	1	0	3	.167	.167	.167	.333	0	-1	-1	111	421	0	.200	0	0	0	0	/C	0.0
Total	8	304	574	53	128	28	3	11	56	49	127	.223	.286	.340	.626	68	-21	-26	107	99	51	.553	3	4	-2	-15	C	-2.5

■ **JOHNNY SCHAIVE** Schaive, John Edward b: 2/25/34, Springfield, Ill. BR/TR, 5'8", 175 lbs. Deb: 9/19/58

YEAR	TM/L	G	AB	R	H	2B	3B	HR	RBI	BB	SO	AVG	OBP	SLG	PRO	/A	BR	/A	PF	CHI	RC	TA	SB	CS	SBR	FR	POS	TPR
1958	Was-A	7	24	1	6	0	0	0	1	1	4	.250	.280	.250	.530	49	-2	-2	97	67	1	.333	0	0	0	0	/2	0.0
1959	Was-A	16	59	3	9	2	0	0	2	0	7	.153	.167	.186	.353	-3	-8	-8	100	73	2	.240	0	0	0	-1	2	-0.8
1960	Was-A	6	12	1	3	1	0	0	0	0	3	.250	.250	.333	.583	55	-1	-1	102	0	1	.400	0	0	0	0	/2	0.0
1962	Was-A	82	225	20	57	15	1	6	29	6	25	.253	.273	.409	.682	80	-7	-7	101	105	21	.544	0	1	-1	2	3/2	-0.3
1963	Was-A	3	3	0	0	0	0	0	0	0	1	.000	.000	.000	.000	-99	-1	-1	98	0	0	.000	0	0	0	0	H	0.0
Total	5	114	323	25	75	18	1	6	32	7	40	.232	.251	.350	.601	60	-19	-19	100	91	24	.486	0	1	-1	2	/32	-1.1

■ **ROY SCHALK** Schalk, Le Roy John b: 11/9/08, Chicago, Ill. BR/TR, 5'10", 168 lbs. Deb: 9/17/32

YEAR	TM/L	G	AB	R	H	2B	3B	HR	RBI	BB	SO	AVG	OBP	SLG	PRO	/A	BR	/A	PF	CHI	RC	TA	SB	CS	SBR	FR	POS	TPR
1932	NY-A	3	12	3	3	1	0	0	0	2	2	.250	.357	.333	.690	84	-0	-0	95	0	2	.667	0	0	0	0	/2	0.0
1944	Chi-A	146	587	47	129	14	4	1	44	45	52	.220	.276	.262	.539	54	-35	-35	100	89	43	.428	5	4	-1	-9	*2/S	-4.2
1945	Chi-A	133	513	50	127	23	1	1	65	32	41	.248	.293	.302	.595	76	-18	-16	95	**158**	45	.472	3	6	-3	7	*2	-0.9
Total	3	282	1112	100	259	38	5	2	109	79	95	.233	.285	.281	.566	64	-53	-50	98	120	90	.459	8	10	-4	-3	2/S	-5.1

■ **RAY SCHALK** Schalk, Raymond William "Cracker" b: 8/12/1892, Harvey, Ill. d: 5/19/70, Chicago, Ill. BR/TR, 5'9", 165 lbs. Deb: 8/11/12 MCH

YEAR	TM/L	G	AB	R	H	2B	3B	HR	RBI	BB	SO	AVG	OBP	SLG	PRO	/A	BR	/A	PF	CHI	RC	TA	SB	CS	SBR	FR	POS	TPR
1912	Chi-A	23	63	7	18	2	0	0	8	3		.286	.357	.317	.675	94	-0	-0	99	133	8	.644	2			-1	C	0.1
1913	Chi-A	129	401	38	98	15	5	1	38	27	36	.244	.297	.314	.611	83	-12	-9	95	105	40	.561	14			0	*C	0.0
1914	Chi-A	135	392	30	106	13	2	0	36	38	24	.270	.347	.314	.661	96	1	-1	103	110	50	.650	24	11	1	6	*C	1.6
1915	Chi-A	135	413	46	110	14	4	1	54	62	21	.266	.366	.327	.693	110	6	7	98	133	51	.670	15	18	-6	-6	*C	0.5
1916	Chi-A	129	410	36	95	12	9	0	41	41	31	.232	.311	.305	.616	79	-7	-11	108	117	45	.616	30	13	1	17	*C	1.2
1917	Chi-A	140	424	48	96	12	5	2	51	59	27	.226	.331	.292	.623	92	-3	-2	98	141	47	.637	19			1	*C	1.1
1918	Chi-A	108	333	35	73	6	3	0	22	36	22	.219	.301	.255	.556	67	-12	-12	101	94	29	.523	12			-7	*C	-1.0
1919	Chi-A	131	394	57	111	9	3	0	34	51	25	.282	.367	.320	.687	89	-1	-4	105	98	50	.671	11			-5	*C	-0.1
1920	Chi-A	151	485	64	131	25	5	1	61	68	19	.270	.362	.348	.711	93	-6	-3	96	125	67	.696	10	4	1	-0	*C	0.9
1921	Chi-A	128	416	32	105	24	4	0	47	40	36	.252	.328	.329	.658	69	-20	-19	99	118	47	.594	3	4	-2	8	*C	-0.7
1922	Chi-A	142	442	57	124	22	3	4	60	67	36	.281	.379	.371	.750	95	-0	-1	101	122	68	.764	12	4	1	15	*C	1.9
1923	Chi-A	123	382	42	87	12	2	1	44	39	28	.228	.306	.277	.583	55	-25	-24	98	138	35	.518	6	4	-1	-1	*C	-1.6
1924	Chi-A	57	153	15	30	4	2	1	11	21	10	.196	.301	.268	.569	49	-12	-11	97	83	13	.508	1	5	-3	6	C	-0.3
1925	Chi-A	125	343	44	94	18	1	0	52	57	27	.274	.382	.332	.714	86	-7	-4	96	153	49	.728	11	5	0	-2	*C	0.2
1926	Chi-A	82	226	26	60	9	1	0	32	27	11	.265	.349	.314	.663	81	-8	-5	92	153	27	.629	5	1	1	-6	C	-0.4
1927	Chi-A	16	26	2	6	2	0	0	2	2	1	.231	.286	.308	.593	53	-2	-2	102	83	2	.500	0	0	0	0	CM	0.0
1928	Chi-A	2	1	0	1	0	0	0	1	0	0	1.000	1.000	1.000	2.000	431	0	0	99	343	1	—	1	0	0	0	/CM	0.1
1929	NY-N	5	2	0	0	0	0	0	0	0	1	.000	.000	.000	.000	-99	-1	-1	100	0	0	.000	0			-0	/C	0.0
Total	18	1761	5306	579	1345	199	49	11	594	638	355	.253	.340	.316	.656	83	-108	-101	99	122	630	.632	176	69		26	*C	3.5

■ **BIFF SCHALLER** Schaller, Walter b: 9/23/1889, Chicago, Ill. d: 10/9/39, Emeryville, Cal. BL/TR, 5'11", 168 lbs. Deb: 4/30/11

YEAR	TM/L	G	AB	R	H	2B	3B	HR	RBI	BB	SO	AVG	OBP	SLG	PRO	/A	BR	/A	PF	CHI	RC	TA	SB	CS	SBR	FR	POS	TPR
1911	Det-A	40	60	8	8	0	1	1	7	4		.133	.200	.217	.417	15	-7	-8	108	148	3	.365	1			-0	O/1	-0.8
1913	Chi-A	36	96	12	21	3	0	0	4	20	16	.219	.353	.250	.603	81	-2	-1	95	59	10	.653	5			-7	O	-0.9
Total	2	76	156	20	29	3	1	1	11	24	16	.186	.298	.237	.536	55	-9	-9	100	91	13	.535	6			-7	/O1	-1.7

■ **BOBBY SCHANG** Schang, Robert Martin b: 12/7/1886, Wales Center, N.Y. d: 8/29/66, Sacramento, Cal. BR/TR, 5'7", 165 lbs. Deb: 9/23/14

YEAR	TM/L	G	AB	R	H	2B	3B	HR	RBI	BB	SO	AVG	OBP	SLG	PRO	/A	BR	/A	PF	CHI	RC	TA	SB	CS	SBR	FR	POS	TPR
1914	Pit-N	11	35	0	8	1	1	0	1	0	10	.229	.229	.314	.543	66	-2	-2	92	33	2	.407	0			-1	C	-0.1
1915	Pit-N	56	125	13	23	6	3	0	4	14	32	.184	.271	.280	.551	68	-5	-5	99	44	10	.500	2	2	-1	-0	C	-0.2
	NY-N	12	21	1	3	0	0	0	1	4	5	.143	.280	.143	.423	32	-2	-1	91	127	1	.444	1			-0	/C	0.0
	Yr	68	146	14	26	6	3	0	5	18	37	.178	.273	.260	.533	63	-6	-6	97	59	12	.492	3	2	-0	-1		-0.2
1927	StL-N	3	5	0	1	0	0	0	0	0	0	.200	.200	.200	.400	7	-1	-1	107	0	0	.250	0			0	/C	0.0
Total	3	82	186	14	35	7	4	0	6	18	47	.188	.263	.269	.532	62	-9	-8	97	51	14	.471	3	2		-1	/C	-0.3

■ **WALLY SCHANG** Schang, Walter Henry b: 8/22/1889, S.Wales, N.Y. d: 3/6/65, St.Louis, Mo. BB/TR, 5'10", 180 lbs. Deb: 5/01/13 C

YEAR	TM/L	G	AB	R	H	2B	3B	HR	RBI	BB	SO	AVG	OBP	SLG	PRO	/A	BR	/A	PF	CHI	RC	TA	SB	CS	SBR	FR	POS	TPR
1913	Phi-A	79	207	32	55	16	3	3	30	34	44	.266	.392	.415	.807	141	11	12	97	112	34	.875	4			-3	C	1.5
1914	Phi-A	107	307	44	88	11	8	3	45	32	33	.287	.371	.404	.775	137	13	13	97	127	47	.761	7	7	-2	1	*C	2.2
1915	Phi-A	116	359	64	89	9	11	1	44	66	47	.248	.385	.343	.728	123	12	13	96	121	55	.810	18	3	4	5	3OC	2.5
1916	Phi-A	110	338	41	90	15	8	7	38	38	44	.266	.358	.420	.778	136	14	14	98	85	57	.823	14			5	OC	1.9
1917	Phi-A	118	316	41	90	14	9	3	36	29	24	.285	.362	.415	.776	146	14	16	94	92	49	.774	6			2	C3/O	2.6
1918	Bos-A	88	225	36	55	7	1	0	20	46	35	.244	.377	.284	.662	105	3	4	95	114	26	.682	4			-6	CO/3S	0.2
1919	Bos-A	113	330	43	101	16	3	0	55	71	42	.306	.436	.373	.809	140	18	22	91	162	58	.934	15			4	*C	3.2
1920	Bos-A	122	387	58	118	30	7	4	51	64	37	.305	.413	.450	.862	134	18	21	96	96	75	.913	7	7	-2	8	CO	2.7
1921	NY-A	134	424	77	134	30	5	6	55	78	35	.316	.428	.453	.881	121	20	18	103	90	88	.959	7	4	-0	-9	*C	1.2
1922	NY-A	124	408	46	130	21	7	1	53	53	36	.319	.405	.412	.816	111	10	9	102	113	72	.842	12	6	0	-5	*C	0.7
1923	NY-A	84	272	39	75	8	2	2	29	27	17	.276	.360	.342	.702	82	-5	-6	104	100	36	.663	3	2	-0	-6	C	-0.6
1924	NY-A	114	356	46	104	19	7	5	52	48	43	.292	.382	.427	.809	109	5	6	99	103	59	.798	2	6	-3	-3	*C	0.6
1925	NY-A	73	167	17	40	8	1	2	24	17	9	.240	.310	.335	.645	66	-10	-9	96	130	18	.594	3	1	0	2	C	-0.2
1926	StL-A	103	285	36	94	19	5	8	50	32	20	.330	.405	.516	.921	138	16	16	101	99	59	.959	5	5	-2	7	C/O	2.5
1927	StL-A	97	264	40	84	15	2	5	42	41	33	.318	.414	.447	.861	116	11	8	106	105	50	.911	3	0	1	5	C	1.5
1928	StL-A	91	245	41	70	10	5	3	39	68	26	.286	.448	.404	.852	121	14	12	104	124	52	1.011	8	2	1	2	C	2.0
1929	StL-A	94	249	43	59	10	5	5	36	74	22	.237	.424	.378	.802	108	7	8	100	113	46	.907	1	4	-2	1	C	1.3
1930	Phi-A	45	92	16	16	4	1	1	9	17	15	.174	.309	.272	.581	49	-7	-7	99	107	9	.566	0	0	0	-1	C	-0.4
1931	Det-A	30	76	9	14	2	0	0	2	14	11	.184	.311	.211	.522	38	-6	-7	104	41	6	.500	1	0	0	1	C	-0.2
Total	19	1842	5307	769	1506	264	90	59	710	849	573	.284	.393	.401	.794	118	156	163	99	109	897	.832	120	47		9	*CO/3S	25.2

■ **ART SCHAREIN** Scharein, Arthur Otto "Scoop" b: 6/30/05, Decatur, Ill. d: 7/2/69, San Antonio, Tex. BR/TR, 5'11", 155 lbs. Deb: 7/06/32

YEAR	TM/L	G	AB	R	H	2B	3B	HR	RBI	BB	SO	AVG	OBP	SLG	PRO	/A	BR	/A	PF	CHI	RC	TA	SB	CS	SBR	FR	POS	TPR
1932	StL-A	81	303	43	92	19	2	0	42	25	10	.304	.363	.380	.742	92	-3	-3	100	125	41	.671	4	8	-4	9	3/S2	0.8
1933	StL-A	123	471	49	96	13	3	0	26	41	21	.204	.269	.244	.513	32	-43	-53	115	80	32	.427	7	9	-3	13	3S/2	-3.1
1934	StL-A	1	2	0	1	0	0	0	2	0	0	.500	.500	.500	1.000	153	0	0	104	668	0	1.000	0	0	0	0	H	0.0
Total	3	205	776	92	189	32	5	0	70	66	31	.244	.306	.298	.604	54	-45	-55	109	99	73	.517	11	17	-7	23	3/S2	-2.3

■ **GEORGE SCHAREIN** Scharein, George Albert "Tom" b: 11/21/14, Decatur, Ill. d: 12/23/81, Decatur, Ill. BR/TR, 6'1", 174 lbs. Deb: 4/19/37

YEAR	TM/L	G	AB	R	H	2B	3B	HR	RBI	BB	SO	AVG	OBP	SLG	PRO	/A	BR	/A	PF	CHI	RC	TA	SB	CS	SBR	FR	POS	TPR
1937	Phi-N	146	511	44	123	20	1	0	57	36	47	.241	.293	.284	.577	53	-30	-35	108	142	44	.491	13			9	*S	-1.4
1938	Phi-N	117	390	47	93	16	4	1	29	16	33	.238	.268	.308	.576	58	-23	-23	100	85	32	.482	11			-7	S2/3	-2.2
1939	Phi-N	118	399	35	95	17	1	1	33	13	40	.238	.262	.293	.555	52	-29	-26	94	101	31	.432	4			-19	*S	-3.8
1940	Phi-N	7	17	0	5	0	0	0	0	0	3	.294	.294	.294	.588	65	-1	-1	97	0	1	.417	0			0	/S	0.0

YEAR	TM/L	G	AB	R	H	2B	3B	HR	RBI	BB	SO	AVG	OBP	SLG	PRO	/A	BR	/A	PF	CHI	RC	TA	SB	CS	SBR	FR	POS	TPR
Total	4	388	1317	126	316	53	6	2	119	65	123	.240	.277	.294	.571	54	-82	-85	101	111	108	.482	28			-18	S/23	-7.4
■ **NICK SCHARF** Scharf, Edward T. b: 1859, Baltimore, Md. d: 3/12/37, Baltimore, Md. Deb: 5/18/1882																												
1882	Bal-a	10	39	4	8	1	1	1		0		.205	.205	.359	.564	94	-1	-0	92	0	3	.452				0	/O3	0.0
1883	Bal-a	3	13	1	2	1	0	0		1		.154	.214	.231	.445	41	-1	-1	107	0	1	.364				0	/S	0.0
Total	2	13	52	5	10	2	1	1		1		.192	.208	.327	.534	78	-1	-1	96	0	4	.429				0	/OS3	0.0
■ **AL SCHEER** Scheer, Allan G. b: 10/21/1888, Dayton, Ohio d: 5/6/59, Logansport, Ind. BL/TR, 5'9", 165 lbs. Deb: 8/02/13																												
1913	Bro-N	6	22	3	5	0	0	0	0	2	4	.227	.292	.227	.519	47	-1	-2	104	0	2	.471	1			-2	/O	-0.3
1914	Ind-F	120	363	63	111	23	6	3	45	49	39	.306	.388	.427	.815	120	17	12	111	99	66	.845	9			-7	*O/2S	0.0
1915	New-F	155	546	75	146	25	14	2	60	65	38	.267	.345	.375	.721	120	10	14	94	109	85	.753	31			-2	*O	0.4
Total	3	281	931	141	262	48	20	5	105	116	81	.281	.361	.392	.753	119	25	24	101	102	153	.780	41			-11	O/2S	0.1
■ **HEINIE SCHEER** Scheer, Henry b: 7/31/1900, New York, N.Y. d: 3/21/76, New Haven, Conn. BR/TR, 5'8", 146 lbs. Deb: 4/20/22																												
1922	Phi-A	51	135	10	23	3	0	4	12	3	25	.170	.188	.281	.470	20	-16	-17	104	86	7	.375	1	0	0	-1	23	-1.4
1923	Phi-A	69	210	26	50	8	1	2	21	17	41	.238	.301	.314	.616	62	-12	-12	100	100	21	.537	3	4	-2	-1	2	-1.1
Total	2	120	345	36	73	11	1	6	33	20	66	.212	.259	.301	.560	46	-28	-29	102	94	28	.471	4	4	-1	-2	/23	-2.5
■ **FRITZ SCHEEREN** Scheeren, Frederick "Dutch" b: 9/8/1891, Kokomo, Ind. d: 6/17/73, Oil City, Pa. BR/TR, 6', 180 lbs. Deb: 9/14/14																												
1914	Pit-N	11	31	4	9	0	1	1	2	1	6	.290	.313	.452	.764	137	1	1	92	43	4	.727	1			-3	O	-0.1
1915	Pit-N	4	3	0	0	0	0	0	0	0	0	.000	.000	.000	.000	-99	-1	-1	99	0	0	.000	0			-0	/O	0.0
Total	2	15	34	4	9	0	1	1	2	1	6	.265	.286	.412	.697	115	0	0	93	39	4	.640	1			-3	/O	-0.1
■ **BOB SCHEFFING** Scheffing, Robert Boden b: 8/11/13, Overland, Mo. d: 10/26/85, Phoenix, Ariz. BR/TR, 6'2", 180 lbs. Deb: 4/27/41 MC																												
1941	Chi-N	51	132	9	32	8	0	1	20	5	19	.242	.270	.326	.596	72	-6	-5	94	157	10	.476	2			2	C	0.0
1942	Chi-N	44	102	7	20	3	0	2	12	7	11	.196	.248	.284	.532	58	-6	-6	96	127	7	.447	2			1	C	-0.3
1946	Chi-N	63	115	8	32	4	1	0	18	12	18	.278	.346	.330	.677	98	-1	-0	94	177	13	.575	0			-2	C	0.0
1947	Chi-N	110	363	33	96	11	5	5	50	25	25	.264	.312	.364	.675	78	-12	-12	101	126	39	.570	2			4	C	-0.5
1948	Chi-N	102	293	23	88	18	2	5	45	22	27	.300	.351	.427	.778	118	3	6	93	120	44	.701	0			1	C	1.3
1949	Chi-N	55	149	12	40	6	1	3	19	9	9	.268	.314	.383	.697	91	-3	-2	94	109	16	.578	0			1	C	0.0
1950	Chi-N	12	16	0	3	1	0	0	1	0	2	.188	.188	.250	.438	13	-2	-2	105	96	1	.308	0			0	/C	-0.1
	Cin-N	21	47	4	13	0	0	2	6	4	2	.277	.333	.404	.738	89	-1	-1	105	93	5	.605	0			-1	C	0.0
	Yr	33	63	4	16	1	0	2	7	4	4	.254	.299	.365	.664	70	-3	-3	105	97	6	.529	0			-0		-0.1
1951	Cin-N	47	122	9	31	2	0	2	14	16	9	.254	.345	.320	.665	80	-3	-3	101	120	15	.602	0	0	0	-2	C	-0.4
	StL-N	12	18	0	2	0	0	0	2	3	5	.111	.238	.111	.349	-3	-3	-3	101	387	1	.294	0	0	0	0	C	-0.2
	Yr	59	140	9	33	2	0	2	16	19	14	.236	.331	.293	.624	69	-5	-6	101	177	15	.565	0	0	0	-2		-0.6
Total	8	517	1357	105	357	53	9	20	187	103	127	.263	.316	.360	.676	86	-32	-27	97	132	150	.599	6	0		4	C	-0.2
■ **TED SCHEFFLER** Scheffler, Theodore J. b: 4/5/1864, New York, N.Y. d: 2/24/49, Jamaica, N.Y. BR/TR, 5'10", 160 lbs. Deb: 1888																												
1888	Det-N	27	94	17	19	3	1	0	4	9	9	.202	.286	.255	.541	77	-2	-2	98	61	8	.520	4			0	O	-0.1
1890	Roc-a	119	445	111	109	12	6	3		78		.245	.373	.319	.692	115	8	14	93	0	84	.923	77			7	*O/C	1.3
Total	2	146	539	128	128	15	7	3	4	87	9	.237	.359	.308	.667	109	6	12	93	10	92	.849	81			7	O/C	1.2
■ **FRANK SCHEIBECK** Scheibeck, Frank S. b: 6/28/1865, Detroit, Mich. d: 10/22/56, Detroit, Mich. BR/TR, 5'7", 145 lbs. Deb: 5/09/1887																												
1887	Cle-a	3	9	2	2	0	0	0		2		.222	.364	.222	.586	69	-0	-0	98	0	1	.571	0			0	/S3P	0.0
1888	Det-N	1	4	0	0	0	0	0	0	0	0	.000	.000	.000	.000	-99	-1	-1	98	0	0	.000	0			0	/S	0.0
1890	Tol-a	134	485	72	117	13	5	1		76		.241	.348	.295	.642	90	-2	-4	103	0	71	.758	57			-3	*S	0.0
1894	Pit-N	28	102	20	36	2	3	1	10	11	9	.353	.416	.461	.877	120	2	4	94	56	23	.985	7			-5	S/O32	0.0
	Was-N	52	196	49	45	2	4	0	17	45	24	.230	.384	.281	.664	65	-9	-8	98	75	26	.762	11			4	S	0.0
	Yr	80	298	69	81	4	7	1	27	56	33	.272	.394	.342	.736	83	-7	-5	97	69	48	.829	18			-1		0.0
1895	Was-N	48	167	17	31	5	2	0	25	17	21	.186	.265	.240	.504	31	-17	-18	103	175	12	.463	5			-5	S/32	-1.5
1899	Was-N	27	94	19	27	4	1	0	9	11		.287	.368	.351	.719	105	0	1	96	85	14	.746	5			0	S	0.1
1901	Cle-A	93	329	33	70	11	3	0	38	18		.213	.254	.264	.518	48	-24	-21	95	141	23	.417	3			-14	S	-2.7
1906	Det-A	3	10	1	1	0	0	0	0	2		.100	.250	.100	.350	11	-1	-1	108	0	0	.333	0			0	/2	0.0
Total	8	389	1396	213	329	37	18	2	99	182	54	.236	.328	.292	.620	71	-51	-48	99	72	171	.644	88			-23	S/O23P	-4.1
■ **RICHIE SCHEINBLUM** Scheinblum, Richard Alan b: 11/5/42, New York, N.Y. BB/TR, 6'1", 180 lbs. Deb: 9/01/65																												
1965	Cle-A	4	1	1	0	0	0	0	0	0	0	.000	.000	.000	.000	-99	-0	-0	98	0	0	.000	0	0	0	0	H	0.0
1967	Cle-A	18	66	8	21	4	2	0	6	5	10	.318	.366	.439	.806	137	3	3	100	91	10	.723	0	2	-1	-0	O	0.1
1968	Cle-A	19	55	3	12	5	0	0	5	5	8	.218	.295	.309	.604	82	-1	-1	101	126	5	.511	0	0	0	1	O	0.0
1969	Cle-A	102	199	13	37	5	1	1	13	19	30	.186	.257	.236	.493	41	-16	-15	94	104	11	.384	0	2	-1	-2	O	-2.0
1971	Was-A	27	49	5	7	3	0	0	4	8	5	.143	.263	.204	.467	37	-4	-4	92	163	3	.409	0	0	0	3	O	0.0
1972	KC-A	134	450	60	135	21	4	8	66	58	40	.300	.385	.418	.803	138	23	23	100	133	71	.746	0	1	-1	-3	*O	1.8
1973	Cin-N	29	54	5	12	2	0	1	8	10	4	.222	.344	.315	.659	90	-1	-0	93	161	6	.628	0	0	0	-2	O	-0.3
	Cal-A	77	229	28	75	10	2	3	21	35	27	.328	.419	.428	.847	145	13	15	96	77	42	.837	0	0	0	-2	O/D	1.1
1974	Cal-A	10	26	1	4	0	0	0	2	1	2	.154	.185	.154	.339	-2	-3	-3	92	197	0	.208	0	0	0	-1	/OD	-0.4
	KC-A	36	83	7	15	2	0	0	2	8	8	.181	.253	.205	.458	31	-7	-8	106	46	4	.342	0	1	-1	-1	D/O	-0.9
	Yr	46	109	8	19	2	0	0	4	9	10	.174	.237	.193	.430	24	-10	-11	103	83	5	.316	0	1	-1	-2		-1.3
	StL-N	6	6	0	2	0	0	0	0	0	1	.333	.333	.333	.667	84	-0	-0	104	0	1	.500	0	0	0	0	H	0.0
Total	8	462	1218	131	320	52	9	13	127	149	135	.263	.346	.352	.698	104	6	9	98	112	153	.646	0	6	-4	-8	O/D	-0.6
■ **DANNY SCHELL** Schell, Clyde Daniel b: 12/26/27, Fostoria, Mich. d: 5/11/72, Mayville, Mich. BR/TR, 6'1", 195 lbs. Deb: 4/13/54																												
1954	Phi-N	92	272	25	77	14	3	7	33	17	31	.283	.330	.434	.764	99	-2	-1	99	93	34	.652	0	3	-2	0	O	-0.4
1955	Phi-N	2	2	0	0	0	0	0	0	0	1	.000	.000	.000	.000	-98	-1	-1	102	0	0	.000	0	0	0	0	H	0.0
Total	2	94	274	25	77	14	3	7	33	17	32	.281	.328	.431	.758	97	-2	-2	99	93	34	.685	0	3	-2	0	/O	-0.4
■ **AL SCHELLHASE** Schellhase, Albert Herman "Schelley" b: 9/13/1864, Evansville, Ind. d: 1/3/19, Evansville, Ind. TR , Deb: 5/07/1890																												
1890	Bos-N	9	29	1	4	0	0	0	1	1	10	.138	.167	.138	.305	-9	-4	-4	111	75	1	.200	0			0	/OCS3	-0.3
1891	Lou-a	7	20	4	3	0	0	0	1	1	2	.150	.190	.150	.340	-1	-3	-2	90	96	1	.412	3			0	/C	-0.1
Total	2	16	49	5	7	0	0	0	2	2	12	.143	.176	.143	.319	-6	-7	-7	102	84	2	.286	3			0	/CO3S	-0.4
■ **FRED SCHEMANSKE** Schemanske, Frederick George "Buck" b: 4/28/03, Detroit, Mich. d: 2/18/60, Detroit, Mich. BR/TR, 6'2", 190 lbs. Deb: 9/15/23																												
1923	Was-A	2	2	0	2	0	0	0	2	1	0	1.000	1.000	1.000	2.000	452	1	1	95	342	2	—	0	0	0	0	/P	0.1
■ **MIKE SCHEMER** Schemer, Michael "Lefty" b: 11/20/17, Baltimore, Md. d: 4/22/83, Miami, Fla. BL/TL, 6', 180 lbs. Deb: 8/08/45																												
1945	NY-N	31	108	10	36	3	1	1	10	6	1	.333	.368	.407	.776	116	2	2	100	74	14	.667	2			1	1	0.2
1946	NY-N	1	1	0	0	0	0	0	0	0	0	.000	.000	.000	.000	-99	-0	-0	102	0	0	.000	0			0	H	0.0
Total	2	32	109	10	36	3	1	1	10	6	1	.330	.365	.404	.769	114	2	2	100	73	14	.712	2			1	/1	0.2
■ **BILL SCHENCK** Schenck, William G. b: Brooklyn, N.Y. 5'7", 171 lbs. Deb: 5/29/1882																												
1882	Lou-a	60	231	37	60	11	3	0		8		.260	.285	.333	.618	115	2	4	94	0	22	.497				-6	*3/SP	-0.3
1884	Ric-a	42	151	14	31	4	0	3		1		.205	.216	.291	.507	67	-5	-5	99	0	10	.383				-2	S/2	-0.6
1885	Bro-a	1	4	0	0	0	0	0		0		.000	.000	.000	.000	-96	-1	-1	104	0	0	.000				0	/3	0.0
Total	3	103	386	51	91	15	3	3		9		.236	.255	.313	.569	93	-5	-2	96	0	32	.444				-8	/3S2P	-0.9
■ **HANK SCHENZ** Schenz, Henry Leonard b: 4/11/19, New Richmond, Ohio BR/TR, 5'9.5", 175 lbs. Deb: 9/18/46																												
1946	Chi-N	6	11	0	2	0	0	0	1	0	0	.182	.182	.182	.364	4	-1	-1	94	187	0	.333	1			0	/3	0.0
1947	Chi-N	7	14	2	1	0	0	0	0	2	1	.071	.235	.071	.307	-15	-2	-2	101	0	1	.308	0			0	/3	-0.1
1948	Chi-N	96	337	43	88	17	1	1	14	18	15	.261	.306	.326	.633	77	-14	-11	93	46	34	.529	3			-0	2/3	-0.5
1949	Chi-N	7	14	2	6	0	0	0	1	1	0	.429	.467	.429	.895	150	1	1	94	63	3	1.125	2			0	/3	0.1
1950	Pit-N	58	101	17	23	4	2	1	5	6	7	.228	.271	.337	.608	57	-6	-7	103	52	8	.488	0			0	23/S	-0.5

YEAR	TM/L	G	AB	R	H	2B	3B	HR	RBI	BB	SO	AVG	OBP	SLG	PRO	/A	BR	/A	PF	CHI	RC	TA	SB	CS	SBR	FR	POS	TPR
1951	Pit-N	25	61	5	13	1	0	0	3	0	2	.213	.226	.230	.455	21	-7	-7	107	83	3	.300	0	2	-1	1	2/3	-0.6
	NY-N	8	0	1	0	0	0	0	0	0	0	—	—	—	—	—	0	0	102	—	—	—	0	0	0	0	R	0.0
	Yr	33	61	6	13	1	0	0	3	0	2	.213	.226	.230	.455	22	-7	-7	105	65	3	.300	0	2	-1	1		-0.6
Total	6	207	538	70	133	22	3	2	24	27	25	.247	.291	.310	.601	64	-29	-27	97	53	52	.506	6	2		1	2/3S	-1.6
■ **JOE SCHEPNER** Schepner, Joseph Maurice "Gentleman Joe" b: 8/10/1895, Aliquippa, Pa. d: 7/25/59, Mobile, Ala. BR/TR, 5'10", 160 lbs. Deb: 9/11/19																												
1919	StL-A	14	48	2	10	4	0	0	6	1	5	.208	.224	.292	.516	46	-4	-4	97	155	3	.395	0			1	3	-0.1
■ **BOB SCHERBARTH** Scherbarth, Robert Elmer b: 1/18/26, Milwaukee, Wis. BR/TR, 6', 180 lbs. Deb: 4/23/50																												
1950	Bos-A	1	0	0	0	0	0	0	0	0	0	—	—	—	—	—	0	0	114	—	—	—	0	0	0	0	/C	0.0
■ **HARRY SCHERER** Scherer, Harry Deb: 7/24/1889																												
1889	Lou-a	1	3	0	1	0	0	0	0	0	0	.333	.333	.333	.667	96	-0	-0	96	0	0	.500	0			0	/O	0.0
■ **LOU SCHIAPPACASSE** Schiappacasse, Louis Joseph b: 3/29/1881, Ann Arbor, Mich. d: 9/20/10, Ann Arbor, Mich. BR/TR, Deb: 9/07/02																												
1902	Det-A	2	5	0	0	0	0	0	1	1		.000	.167	.000	.167	-51	-1	-1	99	0	0	.200	0			0	/O	0.0
■ **MORRIE SCHICK** Schick, Maurice Francis b: 4/17/1892, Chicago, Ill. d: 10/25/79, Hazel Crest, Ill. BR/TR, 5'11", 170 lbs. Deb: 4/15/17																												
1917	Chi-N	14	34	3	5	0	0	0	3	3	10	.147	.216	.147	.363	12	-3	-4	105	231	1	.276	0			1	O	-0.3
■ **CHUCK SCHILLING** Schilling, Charles Thomas b: 10/25/37, Brooklyn, N.Y. BR/TR, 5'10", 160 lbs. Deb: 4/11/61																												
1961	Bos-A	158	646	87	167	25	2	5	62	78	77	.259	.340	.327	.667	78	-17	-19	102	93	76	.604	7	6	-2	17	*2	1.6
1962	Bos-A	119	413	48	95	17	1	7	35	29	48	.230	.287	.327	.614	63	-21	-22	102	89	38	.512	1	0	0	-2	*2	-1.4
1963	Bos-A	146	576	63	135	25	0	8	33	41	72	.234	.291	.319	.610	67	-22	-26	106	70	54	.513	3	2	-0	-7	*2	-2.4
1964	Bos-A	47	163	18	32	6	0	0	7	15	22	.196	.264	.233	.497	39	-13	-13	102	80	11	.396	0	1	-1	-2	2	-1.1
1965	Bos-A	71	171	14	41	3	2	3	9	13	17	.240	.293	.333	.627	72	-5	-7	107	57	15	.504	0	1	-1	-2	2	-0.7
Total	5	541	1969	230	470	76	5	23	146	176	236	.239	.305	.317	.622	68	-78	-87	103	81	193	.543	11	10	-3	4	2	-4.0
■ **BILL SCHINDLER** Schindler, William Gibbons b: 7/10/1896, Perryville, Mo. d: 2/6/79, Perryville, Mo. BR/TR, 5'11", 160 lbs. Deb: 9/03/20																												
1920	StL-N	1	2	0	0	0	0	0	0	0	1	.000	.000	.000	.000	-99	-1	-1	98	0	0	.000	0	0	0	0	/C	0.0
■ **DUTCH SCHIRICK** Schirick, Harry Ernest b: 6/15/1890, Ruby, N.Y. d: 11/12/68, Kingston, N.Y. BR/TR, 5'8", 160 lbs. Deb: 9/17/14																												
1914	StL-A	1	0	0	0	0	0	0	0	1	0	—	1.000	—	1.000	208	0	0	98	0	2	—	2			0	H	0.1
■ **LARRY SCHLAFLY** Schlafly, Harry Linton b: 9/20/1878, Port Washington, Ohio d: 6/27/19, Canton, Ohio BR/TR, 5'11", 182 lbs. Deb: 9/18/02 M																												
1902	Chi-N	10	31	5	10	0	3	0	5	6		.323	.432	.516	.949	203	4	4	96	110	8	1.143	2			0	/O23	0.4
1906	Was-A	123	426	60	105	13	8	2	30	50		.246	.326	.329	.654	117	5	9	91	79	56	.682	29			15	*2	2.3
1907	Was-A	24	74	10	10	0	0	1	4	22		.135	.333	.176	.509	72	-1	-0	90	95	7	.656	7			-6	2	-0.6
1914	Buf-F	51	127	16	33	7	1	2	19	12	22	.260	.324	.378	.702	96	-0	-1	104	127	17	.670	3			3	2/1C3OM	0.2
Total	4	208	658	91	158	20	12	5	58	90	22	.240	.332	.330	.661	113	7	12	94	92	88	.696	41			13	2/1O3C	2.3
■ **ADMIRAL SCHLEI** Schlei, George Henry b: 1/12/1878, Cincinnati, Ohio d: 1/24/58, Huntington, W.Va. BR/TR, 5'8.5", 179 lbs. Deb: 4/24/04																												
1904	Cin-N	97	291	25	69	8	3	0	32	17		.237	.279	.285	.564	67	-8	-13	114	141	26	.482	7			2	C	-0.2
1905	Cin-N	99	314	32	71	8	3	1	36	22		.226	.277	.280	.557	66	-12	-13	103	138	28	.490	9			6	C/1	0.1
1906	Cin-N	116	388	44	95	13	8	4	54	29		.245	.297	.351	.648	90	1	-6	115	136	44	.587	7			7	C1	0.9
1907	Cin-N	84	246	28	67	3	2	0	27	28		.272	.347	.301	.648	110	3	4	95	138	28	.598	5			3	C/1O	1.3
1908	Cin-N	92	300	31	66	6	4	1	22	22		.220	.273	.277	.550	76	-7	-8	103	100	22	.457	2			-1	C	-0.4
1909	NY-N	92	279	25	68	12	0	0	30	40		.244	.343	.287	.629	92	1	-1	105	136	28	.597	4			-2	C	0.4
1910	NY-N	55	99	10	19	2	1	0	8	14	10	.192	.304	.232	.537	60	-5	-4	95	121	9	.538	4			-4	C	-0.5
1911	NY-N	1	1	0	0	0	0	0	0	0	1	.000	.000	.000	.000	-98	-0	-0	102	0	0	.000	0			0	H	0.0
Total	8	636	1918	195	455	52	21	6	209	172	11	.237	.301	.296	.597	81	-29	-42	106	131	184	.534	38			12	C/1O	1.6
■ **RUDY SCHLESINGER** Schlesinger, William Cordes b: 11/5/41, Cincinnati, Ohio BR/TR, 6'2", 175 lbs. Deb: 5/04/65																												
1965	Bos-A	1	1	0	0	0	0	0	0	0	0	.000	.000	.000	.000	-93	-0	-0	107	0	0	.000	0	0	0	0	H	0.0
■ **DUTCH SCHLIEBNER** Schliebner, Frederick Paul b: 5/19/1891, Charlottenburg, Germany d: 4/15/75, Toledo, Ohio BR/TR, 5'10", 180 lbs. Deb: 4/17/23																												
1923	Bro-N	19	76	11	19	4	0	0	4	5	7	.250	.296	.303	.599	60	-5	-4	98	65	7	.509	1	0	0	1	1	-0.3
	StL-A	127	444	50	122	19	6	4	52	39	60	.275	.339	.372	.710	84	-9	-11	104	102	58	.651	3	2	-0	-1	*1	-1.7
Total	1	146	520	61	141	23	6	4	56	44	67	.271	.333	.362	.694	80	-13	-16	103	97	65	.630	4	2	0	-0	1	-2.0
■ **JAY SCHLUETER** Schlueter, Jay D b: 7/31/49, Phoenix, Ariz. BR/TR, 6', 182 lbs. Deb: 6/18/71																												
1971	Hou-N	7	3	1	1	0	0	0	0	0	1	.333	.333	.333	.667	97	-0	-0	93	0	0	.500	0	0	0	-0	/O	0.0
■ **NORM SCHLUETER** Schlueter, Norman John "Duke" b: 9/25/16, Belleville, Ill. BR/TR, 5'10", 175 lbs. Deb: 5/28/38																												
1938	Chi-A	35	118	11	27	5	1	0	7	4	15	.229	.254	.288	.542	36	-12	-12	98	70	9	.429	1	0	0	1	C	-0.8
1939	Chi-A	34	56	5	13	2	1	0	8	1	11	.232	.246	.304	.549	37	-5	-6	107	159	3	.426	2	0	1	-1	C	-0.3
1944	Cle-A	49	122	2	15	4	0	0	11	12	22	.123	.201	.156	.357	3	-15	-15	100	209	4	.277	0	2	-1	-2	C	-1.5
Total	3	118	296	18	55	11	2	0	26	17	48	.186	.230	.236	.467	24	-33	-33	100	145	16	.366	3	2	-0	-2	C	-2.6
■ **RAY SCHMANDT** Schmandt, Raymond Henry b: 1/25/1896, St.Louis, Mo. d: 2/1/69, St.Louis, Mo. BR/TR, 6'1", 175 lbs. Deb: 6/24/15																												
1915	StL-A	3	4	0	0	0	0	0	0	0	1	.000	.000	.000	.000	-99	-1	-1	96	0	0	.000	0			0	/1	0.0
1918	Bro-N	34	114	11	35	5	4	0	18	7	7	.307	.347	.421	.768	132	4	4	101	142	16	.709	1			1	2	0.8
1919	Bro-N	47	127	8	21	4	0	0	10	4	13	.165	.191	.197	.388	18	-13	-12	94	155	4	.274	0			0	21/3	-1.2
1920	Bro-N	28	63	7	15	2	1	0	7	3	4	.238	.273	.302	.574	58	-3	-4	111	143	5	.469	1	1	-0	0	1	-0.3
1921	Bro-N	95	350	42	107	8	5	1	43	11	22	.306	.329	.366	.694	80	-8	-10	105	123	41	.579	3	4	-2	-1	1	-1.4
1922	Bro-N	110	396	54	106	17	3	2	44	21	28	.268	.306	.341	.647	70	-20	-17	95	111	41	.551	6	6	-2	5	*1	-1.4
Total	6	317	1054	122	284	36	13	3	122	46	75	.269	.301	.337	.638	73	-41	-40	100	125	108	.530	11	11		5	1/23	-3.5
■ **GEORGE SCHMEES** Schmees, George Edward "Rocky" b: 9/6/24, Cincinnati, Ohio BL/TL, 6', 190 lbs. Deb: 4/15/52																												
1952	StL-A	34	61	9	8	1	1	0	3	2	18	.131	.159	.180	.339	-6	-9	-9	97	102	2	.245	0	0	0	-1	O/1	-1.0
	Bos-A	42	64	8	13	3	0	0	3	10	11	.203	.311	.250	.561	54	-3	-4	107	70	5	.491	0	1	-1	-6	O/P1	-1.1
	Yr	76	125	17	21	4	1	0	6	12	29	.168	.241	.216	.457	27	-12	-13	103	86	7	.368	0	1	-1	-7		-2.1
Total	1	76	125	17	21	4	1	0	6	12	29	.168	.241	.216	.457	27	-12	-13	102	85	7	.368	0	1	-1	-7	/O1P	-2.1
■ **BOSS SCHMIDT** Schmidt, Charles b: 9/12/1880, Coal Hill, Ark. d: 11/14/32, Clarksville, Ark. BB/TR, 5'11", 200 lbs. Deb: 4/30/06																												
1906	Det-A	68	216	13	47	4	3	0	10	6		.218	.239	.264	.503	54	-10	-12	108	64	14	.379	1			8	C	0.1
1907	Det-A	104	349	32	85	6	6	0	23	5		.244	.254	.295	.549	75	-10	-11	102	80	29	.439	8			4	*C	0.3
1908	Det-A	122	419	45	111	14	3	1	38	16		.265	.292	.320	.612	100	-0	-1	101	106	39	.503	5			7	*C	2.0
1909	Det-A	84	253	21	53	8	2	1	28	7		.209	.240	.269	.508	55	-12	-15	110	152	17	.425	7			-6	C/O	-1.5
1910	Det-A	71	197	22	51	7	7	1	23	2		.259	.277	.381	.658	104	-0	-1	102	109	21	.562	2			1	C	0.8
1911	Det-A	28	46	4	13	2	1	0	2	0		.283	.298	.370	.667	79	-1	-2	108	40	5	.545	0			-0	/CO	0.0
Total	6	477	1480	137	360	41	22	3	124	36		.243	.265	.307	.571	79	-34	-40	104	100	125	.464	23			13	C/O	1.7
■ **BUTCH SCHMIDT** Schmidt, Charles John "Butcher Boy" b: 7/19/1886, Baltimore, Md. d: 9/4/52, Baltimore, Md. BL/TL, 6'1.5", 200 lbs. Deb: 5/11/09																												
1909	NY-A	1	2	0	0	0	0	0	0	0		.000	.000	.000	.000	-99	-0	-0	99	0	0	.000	0			-0	/P	0.0
1913	Bos-N	22	78	6	24	2	2	1	14	2	5	.308	.333	.423	.756	122	1	2	95	141	11	.685	1			1	1	0.1
1914	Bos-N	147	537	67	153	17	9	1	71	43	55	.285	.350	.356	.706	106	7	4	104	141	71	.674	14			3	*1	0.6
1915	Bos-N	127	458	46	115	26	7	2	60	36	59	.251	.318	.352	.670	104	1	2	98	145	52	.592	3	10	-5	-3	*1	-1.3
Total	4	297	1075	119	292	45	18	4	145	81	119	.272	.335	.358	.693	106	9	8	101	142	134	.637	18	10		1	1/P	-0.6
■ **DAVE SCHMIDT** Schmidt, David Frederick b: 12/22/56, Mesa, Ariz. BR/TR, 6'1", 190 lbs. Deb: 4/28/81																												
1981	Bos-A	15	42	6	10	1	0	2	3	7	17	.238	.347	.405	.752	109	1	1	106	51	6	.727	0	0	0	-0	C	0.1

YEAR	TM/L	G	AB	R	H	2B	3B	HR	RBI	BB	SO	AVG	OBP	SLG	PRO	/A	BR	/A	PF	CHI	RC	TA	SB	CS	SBR	FR	POS	TPR
■ **MIKE SCHMIDT**	Schmidt, Michael Jack b: 9/27/49, Dayton, Ohio BR/TR, 6'2", 195 lbs. Deb: 9/12/72																											
1972	Phi-N	13	34	2	7	0	0	1	3	5	15	.206	.325	.294	.619	79	-1	-1	97	95	4	.593	0	0	0	1	3/2	0.0
1973	Phi-N	132	367	43	72	11	0	18	52	62	136	.196	.326	.373	.700	87	-2	-6	108	109	48	.708	8	2	1	5	*3/21S	-0.2
1974	Phi-N	162	568	108	160	28	7	**36**	116	106	138	.282	.398	**.546**	.944	157	**48**	46	103	113	**130**	1.045	23	12	-0	26	*3	**7.0**
1975	Phi-N	158	562	93	140	34	3	**38**	95	101	180	.249	.367	.523	.890	143	34	33	101	95	113	.971	29	12	2	**26**	*3S	6.2
1976	Phi-N	160	584	112	153	31	4	**38**	107	100	149	.262	.380	.524	.904	144	43	37	107	94	121	.964	14	9	-1	**25**	*3	**6.1**
1977	Phi-N	154	544	114	149	27	11	38	101	104	122	.274	.399	.574	.972	157	46	45	100	101	129	1.065	15	8	-0	29	*3/S2	**7.2**
1978	Phi-N	145	513	93	129	27	2	21	78	91	103	.251	.368	.435	.803	117	18	15	105	115	90	.855	19	6	2	11	*3/S	2.8
1979	Phi-N	160	541	109	137	25	4	45	114	**120**	115	.253	.392	.564	.955	162	45	47	97	109	123	**1.036**	9	5	-0	20	*3/S	**6.1**
1980	Phi-N	150	548	104	157	25	8	**48**	**121**	89	119	.286	.388	**.624**	**1.012**	**166**	**56**	**51**	107	104	**137**	**1.107**	12	5	1	21	*3	**7.4**
1981	Phi-N	102	354	**78**	112	19	2	**31**	**91**	**73**	71	.316	**.439**	**.644**	**1.083**	**182**	**50**	**45**	112	118	**102**	**1.243**	12	4	1	22	*3	**6.6**
1982	Phi-N	148	514	108	144	26	3	35	87	**107**	131	.280	**.407**	**.547**	**.954**	**176**	**47**	**52**	94	94	118	**1.044**	14	7	0	18	*3	**6.8**
1983	Phi-N	154	534	104	136	16	4	**40**	109	**128**	148	.255	**.402**	.524	.926	**153**	43	**43**	101	114	117	1.005	7	8	-3	21	*3/S	**5.7**
1984	Phi-N	151	528	93	146	23	3	**36**	**106**	92	116	.277	.388	.536	**.924**	**154**	41	**40**	102	108	108	.950	5	7	-3	13	*3/1S	5.1
1985	Phi-N	158	549	89	152	31	5	33	93	87	117	.277	.379	.532	.911	149	39	37	102	97	113	.934	1	3	-2	-2	*13/S	3.2
1986	Phi-N	160	552	97	160	29	1	**37**	**119**	89	84	.290	.395	**.547**	**.942**	**151**	**44**	**41**	104	117	122	.993	1	2	-1	-3	*31	3.4
1987	Phi-N	147	522	88	153	28	0	35	113	83	80	.293	.392	.548	.940	140	35	32	104	122	111	.964	2	1	0	10	*3/1S	4.0
1988	Phi-N	108	390	52	97	21	2	12	62	49	42	.249	.342	.405	.747	112	7	7	101	135	55	.711	3	0	1	-2	*3/1	0.5
Total	17	2362	8204	1487	2204	401	59	542	1567	1486	1866	.269	.386	.530	.916	148	594	563	103	108	1741	.998	174	91	-2	241	*31/S2	77.9
■ **BOB SCHMIDT**	Schmidt, Robert Benjamin b: 4/22/33, St.Louis, Mo. BR/TR, 6'2", 205 lbs. Deb: 4/16/58																											
1958	SF-N	127	393	46	96	20	2	14	54	33	59	.244	.308	.412	.720	88	-7	-7	100	109	44	.625	0	1	-1	-4	*C	-0.5
1959	SF-N	71	181	17	44	7	1	5	20	13	24	.243	.297	.376	.673	82	-6	-5	95	97	19	.573	0	2	-1	-6	C	-0.7
1960	SF-N	110	344	31	92	12	1	8	37	26	51	.267	.319	.378	.697	100	-5	-1	90	97	39	.593	0	3	-2	-3	*C	0.0
1961	SF-N	2	6	0	1	0	0	0	1	0	1	.167	.167	.167	.333	-11	-1	-1	98	403	0	.200	0	0	0	0	/C	0.0
	Cin-N	27	70	4	9	0	0	1	4	8	14	.129	.218	.171	.389	5	-10	-10	104	108	2	.303	0	0	0	-1	C	-0.8
	Yr	29	76	4	10	0	0	1	5	8	15	.132	.214	.171	.385	4	-11	-11	104	142	2	.296	0	0	0	-1		-0.8
1962	Was-A	88	256	28	62	14	0	10	31	14	37	.242	.284	.414	.698	85	-6	-7	101	90	30	.614	0	0	0	-3	C	-0.4
1963	Was-A	9	15	3	3	1	0	0	0	3	5	.200	.333	.267	.600	72	-0	-0	98	0	1	.538	0	0	0	-0	/C	0.0
1965	NY-A	20	40	4	10	1	0	1	3	3	8	.250	.302	.350	.652	84	-1	-1	101	73	4	.567	0	0	0	1	C	0.1
Total	7	454	1305	133	317	55	4	39	150	100	199	.243	.299	.381	.680	84	-36	-32	97	100	141	.606	0	6	-4	-15	C	-2.3
■ **WALTER SCHMIDT**	Schmidt, Walter Joseph b: 3/20/1887, Coal Hill, Ark. d: 7/4/73, Modesto, Cal. BR/TR, 5'9", 159 lbs. Deb: 4/13/16																											
1916	Pit-N	64	184	16	35	1	2	2	15	10	13	.190	.236	.250	.486	47	-11	-12	105	115	12	.403	3			4	C	-0.5
1917	Pit-N	72	183	9	45	7	0	0	17	11	11	.246	.296	.284	.580	79	-5	-4	100	126	16	.500	4			3	C	0.2
1918	Pit-N	105	323	31	77	6	3	0	27	17	19	.238	.281	.276	.556	66	-12	-14	106	115	27	.467	7			8	*C	0.4
1919	Pit-N	85	267	23	67	9	2	0	29	23	9	.251	.310	.300	.610	80	-5	-6	105	141	26	.540	5			-5	C	-0.6
1920	Pit-N	94	310	22	86	8	4	0	20	24	15	.277	.337	.329	.666	91	-3	-3	101	76	36	.612	9	3	1	-2	C	0.3
1921	Pit-N	114	393	30	111	9	3	0	38	12	13	.282	.307	.321	.628	64	-19	-20	103	111	38	.521	10	6	-1	-0	*C	-1.3
1922	Pit-N	40	152	21	50	11	1	0	22	1	5	.329	.333	.414	.748	89	-2	-3	104	122	20	.641	2	1	0	-1	C	-0.3
1923	Pit-N	97	335	39	83	7	2	0	37	22	12	.248	.300	.281	.581	56	-22	-20	97	139	29	.502	10	5	0	-1	C	-1.5
1924	Pit-N	58	177	16	43	3	2	1	20	13	5	.243	.295	.299	.594	56	-10	-11	106	130	17	.533	6	1	1	-1	C	-0.9
1925	StL-N	37	87	9	22	2	1	0	9	4	3	.253	.293	.299	.592	51	-6	-7	102	123	8	.492	1	0	0	1	C	-0.3
Total	10	766	2411	216	619	63	20	3	234	137	105	.257	.301	.303	.604	68	-94	-101	103	118	231	.520	57	16		5	C	-4.5
■ **HANK SCHMULBACH**	Schmulbach, Henry Alrives b: 1/17/25, E.St.Louis, Ill. BL/TR, 5'11", 165 lbs. Deb: 9/27/43																											
1943	StL-A	1	0	1	0	0	0	0	0	0	0	—	—	—	—	—	0	0	100	—	—	—	0	0	0	0	R	0.0
■ **DAVE SCHNECK**	Schneck, David Lee b: 6/18/49, Allentown, Pa. BL/TL, 5'10", 200 lbs. Deb: 7/14/72																											
1972	NY-N	37	123	7	23	3	2	3	10	10	26	.187	.254	.317	.571	64	-7	-6	95	86	10	.485	0	1	-1	-0	O	-0.8
1973	NY-N	13	36	2	7	0	1	0	0	1	4	.194	.216	.250	.466	29	-3	-4	101	0	1	.323	0	0	0	1	O	-0.3
1974	NY-N	93	254	23	52	11	1	5	25	16	43	.205	.255	.315	.570	59	-15	-15	99	102	21	.495	4	1	1	6	O	-1.1
Total	3	143	413	32	82	14	4	8	35	27	73	.199	.251	.310	.561	58	-25	-24	98	88	32	.482	4	2	0	7	O	-2.2
■ **RED SCHOENDIENST**	Schoendienst, Albert Fred b: 2/2/23, Germantown, Ill. BB/TR, 6', 170 lbs. Deb: 4/17/45 MC																											
1945	StL-N	137	565	89	157	22	6	1	47	21	17	.278	.305	.343	.648	80	-17	-17	100	88	59	.585	**26**			6	*OS/2	-1.4
1946	StL-N	142	606	94	170	28	5	0	34	37	27	.281	.322	.343	.665	83	-10	-14	107	54	67	.575	12			-1	*23/S	-1.1
1947	StL-N	151	659	91	167	25	9	3	48	48	27	.253	.304	.332	.636	65	-30	-35	106	67	65	.537	6			-4	*2/3O	-2.2
1948	StL-N	119	408	64	111	21	4	4	36	28	16	.272	.319	.373	.691	86	-8	-9	101	82	49	.597	1			4	2	0.3
1949	StL-N	151	640	102	190	25	2	3	54	51	18	.297	.351	.356	.707	82	-8	-17	110	76	82	.628	8			**23**	*2S/3O	1.3
1950	StL-N	153	642	81	177	**43**	9	7	63	33	32	.276	.313	.403	.717	84	-14	-16	103	77	79	.619	3			8	*2S/3	-0.3
1951	StL-N	135	553	88	160	32	7	6	54	35	23	.289	.335	.405	.740	97	-2	-3	101	83	75	.644	0	1	-1	13	*2/S	1.5
1952	StL-N	152	620	91	188	40	7	7	67	42	30	.303	.347	.424	.772	115	10	11	98	89	89	.690	9	6	-1	**28**	*23/S	4.5
1953	StL-N	146	564	107	193	35	5	15	79	60	23	.342	.405	.502	.907	133	30	29	102	100	114	.880	3	3	-1	24	*2	**5.4**
1954	StL-N	148	610	98	192	38	8	5	79	54	22	.315	.371	.428	.799	107	7	7	100	108	96	.732	4	2	0	**30**	*2	4.4
1955	StL-N	145	553	68	148	21	3	11	51	54	28	.268	.337	.376	.713	89	-8	-8	101	91	70	.648	7	7	-2	-14	*2	-1.1
1956	StL-N	40	153	22	48	9	0	0	15	13	5	.314	.367	.373	.740	101	0	1	99	118	21	.648	0	1	-1	4	2	0.7
	NY-N	92	334	39	99	12	3	2	14	28	10	.296	.354	.368	.723	97	-2	-1	97	47	42	.621	1	2	-1	-7	2	-0.1
	Yr	132	487	61	147	21	3	2	29	41	15	.302	.358	.370	.728	98	-1	-0	98	69	64	.633	1	3	-2	-3		0.6
1957	NY-N	57	254	35	78	8	4	9	33	10	8	.307	.338	.476	.815	113	5	4	102	80	40	.746	2	1	0	2	2	1.1
	Mil-N	93	394	56	122	23	4	6	32	23	7	.310	.349	.434	.783	121	5	9	90	62	59	.701	2	3	-1	10	2/O	2.5
	Yr	150	648	91	**200**	31	8	15	65	33	15	.309	.345	.451	.796	118	10	14	95	69	100	.725	4	4	-1	12		3.6
1958	Mil-N	106	427	47	112	23	1	1	24	31	21	.262	.314	.328	.642	79	-18	-12	89	67	44	.540	3	1	0	1	*2	-0.4
1959	Mil-N	5	3	0	0	0	0	0	0	0	0	.000	.000	.000	.000	-99	-1	-1	95	0	0	.000	0	0	0	0	/2	0.0
1960	Mil-N	68	226	21	58	9	1	1	19	17	13	.257	.311	.319	.630	80	-8	-6	91	103	23	.532	1	0	0	-4	2	-0.4
1961	StL-N	72	120	9	36	9	0	1	12	12	6	.300	.364	.400	.764	91	1	-1	113	95	18	.718	1	0	0	0	2	0.3
1962	StL-N	98	143	21	43	4	0	2	12	9	12	.301	.346	.371	.717	85	-1	-3	109	80	17	.594	0	0	0	0	2/3	0.0
1963	StL-N	6	5	0	0	0	0	0	0	0	1	.000	.000	.000	.000	-93	-1	-1	107	0	0	.000	0	0	0	0	H	0.0
Total	19	2216	8479	1223	2449	427	78	84	773	606	346	.289	.338	.387	.725	93	-70	-82	101	81	1109	.660	89	27		123	*2O/S3	15.0
■ **JUMBO SCHOENECK**	Schoeneck, Louis N. b: 3/3/1862, Chicago, Ill. d: 1/20/30, Chicago, Ill. BR/TR, 6'3", 223 lbs. Deb: 4/20/1884																											
1884	CP-U	90	366	56	116	22	2	2		8		.317	.332	.404	.736	149	17	17	99	0	50	.624	0			0	*1	1.4
	Bal-U	16	60	5	15	2	0	0		0		.250	.250	.283	.533	72	-1	-2	110	0	4	.378	0			2	1/S	0.0
	Yr	106	426	61	131	24	2	2		8		.308	.320	.387	.708	137	16	15	101	0	54	.586	0			2		1.4
1888	Ind-N	48	169	15	40	4	0	0	20	9	24	.237	.283	.260	.544	80	-4	-3	95	166	16	.512	11			-1	1/P	-0.8
1889	Ind-N	16	62	3	15	2	2	0	8	3	3	.242	.299	.339	.637	73	-2	-3	109	116	7	.574	1			0	1	-0.1
Total	3	170	657	79	186	30	4	2	28	20	27	.283	.308	.350	.658	115	10	9	100	55	77	.565	12			0	1/PS	0.5
■ **DICK SCHOFIELD**	Schofield, John Richard "Ducky" b: 1/7/35, Springfield, Ill. BB/TR, 5'9", 163 lbs. Deb: 7/03/53																											
1953	StL-N	33	39	9	7	0	0	2	4	2	11	.179	.220	.333	.553	41	-3	-4	102	82	3	.469	0	0	0	1	S	0.0
1954	StL-N	43	7	17	1	0	1	0	1	0	3	.143	.143	.429	.571	42	-1	-1	100	131	-1	.500	1	1	-0	0	S	0.0
1955	StL-N	12	4	3	0	0	0	0	0	0	1	.000	.000	.000	.000	-99	-1	-1	101	0	0	.000	0	0	0	0	/S	0.0
1956	StL-N	16	30	3	3	2	0	0	1	0	6	.100	.100	.167	.267	-30	-5	-5	99	84	0	.179	0	0	0	-0	/S	-0.4
1957	StL-N	65	56	10	9	0	0	0	1	7	13	.161	.254	.161	.415	15	-7	-7	101	46	2	.327	1	3	-2	1	S	-0.6
1958	StL-N	39	108	16	23	4	0	1	8	23	15	.213	.351	.278	.629	65	-4	-5	106	100	12	.602	0	2	-1	-4	S	-0.8
	Pit-N	26	27	4	4	0	1	0	2	3	6	.148	.233	.222	.456	23	-3	-3	95	138	1	.375	0	1	-1	0	/S3	-0.2
	Yr	65	135	20	27	4	1	1	10	26	21	.200	.329	.267	.596	59	-7	-7	102	117	14	.559	0	3	-2	-4		-1.0
1959	Pit-N	81	145	21	34	10	1	1	9	16	22	.234	.311	.338	.648	70	-6	-6	103	70	16	.579	1	1	-0	-1	2/SO	-0.4

YEAR	TM/L	G	AB	R	H	2B	3B	HR	RBI	BB	SO	AVG	OBP	SLG	PRO	/A	BR	/A	PF	CHI	RC	TA	SB	CS	SBR	FR	POS	TPR
1960	Pit-N	65	102	9	34	4	1	0	10	16	20	.333	.429	.392	.821	127	5	5	99	101	18	.814	0	1	-1	4	S2/3	1.0
1961	Pit-N	60	78	16	15	2	1	0	2	10	19	.192	.284	.244	.528	42	-6	-6	99	42	6	.446	0	1	-1	1	3/S2O	-0.4
1962	Pit-N	54	104	19	30	3	0	2	10	17	22	.288	.388	.375	.763	104	2	1	102	88	17	.747	0	1	-1	-0	3/2S	0.1
1963	Pit-N	138	541	54	133	18	2	3	32	69	83	.246	.334	.303	.638	86	-8	-7	99	69	58	.564	2	4	-2	18	*S2/3	2.3
1964	Pit-N	121	398	50	98	22	5	3	36	54	60	.246	.346	.349	.696	96	0	-0	101	102	52	.659	1	2	-1	16	*S	2.3
1965	Pit-N	31	109	13	25	5	0	0	6	15	19	.229	.323	.275	.598	70	-4	-4	100	85	11	.535	1	0	0	4	S	0.3
	SF-N	101	379	39	77	10	1	2	19	33	50	.203	.272	.251	.523	44	-25	-30	111	83	26	.425	2	4	-2	-19	S	-4.3
	Yr	132	488	52	102	15	1	2	25	48	69	.209	.284	.256	.540	49	-29	-34	108	84	37	.451	3	4	-2	-16		-4.0
1966	SF-N	11	16	4	1	0	0	0	0	2	2	.063	.167	.063	.229	-34	-3	-3	97	0	0	.200	0	0	0	-0	/S	-0.2
	NY-A	25	58	5	9	2	0	0	2	9	8	.155	.269	.190	.458	37	-5	-4	94	76	4	.408	0	0	0	-1	S	-0.4
	LA-N	20	70	10	18	0	0	0	4	8	8	.257	.350	.257	.607	74	-2	-2	97	99	7	.527	1	1	-0	-0	3/S	-0.2
1967	LA-N	84	232	23	50	10	1	2	15	31	40	.216	.308	.293	.601	83	-7	-4	88	84	20	.518	1	2	-1	1	S/23	0.4
1968	StL-N	69	127	14	28	7	1	1	8	13	31	.220	.303	.315	.618	90	-2	-1	95	78	12	.549	1	2	-1	-4	S2	0.0
1969	Bos-A	94	226	30	58	9	3	2	20	29	44	.257	.351	.350	.701	92	-0	-2	105	94	29	.647	0	2	-1	1	2S/3O	0.0
1970	Bos-A	76	139	16	26	1	2	1	14	21	26	.187	.298	.245	.543	46	-9	-11	111	153	10	.459	0	1	-1	-3	23/S	-1.2
1971	Mil-A	23	28	2	3	2	0	0	1	2	8	.107	.194	.179	.372	6	-4	-4	103	82	1	.320	0	0	0	-1	3/S2	-0.4
	StL-N	34	60	7	13	2	0	1	6	10	9	.217	.347	.300	.647	84	-1	-1	101	116	7	.612	0	0	0	1	S2/3	0.3
Total	19	1321	3083	394	699	113	20	21	211	390	526	.227	.319	.297	.615	73	-100	-104	101	87	311	.556	12	29	-14	14	S2/3O	-2.8

■ **DICK SCHOFIELD** Schofield, Richard Craig b: 11/21/62, Springfield, Ill. BR/TR, 5'10", 175 lbs. Deb: 9/08/83

YEAR	TM/L	G	AB	R	H	2B	3B	HR	RBI	BB	SO	AVG	OBP	SLG	PRO	/A	BR	/A	PF	CHI	RC	TA	SB	CS	SBR	FR	POS	TPR
1983	Cal-A	21	54	4	11	2	0	3	4	6	8	.204	.295	.407	.702	95	-1	-0	96	50	6	.644	0	0	0	3	S	0.3
1984	Cal-A	140	400	39	77	10	3	4	21	33	79	.192	.264	.262	.527	46	-29	-30	101	72	29	.449	5	2	0	7	*S	-1.1
1985	Cal-A	147	438	50	96	19	3	8	41	35	70	.219	.289	.331	.620	69	-19	-19	101	96	43	.562	11	4	1	16	*S	0.9
1986	Cal-A	139	458	67	114	17	6	13	57	48	55	.249	.327	.397	.724	101	-2	1	96	103	63	.723	23	5	4	10	*S	2.1
1987	Cal-A	134	479	52	120	17	3	9	46	37	63	.251	.307	.355	.662	76	-16	-16	99	95	56	.623	19	3	4	-20	*S/2D	-2.4
1988	Cal-A	155	527	61	126	11	6	6	34	40	57	.239	.304	.317	.621	79	-18	-14	94	73	55	.574	20	5	3	21	*S	1.8
Total	6	736	2356	273	544	76	21	43	203	199	332	.231	.299	.336	.635	75	-84	-78	98	87	254	.599	78	19	12	36	S/2D	1.6

■ **OTTO SCHOMBERG** Schomberg, Otto H. (born Otto H. Shambrick) b: 11/14/1864, Milwaukee, Wis. d: 5/3/27, Ottawa, Kan. TL , Deb: 7/07/1886

YEAR	TM/L	G	AB	R	H	2B	3B	HR	RBI	BB	SO	AVG	OBP	SLG	PRO	/A	BR	/A	PF	CHI	RC	TA	SB	CS	SBR	FR	POS	TPR
1886	Pit-a	72	246	53	67	6	6	1		57		.272	.417	.358	.775	158	17	21	93	0	41	.872	7			-7	1	0.9
1887	Ind-N	112	419	91	129	18	16	5	83	56	32	.308	.397	.463	.860	146	25	28	96	118	88	.955	21			-10	*1/O	0.0
1888	Ind-N	30	112	11	24	5	1	1	10	10	12	.214	.290	.304	.594	96	-1	0	95	93	12	.591	6			0	O1	0.0
Total	3	214	777	155	220	29	23	7	93	123	44	.283	.389	.407	.796	144	41	48	95	75	140	.871	34			-17	1/O	0.9

■ **JERRY SCHOONMAKER** Schoonmaker, Jerald Lee b: 12/14/33, Seymour, Mo. BR/TR, 5'11", 190 lbs. Deb: 6/11/55

YEAR	TM/L	G	AB	R	H	2B	3B	HR	RBI	BB	SO	AVG	OBP	SLG	PRO	/A	BR	/A	PF	CHI	RC	TA	SB	CS	SBR	FR	POS	TPR
1955	Was-A	20	46	5	7	0	1	1	4	5	11	.152	.235	.261	.496	37	-4	-4	91	99	3	.450	1	0	0	-1	O	-0.5
1957	Was-A	30	23	5	2	1	0	0	0	2	11	.087	.160	.130	.290	-20	-4	-4	98	0	1	.238	0	0	0	-2	O	-0.6
Total	2	50	69	10	9	1	1	1	4	7	22	.130	.211	.217	.428	17	-8	-8	93	67	4	.383	1	0	0	-3	/O	-1.1

■ **PAUL SCHRAMKA** Schramka, Paul Edward b: 3/22/28, Milwaukee, Wis. BL/TL, 6', 185 lbs. Deb: 4/14/53

YEAR	TM/L	G	AB	R	H	2B	3B	HR	RBI	BB	SO	AVG	OBP	SLG	PRO	/A	BR	/A	PF	CHI	RC	TA	SB	CS	SBR	FR	POS	TPR
1953	Chi-N	2	0	0	0	0	0	0	0	0	0	—	—	—	—	—	0	0	103	—	—	—	0	0	0	-0	/O	0.0

■ **OSSEE SCHRECKENGOST** Schreckengost, Ossee Freeman (a.k.a. Ossee Schreck) b: 4/11/1875, New Bethlehem, Pa. d: 7/9/14, Philadelphia, Pa. BR/TR, 5'10", 180 lbs. Deb: 9/08/1897

YEAR	TM/L	G	AB	R	H	2B	3B	HR	RBI	BB	SO	AVG	OBP	SLG	PRO	/A	BR	/A	PF	CHI	RC	TA	SB	CS	SBR	FR	POS	TPR
1897	Lou-N	1	3	0	0	0	0	0	0	0		.000	.000	.000	.000	-99	-1	-1	95	0	0	.000	0			0	/C	0.0
1898	Cle-N	10	35	5	11	2	3	0	10	0		.314	.314	.543	.857	154	2	2	96	159	6	.833	1			0	/C	0.2
1899	StL-N	6	8	0	0	0	0	0	0	1		.000	.111	.000	.111	-63	-2	-2	108	0	0	.125	0			0	/1O	-0.1
	Cle-N	43	150	15	47	8	3	0	10	6		.313	.344	.407	.751	121	1	4	89	51	23	.699	4			6	C/1SO	1.0
	StL-N	66	269	42	77	12	2	2	37	14		.286	.324	.368	.692	85	-3	-6	108	104	38	.667	14			-4	1C/2	-0.6
	Yr	115	427	57	124	20	5	2	47	21		.290	.327	.375	.701	94	-4	-4	101	79	60	.663	18			2		0.3
1901	Bos-A	86	280	37	85	13	5	0	38	19		.304	.348	.386	.734	108	2	3	97	111	41	.682	6			9	C/1	1.7
1902	Cle-A	18	74	5	25	0	0	0	9	0		.338	.338	.338	.676	92	-1	-1	97	126	9	.551	2			-1	1	0.0
	Phi-A	79	284	45	92	17	2	2	43	9		.324	.345	.419	.764	104	4	1	108	116	43	.682	3			13	C/1O	1.9
	Yr	97	358	50	117	17	2	2	52	9		.327	.343	.402	.746	101	3	-0	106	119	52	.656	5			13		1.9
1903	Phi-A	92	306	26	78	13	4	3	30	11		.255	.281	.353	.634	88	-4	-5	104	92	31	.522	0			8	C1	1.2
1904	Phi-A	95	311	23	58	9	1	1	21	5		.186	.199	.232	.431	37	-22	-22	102	104	15	.316	3			-6	C/1	-2.1
1905	Phi-A	122	416	30	113	19	6	0	45	3		.272	.277	.346	.623	91	-2	-6	109	111	43	.515	9			-10	*C/1	-0.5
1906	Phi-A	98	338	29	96	20	1	1	41	10		.284	.305	.358	.663	117	2	5	94	123	39	.562	5			9	C/1	2.2
1907	Phi-A	101	356	30	97	16	3	0	38	17		.272	.306	.334	.640	100	2	-1	106	116	39	.541	4			13	C/1	2.3
1908	Phi-A	71	207	16	46	7	1	0	16	6		.222	.244	.266	.510	63	-8	-9	108	109	13	.385	1			6	C/1	0.3
	Chi-A	6	16	1	3	0	0	0	0	1		.188	.235	.188	.423	42	-1	-1	94	0	1	.308	0			-2	/C	-0.1
	Yr	77	223	17	49	7	1	0	16	7		.220	.243	.260	.504	61	-9	-10	106	102	14	.379	1			4		0.2
Total	11	894	3053	304	828	136	31	9	338	102		.271	.295	.345	.640	91	-30	-40	103	107	341	.543	52			41	C/1O2S	7.4

■ **HANK SCHREIBER** Schreiber, Henry Walter b: 7/12/1891, Cleveland, Ohio d: 2/23/68, Indianapolis, Ind. BR/TR, 5'11", 165 lbs. Deb: 4/14/14

YEAR	TM/L	G	AB	R	H	2B	3B	HR	RBI	BB	SO	AVG	OBP	SLG	PRO	/A	BR	/A	PF	CHI	RC	TA	SB	CS	SBR	FR	POS	TPR
1914	Chi-A	1	2	0	0	0	0	0	0	0	1	.000	.000	.000	.000	-97	-0	-0	103	0	0	.000	0			-0	/O	0.0
1917	Bos-N	2	7	1	2	0	0	0	0	0	1	.286	.286	.286	.571	78	-0	-0	96	0	1	.400	0			0	/S3	0.0
1919	Cin-N	19	58	5	13	4	0	0	4	0	12	.224	.224	.293	.517	52	-3	-4	105	91	4	.378	0			0	3/S	-0.2
1921	NY-N	4	6	2	2	0	0	0	2	1	1	.333	.429	.333	.762	107	0	0	98	367	1	.750	0	0	0	0	/2S3	0.1
1926	Chi-N	10	18	2	1	1	0	0	0	0	1	.056	.056	.111	.167	-53	-4	-4	106	0	0	.118	0			0	/S32	-0.3
Total	5	36	91	10	18	5	0	0	6	1	16	.198	.207	.253	.459	32	-8	-8	104	86	5	.329	0	0		1	/3S2O	-0.4

■ **TED SCHREIBER** Schreiber, Theodore Henry b: 7/11/38, Brooklyn, N.Y. BR/TR, 5'11", 175 lbs. Deb: 4/14/63

YEAR	TM/L	G	AB	R	H	2B	3B	HR	RBI	BB	SO	AVG	OBP	SLG	PRO	/A	BR	/A	PF	CHI	RC	TA	SB	CS	SBR	FR	POS	TPR
1963	NY-N	39	50	1	8	0	0	0	2	4	14	.160	.236	.160	.396	17	-5	-5	99	105	2	.295	0	1	-1	1	3/S2	-0.4

■ **POP SCHRIVER** Schriver, William Frederick b: 7/11/1865, Brooklyn, N.Y. d: 12/27/32, Brooklyn, N.Y. BR/TR, 5'9.5", 172 lbs. Deb: 4/29/1886

YEAR	TM/L	G	AB	R	H	2B	3B	HR	RBI	BB	SO	AVG	OBP	SLG	PRO	/A	BR	/A	PF	CHI	RC	TA	SB	CS	SBR	FR	POS	TPR
1886	Bro-a	8	21	2	1	0	0	0		2		.048	.130	.048	.178	-42	-3	-3	100	0	0	.150	0			0	/OC	-0.2
1888	Phi-N	40	134	15	26	5	2	1	23	7	21	.194	.250	.284	.534	63	-4	-6	114	201	10	.463	2			0	C/S3O	-0.5
1889	Phi-N	55	211	24	56	10	0	1	19	16	8	.265	.323	.327	.650	80	-5	-6	104	80	25	.594	5			7	C/23	0.1
1890	Phi-N	57	223	37	61	9	6	0	35	22	15	.274	.339	.368	.706	100	2	-1	108	131	32	.698	9			0	C1/32O	0.0
1891	Chi-N	27	90	15	30	1	4	1	21	10	9	.333	.412	.467	.878	149	7	6	106	136	18	.917	1			0	C/1	0.5
1892	Chi-N	92	326	40	73	10	6	1	34	27	25	.224	.297	.301	.598	89	-7	-3	92	105	31	.538	4			-3	CO	-0.1
1893	Chi-N	64	229	49	65	8	3	4	34	14	9	.284	.336	.397	.733	93	-2	-3	104	90	33	.689	4			3	C/O	0.3
1894	Chi-N	96	349	55	96	12	3	3	47	29	21	.275	.341	.352	.694	64	-17	-23	108	98	46	.660	9			2	*C/S31	-0.9
1895	NY-N	24	92	16	29	2	1	1	16	9	10	.315	.382	.391	.774	108	1	1	95	121	15	.778	3			0	C/1	0.1
1897	Cin-N	61	178	29	54	12	4	1	30	19		.303	.374	.433	.806	107	4	2	107	110	31	.806	3			-10	C	0.0
1898	Pit-N	95	315	25	72	15	3	0	32	23		.229	.285	.295	.581	70	-13	-12	98	106	27	.486	0			-6	C/1	-0.9
1899	Pit-N	91	301	31	85	19	5	1	49	23		.282	.339	.389	.728	103	1	1	99	125	42	.681	4			1	C/1	0.7
1900	Pit-N	37	92	12	27	7	0	1	12	10		.293	.363	.402	.765	110	2	1	103	94	14	.723	0			0	C/1	0.1
1901	StL-N	53	166	17	45	7	3	1	23	12		.271	.320	.367	.688	105	0	1	97	120	21	.620	2			1	C1	0.4
Total	14	800	2727	367	720	117	40	16	375	223	118	.264	.327	.354	.681	89	-35	-44	102	112	344	.630	46			-5	C/1O32S	-0.4

■ **BOB SCHRODER** Schroder, Robert James b: 12/30/44, Ridgefield, N.J. BL/TR, 6', 175 lbs. Deb: 4/20/65

YEAR	TM/L	G	AB	R	H	2B	3B	HR	RBI	BB	SO	AVG	OBP	SLG	PRO	/A	BR	/A	PF	CHI	RC	TA	SB	CS	SBR	FR	POS	TPR
1965	SF-N	31	9	4	2	0	0	0	1	1	1	.222	.300	.222	.522	45	-1	-1	111	207	1	.429	0	0	0	0	/23	0.0
1966	SF-N	10	33	0	8	0	0	0	2	0	2	.242	.242	.242	.485	36	-3	-3	97	105	2	.308	0	0	0	-0	/S	-0.2
1967	SF-N	62	135	20	31	4	0	0	7	15	15	.230	.307	.259	.566	63	-6	-6	101	83	12	.486	1	0	0	2	2/3	0.0
1968	SF-N	35	44	5	7	1	1	0	2	7	3	.159	.288	.227	.516	58	-2	-2	98	84	3	.474	0	0	0	-1	2/S3	-0.1
Total	4	138	221	29	48	5	1	0	12	23	21	.217	.294	.249	.543	57	-11	-11	100	91	18	.460	1	0	0	2	/2S3	-0.3

YEAR	TM/L	G	AB	R	H	2B	3B	HR	RBI	BB	SO	AVG	OBP	SLG	PRO	/A	BR	/A	PF	CHI	RC	TA	SB	CS	SBR	FR	POS	TPR
■ **BILL SCHROEDER**	Schroeder, Alfred William b: 9/7/58, Baltimore, Md. BR/TR, 6'2", 200 lbs. Deb: 7/13/83																											
1983	Mil-A	23	73	7	13	2	1	3	7	3	23	.178	.221	.356	.577	61	-5	-4	92	78	6	.492	0	1	-1	1	C	-0.1
1984	Mil-A	61	210	29	54	6	0	14	25	8	54	.257	.291	.486	.777	121	2	4	92	69	27	.687	0	1	-1	7	C/1D	1.4
1985	Mil-A	53	194	18	47	8	0	8	25	12	61	.242	.293	.407	.700	85	-3	-4	105	98	22	.608	0	1	-1	4	C/1D	0.1
1986	Mil-A	64	217	32	46	14	0	7	19	9	59	.212	.263	.373	.636	70	-9	-10	102	74	22	.557	1	0	0	5	C1D	-0.2
1987	Mil-A	75	250	35	83	12	0	14	42	16	56	.332	.379	.548	.927	140	15	14	102	94	52	.936	5	2	0	10	C/1D	2.7
1988	Mil-A	41	122	9	19	2	0	5	10	6	36	.156	.208	.295	.503	38	-10	-11	103	78	6	.404	0	0	0	3	C1/D	-0.6
Total	6	317	1066	130	262	44	1	51	128	54	289	.246	.292	.432	.725	95	-10	-11	100	83	134	.659	6	5	-1	31	C/1D	3.3
■ **RICH SCHU**	Schu, Rick Spencer b: 1/26/62, Philadelphia, Pa. BR/TR, 6', 170 lbs. Deb: 9/01/84																											
1984	Phi-N	17	29	12	8	2	1	2	5	6	6	.276	.400	.621	1.021	180	3	3	102	82	8	1.143	0	0	0	1	3	0.4
1985	Phi-N	112	416	54	105	21	4	7	24	38	78	.252	.318	.373	.691	91	-4	-5	102	55	49	.627	8	6	-1	-7	*3	-1.3
1986	Phi-N	92	208	32	57	10	1	8	25	18	44	.274	.338	.447	.785	110	4	3	104	85	32	.747	2	2	-1	-1	3	0.0
1987	Phi-N	92	196	24	46	6	3	7	23	20	36	.235	.312	.403	.715	84	-4	-5	104	92	25	.660	0	2	-1	2	31	-0.6
1988	Bal-A	89	270	22	69	9	4	4	20	21	49	.256	.316	.363	.679	94	-4	-2	95	72	30	.604	6	4	-1	2	3/1D	0.0
Total	5	402	1119	144	285	48	13	28	97	103	213	.255	.323	.396	.718	96	-5	-6	101	72	144	.668	16	14	-4	-4	3/1D	-1.5
■ **HEINIE SCHUBLE**	Schuble, Henry George b: 11/1/06, Houston, Tex. BR/TR, 5'9", 152 lbs. Deb: 7/08/27																											
1927	StL-N	65	218	29	56	6	2	4	28	7	27	.257	.283	.358	.641	66	-10	-12	107	109	21	.531	0			-0	S	-0.5
1929	Det-A	92	258	35	60	11	7	2	28	19	23	.233	.288	.353	.640	66	-15	-14	97	99	27	.570	3	2	-0	-13	S/3	-1.7
1932	Det-A	102	340	58	92	20	6	5	52	24	37	.271	.319	.409	.728	86	-7	-8	102	113	45	.700	14	5	1	4	3S	0.3
1933	Det-A	49	96	12	21	4	1	0	6	5	17	.219	.257	.281	.539	40	-8	-9	107	74	7	.453	2	0	1	-1	3/S2	-0.6
1934	Det-A	11	15	2	4	2	0	0	2	1	4	.267	.313	.400	.712	85	-0	-0	98	111	2	.636	0	0	0	0	/S32	0.0
1935	Det-A	11	8	3	2	0	0	0	0	1	0	.250	.333	.250	.583	55	-1	-0	97	0	1	.500	0	0	0	0	/32	0.0
1936	StL-N	2	0	0	0	0	0	0	0	0	0	—	—	—	—	—	0	0	94	—	—	—	0			0	/3	0.0
Total	7	332	935	139	235	43	16	11	116	57	108	.251	.296	.367	.663	71	-41	-43	102	103	103	.595	19	7		-9	S3/2	-2.5
■ **WES SCHULMERICH**	Schulmerich, Edward Wesley b: 4/21/01, Hillsboro, Ore. d: 6/26/85, Corvallis, Ore. BR/TR, 5'11", 210 lbs. Deb: 5/01/31																											
1931	Bos-N	95	327	36	101	17	7	2	43	28	30	.309	.363	.422	.785	112	5	5	99	109	51	.735	0			-2	O	0.0
1932	Bos-N	119	404	47	105	22	5	11	57	27	61	.260	.314	.421	.735	102	-3	0	93	104	55	.692	5			2	*O	-0.4
1933	Bos-N	29	85	10	21	6	1	1	13	5	10	.247	.289	.376	.665	92	-1	-1	96	140	10	.569	0			0	O	-0.1
	Phi-N	97	365	53	122	19	4	8	59	32	45	.334	.394	.474	.868	125	23	15	118	119	69	.830	1			-3	O	0.6
	Yr	126	450	63	143	25	5	9	72	37	55	.318	.375	.456	.830	121	21	14	113	125	78	.779	1			-3		0.5
1934	Phi-N	15	52	2	13	1	0	0	1	4	8	.250	.316	.269	.585	54	-3	-3	108	26	4	.463	0			-1	O	-0.4
	Cin-N	74	209	21	55	8	3	5	19	22	43	.263	.333	.402	.735	95	-1	-1	101	69	28	.669	1			-3	O	-0.6
	Yr	89	261	23	68	9	3	5	20	26	51	.261	.330	.375	.705	87	-4	-5	102	62	33	.633	1			-4		-1.0
Total	4	429	1442	169	417	73	20	27	192	118	197	.289	.347	.424	.771	107	19	15	103	103	217	.724	7			-7	O	-0.9
■ **ART SCHULT**	Schult, Arthur William "Dutch" b: 6/20/28, Brooklyn, N.Y. BR/TR, 6'3", 210 lbs. Deb: 5/17/53																											
1953	NY-A	7	0	3	0	0	0	0	0	0	0	—	—	—	—	—	0	0	93	—	—	—	0	0	0	0	R	0.0
1956	Cin-N	5	7	3	3	0	0	0	2	1	1	.429	.500	.429	.929	141	1	1	108	282	2	1.000	0	0	0	-0	/O	0.0
1957	Cin-N	21	34	4	9	2	0	0	4	0	2	.265	.286	.324	.609	60	-2	-2	105	151	3	.462	0	0	0	0	/O	-0.1
	Was-A	77	247	30	65	14	0	4	35	14	30	.263	.305	.368	.674	85	-6	-6	98	134	26	.555	0	1	-1	1	1O	-0.7
1959	Chi-N	42	118	17	32	7	0	2	14	7	14	.271	.323	.381	.704	88	-2	-2	98	111	13	.587	0	0	0	-1	1O	-0.4
1960	Chi-N	12	15	1	2	1	0	0	1	1	3	.133	.188	.200	.387	6	-2	-2	98	135	1	.308	0	0	0	-1	/O1	-0.2
Total	5	164	421	58	111	24	0	6	56	23	50	.264	.308	.363	.671	82	-12	-11	99	132	261	.579	0	1	-1	-1	/1O	-1.4
■ **FRANK SCHULTE**	Schulte, Frank M. "Wildfire" b: 9/17/1882, Cohocton, N.Y. d: 10/2/49, Oakland, Cal. BL/TR, 5'11", 170 lbs. Deb: 9/21/04																											
1904	Chi-N	20	84	16	24	4	3	2	13	2		.286	.302	.476	.779	140	3	3	101	89	13	.717	1			-1	O	0.2
1905	Chi-N	123	493	67	135	15	14	1	47	32		.274	.318	.367	.685	101	3	0	105	78	64	.640	16			-17	*O	-2.5
1906	Chi-N	146	563	77	158	18	**13**	7	60	31		.281	.318	.396	.714	117	13	9	107	86	81	.689	25			-3	*O	0.4
1907	Chi-N	97	342	44	98	14	7	2	32	22		.287	.330	.386	.716	119	9	7	106	93	47	.660	7			7	O	1.2
1908	Chi-N	102	386	42	91	20	2	1	43	29		.236	.289	.306	.595	87	-4	-6	106	131	37	.549	15			4	*O	-0.2
1909	Chi-N	140	538	57	142	16	11	4	60	24		.264	.298	.357	.655	104	0	-0	101	103	61	.609	23			-14	*O	-2.0
1910	Chi-N	151	559	93	168	29	15	**10**	68	39	57	.301	.349	.460	.809	135	22	21	101	88	97	.821	22			-9	*O	0.6
1911	Chi-N	154	577	105	173	30	21	**21**	**107**	76	68	.300	.384	**.534**	.918	**161**	**41**	**43**	97	86	**127**	1.015	23			-9	*O	3.0
1912	Chi-N	139	553	90	146	27	11	13	64	53	70	.264	.336	.423	.759	103	3	1	104	70	84	.764	17			-11	*O	-1.3
1913	Chi-N	132	497	85	138	28	6	9	68	39	68	.278	.336	.412	.749	115	7	8	99	113	73	.752	21			-15	*O	-0.8
1914	Chi-N	137	465	54	112	22	7	5	61	39	55	.241	.306	.351	.657	97	-4	-3	98	127	53	.632	16			-13	*O	-2.0
1915	Chi-N	151	550	66	137	20	6	12	62	49	68	.249	.313	.373	.686	105	4	3	102	104	66	.640	19	17	-5	10	*O	0.4
1916	Chi-N	72	230	31	68	11	1	5	27	20	35	.296	.352	.417	.769	116	9	5	117	97	37	.772	9			-4	O	0.0
	Pit-N	55	177	12	45	5	3	0	14	17	19	.254	.323	.316	.639	92	-0	-1	105	99	20	.598	5			-4	O	-0.6
	Yr	127	407	43	113	16	4	5	41	37	54	.278	.339	.373	.713	106	9	4	112	98	56	.694	14			-8		-0.6
1917	Pit-N	30	103	11	22	5	1	0	7	10	14	.214	.283	.282	.565	74	-3	-3	100	95	9	.543	5			-2	O	-0.6
	Phi-N	64	149	21	32	10	0	1	15	16	22	.215	.299	.302	.601	79	-2	-4	108	120	14	.573	4			-11	O	-1.7
	Yr	94	252	32	54	15	1	1	22	26	36	.214	.293	.294	.587	76	-6	-7	105	113	23	.561	9			-12		-2.3
1918	Was-A	93	267	35	77	14	3	0	44	47	36	.288	.406	.363	.770	127	13	12	104	165	41	.816	5			-1	O	0.8
Total	15	1806	6533	906	1766	288	124	93	792	545	512	.270	.330	.395	.725	113	115	96	103	100	925	.710	233	17		-90	*O	-5.1
■ **FRED SCHULTE**	Schulte, Fred William "Fritz" (born Fred William Schult) b: 1/13/01, Belvidere, Ill. d: 5/20/83, Belvidere, Ill. BR/TR, 6'1", 183 lbs. Deb: 4/15/27																											
1927	StL-A	60	189	32	60	16	5	3	34	20	14	.317	.383	.503	.885	121	7	6	106	109	36	.930	5	0	2	-0	O	0.2
1928	StL-A	146	556	90	159	44	6	7	85	51	60	.286	.347	.424	.771	98	1	-2	104	120	83	.731	6	5	-1	11	*O	0.0
1929	StL-A	121	446	63	137	24	5	3	71	59	44	.307	.389	.404	.793	105	5	5	100	136	74	.795	8	3	1	10	*O	0.9
1930	StL-A	113	392	59	109	23	5	5	62	41	44	.278	.348	.401	.748	83	-6	-11	108	122	55	.725	12	8	-1	-6	O/1	-2.0
1931	StL-A	134	553	100	168	32	7	9	65	56	49	.304	.369	.436	.805	108	9	7	102	71	89	.774	6	8	-3	-0	*O	-0.4
1932	StL-A	146	565	106	166	35	6	9	73	71	44	.294	.373	.425	.797	106	6	6	100	97	90	.775	5	9	-4	-6	*O/1	-0.8
1933	Was-A	144	550	98	162	30	7	5	87	61	27	.295	.366	.402	.768	108	3	7	96	125	81	.733	10	12	-4	12	*O	0.9
1934	Was-A	136	524	72	156	32	6	3	73	53	34	.298	.363	.399	.762	95	-2	-3	101	118	76	.709	3	7	-3	-4	*O	-1.1
1935	Was-A	76	226	33	60	6	4	2	0	0	0	.265	.265	.354	.619	64	-14	-12	92	0	19	.473	0	3	-2	-8	O	-2.0
1936	Pit-N	74	238	28	62	7	3	1	17	20	20	.261	.320	.328	.648	77	-8	-7	98	74	26	.556	1			-1	O	-0.9
1937	Pit-N	29	20	5	2	0	0	0	3	4	3	.100	.280	.100	.380	7	-2	-3	102	541	1	.389	0			-1	/O	-0.3
Total	11	1179	4259	686	1241	249	54	47	570	436	339	.291	.358	.408	.767	98	-3	-9	101	106	630	.729	56	55		7	*O/1	-5.5
■ **HAM SCHULTE**	Schulte, Herman Joseph (born Herman Joseph Schultehenrich) b: 9/1/12, St.Charles, Mo. BR/TR, 5'8.5", 158 lbs. Deb: 4/16/40																											
1940	Phi-N	120	436	44	103	18	2	1	21	32	30	.236	.288	.294	.582	63	-23	-21	97	63	40	.485	3			-9	*2/S	-2.2
■ **JOHNNY SCHULTE**	Schulte, John Clement b: 9/8/1896, Fredericktown, Mo. d: 6/28/78, St.Louis, Mo. BL/TR, 5'11", 190 lbs. Deb: 4/18/23 C																											
1923	StL-A	7	3	1	0	0	0	0	1	4	0	.000	.571	.000	.571	57	0	0	104	0	1	1.333	0	0	0	0	/C1	0.0
1927	StL-N	64	156	35	45	8	2	9	32	47	19	.288	.456	.538	.994	154	17	15	107	101	41	1.198	1			-1	C	1.8
1928	Phi-N	65	113	14	28	2	2	4	17	15	12	.248	.336	.407	.743	90	-1	-2	104	104	16	.718	0			2	C	0.2
1929	Chi-N	31	69	6	18	3	0	0	9	7	11	.261	.329	.304	.633	57	-4	-5	101	147	7	.549	0			-0	C	-0.1
1932	StL-A	15	24	2	5	2	0	0	3	1	6	.208	.240	.292	.532	37	-2	-2	100	144	2	.421	0	0	0	0	/C	-0.1
	Bos-N	10	9	1	2	0	0	1	2	2	1	.222	.364	.556	.919	153	1	1	93	93	2	1.000	0			0	C	0.1
Total	5	192	374	59	98	15	4	14	64	76	49	.262	.388	.436	.824	110	10	8	104	110	68	.873	1	0		2	C/1	1.9
■ **JACK SCHULTE**	Schulte, John Herman Frank b: 11/15/1881, Cincinnati, Ohio d: 8/17/75, Roseville, Mich. BR/TR, 5'9", 180 lbs. Deb: 8/19/06																											
1906	Bos-N	2	7	0	0	0	0	0	0	0		.000	.000	.000	.000	-99	-2	-2	100	0	0	.000	0			0	/S	-0.1

YEAR	TM/L	G	AB	R	H	2B	3B	HR	RBI	BB	SO	AVG	OBP	SLG	PRO	/A	BR	/A	PF	CHI	RC	TA	SB	CS	SBR	FR	POS	TPR
■ LEN SCHULTE	Schulte, Leonard Bernard (born Leonard Bernard Schultehenrich) b: 12/5/16, St.Charles, Mo. d: 5/6/86, Orlando, Fla. BR/TR, 5'10", 160 lbs. Deb: 9/27/44																											
1944	StL-A	1	0	0	0	0	0	0	0	1	0	—	1.000	—	1.000	195	0	0	102	0	0	—	0	0	0	0	H	0.0
1945	StL-A	119	430	37	106	16	1	0	36	24	35	.247	.286	.288	.575	58	-19	-26	115	107	36	.443	0	3	-2	-5	32S	-3.2
1946	StL-A	4	5	1	2	0	0	0	2	0	0	.400	.400	.400	.800	127	0	0	98	380	0	.500	0	0	0	0	/23	0.0
Total	3	124	435	38	108	16	1	0	38	25	35	.248	.289	.290	.579	59	-18	-25	115	110	37	.456	0	3	-2	-5	/32S	-3.2
■ HOWIE SCHULTZ	Schultz, Howard Henry "Stretch" or "Steeple" b: 7/3/22, St.Paul, Minn. BR/TR, 6'6", 200 lbs. Deb: 8/16/43																											
1943	Bro-N	45	182	20	49	12	0	1	34	6	24	.269	.300	.352	.652	88	-3	-3	100	187	18	.543	3			1	1	-0.3
1944	Bro-N	138	526	59	134	32	3	11	83	24	67	.255	.290	.390	.680	91	-9	-9	99	128	55	.579	6			1	*1	-1.9
1945	Bro-N	39	142	18	34	8	2	1	19	10	14	.239	.294	.345	.639	81	-5	-4	96	129	14	.554	2			-1	1	-0.5
1946	Bro-N	90	249	27	63	14	1	3	27	16	34	.253	.298	.353	.652	82	-6	-7	103	104	26	.558	2			-0	1	-1.5
1947	Bro-N	2	1	0	0	0	0	0	0	0	0	.000	.000	.000	.000	-96	-0	-0	105	0	0	.000	0			0	/1	0.0
	Phi-N	114	403	30	90	19	1	6	35	21	70	.223	.264	.320	.584	54	-27	-27	100	90	33	.467	0			-2	*1	-3.5
	Yr	116	404	30	90	19	1	6	35	21	70	.223	.263	.319	.582	54	-28	-28	100	88	32	.466	0			-2		-3.5
1948	Phi-N	6	13	0	1	0	0	0	1	1	2	.077	.143	.077	.220	-42	-3	-2	94	375	0	.167	0			0	/1	-0.2
	Cin-N	36	72	9	12	0	0	2	9	4	7	.167	.211	.250	.461	23	-8	-8	103	141	4	.393	2			0	1	-0.7
	Yr	42	85	9	13	0	0	2	10	5	9	.153	.200	.224	.424	14	-10	-11	102	183	4	.356	2			0		-0.9
Total	6	470	1588	163	383	85	7	24	208	82	218	.241	.281	.349	.630	74	-61	-61	100	124	150	.545	15			-1	1	-8.6
■ JOHN SCHULTZ	Schultz, John b: St.Louis, Mo. Deb: 8/07/1891																											
1891	StL-a	1	2	0	0	0	0	0	0	0	0	.000	.000	.000	.000	-88	-1	-1	114	0	0	.000	0			0	/C	0.0
■ JOE SCHULTZ	Schultz, Joseph Charles Jr. "Dode" b: 8/29/18, Chicago, Ill. BL/TR, 5'11", 180 lbs. Deb: 9/27/39 MC																											
1939	Pit-N	4	14	3	4	2	0	0	2	2	0	.286	.375	.429	.804	116	0	0	100	125	2	.800	0			0	/C	0.0
1940	Pit-N	16	36	2	7	0	1	0	4	2	1	.194	.237	.250	.487	36	-3	-3	95	165	2	.379	0			0	C	-0.2
1941	Pit-N	2	2	1	1	0	0	0	0	0	0	.500	.500	.500	1.000	178	0	0	103	0	1	1.000	0			0	/C	0.0
1943	StL-A	46	92	6	22	5	0	0	8	9	8	.239	.307	.293	.600	76	-3	-3	100	108	8	.480	0	1	-1	0	C	-0.1
1944	StL-A	3	8	1	2	0	0	0	0	0	1	.250	.250	.250	.500	42	-1	-1	102	0	1	.333	0	0	0	-0	/C	0.0
1945	StL-A	41	44	1	13	2	0	0	8	3	1	.295	.340	.341	.681	85	-0	-1	115	193	5	.563	0	0	0	-0	/C	0.0
1946	StL-A	42	57	1	22	4	0	0	14	11	2	.386	.485	.456	.941	167	6	6	98	205	14	1.028	0	0	0	-1	C	0.6
1947	StL-A	43	38	3	7	0	0	1	1	4	5	.184	.262	.263	.525	45	-3	-3	102	28	3	.438	0	0	0	0	H	-0.2
1948	StL-A	43	37	0	7	0	0	0	9	6	3	.189	.302	.189	.492	31	-3	-4	106	434	2	.419	0	0	0	0	H	-0.3
Total	9	240	328	18	85	13	1	1	46	37	21	.259	.334	.314	.648	81	-7	-7	102	170	38	.571	0	1		-1	/C	-0.2
■ JOE SCHULTZ	Schultz, Joseph Charles Sr. "Germany" b: 7/24/1893, Pittsburgh, Pa. d: 4/13/41, Columbia, S.C. BR/TR, 5'11.5", 172 lbs. Deb: 9/28/12																											
1912	Bos-N	4	12	1	3	1	0	0	4	0	2	.250	.250	.333	.583	55	-1	-1	107	337	1	.444	0			0	/2	0.0
1913	Bos-N	9	18	2	4	0	0	0	1	2	7	.222	.333	.222	.556	64	-1	-1	95	91	2	.500	0			-0	/O2	0.0
1915	Bro-N	56	120	13	35	3	2	0	4	10	18	.292	.346	.350	.696	109	2	1	101	36	14	.618	3	4	-2	1	3/S	0.3
	Chi-N	7	8	1	2	0	0	0	3	0	2	.250	.250	.250	.500	50	-0	-0	102	573	1	.333	0			0	/2	0.0
	Yr	63	128	14	37	3	2	0	7	10	20	.289	.341	.344	.684	106	1	1	101	96	15	.600	3	4	-2	1		0.3
1916	Pit-N	77	204	18	53	8	2	0	22	7	14	.260	.298	.319	.616	85	-3	-4	105	134	22	.543	6			-7	23/OS	-1.1
1919	StL-N	88	229	24	58	9	1	2	21	11	7	.253	.287	.328	.615	90	-5	-3	94	101	22	.526	4			-4	O/23	-1.0
1920	StL-N	99	320	38	84	5	5	0	32	21	11	.262	.308	.309	.617	79	-9	-8	98	125	31	.521	5	4	-1	-4	O	-1.8
1921	StL-N	92	275	37	85	20	3	6	45	15	11	.309	.347	.469	.816	120	5	7	95	112	44	.772	4	3	-1	-4	O/31	0.0
1922	StL-N	112	344	50	108	13	4	2	64	19	10	.314	.350	.392	.742	90	-5	-5	101	159	48	.662	3	1	0	-9	O	-1.6
1923	StL-N	2	7	0	2	0	0	0	1	1	0	.286	.375	.286	.661	85	-0	-0	90	186	1	.600	0	0	0	0	/O	0.0
1924	StL-N	12	12	0	2	0	0	0	2	3	0	.167	.333	.167	.500	37	-1	-1	103	365	1	.500	0	0	0	-1	/O	-0.1
	Phi-N	88	284	35	80	15	1	5	29	20	18	.282	.329	.394	.723	86	-3	-6	108	83	37	.670	6	2	1	-7	O	-1.3
	Yr	100	296	35	82	15	1	5	31	23	18	.277	.329	.385	.714	85	-4	-7	107	121	38	.662	6	2	1	-8		-1.4
1925	Phi-N	24	64	10	22	6	0	0	8	4	1	.344	.382	.438	.820	94	1	-1	116	102	10	.767	1	1	-0	-2	O	-0.3
	Cin-N	33	62	6	20	3	1	0	13	3	1	.323	.354	.403	.757	95	-1	-0	97	185	9	.721	3	1	0	-3	O/2	-0.3
	Yr	57	126	16	42	9	1	0	21	7	2	.333	.368	.421	.789	96	0	-1	105	152	19	.744	4	2	0	-5		-0.6
Total	11	703	1959	235	558	83	19	15	249	116	102	.285	.327	.370	.696	92	-21	-22	100	121	242	.622	35	16		-40	O/321S	-7.2
■ BILL SCHUSTER	Schuster, William Charles "Broadway Bill" b: 8/4/12, Buffalo, N.Y. d: 6/28/87, El Monte, Cal. BR/TR, 5'9", 164 lbs. Deb: 9/29/37																											
1937	Pit-N	3	6	2	3	0	0	0	1	1	0	.500	.571	.500	1.071	189	1	1	102	120	2	1.333	0			0	/S	0.1
1939	Bos-N	2	3	0	0	0	0	0	0	0	1	.000	.000	.000	.000	-99	-1	-1	92	0	0	.000	0			0	/S3	0.0
1943	Chi-N	13	51	3	15	2	1	0	0	3	2	.294	.333	.373	.706	105	0	0	99	0	6	.579	0			-1	S	0.1
1944	Chi-N	60	154	14	34	7	1	1	14	12	16	.221	.277	.299	.576	62	-8	-8	101	102	12	.492	4			1	S/2	-0.1
1945	Chi-N	45	47	8	9	2	1	0	2	7	4	.191	.296	.277	.573	60	-2	-2	99	53	4	.537	2			-0	S/23	0.0
Total	5	123	261	27	61	11	3	1	17	23	23	.234	.296	.310	.606	71	-10	-10	100	73	23	.542	6			-0	/S23	0.1
■ RANDY SCHWARTZ	Schwartz, Douglas Randall b: 2/9/44, Los Angeles, Cal. BL/TL, 6'3", 230 lbs. Deb: 9/08/65																											
1965	KC-A	6	7	0	2	0	0	0	1	0	4	.286	.286	.286	.571	65	-0	-0	97	207	1	.400	0	0	0	0	/1	0.0
1966	KC-A	10	11	0	1	0	0	0	1	1	3	.091	.167	.091	.258	-25	-2	-2	94	420	0	.200	0	0	0	0	/1	-0.1
Total	2	16	18	0	3	0	0	0	2	1	7	.167	.211	.167	.377	10	-2	-2	95	342	1	.267	0	0	0	0	/1	-0.1
■ BILL SCHWARTZ	Schwartz, William August "Pop" or "Scooper Bill" b: 4/3/1864, Jamestown, Ky. d: 12/22/40, Newport, Ky. BR/TR, Deb: 5/03/1883																											
1883	Col-a	2	4	0	1	0	0	0		0		.250	.250	.250	.500	71	-0	-0	87	0	0	.333				0	/1C	0.0
1884	Cin-U	29	106	14	25	4	0	1		3		.236	.257	.302	.559	82	-1	-3	108	0	8	.432	0			0	C/O3	-0.1
Total	2	31	110	14	26	4	0	1		3		.236	.257	.300	.557	81	-1	-3	107	0	9	.429	0			0	/CO31	-0.1
■ BILL SCHWARTZ	Schwartz, William Charles "Blab" b: 4/22/1884, Cleveland, Ohio d: 8/29/61, Nashville, Tenn. TR , 6'2", 185 lbs. Deb: 5/02/04																											
1904	Cle-A	24	86	5	13	2	0	0	0	0		.151	.151	.174	.326	4	-9	-9	102	0	3	.260	4			-1	1/3	-1.1
■ BILL SCHWARZ	Schwarz, William De Witt b: 1/30/1891, Birmingham, Ala. d: 6/24/49, Jacksonville, Fla TR , Deb: 8/20/14																											
1914	NY-A	1	1	0	0	0	0	0	0	0	1	.000	.000	.000	.000	-99	-0	-0	100	0	0	.000	0			0	/C	0.0
■ AL SCHWEITZER	Schweitzer, Albert Caspar "Cheese" b: 12/23/1882, Cleveland, Ohio d: 1/27/69, Newark, Ohio BR/TR, 5'6", 170 lbs. Deb: 4/30/08																											
1908	StL-A	64	182	22	53	4	2	1	14	20		.291	.361	.352	.713	130	7	7	103	78	25	.698	6			8	O	1.3
1909	StL-A	27	76	7	17	2	0	0	2	5		.224	.298	.250	.548	80	-2	-1	92	41	6	.508	3			1	O	-0.1
1910	StL-A	113	379	37	87	11	2	2	37	36		.230	.303	.285	.588	89	-6	-4	94	122	40	.596	26			-4	*O	-1.3
1911	StL-A	76	237	31	51	11	4	0	34	43		.215	.338	.295	.633	81	-6	-4	95	167	28	.677	12			-1	O	-1.0
Total	4	280	874	97	208	28	8	3	87	104		.238	.325	.299	.623	95	-7	-3	96	119	99	.631	47			4	O	-1.1
■ PI SCHWERT	Schwert, Pius Louis b: 11/22/1892, Angola, N.Y. d: 3/11/41, Washington, D.C. BR/TR, 5'10.5", 160 lbs. Deb: 10/06/14																											
1914	NY-A	2	5	0	0	0	0	0	0	2	2	.000	.286	.000	.286	-13	-1	-1	100	0	0	.400	0			0	/C	0.0
1915	NY-A	9	18	6	5	3	0	0	6	1	6	.278	.316	.444	.760	129	0	0	98	255	3	.692	0			0	/C	0.2
Total	2	11	23	6	5	3	0	0	6	3	8	.217	.308	.348	.656	98	-0	-0	99	186	3	.611	0			0	/C	0.2
■ ART SCHWIND	Schwind, Arthur Edwin b: 11/4/1889, Ft.Wayne, Ind. d: 1/13/68, Sullivan, Ill. BB/TR, 5'8", 150 lbs. Deb: 10/03/12																											
1912	Bos-N	1	2	0	1	0	0	0	0	0	0	.500	.500	.500	1.000	162	0	0	107	0	0	1.000	0			0	/3	0.0
■ JERRY SCHYPINSKI	Schypinski, Gerald Albert b: 9/16/31, Detroit, Mich. BL/TR, 5'10", 170 lbs. Deb: 8/31/55																											
1955	KC-A	22	69	7	15	2	0	0	5	1	6	.217	.229	.246	.475	27	-7	-7	101	110	4	.327	0	0	0	-1	S/2	-0.5
■ MIKE SCIOSCIA	Scioscia, Michael Lorri b: 11/27/58, Upper Darby, Pa. BL/TR, 6'2", 200 lbs. Deb: 4/20/80																											
1980	LA-N	54	134	8	34	5	1	1	8	12	9	.254	.315	.328	.643	82	-4	-3	97	67	15	.559	1	0	0	-7	C	-0.9
1981	LA-N	93	290	27	80	10	0	2	29	36	18	.276	.358	.331	.689	98	-0	1	98	112	34	.605	0	2	-1	-8	C	-0.7
1982	LA-N	129	365	31	80	11	1	5	38	44	31	.219	.305	.296	.601	73	-15	-12	95	121	34	.529	2	0	1	-16	*C	-2.7
1983	LA-N	12	35	3	11	3	0	1	7	5	2	.314	.400	.486	.886	144	2	2	100	138	7	.880	0	0	0	-1	C	0.2

YEAR	TM/L	G	AB	R	H	2B	3B	HR	RBI	BB	SO	AVG	OBP	SLG	PRO	/A	BR	/A	PF	CHI	RC	TA	SB	CS	SBR	FR	POS	TPR
1984	LA-N	114	341	29	93	18	0	5	38	52	26	.273	.371	.370	.740	105	6	4	104	106	48	.699	2	1	0	-5	*C	0.2
1985	LA-N	141	429	47	127	26	3	7	53	77	21	.296	.409	.420	.829	142	22	26	93	105	78	.841	3	3	-1	-1	*C	3.0
1986	LA-N	122	374	36	94	18	1	5	26	62	23	.251	.362	.345	.707	102	0	3	94	72	49	.670	3	3	-1	0	*C	0.5
1987	LA-N	142	461	44	122	26	1	6	38	55	23	.265	.344	.364	.709	96	-7	-2	92	82	58	.649	7	4	-0	-2	*C	0.7
1988	LA-N	130	408	29	105	18	0	3	35	38	31	.257	.321	.324	.644	80	-7	-10	106	99	40	.531	0	3	-2	-8	*C	-1.4
Total	9	937	2837	254	746	135	7	35	272	381	184	.263	.353	.352	.705	100	-2	9	97	97	361	.665	18	16	-4	-48	C	-1.1
■ **LOU SCOFFIC**	Scoffic, Louis "Weaser" b: 5/20/13, Herrin, Ill. BR/TR, 5'10", 182 lbs. Deb: 4/16/36																											
1936	StL-N	4	7	2	3	0	0	0	2	1	2	.429	.500	.429	.929	161	1	1	94	236	2	1.000	0			-0	/O	0.0
■ **DARYL SCONIERS**	Sconiers, Daryl Anthony b: 10/3/58, San Bernardino, Cal. BL/TL, 6'2", 185 lbs. Deb: 9/13/81																											
1981	Cal-A	15	52	6	14	1	1	1	7	1	10	.269	.283	.385	.668	87	-1	-1	104	119	6	.553	0	0	0	0	1/D	-0.1
1982	Cal-A	12	13	0	2	0	0	0	2	2	1	.154	.267	.154	.421	19	-1	-1	100	400	0	.308	0	0	0	0	/1D	0.0
1983	Cal-A	106	314	49	86	19	3	8	46	17	41	.274	.311	.430	.741	106	-0	2	96	113	39	.653	4	2	0	-4	1D/O	-0.4
1984	Cal-A	57	160	14	39	4	0	4	17	13	17	.244	.301	.344	.644	77	-5	-5	101	101	15	.535	1	2	-1	-1	1/D	-0.9
1985	Cal-A	44	98	14	28	6	1	2	12	15	18	.286	.381	.429	.809	120	3	3	101	99	17	.808	2	1	0	-0	D/1	0.2
Total	5	234	637	83	169	30	5	15	84	48	87	.265	.317	.399	.716	98	-4	-3	99	114	77	.651	7	5	-1	-6	1/DO	-1.2
■ **SCOTT**	Scott Deb:7/16/1884																											
1884	Bal-U	13	53	10	12	1	1	1		2		.226	.255	.340	.594	90	-0	-1	110	0	5	.488	0			0	O/3	0.0
■ **TONY SCOTT**	Scott, Anthony b: 9/18/51, Cincinnati, Ohio BB/TR, 6', 164 lbs. Deb: 9/01/73																											
1973	Mon-N	11	1	2	0	0	0	0	0	0	1	.000	.000	.000	.000	-96	-0	-0	104	0	0	.000	0	0	0	-1	/O	-0.1
1974	Mon-N	19	7	2	2	0	0	0	1	1	3	.286	.375	.286	.661	83	-0	-0	104	193	1	.667	1	1	-0	-5	O	-0.6
1975	Mon-N	92	143	19	26	4	2	0	11	12	38	.182	.259	.238	.497	36	-12	-13	108	125	8	.425	5	6	-2	-9	O	-2.7
1977	StL-N	95	292	38	85	16	3	3	41	33	48	.291	.369	.397	.766	110	3	5	96	131	42	.743	13	10	-2	-1	O	0.0
1978	StL-N	96	219	28	50	5	2	1	14	14	41	.228	.281	.283	.564	61	-12	-11	95	85	16	.461	5	6	-2	-9	O	-2.6
1979	StL-N	153	587	69	152	22	10	6	68	34	92	.259	.305	.361	.666	77	-16	-19	105	119	62	.619	37	17	1	11	*O	-1.2
1980	StL-N	143	415	51	104	19	3	0	28	35	68	.251	.310	.311	.621	72	-14	-15	103	86	40	.568	22	10	1	-8	*O	-2.9
1981	StL-N	45	176	21	40	5	2	2	17	5	22	.227	.253	.313	.565	59	-10	-10	102	112	12	.486	10	7	-1	-2	O	-1.5
	Hou-N	55	225	28	66	13	2	2	22	15	32	.293	.338	.396	.733	122	2	5	88	87	31	.687	8	3	1	-2	O	0.2
	Yr	100	401	49	106	18	4	4	39	20	54	.264	.301	.359	.660	92	-8	-5	94	99	44	.598	18	10	-1	-3		-1.3
1982	Hou-N	132	460	43	110	16	3	1	29	15	56	.239	.265	.293	.558	57	-27	-27	99	82	35	.463	18	4	3	4	*O	-2.2
1983	Hou-N	80	186	20	42	6	1	2	17	11	39	.226	.269	.301	.570	64	-11	-9	90	108	16	.486	5	4	-1	-6	O	-1.6
1984	Hou-N	25	21	2	4	1	0	0	0	4	3	.190	.320	.238	.558	64	-1	-1	93	0	2	.529	0	0	0	-1	/O	-0.1
	Mon-N	45	71	8	18	4	0	0	5	7	21	.254	.321	.310	.630	85	-2	-1	91	89	7	.545	1	1	-0	-2	O	-0.3
	Yr	70	92	10	22	5	0	0	5	11	24	.239	.320	.293	.614	80	-3	-2	92	57	9	.542	1	1	-0	-2		-0.4
Total	11	991	2803	331	699	111	28	17	253	186	464	.249	.300	.327	.627	74	-100	-97	99	102	272	.572	125	69	-4	-29	O	-15.6
■ **DONNIE SCOTT**	Scott, Donald Malcolm b: 8/16/61, Dunedin, Fla. BB/TR, 5'11", 185 lbs. Deb: 9/30/83																											
1983	Tex-A	2	4	0	0	0	0	0	0	0	0	.000	.000	.000	.000	-99	-1	-1	101	0	0	.000	0	0	0	0	/C	0.0
1984	Tex-A	81	235	16	52	9	0	3	20	20	44	.221	.282	.298	.580	61	-12	-12	100	101	20	.476	0	1	-1	-5	C	-1.2
1985	Sea-A	80	185	18	41	13	0	4	23	15	41	.222	.280	.357	.637	77	-7	-6	95	117	19	.554	1	1	-0	-5	C	-0.7
Total	3	163	424	34	93	22	0	7	43	35	85	.219	.279	.321	.600	66	-21	-19	98	107	38	.512	1	2	-1	-10	C	-1.9
■ **PETE SCOTT**	Scott, Floyd John b: 12/21/1898, Woodland, Cal. d: 5/3/53, Daly City, Cal. BR/TR, 5'11.5", 175 lbs. Deb: 4/13/26																											
1926	Chi-N	77	189	34	54	13	1	3	34	22	31	.286	.363	.413	.776	102	3	1	106	135	29	.770	3			-1	O/3	-0.1
1927	Chi-N	71	156	28	49	18	1	0	21	19	18	.314	.392	.442	.834	123	6	6	100	106	27	.841	1			-3	O	0.1
1928	Pit-N	60	177	33	55	10	4	5	33	18	14	.311	.378	.497	.875	119	7	5	107	114	33	.885	1			2	O/1	0.4
Total	3	208	522	95	158	41	6	8	88	59	63	.303	.377	.450	.827	114	15	11	104	119	88	.830	5			-1	O/13	0.4
■ **GEORGE SCOTT**	Scott, George Charles "Boomer" b: 3/23/44, Greenville, Miss. BR/TR, 6'2", 200 lbs. Deb: 4/12/66																											
1966	Bos-A	162	601	73	147	18	7	27	90	65	152	.245	.326	.433	.759	106	12	6	109	117	81	.704	4	0	1	3	*1/3	0.5
1967	Bos-A	159	565	74	171	21	7	19	82	63	119	.303	.377	.465	.842	129	34	24	115	109	97	.819	10	8	-2	-4	*1/3	0.8
1968	Bos-A	124	350	23	60	14	0	3	25	26	88	.171	.239	.237	.476	44	-23	-23	101	116	18	.380	3	5	-2	-2	*1/3	-3.6
1969	Bos-A	152	549	63	139	14	5	16	52	61	74	.253	.332	.384	.717	95	-0	-3	105	82	69	.654	4	3	-1	-4	*31	-0.9
1970	Bos-A	127	480	50	142	24	5	16	63	44	95	.296	.357	.467	.824	113	16	10	111	96	74	.757	4	11	-5	-4	31	-0.1
1971	Bos-A	146	537	72	141	16	4	24	78	41	102	.263	.321	.441	.762	108	8	5	106	105	69	.671	0	3	-2	-8	*1	-1.2
1972	Mil-A	152	578	71	154	24	4	20	88	43	130	.266	.322	.426	.747	127	13	16	95	127	76	.691	16	4	2	-5	*13	0.0
1973	Mil-A	158	604	98	185	30	4	24	107	61	94	.306	.372	.488	.860	147	32	35	96	121	106	.828	9	5	-0	6	*1/D	3.1
1974	Mil-A	158	604	74	170	36	2	17	82	59	90	.281	.348	.432	.780	121	18	16	102	109	84	.709	9	9	-3	5	*1/D	1.2
1975	Mil-A	158	617	86	176	26	4	**36**	**109**	51	97	.285	.343	.515	.858	140	29	29	100	104	99	.801	6	5	-1	5	*1D/3	2.5
1976	Mil-A	156	606	73	166	21	5	18	77	53	118	.274	.337	.414	.752	120	14	15	99	93	82	.672	0	1	-1	-2	*1	0.4
1977	Bos-A	157	584	103	157	26	5	33	95	57	112	.269	.340	.500	.840	107	19	6	117	102	93	.788	1	1	-0	1	*1	-0.1
1978	Bos-A	120	412	51	96	16	4	12	54	44	86	.233	.307	.379	.686	85	-5	-9	107	113	44	.598	1	1	-0	-3	*1/D	-1.6
1979	Bos-A	45	156	18	35	9	1	4	23	17	22	.224	.301	.372	.672	75	-5	-6	107	129	14	.564	0	0	0	3	1	-0.5
	KC-A	44	146	19	39	8	2	1	20	12	32	.267	.331	.370	.701	84	-2	-3	105	135	15	.575	1	1	-0	-0	1/3D	-0.5
	NY-A	16	44	9	14	3	1	1	6	2	7	.318	.348	.500	.848	131	1	2	96	92	8	.833	1	0	0	0	D/1	0.2
	Yr	105	346	46	88	20	4	6	49	31	61	.254	.319	.387	.707	86	-5	-8	105	128	46	.653	2	1	0	2		-0.8
Total	14	2034	7433	957	1992	306	60	271	1051	699	1418	.268	.335	.435	.770	112	161	117	105	108	1027	.737	69	57	-14	-7	*13/D	0.2
■ **JIM SCOTT**	Scott, James Walter b: 9/22/1888, Shenandoah, Pa. d: 5/12/72, S.Pasadena, Fla. BR/TR, 5'9.5", 165 lbs. Deb: 4/22/14																											
1914	Pit-F	8	24	2	6	1	0	0	1	5	0	.250	.379	.292	.671	99	0	0	94	52	3	.722	1			0	/S	0.0
■ **JOHN SCOTT**	Scott, John Henry b: 1/24/52, Jackson, Miss. BR/TR, 6'2", 165 lbs. Deb: 9/07/74																											
1974	SD-N	14	15	3	1	0	0	0	0	0	4	.067	.067	.067	.133	-67	-3	-3	93	0	0	.143	1	0	0	-1	/O	-0.3
1975	SD-N	25	9	6	0	0	0	0	0	0	2	.000	.000	.000	.000	-99	-2	-2	100	0	0	.222	2	0	1	-0	/O	-0.1
1977	Tor-A	79	233	26	56	9	0	2	15	8	39	.240	.266	.305	.570	54	-15	-15	103	77	17	.471	10	8	-2	-2	O/D	-2.1
Total	3	118	257	35	57	9	0	2	15	8	45	.222	.245	.280	.525	42	-20	-21	102	70	17	.439	13	8	-1	-3	/OD	-2.5
■ **LE GRANT SCOTT**	Scott, Le Grant Edward b: 7/25/10, Cleveland, Ohio BL/TL, 5'8.5", 170 lbs. Deb: 4/19/39																											
1939	Phi-N	76	232	31	65	15	1	1	26	22	14	.280	.343	.366	.709	96	-3	-1	94	108	29	.647	5			1	O	0.0
■ **EVERETT SCOTT**	Scott, Lewis Everett "Deacon" b: 11/19/1892, Bluffton, Ind. d: 11/2/60, Fort Wayne, Ind. BR/TR, 5'8", 148 lbs. Deb: 4/14/14																											
1914	Bos-A	144	539	66	129	15	6	2	37	32	43	.239	.286	.301	.586	78	-17	-16	98	88	48	.486	9	14	-6	-15	*S	-2.4
1915	Bos-A	100	359	25	72	11	0	0	28	17	21	.201	.237	.231	.468	40	-27	-27	99	117	22	.354	4	7	-3	-7	*S	-3.0
1916	Bos-A	123	366	37	85	19	2	0	27	23	24	.232	.283	.295	.578	79	-13	-10	94	89	37	.505	8			-2	*S/23	-0.2
1917	Bos-A	157	528	40	127	24	7	0	50	20	46	.241	.268	.313	.581	71	-17	-22	108	111	49	.491	12			10	*S	-0.5
1918	Bos-A	126	443	40	98	11	5	0	43	12	16	.221	.242	.269	.510	57	-26	-24	95	134	32	.412	11			16	*S	0.0
1919	Bos-A	138	507	41	141	19	0	0	38	19	26	.278	.306	.316	.621	81	-18	-13	91	88	50	.514	8			9	*S	0.7
1920	Bos-A	154	569	41	153	21	12	4	61	21	15	.269	.300	.369	.669	80	-21	-18	96	98	60	.560	4	11	-5	16	*S	0.6
1921	Bos-A	154	576	65	151	21	9	1	62	27	21	.262	.295	.335	.630	61	-35	-35	100	111	55	.518	5	9	-4	**38**	*S	1.7
1922	NY-A	154	557	64	150	23	5	3	45	23	22	.269	.304	.345	.649	68	-26	-27	102	82	59	.541	2	3	-1	19	*S	0.7
1923	NY-A	152	533	48	131	16	4	6	60	13	19	.246	.266	.325	.591	53	-37	-40	104	107	45	.467	1	3	-2	-10	*S	-3.5
1924	NY-A	153	548	56	137	12	6	4	64	21	15	.250	.278	.316	.593	53	-40	-39	99	114	47	.471	3	7	-3	9	*S	-1.6
1925	NY-A	22	60	3	13	0	0	0	4	2	2	.217	.242	.217	.459	18	-8	-7	96	103	3	.313	0	1	-1	-1	S	-0.5
	Was-A	33	103	10	28	6	1	0	18	4	4	.272	.299	.350	.649	65	-6	-6	98	167	10	.532	1	2	-1	-4	S/3	-0.4
	Yr	55	163	13	41	6	1	0	22	6	6	.252	.278	.301	.579	48	-13	-13	97	143	13	.448	1	3	-2	-5		-0.9
1926	Chi-A	40	143	15	36	10	1	0	13	9	8	.252	.296	.336	.632	70	-8	-6	92	94	14	.527	1	3	-2	1	S	-0.3
	Cin-N	4	6	1	4	0	0	0	1	0	0	.667	.667	.667	1.333	273	1	1	95	86	2	2.000	0			-0	/S	0.1

YEAR	TM/L	G	AB	R	H	2B	3B	HR	RBI	BB	SO	AVG	OBP	SLG	PRO	/A	BR	/A	PF	CHI	RC	TA	SB	CS	SBR	FR	POS	TPR
Total	13	1654	5837	552	1455	208	58	20	551	243	282	.249	.281	.315	.596	65	-297	-288	99	104	532	.488	69	60		78	*S/32	-8.6
■ MILT SCOTT	Scott, Milton Parker "Mikado Milt" b: 1/17/1866, Chicago, Ill. d: 11/3/38, Baltimore, Md. 5'9", 160 lbs. Deb: 9/30/1882																											
1882	Chi-N	1	5	1	2	0	0	0	0	0	0	.400	.400	.400	.800	156	0	0	101	0	1	.667				0	/1	0.0
1884	Det-N	110	438	29	108	17	5	3	50	9	62	.247	.262	.329	.591	90	-8	-4	94	119	39	.464				-2	*1	-1.5
1885	Det-N	38	148	14	39	7	0	0	12	4	16	.264	.283	.311	.594	94	-1	-1	97	96	13	.459				2	1	-0.5
	Pit-a	55	210	15	52	7	1	0		5		.248	.272	.290	.562	75	-5	-7	106	0	17	.430				3	1	-0.7
1886	Bal-a	137	484	48	92	11	4	2		22		.190	.239	.242	.481	58	-26	-19	91	0	31	.406	11			9	*1/P	-1.4
Total	4	341	1285	107	293	42	10	5	62	40	78	.228	.257	.288	.545	77	-40	-30	95	51	101	.435	11			11	1/P	-4.1
■ ROD SCOTT	Scott, Rodney Darrell b: 10/16/53, Indianapolis, Ind. BB/TR, 6', 160 lbs. Deb: 4/11/75																											
1975	KC-A	48	15	13	1	0	0	0	0	1	3	.067	.125	.067	.192	-44	-3	-3	102	0	0	.375	4	2	0	0	D/2SR	-0.1
1976	Mon-N	7	10	3	4	0	0	0	0	1	1	.400	.455	.400	.855	143	1	1	100	0	2	1.167	2	0	1	0	/2S	0.2
1977	Oak-A	133	364	56	95	4	4	0	20	43	50	.261	.344	.294	.638	80	-10	-8	95	74	41	.646	33	18	-1	-5	2S/3OD	0.0
1978	Chi-N	78	227	41	64	5	1	0	15	43	41	.282	.403	.313	.716	93	4	1	110	84	35	.814	27	10	2	6	3O/2S	0.9
1979	Mon-N	151	562	69	134	12	5	3	42	66	82	.238	.321	.294	.614	67	-23	-24	102	101	61	.613	39	12	5	-7	*2S	-1.5
1980	Mon-N	154	567	84	127	13	**13**	0	46	70	75	.224	.310	.293	.603	70	-22	-21	99	116	60	.648	63	13	11	-7	*2S	-0.6
1981	Mon-N	95	336	43	69	9	3	0	26	50	35	.205	.310	.250	.560	61	-16	-15	99	129	32	.587	30	7	5	-12	2	-1.6
1982	Mon-N	14	25	2	5	0	0	0	1	3	2	.200	.286	.200	.486	36	-2	-2	105	78	2	.650	5	0	2	-1	2	0.0
	NY-A	10	26	5	5	0	0	0	0	4	2	.192	.300	.192	.492	40	-2	-2	96	0	2	.500	2	0	1	0	/S2	0.0
Total	8	690	2132	316	504	43	26	3	150	281	291	.236	.328	.285	.613	71	-74	-75	101	100	235	.653	205	62	24	-24	2S/3DO	-2.7
■ JIM SCRANTON	Scranton, James Dean b: 4/5/60, Torrance, Cal. BR/TR, 6', 175 lbs. Deb: 9/05/84																											
1984	KC-A	2	2	0	0	0	0	0	0	0	0	.000	.000	.000	.000	-99	-1	-1	99	0	0	.000	0	0	0	0	/S3	0.0
1985	KC-A	6	4	1	0	0	0	0	0	0	0	.000	.000	.000	.000	-98	-1	-1	102	0	0	.000	0	0	0	0	/S	0.0
Total	2	8	6	1	0	0	0	0	0	0	0	.000	.000	.000	.000	-99	-2	-2	101	0	0	.000	0	0	0	0	/S3	0.0
■ CHUCK SCRIVENER	Scrivener, Wayne Allison b: 10/3/47, Alexandria, Va. BR/TR, 5'9", 170 lbs. Deb: 9/18/75																											
1975	Det-A	4	16	0	4	1	0	0	0	0	1	.250	.250	.313	.563	56	-1	-1	104	0	1	.500	1	0	0	0	/3S	0.0
1976	Det-A	80	222	28	49	7	1	2	16	19	34	.221	.282	.288	.570	65	-9	-10	104	88	19	.480	1	0	0	6	2S/3	0.0
1977	Det-A	61	72	10	6	0	0	0	2	5	9	.083	.143	.083	.226	-35	-14	-14	105	132	1	.164	0	0	0	1	S/23	-0.5
Total	3	145	310	38	59	8	1	2	18	24	44	.190	.249	.242	.490	40	-24	-25	104	94	22	.401	2	0	1	7	/S23	-0.5
■ KEN SEARS	Sears, Kenneth Eugene "Ziggy" b: 7/6/17, Streator, Ill. d: 7/17/68, Bridgeport, Tex. BL/TR, 6'1", 200 lbs. Deb: 5/02/43																											
1943	NY-A	60	187	22	52	7	0	2	22	11	18	.278	.328	.348	.676	101	-1	-0	96	113	21	.567	1	3	-2	-1	C	0.0
1946	StL-A	7	15	1	5	0	0	0	1	3	0	.333	.444	.333	.778	122	1	1	98	76	2	.727	0	0	0	-0	/C	0.1
Total	2	67	202	23	57	7	0	2	23	14	18	.282	.338	.347	.684	103	-0	1	97	110	23	.591	1	3	-2	-1	/C	0.1
■ JIMMY SEBRING	Sebring, James Dennison b: 3/22/1882, Liberty, Pa. d: 12/22/09, Williamsport, Pa. BL/TL, 6', 180 lbs. Deb: 9/08/02																											
1902	Pit-N	19	80	15	26	4	4	0	15	5		.325	.365	.475	.840	153	5	5	105	121	15	.833	2			2	O	0.6
1903	Pit-N	124	506	71	140	16	13	4	64	32		.277	.320	.383	.703	97	-0	-3	105	96	70	.672	20			12	*O	0.1
1904	Pit-N	80	305	28	82	11	7	0	32	17		.269	.307	.351	.658	106	1	2	99	116	36	.592	8			-0	O	-0.1
	Cin-N	56	222	22	50	9	2	0	24	14		.225	.271	.284	.555	64	-7	-11	114	123	20	.494	8			-2	O	-1.5
	Yr	136	527	50	132	20	9	0	56	31		.250	.292	.323	.615	87	-6	-9	106	120	56	.549	16			-2		-1.6
1905	Cin-N	58	217	31	62	10	5	2	28	14		.286	.329	.406	.735	117	5	4	103	110	33	.729	11			4	O	0.4
1909	Bro-N	25	81	11	8	1	1	0	5	11		.099	.207	.136	.342	7	-9	-8	99	169	3	.342	3			0	O	-0.9
	Was-A	1	0	0	0	0	0	0	0	0		—	—	—	—	—	0	0	90	—	—	—	0			0	/O	0.0
Total	5	363	1411	178	368	51	32	6	168	93		.261	.307	.355	.662	95	-4	-12	104	112	180	.619	52			16	O	-1.4
■ FRANK SECORY	Secory, Frank Edward b: 8/24/12, Mason City, Iowa BR/TR, 6'1", 200 lbs. Deb: 4/28/40 U																											
1940	Det-A	1	1	0	0	0	0	0	0	0	1	.000	.000	.000	.000	-90	-0	-0	111	0	0	.000	0	0	0	0	H	0.0
1942	Cin-N	2	5	1	0	0	0	0	1	3	2	.000	.375	.000	.375	14	-0	-0	101	0	0	.600	0			0	/O	0.0
1944	Chi-N	22	56	10	18	1	0	4	17	6	8	.321	.387	.554	.941	161	4	4	101	142	13	1.000	1			0	O	0.3
1945	Chi-N	35	57	4	9	1	0	0	6	2	7	.158	.186	.175	.362	1	-8	-8	99	208	2	.240	0			-2	O	-0.9
1946	Chi-N	33	43	6	10	3	0	3	12	6	6	.233	.327	.512	.838	144	2	2	94	144	7	.824	0			-3	/O	0.0
Total	5	93	162	21	37	5	0	7	36	17	24	.228	.302	.389	.691	95	-2	-2	98	157	22	.643	1	0		-4	/O	-0.6
■ CHARLIE SEE	See, Charles Henry "Chad" b: 10/13/1896, Pleasantville, N.Y d: 7/19/48, Bridgeport, Conn. BL/TR, 5'10.5", 175 lbs. Deb: 8/06/19																											
1919	Cin-N	8	14	1	4	0	0	0	1	1	0	.286	.333	.286	.619	83	-0	-0	105	97	1	.500	0			-1	/O	-0.1
1920	Cin-N	47	82	9	25	4	0	0	15	1	7	.305	.329	.354	.683	107	-0	0	90	200	9	.557	2	4	-2	4	O/P	0.2
1921	Cin-N	37	106	11	26	5	1	1	7	7	5	.245	.298	.340	.638	68	-5	-5	101	66	11	.573	3	2	-0	-1	O	-0.7
Total	3	92	202	21	55	9	1	1	23	9	12	.272	.313	.342	.655	83	-6	-5	97	121	21	.562	5	6		2	/OP	-0.6
■ LARRY SEE	See, Ralph Laurence b: 6/20/60, Norwalk, Cal. BR/TR, 6'1", 195 lbs. Deb: 9/03/86																											
1986	LA-N	13	20	1	5	2	0	0	2	2	7	.250	.318	.350	.668	89	-0	-0	94	114	2	.600	0	0	0	0	/1	0.0
1988	Tex-A	13	23	0	3	0	0	0	0	1	8	.130	.167	.130	.297	-15	-4	-4	101	0	1	.200	0	0	0	0	/C1/3D	-0.3
Total	2	26	43	1	8	2	0	0	2	3	15	.186	.239	.233	.472	32	-4	-4	98	54	3	.371	0	0	0	1	/1DC3	-0.3
■ BOB SEEDS	Seeds, Robert Ira "Suitcase Bob" b: 2/24/07, Ringgold, Tex. BR/TR, 6', 180 lbs. Deb: 4/19/30																											
1930	Cle-A	85	277	37	79	11	3	3	32	12	22	.285	.315	.379	.694	72	-11	-13	105	93	32	.587	1	3	-2	1	O	-1.4
1931	Cle-A	48	134	26	41	4	1	1	10	11	11	.306	.359	.373	.732	87	-1	-2	106	62	18	.667	1	0	0	-4	O/1	-0.7
1932	Cle-A	2	4	0	0	0	0	0	0	0	0	.000	.000	.000	.000	-92	-1	-1	108	0	0	.000	0	0	0	-0	/O	-0.1
	Chi-A	116	434	53	126	18	6	2	45	31	37	.290	.342	.373	.715	97	-9	-1	87	92	55	.638	5	7	-3	-3	*O	-1.0
	Yr	118	438	53	126	18	6	2	45	31	37	.288	.339	.370	.709	95	-11	-3	88	90	54	.630	5	7	-3	-4		-1.1
1933	Bos-A	82	230	26	56	13	4	0	23	21	20	.243	.310	.335	.644	70	-10	-10	101	100	24	.565	1	3	-2	-4	1O	-1.8
1934	Bos-A	8	6	0	1	0	0	0	1	0	1	.167	.167	.167	.333	-13	-1	-1	106	334	0	.200	0	0	0	-0	/O	0.0
	Cle-A	61	186	28	46	8	1	0	18	21	13	.247	.327	.301	.628	63	-10	-10	101	107	20	.567	2	1	0	-5	O	-1.4
	Yr	69	192	28	47	8	1	0	19	21	14	.245	.322	.297	.619	60	-11	-11	101	138	20	.555	2	1	0	-5		-1.4
1936	NY-A	13	42	12	11	1	0	4	10	5	3	.262	.340	.571	.912	128	1	1	95	90	8	1.000	3	1	0	0	/O3	0.2
1938	NY-N	81	296	35	86	12	3	9	52	20	33	.291	.338	.443	.780	109	4	3	103	121	44	.697	0			-2	O	0.0
1939	NY-N	63	173	33	46	5	1	5	26	22	31	.266	.352	.393	.745	101	0	0	99	115	25	.708	1			-7	O	-0.6
1940	NY-N	56	155	18	45	5	2	4	16	17	19	.290	.371	.426	.797	119	4	4	100	76	25	.754	0			-3	O	0.0
Total	9	615	1937	268	537	77	21	28	233	160	190	.277	.336	.382	.718	90	-33	-30	99	98	251	.651	14	15		-28	O/13	-6.8
■ PAT SEEREY	Seerey, James Patrick b: 3/17/23, Wilburton, Okla. d: 4/28/86, Jennings, Mo. BR/TR, 5'10", 200 lbs. Deb: 6/09/43																											
1943	Cle-A	26	72	8	16	3	0	1	5	4	19	.222	.263	.306	.569	73	-3	-3	90	73	5	.441	0	0	0	1	O	-0.1
1944	Cle-A	101	342	39	80	16	0	15	39	19	99	.234	.276	.412	.689	95	-4	-4	100	76	36	.588	0	2	-1	4	O	-0.3
1945	Cle-A	126	414	56	98	22	2	14	56	66	97	.237	.342	.401	.743	117	8	9	99	99	60	.713	1	2	-1	-7	*O	-0.3
1946	Cle-A	117	404	57	91	17	2	26	62	65	101	.225	.334	.470	.804	139	11	17	89	93	64	.787	2	3	-1	-11	*O	-0.1
1947	Cle-A	82	216	24	37	4	1	11	29	34	66	.171	.284	.352	.636	79	-8	-7	96	98	22	.588	0	1	-1	-9	O	-1.9
1948	Cle-A	10	23	7	6	0	0	1	6	7	8	.261	.433	.391	.825	122	1	1	99	169	4	.842	0	0	0	-2	/O	0.0
	Chi-A	95	340	44	78	11	0	18	64	61	94	.229	.347	.421	.767	108	1	3	95	116	53	.756	0	0	0	2	O	0.1
	Yr	105	363	51	84	11	0	19	70	68	102	.231	.353	.419	.771	109	2	4	96	123	58	.767	0	0	0	-1		0.1
1949	Chi-A	4	4	1	0	0	0	0	0	3	1	.000	.429	.000	.429	19	-0	-0	98	0	0	.750	0	0	0	-1	/O	0.0
Total	7	561	1815	236	406	73	5	86	261	259	485	.224	.321	.412	.733	110	6	17	95	97	246	.713	3	8	-4	-23	O	-2.6
■ EMMETT SEERY	Seery, John Emmett b: 2/13/1861, Princeville, Ill. BL/TR, Deb: 4/17/1884																											
1884	Bal-U	105	463	113	144	25	7	2		20		.311	.340	.408	.748	137	24	17	110	0	66	.655	0			4	*O/C3	1.6
	KC-U	1	4	2	2	1	0	0		1		.500	.600	.750	1.350	407	1	1	87	0	2	2.000	0			0	/O	0.1
	Yr	106	467	115	146	26	7	2		21		.313	.342	.411	.753	139	25	18	110	0	67	.664	0			4		1.7

YEAR	TM/L	G	AB	R	H	2B	3B	HR	RBI	BB	SO	AVG	OBP	SLG	PRO	/A	BR	/A	PF	CHI	RC	TA	SB	CS	SBR	FR	POS	TPR
1885	StL-N	59	216	20	35	7	0	1	14	16	37	.162	.220	.208	.428	42	-14	-12	92	107	10	.337				5	O/3	-0.7
1886	StL-N	126	453	73	108	22	6	2	48	57	82	.238	.324	.327	.650	104	1	5	95	108	57	.664	24			-3	*O/P	0.3
1887	Ind-N	122	465	104	104	18	15	4	28	71	68	.224	.331	.353	.684	96	-3	0	96	43	72	.795	48			7	*O/S	0.7
1888	Ind-N	133	500	87	110	20	10	5	50	64	73	.220	.316	.330	.646	114	7	10	95	88	79	.808	80			11	*O/S	1.9
1889	Ind-N	127	526	123	165	26	12	8	59	67	59	.314	.401	.454	.856	130	30	22	109	58	106	.928	19			1	*O	1.6
1890	Bro-P	104	394	78	88	12	7	1	50	70	36	.223	.348	.297	.645	71	-12	-16	106	121	57	.771	44			7	*O	-1.0
1891	CM-a	97	372	77	106	15	10	4	36	81	52	.285	.423	.411	.834	127	25	17	112	54	75	.981	19			1	*O	1.2
1892	Lou-N	42	154	18	31	6	1	0	15	24	19	.201	.309	.253	.562	78	-4	-2	92	125	14	.561	6			3	O	0.0
Total	9	916	3547	695	893	152	68	27	300	471	426	.252	.345	.356	.701	107	55	42	102	72	538	.756	240			35	O/3CSP	5.7
■ **KAL SEGRIST**	Segrist, Kal Hill b: 4/14/31, Greenville, Tex. BR/TR, 6', 180 lbs. Deb: 7/16/52																											
1952	NY-A	13	23	3	1	0	0	0	1	3	1	.043	.154	.043	.197	-44	-4	-4	98	374	0	.182	0	0	0	1	2/3	-0.2
1955	Bal-A	7	9	1	3	0	0	0	0	2	0	.333	.455	.333	.788	128	0	0	90	0	1	.714	0	0	0	0	/312	0.1
Total	2	20	32	4	4	0	0	0	1	5	1	.125	.243	.125	.368	4	-4	-4	95	262	2	.310	0	0	0	1	/231	-0.1
■ **KURT SEIBERT**	Seibert, Kurt Elliott b: 10/16/55, Cheverly, Md. BB/TR, 6', 165 lbs. Deb: 9/03/79																											
1979	Chi-N	7	2	2	0	0	0	0	0	0	1	.000	.000	.000	.000	-89	-1	-1	112	0	0	.000	0	0	0	0	/2	0.0
■ **RICKY SEILHEIMER**	Seilheimer, Ricky Allen b: 8/30/60, Brenham, Tex. BL/TR, 5'11", 185 lbs. Deb: 7/05/80																											
1980	Chi-A	21	52	4	11	3	1	1	3	4	15	.212	.268	.365	.633	74	-2	-2	97	53	5	.585	1	0	0	-2	C	-0.2
■ **KEVIN SEITZER**	Seitzer, Kevin Lee b: 3/26/62, Springfield, Ill. BR/TR, 5'11", 180 lbs. Deb: 9/03/86																											
1986	KC-A	28	96	16	31	4	1	2	11	19	14	.323	.440	.448	.888	144	7	7	100	95	21	.969	0	0	0	1	1/O3	0.6
1987	KC-A	161	641	105	**207**	33	8	15	83	80	85	.323	.400	.470	.869	126	31	27	104	85	120	.861	12	7	-1	5	*31/OD	2.4
1988	KC-A	149	559	90	170	32	5	5	60	72	64	.304	.389	.406	.795	119	20	18	103	95	89	.765	10	8	-2	8	*3/OD	2.5
Total	3	338	1296	211	408	69	14	22	154	171	163	.315	.398	.441	.839	124	58	52	103	90	230	.842	22	15	-2	14	3/1OD	5.5
■ **KIP SELBACH**	Selbach, Albert Karl b: 3/24/1872, Columbus, Ohio d: 2/17/56, Columbus, Ohio BR/TR, 5'7", 190 lbs. Deb: 4/24/1894																											
1894	Was-N	97	372	69	114	21	17	7	71	51	20	.306	.390	.511	.901	120	10	11	98	98	84	1.016	21			-6	OS	0.0
1895	Was-N	129	516	115	166	21	**22**	6	55	69	28	.322	.403	.483	.885	126	23	20	103	55	116	1.000	31			12	*O/S2	1.8
1896	Was-N	127	487	100	148	17	13	5	100	76	28	.304	.405	.423	.828	127	18	22	95	125	106	.997	49			7	*O	1.7
1897	Was-N	124	486	113	152	25	16	5	59	80		.313	.414	.461	.875	131	26	25	101	62	115	1.060	46			12	*O	2.3
1898	Was-N	132	515	88	156	28	11	3	60	64		.303	.383	.417	.801	130	23	21	102	72	94	.855	25			18	*O/S	2.8
1899	Cin-N	140	521	104	154	27	11	3	87	70		.296	.382	.407	.789	113	16	11	106	116	98	.880	38			15	*O	1.5
1900	NY-N	141	523	98	176	29	12	4	68	72		.337	.417	.461	.878	149	34	36	97	81	118	1.006	36			7	*O	2.8
1901	NY-N	125	502	89	145	29	6	1	56	45		.289	.347	.376	.724	123	8	14	91	86	70	.678	8			-16	*O	-1.4
1902	Bal-A	128	503	86	161	27	9	3	60	58		.320	.390	.427	.818	126	21	19	102	78	95	.863	22			6	*O	1.6
1903	Was-A	140	533	68	134	23	12	3	49	41		.251	.305	.356	.661	95	0	-4	105	78	66	.629	20			13	*O/3	0.1
1904	Was-A	48	178	15	49	8	4	0	14	24		.275	.361	.365	.727	144	8	9	93	69	27	.760	9			-1	O	0.6
	Bos-A	98	376	50	97	19	8	0	30	48		.258	.342	.351	.693	117	11	9	105	73	50	.681	10			0	O	0.3
	Yr	146	554	65	146	27	12	0	44	72		.264	.348	.356	.704	125	18	18	101	72	77	.706	19			-1		0.9
1905	Bos-A	121	418	54	103	16	6	4	47	67		.246	.351	.342	.693	122	13	13	100	115	56	.705	12			0	O	0.8
1906	Bos-A	60	228	15	48	9	2	0	23	18		.211	.268	.268	.536	71	-8	-7	98	132	19	.478	7			-0	O	-1.0
Total	13	1610	6158	1064	1803	299	149	44	779	783	76	.293	.374	.411	.785	122	202	200	100	87	1113	.842	334			66	*O/S23	13.9
■ **GEORGE SELKIRK**	Selkirk, George Alexander "Twinkletoes" b: 1/4/1899, Huntsville, Ont., Canada d: 1/19/87, Ft.Lauderdale, Fla BL/TR, 6'1", 182 lbs. Deb: 8/12/34																											
1934	NY-A	46	176	23	55	7	1	5	38	15	17	.313	.370	.449	.819	115	2	4	96	138	29	.787	1	1	-0	-1	O	0.2
1935	NY-A	128	491	64	153	29	12	11	94	44	36	.312	.372	.487	.859	130	14	19	93	120	87	.835	2	7	-4	2	*O	1.4
1936	NY-A	137	493	93	152	28	9	18	107	94	60	.308	.420	.511	.931	136	24	29	95	116	111	1.034	13	7	-0	1	*O	2.2
1937	NY-A	78	256	49	84	13	5	18	68	34	24	.328	.411	.629	1.040	155	22	21	102	108	68	1.178	8	2	1	1	O	1.9
1938	NY-A	99	335	58	85	12	5	10	62	68	52	.254	.384	.409	.793	94	1	-2	105	128	58	.854	9	4	0	-3	O	-0.3
1939	NY-A	128	418	103	128	17	4	21	101	103	49	.306	.452	.517	.969	161	35	41	91	125	110	1.138	12	5	1	-6	*O	2.9
1940	NY-A	118	379	68	102	17	5	19	71	84	43	.269	.406	.491	.896	133	20	21	99	108	83	.965	3	6	-3	-1	*O	0.8
1941	NY-A	70	164	30	36	5	0	6	25	28	30	.220	.340	.360	.700	87	-3	-3	98	115	22	.687	1	0	0	-4	O	-0.8
1942	NY-A	42	78	15	15	3	0	0	10	16	8	.192	.330	.231	.561	59	-4	-4	99	196	7	.531	0	0	0	-2	O	-0.6
Total	9	846	2790	503	810	131	41	108	576	486	319	.290	.400	.483	.883	129	111	126	97	121	575	.946	49	32	-5	-12	O	7.7
■ **RUBE SELLERS**	Sellers, Oliver b: 3/7/1881, Duquesne, Pa. d: 1/14/52, Pittsburgh, Pa. BR/TR, 5'10", 180 lbs. Deb: 8/12/10																											
1910	Bos-N	12	32	3	5	0	0	0	2	6	5	.156	.289	.156	.446	27	-3	-3	114	139	2	.444	1			-2	/O	-0.5
■ **FRANK SELLMAN**	Sellman, Frank C. (Also Played Under Name Of Frank C. Williams 1871-74) b: Baltimore, Md. Deb: 5/04/1871																											
1871	Kek-n	14	69	12	15							.217															3/CS	
1872	Oly-n	8	40	3	11							.275															/C3	
1873	Mar-n	1	5	1	1							.200															/P	
1874	Bal-n	12	58	9	16							.276															/SCO	
Total	4 n	35	172	25	43							.250															/SCO	
■ **CAREY SELPH**	Selph, Carey Isom b: 12/5/01, Donaldson, Ark. d: 2/24/76, Houston, Tex. BR/TR, 5'9.5", 175 lbs. Deb: 5/25/29																											
1929	StL-N	25	51	8	12	1	1	0	7	6	4	.235	.316	.294	.610	53	-4	-4	98	160	5	.564	1			-1	2	-0.3
1932	Chi-A	116	396	50	112	19	8	0	51	31	9	.283	.341	.371	.712	97	-9	-2	87	116	50	.652	7	6	-2	-9	32	-0.5
Total	2	141	447	58	124	20	9	0	58	37	13	.277	.338	.362	.701	91	-13	-5	89	121	55	.641	8	6		-10	/32	-0.8
■ **MIKE SEMBER**	Sember, Michael David b: 2/24/53, Hammond, Ind. BR/TR, 6', 185 lbs. Deb: 8/18/77																											
1977	Chi-N	3	4	0	1	0	0	0	0	0	2	.250	.250	.250	.500	30	-0	-0	114	0	0	.333	0	0	0	0	/2	0.0
1978	Chi-N	9	3	2	1	0	0	0	0	1	1	.333	.500	.333	.833	124	0	0	110	0	1	1.000	0	0	0	0	/3S	0.0
Total	2	12	7	2	2	0	0	0	0	1	3	.286	.375	.286	.661	74	-0	-0	112	0	1	.600	0	0	0	0	/3S2	0.0
■ **ANDY SEMINICK**	Seminick, Andrew Wasil b: 9/12/20, Pierce, W.Va. BR/TR, 5'11", 187 lbs. Deb: 9/14/43 C																											
1943	Phi-N	22	72	9	13	2	0	2	5	7	22	.181	.253	.292	.545	61	-4	-4	94	67	5	.452	0			2	C/O	0.0
1944	Phi-N	22	63	9	14	2	1	0	4	6	17	.222	.300	.286	.586	65	-3	-3	100	80	5	.529	2			1	C/O	-0.1
1945	Phi-N	80	188	18	45	7	2	6	26	18	38	.239	.313	.394	.706	99	-2	-1	96	98	23	.655	3			-1	C/3O	0.0
1946	Phi-N	124	406	55	107	15	5	12	52	39	86	.264	.334	.414	.748	118	5	7	95	95	52	.670	2			17	*C	2.9
1947	Phi-N	111	337	48	85	16	2	13	50	58	69	.252	.370	.427	.797	111	6	6	100	101	56	.808	4			-1	*C	0.8
1948	Phi-N	125	391	49	88	11	3	13	44	58	68	.225	.328	.368	.696	94	-6	-3	94	90	49	.665	4			9	*C	1.5
1949	Phi-N	109	334	52	81	11	2	24	68	69	74	.243	.380	.503	.883	134	17	17	101	107	67	.920	0			11	C	3.0
1950	Phi-N	130	393	55	113	15	3	24	68	68	50	.288	.400	.524	.925	145	25	26	97	94	84	.959	0			-2	*C	2.7
1951	Phi-N	101	291	42	66	8	1	11	37	63	67	.227	.370	.375	.744	104	2	4	97	101	46	.762	1	0	0	4	C	0.8
1952	Cin-N	108	336	38	86	16	1	14	50	35	65	.256	.330	.435	.764	111	4	4	100	104	48	.708	1	3	-2	2	C	0.7
1953	Cin-N	119	387	46	91	12	0	19	64	49	82	.235	.323	.413	.736	91	-6	-5	99	115	53	.688	2	2	-1	7	*C	0.7
1954	Cin-N	86	247	25	58	9	4	7	30	48	39	.235	.364	.389	.752	93	-0	-2	104	101	37	.741	0	0	0	0	C	0.0
1955	Cin-N	6	15	1	2	0	0	1	1	0	3	.133	.133	.333	.467	18	-2	-2	106	51	1	.385	0	0	0	0	/C	-0.1
	Phi-N	93	289	32	71	12	1	11	34	32	59	.246	.333	.408	.742	94	-2	-3	102	91	39	.689	1	2	-1	14	C	1.2
	Yr	99	304	33	73	12	1	12	35	32	62	.240	.325	.405	.729	90	-4	-4	102	89	39	.672	1	2	-1	14		1.1
1956	Phi-N	60	161	16	32	3	1	7	23	31	38	.199	.332	.360	.692	91	-3	-1	94	123	19	.679	3	0	1	1	C	0.2
1957	Phi-N	8	11	0	1	0	0	0	0	1	3	.091	.167	.091	.258	-29	-2	-2	98	0	0	.182	0	0	0	0	/C	-0.1
Total	15	1304	3921	495	953	139	26	164	556	582	780	.243	.347	.417	.764	107	30	40	98	99	584	.766	23	7		64	*C/O3	14.2
■ **SONNY SENERCHIA**	Senerchia, Emanuel Robert b: 4/6/31, Newark, N.J. BR/TR, 6'1", 195 lbs. Deb: 8/22/52																											
1952	Pit-N	29	100	5	22	5	0	3	11	4	21	.220	.250	.360	.610	67	-5	-5	100	95	8	.494	0	3	-2	-1	3	-0.6

YEAR	TM/L	G	AB	R	H	2B	3B	HR	RBI	BB	SO	AVG	OBP	SLG	PRO	/A	BR	/A	PF	CHI	RC	TA	SB	CS	SBR	FR	POS	TPR
■ **COUNT SENSENDERFER** Sensenderfer, John Phillips Jenkins b: 12/28/1847, Philadelphia, Pa. d: 5/3/03, Philadelphia, Pa. 5'9", 170 lbs. Deb: 5/20/1871																												
1871	Ath-n	25	127	38	43							.339															*O	
1872	Ath-n	1	5	2	2							.400															/O	
1873	Ath-n	19	88	12	22							.250															O	
1874	Ath-n	4	16	3	4							.250															/O	
Total	4 n	49	236	55	71							.301															/O	
■ **PAUL SENTELL** Sentell, Leopold Theodore b: 8/27/1879, New Orleans, La. d: 4/27/23, Cincinnati, Ohio TR, 5'9", 176 lbs. Deb: 4/12/06																												
1906	Phi-N	63	192	19	44	5	1	1	14	14		.229	.282	.281	.563	84	-5	-3	92	90	20	.561	15			-8	32/OS	-1.4
1907	Phi-N	3	3	0	0	0	0	0	0	1		.000	.250	.000	.250	-19	-0	-0	104	0	0	.333	0			0	/SO	0.0
Total	2	66	195	19	44	5	1	1	14	15		.226	.281	.277	.558	82	-5	-4	92	88	20	.556	15			-8	/32SO	-1.4
■ **TED SEPKOWSKI** Sepkowski, Theodore Walter (born Theodore Walter Sczepkowski) b: 11/9/23, Baltimore, Md. BL/TR, 5'11", 190 lbs. Deb: 9/09/42																												
1942	Cle-A	5	10	0	1	0	0	0	0	0	3	.100	.100	.100	.200	-48	-2	-2	92	0	0	.111	0	0	0	0	/2	-0.1
1946	Cle-A	2	8	2	4	1	0	0	1	0	0	.500	.500	.625	1.125	240	1	1	89	78	3	1.250	0	0	0	-0	/3	0.1
1947	Cle-A	10	8	0	1	1	0	0	0	1	1	.125	.222	.250	.472	32	-1	-1	96	0	1	.429	0	0	0	-0	/O	0.0
	NY-A	2	0	1	0	0	0	0	0	0	0	—	—	—	—	—	0	0	97	—	1	.000	0	1	-1	0	R	0.0
	Yr	12	8	1	1	1	0	0	0	1	1	.125	.222	.250	.472	32	-1	-1	96	0	0	.375	0	1	-1	-0		0.0
Total	3	19	26	3	6	2	0	0	1	1	4	.231	.259	.308	.567	63	-2	-1	92	23	4	.429	0	1	-1	-1	/32O	0.0
■ **BILL SERENA** Serena, William Robert b: 10/2/24, Alameda, Cal. BR/TR, 5'9.5", 175 lbs. Deb: 9/16/49																												
1949	Chi-N	12	37	3	8	3	0	1	7	7	9	.216	.341	.378	.719	98	-0	0	94	155	5	.700	0			-0	3	0.0
1950	Chi-N	127	435	56	104	20	4	17	61	65	75	.239	.339	.421	.760	94	-1	-4	105	103	64	.733	1			-6	*3	-0.9
1951	Chi-N	13	39	8	13	3	1	1	4	11	4	.333	.490	.538	1.029	181	5	5	97	66	11	1.179	0	2	-1	0	3	0.4
1952	Chi-N	122	390	49	107	21	5	15	61	39	83	.274	.345	.469	.814	120	12	10	103	104	62	.761	1	0	0	-7	32	0.7
1953	Chi-N	93	275	30	69	10	5	10	52	41	46	.251	.350	.433	.783	100	1	0	103	136	43	.749	0	0	0	-7	23	-0.4
1954	Chi-N	41	63	8	10	0	1	4	13	14	18	.159	.321	.381	.701	81	-2	-2	101	142	8	.709	0	0	0	0	3/2	-0.1
Total	6	408	1239	154	311	57	16	48	198	177	235	.251	.348	.439	.787	105	15	10	103	113	193	.783	2	2		-21	32	-0.3
■ **PAUL SERNA** Serna, Paul David b: 11/16/58, El Centro, Cal. BR/TR, 5'8", 170 lbs. Deb: 9/01/81																												
1981	Sea-A	30	94	11	24	2	0	4	9	3	11	.255	.293	.404	.697	99	-0	-0	100	70	11	.616	2	3	-1	1	S/2	0.1
1982	Sea-A	65	169	15	38	3	0	3	8	4	13	.225	.247	.296	.543	44	-12	-14	109	54	10	.393	0	5	-3	1	S23/D	-1.2
Total	2	95	263	26	62	5	0	7	17	7	24	.236	.264	.335	.598	62	-13	-14	106	60	21	.469	2	8	-4	2	/S23D	-1.1
■ **WALTER SESSI** Sessi, Walter Anthony "Watsie" b: 7/23/18, Finleyville, Pa. BL/TL, 6'3", 225 lbs. Deb: 9/18/41																												
1941	StL-N	5	13	2	0	0	0	0	0	1	2	.000	.071	.000	.071	-72	-3	-3	110	0	0	.071	0			-1	/O	-0.4
1946	StL-N	15	14	2	2	0	0	1	2	1	4	.143	.200	.357	.557	53	-1	-1	107	93	1	.500	0			0	H	0.0
Total	2	20	27	4	2	0	0	1	2	2	6	.074	.138	.185	.323	-8	-4	-4	108	48	1	.280	0			-1	/O	-0.4
■ **JOHN SEVCIK** Sevcik, John Joseph b: 7/11/42, Oak Park, Ill. BR/TR, 6'2", 205 lbs. Deb: 4/24/65																												
1965	Min-A	12	16	1	1	1	0	0	0	1	5	.063	.118	.125	.243	-31	-3	-3	101	0	0	.188	0	0	0	-1	C	-0.2
■ **HANK SEVEREID** Severeid, Henry Levai b: 6/1/1891, Story City, Iowa d: 12/17/68, San Antonio, Tex. BR/TR, 6', 175 lbs. Deb: 5/15/11																												
1911	Cin-N	37	56	5	17	6	1	0	10	3	6	.304	.350	.446	.796	133	1	2	92	135	8	.744	0			-0	C	0.3
1912	Cin-N	50	114	10	27	0	3	0	13	8	11	.237	.287	.289	.576	63	-7	-6	92	133	10	.471	0			-2	C/1O	-0.6
1913	Cin-N	8	6	0	0	0	0	0	0	1	1	.000	.143	.000	.143	-56	-1	-1	102	0	0	.167	0			-0	/CO	-0.1
1915	StL-A	80	203	12	45	6	1	1	22	16	25	.222	.279	.276	.554	69	-9	-8	96	127	16	.465	2	1	0	-1	C	-0.4
1916	StL-A	100	293	23	80	8	2	0	34	26	17	.273	.341	.314	.655	102	-1	1	95	132	33	.587	3			-5	C/13	0.0
1917	StL-A	143	501	45	133	23	4	1	57	28	20	.265	.306	.333	.639	100	-5	-2	95	123	51	.549	6			1	*C/1	1.1
1918	StL-A	51	133	8	34	4	0	0	11	18	4	.256	.357	.286	.643	95	-0	0	99	106	14	.636	4			0	C	0.5
1919	StL-A	112	351	16	87	12	2	0	36	21	13	.248	.298	.293	.591	68	-16	-14	97	127	30	.492	2			2	*C	-0.7
1920	StL-A	123	422	46	117	14	5	2	49	33	11	.277	.336	.348	.684	73	-11	-18	111	112	51	.614	5	3	-0	2	*C	-0.5
1921	StL-A	143	472	66	153	23	7	2	78	42	9	.324	.379	.415	.795	102	2	2	101	132	76	.763	7	2	1	1	*C	0.8
1922	StL-A	137	517	49	166	32	7	3	78	28	12	.321	.356	.427	.783	98	2	-2	106	124	77	.704	1	4	-2	6	*C	0.5
1923	StL-A	122	432	50	133	27	6	3	51	31	11	.308	.356	.419	.775	99	1	-1	104	94	66	.722	3	0	1	8	*C	1.5
1924	StL-A	137	432	37	133	23	2	4	48	36	15	.308	.362	.398	.761	90	-3	-7	107	86	62	.689	1	6	-3	0	*C	-0.2
1925	StL-A	34	109	15	40	9	0	1	21	11	2	.367	.425	.477	.902	119	5	4	108	128	22	.887	0	2	-1	1	C	0.5
	Was-A	50	110	11	39	8	1	0	14	13	6	.355	.423	.445	.868	123	4	4	98	96	21	.873	0	0	0	2	C	0.8
	Yr	84	219	26	79	17	1	1	35	24	8	.361	.424	.461	.885	122	9	8	102	110	43	.880	0	2	-1	3		1.3
1926	Was-A	22	34	2	7	1	0	0	4	3	2	.206	.270	.235	.506	33	-3	-3	98	170	2	.407	0	0	0	0	C	-0.1
	NY-A	41	127	13	34	8	1	0	13	13	4	.268	.336	.346	.682	79	-4	-4	99	100	15	.617	1	1	-0	1	C	0.0
	Yr	63	161	15	41	9	1	0	17	16	6	.255	.322	.323	.645	69	-7	-7	99	127	17	.570	1	1	-0	1		-0.1
Total	15	1390	4312	408	1245	204	42	17	539	331	169	.289	.342	.367	.709	92	-44	-54	101	116	556	.638	35	19		15	*C/1O3	3.4
■ **RICH SEVERSON** Severson, Richard Allen b: 1/18/45, Artesia, Cal. BR/TR, 6', 174 lbs. Deb: 4/10/70																												
1970	KC-A	77	240	22	60	11	1	1	22	16	33	.250	.300	.317	.616	71	-10	-9	98	113	23	.503	0	0	0	1	S2	-0.1
1971	KC-A	16	30	4	9	0	2	0	1	3	5	.300	.364	.433	.797	127	1	1	99	31	5	.762	0	0	0	0	/2S3	0.2
Total	2	93	270	26	69	11	3	1	23	19	38	.256	.307	.330	.637	77	-9	-8	98	103	28	.542	0	0	0	1	/S23	0.1
■ **GEORGE SEWARD** Seward, George E. b: St.Louis, Mo. 5'7.5", 145 lbs. Deb: 5/19/1875																												
1875	StL-n	24	95	12	20							.211															C/O2	
1876	NY-N	1	3	0	0	0	0	0	0	0	0	.000	.000	.000	.000	-99	-1	-1	87	0	0	.000				0	/2	0.0
1882	StL-a	38	144	23	31	1	1	0		12		.215	.276	.236	.512	74	-3	-3	100	0	10	.407				1	O/C	-0.2
Total	2	39	147	23	31	1	1	0	0	12	0	.211	.270	.231	.502	71	-4	-4	100	0	10	.397				1	/OC2	-0.2
■ **LUKE SEWELL** Sewell, James Luther b: 1/5/01, Titus, Ala. d: 5/14/87, Akron, Ohio BR/TR, 5'9", 160 lbs. Deb: 6/30/21 MC																												
1921	Cle-A	3	6	0	0	0	0	0	1	0	3	.000	.000	.000	.000	-99	-2	-2	99	0	0	.000	0	0	0	-0	/C	-0.1
1922	Cle-A	41	87	14	23	5	0	0	10	5	8	.264	.312	.322	.634	64	-4	-5	102	128	9	.538	1	1	-0	-4	C	-0.7
1923	Cle-A	10	10	2	2	0	1	0	1	1	0	.200	.273	.400	.673	75	-0	-0	101	85	1	.625	0	0	0	-0	/C	0.0
1924	Cle-A	63	165	27	48	9	1	0	17	22	13	.291	.387	.358	.745	96	-1	0	97	95	25	.735	1	0	0	0	C	0.4
1925	Cle-A	74	220	30	51	10	2	0	18	33	18	.232	.337	.295	.633	58	-12	-14	106	93	25	.624	6	1	1	0	C/O	-0.8
1926	Cle-A	126	433	41	103	16	4	0	46	36	27	.238	.302	.293	.596	56	-28	-28	100	126	42	.529	9	3	1	0	*C	-1.7
1927	Cle-A	128	470	52	138	27	6	0	53	20	23	.294	.328	.377	.705	85	-13	-11	97	102	56	.617	4	0	1	10	*C	0.4
1928	Cle-A	122	411	52	111	16	9	3	52	26	27	.270	.318	.375	.693	77	-12	-15	106	109	49	.612	3	4	-2	15	*C	0.6
1929	Cle-A	124	406	41	96	16	3	1	39	29	26	.236	.287	.298	.585	51	-30	-30	100	108	36	.494	6	6	-2	-3	*C	-2.2
1930	Cle-A	76	292	40	75	21	2	1	43	14	9	.257	.293	.353	.646	60	-17	-19	105	137	30	.562	5	2	0	5	C	-0.6
1931	Cle-A	108	375	45	103	30	4	1	53	36	17	.275	.341	.384	.725	85	-5	-9	106	119	51	.670	1	1	-0	-3	*C	-0.3
1932	Cle-A	87	300	36	76	20	2	2	52	38	24	.253	.337	.353	.691	73	-9	-13	108	155	37	.646	4	5	-2	0	C	-0.8
1933	Was-A	141	474	65	125	30	4	2	61	48	24	.264	.335	.357	.692	87	-11	-8	96	116	60	.647	7	2	1	-13	*C	-1.2
1934	Was-A	72	207	21	49	7	3	2	21	22	10	.237	.313	.329	.642	65	-11	-11	101	95	22	.572	0	1	-1	-1	C/O123	-0.8
1935	Chi-A	118	421	52	120	19	3	2	67	32	18	.285	.336	.359	.694	73	-13	-18	109	145	51	.614	3	2	-0	13	*C	-0.1
1936	Chi-A	128	451	59	113	20	5	5	73	54	16	.251	.332	.350	.682	69	-23	-22	99	137	56	.659	11	2	2	13	*C	0.3
1937	Chi-A	122	412	51	111	21	6	1	61	46	18	.269	.343	.357	.700	75	-14	-16	103	139	51	.644	4	5	-2	4	*C	-0.4
1938	Chi-A	65	211	23	45	4	1	0	27	20	20	.213	.284	.242	.526	34	-22	-21	98	179	16	.434	0	0	0	2	C	-1.5
1939	Cle-A	16	20	1	3	1	0	0	1	3	1	.150	.261	.200	.461	20	-2	-2	98	84	1	.412	0	0	0	0	C/1	0.0
1942	StL-A	6	12	1	1	0	0	0	0	1	5	.083	.154	.083	.237	-31	-2	-2	104	0	0	.167	0	0	0	0	/CM	-0.1
Total	20	1630	5383	653	1393	272	56	20	696	486	307	.259	.323	.341	.665	70	-231	-246	102	123	619	.600	65	35	-2	37	*C/O132	-9.6
■ **JOE SEWELL** Sewell, Joseph Wheeler b: 10/9/1898, Titus, Ala. BL/TR, 5'6.5", 155 lbs. Deb: 9/10/20 CH																												
1920	Cle-A	22	70	14	23	4	1	0	12	9	4	.329	.412	.414	.827	115	2	2	104	145	13	.851	1	0	0	2	S	0.6

YEAR	TM/L	G	AB	R	H	2B	3B	HR	RBI	BB	SO	AVG	OBP	SLG	PRO	/A	BR	/A	PF	CHI	RC	TA	SB	CS	SBR	FR	POS	TPR
1921	Cle-A	154	572	101	182	36	12	4	93	80	17	.318	.412	.444	.856	119	19	20	99	127	109	.889	7	6	-2	-3	*S	3.2
1922	Cle-A	153	558	80	167	28	7	2	83	73	20	.299	.386	.385	.771	100	4	3	102	**142**	86	.754	10	12	-4	-6	*S2	0.8
1923	Cle-A	153	553	98	195	41	10	3	109	98	12	.353	.456	.479	.935	145	43	42	101	144	128	1.041	9	6	-1	5	*S	5.7
1924	Cle-A	153	594	99	188	**45**	5	4	104	67	13	.316	.388	.429	.817	114	10	13	97	136	102	.801	3	2	-0	**21**	*S	4.6
1925	Cle-A	155	608	78	204	37	7	1	98	64	4	.336	.402	.424	.827	103	11	5	106	133	106	.812	7	6	-2	**16**	*S/2	**3.9**
1926	Cle-A	154	578	91	187	41	5	4	85	65	6	.324	.399	.433	.832	117	16	16	100	117	104	.854	17	7	1	3	*S	3.1
1927	Cle-A	153	569	83	180	48	5	1	92	51	7	.316	.382	.424	.805	112	8	11	97	**133**	91	.781	3	0	1	5	*S	2.7
1928	Cle-A	155	588	79	190	40	2	4	70	58	9	.323	.391	.418	.809	106	12	8	106	99	100	.797	7	1	2	**23**	*S3	4.3
1929	Cle-A	152	578	90	182	38	3	7	73	48	4	.315	.372	.427	.800	105	5	5	100	90	93	.761	6	6	-2	15	*3	2.5
1930	Cle-A	109	353	44	102	17	6	0	48	42	3	.289	.374	.371	.745	85	-4	-7	105	122	51	.706	1	4	-2	-1	3	-0.5
1931	NY-A	130	484	102	146	22	1	6	64	61	8	.302	.390	.388	.778	107	6	8	98	105	78	.764	1	1	-0	-5	*3/2	0.9
1932	NY-A	125	503	95	137	21	3	11	68	56	3	.272	.349	.392	.740	96	-6	-2	95	105	71	.696	0	2	-1	0	*3	0.4
1933	NY-A	135	524	87	143	18	1	2	54	71	4	.273	.361	.323	.683	90	-11	-4	91	109	65	.634	2	2	-1	4	*3	0.9
Total	14	1903	7132	1141	2226	436	68	49	1053	843	114	.312	.391	.413	.804	109	116	118	100	121	1199	.794	74	55	-11	80	*S3/2	33.1

■ **TOMMY SEWELL** Sewell, Thomas Wesley b: 4/16/06, Titus, Ala. d: 7/30/56, Montgomery, Ala. BL/TR, 5'7.5", 155 lbs. Deb: 6/21/27

YEAR	TM/L	G	AB	R	H	2B	3B	HR	RBI	BB	SO	AVG	OBP	SLG	PRO	/A	BR	/A	PF	CHI	RC	TA	SB	CS	SBR	FR	POS	TPR
1927	Chi-N	1	1	0	0	0	0	0	0	0	0	.000	.000	.000	.000	-99	-0	-0	100	0	0	.000	0			0	H	0.0

■ **JIMMY SEXTON** Sexton, Jimmy Dale b: 12/15/51, Mobile, Ala. BR/TR, 5'10", 175 lbs. Deb: 9/02/77

YEAR	TM/L	G	AB	R	H	2B	3B	HR	RBI	BB	SO	AVG	OBP	SLG	PRO	/A	BR	/A	PF	CHI	RC	TA	SB	CS	SBR	FR	POS	TPR
1977	Sea-A	14	37	5	8	1	1	1	3	2	6	.216	.256	.378	.635	73	-2	-1	96	70	3	.548	1	1	-0	0	S	0.0
1978	Hou-N	88	141	17	29	3	2	2	6	13	28	.206	.273	.298	.571	63	-8	-7	95	50	14	.623	16	2	4	-8	S/32	-0.6
1979	Hou-N	52	43	8	9	0	0	0	1	7	7	.209	.320	.209	.529	52	-3	-2	90	44	3	.459	1	3	-2	-0	S/32	-0.2
1981	Oak-A	7	3	3	0	0	0	0	0	0	2	.000	.000	.000	.000	-99	-1	-1	96	0	0	.667	2	0	1	0	/3D	0.0
1982	Oak-A	69	139	19	34	4	0	2	14	9	24	.245	.295	.317	.612	72	-6	-5	95	112	16	.667	16	0	5	-6	S/3D	-0.2
1983	StL-N	6	9	1	1	1	0	0	0	1	4	.111	.200	.222	.422	17	-1	-1	98	0	0	.375	0	0	0	0	/S3	0.0
Total	6	236	372	53	81	9	3	5	24	32	71	.218	.281	.298	.580	64	-20	-18	95	72	37	.606	36	6	7	-14	S/3D2	-1.0

■ **TOM SEXTON** Sexton, Thomas W. b: 3/14/1865, Rock Island, Ill. d: 2/8/34, Rock Island, Ill. Deb: 9/27/1884

YEAR	TM/L	G	AB	R	H	2B	3B	HR	RBI	BB	SO	AVG	OBP	SLG	PRO	/A	BR	/A	PF	CHI	RC	TA	SB	CS	SBR	FR	POS	TPR
1884	Mil-U	12	47	9	11	2	0	0		4		.234	.294	.277	.571	94	-0	-0	100	0	4	.472	0			0	S	0.0

■ **SOCKS SEYBOLD** Seybold, Ralph Orlando b: 11/23/1870, Washingtonville, O d: 12/22/21, Greensburg, Pa. BR/TR, 5'11", 175 lbs. Deb: 8/20/1899

YEAR	TM/L	G	AB	R	H	2B	3B	HR	RBI	BB	SO	AVG	OBP	SLG	PRO	/A	BR	/A	PF	CHI	RC	TA	SB	CS	SBR	FR	POS	TPR
1899	Cin-N	22	85	13	19	5	1	0	8	6		.224	.275	.306	.581	58	-5	-5	106	100	8	.515	2			0	O	-0.4
1901	Phi-A	114	449	74	150	24	14	8	90	40		.334	.389	.503	.892	148	28	28	100	120	96	.940	15			1	*O1	2.5
1902	Phi-A	137	522	91	165	27	12	**16**	97	43		.316	.368	.506	.874	131	28	22	108	109	102	.877	6			4	*O	1.6
1903	Phi-A	137	522	76	156	**45**	8	8	84	38		.299	.346	.462	.808	138	26	24	104	121	87	.776	5			-5	*O1	1.1
1904	Phi-A	143	510	56	149	26	9	3	64	42		.292	.346	.396	.742	135	21	20	102	120	76	.709	12			-5	*O1	0.8
1905	Phi-A	132	488	64	132	37	4	6	59	42		.270	.328	.400	.728	121	17	12	109	105	67	.680	5			-0	*O	0.6
1906	Phi-A	116	411	41	130	23	2	5	59	30		.316	.363	.418	.781	157	21	24	94	117	67	.751	9			-13	*O	0.7
1907	Phi-A	147	564	58	153	29	4	5	92	40		.271	.320	.363	.683	113	12	8	106	144	70	.620	10			1	*O	0.1
1908	Phi-A	48	130	5	28	2	0	0	3	12		.215	.282	.231	.512	64	-4	-5	108	38	9	.431	2			2	O	-0.4
Total	9	996	3681	478	1082	218	54	51	556	293		.294	.346	.424	.770	129	145	128	104	116	583	.739	66			-16	O/1	6.6

■ **CY SEYMOUR** Seymour, James Bentley b: 12/9/1872, Albany, N.Y. d: 9/20/19, New York, N.Y. BL/TL, 6', 200 lbs. Deb: 4/22/1896

YEAR	TM/L	G	AB	R	H	2B	3B	HR	RBI	BB	SO	AVG	OBP	SLG	PRO	/A	BR	/A	PF	CHI	RC	TA	SB	CS	SBR	FR	POS	TPR
1896	NY-N	12	32	2	7	0	0	0	0	0	7	.219	.219	.219	.438	17	-4	-4	99	0	2	.280	0			0	P/O	0.0
1897	NY-N	44	137	13	33	5	1	2	14	4		.241	.262	.336	.598	60	-8	-8	98	79	13	.510	3			9	P/O	0.0
1898	NY-N	80	297	41	82	5	2	4	23	9		.276	.300	.347	.646	92	-6	-3	95	62	34	.563	8			9	PO/2	0.0
1899	NY-N	50	159	25	52	3	2	2	27	4		.327	.344	.409	.752	111	1	2	97	117	24	.664	2			5	P/O13	0.0
1900	NY-N	23	40	9	12	0	0	0	2	3		.300	.349	.300	.649	84	-1	-1	97	52	4	.536	0			0	P/O1	0.0
1901	Bal-A	134	547	84	166	19	8	1	77	28		.303	.337	.373	.710	93	-1	-7	107	113	84	.709	38			15	*O/1	0.6
1902	Bal-A	72	280	38	75	8	8	3	41	18		.268	.312	.386	.698	92	-3	-3	102	122	38	.673	12			2	O	-0.5
	Cin-N	62	244	27	83	8	2	2	37	12		.340	.371	.414	.785	132	12	9	110	127	41	.752	8			-1	O/P3	0.4
1903	Cin-N	135	558	85	191	25	15	7	72	33		.342	.379	.478	.858	134	31	24	109	71	113	.886	25			12	*O	2.6
1904	Cin-N	131	531	71	166	26	13	5	58	29		.313	.348	.439	.787	126	25	17	114	76	87	.748	11			3	*O	1.5
1905	Cin-N	149	581	95	**219**	**40**	**21**	8	**121**	51		**.377**	**.427**	**.559**	**.987**	**190**	**66**	**64**	103	116	**152**	1.097	21			6	*O	6.0
1906	Cin-N	79	307	35	79	7	2	4	38	24		.257	.311	.332	.643	89	1	-4	115	107	35	.592	9			-21	O	-3.0
	NY-N	72	269	35	86	12	3	4	42	18		.320	.362	.431	.794	150	14	14	100	115	51	.842	20			2	O	1.6
	Yr	151	576	70	165	19	5	8	80	42		.286	.335	.378	.713	116	15	10	108	112	85	.703	29			-19		-1.4
1907	NY-N	131	473	46	139	25	8	3	75	36		.294	.344	.400	.743	128	18	15	105	152	74	.737	21			-5	*O	0.6
1908	NY-N	156	587	60	157	23	2	5	92	30		.267	.303	.339	.642	103	3	1	104	**175**	63	.574	18			21	*O	2.3
1909	NY-N	80	280	37	87	12	5	1	30	25		.311	.369	.400	.769	134	13	11	105	97	45	.788	14			2	O	1.2
1910	NY-N	79	287	32	76	9	4	1	40	23	18	.265	.324	.334	.658	97	-3	-2	95	144	34	.621	10			-3	O	-0.7
1913	Bos-N	39	73	2	13	2	0	0	10	7	7	.178	.259	.205	.465	36	-6	-6	95	242	4	.417	2			1	O	-0.4
Total	16	1528	5682	737	1723	229	96	52	799	354	32	.303	.345	.405	.749	118	152	119	105	114	899	.728	222			54	*OP/132	12.2

■ **TILLIE SHAFER** Shafer, Arthur Joseph b: 3/22/1889, Los Angeles, Cal. d: 1/10/62, Los Angeles, Cal. BB/TR, 5'10", 165 lbs. Deb: 09

YEAR	TM/L	G	AB	R	H	2B	3B	HR	RBI	BB	SO	AVG	OBP	SLG	PRO	/A	BR	/A	PF	CHI	RC	TA	SB	CS	SBR	FR	POS	TPR
1909	NY-N	38	84	11	15	2	1	0	7	14		.179	.296	.226	.522	60	-3	-4	105	134	7	.565	6			0	32/O	-0.3
1910	NY-N	29	21	5	4	1	0	0	1	0	6	.190	.190	.238	.429	26	-2	-2	95	70	1	.294	0			0	/32S	-0.1
1912	NY-N	78	163	48	47	4	1	0	23	30	19	.288	.408	.325	.733	98	3	2	104	146	31	.931	22			1	S2/3	0.5
1913	NY-N	138	508	74	146	17	12	5	52	61	55	.287	.369	.398	.767	116	14	12	103	92	82	.829	32			-2	32SO	0.9
Total	4	283	776	138	212	24	14	5	83	105	80	.273	.366	.360	.725	104	11	8	103	108	121	.801	60			-1	3/2SO	1.0

■ **RALPH SHAFER** Shafer, Ralph Newton b: 3/17/1894, Cincinnati, Ohio d: 2/5/50, Akron, Ohio 5'11", Deb: 7/25/14

YEAR	TM/L	G	AB	R	H	2B	3B	HR	RBI	BB	SO	AVG	OBP	SLG	PRO	/A	BR	/A	PF	CHI	RC	TA	SB	CS	SBR	FR	POS	TPR
1914	Pit-N	1	0	0	0	0	0	0	0	0	0	—	—	—	—	—	0	0	92	—	—	—	0			0	H	0.0

■ **SHAFFER** Shaffer Deb:9/15/1875

YEAR	TM/L	G	AB	R	H	2B	3B	HR	RBI	BB	SO	AVG	OBP	SLG	PRO	/A	BR	/A	PF	CHI	RC	TA	SB	CS	SBR	FR	POS	TPR
1875	Atl-n	1	4	0	0							.000															/O	

■ **FRANK SHAFFER** Shaffer, Frank Deb: 4/24/1884

YEAR	TM/L	G	AB	R	H	2B	3B	HR	RBI	BB	SO	AVG	OBP	SLG	PRO	/A	BR	/A	PF	CHI	RC	TA	SB	CS	SBR	FR	POS	TPR
1884	Alt-U	19	74	11	21	2	0	0		3		.284	.312	.311	.622	110	1	1	101	0	7	.491	0			0	O/C3	0.1
	KC-U	44	164	18	28	3	2	0		15		.171	.240	.213	.454	63	-7	-4	87	0	9	.368	0			-1	O/C2S3	-0.4
	Bal-U	3	13	1	1	0	0	0		0		.077	.077	.077	.154	-43	-2	-2	110	0	0	.083	0			0	/O	-0.1
	Yr	66	251	30	50	5	2	0		18		.199	.253	.235	.488	71	-8	-5	92	0	15	.383	0			-1		-0.4
Total	1	66	251	30	50	5	2	0		18		.199	.253	.235	.488	71	-8	-5	92	0	16	.383	0			-1	/OC3S2	-0.4

■ **ORATOR SHAFFER** Shaffer, George b: 1852, Philadelphia, Pa. BL/TR, 5'9", 165 lbs. Deb: 5/23/1874

YEAR	TM/L	G	AB	R	H	2B	3B	HR	RBI	BB	SO	AVG	OBP	SLG	PRO	/A	BR	/A	PF	CHI	RC	TA	SB	CS	SBR	FR	POS	TPR
1874	Har-n	9	35	6	7							.200															/O	
	Mut-n	1	6	1	1							.167															/O	
	Yr	10	41	7	8							.195																
1875	Phi-n	18	79	11	19							.241															O/31	
1877	Lou-N	61	260	38	74	9	5	3	34	9	17	.285	.309	.392	.701	90	6	-7	132	110	32	.597				13	*O/1	0.4
1878	Ind-N	63	266	48	90	19	6	0	30	13	20	.338	.369	.455	.824	**196**	20	**25**	87	74	46	.761				5	*O	2.3
1879	Chi-N	73	316	53	96	13	0	0	35	6	28	.304	.317	.345	.662	113	6	4	105	108	35	.523				19	*O/3	1.8
1880	Cle-N	83	338	62	90	14	9	0	21	17	36	.266	.301	.361	.662	125	8	9	99	56	38	.560				15	*O	2.0
1881	Cle-N	85	343	48	88	13	6	1	34	23	20	.257	.303	.338	.641	105	1	3	96	105	36	.545				-1	*O	0.0
1882	Cle-N	84	313	37	67	14	2	3	28	27	27	.214	.276	.300	.577	95	-4	1	90	97	27	.492				-12	*O	-1.1
1883	Buf-N	95	401	67	117	11	3	0	41	27	39	.292	.336	.334	.671	105	3	3	100	112	46	.567				18	*O	2.0
1884	StL-U	106	467	130	168	**40**	10	2		30		.360	.398	.501	.899	195	49	47	104	0	96	.883	0			-2	*O/21	3.7
1885	StL-N	69	257	30	50	11	2	0	18	19	31	.195	.250	.253	.503	68	-10	-7	92	102	17	.406				9	O	0.0
	Phi-a	2	9	1	2	0	1	0		1		.222	.300	.444	.744	131	0	0	103	0	1	.714				0	/O	0.0

YEAR	TM/L	G	AB	R	H	2B	3B	HR	RBI	BB	SO	AVG	OBP	SLG	PRO	/A	BR	/A	PF	CHI	RC	TA	SB	CS	SBR	FR	POS	TPR
1886	Phi-a	21	82	15	22	3	3	0		8		.268	.333	.378	.711	125	2	2	100	0	12	.700	3			0	O	0.2
1890	Phi-a	100	390	55	110	15	5	1		47		.282	.367	.354	.720	118	9	10	97	0	63	.782	29			1	*O/1	0.6
Total	2 n	28	120	18	27							.225															*O/1	
Total	11	842	3442	584	974	162	52	10	241	227	218	.283	.328	.369	.697	123	89	89	100	69	448	.622	32			66	O/123	11.9
■ **TAYLOR SHAFFER** Shaffer, Taylor b: 7/1870, Philadelphia, Pa. Deb: 4/17/1890																												
1890	Phi-a	69	261	28	45	3	4	0		28		.172	.258	.215	.472	42	-19	-17	97	0	20	.486	19			8	2	-0.5
■ **ART SHAMSKY** Shamsky, Arthur Louis b: 10/14/41, St.Louis, Mo. BL/TL, 6'1", 168 lbs. Deb: 4/17/65																												
1965	Cin-N	64	96	13	25	4	3	2	10	10	29	.260	.330	.427	.757	108	1	1	104	88	15	.732	1	0	0	0	O/1	0.1
1966	Cin-N	96	234	41	54	5	0	21	47	32	45	.231	.323	.521	.845	114	9	5	114	107	39	.824	0	2	-1	-5	O	-0.2
1967	Cin-N	76	147	6	29	3	1	3	13	15	34	.197	.276	.293	.569	58	-7	-9	109	104	12	.492	0	1	-1	-2	O	-1.3
1968	NY-N	116	345	30	82	14	4	12	48	21	58	.238	.295	.406	.701	106	3	2	102	115	41	.628	1	0	0	-1	O1	-0.3
1969	NY-N	100	303	42	91	9	3	14	47	36	32	.300	.380	.488	.869	141	17	17	100	99	57	.858	1	2	-1	-4	O/1	0.7
1970	NY-N	122	403	48	118	19	2	11	49	49	33	.293	.374	.432	.805	111	9	7	104	92	64	.764	1	1	-0	1	O1	0.0
1971	NY-N	68	135	13	25	6	2	5	18	21	18	.185	.299	.370	.670	92	-2	-1	96	113	14	.624	1	1	-0	2	O/1	-0.1
1972	Chi-N	15	16	1	2	0	0	0	1	3	3	.125	.263	.125	.388	12	-2	-2	114	205	1	.357	0	0	0	0	/1	-0.1
	Oak-A	8	7	0	0	0	0	0	0	1	2	.000	.125	.000	.125	-63	-1	-1	97	0	0	.143	0	0	0	0	H	-0.1
Total	8	665	1686	194	426	60	15	68	233	188	254	.253	.333	.427	.760	108	27	19	104	103	243	.732	5	7	-3	-9	O/1	-1.3
■ **WALLY SHANER** Shaner, Walter Dedaker "Skinny" b: 5/24/1900, Lynchburg, Va. BR/TR, 6'2", 195 lbs. Deb: 5/04/23																												
1923	Cle-A	3	4	1	1	0	0	0	0	1	1	.250	.400	.250	.650	73	-0	-0	101	0	0	.667	0	0	0	-1	/O3	0.0
1926	Bos-A	69	191	20	54	12	2	0	21	17	13	.283	.348	.366	.714	85	-4	-4	101	102	25	.657	1	0	0	-1	O	-0.7
1927	Bos-A	122	406	54	111	33	6	3	49	21	35	.273	.311	.406	.717	90	-11	-8	95	94	49	.671	11	0	3	-0	*O/1	-1.4
1929	Cin-N	13	28	5	9	0	0	1	4	4	5	.321	.406	.429	.835	108	0	0	99	91	5	.895	1			0	/1O	0.0
Total	4	207	629	80	175	45	8	4	74	43	54	.278	.327	.394	.722	89	-14	-11	97	95	80	.676	13	<u>0</u>		-1	O/13	-2.1
■ **HOWIE SHANKS** Shanks, Howard Samuel "Hank" b: 7/21/1890, Chicago, Ill. d: 7/30/41, Monaca, Pa. BR/TR, 5'11", 170 lbs. Deb: 5/09/12 C																												
1912	Was-A	115	399	52	92	14	7	1	48	40		.231	.305	.308	.614	76	-13	-12	99	130	45	.609	21			0	*O	-1.8
1913	Was-A	109	390	38	99	11	5	1	37	15	40	.254	.287	.315	.602	72	-13	-16	106	106	39	.567	24			3	*O	-1.9
1914	Was-A	143	500	44	112	22	10	4	64	29	51	.224	.269	.332	.601	80	-14	-15	101	138	47	.532	18	16	-4	6	*O	-2.3
1915	Was-A	141	492	52	123	19	8	0	47	30	42	.250	.297	.321	.618	84	-11	-11	101	103	48	.530	12	14	-5	5	O32	-1.3
1916	Was-A	140	471	51	119	15	7	1	48	41	34	.253	.317	.321	.637	91	-5	-5	100	114	54	.599	23	12	-0	10	O3/S1	0.2
1917	Was-A	126	430	45	87	15	5	0	28	33	37	.202	.269	.260	.529	67	-20	-16	92	92	35	.484	15			9	SO/1	-0.5
1918	Was-A	120	436	42	112	19	4	1	56	31	21	.257	.312	.326	.638	89	-5	-7	104	144	50	.617	23			-3	O2/3	-1.1
1919	Was-A	135	491	33	122	8	7	1	54	25	48	.248	.289	.299	.588	67	-23	-22	98	133	47	.509	13			-18	S2/O	-3.1
1920	Was-A	128	444	56	119	16	7	4	37	29	43	.268	.316	.363	.678	84	-14	-11	95	75	51	.613	11	6	-0	-3	3O1/2S	-1.2
1921	Was-A	154	562	81	170	25	**19**	6	69	57	38	.302	.370	.447	.816	109	6	7	99	90	93	.801	11	10	-3	5	*3/2	2.0
1922	Was-A	84	272	35	77	10	9	1	32	25	25	.283	.352	.397	.749	103	-2	1	92	103	41	.733	6	0	2	6	3O	1.2
1923	Bos-A	131	464	38	118	19	5	3	57	19	37	.254	.285	.336	.621	62	-26	-27	102	120	44	.517	6	6	-2	-9	32/OS	-2.6
1924	Bos-A	72	193	22	50	16	3	0	25	21	12	.259	.332	.373	.705	79	-6	-7	104	115	25	.657	1	0	0	1	S3/O12	0.0
1925	NY-A	66	155	15	40	3	1	1	18	20	15	.258	.343	.310	.653	69	-7	-6	96	118	18	.600	1	0	0	-3	32/O	-0.6
Total	14	1664	5699	604	1440	212	97	24	620	415	<u>443</u>	.253	.308	.337	.644	82	-154	-148	99	112	637	.591	185	<u>64</u>		10	O3S2/1	-13.0
■ **DOC SHANLEY** Shanley, Harry Root b: 1890, Granbury, Tex. d: 12/13/34, St.Petersburg, Fla BR/TR, 6', 174 lbs. Deb: 9/15/12																												
1912	StL-A	5	8	1	0	0	0	0	1	2		.000	.200	.000	.200	-42	-1	-1	99	0	0	.250	0			0	/S	0.0
■ **JIM SHANLEY** Shanley, James H. b: New York d: 11/4/04, Brooklyn, N.Y. Deb: 5/03/1876																												
1876	NY-N	2	8	0	1	0	0	0	0	0	0	.125	.125	.125	.250	-19	-1	-1	87	0	0	.143				0	/O	0.0
■ **WARREN SHANNABROOK** Shannabrook, Warren H. b: 11/30/1880, Massillon, Ohio d: 3/10/64, N.Canton, Ohio BR/TR, 6', 170 lbs. Deb: 8/13/06																												
1906	Was-A	1	2	0	0	0	0	0	0	0		.000	.000	.000	.000	-99	-0	-0	91	0	0	.000	0			0	/3	0.0
■ **DAN SHANNON** Shannon, Daniel W. b: 3/23/1865, Bridgeport, Conn. d: 10/25/13, Bridgeport, Conn. 175 lbs. Deb: 4/17/1889 M																												
1889	Lou-a	121	498	90	128	22	12	4	48	42	52	.257	.315	.373	.688	102	-3	1	96	61	68	.686	26			2	*2M	0.4
1890	Phi-P	19	75	15	18	5	1	1	16	4	12	.240	.278	.373	.652	73	-3	-3	102	144	9	.632	4			-7	2	-0.7
	NY-P	83	324	59	70	7	8	3	44	25	34	.216	.274	.315	.589	54	-20	-25	109	111	35	.587	21			-2	2/S	-1.7
	Yr	102	399	74	88	12	9	4	60	29	46	.221	.275	.326	.601	57	-23	-28	108	118	44	.595	25			-9		-2.4
1891	Was-a	19	67	7	9	2	0	0	3	6	9	.134	.205	.164	.370	8	-8	-7	95	80	3	.345	3			0	S/2M	-0.5
Total	3	242	964	171	225	36	21	8	111	77	107	.233	.291	.339	.630	76	-33	-35	101	85	115	.621	54			-7	2/S	-2.5
■ **FRANK SHANNON** Shannon, John Francis b: 12/3/1873, San Francisco, Cal. d: 2/27/34, Boston, Mass. 5'3", 155 lbs. Deb: 10/01/1892																												
1892	Was-N	1	4	0	1	0	0	0	2	0	2	.250	.250	.250	.500	50	-0	-0	105	626	0	.333	0			0	/S	0.0
1896	Lou-N	31	115	14	18	1	1	1	15	13	15	.157	.248	.209	.457	23	-13	-12	98	170	7	.423	3			0	S/3	-1.0
Total	2	32	119	14	19	1	1	1	17	13	17	.160	.248	.210	.458	24	-13	-13	98	183	7	.420	3			0	/S3	-1.0
■ **JOE SHANNON** Shannon, Joseph Aloysius b: 2/11/1897, Jersey City, N.J. d: 7/28/55, Jersey City, N.J. BR/TR, 5'11", 170 lbs. Deb: 7/07/15																												
1915	Bos-N	5	10	3	2	0	0	0	1	0	3	.200	.200	.200	.400	22	-1	-1	98	191	1	.250	0			-1	/O2	-0.2
■ **RED SHANNON** Shannon, Maurice Joseph b: 2/11/1897, Jersey City, N.J. d: 4/12/70, Jersey City, N.J. BB/TR, 5'11", 170 lbs. Deb: 10/07/15																												
1915	Bos-N	1	3	0	0	0	0	0	0	0	0	.000	.000	.000	.000	-99	-1	-1	98	0	0	.000	0			0	/2	0.0
1917	Phi-A	11	35	8	10	0	0	0	7	6	9	.286	.390	.286	.676	114	1	1	94	256	4	.720	2			0	S	0.2
1918	Phi-A	72	225	23	54	6	5	0	16	42	52	.240	.367	.311	.678	100	3	2	104	85	28	.702	5			4	S2	1.1
1919	Phi-A	39	155	14	42	7	2	0	14	12	28	.271	.331	.342	.673	84	-2	-3	106	84	18	.628	4			-1	2	0.0
	Bos-A	80	290	36	75	11	7	0	17	17	42	.259	.313	.345	.658	93	-6	-3	91	63	32	.605	7			-3	2	0.1
	Yr	119	445	50	117	18	9	0	31	29	70	.263	.320	.344	.663	90	-9	-6	96	71	50	.613	11			-4		0.1
1920	Was-A	63	222	30	64	8	7	0	30	22	32	.288	.352	.387	.740	101	-1	0	95	125	30	.675	2	5	-2	-5	S23	-0.2
	Phi-A	24	88	4	15	1	1	0	3	4	12	.170	.207	.205	.411	10	-12	-11	94	60	4	.311	1	1	-0	0	S	-0.8
	Yr	87	310	34	79	9	8	0	33	26	44	.255	.313	.335	.648	76	-13	-10	95	108	32	.561	3	6	-3	-5		-1.0
1921	Phi-A	1	1	0	0	0	0	0	0	0	0	.000	.000	.000	.000	-97	-0	-0	103	0	0	.000	0	0	0	0	H	0.0
1926	Chi-N	19	51	9	17	5	0	0	4	6	3	.333	.414	.431	.845	120	2	2	106	63	9	.853	0			1	S	0.4
Total	7	310	1070	124	277	38	22	0	91	109	178	.259	.334	.336	.670	90	-16	-13	98	90	125	.627	21	<u>6</u>		-4	2S/3	0.8
■ **MIKE SHANNON** Shannon, Thomas Michael "Moonman" b: 7/5/39, St.Louis, Mo. BR/TR, 6'3", 195 lbs. Deb: 9/11/62																												
1962	StL-N	10	15	3	2	0	0	0	0	1	3	.133	.188	.133	.321	-11	-2	-3	109	0	0	.231	0	0	0	-1	/O	-0.3
1963	StL-N	32	26	3	8	0	0	1	2	0	6	.308	.333	.423	.756	108	0	0	107	60	3	.600	0	1	-1	-5	O	-0.7
1964	StL-N	88	253	30	66	8	2	9	43	19	54	.261	.313	.415	.728	92	1	-3	112	134	32	.660	4	0	1	-6	O	-1.0
1965	StL-N	124	244	32	54	17	3	3	25	28	46	.221	.307	.352	.659	80	-5	-7	107	109	26	.593	2	1	0	0	*O/C	-0.9
1966	StL-N	137	459	61	132	20	6	16	64	37	106	.288	.341	.462	.803	121	12	12	100	106	70	.751	8	4	0	8	*O/C	1.7
1967	StL-N	130	482	53	118	18	3	12	77	37	89	.245	.304	.369	.673	91	-6	-6	101	**152**	52	.582	2	4	-2	-9	*3/O	-2.5
1968	StL-N	156	576	62	153	29	2	15	79	37	114	.266	.312	.401	.713	119	8	11	95	123	70	.622	1	2	-1	-7	*3	0.3
1969	StL-N	150	551	51	140	15	5	12	55	49	87	.254	.316	.365	.681	91	-8	-7	100	95	63	.594	1	4	-2	-19	*3	-2.8
1970	StL-N	55	174	18	37	9	2	0	22	16	20	.213	.279	.287	.566	49	-12	-13	106	171	14	.475	1	1	-0	-6	3	-2.0
Total	9	882	2780	313	710	116	23	68	367	224	525	.255	.313	.387	.700	97	-11	-16	101	121	331	.636	19	17	-5	-44	3O/C	-8.2
■ **OWEN SHANNON** Shannon, Owen Dennis Ignatius b: 12/22/1885, Omaha, Neb. d: 4/10/18, Omaha, Neb. BR/TR, Deb: 03																												
1903	StL-A	9	28	1	6	2	0	0	3	1		.214	.241	.286	.527	62	-1	-1	95	135	2	.409	0			0	/C1	0.0
1907	Was-A	4	7	0	1	0	0	0	0	0		.143	.143	.143	.286	-9	-1	-1	90	0	0	.167	0			-0	/C	0.0
Total	2	13	35	1	7	2	0	0	3	1		.200	.222	.257	.479	49	-2	-2	94	109	2	.357	0			-0	/C1	0.0

YEAR	TM/L	G	AB	R	H	2B	3B	HR	RBI	BB	SO	AVG	OBP	SLG	PRO	/A	BR	/A	PF	CHI	RC	TA	SB	CS	SBR	FR	POS	TPR
■ **WALLY SHANNON**	Shannon, Walter Charles b: 1/23/34, Cleveland, Ohio BL/TR, 6', 178 lbs. Deb: 7/09/59																											
1959	StL-N	47	95	5	27	5	0	0	5	0	12	.284	.292	.337	.629	64	-5	-5	105	63	9	.485	0	0	0	0	S2	-0.2
1960	StL-N	18	23	2	4	0	0	0	1	3	6	.174	.296	.174	.470	30	-2	-2	108	101	1	.421	0	0	0	0	2/S	0.0
Total	2	65	118	7	31	5	0	0	6	3	18	.263	.293	.305	.598	57	-7	-7	105	72	11	.471	0	0	0	1	/2S	-0.2
■ **SPIKE SHANNON**	Shannon, William Porter b: 2/7/1878, Pittsburgh, Pa. d: 5/16/40, Minneapolis, Minn. BB/TR, 5'11", 180 lbs. Deb: 4/15/04																											
1904	StL-N	134	500	84	140	10	3	1	26	50		.280	.345	.318	.663	109	6	7	99	57	68	.675	34			12	*O	1.4
1905	StL-N	140	544	73	146	16	3	0	41	47		.268	.327	.309	.635	101	-4	2	91	75	65	.608	27			0	*O	-0.8
1906	StL-N	80	302	36	78	4	0	0	25	36		.258	.337	.272	.609	91	-1	-1	101	98	34	.594	15			-6	O	-0.9
	NY-N	76	287	42	73	5	1	0	25	34		.254	.333	.279	.612	93	-1	-1	100	98	33	.617	18			-7	O	-1.0
	Yr	156	589	78	151	9	1	0	50	70		.256	.335	.275	.610	92	-2	-2	100	99	67	.605	33			-13		-1.9
1907	NY-N	155	585	**104**	155	12	5	1	33	82		.265	.355	.308	.663	105	10	7	105	59	78	.686	33			-0	*O	0.1
1908	NY-N	77	268	34	60	2	1	1	21	28		.224	.297	.250	.547	74	-6	-7	104	122	23	.519	13			-9	O	-1.9
	Pit-N	32	127	10	25	0	2	0	12	9		.197	.250	.228	.478	58	-6	-6	95	140	8	.422	5			1	O	-0.5
	Yr	109	395	44	85	2	3	1	33	37		.215	.282	.243	.525	69	-12	-13	102	128	31	.487	18			-8		-2.4
Total	5	694	2613	383	677	49	15	3	183	286		.259	.332	.293	.625	96	-2	0	99	81	309	.618	145			-10	O	-3.6
■ **BILLY SHANTZ**	Shantz, Wilmer Ebert b: 7/31/27, Pottstown, Pa. BR/TR, 6'1", 160 lbs. Deb: 4/13/54																											
1954	Phi-A	51	164	13	42	9	3	1	17	17	23	.256	.326	.366	.692	91	-3	-2	98	102	19	.606	0	0	0	2	C	0.2
1955	KC-A	79	217	18	56	4	1	1	12	11	14	.258	.294	.300	.593	59	-12	-13	101	66	18	.455	0	0	0	3	C	-0.6
1960	NY-A	1	0	0	0	0	0	0	0	0	0	—	—	—	—	—	0	0	94	—	—	—	0	0	0	0	/C	0.0
Total	3	131	381	31	98	13	4	2	29	28	37	.257	.308	.328	.636	72	-15	-15	100	82	56	.541	0	0	0	5	C	-0.4
■ **RALPH SHARMAN**	Sharman, Ralph Edward "Bally" b: 4/11/1895, Cleveland, Ohio d: 5/24/18, Camp Sheridan, Ala BR/TR, 5'11", 176 lbs. Deb: 9/10/17																											
1917	Phi-A	13	37	2	11	2	1	0	2	3	2	.297	.366	.405	.771	145	2	2	94	48	6	.769	1			-1	O	0.0
■ **DICK SHARON**	Sharon, Richard Louis b: 4/15/50, San Mateo, Cal. BR/TR, 6'2", 195 lbs. Deb: 5/13/73																											
1973	Det-A	91	178	20	43	9	0	7	16	10	31	.242	.282	.410	.692	92	-3	-3	101	67	20	.607	2	0	1	-10	O	-1.5
1974	Det-A	60	129	12	28	4	0	2	10	14	29	.217	.294	.295	.588	66	-5	-6	106	89	11	.519	4	4	-1	-6	O	-1.4
1975	SD-N	91	160	14	31	7	0	4	20	26	35	.194	.306	.313	.619	72	-6	-6	100	125	15	.555	0	2	-1	-8	O	-1.7
Total	3	242	467	46	102	20	0	13	46	50	95	.218	.294	.345	.639	78	-13	-14	102	94	46	.576	6	6	-2	-24	O	-4.6
■ **BILL SHARP**	Sharp, William Howard b: 1/18/50, Lima, Ohio BL/TL, 5'10", 178 lbs. Deb: 5/26/73																											
1973	Chi-A	77	196	23	54	8	3	4	22	19	28	.276	.349	.408	.757	110	3	3	102	94	28	.707	2	3	-1	-2	O/D	-0.2
1974	Chi-A	100	320	45	81	13	2	4	24	25	37	.253	.311	.344	.655	87	-5	-6	102	77	33	.546	0	3	-2	0	O	-1.0
1975	Chi-A	18	35	1	7	0	0	0	4	2	3	.200	.243	.200	.443	26	-3	-3	103	220	2	.321	0	0	0	-3	O	-0.7
	Mil-A	125	373	37	95	27	3	1	34	19	26	.255	.293	.351	.644	81	-10	-10	100	97	36	.521	0	3	-2	-3	*O	-1.8
	Yr	143	408	38	102	27	3	1	38	21	29	.250	.288	.338	.627	76	-13	-14	100	114	38	.503	0	3	-2	-6		-2.5
1976	Mil-A	78	180	16	44	4	0	0	11	10	15	.244	.288	.267	.555	64	-8	-8	99	88	13	.423	1	3	-2	0	O/D	-1.0
Total	4	398	1104	122	281	52	8	9	95	75	109	.255	.306	.341	.647	84	-23	-24	101	93	113	.550	3	12	-6	-8	O/D	-4.7
■ **BUD SHARPE**	Sharpe, Bayard Heston b: 8/6/1881, West Chester, Pa. d: 5/31/16, Haddock, Ga. BL/TR, Deb: 4/14/05																											
1905	Bos-N	46	170	8	31	3	2	0	11	7		.182	.215	.224	.438	33	-14	-13	97	107	8	.324	0			0	O/C1	-1.6
1910	Bos-N	115	439	30	105	14	3	0	29	14	31	.239	.264	.285	.549	53	-24	-31	114	86	34	.431	4			6	*1	-2.6
	Pit-N	4	16	2	3	0	1	0	1	0	2	.188	.188	.313	.500	41	-1	-1	112	74	1	.385	0			0	/1	-0.1
	Yr	119	455	32	108	14	4	0	30	14	33	.237	.262	.286	.547	52	-25	-32	114	86	35	.429	4			6		-2.7
Total	2	165	625	40	139	17	6	0	41	21	33	.222	.249	.269	.518	48	-39	-46	109	91	44	.399	4			6	1/OC	-4.3
■ **MIKE SHARPERSON**	Sharperson, Michael Tyrone b: 10/4/61, Orangeburg, S.C. BR/TR, 6'1", 175 lbs. Deb: 4/06/87																											
1987	Tor-A	32	96	4	20	4	1	0	9	7	15	.208	.269	.271	.540	44	-8	-8	101	138	7	.456	2	1	0	-3	2	-0.7
	LA-N	10	33	7	9	2	0	0	1	4	5	.273	.351	.333	.685	90	-1	-0	92	36	4	.600	0	0	0	0	/32	0.0
1988	LA-N	46	59	8	16	1	0	0	4	1	12	.271	.295	.288	.583	64	-2	-3	106	94	5	.422	0	1	-1	-1	2/3S	-0.3
Total	2	88	188	19	45	7	1	0	14	12	32	.239	.292	.287	.579	58	-11	-11	101	106	16	.479	2	2	-1	-3	/23S	-1.0
■ **JACK SHARROTT**	Sharrott, John Henry b: 8/13/1869, Bangor, Me. d: 12/31/27, Los Angeles, Cal. BR/TR, 5'9", 165 lbs. Deb: 4/22/1890																											
1890	NY-N	32	109	16	22	3	2	0	14	0	14	.202	.202	.266	.468	39	-9	-8	95	146	7	.402	6			0	P/O	0.0
1891	NY-N	10	30	5	10	2	0	1	7	1	2	.333	.355	.500	.855	160	2	2	94	113	7	.950	3			0	P	0.0
1892	NY-N	4	8	1	1	0	0	0	0	0	1	.125	.125	.125	.250	-24	-1	-1	98	0	0	.143	0			0	/OP	0.0
1893	Phi-N	50	152	25	38	4	3	1	22	8	14	.250	.287	.336	.623	67	-8	-8	100	111	17	.570	6			-5	OP	-1.1
Total	4	96	299	47	71	9	5	2	43	9	31	.237	.260	.321	.581	64	-16	-15	97	121	31	.526	15			-5	/PO	-1.1
■ **SHAG SHAUGHNESSY**	Shaughnessy, Francis Joseph b: 4/8/1883, Amboy, Ill. d: 5/15/69, Montreal, Que., Can BR/TR, 6'1.5", 185 lbs. Deb: 4/17/05 C																											
1905	Was-A	1	3	0	0	0	0	0	0	0		.000	.000	.000	.000	-96	-1	-1	104	0	0	.000	0			0	/O	0.0
1908	Phi-A	8	29	2	9	0	0	0	1	2		.310	.355	.310	.665	111	1	0	108	44	4	.700	3			-0	/O	0.0
Total	2	9	32	2	9	0	0	0	1	2		.281	.324	.281	.605	92	-0	-0	107	40	4	.609	3			0	/O	0.0
■ **AL SHAW**	Shaw, Albert Simpson b: 3/1/1881, Toledo, Ill. d: 12/30/74, Danville, Ill. BL/TR, 5'8.5", 165 lbs. Deb: 9/28/07																											
1907	StL-N	9	25	2	7	0	0	0	1	3		.280	.357	.280	.637	106	0	0	96	54	3	.611	1			-1	/O	0.0
1908	StL-N	107	367	40	97	13	4	1	19	25		.264	.311	.330	.641	114	3	5	94	60	39	.574	9			-14	O/S3	-1.1
1909	StL-N	114	331	45	82	12	7	2	34	55		.248	.355	.344	.699	123	9	10	96	103	45	.739	15			-3	O	0.4
1914	Bro-F	112	376	81	122	27	7	5	49	44	59	.324	.395	.473	.869	147	24	23	101	93	83	.969	24			-3	*O	1.6
1915	KC-F	132	448	67	126	22	10	6	67	46	45	.281	.348	.415	.763	130	14	16	97	121	73	.767	15			-14	*O	-0.4
Total	5	474	1547	235	434	74	28	14	170	173	104	.281	.353	.392	.745	130	49	54	97	95	243	.757	64			-35	O/S3	0.5
■ **AL SHAW**	Shaw, Alfred "Shoddy" b: 10/3/1874, Burslem, England d: 3/25/58, Uhrichsville, Ohio BR/TR, 5'8", 170 lbs. Deb: 6/08/01																											
1901	Det-A	55	171	20	46	7	0	1	23	10		.269	.309	.327	.637	71	-5	-7	110	123	18	.544	2			-3	C/13S	-0.6
1907	Bos-A	76	198	10	38	1	3	0	1	18		.192	.259	.227	.487	56	-9	-9	101	8	13	.419	4			8	C/1	0.6
1908	Chi-A	32	49	0	4	1	0	0	2	2		.082	.118	.102	.220	-29	-7	-6	94	150	1	.156	0			-3	C	-0.7
1909	Bos-N	18	41	1	4	0	0	0	0	5		.098	.213	.098	.310	-3	-5	-5	96	0	1	.270	0			1	C	-0.2
Total	4	181	459	31	92	9	3	1	26	35		.200	.259	.240	.498	51	-25	-27	103	64	33	.414	6			3	C/13S	-0.9
■ **BEN SHAW**	Shaw, Benajmin Nathaniel b: 6/18/1893, La Center, Ky. d: 3/16/59, Aurora, Ohio BR/TR, 5'11.5", 190 lbs. Deb: 4/11/17																											
1917	Pit-N	2	2	0	0	0	0	0	0	0	0	.000	.000	.000	.000	-99	-0	-0	100	0	0	.000	0			0	H	0.0
1918	Pit-N	21	36	5	7	1	0	0	2	2	2	.194	.275	.222	.497	49	-2	-2	106	95	2	.414	0			0	/1C	-0.1
Total	2	23	38	5	7	1	0	0	2	2	2	.184	.262	.211	.472	42	-2	-3	106	90	2	.387	0			0	/1C	-0.1
■ **HUNKY SHAW**	Shaw, Royal N b: 9/29/1884, Yakima, Wash. d: 7/3/69, Yakima, Wash. BB/TR, 5'8", 165 lbs. Deb: 5/16/08																											
1908	Pit-N	1	1	0	0	0	0	0	0	0		.000	.000	.000	.000	-99	-0	-0	95	0	0	.000	0			0	H	0.0
■ **MARTY SHAY**	Shay, Arthur Joseph b: 4/25/1896, Boston, Mass. d: 2/20/51, Worcester, Mass. BR/TR, 5'7.5", 148 lbs. Deb: 9/16/16																											
1916	Chi-N	2	7	0	2	0	0	0	0	0	1	.286	.286	.286	.571	65	-0	-0	117	0	1	.400	0			-0	/S	0.0
1924	Bos-N	19	68	4	16	3	1	0	2	5	5	.235	.297	.309	.606	67	-4	-3	94	35	6	.547	2	1	0	-2	2/S	-0.5
Total	2	21	75	4	18	3	1	0	2	5	6	.240	.296	.307	.603	66	-4	-3	96	32	7	.534	2	1		-2	/2S	-0.5
■ **DANNY SHAY**	Shay, Daniel C. b: 11/8/1876, Springfield, Ohio d: 12/1/27, Kansas City, Mo. TR , 5'10", Deb: 4/30/01																											
1901	Cle-A	19	75	4	17	2	2	0	10	2		.227	.247	.307	.553	57	-5	-4	95	145	6	.431	0			-3	S	-0.5
1904	StL-N	99	340	45	87	11	1	1	18	39		.256	.332	.303	.635	100	1	1	99	66	47	.704	36			-7	S/2	-0.5
1905	StL-N	78	281	30	67	12	1	0	28	35		.238	.323	.288	.611	93	-4	-1	91	115	30	.593	11			-15	2S	-1.3
1907	NY-N	35	79	10	15	1	1	1	6	12		.190	.297	.266	.563	74	-2	-2	105	95	8	.594	5			-3	2/SO	-0.4
Total	4	231	775	89	186	26	5	2	62	88		.240	.317	.294	.612	90	-9	-6	96	94	92	.625	52			-28	S/2O	-2.7

YEAR	TM/L	G	AB	R	H	2B	3B	HR	RBI	BB	SO	AVG	OBP	SLG	PRO	/A	BR	/A	PF	CHI	RC	TA	SB	CS	SBR	FR	POS	TPR
■ GERRY SHEA	Shea, Gerald J. b: 7/26/1881, St.Louis, Mo. d: 5/3/64, Berkeley, Mo. TR , 5'7", 160 lbs. Deb: 10/01/05																											
1905	StL-N	2	6	0	2	0	0	0	0	0		.333	.333	.333	.667	111	-0	0	91	0	1	.500	0			0	/C	0.0
■ NAP SHEA	Shea, John Edward "Napoleon" b: 5/23/1874, Ware, Mass. d: 7/8/68, Bloomfield Hills, Mich. BR/TR, 5'5", 155 lbs. Deb: 9/11/02																											
1902	Phi-N	3	8	1	1	0	0	0	0	1		.125	.222	.125	.347	8	-1	-1	105	0	0	.286	0			0	/C	0.0
■ MERV SHEA	Shea, Mervyn David John b: 9/5/1900, San Francisco, Cal d: 1/27/53, Sacramento, Cal. BR/TR, 5'11", 175 lbs. Deb: 4/23/27 C																											
1927	Det-A	34	85	5	15	6	3	0	9	7	15	.176	.239	.318	.557	40	-8	-9	108	111	6	.486	0	0	0	0	C	-0.6
1928	Det-A	39	85	8	20	2	3	0	9	9	11	.235	.316	.329	.645	70	-4	-4	99	110	9	.597	2	2	-1	-0	C	-0.1
1929	Det-A	50	162	23	47	6	0	3	24	19	18	.290	.365	.383	.747	95	-1	-1	97	116	23	.716	2	1	0	1	C	0.4
1933	Bos-A	16	56	1	8	3	0	0	8	4	7	.143	.200	.196	.396	5	-8	-8	101	243	2	.313	0	0	0	1	C	-0.5
	StL-A	94	279	26	73	11	1	1	27	43	26	.262	.360	.319	.679	71	-6	-12	115	98	35	.650	2	0	1	9	C	0.2
	Yr	110	335	27	81	14	1	1	35	47	33	.242	.335	.299	.634	61	-14	-20	113	121	37	.587	2	0	1	11		-0.3
1934	Chi-A	62	176	8	28	3	0	0	5	24	19	.159	.260	.176	.436	14	-22	-22	99	54	9	.369	0	1	-1	5	C	-1.0
1935	Chi-A	46	122	8	28	2	0	0	13	30	9	.230	.382	.246	.627	60	-5	-6	109	147	14	.638	0	0	0	5	C	0.0
1936	Chi-A	14	24	3	3	0	0	0	2	6	5	.125	.300	.125	.425	9	-3	-3	99	216	1	.429	0	0	0	1	C	0.0
1937	Chi-A	25	71	7	15	1	0	0	5	15	10	.211	.349	.225	.574	47	-5	-5	103	107	7	.571	1	0	0	1	C	-0.1
1938	Bro-N	48	120	14	22	5	0	0	12	28	20	.183	.338	.225	.563	60	-6	-5	96	161	11	.560	1			-2	C	-0.4
1939	Det-A	4	2	0	0	0	0	0	0	0	1	.000	.000	.000	.000	-90	-1	-1	111	0	0	.000	0	0	0	0	/C	0.0
1944	Phi-N	7	15	2	4	0	0	1	1	4	4	.267	.421	.467	.888	149	1	1	100	36	3	.917	0			0	/C	0.2
Total	11	439	1197	105	263	39	7	5	115	189	145	.220	.327	.277	.603	57	-67	-75	104	116	122	.563	8	4		22	C	-1.9
■ DANNY SHEAFFER	Sheaffer, Danny Todd b: 8/2/61, Jacksonville, Fla. BR/TR, 6' ", 185 lbs. Deb: 4/09/87																											
1987	Bos-A	25	66	5	8	1	0	1	5	0	14	.121	.121	.182	.303	-21	-11	-11	99	133	1	.200	0	0	0	0	C	-0.8
■ DAVE SHEAN	Shean, David William b: 7/9/1883, Arlington, Mass. d: 5/22/63, Boston, Mass. BR/TR, 5'11", 175 lbs. Deb: 9/10/06																											
1906	Phi-A	22	75	7	16	3	2	0	3	5		.213	.262	.307	.569	85	-2	-1	94	48	8	.576	6			-2	2	-0.3
1908	Phi-N	14	48	4	7	2	0	0	2	1		.146	.163	.188	.351	13	-5	-5	100	87	1	.268	1			-0	S	-0.5
1909	Phi-N	36	112	14	26	2	2	0	4	14		.232	.323	.286	.609	85	-1	-2	106	46	11	.581	3			1	21/OS	0.0
	Bos-N	75	267	32	66	11	4	1	29	17		.247	.297	.330	.627	100	-2	-1	96	123	29	.602	14			0	2	-0.1
	Yr	111	379	46	92	13	6	1	33	31		.243	.305	.317	.622	95	-3	-3	100	98	40	.596	17			1		-0.1
1910	Bos-N	150	543	52	130	12	7	3	36	42	45	.239	.294	.304	.598	65	-19	-28	114	76	53	.540	16			**42**	*2	1.9
1911	Chi-N	54	145	17	28	4	0	0	15	8	15	.193	.240	.221	.461	30	-14	-13	97	158	9	.385	4			3	2S/3	-1.0
1912	Bos-N	4	10	1	3	0	0	0	0	1	2	.300	.417	.300	.717	91	0	0	107	0	1	.714	0			-0	/S	0.0
1917	Cin-N	131	442	36	93	9	5	2	35	22	39	.210	.249	.267	.516	63	-22	-18	92	111	31	.433	10			13	*2	0.2
1918	Bos-A	115	425	58	112	16	3	0	34	40	25	.264	.331	.315	.646	100	-2	0	95	82	51	.601	11			-8	*2	-0.1
1919	Bos-A	29	100	4	14	0	0	0	8	5	7	.140	.189	.140	.329	-8	-14	-13	91	211	3	.244	1			-1	2	-1.2
Total	9	630	2167	225	495	59	23	6	166	155	133	.228	.283	.285	.568	70	-80	-81	100	99	197	.508	66			47	2/S103	-1.1
■ RAY SHEARER	Shearer, Ray Solomon b: 9/19/29, Jacobus, Pa. d: 4/1982, Manchester, Pa. BR/TR, 6', 200 lbs. Deb: 9/18/57																											
1957	Mil-N	2	2	1	1	0	0	0	0	1	1	.500	.667	.500	1.167	243	1	1	90	0	1	2.000	0	0	0	-0	/O	0.0
■ JOHN SHEARON	Shearon, John M. b: 1870, Pittsburgh, Pa. d: 2/1/23, Bradford, Pa. Deb: 7/28/1891																											
1891	Cle-N	30	124	10	30	1	1	0	13	1	15	.242	.248	.266	.514	49	-8	-9	105	117	10	.426	6			0	O/P	-0.7
1896	Cle-N	16	64	6	11	0	1	0	3	4	6	.172	.221	.203	.424	12	-8	-9	110	68	4	.377	3			0	O	-0.7
Total	2	46	188	16	41	1	2	0	16	5	21	.218	.238	.245	.483	35	-16	-18	107	100	14	.408	9			0	/OP	-1.4
■ JIMMY SHECKARD	Sheckard, Samuel James Tilden b: 11/23/1878, Upper Chanceford, Pa. d: 1/15/47, Lancaster, Pa. BL/TR, 5'9", 175 lbs. Deb: 9/14/1897																											
1897	Bro-N	13	49	12	14	3	2	3	14	6		.286	.364	.612	.976	155	4	3	102	111	13	1.171	5			0	S/O	0.3
1898	Bro-N	105	408	51	113	17	9	4	64	37		.277	.349	.392	.741	122	8	11	95	108	60	.722	8			-5	*O/3	0.0
1899	Bal-N	147	536	104	158	18	10	3	75	56		.295	.380	.382	.763	104	11	5	108	114	110	.942	**77**			21	*O/1	1.4
1900	Bro-N	85	273	74	82	19	10	1	39	42		.300	.394	.454	.848	127	14	11	108	98	62	1.026	30			-0	O	0.3
1901	Bro-N	133	554	116	196	29	**19**	11	104	47		.354	.404	**.534**	.939	164	50	46	106	93	137	1.056	35			3	*O3	3.5
1902	Bal-A	4	15	3	4	1	0	0	0	1		.267	.313	.333	.646	79	-0	-0	102	0	2	.727	2			0	/O	0.0
	Bro-N	123	486	86	129	20	10	4	37	57		.265	.343	.372	.715	129	14	17	95	57	72	.731	23			9	*O	1.7
1903	Bro-N	139	515	99	171	29	9	**9**	75	75		.332	.417	.476	.893	155	40	**39**	101	85	**133**	1.125	**67**			**30**	*O	**5.7**
1904	Bro-N	143	507	70	121	23	6	1	46	56		.239	.314	.314	.628	101	-1	2	95	110	58	.611	21			4	*O/2	0.0
1905	Bro-N	130	480	58	140	20	11	3	41	61		.292	.372	.398	.769	137	20	23	96	63	81	.809	23			25	*O	3.9
1906	Chi-N	149	549	90	144	27	10	1	45	67		.262	.343	.353	.696	112	13	9	107	80	79	.719	30			-10	*O	-0.3
1907	Chi-N	143	484	76	129	23	1	1	36	76		.267	.366	.324	.690	112	14	10	106	90	71	.744	31			-19	*O	-1.5
1908	Chi-N	115	403	54	93	18	3	2	22	62		.231	.333	.305	.639	100	5	3	106	63	46	.655	18			-28	*O	-3.0
1909	Chi-N	148	525	81	134	29	5	1	43	72		.255	.346	.335	.681	112	10	9	101	84	64	.675	15			1	*O	0.5
1910	Chi-N	144	507	82	130	27	6	5	51	83	53	.256	.366	.363	.729	112	11	10	101	86	78	.780	22			13	*O	1.8
1911	Chi-N	156	539	**121**	149	26	11	4	50	**147**	58	.276	**.434**	.388	.822	135	32	35	97	68	106	1.003	32			18	*O	**4.7**
1912	Chi-N	146	523	85	128	22	10	3	47	**122**	81	.245	.392	.342	.735	98	8	5	104	74	76	.813	15			13	*O	1.2
1913	StL-N	52	136	18	27	2	1	0	17	41	25	.199	.388	.228	.616	84	-1	1	93	199	14	.716	5			-2	O	-0.2
	Cin-N	47	116	16	22	1	3	0	7	27	16	.190	.343	.250	.593	70	-3	-3	102	88	12	.660	6			-4	O	-0.7
	Yr	99	252	34	49	3	4	0	24	68	41	.194	.368	.238	.606	77	-4	-3	97	148	26	.690	11			-6		-0.9
Total	17	2122	7605	1296	2084	354	136	56	813	1135	233	.274	.371	.378	.750	121	246	233	101	87	1274	.819	465			67	*O/3S21	19.3
■ DAN SHEEHAN	Sheehan, Daniel b: 12/18/1872, Cleveland, Ohio 5'6", 142 lbs. Deb: 8/02/00																											
1900	NY-N	1	2	0	0	0	0	0	0	0		.000	.000	.000	.000	-99	-1	-1	97	0	0	.000	0			0	/S	0.0
■ JIM SHEEHAN	Sheehan, James Thomas "Big Jim" b: 6/3/13, New Haven, Conn. BR/TR, 6'2", 196 lbs. Deb: 9/26/36																											
1936	NY-N	1	4	0	0	0	0	0	0	0	2	.000	.000	.000	.000	-99	-1	-1	100	0	0	.000	0			0	/C	0.0
■ JACK SHEEHAN	Sheehan, John Thomas b: 4/15/1893, Chicago, Ill. d: 5/29/87, W.Palm Beach, Fla. BB/TR, 5'8.5", 165 lbs. Deb: 9/11/20																											
1920	Bro-N	3	5	0	2	1	0	0	0	1	0	.400	.500	.600	1.100	193	1	1	111	0	2	1.333	0	0	0	0	/S3	0.1
1921	Bro-N	5	12	2	0	0	0	0	0	0	1	.000	.000	.000	.000	-96	-3	-3	105	0	0	.000	0	0	0	0	/2S3	-0.2
Total	2	8	17	2	2	1	0	0	0	1	1	.118	.167	.176	.343	-6	-3	-3	107	0	2	.267	0	0	0	0	/S23	-0.1
■ TOMMY SHEEHAN	Sheehan, Thomas H. b: 11/6/1877, Sacramento, Cal. d: 5/22/59, Panama City, Pan. TR , 5'8", 160 lbs. Deb: 4/12/06																											
1906	Pit-N	95	315	28	76	6	3	1	34	18		.241	.282	.289	.571	77	-8	-9	104	135	30	.510	13			-3	3	-1.6
1907	Pit-N	75	226	23	62	2	3	0	25	23		.274	.341	.310	.651	101	2	1	105	135	28	.628	10			-2	3S	0.0
1908	Bro-N	146	468	45	100	18	2	0	29	53		.214	.294	.261	.554	83	-9	-7	95	93	37	.500	9			-6	*3	-1.0
Total	3	316	1009	96	238	26	8	1	88	94		.236	.301	.280	.581	86	-15	-15	100	115	95	.530	32			-11	3/S	-2.6
■ BIFF SHEEHAN	Sheehan, Timothy James b: 2/13/1868, Hartford, Conn. d: 10/21/23, Hartford, Conn. 5'9", 165 lbs. Deb: 7/22/1895																											
1895	StL-N	52	180	24	57	3	6	1	18	20	6	.317	.394	.417	.811	112	4	4	100	66	33	.854	7			-1	O1	0.0
1896	StL-N	6	19	0	3	0	0	0	1	4	0	.158	.304	.158	.462	27	-2	-2	95	98	1	.438	0			0	/O	0.0
Total	2	58	199	24	60	3	6	1	19	24	6	.302	.385	.392	.777	104	2	2	99	69	34	.806	7			-1	/O1	0.0
■ EARL SHEELY	Sheely, Earl Homer "Whitey" b: 2/12/1893, Bushnell, Ill. d: 9/16/52, Seattle, Wash. BR/TR, 6'3.5", 195 lbs. Deb: 4/14/21																											
1921	Chi-A	154	563	68	171	25	6	11	95	57	34	.304	.375	.428	.803	105	4	5	99	121	90	.771	4	9	-4	6	*1	0.5
1922	Chi-A	149	526	72	167	37	4	6	80	60	27	.317	.393	.437	.830	115	14	13	101	118	92	.819	4	6	-2	2	*1	0.0
1923	Chi-A	156	570	74	169	25	3	4	88	79	30	.296	.387	.372	.759	102	3	5	98	142	87	.741	5	5	-2	-1	*1	-0.4
1924	Chi-A	146	535	84	171	34	3	3	103	95	28	.320	.426	.411	.837	120	18	21	97	143	102	.886	7	4	-0	-11	*1	0.2
1925	Chi-A	153	600	93	189	43	3	9	111	68	23	.315	.389	.442	.831	116	10	14	96	122	106	.824	3	3	-1	-5	*1	0.4
1926	Chi-A	145	525	77	157	40	2	6	89	75	13	.299	.394	.417	.811	122	11	18	92	135	92	.824	3	1	0	0	*1	1.1
1927	Chi-A	45	129	11	27	3	0	2	16	20	5	.209	.320	.279	.599	55	-8	-8	102	127	13	.569	1	0	0	-1	1	-0.9
1929	Pit-N	139	485	63	142	22	4	6	88	75	24	.293	.392	.392	.784	92	-1	-4	103	**148**	77	.802	6			-2	*1	-1.1

YEAR	TM/L	G	AB	R	H	2B	3B	HR	RBI	BB	SO	AVG	OBP	SLG	PRO	/A	BR	/A	PF	CHI	RC	TA	SB	CS	SBR	FR	POS	TPR
1931	Bos-N	147	538	30	147	15	2	1	77	34	21	.273	.319	.314	.633	71	-21	-21	99	**163**	56	.524	0			-2	*1	-3.4
Total	9	1234	4471	572	1340	244	27	48	747	563	205	.300	.383	.399	.782	104	30	42	98	136	716	.765	33	28		-14	*1	-3.6
■ **BUD SHEELY** Sheely, Hollis Kimball b: 11/26/20, Spokane, Wash. d: 10/17/85, Sacramento, Cal. BL/TR, 6'1", 200 lbs. Deb: 7/26/51																												
1951	Chi-A	34	89	2	16	2	0	0	7	6	7	.180	.240	.202	.442	21	-10	-10	97	139	5	.333	0	0	0	-1	C	-0.8
1952	Chi-A	36	75	1	18	2	0	0	3	12	7	.240	.352	.267	.619	74	-2	-2	100	56	8	.550	0	1	-1	-3	C	-0.3
1953	Chi-A	31	46	4	10	1	0	0	2	9	8	.217	.345	.239	.585	57	-2	-3	106	67	5	.541	0	0	0	-1	C	-0.2
Total	3	101	210	7	44	5	0	0	12	27	22	.210	.305	.233	.539	49	-14	-14	100	92	17	.464	0	1	-1	-5	/C	-1.3
■ **CHUCK SHEERIN** Sheerin, Charles Joseph b: 4/17/09, Brooklyn, N.Y. d: 9/27/86, Valley Stream, N.Y. BR/TR, 5'11.5", 198 lbs. Deb: 4/21/36																												
1936	Phi-N	39	72	4	19	4	0	0	4	7	18	.264	.329	.319	.649	70	-2	-3	108	62	8	.545	0			0	23/S	0.0
■ **LARRY SHEETS** Sheets, Larry Kent b: 12/6/59, Staunton, Va. BL/TR, 6'3", 217 lbs. Deb: 9/18/84																												
1984	Bal-A	8	16	3	7	1	0	1	2	1	3	.438	.471	.688	1.158	229	2	3	94	57	5	1.333	0	0	0	0	/O	0.2
1985	Bal-A	113	328	43	86	8	0	17	50	28	52	.262	.324	.442	.766	109	3	3	99	101	43	.678	0	1	-1	-3	D/O1	0.0
1986	Bal-A	112	338	42	92	17	1	18	60	21	56	.272	.319	.488	.807	118	7	7	99	109	47	.725	2	0	1	-1	DO/C13	0.5
1987	Bal-A	135	469	74	148	23	0	31	94	31	67	.316	.362	.563	.925	144	26	28	98	105	90	.885	1	1	-0	-5	*O/1D	1.7
1988	Bal-A	136	452	38	104	19	1	10	47	42	72	.230	.304	.343	.647	85	-11	-9	95	103	45	.559	1	6	-3	-1	OD/1	-1.4
Total	5	504	1603	200	437	68	2	77	253	123	250	.273	.329	.462	.791	116	27	32	97	104	230	.743	4	8	-4	-10	OD/1C3	1.0
■ **GARY SHEFFIELD** Sheffield, Gary Antonian b: 11/18/68, Tampa, Fla. BR/TR, 5'11", 190 lbs. Deb: 9/03/88																												
1988	Mil-A	24	80	12	19	1	0	4	12	7	7	.237	.299	.400	.699	91	-1	-1	103	108	8	.627	3	1	0	-2	S	-0.1
■ **JOHN SHELBY** Shelby, John T. b: 2/23/58, Lexington, Ky. BB/TR, 6'1", 175 lbs. Deb: 9/15/81																												
1981	Bal-A	7	2	2	0	0	0	0	0	0	1	.000	.000	.000	.000	-99	-1	-1	99	0	0	1.000	2	0	1	-2	/O	-0.1
1982	Bal-A	26	35	8	11	3	0	1	2	0	5	.314	.314	.486	.800	116	1	1	100	40	5	.680	0	1	-1	-6	O	-0.6
1983	Bal-A	126	325	52	84	15	2	5	27	18	64	.258	.297	.363	.660	81	-9	-9	100	79	37	.616	15	2	3	-7	*O/D	-1.3
1984	Bal-A	128	383	44	80	12	5	6	30	20	71	.209	.248	.313	.561	57	-24	-22	94	87	31	.489	12	4	1	1	*O	-2.3
1985	Bal-A	69	205	28	58	6	2	7	27	7	44	.283	.307	.434	.741	101	-1	-0	99	97	26	.664	5	1	1	5	O/2D	0.4
1986	Bal-A	135	404	54	92	14	4	11	49	18	75	.228	.264	.364	.628	70	-18	-17	99	108	39	.576	18	6	2	-5	*O/D	-2.3
1987	Bal-A	21	32	4	6	0	0	1	3	1	13	.188	.212	.281	.493	31	-3	-3	98	100	2	.370	0	1	-1	-3	O/D	-0.6
	LA-N	120	476	61	132	26	0	21	69	31	97	.277	.323	.464	.787	115	2	7	92	93	70	.749	16	6	1	5	*O	0.8
1988	LA-N	140	494	65	130	23	6	10	64	44	128	.263	.323	.395	.718	99	3	-1	106	116	62	.668	16	5	2	-1	*O	-0.3
Total	8	772	2356	318	593	99	19	62	271	139	498	.252	.294	.389	.683	87	-49	-44	98	97	272	.634	84	26	10	-13	O/D2	-6.3
■ **BOB SHELDON** Sheldon, Bob Mitchell b: 11/27/50, Montebello, Cal. BL/TR, 6', 170 lbs. Deb: 4/10/74																												
1974	Mil-A	10	17	4	2	1	1	0	0	4	2	.118	.286	.294	.580	65	-1	-1	102	0	2	.563	0	1	-1	0	/2D	0.0
1975	Mil-A	53	181	17	52	3	3	0	14	13	14	.287	.342	.337	.679	92	-2	-2	100	90	20	.555	0	3	-2	3	2/D	0.1
1977	Mil-A	31	64	9	13	4	1	0	3	6	9	.203	.271	.297	.568	58	-4	-4	95	63	6	.490	0	0	0	0	D/2	-0.2
Total	3	94	262	30	67	8	5	0	17	23	25	.256	.321	.324	.645	82	-6	-6	99	77	27	.553	0	4	-2	3	/2D	-0.1
■ **HUGH SHELLEY** Shelley, Hubert Leneirre b: 10/26/10, Rogers, Tex. d: 6/16/78, Beaumont, Tex. BR/TR, 6', 170 lbs. Deb: 6/25/35																												
1935	Det-A	7	8	1	2	0	0	0	1	2	1	.250	.400	.250	.650	74	-0	-0	97	170	1	.667	0	0	0	-1	/O	-0.1
■ **SKEETER SHELTON** Shelton, Andrew Kemper b: 6/29/1888, Huntington, W.Va. d: 1/9/54, Huntington, W.Va. BR/TR, 5'11", 175 lbs. Deb: 8/25/15																												
1915	NY-A	10	40	1	1	0	0	0	0	2	10	.025	.071	.025	.096	-72	-8	-8	98	0	0	.077	0			1	O	-0.8
■ **STEVE SHEMO** Shemo, Stephen Michael b: 4/9/15, Swoyersville, Pa. BR/TR, 5'11", 175 lbs. Deb: 4/18/44																												
1944	Bos-N	18	31	3	9	2	0	0	1	1	3	.290	.313	.355	.667	93	-1	-0	95	33	4	.545	0			1	2/3	0.3
1945	Bos-N	17	46	4	11	1	0	0	7	1	3	.239	.255	.261	.516	39	-4	-4	112	202	3	.371	0			-1	2/3S	-0.3
Total	2	35	77	7	20	3	0	0	8	2	6	.260	.278	.299	.577	58	-4	-5	105	134	7	.439	0			0	/23S	0.0
■ **JACK SHEPARD** Shepard, Jack Leroy b: 5/13/32, Clovis, Cal. BR/TR, 6'2", 195 lbs. Deb: 6/19/53																												
1953	Pit-N	2	4	0	1	0	0	0	0	0	2	.250	.250	.250	.500	30	-0	-0	102	0	0	.333	0	0	0	0	/C	0.0
1954	Pit-N	82	227	24	69	8	2	3	22	26	33	.304	.375	.396	.772	105	1	2	97	87	33	.690	0	0	0	8	C	1.2
1955	Pit-N	94	264	24	63	10	2	2	23	33	25	.239	.323	.314	.638	72	-11	-10	97	105	27	.560	1	0	0	3	C	-0.3
1956	Pit-N	100	256	24	62	11	2	7	30	25	37	.242	.310	.383	.692	83	-6	-6	102	107	29	.611	1	1	-0	-4	C/1	-0.8
Total	4	278	751	72	195	29	6	12	75	84	97	.260	.334	.362	.696	86	-16	-14	99	99	90	.634	2	1	0	7	C/1	0.1
■ **RAY SHEPARDSON** Shepardson, Raymond Francis b: 5/3/1897, Little Falls, N.Y. d: 11/8/75, Little Falls, N.Y. BR/TR, 5'11.5", 170 lbs. Deb: 9/19/24																												
1924	StL-N	3	6	1	0	0	0	0	0	0	3	.000	.000	.000	.000	-98	-2	-2	103	0	0	.000	0	0	0	0	/C	-0.1
■ **RON SHEPHERD** Shepherd, Ronald Wayne b: 10/27/60, Longview, Tex. BR/TR, 6'4", 175 lbs. Deb: 9/05/84																												
1984	Tor-A	12	4	0	0	0	0	0	0	0	3	.000	.000	.000	.000	-99	-1	-1	102	0	0	.000	0	1	-1	-1	/OD	-0.2
1985	Tor-A	38	35	7	4	2	0	0	1	2	12	.114	.162	.171	.334	-8	-5	-5	101	66	1	.344	3	0	1	-3	OD	-0.6
1986	Tor-A	65	69	16	14	4	0	2	4	3	22	.203	.236	.348	.584	54	-4	-5	105	53	6	.482	0	0	0	-8	OD	-1.3
Total	3	115	108	23	18	6	0	2	5	5	37	.167	.204	.278	.481	29	-11	-11	104	55	7	.413	3	1	0	-12	/OD	-2.1
■ **JOHN SHEPPARD** Sheppard, John b: Baltimore, Md. Deb: 6/27/1873																												
1873	Mar-n	2	7	0	0							.000															/CO	
■ **SHERIDAN** Sheridan Deb:10/09/1875																												
1875	Atl-n	1	4	0	0							.000															/O	
■ **RED SHERIDAN** Sheridan, Eugene Anthony b: 11/14/1896, Brooklyn, N.Y. d: 11/25/75, Queens Village, N.Y. BR/TR, 5'10.5", 160 lbs. Deb: 7/03/18																												
1918	Bro-N	2	4	0	1	0	0	0	0	1	0	.250	.400	.250	.650	98	0	0	101	0	1	1.000	1			0	/2	0.0
1920	Bro-N	3	2	0	0	0	0	0	0	0	1	.000	.000	.000	.000	-90	-1	-1	111	0	0	.000	0	0	0	0	/S	0.0
Total	2	5	6	0	1	0	0	0	0	1	1	.167	.286	.167	.452	35	-0	-0	104	0	1	.600	1	0		0	/S2	0.0
■ **NEILL SHERIDAN** Sheridan, Neill Rawlins "Wild Horse" b: 11/20/21, Sacramento, Cal. BR/TR, 6'1.5", 195 lbs. Deb: 9/19/48																												
1948	Bos-A	2	1	0	0	0	0	0	0	0	1	.000	.000	.000	.000	-99	-0	-0	100	0	0	.000	0	0	0	0	H	0.0
■ **PAT SHERIDAN** Sheridan, Patrick Arthur b: 12/4/57, Ann Arbor, Mich. BL/TR, 6'3", 175 lbs. Deb: 9/16/81																												
1981	KC-A	3	1	0	0	0	0	0	0	0	1	.000	.000	.000	.000	-99	-0	-0	99	0	0	.000	0	0	0	-1	/O	0.0
1983	KC-A	109	333	43	90	12	2	7	36	20	64	.270	.312	.381	.693	88	-5	-6	101	95	41	.639	12	3	2	3	*O	-0.1
1984	KC-A	138	481	64	136	24	4	8	53	41	91	.283	.340	.399	.740	105	3	3	99	100	68	.709	19	6	2	-2	*O	-0.1
1985	KC-A	78	206	18	47	9	2	3	17	23	38	.228	.309	.335	.644	75	-7	-7	102	86	23	.627	11	3	2	-6	O/D	-1.2
1986	Det-A	98	236	41	56	9	1	6	19	21	57	.237	.302	.360	.662	84	-6	-5	95	73	27	.627	9	2	2	-6	O/D	-1.1
1987	Det-A	141	421	57	109	19	3	6	49	44	90	.259	.330	.361	.692	87	-9	-7	97	115	50	.648	18	13	-2	-8	*O	-2.0
1988	Det-A	127	347	47	88	9	5	11	47	44	64	.254	.341	.403	.744	114	4	7	94	108	48	.716	8	6	-1	-8	*O/D	-0.4
Total	7	694	2025	270	526	82	17	41	221	193	405	.260	.326	.378	.704	94	-20	-15	98	99	256	.677	77	33	3	-29	O/D	-4.9
■ **ED SHERLING** Sherling, Edward Creech "Shine" b: 7/17/1897, Coalsburg, Pa. d: 11/16/65, Enterprise, Cal. BR/TR, 6'1", 185 lbs. Deb: 8/13/24																												
1924	Phi-A	4	2	2	1	1	0	0	0	0	0	.500	.500	1.000	1.500	283	0	0	99	0	1	2.000	0	0	0	0	H	0.0
■ **MONK SHERLOCK** Sherlock, John Clinton b: 10/26/04, Buffalo, N.Y. d: 11/26/85, Buffalo, N.Y. BR/TR, 5'10", 175 lbs. Deb: 4/20/30																												
1930	Phi-N	92	299	51	97	18	2	0	38	27	28	.324	.380	.398	.778	84	-5	-7	106	110	45	.723	0			2	1/2O	-0.6
■ **VINCE SHERLOCK** Sherlock, Vincent Thomas "Baldy" b: 3/27/09, Buffalo, N.Y. BR/TR, 6', 180 lbs. Deb: 9/18/35																												
1935	Bro-N	9	26	4	12	1	0	0	6	1	2	.462	.481	.500	.981	175	2	3	94	166	7	1.071	1			1	/2	0.4
■ **DENNIS SHERRILL** Sherrill, Dennis Lee b: 3/3/56, Miami, Fla. BR/TR, 6', 165 lbs. Deb: 9/04/78																												
1978	NY-A	2	1	1	0	0	0	0	0	0	1	.000	.000	.000	.000	-99	-0	-0	99	0	0	.000	0	0	0	0	/3D	0.0
1980	NY-A	3	4	0	1	0	0	0	0	0	1	.250	.250	.250	.500	38	-0	-0	99	0	0	.250	0	0	0	0	/S2	0.0
Total	2	5	5	1	1	0	0	0	0	0	2	.200	.200	.200	.400	11	-1	-1	99	0	0	.200	0	0	0	0	/S2D3	0.0

YEAR	TM/L	G	AB	R	H	2B	3B	HR	RBI	BB	SO	AVG	OBP	SLG	PRO	/A	BR	/A	PF	CHI	RC	TA	SB	CS	SBR	FR	POS	TPR
■ NORM SHERRY	Sherry, Norman Burt b: 7/16/31, New York, N.Y. BR/TR, 5'11", 180 lbs. Deb: 4/12/59 MC																											
1959	LA-N	2	3	0	1	0	0	0	2	0	0	.333	.500	.333	.833	125	0	0	102	809	0	.667	0	0	0	0	/C	0.0
1960	LA-N	47	138	22	39	4	1	8	19	12	29	.283	.353	.500	.853	113	6	3	115	83	25	.832	0	0	0	1	C	0.6
1961	LA-N	47	121	10	31	2	0	5	21	9	30	.256	.308	.397	.704	83	-3	-3	102	134	13	.588	0	0	0	0	C	0.1
1962	LA-N	35	88	7	16	2	0	3	16	6	17	.182	.242	.307	.549	50	-7	-6	93	175	6	.459	0	0	0	-2	C	-0.6
1963	NY-N	63	147	6	20	1	0	2	11	10	26	.136	.206	.184	.390	13	-16	-16	99	140	5	.308	1	0	0	-4	C	-1.9
Total	5	194	497	45	107	9	1	18	69	37	102	.215	.280	.346	.627	69	-20	-22	103	134	49	.551	1	0	0	-4	C	-1.8
■ BARRY SHETRONE	Shetrone, Barry Stevan b: 7/6/38, Baltimore, Md. BL/TR, 6'2", 190 lbs. Deb: 7/27/59																											
1959	Bal-A	33	79	8	16	1	1	0	5	5	9	.203	.250	.241	.491	36	-7	-7	97	104	6	.429	3	0	1	-3	O	-0.9
1960	Bal-A	1	0	1	0	0	0	0	0	0	0	—	—	—	—	—	0	0	102	—	—	—	0	0	0	0	R	0.0
1961	Bal-A	3	7	0	1	0	0	0	1	0	2	.143	.143	.143	.286	-24	-1	-1	97	392	0	.167	0	0	0	-0	/O	-0.1
1962	Bal-A	21	24	3	6	1	0	1	1	0	5	.250	.250	.417	.667	80	-1	-1	95	30	3	.556	0	0	0	-0	/O	0.0
1963	Was-A	2	2	0	0	0	0	0	0	0	0	.000	.000	.000	.000	-99	-1	-1	98	0	0	.000	0	0	0	0	H	0.0
Total	5	60	112	12	23	2	1	1	7	5	16	.205	.239	.268	.507	40	-10	-9	96	104	14	.427	3	0	1	-3	/O	-1.0
■ JOHN SHETZLINE	Shetzline, John Henry b: 1850, Philadelphia, Pa. d: 12/15/1892, Philadelphia, Pa. 5'11.5", 190 lbs. Deb: 5/02/1882																											
1882	Bal-a	73	282	23	62	8	3	0		5		.220	.233	.270	.503	75	-9	-6	92	0	18	.368				3	32/OS	-0.2
■ JIMMY SHEVLIN	Shevlin, James Cornelius b: 7/9/09, Cincinnati, Ohio d: 10/30/74, Ft.Lauderdale, Fla BL/TL, 5'10.5", 155 lbs. Deb: 6/29/30																											
1930	Det-A	28	14	4	2	0	0	0	2	2	3	.143	.250	.143	.393	2	-2	-2	105	332	1	.333	0	0	0	-0	1	-0.4
1932	Cin-N	7	24	3	5	2	0	0	4	4	0	.208	.345	.292	.636	76	-1	-1	96	217	3	.842	4			-0	/1	0.0
1934	Cin-N	18	39	6	12	2	0	0	6	6	5	.308	.400	.359	.759	104	1	1	101	154	6	.714	0			-0	1	0.0
Total	3	53	77	13	19	4	0	0	12	12	8	.247	.356	.299	.654	76	-2	-2	100	206	9	.678	4	0		-0	/1	-0.4
■ PETE SHIELDS	Shields, Francis Leroy b: 9/21/1891, Swiftwater, Miss. d: 2/11/61, Jackson, Miss. BR/TR, 6', 175 lbs. Deb: 4/14/15																											
1915	Cle-A	23	72	4	15	6	0	0	6	4	14	.208	.250	.292	.542	60	-4	-4	104	97	5	.467	3	3	-1	-0	1	-0.6
■ JIM SHILLING	Shilling, James Robert b: 5/14/14, Tulsa, Okla. d: 9/12/86, Tulsa, Okla. BR/TR, 5'11", 175 lbs. Deb: 4/21/39																											
1939	Cle-A	31	98	8	27	7	2	0	12	7	9	.276	.324	.388	.712	83	-3	-3	98	107	12	.622	1	0	0	-2	2/S	-0.2
	Phi-N	11	33	3	10	1	3	0	4	1	4	.303	.324	.515	.839	130	1	1	94	86	5	.720	0			-1	/2S3O	0.0
Total	1	42	131	11	37	8	5	0	16	8	13	.282	.324	.420	.744	94	-2	-2	97	102	17	.667	1	0		-3	/2S3O	-0.2
■ GINGER SHINAULT	Shinault, Enoch Erskine b: 9/7/1892, Benton, Ark. d: 12/29/30, Denver, Colo. BR/TR, 5'11", 170 lbs. Deb: 7/04/21																											
1921	Cle-A	22	29	5	11	1	0	0	4	6	5	.379	.486	.414	.900	132	2	2	99	114	7	1.056	1	0	0	-1	C	0.2
1922	Cle-A	13	15	1	2	1	0	0	0	0	2	.133	.133	.200	.333	-14	-3	-3	102	0	0	.231	0	0	0	0	C	-0.1
Total	2	35	44	6	13	2	0	0	4	6	7	.295	.380	.341	.721	86	-1	-1	100	80	7	.710	1	0	0	-1	/C	0.1
■ BILLY SHINDLE	Shindle, William b: 12/5/1860, Gloucester, N.J. d: 6/3/36, Lakeland, N.J. TR, 5'8.5", 155 lbs. Deb: 10/04/1886																											
1886	Det-N	7	26	4	7	0	0	0	4	0	5	.269	.269	.269	.538	59	-1	-1	109	186	2	.474	2			0	/S	0.0
1887	Det-N	22	84	17	24	3	2	0	12	7	10	.286	.341	.369	.710	97	0	-0	102	122	15	.850	13			0	3/O	0.0
1888	Bal-a	135	514	61	107	14	8	1	53	20		.208	.249	.272	.521	72	-17	-14	96	117	49	.541	52			**36**	*3	2.0
1889	Bal-a	138	567	122	178	24	7	3	64	42	37	.314	.369	.397	.765	121	15	15	100	69	106	.848	56			18	*3	2.9
1890	Phi-P	132	584	127	188	21	21	10	90	40	30	.322	.369	.481	.851	125	21	18	102	70	126	.949	51			2	*S/3	2.2
1891	Phi-N	103	415	68	87	13	1	0	38	33	39	.210	.278	.246	.523	57	-23	-20	95	115	34	.482	17			5	*3/S	-0.9
1892	Bal-N	143	619	100	156	20	18	3	50	35	34	.252	.301	.357	.658	101	-2	-1	100	58	75	.622	24			36	*3/S	3.9
1893	Bal-N	125	521	100	136	22	11	1	75	66	17	.261	.353	.351	.704	83	-7	-13	107	97	72	.712	17			8	*3	-0.3
1894	Bro-N	116	476	94	141	22	9	4	96	29	20	.296	.344	.405	.750	87	-15	-9	94	137	75	.737	19			2	*3	-0.6
1895	Bro-N	116	477	91	133	21	2	3	69	47	28	.279	.357	.350	.707	90	-9	-4	94	97	67	.703	17			0	*3	-0.1
1896	Bro-N	131	516	75	144	24	9	1	61	24	20	.279	.316	.366	.682	93	-15	-4	87	97	69	.648	24			-14	*3	-0.9
1897	Bro-N	134	542	83	154	32	6	3	105	35		.284	.336	.382	.718	90	-7	-9	102	151	79	.701	23			-13	*3	-1.8
1898	Bro-N	120	466	50	105	10	3	1	41	10		.225	.249	.266	.516	53	-30	-27	95	103	32	.393	3			5	*3	-1.7
Total	13	1422	5807	992	1560	226	97	30	758	388	240	.269	.323	.356	.679	91	-91	-70	98	100	803	.671	318			85	*3S/O	4.7
■ RAY SHINES	Shines, Anthony Raymond b: 7/18/56, Durham, N.C. BB/TR, 6'1", 210 lbs. Deb: 9/09/83																											
1983	Mon-N	3	2	0	1	0	0	0	0	0	0	.500	.500	.500	1.000	175	0	0	102	0	1	1.000	0	0	0	-0	/O	0.0
1984	Mon-N	12	20	0	6	1	0	0	2	0	3	.300	.300	.350	.650	90	-1	-0	91	112	2	.500	0	0	0	0	/13	0.0
1985	Mon-N	47	50	0	6	0	0	0	3	4	9	.120	.185	.120	.305	-14	-7	-7	94	199	1	.213	0	1	-1	0	/1P	-0.7
1987	Mon-N	6	9	0	2	0	0	0	0	1	0	.222	.364	.222	.586	56	-0	-0	106	0	1	.625	1	0	0	0	/1	0.0
Total	4	68	81	0	15	1	0	0	5	5	12	.185	.241	.198	.439	25	-8	-8	95	149	4	.338	1	1	-0	0	/1P3O	-0.7
■ RALPH SHINNERS	Shinners, Ralph Peter b: 10/4/1895, Monches, Wis. d: 7/23/62, Milwaukee, Wis. BR/TR, 6', 180 lbs. Deb: 4/12/22																											
1922	NY-N	56	135	16	34	4	2	0	15	5	22	.252	.308	.311	.619	58	-8	-9	104	125	12	.528	3	5	-2	-2	O	-1.2
1923	NY-N	33	13	5	2	1	0	0	0	2	1	.154	.267	.231	.497	32	-1	-1	101	0	1	.455	0	0	0	-1	/O	-0.2
1925	StL-N	74	251	39	74	9	2	7	36	12	19	.295	.330	.430	.760	91	-3	-4	102	99	35	.709	8	5	-1	-0	O	-0.6
Total	3	163	399	60	110	14	4	7	51	19	42	.276	.320	.383	.703	78	-13	-14	102	104	48	.635	11	10	-3	-3	O	-2.0
■ TIM SHINNICK	Shinnick, Timothy James "Dandy" or "Good Eye" b: 11/6/1867, Exeter, N.H. d: 5/18/44, Exeter, N.H. BB/TR, 6', 150 lbs. Deb: 4/19/1890																											
1890	Lou-a	133	493	87	126	16	11	1		62		.256	.348	.339	.687	98	5	-1	107	0	82	.815	62			-25	*2/3	-1.8
1891	Lou-a	128	443	79	98	10	11	1	54	54	47	.221	.314	.300	.614	87	-11	-4	90	117	54	.664	36			-23	*2/3S	-1.5
Total	2	261	936	166	224	26	22	2	54	116	47	.239	.332	.321	.653	93	-7	-5	99	55	136	.742	98			-48	2/3S	-3.3
■ BILL SHIPKE	Shipke, William Martin "Skipper Bill" or "Muskrat Bill" (born Shipkrethaver) b: 11/18/1882, St.Louis, Mo. d: 9/10/40, Omaha, Neb. TR, 5'7", 145 lbs. Deb: 4/23/06																											
1906	Cle-A	2	6	0	0	0	0	0	0	0		.000	.000	.000	.000	-97	-1	-1	103	0	0	.000	0			0	/2	0.0
1907	Was-A	64	189	17	37	3	2	1	9	15		.196	.255	.249	.504	69	-8	-6	90	64	14	.447	6			4	3	0.2
1908	Was-A	111	341	40	71	7	8	0	20	38		.208	.288	.276	.563	89	-4	-3	95	80	30	.544	15			-2	*3/2	0.3
1909	Was-A	9	16	2	2	1	0	0	0	2		.125	.222	.188	.410	33	-1	-1	90	0	1	.357	0			0	/3S	0.0
Total	4	186	552	59	110	11	10	1	29	55		.199	.272	.261	.533	79	-15	-11	93	71	45	.498	21			3	3/2S	0.5
■ CRAIG SHIPLEY	Shipley, Craig Barry b: 1/7/63, Parramatta, Australia BR/TR, 6'1", 175 lbs. Deb: 6/22/86																											
1986	LA-N	12	27	3	3	1	0	0	4	2	5	.111	.200	.148	.348	-3	-4	-4	94	399	1	.280	0	0	0	0	S/23	-0.2
1987	LA-N	26	35	3	9	1	0	0	2	0	6	.257	.257	.286	.543	48	-3	-2	92	80	2	.357	0	0	0	0	S/3	0.0
Total	2	38	62	6	12	2	0	0	6	2	11	.194	.231	.226	.457	25	-7	-6	93	227	3	.327	0	0	0	0	/S32	-0.2
■ ART SHIRES	Shires, Charles Arthur "Art The Great" b: 8/13/07, Italy, Tex. d: 7/13/67, Italy, Tex. BL/TR, 6'1", 195 lbs. Deb: 8/20/28																											
1928	Chi-A	33	123	20	42	6	1	1	11	13	10	.341	.409	.431	.840	122	4	4	99	71	21	.798	0	3	-2	2	1	0.2
1929	Chi-A	100	353	41	110	20	7	3	41	32	20	.312	.370	.433	.804	112	3	6	95	88	56	.766	4	5	-2	2	1/2	-0.5
1930	Chi-A	37	128	14	33	5	1	1	18	6	6	.258	.291	.336	.627	57	-8	-9	103	130	13	.537	2	0	1	-1	1	-1.1
	Was-A	38	84	11	31	5	0	1	19	5	5	.369	.404	.464	.869	118	3	2	101	150	15	.804	1	3	-2	0	1	0.0
	Yr	75	212	25	64	10	1	2	37	11	11	.302	.336	.387	.723	81	-6	-6	102	142	27	.636	3	3	-1	-1		-1.1
1932	Bos-N	82	298	32	71	9	3	5	30	25	21	.238	.299	.339	.638	76	-12	-9	93	98	32	.564	1			-2	1	-1.5
Total	4	290	986	118	287	45	12	11	119	81	62	.291	.347	.395	.741	96	-10	-5	96	99	137	.677	8	11		1	1/2	-2.9
■ BART SHIRLEY	Shirley, Barton Arvin b: 1/4/40, Corpus Christi, Tex. BR/TR, 5'10", 183 lbs. Deb: 9/14/64																											
1964	LA-N	18	62	6	17	1	1	0	7	4	8	.274	.318	.323	.641	88	-1	-1	92	144	5	.490	0	0	0	-1	3/S	-0.1
1966	LA-N	12	5	2	1	0	0	0	0	0	2	.200	.200	.200	.400	12	-1	-1	97	0	0	.250	0	0	0	0	/S	0.0
1967	NY-N	6	12	1	0	0	0	0	0	0	5	.000	.000	.000	.000	-99	-3	-3	99	0	0	.000	0	0	0	0	/2	-0.2
1968	LA-N	39	83	6	15	3	0	0	4	10	13	.181	.269	.217	.486	52	-5	-4	91	94	4	.378	0	1	-1	0	S2	0.0
Total	4	75	162	15	33	4	1	0	11	14	28	.204	.267	.241	.508	53	-10	-9	92	103	10	.393	0	1	-1	-0	/S23	-0.3
■ MULE SHIRLEY	Shirley, Ernest Raeford b: 5/24/01, Snow Hill, N.C. d: 8/4/55, Goldsboro, N.C. BL/TL, 5'11", 180 lbs. Deb: 5/06/24																											
1924	Was-A	30	77	12	18	2	2	0	16	3	7	.234	.262	.312	.574	48	-6	-6	98	220	7	.458	0	0	0	-0	1	-0.6

YEAR	TM/L	G	AB	R	H	2B	3B	HR	RBI	BB	SO	AVG	OBP	SLG	PRO	/A	BR	/A	PF	CHI	RC	TA	SB	CS	SBR	FR	POS	TPR
1925	Was-A	14	23	2	3	1	0	0	2	1	7	.130	.167	.174	.341	-14	-4	-4	98	167	1	.250	0	0	0	0	/1	-0.3
Total	2	44	100	14	21	3	2	0	18	4	14	.210	.240	.280	.520	34	-10	-10	98	208	7	.405	0	0	0	0	/1	-0.9
■ IVEY SHIVER Shiver, Ivey Merwin "Chick" b: 1/22/07, Sylvester, Ga. d: 8/31/72, Savannah, Ga. BR/TR, 6'1.5", 190 lbs. Deb: 4/14/31																												
1931	Det-A	2	9	2	1	0	0	0	0	0	3	.111	.111	.111	.222	-40	-2	-2	104	0	0	.125	0	0	0	-0	/O	-0.1
1934	Cin-N	19	59	6	12	1	0	2	6	3	15	.203	.242	.322	.564	49	-4	-4	101	86	5	.489	1			-2	O	-0.6
Total	2	21	68	8	13	1	0	2	6	3	18	.191	.225	.294	.519	37	-6	-6	101	75	5	.436	1	0		-3	/O	-0.7
■ GEORGE SHOCH Shoch, George Quintus b: 1/6/1859, Philadelphia, Pa. d: 9/30/37, Philadelphia, Pa. BR/TR, Deb: 9/10/1886																												
1886	Was-N	26	95	11	28	2	1	1	18	2	13	.295	.309	.368	.678	113	0	1	94	157	12	.582	2			0	O/S	0.1
1887	Was-N	70	264	47	63	9	1	1	18	21	16	.239	.304	.292	.596	71	-11	-9	95	73	33	.652	29			5	O/S2	-0.1
1888	Was-N	90	317	46	58	6	3	2	24	25	22	.183	.262	.240	.502	65	-12	-10	96	111	27	.514	23			5	SO/2P	-0.3
1889	Was-N	30	109	12	26	2	0	0	11	20	5	.239	.385	.257	.642	90	-1	1	92	113	15	.759	9			0	O/S	0.1
1891	CM-a	34	127	29	40	7	1	1	16	18	5	.315	.435	.409	.845	130	9	6	112	81	29	1.046	12			0	S/3	0.5
1892	Bal-N	76	308	42	85	15	3	1	50	24	19	.276	.340	.354	.694	112	4	5	100	132	43	.686	14			-4	SO/3	0.3
1893	Bro-N	94	327	53	86	17	1	2	54	48	13	.263	.366	.339	.705	99	-3	3	91	129	45	.718	9			-11	O3S/2	-0.7
1894	Bro-N	64	239	47	77	6	5	1	37	26	6	.322	.400	.402	.802	101	-1	2	94	105	46	.883	16			-2	O3/2S	-0.1
1895	Bro-N	61	216	49	56	9	7	0	29	32	6	.259	.368	.366	.733	97	-2	1	94	105	32	.769	7			1	O2/S3	0.0
1896	Bro-N	76	250	36	73	7	4	1	28	33	10	.292	.381	.364	.745	113	1	7	87	88	40	.780	11			-14	2O/3S	-0.4
1897	Bro-N	85	284	42	79	9	2	0	38	49		.278	.393	.324	.717	92	0	-1	102	123	40	.741	6			8	2S/O	1.1
Total	11	706	2536	414	671	89	28	10	323	298	115	.265	.355	.334	.688	96	-14	6	96	110	360	.718	138			-13	OS2/3P	0.5
■ COSTEN SHOCKLEY Shockley, John Costen b: 2/8/42, Georgetown, Del. BL/TL, 6'2", 200 lbs. Deb: 7/17/64																												
1964	Phi-N	11	35	4	8	0	0	1	2	2	8	.229	.270	.314	.585	65	-2	-2	99	59	3	.464	0	0	0	-0	/1	-0.1
1965	Cal-A	40	107	5	20	2	0	2	17	9	16	.187	.256	.262	.518	49	-7	-7	98	207	7	.427	0	0	0	0	1/O	-0.8
Total	2	51	142	9	28	2	0	3	19	11	24	.197	.260	.275	.534	53	-9	-9	98	172	10	.440	0	0	0	-0	/1O	-0.9
■ CHARLIE SHOEMAKER Shoemaker, Charles Landis b: 8/10/39, Los Angeles, Cal. BL/TR, 5'10", 155 lbs. Deb: 9/09/61																												
1961	KC-A	7	26	5	10	2	0	0	1	2	2	.385	.429	.462	.890	135	1	1	102	33	5	.824	0	0	0	1	/2	0.3
1962	KC-A	5	11	1	2	0	0	0	0	0	2	.182	.182	.182	.364	-2	-2	-2	100	0	0	.222	0	0	0	0	/2	0.0
1964	KC-A	16	52	6	11	2	2	0	3	0	9	.212	.212	.327	.538	45	-4	-4	105	75	4	.415	0	0	0	1	2	0.0
Total	3	28	89	12	23	4	2	0	4	2	13	.258	.275	.348	.623	67	-4	-4	103	53	9	.500	0	0	0	2	/2	0.3
■ STRICK SHOFNER Shofner, Frank Strickland b: 7/23/19, Crawford, Tex. BL/TR, 5'10.5", 187 lbs. Deb: 4/19/47																												
1947	Bos-A	5	13	1	2	0	1	0	0	0	3	.154	.154	.308	.462	25	-1	-1	108	0	1	.364	0	0	0	0	/3	-0.1
■ EDDIE SHOKES Shokes, Edward Christopher b: 1/27/20, Charleston, S.C. BL/TL, 6', 170 lbs. Deb: 6/09/41																												
1941	Cin-N	1	1	0	0	0	0	0	0	0	1	.000	.000	.000	.000	-99	-0	-0	99	0	0	.000	0			0	H	0.0
1946	Cin-N	31	83	3	10	1	0	0	5	18	21	.120	.277	.133	.410	17	-8	-9	104	170	4	.405	1			-0	1	-1.2
Total	2	32	84	3	10	1	0	0	5	18	22	.119	.275	.131	.405	16	-9	-9	104	168	4	.400	1			-0	/1	-1.2
■ RAY SHOOK Shook, Raymond Curtis b: 11/18/1889, Perry, Ohio d: 9/16/70, South Bend, Ind. BR/TR, 5'7.5", 155 lbs. Deb: 4/16/16																												
1916	Chi-A	1	0	0	0	0	0	0	0	0	0	—	—	—	—	—	0	0	108	—	—	—	0			0	R	0.0
■ RON SHOOP Shoop, Ronald Lee b: 9/19/31, Rural Valley, Pa. BR/TR, 5'11", 180 lbs. Deb: 8/22/59																												
1959	Det-A	3	7	1	1	0	0	0	1	0	1	.143	.143	.143	.286	-19	-1	-1	111	394	0	.143	0	0	0	0	/C	0.0
■ TOM SHOPAY Shopay, Thomas Michael b: 2/21/45, Bristol, Conn. BL/TR, 5'9.5", 160 lbs. Deb: 9/17/67																												
1967	NY-A	8	27	2	8	1	0	2	6	1	5	.296	.321	.556	.877	164	2	2	94	119	5	.947	2	0	1	0	/O	0.3
1969	NY-A	28	48	2	4	0	1	0	0	2	10	.083	.120	.125	.245	-33	-8	-8	95	0	1	.174	0	1	-1	1	O	-0.8
1971	Bal-A	47	74	10	19	2	0	0	5	3	7	.257	.286	.284	.569	60	-4	-4	103	97	6	.448	2	1	0	-1	O	-0.5
1972	Bal-A	49	40	3	9	0	0	0	2	5	12	.225	.311	.225	.536	63	-2	-2	98	93	3	.452	0	0	0	-0	/O	-0.1
1975	Bal-A	40	31	4	5	1	0	0	2	4	7	.161	.257	.194	.451	32	-3	-2	91	128	2	.464	3	0	1	-4	O/CD	-0.5
1976	Bal-A	14	20	4	4	0	0	0	1	3	3	.200	.304	.200	.504	51	-1	-1	98	96	2	.500	1	0	0	-4	O/C	-0.5
1977	Bal-A	67	69	15	13	3	0	1	4	8	7	.188	.273	.275	.548	54	-5	-4	93	72	5	.508	3	3	-1	-11	O/D	-1.7
Total	7	253	309	40	62	7	1	3	20	26	51	.201	.263	.259	.522	50	-21	-20	96	81	23	.464	11	5	0	-19	O/DC	-3.8
■ DAVE SHORT Short, David Orvis b: 5/11/17, Magnolia, Ark. d: 11/22/83, Shreveport, La. BL/TR, 5'11.5", 162 lbs. Deb: 9/16/40																												
1940	Chi-A	4	3	1	1	0	0	0	0	1	2	.333	.500	.333	.833	116	0	0	104	0	1	1.000	0	0	0	0	H	0.0
1941	Chi-A	3	8	0	0	0	0	0	0	2	1	.000	.200	.000	.200	-46	-2	-2	94	0	0	.250	0	0	0	-0	/O	-0.1
Total	2	7	11	1	1	0	0	0	0	3	3	.091	.286	.091	.377	3	-1	-1	96	0	1	.400	0	0	0	-0	/O	-0.1
■ CHICK SHORTEN Shorten, Charles Henry b: 4/19/1892, Scranton, Pa. d: 10/23/65, Scranton, Pa. BL/TL, 6', 175 lbs. Deb: 9/22/15																												
1915	Bos-A	6	14	1	3	1	0	0	0	0	2	.214	.214	.286	.500	50	-1	-1	99	0	1	.364	0			-0	/O	-0.1
1916	Bos-A	53	112	14	33	2	1	0	11	10	8	.295	.352	.330	.683	112	1	2	94	106	14	.608	1			-7	O	-0.7
1917	Bos-A	69	168	12	30	4	2	0	16	10	10	.179	.229	.226	.455	36	-13	-14	108	151	9	.370	2			-4	O	-2.3
1919	Det-A	95	270	37	85	9	3	0	22	22	13	.315	.366	.370	.737	115	3	5	93	80	40	.686	5			-7	O	-0.6
1920	Det-A	116	364	35	105	9	6	1	40	28	14	.288	.339	.354	.694	81	-8	-10	103	106	44	.605	2	4	-2	-1	O	-2.0
1921	Det-A	92	217	33	59	11	3	0	23	20	11	.272	.333	.350	.684	78	-8	-7	96	104	26	.609	2	3	-1	-3	O	-1.4
1922	StL-A	55	131	22	36	12	5	2	16	16	8	.275	.354	.489	.842	111	3	2	106	82	23	.833	0	1	-1	-2	O	-0.2
1924	Cin-N	41	69	7	19	3	0	0	6	4	2	.275	.315	.319	.634	70	-3	-3	101	99	7	.520	0	0	0	-4	O	-0.6
Total	8	527	1345	161	370	51	20	3	134	110	68	.275	.330	.349	.680	86	-26	-26	100	102	163	.603	12	8		-28	O	-7.9
■ BURT SHOTTON Shotton, Burton Edwin "Barney" b: 10/18/1884, Brownhelm, Ohio d: 7/29/62, Lake Wales, Fla. BL/TR, 5'11", 175 lbs. Deb: 9/13/09 MC																												
1909	StL-A	17	61	5	16	0	1	0	0	5		.262	.328	.295	.623	106	-0	1	92	0	7	.600	3			2	O	0.2
1911	StL-A	139	572	84	146	11	8	0	36	51		.255	.317	.302	.620	77	-20	-16	95	61	62	.589	26			0	*O	-2.6
1912	StL-A	154	580	87	168	15	8	2	40	86		.290	.390	.353	.743	114	14	15	99	55	92	.813	35			1	*O	0.6
1913	StL-A	147	549	105	163	23	8	1	28	**99**	63	.297	.405	.373	.779	134	24	28	95	41	95	.902	43			12	*O	3.3
1914	StL-A	154	579	82	156	19	9	0	38	64	66	.269	.344	.333	.678	106	3	5	98	65	69	.662	40	29	-5	-5	*O	-1.5
1915	StL-A	156	559	93	158	18	11	1	30	118	62	.283	.409	.360	.769	136	27	31	96	43	87	.841	43	32	-6	-0	*O	1.6
1916	StL-A	157	618	97	174	23	6	1	36	**111**	67	.282	.391	.343	.734	127	21	24	95	52	88	.771	41	28	-5	11	*O	2.9
1917	StL-A	118	398	47	89	9	1	1	20	62	47	.224	.330	.259	.589	84	-7	-5	95	72	38	.589	16			-9	*O	-2.2
1918	Was-A	126	505	68	132	16	7	0	21	67	28	.261	.349	.321	.670	98	3	0	104	42	61	.684	25			2	*O	-0.4
1919	StL-N	85	270	35	77	13	5	1	20	22	25	.285	.341	.381	.723	124	6	7	94	73	39	.736	16			-5	O	0.0
1920	StL-N	62	180	28	41	5	0	1	12	18	14	.228	.305	.272	.577	68	-7	-7	98	89	17	.529	5	1	1	-2	O	-1.0
1921	StL-N	38	48	9	12	1	1	1	7	7	4	.250	.357	.375	.732	99	-0	0	95	122	6	.684	0	2	-1	0	O	0.0
1922	StL-N	34	30	5	6	1	0	0	2	4	6	.200	.294	.233	.527	37	-3	-3	101	100	2	.440	0	1	-1	-1	/O	-0.4
1923	StL-N	1	0	1	0	0	0	0	0	0	0	—	—	—	—	—	0	0	90	—	—	—	0	0	0	0	R	0.0
Total	14	1388	4949	746	1338	154	65	9	290	714	382	.270	.365	.333	.698	109	61	81	97	56	665	.723	293	93		5	*O	0.5
■ JOHN SHOUPE Shoupe, John F. b: 9/30/1851, Cincinnati, Ohio d: 2/13/20, Cincinnati, Ohio BL/TL, 5'7", 140 lbs. Deb: 5/03/1879																												
1879	Tro-N	11	44	5	4	0	0	0	1	0	3	.091	.091	.091	.182	-43	-6	-6	93	89	0	.100				0	S/2	-0.5
1882	StL-a	2	7	1	0	0	0	0		0		.000	.000	.000	.000	-99	-1	-1	100	0	0	.000				0	/2	0.0
1884	Was-U	1	4	1	3	0	0	0		0		.750	.750	.750	1.500	423	1	1	97	0	2	3.000	0			0	/O	0.1
Total	3	14	55	7	7	0	0	0	1	0	3	.127	.127	.127	.255	-16	-7	-6	94	72	3	.146	0			0	/S2O	-0.4
■ JOHN SHOVLIN Shovlin, John Joseph "Brode" b: 1/14/1891, Drifton, Pa. d: 2/16/76, Bethesda, Md. BR/TR, 5'7", 163 lbs. Deb: 6/21/11																												
1911	Pit-N	2	1	1	0	0	0	0	0	0	1	.000	.000	.000	.000	-99	-0	-0	101	0	0	.000	0			0	H	0.0
1919	StL-A	9	35	4	7	0	0	0	1	5	2	.200	.300	.200	.500	43	-3	-2	97	45	2	.429	0			-0	/2	-0.1
1920	StL-A	7	7	2	2	0	0	0	2	0	0	.286	.286	.286	.571	46	-0	-1	111	351	1	.400	0	0	0	0	/S	0.0
Total	3	18	43	7	9	0	0	0	3	5	3	.209	.292	.209	.501	41	-3	-3	99	88	3	.412	0	0		-0	/2S	-0.1

YEAR	TM/L	G	AB	R	H	2B	3B	HR	RBI	BB	SO	AVG	OBP	SLG	PRO	/A	BR	/A	PF	CHI	RC	TA	SB	CS	SBR	FR	POS	TPR
■ GEORGE SHUBA	Shuba, George Thomas "Shotgun" b: 12/13/24, Youngstown, Ohio BL/TR, 5'11", 180 lbs. Deb: 7/02/48																											
1948	Bro-N	63	161	21	43	6	0	4	32	34	31	.267	.395	.379	.774	106	4	3	104	164	27	.800	1			-9	O	-1.0
1949	Bro-N	1	1	0	0	0	0	0	0	0	0	.000	.000	.000	.000	-99	-0	-0	102	0	0	.000	0			0	H	0.0
1950	Bro-N	34	111	15	23	8	2	3	12	13	22	.207	.302	.396	.698	77	-3	-4	107	87	14	.685	2			3	O	-0.1
1952	Bro-N	94	256	40	78	12	1	9	40	38	29	.305	.395	.465	.859	135	14	13	102	107	47	.836	1	3	-2	-6	O	0.4
1953	Bro-N	74	169	19	43	12	1	5	23	17	20	.254	.326	.426	.752	91	-2	-3	104	103	23	.684	1	2	-1	-7	O	-1.1
1954	Bro-N	45	65	3	10	5	0	2	10	7	10	.154	.247	.323	.570	46	-5	-5	101	146	5	.518	0	0	0	-2	O	-0.7
1955	Bro-N	44	51	8	14	2	0	1	8	11	10	.275	.422	.373	.794	108	2	1	104	147	9	.821	0	0	0	-2	/O	0.0
Total	7	355	814	106	211	45	4	24	125	120	122	.259	.359	.413	.771	103	9	5	103	121	125	.766	5	5		-24	O	-2.5
■ FRANK SHUGART	Shugart, Frank Harry (born Frank Harry Shugarts) b: 12/10/1866, Luthersburg, Pa. d: 9/9/44, Clearfield, Pa. BR/TR, 5'8", 170 lbs. Deb: 8/23/1890																											
1890	Chi-P	29	106	8	20	5	5	0	15	5	13	.189	.232	.330	.562	49	-8	-9	104	117	10	.535	5			0	S/O	-0.6
1891	Pit-N	75	320	57	88	19	8	1	33	20	26	.275	.324	.394	.717	109	3	3	101	66	49	.733	21			2	S	0.8
1892	Pit-N	137	554	94	148	19	14	0	62	47	48	.267	.329	.352	.681	115	5	10	94	94	75	.675	28			4	*S/CO	1.9
1893	Pit-N	52	210	37	55	7	3	1	32	19	15	.262	.332	.338	.670	75	-6	-8	106	121	28	.677	12			-4	S	-0.8
	StL-N	59	246	41	69	10	4	0	28	22	10	.280	.354	.354	.708	91	-3	-3	99	85	36	.723	13			0	OS/3	-0.1
	Yr	111	456	78	124	17	7	1	60	41	25	.272	.344	.346	.690	83	-9	-11	103	103	65	.702	25			-4		-0.9
1894	StL-N	133	527	103	154	19	18	7	72	38	37	.292	.348	.436	.784	89	-10	-12	101	84	90	.794	21			-4	*O/S3	-1.8
1895	Lou-N	113	473	61	125	14	13	4	70	31	25	.264	.315	.374	.689	83	-16	-12	95	100	62	.649	14			-24	*SO	-2.2
1897	Phi-N	40	163	20	41	8	2	5	25	8		.252	.287	.417	.704	90	-4	-3	96	93	21	.664	5			-5	S	-0.5
1901	Chi-A	107	415	62	104	9	12	2	47	28		.251	.298	.345	.643	80	-12	-11	99	105	47	.588	12			-9	*S	-1.1
Total	8	745	3014	483	804	110	79	20	384	218	174	.267	.322	.376	.698	91	-51	-45	99	93	418	.683	131			-40	SO/3C	-4.4
■ VINCE SHUPE	Shupe, Vincent William b: 9/5/21, E.Canton, Ohio d: 4/5/62, Canton, Ohio BL/TL, 5'11", 180 lbs. Deb: 7/07/45																											
1945	Bos-N	78	283	22	76	8	0	0	15	17	16	.269	.312	.297	.609	62	-11	-16	112	62	26	.488	3			-1	1	-1.9
■ ED SICKING	Sicking, Edward Joseph b: 3/30/1897, St.Bernard, Ohio d: 8/30/78, Cincinnati, Ohio BR/TR, 5'9.5", 165 lbs. Deb: 8/26/16																											
1916	Chi-N	1	1	0	0	0	0	0	0	0	0	.000	.000	.000	.000	-86	-0	-0	117	0	0	.000	0			0	H	0.0
1918	NY-N	46	132	9	33	4	0	0	12	6	11	.250	.283	.280	.563	74	-5	-4	98	123	10	.455	2			-3	32/S	-0.6
1919	NY-N	6	15	2	5	0	0	0	3	1	0	.333	.412	.333	.745	126	1	1	100	233	2	.700	0			1	/S	0.2
	Phi-N	61	185	16	40	2	1	0	15	8	17	.216	.253	.238	.490	46	-12	-12	104	133	12	.393	4			3	S2	-0.8
	Yr	67	200	18	45	2	1	0	18	9	17	.225	.265	.245	.510	52	-11	-12	103	145	14	.413	4			4		-0.6
1920	NY-N	46	134	11	23	3	1	0	9	10	10	.172	.234	.209	.443	28	-12	-12	100	124	7	.398	6	2	1	0	32/S	-1.0
	Cin-N	37	123	12	33	3	0	0	17	13	5	.268	.338	.293	.631	92	-2	-1	90	183	12	.548	2	3	-1	-3	2/S3	-0.3
	Yr	83	257	23	56	6	1	0	26	23	15	.218	.285	.249	.534	57	-15	-13	95	152	19	.466	8	5	-1	-3		-1.3
1927	Pit-N	6	7	1	1	1	0	0	3	1	0	.143	.250	.286	.536	42	-1	-1	102	525	1	.500	0			-0	/2	0.0
Total	5	203	597	51	135	13	2	0	59	39	43	.226	.277	.255	.532	58	-31	-30	98	147	45	.445	14	5		-3	/2S3	-2.5
■ NORM SIEBERN	Siebern, Norman Leroy b: 7/26/33, St.Louis, Mo. BL/TR, 6'2", 200 lbs. Deb: 6/15/56																											
1956	NY-A	54	162	27	33	1	4	4	21	19	38	.204	.287	.333	.621	64	-9	-9	99	119	16	.556	1	1	-0	-2	O	-1.3
1958	NY-A	134	460	79	138	19	5	14	55	66	87	.300	.389	.454	.843	128	21	20	103	90	82	.834	5	8	-3	2	*O	1.0
1959	NY-A	120	380	52	103	17	0	11	53	41	71	.271	.345	.403	.748	113	3	6	93	112	56	.708	3	1	0	-3	O/1	0.0
1960	KC-A	144	520	69	145	31	6	19	69	72	68	.279	.369	.471	.840	127	19	20	99	95	93	.831	0	0	0	0	O1	1.2
1961	KC-A	153	560	68	166	36	5	18	98	82	91	.296	.387	.475	.862	127	24	23	102	127	108	.873	2	4	-2	-1	*1O	0.8
1962	KC-A	162	600	114	185	25	6	25	117	110	88	.308	.416	.495	.911	144	41	41	100	120	**129**	.958	3	1	0	4	*1	3.4
1963	KC-A	152	556	80	151	25	2	16	83	79	82	.272	.362	.410	.772	108	14	8	108	133	85	.735	1	4	-2	0	*1O	0.2
1964	Bal-A	150	478	92	117	24	2	12	56	**106**	87	.245	.384	.379	.763	108	13	10	105	112	78	.789	2	3	-1	4	*1	0.8
1965	Bal-A	106	297	44	76	13	4	8	32	50	49	.256	.365	.407	.772	119	9	9	100	92	47	.769	1	2	-1	1	1	0.5
1966	Cal-A	125	336	29	83	14	1	5	41	63	61	.247	.366	.339	.705	105	4	5	99	133	45	.681	0	1	-1	0	1	0.1
1967	SF-N	46	58	6	9	1	1	0	4	14	13	.155	.319	.207	.526	53	-3	-3	101	138	5	.531	0	0	0	-0	1/O	-0.3
	Bos-A	33	44	2	9	0	2	0	7	6	8	.205	.300	.295	.595	67	-1	-2	115	225	4	.528	0	0	0	0	1/O	-0.2
1968	Bos-A	27	30	0	2	0	0	0	0	0	5	.067	.067	.067	.133	-59	-6	-6	101	0	0	.069	0	0	0	-1	/1O	-0.7
Total	12	1406	4481	662	1217	206	38	132	636	708	748	.272	.372	.423	.795	117	129	122	101	115	749	.800	18	25	-10	6	1O	5.5
■ DICK SIEBERT	Siebert, Richard Walther b: 2/19/12, Fall River, Mass. d: 12/9/78, Minneapolis, Minn. BL/TL, 6', 170 lbs. Deb: 9/07/32																											
1932	Bro-N	6	7	1	2	0	0	0	0	2	2	.286	.444	.286	.730	106	0	0	96	0	1	.800	0			0	/1	0.0
1936	Bro-N	2	2	0	0	0	0	0	0	0	0	.000	.000	.000	.000	-95	-1	-1	105	0	0	.000	0			0	/O	0.0
1937	StL-N	22	38	3	7	2	0	0	2	4	8	.184	.279	.237	.516	41	-3	-3	101	80	3	.484	1			-0	/1	-0.3
1938	StL-N	1	1	0	1	0	0	0	0	0	0	1.000	1.000	1.000	2.000	406	0	0	111	0	1	—	0			0	H	0.0
	Phi-A	48	194	24	55	8	3	0	28	10	9	.284	.329	.356	.684	71	-9	-9	101	145	22	.592	2	3	-1	-2	1	-1.6
1939	Phi-A	101	402	58	118	28	3	6	47	21	22	.294	.329	.423	.751	93	-7	-5	97	89	56	.670	4	1	1	0	1	-1.2
1940	Phi-A	154	595	69	170	31	6	5	77	33	34	.286	.325	.383	.709	87	-16	-12	96	117	74	.612	8	6	-1	6	*1	-1.3
1941	Phi-A	123	467	63	156	28	8	5	79	37	22	.334	.385	.460	.846	122	15	14	101	124	82	.780	1	4	-2	2	*1	1.0
1942	Phi-A	153	612	57	159	25	7	2	74	24	17	.260	.291	.333	.624	78	-22	-19	96	132	59	.504	4	5	-2	-2	*1	-2.5
1943	Phi-A	146	558	50	140	26	7	1	72	33	21	.251	.295	.328	.623	81	-14	-15	101	150	50	.505	6	7	-2	5	*1	-1.7
1944	Phi-A	132	468	52	143	27	5	6	52	62	17	.306	.387	.423	.810	130	20	20	101	89	83	.794	2	0	1	-7	1O	0.8
1945	Phi-A	147	573	62	153	29	1	7	51	50	33	.267	.327	.358	.685	105	-2	3	94	86	68	.593	2	7	-4	10	*1	0.4
Total	11	1035	3917	439	1104	204	40	32	482	276	185	.282	.331	.379	.710	96	-36	-26	98	114	500	.632	30	33		12	1/O	-6.4
■ FRED SIEFKE	Siefke, Frederick Edwin b: 3/27/1870, New York, N.Y. d: 4/18/1893, New York, N.Y. Deb: 5/02/1890																											
1890	BB-a	16	58	1	8	2	0	0		5		.138	.206	.172	.379	13	-6	-6	100	0	3	.340	2			0	3	-0.5
■ JOHN SIEGEL	Siegel, John b: York, Pa. Deb: 6/09/1884																											
1884	Phi-U	8	31	4	7	2	0	0		1		.226	.250	.290	.540	89	-1	-0	93	0	2	.417	0			0	/3	0.0
■ JOHNNY SIEGLE	Siegle, John Herbert b: 7/8/1874, Urbana, Ohio d: 2/12/68, Urbana, Ohio BR/TR, 5'10", 165 lbs. Deb: 9/15/05																											
1905	Cin-N	17	56	9	17	1	2	1	8	7		.304	.381	.446	.827	144	3	3	103	101	10	.821	0			1	O	0.3
1906	Cin-N	22	68	4	8	2	2	0	7	3		.118	.155	.206	.361	12	-7	-8	115	182	2	.283	0			4	O	-0.4
Total	2	39	124	13	25	3	4	1	15	10		.202	.261	.315	.576	71	-4	-5	109	144	12	.495	0			5	/O	-0.1
■ OSCAR SIEMER	Siemer, Oscar Sylvester "Cotton" b: 8/14/01, St.Louis, Mo. d: 12/5/59, St.Louis, Mo. BR/TR, 5'9", 162 lbs. Deb: 5/20/25																											
1925	Bos-N	16	46	5	14	0	1	1	6	1	0	.304	.319	.413	.732	91	-1	-1	94	97	6	.625	0	0	0	-0	C	0.0
1926	Bos-N	31	73	3	15	1	0	0	5	2	7	.205	.227	.219	.446	24	-8	-7	86	108	4	.310	0			2	C	-0.3
Total	2	47	119	8	29	1	1	1	11	3	7	.244	.262	.294	.556	52	-9	-8	89	104	10	.422	0	0		2	/C	-0.3
■ RUBEN SIERRA	Sierra, Ruben Angel (Garcia) b: 10/6/65, Rio Piedras, P.R. BB/TR, 6'1", 175 lbs. Deb: 6/01/86																											
1986	Tex-A	113	382	50	101	13	10	16	55	22	65	.264	.306	.476	.783	115	4	6	96	95	51	.714	7	8	-3	-1	*O/D	0.0
1987	Tex-A	158	643	97	169	35	4	30	109	39	114	.263	.307	.470	.777	99	1	-2	104	107	85	.714	16	11	-2	3	*O	-0.4
1988	Tex-A	156	615	77	156	32	2	23	91	44	91	.254	.305	.424	.729	101	-0	-1	101	116	77	.678	18	4	3	3	*O/D	0.2
Total	3	427	1640	224	426	80	16	69	255	105	270	.260	.306	.454	.760	103	5	3	101	108	213	.715	41	23	-2	4	O/D	-0.2
■ ROY SIEVERS	Sievers, Roy Edward "Squirrel" b: 11/18/26, St.Louis, Mo. BR/TR, 6'1", 195 lbs. Deb: 4/21/49 C																											
1949	StL-A	140	471	84	144	28	1	16	91	70	75	.306	.398	.471	.869	130	20	20	100	118	89	.850	1	5	-3	-0	*O/3	1.3
1950	StL-A	113	370	46	88	20	4	10	57	34	42	.238	.305	.395	.700	73	-14	-18	107	112	43	.618	1	3	-2	1	O3	-1.8
1951	StL-A	31	89	10	20	2	1	1	11	9	21	.225	.303	.303	.606	61	-4	-5	105	131	8	.507	0	0	0	1	O	-0.4
1952	StL-A	11	30	3	6	3	0	0	5	1	4	.200	.226	.300	.526	47	-2	-2	97	207	2	.400	0	0	0	-0	/1	-0.2
1953	StL-A	92	285	37	77	15	0	8	35	32	47	.270	.344	.407	.751	96	1	-2	107	93	40	.679	0	1	-1	-0	1	-0.3
1954	Was-A	145	514	75	119	26	6	24	102	80	77	.232	.337	.446	.783	115	8	9	98	136	78	.758	2	1	0	3	*O/1	0.9
1955	Was-A	144	509	74	138	20	8	25	106	73	66	.271	.367	.489	.856	141	20	26	91	129	90	.838	1	2	-1	-5	*O1/3	1.2
1956	Was-A	152	550	92	139	27	2	29	95	100	88	.253	.373	.467	.840	118	17	15	102	109	100	.856	0	0	0	-3	O1	0.5

YEAR	TM/L	G	AB	R	H	2B	3B	HR	RBI	BB	SO	AVG	OBP	SLG	PRO	/A	BR	/A	PF	CHI	RC	TA	SB	CS	SBR	FR	POS	TPR
1957	Was-A	152	572	99	172	23	5	**42**	**114**	76	55	.301	.389	.579	.968	165	47	49	98	104	131	1.012	1	1	-0	-1	*O1	4.1
1958	Was-A	148	550	85	162	18	1	39	108	53	63	.295	.361	.544	.904	150	32	35	97	110	106	.893	3	1	0	0	*O1	2.7
1959	Was-A	115	385	55	93	19	0	21	49	53	62	.242	.336	.455	.791	115	8	8	100	83	59	.762	1	1	-0	2	1O	0.9
1960	Chi-A	127	444	87	131	22	0	28	93	74	69	.295	.399	.534	.933	148	32	31	101	116	95	.963	1	1	-0	-7	*1/O	1.7
1961	Chi-A	141	492	76	145	26	6	27	92	61	62	.295	.379	.537	.916	143	29	29	99	107	101	.927	1	0	0	1	*1	1.8
1962	Phi-N	144	477	61	125	19	5	21	80	56	80	.262	.348	.455	.803	120	9	12	95	113	78	.781	2	1	0	2	*1/O	1.0
1963	Phi-N	138	450	46	108	19	2	19	82	43	72	.240	.313	.418	.731	106	4	3	103	141	60	.674	0	2	-1	4	*1	0.3
1964	Phi-N	49	120	7	22	3	1	4	16	13	20	.183	.269	.325	.594	67	-5	-5	99	129	10	.510	0	0	0	-1	1	-0.7
	Was-A	33	58	5	10	1	0	4	11	9	14	.172	.284	.397	.680	86	-1	-1	101	133	7	.653	0	0	0	-0	1	-0.1
1965	Was-A	12	21	3	4	1	0	0	0	4	3	.190	.320	.238	.558	61	-1	-1	100	0	2	.500	0	0	0	0	/1	0.0
Total	17	1887	6387	945	1703	292	42	318	1147	841	920	.267	.357	.475	.831	124	198	203	99	115	1097	.837	14	19	-7	-3	1O/3	12.9

■ **FRANK SIFFELL** Siffell, Frank b: 1860, Germany d: 10/26/09, Philadelphia, Pa. Deb: 6/14/1884

YEAR	TM/L	G	AB	R	H	2B	3B	HR	RBI	BB	SO	AVG	OBP	SLG	PRO	/A	BR	/A	PF	CHI	RC	TA	SB	CS	SBR	FR	POS	TPR
1884	Phi-a	7	17	3	3	1	0	0		0		.176	.222	.235	.458	45	-1	-1	114	0	1	.357				0	/C	0.0
1885	Phi-a	3	10	0	1	0	0	0		0		.100	.100	.100	.200	-35	-1	-2	103	0	0	.111				0	/CO	0.0
Total	2	10	27	3	4	1	0	0		0		.148	.179	.185	.364	17	-2	-3	110	0	1	.261				0	/CO	0.0

■ **FRANK SIGAFOOS** Sigafoos, Francis Leonard b: 3/21/04, Easton, Pa. d: 4/12/68, Indianapolis, Ind. BR/TR, 5'9", 170 lbs. Deb: 9/03/26

YEAR	TM/L	G	AB	R	H	2B	3B	HR	RBI	BB	SO	AVG	OBP	SLG	PRO	/A	BR	/A	PF	CHI	RC	TA	SB	CS	SBR	FR	POS	TPR
1926	Phi-A	13	43	4	11	0	0	0	2	0	3	.256	.256	.256	.512	29	-4	-5	118	62	3	.344	0	0	0	-1	S	-0.4
1929	Det-A	14	23	3	4	1	0	0	2	5	4	.174	.321	.217	.539	42	-2	-2	97	137	2	.476	0	2	-1	-1	/3S	-0.2
	Chi-A	7	3	1	1	0	0	0	1	2	1	.333	.600	.333	.933	155	0	1	95	342	1	1.500	0	0	0	0	/2	0.1
	Yr	21	26	4	5	1	0	0	3	7	5	.192	.364	.231	.594	58	-1	-1	96	212	2	.565	0	2	-1	-1		-0.1
1931	Cin-N	21	65	6	11	2	0	0	8	0	6	.169	.182	.200	.382	3	-9	-8	95	219	3	.259	0			0	3/S	-0.6
Total	3	55	134	14	27	3	0	0	13	7	14	.201	.246	.224	.470	24	-14	-15	102	160	8	.349	0	2		-1	/3S2	-1.1

■ **PADDY SIGLIN** Siglin, Wesley Peter b: 9/24/1891, Aurelia, Iowa d: 8/5/56, Oakland, Cal. BR/TR, 5'10", 160 lbs. Deb: 9/12/14

YEAR	TM/L	G	AB	R	H	2B	3B	HR	RBI	BB	SO	AVG	OBP	SLG	PRO	/A	BR	/A	PF	CHI	RC	TA	SB	CS	SBR	FR	POS	TPR
1914	Pit-N	14	39	4	6	0	0	0	2	4	6	.154	.233	.154	.386	17	-4	-4	92	121	2	.333	1			-2	2	-0.5
1915	Pit-N	6	7	1	2	0	0	0	0	1	2	.286	.375	.286	.661	102	0	0	99	0	1	.800	1			0	/2	0.0
1916	Pit-N	3	4	0	1	0	0	0	0	0	2	.250	.250	.250	.500	51	-0	-0	105	0	0	.333	0			-1	/2	0.0
Total	3	23	50	5	9	0	0	0	2	5	10	.180	.255	.180	.435	33	-4	-4	94	94	3	.390	2			-3	/2	-0.5

■ **TRIPP SIGMAN** Sigman, Wesley Triplett b: 1/17/1899, Mooresville, N.C. d: 3/8/71, Augusta, Ga. BL/TR, 6', 180 lbs. Deb: 9/18/29

YEAR	TM/L	G	AB	R	H	2B	3B	HR	RBI	BB	SO	AVG	OBP	SLG	PRO	/A	BR	/A	PF	CHI	RC	TA	SB	CS	SBR	FR	POS	TPR
1929	Phi-N	10	29	8	15	1	0	2	9	3	1	.517	.563	.759	1.321	204	6	5	110	110	12	1.786	0			-2	O	0.2
1930	Phi-N	52	100	15	27	4	1	4	6	6	9	.270	.324	.450	.774	80	-3	-4	106	36	14	.740	1			-1	O	-0.4
Total	2	62	129	23	42	5	1	6	15	9	10	.326	.379	.519	.898	108	3	2	107	53	26	.908	1			-3	/O	-0.2

■ **EDDIE SILBER** Silber, Edward James b: 6/6/14, Philadelphia, Pa. d: 10/26/76, Dunedin, Fla. BR/TR, 5'11", 170 lbs. Deb: 9/03/37

YEAR	TM/L	G	AB	R	H	2B	3B	HR	RBI	BB	SO	AVG	OBP	SLG	PRO	/A	BR	/A	PF	CHI	RC	TA	SB	CS	SBR	FR	POS	TPR
1937	StL-A	22	83	10	26	2	0	0	4	5	13	.313	.352	.337	.690	76	-3	-3	99	50	9	.559	0	2	-1	-6	O	-0.9
1939	StL-A	1	1	0	0	0	0	0	0	0	1	.000	.000	.000	.000	-99	-0	-0	100	0	0	.000	0	0	0	0	H	0.0
Total	2	23	84	10	26	2	0	0	4	5	14	.310	.348	.333	.682	74	-3	-3	99	49	9	.550	0	2	-1	-6	/O	-0.9

■ **ED SILCH** Silch, Edward "Baldy" b: 2/22/1865, St.Louis, Mo. d: 1/15/1895, St.Louis, Mo. TR , Deb: 1888

YEAR	TM/L	G	AB	R	H	2B	3B	HR	RBI	BB	SO	AVG	OBP	SLG	PRO	/A	BR	/A	PF	CHI	RC	TA	SB	CS	SBR	FR	POS	TPR
1888	Bro-a	14	48	5	13	4	0	0	3	4		.271	.327	.354	.681	116	1	1	105	54	7	.714	4			0	O	0.1

■ **DANNY SILVA** Silva, Daniel James b: 10/5/1896, Everett, Mass. d: 4/4/74, Hyannis, Mass. BR/TR, 6', 170 lbs. Deb: 8/11/19

YEAR	TM/L	G	AB	R	H	2B	3B	HR	RBI	BB	SO	AVG	OBP	SLG	PRO	/A	BR	/A	PF	CHI	RC	TA	SB	CS	SBR	FR	POS	TPR
1919	Was-A	1	4	0	1	0	0	0	0	0	0	.250	.250	.250	.500	41	-0	-0	98	0	0	.333	0			0	/3	0.0

■ **AL SILVERA** Silvera, Aaron Albert b: 8/26/35, San Diego, Cal. BR/TR, 6', 180 lbs. Deb: 6/12/55

YEAR	TM/L	G	AB	R	H	2B	3B	HR	RBI	BB	SO	AVG	OBP	SLG	PRO	/A	BR	/A	PF	CHI	RC	TA	SB	CS	SBR	FR	POS	TPR
1955	Cin-N	13	7	3	1	0	0	0	2	0	1	.143	.143	.143	.286	-23	-1	-1	106	810	0	.167	0	0	0	-0	/O	-0.1
1956	Cin-N	1	0	0	0	0	0	0	0	0	0	—	—	—	—	—	0	0	108	—	—	—	0	0	0	0	R	0.0
Total	2	14	7	3	1	0	0	0	2	0	1	.143	.143	.143	.286	-23	-1	-1	106	810	0	.167	0	0	0	-0	/O	-0.1

■ **CHARLIE SILVERA** Silvera, Charles Anthony Ryan "Swede" b: 10/13/24, San Francisco, Cal BR/TR, 5'10", 175 lbs. Deb: 9/29/48 C

YEAR	TM/L	G	AB	R	H	2B	3B	HR	RBI	BB	SO	AVG	OBP	SLG	PRO	/A	BR	/A	PF	CHI	RC	TA	SB	CS	SBR	FR	POS	TPR
1948	NY-A	4	14	1	8	0	1	0	1	0	1	.571	.571	.714	1.286	240	3	3	100	34	6	1.667	0	0	0	0	/C	0.3
1949	NY-A	58	130	8	41	2	0	0	13	18	5	.315	.403	.331	.733	95	0	0	100	104	18	.674	2	1	0	-1	C	0.2
1950	NY-A	18	25	2	4	0	0	0	1	1	2	.160	.192	.160	.352	-9	-4	-4	99	86	1	.238	0	0	0	0	C	-0.2
1951	NY-A	18	51	5	14	3	0	1	7	5	3	.275	.339	.392	.731	106	-0	0	92	109	5	.581	0	0	0	1	C	0.3
1952	NY-A	20	55	4	18	3	0	0	11	5	2	.327	.383	.382	.765	116	1	1	98	196	7	.634	0	3	-2	0	C	0.1
1953	NY-A	42	82	11	23	3	1	0	12	9	5	.280	.352	.341	.693	95	-1	-0	93	159	11	.617	0	1	-1	-1	C/3	0.0
1954	NY-A	20	37	1	10	1	0	0	4	3	2	.270	.341	.297	.639	77	-1	-1	99	138	3	.500	0	1	-1	1	C	0.0
1955	NY-A	14	26	1	5	0	0	0	1	6	4	.192	.344	.192	.536	48	-2	-2	98	75	2	.524	0	0	0	0	C	0.0
1956	NY-A	7	9	0	2	0	0	0	0	2	3	.222	.364	.222	.586	59	-0	-0	99	0	1	.500	0	0	0	0	/C	0.0
1957	Chi-N	26	53	1	11	3	0	0	2	4	5	.208	.263	.264	.527	44	-4	-4	96	59	3	.409	0	0	0	1	C	-0.1
Total	10	227	482	34	136	15	2	1	52	53	32	.282	.356	.328	.683	87	-9	-7	97	115	58	.607	2	6	-3	2	C/3	0.6

■ **LUIS SILVERIO** Silverio, Luis Pascual (Delmonte) b: 10/23/56, Villa Gonzalez, D.R BR/TR, 5'11", 165 lbs. Deb: 9/09/78

YEAR	TM/L	G	AB	R	H	2B	3B	HR	RBI	BB	SO	AVG	OBP	SLG	PRO	/A	BR	/A	PF	CHI	RC	TA	SB	CS	SBR	FR	POS	TPR
1978	KC-A	8	11	7	6	2	1	0	3	2	3	.545	.615	.909	1.524	317	3	3	102	118	6	2.167	1	1	-0	-2	/OD	0.1

■ **TOM SILVERIO** Silverio, Tomas Roberto (Veloz) b: 10/14/45, Santiago, D.R. BL/TL, 5'10", 170 lbs. Deb: 4/30/70

YEAR	TM/L	G	AB	R	H	2B	3B	HR	RBI	BB	SO	AVG	OBP	SLG	PRO	/A	BR	/A	PF	CHI	RC	TA	SB	CS	SBR	FR	POS	TPR
1970	Cal-A	15	15	1	0	0	0	0	0	2	4	.000	.118	.000	.118	-71	-3	-3	92	0	0	.125	0	1	-1	-2	/O1	-0.5
1971	Cal-A	3	3	0	1	0	0	0	0	0	0	.333	.333	.333	.667	91	-0	-0	99	0	0	.500	0	0	0	-0	/O	0.0
1972	Cal-A	13	12	1	2	0	0	0	0	0	5	.167	.167	.167	.333	-1	-1	-1	88	0	0	.200	0	0	0	-1	/O	-0.2
Total	3	31	30	2	3	0	0	0	0	2	9	.100	.156	.100	.256	-28	-5	-5	91	0	1	.179	0	1	-1	-3	/O1	-0.7

■ **KEN SILVESTRI** Silvestri, Kenneth Joseph "Hawk" b: 5/3/16, Chicago, Ill. BB/TR, 6'1", 200 lbs. Deb: 4/18/39 MC

YEAR	TM/L	G	AB	R	H	2B	3B	HR	RBI	BB	SO	AVG	OBP	SLG	PRO	/A	BR	/A	PF	CHI	RC	TA	SB	CS	SBR	FR	POS	TPR
1939	Chi-A	22	75	6	13	3	0	2	5	6	13	.173	.244	.293	.537	34	-7	-8	107	60	6	.460	0	1	-1	-1	C	-0.7
1940	Chi-A	28	24	5	6	2	0	2	10	4	7	.250	.357	.583	.940	134	1	1	104	181	4	.900	0	0	0	0	/C	0.1
1941	NY-A	17	40	6	10	5	0	1	4	7	6	.250	.362	.450	.812	116	1	1	98	67	7	.806	0	0	0	-1	C	0.1
1946	NY-A	13	21	4	6	1	0	0	1	3	7	.286	.375	.333	.708	99	0	0	100	54	3	.667	0	0	0	0	C	0.1
1947	NY-A	3	10	0	2	0	0	0	0	2	2	.200	.333	.200	.533	52	-1	-1	97	0	1	.500	0	0	0	0	/C	0.0
1949	Phi-N	4	4	1	0	0	0	0	0	2	1	.000	.333	.000	.333	-3	-0	-0	101	0	0	.500	0			0	/C2S	0.0
1950	Phi-N	11	20	2	5	0	1	0	4	4	3	.250	.400	.350	.750	102	0	0	97	220	3	.706	0			0	/C	0.0
1951	Phi-N	4	9	2	2	0	0	0	1	3	2	.222	.417	.222	.639	79	-0	-0	97	193	1	.714	0	0	0	0	/C2	0.0
Total	8	102	203	26	44	11	1	5	25	31	41	.217	.326	.355	.681	78	-6	-7	102	94	25	.656	0	1		-2	/C2S	-0.4

■ **AL SIMMONS** Simmons, Aloysius Harry "Bucketfoot Al" (born Aloys Szymanski) b: 5/22/02, Milwaukee, Wis. d: 5/26/56, Milwaukee, Wis. BR/TR, 5'11", 190 lbs. Deb: 4/15/24 CH

YEAR	TM/L	G	AB	R	H	2B	3B	HR	RBI	BB	SO	AVG	OBP	SLG	PRO	/A	BR	/A	PF	CHI	RC	TA	SB	CS	SBR	FR	POS	TPR
1924	Phi-A	152	594	69	183	31	9	8	102	30	60	.308	.343	.431	.774	100	-4	-3	99	128	84	.714	16	15	-4	-1	*O	-1.7
1925	Phi-A	153	654	122	**253**	43	12	24	129	35	41	.387	.419	**.599**	1.018	152	51	49	103	89	**155**	1.048	7	14	-6	-3	*O	2.4
1926	Phi-A	147	583	90	199	53	10	19	109	48	49	.341	.392	.564	.957	125	37	23	118	102	127	.995	10	6	-1	-9	*O	0.3
1927	Phi-A	106	406	86	159	36	11	15	108	31	30	.392	.436	.645	1.081	184	44	46	97	124	108	1.231	10	0	3	-0	*O	3.6
1928	Phi-A	119	464	78	163	33	9	15	107	31	30	.351	.396	.558	.954	144	30	29	103	128	100	.964	1	4	-2	3	*O	2.2
1929	Phi-A	143	581	114	212	41	9	34	**157**	31	38	.365	.398	.642	1.040	150	50	43	109	120	145	1.102	4	2	0	17	*O	**5.0**
1930	Phi-A	138	554	**152**	211	41	16	36	165	39	34	**.381**	.423	.708	1.130	182	64	65	99	116	163	1.278	9	2	2	5	*O	5.8
1931	Phi-A	128	513	105	200	37	13	22	128	47	45	**.390**	.444	.641	1.085	174	60	56	105	113	145	1.209	3	3	-1	7	*O	4.9
1932	Phi-A	154	670	144	**216**	28	9	35	151	47	76	.322	.368	.548	.915	118	30	17	114	103	134	.919	4	2	0	-6	*O	0.4
1933	Chi-A	146	605	85	200	29	10	14	119	39	49	.331	.373	.481	.854	124	20	19	101	126	109	.830	5	1	1	2	*O	1.5
1934	Chi-A	138	558	102	192	36	7	18	104	53	58	.344	.403	.530	.933	140	31	32	99	105	120	.962	3	2	-0	6	*O	3.3
1935	Chi-A	128	525	68	140	22	7	16	79	33	43	.267	.313	.427	.739	82	-11	-17	109	104	68	.673	4	6	-2	-4	*O	-2.3
1936	Det-A	143	568	96	186	38	6	13	112	49	35	.327	.383	.484	.867	118	10	14	95	118	105	.860	6	4	-1	-8	*O/1	0.2
1937	Was-A	103	419	60	117	21	10	8	84	27	35	.279	.329	.434	.763	96	-8	-4	94	148	60	.711	3	2	-0	5	*O	-0.2
1938	Was-A	125	470	79	142	23	6	21	95	38	40	.302	.357	.511	.868	121	8	12	95	108	86	.857	2	1	0	-6	*O	0.5

YEAR	TM/L	G	AB	R	H	2B	3B	HR	RBI	BB	SO	AVG	OBP	SLG	PRO	/A	BR	/A	PF	CHI	RC	TA	SB	CS	SBR	FR	POS	TPR
1939	Bos-N	93	330	39	93	17	5	7	43	22	40	.282	.331	.427	.758	111	0	4	92	99	43	.660	0			-3	O	0.0
	Cin-N	9	21	0	3	0	0	0	1	2	3	.143	.217	.143	.360	-1	-3	-3	103	122	1	.278	0			1	/O	-0.1
	Yr	102	351	39	96	17	5	7	44	24	43	.274	.324	.410	.734	104	-3	0	93	102	49	.667	0			-1		-0.1
1940	Phi-A	37	81	7	25	4	0	1	19	4	8	.309	.341	.395	.736	94	-1	-1	96	196	10	.600	0	0	0	2	O	0.0
1941	Phi-A	9	24	1	3	1	0	0	1	1	2	.125	.160	.167	.327	-13	-4	-4	101	89	0	.217	0	0	0	1	/O	-0.3
1943	Bos-A	40	133	9	27	5	0	1	12	8	21	.203	.248	.263	.511	48	-9	-9	104	115	8	.391	0	1	-1	-2	O	-1.3
1944	Phi-A	4	6	1	3	0	0	0	2	0	0	.500	.500	.500	1.000	184	1	1	101	241	1	.750	0	0	0	-0	/O	0.0
Total	20	2215	8759	1507	2927	539	149	307	1827	615	737	.334	.380	.535	.915	130	399	367	103	115	1771	.918	87	65		6	*O/1	24.2
■ **HACK SIMMONS**	Simmons, George Washington b: 1/29/1885, Brooklyn, N.Y. d: 4/26/42, Arverne, N.Y. BR/TR, 5'8", 179 lbs. Deb: 4/15/10																											
1910	Det-A	42	110	12	25	3	1	0	9	10		.227	.303	.273	.576	79	-2	-2	102	111	10	.506	1			-1	1/3O	-0.2
1912	NY-A	110	401	45	96	17	2	0	41	33		.239	.308	.292	.600	71	-14	-15	101	119	41	.577	19			-17	21/S	-3.3
1914	Bal-F	114	352	50	95	16	5	1	38	32	26	.270	.331	.352	.683	97	-2	-1	99	108	46	.634	7			-3	O2/1S3	-0.7
1915	Bal-F	39	88	8	18	7	1	1	14	10	9	.205	.286	.341	.627	79	-2	-3	107	153	10	.586	1			0	2O	-0.2
Total	4	305	951	115	234	43	9	2	102	85	35	.246	.314	.317	.630	82	-20	-21	101	117	106	.590	28			-21	2/O13S	-4.4
■ **JOHN SIMMONS**	Simmons, John Earl b: 7/7/24, Birmingham, Ala. BR/TR, 6'1.5", 192 lbs. Deb: 4/22/49																											
1949	Was-A	62	93	12	20	0	0	0	5	11	6	.215	.298	.215	.513	40	-8	-7	91	86	6	.403	0	0	0	-5	O	-1.2
■ **JOE SIMMONS**	Simmons, Joseph S. b: 6/13/1845, New York, N.Y. 5'9", 166 lbs. Deb: 5/08/1871 M																											
1871	Chi-n	27	134	29	27							.201															*O/1	
1872	Cle-n	17	87	11	20							.230															1/O	
1875	Wes-n	13	56	5	9							.161															O/1M	
Total	3 n	57	277	45	56							.202															O/1M	
■ **NELSON SIMMONS**	Simmons, Nelson Bernard b: 6/27/63, Washington, D.C. BB/TR, 6'1", 185 lbs. Deb: 9/04/84																											
1984	Det-A	9	30	4	13	2	0	0	3	2	5	.433	.469	.500	.969	175	3	3	96	80	6	.947	1	0	0	-1	/OD	0.2
1985	Det-A	75	251	31	60	11	0	10	33	26	41	.239	.310	.402	.713	88	-3	-5	106	100	32	.656	1	0	0	-2	OD	-0.6
1987	Bal-A	16	49	3	13	1	1	1	4	3	8	.265	.308	.388	.695	86	-1	-1	98	73	5	.550	0	1	-1	1	O/D	0.0
Total	3	100	330	38	86	14	1	11	40	31	54	.261	.324	.409	.733	95	-1	-3	104	94	43	.677	2	1	0	-2	/OD	-0.4
■ **TED SIMMONS**	Simmons, Ted Lyle b: 8/9/49, Highland Park, Mich. BB/TR, 5'11", 193 lbs. Deb: 9/21/68																											
1968	StL-N	2	3	0	1	0	0	0	0	1	1	.333	.500	.333	.833	162	0	0	95	0	1	1.000	0	0	0	0	/C	0.0
1969	StL-N	5	14	0	3	0	1	0	3	1	1	.214	.267	.357	.624	74	-1	-1	100	241	1	.545	0	0	0	0	/C	0.0
1970	StL-N	82	284	29	69	8	2	3	24	37	37	.243	.334	.317	.651	71	-9	-11	106	96	31	.590	2	2	-1	6	C	-0.1
1971	StL-N	133	510	64	155	32	4	7	77	36	50	.304	.353	.424	.777	118	12	12	101	140	71	.677	1	3	-2	2	*C	1.6
1972	StL-N	152	594	70	180	36	6	16	96	29	57	.303	.338	.465	.802	120	18	14	105	129	86	.708	1	3	-2	19	*C1	4.1
1973	StL-N	161	619	62	192	36	2	13	91	61	47	.310	.374	.438	.812	137	21	28	91	125	94	.734	2	2	-1	20	*C/1O	5.7
1974	StL-N	152	599	66	163	33	6	20	103	47	35	.272	.331	.447	.779	112	11	8	104	128	83	.701	0	0	0	10	*C1	2.4
1975	StL-N	157	581	80	193	32	3	18	100	63	35	.332	.398	.491	.889	141	36	34	103	121	108	.852	1	3	-2	-5	*C/1O	3.3
1976	StL-N	150	546	60	159	35	3	5	75	73	35	.291	.375	.394	.769	114	15	12	104	**133**	80	.715	0	7	-4	10	*C1/O3	2.3
1977	StL-N	150	516	82	164	25	3	21	95	79	37	.318	.410	.500	.910	149	33	36	96	121	100	.902	2	6	-3	-0	*C/O	3.1
1978	StL-N	152	516	71	148	40	5	22	80	77	39	.287	.383	.512	.894	156	33	37	95	98	98	.889	1	1	-0	4	*CO	4.4
1979	StL-N	123	448	68	127	22	0	26	87	61	34	.283	.374	.507	.881	132	24	21	105	120	84	.880	0	1	-1	-3	*C	2.0
1980	StL-N	145	495	84	150	33	2	21	98	59	45	.303	.379	.505	.885	141	30	28	103	126	94	.872	1	0	0	5	*C/O	3.7
1981	Mil-A	100	380	45	82	13	3	14	61	23	32	.216	.266	.376	.642	87	-9	-8	96	137	36	.547	0	1	-1	1	CD/1	-0.3
1982	Mil-A	137	539	73	145	29	0	23	97	32	40	.269	.312	.451	.763	113	3	7	94	132	70	.669	0	0	0	7	*CD	2.0
1983	Mil-A	153	600	76	185	39	3	13	108	41	51	.308	.355	.448	.803	130	15	22	92	**145**	89	.718	4	2	0	5	CD	3.0
1984	Mil-A	132	497	44	110	23	2	4	52	30	40	.221	.270	.300	.570	63	-29	-24	92	**131**	36	.451	3	0	1	2	D13	-2.3
1985	Mil-A	143	528	60	144	28	2	12	76	57	32	.273	.345	.402	.746	99	3	-0	105	129	71	.674	1	1	-0	1	D1C/3	0.0
1986	Atl-N	76	127	14	32	5	0	4	25	12	14	.252	.321	.386	.707	92	-1	-1	102	163	16	.656	1	0	0	1	1C/3	0.0
1987	Atl-N	73	177	20	49	8	0	4	30	21	23	.277	.354	.390	.743	89	-0	-2	108	148	24	.684	1	1	-0	1	1C/3	-0.1
1988	Atl-N	78	107	6	21	6	0	2	11	15	9	.196	.295	.308	.603	70	-4	-4	104	113	10	.533	0	0	0	0	1C	-0.4
Total	21	2456	8680	1074	2472	483	47	248	1389	855	694	.285	.352	.437	.789	118	201	208	99	127	1284	.754	21	33	-14	86	*CD1/O3	34.4
■ **HANK SIMON**	Simon, Henry Joseph b: 8/25/1862, Hawkinsville, N.Y. d: 1/1/25, Albany, N.Y. BR/TR, Deb: 10/07/1887																											
1887	Cle-a	3	10	1	1	0	0	0		0		.100	.100	.100	.200	-45	-2	-2	98	0	0	.111	0			0	/O	-0.1
1890	BB-a	89	373	66	96	17	11	0		34		.257	.321	.362	.683	103	1	1	100	0	52	.697	23			6	O	0.2
	Syr-a	38	156	33	47	5	3	2		17		.301	.370	.410	.780	147	6	9	90	0	29	.853	12			-3	O	0.4
	Yr	127	529	99	143	22	14	2	0	51		.270	.336	.376	.712	115	7	9	97	0	81	.741	35			4		0.6
Total	2	130	539	100	144	22	14	2	0	51		.267	.332	.371	.703	112	5	8	97	0	81	.727	35			4	O	0.5
■ **MIKE SIMON**	Simon, Michael Edward b: 4/13/1883, Hayden, Ind. d: 6/10/63, Los Angeles, Cal. BR/TR, 5'11", 188 lbs. Deb: 09																											
1909	Pit-N	12	18	2	3	0	0	0	2	1		.167	.211	.167	.377	17	-2	-2	105	243	1	.267	0			-0	/C	-0.1
1910	Pit-N	22	50	3	10	0	1	0	5	1	2	.200	.216	.240	.456	29	-4	-5	112	145	3	.350	1			0	C	-0.3
1911	Pit-N	71	215	19	49	4	3	0	22	10	14	.228	.275	.274	.550	54	-14	-14	101	126	16	.446	1			1	C	-0.7
1912	Pit-N	42	113	10	34	2	1	0	11	5	9	.301	.331	.336	.667	84	-3	-3	99	97	12	.557	1			-3	C	-0.2
1913	Pit-N	92	255	23	63	6	2	1	17	10	15	.247	.281	.298	.579	68	-12	-11	96	78	21	.474	3			1	C	-0.3
1914	StL-F	93	276	21	57	11	2	0	21	18	21	.207	.255	.261	.516	45	-19	-21	106	105	20	.420	2			10	C	-0.7
1915	Bro-F	47	142	7	25	5	1	0	12	9	12	.176	.225	.225	.451	34	-12	-11	98	135	8	.359	1			-5	C	-1.6
Total	7	379	1069	85	241	28	10	1	90	54	73	.225	.267	.273	.540	54	-65	-66	101	110	82	.436	9			4	C	-3.9
■ **SYL SIMON**	Simon, Sylvester Adam "Sammy" b: 12/14/1897, Evansville, Ind. d: 2/28/73, Chandler, Ind. BR/TR, 5'10.5", 170 lbs. Deb: 10/01/23																											
1923	StL-A	1	1	0	0	0	0	0	0	0	0	.000	.000	.000	.000	-96	-0	-0	104	0	0	.000	0	0	0	0	H	0.0
1924	StL-A	23	32	5	8	1	1	0	6	3	5	.250	.314	.344	.658	65	-2	-2	107	180	4	.583	0	0	0	-0	/3S	0.0
Total	2	24	33	5	8	1	1	0	6	3	5	.242	.306	.333	.639	61	-2	-2	107	175	4	.560	0	0	0	-0	/3S	0.0
■ **MEL SIMONS**	Simons, Melbern Ellis "Butch" b: 7/1/1900, Carlyle, Ill. d: 11/10/74, Paducah, Ky. BL/TR, 5'10", 175 lbs. Deb: 4/14/31																											
1931	Chi-A	68	189	24	52	9	0	0	12	12	17	.275	.318	.323	.641	75	-8	-6	92	65	20	.536	1	1	-0	-6	O	-1.4
1932	Chi-A	7	5	0	0	0	0	0	0	0	1	.000	.000	.000	.000	-99	-1	-1	87	0	0	.000	0	0	0	-3	/O	-0.3
Total	2	75	194	24	52	9	0	0	12	12	18	.268	.311	.314	.625	70	-10	-8	92	63	20	.517	1	1	-0	-8	/O	-1.7
■ **HARRY SIMPSON**	Simpson, Harry Leon "Suitcase" or "Goody" b: 12/3/25, Atlanta, Ga. d: 4/3/79, Akron, Ohio BL/TR, 6'1", 180 lbs. Deb: 4/21/51																											
1951	Cle-A	122	332	51	76	7	0	7	24	45	48	.229	.325	.313	.638	77	-12	-9	95	69	36	.588	6	4	-1	-6	O1	-1.9
1952	Cle-A	146	545	66	145	21	10	10	65	56	82	.266	.337	.396	.733	114	2	8	91	101	75	.676	5	3	-0	-2	*O1	0.0
1953	Cle-A	82	242	25	55	3	1	7	22	18	27	.227	.284	.335	.618	70	-12	-11	95	80	23	.518	0	0	0	-7	O/1	-1.9
1955	Cle-A	3	1	1	0	0	0	0	0	2	0	.000	.667	.000	.667	88	0	0	104	0	0	2.000	0	0	0	0	H	0.0
	KC-A	112	396	42	119	16	7	5	52	34	61	.301	.359	.414	.773	106	4	3	101	110	57	.695	3	5	-2	-2	*O/1	-0.5
	Yr	115	397	43	119	16	7	5	52	36	61	.300	.361	.413	.774	106	4	3	101	108	57	.700	3	5	-2	-2		-0.5
1956	KC-A	141	543	76	159	22	**11**	21	105	47	82	.293	.350	.490	.840	119	13	12	101	126	87	.778	2	3	-1	-10	*O1	-0.5
1957	KC-A	50	179	24	53	9	6	6	24	12	28	.296	.340	.514	.854	132	6	7	99	88	28	.770	0	1	-1	0	1O	0.5
	NY-A	75	224	27	56	7	3	7	39	19	36	.250	.309	.402	.710	99	-3	-1	94	139	27	.632	1	0	0	-2	O1	-0.5
	Yr	125	403	51	109	16	**9**	13	63	31	64	.270	.323	.452	.774	114	4	6	96	119	59	.711	1	1	-0	-2		0.0
1958	NY-A	24	51	1	11	2	1	0	6	6	12	.216	.310	.294	.604	65	-2	-2	103	160	5	.537	0	0	0	-2	O	-0.5
	KC-A	78	212	21	56	7	1	7	27	26	33	.264	.345	.406	.750	100	2	0	106	101	31	.704	0	2	-1	1	1O	-0.1
	Yr	102	263	22	67	9	2	7	33	32	45	.255	.338	.384	.722	94	-0	-2	105	117	36	.673	0	2	-1	-1		-0.6
1959	KC-A	8	14	1	4	0	0	1	2	2	4	.286	.412	.500	.912	147	1	1	101	79	3	1.000	0	0	0	0	/1	0.1
	Chi-A	38	75	5	14	5	1	2	13	4	14	.187	.228	.360	.588	61	-5	-4	97	155	6	.500	0	0	0	-2	O/1	-0.6
	Yr	46	89	6	18	5	1	3	15	6	18	.202	.260	.382	.642	76	-4	-3	97	144	9	.569	0	0	0	-2		-0.5

YEAR	TM/L	G	AB	R	H	2B	3B	HR	RBI	BB	SO	AVG	OBP	SLG	PRO	/A	BR	/A	PF	CHI	RC	TA	SB	CS	SBR	FR	POS	TPR
	Pit-N	9	15	3	4	2	0	0	2	0	2	.267	.267	.400	.667	72	-1	-1	103	135	2	.545	0	0	0	-0	/O	0.0
Total	8	888	2829	343	752	101	41	73	381	271	429	.266	.332	.408	.740	103	-6	3	97	106	380	.693	17	18	-6	-33	O1	-5.9
■ **JOE SIMPSON** Simpson, Joe Allen b: 12/31/51, Purcell, Okla. BL/TL, 6'3", 175 lbs. Deb: 9/02/75																												
1975	LA-N	9	6	3	2	0	0	0	0	0	2	.333	.333	.333	.667	90	-0	-0	95	0	1	.500	0	0	0	-2	/O	-0.1
1976	LA-N	23	30	2	4	1	0	0	0	1	6	.133	.161	.167	.328	-7	-4	-4	100	0	1	.222	0	1	-1	-4	O	-1.0
1977	LA-N	29	23	2	4	0	0	0	1	2	6	.174	.240	.174	.414	13	-3	-3	100	100	1	.333	1	1	-0	-6	O/1	-1.0
1978	LA-N	10	5	1	2	0	0	0	1	0	2	.400	.400	.400	.800	125	0	0	99	198	1	.667	0	0	0	-3	O	-0.2
1979	Sea-A	120	265	29	75	11	0	2	27	11	21	.283	.314	.347	.661	78	-8	-8	100	106	28	.556	6	3	0	-7	*O	-1.8
1980	Sea-A	129	365	42	91	15	3	3	34	28	43	.249	.305	.332	.636	72	-13	-14	103	102	39	.588	17	4	3	-8	*O/1	-2.1
1981	Sea-A	91	288	32	64	11	3	2	30	15	41	.222	.263	.302	.565	63	-14	-14	100	126	24	.500	12	3	2	-4	O	-1.9
1982	Sea-A	105	296	39	76	14	4	2	23	22	48	.257	.313	.351	.664	75	-7	-11	109	84	30	.579	8	14	-6	-3	O	-2.2
1983	KC-A	91	119	16	20	2	2	0	8	11	21	.168	.250	.218	.468	30	-11	-11	101	120	7	.396	1	1	-0	-0	1O/PD	-1.4
Total	9	607	1397	166	338	54	12	9	124	90	190	.242	.291	.317	.608	66	-61	-66	103	103	132	.538	45	27	-3	-36	O/1PD	-11.7
■ **MARTY SIMPSON** Simpson, Martin b: Baltimore, Md. Deb: 5/14/1873																												
1873	Mar-n	3	11	2	0							.000															/2C	
■ **DICK SIMPSON** Simpson, Richard Charles b: 7/28/43, Washington, D.C. BR/TR, 6'4", 176 lbs. Deb: 9/21/62																												
1962	LA-A	6	8	1	2	1	0	0	1	2	3	.250	.400	.375	.775	108	0	0	102	132	1	.833	0	0	0	-0	/O	0.0
1964	LA-A	21	50	11	7	1	0	2	4	8	15	.140	.259	.280	.539	56	-3	-3	89	85	4	.522	2	2	-1	-1	O	-0.4
1965	Cal-A	8	27	2	6	1	0	0	3	2	8	.222	.276	.259	.535	54	-2	-2	98	181	2	.455	1	0	0	-1	/O	-0.2
1966	Cin-N	92	84	26	20	2	0	4	14	10	32	.238	.333	.405	.738	91	1	-1	114	128	12	.708	0	1	-1	-17	O	-2.1
1967	Cin-N	44	54	8	14	3	0	1	6	7	11	.259	.344	.370	.715	96	0	-0	109	108	7	.643	0	1	-1	-2	O	-0.3
1968	StL-N	26	56	11	13	0	0	3	8	8	21	.232	.328	.393	.721	121	1	1	95	109	7	.667	0	1	-1	-3	O	-0.3
	Hou-N	59	177	25	33	7	2	3	11	20	61	.186	.284	.299	.583	76	-5	-5	99	75	15	.540	4	4	-1	-5	O	-1.4
	Yr	85	233	36	46	7	2	6	19	28	82	.197	.294	.322	.616	87	-4	-3	98	86	23	.572	4	5	-2	-7		-1.7
1969	NY-A	6	11	2	3	2	0	0	4	3	6	.273	.429	.455	.883	154	1	1	95	321	2	1.000	0	0	0	-0	/O	0.0
	Sea-A	26	51	8	9	2	0	2	5	4	17	.176	.236	.333	.570	59	-3	-3	98	87	4	.533	3	1	0	-2	O	-0.5
	Yr	32	62	10	12	4	0	2	9	7	23	.194	.275	.355	.630	77	-2	-2	98	141	6	.604	3	1	0	-3		-0.5
Total	7	288	518	94	107	19	2	15	56	64	174	.207	.301	.338	.639	83	-10	-11	101	105	54	.603	10	10	-3	-31	O	-5.2
■ **DUKE SIMS** Sims, Duane B b: 6/5/41, Salt Lake City, Ut. BL/TR, 6'2", 197 lbs. Deb: 9/22/64																												
1964	Cle-A	2	6	0	0	0	0	0	0	0	2	.000	.000	.000	.000	-97	-2	-2	103	0	0	.000	0	0	0	0	/C	-0.1
1965	Cle-A	48	118	9	21	0	0	6	15	15	33	.178	.271	.331	.601	71	-5	-5	98	109	11	.545	0	0	0	-3	C	-0.4
1966	Cle-A	52	133	12	35	2	2	6	19	11	31	.263	.338	.444	.781	121	4	4	101	104	19	.725	0	1	-1	-8	C	-0.2
1967	Cle-A	88	272	25	55	8	2	12	37	30	64	.202	.295	.379	.674	98	-1	-1	100	111	30	.628	3	3	-1	7	C	1.2
1968	Cle-A	122	361	48	90	21	0	11	44	62	68	.249	.367	.399	.766	131	16	16	101	106	54	.752	1	3	-2	-5	C1/O	1.3
1969	Cle-A	114	326	40	77	8	0	18	45	66	80	.236	.374	.426	.801	131	12	15	94	94	57	.838	1	2	-1	9	*C/O1	3.0
1970	Cle-A	110	345	46	91	12	0	23	56	46	59	.264	.360	.499	.859	117	16	9	115	94	63	.852	0	4	-2	4	CO1	0.9
1971	LA-N	90	230	23	63	7	2	6	25	30	39	.274	.360	.400	.760	116	5	5	99	92	34	.715	0	1	-1	-4	C	0.2
1972	LA-N	51	151	7	29	7	0	2	11	17	23	.192	.278	.278	.556	62	-8	-7	94	94	11	.469	0	0	0	-3	C	-0.8
	Det-A	38	98	11	31	4	0	4	19	19	18	.316	.432	.480	.912	151	10	8	113	135	22	.985	0	0	0	1	C/O	1.0
1973	Det-A	80	252	31	61	10	0	8	30	30	36	.242	.327	.377	.704	97	-1	-1	101	99	32	.646	1	2	-1	6	C/O	0.6
	NY-A	4	9	3	3	0	0	1	1	3	1	.333	.500	.667	1.167	225	2	2	101	44	3	1.500	0	0	0	0	/CD	0.2
	Yr	84	261	34	64	10	0	9	31	33	37	.245	.334	.387	.721	102	1	1	101	98	36	.688	1	2	-1	6		0.8
1974	NY-A	5	15	1	2	1	0	0	2	1	5	.133	.188	.200	.387	12	-2	-2	96	262	1	.308	0	0	0	0	/CD	-0.1
	Tex-A	39	106	7	22	0	0	3	6	8	24	.208	.282	.292	.575	68	-5	-4	96	59	9	.483	0	0	0	1	C/OD	-0.1
	Yr	44	121	8	24	1	0	3	8	9	29	.198	.271	.281	.552	61	-6	-6	96	88	9	.460	0	0	0	1		-0.2
Total	11	843	2422	263	580	80	6	100	310	338	483	.239	.341	.401	.742	110	42	38	101	100	346	.726	6	16	-8	6	C/1OD	6.7
■ **GREG SIMS** Sims, Gregory Emmett b: 6/28/46, San Francisco, Cal BB/TR, 6', 190 lbs. Deb: 4/15/66																												
1966	Hou-N	7	6	1	1	0	0	0	0	1	3	.167	.286	.167	.452	30	-1	-1	97	0	0	.400	0	0	0	-0	/O	0.0
■ **MATT SINATRO** Sinatro, Matthew Stephen b: 3/22/60, Hartford, Conn. BR/TR, 5'9", 174 lbs. Deb: 9/22/81																												
1981	Atl-N	12	32	4	9	1	1	0	4	5	4	.281	.378	.375	.753	115	1	1	100	131	5	.783	1	0	0	2	C	0.3
1982	Atl-N	37	81	10	11	2	0	1	4	4	9	.136	.176	.198	.374	4	-10	-11	107	83	2	.270	0	1	-1	0	C	-1.1
1983	Atl-N	7	12	0	2	0	0	0	2	2	1	.167	.286	.167	.452	27	-1	-1	106	396	1	.400	0	0	0	0	/C	0.0
1984	Atl-N	2	4	0	0	0	0	0	0	0	0	.000	.000	.000	.000	-91	-1	-1	110	0	0	.000	0	0	0	0	/C	0.0
1987	Oak-A	6	3	0	0	0	0	0	0	0	1	.000	.000	.000	.000	-99	-1	-1	91	0	0	.000	0	0	0	0	/C	0.0
1988	Oak-A	10	9	1	3	2	0	0	5	0	1	.333	.333	.556	.889	152	0	1	95	398	1	.625	0	0	0	-0	/C	0.1
Total	6	74	141	15	25	5	1	1	15	11	16	.177	.237	.248	.485	35	-12	-13	104	138	9	.395	1	1	-0	2	/C	-0.7
■ **HOSEA SINER** Siner, Hosea John b: 3/20/1885, Shelburn, Ind. d: 6/10/48, Sullivan, Ind. BR/TR, 5'10.5", 185 lbs. Deb: 09																												
1909	Bos-N	10	23	1	3	0	0	0	1	2		.130	.200	.130	.330	3	-3	-2	96	121	1	.250	0			0	/32S	-0.2
■ **KEN SINGLETON** Singleton, Kenneth Wayne b: 6/10/47, New York, N.Y. BB/TR, 6'4", 210 lbs. Deb: 6/24/70																												
1970	NY-N	69	198	22	52	8	0	5	26	30	48	.263	.362	.379	.741	95	0	-1	104	112	28	.704	1	1	-0	-1	O	-0.3
1971	NY-N	115	298	34	73	5	0	13	46	61	64	.245	.377	.393	.769	122	9	11	96	120	45	.756	0	1	-1	-7	O	0.0
1972	Mon-N	142	507	77	139	23	2	14	50	70	99	.274	.364	.410	.775	117	15	13	102	87	75	.731	5	10	-5	-2	*O	0.0
1973	Mon-N	162	560	100	169	26	2	23	103	123	91	.302	**.429**	.479	.908	145	45	42	104	130	113	.927	2	8	-4	2	*O	3.3
1974	Mon-N	148	511	68	141	20	2	9	74	93	84	.276	.387	.376	.763	109	13	10	104	133	77	.744	5	2	0	-10	*O	-0.4
1975	Bal-A	155	586	88	176	37	4	15	55	118	82	.300	.418	.454	.872	162	41	49	91	60	118	.915	3	5	-2	-8	*O	3.5
1976	Bal-A	154	544	62	151	25	2	13	70	79	76	.278	.369	.403	.772	129	20	21	98	110	82	.733	2	2	-1	-3	*OD	1.6
1977	Bal-A	152	536	90	176	24	0	24	99	107	101	.328	.442	.507	.949	170	49	54	93	121	124	1.013	0	1	-1	-6	*O/D	4.1
1978	Bal-A	149	502	67	147	21	2	20	81	98	94	.293	.410	.462	.872	160	34	40	91	112	100	.900	0	0	0	-14	*O/D	2.3
1979	Bal-A	159	570	93	168	29	1	35	111	109	118	.295	.409	.533	.942	156	44	47	97	111	127	.995	3	1	0	-9	*OD	3.1
1980	Bal-A	156	583	85	177	28	3	24	104	92	94	.304	.399	.485	.885	140	35	35	101	121	113	.881	0	2	-1	-19	*O/D	1.2
1981	Bal-A	103	363	48	101	16	1	13	49	61	59	.278	.382	.435	.817	136	18	19	99	103	57	.774	0	0	0	-6	OD	1.1
1982	Bal-A	156	561	71	141	27	2	14	77	86	93	.251	.353	.381	.734	102	3	4	100	127	75	.679	0	1	-1	-0	*D/O	0.2
1983	Bal-A	151	507	52	140	21	3	18	84	99	83	.276	.395	.436	.831	128	24	24	100	122	86	.821	0	2	-1	0	*D	2.2
1984	Bal-A	111	363	28	78	7	1	6	36	37	60	.215	.287	.289	.577	64	-19	-17	94	117	27	.466	0	0	0	0	*D	-1.6
Total	15	2082	7189	985	2029	317	25	246	1065	1263	1246	.282	.391	.436	.827	132	332	350	98	112	1247	.850	21	36	-15	-83	*OD	20.3
■ **FRED SINGTON** Sington, Frederick William b: 2/24/10, Brimingham, Ala. BR/TR, 6'2", 215 lbs. Deb: 9/23/34																												
1934	Was-A	9	35	2	10	2	0	0	6	4	3	.286	.359	.343	.702	81	-1	-1	101	177	4	.615	0	1	-1	-1	/O	-0.2
1935	Was-A	20	22	1	4	0	0	0	3	5	1	.182	.333	.182	.515	40	-2	-2	92	255	2	.500	0	0	0	0	/O	-0.1
1936	Was-A	25	94	13	30	8	0	1	28	15	9	.319	.413	.436	.849	113	2	2	98	218	18	.875	0	0	0	-2	O	0.0
1937	Was-A	78	228	27	54	15	4	3	36	37	33	.237	.348	.377	.726	88	-6	-4	94	130	32	.720	1	1	-0	-6	O	-1.1
1938	Bro-N	17	53	10	19	6	1	2	5	13	5	.358	.493	.623	1.115	214	8	9	96	47	18	1.412	1			-2	O	0.6
1939	Bro-N	32	84	13	23	5	0	1	7	15	15	.274	.384	.369	.753	96	1	0	107	75	11	.687	0			-1	O	0.0
Total	6	181	516	66	140	36	5	7	85	89	66	.271	.382	.401	.783	104	3	5	97	136	85	.784	2	2		-12	O	-0.8
■ **DICK SIPEK** Sipek, Richard Francis b: 1/16/23, Chicago, Ill. BL/TR, 5'9", 170 lbs. Deb: 4/28/45																												
1945	Cin-N	82	156	14	38	6	2	0	13	9	15	.244	.302	.308	.609	74	-6	-5	94	94	14	.500	0			-1	O	-0.7
■ **JOHN SIPIN** Sipin, John White b: 8/29/46, Watsonville, Cal. BR/TR, 6'1.5", 175 lbs. Deb: 5/24/69																												
1969	SD-N	68	229	22	51	12	2	2	9	8	44	.223	.252	.319	.571	61	-13	-12	97	46	18	.464	2	0	1	-1	2	-0.8

YEAR	TM/L	G	AB	R	H	2B	3B	HR	RBI	BB	SO	AVG	OBP	SLG	PRO	/A	BR	/A	PF	CHI	RC	TA	SB	CS	SBR	FR	POS	TPR
■ GEORGE SISLER Sisler, George Harold "Georgeous George" b: 3/24/1893, Manchester, Ohio d: 3/26/73, Richmond Heights, Mo. BL/TL, 5'11", 170 lbs. Deb: 6/28/15 MCH																												
1915	StL-A	81	274	28	78	10	2	3	29	7	27	.285	.307	.369	.676	107	-1	0	96	91	32	.585	10	9	-2	-1	1OP	-0.4
1916	StL-A	151	580	83	177	21	11	4	76	40	37	.305	.355	.400	.755	133	17	20	95	118	84	.725	34	26	-5	-2	*1/PO3	1.7
1917	StL-A	135	539	60	190	30	9	2	52	30	19	.353	.390	.453	.843	166	34	37	95	66	104	.900	37			4	*1/2	4.0
1918	StL-A	114	452	69	154	21	9	2	41	40	17	.341	.400	.440	.841	155	29	29	99	64	92	.970	**45**			9	*1/P	3.4
1919	StL-A	132	511	96	180	31	15	10	83	27	20	.352	.390	.530	.921	162	36	38	97	106	112	1.000	28			11	*1	4.0
1920	StL-A	154	631	137	**257**	49	18	19	122	46	19	**.407**	.449	.632	1.082	166	73	63	111	90	176	1.251	42	17	**2**	15	*1/P	7.7
1921	StL-A	138	582	125	216	38	18	11	104	34	27	.371	.411	.555	.966	143	37	36	101	96	132	1.053	**35**	11	**4**	10	*1	4.4
1922	StL-A	142	586	**134**	**246**	42	**18**	8	105	49	14	**.420**	.467	.594	1.061	166	**64**	**60**	106	97	**162**	1.256	**51**	19	**4**	10	*1	**5.9**
1924	StL-A	151	636	94	194	27	10	9	74	31	29	.305	.340	.421	.762	89	-7	-13	107	73	87	.699	19	17	-5	1	*1M	-2.1
1925	StL-A	150	649	100	224	21	15	12	105	27	24	.345	.371	.479	.851	106	12	4	108	97	110	.799	11	12	-4	10	*1/PM	0.6
1926	StL-A	150	613	78	178	21	12	7	71	30	30	.290	.327	.398	.725	88	-13	-13	101	88	79	.652	12	8	-1	-3	*1/PM	-2.2
1927	StL-A	149	614	87	201	32	8	5	97	24	15	.327	.357	.430	.787	98	2	-4	106	111	90	.772	**27**	0	8	12	*1	0.2
1928	Was-A	20	49	1	12	1	0	0	2	1	2	.245	.260	.265	.525	38	-4	-4	102	53	3	.368	0	1	-1	-1	/1O	-0.5
	Bos-N	118	491	71	167	26	4	4	68	30	15	.340	.380	.434	.814	116	9	11	97	95	78	.790	11			4	*1/P	0.2
1929	Bos-N	154	629	67	205	40	8	2	79	33	17	.326	.363	.424	.788	101	-6	0	94	95	94	.731	6			3	*1	-0.3
1930	Bos-N	116	431	54	133	15	7	3	67	23	15	.309	.346	.397	.743	82	-14	-12	97	131	58	.681	7			4	*1	-1.1
Total	15	2055	8267	1284	2812	425	164	101	1175	472	327	.340	.379	.468	.847	124	268	253	101	94	1492	.854	375	120		85	*1/OP23	25.5
■ DICK SISLER Sisler, Richard Allan b: 11/2/20, St.Louis, Mo. BL/TR, 6'2", 205 lbs. Deb: 4/16/46 MC																												
1946	StL-N	83	235	17	61	11	2	3	42	14	28	.260	.307	.362	.668	84	-4	-6	107	167	26	.567	0			-5	1O	-1.4
1947	StL-N	46	74	4	15	2	1	0	9	3	8	.203	.234	.257	.491	28	-7	-8	106	175	5	.373	0			-1	1/O	-0.9
1948	Phi-N	121	446	60	122	21	3	11	56	47	46	.274	.344	.408	.752	109	1	5	94	103	66	.704	1			-4	*1	0.0
1949	Phi-N	121	412	42	119	19	6	7	50	25	38	.289	.333	.415	.748	99	-1	-2	101	98	57	.664	0			-5	1	-0.5
1950	Phi-N	141	523	79	155	29	4	13	83	64	50	.296	.373	.442	.815	116	11	13	97	126	88	.781	1			4	*O	1.1
1951	Phi-N	125	428	46	123	20	5	8	52	40	39	.287	.351	.414	.765	108	3	5	97	100	63	.696	1	0	0	-1	*O	0.1
1952	Cin-N	11	27	3	5	1	1	0	4	3	5	.185	.267	.296	.563	56	-2	-2	100	195	2	.500	0	0	0	-1	/O	-0.2
	StL-N	119	418	48	109	14	5	13	60	29	35	.261	.312	.411	.723	101	-2	-1	98	113	53	.644	3	3	-1	4	*1	-0.1
	Yr	130	445	51	114	15	6	13	64	32	40	.256	.309	.404	.713	98	-3	-2	98	121	56	.635	3	3	-1	3		-0.3
1953	StL-N	32	43	3	11	1	1	0	4	1	4	.256	.273	.326	.598	54	-3	-3	102	111	4	.455	0	0	0	0	1	-0.2
Total	8	799	2606	302	720	118	28	55	360	226	253	.276	.336	.406	.743	101	-4	2	98	117	365	.688	6	3		-8	1O	-2.1
■ SIBBY SISTI Sisti, Sebastian Daniel b: 7/26/20, Buffalo, N.Y. BR/TR, 5'11", 175 lbs. Deb: 7/21/39																												
1939	Bos-N	63	215	19	49	7	1	1	11	12	38	.228	.269	.284	.552	53	-16	-13	92	63	16	.450	4			3	23S	-0.8
1940	Bos-N	123	459	73	115	19	5	6	34	36	64	.251	.311	.353	.664	84	-11	-10	99	72	53	.592	4			2	*32	-0.7
1941	Bos-N	140	541	72	140	24	3	1	45	38	76	.259	.309	.320	.628	83	-17	-12	93	98	54	.535	7			-4	*3/2S	-1.5
1942	Bos-N	129	407	50	86	11	4	4	35	45	55	.211	.296	.287	.584	74	-14	-12	95	101	36	.517	5			-2	*2/O	-0.4
1946	Bos-N	1	0	0	0	0	0	0	0	0	0	—	—	—	—	—	0	0	95	—	—	—	0			0	/3	0.0
1947	Bos-N	56	153	22	43	8	0	2	15	20	17	.281	.371	.373	.744	101	0	1	97	88	22	.711	2			-5	S/2	0.0
1948	Bos-N	83	221	30	54	6	2	0	21	31	34	.244	.340	.290	.630	71	-8	-8	102	123	24	.561	0			-1	2S	-0.2
1949	Bos-N	101	268	39	69	12	0	5	22	34	42	.257	.343	.358	.701	91	-4	-3	97	75	33	.635	1			-7	O2S/3	-0.8
1950	Bos-N	69	105	21	18	3	1	2	11	16	19	.171	.287	.276	.563	57	-8	-6	86	121	9	.522	1			-4	S23/1O	-0.6
1951	Bos-N	114	362	46	101	20	2	2	38	32	50	.279	.341	.362	.703	91	-5	-4	98	107	46	.624	4	5	-2	-3	S2/31O	-0.2
1952	Bos-N	90	245	19	52	10	1	4	24	14	43	.212	.255	.310	.565	59	-15	-14	95	106	19	.455	2	0	1	-6	2OS/3	-1.7
1953	Mil-N	38	23	8	5	1	0	0	4	5	2	.217	.357	.261	.618	68	-1	-1	94	260	2	.579	0	0	0	-1	2/S3	0.0
1954	Mil-N	9	0	2	0	0	0	0	0	0	0	—	—	—	—	—	0	0	93	—	—	—	0	0	0	0	R	0.0
Total	13	1016	2999	401	732	121	19	27	260	283	440	.244	.313	.324	.637	79	-98	-82	96	95	354	.573	30	5		-27	23S/O1	-6.9
■ ED SIXSMITH Sixsmith, Edward b: 2/26/1863, Philadelphia, Pa. d: 12/12/26, Philadelphia, Pa. BR/TR, Deb: 9/11/1884																												
1884	Phi-N	1	2	0	0	0	0	0	0	0	0	.000	.000	.000	.000	-99	-0	-0	92	0	0	.000				0	/C	0.0
■ TED SIZEMORE Sizemore, Theodore Crawford b: 4/15/45, Gadsden, Ala. BR/TR, 5'10", 165 lbs. Deb: 4/07/69																												
1969	LA-N	159	590	69	160	20	5	4	46	45	40	.271	.328	.342	.670	89	-9	-8	99	88	66	.576	5	5	-2	-4	*2S/O	0.1
1970	LA-N	96	340	40	104	10	1	1	34	34	19	.306	.369	.350	.719	105	-2	3	90	110	42	.627	5	1	1	-11	2/OS	0.2
1971	StL-N	135	478	53	126	14	5	3	42	42	26	.264	.324	.333	.657	86	-8	-8	101	104	50	.557	4	6	-2	3	2SO/3	0.1
1972	StL-N	120	439	53	116	17	4	2	38	37	36	.264	.327	.335	.662	84	-6	-9	105	104	49	.582	8	3	1	6	*2	0.6
1973	StL-N	142	521	69	147	22	1	1	54	68	34	.282	.367	.334	.701	105	-0	6	91	118	69	.646	6	4	-1	11	*2/3	2.2
1974	StL-N	129	504	68	126	17	0	2	47	70	37	.250	.341	.296	.637	77	-12	-14	104	103	55	.578	8	4	0	16	*2/SO	0.9
1975	StL-N	153	562	56	135	23	1	3	49	45	37	.240	.299	.301	.600	65	-25	-27	103	113	51	.491	1	5	-3	-19	*2	-4.3
1976	LA-N	84	266	18	64	8	1	0	18	15	22	.241	.281	.278	.559	59	-14	-14	100	94	21	.433	2	3	-1	-4	2/3C	-1.6
1977	Phi-N	152	519	64	146	20	3	4	47	52	40	.281	.348	.355	.702	89	-7	-7	100	96	56	.599	8	11	-4	14	*2	1.1
1978	Phi-N	108	351	38	77	12	0	0	25	25	29	.219	.273	.254	.527	45	-24	-26	105	111	23	.426	8	1	2	12	*2	-0.5
1979	Chi-N	98	330	36	82	17	0	2	24	32	25	.248	.321	.318	.639	67	-11	-16	112	87	34	.552	3	3	-1	23	2	1.3
	Bos-A	26	88	12	23	7	0	1	6	4	5	.261	.301	.375	.676	76	-2	-3	107	64	8	.549	1	0	0	-0	2/C	-0.1
1980	Bos-A	9	23	1	5	1	0	0	0	0	0	.217	.217	.261	.478	30	-2	-2	102	0	1	.316	0	0	0	1	/2	0.0
Total	12	1411	5011	577	1311	188	21	23	430	469	350	.262	.327	.321	.649	80	-123	-126	101	102	526	.576	59	46	-10	48	*2/SO3C	-0.0
■ FRANK SKAFF Skaff, Francis Michael b: 9/30/13, La Crosse, Wis. d: 4/12/88, Towson, Md. BR/TR, 5'10", 185 lbs. Deb: 9/11/35 MC																												
1935	Bro-N	6	11	4	6	1	1	0	3	0	2	.545	.545	.818	1.364	278	2	2	94	120	4	1.500	0			0	/3	0.3
1943	Phi-A	32	64	8	18	2	1	1	8	6	11	.281	.343	.391	.733	113	1	1	101	104	9	.674	0	0	0	0	1/3S	0.1
Total	2	38	75	12	24	3	2	1	11	6	13	.320	.370	.453	.824	137	3	3	100	106	14	.784	0	0		1	/13S	0.4
■ DAVE SKAGGS Skaggs, David Lindsey b: 6/12/51, Santa Monica, Cal. BR/TR, 6'2", 200 lbs. Deb: 4/17/77																												
1977	Bal-A	80	216	22	62	9	1	1	24	20	34	.287	.347	.352	.699	98	-2	-0	93	120	28	.615	0	0	0	2	C	0.3
1978	Bal-A	36	86	6	13	1	1	0	2	9	14	.151	.232	.186	.418	21	-9	-8	91	49	4	.333	0	1	-1	1	C	-0.6
1979	Bal-A	63	137	9	34	8	0	1	14	13	14	.248	.313	.328	.642	75	-5	-4	97	112	13	.523	0	0	0	0	C	0.0
1980	Bal-A	2	5	0	1	0	0	0	0	0	1	.200	.200	.200	.400	10	-1	-1	101	0	0	.250	0	0	0	0	/C	0.0
	Cal-A	24	66	7	13	0	0	1	9	9	13	.197	.293	.242	.536	51	-4	-4	96	185	5	.463	0	0	0	-4	C	-0.6
	Yr	26	71	7	14	0	0	1	9	9	14	.197	.287	.239	.527	48	-5	-5	96	170	5	.448	0	0	0	-4		-0.6
Total	4	205	510	44	123	18	2	3	49	51	76	.241	.310	.302	.612	72	-21	-17	94	114	50	.527	0	1	-1	-1	C	-0.9
■ BUD SKETCHLEY Sketchley, Harry Clement b: 3/30/19, Virden, Man., Can. d: 12/19/79, Los Angeles, Cal. BL/TL, 5'10", 180 lbs. Deb: 4/14/42																												
1942	Chi-A	13	36	1	7	1	0	0	3	7	4	.194	.326	.222	.548	56	-2	-2	99	132	3	.500	0	1	-1	-2	O	-0.4
■ ROE SKIDMORE Skidmore, Robert Roe b: 10/30/45, Decatur, Ill. BR/TR, 6'3", 188 lbs. Deb: 9/17/70																												
1970	Chi-N	1	1	0	1	0	0	0	0	0	0	1.000	1.000	1.000	2.000	365	0	0	120	0	1	—	0	0	0	0	H	0.0
■ BILL SKIFF Skiff, William Franklin b: 10/16/1895, New Rochelle, N.Y. d: 12/25/76, Bronxville, N.Y. BR/TR, 5'10", 170 lbs. Deb: 5/17/21																												
1921	Pit-N	16	45	7	13	2	0	0	11	0	4	.289	.289	.333	.622	62	-2	-3	103	269	4	.485	1	1	-0	0	C	-0.1
1926	NY-A	6	11	0	1	0	0	0	0	0	1	.091	.091	.091	.182	-53	-2	-2	99	0	0	.100	0	0	0	0	/C	-0.1
Total	2	22	56	7	14	2	0	0	11	0	5	.250	.250	.286	.536	40	-5	-5	103	216	4	.395	1	1	-0	0	/C	-0.2
■ AL SKINNER Skinner, Al Deb: 7/12/1884																												
1884	Bal-U	1	3	0	1	0	0	0		0		.333	.333	.333	.667	114	0	0	110	0	0	.500	0			0	/O	0.0
	CP-U	1	3	1	1	0	0	0		0		.333	.333	.333	.667	127	0	0	99	0	0	.500	0			0	/O	0.0
	Yr	2	6	1	2	0	0	0		0		.333	.333	.333	.667	120	0	0	105	0	1	.500	0			0		0.0
Total	1	2	6	1	2	0	0	0		0		.333	.333	.333	.667	120	0	0	105	0	1	.500	0			0	/O	0.0
■ CAMP SKINNER Skinner, Elisha Harrison b: 6/25/1897, Douglasville, Ga. d: 8/4/44, Douglasville, Ga. BL/TR, 5'11", 165 lbs. Deb: 5/02/22																												
1922	NY-A	27	33	1	6	0	0	0	2	0	4	.182	.206	.182	.388	2	-5	-5	102	119	1	.296	1	0	0	-0	/O	-0.4

YEAR	TM/L	G	AB	R	H	2B	3B	HR	RBI	BB	SO	AVG	OBP	SLG	PRO	/A	BR	/A	PF	CHI	RC	TA	SB	CS	SBR	FR	POS	TPR
1923	Bos-A	7	13	1	3	2	0	0	1	0	0	.231	.231	.385	.615	59	-1	-1	102	68	1	.500	0	0	0	-1	/O	-0.1
Total	2	34	46	2	9	2	0	0	3	0	4	.196	.213	.239	.452	18	-6	-6	102	105	2	.351	1	0	0	-1	/O	-0.5
■ JOEL SKINNER	Skinner, Joel Patrick b: 2/21/61, La Jolla, Cal. BR/TR, 6'4", 198 lbs. Deb: 6/12/83																											
1983	Chi-A	6	11	2	3	0	0	0	1	0	1	.273	.273	.273	.545	49	-1	-1	103	130	0	.300	0	0	0	-0	/C	0.0
1984	Chi-A	43	80	4	17	2	0	0	3	7	19	.213	.276	.237	.513	39	-6	-7	111	63	5	.415	1	0	0	-4	C	-0.7
1985	Chi-A	22	44	9	15	4	1	1	5	5	13	.341	.408	.545	.954	158	4	4	100	73	9	.935	0	0	0	0	C	0.5
1986	NY-A	54	166	6	43	4	0	1	17	7	40	.259	.289	.301	.590	60	-9	-9	103	128	13	.435	0	4	-2	0	C	-0.8
	Chi-A	60	149	17	30	5	1	4	20	9	43	.201	.252	.329	.580	57	-9	-9	101	131	13	.496	1	0	0	1	C	-0.4
	Yr	114	315	23	73	9	1	5	37	16	83	.232	.271	.314	.585	59	-18	-18	102	130	27	.472	1	4	-2	1		-1.2
1987	NY-A	64	139	9	19	4	0	3	14	8	46	.137	.189	.230	.419	11	-18	-17	98	136	5	.318	0	0	0	-5	C	-1.6
1988	NY-A	88	251	23	57	15	0	4	23	14	72	.227	.268	.335	.603	71	-11	-10	96	95	22	.490	0	0	0	-6	C/O1	-1.2
Total	6	337	840	70	184	34	2	13	83	50	234	.219	.265	.311	.575	57	-50	-50	100	111	67	.473	2	4	-2	-14	C/O1	-4.2
■ BOB SKINNER	Skinner, Robert Ralph b: 10/3/31, La Jolla, Cal. BL/TR, 6'4", 190 lbs. Deb: 4/13/54 MC																											
1954	Pit-N	132	470	67	117	15	9	8	46	47	59	.249	.317	.370	.687	81	-15	-13	97	93	56	.618	4	0	1	0	*1/O	-1.5
1956	Pit-N	113	233	29	47	8	3	5	29	26	50	.202	.285	.326	.611	62	-12	-13	102	135	22	.539	1	1	-0	-8	O1/3	-2.3
1957	Pit-N	126	387	58	118	12	6	13	45	38	50	.305	.370	.468	.838	131	13	16	94	85	70	.840	10	4	1	-0	O/13	1.3
1958	Pit-N	144	529	93	170	33	9	13	70	58	55	.321	.390	.491	.882	138	25	28	95	102	102	.888	12	4	1	1	*O	2.6
1959	Pit-N	143	547	78	153	18	4	13	61	67	65	.280	.358	.399	.757	98	2	0	103	102	81	.725	10	7	-1	1	*O/1	-0.1
1960	Pit-N	145	571	83	156	33	6	15	86	59	86	.273	.342	.431	.773	111	8	8	99	127	82	.727	11	8	-2	-1	*O	0.1
1961	Pit-N	119	381	61	102	20	3	3	42	51	49	.268	.360	.360	.720	92	-3	-2	99	116	51	.672	3	5	-2	-1	O	-1.1
1962	Pit-N	144	510	87	154	29	7	20	75	76	89	.302	.397	.504	.901	137	30	29	102	99	106	.940	10	4	1	-10	*O	1.2
1963	Pit-N	34	122	18	33	5	5	0	8	13	22	.270	.341	.393	.734	112	2	2	99	71	16	.684	4	1	1	-0	O	0.1
	Cin-N	72	194	25	49	10	2	3	17	21	42	.253	.332	.371	.703	98	1	-0	104	88	23	.627	1	2	-1	-1	O	-0.4
	Yr	106	316	43	82	15	7	3	25	34	64	.259	.335	.380	.715	103	3	2	102	83	41	.663	5	3	-0	-1		-0.3
1964	Cin-N	25	59	6	13	3	0	3	5	4	12	.220	.270	.424	.694	89	-1	-1	103	60	7	.617	0	0	0	0	O	0.0
	StL-N	55	118	10	32	5	0	1	16	11	20	.271	.333	.339	.672	80	-1	-3	112	153	14	.593	0	0	0	-2	O	-0.5
	Yr	80	177	16	45	8	0	4	21	15	32	.254	.313	.367	.680	83	-2	-4	109	124	21	.606	0	0	0	-1		-0.5
1965	StL-N	80	152	25	47	5	4	5	26	12	30	.309	.360	.493	.853	129	7	6	107	120	26	.800	1	0	0	-5	O	0.1
1966	StL-N	49	45	2	7	1	0	1	5	2	17	.156	.208	.244	.453	25	-5	-5	100	150	2	.368	0	0	0	0	H	-0.4
Total	12	1381	4318	642	1198	197	58	103	531	485	646	.277	.353	.421	.774	108	51	52	100	106	656	.757	67	36	-2	-25	O1/3	-0.9
■ LOU SKIZAS	Skizas, Louis Peter "The Nervous Greek" b: 6/2/32, Chicago, Ill. BR/TR, 5'11", 175 lbs. Deb: 4/19/56																											
1956	NY-A	6	6	0	1	0	0	0	1	0	2	.167	.167	.167	.333	-12	-1	-1	99	374	0	.200	0	0	0	0	H	0.0
	KC-A	83	297	39	94	11	3	11	39	15	17	.316	.349	.485	.834	117	6	6	101	84	45	.747	3	1	0	3	O	0.5
	Yr	89	303	39	95	11	3	11	40	15	19	.314	.346	.479	.824	115	5	5	101	108	45	.734	3	1	0	3		0.5
1957	KC-A	119	376	34	92	14	1	18	44	27	15	.245	.299	.431	.730	98	-3	-3	99	80	47	.664	5	2	0	-5	O3	-1.0
1958	Det-A	23	33	4	8	2	0	1	2	5	1	.242	.342	.394	.736	98	0	-0	104	50	4	.692	0	0	0	-2	/O3	-0.1
1959	Chi-A	8	13	3	1	0	0	0	0	3	2	.077	.250	.077	.327	-6	-2	-2	97	0	0	.308	0	0	0	-1	/O	-0.2
Total	4	239	725	80	196	27	4	30	86	50	37	.270	.319	.443	.762	103	0	1	100	81	97	.715	8	3	1	-4	O/3	-0.8
■ BILL SKOWRON	Skowron, William Joseph "Moose" b: 12/18/30, Chicago, Ill. BR/TR, 5'11", 195 lbs. Deb: 4/13/54																											
1954	NY-A	87	215	37	73	12	9	7	41	19	18	.340	.396	.577	.972	166	18	18	99	107	47	.967	2	1	0	1	1/32	1.7
1955	NY-A	108	288	46	92	17	3	12	61	21	32	.319	.372	.524	.896	142	14	15	98	122	52	.846	1	1	-0	1	1/3	1.2
1956	NY-A	134	464	78	143	21	6	23	90	50	60	.308	.383	.528	.911	140	24	25	99	107	90	.894	4	4	-1	6	*1/3	2.5
1957	NY-A	122	457	54	139	15	5	17	88	31	60	.304	.352	.470	.823	131	13	17	94	133	70	.748	3	2	-0	4	*1	1.9
1958	NY-A	126	465	61	127	22	3	14	73	28	69	.273	.320	.424	.744	100	1	-1	103	125	59	.648	1	1	-0	-0	*1/3	-0.4
1959	NY-A	74	282	39	84	13	5	15	59	20	47	.298	.351	.539	.890	152	14	17	93	125	50	.846	1	0	0	-0	1	1.7
1960	NY-A	146	538	63	166	34	3	26	91	38	95	.309	.356	.528	.884	144	25	28	94	100	95	.832	2	3	-1	7	*1	2.5
1961	NY-A	150	561	76	150	23	4	28	89	35	108	.267	.320	.472	.792	113	4	7	96	102	78	.713	0	0	0	-2	*1	-0.8
1962	NY-A	140	478	63	129	16	6	23	80	36	99	.270	.328	.473	.800	120	7	11	94	108	71	.736	0	1	-1	-4	*1	-0.2
1963	LA-N	89	237	19	48	8	0	4	19	13	49	.203	.253	.287	.540	58	-14	-12	95	100	15	.420	0	1	-1	-3	1/3	-1.8
1964	Was-A	73	262	28	71	10	0	13	41	11	56	.271	.308	.458	.766	109	2	2	101	111	35	.677	0	0	0	-1	1	0.0
	Chi-A	73	273	19	80	11	3	4	38	19	36	.293	.341	.399	.741	110	2	3	96	136	36	.645	0	0	0	-2	1	0.0
	Yr	146	535	47	151	21	3	17	79	30	92	.282	.325	.428	.753	109	4	5	98	124	74	.673	0	0	0	-3		0.0
1965	Chi-A	146	559	63	153	24	3	18	78	32	77	.274	.319	.424	.743	119	5	10	92	113	68	.638	1	3	-2	-4	*1	-0.1
1966	Chi-A	120	337	27	84	15	2	6	29	26	45	.249	.309	.359	.668	97	-4	-2	94	88	35	.570	1	1	-0	3	1	-0.2
1967	Chi-A	8	8	0	0	0	0	0	1	0	1	.000	.000	.000	.000	-99	-2	-2	94	0	0	.000	0	0	0	0	H	-0.1
	Cal-A	62	123	8	27	2	1	1	10	4	18	.220	.267	.276	.544	64	-6	-5	96	113	8	.416	0	0	0	-0	1	-0.8
	Yr	70	131	8	27	2	1	1	11	4	19	.206	.252	.260	.511	54	-8	-7	95	100	8	.385	0	0	0	-0		-0.9
Total	14	1658	5547	681	1566	243	53	211	888	383	870	.282	.335	.459	.794	121	104	132	96	112	810	.750	16	18	-6	5	*1/32	7.1
■ BOB SKUBE	Skube, Robert Jacob b: 10/8/57, Northridge, Cal. BL/TL, 6', 180 lbs. Deb: 9/17/82																											
1982	Mil-A	4	3	0	2	0	0	0	0	0	0	.667	.667	.667	1.333	285	1	1	94	0	1	2.000	0	0	0	-0	/OD	0.0
1983	Mil-A	12	25	2	5	1	1	0	9	4	7	.200	.310	.320	.630	81	-1	-1	92	440	2	.545	0	0	0	-0	/O1D	0.0
Total	2	16	28	2	7	1	1	0	9	4	7	.250	.344	.357	.701	101	-0	0	92	399	4	.609	0	0	0	-1	/OD1	0.0
■ GORDON SLADE	Slade, Gordon Leigh "Oskie" b: 10/9/04, Salt Lake City, Utah d: 1/2/74, Long Beach, Cal. BR/TR, 5'10.5", 160 lbs. Deb: 4/21/30																											
1930	Bro-N	25	37	8	8	2	0	1	2	3	5	.216	.275	.351	.626	50	-3	-3	101	43	4	.552	0			1	S	0.0
1931	Bro-N	85	272	27	65	13	2	1	29	23	28	.239	.310	.313	.623	67	-12	-12	101	117	28	.556	2			11	S/3	0.5
1932	Bro-N	79	250	23	60	15	1	1	23	11	26	.240	.280	.320	.600	64	-14	-12	96	103	23	.511	3			6	S3	0.0
1933	StL-N	39	62	6	7	1	0	0	3	6	7	.113	.191	.129	.320	-7	-9	-9	102	141	2	.259	1			-1	S/2	-0.7
1934	Cin-N	138	555	61	158	19	8	4	52	25	34	.285	.320	.369	.690	83	-13	-13	101	83	66	.588	6			1	S2	-0.6
1935	Cin-N	71	196	22	55	10	0	1	14	16	16	.281	.341	.347	.688	91	-4	-2	93	71	24	.589	0			-3	S2/O3	-0.1
Total	6	437	1372	147	353	60	11	8	123	84	116	.257	.307	.335	.641	73	-54	-52	99	93	146	.556	12			16	S/23O	-0.9
■ ART SLADEN	Sladen, Arthur b: 10/28/1860, Dracut, Mass. d: 2/28/14, Dracut, Mass. Deb: 4/17/1884																											
1884	Bos-U	2	7	0	0	0	0	0		0		.000	.000	.000	.000	-99	-1	-1	98	0	0	.000	0			0	/O	0.0
■ JIMMY SLAGLE	Slagle, James Franklin "Rabbit" or "Shorty" b: 7/11/1873, Worthville, Pa. d: 5/10/56, Chicago, Ill. BL/TR, 5'7", 144 lbs. Deb: 4/17/1899																											
1899	Was-N	147	599	92	163	15	8	0	41	55		.272	.338	.324	.662	88	-11	-7	96	56	75	.633	22			21	*O	0.4
1900	Phi-N	141	574	115	165	16	9	0	45	60		.287	.355	.347	.702	98	-1	1	98	62	85	.716	34			-3	*O	-1.2
1901	Phi-N	48	183	20	37	6	2	1	20	16		.202	.266	.273	.540	57	-9	-10	103	134	15	.486	5			2	O	-1.2
	Bos-N	66	255	35	69	7	0	0	7	34		.271	.356	.298	.654	83	-0	-5	112	27	33	.667	14			-8	O	-1.8
	Yr	114	438	55	106	13	2	1	27	50		.242	.320	.288	.607	73	-10	-15	108	73	48	.587	19			-5		-3.0
1902	Chi-N	115	454	64	143	11	4	0	28	53		.315	.387	.357	.743	138	19	21	96	52	80	.820	40			1	*O	1.5
1903	Chi-N	139	543	104	162	20	6	0	44	81		.298	.389	.357	.747	121	15	19	95	63	91	.808	33			16	*O	2.5
1904	Chi-N	120	481	73	125	12	10	1	31	41		.260	.318	.333	.651	102	2	2	101	60	61	.643	28			-4	*O	-0.6
1905	Chi-N	155	568	96	153	19	4	0	37	97		.269	.376	.317	.693	105	12	8	105	63	80	.733	27			17	*O	1.5
1906	Chi-N	127	498	71	119	8	6	0	33	63		.239	.324	.279	.604	85	-3	-7	107	75	55	.599	25			10	*O	0.0
1907	Chi-N	136	489	71	126	6	6	0	32	76		.258	.358	.294	.652	100	8	4	106	73	63	.683	28			-17	*O	-1.9
1908	Chi-N	104	352	38	78	4	1	0	26	43		.222	.306	.239	.545	72	-7	-10	106	126	30	.526	17			3	*O	-0.8
Total	10	1298	4996	779	1340	124	56	2	344	619		.268	.349	.317	.666	98	23	17	101	68	667	.678	273			38	*O	-1.6
■ JACK SLATTERY	Slattery, John Terrence b: 1/6/1878, S.Boston, Mass. d: 7/17/49, Boston, Mass. TR, 6'2", 191 lbs. Deb: 9/28/01 M																											
1901	Bos-A	1	3	1	1	0	0	0	1	1		.333	.500	.333	.833	141	0	0	97	322	1	1.000	0			0	/C	0.0
1903	Cle-A	4	11	1	0	0	0	0	0	0		.000	.000	.000	.000	-99	-3	-3	96	0	0	.000	0			0	/1	-0.2
	Chi-A	63	211	8	46	3	2	0	20	2		.218	.225	.251	.477	48	-14	-12	92	136	13	.345	2			-1	C/1	-0.6

YEAR	TM/L	G	AB	R	H	2B	3B	HR	RBI	BB	SO	AVG	OBP	SLG	PRO	/A	BR	/A	PF	CHI	RC	TA	SB	CS	SBR	FR	POS	TPR
	Yr	67	222	9	46	3	2	0	20	2		.207	.214	.239	.453	40	-17	-15	92	128	12	.324	2			-1		-0.8
1906	StL-N	3	7	0	2	0	0	0	0	1		.286	.375	.286	.661	108	0	0	101	0	1	.600	0			-0	/C	0.0
1909	Was-A	32	56	4	12	2	0	0	6	2		.214	.254	.250	.504	66	-3	-2	90	165	4	.409	1			0	1/C	-0.1
Total	4	103	288	14	61	5	2	0	27	6		.212	.231	.243	.474	48	-19	-16	92	136	18	.352	3			-2	/C1	-0.9
■ **MIKE SLATTERY**	Slattery, Michael J. b: 11/26/1866, Boston, Mass. d: 10/16/04, Boston, Mass. BL/TL, 6'2", 210 lbs. Deb: 4/19/1884																											
1884	Bos-U	106	413	60	86	6	2	0		4		.208	.216	.232	.448	52	-20	-19	98	0	21	.306	0			6	*O1	-1.2
1888	NY-N	103	391	50	96	12	6	1	35	13	28	.246	.272	.315	.586	95	-5	-2	93	101	41	.553	26			-1	*O	-0.3
1889	NY-N	12	48	7	14	2	0	1	12	4	3	.292	.346	.396	.742	103	0	0	105	172	7	.735	2			0	O	0.0
1890	NY-P	97	411	80	126	20	11	5	67	27	25	.307	.352	.445	.798	105	7	0	109	98	73	.807	18			-9	*O	-0.9
1891	Cin-N	41	158	24	33	3	2	1	16	10	10	.209	.256	.272	.528	61	-9	-7	91	103	12	.432	1			-2	O	-0.9
	Was-a	15	60	8	17	1	0	0	5	4	5	.283	.358	.300	.658	96	-0	0	95	71	9	.721	6			0	O	0.0
Total	5	374	1481	229	372	44	21	8	135	62	71	.251	.284	.325	.610	85	-28	-28	99	74	163	.544	53			-6	O/1	-3.3
■ **DON SLAUGHT**	Slaught, Donald Martin b: 9/11/58, Long Beach, Cal. BR/TR, 6'1", 190 lbs. Deb: 7/06/82																											
1982	KC-A	43	115	14	32	6	0	3	8	9	12	.278	.331	.409	.739	102	0	0	100	57	15	.651	0	0	0	-3	C	0.0
1983	KC-A	83	276	21	86	13	4	0	28	11	27	.312	.338	.388	.726	98	-1	-1	101	102	34	.608	3	1	0	6	C/D	0.9
1984	KC-A	124	409	48	108	27	4	4	42	20	55	.264	.302	.379	.681	88	-8	-7	99	100	46	.573	0	0	0	-1	*C/D	0.0
1985	Tex-A	102	343	34	96	17	4	8	35	20	41	.280	.331	.423	.753	97	2	-2	108	82	46	.680	5	4	-1	-6	*C	-0.3
1986	Tex-A	95	314	39	83	17	1	13	46	16	59	.264	.310	.449	.759	110	1	3	96	102	42	.685	3	2	-0	-8	C/D	0.0
1987	Tex-A	95	237	25	53	15	2	8	16	24	51	.224	.298	.405	.703	82	-5	-7	104	53	27	.624	0	3	-2	-16	C/D	-1.6
1988	NY-A	97	322	33	91	25	1	9	43	24	54	.283	.338	.450	.788	124	7	9	96	99	47	.718	1	0	0	-6	C/D	0.7
Total	7	639	2016	214	549	120	16	45	218	124	299	.272	.320	.415	.735	99	-3	-4	100	89	257	.665	12	10	-2	-33	C/D	-0.3
■ **ENOS SLAUGHTER**	Slaughter, Enos Bradsher "Country" b: 4/27/16, Roxboro, N.C. BL/TR, 5'9.5", 180 lbs. Deb: 4/19/38 H																											
1938	StL-N	112	395	59	109	20	10	8	58	32	38	.276	.330	.438	.768	99	4	-2	111	106	57	.694	1			1	O	-0.2
1939	StL-N	149	604	95	193	**52**	5	12	86	44	53	.320	.371	.482	.852	121	22	18	105	102	108	.810	2			15	*O	3.0
1940	StL-N	140	516	96	158	25	13	17	73	50	35	.306	.370	.504	.874	136	26	25	102	89	99	.884	8			0	*O	2.0
1941	StL-N	113	425	71	132	22	9	13	76	53	28	.311	.390	.496	.886	135	27	22	110	112	86	.906	4			-13	*O	0.4
1942	StL-N	152	591	100	**188**	31	**17**	13	98	88	30	**.318**	.412	.494	.906	152	**50**	44	108	106	**128**	.966	9			2	*O	4.5
1946	StL-N	156	609	100	183	30	8	18	**130**	69	41	.300	.374	.465	.838	129	29	24	107	152	110	.838	9			2	*O	2.4
1947	StL-N	147	551	100	162	31	13	10	86	59	27	.294	.366	.452	.818	109	12	8	106	117	93	.792	4			6	*O	0.8
1948	StL-N	146	549	91	176	27	11	11	90	81	29	.321	.409	.470	.879	136	31	30	101	123	110	.896	4			-11	*O	0.9
1949	StL-N	151	568	92	191	34	**13**	13	96	79	37	.336	.418	.511	.929	134	40	32	110	117	127	.971	3			-1	*O	2.2
1950	StL-N	148	556	82	161	26	7	10	101	66	33	.290	.367	.415	.782	102	5	3	103	**158**	87	.742	3			-6	*O	-0.7
1951	StL-N	123	409	48	115	17	8	4	64	67	25	.281	.386	.391	.777	109	8	8	101	**147**	67	.775	7	2	1	-2	*O	0.3
1952	StL-N	140	510	73	153	17	12	11	101	70	25	.300	.386	.445	.831	132	22	23	98	**161**	93	.824	6	1	1	0	*O	2.2
1953	StL-N	143	492	64	143	34	9	6	89	80	28	.291	.395	.433	.828	114	14	13	102	**153**	90	.832	4	4	-1	-10	*O	-0.3
1954	NY-A	69	125	19	31	4	2	1	19	28	8	.248	.386	.336	.722	100	1	1	99	160	18	.729	0	2	-1	-7	O	-0.7
1955	NY-A	10	9	1	1	0	0	0	1	1	1	.111	.200	.111	.311	-15	-1	-1	98	373	0	.250	0	0	0	0	H	0.0
	KC-A	108	267	49	86	12	4	5	34	40	17	.322	.414	.453	.867	131	14	13	101	93	50	.859	2	3	-1	-6	O	0.2
	Yr	118	276	50	87	12	4	5	35	41	18	.315	.408	.442	.850	127	12	12	101	120	50	.835	2	3	-1	-6		0.2
1956	KC-A	91	223	37	62	14	3	2	23	29	20	.278	.364	.395	.758	99	0	0	101	91	33	.713	1	0	0	-4	O	-0.5
	NY-A	24	83	15	24	4	2	0	4	5	6	.289	.330	.386	.715	89	-2	-1	99	47	11	.633	1	1	-0	-2	O	-0.4
	Yr	115	306	52	86	18	5	2	27	34	26	.281	.355	.392	.747	97	-1	-1	100	83	46	.710	2	1	0	-6		-0.9
1957	NY-A	96	209	24	53	7	1	5	34	40	19	.254	.373	.368	.742	110	2	4	94	146	30	.718	0	2	-1	-6	O	-0.6
1958	NY-A	77	138	21	42	4	1	4	19	21	16	.304	.396	.435	.831	125	6	6	103	106	25	.838	2	0	1	-6	O	-0.1
1959	NY-A	74	99	10	17	2	0	6	21	13	19	.172	.268	.374	.642	80	-4	-3	93	150	10	.607	1	0	0	-6	O	-0.9
	Mil-N	11	18	0	3	0	0	0	1	3	3	.167	.286	.167	.452	26	-2	-2	95	135	1	.400	0	0	0	-1	/O	-0.2
Total	19	2380	7946	1247	2383	413	148	169	1304	1018	538	.300	.382	.453	.835	122	306	265	104	125	1432	.847	71	15		-56	*O	14.3
■ **SCOTTIE SLAYBACK**	Slayback, Elbert b: 10/5/01, Paducah, Ky. d: 11/30/79, Cincinnati, Ohio BR/TR, 5'8", 165 lbs. Deb: 9/26/26																											
1926	NY-N	2	8	0	0	0	0	0	0	0	0	.000	.000	.000	.000	-99	-2	-2	98	0	0	.000	0			0	/2	-0.1
■ **BRUCE SLOAN**	Sloan, Bruce Adams "Fatso" b: 10/4/14, Mc Alester, Okla. d: 9/24/73, Oklahoma City, Okla. BL/TL, 5'9", 195 lbs. Deb: 4/29/44																											
1944	NY-N	59	104	7	28	4	1	1	9	13	8	.269	.350	.356	.706	96	0	-0	104	81	13	.625	0			-5	O	-0.6
■ **TOD SLOAN**	Sloan, Yale Yeastman b: 12/24/1890, Madisonville, Tenn d: 9/12/56, Akron, Ohio BL/TR, 6', 175 lbs. Deb: 9/22/13																											
1913	StL-A	7	26	2	7	1	0	0	2	1	9	.269	.321	.308	.629	88	-1	-0	95	94	3	.579	1			2	/O	0.1
1917	StL-A	109	313	32	72	6	2	2	25	28	34	.230	.307	.281	.589	84	-7	-5	95	95	28	.544	8			-7	O	-1.8
1919	StL-A	27	63	9	15	1	3	0	6	12	3	.238	.368	.349	.718	105	1	1	97	99	8	.729	0			-1	O	-0.1
Total	3	143	402	43	94	8	5	2	33	41	46	.234	.319	.294	.612	88	-7	-5	95	96	39	.575	9			-6	O	-1.8
■ **RON SLOCUM**	Slocum, Ronald Reece b: 7/2/45, Modesto, Cal. BR/TR, 6'2", 185 lbs. Deb: 9/08/69																											
1969	SD-N	13	24	6	7	1	0	1	5	0	5	.292	.292	.458	.750	111	0	0	97	143	3	.647	0	0	0	0	/23S	0.1
1970	SD-N	60	71	8	10	2	2	1	11	8	24	.141	.237	.268	.505	37	-7	-6	95	194	4	.438	0	1	-1	1	CS3/2	-0.2
1971	SD-N	7	18	1	0	0	0	0	0	0	8	.000	.053	.000	.053	-87	-4	-4	96	0	0	.056	0	0	0	1	/3	-0.3
Total	3	80	113	15	17	3	2	2	16	8	37	.150	.220	.265	.485	33	-11	-10	96	154	8	.412	0	1	-1	1	/3CS2	-0.4
■ **CRAIG SMAJSTRLA**	Smajstrla, Craig Lee b: 6/19/62, Houston, Tex. BR/TR, 5'8", 160 lbs. Deb: 9/06/88																											
1988	Hou-N	8	3	2	0	0	0	0	0	0	1	.000	.000	.000	.000	-99	-1	-1	93	0	0	.000	0	0	0	0	/2	0.0
■ **CHARLIE SMALL**	Small, Charles Albert b: 10/24/05, Auburn, Me. d: 1/14/53, Auburn, Me. BL/TR, 5'11", 180 lbs. Deb: 7/07/30																											
1930	Bos-A	25	18	1	3	1	0	0	0	2	5	.167	.250	.222	.472	22	-2	-2	93	0	1	.467	1	0	0	-0	/O	-0.1
■ **HANK SMALL**	Small, George Henry b: 7/31/53, Atlanta, Ga. BR/TR, 6'3", 205 lbs. Deb: 9/27/78																											
1978	Atl-N	1	4	0	0	0	0	0	0	0	0	.000	.000	.000	.000	-89	-1	-1	112	0	0	.000	0	0	0	0	/1	0.0
■ **JIM SMALL**	Small, James Arthur b: 3/8/37, Portland, Ore. BL/TL, 6'1.5", 180 lbs. Deb: 6/22/55																											
1955	Det-A	12	4	2	0	0	0	0	0	1	1	.000	.200	.000	.200	-44	-1	-1	97	0	0	.250	0	0	0	-1	/O	-0.1
1956	Det-A	58	91	13	29	4	2	0	10	6	10	.319	.361	.407	.767	106	0	1	97	101	14	.683	0	0	0	-2	O	-0.2
1957	Det-A	36	42	7	9	2	0	0	0	2	11	.214	.250	.262	.512	37	-3	-4	107	0	2	.361	0	2	-1	-3	O	-0.8
1958	KC-A	2	4	0	0	0	0	0	0	1	0	.000	.200	.000	.200	-38	-1	-1	106	0	0	.250	0	0	0	0	/O	0.0
Total	4	108	141	22	38	6	2	0	10	10	22	.270	.318	.340	.658	76	-5	-5	100	65	16	.552	0	2	-1	-6	/O	-1.1
■ **ROY SMALLEY**	Smalley, Roy Frederick Jr. b: 10/25/52, Los Angeles, Cal. BB/TR, 6'1", 185 lbs. Deb: 4/30/75																											
1975	Tex-A	78	250	22	57	8	0	3	33	30	42	.228	.311	.296	.607	72	-9	-9	100	153	25	.543	4	0	1	6	S2/C	0.5
1976	Tex-A	41	129	15	29	2	0	1	8	29	27	.225	.367	.264	.631	85	-1	-1	102	85	15	.625	2	0	1	-2	2/S	0.0
	Min-A	103	384	46	104	16	3	2	36	47	79	.271	.353	.344	.697	106	4	5	98	106	49	.622	0	4	-2	8	*S	1.7
	Yr	144	513	61	133	18	3	3	44	76	106	.259	.357	.324	.681	101	3	4	99	100	65	.629	2	4	-2	6		1.7
1977	Min-A	150	584	93	135	21	5	6	56	74	89	.231	.319	.315	.634	71	-20	-22	103	106	62	.567	5	5	-2	22	*S	1.5
1978	Min-A	158	586	80	160	31	3	19	77	85	70	.273	.366	.433	.800	131	20	25	94	104	92	.760	2	8	-4	19	*S	5.2
1979	Min-A	162	621	94	168	28	3	24	95	80	80	.271	.357	.441	.799	105	13	5	109	101	101	.774	2	3	-1	**33**	*S/1	**5.4**
1980	Min-A	133	486	64	135	24	1	12	63	65	63	.278	.365	.405	.771	102	9	3	109	112	72	.724	3	3	-1	26	*S/1D	3.7
1981	Min-A	56	167	24	44	7	1	7	22	31	24	.263	.379	.443	.822	130	9	8	105	91	27	.802	0	0	0	-4	SD/1	0.7
1982	Min-A	4	13	2	2	1	0	0	0	3	4	.154	.313	.231	.543	52	-1	-1	100	0	1	.545	0	0	0	-1	/S	0.0
	NY-A	142	486	55	125	14	2	20	67	68	100	.257	.348	.418	.766	113	7	9	96	104	75	.740	0	1	-1	4	S3/2D	1.9
	Yr	146	499	57	127	15	2	20	67	71	104	.255	.347	.413	.760	112	6	9	97	101	76	.735	0	1	-1	3		1.9
1983	NY-A	130	451	70	124	24	1	18	62	58	68	.275	.360	.452	.812	124	14	15	99	96	75	.788	3	3	-1	6	S31	2.4
1984	NY-A	67	209	17	50	8	1	7	26	15	35	.239	.290	.388	.678	91	-5	-3	94	102	23	.594	2	1	0	2	3S/1D	0.0

YEAR	TM/L	G	AB	R	H	2B	3B	HR	RBI	BB	SO	AVG	OBP	SLG	PRO	/A	BR	/A	PF	CHI	RC	TA	SB	CS	SBR	FR	POS	TPR
	Chi-A	47	135	15	23	4	0	4	13	22	30	.170	.287	.289	.576	54	-7	-9	111	102	12	.544	1	1	-0	-3	3/S1D	-1.1
	Yr	114	344	32	73	12	1	11	39	37	65	.212	.289	.349	.638	75	-12	-12	101	102	37	.584	3	2	-0	-1		-1.1
1985	Min-A	129	388	57	100	20	0	12	45	60	65	.258	.359	.402	.761	105	6	4	103	93	58	.728	0	2	-1	-1	DS3/1	0.4
1986	Min-A	143	459	59	113	20	4	20	57	68	80	.246	.343	.438	.781	103	8	3	108	87	70	.752	1	3	-2	-0	*DS/3	0.1
1987	Min-A	110	309	32	85	16	1	8	34	36	52	.275	.353	.411	.764	107	2	4	96	90	46	.719	2	0	1	-0	D3/S	0.3
Total	13	1653	5657	745	1454	244	25	163	694	771	908	.257	.348	.395	.743	103	49	35	102	102	801	.718	27	34	-12	114	*SD3/21C	22.7
■ ROY SMALLEY Smalley, Roy Frederick Sr. b: 6/9/26, Springfield, Mo. BR/TR, 6'3", 190 lbs. Deb: 4/20/48																												
1948	Chi-N	124	361	25	78	11	4	4	36	23	76	.216	.265	.302	.567	57	-24	-21	93	111	27	.452	0			12	*S	0.4
1949	Chi-N	135	477	57	117	21	10	8	35	36	77	.245	.304	.382	.685	88	-13	-9	94	65	54	.602	2			16	*S	2.0
1950	Chi-N	154	557	58	128	21	9	21	85	49	114	.230	.297	.413	.710	81	-15	-18	105	114	68	.648	2			**21**	*S	1.8
1951	Chi-N	79	238	24	55	7	4	8	31	25	53	.231	.304	.395	.699	89	-5	-4	97	102	29	.630	0	0	0	-2	S	0.0
1952	Chi-N	87	261	36	58	14	1	5	30	29	58	.222	.305	.341	.646	76	-8	-9	103	113	29	.577	0	0	0	-15	S	-2.2
1953	Chi-N	82	253	20	63	9	0	6	25	28	57	.249	.329	.356	.684	76	-8	-9	103	90	32	.619	0	0	0	-7	S	-0.8
1954	Mil-N	25	36	5	8	0	0	1	7	4	9	.222	.317	.306	.623	68	-2	-2	93	197	3	.533	0	0	0	1	/S21	0.0
1955	Phi-N	92	260	33	51	11	1	7	39	39	58	.196	.306	.327	.633	67	-12	-12	102	149	26	.573	0	0	0	-15	S/23	-2.4
1956	Phi-N	65	168	14	38	9	3	0	16	23	29	.226	.323	.315	.638	77	-6	-5	94	128	18	.575	0	0	0	-4	S	-0.4
1957	Phi-N	28	31	5	5	0	1	1	1	1	9	.161	.212	.323	.535	42	-3	-3	98	32	2	.462	0	0	0	-1	S	-0.2
1958	Phi-N	1	2	0	0	0	0	0	0	0	1	.000	.000	.000	.000	-99	-1	-1	98	0	0	.000	0	0	0	0	/S	0.0
Total	11	872	2644	277	601	103	33	61	305	257	541	.227	.300	.360	.661	76	-95	-92	99	106	288	.603	4	0		5	S/213	-1.8
■ WILL SMALLEY Smalley, William Darwin "Deacon" b: 6/27/1871, Oakland, Cal. d: 10/11/1891, Bay City, Mich. BR/TR, Deb: 4/19/1890																												
1890	Cle-N	136	502	62	107	11	1	0	42	60	44	.213	.303	.239	.542	65	-23	-18	94	112	40	.494	10			17	*3	0.4
1891	Was-a	11	38	5	6	0	1	0	3	5	2	.158	.256	.211	.466	37	-3	-3	95	111	2	.406	0			0	/32	-0.1
Total	2	147	540	67	113	11	2	0	45	65	46	.209	.300	.237	.537	63	-26	-20	94	112	43	.487	10			17	3/2	0.3
■ JOE SMAZA Smaza, Joseph Paul b: 7/7/23, Detroit, Mich. d: 5/30/79, Royal Oak, Mich. BL/TL, 5'11", 175 lbs. Deb: 9/18/46																												
1946	Chi-A	2	5	2	1	0	0	0	0	0	0	.200	.200	.200	.400	12	-1	-1	97	0	0	.250	0	0	0	-0	/O	0.0
■ BILL SMILEY Smiley, William B. b: 1856, Baltimore, Md. d: 7/11/1884, Baltimore, Md. Deb: 10/13/1874																												
1874	Bal-n	2	7	0	0							.000															/3	
1882	StL-a	59	240	30	51	4	2	0		6		.213	.232	.246	.478	61	-10	-9	100	0	14	.344				-6	*2/O	-1.0
	Bal-a	16	61	3	9	0	0	0		0		.148	.148	.148	.295	-0	-6	-6	92	0	1	.173				-0	2/S	-0.3
	Yr	75	301	33	60	4	2	0		6		.199	.215	.226	.441	50	-16	-15	98	0	15	.307				-6		-1.3
■ EDGAR SMITH Smith, Albert Edgar b: 10/15/1860, North Haven, Conn. TR , 6', 200 lbs. Deb: 7/06/1883																												
1883	Bos-N	30	115	10	25	5	3	0	16	5	11	.217	.250	.313	.563	66	-4	-5	106	157	9	.456				-1	O/C	-0.4
■ ALECK SMITH Smith, Alexander Benjamin "Broadway Aleck" b: 1871, New York, N.Y. d: 7/9/19, New York, N.Y. TR , Deb: 4/23/1897																												
1897	Bro-N	66	237	36	71	13	1	1	39	4		.300	.317	.376	.692	83	-6	-6	102	124	33	.645	12			-6	CO/1	-0.5
1898	Bro-N	52	199	25	52	6	5	0	23	3		.261	.276	.342	.618	83	-6	-5	95	104	21	.537	7			0	OC/321	-0.3
1899	Bro-N	17	61	6	11	0	1	0	6	2		.180	.206	.213	.419	16	-7	-7	105	144	3	.300	0			0	C	-0.6
	Bal-N	41	120	17	46	6	4	0	25	4		.383	.417	.500	.917	143	8	7	108	128	29	1.000	7			0	C/O1	0.6
	Yr	58	181	23	57	6	5	0	31	6		.315	.347	.403	.751	101	2	-0	107	135	28	.718	7			0		0.0
1900	Bro-N	7	25	2	6	0	0	0	3	1		.240	.269	.240	.509	40	-2	-2	108	159	2	.474	2			0	/3C	-0.1
1901	NY-N	26	78	5	11	0	0	0	6	0		.141	.141	.141	.282	-19	-11	-10	91	183	2	.194	2			1	C	-0.6
1902	Bal-A	41	145	10	34	3	0	0	21	8		.234	.275	.255	.530	48	-10	-10	102	191	12	.450	5			-1	C/1O23	-0.8
1903	Bos-A	11	33	4	10	1	0	0	4	0		.303	.303	.333	.636	83	-0	-1	112	131	3	.478	0			1	C	0.1
1904	Chi-N	10	29	2	6	1	0	0	1	3		.207	.281	.241	.523	63	-1	-1	101	52	2	.478	1			-0	/OC3	-0.1
1906	NY-N	16	28	0	5	0	0	0	2	1		.179	.207	.179	.385	22	-2	-2	100	146	1	.304	1			0	/C1O	-0.1
Total	9	287	955	107	252	30	11	1	130	26		.264	.288	.321	.609	71	-37	-38	101	136	108	.535	37			-6	C/O132	-2.4
■ AL SMITH Smith, Alphonse Eugene "Fuzzy" b: 2/7/28, Kirkwood, Mo. BR/TR, 6'0.5", 189 lbs. Deb: 7/10/53																												
1953	Cle-A	47	150	28	36	9	0	3	14	20	25	.240	.341	.360	.701	94	-2	-1	95	82	21	.693	2	0	1	-5	O/3	-0.6
1954	Cle-A	131	481	101	135	29	6	11	50	88	65	.281	.399	.435	.834	121	22	18	106	75	90	.857	2	9	-5	-0	*O3/S	1.0
1955	Cle-A	154	607	**123**	186	27	4	22	77	93	77	.306	.411	.473	.884	132	35	31	104	70	128	.942	11	6	-0	-7	*O3/S2	1.9
1956	Cle-A	141	526	87	144	26	5	16	71	84	72	.274	.382	.433	.815	113	13	12	101	92	90	.815	6	3	0	-1	*O3/2	0.5
1957	Cle-A	135	507	78	125	23	5	11	49	79	70	.247	.353	.377	.729	98	1	0	102	83	73	.724	12	6	0	-6	3O	-0.6
1958	Chi-A	139	480	61	121	23	5	12	58	48	77	.252	.326	.396	.722	100	-2	-0	98	105	59	.649	3	3	-1	-3	*O/3	-1.3
1959	Chi-A	129	472	65	112	16	4	17	55	46	74	.237	.312	.396	.708	96	-5	-3	97	93	58	.653	7	5	-1	7	*O/3	-0.2
1960	Chi-A	142	536	80	169	31	3	12	72	50	65	.315	.377	.451	.828	122	17	17	101	103	89	.781	8	3	1	-6	*O	0.6
1961	Chi-A	147	532	88	148	29	4	28	93	56	67	.278	.352	.506	.858	127	18	19	99	105	91	.825	4	4	-1	-4	3O	1.6
1962	Chi-A	142	511	62	149	23	8	16	82	57	60	.292	.366	.462	.828	128	15	19	95	117	83	.783	3	3	-1	-15	*3O	0.3
1963	Bal-A	120	368	45	100	17	1	10	39	32	74	.272	.335	.405	.740	113	3	6	94	91	49	.684	9	0	3	-4	O	0.1
1964	Cle-A	61	136	15	22	1	1	4	9	8	32	.162	.214	.272	.486	33	-12	-13	103	78	7	.383	0	1	-1	-4	O/3	-1.9
	Bos-A	29	51	10	11	4	0	2	7	13	10	.216	.385	.412	.796	120	2	2	102	110	9	.854	0	0	0	-1	3/O	0.1
	Yr	90	187	25	33	5	1	6	16	21	42	.176	.267	.310	.577	58	-10	-11	102	89	17	.519	0	1	-1	-5		-1.8
Total	12	1517	5357	843	1458	258	46	164	676	674	768	.272	.360	.429	.790	113	106	106	100	92	846	.787	67	43	-6	-47	*O3/S2	1.5
■ TONY SMITH Smith, Anthony b: 5/14/1884, Chicago, Ill. d: 2/27/64, Galveston, Tex. BR/TR, 5'9", 150 lbs. Deb: 8/12/07																												
1907	Was-A	51	139	12	26	1	1	0	8	18		.187	.280	.209	.489	64	-6	-4	90	99	9	.442	3			-9	S	-1.2
1910	Bro-N	106	321	31	58	10	1	1	16	69	53	.181	.329	.227	.556	66	-12	-10	95	75	30	.582	9			7	*S/3	0.1
1911	Bro-N	13	40	3	6	1	0	0	2	8	7	.150	.292	.175	.467	33	-3	-3	97	98	2	.471	1			-0	S/2	-0.2
Total	3	170	500	46	90	12	2	1	26	95	60	.180	.313	.218	.531	63	-21	-17	94	83	41	.534	13			-3	S/32	-1.3
■ KLONDIKE SMITH Smith, Armstrong Frederick b: 1/4/1887, London, England d: 11/15/59, Springfield, Mass. BL/TL, 5'9", 160 lbs. Deb: 9/28/12																												
1912	NY-A	7	27	0	5	1	0	0	0	0		.185	.185	.222	.407	16	-3	-3	101	0	1	.318	1			-1	/O	-0.4
■ BILLY SMITH Smith, Billy Edward b: 7/14/53, Jonesboro, La. BB/TR, 6'2.5", 185 lbs. Deb: 4/13/75																												
1975	Cal-A	59	143	10	29	5	1	0	14	12	27	.203	.265	.252	.516	49	-10	-9	95	149	10	.419	1	3	-2	-5	S/13D	-1.1
1976	Cal-A	13	8	0	3	0	0	0	0	0	2	.375	.375	.375	.750	131	0	0	92	0	1	.600	0	0	0	0	S/D	0.1
1977	Bal-A	109	367	44	79	12	2	5	29	33	71	.215	.282	.300	.582	63	-21	-17	93	92	33	.502	3	2	-0	5	*2/S13	-0.3
1978	Bal-A	85	250	29	65	12	2	5	30	27	40	.260	.335	.384	.719	112	1	4	91	107	34	.679	3	0	1	-2	2/S	0.8
1979	Bal-A	68	189	18	47	9	4	6	33	15	33	.249	.311	.434	.745	101	-1	-0	97	127	27	.699	1	0	0	-5	2/S	0.0
1981	SF-N	36	61	6	11	0	0	1	5	9	16	.180	.286	.230	.515	45	-4	-4	105	115	5	.451	0	0	0	-1	S/23	-0.2
Total	6	370	1018	107	234	38	9	17	111	96	189	.230	.299	.335	.634	79	-35	-27	94	111	110	.568	8	5	-1	-7	2/S13D	-0.7
■ BOBBY GENE SMITH Smith, Bobby Gene b: 5/28/34, Hood River, Ore. BR/TR, 5'11", 180 lbs. Deb: 4/16/57																												
1957	StL-N	93	185	24	39	7	1	3	18	13	35	.211	.263	.308	.571	64	-12	-13	101	113	14	.467	1	1	-0	-3	O	-1.8
1958	StL-N	28	88	8	25	3	0	2	5	2	18	.284	.308	.386	.694	77	-2	-3	106	52	11	.594	1	0	0	2	O	-0.1
1959	StL-N	43	60	11	13	1	1	1	7	1	9	.217	.230	.317	.546	42	-5	-5	105	129	4	.408	0	0	0	-4	O	-0.9
1960	Phi-N	98	217	24	62	5	2	4	27	10	28	.286	.317	.382	.700	84	-3	-5	107	115	24	.579	2	3	-1	-2	O/3	-1.0
1961	Phi-N	79	174	16	44	7	0	2	18	15	32	.253	.316	.328	.643	76	-7	-6	94	115	17	.537	0	1	-1	5	O	-0.3
1962	NY-N	8	22	1	3	0	1	0	2	3	2	.136	.240	.227	.467	25	-2	-2	104	158	1	.381	0	1	-1	0	/O	-0.2
	Chi-N	13	29	3	5	0	0	1	2	2	6	.172	.226	.276	.502	32	-3	-3	106	72	2	.400	0	1	-1	-0	/O	-0.3
	StL-N	91	130	13	30	9	0	0	12	7	14	.231	.270	.300	.570	49	-9	-10	109	121	9	.443	1	1	-0	-15	O	-2.9
	Yr	112	181	17	38	9	1	1	16	12	22	.210	.259	.287	.546	43	-14	-16	108	120	12	.430	1	3	-2	-15		-3.4
1965	Cal-A	23	57	1	13	3	0	0	5	2	10	.228	.267	.281	.547	57	-3	-3	98	130	4	.422	0	1	-1	-1	O	-0.4
Total	7	476	962	101	234	35	5	13	96	55	154	.243	.286	.331	.617	64	-47	-50	103	111	86	.517	5	9	-4	-18	O/3	-7.9

YEAR	TM/L	G	AB	R	H	2B	3B	HR	RBI	BB	SO	AVG	OBP	SLG	PRO	/A	BR	/A	PF	CHI	RC	TA	SB	CS	SBR	FR	POS	TPR
■ BRICK SMITH	Smith, Brick Dudley b: 5/2/59, Charlotte, N.C. BR/TR, 6'4", 225 lbs. Deb: 9/13/87																											
1987	Sea-A	5	8	1	1	0	0	0	0	2	4	.125	.300	.125	.425	19	-1	-1	103	0	0	.429	0	0	0	0	/1D	0.0
1988	Sea-A	4	10	1	1	0	0	0	1	0	1	.100	.100	.100	.200	-41	-2	-2	108	398	0	.111	0	0	0	0	/1	-0.1
Total	2	9	18	2	2	0	0	0	1	2	5	.111	.200	.111	.311	-11	-3	-3	105	199	1	.250	0	0	0	0	/1D	-0.1
■ BERNIE SMITH	Smith, Calvin Bernard b: 9/4/41, Ponchatoula, La. BR/TR, 5'9", 164 lbs. Deb: 7/31/70																											
1970	Mil-A	44	76	8	21	3	1	1	6	11	12	.276	.382	.382	.764	113	2	2	98	76	11	.729	1	3	-2	-7	O	-0.7
1971	Mil-A	15	36	1	5	1	0	1	3	0	5	.139	.162	.250	.412	15	-4	-4	103	102	1	.313	0	0	0	-2	O	-0.7
Total	2	59	112	9	26	4	1	2	9	11	17	.232	.317	.339	.657	83	-2	-2	100	83	12	.589	1	3	-2	-9	/O	-1.4
■ REGGIE SMITH	Smith, Carl Reginald b: 4/2/45, Shreveport, La. BB/TR, 6', 180 lbs. Deb: 9/18/66																											
1966	Bos-A	6	26	1	4	1	0	0	0	0	5	.154	.154	.192	.346	-1	-3	-4	109	0	1	.227	0	0	0	1	/O	-0.2
1967	Bos-A	158	565	78	139	24	6	15	61	57	95	.246	.316	.389	.706	94	5	-4	115	98	71	.670	16	6	1	7	*O/2	0.0
1968	Bos-A	155	558	78	148	**37**	5	15	69	64	77	.265	.345	.430	.775	133	23	22	101	110	80	.753	22	18	-4	4	*O	1.8
1969	Bos-A	143	543	87	168	29	7	25	93	54	67	.309	.373	.527	.900	142	34	31	105	110	99	.866	7	13	-6	-1	*O	2.1
1970	Bos-A	147	580	109	176	32	7	22	74	51	60	.303	.364	.497	.860	122	26	19	111	90	102	.833	10	7	-1	8	*O	2.0
1971	Bos-A	159	618	85	175	**33**	2	30	96	63	82	.283	.354	.489	.843	130	28	24	106	96	106	.826	11	3	2	5	*O	2.7
1972	Bos-A	131	467	75	126	25	4	21	74	68	63	.270	.367	.475	.843	142	29	26	105	115	85	.875	15	4	2	4	*O	3.2
1973	Bos-A	115	423	79	128	23	2	21	69	68	49	.303	.400	.515	.916	148	33	29	106	102	88	.942	3	2	-0	2	*O/1D	2.9
1974	StL-N	143	517	79	160	26	9	23	100	71	70	.309	.394	.528	.922	151	38	36	104	115	105	.928	4	3	-1	6	*O/1	3.7
1975	StL-N	135	477	67	144	26	3	19	76	63	59	.302	.387	.488	.875	137	27	25	103	103	87	.865	9	7	-2	-3	O1/3	1.5
1976	StL-N	47	170	20	37	7	1	8	23	14	28	.218	.281	.412	.693	91	-2	-3	104	96	18	.619	1	2	-1	4	1O3	0.0
	LA-N	65	225	35	63	8	4	10	26	18	42	.280	.336	.484	.821	131	8	8	100	73	36	.783	2	0	1	3	O/3	1.0
	Yr	112	395	55	100	15	5	18	49	32	70	.253	.312	.453	.766	114	6	5	101	84	56	.718	3	2	-0	7		1.0
1977	LA-N	148	488	104	150	27	4	32	87	104	76	.307	**.432**	.576	1.008	168	50	50	100	94	129	**1.135**	7	5	-1	-8	*O	3.7
1978	LA-N	128	447	82	132	27	2	29	93	70	90	.295	.392	.559	.951	**165**	38	38	99	112	102	1.025	12	5	1	-6	*O	3.0
1979	LA-N	68	234	41	64	13	1	10	32	31	50	.274	.363	.466	.829	125	8	8	100	93	39	.822	6	5	-1	8	O	1.4
1980	LA-N	92	311	47	100	13	0	15	55	41	63	.322	.402	.508	.910	158	22	24	97	109	64	.928	5	6	-2	7	O	2.6
1981	LA-N	41	35	5	7	1	0	1	8	7	8	.200	.333	.314	.648	86	-1	-0	98	224	3	.563	0	0	0	0	/1	0.0
1982	SF-N	106	349	51	99	11	0	18	56	46	46	.284	.367	.470	.837	142	15	18	94	101	61	.838	7	0	2	4	1	2.0
Total	17	1987	7033	1123	2020	363	57	314	1092	890	1030	.287	.370	.489	.859	136	379	349	104	103	1277	.881	137	86	-11	44	*O1/3D2	33.4
■ CHARLIE SMITH	Smith, Charles J. b: 12/11/1840, Brooklyn, N.Y. d: 11/15/1897, Great Neck, N.Y. 5'10.5", 150 lbs. Deb: 5/18/1871																											
1871	Mut-n	14	72	15	17							.236															3/2	
■ POP SMITH	Smith, Charles Marvin b: 10/12/1856, Digby, N.S., Canada d: 4/18/27, Boston, Mass. BR/TR, 5'11", 170 lbs. Deb: 5/01/1880																											
1880	Cin-N	83	334	35	69	10	9	0	27	6	36	.207	.221	.290	.511	72	-10	-9	99	98	22	.389				-11	*2	-1.6
1881	Cle-N	10	34	1	4	0	0	0	3	0	8	.118	.118	.118	.235	-27	-5	-5	96	260	0	.133				0	3	-0.3
	Wor-N	11	41	1	3	0	0	0	2	3	5	.073	.136	.073	.210	-31	-6	-6	105	236	0	.158				0	/OI	-0.5
	Buf-N	3	11	3	0	0	0	0	1	3	5	.000	.214	.000	.214	-27	-2	-2	101	0	0	.273				0	/2	0.0
	Yr	24	86	5	7	0	0	0	6	6	18	.081	.141	.081	.223	-28	-12	-12	101	237	1	.165				0		-0.8
1882	Bal-a	1	3	0	0	0	0	0		0		.000	.000	.000	.000	-99	-1	-1	92	0	0	.000				0	/O	0.0
	Lou-a	3	11	1	2	0	0	0		0		.182	.182	.182	.364	25	-1	-1	94	0	0	.222				0	/S	0.0
	Yr	4	14	1	2	0	0	0		0		.143	.143	.143	.286	-4	-1	-1	93	0	0	.167				0		0.0
1883	Col-a	97	405	82	106	14	**17**	4		22		.262	.300	.410	.710	145	12	20	87	0	51	.629				16	*23/P	**3.2**
1884	Col-a	108	445	78	106	18	10	6		20		.238	.289	.364	.653	118	7	9	97	0	48	.572				27	*2	3.5
1885	Pit-a	106	453	85	113	11	13	0		25		.249	.293	.331	.624	94	-0	-4	106	0	45	.524				31	*2	2.8
1886	Pit-a	126	483	75	105	20	9	2		42		.217	.288	.308	.597	96	-6	0	93	0	55	.622	38			15	*S2/C	1.8
1887	Pit-N	122	456	69	98	12	7	2	54	30	48	.215	.283	.285	.568	64	-24	-19	93	125	46	.567	30			-7	*2S	-1.8
1888	Pit-N	131	481	61	99	15	2	4	52	22	78	.206	.248	.270	.518	71	-17	-14	95	139	42	.508	37			-1	S2	-1.0
1889	Pit-N	72	258	26	54	10	2	5	27	24	38	.209	.292	.322	.613	82	-10	-5	89	84	28	.613	12			1	S/23O	0.0
	Bos-N	59	208	21	54	13	4	0	32	23	30	.260	.345	.361	.705	97	0	-1	102	130	30	.734	11			-1	S	0.0
	Yr	131	466	47	108	23	6	5	59	47	68	.232	.315	.339	.655	89	-10	-5	95	105	59	.665	23			-0		0.0
1890	Bos-N	134	463	82	106	16	12	1	53	80	81	.229	.353	.322	.675	90	3	-5	111	107	68	.776	39			-28	*2/S	-2.5
1891	Was-a	27	90	13	16	2	2	0	13	13	16	.178	.295	.244	.540	60	-5	-4	95	174	7	.527	2			0	2/S3	-0.2
Total	12	1093	4176	633	935	141	87	24	264	313	345	.224	.288	.317	.604	89	-63	-45	97	70	445	.575	169			42	2S/3OPIC	3.4
■ CHARLEY SMITH	Smith, Charles William b: 9/15/37, Charleston, S.C. BR/TR, 6'1", 170 lbs. Deb: 9/08/60																											
1960	LA-N	18	60	2	10	1	1	0	5	1	15	.167	.180	.217	.397	7	-8	-9	115	156	3	.280	0	0	0	2	3	-0.6
1961	LA-N	9	24	4	6	1	0	2	3	1	6	.250	.280	.542	.822	109	0	0	102	64	4	.778	0	0	0	0	/3S	0.1
	Phi-N	112	411	43	102	13	4	9	47	23	76	.248	.296	.365	.661	79	-16	-12	94	109	43	.566	3	4	-2	2	3S	-1.4
	Yr	121	435	47	108	14	4	11	50	24	82	.248	.295	.375	.670	81	-15	-12	94	106	47	.577	3	4	-2	2		-1.3
1962	Chi-A	65	145	11	30	4	0	2	17	9	32	.207	.258	.276	.534	46	-12	-11	95	147	9	.410	0	1	-1	-4	3	-1.4
1963	Chi-A	4	7	0	2	0	1	0	1	0	2	.286	.286	.571	.857	128	0	0	104	105	1	.667	0	0	0	0	/S	0.1
1964	Chi-A	2	7	1	1	0	1	0	0	1	1	.143	.250	.429	.679	89	-0	-0	96	0	0	.571	0	0	0	0	/3	0.0
	NY-N	127	443	44	106	12	0	20	58	19	101	.239	.275	.402	.677	92	-8	-6	95	102	47	.582	2	2	-1	-3	3SO	-1.2
1965	NY-N	135	499	49	122	20	3	16	62	17	123	.244	.275	.393	.668	86	-11	-11	100	107	50	.560	2	1	0	9	*3/S2	-0.6
1966	StL-N	116	391	34	104	13	4	10	43	22	81	.266	.305	.396	.702	93	-4	-4	100	100	45	.596	0	2	-1	-6	*3/S	-1.3
1967	NY-A	135	425	38	95	15	3	9	38	32	110	.224	.279	.336	.616	86	-10	-8	94	93	37	.509	0	2	-1	5	*3	-0.1
1968	NY-A	46	70	2	16	4	1	1	7	5	18	.229	.280	.357	.637	91	-1	-1	101	107	7	.536	0	0	0	0	3	0.0
1969	Chi-N	2	2	0	0	0	0	0	0	0	0	.000	.000	.000	.000	-94	-1	-1	107	0	0	.000	0	0	0	0	H	0.0
Total	10	771	2484	228	594	83	18	69	281	130	565	.239	.281	.370	.651	83	-70	-61	97	106	246	.563	7	12	-5	6	3/SO2	-6.4
■ CHRIS SMITH	Smith, Christopher William b: 7/18/57, Torrance, Cal. BB/TR, 6', 185 lbs. Deb: 5/14/81																											
1981	Mon-N	7	7	0	0	0	0	0	0	0	2	.000	.000	.000	.000	-99	-2	-2	99	0	0	.000	0	0	0	0	/2	-0.1
1982	Mon-N	2	2	0	0	0	0	0	0	0	1	.000	.000	.000	.000	-95	-1	-1	105	0	0	.000	0	0	0	0	/H	0.0
1983	SF-N	22	67	13	22	6	1	1	11	7	12	.328	.408	.493	.900	147	5	4	101	121	14	.933	0	0	0	-0	1/O3	0.3
Total	3	31	76	13	22	6	1	1	11	7	15	.289	.365	.434	.799	120	2	2	101	108	14	.778	0	0	0	-0	/1O32	0.2
■ EARL SMITH	Smith, Earl Calvin b: 3/14/28, Sunnyside, Wash. BR/TR, 6', 185 lbs. Deb: 4/14/55																											
1955	Pit-N	5	16	1	1	0	0	0	0	4	2	.063	.286	.063	.348	-1	-2	-2	97	0	1	.400	0	0	0	0	/O	-0.1
■ EARL SMITH	Smith, Earl Leonard "Sheriff" b: 1/20/1891, Oak Hill, Ohio d: 3/14/43, Portsmouth, Ohio BB/TR, 5'11", 170 lbs. Deb: 9/12/16																											
1916	Chi-N	14	27	2	7	1	1	0	4	2	5	.259	.310	.370	.681	93	0	-0	117	159	4	.650	1			-3	/O	-0.3
1917	StL-A	52	199	31	56	7	7	0	10	15	21	.281	.332	.387	.719	126	4	5	95	45	27	.678	5			8	O	1.0
1918	StL-A	89	286	28	77	10	5	0	32	13	16	.269	.303	.339	.642	95	-3	-3	99	120	33	.593	13			-5	O	-1.3
1919	StL-A	88	252	21	63	12	5	1	36	18	27	.250	.300	.349	.649	84	-7	-6	97	143	27	.566	1			8	O	-0.2
1920	StL-A	103	353	45	108	21	8	3	55	13	18	.306	.336	.436	.772	93	0	-5	111	118	51	.727	11	4	1	-1	3O	0.0
1921	StL-A	25	78	7	26	4	2	2	14	3	4	.333	.366	.513	.879	121	2	2	101	104	14	.846	0	0	0	-1	3/O	0.2
	Was-A	59	180	20	39	5	2	2	12	10	19	.217	.266	.300	.566	45	-16	-15	99	68	15	.475	1	0	0	3	O/3	-1.4
	Yr	84	258	27	65	9	4	4	26	13	23	.252	.296	.364	.660	68	-13	-13	99	80	28	.575	1	0	0	2		-1.2
1922	Was-A	65	205	22	53	12	2	1	23	8	17	.259	.293	.351	.644	73	-10	-8	92	110	20	.551	4	4	-1	2	O/3	-0.9
Total	7	495	1580	176	429	72	32	9	186	82	127	.272	.311	.375	.686	89	-30	-31	100	106	191	.620	36	8		11	O/3	-2.9
■ EARL SMITH	Smith, Earl Sutton "Oil" b: 2/14/1897, Hot Springs, Ark. d: 6/8/63, Little Rock, Ark. BL/TR, 5'10.5", 180 lbs. Deb: 4/24/19																											
1919	NY-N	21	36	5	9	2	1	0	8	3	3	.250	.308	.361	.669	101	-0	0	100	239	4	.630	1			-1	C/2	0.0
1920	NY-N	91	262	20	77	7	1	1	30	18	16	.294	.344	.340	.684	97	-1	-1	100	126	31	.610	5	2	0	-2	C	0.3
1921	NY-N	89	229	35	77	8	4	10	51	27	8	.336	.409	.537	.946	152	16	17	98	122	50	1.000	4	3	-1	-4	C	1.7
1922	NY-N	90	234	29	65	11	4	9	39	37	12	.278	.383	.474	.858	116	7	6	104	99	44	.894	1	1	-0	-6	C	0.0

YEAR	TM/L	G	AB	R	H	2B	3B	HR	RBI	BB	SO	AVG	OBP	SLG	PRO	/A	BR	/A	PF	CHI	RC	TA	SB	CS	SBR	FR	POS	TPR
1923	NY-N	24	34	2	7	1	1	1	4	4	1	.206	.289	.382	.672	75	-1	-1	101	88	4	.630	0	0	0	-1	C	0.0
	Bos-N	72	191	22	55	15	1	3	19	22	10	.288	.364	.424	.789	108	2	2	100	74	30	.759	0	1	-1	3	C	0.7
	Yr	96	225	24	62	16	2	4	23	26	11	.276	.353	.418	.771	103	1	1	100	79	34	.738	0	1	-1	2		0.7
1924	Bos-N	33	59	1	16	3	0	0	8	6	3	.271	.338	.322	.660	83	-2	-1	94	154	6	.568	0	1	-1	1	C	0.0
	Pit-N	39	111	12	41	10	1	4	21	13	4	.369	.435	.586	1.021	161	11	10	106	99	29	1.143	2	0	1	-1	C	1.0
	Yr	72	170	13	57	13	1	4	29	19	7	.335	.402	.494	.896	138	10	9	101	126	34	.921	2	1	0	1		1.0
1925	Pit-N	109	329	34	103	22	3	8	64	31	13	.313	.374	.471	.845	112	7	6	102	127	59	.841	4	1	1	-5	C	0.6
1926	Pit-N	105	292	29	101	17	2	2	46	28	7	.346	.407	.438	.845	113	12	7	112	119	52	.832	1			-4	C	0.7
1927	Pit-N	66	189	16	51	3	1	5	25	21	11	.270	.346	.376	.722	91	-2	-2	102	102	25	.674	0			-3	C	0.0
1928	Pit-N	32	85	8	21	6	0	2	11	11	7	.247	.333	.388	.722	82	-2	-2	107	100	11	.688	0			-1	C	-0.1
	StL-N	24	58	3	13	2	0	0	7	5	4	.224	.286	.259	.544	43	-5	-5	100	166	4	.444	0			0	C	-0.2
	Yr	56	143	11	34	8	0	2	18	16	11	.238	.314	.336	.650	67	-6	-7	104	130	15	.587	0			-1		-0.3
1929	StL-N	57	145	9	50	8	0	1	22	18	6	.345	.417	.421	.838	110	3	3	98	118	26	.832	0			0	C	0.7
1930	StL-N	8	10	0	0	0	0	0	0	3	1	.000	.231	.000	.231	-36	-2	-2	105	0	0	.300	0			0	/C	-0.1
Total	12	860	2264	225	686	115	19	46	355	247	106	.303	.374	.432	.806	110	45	37	102	115	377	.790	18	9		-23	C/2	5.3

■ **EDGAR SMITH** Smith, Edgar Eugene b: 6/12/1862, Providence, R.I. d: 11/3/1892, Providence, R.I. BR/TR, 5'10", 160 lbs. Deb: 5/25/1883

YEAR	TM/L	G	AB	R	H	2B	3B	HR	RBI	BB	SO	AVG	OBP	SLG	PRO	/A	BR	/A	PF	CHI	RC	TA	SB	CS	SBR	FR	POS	TPR
1883	Pro-N	2	9	2	2	1	0	0	1	0	2	.222	.222	.333	.556	66	-0	-0	101	111	1	.429				0	/1O	0.0
	Phi-N	1	4	1	3	0	0	0	1	0	0	.750	.750	.750	1.500	397	1	1	90	118	2	3.000				0	/PO	0.0
	Yr	3	13	3	5	1	0	0	2	0	2	.385	.385	.462	.846	160	1	1	97	150	2	.750				0		0.0
1884	Was-a	14	57	5	5	0	1	0		1		.088	.103	.123	.226	-29	-7	-6	88	0	1	.154				0	O/P	-0.5
1885	Pro-N	1	4	0	1	0	0	0	0	0	0	.250	.250	.250	.500	68	-0	-0	91	0	0	.333				0	/P	0.0
1890	Cle-N	8	24	2	7	0	1	0	4	4	1	.292	.393	.375	.768	135	1	1	94	134	4	.765	0			0	/PO	0.0
Total	4	26	98	10	18	1	2	0	6	5	3	.184	.223	.235	.458	49	-6	-5	91	51	8	.350	0			0	/OP1	-0.5

■ **MAYO SMITH** Smith, Edward Mayo b: 1/17/15, New London, Mo. d: 11/24/77, Boynton Beach, Fla BL/TR, 6', 183 lbs. Deb: 6/24/45 M

YEAR	TM/L	G	AB	R	H	2B	3B	HR	RBI	BB	SO	AVG	OBP	SLG	PRO	/A	BR	/A	PF	CHI	RC	TA	SB	CS	SBR	FR	POS	TPR
1945	Phi-A	73	203	18	43	5	0	0	11	36	13	.212	.333	.236	.570	71	-7	-5	94	83	19	.521	0	1	-1	-6	O	-1.5

■ **MIKE SMITH** Smith, Elmer Ellsworth b: 3/23/1868, Pittsburgh, Pa. d: 11/5/45, Pittsburgh, Pa. BL/TL, 5'11", 178 lbs. Deb: 5/31/1886

YEAR	TM/L	G	AB	R	H	2B	3B	HR	RBI	BB	SO	AVG	OBP	SLG	PRO	/A	BR	/A	PF	CHI	RC	TA	SB	CS	SBR	FR	POS	TPR
1886	Cin-a	10	32	7	9	1	1	0		9		.281	.439	.375	.814	165	3	3	96	0	5	.913	0			0	P/O	0.0
1887	Cin-a	52	186	26	47	10	6	0		11		.253	.298	.371	.669	81	-3	-6	108	0	23	.619	5			-6	P/O	0.0
1888	Cin-a	40	129	15	29	4	1	0	9	20		.225	.329	.271	.600	96	0	0	101	77	12	.570	2			-5	P/O	0.0
1889	Cin-a	29	83	12	23	3	1	2	17	7	18	.277	.348	.410	.757	112	2	1	105	122	12	.733	1			0	P	0.0
1892	Pit-N	138	511	86	140	16	14	4	63	82	43	.274	.375	.384	.759	141	22	27	94	99	84	.811	22			-7	*OP	1.5
1893	Pit-N	128	518	121	179	26	23	7	103	77	23	.346	.435	.525	.960	147	43	37	106	102	133	1.121	26			2	*O	2.7
1894	Pit-N	125	489	128	174	33	19	6	72	65	12	.356	.436	.538	.974	144	29	35	94	68	132	1.162	33			3	*O/P	2.3
1895	Pit-N	124	480	88	145	14	12	1	81	55	25	.302	.381	.387	.768	104	2	5	97	115	86	.839	34			-5	*O	-0.7
1896	Pit-N	122	484	121	175	21	14	7	94	74	18	.362	.454	.506	.960	167	42	48	93	90	129	1.165	33			10	*O	4.1
1897	Pit-N	123	467	99	145	19	17	6	54	70		.310	.408	.463	.871	134	24	25	98	60	101	.988	25			1	*O	1.4
1898	Cin-N	123	486	79	166	21	10	1	66	69		.342	.423	.432	.856	138	33	27	108	81	100	.934	20			2	*O/P	2.0
1899	Cin-N	87	339	65	101	13	6	1	24	47		.298	.383	.381	.764	106	8	4	106	48	55	.782	10			-4	O	-0.3
1900	Cin-N	29	111	14	31	4	4	1	18	18		.279	.380	.414	.794	132	4	5	92	101	20	.863	5			-1	O	0.2
	NY-N	85	312	47	81	9	7	2	34	24		.260	.313	.353	.665	88	-6	-5	97	97	40	.641	14			-5	O	-1.5
	Yr	114	423	61	112	13	11	3	52	42		.265	.331	.369	.700	99	-3	0	96	99	59	.698	19			-6		-1.3
1901	Pit-N	4	4	0	0	0	0	0	0	2		.000	.333	.000	.333	3	-0	-0	101	0	0	.500	0			0	/O	0.0
	Bos-N	16	57	5	10	2	1	0	3	6		.175	.254	.246	.500	42	-4	-5	112	76	4	.468	2			1	O	-0.4
	Yr	20	61	5	10	2	1	0	3	8		.164	.261	.230	.490	41	-4	-5	109	61	4	.471	2			1		-0.4
Total	14	1235	4688	913	1455	196	136	38	638	636	139	.310	.397	.435	.831	128	198	203	100	82	936	.909	232			-13	*OP	11.3

■ **ELMER SMITH** Smith, Elmer John b: 9/21/1892, Sandusky, Ohio d: 8/3/84, Columbia, Ky. BL/TR, 5'10", 165 lbs. Deb: 9/20/14

YEAR	TM/L	G	AB	R	H	2B	3B	HR	RBI	BB	SO	AVG	OBP	SLG	PRO	/A	BR	/A	PF	CHI	RC	TA	SB	CS	SBR	FR	POS	TPR
1914	Cle-A	13	53	5	17	3	0	0	8	2	11	.321	.345	.377	.723	115	1	1	102	144	7	.622	1	1	-0	2	O	0.1
1915	Cle-A	144	476	37	118	23	12	3	67	36	75	.248	.301	.366	.666	96	-3	-5	104	125	53	.596	10	11	-4	-4	*O	-2.0
1916	Cle-A	79	213	25	59	15	3	3	40	18	35	.277	.336	.418	.754	127	6	6	100	146	32	.721	3			-6	O	-0.3
	Was-A	45	168	12	36	10	3	2	27	18	28	.214	.298	.345	.643	93	-2	-2	100	133	19	.621	4			-2	O	-0.6
	Yr	124	381	37	95	25	6	5	67	36	63	.249	.319	.386	.705	112	4	4	100	142	51	.675	7			-7		-0.9
1917	Was-A	35	117	8	26	4	3	0	17	5	14	.222	.260	.308	.568	79	-4	-3	92	169	10	.473	1			-0	O	-0.5
	Cle-A	64	161	21	42	5	1	3	22	13	18	.261	.316	.360	.676	93	1	-2	114	118	20	.647	6			-3	O	-0.8
	Yr	99	278	29	68	9	4	3	39	18	32	.245	.293	.338	.631	87	-4	-6	106	138	29	.571	7			-4		-1.3
1919	Cle-A	114	395	60	110	24	6	9	54	41	30	.278	.354	.438	.792	114	11	7	107	100	64	.821	15			-9	*O	-0.9
1920	Cle-A	129	456	82	144	37	10	12	103	53	35	.316	.391	.520	.910	135	25	23	104	135	93	.943	5	4	-1	-13	*O	-0.1
1921	Cle-A	129	431	98	125	28	9	16	85	56	46	.290	.374	.508	.882	124	14	14	99	109	83	.899	0	2	-1	-14	*O	-1.0
1922	Bos-A	73	231	43	66	13	6	6	32	25	21	.286	.358	.472	.830	119	4	6	96	90	39	.804	0	3	-2	-1	O	-0.1
	NY-A	21	27	1	5	0	0	1	5	3	5	.185	.267	.296	.563	46	-2	-2	102	163	2	.500	0	0	0	-2	O	-0.4
	Yr	94	258	44	71	13	6	7	37	28	26	.275	.348	.453	.802	110	2	3	97	107	41	.768	0	3	-2	-3		-0.5
1923	NY-A	70	183	30	56	6	2	7	35	21	21	.306	.377	.475	.853	118	6	5	104	111	34	.867	3	1	0	-3	O	-0.2
1925	Cin-N	96	284	47	77	13	7	8	46	28	20	.271	.339	.451	.789	102	-1	0	97	108	43	.769	6	5	-1	-8	O	-0.9
Total	10	1012	3195	469	881	181	62	70	541	319	359	.276	.344	.437	.781	113	55	47	102	120	498	.762	54	27		-64	O	-7.7

■ **MIKE SMITH** Smith, Elwood Hope b: 11/16/04, Norfolk, Va. d: 5/31/81, Chesapeake, Va. BL/TR, 5'11.5", 170 lbs. Deb: 9/04/26

YEAR	TM/L	G	AB	R	H	2B	3B	HR	RBI	BB	SO	AVG	OBP	SLG	PRO	/A	BR	/A	PF	CHI	RC	TA	SB	CS	SBR	FR	POS	TPR
1926	NY-N	4	7	0	1	0	0	0	0	0	2	.143	.143	.143	.286	-23	-1	-1	98	0	0	.167	0			0	/O	0.0

■ **CARR SMITH** Smith, Emamuel Carr b: 4/8/01, Kernersville, N.C. BR/TR, 6', 175 lbs. Deb: 9/23/23

YEAR	TM/L	G	AB	R	H	2B	3B	HR	RBI	BB	SO	AVG	OBP	SLG	PRO	/A	BR	/A	PF	CHI	RC	TA	SB	CS	SBR	FR	POS	TPR
1923	Was-A	5	9	0	1	1	0	0	1	0	0	.111	.111	.222	.333	-14	-2	-1	95	171	0	.250	0	0	0	-1	/O	-0.2
1924	Was-A	5	10	1	2	0	0	0	0	0	3	.200	.200	.200	.400	3	-1	-1	98	0	0	.250	0	0	0	-1	/O	-0.2
Total	2	10	19	1	3	1	0	0	1	0	3	.158	.158	.211	.368	-5	-3	-3	97	81	1	.250	0	0	0	-3	/O	-0.4

■ **ERNIE SMITH** Smith, Ernest Henry "Kansas City Kid" b: 10/11/1899, Totowa, N.J. d: 4/6/73, Brooklyn, N.Y. BR/TR, 5'8", 155 lbs. Deb: 4/17/30

YEAR	TM/L	G	AB	R	H	2B	3B	HR	RBI	BB	SO	AVG	OBP	SLG	PRO	/A	BR	/A	PF	CHI	RC	TA	SB	CS	SBR	FR	POS	TPR
1930	Chi-A	24	79	5	19	3	0	0	3	5	6	.241	.286	.278	.564	43	-7	-7	103	45	7	.483	2	0	1	-3	S	-0.6

■ **FRANK SMITH** Smith, Frank L. b: 11/24/1857, Canada d: 10/11/28, Canandaigua, N.Y. Deb: 8/06/1884

YEAR	TM/L	G	AB	R	H	2B	3B	HR	RBI	BB	SO	AVG	OBP	SLG	PRO	/A	BR	/A	PF	CHI	RC	TA	SB	CS	SBR	FR	POS	TPR
1884	Pit-a	10	36	3	9	0	1	0		0		.250	.250	.306	.556	85	-1	-1	97	0	3	.407				0	/CO	0.0

■ **FRED SMITH** Smith, Fred Vincent b: 7/29/1886, Cleveland, Ohio d: 5/28/61, Cleveland, Ohio BR/TR, 5'11.5", 185 lbs. Deb: 4/17/13

YEAR	TM/L	G	AB	R	H	2B	3B	HR	RBI	BB	SO	AVG	OBP	SLG	PRO	/A	BR	/A	PF	CHI	RC	TA	SB	CS	SBR	FR	POS	TPR
1913	Bos-N	92	285	35	65	9	3	0	27	29	55	.228	.302	.281	.582	71	-12	-10	95	123	26	.532	7			-3	32S/O	-1.3
1914	Buf-F	145	473	48	104	12	10	2	45	49	78	.220	.293	.300	.593	67	-18	-21	104	112	51	.583	24			-8	*3S/1	-2.6
1915	Buf-F	35	114	8	27	2	4	0	11	13	0	.237	.315	.325	.640	90	-1	-1	100	109	13	.598	2			6	S/3	0.8
	Bro-F	110	385	41	95	16	6	5	58	25	0	.247	.293	.358	.651	94	-5	-4	98	139	48	.634	21			-29	S3	-2.8
	Yr	145	499	49	122	18	10	5	69	38	0	.244	.298	.351	.649	93	-6	-5	98	133	60	.626	23			-23		-2.0
1917	StL-N	56	165	11	30	0	2	1	17	17	22	.182	.262	.224	.487	49	-9	-10	102	164	10	.437	4			7	3/2S	-0.3
Total	4	438	1422	143	321	39	25	8	158	133	155	.226	.293	.305	.598	75	-45	-45	100	127	148	.569	58			-28	3S/201	-6.2

■ **GEORGE SMITH** Smith, George Cornelius b: 7/7/37, St.Petersburg, Fla. d: 6/15/87, St.Petersburg, Fla. BR/TR, 5'10", 170 lbs. Deb: 8/04/63

YEAR	TM/L	G	AB	R	H	2B	3B	HR	RBI	BB	SO	AVG	OBP	SLG	PRO	/A	BR	/A	PF	CHI	RC	TA	SB	CS	SBR	FR	POS	TPR
1963	Det-A	52	171	16	37	8	2	0	17	18	34	.216	.298	.287	.585	63	-8	-8	104	145	16	.529	4	0	1	-1	2	-0.4
1964	Det-A	5	7	1	2	0	0	0	2	1	4	.286	.375	.286	.661	91	-0	-0	96	424	1	.800	1	0	0	0	/2	0.0
1965	Det-A	32	53	6	5	0	0	1	1	3	18	.094	.143	.151	.294	-16	-8	-8	105	38	1	.220	0	0	0	-1	2/S3	-0.8
1966	Bos-A	128	403	41	86	19	4	8	37	37	86	.213	.284	.340	.624	72	-11	-16	109	96	39	.555	4	0	1	2	*2S	-0.1
Total	4	217	634	64	130	27	6	9	57	59	142	.205	.278	.309	.587	63	-27	-32	107	109	57	.524	9	0	3	-0	2/S3	-1.3

■ **HEINIE SMITH** Smith, George Henry b: 10/24/1871, Pittsburgh, Pa. d: 6/25/39, Buffalo, N.Y. BR/TR, 5'9.5", 160 lbs. Deb: 9/08/1897 M

YEAR	TM/L	G	AB	R	H	2B	3B	HR	RBI	BB	SO	AVG	OBP	SLG	PRO	/A	BR	/A	PF	CHI	RC	TA	SB	CS	SBR	FR	POS	TPR
1897	Lou-N	21	76	7	20	3	0	1	7	3		.263	.300	.342	.642	75	-3	-3	95	72	8	.554	1			0	2	-0.1

YEAR	TM/L	G	AB	R	H	2B	3B	HR	RBI	BB	SO	AVG	OBP	SLG	PRO	/A	BR	/A	PF	CHI	RC	TA	SB	CS	SBR	FR	POS	TPR
1898	Lou-N	35	121	14	23	4	0	0	13	6		.190	.240	.223	.463	36	-10	-9	96	148	8	.418	6			-12	2	-1.8
1899	Pit-N	15	53	9	15	3	1	0	12	5		.283	.345	.377	.722	102	0	0	99	188	8	.711	2			0	2/S	0.0
1901	NY-N	9	29	5	6	2	1	1	4	1		.207	.233	.448	.682	106	-0	-0	91	84	3	.652	1			-4	/2P	-0.2
1902	NY-N	138	511	46	129	19	2	0	33	17		.252	.277	.297	.574	79	-13	-13	100	80	52	.526	32			3	*2M	0.0
1903	Det-A	93	336	36	75	11	3	1	22	19		.223	.265	.283	.548	68	-13	-12	97	82	29	.483	12			0	2	-1.0
Total	6	311	1126	117	268	42	7	3	91	51		.238	.273	.296	.569	72	-40	-37	98	93	109	.514	54			-13	2/PS	-3.1
■ **GERMANY SMITH**	Smith, George J. b: 4/21/1863, Pittsburgh, Pa. d: 12/1/27, Altoona, Pa. BR/TR, 6', 175 lbs. Deb: 4/17/1884																											
1884	Alt-U	25	108	9	34	8	1	0		1		.315	.321	.407	.729	143	5	4	101	0	14	.608	0			0	S/P	0.4
	Cle-N	72	291	31	74	14	4	4	26	2	45	.254	.259	.371	.631	94	-2	-3	102	79	29	.507				-2	2S	-0.3
1885	Bro-a	108	419	63	108	17	11	4		10		.258	.275	.379	.655	104	3	0	104	0	45	.543				**37**	*S	3.4
1886	Bro-a	105	426	66	105	17	6	2		19		.246	.279	.329	.607	91	-5	-5	100	0	46	.564	22			13	*S/OC	1.1
1887	Bro-a	103	435	79	128	19	16	4		13		.294	.316	.439	.755	113	4	5	99	0	70	.752	26			**32**	*S/3	2.8
1888	Bro-a	103	402	47	86	10	7	3	61	22		.214	.255	.296	.551	75	-10	-12	105	151	38	.532	27			3	*S/2	-0.3
1889	Bro-a	121	446	89	103	22	3	3	53	40	42	.231	.296	.314	.610	79	-14	-11	96	104	53	.630	35			10	*S/O	0.6
1890	Bro-N	129	481	76	92	6	5	1	47	42	23	.191	.260	.231	.491	45	-33	-33	100	127	36	.463	24			-2	*S	-3.2
1891	Cin-N	138	512	50	103	11	5	3	53	38	32	.201	.258	.260	.517	57	-31	-24	91	111	39	.460	16			9	*S	-0.7
1892	Cin-N	139	506	58	121	13	6	8	63	42	52	.239	.297	.336	.633	90	-5	-7	103	102	58	.600	19			21	*S	1.9
1893	Cin-N	130	500	63	118	18	6	4	56	38	20	.236	.293	.320	.613	63	-26	-28	101	91	52	.560	14			19	*S	-0.3
1894	Cin-N	127	482	73	127	33	5	3	76	41	28	.263	.324	.371	.695	69	-25	-25	100	114	64	.668	15			13	*S	-0.3
1895	Cin-N	127	503	75	151	23	6	4	74	34	24	.300	.345	.394	.738	85	-7	-13	108	104	75	.696	13			-3	*S	-0.4
1896	Cin-N	120	456	65	131	22	9	2	71	28	22	.287	.330	.388	.718	86	-7	-11	105	114	67	.702	22			-14	*S	-2.0
1897	Bro-N	112	428	47	86	17	3	0	29	14		.201	.233	.255	.488	30	-43	-44	102	79	26	.374	1			-14	*S	-4.8
1898	StL-N	51	157	16	25	2	1	1	9	24		.159	.275	.204	.479	38	-11	-13	106	78	9	.439	1			-14	S	-2.2
Total	15	1710	6552	907	1592	252	94	46	618	408	288	.243	.289	.331	.620	76	-207	-220	101	85	723	.570	235			107	*S/23OCP	-4.3
■ **HAL SMITH**	Smith, Harold Raymond "Cura" b: 6/1/31, Barling, Ark. BR/TR, 5'10.5", 186 lbs. Deb: 5/02/56 C																											
1956	StL-N	75	227	27	64	12	0	5	23	15	22	.282	.326	.401	.727	95	-2	-2	99	92	28	.629	1	0	0	3	C	0.3
1957	StL-N	100	333	25	93	12	3	2	37	18	18	.279	.316	.351	.668	79	-10	-10	101	125	35	.546	2	2	-1	5	C	0.0
1958	StL-N	77	220	13	50	4	1	1	24	14	14	.227	.274	.268	.542	41	-17	-19	106	160	16	.415	0	0	0	1	C	-1.4
1959	StL-N	142	452	35	122	15	3	13	50	15	28	.270	.295	.403	.698	80	-12	-14	105	91	47	.573	2	6	-3	-13	*C	-2.1
1960	StL-N	127	337	20	77	16	0	2	28	29	33	.228	.292	.294	.585	56	-18	-21	108	108	27	.478	1	0	0	-16	*C	-3.2
1961	StL-N	45	125	6	31	4	1	0	10	11	12	.248	.314	.296	.610	56	-6	-9	113	109	12	.505	0	0	0	-6	C	-1.0
1965	Pit-N	4	3	0	0	0	0	0	0	0	1	.000	.000	.000	.000	-99	-1	-1	100	0	0	.000	0	0	0	-0	/C	0.0
Total	7	570	1697	126	437	63	8	23	172	102	128	.258	.301	.345	.646	69	-66	-76	105	111	165	.549	6	8	-3	-27	C	-7.4
■ **HAL SMITH**	Smith, Harold Wayne b: 12/7/30, W.Frankfort, Ill. BR/TR, 6', 195 lbs. Deb: 4/11/55																											
1955	Bal-A	135	424	41	115	23	4	4	52	30	21	.271	.322	.373	.695	96	-9	-3	90	114	47	.582	1	3	-2	-1	*C	-0.1
1956	Bal-A	77	229	16	60	14	0	3	18	17	22	.262	.316	.362	.678	84	-7	-6	94	73	22	.551	1	0	0	2	C	-0.1
	KC-A	37	142	15	39	9	2	2	24	3	12	.275	.290	.408	.698	82	-4	-4	101	143	16	.585	1	1	-0	5	C	0.1
	Yr	114	371	31	99	23	2	5	42	20	34	.267	.306	.380	.686	83	-12	-10	96	96	44	.596	2	1	0	8		0.0
1957	KC-A	107	360	41	109	26	0	13	41	14	44	.303	.331	.483	.814	121	8	8	99	76	52	.718	2	2	-1	9	*C	2.2
1958	KC-A	99	315	32	86	19	2	5	46	25	47	.273	.330	.394	.724	93	-1	-3	106	133	41	.643	0	0	0	-3	3C1	-0.4
1959	KC-A	108	292	36	84	12	0	5	31	34	39	.288	.368	.380	.748	104	3	3	101	97	42	.688	0	3	-2	1	3C	0.3
1960	Pit-N	77	258	37	76	18	2	11	45	22	48	.295	.355	.508	.862	134	11	11	99	111	45	.825	1	1	-0	1	C	1.5
1961	Pit-N	67	193	12	43	10	0	3	26	11	38	.223	.268	.321	.590	56	-12	-12	99	148	16	.474	0	0	0	-1	C	-0.7
1962	Hou-N	109	345	32	81	14	0	12	35	24	55	.235	.288	.380	.668	84	-12	-8	93	83	35	.567	0	0	0	12	C/31	0.4
1963	Hou-N	31	58	1	14	2	0	0	4	2	15	.241	.290	.276	.566	69	-3	-2	92	52	4	.417	0	0	0	1	C	0.0
1964	Cin-N	32	66	6	8	1	0	0	3	12	20	.121	.256	.136	.393	14	-7	-7	103	137	2	.344	1	0	0	1	C	-0.5
Total	10	879	2682	269	715	148	10	58	323	196	361	.267	.320	.394	.714	95	-33	-24	97	105	323	.642	7	10	-4	27	C3/1	2.7
■ **HARRY SMITH**	Smith, Harry Thomas b: 10/31/1874, Yorkshire, England d: 2/17/33, Salem, N.J. BR/TR, Deb: 7/11/01 M																											
1901	Phi-A	11	34	3	11	1	0	0	3	2		.324	.361	.353	.714	100	0	0	100	79	5	.652	1			0	/CO	0.1
1902	Pit-N	50	185	14	35	4	1	0	12	4		.189	.206	.222	.428	32	-14	-16	105	103	10	.327	4			-6	C	-1.7
1903	Pit-N	61	212	15	37	3	2	0	19	12		.175	.219	.208	.426	22	-21	-22	105	139	10	.331	2			-6	C/O	-2.2
1904	Pit-N	47	141	17	35	3	1	0	18	16		.248	.325	.284	.609	91	-1	-1	99	165	15	.575	5			-2	C/O	0.1
1905	Pit-N	1	3	0	0	0	0	0	1	0		.000	.000	.000	.000	-96	-1	-1	104	0	0	.333	1			0	/C	0.0
1906	Pit-N	1	1	0	0	0	0	0	0	0		.000	.000	.000	.000	-96	-0	-0	104	0	0	.000	0			0	/C	0.0
1907	Pit-N	18	38	4	10	1	0	0	1	4		.263	.333	.289	.623	93	0	-0	105	34	4	.536	0			-1	C	0.1
1908	Bos-N	41	130	13	32	2	2	1	16	7		.246	.285	.315	.600	90	-1	-2	104	140	12	.510	2			1	C	0.1
1909	Bos-N	43	113	9	19	4	1	0	4	5		.168	.203	.221	.425	34	-9	-9	96	58	5	.351	3			2	CM	-0.4
1910	Bos-N	70	147	8	35	4	0	1	15	5	14	.238	.263	.286	.549	53	-8	-10	114	116	12	.464	5			-0	C	-0.8
Total	10	343	1004	83	214	22	7	2	89	55	14	.213	.254	.255	.509	53	-55	-60	104	117	73	.423	23			-12	C/O	-4.7
■ **HARRY SMITH**	Smith, Harry W. b: 2/5/1856, N.Vernon, Ind. d: 6/4/1898, N.Vernon, Ind. BR/TR, 6', 175 lbs. Deb: 5/08/1877																											
1877	Chi-N	24	94	7	19	1	0	0	3	4	6	.202	.235	.213	.447	43	-6	-6	98	52	5	.320				0	2O	-0.4
	Cin-N	10	36	4	9	2	1	0	3	1	5	.250	.270	.361	.631	119	-0	1	82	78	4	.519				0	/C2O	0.1
	Yr	34	130	11	28	3	1	0	6	5	11	.215	.244	.254	.498	61	-6	-5	93	61	8	.373				0		-0.3
1889	Lou-a	1	2	0	1	0	0	0	1	0	1	.500	.500	.500	1.000	197	0	0	96	286	1	1.000	0			0	/OC	0.0
Total	2	35	132	11	29	3	1	0	7	5	12	.220	.248	.258	.506	63	-6	-5	94	62	9	.379	0			0	/2OC	-0.3
■ **HARVEY SMITH**	Smith, Harvey Fetterhoff b: 7/24/1871, Union Deposit, Pa d: 11/12/62, Harrisburg, Pa. BL/TR, 5'8", 160 lbs. Deb: 8/19/1896																											
1896	Was-N	36	131	21	36	7	2	0	17	12	7	.275	.345	.359	.704	92	-2	-1	95	106	20	.737	9			1	3	0.1
■ **HAPPY SMITH**	Smith, Henry Joseph b: 7/14/1883, Coquille, Ore. d: 2/26/61, San Jose, Cal. BL/TR, 6', 185 lbs. Deb: 4/15/10																											
1910	Bro-N	35	76	6	18	2	0	0	5	4	14	.237	.275	.263	.538	60	-4	-4	95	87	6	.483	4			2	O	-0.1
■ **JACK SMITH**	Smith, Jack b: 6/23/1895, Chicago, Ill. d: 5/2/72, Westchester, Ill. BL/TL, 5'8", 165 lbs. Deb: 9/30/15																											
1915	StL-N	4	16	2	3	0	1	0	0	1	5	.188	.235	.313	.548	65	-1	-1	100	0	1	.462	0			-1	/O	-0.1
1916	StL-N	130	357	43	87	6	5	6	34	20	50	.244	.291	.339	.630	97	-3	-2	97	97	37	.591	24	16	-2	-3	*O	-1.0
1917	StL-N	137	462	64	137	16	11	3	34	38	65	.297	.351	.398	.750	128	16	15	102	69	70	.763	25			-5	*O	0.7
1918	StL-N	42	166	24	35	2	1	0	4	7	21	.211	.260	.235	.495	55	-9	-8	93	37	11	.420	5			5	O	-0.6
1919	StL-N	119	408	47	91	16	3	0	15	26	29	.223	.271	.277	.548	69	-17	-15	94	53	37	.536	30			2	*O	-1.8
1920	StL-N	91	313	53	104	22	5	1	28	25	23	.332	.385	.444	.829	141	15	16	98	76	53	.826	14	9	-1	-4	O	0.6
1921	StL-N	116	411	86	135	22	9	7	33	21	24	.328	.361	.477	.838	126	11	14	95	56	69	.809	11	6	-0	-8	*O	0.0
1922	StL-N	143	510	117	158	23	12	8	46	50	30	.310	.375	.449	.824	110	9	8	101	65	88	.836	18	7	1	-4	*O	0.0
1923	StL-N	124	407	98	126	16	6	5	41	27	20	.310	.356	.415	.771	114	1	7	90	78	61	.788	32	11	3	3	*O	0.8
1924	StL-N	124	459	91	130	18	6	2	33	33	27	.283	.333	.362	.694	84	-9	-10	103	71	54	.649	24	16	-2	11	*O	-0.3
1925	StL-N	80	243	53	61	11	4	4	31	19	13	.251	.308	.379	.687	73	-10	-11	102	106	31	.717	20	2	5	3	O	-0.4
1926	StL-N	1	1	0	0	0	0	0	0	0	1	.000	.000	.000	.000	-98	-0	-0	102	0	0	.000	0			0	H	0.0
	Bos-N	96	322	46	100	15	2	2	25	28	12	.311	.369	.388	.758	120	2	9	86	66	46	.748	11			4	O	0.9
	Yr	97	323	46	100	15	2	2	25	28	13	.310	.368	.387	.755	120	2	8	86	65	46	.744	11			4		0.9
1927	Bos-N	84	183	27	58	6	4	1	24	16	12	.317	.375	.410	.785	118	3	5	93	108	28	.800	8			0	O	0.3
1928	Bos-N	96	254	30	71	9	2	1	32	21	14	.280	.335	.343	.677	79	-8	-7	97	127	29	.623	6			-4	O	-1.2
1929	Bos-N	19	20	2	5	0	0	0	2	2	2	.250	.318	.250	.568	46	-2	-2	94	137	2	.467	0			-3	/O	-0.4
Total	15	1406	4532	783	1301	182	71	40	382	334	348	.287	.339	.385	.724	103	-2	17	97	75	618	.706	228	67		-5	*O	-2.5
■ **STUB SMITH**	Smith, James A. b: 11/26/1876, Elmwood, Ill. BL/TR, 145 lbs. Deb: 9/10/1898																											
1898	Bos-N	3	10	1	1	0	0	0	0	0		.100	.100	.100	.200	-40	-2	-2	104	0	0	.111	0			0	/S	-0.1

YEAR	TM/L	G	AB	R	H	2B	3B	HR	RBI	BB	SO	AVG	OBP	SLG	PRO	/A	BR	/A	PF	CHI	RC	TA	SB	CS	SBR	FR	POS	TPR
■ **RED SMITH**	Smith, James Carlisle b: 4/6/1890, Greenville, S.C. d: 10/11/66, Atlanta, Ga. BR/TR, 5'11", 165 lbs. Deb: 9/05/11																											
1911	Bro-N	28	111	10	29	6	1	0	19	5	13	.261	.299	.333	.632	79	-4	-3	97	167	12	.585	5			0	3	-0.1
1912	Bro-N	128	486	75	139	28	6	4	57	54	51	.286	.362	.393	.755	112	5	8	95	91	77	.781	22			10	*3	1.8
1913	Bro-N	151	540	70	160	**40**	10	6	76	45	67	.296	.358	.441	.799	122	18	15	104	114	90	.821	22			-2	*3	1.2
1914	Bro-N	90	330	39	81	10	8	4	48	30	26	.245	.310	.361	.671	98	-1	-1	101	141	39	.647	11			16	3	2.0
	Bos-N	60	207	30	65	17	1	3	37	28	24	.314	.403	.449	.853	147	14	13	104	139	39	.901	4			2	3	1.8
	Yr	150	537	69	146	27	9	7	85	58	50	.272	.347	.395	.742	118	13	12	102	141	78	.739	15			18		3.8
1915	Bos-N	157	549	66	145	34	4	2	65	67	49	.264	.345	.352	.697	113	9	10	98	132	71	.663	10	5	0	-6	*3	1.2
1916	Bos-N	150	509	48	132	16	10	3	60	53	55	.259	.333	.348	.680	117	6	10	93	131	66	.653	13			-6	*3	0.7
1917	Bos-N	147	505	60	149	31	6	2	62	53	61	.295	.369	.392	.761	139	21	23	96	120	78	.767	16			-25	*3	-0.3
1918	Bos-N	119	429	55	128	20	3	2	65	45	47	.298	.373	.373	.746	136	16	19	94	157	63	.728	8			4	*3	2.7
1919	Bos-N	87	241	24	59	6	0	1	25	40	22	.245	.359	.282	.641	96	1	1	98	137	27	.643	6			-2	O3	-0.2
Total	9	1117	3907	477	1087	208	49	27	514	420	415	.278	.354	.377	.731	119	85	96	98	128	562	.724	117	5		-9	*3/O	10.8
■ **HARRY SMITH**	Smith, James Harry b: 5/15/1890, Baltimore, Md. d: 4/1/22, Charlotte, N.C. BR/TR, 5'10", 180 lbs. Deb: 9/21/14																											
1914	NY-N	5	7	0	3	0	0	0	2	3	1	.429	.600	.429	1.029	217	1	1	96	242	2	1.750	1			-1	/C	0.1
1915	NY-N	21	32	1	4	0	1	0	3	6	12	.125	.263	.188	.451	41	-2	-2	91	191	1	.414	0	1	-1	-1	C	-0.2
	Bro-F	28	65	5	13	0	0	1	4	7	16	.200	.278	.246	.524	57	-3	-3	98	76	5	.481	2			-2	C/O	-0.4
1917	Cin-N	8	17	0	2	0	0	0	1	2	7	.118	.211	.118	.328	2	-2	-2	92	193	1	.267	0			0	/C	-0.1
1918	Cin-N	13	27	4	5	1	2	0	4	3	6	.185	.267	.370	.637	96	-0	-0	97	151	3	.636	1			0	/CO	0.0
Total	4	75	148	10	27	1	3	1	14	21	42	.182	.284	.250	.534	64	-7	-6	95	138	12	.508	4	1		-3	/CO	-0.6
■ **JIMMY SMITH**	Smith, James Lawrence "Greenfield Jimmy" b: 5/15/1895, Pittsburgh, Pa. d: 1/1/74, Pittsburgh, Pa. BB/TR, 5'9", 152 lbs. Deb: 9/26/14																											
1914	Chi-F	3	6	1	3	1	0	0	1	0	0	.500	.500	.667	1.167	255	1	1	91	90	2	1.333	0			0	/S	0.1
1915	Chi-F	95	318	32	69	11	4	4	30	14	0	.217	.250	.314	.564	68	-14	-13	97	97	27	.474	4			-8	S/2	-1.5
	Bal-F	33	108	9	19	1	1	1	11	11	0	.176	.252	.231	.484	41	-7	-8	107	142	7	.438	3			7	S	0.1
	Yr	128	426	41	88	12	5	5	41	25	0	.207	.251	.293	.544	61	-22	-22	100	109	34	.464	7			-2		-1.4
1916	Pit-N	36	96	4	18	1	1	0	5	6	22	.188	.257	.219	.476	45	-6	-6	105	95	6	.385	0			-3	S/3	-0.8
1917	NY-N	36	96	12	22	5	1	0	9	9	18	.229	.295	.302	.597	86	-2	-1	97	120	10	.595	6			0	2/S	0.0
1918	Bos-N	34	102	8	23	3	4	1	14	3	13	.225	.255	.363	.617	93	-2	-1	94	132	10	.532	1			0	2/SO3	0.0
1919	Cin-N	28	40	9	11	1	3	1	10	4	8	.275	.341	.525	.866	150	3	2	105	162	7	.897	1			-3	/3S2O	0.0
1921	Phi-N	67	247	31	57	8	1	4	22	11	28	.231	.266	.320	.586	54	-16	-17	102	90	19	.470	2	8	-4	9	2	-1.1
1922	Phi-N	38	114	13	25	1	0	1	6	5	9	.219	.258	.254	.513	29	-11	-14	113	66	7	.391	1	3	-2	4	S2/3	-0.8
Total	8	370	1127	119	247	32	15	12	108	63	98	.219	.264	.306	.570	62	-56	-58	101	104	95	.485	18	11		5	S2/3O	-4.0
■ **JIM SMITH**	Smith, James Lorne b: 9/8/54, Santa Monica, Cal. BR/TR, 6'3", 185 lbs. Deb: 4/12/82																											
1982	Pit-N	42	42	5	10	2	1	0	4	5	7	.238	.319	.333	.652	75	-1	-1	110	112	5	.576	0	1	-1	1	S/23	0.1
■ **JOHN SMITH**	Smith, John b: Baltimore, Md. Deb: 4/14/1873																											
1873	Mar-n	5	21	1	4							.190															/SO2M	
1874	Bal-n	5	19	1	3							.158															/SO	
1875	NH-n	1	4	0	0							.000															/S	
Total	3 n	11	44	2	7							.159															/S	
■ **JOHN SMITH**	Smith, John J. b: San Francisco, Cal. 5'11", 210 lbs. Deb: 5/01/1882																											
1882	Tro-N	35	149	27	36	4	3	0	14	3	24	.242	.257	.309	.565	84	-3	-2	95	98	12	.434				-0	1	-0.7
	Wor-N	19	70	10	17	3	2	0	5	5	10	.243	.293	.343	.636	103	0	0	100	71	7	.547				0	1	0.0
	Yr	54	219	37	53	7	5	0	19	8	34	.242	.269	.320	.588	91	-3	-2	97	91	19	.470				-0		-0.7
Total	1	54	219	37	53	7	5	0	19	8	34	.242	.269	.320	.588	91	-3	-2	97	89	19	.470				-0	/1	-0.7
■ **JACK SMITH**	Smith, John Joseph (born John Joseph Coffey) b: 8/8/1893, Oswayo, Pa. d: 12/4/62, New York, N.Y. TR , 5'9", Deb: 5/18/12																											
1912	Det-A	1	0	0	0	0	0	0	0	0		—	—	—	—	—	0	0	95	—	—	—	0			0	/3	0.0
■ **JOHN SMITH**	Smith, John Marshall b: 9/27/06, Washington, D.C. d: 5/9/82, Silver Spring, Md. BB/TR, 6'1", 180 lbs. Deb: 9/17/31																											
1931	Bos-A	4	15	2	2	0	0	0	1	2	1	.133	.235	.133	.369	-1	-2	-2	94	175	1	.385	1	0	0	0	/1	-0.1
■ **JUD SMITH**	Smith, Judson Grant b: 1/13/1869, Green Oak, Mich. d: 12/7/47, Los Angeles, Cal. BR/TR, Deb: 5/21/1893																											
1893	Cin-N	17	43	7	10	1	0	1	5	9	5	.233	.365	.326	.691	85	-1	-1	101	80	6	.727	1			0	/O3S	0.0
	StL-N	4	13	1	1	0	0	0	0	1	2	.077	.200	.077	.277	-24	-2	-2	99	0	0	.250	0			0	/3	-0.1
	Yr	21	56	8	11	1	0	1	5	10	7	.196	.328	.268	.596	60	-3	-3	101	69	5	.600	1			0		-0.1
1896	Pit-N	10	35	6	12	2	1	0	4	2	2	.343	.395	.457	.852	135	1	2	93	72	8	.957	3			0	3	0.1
1898	Was-N	66	234	33	71	7	5	3	28	22		.303	.378	.415	.792	127	9	9	102	81	42	.834	11			-9	3S/12	0.1
1901	Pit-N	6	21	1	3	1	0	0	0	3		.143	.250	.190	.440	30	-2	-2	101	0	1	.389	0			1	/3	0.0
Total	4	103	346	48	97	11	6	4	37	37	9	.280	.363	.382	.745	111	6	6	101	72	56	.771	15			-8	/3SO12	0.1
■ **KEITH SMITH**	Smith, Keith Lavarne b: 5/3/53, Palmetto, Fla. BR/TR, 5'9", 178 lbs. Deb: 8/02/77																											
1977	Tex-A	23	67	13	16	4	0	2	6	4	7	.239	.301	.388	.689	83	-1	-2	105	74	9	.667	2	0	1	-1	O	-0.2
1979	StL-N	6	13	1	3	0	0	0	0	0	1	.231	.231	.231	.462	25	-1	-1	105	0	0	.273	0	1	-1	1	/O	0.0
1980	StL-N	24	31	3	4	1	0	0	2	2	2	.129	.182	.161	.343	-3	-4	-4	103	158	1	.241	0	0	0	-1	/O	-0.5
Total	3	53	111	17	23	5	0	2	8	6	10	.207	.261	.306	.567	53	-7	-8	104	89	10	.484	2	1	0	-1	/O	-0.7
■ **KEN SMITH**	Smith, Kenneth Earl b: 2/12/58, Youngstown, Ohio BL/TR, 6'1", 195 lbs. Deb: 9/22/81																											
1981	Atl-N	5	3	0	1	1	0	0	0	0	1	.333	.333	.667	1.000	179	0	0	100	0	1	1.000	0	0	0	0	/1	0.0
1982	Atl-N	48	41	6	12	1	0	0	3	6	13	.293	.383	.317	.700	91	0	-0	107	90	6	.655	0	0	0	-1	/1O	-0.1
1983	Atl-N	30	12	2	2	0	0	1	2	1	5	.167	.231	.417	.647	72	-0	-1	106	99	1	.700	1	0	0	0	1	0.0
Total	3	83	56	8	15	2	0	1	5	7	19	.268	.349	.357	.706	92	-0	-0	106	88	8	.683	1	0	0	-1	/1O	-0.1
■ **PADDY SMITH**	Smith, Lawrence Patrick b: 5/16/1894, Pelham, N.Y. BL/TR, 6', 195 lbs. Deb: 7/06/20																											
1920	Bos-A	2	2	0	0	0	0	0	0	0	1	.000	.000	.000	.000	-99	-1	-1	96	0	0	.000	0	0	0	0	/C	0.0
■ **BULL SMITH**	Smith, Lewis Oscar b: 8/20/1880, Plum, W.Va. d: 5/1/28, Charleston, W.Va. BR/TR, 6', 180 lbs. Deb: 8/30/04																											
1904	Pit-N	13	42	2	6	0	1	0	0	1		.143	.163	.190	.353	10	-4	-4	99	0	1	.250	0			-1	O	-0.5
1906	Chi-N	1	1	0	0	0	0	0	0	0		.000	.000	.000	.000	-94	-0	-0	107	0	0	.000	0			0	H	0.0
1911	Was-A	1	0	0	0	0	0	0	0	0		—	—	—	—	—	0	0	97	—	—	—	0			0	R	0.0
Total	3	15	43	2	6	0	1	0	0	1		.140	.159	.186	.345	7	-5	-5	99	0	1	.243	0			-1	/O	-0.5
■ **LEO SMITH**	Smith, Lionel H. b: 5/13/1859, Brooklyn, N.Y. d: 8/30/35, Brooklyn, N.Y. 5'6", 142 lbs. Deb: 8/28/1890																											
1890	Roc-a	35	112	11	21	1	3	0		14		.188	.283	.250	.533	64	-5	-4	93	0	8	.484	1			3	S	0.1
■ **LONNIE SMITH**	Smith, Lonnie b: 12/22/55, Chicago, Ill. BR/TR, 5'9", 170 lbs. Deb: 9/02/78																											
1978	Phi-N	17	4	6	0	0	0	0	0	4	3	.000	.500	.000	.500	48	0	0	105	0	2	2.000	4	0	1	-3	O	-0.1
1979	Phi-N	17	30	4	5	2	0	0	3	1	7	.167	.194	.233	.427	16	-4	-3	97	170	1	.385	2	1	0	-0	O	-0.3
1980	Phi-N	100	298	69	101	14	4	3	20	26	48	.339	.399	.443	.842	125	15	12	107	56	54	.907	33	13	2	-11	O	0.0
1981	Phi-N	62	176	40	57	14	3	2	11	18	14	.324	.402	.472	.874	131	11	9	112	48	35	.977	21	10	0	4	O	1.2
1982	StL-N	156	592	**120**	182	35	8	8	69	64	74	.307	.383	.434	.818	124	24	21	103	102	102	.890	68	26	5	6	*O	3.2
1983	StL-N	130	492	83	158	31	5	8	45	41	55	.321	.384	.453	.837	134	21	22	98	76	85	.871	43	18	2	-1	*O	2.2
1984	StL-N	145	504	77	126	20	4	6	49	70	90	.250	.352	.341	.693	97	-1	0	99	107	70	.756	50	13	7	-11	*O	-0.8
1985	StL-N	28	96	15	25	2	2	0	7	15	20	.260	.377	.323	.700	102	1	1	96	92	13	.772	12	6	0	-2	O	-0.1
	KC-A	120	448	77	115	23	4	6	41	41	69	.257	.325	.366	.691	87	-7	-8	102	95	60	.728	40	7	8	-9	*O	-0.9
1986	KC-A	134	508	80	146	25	7	8	44	46	78	.287	.358	.411	.770	110	8	8	100	80	77	.764	26	9	2	-2	*OD	0.5
1987	KC-A	48	167	26	42	7	1	3	8	24	31	.251	.359	.359	.718	89	-1	-2	104	49	24	.746	9	4	0	-3	OD	-0.4

YEAR	TM/L	G	AB	R	H	2B	3B	HR	RBI	BB	SO	AVG	OBP	SLG	PRO	/A	BR	/A	PF	CHI	RC	TA	SB	CS	SBR	FR	POS	TPR
1988	Atl-N	43	114	14	27	3	0	3	9	10	25	.237	.298	.342	.640	80	-2	-3	104	75	12	.596	4	2	0	-2	O	-0.6
Total	11	1000	3429	611	984	176	38	47	306	360	514	.287	.364	.402	.766	110	65	58	102	85	535	.825	312	109	28	-32	O/D	3.9
■ RED SMITH	Smith, Marvin Harold b: 7/17/1900, Ashley, Ill. d: 2/19/61, Los Angeles, Cal. BL/TR, 5'7", 165 lbs. Deb: 4/14/25																											
1925	Phi-A	20	14	1	4	0	0	0	1	2	5	.286	.375	.286	.661	67	-1	-1	103	84	2	.600	0	0	0	0	S/3	0.2
■ MILT SMITH	Smith, Milton b: 3/27/29, Columbus, Ga. BR/TR, 5'10", 165 lbs. Deb: 7/21/55																											
1955	Cin-N	36	102	15	20	3	1	3	8	13	24	.196	.293	.333	.626	62	-5	-6	106	75	10	.575	2	2	-1	-0	3/2	-0.5
■ NATE SMITH	Smith, Nathaniel Beverly b: 4/26/35, Chicago, Ill. BR/TR, 5'11", 170 lbs. Deb: 9/19/62																											
1962	Bal-A	5	9	3	2	1	0	0	0	1	4	.222	.364	.333	.697	94	-0	0	95	0	1	.714	0	0	0	-0	/C	0.0
■ OLLIE SMITH	Smith, Oliver H. b: 1868, Mt.Vernon, Ohio BL , Deb: 7/11/1894																											
1894	Lou-N	38	134	26	40	6	1	3	20	27	15	.299	.427	.425	.852	122	3	7	88	80	31	1.064	13			-3	O	0.1
■ OZZIE SMITH	Smith, Osborne Earl b: 12/26/54, Mobile, Ala. BB/TR, 5'11", 150 lbs. Deb: 4/07/78																											
1978	SD-N	159	590	69	152	17	6	1	46	47	43	.258	.312	.312	.624	81	-19	-14	93	103	61	.588	40	12	5	33	*S	3.8
1979	SD-N	156	587	77	124	18	6	0	27	37	37	.211	.260	.262	.523	45	-46	-43	96	74	42	.459	28	7	4	24	*S	0.0
1980	SD-N	158	609	67	140	18	5	0	35	71	49	.230	.315	.276	.591	71	-25	-20	93	73	62	.611	57	15	8	**43**	*S	5.0
1981	SD-N	110	450	53	100	11	2	0	21	41	37	.222	.294	.256	.550	61	-24	-21	93	62	36	.495	22	12	-1	**28**	*S	1.9
1982	StL-N	140	488	58	121	24	1	2	43	68	32	.248	.342	.314	.656	82	-8	-10	103	108	58	.649	25	5	5	**34**	*S	4.0
1983	StL-N	159	552	69	134	30	6	3	50	64	36	.243	.323	.335	.658	84	-12	-11	98	104	65	.653	34	7	6	20	*S	3.0
1984	StL-N	124	412	53	106	20	5	1	44	56	17	.257	.349	.337	.686	95	-2	-1	99	124	55	.723	35	7	6	**31**	*S	5.1
1985	StL-N	158	537	70	148	22	3	6	54	65	27	.276	.356	.361	.717	106	3	5	96	104	73	.712	31	8	5	14	*S	3.8
1986	StL-N	153	514	67	144	19	4	0	54	79	27	.280	.378	.333	.711	95	2	0	103	128	73	.733	31	7	5	-11	*S	0.8
1987	StL-N	158	600	104	182	40	4	0	75	89	36	.303	.394	.383	.778	109	10	11	99	125	102	.833	43	9	8	22	*S	5.8
1988	StL-N	153	575	80	155	27	1	3	51	74	43	.270	.354	.336	.689	95	2	-1	104	97	80	.745	57	9	**12**	**24**	*S	4.8
Total	11	1628	5914	767	1506	246	43	16	500	691	384	.255	.335	.319	.654	84	-121	-104	98	100	707	.665	403	98	62	262	*S	38.0
■ KEITH SMITH	Smith, Patrick Keith b: 10/20/61, Los Angeles, Cal. BB/TR, 6'1", 175 lbs. Deb: 4/12/84																											
1984	NY-A	2	4	0	0	0	0	0	0	0	2	.000	.200	.000	.200	-42	-1	-1	94	0	0	.250	0	0	0	0	/S	0.0
1985	NY-A	4	0	1	0	0	0	0	0	0	0	—	—	—	—	—	0	0	96	—	—	—	0	0	0	0	/S	0.0
Total	2	6	4	1	0	0	0	0	0	0	2	.000	.200	.000	.200	-42	-1	-1	94	0	0	.250	0	0	0	0	/S	0.0
■ PAUL SMITH	Smith, Paul Leslie b: 3/19/31, New Castle, Pa. BL/TL, 5'8", 165 lbs. Deb: 4/14/53																											
1953	Pit-N	118	389	41	110	12	7	4	44	24	23	.283	.329	.380	.710	83	-9	-10	102	107	50	.620	3	0	1	-1	1O	-1.0
1957	Pit-N	81	150	12	38	4	0	3	11	12	17	.253	.313	.340	.653	80	-5	-4	94	76	15	.538	0	2	-1	-3	O/1	-0.9
1958	Pit-N	6	3	0	1	0	0	0	0	3	0	.333	.667	.333	1.000	184	1	1	95	0	1	2.000	0	0	0	0	H	0.1
	Chi-N	18	20	1	3	0	0	0	1	3	4	.150	.261	.150	.411	12	-2	-2	101	138	1	.353	0	0	0	0	/1	-0.2
	Yr	24	23	1	4	0	0	0	1	6	4	.174	.345	.174	.519	43	-2	-2	99	103	2	.526	0	0	0	0		-0.1
Total	3	223	562	54	152	16	7	7	56	42	44	.270	.326	.361	.687	81	-16	-15	100	99	67	.612	3	2	-0	-4	/1O	-2.0
■ PAUL SMITH	Smith, Paul Stoner b: 5/7/1888, Mt.Zion, Ill. d: 7/3/58, Decatur, Ill. BL/TR, 6'1", 190 lbs. Deb: 9/19/16																											
1916	Cin-N	10	44	5	10	0	1	0	1	1	8	.227	.244	.273	.517	60	-2	-2	98	29	4	.471	3			-1	O	-0.3
■ RAY SMITH	Smith, Raymond Edward b: 9/18/55, Glendale, Cal. BR/TR, 6'1", 185 lbs. Deb: 4/09/81																											
1981	Min-A	15	40	4	8	1	0	1	1	0	3	.200	.200	.300	.500	40	-3	-3	105	26	2	.375	0	0	0	1	C	-0.1
1982	Min-A	9	23	1	5	0	1	0	1	1	3	.217	.250	.304	.554	51	-2	-2	100	57	2	.444	0	0	0	0	/C	0.0
1983	Min-A	59	152	11	34	5	0	0	8	10	12	.224	.276	.257	.533	45	-11	-12	105	80	11	.418	1	0	0	3	C	-0.5
Total	3	83	215	16	47	6	1	1	10	11	18	.219	.260	.270	.530	45	-15	-16	105	68	15	.413	1	0	0	4	/C	-0.6
■ DICK SMITH	Smith, Richard Arthur b: 5/17/39, Lebanon, Ore. BR/TR, 6'2", 205 lbs. Deb: 7/20/63																											
1963	NY-N	20	42	4	10	0	1	0	3	5	10	.238	.319	.286	.605	76	-1	-1	99	105	4	.588	3	2	-0	-1	O/1	-0.2
1964	NY-N	46	94	14	21	6	1	0	3	1	29	.223	.247	.309	.556	58	-6	-5	95	42	7	.494	6	2	1	-3	1O	-0.8
1965	LA-N	10	6	0	0	0	0	0	1	0	3	.000	.000	.000	.000	-99	-2	-1	91	0	0	.000	0	0	0	-3	/O	-0.4
Total	3	76	142	18	31	6	2	0	7	6	42	.218	.260	.289	.549	57	-8	-8	96	60	11	.504	9	4	0	-6	/O1	-1.4
■ DICK SMITH	Smith, Richard Harrison b: 7/21/27, Blandburg, Pa. BR/TR, 5'8", 160 lbs. Deb: 9/14/51																											
1951	Pit-N	12	46	2	8	0	0	0	4	8	8	.174	.296	.174	.470	28	-4	-5	107	186	3	.400	0	2	-1	1	3	-0.4
1952	Pit-N	29	66	8	7	1	0	0	5	9	3	.106	.213	.121	.335	-5	-9	-9	100	244	2	.283	0	0	0	0	3/2S	-0.8
1953	Pit-N	13	43	4	7	0	1	0	2	6	6	.163	.265	.209	.475	25	-5	-5	102	87	2	.395	0	1	-1	-1	S	-0.4
1954	Pit-N	12	31	2	3	1	1	0	0	6	5	.097	.243	.194	.437	16	-4	-4	97	0	2	.414	0	0	0	-0	/3	-0.3
1955	Pit-N	4	0	1	0	0	0	0	0	1	0	—	1.000	—	1.194	249	0	0	97	0	0	—	0	0	0	0	/S	0.0
Total	5	70	186	17	25	2	2	0	11	30	22	.134	.255	.167	.421	15	-22	-22	101	151	9	.372	0	3	-2	1	/3S2	-1.9
■ DICK SMITH	Smith, Richard Kelly b: 8/25/44, Lincolnton, N.C. BR/TR, 6'5", 200 lbs. Deb: 8/20/69																											
1969	Was-A	21	28	2	3	0	0	0	0	4	7	.107	.242	.107	.350	1	-4	-4	97	0	1	.320	0	0	0	-2	/O	-0.5
■ RED SMITH	Smith, Richard Paul b: 5/18/04, Brokaw, Wis. BR/TR, 5'10", 185 lbs. Deb: 5/31/27 C																											
1927	NY-N	1	0	0	0	0	0	0	0	0	0	—	—	—	—	—	0	0	100	—	—	—	0			0	/C	0.0
■ BOB SMITH	Smith, Robert Eldridge b: 4/22/1895, Rogersville, Tenn. d: 7/19/87, Waycross, Ga. BR/TR, 5'10", 175 lbs. Deb: 4/19/23																											
1923	Bos-N	115	375	30	94	16	3	0	40	17	35	.251	.285	.309	.594	57	-24	-23	100	121	32	.476	4	9	-4	3	*S/2	-1.5
1924	Bos-N	106	347	32	79	12	3	2	38	15	26	.228	.260	.297	.556	52	-25	-23	94	127	27	.456	5	2	0	0	S3	-1.3
1925	Bos-N	58	174	17	49	9	4	0	23	5	6	.282	.302	.379	.681	78	-7	-6	94	124	19	.575	2	2	-1	-1	S2P/O	-0.2
1926	Bos-N	40	84	10	25	6	2	0	13	2	4	.298	.314	.417	.731	110	-1	1	86	128	10	.627	0			2	P	0.0
1927	Bos-N	54	109	10	27	3	1	1	10	2	4	.248	.261	.321	.582	59	-7	-6	93	92	9	.451	0			2	P	0.0
1928	Bos-N	39	92	11	23	2	0	1	8	1	6	.250	.258	.304	.562	48	-7	-7	97	92	7	.449	2			2	P	0.0
1929	Bos-N	39	99	12	17	4	2	1	8	2	8	.172	.188	.283	.471	16	-14	-13	94	88	5	.378	1			2	P/S	0.0
1930	Bos-N	39	81	7	19	2	0	0	4	0	5	.235	.235	.259	.494	20	-10	-10	97	66	5	.339	0			1	P	0.0
1931	Chi-N	36	87	7	19	2	0	0	4	5	2	.218	.261	.241	.502	37	-8	-7	96	68	6	.382	0			1	P	0.0
1932	Chi-N	36	42	5	10	4	1	0	4	0	2	.238	.238	.381	.619	61	-2	-2	104	93	4	.531	1			1	P/2	0.0
1933	Cin-N	23	25	2	5	1	0	0	1	1	0	.200	.231	.240	.471	35	-2	-2	99	63	1	.381	1			-0	P/S	0.0
	Bos-N	14	20	1	4	0	1	0	2	0	1	.200	.200	.300	.500	43	-2	-1	96	125	1	.375	0			1	P	0.0
	Yr	37	45	3	9	1	1	0	3	1	1	.200	.217	.267	.484	38	-4	-4	98	88	3	.389	1			1		0.0
1934	Bos-N	42	36	5	9	1	0	0	3	0	1	.250	.250	.278	.528	48	-3	-2	86	108	3	.370	0			1	P	0.0
1935	Bos-N	47	63	3	17	0	0	0	4	1	5	.270	.281	.270	.551	51	-4	-4	96	85	4	.367	0			-1	P	0.0
1936	Bos-N	35	45	1	10	2	0	0	4	0	4	.222	.222	.267	.489	33	-4	-4	95	118	3	.333	0			1	P	0.0
1937	Bos-N	19	10	1	2	0	0	0	0	1	1	.200	.273	.200	.473	33	-1	-1	90	0	1	.375	0			-1	P	0.0
Total	15	742	1689	154	409	64	17	5	166	52	110	.242	.265	.309	.574	53	-122	-112	95	108	136	.457	16	13		14	PS/230	-3.0
■ JOE SMITH	Smith, Salvatore (born Salvatore Persico) b: 12/29/1893, New York, N.Y. d: 1/12/74, Yonkers, N.Y. BR/TR, 5'7", 170 lbs. Deb: 7/07/13																											
1913	NY-A	14	32	1	5	0	0	0	2	1	14	.156	.182	.156	.338	-1	-4	-4	101	142	1	.259	1			1	C	-0.1
■ SKYROCKET SMITH	Smith, Samuel J. b: 3/19/1868, St.Louis, Mo. d: 4/26/16, St.Louis, Mo. BR , Deb: 1888																											
1888	Lou-a	58	206	27	49	9	4	1	31	24		.238	.349	.335	.683	135	7	10	91	136	26	.694	5			-0	1	0.5
■ SYD SMITH	Smith, Sydney E. b: 8/31/1883, Smithville, S.C. d: 6/5/61, Orangeburg, S.C. BR/TR, 5'10", 190 lbs. Deb: 4/14/08																											
1908	Phi-A	46	128	8	26	8	0	1	10	4		.203	.227	.289	.516	64	-5	-6	108	94	8	.402	0			3	C/1O	0.0
	StL-A	27	76	6	14	4	0	0	5	4		.184	.225	.237	.462	50	-4	-4	103	104	4	.387	2			3	C	0.1
	Yr	73	204	14	40	12	0	1	15	8		.196	.226	.270	.496	59	-9	-10	106	99	12	.396	2			5		0.1
1910	Cle-A	9	27	1	9	1	0	0	3	3		.333	.400	.370	.770	142	1	1	100	111	4	.722	0			-0	/C	0.2
1911	Cle-A	58	154	8	46	8	1	1	21	11		.299	.353	.383	.736	102	1	0	103	114	21	.667	0			5	C/13	1.1

YEAR	TM/L	G	AB	R	H	2B	3B	HR	RBI	BB	SO	AVG	OBP	SLG	PRO	/A	BR	/A	PF	CHI	RC	TA	SB	CS	SBR	FR	POS	TPR
1914	Pit-N	5	11	1	3	0	0	0	1	0	1	.273	.273	.273	.545	67	-1	-0	92	121	1	.375	0			-0	/C	0.0
1915	Pit-N	1	1	0	0	0	0	0	0	0	0	.000	.000	.000	.000	-99	-0	-0	99	0	0	.000	0			0	H	0.0
Total	5	146	397	24	98	21	1	2	40	22	1	.247	.290	.320	.610	83	-7	-9	104	106	38	.512	2			10	C/13O	1.4
■ TOM SMITH	Smith, Thomas N. b: 1851, Guelph, Ontario, Canada d: 3/28/1889, Detroit, Mich. Deb: 9/15/1875																											
1875	Atl-n	3	14	0	1							.071															/2	
1882	Phi-a	20	65	10	6	0	0	0		12		.092	.234	.092	.326	12	-5	-7	112	0	1	.305				0	3/SO2	-0.5
■ TOMMY SMITH	Smith, Tommy Alexander b: 8/1/48, Albermarle, N.C. BL/TR, 6'4", 210 lbs. Deb: 9/06/73																											
1973	Cle-A	14	41	6	10	2	0	2	3	1	2	.244	.262	.439	.701	97	-1	-0	97	49	4	.625	1	0	0	-0	O	0.0
1974	Cle-A	23	31	4	3	1	0	0	0	2	7	.097	.176	.129	.306	-11	-4	-4	101	0	1	.250	0	0	0	-2	O/D	-0.6
1975	Cle-A	8	8	0	1	0	0	0	2	0	1	.125	.125	.125	.250	-29	-1	-1	100	768	0	.143	0	0	0	-1	/OD	-0.1
1976	Cle-A	55	164	17	42	3	1	2	12	8	8	.256	.291	.323	.614	80	-4	-4	100	78	16	.548	8	0	2	-2	O/D	-0.4
1977	Sea-A	21	27	1	7	1	1	0	4	0	6	.259	.259	.370	.630	72	-1	-1	96	159	2	.476	0	1	-1	-2	O	-0.3
Total	5	121	271	28	63	7	2	4	21	11	24	.232	.265	.317	.582	68	-12	-12	99	92	23	.512	9	1	2	-6	/OD	-1.4
■ VINNIE SMITH	Smith, Vincent Ambrose b: 12/7/15, Richmond, Va. d: 12/14/79, Virginia Beach, Va BR/TR, 6'1", 176 lbs. Deb: 9/10/41 U																											
1941	Pit-N	9	33	3	10	1	0	0	5	1	5	.303	.324	.333	.657	83	-1	-1	103	164	3	.462	0			-0	/C	0.0
1946	Pit-N	7	21	2	4	0	0	0	0	1	5	.190	.227	.190	.418	19	-2	-2	103	0	1	.278	0			0	/C	-0.1
Total	2	16	54	5	14	1	0	0	5	2	10	.259	.286	.278	.563	58	-3	-3	103	100	3	.415	0			-0	/C	-0.1
■ WALLY SMITH	Smith, Wallace H. b: 3/13/1889, Philadelphia, Pa. d: 6/10/30, Florence, Ariz. BR/TR, 5'11.5", 180 lbs. Deb: 4/17/11																											
1911	StL-N	81	194	23	42	6	5	2	19	21	33	.216	.303	.330	.633	76	-6	-7	101	92	21	.612	5			-1	3S/2O	-0.5
1912	StL-N	75	219	22	56	5	5	0	26	29	27	.256	.351	.324	.675	85	-4	-3	100	123	26	.656	4			2	3S/1	0.0
1914	Was-A	45	97	11	19	4	1	0	8	3	12	.196	.235	.258	.493	48	-6	-7	101	120	6	.402	3	4	-2	-1	2/1S3O	-0.8
Total	3	201	510	56	117	15	11	2	53	53	72	.229	.312	.314	.625	75	-16	-17	100	111	53	.587	12	4		0	/3S21O	-1.3
■ WIB SMITH	Smith, Wilbur Floyd b: 8/30/1886, Evart, Mich. d: 11/18/59, Fargo, N.D. BL/TR, 5'10.5", 165 lbs. Deb: 5/31/09																											
1909	StL-A	17	42	3	8	0	0	0	2	0		.190	.190	.190	.381	22	-4	-3	92	96	1	.235	0			1	C/1	-0.1
■ RED SMITH	Smith, Willard Jehu b: 4/11/1892, Logansport, Ind. d: 7/17/72, Noblesville, Ind. BR/TR, 5'8", 165 lbs. Deb: 9/17/17																											
1917	Pit-N	11	21	1	3	1	0	0	2	3	4	.143	.250	.190	.440	36	-2	-1	100	193	1	.444	1			0	/C	0.0
1918	Pit-N	15	24	1	4	1	0	0	3	3	0	.167	.259	.208	.468	41	-2	-2	106	227	1	.400	0			1	C	0.0
Total	2	26	45	2	7	2	0	0	5	6	4	.156	.255	.200	.455	39	-3	-3	103	211	2	.421	1			1	/C	0.0
■ BILL SMITH	Smith, William E. b: E.Liverpool, Ohio Deb: 9/17/1884																											
1884	Cle-N	1	3	0	0	0	0	0	0	0	2	.000	.000	.000	.000	-98	-1	-1	102	0	0	.000				0	/O	0.0
■ BILL SMITH	Smith, William J. b: Baltimore, Md. d: 8/9/1886, Deb: 4/14/1873 M																											
1873	Mar-n	4	16	1	1							.063															/OC	
■ WILLIE SMITH	Smith, Willie b: 2/11/39, Anniston, Ala. BL/TL, 6', 182 lbs. Deb: 6/18/63																											
1963	Det-A	17	8	2	1	0	0	0	0	0	1	.125	.125	.125	.250	-29	-1	-1	104	0	0	.143	0	0	0	0	P	0.0
1964	LA-A	118	359	46	108	14	6	11	51	8	39	.301	.320	.465	.785	130	6	10	89	108	49	.697	7	5	-1	-6	OP	0.2
1965	Cal-A	136	459	52	120	14	9	14	57	32	60	.261	.311	.423	.734	109	3	4	98	102	58	.670	9	8	-2	-3	*O/1	-0.6
1966	Cal-A	90	195	18	36	3	2	1	20	12	37	.185	.243	.236	.479	39	-15	-15	99	171	12	.390	1	0	0	-4	O	-2.2
1967	Cle-A	21	32	0	7	2	0	0	2	1	10	.219	.242	.281	.524	54	-2	-2	100	93	1	.357	0	2	-1	-1	/O1	-0.4
1968	Cle-A	33	42	1	6	2	0	0	3	3	14	.143	.217	.190	.408	24	-4	-4	101	161	2	.324	0	0	0	-0	/1PO	-0.4
	Chi-N	55	142	13	39	8	2	5	25	12	33	.275	.335	.465	.800	123	6	4	112	130	23	.760	0	0	0	-6	O/1P	-0.3
1969	Chi-N	103	195	21	48	9	1	9	25	25	49	.246	.332	.441	.773	108	4	2	107	89	29	.747	1	0	0	-8	O1	-0.9
1970	Chi-N	87	167	15	36	9	1	5	24	11	32	.216	.268	.371	.639	58	-8	-12	120	121	17	.567	2	1	0	-1	1/O	-1.6
1971	Cin-N	31	55	3	9	2	0	1	4	3	9	.164	.207	.255	.461	31	-5	-5	96	96	2	.340	0	0	0	-0	1	-0.6
Total	9	691	1654	171	410	63	21	46	211	107	284	.248	.297	.395	.692	93	-17	-19	101	115	194	.624	20	16	-4	-28	O/1P	-6.8
■ HOMER SMOOT	Smoot, Homer Vernon "Doc" b: 3/26/1878, Galestown, Md. d: 3/25/28, Salisbury, Md. BL/TR, 5'10", 180 lbs. Deb: 4/17/02																											
1902	StL-N	129	518	58	161	19	4	3	48	23		.311	.340	.380	.720	131	13	16	95	78	76	.672	20			-1	*O	0.6
1903	StL-N	129	500	67	148	22	8	4	49	32		.296	.338	.396	.734	115	6	9	96	72	75	.702	17			-1	*O	0.0
1904	StL-N	137	520	58	146	23	6	3	66	37		.281	.329	.365	.694	117	9	10	99	117	72	.668	23			2	*O	0.7
1905	StL-N	139	534	73	166	21	16	4	58	33		.311	.351	.433	.784	148	21	27	91	80	91	.774	21			0	*O	1.8
1906	StL-N	86	343	41	85	9	10	0	31	11		.248	.271	.332	.604	89	-5	-6	101	95	33	.496	3			-2	O	-1.0
	Cin-N	60	220	11	57	8	1	1	17	13		.259	.300	.318	.619	82	-2	-5	115	90	22	.509	0			9	O	0.3
	Yr	146	563	52	142	17	11	1	48	24		.252	.283	.327	.610	86	-7	-11	107	94	54	.501	3			7		-0.7
Total	5	680	2635	308	763	102	45	15	269	149		.290	.328	.380	.707	118	43	51	98	88	367	.659	84			7	O	2.4
■ HENRY SMOYER	Smoyer, Henry Neitz "Hennie" (born Henry Neitz Smowery) b: 4/24/1890, Fredricksburg, Pa. d: 2/28/58, Dubois, Pa. BR/TR, 5'6", Deb: 8/14/12																											
1912	StL-A	6	14	1	3	0	0	0	0	2		.214	.313	.214	.527	52	-1	-1	99	0	1	.455	0			0	/S3	0.0
■ FRANK SMYKAL	Smykal, Frank John (born Frank John Smejkal) b: 10/13/1889, Chicago, Ill. d: 8/11/50, Chicago, Ill. BR/TR, 5'7", 150 lbs. Deb: 8/30/16																											
1916	Pit-N	6	10	1	3	0	0	0	2	3	1	.300	.500	.300	.800	142	1	1	105	265	2	1.143	1			0	/S3	0.1
■ CLANCY SMYRES	Smyres, Clarence Melvin b: 5/24/22, Culver City, Cal. BB/TR, 5'11.5", 175 lbs. Deb: 4/18/44																											
1944	Bro-N	5	2	1	0	0	0	0	0	0	0	.000	.000	.000	.000	-99	-1	-1	99	0	0	.000	0			0	H	0.0
■ RED SMYTH	Smyth, James Daniel b: 1/30/1893, Holly Springs, Miss. d: 4/14/58, Inglewood, Cal. BL/TR, 5'9", 152 lbs. Deb: 8/11/15																											
1915	Bro-N	19	22	3	3	1	0	0	3	4	2	.136	.269	.182	.451	37	-2	-2	101	286	1	.429	1	2	-1	-1	/O	-0.3
1916	Bro-N	2	5	0	0	0	0	0	0	0	3	.000	.000	.000	.000	-97	-1	-1	103	0	0	.000	0			0	/2	0.0
1917	Bro-N	29	24	5	3	0	0	0	1	4	6	.125	.250	.125	.375	16	-2	-2	104	129	1	.333	0			-1	/3O	-0.2
	StL-N	38	72	5	15	0	2	0	4	4	9	.208	.269	.264	.533	63	-3	-3	102	81	5	.491	3			-6	O	-1.1
	Yr	67	96	10	18	0	2	0	5	8	15	.188	.264	.229	.493	51	-5	-5	102	104	6	.449	3			-7		-1.3
1918	StL-N	40	113	19	24	1	2	0	4	16	11	.212	.315	.257	.572	80	-3	-2	93	52	10	.551	3			-1	O2	-0.3
Total	4	128	236	32	45	2	4	0	12	28	31	.191	.285	.233	.518	60	-11	-10	98	90	17	.482	7	2		-8	/O23	-1.9
■ JOHN SNEED	Sneed, Jonathon L. b: Columbus, Ohio d: 1/4/1899, Memphis, Tenn. Deb: 5/01/1884																											
1884	Ind-a	27	102	14	22	4	0	1		6		.216	.259	.284	.544	83	-2	-2	96	0	8	.438				0	O	0.0
1890	Tol-a	9	30	3	6	0	0	0		8		.200	.368	.200	.568	69	-1	-1	103	0	4	.792	5			2	/O	0.1
	Col-a	128	484	114	141	13	15	2		63		.291	.383	.393	.776	133	21	21	99	0	90	.878	39			-9	*O/S	0.5
	Yr	137	514	117	147	13	15	2	0	71		.286	.382	.381	.763	129	20	21	99	0	94	.872	44			-6		0.6
1891	Col-a	99	366	66	94	9	6	1	61	55	29	.257	.366	.322	.688	112	3	9	89	154	53	.754	24			-8	*O	-0.1
Total	3	263	982	197	263	26	21	4	61	132	29	.268	.364	.349	.714	118	21	29	95	59	155	.779	68			-14	O/S	0.5
■ CHARLIE SNELL	Snell, Charles Anthony (born Charles Anthony Schnell) b: 11/29/1893, Hampstead, Md. d: 4/4/88, Reading, Pa. BR/TR, 5'11", 160 lbs. Deb: 7/19/12																											
1912	StL-A	8	19	0	4	1	0	0	0	3		.211	.348	.263	.611	76	-0	-0	99	0	2	.600	0			0	/C	0.1
■ WALLY SNELL	Snell, Walter Henry "Doc" b: 5/19/1889, W.Bridgewater, Mass. d: 7/23/80, Providence, R.I. BR/TR, 5'10", 170 lbs. Deb: 8/01/13																											
1913	Bos-A	5	8	1	3	0	0	0	0	0	0	.375	.375	.375	.750	116	0	0	103	0	1	.800	1			0	/C	0.0
■ DUKE SNIDER	Snider, Edwin Donald "The Silver Fox" b: 9/19/26, Los Angeles, Cal. BL/TR, 6', 179 lbs. Deb: 4/17/47 H																											
1947	Bro-N	40	83	6	20	3	1	0	5	3	24	.241	.276	.301	.577	51	-6	-6	105	74	7	.492	2			-2	O	-0.9
1948	Bro-N	53	160	22	39	6	6	5	21	12	27	.244	.297	.450	.747	95	-1	-2	104	90	21	.704	4			-1	O	-0.6
1949	Bro-N	146	552	100	161	28	7	23	92	56	92	.292	.361	.493	.854	125	20	19	102	104	100	.862	12			-3	*O	0.7
1950	Bro-N	152	620	109	**199**	31	10	31	107	58	79	.321	.379	.553	.932	133	36	30	107	91	131	.970	16			4	*O	2.8
1951	Bro-N	150	606	96	168	26	6	29	101	62	97	.277	.344	.483	.828	123	15	17	98	109	96	.783	14	10	-2	-5	*O	0.6
1952	Bro-N	144	534	80	162	25	7	21	92	55	77	.303	.368	.494	.863	135	26	25	102	112	96	.830	7	4	-0	-0	*O	2.1

YEAR	TM/L	G	AB	R	H	2B	3B	HR	RBI	BB	SO	AVG	OBP	SLG	PRO	/A	BR	/A	PF	CHI	RC	TA	SB	CS	SBR	FR	POS	TPR
1953	Bro-N	153	590	**132**	198	38	4	42	126	82	90	.336	.419	**.627**	**1.046**	162	59	56	104	105	161	1.152	16	7	1	-7	*O	4.1
1954	Bro-N	149	584	**120**	199	39	10	40	130	84	96	.341	.427	.647	1.074	173	**65**	**64**	101	99	**161**	1.171	6	6	-2	-9	*O	4.6
1955	Bro-N	148	538	**126**	166	34	6	42	**136**	104	87	.309	.421	.628	1.050	167	59	55	104	126	145	1.165	9	7	-2	-5	*O	4.5
1956	Bro-N	151	542	112	158	33	2	**43**	101	**99**	101	.292	**.402**	**.598**	**1.000**	**160**	**50**	**48**	103	100	**128**	**1.060**	3	3	-1	-5	*O	3.8
1957	Bro-N	139	508	91	139	25	7	40	92	77	104	.274	.370	.587	.957	130	37	25	116	97	106	.972	3	4	-2	-12	*O	0.8
1958	LA-N	106	327	45	102	12	3	15	58	32	49	.312	.375	.505	.880	124	14	12	105	114	59	.840	2	2	-1	-4	O	0.4
1959	LA-N	126	370	59	114	11	2	23	88	58	71	.308	.402	.535	.937	144	26	25	102	133	78	.955	1	5	-3	-9	*O	1.1
1960	LA-N	101	235	38	57	13	5	14	36	46	54	.243	.369	.519	.888	121	13	9	115	89	46	.919	1	0	0	-6	O	0.0
1961	LA-N	85	233	35	69	8	3	16	56	29	43	.296	.376	.562	.939	142	15	14	102	126	48	.947	1	1	-0	3	O	1.3
1962	LA-N	80	158	28	44	11	3	5	30	36	32	.278	.418	.481	.899	152	11	12	93	130	34	.975	2	0	1	-1	O	0.9
1963	NY-N	129	354	44	86	8	3	14	45	56	74	.243	.348	.401	.749	116	8	8	99	103	53	.734	0	1	-1	-9	*O	-0.7
1964	SF-N	91	167	16	35	7	0	4	17	22	40	.210	.302	.323	.625	76	-5	-5	100	106	17	.567	0	0	0	-6	O	-1.2
Total	18	2143	7161	1259	2116	358	85	407	1333	971	1237	.295	.381	.540	.921	139	441	407	104	107	1487	.972	99	50		-79	*O	24.3
■ VAN SNIDER	Snider, Van Voorhees b: 8/11/63, Birmingham, Ala. BL/TR, 6'3", 185 lbs. Deb: 9/02/88																											
1988	Cin-N	11	28	4	6	1	0	1	6	0	13	.214	.214	.357	.571	58	-2	-2	105	185	2	.435	0	1	-1	-0	/O	-0.2
■ ROXY SNIPES	Snipes, Wyatt Eure "Rock" b: 10/28/1896, Marion, S.C. d: 5/1/41, Fayetteville, N.C. BL/TR, 6', 185 lbs. Deb: 7/15/23																											
1923	Chi-A	1	1	0	0	0	0	0	0	0	0	.000	.000	.000	.000	-99	-0	-0	98	0	0	.000	0	0	0	0	H	0.0
■ CHAPPIE SNODGRASS	Snodgrass, Amzie Beal b: 3/18/1870, Springfield, Ohio d: 9/9/51, New York, N.Y. BR/TR, 5'10", 165 lbs. Deb: 5/15/01																											
1901	Bal-A	3	10	0	1	0	0	0	1	0		.100	.100	.100	.200	-41	-2	-2	107	316	0	.111	0			0	/O	-0.1
■ FRED SNODGRASS	Snodgrass, Frederick Carlisle "Snow" b: 10/19/1887, Ventura, Cal. d: 4/5/74, Ventura, Cal. BR/TR, 5'11.5", 175 lbs. Deb: 6/04/08																											
1908	NY-N	6	4	2	1	0	0	0	1	0		.250	.250	.250	.500	59	-0	-0	104	384	0	.667	1			-0	/C	0.0
1909	NY-N	28	70	10	21	5	0	1	6	7		.300	.387	.414	.802	144	4	4	105	68	15	1.000	10			-2	O/C1	0.2
1910	NY-N	123	396	69	127	22	8	2	44	71	52	.321	.440	.432	.871	162	32	34	95	88	90	1.071	33			-5	*O/1C3	2.7
1911	NY-N	151	534	83	157	27	10	1	77	72	59	.294	.393	.388	.781	116	16	14	102	119	102	.915	51			4	*O/13	1.3
1912	NY-N	146	535	91	144	24	9	3	69	70	65	.269	.362	.364	.727	95	1	-2	104	110	87	.808	43			-1	*O1/2	-0.6
1913	NY-N	141	457	65	133	21	6	3	49	53	44	.291	.373	.383	.756	113	11	10	103	99	72	.809	27			-1	*O/12	0.6
1914	NY-N	113	392	54	103	20	4	0	44	37	43	.263	.336	.334	.670	104	0	2	96	124	50	.689	25			4	O1/23	0.4
1915	NY-N	80	252	36	49	9	0	0	20	35	33	.194	.307	.230	.537	70	-9	-7	91	134	19	.512	11	12	-4	-1	O	-1.5
	Bos-N	23	79	10	22	2	0	0	9	7	9	.278	.352	.304	.656	101	0	0	98	152	8	.541	0	4	-2	1	O/1	-0.1
	Yr	103	331	46	71	11	0	0	29	42	42	.215	.318	.248	.565	78	-9	-6	93	139	27	.518	11	16	-6	-0		-1.6
1916	Bos-N	112	382	33	95	13	5	1	32	34	54	.249	.318	.317	.635	103	-1	2	93	104	45	.606	14			10	*O	0.8
Total	9	923	3101	453	852	143	42	11	351	386	359	.275	.367	.359	.725	112	54	58	99	110	488	.785	215	16		9	O/1C23	3.8
■ CHARLIE SNOW	Snow, Charles M. b: 8/3/1849, Lowell, Mass. Deb: 10/01/1874																											
1874	Atl-n	1	1	0	0							.000															/O	
■ BERNIE SNYDER	Snyder, Bernard Austin b: 8/25/13, Philadelphia, Pa. BR/TR, 6', 165 lbs. Deb: 9/15/35																											
1935	Phi-A	10	32	5	11	1	0	0	3	1	2	.344	.364	.375	.739	91	-0	-0	100	85	4	.619	0	0	0	-1	/2S	0.0
■ CHARLES SNYDER	Snyder, Charles b: Camden, N.J. d: 3/10/01, Philadelphia, Pa. TR , Deb: 9/19/1890																											
1890	Phi-a	9	33	5	9	1	0	0		2		.273	.314	.303	.617	87	-1	-1	97	0	3	.500	0			0	/OC	0.0
■ POP SNYDER	Snyder, Charles N. b: 10/6/1854, Washington, D.C. d: 10/29/24, Washington, D.C. BR/TR, 5'11.5", 184 lbs. Deb: 6/16/1873 M																											
1873	Nat-n	28	118	16	18							.153															C/O	
1874	Bal-n	39	168	23	32							.190															C	
1875	Phi-n	66	206	39	62							.301															*C/O	
1876	Lou-N	56	224	21	44	4	1	1	9	2	7	.196	.204	.237	.440	44	-12	-14	104	55	11	.306				5	*C/O	-0.4
1877	Lou-N	61	248	23	64	7	2	2	28	3	14	.258	.267	.327	.594	65	-4	-16	132	111	22	.457				11	*C/OS	-0.1
1878	Bos-N	60	226	21	48	5	0	0	14	1	19	.212	.216	.235	.450	44	-12	-15	108	91	12	.303				11	*C/O	-0.1
1879	Bos-N	81	329	42	78	16	3	2	35	5	31	.237	.249	.322	.571	81	-5	-8	107	112	27	.442				21	*C/O	1.1
1881	Bos-N	62	219	14	50	8	0	0	16	3	23	.228	.239	.265	.504	63	-10	-8	91	96	14	.361				1	*C/OS2	-0.6
1882	Cin-a	72	309	49	90	12	2	1		9		.291	.311	.353	.664	113	7	3	109	0	35	.539				13	*C/1OM	1.5
1883	Cin-a	58	250	38	64	14	6	0		8		.256	.279	.360	.639	101	1	-0	103	0	26	.527				11	C/SM	1.3
1884	Cin-a	67	268	32	69	9	9	0		7		.257	.276	.358	.635	102	2	-0	106	0	27	.518				25	C/1OM	2.6
1885	Cin-a	39	152	13	36	4	3	1		6		.237	.270	.322	.593	86	-2	-3	104	0	14	.483				4	C/1	0.6
1886	Cin-a	60	220	33	41	8	3	0		13		.186	.242	.250	.492	58	-11	-10	96	0	16	.458	11			-1	C1/O	-0.7
1887	Cle-a	74	282	33	72	12	6	0		9		.255	.281	.340	.621	76	-10	-9	98	0	29	.529	5			21	C1	1.9
1888	Cle-a	64	237	22	51	7	3	0	14	6		.215	.238	.270	.508	67	-9	-8	97	67	18	.430	9			14	C/1O	1.1
1889	Cle-N	22	83	5	16	3	0	0	12	2	12	.193	.221	.229	.450	26	-8	-9	103	192	5	.388	4			0	C	-0.6
1890	Cle-P	13	48	5	9	1	0	0	12	1	9	.188	.220	.208	.428	17	-6	-5	92	328	2	.333	1			0	C	-0.3
1891	Was-a	8	27	4	5	0	1	0	2	0	3	.185	.241	.259	.501	47	-2	-2	95	83	2	.409	0			0	/1COM	-0.1
Total	3 n	133	492	78	112							.228															/1COM	
Total	15	797	3122	355	737	110	39	7	142	75	118	.236	.256	.303	.559	74	-82	-102	104	53	260	.445	30			136	C/1OS2	7.2
■ REDLEG SNYDER	Snyder, Emanuel Sebastian (born Emanuel Sebastian Schneider) b: 12/12/1854, Camden, N.J. d: 11/24/32, Camden, N.J. BR/TR, 5'10", 175 lbs. Deb: 4/25/1876																											
1876	Cin-N	55	205	10	31	3	1	0	12	1	19	.151	.155	.176	.331	11	-19	-15	90	115	6	.213				-7	*O	-1.9
1884	WiL-U	17	52	4	10	0	0	0		1		.192	.208	.192	.400	35	-3	-4	103	0	2	.262	0			0	1/O	-0.2
Total	2	72	257	14	41	3	1	0	12	2	19	.160	.166	.179	.345	17	-22	-19	92	91	8	.222	0			-7	/O1	-2.1
■ COONEY SNYDER	Snyder, Frank C. b: Toronto, Ontario, Canada d: 3/9/17, Toronto, Ont., Can. Deb: 5/19/1898																											
1898	Lou-N	17	61	4	10	0	0	0	6	3		.164	.215	.164	.379	11	-7	-6	96	185	2	.275	0			0	C	-0.5
■ FRANK SNYDER	Snyder, Frank Elton "Pancho" b: 5/27/1893, San Antonio, Tex. d: 1/5/62, San Antonio, Tex. BR/TR, 6'2", 185 lbs. Deb: 8/25/12 C																											
1912	StL-N	11	18	2	2	0	0	0	0	2	7	.111	.200	.111	.311	-14	-3	-3	100	0	1	.313	1			1	C	0.0
1913	StL-N	7	21	1	4	0	1	0	2	0	4	.190	.190	.286	.476	38	-2	-2	93	121	1	.353	0			1	/C	0.0
1914	StL-N	100	326	19	75	15	4	1	25	13	28	.230	.262	.310	.572	67	-13	-15	104	87	27	.462	1			2	C	-0.9
1915	StL-N	144	473	41	141	22	7	2	55	39	49	.298	.353	.387	.740	123	13	13	100	111	65	.669	3	6	-3	12	*C	3.3
1916	StL-N	132	406	23	105	12	4	0	39	18	31	.259	.290	.308	.598	87	-8	-7	97	124	39	.498	7			10	C1	0.6
1917	StL-N	115	313	18	74	9	2	1	33	27	43	.236	.301	.288	.589	80	-7	-7	102	137	27	.515	4			6	C/2	0.4
1918	StL-N	39	112	5	28	7	1	0	10	6	13	.250	.288	.330	.618	95	-2	-1	93	102	11	.560	4			2	C/1	0.3
1919	StL-N	50	154	7	28	4	2	0	14	5	13	.182	.213	.234	.446	36	-12	-11	94	151	8	.349	2			1	C/1	-0.7
	NY-N	32	92	7	21	6	0	0	11	8	9	.228	.297	.293	.591	78	-2	-2	100	158	8	.521	1			-3	C	-0.3
	Yr	82	246	14	49	10	2	0	25	13	22	.199	.245	.256	.501	53	-15	-14	96	156	16	.411	3			-2		-1.0
1920	NY-N	87	264	26	66	13	4	3	27	17	18	.250	.295	.364	.659	89	-4	-4	100	99	29	.575	2	2	-1	-3	C	-0.1
1921	NY-N	108	309	36	99	13	2	8	45	27	24	.320	.382	.453	.835	123	9	10	98	101	53	.813	3	4	-2	-5	*C	1.0
1922	NY-N	104	318	34	109	21	5	5	51	23	25	.343	.387	.487	.875	120	11	9	104	105	58	.836	1	5	-3	-8	C	0.0
1923	NY-N	120	402	37	103	13	6	5	63	24	29	.256	.298	.356	.654	71	-17	-18	101	140	43	.570	5	3	-0	-8	*C	-1.8
1924	NY-N	118	354	37	107	18	3	5	53	30	43	.302	.357	.412	.769	116	3	7	91	120	53	.725	3	0	1	-13	*C	-0.2
1925	NY-N	107	325	21	78	9	1	11	51	20	49	.240	.286	.375	.662	68	-17	-16	99	117	35	.579	0	0	0	-2	C	-1.2
1926	NY-N	55	148	10	32	3	2	5	16	13	13	.216	.280	.365	.644	74	-6	-6	98	80	15	.578	0			-8	C	-1.1
1927	StL-N	63	194	7	50	5	0	1	30	9	18	.258	.291	.299	.590	54	-11	-13	107	172	17	.465	0			-1	C	-0.9
Total	16	1392	4229	331	1122	170	44	47	525	281	416	.265	.313	.360	.672	89	-69	-66	99	118	489	.592	37	20		-15	*C/12	-1.6
■ JERRY SNYDER	Snyder, Gerald George b: 7/21/29, Jenks, Okla. BR/TR, 6', 170 lbs. Deb: 5/08/52																											
1952	Was-A	36	57	5	9	2	0	0	2	5	8	.158	.226	.193	.419	17	-6	-6	100	68	3	.347	1	0	0	-1	2/S	-0.5
1953	Was-A	29	62	10	21	4	0	0	4	5	8	.339	.388	.403	.791	121	1	2	94	59	9	.705	1	1	-0	-2	S/2	0.1

YEAR	TM/L	G	AB	R	H	2B	3B	HR	RBI	BB	SO	AVG	OBP	SLG	PRO	/A	BR	/A	PF	CHI	RC	TA	SB	CS	SBR	FR	POS	TPR
1954	Was-A	64	154	17	36	3	1	0	17	15	18	.234	.302	.266	.568	57	-9	-9	98	157	13	.484	3	0	1	-2	S/2	-0.5
1955	Was-A	46	107	7	24	5	0	0	5	6	6	.224	.265	.271	.537	49	-8	-7	91	64	7	.409	1	1	-0	1	2S	-0.2
1956	Was-A	43	148	14	40	3	1	2	14	10	9	.270	.321	.345	.665	74	-5	-6	102	92	15	.553	1	0	0	1	S/2	0.0
1957	Was-A	42	93	6	14	1	0	1	4	4	9	.151	.186	.194	.379	4	-12	-12	98	75	3	.265	0	1	-1	1	S2/3	-0.9
1958	Was-A	6	9	1	1	0	0	0	1	1	1	.111	.200	.111	.311	-12	-1	-1	97	401	0	.250	0	0	0	0	/2S	0.0
Total	7	266	630	60	145	18	2	3	47	46	59	.230	.284	.279	.563	54	-42	-40	98	100	51	.471	7	3	0	-1	S/23	-2.0
■ **JIM SNYDER**	Snyder, James C. A. b: 8/27/1849, New York d: 12/1/22, Queens, N.Y. 5'7", 130 lbs. Deb: 5/07/1872																											
1872	Eck-n	26	109	15	30							.275															S/OC	
■ **CORY SNYDER**	Snyder, James Cory b: 11/11/62, Inglewood, Cal. BR/TR, 6'4", 175 lbs. Deb: 6/13/86																											
1986	Cle-A	103	416	58	113	21	1	24	69	16	123	.272	.299	.500	.799	116	6	7	98	104	58	.720	2	3	-1	-4	OS3/D	0.1
1987	Cle-A	157	577	74	136	24	2	33	82	31	166	.236	.276	.456	.732	88	-10	-12	103	92	74	.674	5	1	1	5	*OS	-0.8
1988	Cle-A	142	511	71	139	24	3	26	75	42	101	.272	.329	.483	.812	122	15	14	102	94	79	.766	5	1	1	11	*O	2.3
Total	3	402	1504	203	388	69	6	83	226	89	390	.258	.300	.477	.778	107	11	9	101	96	211	.725	12	5	1	11	O/S3D	1.6
■ **JIM SNYDER**	Snyder, James Robert b: 8/15/32, Dearbon, Mich. BR/TR, 6'1", 185 lbs. Deb: 9/15/61 MC																											
1961	Min-A	3	5	0	0	0	0	0	0	0	1	.000	.000	.000	.000	-94	-1	-1	106	0	0	.000	0	0	0	0	/2	0.0
1962	Min-A	12	10	1	1	0	0	0	1	0	0	.100	.100	.100	.200	-44	-2	-2	105	397	0	.100	0	1	-1	-0	/21	-0.2
1964	Min-A	26	71	3	11	2	0	1	9	4	11	.155	.211	.225	.436	21	-8	-8	101	201	3	.328	0	0	0	-1	2	-0.6
Total	3	41	86	4	12	2	0	1	10	4	12	.140	.187	.198	.384	6	-11	-11	102	211	3	.278	0	1	-1	-2	/21	-0.8
■ **JACK SNYDER**	Snyder, John William b: 10/1886, Lincoln Township, Pa. d: 12/13/81, Brownsville, Pa. BR/TR, 5'9", 168 lbs. Deb: 6/13/14																											
1914	Buf-F	1	0	0	0	0	0	0	0	1	0	—	1.000	—	1.198	245	0	0	104	0	0	—	0			0	/C	0.0
1917	Bro-N	7	11	1	3	0	0	0	1	0	2	.273	.273	.273	.545	65	-0	-0	104	129	1	.375	0			0	/C	0.0
Total	2	8	11	1	3	0	0	0	1	1	2	.273	.333	.273	.606	83	-0	-0	104	118	1	.500	0			0	/C	0.0
■ **JOSH SNYDER**	Snyder, Joshua M. b: 3/1844, Brooklyn, N.Y. d: 4/21/1881, Brooklyn, N.Y. Deb: 5/18/1872																											
1872	Eck-n	9	41	3	7							.171															/O	
■ **RUSS SNYDER**	Snyder, Russell Henry b: 6/22/34, Oak, Neb. BL/TR, 6'1", 190 lbs. Deb: 4/18/59																											
1959	KC-A	73	243	41	76	13	2	3	21	19	29	.313	.367	.420	.787	114	5	5	101	74	38	.746	6	2	1	6	O	0.8
1960	KC-A	125	304	45	79	10	5	4	26	20	28	.260	.308	.365	.673	82	-8	-8	99	83	34	.599	7	3	0	-7	O	-1.8
1961	Bal-A	115	312	46	91	13	5	1	13	20	32	.292	.334	.375	.709	92	-5	-4	97	42	39	.623	5	3	-0	-12	*O	-1.9
1962	Bal-A	139	416	47	127	19	4	9	40	17	46	.305	.336	.435	.771	112	2	5	95	76	58	.685	7	4	-0	0	*O	0.0
1963	Bal-A	148	429	51	110	21	2	7	36	40	48	.256	.323	.364	.686	98	-4	-1	94	85	53	.657	18	5	2	-3	*O	-0.6
1964	Bal-A	56	93	11	27	3	0	1	7	11	22	.290	.365	.355	.720	96	1	-0	105	82	12	.638	0	2	-1	-9	O	-1.2
1965	Bal-A	132	345	49	93	11	2	1	29	27	38	.270	.324	.322	.646	84	-7	-7	100	106	36	.544	3	4	-2	-1	*O	-1.3
1966	Bal-A	117	373	66	114	21	5	3	41	38	37	.306	.370	.413	.783	123	12	12	101	106	57	.721	2	1	0	-5	*O	0.4
1967	Bal-A	108	275	40	65	8	2	4	23	32	48	.236	.318	.324	.642	95	-3	-1	95	95	31	.596	5	2	0	1	O	-0.1
1968	Chi-A	38	82	2	11	2	0	1	5	4	16	.134	.174	.195	.370	12	-9	-9	101	113	3	.274	0	0	0	-5	O	-1.6
	Cle-A	68	217	30	61	8	2	2	23	25	21	.281	.355	.364	.719	117	5	5	101	116	29	.648	1	1	-0	5	O/1	0.9
	Yr	106	299	32	72	10	2	3	28	29	37	.241	.308	.318	.626	89	-3	-4	101	116	30	.536	1	1	-0	1		-0.7
1969	Cle-A	122	266	26	66	10	0	2	24	25	33	.248	.313	.308	.621	79	-9	-7	94	109	26	.529	3	2	-0	-3	O	-1.3
1970	Mil-A	124	276	34	64	11	0	4	31	16	40	.232	.274	.315	.589	63	-15	-14	98	127	23	.471	1	3	-2	-13	*O	-3.4
Total	12	1365	3631	488	984	150	29	42	319	294	438	.271	.327	.363	.690	95	-34	-23	98	92	441	.625	58	32	-2	-46	*O/1	-11.1
■ **CHIEF SOCKALEXIS**	Sockalexis, Lewis M. b: 10/24/1871, Old Town, Maine d: 12/24/13, Burlington, Maine BL/TR, 5'11", 185 lbs. Deb: 4/22/1897																											
1897	Cle-N	66	278	43	94	9	8	3	42	18		.338	.385	.460	.845	113	10	5	111	79	57	.897	16			2	O	0.1
1898	Cle-N	21	67	11	15	2	0	0	10	1		.224	.246	.254	.500	47	-5	-4	96	178	4	.365	0			0	O	-0.3
1899	Cle-N	7	22	0	6	1	0	0	3	1		.273	.304	.318	.623	82	-1	-0	89	131	2	.500	0			0	/O	0.0
Total	3	94	367	54	115	12	8	3	55	20		.313	.355	.414	.770	102	4	-0	107	100	63	.762	16			2	/O	-0.2
■ **BILL SODD**	Sodd, William b: 9/18/14, Ft.Worth, Tex. BR/TR, 6'2", 210 lbs. Deb: 9/27/37																											
1937	Cle-A	1	1	0	0	0	0	0	0	0	1	.000	.000	.000	.000	-99	-0	-0	98	0	0	.000	0	0	0	0	H	0.0
■ **ERIC SODERHOLM**	Soderholm, Eric Thane b: 9/24/48, Cortland, N.Y. BR/TR, 5'11", 187 lbs. Deb: 9/03/71																											
1971	Min-A	21	64	9	10	4	0	1	4	10	17	.156	.299	.266	.564	59	-3	-3	104	82	6	.536	0	1	-1	-4	3	-0.9
1972	Min-A	93	287	28	54	10	0	13	39	19	48	.188	.246	.359	.605	73	-9	-11	107	115	24	.529	3	3	-1	-3	3	-1.4
1973	Min-A	35	111	22	33	7	2	1	9	21	16	.297	.414	.423	.837	131	6	6	104	71	20	.833	1	2	-1	-1	3/S	0.3
1974	Min-A	141	464	63	128	18	3	10	51	48	68	.276	.350	.392	.742	112	8	8	101	95	63	.686	7	3	0	3	*3/S	1.3
1975	Min-A	117	419	62	120	17	2	11	58	53	66	.286	.367	.415	.782	112	12	8	107	110	62	.723	3	5	-2	11	*3/D	1.9
1977	Chi-A	130	460	77	129	20	3	25	67	47	47	.280	.352	.500	.852	130	18	18	99	89	77	.809	2	4	-2	3	*3/D	1.6
1978	Chi-A	143	457	57	118	17	1	20	67	39	44	.258	.322	.431	.753	109	5	4	101	103	61	.684	2	2	-1	13	*3D/2	1.6
1979	Chi-A	56	210	31	53	8	2	6	34	19	19	.252	.314	.395	.710	88	-3	-4	102	137	24	.611	0	1	-1	13	3	0.9
	Tex-A	63	147	15	40	6	0	4	19	12	9	.272	.331	.395	.726	95	-1	-1	100	104	19	.634	0	0	0	4	3D/1	0.3
	Yr	119	357	46	93	14	2	10	53	31	28	.261	.321	.395	.716	91	-4	-5	101	121	46	.641	0	1	-1	16		1.2
1980	NY-A	95	275	38	79	13	1	11	35	27	25	.287	.353	.462	.815	122	8	8	99	85	43	.756	0	0	0	-1	D3	0.7
Total	9	894	2894	402	764	120	14	102	383	295	359	.264	.337	.421	.758	109	41	34	102	100	398	.719	18	21	-7	35	3/D1S2	6.3
■ **RICK SOFIELD**	Sofield, Richard Michael b: 12/16/56, Cheyenne, Wyo. BL/TR, 6'1", 195 lbs. Deb: 4/06/79																											
1979	Min-A	35	93	8	28	5	0	0	12	12	27	.301	.381	.355	.736	92	1	-1	109	140	12	.671	2	3	-1	-3	O	-0.6
1980	Min-A	131	417	52	103	18	4	9	49	24	92	.247	.291	.374	.665	74	-12	-16	109	104	46	.578	4	5	-2	-17	*O/D	-3.7
1981	Min-A	41	102	9	18	2	0	0	5	8	22	.176	.236	.196	.432	25	-10	-10	105	98	4	.341	3	2	-0	-1	O	-1.2
Total	3	207	612	69	149	25	4	9	66	44	141	.243	.296	.342	.638	70	-21	-27	108	109	62	.552	9	10	-3	-21	O/D	-5.5
■ **TONY SOLAITA**	Solaita, Tolia b: 1/15/47, Nuuyli, Amer.Somoa BL/TL, 6', 210 lbs. Deb: 9/16/68																											
1968	NY-A	1	1	0	0	0	0	0	0	0	1	.000	.000	.000	.000	-99	-0	-0	101	0	0	.000	0	0	0	0	/1	0.0
1974	KC-A	96	239	31	64	12	0	7	30	35	70	.268	.364	.406	.769	114	7	5	106	100	36	.739	0	3	-2	-0	1D/O	0.0
1975	KC-A	93	231	35	60	11	0	16	44	39	79	.260	.371	.515	.886	146	15	14	102	101	45	.899	0	1	-1	1	D1	1.3
1976	KC-A	31	68	4	16	4	0	0	9	6	17	.235	.297	.294	.591	74	-2	-2	100	173	7	.500	0	0	0	0	D/1	-0.2
	Cal-A	63	215	25	58	9	0	9	33	34	44	.270	.369	.437	.807	147	10	12	92	107	36	.796	1	1	-0	3	1/D	1.3
	Yr	94	283	29	74	13	0	9	42	40	61	.261	.353	.403	.756	128	8	10	95	130	42	.724	1	1	-0	3		1.1
1977	Cal-A	116	324	40	78	15	0	14	53	56	77	.241	.353	.417	.769	115	5	7	95	119	49	.753	1	3	-2	3	1/D	0.3
1978	Cal-A	60	94	10	21	3	0	1	14	16	25	.223	.336	.287	.624	76	-2	-3	102	184	10	.573	0	0	0	0	D1	-0.2
1979	Mon-N	29	42	5	12	4	0	1	7	11	16	.286	.434	.452	.886	139	3	3	102	126	9	1.000	0	0	0	-0	1	0.2
	Tor-A	36	102	14	27	8	1	2	13	17	16	.265	.370	.422	.791	109	2	2	103	102	17	.779	0	0	0	0	D/1	0.1
Total	7	525	1316	164	336	66	1	50	203	214	345	.255	.361	.421	.782	120	38	39	99	116	209	.781	2	8	-4	6	1D/O	2.8
■ **MOSE SOLOMON**	Solomon, Morris Hirsch "The Rabbi Of Swat" b: 12/8/1900, New York, N.Y. d: 6/25/66, Miami, Fla. BL/TL, 5'9.5", 180 lbs. Deb: 9/30/23																											
1923	NY-N	2	8	0	3	1	0	0	1	0	1	.375	.375	.500	.875	127	0	0	101	90	1	.800	0	0	0	-0	/O	0.0
■ **MOOSE SOLTERS**	Solters, Julius Joseph (born Julius Joseph Soltesz) b: 3/22/06, Pittsburgh, Pa. d: 9/28/75, Pittsburgh, Pa. BR/TR, 6', 190 lbs. Deb: 4/17/34																											
1934	Bos-A	101	365	61	109	25	4	7	58	18	50	.299	.333	.447	.780	94	-2	-5	106	105	54	.735	9	4	0	5	O	0.0
1935	Bos-A	24	79	15	19	6	1	0	8	2	7	.241	.268	.342	.610	53	-5	-6	108	101	7	.508	1	1	-0	2	O	-0.4
	StL-A	127	552	79	182	39	6	18	104	34	35	.330	.369	.520	.889	120	20	15	107	91	106	.892	10	1	2	19	*O	3.2
	Yr	151	631	94	201	45	7	18	112	36	42	.319	.356	.498	.854	111	14	8	107	94	112	.838	11	2	2	21		2.8
1936	StL-A	152	628	100	183	45	7	17	134	41	76	.291	.336	.467	.802	93	-7	-10	103	134	99	.760	3	0	1	11	*O	-0.1
1937	Cle-A	152	589	90	190	42	11	20	109	42	56	.323	.372	.533	.905	128	20	22	98	106	113	.897	6	9	-4	1	*O	1.3
1938	Cle-A	67	199	30	40	6	3	2	22	13	28	.201	.250	.291	.541	36	-21	-20	99	116	15	.469	4	1	1	0	O	-1.7
1939	Cle-A	41	102	19	28	7	2	2	19	9	15	.275	.333	.441	.775	99	-1	-1	98	126	15	.737	2	1	0	-4	O	-0.4

YEAR	TM/L	G	AB	R	H	2B	3B	HR	RBI	BB	SO	AVG	OBP	SLG	PRO	/A	BR	/A	PF	CHI	RC	TA	SB	CS	SBR	FR	POS	TPR
	StL-A	40	131	14	27	6	1	0	14	10	20	.206	.262	.267	.530	36	-13	-13	100	135	9	.434	1	0	0	-1	O	-1.2
	Yr	81	233	33	55	13	3	2	33	19	35	.236	.294	.343	.637	63	-14	-13	99	132	24	.564	3	1	0	-4		-1.6
1940	Chi-A	116	428	65	132	28	3	12	80	27	54	.308	.351	.472	.823	107	6	4	104	124	70	.754	3	3	-1	6	*O	0.1
1941	Chi-A	76	251	24	65	9	4	4	43	18	31	.259	.311	.375	.686	86	-8	-5	94	144	28	.592	3	2	-0	-1	O	-0.9
1943	Chi-A	42	97	6	15	0	0	1	8	7	5	.155	.212	.186	.397	16	-10	-10	101	139	3	.281	0	1	-1	-4	O	-1.6
Total	9	938	3421	503	990	213	42	83	599	221	377	.289	.334	.449	.783	97	-21	-31	102	117	519	.735	42	23	-1	34	O	-1.7
■ **JOCK SOMERLOTT** Somerlott, John Wesley b: 10/26/1882, Flint, Ind. d: 4/21/65, Butler, Ind. TR, 6', 160 lbs. Deb: 9/19/10																												
1910	Was-A	16	63	6	14	0	0	0	2	3		.222	.258	.222	.480	50	-4	-4	101	56	4	.388	2			1	1	-0.2
1911	Was-A	13	40	2	7	0	0	0	2	2		.175	.233	.175	.408	15	-5	-4	97	97	2	.303	0			1	1	-0.3
Total	2	29	103	8	21	0	0	0	4	5		.204	.248	.204	.452	36	-8	-8	99	72	5	.354	2			1	/1	-0.5
■ **KID SOMERS** Somers, William b: Toronto, Ont., Canada d: 10/16/1895, Toronto, Ont., Can. TR, Deb: N/A.																												
1893	StL-N	2	1	1	0	0	0	0	0	0	0	.000	.500	.000	.500	40	0	0	99	0	0	1.000	0			0	/OC	0.0
■ **ED SOMERVILLE** Somerville, Edward b: Philadelphia, Pa. d: 9/30/1877, Hamilton, Ont., Canada BR/TR, Deb: 4/30/1875																												
1875	Cen-n	14	59	5	13							.220															2	
	NH-n	33	145	16	30							.207															2/1S3	
	Yr	47	204	21	43							.211																
1876	Lou-N	64	256	29	48	5	1	0	14	1	6	.188	.191	.215	.406	34	-17	-18	104	88	11	.269				**28**	*2	0.8
■ **JOE SOMMER** Sommer, Joseph John b: 11/20/1858, Covington, Ky. d: 1/16/38, Cincinnati, Ohio BR/TR, Deb: 7/08/1880																												
1880	Cin-N	24	88	10	16	1	0	0	6	0	2	.182	.182	.193	.375	27	-6	-6	99	131	3	.236				0	O/S3C	-0.6
1882	Cin-a	80	354	82	102	12	6	1		24		.288	.333	.364	.698	124	13	9	109	0	44	.607				4	*O	1.0
1883	Cin-a	97	413	79	115	5	7	3		20		.278	.312	.346	.658	108	5	3	103	0	46	.547				-1	*O/3P	0.2
1884	Bal-a	107	479	96	129	11	10	4		8		.269	.293	.359	.652	116	7	8	99	0	52	.537				-0	*3/O2	0.7
1885	Bal-a	110	471	84	118	23	6	1		24		.251	.291	.331	.622	93	-0	-5	106	0	47	.518				13	*O/S3P1	0.2
1886	Bal-a	139	560	79	117	18	4	1		24		.209	.245	.261	.506	66	-26	-17	91	0	45	.460	31			8	*O23/SP	-1.0
1887	Bal-a	131	463	88	123	11	5	0		63		.266	.358	.311	.670	93	-3	0	96	0	64	.706	29			1	*O23/SP	-0.1
1888	Bal-a	79	297	31	65	10	0	0	35	18		.219	.266	.253	.518	72	-10	-8	96	148	24	.461	13			-3	OS/21	-1.1
1889	Bal-a	106	386	51	85	13	2	1	36	42	49	.220	.298	.272	.570	65	-17	-16	100	97	38	.551	18			10	*O/S	-0.8
1890	Cle-N	9	35	4	8	1	0	0	0	2	2	.229	.270	.257	.527	59	-2	-2	94	0	2	.407	0			0	/OP	0.0
	BB-a	38	129	13	33	4	2	0		13		.256	.324	.318	.642	91	-1	-1	100	0	17	.667	10			0	O	0.0
Total	10	920	3675	617	911	109	42	11	77	238	53	.248	.297	.309	.607	90	-40	-36	99	25	380	.541	101			31	O3/2SP1C	-1.5
■ **PETE SOMMERS** Sommers, Joseph Andrews b: 10/26/1866, Cleveland, Ohio d: 7/22/08, Cleveland, Ohio BR/TL, 5'11.5", 181 lbs. Deb: 4/27/1887																												
1887	NY-a	33	116	9	21	3	0	1		7		.181	.234	.233	.467	36	-10	-8	88	0	8	.432	6			0	C/O1	-0.5
1888	Bos-N	4	13	1	3	1	0	0	0	0	3	.231	.231	.308	.538	68	-0	-1	106	0	1	.400	0			0	/C	0.0
1889	Chi-N	12	45	5	10	5	0	0	8	2	8	.222	.271	.333	.604	70	-2	-2	99	162	4	.514	0			0	C/O	-0.1
	Ind-N	23	84	12	21	2	2	2	14	1	16	.250	.267	.393	.660	78	-2	-3	109	107	10	.587	2			0	C/O	-0.2
	Yr	35	129	17	31	7	2	2	22	3	24	.240	.269	.372	.641	75	-4	-5	105	131	14	.561	2			0		-0.3
1890	NY-N	17	47	4	5	1	1	0	1	4	13	.106	.192	.170	.363	7	-5	-5	95	38	2	.310	0			0	C/1O	-0.4
	Cle-N	9	34	4	7	1	1	0	1	2	3	.206	.250	.294	.544	64	-2	-1	94	31	3	.444	0			0	/CO	0.0
	Yr	26	81	8	12	2	2	0	2	6	16	.148	.216	.222	.438	31	-7	-7	95	37	4	.362	0			0		-0.4
Total	4	98	339	35	67	13	4	3	24	16	43	.198	.242	.286	.528	53	-22	-20	97	56	27	.460	8			0	/CO1	-1.2
■ **BILL SOMMERS** Sommers, William Dunn b: 2/17/23, Brooklyn, N.Y. BR/TR, 6', 180 lbs. Deb: 4/25/50																												
1950	StL-A	65	137	24	35	5	1	0	14	25	14	.255	.370	.307	.677	70	-4	-6	107	115	17	.620	0	1	-1	-4	32	-0.9
■ **BILL SORRELL** Sorrell, William b: 10/14/40, Morehead, Ky. BL/TR, 6', 190 lbs. Deb: 9/02/65																												
1965	Phi-N	10	13	2	5	0	0	1	2	2	1	.385	.467	.615	1.082	213	2	2	95	75	4	1.250	0	0	0	0	/3	0.2
1967	SF-N	18	17	1	3	1	0	0	1	3	2	.176	.300	.235	.535	55	-1	-1	101	104	2	.500	0	0	0	-2	/O	-0.2
1970	KC-A	57	135	12	36	2	0	4	14	10	13	.267	.317	.370	.688	90	-2	-2	98	91	15	.587	1	0	0	-3	3/O1	-0.5
Total	3	85	165	15	44	3	0	5	17	15	16	.267	.328	.376	.704	96	-1	-1	98	91	20	.619	1	0	0	-5	/3O1	-0.5
■ **CHICK SORRELLS** Sorrells, Raymond Edwin b: 7/31/1896, Stringtown, Okla. d: 7/20/83, Terrell, Tex. BR/TR, 5'9", 155 lbs. Deb: 9/18/22																												
1922	Cle-A	2	1	0	0	0	0	0	0	0	0	.000	.000	.000	.000	-98	-0	-0	102	0	0	.000	0	0	0	0	/S	0.0
■ **DENNY SOTHERN** Sothern, Dennis Elwood b: 1/20/04, Washington, D.C. d: 12/7/77, Durham, N.C. BR/TR, 5'11", 175 lbs. Deb: 9/10/26																												
1926	Phi-N	14	53	5	13	1	0	3	10	4	10	.245	.310	.434	.744	95	-0	-1	103	114	7	.700				2	O	0.0
1928	Phi-N	141	579	82	165	27	5	5	38	34	53	.285	.327	.375	.702	80	-15	-18	104	62	69	.652	17			5	*O	-1.7
1929	Phi-N	76	294	52	90	21	3	5	27	16	24	.306	.346	.449	.795	87	-3	-7	110	64	44	.799	13			0	O	-1.1
1930	Phi-N	90	347	66	97	26	1	5	36	22	37	.280	.326	.403	.730	71	-14	-18	106	82	45	.680	6			3	O	-1.8
	Pit-N	17	51	4	9	4	0	1	4	3	4	.176	.222	.314	.536	29	-6	-6	97	73	3	.500	2			0	O	-0.5
	Yr	107	398	70	106	30	1	6	40	25	41	.266	.313	.392	.705	66	-21	-24	104	81	48	.654	8			3		-2.3
1931	Bro-N	19	31	10	5	1	0	0	0	4	8	.161	.257	.194	.451	23	-3	-3	101	0	2	.385	0			-1	O	-0.4
Total	5	357	1355	219	379	80	9	19	115	83	136	.280	.325	.394	.719	77	-42	-53	105	68	170	.678	38			9	O	-5.5
■ **BUD SOUCHOCK** Souchock, Stephen b: 3/3/19, Yatesboro, Pa. BR/TR, 6'2.5", 203 lbs. Deb: 5/25/46																												
1946	NY-A	47	86	15	26	3	3	2	10	7	13	.302	.362	.477	.838	132	4	3	100	81	15	.778	0	3	-2	-1	1	0.0
1948	NY-A	44	118	11	24	3	1	3	11	7	13	.203	.248	.322	.570	51	-9	-9	100	79	9	.490	3	0	1	-1	1	-0.7
1949	Chi-A	84	252	29	59	13	5	7	37	25	38	.234	.303	.409	.712	89	-6	-6	98	102	32	.665	5	2	0	-1	O1	-0.6
1951	Det-A	91	188	33	46	10	3	11	28	18	27	.245	.314	.505	.819	113	3	2	106	78	27	.750	0	2	-1	-9	O/312	-0.9
1952	Det-A	92	265	40	66	16	4	13	45	21	28	.249	.304	.487	.791	119	4	4	99	100	34	.699	1	0	0	-1	O3/1	0.2
1953	Det-A	89	278	29	84	13	3	11	46	8	35	.302	.326	.489	.816	121	5	6	98	101	42	.737	5	1	1	-4	O/1	0.0
1954	Det-A	25	39	6	7	0	1	3	8	2	10	.179	.220	.462	.681	83	-1	-1	100	112	3	.618	1	1	-0	-2	/O3	-0.3
1955	Det-A	1	1	0	1	0	0	0	1	0	0	1.000	1.000	1.000	2.000	453	0	0	97	373	1	—	0	0	0	0	H	0.0
Total	8	473	1227	163	313	58	20	50	186	88	164	.255	.307	.457	.764	105	-0	-0	100	94	163	.724	15	9	-1	-18	O/132	-2.3
■ **CLYDE SOUTHWICK** Southwick, Clyde Aubra b: 11/3/1886, Maxwell, Iowa d: 10/14/61, Freeport, Ill. BL/TR, 6', 180 lbs. Deb: 8/22/11																												
1911	StL-A	4	12	3	3	0	0	0	0	1		.250	.308	.250	.558	59	-1	-1	95	0	1	.444	0			0	/C	0.0
■ **BILL SOUTHWORTH** Southworth, William Frederick b: 11/10/45, Madison, Wis. BR/TR, 6'2", 205 lbs. Deb: 10/02/64																												
1964	Mil-N	3	7	2	2	0	0	1	2	0	3	.286	.444	.714	1.159	228	1	1	97	103	2	1.400	0	0	0	0	/3	0.1
■ **BILLY SOUTHWORTH** Southworth, William Harrison b: 3/9/1893, Harvard, Neb. d: 11/15/69, Columbus, Ohio BL/TR, 5'9", 170 lbs. Deb: 8/04/13 MC																												
1913	Cle-A	1	0	0	0	0	0	0	0	0	0	—	—	—	—	—	0	0	106	—	—	—	0			-0	/O	0.0
1915	Cle-A	60	177	25	39	2	5	0	8	36	12	.220	.352	.288	.640	88	-0	-1	104	53	18	.636	2	2	-1	3	O	0.0
1918	Pit-N	64	246	37	84	5	7	2	43	26	9	.341	.409	.443	.852	151	18	16	106	136	49	.963	19			7	O	2.2
1919	Pit-N	121	453	56	127	14	**14**	4	61	32	22	.280	.329	.400	.729	113	9	7	105	118	64	.727	23			5	*O	0.7
1920	Pit-N	146	546	64	155	17	13	2	53	52	20	.284	.348	.374	.722	106	6	5	101	103	68	.675	23	25	-8	8	*O	-0.2
1921	Bos-N	141	569	86	175	25	15	7	79	36	13	.308	.351	.441	.792	117	6	12	93	102	84	.751	22	20	-5	4	*O	0.3
1922	Bos-N	43	158	27	51	4	4	4	18	18	1	.323	.392	.475	.867	130	5	7	94	77	30	.898	4	1	1	4	O	0.9
1923	Bos-N	153	611	95	195	29	16	6	78	61	23	.319	.383	.448	.831	119	17	17	100	83	103	.813	14	16	-5	5	*O/2	1.1
1924	NY-N	94	281	40	72	13	0	3	36	32	16	.256	.332	.335	.667	87	-8	-4	91	127	32	.591	1	6	-3	-2	O	-1.0
1925	NY-N	123	473	79	138	19	5	6	44	51	11	.292	.363	.391	.754	94	-4	-3	99	82	66	.701	6	13	-6	-10	*O	-2.1
1926	NY-N	36	116	23	38	6	1	5	30	7	1	.328	.366	.526	.892	141	6	6	98	137	21	.885	1			-1	O	0.4
	StL-N	99	391	76	124	22	6	11	69	26	9	.317	.364	.488	.853	125	14	13	102	113	67	.873	13			-4	O	0.5
	Yr	135	507	99	162	28	7	16	99	33	10	.320	.365	.497	.862	129	19	19	101	120	88	.875	14			-4		0.9
1927	StL-N	92	306	52	92	15	5	2	39	23	7	.301	.350	.402	.752	94	0	-3	107	106	42	.729	10			-9	O	-1.5
1929	StL-N	19	32	1	6	2	0	0	3	2	4	.188	.235	.250	.485	21	-4	-4	98	128	2	.385	0			-0	/OM	-0.3

YEAR	TM/L	G	AB	R	H	2B	3B	HR	RBI	BB	SO	AVG	OBP	SLG	PRO	/A	BR	/A	PF	CHI	RC	TA	SB	CS	SBR	FR	POS	TPR
Total	13	1192	4359	661	1296	173	91	52	561	402	148	.297	.359	.415	.773	111	65	67	100	102	650	.750	138	83		9	*O/2	1.0
■ **LEN SOWDERS**	Sowders, Leonard b: 6/29/1861, Louisville, Ky. d: 11/19/1888, Indianapolis, Ind. Deb: 9/10/1886																											
1886	Bal-a	23	76	10	20	3	1	0	12			.263	.364	.329	.693	132	2	4	91	0	12	.768	6			0	O/1	0.3
■ **DICK SPALDING**	Spalding, Charles Harry b: 10/13/1893, Philadelphia, Pa. d: 2/3/50, Philadelphia, Pa. BL/TL, 5'11", 185 lbs. Deb: 4/18/27 C																											
1927	Phi-N	115	442	68	131	16	3	0	25	38	40	.296	.352	.346	.698	91	-7	-5	96	61	54	.630	5			-1	*O	-1.0
1928	Was-A	16	23	1	8	0	0	0	0	0	4	.348	.348	.348	.696	82	-1	-1	102	0	2	.471	0	2	-1	-4	O	-0.5
Total	2	131	465	69	139	16	3	0	25	38	44	.299	.352	.346	.698	90	-7	-5	97	58	56	.622	5	2		-5	O	-1.5
■ **AL SPANGLER**	Spangler, Albert Donald b: 7/8/33, Philadelphia, Pa. BL/TL, 6', 175 lbs. Deb: 9/16/59 C																											
1959	Mil-N	6	12	3	5	0	1	0	0	1	1	.417	.462	.583	1.045	185	1	1	95	0	4	1.286	1	0	0	-0	/O	0.1
1960	Mil-N	101	105	26	28	5	2	0	6	14	17	.267	.358	.352	.711	105	-0	1	91	66	15	.725	6	2	1	-19	O	-2.0
1961	Mil-N	68	97	23	26	2	0	0	6	28	9	.268	.432	.289	.721	104	1	3	92	86	15	.822	4	2	0	-6	O	-0.5
1962	Hou-N	129	418	51	119	10	9	5	35	70	46	.285	.391	.388	.779	118	9	13	93	79	69	.791	7	6	-2	-5	*O	0.0
1963	Hou-N	120	430	52	121	25	4	4	27	50	38	.281	.358	.386	.744	124	9	13	92	67	60	.689	5	8	-3	4	*O	0.8
1964	Hou-N	135	449	51	110	18	5	4	38	41	43	.245	.314	.334	.648	86	-10	-8	96	98	48	.572	7	8	-3	-10	*O	-2.5
1965	Hou-N	38	112	18	24	1	1	1	7	14	8	.214	.302	.268	.569	70	-5	-4	89	88	10	.500	1	1	-0	-3	O	-0.7
	Cal-A	51	96	17	25	1	0	0	1	8	9	.260	.317	.271	.588	70	-4	-3	98	16	10	.535	4	0	1	-2	O	-0.5
1966	Cal-A	6	9	2	6	0	0	0	0	2	2	.667	.727	.667	1.394	307	3	3	99	0	5	2.667	0	0	0	-1	/O	0.2
1967	Chi-N	62	130	18	33	7	0	0	13	23	17	.254	.366	.308	.674	93	0	-0	102	135	16	.650	2	2	-1	-2	O	-0.4
1968	Chi-N	88	177	21	48	9	3	2	18	20	24	.271	.348	.390	.738	108	5	3	112	101	24	.672	0	1	-1	-3	O	-0.3
1969	Chi-N	82	213	23	45	8	1	4	23	21	16	.211	.285	.315	.600	64	-9	-11	107	117	20	.520	0	2	-1	-7	O	-2.3
1970	Chi-N	21	14	2	2	1	0	1	1	3	3	.143	.294	.429	.723	76	-0	-1	120	43	2	.750	0	0	0	-1	/O	-0.1
1971	Chi-N	5	5	0	2	0	0	0	0	0	1	.400	.400	.400	.800	116	0	0	110	0	1	.667	0	0	0	0	H	0.0
Total	13	912	2267	307	594	87	26	21	175	295	234	.262	.350	.351	.701	100	0	10	97	86	298	.668	37	32	-8	-55	O	-8.2
■ **BOB SPEAKE**	Speake, Robert Charles "Spook" b: 8/22/30, Springfield, Mo. BL/TL, 6'1", 178 lbs. Deb: 4/16/55																											
1955	Chi-N	95	261	36	57	9	5	12	43	28	71	.218	.301	.429	.730	91	-4	-4	100	118	34	.699	3	4	-2	-5	O/1	-1.1
1957	Chi-N	129	418	65	97	14	5	16	50	38	68	.232	.301	.404	.705	91	-8	-6	96	95	51	.652	5	6	-2	6	O1	-0.7
1958	SF-N	66	71	9	15	3	0	3	10	13	15	.211	.333	.380	.714	88	-1	-1	100	115	9	.690	0	1	-1	-0	O	-0.1
1959	SF-N	15	11	0	1	0	0	0	1	1	4	.091	.167	.091	.258	-30	-2	-2	95	404	0	.182	0	0	0	0	H	-0.1
Total	4	305	761	110	170	26	10	31	104	80	158	.223	.302	.406	.708	89	-15	-13	98	109	95	.668	8	11	-4	1	O/1	-2.0
■ **TRIS SPEAKER**	Speaker, Tristram E "The Grey Eagle" b: 4/4/1888, Hubbard, Tex. d: 12/8/58, Lake Whitney, Tex. BL/TL, 5'11.5", 193 lbs. Deb: 9/14/07 MH																											
1907	Bos-A	7	19	0	3	0	0	0	1	1		.158	.200	.158	.358	15	-2	-2	101	119	1	.250	0			0	/O	-0.1
1908	Bos-A	31	118	12	26	2	3	0	9	4		.220	.246	.288	.534	77	-3	-3	98	105	8	.435	2			0	O	-0.4
1909	Bos-A	143	544	73	168	26	13	7	77	38		.309	.362	.443	.805	141	32	26	109	109	97	.854	35			20	*O	4.5
1910	Bos-A	141	538	92	183	20	14	7	65	52		.340	.404	.468	.873	175	45	46	99	85	115	.972	35			7	*O	5.0
1911	Bos-A	141	510	88	167	34	13	8	70	59		.327	.411	.492	.903	153	36	36	99	91	113	1.015	25			2	*O	2.7
1912	Bos-A	153	580	136	222	**53**	12	**10**	90	82		.383	**.464**	.567	1.031	182	**73**	67	107	80	**175**	1.310	52			17	*O	**7.3**
1913	Bos-A	141	520	94	189	35	22	3	71	65	22	.363	.441	.533	.974	179	56	54	103	85	136	1.193	46			22	*O	**7.1**
1914	Bos-A	158	571	100	**193**	**46**	18	4	90	77	25	.338	.423	**.503**	**.926**	**182**	**55**	**57**	98	109	**124**	1.015	42	29	-5	23	*O/P1	**7.0**
1915	Bos-A	150	547	108	176	25	12	0	69	81	14	.322	.416	.411	.827	149	35	36	99	100	97	.864	29	25	-6	11	*O	3.4
1916	Cle-A	151	546	102	**211**	**41**	8	2	79	82	20	**.386**	**.470**	**.502**	**.972**	**192**	**65**	**65**	100	97	132	1.091	35	27	-6	5	*O	**6.6**
1917	Cle-A	142	523	90	184	42	11	2	60	67	14	.352	.432	.486	.918	157	51	42	114	80	118	1.056	30			5	*O	4.2
1918	Cle-A	127	471	73	150	**33**	11	0	61	64	9	.318	.403	.435	.839	142	31	27	108	104	90	.931	27			7	*O	3.0
1919	Cle-A	134	494	83	146	38	12	2	63	73	12	.296	.395	.433	.828	124	23	19	107	100	89	.891	15			15	*OM	2.6
1920	Cle-A	150	552	137	214	**50**	11	8	107	97	13	.388	.483	.562	1.045	170	66	63	104	108	152	1.202	10	13	-5	5	*OM	4.7
1921	Cle-A	132	506	107	183	**52**	14	3	75	68	12	.362	.439	.538	.977	149	38	39	99	97	121	1.052	2	4	-2	4	*OM	2.8
1922	Cle-A	131	426	85	161	**48**	8	11	71	77	11	.378	**.474**	.606	1.080	177	53	52	102	89	127	**1.284**	8	3	1	5	*OM	4.7
1923	Cle-A	150	574	133	218	**59**	11	17	**130**	93	15	.380	.469	.610	1.079	181	71	70	101	107	166	1.252	10	9	-2	5	*OM	5.6
1924	Cle-A	135	486	94	167	36	9	9	65	72	13	.344	.432	.510	.943	148	32	35	97	80	109	1.009	5	7	-3	1	*OM	2.2
1925	Cle-A	117	429	79	167	35	5	12	87	70	12	.389	**.479**	.578	1.057	157	47	43	106	109	123	1.239	5	2	0	6	*OM	3.6
1926	Cle-A	150	539	96	164	52	8	7	86	94	15	.304	.408	.469	.877	129	24	25	100	113	110	.939	6	1	1	6	*OM	2.0
1927	Was-A	141	523	71	171	43	6	2	73	55	8	.327	.395	.444	.839	121	14	17	97	108	91	.852	9	0	3	7	*O1	1.4
1928	Phi-A	64	191	28	51	23	2	3	29	10	5	.267	.310	.455	.766	96	-1	-2	103	104	27	.738	5	1	1	4	O	0.0
Total	22	2789	10207	1881	3514	793	223	117	1528	1381	220	.344	.427	.500	.927	156	841	809	102	98	2320	1.030	433	121		177	*O/1P	79.9
■ **HORACE SPEED**	Speed, Horace Arthur b: 10/4/51, Los Angeles, Cal. BR/TR, 6'1", 180 lbs. Deb: 4/10/75																											
1975	SF-N	17	15	2	2	1	0	0	1	1	8	.133	.235	.200	.435	21	-2	-2	102	129	1	.385	0	0	0	-2	/O	-0.3
1978	Cle-A	70	106	13	24	4	1	0	4	14	31	.226	.322	.283	.605	77	-4	-3	93	53	9	.516	2	4	-2	-10	O/D	-1.6
1979	Cle-A	26	14	6	2	0	0	0	1	5	7	.143	.368	.143	.511	42	-1	-1	106	192	1	.692	2	1	0	-5	O	-0.5
Total	3	113	135	21	28	5	1	0	6	20	46	.207	.318	.259	.578	66	-6	-5	96	78	11	.545	4	5	-2	-17	/OD	-2.4
■ **CHRIS SPEIER**	Speier, Chris Edward b: 6/28/50, Alameda, Cal. BR/TR, 6'1", 175 lbs. Deb: 4/07/71																											
1971	SF-N	157	601	74	141	17	6	8	46	56	90	.235	.307	.323	.630	79	-16	-16	100	91	58	.541	4	7	-3	-4	*S	-0.2
1972	SF-N	150	562	74	151	25	2	15	71	82	92	.269	.365	.400	.765	117	15	15	100	104	87	.754	9	4	0	-0	*S	3.4
1973	SF-N	153	542	58	135	17	4	11	71	66	69	.249	.333	.356	.689	87	-6	-9	105	129	63	.616	4	5	-2	-10	*S/2	0.0
1974	SF-N	141	501	55	125	19	5	9	53	62	64	.250	.337	.361	.698	88	-3	-7	108	100	64	.649	3	2	-0	6	*S/2	1.4
1975	SF-N	141	487	60	132	30	5	10	69	70	50	.271	.364	.415	.779	114	11	10	102	117	73	.743	4	5	-2	3	*S/3	2.8
1976	SF-N	145	495	51	112	18	4	3	40	60	52	.226	.315	.297	.612	72	-15	-17	103	101	47	.531	2	2	-1	6	*S/231	0.1
1977	SF-N	6	17	1	3	1	0	0	0	0	3	.176	.176	.235	.412	9	-2	-2	104	0	1	.286	0	0	0	-0	/S	-0.1
	Mon-N	139	531	58	125	30	6	5	38	67	78	.235	.322	.343	.665	80	-15	-14	98	82	59	.595	1	2	-1	-5	*S	0.0
	Yr	145	548	59	128	31	6	5	38	67	81	.234	.318	.339	.658	78	-18	-16	99	78	60	.585	1	2	-1	-5		-0.1
1978	Mon-N	150	501	47	126	18	3	5	51	60	75	.251	.333	.329	.662	89	-8	-6	96	115	56	.584	1	0	0	0	*S	0.7
1979	Mon-N	113	344	31	78	13	1	7	26	43	45	.227	.318	.331	.649	76	-10	-11	102	76	35	.573	0	0	0	-8	*S	-0.8
1980	Mon-N	128	388	35	103	14	4	1	32	52	38	.265	.352	.330	.682	92	-3	-2	99	97	45	.604	0	3	-2	-4	*S/3	0.7
1981	Mon-N	96	307	33	69	10	2	2	25	38	29	.225	.310	.290	.600	72	-11	-10	99	103	27	.514	1	2	-1	-9	S	-1.0
1982	Mon-N	156	530	41	136	26	4	7	60	47	67	.257	.318	.360	.679	85	-7	-11	105	111	58	.581	1	6	-3	-21	*S	-2.4
1983	Mon-N	88	261	31	67	12	2	2	22	29	37	.257	.336	.341	.677	86	-4	-4	102	92	31	.613	2	1	0	-12	S3/2	-0.9
1984	Mon-N	25	40	1	6	0	0	0	1	1	8	.150	.171	.150	.321	-10	-6	-5	91	65	1	.200	0	0	0	-1	S/3	-0.4
	StL-N	38	118	9	21	7	1	3	8	9	19	.178	.242	.331	.573	60	-7	-7	99	65	9	.485	0	0	0	7	S/3	0.4
	Yr	63	158	10	27	7	1	3	9	10	27	.171	.225	.285	.510	44	-12	-12	96	66	10	.415	0	0	0	6		0.0
	Min-A	12	33	2	7	0	0	0	1	3	7	.212	.278	.212	.490	36	-3	-3	106	57	2	.370	0	0	0	-2	S	-0.3
1985	Chi-N	106	218	16	53	11	0	4	24	17	34	.243	.298	.349	.646	69	-6	-10	116	109	21	.537	1	3	-2	6	S32	0.0
1986	Chi-N	95	155	21	44	8	0	6	23	15	32	.284	.351	.452	.802	112	4	3	107	104	24	.752	2	2	-1	1	3S/2	0.4
1987	SF-N	111	317	39	79	13	0	11	39	42	51	.249	.343	.394	.737	98	-2	-0	96	98	43	.702	4	7	-3	4	23S	0.3
1988	SF-N	82	171	26	37	9	1	3	18	23	39	.216	.313	.333	.646	91	-3	-2	94	109	17	.583	3	3	-1	0	23/S	0.0
Total	18	2232	7119	763	1750	298	50	112	718	842	979	.246	.329	.349	.677	87	-97	-111	101	101	821	.627	42	54	-20	-43	*S32/1	4.1
■ **BOB SPENCE**	Spence, John Robert b: 2/10/46, San Diego, Cal. BL/TR, 6'4", 215 lbs. Deb: 9/05/69																											
1969	Chi-A	12	26	0	4	1	0	0	3	0	9	.154	.154	.192	.346	-3	-4	-4	108	241	1	.227	0	0	0	-0	/1	-0.4
1970	Chi-A	46	130	11	29	4	1	4	15	11	32	.223	.289	.362	.650	74	-4	-5	106	103	14	.567	0	0	0	1	1	-0.5
1971	Chi-A	14	27	2	4	0	0	0	1	5	6	.148	.281	.148	.429	25	-3	-2	98	102	1	.375	0	0	0	-0	/1	-0.2
Total	3	72	183	13	37	5	1	4	19	16	47	.202	.270	.306	.576	57	-10	-11	105	121	16	.497	0	0	0	1	/1	-1.1
■ **STAN SPENCE**	Spence, Stanley Orville b: 3/20/15, S.Portsmouth, Ky. d: 1/9/83, Kinston, N.C. BL/TL, 5'10.5", 180 lbs. Deb: 6/08/40																											
1940	Bos-A	51	68	5	19	2	1	2	13	4	9	.279	.319	.426	.746	91	-1	-1	101	134	9	.647	0	1	-1	-5	O	-0.6

YEAR	TM/L	G	AB	R	H	2B	3B	HR	RBI	BB	SO	AVG	OBP	SLG	PRO	/A	BR	/A	PF	CHI	RC	TA	SB	CS	SBR	FR	POS	TPR
1941	Bos-A	86	203	22	47	10	3	2	28	18	14	.232	.304	.340	.643	68	-9	-10	103	132	22	.572	1	0	0	-1	O/1	-1.3
1942	Was-A	149	629	94	203	27	**15**	4	79	62	16	.323	.384	.432	.817	135	25	28	96	87	111	.782	5	2	0	-6	*O	1.2
1943	Was-A	149	570	72	152	23	10	12	88	84	39	.267	.366	.405	.771	121	20	17	104	116	93	.766	8	1	2	-1	*O	1.4
1944	Was-A	153	592	83	187	31	8	18	100	69	28	.316	.391	.486	.877	167	38	46	90	112	118	.873	3	7	-3	16	*O/1	5.5
1946	Was-A	152	578	83	169	50	10	16	87	62	31	.292	.365	.497	.861	151	28	34	92	105	104	.823	1	7	-4	4	*O	2.7
1947	Was-A	147	506	62	141	22	6	16	73	81	41	.279	.378	.441	.819	131	19	21	97	101	89	.810	2	2	-1	3	*O	1.8
1948	Bos-A	114	391	71	92	17	4	12	61	82	33	.235	.368	.391	.759	102	2	2	100	111	62	.763	0	2	-1	-2	O1	-0.2
1949	Bos-A	7	20	3	3	1	0	0	1	6	1	.150	.346	.200	.546	43	-1	-2	107	86	2	.588	0	0	0	1	/O	0.0
	StL-A	104	314	46	77	13	3	13	45	52	36	.245	.356	.430	.786	108	3	3	100	89	50	.766	1	1	-0	7	O/1	0.7
	Yr	111	334	49	80	14	3	13	46	58	37	.240	.355	.416	.771	103	1	1	100	89	52	.755	1	1	-0	8		0.7
Total	9	1112	3871	541	1090	196	60	95	575	520	248	.282	.369	.437	.806	128	124	139	97	105	660	.800	21	23	-8	17	O/1	11.2

■ SPENCER Spencer Deb:6/03/1872

YEAR	TM/L	G	AB	R	H	2B	3B	HR	RBI	BB	SO	AVG	OBP	SLG	PRO	/A	BR	/A	PF	CHI	RC	TA	SB	CS	SBR	FR	POS	TPR
1872	Nat-n	2	10	3	2							.200															/S	

■ CHET SPENCER Spencer, Chester Arthur b: 3/4/1883, S.Webster, Ohio d: 11/10/38, Portsmouth, Ohio BL/TR, 6', 180 lbs. Deb: 8/22/06

YEAR	TM/L	G	AB	R	H	2B	3B	HR	RBI	BB	SO	AVG	OBP	SLG	PRO	/A	BR	/A	PF	CHI	RC	TA	SB	CS	SBR	FR	POS	TPR
1906	Bos-N	8	27	1	4	1	0	0	0	0		.148	.148	.185	.333	5	-3	-3	100	0	1	.217	0			-0	/O	-0.3

■ DARYL SPENCER Spencer, Daryl Dean "Big Dee" b: 7/13/29, Wichita, Kan. BR/TR, 6'2.5", 185 lbs. Deb: 9/17/52

YEAR	TM/L	G	AB	R	H	2B	3B	HR	RBI	BB	SO	AVG	OBP	SLG	PRO	/A	BR	/A	PF	CHI	RC	TA	SB	CS	SBR	FR	POS	TPR
1952	NY-N	7	17	0	5	0	1	0	3	1	4	.294	.333	.412	.745	103	0	0	102	167	2	.667	0	0	0	0	/S3	0.0
1953	NY-N	118	408	55	85	18	5	20	56	42	74	.208	.287	.424	.711	84	-12	-11	98	96	49	.651	0	1	-1	0	S32	-0.6
1956	NY-N	146	489	46	108	13	2	14	42	35	65	.221	.277	.342	.619	67	-25	-23	97	85	45	.523	1	3	-2	-11	2S3	-2.6
1957	NY-N	148	534	65	133	31	2	11	50	50	50	.249	.315	.376	.691	83	-12	-13	102	90	62	.612	3	1	0	10	*S2/3	0.5
1958	SF-N	148	539	71	138	20	5	17	74	73	60	.256	.348	.406	.754	99	0	-0	100	120	77	.708	1	0	0	-3	*S2	0.7
1959	SF-N	152	555	59	147	20	1	12	62	58	67	.265	.334	.369	.704	91	-9	-6	95	106	69	.635	5	0	2	-3	*2/S	0.4
1960	StL-N	148	507	70	131	20	3	16	58	81	74	.258	.366	.404	.770	102	10	4	108	95	77	.745	1	1	-0	-14	*S2	-0.3
1961	StL-N	37	130	19	33	4	0	4	21	23	17	.254	.366	.377	.743	86	0	-2	113	142	17	.695	1	0	0	-1	S	0.0
	LA-N	60	189	27	46	7	0	8	27	20	35	.243	.329	.407	.736	92	-2	-2	102	108	25	.678	0	1	-1	3	3/S	-0.2
	Yr	97	319	46	79	11	0	12	48	43	52	.248	.344	.395	.739	90	-1	-4	106	122	46	.707	1	1	-0	1		-0.2
1962	LA-N	77	157	24	37	5	1	2	12	32	31	.236	.365	.318	.684	92	-2	-0	93	84	19	.646	0	0	0	0	3S	0.2
1963	LA-N	7	9	0	1	0	0	0	0	3	2	.111	.333	.111	.444	36	-1	-1	95	0	1	.444	0	0	0	0	/3	0.0
	Cin-N	50	155	21	37	7	0	1	23	31	37	.239	.369	.303	.672	92	1	-0	104	197	21	.678	1	0	0	-2	3	-0.1
	Yr	57	164	21	38	7	0	1	23	34	39	.232	.367	.293	.660	90	0	-0	103	173	22	.667	1	0	0	-2		-0.1
Total	10	1098	3689	457	901	145	20	105	428	449	516	.244	.329	.380	.709	89	-51	-54	101	105	465	.674	13	7	-0	-21	S23	-2.0

■ TUBBY SPENCER Spencer, Edward Russell b: 1/26/1884, Oil City, Pa. d: 2/1/45, San Francisco, Cal. BR/TR, 5'10", 215 lbs. Deb: 7/23/05

YEAR	TM/L	G	AB	R	H	2B	3B	HR	RBI	BB	SO	AVG	OBP	SLG	PRO	/A	BR	/A	PF	CHI	RC	TA	SB	CS	SBR	FR	POS	TPR
1905	StL-A	35	115	6	27	1	2	0	11	7		.235	.279	.278	.557	86	-3	-2	91	123	10	.466	2			3	C	0.5
1906	StL-A	58	188	15	33	6	1	0	17	7		.176	.205	.218	.423	34	-14	-14	98	151	9	.335	4			-0	C	-1.0
1907	StL-A	71	230	27	61	11	1	1	25	7		.265	.287	.335	.622	102	-1	-0	98	112	23	.503	1			0	C	0.6
1908	StL-A	91	286	19	60	6	1	0	28	17		.210	.254	.238	.492	60	-12	-12	103	155	17	.381	1			8	C	0.4
1909	Bos-A	28	74	6	12	1	0	0	9	6		.162	.225	.176	.401	24	-6	-7	109	267	3	.339	2			-0	C	-0.5
1911	Phi-N	11	32	2	5	1	0	1	3	3	7	.156	.229	.281	.510	39	-3	-3	108	84	2	.444	0			0	C	-0.1
1916	Det-A	19	54	7	20	1	1	1	10	6	6	.370	.443	.481	.924	170	5	5	105	123	13	1.029	2			-2	C	0.4
1917	Det-A	70	192	13	46	8	3	0	22	15	15	.240	.324	.313	.637	97	-1	-0	98	132	19	.575	0			-4	C	0.0
1918	Det-A	66	155	11	34	8	1	0	8	19	18	.219	.313	.284	.596	83	-3	-3	97	66	14	.545	1			-1	C/1	0.0
Total	9	449	1326	106	298	43	10	3	133	87	46	.225	.279	.279	.558	76	-37	-36	99	133	109	.469	13			3	C/1	0.3

■ TOM SPENCER Spencer, Hubert Thomas b: 2/28/51, Gallipolis, Ohio BR/TR, 6', 170 lbs. Deb: 7/17/78 C

YEAR	TM/L	G	AB	R	H	2B	3B	HR	RBI	BB	SO	AVG	OBP	SLG	PRO	/A	BR	/A	PF	CHI	RC	TA	SB	CS	SBR	FR	POS	TPR
1978	Chi-A	29	65	3	12	1	0	0	4	2	9	.185	.209	.200	.409	15	-7	-7	101	122	2	.273	0	1	-1	-0	O/D	-0.8

■ JIM SPENCER Spencer, James Lloyd b: 7/30/47, Hanover, Pa. BL/TL, 6'2", 195 lbs. Deb: 9/07/68

YEAR	TM/L	G	AB	R	H	2B	3B	HR	RBI	BB	SO	AVG	OBP	SLG	PRO	/A	BR	/A	PF	CHI	RC	TA	SB	CS	SBR	FR	POS	TPR
1968	Cal-A	19	68	2	13	1	0	0	5	3	10	.191	.236	.206	.442	37	-5	-5	94	156	3	.316	0	0	0	0	1	-0.5
1969	Cal-A	113	386	39	98	14	3	10	31	26	53	.254	.304	.383	.688	92	-6	-5	99	71	45	.602	1	0	0	-3	*1	-1.5
1970	Cal-A	146	511	61	140	20	4	12	68	28	61	.274	.312	.399	.711	103	-5	0	92	117	61	.607	0	2	-1	-2	*1	-1.0
1971	Cal-A	148	510	50	121	21	2	18	59	48	63	.237	.307	.392	.699	98	-3	-2	99	97	59	.618	0	1	-1	2	*1	-0.8
1972	Cal-A	82	212	13	47	5	0	1	14	12	25	.222	.263	.259	.523	63	-12	-9	88	101	13	.385	0	1	-1	-5	1O	-2.1
1973	Cal-A	29	87	10	21	4	2	2	11	9	9	.241	.320	.402	.722	106	0	1	96	105	11	.652	0	0	0	-0	1/D	0.0
	Tex-A	102	352	35	94	12	3	4	43	34	41	.267	.333	.352	.686	96	-3	-2	97	127	40	.591	0	3	-2	3	1/D	-0.5
	Yr	131	439	45	115	16	5	6	54	43	50	.262	.331	.362	.693	98	-3	-1	97	123	52	.609	0	3	-2	3		-0.5
1974	Tex-A	118	352	36	98	11	4	7	44	22	27	.278	.326	.392	.718	110	2	4	96	109	44	.621	1	2	-1	3	1D	0.4
1975	Tex-A	132	403	50	107	18	1	11	47	35	43	.266	.327	.397	.724	104	1	2	100	94	51	.644	0	1	-1	7	1D	0.3
1976	Chi-A	150	518	53	131	13	2	14	70	49	52	.253	.319	.367	.685	101	-0	0	99	118	60	.613	6	4	-1	7	*1/D	0.0
1977	Chi-A	128	470	56	116	16	1	18	69	36	50	.247	.303	.400	.703	90	-7	-7	99	115	55	.619	1	2	-1	3	*1	-1.1
1978	NY-A	71	150	12	34	9	1	7	24	15	32	.227	.297	.440	.737	106	0	1	99	109	18	.669	0	1	-1	0	D1	0.0
1979	NY-A	106	295	60	85	15	3	23	53	38	25	.288	.369	.593	.963	162	22	24	96	83	60	.951	0	2	-1	0	D1	2.0
1980	NY-A	97	259	38	61	9	0	13	43	30	44	.236	.317	.421	.738	101	-0	0	99	113	34	.688	1	0	0	0	1D	-0.4
1981	NY-A	25	63	6	9	2	0	2	4	9	7	.143	.250	.270	.520	50	-4	-4	100	68	4	.456	0	0	0	1	1	-0.3
	Oak-A	54	171	14	35	6	0	2	9	10	20	.205	.249	.275	.523	53	-11	-10	96	66	11	.411	1	0	0	-1	1	-1.2
	Yr	79	234	20	44	8	0	4	13	19	27	.188	.249	.274	.523	52	-15	-14	97	68	16	.431	1	0	0	0		-1.5
1982	Oak-A	33	101	6	17	3	1	2	5	3	20	.168	.192	.277	.470	29	-10	-10	95	59	5	.356	0	0	0	-1	1	-1.1
Total	15	1553	4908	541	1227	179	27	146	599	407	582	.250	.310	.387	.696	98	-41	-23	97	103	574	.630	11	19	-8	15	*1D/O	-7.8

■ BEN SPENCER Spencer, Lloyd Benjamin b: 5/15/1890, Patapsco, Md. d: 9/1/70, Finksburg, Md. BL/TL, 5'8", 160 lbs. Deb: 9/08/13

YEAR	TM/L	G	AB	R	H	2B	3B	HR	RBI	BB	SO	AVG	OBP	SLG	PRO	/A	BR	/A	PF	CHI	RC	TA	SB	CS	SBR	FR	POS	TPR
1913	Was-A	8	21	2	6	1	1	0	2	2	4	.286	.348	.429	.776	120	1	0	106	79	3	.733	0			-1	/O	0.0

■ ROY SPENCER Spencer, Roy Hampton b: 2/22/1900, Scranton, N.C. d: 2/8/73, Port Charlotte, Fla BR/TR, 5'10", 168 lbs. Deb: 4/19/25

YEAR	TM/L	G	AB	R	H	2B	3B	HR	RBI	BB	SO	AVG	OBP	SLG	PRO	/A	BR	/A	PF	CHI	RC	TA	SB	CS	SBR	FR	POS	TPR
1925	Pit-N	14	28	1	6	1	0	0	2	1	3	.214	.241	.250	.491	25	-3	-3	102	102	2	.409	1	0	0	-0	C	-0.2
1926	Pit-N	28	43	5	17	3	0	0	4	1	0	.395	.409	.465	.874	120	2	1	112	69	8	.808	0			-0	C	0.1
1927	Pit-N	38	92	9	26	3	1	0	13	3	3	.283	.305	.337	.642	70	-4	-4	102	147	9	.515	0			-2	C	-0.2
1929	Was-A	50	116	18	18	4	0	1	9	8	15	.155	.222	.216	.438	13	-15	-15	100	110	6	.357	0	0	0	1	C	-0.9
1930	Was-A	93	321	32	82	11	4	0	36	18	27	.255	.303	.315	.618	56	-21	-21	101	118	32	.527	3	0	1	3	C	-0.8
1931	Was-A	145	483	48	133	16	3	1	60	35	21	.275	.327	.327	.654	72	-19	-19	101	123	53	.557	0	0	0	-14	*C	-2.0
1932	Was-A	102	317	28	78	9	0	1	41	24	17	.246	.301	.284	.585	53	-22	-22	100	148	28	.479	0	1	-1	-14	C	-2.8
1933	Cle-A	75	227	26	46	5	2	0	23	23	17	.203	.282	.242	.524	38	-19	-21	105	139	17	.442	0	0	0	4	C	-1.2
1934	Cle-A	5	7	0	1	1	0	0	2	0	1	.143	.143	.286	.429	8	-1	-1	101	334	0	.333	0	0	0	0	/C	0.0
1936	NY-N	19	18	3	5	1	0	0	3	2	3	.278	.350	.333	.683	84	-0	-0	100	177	2	.615	0			0	C	0.0
1937	Bro-N	51	117	5	24	2	2	0	4	8	17	.205	.256	.256	.512	38	-10	-10	104	48	8	.396	0			-2	C	-1.0
1938	Bro-N	16	45	2	12	1	1	0	6	5	6	.267	.340	.333	.673	90	-1	-0	96	145	5	.588	0			-1	C	0.0
Total	12	636	1814	177	448	57	13	3	203	128	130	.247	.301	.298	.598	56	-113	-117	101	124	171	.499	4	1		-25	C	-9.0

■ VERN SPENCER Spencer, Vernon Murray b: 2/23/1896, Wixom, Mich. d: 6/3/71, Wixon, Mich. BL/TR, 5'7", 165 lbs. Deb: 7/04/20

YEAR	TM/L	G	AB	R	H	2B	3B	HR	RBI	BB	SO	AVG	OBP	SLG	PRO	/A	BR	/A	PF	CHI	RC	TA	SB	CS	SBR	FR	POS	TPR
1920	NY-N	45	140	15	28	2	3	0	19	11	17	.200	.258	.257	.515	49	-9	-9	100	204	9	.443	4	3	-1	-2	O	-1.4

■ PAUL SPERAW Speraw, Paul Bachman "Polly" or "Birdie" b: 10/5/1893, Annville, Pa. d: 2/22/62, Cedar Rapids, Iowa BR/TR, 5'8.5", 145 lbs. Deb: 9/15/20

YEAR	TM/L	G	AB	R	H	2B	3B	HR	RBI	BB	SO	AVG	OBP	SLG	PRO	/A	BR	/A	PF	CHI	RC	TA	SB	CS	SBR	FR	POS	TPR
1920	StL-A	1	2	0	0	0	0	0	0	0	0	.000	.000	.000	.000	-90	-1	-1	111	0	0	.000	0	0	0	0	/3	0.0

■ ED SPERBER Sperber, Edwin George b: 1/21/1895, Cincinnati, Ohio d: 1/5/76, Cincinnati, Ohio BL/TL, 5'11", 175 lbs. Deb: 4/16/24

YEAR	TM/L	G	AB	R	H	2B	3B	HR	RBI	BB	SO	AVG	OBP	SLG	PRO	/A	BR	/A	PF	CHI	RC	TA	SB	CS	SBR	FR	POS	TPR
1924	Bos-N	24	59	8	17	2	0	1	12	10	9	.288	.400	.373	.773	115	1	2	94	175	10	.837	3	1	0	-3	O	-0.1
1925	Bos-N	2	2	0	0	0	0	0	0	0	0	.000	.000	.000	.000	-99	-1	-1	94	0	0	.000	0	0	0	0	H	0.0
Total	2	26	61	8	17	2	0	1	12	10	9	.279	.389	.361	.750	108	1	1	94	170	10	.800	3	1	0	-3	/O	-0.1

YEAR	TM/L	G	AB	R	H	2B	3B	HR	RBI	BB	SO	AVG	OBP	SLG	PRO	/A	BR	/A	PF	CHI	RC	TA	SB	CS	SBR	FR	POS	TPR
■ ROB SPERRING	Sperring, Robert Walter b: 10/10/49, San Francisco, Cal. BR/TR, 6'1", 185 lbs. Deb: 8/11/74																											
1974	Chi-N	42	107	9	22	3	0	1	5	9	28	.206	.267	.262	.529	48	-7	-7	100	62	8	.437	1	2	-1	-2	2/S	-0.7
1975	Chi-N	65	144	25	30	4	1	1	9	16	31	.208	.292	.271	.563	55	-8	-9	104	83	11	.471	0	2	-1	-0	32S/O	-0.8
1976	Chi-N	43	93	8	24	3	0	0	7	9	25	.258	.324	.290	.614	69	-3	-4	109	100	9	.493	0	2	-1	-1	3S/2O	-0.5
1977	Hou-N	58	129	6	24	3	0	1	9	12	23	.186	.255	.233	.488	34	-12	-11	93	109	8	.385	0	0	0	-2	S23	-0.8
Total	4	208	473	48	100	13	1	3	30	46	107	.211	.283	.262	.545	51	-31	-31	101	89	35	.449	1	6	-3	-6	/2S3O	-2.8
■ STAN SPERRY	Sperry, Stanley Kenneth b: 2/19/14, Evansville, Wis. d: 9/27/62, Evansville, Wis. BL/TR, 5'10.5", 164 lbs. Deb: 7/28/36																											
1936	Phi-N	20	37	2	5	3	0	0	4	3	5	.135	.200	.216	.416	11	-5	-5	108	177	2	.333	0			0	2	-0.3
1938	Phi-A	60	253	28	69	6	3	0	27	15	9	.273	.313	.320	.634	58	-16	-16	101	99	25	.522	1	2	-1	-5	2	-1.8
Total	2	80	290	30	74	9	3	0	31	18	14	.255	.299	.307	.606	52	-21	-21	102	109	27	.495	1	2		-5	/2	-2.1
■ HARRY SPIES	Spies, Henry b: 6/12/1866, New Orleans, La. d: 7/8/42, Los Angeles, Cal. 5'11.5", 170 lbs. Deb: 4/20/1895																											
1895	Cin-N	14	50	2	11	0	1	0	5	3	2	.220	.264	.260	.524	34	-5	-5	108	107	4	.410	0			0	C/1	-0.3
	Lou-N	72	276	42	74	14	7	2	35	11	19	.268	.313	.391	.704	87	-8	-6	95	87	36	.644	4			-1	1C/S	-0.4
	Yr	86	326	44	85	14	8	2	40	14	21	.261	.305	.371	.677	78	-13	-11	97	92	39	.606	4			-1		-0.7
Total	1	86	326	44	85	14	8	2	40	14	21	.261	.305	.371	.677	78	-13	-11	97	90	39	.606	4			-1	/1CS	-0.7
■ ED SPIEZIO	Spiezio, Edward Wayne b: 10/31/41, Joliet, Ill. BR/TR, 5'11", 180 lbs. Deb: 7/23/64																											
1964	StL-N	12	12	0	4	0	0	0	0	0	1	.333	.333	.333	.667	79	-0	-0	112	0	1	.500	0	0	0	0	H	0.0
1965	StL-N	10	18	0	3	0	0	0	5	1	4	.167	.250	.167	.417	19	-2	-2	107	691	1	.333	0	0	0	0	/3	-0.1
1966	StL-N	26	73	4	16	5	1	2	10	5	11	.219	.269	.397	.666	83	-2	-2	100	120	6	.565	1	0	0	-1	3	-0.2
1967	StL-N	55	105	9	22	2	0	3	10	7	18	.210	.265	.314	.580	65	-5	-5	101	99	8	.494	2	1	0	-3	3/O	-0.9
1968	StL-N	29	51	1	8	0	0	0	2	5	6	.157	.232	.157	.389	19	-5	-5	95	105	2	.311	1	1	-0	1	O/3	-0.5
1969	SD-N	121	355	29	83	9	0	13	43	38	64	.234	.315	.369	.684	94	-4	-3	97	101	41	.617	1	2	-1	-2	3/O	-0.5
1970	SD-N	110	316	45	90	18	1	12	42	43	42	.285	.377	.462	.839	130	11	13	95	90	57	.845	4	0	1	-1	3	1.1
1971	SD-N	97	308	16	71	10	1	7	36	22	50	.231	.290	.338	.628	80	-9	-8	96	117	29	.544	6	5	-1	3	3/O	-0.5
1972	SD-N	20	29	2	4	2	0	0	4	1	6	.138	.167	.207	.374	6	-4	-3	88	274	1	.296	1	0	0	0	/3	-0.2
	Chi-A	74	277	20	66	10	1	2	22	13	43	.238	.277	.303	.581	68	-10	-11	106	104	22	.450	0	1	-1	9	3	0.0
Total	9	554	1544	126	367	56	4	39	174	135	245	.238	.306	.355	.661	87	-30	-26	98	112	168	.598	16	10	-1	6	3/O	-1.8
■ CHARLIE SPIKES	Spikes, Leslie Charles b: 1/23/51, Bogalusa, La. BR/TR, 6'3", 215 lbs. Deb: 9/01/72																											
1972	NY-A	14	34	2	5	1	0	0	3	1	13	.147	.171	.176	.348	4	-4	-4	92	209	1	.233	0	1	-1	0	/O	-0.4
1973	Cle-A	140	506	68	120	12	3	23	73	45	103	.237	.306	.409	.715	103	-2	0	97	106	62	.653	5	3	-0	2	*OD	0.0
1974	Cle-A	155	568	63	154	23	1	22	80	34	100	.271	.320	.431	.752	114	9	8	101	103	74	.679	10	7	-1	-2	*O	0.1
1975	Cle-A	111	345	41	79	13	3	11	33	30	51	.229	.291	.380	.670	89	-6	-6	100	77	35	.594	7	6	-2	0	*O/D	-0.9
1976	Cle-A	101	334	34	79	11	5	3	31	23	50	.237	.296	.326	.622	82	-8	-8	100	101	32	.536	5	6	-2	-2	O/D	-1.4
1977	Cle-A	32	95	13	22	2	0	3	11	11	17	.232	.324	.347	.671	85	-2	-2	98	104	10	.582	0	2	-1	-4	O/D	-0.7
1978	Det-A	10	28	1	7	1	0	0	2	2	6	.250	.344	.286	.629	73	-1	-1	108	99	3	.571	0	0	0	-1	/O	-0.2
1979	Atl-N	66	93	12	26	8	0	3	21	5	30	.280	.316	.462	.779	100	1	-0	109	160	13	.686	0	0	0	-4	O	-0.4
1980	Atl-N	41	36	6	10	1	0	0	2	3	18	.278	.350	.306	.656	83	-1	-1	101	72	4	.577	0	0	0	-2	/O	-0.2
Total	9	670	2039	240	502	72	12	65	256	154	388	.246	.306	.389	.695	97	-13	-13	100	103	233	.638	27	25	-7	-13	O/D	-4.1
■ HARRY SPILMAN	Spilman, William Harry b: 7/18/54, Albany, Ga. BL/TR, 6'1", 180 lbs. Deb: 9/11/78																											
1978	Cin-N	4	4	1	1	0	0	0	0	0	1	.250	.250	.250	.500	39	-0	-0	103	0	0	.333	0	0	0	0	H	0.0
1979	Cin-N	43	56	7	12	3	0	0	5	7	5	.214	.323	.268	.591	65	-3	-2	97	132	5	.533	0	0	0	-0	1/3	-0.3
1980	Cin-N	65	101	14	27	4	0	4	19	9	19	.267	.333	.426	.759	109	1	1	102	137	14	.697	0	0	0	-1	1/OC3	0.0
1981	Cin-N	23	24	4	4	1	0	0	3	3	7	.167	.259	.208	.468	34	-2	-2	101	236	1	.381	0	0	0	-1	/31	-0.2
	Hou-N	28	34	5	10	0	0	0	1	2	3	.294	.333	.294	.627	90	-1	-0	88	39	3	.462	0	1	-1	-0	1	-0.1
	Yr	51	58	9	14	1	0	0	4	5	10	.241	.302	.259	.560	64	-3	-2	94	132	4	.435	0	1	-1	-1		-0.3
1982	Hou-N	38	61	7	17	2	0	3	11	5	10	.279	.333	.459	.792	121	1	1	99	117	9	.733	0	0	0	-0	1	0.0
1983	Hou-N	42	78	7	13	3	0	1	9	5	12	.167	.217	.244	.460	30	-8	-7	90	162	4	.358	0	0	0	-1	1/C	-0.8
1984	Hou-N	32	72	14	19	2	0	2	15	12	10	.264	.369	.375	.744	118	1	2	93	178	11	.722	0	0	0	-0	1/C	0.1
1985	Hou-N	44	66	3	9	1	0	1	4	3	7	.136	.174	.197	.371	4	-9	-8	96	100	2	.271	0	0	0	-0	1/C	-0.9
1986	Det-A	24	49	6	12	2	0	3	8	3	8	.245	.288	.469	.758	108	0	0	95	100	6	.684	0	0	0	0	D/3C1	0.0
	SF-N	58	94	12	27	7	0	2	22	12	13	.287	.368	.426	.793	123	2	3	96	191	16	.776	0	0	0	-0	1/3C20	0.2
1987	SF-N	83	90	5	24	5	0	1	14	9	20	.267	.333	.356	.689	86	-2	-2	96	160	10	.600	1	1	-0	0	3/1C	-0.1
1988	SF-N	40	40	4	7	1	1	1	3	4	6	.175	.250	.325	.575	68	-2	-2	94	75	3	.515	0	0	0	0	/1CO	-0.1
	Hou-N	7	5	0	0	0	0	0	0	0	3	.000	.000	.000	.000	-99	-1	-1	93	0	0	.000	0	0	0	0	/1	0.0
	Yr	47	45	4	7	1	1	1	3	4	9	.156	.224	.289	.513	49	-3	-3	94	65	3	.447	0	0	0	0		-0.1
Total	11	531	774	89	182	31	1	18	114	74	124	.235	.304	.348	.652	84	-21	-17	96	140	86	.584	1	2	-1	-4	1/3CDO2	-2.2
■ HAL SPINDEL	Spindel, Harold Stewart b: 5/27/13, Chandler, Okla. BR/TR, 6', 185 lbs. Deb: 4/23/39																											
1939	StL-A	48	119	13	32	3	1	0	11	8	7	.269	.315	.311	.626	60	-7	-7	100	100	11	.489	0	2	-1	1	C	-0.4
1945	Phi-N	36	87	7	20	3	0	0	8	6	7	.230	.280	.264	.544	54	-6	-5	96	121	7	.426	0			-0	C	-0.4
1946	Phi-N	1	3	0	1	0	0	0	1	0	0	.333	.333	.333	.667	94	-0	-0	95	373	0	.333	0			0	/C	0.0
Total	3	85	209	20	53	6	1	0	20	14	14	.254	.300	.292	.592	58	-13	-12	99	112	17	.472	0	2		1	/C	-0.8
■ ANDY SPOGNARDI	Spognardi, Andrea Ettore b: 10/18/08, Boston, Mass. BR/TR, 5'9.5", 160 lbs. Deb: 9/02/32																											
1932	Bos-A	17	34	9	10	1	0	0	1	6	6	.294	.400	.324	.724	92	-0	-0	97	30	5	.708	0	0	0	-0	/2S3	0.0
■ AL SPOHRER	Spohrer, Alfred Ray b: 12/3/02, Philadelphia, Pa. d: 7/17/72, Plymouth, N.H. BR/TR, 5'10.5", 175 lbs. Deb: 4/13/28																											
1928	NY-N	2	2	0	0	0	0	0	0	0	0	.000	.000	.000	.000	-98	-1	-1	102	0	0	.000	0			0	/C	0.0
	Bos-N	51	124	15	27	3	0	0	9	5	11	.218	.254	.242	.496	31	-13	-12	97	107	7	.381	1			-1	C	-0.9
	Yr	53	126	15	27	3	0	0	9	5	11	.214	.250	.238	.488	29	-13	-13	97	103	7	.374	1			-1		-0.9
1929	Bos-N	114	342	42	93	21	8	2	48	26	35	.272	.327	.398	.725	84	-12	-9	94	116	44	.663	1			2	*C	0.2
1930	Bos-N	112	356	44	113	22	8	2	37	22	24	.317	.361	.441	.802	95	-4	-3	97	78	55	.757	3			-9	*C	-0.4
1931	Bos-N	114	350	23	84	17	5	0	27	22	27	.240	.285	.317	.602	62	-19	-19	99	87	32	.508	2			-5	*C	-1.7
1932	Bos-N	104	335	31	90	12	2	0	33	15	26	.269	.300	.316	.616	71	-16	-13	93	116	32	.502	2			2	*C	-0.6
1933	Bos-N	67	184	11	46	6	1	1	12	11	13	.250	.292	.310	.602	75	-7	-6	96	75	17	.504	3			-2	C	-0.5
1934	Bos-N	100	265	25	59	15	0	0	17	14	18	.223	.262	.279	.541	52	-21	-16	86	83	19	.416	1			0	C	-1.1
1935	Bos-N	92	260	22	63	7	1	1	16	9	12	.242	.273	.288	.562	53	-18	-16	96	74	20	.422	0			-1	C	-1.6
Total	8	756	2218	213	575	103	25	6	199	124	166	.259	.301	.336	.637	70	-110	-94	95	92	226	.539	13			-13	C	-6.6
■ JIM SPOTTS	Spotts, James Russell b: 4/10/09, Honey Brook, Pa. d: 6/15/64, Medford, N.J. BR/TR, 5'10.5", 175 lbs. Deb: 4/23/30																											
1930	Phi-N	3	2	1	0	0	0	0	0	0	1	.000	.000	.000	.000	-95	-1	-1	106	0	0	.000	0			0	/C	0.0
■ CHARLIE SPRAGUE	Sprague, Charles Wellington b: 10/10/1864, Cleveland, Ohio d: 12/31/12, Des Moines, Iowa 5'11", 150 lbs. Deb: 9/17/1887																											
1887	Chi-N	3	13	0	2	0	0	0	0	0	2	.154	.154	.154	.308	-12	-2	-2	116	0	0	.182	0			0	/PO	0.0
1889	Cle-N	2	7	2	1	0	0	0	1	1	0	.143	.250	.143	.393	12	-1	-1	103	304	1	.500	1			0	/P	0.0
1890	Tol-a	55	199	25	47	5	6	1		16		.236	.303	.337	.639	88	-3	-4	103	0	24	.632	10			-3	OP	-0.7
Total	3	60	219	27	50	5	6	1	1	17	2	.228	.293	.320	.613	79	-5	-7	103	10	25	.598	11			-3	/OP	-0.7
■ HARRY SPRATT	Spratt, Henry Lee b: 7/10/1887, Broadford, Va. d: 7/3/69, Washington, D.C. BL/TR, 5'8.5", 175 lbs. Deb: 4/13/11																											
1911	Bos-N	62	154	22	37	4	4	2	13	13	25	.240	.299	.357	.657	81	-4	-5	103	72	17	.590	1			-1	S/23O	-0.4
1912	Bos-N	27	89	6	23	3	2	3	15	7	11	.258	.313	.438	.751	97	-0	-1	107	105	12	.727	2			-2	S	0.0
Total	2	89	243	28	60	7	6	5	28	20	36	.247	.304	.387	.691	87	-4	-6	105	84	29	.639	3			-4	/S2O3	-0.4
■ GEORGE SPRIGGS	Spriggs, George Herman b: 5/22/41, Newell, Md. BL/TR, 5'11", 175 lbs. Deb: 9/15/65																											
1965	Pit-N	9	2	5	1	0	0	0	0	0	0	.500	.500	.500	1.000	183	0	0	100	0	1	3.000	2	0	1	-0	/O	0.0

YEAR	TM/L	G	AB	R	H	2B	3B	HR	RBI	BB	SO	AVG	OBP	SLG	PRO	/A	BR	/A	PF	CHI	RC	TA	SB	CS	SBR	FR	POS	TPR
1966	Pit-N	9	7	0	1	0	0	0	0	0	3	.143	.143	.143	.286	-20	-1	-1	101	0	0	.167	0	0	0	0	H	0.0
1967	Pit-N	38	57	14	10	1	1	0	5	6	20	.175	.254	.228	.482	39	-4	-4	100	159	4	.468	3	0	1	-2	O	-0.6
1969	KC-A	23	29	4	4	2	1	0	0	3	8	.138	.242	.276	.518	43	-2	-2	103	0	2	.480	0	0	0	-1	/O	-0.3
1970	KC-A	51	130	12	27	2	3	1	7	14	32	.208	.285	.292	.577	60	-7	-7	98	69	12	.528	4	3	-1	-1	O	-0.9
Total	5	130	225	35	43	5	5	1	12	23	63	.191	.269	.271	.540	51	-15	-15	99	80	19	.508	9	3	1	-4	/O	-1.8
■ **JOE SPRINZ** Sprinz, Joseph Conrad "Mule" b: 8/3/02, St.Louis, Mo. BR/TR, 5'11", 185 lbs. Deb: 7/16/30																												
1930	Cle-A	17	45	5	8	1	0	0	2	4	4	.178	.245	.200	.445	14	-6	-6	105	74	2	.351	0	0	0	1	C	-0.2
1931	Cle-A	1	3	0	0	0	0	0	0	0	0	.000	.000	.000	.000	-94	-1	-1	106	0	0	.000	0	0	0	0	/C	0.0
1933	StL-N	3	5	1	1	0	0	0	0	1	1	.200	.333	.200	.533	54	-0	-0	102	0	0	.400	0			0	/C	0.0
Total	3	21	53	6	9	1	0	0	2	5	5	.170	.241	.189	.430	12	-7	-7	105	62	3	.333	0	0		1	/C	-0.2
■ **FREDDY SPURGEON** Spurgeon, Fred b: 10/9/1900, Wabash, Ind. d: 11/5/70, Kalamazoo, Mich. BR/TR, 5'11.5", 160 lbs. Deb: 9/19/24																												
1924	Cle-A	3	7	0	1	1	0	0	0	0	0	.143	.250	.286	.536	39	-1	-1	97	0	1	.500	0	0	0	-1	/2	0.0
1925	Cle-A	107	376	50	108	9	3	0	32	15	21	.287	.315	.327	.642	59	-21	-25	106	87	39	.537	8	4	0	-3	32/S	-2.0
1926	Cle-A	149	614	101	181	31	3	0	49	27	36	.295	.327	.355	.682	78	-21	-20	100	73	73	.584	7	2	1	-6	*2	-1.8
1927	Cle-A	57	179	30	45	6	1	1	19	18	14	.251	.323	.313	.636	68	-9	-8	97	109	19	.619	8	0	2	-1	2	-0.6
Total	4	316	1176	181	335	47	7	1	100	60	71	.285	.322	.339	.661	70	-52	-54	101	83	132	.574	23	6	3	-11	2/3S	-4.4
■ **ED SPURNEY** Spurney, Edward Frederick b: 1/9/1872, Cleveland, Ohio d: 10/12/32, Cleveland, Ohio Deb: 6/26/1891																												
1891	Pit-N	3	7	2	2	1	0	0	0	2	1	.286	.444	.429	.873	155	1	1	101	0	1	1.000	0			0	/S	0.1
■ **MIKE SQUIRES** Squires, Michael Lynn b: 3/5/52, Kalamazoo, Mich. BL/TL, 5'11", 185 lbs. Deb: 9/01/75																												
1975	Chi-A	20	65	5	15	0	0	0	4	8	5	.231	.315	.231	.546	54	-3	-4	103	102	5	.500	3	0	1	-0	1	-0.3
1977	Chi-A	3	3	0	0	0	0	0	0	0	1	.000	.000	.000	.000	-99	-1	-1	99	0	0	.000	0	0	0	0	/1	0.0
1978	Chi-A	46	150	25	42	9	2	0	19	16	21	.280	.349	.367	.716	101	1	0	101	139	20	.664	4	4	-1	-1	1	-0.3
1979	Chi-A	122	295	44	78	10	1	2	22	22	9	.264	.320	.325	.645	73	-10	-11	102	83	30	.582	15	5	2	2	*1/O	-1.3
1980	Chi-A	131	343	38	97	11	3	2	33	33	24	.283	.347	.350	.697	95	-3	-2	97	102	41	.621	8	9	-3	4	*1/C	-0.7
1981	Chi-A	92	294	35	78	9	0	0	25	22	17	.265	.316	.296	.612	78	-8	-8	100	113	29	.520	7	2	1	0	1/O	-0.9
1982	Chi-A	116	195	33	52	9	3	1	21	14	13	.267	.316	.359	.675	87	-4	-3	97	115	21	.580	3	3	-1	3	*1	-0.3
1983	Chi-A	144	153	21	34	4	1	1	11	22	11	.222	.328	.281	.609	67	-6	-6	103	93	15	.565	3	3	-1	-1	*1/3D	-1.2
1984	Chi-A	104	82	9	15	1	0	0	6	6	7	.183	.239	.195	.434	20	-9	-10	111	150	4	.343	2	2	-1	-3	13/OP	-1.7
1985	Chi-A	2	0	1	0	0	0	0	0	0	0	—	—	—	—	—	0	0	100	—	—	—	0	0	0	0	/R	0.0
Total	10	780	1580	211	411	53	10	6	141	143	108	.260	.323	.318	.641	78	-43	-44	100	107	170	.581	45	28	-3	4	1/3DOCP	-6.7
■ **MARV STAEHLE** Staehle, Marvin Gustave b: 3/13/42, Oak Park, Ill. BL/TR, 5'10", 165 lbs. Deb: 9/15/64																												
1964	Chi-A	6	5	0	2	0	0	0	2	0	0	.400	.400	.400	.800	129	0	0	96	424	1	1.000	1	0	0	0	H	0.0
1965	Chi-A	7	7	0	3	0	0	0	2	0	0	.429	.429	.429	.857	157	0	0	92	277	1	.750	0	0	0	0	H	0.0
1966	Chi-A	8	15	2	2	0	0	0	0	4	2	.133	.316	.133	.449	37	-1	-1	94	0	1	.538	1	0	0	0	/2	0.0
1967	Chi-A	32	54	1	6	1	0	0	1	4	8	.111	.172	.130	.302	-10	-7	-7	94	60	1	.235	1	1	-0	0	2/S	-0.6
1969	Mon-N	6	17	4	7	2	0	1	1	2	0	.412	.474	.706	1.180	226	3	3	100	27	6	1.400	0	0	0	0	/2	0.3
1970	Mon-N	104	321	41	70	9	1	0	26	39	21	.218	.309	.252	.561	52	-21	-21	100	125	27	.477	1	3	-2	-3	2/S	-1.4
1971	Atl-N	22	36	5	4	0	0	0	1	5	4	.111	.238	.111	.349	2	-5	-5	110	102	1	.294	0	0	0	1	/23	-0.3
Total	7	185	455	53	94	12	1	1	33	54	35	.207	.296	.244	.540	50	-30	-30	100	112	38	.471	4	4	-1	-2	2/S3	-2.0
■ **HEINIE STAFFORD** Stafford, Henry Alexander b: 11/1/1891, Orleans, Vt. d: 1/29/72, Lake Worth, Fla. TR , 5'7", 160 lbs. Deb: 10/05/16																												
1916	NY-N	1	1	0	0	0	0	0	0	0	0	.000	.000	.000	.000	-99	-0	-0	96	0	0	.000	0			0	H	0.0
■ **GENERAL STAFFORD** Stafford, James Joseph "Jamsey" b: 7/9/1868, Webster, Mass. d: 9/11/23, Worcester, Mass. BR/TR, 5'8", 165 lbs. Deb: 8/27/1890																												
1890	Buf-P	15	49	11	7	1	0	0	3	7	8	.143	.250	.163	.413	14	-6	-5	92	103	3	.405	2			0	P/O	0.0
1893	NY-N	67	281	58	79	7	4	5	27	25	31	.281	.344	.388	.732	93	-2	-4	104	57	45	.767	19			-8	O	-1.1
1894	NY-N	14	46	10	10	1	1	0	4	10	7	.217	.368	.283	.651	61	-3	-3	100	86	6	.722	2			0	/3O21	-0.1
1895	NY-N	123	463	79	129	12	5	3	73	40	32	.279	.344	.346	.689	84	-13	-8	95	123	71	.743	42			-10	*2O/3	-0.9
1896	NY-N	59	230	28	66	9	1	0	40	13	18	.287	.333	.335	.668	79	-7	-6	99	153	31	.659	15			-4	O/S	-1.1
1897	NY-N	7	23	0	2	0	0	0	3	3		.087	.192	.087	.279	-24	-4	-4	98	439	0	.238	0			-2	/OS	-0.4
	Lou-N	111	432	68	120	16	5	7	53	31		.278	.330	.387	.717	95	-6	-3	95	87	61	.689	14			-11	*S/O3	-0.9
	Yr	118	455	68	122	16	5	7	56	34		.268	.323	.371	.695	89	-10	-7	95	112	61	.661	14			-13		-1.3
1898	Lou-N	49	181	26	54	3	0	1	25	19		.298	.365	.331	.696	107	1	2	96	127	25	.677	7			0	2O/3	0.2
	Bos-N	37	123	21	32	2	0	1	8	4		.260	.289	.301	.590	69	-5	-5	104	60	12	.495	3			0	O/1	-0.4
	Yr	86	304	47	86	5	0	2	33	23		.283	.335	.319	.654	91	-3	-3	100	100	37	.601	10			0		-0.2
1899	Bos-N	55	182	29	55	4	2	3	40	7		.302	.328	.396	.724	96	-0	-2	105	151	27	.693	9			-6	O/2S	-0.8
	Was-N	31	118	11	29	5	1	1	14	5		.246	.276	.331	.607	71	-5	-5	96	108	12	.539	4			0	2S/3	-0.3
	Yr	86	300	40	84	9	3	4	54	12		.280	.308	.370	.678	86	-6	-7	102	138	39	.630	13			-6		-1.1
Total	8	568	2128	341	583	60	19	21	290	164	96	.274	.331	.350	.680	85	-50	-42	98	111	294	.674	117			-41	O2S/3P1	-5.8
■ **BOB STAFFORD** Stafford, Robert M. b: Oak Ridge, N.C. Deb: 10/12/1890																												
1890	Phi-a	1	2	0	0	0	0	0		0		.000	.000	.000	.000	-99	-0	-0	97	0	0	.000	0			0	/O	0.0
■ **STEVE STAGGS** Staggs, Stephen Robert b: 5/6/51, Anchorage, Alaska BR/TR, 5'9", 150 lbs. Deb: 7/01/77																												
1977	Tor-A	72	290	37	75	11	6	2	28	36	38	.259	.340	.359	.699	88	-3	-4	103	87	36	.642	5	9	-4	-6	2	-0.7
1978	Oak-A	47	78	10	19	2	2	0	0	19	17	.244	.392	.321	.712	102	1	1	101	0	11	.742	2	3	-1	-5	2/S3D	-0.2
Total	2	119	368	47	94	13	8	2	28	55	55	.255	.352	.351	.703	92	-2	-3	102	67	47	.668	7	12	-5	-11	2/D3S	-0.9
■ **CHICK STAHL** Stahl, Charles Sylvester b: 1/10/1873, Avila, Ind. d: 3/28/07, W.Baden, Ind. BL/TL, 5'10", 160 lbs. Deb: 4/19/1897 M																												
1897	Bos-N	114	469	112	166	30	13	4	97	38		.354	.406	.499	.905	131	27	21	107	122	105	.967	18			-2	*O	0.9
1898	Bos-N	125	467	72	144	21	8	3	52	46		.308	.375	.407	.782	122	17	14	104	84	75	.762	6			-1	*O	0.5
1899	Bos-N	148	576	122	202	23	18	8	53	72		.351	.426	.495	.921	148	45	40	105	46	139	1.053	33			8	*O/P	3.4
1900	Bos-N	136	553	88	163	23	16	5	82	34		.295	.336	.421	.757	92	6	-10	120	99	89	.754	27			-2	*O	-2.2
1901	Bos-A	131	515	105	156	20	16	6	72	54		.303	.369	.439	.808	129	18	20	97	90	96	.861	29			-7	*O	1.0
1902	Bos-A	127	508	92	164	22	11	2	58	37		.323	.369	.421	.790	121	14	14	99	84	90	.799	24			-1	*O	0.5
1903	Bos-A	77	299	60	82	12	6	2	44	28		.274	.336	.375	.711	103	6	1	112	129	42	.691	10			-4	O	-0.6
1904	Bos-A	157	587	83	170	27	**19**	3	67	64		.290	.359	.416	.775	141	32	29	105	95	94	.765	11			-17	*O	0.3
1905	Bos-A	134	500	61	129	17	4	0	47	50		.258	.325	.308	.633	103	3	3	100	115	57	.598	18			-13	*O	-1.7
1906	Bos-A	155	595	62	170	24	6	4	51	47		.286	.338	.366	.704	125	15	17	98	71	80	.654	13			-5	*OM	0.6
Total	10	1304	5069	857	1546	219	117	37	623	470		.305	.365	.416	.781	123	183	150	104	91	869	.789	189			-43	*O/P	2.7
■ **JAKE STAHL** Stahl, Garland b: 4/13/1879, Elkhart, Ill. d: 9/18/22, Monrovia, Cal. BR/TR, 6'2", 195 lbs. Deb: 4/20/03 M																												
1903	Bos-A	40	92	14	22	3	5	2	8	4		.239	.271	.446	.716	102	1	-0	112	61	12	.657	1			-1	C/O	0.2
1904	Was-A	142	520	54	136	29	12	3	50	21		.262	.290	.381	.671	123	7	11	93	96	66	.635	25			0	*1O	1.3
1905	Was-A	141	501	66	125	22	12	5	66	28		.250	.289	.371	.660	106	5	2	104	124	67	.678	41			1	*1M	0.1
1906	Was-A	137	482	38	107	9	8	0	51	21		.222	.254	.274	.528	73	-18	-14	91	143	42	.488	30			-2	*1M	-2.1
1908	NY-A	75	274	34	70	18	5	2	42	11		.255	.284	.380	.664	123	4	5	95	152	33	.642	16			-0	O/1	0.2
	Bos-A	78	262	29	64	9	11	0	23	20		.244	.298	.363	.660	119	4	5	98	93	31	.652	14			-0	1	0.3
	Yr	153	536	63	134	27	16	2	65	31		.250	.291	.371	.662	121	8	10	97	123	64	.647	30			-0		0.5
1909	Bos-A	127	435	62	128	19	12	6	60	43		.294	.377	.434	.812	143	28	24	109	118	76	.857	16			-8	*1	1.7
1910	Bos-A	144	531	68	144	19	16	**10**	77	42		.271	.334	.424	.758	138	21	21	99	118	82	.767	22			-7	*1	2.1
1912	Bos-A	95	326	40	98	21	6	3	60	31		.301	.372	.429	.801	121	12	9	107	137	57	.833	13			-2	1M	0.8
1913	Bos-A	2	2	0	0	0	0	0	0	0	1	.000	.000	.000	.000	-97	-0	-1	103	0	0	.000	0			0	HM	0.0
Total	9	981	3425	405	894	149	87	31	437	221	1	.261	.311	.382	.694	118	63	62	100	120	466	.687	178			-19	1/OC	4.6

YEAR	TM/L	G	AB	R	H	2B	3B	HR	RBI	BB	SO	AVG	OBP	SLG	PRO	/A	BR	/A	PF	CHI	RC	TA	SB	CS	SBR	FR	POS	TPR
■ LARRY STAHL	Stahl, Larry Floyd b: 6/29/41, Belleville, Ill. BL/TL, 6', 175 lbs. Deb: 9/11/64																											
1964	KC-A	15	46	7	12	1	0	3	6	1	10	.261	.277	.478	.755	101	0	-0	105	82	6	.676	0	0	0	1	O	0.1
1965	KC-A	28	81	9	16	2	1	4	14	5	16	.198	.253	.395	.648	84	-2	-2	97	132	8	.591	1	0	0	2	O	0.0
1966	KC-A	119	312	37	78	11	5	5	34	17	63	.250	.291	.365	.656	93	-6	-4	94	111	34	.578	5	3	-0	-5	O	-1.3
1967	NY-N	71	155	9	37	5	0	1	18	8	25	.239	.285	.290	.575	66	-7	-7	99	155	12	.463	2	2	-1	4	O	-0.5
1968	NY-N	53	183	15	43	7	2	3	10	21	38	.235	.314	.344	.658	95	-0	-1	102	60	22	.617	3	0	1	7	O/1	0.6
1969	SD-N	95	162	10	32	6	2	3	10	17	31	.198	.278	.315	.593	68	-8	-7	97	67	13	.522	3	3	-1	-3	O1	-1.3
1970	SD-N	52	66	5	12	2	0	0	3	2	14	.182	.206	.212	.418	13	-8	-8	95	83	3	.321	2	2	-1	-4	O	-1.2
1971	SD-N	114	308	27	78	13	4	8	36	26	59	.253	.311	.399	.711	104	-1	1	96	100	37	.637	4	3	-1	7	O/1	0.4
1972	SD-N	107	297	31	67	9	3	7	20	31	67	.226	.299	.347	.646	94	-7	-3	88	66	31	.572	1	3	-2	-1	O/1	-0.9
1973	Cin-N	76	111	17	25	2	2	2	12	14	34	.225	.317	.333	.651	86	-3	-2	93	112	13	.609	1	0	0	-4	O/1	-0.7
Total	10	730	1721	167	400	58	19	36	163	142	357	.232	.293	.351	.644	87	-41	-32	95	94	180	.578	22	16	-3	5	O/1	-4.8
■ ROY STAIGER	Staiger, Roy Joseph b: 1/6/50, Tulsa, Okla. BR/TR, 6', 195 lbs. Deb: 9/12/75																											
1975	NY-N	13	19	2	3	1	0	0	0	0	4	.158	.158	.211	.368	2	-3	-2	95	0	0	.222	0	0	0	0	3	-0.1
1976	NY-N	95	304	23	67	8	1	2	26	25	35	.220	.282	.273	.555	63	-17	-14	92	112	23	.452	3	3	-1	13	3/S	-0.2
1977	NY-N	40	123	16	31	9	0	2	11	4	20	.252	.276	.374	.650	75	-5	-5	96	85	12	.543	1	0	0	1	3/S	-0.2
1979	NY-A	4	11	1	3	1	0	0	1	1	0	.273	.333	.364	.697	92	-0	-0	96	96	1	.556	0	0	0	0	/3	0.0
Total	4	152	457	42	104	19	1	4	38	30	59	.228	.277	.300	.576	65	-24	-21	93	100	36	.482	4	3	-1	15	3/S	-0.5
■ TUCK STAINBACK	Stainback, George Tucker b: 8/4/10, Los Angeles, Cal. BR/TR, 5'11.5", 175 lbs. Deb: 4/17/34																											
1934	Chi-N	104	359	47	110	14	3	2	46	8	42	.306	.327	.379	.706	90	-6	-5	98	117	45	.609	7			-7	O/3	-1.6
1935	Chi-N	47	94	16	24	4	0	3	11	0	13	.255	.271	.394	.664	77	-3	-3	99	86	9	.548	1			-6	O	-0.9
1936	Chi-N	44	75	13	13	3	0	1	5	6	14	.173	.235	.253	.488	30	-7	-8	105	80	5	.413	1			-4	O	-1.2
1937	Chi-N	72	160	18	37	7	1	0	14	7	16	.231	.268	.287	.555	50	-11	-11	103	110	12	.445	3			0	O	-1.3
1938	StL-N	6	10	2	0	0	0	0	0	0	3	.000	.000	.000	.000	-90	-3	-3	111	0	0	.000	0			1	/O	-0.1
	Phi-N	30	81	9	21	3	0	1	11	3	3	.259	.294	.333	.627	72	-3	-3	100	133	8	.525	1			-2	O	-0.5
	Bro-N	35	104	15	34	6	3	0	20	2	4	.327	.346	.442	.788	121	2	2	96	157	16	.704	1			-0	O	0.2
	Yr	71	195	26	55	9	3	1	31	5	10	.282	.307	.374	.681	87	-4	-4	99	135	23	.582	2			-2		-0.4
1939	Bro-N	68	201	22	54	7	0	3	19	4	23	.269	.290	.348	.638	66	-9	-10	107	88	21	.517	0			-4	O	-1.4
1940	Det-A	15	40	4	9	2	0	0	1	1	9	.225	.262	.275	.537	35	-4	-4	111	33	3	.394	0	0	0	4	/O	0.0
1941	Det-A	94	200	19	49	8	1	2	10	3	21	.245	.260	.325	.585	51	-14	-15	106	50	18	.487	6	3	0	-17	O	-3.6
1942	NY-A	15	10	0	2	0	0	0	0	0	2	.200	.200	.200	.400	13	-1	-1	99	0	0	.250	0	0	0	-0	/O	-0.1
1943	NY-A	71	231	31	60	11	2	0	10	7	16	.260	.285	.325	.609	81	-7	-6	96	49	21	.486	3	3	-1	0	O	-0.9
1944	NY-A	30	78	13	17	3	0	0	5	3	7	.218	.247	.256	.503	41	-6	-6	106	90	6	.393	1	0	0	-3	O	-1.0
1945	NY-A	95	327	40	84	12	2	5	32	13	20	.257	.289	.352	.641	80	-7	-10	107	89	33	.518	0	4	-2	6	O	-0.9
1946	Phi-A	91	291	35	71	10	2	0	20	7	20	.244	.264	.292	.556	53	-18	-19	104	89	23	.430	3	2	-0	2	O	-2.2
Total	13	817	2261	284	585	90	14	17	204	64	213	.259	.284	.333	.618	68	-97	-105	103	90	219	.510	27	12		-30	O/3	-15.5
■ GALE STALEY	Staley, George Gaylord b: 5/2/1899, De Pere, Wis. BL/TR, 5'8.5", 167 lbs. Deb: 9/16/25																											
1925	Chi-N	7	26	2	11	2	0	0	3	2	1	.423	.464	.500	.964	150	2	2	97	84	6	.938	0	1	-1	1	/2	0.2
■ VIRGIL STALLCUP	Stallcup, Thomas Virgil "Red" b: 1/3/22, Ravensford, N.C. BR/TR, 6'3", 185 lbs. Deb: 4/18/47																											
1947	Cin-N	8	1	1	0	0	0	0	0	0	1	.000	.000	.000	.000	-99	-0	-0	91	0	0	.000	0			0	/S	0.0
1948	Cin-N	149	539	40	123	30	4	3	65	18	52	.228	.253	.315	.569	51	-37	-39	103	139	40	.442	2			-1	*S	-2.4
1949	Cin-N	141	575	49	146	28	5	3	45	9	44	.254	.268	.336	.604	64	-33	-30	96	89	49	.466	1			-10	*S	-2.4
1950	Cin-N	136	483	44	121	23	2	8	54	17	39	.251	.276	.356	.632	62	-26	-29	105	106	44	.513	4			-9	*S	-2.2
1951	Cin-N	121	428	33	103	17	2	8	49	6	40	.241	.251	.346	.597	59	-26	-26	101	110	34	.462	2	4	-2	-5	*S	-2.3
1952	Cin-N	2	1	0	0	0	0	0	0	0	0	.000	.000	.000	.000	-99	-0	-0	100	0	0	.000	0	0	0	0	/S	0.0
	StL-N	29	31	4	4	1	0	0	1	1	5	.129	.156	.161	.318	-12	-5	-5	98	78	1	.214	0	0	0	0	S	-0.3
	Yr	31	32	4	4	1	0	0	1	1	5	.125	.152	.156	.308	-15	-5	-5	98	73	1	.207	0	0	0	0		-0.3
1953	StL-N	1	1	0	0	0	0	0	0	0	0	.000	.000	.000	.000	-99	-0	-0	102	0	0	.000	0	0	0	0	H	0.0
Total	7	587	2059	171	497	99	13	22	214	51	181	.241	.260	.334	.595	58	-127	-129	101	110	168	.479	9	4		-25	S	-9.6
■ GEORGE STALLER	Staller, George Walborn "Stopper" b: 4/1/16, Rutherford Heights, Pa. BL/TL, 5'11", 190 lbs. Deb: 9/14/43 C																											
1943	Phi-A	21	85	14	23	1	3	3	12	5	6	.271	.326	.459	.785	127	3	2	101	81	13	.746	1	0	0	-1	O	0.1
■ GEORGE STALLINGS	Stallings, George Tweedy "Gentleman George" b: 11/17/1867, Augusta, Ga. d: 5/13/29, Haddock, Ga. BR/TR, 6'1", 187 lbs. Deb: 5/22/1890 M																											
1890	Bro-N	4	11	1	0	0	0	0	0	1	3	.000	.154	.000	.154	-53	-2	-2	100	0	0	.182	0			0	/C	-0.1
1897	Phi-N	2	9	1	2	1	0	0	0	0		.222	.222	.333	.556	49	-1	-1	96	0	1	.429	0			0	/O1M	0.0
1898	Phi-N	1	0	1	0	0	0	0	0	0		—	—	—	—	—	0	0	95	—	—	—	0			0	/HM	0.0
Total	3	7	20	3	2	1	0	0	0	1	3	.100	.182	.150	.332	-6	-3	-3	98	0	1	.278	0			0	/C1O	-0.1
■ OSCAR STANAGE	Stanage, Oscar Harland b: 3/17/1883, Tulare, Cal. d: 11/11/64, Detroit, Mich. BR/TR, 5'11", 190 lbs. Deb: 5/19/06 C																											
1906	Cin-N	1	1	0	0	0	0	0	0	0		.000	.000	.000	.000	-87	-0	-0	115	0	0	.000	0			0	/C	0.0
1909	Det-A	77	252	17	66	8	6	0	21	11		.262	.298	.341	.639	92	-0	-3	110	94	25	.543	2			-6	C	-0.2
1910	Det-A	88	275	24	57	7	4	2	25	20		.207	.266	.284	.550	71	-9	-10	102	110	21	.463	1			1	C	0.0
1911	Det-A	141	503	45	133	13	7	3	51	20		.264	.297	.336	.633	71	-17	-23	108	97	51	.527	3			0	*C	-0.5
1912	Det-A	119	394	35	103	9	4	0	41	34		.261	.326	.305	.631	85	-9	-7	95	114	40	.553	3			-10	*C	-0.4
1913	Det-A	80	241	19	54	13	2	0	21	21	35	.224	.292	.295	.586	72	-9	-9	99	105	22	.529	5			-2	C	-0.4
1914	Det-A	122	400	16	77	8	4	0	25	24	58	.192	.242	.233	.474	42	-29	-29	102	101	25	.373	2	1	0	-13	*C	-3.7
1915	Det-A	100	300	27	67	9	2	1	31	20	41	.223	.274	.277	.551	60	-14	-17	108	123	25	.466	5	1	1	-15	*C	-2.4
1916	Det-A	94	291	16	69	17	3	0	30	17	48	.237	.286	.316	.602	77	-8	-9	105	116	28	.518	3			-14	C	-2.0
1917	Det-A	99	297	19	61	14	1	0	30	20	35	.205	.262	.259	.522	61	-15	-14	98	140	21	.436	3			-6	C	-1.4
1918	Det-A	54	186	9	47	4	0	1	14	11	18	.253	.294	.290	.585	79	-6	-5	97	90	16	.482	2			-2	C/1S	-0.2
1919	Det-A	38	120	9	29	4	1	1	15	7	12	.242	.295	.317	.611	77	-5	-4	93	133	11	.527	1			-1	C/1	-0.2
1920	Det-A	78	238	12	55	17	0	0	17	14	21	.231	.277	.303	.579	52	-16	-17	103	83	21	.475	0	0	0	-5	C	-1.5
1925	Det-A	3	5	0	1	0	0	0	0	0	0	.200	.200	.200	.400	2	-1	-1	99	0	0	.250	0	0	0	0	/C	0.0
Total	14	1094	3503	248	819	123	34	8	321	219	268	.234	.284	.295	.579	69	-138	-147	102	108	305	.487	30	2		-73	*C/1S	-12.9
■ PETE STANICEK	Stanicek, Peter Louis b: 4/18/63, Harvey, Ill. BB/TR, 5'11", 175 lbs. Deb: 9/01/87																											
1987	Bal-A	30	113	9	31	3	0	0	9	8	19	.274	.333	.301	.634	73	-4	-4	98	112	13	.612	8	1	2	-1	2D/3	-0.1
1988	Bal-A	83	261	29	60	7	1	4	17	28	45	.230	.314	.310	.624	79	-8	-6	95	73	25	.579	12	6	0	-1	O2/D	-0.7
Total	2	113	374	38	91	10	1	4	26	36	64	.243	.320	.307	.627	77	-12	-10	96	84	38	.592	20	7	2	-2	/O2D3	-0.8
■ STEVE STANICEK	Stanicek, Stephen Blair b: 6/19/61, Lake Forest, Ill. BR/TR, 6' ", 190 lbs. Deb: 9/16/87																											
1987	Mil-A	4	7	2	2	0	0	0	0	0	2	.286	.286	.286	.571	52	-0	-0	102	0	1	.400	0	0	0	0	/D	0.0
■ JERRY STANDAERT	Standaert, Jerome John b: 11/2/01, Chicago, Ill. d: 8/4/64, Chicago, Ill. BR/TR, 5'10", 168 lbs. Deb: 4/16/25																											
1925	Bro-N	1	1	0	0	0	0	0	0	0	1	.000	.000	.000	.000	-99	-0	-0	94	0	0	.000	0	0	0	0	H	0.0
1926	Bro-N	66	113	13	39	8	2	0	14	5	7	.345	.378	.451	.829	123	3	3	99	95	19	.770	0			-2	23/S	0.3
1929	Bos-A	19	18	1	3	2	0	0	4	3	2	.167	.286	.278	.563	45	-1	-2	102	274	2	.533	0	0	0	0	1	-0.2
Total	3	86	132	14	42	10	2	0	18	8	10	.318	.362	.424	.786	110	2	2	100	121	20	.722	0	0		-2	/231S	0.1
■ TOM STANKARD	Stankard, Thomas Francis b: 3/20/1882, Waltham, Mass. d: 6/13/58, Waltham, Mass. BR/TR, 6', 190 lbs. Deb: 7/02/04																											
1904	Pit-N	2	2	0	0	0	0	0	0	0		.000	.000	.000	.000	-99	-0	-0	99	0	0	.000	0			0	/S3	0.0
■ EDDIE STANKY	Stanky, Edward Raymond "The Brat" or "Muggsy" b: 9/3/16, Philadelphia, Pa. BR/TR, 5'8", 170 lbs. Deb: 4/21/43 MC																											
1943	Chi-N	142	510	92	125	15	1	0	47	92	42	.245	.363	.278	.641	87	-4	-3	99	127	58	.603	4			18	*2S/3	2.1
1944	Chi-N	13	25	4	6	0	1	0	0	2	2	.240	.296	.320	.616	73	-1	-1	101	0	2	.550	1			0	/2S3	0.0

YEAR	TM/L	G	AB	R	H	2B	3B	HR	RBI	BB	SO	AVG	OBP	SLG	PRO	/A	BR	/A	PF	CHI	RC	TA	SB	CS	SBR	FR	POS	TPR
	Bro-N	89	261	32	72	9	2	0	16	44	13	.276	.382	.326	.708	102	3	3	99	67	37	.693	3			-17	2S/3	-0.3
	Yr	102	286	36	78	9	3	0	16	46	15	.273	.375	.325	.701	99	2	2	99	59	39	.682	4			-16		-0.3
1945	Bro-N	153	555	**128**	143	29	5	1	39	**148**	42	.258	.417	.333	.751	115	18	21	96	64	93	.819	6			10	*2/S	4.3
1946	Bro-N	144	483	98	132	24	7	0	36	**137**	56	.273	**.436**	.352	.788	122	26	24	103	76	90	.890	8			-1	*2	2.9
1947	Bro-N	146	559	97	141	24	5	3	53	103	39	.252	.373	.329	.702	84	-5	-9	105	90	78	.694	3			12	*2	1.9
1948	Bos-N	67	247	49	79	14	2	2	29	61	13	.320	.455	.417	.872	135	17	17	102	88	52	.965	3			2	2	2.3
1949	Bos-N	138	506	90	144	24	5	1	42	113	41	.285	.417	.358	.775	114	14	16	97	83	86	.808	3			-6	*2	1.5
1950	NY-N	152	527	115	158	25	5	8	51	**144**	50	.300	**.460**	.412	.872	133	35	37	98	72	116	1.013	9			6	*2	4.5
1951	NY-N	145	515	88	127	17	2	14	43	127	63	.247	.401	.369	.770	107	13	12	102	69	90	.832	8	5	-1	4	*2	2.0
1952	StL-N	53	83	13	19	4	0	0	7	19	9	.229	.373	.277	.650	84	-1	-1	98	119	11	.656	0	0	0	3	2M	0.3
1953	StL-N	17	30	5	8	0	0	0	1	6	4	.267	.405	.267	.672	79	-0	-1	102	49	4	.682	0	0	0	1	/2M	0.1
Total	11	1259	4301	811	1154	185	35	29	364	996	374	.268	.410	.348	.758	109	113	115	100	82	717	.817	48	5		32	*2/S3	21.6
■ **FRED STANLEY**	Stanley, Frederick Blair b: 8/13/47, Farnhamville, Iowa BR/TR, 5'10", 165 lbs. Deb: 9/11/69																											
1969	Sea-A	17	43	2	12	2	1	0	4	3	8	.279	.326	.372	.698	96	-0	-0	98	100	6	.645	1	0	0	-1	S/2	0.0
1970	Mil-A	6	0	1	0	0	0	0	0	0	0	—	—	—	—	—	0	0	98	—	—	—	0	0	0	0	/2	0.0
1971	Cle-A	60	129	14	29	4	0	2	12	27	25	.225	.363	.302	.665	85	-0	-1	106	109	16	.654	1	0	0	-4	S/2	0.1
1972	Cle-A	6	12	1	2	1	0	0	0	2	3	.167	.286	.250	.536	56	-1	-1	107	0	1	.455	0	0	0	-0	/S2	0.0
	SD-N	39	85	15	17	2	0	0	2	12	19	.200	.306	.224	.530	60	-5	-4	88	43	7	.485	1	0	0	-3	2S/3	-0.2
1973	NY-A	26	66	6	14	0	1	1	5	7	16	.212	.288	.288	.576	62	-3	-3	101	89	6	.500	0	0	0	1	S/2	0.1
1974	NY-A	33	38	2	7	0	0	0	3	3	2	.184	.244	.184	.428	26	-4	-3	96	168	1	.314	1	2	-1	-0	S2	-0.2
1975	NY-A	117	252	34	56	5	1	0	15	21	27	.222	.285	.250	.535	53	-15	-15	99	91	18	.429	3	1	0	-7	S2/3	-1.2
1976	NY-A	110	260	32	62	2	2	1	20	34	29	.238	.329	.273	.602	78	-6	-6	99	104	26	.527	1	0	0	-9	*S/2	-0.7
1977	NY-A	48	46	6	12	0	0	1	7	8	6	.261	.370	.326	.696	93	-0	-0	99	154	6	.686	1	1	-0	-1	S/32	0.4
1978	NY-A	81	160	14	35	7	0	1	9	25	31	.219	.324	.281	.606	73	-5	-5	99	74	16	.547	0	0	0	-4	S2/3	-0.2
1979	NY-A	57	100	9	20	1	0	2	14	5	17	.200	.238	.270	.508	38	-9	-8	96	163	6	.390	0	1	-1	4	S3/21O	0.0
1980	NY-A	49	86	13	18	3	0	0	5	5	5	.209	.269	.244	.513	42	-7	-7	99	93	6	.412	0	0	0	1	S23	-0.2
1981	Oak-A	66	145	15	28	4	0	0	7	15	23	.193	.269	.221	.489	44	-10	-10	96	86	11	.419	2	0	1	-15	S/2	-2.0
1982	Oak-A	101	228	33	44	7	0	2	17	29	32	.193	.287	.250	.537	51	-15	-14	95	108	17	.460	0	1	-1	-12	S/2	-1.7
Total	14	816	1650	197	356	38	5	10	120	196	243	.216	.302	.263	.565	62	-82	-77	98	99	150	.497	11	6	-0	-50	S2/3O1	-5.8
■ **JIM STANLEY**	Stanley, James F. b: 1889, 5'6", 148 lbs. Deb: 4/19/14																											
1914	Chi-F	54	98	13	19	3	0	0	4	19	14	.194	.325	.224	.549	65	-4	-3	91	66	9	.544	2			1	S/32O	0.1
■ **JOE STANLEY**	Stanley, Joseph b: New Jersey Deb: 4/24/1884																											
1884	Bal-U	6	21	3	5	1	0	0		0		.238	.238	.286	.524	69	-1	-1	110	0	1	.375	0			0	/O	0.0
■ **JOE STANLEY**	Stanley, Joseph Bernard b: 4/2/1881, Washington, D.C. d: 9/13/67, Detroit, Mich. BB/TR, 5'9.5", 150 lbs. Deb: 9/11/1897																											
1897	Was-N	1	1	0	0	0	0	0	0	0		.000	.000	.000	.000	-99	-0	-0	101	0	0	.000	0			0	/P	0.0
1902	Was-A	3	12	2	4	0	0	0	1	0		.333	.333	.333	.667	88	-0	-0	99	87	1	.500	0			0	/O	0.0
1903	Bos-N	86	308	40	77	12	5	1	47	18		.250	.291	.331	.623	82	-9	-7	96	147	33	.563	10			13	O/PS	0.1
1904	Bos-N	3	8	0	0	0	0	0	0	0		.000	.000	.000	.000	-99	-2	-2	97	0	0	.000	0			0	/O	-0.1
1905	Was-A	28	92	13	24	2	1	1	17	7		.261	.313	.337	.650	104	1	0	104	182	11	.618	4			-3	O	-0.3
1906	Was-A	73	221	18	36	0	4	0	9	20		.163	.232	.199	.431	40	-15	-13	91	74	12	.378	6			2	O/P	-1.5
1909	Chi-N	22	52	4	7	1	0	0	2	6		.135	.224	.154	.378	18	-5	-5	101	91	2	.311	0			-1	O	-0.7
Total	7	216	694	77	148	15	10	2	76	51		.213	.267	.272	.539	66	-30	-27	96	121	60	.476	20			10	O/PS	-2.5
■ **MICKEY STANLEY**	Stanley, Mitchell Jack b: 7/20/42, Grand Rapids, Mich BR/TR, 6'1", 185 lbs. Deb: 9/13/64																											
1964	Det-A	4	11	3	3	0	0	0	1	0	1	.273	.273	.273	.545	55	-1	-1	96	141	1	.333	0	0	0	-0	/O	0.0
1965	Det-A	30	117	14	28	6	0	3	13	3	12	.239	.258	.368	.626	72	-4	-5	105	106	11	.516	1	0	0	4	O	-0.1
1966	Det-A	92	235	28	68	15	4	3	19	17	20	.289	.337	.426	.763	115	5	4	102	73	33	.692	2	1	0	6	O	0.8
1967	Det-A	145	333	38	70	7	3	7	24	29	46	.210	.273	.312	.586	73	-12	-11	99	80	30	.526	9	2	2	-2	*O/1	-1.7
1968	Det-A	153	583	88	151	16	6	11	60	42	57	.259	.313	.364	.677	98	3	-1	106	111	62	.573	4	3	-1	0	*O1/S2	-0.7
1969	Det-A	149	592	73	139	28	1	16	70	52	56	.235	.299	.367	.665	82	-13	-15	103	102	64	.592	8	4	0	-9	*OS/1	-2.5
1970	Det-A	142	568	83	143	21	11	13	47	45	56	.252	.307	.396	.703	90	-7	-10	103	69	67	.629	10	1	2	-1	*O/1	-1.4
1971	Det-A	139	401	43	117	14	5	7	41	24	44	.292	.332	.404	.736	112	3	5	96	91	52	.636	1	3	-2	1	*O	0.0
1972	Det-A	142	435	45	102	16	6	14	55	29	49	.234	.282	.395	.678	89	-2	-8	113	107	45	.580	1	0	0	0	*O	-1.2
1973	Det-A	157	602	81	147	23	5	17	57	48	65	.244	.300	.384	.684	91	-8	-9	101	84	68	.594	0	4	-2	6	*O	-0.9
1974	Det-A	99	394	40	87	13	2	8	34	26	63	.221	.271	.325	.596	67	-16	-18	106	84	32	.492	5	3	-0	0	O1/2	-2.1
1975	Det-A	52	164	26	42	7	3	3	19	15	27	.256	.322	.390	.712	97	-0	-1	104	100	21	.648	1	1	-0	0	O1/3D	-0.2
1976	Det-A	84	214	34	55	17	1	4	29	14	19	.257	.303	.402	.705	101	1	-0	104	114	25	.614	2	0	1	-4	O13/S2D	-0.4
1977	Det-A	75	222	30	51	9	1	8	23	18	30	.230	.287	.387	.675	78	-6	-7	105	83	24	.588	0	0	0	-4	O/1SD	-1.3
1978	Det-A	53	151	15	40	9	0	3	8	9	19	.265	.306	.384	.690	86	-2	-3	108	47	17	.583	0	1	-1	-7	O1	-1.1
Total	15	1516	5022	641	1243	201	48	117	500	371	564	.248	.300	.377	.677	89	-59	-80	104	91	549	.608	44	23	-1	-10	*O/1S3D2	-12.8
■ **MIKE STANLEY**	Stanley, Robert Michael b: 6/25/63, Ft.Lauderdale, Fla BR/TR, 6'1", 185 lbs. Deb: 6/24/86																											
1986	Tex-A	15	30	4	10	3	0	1	1	3	7	.333	.394	.533	.927	158	2	2	96	21	7	1.000	1	0	0	-1	/3COD	0.2
1987	Tex-A	78	216	34	59	8	1	6	37	31	48	.273	.367	.403	.770	102	2	1	104	141	33	.748	3	0	1	-12	C1/OD	-0.5
1988	Tex-A	94	249	21	57	8	0	3	27	37	62	.229	.329	.297	.626	76	-7	-7	101	129	26	.561	0	0	0	-7	CD/13	-1.1
Total	3	187	495	59	126	19	1	10	65	71	117	.255	.349	.358	.707	92	-2	-3	102	128	66	.675	4	0	1	-19	C/D13O	-1.4
■ **JACK STANSBURY**	Stansbury, John James b: 12/6/1885, Phillipsburg, N.J. d: 12/26/70, Easton, Pa. BR/TR, 5'9", 165 lbs. Deb: 6/30/18																											
1918	Bos-A	20	47	3	6	1	0	0	2	6	3	.128	.241	.149	.390	18	-5	-4	95	104	2	.341	0			-0	3/O	-0.4
■ **BUCK STANTON**	Stanton, George Washington b: 6/19/06, Stantonsburg, N.C BL/TL, 5'10", 150 lbs. Deb: 9/05/31																											
1931	StL-A	13	15	3	3	2	0	0	0	0	6	.200	.200	.333	.533	37	-1	-1	102	0	1	.417	0	0	0	0	/O	-0.1
■ **HARRY STANTON**	Stanton, Harry Andrew b: St.Louis, Mo. TR , Deb: 10/14/00																											
1900	StL-N	1	0	0	0	0	0	0	0	0		—	—	—	—	—	0	0	93	—	—	—	0			0	/C	0.0
■ **LEROY STANTON**	Stanton, Leroy Bobby b: 4/10/46, Latta, S.C. BR/TR, 6'1", 195 lbs. Deb: 9/10/70																											
1970	NY-N	4	4	0	1	0	1	0	0	0	0	.250	.250	.750	1.000	151	0	0	104	0	0	.750	0	0	0	-0	/O	0.0
1971	NY-N	5	21	2	4	1	0	0	2	2	4	.190	.261	.238	.499	44	-2	-1	96	140	1	.389	0	0	0	0	/O	-0.1
1972	Cal-A	127	402	44	101	15	3	12	39	22	100	.251	.297	.393	.690	118	1	5	88	84	42	.581	2	3	-1	1	*O	0.2
1973	Cal-A	119	306	41	72	9	2	8	34	27	88	.235	.301	.356	.658	88	-7	-5	96	100	31	.571	3	3	-1	-8	*O	-1.6
1974	Cal-A	118	415	48	111	21	2	11	62	33	107	.267	.329	.407	.736	120	5	9	92	123	54	.676	10	8	-2	6	*O	1.0
1975	Cal-A	137	440	67	115	20	3	14	82	52	85	.261	.347	.416	.763	121	9	12	95	140	66	.764	18	6	2	1	*O/D	1.2
1976	Cal-A	93	231	12	44	13	1	2	25	24	57	.190	.270	.281	.551	67	-11	-9	92	135	16	.455	2	6	-3	-10	O/D	-2.4
1977	Sea-A	133	454	56	125	24	1	27	90	42	115	.275	.343	.511	.854	134	17	19	96	116	79	.825	0	1	-1	1	OD	1.7
1978	Sea-A	93	302	24	55	11	0	3	24	34	80	.182	.267	.248	.515	45	-21	-22	102	113	21	.439	1	0	0	-1	DO	-2.4
Total	9	829	2575	294	628	114	13	77	358	236	636	.244	.313	.388	.701	104	-9	9	94	116	310	.654	36	27	-5	-9	O/D	-2.4
■ **TOM STANTON**	Stanton, Thomas Patrick b: 10/25/1874, St.Louis, Mo. d: 1/17/57, St.Louis, Mo. BB/TR, 5'10", 175 lbs. Deb: 4/19/04																											
1904	Chi-N	1	3	0	0	0	0	0	0	0		.000	.000	.000	.000	-99	-1	-1	101	0	0	.000	0			0	/C	0.0
■ **JOE STAPLES**	Staples, Joseph F. b: Buffalo, N.Y. Deb: 1885																											
1885	Buf-N	7	22	0	1	0	0	0	0	0	9	.045	.045	.045	.091	-71	-4	-4	99	0	0	.048	0			0	/O2	-0.3
■ **DAVE STAPLETON**	Stapleton, David Leslie b: 1/16/54, Fairhope, Ala. BR/TR, 6'1", 178 lbs. Deb: 5/30/80																											
1980	Bos-A	106	449	61	144	33	5	7	45	13	32	.321	.341	.463	.805	116	10	9	102	74	67	.710	3	2	-0	5	2/1O3D	1.8
1981	Bos-A	93	355	45	101	17	1	10	42	21	22	.285	.326	.423	.749	108	6	3	106	93	45	.639	0	4	-2	-2	S321/D	0.1

YEAR	TM/L	G	AB	R	H	2B	3B	HR	RBI	BB	SO	AVG	OBP	SLG	PRO	/A	BR	/A	PF	CHI	RC	TA	SB	CS	SBR	FR	POS	TPR
1982	Bos-A	150	538	66	142	28	1	14	65	31	40	.264	.308	.398	.705	84	-7	-14	110	104	58	.590	2	4	-2	8	*1S/23OD	-0.6
1983	Bos-A	151	542	54	134	31	1	10	66	40	44	.247	.301	.363	.665	81	-14	-14	101	116	56	.561	1	1	-0	2	*1/2	-1.8
1984	Bos-A	13	39	4	9	2	0	0	1	3	3	.231	.286	.282	.568	52	-2	-3	110	36	3	.438	0	0	0	1	1/D	-0.2
1985	Bos-A	30	66	4	15	6	0	0	2	4	11	.227	.271	.318	.590	59	-4	-4	102	38	6	.481	0	0	0	2	2/1D	-0.1
1986	Bos-A	39	39	4	5	1	0	0	3	2	10	.128	.171	.154	.325	-10	-6	-6	100	199	1	.229	0	0	0	1	1/23	-0.5
Total	7	582	2028	238	550	118	8	41	224	114	162	.271	.312	.398	.710	91	-17	-29	105	97	236	.627	6	11	-5	16	12/S3DO	-1.3
■ **WILLIE STARGELL** Stargell, Wilver Dornel b: 3/6/40, Earlsboro, Okla. BL/TL, 6'2", 188 lbs. Deb: 9/16/62 CH																												
1962	Pit-N	10	31	1	9	3	1	0	4	3	10	.290	.353	.452	.805	112	1	1	102	113	5	.739	0	1	-1	-0	/O	0.0
1963	Pit-N	108	304	34	74	11	6	11	47	19	85	.243	.292	.428	.720	106	1	1	99	121	36	.634	0	2	-1	-7	O1	-1.1
1964	Pit-N	117	421	53	115	19	7	21	78	17	92	.273	.305	.501	.806	121	10	10	101	119	62	.736	1	1	-0	-7	O1	0.0
1965	Pit-N	144	533	68	145	25	8	27	107	39	127	.272	.330	.501	.831	131	20	20	100	130	87	.791	1	1	-0	-3	*O/1	1.3
1966	Pit-N	140	485	84	153	30	0	33	102	48	109	.315	.384	.581	.965	163	41	41	101	115	107	.988	2	3	-1	-8	*O1	2.8
1967	Pit-N	134	462	54	125	18	6	20	73	67	103	.271	.367	.465	.832	137	23	23	100	112	78	.819	1	0	0	-3	O1	1.5
1968	Pit-N	128	435	57	103	15	1	24	67	47	105	.237	.320	.441	.761	125	14	13	101	109	61	.727	5	0	2	-9	*O1	0.0
1969	Pit-N	145	522	89	160	31	6	29	92	61	120	.307	.385	.556	.941	170	41	45	95	100	112	.962	1	0	0	-9	*O1	2.9
1970	Pit-N	136	474	70	125	18	3	31	85	44	119	.264	.333	.511	.843	127	13	15	97	100	77	.799	0	1	-1	-1	*O/1	0.7
1971	Pit-N	141	511	104	151	26	0	**48**	125	83	154	.295	.401	.628	1.029	**189**	59	59	99	116	131	1.117	0	0	0	-5	*O	**5.2**
1972	Pit-N	138	495	75	145	28	2	33	112	65	129	.293	.377	.558	.935	158	40	38	103	125	105	.961	1	1	-0	-3	*1O	2.8
1973	Pit-N	148	522	106	156	**43**	3	**44**	**119**	80	129	.299	.395	**.646**	**1.041**	**200**	**58**	**63**	92	104	136	**1.129**	0	0	0	1	*O	5.8
1974	Pit-N	140	508	90	153	37	4	25	96	87	106	.301	.409	.537	**.947**	**167**	44	46	98	113	115	1.003	0	2	-1	-3	*O/1	3.8
1975	Pit-N	124	461	71	136	32	2	22	90	58	109	.295	.377	.516	.894	147	28	28	99	121	91	.895	0	0	0	-7	*1	1.5
1976	Pit-N	117	428	54	110	20	3	20	65	50	101	.257	.342	.458	.800	125	13	13	100	104	70	.786	2	0	1	-7	*1	0.1
1977	Pit-N	63	186	29	51	12	0	13	35	31	55	.274	.386	.548	.935	144	13	12	103	99	39	.971	0	1	-1	-3	1	0.6
1978	Pit-N	122	390	60	115	18	2	28	97	50	93	.295	.385	.567	.951	155	32	30	105	126	85	.986	3	2	-0	-2	*1	2.4
1979	Pit-N	126	424	60	119	19	0	32	82	47	105	.281	.357	.552	.908	136	24	21	106	98	81	.899	0	1	-1	-5	*1	1.0
1980	Pit-N	67	202	28	53	10	1	11	38	26	52	.262	.352	.485	.837	127	8	8	103	115	35	.834	0	0	0	-3	1	0.3
1981	Pit-N	38	60	2	17	4	0	0	9	5	9	.283	.338	.350	.688	100	-0	-0	96	168	8	.605	0	0	0	-0	/1	0.0
1982	Pit-N	74	73	6	17	4	0	3	17	10	24	.233	.325	.411	.736	95	0	-1	110	171	10	.702	0	0	0	0	/1	0.0
Total	21	2360	7927	1195	2232	423	55	475	1540	937	1936	.282	.363	.529	.892	148	483	486	100	114	1531	.914	17	16	-5	-85	*O1	31.6
■ **MATT STARK** Stark, Matthew Scott b: 1/21/65, Whittier, Cal. BR/TR, 6'4", 225 lbs. Deb: 4/08/87																												
1987	Tor-A	5	12	0	1	0	0	0	0	0	0	.083	.083	.083	.167	-55	-3	-3	101	0	-0	.077	0	0	0	0	/C	-0.1
■ **DOLLY STARK** Stark, Monroe Randolph b: 1/19/1885, Ripley, Miss. d: 12/1/24, Memphis, Tenn. BR/TR, 5'9", 160 lbs. Deb: 9/12/09																												
1909	Cle-A	19	60	4	12	0	0	0	1	6		.200	.273	.200	.473	49	-3	-3	102	33	4	.458	4			-2	S	-0.5
1910	Bro-N	30	103	7	17	3	0	0	8	7	19	.165	.225	.194	.419	24	-10	-10	95	142	5	.349	2			2	S	-0.6
1911	Bro-N	70	193	25	57	4	1	0	19	20	24	.295	.370	.326	.697	99	-0	1	97	102	26	.676	6			-2	S2/3	0.0
1912	Bro-N	8	22	2	4	0	0	0	2	1	3	.182	.217	.182	.399	10	-3	-3	95	168	1	.389	2			-1	/S	-0.2
Total	4	127	378	38	90	7	1	0	30	34	46	.238	.308	.262	.570	66	-16	-15	97	105	37	.524	14			-4	/S23	-1.3
■ **GEORGE STARNAGLE** Starnagle, George Henry (born George Henry Steuernagel) b: 10/6/1873, Belleville, Ill. d: 2/15/46, Belleville, Ill. BR/TR, 5'11", 175 lbs. Deb: 9/14/02																												
1902	Cle-A	1	3	0	0	0	0	0	0	0		.000	.000	.000	.000	-99	-1	-1	97	0	0	.000	0			0	/C	0.0
■ **CHARLIE STARR** Starr, Charles Watkin b: 8/30/1878, Pike Co., Ohio d: 10/18/37, Pasadena, Cal. TR , Deb: 4/29/05																												
1905	StL-A	26	97	9	20	0	0	0	6	7		.206	.260	.206	.466	55	-5	-4	91	113	5	.351	0			-2	2/3	-0.6
1908	Pit-N	20	59	8	11	2	0	0	8	13		.186	.333	.220	.554	84	-1	-0	95	241	6	.667	6			-1	2/S3	0.0
1909	Bos-N	61	216	16	48	2	3	0	6	31		.222	.333	.259	.593	89	-2	-1	96	34	20	.589	7			0	2/S3	-0.1
	Phi-N	3	3	0	0	0	0	0	0	0		.000	.000	.000	.000	-94	-1	-1	106	0	0	.000	0			0	H	0.0
	Yr	64	219	16	48	2	3	0	6	31		.219	.329	.256	.585	86	-3	-2	97	33	20	.579	7			0		-0.1
Total	3	110	375	33	79	4	3	0	20	51		.211	.313	.237	.551	78	-8	-6	95	88	32	.534	13			-3	/2S3	-0.7
■ **CHICK STARR** Starr, William b: 2/26/11, Brooklyn, N.Y. BR/TR, 6'1", 175 lbs. Deb: 8/23/35																												
1935	Was-A	12	24	1	5	0	0	0	1	0	1	.208	.208	.208	.417	9	-3	-3	92	68	1	.263	0	0	0	-1	C	-0.2
1936	Was-A	1	0	0	0	0	0	0	0	0	0	—	—	—	—	—	0	0	98	—	—	—	0	0	0	0	/C	0.0
Total	2	13	24	1	5	0	0	0	1	0	1	.208	.208	.208	.417	9	-3	-3	92	68	2	.263	0	0	0	-1	/C	-0.2
■ **JOE START** Start, Joseph "Old Reliable" or "Rocks" b: 10/14/1842, New York, N.Y. d: 3/27/27, Providence, R.I. BL/TL, 5'9", 165 lbs. Deb: 5/18/1871 M																												
1871	Mut-n	33	165	35	56							.339															*1	
1872	Mut-n	55	281	62	77							.274															*1	
1873	Mut-n	53	262	44	66							.252															*1M	
1874	Mut-n	63	321	68	93							.290															*1	
1875	Mut-n	69	324	57	90							.278															*1	
1876	NY-N	56	264	40	73	6	0	0	21	1	2	.277	.279	.299	.578	107	-2	3	87	78	23	.419				3	*1	0.6
1877	Har-N	60	271	55	90	3	6	1	21	6	2	.332	.347	.399	.745	150	10	14	89	62	38	.630				-3	*1	0.8
1878	Chi-N	61	285	58	**100**	12	5	1	27	2	3	.351	.355	.439	.794	148	17	14	108	63	46	.686				-2	*1	1.3
1879	Pro-N	66	317	70	101	11	5	2	37	7	4	.319	.333	.404	.737	140	14	13	102	84	44	.625				0	*1/O	0.7
1880	Pro-N	82	345	53	96	14	6	0	27	13	20	.278	.304	.354	.658	127	8	10	96	78	38	.542				-4	*1	0.2
1881	Pro-N	79	348	56	114	12	6	0	29	9	7	.328	.345	.397	.741	142	12	16	93	64	49	.628				-4	*1	0.0
1882	Pro-N	82	356	58	117	8	10	0	48	11	7	.329	.349	.407	.756	134	16	13	106	98	52	.653				1	*1	0.0
1883	Pro-N	87	370	63	105	16	7	1	57	22	16	.284	.324	.373	.697	111	5	5	101	135	46	.604				-1	*1	-0.6
1884	Pro-N	93	381	80	105	10	5	2	32	35	25	.276	.337	.344	.680	113	7	6	102	77	45	.601				0	*1	-0.2
1885	Pro-N	101	374	47	103	11	4	0	41	39	10	.275	.344	.326	.670	129	9	13	91	124	43	.594				0	*1	-0.3
1886	Was-N	31	122	10	27	4	1	0	17	5	13	.221	.252	.270	.522	63	-6	-5	94	161	10	.442	4			-2	1	-1.0
Total	5 n	273	1353	266	382							.282															1	
Total	11	798	3433	590	1031	107	55	7	357	150	109	.300	.330	.370	.699	127	90	102	97	91	432	.592	4			-10	*1/O	1.5
■ **JOE STATON** Staton, Joseph b: 3/8/48, Seattle, Wash. BL/TL, 6'3", 175 lbs. Deb: 9/05/72																												
1972	Det-A	6	2	1	0	0	0	0	0	0	1	.000	.000	.000	.000	-88	-0	-1	113	0	0	.000	0	1	-1	0	/1	-0.1
1973	Det-A	9	17	2	4	0	0	0	3	0	3	.235	.235	.235	.471	33	-2	-2	101	295	1	.385	1	0	0	0	/1	-0.1
Total	2	15	19	3	4	0	0	0	3	0	4	.211	.211	.211	.421	19	-2	-2	102	264	1	.313	1	1	-0	0	/1	-0.2
■ **JIGGER STATZ** Statz, Arnold John b: 10/20/1897, Waukegan, Ill. d: 3/16/88, Corona Del Mar, Cal. BR/TR, 5'7.5", 150 lbs. Deb: 7/30/19																												
1919	NY-N	21	60	7	18	2	1	0	6	3	8	.300	.333	.367	.700	111	1	1	100	106	7	.643	2			-1	O/2	0.0
1920	NY-N	16	30	0	4	0	1	0	5	2	9	.133	.188	.200	.387	11	-3	-3	100	323	1	.296	0	1	-1	-2	O	-0.6
	Bos-A	2	3	0	0	0	0	0	0	0	0	.000	.000	.000	.000	-99	-1	-1	96	0	0	.000	0	0	0	-1	/O	-0.1
1922	Chi-N	110	462	77	137	19	5	1	34	41	31	.297	.355	.366	.721	91	-9	-5	95	61	60	.672	16	13	-3	6	*O	-0.6
1923	Chi-N	154	655	110	209	33	8	10	70	56	42	.319	.375	.440	.815	110	14	10	104	67	105	.802	29	23	-5	15	*O	1.3
1924	Chi-N	135	549	69	152	22	5	3	49	37	50	.277	.325	.352	.676	80	-14	-15	101	78	63	.603	13	9	-2	13	*O/2	-0.5
1925	Chi-N	38	148	21	38	6	3	2	14	11	16	.257	.317	.378	.695	79	-5	-5	97	77	19	.664	4	0	1	4	O	0.0
1927	Bro-N	130	507	64	139	24	7	1	21	26	43	.274	.310	.355	.665	76	-17	-18	103	43	54	.587	10			11	*O/2	-1.1
1928	Bro-N	77	171	28	40	8	1	0	16	18	12	.234	.311	.292	.603	59	-10	-10	99	114	16	.550	3			-2	O/2	-1.3
Total	8	683	2585	376	737	114	31	17	215	194	211	.285	.337	.373	.710	87	-45	-47	101	71	325	.657	77	46		43	O/2	-2.9
■ **RUSTY STAUB** Staub, Daniel Joseph b: 4/1/44, New Orleans, La. BL/TR, 6'2", 190 lbs. Deb: 4/09/63 C																												
1963	Hou-N	150	513	43	115	17	4	6	45	59	58	.224	.310	.308	.618	85	-13	-8	92	110	51	.544	0	0	0	-1	*1O	-1.4
1964	Hou-N	89	292	26	63	10	2	8	35	21	31	.216	.275	.346	.621	77	-10	-9	96	117	27	.534	1	1	-0	-0	1O	-1.2
1965	Hou-N	131	410	43	105	20	1	14	63	52	57	.256	.343	.412	.755	126	7	13	89	124	56	.702	3	0	1	6	*O/1	1.6
1966	Hou-N	153	554	60	155	28	3	13	81	58	61	.280	.349	.412	.761	113	9	10	97	135	79	.700	2	1	0	11	*O/1	1.8

YEAR	TM/L	G	AB	R	H	2B	3B	HR	RBI	BB	SO	AVG	OBP	SLG	PRO	/A	BR	/A	PF	CHI	RC	TA	SB	CS	SBR	FR	POS	TPR
1967	Hou-N	149	546	71	182	**44**	1	10	74	60	47	.333	.402	.473	.875	160	36	40	94	113	100	.838	0	4	-2	7	*O	4.1
1968	Hou-N	161	591	54	172	37	1	6	72	73	57	.291	.376	.387	.763	131	24	24	99	118	88	.723	2	0	1	-2	*1O	1.8
1969	Mon-N	158	549	89	166	26	5	29	79	110	61	.302	.427	.526	.953	165	53	52	100	89	128	1.028	3	4	-2	6	*O	5.0
1970	Mon-N	160	569	98	156	23	7	30	94	112	93	.274	.396	.497	.894	138	33	33	100	104	117	.951	12	11	-3	-1	*O	2.1
1971	Mon-N	162	599	94	186	34	6	19	97	74	42	.311	.394	.482	.877	149	39	39	99	121	111	.868	9	5	-0	3	*O	3.8
1972	NY-N	66	239	32	70	11	0	9	38	31	13	.293	.379	.452	.831	142	11	13	95	122	41	.806	0	1	-1	-1	O	0.9
1973	NY-N	152	585	77	163	36	1	15	76	74	52	.279	.363	.421	.783	116	14	14	101	101	89	.738	1	1	-0	10	*O	1.7
1974	NY-N	151	561	65	145	22	2	19	78	77	39	.258	.351	.406	.757	112	9	9	99	112	78	.708	2	1	0	8	*O	1.2
1975	NY-N	155	574	93	162	30	4	19	105	77	55	.282	.376	.448	.823	134	22	26	95	137	97	.802	2	0	1	3	*O	2.5
1976	Det-A	161	589	73	176	28	3	15	96	83	49	.299	.392	.433	.825	136	33	31	104	118	99	.796	3	1	0	-9	*OD	2.0
1977	Det-A	158	623	84	173	34	3	22	101	59	47	.278	.341	.448	.789	108	11	7	105	112	89	.711	1	1	-0	0	*D	0.6
1978	Det-A	162	642	75	175	30	1	24	121	76	35	.273	.352	.435	.787	111	17	11	108	131	96	.734	3	1	0	0	*D	1.2
1979	Det-A	68	246	32	58	12	1	9	40	32	18	.236	.336	.402	.738	102	-0	1	96	129	33	.695	1	0	0	0	D	0.1
	Mon-N	38	86	9	23	3	0	3	14	14	10	.267	.370	.407	.777	109	2	1	102	126	13	.742	0	0	0	-1	1/O	0.0
1980	Tex-A	109	340	42	102	23	2	9	55	39	18	.300	.375	.459	.834	127	13	13	100	117	55	.776	1	1	-0	1	D1O	1.1
1981	NY-N	70	161	9	51	9	0	5	21	22	12	.317	.402	.466	.868	145	10	10	101	92	30	.853	1	0	0	-2	1	0.8
1982	NY-N	112	219	11	53	9	0	3	27	24	10	.242	.317	.324	.641	81	-6	-5	99	132	22	.540	0	0	0	-1	O1	-0.7
1983	NY-N	104	115	5	34	6	0	3	28	14	10	.296	.377	.426	.803	124	4	4	99	191	18	.753	0	0	0	-1	/1O	0.2
1984	NY-N	78	72	2	19	4	0	1	18	4	9	.264	.303	.361	.664	86	-1	-1	100	243	8	.556	0	0	0	0	/1	0.0
1985	NY-N	54	45	2	12	3	0	1	8	10	4	.267	.400	.400	.800	128	2	2	97	152	8	.824	0	0	0	-0	/O	0.2
Total	23	2951	9720	1189	2716	499	47	292	1466	1255	888	.279	.366	.431	.797	124	318	331	99	118	1534	.791	47	33	-6	35	*OD1	29.4
■ DAN STEARNS	Stearns, Daniel Eckford b: 10/17/1861, Buffalo, N.Y. d: 6/28/44, Glendale, Cal. BL/TR, 6'1", 185 lbs. Deb: 8/17/1880																											
1880	Buf-N	28	104	8	19	6	1	0	13	3	23	.183	.206	.260	.465	62	-5	-3	91	179	6	.353				-3	O/C3S	-0.6
1881	Det-N	3	11	1	1	1	0	0	0	0	2	.091	.091	.182	.273	-15	-1	-2	106	0	0	.200				0	/S	0.0
1882	Cin-a	49	214	28	55	10	2	0		6		.257	.277	.322	.600	93	0	-2	109	0	20	.472				-3	1O/2S	-0.4
1883	Bal-a	93	382	54	94	10	9	1		**34**		.246	.308	.327	.635	98	3	-1	107	0	39	.552				3	*1/O	-0.5
1884	Bal-a	100	396	61	94	12	3	3		28		.237	.298	.306	.603	101	1	2	99	0	37	.513				4	*1/2	0.1
1885	Bal-a	67	253	40	47	3	8	1		38		.186	.306	.273	.579	82	-2	-4	106	0	22	.549				2	1/OC	-0.6
	Buf-N	30	105	7	21	6	1	0	9	8	23	.200	.257	.276	.533	73	-3	-3	99	110	8	.440				0	S1/C	-0.2
1889	KC-a	139	560	96	160	24	13	2	87	56	69	.286	.351	.386	.736	106	9	3	106	119	102	.848	67			1	*1/3	-0.5
Total	7	509	2025	295	491	72	37	7	109	173	117	.242	.306	.325	.631	95	2	-11	104	47	233	.593	67			4	1/OSC32	-2.7
■ JOHN STEARNS	Stearns, John Hardin b: 8/21/51, Denver, Col. BR/TR, 6', 185 lbs. Deb: 9/22/74																											
1974	Phi-N	1	2	0	1	0	0	0	0	0	0	.500	.500	.500	1.000	175	0	0	103	0	1	1.000	0	0	0	0	/C	0.0
1975	NY-N	59	169	25	32	5	1	3	10	17	15	.189	.271	.284	.555	57	-11	-10	95	68	13	.493	4	1	1	6	C	0.0
1976	NY-N	32	103	13	27	6	0	2	10	16	11	.262	.367	.379	.745	122	2	3	92	87	14	.695	1	2	-1	0	C	0.4
1977	NY-N	139	431	52	108	25	1	12	55	77	76	.251	.373	.397	.770	111	7	9	96	108	64	.763	9	8	-2	6	*C/1	1.1
1978	NY-N	143	477	65	126	24	1	15	73	70	57	.264	.368	.413	.781	120	13	14	98	122	75	.800	25	13	-0	24	*C/3	4.3
1979	NY-N	155	538	58	131	29	2	9	66	52	57	.243	.315	.355	.670	87	-13	-10	95	122	54	.591	15	15	-5	20	*C13/O	0.7
1980	NY-N	91	319	42	91	25	1	0	45	33	24	.285	.354	.370	.724	107	2	3	96	154	44	.674	7	3	0	7	C1/3	1.2
1981	NY-N	80	273	25	74	12	1	1	24	24	17	.271	.330	.333	.663	88	-4	-4	101	102	30	.602	12	2	2	2	C/13	0.1
1982	NY-N	98	352	46	103	25	3	4	28	30	35	.293	.352	.415	.766	115	6	7	99	71	51	.739	17	7	1	8	C3	1.6
1983	NY-N	4	0	2	0	0	0	0	0	0	0	—	—	—	—	—	0	0	99	—	—	—	0	0	0	0	/R	0.0
1984	NY-N	8	17	6	3	1	0	0	1	4	2	.176	.333	.235	.569	62	-1	-1	100	98	2	.643	1	0	0	0	/C1	0.0
Total	11	810	2681	334	696	152	10	46	312	323	294	.260	.345	.375	.720	102	2	13	97	110	398	.710	91	51	-3	73	C/13O	9.4
■ STEDRONSKY	Stedronsky b:Troy, N.Y. Deb: 9/25/1879																											
1879	Chi-N	4	12	0	1	0	0	0	0	0	3	.083	.083	.083	.167	-43	-2	-2	105	0	0	.091				0	/3	-0.1
■ FARMER STEELMAN	Steelman, Morris James b: 6/29/1875, Millville, N.J. d: 9/16/44, Merchantville, N.J. TR , Deb: 9/15/1899																											
1899	Lou-N	4	15	2	1	0	1	0	2	2		.067	.176	.200	.376	4	-2	-2	103	217	1	.357	0			0	/C	-0.1
1900	Bro-N	1	4	0	0	0	0	0	0	0		.000	.000	.000	.000	-93	-1	-1	108	0	0	.000	0			0	/C	0.0
1901	Bro-N	1	3	0	1	0	0	0	0	0		.333	.333	.333	.667	90	-0	-0	106	0	0	.500	0			0	/C	0.0
	Phi-A	27	88	5	23	2	0	0	7	10		.261	.337	.284	.621	75	-2	-2	100	88	10	.600	4			1	CO	0.0
1902	Phi-A	10	32	1	6	1	0	0	6	2		.188	.235	.219	.454	25	-3	-3	108	283	2	.423	2			1	/CO	-0.2
Total	4	43	142	8	31	3	1	0	15	14		.218	.288	.254	.542	51	-9	-9	103	141	13	.505	6			2	/CO	-0.3
■ JIM STEELS	Steels, James Earl b: 5/30/61, Bentonia, Miss. BL/TL, 5'10", 185 lbs. Deb: 4/06/87																											
1987	SD-N	62	68	9	13	1	1	0	6	11	14	.191	.304	.235	.539	47	-5	-5	97	150	5	.508	3	2	-0	-6	O	-1.1
1988	Tex-A	36	53	4	10	1	0	0	5	0	15	.189	.189	.208	.396	11	-6	-6	101	181	2	.302	2	0	1	-5	O/1D	-1.1
Total	2	98	121	13	23	2	1	0	11	11	29	.190	.258	.223	.481	32	-11	-11	98	162	8	.430	5	2	0	-11	/OD1	-2.2
■ GENE STEERE	Steere, Frederick Eugene b: 8/16/1872, S.Scituate, R.I. d: 3/13/42, San Francisco, Cal Deb: 8/29/1894																											
1894	Pit-N	10	39	3	8	0	0	0	4	2	1	.205	.244	.205	.449	11	-6	-5	94	141	3	.387	2			0	S	-0.3
■ JOHN STEFERO	Stefero, John Robert b: 9/22/59, Sumter, S.C. BL/TR, 5'8", 185 lbs. Deb: 6/24/83																											
1983	Bal-A	9	11	2	5	1	0	0	4	3	2	.455	.571	.545	1.117	209	2	2	100	261	4	1.500	0	0	0	0	/C	0.2
1986	Bal-A	52	120	14	28	2	0	2	13	16	25	.233	.324	.300	.624	73	-4	-4	99	123	12	.553	0	1	-1	-3	C/2	-0.3
1987	Mon-N	18	56	4	11	0	0	1	3	3	17	.196	.237	.250	.487	28	-6	-6	106	70	3	.362	0	0	0	-2	C	-0.6
Total	3	79	187	20	44	3	0	3	20	22	44	.235	.316	.299	.615	67	-8	-8	101	117	19	.534	0	1	-1	-5	/C2	-0.7
■ DAVE STEGMAN	Stegman, David William b: 1/30/54, Inglewood, Cal. BR/TR, 5'11", 190 lbs. Deb: 9/04/78																											
1978	Det-A	8	14	3	4	2	0	1	3	1	2	.286	.333	.643	.976	156	1	1	108	99	2	.909	0	0	0	-1	/O	0.0
1979	Det-A	12	31	6	6	0	0	3	5	2	3	.194	.242	.484	.726	94	-1	-1	96	80	3	.692	1	1	-0	2	O	0.0
1980	Det-A	65	130	12	23	5	0	2	9	14	23	.177	.257	.262	.518	40	-10	-11	105	88	10	.454	1	1	-0	-10	O/D	-2.2
1982	NY-A	2	0	0	0	0	0	0	0	0	0	—	—	—	—	—	0	0	96	—	—	—	0	0	0	0	/D	0.0
1983	Chi-A	30	53	5	9	2	0	0	4	10	9	.170	.302	.208	.509	42	-4	-4	103	142	4	.457	0	1	-1	-6	O	-1.0
1984	Chi-A	55	92	13	24	1	2	2	11	4	18	.261	.306	.380	.687	80	-2	-3	111	107	11	.638	3	0	1	-8	O/D	-1.0
Total	6	172	320	39	66	10	2	8	32	31	55	.206	.280	.325	.605	62	-15	-18	106	102	40	.550	5	3	-0	-23	O/D	-4.2
■ JUSTIN STEIN	Stein, Justin Marion "Ott" b: 8/9/11, St.Louis, Mo. BR/TR, 5'11", 180 lbs. Deb: 5/28/38																											
1938	Phi-N	11	39	6	10	0	1	0	2	2	4	.256	.293	.308	.600	65	-2	-2	100	60	4	.483	0			-0	/32	-0.1
	Cin-N	11	18	3	6	1	0	0	1	0	1	.333	.333	.389	.722	100	-0	-0	98	52	2	.538	0			0	/S2	0.0
	Yr	22	57	9	16	1	1	0	3	2	5	.281	.305	.333	.638	76	-2	-2	99	59	6	.500	0			-0		-0.1
Total	1	22	57	9	16	1	1	0	3	2	5	.281	.305	.333	.638	76	-2	-2	99	58	6	.500	0			-0	/S32	-0.1
■ BILL STEIN	Stein, William Allen b: 1/21/47, Battle Creek, Mich. BR/TR, 5'10", 170 lbs. Deb: 9/06/72																											
1972	StL-N	14	35	2	11	0	1	2	3	0	7	.314	.314	.543	.857	133	1	1	105	49	6	.833	1	0	0	-1	/3O	0.0
1973	StL-N	32	55	4	12	2	0	0	2	7	18	.218	.306	.255	.561	63	-3	-2	91	57	5	.488	0	0	0	-1	O/13	-0.3
1974	Chi-A	13	43	5	12	1	0	0	5	7	8	.279	.380	.302	.682	97	0	0	102	154	5	.588	0	0	0	-0	3/D	0.0
1975	Chi-A	76	226	23	61	7	1	3	21	18	32	.270	.327	.350	.676	88	-3	-4	103	92	25	.578	2	2	-1	-2	23D/O	-0.4
1976	Chi-A	117	392	32	105	15	2	4	36	22	67	.268	.310	.347	.657	93	-4	-4	99	93	41	.552	4	2	0	3	23/1SOD	0.2
1977	Sea-A	151	556	53	144	26	5	13	67	29	79	.259	.302	.394	.696	91	-10	-8	96	105	62	.595	3	4	-2	-11	*3/SD	-2.3
1978	Sea-A	114	403	41	105	24	4	4	37	37	56	.261	.323	.370	.692	93	-3	-4	102	93	48	.607	1	0	0	-5	*3/D	-0.9
1979	Sea-A	88	250	28	62	9	2	7	27	17	28	.248	.301	.384	.685	83	-6	-6	100	89	26	.577	1	2	-1	-0	32/S	-0.4
1980	Sea-A	67	198	16	53	5	1	5	27	16	25	.268	.326	.379	.704	90	-2	-3	103	117	24	.616	1	1	-0	2	32/1D	-0.1
1981	Tex-A	53	115	21	38	6	0	2	22	7	15	.330	.369	.435	.804	144	4	6	91	154	16	.690	1	2	-1	2	1/O32S	0.6
1982	Tex-A	85	184	14	44	8	0	1	16	12	23	.239	.293	.299	.592	68	-9	-7	93	110	16	.479	0	0	0	5	23/S1OD	0.0

YEAR	TM/L	G	AB	R	H	2B	3B	HR	RBI	BB	SO	AVG	OBP	SLG	PRO	/A	BR	/A	PF	CHI	RC	TA	SB	CS	SBR	FR	POS	TPR
1983	Tex-A	78	232	21	72	15	1	2	33	8	31	.310	.333	.409	.743	102	1	0	101	128	30	.625	2	3	-1	2	213/D	0.1
1984	Tex-A	27	43	3	12	1	0	0	3	5	9	.279	.354	.302	.656	84	-1	-1	100	92	5	.563	0	0	0	-1	2/13D	0.0
1985	Tex-A	44	79	5	20	3	1	1	12	1	15	.253	.272	.354	.626	64	-3	-4	108	154	7	.492	0	0	0	0	3/12OD	-0.4
Total	14	959	2811	268	751	122	18	44	311	186	413	.267	.316	.370	.686	91	-39	-36	99	104	315	.605	16	16	-5	-8	32/1DOS	-3.9
■ **TERRY STEINBACH**	Steinbach, Terry Lee b: 3/2/62, New Ulm, Minn. BR/TR, 6'1", 195 lbs. Deb: 9/12/86																											
1986	Oak-A	6	15	3	5	0	0	2	4	1	0	.333	.375	.733	1.108	207	2	2	94	94	4	1.200	0	0	0	-0	/C	0.2
1987	Oak-A	122	391	66	111	16	3	16	56	32	66	.284	.352	.463	.815	126	8	13	91	98	62	.764	1	2	-1	-3	*C3/1D	1.6
1988	Oak-A	104	351	42	93	19	1	9	51	33	47	.265	.338	.402	.740	112	3	6	95	121	47	.675	3	0	1	-8	C1/3OD	0.1
Total	3	232	757	111	209	35	4	27	111	66	113	.276	.346	.440	.786	121	13	21	93	108	113	.742	4	2	0	-11	C/13DO	1.9
■ **HANK STEINBACHER**	Steinbacher, Henry John b: 3/22/13, Sacramento, Cal. d: 4/3/77, Sacramento, Cal. BL/TR, 5'11", 180 lbs. Deb: 4/21/37																											
1937	Chi-A	26	73	13	19	4	1	1	9	4	7	.260	.299	.384	.682	69	-4	-4	103	99	9	.630	2	0	1	-3	O	-0.5
1938	Chi-A	106	399	59	132	23	8	4	61	41	19	.331	.393	.459	.852	115	8	10	98	108	72	.833	1	3	-2	-3	*O	0.4
1939	Chi-A	71	111	16	19	2	1	1	15	21	8	.171	.303	.234	.537	37	-10	-11	107	175	9	.505	0	0	0	-3	O	-1.3
Total	3	203	583	88	170	29	10	6	85	66	34	.292	.364	.407	.770	93	-5	-5	100	120	90	.734	3	3	-1	-9	O	-1.4
■ **GENE STEINBRENNER**	Steinbrenner, Eugene Gass b: 11/17/1892, Pittsburgh, Pa. d: 4/25/70, Pittsburgh, Pa. TR, 5'8.5", 155 lbs. Deb: 4/25/12																											
1912	Phi-N	3	9	0	2	1	0	0	1	0	3	.222	.222	.333	.556	51	-1	-1	100	112	1	.429	0			0	/2	0.0
■ **BILL STEINECKE**	Steinecke, William Robert b: 2/7/07, Cincinnati, Ohio d: 7/29/86, St.Augustine, Fla BR/TR, 5'8.5", 175 lbs. Deb: 9/16/31																											
1931	Pit-N	4	4	0	0	0	0	0	0	0	1	.000	.000	.000	.000	-99	-1	-1	101	0	0	.000	0			0	/C	0.0
■ **BEN STEINER**	Steiner, Benajmin Saunders b: 7/28/21, Alexandria, Va. BL/TR, 5'11", 165 lbs. Deb: 4/17/45																											
1945	Bos-A	78	304	39	78	8	3	3	20	31	29	.257	.327	.332	.660	97	-3	-1	95	63	35	.606	10	6	-1	0	2	0.0
1946	Bos-A	3	4	1	1	0	0	0	0	0	0	.250	.250	.250	.500	35	-0	-0	114	0	0	.333	0	0	0	0	/3	0.0
1947	Det-A	1	0	1	0	0	0	0	0	0	0	—	—	—	—	—	0	0	104	—	—	—	0	0	0	0	R	0.0
Total	3	82	308	41	79	8	3	3	20	31	29	.256	.326	.331	.658	96	-3	-2	95	62	36	.613	10	6	-1	0	/23	0.0
■ **RED STEINER**	Steiner, James Harry b: 1/7/15, Los Angeles, Cal. BL/TR, 6', 185 lbs. Deb: 5/11/45																											
1945	Cle-A	12	20	0	3	0	0	0	2	1	4	.150	.190	.150	.340	-1	-3	-3	99	241	0	.222	0	0	0	0	/C	-0.1
	Bos-A	26	59	6	12	1	0	0	4	14	2	.203	.356	.220	.577	72	-2	-1	95	111	6	.551	0	0	0	-1	C	0.0
	Yr	38	79	6	15	1	0	0	6	15	6	.190	.319	.203	.522	55	-4	-4	96	159	6	.470	0	0	0	-0		-0.1
Total	1	38	79	6	15	1	0	0	6	15	6	.190	.319	.203	.522	55	-4	-4	96	140	6	.470	0	0	0	-0	/C	-0.1
■ **HARRY STEINFELDT**	Steinfeldt, Harry M. b: 9/29/1877, St.Louis, Mo. d: 8/17/14, Bellevue, Ky. BR/TR, 5'9.5", 180 lbs. Deb: 4/22/1898																											
1898	Cin-N	88	308	47	91	18	6	0	43	27		.295	.352	.393	.745	108	6	3	108	110	47	.724	9			0	2O3/S1	0.3
1899	Cin-N	107	386	62	94	16	8	0	43	40		.244	.318	.326	.644	75	-10	-14	106	111	47	.640	19			-12	32/SO	-2.1
1900	Cin-N	134	510	57	125	29	7	2	66	27		.245	.283	.341	.624	80	-19	-13	92	117	55	.558	14			**33**	32/OS	2.2
1901	Cin-N	105	382	40	95	18	7	6	47	28		.249	.300	.380	.680	104	-2	1	95	98	48	.638	10			6	32	1.4
1902	Cin-N	129	479	53	133	20	7	1	49	24		.278	.312	.355	.667	98	3	-2	110	100	58	.595	12			21	*3/O	2.6
1903	Cin-N	118	439	71	137	**32**	12	6	83	47		.312	.379	.481	.859	134	26	20	109	123	84	.874	6			4	*3S	2.4
1904	Cin-N	99	349	35	85	11	6	1	52	29		.244	.302	.318	.620	81	-3	-9	114	170	39	.591	16			-5	3	-0.9
1905	Cin-N	114	384	49	104	16	9	1	39	30		.271	.324	.367	.691	104	3	2	103	96	52	.664	15			9	*3/12O	1.9
1906	Chi-N	151	539	81	**176**	27	10	3	**83**	47		.327	.381	.430	.811	146	33	29	107	133	102	.848	29			-19	*3/2	0.6
1907	Chi-N	152	542	52	144	25	5	1	70	37		.266	.313	.336	.648	99	2	-1	106	152	64	.598	19			-8	*3	-0.9
1908	Chi-N	150	539	63	130	20	6	1	62	36		.241	.289	.306	.595	87	-5	-9	106	150	49	.521	12			-10	*3	-1.6
1909	Chi-N	151	528	73	133	27	6	2	59	57		.252	.331	.337	.668	108	6	5	101	124	64	.663	22			-2	*3	0.7
1910	Chi-N	129	448	70	113	21	1	2	58	36	29	.252	.323	.317	.640	86	-7	-8	101	145	51	.594	10			-0	*3	-0.7
1911	Bos-N	19	63	5	16	4	0	1	8	6	3	.254	.338	.365	.703	94	-0	-1	103	104	8	.681	1			-0	3	0.0
Total	14	1646	5896	758	1576	284	90	27	762	471	32	.267	.324	.360	.683	101	33	5	104	126	768	.650	194			18	*32/OS1	5.9
■ **BILL STELLBAUER**	Stellbauer, William Jennings b: 3/20/1894, Bremond, Tex. d: 2/16/74, New Braunfels, Tex BR/TR, 5'10", 175 lbs. Deb: 4/12/16																											
1916	Phi-A	25	48	2	13	2	1	0	5	6	7	.271	.352	.354	.706	114	1	1	98	105	7	.714	2			-3	O	-0.3
■ **RICK STELMASZEK**	Stelmaszek, Richard Francis b: 10/8/48, Chicago, Ill. BL/TR, 6'1", 195 lbs. Deb: 6/25/71 C																											
1971	Was-A	6	9	0	0	0	0	0	0	0	3	.000	.000	.000	.000	-99	-2	-2	92	0	0	.000	0	0	0	0	/C	-0.1
1973	Tex-A	7	9	0	1	0	0	0	0	1	2	.111	.200	.111	.311	-11	-1	-1	97	0	0	.250	0	0	0	0	/C	0.0
	Cal-A	22	26	2	4	1	0	0	3	6	7	.154	.313	.192	.505	47	-2	-2	96	236	2	.478	0	0	0	-4	C	-0.4
	Yr	29	35	2	5	1	0	0	3	7	9	.143	.286	.171	.457	33	-3	-3	96	179	2	.419	0	0	0	-4		-0.4
1974	Chi-N	25	44	2	10	2	0	1	7	10	6	.227	.370	.341	.711	100	0	0	100	150	6	.694	0	0	0	-1	C	0.0
Total	3	60	88	4	15	3	0	1	10	17	18	.170	.305	.239	.543	55	-5	-5	98	149	8	.507	0	0	0	-5	/C	-0.5
■ **FRED STEM**	Stem, Frederick Boothe b: 9/22/1885, Oxford, N.C. d: 9/5/64, Darlington, S.C. BL/TR, 6'2", 160 lbs. Deb: 9/15/08																											
1908	Bos-N	20	72	9	20	0	1	0	3	2		.278	.297	.306	.603	91	-1	-1	104	53	7	.481	1			1	1	0.0
1909	Bos-N	73	245	13	51	2	3	0	11	12		.208	.254	.241	.495	57	-13	-12	96	69	15	.407	5			6	1	-0.8
Total	2	93	317	22	71	2	4	0	14	14		.224	.263	.256	.519	65	-14	-13	98	66	22	.423	6			7	/1	-0.8
■ **CASEY STENGEL**	Stengel, Charles Dillon "The Old Professor" b: 7/30/1889, Kansas City, Mo. d: 9/29/75, Glendale, Cal. BL/TL, 5'11", 175 lbs. Deb: 9/17/12 MCH																											
1912	Bro-N	17	57	9	18	1	0	1	13	15	9	.316	.466	.386	.852	141	4	4	95	168	13	1.103	5			-1	O	0.2
1913	Bro-N	124	438	60	119	16	8	7	43	56	58	.272	.356	.393	.748	109	8	6	104	83	65	.777	19			8	*O	1.3
1914	Bro-N	126	412	55	130	13	10	4	60	56	55	.316	**.404**	.425	.829	145	26	25	101	119	76	.904	19			-11	*O	1.2
1915	Bro-N	132	459	52	109	20	12	3	50	34	46	.237	.294	.353	.647	94	-3	-4	101	114	48	.567	5	10	-5	-6	*O	-2.0
1916	Bro-N	127	462	66	129	27	8	8	53	33	51	.279	.329	.424	.753	126	15	14	103	98	70	.724	11			-4	*O	0.6
1917	Bro-N	150	549	69	141	23	12	6	73	60	62	.257	.336	.375	.711	114	12	10	104	133	72	.708	18			6	*O	1.2
1918	Pit-N	39	122	18	30	4	1	1	12	16	14	.246	.343	.320	.663	97	1	0	106	108	16	.739	11			1	O	0.0
1919	Pit-N	89	321	38	94	10	10	4	43	35	35	.293	.364	.424	.788	130	15	13	105	108	53	.811	12			1	O	1.1
1920	Phi-N	129	445	53	130	25	6	9	50	38	35	.292	.356	.436	.792	116	15	10	109	89	66	.747	7	13	-6	-3	*O	-0.5
1921	Phi-N	24	59	7	18	3	1	0	4	6	7	.305	.369	.390	.759	99	0	0	102	64	9	.714	1	1	-0	2	O	0.1
	NY-N	18	22	4	5	1	0	0	2	1	5	.227	.261	.273	.534	42	-2	-2	98	122	1	.389	0	1	-1	-3	/O	-0.5
	Yr	42	81	11	23	4	1	0	6	7	12	.284	.341	.358	.699	85	-2	-2	100	90	10	.617	1	2	-1	-1		-0.4
1922	NY-N	84	250	48	92	8	10	7	48	21	17	.368	.436	.564	1.000	151	21	20	104	104	62	1.094	4	2	0	-7	O	1.0
1923	NY-N	75	218	39	74	11	5	5	43	20	18	.339	.400	.505	.905	135	12	11	101	121	45	.945	6	2	1	-3	O	0.7
1924	Bos-N	131	461	57	129	20	6	5	39	45	39	.280	.348	.382	.730	102	-2	2	94	76	61	.687	13	13	-4	-9	*O	-1.3
1925	Bos-N	12	13	0	1	0	0	0	2	1	2	.077	.143	.077	.220	-45	-3	-3	94	711	0	.154	0	1	-1	-0	/O	-0.2
Total	14	1277	4288	575	1219	182	89	60	535	437	453	.284	.356	.410	.766	118	118	106	102	106	654	.760	131	43		-29	*O	2.9
■ **MIKE STENHOUSE**	Stenhouse, Michael Steven b: 5/29/58, Pueblo, Colo. BL/TR, 6'1", 195 lbs. Deb: 10/03/82																											
1982	Mon-N	1	1	0	0	0	0	0	0	0	1	.000	.000	.000	.000	-95	-0	-0	105	0	0	.000	0	0	0	0	/H	0.0
1983	Mon-N	24	40	2	5	1	0	0	2	4	10	.125	.205	.150	.355	-0	-5	-5	102	132	1	.270	0	0	0	-2	/O1	-0.8
1984	Mon-N	80	175	14	32	8	0	4	16	26	32	.183	.292	.297	.589	72	-8	-6	91	98	16	.534	0	0	0	-2	O1	-1.0
1985	Min-A	81	179	23	40	5	0	5	21	29	18	.223	.332	.335	.667	81	-3	-4	103	111	22	.634	1	0	0	-1	DO/1	-0.5
1986	Bos-A	21	21	1	2	1	0	0	1	12	5	.095	.424	.143	.567	65	-0	-0	100	133	3	.750	0	0	0	-0	/O1	0.0
Total	5	207	416	40	79	15	0	9	40	71	66	.190	.309	.291	.600	69	-17	-16	98	109	41	.574	1	0	0	-6	/O1D	-2.3
■ **RENNIE STENNETT**	Stennett, Renaldo Antonio (Porte) b: 4/5/51, Colon, Panama BR/TR, 5'11", 160 lbs. Deb: 7/10/71																											
1971	Pit-N	50	153	24	54	5	4	1	15	7	9	.353	.381	.458	.839	138	7	7	99	84	26	.765	1	1	-0	3	2	1.2
1972	Pit-N	109	370	43	106	14	5	3	30	9	43	.286	.307	.376	.683	91	-4	-5	103	83	37	.544	4	3	-1	10	2O/S	0.6
1973	Pit-N	128	466	45	113	18	3	10	55	16	63	.242	.268	.358	.626	78	-19	-15	92	114	42	.508	2	3	-1	10	2S/O	0.3
1974	Pit-N	157	673	84	196	29	3	7	56	32	51	.291	.325	.374	.700	98	-6	-4	98	70	77	.586	8	9	-3	12	*2/O	1.3
1975	Pit-N	148	616	89	176	25	7	7	62	33	42	.286	.326	.383	.709	97	-4	-4	99	82	74	.606	5	4	-1	13	*2	1.5

YEAR	TM/L	G	AB	R	H	2B	3B	HR	RBI	BB	SO	AVG	OBP	SLG	PRO	/A	BR	/A	PF	CHI	RC	TA	SB	CS	SBR	FR	POS	TPR
1976	Pit-N	157	654	59	168	31	9	2	60	19	32	.257	.279	.341	.620	75	-23	-23	100	107	59	.515	18	6	2	19	*2/S	0.5
1977	Pit-N	116	453	53	152	20	4	5	51	29	24	.336	.378	.430	.809	113	11	9	103	103	71	.779	28	18	-2	-13	*2	0.1
1978	Pit-N	106	333	30	81	9	2	3	35	13	22	.243	.276	.309	.585	60	-17	-19	105	124	26	.458	2	1	0	-1	2/3	-1.5
1979	Pit-N	108	319	31	76	13	2	0	24	24	25	.238	.292	.292	.583	56	-18	-20	106	102	25	.457	1	4	-2	3	*2	-1.2
1980	SF-N	120	397	34	97	13	2	2	37	22	31	.244	.287	.302	.590	68	-19	-17	96	116	32	.471	4	4	-1	-9	*2	-2.0
1981	SF-N	38	87	8	20	0	0	1	7	3	6	.230	.264	.264	.528	48	-6	-6	105	106	6	.408	2	1	0	-1	2	-0.6
Total	11	1237	4521	500	1239	177	41	41	432	207	348	.274	.308	.359	.667	85	-98	-96	100	97	475	.575	75	54	-10	45	*2/SO3	0.2

■ JAKE STENZEL Stenzel, Jacob Charles (born Jacob Charles Stelzle) b: 6/24/1867, Cincinnati, Ohio d: 1/6/1919, Cincinnati, Ohio BR/TR, 5'10", 168 lbs. Deb. 6/16/1890

YEAR	TM/L	G	AB	R	H	2B	3B	HR	RBI	BB	SO	AVG	OBP	SLG	PRO	/A	BR	/A	PF	CHI	RC	TA	SB	CS	SBR	FR	POS	TPR
1890	Chi-N	11	41	3	11	1	0	0	3	1	0	.268	.286	.293	.578	65	-2	-2	109	75	4	.433	0			0	/OC	-0.1
1892	Pit-N	3	9	0	0	0	0	0	0	1	3	.000	.100	.000	.100	-73	-2	-2	94	0	0	.222	1			0	/OC	-0.1
1893	Pit-N	60	224	57	81	13	4	4	37	24	17	.362	.423	.509	.932	140	16	13	106	80	56	1.077	16			-1	OC/S2	0.8
1894	Pit-N	131	522	148	185	39	20	13	121	75	13	.354	.441	.580	1.022	156	40	46	94	86	165	1.320	61			-4	*O	2.5
1895	Pit-N	129	514	114	192	38	13	7	97	57	25	.374	.447	.539	.986	161	44	47	97	80	151	1.236	53			-7	*O	2.3
1896	Pit-N	114	479	104	173	26	14	2	82	32	13	.361	.409	.486	.896	148	26	31	93	95	122	1.075	57			-4	*O/1	1.6
1897	Bal-N	131	536	113	189	**43**	7	5	116	36		.353	.404	.487	.891	144	28	32	95	130	137	1.084	69			-11	*O	1.0
1898	Bal-N	35	138	33	35	5	2	0	22	12		.254	.340	.319	.659	89	-1	-2	103	145	17	.641	4			-3	O	-0.5
	StL-N	108	404	64	114	15	11	1	33	41		.282	.365	.381	.747	110	10	6	106	61	66	.786	21			-3	*O	-0.2
	Yr	143	542	97	149	20	13	1	55	53		.275	.359	.365	.724	105	9	5	105	83	82	.748	25			-5		-0.7
1899	StL-N	35	128	21	35	9	0	1	19	16		.273	.367	.367	.735	97	1	-0	108	123	21	.796	8			0	O	0.0
	Cin-N	9	29	5	9	1	0	0	3	4		.310	.412	.345	.757	105	1	1	106	94	5	.850	2			0	/O	0.0
	Yr	44	157	26	44	10	0	1	22	20		.280	.376	.363	.739	98	2	0	107	120	26	.805	10			0		0.0
Total	9	766	3024	662	1024	190	71	33	533	299	71	.339	.408	.481	.889	138	160	171	98	94	742	1.051	292			-33	O/C12S	7.3

■ GENE STEPHENS Stephens, Glen Eugene b: 1/20/33, Gravette, Ark. BL/TR, 6'3.5", 175 lbs. Deb: 4/16/52

YEAR	TM/L	G	AB	R	H	2B	3B	HR	RBI	BB	SO	AVG	OBP	SLG	PRO	/A	BR	/A	PF	CHI	RC	TA	SB	CS	SBR	FR	POS	TPR
1952	Bos-A	21	53	10	12	5	0	0	5	3	8	.226	.268	.321	.589	59	-3	-3	107	110	4	.545	4	2	0	-1	O	-0.4
1953	Bos-A	78	221	30	45	6	2	3	18	29	56	.204	.302	.290	.591	55	-12	-15	109	91	22	.544	3	3	-1	-11	O	-2.8
1955	Bos-A	109	157	25	46	9	4	3	18	20	34	.293	.380	.459	.838	100	6	0	124	83	29	.839	0	0	0	-13	O	-1.6
1956	Bos-A	104	63	22	17	2	0	1	7	12	12	.270	.387	.349	.736	93	0	-0	103	105	9	.708	0	1	-1	-19	O	-2.2
1957	Bos-A	120	173	25	46	6	4	3	26	26	20	.266	.362	.399	.761	98	2	0	110	132	26	.731	0	2	-1	-20	O	-2.7
1958	Bos-A	134	270	38	59	10	1	9	25	22	46	.219	.280	.363	.643	72	-10	-11	105	80	27	.560	1	2	-1	-13	*O	-3.4
1959	Bos-A	92	270	34	75	13	1	3	39	29	33	.278	.356	.367	.723	94	0	-2	106	142	38	.685	5	2	0	1	O	-0.4
1960	Bos-A	35	109	9	25	4	0	2	11	14	22	.229	.317	.321	.638	71	-4	-4	103	105	13	.635	5	1	1	-0	O	-0.4
	Bal-A	84	193	38	46	11	0	5	11	25	25	.238	.329	.373	.702	88	-3	-3	102	49	26	.685	4	2	0	-3	O	-0.9
	Yr	119	302	47	71	15	0	7	22	39	47	.235	.325	.354	.679	82	-7	-8	102	67	39	.667	9	3	1	-4		-1.3
1961	Bal-A	32	58	4	11	2	0	0	2	14	7	.190	.347	.224	.571	58	-3	-3	97	60	6	.583	1	1	-0	-4	O	-0.7
	KC-A	62	183	22	38	6	1	4	26	16	27	.208	.279	.317	.596	58	-11	-11	102	145	17	.530	3	2	-0	5	O	-0.8
	Yr	94	241	26	49	8	1	4	28	30	34	.203	.297	.295	.591	58	-14	-14	100	117	23	.543	4	3	-1	1		-1.5
1962	KC-A	5	4	0	0	0	0	0	0	1	1	.000	.200	.000	.200	-41	-1	-1	100	0	0	.250	0	0	0	0	H	0.0
1963	Chi-A	6	18	5	7	0	0	1	2	1	3	.389	.421	.556	.977	164	2	2	104	64	4	1.000	0	0	0	1	/O	0.2
1964	Chi-A	82	141	21	33	4	2	3	17	21	28	.234	.341	.355	.696	98	-1	0	96	122	18	.667	1	2	-1	-4	O	-0.6
Total	12	964	1913	283	460	78	15	37	207	233	322	.240	.327	.355	.682	81	-37	-51	106	103	239	.647	27	20	-4	-83	O	-16.7

■ JIM STEPHENS Stephens, James Walter "Little Nemo" b: 12/10/1883, Salineville, Ohio d: 1/2/65, Oxford, Ala. BR/TR, 5'6.5", 157 lbs. Deb: 4/11/07

YEAR	TM/L	G	AB	R	H	2B	3B	HR	RBI	BB	SO	AVG	OBP	SLG	PRO	/A	BR	/A	PF	CHI	RC	TA	SB	CS	SBR	FR	POS	TPR
1907	StL-A	58	173	15	35	6	3	0	11	15		.202	.266	.272	.538	75	-5	-5	98	84	14	.471	3			0	C	0.0
1908	StL-A	47	150	14	30	4	1	0	6	9		.200	.245	.240	.485	58	-6	-7	103	63	8	.375	0			4	C	0.1
1909	StL-A	79	223	18	49	5	0	3	18	13		.220	.278	.283	.561	84	-6	-4	92	96	18	.494	5			6	C	0.8
1910	StL-A	99	289	24	62	3	7	0	23	16		.215	.261	.273	.534	71	-11	-10	94	108	22	.436	2			10	C	1.1
1911	StL-A	70	212	11	49	5	5	0	17	17		.231	.300	.302	.602	72	-9	-8	95	90	19	.528	1			4	C	0.4
1912	StL-A	74	205	13	51	7	5	0	22	7		.249	.274	.332	.605	74	-8	-8	99	108	19	.506	3			1	C	0.0
Total	6	427	1252	95	276	30	21	3	97	77		.220	.272	.285	.557	73	-46	-41	96	94	100	.470	14			25	C	2.4

■ VERN STEPHENS Stephens, Vernon Decatur "Junior" or "Buster" b: 10/23/20, Mc Alister, N.Mex. d: 11/3/68, Long Beach, Cal. BR/TR, 5'10", 185 lbs. Deb: 9/13/41

YEAR	TM/L	G	AB	R	H	2B	3B	HR	RBI	BB	SO	AVG	OBP	SLG	PRO	/A	BR	/A	PF	CHI	RC	TA	SB	CS	SBR	FR	POS	TPR
1941	StL-A	3	2	0	1	0	0	0	0	0	0	.500	.500	.500	1.000	165	0	0	100	0	1	1.000	0	0	0	0	/S	0.0
1942	StL-A	145	575	84	169	26	6	14	92	41	53	.294	.341	.433	.774	112	10	8	104	118	83	.686	1	3	-2	-11	*S	0.2
1943	StL-A	137	512	75	148	27	3	22	91	54	73	.289	.357	.482	.839	144	26	26	100	112	90	.806	3	2	-0	-21	*SO	0.6
1944	StL-A	145	559	91	164	32	1	20	**109**	62	54	.293	.365	.462	.826	133	25	23	102	131	101	.808	2	2	-1	-5	*S	2.7
1945	StL-A	149	571	90	165	27	3	**24**	89	55	70	.289	.352	.473	.825	120	25	15	115	100	98	.785	2	1	0	-17	*S/3	0.4
1946	StL-A	115	450	67	138	19	4	14	64	35	49	.307	.357	.460	.817	130	15	16	98	104	73	.745	0	1	-1	1	*S	1.8
1947	StL-A	150	562	74	157	18	4	15	83	70	61	.279	.359	.406	.765	110	9	8	102	119	88	.736	8	4	0	14	*S	2.3
1948	Bos-A	155	635	114	171	25	8	29	137	77	56	.269	.350	.471	.821	117	12	12	100	115	103	.775	1	0	0	10	*S	2.3
1949	Bos-A	155	610	113	177	31	2	39	**159**	101	73	.290	.391	.539	.930	135	37	31	107	129	132	.952	2	2	-1	3	*S	3.4
1950	Bos-A	149	628	125	185	34	6	30	**144**	65	43	.295	.361	.511	.872	106	16	3	114	128	114	.834	1	0	0	4	*S	1.4
1951	Bos-A	109	377	62	113	21	2	17	78	38	33	.300	.364	.501	.865	123	15	11	108	116	62	.792	1	2	-1	20	3/S	2.7
1952	Bos-A	92	295	35	75	13	2	7	44	39	31	.254	.343	.383	.726	95	1	-2	107	123	40	.674	2	2	-1	3	S3	0.4
1953	Chi-A	44	129	14	24	6	0	1	14	13	18	.186	.261	.256	.516	38	-11	-12	106	144	9	.444	2	0	1	-1	3/S	-1.3
	StL-A	46	165	16	53	8	0	4	17	18	24	.321	.388	.442	.830	116	6	4	107	75	28	.765	0	0	0	-3	3	0.0
	Yr	90	294	30	77	14	0	5	31	31	42	.262	.332	.361	.693	82	-5	-8	106	110	37	.621	2	0	1	-3		-1.3
1954	Bal-A	101	365	31	104	17	1	8	46	17	36	.285	.317	.403	.719	101	-3	-1	95	104	46	.612	0	3	-2	-6	3	-1.5
1955	Bal-A	3	6	0	1	0	0	0	0	0	0	.167	.286	.167	.452	27	-1	-1	90	0	0	.400	0	0	0	0	/3	0.0
	Chi-A	22	56	10	14	3	0	3	7	7	11	.250	.333	.464	.798	112	1	1	101	75	9	.767	0	0	0	-1	3	0.1
	Yr	25	62	10	15	3	0	3	7	7	11	.242	.329	.435	.764	105	0	0	99	66	9	.729	0	0	0	-1		0.0
Total	15	1720	6497	1001	1859	307	42	247	1174	692	685	.286	.355	.460	.816	118	184	144	105	116	1076	.797	25	22	-6	-9	*S3/O	15.4

■ RIGGS STEPHENSON Stephenson, Jackson Riggs "Old Hoss" b: 1/5/1898, Akron, Ala. d: 11/15/85, Tuscaloosa, Ala. BR/TR, 5'10", 185 lbs. Deb: 4/13/21

YEAR	TM/L	G	AB	R	H	2B	3B	HR	RBI	BB	SO	AVG	OBP	SLG	PRO	/A	BR	/A	PF	CHI	RC	TA	SB	CS	SBR	FR	POS	TPR
1921	Cle-A	65	206	45	68	17	2	2	34	23	15	.330	.408	.461	.869	122	7	7	99	115	40	.906	4	1	1	-7	2/3	0.3
1922	Cle-A	86	233	47	79	24	5	2	32	27	18	.339	.421	.511	.932	139	15	14	102	92	52	1.006	3	0	1	-4	32/O	1.6
1923	Cle-A	91	301	48	96	20	6	5	65	15	25	.319	.357	.475	.832	117	6	6	101	141	50	.795	6	5	-1	6	2/O3	1.2
1924	Cle-A	71	240	33	89	20	0	4	44	27	10	.371	.439	.504	.943	148	16	17	97	109	53	.987	1	2	-1	-13	2/O	0.4
1925	Cle-A	19	54	8	16	3	1	1	9	7	3	.296	.387	.444	.832	104	1	0	106	112	10	.846	1	1	-0	0	O	0.0
1926	Chi-N	82	281	40	95	18	3	3	44	31	16	.338	.404	.456	.859	123	13	11	106	113	51	.866	2			-8	O	0.0
1927	Chi-N	152	579	101	199	**46**	9	7	82	65	28	.344	.415	.491	.906	142	36	36	100	100	117	.955	8			-0	*O/3	2.9
1928	Chi-N	137	512	75	166	36	9	8	90	68	29	.324	.407	.477	.883	138	24	28	95	127	99	.934	8			-2	*O	2.0
1929	Chi-N	136	495	91	179	36	6	17	110	67	21	.362	.445	.562	1.006	146	39	38	101	117	123	1.146	10			-6	*O	1.8
1930	Chi-N	109	341	56	125	21	1	5	68	32	20	.367	.421	.478	.899	111	11	8	105	132	67	.912	2			-8	O	-0.4
1931	Chi-N	80	263	34	84	14	4	1	52	37	14	.319	.405	.414	.820	126	9	11	96	165	47	.827	1			-6	O	0.1
1932	Chi-N	147	583	86	189	49	4	4	85	54	27	.324	.383	.443	.826	117	19	16	104	124	102	.805	3			-11	*O	-0.5
1933	Chi-N	97	346	45	114	17	4	4	51	34	16	.329	.397	.436	.834	142	18	19	97	120	60	.799	5			-3	O	1.1
1934	Chi-N	38	74	5	16	0	0	0	7	7	5	.216	.293	.216	.509	39	-6	-6	98	158	5	.400	0			1	O	-0.5
Total	14	1310	4508	714	1515	321	54	63	773	494	247	.336	.407	.473	.880	129	208	205	100	121	876	.906	54	9		-60	O2/3	10.0

■ JOHN STEPHENSON Stephenson, John Herman b: 4/13/41, S.Portsmouth, Ky. BL/TR, 5'11", 180 lbs. Deb: 4/14/64

YEAR	TM/L	G	AB	R	H	2B	3B	HR	RBI	BB	SO	AVG	OBP	SLG	PRO	/A	BR	/A	PF	CHI	RC	TA	SB	CS	SBR	FR	POS	TPR
1964	NY-N	37	57	2	9	0	0	1	2	4	18	.158	.226	.211	.436	25	-6	-5	95	55	3	.354	0	0	0	-2	3/O	-0.8
1965	NY-N	62	121	9	26	5	0	4	15	8	19	.215	.264	.355	.619	73	-5	-5	100	113	9	.495	0	1	-1	-5	C/O	-0.8
1966	NY-N	63	143	17	28	1	1	1	11	8	28	.196	.248	.238	.486	38	-12	-11	94	125	7	.361	0	0	0	-4	C/O	-1.4
1967	Chi-N	18	49	3	11	3	1	0	5	1	6	.224	.255	.327	.581	64	-2	-2	102	129	4	.462	0	0	0	1	C	0.0
1968	Chi-N	2	2	0	0	0	0	0	0	0	0	.000	.000	.000	.000	-89	-0	-0	112	0	0	.000	0	0	0	0	H	0.0

YEAR	TM/L	G	AB	R	H	2B	3B	HR	RBI	BB	SO	AVG	OBP	SLG	PRO	/A	BR	/A	PF	CHI	RC	TA	SB	CS	SBR	FR	POS	TPR
1969	SF-N	22	27	2	6	2	0	0	3	0	4	.222	.222	.296	.519	44	-2	-2	101	150	1	.348	0	0	0	-0	/C3	-0.1
1970	SF-N	23	43	3	3	1	0	0	6	2	7	.070	.111	.093	.204	-47	-9	-9	96	582	0	.146	0	0	0	0	/CO	-0.7
1971	Cal-A	98	279	24	61	17	0	3	25	22	21	.219	.283	.312	.595	69	-12	-11	99	106	24	.493	0	0	0	-12	C	-2.0
1972	Cal-A	66	146	14	40	3	1	2	17	11	8	.274	.342	.349	.691	120	1	3	88	125	16	.584	0	0	0	-8	C	-0.4
1973	Cal-A	60	122	9	30	5	0	1	9	7	7	.246	.292	.311	.604	73	-5	-4	96	86	11	.479	0	0	0	-16	C	-1.9
Total	10	451	989	83	214	37	3	12	93	63	118	.216	.272	.296	.568	63	-52	-47	96	129	75	.472	0	1	-1	-45	C/3O	-8.1
■ JOE STEPHENSON	Stephenson, Joseph Chester b: 6/30/21, Detroit, Mich. BR/TR, 6'2", 185 lbs. Deb: 9/19/43																											
1943	NY-N	9	24	4	6	1	0	0	1	0	5	.250	.250	.292	.542	59	-1	-1	96	52	2	.389	0			0	/C	0.0
1944	Chi-N	4	8	1	1	0	0	0	0	1	3	.125	.222	.125	.347	-0	-1	-1	101	0	0	.375	1			0	/C	0.0
1947	Chi-A	16	35	3	5	0	0	0	3	1	7	.143	.211	.143	.353	-1	-5	-5	97	221	1	.267	0	0	0	-0	C	-0.3
Total	3	29	67	8	12	1	0	0	4	2	15	.179	.225	.194	.419	20	-7	-7	97	136	3	.327	1	0		-0	/C	-0.3
■ DUMMY STEPHENSON	Stephenson, Reuben Crandol b: 9/22/1869, Petersburg, N.J. d: 12/1/24, Trenton, N.J. 5'11.5", 180 lbs. Deb: 9/09/1892																											
1892	Phi-N	8	37	4	10	3	0	0	5	0	2	.270	.289	.351	.641	91	-0	-1	104	102	4	.519	0			0	/O	0.0
■ BOB STEPHENSON	Stephenson, Robert Lloyd b: 8/11/28, Blair, Okla. BR/TR, 6', 165 lbs. Deb: 4/14/55																											
1955	StL-N	67	111	19	27	3	0	0	6	5	18	.243	.276	.270	.546	45	-9	-9	101	81	8	.416	2	1	0	0	S/23	-0.5
■ WALTER STEPHENSON	Stephenson, Walter Mc Queen "Tarzan" b: 3/27/11, Saluda, N.C. BR/TR, 6', 180 lbs. Deb: 4/29/35																											
1935	Chi-N	16	26	2	10	1	1	0	2	1	5	.385	.407	.500	.907	144	2	2	99	55	6	.875	0			0	/C	0.1
1936	Chi-N	6	12	0	1	0	0	0	1	0	5	.083	.083	.083	.167	-52	-3	-3	105	354	0	.083	0			0	/C	-0.1
1937	Phi-N	10	23	1	6	0	0	0	2	2	3	.261	.320	.261	.581	55	-1	-1	108	120	2	.444	0			0	/C	0.0
Total	3	32	61	3	17	1	1	0	5	3	13	.279	.313	.328	.640	70	-2	-3	104	137	7	.511	0			0	/C	0.0
■ DUTCH STERRETT	Sterrett, Charles Hurlbut b: 10/1/1889, Milroy, Pa. d: 12/ 8, 5 Baltimore, Md. BR/TR, 5'11.5", 165 lbs. Deb: 6/20/12																											
1912	NY-A	66	230	30	61	4	7	1	32	11		.265	.310	.357	.667	89	-4	-4	101	128	28	.621	8			-2	O1C/2	-0.6
1913	NY-A	21	35	0	6	0	0	0	3	1	5	.171	.216	.171	.388	14	-4	-4	101	178	1	.310	1			0	/1C	-0.3
Total	2	87	265	30	67	4	7	1	35	12	5	.253	.298	.332	.630	80	-7	-8	101	135	29	.576	9			-2	/O1C2	-0.9
■ CHUCK STEVENS	Stevens, Charles Augustus b: 7/10/18, Van Houten, N.Mex BB/TL, 6'1", 180 lbs. Deb: 9/16/41																											
1941	StL-A	4	13	2	2	0	0	0	2	0	1	.154	.154	.154	.308	-18	-2	-2	100	354	0	.182	0	0	0	0	/1	-0.1
1946	StL-A	122	432	53	107	17	4	3	27	47	62	.248	.324	.326	.651	84	-10	-9	98	70	46	.567	4	6	-2	3	*1	-1.5
1948	StL-A	85	287	34	75	12	4	1	26	41	26	.261	.354	.341	.695	81	-5	-8	106	89	39	.650	2	2	-1	-0	1	-0.4
Total	3	211	732	89	184	29	8	4	55	88	89	.251	.333	.329	.663	81	-17	-19	101	82	86	.603	6	8	-3	3	1	-2.0
■ ED STEVENS	Stevens, Edward Lee "Big Ed" b: 1/12/25, Galveston, Tex. BL/TL, 6'1", 190 lbs. Deb: 8/09/45																											
1945	Bro-N	55	201	29	55	14	3	4	29	32	20	.274	.376	.433	.809	130	7	8	96	104	35	.805	0			-1	1	0.5
1946	Bro-N	103	310	34	75	13	7	10	60	27	44	.242	.303	.426	.728	103	0	-1	103	138	40	.674	2			-1	1	-0.9
1947	Bro-N	5	13	0	2	1	0	0	0	1	5	.154	.214	.231	.445	17	-2	-2	105	0	1	.364	0			0	/1	-0.1
1948	Pit-N	128	429	47	109	19	6	10	69	35	53	.254	.313	.396	.710	87	-7	-9	104	129	54	.647	4			6	*1	-0.3
1949	Pit-N	67	221	22	58	10	1	4	32	22	24	.262	.332	.371	.703	88	-4	-4	101	128	29	.642	1			4	1	0.0
1950	Pit-N	17	46	2	9	2	0	0	3	4	5	.196	.260	.239	.499	31	-5	-5	103	105	3	.395	0			0	1	-0.4
Total	6	375	1220	134	308	59	17	28	193	121	151	.252	.322	.398	.719	95	-9	-11	102	125	162	.676	7			8	1	-1.2
■ R. C. STEVENS	Stevens, R C b: 7/22/34, Moultrie, Ga. BL/TR, 6'5", 219 lbs. Deb: 4/15/58																											
1958	Pit-N	59	90	16	24	3	1	7	18	5	25	.267	.320	.556	.875	133	3	3	95	105	17	.864	0	0	0	-0	1	0.0
1959	Pit-N	3	7	2	2	0	0	1	1	0	0	.286	.286	.714	1.000	151	0	0	103	50	1	1.000	0	0	0	0	/1	0.0
1960	Pit-N	9	3	1	0	0	0	0	0	0	1	.000	.000	.000	.000	-99	-1	-1	99	0	0	.000	0	0	0	0	/1	0.0
1961	Was-A	33	62	2	8	1	0	0	2	7	15	.129	.217	.145	.363	-1	-9	-8	95	87	2	.298	1	0	0	-0	1	-1.0
Total	4	104	162	21	34	4	1	8	21	12	41	.210	.273	.395	.668	79	-6	-5	95	94	20	.603	1	0	0	-1	/1	-1.0
■ BOBBY STEVENS	Stevens, Robert Jordan b: 4/17/07, Chevy Chase, Md. BL/TR, 5'8", 149 lbs. Deb: 7/03/31																											
1931	Phi-N	12	35	3	12	0	0	0	4	2	2	.343	.410	.343	.753	98	1	0	106	119	5	.696	0			0	S	0.1
■ ACE STEWART	Stewart, Asa b: 2/14/1869, Terre Haute, Ind. d: 4/17/12, Terre Haute, Ind. BR/TR, 5'10", 176 lbs. Deb: 4/18/1895																											
1895	Chi-N	97	365	52	88	8	10	8	76	39	40	.241	.314	.384	.698	79	-11	-13	103	132	50	.697	14			-10	*2	-1.3
■ TUFFY STEWART	Stewart, Charles Eugene b: 7/31/1883, Chicago, Ill. d: 11/18/34, Chicago, Ill. BL/TL, 5'10", 167 lbs. Deb: 8/08/13																											
1913	Chi-N	9	8	1	1	1	0	0	2	2	5	.125	.300	.250	.550	59	-0	-0	99	363	1	.714	1			0	/O	0.0
1914	Chi-N	2	1	0	0	0	0	0	0	0	0	.000	.000	.000	.000	-99	-0	-0	98	0	0	.000	0			0	H	0.0
Total	2	11	9	1	1	1	0	0	2	2	5	.111	.273	.222	.495	43	-1	-1	99	330	1	.625	1			0	/O	0.0
■ BUD STEWART	Stewart, Edward Perry b: 6/15/16, Sacramento, Cal. BL/TR, 5'11", 160 lbs. Deb: 4/19/41																											
1941	Pit-N	73	172	27	46	7	0	0	10	12	17	.267	.315	.308	.623	74	-5	-6	103	68	18	.535	3			-1	O	-0.8
1942	Pit-N	82	183	21	40	8	4	0	20	22	16	.219	.302	.306	.608	78	-5	-5	101	132	18	.548	2			-3	O3/2	-0.8
1948	NY-A	6	5	1	1	1	0	0	0	0	0	.200	.200	.400	.600	57	-0	-0	100	0	0	.500	0	0	0	0	H	0.0
	Was-A	118	401	56	112	17	13	7	69	49	27	.279	.361	.439	.800	109	6	4	103	121	66	.778	8	9	-3	-1	*O	-0.3
	Yr	124	406	57	113	18	13	7	69	49	27	.278	.359	.438	.797	108	6	4	103	115	66	.775	8	9	-3	-1		-0.3
1949	Was-A	118	388	58	110	23	4	8	43	49	33	.284	.368	.425	.793	120	5	10	91	78	65	.780	6	4	-1	-4	*O	0.2
1950	Was-A	118	378	46	101	15	6	4	35	46	33	.267	.348	.370	.719	85	-9	-8	99	79	53	.676	5	4	-1	-1	*O	-1.0
1951	Chi-A	95	217	40	60	13	5	6	40	29	9	.276	.367	.465	.832	128	7	8	97	120	36	.792	1	6	-3	-7	O	-0.3
1952	Chi-A	92	225	23	60	10	0	5	30	28	17	.267	.350	.378	.728	103	1	1	100	112	34	.705	3	0	1	-6	O	-0.5
1953	Chi-A	53	59	16	16	2	0	2	13	14	3	.271	.411	.407	.818	115	2	2	106	160	11	.886	1	0	0	-5	O	-0.2
1954	Chi-A	18	13	0	1	0	0	0	0	3	2	.077	.250	.077	.327	-7	-2	-2	104	0	0	.267	0	0	0	-0	/O	-0.1
Total	9	773	2041	288	547	96	32	32	260	252	157	.268	.351	.393	.744	101	-0	3	99	101	301	.719	29	23		-27	O/32	-3.8
■ GLEN STEWART	Stewart, Glen Weldon "Gabby" b: 9/29/12, Tullahoma, Tenn. BR/TR, 6', 175 lbs. Deb: 6/26/40																											
1940	NY-N	15	29	1	4	1	0	0	0	1	2	.138	.167	.172	.339	-6	-4	-4	100	0	1	.222	0			0	/3S	-0.3
1943	Phi-N	110	336	23	71	10	1	2	24	32	41	.211	.284	.265	.549	63	-17	-15	94	91	26	.454	1			-22	S2/1C	-3.1
1944	Phi-N	118	377	32	83	11	5	0	29	28	40	.220	.274	.276	.550	55	-22	-23	100	100	27	.429	0			0	3S/2	-1.4
Total	3	243	742	56	158	22	6	2	53	61	83	.213	.275	.267	.541	56	-44	-42	97	92	54	.438	1			-22	S/321C	-4.8
■ JIMMY STEWART	Stewart, James Franklin b: 6/11/39, Opelika, Ala. BB/TR, 6', 165 lbs. Deb: 9/03/63																											
1963	Chi-N	13	37	1	11	2	0	0	1	1	7	.297	.316	.351	.667	87	-0	-1	105	32	4	.556	1	1	-0	0	/S2	0.0
1964	Chi-N	132	415	59	105	17	0	3	33	49	61	.253	.335	.316	.650	80	-7	-10	105	97	47	.594	10	8	-2	7	2S/O3	0.4
1965	Chi-N	116	282	26	63	9	4	0	19	30	53	.223	.303	.284	.586	65	-12	-13	102	98	27	.556	13	3	2	-3	OS	-1.0
1966	Chi-N	57	90	4	16	4	1	0	4	7	12	.178	.253	.244	.497	39	-7	-7	100	76	6	.416	1	1	-0	1	O/2S3	-0.6
1967	Chi-N	6	6	1	1	0	0	0	1	0	0	.167	.167	.167	.333	-4	-1	-1	102	414	0	.200	0	0	0	0	H	0.0
	Chi-A	24	18	5	3	0	0	0	1	1	6	.167	.211	.167	.377	14	-2	-2	94	139	1	.333	1	0	0	-2	/O2S	-0.2
1969	Cin-N	119	221	26	56	3	4	4	24	19	33	.253	.313	.357	.670	88	-4	-4	99	106	25	.600	4	2	0	-10	O2/3S	-1.6
1970	Cin-N	101	105	15	28	3	1	1	8	8	13	.267	.325	.343	.667	76	-3	-4	104	80	12	.610	5	3	-0	-15	O2/3C1	-1.9
1971	Cin-N	80	82	7	19	2	2	0	9	9	12	.232	.308	.305	.613	77	-3	-2	96	147	8	.561	3	1	0	-7	O/32	-0.9
1972	Hou-N	68	96	14	21	5	2	0	9	6	9	.219	.265	.313	.577	60	-5	-5	106	123	8	.474	0	1	-1	-3	O/123	-1.0
1973	Hou-N	61	68	6	13	0	0	0	3	9	12	.191	.295	.191	.486	39	-5	-5	95	93	5	.411	0	0	0	-1	/3O2	-0.5
Total	10	777	1420	164	336	45	14	8	112	139	218	.237	.308	.305	.613	71	-49	-53	102	100	142	.559	38	20	-1	-32	O2S/31C	-7.3
■ STUFFY STEWART	Stewart, John Franklin b: 1/31/1894, Jasper, Fla. d: 12/30/80, Lake City, Fla. BR/TR, 5'9.5", 160 lbs. Deb: 9/03/16																											
1916	StL-N	9	17	0	3	0	0	0	1	0	3	.176	.176	.176	.353	9	-2	-2	97	132	1	.214	0			1	/2	0.0
1917	StL-N	13	9	4	0	0	0	0	0	0	4	.000	.000	.000	.000	-98	-2	-2	102	0	0	.000	0			-2	/O2	-0.4
1922	Pit-N	3	13	3	2	0	0	0	0	0	1	.154	.154	.154	.308	-20	-2	-2	104	0	0	.182	0	0	0	-1	/2	-0.2
1923	Bro-N	4	11	3	4	1	0	1	1	1	1	.364	.417	.727	1.144	201	1	1	98	32	3	1.286	0	0	0	0	/2	0.1

YEAR	TM/L	G	AB	R	H	2B	3B	HR	RBI	BB	SO	AVG	OBP	SLG	PRO	/A	BR	/A	PF	CHI	RC	TA	SB	CS	SBR	FR	POS	TPR
1925	Was-A	7	17	3	6	1	0	0	3	1	2	.353	.389	.412	.801	105	0	0	98	143	3	.818	1	0	0	0	/32	0.1
1926	Was-A	62	63	27	17	6	1	0	9	6	6	.270	.333	.397	.730	92	-1	-1	98	122	8	.780	8	4	0	-0	2/3	0.0
1927	Was-A	56	129	24	31	6	2	0	4	8	15	.240	.285	.318	.603	58	-9	-8	97	32	12	.622	12	0	4	0	2/3	-0.5
1929	Was-A	22	6	10	0	0	0	0	0	1	0	.000	.143	.000	.143	-60	-1	-1	100	0	0	.143	0	1	-1	0	/2	-0.1
Total	8	176	265	74	63	14	3	1	18	17	32	.238	.284	.325	.608	61	-16	-15	98	64	27	.599	21	5		-2	/23O	-1.0
■ MARK STEWART	Stewart, Mark "Big Slick" b: 10/11/1889, Whitlock, Tenn. d: 1/17/32, Memphis, Tenn. BL/TR, 6'1", 180 lbs. Deb: 10/04/13																											
1913	Cin-N	1	1	0	0	0	0	0	0	0	0	.000	.000	.000	.000	-98	-0	-0	102	0	0	.000	0			0	/C	0.0
■ NEB STEWART	Stewart, Walter Nesbitt b: 5/21/18, S.Charleston, Ohio BR/TR, 6'1", 195 lbs. Deb: 9/08/40																											
1940	Phi-N	10	31	3	4	0	0	0	0	1	5	.129	.156	.129	.285	-21	-5	-5	97	0	1	.179	0			1	/O	-0.4
■ BILL STEWART	Stewart, William Wayne b: 4/15/28, Bay City, Mich. BR/TR, 5'11", 200 lbs. Deb: 4/17/55																											
1955	KC-A	11	18	2	2	1	0	0	0	1	6	.111	.158	.167	.325	-13	-3	-3	101	0	1	.250	0	0	0	-0	/O	-0.3
■ ROYLE STILLMAN	Stillman, Royle Eldon b: 1/2/51, Santa Monica, Cal. BL/TL, 5'11", 180 lbs. Deb: 6/22/75																											
1975	Bal-A	13	14	1	6	0	0	0	1	1	3	.429	.467	.429	.895	170	1	1	91	64	3	.875	0	0	0	-0	/O	0.1
1976	Bal-A	20	22	0	2	0	0	0	1	3	4	.091	.200	.091	.291	-13	-3	-3	98	192	1	.250	0	0	0	0	/1D	-0.2
1977	Chi-A	56	119	18	25	7	1	3	13	17	21	.210	.309	.361	.670	82	-3	-3	99	99	14	.646	2	1	0	-3	OD/1	-0.6
Total	3	89	155	19	33	7	1	3	15	21	28	.213	.307	.329	.636	77	-5	-5	98	109	18	.597	2	1	0	-3	/OD1	-0.7
■ KURT STILLWELL	Stillwell, Kurt Andrew b: 6/4/65, Glendale, Cal. BB/TR, 5'11", 165 lbs. Deb: 4/13/86																											
1986	Cin-N	104	279	31	64	6	1	0	26	30	47	.229	.309	.258	.567	56	-15	-17	104	144	24	.495	6	2	1	-3	S	-1.1
1987	Cin-N	131	395	54	102	20	7	4	33	32	50	.258	.317	.375	.692	80	-10	-12	104	82	46	.612	4	6	-2	-7	S23	-1.4
1988	KC-A	128	459	63	115	28	5	10	53	47	76	.251	.324	.399	.723	98	1	-1	103	101	60	.671	6	5	-1	-4	*S	0.0
Total	3	363	1133	148	281	54	13	14	112	109	173	.248	.318	.356	.674	81	-25	-30	104	105	131	.614	16	13	-3	-14	S/23	-2.5
■ RON STILLWELL	Stillwell, Ronald Roy b: 12/3/39, Los Angeles, Cal. BR/TR, 5'11", 165 lbs. Deb: 7/03/61																											
1961	Was-A	8	16	3	2	1	0	0	1	1	4	.125	.176	.188	.364	-3	-2	-2	95	131	1	.286	0	0	0	0	/S	-0.1
1962	Was-A	6	22	5	6	0	0	0	2	2	2	.273	.333	.273	.606	65	-1	-1	101	140	2	.500	0	0	0	1	/2S	0.0
Total	2	14	38	8	8	1	0	0	3	3	6	.211	.268	.237	.505	37	-3	-3	98	136	3	.400	0	0	0	1	/2S	-0.1
■ CRAIG STIMAC	Stimac, Craig Steven b: 11/18/54, Oak Park, Ill. BR/TR, 6'2", 185 lbs. Deb: 8/12/80																											
1980	SD-N	20	50	5	11	2	0	0	7	1	6	.220	.235	.260	.495	41	-4	-4	93	213	3	.359	0	0	0	-1	C/3	-0.4
1981	SD-N	9	9	0	1	0	0	0	0	0	3	.111	.111	.111	.222	-40	-2	-2	93	0	0	.125	0	0	0	0	/H	-0.1
Total	2	29	59	5	12	2	0	0	7	1	9	.203	.217	.237	.454	29	-6	-5	93	181	4	.319	0	0	0	-1	/C3	-0.5
■ BOB STINSON	Stinson, Gorrell Robert b: 10/11/45, Elkin, N.C. BB/TR, 5'11", 180 lbs. Deb: 9/23/69																											
1969	LA-N	4	8	1	3	0	0	0	2	0	2	.375	.375	.375	.750	112	0	0	99	267	0	.429	0	1	-1	0	/C	0.0
1970	LA-N	4	3	1	0	0	0	0	0	0	1	.000	.000	.000	.000	-99	-1	-1	90	0	0	.000	0	0	0	0	/C	0.0
1971	StL-N	17	19	3	4	1	0	0	1	1	7	.211	.250	.263	.513	45	-1	-1	101	81	1	.400	0	0	0	-1	/CO	-0.1
1972	Hou-N	27	35	3	6	1	0	0	2	1	6	.171	.216	.200	.416	18	-4	-4	106	117	2	.310	0	0	0	-2	C/O	-0.4
1973	Mon-N	48	111	12	29	6	1	3	12	17	15	.261	.374	.414	.788	114	3	3	104	88	18	.776	0	1	-1	-0	C/3	0.4
1974	Mon-N	38	87	4	15	2	0	1	6	15	16	.172	.294	.230	.524	46	-6	-6	104	101	6	.474	1	1	-0	3	C	-0.2
1975	KC-A	63	147	18	39	9	1	1	9	18	29	.265	.349	.361	.710	99	1	0	102	62	20	.670	1	0	0	-1	C/1O2D	0.1
1976	KC-A	79	209	26	55	7	1	2	25	25	29	.263	.345	.335	.680	100	1	1	100	126	25	.619	3	1	0	-5	C	-0.1
1977	Sea-A	105	297	27	80	11	1	8	32	37	50	.269	.362	.394	.756	110	3	5	96	90	41	.696	0	3	-2	0	C/D	0.6
1978	Sea-A	124	364	46	94	14	3	11	55	45	42	.258	.349	.404	.753	109	6	5	102	121	52	.712	2	1	0	-9	*C/D	0.0
1979	Sea-A	95	247	19	60	8	0	6	28	33	38	.243	.342	.348	.690	86	-4	-4	100	103	30	.633	1	2	-1	-5	C	-0.5
1980	Sea-A	48	107	6	23	2	0	1	8	9	19	.215	.282	.262	.544	48	-7	-8	103	101	8	.442	0	0	0	-4	C	-0.9
Total	12	652	1634	166	408	61	7	33	180	201	254	.250	.340	.356	.696	93	-9	-10	101	103	205	.658	8	10	-4	-24	C/OD213	-1.1
■ GAT STIRES	Stires, Garrett b: 10/13/1849, Hunterdon Co., N.J d: 6/13/33, Byron, Ill. 5'8", 180 lbs. Deb: 5/06/1871																											
1871	Rok-n	25	118	23	32							.271															*O	
■ SNUFFY STIRNWEISS	Stirnweiss, George Henry b: 10/26/18, New York, N.Y. d: 9/15/58, Newark Bay, N.J. BR/TR, 5'8.5", 175 lbs. Deb: 4/22/43																											
1943	NY-A	83	274	34	60	8	4	1	25	47	37	.219	.333	.288	.622	86	-5	-3	96	113	28	.591	11	9	-2	-0	S/2	-0.5
1944	NY-A	154	643	**125**	**205**	35	**16**	8	43	73	87	.319	.389	.460	.849	134	35	30	106	42	**128**	.934	**55**	11	**10**	19	*2	6.6
1945	NY-A	152	632	**107**	**195**	32	**22**	10	64	78	62	**.309**	.385	**.476**	**.862**	140	**39**	**34**	107	60	**121**	.892	**33**	17	-0	26	*2	6.4
1946	NY-A	129	487	75	122	19	7	0	37	66	58	.251	.340	.318	.658	84	-8	-9	100	96	57	.624	18	6	**2**	7	32/S	1.1
1947	NY-A	148	571	102	146	18	8	5	41	89	47	.256	.358	.342	.700	98	-1	1	97	63	76	.660	5	3	-0	-9	*2	0.0
1948	NY-A	141	515	90	130	20	7	3	32	86	62	.252	.360	.336	.696	86	-8	-8	100	63	68	.659	5	4	-1	-13	*2	-1.8
1949	NY-A	70	157	29	41	8	2	0	11	29	20	.261	.380	.338	.717	90	-1	-1	100	71	23	.717	3	2	-0	1	2/3	0.0
1950	NY-A	7	2	0	0	0	0	0	0	0	0	.000	.000	.000	.000	-99	-1	-1	99	0	0	.000	0	0	0	0	/2	0.0
	StL-A	93	326	32	71	16	2	1	24	51	49	.218	.324	.288	.612	54	-20	-24	107	87	33	.558	3	3	-1	-7	23/S	-2.6
	Yr	100	328	32	71	16	2	1	24	51	49	.216	.322	.287	.608	53	-21	-24	106	81	33	.554	3	3	-1	-7		-2.6
1951	Cle-A	50	88	10	19	1	0	1	4	22	25	.216	.373	.261	.634	78	-2	-1	95	55	11	.648	1	0	0	1	2/3	0.0
1952	Cle-A	1	0	0	0	0	0	0	0	0	0	—	—	—	—	—	0	0	91	—	—	—	0	0	0	0	/3	0.0
Total	10	1028	3695	604	989	157	68	29	281	541	447	.268	.362	.371	.733	102	28	18	102	69	556	.742	134	55	7	25	23/S	9.2
■ JACK STIVETTS	Stivetts, John Elmer "Happy Jack" b: 3/31/1868, Ashland, Pa. d: 4/18/30, Ashland, Pa. BR/TR, 6'2", 185 lbs. Deb: 6/26/1889																											
1889	StL-a	27	79	12	18	2	2	0	7	3	13	.228	.265	.304	.569	56	-4	-5	112	83	7	.459	0			0	P/O	0.0
1890	StL-a	67	226	36	65	15	6	7		16		.288	.337	.500	.837	129	12	6	116	0	40	.820	2			4	PO/1	0.0
1891	StL-a	85	302	45	92	10	2	7	54	10	32	.305	.331	.421	.752	103	5	-2	114	105	44	.681	4			3	PO	0.0
1892	Bos-N	70	240	40	71	14	2	3	36	27	28	.296	.369	.408	.778	121	11	6	113	103	40	.793	8			8	PO/1	0.0
1893	Bos-N	49	172	32	51	5	6	3	25	12	14	.297	.342	.448	.790	108	2	1	103	80	29	.785	6			-1	P/O3	0.0
1894	Bos-N	68	244	55	80	12	7	8	64	16	21	.328	.369	.533	.902	103	5	-1	113	115	50	.909	3			-2	PO/1	0.0
1895	Bos-N	46	158	20	30	6	4	0	24	6	18	.190	.220	.278	.498	28	-17	-18	103	152	10	.398	1			-0	P/1O	0.0
1896	Bos-N	67	221	42	76	9	6	3	49	12	10	.344	.380	.480	.860	119	8	5	108	123	43	.848	4			-3	PO/13	0.0
1897	Bos-N	61	199	41	73	9	9	2	37	15		.367	.417	.533	.949	142	14	12	107	97	46	.992	2			0	OP/21	1.0
1898	Bos-N	41	111	16	28	1	1	2	16	10		.252	.314	.333	.647	85	-2	-2	104	113	12	.578	1			0	O1/S2P	-0.1
1899	Cle-N	18	39	8	8	1	1	0	2	6		.205	.326	.282	.608	78	-1	-1	89	56	4	.581	0			0	/OPS3	0.0
Total	11	599	1991	347	592	84	46	35	314	133	136	.297	.344	.438	.783	105	33	1	110	95	325	.748	31			9	PO/1S32	0.9
■ MILT STOCK	Stock, Milton Joseph b: 7/11/1893, Chicago, Ill. d: 7/16/77, Montrose, Ala. BR/TR, 5'8", 154 lbs. Deb: 9/29/13 C																											
1913	NY-N	7	17	2	3	1	0	0	1	2	1	.176	.263	.235	.498	42	-1	-1	103	91	1	.571	2			0	/S	0.0
1914	NY-N	115	365	52	96	17	1	3	41	34	21	.263	.333	.340	.672	105	0	2	96	112	44	.643	11			9	*3/S	1.7
1915	Phi-N	69	227	37	59	7	3	1	15	22	26	.260	.325	.330	.656	92	-0	-2	107	75	26	.606	6	2	1	-2	3/S	0.0
1916	Phi-N	132	509	61	143	25	6	1	43	27	33	.281	.320	.360	.679	113	4	6	96	88	56	.594	21	26	-9	-2	*3S	0.7
1917	Phi-N	150	564	76	149	27	6	3	53	51	34	.264	.326	.349	.676	100	5	0	108	95	71	.660	25			-5	*3S	-0.6
1918	Phi-N	123	481	62	132	14	1	1	42	35	22	.274	.325	.314	.639	87	-2	-7	109	99	54	.593	20			-4	*3	-1.0
1919	StL-N	135	492	56	151	16	4	0	52	49	21	.307	.371	.356	.727	126	13	16	94	122	70	.710	17			9	23	3.0
1920	StL-N	155	639	85	204	28	6	0	76	40	27	.319	.360	.382	.742	116	11	13	98	116	86	.664	15	17	-6	-8	*3	0.7
1921	StL-N	149	587	96	180	27	6	3	84	48	26	.307	.360	.388	.748	103	-1	4	95	115	85	.702	11	3	2	-23	*3	-1.6
1922	StL-N	151	581	85	177	33	9	5	79	42	29	.305	.352	.418	.770	97	-2	-3	101	113	83	.702	7	12	-5	-9	*3/S	-0.4
1923	StL-N	151	603	63	174	33	3	2	96	40	21	.289	.334	.363	.697	93	-14	-6	90	**159**	74	.618	9	6	-1	-14	*3/2	-1.6
1924	Bro-N	142	561	66	136	14	4	2	52	26	32	.242	.277	.292	.570	53	-37	-37	99	118	45	.448	3	8	-4	-20	*3	-5.0
1925	Bro-N	146	615	98	202	28	9	1	62	38	28	.328	.368	.408	.776	104	-1	4	94	83	93	.717	8	1	2	-4	*2/3	0.0
1926	Bro-N	3	8	0	0	0	0	0	0	1	0	.000	.111	.000	.111	-68	-2	-2	99	0	0	.125	0			-0	/2	-0.1
Total	14	1628	6249	839	1806	270	58	22	696	455	321	.289	.339	.361	.700	98	-28	-12	98	110	789	.638	155	75		-72	*32/S	-4.2

YEAR	TM/L	G	AB	R	H	2B	3B	HR	RBI	BB	SO	AVG	OBP	SLG	PRO	/A	BR	/A	PF	CHI	RC	TA	SB	CS	SBR	FR	POS	TPR
■ LEN STOCKWELL Stockwell, Leonard Clark b: 8/25/1859, Cordova, Ill. d: 1/28/05, Niles, Cal. TR , 5'11", 165 lbs. Deb: 5/17/1879																												
1879	Cle-N	2	6	0	0	0	0	0	0	0	2	.000	.000	.000	.000	-99	-1	-1	99	0	0	.000				0	/O	0.0
1884	Lou-a	2	9	0	1	0	0	0		0		.111	.111	.111	.222	-29	-1	-1	89	0	0	.125				0	/OC	0.0
1890	Cle-N	2	7	2	2	1	0	0	0	0	3	.286	.286	.429	.714	117	0	0	94	0	1	.600	0			0	/O1	0.0
Total	3	6	22	2	3	1	0	0	0	0	5	.136	.136	.182	.318	0	-2	-2	93	0	1	.211	0			0	/O1C	0.0
■ STODDARD Stoddard Deb:9/25/1875																												
1875	Atl-n	2	9	1	1							.111															/O	
■ AL STOKES Stokes, Albert John (born Albert John Stacek) b: 1/1/1900, Chicago, Ill. BR/TR, 5'10", 170 lbs. Deb: 5/10/25																												
1925	Bos-A	17	52	7	11	0	1	0	1	4	8	.212	.268	.250	.518	34	-5	-5	95	26	4	.415	0	0	0	1	C	-0.2
1926	Bos-A	30	86	7	14	3	3	0	6	8	28	.163	.234	.267	.501	30	-9	-9	101	89	6	.431	0	0	0	0	C	-0.6
Total	2	47	138	14	25	3	4	0	7	12	36	.181	.247	.261	.508	31	-15	-14	99	65	9	.425	0	0	0	1	/C	-0.8
■ GENE STONE Stone, Eugene Daniel b: 1/16/44, Burbank, Cal. BL/TL, 5'11", 190 lbs. Deb: 5/13/69																												
1969	Phi-N	18	28	4	6	0	1	0	0	4	9	.214	.313	.286	.598	70	-1	-1	98	0	3	.545	0	0	0	-0	/1	-0.1
■ GEORGE STONE Stone, George Robert b: 9/3/1877, Lost Nation, Iowa d: 1/3/45, Clinton, Iowa BL/TL, 5'9", 175 lbs. Deb: 4/20/03																												
1903	Bos-A	2	2	0	0	0	0	0	0	0		.000	.000	.000	.000	-89	-0	-0	112	0	0	.000	0			0	H	0.0
1905	StL-A	154	632	76	**187**	25	13	7	52	44		.296	.342	.410	.752	154	27	33	91	57	100	.739	26			-1	*O	2.6
1906	StL-A	154	581	91	208	25	20	6	71	52		**.358**	**.411**	**.501**	**.912**	**191**	**57**	**58**	98	80	**137**	**1.013**	35			6	*O	6.2
1907	StL-A	155	596	77	191	13	11	4	59	59		.320	.382	.399	.781	155	35	37	98	81	102	.790	23			-3	*O	2.7
1908	StL-A	148	588	89	165	21	8	5	31	55		.281	.342	.369	.711	129	22	20	103	43	79	.690	20			5	*O	2.0
1909	StL-A	83	310	33	89	5	4	1	15	24		.287	.340	.339	.679	125	5	8	92	51	37	.624	8			-12	O	-0.7
1910	StL-A	152	562	60	144	17	12	0	40	48		.256	.315	.329	.644	108	1	4	94	77	65	.605	20			0	*O	-0.2
Total	7	848	3271	426	984	106	68	23	268	282		.301	.356	.396	.752	146	147	160	96	66	520	.748	132			-5	O	12.6
■ RON STONE Stone, Harry Ronald b: 9/9/42, Corning, Cal. BL/TL, 6'2", 185 lbs. Deb: 4/13/66																												
1966	KC-A	26	22	2	6	1	0	0	0	0	2	.273	.273	.318	.591	74	-1	-1	94	0	2	.471	1	1	-0	-1	/O1	-0.2
1969	Phi-N	103	222	22	53	7	1	1	24	29	28	.239	.335	.293	.627	78	-6	-5	98	141	21	.552	3	1	0	-5	O	-1.3
1970	Phi-N	123	321	30	84	12	5	3	39	38	45	.262	.342	.358	.700	91	-5	-3	96	122	40	.641	5	6	-2	-5	O/1	-1.5
1971	Phi-N	95	185	16	42	8	1	2	23	25	36	.227	.319	.314	.633	78	-4	-5	103	146	19	.570	2	2	-1	-3	O/1	-1.1
1972	Phi-N	41	54	3	9	0	1	0	3	9	11	.167	.286	.204	.489	42	-4	-4	97	112	3	.417	0	0	0	1	O	-0.3
Total	5	388	804	73	194	28	8	6	89	101	122	.241	.329	.318	.647	81	-20	-18	98	129	85	.597	11	10	-3	-13	O/1	-4.4
■ JEFF STONE Stone, Jeffrey Glen b: 12/26/60, Kennett, Mo. BL/TR, 6', 175 lbs. Deb: 9/09/83																												
1983	Phi-N	9	4	2	3	0	2	0	3	0	1	.750	.750	1.750	2.500	568	2	2	101	170	7	11.000	4	0	1	-0	/O	0.3
1984	Phi-N	51	185	27	67	4	6	1	15	9	26	.362	.398	.465	.863	139	10	10	102	67	37	.992	27	5	5	-5	O	0.9
1985	Phi-N	88	264	36	70	4	3	3	11	15	50	.265	.307	.337	.644	78	-7	-8	102	45	28	.594	15	5	2	-9	O	-1.7
1986	Phi-N	82	249	32	69	6	4	6	19	20	52	.277	.341	.406	.746	101	2	0	104	64	36	.762	19	6	2	3	O	0.5
1987	Phi-N	66	125	19	32	7	1	1	16	8	38	.256	.316	.352	.668	74	-4	-5	104	136	14	.604	3	1	0	-1	O	-0.6
1988	Bal-A	26	61	4	10	1	0	0	1	4	11	.164	.215	.180	.396	13	-7	-7	95	36	2	.345	4	1	1	-3	O/D	-0.8
Total	6	322	888	120	251	22	16	11	65	56	178	.283	.332	.381	.713	94	-4	-7	102	68	125	.723	72	18	11	-14	O/D	-1.4
■ JOHN STONE Stone, John Thomas "Rocky" b: 10/10/05, Lynchburg, Tenn. d: 11/30/55, Shelbyville, Tenn. BL/TR, 6'1", 178 lbs. Deb: 8/31/28																												
1928	Det-A	26	113	20	40	10	3	2	21	5	8	.354	.387	.549	.935	144	6	7	99	91	24	.945	1	0	0	-2	O	0.3
1929	Det-A	51	150	23	39	11	2	2	15	11	13	.260	.311	.400	.711	84	-5	-4	97	78	19	.643	1	1	-0	-2	O	-0.6
1930	Det-A	126	422	60	132	29	11	3	56	32	49	.313	.363	.455	.818	101	3	0	105	92	67	.773	6	9	-4	1	*O	-0.6
1931	Det-A	147	584	86	191	28	11	10	76	56	48	.327	.388	.464	.852	119	20	16	104	88	103	.842	13	13	-4	4	*O	0.7
1932	Det-A	145	582	106	173	35	12	17	108	58	64	.297	.361	.486	.847	115	13	12	102	115	103	.837	2	1	0	7	*O	1.2
1933	Det-A	148	574	86	161	33	11	11	80	54	37	.280	.344	.434	.778	99	3	-2	107	100	86	.734	1	4	-2	-3	*O	-1.0
1934	Was-A	113	419	77	132	28	7	7	67	52	26	.315	.395	.465	.860	120	14	13	101	106	79	.869	1	2	-1	6	*O	1.5
1935	Was-A	125	455	78	143	27	18	1	78	39	29	.314	.372	.459	.832	125	9	14	92	125	77	.804	4	5	-2	-1	*O	1.0
1936	Was-A	123	437	95	149	22	11	15	90	60	26	.341	.421	.545	.965	140	25	27	98	105	104	1.063	8	0	2	4	*O	2.7
1937	Was-A	139	542	84	179	33	15	6	88	66	36	.330	.403	.480	.883	129	19	23	94	115	107	.905	6	4	-1	6	*O	2.1
1938	Was-A	56	213	24	52	12	4	3	28	30	16	.244	.337	.380	.718	84	-7	-5	95	107	29	.698	2	1	0	-2	O	-0.6
Total	11	1199	4491	739	1391	268	105	77	707	463	352	.310	.376	.468	.843	116	101	102	100	104	798	.834	45	40	-10	18	*O	6.7
■ TIGE STONE Stone, William Arthur b: 9/18/01, Macon, Ga. d: 1/1/60, Jacksonville, Fla. 5'8", 145 lbs. Deb: 8/23/23																												
1923	StL-N	5	1	0	1	0	0	0	0	2	0	1.000	1.000	1.000	2.000	476	1	1	90	0	1	—	0	0	0	-2	/OP	0.0
■ JOHN STONEHAM Stoneham, John Andrew b: 11/8/08, Wood River, Ill. BL/TR, 5'9.5", 168 lbs. Deb: 9/18/33																												
1933	Chi-A	10	25	4	3	0	0	1	3	2	2	.120	.185	.240	.425	12	-3	-3	101	111	1	.364	0	0	0	-2	/O	-0.4
■ HOWIE STORIE Storie, Howard Edward "Sponge" b: 5/15/11, Pittsfield, Mass. d: 7/27/68, Pittsfield, Mass. BR/TR, 5'10", 175 lbs. Deb: 9/07/31																												
1931	Bos-A	6	17	2	2	0	0	0	0	3	2	.118	.250	.118	.368	-1	-2	-2	94	0	1	.333	0	0	0	0	/C	-0.1
1932	Bos-A	6	8	0	3	0	0	0	0	0	0	.375	.375	.375	.750	98	-0	-0	97	0	1	.600	0	0	0	0	/C	0.0
Total	2	12	25	2	5	0	0	0	0	3	2	.200	.286	.200	.486	31	-2	-2	95	0	2	.400	0	0	0	0	/C	-0.1
■ ALAN STORKE Storke, Alan Marshall b: 9/27/1884, Auburn, N.Y. d: 3/18/10, Newton, Mass. TR , Deb: 9/24/06																												
1906	Pit-N	5	12	1	3	1	0	0	1	1		.250	.308	.333	.641	98	0	-0	104	91	2	.667	1			0	/3S	0.0
1907	Pit-N	112	357	24	92	6	6	1	39	16		.258	.290	.317	.606	87	-4	-6	105	127	35	.509	6			-3	31/2S	-1.0
1908	Pit-N	64	202	20	51	5	3	1	12	9		.252	.284	.322	.606	101	-1	-0	95	68	19	.517	4			-5	1/32	-0.6
1909	Pit-N	37	118	12	30	5	2	0	12	7		.254	.302	.331	.632	93	-1	-1	105	112	12	.545	1			-1	13	-0.2
	StL-N	48	174	11	49	5	0	0	10	12		.282	.328	.310	.638	103	-0	1	96	69	19	.568	5			-6	S/21	-0.5
	Yr	85	292	23	79	10	2	0	22	19		.271	.317	.318	.636	99	-1	-1	100	89	30	.559	6			-7		-0.7
Total	4	266	863	68	225	22	11	2	74	45		.261	.298	.319	.617	94	-7	-7	101	99	86	.530	17			-15	/13S2	-2.3
■ LIN STORTI Storti, Lindo Ivan b: 12/5/06, Santa Monica, Cal. d: 7/24/82, Ontario, Cal. BB/TR, 5'11", 165 lbs. Deb: 9/18/30																												
1930	StL-A	7	28	6	9	1	1	0	2	2	6	.321	.367	.429	.795	93	0	-0	108	59	4	.737	0	0	0	1	/2	0.1
1931	StL-A	86	273	32	60	15	4	3	26	15	50	.220	.263	.337	.600	55	-18	-19	102	85	24	.502	0	2	-1	-0	3/2	-1.4
1932	StL-A	53	193	19	50	11	2	3	26	5	20	.259	.278	.383	.661	70	-9	-9	100	105	20	.559	1	0	0	5	3	0.0
1933	StL-A	70	210	26	41	7	4	3	21	25	31	.195	.281	.310	.590	49	-14	-18	115	95	19	.538	2	2	-1	8	32	-0.8
Total	4	216	704	83	160	34	11	9	75	47	107	.227	.277	.345	.622	59	-41	-47	106	92	68	.536	3	4	-2	14	3/2	-2.1
■ TOM STOUCH Stouch, Thomas Carl b: 12/2/1870, Perryville, Ohio d: 10/7/56, Lancaster, Pa. BR/TR, 6'2", 165 lbs. Deb: 7/07/1898																												
1898	Lou-N	4	16	4	5	1	0	0	6	1		.313	.353	.375	.728	115	0	0	96	291	2	.636	0			0	/2	0.0
■ GEORGE STOVALL Stovall, George Thomas "Firebrand" b: 11/23/1878, Independence, Mo. d: 11/5/51, Burlington, Iowa BR/TR, 6'2", 180 lbs. Deb: 7/04/04 M																												
1904	Cle-A	52	181	18	54	10	1	1	31	2		.298	.306	.381	.687	117	3	3	102	164	23	.583	3			-2	1/2O3	0.2
1905	Cle-A	112	423	41	115	31	1	1	47	13		.272	.294	.357	.651	108	2	2	100	115	49	.575	13			1	12/O	0.2
1906	Cle-A	116	443	54	121	19	5	0	37	8		.273	.286	.339	.625	94	-3	-4	103	92	48	.537	15			-1	132	-0.5
1907	Cle-A	124	466	38	110	17	6	1	36	18		.236	.264	.305	.569	89	-10	-6	93	94	42	.486	13			-2	*1	-1.0
1908	Cle-A	138	534	71	156	29	6	2	45	17		.292	.314	.380	.694	120	14	10	106	78	66	.619	14			4	*1/OS	1.2
1909	Cle-A	145	565	60	139	17	10	2	49	6		.246	.259	.322	.581	82	-13	-15	102	97	51	.509	25			8	*1	-0.7
1910	Cle-A	142	521	47	136	19	4	0	52	14		.261	.284	.313	.597	87	-10	-9	100	120	52	.509	16			7	*1/2	0.3
1911	Cle-A	126	458	48	124	17	7	0	79	21		.271	.306	.338	.644	77	-14	-15	103	**176**	50	.566	11			3	*1/2M	-0.9
1912	StL-A	115	398	35	101	17	5	0	45	14		.254	.286	.322	.608	75	-15	-14	99	120	39	.529	11			1	1M	-1.2
1913	StL-A	89	303	34	87	14	3	1	24	7	23	.287	.305	.363	.669	100	-3	-2	95	75	34	.579	7			5	1M	0.3
1914	KC-F	124	450	51	128	20	5	7	75	23	35	.284	.319	.398	.717	110	1	4	95	138	62	.646	6			3	*1/3M	1.0
1915	KC-F	130	480	48	111	21	3	0	44	29	36	.231	.275	.287	.563	69	-20	-18	97	122	43	.474	8			7	*1M	-1.0

YEAR	TM/L	G	AB	R	H	2B	3B	HR	RBI	BB	SO	AVG	OBP	SLG	PRO	/A	BR	/A	PF	CHI	RC	TA	SB	CS	SBR	FR	POS	TPR
Total	12	1413	5222	545	1382	231	56	15	564	172	94	.265	.290	.339	.629	92	-68	-65	100	114	557	.546	142			34	*1/23OS	-2.1
■ HARRY STOVEY	Stovey, Harry Duffield (born Harry Duffield Stowe) b: 12/20/1856, Philadelphia, Pa. d: 9/20/37, New Bedford, Mass BR/TR, 5'11.5", 175 lbs. Deb: 5/01/1880 M																											
1880	Wor-N	83	355	76	94	21	**14**	**6**	28	12	46	.265	.289	.454	.742	131	17	11	113	49	48	.663				-6	O1/P	0.2
1881	Wor-N	75	341	57	92	25	7	2	30	12	23	.270	.295	.402	.696	111	6	4	105	63	41	.598				-2	*1OM	-0.5
1882	Wor-N	84	360	90	104	13	10	5	26	22	34	.289	.330	.422	.752	139	16	16	100	45	51	.680				3	1O	1.0
1883	Phi-a	94	421	**110**	127	**31**	6	**14**		26		.302	.342	**.504**	.846	165	31	30	103	0	74	.810				0	*1/OP	1.9
1884	Phi-a	104	448	**124**	146	22	**23**	10		26		.326	.368	.545	.913	173	**46**	36	114	0	92	**.907**				-1	*1	2.7
1885	Phi-a	112	486	**130**	153	27	9	**13**		39		.315	.371	.488	.858	167	40	37	103	0	90	.841				4	*1OM	2.8
1886	Phi-a	123	489	115	144	28	11	**7**		64		.294	.377	.440	.817	158	33	33	100	0	109	**1.009**	**68**			2	O1/P	2.6
1887	Phi-a	124	497	125	142	31	12	4		56		.286	.366	.421	.787	122	15	15	99	0	106	.975	74			4	O1	1.3
1888	Phi-a	130	530	127	152	25	**20**	9	65	62		.287	.365	.460	.825	166	40	39	101	63	124	1.048	87			2	*O1	3.3
1889	Phi-a	137	556	**152**	171	38	13	**19**	**119**	77	68	.308	.393	**.525**	.918	167	45	47	98	86	143	1.125	63			17	*O/1	**4.9**
1890	Bos-P	118	481	142	143	25	12	11	83	81	38	.297	.404	.468	.872	126	25	19	107	78	133	**1.207**	**97**			-1	*O/1	1.0
1891	Bos-N	134	544	118	152	31	**20**	**16**	95	78	69	.279	.372	**.498**	.870	139	37	26	112	77	125	1.041	57			11	*O/1	2.7
1892	Bos-N	38	146	21	24	8	1	0	12	14	19	.164	.252	.233	.484	43	-9	-12	113	115	14	.582	20			-0	O	-1.2
	Bal-N	74	283	58	77	14	11	4	55	40	32	.272	.364	.442	.806	146	16	16	100	131	54	.903	20			-3	O1	0.9
	Yr	112	429	79	101	22	12	4	67	54	51	.235	.326	.371	.697	108	7	4	104	126	67	.784	40			-4		-0.3
1893	Bal-N	8	26	4	4	2	0	0	5	8	3	.154	.353	.231	.584	54	-1	-2	107	233	3	.682	1			0	/O	0.0
	Bro-N	48	175	43	44	6	6	1	29	44	11	.251	.402	.371	.773	119	4	7	91	103	36	1.000	22			-5	O	0.0
	Yr	56	201	47	48	8	6	1	34	52	14	.239	.395	.353	.748	109	3	6	93	126	38	.954	23			-5		0.0
Total	14	1486	6138	1492	1769	347	175	121	547	661	343	.288	.360	.461	.821	144	360	323	104	49	1244	.922	509			24	O1/P	23.6
■ RAY STOVIAK	Stoviak, Raymond Thomas b: 6/6/15, Scottdale, Pa. BL/TL, 6'1", 195 lbs. Deb: 6/05/38																											
1938	Phi-N	10	10	1	0	0	0	0	0	0	3	.000	.000	.000	.000	-99	-3	-3	100	0	0	.000	0			-1	/O	-0.3
■ JOE STRAIN	Strain, Joseph Allan b: 4/30/54, Denver, Colo. BR/TR, 5'10", 169 lbs. Deb: 6/28/79																											
1979	SF-N	67	257	27	62	8	1	1	12	13	21	.241	.286	.292	.578	63	-15	-12	92	64	22	.485	8	4	0	-3	2/3	-1.1
1980	SF-N	77	189	26	54	6	0	0	16	10	10	.286	.322	.317	.639	83	-5	-4	96	106	18	.490	1	2	-1	-3	2/3S	-0.4
1981	Chi-N	25	74	7	14	1	0	0	1	5	7	.189	.250	.203	.453	28	-7	-7	104	26	4	.344	0	0	0	3	2	-0.2
Total	3	169	520	60	130	15	1	1	29	28	38	.250	.293	.288	.582	65	-27	-24	95	74	43	.481	9	6	-1	-3	2/3S	-1.7
■ PAUL STRAND	Strand, Paul Edward b: 12/19/1893, Carbonado, Wash. d: 7/2/74, Salt Lake City, Utah BR/TL, 6'0.5", 190 lbs. Deb: 5/15/13																											
1913	Bos-N	7	6	0	1	0	0	0	0	0	0	.167	.167	.167	.333	-5	-1	-1	95	0	0	.200	0			0	/P	0.0
1914	Bos-N	18	24	2	8	2	0	0	3	0	2	.333	.333	.417	.750	118	0	0	104	109	3	.625	0			-0	P	0.0
1915	Bos-N	24	22	3	2	0	0	0	2	0	4	.091	.091	.091	.182	-46	-4	-4	98	382	0	.100	0			-2	/PO	-0.4
1924	Phi-A	47	167	15	38	9	4	0	13	4	9	.228	.254	.329	.584	50	-13	-13	99	78	13	.485	3	3	-1	-4	O	-2.0
Total	4	96	219	20	49	11	4	0	18	4	15	.224	.244	.311	.555	47	-17	-17	100	109	17	.445	3	3		-6	/OP	-2.4
■ LARRY STRANDS	Strands, John Lawrence b: 12/5/1885, Chicago, Ill. d: 1/19/57, Forest Park, Ill. BR/TR, 5'10.5", 165 lbs. Deb: 4/25/15																											
1915	New-F	35	75	7	14	3	1	1	11	6	11	.187	.247	.293	.540	63	-4	-3	94	159	6	.475	1			0	3/2O	-0.3
■ SAMMY STRANG	Strang, Samuel Nicklin (born Samuel Strang Nicklin) b: 12/16/1876, Chattanooga, Tenn. d: 3/13/32, Chattanooga, Tenn. BB/TR, 5'8", 160 lbs. Deb: 7/10/1896																											
1896	Lou-N	14	46	6	12	0	0	0	7	6	6	.261	.346	.261	.607	64	-2	-2	98	168	6	.647	4			0	S	-0.1
1900	Chi-N	27	102	15	29	3	0	0	9	8		.284	.336	.314	.650	89	-2	-1	93	93	11	.562	1			0	3/S2	0.0
1901	NY-N	135	493	55	139	14	6	1	34	59		.282	.359	.341	.699	116	6	12	91	71	76	.754	40			-1	32/OS	1.8
1902	Chi-A	137	536	108	158	18	5	3	46	76		.295	.382	.364	.746	115	10	14	95	64	91	.817	38			5	*3	1.4
	Chi-N	3	11	1	4	0	0	0	0	0		.364	.364	.364	.727	132	0	0	96	0	2	.714	1			-0	/23	0.0
1903	Bro-N	135	508	101	138	21	5	0	37	75		.272	.365	.333	.698	100	4	3	101	62	81	.784	46			-7	*3/O2	-0.2
1904	Bro-N	77	271	28	52	11	0	1	9	45		.192	.307	.244	.551	76	-7	-5	95	42	26	.580	16			-21	23/S	-2.5
1905	NY-N	111	294	51	76	9	4	3	29	58		.259	.381	.347	.728	118	10	10	101	91	49	.839	23			3	2O/S13	1.3
1906	NY-N	113	313	50	100	16	4	4	49	54		.319	.420	.435	.854	169	27	27	100	121	68	.991	21			11	2O/S31	4.0
1907	NY-N	123	306	56	77	20	4	4	30	60		.252	.374	.382	.757	132	16	14	105	88	53	.865	21			-1	O2/31S	1.3
1908	NY-N	28	53	8	5	0	0	0	2	23		.094	.368	.094	.463	50	-1	-1	104	154	4	.688	5			-0	2/OS	-0.1
Total	10	903	2933	479	790	112	28	16	252	464	6	.269	.369	.343	.712	114	62	71	98	79	466	.787	216			-11	32O/S1	6.9
■ ALAN STRANGE	Strange, Alan Cochrane "Inky" b: 11/7/09, Philadelphia, Pa. BR/TR, 5'9", 162 lbs. Deb: 4/17/34																											
1934	StL-A	127	430	39	100	17	2	1	45	48	28	.233	.310	.288	.598	53	-28	-31	104	118	41	.529	3	1	0	0	*S	-1.9
1935	StL-A	49	147	8	34	6	1	0	17	17	7	.231	.311	.286	.597	52	-10	-11	107	137	14	.522	0	0	0	3	S	-0.4
	Was-A	20	54	3	10	2	1	0	5	4	1	.185	.241	.259	.501	32	-6	-5	92	121	4	.409	0	0	0	1	S	-0.2
	Yr	69	201	11	44	8	2	0	22	21	8	.219	.293	.279	.571	47	-15	-16	102	135	18	.490	0	0	0	4		-0.6
1940	StL-A	54	167	26	31	8	3	0	6	22	12	.186	.284	.269	.554	42	-14	-15	106	48	14	.493	2	1	0	2	S/2	-0.8
1941	StL-A	45	112	14	26	4	0	0	11	15	5	.232	.323	.268	.591	58	-6	-6	100	130	10	.500	1	0	0	-4	S/13	-0.8
1942	StL-A	19	37	3	10	2	0	0	5	3	1	.270	.325	.324	.649	80	-1	-1	104	147	4	.517	0	1	-1	0	3/S2	0.0
Total	5	314	947	93	211	39	7	1	89	109	54	.223	.304	.282	.586	51	-65	-70	104	111	86	.518	6	3	0	3	S/321	-4.1
■ ASA STRATTON	Stratton, Asa Evans b: 2/10/1853, Grafton, Mass. d: 8/14/25, Fitchburg, Mass. Deb: 6/17/1881																											
1881	Wor-N	1	4	0	1	0	0	0	0	0	2	.250	.250	.250	.500	55	-0	-0	105	0	0	.333				0	/S	0.0
■ SCOTT STRATTON	Stratton, C. Scott b: 10/2/1869, Campbellsburg, Ky. d: 3/8/39, Louisville, Ky. BL/TR, 6', 180 lbs. Deb: 1888																											
1888	Lou-a	67	249	35	64	8	1	1	29	12		.257	.310	.309	.619	112	1	4	91	111	28	.573	10			-5	OP	-0.1
1889	Lou-a	62	229	30	66	7	5	4	34	13	36	.288	.332	.415	.747	119	3	5	96	93	36	.736	10			0	OP1	0.4
1890	Lou-a	55	189	29	61	3	5	0		16		.323	.385	.392	.776	123	8	5	107	0	32	.789	8			7	P/O	0.0
1891	Pit-N	2	8	1	1	0	0	0	0	0	3	.125	.125	.125	.250	-26	-1	-1	101	0	0	.143	0			0	/P	0.0
	Lou-a	34	115	9	27	2	0	0	8	11	13	.235	.307	.252	.559	69	-5	-3	90	80	12	.557	8			0	P/1O	0.0
1892	Lou-N	63	219	22	56	2	9	0	23	17	21	.256	.318	.347	.665	112	1	3	92	95	28	.644	9			2	PO/1	0.0
1893	Lou-N	61	221	34	50	8	5	0	16	25	15	.226	.308	.308	.615	68	-11	-9	96	64	23	.585	6			6	PO/1	0.0
1894	Lou-N	13	37	9	12	1	2	0	4	4	2	.324	.390	.459	.850	120	0	1	88	65	7	.880	1			0	/PO	0.0
	Chi-N	23	96	29	36	5	4	3	23	6	1	.375	.417	.604	1.022	135	7	5	108	100	26	1.133	3			0	P/O1	0.0
	Yr	36	133	38	48	6	6	3	27	10	3	.361	.410	.564	.974	134	7	7	100	89	33	1.059	4			0		0.0
1895	Chi-N	10	24	3	7	1	1	0	2	4	2	.292	.393	.417	.810	107	1	0	103	56	4	.882	1			0	/PO	0.0
Total	8	390	1387	201	380	37	32	8	139	108	93	.274	.334	.364	.699	106	2	10	96	76	196	.682	56			11	PO/1	0.3
■ JOE STRAUB	Straub, Joseph b: 1/19/1858, Germany d: 2/13/29, Pueblo, Colo. BR/TR, 5'10", 160 lbs. Deb: 6/24/1880																											
1880	Tro-N	3	12	1	3	0	0	0	3	1	3	.250	.308	.250	.558	83	-0	-0	110	351	1	.444				0	/C	0.0
1882	Phi-a	8	32	2	6	2	0	0		1		.188	.212	.250	.462	49	-1	-2	112	0	2	.346				0	/CO	-0.1
1883	Col-a	27	100	4	13	0	0	0		4		.130	.163	.130	.293	-5	-11	-9	87	0	2	.195				0	C1/O	-0.7
Total	3	38	144	7	22	2	0	0	3	6	3	.153	.187	.167	.353	17	-13	-11	95	30	5	.246				0	/C1O	-0.8
■ JOE STRAUSS	Strauss, Josef "Dutch" or "The Socker" b: 3/17/1844, Gecse, Hungary d: 6/25/06, Cincinnati, Ohio BR/TR, Deb: 7/27/1884																											
1884	KC-U	16	60	4	12	3	0	0		1		.200	.213	.250	.463	64	-3	-1	87	0	3	.333	0			0	O/C23	0.0
1885	Lou-a	2	6	0	1	0	0	0		0		.167	.167	.167	.333	7	-1	-1	102	0	0	.200				0	/OC	0.0
1886	Lou-a	74	297	36	64	5	6	1		8		.215	.239	.283	.521	60	-13	-16	108	0	27	.506	25			2	O/PC	-1.4
	Bro-a	9	36	6	9	1	1	0		1		.250	.270	.333	.604	90	-1	-1	100	0	4	.630	4			-0	/OC	0.0
	Yr	83	333	42	73	6	7	1		9		.219	.242	.288	.530	63	-13	-17	107	0	31	.519	29			1		-1.4
Total	3	101	399	46	86	9	7	1		10		.216	.237	.281	.517	62	-16	-19	104	0	35	.486	29			1	/OCP23	-1.4
■ DARRYL STRAWBERRY	Strawberry, Darryl Eugene b: 3/12/62, Los Angeles, Cal. BL/TL, 6'6", 190 lbs. Deb: 5/06/83																											
1983	NY-N	122	420	63	108	15	7	26	74	47	128	.257	.338	.512	.849	134	17	17	99	102	74	.882	19	6	2	0	*O	1.8
1984	NY-N	147	522	75	131	27	4	26	97	75	131	.251	.345	.467	.812	126	18	18	100	125	87	.850	27	8	3	6	*O	2.3

YEAR	TM/L	G	AB	R	H	2B	3B	HR	RBI	BB	SO	AVG	OBP	SLG	PRO	/A	BR	/A	PF	CHI	RC	TA	SB	CS	SBR	FR	POS	TPR
1985	NY-N	111	393	78	109	15	4	29	79	73	96	.277	.392	.557	.949	167	34	35	97	109	87	1.049	26	11	1	1	*O	3.5
1986	NY-N	136	475	76	123	27	5	27	93	72	141	.259	.363	.507	.871	144	24	27	96	117	92	.943	28	12	1	-1	*O	2.6
1987	NY-N	154	532	108	151	32	5	39	104	97	122	.284	.401	.583	.984	159	45	46	99	99	132	1.134	36	12	4	-2	*O	4.1
1988	NY-N	153	543	101	146	27	3	**39**	101	85	127	.269	.371	**.545**	**.916**	**177**	42	48	90	104	111	**.990**	29	14	0	2	*O	**4.9**
Total	6	823	2885	501	768	143	28	186	548	449	745	.266	.369	.529	.898	151	179	192	97	109	583	.988	165	63	12	6	O	19.2

■ **GABBY STREET** Street, Charles Evard "Old Sarge" b: 9/30/1882, Huntsville, Ala. d: 2/6/51, Joplin, Mo. BR/TR, 5'11", 180 lbs. Deb: 9/13/04 M

YEAR	TM/L	G	AB	R	H	2B	3B	HR	RBI	BB	SO	AVG	OBP	SLG	PRO	/A	BR	/A	PF	CHI	RC	TA	SB	CS	SBR	FR	POS	TPR
1904	Cin-N	11	33	1	4	1	0	0	0	1		.121	.147	.152	.299	-6	-4	-5	114	0	1	.276	2			0	C	-0.3
1905	Cin-N	2	2	0	0	0	0	0	0	0		.000	.000	.000	.000	-97	-0	-0	103	0	0	.000	0			0	/C	0.0
	Bos-N	3	12	0	2	0	0	0	0	0		.167	.167	.167	.333	0	-1	-1	97	0	1	.300	1			0	/C	0.0
	Cin-N	29	91	8	23	5	1	0	8	6		.253	.299	.330	.629	86	-1	-2	103	93	9	.544	1			2	C	0.3
	Yr	34	105	8	25	5	1	0	8	6		.238	.279	.305	.584	74	-3	-4	103	79	10	.500	2			2		0.3
1908	Was-A	131	394	31	81	12	7	1	32	40		.206	.279	.279	.558	87	-6	-4	95	106	31	.495	5			2	*C	1.2
1909	Was-A	137	407	25	86	12	1	0	29	26		.211	.262	.246	.508	67	-18	-14	90	112	25	.405	2			7	*C	0.4
1910	Was-A	89	257	13	52	6	0	1	16	23		.202	.273	.237	.510	60	-11	-12	101	92	17	.424	1			5	C	0.3
1911	Was-A	72	216	16	48	7	1	0	14	14		.222	.270	.264	.533	51	-15	-14	97	83	16	.446	4			11	C	0.5
1912	NY-A	28	88	4	16	1	1	0	6	7		.182	.258	.216	.474	35	-7	-7	101	105	5	.403	1			1	C	-0.2
1931	StL-N	1	1	0	0	0	0	0	0	0	0	.000	.000	.000	.000	-94	-0	-0	107	0	0	.000	0			0	/CM	0.0
Total	8	503	1501	98	312	44	11	2	105	117	0	.208	.268	.256	.524	65	-66	-60	96	98	106	.441	17			28	C	2.2

■ **WALT STREULI** Streuli, Walter Herbert b: 9/26/35, Memphis, Tenn. BR/TR, 6'2", 195 lbs. Deb: 9/25/54

YEAR	TM/L	G	AB	R	H	2B	3B	HR	RBI	BB	SO	AVG	OBP	SLG	PRO	/A	BR	/A	PF	CHI	RC	TA	SB	CS	SBR	FR	POS	TPR
1954	Det-A	1	0	0	0	0	0	0	0	1	0	—	1.000	—	1.256	257	0	0	100	0	0	—	0	0	0	0	/C	0.0
1955	Det-A	2	4	1	1	1	0	0	1	0	0	.250	.250	.500	.750	101	-0	-0	97	187	1	.667	0	0	0	0	/C	0.0
1956	Det-A	3	8	0	2	1	0	0	1	1	2	.250	.333	.375	.708	90	-0	-0	97	124	1	.667	0	0	0	0	/C	0.0
Total	3	6	12	1	3	2	0	0	2	2	2	.250	.357	.417	.774	108	0	0	97	133	2	.778	0	0	0	0	/C	0.0

■ **CUB STRICKER** Stricker, John A. (born John A. Streaker) b: 2/15/1860, Philadelphia, Pa. d: 11/19/37, Philadelphia, Pa. BR/TR, 5'3", 138 lbs. Deb: 5/02/1882 M

YEAR	TM/L	G	AB	R	H	2B	3B	HR	RBI	BB	SO	AVG	OBP	SLG	PRO	/A	BR	/A	PF	CHI	RC	TA	SB	CS	SBR	FR	POS	TPR
1882	Phi-a	72	272	34	59	6	1	0		15		.217	.258	.246	.504	63	-8	-12	112	0	18	.385				**20**	*2/PO	1.2
1883	Phi-a	89	330	67	90	8	0	1		19		.273	.312	.306	.618	97	0	-1	103	0	32	.500				-26	*2/C	-2.2
1884	Phi-a	107	399	59	92	16	11	1		19		.231	.267	.333	.601	85	-1	-10	114	0	36	.498				-38	*2/OCP	-4.2
1885	Phi-a	106	398	71	93	9	3	1		21		.234	.284	.279	.563	78	-8	-10	103	0	32	.456				-15	*2	-1.8
1887	Cle-a	131	534	122	141	19	4	2		53		.264	.334	.326	.660	89	-8	-6	98	0	89	.804	86			7	*2/SP	0.2
1888	Cle-a	127	493	80	115	13	6	1	33	50		.233	.311	.290	.602	99	-0	2	97	65	65	.685	60			18	*2/OP	2.2
1889	Cle-N	136	566	83	142	10	4	1	47	58	18	.251	.323	.288	.611	71	-19	-22	103	73	64	.601	32			-0	*2/S	-0.9
1890	Cle-P	127	544	93	133	19	8	2	65	54	16	.244	.318	.320	.638	79	-21	-12	92	95	65	.625	24			-0	*2S	-0.5
1891	Bos-a	139	514	96	111	15	4	0	46	63	34	.216	.309	.261	.569	67	-21	-20	99	101	59	.638	54			**27**	*2	1.5
1892	StL-N	28	98	12	20	1	0	0	11	10	7	.204	.297	.214	.512	60	-5	-4	95	164	8	.500	5			-5	2/SM	-0.7
	Bal-N	75	269	45	71	5	5	3	37	32	18	.264	.344	.353	.698	113	5	5	100	111	38	.712	13			-16	2	-0.9
	Yr	103	367	57	91	6	5	3	48	42	25	.248	.332	.316	.648	99	0	1	99	127	46	.652	18			-21		-1.6
1893	Was-N	59	218	28	40	7	1	0	20	20	12	.183	.252	.225	.477	32	-22	-18	90	112	14	.410	4			6	2O/S3	-1.0
Total	11	1196	4635	790	1107	128	47	12	259	414	105	.239	.306	.294	.600	80	-107	-107	100	54	521	.593	278			-23	*2/SOP3C	-7.1

■ **GEORGE STRICKLAND** Strickland, George Bevan "Bo" b: 1/10/26, New Orleans, La. BR/TR, 6'1", 175 lbs. Deb: 5/07/50 MC

YEAR	TM/L	G	AB	R	H	2B	3B	HR	RBI	BB	SO	AVG	OBP	SLG	PRO	/A	BR	/A	PF	CHI	RC	TA	SB	CS	SBR	FR	POS	TPR
1950	Pit-N	23	27	0	3	0	0	0	2	3	8	.111	.226	.111	.337	-8	-4	-4	103	257	1	.292	0			-1	S/3	-0.2
1951	Pit-N	138	454	59	98	12	7	9	47	65	83	.216	.318	.333	.651	71	-15	-19	107	102	52	.608	4	2	0	2	*S2	-0.5
1952	Pit-N	76	232	17	41	6	2	5	22	21	45	.177	.248	.284	.533	47	-17	-17	100	106	17	.465	4	2	0	4	2S/13	-1.0
	Cle-A	31	88	8	19	4	0	1	8	14	15	.216	.324	.295	.619	80	-3	-2	91	103	10	.580	0	0	0	2	S/2	0.2
1953	Cle-A	123	419	43	119	17	4	5	47	51	52	.284	.362	.379	.741	105	1	4	95	102	63	.691	0	0	0	12	*S/1	2.5
1954	Cle-A	112	361	42	77	12	3	6	37	55	62	.213	.319	.313	.632	69	-12	-15	106	109	39	.580	2	1	0	-13	*S	-1.9
1955	Cle-A	130	388	34	81	9	5	2	34	49	60	.209	.302	.273	.575	53	-24	-26	104	113	35	.505	1	0	0	9	*S	-0.2
1956	Cle-A	85	171	22	36	1	2	3	17	22	27	.211	.301	.292	.593	56	-11	-11	101	108	15	.507	0	1	-1	-4	2S3	-0.9
1957	Cle-A	89	201	21	47	8	2	1	19	26	29	.234	.325	.308	.633	73	-7	-7	102	115	20	.549	0	3	-2	-4	2S3	-0.7
1959	Cle-A	132	441	55	105	15	2	3	48	52	64	.238	.318	.302	.620	74	-16	-14	97	**136**	45	.541	1	1	-0	-8	3S/2	-1.9
1960	Cle-A	32	42	4	7	0	0	1	3	4	8	.167	.255	.238	.493	35	-4	-4	98	90	3	.417	0	0	0	-0	S3/2	-0.2
Total	10	971	2824	305	633	84	27	36	284	362	453	.224	.315	.311	.626	70	-112	-116	101	113	299	.574	12	10		-1	S23/1	-4.8

■ **GEORGE STRIEF** Strief, George Andrew b: 10/16/1856, Cincinnati, Ohio d: 4/1/46, Cleveland, Ohio 5'7", 172 lbs. Deb: 5/01/1879

YEAR	TM/L	G	AB	R	H	2B	3B	HR	RBI	BB	SO	AVG	OBP	SLG	PRO	/A	BR	/A	PF	CHI	RC	TA	SB	CS	SBR	FR	POS	TPR
1879	Cle-N	71	264	24	46	7	1	0	15	10	23	.174	.204	.208	.413	37	-17	-17	99	98	12	.298				0	O2	-1.7
1882	Pit-a	79	297	45	58	9	6	2		13		.195	.229	.286	.515	75	-8	-7	97	0	20	.410				-4	*2/S	-0.4
1883	StL-a	82	302	22	68	9	0	1		12		.225	.255	.265	.520	63	-10	-14	108	0	21	.393				5	*2O	-0.6
1884	StL-a	48	184	22	37	5	2	2		13		.201	.254	.283	.536	70	-4	-7	110	0	14	.442				-4	O/21	-0.9
	KC-U	15	56	5	6	5	0	0		4		.107	.167	.196	.363	26	-4	-3	87	0	2	.300	0			0	2	-0.2
	CP-U	15	53	6	11	5	0	0		3		.208	.250	.302	.552	86	-1	-1	99	0	4	.452	0			0	2	0.0
	Yr	30	109	11	17	10	0	0		7		.156	.207	.248	.455	57	-5	-4	93	0	6	.370	0			0		-0.2
	Cle-N	8	29	2	7	2	0	0	0	0	5	.241	.241	.310	.552	71	-1	-1	102	0	2	.409				0	/O32	0.0
1885	Phi-a	44	175	19	48	8	5	0		9		.274	.310	.377	.687	115	4	3	103	0	21	.591				0	3S/O2	0.2
Total	5	362	1360	145	281	50	14	5	15	64	28	.207	.242	.275	.517	68	-43	-47	102	19	95	.406	0			-2	2O/3S1	-3.6

■ **JOHN STRIKE** Strike, John b: 1865, Pennsylvania Deb: 5/18/1882

YEAR	TM/L	G	AB	R	H	2B	3B	HR	RBI	BB	SO	AVG	OBP	SLG	PRO	/A	BR	/A	PF	CHI	RC	TA	SB	CS	SBR	FR	POS	TPR
1882	Lou-a	32	110	17	18	6	1	0		9		.164	.227	.236	.463	60	-5	-4	94	0	6	.380				-3	C/O2S1	-0.5
1886	Phi-N	2	7	0	0	0	0	0	0	0	4	.000	.000	.000	.000	-99	-2	-2	98	0	0	.000	0			0	/PO	0.0
Total	2	34	117	17	18	6	1	0	0	9	4	.154	.214	.222	.437	49	-6	-5	94	0	6	.354	0			-3	/CO2P1S	-0.5

■ **LOU STRINGER** Stringer, Louis Bernard b: 5/13/17, Grand Rapids, Mich BR/TR, 5'11", 173 lbs. Deb: 4/15/41

YEAR	TM/L	G	AB	R	H	2B	3B	HR	RBI	BB	SO	AVG	OBP	SLG	PRO	/A	BR	/A	PF	CHI	RC	TA	SB	CS	SBR	FR	POS	TPR
1941	Chi-N	145	512	59	126	31	4	5	53	59	86	.246	.324	.352	.676	96	-6	-2	94	100	62	.619	3			17	*2/S	2.4
1942	Chi-N	121	406	45	96	10	5	9	41	31	55	.236	.292	.352	.644	92	-7	-5	96	89	42	.560	3			7	*2/3	1.1
1946	Chi-N	80	209	26	51	3	1	3	19	26	34	.244	.328	.311	.639	87	-5	-3	94	96	22	.558	0			-6	2/S3	-0.6
1948	Bos-A	4	11	1	1	0	0	1	1	0	3	.091	.091	.364	.455	18	-1	-1	100	48	0	.364	0	0	0	0	/2	0.0
1949	Bos-A	35	41	10	11	4	0	1	6	5	10	.268	.348	.439	.787	100	0	-0	107	98	6	.742	0	0	0	1	/2	0.1
1950	Bos-A	24	17	7	5	1	0	0	2	0	4	.294	.294	.353	.647	57	-1	-1	114	115	2	.538	1	0	0	0	/32S	0.0
Total	6	409	1196	148	290	49	10	19	122	121	192	.242	.313	.348	.660	92	-20	-14	95	95	135	.601	7	0		20	2/S3	3.0

■ **JOE STRIPP** Stripp, Joseph Valentine "Jersey Joe" b: 2/3/03, Harrison, N.J. BR/TR, 5'11.5", 175 lbs. Deb: 7/02/28

YEAR	TM/L	G	AB	R	H	2B	3B	HR	RBI	BB	SO	AVG	OBP	SLG	PRO	/A	BR	/A	PF	CHI	RC	TA	SB	CS	SBR	FR	POS	TPR
1928	Cin-N	42	139	18	40	7	3	1	17	8	8	.288	.340	.403	.743	97	-1	-1	96	103	19	.677	0			-6	O3/S	-0.6
1929	Cin-N	64	187	24	40	3	2	3	20	24	15	.214	.313	.299	.613	53	-14	-14	99	105	19	.578	2			-4	3/2	-1.1
1930	Cin-N	130	464	74	142	37	6	3	64	51	37	.306	.377	.431	.808	105	-3	5	90	108	75	.832	15			-3	13	0.0
1931	Cin-N	105	426	71	138	26	2	3	42	21	31	.324	.359	.415	.774	113	4	7	95	85	64	.712	5			1	3/1	1.2
1932	Bro-N	138	534	94	162	36	9	6	64	36	30	.303	.350	.438	.788	115	8	10	96	100	84	.769	14			16	31	3.1
1933	Bro-N	141	537	69	149	20	7	1	51	26	23	.277	.312	.346	.658	91	-9	-7	97	107	59	.548	5			5	*3	0.2
1934	Bro-N	104	384	50	121	19	6	1	40	22	20	.315	.354	.404	.757	108	1	4	95	93	55	.659	2			-4	3/1S	0.6
1935	Bro-N	109	373	44	114	13	5	3	43	22	15	.306	.344	.391	.736	104	-1	2	94	100	49	.625	2			3	31/O	0.7
1936	Bro-N	110	439	51	139	31	1	1	60	22	12	.317	.351	.399	.749	97	1	-2	105	126	62	.645	2			6	*3	1.2
1937	Bro-N	90	300	37	73	10	2	1	26	20	18	.243	.291	.300	.591	58	-16	-18	104	101	25	.464	1			-1	31/S	-1.6
1938	StL-N	54	199	24	57	7	0	0	18	18	10	.286	.349	.322	.670	77	-3	-6	111	104	23	.557	0			1	3	-0.5
	Bos-N	59	229	19	63	10	0	1	19	10	7	.275	.305	.332	.637	85	-8	-4	88	92	24	.518	2			-2	3	-0.7
	Yr	113	428	43	120	17	0	1	37	28	17	.280	.326	.327	.653	81	-11	-11	99	98	49	.548	2			-0		-1.2
Total	11	1146	4211	575	1238	219	43	24	464	280	226	.294	.340	.384	.724	96	-42	-24	97	103	555	.659	50			11	31/OS2	2.5

YEAR	TM/L	G	AB	R	H	2B	3B	HR	RBI	BB	SO	AVG	OBP	SLG	PRO	/A	BR	/A	PF	CHI	RC	TA	SB	CS	SBR	FR	POS	TPR
■ ALLIE STROBEL Strobel, Albert Irving b: 6/11/1884, Boston, Mass. d: 2/10/55, Hollywood, Fla. TR , 6', 160 lbs. Deb: 8/29/05																												
1905	Bos-N	5	19	1	2	0	0	0	2	0		.105	.105	.105	.211	-38	-3	-3	97	355	0	.118	0			0	/3O	-0.2
1906	Bos-N	100	317	28	64	10	3	1	24	29		.202	.269	.262	.531	67	-12	-12	100	104	23	.451	2			-11	2/SO	-2.5
Total	2	105	336	29	66	10	3	1	26	29		.196	.260	.253	.513	61	-15	-15	100	117	24	.430	2			-11	/2S3O	-2.7
■ JIM STRONER Stroner, James M. b: 9/26/1892, Chicago, Ill. d: 11/16/71, Chicago, Ill. BR/TR, 5'10", 175 lbs. Deb: 5/01/29																												
1929	Pit-N	6	8	0	3	1	0	0	0	1	0	.375	.444	.500	.944	129	0	0	103	0	2	1.000	0			0	/3	0.1
■ ED STROUD Stroud, Edwin Marvin b: 10/31/39, Lapine, Ala. BL/TR, 5'11", 180 lbs. Deb: 9/11/66																												
1966	Chi-A	12	36	3	6	2	0	0	1	2	8	.167	.231	.222	.453	33	-3	-3	94	52	2	.467	3	0	1	-0	O	-0.2
1967	Chi-A	20	27	6	8	0	1	0	3	1	5	.296	.345	.370	.715	119	0	1	94	125	3	.826	7	2	1	0	O	0.1
	Was-A	87	204	36	41	5	3	1	10	25	29	.201	.291	.270	.561	65	-8	-8	102	72	17	.514	8	6	-1	-8	O	-2.2
	Yr	107	231	42	49	5	4	1	13	26	34	.212	.297	.281	.579	71	-8	-8	101	83	20	.557	15	8	-0	-8		-2.1
1968	Was-A	105	306	41	73	10	10	4	23	20	50	.239	.285	.376	.661	108	-1	1	91	78	30	.583	9	3	1	-4	O	-0.5
1969	Was-A	123	206	35	52	5	6	4	29	30	33	.252	.353	.393	.746	112	3	4	97	125	31	.772	12	2	2	-13	O	-0.8
1970	Was-A	129	433	69	115	11	5	5	32	40	79	.266	.332	.349	.681	91	-7	-5	96	78	51	.658	29	8	4	-3	*O	-0.9
1971	Chi-A	53	141	19	25	4	3	0	2	11	20	.177	.237	.248	.485	38	-12	-11	98	23	7	.403	4	5	-2	-8	O	-2.4
Total	6	529	1353	209	320	37	28	14	100	129	224	.237	.307	.336	.643	87	-28	-22	96	79	141	.625	72	26	6	-36	O	-6.9
■ STEVE STROUGHTER Stroughter, Stephen Lewis b: 3/15/52, Visalia, Cal. BL/TR, 6'2", 190 lbs. Deb: 4/07/82																												
1982	Sea-A	26	47	4	8	1	0	1	3	3	9	.170	.235	.255	.491	32	-4	-5	109	80	3	.410	0	0	0	1	/OD	-0.3
■ AMOS STRUNK Strunk, Amos Aaron b: 1/22/1889, Philadelphia, Pa. d: 7/22/79, Llanerch, Pa. BL/TL, 5'11.5", 175 lbs. Deb: 9/24/08																												
1908	Phi-A	12	34	4	8	1	0	0	0	4		.235	.316	.265	.580	85	-0	-0	108	0	3	.500	0			-0	O	-0.1
1909	Phi-A	11	35	1	4	0	0	0	2	1		.114	.139	.114	.253	-20	-5	-5	102	193	1	.226	2			-1	/O	-0.6
1910	Phi-A	16	48	9	16	0	1	0	2	3		.333	.373	.375	.748	131	2	2	102	41	8	.781	4			1	O	0.3
1911	Phi-A	74	215	42	55	7	2	1	21	35		.256	.363	.321	.683	98	-1	1	93	99	31	.738	13			4	O/1	0.1
1912	Phi-A	120	412	58	119	13	12	3	63	47		.289	.366	.400	.766	120	10	11	99	123	72	.833	29			2	*O	0.5
1913	Phi-A	94	292	30	89	11	12	0	46	29	23	.305	.368	.425	.792	136	11	12	97	132	49	.823	14			-3	O	0.5
1914	Phi-A	122	404	58	111	15	3	2	45	57	38	.275	.364	.342	.706	115	8	9	97	120	53	.698	25	22	-6	4	*O	0.0
1915	Phi-A	132	485	76	144	28	16	1	45	56	45	.297	.371	.427	.798	144	22	24	96	70	78	.781	17	19	-6	16	*O1	2.9
1916	Phi-A	150	544	71	172	30	9	3	49	66	59	.316	.393	.421	.814	147	30	32	98	71	91	.808	21	23	-8	9	*O/1	3.5
1917	Phi-A	148	540	83	152	26	7	1	45	68	37	.281	.363	.361	.724	129	15	19	94	78	76	.722	16			-5	*O	0.5
1918	Bos-A	114	413	50	106	18	9	0	35	36	13	.257	.316	.344	.660	104	-1	1	95	95	50	.645	20			-0	*O	-0.5
1919	Bos-A	48	184	27	50	11	3	0	17	13	13	.272	.323	.364	.687	101	-2	-0	91	97	22	.627	3			2	O	-0.1
	Phi-A	60	194	15	41	6	4	0	13	23	15	.211	.298	.284	.582	60	-9	-11	106	87	17	.536	3			-1	O	-1.5
	Yr	108	378	42	91	17	7	0	30	36	28	.241	.310	.323	.633	78	-11	-11	99	93	39	.578	6			1		-1.6
1920	Phi-A	58	202	23	60	9	3	0	20	21	9	.297	.363	.371	.735	101	-1	1	94	95	26	.649	0	6	-4	-5	O	-1.1
	Chi-A	53	188	33	45	8	1	1	16	28	15	.239	.338	.309	.646	75	-7	-6	96	94	21	.608	1	0	0	-3	O	-1.2
	Yr	111	390	56	105	17	4	1	36	49	24	.269	.351	.341	.692	88	-8	-5	95	95	48	.629	1	6	-3	-8		-2.3
1921	Chi-A	121	401	68	133	19	10	3	69	38	27	.332	.391	.451	.842	115	9	9	99	124	69	.817	7	10	-4	-5	*O	-0.8
1922	Chi-A	92	311	36	90	11	4	0	33	33	28	.289	.358	.350	.708	84	-6	-6	101	108	40	.665	9	6	-1	4	O/1	-0.8
1923	Chi-A	54	54	7	17	0	0	0	8	8	5	.315	.403	.315	.718	92	-0	-0	98	161	8	.703	1	0	0	0	/O1	0.0
1924	Chi-A	1	1	0	0	0	0	0	0	0	0	.000	.000	.000	.000	-99	-0	-0	97	0	0	.000	0	0	0	0	H	0.0
	Phi-A	30	42	5	6	0	0	0	1	7	4	.143	.265	.143	.408	7	-6	-6	99	55	2	.361	0	0	0	-3	/O	-0.8
	Yr	31	43	5	6	0	0	0	1	7	4	.140	.260	.140	.400	5	-6	-6	99	53	2	.351	0	0	0	-3		-0.8
Total	17	1510	4999	696	1418	213	96	15	530	573	331	.284	.359	.374	.732	113	68	87	97	97	720	.719	185	86		16	*O/1	0.8
■ AL STRUVE Struve, Al b: St.Louis, Mo. Deb: 6/22/1884																												
1884	StL-a	2	7	2	2	0	0	0		0		.286	.286	.286	.571	82	-0	-0	110	0	1	.400				0	/OC	0.0
■ LUKE STUART Stuart, Luther Lane b: 5/23/1892, Alamance Co., N.C. d: 6/15/47, Winston-Salem, N.C. BR/TR, 5'8", 165 lbs. Deb: 7/28/21																												
1921	StL-A	3	3	2	1	0	0	1	2	0	1	.333	.333	1.333	1.667	306	1	1	101	98	1	2.000	0	0	0	0	/2	0.1
■ DICK STUART Stuart, Richard Lee "Dr. Strangeglove" b: 11/7/32, San Francisco, Cal. BR/TR, 6'4", 212 lbs. Deb: 7/10/58																												
1958	Pit-N	67	254	38	68	12	5	16	48	11	75	.268	.311	.543	.854	127	6	8	95	109	41	.802	0	0	0	-1	1	0.3
1959	Pit-N	118	397	64	118	15	2	27	78	42	86	.297	.367	.549	.916	136	22	20	103	105	78	.904	1	1	-0	-2	*1/O	1.0
1960	Pit-N	122	438	48	114	17	5	23	83	39	107	.260	.321	.479	.800	116	8	8	99	123	63	.735	0	0	0	0	*1	0.3
1961	Pit-N	138	532	83	160	28	8	35	117	34	121	.301	.347	.581	.928	142	28	29	99	121	97	.874	0	3	-2	-2	*1/O	1.6
1962	Pit-N	114	394	52	90	11	4	16	64	32	94	.228	.290	.398	.688	81	-11	-12	102	125	44	.608	0	1	-1	1	*1	-1.4
1963	Bos-A	157	612	81	160	25	4	42	**118**	44	144	.261	.312	.521	.833	122	20	16	106	118	91	.765	0	0	0	8	*1	2.0
1964	Bos-A	156	603	73	168	27	1	33	114	37	130	.279	.323	.491	.814	121	16	15	102	130	93	.753	0	0	0	1	*1	1.2
1965	Phi-N	149	538	53	126	19	1	28	95	39	136	.234	.290	.429	.719	105	-2	1	95	128	66	.649	1	0	0	4	*1/3	-0.1
1966	NY-N	31	87	7	19	0	0	4	13	9	26	.218	.292	.356	.648	84	-2	-2	94	127	8	.541	0	1	-1	1	1	-0.2
	LA-N	38	91	4	24	1	0	3	9	11	17	.264	.356	.374	.729	106	1	1	97	88	12	.662	0	1	-1	0	1	0.0
	Yr	69	178	11	43	1	0	7	22	20	43	.242	.325	.365	.690	96	-2	-1	96	107	21	.621	0	2	-1	1		-0.2
1969	Cal-A	22	51	3	8	2	0	1	4	3	21	.157	.204	.255	.459	28	-5	-5	99	100	2	.356	0	0	0	-0	1	-0.6
Total	10	1112	3997	506	1055	157	30	228	743	301	957	.264	.319	.489	.808	117	81	80	100	120	595	.773	2	7	-4	9	*1/O3	4.1
■ BILL STUART Stuart, William Alexander "Chauncey" b: 8/28/1873, Boalsburg, Pa. d: 10/14/28, Fort Worth, Tex. 5'11", 170 lbs. Deb: 8/15/1895																												
1895	Pit-N	19	77	5	19	3	0	0	10	2	6	.247	.275	.286	.561	48	-6	-6	97	135	7	.466	2			0	S/2	-0.4
1899	NY-N	1	3	0	0	0	0	0	0	0		.000	.000	.000	.000	-99	-1	-1	97	0	0	.000	0			0	/2	0.0
Total	2	20	80	5	19	3	0	0	10	2	6	.237	.265	.275	.540	43	-7	-6	97	130	7	.443	2			0	/S2	-0.4
■ FRANKLIN STUBBS Stubbs, Franklin Lee b: 10/21/60, Richland, N.C. BL/TL, 6'2", 215 lbs. Deb: 4/28/84																												
1984	LA-N	87	217	22	42	2	3	8	17	24	63	.194	.274	.341	.615	69	-9	-10	104	68	22	.565	2	2	-1	-1	1O	-1.4
1985	LA-N	10	9	0	2	0	0	0	2	0	3	.222	.222	.222	.444	27	-1	-1	93	398	0	.286	0	0	0	0	/1	0.0
1986	LA-N	132	420	55	95	11	1	23	58	37	107	.226	.292	.421	.713	100	-5	-2	94	94	51	.666	7	1	2	-9	*O1	-1.2
1987	LA-N	129	386	48	90	16	3	16	52	31	85	.233	.292	.415	.706	92	-10	-6	92	100	47	.658	8	1	2	7	*1O	-0.3
1988	LA-N	115	242	30	54	13	0	8	34	23	61	.223	.293	.376	.669	86	-3	-5	106	118	28	.646	11	3	2	0	1O	-0.7
Total	5	473	1274	155	283	42	7	55	163	115	319	.222	.289	.396	.684	89	-27	-23	97	98	147	.650	28	7	4	-3	1O	-3.6
■ MOOSE STUBING Stubing, Lawrence George b: 3/31/38, Bronx, N.Y. BL/TL, 6'3", 220 lbs. Deb: 4/14/67 MC																												
1967	Cal-A	5	5	0	0	0	0	0	0	0	4	.000	.000	.000	.000	-99	-1	-1	96	0	0	.000	0	0	0	0	H	0.0
■ SY STUDLEY Studley, Seymour L. "Warhorse" b: Washington, D.C. d: 1873, Washington, D.C. Deb: 4/20/1872																												
1872	Nat-n	5	22	3	3							.136															/O	
■ GEORGE STUMPF Stumpf, George Frederick b: 12/15/10, New Orleans, La. BL/TL, 5'8", 155 lbs. Deb: 9/19/31																												
1931	Bos-A	7	28	2	7	1	1	0	4	1	2	.250	.276	.357	.633	70	-2	-1	94	135	3	.524	0	0	0	-1	/O	-0.1
1932	Bos-A	79	169	18	34	2	2	1	18	18	21	.201	.278	.254	.533	40	-15	-14	97	131	13	.456	1	1	-0	-9	O	-2.4
1933	Bos-A	22	41	8	14	3	0	0	5	4	2	.341	.400	.415	.815	115	1	1	101	98	8	.926	4	0	1	-3	O	0.0
1936	Chi-A	10	22	3	6	1	0	0	5	2	1	.273	.333	.318	.652	62	-1	-1	99	231	2	.563	0	0	0	1	/O	0.0
Total	4	118	260	31	61	7	3	1	32	25	26	.235	.302	.296	.598	57	-17	-16	97	135	26	.535	5	1	1	-12	/O	-2.5
■ BILL STUMPF Stumpf, William Frederick b: 3/21/1892, Baltimore, Md. d: 2/14/66, Crownsville, Md. BR/TR, 6'0.5", 175 lbs. Deb: 5/11/12																												
1912	NY-A	40	129	8	31	0	0	0	10	6		.240	.279	.240	.520	48	-8	-9	101	108	10	.439	5			-5	S/231O	-1.0
1913	NY-A	12	29	5	6	1	0	0	1	3	3	.207	.281	.241	.523	53	-2	-2	101	51	2	.435	0			-1	/S2O	-0.1
Total	2	52	158	13	37	1	0	0	11	9	3	.234	.280	.241	.520	49	-10	-10	101	97	12	.438	5			-5	/S23O1	-1.1

YEAR	TM/L	G	AB	R	H	2B	3B	HR	RBI	BB	SO	AVG	OBP	SLG	PRO	/A	BR	/A	PF	CHI	RC	TA	SB	CS	SBR	FR	POS	TPR
■ **GUY STURDY**	Sturdy, Guy R. b: 8/7/1899, Sherman, Tex. d: 5/4/65, Marshall, Tex. BL/TL, 6'0.5", 180 lbs. Deb: 9/30/27																											
1927	StL-A	5	21	5	9	1	0	0	5	1	0	.429	.455	.476	.931	134	1	1	106	160	4	1.083	2	0	1	0	/1	0.1
1928	StL-A	54	45	3	10	1	0	1	8	8	4	.222	.340	.311	.651	69	-2	-2	104	162	5	.657	1	0	0	0	/1	-0.1
Total	2	59	66	8	19	2	0	1	13	9	4	.288	.373	.364	.737	90	-0	-1	104	161	10	.766	3	0	1	0	/1	0.0
■ **BOBBY STURGEON**	Sturgeon, Robert Howard b: 8/6/19, Clinton, Ind. BR/TR, 6', 175 lbs. Deb: 4/16/40																											
1940	Chi-N	7	21	1	4	1	0	0	2	0	1	.190	.190	.238	.429	18	-2	-2	100	148	1	.278	0			1	/S	0.0
1941	Chi-N	129	433	45	106	15	3	0	25	9	30	.245	.260	.293	.553	59	-26	-23	94	71	31	.418	5			-3	*S/23	-1.5
1942	Chi-N	63	162	8	40	7	1	0	7	4	13	.247	.269	.302	.572	70	-7	-6	96	53	13	.452	2			3	2S/3	0.1
1946	Chi-N	100	294	26	87	12	2	1	21	10	18	.296	.319	.361	.680	98	-4	-2	94	72	33	.547	0			-2	S2	0.2
1947	Chi-N	87	232	16	59	10	5	0	21	7	12	.254	.276	.341	.617	62	-13	-13	101	98	19	.473	0			4	S2/3	-0.2
1948	Bos-N	34	78	10	17	3	1	0	4	4	5	.218	.256	.282	.538	45	-6	-6	102	68	5	.413	0			0	2/S3	-0.4
Total	6	420	1220	106	313	48	12	1	80	34	79	.257	.277	.318	.595	69	-58	-53	96	75	103	.473	7			2	S2/3	-1.8
■ **DEAN STURGIS**	Sturgis, Dean Donnell b: 12/1/1892, Beloit, Kan. d: 6/4/50, Uniontown, Pa. BR/TR, 6'1", 180 lbs. Deb: 5/01/14																											
1914	Phi-A	4	4	1	1	0	0	0	0	1	2	.250	.400	.250	.650	98	0	0	97	0	0	.667	0			0	/C	0.0
■ **JOHNNY STURM**	Sturm, John Peter Joseph b: 1/23/16, St.Louis, Mo. BL/TL, 6'1", 185 lbs. Deb: 4/15/41																											
1941	NY-A	124	524	58	125	17	3	3	36	37	50	.239	.293	.300	.592	58	-33	-31	98	74	46	.483	3	5	-2	-2	*1	-3.7
■ **GEORGE STUTZ**	Stutz, George "Kid" or "Satan" b: 2/12/1893, Philadelphia, Pa. d: 12/29/30, Philadelphia, Pa. BL/TR, 5'5", 150 lbs. Deb: 8/17/26																											
1926	Phi-N	6	9	0	0	0	0	0	0	0	2	.000	.000	.000	.000	-97	-2	-3	103	0	0	.000	0			0	/S	-0.1
■ **LENA STYLES**	Styles, William Graves b: 11/27/1899, Gurley, Ala. d: 3/14/56, Gurley, Ala. BR/TR, 6'1", 185 lbs. Deb: 9/10/19																											
1919	Phi-A	8	22	0	6	1	0	0	5	1	6	.273	.304	.318	.623	71	-1	-1	106	259	2	.500	0			1	/C	0.1
1920	Phi-A	24	50	5	13	3	1	0	5	6	7	.260	.339	.360	.699	91	-1	-1	94	98	7	.676	1	0	0	1	/C1	0.1
1921	Phi-A	4	5	0	1	0	0	0	0	0	2	.200	.200	.200	.400	2	-1	-1	103	0	0	.250	0	0	0	0	/C	0.0
1930	Cin-N	7	12	2	3	0	1	0	1	1	2	.250	.357	.417	.774	95	-0	-0	90	69	2	.778	0			0	/C1	0.0
1931	Cin-N	34	87	7	21	3	0	0	5	8	7	.241	.313	.276	.588	62	-5	-4	95	74	8	.500	0			0	C	-0.1
Total	5	77	176	14	44	7	2	0	16	16	24	.250	.320	.313	.632	72	-7	-6	96	101	19	.561	1	0		2	/C1	0.1
■ **NEIL STYNES**	Stynes, Cornelius William b: 12/10/1868, Arlington, Mass. d: 3/26/44, Somerville, Mass. 6', 165 lbs. Deb: 9/08/1890																											
1890	Cle-P	2	8	0	0	0	0	0	0	0	0	.000	.000	.000	.000	-99	-2	-2	92	0	0	.000	0			0	/C	-0.1
■ **KEN SUAREZ**	Suarez, Kenneth Raymond b: 4/12/43, Tampa, Fla. BR/TR, 5'9", 175 lbs. Deb: 4/14/66																											
1966	KC-A	35	69	5	10	0	1	0	2	15	26	.145	.298	.174	.472	42	-5	-4	94	70	5	.483	2	0	1	-0	C	-0.2
1967	KC-A	39	63	7	15	5	0	2	9	16	21	.238	.392	.413	.805	139	4	4	100	117	12	.878	1	0	0	-2	C	0.4
1968	Cle-A	17	10	1	1	0	0	0	0	1	3	.100	.182	.100	.282	-13	-1	-1	101	0	0	.200	0	0	0	-1	C/23O	-0.1
1969	Cle-A	36	85	7	25	5	0	1	9	15	12	.294	.400	.388	.788	128	3	4	94	100	13	.754	1	0	0	3	C	0.9
1971	Cle-A	50	123	10	25	7	0	1	9	18	15	.203	.315	.285	.599	67	-4	-5	106	97	12	.545	0	1	-1	3	C	0.0
1972	Tex-A	25	33	2	5	1	0	0	4	1	4	.152	.176	.182	.358	7	-4	-4	94	279	1	.241	0	0	0	-0	C	-0.3
1973	Tex-A	93	278	25	69	11	0	1	27	33	16	.248	.339	.299	.637	83	-6	-5	97	123	29	.552	1	2	-1	3	C	0.0
Total	7	295	661	57	150	29	1	5	60	99	97	.227	.334	.297	.630	82	-13	-12	98	114	71	.586	5	3	-0	5	C/O32	0.7
■ **LUIS SUAREZ**	Suarez, Luis Abelardo b: 8/24/16, Alto Songo, Cuba BR/TR, 5'11", 170 lbs. Deb: 5/28/44																											
1944	Was-A	1	2	0	0	0	0	0	0	0	0	.000	.000	.000	.000	-99	-1	-0	90	0	0	.000	0	0	0	0	/3	0.0
■ **TONY SUCK**	Suck, Anthony (born Charles Anthony Zuck) b: 6/11/1858, Chicago.Ill. d: 1/29/1895, Chicago, Ill. Deb: N/A.																											
1883	Buf-N	2	7	1	0	0	0	0	0	1	4	.000	.125	.000	.125	-58	-1	-1	100	0	0	.143				0	/OC	0.0
1884	CP-U	53	188	18	28	2	0	0		13		.149	.204	.160	.364	25	-14	-14	99	0	6	.269	0			0	CSO/3	-1.1
	Bal-U	3	10	2	3	0	0	0		0		.300	.300	.300	.600	94	0	-0	110	0	1	.429	0			0	/C	0.0
	Yr	56	198	20	31	2	0	0		13		.157	.209	.167	.375	28	-14	-14	100	0	7	.275	0			0		-1.1
Total	2	58	205	21	31	2	0	0	0	14	4	.151	.205	.161	.366	25	-15	-15	100	0	7	.270	0			0	/CSO3	-1.1
■ **BILL SUDAKIS**	Sudakis, William Paul "Suds" b: 3/27/46, Joliet, Ill. BB/TR, 6'1", 190 lbs. Deb: 9/03/68																											
1968	LA-N	24	87	11	24	4	2	3	12	15	14	.276	.382	.471	.854	171	6	7	91	97	15	.851	1	0	0	0	3	0.8
1969	LA-N	132	462	50	108	17	5	14	53	40	94	.234	.296	.383	.679	90	-8	-7	99	99	52	.605	3	2	-0	13	*3	0.6
1970	LA-N	94	269	37	71	11	0	14	44	35	46	.264	.355	.461	.816	130	6	10	90	103	45	.810	4	0	1	-3	C3/O1	0.8
1971	LA-N	41	83	10	16	3	0	3	7	12	22	.193	.302	.337	.639	82	-2	-2	99	77	8	.569	0	1	-1	-0	C/31O	-0.2
1972	NY-N	18	49	3	7	0	0	1	7	6	14	.143	.236	.204	.440	27	-5	-4	95	221	3	.372	0	0	0	1	/1C	-0.3
1973	Tex-A	82	235	32	60	11	0	15	43	23	53	.255	.322	.494	.815	131	7	8	97	105	36	.764	0	1	-1	-5	31/COD	0.1
1974	NY-A	89	259	26	60	8	0	7	39	25	48	.232	.302	.344	.645	89	-5	-4	96	139	29	.572	0	0	0	1	D1/3C	-0.3
1975	Cal-A	30	58	4	7	2	0	1	6	12	15	.121	.282	.207	.489	42	-4	-4	95	154	4	.500	1	1	-0	-0	D/C1	-0.4
	Cle-A	20	46	4	9	0	0	1	3	4	7	.196	.260	.261	.521	48	-3	-3	100	77	3	.421	0	1	-1	-0	1/C	-0.4
	Yr	50	104	8	16	2	0	2	9	16	22	.154	.273	.231	.503	45	-8	-7	97	126	7	.467	1	2	-1	-1		-0.8
Total	8	530	1548	177	362	56	7	59	214	172	313	.234	.313	.393	.707	102	-8	1	96	111	194	.669	9	6	-1	6	3/C1DO	0.7
■ **PETE SUDER**	Suder, Peter "Pecky" b: 4/16/16, Aliquippa, Pa. BR/TR, 6', 175 lbs. Deb: 4/15/41																											
1941	Phi-A	139	531	45	130	20	9	4	52	19	47	.245	.271	.339	.610	60	-32	-32	101	98	43	.468	1	3	-2	-11	*3/S	-3.6
1942	Phi-A	128	476	46	122	20	4	4	54	24	39	.256	.293	.340	.634	81	-15	-13	96	112	43	.505	4	4	-1	-12	S32	-2.2
1943	Phi-A	131	475	30	105	14	5	3	41	14	40	.221	.243	.291	.534	55	-28	-29	101	104	31	.397	1	1	-0	-11	23/S	-3.8
1946	Phi-A	128	455	38	128	20	3	2	50	18	37	.281	.309	.352	.660	81	-11	-13	104	117	48	.525	1	1	-0	-12	S32/1O	-2.1
1947	Phi-A	145	528	45	127	28	4	5	60	35	44	.241	.290	.337	.627	74	-20	-20	100	117	51	.514	0	3	-2	-19	*2/S3	-3.5
1948	Phi-A	148	519	64	125	23	5	7	60	60	60	.241	.321	.345	.666	76	-18	-19	102	103	60	.592	1	3	-2	-1	*2	-1.7
1949	Phi-A	118	445	44	119	24	6	10	75	23	35	.267	.306	.416	.722	91	-10	-9	99	122	52	.605	0	1	-1	1	23/S	-0.6
1950	Phi-A	77	248	34	61	10	0	8	35	23	31	.246	.310	.383	.693	85	-10	-6	90	102	29	.609	2	2	-1	-0	23S/1	-0.3
1951	Phi-A	123	440	46	108	18	1	1	42	30	42	.245	.295	.298	.593	57	-25	-28	106	112	37	.474	5	5	-2	3	*2S/3	-2.0
1952	Phi-A	74	228	22	55	7	2	1	20	16	17	.241	.291	.303	.594	59	-11	-14	111	104	21	.483	1	1	-0	-5	2S3	-1.7
1953	Phi-A	115	454	44	130	11	3	4	35	17	35	.286	.312	.350	.662	77	-14	-16	102	77	48	.531	3	3	-1	1	32/S	-1.6
1954	Phi-A	69	205	8	41	11	1	0	16	7	16	.200	.226	.263	.490	34	-19	-19	98	112	11	.359	0	0	0	-1	23/S	-2.0
1955	KC-A	26	81	3	17	4	1	0	1	2	13	.210	.229	.284	.513	37	-7	-8	101	16	5	.379	0	1	-1	-2	2	-0.8
Total	13	1421	5085	469	1268	210	44	49	541	288	456	.249	.291	.337	.627	70	-220	-225	101	105	478	.527	19	28	-11	-69	23S/1O	-25.9
■ **JOE SUGDEN**	Sugden, Joseph b: 7/31/1870, Philadelphia, Pa. d: 6/28/59, Philadelphia, Pa. BB/TR, 5'10", 180 lbs. Deb: 7/20/1893 C																											
1893	Pit-N	27	92	20	24	4	3	0	12	10	11	.261	.340	.370	.709	85	-1	-2	106	97	12	.676	1			0	C	-0.1
1894	Pit-N	39	139	23	46	13	2	2	23	14	2	.331	.404	.496	.900	125	4	6	94	86	30	.957	3			0	C/3SO	0.4
1895	Pit-N	49	155	28	48	4	1	1	17	16	12	.310	.385	.368	.753	100	0	1	97	79	24	.748	4			-3	C	0.2
1896	Pit-N	80	301	42	89	5	7	0	36	19	9	.296	.348	.359	.706	95	-5	-1	93	98	40	.646	5			4	C/1O	0.7
1897	Pit-N	84	288	31	64	6	4	0	38	18		.222	.275	.271	.546	47	-22	-21	98	143	25	.482	9			2	C/1	-0.7
1898	StL-N	89	289	29	73	7	1	0	34	23		.253	.314	.284	.598	70	-9	-11	106	125	28	.523	5			7	CO/1	0.0
1899	Cle-N	76	250	19	69	5	1	0	14	11		.276	.307	.304	.611	78	-10	-6	89	56	25	.492	2			18	C/O13	1.4
1901	Chi-A	48	153	21	42	7	1	0	19	13		.275	.331	.333	.665	87	-2	-2	99	118	19	.613	4			-0	C/1	0.1
1902	StL-A	68	200	25	50	7	2	0	15	20		.250	.318	.305	.623	73	-6	-7	102	81	21	.553	2			-3	C/1P	-0.3
1903	StL-A	79	241	18	51	4	0	0	22	25		.212	.286	.228	.514	60	-11	-10	95	144	17	.442	4			1	C/1	0.0
1904	StL-A	105	348	25	93	6	3	0	30	28		.267	.322	.302	.624	106	1	3	95	109	37	.545	6			3	C1	1.6
1905	StL-A	90	266	21	46	4	0	0	23	23		.173	.239	.188	.427	41	-18	-15	91	164	13	.345	3			9	C/1	0.1
1912	Det-A	1	4	1	1	0	0	0	0	0		.250	.250	.250	.500	45	-0	-0	95	0	0	.333	0			0	/1	0.0
Total	13	835	2726	303	696	72	25	3	283	220	34	.255	.315	.303	.618	79	-80	-67	97	112	290	.548	48			37	C/1O3SP	3.4
■ **GUS SUHR**	Suhr, August Richard b: 1/3/06, San Francisco, Cal. BL/TR, 6', 180 lbs. Deb: 4/15/30																											
1930	Pit-N	151	542	93	155	26	14	17	107	80	56	.286	.380	.480	.860	109	6	9	97	121	99	.912	11			-6	*1	-0.3

YEAR	TM/L	G	AB	R	H	2B	3B	HR	RBI	BB	SO	AVG	OBP	SLG	PRO	/A	BR	/A	PF	CHI	RC	TA	SB	CS	SBR	FR	POS	TPR
1931	Pit-N	87	270	26	57	13	4	4	32	38	25	.211	.308	.333	.642	72	-10	-10	101	112	30	.620	4			-4	1	-1.9
1932	Pit-N	154	581	78	153	31	16	5	81	63	39	.263	.337	.398	.735	97	-2	-1	99	130	82	.708	7			-10	*1	-1.9
1933	Pit-N	154	566	72	151	31	11	10	75	72	52	.267	.350	.413	.763	124	14	17	95	113	87	.723	2			-4	*1	1.1
1934	Pit-N	151	573	67	162	36	13	13	103	66	52	.283	.360	.459	.819	112	14	10	105	130	98	.792	4			-5	*1	-0.6
1935	Pit-N	153	529	68	144	33	12	10	81	70	54	.272	.357	.437	.794	105	10	5	107	114	89	.785	6			-7	*1/O	-0.5
1936	Pit-N	156	583	111	182	33	12	11	118	95	34	.312	.410	.467	.877	139	32	34	98	145	119	.908	8			-4	*1	1.7
1937	Pit-N	151	575	69	160	28	14	5	97	83	42	.278	.369	.402	.771	107	9	8	102	**151**	92	.745	2			-4	*1	-0.3
1938	Pit-N	145	530	82	156	35	14	3	64	87	37	.294	.394	.430	.824	126	22	22	100	103	97	.831	4			-9	*1	0.1
1939	Pit-N	63	204	23	59	10	2	1	31	25	23	.289	.367	.373	.739	99	0	1	100	144	31	.724	4			-3	1	-0.7
	Phi-N	60	198	21	63	12	2	3	24	34	14	.318	.421	.444	.865	141	11	12	94	92	40	.912	1			0	1	0.6
	Yr	123	402	44	122	22	4	4	55	59	37	.303	.394	.408	.802	119	11	13	97	120	71	.815	5			-2		-0.1
1940	Phi-N	10	25	4	4	0	0	2	5	5	5	.160	.300	.400	.700	94	-0	-0	97	116	3	.714	0			0	/1	0.0
Total	11	1435	5176	714	1446	288	114	84	818	718	433	.279	.368	.428	.796	113	106	105	100	125	867	.803	53			-53	*1/O	-2.7
■ **CLYDE SUKEFORTH** Sukeforth, Clyde Leroy "Sukey" b: 11/30/01, Washington, Me. BL/TR, 5'10", 155 lbs. Deb: 5/23/26 MC																												
1926	Cin-N	1	1	0	0	0	0	0	0	0	1	.000	.000	.000	.000	-99	-0	-0	95	0	0	.000	0			0	H	0.0
1927	Cin-N	38	58	12	11	2	0	0	2	7	2	.190	.277	.224	.501	36	-5	-5	100	54	4	.468	2			-1	C	-0.3
1928	Cin-N	33	53	5	7	2	1	0	3	3	5	.132	.179	.208	.386	1	-8	-8	96	97	2	.304	0			0	C	-0.5
1929	Cin-N	84	237	31	84	16	2	1	33	17	6	.354	.398	.451	.849	111	4	4	99	103	41	.863	8			3	C	1.2
1930	Cin-N	94	296	30	84	9	3	1	19	17	12	.284	.325	.345	.669	69	-18	-13	90	62	33	.571	1			1	C	-0.6
1931	Cin-N	112	351	22	90	15	4	0	25	38	13	.256	.334	.322	.656	81	-10	-8	95	79	40	.590	0			2	*C	-0.1
1932	Bro-N	59	111	14	26	4	4	0	12	6	10	.234	.280	.342	.622	69	-5	-5	96	117	11	.541	1			-0	C	-0.3
1933	Bro-N	20	36	1	2	0	0	0	0	2	1	.056	.105	.056	.161	-55	-7	-7	97	0	0	.111	0			0	C	-0.5
1934	Bro-N	27	43	5	7	1	0	0	1	1	6	.163	.182	.186	.368	-1	-6	-6	95	45	1	.243	0			-0	C	-0.5
1945	Bro-N	18	51	2	15	1	0	0	1	4	1	.294	.345	.314	.659	88	-1	-1	96	22	6	.556	0			-1	C	-0.1
Total	10	486	1237	122	326	50	14	2	96	95	57	.264	.319	.331	.650	71	-57	-48	95	77	138	.573	12			4	C	-1.7
■ **GUY SULARZ** Sularz, Guy Patrick b: 11/7/55, Minneapolis, Minn. BR/TR, 5'11", 165 lbs. Deb: 9/02/80																												
1980	SF-N	25	65	3	16	1	1	0	3	9	6	.246	.338	.292	.630	81	-2	-1	96	62	7	.569	1	0	0	-1	2/3	0.0
1981	SF-N	10	20	0	4	0	0	0	2	2	4	.200	.304	.200	.504	43	-1	-1	105	196	1	.412	0	1	-1	-0	/23	-0.1
1982	SF-N	63	101	15	23	3	0	1	7	9	11	.228	.291	.287	.578	66	-5	-4	94	86	9	.512	3	0	1	-1	S3/2	0.0
1983	SF-N	10	20	3	2	0	0	0	0	3	2	.100	.217	.100	.317	-9	-3	-3	101	0	0	.263	0	0	0	-1	/S3	-0.2
Total	4	108	206	21	45	4	1	1	12	23	23	.218	.300	.262	.562	61	-11	-10	96	81	18	.503	4	1	1	-2	/S23	-0.3
■ **ERNIE SULIK** Sulik, Ernest Richard "Dave" b: 7/7/10, San Francisco, Cal. d: 5/31/63, Oakland, Cal. BL/TL, 5'10", 178 lbs. Deb: 4/15/36																												
1936	Phi-N	122	404	69	116	14	4	6	36	40	22	.287	.353	.386	.739	91	-0	-5	108	73	57	.674	4			-1	*O	-0.9
■ **SULLIVAN** Sullivan b:Bristol, R.I. Deb: 5/14/1875																												
1875	NH-n	2	10	3	3							.300															/O	
■ **ANDY SULLIVAN** Sullivan, Andrew R. b: 8/30/1884, Southborough, Mass d: 2/14/20, Framingham, Mass. TR , Deb: 9/13/04																												
1904	Bos-N	1	1	0	0	0	0	0	0	1		.000	.500	.000	.500	64	0	0	97	0	0	1.000	0			0	/S	0.0
■ **JACKIE SULLIVAN** Sullivan, Carl Mancel b: 2/22/18, Princeton, Tex. BR/TR, 5'11", 172 lbs. Deb: 7/06/44																												
1944	Det-A	1	1	0	0	0	0	0	0	0	0	.000	.000	.000	.000	-95	-0	-0	105	0	0	.000	0	0	0	0	/2	0.0
■ **DAN SULLIVAN** Sullivan, Daniel C. "Link" b: 5/9/1857, Providence, R.I. d: 10/26/1893, Providence, R.I. TR , 5'11", 194 lbs. Deb: 5/02/1882																												
1882	Lou-a	67	286	44	78	8	2	0		9		.273	.295	.315	.610	113	2	4	94	0	27	.476				9	*C3/OS	1.2
1883	Lou-a	37	147	8	31	5	2	0		3		.211	.227	.272	.499	64	-6	-5	94	0	9	.371				-2	C/O3S	-0.3
1884	Lou-a	63	247	27	59	8	6	0		9		.239	.268	.320	.588	105	-2	2	89	0	22	.473				-20	C/O	-1.1
1885	Lou-a	13	44	3	8	1	0	0		2		.182	.234	.205	.439	41	-3	-3	102	0	2	.333				0	C	-0.2
	StL-a	17	60	4	7	2	0	0		6		.117	.197	.150	.347	13	-6	-5	93	0	2	.283				0	C/1	-0.4
	Yr	30	104	7	15	3	0	0		8		.144	.212	.173	.385	25	-8	-8	97	0	4	.303				0		-0.6
1886	Pit-a	1	4	0	0	0	0	0		0		.000	.000	.000	.000	-99	-1	-1	93	0	0	.000	0			0	/C	0.0
Total	5	198	788	86	183	24	10	0		29		.232	.261	.288	.549	87	-16	-7	93	0	62	.426	0			-14	C/3O1S	-0.8
■ **DENNY SULLIVAN** Sullivan, Dennis J. b: 6/26/1858, Boston, Mass. d: 12/31/25, Boston, Mass. TR , Deb: 8/25/1879																												
1879	Pro-N	5	19	5	5	2	0	0	2	1	1	.263	.300	.368	.668	117	0	0	102	100	2	.571				0	/3O	0.0
1880	Bos-N	1	4	1	1	0	0	0	1	0	1	.250	.250	.250	.500	76	-0	-0	92	372	0	.333				0	/C	0.0
Total	2	6	23	6	6	2	0	0	3	1	2	.261	.292	.348	.639	111	0	0	100	146	2	.529				0	/3CO	0.0
■ **DENNY SULLIVAN** Sullivan, Dennis William b: 9/28/1882, Hillsboro, Wis. d: 6/2/56, W.Los Angeles, Cal BL/TR, Deb: 4/22/05																												
1905	Was-A	3	11	0	0	0	0	0	0	1		.000	.083	.000	.083	-69	-2	-2	104	0	0	.091	0			0	/O	-0.1
1907	Bos-A	144	551	73	135	18	0	1	26	44		.245	.301	.283	.584	87	-6	-7	101	56	53	.519	16			-5	*O	-2.1
1908	Bos-A	101	353	33	85	7	7	0	25	14		.241	.270	.300	.570	89	-6	-5	98	90	31	.504	15			1	O	-1.0
	Cle-A	4	6	0	0	0	0	0	0	0		.000	.000	.000	.000	-94	-1	-1	106	0	0	.000	0			0	/O	-0.1
	Yr	105	359	33	85	7	7	0	25	14		.237	.265	.295	.561	85	-7	-6	99	88	31	.493	15			1		-1.1
1909	Cle-A	3	2	0	1	0	0	0	0	0		.500	.500	.500	1.000	211	0	0	102	0	0	1.000	0			0	/O	0.0
Total	4	255	923	106	221	25	7	1	51	59		.239	.285	.285	.570	85	-15	-15	100	68	85	.503	31			-4	O	-3.3
■ **HAYWOOD SULLIVAN** Sullivan, Haywood Cooper b: 12/15/30, Donalsonville, Ga. BR/TR, 6'4", 210 lbs. Deb: 9/20/55 M																												
1955	Bos-A	2	6	1	0	0	0	0	0	0	1	.000	.000	.000	.000	-81	-2	-2	124	0	0	.000	0	0	0	0	/C	-0.1
1957	Bos-A	2	1	0	0	0	0	0	0	0	0	.000	.000	.000	.000	-91	-0	-0	110	0	0	.000	0	0	0	0	/C	0.0
1959	Bos-A	4	2	0	0	0	0	0	0	1	1	.000	.333	.000	.333	-0	-0	-0	106	0	0	.500	0	0	0	0	/C	0.0
1960	Bos-A	52	124	9	20	1	0	3	10	16	24	.161	.257	.242	.499	35	-11	-12	103	100	8	.430	0	0	0	-4	C	-1.3
1961	KC-A	117	331	42	80	16	2	6	40	46	45	.242	.334	.356	.691	83	-7	-7	102	115	41	.635	1	0	0	1	C1/O	-0.8
1962	KC-A	95	274	33	68	7	2	4	29	31	54	.248	.327	.332	.659	78	-8	-8	100	112	31	.585	1	0	0	-1	C/1	-0.3
1963	KC-A	40	113	9	24	6	1	0	8	15	15	.212	.305	.283	.588	61	-5	-6	108	105	9	.495	0	0	0	3	C	-0.2
Total	7	312	851	94	192	30	5	13	87	109	140	.226	.314	.318	.633	70	-33	-36	102	109	89	.576	2	0	1	-1	C/1O	-2.7
■ **JOHN SULLIVAN** Sullivan, John Eugene b: 2/16/1873, Illinois d: 6/5/24, St.Paul, Minn. TR , Deb: 4/19/05																												
1905	Det-A	13	32	4	5	0	0	0	4	4		.156	.250	.156	.406	32	-2	-2	98	285	1	.333	0			0	C	0.0
1908	Pit-N	1	1	0	0	0	0	0	0	0		.000	.000	.000	.000	-99	-0	-0	95	0	0	.000	0			0	/C	0.0
Total	2	14	33	4	5	0	0	0	4	4		.152	.243	.152	.395	28	-2	-2	98	278	1	.321	0			0	/C	0.0
■ **CHUB SULLIVAN** Sullivan, John Frank b: 1/12/1856, Boston, Mass. d: 9/12/1881, Boston, Mass. BR/TR, 6', 164 lbs. Deb: 9/24/1877																												
1877	Cin-N	8	32	4	8	0	0	0	4	1	0	.250	.273	.250	.523	80	-1	-0	82	173	2	.375				0	/1	0.0
1878	Cin-N	61	244	29	63	4	2	0	20	2	9	.258	.264	.291	.555	86	-5	-3	95	97	19	.403				5	*1	0.4
1880	Wor-N	43	166	22	43	6	3	0	0	4	6	.259	.276	.331	.608	93	1	-2	113	0	16	.480				2	1	-0.1
Total	3	112	442	55	114	10	5	0	24	7	15	.258	.269	.303	.573	89	-5	-5	101	66	37	.430				7	1	0.3
■ **JOHN SULLIVAN** Sullivan, John Lawrence b: 3/21/1890, Williamsport, Pa. d: 4/1/66, Milton, Pa. BR/TR, 5'11", 180 lbs. Deb: 4/18/20																												
1920	Bos-N	81	250	36	74	14	4	1	28	29	29	.296	.374	.396	.770	126	8	9	96	106	39	.747	3	2	-0	-3	O/1	0.1
1921	Bos-N	5	5	0	0	0	0	0	0	0	0	.000	.000	.000	.000	-99	-1	-1	93	0	0	.000	0	0	0	0	H	0.0
	Chi-N	76	240	28	79	14	4	4	41	19	26	.329	.381	.471	.852	116	8	6	107	120	42	.819	3	5	-2	-8	O	-0.6
	Yr	81	245	28	79	14	4	4	41	19	26	.322	.374	.461	.835	113	7	5	106	113	41	.795	3	5	-2	-8		-0.6
Total	2	162	495	64	153	28	8	5	69	48	55	.309	.374	.428	.802	119	14	13	101	112	80	.771	6	7	-2	-11	O/1	-0.5
■ **JOHN SULLIVAN** Sullivan, John Paul b: 11/2/20, Chicago, Ill. BR/TR, 5'10", 170 lbs. Deb: 6/07/42																												
1942	Was-A	94	357	38	84	16	1	0	42	25	30	.235	.285	.286	.571	64	-19	-17	96	148	31	.464	2	0	1	-8	S	-2.0
1943	Was-A	134	456	49	95	12	2	1	55	57	59	.208	.298	.250	.548	59	-21	-23	104	**175**	39	.481	6	2	1	3	*S	-1.9

YEAR	TM/L	G	AB	R	H	2B	3B	HR	RBI	BB	SO	AVG	OBP	SLG	PRO	/A	BR	/A	PF	CHI	RC	TA	SB	CS	SBR	FR	POS	TPR
1944	Was-A	138	471	49	118	12	1	0	30	52	43	.251	.325	.280	.605	82	-14	-8	90	84	46	.510	3	3	-1	-17	*S	-1.9
1947	Was-A	49	133	13	34	0	1	0	5	22	14	.256	.361	.271	.632	80	-3	-2	97	51	15	.569	0	2	-1	-1	S/2	-0.4
1948	Was-A	85	173	25	36	4	1	0	12	22	25	.208	.297	.243	.540	43	-13	-14	103	96	14	.471	2	2	-1	-8	S/2	-2.1
1949	StL-A	105	243	29	55	8	3	0	18	38	35	.226	.331	.284	.615	64	-12	-12	100	89	25	.569	5	2	0	-7	S3/2	-1.7
Total	6	605	1833	203	422	52	9	1	162	216	206	.230	.312	.270	.582	66	-83	-77	97	118	169	.511	18	11	-1	-39	S/32	-10.0

■ JOHN SULLIVAN Sullivan, John Peter b: 1/3/41, Somerville, N.J. BL/TR, 6', 195 lbs. Deb: 9/20/63 C

YEAR	TM/L	G	AB	R	H	2B	3B	HR	RBI	BB	SO	AVG	OBP	SLG	PRO	/A	BR	/A	PF	CHI	RC	TA	SB	CS	SBR	FR	POS	TPR
1963	Det-A	3	5	0	0	0	0	0	0	2	1	.000	.286	.000	.286	-11	-1	-1	104	0	0	.333	0	0	0	0	/C	0.0
1964	Det-A	2	3	0	0	0	0	0	0	0	1	.000	.000	.000	.000	-99	-1	-1	96	0	0	.000	0	0	0	0	/C	0.0
1965	Det-A	34	86	5	23	0	0	2	11	9	13	.267	.344	.337	.681	89	-0	-1	105	130	11	.609	0	0	0	3	C	0.4
1967	NY-N	65	147	4	32	5	0	0	6	6	26	.218	.248	.252	.500	44	-11	-11	99	67	9	.361	0	2	-1	-4	C	-1.3
1968	Phi-N	12	18	0	4	0	0	0	1	2	4	.222	.300	.222	.522	60	-1	-1	97	105	1	.429	0	0	0	0	/C	0.0
Total	5	116	259	9	59	5	0	2	18	19	45	.228	.283	.270	.553	58	-13	-14	101	89	21	.446	0	2	-1	-1	/C	-0.9

■ JOE SULLIVAN Sullivan, Joseph Daniel b: 1/6/1870, Charlestown, Mass. d: 11/2/1897, Charlestown, Mass. Deb: 4/27/1893

YEAR	TM/L	G	AB	R	H	2B	3B	HR	RBI	BB	SO	AVG	OBP	SLG	PRO	/A	BR	/A	PF	CHI	RC	TA	SB	CS	SBR	FR	POS	TPR
1893	Was-N	128	508	72	135	16	13	2	64	36	24	.266	.324	.360	.685	93	-13	-3	90	95	63	.627	7			-32	*S	-2.5
1894	Was-N	17	60	7	15	3	0	0	5	6	2	.250	.357	.300	.657	63	-3	-3	98	78	8	.689	3			0	/2S3O	-0.1
	Phi-N	75	304	63	107	10	8	3	63	23	10	.352	.407	.467	.874	118	6	9	95	117	63	.914	10			-15	S	-0.1
	Yr	92	364	70	122	13	8	3	68	29	12	.335	.398	.440	.838	108	3	6	96	111	71	.872	13			-15		-0.2
1895	Phi-N	94	373	75	126	7	3	2	50	24	20	.338	.395	.389	.783	106	4	5	99	94	65	.789	15			-23	*S/O	-0.9
1896	Phi-N	48	191	45	48	5	3	2	24	18	12	.251	.347	.340	.687	82	-4	-5	102	94	26	.713	9			-3	O/S3	-0.8
	StL-N	51	212	25	62	4	2	2	21	9	12	.292	.351	.358	.709	94	-3	-1	95	64	29	.667	5			-3	O/2	-0.6
	Yr	99	403	70	110	9	5	4	45	27	24	.273	.349	.350	.699	88	-7	-6	98	79	55	.689	14			-6		-1.4
Total	4	413	1648	287	493	45	29	11	227	116	80	.299	.363	.382	.744	98	-13	2	95	94	254	.729	49			-76	S/O23	-5.0

■ MARC SULLIVAN Sullivan, Marc Cooper b: 7/25/58, Quincy, Mass. BR/TR, 6'4", 205 lbs. Deb: 10/01/82

YEAR	TM/L	G	AB	R	H	2B	3B	HR	RBI	BB	SO	AVG	OBP	SLG	PRO	/A	BR	/A	PF	CHI	RC	TA	SB	CS	SBR	FR	POS	TPR
1982	Bos-A	2	6	0	2	0	0	0	0	0	2	.333	.333	.333	.667	76	-0	-0	110	0	1	.500	0	0	0	0	/C	0.0
1984	Bos-A	2	6	1	3	0	0	0	1	1	0	.500	.571	.500	1.071	181	1	1	110	133	2	1.333	0	0	0	0	/C	0.1
1985	Bos-A	32	69	10	12	2	0	2	3	6	15	.174	.240	.290	.530	43	-5	-6	102	46	5	.456	0	0	0	1	C	-0.2
1986	Bos-A	41	119	15	23	4	0	1	14	7	32	.193	.262	.252	.514	42	-9	-9	100	169	9	.423	0	0	0	3	C	-0.3
1987	Bos-A	60	160	11	27	5	0	2	10	4	43	.169	.199	.237	.436	16	-19	-19	99	91	7	.319	0	0	0	0	C	-1.3
Total	5	137	360	37	67	11	0	5	28	18	92	.186	.237	.258	.495	34	-33	-33	100	108	23	.393	0	0	0	5	C	-1.7

■ MARTY SULLIVAN Sullivan, Martin C. b: 10/20/1862, Lowell, Mass. d: 1/6/1894, Lowell, Mass. BR/TR, Deb: 4/30/1887

YEAR	TM/L	G	AB	R	H	2B	3B	HR	RBI	BB	SO	AVG	OBP	SLG	PRO	/A	BR	/A	PF	CHI	RC	TA	SB	CS	SBR	FR	POS	TPR
1887	Chi-N	115	472	98	134	13	16	7	77	36	53	.284	.340	.424	.764	97	8	-5	116	95	82	.814	35			-8	*O/P	-1.0
1888	Chi-N	75	314	40	74	12	6	7	39	15	32	.236	.273	.379	.652	101	2	-0	107	86	36	.600	9			5	O	0.3
1889	Ind-N	69	256	45	73	11	3	4	35	50	31	.285	.404	.398	.802	116	11	7	109	97	48	.918	15			-5	O/1	0.0
1890	Bos-N	121	505	82	144	19	7	6	61	56	48	.285	.357	.386	.743	107	12	4	111	76	83	.787	33			2	*O/3	0.2
1891	Bos-N	17	67	15	15	1	0	2	7	5	3	.224	.288	.328	.616	72	-2	-3	112	74	9	.673	7			0	O	-0.2
	Cle-N	1	4	0	1	0	0	0	1	0	1	.250	.250	.250	.500	45	-0	-0	105	297	0	.333	0			0	/O	0.0
	Yr	18	71	15	16	1	0	2	8	5	4	.225	.286	.324	.610	71	-2	-3	111	91	9	.655	7			0		-0.2
Total	5	398	1618	280	441	56	32	26	220	162	168	.273	.341	.395	.736	103	32	2	111	87	258	.771	99			-7	O/13P	-0.7

■ MIKE SULLIVAN Sullivan, Michael Joseph b: 6/10/1860, Webster, Mass. d: 3/21/29, Webster, Mass. BR/TR, 5'8.5", 165 lbs. Deb: 1888

YEAR	TM/L	G	AB	R	H	2B	3B	HR	RBI	BB	SO	AVG	OBP	SLG	PRO	/A	BR	/A	PF	CHI	RC	TA	SB	CS	SBR	FR	POS	TPR
1888	Phi-a	28	112	20	31	5	6	1	19	3		.277	.296	.455	.751	141	5	4	101	107	18	.790	10			0	O3	0.4

■ PAT SULLIVAN Sullivan, Patrick B. b: 12/22/1862, Milwaukee, Wis. TR , 5'11", 165 lbs. Deb: 8/30/1884

YEAR	TM/L	G	AB	R	H	2B	3B	HR	RBI	BB	SO	AVG	OBP	SLG	PRO	/A	BR	/A	PF	CHI	RC	TA	SB	CS	SBR	FR	POS	TPR
1884	KC-U	31	114	15	22	2	1	1		4		.193	.220	.254	.475	69	-5	-2	87	0	7	.359	0			-2	3/OCP	-0.2

■ RUSS SULLIVAN Sullivan, Russell Guy b: 2/19/23, Fredericksburg, Va BL/TR, 6', 196 lbs. Deb: 9/08/51

YEAR	TM/L	G	AB	R	H	2B	3B	HR	RBI	BB	SO	AVG	OBP	SLG	PRO	/A	BR	/A	PF	CHI	RC	TA	SB	CS	SBR	FR	POS	TPR
1951	Det-A	7	26	2	5	1	0	1	1	2	1	.192	.250	.346	.596	57	-2	-2	106	30	2	.524	0	0	0	0	/O	-0.1
1952	Det-A	15	52	7	17	2	1	3	5	3	5	.327	.375	.577	.952	164	4	4	99	48	12	1.000	1	0	0	-2	O	0.2
1953	Det-A	23	72	7	18	5	1	1	6	13	5	.250	.379	.389	.768	110	1	2	98	72	11	.741	0	0	0	2	O	0.3
Total	3	45	150	16	40	8	2	5	12	18	11	.267	.357	.447	.803	119	4	4	99	57	25	.781	1	0	0	-0	/O	0.4

■ SUTER SULLIVAN Sullivan, Suter G. b: 10/14/1872, Baltimore, Md. d: 4/19/25, Baltimore, Md. Deb: 7/24/1898

YEAR	TM/L	G	AB	R	H	2B	3B	HR	RBI	BB	SO	AVG	OBP	SLG	PRO	/A	BR	/A	PF	CHI	RC	TA	SB	CS	SBR	FR	POS	TPR
1898	StL-N	42	144	10	32	3	0	0	12	13		.222	.300	.243	.543	55	-7	-8	106	106	11	.464	1			0	SO/21P	-0.7
1899	Cle-N	127	473	37	116	16	3	0	55	25		.245	.293	.292	.585	70	-24	-16	89	130	46	.521	16			5	*30/S12	-0.9
Total	2	169	617	47	148	19	3	0	67	38		.240	.295	.280	.575	66	-31	-24	93	124	57	.507	17			5	3/OS21P	-1.6

■ TOM SULLIVAN Sullivan, Thomas Brandon b: 12/19/06, Nome, Alaska d: 8/16/44, Seattle, Wash. BR/TR, 6', 190 lbs. Deb: 6/14/25

YEAR	TM/L	G	AB	R	H	2B	3B	HR	RBI	BB	SO	AVG	OBP	SLG	PRO	/A	BR	/A	PF	CHI	RC	TA	SB	CS	SBR	FR	POS	TPR
1925	Cin-N	1	1	0	0	0	0	0	0	0	0	.000	.000	.000	.000	-99	-0	-0	97	0	0	.000	0	0	0	0	/C	0.0

■ SLEEPER SULLIVAN Sullivan, Thomas Jefferson "Old Iron Hands" b: St.Louis, Mo. d: 9/25/1899, Camden, N.J. TR , 175 lbs. Deb: 5/03/1881

YEAR	TM/L	G	AB	R	H	2B	3B	HR	RBI	BB	SO	AVG	OBP	SLG	PRO	/A	BR	/A	PF	CHI	RC	TA	SB	CS	SBR	FR	POS	TPR
1881	Buf-N	35	121	13	23	4	0	0	15	1	21	.190	.197	.223	.420	31	-9	-9	101	193	5	.286				-14	C/O	-2.2
1882	StL-a	51	188	24	34	3	3	0		3		.181	.194	.229	.422	42	-11	-11	100	0	9	.299				-17	C/P	-2.5
1883	StL-a	8	27	2	6	0	1	0		0		.222	.222	.296	.519	61	-1	-1	108	0	2	.381				0	/CO	0.0
1884	StL-U	2	9	0	1	0	0	0		0		.111	.111	.111	.222	-24	-1	-1	104	0	0	.125	0			0	/OCP	0.0
Total	4	96	345	39	64	7	4	0	15	4	21	.186	.195	.229	.424	38	-23	-23	101	67	16	.295	0			-31	/COP	-4.7

■ TED SULLIVAN Sullivan, Timothy Paul b: 1851, County Clare, Ireland d: 7/5/29, Washington, D.C. Deb: 9/09/1884 M

YEAR	TM/L	G	AB	R	H	2B	3B	HR	RBI	BB	SO	AVG	OBP	SLG	PRO	/A	BR	/A	PF	CHI	RC	TA	SB	CS	SBR	FR	POS	TPR
1884	KC-U	3	9	0	3	0	0	0		1		.333	.400	.333	.733	173	1	1	87	0	1	.667	0			0	/OSM	0.1

■ BILL SULLIVAN Sullivan, William b: 7/4/1853, Holyoke, Mass. d: 11/13/1884, Holyoke, Mass. Deb: 8/09/1878

YEAR	TM/L	G	AB	R	H	2B	3B	HR	RBI	BB	SO	AVG	OBP	SLG	PRO	/A	BR	/A	PF	CHI	RC	TA	SB	CS	SBR	FR	POS	TPR
1878	Chi-N	2	6	1	1	0	0	0	0	0	0	.167	.167	.167	.333	9	-1	-1	108	0	0	.200				0	/O	0.0

■ BILLY SULLIVAN Sullivan, William Joseph Jr. b: 10/23/10, Chicago, Ill. BL/TR, 6', 170 lbs. Deb: 6/09/31

YEAR	TM/L	G	AB	R	H	2B	3B	HR	RBI	BB	SO	AVG	OBP	SLG	PRO	/A	BR	/A	PF	CHI	RC	TA	SB	CS	SBR	FR	POS	TPR
1931	Chi-A	92	363	48	100	16	5	2	33	20	14	.275	.315	.364	.679	84	-12	-8	92	84	41	.588	4	4	-1	-3	3/O1	-0.6
1932	Chi-A	93	307	31	97	16	1	1	45	20	9	.316	.358	.384	.742	106	-3	2	87	125	41	.653	1	3	-2	1	13/CO	-0.2
1933	Chi-A	54	125	9	24	0	1	0	13	10	5	.192	.252	.208	.460	23	-14	-14	101	167	7	.356	0	0	0	-1	1/C	-1.4
1935	Cin-N	85	241	29	64	9	4	2	36	19	16	.266	.324	.361	.685	90	-5	-3	93	140	29	.615	4			1	13/2	-0.1
1936	Cle-A	93	319	39	112	32	6	2	48	16	9	.351	.382	.508	.890	112	8	5	106	92	61	.876	5	2	0	3	C/31O	1.2
1937	Cle-A	72	168	26	48	12	3	3	22	17	7	.286	.355	.446	.801	103	-0	0	98	90	26	.758	1	4	-2	1	C/13	0.1
1938	StL-A	111	375	35	104	16	1	7	49	20	10	.277	.316	.381	.697	74	-16	-16	100	101	45	.623	8	5	-1	8	C/1	-0.6
1939	StL-A	118	332	53	96	17	5	5	50	34	18	.289	.362	.416	.778	98	-1	-1	100	110	49	.719	3	3	-1	4	OC/1	0.1
1940	Det-A	78	220	36	68	14	4	3	41	31	11	.309	.399	.450	.849	108	7	4	111	137	44	.870	2	0	1	5	C/3	1.2
1941	Det-A	85	234	29	66	15	1	3	29	35	11	.282	.375	.393	.769	97	2	-0	106	102	36	.722	0	3	-2	5	C	0.7
1942	Bro-N	43	101	11	27	2	1	1	14	12	6	.267	.345	.337	.682	98	0	0	102	140	13	.627	1			-1	C	0.0
1947	Pit-N	38	55	1	14	3	0	0	8	6	3	.255	.328	.309	.637	69	-2	-2	101	174	6	.571	1			0	C	-0.1
Total	12	962	2840	347	820	152	32	29	388	240	119	.289	.346	.395	.742	92	-36	-33	99	113	397	.687	30	24		22	C13/O2	0.3

■ BILLY SULLIVAN Sullivan, William Joseph Sr. b: 2/1/1875, Oakland, Wis. d: 1/28/65, Newberg,Ore. BR/TR, 5'9", 155 lbs. Deb: 9/13/1899 M

YEAR	TM/L	G	AB	R	H	2B	3B	HR	RBI	BB	SO	AVG	OBP	SLG	PRO	/A	BR	/A	PF	CHI	RC	TA	SB	CS	SBR	FR	POS	TPR
1899	Bos-N	22	74	10	20	2	0	2	12	1		.270	.308	.378	.686	86	-1	-2	105	108	9	.630	2			0	C	-0.1
1900	Bos-N	72	238	36	65	6	0	8	41	9		.273	.300	.399	.699	78	-3	-10	120	108	30	.624	4			-5	C/S2	-0.7
1901	Chi-A	98	367	54	90	15	6	4	56	10		.245	.265	.351	.617	72	-15	-14	99	128	38	.545	12			-1	C/3	-0.5
1902	Chi-A	76	263	36	64	12	3	1	26	6		.243	.260	.323	.583	65	-14	-12	95	97	26	.513	11			0	C/1O	-0.5
1903	Chi-A	32	111	10	21	4	0	1	7	5		.189	.224	.252	.476	48	-7	-6	92	83	7	.400	3			-1	C	-0.3
1904	Chi-A	108	371	29	85	18	4	1	44	12		.229	.253	.307	.561	79	-9	-9	99	143	32	.479	11			-6	*C	-0.3
1905	Chi-A	98	323	25	65	10	3	2	26	13		.201	.232	.269	.501	63	-15	-13	97	100	24	.442	14			-2	C/13	-0.6
1906	Chi-A	118	387	37	83	18	4	1	33	22		.214	.257	.289	.546	79	-12	-9	92	106	32	.474	10			-11	*C	-1.1
1907	Chi-A	112	329	30	59	8	4	0	36	21		.179	.229	.228	.457	45	-19	-20	104	172	19	.378	6			-7	*C/2	-1.9

YEAR	TM/L	G	AB	R	H	2B	3B	HR	RBI	BB	SO	AVG	OBP	SLG	PRO	/A	BR	/A	PF	CHI	RC	TA	SB	CS	SBR	FR	POS	TPR
1908	Chi-A	137	430	40	82	8	4	0	29	22		.191	.230	.228	.458	54	-23	-20	94	111	24	.388	15			-20	*C	-2.9
1909	Chi-A	97	265	11	43	3	0	0	16	17		.162	.226	.174	.400	27	-22	-21	97	134	12	.347	9			-5	CM	-2.1
1910	Chi-A	45	142	10	26	4	1	0	6	7		.183	.227	.225	.452	44	-10	-9	95	69	7	.345	0			2	C	-0.2
1911	Chi-A	89	256	26	55	9	3	0	31	16		.215	.266	.273	.540	52	-17	-16	97	150	19	.443	1			-14	C	-1.9
1912	Chi-A	39	91	9	19	2	1	0	15	9		.209	.287	.253	.540	55	-5	-5	99	218	7	.458	0			-1	C	-0.1
1914	Chi-A	1	0	0	0	0	0	0	0	0	0	—	—	—	—	—	0	0	103	—	—	—	0			0	/C	0.0
1916	Det-A	1	0	0	0	0	0	0	0	0	0	—	—	—	—	—	0	0	105	—	—	—	0			0	/C	0.0
Total	16	1145	3647	363	777	119	33	20	378	170	0	.213	.250	.280	.531	62	-172	-168	99	123	303	.454	98			-70	*C/1032S	-13.2

■ HOMER SUMMA Summa, Homer Wayne b: 11/3/1898, Gentry, Mo. d: 1/29/66, Los Angeles, Cal. BL/TR, 5'10.5", 170 lbs. Deb: 9/13/20

YEAR	TM/L	G	AB	R	H	2B	3B	HR	RBI	BB	SO	AVG	OBP	SLG	PRO	/A	BR	/A	PF	CHI	RC	TA	SB	CS	SBR	FR	POS	TPR
1920	Pit-N	10	22	1	7	1	1	0	1	3	1	.318	.400	.455	.855	144	1	1	101	39	4	.933	1	0	0	1	/O	0.3
1922	Cle-A	12	46	9	16	3	3	1	6	1	1	.348	.400	.609	1.009	157	4	4	102	71	11	1.065	1	1	-0	-1	O	0.2
1923	Cle-A	137	525	92	172	27	6	3	69	33	20	.328	.374	.419	.793	107	6	5	101	105	80	.732	9	13	-5	-15	*O	-2.6
1924	Cle-A	111	390	55	113	21	6	2	38	11	16	.290	.311	.390	.701	83	-13	-11	97	79	46	.602	4	2	0	-9	O	-2.5
1925	Cle-A	75	224	28	74	10	1	0	25	13	6	.330	.375	.384	.759	87	-2	-4	106	97	33	.691	3	2	-0	-10	O/3	-1.7
1926	Cle-A	154	581	74	179	31	6	4	76	47	9	.308	.368	.403	.771	101	1	1	100	111	88	.741	15	8	-0	2	*O	-0.7
1927	Cle-A	145	574	73	164	41	7	4	74	32	18	.286	.331	.402	.734	92	-10	-8	97	97	75	.673	6	0	2	-15	*O	-3.0
1928	Cle-A	134	504	60	143	26	3	3	57	20	15	.284	.319	.365	.684	75	-16	-20	106	103	59	.590	4	2	0	-8	*O	-3.3
1929	Phi-A	37	81	12	22	4	0	0	10	2	1	.272	.298	.321	.619	54	-5	-6	109	132	8	.500	1	1	-0	-2	O	-0.8
1930	Phi-A	25	54	10	15	2	1	1	5	4	1	.278	.339	.407	.746	89	-1	-1	99	66	8	.692	0	0	0	-0	O	-0.1
Total	10	840	3001	414	905	166	34	18	361	166	88	.302	.346	.398	.743	92	-35	-39	101	100	411	.677	44	29	-4	-56	O/3	-14.2

■ CHAMP SUMMERS Summers, John Junior b: 6/15/46, Bremerton, Wash. BL/TR, 6'2", 205 lbs. Deb: 5/04/74

YEAR	TM/L	G	AB	R	H	2B	3B	HR	RBI	BB	SO	AVG	OBP	SLG	PRO	/A	BR	/A	PF	CHI	RC	TA	SB	CS	SBR	FR	POS	TPR
1974	Oak-A	20	24	2	3	1	0	0	3	1	5	.125	.160	.167	.327	-6	-3	-3	100	295	1	.238	0	0	0	-4	O/D	-0.8
1975	Chi-N	76	91	14	21	5	1	1	16	10	13	.231	.314	.341	.654	78	-2	-3	104	182	10	.575	0	0	0	-5	O	-0.8
1976	Chi-N	83	126	11	26	2	0	3	13	13	31	.206	.286	.294	.579	59	-6	-7	109	109	11	.505	1	0	0	-5	O1/C	-1.4
1977	Cin-N	59	76	11	13	4	0	3	6	6	16	.171	.241	.342	.583	54	-5	-5	100	69	6	.500	0	0	0	-1	O/3	-0.6
1978	Cin-N	13	35	4	9	2	0	1	3	7	4	.257	.381	.400	.781	115	1	1	103	70	5	.793	2	1	0	-2	O	-0.1
1979	Cin-N	27	60	10	12	2	1	1	11	13	15	.200	.351	.317	.668	86	-1	-1	97	198	7	.660	0	1	-1	-2	O/1	-0.3
	Det-A	90	246	47	77	12	1	20	51	40	33	.313	.415	.614	1.029	180	26	27	96	93	63	1.123	7	6	-2	-11	OD/1	1.1
1980	Det-A	120	347	61	103	19	1	17	60	52	52	.297	.396	.504	.900	137	23	20	105	104	69	.918	4	3	-1	-10	DO/1	0.9
1981	Det-A	64	165	16	42	8	0	3	21	19	35	.255	.342	.358	.700	97	1	-0	105	121	22	.661	1	1	-0	-3	DO	-0.3
1982	SF-N	70	125	15	31	5	0	4	19	16	17	.248	.347	.384	.731	111	1	2	94	124	17	.677	0	1	-1	-4	O/1	-0.3
1983	SF-N	29	22	3	3	0	0	0	3	7	8	.136	.345	.136	.481	38	-1	-2	101	396	1	.455	0	0	0	0	/O	-0.1
1984	SD-N	47	54	5	10	3	0	1	12	4	15	.185	.254	.296	.551	55	-3	-3	99	248	4	.457	0	0	0	-0	/1	-0.3
Total	11	698	1371	199	350	63	4	54	218	188	244	.255	.353	.425	.778	112	29	26	102	126	215	.777	15	13	-3	-48	OD/13C	-3.0

■ CARL SUMNER Sumner, Carl Ringdahl "Lefty" b: 9/28/08, Cambridge, Mass. BL/TL, 5'8", 170 lbs. Deb: 7/28/28

YEAR	TM/L	G	AB	R	H	2B	3B	HR	RBI	BB	SO	AVG	OBP	SLG	PRO	/A	BR	/A	PF	CHI	RC	TA	SB	CS	SBR	FR	POS	TPR
1928	Bos-A	16	29	6	8	1	1	0	3	5	6	.276	.382	.379	.762	102	0	0	98	94	5	.762	0	0	0	-3	O	-0.2

■ ART SUNDAY Sunday, Arthur (born August Wacher) b: 1/21/1862, Springfield, Ohio BL, 5'9", 193 lbs. Deb: 5/05/1890

YEAR	TM/L	G	AB	R	H	2B	3B	HR	RBI	BB	SO	AVG	OBP	SLG	PRO	/A	BR	/A	PF	CHI	RC	TA	SB	CS	SBR	FR	POS	TPR
1890	Bro-P	24	83	26	22	5	1	0	13	15	9	.265	.419	.349	.768	102	2	1	106	125	12	.836	0			0	O	0.1

■ BILLY SUNDAY Sunday, William Ashley "Parson" or "The Evangelist" b: 11/9/1862, Ames, Iowa d: 11/6/35, Chicago, Ill. BL, 5'10", 160 lbs. Deb: 5/22/1883

YEAR	TM/L	G	AB	R	H	2B	3B	HR	RBI	BB	SO	AVG	OBP	SLG	PRO	/A	BR	/A	PF	CHI	RC	TA	SB	CS	SBR	FR	POS	TPR
1883	Chi-N	14	54	6	13	4	0	0	5	1	18	.241	.255	.315	.569	66	-2	-3	109	104	4	.439				0	O	-0.1
1884	Chi-N	43	176	25	39	4	1	4	28	4	36	.222	.239	.324	.563	70	-5	-7	108	142	14	.445				-11	O	-1.6
1885	Chi-N	46	172	36	44	3	3	2	20	12	33	.256	.304	.343	.647	96	2	-2	114	109	18	.555				-8	O	-1.0
1886	Chi-N	28	103	16	25	2	2	0	6	7	26	.243	.291	.301	.592	69	-2	-5	116	64	12	.615	10			0	O	-0.3
1887	Chi-N	50	199	41	58	6	6	3	32	21	20	.291	.362	.427	.789	103	6	0	116	93	44	1.000	34			-7	O	-0.5
1888	Pit-N	120	505	69	119	14	3	0	15	12	36	.236	.256	.275	.532	75	-16	-13	95	33	55	.580	71			15	*O	0.1
1889	Pit-N	81	321	62	77	10	6	2	25	27	33	.240	.307	.327	.634	88	-9	-3	89	71	48	.750	47			10	O	0.3
1890	Pit-N	86	358	58	92	9	2	1	33	32	20	.257	.327	.302	.628	97	-6	1	88	77	56	.763	58			16	O/P	1.4
	Phi-N	31	119	26	31	3	1	0	6	18	7	.261	.367	.303	.669	91	1	-1	108	53	23	.932	26			0	O	0.0
	Yr	117	477	84	123	12	3	1	39	50	27	.258	.337	.302	.639	95	-5	0	93	72	79	.805	84			16		1.4
Total	8	499	2007	339	498	55	24	12	170	134	229	.248	.300	.317	.617	86	-32	-32	100	74	275	.683	246			15	O/P	-1.7

■ JIM SUNDBERG Sundberg, James Howard b: 5/18/51, Galesburg, Ill. BR/TR, 6', 190 lbs. Deb: 4/04/74

YEAR	TM/L	G	AB	R	H	2B	3B	HR	RBI	BB	SO	AVG	OBP	SLG	PRO	/A	BR	/A	PF	CHI	RC	TA	SB	CS	SBR	FR	POS	TPR
1974	Tex-A	132	368	45	91	13	3	3	36	62	61	.247	.356	.323	.679	101	1	3	96	111	43	.616	2	4	-2	9	*C	1.5
1975	Tex-A	155	472	45	94	9	0	6	36	51	77	.199	.283	.256	.539	53	-28	-28	100	100	35	.453	3	1	0	6	*C	-1.7
1976	Tex-A	140	448	33	102	24	2	3	34	37	61	.228	.287	.310	.597	73	-14	-16	102	88	39	.488	0	0	0	17	*C	0.6
1977	Tex-A	149	453	61	132	20	3	6	65	53	77	.291	.368	.389	.757	102	6	3	105	133	67	.702	2	3	-1	0	*C	0.5
1978	Tex-A	149	518	54	144	23	6	6	58	64	70	.278	.361	.380	.741	113	7	10	96	109	69	.670	2	5	-2	16	*C/D	2.8
1979	Tex-A	150	495	50	136	23	4	5	64	51	51	.275	.348	.368	.716	94	-3	-3	100	125	62	.636	3	3	-1	9	*C	1.1
1980	Tex-A	151	505	59	138	24	1	10	63	64	67	.273	.356	.384	.740	103	3	3	100	110	69	.680	2	2	-1	15	*C	2.5
1981	Tex-A	102	339	42	94	17	2	3	28	50	48	.277	.372	.366	.738	124	8	12	91	84	48	.694	2	5	-2	11	C/O	2.5
1982	Tex-A	139	470	37	118	22	5	10	47	49	57	.251	.323	.383	.706	100	-4	0	93	91	57	.629	2	6	-3	20	*C/O	2.4
1983	Tex-A	131	378	30	76	14	0	2	28	35	64	.201	.272	.254	.526	45	-27	-28	101	107	26	.424	0	4	-2	-4	*C	-2.7
1984	Mil-A	110	348	43	91	19	4	7	43	38	63	.261	.334	.399	.734	111	1	5	92	107	48	.677	1	1	-0	14	*C	2.5
1985	KC-A	115	367	38	90	12	4	10	35	33	67	.245	.309	.381	.691	86	-6	-7	102	82	42	.604	0	2	-1	10	*C	0.6
1986	KC-A	140	429	41	91	9	1	12	42	57	91	.212	.305	.322	.626	72	-16	-16	100	96	44	.566	1	1	-0	12	*C	0.2
1987	Chi-N	61	139	9	28	2	0	4	15	19	40	.201	.306	.302	.608	61	-7	-8	101	111	13	.553	0	0	0	0	C	-0.2
1988	Chi-N	24	54	8	13	1	0	2	9	8	15	.241	.339	.370	.709	99	0	0	104	138	7	.667	0	0	0	1	C	0.2
	Tex-A	38	91	13	26	4	0	4	13	5	17	.286	.323	.462	.784	116	2	2	101	96	13	.701	0	0	0	-3	C	0.0
Total	15	1886	5874	608	1464	236	35	93	616	676	926	.249	.329	.349	.678	90	-80	-69	99	104	684	.622	20	37	-16	132	*C/OD	12.8

■ B.J. SURHOFF Surhoff, William James b: 8/4/64, Bronx, N.Y. BL/TR, 6'1", 185 lbs. Deb: 4/08/87

YEAR	TM/L	G	AB	R	H	2B	3B	HR	RBI	BB	SO	AVG	OBP	SLG	PRO	/A	BR	/A	PF	CHI	RC	TA	SB	CS	SBR	FR	POS	TPR
1987	Mil-A	115	395	50	118	22	3	7	68	36	30	.299	.357	.423	.780	104	4	3	102	144	56	.713	11	10	-3	18	C3/1D	2.4
1988	Mil-A	139	493	47	121	21	0	5	38	31	49	.245	.294	.318	.613	69	-19	-21	103	90	46	.544	21	6	3	8	*C3/1SO	-0.5
Total	2	254	888	97	239	43	3	12	106	67	79	.269	.323	.365	.687	85	-14	-18	103	114	102	.629	32	16	0	26	C/3D1OS	1.9

■ GEORGE SUSCE Susce, George Cyril Methodius "Good Kid" b: 8/13/08, Pittsburgh, Pa. d: 2/25/86, Sarasota, Fla. BR/TR, 5'11.5", 200 lbs. Deb: 4/23/29 C

YEAR	TM/L	G	AB	R	H	2B	3B	HR	RBI	BB	SO	AVG	OBP	SLG	PRO	/A	BR	/A	PF	CHI	RC	TA	SB	CS	SBR	FR	POS	TPR
1929	Phi-N	17	17	5	5	3	0	1	1	1	2	.294	.368	.647	1.015	133	1	1	110	24	4	1.083	0			0	C	0.2
1932	Det-A	2	0	0	0	0	0	0	0	0	0	—	—	—	—	—	0	0	102	—	—	—	0	0	0	0	/C	0.0
1939	Pit-N	31	75	8	17	3	1	1	4	12	5	.227	.333	.333	.667	80	-2	-2	100	52	8	.578	0			0	C	0.0
1940	StL-A	61	113	6	24	4	0	0	13	9	9	.212	.282	.248	.530	37	-10	-11	106	168	7	.412	1	0	0	-6	C	-1.0
1941	Cle-A	1	0	0	0	0	0	0	0	0	0	—	—	—	—	—	0	0	101	—	—	—	0	0	0	0	/C	0.0
1942	Cle-A	2	1	1	1	0	0	0	0	1	0	1.000	1.000	1.000	2.000	506	1	1	92	0	1	—	0	0	0	0	/C	0.1
1943	Cle-A	3	1	0	0	0	0	0	0	0	0	.000	.000	.000	.000	-99	-0	-0	90	0	0	.000	0	0	0	0	/C	0.0
1944	Cle-A	29	61	3	14	1	0	0	4	2	5	.230	.254	.246	.500	43	-5	-5	100	96	4	.354	0	0	0	-1	C	-0.3
Total	8	146	268	23	61	11	1	2	22	25	21	.228	.301	.299	.599	59	-15	-16	103	108	35	.524	1	0		-6	C	-1.0

■ PETE SUSKO Susko, Peter Jonathan b: 7/2/04, Laura, Ohio d: 5/22/78, Jacksonville, Fla. BL/TL, 5'11", 172 lbs. Deb: 8/01/34

YEAR	TM/L	G	AB	R	H	2B	3B	HR	RBI	BB	SO	AVG	OBP	SLG	PRO	/A	BR	/A	PF	CHI	RC	TA	SB	CS	SBR	FR	POS	TPR
1934	Was-A	58	224	25	64	5	3	2	25	18	10	.286	.342	.362	.703	81	-6	-6	101	98	28	.628	3	4	-2	-1	1	-1.7

■ BUTCH SUTCLIFFE Sutcliffe, Charles Inigo b: 7/22/15, Fall River, Mass. BR/TR, 5'8.5", 165 lbs. Deb: 8/28/38

YEAR	TM/L	G	AB	R	H	2B	3B	HR	RBI	BB	SO	AVG	OBP	SLG	PRO	/A	BR	/A	PF	CHI	RC	TA	SB	CS	SBR	FR	POS	TPR
1938	Bos-N	4	4	1	1	0	0	0	2	2	1	.250	.500	.250	.750	127	0	0	88	723	1	.750	0			0	/C	0.1

■ SY SUTCLIFFE Sutcliffe, Elmer Ellsworth b: 4/15/1862, Wheaton, Ill. d: 2/13/1893, Wheaton, Ill. BL, 6'2", 170 lbs. Deb: 10/02/1884

YEAR	TM/L	G	AB	R	H	2B	3B	HR	RBI	BB	SO	AVG	OBP	SLG	PRO	/A	BR	/A	PF	CHI	RC	TA	SB	CS	SBR	FR	POS	TPR
1884	Chi-N	4	15	4	3	1	0	0	2	2	4	.200	.294	.267	.561	72	-0	-1	108	175	1	.500				0	/C	0.0
1885	Chi-N	11	43	5	8	1	1	0	4	2	5	.186	.222	.256	.478	48	-2	-3	114	129	3	.371				0	C	-0.2

YEAR	TM/L	G	AB	R	H	2B	3B	HR	RBI	BB	SO	AVG	OBP	SLG	PRO	/A	BR	/A	PF	CHI	RC	TA	SB	CS	SBR	FR	POS	TPR
	StL-N	16	49	2	6	1	0	0	4	5	10	.122	.204	.143	.347	15	-4	-4	92	199	1	.279				0	C/O	-0.3
	Yr	27	92	7	14	2	1	0	8	7	15	.152	.212	.196	.408	32	-7	-7	101	175	4	.321				0		-0.5
1888	Det-N	49	191	17	49	5	3	0	23	5	14	.257	.276	.314	.590	91	-2	-2	98	140	19	.500	6			0	SC/102	-0.1
1889	Cle-N	46	161	17	40	3	2	1	21	14	6	.248	.309	.311	.619	72	-5	-6	103	121	17	.570	5			9	C/1O	0.3
1890	Cle-P	99	386	62	127	14	8	2	60	33	16	.329	.382	.422	.804	127	9	15	92	99	68	.795	10			-6	CO/S3	1.0
1891	Was-a	53	201	29	71	8	3	2	33	17	17	.353	.409	.453	.862	157	13	14	95	104	42	.908	8			-0	OC/S3	1.1
1892	Bal-N	66	276	41	77	10	7	1	27	14	15	.279	.316	.377	.693	111	3	3	100	74	38	.658	12			-8	1	-0.8
Total	7	344	1322	177	381	43	24	6	174	92	87	.288	.336	.371	.707	109	10	16	97	109	188	.665	41			-4	C/1OS32	1.0
■ **GARY SUTHERLAND** Sutherland, Gary Lynn b: 9/27/44, Glendale, Cal. BR/TR, 6', 185 lbs. Deb: 9/17/66																												
1966	Phi-N	3	3	0	0	0	0	0	0	0	0	.000	.000	.000	.000	-99	-1	-1	101	0	0	.000	0	0	0	0	/S	0.0
1967	Phi-N	103	231	23	57	12	1	1	19	17	22	.247	.298	.320	.619	74	-7	-8	104	102	20	.497	0	3	-2	1	SO	-0.2
1968	Phi-N	67	138	16	38	7	0	0	15	8	15	.275	.315	.326	.641	95	-1	-1	97	140	14	.520	0	0	0	0	2S3/O	0.1
1969	Mon-N	141	544	63	130	26	1	3	35	37	31	.239	.290	.307	.597	67	-24	-24	100	84	46	.486	5	7	-3	10	*2S/O	-0.3
1970	Mon-N	116	359	37	74	10	0	3	26	31	22	.206	.273	.259	.532	43	-29	-29	100	99	26	.434	2	2	-1	-4	2S/3	-1.9
1971	Mon-N	111	304	25	78	7	2	4	26	18	12	.257	.302	.332	.635	81	-8	-8	99	94	28	.515	3	4	-2	-2	2S/O3	-0.2
1972	Hou-N	5	8	0	1	0	0	0	1	0	0	.125	.125	.125	.250	-27	-1	-1	106	411	0	.143	0	0	0	0	/23	0.0
1973	Hou-N	16	54	8	14	5	0	0	3	3	5	.259	.298	.352	.650	84	-2	-1	95	63	5	.524	0	0	0	-0	2/S	0.0
1974	Det-A	149	619	60	157	20	1	5	49	26	37	.254	.284	.313	.597	68	-23	-28	106	89	51	.459	1	3	-2	-13	*2S/3	-3.6
1975	Det-A	129	503	51	130	12	3	6	39	45	41	.258	.323	.330	.653	82	-10	-12	104	72	53	.552	0	2	-1	-3	*2	-1.1
1976	Det-A	42	117	10	24	5	2	0	6	7	12	.205	.250	.282	.532	54	-7	-7	104	70	7	.404	0	1	-1	2	2	-0.3
	Mil-A	59	115	9	25	2	0	1	9	8	7	.217	.274	.261	.535	58	-6	-6	99	105	7	.394	0	2	-1	-5	2/1D	-0.9
	Yr	101	232	19	49	7	2	1	15	15	19	.211	.262	.272	.534	56	-13	-13	101	91	15	.409	0	3	-2	-3		-1.2
1977	SD-N	80	103	5	25	3	0	1	11	7	15	.243	.291	.301	.592	67	-6	-4	88	129	9	.469	0	0	0	-3	23/1	-0.5
1978	StL-N	10	6	1	1	0	0	0	0	0	0	.167	.167	.167	.333	-7	-1	-1	95	0	0	.200	0	0	0	0	/2	0.0
Total	13	1031	3104	308	754	109	10	24	239	207	219	.243	.292	.308	.600	69	-125	-131	102	91	267	.498	11	24	-11	-16	2S/3OD1	-8.9
■ **LEO SUTHERLAND** Sutherland, Leonardo (Cantin) b: 4/6/58, Santiago, Cuba BL/TL, 5'10", 165 lbs. Deb: 8/11/80																												
1980	Chi-A	34	89	9	23	3	0	0	5	1	11	.258	.267	.292	.559	55	-6	-5	97	75	7	.449	4	1	1	-1	O	-0.6
1981	Chi-A	11	12	6	2	0	0	0	0	3	1	.167	.333	.167	.500	48	-1	-1	100	0	1	.636	2	1	0	-2	/O	-0.2
Total	2	45	101	15	25	3	0	0	5	4	12	.248	.276	.277	.553	55	-6	-6	97	64	8	.487	6	2	1	-3	/O	-0.8
■ **EZRA SUTTON** Sutton, Ezra Ballou b: 9/17/1850, Palmyra, N.Y. d: 6/20/07, Braintree, Mass. BR/TR, 5'8.5", 153 lbs. Deb: 5/04/1871																												
1871	Cle-n	29	130	35	45							.346															*3	
1872	Cle-n	21	110	30	31							.282															3	
1873	Ath-n	51	258	52	82							.318															*3/S2	
1874	Ath-n	55	246	54	85							.346															3S	
1875	Ath-n	75	357	85	117							.328															*3/1O	
1876	Phi-N	54	236	45	70	12	7	1	31	3	2	.297	.305	.419	.725	141	9	10	99	109	31	.614				0	12/3O	0.9
1877	Bos-N	58	253	43	74	10	6	0	39	4	10	.292	.304	.379	.683	105	4	1	108	146	30	.559				-5	S3	-0.1
1878	Bos-N	60	239	31	54	9	3	1	29	2	14	.226	.232	.301	.534	69	-7	-9	108	134	17	.400				-2	*3/S	-0.7
1879	Bos-N	84	339	54	84	13	4	0	34	2	18	.248	.252	.310	.562	78	-6	-9	107	116	27	.420				-13	S3	-1.5
1880	Bos-N	76	288	41	72	9	2	0	25	7	7	.250	.268	.295	.563	99	-3	0	92	110	23	.426				1	S3	0.3
1881	Bos-N	83	333	43	97	12	4	0	31	13	9	.291	.318	.351	.669	120	4	8	91	88	38	.551				-5	*3/S	0.8
1882	Bos-N	81	319	44	80	8	1	2	38	24	25	.251	.303	.301	.604	92	-1	-3	103	133	30	.502				-7	*3/S	-0.8
1883	Bos-N	94	414	101	134	28	15	3	73	17	12	.324	.350	.486	.836	142	24	20	106	106	72	.779				-1	*3/OS	1.8
1884	Bos-N	110	468	102	**162**	28	7	3	61	29	22	.346	.384	.455	.839	166	33	35	98	83	84	.791				-2	*3	2.4
1885	Bos-N	110	457	78	143	23	8	4	47	17	25	.313	.338	.425	.762	155	21	25	94	70	67	.672				3	*3S/21	2.7
1886	Bos-N	116	499	83	138	21	6	3	48	26	21	.277	.312	.361	.673	107	2	4	97	71	63	.620	18			-2	OS32	0.3
1887	Bos-N	77	326	58	99	14	9	3	46	13	6	.304	.342	.429	.771	118	6	7	98	91	55	.775	17			24	SO23	2.5
1888	Bos-N	28	110	16	24	3	1	1	16	7	3	.218	.277	.291	.568	79	-2	-3	106	173	12	.593	10			0	3/S	-0.2
Total	5 n	231	1101	256	360							.327															3/S	
Total	13	1031	4281	739	1231	190	73	21	518	164	174	.288	.315	.381	.696	118	86	87	100	102	550	.606	45			-9	3S/O21	8.4
■ **DALE SVEUM** Sveum, Dale Curtis b: 11/23/63, Richmond, Cal. BB/TR, 6'2", 185 lbs. Deb: 5/12/86																												
1986	Mil-A	91	317	35	78	13	2	7	35	32	63	.246	.317	.366	.683	84	-6	-7	102	104	37	.614	4	3	-1	-4	32S	-1.0
1987	Mil-A	153	535	86	135	27	3	25	95	40	133	.252	.306	.454	.760	96	-2	-4	102	119	70	.686	2	6	-3	-12	*S2	-1.0
1988	Mil-A	129	467	41	113	14	4	9	51	21	122	.242	.276	.347	.623	71	-17	-19	103	109	45	.514	1	0	0	-12	*S/2D	-2.4
Total	3	373	1319	162	326	54	9	41	181	93	318	.247	.298	.395	.693	85	-25	-30	103	112	152	.619	7	9	-3	-27	S/32D	-4.4
■ **HARRY SWACINA** Swacina, Harry Joseph "Swats" b: 8/22/1881, St.Louis, Mo. d: 6/21/44, Birmingham, Ala. BR/TR, 6'2", 190 lbs. Deb: 9/13/07																												
1907	Pit-N	26	95	9	19	1	1	0	10	4		.200	.232	.232	.464	45	-6	-6	105	182	5	.355	1			-0	1	-0.7
1908	Pit-N	53	176	7	38	6	1	0	13	5		.216	.238	.261	.499	64	-8	-7	95	108	11	.399	4			-4	1	-1.4
1914	Bal-F	158	617	70	173	26	8	0	90	14	23	.280	.296	.348	.645	85	-14	-14	99	160	72	.550	15			10	*1	0.0
1915	Bal-F	85	301	24	74	13	1	1	38	9	11	.246	.268	.306	.573	65	-12	-15	107	147	29	.485	9			5	1/2	-0.9
Total	4	322	1189	110	304	46	11	1	151	32	34	.256	.275	.315	.591	74	-40	-41	101	151	117	.493	29			10	1/2	-3.0
■ **ANDY SWAN** Swan, Andrew J. Deb: 7/23/1884																												
1884	Was-a	5	21	3	3	1	0	0		0		.143	.143	.190	.333	10	-2	-2	88	0	1	.222				0	/1O	-0.1
	Ric-a	3	10	2	5	0	0	0		0		.500	.500	.500	1.000	235	1	1	99	0	3	1.000				0	/1	0.1
	Yr	8	31	5	8	1	0	0		0		.258	.258	.290	.548	88	-1	-0	92	0	2	.391				0		0.0
Total	1	8	31	5	8	1	0	0		0		.258	.258	.290	.548	88	-1	-0	92	0	3	.391				0	/1O	0.0
■ **MARTY SWANDELL** Swandell, John Martin b: 1845, Brooklyn, N.Y. 5'10.5", 146 lbs. Deb: 5/07/1872																												
1872	Eck-n	14	58	6	12							.207															/3O12	
1873	Res-n	2	10	1	1							.100															/1O	
Total	2 n	16	68	7	13							.191															/1O	
■ **PINKY SWANDER** Swander, Edward O. b: 7/4/1880, Portsmouth, Ohio d: 10/24/44, Springfield, Mass. BL/TR, 5'9", 180 lbs. Deb: 03																												
1903	StL-A	14	51	9	14	2	2	0	6	10		.275	.393	.392	.786	146	3	3	95	93	8	.811	0			1	O	0.3
1904	StL-A	1	1	0	0	0	0	0	0	0		.000	.000	.000	.000	-99	-0	-0	95	0	0	.000	0			0	H	0.0
Total	2	15	52	9	14	2	2	0	6	10		.269	.387	.385	.772	142	3	3	95	92	8	.789	0			1	/O	0.3
■ **EVAR SWANSON** Swanson, Ernest Evar b: 10/15/02, De Kalb, Ill. d: 7/17/73, Galesburg, Ill. BR/TR, 5'9", 170 lbs. Deb: 4/18/29																												
1929	Cin-N	148	574	100	172	35	12	4	43	41	47	.300	.353	.423	.776	92	-8	-8	99	61	84	.803	33			-2	*O	-2.0
1930	Cin-N	95	301	43	93	15	3	2	22	11	17	.309	.335	.399	.734	85	-11	-7	90	60	39	.654	4			3	O	-0.8
1932	Chi-A	14	52	9	16	3	1	0	8	8	3	.308	.400	.404	.804	125	1	2	87	135	9	.865	3	1	0	-2	O	0.0
1933	Chi-A	144	539	102	165	25	7	1	63	93	35	.306	.411	.384	.795	111	14	13	101	106	92	.836	19	11	-1	-8	*O	0.0
1934	Chi-A	117	426	71	127	9	5	0	34	59	31	.298	.385	.343	.727	90	-4	-4	99	79	61	.715	10	3	1	-6	*O	-0.9
Total	5	518	1892	325	573	87	28	7	170	212	133	.303	.376	.390	.766	97	-9	-3	98	81	285	.771	69	15		-16	O	-3.7
■ **KARL SWANSON** Swanson, Karl Edward b: 12/17/03, N.Henderson, Ill. BL/TR, 5'10", 155 lbs. Deb: 8/12/28																												
1928	Chi-A	22	64	2	9	1	0	0	6	4	7	.141	.191	.156	.347	-8	-10	-10	99	206	3	.309	3	0	1	-1	2	-0.8
1929	Chi-A	2	1	0	0	0	0	0	0	0	0	.000	.000	.000	.000	-99	-0	-0	95	0	0	.000	0	0	0	0	H	0.0
Total	2	24	65	2	9	1	0	0	6	4	7	.138	.188	.154	.342	-9	-10	-10	99	203	3	.304	3	0	1	-1	/2	-0.8
■ **STAN SWANSON** Swanson, Stanley Lawrence b: 5/19/44, Yuba City, Cal. BR/TR, 5'11", 168 lbs. Deb: 6/23/71																												
1971	Mon-N	49	106	14	26	3	0	2	11	10	13	.245	.310	.330	.641	82	-3	-2	99	109	11	.548	1	3	-2	-5	O	-1.0

YEAR	TM/L	G	AB	R	H	2B	3B	HR	RBI	BB	SO	AVG	OBP	SLG	PRO	/A	BR	/A	PF	CHI	RC	TA	SB	CS	SBR	FR	POS	TPR
■ **BILL SWANSON** Swanson, William Andrew b: 10/12/1888, New York, N.Y. d: 10/14/54, New York, N.Y. BB/TR, 5'6", 156 lbs. Deb: 9/02/14																												
1914	Bos-A	11	20	0	4	2	0	0	0	3	4	.200	.304	.300	.604	84	-0	-0	98	0	2	.529	0	1	-1	-1	/23S	-0.1
■ **ED SWARTWOOD** Swartwood, Cyrus Edward b: 1/12/1859, Rockford, Ill. d: 5/15/24, Pittsburgh, Pa. TR , 198 lbs. Deb: 8/11/1881																												
1881	Buf-N	1	3	0	1	0	0	0	0	1	0	.333	.500	.333	.833	165	0	0	101	0	1	1.000				0	/O	0.0
1882	Pit-a	76	325	**86**	107	**18**	11	5		21		.329	.370	.498	.868	196	30	32	97	0	61	.839				-8	*O/1	2.1
1883	Pit-a	94	413	86	**147**	24	8	3		24		**.356**	**.391**	.475	**.866**	**190**	**35**	**39**	94	0	**79**	**.827**				1	1O/C	3.1
1884	Pit-a	102	399	74	115	19	6	0		33		.288	.365	.366	.731	147	20	22	97	0	55	.683				-6	*O1/3P	1.4
1885	Bro-a	99	399	80	106	8	9	0		36		.266	.334	.331	.665	109	7	5	104	0	45	.590				-6	*O/1SC	-0.5
1886	Bro-a	122	471	95	132	13	10	3		**70**		.280	.377	.369	.746	136	23	22	100	0	82	.838	37			5	*O/C	2.1
1887	Bro-a	91	363	72	92	14	8	1		46		.253	.342	.344	.687	95	-2	-1	99	0	54	.749	29			1	O	-0.2
1890	Tol-a	126	462	106	151	23	11	3		80		.327	**.442**	.444	.885	160	42	40	103	0	117	1.135	53			5	*O/P	3.3
1892	Pit-N	13	42	8	10	1	0	0	4	13	11	.238	.418	.262	.680	116	2	2	94	118	5	.781	1			0	O	0.2
Total	9	724	2877	607	861	120	63	15	4	324	11	.299	.378	.400	.779	145	157	162	99	2	498	.812	120			-7	O/1CPS3	11.5
■ **CHARLIE SWEASY** Sweasy, Charles James (born Charles James Swasey) b: 11/2/1847, Newark, N.J. BR/TR, 5'9", 172 lbs. Deb: 5/19/1871 M																												
1871	Oly-n	5	20	4	4							.200															/2	
1872	Cle-n	11	54	8	12							.222															2/O	
1873	Bos-n	1	5	0	1							.200															/2	
1874	Bal-n	8	34	2	8							.235															/2O	
	Atl-n	10	39	4	5							.128															2	
	Yr	18	73	6	13							.178																
1875	RS-n	18	72	5	12							.167															2M	
1876	Cin-N	56	225	18	46	5	2	0	10	2	5	.204	.211	.244	.456	57	-11	-8	90	65	12	.318				1	*2/O	-0.4
1878	Pro-N	55	212	23	37	3	0	0	8	7	23	.175	.201	.189	.390	29	-16	-15	98	69	8	.269				-9	*2	-1.8
Total	5 n	53	224	23	42							.188															*2	
Total	2	111	437	41	83	8	2	0	18	9	28	.190	.206	.217	.424	43	-27	-22	93	67	20	.294				-8	2/O	-2.2
■ **BUCK SWEENEY** Sweeney, Charles Francis b: 4/15/1890, Pittsburgh, Pa d: 3/13/55, Pittsburgh, Pa. Deb: 9/28/14																												
1914	Phi-A	1	1	0	0	0	0	0	0	0	1	.000	.000	.000	.000	-99	-0	-0	97	0	0	.000	0			-0	/O	0.0
■ **CHARLIE SWEENEY** Sweeney, Charles J. b: 4/13/1863, San Francisco, Cal d: 4/4/02, San Francisco, Cal. BR , 5'10.5", 181 lbs. Deb: 5/11/1882																												
1882	Pro-N	1	4	0	0	0	0	0	0	0	1	.000	.000	.000	.000	-94	-1	-1	106	0	0	.000				0	/O	0.0
1883	Pro-N	22	87	9	19	3	0	0	15	2	10	.218	.236	.253	.489	48	-5	-5	101	241	5	.353				0	P/O	0.0
1884	Pro-N	41	168	24	50	9	0	1	19	11	17	.298	.341	.369	.710	121	5	4	102	106	22	.619				2	PO/1	0.0
	StL-U	45	171	31	54	14	2	1		10		.316	.354	.439	.792	161	12	11	104	0	27	.726	0			6	PO/1	0.0
1885	StL-N	71	267	27	55	7	1	0	24	12	33	.206	.240	.240	.480	60	-13	-10	92	138	16	.358				-2	OP	-0.6
1886	StL-N	17	64	4	16	2	0	0	7	3	10	.250	.284	.281	.565	76	-2	-2	95	134	5	.438	0			0	P/OS	0.0
1887	Cle-a	36	133	22	30	4	4	0		21		.226	.331	.316	.647	85	-2	-2	98	0	18	.718	11			0	1O/PS3	0.0
Total	6	233	894	117	224	39	7	2	65	59	71	.251	.297	.317	.614	94	-7	-5	98	92	93	.527	11			5	P/O1S3	-0.6
■ **DAN SWEENEY** Sweeney, Daniel J. b: 1/28/1868, Philadelphia, Pa. d: 7/13/13, Louisville, Ky. 5'5", 160 lbs. Deb: 4/18/1895																												
1895	Lou-N	22	90	18	24	5	0	1	16	17	2	.267	.389	.356	.744	100	0	1	95	110	14	.788	2			0	O	0.1
■ **JEFF SWEENEY** Sweeney, Edward Francis "Ed" b: 7/19/1888, Chicago, Ill. d: 7/4/47, Chicago, Ill. BR/TR, 6'1", 200 lbs. Deb: 5/16/08																												
1908	NY-A	32	82	4	12	2	0	0	2	5		.146	.195	.171	.366	22	-7	-7	95	54	3	.271	0			-4	C/1O	-0.8
1909	NY-A	67	176	19	47	3	0	0	21	16		.267	.328	.284	.612	94	-1	-1	99	162	17	.535	3			-5	C/1	0.0
1910	NY-A	78	215	25	43	4	4	0	13	17		.200	.271	.256	.527	61	-9	-10	107	87	18	.512	12			-7	C	-1.0
1911	NY-A	83	229	17	53	6	5	0	18	14		.231	.299	.301	.600	61	-10	-14	111	88	24	.563	8			-7	C	-1.0
1912	NY-A	110	351	37	94	12	1	0	30	27		.268	.325	.308	.633	80	-8	-9	101	93	37	.560	6			5	*C	0.7
1913	NY-A	117	351	35	93	10	2	2	40	37	41	.265	.348	.322	.670	96	-0	-1	101	119	42	.655	11			10	*C/1O	1.8
1914	NY-A	87	258	25	55	8	1	1	22	35	30	.213	.316	.264	.580	75	-7	-7	100	116	26	.603	19	6	2	11	C	1.3
1915	NY-A	53	137	12	26	2	0	0	5	25	12	.190	.319	.204	.523	58	-6	-6	98	61	11	.500	3	3	-1	2	C	0.0
1919	Pit-N	17	42	0	4	1	0	0	0	5	6	.095	.191	.119	.311	-5	-5	-6	105	0	1	.289	1			-1	C	-0.5
Total	9	644	1841	174	427	48	13	3	151	181	89	.232	.310	.277	.587	73	-53	-59	102	100	179	.550	63	9		5	C/1O	0.5
■ **HANK SWEENEY** Sweeney, Henry Leon b: 12/28/15, Franklin, Tenn. d: 5/6/80, Columbia, Tenn. BL/TL, 6', 185 lbs. Deb: 10/01/44																												
1944	Pit-N	1	2	0	0	0	0	0	0	0	1	.000	.000	.000	.000	-95	-1	-1	105	0	0	.000	0			0	/1	0.0
■ **JERRY SWEENEY** Sweeney, Jeremiah H. b: 1860, Boston, Mass. d: 8/25/1891, Boston, Mass. 5'9.5", 157 lbs. Deb: 8/22/1884																												
1884	KC-U	31	129	16	34	3	0	0		4		.264	.286	.287	.573	108	-1	2	87	0	11	.432	0			3	1	0.3
■ **ROONEY SWEENEY** Sweeney, John J. b: 1860, d: 6/1/1889, New York, N.Y. 5'8", 155 lbs. Deb: 1883																												
1883	Bal-a	25	101	13	21	5	2	0		4		.208	.238	.297	.535	67	-3	-4	107	0	7	.425				-2	C/O	-0.3
1884	Bal-U	48	186	37	42	7	1	0		15		.226	.284	.274	.558	81	-2	-5	110	0	15	.458	0			-4	CO/3	-0.5
1885	StL-N	3	11	1	1	0	0	0	0	0	4	.091	.091	.091	.182	-44	-2	-2	92	0	0	.100				0	/OC	0.0
Total	3	76	298	51	64	12	3	0	0	19	4	.215	.262	.275	.537	72	-6	-10	109	0	22	.432				-6	/CO3	-0.8
■ **PETE SWEENEY** Sweeney, Peter Jay b: 12/31/1863, California d: 8/22/01, San Francisco, Cal BR/TR, Deb: 1888																												
1888	Was-N	11	44	3	8	0	1	0	5	0	4	.182	.182	.227	.409	32	-3	-3	96	190	2	.278	0			0	/3O	-0.2
1889	Was-N	49	193	13	44	7	3	1	23	11	26	.228	.284	.311	.595	73	-9	-6	92	115	20	.557	8			-10	3/2O	-1.1
	StL-a	9	38	8	14	2	0	0	8	1	5	.368	.415	.421	.836	125	2	1	112	126	8	.875	2			0	/3O	0.1
1890	StL-a	49	190	23	34	3	2	0		17		.179	.271	.216	.487	39	-12	-17	116	0	14	.468	8			-5	23/1O	-2.0
	Lou-a	2	7	1	1	1	0	0		1		.143	.250	.286	.536	56	-0	-0	107	0	1	.667	1			0	/S	0.0
	Phi-a	14	49	5	8	1	1	0		7		.163	.281	.224	.505	52	-3	-3	97	0	3	.463	0			0	/2O3	-0.1
	Yr	65	246	29	43	5	3	0	0	25		.175	.272	.220	.492	42	-15	-20	112	0	18	.473	9			-5		-2.1
Total	3	134	521	53	109	14	7	1	36	37	35	.209	.280	.269	.548	59	-25	-28	103	66	47	.510	19			-16	/32O1S	-3.3
■ **BILL SWEENEY** Sweeney, William John b: 3/6/1886, Covington, Ky. d: 5/26/48, Cambridge, Mass. BR/TR, 5'11", 175 lbs. Deb: 6/14/07																												
1907	Chi-N	3	10	1	1	0	0	0	1	1		.100	.182	.100	.282	-10	-1	-1	106	386	0	.333	1			0	/S	0.0
	Bos-N	58	191	24	50	2	0	0	18	15		.262	.316	.272	.588	91	-3	-2	95	134	19	.532	8			5	3SO/21	0.3
	Yr	61	201	25	51	2	0	0	19	16		.254	.309	.264	.572	85	-4	-3	96	152	20	.520	9			5		0.3
1908	Bos-N	127	418	44	102	15	3	0	40	45		.244	.317	.294	.612	94	0	-1	104	127	43	.585	17			14	*3/S2	1.8
1909	Bos-N	138	493	44	120	19	3	1	36	37		.243	.296	.300	.596	90	-8	-6	96	92	49	.563	25			3	*3S	0.0
1910	Bos-N	150	499	43	133	22	4	5	46	61	28	.267	.349	.357	.705	93	4	-5	114	85	71	.727	25			-5	*S31	-0.5
1911	Bos-N	137	523	92	164	33	6	3	63	77	26	.314	.404	.417	.820	125	23	21	103	90	101	.919	33			13	*2	3.0
1912	Bos-N	153	593	84	204	31	13	1	100	68	34	.344	.416	.445	.861	126	31	25	107	111	123	.936	27			**26**	*2	4.4
1913	Bos-N	139	502	65	129	17	6	0	47	66	50	.257	.347	.315	.662	95	-4	-1	95	115	59	.657	18			-4	*2	-0.8
1914	Chi-N	134	463	45	101	14	5	1	38	53	15	.218	.298	.276	.575	73	-16	-15	98	111	44	.550	18			12	*2	-0.3
Total	8	1039	3692	442	1004	153	40	11	389	423	153	.272	.349	.344	.693	101	26	14	102	106	509	.698	172			63	23S/1O	7.9
■ **BILL SWEENEY** Sweeney, William Joseph b: 12/29/04, Cleveland, Ohio d: 4/18/57, San Diego, Cal. BR/TR, 5'11", 180 lbs. Deb: 4/13/28 C																												
1928	Det-A	89	309	47	78	15	5	0	19	15	28	.252	.287	.333	.620	63	-17	-17	99	63	28	.542	12	9	-2	2	1/O	-2.0
1930	Bos-A	88	243	32	75	13	0	4	30	9	15	.309	.333	.412	.745	94	-5	-2	93	89	32	.667	5	3	-0	1	1/3	-0.7
1931	Bos-A	131	498	48	147	30	3	1	58	20	30	.295	.322	.373	.696	88	-13	-9	94	103	56	.581	5	12	-6	9	*1	-1.6
Total	3	308	1050	127	300	58	8	5	107	44	73	.286	.314	.370	.685	82	-36	-28	95	88	117	.588	22	24	-8	11	1/O3	-4.3
■ **RICK SWEET** Sweet, Ricky Joe b: 9/7/52, Longview, Wash. BB/TR, 6'1", 200 lbs. Deb: 4/08/78 C																												
1978	SD-N	88	226	15	50	8	0	1	11	27	22	.221	.307	.270	.577	67	-11	-9	93	68	19	.489	1	4	-2	-5	C	-1.3
1982	NY-N	3	3	0	1	0	0	0	0	0	1	.333	.333	.333	.667	88	-0	-0	99	0	0	.500	0	0	0	0	/H	0.0
	Sea-A	88	258	29	66	6	1	4	24	20	24	.256	.314	.333	.648	71	-8	-11	109	98	29	.572	3	0	1	-8	C	-1.2

YEAR	TM/L	G	AB	R	H	2B	3B	HR	RBI	BB	SO	AVG	OBP	SLG	PRO	/A	BR	/A	PF	CHI	RC	TA	SB	CS	SBR	FR	POS	TPR
1983	Sea-A	93	249	18	55	9	0	1	22	13	26	.221	.260	.269	.529	46	-18	-18	100	123	15	.396	2	2	-1	-2	C	-1.6
Total	3	272	736	62	172	23	1	6	57	60	73	.234	.294	.292	.586	62	-37	-38	101	96	63	.489	6	6	-2	-14	C	-4.1

■ HAM SWEIGERT   Sweigert, Hampton   Deb: 10/12/1890

YEAR	TM/L	G	AB	R	H	2B	3B	HR	RBI	BB	SO	AVG	OBP	SLG	PRO	/A	BR	/A	PF	CHI	RC	TA	SB	CS	SBR	FR	POS	TPR
1890	Phi-a	1	1	0	0	0	0	0	1			.000	.500	.000	.500	53	0	0	97	0	1	2.000	1			0	/O	0.0

■ AUGIE SWENTOR   Swentor, August William   b: 11/21/1899, Seymour, Conn.   d: 11/10/69, Waterbury, Conn.   BR/TR, 6', 185 lbs.   Deb: 9/12/22

| 1922 | Chi-A | 1 | 1 | 0 | 0 | 0 | 0 | 0 | 0 | 0 | 0 | .000 | .000 | .000 | .000 | -99 | 0 | -0 | 101 | 0 | 0 | .000 | 0 | 0 | 0 | 0 | H | 0.0 |

■ POP SWETT   Swett, William E.   b: 4/16/1870, San Francisco, Cal   d: 11/22/34, San Francisco, Cal   Deb: 5/03/1890

| 1890 | Bos-P | 37 | 94 | 16 | 18 | 4 | 3 | 1 | 12 | 16 | 26 | .191 | .321 | .330 | .651 | 71 | -3 | -4 | 107 | 97 | 12 | .697 | 4 | | | 0 | C/O | -0.2 |

■ BOB SWIFT   Swift, Robert Virgil   b: 3/6/15, Salina, Kan.   d: 10/17/66, Detroit, Mich.   BR/TR, 5'11.5", 180 lbs.   Deb: 4/16/40   MC

1940	StL-A	130	398	37	97	20	1	0	39	28	39	.244	.295	.299	.594	51	-27	-30	106	118	36	.482	1	0	0	-13	*C	-3.1
1941	StL-A	63	170	13	44	7	0	0	21	22	11	.259	.344	.300	.644	71	-6	-6	100	146	19	.573	2	0	1	-2	C	-0.3
1942	StL-A	29	76	3	15	4	0	0	8	3	5	.197	.228	.289	.517	43	-6	-6	104	113	5	.391	0	2	-1	-0	C	-0.4
	Phi-A	60	192	9	44	3	0	0	15	13	17	.229	.278	.245	.523	49	-13	-12	96	112	13	.396	1	2	-1	0	C	-0.5
	Yr	89	268	12	59	7	0	1	23	16	22	.220	.264	.257	.522	47	-19	-19	99	114	18	.396	1	4	-2	-0		-0.9
1943	Phi-A	77	224	16	43	5	1	1	11	35	16	.192	.301	.237	.538	57	-11	-11	101	72	17	.461	0	0	0	-1	C	-0.8
1944	Det-A	80	247	15	63	11	1	1	19	27	27	.255	.331	.320	.651	82	-4	-5	105	84	27	.565	2	0	1	4	C	0.5
1945	Det-A	95	279	19	65	5	0	0	24	26	22	.233	.298	.251	.549	57	-14	-16	106	124	22	.439	1	0	1	0	C	-0.7
1946	Det-A	42	107	13	25	2	0	2	10	14	7	.234	.322	.308	.631	71	-3	-4	108	97	11	.547	0	0	0	-2	C	-0.4
1947	Det-A	97	279	23	70	11	1	0	21	33	16	.251	.330	.301	.631	73	-8	-10	104	89	29	.543	2	2	-1	-3	C	-0.5
1948	Det-A	113	292	23	65	6	0	4	33	51	29	.223	.338	.284	.622	69	-13	-11	96	117	32	.572	1	0	0	-15	*C	-1.7
1949	Det-A	74	189	16	45	6	0	2	18	26	20	.238	.330	.302	.632	63	-9	-11	108	98	21	.568	0	0	0	-6	C	-1.2
1950	Det-A	67	132	14	30	4	0	0	9	25	6	.227	.350	.303	.653	71	-6	-5	97	68	15	.596	0	0	0	-8	C	-0.8
1951	Det-A	44	104	8	20	0	0	0	5	12	10	.192	.276	.192	.468	27	-10	-11	106	89	7	.381	0	0	0	-9	C	-0.9
1952	Det-A	28	58	3	8	1	0	0	4	7	7	.138	.242	.155	.396	38	12	-7	99	166	2	.309	0	0	0	-0	C	-0.5
1953	Det-A	2	3	0	1	1	0	0	1	2	1	.333	.600	.667	1.267	247	1	1	98	185	2	2.000	0	0	0	0	/C	0.1
Total	14	1001	2750	212	635	86	3	14	238	324	233	.231	.313	.280	.592	61	-135	-144	103	105	256	.521	10	6	-1	-47	C	-11.2

■ CHARLIE SWINDELLS   Swindells, Charles Jay "Swin"   b: 10/26/1878, Rockford, Ill.   d: 7/22/40, Portland, Ore.   TR, 5'11.5", 180 lbs.   Deb: 9/07/04

| 1904 | StL-N | 3 | 8 | 0 | 1 | 0 | 0 | 0 | 0 | 0 | | .125 | .125 | .250 | .250 | -22 | -1 | -1 | 99 | 0 | 0 | .143 | 0 | | | | /C | 0.0 |

■ STEVE SWISHER   Swisher, Steven Eugene   b: 8/9/51, Parkersburg, W.Va.   BR/TR, 6'2", 205 lbs.   Deb: 6/14/74

1974	Chi-N	90	280	21	60	5	0	5	27	37	63	.214	.310	.286	.596	67	-11	-11	100	110	25	.517	0	3	-2	-10	C	-1.9
1975	Chi-N	93	254	20	54	16	2	1	22	30	57	.213	.306	.303	.609	67	-10	-12	104	106	22	.521	1	0	0	-10	C	-1.8
1976	Chi-N	109	377	25	89	13	3	5	42	20	82	.236	.278	.326	.604	65	-15	-19	109	117	33	.490	2	1	0	-0	*C	-1.4
1977	Chi-N	74	205	21	39	7	0	5	15	9	47	.190	.231	.298	.529	36	-18	-21	114	79	14	.426	0	1	0	0	C	-2.3
1978	StL-N	45	115	11	32	5	1	1	10	8	14	.278	.331	.365	.696	99	-1	-0	95	88	13	.584	1	0	0	2	C	0.3
1979	StL-N	38	73	4	11	1	1	1	3	6	11	.151	.215	.233	.448	21	-8	-8	105	59	4	.359	0	0	0	-1	C	-0.8
1980	StL-N	18	24	2	6	1	0	0	2	1	7	.250	.280	.292	.572	58	-1	-1	103	113	1	.400	0	0	0	-1	/C	0.0
1981	SD-N	16	28	2	4	0	0	0	2	0	11	.143	.200	.143	.343	-2	-4	-3	93	0	1	.240	0	0	0	-2	C	-0.2
1982	SD-N	26	58	2	10	1	0	2	5	3	24	.172	.238	.293	.531	52	-4	-4	92	51	4	.458	0	0	0	-1	C	-0.3
Total	9	509	1414	108	305	49	7	20	124	118	322	.216	.281	.303	.584	60	-72	-80	104	98	117	.504	4	4	-1	-19	C	-8.4

■ RON SWOBODA   Swoboda, Ronald Alan "Rocky"   b: 6/30/44, Baltimore, Md.   BR/TR, 6'2", 195 lbs.   Deb: 4/12/65

1965	NY-N	135	399	52	91	15	3	19	50	33	102	.228	.292	.424	.716	99	-	2	100	92	47	.645	2	3	-1	-0	*O	-0.6
1966	NY-N	112	342	34	76	9	4	8	50	31	76	.222	.296	.342	.638	82	-11	-8	94	149	34	.567	4	2	0	-4	O	-1.5
1967	NY-N	134	449	47	126	17	3	13	53	41	96	.281	.342	.419	.761	118	10	10	99	99	65	.704	3	1	0	2	*O1	0.7
1968	NY-N	132	450	46	109	14	6	11	59	52	113	.242	.326	.373	.699	107	6	5	102	126	55	.652	8	1	2	-5	O	-0.5
1969	NY-N	109	327	38	77	10	2	9	52	43	90	.235	.328	.361	.689	92	-3	-3	100	144	39	.628	1	0	-0	-1	O	-0.9
1970	NY-N	115	245	29	57	8	2	9	40	40	72	.233	.343	.392	.734	93	-1	-2	104	126	33	.698	2	4	-2	-14	*O	-2.1
1971	Mon-N	39	75	7	19	4	3	0	6	11	16	.253	.364	.387	.750	114	2	2	99	84	10	.700	0	1	-1	-1	O	0.0
	NY-A	54	138	17	36	2	1	2	20	27	35	.261	.393	.333	.726	111	3	4	97	157	20	.717	0	0	0	-4	O	-0.1
1972	NY-A	63	113	9	28	8	1	0	12	17	29	.248	.346	.336	.691	115	1	2	92	119	14	.644	1	0	-1	-2	O/1	-0.1
1973	NY-A	35	43	6	5	0	0	1	2	4	18	.116	.191	.186	.378	7	-5	-5	101	71	2	.316	0	0	0	-4	O/D	-1.0
Total	9	928	2581	285	624	87	24	73	344	299	647	.242	.325	.379	.704	100	0	2	99	121	320	.669	20	14	-2	-33	O/1D	-6.1

■ LOU SYLVESTER   Sylvester, Louis J.   b: 2/14/1855, Springfield, Ill.   BR/TR, 5'3", 165 lbs.   Deb: 4/18/1884

1884	Cin-U	82	333	67	89	13	8	2		18		.267	.305	.372	.677	119	10	5	108	0	39	.582	0			1	*O/PS	0.4
1886	Lou-a	45	154	41	35	5	3	0		29		.227	.350	.299	.648	98	2	0	108	0	18	.655	3		-0	0	O	0.0
	Cin-a	17	55	10	10	0	0	3		7		.182	.286	.345	.631	103	0	0	96	0	6	.644	2			1	O	0.1
	Yr	62	209	51	45	5	3	3		36		.215	.333	.311	.644	100	2	1	105	0	24	.652	5			1		0.1
1887	StL-a	29	112	20	25	4	3	1		13		.223	.340	.339	.649	76	-2	-5	110	0	16	.747	13			0	O/2	-0.3
Total	3	173	654	138	159	22	14	6		67		.243	.315	.347	.662	104	12	2	107	0	79	.634	18			2	O/PS2	0.2

■ JOE SZEKELY   Szekely, Joseph   b: 2/2/25, Cleveland, Ohio   BR/TR, 5'11", 180 lbs.   Deb: 9/13/53

| 1953 | Cin-N | 5 | 13 | 0 | 1 | 0 | 0 | 0 | 0 | 0 | 3 | .077 | .077 | .077 | .154 | -60 | -3 | -3 | 99 | 0 | 0 | .077 | 0 | 0 | 0 | 1 | /O | -0.1 |

■ KEN SZOTKIEWICZ   Szotkiewicz, Kenneth John   b: 2/25/47, Wilmington, Del.   BL/TR, 6', 165 lbs.   Deb: 4/07/70

| 1970 | Det-A | 47 | 84 | 9 | 9 | 1 | 0 | 3 | 9 | 12 | 29 | .107 | .219 | .226 | .445 | 22 | -9 | -9 | 103 | 130 | 5 | .408 | 0 | 0 | 0 | -2 | S | -0.7 |

■ JERRY TABB   Tabb, Jerry Lynn   b: 3/17/52, Altus, Okla.   BL/TR, 6'2", 195 lbs.   Deb: 9/08/76

1976	Chi-N	11	24	2	7	0	0	0	3	2	2	.292	.370	.292	.662	82	-0	-0	109	0	3	.588	0	0	0	-1	/1	0.0
1977	Oak-A	51	144	8	32	3	0	6	19	10	26	.222	.273	.368	.641	77	-6	-5	95	106	13	.534	0	1	-1	0	1/D	-0.6
1978	Oak-A	12	9	0	1	0	0	0	1	2	5	.111	.273	.111	.384	12	-1	-1	101	395	0	.375	0	0	0	-0	1/D	0.0
Total	3	74	177	10	40	3	0	6	23	14	33	.226	.286	.345	.631	74	-7	-6	97	108	16	.551	0	1	-1	-0	1/D	-0.6

■ PAT TABLER   Tabler, Patrick Sean   b: 2/2/58, Hamilton, Ohio   BR/TR, 6'3", 175 lbs.   Deb: 8/21/81

1981	Chi-N	35	101	11	19	3	1	1	13	26	.188	.281	.267	.548	54	-6	-6	104	65	7	.460	0	1	-1	5	2	0.1
1982	Chi-N	25	85	9	20	4	2	1	7	6	20	.235	.293	.365	.658	80	-2	-2	103	81	9	.559	0	0	0	3	-0.4
1983	Cle-A	124	430	56	125	23	5	6	65	56	63	.291	.374	.400	.783	110	11	8	105	134	63	.719	2	4	-2	-6	O3/2D	0.0
1984	Cle-A	144	473	66	137	21	3	10	68	47	62	.290	.358	.410	.768	106	8	5	106	124	68	.700	3	3	0	-10	103/2D	-0.9
1985	Cle-A	117	404	47	111	18	3	5	59	27	55	.275	.323	.371	.695	95	-6	-3	94	142	43	.570	6	4	-3	1D/32	-0.9
1986	Cle-A	130	473	61	154	29	2	6	48	29	75	.326	.368	.433	.802	121	12	14	98	87	74	.725	3	1	0	-1	*1D	0.5
1987	Cle-A	151	553	66	170	34	3	11	86	51	84	.307	.372	.439	.812	112	11	13	101	132	93	.780	5	2	0	-4	1D	0.5
1988	Cle-A	41	143	16	32	5	1	1	17	23	27	.224	.335	.294	.629	77	-3	-4	102	159	15	.588	1	0	0	-3	D1	-0.3
	KC-A	89	301	37	93	17	2	1	49	23	41	.309	.362	.389	.751	107	4	3	103	162	42	.664	2	3	-1	-3	DO/13	-0.1
	Yr	130	444	53	125	22	3	2	66	46	68	.282	.353	.358	.711	97	1	-0	103	162	58	.643	3	3	-1	-4		-0.4
Total	8	856	2963	369	861	154	22	42	404	275	453	.291	.355	.400	.755	105	32	25	102	125	415	.703	16	18	-6	-13	1DO/32	-1.8

■ GREG TABOR   Tabor, Gregory Steven   b: 5/21/61, Castro Valley, Cal.   BR/TR, 6' ", 165 lbs.   Deb: 9/10/87

| 1987 | Tex-A | 9 | 9 | 4 | 1 | 1 | 0 | 0 | 1 | 0 | 4 | .111 | .111 | .222 | .333 | -14 | -1 | -1 | 104 | 200 | 0 | .250 | 0 | 0 | 0 | 0 | /2D | 0.0 |

■ JIM TABOR   Tabor, James Reubin "Rawhide"   b: 11/5/13, Owens Crossroads, Ala.   d: 8/22/53, Sacramento, Cal.   BR/TR, 6'2", 175 lbs.   Deb: 8/02/38

1938	Bos-A	19	57	8	18	3	2	1	8	1	6	.316	.328	.491	.819	100	-0	-0	102	87	8	.725	0	1		-1	3/S	0.1
1939	Bos-A	149	577	76	167	33	8	14	95	40	54	.289	.337	.447	.784	91	-3	-10	108	109	82	.724	16	10	-1	8	*3	-0.6
1940	Bos-A	120	459	73	131	28	6	21	81	42	58	.285	.345	.510	.855	118	11	10	101	101	81	.845	14	10	-2	9	*3	2.2
1941	Bos-A	126	498	65	139	29	3	16	101	36	48	.279	.328	.446	.773	100	-0	-2	103	135	69	.714	17	9	-0	-3	*3	0.1
1942	Bos-A	139	508	56	128	34	2	12	75	37	47	.252	.303	.366	.669	84	-10	-12	104	121	53	.567	6	13	-6	-7	*3	-2.3

YEAR	TM/L	G	AB	R	H	2B	3B	HR	RBI	BB	SO	AVG	OBP	SLG	PRO	/A	BR	/A	PF	CHI	RC	TA	SB	CS	SBR	FR	POS	TPR
1943	Bos-A	137	537	57	130	26	3	13	85	43	54	.242	.299	.374	.674	93	-4	-7	104	137	59	.592	7	7	-2	-4	*3/O	-1.1
1944	Bos-A	116	438	58	125	25	3	13	72	31	38	.285	.334	.445	.779	124	10	11	98	113	63	.700	4	4	-1	-0	*3	1.0
1946	Phi-N	124	463	53	124	15	2	10	50	36	51	.268	.322	.374	.696	102	-3	-0	95	97	56	.610	3			-2	*3	0.0
1947	Phi-N	75	251	27	59	14	0	4	31	20	21	.235	.297	.339	.635	68	-12	-12	100	118	25	.548	2			-4	3	-1.7
Total	9	1005	3788	473	1021	191	29	104	598	286	377	.270	.322	.418	.739	99	-12	-22	102	116	496	.687	69	54		-4	3/OS	-2.4
■ **DOUG TAITT**	Taitt, Douglas John "Poco" b: 8/3/02, Bay City, Mich. d: 12/12/70, Portland, Ore. BL/TR, 6', 176 lbs. Deb: 4/10/28																											
1928	Bos-A	143	482	51	144	28	14	3	61	36	32	.299	.350	.434	.784	107	2	4	98	98	74	.756	13	6	0	2	*O/P	0.0
1929	Bos-A	26	65	6	18	4	0	0	6	8	5	.277	.365	.338	.703	81	-1	-2	102	93	8	.646	0	1	-1	-0	O	-0.2
	Chi-A	47	124	11	21	7	0	0	12	8	13	.169	.220	.226	.446	16	-16	-15	95	147	7	.350	0	0	0	-2	O	-1.6
	Yr	73	189	17	39	11	0	0	18	16	18	.206	.272	.265	.536	40	-17	-17	97	129	14	.444	0	1	-1	-2		-1.8
1931	Phi-N	38	151	13	34	4	2	1	15	4	14	.225	.245	.298	.543	43	-12	-13	106	114	11	.419	0			2	O	-1.2
1932	Phi-N	4	2	0	0	0	0	0	1	2	0	.000	.500	.000	.500	43	0	0	112	0	0	1.000	0			0	H	0.0
Total	4	258	824	81	217	43	16	4	95	58	64	.263	.314	.369	.683	79	-27	-26	99	107	100	.616	13	7		3	O/P	-3.0
■ **BOB TALBOT**	Talbot, Robert Dale b: 6/6/27, Visalia, Cal. BR/TR, 6', 170 lbs. Deb: 9/16/53																											
1953	Chi-N	8	30	5	10	0	1	0	0	0	4	.333	.333	.400	.733	88	-0	-1	103	0	3	.591	1	0	0	4	/O	0.3
1954	Chi-N	114	403	45	97	15	4	1	19	16	25	.241	.275	.305	.580	51	-29	-30	101	59	32	.456	3	6	-3	-10	*O	-4.6
Total	2	122	433	50	107	15	5	1	19	16	29	.247	.279	.312	.591	53	-30	-30	101	55	36	.467	4	6	-2	-6	O	-4.3
■ **TIM TALTON**	Talton, Marion Lee b: 1/14/39, Pikeville, N.C. BL/TR, 6'3", 200 lbs. Deb: 7/08/66																											
1966	KC-A	37	53	8	18	3	1	2	6	1	5	.340	.364	.547	.911	168	4	4	94	72	10	.861	0	1	-1	0	C/1	0.4
1967	KC-A	46	59	7	15	3	1	0	5	7	13	.254	.333	.339	.672	100	0	0	100	104	6	.563	0	0	0	-1	C/1	0.1
Total	2	83	112	15	33	6	2	2	11	8	18	.295	.347	.438	.785	131	4	4	97	90	16	.690	0	1	-1	-1	/C1	0.5
■ **JOHN TAMARGO**	Tamargo, John Felix b: 11/7/51, Tampa, Fla. BB/TR, 5'10", 170 lbs. Deb: 9/03/76																											
1976	StL-N	10	10	2	3	0	0	0	1	3	0	.300	.462	.300	.762	115	1	0	104	128	2	.750	0	0	0	0	/C	0.1
1977	StL-N	4	4	0	0	0	0	0	0	0	2	.000	.000	.000	.000	-99	-1	-1	96	0	0	.000	0	0	0	0	/C	0.0
1978	StL-N	6	6	0	0	0	0	0	0	0	2	.000	.000	.000	.000	-99	-2	-2	95	0	0	.000	0	0	0	0	/C	-0.1
	SF-N	36	92	6	22	4	1	1	8	18	7	.239	.364	.337	.701	106	0	1	92	93	12	.694	1	1	-0	1	C	0.3
	Yr	42	98	6	22	4	1	1	8	18	9	.224	.345	.316	.661	93	-1	-0	92	80	12	.641	1	1	-0	1		0.2
1979	SF-N	30	60	7	12	3	0	2	6	4	8	.200	.250	.350	.600	67	-3	-3	92	88	6	.521	0	0	0	-0	C	-0.2
	Mon-N	12	21	0	8	2	0	0	5	3	3	.381	.458	.476	.935	152	2	2	102	198	5	1.000	0	0	0	1	/C	0.2
	Yr	42	81	7	20	5	0	2	11	7	11	.247	.307	.383	.690	91	-2	-1	95	121	10	.623	0	0	0	0		0.0
1980	Mon-N	37	51	4	14	3	0	1	13	6	5	.275	.351	.392	.743	108	1	1	99	224	8	.703	0	0	0	1	C	0.2
Total	5	135	244	19	59	12	1	4	33	34	27	.242	.335	.348	.683	94	-3	-1	95	126	32	.645	1	1	-0	2	/C	0.5
■ **LEO TANKERSLEY**	Tankersley, Lawrence William b: 6/8/01, Terrell, Tex. d: 9/18/80, Dallas, Tex. BR/TR, 6', 176 lbs. Deb: 7/02/25																											
1925	Chi-A	1	3	0	0	0	0	0	0	0	0	.000	.000	.000	.000	-99	-1	-1	96	0	0	.000	0	0	0	0	/C	0.0
■ **JESSE TANNEHILL**	Tannehill, Jesse Niles "Powder" b: 7/14/1874, Dayton, Ky. d: 9/22/56, Dayton, Ky. BB/TL, 5'8", 150 lbs. Deb: 6/17/1894 C																											
1894	Cin-N	5	11	0	0	0	0	0	1	1	2	.000	.083	.000	.083	-78	-3	-3	100	0	0	.091	0			0	/P	0.0
1897	Pit-N	56	184	22	49	8	2	0	22	18		.266	.338	.332	.670	81	-5	-4	98	105	23	.630	4			3	OP	-0.2
1898	Pit-N	60	152	25	44	9	3	1	17	7		.289	.321	.408	.729	114	1	2	98	79	22	.676	4			4	P/O	0.0
1899	Pit-N	47	132	17	34	5	3	0	10	8		.258	.310	.341	.651	82	-4	-3	99	68	15	.582	2			4	P/O	0.0
1900	Pit-N	34	110	19	37	7	0	0	17	5		.336	.365	.400	.765	110	2	1	103	121	17	.699	2			0	P/O	0.0
1901	Pit-N	42	135	19	33	3	3	1	12	6		.244	.277	.333	.610	78	-4	-4	101	84	13	.500	0			-2	PO	0.0
1902	Pit-N	44	148	27	43	6	1	1	17	12		.291	.344	.365	.709	115	4	3	105	103	20	.657	3			1	PO	0.0
1903	NY-A	40	111	18	26	6	2	1	13	8		.234	.286	.351	.637	92	-1	-1	100	112	12	.565	1			-0	P/O	0.0
1904	Bos-A	45	122	14	24	2	6	0	6	9		.197	.252	.311	.563	76	-3	-3	105	59	10	.490	1			2	P/O	0.0
1905	Bos-A	37	93	11	21	2	0	1	12	16		.226	.339	.280	.619	99	1	1	100	148	9	.597	1			2	P	0.0
1906	Bos-A	31	79	12	22	2	2	0	4	6		.278	.329	.354	.684	118	1	2	98	52	10	.614	1			0	P	0.0
1907	Bos-A	21	51	2	10	3	1	0	6	2		.196	.226	.294	.521	67	-2	-2	101	143	3	.415	0			0	P	0.0
1908	Bos-A	1	2	0	1	0	0	0	0	0		.500	.500	.500	1.000	233	0	0	98	0	0	1.000	0			0	/P	0.0
	Was-A	26	43	1	11	1	0	0	3	2		.256	.289	.279	.568	91	-1	-0	95	94	3	.438	0			1	P	0.2
	Yr	27	45	1	12	1	0	0	3	2		.267	.298	.289	.587	97	-0	-0	96	90	4	.455	0			2		0.2
1909	Was-A	16	36	2	6	1	0	0	1	5		.167	.286	.194	.480	58	-2	-1	90	55	2	.433	0			-1	/OP	-0.1
1911	Cin-N	1	1	0	0	0	0	0	0	0	1	.000	.000	.000	.000	-99	-0	-0	92	0	0	.000	0			0	/P	0.0
Total	15	506	1410	189	361	55	23	5	141	105	3	.256	.310	.338	.648	92	-15	-15	100	93	159	.578	19			15	P/O	-0.1
■ **LEE TANNEHILL**	Tannehill, Lee Ford b: 10/26/1880, Dayton, Ky. d: 2/16/38, Live Oak, Fla. BR/TR, 5'11", 170 lbs. Deb: 4/22/03																											
1903	Chi-A	138	503	48	113	14	3	2	50	25		.225	.261	.276	.538	68	-22	-17	92	127	40	.446	10			-5	*S	-1.5
1904	Chi-A	153	547	50	125	31	5	0	61	20		.229	.256	.303	.559	79	-14	-13	99	140	47	.474	14			**25**	*3	2.0
1905	Chi-A	142	480	38	96	17	2	0	39	45		.200	.269	.244	.512	67	-18	-16	97	121	34	.443	8			27	*3	1.8
1906	Chi-A	116	378	26	69	8	3	0	33	31		.183	.244	.220	.464	51	-22	-18	92	148	23	.392	7			**27**	3S	1.7
1907	Chi-A	33	108	9	26	2	0	0	11	8		.241	.293	.259	.552	75	-2	-3	104	143	9	.476	3			1	3	0.0
1908	Chi-A	141	482	44	104	15	3	0	35	25		.216	.254	.259	.514	73	-16	-13	94	107	32	.413	6			20	*3/S	1.8
1909	Chi-A	155	531	39	118	21	5	0	47	31		.222	.269	.281	.550	76	-17	-15	97	124	41	.472	12			10	3S	0.0
1910	Chi-A	67	230	17	51	10	0	1	21	11		.222	.263	.278	.542	73	-9	-7	95	118	18	.447	3			3	S1/3	-0.2
1911	Chi-A	141	516	60	131	17	6	0	49	32		.254	.300	.310	.610	73	-21	-19	97	106	49	.504	0			**30**	*S2/31	2.0
1912	Chi-A	3	3	0	0	0	0	0	0	1		.000	.400	.000	.400	17	-0	-0	99	0	0	.667	0			-0	/3	0.0
Total	10	1089	3778	331	833	135	27	3	346	229		.220	.267	.273	.539	71	-141	-123	96	124	293	.452	63			138	3S/12	7.6
■ **CHUCK TANNER**	Tanner, Charles William b: 7/4/29, New Castle, Pa. BL/TL, 6', 185 lbs. Deb: 4/12/55 M																											
1955	Mil-N	97	243	27	60	9	3	6	27	27	32	.247	.322	.383	.705	93	-5	-2	93	98	28	.619	0	0	0	-6	O	-0.9
1956	Mil-N	60	63	6	15	2	0	1	4	10	10	.238	.342	.317	.660	80	-2	-1	99	73	7	.588	0	0	0	-3	/O	-0.4
1957	Mil-N	22	69	5	17	3	0	2	6	5	4	.246	.297	.377	.674	88	-2	-1	90	78	8	.585	0	0	0	-1	O	-0.2
	Chi-N	95	318	42	91	16	2	7	42	23	20	.286	.338	.415	.753	105	0	2	96	114	44	.668	0	2	-1	-11	O	-1.2
	Yr	117	387	47	108	19	2	9	48	28	24	.279	.331	.408	.739	102	-2	1	95	108	52	.655	0	2	-1	-12		-1.4
1958	Chi-N	73	103	10	27	6	0	4	17	9	10	.262	.321	.437	.758	98	-0	-1	101	123	14	.705	1	0	0	-2	O	-0.2
1959	Cle-A	14	48	6	12	2	0	1	5	2	9	.250	.280	.354	.634	76	-2	-2	97	98	4	.500	0	0	0	-1	O	-0.2
1960	Cle-A	21	25	2	7	1	0	0	4	4	6	.280	.379	.320	.699	93	-0	-0	98	196	3	.684	1	0	0	-1	/O	0.0
1961	LA-A	7	8	0	1	0	0	0	0	2	2	.125	.300	.125	.425	16	-1	-1	111	0	0	.429	0	0	0	-0	/O	0.0
1962	LA-A	7	8	0	1	0	0	0	0	0	0	.125	.125	.125	.250	-32	-1	-1	102	0	0	.125	0	0	0	-1	/O	-0.1
Total	8	396	885	98	231	39	5	21	105	82	93	.261	.325	.388	.713	94	-13	-8	96	104	109	.653	2	2	-1	-26	O	-3.2
■ **WALTER TAPPAN**	Tappan, Walter Van Dorn "Tap" b: 10/8/1890, Carlinville, Ill. d: 12/19/67, Lynwood, Cal. BR/TR, 5'8", 158 lbs. Deb: 4/16/14																											
1914	KC-F	18	39	1	8	1	0	1	3	1	0	.205	.225	.308	.533	54	-3	-2	95	72	3	.452	1			0	/S32	-0.1
■ **EL TAPPE**	Tappe, Elvin Walter b: 5/21/27, Quincy, Ill. BR/TR, 5'11", 180 lbs. Deb: 4/24/54 MC																											
1954	Chi-N	46	119	5	22	3	0	0	4	10	9	.185	.248	.210	.458	21	-14	-14	101	63	7	.354	0	0	0	-2	C	-1.4
1955	Chi-N	2	0	0	0	0	0	0	0	0	0	—	—	—	—	—	0	0	100	—	—	—	0	0	0	0	/C	0.0
1956	Chi-N	3	1	0	0	0	0	0	0	1	0	.000	.500	.000	.500	51	0	0	99	0	0	1.000	0	0	0	0	/C	0.0
1958	Chi-N	17	28	2	6	0	0	0	4	3	1	.214	.290	.214	.505	36	-2	-2	101	275	1	.375	0	0	0	-1	C	-0.1
1960	Chi-N	51	103	11	24	7	0	0	3	11	12	.233	.313	.301	.614	70	-4	-4	98	39	10	.524	0	1	-1	-8	C	-0.9
1962	Chi-N	26	53	3	11	0	0	0	6	4	3	.208	.288	.208	.496	34	-5	-5	106	215	3	.386	0	0	0	-3	CM	-0.6
Total	6	145	304	21	63	10	0	0	17	29	25	.207	.283	.240	.523	41	-25	-25	101	101	28	.430	0	1	-1	-13	C	-3.0
■ **TED TAPPE**	Tappe, Theodore Nash b: 2/2/31, Seattle, Wash. BL/TR, 6'3", 185 lbs. Deb: 9/14/50																											
1950	Cin-N	7	5	1	1	0	0	1	1	1	1	.200	.333	.800	1.133	179	1	1	105	55	1	1.250	0			0	H	0.1

YEAR	TM/L	G	AB	R	H	2B	3B	HR	RBI	BB	SO	AVG	OBP	SLG	PRO	/A	BR	/A	PF	CHI	RC	TA	SB	CS	SBR	FR	POS	TPR
1951	Cin-N	4	3	0	1	0	0	0	0	0	0	.333	.333	.333	.667	79	-0	-0	101	0	0	.500	0	0	0	0	H	0.0
1955	Chi-N	23	50	12	13	2	0	4	10	11	11	.260	.413	.540	.953	151	4	4	100	104	12	1.081	0	0	0	-2	O	0.1
Total	3	34	58	13	15	2	0	5	11	12	12	.259	.403	.552	.955	150	5	5	100	95	14	1.070	0	0		-2	/O	0.2
■ **ARLIE TARBERT** Tarbert, Wilbur Arlington b: 9/10/04, Cleveland, Ohio d: 11/27/46, Cleveland, Ohio BR/TR, 6', 160 lbs. Deb: 6/18/27																												
1927	Bos-A	33	69	5	13	1	0	0	5	3	12	.188	.253	.203	.456	21	-8	-8	95	119	4	.357	0	0	0	-5	O	-1.3
1928	Bos-A	6	17	1	3	1	0	0	2	1	1	.176	.222	.235	.458	21	-2	-2	98	172	1	.429	1	0	0	-1	/O	-0.2
Total	2	39	86	6	16	2	0	0	7	4	13	.186	.247	.209	.457	21	-10	-10	95	129	5	.371	1	0	0	-5	/O	-1.5
■ **DAN TARTABULL** Tartabull, Danilo (Mora) b: 10/30/62, San Juan, P.R. BR/TR, 6'1.5", 185 lbs. Deb: 9/07/84																												
1984	Sea-A	10	20	3	6	1	0	2	7	2	3	.300	.391	.650	1.041	178	2	2	102	147	5	1.143	0	0	0	1	/S2	0.3
1985	Sea-A	19	61	8	20	7	1	1	7	8	14	.328	.406	.525	.930	161	5	5	95	79	14	.976	1	0	0	2	S/3	0.8
1986	Sea-A	137	511	76	138	25	6	25	96	61	157	.270	.349	.489	.838	120	18	15	105	125	85	.808	4	8	-4	-1	*O2/3D	0.8
1987	KC-A	158	582	95	180	27	3	34	101	79	136	.309	.393	.541	.934	140	39	35	104	102	124	.962	9	4	0	-10	*O/D	2.0
1988	KC-A	146	507	80	139	38	3	26	102	76	119	.274	.373	.515	.888	142	32	30	103	122	99	.911	8	5	-1	-7	*OD	1.9
Total	5	470	1681	262	483	98	13	88	313	226	429	.287	.374	.518	.892	135	96	87	104	115	327	.919	22	17	-4	-16	O/2SD3	5.8
■ **JOSE TARTABULL** Tartabull, Jose Milages (Guzman) b: 11/27/38, Cienfuegos, Cuba BL/TL, 5'11", 165 lbs. Deb: 4/10/62																												
1962	KC-A	107	310	49	86	6	5	0	22	20	19	.277	.323	.329	.652	76	-10	-10	100	86	36	.617	19	5	3	-1	O	-1.1
1963	KC-A	79	242	27	58	8	5	1	19	17	17	.240	.290	.326	.616	67	-9	-11	108	97	26	.599	16	1	4	-7	O	-1.7
1964	KC-A	104	100	9	20	2	0	0	3	5	12	.200	.238	.220	.458	27	-10	-10	105	58	6	.387	4	0	1	-12	O	-2.4
1965	KC-A	68	218	28	68	11	4	1	19	18	20	.312	.364	.413	.777	124	6	7	97	85	33	.748	11	5	0	10	O	1.5
1966	KC-A	37	127	13	30	2	3	0	4	11	13	.236	.297	.299	.596	76	-4	-4	94	45	13	.582	8	1	2	2	O	-0.1
	Bos-A	68	195	28	54	7	4	0	11	6	11	.277	.299	.354	.652	79	-4	-6	109	67	20	.581	11	3	2	1	O	-0.5
	Yr	105	322	41	84	9	7	0	15	17	24	.261	.298	.332	.630	78	-8	-10	104	60	34	.581	19	4	3	2		-0.6
1967	Bos-A	115	247	36	55	1	2	0	10	23	26	.223	.289	.243	.532	51	-12	-16	115	69	18	.441	6	6	-2	-11	O	-3.5
1968	Bos-A	72	139	24	39	6	0	0	6	6	5	.281	.310	.324	.634	92	-1	-2	101	57	14	.515	2	3	-1	-4	O	-0.9
1969	Oak-A	75	266	28	71	11	1	0	11	9	11	.267	.291	.316	.607	76	-11	-9	92	53	24	.480	3	4	-2	2	O	-0.9
1970	Oak-A	24	13	5	3	2	0	0	2	0	2	.231	.231	.385	.615	69	-1	-1	97	162	1	.600	1	0	0	-2	/O	-0.1
Total	9	749	1857	247	484	56	24	2	107	115	136	.261	.304	.320	.624	75	-56	-61	102	72	192	.565	81	28	8	-24	O	-9.7
■ **LA SCHELLE TARVER** Tarver, La Schelle b: 1/30/59, Modesto, Cal. BL/TL, 5'11", 165 lbs. Deb: 7/12/86																												
1986	Bos-A	13	25	3	3	0	0	0	1	1	4	.120	.154	.120	.274	-24	-4	-4	100	133	0	.174	0	1	-1	-1	/O	-0.5
■ **WILLIE TASBY** Tasby, Willie b: 1/8/33, Shreveport, La. BR/TR, 5'11", 170 lbs. Deb: 9/09/58																												
1958	Bal-A	18	50	6	10	3	0	1	1	7	15	.200	.310	.320	.630	78	-2	-1	94	21	5	.610	1	1	-0	-1	O	-0.3
1959	Bal-A	142	505	69	126	16	5	13	48	34	80	.250	.305	.378	.683	89	-10	-8	97	84	57	.597	3	5	-2	-3	*O	-1.9
1960	Bal-A	39	85	9	18	2	1	0	3	9	12	.212	.295	.259	.554	50	-6	-6	102	53	7	.478	1	0	0	-5	O	-1.1
	Bos-A	105	385	68	108	17	1	7	37	51	54	.281	.372	.384	.756	102	4	3	103	91	58	.721	3	1	0	-2	*O	-0.2
	Yr	144	470	77	126	19	2	7	40	60	66	.268	.358	.362	.720	93	-1	-3	103	81	65	.678	4	1	1	-6		-1.3
1961	Was-A	141	494	54	124	13	2	17	63	58	94	.251	.332	.389	.721	97	-6	-2	95	104	60	.648	4	10	-5	-6	*O	-1.8
1962	Was-A	11	34	4	7	0	0	0	0	2	6	.206	.250	.206	.456	24	-4	-4	101	0	2	.321	0	0	0	-2	O	-0.5
	Cle-A	75	199	25	48	7	0	4	17	25	41	.241	.326	.337	.663	81	-6	-5	98	85	22	.582	0	2	-1	-5	O/3	-1.3
	Yr	86	233	29	55	7	0	4	17	27	47	.236	.315	.318	.633	72	-9	-9	98	74	23	.546	0	2	-1	-7		-1.8
1963	Cle-A	52	116	11	26	3	1	4	5	15	25	.224	.318	.371	.689	95	-1	-1	97	38	13	.615	0	1	-1	-5	O/2	-0.6
Total	6	583	1868	246	467	61	10	46	174	201	327	.250	.328	.367	.695	90	-29	-24	98	83	224	.642	12	20	-8	-27	O/23	-7.7
■ **POP TATE** Tate, Edward Christopher "Dimples" b: 12/22/1860, Richmond, Va. d: 6/25/32, Richmond, Va. BR/TL, Deb: 1885																												
1885	Bos-N	4	13	1	2	0	0	0	2	1	3	.154	.214	.154	.368	22	-1	-1	94	348	0	.273				0	/C	0.0
1886	Bos-N	31	106	13	24	3	1	0	3	7	17	.226	.274	.274	.548	69	-4	-4	97	34	8	.439	0			-3	C	-0.3
1887	Bos-N	60	231	34	60	5	3	0	27	8	9	.260	.296	.307	.604	71	-9	-8	98	120	24	.526	7			17	C/O	1.2
1888	Bos-N	41	148	18	34	7	1	1	6	8	7	.230	.278	.311	.589	85	-2	-3	106	45	14	.518	3			-6	C/O	-0.6
1889	Bal-a	72	253	28	46	6	3	1	27	13	37	.182	.236	.241	.477	38	-21	-20	100	123	16	.401	4			-5	C1	-1.5
1890	BB-a	19	71	7	13	1	1	0		4		.183	.284	.225	.509	52	-4	-4	100	0	6	.500	3			0	C/1	-0.2
Total	6	227	822	101	179	22	9	2	65	41	73	.218	.269	.274	.543	60	-40	-40	100	89	68	.467	17			2	C/1O	-1.4
■ **BENNIE TATE** Tate, Henry Bennett b: 12/3/01, Whitwell, Tenn. d: 10/27/73, W.Frankfort, Ill. BL/TR, 5'8", 165 lbs. Deb: 4/29/24																												
1924	Was-A	21	43	2	13	2	0	0	7	1	2	.302	.318	.349	.667	73	-2	-2	98	154	5	.533	0	0	0	0	C	0.0
1925	Was-A	16	27	0	13	3	0	0	7	2	2	.481	.517	.593	1.110	185	3	3	98	146	8	1.200	0	1	-1	1	C	0.4
1926	Was-A	59	142	17	38	5	2	1	13	15	1	.268	.338	.352	.690	82	-4	-4	98	83	18	.625	0	0	0	1	C	0.0
1927	Was-A	61	131	12	41	5	1	1	24	8	4	.313	.357	.389	.746	97	-1	-1	97	148	18	.667	0	0	0	0	C	0.1
1928	Was-A	57	122	10	30	6	0	0	15	10	4	.246	.303	.295	.598	57	-7	-8	102	143	10	.479	0	4	-2	2	C	-0.4
1929	Was-A	81	265	26	78	12	3	0	30	16	8	.294	.335	.362	.697	80	-8	-8	100	107	31	.594	2	5	-2	3	C	0.0
1930	Was-A	14	20	1	5	0	0	0	2	0	1	.250	.250	.250	.500	27	-2	-2	101	133	1	.333	0	0	0	0	/C	0.0
	Chi-A	72	230	26	73	11	2	0	27	18	10	.317	.367	.383	.750	88	-3	-4	103	102	33	.684	2	1	0	0	C	0.2
	Yr	86	250	27	78	11	2	0	29	18	11	.312	.358	.372	.730	83	-5	-6	102	108	34	.653	2	1	0	0		0.2
1931	Chi-A	89	273	27	73	12	3	0	22	26	10	.267	.331	.333	.664	81	-10	-6	92	80	31	.587	1	1	-0	6	C	0.5
1932	Chi-A	4	10	1	1	0	0	0	0	1	0	.100	.182	.100	.282	-29	-2	-2	87	0	0	.222	0	0	0	0	/C	0.0
	Bos-A	81	273	21	67	12	5	2	26	20	6	.245	.297	.348	.645	69	-14	-13	97	86	28	.556	0	1	-1	6	C	-0.2
	Yr	85	283	22	68	12	5	2	26	21	6	.240	.293	.339	.632	66	-16	-14	96	82	28	.542	0	1	-1	6		-0.2
1934	Chi-N	11	24	1	3	0	0	0	0	1	3	.125	.160	.125	.285	-23	-4	-4	98	0	0	.174	0			0	/C	-0.3
Total	10	566	1560	144	435	68	16	4	173	118	51	.279	.330	.351	.681	78	-54	-49	98	102	183	.589	5	13		19	C	0.3
■ **HUGHIE TATE** Tate, Hugh Henry b: 5/19/1880, Everett, Pa. d: 8/7/56, Greenville, Pa. BR/TR, 5'11", 190 lbs. Deb: 9/21/05																												
1905	Was-A	4	13	1	4	0	1	0	2	0		.308	.308	.462	.769	139	1	0	104	119	2	.778	1			-0	/O	0.0
■ **LEE TATE** Tate, Lee Willie "Skeeter" b: 3/18/32, Black Rock, Ark. BR/TR, 5'10", 165 lbs. Deb: 9/12/58																												
1958	StL-N	10	35	4	7	2	0	0	1	4	3	.200	.282	.257	.539	41	-3	-3	106	47	3	.448	0	0	0	-2	/S	-0.3
1959	StL-N	41	50	5	7	1	1	1	4	5	7	.140	.232	.260	.492	29	-5	-5	105	101	3	.422	0	0	0	-0	S/23	-0.3
Total	2	51	85	9	14	3	1	1	5	9	10	.165	.253	.259	.511	34	-8	-8	105	79	5	.438	0	0	0	-2	/S32	-0.6
■ **JARVIS TATUM** Tatum, Jarvis b: 10/11/46, Fresno, Cal. BR/TR, 6', 185 lbs. Deb: 9/07/68																												
1968	Cal-A	17	51	7	9	1	0	0	2	0	9	.176	.176	.196	.373	14	-5	-5	94	86	2	.233	0	0	0	1	O	-0.5
1969	Cal-A	10	22	2	7	0	0	0	0	0	6	.318	.318	.318	.636	79	-1	-1	99	0	2	.412	0	1	-1	-1	/O	-0.2
1970	Cal-A	75	181	28	43	7	0	0	6	17	35	.238	.303	.276	.579	66	-9	-7	92	49	15	.476	1	0	0	-1	O	-1.0
Total	3	102	254	37	59	8	0	0	8	17	50	.232	.280	.264	.544	58	-15	-13	93	52	18	.423	1	1	-0	-1	/O	-1.7
■ **TOMMY TATUM** Tatum, V T b: 7/16/19, Boyd, Tex. BR/TR, 6', 185 lbs. Deb: 8/01/41																												
1941	Bro-N	8	12	1	2	1	0	0	1	1	3	.167	.231	.250	.481	34	-1	-1	103	120	1	.400	0			-1	/O	-0.1
1947	Bro-N	4	6	0	0	0	0	0	0	0	1	.000	.000	.000	.000	-96	-2	-2	105	0	0	.000	0			-1	/O	-0.2
	Cin-N	69	176	19	48	5	2	1	16	16	16	.273	.333	.341	.674	87	-5	-3	91	94	21	.638	7			6	O/2	0.2
	Yr	73	182	19	48	5	2	1	16	16	17	.264	.323	.330	.653	80	-7	-5	92	89	20	.610	7			6		0.0
Total	2	81	194	20	50	6	2	1	17	17	20	.258	.318	.325	.642	78	-8	-6	92	93	22	.596	7			5	/O2	-0.1
■ **FRED TAUBY** Tauby, Fred Joseph (born Fred Joseph Taubensee) b: 3/27/06, Canton, Ohio d: 11/23/55, Concordia, Cal. BR/TR, 5'9.5", 168 lbs. Deb: 9/01/35																												
1935	Chi-A	13	32	5	4	1	0	0	2	2	3	.125	.176	.156	.333	-12	-5	-6	109	136	1	.250	0	0	0	2	/O	-0.3
1937	Phi-N	11	20	2	0	0	0	0	3	0	5	.000	.000	.000	.000	-93	-5	-6	108	0	0	.050	1			-2	/O	-0.7
Total	2	24	52	7	4	1	0	0	5	2	8	.077	.111	.096	.207	-41	-11	-12	109	86	1	.167	1	0		-0	/O	-1.0
■ **DON TAUSSIG** Taussig, Donald Franklin b: 2/19/32, New York, N.Y. BR/TR, 6', 180 lbs. Deb: 4/23/58																												
1958	SF-N	39	50	10	10	0	0	1	4	3	8	.200	.245	.260	.505	34	-5	-5	100	103	3	.400	0	0	0	-10	O	-1.5

YEAR	TM/L	G	AB	R	H	2B	3B	HR	RBI	BB	SO	AVG	OBP	SLG	PRO	/A	BR	/A	PF	CHI	RC	TA	SB	CS	SBR	FR	POS	TPR
1961	StL-N	98	188	27	54	14	5	2	25	16	34	.287	.343	.447	.790	95	2	-1	113	112	28	.723	2	2	-1	-6	O	-1.2
1962	Hou-N	16	25	1	5	0	0	1	1	2	11	.200	.259	.320	.579	59	-2	-1	93	36	2	.476	0	0	0	1	/O	0.0
Total	3	153	263	38	69	14	5	4	30	21	53	.262	.317	.399	.716	82	-5	-8	109	103	33	.650	2	2	-1	-15	O	-2.7

■ **JACKIE TAVENER** Tavener, John Adam "Rabbit" b: 12/27/1897, Celina, Ohio d: 9/14/69, Fort Worth, Tex. BL/TR, 5'5", 138 lbs. Deb: 9/24/21

YEAR	TM/L	G	AB	R	H	2B	3B	HR	RBI	BB	SO	AVG	OBP	SLG	PRO	/A	BR	/A	PF	CHI	RC	TA	SB	CS	SBR	FR	POS	TPR
1921	Det-A	2	4	0	0	0	0	0	0	0	1	.000	.000	.000	.000	-99	-1	-1	96	0	0	.000	0	0	0	0	/S	0.0
1925	Det-A	134	453	45	111	11	11	0	47	39	60	.245	.309	.318	.627	60	-28	-28	99	109	47	.552	5	4	-1	-6	*S	-1.2
1926	Det-A	156	532	65	141	22	14	1	58	52	53	.265	.332	.365	.696	84	-15	-13	97	100	66	.641	8	7	-2	8	*S	0.5
1927	Det-A	116	419	60	115	22	9	5	59	36	38	.274	.333	.406	.739	84	-7	-12	108	108	56	.747	20	0	6	0	*S	0.0
1928	Det-A	132	473	59	123	24	15	5	52	33	51	.260	.314	.406	.720	88	-10	-9	99	88	60	.676	13	8	-1	9	*S	1.1
1929	Cle-A	92	250	25	53	9	4	2	27	26	28	.212	.286	.304	.590	52	-18	-18	100	113	22	.512	1	4	-2	17	*S	0.4
Total	6	632	2131	254	543	88	53	13	243	186	231	.255	.317	.364	.681	76	-79	-81	100	102	252	.632	47	23	0	28	S	0.8

■ **ALEX TAVERAS** Taveras, Alejandro Antonio (Betances) b: 10/9/55, Santiago, D.R. BR/TR, 5'10", 155 lbs. Deb: 9/09/76

YEAR	TM/L	G	AB	R	H	2B	3B	HR	RBI	BB	SO	AVG	OBP	SLG	PRO	/A	BR	/A	PF	CHI	RC	TA	SB	CS	SBR	FR	POS	TPR
1976	Hou-N	14	46	3	10	0	0	0	2	2	1	.217	.250	.217	.467	39	-4	-3	86	77	2	.325	1	2	-1	1	/2S	-0.2
1982	LA-N	11	3	1	1	1	0	0	2	0	1	.333	.333	.667	1.000	183	0	0	95	392	1	1.000	0	0	0	0	/23S	0.1
1983	LA-N	10	4	0	0	0	0	0	0	0	1	.000	.000	.000	.000	-99	-1	-1	100	0	0	.000	0	0	0	-0	/S23	0.0
Total	3	35	53	4	11	1	0	0	4	2	3	.208	.236	.226	.463	36	-5	-4	88	89	3	.341	1	2	-1	0	/2S3	-0.1

■ **FRANK TAVERAS** Taveras, Franklin Crisostomo (Fabian) b: 12/24/49, Las Matas De Santa Cruz, D.R. BR/TR, 6', 155 lbs. Deb: 9/25/71

YEAR	TM/L	G	AB	R	H	2B	3B	HR	RBI	BB	SO	AVG	OBP	SLG	PRO	/A	BR	/A	PF	CHI	RC	TA	SB	CS	SBR	FR	POS	TPR
1971	Pit-N	1	0	0	0	0	0	0	0	0	0	—	—	—	—	—	0	0	99	—	—	—	0	0	0	0	R	0.0
1972	Pit-N	4	3	0	0	0	0	0	0	1	1	.000	.250	.000	.250	-23	-0	-0	103	0	0	.250	0	0	0	0	/S	0.0
1974	Pit-N	126	333	33	82	4	2	0	26	25	41	.246	.303	.270	.573	63	-17	-16	98	111	29	.496	13	4	2	-8	*S	-0.8
1975	Pit-N	134	378	44	80	9	4	0	23	37	42	.212	.285	.257	.542	52	-24	-24	99	92	32	.500	17	6	2	-3	*S	-1.0
1976	Pit-N	144	519	76	134	8	6	0	24	44	79	.258	.321	.297	.618	76	-15	-15	100	61	56	.639	58	11	11	7	*S	1.6
1977	Pit-N	147	544	72	137	20	10	1	29	38	71	.252	.308	.331	.639	70	-22	-24	103	65	61	.681	**70**	18	**10**	-10	*S	-0.2
1978	Pit-N	157	654	81	182	31	9	0	38	29	60	.278	.314	.353	.667	82	-13	-17	105	58	72	.621	46	25	-1	-25	*S	-3.2
1979	Pit-N	11	45	4	11	3	0	0	1	0	2	.244	.244	.311	.556	48	-3	-3	106	29	3	.432	2	1	0	-0	S	-0.2
	NY-N	153	635	89	167	26	9	1	33	33	72	.263	.301	.337	.639	78	-23	-19	95	58	63	.584	42	19	1	-14	*S	-1.6
	Yr	164	680	93	178	29	9	1	34	33	74	.262	.298	.335	.633	76	-26	-23	96	56	67	.576	44	20	1	-14		-1.8
1980	NY-N	141	562	65	157	27	0	0	25	23	64	.279	.309	.327	.636	81	-17	-14	96	57	53	.548	32	18	-1	-27	*S	-2.8
1981	NY-N	84	283	30	65	11	3	0	11	12	36	.230	.266	.290	.556	57	-16	-16	101	53	23	.498	16	4	2	-11	S	-1.7
1982	Mon-N	48	87	9	14	5	1	0	4	7	6	.161	.223	.241	.465	28	-8	-9	105	75	5	.427	4	0	1	-3	S2	-0.7
Total	11	1150	4043	503	1029	144	44	2	214	249	474	.255	.302	.313	.615	71	-159	-158	100	66	398	.589	300	106	26	-93	*S/2	-10.6

■ **TAYLOR** Taylor Deb:9/10/1874

YEAR	TM/L	G	AB	R	H	2B	3B	HR	RBI	BB	SO	AVG	OBP	SLG	PRO	/A	BR	/A	PF	CHI	RC	TA	SB	CS	SBR	FR	POS	TPR
1874	Bal-n	13	51	3	10							.196															1	

■ **TONY TAYLOR** Taylor, Antonio Nemesio (Sanchez) b: 12/19/35, Central Alara, Cuba BR/TR, 5'9", 170 lbs. Deb: 4/15/58 C

YEAR	TM/L	G	AB	R	H	2B	3B	HR	RBI	BB	SO	AVG	OBP	SLG	PRO	/A	BR	/A	PF	CHI	RC	TA	SB	CS	SBR	FR	POS	TPR
1958	Chi-N	140	497	63	117	15	3	6	27	40	93	.235	.301	.314	.615	63	-26	-26	101	65	50	.567	21	6	3	12	*2/3	-0.4
1959	Chi-N	150	624	96	175	30	8	8	38	45	86	.280	.335	.393	.727	94	-6	-5	98	50	84	.685	23	9	2	12	*2/S	2.0
1960	Chi-N	19	76	14	20	3	3	1	9	8	12	.263	.341	.421	.762	109	1	1	98	90	12	.754	2	0	1	2	2	0.5
	Phi-N	127	505	66	145	22	4	4	35	33	86	.287	.333	.370	.704	86	-5	-10	107	69	62	.646	24	11	1	1	*2/3	0.2
	Yr	146	581	80	165	25	7	5	44	41	98	.284	.334	.377	.711	89	-4	-9	106	72	74	.661	26	11	1	2		0.7
1961	Phi-N	106	400	47	100	17	3	2	26	29	59	.250	.304	.322	.626	71	-19	-16	94	82	38	.543	11	5	0	7	2/3	0.3
1962	Phi-N	152	625	87	162	21	5	7	43	68	82	.259	.337	.342	.679	87	-14	-9	95	62	76	.638	20	9	1	-12	*2/S	-0.7
1963	Phi-N	157	640	102	180	20	10	5	49	42	99	.281	.332	.367	.700	99	1	-1	103	73	79	.640	23	9	2	7	*23	1.8
1964	Phi-N	154	570	62	143	13	6	4	46	46	74	.251	.321	.316	.637	81	-14	-13	99	104	60	.569	13	7	-0	-22	*2	-2.3
1965	Phi-N	106	323	41	74	14	3	3	27	22	58	.229	.303	.319	.621	79	-10	-8	95	100	32	.548	5	4	-1	-1	2/3	-0.6
1966	Phi-N	125	434	47	105	14	8	5	40	31	56	.242	.294	.346	.640	76	-13	-14	101	102	42	.548	8	4	0	-2	23	-1.3
1967	Phi-N	132	462	55	110	16	6	2	34	42	74	.238	.308	.312	.620	75	-12	-15	104	96	42	.535	10	9	-2	-3	132/S	-2.3
1968	Phi-N	145	547	59	137	20	2	3	38	39	60	.250	.304	.311	.615	87	-10	-8	97	95	54	.552	22	5	4	12	*3/21	0.8
1969	Phi-N	138	557	68	146	24	5	3	30	42	62	.262	.318	.339	.658	86	-12	-10	98	54	60	.587	19	10	-0	0	321	-0.6
1970	Phi-N	124	439	74	132	26	9	9	55	50	67	.301	.376	.462	.838	128	15	17	96	95	71	.798	9	11	-4	-4	23O/S	1.3
1971	Phi-N	36	107	9	25	2	1	1	5	9	10	.234	.293	.299	.592	66	-4	-5	103	58	9	.494	2	2	-1	2	23/1	-0.2
	Det-A	55	181	27	52	10	2	3	19	12	11	.287	.335	.414	.749	116	2	3	96	92	25	.694	5	1	1	3	2/3	0.9
1972	Det-A	78	228	33	69	12	4	1	20	14	34	.303	.348	.404	.752	109	6	3	113	88	31	.673	5	1	1	-2	2/31	0.7
1973	Det-A	84	275	35	63	9	3	5	24	17	29	.229	.276	.338	.615	72	-11	-11	101	87	24	.533	9	5	-0	-4	2/13OD	-1.3
1974	Phi-N	62	64	5	21	4	0	2	13	6	6	.328	.394	.484	.879	140	4	4	103	136	12	.844	0	0	0	0	/132	0.4
1975	Phi-N	79	103	13	25	5	1	1	17	17	18	.243	.355	.340	.695	92	-0	-1	101	173	12	.659	3	3	-1	2	3/12	0.1
1976	Phi-N	26	23	2	6	1	0	0	3	1	7	.261	.320	.304	.624	73	-1	-1	107	165	2	.529	0	0	0	0	/23	0.0
Total	19	2195	7680	1005	2007	298	86	75	598	613	1083	.261	.322	.352	.674	87	-128	-124	100	81	876	.627	234	111	4	6	*23/1OSD	-0.7

■ **BEN TAYLOR** Taylor, Benjamin Eugene b: 9/30/27, Metropolis, Ill. BL/TL, 6', 175 lbs. Deb: 7/29/51

YEAR	TM/L	G	AB	R	H	2B	3B	HR	RBI	BB	SO	AVG	OBP	SLG	PRO	/A	BR	/A	PF	CHI	RC	TA	SB	CS	SBR	FR	POS	TPR
1951	StL-A	33	93	14	24	2	1	3	6	9	22	.258	.337	.398	.734	94	-0	-1	105	47	12	.671	1	1	-0	1	1	0.0
1952	Det-A	7	18	0	3	0	0	0	0	0	5	.167	.167	.167	.333	-7	-3	-3	99	0	0	.188	0	0	0	0	/1	-0.2
1955	Mil-N	12	10	2	1	0	0	0	0	2	4	.100	.250	.100	.350	-3	-1	-1	93	0	0	.333	0	0	0	0	/1	0.0
Total	3	52	121	16	28	2	1	3	6	11	31	.231	.306	.339	.645	73	-4	-5	103	36	13	.585	1	1	-0	1	/1	-0.2

■ **CHINK TAYLOR** Taylor, C L b: 2/9/1898, Burnet, Tex. d: 7/7/80, Temple, Tex. BR/TR, 5'9", 160 lbs. Deb: 4/18/25

YEAR	TM/L	G	AB	R	H	2B	3B	HR	RBI	BB	SO	AVG	OBP	SLG	PRO	/A	BR	/A	PF	CHI	RC	TA	SB	CS	SBR	FR	POS	TPR
1925	Chi-N	8	6	2	0	0	0	0	0	0	0	.000	.000	.000	.000	-99	-2	-2	97	0	0	.000	0	0	0	-1	/O	-0.1

■ **CARL TAYLOR** Taylor, Carl Means b: 1/20/44, Sarasota, Fla. BR/TR, 6'2", 200 lbs. Deb: 4/11/68

YEAR	TM/L	G	AB	R	H	2B	3B	HR	RBI	BB	SO	AVG	OBP	SLG	PRO	/A	BR	/A	PF	CHI	RC	TA	SB	CS	SBR	FR	POS	TPR
1968	Pit-N	44	71	5	15	1	0	0	7	10	10	.211	.309	.225	.534	62	-3	-3	101	184	5	.450	1	0	0	-2	C/O	-0.4
1969	Pit-N	104	221	30	77	10	1	4	33	31	36	.348	.435	.457	.892	159	16	18	95	117	45	.894	0	1	-1	-1	O1	1.2
1970	StL-N	104	245	39	61	12	2	6	45	41	30	.249	.359	.388	.747	94	1	-1	106	155	34	.721	5	2	0	-3	O1/3	-0.6
1971	Pit-N	7	12	1	2	0	1	0	0	0	5	.167	.167	.333	.500	39	-1	-1	99	0	0	.364	0	0	0	-2	/O	-0.2
	KC-A	20	39	3	7	0	0	0	3	5	13	.179	.273	.179	.452	31	-3	-3	99	175	2	.353	0	1	-1	0	O	-0.4
1972	KC-A	63	113	17	30	2	1	0	11	17	16	.265	.366	.301	.667	100	1	1	100	135	14	.644	4	1	1	-2	C/O13	0.0
1973	KC-A	69	145	18	33	6	1	0	16	32	20	.228	.367	.283	.650	78	-1	-3	109	153	17	.636	2	2	-1	-4	C/1D	-0.5
Total	6	411	846	113	225	31	6	10	115	136	130	.266	.371	.352	.723	102	10	7	102	143	117	.714	12	7	-1	-14	CO/13D	-0.9

■ **DANNY TAYLOR** Taylor, Daniel Turney b: 12/23/1900, Lash, Pa. d: 10/11/72, Latrobe, Pa. BR/TR, 5'10", 190 lbs. Deb: 6/30/26

YEAR	TM/L	G	AB	R	H	2B	3B	HR	RBI	BB	SO	AVG	OBP	SLG	PRO	/A	BR	/A	PF	CHI	RC	TA	SB	CS	SBR	FR	POS	TPR
1926	Was-A	21	50	10	15	0	1	1	5	5	7	.300	.364	.400	.764	101	-0	0	98	74	7	.703	1	2	-1	-2	O	-0.2
1929	Chi-N	2	3	0	0	0	0	0	0	1	1	.000	.250	.000	.250	-32	-1	-1	101	0	0	.333	0			-0	/O	0.0
1930	Chi-N	74	219	43	62	14	3	2	37	27	34	.283	.364	.402	.766	81	-5	-7	105	136	32	.777	6			-5	O	-1.2
1931	Chi-N	88	270	48	81	13	6	5	41	31	46	.300	.372	.448	.820	125	8	9	96	107	47	.825	4			-6	O	0.0
1932	Chi-N	6	22	3	5	2	0	0	3	3	1	.227	.320	.318	.638	69	-1	-1	104	163	2	.647	1			0	/O	0.0
	Bro-N	105	395	84	128	22	7	11	48	33	41	.324	.378	.499	.876	139	18	21	96	79	76	.914	13			0	O	1.3
	Yr	111	417	87	133	24	7	11	51	36	42	.319	.374	.489	.864	135	18	20	96	85	78	.898	14			0		1.3
1933	Bro-N	103	358	75	102	21	9	9	40	47	45	.285	.368	.469	.837	142	18	19	97	79	64	.856	11			-0	O	1.4
1934	Bro-N	120	405	62	121	24	6	7	57	63	47	.299	.396	.440	.835	130	16	19	95	105	74	.864	12			-9	*O	0.4
1935	Bro-N	112	352	51	102	19	5	7	59	46	32	.290	.372	.432	.804	123	8	12	94	123	60	.794	6			-9	O	-0.1
1936	Bro-N	43	116	12	34	6	0	2	15	11	14	.293	.359	.397	.756	98	1	-0	105	102	16	.698	2			-3	O	-0.4
Total	9	674	2190	388	650	121	37	44	305	267	268	.297	.374	.446	.821	123	62	71	97	102	379	.844	56	2		-34	O	1.2

■ **DWIGHT TAYLOR** Taylor, Dwight Bernard b: 3/24/60, Los Angeles, Cal. BL/TL, 5'9", 166 lbs. Deb: 4/14/86

YEAR	TM/L	G	AB	R	H	2B	3B	HR	RBI	BB	SO	AVG	OBP	SLG	PRO	/A	BR	/A	PF	CHI	RC	TA	SB	CS	SBR	FR	POS	TPR
1986	KC-A	4	2	1	0	0	0	0	0	0	0	.000	.000	.000	.000	-99	-1	-1	100	0	0	.000	0	0	0	-0	/OD	0.0

YEAR	TM/L	G	AB	R	H	2B	3B	HR	RBI	BB	SO	AVG	OBP	SLG	PRO	/A	BR	/A	PF	CHI	RC	TA	SB	CS	SBR	FR	POS	TPR
■ ED TAYLOR	Taylor, Edward James b: 11/17/01, Chicago, Ill. BR/TR, 5'6.5", 160 lbs. Deb: 4/14/26																											
1926	Bos-N	92	272	37	73	8	2	0	33	38	26	.268	.368	.313	.681	98	-4	2	86	134	34	.663	4			-2	3S	0.3
■ FRED TAYLOR	Taylor, Frederick Rankin b: 12/3/24, Zanesville, Ohio BL/TR, 6'3", 201 lbs. Deb: 9/12/50																											
1950	Was-A	6	16	1	2	0	0	0	0	1	2	.125	.176	.125	.301	-22	-3	-3	99	0	0	.214	0	0	0	0	/1	-0.2
1951	Was-A	6	12	1	2	1	0	0	0	0	4	.167	.167	.250	.417	12	-2	-1	95	0	1	.300	0	0	0	0	/1	-0.1
1952	Was-A	10	19	3	5	1	0	0	4	3	2	.263	.364	.316	.679	90	-0	-0	100	249	3	.643	0	0	0	0	/1	0.0
Total	3	22	47	5	9	2	0	0	4	4	8	.191	.255	.234	.489	32	-5	-5	99	107	3	.395	0	0	0	0	/1	-0.3
■ GEORGE TAYLOR	Taylor, George Edward "Live" b: 2/3/1855, Belfast, Me. d: 2/19/1888, San Francisco, Cal Deb: 5/01/1884																											
1884	Pit-a	41	152	22	32	4	1	0		6		.211	.255	.250	.505	70	-5	-4	97	0	10	.392				-1	O	-0.4
■ HARRY TAYLOR	Taylor, Harry Leonard b: 4/4/1866, Halsey Valley, N.Y. d: 7/12/55, Buffalo, N.Y. BL, 6'2", 160 lbs. Deb: 4/18/1890																											
1890	Lou-a	134	553	115	169	7	7	0		68		.306	.382	.344	.725	109	14	7	107	0	92	.789	45			0	*1S/2C	0.3
1891	Lou-a	93	356	81	105	7	4	2	37	55	33	.295	.397	.354	.751	131	11	17	90	78	57	.801	15			3	1/32C	1.3
1892	Lou-N	125	493	66	128	7	1	0	34	58	23	.260	.342	.278	.620	98	-3	3	92	67	56	.611	24			1	O12/3S	0.1
1893	Bal-N	88	360	50	102	9	1	1	54	32	11	.283	.347	.322	.669	75	-9	-14	107	132	50	.678	24			-2	*1	-1.3
Total	4	440	1762	312	504	30	13	3	125	213	67	.286	.367	.323	.690	102	12	14	99	61	256	.717	108			2	1/O2S3C	0.4
■ HARRY TAYLOR	Taylor, Harry Warren b: 12/26/07, Mc Keesport, Pa. d: 4/27/69, Toledo, Ohio BL/TL, 6'1.5", 185 lbs. Deb: 4/14/32																											
1932	Chi-N	10	8	1	1	0	0	0	0	1	1	.125	.222	.125	.347	-4	-1	-1	104	0	0	.286	0			0	/1	0.0
■ SANDY TAYLOR	Taylor, James B. 5'10.5", 175 lbs. Deb: 1879																											
1879	Tro-N	24	97	10	21	4	0	0	8	1	8	.216	.224	.258	.482	63	-4	-3	93	119	6	.342				-3	O	-0.6
■ ZACK TAYLOR	Taylor, James Wren b: 7/27/1898, Yulee, Fla. d: 9/19/74, Orlando, Fla. BR/TR, 5'11.5", 180 lbs. Deb: 6/15/20 MC																											
1920	Bro-N	9	13	3	5	2	0	0	5	0	2	.385	.385	.538	.923	147	1	1	111	276	2	.778	0	1	-1	-0	/C	0.1
1921	Bro-N	30	102	6	20	0	2	0	8	1	8	.196	.212	.235	.447	17	-12	-13	105	122	5	.341	2	0	1	1	C	-0.8
1922	Bro-N	7	14	0	3	0	0	0	2	1	1	.214	.267	.214	.481	27	-2	-1	95	233	1	.364	0	0	0	0	/C	0.0
1923	Bro-N	96	337	29	97	11	6	0	46	9	13	.288	.312	.356	.668	78	-12	-11	98	135	36	.547	2	5	-2	12	C	0.3
1924	Bro-N	99	345	36	100	9	4	1	39	14	14	.290	.319	.348	.667	80	-10	-10	99	116	38	.549	0	1	-1	7	C	-0.1
1925	Bro-N	109	352	33	109	16	4	3	44	17	19	.310	.343	.403	.747	96	-5	-2	94	104	48	.658	0	0	0	10	C	1.1
1926	Bos-N	125	432	36	110	22	3	0	42	28	27	.255	.303	.319	.622	78	-20	-12	86	105	41	.525	1			11	*C	0.3
1927	Bos-N	30	96	8	23	2	1	1	14	8	5	.240	.298	.313	.611	68	-5	-4	93	148	9	.521	0			4	C	0.2
	NY-N	83	258	18	60	7	3	0	21	17	20	.233	.283	.283	.566	52	-18	-17	100	101	21	.470	2			-12	C	-2.3
	Yr	113	354	26	83	9	4	1	35	25	25	.234	.287	.291	.578	56	-22	-21	98	115	30	.483	2			-7		-2.1
1928	Bos-N	125	399	36	100	15	1	2	30	33	29	.251	.313	.308	.621	65	-21	-20	97	83	39	.538	2			-2	*C	-1.3
1929	Bos-N	34	101	8	25	7	0	0	10	7	9	.248	.303	.317	.620	57	-7	-6	94	107	10	.526	0			1	C	-0.2
	Chi-N	64	215	29	59	16	3	1	31	19	18	.274	.336	.391	.727	79	-7	-7	101	122	28	.667	0			-0	C	-0.2
	Yr	98	316	37	84	23	3	1	41	26	27	.266	.326	.367	.693	72	-14	-14	99	118	38	.621	0			0		-0.4
1930	Chi-N	32	95	12	22	2	1	1	11	2	12	.232	.255	.305	.560	33	-10	-11	105	118	7	.438	0			1	C	-0.7
1931	Chi-N	8	4	0	1	0	0	0	0	2	1	.250	.500	.250	.750	112	0	0	96	0	1	1.000	0			0	/C	0.1
1932	Chi-N	21	30	2	6	1	0	0	3	1	4	.200	.226	.233	.459	23	-3	-3	104	159	2	.333	0			0	C	-0.2
1933	Chi-N	16	11	0	0	0	0	0	0	0	1	.000	.000	.000	.000	-99	-3	-3	97	0	0	.000	0			0	C	-0.1
1934	NY-A	4	7	0	1	0	0	0	0	0	1	.143	.143	.143	.286	-27	-1	-1	96	0	0	.167	0	0	0	0	/C	0.0
1935	Bro-N	26	54	2	7	3	0	0	5	2	8	.130	.175	.185	.361	-3	-8	-7	94	180	1	.255	0			0	C	-0.6
Total	16	918	2865	258	748	113	28	9	311	161	192	.261	.304	.329	.634	68	-143	-129	96	112	289	.531	9	7		33	C	-4.4
■ JOE TAYLOR	Taylor, Joe Cephus b: 3/2/26, Chapman, Ala. BR/TR, 6'1", 185 lbs. Deb: 8/26/54																											
1954	Phi-A	18	58	5	13	1	1	1	8	2	9	.224	.250	.328	.578	58	-4	-4	98	138	4	.438	0	1	-1	-1	O	-0.5
1957	Cin-N	33	107	14	28	7	0	4	9	6	24	.262	.301	.439	.740	91	-1	-2	105	63	13	.646	0	1	-1	3	O	0.0
1958	StL-N	18	23	2	7	3	0	1	3	2	4	.304	.360	.565	.925	132	1	1	106	77	5	.938	0	0	0	0	/O	0.1
	Bal-A	36	77	11	21	4	0	2	9	7	19	.273	.333	.403	.736	108	0	1	94	97	9	.623	0	0	0	-1	O	-0.1
1959	Bal-A	14	32	2	5	1	0	1	2	11	5	.156	.372	.281	.653	85	-0	-0	97	66	4	.741	0	0	0	-3	O	-0.3
Total	4	119	297	34	74	16	1	9	31	28	61	.249	.314	.401	.715	92	-4	-4	100	87	35	.653	0	2	-1	-2	/O	-0.8
■ LEO TAYLOR	Taylor, Leo Thomas "Chink" b: 5/13/01, Walla Walla, Wash. d: 5/20/82, Seattle, Wash. BR/TR, 5'10.5", 150 lbs. Deb: 5/03/23																											
1923	Chi-A	1	0	0	0	0	0	0	0	0	0	—	—	—	—	—	0	0	98	—	—	—	0	0	0	0	R	0.0
■ OAK TAYLOR	Taylor, Oak b: Cincinnati, Ohio Deb: 1877																											
1877	Har-N	2	8	0	3	0	0	0	0	0	2	.375	.375	.375	.750	153	0	0	89	0	1	.600				0	/O	0.0
■ HAWK TAYLOR	Taylor, Robert Dale b: 4/3/39, Metropolis, Ill. BR/TR, 6'1", 187 lbs. Deb: 6/09/57																											
1957	Mil-N	7	1	2	0	0	0	0	0	0	0	.000	.000	.000	.000	-99	-0	-0	90	0	0	.000	0	0	0	0	/C	0.0
1958	Mil-N	4	8	1	1	1	0	0	0	0	3	.125	.125	.250	.375	-4	-1	-1	89	0	0	.286	0	0	0	-1	/O	-0.1
1961	Mil-N	20	26	1	5	0	0	1	1	3	11	.192	.276	.308	.584	59	-2	-1	92	37	2	.500	0	1	-1	0	/OC	-0.1
1962	Mil-N	20	47	3	12	0	0	0	2	2	10	.255	.286	.255	.541	47	-3	-3	99	66	3	.389	0	1	-1	1	O	-0.3
1963	Mil-N	16	29	1	2	0	0	0	0	1	12	.069	.100	.069	.169	-50	-6	-6	101	0	0	.107	0	0	0	-0	/O	-0.6
1964	NY-N	92	225	20	54	8	0	4	23	8	33	.240	.272	.329	.601	72	-10	-8	95	110	19	.472	0	0	0	2	CO	-0.5
1965	NY-N	25	46	5	7	0	0	4	10	1	8	.152	.170	.413	.583	58	-3	-3	100	134	2	.488	0	0	0	-1	C/1	-0.3
1966	NY-N	53	109	5	19	2	0	3	12	3	19	.174	.204	.275	.479	34	-10	-9	94	129	4	.351	0	1	-1	-1	C1	-1.1
1967	NY-N	13	37	3	9	3	0	0	4	2	8	.243	.282	.324	.606	74	-1	-1	99	138	3	.500	0	0	0	-1	C	-0.1
	Cal-A	23	52	5	16	3	0	1	3	4	8	.308	.357	.423	.780	136	2	2	96	50	8	.703	0	0	0	1	C	0.4
1969	KC-A	64	89	7	24	5	0	3	21	6	18	.270	.316	.427	.743	103	0	0	103	179	11	.638	0	0	0	-3	O/C	-0.2
1970	KC-A	57	55	3	9	3	0	0	6	6	16	.164	.258	.218	.476	33	-5	-5	98	202	3	.404	0	0	0	0	/C1	-0.4
Total	11	394	724	56	158	25	0	16	82	36	146	.218	.259	.319	.578	63	-39	-36	97	116	57	.475	0	3	-2	-4	C/O1	-3.3
■ BOB TAYLOR	Taylor, Robert Lee b: 3/20/44, Leland, Miss. BL/TR, 5'9", 170 lbs. Deb: 4/09/70																											
1970	SF-N	63	84	12	16	0	0	2	10	12	13	.190	.320	.262	.582	60	-5	-4	96	139	8	.535	0	0	0	-4	O/C	-0.8
■ SAMMY TAYLOR	Taylor, Samuel Douglas b: 2/27/33, Woodruff, S.C. BL/TR, 6'2", 185 lbs. Deb: 4/27/58																											
1958	Chi-N	96	301	30	78	12	2	6	36	27	46	.259	.320	.372	.692	82	-8	-8	101	114	35	.605	2	1	0	-7	C	-1.0
1959	Chi-N	110	353	41	95	13	2	13	43	35	47	.269	.337	.428	.765	104	1	2	98	91	51	.712	1	0	0	-3	*C	0.5
1960	Chi-N	74	150	14	31	9	0	3	17	6	18	.207	.242	.327	.569	55	-10	-9	98	119	10	.448	0	1	-1	-5	C	-1.3
1961	Chi-N	89	235	26	56	8	2	8	23	23	39	.238	.317	.391	.708	87	-5	-5	100	80	29	.643	0	0	0	-3	C	0.0
1962	Chi-N	7	15	0	2	1	0	0	1	3	3	.133	.278	.200	.478	29	-1	-2	106	131	1	.429	0	0	0	-1	/C	-0.1
	NY-N	68	158	12	35	4	2	3	20	23	17	.222	.328	.329	.657	74	-5	-6	104	129	18	.606	0	0	0	-2	C	-0.6
	Yr	75	173	12	37	5	2	3	21	26	20	.214	.323	.318	.641	70	-6	-7	104	131	19	.593	0	0	0	-2		-0.7
1963	NY-N	22	35	3	9	0	1	0	6	5	7	.257	.350	.314	.664	93	-0	-0	99	229	3	.552	0	0	0	-1	C	0.0
	Cin-N	3	6	0	0	0	0	0	0	0	2	.000	.000	.000	.000	-96	-2	-2	104	0	0	.000	0	0	0	0	/C	-0.1
	Yr	25	41	3	9	0	1	0	6	5	9	.220	.304	.268	.573	66	-2	-2	100	211	4	.500	0	0	0	-1		-0.1
	Cle-A	4	10	1	3	0	0	0	1	0	2	.300	.300	.300	.600	71	-0	-0	97	139	1	.429	0	0	0	0	/C	0.0
Total	6	473	1263	127	309	47	9	33	147	122	181	.245	.315	.375	.690	84	-29	-29	100	107	147	.634	3	2	-0	-21	C	-2.6
■ TOMMY TAYLOR	Taylor, Thomas Livingstone Carlton b: 9/17/1892, Mexia, Tex. d: 4/5/56, Greenville, Miss. BR/TR, 5'8.5", 160 lbs. Deb: 7/09/24																											
1924	Was-A	26	73	11	19	3	1	0	10	2	8	.260	.289	.329	.618	60	-5	-4	98	138	7	.537	2	0	1	-3	3/2O	-0.4
■ BILLY TAYLOR	Taylor, William H. b: 1868, Butler, Ky. d: 9/12/05, Cincinnati, Ohio Deb: 9/19/1898																											
1898	Lou-N	9	24	2	6	1	0	0	2	1		.250	.308	.292	.599	77	-1	-1	96	86	3	.556	1			0	/32	0.0
■ BILLY TAYLOR	Taylor, William Henry "Bollicky Bill" b: 1855, Washington, D.C. d: 5/14/1900, Jacksonville, Fla. TR, 5'11.5", 204 lbs. Deb: 1881																											
1881	Wor-N	6	28	3	3	1	0	0	2	0	2	.107	.107	.143	.250	-21	-4	-4	105	150	0	.160				0	/OP3	-0.3

YEAR	TM/L	G	AB	R	H	2B	3B	HR	RBI	BB	SO	AVG	OBP	SLG	PRO	/A	BR	/A	PF	CHI	RC	TA	SB	CS	SBR	FR	POS	TPR
	Det-N	1	4	0	2	2	0	0	1	0	0	.500	.500	1.000	1.500	338	1	1	106	88	2	2.000				0	/3	0.1
	Cle-N	24	103	6	25	1	0	0	12	0	8	.243	.243	.252	.495	58	-5	-5	96	170	6	.333				-1	O/P	-0.5
	Yr	31	135	9	30	4	0	0	15	0	10	.222	.222	.252	.474	49	-8	-7	98	171	8	.324				-1		-0.7
1882	Pit-a	70	299	40	84	16	12	4		7		.281	.297	.455	.752	155	15	16	97	0	41	.665				-7	C13/OP	0.8
1883	Pit-a	83	369	43	96	13	7	2		9		.260	.278	.350	.627	108	-0	4	94	0	37	.505				-14	OCP/1	-0.6
1884	StL-U	43	186	44	68	23	1	3		7		.366	.389	.548	.937	206	21	20	104	0	41	.924	0			-1	P1/O	0.0
	Phi-a	30	111	8	28	6	2	0		2		.252	.272	.342	.614	89	0	-2	114	0	11	.494				2	P	0.0
1885	Phi-a	6	21	0	4	0	0	0		0		.190	.190	.190	.381	22	-2	-2	103	0	1	.235				0	/P	0.0
1886	Bal-a	10	39	4	12	0	1	0		1		.308	.325	.359	.684	128	1	1	91	0	5	.593	1			0	/P1C	0.0
1887	Phi-a	1	4	0	1	0	0	0		0		.250	.250	.250	.500	41	-0	-0	99	0	0	.333	0			0	/P	0.0
Total	7	274	1164	148	323	62	23	9	15	26	10	.277	.294	.393	.687	125	27	29	99	18	144	.578	1			-21	P/OC13	-0.5

■ BILL TAYLOR Taylor, William Michael b: 12/30/29, Alhambra, Cal. BL/TR, 6'3", 212 lbs. Deb: 4/14/54

YEAR	TM/L	G	AB	R	H	2B	3B	HR	RBI	BB	SO	AVG	OBP	SLG	PRO	/A	BR	/A	PF	CHI	RC	TA	SB	CS	SBR	FR	POS	TPR
1954	NY-N	55	65	4	12	1	0	2	10	3	15	.185	.243	.292	.535	37	-6	-6	105	157	5	.453	0	0	0	-3	/O	-0.9
1955	NY-N	65	64	9	17	4	0	4	12	1	16	.266	.277	.516	.793	106	0	0	99	108	8	.680	0	0	0	-1	/O	0.0
1956	NY-N	1	4	0	1	1	0	0	0	0	1	.250	.250	.500	.750	98	-0	-0	97	0	1	.667	0	0	0	-0	/O	0.0
1957	NY-N	11	9	0	0	0	0	0	0	1	2	.000	.100	.000	.100	-69	-2	-2	102	0	0	.111	0	0	0	0	H	-0.1
	Det-A	9	23	4	8	2	0	1	3	0	3	.348	.348	.565	.913	136	1	1	107	74	5	.867	0	0	0	-1	/O	0.0
1958	Det-A	8	8	0	3	0	0	0	1	0	2	.375	.375	.375	.750	103	0	0	104	134	1	.600	0	0	0	-0	/O	0.0
Total	5	149	173	17	41	8	0	7	26	5	39	.237	.267	.405	.671	73	-7	-7	103	116	19	.583	0	0	0	-5	/O	-1.0

■ BIRDIE TEBBETTS Tebbetts, George Robert b: 11/10/12, Burlington, Vt. BR/TR, 5'11.5", 170 lbs. Deb: 9/16/36 M

YEAR	TM/L	G	AB	R	H	2B	3B	HR	RBI	BB	SO	AVG	OBP	SLG	PRO	/A	BR	/A	PF	CHI	RC	TA	SB	CS	SBR	FR	POS	TPR
1936	Det-A	10	33	7	10	1	2	1	4	5	3	.303	.395	.545	.940	136	1	2	95	62	7	1.000	0	0	0	-1	C	0.1
1937	Det-A	50	162	15	31	4	3	2	16	10	13	.191	.238	.290	.528	30	-17	-20	109	103	12	.435	0	0	0	-1	C	-1.5
1938	Det-A	53	143	16	42	6	2	1	25	12	13	.294	.348	.385	.733	83	-4	-4	100	146	19	.660	1	2	-1	-1	C	-0.3
1939	Det-A	106	341	37	89	22	2	4	53	25	20	.261	.315	.372	.688	68	-13	-19	111	129	40	.598	2	1	0	-3	*C	-1.3
1940	Det-A	111	379	46	112	24	4	4	46	35	14	.296	.357	.412	.768	88	-1	-7	111	99	55	.698	4	5	-2	9	*C	0.8
1941	Det-A	110	359	28	102	19	4	2	47	38	29	.284	.354	.376	.730	88	-3	-6	106	118	50	.658	1	2	-1	7	C	0.5
1942	Det-A	99	308	24	76	11	0	1	27	39	17	.247	.335	.292	.627	69	-8	-13	113	102	33	.560	4	0	1	2	C	0.2
1946	Det-A	87	280	20	68	11	2	1	34	28	23	.243	.312	.307	.619	68	-10	-13	108	145	26	.511	1	3	-2	-5	C	-1.5
1947	Det-A	20	53	1	5	1	0	0	2	3	3	.094	.143	.113	.256	-27	-9	-9	104	123	1	.176	0	1	-1	-1	C	-0.9
	Bos-A	90	291	22	87	10	0	1	28	21	30	.299	.346	.344	.690	86	-3	-6	108	100	34	.569	2	4	-2	-1	C	-0.1
	Yr	110	344	23	92	11	0	1	30	24	33	.267	.315	.308	.623	69	-12	-15	107	105	33	.498	2	5	-2	-2		-1.0
1948	Bos-A	128	446	54	125	26	2	5	68	62	32	.280	.371	.381	.752	100	1	1	100	124	63	.693	5	2	0	-2	*C	0.7
1949	Bos-A	122	403	42	109	14	0	5	48	62	22	.270	.369	.342	.712	83	-5	-9	107	108	55	.676	8	1	**2**	-2	*C	-0.2
1950	Bos-A	79	268	33	83	10	1	8	45	29	26	.310	.377	.444	.821	96	4	-2	114	109	43	.749	1	1	-0	-1	C	0.0
1951	Cle-A	55	137	8	36	6	0	2	18	8	7	.263	.308	.350	.659	82	-5	-4	95	119	14	.543	0	0	0	1	C	0.0
1952	Cle-A	42	101	4	25	4	0	1	8	12	9	.248	.339	.317	.656	92	-2	-1	91	85	11	.561	0	1	-1	-1	C	0.0
Total	14	1162	3704	357	1000	169	22	38	469	389	261	.270	.341	.358	.700	80	-74	-108	107	114	461	.643	29	23	-5	-1	*C	-3.5

■ PUSSY TEBEAU Tebeau, Charles Alston b: 2/22/1870, Worcester, Mass. d: 3/25/50, Pittsfield, Mass. BR/TR, 5'10", 175 lbs. Deb: 7/22/1895

YEAR	TM/L	G	AB	R	H	2B	3B	HR	RBI	BB	SO	AVG	OBP	SLG	PRO	/A	BR	/A	PF	CHI	RC	TA	SB	CS	SBR	FR	POS	TPR
1895	Cle-N	2	6	3	3	0	0	0	1	2	1	.500	.625	.500	1.125	202	1	1	97	95	3	2.000	1			0	/O	0.1

■ WHITE WINGS TEBEAU Tebeau, George E. b: 12/26/1861, St.Louis, Mo. d: 2/4/23, Denver, Colo. BR/TR, 5'9", 175 lbs. Deb: 4/16/1887

YEAR	TM/L	G	AB	R	H	2B	3B	HR	RBI	BB	SO	AVG	OBP	SLG	PRO	/A	BR	/A	PF	CHI	RC	TA	SB	CS	SBR	FR	POS	TPR
1887	Cin-a	85	318	57	94	12	5	4		31		.296	.364	.403	.766	107	7	2	108	0	62	.888	37			2	O/P	0.1
1888	Cin-a	121	411	72	94	12	12	3	51	61		.229	.338	.338	.676	119	12	11	101	105	61	.770	37			1	*O	0.7
1889	Cin-a	135	496	110	125	21	11	7	70	69	62	.252	.350	.381	.731	105	8	3	105	101	90	.876	61			-8	*O/1	-0.7
1890	Tol-a	94	381	71	102	16	10	1		51		.268	.359	.370	.729	114	9	7	103	0	72	.896	55			1	*O/P	0.3
1894	Was-N	61	222	41	50	10	6	0	28	37	20	.225	.341	.324	.665	64	-13	-12	98	109	31	.744	17			-8	O	-1.8
	Cle-N	40	150	32	47	9	4	0	25	25	18	.313	.411	.427	.838	94	2	-2	111	110	31	.951	9			-1	O1/3	-0.2
	Yr	101	372	73	97	19	10	0	53	62	38	.261	.369	.366	.735	77	-11	-14	103	110	61	.822	26			-9		-2.0
1895	Cle-N	91	337	57	110	16	6	0	68	50	28	.326	.415	.409	.824	119	10	12	97	140	64	.885	12			-10	O1	0.0
Total	6	627	2315	440	622	96	54	15	242	324	128	.269	.364	.376	.740	106	35	23	103	79	410	.854	228			-23	O/1P3	-1.6

■ PATSY TEBEAU Tebeau, Oliver Wendell b: 12/5/1864, St.Louis, Mo. d: 5/15/18, St.Louis, Mo. BR/TR, 5'8", 163 lbs. Deb: 9/20/1887 M

YEAR	TM/L	G	AB	R	H	2B	3B	HR	RBI	BB	SO	AVG	OBP	SLG	PRO	/A	BR	/A	PF	CHI	RC	TA	SB	CS	SBR	FR	POS	TPR
1887	Chi-N	20	68	8	11	3	0	0	10	4	4	.162	.208	.206	.414	14	-7	-9	116	220	5	.456	8			0	3	-0.7
1889	Cle-N	136	521	72	147	20	6	8	76	37	41	.282	.332	.390	.722	100	1	-2	103	106	78	.717	26			-1	*3	0.5
1890	Cle-P	110	450	86	135	26	6	5	74	34	20	.300	.353	.418	.771	117	4	10	92	102	73	.759	14			13	*3M	2.5
1891	Cle-N	61	249	38	65	8	3	1	41	16	13	.261	.313	.329	.643	85	-4	-5	105	149	30	.614	12			6	3/OM	0.3
1892	Cle-N	86	340	47	83	13	3	2	49	23	34	.244	.307	.318	.625	88	-4	-5	103	140	36	.564	6			-2	3/21SM	-0.1
1893	Cle-N	116	486	90	160	32	8	2	102	32	11	.329	.375	.440	.816	114	11	8	104	134	90	.825	19			6	13/2M	1.2
1894	Cle-N	125	523	82	158	23	7	3	89	35	35	.302	.347	.390	.737	71	-18	-29	111	122	83	.740	30			-6	*12/3SM	-2.5
1895	Cle-N	63	264	50	84	13	2	2	52	16	18	.318	.362	.405	.767	103	-0	1	97	136	43	.739	8			-2	1/23M	0.0
1896	Cle-N	132	543	56	146	22	6	2	94	21	22	.269	.300	.343	.642	64	-24	-32	110	150	63	.579	20			5	*1/32SPM	-2.0
1897	Cle-N	109	412	62	110	15	9	0	59	30		.267	.323	.347	.670	71	-12	-20	111	123	51	.623	11			-1	*12/3SM	-1.8
1898	Cle-N	131	477	53	123	11	4	1	63	53		.258	.341	.304	.645	92	-5	-2	96	136	52	.593	5			1	12/S3M	0.0
1899	StL-N	77	281	27	69	10	3	1	26	18		.246	.303	.313	.616	66	-11	-14	108	89	29	.547	5			-4	1S/32M	-1.5
1900	StL-N	1	4	0	0	0	0	0	0	0		.000	.000	.000	.000	-99	-1	-1	93	0	0	.000	0			0	/SM	0.0
Total	13	1167	4618	671	1291	196	57	27	735	319	198	.280	.332	.364	.696	86	-70	-100	104	127	633	.663	164			15	13/2SPO	-4.1

■ DICK TEED Teed, Richard Leroy b: 3/8/26, Springfield, Mass. BB/TR, 5'11", 180 lbs. Deb: 7/24/53

YEAR	TM/L	G	AB	R	H	2B	3B	HR	RBI	BB	SO	AVG	OBP	SLG	PRO	/A	BR	/A	PF	CHI	RC	TA	SB	CS	SBR	FR	POS	TPR
1953	Bro-N	1	1	0	0	0	0	0	0	0	1	.000	.000	.000	.000	-96	-0	-0	104	0	0	.000	0	0	0	0	H	0.0

■ WILFREDO TEJADA Tejada, Wilfredo Aristides (Andujar) b: 11/12/62, Santo Domingo, D.R. BR/TR, 6', 175 lbs. Deb: 9/09/86

YEAR	TM/L	G	AB	R	H	2B	3B	HR	RBI	BB	SO	AVG	OBP	SLG	PRO	/A	BR	/A	PF	CHI	RC	TA	SB	CS	SBR	FR	POS	TPR
1986	Mon-N	10	25	1	6	1	0	0	2	2	8	.240	.296	.280	.576	61	-1	-1	98	114	2	.450	0	0	0	-1	C	-0.1
1988	Mon-N	8	15	1	4	2	0	0	2	0	4	.267	.267	.400	.667	84	-0	-0	106	133	2	.545	0	0	0	0	/C	0.0
Total	2	18	40	2	10	3	0	0	4	2	12	.250	.286	.325	.611	70	-2	-2	100	121	4	.500	0	0	0	-1	/C	-0.1

■ JOHNNY TEMPLE Temple, John Ellis b: 8/8/28, Lexington, N.C. BR/TR, 5'11", 175 lbs. Deb: 4/15/52 C

YEAR	TM/L	G	AB	R	H	2B	3B	HR	RBI	BB	SO	AVG	OBP	SLG	PRO	/A	BR	/A	PF	CHI	RC	TA	SB	CS	SBR	FR	POS	TPR
1952	Cin-N	30	97	8	19	3	0	1	5	5	1	.196	.235	.258	.493	37	-8	-8	100	70	5	.390	2	1	0	-1	2	-0.8
1953	Cin-N	63	110	14	29	4	0	1	9	7	12	.264	.314	.327	.641	68	-5	-5	99	90	12	.556	1	0	0	2	2	0.0
1954	Cin-N	146	505	60	155	14	8	0	44	62	24	.307	.385	.366	.751	93	0	-2	104	96	77	.742	21	7	2	-4	*2	0.4
1955	Cin-N	150	588	94	165	20	3	0	50	80	32	.281	.368	.325	.693	81	-9	-13	106	94	79	.672	19	4	3	-1	*2/S	0.2
1956	Cin-N	154	632	88	180	18	3	2	41	58	40	.285	.346	.332	.678	77	-13	-20	108	71	76	.605	14	4	2	-4	*2/O	-0.8
1957	Cin-N	145	557	85	158	24	4	0	37	**94**	34	.284	.391	.341	.732	94	4	-0	105	71	86	.752	19	5	**3**	-18	*2	-0.3
1958	Cin-N	141	542	82	166	31	6	3	47	91	41	.306	.406	.402	.808	107	16	10	107	76	96	.827	15	8	-0	-13	*2/1	0.4
1959	Cin-N	149	598	102	186	35	6	8	67	72	40	.311	.387	.430	.817	114	17	14	103	83	104	.810	14	3	2	-25	*2	0.3
1960	Cle-A	98	381	50	102	13	1	2	19	32	20	.268	.326	.323	.649	78	-12	-11	98	61	41	.572	11	5	0	-15	23	-2.0
1961	Cle-A	129	518	73	143	22	3	3	30	61	36	.276	.352	.347	.700	91	-7	-5	96	55	65	.638	9	5	-0	-21	*2	-1.0
1962	Bal-A	78	270	28	71	8	1	1	17	36	22	.263	.352	.311	.663	85	-6	-4	95	79	33	.621	7	4	-0	0	2	0.1
	Hou-N	31	95	14	25	4	0	0	12	7	11	.263	.314	.305	.619	72	-4	-3	93	163	10	.514	1	0	0	-1	2/3	0.0
1963	Hou-N	100	322	22	85	12	1	1	17	41	24	.264	.347	.317	.664	100	-2	1	92	69	40	.620	7	2	1	-14	23	-0.8
1964	Cin-N	6	3	0	0	0	0	0	0	2	1	.000	.400	.000	.400	23	-0	-0	103	0	0	.667	0	0	0	0	H	0.0
Total	13	1420	5218	720	1484	208	36	22	395	648	338	.284	.365	.351	.716	91	-30	-46	102	78	725	.696	140	48	13	-116	*2/31OS	-4.3

■ GARRY TEMPLETON Templeton, Garry Lewis b: 3/24/56, Lockney, Tex. BB/TR, 5'11", 175 lbs. Deb: 8/09/76

YEAR	TM/L	G	AB	R	H	2B	3B	HR	RBI	BB	SO	AVG	OBP	SLG	PRO	/A	BR	/A	PF	CHI	RC	TA	SB	CS	SBR	FR	POS	TPR
1976	StL-N	53	213	32	62	8	2	1	17	7	33	.291	.317	.362	.678	89	-3	-4	104	87	24	.604	11	7	-1	2	S	0.3
1977	StL-N	153	621	94	200	19	**18**	8	79	15	70	.322	.339	.449	.788	114	6	10	96	111	85	.711	28	24	-6	3	*S	2.7
1978	StL-N	155	647	82	181	31	**13**	2	47	22	87	.280	.304	.377	.682	94	-11	-7	95	66	74	.622	34	11	4	27	*S	3.8

YEAR	TM/L	G	AB	R	H	2B	3B	HR	RBI	BB	SO	AVG	OBP	SLG	PRO	/A	BR	/A	PF	CHI	RC	TA	SB	CS	SBR	FR	POS	TPR
1979	StL-N	154	672	105	**211**	32	**19**	9	62	18	91	.314	.333	.458	.791	109	10	6	105	70	100	.737	26	10	2	**26**	*S	5.0
1980	StL-N	118	504	83	161	19	9	4	43	18	43	.319	.343	.417	.760	108	6	5	103	74	66	.698	31	15	0	31	*S	5.0
1981	StL-N	80	333	47	96	16	8	1	33	14	55	.288	.317	.393	.710	99	-1	-1	102	102	37	.605	8	12	-5	14	S	1.7
1982	SD-N	141	563	76	139	25	8	6	64	26	82	.247	.281	.352	.633	83	-19	-14	92	123	49	.549	27	16	-2	-22	*S	-2.8
1983	SD-N	126	460	39	121	20	2	3	40	21	57	.263	.295	.335	.630	75	-17	-16	99	99	42	.529	16	6	1	-15	*S	-1.9
1984	SD-N	148	493	40	127	19	3	2	35	39	81	.258	.313	.320	.634	80	-14	-13	99	84	48	.544	8	3	1	-23	*S	-1.9
1985	SD-N	148	546	63	154	30	2	6	55	41	88	.282	.333	.377	.711	97	-1	-2	102	100	69	.655	16	6	1	-9	*S	0.2
1986	SD-N	147	510	42	126	21	2	2	44	35	86	.247	.297	.308	.605	70	-23	-20	95	108	44	.506	10	5	0	-21	*S	-2.8
1987	SD-N	148	510	42	113	13	5	5	48	42	92	.222	.282	.296	.578	55	-34	-32	97	115	42	.501	14	3	2	1	*S	-1.0
1988	SD-N	110	362	35	90	15	7	3	36	20	50	.249	.288	.354	.642	85	-8	-7	97	105	36	.557	8	2	1	-4	*S/3	-0.2
Total	13	1681	6434	780	1781	268	98	52	603	318	915	.277	.312	.373	.685	90	-108	-96	98	95	718	.620	237	120	-1	12	*S/3	8.1
■ GENE TENACE	Tenace, Fury Gene (born Fiore Gino Tennaci) b: 10/10/46, Russellton, Pa. BR/TR, 6', 190 lbs. Deb: 5/29/69 C																											
1969	Oak-A	16	38	1	6	0	0	1	2	1	15	.158	.200	.237	.437	24	-4	-4	92	67	2	.344	0	0	0	-3	C	-0.6
1970	Oak-A	38	105	19	32	6	0	7	20	23	30	.305	.430	.562	.992	177	11	11	97	101	26	1.065	0	2	-1	1	C	1.2
1971	Oak-A	65	179	26	49	7	0	7	25	29	34	.274	.381	.430	.811	129	8	8	101	104	31	.821	2	1	0	-0	C/O	1.0
1972	Oak-A	82	227	22	51	5	3	5	32	24	42	.225	.307	.339	.646	95	-2	-1	97	145	24	.578	0	0	0	-1	C/O123	-0.2
1973	Oak-A	160	510	83	132	18	2	24	84	101	94	.259	.391	.443	.834	154	27	37	87	113	94	.863	2	2	-1	-12	*1C/2D	1.7
1974	Oak-A	158	484	71	102	17	1	26	73	**110**	105	.211	.370	.411	.781	124	19	19	100	106	78	.805	2	9	-5	-17	*1C/2	-0.4
1975	Oak-A	158	498	83	127	17	0	29	87	106	127	.255	.398	.464	.862	153	32	37	93	107	100	.930	7	4	-0	-42	*C1/D	-0.5
1976	Oak-A	128	417	64	104	19	1	22	66	81	91	.249	.376	.458	.835	144	25	25	100	101	76	.867	5	4	-1	-16	1C/D	0.7
1977	SD-N	147	437	66	102	24	4	15	61	**125**	119	.233	.417	.410	.827	140	21	30	88	111	87	.939	5	3	-0	-9	C13	1.7
1978	SD-N	142	401	60	90	18	4	16	61	101	98	.224	.394	.409	.803	135	18	22	93	114	73	.879	6	5	-1	-4	1C/3	1.6
1979	SD-N	151	463	61	122	16	4	20	67	105	106	.263	.407	.445	.852	137	25	28	96	102	91	.904	2	6	-3	-4	C1	2.0
1980	SD-N	133	316	46	70	11	1	17	50	92	63	.222	.403	.424	.827	141	18	21	93	107	58	.897	4	4	-1	-12	*C1	0.9
1981	StL-N	58	129	26	30	7	0	5	22	38	26	.233	.421	.403	.824	132	8	8	102	129	26	.940	0	0	0	-2	C/1	0.7
1982	StL-N	66	124	18	32	9	0	7	18	36	31	.258	.439	.500	.939	157	13	12	103	85	31	1.096	1	1	-0	-2	C/1	1.0
1983	Pit-N	53	62	7	11	5	0	0	6	12	17	.177	.346	.258	.604	68	-2	-2	103	148	7	.615	0	1	-1	-1	1/CO	-0.4
Total	15	1555	4390	653	1060	179	20	201	674	984	998	.241	.391	.429	.819	137	218	251	95	109	805	.888	36	42	-14	-124	C1/3OD2	10.4
■ TOM TENNANT	Tennant, Thomas Francis b: 7/3/1882, Monroe, Wis. d: 2/15/55, San Carlos, Cal. BL/TL, 5'11", 165 lbs. Deb: 4/18/12																											
1912	StL-A	2	2	1	0	0	0	0	0	0		.000	.000	.000	.000	-99	-1	-1	99	0	0	.000	0			0	H	0.0
■ FRED TENNEY	Tenney, Frederick b: 11/26/1871, Georgetown, Mass. d: 7/3/52, Boston, Mass. BL/TL, 5'9", 155 lbs. Deb: 6/16/1894 M																											
1894	Bos-N	27	86	23	34	7	1	2	21	12	9	.395	.469	.570	1.039	134	8	5	113	105	26	1.288	6			0	C/O1	0.4
1895	Bos-N	49	173	35	47	9	1	1	21	24	5	.272	.360	.353	.713	84	-3	-4	103	93	25	.722	6			0	OC	-0.2
1896	Bos-N	88	348	64	117	14	3	2	49	36	12	.336	.400	.411	.811	108	9	5	108	100	66	.857	18			-5	OC	-0.3
1897	Bos-N	132	566	125	180	24	3	1	85	49		.318	.376	.376	.753	95	3	-4	107	102	95	.777	34			5	*1/O	0.0
1898	Bos-N	117	488	106	160	25	5	0	62	33		.328	.370	.400	.770	119	14	12	104	85	83	.765	23			5	*1/C	1.5
1899	Bos-N	150	603	115	209	19	17	1	67	63		.347	.410	.439	.850	130	31	26	105	68	123	.909	28			9	*1	3.4
1900	Bos-N	112	437	77	122	13	5	1	56	39		.279	.338	.339	.677	74	-5	-19	120	123	57	.648	17			8	*1	-0.8
1901	Bos-N	115	451	66	127	13	1	1	22	37		.282	.336	.322	.658	84	-3	-10	112	44	55	.608	15			4	*1/C	-0.4
1902	Bos-N	134	489	88	154	18	3	2	30	73		.315	.404	.376	.780	150	29	31	95	53	85	.830	21			13	*1	4.0
1903	Bos-N	122	447	79	140	22	3	3	41	70		.313	.406	.396	.802	137	21	24	96	68	82	.873	21			6	*1	2.5
1904	Bos-N	147	533	76	144	17	9	1	37	57		.270	.341	.341	.682	117	9	12	97	78	69	.658	17			7	*1/O	1.3
1905	Bos-N	149	549	84	158	18	3	0	28	67		.288	.365	.332	.697	114	10	12	97	47	75	.680	17			20	*1/PM	2.6
1906	Bos-N	143	544	61	154	12	8	1	28	58		.283	.352	.340	.692	118	13	12	100	47	73	.667	17			10	*1M	1.8
1907	Bos-N	150	554	83	151	18	8	0	26	82		.273	.366	.334	.700	128	17	20	95	47	75	.700	15			9	*1M	2.8
1908	NY-N	156	583	**101**	149	20	1	2	49	72		.256	.337	.304	.641	103	7	5	104	91	64	.613	17			10	*1	1.2
1909	NY-N	101	375	43	88	8	2	3	30	52		.235	.333	.291	.623	90	-0	-3	105	89	38	.599	8			3	1	-0.1
1911	Bos-N	102	369	52	97	13	4	1	36	50	17	.263	.352	.328	.680	88	-3	-5	103	104	45	.651	5			0	1/OM	-0.8
Total	17	1994	7595	1278	2231	270	77	22	688	874	43	.294	.367	.358	.726	110	157	120	103	75	1136	.725	285			102	*1O/CP	18.9
■ FRED TENNEY	Tenney, Frederick Clay b: 7/9/1859, Marlboro, N.H. d: 6/15/19, Fall River, Mass. Deb: 4/28/1884																											
1884	Was-U	32	119	17	28	3	1	0		6		.235	.272	.277	.549	89	-2	-1	97	0	9	.429	0			0	O/1	0.0
	Bos-U	4	17	1	2	0	0	0		0		.118	.118	.118	.235	-21	-2	-2	98	0	0	.133	0			0	/P	0.0
	WiL-U	1	3	0	0	0	0	0		0		.000	.000	.000	.000	-97	-1	-1	103	0	0	.000	0			0	/P	0.0
	Yr	37	139	18	30	3	1	0		6		.216	.248	.252	.500	72	-4	-4	97	0	9	.376	0			0		0.0
Total	1	37	139	18	30	3	1	0		6		.216	.248	.252	.500	72	-4	-4	97	0	9	.376	0			0	/O1P	0.0
■ FRANK TEPEDINO	Tepedino, Frank Ronald b: 11/23/47, Brooklyn, N.Y. BL/TL, 5'11", 185 lbs. Deb: 5/12/67																											
1967	NY-A	9	5	0	2	0	0	0	0	1	1	.400	.500	.400	.900	179	1	1	94	0	1	1.000	0	0	0	0	/1	0.1
1969	NY-A	13	39	6	9	0	0	0	4	4	4	.231	.302	.231	.533	53	-2	-2	95	178	3	.438	1	0	0	-2	O	-0.3
1970	NY-A	16	19	2	6	2	0	0	2	1	2	.316	.350	.421	.771	121	0	0	92	101	2	.600	0	1	-1	-0	/1O	0.0
1971	NY-A	6	6	0	0	0	0	0	0	0	0	.000	.000	.000	.000	-99	-2	-2	97	0	0	.000	0	0	0	-0	/O	-0.1
	Mil-A	53	106	11	21	1	0	2	7	4	17	.198	.234	.264	.498	40	-8	-9	103	84	6	.398	2	2	-1	1	1	-0.9
	Yr	59	112	11	21	1	0	2	7	4	17	.188	.222	.250	.472	33	-10	-10	102	75	6	.372	2	2	-1	1		-1.0
1972	NY-A	8	8	0	0	0	0	0	0	0	1	.000	.000	.000	.000	-99	-2	-2	92	0	0	.000	0	0	0	0	H	-0.1
1973	Atl-N	74	148	20	45	5	0	4	29	13	21	.304	.360	.419	.779	102	3	1	113	157	21	.688	0	0	0	0	1	-0.1
1974	Atl-N	78	169	11	39	5	1	0	16	9	13	.231	.274	.272	.546	51	-11	-12	105	134	11	.413	1	2	-1	1	1	-1.4
1975	Atl-N	8	7	0	0	0	0	0	0	1	2	.000	.125	.000	.125	-66	-2	-2	95	0	0	.125	0	0	0	0	H	-0.1
Total	8	265	507	50	122	13	1	6	58	33	61	.241	.290	.306	.595	63	-23	-26	105	126	44	.496	4	5	-2	-0	1/O	-2.9
■ JOE TEPSIC	Tepsic, Joseph John b: 9/18/23, Slovan, Pa. BR/TR, 5'9", 170 lbs. Deb: 7/12/46																											
1946	Bro-N	15	5	2	0	0	0	0	0	1	1	.000	.167	.000	.167	-49	-1	-1	103	0	0	.200	0			-0	/O	0.0
■ JERRY TERRELL	Terrell, Jerry Wayne b: 7/13/46, Waseca, Minn. BR/TR, 5'11", 165 lbs. Deb: 4/14/73																											
1973	Min-A	124	438	43	116	15	2	1	32	21	56	.265	.300	.315	.615	71	-16	-18	104	89	42	.520	13	7	-0	-5	S32/OD	-1.1
1974	Min-A	116	229	43	56	4	6	0	19	11	27	.245	.279	.314	.594	70	-9	-9	101	104	19	.475	3	2	-0	1	S23D/O1	-0.4
1975	Min-A	108	385	48	110	16	2	1	36	19	27	.286	.324	.345	.670	83	-6	-9	107	102	41	.546	4	4	-1	2	S213/OD	-0.3
1976	Min-A	89	171	29	42	3	1	0	8	9	15	.246	.287	.275	.562	66	-7	-7	98	65	14	.504	11	2	2	-1	23SD/O	-0.3
1977	Min-A	93	214	32	48	6	0	1	20	11	21	.224	.265	.266	.532	44	-16	-17	103	132	13	.436	10	4	1	3	32/S1OD	-1.1
1978	KC-A	73	133	14	27	1	0	0	8	4	13	.203	.226	.211	.437	23	-13	-14	102	113	6	.351	8	4	0	-2	23S/1	-1.4
1979	KC-A	31	40	5	12	3	0	1	2	1	1	.300	.317	.450	.767	99	0	-0	105	37	5	.667	1	0	0	0	3/2PS	0.1
1980	KC-A	23	16	4	1	0	0	0	0	0	0	.063	.063	.063	.125	-67	-4	-4	98	0	0	.067	0	0	0	-2	/O12PD	-0.5
Total	8	657	1626	218	412	48	11	4	125	76	160	.253	.289	.304	.593	65	-71	-77	103	97	141	.506	50	23	1	-3	3S2/D1OP	-5.0
■ TOM TERRELL	Terrell, John Thomas b: 1866, Louisville, Ky. d: 7/9/1893, Louisville, Ky. Deb: 10/05/1886																											
1886	Lou-a	1	4	0	1	0	0	0		0		.250	.250	.250	.500	54	-0	-0	108	0	0	.333	0			0	/OC	0.0
■ TERRY	Terry Deb:4/26/1875																											
1875	Nat-n	6	24	0	2							.083															/O1	
■ BILL TERRY	Terry, William Harold "Memphis Bill" b: 10/30/1898, Atlanta, Ga. BL/TL, 6'1", 200 lbs. Deb: 9/24/23 MH																											
1923	NY-N	3	7	1	1	0	0	0	0	2	2	.143	.333	.143	.476	29	-1	-1	101	0	0	.500	0	0	0	0	/1	0.0
1924	NY-N	77	163	26	39	7	2	5	24	17	18	.239	.311	.399	.710	97	-3	-1	91	109	21	.664	1	1	-0	-1	1	-0.3
1925	NY-N	133	489	75	156	31	6	11	70	42	52	.319	.374	.474	.848	116	11	12	99	96	86	.825	4	5	-2	4	*1	0.1
1926	NY-N	98	225	26	65	12	5	5	43	22	17	.289	.352	.453	.806	118	4	5	98	127	35	.794	3			3	1O	0.6
1927	NY-N	150	580	101	189	32	13	20	121	46	53	.326	.377	.529	.907	141	31	31	100	122	112	.910	1			5	*1	2.5

YEAR	TM/L	G	AB	R	H	2B	3B	HR	RBI	BB	SO	AVG	OBP	SLG	PRO	/A	BR	/A	PF	CHI	RC	TA	SB	CS	SBR	FR	POS	TPR
1928	NY-N	149	568	100	185	36	11	17	101	64	36	.326	.394	.518	.912	134	30	28	102	110	114	.953	7			-2	*1	1.0
1929	NY-N	150	607	103	226	39	5	14	117	48	35	.372	.418	.522	.941	132	30	31	100	118	128	.984	10			6	*1/O	2.6
1930	NY-N	154	633	139	**254**	39	15	23	129	57	33	**.401**	.452	.619	1.071	159	58	60	98	93	170	1.208	8			13	*1	5.7
1931	NY-N	153	611	**121**	213	43	**20**	9	112	47	36	.349	.397	.529	.926	152	39	42	97	121	130	.955	8			9	*1	**3.8**
1932	NY-N	154	643	124	225	42	11	28	117	32	23	.350	.382	.580	.962	157	46	48	99	101	142	.981	4			13	*1M	5.1
1933	NY-N	123	475	68	153	20	5	6	58	40	23	.322	.375	.423	.798	129	17	18	99	105	77	.735	3			2	*1M	1.8
1934	NY-N	153	602	109	213	30	6	8	83	60	47	.354	.414	.463	.878	137	31	33	98	95	122	.859	0			6	*1M	2.5
1935	NY-N	145	596	91	203	32	8	6	64	41	55	.341	.383	.451	.834	128	20	23	96	77	104	.781	7			5	*1M	2.4
1936	NY-N	79	229	36	71	10	5	2	39	19	19	.310	.363	.424	.786	111	4	3	100	134	35	.703	0			1	1M	0.0
Total	14	1721	6428	1120	2193	373	112	154	1078	537	449	.341	.393	.506	.899	137	318	332	98	106	1275	.907	56	6		65	*1/O	27.8
■ ADONIS TERRY	Terry, William H. b: 8/7/1864, Westfield, Mass. d: 2/24/15, Milwaukee, Wis. BR/TR, 168 lbs. Deb: 5/01/1884																											
1884	Bro-a	68	240	16	56	10	3	0		8		.233	.258	.300	.558	86	-4	-3	98	0	19	.435				-4	PO	0.0
1885	Bro-a	71	264	23	45	1	3	1		10		.170	.201	.208	.409	30	-20	-21	104	0	11	.297				4	OP/3	-1.8
1886	Bro-a	75	299	34	71	8	9	2		10		.237	.265	.344	.609	92	-4	-4	100	0	33	.575	17			0	POS	-0.2
1887	Bro-a	86	352	56	103	6	10	3		16		.293	.323	.392	.715	102	-0	0	99	0	55	.727	27			3	OP/S	0.7
1888	Bro-a	30	115	13	29	6	0	0	8	5		.252	.283	.304	.588	87	-1	-2	105	72	12	.547	7			0	P/O1	0.0
1889	Bro-a	49	160	29	48	6	6	2	26	14	14	.300	.356	.450	.806	137	6	7	96	95	29	.839	8			6	P1	0.0
1890	Bro-N	99	363	63	101	17	9	4	59	40	34	.278	.356	.408	.764	124	11	11	100	114	66	.855	32			-1	OP/1	1.5
1891	Bro-N	30	91	10	19	7	1	0	6	9	26	.209	.301	.308	.609	81	-2	-2	97	62	10	.611	4			0	P/O	0.0
1892	Bal-N	1	4	0	0	0	0	0	0	0	1	.000	.000	.000	.000	-99	-1	-1	100	0	0	.000	0			0	/P	0.0
	Pit-N	31	100	10	16	0	4	2	11	10	11	.160	.236	.300	.536	68	-5	-4	94	94	8	.500	2			0	P/O	0.0
	Yr	32	104	10	16	0	4	2	11	10	12	.154	.228	.288	.517	61	-6	-5	94	91	7	.477	2			0		0.0
1893	Pit-N	26	71	9	18	4	3	0	11	3	11	.254	.293	.394	.688	79	-2	-3	106	108	9	.623	1			0	P	0.0
1894	Pit-N	1	0	0	0	0	0	0	0	0	0	—	—	—	—	—	0	0	94	—	—	—	0			0	/P	0.0
	Chi-N	30	95	19	33	4	2	0	17	11	12	.347	.415	.432	.847	99	1	-0	108	114	19	.887	3			0	P/O1	0.0
	Yr	31	95	19	33	4	2	0	17	11	12	.347	.415	.432	.847	99	1	0	107	111	19	.887	3			0		0.0
1895	Chi-N	40	137	18	30	3	2	1	10	2	17	.219	.236	.292	.528	36	-13	-14	103	65	10	.411	1			3	P/OS	0.0
1896	Chi-N	30	99	14	26	4	2	0	15	8	12	.263	.324	.343	.668	72	-3	-5	108	127	13	.644	4			0	P	0.0
1897	Chi-N	1	3	1	0	0	0	0	0	0		.000	.000	.000	.000	-99	-1	-1	100	0	0	.000	0			0	/P	0.0
Total	14	668	2393	315	595	76	54	15	163	146	138	.249	.295	.344	.639	88	-38	-41	101	51	301	.605	106			11	PO/S13	0.2
■ ZEB TERRY	Terry, Zebulon Alexander b: 6/17/1891, Denison, Tex. d: 3/16/88, Los Angeles, Cal. BR/TR, 5′8″, 129 lbs. Deb: 4/12/16																											
1916	Chi-A	94	269	20	51	8	4	0	17	33	36	.190	.292	.249	.541	58	-12	-14	108	91	23	.505	4			-6	S	-1.4
1917	Chi-A	2	1	0	0	0	0	0	0	2	0	.000	.667	.000	.667	107	0	0	98	0	0	2.000	0			0	/S	0.0
1918	Bos-N	28	105	17	32	2	2	0	8	8	14	.305	.360	.362	.722	128	3	3	94	84	14	.658	1			1	S	0.5
1919	Pit-N	129	472	46	107	12	6	0	27	31	26	.227	.280	.278	.558	65	-18	-21	105	85	39	.488	12			-35	*S	-5.7
1920	Chi-N	133	496	56	139	26	9	0	52	44	22	.280	.341	.369	.710	105	3	4	99	106	61	.646	12	16	-6	7	S2	1.0
1921	Chi-N	123	488	59	134	18	1	2	45	27	19	.275	.318	.328	.646	67	-20	-24	107	96	49	.523	1	13	-8	4	*2	-2.5
1922	Chi-N	131	496	56	142	24	2	0	67	34	16	.286	.335	.343	.677	79	-18	-14	95	**146**	56	.570	2	11	-6	2	*2/S3	-1.7
Total	7	640	2327	254	605	90	24	2	216	179	133	.260	.318	.322	.640	78	-61	-66	102	105	243	.556	32	40		-27	S2/3	-9.8
■ WAYNE TERWILLIGER	Terwilliger, Willard Wayne "Twig" b: 6/27/25, Clare, Mich. BR/TR, 5′11″, 165 lbs. Deb: 8/06/49 C																											
1949	Chi-N	36	112	11	25	2	1	2	10	16	22	.223	.326	.313	.638	76	-4	-3	94	92	13	.591	0			4	2	0.2
1950	Chi-N	133	480	63	116	22	3	10	32	43	63	.242	.311	.363	.673	73	-17	-20	105	62	56	.632	13			-2	*2/13O	-1.8
1951	Chi-N	50	192	26	41	6	0	0	10	29	21	.214	.317	.245	.562	55	-12	-11	97	73	17	.503	3	1	0	1	2	-0.8
	Bro-N	37	50	11	14	1	0	0	4	8	7	.280	.390	.300	.690	90	-0	-0	98	103	7	.676	1	0	0	2	2/3	0.3
	Yr	87	242	37	55	7	0	0	14	37	28	.227	.332	.256	.588	62	-12	-11	98	86	25	.550	4	1	1	2		-0.5
1953	Was-A	134	464	62	117	24	4	4	46	64	65	.252	.343	.347	.690	92	-8	-4	94	100	58	.637	7	4	-0	-0	*2	0.3
1954	Was-A	106	337	42	70	10	1	3	24	32	40	.208	.282	.270	.552	53	-22	-22	98	91	27	.466	3	3	-1	-2	23/S	-2.1
1955	NY-N	80	257	29	66	16	1	1	18	36	42	.257	.350	.339	.689	85	-5	-4	99	81	30	.612	2	4	-2	7	2/S3	0.8
1956	NY-N	14	18	0	4	1	0	0	0	0	5	.222	.222	.278	.500	34	-2	-2	97	0	1	.357	0	0	0	-0	/2	-0.1
1959	KC-A	74	180	27	48	11	0	2	18	19	31	.267	.337	.361	.698	91	-2	-2	101	100	23	.632	2	2	-1	1	2/S3	0.1
1960	KC-A	2	1	0	0	0	0	0	0	0	0	.000	.000	.000	.000	-99	-0	-0	99	0	0	.000	0	0	0	0	/2	0.0
Total	9	666	2091	271	501	93	10	22	162	247	296	.240	.323	.325	.648	75	-72	-68	99	84	230	.604	31	14		10	2/3SO1	-3.1
■ AL TESCH	Tesch, Albert John "Tiny" b: 1/27/1891, Jersey City, N.J. d: 8/3/47, Jersey City, N.J. BB/TR, 5′10″, 155 lbs. Deb: 8/21/15																											
1915	Bro-F	8	7	2	2	1	0	0	2	0	0	.286	.286	.429	.714	113	0	0	98	240	1	.600	0			0	/2	0.0
■ NICK TESTA	Testa, Nicholas b: 6/29/28, New York, N.Y. BR/TR, 5′8″, 180 lbs. Deb: 4/23/58 C																											
1958	SF-N	1	0	0	0	0	0	0	0	0	0	—	—	—	—	—	0	0	100	—	—	—	0	0	0	0	/C	0.0
■ DICK TETTELBACH	Tettelbach, Richard Morley "Tut" b: 6/26/29, New Haven, Conn. BR/TR, 6′, 195 lbs. Deb: 9/25/55																											
1955	NY-A	2	5	0	0	0	0	0	0	0	0	.000	.000	.000	.000	-99	-1	-1	98	0	0	.000	0	0	0	0	/O	-0.1
1956	Was-A	18	64	10	10	1	2	1	9	14	15	.156	.308	.281	.589	55	-4	-4	102	141	7	.582	0	1	-1	1	O	-0.4
1957	Was-A	9	11	2	2	0	0	0	1	4	2	.182	.400	.182	.582	66	-0	-0	98	198	1	.667	0	0	0	0	/O	0.0
Total	3	29	80	12	12	1	2	1	10	18	17	.150	.306	.250	.556	49	-6	-6	101	143	8	.551	0	1	-1	1	/O	-0.5
■ MICKEY TETTLETON	Tettleton, Mickey Lee b: 9/16/60, Okalhoma City, Okla. BB/TR, 6′2″, 200 lbs. Deb: 6/30/84																											
1984	Oak-A	33	76	10	20	2	1	1	5	11	21	.263	.356	.355	.712	107	0	1	92	66	10	.644	0	0	0	1	C	0.4
1985	Oak-A	78	211	23	53	12	0	3	15	28	59	.251	.344	.351	.695	98	-2	0	93	72	26	.639	2	2	-1	-4	C/D	0.0
1986	Oak-A	90	211	26	43	9	0	10	35	39	51	.204	.331	.389	.719	103	-1	1	94	124	31	.750	7	1	2	-8	C	0.0
1987	Oak-A	82	211	19	41	3	0	8	26	30	65	.194	.295	.322	.617	71	-11	-8	91	113	22	.569	1	1	-0	-2	C/1D	-0.3
1988	Bal-A	86	283	31	74	11	1	11	37	28	70	.261	.332	.424	.756	116	4	5	95	96	38	.685	0	1	-1	9	C	1.7
Total	5	369	992	109	231	37	2	33	118	136	266	.233	.328	.374	.702	99	-9	0	93	98	126	.674	10	5	0	-4	C/D1	1.8
■ TIM TEUFEL	Teufel, Timothy Shawn b: 7/7/58, Greenwich, Conn. BR/TR, 6′, 175 lbs. Deb: 9/03/83																											
1983	Min-A	21	78	11	24	7	1	3	6	2	8	.308	.325	.538	.863	126	3	3	105	47	13	.800	0	0	0	0	2/SD	0.3
1984	Min-A	157	568	76	149	30	3	14	61	76	73	.262	.351	.400	.751	102	7	3	106	96	79	.695	1	3	-2	-11	*2	-0.1
1985	Min-A	138	434	58	113	24	3	10	50	48	70	.260	.338	.399	.737	98	1	-1	103	98	58	.677	4	2	0	-19	*2/D	-1.4
1986	NY-N	93	279	35	69	20	1	4	31	32	42	.247	.327	.369	.696	96	-3	-2	96	107	34	.628	1	2	-1	-9	2/13	-1.0
1987	NY-N	97	299	55	92	29	0	14	61	44	53	.308	.400	.545	.945	150	21	22	99	119	66	.981	3	2	-0	-8	2/1	1.5
1988	NY-N	90	273	35	64	20	0	4	31	29	41	.234	.310	.352	.662	99	-4	-0	90	115	30	.583	0	1	-1	-0	2/1	0.1
Total	6	596	1931	270	511	130	8	49	240	231	287	.265	.346	.416	.762	108	25	24	100	102	279	.733	9	10	-3	-47	2/1D3S	-0.6
■ GEORGE TEXTOR	Textor, George Bernhardt b: 12/27/1888, Newport, Ky. d: 3/10/54, Massillon, Ohio BB/TR, 5′10.5″, 174 lbs. Deb: 4/19/14																											
1914	Ind-F	22	57	2	10	0	0	0	4	2	9	.175	.203	.175	.379	8	-7	-7	111	144	2	.255	0			1	C	-0.5
1915	New-F	3	6	1	2	0	0	0	0	0	0	.333	.333	.333	.667	104	-0	0	94	0	1	.500	0			0	/C	0.0
Total	2	25	63	3	12	0	0	0	4	2	9	.190	.215	.190	.406	16	-7	-7	109	131	3	.275	0			1	/C	-0.5
■ MOE THACKER	Thacker, Morris Benton b: 5/21/34, Louisville, Ky. BR/TR, 6′3″, 205 lbs. Deb: 4/20/58																											
1958	Chi-N	11	24	4	6	1	0	2	3	1	7	.250	.280	.542	.822	110	0	0	101	65	3	.737	0	0	0	-0	/C	0.0
1960	Chi-N	54	90	5	14	1	0	0	6	14	20	.156	.269	.167	.436	23	-9	-9	98	162	4	.375	1	1	-0	-6	C	-1.3
1961	Chi-N	25	35	3	6	0	0	0	2	11	11	.171	.383	.171	.554	54	-2	-2	100	134	3	.600	0	0	0	-0	C	0.0
1962	Chi-N	65	107	8	20	5	0	0	9	14	40	.187	.287	.234	.521	39	-9	-9	106	142	8	.444	0	1	-1	-6	C	-1.4
1963	StL-N	3	4	0	0	0	0	0	0	0	3	.000	.000	.000	.000	-93	-1	-1	107	0	0	.000	0	0	0	0	/C	0.0
Total	5	158	260	20	46	7	0	2	20	40	81	.177	.291	.227	.518	41	-20	-21	102	139	18	.472	1	2	-1	-12	C	-2.7
■ AL THAKE	Thake, Albert b: 10/1/1849, England d: 9/1/1872, Hamilton, N.Y. 6′, Deb: 6/13/1872																											
1872	Atl-n	17	73	12	20							.274															O/2	

YEAR	TM/L	G	AB	R	H	2B	3B	HR	RBI	BB	SO	AVG	OBP	SLG	PRO	/A	BR	/A	PF	CHI	RC	TA	SB	CS	SBR	FR	POS	TPR
■ **RON THEOBALD**	Theobald, Ronald Merrill b: 7/28/43, Oakland, Cal. BR/TR, 5'8", 165 lbs. Deb: 4/12/71																											
1971	Mil-A	126	388	50	107	12	2	1	23	38	39	.276	.345	.325	.670	88	-4	-5	103	73	46	.608	11	8	-2	0	*2/S3	-0.1
1972	Mil-A	125	391	45	86	11	0	1	19	68	38	.220	.343	.256	.598	84	-6	-4	95	79	37	.536	0	7	-4	-5	*2	-0.6
Total	2	251	779	95	193	23	2	2	42	106	77	.248	.344	.290	.634	86	-10	-9	99	76	83	.574	11	15	-6	-4	2/3S	-0.7
■ **GEORGE THEODORE**	Theodore, George Basil b: 11/13/47, Salt Lake City, Ut. BR/TR, 6'4", 190 lbs. Deb: 4/14/73																											
1973	NY-N	45	116	14	30	4	0	1	15	10	13	.259	.323	.319	.642	78	-3	-3	101	151	11	.527	1	0	0	1	O/1	-0.3
1974	NY-N	60	76	7	12	1	0	1	1	8	14	.158	.247	.211	.458	29	-7	-7	99	20	3	.352	0	0	0	-4	1O	-1.2
Total	2	105	192	21	42	5	0	2	16	18	27	.219	.292	.276	.568	59	-10	-10	100	98	14	.471	1	0	0	-3	/O1	-1.5
■ **TOMMY THEVENOW**	Thevenow, Thomas Joseph b: 9/6/03, Madison, Ind. d: 7/29/57, Madison, Ind. BR/TR, 5'10", 155 lbs. Deb: 9/04/24																											
1924	StL-N	23	89	4	18	4	1	0	7	1	6	.202	.211	.270	.481	27	-9	-9	103	108	4	.351	1	3	-2	0	S	-0.8
1925	StL-N	50	175	17	47	7	2	0	17	7	12	.269	.301	.331	.632	60	-10	-11	102	104	18	.539	3	0	1	-1	S	-0.6
1926	StL-N	156	563	64	144	15	5	2	63	27	26	.256	.291	.311	.602	61	-30	-32	102	121	50	.504	8			17	*S	-0.3
1927	StL-N	59	191	23	37	6	1	0	4	14	8	.194	.249	.236	.484	28	-19	-21	107	31	11	.396	2			-0	S	-1.4
1928	StL-N	69	171	11	35	8	3	0	13	20	12	.205	.288	.287	.575	51	-12	-12	100	94	15	.507	0			-4	S/31	-0.6
1929	Phi-N	90	317	30	72	11	0	0	35	25	25	.227	.288	.262	.550	34	-31	-36	110	144	25	.461	3			-14	S	-3.3
1930	Phi-N	156	573	57	164	21	1	0	78	23	26	.286	.316	.326	.642	53	-40	-46	106	144	58	.521	1			-4	*S	-3.0
1931	Pit-N	120	404	35	86	12	1	0	38	28	22	.213	.266	.248	.513	38	-34	-35	101	135	28	.406	0			-0	*S	-2.5
1932	Pit-N	59	194	12	46	3	3	0	26	7	12	.237	.264	.284	.547	47	-14	-14	99	176	15	.419	0			-5	S3	-1.4
1933	Pit-N	73	253	20	79	5	1	0	34	3	5	.312	.320	.340	.660	93	-4	-3	95	149	25	.495	2			-6	2/S3	-0.3
1934	Pit-N	122	446	37	121	16	2	0	54	20	20	.271	.306	.316	.622	63	-21	-24	105	**138**	41	.479	0			-14	23/S	-2.5
1935	Pit-N	110	408	38	97	9	9	0	47	12	23	.238	.261	.304	.565	48	-28	-32	107	137	30	.426	1			-2	3S/2	-2.9
1936	Cin-N	106	321	25	75	7	2	0	36	15	23	.234	.268	.268	.536	46	-25	-23	97	148	21	.396	2			2	S23	-1.3
1937	Bos-N	21	34	5	4	0	1	0	2	4	2	.118	.211	.176	.387	7	-4	-4	90	120	2	.333	0			-0	S/32	-0.2
1938	Pit-N	15	25	2	5	0	0	0	2	4	0	.200	.333	.200	.533	50	-1	-1	100	145	2	.500	0			1	/2S3	0.0
Total	15	1229	4164	380	1030	124	32	2	456	210	222	.247	.285	.294	.579	51	-284	-302	103	131	346	.468	23	3		-30	S23/1	-21.1
■ **ANDRES THOMAS**	Thomas, Andres Perez (born Andres Perez (Thomas)) b: 11/10/63, Boca Chica, D.R. BR/TR, 6'1", 170 lbs. Deb: 9/03/85																											
1985	Atl-N	15	18	6	5	0	0	0	2	0	2	.278	.278	.278	.556	52	-1	-1	106	159	1	.357	0	0	0	0	S	0.0
1986	Atl-N	102	323	26	81	17	2	6	32	8	49	.251	.269	.372	.640	73	-12	-13	102	92	26	.504	4	6	-2	20	S	1.5
1987	Atl-N	82	324	29	75	11	0	5	39	14	50	.231	.268	.312	.579	49	-22	-26	108	137	25	.471	6	5	-1	8	S	-0.9
1988	Atl-N	153	606	54	153	22	2	13	68	14	95	.252	.271	.360	.630	76	-18	-21	104	112	54	.507	7	3	0	-9	*S	-2.0
Total	4	352	1271	115	314	50	4	24	141	36	196	.247	.269	.349	.619	67	-53	-60	105	114	106	.506	17	14	-3	19	S	-1.4
■ **PINCH THOMAS**	Thomas, Chester David b: 1/24/1888, Camp Point, Ill. d: 12/24/53, Modesto, Cal. BL/TR, 5'9.5", 173 lbs. Deb: 4/24/12																											
1912	Bos-A	13	30	0	6	0	0	0	5	2		.200	.250	.200	.450	27	-3	-3	107	278	2	.375	1			-1	C	-0.1
1913	Bos-A	38	91	6	26	1	2	1	15	2	11	.286	.309	.374	.682	96	-1	-1	103	144	10	.585	1			0	C	0.1
1914	Bos-A	63	130	9	25	1	0	0	5	18	17	.192	.291	.200	.491	49	-8	-7	98	72	8	.429	1			-5	C/1	-0.8
1915	Bos-A	86	203	21	48	4	4	0	21	13	20	.236	.286	.296	.581	74	-7	-7	99	119	18	.490	3	2	-0	-6	C	-0.6
1916	Bos-A	99	216	21	57	10	1	1	21	33	13	.264	.364	.333	.697	117	4	5	94	100	30	.692	4			-14	C	-0.5
1917	Bos-A	83	202	24	48	7	0	0	24	27	9	.238	.333	.272	.606	79	-3	-5	108	157	19	.558	2			-4	C	-0.2
1918	Cle-A	32	73	2	18	0	1	0	5	6	6	.247	.304	.274	.578	69	-2	-3	108	91	6	.473	0			-0	C	0.0
1919	Cle-A	34	46	2	5	0	0	0	2	4	3	.109	.180	.109	.289	-17	-7	-8	107	145	1	.220	0			-1	C	-0.7
1920	Cle-A	9	9	2	3	1	0	0	0	3	1	.333	.500	.444	.944	146	1	1	104	0	2	1.167	0	0	0	-0	/C	0.1
1921	Cle-A	21	35	1	9	3	0	0	4	10	2	.257	.422	.343	.765	98	0	0	99	114	6	.846	0	0	0	-1	C	0.0
Total	10	478	1035	88	245	27	8	2	102	118	82	.237	.318	.284	.602	78	-25	-26	101	121	104	.542	12	2		-32	C/1	-2.7
■ **DAN THOMAS**	Thomas, Danny Lee b: 5/9/51, Birmingham, Ala. d: 6/12/80, Mobile, Ala. BR/TR, 6'2", 190 lbs. Deb: 9/02/76																											
1976	Mil-A	32	105	13	29	5	1	4	15	14	28	.276	.372	.457	.829	143	6	6	99	98	18	.823	1	2	-1	-1	O	0.3
1977	Mil-A	22	70	11	19	3	2	2	11	8	11	.271	.354	.457	.812	125	2	2	95	115	11	.759	0	2	-1	0	/OD	0.1
Total	2	54	175	24	48	8	3	6	26	22	39	.274	.365	.457	.822	136	8	8	97	104	29	.803	1	4	-2	-1	/OD	0.4
■ **DERRELL THOMAS**	Thomas, Derrell Osbon b: 1/14/51, Los Angeles, Cal. BB/TR, 6', 160 lbs. Deb: 9/14/71																											
1971	Hou-N	5	5	0	0	0	0	0	0	0	2	.000	.000	.000	.000	-99	-1	-1	93	0	-0	.000	0	1	-1	0	/2	-0.1
1972	SD-N	130	500	48	115	15	5	5	36	41	73	.230	.291	.310	.601	80	-19	-12	88	92	45	.517	9	9	-3	-12	2S/O	-1.7
1973	SD-N	113	404	41	96	7	1	0	22	34	52	.238	.300	.260	.560	60	-23	-20	94	86	35	.495	15	5	2	1	S2	-0.5
1974	SD-N	141	523	48	129	24	6	3	41	51	58	.247	.315	.333	.647	87	-13	-9	93	92	54	.566	7	8	-3	-5	*23O/S	-1.2
1975	SF-N	144	540	99	149	21	9	6	48	57	56	.276	.348	.381	.730	101	2	1	102	88	75	.715	28	13	1	1	*2/O	0.9
1976	SF-N	81	272	38	63	5	4	2	19	29	26	.232	.315	.301	.616	73	-8	-9	103	85	26	.556	10	11	-4	7	2/OS3	-0.1
1977	SF-N	148	506	75	135	13	10	8	44	46	70	.267	.330	.379	.710	86	-7	-10	104	83	63	.651	15	13	-3	4	O2S/31	-0.6
1978	SD-N	128	352	36	80	10	2	3	26	35	37	.227	.303	.293	.595	72	-15	-12	93	92	34	.543	11	6	-0	-7	O231	-2.0
1979	LA-N	141	406	47	104	15	4	5	44	41	49	.256	.332	.350	.682	86	-7	-7	100	111	49	.652	18	5	2	-4	*O3/2S1	-1.1
1980	LA-N	117	297	32	79	18	3	1	22	26	48	.266	.327	.357	.684	94	-3	-2	97	80	33	.603	7	9	-3	-12	OS2/C3	-1.3
1981	LA-N	80	218	25	54	4	0	4	24	25	23	.248	.325	.321	.646	86	-4	-4	98	115	25	.607	7	2	1	-3	2SO3	-0.1
1982	LA-N	66	98	13	26	2	1	0	2	10	12	.265	.333	.306	.639	85	-2	-2	95	26	10	.545	2	3	-1	-7	O23/S	-0.9
1983	LA-N	118	192	38	48	6	6	2	8	27	36	.250	.348	.375	.723	100	1	1	100	41	27	.728	9	3	1	-11	OS/23	-1.0
1984	Mon-N	108	243	26	62	12	2	0	20	20	33	.255	.312	.321	.633	85	-7	-4	91	100	23	.510	0	4	-2	-25	SO2/31	-2.8
	Cal-A	14	29	3	4	0	1	0	2	3	4	.138	.219	.207	.426	18	-3	-3	101	133	1	.346	0	0	0	-2	/OS3	-0.4
1985	Phi-N	63	92	16	19	2	0	4	12	11	14	.207	.291	.359	.650	79	-2	-3	102	106	10	.605	2	0	1	-1	S/OC23	-0.1
Total	15	1597	4677	585	1163	154	54	43	370	456	593	.249	.319	.332	.651	84	-114	-97	97	89	509	.603	140	92	-13	-77	2OS3/1C	-13.0
■ **FRANK THOMAS**	Thomas, Frank Joseph b: 6/11/29, Pittsburgh, Pa. BR/TR, 6'3", 200 lbs. Deb: 8/17/51																											
1951	Pit-N	39	148	21	39	9	2	2	16	9	15	.264	.306	.392	.698	81	-3	-4	107	99	16	.578	0	2	-1	4	O	-0.2
1952	Pit-N	6	21	1	2	0	0	0	0	1	1	.095	.136	.095	.232	-35	-4	-4	100	0	0	.143	0	0	0	0	/O	-0.3
1953	Pit-N	128	455	68	116	22	1	30	102	50	93	.255	.331	.505	.837	112	8	7	102	127	76	.802	1	2	-1	3	*O	0.3
1954	Pit-N	153	577	81	172	32	7	23	94	51	74	.298	.365	.497	.863	126	18	21	97	110	106	.842	3	2	-0	3	*O	1.7
1955	Pit-N	142	510	72	125	16	2	25	72	60	76	.245	.327	.431	.758	102	-1	1	97	105	72	.714	2	0	1	6	*O	0.5
1956	Pit-N	157	588	69	166	24	3	25	80	36	61	.282	.329	.461	.790	107	7	5	102	104	80	.695	0	5	-3	-13	*3O/2	-1.3
1957	Pit-N	151	594	72	172	30	1	23	89	44	66	.290	.342	.460	.801	120	10	15	94	114	90	.736	3	1	0	2	1O3	1.0
1958	Pit-N	149	562	89	158	26	4	35	109	42	79	.281	.339	.528	.867	132	18	22	95	119	95	.816	0	1	-1	-30	*3/O1	-0.7
1959	Cin-N	108	374	41	84	18	2	12	47	27	56	.225	.282	.380	.662	72	-15	-16	103	107	37	.564	0	2	-1	-9	3O1	-3.0
1960	Chi-N	135	479	54	114	12	1	21	64	28	74	.238	.280	.399	.679	85	-12	-11	98	102	51	.584	1	0	0	-9	1O3	-2.5
1961	Chi-N	15	50	7	13	2	0	2	6	2	8	.260	.288	.420	.708	85	-1	-1	100	90	5	.575	0	0	0	-1	O/1	-0.2
	Mil-N	124	423	58	120	13	3	25	67	29	70	.284	.338	.506	.844	131	11	15	92	93	66	.777	2	4	-2	-6	*O1	0.1
	Yr	139	473	65	133	15	3	27	73	31	78	.281	.333	.497	.830	125	10	14	93	94	72	.761	2	4	-2	-6		-0.1
1962	NY-N	156	571	69	152	23	3	34	94	48	95	.266	.332	.496	.827	114	13	10	104	98	91	.784	2	1	0	2	*O13	0.5
1963	NY-N	126	420	34	109	9	1	15	60	33	48	.260	.318	.393	.711	104	2	2	99	122	46	.602	0	0	0	3	O1/3	0.0
1964	NY-N	60	197	19	50	6	1	3	19	10	29	.254	.297	.340	.637	83	-6	-4	95	103	19	.526	1	1	-0	2	O1/3	-0.3
	Phi-N	39	143	20	42	11	0	7	26	5	12	.294	.318	.517	.835	132	5	5	99	114	22	.752	0	1	-1	-1	1	0.2
	Yr	99	340	39	92	17	1	10	45	15	41	.271	.305	.415	.720	104	-1	1	97	108	43	.628	1	2	-1	1		-0.1
1965	Phi-N	35	77	7	20	4	0	1	7	4	10	.260	.296	.351	.647	86	-2	-1	95	97	7	.517	0	0	0	-1	O1/3	-0.3
	Hou-N	23	58	7	10	2	0	3	9	3	15	.172	.213	.362	.575	66	-3	-3	89	124	5	.500	0	0	0	-0	1/3O	-0.3
	Mil-N	15	33	3	7	3	0	0	1	2	11	.212	.257	.303	.560	55	-2	-2	104	41	3	.462	0	0	0	-1	/1O	-0.2
	Yr	73	168	17	37	9	0	4	17	9	36	.220	.260	.345	.605	73	-7	-6	95	97	16	.511	0	0	0	-2		-0.8
1966	Chi-N	5	5	0	0	0	0	0	0	0	1	.000	.000	.000	.000	-99	-1	-1	100	0	0	.000	0	0	0	0	H	0.0
Total	16	1766	6285	792	1671	262	31	286	962	484	894	.266	.323	.454	.777	108	40	53	98	108	886	.734	15	22	-9	-47	*O31/2	-5.0

YEAR	TM/L	G	AB	R	H	2B	3B	HR	RBI	BB	SO	AVG	OBP	SLG	PRO	/A	BR	/A	PF	CHI	RC	TA	SB	CS	SBR	FR	POS	TPR
■ FRED THOMAS	Thomas, Frederick Harvey "Tommy" b: 12/19/1892, Milwaukee, Wis. d: 1/15/86, Rice Lake, Wis. BR/TR, 5'10", 160 lbs. Deb: 4/22/18																											
1918	Bos-A	44	144	19	37	2	1	1	11	15	20	.257	.331	.306	.637	97	-1	-0	95	87	16	.598	4			-1	3/S	0.0
1919	Phi-A	124	453	42	96	11	10	2	23	43	52	.212	.283	.294	.577	59	-23	-27	106	64	41	.532	12			-7	*3	-2.4
1920	Phi-A	76	255	27	59	6	3	1	11	26	17	.231	.307	.290	.598	63	-15	-12	94	51	25	.550	8	4	0	0	3S	-0.6
	Was-A	3	7	0	1	0	0	0	0	0	1	.143	.143	.143	.286	-25	-1	-1	95	0	0	.143	0	1	-1	0	/3	-0.1
	Yr	79	262	27	60	6	3	1	11	26	18	.229	.303	.286	.590	60	-16	-14	94	50	24	.536	8	5	-1	0		-0.7
Total	3	247	859	88	193	19	14	4	45	84	90	.225	.297	.293	.591	65	-40	-41	100	63	81	.544	24	5		-7	3/S	-3.1
■ GEORGE THOMAS	Thomas, George Edward b: 11/29/37, Minneapolis, Minn. BR/TR, 6'3.5", 190 lbs. Deb: 9/11/57 C																											
1957	Det-A	1	1	0	0	0	0	0	0	0	1	.000	.000	.000	.000	-93	-0	-0	107	0	0	.000	0	0	0	0	/3	0.0
1958	Det-A	1	0	0	0	0	0	0	0	0	0	—	—	—	—	—	0	0	104	—	—	—	0	0	0	-0	/O	0.0
1961	Det-A	17	6	2	0	0	0	0	0	0	4	.000	.000	.000	.000	-99	-2	-2	96	0	0	.000	0	0	0	-1	/OS	-0.2
	LA-A	79	282	39	79	12	1	13	59	21	66	.280	.337	.468	.805	101	4	-0	111	138	43	.750	3	6	-3	-4	O3	-0.5
	Yr	96	288	41	79	12	1	13	59	21	70	.274	.330	.458	.788	100	2	-1	109	113	42	.729	3	6	-3	-5		-0.7
1962	LA-A	56	181	13	43	10	2	4	12	21	37	.238	.320	.381	.701	86	-3	-4	102	59	23	.645	0	0	0	3	O	-0.2
1963	LA-A	53	167	14	35	7	1	4	15	9	32	.210	.254	.335	.590	70	-8	-7	91	92	14	.485	0	0	0	-4	O3/1	-1.2
	Det-A	49	109	13	26	4	1	1	11	11	22	.239	.314	.321	.635	76	-3	-3	104	121	12	.576	2	1	0	0	O/2	-0.4
	Yr	102	276	27	61	11	2	5	26	20	54	.221	.279	.330	.608	72	-11	-10	97	107	27	.530	2	1	0	-4		-1.6
1964	Det-A	105	308	39	88	15	2	12	44	18	53	.286	.331	.464	.796	124	7	8	96	104	47	.740	4	1	1	3	O/3	0.8
1965	Det-A	79	169	19	36	5	1	3	10	12	39	.213	.273	.308	.581	61	-8	-9	105	68	13	.486	2	3	-1	-2	O/2	-1.5
1966	Bos-A	69	173	25	41	4	0	5	20	23	33	.237	.333	.347	.680	88	-0	-2	109	112	20	.619	1	0	0	1	O/3C1	-0.2
1967	Bos-A	65	89	10	19	2	0	1	6	3	23	.213	.255	.270	.525	48	-5	-6	115	93	6	.408	0	1	-1	-9	O/1C	-1.9
1968	Bos-A	12	10	3	2	0	0	1	1	1	3	.200	.273	.500	.773	130	0	0	101	54	2	.875	1	0	0	-2	/O	-0.1
1969	Bos-A	29	51	9	18	3	1	0	8	3	11	.353	.400	.451	.851	131	3	2	105	140	10	.818	0	0	0	-3	O1/C3	-0.1
1970	Bos-A	38	99	13	34	8	0	2	13	11	12	.343	.420	.485	.904	134	7	6	111	97	20	.897	0	0	0	-4	O/3	0.1
1971	Bos-A	9	13	0	1	0	0	0	1	1	4	.077	.143	.077	.220	-34	-2	-2	106	408	0	.167	0	0	0	-2	/O	-0.4
	Min-A	23	30	4	8	1	0	0	2	4	3	.267	.353	.300	.653	83	-0	-1	104	91	4	.591	0	0	0	-4	O/13	-0.4
	Yr	32	43	4	9	1	0	0	3	5	7	.209	.292	.233	.524	48	-3	-3	104	193	3	.441	0	0	0	-6		-0.8
Total	13	685	1688	203	430	71	9	46	202	138	343	.255	.318	.389	.707	92	-12	-20	104	103	213	.650	13	12	-3	-28	O/31C2S	-6.2
■ HERB THOMAS	Thomas, Herbert Mark b: 5/26/02, Sampson City, Fla. BR/TR, 5'4.5", 157 lbs. Deb: 8/28/24																											
1924	Bos-N	32	127	12	28	4	1	1	8	9	8	.220	.288	.291	.579	59	-8	-7	94	70	11	.535	5	2	0	10	O	0.3
1925	Bos-N	5	17	2	4	0	1	0	0	2	0	.235	.350	.353	.703	86	-0	-0	94	0	2	.643	0	1	-1	-1	/2	-0.1
1927	Bos-N	24	74	11	17	6	1	0	6	3	9	.230	.269	.338	.607	66	-4	-4	93	84	7	.544	2			-1	2/S	-0.4
	NY-N	13	17	2	3	1	1	0	1	1	1	.176	.263	.353	.616	64	-1	-1	100	58	2	.571	0			0	/OS	0.0
	Yr	37	91	13	20	7	2	0	7	4	10	.220	.268	.341	.609	65	-5	-5	95	77	8	.549	2			-1		-0.4
Total	3	74	235	27	52	11	4	1	15	15	18	.221	.285	.315	.600	64	-14	-12	94	68	21	.548	7	3		9	/O2S	-0.2
■ IRA THOMAS	Thomas, Ira Felix b: 1/22/1881, Ballston Spa, N.Y. d: 10/11/58, Philadelphia, Pa. BR/TR, 6'2", 200 lbs. Deb: 5/18/06 C																											
1906	NY-A	44	115	12	23	1	2	0	15	8		.200	.252	.243	.496	47	-6	-8	120	195	8	.413	2			-4	C	-0.9
1907	NY-A	80	208	20	40	5	4	1	24	10		.192	.229	.269	.499	55	-9	-11	109	145	14	.423	5			1	C/1	-0.4
1908	Det-A	40	101	6	31	1	0	0	8	5		.307	.340	.317	.656	115	2	2	101	94	11	.529	0			2	C	0.7
1909	Phi-A	84	256	22	57	9	3	0	31	18		.223	.292	.281	.573	80	-5	-6	102	166	21	.508	4			6	C	0.8
1910	Phi-A	60	180	14	50	8	2	1	19	6		.278	.301	.361	.662	105	1	0	102	103	20	.562	2			3	C	1.0
1911	Phi-A	103	297	33	81	14	3	0	39	23		.273	.341	.340	.682	97	-3	-0	93	130	36	.630	4			-9	*C	0.3
1912	Phi-A	46	139	14	30	4	2	1	13	8		.216	.268	.295	.563	61	-7	-7	99	99	12	.495	3			-1	C	-0.3
1913	Phi-A	22	53	3	15	4	1	0	6	4	8	.283	.333	.396	.730	117	1	1	97	102	7	.658	0			-1	C	0.2
1914	Phi-A	2	3	0	0	0	0	0	0	0	0	.000	.000	.000	.000	-99	-1	-1	97	0	0	.000	0			0	/C	0.0
1915	Phi-A	1	0	0	0	0	0	0	0	0	0	—	—	—	—	—	0	0	96	—	—	—	0			0	/C	0.0
Total	10	482	1352	124	327	46	17	3	155	82	8	.242	.294	.308	.601	81	-29	-31	102	134	128	.522	20			-3	C/1	1.4
■ GORMAN THOMAS	Thomas, James Gorman b: 12/12/50, Charleston, S.C. BR/TR, 6'2", 210 lbs. Deb: 4/06/73																											
1973	Mil-A	59	155	16	29	7	1	2	11	14	61	.187	.254	.284	.538	54	-10	-9	96	86	11	.474	5	5	-2	-5	O/3D	-1.7
1974	Mil-A	17	46	10	12	4	0	2	11	8	15	.261	.370	.478	.849	139	3	2	102	154	9	.944	4	0	1	-1	O/D	0.2
1975	Mil-A	121	240	34	43	12	2	10	28	31	84	.179	.273	.371	.644	80	-7	-7	100	90	25	.611	4	2	0	-6	*O/D	-1.6
1976	Mil-A	99	227	27	45	9	2	8	36	31	67	.198	.297	.361	.659	93	-2	-2	99	130	24	.604	2	3	-1	-0	O/3D	-0.5
1978	Mil-A	137	452	70	111	24	1	32	86	73	133	.246	.353	.515	.868	134	24	21	106	105	85	.886	3	4	-2	-12	*O	0.5
1979	Mil-A	156	557	97	136	29	0	**45**	123	98	175	.244	.359	.539	.898	138	30	30	100	115	110	.924	1	5	-3	-3	*O/D	1.7
1980	Mil-A	162	628	78	150	26	3	38	105	58	170	.239	.305	.471	.777	116	5	10	95	106	91	.743	8	5	-1	-4	*O/D	0.2
1981	Mil-A	103	363	54	94	22	0	21	65	50	85	.259	.352	.493	.845	147	19	21	96	107	63	.839	4	5	-2	4	O/D	2.1
1982	Mil-A	158	567	96	139	29	1	**39**	112	84	143	.245	.347	.506	.853	139	24	28	94	117	100	.849	3	7	-3	3	*O	2.2
1983	Mil-A	46	164	21	30	6	1	5	18	23	50	.183	.287	.323	.610	74	-7	-5	92	110	15	.560	2	1	0	3	O	-0.2
	Cle-A	106	371	51	82	17	0	17	51	57	98	.221	.326	.404	.731	95	0	-2	105	101	51	.722	8	3	1	7	*O	0.4
	Yr	152	535	72	112	23	1	22	69	80	148	.209	.314	.379	.694	89	-7	-8	101	104	68	.680	10	4	1	10		0.2
1984	Sea-A	35	108	6	17	3	0	1	13	28	27	.157	.336	.213	.549	54	-5	-6	102	203	9	.536	0	3	-2	-4	O/D	-1.2
1985	Sea-A	135	484	76	104	16	1	32	87	84	126	.215	.332	.450	.783	118	8	12	95	116	74	.779	3	2	-0	0	*D	1.1
1986	Sea-A	57	170	24	33	4	0	10	26	27	55	.194	.308	.394	.702	86	-2	-3	105	107	21	.681	1	2	-1	0	D	-0.4
	Mil-A	44	145	21	26	4	1	6	10	31	50	.179	.324	.345	.669	81	-3	-3	102	60	17	.669	2	2	-1	-0	D/1	-0.4
	Yr	101	315	45	59	8	1	16	36	58	105	.187	.316	.371	.687	84	-5	-7	104	87	40	.681	3	4	-2	-0		-0.8
Total	13	1435	4677	681	1051	212	13	268	782	697	1339	.225	.328	.448	.775	114	76	86	98	111	706	.777	50	49	-14	-20	*OD/13	2.4
■ LEE THOMAS	Thomas, James Leroy b: 2/5/36, Peoria, Ill. BL/TR, 6'2", 195 lbs. Deb: 4/22/61 C																											
1961	NY-A	2	2	0	1	0	0	0	0	0	0	.500	.500	.500	1.000	175	0	0	96	0	1	1.000	0	0	0	0	H	0.0
	LA-A	130	450	77	128	11	5	24	70	47	74	.284	.355	.491	.846	111	14	7	111	95	75	.796	0	5	-3	2	O1	0.0
	Yr	132	452	77	129	11	5	24	70	47	74	.285	.355	.491	.846	111	14	7	111	94	75	.797	0	5	-3	2		0.0
1962	LA-A	160	583	88	169	21	2	26	104	55	74	.290	.357	.467	.824	117	16	14	102	120	96	.787	6	1	1	-7	1O	0.0
1963	LA-A	149	528	52	116	12	6	9	55	53	82	.220	.302	.316	.618	80	-18	-12	91	121	52	.553	6	0	2	-1	*1O	-1.7
1964	LA-A	47	172	14	47	8	1	2	24	18	22	.273	.342	.366	.708	110	-0	2	89	156	23	.646	1	0	0	-1	O/1	0.0
	Bos-A	107	401	44	103	19	2	13	42	34	29	.257	.321	.411	.733	100	1	-0	102	92	50	.655	2	1	0	2	*O/1	-0.1
	Yr	154	573	58	150	27	3	15	66	52	51	.262	.328	.398	.725	103	0	2	98	113	74	.655	3	1	0	1		-0.1
1965	Bos-A	151	521	74	141	27	4	22	75	72	42	.271	.362	.464	.827	124	23	19	107	103	87	.812	6	2	1	3	*1O	1.6
1966	Atl-N	39	126	11	25	1	1	6	15	10	15	.198	.263	.365	.628	73	-5	-5	99	98	13	.569	1	1	-0	0	1	-0.6
	Chi-N	75	149	15	36	4	0	1	9	14	15	.242	.319	.289	.608	70	-5	-5	100	82	14	.517	0	0	0	-1	1O	-0.8
	Yr	114	275	26	61	5	1	7	24	24	30	.222	.294	.324	.617	72	-10	-10	100	89	27	.541	1	1	-0	-1		-1.4
1967	Chi-N	77	191	16	42	4	1	2	23	15	22	.220	.287	.283	.570	63	-9	-9	102	159	16	.480	1	0	0	-4	O1	-1.6
1968	Hou-N	90	201	14	39	4	0	1	11	14	22	.194	.250	.229	.479	45	-13	-13	99	95	11	.373	2	1	0	-1	O/1	-1.9
Total	8	1027	3324	405	847	111	22	106	428	332	397	.255	.328	.397	.725	99	3	-3	101	111	438	.685	25	11	1	-9	O1	-5.1
■ BUD THOMAS	Thomas, John Tillman b: 3/10/29, Sedalia, Mo. BR/TR, 6', 180 lbs. Deb: 9/02/51																											
1951	StL-A	14	20	3	7	0	0	1	1	0	3	.350	.350	.500	.850	122	1	1	105	27	4	.923	2	0	1	-1	S	0.1
■ KITE THOMAS	Thomas, Keith Marshall b: 4/27/24, Kansas City, Kan. BR/TR, 6'1.5", 195 lbs. Deb: 4/19/52																											
1952	Phi-A	75	116	24	29	6	1	6	18	20	27	.250	.365	.474	.839	119	5	3	111	92	20	.826	0	1	-1	-5	O	-0.2
1953	Phi-A	24	49	1	6	0	0	0	2	3	6	.122	.173	.122	.296	-19	-8	-8	102	123	1	.200	0	0	0	-1	O	-0.9
	Was-A	38	58	10	17	3	2	1	12	11	7	.293	.414	.466	.880	145	3	4	94	148	11	.848	0	0	0	-2	/OC	0.2
	Yr	62	107	11	23	3	2	1	14	14	13	.215	.311	.308	.620	70	-5	-4	97	140	10	.539	0	0	0	-3		-0.7
Total	2	137	223	35	52	9	3	7	32	34	40	.233	.340	.395	.734	96	0	-1	105	113	32	.701	0	1	-1	-7	/OC	-0.9

YEAR	TM/L	G	AB	R	H	2B	3B	HR	RBI	BB	SO	AVG	OBP	SLG	PRO	/A	BR	/A	PF	CHI	RC	TA	SB	CS	SBR	FR	POS	TPR
■ **LEO THOMAS**	Thomas, Leo Raymond "Tommy" b: 7/26/23, Turlock, Cal. BR/TR, 5'11.5", 178 lbs. Deb: 4/29/50																											
1950	StL-A	35	121	19	24	6	0	1	9	20	14	.198	.312	.273	.585	47	-9	-10	107	91	11	.520	0	1	-1	-5	3	-1.5
1952	StL-A	41	124	12	29	5	1	0	12	17	7	.234	.336	.290	.626	77	-4	-3	97	124	13	.576	2	0	1	3	3/S2	0.0
	Chi-A	19	24	1	4	0	0	0	6	6	4	.167	.333	.167	.500	42	-2	-2	100	560	2	.476	0	0	0	0	/3	0.0
	Yr	60	148	13	33	5	1	0	18	23	11	.223	.335	.270	.606	71	-5	-5	98	265	17	.578	2	0	1	3		0.0
Total	2	95	269	32	57	11	1	1	27	43	25	.212	.325	.271	.596	60	-14	-15	102	151	27	.561	2	1	0	-2	/3S2	-1.5
■ **RAY THOMAS**	Thomas, Raymond Joseph b: 7/9/10, Dover, N.H. BR/TR, 5'10.5", 175 lbs. Deb: 7/21/38																											
1938	Bro-N	1	3	1	1	0	0	0	0	0	0	.333	.333	.333	.667	88	-0	-0	96	0	0	.500	0			0	/C	0.0
■ **RED THOMAS**	Thomas, Robert William b: 4/25/1898, Hargrove, Ala. d: 3/29/62, Fremont, Ohio BR/TR, 5'11", 165 lbs. Deb: 9/13/21																											
1921	Chi-N	8	30	5	8	3	0	1	5	4	5	.267	.371	.467	.838	113	1	1	107	104	5	.826	0	1	-1	1	/O	0.1
■ **ROY THOMAS**	Thomas, Roy Allen b: 3/24/1874, Norristown, Pa. d: 11/20/59, Norristown, Pa. BL/TL, 5'11", 150 lbs. Deb: 4/14/1899																											
1899	Phi-N	150	547	137	178	12	4	0	47	115		.325	.455	.362	.817	132	32	35	97	64	112	1.003	42			7	*O1	2.9
1900	Phi-N	140	531	**132**	168	4	3	0	33	**115**		.316	.438	.335	.773	120	22	24	98	50	97	.909	37			-3	*O/P	0.8
1901	Phi-N	129	479	102	148	5	2	1	28	**100**		.309	.428	.334	.762	122	23	21	103	50	82	.867	27			-7	*O	0.1
1902	Phi-N	138	500	89	143	4	7	0	24	**107**		.286	**.412**	.322	.734	123	25	22	105	45	75	.798	17			10	*O	2.2
1903	Phi-N	130	477	88	156	11	2	1	27	**107**		.327	**.450**	.365	.815	147	31	37	92	42	88	.928	17			9	*O	3.3
1904	Phi-N	139	496	92	144	6	6	3	29	**102**		.290	.411	.345	.756	148	28	33	93	51	84	.855	28			10	*O	3.9
1905	Phi-N	147	562	118	178	11	6	0	31	93		.317	.414	.358	.771	128	29	25	104	46	95	.826	23			11	*O	2.7
1906	Phi-N	142	493	81	125	10	7	0	16	**107**		.254	.387	.302	.689	128	17	22	92	34	68	.755	22			9	*O	3.1
1907	Phi-N	121	419	70	102	15	3	1	23	**83**		.243	.369	.301	.669	108	11	9	104	60	52	.694	11			7	*O	1.2
1908	Phi-N	6	24	2	4	0	0	0	0	2		.167	.231	.167	.397	29	-2	-2	100	0	1	.300	0			0	/O	-0.1
	Pit-N	102	386	52	99	11	10	1	24	49		.256	.340	.345	.685	128	10	12	95	60	48	.672	11			4	*O	1.7
	Yr	108	410	54	103	11	10	1	24	51		.251	.334	.334	.668	122	9	11	95	56	48	.648	11			4		1.6
1909	Bos-N	82	281	36	74	9	1	0	11	47		.263	.369	.302	.671	114	6	7	96	50	32	.662	5			3	O	0.8
1910	Phi-N	23	71	7	13	0	2	0	4	7	5	.183	.266	.239	.505	50	-5	-4	96	82	6	.500	4			-1	O	-0.5
1911	Phi-N	21	30	5	5	2	0	0	2	8	6	.167	.342	.233	.575	58	-1	-2	108	97	2	.600	0			0	O	-0.1
Total	13	1470	5296	1011	1537	100	53	7	299	1042	11	.290	.408	.333	.741	126	226	239	98	50	841	.816	244			60	*O/1P	22.0
■ **VALMY THOMAS**	Thomas, Valmy b: 10/21/28, Santurce, P.R. BR/TR, 5'9", 165 lbs. Deb: 4/16/57																											
1957	NY-N	88	241	30	60	10	3	6	31	16	29	.249	.298	.390	.688	81	-6	-7	102	115	28	.597	0	0	0	-14	C	-1.6
1958	SF-N	63	143	14	37	5	0	3	16	13	24	.259	.325	.357	.681	80	-4	-4	100	110	17	.600	1	0	0	-1	C	-0.1
1959	Phi-N	66	140	5	28	2	0	1	7	9	19	.200	.253	.236	.489	31	-14	-14	99	79	7	.370	1	0	0	-6	C/3	-1.5
1960	Bal-A	8	16	0	1	0	0	0	0	1	0	.063	.118	.063	.180	-49	-3	-3	102	0	-0	.111	0	1	-1	-0	/C	-0.3
1961	Cle-A	27	86	7	18	3	0	2	6	6	7	.209	.261	.314	.575	55	-6	-6	96	71	5	.440	0	0	0	3	C	-0.2
Total	5	252	626	56	144	20	3	12	60	45	79	.230	.285	.329	.614	63	-33	-33	100	97	57	.522	2	1	0	-18	C/3	-3.7
■ **BILL THOMAS**	Thomas, William Miskey b: 12/8/1877, Norristown, Pa. d: 1/14/50, Evansburg, Pa. TR, 5'10", 190 lbs. Deb: 5/01/02																											
1902	Phi-N	6	17	1	2	0	0	0	0	1		.118	.167	.118	.284	-11	-2	-2	105	0	0	.200	0			-0	/O12	-0.2
■ **WALT THOMAS**	Thomas, William Walter "Tommy" b: 4/28/1884, Foot-Of-Ten, Pa. d: 6/6/50, Altoona, Pa. BR/TR, 5'8", Deb: 9/18/08																											
1908	Bos-N	5	13	2	2	0	0	0	1	3		.154	.313	.154	.466	50	-1	-1	104	192	1	.636	2			1	/S	0.0
■ **ART THOMASON**	Thomason, Arthur Wilson b: 2/12/1889, Liberty, Mo. d: 5/2/44, Kansas City, Mo. BL/TL, 5'8", 150 lbs. Deb: 8/10/10																											
1910	Cle-A	20	70	3	12	0	1	0	2	5		.171	.227	.200	.427	34	-5	-5	100	54	4	.379	3			1	O	-0.5
■ **GARY THOMASSON**	Thomasson, Gary Leah b: 7/29/51, San Diego, Cal. BL/TL, 6'1", 180 lbs. Deb: 9/05/72																											
1972	SF-N	10	27	5	9	1	1	0	1	1	7	.333	.357	.444	.802	127	1	1	100	34	4	.684	0	0	0	-1	/1O	0.0
1973	SF-N	112	235	35	67	10	4	4	30	22	43	.285	.346	.413	.759	104	3	2	105	111	36	.716	2	0	1	-2	1O	-0.3
1974	SF-N	120	315	41	77	14	3	2	29	38	56	.244	.326	.327	.653	77	-7	-10	108	103	35	.597	7	1	2	1	O1	-1.1
1975	SF-N	114	326	44	74	12	3	7	32	37	48	.227	.308	.347	.654	80	-8	-9	102	92	38	.625	9	3	1	10	O1	-0.1
1976	SF-N	103	328	45	85	20	5	8	38	30	45	.259	.323	.424	.747	107	4	2	103	90	45	.712	8	3	1	1	O1	0.0
1977	SF-N	145	446	63	114	24	6	17	71	75	102	.256	.364	.451	.815	112	12	9	104	113	78	.854	16	4	2	1	*O1	0.7
1978	Oak-A	47	154	17	31	4	1	5	16	15	44	.201	.272	.338	.610	70	-6	-6	101	96	14	.559	4	1	1	1	O/1	-0.6
	NY-A	55	116	20	32	4	1	3	20	13	22	.276	.349	.405	.754	113	2	2	99	141	17	.698	0	2	-1	1	O/D	0.0
	Yr	102	270	37	63	8	2	8	36	28	66	.233	.305	.367	.672	88	-4	-4	100	121	32	.624	4	3	-1	1		-0.6
1979	LA-N	115	315	39	78	11	1	14	45	43	70	.248	.340	.422	.762	107	3	3	100	102	47	.742	4	2	0	-1	*O/1	0.0
1980	LA-N	80	111	6	24	3	0	1	12	17	26	.216	.326	.270	.596	70	-4	-4	97	144	10	.533	0	0	0	-6	O/1	-1.0
Total	9	901	2373	315	591	103	25	61	294	291	463	.249	.332	.391	.723	97	-2	-10	103	105	324	.707	50	16	5	4	O1/D	-2.4
■ **BOBBY THOMPSON**	Thompson, Bobby La Rue b: 11/3/53, Charlotte, N.C. BB/TR, 5'11", 175 lbs. Deb: 4/16/78																											
1978	Tex-A	64	120	23	27	3	3	2	12	9	26	.225	.290	.350	.640	82	-3	-3	96	99	13	.632	7	2	1	-2	O/D	-0.4
■ **TIM THOMPSON**	Thompson, Charles Lemoine b: 3/1/24, Coalport, Pa. BL/TR, 5'11", 190 lbs. Deb: 4/28/54 C																											
1954	Bro-N	10	13	2	2	1	0	0	1	1	1	.154	.214	.231	.445	16	-2	-2	101	131	1	.364	0	0	0	-0	/CO	-0.1
1956	KC-A	92	268	21	73	13	2	1	27	17	23	.272	.321	.347	.668	75	-9	-10	101	105	29	.562	2	4	-2	10	C	0.0
1957	KC-A	81	230	25	47	10	0	7	19	18	26	.204	.262	.339	.601	64	-12	-12	99	76	20	.516	0	0	0	5	C	-0.3
1958	Det-A	4	6	1	1	0	0	0	0	3	2	.167	.444	.167	.611	73	0	0	104	0	1	.800	0	0	0	0	/C	0.0
Total	4	187	517	49	123	24	2	8	47	39	52	.238	.294	.338	.632	69	-23	-23	100	91	51	.548	2	4	-2	15	C/O	-0.4
■ **DANNY THOMPSON**	Thompson, Danny Leon b: 2/1/47, Wichita, Kan. d: 12/10/76, Rochester, Minn. BR/TR, 6', 183 lbs. Deb: 6/25/70																											
1970	Min-A	96	302	25	66	9	0	0	22	7	39	.219	.236	.248	.485	34	-27	-27	98	119	17	.339	0	0	0	-6	23/S	-2.4
1971	Min-A	48	57	10	15	2	0	0	7	7	12	.263	.344	.298	.642	80	-1	-1	104	168	5	.511	0	0	0	-2	3/2S	-0.3
1972	Min-A	144	573	54	158	22	6	4	48	34	57	.276	.319	.356	.675	94	-0	-5	107	89	63	.561	3	4	-2	-10	*S	0.0
1973	Min-A	99	347	29	78	13	2	1	36	16	41	.225	.263	.282	.545	52	-22	-23	104	140	24	.418	1	0	0	-5	S/3D	-1.5
1974	Min-A	97	264	25	66	6	1	4	25	22	29	.250	.313	.326	.638	83	-5	-6	101	100	24	.519	1	1	-0	-3	S/3D	-0.1
1975	Min-A	112	355	25	96	11	2	5	37	18	30	.270	.306	.355	.661	80	-7	-10	107	101	37	.535	0	3	-2	-6	*S/32D	-0.7
1976	Min-A	34	124	9	29	4	0	0	6	3	8	.234	.258	.266	.524	54	-7	-7	98	70	9	.392	1	1	-0	2	S	-0.2
	Tex-A	64	196	12	42	3	0	1	13	13	19	.214	.267	.245	.512	49	-12	-13	102	98	13	.398	2	2	-1	-3	32S/D	-1.5
	Yr	98	320	21	71	7	0	1	19	16	27	.222	.263	.253	.516	51	-19	-20	101	89	21	.397	3	3	-1	-1		-1.7
Total	7	694	2218	189	550	70	11	15	194	120	235	.248	.289	.310	.599	69	-82	-91	104	106	192	.489	8	11	-4	-33	S3/2D	-6.7
■ **DON THOMPSON**	Thompson, Donald Newlin b: 12/28/23, Swepsonville, N.C. BL/TL, 6', 185 lbs. Deb: 4/24/49																											
1949	Bos-N	7	11	0	2	0	0	0	0	0	2	.182	.182	.182	.364	-2	-2	-2	97	0	0	.222	0			-0	/O	-0.1
1951	Bro-N	80	118	25	27	3	0	0	6	12	12	.229	.305	.254	.560	53	-8	-7	98	77	8	.450	2	8	-4	-12	O	-2.5
1953	Bro-N	96	153	25	37	5	0	1	12	14	13	.242	.310	.294	.604	56	-9	-10	104	97	13	.496	2	3	-1	-15	O	-2.8
1954	Bro-N	34	25	2	1	0	0	0	1	5	5	.040	.226	.040	.266	-25	-5	-5	101	394	1	.292	0	0	0	-10	O	-1.5
Total	4	217	307	52	67	8	0	1	19	31	32	.218	.296	.254	.550	46	-23	-23	101	113	22	.462	4	11		-38	O	-6.9
■ **FRANK THOMPSON**	Thompson, Frank Deb: N/A.																											
1875	Nat-n	11	42	3	4							.095															C/O	
	Atl-n	1	5	1	2							.400															O	
	Yr	12	47	4	6							.128																
■ **FRANK THOMPSON**	Thompson, Frank E b: 7/2/1895, Springfield, Mo. d: 6/27/40, Jasper Co., Mo. BR/TR, 5'8", 155 lbs. Deb: 5/06/20																											
1920	StL-A	22	53	7	9	0	0	0	5	13	10	.170	.343	.170	.513	35	-4	-5	111	195	4	.533	1	1	-0	-1	3/2	-0.4
■ **HANK THOMPSON**	Thompson, Henry Curtis b: 12/8/25, Oklahoma City, Okla d: 9/30/69, Fresno, Cal. BL/TR, 5'9", 174 lbs. Deb: 7/17/47																											
1947	StL-A	27	78	10	20	1	1	0	5	10	7	.256	.341	.295	.636	76	-2	-2	102	80	8	.574	2	1	0	1	2	0.0
1949	NY-N	75	275	51	77	10	4	9	34	42	30	.280	.377	.444	.821	118	8	8	102	91	50	.854	5			-4	2/3	0.6

YEAR	TM/L	G	AB	R	H	2B	3B	HR	RBI	BB	SO	AVG	OBP	SLG	PRO	/A	BR	/A	PF	CHI	RC	TA	SB	CS	SBR	FR	POS	TPR
1950	NY-N	148	512	82	148	17	6	20	91	83	60	.289	.391	.463	.854	126	20	21	98	121	97	.885	8			7	*3O	2.6
1951	NY-N	87	264	37	62	8	4	8	33	43	23	.235	.342	.386	.728	94	-1	-2	102	101	36	.692	1	2	-1	-6	3	-0.8
1952	NY-N	128	423	67	110	13	9	17	67	50	38	.260	.344	.454	.798	117	11	9	102	108	68	.772	4	4	-1	-1	O3/2	0.6
1953	NY-N	114	388	80	117	15	8	24	74	60	39	.302	.400	.567	.967	152	28	29	98	101	93	1.032	6	5	-1	-5	*3/O2	1.9
1954	NY-N	136	448	76	118	18	1	26	86	90	58	.263	.392	.482	.874	120	20	16	105	117	92	.932	3	0	1	2	*3/2O	2.0
1955	NY-N	135	432	65	106	13	1	17	63	84	56	.245	.373	.398	.771	106	6	7	99	117	71	.787	2	2	-1	8	*3/2S	1.3
1956	NY-N	83	183	24	43	9	0	8	29	31	26	.235	.349	.415	.764	107	2	2	97	123	29	.769	2	1	0	1	3O/S	0.2
Total	9	933	3003	492	801	104	34	129	482	493	337	.267	.374	.453	.827	118	90	88	101	110	545	.860	33	15		2	3O2/S	8.4
■ SHAG THOMPSON	Thompson, James Alfred b: 4/29/1893, Haw River, N.C. BL/TR, 5'8.5", 165 lbs. Deb: 6/08/14																											
1914	Phi-A	16	29	3	5	0	1	0	2	7	8	.172	.351	.241	.593	81	-0	-0	97	107	3	.667	1			2	/O	0.1
1915	Phi-A	17	33	5	11	2	0	0	2	4	6	.333	.405	.394	.799	145	2	2	96	52	5	.739	0	1	-1	1	/O	0.2
1916	Phi-A	15	17	4	0	0	0	0	0	7	6	.000	.292	.000	.292	-12	-2	-2	98	0	0	.471	1			-0	/O	-0.2
Total	3	48	79	12	16	2	1	0	4	18	20	.203	.357	.253	.610	86	-1	-0	97	60	8	.641	2	1		2	/O	0.1
■ JASON THOMPSON	Thompson, Jason Dolph b: 7/6/54, Hollywood, Cal. BL/TL, 6'4", 200 lbs. Deb: 4/23/76																											
1976	Det-A	123	412	45	90	12	1	17	54	68	72	.218	.331	.376	.707	103	4	3	104	103	53	.677	2	4	-2	0	*1	-0.4
1977	Det-A	158	585	87	158	24	5	31	105	73	91	.270	.352	.487	.839	120	21	17	105	117	100	.810	0	1	-1	-7	*1	0.0
1978	Det-A	153	589	79	169	25	3	26	96	74	96	.287	.367	.472	.839	125	27	21	108	113	104	.817	0	0	0	-5	*1	1.0
1979	Det-A	145	492	58	121	16	1	20	79	70	90	.246	.341	.404	.746	104	1	3	96	120	68	.705	2	0	1	1	*1	-0.2
1980	Det-A	36	126	10	27	5	0	4	20	13	26	.214	.293	.349	.642	71	-4	-5	105	139	12	.558	0	1	-1	1	1	-0.7
	Cal-A	102	312	59	99	14	0	17	70	70	60	.317	.442	.526	.968	171	31	33	96	127	76	1.068	2	0	1	-2	1D	2.8
	Yr	138	438	69	126	19	0	21	90	83	86	.288	.402	.475	.877	142	27	28	98	131	88	.916	2	1	0	-2		2.1
1981	Pit-N	86	223	36	54	13	0	15	42	59	49	.242	.401	.502	.903	162	18	19	96	105	48	.977	0	0	0	-4	1	1.3
1982	Pit-N	156	550	87	156	32	0	31	101	101	107	.284	.397	.511	.908	138	41	33	110	112	117	.951	1	0	0	-2	*1	2.5
1983	Pit-N	152	517	70	134	20	1	18	76	99	128	.259	.379	.406	.785	114	16	14	103	116	84	.783	1	0	0	-8	*1	0.0
1984	Pit-N	154	543	61	138	22	0	17	74	87	73	.254	.359	.389	.748	117	9	13	94	117	78	.718	0	0	0	-9	*1	0.0
1985	Pit-N	123	402	42	97	17	1	12	61	84	58	.241	.372	.378	.751	108	9	7	103	132	61	.754	0	0	0	1	*1	0.5
1986	Mon-N	30	51	6	10	4	0	0	4	18	12	.196	.406	.275	.680	93	1	1	98	114	7	.762	0	1	-1	-1	1	0.0
Total	11	1418	4802	640	1253	204	12	208	782	816	862	.261	.369	.438	.808	121	172	159	102	117	809	.826	8	7	-2	-34	*1/D	6.8
■ TUG THOMPSON	Thompson, John P. b: London, Ontario, Canada d: 6/27/1895, Wilmington, Del. BL , 160 lbs. Deb: 8/31/1882																											
1882	Cin-a	1	5	0	1	0	0	0		0		.200	.200	.200	.400	32	-0	-0	109	0	0	.250				0	/O	0.0
1884	Ind-a	24	97	10	20	3	0	0		2		.206	.222	.237	.459	54	-5	-4	96	0	5	.325				0	OC	-0.3
Total	2	25	102	10	21	3	0	0		2		.206	.221	.235	.456	53	-5	-5	97	0	5	.321				0	/OC	-0.3
■ FRESCO THOMPSON	Thompson, Lafayette Fresco "Tommy" b: 6/6/02, Centerville, Ala. d: 11/20/68, Fullerton, Cal. BR/TR, 5'8", 150 lbs. Deb: 9/05/25																											
1925	Pit-N	14	37	4	9	2	1	0	8	4	1	.243	.317	.351	.668	69	-2	-2	102	219	4	.655	2	1	0	-0	2	-0.1
1926	NY-N	2	8	1	5	0	0	0	1	2	0	.625	.700	.625	1.325	265	2	2	98	60	4	2.667	1			0	/2	0.2
1927	Phi-N	153	597	78	181	32	14	1	70	34	36	.303	.343	.409	.752	104	-0	2	96	105	81	.719	19			-4	*2	-0.2
1928	Phi-N	152	634	99	182	34	11	3	50	42	27	.287	.332	.390	.722	85	-12	-15	104	61	80	.684	19			9	*2	-0.3
1929	Phi-N	148	623	115	202	41	3	4	53	75	34	.324	.398	.419	.817	94	5	-4	110	57	104	.838	16			10	*2	0.9
1930	Phi-N	122	478	77	135	34	4	4	46	35	29	.282	.331	.395	.727	71	-20	-24	106	81	61	.673	7			-1	*2	-1.0
1931	Bro-N	74	181	26	48	6	1	1	21	23	16	.265	.351	.326	.677	82	-3	-4	101	121	22	.662	5			0	2S/3	0.0
1932	Bro-N	3	1	0	0	0	0	0	0	0	0	.000	.000	.000	.000	-99	-0	-0	96	0	0	.000	0			0	H	0.0
1934	NY-N	1	1	0	0	0	0	0	0	0	0	.000	.000	.000	.000	-99	-0	-0	98	0	0	.000	0			0	H	0.0
Total	9	669	2560	400	762	149	34	13	249	215	143	.298	.353	.398	.751	88	-30	-46	104	80	357	.727	69	1		15	2/S3	-0.5
■ MILT THOMPSON	Thompson, Milton Bernard b: 1/5/59, Washington, D.C. BL/TR, 5'11", 170 lbs. Deb: 9/04/84																											
1984	Atl-N	25	99	16	30	1	0	2	4	11	11	.303	.373	.374	.746	101	2	1	110	32	16	.861	14	2	3	2	O	0.5
1985	Atl-N	73	182	17	55	7	2	0	6	7	36	.302	.339	.363	.701	90	-1	-2	106	36	23	.644	9	4	0	-4	O	-0.7
1986	Phi-N	96	299	38	75	7	1	6	23	26	62	.251	.313	.341	.654	77	-8	-10	104	76	34	.638	19	4	3	-1	O	-0.8
1987	Phi-N	150	527	86	159	26	9	7	43	42	87	.302	.353	.425	.778	101	4	1	104	71	85	.815	46	10	8	-0	*O	0.2
1988	Phi-N	122	378	53	109	16	2	2	33	39	59	.288	.356	.357	.714	104	4	3	101	94	48	.671	17	9	-0	1	*O	0.0
Total	5	466	1485	210	428	57	14	17	109	125	255	.288	.346	.380	.725	96	0	-7	104	71	207	.730	105	29	14	-3	O	-0.8
■ ROB THOMPSON	Thompson, Robert Randall b: 5/10/62, W.Palm Beach, Fla. BR/TR, 5'11", 165 lbs. Deb: 4/08/86																											
1986	SF-N	149	549	73	149	27	3	7	47	42	112	.271	.329	.370	.699	96	-6	-3	96	85	64	.615	12	15	-5	-1	*2/S	-0.7
1987	SF-N	132	420	62	110	26	5	10	44	40	91	.262	.338	.419	.757	103	-1	2	96	85	58	.729	16	11	-2	4	*2	0.6
1988	SF-N	138	477	66	126	24	6	7	48	40	111	.264	.326	.384	.710	110	2	5	94	96	62	.664	14	5	1	-6	*2	0.4
Total	3	419	1446	201	385	77	14	24	139	122	314	.266	.331	.389	.719	103	-5	4	95	89	184	.676	42	31	-6	-4	2/S	0.3
■ TOMMY THOMPSON	Thompson, Rupert Lockhart b: 5/19/10, Elkhart, Ill. d: 5/24/71, Auburn, Cal. BL/TR, 5'9.5", 155 lbs. Deb: 9/03/33																											
1933	Bos-N	24	97	6	18	1	0	0	6	4	6	.186	.218	.196	.414	20	-10	-10	96	114	4	.274	0			3	O	-0.8
1934	Bos-N	105	343	40	91	12	3	0	37	13	19	.265	.300	.318	.618	76	-17	-10	86	122	34	.498	2			9	O	-0.4
1935	Bos-N	112	297	34	81	7	1	4	30	36	17	.273	.353	.343	.697	92	-4	-2	96	95	36	.616	2			1	O	-0.3
1936	Bos-N	106	266	37	76	9	0	4	36	31	12	.286	.362	.365	.727	101	-0	1	95	117	38	.677	3			1	O1	0.0
1938	Chi-A	19	18	2	2	0	0	0	2	1	2	.111	.158	.111	.269	-32	-4	-4	98	338	0	.188	0	0	0	0	/1	-0.2
1939	Chi-A	1	0	0	0	0	0	0	1	0	0	—	—	—	—	—	0	-0	107	—	0	—	0	0	0	0	H	0.0
	StL-A	30	86	23	26	5	0	1	7	23	7	.302	.455	.395	.850	119	4	4	100	64	18	.967	0	0	0	-1	O	0.2
	Yr	31	86	23	26	5	0	1	8	23	7	.302	.455	.395	.850	118	4	4	101	62	19	.967	0	0	0	-1		0.2
Total	6	397	1107	142	294	34	4	9	119	108	63	.266	.335	.328	.663	84	-30	-20	93	111	130	.597	7	0		13	O/1	-1.5
■ SAM THOMPSON	Thompson, Samuel Luther "Big Sam" b: 3/5/1860, Danville, Ind. d: 11/7/22, Detroit, Mich. BL/TL, 6'2", 207 lbs. Deb: 1885																											
1885	Det-N	63	254	58	77	11	9	7	44	16	22	.303	.344	.500	.844	175	19	20	97	99	45	.808				6	O/3	2.2
1886	Det-N	122	503	101	156	18	13	8	89	35	31	.310	.355	.445	.800	131	25	18	109	124	86	.784	13			7	*O	2.4
1887	Det-N	127	545	118	**203**	29	**23**	11	**166**	32	19	**.372**	.416	**.571**	.987	171	**53**	**51**	102	143	**142**	1.094	22			2	*O	**4.5**
1888	Det-N	56	238	51	67	10	8	6	40	23	10	.282	.352	.466	.819	164	17	17	98	96	42	.830	5			-8	O	0.8
1889	Phi-N	128	533	103	158	36	4	**20**	111	36	22	.296	.348	.492	.839	129	22	18	104	99	102	.875	24			-7	*O	0.5
1890	Phi-N	132	549	116	**172**	**41**	9	4	102	42	29	.313	.371	.443	.813	129	26	19	108	116	102	.844	25			-1	*O	1.4
1891	Phi-N	133	554	108	163	23	10	7	90	52	20	.294	.363	.410	.773	134	19	23	95	102	95	.808	29			19	*O	3.1
1892	Phi-N	153	609	109	186	28	11	9	104	59	19	.305	.377	.432	.809	140	34	30	104	106	112	.853	28			3	*O	2.6
1893	Phi-N	131	600	130	**222**	**37**	13	11	126	50	17	.370	.424	.530	.954	155	45	46	100	87	146	1.037	18			-12	*O/1	2.3
1894	Phi-N	99	437	108	178	29	27	13	141	40	13	.407	.458	.686	1.145	**184**	51	55	95	110	152	1.409	24			-5	*O	3.3
1895	Phi-N	119	538	131	211	45	21	**18**	**165**	31	11	.392	.430	**.654**	1.085	182	59	60	99	109	167	1.269	27			10	*O	4.8
1896	Phi-N	119	517	103	154	28	7	12	100	28	13	.298	.341	.449	.790	107	5	3	102	95	85	.766	12			18	*O	1.0
1897	Phi-N	3	13	2	3	0	1	0	3	1		.231	.286	.385	.670	81	-0	-0	96	151	1	.600	0			0	/O	0.0
1898	Phi-N	14	63	14	22	5	3	1	15	4		.349	.388	.571	.959	187	6	6	95	100	15	1.024	2			0	O	0.6
1906	Det-A	8	31	4	7	0	1	0	3	1		.226	.250	.290	.540	65	-1	-1	108	117	2	.417	0			-0	/O	-0.1
Total	15	1407	5984	1256	1979	340	160	127	1299	450	226	.331	.384	.505	.888	148	376	364	101	108	1296	.939	229			32	*O/13	29.4
■ HOMER THOMPSON	Thompson, Thomas Homer b: 6/1/1892, Spring City, Tenn. d: 9/12/57, Atlanta, Ga. BR/TR, 5'9", 160 lbs. Deb: 10/05/12																											
1912	NY-A	1	0	0	0	0	0	0	0	0		—	—	—	—	—	0	0	101	—	—	—	0			0	/C	0.0
■ SCOT THOMPSON	Thompson, Vernon Scot b: 12/7/55, Grove City, Pa. BL/TL, 6'3", 195 lbs. Deb: 9/03/78																											
1978	Chi-N	19	36	7	15	3	0	0	2	2	4	.417	.447	.500	.947	149	3	3	110	44	8	.952	0	0	0	-1	/O1	0.2
1979	Chi-N	128	346	36	100	13	5	2	29	17	37	.289	.324	.373	.697	80	-5	-10	112	85	40	.588	4	3	-1	-4	*O	-1.7
1980	Chi-N	102	226	26	48	10	1	2	13	28	31	.212	.302	.292	.594	63	-10	-11	106	71	19	.532	6	6	-2	-5	O1	-2.2
1981	Chi-N	57	115	8	19	5	0	0	8	7	8	.165	.213	.209	.422	19	-12	-13	104	131	6	.337	2	0	1	-3	O/1	-1.6

YEAR	TM/L	G	AB	R	H	2B	3B	HR	RBI	BB	SO	AVG	OBP	SLG	PRO	/A	BR	/A	PF	CHI	RC	TA	SB	CS	SBR	FR	POS	TPR
1982	Chi-N	49	74	11	27	5	1	0	7	5	4	.365	.405	.459	.865	137	4	4	103	81	13	.780	0	1	-1	-0	O/1	0.2
1983	Chi-N	53	88	4	17	3	1	0	10	3	14	.193	.220	.250	.470	30	-8	-9	101	180	4	.333	0	0	0	-6	O/1	-1.5
1984	SF-N	120	245	30	75	7	1	1	31	30	26	.306	.382	.355	.737	113	4	5	96	135	32	.663	5	3	-0	-2	1/O	0.0
1985	SF-N	64	111	8	23	5	0	0	6	2	10	.207	.221	.252	.473	34	-10	-9	93	85	5	.323	0	0	0	-0	1	-1.0
	Mon-N	34	32	2	9	1	0	0	4	3	7	.281	.343	.313	.655	90	-1	-0	94	159	3	.542	0	0	0	-0	/1O	0.0
	Yr	98	143	10	32	6	0	0	10	5	17	.224	.250	.266	.516	47	-11	-10	93	112	10	.384	0	0	0	-1		-1.0
Total	8	626	1273	132	333	52	9	5	110	97	141	.262	.315	.328	.643	76	-35	-41	104	103	131	.560	17	13	-3	-21	O1	-7.6

■ **BOBBY THOMSON** Thomson, Robert Brown "The Staten Island Scot" b: 10/25/23, Glasgow, Scotland BR/TR, 6'2", 180 lbs. Deb: 9/09/46

YEAR	TM/L	G	AB	R	H	2B	3B	HR	RBI	BB	SO	AVG	OBP	SLG	PRO	/A	BR	/A	PF	CHI	RC	TA	SB	CS	SBR	FR	POS	TPR
1946	NY-N	18	54	8	17	4	1	2	9	4	5	.315	.362	.537	.899	151	3	3	102	96	10	.868	0			0	3	0.4
1947	NY-N	138	545	105	154	26	5	29	85	40	78	.283	.336	.508	.844	121	13	13	101	92	92	.801	1			5	*O/2	1.4
1948	NY-N	138	471	75	117	20	2	16	63	30	77	.248	.296	.401	.697	87	-10	-10	100	100	53	.604	2			9	*O	-0.9
1949	NY-N	156	641	99	198	35	9	27	109	44	45	.309	.355	.518	.873	129	25	24	102	96	115	.847	10			13	*O	2.7
1950	NY-N	149	563	79	142	22	7	25	85	55	45	.252	.324	.449	.774	103	-1	0	98	102	81	.726	3			6	*O	0.1
1951	NY-N	148	518	89	152	27	8	32	101	73	57	.293	.385	.562	.947	149	37	36	102	103	113	.969	5	5	-2	-11	O3	2.0
1952	NY-N	153	608	89	164	29	**14**	24	108	52	74	.270	.331	.482	.813	120	16	15	102	122	97	.766	5	2	0	5	3O	2.1
1953	NY-N	154	608	80	175	22	6	26	106	43	57	.288	.338	.472	.810	110	6	7	98	120	95	.744	4	2	0	-2	*O	0.0
1954	Mil-N	43	99	7	23	3	0	2	15	12	29	.232	.315	.323	.639	72	-5	-4	93	155	10	.557	0	0	0	-0	O	-0.4
1955	Mil-N	101	343	40	88	12	3	12	56	34	52	.257	.324	.414	.738	101	-3	-0	93	127	45	.669	2	1	0	-2	O	-0.3
1956	Mil-N	142	451	59	106	10	4	20	74	43	75	.235	.304	.408	.712	90	-8	-7	99	128	55	.645	2	4	-2	-5	*O/3	-1.8
1957	Mil-N	41	148	15	35	5	3	4	23	8	27	.236	.285	.392	.677	88	-5	-3	90	139	17	.609	2	1	0	-1	O	-0.4
	NY-N	81	215	24	52	7	4	8	38	19	39	.242	.303	.423	.727	91	-3	-3	102	137	26	.649	1	2	-1	-6	O/3	-1.2
	Yr	122	363	39	87	12	7	12	61	27	66	.240	.296	.410	.706	89	-7	-7	98	139	43	.635	3	3	-1	-7		-1.6
1958	Chi-N	152	547	67	155	27	5	21	82	56	76	.283	.354	.466	.820	114	11	11	101	109	87	.768	0	2	-1	-3	*O/3	0.2
1959	Chi-N	122	374	55	97	15	2	11	52	35	50	.259	.326	.398	.724	93	-5	-4	98	115	48	.654	1	0	0	3	*O	-0.1
1960	Bos-A	40	114	12	30	3	1	5	20	11	15	.263	.328	.439	.767	102	1	0	103	120	15	.685	0	1	-1	3	O/1	0.1
	Bal-A	3	6	0	0	0	0	0	0	0	3	.000	.000	.000	.000	-98	-2	-2	102	0	0	.000	0	0	0	-1	/O	-0.2
	Yr	43	120	12	30	3	1	5	20	11	18	.250	.313	.417	.730	93	-1	-2	103	115	16	.663	0	1	-1	2		-0.1
Total	15	1779	6305	903	1705	267	74	264	1026	559	804	.270	.333	.462	.795	111	73	77	100	112	958	.767	38	20		13	*O3/21	3.7

■ **DICKIE THON** Thon, Richard William b: 6/20/58, South Bend, Ind BR/TR, 5'11", 160 lbs. Deb: 5/22/79

YEAR	TM/L	G	AB	R	H	2B	3B	HR	RBI	BB	SO	AVG	OBP	SLG	PRO	/A	BR	/A	PF	CHI	RC	TA	SB	CS	SBR	FR	POS	TPR
1979	Cal-A	35	56	6	19	3	0	0	8	5	10	.339	.393	.393	.786	122	1	2	93	140	8	.692	0	0	0	0	2/S3	0.4
1980	Cal-A	80	267	32	68	12	2	0	15	10	28	.255	.284	.315	.599	67	-13	-12	96	70	23	.488	7	5	-1	-4	S2D3/1	-1.3
1981	Hou-N	49	95	13	26	6	0	0	3	9	13	.274	.337	.337	.673	104	-1	0	88	37	11	.644	6	1	1	-3	2S/3	0.2
1982	Hou-N	136	496	73	137	31	**10**	3	36	37	48	.276	.328	.397	.725	103	1	1	99	70	69	.733	37	8	6	9	*S/32	2.6
1983	Hou-N	154	619	81	177	28	9	20	79	54	73	.286	.345	.457	.802	134	16	23	90	88	95	.794	34	16	1	18	*S	5.6
1984	Hou-N	5	17	3	6	0	1	0	1	0	4	.353	.389	.471	.859	152	1	1	93	49	2	.692	0	1	-1	1	/S	0.2
1985	Hou-N	84	251	26	63	6	1	6	29	18	50	.251	.301	.355	.656	86	-6	-5	96	108	27	.596	8	3	1	6	S	0.8
1986	Hou-N	106	278	24	69	13	1	3	21	29	49	.248	.319	.335	.654	78	-7	-8	103	82	28	.577	6	5	-1	-7	*S	-0.5
1987	Hou-N	32	66	6	14	1	0	1	3	16	13	.212	.366	.273	.639	78	-2	-1	93	57	8	.698	3	0	1	-2	S	0.1
1988	SD-N	95	258	36	68	12	2	1	18	33	49	.264	.349	.337	.687	100	0	1	97	80	34	.707	19	4	3	-2	S/23	0.8
Total	10	776	2403	300	647	112	26	34	213	211	337	.269	.330	.380	.710	101	-11	3	95	81	307	.693	120	43	10	17	S/23D1	8.9

■ **JACK THONEY** Thoney, John "Bullet Jack" (born John Thoeny) b: 12/8/1879, Ft.Thomas, Ky. d: 10/24/48, Covington, Ky. BR/TR, 5'10", 175 lbs. Deb: 4/26/02

YEAR	TM/L	G	AB	R	H	2B	3B	HR	RBI	BB	SO	AVG	OBP	SLG	PRO	/A	BR	/A	PF	CHI	RC	TA	SB	CS	SBR	FR	POS	TPR
1902	Cle-A	28	105	14	30	7	1	0	11	9		.286	.342	.371	.714	103	0	1	97	98	15	.693	4			-3	2S/O	0.0
	Bal-A	3	11	1	0	0	0	0	0	1		.000	.083	.000	.083	-74	-3	-3	102	0	0	.182	1			-0	/3	-0.2
	Yr	31	116	15	30	7	1	0	11	10		.259	.317	.336	.654	85	-3	-2	97	92	14	.628	5			-3		-0.2
1903	Cle-A	32	122	10	25	3	0	1	9	2		.205	.218	.254	.472	44	-8	-8	96	97	8	.412	7			2	O/23	-0.7
1904	Was-A	17	70	6	21	3	0	0	6	1		.300	.310	.343	.653	117	1	1	93	82	8	.551	2			1	O	0.1
	NY-A	36	128	17	24	4	2	0	12	8		.188	.235	.250	.485	49	-6	-8	112	143	10	.471	9			2	3O	-0.5
	Yr	53	198	23	45	7	2	0	18	9		.227	.261	.283	.544	70	-6	-7	106	125	18	.497	11			3		-0.4
1908	Bos-A	109	416	58	106	5	9	2	30	13		.255	.277	.325	.602	99	-2	-2	98	85	40	.529	16			10	*O	0.4
1909	Bos-A	13	40	1	5	1	0	0	3	2		.125	.167	.150	.317	0	-5	-5	109	193	1	.286	2			1	O	-0.4
1911	Bos-A	26	20	5	5	0	0	0	2	0		.250	.250	.250	.500	40	-2	-2	99	135	1	.400	1			0	H	-0.1
Total	6	264	912	112	216	23	12	3	73	36		.237	.266	.298	.564	77	-25	-25	100	101	84	.503	42			13	O/32S	-1.4

■ **ANDY THORNTON** Thornton, Andre b: 8/13/49, Tuskegee, Ala. BR/TR, 6'3", 200 lbs. Deb: 7/28/73

YEAR	TM/L	G	AB	R	H	2B	3B	HR	RBI	BB	SO	AVG	OBP	SLG	PRO	/A	BR	/A	PF	CHI	RC	TA	SB	CS	SBR	FR	POS	TPR
1973	Chi-N	17	35	3	7	3	0	0	2	7	9	.200	.333	.286	.619	67	-1	-1	108	80	4	.586	0	0	0	1	/1	0.0
1974	Chi-N	107	303	41	79	16	4	10	46	48	50	.261	.369	.439	.808	125	11	11	100	109	51	.810	2	1	0	7	1/3	1.4
1975	Chi-N	120	372	70	109	21	4	18	60	88	63	.293	.433	.516	.949	156	35	33	104	96	89	1.059	3	2	-0	6	*1/3	3.3
1976	Chi-N	27	85	8	17	6	0	2	14	20	14	.200	.364	.341	.706	92	1	-0	109	157	13	.779	2	0	1	1	1	0.0
	Mon-N	69	183	20	35	5	2	9	24	28	32	.191	.308	.388	.696	96	-1	-1	100	94	24	.693	2	1	0	2	1O	-0.1
	Yr	96	268	28	52	11	2	11	38	48	46	.194	.327	.373	.700	96	0	-1	103	113	37	.720	4	1	1	2		-0.1
1977	Cle-A	131	433	77	114	20	5	28	70	70	82	.263	.379	.527	.906	147	27	29	98	91	89	.940	3	4	-2	-2	*1/D	1.8
1978	Cle-A	145	508	97	133	22	4	33	105	93	72	.262	.382	.516	.898	**161**	36	40	93	122	99	.915	4	7	-3	5	*1	3.6
1979	Cle-A	143	515	89	120	31	1	26	93	90	93	.233	.351	.449	.800	108	11	7	106	123	86	.811	5	4	-1	-4	*1D	-0.4
1981	Cle-A	69	226	22	54	12	0	6	30	23	37	.239	.309	.372	.681	102	-1	0	93	115	23	.585	3	1	0	1	D1	0.1
1982	Cle-A	161	589	90	161	26	1	32	116	109	81	.273	.389	.484	.872	138	34	33	100	129	109	.882	6	7	-2	1	*D/1	3.1
1983	Cle-A	141	508	78	143	27	1	17	77	87	72	.281	.389	.439	.828	121	22	18	105	116	90	.838	4	2	0	2	*D1	1.9
1984	Cle-A	155	587	91	159	26	0	33	99	91	79	.271	.371	.484	.854	127	29	24	106	109	108	.867	6	5	-1	0	*D1	2.2
1985	Cle-A	124	461	49	109	13	0	22	88	47	75	.236	.307	.408	.715	100	-5	-1	94	**146**	56	.647	3	2	-0	0	*D	0.0
1986	Cle-A	120	401	49	92	14	0	17	66	65	67	.229	.338	.392	.730	101	1	2	98	129	55	.707	4	1	1	0	*D	0.2
1987	Cle-A	36	85	8	10	2	0	0	5	10	25	.118	.211	.141	.352	-3	-13	-13	103	166	3	.303	1	0	0	0	D	-1.1
Total	14	1565	5291	792	1342	244	22	253	895	876	851	.254	.364	.452	.815	123	185	182	100	118	900	.841	48	37	-8	18	D1/O3	16.0

■ **LOU THORNTON** Thornton, Louis b: 4/26/63, Montgomery, Ala. BL/TR, 6'2", 185 lbs. Deb: 4/08/85

YEAR	TM/L	G	AB	R	H	2B	3B	HR	RBI	BB	SO	AVG	OBP	SLG	PRO	/A	BR	/A	PF	CHI	RC	TA	SB	CS	SBR	FR	POS	TPR
1985	Tor-A	56	72	18	17	1	1	1	8	2	24	.236	.267	.319	.586	59	-4	-4	101	122	6	.474	1	0	0	-8	OD	-1.1
1987	Tor-A	12	2	5	1	0	0	0	0	1	0	.500	.667	.500	1.167	216	1	0	101	0	0	.667	0	1	-1	-2	/OD	-0.1
1988	Tor-A	11	2	1	0	0	0	0	0	0	0	.000	.000	.000	.000	-99	-1	-1	100	0	0	.000	0	0	0	-4	O/D	-0.4
Total	3	79	76	24	18	1	1	1	8	3	24	.237	.275	.316	.591	61	-4	-4	101	114	6	.492	1	1	-0	-13	/OD	-1.6

■ **OTIS THORNTON** Thornton, Otis Benjamin b: 6/30/45, Docena, Ala. BR/TR, 6'1", 186 lbs. Deb: 7/06/73

YEAR	TM/L	G	AB	R	H	2B	3B	HR	RBI	BB	SO	AVG	OBP	SLG	PRO	/A	BR	/A	PF	CHI	RC	TA	SB	CS	SBR	FR	POS	TPR
1973	Hou-N	2	3	0	0	0	0	0	1	0	2	.000	.000	.000	.000	-99	-1	-1	95	0	0	.000	0	0	0	0	/C	0.0

■ **WALTER THORNTON** Thornton, Walter Miller b: 2/18/1875, Lewiston, Maine d: 7/14/60, Los Angeles, Cal. TL, 6'1", 180 lbs. Deb: 7/01/1895

YEAR	TM/L	G	AB	R	H	2B	3B	HR	RBI	BB	SO	AVG	OBP	SLG	PRO	/A	BR	/A	PF	CHI	RC	TA	SB	CS	SBR	FR	POS	TPR
1895	Chi-N	8	22	4	7	1	0	1	7	3	1	.318	.400	.500	.900	129	1	1	103	140	5	.933	0			0	/P1	0.0
1896	Chi-N	9	22	6	8	0	1	0	1	5	2	.364	.481	.455	.936	139	2	2	108	29	6	1.214	2			0	/PO	0.0
1897	Chi-N	75	265	39	85	9	6	0	55	30		.321	.401	.400	.802	114	7	7	100	155	49	.861	13			-12	OP	-0.7
1898	Chi-N	62	210	34	62	5	2	0	14	22		.295	.362	.338	.700	101	2	1	103	60	29	.682	8			0	OP	0.1
Total	4	154	519	83	162	15	9	1	77	60	3	.312	.390	.382	.771	111	12	10	102	111	89	.804	23			-12	/OP1	-0.6

■ **BOB THORPE** Thorpe, Benjamin Robert b: 11/19/26, Caryville, Fla. BR/TR, 6'1.5", 190 lbs. Deb: 4/19/51

YEAR	TM/L	G	AB	R	H	2B	3B	HR	RBI	BB	SO	AVG	OBP	SLG	PRO	/A	BR	/A	PF	CHI	RC	TA	SB	CS	SBR	FR	POS	TPR
1951	Bos-N	2	2	1	1	0	1	0	1	0	0	.500	.500	1.500	2.000	425	1	1	98	129	2	3.000	0	0	0	0	H	0.1
1952	Bos-N	81	292	20	76	8	2	3	26	5	42	.260	.275	.332	.607	71	-13	-12	95	96	26	.473	3	1	0	2	O	-1.1
1953	Mil-N	27	37	1	6	1	0	0	5	1	6	.162	.184	.189	.373	-3	-6	-5	94	279	1	.250	0	1	-1	-6	O	-1.1
Total	3	110	331	22	83	9	3	3	32	6	48	.251	.266	.323	.590	65	-18	-16	95	116	28	.468	3	2	-0	-4	/O	-2.1

■ **JIM THORPE** Thorpe, James Francis b: 5/28/1887, Prague, Okla. d: 3/28/53, Long Beach, Cal. BR/TR, 6'1", 185 lbs. Deb: 4/14/13

YEAR	TM/L	G	AB	R	H	2B	3B	HR	RBI	BB	SO	AVG	OBP	SLG	PRO	/A	BR	/A	PF	CHI	RC	TA	SB	CS	SBR	FR	POS	TPR
1913	NY-N	19	35	6	5	0	0	1	2	1	9	.143	.167	.229	.395	12	-4	-4	103	66	1	.367	2			0	/O	-0.3

YEAR	TM/L	G	AB	R	H	2B	3B	HR	RBI	BB	SO	AVG	OBP	SLG	PRO	/A	BR	/A	PF	CHI	RC	TA	SB	CS	SBR	FR	POS	TPR
1914	NY-N	30	31	5	6	1	0	0	2	0	4	.194	.194	.226	.419	26	-3	-3	96	104	1	.320	1			-1	/O	-0.4
1915	NY-N	17	52	8	12	3	1	0	1	2	16	.231	.259	.327	.586	84	-2	-1	91	22	5	.548	4	2	0	-2	O	-0.3
1917	Cin-N	77	251	29	62	2	8	4	36	6	35	.247	.267	.367	.634	101	-3	-1	92	133	26	.582	11			0	O	-0.3
	NY-N	26	57	12	11	3	2	0	4	8	10	.193	.303	.316	.619	93	-1	-0	97	86	6	.609	1			-3	O	-0.3
	Yr	103	308	41	73	5	10	4	40	14	45	.237	.275	.357	.632	99	-4	-1	93	123	32	.587	12			-3		-0.6
1918	NY-N	58	113	15	28	4	4	1	11	4	18	.248	.286	.381	.666	105	-0	0	98	90	12	.612	3			-9	O	-1.1
1919	NY-N	2	3	0	1	0	0	0	1	0	0	.333	.333	.333	.667	101	-0	-0	100	389	0	.500	0			-1	/O	0.0
	Bos-N	60	156	16	51	7	3	1	25	6	30	.327	.360	.429	.789	140	7	7	98	139	25	.781	7			-5	O/1	0.1
	Yr	62	159	16	52	7	3	1	26	6	30	.327	.359	.428	.787	139	6	7	98	153	26	.776	7			-5		0.1
Total	6	289	698	91	176	20	18	7	82	27	122	.252	.286	.362	.648	101	-6	-2	95	112	77	.601	29	2		-19	O/1	-2.6

■ BUCK THRASHER Thrasher, Frank Edward b: 8/6/1889, Watkinsville, Ga. d: 6/12/38, Cleveland, Ohio BL/TR, 5′11″, 182 lbs. Deb: 9/27/16

YEAR	TM/L	G	AB	R	H	2B	3B	HR	RBI	BB	SO	AVG	OBP	SLG	PRO	/A	BR	/A	PF	CHI	RC	TA	SB	CS	SBR	FR	POS	TPR
1916	Phi-A	7	29	4	9	2	1	0	4	2	1	.310	.355	.448	.803	144	1	1	98	95	5	.750	0			-1	/O	0.0
1917	Phi-A	23	77	5	18	2	1	0	2	3	12	.234	.272	.286	.557	75	-3	-2	94	33	6	.441	0			-5	O	-0.9
Total	2	30	106	9	27	4	2	0	6	5	13	.255	.295	.330	.625	95	-2	-1	95	50	11	.519	0			-6	/O	-0.9

■ MARV THRONEBERRY Throneberry, Marvin Eugene "Marvelous Marv" b: 9/2/33, Collierville, Tenn. BL/TL, 6′1″, 190 lbs. Deb: 9/25/55

YEAR	TM/L	G	AB	R	H	2B	3B	HR	RBI	BB	SO	AVG	OBP	SLG	PRO	/A	BR	/A	PF	CHI	RC	TA	SB	CS	SBR	FR	POS	TPR
1955	NY-A	1	2	1	2	1	0	0	3	0	0	1.000	1.000	1.500	2.500	578	1	1	98	373	3	—	1	0	0	0	/1	0.1
1958	NY-A	60	150	30	34	5	2	7	19	19	40	.227	.318	.427	.744	100	0	-0	103	90	21	.714	1	1	-0	-1	1/O	-0.2
1959	NY-A	80	192	27	46	5	0	8	22	18	51	.240	.305	.391	.695	97	-3	-1	93	87	24	.628	0	0	0	-2	1O	-0.3
1960	KC-A	104	236	29	59	9	2	11	41	23	60	.250	.317	.445	.762	105	0	1	99	116	32	.696	0	0	0	-1	1	-0.4
1961	KC-A	40	130	17	31	2	1	6	24	19	30	.238	.336	.408	.743	96	-0	-1	102	132	18	.699	0	0	0	-1	1O	-0.4
	Bal-A	56	96	9	20	3	0	5	11	12	20	.208	.296	.396	.692	85	-3	-2	97	81	11	.641	0	0	0	-4	O1	-0.7
	Yr	96	226	26	51	5	1	11	35	31	50	.226	.319	.403	.722	92	-3	-3	99	104	31	.689	0	0	0	-5		-1.1
1962	Bal-A	9	9	1	0	0	0	0	0	4	6	.000	.308	.000	.308	-9	-1	-1	95	0	0	.444	0	0	0	-0	/O	0.0
	NY-N	116	357	29	87	11	3	16	49	34	83	.244	.309	.426	.735	92	-3	-5	104	97	46	.668	1	3	-2	6	1	-0.3
1963	NY-N	14	14	0	2	1	0	0	1	1	5	.143	.200	.214	.414	19	-1	-1	99	140	1	.333	0	0	0	0	/1	-0.1
Total	7	480	1186	143	281	37	8	53	170	130	295	.237	.313	.416	.729	95	-10	-10	100	101	155	.690	3	4	-2	-3	1/O	-2.3

■ FAYE THRONEBERRY Throneberry, Maynard Faye b: 6/22/31, Memphis, Tenn. BL/TR, 5′11″, 185 lbs. Deb: 4/15/52

YEAR	TM/L	G	AB	R	H	2B	3B	HR	RBI	BB	SO	AVG	OBP	SLG	PRO	/A	BR	/A	PF	CHI	RC	TA	SB	CS	SBR	FR	POS	TPR
1952	Bos-A	98	310	38	80	11	3	5	23	33	67	.258	.331	.361	.693	87	-3	-6	107	68	41	.681	16	7	1	-5	O	-1.2
1955	Bos-A	60	144	20	37	7	3	6	27	14	31	.257	.327	.472	.799	91	2	-3	124	117	23	.761	0	0	0	0	O	-0.3
1956	Bos-A	24	50	6	11	2	0	1	3	3	16	.220	.264	.320	.584	52	-4	-4	103	59	4	.475	0	0	0	-2	O	-0.6
1957	Bos-A	1	1	0	0	0	0	0	0	0	1	.000	.000	.000	.000	-91	-0	-0	110	0	0	.000	0	0	0	0	H	0.0
	Was-A	68	195	21	36	8	2	2	12	17	37	.185	.254	.277	.530	46	-15	-15	98	79	14	.442	0	1	-1	-0	O	-1.9
	Yr	69	196	21	36	8	2	2	12	17	38	.184	.252	.276	.528	45	-15	-15	98	78	14	.439	0	1	-1	-0		-1.9
1958	Was-A	44	87	12	16	1	1	4	7	4	28	.184	.245	.356	.601	65	-5	-4	97	65	8	.528	0	1	-1	-3	O	-0.9
1959	Was-A	117	327	36	82	11	2	10	42	33	61	.251	.325	.388	.713	95	-2	-2	100	105	42	.668	6	4	-1	-4	O	-1.0
1960	Was-A	85	157	18	39	7	1	1	23	18	33	.248	.330	.325	.654	76	-5	-5	102	167	17	.582	1	1	-0	-3	O	-0.9
1961	LA-A	24	31	1	6	1	0	0	0	5	10	.194	.306	.226	.531	40	-2	-3	111	0	2	.462	0	0	0	0	/O	-0.2
Total	8	521	1302	152	307	48	12	29	137	127	284	.236	.309	.358	.666	78	-34	-42	104	94	151	.620	23	14	-2	-16	O	-7.0

■ GARY THURMAN Thurman, Gary Montez b: 11/12/64, Indianapolis, Ind. BR/TR, 5′10″, 170 lbs. Deb: 8/30/87

YEAR	TM/L	G	AB	R	H	2B	3B	HR	RBI	BB	SO	AVG	OBP	SLG	PRO	/A	BR	/A	PF	CHI	RC	TA	SB	CS	SBR	FR	POS	TPR
1987	KC-A	27	81	12	24	2	0	0	5	8	20	.296	.360	.321	.681	81	-2	-2	104	77	10	.683	7	2	1	5	O	0.3
1988	KC-A	35	66	6	11	1	0	0	2	4	20	.167	.214	.182	.396	12	-8	-8	103	66	3	.375	5	1	1	-7	O/D	-1.4
Total	2	62	147	18	35	3	0	0	7	12	40	.238	.296	.259	.554	51	-9	-10	104	72	14	.539	12	3	2	-2	/OD	-1.1

■ BOB THURMAN Thurman, Robert Burns b: 5/14/17, Wichita, Kan. BL/TL, 6′1″, 205 lbs. Deb: 4/14/55

YEAR	TM/L	G	AB	R	H	2B	3B	HR	RBI	BB	SO	AVG	OBP	SLG	PRO	/A	BR	/A	PF	CHI	RC	TA	SB	CS	SBR	FR	POS	TPR
1955	Cin-N	82	152	19	33	2	3	7	22	17	26	.217	.296	.408	.704	80	-4	-5	106	107	16	.622	0	2	-1	-5	O	-1.1
1956	Cin-N	80	139	25	41	5	2	8	22	10	14	.295	.342	.532	.875	121	5	4	108	95	25	.832	0	0	0	-4	O	0.0
1957	Cin-N	74	190	38	47	4	2	16	40	15	33	.247	.306	.542	.848	116	5	4	105	110	31	.815	0	0	0	-2	O	0.0
1958	Cin-N	94	178	23	41	7	4	4	20	20	38	.230	.322	.382	.704	80	-4	-5	107	103	21	.646	1	2	-1	-0	O	-0.7
1959	Cin-N	4	4	1	1	0	0	0	2	0	1	.250	.250	.250	.500	33	-0	-0	103	809	0	.333	0	0	0	0	H	0.0
Total	5	334	663	106	163	18	11	35	106	62	112	.246	.315	.465	.780	98	2	-3	107	108	94	.746	1	4	-2	-12	O	-1.8

■ EDDIE TIEMEYER Tiemeyer, Edward Carl b: 5/9/1885, Cincinnati, Ohio d: 9/27/46, Cincinnati, Ohio BR/TR, 5′11.5″, 185 lbs. Deb: 8/19/06

YEAR	TM/L	G	AB	R	H	2B	3B	HR	RBI	BB	SO	AVG	OBP	SLG	PRO	/A	BR	/A	PF	CHI	RC	TA	SB	CS	SBR	FR	POS	TPR
1906	Cin-N	5	11	3	2	0	0	0	0	1		.182	.250	.182	.432	32	-1	-1	115	0	1	.333	0			0	/3P	0.0
1907	Cin-N	1	0	1	0	0	0	0	0	1		—	1.000	—	1.182	291	0	0	95	0	0	—	0			0	H	0.0
1909	NY-A	3	8	1	3	1	0	0	0	1		.375	.444	.500	.944	199	1	1	99	0	2	1.000	0			0	/1	0.1
Total	3	9	19	5	5	1	0	0	0	3		.263	.364	.316	.679	106	0	0	108	0	2	.643	0			0	/13P	0.1

■ MIKE TIERNAN Tiernan, Michael Joseph "Silent Mike" b: 1/21/1867, Trenton, N.J. d: 11/9/18, New York, N.Y. BL/TL, 5′11″, 165 lbs. Deb: 4/30/1887

YEAR	TM/L	G	AB	R	H	2B	3B	HR	RBI	BB	SO	AVG	OBP	SLG	PRO	/A	BR	/A	PF	CHI	RC	TA	SB	CS	SBR	FR	POS	TPR
1887	NY-N	103	407	82	117	13	12	10	62	32	31	.287	.344	.452	.796	113	11	6	107	95	75	.852	28			-8	*O/P	0.0
1888	NY-N	113	443	75	130	16	8	9	52	42	42	.293	.364	.427	.790	166	28	32	93	76	90	.927	52			-2	*O	2.8
1889	NY-N	122	499	**147**	167	23	14	10	73	**96**	32	.335	.447	.497	.944	158	48	44	105	68	129	1.151	33			-3	*O	3.1
1890	NY-N	133	553	132	168	25	21	**13**	59	68	53	.304	.385	**.495**	**.880**	**167**	**40**	**44**	95	49	130	1.047	56			-16	*O	2.3
1891	NY-N	134	542	111	166	30	12	**16**	73	69	32	.306	.388	.494	**.882**	**169**	39	45	94	59	128	1.045	53			-8	*O	2.6
1892	NY-N	116	450	79	129	16	10	5	66	57	46	.287	.369	.400	.769	137	20	21	98	100	76	.807	20			-4	*O	1.1
1893	NY-N	125	511	114	158	19	12	14	102	72	24	.309	.399	.476	.874	129	25	22	104	87	110	.977	26			-11	*O	0.5
1894	NY-N	112	424	84	117	19	13	5	77	54	21	.276	.359	.417	.777	89	-8	-8	100	117	75	.847	28			-13	*O	-2.1
1895	NY-N	120	476	127	165	23	21	7	70	66	19	.347	.427	.527	.955	156	34	39	95	64	126	1.138	36			-7	*O	1.8
1896	NY-N	133	521	132	192	24	16	7	89	77	18	.369	.452	.516	.968	159	46	47	99	85	141	1.164	35			-5	*O	2.8
1897	NY-N	127	528	123	174	29	10	5	72	61		.330	.400	.451	.851	129	21	23	98	72	114	.960	40			-9	*O	0.3
1898	NY-N	103	415	90	116	15	11	4	49	43		.280	.357	.398	.755	126	10	14	95	72	67	.783	19			-14	*O	-0.5
1899	NY-N	35	137	17	35	4	2	0	7	10		.255	.306	.314	.620	74	-5	-5	97	48	14	.539	2			0	O	-0.3
Total	13	1476	5906	1313	1834	256	162	105	851	747	318	.311	.392	.462	.854	140	309	324	98	77	1274	.969	428			-99	*O/P	14.4

■ COTTON TIERNEY Tierney, James Arthur b: 2/10/1894, Kansas City, Kan. d: 4/18/53, Kansas City, Mo. BR/TR, 5′8″, 175 lbs. Deb: 9/23/20

YEAR	TM/L	G	AB	R	H	2B	3B	HR	RBI	BB	SO	AVG	OBP	SLG	PRO	/A	BR	/A	PF	CHI	RC	TA	SB	CS	SBR	FR	POS	TPR
1920	Pit-N	12	46	4	11	5	0	0	8	3	4	.239	.286	.348	.634	81	-1	-1	101	186	5	.556	1	1	-0	0	2/S	0.0
1921	Pit-N	117	442	49	132	22	8	3	52	24	31	.299	.338	.405	.743	93	-3	-5	103	104	59	.661	4	6	-2	-23	23/OS	-2.8
1922	Pit-N	122	441	58	152	26	14	7	86	22	40	.345	.378	.515	.893	124	17	15	104	124	82	.869	7	8	-3	-26	*2/OS3	-1.3
1923	Pit-N	29	120	22	35	5	2	2	23	2	10	.292	.309	.417	.726	93	-2	-2	97	153	15	.640	2	1	0	-3	2	-0.3
	Phi-N	121	480	68	152	31	1	11	65	24	42	.317	.352	.454	.806	98	6	-3	114	97	75	.744	3	4	-2	15	*2/O3	1.2
	Yr	150	600	90	187	36	3	13	88	26	52	.312	.343	.447	.790	97	4	-4	110	108	90	.722	5	5	-2	13		0.9
1924	Bos-N	136	505	38	131	16	1	6	58	22	37	.259	.296	.331	.626	72	-23	-19	94	117	49	.534	11	8	-2	-13	*23	-3.9
1925	Bro-N	93	265	27	68	14	4	2	39	12	23	.257	.294	.362	.656	71	-14	-11	94	136	27	.550	0	3	-2	-9	3/12	-1.6
Total	6	630	2299	266	681	119	30	31	331	109	187	.296	.332	.415	.746	93	-20	-27	102	117	312	.669	28	31	-10	-57	23/OS1	-8.7

■ BILL TIERNEY Tierney, William J. b: 5/14/1858, Boston, Mass. d: 9/21/1898, Boston, Mass. Deb: 5/02/1882

YEAR	TM/L	G	AB	R	H	2B	3B	HR	RBI	BB	SO	AVG	OBP	SLG	PRO	/A	BR	/A	PF	CHI	RC	TA	SB	CS	SBR	FR	POS	TPR
1882	Cin-a	1	5	1	0	0	0	0		0		.000	.000	.000	.000	-92	-1	-1	109	0	0	.000				0	/1	0.0
1884	Bal-U	1	3	0	1	0	0	0		1		.333	.500	.333	.833	169	0	0	110	0	1	1.000	0			0	/O	0.0
Total	2	2	8	1	1	0	0	0		1		.125	.222	.125	.347	18	-1	-1	110	0	1	.286	0			0	/O1	0.0

■ JOHN TILLEY Tilley, John C. b: 1856, New York, N.Y. Deb: 8/23/1882

YEAR	TM/L	G	AB	R	H	2B	3B	HR	RBI	BB	SO	AVG	OBP	SLG	PRO	/A	BR	/A	PF	CHI	RC	TA	SB	CS	SBR	FR	POS	TPR
1882	Cle-N	15	56	2	5	1	1	0	4	2	11	.089	.121	.143	.264	-18	-7	-6	90	172	1	.196				0	O	-0.5
1884	Tol-a	17	56	5	10	2	0	0		4		.179	.246	.214	.460	52	-3	-3	104	0	3	.370				0	O	-0.2
	StP-U	9	26	2	4	1	0	0		3		.154	.241	.192	.434	48	-1	-1	100	0	1	.364	0			0	/O	0.0
Total	2	41	138	9	19	4	1	0	4	9	11	.138	.196	.181	.377	25	-11	-10	97	67	5	.294	0			0	/O	-0.7

YEAR	TM/L	G	AB	R	H	2B	3B	HR	RBI	BB	SO	AVG	OBP	SLG	PRO	/A	BR	/A	PF	CHI	RC	TA	SB	CS	SBR	FR	POS	TPR
■ **BOB TILLMAN**	Tillman, John Robert b: 3/24/37, Nashville, Tenn. BR/TR, 6'4", 205 lbs. Deb: 4/15/62																											
1962	Bos-A	81	249	28	57	6	4	14	38	19	65	.229	.286	.454	.740	93	-3	-4	102	97	31	.668	0	0	0	-2	C	-0.1
1963	Bos-A	96	307	24	69	10	2	8	32	34	64	.225	.304	.349	.653	78	-7	-9	106	102	33	.584	0	0	0	5	C	-0.2
1964	Bos-A	131	425	43	118	18	1	17	61	49	74	.278	.352	.445	.797	118	12	11	102	108	65	.746	0	0	0	6	*C	2.2
1965	Bos-A	111	368	20	79	10	3	6	35	40	69	.215	.292	.307	.599	65	-14	-17	107	111	32	.507	0	0	0	13	*C	0.3
1966	Bos-A	78	204	12	47	8	0	3	24	22	35	.230	.305	.314	.619	72	-5	-8	109	138	20	.531	0	0	0	0	C	-0.3
1967	Bos-A	30	64	4	12	1	0	1	4	3	18	.188	.224	.250	.474	35	-5	-6	115	88	3	.352	0	0	0	-1	C	-0.5
	NY-A	22	63	5	16	1	0	2	9	7	17	.254	.329	.365	.694	111	0	1	94	129	7	.612	0	0	0	3	C	0.5
	Yr	52	127	9	28	2	0	3	13	10	35	.220	.277	.307	.584	68	-4	-5	106	107	11	.485	0	0	0	2		0.0
1968	Atl-N	86	236	16	52	4	0	5	20	16	55	.220	.278	.301	.579	79	-7	-6	93	98	19	.474	1	0	0	-5	C	-0.8
1969	Atl-N	69	190	18	37	5	0	12	29	18	47	.195	.264	.411	.675	84	-4	-5	104	102	19	.604	0	0	0	-6	C	-0.6
1970	Atl-N	71	223	19	53	5	0	11	30	20	66	.238	.300	.408	.708	84	-5	-6	104	94	28	.645	0	0	0	-6	C	-0.8
Total	9	775	2329	189	540	68	10	79	282	228	510	.232	.302	.371	.673	85	-39	-49	104	106	258	.614	1	0	0	6	C	-0.3
■ **RUSTY TILLMAN**	Tillman, Kerry Jerome b: 8/29/60, Jacksonville, Fla. BR/TR, 6', 185 lbs. Deb: 6/06/82																											
1982	NY-N	12	13	4	2	1	0	0	0	0	4	.154	.154	.231	.385	6	-2	-2	99	0	1	.364	1	0	0	-1	/O	-0.1
1986	Oak-A	22	39	6	10	1	0	1	6	3	11	.256	.310	.359	.668	88	-1	-1	94	141	5	.655	2	0	1	-4	O	-0.3
1988	SF-N	4	4	1	1	0	0	1	3	2	1	.250	.500	1.000	1.500	342	1	1	94	171	2	2.000	0	0	0	-0	/O	0.1
Total	3	38	56	11	13	2	0	2	9	5	16	.232	.295	.375	.670	88	-1	-1	95	114	8	.674	3	0	1	-5	/O	-0.3
■ **RON TINGLEY**	Tingley, Ronald Irvin b: 5/27/59, Presque Isle, Maine BR/TR, 6'2", 160 lbs. Deb: 9/25/82																											
1982	SD-N	8	20	0	2	0	0	0	0	0	7	.100	.100	.100	.200	-48	-4	-4	92	0	0	.111	0	0	0	-0	/C	-0.3
1988	Cle-A	9	24	1	4	0	0	1	2	2	8	.167	.231	.292	.522	45	-2	-2	102	79	1	.429	0	0	0	1	/C	0.0
Total	2	17	44	1	6	0	0	1	2	2	15	.136	.174	.205	.378	6	-6	-5	97	45	2	.282	0	0	0	1	/C	-0.3
■ **JOE TINKER**	Tinker, Joseph Bert b: 7/27/1880, Muscotah, Kan. d: 7/27/48, Orlando, Fla. BR/TR, 5'9", 175 lbs. Deb: 4/17/02 MH																											
1902	Chi-N	131	494	55	129	19	5	2	54	26		.261	.298	.332	.630	100	-3	-1	96	116	58	.595	27			-1	*S/3	0.4
1903	Chi-N	124	460	67	134	21	7	2	70	37		.291	.344	.380	.724	114	5	8	95	127	71	.733	27			0	*S3	1.3
1904	Chi-N	141	488	55	108	12	13	3	41	29		.221	.265	.318	.583	81	-11	-12	101	93	53	.592	41			17	*S/O	0.5
1905	Chi-N	149	547	70	135	18	8	2	66	34		.247	.291	.320	.611	80	-11	-14	105	134	61	.583	31			16	*S	0.5
1906	Chi-N	148	523	75	122	18	4	1	64	43		.233	.292	.289	.580	78	-10	-14	107	**161**	54	.559	30			5	*S/3	-0.1
1907	Chi-N	117	402	36	89	11	3	1	36	25		.221	.267	.271	.538	66	-14	-17	106	124	35	.492	20			9	*S	-0.2
1908	Chi-N	157	548	67	146	22	14	6	68	32		.266	.307	.391	.697	117	13	9	106	115	72	.687	30			**32**	*S	4.5
1909	Chi-N	143	516	56	132	26	11	4	57	17		.256	.280	.372	.652	103	-2	-2	101	104	57	.604	23			17	*S	1.8
1910	Chi-N	134	473	48	136	25	9	3	69	24	35	.288	.322	.397	.719	109	3	3	101	125	66	.688	20			5	*S	1.4
1911	Chi-N	144	536	61	149	24	12	4	69	39	31	.278	.327	.390	.717	104	-2	1	97	112	77	.718	30			**22**	*S	2.8
1912	Chi-N	142	550	80	155	24	7	0	75	38	21	.282	.331	.351	.681	83	-11	-14	104	126	73	.653	25			26	*S	2.5
1913	Cin-N	110	382	47	121	20	13	1	57	20	26	.317	.352	.445	.797	125	12	11	102	122	61	.770	10			13	*SM	**3.1**
1914	Chi-F	126	438	50	112	21	7	2	46	38	30	.256	.315	.349	.664	99	-6	-1	91	107	58	.644	19			7	*SM	1.5
1915	Chi-F	31	67	7	18	2	1	0	9	13	5	.269	.387	.328	.716	116	2	2	97	147	10	.776	3			-1	S/23M	0.3
1916	Chi-N	7	10	0	1	0	0	0	1	1	1	.100	.182	.100	.282	-11	-1	-1	117	397	0	.222	0			0	/S3M	-0.1
Total	15	1804	6434	774	1687	263	114	31	782	416	149	.262	.307	.353	.660	96	-37	-41	101	121	810	.637	336			168	*S/32O	20.2
■ **JIM TIPPER**	Tipper, James b: 6/18/1849, Middletown, Conn. d: 4/19/1895, New Haven, Conn. Deb: 4/26/1872																											
1872	Man-n	24	110	23	29							.264															O/3	
1874	Har-n	45	196	36	60							.306															*O	
1875	NH-n	41	170	9	25							.147															O	
Total	3 n	110	476	68	114							.239															O	
■ **ERIC TIPTON**	Tipton, Eric Gordon "Dukie" or "Blue Devil" b: 4/20/15, Petersburg, Va. BR/TR, 5'11", 190 lbs. Deb: 6/09/39																											
1939	Phi-A	47	104	12	24	4	2	1	14	13	7	.231	.316	.337	.653	69	-5	-5	97	124	11	.595	2	0	1	-5	O	-0.9
1940	Phi-A	2	8	2	1	0	1	0	0	1	1	.125	.222	.375	.597	54	-1	-1	96	0	1	.571	0	0	0	-0	/O	0.0
1941	Phi-A	1	4	0	2	0	0	0	0	0	0	.500	.500	.500	1.000	164	0	0	101	0	1	1.000	0	0	0	0	/O	0.0
1942	Cin-N	63	207	22	46	5	5	4	18	25	14	.222	.309	.353	.662	92	-2	-2	101	80	22	.592	1			1	O	-0.2
1943	Cin-N	140	493	82	142	26	7	9	49	85	36	.288	.395	.424	.819	137	26	26	99	79	88	.825	1			-4	*O	1.9
1944	Cin-N	140	479	62	144	28	3	3	36	59	32	.301	.380	.390	.770	123	13	15	95	67	71	.717	5			0	*O	0.5
1945	Cin-N	108	331	32	80	17	1	5	34	40	37	.242	.327	.344	.671	92	-6	-3	94	91	40	.652	11			-2	O	-0.8
Total	7	501	1626	212	439	80	19	22	151	223	127	.270	.360	.383	.744	113	25	31	97	81	234	.732	20	0		-11	O	0.5
■ **JOE TIPTON**	Tipton, Joe Hicks b: 2/18/23, Mc Caysville, Ga. BR/TR, 5'11", 185 lbs. Deb: 5/02/48																											
1948	Cle-A	47	90	11	26	3	0	1	13	4	10	.289	.333	.356	.689	84	-2	-2	99	125	12	.594	0	0	0	1	C	0.1
1949	Chi-A	67	191	20	39	5	3	3	19	27	17	.204	.306	.309	.615	64	-11	-10	98	96	19	.557	1	1	-0	5	C	-0.2
1950	Phi-A	64	184	15	49	5	1	6	20	19	16	.266	.335	.402	.737	98	-4	-1	90	75	26	.674	0	0	0	1	C	0.2
1951	Phi-A	72	213	23	51	9	0	3	20	51	25	.239	.389	.324	.713	89	1	-1	106	92	32	.739	1	1	-0	6	C	0.9
1952	Phi-A	23	68	6	13	4	0	3	8	15	10	.191	.337	.382	.720	90	0	-1	111	85	10	.732	0	0	0	2	C	0.2
	Cle-A	43	105	15	26	2	0	6	22	21	21	.248	.383	.438	.821	141	5	6	91	128	19	.843	1	0	0	-1	C	0.7
	Yr	66	173	21	39	6	0	9	30	36	31	.225	.365	.416	.781	120	5	5	98	115	29	.804	1	0	0	1		0.9
1953	Cle-A	47	109	17	25	2	0	6	13	19	13	.229	.359	.413	.772	113	2	2	95	76	16	.736	0	0	0	-4	C	0.0
1954	Was-A	54	157	9	35	6	1	1	10	30	30	.223	.354	.293	.647	80	-3	-3	98	77	18	.619	0	1	-1	-1	C	-0.2
Total	7	417	1117	116	264	36	5	29	125	186	142	.236	.351	.355	.706	91	-13	-10	98	92	152	.695	3	3	-1	7	C	1.7
■ **TOM TISCHINSKI**	Tischinski, Thomas Arthur b: 7/12/44, Kansas City, Mo. BR/TR, 5'10", 190 lbs. Deb: 4/11/69																											
1969	Min-A	37	47	2	9	0	0	0	2	8	8	.191	.309	.191	.501	42	-3	-3	102	89	4	.447	0	0	0	-1	C	-0.2
1970	Min-A	24	46	6	9	0	0	1	2	9	6	.196	.327	.261	.588	65	-2	-2	98	54	4	.553	0	0	0	-1	C	-0.2
1971	Min-A	21	23	0	3	2	0	0	2	1	4	.130	.200	.217	.417	17	-3	-3	104	163	1	.318	0	0	0	-0	C	-0.1
Total	3	82	116	8	21	2	0	1	6	18	18	.181	.296	.224	.520	47	-8	-8	101	88	9	.464	0	0	0	-2	/C	-0.5
■ **JOHN TITUS**	Titus, John Franklin "Silent John" b: 2/21/1876, St.Clair, Pa. d: 1/8/43, St.Clair, Pa. BL/TL, 5'9", 156 lbs. Deb: 03																											
1903	Phi-N	72	280	38	80	15	6	2	34	19		.286	.331	.404	.735	120	3	6	92	97	40	.685	5			4	O	.5
1904	Phi-N	146	504	60	148	25	5	4	55	46		.294	.353	.387	.740	141	18	23	93	99	76	.719	15			11	*O	2.9
1905	Phi-N	147	548	99	169	36	14	2	89	69		.308	.386	.436	.822	141	33	30	104	121	99	.842	11			4	*O	2.4
1906	Phi-N	145	484	67	129	22	5	1	57	78		.267	.368	.339	.707	134	16	21	92	132	66	.715	12			11	*O	3.1
1907	Phi-N	145	523	72	144	23	12	3	62	47		.275	.335	.382	.717	122	15	13	104	119	72	.675	9			-8	*O	0.0
1908	Phi-N	149	539	75	154	24	5	2	48	53		.286	.350	.360	.710	129	18	18	100	89	75	.712	27			-14	*O	0.4
1909	Phi-N	151	540	69	146	22	6	3	46	66		.270	.367	.350	.717	116	18	14	106	81	76	.746	23			5	*O	1.4
1910	Phi-N	143	535	91	129	26	5	3	35	93	44	.241	.358	.325	.683	104	3	6	96	59	70	.717	20			-2	*O	0.0
1911	Phi-N	76	236	35	67	14	1	8	26	32	16	.284	.372	.453	.825	121	9	7	108	67	40	.846	3			-2	O	0.3
1912	Phi-N	45	157	43	43	9	5	3	22	33	14	.274	.403	.452	.855	133	8	8	100	98	31	.974	6			-10	O	-0.2
	Bos-N	96	345	56	112	23	6	2	48	49	20	.325	.422	.443	.865	128	20	16	107	108	67	.927	5			-9	O	0.4
	Yr	141	502	99	155	32	11	5	70	82	34	.309	.416	.446	.862	129	28	24	105	105	98	.942	11			-19		0.2
1913	Bos-N	87	269	33	80	14	2	5	38	35	22	.297	.392	.420	.812	139	12	14	95	108	45	.841	4			-11	O	0.2
Total	11	1402	4960	738	1401	253	72	38	560	620	116	.282	.367	.385	.752	127	174	175	100	99	757	.761	140			-21	*O	11.4
■ **JIM TOBIN**	Tobin, James Anthony "Abba Dabba" b: 12/27/12, Oakland, Cal. d: 5/19/69, Oakland, Cal. BR/TR, 6', 185 lbs. Deb: 4/30/37																											
1937	Pit-N	21	34	7	15	4	0	0	6	4	3	.441	.500	.559	1.059	183	4	4	102	114	9	1.095	0			-2	P	0.0
1938	Pit-N	56	103	8	25	6	1	0	11	9	12	.243	.310	.320	.630	73	-4	-4	100	120	11	.538	0			-2	P	0.0
1939	Pit-N	43	74	9	18	3	1	2	11	2	12	.243	.263	.392	.655	74	-3	-3	100	115	8	.554	0			-1	P	0.0
1940	Bos-N	20	43	5	12	3	0	0	3	1	10	.279	.295	.349	.644	78	-1	-1	99	74	4	.485	0			-1	P	0.0
1941	Bos-N	43	103	6	19	5	0	0	9	10	31	.184	.257	.233	.490	41	-8	-7	93	135	6	.398	1			4	P	0.0

YEAR	TM/L	G	AB	R	H	2B	3B	HR	RBI	BB	SO	AVG	OBP	SLG	PRO	/A	BR	/A	PF	CHI	RC	TA	SB	CS	SBR	FR	POS	TPR
1942	Bos-N	47	114	14	28	2	0	6	15	16	23	.246	.344	.421	.765	129	3	4	95	84	17	.852	10			6	P	0.0
1943	Bos-N	46	107	8	30	4	0	2	12	6	16	.280	.319	.374	.692	94	-0	-1	106	94	12	.575	0			2	P/1	0.0
1944	Bos-N	62	116	13	22	5	1	2	18	16	28	.190	.288	.302	.590	70	-5	-4	95	157	11	.526	0			7	P	0.0
1945	Bos-N	41	77	9	11	3	0	3	12	15	22	.143	.290	.299	.589	57	-4	-5	112	130	7	.574	0			2	P	0.0
	Det-A	17	25	2	3	0	0	2	5	1	5	.120	.154	.360	.514	45	-2	-2	106	121	1	.417	0	0	0	1	P	0.0
Total	9	396	796	81	183	35	3	17	102	80	162	.230	.303	.345	.648	82	-20	-20	100	117	85	.600	11	0		17	P/1	0.0
■ TIP TOBIN	Tobin, John Martin "Johnny" b: 9/15/06, Jamaica Plain, d: 8/6/83, Rhinebeck, N.Y. Mass. BR/TR, 6'3", 187 lbs. Deb: 9/22/32																											
1932	NY-N	1	1	0	0	0	0	0	0	0	0	.000	.000	.000	.000	-99	-0	-0	99	0	0	.000	0			0	H	0.0
■ JACKIE TOBIN	Tobin, John Patrick b: 1/8/21, Oakland, Cal. d: 1/18/82, Oakland, Cal. BL/TR, 6', 165 lbs. Deb: 4/20/45																											
1945	Bos-A	84	278	25	70	6	2	0	21	26	24	.252	.320	.288	.608	81	-8	-6	95	95	26	.500	2	6	-3	7	3/2O	0.0
■ JACK TOBIN	Tobin, John Thomas b: 5/4/1892, St.Louis, Mo. d: 12/10/69, St.Louis, Mo. BL/TL, 5'8", 142 lbs. Deb: 4/16/14 C																											
1914	StL-F	139	529	81	143	24	10	7	35	51	53	.270	.334	.393	.728	102	5	1	106	53	80	.723	20			2	*O	-0.3
1915	StL-F	158	625	92	**184**	26	13	6	51	68	42	.294	.364	.406	.770	122	22	18	105	58	109	.800	31			1	*O	1.2
1916	StL-A	77	150	16	32	4	1	0	10	12	13	.213	.272	.253	.525	61	-8	-7	95	94	13	.483	7			-11	O	-2.3
1918	StL-A	122	480	59	133	19	5	0	36	48	26	.277	.349	.338	.686	108	5	5	99	72	60	.657	13			2	*O	0.1
1919	StL-A	127	486	54	159	22	7	6	57	36	24	.327	.376	.438	.814	132	17	19	97	95	82	.792	8			1	*O	1.2
1920	StL-A	147	593	94	202	34	10	4	62	39	23	.341	.383	.452	.835	108	17	7	111	82	101	.817	21	13	-2	1	*O	-0.5
1921	StL-A	150	671	132	236	31	18	8	59	45	22	.352	.395	.487	.882	123	23	23	101	50	125	.855	7	12	-5	3	*O	0.7
1922	StL-A	146	625	122	207	34	8	13	66	56	22	.331	.388	.474	.862	117	21	16	106	61	113	.845	7	9	-3	-14	*O	-1.1
1923	StL-A	151	637	91	202	32	15	13	73	42	13	.317	.363	.476	.839	115	15	12	104	64	108	.808	8	7	-2	-11	*O	-1.4
1924	StL-A	136	569	87	170	30	8	2	48	50	12	.299	.357	.390	.748	87	-6	-12	107	60	79	.685	6	10	-4	-1	*O	-2.5
1925	StL-A	77	193	25	58	11	0	2	27	9	5	.301	.335	.389	.724	77	-5	-7	108	112	26	.679	8	2	1	-7	O/1	-1.5
1926	Was-A	27	33	5	7	0	1	0	3	0	0	.212	.212	.273	.485	26	-4	-4	98	113	2	.346	0	0	0	-1	/O	-0.5
	Bos-A	51	209	26	57	9	0	1	14	16	3	.273	.324	.330	.655	70	-9	-9	101	58	22	.580	6	5	-1	-5	O	-1.8
	Yr	78	242	31	64	9	1	1	17	16	3	.264	.310	.322	.632	65	-13	-13	100	79	24	.546	6	5	-1	-6		-2.3
1927	Bos-A	111	374	52	116	18	3	2	40	36	9	.310	.371	.390	.761	103	-1	2	95	88	54	.725	5	0	2	-8	O	-1.0
Total	13	1619	6174	936	1906	294	99	64	581	508	267	.309	.363	.420	.783	108	93	64	103	69	972	.755	147	58		-50	*O/1	-9.7
■ BILL TOBIN	Tobin, William F. b: 10/10/1854, Hartford, Conn. d: 10/10/12, Hartford, Conn. BL , Deb: 7/21/1880																											
1880	Wor-N	5	16	1	2	0	0	0	3	0	5	.125	.125	.125	.250	-13	-2	-2	113	548	0	.143				0	/1	-0.1
	Tro-N	33	136	14	22	1	1	0	8	4	20	.162	.186	.184	.370	23	-10	-12	110	124	5	.254				-1	1	-1.3
	Yr	38	152	15	24	1	1	0	11	4	25	.158	.179	.178	.357	19	-12	-14	111	194	5	.242				-1		-1.4
Total	1	38	152	15	24	1	1	0	11	4	25	.158	.179	.178	.357	19	-12	-14	111	167	5	.242				-1	/1	-1.4
■ AL TODD	Todd, Alfred Chester b: 1/7/02, Troy, N.Y. d: 3/8/85, Elmira, N.Y. BR/TR, 6'1", 198 lbs. Deb: 4/25/32																											
1932	Phi-N	33	70	8	16	5	0	0	9	1	9	.229	.260	.300	.560	45	-5	-6	112	159	6	.463	1			-1	C	-0.5
1933	Phi-N	73	136	13	28	4	0	0	10	4	18	.206	.239	.235	.475	31	-11	-14	118	117	8	.351	1			2	C/O	-1.1
1934	Phi-N	91	302	33	96	22	2	4	41	10	39	.318	.344	.444	.788	101	3	0	108	101	44	.693	3			7	C	0.9
1935	Phi-N	107	328	40	95	18	3	3	42	19	35	.290	.334	.390	.725	83	-3	-9	114	111	42	.632	3			2	C	-0.5
1936	Pit-N	76	267	28	73	10	5	2	28	11	24	.273	.307	.371	.678	84	-7	-6	98	94	31	.586	4			5	C	0.0
1937	Pit-N	133	514	51	158	18	10	8	86	16	36	.307	.330	.428	.758	102	1	-0	102	130	69	.642	2			7	*C	1.1
1938	Pit-N	133	491	52	130	19	7	7	75	18	31	.265	.296	.375	.671	83	-12	-12	100	132	48	.539	2			7	*C	0.0
1939	Bro-N	86	245	28	68	10	0	5	32	13	16	.278	.317	.380	.696	81	-5	-7	107	109	28	.584	1			2	C	-0.2
1940	Chi-N	104	381	31	97	13	2	6	42	11	29	.255	.283	.346	.629	73	-15	-15	100	104	36	.505	1			1	*C	-0.9
1941	Chi-N	6	6	1	1	0	0	0	0	0	1	.167	.167	.167	.333	-6	-1	-1	94	0	0	.200	0			0	H	0.0
1943	Chi-N	21	45	1	6	0	0	0	1	1	5	.133	.152	.133	.286	-17	-7	-7	99	60	1	.175	0			-2	C	-0.8
Total	11	863	2785	286	768	119	29	35	366	104	243	.276	.307	.377	.684	82	-62	-77	104	115	312	.591	18			29	C/O	-2.0
■ PHIL TODT	Todt, Philip Julius "Hook" b: 8/9/01, St.Louis, Mo. d: 11/15/73, St.Louis, Mo. BL/TL, 6', 175 lbs. Deb: 4/25/24																											
1924	Bos-A	52	103	17	27	8	2	1	14	6	9	.262	.309	.408	.717	81	-3	-4	104	103	13	.636	0	1	-1	-1	1/O	-0.5
1925	Bos-A	141	544	62	151	29	13	11	75	44	29	.278	.343	.439	.782	102	-4	-0	95	98	83	.749	3	2	-0	2	*1	-0.1
1926	Bos-A	154	599	56	153	19	12	7	69	40	38	.255	.306	.362	.669	73	-25	-26	101	104	68	.589	3	2	-0	10	*1	-2.1
1927	Bos-A	140	516	55	122	22	6	6	52	28	23	.236	.280	.337	.617	63	-33	-28	95	92	48	.536	6	0	2	9	*1	-2.3
1928	Bos-A	144	539	61	136	31	8	12	73	26	47	.252	.290	.406	.697	83	-17	-16	98	104	63	.623	6	5	-1	2	*1	-2.2
1929	Bos-A	153	534	49	140	38	10	4	64	31	28	.262	.305	.393	.698	77	-19	-20	102	101	63	.621	6	7	-2	3	*1	-3.9
1930	Bos-A	111	383	49	103	22	5	11	62	24	33	.269	.312	.439	.751	95	-9	-4	93	104	53	.698	4	1	1	2	*1	-1.2
1931	Phi-A	62	197	23	48	14	2	5	44	8	22	.244	.273	.411	.684	74	-8	-9	105	151	22	.600	1	1	-0	-2	1	-1.4
Total	8	957	3415	372	880	183	58	57	453	207	229	.258	.305	.395	.700	81	-117	-107	98	103	412	.630	29	19	-3	23	1/O	-13.7
■ BOBBY TOLAN	Tolan, Robert b: 11/19/45, Los Angeles, Cal. BL/TL, 5'11", 170 lbs. Deb: 9/03/65 C																											
1965	StL-N	17	69	8	13	2	0	0	6	0	4	.188	.200	.217	.417	16	-7	-8	107	176	3	.310	2	1	0	-0	O	-0.9
1966	StL-N	43	93	10	16	5	1	1	6	6	15	.172	.238	.280	.517	43	-7	-7	100	87	6	.438	1	2	-1	-2	O/1	-1.1
1967	StL-N	110	265	35	67	7	3	6	32	19	43	.253	.313	.370	.682	93	-2	-2	101	114	30	.630	12	7	-1	-5	O1	-1.2
1968	StL-N	92	278	28	64	12	1	5	17	13	42	.230	.272	.335	.607	85	-7	-5	95	66	23	.520	9	5	-0	-2	O/1	-1.2
1969	Cin-N	152	637	104	194	25	10	21	93	27	92	.305	.348	.474	.822	130	22	22	99	90	103	.797	26	12	1	-0	*O	1.5
1970	Cin-N	152	589	112	186	34	6	16	80	62	94	.316	.388	.475	.864	125	26	22	104	91	113	.942	**57**	20	5	2	*O	2.2
1972	Cin-N	149	604	88	171	28	5	8	82	44	88	.283	.338	.386	.724	113	4	9	93	126	78	.702	42	15	4	6	*O	1.2
1973	Cin-N	129	457	42	94	14	2	9	51	27	68	.206	.255	.304	.559	58	-29	-25	93	126	33	.479	15	10	-2	-1	*O	-3.5
1974	SD-N	95	357	45	95	16	1	8	40	20	41	.266	.321	.384	.705	103	-2	1	93	102	42	.627	7	9	-3	-1	O	-0.6
1975	SD-N	147	506	58	129	19	4	5	43	28	45	.255	.307	.338	.645	79	-15	-15	100	91	48	.543	11	13	-5	-3	*O1	-2.9
1976	Phi-N	110	272	32	71	7	0	5	35	7	39	.261	.290	.342	.632	73	-8	-10	107	125	25	.533	10	5	0	-8	1O	-2.3
1977	Phi-N	15	16	1	2	0	0	0	1	1	4	.125	.176	.125	.301	-17	-3	-3	100	200	0	.214	0	0	0	0	/1	-0.2
	Pit-N	49	74	7	15	4	0	2	9	4	10	.203	.244	.338	.581	53	-5	-5	103	116	6	.492	1	1	-0	-1	1/O	-0.7
	Yr	64	90	8	17	4	0	2	10	5	14	.189	.232	.300	.532	41	-8	-8	102	139	6	.440	1	1	-0	-1		-0.9
1979	SD-N	22	21	2	4	0	1	0	2	0	2	.190	.190	.286	.476	29	-2	-2	96	132	1	.316	0	0	0	-0	/1O	-0.2
Total	13	1282	4238	572	1121	173	34	86	497	258	587	.265	.317	.382	.699	96	-37	-29	98	105	511	.664	193	100	-2	-15	*O1	-9.9
■ WAYNE TOLLESON	Tolleson, Jimmy Wayne b: 11/22/59, Spartanburg, S.C. BB/TR, 5'9", 160 lbs. Deb: 9/01/81																											
1981	Tex-A	14	24	6	4	0	0	0	1	1	5	.167	.200	.167	.367	7	-3	-3	91	98	1	.350	2	0	1	2	/3S	0.0
1982	Tex-A	38	70	6	8	1	0	0	2	5	14	.114	.173	.129	.302	-17	-11	-10	93	89	2	.234	1	1	-0	0	S/32	-0.7
1983	Tex-A	134	470	64	122	13	2	3	20	40	68	.260	.320	.315	.635	75	-15	-15	101	51	51	.609	33	10	4	-2	*2S/D	-0.7
1984	Tex-A	118	338	35	72	9	2	0	9	27	47	.213	.277	.251	.529	47	-24	-24	100	42	25	.486	22	4	4	-16	*2/S3OD	-2.9
1985	Tex-A	123	323	45	101	9	5	1	18	21	46	.313	.355	.381	.735	94	1	-3	108	57	43	.688	21	12	-1	-3	S23/D	0.0
1986	Chi-A	81	260	39	65	7	3	3	29	38	43	.250	.346	.335	.680	87	-3	-4	101	123	33	.676	13	6	0	-4	3S/OD	-0.7
	NY-A	60	215	22	61	9	2	0	14	14	33	.284	.333	.344	.678	83	-4	-5	103	77	25	.584	4	4	-1	3	S/32	0.0
	Yr	141	475	61	126	16	5	3	43	52	76	.265	.340	.339	.679	85	-7	-8	102	104	59	.641	17	10	-1	-1		-0.7
1987	NY-A	121	349	48	77	4	0	1	22	43	72	.221	.306	.241	.547	50	-24	-23	98	101	29	.475	5	3	-0	-4	*S/3	-2.1
1988	NY-A	21	59	8	15	2	0	0	5	8	12	.254	.343	.288	.631	82	-1	-1	96	117	7	.578	1	0	0	1	2/3S	0.1
Total	8	710	2108	273	525	54	14	8	120	197	340	.249	.315	.299	.615	69	-84	-87	101	74	214	.577	102	40	7	-23	S23/DO	-7.0
■ TIM TOLMAN	Tolman, Timothy Lee b: 4/20/56, Santa Monica, Cal. BR/TR, 6', 190 lbs. Deb: 9/09/81																											
1981	Hou-N	4	8	0	1	0	0	0	0	0	0	.125	.125	.125	.250	-33	-1	-1	88	0	0	.143	0	0	0	-1	/O	-0.1
1982	Hou-N	15	26	4	5	2	0	1	3	4	3	.192	.300	.385	.685	91	-0	-0	99	90	3	.636	0	0	0	-1	/O1	0.0
1983	Hou-N	43	56	4	11	4	0	2	10	6	9	.196	.274	.375	.649	87	-2	-1	90	147	5	.574	0	1	-1	-1	/1O	-0.3
1984	Hou-N	14	17	2	3	1	0	0	0	0	3	.176	.176	.235	.412	16	-2	-2	93	0	1	.286	0	0	0	-0	/O1	-0.2
1985	Hou-N	31	43	4	6	1	0	2	8	1	10	.140	.178	.302	.480	33	-4	-4	96	168	2	.395	0	1	-1	-1	/O1	-0.6

YEAR	TM/L	G	AB	R	H	2B	3B	HR	RBI	BB	SO	AVG	OBP	SLG	PRO	/A	BR	/A	PF	CHI	RC	TA	SB	CS	SBR	FR	POS	TPR
1986	Det-A	16	34	4	6	1	0	0	2	6	4	.176	.300	.206	.506	44	-3	-2	95	114	3	.483	1	1	-0	0	/O1D	-0.2
1987	Det-A	9	12	3	1	1	0	0	1	7	2	.083	.450	.167	.617	77	0	0	97	200	2	.833	0	0	0	-1	/OD	0.0
Total	7	132	196	21	33	10	0	5	24	24	31	.168	.266	.296	.562	59	-12	-10	94	126	16	.509	1	3	-2	-5	/O1D	-1.4

■ CHICK TOLSON Tolson, Charles Julius "Toby" b: 11/6/1898, Washington, D.C. d: 4/16/65, Washington, D.C. BR/TR, 6', 185 lbs. Deb: 7/03/25

YEAR	TM/L	G	AB	R	H	2B	3B	HR	RBI	BB	SO	AVG	OBP	SLG	PRO	/A	BR	/A	PF	CHI	RC	TA	SB	CS	SBR	FR	POS	TPR
1925	Cle-A	3	12	0	3	0	0	0	0	2	1	.250	.357	.250	.607	53	-1	-1	106	0	1	.556	0	0	0	0	/1	0.0
1926	Chi-N	57	80	4	25	6	1	1	8	5	8	.313	.353	.450	.803	108	1	1	106	71	12	.745	0			-0	1	0.0
1927	Chi-N	39	54	6	16	4	0	2	17	4	9	.296	.345	.481	.826	119	1	1	100	186	9	.789	0			0	/1	0.1
1929	Chi-N	32	109	13	28	5	0	1	19	9	16	.257	.325	.330	.655	62	-6	-6	101	167	12	.580	0			-0	1	-0.7
1930	Chi-N	13	20	0	6	1	0	0	1	6	5	.300	.462	.350	.812	95	0	0	105	49	4	1.000	1			0	/1	0.0
Total	5	144	275	23	78	16	1	4	45	26	39	.284	.350	.393	.743	88	-4	-5	103	126	38	.695	1	0		-0	/1	-0.6

■ GEORGE TOMER Tomer, George Clarence b: 11/26/1895, Perry, Iowa d: 12/15/84, Perry, Iowa BL/TR, 6', 180 lbs. Deb: 9/17/13

YEAR	TM/L	G	AB	R	H	2B	3B	HR	RBI	BB	SO	AVG	OBP	SLG	PRO	/A	BR	/A	PF	CHI	RC	TA	SB	CS	SBR	FR	POS	TPR
1913	StL-A	1	1	0	0	0	0	0	0	0	1	.000	.000	.000	.000	-99	-0	-0	95	0	0	.000	0			0	H	0.0

■ PHIL TOMNEY Tomney, Philip Howard "Buster" b: 7/17/1863, Reading, Pa. d: 3/18/1892, Reading, Pa. BR/TR, 5'7", 155 lbs. Deb: 1888

YEAR	TM/L	G	AB	R	H	2B	3B	HR	RBI	BB	SO	AVG	OBP	SLG	PRO	/A	BR	/A	PF	CHI	RC	TA	SB	CS	SBR	FR	POS	TPR
1888	Lou-a	34	120	15	18	3	0	0	4	7		.150	.197	.175	.372	24	-10	-8	91	57	6	.382	11			0	S	-0.7
1889	Lou-a	112	376	61	80	8	5	4	38	46	47	.213	.304	.293	.596	75	-13	-10	96	91	42	.625	26			0	*S	-9.7
1890	Lou-a	108	386	72	107	21	7	1		43		.277	.357	.376	.733	111	9	5	107	0	63	.789	27			18	*S	2.5
Total	3	254	882	148	205	32	12	5	42	96	47	.232	.313	.313	.626	86	-14	-14	100	46	112	.656	64			18	S	-7.9

■ TONY TONNEMAN Tonneman, Charles Richard b: 9/10/1881, Chicago, Ill. d: 8/7/51, Prescott, Ariz. BR/TR, 5'10.5", 175 lbs. Deb: 9/19/11

YEAR	TM/L	G	AB	R	H	2B	3B	HR	RBI	BB	SO	AVG	OBP	SLG	PRO	/A	BR	/A	PF	CHI	RC	TA	SB	CS	SBR	FR	POS	TPR
1911	Bos-A	2	5	0	1	1	0	0	3	1		.200	.333	.400	.733	105	0	0	99	507	1	.750	0			0	/C	0.0

■ BERT TOOLEY Tooley, Albert R. b: 8/30/1886, Howell, Mich. d: 8/17/76, Marshall, Mich. BR/TR, 5'10", 155 lbs. Deb: 4/12/11

YEAR	TM/L	G	AB	R	H	2B	3B	HR	RBI	BB	SO	AVG	OBP	SLG	PRO	/A	BR	/A	PF	CHI	RC	TA	SB	CS	SBR	FR	POS	TPR
1911	Bro-N	119	433	55	89	11	3	1	29	53	63	.206	.295	.252	.547	55	-26	-24	97	93	37	.529	18			-6	*S	-2.6
1912	Bro-N	77	265	34	62	6	5	2	37	19	21	.234	.285	.317	.602	68	-14	-12	95	141	28	.567	12			-15	S	-1.9
Total	2	196	698	89	151	17	8	3	66	72	84	.216	.291	.277	.568	60	-40	-36	96	111	64	.543	30			-21	S	-4.5

■ SPECS TOPORCER Toporcer, George b: 2/9/1899, New York, N.Y. BL/TR, 5'10.5", 165 lbs. Deb: 4/13/21

YEAR	TM/L	G	AB	R	H	2B	3B	HR	RBI	BB	SO	AVG	OBP	SLG	PRO	/A	BR	/A	PF	CHI	RC	TA	SB	CS	SBR	FR	POS	TPR
1921	StL-N	22	53	4	14	1	0	0	2	3	4	.264	.304	.283	.587	59	-3	-3	95	49	5	.487	1	0	0	0	2/S	-0.1
1922	StL-N	116	352	56	114	25	6	3	36	24	18	.324	.370	.455	.825	110	6	5	101	74	60	.787	2	1	0	-6	S/32O	0.5
1923	StL-N	97	303	45	77	11	3	3	35	41	14	.254	.349	.340	.689	91	-7	-2	90	110	38	.659	4	3	-1	-11	2S/13	-0.9
1924	StL-N	70	198	30	62	10	3	1	24	11	14	.313	.362	.409	.771	103	2	1	103	104	29	.705	2	3	-1	-1	3S/2	0.3
1925	StL-N	83	268	38	76	13	4	2	26	36	15	.284	.373	.384	.757	92	-1	-2	102	85	41	.763	7	2	1	-3	S/2	0.1
1926	StL-N	64	88	13	22	3	2	0	9	8	9	.250	.327	.330	.656	75	-3	-3	102	107	10	.606	1			-3	2/S3	-0.3
1927	StL-N	86	290	37	72	13	4	0	19	27	16	.248	.314	.321	.635	66	-12	-15	107	71	30	.578	5			-7	3S/21	-1.5
1928	StL-N	8	14	0	0	0	0	0	0	0	3	.000	.000	.000	.000	-99	-4	-4	100	0	0	.000	0			0	/12	-0.3
Total	8	546	1566	223	437	76	22	9	151	150	93	.279	.347	.373	.720	89	-22	-23	100	87	212	.677	22	9		-30	S2/310	-2.2

■ JEFF TORBORG Torborg, Jeffrey Allen b: 11/26/41, Plainfield, N.J. BR/TR, 6'0.5", 195 lbs. Deb: 5/10/64 MC

YEAR	TM/L	G	AB	R	H	2B	3B	HR	RBI	BB	SO	AVG	OBP	SLG	PRO	/A	BR	/A	PF	CHI	RC	TA	SB	CS	SBR	FR	POS	TPR
1964	LA-N	28	43	4	10	1	1	0	4	3	8	.233	.298	.302	.600	76	-2	-1	92	126	4	.515	0	0	0	-1	C	-0.1
1965	LA-N	56	150	8	36	5	1	3	13	10	26	.240	.292	.347	.639	86	-4	-3	91	88	14	.529	0	0	0	-1	C	-0.1
1966	LA-N	46	120	4	27	3	0	1	13	10	23	.225	.285	.275	.560	58	-7	-6	97	152	9	.439	0	0	0	1	C	-0.4
1967	LA-N	76	196	11	42	4	1	2	12	13	31	.214	.267	.276	.542	63	-11	-9	88	83	13	.423	1	3	-2	-6	C	-1.2
1968	LA-N	37	93	2	15	2	0	0	4	6	10	.161	.212	.183	.395	21	-9	-8	91	99	4	.287	0	0	0	3	C	-0.4
1969	LA-N	51	124	7	23	4	0	0	7	9	17	.185	.241	.218	.458	30	-12	-11	99	104	7	.366	1	0	0	-2	C	-0.9
1970	LA-N	64	134	11	31	8	0	1	17	14	15	.231	.304	.313	.617	73	-6	-5	90	147	13	.538	1	1	-0	-9	C	-1.1
1971	Cal-A	55	123	6	25	5	0	0	5	3	6	.203	.222	.244	.466	32	-11	-11	99	68	6	.327	0	0	0	-6	C	-1.5
1972	Cal-A	59	153	5	32	3	0	0	8	14	21	.209	.280	.229	.509	59	-9	-7	88	96	9	.394	0	0	0	-11	C	-1.9
1973	Cal-A	102	255	20	56	7	0	1	18	21	32	.220	.279	.259	.538	54	-16	-15	96	102	18	.418	0	2	-1	-43	*C	-5.8
Total	10	574	1391	78	297	42	3	8	101	103	189	.214	.270	.265	.535	56	-87	-75	93	104	97	.433	3	6	-3	-75	C	-13.4

■ EARL TORGESON Torgeson, Clifford Earl "The Earl Of Snohomish" b: 1/1/24, Snohomish, Wash. BL/TL, 6'3", 180 lbs. Deb: 4/15/47

YEAR	TM/L	G	AB	R	H	2B	3B	HR	RBI	BB	SO	AVG	OBP	SLG	PRO	/A	BR	/A	PF	CHI	RC	TA	SB	CS	SBR	FR	POS	TPR
1947	Bos-N	128	399	73	112	20	6	16	78	82	59	.281	.403	.481	.885	138	22	23	97	120	83	.973	11			-1	*1	1.5
1948	Bos-N	134	438	70	111	23	5	10	67	81	54	.253	.372	.397	.770	107	7	6	102	123	71	.826	19			3	*1	0.8
1949	Bos-N	25	100	17	26	5	1	4	19	13	4	.260	.345	.450	.795	115	2	2	97	121	15	.805	4			0	1	0.2
1950	Bos-N	156	576	**120**	167	30	3	23	87	119	69	.290	.412	.472	.885	153	31	43	86	95	121	.971	15			-0	*1	3.5
1951	Bos-N	155	581	99	153	21	4	24	92	102	70	.263	.375	.437	.812	120	17	18	98	105	99	.827	20	11	-1	-1	*1	1.3
1952	Bos-N	122	382	49	88	17	0	5	34	81	38	.230	.366	.314	.681	95	-2	1	95	100	51	.689	11	7	-1	0	*1/O	-0.3
1953	Phi-N	111	379	58	104	25	8	11	64	53	57	.274	.366	.470	.836	117	9	10	99	121	70	.848	7	1	2	-2	*1	0.7
1954	Phi-N	135	490	63	133	22	6	5	54	75	52	.271	.368	.371	.740	95	-3	-2	99	114	71	.712	7	1	2	-12	*1	-1.6
1955	Phi-N	47	150	29	40	5	3	1	17	32	20	.267	.396	.360	.756	100	2	2	102	123	22	.746	2	3	-1	-0	1	-0.2
	Det-A	89	300	58	85	10	1	9	50	61	29	.283	.404	.413	.818	124	11	12	97	126	56	.878	9	0	**3**	-1	1	1.0
1956	Det-A	117	318	61	84	9	3	12	42	78	47	.264	.409	.425	.834	125	12	14	97	92	61	.901	6	4	-1	-3	1	0.7
1957	Det-A	30	50	5	12	2	1	1	5	12	10	.240	.387	.380	.767	103	1	1	107	90	8	.795	0	0	0	-1	1	0.0
	Chi-A	86	251	53	74	11	2	7	46	49	44	.295	.410	.438	.848	133	13	13	99	139	47	.883	7	3	0	-4	1/O	0.9
	Yr	116	301	58	86	13	3	8	51	61	54	.286	.406	.429	.835	127	14	14	101	127	56	.872	7	3	0	-4		0.9
1958	Chi-A	96	188	37	50	8	0	10	30	48	29	.266	.415	.468	.883	145	13	14	98	102	39	.973	7	2	1	-2	1	1.1
1959	Chi-A	127	277	40	61	5	3	9	45	62	55	.220	.363	.357	.720	102	1	3	97	141	39	.734	7	6	-2	-4	*1	-0.2
1960	Chi-A	68	57	12	15	2	0	2	9	21	8	.263	.462	.404	.865	134	4	4	101	122	13	1.071	1	0	0	-0	1	0.4
1961	Chi-A	20	15	1	1	0	0	0	1	3	5	.067	.222	.067	.289	-19	-3	-2	99	392	0	.267	0	0	0	0	/1	-0.2
	NY-A	22	18	3	2	0	0	0	0	8	3	.111	.385	.111	.496	41	-1	-1	96	0	1	.556	0	1	-1	0	/1	-0.1
	Yr	42	33	4	3	0	0	0	1	11	8	.091	.318	.091	.409	16	-4	-3	98	196	2	.438	0	1	-1	0		-0.3
Total	15	1668	4969	848	1318	215	46	149	740	980	653	.265	.387	.417	.804	119	139	162	97	114	870	.865	133	39		-28	*1/O	9.5

■ RED TORPHY Torphy, Walter Anthony b: 11/6/1891, Fall River, Mass. d: 2/11/80, Fall River, Mass. BR/TR, 5'11", 169 lbs. Deb: 9/25/20

YEAR	TM/L	G	AB	R	H	2B	3B	HR	RBI	BB	SO	AVG	OBP	SLG	PRO	/A	BR	/A	PF	CHI	RC	TA	SB	CS	SBR	FR	POS	TPR
1920	Bos-N	3	15	1	3	2	0	0	2	0	1	.200	.200	.333	.533	53	-1	-1	96	134	1	.417	0	0	0	0	/1	0.0

■ FRANK TORRE Torre, Frank Joseph b: 12/30/31, Brooklyn, N.Y. BL/TL, 6'4", 200 lbs. Deb: 4/20/56

YEAR	TM/L	G	AB	R	H	2B	3B	HR	RBI	BB	SO	AVG	OBP	SLG	PRO	/A	BR	/A	PF	CHI	RC	TA	SB	CS	SBR	FR	POS	TPR
1956	Mil-N	111	159	17	41	6	0	0	16	11	4	.258	.306	.296	.601	63	-8	-8	99	144	14	.480	1	0	0	0	1	-1.1
1957	Mil-N	129	364	46	99	19	5	5	40	29	19	.272	.341	.393	.734	107	-1	3	90	105	49	.658	0	0	0	-1	*1	-0.8
1958	Mil-N	138	372	41	115	22	5	6	55	42	14	.309	.390	.444	.833	134	12	17	89	124	63	.797	2	0	1	3	*1	1.3
1959	Mil-N	115	263	23	60	15	1	1	33	35	12	.228	.326	.304	.630	73	-11	-9	95	161	28	.567	0	0	0	4	1	-1.1
1960	Mil-N	21	44	2	9	1	0	0	5	3	2	.205	.255	.227	.483	37	-4	-3	91	203	3	.361	0	0	0	0	1	-0.3
1962	Phi-N	108	168	13	52	8	2	0	20	24	6	.310	.408	.381	.789	120	5	6	95	123	26	.744	1	1	-0	2	1	0.5
1963	Phi-N	92	112	8	28	7	2	1	10	11	7	.250	.333	.375	.708	101	1	0	103	93	15	.659	0	0	0	1	1	0.0
Total	7	714	1482	150	404	78	15	13	179	155	64	.273	.352	.372	.724	102	-7	7	93	128	197	.681	4	1	1	8	1	-1.5

■ JOE TORRE Torre, Joseph Paul b: 7/18/40, Brooklyn, N.Y. BR/TR, 6'2", 212 lbs. Deb: 9/25/60 M

YEAR	TM/L	G	AB	R	H	2B	3B	HR	RBI	BB	SO	AVG	OBP	SLG	PRO	/A	BR	/A	PF	CHI	RC	TA	SB	CS	SBR	FR	POS	TPR
1960	Mil-N	2	2	0	1	0	0	0	0	0	1	.500	.500	.500	1.000	193	0	0	91	0	1	1.000	0	0	0	0	H	0.0
1961	Mil-N	113	406	40	113	21	4	10	42	28	60	.278	.331	.424	.755	107	-1	3	92	85	54	.672	3	5	-2	17	*C	2.6
1962	Mil-N	80	220	23	62	8	1	5	26	24	24	.282	.358	.395	.753	103	1	1	99	100	31	.695	1	0	0	10	C	1.3
1963	Mil-N	142	501	57	147	19	4	14	71	42	79	.293	.354	.431	.785	124	16	16	101	118	71	.698	1	5	-3	-0	*C1/O	1.6
1964	Mil-N	154	601	87	193	36	5	20	109	36	67	.321	.366	.498	.864	145	31	34	97	132	99	.785	2	4	-2	-5	C1	2.8
1965	Mil-N	148	523	68	152	21	1	27	80	61	79	.291	.373	.489	.863	135	29	26	104	100	91	.825	0	1	-1	11	*C1	3.9
1966	Atl-N	148	546	83	172	20	3	36	101	60	61	.315	.385	.560	.945	161	43	44	99	105	112	.929	0	4	-2	12	*C1	5.6
1967	Atl-N	135	477	67	132	18	1	20	68	49	75	.277	.348	.444	.792	120	15	13	104	106	68	.721	2	2	-1	3	*C1	2.3
1968	Atl-N	115	424	45	115	11	2	10	55	34	72	.271	.333	.377	.710	121	7	10	93	124	51	.617	1	0	0	-7	C1	0.5
1969	StL-N	159	602	72	174	29	6	18	101	66	85	.289	.364	.447	.811	127	21	21	100	133	99	.776	0	0	0	1	*1C	1.3

YEAR	TM/L	G	AB	R	H	2B	3B	HR	RBI	BB	SO	AVG	OBP	SLG	PRO	/A	BR	/A	PF	CHI	RC	TA	SB	CS	SBR	FR	POS	TPR
1970	StL-N	161	624	89	203	27	9	21	100	70	91	.325	.399	.498	.898	131	35	30	106	110	120	.874	2	2	-1	-5	C3/1	2.6
1971	StL-N	161	634	97	**230**	34	8	24	**137**	63	70	**.363**	.424	.555	.979	174	62	**62**	101	139	**145**	1.000	4	1	1	-17	*3	4.8
1972	StL-N	149	544	71	157	26	6	11	81	54	64	.289	.361	.419	.781	115	16	12	105	135	80	.722	3	0	1	-15	*31	-0.4
1973	StL-N	141	519	67	149	17	2	13	69	65	78	.287	.377	.403	.780	128	13	20	91	118	78	.733	2	0	1	-10	*13	0.4
1974	StL-N	147	529	59	149	28	1	11	70	69	88	.282	.373	.401	.774	112	13	11	104	113	80	.730	1	2	-1	2	*13	0.6
1975	NY-N	114	361	33	89	16	3	6	35	35	55	.247	.317	.357	.674	91	-7	-5	95	92	36	.565	0	0	0	6	31	0.0
1976	NY-N	114	310	36	95	10	3	5	31	21	35	.306	.360	.406	.767	128	7	10	92	85	41	.654	1	3	-2	-1	1/3	0.4
1977	NY-N	26	51	2	9	3	0	1	9	2	10	.176	.208	.294	.502	34	-5	-5	96	200	2	.378	0	0	0	0	1/3M	-0.5
Total	18	2209	7874	996	2342	344	59	252	1185	779	1094	.297	.367	.452	.819	129	298	304	99	115	1258	.799	23	29	-11	2	C13/O	29.8
■ GIL TORRES	Torres, Don Gilberto (Nunez) b: 8/23/15, Regla, Cuba d: 1/11/83, Regla, Cuba BR/TR, 6', 155 lbs. Deb: 4/25/40																											
1940	Was-A	2	0	0	0	0	0	0	0	0	0	—	—	—	—	—	0	0	93	—	—	—	0	0	0	0	/P	0.0
1944	Was-A	134	524	42	140	20	6	0	58	21	24	.267	.297	.328	.625	88	-16	-9	90	124	47	.496	10	7	-1	4	*32/1	-0.7
1945	Was-A	147	562	39	133	12	5	0	48	21	29	.237	.264	.276	.540	61	-32	-28	93	114	40	.409	7	4	-0	-23	*S/3	-4.9
1946	Was-A	63	185	18	47	8	0	0	13	11	12	.254	.296	.297	.593	72	-8	-7	92	90	16	.473	3	2	-0	-5	S3/2P	-0.9
Total	4	346	1271	99	320	40	11	0	119	53	65	.252	.282	.301	.583	73	-56	-44	91	115	1361	.470	20	13	-2	-24	S3/2P1	-6.5
■ FELIX TORRES	Torres, Felix (Sanchez) b: 5/1/32, Ponce, P.R. BR/TR, 5'11", 165 lbs. Deb: 4/10/62																											
1962	LA-A	127	451	44	117	19	4	11	74	28	73	.259	.308	.392	.701	85	-9	-10	102	143	50	.592	0	0	0	-3	*3	-1.1
1963	LA-A	138	463	40	121	32	1	4	51	30	73	.261	.310	.361	.671	96	-8	-3	91	119	48	.555	1	0	0	-2	*3/1	-0.3
1964	LA-A	100	277	25	64	10	0	12	28	13	56	.231	.268	.397	.665	93	-8	-4	89	81	25	.548	1	3	-2	-4	3/1	-0.8
Total	3	365	1191	109	302	61	5	27	153	71	202	.254	.300	.381	.681	91	-24	-17	95	119	123	.592	2	3	-1	-9	3/1	-2.2
■ HECTOR TORRES	Torres, Hector Epitacio (Marroquin) b: 9/16/45, Monterrey, Mexico BR/TR, 6', 175 lbs. Deb: 4/10/68																											
1968	Hou-N	128	466	44	104	11	1	1	24	18	64	.223	.252	.258	.510	54	-27	-26	99	84	29	.373	2	3	-1	-5	*S/2	-1.9
1969	Hou-N	34	69	5	11	1	0	1	8	2	12	.159	.183	.217	.400	12	-8	-8	102	178	2	.279	0	0	0	-3	S	-0.8
1970	Hou-N	31	65	6	16	1	2	0	5	6	8	.246	.310	.323	.633	75	-3	-2	94	92	6	.529	0	0	0	-2	S/2	0.0
1971	Chi-N	31	58	4	13	3	0	0	2	4	10	.224	.274	.276	.550	51	-3	-4	110	51	4	.408	0	0	0	0	S/2	0.0
1972	Mon-N	83	181	14	28	4	1	2	7	13	26	.155	.215	.221	.436	24	-18	-19	102	62	8	.340	0	2	-1	1	2S/OP3	-1.3
1973	Hou-N	38	66	3	6	1	0	0	2	7	13	.091	.189	.106	.295	-17	-10	-10	95	115	1	.231	0	1	-1	-1	S2	-0.8
1975	SD-N	112	352	31	91	12	0	5	26	22	32	.259	.302	.335	.637	77	-12	-11	100	76	34	.522	2	3	-1	7	S32	0.4
1976	SD-N	74	215	8	42	6	0	4	15	16	31	.195	.254	.279	.533	58	-14	-11	89	80	14	.434	2	1	0	-3	S/32	-0.8
1977	Tor-A	91	266	33	64	7	3	5	26	16	33	.241	.286	.346	.632	70	-11	-12	103	96	24	.516	1	1	-0	-6	S2/3	-0.7
Total	9	622	1738	148	375	46	7	18	115	104	229	.216	.262	.281	.543	55	-106	-103	99	85	123	.436	7	11	-5	-12	S2/3OP	-5.9
■ RICARDO TORRES	Torres, Ricardo J. b: 1894, Cuba d: Havana, Cuba BR/TR, 5'11", 160 lbs. Deb: 5/18/20																											
1920	Was-A	16	30	8	10	1	0	0	3	1	4	.333	.355	.367	.722	96	-0	-0	95	96	4	.600	0	0	0	0	/1C	0.0
1921	Was-A	2	3	1	1	0	0	0	0	1	1	.333	.500	.333	.833	118	0	0	99	0	1	1.000	0	0	0	0	/C	0.0
1922	Was-A	4	4	0	0	0	0	0	0	0	1	.000	.000	.000	.000	-99	-1	-1	92	0	0	.000	0	0	0	0	/C	0.0
Total	3	22	37	9	11	1	0	0	3	2	6	.297	.333	.324	.658	78	-1	-1	95	76	4	.538	0	0	0	0	/C1	0.0
■ RUSTY TORRES	Torres, Rosendo (Hernandez) b: 9/30/48, Aquadilla, P.R. BB/TR, 5'10", 175 lbs. Deb: 9/20/71																											
1971	NY-A	9	26	5	10	3	0	2	3	0	8	.385	.385	.731	1.115	217	3	3	97	49	7	1.118	0	1	-1	0	/O	0.3
1972	NY-A	80	199	15	42	7	0	3	13	18	44	.211	.280	.291	.571	76	-7	-6	92	81	16	.472	0	4	-2	-7	O	-1.9
1973	Cle-A	122	312	31	64	8	1	7	28	50	62	.205	.321	.304	.625	79	-8	-7	97	95	32	.592	6	5	-1	-3	*O	-1.4
1974	Cle-A	108	150	19	28	2	0	3	12	13	24	.187	.252	.260	.512	47	-10	-10	101	98	10	.432	2	1	0	-17	O/D	-3.1
1976	Cal-A	120	264	37	54	16	3	6	27	36	39	.205	.300	.356	.656	100	-3	-0	92	93	29	.615	4	4	-1	-5	*O/3D	-0.8
1977	Cal-A	58	77	9	12	1	1	3	10	10	18	.156	.253	.312	.565	56	-5	-5	95	120	6	.500	0	1	-1	-10	O	-1.6
1978	Chi-A	16	44	7	14	3	0	3	6	6	7	.318	.400	.591	.991	174	4	4	101	68	10	1.032	0	1	-1	-1	O	0.2
1979	Chi-A	90	170	26	43	5	0	8	24	23	37	.253	.349	.424	.772	105	2	1	102	96	26	.740	0	0	0	-13	O	-1.3
1980	KC-A	51	72	10	12	0	0	0	3	8	7	.167	.250	.167	.417	17	-8	-8	98	97	3	.328	1	3	-2	-3	O/D	-1.2
Total	9	654	1314	159	279	45	5	35	126	164	246	.212	.303	.334	.637	84	-32	-27	97	93	139	.589	13	20	-8	-58	O/D3	-10.8
■ KELVIN TORVE	Torve, Kelvin Curtis b: 1/10/60, Rapid City, S.Dak. BL/TR, 6'3", 190 lbs. Deb: 6/25/88																											
1988	Min-A	12	16	1	3	0	0	1	2	1	2	.188	.235	.375	.610	64	-1	-1	106	88	1	.500	0	1	-1	0	/1	-0.1
■ CESAR TOVAR	Tovar, Cesar Leonardo "Pepito" (born Cesar Leonard Perez (Tovar)) b: 7/3/40, Caracas, Venez. BR/TR, 5'9", 155 lbs. Deb: 4/12/65																											
1965	Min-A	18	25	3	5	1	0	0	2	2	3	.200	.259	.240	.499	42	-2	-2	101	138	2	.500	2	0	1	-0	/23OS	0.0
1966	Min-A	134	465	57	121	19	5	2	41	44	50	.260	.329	.335	.665	82	-4	-10	111	108	54	.616	16	6	1	-6	2SO	-0.8
1967	Min-A	164	649	98	173	32	7	6	47	46	51	.267	.328	.365	.693	98	4	-1	107	68	80	.636	19	11	-1	3	O32/S	0.2
1968	Min-A	157	613	89	167	31	6	6	47	34	41	.272	.328	.372	.700	105	8	4	106	79	80	.681	35	13	3	4	O3S2/PC1	1.5
1969	Min-A	158	535	99	154	25	5	11	52	37	37	.288	.344	.415	.759	109	7	6	102	82	80	.783	45	12	6	5	*O23	1.7
1970	Min-A	161	650	120	195	**36**	**13**	10	54	52	47	.300	.359	.442	.801	122	17	18	98	61	103	.787	30	15	0	2	*O/23	1.4
1971	Min-A	157	657	94	**204**	29	3	1	45	45	39	.311	.357	.368	.726	102	5	2	104	65	87	.653	18	14	-3	2	*O/32	-0.3
1972	Min-A	141	548	86	145	20	6	2	31	39	39	.265	.329	.334	.663	91	-1	-5	107	73	63	.613	21	10	0	-8	*O	-1.8
1973	Phi-N	97	328	49	88	18	4	1	21	29	35	.268	.337	.357	.694	86	-3	-6	108	70	41	.636	6	4	-1	1	3O2	-0.6
1974	Tex-A	138	562	78	164	24	6	4	58	47	33	.292	.356	.377	.733	116	9	12	96	90	79	.685	13	9	-2	-2	*O/D	0.4
1975	Tex-A	102	427	53	110	16	0	3	28	27	25	.258	.306	.316	.623	76	-13	-13	100	72	40	.539	16	11	-2	-3	DO/2	-1.9
	Oak-A	19	26	5	6	1	0	0	3	3	3	.231	.310	.269	.580	70	-1	-1	93	165	3	.700	4	0	1	0	/23SD	0.0
	Yr	121	453	58	116	17	0	3	31	30	28	.256	.307	.313	.620	77	-15	-14	98	87	46	.560	20	11	-1	-3		-1.9
1976	Oak-A	29	45	1	8	0	0	0	4	4	4	.178	.275	.178	.452	34	-4	-3	100	192	2	.385	1	2	-1	-5	O/D	-1.0
	NY-A	13	39	2	6	1	0	0	2	4	3	.154	.250	.179	.429	27	-3	-3	99	110	2	.353	0	1	-1	0	D/2	-0.3
	Yr	42	84	3	14	1	0	0	6	8	7	.167	.263	.179	.442	31	-7	-7	100	171	4	.370	1	3	-2	-5		-1.3
Total	12	1488	5569	834	1546	253	55	46	435	413	410	.278	.337	.368	.705	99	19	-3	104	78	717	.672	226	108	3	-9	O32/DS1C	-1.5
■ BABE TOWNE	Towne, Jay King b: 3/12/1880, Coon Rapid, Iowa d: 10/29/38, Des Moines, Iowa BL/TR, 5'10", 180 lbs. Deb: 8/01/06																											
1906	Chi-A	14	36	3	10	0	0	0	6	7		.278	.395	.278	.673	124	1	1	92	218	4	.654	0			-1	C	0.2
■ GEORGE TOWNSEND	Townsend, George Hodgson "Sleepy" b: 6/4/1867, Hartsdale, N.Y. d: 3/15/30, New Haven, Conn. BR/TR, 5'7.5", 180 lbs. Deb: 6/25/1887																											
1887	Phi-a	31	109	12	21	3	0	0		3		.193	.214	.220	.434	23	-11	-11	99	0	7	.398	8			0	C/O	-0.8
1888	Phi-a	42	161	13	25	6	0	0	12	4		.155	.181	.193	.373	21	-14	-14	101	118	6	.279	2			-3	C	-1.1
1890	BB-a	18	67	6	16	4	1	0		4		.239	.282	.328	.610	82	-2	-2	100	0	7	.569	3			0	C	-0.1
1891	Bal-a	61	204	29	39	5	4	0	18	20	21	.191	.279	.255	.534	55	-11	-12	101	100	16	.485	3			-8	C/O	-1.4
Total	4	152	541	60	101	18	5	0	30	31	21	.187	.239	.238	.477	43	-38	-38	101	74	36	.414	16			-11	C/O	-3.4
■ JIM TOY	Toy, James Madison b: 2/20/1858, Beaver Falls, Pa. d: 3/13/19, Beaver Falls, Pa. 5'6", 160 lbs. Deb: 4/20/1887																											
1887	Cle-a	109	423	56	94	20	5	1		17		.222	.256	.300	.556	58	-25	-23	98	0	35	.468	8			2	1OC/3S	-1.8
1890	BB-a	44	160	11	29	3	0	0		11		.181	.238	.200	.438	31	-13	-14	100	0	8	.351	2			1	C	-0.6
Total	2	153	583	67	123	23	5	1	0	28		.211	.251	.273	.524	51	-39	-37	98	0	44	.435	10			2	/1CO3S	-2.4
■ JIM TRABER	Traber, James Joseph b: 12/26/61, Columbus, Ohio BL/TL, 6', 194 lbs. Deb: 9/21/84																											
1984	Bal-A	10	21	3	5	0	0	0	2	2	4	.238	.304	.238	.542	56	-1	-1	94	159	2	.412	0	0	0	0	/D	0.0
1986	Bal-A	65	212	28	54	7	0	13	44	18	31	.255	.328	.472	.799	117	4	5	99	126	32	.750	0	0	0	1	1D/O	0.3
1988	Bal-A	103	352	25	78	6	0	10	45	19	42	.222	.263	.324	.587	67	-18	-16	95	124	28	.475	1	2	-1	6	1DO	-1.3
Total	3	178	585	56	137	13	0	23	91	39	77	.234	.289	.374	.663	86	-15	-12	96	126	62	.579	1	2	-1	7	/1DO	-1.0
■ DICK TRACEWSKI	Tracewski, Richard Joseph b: 2/3/35, Eynon, Pa. BR/TR, 5'11", 160 lbs. Deb: 4/12/62 MC																											
1962	LA-N	15	2	3	0	0	0	0	0	2	0	.000	.500	.000	.500	51	0	0	93	0	0	1.000	0	0	0	0	/S	0.0
1963	LA-N	104	217	23	49	2	1	1	10	19	39	.226	.288	.258	.546	62	-11	-10	95	71	16	.443	2	3	-1	4	S2	0.2
1964	LA-N	106	304	31	75	13	4	1	26	31	61	.247	.316	.326	.642	88	-7	-4	92	105	33	.568	3	3	-1	-11	23S	-1.2

YEAR	TM/L	G	AB	R	H	2B	3B	HR	RBI	BB	SO	AVG	OBP	SLG	PRO	/A	BR	/A	PF	CHI	RC	TA	SB	CS	SBR	FR	POS	TPR
1965	LA-N	78	186	17	40	6	0	1	20	25	30	.215	.315	.263	.578	71	-8	-6	91	159	15	.503	2	6	-3	3	32/S	-0.7
1966	Det-A	81	124	15	24	1	1	0	7	10	32	.194	.254	.218	.471	36	-10	-10	102	109	7	.373	1	1	-0	-1	2/S	-0.5
1967	Det-A	74	107	19	30	4	2	1	9	8	20	.280	.330	.383	.714	111	1	1	99	85	14	.633	1	1	-0	0	S23	0.6
1968	Det-A	90	212	30	33	3	1	4	15	24	51	.156	.242	.236	.477	42	-14	-15	106	104	13	.418	3	0	1	-4	S32	-1.5
1969	Det-A	66	79	10	11	2	0	0	4	15	20	.139	.277	.165	.441	25	-7	-8	103	124	5	.437	3	0	1	-3	S2/3	-0.7
Total	8	614	1231	148	262	31	9	8	91	134	253	.213	.291	.272	.563	65	-56	-52	97	107	104	.493	15	14	-4	-12	S23	-3.8
■ **JIM TRACY**	Tracy, James Edwin b: 12/31/55, Hamilton, Ohio BL/TR, 6', 185 lbs. Deb: 7/20/80																											
1980	Chi-N	42	122	12	31	3	3	3	9	13	37	.254	.326	.402	.728	96	0	-1	106	61	16	.681	2	2	-1	-6	O/1	-0.8
1981	Chi-N	45	63	6	15	2	1	0	5	12	14	.238	.360	.302	.662	86	-0	-1	104	103	8	.640	1	0	0	-2	O	-0.2
Total	2	87	185	18	46	5	4	3	14	25	51	.249	.338	.368	.706	93	-0	-1	105	76	24	.671	3	2	-0	-8	/O1	-1.0
■ **JOHN TRAFFLEY**	Traffley, John b: 1862, Chicago, Ill. d: 7/13/1900, Baltimore, Md. 5'9", 180 lbs. Deb: 6/15/1889																											
1889	Lou-a	1	2	0	1	0	0	0	0	0	0	.500	.500	.500	1.000	197	0	0	96	0	1	1.000	0			0	/O	0.0
■ **BILL TRAFFLEY**	Traffley, William F. b: 12/21/1859, Staten Island, N.Y d: 6/24/08, Denver, Colo. BR/TR, 5'11.5", 185 lbs. Deb: 7/27/1878																											
1878	Chi-N	2	9	1	1	0	0	0	1	0	1	.111	.111	.111	.222	-25	-1	-1	108	359	0	.125				0	/C	0.0
1883	Cin-a	30	105	17	21	5	0	0		4		.200	.229	.248	.477	52	-5	-6	103	0	6	.357				-4	C/S	-0.6
1884	Bal-a	53	210	25	37	4	6	0		3		.176	.192	.252	.444	46	-12	-12	99	0	10	.329				-11	C/O1	-1.7
1885	Bal-a	69	254	27	39	4	5	1		17		.154	.215	.220	.436	38	-17	-19	106	0	12	.353				13	CO/2	0.2
1886	Bal-a	25	85	15	18	0	1	0		10		.212	.295	.235	.530	76	-3	-1	91	0	8	.567	8			0	C	0.0
Total	5	179	663	85	116	13	12	1	1	34	1	.175	.220	.235	.455	46	-38	-39	101	5	37	.369	8			-2	C/O2S1	-2.1
■ **WALT TRAGESSER**	Tragesser, Walter Joseph b: 6/14/1887, Lafayette, Ind. d: 12/14/70, Lafayette, Ind. BR/TR, 6', 175 lbs. Deb: 7/30/13																											
1913	Bos-N	2	0	0	0	0	0	0	0	0	0	—	—	—	—	—	0	0	95	—	—	—	0			0	/C	0.0
1915	Bos-N	7	7	1	0	0	0	0	0	0	2	.000	.000	.000	.000	-99	-2	-2	98	0	0	.000	0			0	/C	-0.1
1916	Bos-N	41	54	3	11	1	0	0	4	5	10	.204	.283	.222	.506	61	-3	-2	93	132	4	.419	0			-1	C	-0.1
1917	Bos-N	98	297	23	66	10	2	0	25	15	36	.222	.264	.269	.534	66	-13	-12	96	120	22	.442	5			5	C	-0.1
1918	Bos-N	7	1	0	0	0	0	0	0	0	0	.000	.000	.000	.000	-99	-0	-0	94	0	0	.000	0			0	/C	0.0
1919	Bos-N	20	40	3	7	2	0	0	3	2	10	.175	.233	.225	.458	39	-3	-3	98	130	2	.394	1			1	C	-0.1
	Phi-N	35	114	7	27	7	0	0	8	9	31	.237	.298	.298	.597	77	-3	-3	104	91	10	.552	4			2	C	0.1
	Yr	55	154	10	34	9	0	0	11	11	41	.221	.281	.279	.561	68	-6	-6	102	108	13	.508	5			2		0.0
1920	Phi-N	62	176	17	37	11	1	6	26	4	36	.210	.236	.386	.623	71	-6	-8	109	117	16	.561	4	0	1	1	C	-0.1
Total	7	272	689	54	148	31	3	6	66	35	125	.215	.260	.295	.555	66	-29	-30	100	115	92	.479	14	0		8	C	-0.4
■ **RED TRAMBACK**	Tramback, Stephen Joseph b: 11/1/15, Iselin, Pa. d: 12/28/79, Buffalo, N.Y. BL/TL, 6', 175 lbs. Deb: 9/15/40																											
1940	NY-N	2	4	0	1	0	0	0	0	1	1	.250	.400	.250	.650	83	-0	-0	100	0	1	1.000	1			-0	/O	0.0
■ **ALAN TRAMMELL**	Trammell, Alan Stuart b: 2/21/58, Garden Grove, Cal. BR/TR, 6', 165 lbs. Deb: 9/09/77																											
1977	Det-A	19	43	6	8	0	0	0	0	4	12	.186	.255	.186	.441	22	-5	-5	105	0	2	.333	0	0	0	0	S	-0.1
1978	Det-A	139	448	49	120	14	6	2	34	45	56	.268	.337	.339	.677	84	-5	-9	108	85	52	.592	3	1	0	-0	*S	0.2
1979	Det-A	142	460	68	127	11	4	6	50	43	55	.276	.338	.357	.694	91	-7	-5	96	106	56	.635	17	14	-3	-9	*S	0.0
1980	Det-A	146	560	107	168	21	5	9	65	69	63	.300	.380	.404	.783	109	14	9	105	106	87	.749	12	12	-4	-22	*S	-0.4
1981	Det-A	105	392	52	101	15	3	2	31	49	31	.258	.345	.327	.671	90	-1	-4	105	87	47	.625	10	3	1	11	*S	1.6
1982	Det-A	157	489	66	126	34	3	9	57	52	47	.258	.329	.395	.724	97	-1	-2	100	104	67	.702	19	8	1	-3	*S	1.0
1983	Det-A	142	505	83	161	31	2	14	66	57	64	.319	.388	.471	.859	141	25	28	96	94	96	.900	30	10	3	-10	*S	2.9
1984	Det-A	139	555	85	174	34	5	14	69	60	63	.314	.383	.468	.852	140	27	30	96	88	100	.851	19	13	-2	-2	*SD	3.4
1985	Det-A	149	605	79	156	21	7	13	57	50	71	.258	.317	.380	.697	84	-9	-14	106	74	76	.643	14	5	1	-15	*S	-1.6
1986	Det-A	151	574	107	159	33	7	21	75	59	57	.277	.350	.469	.818	127	17	20	95	95	95	.825	25	12	0	8	*S/D	3.5
1987	Det-A	151	597	109	205	34	3	28	105	60	47	.343	.406	.551	.957	156	45	47	97	108	137	1.020	21	2	5	-4	*S	5.1
1988	Det-A	128	466	73	145	24	1	15	69	46	46	.311	.378	.464	.841	142	22	25	94	107	79	.805	7	4	-0	-10	*S	2.1
Total	12	1568	5694	884	1650	272	46	133	678	594	612	.290	.359	.424	.783	115	121	122	100	95	894	.775	177	84	3	-56	*S/D	17.7
■ **CECIL TRAVIS**	Travis, Cecil Howell b: 8/8/13, Riverdale, Ga. BL/TR, 6'1.5", 185 lbs. Deb: 5/16/33																											
1933	Was-A	18	43	7	13	1	0	0	2	2	5	.302	.348	.326	.673	83	-1	-1	96	48	5	.567	0	0	0	-0	3	0.0
1934	Was-A	109	392	48	125	22	4	1	53	24	37	.319	.361	.403	.764	96	-2	-3	101	110	56	.680	1	5	-3	10	3	0.4
1935	Was-A	138	534	85	170	27	8	0	61	41	28	.318	.377	.399	.776	110	2	8	92	99	82	.730	4	2	0	21	*3O	2.7
1936	Was-A	138	517	77	164	34	10	2	92	39	21	.317	.366	.433	.800	99	-3	-1	98	132	82	.751	4	4	-1	-6	SO/23	-0.4
1937	Was-A	135	526	72	181	27	7	3	66	39	34	.344	.395	.439	.834	116	9	13	94	96	92	.801	3	2	-0	-5	*S	1.3
1938	Was-A	146	567	96	190	30	5	5	67	58	22	.335	.401	.432	.833	114	9	14	95	92	100	.819	6	5	-1	3	*S	2.1
1939	Was-A	130	476	55	139	20	9	5	63	34	25	.292	.342	.403	.745	100	-8	-1	90	105	65	.653	0	3	-2	-3	*S	0.5
1940	Was-A	136	528	60	170	37	11	2	76	48	23	.322	.381	.445	.826	122	11	16	93	121	94	.783	0	1	-1	8	*3S	3.0
1941	Was-A	152	608	106	**218**	39	19	7	101	52	25	.359	.410	.520	.930	148	38	40	98	112	131	.916	2	2	-1	-4	*S3	3.8
1945	Was-A	15	54	4	13	2	1	0	10	4	5	.241	.293	.315	.608	82	-2	-1	93	217	4	.467	0	1	-1	-1	3	-0.1
1946	Was-A	137	465	45	117	22	3	1	56	45	47	.252	.323	.318	.641	86	-12	-8	92	141	47	.539	2	4	-2	-12	S3	-1.6
1947	Was-A	74	204	10	44	4	1	1	10	16	19	.216	.273	.260	.533	50	-14	-13	97	66	14	.419	1	3	-2	-2	3S	-1.6
Total	12	1328	4914	665	1544	265	78	27	657	402	291	.314	.370	.416	.786	109	26	63	95	110	772	.735	23	32	-12	9	S3/O2	10.1
■ **JIM TRAY**	Tray, James b: 2/14/1860, Jackson, Mich. d: 7/28/05, Jackson, Mich. 5'8", 144 lbs. Deb: 9/06/1884																											
1884	Ind-a	6	21	2	6	0	0	0		2		.286	.348	.286	.634	116	0	0	96	0	2	.533				0	/C1	0.0
■ **PIE TRAYNOR**	Traynor, Harold Joseph b: 11/11/1899, Framingham, Mass. d: 3/16/72, Pittsburgh, Pa. BR/TR, 6', 170 lbs. Deb: 9/15/20 MH																											
1920	Pit-N	17	52	6	11	3	1	0	2	3	6	.212	.268	.308	.576	64	-2	-2	101	48	4	.477	1	3	-2	-4	S	-0.7
1921	Pit-N	7	19	0	5	0	0	0	2	1	2	.263	.300	.263	.563	49	-1	-1	103	147	2	.429	0	0	0	-0	/3S	-0.1
1922	Pit-N	142	571	89	161	17	12	4	81	27	28	.282	.319	.375	.694	76	-19	-22	104	133	70	.634	17	3	3	-10	*3S	-1.6
1923	Pit-N	153	616	108	208	19	**19**	12	101	34	19	.338	.377	.489	.866	131	22	25	97	112	112	.874	28	13	1	9	*3/S	3.6
1924	Pit-N	142	545	86	160	26	13	5	82	37	26	.294	.340	.417	.756	96	1	-4	106	131	74	.717	24	18	-4	8	*3	1.0
1925	Pit-N	150	591	114	189	39	14	6	106	52	19	.320	.377	.464	.840	111	12	10	102	137	103	.835	15	9	-1	21	*3/S	3.7
1926	Pit-N	152	574	83	182	25	17	3	92	38	14	.317	.361	.436	.796	101	10	0	112	130	88	.758	8			4	*3/S	0.7
1927	Pit-N	149	573	93	196	32	9	5	106	22	11	.342	.370	.455	.825	118	15	13	102	142	92	.788	11			11	*3/S	3.2
1928	Pit-N	144	569	91	192	38	12	3	124	28	10	.337	.370	.462	.832	109	12	7	107	**172**	93	.806	12			2	*3	1.1
1929	Pit-N	130	540	94	192	27	12	4	108	30	7	.356	.393	.472	.865	109	11	8	103	133	96	.865	13			-3	*3	1.4
1930	Pit-N	130	497	90	182	22	11	9	119	48	19	.366	.423	.509	.932	128	21	23	97	**155**	104	.981	7			7	*3	2.8
1931	Pit-N	155	615	81	183	37	15	2	103	54	28	.298	.354	.416	.771	106	6	5	101	148	93	.731	6			-9	*3	0.6
1932	Pit-N	135	513	74	169	27	10	2	68	32	20	.329	.373	.433	.806	117	12	12	99	113	84	.767	6			-1	*3	2.2
1933	Pit-N	154	624	85	190	27	6	1	82	35	24	.304	.342	.372	.714	110	3	7	95	**139**	80	.609	5			-0	*3	1.1
1934	Pit-N	119	444	62	137	22	10	1	61	21	27	.309	.341	.410	.751	95	-0	-3	105	121	56	.627	3			-9	*3M	-0.2
1935	Pit-N	57	204	24	57	10	3	1	36	10	17	.279	.323	.373	.695	81	-4	-6	107	164	23	.583	2			0	3/1M	-0.3
1937	Pit-N	5	12	3	2	0	0	0	0	0	1	.167	.167	.167	.333	-9	-2	-2	102	0	0	.182	0			0	/3M	-0.1
Total	17	1941	7559	1183	2416	371	164	58	1273	472	278	.320	.362	.435	.797	107	96	71	102	136	1174	.761	158	46		25	*3/S1	18.4
■ **FRED TREACEY**	Treacey, Frederick S. b: 1847, Brooklyn, N.Y. 5'9.5", 145 lbs. Deb: 5/16/1871																											
1871	Chi-n	25	125	39	43							.344															*O	
1872	Ath-n	46	242	53	62							.256															*O	
1873	Phi-n	51	246	49	62							.252															*O	
1874	Chi-n	35	160	18	28							.175															O	
1875	Cen-n	11	48	9	13							.271															O	
	Phi-n	42	179	19	37							.207															O	
	Yr	53	227	28	50							.220																

YEAR	TM/L	G	AB	R	H	2B	3B	HR	RBI	BB	SO	AVG	OBP	SLG	PRO	/A	BR	/A	PF	CHI	RC	TA	SB	CS	SBR	FR	POS	TPR
1876	NY-N	57	256	47	54	5	1	0	18	1	5	.211	.214	.238	.452	58	-13	-8	87	88	13	.307				12	*O	0.3
Total	5 n	210	1000	187	245							.245															*O	
■ **PETE TREACEY** Treacey, Peter b: 1852, Brooklyn, N.Y. Deb: 8/05/1876																												
1876	NY-N	2	5	1	0	0	0	0	0	1	0	.000	.167	.000	.167	-46	-1	-1	87	0	0	.200				0	/S	0.0
■ **RAY TREADAWAY** Treadaway, Edgar Raymond b: 10/31/07, Ragland, Ala. d: 10/12/35, Chattanooga, Tenn. BL/TR, 5'7", 150 lbs. Deb: 9/17/30																												
1930	Was-A	6	19	1	4	2	0	0	1	0	3	.211	.211	.316	.526	31	-2	-2	101	55	1	.400	0	0	0	0	/3	-0.1
■ **GEORGE TREADWAY** Treadway, George B. b: 11/11/1866, Greenup Co., Ky. d: 11/17/28, Riverside, Cal. BL , Deb: 4/27/1893																												
1893	Bal-N	115	458	78	119	16	17	1	67	57	50	.260	.347	.376	.722	88	-4	-10	107	111	70	.758	24			7	*O	-0.5
1894	Bro-N	123	479	124	157	27	26	4	102	72	43	.328	.418	.518	.935	134	21	27	94	115	118	1.084	27			-2	*O/1	1.3
1895	Bro-N	86	339	54	87	14	3	7	54	33	22	.257	.326	.378	.704	88	-9	-5	94	107	46	.683	9			-10	O	-1.8
1896	Lou-N	2	7	0	1	0	0	0	1	1	0	.143	.250	.143	.393	6	-1	-1	98	294	0	.333	0			0	/O1	0.0
Total	4	326	1283	256	364	57	46	12	224	163	115	.284	.368	.428	.796	105	7	11	99	112	233	.849	60			-4	O/1	-1.0
■ **JEFF TREADWAY** Treadway, Hugh Jeffrey b: 1/22/63, Columbus, Ga. BL/TR, 6' ", 175 lbs. Deb: 9/04/87																												
1987	Cin-N	23	84	9	28	4	0	2	4	2	6	.333	.356	.452	.809	109	1	1	104	37	14	.737	1	0	0	-0	2	0.1
1988	Cin-N	103	301	30	76	19	4	2	23	27	30	.252	.320	.362	.682	91	-2	-4	105	80	36	.616	2	0	1	0	2/3	0.0
Total	2	126	385	39	104	23	4	4	27	29	36	.270	.328	.382	.710	95	-0	-3	105	71	50	.642	3	0	1	-0	2/3	0.1
■ **RED TREADWAY** Treadway, Thadford Leon b: 4/28/20, Athalone, N.C. BL/TR, 5'10", 175 lbs. Deb: 7/25/44																												
1944	NY-N	50	170	23	51	5	2	0	5	13	11	.300	.350	.353	.703	95	-0	-1	104	30	22	.620	2			0	O	-0.3
1945	NY-N	88	224	31	54	4	2	4	23	20	13	.241	.303	.330	.634	76	-7	-7	100	93	24	.571	3			-8	O	-1.7
Total	2	138	394	54	105	9	4	4	28	33	24	.266	.323	.340	.663	84	-8	-8	101	66	46	.595	5			-8	/O	-2.0
■ **FRANK TRECHOCK** Trechock, Frank Adam b: 12/24/15, Windber, Pa. BR/TR, 5'10", 175 lbs. Deb: 9/19/37																												
1937	Was-A	1	4	0	2	0	0	0	0	0	1	.500	.500	.500	1.000	162	0	0	94	0	1	1.000	0	0	0	0	/S	0.0
■ **NICK TREMARK** Tremark, Nicholas Joseph b: 10/15/12, Yonkers, N.Y. BL/TL, 5'5", 150 lbs. Deb: 8/09/34																												
1934	Bro-N	17	28	3	7	1	0	0	6	2	2	.250	.300	.286	.586	61	-2	-1	95	270	2	.455	0			-1	/O	-0.2
1935	Bro-N	10	13	1	3	1	0	0	3	1	1	.231	.286	.308	.593	63	-1	-1	94	271	1	.500	0			-1	/O	-0.1
1936	Bro-N	8	32	6	8	2	0	0	1	3	2	.250	.333	.313	.646	71	-1	-1	105	34	3	.560	0			1	/O	0.0
Total	3	35	73	10	18	4	0	0	10	6	5	.247	.313	.301	.614	66	-3	-3	99	164	7	.518	0			-1	/O	-0.3
■ **OVERTON TREMPER** Tremper, Carlton Overton b: 3/22/06, Brooklyn, N.Y. BR/TR, 5'10", 163 lbs. Deb: 6/16/27																												
1927	Bro-N	26	60	4	14	0	0	0	4	0	2	.233	.246	.233	.479	28	-6	-6	103	100	3	.326	0			-5	O	-1.1
1928	Bro-N	10	31	1	6	2	1	0	1	0	1	.194	.194	.323	.516	33	-3	-3	99	36	2	.400	0			-1	/O	-0.3
Total	2	36	91	5	20	2	1	0	5	0	3	.220	.228	.264	.492	30	-9	-9	101	78	5	.352	0			-6	/O	-1.4
■ **GEORGE TRENWITH** Trenwith, George b: Philadelphia, Pa. d: 2/1/1890, Philadelphia, Pa. Deb: 4/30/1875																												
1875	Cen-n	10	46	5	8							.174															3	
	NH-n	6	25	1	5							.200															/3	
	Yr	16	71	6	13							.183																
■ **MIKE TRESH** Tresh, Michael b: 2/23/14, Hazleton, Pa. d: 10/4/66, Detroit, Mich. BR/TR, 5'11", 170 lbs. Deb: 9/04/38																												
1938	Chi-A	10	29	3	7	2	0	0	2	8	4	.241	.405	.310	.716	84	-0	-0	98	75	4	.773	0	0	0	0	C	0.0
1939	Chi-A	119	352	49	91	5	2	0	38	64	30	.259	.377	.284	.661	67	-12	-16	107	128	43	.627	3	2	-0	-8	*C	-1.4
1940	Chi-A	135	480	62	135	15	5	1	64	49	40	.281	.349	.340	.689	76	-13	-16	104	**142**	56	.589	3	10	-5	5	*C	-0.5
1941	Chi-A	115	390	38	98	10	1	0	33	38	27	.251	.319	.282	.601	64	-21	-18	94	106	36	.492	1	0	0	7	*C	-0.3
1942	Chi-A	72	233	21	54	8	1	0	15	28	24	.232	.314	.275	.589	67	-10	-9	99	83	22	.508	2	0	1	1	C	0.0
1943	Chi-A	86	279	20	60	3	0	0	20	37	20	.215	.307	.226	.533	56	-14	-14	101	116	22	.449	2	1	0	2	C	-0.8
1944	Chi-A	93	312	22	81	8	1	0	25	37	15	.260	.342	.292	.634	82	-6	-6	100	101	32	.535	0	3	-2	1	C	0.0
1945	Chi-A	150	458	50	114	12	0	0	47	65	37	.249	.342	.275	.617	84	-9	-6	95	135	48	.553	6	3	0	0	*C	0.5
1946	Chi-A	80	217	28	47	5	2	0	21	36	24	.217	.336	.258	.594	70	-8	-7	97	143	21	.537	0	2	-1	7	C	0.2
1947	Chi-A	90	274	19	66	6	2	0	20	26	26	.241	.309	.277	.586	66	-13	-12	97	97	24	.484	2	0	1	-2	C	-0.5
1948	Chi-A	39	108	10	27	1	0	1	11	9	9	.250	.308	.287	.595	61	-6	-6	95	109	10	.488	0	0	0	2	C	0.0
1949	Cle-A	38	37	4	8	0	0	0	1	5	7	.216	.310	.216	.526	41	-3	-3	98	43	3	.448	0	0	0	-1	C	-0.1
Total	12	1027	3169	326	788	75	14	2	297	402	263	.249	.335	.283	.618	71	-116	-113	99	118	322	.553	19	21	-7	14	*C	-2.9
■ **TOM TRESH** Tresh, Thomas Michael b: 9/20/37, Detroit, Mich. BB/TR, 6'1", 180 lbs. Deb: 9/03/61																												
1961	NY-A	9	8	1	2	0	0	0	0	0	1	.250	.250	.250	.500	35	-1	-1	96	0	0	.286	0	0	0	0	/S	0.0
1962	NY-A	157	622	94	178	26	5	20	93	67	74	.286	.363	.441	.803	123	14	19	94	106	103	.776	4	8	-4	-6	*SO	1.5
1963	NY-A	145	520	91	140	28	5	25	71	83	79	.269	.374	.487	.861	138	29	28	101	96	100	.886	3	3	-1	-8	*O	1.5
1964	NY-A	153	533	75	131	25	5	16	73	73	110	.246	.344	.402	.746	103	6	4	103	120	78	.742	13	0	4	1	*O	0.3
1965	NY-A	156	602	94	168	29	6	26	74	59	92	.279	.348	.477	.825	131	24	24	101	81	101	.798	5	2	0	6	*O	2.5
1966	NY-A	151	537	76	125	12	4	27	68	86	89	.233	.345	.421	.766	127	15	19	94	99	81	.758	5	4	-1	15	O3	3.0
1967	NY-A	130	448	45	98	23	3	14	53	50	86	.219	.303	.377	.680	106	-0	3	94	107	51	.619	1	0	0	-1	*O	-0.1
1968	NY-A	152	507	60	99	18	3	11	52	76	97	.195	.305	.308	.613	85	-7	-8	101	120	51	.584	10	5	0	3	*SO	0.3
1969	NY-A	45	143	13	26	5	2	1	9	17	23	.182	.269	.266	.534	52	-10	-9	95	88	11	.475	2	1	0	-0	S	-0.7
	Det-A	94	331	46	74	13	1	13	37	39	47	.224	.309	.387	.696	91	-3	-5	103	91	41	.648	2	2	-1	-9	SO/3	-1.1
	Yr	139	474	59	100	18	3	14	46	56	70	.211	.297	.350	.647	80	-13	-13	101	90	52	.597	4	3	-1	-9		-1.8
Total	9	1192	4251	595	1041	179	34	153	530	550	698	.245	.337	.411	.748	113	66	75	98	102	618	.735	45	25	-2	1	OS/3	7.2
■ **ALEX TREVINO** Trevino, Alejandro (Castro) b: 8/26/57, Monterrey, Mex. BR/TR, 5'10", 165 lbs. Deb: 9/11/78																												
1978	NY-N	6	12	3	3	0	0	0	0	1	2	.250	.308	.250	.558	58	-1	-1	98	0	1	.400	0	0	0	0	/C3	0.0
1979	NY-N	79	207	24	56	11	1	0	20	20	27	.271	.338	.333	.671	88	-4	-3	95	115	22	.571	2	2	-1	6	C3/2	0.3
1980	NY-N	106	355	26	91	11	2	0	37	13	41	.256	.285	.299	.583	66	-18	-16	96	138	27	.432	0	3	-2	7	C3/2	-0.9
1981	NY-N	56	149	17	39	2	0	0	10	13	19	.262	.325	.275	.600	71	-5	-5	101	96	14	.509	3	0	1	2	C/2O3	-0.1
1982	Cin-N	120	355	24	89	10	3	1	33	34	34	.251	.321	.304	.626	74	-11	-12	102	117	33	.523	3	1	0	-5	*C/3	-1.6
1983	Cin-N	74	167	14	36	8	1	1	13	17	20	.216	.288	.293	.581	60	-9	-9	103	99	14	.493	0	0	0	-6	C/32	-1.3
1984	Cin-N	6	6	0	1	0	0	0	0	0	2	.167	.167	.167	.333	-6	-1	-1	106	0	0	.200	0	0	0	0	/C	0.0
	Atl-N	79	266	36	65	16	0	3	28	16	27	.244	.290	.338	.628	69	-9	-12	110	111	26	.541	5	2	0	6	C	-0.2
	Yr	85	272	36	66	16	0	3	28	16	29	.243	.287	.335	.622	68	-10	-13	109	103	26	.533	5	2	0	6		-0.2
1985	SF-N	57	157	17	34	10	1	6	19	20	24	.217	.305	.408	.713	105	-1	0	93	92	19	.656	0	0	0	2	C/3	0.5
1986	LA-N	89	202	31	53	13	0	4	26	27	35	.262	.352	.386	.738	110	1	3	94	115	28	.684	0	0	0	0	C/1	0.4
1987	LA-N	72	144	16	32	7	1	3	16	6	28	.222	.273	.347	.620	69	-8	-6	92	108	12	.513	1	0	0	-1	C/O3	-0.3
1988	Hou-N	78	193	19	48	17	0	2	13	24	29	.249	.341	.368	.709	111	1	3	93	67	24	.665	5	2	0	-6	C/O	0.1
Total	11	822	2213	227	547	105	9	20	215	191	288	.247	.311	.330	.641	80	-62	-58	98	108	221	.567	19	10	-0	6	C/3201	-3.1
■ **BOBBY TREVINO** Trevino, Carlos (Castro) b: 8/15/43, Monterrey, Mexico BR/TR, 6'2", 185 lbs. Deb: 5/22/68																												
1968	Cal-A	17	40	1	9	1	0	0	1	2	9	.225	.262	.250	.512	59	-2	-2	94	43	3	.375	0	1	-1	1	O	-0.1
■ **GUS TRIANDOS** Triandos, Gus b: 7/30/30, San Francisco, Cal BR/TR, 6'3", 205 lbs. Deb: 8/13/53																												
1953	NY-A	18	51	5	8	2	0	1	6	3	9	.157	.204	.255	.459	25	-6	-5	93	139	3	.372	0	0	0	-0	1/C	-0.5
1954	NY-A	2	1	0	0	0	0	0	0	0	1	.000	.000	.000	.000	-99	-0	-0	99	0	0	.000	0	0	0	0	/C	0.0
1955	Bal-A	140	481	47	133	17	3	12	65	40	55	.277	.335	.399	.734	108	-3	3	90	106	64	.655	0	0	0	1	*1C/3	0.0
1956	Bal-A	131	452	47	126	18	1	21	88	48	73	.279	.351	.462	.813	120	7	11	94	123	68	.746	0	0	0	3	C1	1.3
1957	Bal-A	129	418	44	106	21	1	19	72	38	73	.254	.320	.445	.765	115	3	6	93	117	58	.701	0	0	0	-13	*C	-0.1
1958	Bal-A	137	474	59	116	10	0	30	79	60	65	.245	.331	.456	.787	121	8	12	94	106	67	.732	1	0	0	1	*C	1.5
1959	Bal-A	126	393	43	85	7	1	25	73	65	56	.216	.332	.430	.762	111	4	6	97	118	57	.741	0	0	0	-5	*C	0.7

YEAR	TM/L	G	AB	R	H	2B	3B	HR	RBI	BB	SO	AVG	OBP	SLG	PRO	/A	BR	/A	PF	CHI	RC	TA	SB	CS	SBR	FR	POS	TPR
1960	Bal-A	109	364	36	98	18	0	12	54	41	62	.269	.345	.418	.762	103	3	2	102	112	52	.700	0	0	0	-10	*C	-0.1
1961	Bal-A	115	397	35	97	21	0	17	63	44	60	.244	.321	.426	.747	100	-2	-1	97	114	52	.684	0	0	0	-4	*C	-0.4
1962	Bal-A	66	207	20	33	7	0	6	23	29	43	.159	.263	.280	.543	49	-16	-14	95	120	15	.483	0	0	0	-5	C	-1.5
1963	Det-A	106	327	28	78	13	0	14	41	32	67	.239	.318	.407	.725	98	1	-1	104	98	41	.660	0	0	0	1	C	0.2
1964	Phi-N	73	188	17	47	9	0	8	33	26	41	.250	.344	.426	.770	117	4	4	99	130	27	.723	0	0	0	-1	C/1	0.5
1965	Phi-N	30	82	3	14	2	0	0	4	9	17	.171	.253	.195	.448	30	-8	-7	95	104	4	.352	0	0	0	1	C	-0.5
	Hou-N	24	72	5	13	2	0	2	7	5	14	.181	.244	.292	.535	56	-5	-4	89	107	5	.443	0	0	0	3	C	0.0
	Yr	54	154	8	27	4	0	2	11	14	31	.175	.249	.240	.489	42	-12	-11	92	107	10	.403	0	0	0	3		-0.5
Total	13	1206	3907	389	954	147	6	167	608	440	636	.244	.324	.413	.737	103	-10	11	96	113	514	.703	1	0	0	-29	C1/3	1.1

■ **MANNY TRILLO** Trillo, Jesus Manuel Marcano (born Jesus Manuel Marcano (Trillo)) b: 12/25/50, Caripito, Ven. BR/TR, 6'1", 150 lbs. Deb: 6/28/73

YEAR	TM/L	G	AB	R	H	2B	3B	HR	RBI	BB	SO	AVG	OBP	SLG	PRO	/A	BR	/A	PF	CHI	RC	TA	SB	CS	SBR	FR	POS	TPR
1973	Oak-A	17	12	0	3	2	0	0	3	0	4	.250	.250	.417	.667	97	-0	-0	87	236	1	.500	0	0	0	-0	2	0.0
1974	Oak-A	21	33	3	5	0	0	0	2	2	8	.152	.222	.152	.374	9	-4	-4	100	157	1	.286	0	0	0	-0	2	-0.3
1975	Chi-N	154	545	55	135	12	2	7	70	45	78	.248	.309	.316	.624	71	-19	-22	104	143	53	.518	1	7	-4	19	*2/S	0.0
1976	Chi-N	158	582	42	139	24	3	4	59	53	70	.239	.306	.311	.617	69	-18	-25	109	120	55	.545	17	6	2	17	*2/S	0.1
1977	Chi-N	152	504	51	141	18	5	7	57	44	58	.280	.344	.377	.721	82	-4	-13	114	108	62	.629	3	5	-2	36	*2	2.9
1978	Chi-N	152	552	53	144	17	5	4	55	50	67	.261	.325	.332	.656	76	-11	-18	110	114	59	.553	0	7	-4	**34**	*2	2.2
1979	Phi-N	118	431	40	112	22	1	6	42	20	59	.260	.299	.357	.656	81	-14	-12	97	99	42	.537	4	7	-3	4	*2	-0.2
1980	Phi-N	141	531	68	155	25	9	7	43	32	46	.292	.336	.412	.748	100	5	0	107	72	70	.663	8	3	1	17	*2	2.8
1981	Phi-N	94	349	37	100	14	3	6	36	26	37	.287	.341	.395	.737	97	4	-1	112	92	48	.683	10	4	1	10	2	1.7
1982	Phi-N	149	549	52	149	24	1	0	39	33	53	.271	.316	.319	.635	83	-16	-11	94	89	52	.517	8	10	-4	8	*2	0.0
1983	Cle-A	88	320	33	87	13	1	1	29	21	46	.272	.317	.328	.645	74	-9	-12	105	107	30	.510	1	3	-2	12	2	0.2
	Mon-N	31	121	16	32	8	0	2	16	10	18	.264	.331	.380	.711	95	-1	-1	102	129	16	.637	0	0	0	-2	2	-0.1
1984	SF-N	98	401	45	102	21	1	4	36	25	55	.254	.303	.342	.645	84	-11	-9	96	91	41	.537	0	0	0	3	2/3	-0.2
1985	SF-N	125	451	36	101	16	2	3	25	40	44	.224	.289	.288	.577	66	-23	-19	93	73	40	.486	2	0	1	-3	*2/3	-2.1
1986	Chi-N	81	152	22	45	10	0	1	19	16	21	.296	.363	.382	.745	99	1	0	107	124	21	.667	0	2	-1	-2	31/2	-0.4
1987	Chi-N	108	214	27	63	8	0	8	26	25	37	.294	.368	.444	.812	113	5	4	101	87	34	.750	0	3	-2	-2	132/S	0.0
1988	Chi-N	76	164	15	41	5	0	1	14	8	32	.250	.285	.299	.584	65	-7	-8	104	108	15	.472	2	0	1	0	132/S	-0.7
Total	16	1763	5911	595	1554	239	33	61	571	450	733	.263	.319	.345	.664	81	-123	-150	104	103	639	.584	56	57	-17	151	*23/1S	5.9

■ **COAKER TRIPLETT** Triplett, Herman Coaker b: 12/18/11, Boone, N.C. d: 5/19/ 1987 BR/TR, 5'11", 185 lbs. Deb: 4/19/38

YEAR	TM/L	G	AB	R	H	2B	3B	HR	RBI	BB	SO	AVG	OBP	SLG	PRO	/A	BR	/A	PF	CHI	RC	TA	SB	CS	SBR	FR	POS	TPR
1938	Chi-N	12	36	4	9	2	1	0	2	0	1	.250	.250	.361	.611	63	-2	-2	105	56	3	.448	0			-1	/O	-0.2
1941	StL-N	76	185	29	53	6	3	3	21	18	27	.286	.350	.400	.750	101	3	0	110	91	25	.667	0			-3	O	-0.4
1942	StL-N	64	154	18	42	7	4	1	23	17	15	.273	.345	.390	.735	106	3	1	108	135	20	.667	1			-4	O	-0.3
1943	StL-N	9	25	1	2	0	0	1	4	1	6	.080	.115	.200	.315	-9	-4	-4	105	180	0	.250	0			-0	/O	-0.4
	Phi-N	105	360	45	98	16	4	14	52	28	28	.272	.325	.456	.780	133	9	12	94	91	52	.716	2			-0	O	0.9
	Yr	114	385	46	100	16	4	15	56	29	34	.260	.312	.439	.751	122	5	8	94	100	51	.680	2			-1		0.5
1944	Phi-N	84	184	15	43	5	1	1	25	19	10	.234	.305	.288	.593	68	-8	-8	100	160	15	.487	1			-2	O	-1.3
1945	Phi-N	120	363	36	87	11	1	7	46	40	27	.240	.315	.333	.648	83	-10	-8	96	112	39	.590	6			-4	O	-1.5
Total	6	470	1307	148	334	47	14	27	173	123	114	.256	.320	.375	.694	97	-8	-8	100	113	155	.636	10			-14	O	-3.2

■ **HAL TROSKY** Trosky, Harold Arthur Sr. (born Harold Arthur Troyavesky Sr.) b: 11/11/12, Norway, Iowa d: 6/18/79, Cedar Rapids, Ia. BL/TR, 6'2", 207 lbs. Deb: 9/11/33

YEAR	TM/L	G	AB	R	H	2B	3B	HR	RBI	BB	SO	AVG	OBP	SLG	PRO	/A	BR	/A	PF	CHI	RC	TA	SB	CS	SBR	FR	POS	TPR
1933	Cle-A	11	44	6	13	1	2	1	8	2	12	.295	.340	.477	.818	110	1	0	105	118	7	.774	0	0	0	1	1	0.0
1934	Cle-A	154	625	117	206	45	9	35	142	58	49	.330	.388	.598	.987	151	44	43	101	105	145	1.036	2	2	-1	0	*1	1.4
1935	Cle-A	154	632	84	171	33	7	26	113	46	60	.271	.321	.468	.789	103	-2	-2	99	109	94	.743	1	2	-1	1	*1	-1.5
1936	Cle-A	151	629	124	216	45	9	42	**162**	36	58	.343	.382	.644	1.026	141	42	37	106	105	150	1.077	6	5	-1	1	*1/2	1.4
1937	Cle-A	153	601	104	179	36	9	32	128	65	60	.298	.367	.547	.915	131	22	24	98	109	122	.941	3	1	0	-3	*1	0.3
1938	Cle-A	150	554	106	185	40	9	19	110	67	40	.334	.407	.542	.948	137	30	31	99	106	125	1.008	5	1	1	4	*1	1.4
1939	Cle-A	122	448	89	150	31	4	25	104	52	28	.335	.405	.589	.994	155	33	35	98	106	108	1.039	2	3	-1	7	*1	2.7
1940	Cle-A	140	522	85	154	39	4	25	93	79	45	.295	.392	.529	.920	146	28	34	93	101	116	.960	1	2	-1	-6	*1	1.8
1941	Cle-A	89	310	43	91	17	0	11	51	44	21	.294	.383	.455	.838	120	10	9	101	106	57	.824	1	2	-1	-4	1	0.2
1944	Chi-A	135	497	55	120	32	2	10	70	62	30	.241	.327	.374	.701	100	-0	-0	100	124	62	.640	3	2	-0	-10	*1	-1.8
1946	Chi-A	88	299	22	76	12	3	2	31	34	37	.254	.330	.334	.665	89	-5	-4	97	113	33	.582	4	3	-1	-6	1	-1.5
Total	11	1347	5161	835	1561	331	58	228	1012	545	440	.302	.371	.522	.892	130	202	208	99	108	1018	.903	28	23	-5	-14	*1/2	4.4

■ **MIKE TROST** Trost, Michael J. b: 1866, Philadelphia, Pa. d: 3/24/01, Philadelphia, Pa. TR , 6'0.5", 180 lbs. Deb: 8/21/1890

YEAR	TM/L	G	AB	R	H	2B	3B	HR	RBI	BB	SO	AVG	OBP	SLG	PRO	/A	BR	/A	PF	CHI	RC	TA	SB	CS	SBR	FR	POS	TPR
1890	StL-a	17	51	10	13	2	0	1		6		.255	.345	.353	.698	93	1	-1	116	0	8	.763	4			0	C/O	0.0
1895	Lou-N	3	12	1	1	0	0	0	1	0	1	.083	.083	.083	.167	-59	-3	-3	95	285	0	.182	1			0	/1	-0.1
Total	2	20	63	11	14	2	0	1	1	6	1	.222	.300	.302	.602	67	-2	-3	112	49	8	.633	5			0	/CO1	-0.1

■ **SAM TROTT** Trott, Samuel W. b: 1858, Washington, D.C. d: 6/5/25, Catonsville, Md. BL/TL, 5'9", 190 lbs. Deb: 5/29/1880 M

YEAR	TM/L	G	AB	R	H	2B	3B	HR	RBI	BB	SO	AVG	OBP	SLG	PRO	/A	BR	/A	PF	CHI	RC	TA	SB	CS	SBR	FR	POS	TPR
1880	Bos-N	39	125	14	26	4	1	0	9	3	5	.208	.227	.256	.483	69	-5	-3	92	103	7	.354				4	C/O	0.3
1881	Det-N	6	25	3	5	2	1	0	2	1	3	.200	.231	.360	.591	78	-1	-1	106	74	2	.500				0	/C	0.0
1882	Det-N	32	129	11	31	7	1	0	12	0	13	.240	.240	.310	.550	74	-4	-4	102	103	10	.408				6	C/S2103	0.4
1883	Det-N	75	295	27	72	14	1	0	29	10	23	.244	.269	.298	.567	79	-10	-5	91	117	24	.439				-25	2C/O1	-2.6
1884	Bal-a	71	284	36	73	17	9	2		4		.257	.272	.401	.674	121	5	6	99	0	32	.569				10	C/2O	1.8
1885	Bal-a	21	88	12	24	2	2	0		5		.273	.312	.341	.653	103	1	0	106	0	10	.547				0	C/O2S	0.0
1887	Bal-a	85	300	44	77	16	3	0		27		.257	.322	.330	.652	87	-6	-4	96	0	35	.610	8			0	C2/O1S	0.6
1888	Bal-a	31	108	19	30	11	4	0	22	4		.278	.304	.454	.757	150	5	5	96	134	16	.692	1			-2	C/O21	0.6
Total	8	360	1354	166	338	73	22	2	74	54	44	.250	.280	.340	.621	95	-13	-6	97	56	136	.520	9			-7	C/2O1S3	1.1

■ **QUINCY TROUPPE** Trouppe, Quincy Thomas b: 12/25/12, Dublin, Ga. BB/TR, 6'2.5", 225 lbs. Deb: 4/30/52

YEAR	TM/L	G	AB	R	H	2B	3B	HR	RBI	BB	SO	AVG	OBP	SLG	PRO	/A	BR	/A	PF	CHI	RC	TA	SB	CS	SBR	FR	POS	TPR
1952	Cle-A	6	10	1	1	0	0	0	0	1	3	.100	.182	.100	.282	-22	-2	-2	91	0	0	.200	0	0	0	-0	/C	-0.1

■ **DASHER TROY** Troy, John Joseph b: 5/8/1856, New York, N.Y. d: 3/30/38, Ozone Park, N.Y. BR/TR, Deb: 8/23/1881

YEAR	TM/L	G	AB	R	H	2B	3B	HR	RBI	BB	SO	AVG	OBP	SLG	PRO	/A	BR	/A	PF	CHI	RC	TA	SB	CS	SBR	FR	POS	TPR
1881	Det-N	11	44	2	15	3	0	0	4	3	8	.341	.383	.409	.792	140	3	2	106	74	7	.724				0	/32	0.2
1882	Det-N	40	152	22	37	7	2	0	14	5	10	.243	.268	.316	.583	85	-2	-3	102	100	13	.461				-14	2S	-1.4
	Pro-N	4	17	1	4	0	0	0	1	0	1	.235	.235	.235	.471	49	-1	-1	106	89	1	.308				0	/S	0.0
	Yr	44	169	23	41	7	2	0	15	5	11	.243	.264	.308	.572	81	-3	-4	102	101	14	.445				-14		-1.4
1883	NY-N	85	316	37	68	7	5	0	20	9	33	.215	.237	.269	.506	54	-17	-17	100	83	21	.379				-16	*2S	-3.2
1884	NY-a	107	421	80	111	22	10	2		19		.264	.300	.378	.678	122	10	10	100	0	49	.584				-24	*2	-1.0
1885	NY-a	45	177	24	39	3	3	2		5		.220	.258	.305	.563	95	-4	0	84	0	14	.457				-11	2/OS	-0.7
Total	5	292	1127	166	274	42	20	4	39	41	52	.243	.274	.327	.601	93	-12	-8	98	41	105	.488				-66	2/S3O	-6.1

■ **FRED TRUAX** Truax, Frederick W. b: 1868, d: 12/18/1899, Omaha, Neb. Deb: 8/18/1890

YEAR	TM/L	G	AB	R	H	2B	3B	HR	RBI	BB	SO	AVG	OBP	SLG	PRO	/A	BR	/A	PF	CHI	RC	TA	SB	CS	SBR	FR	POS	TPR
1890	Pit-N	1	3	0	1	0	0	0	1	1	1	.333	.500	.333	.833	168	0	0	88	308	1	1.000	0			0	/O	0.0

■ **HARRY TRUBY** Truby, Harry Garvin "Bird Eye" b: 5/12/1870, Ironton, Ohio d: 3/21/53, Ironton, Ohio TR , 5'11", 185 lbs. Deb: 8/21/1895

YEAR	TM/L	G	AB	R	H	2B	3B	HR	RBI	BB	SO	AVG	OBP	SLG	PRO	/A	BR	/A	PF	CHI	RC	TA	SB	CS	SBR	FR	POS	TPR
1895	Chi-N	33	119	17	40	3	0	0	16	10	7	.336	.402	.361	.763	97	1	0	103	106	21	.797	7			0	2	0.2
1896	Chi-N	29	109	13	28	2	2	2	31	6	5	.257	.314	.367	.681	75	-3	-5	108	198	14	.654	4			0	2	-0.3
	Pit-N	8	32	1	5	0	0	0	3	2	4	.156	.206	.156	.362	-3	-5	-4	93	176	1	.296	1			0	/2	-0.3
	Yr	37	141	14	33	2	2	2	34	8	9	.234	.289	.319	.609	59	-8	-9	105	199	15	.565	5			0		-0.6
Total	2	70	260	31	73	5	2	2	50	18	16	.281	.342	.338	.680	76	-7	-9	104	153	36	.663	12			0	/2	-0.4

■ **FRANK TRUESDALE** Truesdale, Frank Day b: 3/31/1884, St.Louis, Mo. d: 8/27/43, Albuquerque, N.M. BB/TR, 5'8", 145 lbs. Deb: 4/27/10

YEAR	TM/L	G	AB	R	H	2B	3B	HR	RBI	BB	SO	AVG	OBP	SLG	PRO	/A	BR	/A	PF	CHI	RC	TA	SB	CS	SBR	FR	POS	TPR
1910	StL-A	123	415	39	91	7	2	1	25	48		.219	.303	.253	.556	79	-11	-8	94	87	40	.568	29			-10	*2	-2.8
1911	StL-A	1	0	1	0	0	0	0	0	0		—	—	—	—	—	0	0	95	—	—	—	0			0	R	0.0
1914	NY-A	77	217	23	46	4	0	0	13	39	35	.212	.340	.230	.570	72	-5	-5	100	98	18	.566	11	11	-3	7	2/3	-0.1
1918	Bos-A	15	36	6	10	1	0	0	2	4	5	.278	.350	.306	.656	103	0	0	95	66	4	.615	1			-0	2	0.0

YEAR	TM/L	G	AB	R	H	2B	3B	HR	RBI	BB	SO	AVG	OBP	SLG	PRO	/A	BR	/A	PF	CHI	RC	TA	SB	CS	SBR	FR	POS	TPR
Total	4	216	668	69	147	12	2	1	40	91	40	.220	.318	.249	.567	78	-16	-13	96	90	103	.570	41	11		-3	2/3	-2.9
■ ED TRUMBULL	Trumbull, Edward J. (born Edward J. Trembly) b: 11/3/1860, Chicopee, Mass. Deb: 5/10/1884																											
1884	Was-a	25	86	5	10	2	0	0		2		.116	.136	.140	.276	-10	-10	-8	88	0	2	.184				0	OP	-0.7
■ OLLIE TUCKER	Tucker, Oliver Dinwiddie b: 1/27/02, Radiant, Va. d: 7/13/40, Radiant, Va. BL/TR, 5'11", 180 lbs. Deb: 4/17/27																											
1927	Was-A	20	24	1	5	2	0	0	8	4	2	.208	.321	.292	.613	62	-1	-1	97	380	3	.579	0	0	0	-1	/O	-0.1
1928	Cle-A	14	47	5	6	0	0	1	2	7	3	.128	.255	.191	.446	18	-6	-6	106	58	2	.395	0	2	-1	-1	O	-0.8
Total	2	34	71	6	11	2	0	1	10	11	5	.155	.277	.225	.502	32	-7	-7	103	167	5	.452	0	2	-1	-2	/O	-0.9
■ TOMMY TUCKER	Tucker, Thomas Joseph "Foghorn" b: 10/28/1863, Holyoke, Mass. d: 10/22/35, Montague, Mass. BB/TR, 5'11", 165 lbs. Deb: 4/16/1887																											
1887	Bal-a	136	524	114	144	15	9	6		29		.275	.347	.372	.719	107	3	7	96	0	100	.889	85			2	*1	0.5
1888	Bal-a	136	520	74	149	17	12	6	61	16		.287	.330	.400	.730	143	20	23	96	86	85	.768	43			4	*1/OP	1.7
1889	Bal-a	134	527	103	**196**	22	11	5	99	42	26	**.372**	**.450**	.484	**.934**	**170**	**50**	**50**	100	93	**147**	**1.187**	63			-1	*1O	3.2
1890	Bos-N	132	539	104	159	17	8	1	62	56	22	.295	.387	.362	.749	109	18	8	111	84	94	.839	43			-1	*1	-0.1
1891	Bos-N	140	548	103	148	16	5	2	69	37	30	.270	.349	.328	.677	89	2	-9	112	115	74	.680	26			-3	*1/P	-1.4
1892	Bos-N	149	542	85	153	15	7	1	62	45	35	.282	.365	.341	.707	103	13	2	113	103	78	.715	22			-14	*1	-2.0
1893	Bos-N	121	486	83	138	13	2	7	91	27	31	.284	.347	.362	.709	88	-7	-9	103	134	65	.664	8			-11	*1	-1.6
1894	Bos-N	123	500	112	165	24	6	3	100	53	21	.330	.412	.420	.832	91	5	-9	113	133	96	.890	18			3	*1/O	-0.2
1895	Bos-N	125	462	87	115	19	6	3	73	61	29	.249	.360	.335	.695	80	-10	-12	103	132	63	.720	15			5	*1	-0.3
1896	Bos-N	122	474	74	144	27	5	2	72	30	29	.304	.363	.395	.757	94	1	-5	108	110	72	.718	6			5	*1	0.3
1897	Bos-N	4	14	0	3	2	0	0	4	2		.214	.313	.357	.670	73	-0	-1	107	234	2	.636	0			0	/1	0.0
	Was-N	93	352	52	119	18	5	5	61	27		.338	.403	.460	.863	128	16	15	101	107	74	.936	18			-3	*1	0.9
	Yr	97	366	52	122	20	5	5	65	29		.333	.399	.456	.855	126	15	14	102	114	76	.922	18			-3		0.9
1898	Bro-N	73	283	35	79	9	4	1	34	12		.279	.325	.350	.674	101	-2	0	95	107	33	.583	1			7	1	0.7
	StL-N	72	252	18	60	7	2	0	20	18		.238	.322	.282	.603	72	-7	-9	106	87	24	.536	1			-1	1	-0.8
	Yr	145	535	53	139	16	6	1	54	30		.260	.323	.318	.641	86	-9	-9	100	98	57	.561	2			6		-0.1
1899	Cle-N	127	456	40	110	19	3	0	40	24		.241	.295	.296	.591	72	-22	-14	89	93	42	.500	3			-2	*1	-1.2
Total	13	1687	6479	1084	1882	240	85	42	848	479	223	.290	.364	.373	.737	104	80	38	104	98	1048	.766	352			-11	*1/OP	-0.3
■ THURMAN TUCKER	Tucker, Thurman Lowell "Joe E." b: 9/26/17, Gordon, Tex. BL/TR, 5'10.5", 165 lbs. Deb: 4/14/42																											
1942	Chi-A	7	24	2	3	0	1	0	1	0	4	.125	.125	.208	.333	-7	-3	-3	99	70	1	.238	0	0	0	-0	/O	-0.3
1943	Chi-A	139	528	81	124	15	6	3	39	79	72	.235	.336	.303	.639	87	-6	-7	101	81	60	.631	29	17	-2	11	*O	0.0
1944	Chi-A	124	446	59	128	15	6	2	46	57	40	.287	.368	.361	.729	109	7	7	100	101	63	.692	13	12	-3	14	*O	1.5
1946	Chi-A	121	438	62	126	20	3	1	36	54	45	.288	.367	.354	.721	105	3	5	97	88	61	.676	9	10	-3	-2	*O	-0.6
1947	Chi-A	89	254	28	60	9	4	1	17	38	25	.236	.336	.315	.651	84	-6	-4	97	75	31	.646	10	4	1	4	O	-0.1
1948	Cle-A	83	242	52	63	13	2	1	19	31	17	.260	.347	.343	.690	85	-5	-5	99	75	33	.685	11	2	2	-3	O	-0.7
1949	Cle-A	80	197	28	48	5	2	0	14	18	19	.244	.307	.289	.596	60	-12	-11	98	84	19	.513	4	2	0	4	O	-0.7
1950	Cle-A	57	101	13	18	2	0	1	7	14	14	.178	.284	.228	.512	33	-10	-10	98	93	8	.470	1	0	0	-4	O	-1.2
1951	Cle-A	1	1	0	0	0	0	0	0	0	1	.000	.000	.000	.000	-99	-0	-0	95	0	0	.000	0	0	0	0	H	0.0
Total	9	701	2231	325	570	79	24	9	179	291	237	.255	.342	.325	.667	88	-34	-30	99	86	275	.642	77	47	-5	25	O	-2.1
■ JERRY TURBIDY	Turbidy, Jeremiah b: 7/4/1852, Dudley, Mass. d: 9/5/20, Webster, Mass. 5'8", 165 lbs. Deb: 7/27/1884																											
1884	KC-U	13	49	5	11	4	0	0		3		.224	.269	.306	.575	108	-0	1	87	0	4	.474	0			0	S	0.1
■ EDDIE TURCHIN	Turchin, Edward Lawrence "Smiley" b: 2/10/17, New York, N.Y. d: 2/8/82, Brookhaven, N.Y. BR/TR, 5'10", 165 lbs. Deb: 5/09/43																											
1943	Cle-A	11	13	4	3	0	0	0	1	3	1	.231	.375	.231	.606	87	-0	0	90	122	1	.545	0	0	0	0	/3S	0.0
■ PETE TURGEON	Turgeon, Eugene Joseph b: 1/3/1897, Minneapolis, Minn. d: 1/24/77, Wichita Falls, Tex BR/TR, 5'6", 145 lbs. Deb: 9/20/23																											
1923	Chi-N	3	6	1	1	0	0	0	0	0	0	.167	.167	.167	.333	-11	-1	-1	104	0	0	.200	0	0	0	-0	/S	0.0
■ EARL TURNER	Turner, Earl Edwin b: 5/6/23, Pittsfield, Mass. BR/TR, 5'9", 170 lbs. Deb: 9/25/48																											
1948	Pit-N	2	1	0	0	0	0	0	0	0	0	.000	.000	.000	.000	-96	-0	-0	104	0	0	.000	0			0	/C	0.0
1950	Pit-N	40	74	10	18	0	0	3	5	4	13	.243	.282	.365	.647	67	-4	-4	103	54	7	.542	1			-1	C	-0.3
Total	2	42	75	10	18	0	0	3	5	4	13	.240	.278	.360	.638	65	-4	-4	103	53	7	.533	1			-1	/C	-0.3
■ TUCK TURNER	Turner, George A. b: 2/13/1873, W.New Brighton, N.Y. d: 7/16/45, Staten Island, N.Y. BL , Deb: 8/18/1893																											
1893	Phi-N	36	155	32	50	4	3	1	13	9	19	.323	.364	.406	.770	107	1	1	100	55	26	.762	7			-2	O	-0.1
1894	Phi-N	80	339	91	141	21	9	1	82	23	13	.416	.456	.540	.996	149	23	26	95	124	91	1.106	11			-10	O/P	0.9
1895	Phi-N	59	210	51	81	8	6	2	43	25	11	.386	.453	.510	.963	152	17	17	99	106	56	1.140	14			-10	O	0.2
1896	Phi-N	13	32	12	7	2	0	0	0	8	5	.219	.375	.281	.656	75	-1	-1	102	0	6	.920	6			2	/O	0.0
	StL-N	51	203	30	50	7	8	1	27	14	21	.246	.298	.374	.673	82	-7	-5	95	95	25	.634	6			-6	O	-1.2
	Yr	64	235	42	57	9	8	1	27	22	26	.243	.310	.362	.672	81	-8	-6	96	75	31	.674	12			-5		-1.2
1897	StL-N	103	416	58	121	17	12	2	41	35		.291	.350	.404	.754	108	0	5	93	66	63	.725	8			-7	*O	-0.8
1898	StL-N	35	141	20	28	8	0	0	7	14		.199	.280	.255	.536	53	-8	-9	106	51	11	.469	1			0	O	-0.7
Total	6	377	1496	294	478	67	38	7	213	128	69	.320	.377	.429	.806	115	26	35	97	84	278	.818	53			-33	O/P	-1.7
■ JERRY TURNER	Turner, John Webber b: 1/17/54, Texarkana, Ark. BL/TL, 5'9", 180 lbs. Deb: 9/02/74																											
1974	SD-N	17	48	4	14	1	0	0	2	3	5	.292	.333	.313	.646	87	-1	-1	93	51	5	.571	2	1	0	-2	O	-0.2
1975	SD-N	11	22	1	6	0	0	0	0	2	1	.273	.333	.273	.606	70	-1	-1	100	0	2	.471	0	0	0	0	/O	0.0
1976	SD-N	105	281	41	75	16	5	5	37	32	38	.267	.342	.413	.755	128	5	9	89	109	41	.744	12	6	0	-7	O	0.0
1977	SD-N	118	289	43	71	16	1	10	48	31	43	.246	.319	.412	.731	107	-3	2	88	129	38	.711	12	4	1	1	O	0.1
1978	SD-N	106	225	28	63	9	1	8	37	21	32	.280	.349	.436	.785	128	5	7	93	120	34	.753	6	4	-1	-3	O	0.1
1979	SD-N	138	448	55	111	23	2	9	61	34	58	.248	.304	.368	.672	86	-11	-9	96	126	50	.591	4	2	0	-6	*O	-1.9
1980	SD-N	85	153	22	44	5	0	3	18	10	18	.288	.339	.379	.718	108	0	1	93	106	20	.690	8	3	1	-4	O	-0.3
1981	SD-N	33	31	5	7	0	0	2	6	4	3	.226	.314	.419	.734	114	0	0	93	124	4	.654	0	1	-1	-1	/O	0.0
	Chi-A	10	12	1	2	0	0	0	2	1	2	.167	.231	.167	.397	16	-1	-1	100	391	1	.300	0	0	0	0	/O	0.0
1982	Det-A	85	210	21	52	3	0	8	27	20	37	.248	.313	.376	.689	88	-3	-4	100	105	25	.613	1	3	-2	-4	DO	-0.9
1983	SD-N	25	23	1	3	0	0	0	0	1	8	.130	.167	.130	.297	-17	-4	-4	99	0	0	.190	0	0	0	-0	/O	-0.3
Total	10	733	1742	222	448	73	9	45	238	159	245	.257	.322	.387	.709	101	-14	0	93	115	220	.671	45	24	-1	-27	O/D	-3.4
■ SHANE TURNER	Turner, Shane Lee b: 1/8/63, Los Angeles, Cal. BL/TR, 5'10", 180 lbs. Deb: 8/19/88																											
1988	Phi-N	18	35	1	6	0	0	0	1	5	9	.171	.275	.171	.446	30	-3	-3	101	67	2	.367	0	0	0	-0	/3S	-0.2
■ TERRY TURNER	Turner, Terrence Lamont "Cotton Top" b: 2/28/1881, Sandy Lake, Pa. d: 7/18/60, Cleveland, Ohio BR/TR, 5'8", 149 lbs. Deb: 8/25/01 C																											
1901	Pit-N	2	7	0	3	0	0	0	1	0		.429	.429	.429	.857	151	0	0	101	112	1	.750	0			0	/3	0.1
1904	Cle-A	111	404	41	95	9	6	1	45	11		.235	.255	.295	.550	75	-11	-12	102	140	32	.437	5			-2	*S	-1.4
1905	Cle-A	155	586	49	155	16	14	4	72	14		.265	.282	.360	.642	105	1	1	100	122	66	.561	17			-23	*S	-1.8
1906	Cle-A	147	584	85	170	27	7	2	62	35		.291	.331	.372	.703	118	14	12	103	97	83	.674	27			22	*S	3.8
1907	Cle-A	148	524	57	127	20	7	0	46	19		.242	.269	.307	.576	91	-10	-6	93	104	52	.521	27			-18	*S	-2.2
1908	Cle-A	60	201	21	48	11	1	0	19	15		.239	.292	.303	.595	90	-1	-2	106	119	22	.614	18			-2	OS	-0.5
1909	Cle-A	53	208	25	52	7	4	0	16	14		.250	.304	.322	.626	96	-1	-1	102	79	24	.622	14			1	2S	0.0
1910	Cle-A	150	574	71	132	14	6	0	33	53		.230	.301	.275	.576	81	-12	-12	100	68	57	.559	31			-2	S3/2	-1.2
1911	Cle-A	117	417	59	105	16	9	0	28	34		.252	.310	.333	.643	77	-12	-14	103	69	52	.651	29			4	32S	-0.7
1912	Cle-A	103	370	54	114	14	4	0	33	31		.308	.363	.368	.731	108	5	4	101	86	57	.730	19			3	*3	0.5
1913	Cle-A	120	388	60	96	13	4	0	44	55	35	.247	.348	.302	.650	85	-3	-6	106	142	48	.651	13			9	32S	0.7
1914	Cle-A	120	428	43	105	14	9	1	33	44	36	.245	.319	.327	.646	92	-3	-4	102	83	50	.604	17	13	-3	12	*32	0.8
1915	Cle-A	75	262	35	66	14	1	0	14	29	13	.252	.329	.313	.642	89	-2	-4	104	61	29	.599	12	11	-3	-5	23	-1.1
1916	Cle-A	124	428	52	112	15	3	0	38	40	29	.262	.325	.311	.636	91	-5	-5	100	104	52	.595	15			8	32	0.9
1917	Cle-A	69	180	16	37	7	0	0	15	14	19	.206	.263	.244	.507	48	-10	-13	114	122	13	.434	4			2	32/S	-0.7

YEAR	TM/L	G	AB	R	H	2B	3B	HR	RBI	BB	SO	AVG	OBP	SLG	PRO	/A	BR	/A	PF	CHI	RC	TA	SB	CS	SBR	FR	POS	TPR
1918	Cle-A	74	233	24	58	7	2	0	23	22	15	.249	.316	.296	.613	78	-4	-6	108	122	24	.560	6			-0	32/S	-0.5
1919	Phi-A	38	127	7	24	3	0	0	6	5	9	.189	.220	.213	.432	20	-13	-14	106	81	6	.330	2			-0	S2/3	-1.1
Total	17	1666	5921	699	1499	207	77	8	528	435	156	.253	.306	.318	.624	89	-67	-81	102	100	668	.583	256	24		9	S32/O	-4.4
■ **TOM TURNER**	Turner, Thomas Richard b: 9/8/16, Custer Co., Okla. d: 5/14/86, Kennewick, Wash. BR/TR, 6'2", 195 lbs. Deb: 4/25/40																											
1940	Chi-A	37	96	11	20	1	2	0	6	3	12	.208	.240	.260	.500	29	-10	-11	104	87	6	.385	1	0	0	1	C	-0.6
1941	Chi-A	38	126	7	30	5	0	0	8	9	15	.238	.289	.278	.567	54	-9	-8	94	81	10	.465	2	0	1	2	C	-0.2
1942	Chi-A	56	182	18	44	9	1	3	21	19	15	.242	.313	.352	.665	88	-3	-3	99	101	21	.580	0	1	-1	0	C	0.3
1943	Chi-A	51	154	16	37	7	1	2	11	13	21	.240	.299	.338	.637	85	-3	-3	101	69	15	.532	1	0	0	1	C	0.0
1944	Chi-A	36	113	9	26	6	0	2	13	5	16	.230	.263	.336	.599	70	-5	-5	100	107	8	.453	0	1	-1	0	C	-0.2
	StL-A	15	25	2	8	1	0	0	4	2	5	.320	.370	.360	.730	107	0	0	102	160	3	.611	0	0	0	-1	C	0.0
	Yr	51	138	11	34	7	0	2	17	7	21	.246	.283	.341	.623	77	-4	-5	100	124	13	.509	0	1	-1	-1		-0.2
Total	5	233	696	63	165	29	4	7	63	51	84	.237	.290	.320	.611	70	-30	-29	99	91	63	.522	4	2	0	4	C	-0.7
■ **BILL TUTTLE**	Tuttle, William Robert b: 7/4/29, Elwood, Ill. BR/TR, 6', 190 lbs. Deb: 9/10/52																											
1952	Det-A	7	25	2	6	0	0	0	2	0	1	.240	.240	.240	.480	34	-2	-2	99	124	1	.286	0	0	0	1	/O	0.0
1954	Det-A	147	530	64	141	20	11	7	58	62	60	.266	.345	.385	.730	100	-0	0	100	104	69	.663	5	8	-3	-1	*O	-0.7
1955	Det-A	154	603	102	168	23	4	14	78	76	54	.279	.360	.400	.760	108	4	7	97	99	85	.700	6	3	0	9	*O	0.8
1956	Det-A	140	546	61	138	22	4	9	65	38	48	.253	.303	.357	.660	76	-22	-20	97	112	55	.556	5	4	-1	3	*O	-2.3
1957	Det-A	133	451	49	113	12	4	5	47	44	41	.251	.319	.328	.647	72	-14	-18	107	114	45	.545	2	6	-3	-3	*O	-3.2
1958	KC-A	148	511	77	118	14	9	11	51	74	58	.231	.329	.358	.687	84	-7	-10	106	97	59	.632	7	9	-3	9	*O	-1.4
1959	KC-A	126	463	74	139	19	6	7	43	48	38	.300	.371	.413	.783	113	10	10	101	81	71	.740	10	6	-1	6	*O	0.9
1960	KC-A	151	559	75	143	21	3	8	40	66	52	.256	.337	.347	.684	86	-10	-10	99	76	64	.598	1	5	-3	11	*O	-0.7
1961	KC-A	25	84	15	22	2	2	0	8	9	9	.262	.333	.333	.667	77	-2	-3	102	114	10	.578	0	0	0	0	O	-0.2
	Min-A	113	370	38	91	12	3	5	38	43	41	.246	.324	.335	.660	72	-12	-15	106	107	39	.569	1	3	-2	-16	3O/2	-2.9
	Yr	138	454	53	113	14	5	5	46	52	50	.249	.326	.335	.661	73	-14	-18	105	109	49	.574	1	3	-2	-16		-3.1
1962	Min-A	110	123	21	26	4	1	1	13	19	14	.211	.322	.285	.606	62	-6	-6	105	136	12	.554	1	0	0	-26	*O	-3.6
1963	Min-A	16	3	0	0	0	0	0	0	1	0	.000	.250	.000	.250	-23	-0	-0	100	0	0	.200	0	0	0	-3	O	-0.3
Total	11	1270	4268	578	1105	149	47	67	443	480	416	.259	.336	.363	.699	88	-61	-68	101	100	509	.648	38	44	-15	-10	*O/32	-13.6
■ **GUY TUTWILER**	Tutwiler, Guy Isbell "King Tut" b: 7/17/1889, Coalburg, Ala. d: 8/15/30, Birmingham, Ala. BL/TR, 6', 175 lbs. Deb: 8/29/11																											
1911	Det-A	13	32	3	6	2	0	0	3	2		.188	.235	.250	.485	33	-3	-3	108	127	2	.385	0			-0	/2O	-0.3
1913	Det-A	14	47	4	10	0	1	0	7	4	12	.213	.275	.255	.530	56	-3	-3	99	207	4	.486	2			-1	1	-0.2
Total	2	27	79	7	16	2	1	0	10	6	12	.203	.259	.253	.512	46	-6	-6	102	175	5	.444	2			-1	/12O	-0.5
■ **ART TWINEHAM**	Twineham, Arthur W. "Old Hoss" b: 11/26/1866, Galesburg, Ill. BL/TL, 6'1.5", 190 lbs. Deb: 9/11/1893																											
1893	StL-N	14	48	8	15	2	0	0	11	1	2	.313	.340	.354	.694	87	-1	-1	99	177	6	.576	0			0	C	0.0
1894	StL-N	38	127	22	40	4	1	1	16	9	11	.315	.387	.386	.773	88	-2	-2	101	85	20	.759	2			1	C	0.1
Total	2	52	175	30	55	6	1	1	27	10	13	.314	.375	.377	.752	87	-3	-3	101	109	26	.708	2			1	/C	0.1
■ **LARRY TWITCHELL**	Twitchell, Lawrence Grant b: 2/18/1864, Cleveland, Ohio d: 4/23/30, Cleveland, Ohio BR/TR, 6', 185 lbs. Deb: 4/30/1886																											
1886	Det-N	4	16	0	1	0	0	0	0	0	2	.063	.063	.063	.125	-57	-3	-3	109	0	0	.067	0			0	/PO	0.0
1887	Det-N	65	264	44	88	14	6	0	51	8	19	.333	.358	.432	.789	118	7	6	102	141	46	.773	12			-5	OP	0.1
1888	Det-N	131	524	71	128	19	4	5	67	28	45	.244	.286	.324	.611	98	-2	-1	98	137	54	.543	14			-7	*O/P	-0.9
1889	Cle-N	134	549	73	151	16	11	4	95	29	37	.275	.315	.366	.681	89	-7	-10	103	128	70	.628	17			-11	*O/P	-2.2
1890	Cle-P	56	233	33	52	6	3	2	36	17	17	.223	.279	.300	.579	61	-15	-11	92	137	21	.508	4			-10	O	-1.9
	Buf-P	44	172	24	38	3	1	2	17	23	12	.221	.316	.285	.601	69	-9	-6	92	90	17	.575	4			-4	OP/13	-0.8
	Yr	100	405	57	90	9	4	4	53	40	29	.222	.295	.294	.589	64	-23	-17	92	118	38	.537	8			-14		-2.7
1891	Col-a	57	224	32	62	9	4	2	35	20	28	.277	.341	.379	.721	122	2	6	89	118	33	.722	10			-12	O/P	-0.6
1892	Was-N	51	192	20	42	9	5	0	20	11	31	.219	.275	.318	.593	77	-5	-6	105	103	19	.560	8			-4	O/S3	-1.0
1893	Lou-N	45	187	37	58	12	3	2	31	17	20	.310	.377	.439	.815	123	5	6	96	102	34	.845	7			-3	O	0.1
1894	Lou-N	52	210	28	56	16	3	2	32	15	20	.267	.316	.400	.716	83	-10	-5	88	94	30	.695	8			6	O/P	-0.1
Total	9	639	2571	362	676	104	40	19	384	168	231	.263	.313	.357	.670	93	-37	-24	97	121	326	.627	84			-49	O/PS13	-7.3
■ **BABE TWOMBLY**	Twombly, Clarence Edward b: 1/18/1896, Jamaica Plain, Mass. d: 11/23/74, San Clemente, Cal. BL/TR, 5'10", 165 lbs. Deb: 4/14/20																											
1920	Chi-N	78	183	25	43	1	1	2	14	17	20	.235	.303	.284	.588	70	-7	-7	99	93	15	.503	5	9	-4	0	O/2	-1.3
1921	Chi-N	87	175	22	66	8	1	1	18	11	10	.377	.414	.451	.865	121	8	6	107	81	31	.817	4	6	-2	1	O	0.3
Total	2	165	358	47	109	9	2	3	32	28	30	.304	.357	.366	.723	97	1	-1	103	87	46	.640	9	15	-6	1	/O2	-1.0
■ **GEORGE TWOMBLY**	Twombly, George Frederick "Silent George" b: 6/4/1892, Boston, Mass. d: 2/17/75, Lexington, Mass. BR/TR, 5'9", 165 lbs. Deb: 7/09/14																											
1914	Cin-N	68	240	22	56	0	5	0	19	14	27	.233	.284	.275	.559	63	-10	-11	105	110	21	.516	12			-1	O	-1.4
1915	Cin-N	46	66	5	13	0	1	0	5	8	8	.197	.293	.227	.521	57	-3	-3	103	127	5	.518	5	3	-0	-4	O	-0.8
1916	Cin-N	3	5	0	0	0	0	0	0	1	1	.000	.167	.000	.167	-48	-1	-1	98	0	0	.200	0			0	/O	0.0
1917	Bos-N	32	102	8	19	1	1	0	9	18	5	.186	.314	.216	.530	66	-3	-3	96	161	9	.542	4			-3	O/1	-0.8
1919	Was-A	1	4	0	0	0	0	0	0	0	0	.000	.000	.000	.000	-99	-1	-1	98	0	0	.000	0			-0	/O	-0.1
Total	5	150	417	35	88	1	7	0	33	41	41	.211	.289	.247	.536	61	-18	-19	102	124	35	.512	21	3		-8	O/1	-3.1
■ **JIM TYACK**	Tyack, James Frederick b: 1/9/11, Florence, Mont. BL/TR, 6'2", 195 lbs. Deb: 4/20/43																											
1943	Phi-A	54	155	11	40	8	1	0	23	14	9	.258	.320	.323	.642	87	-2	-3	101	168	17	.546	1	1	-0	-1	O	-0.4
■ **FRED TYLER**	Tyler, Frederick Franklin "Clancy" b: 12/16/1891, Derry, N.H. d: 10/14/45, E.Derry, N.H. TR , 5'10.5", 180 lbs. Deb: 4/14/14																											
1914	Bos-N	6	19	2	2	0	0	0	2	1	5	.105	.150	.105	.255	-23	-3	-3	104	363	0	.176	0			0	/C	-0.2
■ **JOHNNIE TYLER**	Tyler, John Anthony "Ty Ty" or "Katz" (born John Tylka) b: 7/30/06, Mt.Pleasant, Pa. d: 7/11/72, Mt.Pleasant, Pa. BB/TR, 6', 175 lbs. Deb: 9/16/34																											
1934	Bos-N	3	6	0	1	0	0	0	1	0	3	.167	.167	.167	.333	-12	-1	-1	86	360	0	.200	0			1	/O	0.0
1935	Bos-N	13	47	7	16	2	1	2	11	4	3	.340	.404	.553	.957	162	4	4	96	131	11	1.000	0			-1	O	0.3
Total	2	16	53	7	17	2	1	2	12	4	6	.321	.379	.509	.889	144	3	3	94	155	11	.889	0			0	/O	0.3
■ **EARL TYREE**	Tyree, Earl Carlton "Ty" b: 3/4/1890, Huntsville, Ill. d: 5/17/54, Rushville, Ill. BR/TR, 5'8", 160 lbs. Deb: 10/05/14																											
1914	Chi-N	1	4	1	0	0	0	0	0	0	0	.000	.000	.000	.000	-99	-1	-1	98	0	0	.000	0			0	/C	0.0
■ **JIM TYRONE**	Tyrone, James Vernon b: 1/29/49, Alice, Tex. BR/TR, 6'1", 185 lbs. Deb: 8/27/72																											
1972	Chi-N	13	8	1	0	0	0	0	0	0	3	.000	.000	.000	.000	-88	-2	-2	114	0	0	.125	1	0	0	0	/O	-0.1
1974	Chi-N	57	81	19	15	0	1	3	3	6	8	.185	.241	.321	.562	56	-5	-5	100	33	6	.478	1	1	-0	-8	O/3	-1.5
1975	Chi-N	11	22	0	5	0	1	0	3	1	4	.227	.261	.318	.579	58	-1	-1	104	166	2	.500	1	1	-0	-1	/O	-0.2
1977	Oak-A	96	294	32	72	11	1	5	26	25	62	.245	.304	.340	.644	79	-10	-8	95	90	31	.561	3	1	0	-0	O/1SD	-1.0
Total	4	177	405	52	92	11	3	8	32	32	77	.227	.284	.328	.612	70	-18	-17	97	81	39	.533	6	3	0	-9	O/DS13	-2.8
■ **WAYNE TYRONE**	Tyrone, Oscar Wayne b: 8/1/50, Alice, Tex. BR/TR, 6'1", 185 lbs. Deb: 7/15/76																											
1976	Chi-N	30	57	3	13	1	0	1	8	3	21	.228	.267	.298	.565	55	-3	-4	109	154	5	.455	0	0	0	-3	/O13	-0.7
■ **TY TYSON**	Tyson, Albert Thomas b: 6/1/1892, Wilkes-Barre, Pa. d: 8/16/53, Buffalo, N.Y. BR/TR, 5'11", 169 lbs. Deb: 4/13/26																											
1926	NY-N	97	335	40	98	16	1	3	35	15	28	.293	.329	.373	.702	90	-6	-5	98	90	40	.629	6			1	O	-0.6
1927	NY-N	43	159	24	42	7	2	1	17	10	19	.264	.308	.352	.660	76	-6	-5	100	103	17	.607	5			-4	O	-1.0
1928	Bro-N	59	210	25	57	11	1	1	21	10	14	.271	.317	.348	.665	74	-8	-8	99	100	23	.588	3			4	O	-0.5
Total	3	199	704	89	197	34	4	5	73	35	61	.280	.320	.361	.681	82	-19	-18	99	96	79	.611	14			1	O	-2.1
■ **TURKEY TYSON**	Tyson, Cecil Washington "Slim" b: 12/6/14, Elm City, N.C. BL/TR, 6'5.5", 225 lbs. Deb: 4/23/44																											
1944	Phi-N	1	1	0	0	0	0	0	0	0	0	.000	.000	.000	.000	-99	-0	-0	100	0	0	.000	0			0	H	0.0
■ **MIKE TYSON**	Tyson, Michael Ray b: 1/13/50, Rocky Mount, N.C. BR/TR, 5'9", 170 lbs. Deb: 9/05/72																											
1972	StL-N	13	37	1	7	1	0	0	0	1	9	.189	.211	.216	.427	20	-4	-4	105	0	2	.290	0	1	-1	1	2/S	-0.2

YEAR	TM/L	G	AB	R	H	2B	3B	HR	RBI	BB	SO	AVG	OBP	SLG	PRO	/A	BR	/A	PF	CHI	RC	TA	SB	CS	SBR	FR	POS	TPR
1973	StL-N	144	469	48	114	15	4	1	33	23	66	.243	.281	.299	.580	67	-25	-20	91	93	37	.453	2	5	-2	-15	*S2	-1.9
1974	StL-N	151	422	35	94	14	5	1	37	22	70	.223	.266	.287	.553	53	-26	-28	104	115	29	.435	4	2	0	-2	*S2	-1.4
1975	StL-N	122	368	45	98	16	3	2	37	24	39	.266	.316	.342	.659	80	-9	-10	103	108	40	.566	5	2	0	-2	S2/3	0.0
1976	StL-N	76	245	26	70	12	9	3	28	16	34	.286	.330	.445	.774	114	5	4	104	91	34	.703	3	1	0	-2	2	0.6
1977	StL-N	138	418	42	103	15	2	7	57	30	48	.246	.300	.342	.642	75	-17	-15	96	139	41	.543	3	4	-2	19	*2	1.1
1978	StL-N	125	377	26	88	16	0	3	26	24	41	.233	.279	.300	.579	65	-19	-17	95	84	29	.459	2	0	1	2	*2	-0.6
1979	StL-N	75	190	18	42	8	2	5	20	13	28	.221	.275	.363	.638	69	-8	-9	105	94	18	.552	2	1	0	4	2	0.0
1980	Chi-N	123	341	34	81	19	3	3	23	15	61	.238	.274	.337	.611	66	-15	-17	106	73	31	.498	1	2	-1	12	*2	0.1
1981	Chi-N	50	92	6	17	2	0	2	8	7	15	.185	.250	.272	.522	46	-6	-7	104	101	7	.453	1	0	0	4	2/S	0.0
Total	10	1017	2959	281	714	118	28	27	269	175	411	.241	.287	.327	.614	70	-124	-123	100	100	268	.522	23	18	-4	20	2S/3	-2.3
■ **BOB UECKER** Uecker, Robert George b: 1/26/35, Milwaukee, Wis. BR/TR, 6'1", 190 lbs. Deb: 4/13/62																												
1962	Mil-N	33	64	5	16	2	0	1	8	7	15	.250	.324	.328	.652	76	-2	-2	99	131	6	.549	0	0	0	3	C	0.2
1963	Mil-N	13	16	3	4	2	0	0	0	2	5	.250	.333	.375	.708	103	0	0	101	0	2	.615	0	0	0	0	/C	0.0
1964	StL-N	40	106	8	21	1	0	1	6	17	24	.198	.315	.236	.550	51	-5	-7	112	88	9	.494	0	1	-1	0	C	-0.6
1965	StL-N	53	145	17	33	7	0	2	10	24	27	.228	.345	.317	.662	83	-1	-3	107	80	18	.632	0	1	-1	4	C	0.3
1966	Phi-N	78	207	15	43	6	0	7	30	22	36	.208	.284	.338	.622	71	-8	-8	101	139	19	.535	0	0	0	-2	C	-0.8
1967	Phi-N	18	35	3	6	2	0	0	7	5	9	.171	.275	.229	.504	44	-2	-3	104	363	2	.433	0	0	0	-0	C	-0.1
	Atl-N	62	158	14	23	2	0	3	13	19	51	.146	.237	.215	.452	29	-14	-15	104	125	8	.381	0	1	-1	2	C	-1.0
	Yr	80	193	17	29	4	0	3	20	24	60	.150	.244	.218	.462	32	-17	-17	104	183	11	.393	0	1	-1	2		-1.1
Total	6	297	731	65	146	22	0	14	74	96	167	.200	.295	.287	.582	61	-33	-37	105	123	64	.523	0	3	-2	7	C	-2.0
■ **FRENCHY UHALT** Uhalt, Bernard Bartholomew b: 4/27/10, Bakersfield, Cal. BL/TR, 5'10", 180 lbs. Deb: 4/17/34																												
1934	Chi-A	57	165	28	40	5	1	0	16	29	12	.242	.359	.285	.644	68	-7	-7	99	114	19	.638	6	5	-1	-1	O	-0.8
■ **TED UHLAENDER** Uhlaender, Theodore Otto b: 10/21/40, Chicago, Heights, Ill. BL/TR, 6'2", 190 lbs. Deb: 9/04/65																												
1965	Min-A	13	22	1	4	0	0	0	1	0	2	.182	.182	.182	.364	4	-3	-3	101	104	1	.278	1	0	0	1	/O	-0.1
1966	Min-A	105	367	39	83	12	2	2	22	27	33	.226	.281	.286	.567	57	-17	-22	111	85	32	.493	10	2	2	6	*O	-1.8
1967	Min-A	133	415	41	107	19	7	6	49	13	45	.258	.285	.381	.666	89	-4	-7	107	116	44	.563	4	4	-1	3	*O	-0.8
1968	Min-A	140	488	52	138	21	5	7	52	28	46	.283	.326	.389	.715	109	8	5	106	108	63	.658	16	7	1	-6	*O	-0.5
1969	Min-A	152	554	93	151	18	2	8	62	44	52	.273	.331	.356	.686	90	-6	-7	102	115	68	.627	15	9	-1	-1	*O	-1.3
1970	Cle-A	141	473	56	127	21	2	11	46	39	44	.268	.326	.391	.717	84	-3	-11	115	85	60	.637	3	6	-3	-1	*O	-2.0
1971	Cle-A	141	500	52	144	20	3	2	47	38	44	.288	.338	.352	.690	91	-3	-6	106	108	59	.588	3	6	-3	1	*O	-1.2
1972	Cin-N	73	113	9	18	3	0	0	6	13	11	.159	.246	.186	.432	26	-11	-10	93	117	5	.333	0	1	-1	-2	O	-1.5
Total	8	898	2932	343	772	114	21	36	285	202	277	.263	.313	.353	.667	85	-38	-61	107	104	330	.592	52	35	-5	1	O	-9.2
■ **GEORGE UHLE** Uhle, George Ernest "The Bull" b: 9/18/1898, Cleveland, Ohio d: 2/26/85, Lakewood, Ohio BR/TR, 6', 190 lbs. Deb: 4/30/19 C																												
1919	Cle-A	26	43	7	13	2	1	0	6	1	5	.302	.318	.395	.714	94	-0	-1	107	128	5	.600	0			0	P	0.0
1920	Cle-A	27	32	4	11	0	0	0	2	2	2	.344	.382	.344	.726	90	-0	-0	104	64	4	.667	1	0	0	0	P	0.0
1921	Cle-A	48	94	21	23	2	3	1	18	6	9	.245	.290	.362	.652	66	-5	-5	99	167	10	.563	0	0	0	-3	P	0.0
1922	Cle-A	56	109	21	29	8	2	0	14	13	6	.266	.350	.376	.726	88	-2	-2	102	122	15	.683	1	2	-1	-3	P	0.0
1923	Cle-A	58	144	23	52	10	3	0	22	7	10	.361	.391	.472	.863	125	5	5	101	111	26	.828	2	1	0	0	P	0.0
1924	Cle-A	59	107	10	33	6	1	1	19	4	8	.308	.339	.411	.751	96	-2	-1	97	134	14	.653	0	1	-1	1	P	0.3
1925	Cle-A	55	101	10	29	3	3	0	13	7	7	.287	.339	.376	.716	77	-3	-4	106	114	13	.639	0	0	0	-3	P	0.0
1926	Cle-A	50	132	16	30	3	0	1	11	10	12	.227	.287	.273	.559	47	-10	-10	100	96	11	.471	2	2	-1	-0	P	0.0
1927	Cle-A	43	79	4	21	7	1	0	14	5	12	.266	.310	.380	.689	80	-3	-2	97	155	9	.603	0	0	0	-1	P	0.0
1928	Cle-A	55	98	9	28	3	2	1	17	8	4	.286	.340	.388	.727	86	-1	-2	106	142	13	.657	0	0	0	2	P	0.0
1929	Det-A	40	108	18	37	1	1	0	13	6	6	.343	.377	.370	.748	96	-1	-0	97	111	15	.648	0	0	0	-3	P	0.0
1930	Det-A	59	117	15	36	4	2	2	21	8	13	.308	.352	.427	.779	92	-1	-2	105	124	18	.716	0	0	0	-3	P	0.0
1931	Det-A	53	90	8	22	6	0	2	7	8	8	.244	.306	.378	.684	76	-3	-3	104	58	10	.609	0	1	-1	-1	P	0.0
1932	Det-A	38	55	2	10	3	1	0	4	6	5	.182	.262	.273	.535	38	-5	-5	102	89	4	.467	0	0	0	-1	P	0.0
1933	Det-A	1	0	0	0	0	0	0	0	0	0	—	—	—	—	—	0	0	107	—	—	—	0	0	0	0	/P	0.0
	NY-N	8	5	1	0	0	0	0	0	1	3	.000	.167	.000	.167	-50	-1	-1	99	0	0	.200	0			0	/P	0.0
	NY-A	12	20	1	8	1	0	0	1	4	2	.400	.500	.450	.950	168	2	2	91	37	5	1.083	0	0	0	-1	P	0.0
1934	NY-A	10	5	1	3	0	1	0	1	0	0	.600	.600	1.000	1.600	321	1	1	96	67	3	2.500	0	0	0	-0	P	0.0
1936	Cle-A	24	21	1	8	1	0	1	4	2	0	.381	.435	.571	1.006	139	2	1	106	86	5	1.077	0	0	0	-0	/P	0.2
Total	17	722	1360	172	393	60	21	9	187	98	112	.289	.339	.384	.722	86	-27	-30	101	115	186	.647	6	7		-15	P	0.5
■ **MAURY UHLER** Uhler, Maurice William b: 12/14/1886, Pikesville, Md. d: 5/4/18, Baltimore, Md. BR/TR, 5'11", 165 lbs. Deb: 4/14/14																												
1914	Cin-N	46	56	12	12	2	0	0	3	5	11	.214	.279	.250	.529	55	-3	-3	105	78	5	.523	4			-8	O	-1.3
■ **CHARLIE UHLIR** Uhlir, Charles Karel b: 7/30/12, Chicago, Ill. BL/TL, 5'7.5", 150 lbs. Deb: 8/03/34																												
1934	Chi-A	14	27	3	4	0	0	0	3	2	6	.148	.207	.148	.355	-7	-4	-4	99	250	1	.261	0	0	0	-1	/O	-0.4
■ **MIKE ULISNEY** Ulisney, Michael Edward "Slugs" b: 9/28/17, Greenwald, Pa. BR/TR, 5'9", 165 lbs. Deb: 5/05/45																												
1945	Bos-N	11	18	4	7	1	0	1	4	1	0	.389	.421	.611	1.032	164	2	2	112	99	5	1.091	0			0	/C	0.2
■ **SCOTT ULLGER** Ullger, Scott Matthew b: 6/10/56, New York, N.Y. BR/TR, 6'2", 186 lbs. Deb: 4/17/83																												
1983	Min-A	35	79	8	15	4	0	0	5	5	21	.190	.247	.241	.488	33	-7	-7	105	103	3	.347	0	2	-1	-0	1/3D	-1.0
■ **GEORGE ULRICH** Ulrich, George F. b: Philadelphia, Pa. Deb: 5/01/1892																												
1892	Was-N	6	24	1	7	1	0	0	0	0	4	.292	.292	.333	.625	87	-0	-1	105	0	3	.588	2			0	/3SC	0.0
1893	Cin-N	1	3	0	0	0	0	0	0	0	0	.000	.250	.000	.250	-30	-1	-1	101	0	0	.667	1			0	/O	0.0
1896	NY-N	14	45	4	8	1	0	0	1	1	1	.178	.229	.200	.429	15	-5	-5	99	32	2	.324	0			0	O/3	-0.4
Total	3	21	72	5	15	2	0	0	1	1	5	.208	.250	.236	.486	35	-6	-6	101	20	5	.421	3			0	/O3CS	-0.4
■ **TOM UMPHLETT** Umphlett, Thomas Mullen b: 5/12/30, Scotland Neck, N.C BR/TR, 6'2", 180 lbs. Deb: 4/16/53																												
1953	Bos-A	137	495	53	140	27	5	3	59	34	30	.283	.331	.376	.707	83	-7	-13	109	114	62	.614	4	2	0	1	*O	-1.5
1954	Was-A	114	342	21	75	8	3	1	33	17	42	.219	.256	.269	.525	45	-27	-26	98	132	21	.390	1	2	-1	-2	*O	-3.2
1955	Was-A	110	323	34	70	10	0	2	19	24	35	.217	.271	.266	.537	49	-25	-22	91	77	24	.432	2	1	0	-5	*O	-3.1
Total	3	361	1160	108	285	45	8	6	111	75	107	.246	.293	.314	.606	64	-59	-60	101	109	107	.506	7	5	-1	-6	O	-7.8
■ **BOB UNGLAUB** Unglaub, Robert Alexander b: 7/31/1881, Baltimore, Md. d: 11/29/16, Baltimore, Md. BR/TR, 5'11", 178 lbs. Deb: 4/15/04 M																												
1904	NY-A	6	19	2	4	0	0	0	2	0		.211	.211	.211	.421	31	-1	-2	112	187	1	.267	0			0	/3S	0.0
	Bos-A	9	13	1	2	1	0	0	2	1		.154	.214	.231	.445	40	-1	-1	105	249	1	.364	0			0	/23S	0.0
	Yr	15	32	3	6	1	0	0	4	1		.188	.212	.219	.431	35	-2	-2	108	236	2	.308	0			0		0.0
1905	Bos-A	43	121	18	27	5	1	0	11	6		.223	.260	.281	.541	73	-4	-4	100	115	10	.447	2			2	3/21	0.0
1907	Bos-A	139	544	49	138	17	13	1	62	23		.254	.284	.338	.622	99	-1	-2	101	126	58	.544	14			-2	*1M	-0.6
1908	Bos-A	72	266	23	70	11	3	1	25	7		.263	.282	.338	.620	105	0	1	98	107	26	.526	6			-0	1	-0.1
	Was-A	72	276	23	85	10	5	0	29	8		.308	.327	.380	.708	139	9	10	95	110	36	.634	8			-1	32/1	1.1
	Yr	144	542	46	155	21	8	1	54	15		.286	.305	.360	.665	122	9	10	97	109	61	.579	14			-2		1.0
1909	Was-A	130	480	43	127	14	9	3	41	22		.265	.301	.350	.651	117	1	6	90	95	53	.589	15			-8	1O2/3	-0.4
1910	Was-A	124	431	29	101	9	4	0	44	21		.234	.270	.274	.544	70	-16	-16	101	141	37	.485	21			5	*1	-0.6
Total	6	595	2150	188	554	67	35	5	216	88		.258	.288	.328	.616	100	-13	-7	97	118	220	.541	66			-5	1/32OS	-0.6
■ **AL UNSER** Unser, Albert Bernard b: 10/12/12, Morrisonville, Ill BR/TR, 6'1", 175 lbs. Deb: 9/14/42																												
1942	Det-A	4	8	2	3	0	0	0	0	0	2	.375	.375	.375	.750	99	0	-0	113	0	1	.500	0	0	0	0	/C	0.1
1943	Det-A	38	101	14	25	5	0	0	4	15	15	.248	.350	.297	.647	85	-1	-1	106	49	11	.575	0	1	-1	2	C	0.2
1944	Det-A	11	25	2	3	0	1	1	5	3	2	.120	.214	.320	.534	49	-2	-2	105	164	2	.500	0	0	0	1	/2C	0.0
1945	Cin-N	67	204	23	54	10	3	3	21	14	24	.265	.318	.387	.705	101	-2	-0	94	83	25	.617	0			2	C	0.3

YEAR	TM/L	G	AB	R	H	2B	3B	HR	RBI	BB	SO	AVG	OBP	SLG	PRO	/A	BR	/A	PF	CHI	RC	TA	SB	CS	SBR	FR	POS	TPR
Total	4	120	338	41	85	15	4	4	30	32	43	.251	.322	.355	.677	92	-4	-4	99	76	39	.601	0	1		5	C/2	0.6

■ DEL UNSER Unser, Delbert Bernard b: 12/9/44, Decatur, Ill. BL/TL, 6'1", 180 lbs. Deb: 4/10/68 C

1968	Was-A	156	635	66	146	13	7	1	30	46	66	.230	.284	.277	.561	77	-22	-17	91	63	52	.470	11	6	-0	15	*O/1	-0.9
1969	Was-A	153	581	69	166	19	**8**	7	57	58	54	.286	.351	.382	.733	108	4	6	97	100	79	.670	8	10	-4	-2	*O	-0.3
1970	Was-A	119	322	37	83	5	1	5	30	30	29	.258	.321	.326	.647	82	-9	-7	96	101	35	.557	1	1	-0	-0	*O	-1.2
1971	Was-A	153	581	63	148	19	6	9	41	59	68	.255	.326	.355	.680	100	-5	-0	92	76	70	.628	11	6	-0	5	*O	0.0
1972	Cle-A	132	383	29	91	12	0	1	17	28	46	.238	.291	.277	.568	65	-14	-17	107	65	31	.459	5	9	-4	7	*O	-1.8
1973	Phi-N	136	440	64	127	20	4	11	52	47	55	.289	.359	.427	.786	108	10	6	108	95	68	.744	5	8	-3	13	*O	0.9
1974	Phi-N	142	454	72	120	18	5	11	61	50	62	.264	.339	.399	.737	102	3	1	103	110	62	.690	6	4	-1	-3	*O	-0.7
1975	NY-N	147	531	65	156	18	2	10	53	37	76	.294	.340	.392	.732	108	1	4	95	88	70	.645	4	3	-1	8	*O	0.6
1976	NY-N	77	276	28	63	13	2	5	25	18	40	.228	.278	.344	.622	83	-9	-7	92	89	26	.534	4	4	-1	-0	O	-1.1
	Mon-N	69	220	29	50	6	2	7	15	11	44	.227	.264	.368	.632	78	-7	-7	100	57	21	.540	3	3	-1	-2	O	-1.3
	Yr	146	496	57	113	19	4	12	40	29	84	.228	.272	.355	.627	80	-17	-14	96	74	48	.542	7	7	-2	-3		-2.4
1977	Mon-N	113	289	33	79	14	1	12	40	33	41	.273	.348	.453	.801	115	5	6	98	96	45	.758	2	5	-2	-5	O1	-0.5
1978	Mon-N	130	179	16	35	5	0	2	15	24	29	.196	.294	.257	.551	58	-10	-9	96	114	15	.497	2	0	1	1	1O	-1.1
1979	Phi-N	95	141	26	42	8	0	6	29	14	33	.298	.361	.482	.844	132	5	6	97	134	24	.816	2	0	1	-5	O1	0.0
1980	Phi-N	96	110	15	29	6	4	0	10	10	21	.264	.325	.391	.716	92	-0	-1	107	92	14	.631	0	1	-1	0	1O	-0.3
1981	Phi-N	62	59	5	9	3	0	0	6	13	9	.153	.306	.203	.509	42	-4	-5	112	196	4	.490	0	0	0	-3	1O	-0.8
1982	Phi-N	19	14	0	0	0	0	0	0	3	2	.000	.176	.000	.176	-50	-3	-3	94	0	0	.200	0	0	0	-1	/1O	-0.3
Total	15	1799	5215	617	1344	179	42	87	481	481	675	.258	.321	.358	.680	94	-56	-44	98	89	616	.616	64	60	-17	28	*O1	-8.8

■ JOHN UPHAM Upham, John Leslie b: 12/29/41, Windsor, Ont., Can. BL/TL, 6', 180 lbs. Deb: 4/16/67

1967	Chi-N	8	3	1	2	0	0	0	0	0	0	.667	.667	.667	1.333	279	1	1	102	0	1	2.000	0	0	0	0	/P	0.0
1968	Chi-N	13	10	0	2	0	0	0	0	0	3	.200	.200	.200	.400	18	-1	-1	112	0	0	.250	0	0	0	-0	/PO	-0.1
Total	2	21	13	1	4	0	0	0	0	0	3	.308	.308	.308	.615	76	-0	-0	110	0	2	.444	0	0	0	-0	/PO	-0.1

■ DIXIE UPRIGHT Upright, R T b: 5/30/26, Kannapolis, N.C. d: 11/13/86, Concord, N.C. BL/TL, 6', 175 lbs. Deb: 4/18/53

1953	StL-A	9	8	3	2	0	0	1	1	1	3	.250	.333	.625	.958	144	1	0	107	46	2	1.000	0	0	0	0	H	0.0

■ WILLIE UPSHAW Upshaw, Willie Clay b: 4/27/57, Blanco, Tex. BL/TL, 6', 185 lbs. Deb: 4/09/78

1978	Tor-A	95	224	26	53	8	2	1	17	21	35	.237	.302	.304	.606	71	-8	-8	100	95	20	.514	4	6	-2	-7	OD1	-1.9
1980	Tor-A	34	61	10	13	3	1	1	5	6	14	.213	.284	.344	.628	71	-2	-2	100	81	7	.583	1	0	0	-0	1D/O	-0.3
1981	Tor-A	61	111	15	19	3	1	4	10	11	16	.171	.252	.324	.576	59	-5	-7	111	82	9	.532	2	1	0	-3	D1O	-1.0
1982	Tor-A	160	580	77	155	25	7	21	75	52	91	.267	.329	.443	.772	101	7	0	109	96	82	.716	8	8	-2	-2	*1/D	-0.7
1983	Tor-A	160	579	99	177	26	7	27	104	61	98	.306	.377	.515	.891	131	34	27	108	109	113	.897	10	7	-1	3	*1/D	2.2
1984	Tor-A	152	569	79	158	31	9	19	84	55	86	.278	.347	.464	.811	120	16	15	102	111	92	.788	10	4	1	-1	*1/D	0.6
1985	Tor-A	148	501	79	138	31	5	15	65	48	71	.275	.344	.447	.791	113	10	9	101	96	76	.753	8	8	-2	2	*1/D	0.0
1986	Tor-A	155	573	85	144	28	6	9	60	78	87	.251	.343	.368	.711	90	-2	-6	105	106	80	.715	23	5	4	4	*1/D	-0.8
1987	Tor-A	150	512	68	125	22	4	15	58	58	78	.244	.325	.391	.715	89	-7	-8	101	95	65	.669	10	11	-4	8	*1	-1.7
1988	Cle-A	149	493	58	121	22	3	11	50	62	66	.245	.332	.369	.701	95	-2	-3	102	94	61	.660	12	9	-2	1	*1	-1.1
Total	10	1264	4203	596	1103	199	45	123	528	452	642	.262	.337	.419	.756	103	39	17	104	100	604	.733	88	59	-9	5	*1/OD	-4.7

■ TOM UPTON Upton, Thomas Herbert "Muscles" b: 12/29/26, Ester, Mo. BR/TR, 6', 160 lbs. Deb: 4/19/50

1950	StL-A	124	389	50	92	5	6	2	30	52	45	.237	.328	.296	.624	57	-22	-26	107	86	42	.570	7	2	1	-11	*S/23	-2.9
1951	StL-A	52	131	9	26	4	3	0	12	12	22	.198	.271	.275	.546	46	-10	-11	105	119	10	.450	1	1	-0	-4	S	-1.1
1952	Was-A	5	5	1	0	0	0	0	0	1	0	.000	.167	.000	.167	-51	-1	-1	100	0	0	.200	0	0	0	0	/S	0.0
Total	3	181	525	60	118	9	9	2	42	65	67	.225	.313	.288	.600	53	-33	-38	106	93	51	.551	8	3	1	-15	S/23	-4.0

■ LUKE URBAN Urban, Louis John b: 3/22/1898, Fall River, Mass. d: 12/7/80, Somerset, Mass. BR/TR, 5'8", 168 lbs. Deb: 7/19/27

1927	Bos-N	35	111	11	32	5	0	0	10	3	6	.288	.313	.333	.646	78	-4	-3	93	95	11	.532	1			2	C	0.1
1928	Bos-N	15	17	0	3	0	0	0	2	0	1	.176	.222	.176	.399	6	-2	-2	97	237	1	.286	0			0	C	-0.1
Total	2	50	128	11	35	5	0	0	12	3	7	.273	.301	.313	.613	68	-7	-6	94	114	12	.495	1			2	/C	0.0

■ BILLY URBANSKI Urbanski, William Michael b: 6/5/03, Linoleumville, N.Y d: 7/12/73, Perth Amboy, N.J. BR/TR, 5'8", 165 lbs. Deb: 7/04/31

1931	Bos-N	82	303	22	72	13	4	0	17	10	32	.238	.274	.307	.581	56	-19	-19	99	69	27	.481	3			1	3S	-1.1
1932	Bos-N	136	563	80	153	25	8	8	46	28	60	.272	.307	.387	.695	92	-12	-7	93	62	68	.622	8			-4	*S	0.0
1933	Bos-N	144	566	65	142	21	4	0	35	33	48	.251	.298	.302	.600	74	-20	-18	96	74	52	.487	4			-2	*S	-1.0
1934	Bos-N	146	605	104	177	30	6	7	53	56	37	.293	.357	.397	.754	119	2	14	86	63	90	.696	4			-7	*S	0.9
1935	Bos-N	132	514	53	118	17	0	4	30	40	32	.230	.286	.286	.572	57	-32	-29	96	72	42	.464	3			-26	*S	-4.8
1936	Bos-N	122	494	55	129	17	5	0	26	31	42	.261	.310	.316	.626	73	-21	-18	95	57	48	.509	2			-4	S3	-1.3
1937	Bos-N	1	1	0	0	0	0	0	0	0	1	.000	.000	.000	.000	-99	-0	-0	90	0	0	.000	0			0	H	0.0
Total	7	763	3046	379	791	123	27	19	207	198	252	.260	.309	.337	.646	81	-103	-77	93	66	327	.562	24			-41	S3	-7.3

■ JOSE URIBE Uribe, Jose Altagracia (Player Under Real Name Of Jose Altagracia Gonzalez (Uribe) In 1984) b: 1/21/59, San Cristobal, D.R. BB/TR, 5'10", 155 lbs. Deb: 9/13/84

1984	StL-N	8	19	4	4	0	0	0	3	0	2	.211	.211	.211	.421	19	-2	-2	99	294	1	.313	1	0	0	1	/S2	0.0
1985	SF-N	147	476	46	113	20	4	3	26	30	57	.237	.285	.315	.601	73	-21	-17	93	65	44	.514	8	2	1	-3	*S/2	-0.7
1986	SF-N	157	453	46	101	15	1	3	43	61	76	.223	.315	.280	.596	68	-20	-17	96	126	43	.575	22	11	0	6	*S	0.3
1987	SF-N	95	309	44	90	16	5	5	30	24	35	.291	.344	.424	.768	106	1	2	96	82	48	.757	12	2	2	16	S	3.1
1988	SF-N	141	493	47	124	10	7	3	35	36	69	.252	.302	.318	.621	83	-14	-10	94	86	48	.542	14	10	-2	-2	*S	-0.4
Total	5	548	1750	187	432	61	17	14	137	151	239	.247	.308	.325	.633	80	-55	-44	95	93	184	.579	57	25	2	18	S/2	2.3

■ LON URY Ury, Louis Newton "Old Sleep" b: 1877, Ft.Scott, Kan. d: 3/4/18, Kansas City, Mo. TR , 6', Deb: 03

1903	StL-N	2	7	0	1	0	0	0	0	0		.143	.143	.143	.286	-18	-1	-1	96	0	0	.167	0			-0	/1	0.0

■ BOB USHER Usher, Robert Royce b: 3/1/25, San Diego, Cal. BR/TR, 6'1.5", 180 lbs. Deb: 4/16/46

1946	Cin-N	92	152	16	31	5	1	1	14	13	27	.204	.271	.270	.541	52	-9	-10	104	119	12	.463	2			-12	O/3	-2.5
1947	Cin-N	9	22	2	4	0	0	1	1	2	2	.182	.250	.318	.568	55	-2	-1	91	37	2	.474	0			0	/O	0.0
1950	Cin-N	106	321	51	83	17	0	6	35	27	38	.259	.316	.368	.684	76	-10	-12	105	99	37	.599	3			3	O	-1.1
1951	Cin-N	114	303	27	63	12	2	5	25	19	36	.208	.257	.310	.567	52	-21	-21	101	89	23	.466	4	5	-2	2	O	-2.3
1952	Chi-N	1	0	0	0	0	0	0	0	1	0	—	1.000	—	1.310	270	0	0	103	0	0	—	0	0	0	0	H	0.0
1957	Cle-A	10	8	1	1	0	0	0	0	1	3	.125	.222	.125	.347	-3	-1	-1	102	0	0	.286	0	0	0	-1	/O3	-0.2
	Was-A	96	295	36	77	7	1	5	27	27	30	.261	.327	.342	.670	85	-7	-6	98	92	34	.580	0	0	0	-2	O	-1.3
	Yr	106	303	37	78	7	1	5	27	28	33	.257	.324	.337	.661	82	-8	-7	98	83	34	.571	0	0	0	-3		-1.5
Total	6	428	1101	133	259	41	4	18	102	90	136	.235	.295	.329	.624	68	-50	-51	101	95	107	.545	9	5		-9	O/3	-7.4

■ DUTCH USSAT Ussat, William August b: 4/11/04, Dayton, Ohio d: 5/29/59, Dayton, Ohio BR/TR, 6'1", 170 lbs. Deb: 9/13/25

1925	Cle-A	1	1	0	0	0	0	0	0	0	0	.000	.000	.000	.000	-94	-0	-0	106	0	0	.000	0	0	0	0	/2	0.0
1927	Cle-A	4	16	4	3	0	1	0	2	0	1	.188	.278	.313	.590	55	-1	-1	97	117	1	.538	0	0	0	0	/3	0.0
Total	2	5	17	4	3	0	1	0	2	0	1	.176	.263	.294	.557	45	-1	-1	97	111	1	.500	0	0	0	0	/32	0.0

■ TEX VACHE Vache, Ernest Lewis b: 11/17/1895, Santa Monica, Cal. d: 6/11/53, Los Angeles, Cal. BR/TR, 6'1", 195 lbs. Deb: 4/16/25

1925	Bos-A	110	252	41	79	15	7	3	48	21	33	.313	.382	.464	.846	120	5	7	95	127	45	.840	2	2	-1	-10	O	-0.7

■ GENE VADEBONCOEUR Vadeboncoeur, Eugene F. b: Louiseville, Que., Can. d: 10/16/35, Haverhill, Mass. 5'6", 150 lbs. Deb: 7/11/1884

1884	Phi-N	4	14	1	3	0	0	0	3	1	2	.214	.267	.214	.481	58	-1	-1	92	351	1	.364				0	/C	0.0

■ HARRY VAHRENHORST Vahrenhorst, Harry Henry "Van" b: 2/13/1885, St.Louis, Mo. d: 10/10/43, St.Louis, Mo. BR/TR, 6'1", 175 lbs. Deb: 9/21/04

1904	StL-A	1	1	0	0	0	0	0	0	0		.000	.000	.000	.000	-99	-0	-0	95	0	0	.000	0			0	H	0.0

■ MIKE VAIL Vail, Michael Lewis b: 11/10/51, San Francisco, Cal. BR/TR, 6'1", 180 lbs. Deb: 8/18/75

1975	NY-N	38	162	17	49	8	1	3	17	9	37	.302	.339	.420	.759	115	2	3	95	75	23	.664	0	0	0	10	O	1.2

YEAR	TM/L	G	AB	R	H	2B	3B	HR	RBI	BB	SO	AVG	OBP	SLG	PRO	/A	BR	/A	PF	CHI	RC	TA	SB	CS	SBR	FR	POS	TPR
1976	NY-N	53	143	8	31	5	1	0	9	6	19	.217	.248	.266	.514	50	-10	-9	92	91	9	.376	0	1	-1	-2	O	-1.3
1977	NY-N	108	279	29	73	12	1	8	35	19	58	.262	.313	.398	.711	93	-5	-3	96	104	30	.595	0	7	-4	0	O	-1.0
1978	Cle-A	14	34	2	8	2	1	0	2	1	9	.235	.257	.353	.610	75	-1	-1	93	66	3	.519	1	1	-0	-0	/OD	-0.1
	Chi-N	74	180	15	60	6	2	4	33	3	24	.333	.344	.456	.800	110	4	2	110	139	25	.669	0	1	-1	-9	O/3	-0.9
1979	Chi-N	87	179	28	60	8	2	7	35	14	27	.335	.383	.520	.903	128	10	8	112	122	34	.856	0	2	-1	-4	O/3	0.1
1980	Chi-N	114	312	30	93	17	2	6	47	14	77	.298	.330	.423	.753	103	3	1	106	124	40	.642	2	5	-2	-5	O	-1.0
1981	Cin-N	31	31	1	5	0	0	0	3	0	9	.161	.161	.161	.323	-8	-4	-4	101	236	1	.185	0	0	0	-1	/O	-0.5
1982	Cin-N	78	189	9	48	10	1	4	29	6	33	.254	.277	.381	.658	80	-5	-6	102	135	18	.527	0	0	0	-1	O	-0.7
1983	SF-N	18	26	1	4	1	0	0	3	0	7	.154	.185	.192	.377	5	-3	-3	101	237	1	.273	0	0	0	-1	/1O	-0.3
	Mon-N	34	53	5	15	2	0	2	4	8	10	.283	.387	.434	.821	125	2	2	102	55	9	.821	0	0	0	1	O/13	0.2
	Yr	52	79	6	19	3	0	2	7	8	17	.241	.326	.354	.680	87	-1	-1	101	122	10	.623	0	0	0	0		-0.1
1984	LA-N	16	16	1	1	0	0	0	2	1	7	.063	.118	.063	.180	-46	-3	-3	104	784	0	.133	0	0	0	-0	/O	-0.3
Total	10	665	1604	146	447	71	11	34	219	81	317	.279	.315	.400	.716	95	-11	-15	102	122	192	.623	3	17	-9	-12	O/13D	-4.6
■ ROY VALDES	Valdes, Rogelio Lazaro (Rojas) b: 2/20/20, Havana, Cuba BR/TR, 5'11", 185 lbs. Deb: 5/03/44																											
1944	Was-A	1	1	0	0	0	0	0	0	0	0	.000	.000	.000	.000	-99	-0	-0	90	0	0	.000	0	0	0	0	H	0.0
■ SANDY VALDESPINO	Valdespino, Hilario (Borroto) b: 1/14/39, San Jose De Las Lajas, Cuba BL/TL, 5'8", 170 lbs. Deb: 4/12/65																											
1965	Min-A	108	245	38	64	8	2	1	22	20	28	.261	.322	.322	.645	83	-5	-5	101	111	26	.568	7	4	-0	0	O	-0.7
1966	Min-A	52	108	11	19	1	1	2	9	4	24	.176	.212	.259	.472	31	-9	-11	111	111	5	.365	2	2	-1	-2	O	-1.4
1967	Min-A	99	97	9	16	2	0	1	3	5	22	.165	.206	.216	.422	23	-9	-10	107	52	4	.349	3	1	0	-14	O	-2.7
1968	Atl-N	36	86	8	20	1	0	1	4	10	20	.233	.320	.279	.599	87	-2	-1	93	62	8	.530	0	0	0	-0	O	-0.2
1969	Hou-N	41	119	17	29	4	0	0	12	15	19	.244	.328	.277	.606	70	-4	-4	102	146	12	.538	2	2	-1	-0	O	-0.6
	Sea-A	20	38	3	8	1	0	0	2	1	7	.211	.250	.237	.487	37	-3	-3	98	89	2	.355	0	1	-1	2	/O	-0.1
1970	Mil-A	8	9	0	0	0	0	0	0	0	4	.000	.000	.000	.000	-99	-2	-2	98	0	0	.000	0	0	0	-0	/O	-0.2
1971	KC-A	18	63	10	20	6	0	2	15	2	5	.317	.338	.508	.846	139	3	3	99	161	10	.756	0	0	0	-2	O	0.0
Total	7	382	765	96	176	23	3	7	67	57	129	.230	.288	.295	.583	66	-32	-34	102	105	67	.502	14	10	-2	-16	O	-5.9
■ JULIO VALDEZ	Valdez, Julio Julian (born Julio Julian Castillo (Valdez) b: 6/3/56, San Cristobal, D.R. BR/TR, 6'2", 160 lbs. Deb: 9/02/80																											
1980	Bos-A	8	19	4	5	1	0	1	4	0	5	.263	.300	.474	.774	106	0	0	102	130	3	.857	2	0	1	2	/S	0.3
1981	Bos-A	17	23	1	5	0	0	0	3	0	2	.217	.217	.217	.435	24	-2	-2	106	235	1	.263	0	1	-1	0	S	-0.1
1982	Bos-A	28	20	3	5	1	0	0	1	0	7	.250	.250	.300	.550	46	-1	-2	110	67	2	.467	1	0	0	1	S/D	0.2
1983	Bos-A	12	25	3	3	0	0	0	0	1	4	.120	.185	.120	.305	-14	-4	-4	101	0	1	.227	0	0	0	-1	/2SD	-0.4
Total	4	65	87	11	18	2	0	1	8	1	18	.207	.233	.264	.498	36	-7	-8	105	104	6	.414	3	1	0	2	/S2D	0.0
■ JOSE VALDIVIELSO	Valdivielso, Jose (Lopez) (born Jose Martinez De Valdivielso (Lopez)) b: 5/22/34, Matanzas, Cuba BR/TR, 6'1", 175 lbs. Deb: 6/21/55																											
1955	Was-A	94	294	32	65	12	5	2	28	21	38	.221	.280	.316	.596	66	-17	-14	91	106	26	.498	1	2	-1	10	S	0.5
1956	Was-A	90	246	18	58	8	2	4	29	29	36	.236	.319	.333	.652	71	-10	-10	102	115	26	.584	3	1	0	3	S	0.1
1959	Was-A	24	14	1	4	0	0	0	0	1	3	.286	.333	.286	.619	72	-1	-1	100	0	1	.500	0	0	0	1	S	0.2
1960	Was-A	117	268	23	57	1	1	2	19	20	36	.213	.277	.246	.524	42	-21	-22	102	103	19	.414	1	2	-1	-1	*S/3	-1.2
1961	Min-A	76	149	15	29	5	0	1	9	8	19	.195	.236	.248	.484	28	-15	-16	106	88	8	.362	1	1	-0	-1	S23	-1.1
Total	5	401	971	89	213	26	8	9	85	79	132	.219	.284	.290	.574	54	-64	-63	99	103	80	.487	6	6	-2	13	S/23	-1.5
■ ELLIS VALENTINE	Valentine, Ellis Clarence b: 7/30/54, Helena, Ark. BR/TR, 6'4", 205 lbs. Deb: 9/03/75																											
1975	Mon-N	12	33	2	12	4	0	1	3	2	4	.364	.400	.576	.976	156	3	3	108	53	7	.955	0	0	0	-2	O	0.0
1976	Mon-N	94	305	36	85	15	2	7	39	30	51	.279	.343	.410	.753	113	5	5	100	103	46	.748	14	1	4	4	O	1.0
1977	Mon-N	127	508	63	149	28	2	25	76	30	58	.293	.333	.504	.837	123	13	14	98	97	78	.783	13	5	1	-3	*O	0.7
1978	Mon-N	151	570	75	165	35	2	25	76	35	88	.289	.333	.489	.822	133	18	21	96	90	90	.780	13	8	-1	12	*O	2.7
1979	Mon-N	146	548	73	151	29	3	21	82	22	74	.276	.305	.454	.759	102	1	-1	102	106	65	.660	11	9	-2	1	*O	-0.5
1980	Mon-N	86	311	40	98	22	2	13	67	25	44	.315	.372	.524	.896	149	19	19	99	134	60	.887	5	5	-2	-2	O	1.3
1981	Mon-N	22	76	8	16	3	0	3	15	6	11	.211	.268	.368	.637	80	-2	-2	99	162	7	.540	0	1	-1	-1	O	-0.4
	NY-N	48	169	15	35	8	1	5	21	5	38	.207	.230	.355	.585	64	-9	-9	101	112	12	.468	0	3	-2	0	O	-1.2
	Yr	70	245	23	51	11	1	8	36	11	49	.208	.242	.359	.601	69	-11	-11	100	130	20	.495	0	4	-2	-1		-1.6
1982	NY-N	111	337	33	97	14	1	8	48	5	38	.288	.300	.407	.707	97	-3	-3	99	117	36	.567	1	3	-2	-1	O	-0.6
1983	Cal-A	86	271	30	65	10	2	13	43	18	48	.240	.287	.435	.723	100	-3	-1	96	107	33	.648	2	1	0	-8	O	-1.0
1985	Tex-A	11	38	5	8	1	0	2	4	2	8	.211	.250	.395	.645	68	-2	-2	108	76	3	.531	0	1	-1	-2	/OD	-0.3
Total	10	894	3166	380	881	169	15	123	474	180	462	.278	.319	.458	.776	113	39	43	99	106	437	.730	59	37	-5	-2	O/D	1.7
■ FRED VALENTINE	Valentine, Fred Lee "Squeaky" b: 1/19/35, Clarksdale, Miss. BB/TR, 6'1", 190 lbs. Deb: 9/07/59																											
1959	Bal-A	12	19	0	6	0	0	0	1	3	4	.316	.409	.316	.725	105	0	0	97	66	2	.643	0	1	-1	-1	/O	-0.1
1963	Bal-A	26	41	5	11	1	0	0	1	8	5	.268	.388	.293	.680	100	0	0	94	35	5	.625	0	0	0	-1	O	0.0
1964	Was-A	102	212	20	48	5	0	4	20	21	44	.226	.305	.307	.612	70	-8	-8	101	110	20	.541	4	2	0	-4	O	-1.5
1965	Was-A	12	29	6	7	0	0	0	1	4	5	.241	.353	.241	.594	72	-1	-1	100	59	3	.652	3	0	1	0	O	0.0
1966	Was-A	146	508	77	140	29	7	16	59	51	63	.276	.353	.455	.808	138	20	23	95	91	81	.805	22	10	1	9	*O/1	2.9
1967	Was-A	151	457	52	107	16	1	11	44	56	76	.234	.331	.346	.677	98	1	0	102	96	58	.673	17	3	3	-11	*O	-1.2
1968	Was-A	37	101	11	24	2	0	3	7	6	11	.238	.294	.347	.640	102	-1	-0	91	68	9	.537	1	0	0	-2	O	-0.2
	Bal-A	47	91	9	17	3	2	2	5	7	20	.187	.253	.330	.582	74	-3	-3	102	59	8	.507	0	0	0	-1	O	-0.6
	Yr	84	192	20	41	5	2	5	12	13	31	.214	.274	.339	.613	87	-4	-3	97	64	19	.539	1	0	0	-4		-0.8
Total	7	533	1458	180	360	56	10	36	138	156	228	.247	.331	.373	.704	105	9	12	98	89	187	.694	47	16	5	-12	O/1	-0.7
■ BOB VALENTINE	Valentine, Robert Deb: 5/20/1876																											
1876	NY-N	1	3	0	0	0	0	0	0	0	0	.000	.000	.000	.000	-99	-1	-1	87	0	0	.000				0	/C	0.0
■ BOBBY VALENTINE	Valentine, Robert John b: 5/13/50, Stamford, Conn. BR/TR, 5'10", 189 lbs. Deb: 9/02/69 MC																											
1969	LA-N	5	0	3	0	0	0	0	0	0	0	—	—	—	—	—	0	0	99	—	—	—	0	0	0	0	R	0.0
1971	LA-N	101	281	32	70	10	2	1	25	15	20	.249	.292	.310	.602	71	-11	-11	99	113	24	.489	5	3	-0	1	S32O	-0.4
1972	LA-N	119	391	42	107	11	2	3	32	27	33	.274	.324	.335	.659	93	-6	-3	94	94	41	.550	5	5	-2	-2	23OS	-0.3
1973	Cal-A	32	126	12	38	5	2	1	13	5	9	.302	.328	.397	.725	108	0	1	96	102	17	.678	6	1	1	3	S/O	0.8
1974	Cal-A	117	371	39	97	10	3	3	39	25	25	.261	.313	.329	.642	92	-7	-4	92	117	39	.552	8	5	-1	-4	OS3/2D	-0.7
1975	Cal-A	26	57	5	16	2	0	0	5	4	3	.281	.339	.316	.654	91	-1	-1	95	107	6	.523	0	2	-1	-1	D/13O	-0.2
	SD-N	7	15	1	2	0	0	1	1	4	0	.133	.316	.333	.649	81	-0	-0	100	48	2	.769	1	0	0	-1	/O	0.0
1976	SD-N	15	49	3	18	4	0	0	4	6	2	.367	.436	.449	.885	171	4	4	89	71	9	.824	0	0	0	1	O/1	0.4
1977	SD-N	44	67	5	12	3	0	1	10	7	10	.179	.257	.269	.525	47	-6	-5	88	191	4	.431	0	1	-1	1	S3/1	-0.2
	NY-N	42	83	8	11	1	0	1	3	6	9	.133	.191	.181	.372	0	-12	-11	96	67	2	.276	0	0	0	-1	1S/3	-1.0
	Yr	86	150	13	23	4	0	2	13	13	19	.153	.221	.220	.441	20	-17	-16	92	132	7	.351	0	0	0	0		-1.2
1978	NY-N	69	160	17	43	7	0	1	18	19	18	.269	.350	.331	.681	93	-1	-1	98	127	18	.592	1	1	-0	-0	2/3	0.1
1979	Sea-A	62	98	9	27	6	0	0	7	22	5	.276	.408	.337	.745	103	2	2	100	81	14	.727	1	2	-1	-1	SO/23C	0.3
Total	10	639	1698	176	441	59	9	12	157	140	134	.260	.319	.326	.646	86	-39	-28	95	107	177	.570	27	20	-4	-4	SO23/1DC	-1.2
■ BENNY VALENZUELA	Valenzuela, Benjamin Beltran "Papelero" b: 6/2/33, Los Mochis, Mexico BR/TR, 5'10", 175 lbs. Deb: 4/27/58																											
1958	StL-N	10	14	0	3	1	0	0	0	1	0	.214	.267	.286	.552	43	-1	-1	106	0	1	.455	0	0	0	0	/3	0.0
■ DAVE VALLE	Valle, David b: 10/30/60, Bayside, N.Y. BR/TR, 6'2", 200 lbs. Deb: 9/07/84																											
1984	Sea-A	13	27	4	8	1	0	1	4	1	5	.296	.321	.444	.766	107	0	0	102	106	4	.684	0	0	0	0	C	0.1
1985	Sea-A	31	70	2	11	1	0	0	4	1	17	.157	.181	.171	.352	-3	-10	-9	95	132	2	.233	0	0	0	-2	C	-0.9
1986	Sea-A	22	53	10	18	3	0	5	15	7	7	.340	.417	.679	1.096	184	7	6	105	117	14	1.162	0	0	0	0	C/1	0.6
1987	Sea-A	95	324	40	83	16	3	12	53	15	46	.256	.295	.435	.731	89	-5	-6	103	119	38	.634	2	0	1	6	CD/1O	0.5
1988	Sea-A	93	290	29	67	15	2	10	50	18	38	.231	.297	.400	.697	87	-3	-6	108	136	31	.603	0	1	-1	8	C/1D	0.5
Total	5	254	764	85	187	36	5	28	126	42	113	.245	.295	.415	.710	88	-11	-15	104	126	90	.633	2	1	0	12	C/D1O	0.8

YEAR	TM/L	G	AB	R	H	2B	3B	HR	RBI	BB	SO	AVG	OBP	SLG	PRO	/A	BR	/A	PF	CHI	RC	TA	SB	CS	SBR	FR	POS	TPR
■ **HECTOR VALLE**	Valle, Hector Jose b: 10/27/40, Vega Baja, P.R. BR/TR, 5'9", 180 lbs. Deb: 6/06/65																											
1965	LA-N	9	13	1	4	0	0	0	2	2	3	.308	.400	.308	.708	112	0	0	91	207	2	.667	0	0	0	0	/C	0.0
■ **ELMER VALO**	Valo, Elmer William b: 3/5/21, Ribnik, Czech. BL/TR, 5'11", 190 lbs. Deb: 9/22/40 C																											
1940	Phi-A	6	23	6	8	0	0	0	0	3	0	.348	.423	.348	.771	107	0	0	96	0	4	.867	2	0	1	1	/O	0.1
1941	Phi-A	15	50	13	21	0	1	2	6	4	2	.420	.463	.580	1.043	173	5	5	101	61	14	1.100	0	0	0	-1	O	0.4
1942	Phi-A	133	459	64	115	13	10	2	40	70	21	.251	.355	.336	.690	98	-1	1	96	90	58	.658	13	8	-1	-2	*O	-1.0
1943	Phi-A	77	249	31	55	6	2	3	18	35	13	.221	.319	.297	.616	80	-5	-6	101	81	24	.544	2	6	-3	-3	O	-1.4
1946	Phi-A	108	348	59	107	21	6	1	31	60	18	.307	.411	.411	.822	125	17	15	104	82	64	.845	9	8	-2	-0	O	0.8
1947	Phi-A	112	370	60	111	12	6	5	36	64	21	.300	.406	.405	.811	126	16	15	100	82	69	.853	11	3	2	-4	*O	0.9
1948	Phi-A	113	383	72	117	17	4	3	46	81	13	.305	.432	.394	.826	119	16	15	102	99	72	.869	10	6	-1	-5	*O	0.5
1949	Phi-A	150	547	86	155	27	12	5	85	119	32	.283	.413	.404	.817	118	18	19	99	119	101	.860	14	11	-2	8	*O	2.0
1950	Phi-A	129	446	62	125	16	5	10	46	82	22	.280	.400	.406	.806	119	7	15	90	77	81	.842	12	7	-1	2	*O	1.3
1951	Phi-A	123	444	75	134	27	8	7	55	75	20	.302	.412	.446	.858	124	23	19	106	95	87	.890	11	6	-0	-2	*O	1.2
1952	Phi-A	129	388	69	109	26	4	5	47	101	16	.281	.432	.407	.839	121	24	18	111	102	76	.910	12	11	-3	-6	*O	0.6
1953	Phi-A	50	85	15	19	3	0	0	9	22	7	.224	.383	.259	.642	74	-2	-2	102	151	10	.638	0	1	-1	-2	O	-0.4
1954	Phi-A	95	224	28	48	11	6	1	33	51	18	.214	.360	.330	.690	91	-1	-1	98	163	31	.709	2	1	0	-1	O	-0.2
1955	KC-A	112	283	50	103	17	4	3	37	52	18	.364	.463	.484	.947	153	25	24	101	95	67	1.032	5	3	-0	0	O	2.0
1956	KC-A	9	9	1	2	0	0	0	2	1	1	.222	.300	.222	.522	39	-1	-1	101	374	1	.429	0	0	0	-0	/O	0.0
	Phi-N	98	291	40	84	13	3	5	37	48	21	.289	.395	.405	.800	123	9	11	94	118	48	.800	7	6	-2	-2	O	0.4
1957	Bro-N	81	161	14	44	10	1	4	26	25	16	.273	.374	.422	.797	98	4	0	116	135	24	.746	0	1	-1	-4	O	-0.5
1958	LA-N	65	101	9	25	2	1	1	14	12	11	.248	.327	.317	.644	68	-4	-4	105	165	11	.557	0	1	-1	-6	O	-1.1
1959	Cle-A	34	24	3	7	0	0	0	5	7	0	.292	.452	.292	.743	112	1	1	97	281	3	.737	0	0	0	-1	/O	0.0
1960	NY-A	8	5	1	0	0	0	0	0	2	1	.000	.286	.000	.286	-17	-1	-1	94	0	0	.400	0	0	0	-1	/O	-0.1
	Was-A	76	64	6	18	3	0	0	16	17	4	.281	.439	.328	.767	109	2	2	102	298	11	.813	0	0	0	-1	/O	0.1
	Yr	84	69	7	18	3	0	0	16	19	5	.261	.427	.304	.731	100	2	1	101	270	11	.774	0	0	0	-2		0.0
1961	Min-A	33	32	0	5	2	0	0	4	3	3	.156	.250	.219	.469	25	-3	-4	106	224	2	.379	0	0	0	0	/O	-0.3
	Phi-N	50	43	4	8	2	0	1	8	8	6	.186	.327	.302	.629	73	-2	-1	94	202	5	.629	0	0	0	-0	/O	-0.1
Total	20	1806	5029	768	1420	228	73	58	601	942	284	.282	.399	.391	.791	114	146	142	101	107	864	.829	110	79	-14	-29	*O	5.2
■ **DEACON Van BUREN**	Van Buren, Edward Eugene b: 12/14/1870, La Salle Co., Ill. d: 6/29/57, Portland, Ore. BL/TR, 5'10", 175 lbs. Deb: 4/21/04																											
1904	Bro-N	1	1	0	1	0	0	0	0	0		1.000	1.000	1.000	2.000	550	0	0	95	0	1	—	0			0	H	0.0
	Phi-N	12	43	2	10	2	0	0	3	3		.233	.283	.279	.562	81	-1	-1	93	97	4	.515	2			1	O	0.0
	Yr	13	44	2	11	2	0	0	3	3		.250	.298	.295	.593	92	-1	-0	93	89	5	.545	2			1		0.0
Total	1	13	44	2	11	2	0	0	3	3		.250	.298	.295	.593	92	-1	-0	93	95	5	.545	2			1	/O	0.0
■ **AL Van CAMP**	Van Camp, Albert Joseph b: 9/7/03, Moline, Ill. d: 2/2/81, Davenport, Iowa BR/TR, 5'11.5", 175 lbs. Deb: 9/11/28																											
1928	Cle-A	5	17	0	4	1	0	0	2	0	1	.235	.235	.294	.529	36	-2	-2	106	137	1	.462	1	0	0	0	/1	-0.1
1931	Bos-A	101	324	34	89	15	4	0	33	20	24	.275	.319	.346	.665	80	-12	-9	94	97	36	.574	3	2	-0	-5	O1	-1.9
1932	Bos-A	34	103	10	23	4	2	0	6	4	17	.223	.252	.301	.553	44	-9	-8	97	65	8	.438	0	0	0	1	1	-0.9
Total	3	140	444	44	116	20	6	0	41	24	42	.261	.301	.333	.634	69	-23	-19	95	91	45	.536	4	2	0	-4	/O1	-2.9
■ **CARL VANDAGRIFT**	Vandagrift, Carl William b: 4/22/1883, Cantrall, Ill. d: 10/9/20, Fort Wayne, Ind. BR/TR, 5'8", 155 lbs. Deb: 5/19/14																											
1914	Ind-F	43	136	25	34	4	0	0	9	9	15	.250	.297	.279	.576	59	-6	-8	111	87	16	.529	7			3	23/S	-0.4
■ **FRED Van DUSEN**	Van Dusen, Frederick William b: 7/31/37, Jackson Heights, N.Y. BL, 6'3", 180 lbs. Deb: 9/11/55																											
1955	Phi-N	1	0	0	0	0	0	0	0	0	0	—	1.000	—	1.279	256	0	0	102	0	0	—	0	0	0	0	H	0.0
■ **BILL Van DYKE**	Van Dyke, William Jennings b: 12/15/1863, Paris, Ill. d: 5/5/33, El Paso, Tex. BR/TR, 5'8", 170 lbs. Deb: 4/17/1890																											
1890	Tol-a	129	502	74	129	14	11	2		25		.257	.294	.341	.634	87	-9	-11	103	0	73	.724	73			-2	*O3/2C	-1.6
1892	StL-N	4	16	2	2	0	0	0	1	0	1	.125	.125	.125	.250	-25	-2	-2	95	157	0	.143	0			0	/O	-0.1
1893	Bos-N	3	12	2	3	1	0	0	1	0	1	.250	.250	.333	.583	54	-1	-1	103	68	1	.556	1			0	/O	0.0
Total	3	136	530	78	134	15	11	2	2	25	2	.253	.288	.334	.622	83	-12	-14	102	6	75	.699	74			-2	O/32C	-1.7
■ **DAVE Van GORDER**	Van Gorder, David Thomas b: 3/27/57, Los Angeles, Cal. BR/TR, 6'2", 205 lbs. Deb: 6/15/82																											
1982	Cin-N	51	137	4	25	3	1	0	7	14	19	.182	.263	.219	.482	35	-11	-12	102	91	8	.397	1	0	0	-2	C	-1.3
1984	Cin-N	38	101	10	23	2	0	0	6	12	17	.228	.310	.248	.557	55	-5	-6	106	94	8	.463	0	0	0	-4	C/1	-0.9
1985	Cin-N	73	151	12	36	7	0	2	24	9	19	.238	.286	.325	.610	67	-6	-7	105	174	13	.488	0	0	0	-6	C	-1.0
1986	Cin-N	9	10	0	0	0	0	0	0	1	2	.000	.091	.000	.091	-70	-2	-2	104	0	0	.091	0	0	0	0	/C	-0.1
1987	Bal-A	12	21	4	5	0	0	1	1	3	6	.238	.333	.381	.714	92	-0	-0	98	36	3	.647	0	0	0	1	C	0.2
Total	5	183	420	30	89	12	1	3	38	39	63	.212	.282	.267	.549	52	-25	-27	104	116	32	.464	1	0	0	-11	C/1	-3.1
■ **GEORGE Van HALTREN**	Van Haltren, George Edward Martin "Rip" b: 3/30/1866, St.Louis, Mo. d: 9/29/45, Oakland, Cal. BL/TL, 5'11", 170 lbs. Deb: 6/27/1887 M																											
1887	Chi-N	45	172	30	35	4	0	3	17	15	15	.203	.271	.279	.550	47	-10	-15	116	97	17	.555	12			0	OP	-1.2
1888	Chi-N	81	318	46	90	9	14	4	34	22	34	.283	.329	.437	.767	136	16	13	107	77	54	.798	21			-3	OP	0.9
1889	Chi-N	134	543	126	168	20	10	9	81	82	41	.309	.405	.433	.838	137	29	30	99	81	109	.933	28			1	*O/S2	2.2
1890	Bro-P	92	376	84	126	8	9	5	54	41	23	.335	.405	.444	.849	122	16	12	106	86	84	.984	35			1	OP/S	0.8
1891	Bal-a	139	566	136	180	14	15	9	83	71	46	.318	.398	.443	.841	142	33	32	101	76	133	1.039	75			-11	OS/P2	1.7
1892	Bal-N	135	556	105	168	20	12	7	57	70	34	.302	.382	.419	.801	145	31	31	100	60	110	.912	49			9	*O/P31SM	3.2
	Pit-N	13	55	10	11	2	2	0	5	6	0	.200	.279	.309	.588	85	-1	-1	94	78	7	.659	6			-2	O	-0.2
	Yr	148	611	115	179	22	14	7	62	76	34	.293	.373	.409	.782	140	29	30	99	62	117	.887	55			7		3.0
1893	Pit-N	124	529	129	179	14	11	3	79	75	25	.338	.422	.423	.846	120	24	17	106	82	113	.966	37			-8	*OS/2	0.4
1894	NY-N	137	519	109	172	22	4	7	104	55	22	.331	.400	.430	.829	102	3	3	100	125	109	.937	43			-5	*O	-0.7
1895	NY-N	131	521	113	177	23	19	8	103	57	29	.340	.408	.503	.911	144	28	33	95	97	123	1.029	32			-7	*O/P	1.2
1896	NY-N	133	562	136	197	18	**21**	5	74	55	36	.351	.410	.484	.894	139	30	32	99	64	131	1.008	39			3	*O/P	2.1
1897	NY-N	129	564	117	186	22	9	3	64	40		.330	.375	.417	.792	113	9	11	98	66	110	.862	50			8	*O	0.7
1898	NY-N	156	654	129	204	28	16	2	68	59		.312	.372	.413	.785	135	23	28	95	64	117	.820	36			-5	*O	1.3
1899	NY-N	151	604	117	182	21	3	2	58	74		.301	.378	.356	.734	107	7	9	97	70	95	.761	31			3	*O	0.2
1900	NY-N	141	571	114	180	30	7	1	51	50		.315	.370	.398	.768	117	12	14	97	60	103	.824	**45**			9	*O/P	1.0
1901	NY-N	135	543	82	182	23	6	1	47	51		.335	.392	.405	.797	147	25	31	91	61	98	.817	24			2	*O/P	1.9
1902	NY-N	24	88	14	23	1	2	0	7	17		.261	.381	.318	.699	119	3	3	100	75	13	.785	6			2	O	0.3
1903	NY-N	84	280	42	72	6	1	0	28	28		.257	.325	.286	.610	72	-8	-10	106	115	31	.587	14			7	O	-0.6
Total	17	1984	8021	1639	2532	285	161	69	1014	868	305	.316	.385	.417	.802	124	268	273	100	77	1557	.880	583			4	*O/PS231	15.2
■ **JOHN VANN**	Vann, John Silas b: 6/7/1893, Fairland, Okla. d: 6/10/58, Shreveport, La. BR/TR, Deb: 6/11/13																											
1913	StL-N	1	1	0	0	0	0	0	0	0	1	.000	.000	.000	.000	-99	-0	-0	93	0	0	.000	0			0	H	0.0
■ **JAY Van NOY**	Van Noy, Jay Lowell b: 11/4/28, Garland, Utah BL/TR, 6'1", 200 lbs. Deb: 6/18/51																											
1951	StL-N	6	7	1	0	0	0	0	0	1	6	.000	.125	.000	.125	-63	-2	-2	101	0	0	.143	0	0	0	0	/O	-0.1
■ **MAURICE Van ROBAYS**	Van Robays, Maurice Rene "Bomber" b: 11/15/14, Detroit, Mich. d: 3/1/65, Detroit, Mich. BR/TR, 6'0.5", 190 lbs. Deb: 9/07/39																											
1939	Pit-N	27	105	13	33	9	0	2	16	6	10	.314	.351	.457	.808	116	2	2	100	111	16	.720	0			-5	O/3	-0.2
1940	Pit-N	145	572	82	156	27	7	11	116	33	58	.273	.316	.402	.718	102	-4	-1	95	**167**	69	.620	2			-5	*O/1	-1.0
1941	Pit-N	129	457	62	129	23	5	4	78	41	29	.282	.343	.381	.723	101	2	1	103	154	57	.624	0			7	*O	0.3
1942	Pit-N	100	328	29	76	13	5	1	46	30	24	.232	.298	.311	.609	78	-9	-9	101	162	30	.508	0			6	O	-0.5
1943	Pit-N	69	236	32	68	17	7	1	35	18	19	.288	.344	.432	.776	118	6	5	104	120	34	.697	0			-4	O	0.0
1946	Pit-N	59	146	14	31	5	3	1	12	11	15	.212	.272	.308	.580	62	-7	-8	103	93	11	.471	0			-5	O/1	-1.4
Total	6	529	1844	232	493	94	27	20	303	139	155	.267	.321	.380	.702	97	-10	-10	100	148	218	.626	2			-7	O/13	-2.8

YEAR	TM/L	G	AB	R	H	2B	3B	HR	RBI	BB	SO	AVG	OBP	SLG	PRO	/A	BR	/A	PF	CHI	RC	TA	SB	CS	SBR	FR	POS	TPR
■ **ANDY Van SLYKE**	Van Slyke, Andrew James b: 12/21/60, Utica, N.Y. BL/TR, 6'1", 190 lbs. Deb: 6/17/83																											
1983	StL-N	101	309	51	81	15	5	8	38	46	64	.262	.360	.421	.780	118	7	8	98	98	50	.828	21	7	2	-4	O3/1	0.3
1984	StL-N	137	361	45	88	16	4	7	50	63	71	.244	.356	.368	.725	105	4	4	99	127	54	.792	28	5	5	-9	O31	-0.3
1985	StL-N	146	424	61	110	25	6	13	55	47	54	.259	.336	.439	.775	120	8	10	96	97	66	.823	34	6	7	-4	*O/1	1.0
1986	StL-N	137	418	48	113	23	7	13	61	47	85	.270	.345	.452	.798	115	10	8	103	107	68	.819	21	8	2	1	*O1	0.7
1987	Pit-N	157	564	93	165	36	11	21	82	56	122	.293	.361	.507	.868	122	21	18	104	96	108	.920	34	8	5	13	*O/1	3.0
1988	Pit-N	154	587	101	169	23	**15**	25	100	57	126	.288	.352	.506	.858	147	31	33	98	114	107	.885	30	9	4	8	*O	4.3
Total	6	832	2663	399	726	138	48	87	386	316	522	.273	.352	.459	.810	123	81	81	100	106	453	.862	168	43	25	5	O/13	9.0
■ **IKE Van ZANDT**	Van Zandt, Charles Isaac b: 1877, Brooklyn, N.Y. d: 9/14/08, Nashua, N.H. BL , Deb: 8/05/01																											
1901	NY-N	3	6	1	1	0	0	0	0	0		.167	.167	.167	.333	-2	-1	-1	91	0	0	.200	0			-1	/PO	0.0
1904	Chi-N	3	11	0	0	0	0	0	0	0		.000	.000	.000	.000	-99	-2	-2	101	0	0	.000	0			0	/O	-0.2
1905	StL-A	94	322	31	75	15	1	1	20	7		.233	.249	.295	.544	81	-10	-7	91	73	26	.441	7			-1	O/P1	-1.2
Total	3	100	339	32	76	15	1	1	20	7		.224	.240	.283	.523	73	-13	-10	92	69	26	.418	7			-2	/OP1	-1.4
■ **DICK Van ZANT**	Van Zant, Richard "Foghorn Dick" b: 11/18/1864 Indiana d: 8/6/12, Center Township, Wayne County, Ind. Deb: 1888																											
1888	Cle-a	10	31	1	8	1	0	0	1	1		.258	.303	.290	.593	96	-0	-0	97	33	3	.522	1			0	3	0.0
■ **EDDIE VARGAS**	Vargas, Hediberto (Rodriguez) b: 2/23/59, Guanica, P.R. BR/TR, 6'4", 205 lbs. Deb: 9/08/82																											
1982	Pit-N	8	8	1	3	1	0	0	3	0	2	.375	.375	.500	.875	129	0	0	110	294	2	.800	0	0	0	0	/1	0.0
1984	Pit-N	18	31	3	7	2	0	0	2	3	5	.226	.294	.290	.584	69	-1	-1	94	87	3	.500	0	0	0	-0	1	-0.1
Total	2	26	39	4	10	3	0	0	5	3	7	.256	.310	.333	.643	83	-1	-1	97	126	4	.552	0	0	0	-0	/1	-0.1
■ **BUCK VARNER**	Varner, Glen Gann b: 8/17/30, Hixson, Tenn. BL/TR, 5'10", 170 lbs. Deb: 9/19/52																											
1952	Was-A	2	4	0	0	0	0	0	0	1	1	.000	.200	.000	.200	-41	-1	-1	100	0	0	.200	0	0	0	-0	/O	0.0
■ **PETE VARNEY**	Varney, Richard Fred b: 4/10/49, Roxbury, Mass. BR/TR, 6'3", 235 lbs. Deb: 8/26/73																											
1973	Chi-A	5	4	0	0	0	0	0	0	1	0	.000	.200	.000	.200	-39	-1	-1	102	0	0	.250	0	0	0	0	/C	0.0
1974	Chi-A	9	28	1	7	0	0	0	2	1	8	.250	.276	.250	.526	51	-2	-2	102	112	2	.381	0	0	0	0	/C	0.0
1975	Chi-A	36	107	12	29	5	1	2	8	6	28	.271	.316	.393	.708	96	-0	-1	103	64	14	.646	2	0	1	4	C/D	0.5
1976	Chi-A	14	41	5	10	2	0	3	5	2	9	.244	.279	.512	.791	129	1	1	99	64	5	.697	0	0	0	-0	C	0.1
	Atl-N	5	10	0	1	0	0	0	0	0	2	.100	.100	.100	.200	-39	-2	-2	111	0	0	.100	0	0	0	0	/C	-0.1
Total	4	69	190	18	47	7	1	5	15	10	47	.247	.289	.374	.662	86	-4	-4	103	66	21	.583	2	0	1	4	/CD	0.5
■ **GARY VARSHO**	Varsho, Gary Andrew b: 6/20/61, Marshfield, Wis. BL/TR, 5'11", 190 lbs. Deb: 7/06/88																											
1988	Chi-N	46	73	6	20	3	0	0	5	1	6	.274	.284	.315	.599	69	-3	-3	104	87	7	.547	5	0	2	-2	O	-0.4
■ **GLENN VAUGHAN**	Vaughan, Glenn Edward "Sparky" b: 2/15/44, Compton, Cal. BB/TR, 5'11", 170 lbs. Deb: 9/20/63																											
1963	Hou-N	9	30	1	5	0	0	0	0	2	5	.167	.219	.167	.385	14	-3	-3	92	0	1	.308	1	0	0	-1	/S3	-0.2
■ **ARKY VAUGHAN**	Vaughan, Joseph Floyd b: 3/9/12, Clifty, Ark. d: 8/30/52, Eagleville, Cal. BL/TR, 5'10.5", 175 lbs. Deb: 4/17/32 H																											
1932	Pit-N	129	497	71	158	15	10	4	61	39	26	.318	.375	.412	.787	112	9	10	99	111	79	.767	10			-19	*S	0.1
1933	Pit-N	152	573	85	180	29	**19**	9	97	64	23	.314	.388	.478	.866	154	35	39	95	128	112	.861	3			-10	*S	4.0
1934	Pit-N	149	558	115	186	41	11	12	94	**94**	38	.333	**.431**	.511	.942	144	44	40	105	112	135	1.043	10			1	*S	4.2
1935	Pit-N	137	499	108	192	34	10	19	99	**97**	18	**.385**	**.491**	**.607**	**1.098**	**181**	**72**	**67**	107	95	**163**	**1.317**	4			-10	*S	**5.9**
1936	Pit-N	156	568	**122**	190	30	11	9	78	**118**	21	.335	**.453**	.474	.927	153	47	49	98	99	137	1.034	6			-12	*S	4.5
1937	Pit-N	126	469	71	151	17	**17**	5	72	54	22	.322	.394	.463	.857	129	22	20	102	114	91	.864	7			10	*SO	3.7
1938	Pit-N	148	541	88	174	35	5	7	68	104	21	.322	.433	.444	.876	141	36	36	100	100	115	.960	14			19	*S	**6.4**
1939	Pit-N	152	595	94	182	30	11	6	62	70	20	.306	.385	.424	.808	117	16	16	100	74	103	.813	12			9	*S	3.4
1940	Pit-N	156	594	**113**	178	40	**15**	7	95	88	25	.300	.393	.453	.846	139	29	32	95	129	113	.884	12			9	*S/3	**5.5**
1941	Pit-N	106	374	69	118	20	7	6	38	50	13	.316	.399	.455	.854	136	21	20	103	74	72	.888	8			-10	S/3	1.8
1942	Bro-N	128	495	82	137	18	4	2	49	51	17	.277	.348	.341	.689	100	2	1	102	110	63	.638	8			-13	*3/S2	-1.1
1943	Bro-N	149	610	**112**	186	39	6	5	66	60	13	.305	.370	.413	.783	126	20	21	100	79	96	.774	**20**			-14	S3	1.7
1947	Bro-N	64	126	24	41	5	2	2	25	27	11	.325	.444	.444	.889	131	8	7	105	149	27	1.000	4			-1	O3	0.5
1948	Bro-N	65	123	19	30	3	0	3	22	21	8	.244	.354	.341	.696	85	-1	-2	104	162	15	.649	0			0	O/3	-0.3
Total	14	1817	6622	1173	2103	356	128	96	926	937	276	.318	.406	.453	.859	136	361	357	100	105	1323	.907	118			-42	*S3/O2	40.3
■ **FRED VAUGHN**	Vaughn, Frederick Thomas "Muscles" b: 10/18/18, Coalinga, Cal. d: 3/2/64, Near Lake Wales, Fla. BR/TR, 5'10", 185 lbs. Deb: 8/20/44																											
1944	Was-A	30	109	10	28	2	1	1	21	9	24	.257	.319	.321	.640	93	-2	-1	90	203	11	.553	2	2	-1	-2	2/3	-0.2
1945	Was-A	80	268	28	63	7	4	1	25	23	48	.235	.298	.302	.600	80	-9	-7	93	108	25	.498	0	3	-2	-11	2/S	-1.9
Total	2	110	377	38	91	9	5	2	46	32	72	.241	.304	.308	.612	83	-11	-8	92	135	36	.517	2	5	-2	-13	2/3S	-2.1
■ **FARMER VAUGHN**	Vaughn, Harry Francis b: 3/1/1864, Rural Dale, Ohio d: 2/21/14, Cincinnati, Ohio BR/TR, 6'3", 177 lbs. Deb: 10/07/1886																											
1886	Cin-a	1	3	0	0	0	0	0		0		.000	.250	.000	.250	-19	-0	-0	96	0	0	.333	0			0	/C	0.0
1888	Lou-a	51	189	15	37	4	2	1	21	4		.196	.216	.254	.470	58	-10	-7	91	126	12	.375	4			0	OC	-0.6
1889	Lou-a	90	360	39	86	11	5	3	45	7	41	.239	.253	.322	.576	68	-18	-15	96	105	34	.496	13			6	CO1/3	-0.2
1890	NY-P	44	166	27	44	7	0	1	22	10	9	.265	.307	.325	.632	65	-7	-10	109	106	19	.574	6			0	CO/32	-0.7
1891	CM-a	76	274	34	78	14	1	1	23	18	20	.285	.331	.354	.685	88	-1	-6	112	66	36	.633	8			1	C/O3P	-0.1
1892	Cin-N	91	346	45	88	10	5	2	50	16	13	.254	.295	.329	.625	88	-5	-6	103	130	38	.558	10			-11	C1O/3	-1.2
1893	Cin-N	121	483	68	135	17	12	1	108	35	17	.280	.332	.371	.703	87	-9	-10	101	172	66	.670	16			-2	CO1	-0.3
1894	Cin-N	72	284	50	88	15	5	8	64	12	11	.310	.338	.482	.820	97	-3	-3	100	112	49	.786	5			3	C1/OS	0.3
1895	Cin-N	92	334	60	102	23	5	1	48	17	10	.305	.339	.413	.752	88	-3	-8	108	95	53	.733	15			8	C1/32	0.5
1896	Cin-N	114	433	71	127	20	9	2	66	16	7	.293	.320	.395	.715	85	-8	-11	105	110	58	.637	7			0	1C	-0.3
1897	Cin-N	54	199	21	58	13	5	0	30	2		.291	.299	.407	.706	81	-5	-7	107	110	25	.603	2			-1	1C	-0.6
1898	Cin-N	78	275	35	84	12	4	1	46	11		.305	.332	.389	.721	101	2	-1	108	126	38	.639	4			-4	1C	-0.3
1899	Cin-N	31	108	9	19	1	0	0	2	3		.176	.198	.185	.383	6	-13	-14	106	31	4	.281	2			0	1/CO	-1.2
Total	13	915	3454	474	946	147	53	21	525	151	128	.274	.306	.365	.672	82	-79	-99	104	115	432	.604	92			-0	C1O/3S2P	-4.7
■ **BOBBY VAUGHN**	Vaughn, Robert b: 6/4/1885, Stamford, N.Y. d: 4/11/65, Seattle, Wash. BR/TR, 5'9", 150 lbs. Deb: 6/12/09																											
1909	NY-A	5	14	1	2	0	0	0	0	1		.143	.200	.143	.343	9	-1	-1	99	0	1	.333	1			-1	/2S	-0.3
1915	StL-F	144	521	69	146	19	9	0	32	58	38	.280	.352	.351	.704	104	7	4	105	61	80	.707	24			6	*2S/3	1.1
Total	2	149	535	70	148	19	9	0	32	59	38	.277	.348	.346	.694	101	5	2	105	59	81	.695	25			4	2/S3	0.8
■ **BOBBY VEACH**	Veach, Robert Hayes b: 6/29/1888, Island, Ky. d: 8/7/45, Detroit, Mich. BL/TR, 5'11", 160 lbs. Deb: 8/06/12																											
1912	Det-A	23	79	8	27	5	1	0	15	5		.342	.388	.430	.819	141	3	4	95	150	14	.808	2			2	O	0.4
1913	Det-A	137	491	54	132	22	10	0	64	53	31	.269	.346	.354	.700	106	4	4	99	139	66	.708	22			-5	*O	-0.8
1914	Det-A	149	531	56	146	19	14	1	72	50	29	.275	.341	.369	.710	111	8	7	102	139	68	.664	20	20	-6	-7	*O	-1.6
1915	Det-A	152	569	81	178	**40**	10	3	**112**	68	43	.313	.390	.434	.824	135	32	26	108	**158**	97	.817	16	19	-7	5	*O	1.7
1916	Det-A	150	566	92	173	33	15	3	91	52	41	.306	.367	.433	.800	134	26	23	105	136	94	.794	24	15	-2	-10	*O	0.4
1917	Det-A	154	571	79	182	31	12	8	**103**	61	44	.319	.393	.457	.850	163	40	42	98	125	108	.905	21			7	*O	4.3
1918	Det-A	127	499	59	139	21	13	3	**78**	35	23	.279	.331	.391	.722	122	8	10	97	134	69	.708	21			0	*O/P	0.4
1919	Det-A	139	538	87	**191**	**45**	**17**	3	101	33	33	.355	.398	.519	.916	167	38	42	93	135	115	.968	19			-7	*O	2.6
1920	Det-A	154	612	92	188	39	15	11	113	36	22	.307	.353	.474	.827	114	13	10	103	130	101	.798	11	7	-1	0	*O	-0.3
1921	Det-A	150	612	110	207	43	13	16	128	48	31	.338	.387	.529	.917	137	27	31	96	125	123	.933	14	10	-2	3	*O	1.8
1922	Det-A	155	618	96	202	34	13	9	126	42	27	.327	.377	.468	.845	122	16	18	98	137	111	.835	9	1	2	13	*O	2.1
1923	Det-A	114	293	45	94	13	3	2	39	29	21	.321	.388	.406	.794	113	5	6	97	107	49	.797	10	3	1	-15	O	-1.5
1924	Bos-A	142	519	77	153	35	9	5	99	47	18	.295	.359	.426	.785	98	0	-3	104	141	81	.749	5	5	-2	-1	*O	-1.3
1925	Bos-A	1	5	0	1	0	0	0	2	1	1	.200	.333	.200	.533	40	-0	-0	95	578	0	.500	0	0	0	0	/O	0.0
	NY-A	56	116	13	41	10	2	0	15	8	0	.353	.400	.474	.874	126	4	4	96	91	20	.823	1	4	-2	-4	O	-0.4
	Was-A	18	37	4	9	3	0	0	8	3	3	.243	.300	.324	.624	60	-2	-2	98	223	4	.536	0	0	0	-3	O	-0.5

YEAR	TM/L	G	AB	R	H	2B	3B	HR	RBI	BB	SO	AVG	OBP	SLG	PRO	/A	BR	/A	PF	CHI	RC	TA	SB	CS	SBR	FR	POS	TPR
	Yr	75	158	17	51	13	2	0	25	12	4	.323	.374	.430	.805	107	1	2	96	138	24	.739	1	4	-2	-7		-0.9
Total	14	1821	6656	953	2063	393	147	64	1166	571	367	.310	.370	.442	.812	127	221	222	100	135	1120	.805	195	84		-23	*O/P	7.3
■ **PEEK-A-BOO VEACH**	Veach, William Walter b: 6/15/1862, Indianapolis, Ind d: 11/12/37, Indianapolis, Ind. Deb: 8/24/1884																											
1884	KC-U	27	82	9	11	1	0	1		9		.134	.220	.183	.403	43	-5	-3	87	0	3	.338	0			0	OP/21	-0.2
1887	Lou-a	1	3	0	0	0	0	0		1		.000	.250	.000	.250	-24	-0	-1	107	0	0	.333	0			0	/P	0.0
1890	Cle-N	64	238	24	56	10	5	0	32	33	28	.235	.336	.319	.655	100	-1	1	94	135	29	.665	9			6	1	0.3
	Pit-N	8	30	6	9	1	1	2	5	8	3	.300	.447	.600	1.047	237	4	5	88	54	8	1.238	0			0	/1	0.4
	Yr	72	268	30	65	11	6	2	37	41	31	.243	.349	.351	.700	114	3	6	93	128	37	.724	9			6		0.7
Total	3	100	353	39	76	12	6	3	37	51	31	.215	.319	.309	.628	99	-2	3	92	96	41	.621	9			6	/1OP2	0.5
■ **COOT VEAL**	Veal, Orville Inman b: 7/9/32, Sandersville, Ga. BR/TR, 6'1", 165 lbs. Deb: 7/30/58																											
1958	Det-A	58	207	29	53	10	2	0	16	14	21	.256	.306	.324	.630	71	-7	-8	104	98	19	.506	1	1	-0	-7	S	-0.7
1959	Det-A	77	89	12	18	1	0	1	15	8	7	.202	.276	.247	.523	40	-7	-8	111	236	7	.437	0	0	0	-0	S	-0.2
1960	Det-A	27	64	8	19	5	1	0	8	11	7	.297	.400	.406	.806	117	2	2	102	120	11	.771	0	0	0	-0	S/32	0.3
1961	Was-A	69	218	21	44	10	0	0	8	19	29	.202	.275	.248	.523	43	-18	-17	95	58	15	.416	1	8	-5	3	S	-1.3
1962	Pit-N	1	1	0	0	0	0	0	0	0	1	.000	.000	.000	.000	-98	-0	-0	102	0	0	.000	0	0	0	0	H	0.0
1963	Det-A	15	32	5	7	0	0	0	4	4	4	.219	.306	.219	.524	48	-2	-2	104	239	2	.379	0	0	0	-1	S	-0.1
Total	6	247	611	75	141	26	3	1	51	56	69	.231	.301	.288	.589	60	-32	-33	101	114	53	.495	2	9	-5	-5	S/32	-2.0
■ **JESUS VEGA**	Vega, Jesus Anthony (Morales) b: 10/14/55, Bayamon, P.R. BR/TR, 6'1", 176 lbs. Deb: 9/05/79																											
1979	Min-A	4	7	0	0	0	0	0	0	0	2	.000	.000	.000	.000	-92	-2	-2	109	0	0	.000	0	0	0	0	/H	-0.1
1980	Min-A	12	30	3	5	0	0	0	4	3	7	.167	.242	.167	.409	13	-3	-4	109	312	1	.346	1	0	0	0	/1D	-0.3
1982	Min-A	71	199	23	53	6	0	5	29	8	19	.266	.295	.372	.667	81	-5	-5	100	130	21	.579	6	1	1	-1	D1/O	-0.4
Total	3	87	236	26	58	6	0	5	33	11	28	.246	.279	.335	.614	67	-11	-11	102	151	23	.527	7	1	2	-1	/D1O	-0.8
■ **RANDY VELARDE**	Velarde, Randy Lee b: 11/24/62, Midland, Tex. BR/TR, 6' ", 185 lbs. Deb: 8/20/87																											
1987	NY-A	8	22	1	4	0	0	0	1	0	6	.182	.182	.182	.364	-3	-3	-3	98	100	1	.211	0	0	0	-0	/S	-0.2
1988	NY-A	48	115	18	20	6	0	5	12	8	24	.174	.240	.357	.597	68	-6	-5	96	85	9	.525	1	1	-0	1	2S3	-0.1
Total	2	56	137	19	24	6	0	5	13	8	30	.175	.231	.328	.560	56	-9	-8	96	87	10	.479	1	1	-0	1	/2S3	-0.3
■ **FREDDIE VELAZQUEZ**	Velazquez, Federico Antonio (Velasquez) b: 12/6/37, Santo Domingo, D.R. BR/TR, 6'1", 185 lbs. Deb: 4/20/69																											
1969	Sea-A	6	16	1	2	2	0	0	2	1	3	.125	.176	.250	.426	18	-2	-2	98	201	0	.313	0	0	0	0	/C	0.0
1973	Atl-N	15	23	2	8	1	0	0	3	1	3	.348	.375	.391	.766	100	0	0	113	134	3	.667	0	0	0	-0	C	0.0
Total	2	21	39	3	10	3	0	0	5	2	6	.256	.293	.333	.626	69	-1	-2	107	162	4	.517	0	0	0	-0	/C	0.0
■ **OTTO VELEZ**	Velez, Otoniel (Franceschi) b: 11/29/50, Ponce, P.R. BR/TR, 6', 170 lbs. Deb: 9/04/73																											
1973	NY-A	23	77	9	15	4	0	2	7	15	24	.195	.326	.325	.651	83	-1	-1	101	90	9	.635	0	1	-1	0	O	-0.2
1974	NY-A	27	67	9	14	1	1	2	10	15	24	.209	.354	.343	.697	106	1	1	96	136	9	.704	0	0	0	-0	1/O3	0.0
1975	NY-A	6	8	0	2	0	0	0	1	2	0	.250	.400	.250	.650	88	0	0	99	192	1	.667	0	0	0	0	/1D	0.0
1976	NY-A	49	94	11	25	6	0	2	10	23	26	.266	.410	.394	.804	137	6	6	99	89	17	.857	0	0	0	-2	O/13D	0.3
1977	Tor-A	120	360	50	92	19	3	16	62	65	87	.256	.371	.458	.829	121	14	12	103	115	64	.842	4	2	0	-3	OD	0.6
1978	Tor-A	91	248	29	66	14	2	9	38	45	41	.266	.383	.448	.831	133	12	12	100	109	43	.824	1	3	-2	6	O/1D	1.5
1979	Tor-A	99	274	45	79	21	0	15	48	46	45	.288	.396	.529	.925	142	19	18	103	97	58	.951	0	1	-1	-6	O/1D	0.7
1980	Tor-A	104	357	54	96	12	3	20	62	54	86	.269	.368	.487	.855	133	16	16	100	105	65	.855	0	0	0	0	D/1	1.6
1981	Tor-A	80	240	32	51	9	2	11	28	55	60	.213	.366	.404	.770	110	9	5	111	86	38	.787	0	3	-2	0	D/1	0.3
1982	Tor-A	28	52	4	10	1	0	1	5	13	15	.192	.354	.269	.623	68	-1	-2	109	118	6	.651	1	0	0	0	D	-0.1
1983	Cle-A	10	25	1	2	0	0	0	1	3	6	.080	.179	.080	.259	-25	-4	-4	105	195	0	.217	0	0	0	0	/D	-0.4
Total	11	637	1802	244	452	87	11	78	272	336	414	.251	.372	.441	.813	122	69	62	103	105	311	.844	6	10	-4	-6	OD/13	4.3
■ **PAT VELTMAN**	Veltman, Arthur Patrick b: 3/24/06, Mobile, Ala. d: 10/1/80, San Antonio, Tex. BR/TR, 6', 175 lbs. Deb: 4/17/26																											
1926	Chi-A	5	4	1	1	0	0	0	0	1	1	.250	.400	.250	.650	79	-0	-0	92	0	0	.667	0	0	0	0	/S	0.0
1928	NY-N	1	3	1	1	0	1	0	0	1	0	.333	.500	1.000	1.500	278	1	1	102	0	2	2.000	0			0	/O	0.1
1929	NY-N	2	1	1	0	0	0	0	0	2	0	.000	.667	.000	.667	81	0	0	100	0	0	2.000	0			0	/C	0.0
1931	Bos-N	1	1	0	0	0	0	0	0	0	0	.000	.000	.000	.000	-99	-0	-0	99	0	0	.000	0			0	H	0.0
1932	NY-N	2	1	0	0	0	0	0	0	0	1	.000	.000	.000	.000	-99	-0	-0	99	0	0	.000	0			0	H	0.0
1934	Pit-N	12	28	1	3	0	0	0	2	0	1	.107	.107	.107	.214	-40	-6	-6	105	240	0	.120	0			-0	C	-0.5
Total	6	23	38	4	5	0	1	0	2	4	3	.132	.214	.184	.398	7	-5	-5	102	160	3	.333	0	0		-0	/COS	-0.4
■ **MAX VENABLE**	Venable, William Mc Kinley b: 6/6/57, Phoenix, Ariz. BL/TR, 5'10", 185 lbs. Deb: 4/08/79																											
1979	SF-N	55	85	12	14	1	1	0	3	10	18	.165	.260	.200	.460	30	-8	-8	92	70	5	.419	3	3	-1	-4	O	-1.2
1980	SF-N	64	138	13	37	5	0	0	10	15	22	.268	.340	.304	.644	85	-3	-2	96	94	16	.613	8	2	1	-5	O	-0.7
1981	SF-N	18	32	2	6	0	2	0	1	4	3	.188	.278	.313	.590	64	-1	-2	105	39	3	.630	3	1	0	0	/O	0.0
1982	SF-N	71	125	17	28	2	1	1	7	7	16	.224	.265	.280	.545	56	-8	-7	94	72	9	.500	9	3	1	-4	O	-1.0
1983	SF-N	94	228	28	50	7	4	6	27	22	34	.219	.296	.364	.660	81	-6	-6	101	106	27	.672	15	2	3	5	O	0.1
1984	Mon-N	38	71	7	17	2	0	2	7	3	7	.239	.280	.352	.632	84	-2	-2	91	88	7	.556	1	0	0	-5	O	-0.6
1985	Cin-N	77	135	21	39	12	3	0	10	6	17	.289	.319	.422	.741	100	1	-0	105	70	18	.733	11	3	2	-1	O	0.0
1986	Cin-N	108	147	17	31	7	1	2	15	17	24	.211	.293	.313	.606	64	-7	-7	104	115	15	.593	7	2	1	-11	O	-1.8
1987	Cin-N	7	7	2	1	0	0	0	2	0	0	.143	.143	.143	.286	-23	-1	-1	104	798	0	.167	0	0	0	-1	/O	-0.1
Total	9	532	968	119	223	36	12	11	82	84	141	.230	.295	.326	.622	73	-36	-35	99	94	101	.607	57	16	8	-25	O	-5.3
■ **VINCE VENTURA**	Ventura, Vincent b: 4/18/17, New York, N.Y. BR/TR, 6'1.5", 190 lbs. Deb: 5/08/45																											
1945	Was-A	18	58	4	12	0	0	0	2	4	4	.207	.258	.207	.465	38	-5	-4	93	60	3	.327	0	0	0	-2	O	-0.6
■ **EMIL VERBAN**	Verban, Emil Matthew "Dutch" or "Antelope" b: 8/27/15, Lincoln, Ill. BR/TR, 5'11", 165 lbs. Deb: 4/18/44																											
1944	StL-N	146	498	51	128	14	2	0	43	19	14	.257	.287	.293	.580	63	-24	-25	101	106	43	.445	0			-5	*2	-1.5
1945	StL-N	155	597	59	166	22	8	0	72	19	15	.278	.304	.342	.645	79	-18	-18	100	125	61	.523	4			-19	*2	-2.4
1946	StL-N	1	1	0	0	0	0	0	0	0	0	.000	.000	.000	.000	-94	-0	-0	107	0	0	.000	0			0	H	0.0
	Phi-N	138	473	44	130	17	5	0	34	21	18	.275	.306	.332	.638	85	-13	-10	95	81	48	.523	5			-7	*2	-1.2
	Yr	139	474	44	130	17	5	0	34	21	18	.274	.305	.331	.636	85	-13	-11	95	80	48	.521	5			-7		-1.2
1947	Phi-N	155	540	50	154	14	8	0	42	23	8	.285	.316	.341	.656	74	-20	-20	100	85	56	.534	5			15	*2	1.2
1948	Phi-N	55	169	14	39	5	1	0	11	11	5	.231	.282	.272	.554	54	-12	-10	94	90	14	.436	0			-3	2	-0.9
	Chi-N	56	248	37	73	15	1	1	16	4	7	.294	.308	.375	.683	90	-6	-4	93	55	28	.570	4			-0	2	0.0
	Yr	111	417	51	112	20	2	1	27	15	12	.269	.297	.333	.631	75	-18	-14	94	73	42	.518	4			-3		-0.9
1949	Chi-N	98	343	38	99	11	1	0	22	8	2	.289	.309	.327	.635	75	-14	-12	94	75	34	.502	3			11	2	0.2
1950	Chi-N	45	37	7	4	1	0	0	1	3	5	.108	.175	.135	.310	-16	-6	-7	105	77	1	.242	0			-0	/2S3O	-0.5
	Bos-N	4	5	1	0	0	0	0	0	0	0	.000	.000	.000	.000	-99	-1	-1	86	0	0	.000	0			-0	/2	-0.1
	Yr	49	42	8	4	1	0	0	1	3	5	.095	.156	.119	.275	-26	-8	-8	103	72	1	.211	0			-1		-0.6
Total	7	853	2911	301	793	99	26	1	241	108	74	.272	.301	.325	.626	73	-116	-108	98	92	286	.513	21			-9	2/SO3	-5.2
■ **GENE VERBLE**	Verble, Gene Kermit "Satchel" b: 6/29/28, Concord, N.C. BR/TR, 5'10", 163 lbs. Deb: 4/17/51																											
1951	Was-A	68	177	16	36	3	2	0	15	18	10	.203	.277	.243	.520	43	-14	-13	95	125	12	.416	1	1	-0	-6	S2/3	-1.6
1953	Was-A	13	21	4	4	0	0	0	2	2	1	.190	.261	.190	.451	25	-2	-2	94	185	1	.333	0	0	0	-1	/S	-0.1
Total	2	81	198	20	40	3	2	0	17	20	11	.202	.275	.237	.513	41	-17	-15	95	131	13	.425	1	1	-0	-7	/S23	-1.7
■ **FRANK VERDI**	Verdi, Frank Michael b: 6/2/26, Brooklyn, N.Y. BR/TR, 5'10.5", 170 lbs. Deb: 5/10/53																											
1953	NY-A	1	0	0	0	0	0	0	0	0	0	—	—	—	—	—	0	0	93	—	—	—	0	0	0	0	/S	0.0
■ **JOHNNY VERGEZ**	Vergez, John Louis b: 7/9/06, Oakland, Cal. BR/TR, 5'8", 165 lbs. Deb: 4/14/31																											
1931	NY-N	152	565	67	157	24	2	13	81	29	65	.278	.320	.396	.716	95	-8	-5	97	112	73	.662	11			-3	*3	0.1
1932	NY-N	118	376	42	98	21	3	6	43	25	36	.261	.310	.380	.690	86	-8	-8	99	99	45	.615	1			5	*3/S	0.7

YEAR	TM/L	G	AB	R	H	2B	3B	HR	RBI	BB	SO	AVG	OBP	SLG	PRO	/A	BR	/A	PF	CHI	RC	TA	SB	CS	SBR	FR	POS	TPR
1933	NY-N	123	458	57	124	21	6	16	72	39	66	.271	.332	.448	.780	123	12	12	99	113	66	.709	1			-7	*3	0.9
1934	NY-N	108	320	31	64	18	1	7	27	28	55	.200	.269	.328	.597	60	-19	-18	98	77	29	.521	1			12	*3	0.1
1935	Phi-N	148	546	56	136	27	4	9	63	46	67	.249	.312	.363	.675	71	-15	-25	114	103	64	.610	8			-4	*3/S	-2.3
1936	Phi-N	15	40	4	11	2	0	1	5	3	11	.275	.326	.400	.726	87	-0	-1	108	93	6	.655	0			1	3	0.1
	StL-N	8	18	1	3	1	0	0	1	1	3	.167	.211	.222	.433	18	-2	-2	94	89	1	.333	0			-0	/3	-0.1
	Yr	23	58	5	14	3	0	1	6	4	14	.241	.290	.345	.635	68	-3	-3	103	96	6	.545	0			1		0.0
Total	6	672	2323	258	593	114	16	52	292	171	303	.255	.311	.385	.696	87	-41	-47	102	103	285	.639	22			3	3/S	-0.5
■ MICKEY VERNON Vernon, James Barton b: 4/22/18, Marcus Hook, Pa. BL/TL, 6'2", 170 lbs. Deb: 7/08/39 MC																												
1939	Was-A	76	276	23	71	15	4	1	30	24	28	.257	.317	.351	.668	78	-12	-8	90	103	31	.578	1	1	-0	-4	1	-1.7
1940	Was-A	5	19	0	3	0	0	0	0	0	3	.158	.158	.158	.316	-19	-3	-3	93	0	0	.176	0	0	0	0	/1	-0.2
1941	Was-A	138	531	73	159	27	11	9	93	43	51	.299	.352	.443	.794	112	6	7	98	133	84	.742	9	3	1	-5	*1	0.0
1942	Was-A	151	621	76	168	34	6	9	86	59	63	.271	.337	.388	.725	108	2	5	96	109	87	.702	25	6	4	-8	*1	0.0
1943	Was-A	145	553	89	148	29	8	7	70	67	55	.268	.357	.387	.744	113	13	11	104	115	83	.745	24	8	2	-8	*1	0.1
1946	Was-A	148	587	88	207	**51**	8	8	85	49	64	**.353**	.403	.508	.910	166	40	46	92	106	120	.898	14	10	-2	-2	*1	3.4
1947	Was-A	154	600	77	159	29	12	7	85	49	42	.265	.320	.388	.709	100	-5	-3	97	130	73	.632	12	12	-4	-4	*1	-1.3
1948	Was-A	150	558	78	135	27	7	3	48	54	43	.242	.310	.332	.641	68	-25	-27	103	89	56	.565	15	11	-2	6	*1	-1.4
1949	Cle-A	153	584	72	170	27	4	18	83	58	51	.291	.357	.443	.801	114	7	9	98	96	96	.765	9	7	-2	19	*1	2.6
1950	Cle-A	28	90	8	17	0	0	0	10	12	10	.189	.284	.189	.473	24	-10	-10	98	203	6	.425	2	0	1	0	1	-0.9
	Was-A	90	327	47	100	17	3	9	65	50	29	.306	.404	.459	.863	122	11	12	99	134	67	.909	6	1	1	3	1	1.0
	Yr	118	417	55	117	17	3	9	75	62	39	.281	.379	.400	.779	101	1	2	99	**152**	72	.793	8	1	2	3		0.1
1951	Was-A	141	546	69	160	30	7	9	87	53	45	.293	.358	.423	.781	116	7	11	95	128	84	.727	7	6	-2	-5	*1	0.2
1952	Was-A	154	569	71	143	33	9	10	80	89	66	.251	.353	.394	.746	107	7	7	100	125	84	.721	7	7	-2	2	*1	-0.2
1953	Was-A	152	608	101	205	**43**	11	15	115	63	57	**.337**	.403	.518	.921	156	40	44	94	114	127	.910	4	6	-2	-3	*1	3.5
1954	Was-A	151	597	90	173	**33**	14	20	97	61	61	.290	.360	.492	.853	134	24	25	98	100	106	.824	1	4	-2	-8	*1	1.1
1955	Was-A	150	538	74	162	23	8	14	85	74	50	.301	.389	.452	.840	138	20	27	91	118	93	.806	0	4	-2	-9	*1	0.9
1956	Bos-A	119	403	67	125	28	4	15	84	57	40	.310	.405	.511	.916	137	24	23	103	125	84	.934	1	0	0	1	*1	1.9
1957	Bos-A	102	270	36	65	18	1	7	38	41	35	.241	.351	.393	.744	94	2	-2	110	118	38	.710	0	0	0	2	1	0.0
1958	Cle-A	119	355	49	104	22	3	8	55	44	56	.293	.374	.439	.814	130	12	14	94	122	58	.768	0	4	-2	-0	1	0.9
1959	Mil-N	74	91	8	20	4	0	3	14	7	20	.220	.283	.363	.645	74	-4	-3	95	135	9	.562	0	0	0	1	1/O	-0.3
1960	Pit-N	9	8	0	1	0	0	0	1	1	0	.125	.222	.125	.347	-2	-1	-1	99	406	0	.286	0	0	0	0	H	0.0
Total	20	2409	8731	1196	2495	490	120	172	1311	955	869	.286	.359	.428	.788	116	154	183	98	116	1387	.772	137	90	-13	-22	*1/O	9.6
■ ZOILO VERSALLES Versalles, Zoilo Casanova (Rodriguez) "Zorro" b: 12/18/39, Veldado, Cuba BR/TR, 5'10", 146 lbs. Deb: 8/01/59																												
1959	Was-A	29	59	4	9	0	0	1	1	4	15	.153	.219	.203	.422	17	-7	-7	100	26	3	.360	1	0	0	2	S	-0.1
1960	Was-A	15	45	2	6	2	2	0	4	2	5	.133	.170	.267	.437	16	-5	-6	102	131	2	.359	0	0	0	0	S	-0.3
1961	Min-A	129	510	65	143	25	5	7	53	25	61	.280	.315	.390	.705	82	-10	-14	106	100	61	.628	16	9	-1	-3	*S	-0.8
1962	Min-A	160	568	69	137	18	3	17	67	37	71	.241	.290	.373	.663	73	-20	-23	105	103	59	.570	5	5	-2	34	*S	1.9
1963	Min-A	159	621	74	162	31	**13**	10	54	33	66	.261	.303	.401	.704	95	-5	-5	100	83	74	.620	7	4	-0	-2	*S	0.1
1964	Min-A	160	659	94	171	33	**10**	20	64	42	88	.259	.312	.431	.743	103	2	1	101	76	91	.700	14	4	2	-14	*S	-1.0
1965	Min-A	160	666	**126**	182	**45**	**12**	19	77	41	122	.273	.322	.462	.785	119	15	14	101	77	102	.772	27	5	**5**	2	*S	3.0
1966	Min-A	137	543	73	135	20	6	7	36	40	85	.249	.308	.346	.655	79	-8	-16	111	70	55	.568	10	12	-4	-18	*S	-3.3
1967	Min-A	160	581	63	116	16	7	6	50	33	113	.200	.250	.282	.532	53	-32	-36	107	117	39	.431	5	3	-0	4	*S	-2.3
1968	LA-N	122	403	29	79	16	3	2	24	26	84	.196	.245	.266	.510	59	-23	-19	91	89	26	.415	6	4	-1	6	*S	0.0
1969	Cle-A	72	217	21	49	11	1	1	13	21	47	.226	.300	.300	.600	72	-9	-8	94	77	19	.517	3	1	0	-3	23/S	-0.7
	Was-A	31	75	9	20	2	1	0	6	3	13	.267	.304	.320	.624	77	-3	-2	97	100	7	.518	1	0	0	1	S/23	0.0
	Yr	103	292	30	69	13	2	1	19	24	60	.236	.301	.305	.606	73	-12	-10	95	85	29	.533	4	1	1	-2		-0.7
1971	Atl-N	66	194	21	37	11	0	5	22	11	40	.191	.234	.325	.559	52	-12	-14	110	115	13	.461	2	1	0	-1	3S/2	-1.2
Total	12	1400	5141	650	1246	230	63	95	471	318	810	.242	.292	.367	.659	82	-116	-133	103	89	552	.593	97	48	0	8	*S/32	-4.7
■ TOM VERYZER Veryzer, Thomas Martin b: 2/11/53, Port Jefferson, N.Y BR/TR, 6'1.5", 175 lbs. Deb: 8/14/73																												
1973	Det-A	18	20	1	6	0	1	0	2	2	4	.300	.364	.400	.764	114	0	0	101	98	3	.714	0	0	0	-0	S	0.2
1974	Det-A	22	55	4	13	2	0	2	9	5	8	.236	.300	.382	.682	90	-0	-1	106	131	7	.643	1	0	0	0	S	0.1
1975	Det-A	128	404	37	102	13	1	5	48	23	76	.252	.301	.327	.628	75	-12	-14	104	125	38	.514	2	6	-3	-8	*S	-1.2
1976	Det-A	97	354	31	83	8	2	1	25	21	44	.234	.289	.277	.566	64	-15	-16	104	97	27	.441	1	4	-2	9	S	-0.3
1977	Det-A	125	350	31	69	12	1	2	28	16	44	.197	.232	.254	.487	31	-33	-35	105	117	21	.366	0	1	-1	5	*S	-1.5
1978	Cle-A	130	421	48	114	18	4	1	32	13	36	.271	.301	.340	.640	86	-12	-8	93	87	42	.513	1	2	-1	-7	*S	-0.5
1979	Cle-A	149	449	41	99	9	3	0	34	34	54	.220	.281	.254	.535	43	-34	-37	106	115	32	.422	2	5	-2	-5	*S	-2.5
1980	Cle-A	109	358	28	97	12	0	2	28	10	25	.271	.306	.321	.627	70	-14	-15	102	90	32	.480	0	5	-3	9	*S	0.0
1981	Cle-A	75	221	13	54	4	0	0	14	10	10	.244	.280	.262	.543	61	-12	-10	93	94	16	.405	1	0	0	-1	S	-0.5
1982	NY-N	40	54	6	18	2	0	0	4	3	4	.333	.368	.370	.739	109	1	1	99	78	7	.649	1	0	0	0	2S	0.3
1983	Chi-N	59	88	5	18	3	0	1	3	3	13	.205	.231	.273	.503	39	-7	-7	101	44	5	.380	0	0	0	1	S3	-0.4
1984	Chi-N	44	74	5	14	1	0	0	4	3	11	.189	.259	.203	.462	28	-7	-7	110	104	4	.349	0	0	0	1	S/32	-0.1
Total	12	996	2848	250	687	84	12	14	231	143	329	.241	.285	.294	.579	61	-144	-150	102	103	235	.467	9	23	-11	5	S/23	-6.4
■ ERNIE VICK Vick, Henry Arthur b: 7/2/1900, Toledo, Ohio d: 7/16/80, Ann Arbor, Mich. BR/TR, 5'9.5", 185 lbs. Deb: 6/29/22																												
1922	StL-N	3	6	1	2	2	0	0	0	0	0	.333	.333	.667	1.000	150	0	0	101	0	1	1.000	0	0	0	0	/C	0.0
1924	StL-N	16	23	2	8	1	0	0	0	3	3	.348	.423	.391	.814	117	1	1	103	0	4	.800	0	0	0	-0	C	0.1
1925	StL-N	14	32	3	6	2	1	0	3	3	1	.188	.257	.313	.570	44	-3	-3	102	107	3	.500	0	0	0	0	/C	-0.1
1926	StL-N	24	51	6	10	2	0	0	4	3	4	.196	.241	.235	.476	28	-5	-5	102	115	3	.366	0			1	C	-0.3
Total	4	57	112	12	26	7	1	0	7	9	8	.232	.289	.313	.602	58	-7	-7	102	82	11	.512	0	0		1	/C	-0.3
■ SAMMY VICK Vick, Samuel Bruce b: 4/12/1895, Batesville, Miss. d: 8/17/86, Memphis, Tenn. BR/TR, 5'10.5", 163 lbs. Deb: 9/20/17																												
1917	NY-A	10	36	4	10	3	0	0	2	1	6	.278	.297	.361	.658	94	-0	-0	107	56	4	.615	2			-2	O	-0.2
1918	NY-A	2	3	1	2	0	0	0	1	0	0	.667	.667	.667	1.333	320	1	1	95	182	1	2.000	0			-0	/O	0.0
1919	NY-A	106	407	59	101	15	9	2	27	35	55	.248	.308	.344	.652	78	-10	-13	106	71	44	.601	9			-8	*O	-2.8
1920	NY-A	51	118	21	26	7	1	0	11	14	20	.220	.313	.297	.610	61	-6	-7	102	110	12	.559	1	1	-0	-6	O	-1.4
1921	Bos-A	44	77	5	20	3	1	0	9	1	10	.260	.269	.325	.594	51	-6	-6	100	123	6	.448	0	1	-1	-2	O	-0.8
Total	5	213	641	90	159	28	11	2	50	51	91	.248	.305	.335	.641	73	-22	-25	104	84	67	.579	12	2		-18	O	-5.2
■ SAM VICO Vico, George Steve b: 8/9/23, San Fernando, Cal. BL/TR, 6'4", 200 lbs. Deb: 4/20/48																												
1948	Det-A	144	521	50	139	23	9	8	58	39	39	.267	.326	.392	.718	94	-9	-7	96	88	63	.619	2	2	-1	0	*1	0.0
1949	Det-A	67	142	15	27	5	2	4	18	21	17	.190	.311	.338	.649	67	-6	-8	108	103	16	.613	0	0	0	-1	1	-0.7
Total	2	211	663	65	166	28	11	12	76	60	56	.250	.323	.380	.703	87	-15	-14	99	91	79	.646	2	2	-1	-1	1	-0.7
■ JOSE VIDAL Vidal, Jose (Nicolas) "Papito" b: 4/3/40, Batey Lechugas, D.R. BR/TR, 6', 190 lbs. Deb: 9/05/66																												
1966	Cle-A	17	32	4	6	1	1	0	3	5	11	.188	.297	.281	.579	66	-1	-1	101	140	3	.519	0	1	-1	-1	O	-0.3
1967	Cle-A	16	34	4	4	0	0	0	0	7	12	.118	.268	.118	.386	18	-3	-3	100	0	1	.333	0	1	-1	1	O	-0.2
1968	Cle-A	37	54	5	9	0	0	2	5	2	15	.167	.196	.278	.474	42	-4	-4	101	102	3	.444	3	0	1	-6	O/1	-1.1
1969	Sea-A	18	26	7	5	0	1	1	2	4	8	.192	.323	.385	.707	99	-0	-0	98	62	3	.727	1	1	-0	-0	/O	0.0
Total	4	88	146	20	24	1	2	3	10	18	46	.164	.261	.260	.521	53	-8	-9	100	78	11	.488	4	3	-1	-7	/O1	-1.6
■ CHARLIE VINSON Vinson, Charles Anthony "Chuck" b: 1/5/44, Washington, D.C. BL/TL, 6'3", 207 lbs. Deb: 9/19/66																												
1966	Cal-A	13	22	3	4	2	0	1	6	5	9	.182	.357	.409	.766	121	1	1	99	210	4	.833	0	0	0	0	1	0.0
■ RUBE VINSON Vinson, Ernest Augustus b: 3/20/1879, Dover, Del. d: 10/12/51, Chester, Pa. 5'9", 168 lbs. Deb: 9/27/04																												
1904	Cle-A	15	49	12	15	1	0	0	2	10		.306	.424	.327	.750	140	3	3	102	49	8	.824	2			1	O	0.3
1905	Cle-A	39	134	12	26	3	1	0	9	7		.194	.234	.231	.465	50	-8	-7	100	106	8	.389	4			2	O	-0.7
1906	Chi-A	10	24	2	6	0	0	0	3	2		.250	.308	.250	.558	84	-1	-0	92	182	2	.500	1			-1	/O	-0.1

YEAR	TM/L	G	AB	R	H	2B	3B	HR	RBI	BB	SO	AVG	OBP	SLG	PRO	/A	BR	/A	PF	CHI	RC	TA	SB	CS	SBR	FR	POS	TPR
Total	3	64	207	26	47	4	1	0	14	19		.227	.292	.256	.548	77	-5	-5	99	100	18	.494	7			2	/O	-0.5
■ **JIM VIOX**	Viox, James Harry b: 12/30/1890, Lockland, Ohio d: 1/6/69, Erlanger, Ky. BR/TR, 5'7", 150 lbs. Deb: 5/09/12																											
1912	Pit-N	33	70	8	13	2	3	1	7	3	9	.186	.219	.343	.562	53	-5	-5	99	87	6	.509	2			-1	3/SO2	-0.4
1913	Pit-N	137	492	86	156	32	8	2	65	64	28	.317	.399	.427	.826	142	25	28	96	116	88	.866	14			-34	*2S	-0.9
1914	Pit-N	143	506	52	134	18	5	1	57	63	33	.265	.351	.326	.677	110	3	8	92	130	60	.648	9			-21	*2/SO	-1.5
1915	Pit-N	150	503	56	129	17	8	2	45	75	31	.256	.357	.334	.691	111	9	10	99	101	63	.678	12	8	-1	-22	*23/O	-1.3
1916	Pit-N	43	132	12	33	7	0	1	17	17	11	.250	.340	.326	.666	100	1	1	105	147	16	.636	2			-6	23	-0.4
Total	5	506	1703	214	465	76	24	7	191	222	112	.273	.361	.358	.719	117	33	41	96	117	233	.709	39	8		-84	2/3SO	-4.5
■ **BILL VIRDON**	Virdon, William Charles b: 6/9/31, Hazel Park, Mich. BL/TR, 6', 175 lbs. Deb: 4/12/55 MC																											
1955	StL-N	144	534	58	150	18	6	17	68	36	64	.281	.327	.433	.760	99	-1	-2	101	100	73	.678	2	4	-2	-8	*O	-1.3
1956	StL-N	24	71	10	15	2	0	2	9	5	8	.211	.273	.324	.597	60	-4	-4	99	131	6	.509	0	1	-1	1	O	-0.3
	Pit-N	133	509	67	170	21	10	8	37	33	63	.334	.376	.462	.837	121	17	15	102	64	84	.770	6	6	-2	0	*O	0.9
	Yr	157	580	77	185	23	10	10	46	38	71	.319	.363	.445	.808	114	13	12	102	75	90	.734	6	7	-2	2		0.6
1957	Pit-N	144	561	59	141	28	11	8	50	33	69	.251	.293	.383	.676	85	-17	-13	94	92	62	.582	3	3	-1	5	*O	-1.2
1958	Pit-N	144	604	75	161	24	11	9	46	52	70	.267	.326	.387	.713	92	-11	-7	95	63	78	.647	5	3	-0	3	*O	-0.8
1959	Pit-N	144	519	67	132	24	2	8	41	55	65	.254	.328	.355	.683	79	-13	-15	103	81	62	.623	7	4	-0	17	*O	0.0
1960	Pit-N	120	409	60	108	16	9	8	40	40	44	.264	.330	.406	.735	101	-0	0	99	85	57	.697	8	2	1	2	*O	0.0
1961	Pit-N	146	599	81	156	22	8	9	58	49	45	.260	.316	.369	.685	82	-16	-16	99	83	71	.604	5	8	-3	4	*O	-2.2
1962	Pit-N	156	663	82	164	27	**10**	6	47	36	65	.247	.287	.345	.633	67	-30	-32	102	65	62	.519	5	13	-6	-1	*O	-4.8
1963	Pit-N	142	554	58	149	22	6	8	53	43	55	.269	.322	.374	.695	101	-0	0	99	102	68	.608	1	2	-1	-2	*O	-1.1
1964	Pit-N	145	473	59	115	11	3	3	27	30	48	.243	.288	.298	.586	65	-21	-22	101	74	38	.459	1	5	-3	1	*O	-2.8
1965	Pit-N	135	481	58	134	22	5	4	24	30	49	.279	.322	.370	.692	95	-4	-4	100	53	58	.598	4	3	-1	-10	*O	-1.9
1968	Pit-N	6	3	1	1	0	0	1	2	0	2	.333	.333	1.333	1.667	378	1	1	101	120	1	2.000	0	0	0	-1	/O	0.0
Total	12	1583	5980	735	1596	237	81	91	502	442	647	.267	.318	.379	.697	89	-100	-96	99	79	721	.623	47	54	-18	11	*O	-15.5
■ **OZZIE VIRGIL**	Virgil, Osvaldo Jose Jr. b: 12/7/56, Mayaguez, P.R. BR/TR, 6'1", 180 lbs. Deb: 10/05/80																											
1980	Phi-N	1	5	1	1	1	0	0	0	0	1	.200	.200	.400	.600	59	-0	-0	107	0	0	.500	0	0	0	0	/C	0.0
1981	Phi-N	6	6	0	0	0	0	0	0	0	2	.000	.000	.000	.000	-89	-2	-2	112	0	0	.000	0	0	0	0	/C	-0.1
1982	Phi-N	49	101	11	24	6	0	3	8	10	26	.238	.306	.386	.692	99	-1	-0	94	65	11	.605	0	1	-1	-3	C	-0.3
1983	Phi-N	55	140	11	30	7	0	6	23	8	34	.214	.272	.393	.664	81	-4	-4	101	125	12	.550	0	2	-1	0	C	-0.3
1984	Phi-N	141	456	61	119	21	2	18	68	45	91	.261	.334	.434	.768	112	8	7	102	106	62	.697	1	1	-0	-8	*C	0.3
1985	Phi-N	131	426	47	105	16	3	19	55	49	85	.246	.331	.432	.763	110	6	5	102	91	59	.710	0	0	0	11	*C	2.1
1986	Atl-N	114	359	45	80	9	0	15	48	63	73	.223	.345	.373	.718	96	0	-1	102	109	49	.701	1	0	0	17	*C	1.9
1987	Atl-N	123	429	57	106	13	1	27	72	47	81	.247	.331	.471	.802	101	5	0	108	103	63	.749	0	1	-1	19	*C	2.8
1988	Atl-N	107	320	23	82	10	0	9	31	22	54	.256	.314	.372	.686	92	-2	-3	104	85	36	.597	2	0	1	-1	C	0.1
Total	9	727	2242	256	547	83	6	97	305	244	447	.244	.326	.416	.742	101	11	2	103	99	293	.708	4	5	-2	35	C	6.5
■ **OZZIE VIRGIL**	Virgil, Osvaldo Jose Sr. (Pichardo) b: 5/17/33, Montecristi, D.R. BR/TR, 6'1", 174 lbs. Deb: 9/23/56 C																											
1956	NY-N	3	12	2	5	1	1	0	2	0	0	.417	.417	.667	1.083	190	1	1	97	108	4	1.286	1	0	0	0	/3	0.2
1957	NY-N	96	226	26	53	0	2	4	24	14	27	.235	.279	.305	.584	56	-14	-14	102	123	17	.462	2	3	-1	-1	3O/S	-1.5
1958	Det-A	49	193	19	47	10	2	3	19	8	20	.244	.274	.363	.636	71	-7	-8	104	102	18	.523	1	0	0	1	3	-0.5
1960	Det-A	62	132	16	30	4	2	3	13	4	14	.227	.250	.356	.606	61	-7	-8	102	91	11	.495	1	1	-0	-3	3/2SC	-0.9
1961	Det-A	20	30	1	4	0	0	1	1	1	5	.133	.161	.233	.395	4	-4	-4	96	39	1	.286	0	0	0	-2	/3C2S	-0.4
	KC-A	11	21	1	3	0	0	0	0	0	3	.143	.143	.143	.286	-23	-4	-4	102	0	-0	.130	0	0	0	0	/3C	-0.2
	Yr	31	51	2	7	0	0	1	1	1	8	.137	.154	.196	.350	-7	-8	-8	98	26	1	.224	0	0	0	-2		-0.6
1962	Bal-A	1	0	0	0	0	0	0	0	1	0	—	1.000	—	1.196	258	0	0	95	0	0	—	0	0	0	0	H	0.0
1965	Pit-N	39	49	3	13	2	0	1	5	2	10	.265	.294	.367	.661	85	-1	-1	100	99	5	.541	0	0	0	0	C/32	0.0
1966	SF-N	42	89	7	19	2	0	2	9	4	12	.213	.247	.303	.551	54	-6	-6	97	115	6	.432	1	1	-0	-1	C3/120	-0.7
1969	SF-N	1	1	0	0	0	0	0	0	0	0	.000	.000	.000	.000	-99	-0	-0	101	0	0	.000	0	0	0	0	H	0.0
Total	9	324	753	75	174	19	7	14	73	34	91	.231	.264	.331	.595	60	-42	-43	101	102	61	.495	6	5	-1	-6	3/CO2S1	-4.0
■ **JAKE VIRTUE**	Virtue, Jacob Kitchline "Guesses" b: 3/2/1865, Philadelphia, Pa. d: 2/3/43, Camden, N.J. BB/TR, 5'9.5", 165 lbs. Deb: 7/21/1890																											
1890	Cle-N	62	223	39	68	6	5	2	25	49	15	.305	.432	.404	.836	156	16	19	94	76	44	.961	9			1	1	1.3
1891	Cle-N	139	517	82	135	19	14	2	72	75	40	.261	.363	.364	.727	109	12	7	105	110	76	.749	15			-10	*1	-0.5
1892	Cle-N	147	557	98	157	15	20	2	89	84	68	.282	.380	.391	.771	131	26	24	103	129	90	.800	14			-6	*1	0.6
1893	Cle-N	97	378	87	100	16	10	1	60	54	14	.265	.358	.368	.726	91	-2	-5	104	123	55	.737	11			2	10/S3P	-0.2
1894	Cle-N	29	89	15	23	4	1	0	10	13	3	.258	.359	.326	.685	61	-4	-6	111	95	11	.667	1			0	O/21P	-0.4
Total	5	474	1764	321	483	60	50	7	256	275	140	.274	.376	.376	.753	114	48	39	103	113	276	.784	50			-13	1/O3S2P	0.8
■ **JOE VISNER**	Visner, Joseph Paul (born Joseph Paul Vezina) b: 9/27/1859, Minneapolis, Minn. BL/TR, 5'11", 180 lbs. Deb: 1885																											
1885	Bal-a	4	13	2	3	0	0	0		2		.231	.333	.231	.564	79	-0	-0	106	0	1	.500				0	/O	0.0
1889	Bro-a	80	295	56	76	12	10	8	68	36	36	.258	.346	.447	.794	133	10	12	96	132	51	.845	13			-12	CO	0.4
1890	Pit-P	127	521	110	138	15	**22**	3	71	76	44	.265	.367	.395	.762	115	5	14	92	80	84	.804	18			-10	*O	0.0
1891	Was-a	18	68	13	19	2	3	1	7	8	7	.279	.355	.441	.796	137	2	3	95	65	12	.816	2			0	O/C3	0.3
	StL-a	6	27	2	4	0	1	0	1	0	3	.148	.148	.222	.370	6	-3	-4	114	51	1	.261	0			0	/O	-0.2
	Yr	24	95	15	23	2	4	1		8	10	.242	.301	.379	.680	97	-1	-1	100	64	12	.639	2			0		0.1
Total	4	235	924	183	240	29	36	12	147	122	90	.260	.353	.408	.762	118	14	25	94	93	149	.795	33			-22	O/C3	0.5
■ **OSSIE VITT**	Vitt, Oscar Joseph b: 1/4/1890, San Francisco, Cal. d: 1/31/63, Oakland, Cal. BR/TR, 5'10", 150 lbs. Deb: 4/11/12 M																											
1912	Det-A	73	273	39	67	4	4	0	19	18		.245	.297	.289	.586	72	-12	-10	95	82	28	.563	17			1	O32	-1.1
1913	Det-A	99	359	45	86	11	3	2	33	31	18	.240	.304	.304	.607	79	-10	-10	99	108	36	.538	5			-5	23/O	-1.7
1914	Det-A	66	195	35	49	7	0	0	8	31	8	.251	.354	.287	.641	91	-0	-1	102	54	24	.630	10	8	-2	1	23/OS	-0.1
1915	Det-A	152	560	116	140	18	13	1	48	80	22	.250	.348	.334	.682	96	4	-2	108	83	74	.678	26	18	-3	14	*3/2	1.7
1916	Det-A	153	597	88	135	17	12	0	42	75	28	.226	.314	.295	.608	79	-12	-15	105	75	65	.584	18			**27**	*3/S	2.0
1917	Det-A	140	512	65	130	13	6	0	47	56	15	.254	.329	.303	.631	95	-4	-2	98	115	58	.602	18			-15	*3	-1.0
1918	Det-A	81	267	29	64	5	2	0	17	32	6	.240	.321	.273	.594	82	-6	-5	97	87	27	.542	5			-3	3/2O	-0.7
1919	Bos-A	133	469	64	114	10	3	0	40	44	11	.243	.309	.277	.587	71	-21	-15	91	118	47	.518	9			19	*3	1.3
1920	Bos-A	87	296	50	65	10	4	1	28	43	10	.220	.321	.291	.611	65	-15	-13	96	113	31	.574	5	4	-1	4	32	-0.4
1921	Bos-A	78	232	29	44	11	1	0	13	45	13	.190	.321	.246	.567	47	-18	-18	100	78	22	.542	1	2	-1	-5	3/O1	-1.6
Total	10	1062	3760	560	894	106	48	4	295	455	131	.238	.322	.295	.617	79	-92	-90	100	93	412	.583	114	32		38	32/OS1	-1.6
■ **OTTO VOGEL**	Vogel, Otto Henry b: 10/26/1899, Mendota, Ill. d: 7/19/69, Iowa City, Iowa BR/TR, 6', 195 lbs. Deb: 6/05/23																											
1923	Chi-N	41	81	10	17	0	1	1	6	7	11	.210	.297	.272	.568	49	-6	-6	104	84	7	.507	2	3	-1	-3	O/3	-1.0
1924	Chi-N	70	172	28	46	11	2	1	24	10	26	.267	.319	.372	.691	84	-4	-4	101	131	20	.623	4	4	-1	-1	O/3	-0.6
Total	2	111	253	38	63	11	3	2	30	17	37	.249	.312	.340	.652	72	-9	-10	102	115	27	.584	6	7	-2	-4	/O3	-1.6
■ **CLYDE VOLLMER**	Vollmer, Clyde Frederick b: 9/24/21, Cincinnati, Ohio BR/TR, 6'1", 185 lbs. Deb: 5/31/42																											
1942	Cin-N	12	43	2	4	0	0	1	4	1	5	.093	.114	.163	.276	-19	-7	-7	101	148	1	.205	0			1	O	-0.5
1946	Cin-N	9	22	1	4	0	0	0	1	1	3	.182	.217	.182	.399	13	-2	-3	104	93	1	.389	2			-2	/O	-0.4
1947	Cin-N	78	155	19	34	10	0	1	13	9	18	.219	.267	.303	.570	56	-11	-9	91	96	13	.463	0			-5	O	-1.6
1948	Cin-N	7	9	0	1	0	0	0	0	0	1	.111	.200	.111	.311	-13	-1	-1	103	0	0	.222	0			-1	/O	-0.2
	Was-A	1	5	1	2	0	0	0	0	0	1	.400	.400	.400	.800	110	0	0	103	0	1	.667	0	0	0	0	/O	0.0
1949	Was-A	129	443	58	112	17	1	14	59	53	62	.253	.335	.391	.726	100	-7	-1	91	96	59	.662	1	2	-1	-0	*O	-0.4
1950	Was-A	6	14	4	4	0	0	0	1	2	3	.286	.375	.286	.661	72	-1	-0	99	86	2	.700	1	0	0	0	/O	0.0
	Bos-A	57	169	35	48	10	0	7	37	21	35	.284	.363	.467	.831	97	2	-1	114	128	29	.802	1	0	0	-2	O	-0.2
	Yr	63	183	39	52	10	0	7	38	23	38	.284	.364	.454	.818	96	2	-2	113	125	31	.794	2	0	1	-2		-0.2
1951	Bos-A	115	386	66	97	9	2	22	85	55	66	.251	.346	.456	.802	107	7	3	108	126	59	.751	0	0	0	-4	*O	-0.4

YEAR	TM/L	G	AB	R	H	2B	3B	HR	RBI	BB	SO	AVG	OBP	SLG	PRO	/A	BR	/A	PF	CHI	RC	TA	SB	CS	SBR	FR	POS	TPR
1952	Bos-A	90	250	35	66	12	4	11	50	39	47	.264	.370	.476	.846	126	12	9	107	123	42	.815	2	2	-1	0	O	0.7
1953	Bos-A	1	0	0	0	0	0	0	0	1	0	—	1.000	—	1.476	284	0	0	109	0	0	—	0	0	0	0	H	0.0
	Was-A	118	408	54	106	15	3	11	74	48	59	.260	.342	.392	.734	104	-1	2	94	145	58	.681	0	2	-1	3	*O	0.0
	Yr	119	408	54	106	15	3	11	74	49	59	.260	.343	.392	.736	104	-1	2	95	143	58	.684	0	2	-1	3		0.0
1954	Was-A	62	117	8	30	4	0	2	15	12	28	.256	.331	.342	.673	86	-2	-2	98	124	13	.589	0	0	0	-4	O	-0.6
Total	10	685	2021	283	508	77	10	69	339	243	328	.251	.335	.402	.737	98	-11	-11	100	119	278	.705	7	6		-13	O	-3.6
■ **FRITZ Von KOLNITZ**	Von Kolnitz, Alfred Holmes b: 5/20/1893, Charleston, S.C. d: 3/18/48, Mount Pleasant, S.C. BR/TR, 5'10.5", 175 lbs. Deb: 4/18/14																											
1914	Cin-N	41	104	8	23	2	0	0	6	6	16	.221	.270	.240	.511	50	-6	-7	105	87	7	.444	4			-3	3O/C1	-0.9
1915	Cin-N	50	78	6	15	4	1	0	6	7	11	.192	.259	.269	.528	58	-4	-4	103	109	5	.439	1	3	-2	0	3/S1CO	-0.4
1916	Chi-A	24	44	1	10	3	0	0	7	2	6	.227	.261	.295	.556	62	-2	-2	108	192	3	.441	0			0	3	-0.1
Total	3	115	226	15	48	9	1	0	19	15	33	.212	.264	.261	.526	55	-12	-13	105	115	16	.442	5	3		-2	/3OS1C	-1.4
■ **JOE VOSMIK**	Vosmik, Joseph Franklin b: 4/4/10, Cleveland, Ohio d: 1/27/62, Cleveland, Ohio BR/TR, 6', 185 lbs. Deb: 9/13/30																											
1930	Cle-A	9	26	1	6	2	0	0	4	1	1	.231	.259	.308	.567	41	-2	-2	105	166	2	.450	0	0	0	1	/O	0.0
1931	Cle-A	149	591	80	189	36	14	7	117	38	30	.320	.363	.464	.827	109	12	7	106	139	97	.785	7	7	-2	4	*O	0.0
1932	Cle-A	153	621	106	194	39	12	10	97	58	42	.312	.376	.462	.838	107	14	7	108	109	109	.819	2	3	-1	1	*O	0.0
1933	Cle-A	119	438	53	115	20	10	4	56	42	13	.263	.331	.381	.713	84	-8	-11	105	106	56	.652	0	2	-1	7	*O	-0.8
1934	Cle-A	104	405	71	138	33	2	6	78	35	10	.341	.393	.477	.870	123	14	13	101	131	76	.854	1	1	-0	-2	*O	0.9
1935	Cle-A	152	620	93	**216**	**47**	**20**	10	110	59	30	.348	.408	.537	.946	144	38	39	99	99	137	.983	2	1	0	3	*O	3.7
1936	Cle-A	138	506	76	145	29	7	7	94	79	21	.287	.383	.413	.796	91	-1	-6	106	135	85	.809	5	1	1	-4	*O	-1.1
1937	StL-A	144	594	81	193	47	9	4	93	49	38	.325	.377	.455	.832	110	8	9	99	109	102	.797	2	3	-1	7	*O	0.8
1938	Bos-A	146	621	121	**201**	37	6	9	86	59	26	.324	.384	.446	.830	105	7	5	102	84	107	.799	0	3	-2	3	*O	0.6
1939	Bos-A	145	554	89	153	29	6	7	84	66	33	.276	.356	.388	.744	83	-7	-15	108	127	73	.668	4	3	-1	-5	*O	-2.2
1940	Bro-N	116	404	45	114	14	6	1	42	22	21	.282	.321	.354	.675	80	-8	-12	108	107	45	.557	0			-1	O	-1.6
1941	Bro-N	25	56	0	11	0	0	0	4	4	4	.196	.250	.196	.446	26	-5	-6	103	131	3	.319	0			-6	O	-1.2
1944	Was-A	14	36	2	7	2	0	0	9	2	3	.194	.237	.250	.487	44	-3	-2	90	361	2	.367	0	0	0	-3	O	-0.5
Total	13	1414	5472	818	1682	335	92	65	874	514	272	.307	.369	.438	.807	103	58	26	104	116	895	.774	23	24		5	*O	-1.4
■ **ALEX VOSS**	Voss, Alexander b: 1855, Roswell, Ga. d: 8/31/06, Cincinnati, Ohio BR/TR, 6'1", 180 lbs. Deb: 4/17/1884																											
1884	Was-U	63	245	33	47	9	0	0		5		.192	.208	.229	.437	49	-13	-12	97	0	12	.308	0			0	P31O/S	-0.9
	KC-U	14	45	1	4	0	0	0		0		.089	.089	.089	.178	-46	-6	-5	87	0	0	.098	0			0	/OP	-0.4
	Yr	77	290	34	51	9	0	0		5		.176	.190	.207	.397	36	-19	-17	95	0	12	.272	0			0		-1.3
Total	1	77	290	34	51	9	0	0		5		.176	.190	.207	.397	36	-19	-17	95	0	12	.272	0			0	/PO31S	-1.3
■ **BILL VOSS**	Voss, William Edward b: 10/31/43, Glendale, Cal. BL/TL, 6'2", 160 lbs. Deb: 9/14/65																											
1965	Chi-A	11	33	4	6	0	1	1	3	3	5	.182	.250	.333	.583	70	-2	-1	92	89	3	.519	0	0	0	-1	O	-0.3
1966	Chi-A	2	2	0	0	0	0	0	0	0	2	.000	.000	.000	.000	-99	-1	-0	94	0	0	.000	0	0	0	-0	/O	0.0
1967	Chi-A	13	22	4	2	0	0	0	0	0	1	.091	.091	.091	.182	-49	-4	-4	94	0	0	.136	1	1	-0	-2	O	-0.6
1968	Chi-A	61	167	14	26	2	1	2	15	16	34	.156	.238	.216	.453	38	-12	-12	101	153	9	.407	5	3	-0	-3	O	-2.1
1969	Cal-A	133	349	33	91	11	4	2	40	35	40	.261	.328	.332	.661	86	-7	-6	99	132	38	.578	5	3	-0	0	*O/1	-0.9
1970	Cal-A	80	181	21	44	4	3	3	30	23	18	.243	.335	.348	.683	97	-2	-0	92	169	22	.638	2	1	0	1	O	-0.1
1971	Mil-A	97	275	31	69	4	0	10	30	24	45	.251	.313	.375	.688	91	-3	-3	103	92	33	.616	2	2	-1	-2	O	-0.8
1972	Mil-A	27	36	1	3	1	0	0	1	5	4	.083	.195	.111	.306	-8	-5	-5	95	104	1	.243	0	1	-1	-2	O	-0.8
	Oak-A	40	97	10	22	5	1	1	5	9	16	.227	.299	.330	.629	90	-2	-1	97	60	10	.545	0	0	0	-0	O	-0.2
	Yr	67	133	11	25	6	1	1	6	14	20	.188	.270	.271	.541	64	-6	-6	96	79	10	.459	0	1	-1	-3		-1.0
	StL-N	11	15	1	4	2	0	0	3	2	2	.267	.353	.400	.753	108	0	0	105	205	2	.667	0	0	0	0	/O	0.0
Total	8	475	1177	119	267	29	10	19	127	117	167	.227	.300	.317	.617	77	-36	-34	99	122	117	.554	15	11	-2	-10	O/1	-5.8
■ **PHIL VOYLES**	Voyles, Philip Vance b: 5/12/1900, Murphy, N.C. d: 11/3/72, Marlboro, Mass. BL/TR, 5'11.5", 175 lbs. Deb: 9/04/29																											
1929	Bos-N	20	68	9	16	0	2	0	14	6	8	.235	.297	.294	.591	50	-6	-5	94	244	6	.500	0			-1	O	-0.6
■ **GEORGE VUKOVICH**	Vukovich, George Stephen b: 6/24/56, Chicago, Ill. BL/TR, 6', 198 lbs. Deb: 4/13/80																											
1980	Phi-N	78	58	6	13	1	1	0	8	6	9	.224	.297	.276	.573	57	-3	-3	107	198	5	.478	0	0	0	-9	O	-1.4
1981	Phi-N	20	26	5	10	0	0	1	4	1	0	.385	.407	.500	.907	139	2	1	112	98	6	.938	1	0	0	-2	/O	0.0
1982	Phi-N	123	335	41	91	18	2	6	42	32	47	.272	.335	.391	.726	109	1	4	94	111	41	.642	2	9	-5	-3	*O	-0.5
1983	Cle-A	124	312	31	77	13	2	3	44	24	37	.247	.305	.330	.635	71	-11	-13	105	154	30	.534	3	4	-2	-15	*O	-3.0
1984	Cle-A	134	437	38	133	22	5	9	60	34	61	.304	.356	.439	.795	112	11	8	106	109	66	.717	1	4	-2	14	*O	1.6
1985	Cle-A	149	434	43	106	22	0	8	45	30	75	.244	.295	.350	.645	80	-15	-11	94	101	43	.546	2	2	-1	-11	*O	-2.4
Total	6	628	1602	164	430	76	10	27	203	127	229	.268	.324	.379	.703	93	-15	-15	100	119	191	.623	9	19	-9	-26	O	-5.7
■ **JOHN VUKOVICH**	Vukovich, John Christopher b: 7/31/47, Sacramento, Cal. BR/TR, 6'1", 187 lbs. Deb: 9/11/70 MC																											
1970	Phi-N	3	8	1	1	0	0	0	0	1	0	.125	.222	.125	.347	-5	-1	-1	96	0	0	.286	0	0	0	-0	/S3	0.0
1971	Phi-N	74	217	11	36	5	0	0	14	12	34	.166	.213	.189	.402	14	-24	-25	103	139	9	.301	2	1	0	5	3	-2.1
1973	Mil-A	55	128	10	16	3	0	2	9	9	40	.125	.182	.195	.378	7	-16	-15	96	114	5	.296	0	2	-1	-4	31/S	-2.2
1974	Mil-A	38	80	5	15	1	0	3	11	1	16	.188	.198	.313	.510	44	-6	-6	102	127	4	.412	2	1	0	-2	S32/1	-0.6
1975	Cin-N	31	38	4	8	3	0	0	2	4	5	.211	.286	.289	.575	57	-2	-2	104	70	4	.500	0	0	0	-2	3	-0.4
1976	Phi-N	4	8	2	1	0	0	1	2	0	2	.125	.125	.500	.625	66	-0	-0	107	110	1	.571	0	0	0	0	/31	0.0
1977	Phi-N	2	2	0	0	0	0	0	0	0	1	.000	.000	.000	.000	-99	-1	-1	100	0	0	.000	0	0	0	0	H	0.0
1979	Phi-N	10	15	0	3	1	0	0	1	0	3	.200	.200	.267	.467	27	-2	-1	97	99	1	.333	0	0	0	0	/32	-0.1
1980	Phi-N	49	62	4	10	1	1	0	5	2	7	.161	.200	.210	.410	13	-7	-8	107	152	2	.291	0	1	-1	3	3/2S1	-0.3
1981	Phi-N	11	1	0	0	0	0	0	0	0	1	.000	.000	.000	.000	-89	-0	-0	112	0	0	.000	0	0	0	0	/312	0.0
Total	10	277	559	37	90	14	1	6	44	29	109	.161	.205	.222	.427	20	-59	-60	102	124	25	.335	4	5	-2	0	3/21S	-5.7
■ **FRANK WADDEY**	Waddey, Frank Orum b: 8/21/05, Memphis, Tenn. BL/TL, 5'10.5", 185 lbs. Deb: 4/16/31																											
1931	StL-A	14	22	3	6	1	0	0	2	2	3	.273	.333	.318	.652	70	-1	-1	102	94	2	.563	0	0	0	-2	/O	-0.2
■ **HAM WADE**	Wade, Abraham Lincoln b: 12/20/1880, Spring City, Pa. d: 7/21/68, Riverside, N.J. BR/TR, 5'8", 155 lbs. Deb: 9/09/07																											
1907	NY-N	1	0	0	0	0	0	0	0	0		—	—	—	—	—	0	0	105	—	—	—	0			0	/O	0.0
■ **GALE WADE**	Wade, Galeard Lee b: 1/20/29, Hollister, Mo. BL/TR, 6'1.5", 185 lbs. Deb: 4/11/55																											
1955	Chi-N	9	33	5	6	1	0	1	1	4	3	.182	.270	.303	.573	52	-2	-2	100	33	3	.500	0	0	0	-1	/O	-0.3
1956	Chi-N	10	12	0	0	0	0	0	0	1	0	.000	.077	.000	.077	-78	-3	-3	99	0	-0	.071	0	0	0	0	/O	-0.2
Total	2	19	45	5	6	1	0	1	1	5	3	.133	.220	.222	.442	18	-5	-5	99	24	3	.366	0	0	0	-1	/O	-0.5
■ **RIP WADE**	Wade, Richard Frank b: 1/12/1898, Duluth, Minn. d: 6/16/57, Sandstone, Minn. BL/TR, 5'11", 174 lbs. Deb: 4/19/23																											
1923	Was-A	33	69	8	16	2	2	2	14	5	10	.232	.284	.406	.690	85	-2	-2	95	141	8	.623	0	0	0	-2	O	-0.5
■ **WOODY WAGENHORST**	Wagenhorst, Elwood Otto b: 6/3/1863, Kutztown, Pa. d: 2/12/46, Deb: 1888																											
1888	Phi-N	2	8	2	1	0	0	0	0	0	1	.125	.125	.125	.250	-17	-1	-1	114	0	0	.143	0			0	/3	0.0
■ **BUTTS WAGNER**	Wagner, Albert b: 9/23/1880, Mansfield, Pa. d: 11/26/28, Pittsburgh, Pa. 5'10", 170 lbs. Deb: 4/27/1898																											
1898	Was-N	63	223	20	50	11	2	1	31	14		.224	.279	.305	.584	68	-9	-10	102	135	21	.514	4			-6	3O/S2	-1.3
	Bro-N	11	38	2	9	1	1	0	3	2		.237	.275	.316	.591	75	-1	-1	95	76	3	.483	0			-1	3	-0.1
	Yr	74	261	22	59	12	3	1	34	16		.226	.279	.307	.585	69	-10	-11	101	128	24	.510	4			-7		-1.4
Total	1	74	261	22	59	12	3	1	34	16		.226	.279	.307	.585	69	-10	-11	101	126	24	.510	4			-7	/3OS2	-1.4
■ **HEINIE WAGNER**	Wagner, Charles F. b: 9/23/1880, New York, N.Y. d: 3/20/43, New Rochelle, N.Y. BR/TR, 5'9", 183 lbs. Deb: 7/01/02 MC																											
1902	NY-N	17	56	4	12	1	0	0	2	0		.214	.214	.232	.446	39	-4	-4	100	53	4	.364	3			-2	S	-0.5
1906	Bos-A	9	32	1	9	0	0	0	4	1		.281	.303	.281	.584	87	-1	-0	98	165	3	.522	2			0	/2	0.0
1907	Bos-A	111	385	29	82	10	4	2	21	31		.213	.272	.275	.547	75	-10	-10	101	68	35	.518	20			2	*S/23	-0.6

YEAR	TM/L	G	AB	R	H	2B	3B	HR	RBI	BB	SO	AVG	OBP	SLG	PRO	/A	BR	/A	PF	CHI	RC	TA	SB	CS	SBR	FR	POS	TPR
1908	Bos-A	153	526	62	130	11	5	1	46	27		.247	.284	.293	.577	91	-6	-5	98	112	47	.508	20			30	*S	3.2
1909	Bos-A	124	430	53	110	16	7	1	49	35		.256	.316	.333	.649	96	2	-2	109	132	49	.622	18			4	*S/2	0.6
1910	Bos-A	142	491	61	134	26	7	1	52	44		.273	.335	.360	.696	119	10	10	99	109	68	.697	26			-17	*S	-0.5
1911	Bos-A	80	261	34	67	13	8	1	38	29		.257	.340	.379	.719	102	0	0	99	126	38	.758	15			-2	2S	0.1
1912	Bos-A	144	504	75	138	25	6	2	68	62		.274	.358	.359	.717	98	5	-0	107	124	72	.732	21			-15	*S	-0.1
1913	Bos-A	110	365	43	83	14	8	2	34	40	29	.227	.316	.326	.642	85	-6	-7	103	99	38	.621	9			-0	*S/2	0.2
1915	Bos-A	84	267	38	64	11	2	0	29	37	34	.240	.339	.296	.635	91	-2	-2	99	127	30	.614	8	4	0	-10	2/3O	-1.3
1916	Bos-A	6	8	2	4	1	0	0	0	3	0	.500	.636	.625	1.261	298	2	2	94	0	4	2.500	2			-0	/32S	0.2
1918	Bos-A	3	8	0	1	0	0	0	0	1	0	.125	.222	.125	.347	5	-1	-1	95	0	0	.286	0			0	/23	0.0
Total	12	983	3333	402	834	128	47	10	343	310	63	.250	.318	.326	.644	95	-11	-19	102	111	390	.624	144	4		-10	S2/3O	1.3

■ **HAL WAGNER** Wagner, Harold Edward b: 7/2/15, E.Riverton, N.J. d: 8/7/79, Riverside, N.J. BL/TR, 6', 165 lbs. Deb: 10/03/37

YEAR	TM/L	G	AB	R	H	2B	3B	HR	RBI	BB	SO	AVG	OBP	SLG	PRO	/A	BR	/A	PF	CHI	RC	TA	SB	CS	SBR	FR	POS	TPR
1937	Phi-A	1	0	0	0	0	0	0	0	0	0	—	—	—	—	—	0	0	94	—	—	—	0	0	0	0	/C	0.0
1938	Phi-A	33	88	10	20	2	1	0	8	8	9	.227	.299	.273	.572	44	-8	-8	101	113	8	.485	0	0	0	-0	C	-0.6
1939	Phi-A	5	8	0	1	0	0	0	0	0	3	.125	.125	.125	.250	-37	-2	-2	97	0	0	.143	0	0	0	0	/C	0.0
1940	Phi-A	34	75	9	19	5	1	0	10	11	6	.253	.356	.347	.703	87	-2	-1	96	139	10	.655	0	0	0	1	C	0.1
1941	Phi-A	46	131	18	29	8	2	1	15	19	9	.221	.320	.336	.656	73	-5	-5	101	113	16	.621	1	0	0	2	C	0.0
1942	Phi-A	104	288	26	68	17	1	1	30	24	29	.236	.304	.313	.616	76	-10	-9	96	114	28	.524	1	0	0	0	C	0.3
1943	Phi-A	111	289	22	69	17	1	1	26	36	17	.239	.327	.315	.642	87	-4	-4	101	101	31	.569	3	3	-1	-1	C	0.0
1944	Phi-A	5	4	0	1	0	0	0	0	0	0	.250	.250	.250	.500	43	-0	-0	101	0	0	.333	0	0	0	0	/C	0.0
	Bos-A	66	223	21	74	13	4	1	38	29	14	.332	.418	.439	.857	148	14	15	98	138	45	.868	1	1	-0	2	C	2.1
	Yr	71	227	21	75	13	4	1	38	29	14	.330	.415	.436	.852	146	14	15	98	129	45	.858	1	1	-0	2		2.1
1946	Bos-A	117	370	39	85	12	2	6	52	69	32	.230	.354	.322	.675	78	-3	-10	114	144	48	.659	3	1	0	-8	*C	-1.2
1947	Bos-A	21	65	5	15	3	0	0	6	9	5	.231	.324	.277	.601	63	-3	-3	108	123	7	.529	0	0	0	-0	C	-0.1
	Det-A	71	191	19	55	10	0	5	33	28	16	.288	.382	.419	.801	118	6	5	104	128	33	.784	0	1	-1	-2	C	0.8
	Yr	92	256	24	70	13	0	5	39	37	21	.273	.367	.383	.750	104	4	2	105	128	40	.720	0	1	-1	-3		0.7
1948	Det-A	54	109	10	22	3	0	0	10	20	11	.202	.326	.229	.555	51	-7	-7	96	135	10	.517	1	0	0	-5	C	-0.7
	Phi-N	3	4	0	0	0	0	0	0	0	0	.000	.000	.000	.000	-99	-1	-1	94	0	0	.000	0			0	/C	0.0
1949	Phi-N	1	4	0	0	0	0	0	0	0	1	.000	.000	.000	.000	-99	-1	-1	101	0	0	.000	0			0	/C	0.0
Total	12	672	1849	179	458	90	12	15	228	253	152	.248	.343	.334	.677	86	-24	-30	103	124	625	.641	10	6		-12	C	0.7

■ **HONUS WAGNER** Wagner, John Peter "The Flying Dutchman" b: 2/24/1874, Mansfield, Pa. d: 12/6/55, Carnegie, Pa. BR/TR, 5'11", 200 lbs. Deb: 7/19/1897 MCH

YEAR	TM/L	G	AB	R	H	2B	3B	HR	RBI	BB	SO	AVG	OBP	SLG	PRO	/A	BR	/A	PF	CHI	RC	TA	SB	CS	SBR	FR	POS	TPR
1897	Lou-N	61	237	37	80	17	4	2	39	15		.338	.379	.468	.848	132	8	10	95	103	51	.930	19			5	O/2	0.9
1898	Lou-N	151	588	80	176	29	3	10	105	31		.299	.340	.410	.750	121	11	14	96	124	93	.738	27			-6	132	0.9
1899	Lou-N	147	571	98	192	43	13	7	113	40		.336	.391	.494	.885	140	33	30	103	121	128	.976	37			2	3O/21	2.5
1900	Pit-N	135	527	107	201	**45**	**22**	4	100	41		**.381**	.426	**.573**	**.999**	172	**53**	50	103	96	**148**	**1.169**	38			0	*O/321P	3.6
1901	Pit-N	140	549	101	194	37	11	6	**126**	53		.353	.410	.494	.904	163	44	44	101	155	135	1.051	**49**			3	SO3/2	4.5
1902	Pit-N	136	534	**105**	176	**30**	16	3	**91**	43		.330	.380	**.463**	.842	**154**	37	**34**	105	130	**112**	**.927**	**42**			9	OS1/P2	4.0
1903	Pit-N	129	512	97	182	30	**19**	5	101	44		**.355**	.406	.518	.924	158	41	38	105	123	130	1.076	46			13	*S1/O	5.4
1904	Pit-N	132	490	97	171	**44**	14	4	75	59		**.349**	**.419**	**.520**	**.939**	**193**	**53**	**53**	99	99	**132**	**1.150**	**53**			-5	*S/O12	**4.9**
1905	Pit-N	147	548	114	199	32	14	6	101	54		.363	.420	.505	.926	171	52	49	104	126	144	**1.112**	57			18	*S/O	**7.0**
1906	Pit-N	142	516	**103**	175	**38**	9	2	71	58		**.339**	.406	.459	**.865**	165	**43**	41	104	113	**121**	1.021	53			14	*S/O3	**6.6**
1907	Pit-N	142	515	98	180	**38**	14	6	82	46		**.350**	**.403**	**.513**	**.915**	**180**	**50**	**48**	105	117	**134**	**1.107**	**61**			-1	*S/1	**5.8**
1908	Pit-N	151	568	100	**201**	**39**	**19**	10	**109**	54		**.354**	**.410**	**.542**	**.952**	**217**	**65**	**68**	95	119	**145**	**1.131**	**53**			-5	*S	**6.8**
1909	Pit-N	137	495	92	168	**39**	10	5	**100**	66		**.339**	**.420**	**.489**	**.909**	**176**	**49**	**46**	105	150	**114**	**1.058**	35			10	*S/O	**6.2**
1910	Pit-N	150	556	90	**178**	34	8	4	81	59	47	.320	.390	.432	.822	125	28	20	112	119	103	.868	24			2	*S1/2	2.8
1911	Pit-N	130	473	87	158	23	16	9	89	67	34	**.334**	.423	.507	**.930**	159	39	38	101	119	109	1.057	20			-3	*S1/O	3.8
1912	Pit-N	145	558	91	181	35	20	7	**102**	59	38	.324	.395	.496	.891	145	32	33	99	122	118	.976	26			19	*S	**6.3**
1913	Pit-N	114	413	51	124	18	4	3	56	26	40	.300	.349	.385	.734	114	5	7	96	123	60	.730	21			-0	*S	1.4
1914	Pit-N	150	552	60	139	15	9	1	50	51	51	.252	.317	.317	.634	96	-7	-2	92	108	60	.608	23			5	*S3/1	0.8
1915	Pit-N	156	566	68	155	32	17	6	78	39	64	.274	.325	.422	.747	127	15	16	99	123	79	.714	22	15	-2	-3	*S21	1.5
1916	Pit-N	123	432	45	124	15	9	1	39	34	36	.287	.350	.370	.721	116	11	9	105	97	61	.692	11			-12	*S1	0.1
1917	Pit-N	74	230	15	61	7	1	0	24	24	17	.265	.337	.304	.642	98	0	0	100	132	25	.592	5			-2	13/2SM	-0.2
Total	21	2792	10430	1736	3415	640	252	101	1732	963	327	.327	.387	.466	.853	150	663	646	101	120	2203	.939	722	15		63	*SO13/2P	75.6

■ **JOE WAGNER** Wagner, Joseph Bernard b: 4/24/1889, New York, N.Y. d: 11/15/48, Bronx, N.Y. 5'11", 165 lbs. Deb: 4/25/15

YEAR	TM/L	G	AB	R	H	2B	3B	HR	RBI	BB	SO	AVG	OBP	SLG	PRO	/A	BR	/A	PF	CHI	RC	TA	SB	CS	SBR	FR	POS	TPR
1915	Cin-N	75	197	17	35	5	2	0	13	8	35	.178	.210	.223	.433	30	-17	-17	103	113	9	.333	4	6	-2	6	2S/3	-1.4

■ **LEON WAGNER** Wagner, Leon Lamar b: 5/13/34, Chattanooga, Tenn. BL/TR, 6'1", 195 lbs. Deb: 6/22/58

YEAR	TM/L	G	AB	R	H	2B	3B	HR	RBI	BB	SO	AVG	OBP	SLG	PRO	/A	BR	/A	PF	CHI	RC	TA	SB	CS	SBR	FR	POS	TPR
1958	SF-N	74	221	31	70	9	0	13	35	18	34	.317	.371	.534	.905	136	11	11	100	92	45	.908	1	0	0	-4	O	0.6
1959	SF-N	87	129	20	29	4	3	5	22	25	24	.225	.363	.419	.782	113	2	3	95	129	20	.788	0	0	0	-2	O	0.0
1960	StL-N	39	98	12	21	2	0	4	11	17	17	.214	.336	.357	.693	83	-1	-2	108	95	12	.671	0	1	-1	-1	O	-0.4
1961	LA-A	133	453	74	127	19	2	28	79	48	65	.280	.353	.517	.870	116	17	10	111	97	85	.873	5	1	1	-2	*O	0.5
1962	LA-A	160	612	96	164	21	5	37	107	50	87	.268	.328	.500	.828	117	14	12	102	108	101	.803	7	5	-1	-7	*O	0.0
1963	LA-A	149	550	73	160	11	1	26	90	49	73	.291	.356	.456	.813	138	19	25	91	117	90	.776	5	7	-3	-6	*O	1.2
1964	Cle-A	163	641	94	162	19	2	31	100	56	121	.253	.319	.434	.752	104	5	3	103	110	89	.717	14	2	3	-7	*O	-0.7
1965	Cle-A	144	517	91	152	18	1	28	79	60	52	.294	.371	.495	.866	146	30	31	98	98	99	.887	12	2	2	-13	*O	1.6
1966	Cle-A	150	549	70	153	20	0	23	66	46	69	.279	.336	.441	.776	119	14	13	101	91	80	.717	5	2	0	-12	*O	-0.3
1967	Cle-A	135	433	56	105	15	1	15	54	37	76	.242	.320	.386	.705	107	4	4	100	106	55	.652	3	3	-1	-12	*O	-1.3
1968	Cle-A	38	49	5	9	4	0	0	6	6	6	.184	.273	.265	.538	63	-2	-2	101	198	3	.452	0	0	0	-4	O	-0.6
	Chi-A	69	162	14	46	8	0	1	18	21	31	.284	.366	.352	.718	117	4	4	101	128	22	.672	2	1	0	-10	O	-0.8
	Yr	107	211	19	55	12	0	1	24	27	37	.261	.345	.332	.676	105	2	2	101	155	26	.623	2	1	0	-14		-1.4
1969	SF-N	11	12	0	4	0	0	0	2	2	1	.333	.467	.333	.800	126	1	1	101	200	2	.875	0	0	0	0	/O	0.1
Total	12	1352	4426	636	1202	150	15	211	669	435	656	.272	.343	.455	.798	120	118	113	101	106	703	.784	54	24	2	-77	*O	-0.1

■ **MARK WAGNER** Wagner, Mark Duane b: 3/4/54, Conneaut, Ohio BR/TR, 6', 165 lbs. Deb: 8/20/76

YEAR	TM/L	G	AB	R	H	2B	3B	HR	RBI	BB	SO	AVG	OBP	SLG	PRO	/A	BR	/A	PF	CHI	RC	TA	SB	CS	SBR	FR	POS	TPR
1976	Det-A	39	115	9	30	2	3	0	12	6	18	.261	.298	.330	.628	81	-3	-3	104	121	11	.500	0	2	-1	3	S	0.2
1977	Det-A	22	48	4	7	0	1	1	3	4	12	.146	.226	.250	.476	28	-5	-5	105	79	3	.405	0	1	-1	0	S/2	-0.2
1978	Det-A	39	109	10	26	1	2	0	6	3	11	.239	.272	.284	.556	53	-6	-7	108	76	8	.430	1	0	0	0	S/2	-0.3
1979	Det-A	75	146	16	40	3	0	1	13	16	25	.274	.346	.315	.661	83	-4	-3	96	102	17	.591	3	2	-0	1	S2/3	0.4
1980	Det-A	45	72	5	17	1	0	0	3	7	11	.236	.304	.250	.554	51	-4	-5	105	65	6	.446	0	1	-1	-4	S/32	-0.6
1981	Tex-A	50	85	15	22	4	1	1	14	8	13	.259	.323	.365	.687	107	-0	1	91	161	10	.606	1	1	-0	3	S/23	0.7
1982	Tex-A	60	179	14	43	4	1	0	8	10	28	.240	.280	.274	.554	57	-11	-10	93	65	13	.423	1	0	0	0	S	-0.3
1983	Tex-A	2	2	0	0	0	0	0	0	0	1	.000	.000	.000	.000	-99	-1	-1	101	0	0	.000	0	0	0	0	/S	0.0
1984	Oak-A	82	87	8	20	5	1	0	12	7	11	.230	.287	.310	.598	71	-4	-3	92	177	7	.500	2	0	1	-4	S3/2PD	-0.1
Total	9	414	843	81	205	20	9	3	71	61	130	.243	.297	.299	.596	67	-38	-36	98	103	76	.498	8	7	-2	0	S/23DP	-0.2

■ **BILL WAGNER** Wagner, William Joseph b: 1/2/1894, Jessup, Iowa d: 1/11/51, Waterloo, Iowa BR/TR, 6', 187 lbs. Deb: 7/16/14

YEAR	TM/L	G	AB	R	H	2B	3B	HR	RBI	BB	SO	AVG	OBP	SLG	PRO	/A	BR	/A	PF	CHI	RC	TA	SB	CS	SBR	FR	POS	TPR
1914	Pit-N	3	1	0	0	0	0	0	0	0	0	.000	.000	.000	.000	-99	-0	-0	92	0	0	.000	0			0	/C	0.0
1915	Pit-N	5	5	0	0	0	0	0	0	1	2	.000	.167	.000	.167	-48	-1	-1	99	0	0	.200	0			0	/C	0.0
1916	Pit-N	19	38	2	9	0	2	0	2	5	8	.237	.326	.342	.668	100	0	0	105	61	4	.621	0			1	C	0.2
1917	Pit-N	53	151	15	31	7	2	0	9	11	22	.205	.264	.278	.542	67	-6	-6	100	83	11	.458	1			2	C1	-0.2
1918	Bos-N	13	47	2	10	0	0	1	7	4	5	.213	.275	.277	.551	73	-2	-1	94	169	3	.459	0			-1	C	-0.1
Total	5	93	242	19	50	7	4	1	18	21	37	.207	.273	.281	.554	70	-9	-8	99	94	19	.474	1			2	/C1	-0.1

■ **KERMIT WAHL** Wahl, Kermit Emerson b: 11/18/22, Columbia, S.Dak. d: 9/16/87, Tucson, Ariz. BR/TR, 5'11", 170 lbs. Deb: 6/23/44

YEAR	TM/L	G	AB	R	H	2B	3B	HR	RBI	BB	SO	AVG	OBP	SLG	PRO	/A	BR	/A	PF	CHI	RC	TA	SB	CS	SBR	FR	POS	TPR
1944	Cin-N	4	1	0	0	0	0	0	0	0	0	.000	.000	.000	.000	-99	-0	-0	95	0	0	.000	0			0	/3	0.0
1945	Cin-N	71	194	18	39	8	2	0	10	23	22	.201	.286	.263	.549	56	-12	-11	94	68	16	.481	2			-1	2S/3	-0.5

YEAR	TM/L	G	AB	R	H	2B	3B	HR	RBI	BB	SO	AVG	OBP	SLG	PRO	/A	BR	/A	PF	CHI	RC	TA	SB	CS	SBR	FR	POS	TPR
1947	Cin-N	39	81	8	14	0	0	1	4	6	12	.173	.239	.210	.449	22	-9	-8	91	74	4	.353	0			-1	3/S2	-0.8
1950	Phi-A	89	280	26	72	12	3	2	27	30	30	.257	.331	.343	.674	81	-12	-7	90	91	32	.587	1	1	-0	1	3S/2	-0.6
1951	Phi-A	20	59	4	11	2	0	0	6	9	5	.186	.294	.220	.514	38	-5	-5	106	165	4	.440	0	0	0	3	3	-0.2
	StL-A	8	27	2	9	1	1	0	3	0	3	.333	.333	.444	.778	104	0	0	105	89	4	.632	0	0	0	0	/3	0.0
	Yr	28	86	6	20	3	1	0	9	9	8	.233	.305	.291	.596	58	-5	-5	106	149	8	.507	0	0	0	3		-0.2
Total	5	231	642	58	145	23	6	3	50	68	72	.226	.302	.294	.596	63	-38	-32	93	89	60	.525	3	1		2	3/S2	-2.1
■ **EDDIE WAITKUS** Waitkus, Edward Stephen b: 9/4/19, Cambridge, Mass. d: 9/15/72, Jamaica Plain, Mass. BL/TL, 6', 170 lbs. Deb: 4/15/41																												
1941	Chi-N	12	28	1	5	0	0	0	0	0	3	.179	.207	.179	.385	10	-3	-3	94	0	1	.250	0			-1	/1	-0.4
1946	Chi-N	113	441	50	134	24	5	4	55	23	14	.304	.340	.408	.748	119	5	8	94	109	60	.657	3			4	*1	0.3
1947	Chi-N	130	514	60	150	28	6	2	35	32	17	.292	.336	.381	.717	89	-8	-8	101	68	66	.626	3			7	*1	-0.9
1948	Chi-N	139	562	87	166	27	10	7	44	43	19	.295	.348	.416	.764	114	4	9	93	62	81	.711	11			5	*1O	1.2
1949	Phi-N	54	209	41	64	16	3	1	28	33	12	.306	.403	.426	.829	122	8	8	101	101	38	.851	3			-3	1	0.5
1950	Phi-N	154	641	102	182	32	5	2	44	55	29	.284	.341	.359	.700	87	-14	-11	97	64	79	.612	3			-2	*1	-1.9
1951	Phi-N	145	610	65	157	27	4	1	46	53	22	.257	.317	.320	.636	74	-24	-21	97	79	64	.534	0	3	-2	-1	*1	-2.6
1952	Phi-N	146	499	51	144	29	4	2	49	64	23	.289	.371	.375	.745	106	7	6	101	101	75	.700	2	2	-1	1	*1	0.2
1953	Phi-N	81	247	24	72	9	2	1	16	13	23	.291	.330	.356	.686	80	-8	-7	99	69	30	.575	1	1	-0	-1	1	-0.8
1954	Bal-A	95	311	35	88	17	4	2	33	28	25	.283	.344	.383	.727	104	-1	1	95	100	41	.638	0	1	-1	2	1	0.0
1955	Bal-A	38	85	2	22	1	1	0	9	11	10	.259	.344	.294	.638	81	-3	-2	90	134	9	.594	2	0	1	0	1	-0.1
	Phi-N	33	107	10	30	5	0	2	14	17	7	.280	.379	.383	.762	101	1	1	102	121	15	.707	0	1	-1	-0	1	-0.1
Total	11	1140	4254	528	1214	215	44	24	373	372	204	.285	.344	.374	.718	96	-35	-20	97	83	560	.655	28	8		12	*1/O	-4.6
■ **CHARLIE WAITT** Waitt, Charles C. b: 10/14/1853, Hallowell, Me. d: 10/21/12, San Francisco, Cal. 5'11", 165 lbs. Deb: 5/25/1875																												
1875	StL-n	31	122	14	26							.213															O/1	
1877	Chi-N	10	41	2	4	0	0	0	2	0	3	.098	.098	.098	.195	-39	-6	-6	98	173	0	.108				0	O	-0.5
1882	Bal-a	72	250	19	39	4	0	0		13		.156	.198	.172	.370	28	-19	-16	92	0	9	.265				-1	*O	-1.5
1883	Phi-N	1	3	0	1	0	0	0	0	0	1	.333	.333	.333	.667	115	0	0	90	0	0	.500				0	/O	0.0
Total	3	83	294	21	44	4	0	0	2	13	4	.150	.186	.163	.349	19	-25	-22	93	23	9	.244				-1	O/1	-2.0
■ **HOWARD WAKEFIELD** Wakefield, Howard John b: 4/2/1884, Bucyrus, Ohio d: 4/16/41, Chicago, Ill. BR/TR, 6'1", 205 lbs. Deb: 9/18/05																												
1905	Cle-A	10	26	3	4	0	0	0	1	0		.154	.154	.154	.308	-1	-3	-3	100	89	1	.182	0			-0	/C	-0.2
1906	Was-A	77	211	17	59	9	2	1	21	7		.280	.303	.355	.658	118	1	3	91	98	25	.579	6			0	C	0.9
1907	Cle-A	26	37	4	5	2	0	0	3	3		.135	.200	.189	.389	27	-3	-3	93	153	1	.313	0			-1	C	-0.2
Total	3	113	274	24	68	11	2	1	25	10		.248	.275	.314	.589	94	-5	-2	92	105	27	.495	6			-1	/C	0.5
■ **DICK WAKEFIELD** Wakefield, Richard Cummings b: 5/6/21, Chicago, Ill. d: 8/26/85, Redford Twp., Mich. BL/TR, 6'4", 210 lbs. Deb: 6/26/41																												
1941	Det-A	7	7	0	1	0	0	0	0	0	1	.143	.143	.143	.286	-23	-1	-1	106	0	0	.167	0	0	0	-0	/O	-0.1
1943	Det-A	155	633	91	**200**	**38**	8	7	79	62	60	.316	.377	.434	.811	130	29	25	106	94	101	.740	4	5	-2	-6	*O	1.3
1944	Det-A	78	276	53	98	15	5	12	53	55	29	.355	.464	.576	1.040	186	37	35	105	104	79	1.173	2	2	-1	-4	O	2.9
1946	Det-A	111	396	64	106	11	5	12	59	59	55	.268	.364	.412	.776	107	10	5	108	115	63	.753	3	5	-2	0	*O	-0.1
1947	Det-A	112	368	59	104	15	5	8	51	80	44	.283	.412	.416	.828	125	19	17	104	108	69	.851	1	4	-2	-1	*O	1.0
1948	Det-A	110	322	50	89	20	5	11	53	70	55	.276	.406	.472	.878	138	17	18	96	97	67	.925	0	1	-1	-0	O	1.3
1949	Det-A	59	126	17	26	3	1	6	19	32	24	.206	.367	.389	.756	93	0	-1	108	97	20	.779	0	0	0	1	O	0.0
1950	NY-A	3	2	0	1	0	0	0	1	1	1	.500	.667	.500	1.167	203	0	0	99	345	1	2.000	0	0	0	0	H	0.0
1952	NY-N	3	2	0	0	0	0	0	0	1	1	.000	.333	.000	.333	-0	-0	-0	102	0	0	.333	0	0	0	0	H	0.0
Total	9	638	2132	334	625	102	29	56	315	360	270	.293	.396	.447	.843	130	110	98	104	102	401	.870	10	17	-7	-10	O	6.3
■ **ED WALCZAK** Walczak, Edwin Joseph "Husky" b: 9/21/18, Artic, R.I. BR/TR, 5'11", 180 lbs. Deb: 9/03/45																												
1945	Phi-N	20	57	6	12	3	0	0	2	6	9	.211	.286	.263	.549	55	-4	-3	96	46	4	.447	0			-0	2/S	-0.1
■ **FRED WALDEN** Walden, Thomas Fred b: 6/25/1890, Fayette, Mo. d: 9/27/55, Jefferson Barracks, Mo. BR/TR, Deb: 6/03/12																												
1912	StL-A	1	0	0	0	0	0	0	0	0		—	—	—	—	—	0	0	99	—	—	—	0			0	/C	0.0
■ **IRV WALDRON** Waldron, Irving J. b: 1/21/1876, Hillside, N.Y. d: 7/22/44, Worcester, Mass. BR/TR, Deb: 4/25/01																												
1901	Mil-A	62	266	48	79	8	6	0	29	16		.297	.337	.372	.709	103	-1	1	95	80	38	.679	12			2	O	0.3
	Was-A	79	332	54	107	14	3	0	23	22		.322	.364	.383	.747	111	5	5	99	50	50	.698	8			1	O	0.4
	Yr	141	598	102	186	22	9	0	52	38		.311	.352	.378	.730	107	4	7	97	64	89	.689	20			3		0.7
Total	1	141	598	102	186	22	9	0	52	38		.311	.352	.378	.730	107	4	7	97	63	89	.689	20			3	O	0.7
■ **JIM WALEWANDER** Walewander, James b: 5/2/62, Chicago, Ill. BB/TR, 5'10", 160 lbs. Deb: 5/31/87																												
1987	Det-A	53	54	24	13	3	1	1	4	7	6	.241	.328	.389	.717	93	-1	-0	97	66	7	.682	2	1	0	0	23/SD	0.1
1988	Det-A	88	175	23	37	5	0	0	6	12	26	.211	.262	.240	.502	44	-13	-12	94	57	13	.455	11	4	1	-4	2/S3D	-1.1
Total	2	141	229	47	50	8	1	1	10	19	32	.218	.278	.275	.553	57	-14	-13	95	59	19	.514	13	5	1	-4	/23DS	-1.0
■ **RUBE WALKER** Walker, Albert Bluford b: 5/16/26, Lenoir, N.C. BL/TR, 6', 175 lbs. Deb: 4/20/48 C																												
1948	Chi-N	79	171	17	47	8	0	5	26	24	17	.275	.371	.409	.780	119	3	5	93	115	25	.727	0			1	C	0.9
1949	Chi-N	56	172	11	42	4	1	3	22	9	18	.244	.282	.331	.613	68	-9	-8	94	126	15	.493	0			1	C	-0.5
1950	Chi-N	74	213	19	49	7	1	6	16	18	34	.230	.290	.357	.647	66	-10	-11	105	66	22	.563	0			2	C	-0.7
1951	Chi-N	37	107	9	25	4	0	2	5	12	13	.234	.311	.327	.638	74	-4	-4	97	47	11	.547	0	0	0	-0	C	-0.3
	Bro-N	36	74	6	18	4	0	2	9	6	14	.243	.300	.378	.678	83	-2	-2	98	102	8	.576	0	0	0	1	C	0.0
	Yr	73	181	15	43	8	0	4	14	18	27	.238	.307	.348	.655	78	-6	-6	98	75	20	.574	0	0	0	1		-0.3
1952	Bro-N	46	139	9	36	8	0	1	19	8	17	.259	.304	.338	.642	77	-4	-5	102	148	14	.528	0	0	0	1	C	-0.2
1953	Bro-N	43	95	5	23	6	0	3	9	7	11	.242	.301	.400	.701	78	-3	-3	104	75	12	.630	0	0	0	1	C	0.0
1954	Bro-N	50	155	12	28	7	0	5	23	24	17	.181	.294	.323	.617	60	-9	-9	101	139	15	.568	0	0	0	5	C	-0.2
1955	Bro-N	48	103	6	26	5	0	2	13	15	11	.252	.347	.359	.707	84	-1	-2	104	122	11	.624	1	0	0	0	C	0.0
1956	Bro-N	54	146	5	31	6	1	3	20	7	18	.212	.248	.329	.577	52	-10	-10	103	148	11	.462	0	1	-1	0	C	-0.9
1957	Bro-N	60	166	12	30	8	0	2	23	15	33	.181	.249	.265	.514	33	-15	-18	116	191	10	.427	2	0	1	2	C	-1.2
1958	LA-N	25	44	3	5	2	0	1	7	5	10	.114	.204	.227	.431	13	-6	-6	105	222	2	.366	0	0	0	-0	C	-0.5
Total	11	608	1585	114	360	69	3	35	192	150	213	.227	.296	.341	.637	68	-70	-74	102	121	158	.568	3	1		13	C	-3.6
■ **TONY WALKER** Walker, Anthony Bruce b: 7/1/59, San Diego, Cal. BR/TR, 6'2", 205 lbs. Deb: 4/08/86																												
1986	Hou-N	84	90	19	20	7	0	2	10	11	15	.222	.307	.367	.674	83	-2	-2	103	102	10	.724	11	3	2	-11	O	-1.3
■ **FRANK WALKER** Walker, Charles Franklin b: 9/22/1894, Enoree, S.C. d: 9/16/74, Bristol, Tenn. BR/TR, 5'11", 165 lbs. Deb: 9/06/17																												
1917	Det-A	2	2	0	0	0	0	0	0	0	1	.000	.000	.000	.000	-99	-0	-0	98	0	0	.000	0			0	H	0.0
1918	Det-A	55	167	10	33	10	3	1	20	7	29	.198	.234	.311	.546	67	-8	-8	97	133	12	.470	3			0	O	-1.0
1920	Phi-A	24	91	10	21	2	2	0	10	5	14	.231	.286	.297	.582	58	-6	-5	94	138	7	.472	0	2	-1	0	O	-0.7
1921	Phi-A	19	66	6	15	3	0	1	6	8	11	.227	.311	.318	.629	59	-4	-4	103	87	7	.588	1	0	0	1	O	-0.3
1925	NY-N	39	81	12	18	1	0	1	5	9	11	.222	.308	.272	.579	50	-6	-6	99	71	7	.516	1	1	-0	0	O	-0.5
Total	5	139	407	38	87	16	5	3	41	29	66	.214	.273	.300	.572	58	-25	-23	98	113	34	.495	5	3		2	O	-2.5
■ **TILLY WALKER** Walker, Clarence William b: 9/4/1887, Telford, Tenn. d: 9/20/59, Chattanooga, Tenn BR/TR, 5'11", 165 lbs. Deb: 4/12/11																												
1911	Was-A	95	356	44	99	6	4	2	39	15		.278	.311	.334	.645	83	-10	-9	97	112	41	.576	12			0	O	-1.5
1912	Was-A	36	110	22	30	2	1	0	9	8		.273	.333	.309	.642	85	-2	-2	99	88	15	.688	11			-3	O/2	-0.6
1913	StL-A	23	85	7	25	4	1	0	11	2	9	.294	.310	.365	.675	102	-1	-0	95	134	11	.633	5			-1	O	-0.2
1914	StL-A	151	517	67	154	24	16	6	78	51	72	.298	.365	.441	.806	146	25	26	98	126	87	.821	29	17	-2	22	*O	4.1
1915	StL-A	144	510	53	137	20	7	5	49	36	77	.269	.323	.365	.688	111	2	4	96	85	62	.633	20	17	-4	10	*O	0.2
1916	Bos-A	128	467	68	124	29	11	3	46	23	45	.266	.303	.394	.697	117	2	5	94	87	61	.650	14			-8	*O	-1.1
1917	Bos-A	106	337	41	83	18	7	2	37	25	38	.246	.300	.359	.659	93	-1	-4	108	105	38	.602	6			4	O	-0.5
1918	Phi-A	114	414	56	122	20	0	**11**	48	41	44	.295	.360	.423	.782	131	17	15	104	89	64	.771	8			9	*O	2.0

YEAR	TM/L	G	AB	R	H	2B	3B	HR	RBI	BB	SO	AVG	OBP	SLG	PRO	/A	BR	/A	PF	CHI	RC	TA	SB	CS	SBR	FR	POS	TPR
1919	Phi-A	125	456	47	133	30	6	10	64	26	41	.292	.330	.450	.779	111	8	5	106	101	68	.740	8			3	*O	0.0
1920	Phi-A	149	585	79	157	23	7	17	82	41	59	.268	.321	.419	.739	101	-7	-2	94	94	80	.691	8	3	1	-7	*O	-2.0
1921	Phi-A	142	556	89	169	32	5	23	101	73	41	.304	.389	.504	.892	122	22	19	103	95	111	.921	3	4	-2	12	*O	1.6
1922	Phi-A	153	565	111	160	31	4	37	99	61	64	.283	.357	.549	.906	128	24	20	104	89	110	.922	4	6	-2	4	*O	1.1
1923	Phi-A	52	109	12	30	5	2	2	16	14	11	.275	.368	.413	.781	105	1	1	100	107	17	.765	1	2	-1	-2	O	-0.3
Total	13	1418	5067	696	1423	244	71	118	679	416	501	.281	.339	.427	.766	115	79	79	100	98	762	.742	129	49		44	*O/2	2.8

■ **CHICO WALKER** Walker, Cleotha b: 11/25/57, Jackson, Miss. BB/TR, 5'9", 170 lbs. Deb: 9/02/80

YEAR	TM/L	G	AB	R	H	2B	3B	HR	RBI	BB	SO	AVG	OBP	SLG	PRO	/A	BR	/A	PF	CHI	RC	TA	SB	CS	SBR	FR	POS	TPR
1980	Bos-A	19	57	3	12	0	0	1	5	6	10	.211	.297	.263	.560	54	-3	-4	102	108	5	.521	3	2	-0	1	2/D	-0.2
1981	Bos-A	6	17	3	6	0	0	0	2	1	2	.353	.389	.353	.742	108	0	0	106	130	2	.538	0	2	-1	-0	/2	0.0
1983	Bos-A	4	5	2	2	0	2	0	1	0	0	.400	.400	1.200	1.600	317	1	1	101	65	2	2.000	0	0	0	0	/O	0.1
1984	Bos-A	3	2	0	0	0	0	0	1	0	1	.000	.000	.000	.000	-91	-1	-1	110	0	0	.000	0	0	0	0	/2	0.0
1985	Chi-N	21	12	3	1	0	0	0	0	0	5	.083	.083	.083	.167	-46	-2	-3	116	0	0	.182	1	0	0	-2	/O2	-0.4
1986	Chi-N	28	101	21	28	3	2	1	7	10	20	.277	.342	.376	.719	92	-0	-1	107	69	14	.788	15	4	2	-1	O	0.0
1987	Chi-N	47	105	15	21	4	0	0	7	12	23	.200	.282	.238	.520	39	-9	-9	101	112	8	.539	11	4	1	-6	O/3	-1.4
1988	Cal-A	33	78	8	12	1	0	0	2	6	15	.154	.214	.167	.381	9	-9	-9	94	61	3	.304	2	1	0	-2	O/23	-1.0
Total	8	161	377	55	82	8	4	2	25	35	76	.218	.286	.276	.562	54	-23	-24	102	86	34	.555	32	13	2	-10	/O2D3	-2.9

■ **DUANE WALKER** Walker, Duane Allen b: 3/13/57, Pasadena, Tex. BL/TL, 6', 185 lbs. Deb: 5/25/82

YEAR	TM/L	G	AB	R	H	2B	3B	HR	RBI	BB	SO	AVG	OBP	SLG	PRO	/A	BR	/A	PF	CHI	RC	TA	SB	CS	SBR	FR	POS	TPR
1982	Cin-N	86	239	26	52	10	0	5	22	27	58	.218	.302	.322	.624	73	-8	-9	102	94	26	.602	9	3	1	0	O	-0.8
1983	Cin-N	109	225	14	53	12	1	2	29	20	43	.236	.298	.324	.622	70	-8	-9	103	145	23	.566	6	3	0	-1	O	-1.1
1984	Cin-N	83	195	35	57	10	3	10	28	33	35	.292	.395	.528	.923	149	15	14	106	82	43	1.007	7	3	0	-5	O	0.7
1985	Cin-N	37	48	5	8	2	1	2	6	6	18	.167	.259	.375	.634	72	-2	-2	105	100	5	.610	1	0	0	-1	O	-0.3
	Tex-A	53	132	14	23	2	0	5	11	15	29	.174	.264	.303	.567	50	-8	-10	108	79	11	.518	2	1	0	1	OD	-0.8
1988	StL-N	24	22	1	4	1	0	0	3	2	7	.182	.250	.227	.477	36	-2	-2	104	240	1	.368	0	0	0	-2	/O1	-0.3
Total	5	392	861	95	197	37	5	24	99	103	190	.229	.313	.367	.680	85	-13	-18	104	106	109	.662	25	10	2	-7	O/D1	-2.6

■ **ERNIE WALKER** Walker, Ernest Robert b: 9/17/1890, Blossburg, Ala. d: 4/1/65, Pell City, Ala. BL/TR, 6', 165 lbs. Deb: 4/13/13

YEAR	TM/L	G	AB	R	H	2B	3B	HR	RBI	BB	SO	AVG	OBP	SLG	PRO	/A	BR	/A	PF	CHI	RC	TA	SB	CS	SBR	FR	POS	TPR
1913	StL-A	7	14	0	3	0	0	0	2	0	5	.214	.214	.214	.429	27	-1	-1	95	237	1	.273	0			0	/O	0.0
1914	StL-A	71	131	19	39	5	3	1	14	13	26	.298	.366	.405	.770	135	5	5	98	94	20	.760	6	4	-1	-6	O	-0.3
1915	StL-A	50	109	15	23	4	2	0	9	23	32	.211	.348	.284	.633	93	-0	0	96	99	10	.628	5	8	-3	-7	O	-1.2
Total	3	128	254	34	65	9	5	1	25	36	63	.256	.351	.343	.693	111	3	4	97	103	31	.672	11	12		-13	/O	-1.5

■ **DIXIE WALKER** Walker, Fred "The People's Cherce" b: 9/24/10, Villa Rica, Ga. d: 5/17/82, Birmingham, Ala. BL/TR, 6'1", 175 lbs. Deb: 4/28/31 C

YEAR	TM/L	G	AB	R	H	2B	3B	HR	RBI	BB	SO	AVG	OBP	SLG	PRO	/A	BR	/A	PF	CHI	RC	TA	SB	CS	SBR	FR	POS	TPR
1931	NY-A	2	10	1	3	2	0	0	1	0	4	.300	.300	.500	.800	109	0	0	98	57	1	.714	0	0	0	-0	/O	0.0
1933	NY-A	98	328	68	90	15	7	15	51	26	28	.274	.330	.500	.830	129	6	10	91	81	54	.804	2	2	-1	8	O	1.4
1934	NY-A	17	17	2	2	0	0	0	0	1	3	.118	.167	.118	.284	-27	-3	-3	96	0	0	.200	0	0	0	-0	/O	-0.2
1935	NY-A	8	13	1	2	1	0	0	1	0	1	.154	.154	.231	.385	-2	-2	-2	93	113	0	.273	0	0	0	-1	/O	-0.1
1936	NY-A	6	20	3	7	0	2	1	5	1	3	.350	.381	.700	1.081	170	2	2	95	95	5	1.143	1	1	-0	-1	/O	0.1
	Chi-A	26	70	12	19	2	0	0	11	14	6	.271	.400	.300	.700	76	-2	-2	99	170	10	.725	1	0	0	2	O	0.0
	Yr	32	90	15	26	2	2	1	16	15	9	.289	.396	.389	.785	96	-0	0	98	159	15	.815	2	1	0	1		0.1
1937	Chi-A	154	593	105	179	28	**16**	9	95	78	26	.302	.383	.449	.832	106	9	6	103	107	105	.829	1	2	-1	-14	*O	-1.2
1938	Det-A	127	454	84	140	27	6	6	43	65	32	.308	.396	.434	.830	108	7	7	100	69	81	.843	5	4	-1	-3	*O	0.2
1939	Det-A	43	154	30	47	4	5	4	19	15	8	.305	.367	.474	.841	102	3	0	111	77	26	.814	4	1	1	3	O	0.3
	Bro-N	61	225	27	63	6	4	2	38	20	10	.280	.339	.369	.708	84	-3	-5	107	160	28	.619	1			0	O	-0.5
1940	Bro-N	143	556	75	171	37	8	6	66	42	21	.308	.357	.435	.793	109	13	7	108	100	88	.735	3			3	*O	0.6
1941	Bro-N	148	531	88	165	32	8	9	71	70	18	.311	.391	.452	.843	133	27	25	103	98	99	.844	4			10	*O	2.9
1942	Bro-N	118	393	57	114	28	1	6	54	47	15	.290	.367	.412	.780	126	14	13	102	111	64	.751	1			-1	*O	1.0
1943	Bro-N	138	540	83	163	32	6	5	71	49	24	.302	.363	.411	.774	124	16	16	100	115	82	.716	3			2	*O	1.4
1944	Bro-N	147	535	77	191	37	8	13	91	72	27	**.357**	.434	.529	.963	172	51	52	99	103	128	1.034	6			-3	*O	3.8
1945	Bro-N	154	607	102	182	42	9	8	**124**	75	16	.300	.381	.438	.820	133	23	27	96	**157**	105	.809	6			11	*O	3.0
1946	Bro-N	150	576	80	184	29	9	9	116	67	28	.319	.391	.448	.839	134	29	27	103	**161**	104	.848	14			-12	*O	1.3
1947	Bro-N	148	529	77	162	31	3	9	94	97	26	.306	.415	.427	.842	118	22	19	105	**146**	101	.878	6			-14	*O	0.0
1948	Pit-N	129	408	39	129	19	3	2	54	52	18	.316	.393	.392	.786	108	9	7	104	122	66	.745	1			-18	*O	-1.8
1949	Pit-N	88	181	26	51	4	1	1	18	26	11	.282	.372	.331	.703	89	-1	-2	101	108	24	.642	0			-6	O/1	-0.9
Total	18	1905	6740	1037	2064	376	96	105	1023	817	325	.306	.383	.437	.820	121	219	205	102	117	1171	.819	59	10		-32	*O/1	11.3

■ **GEE WALKER** Walker, Gerald Holmes b: 3/19/08, Gulfport, Miss. d: 3/20/81, Whitfield, Miss. BR/TR, 5'11", 188 lbs. Deb: 4/14/31 C

YEAR	TM/L	G	AB	R	H	2B	3B	HR	RBI	BB	SO	AVG	OBP	SLG	PRO	/A	BR	/A	PF	CHI	RC	TA	SB	CS	SBR	FR	POS	TPR
1931	Det-A	59	189	20	56	17	2	1	28	14	21	.296	.345	.423	.768	97	-0	-1	104	111	26	.743	10	7	-1	-1	O	-0.5
1932	Det-A	127	480	71	155	32	6	8	78	13	38	.323	.345	.465	.809	106	4	2	102	108	78	.813	30	6	**5**	-4	*O	0.0
1933	Det-A	127	483	68	135	29	7	9	64	15	49	.280	.304	.424	.728	86	-8	-13	107	94	61	.695	26	9	**2**	0	*O	-1.2
1934	Det-A	98	347	54	104	19	2	6	39	19	20	.300	.340	.418	.758	97	-4	-3	98	80	49	.738	20	9	1	4	O	0.1
1935	Det-A	98	362	52	109	22	6	7	53	15	21	.301	.329	.453	.782	104	-2	0	97	97	52	.720	6	4	-1	-1	O	-0.1
1936	Det-A	134	550	105	194	55	5	12	93	23	30	.353	.387	.536	.924	132	20	24	95	96	112	.942	17	8	0	6	*O	2.3
1937	Det-A	151	635	105	213	42	4	18	113	41	74	.335	.380	.499	.880	110	18	9	109	111	121	.900	23	7	3	-6	*O	0.0
1938	Chi-A	120	442	69	135	23	6	16	87	38	32	.305	.360	.493	.854	114	6	8	98	113	79	.852	9	4	0	-10	*O	-0.1
1939	Chi-A	149	598	95	174	30	11	13	111	28	43	.291	.330	.443	.773	90	-6	-12	107	131	84	.711	17	6	2	9	*O	-0.4
1940	Was-A	140	595	87	175	29	7	13	96	24	58	.294	.325	.432	.757	101	-7	-1	93	113	84	.700	21	4	4	-1	*O	-0.7
1941	Cle-A	121	445	56	126	26	11	6	48	18	46	.283	.313	.431	.744	94	-5	-6	101	83	56	.656	12	6	0	-4	*O	-1.5
1942	Cin-N	119	422	40	97	20	2	5	50	31	44	.230	.290	.322	.613	78	-12	-12	101	125	40	.553	11			-1	*O	-1.6
1943	Cin-N	114	429	48	105	23	2	3	54	12	38	.245	.270	.329	.599	73	-17	-16	99	132	35	.481	6			-12	*O	-3.4
1944	Cin-N	121	478	56	133	21	3	5	62	23	48	.278	.318	.366	.684	97	-6	-3	95	124	53	.583	7			-1	*O	-1.3
1945	Cin-N	106	316	28	80	11	2	2	21	16	38	.253	.289	.320	.609	73	-14	-11	94	68	29	.519	8			-8	O/3	-2.2
Total	15	1784	6771	954	1991	399	76	124	997	330	600	.294	.331	.430	.761	99	-33	-35	100	107	959	.723	223	70		-28	*O/3	-10.6

■ **GREG WALKER** Walker, Gregory Lee b: 10/6/59, Douglas, Ga. BL/TR, 6'3", 205 lbs. Deb: 9/18/82

YEAR	TM/L	G	AB	R	H	2B	3B	HR	RBI	BB	SO	AVG	OBP	SLG	PRO	/A	BR	/A	PF	CHI	RC	TA	SB	CS	SBR	FR	POS	TPR
1982	Chi-A	11	17	3	7	2	1	2	7	2	3	.412	.474	1.000	1.474	300	4	4	97	122	8	1.900	0	0	0	0	/D	0.4
1983	Chi-A	118	307	32	83	16	3	10	55	28	57	.270	.335	.440	.775	108	4	3	103	130	46	.732	2	1	0	-1	1D	0.0
1984	Chi-A	136	442	62	130	29	2	24	75	35	66	.294	.349	.532	.880	126	22	16	111	97	79	.859	8	5	-1	-6	*1D	0.4
1985	Chi-A	163	601	77	155	38	4	24	92	44	100	.258	.311	.454	.765	106	3	4	100	108	81	.698	5	2	0	-1	*1/D	-0.6
1986	Chi-A	78	282	37	78	10	6	13	51	29	44	.277	.348	.493	.841	126	10	10	101	121	48	.814	1	2	-1	-3	1/D	0.0
1987	Chi-A	157	566	85	145	33	2	27	94	75	112	.256	.348	.465	.813	105	12	5	109	116	93	.795	2	1	0	-11	*1/D	-2.0
1988	Chi-A	99	377	45	93	22	1	8	42	29	77	.247	.306	.374	.680	92	-6	-5	97	107	43	.592	0	1	-1	-9	1	-2.0
Total	7	762	2592	341	691	150	19	108	416	242	459	.267	.333	.464	.797	111	51	38	104	112	399	.770	18	12	-2	-31	1/D	-3.8

■ **HARRY WALKER** Walker, Harry William "Harry The Hat" b: 10/22/16, Pascagoula, Miss. BL/TR, 6'2", 175 lbs. Deb: 9/25/40 MC

YEAR	TM/L	G	AB	R	H	2B	3B	HR	RBI	BB	SO	AVG	OBP	SLG	PRO	/A	BR	/A	PF	CHI	RC	TA	SB	CS	SBR	FR	POS	TPR
1940	StL-N	7	27	2	5	2	0	0	6	0	2	.185	.185	.259	.444	21	-3	-3	102	324	1	.318	0			3	/O	0.0
1941	StL-N	7	15	3	4	1	0	0	1	2	1	.267	.353	.333	.686	85	-0	-0	110	72	2	.636	0			-1	/O	-0.1
1942	StL-N	74	191	38	60	12	2	0	16	11	14	.314	.355	.398	.753	111	4	3	108	78	28	.682	2			1	O/2	0.3
1943	StL-N	148	564	76	166	28	6	2	53	40	24	.294	.341	.376	.717	102	4	1	105	93	76	.638	5			5	*O/2	0.1
1946	StL-N	112	346	53	82	14	6	3	27	30	29	.237	.300	.338	.638	76	-9	-12	107	80	37	.599	12			7	O/1	-0.7
1947	StL-N	10	25	2	5	1	0	0	0	4	2	.200	.310	.240	.550	45	-2	-2	106	0	2	.476	0			-2	O	-0.3
	Phi-N	130	488	79	181	28	16	1	41	59	37	.371	.443	.500	.943	150	37	37	100	59	111	1.013	13			9	*O/1	4.0
	Yr	140	513	81	186	29	**16**	1	41	63	39	**.363**	.436	.487	.924	144	35	35	100	55	113	.982	13			7		3.7
1948	Phi-N	112	332	34	97	11	2	2	23	33	30	.292	.358	.355	.713	99	-2	0	94	69	44	.655	4			5	O/13	0.0
1949	Chi-N	42	159	20	42	6	3	1	14	11	6	.264	.312	.358	.670	84	-5	-4	94	93	18	.588	2			-4	O	-0.9
	Cin-N	86	314	53	100	15	2	1	23	34	17	.318	.385	.389	.774	113	5	6	96	71	48	.727	4			1	O/1	0.3
	Yr	128	473	73	142	21	5	2	37	45	23	.300	.361	.378	.739	103	-0	3	95	79	67	.682	6			-2		-0.6

YEAR	TM/L	G	AB	R	H	2B	3B	HR	RBI	BB	SO	AVG	OBP	SLG	PRO	/A	BR	/A	PF	CHI	RC	TA	SB	CS	SBR	FR	POS	TPR
1950	StL-N	60	150	17	31	5	0	0	7	18	12	.207	.292	.240	.532	40	-12	-13	103	75	11	.446	0			-1	O/1	-1.5
1951	StL-N	8	26	6	8	1	0	0	2	2	1	.308	.357	.346	.703	89	-0	-0	101	86	3	.611	0	0	0	-1	/O1	-0.1
1955	StL-N	11	14	2	5	2	0	0	1	1	0	.357	.400	.500	.900	136	1	1	101	58	3	.889	0	0	0	1	/OM	0.2
Total	11	807	2651	385	786	126	37	10	214	245	175	.296	.358	.383	.741	103	17	14	101	78	386	.702	42	0		23	O/123	1.3
■ **HUB WALKER** Walker, Harvey Willos b: 8/17/06, Gulfport, Miss. d: 11/26/82, San Jose, Cal. BL/TR, 5'10.5", 175 lbs. Deb: 4/15/31																												
1931	Det-A	90	252	27	72	13	1	0	16	23	25	.286	.355	.345	.700	82	-5	-6	104	61	34	.685	10	1	2	-4	O	-1.0
1935	Det-A	9	25	4	4	3	0	0	1	3	4	.160	.250	.280	.530	38	-2	-2	97	48	2	.476	0	0	0	0	/O	-0.1
1936	Cin-N	92	258	49	71	18	1	4	23	35	32	.275	.366	.399	.765	110	3	4	97	71	41	.775	8			-2	O/C1	0.0
1937	Cin-N	78	221	33	55	9	4	1	19	34	24	.249	.349	.339	.688	96	-3	-0	91	88	28	.674	7			0	O/2	-0.1
1945	Det-A	28	23	4	3	0	0	0	1	9	4	.130	.375	.130	.505	46	-1	-1	106	121	2	.619	1	0	0	-2	/O	-0.3
Total	5	297	779	117	205	43	6	5	60	104	89	.263	.354	.353	.707	92	-8	-5	98	74	106	.714	26	1		-7	O/21C	-1.5
■ **JOHNNY WALKER** Walker, John Miles b: 12/11/1896, Toulon, Ill. d: 8/19/76, Hollywood, Fla. BR/TR, 6', 175 lbs. Deb: 9/19/19																												
1919	Phi-A	3	9	0	0	0	0	0	0	0	2	.000	.000	.000	.000	-95	-2	-2	106	0	0	.000	0			1	/C	-0.1
1920	Phi-A	9	22	0	5	1	0	0	5	0	1	.227	.227	.273	.500	34	-2	-2	94	293	1	.353	0	0	0	1	/C	0.0
1921	Phi-A	113	423	41	109	14	5	2	46	9	29	.258	.278	.329	.607	53	-30	-32	103	111	39	.497	5	0	2	-6	1/C	-3.4
Total	3	125	454	41	114	15	5	2	51	9	32	.251	.270	.319	.590	49	-35	-36	103	117	40	.476	5	0		-5	/1C	-3.5
■ **SPEED WALKER** Walker, Joseph Richard b: 1/23/1898, Munhall, Pa. d: 6/20/59, W.Mifflin, Pa. BR/TR, 6', 170 lbs. Deb: 9/15/23																												
1923	StL-N	2	7	1	2	0	0	0	0	0	1	.286	.286	.286	.571	57	-0	-0	90	0	1	.400	0	0	0	0	/1	0.0
■ **FLEET WALKER** Walker, Moses Fleetwood b: 10/7/1856, Mt.Pleasant, Ohio d: 5/11/24, Cleveland, Ohio BR/TR, Deb: 5/01/1884																												
1884	Tol-a	42	152	23	40	2	3	0		8		.263	.325	.316	.641	109	3	2	104	0	16	.554				-7	C/O	-0.1
■ **OSCAR WALKER** Walker, Oscar b: 3/18/1854, Brooklyn, N.Y. d: 5/30/1889, Brooklyn, N.Y. BL/TL, 5'10", 166 lbs. Deb: 9/17/1875																												
1875	Atl-n	1	3	0	0							.000															/O	
1879	Buf-N	72	287	35	79	15	6	1	35	8	38	.275	.295	.380	.675	105	6	0	114	116	33	.563				3	*1	-0.2
1880	Buf-N	34	126	12	29	4	2	1	15	6	18	.230	.265	.317	.583	106	-0	1	91	135	11	.474				-2	1O	-0.1
1882	StL-a	76	318	48	76	15	7	**7**		10		.239	.262	.396	.658	119	6	6	100	0	34	.562				8	*O/21	1.2
1884	Bro-a	95	382	59	103	12	8	2		9		.270	.292	.359	.651	117	5	7	98	0	41	.534				1	O1	0.5
Total	4	277	1113	154	287	46	23	11	50	33	56	.258	.281	.370	.651	113	17	14	102	45	119	.542				10	O1/2	1.4
■ **WALT WALKER** Walker, Walter S. b: Ionia, Mich. Deb: 1885																												
1885	Bal-a	4	13	1	0	0	0	0		0		.000	.000	.000	.000	-94	-3	-3	106	0	0	.000				0	/O	-0.2
■ **WELDAY WALKER** Walker, Welday Wilberforce b: 6/1859, Steubenville, Ohio d: 11/23/37, Steubenville, Ohio Deb: 7/15/1884																												
1884	Tol-a	5	18	1	4	1	0	0		0		.222	.222	.278	.500	62	-1	-1	104	0	1	.357				0	/O	0.0
■ **CURT WALKER** Walker, William Curtis b: 7/3/1896, Beeville, Tex. d: 12/9/55, Beeville, Tex. BL/TR, 5'9.5", 170 lbs. Deb: 9/17/19																												
1919	NY-A	1	1	0	0	0	0	0	0	0	0	.000	.000	.000	.000	-95	-0	-0	106	0	0	.000	0			0	H	0.0
1920	NY-N	8	14	0	1	0	0	0	0	1	3	.071	.133	.071	.205	-40	-3	-2	100	0	0	.154	0	0	0	-1	/O	-0.3
1921	NY-N	64	192	30	55	13	5	3	35	15	8	.286	.338	.453	.791	110	2	2	98	134	29	.757	4	3	-1	3	O	0.2
	Phi-N	21	77	11	26	2	1	0	8	5	5	.338	.378	.390	.768	102	1	0	102	104	11	.660	0	2	-1	-3	O	-0.4
	Yr	85	269	41	81	15	6	3	43	20	13	.301	.349	.435	.784	108	2	3	99	128	40	.731	4	5	-2	0		-0.2
1922	Phi-N	148	581	102	196	36	11	12	89	56	46	.337	.399	.499	.899	115	26	15	113	101	118	.928	11	4	1	3	*O	1.3
1923	Phi-N	140	527	66	148	26	5	5	66	45	31	.281	.337	.378	.715	78	-9	-19	114	111	66	.655	12	12	-4	3	*O/1	-2.3
1924	Phi-N	24	71	11	21	6	1	1	8	7	4	.296	.359	.451	.810	108	2	1	108	83	11	.765	0	1	-1	-4	O	-0.4
	Cin-N	109	397	55	119	21	10	4	46	44	15	.300	.371	.433	.804	114	9	9	101	97	65	.792	7	5	-1	2	*O	0.7
	Yr	133	468	66	140	27	11	5	54	51	19	.299	.369	.436	.805	113	10	9	102	95	76	.787	7	6	-2	-2		0.3
1925	Cin-N	145	509	86	162	22	16	6	71	57	31	.318	.387	.460	.847	118	13	15	97	102	91	.852	14	11	-2	1	*O	0.8
1926	Cin-N	155	571	83	175	24	20	6	78	60	31	.306	.372	.450	.823	127	16	20	95	104	95	.808	3			-7	*O	0.7
1927	Cin-N	146	527	60	154	16	10	6	80	47	19	.292	.350	.395	.745	99	-1	-0	100	126	72	.697	5			3	*O	-0.2
1928	Cin-N	123	427	64	119	15	12	6	73	49	14	.279	.354	.412	.766	104	-0	2	96	137	63	.795	19			4	*O	0.1
1929	Cin-N	141	492	76	154	28	15	7	83	85	17	.313	.416	.474	.890	121	18	19	99	119	99	.997	17			-2	*O	0.4
1930	Cin-N	134	472	74	145	26	11	8	51	64	30	.307	.391	.460	.851	116	5	13	90	74	85	.875	4			-6	*O	-0.1
Total	12	1359	4858	718	1475	235	117	64	688	535	254	.304	.374	.440	.813	109	79	74	101	108	805	.811	96	38		-5	*O/1	0.5
■ **WALL** Wall Deb:9/13/1873																												
1873	Nat-n	1	4	1	1							.250															/S	
■ **JOE WALL** Wall, Joseph Francis "Gummy" b: 7/24/1873, Brooklyn, N.Y. d: 7/17/36, Brooklyn, N.Y. BL/TL, Deb: 9/22/01																												
1901	NY-N	4	8	0	4	0	0	0	1	0		.500	.500	.500	1.000	212	1	1	91	84	2	1.000	0			0	/CO	0.1
1902	NY-N	6	14	2	5	2	0	0	0	2		.357	.438	.500	.938	192	2	2	100	0	3	1.000	0			0	/O	0.2
	Bro-N	5	18	0	3	0	0	0	0	3		.167	.286	.167	.452	44	-1	-1	95	0	1	.400	0			-0	/C	0.0
	Yr	11	32	2	8	2	0	0	0	5		.250	.351	.313	.664	110	1	1	98	0	4	.625	0			0		0.2
Total	2	15	40	2	12	2	0	0	1	5		.300	.378	.350	.728	130	1	2	96	15	6	.679	0			0	/CO	0.3
■ **JACK WALLACE** Wallace, Clarence Eugene b: 8/6/1890, Winnfield, La. d: 10/15/60, Winnfield, La. BR/TR, 5'10.5", 175 lbs. Deb: 9/27/15																												
1915	Chi-N	2	7	1	2	0	0	0	1	0	2	.286	.375	.286	.661	99	0	0	102	202	1	.600	0			0	/C	0.0
■ **DON WALLACE** Wallace, Donald Allen b: 8/25/40, Sapulpa, Okla. BL/TR, 5'8", 165 lbs. Deb: 4/12/67																												
1967	Cal-A	23	6	2	0	0	0	0	0	3	2	.000	.333	.000	.333	6	-1	-0	96	0	0	.429	0	1	-1	0	/213	0.0
■ **DOC WALLACE** Wallace, Frederick Renshaw "Jesse" b: 9/30/1893, Church Hill, Md. d: 12/31/64, Haverford, Pa. TR , 5'6.5", 135 lbs. Deb: 5/02/19																												
1919	Phi-N	2	4	0	1	0	0	0	0	0	1	.250	.250	.250	.500	49	-0	-0	104	0	0	.333	0			0	/S	0.0
■ **JIM WALLACE** Wallace, James L. b: 11/14/1881, Boston, Mass. d: 5/16/53, Revere, Mass. BL/TL, Deb: 8/24/05																												
1905	Pit-N	7	29	3	6	1	0	0	3	3		.207	.281	.241	.523	56	-1	-2	104	129	3	.522	2			-0	/O	-0.1
■ **BOBBY WALLACE** Wallace, Roderick John b: 11/4/1873, Pittsburgh, Pa. d: 11/3/60, Torrance, Cal. BR/TR, 5'8", 170 lbs. Deb: 9/15/1894 MUCH																												
1894	Cle-N	4	13	0	2	1	0	0	1	0	1	.154	.154	.231	.385	-7	-2	-3	111	92	0	.273	0			0	/P	0.0
1895	Cle-N	30	98	16	21	2	3	0	10	6	17	.214	.274	.296	.570	50	-8	-7	97	96	8	.481	0			0	P	0.0
1896	Cle-N	45	149	19	35	6	3	1	17	11	21	.235	.287	.336	.623	60	-8	-10	110	92	15	.553	2			0	OP/1	-0.8
1897	Cle-N	130	516	99	173	33	21	4	112	48		.335	.394	.504	.898	125	27	18	111	128	111	.945	14			3	*3/O	1.8
1898	Cle-N	154	593	81	160	25	13	3	99	63		.270	.343	.371	.714	112	6	10	96	126	80	.677	7			16	*32	2.7
1899	StL-N	151	577	91	170	28	14	12	108	54		.295	.357	.454	.811	115	18	11	108	118	102	.823	17			34	*S3	4.5
1900	StL-N	126	485	70	130	25	9	4	70	40		.268	.324	.381	.705	103	-3	2	93	118	64	.654	7			3	*S/3	1.6
1901	StL-N	134	550	69	178	34	15	2	91	20		.324	.347	.451	.798	137	20	23	97	127	94	.761	15			**25**	*S	**5.2**
1902	StL-A	133	494	71	141	32	9	1	63	45		.285	.345	.393	.738	104	4	3	102	112	75	.728	18			12	*S/PO	2.4
1903	StL-A	135	511	63	136	21	7	1	54	28		.266	.304	.341	.645	100	-3	0	95	116	57	.565	10			17	*S	2.4
1904	StL-A	139	541	57	149	29	4	2	69	42		.275	.328	.355	.683	125	12	15	95	125	71	.648	20			7	*S	2.5
1905	StL-A	156	587	67	159	25	9	1	59	45		.271	.323	.349	.672	126	10	16	91	107	72	.614	13			21	*S	**4.5**
1906	StL-A	139	476	64	123	21	7	2	67	58		.258	.339	.345	.683	119	10	12	98	152	65	.697	24			-2	*S	1.2
1907	StL-A	147	538	56	138	20	7	0	70	54		.257	.324	.320	.644	110	6	7	98	**154**	62	.605	16			12	*S	2.4
1908	StL-A	137	487	59	123	24	4	1	60	52		.253	.325	.324	.649	110	8	7	103	**148**	51	.591	5			11	*S	2.4
1909	StL-A	116	403	36	96	12	2	0	35	38		.238	.310	.278	.588	94	-5	-2	92	128	36	.524	7			4	S3	0.6
1910	StL-A	138	508	47	131	19	7	0	37	49		.258	.324	.323	.647	109	2	5	94	80	57	.599	12			12	S3	2.2
1911	StL-A	125	410	35	95	12	2	0	31	46		.232	.312	.271	.583	66	-19	-16	95	96	37	.530	8			-1	*S/2M	-0.5
1912	StL-A	99	323	39	78	14	5	0	31	43		.241	.332	.316	.648	87	-5	-5	99	103	35	.608	3			-3	S3/2M	0.0
1913	StL-A	55	147	11	31	5	0	0	21	14	16	.211	.293	.245	.538	60	-8	-7	95	207	11	.466	1			-3	S/3	-0.6
1914	StL-A	26	73	3	16	2	1	0	5	5	13	.219	.269	.274	.543	65	-3	-3	98	94	6	.448	1	1	-0	-2	S/3	-0.3

YEAR	TM/L	G	AB	R	H	2B	3B	HR	RBI	BB	SO	AVG	OBP	SLG	PRO	/A	BR	/A	PF	CHI	RC	TA	SB	CS	SBR	FR	POS	TPR
1915	StL-A	9	13	1	3	0	1	0	4	5	0	.231	.444	.385	.829	155	1	1	96	272	2	.909	0	1	-1	0	/S	0.2
1916	StL-A	14	18	0	5	0	0	0	1	2	1	.278	.350	.278	.628	93	-0	-0	95	71	2	.538	0			0	/3S	0.1
1917	StL-N	8	10	0	1	0	0	0	2	0	1	.100	.100	.100	.200	-38	-2	-2	102	771	0	.111	0			0	/3S	-0.1
1918	StL-N	32	98	3	15	1	0	0	4	6	9	.153	.202	.163	.365	13	-10	-9	93	95	4	.277	1			4	2S/3	-0.4
Total	25	2382	8618	1057	2309	391	143	34	1121	774	79	.268	.330	.358	.688	106	48	65	98	123	1117	.647	201	2		170	*S3/P2O1	34.0
■ **TIM WALLACH**	Wallach, Timothy Charles b: 9/14/57, Huntington Park, Cal. BR/TR, 6'3", 220 lbs. Deb: 9/06/80																											
1980	Mon-N	5	11	1	2	0	0	1	2	1	5	.182	.250	.455	.705	93	-0	-0	99	99	1	.667	0	0	0	-1	/O1	0.0
1981	Mon-N	71	212	19	50	9	1	4	13	15	37	.236	.299	.344	.643	83	-5	-5	99	60	22	.554	0	1	-1	-4	O13	-1.2
1982	Mon-N	158	596	89	160	31	3	28	97	36	81	.268	.314	.471	.786	111	11	7	105	106	84	.719	6	4	-1	-8	*3/O1	-0.4
1983	Mon-N	156	581	54	156	33	3	19	70	55	97	.269	.338	.434	.772	111	9	8	102	91	85	.716	0	3	-2	-9	*3	-0.8
1984	Mon-N	160	582	55	143	25	4	18	72	50	101	.246	.313	.395	.708	107	-3	3	91	101	70	.633	3	7	-3	17	*3/S	1.7
1985	Mon-N	155	569	70	148	36	3	22	81	38	79	.260	.312	.450	.762	118	6	10	94	102	73	.689	9	9	-3	37	*3	4.6
1986	Mon-N	134	480	50	112	22	1	18	71	44	72	.233	.311	.396	.707	96	-5	-4	98	118	57	.649	8	4	0	13	*3	0.7
1987	Mon-N	153	593	89	177	**42**	4	26	123	37	98	.298	.347	.514	.861	117	19	14	106	136	105	.838	9	5	-0	-0	*3/P	1.2
1988	Mon-N	159	592	52	152	32	5	12	69	38	88	.257	.305	.389	.693	93	-3	-7	106	106	64	.587	2	6	-3	11	*3/2	0.1
Total	9	1151	4216	479	1100	230	24	148	598	314	658	.261	.319	.432	.751	107	28	27	100	106	560	.699	37	39	-12	55	*3/O12PS	5.9
■ **JACK WALLAESA**	Wallaesa, John b: 8/31/19, Easton, Pa. d: 12/27/86, Easton, Pa. BB/TR, 6'3", 191 lbs. Deb: 9/22/40																											
1940	Phi-A	6	20	0	3	0	0	0	2	0	2	.150	.150	.150	.300	-23	-4	-3	96	241	0	.176	0	0	0	-1	/S	-0.3
1942	Phi-A	36	117	13	30	4	1	2	13	8	26	.256	.315	.359	.674	93	-2	-1	96	95	14	.584	0	1	-1	-4	S	-0.3
1946	Phi-A	63	194	16	38	4	2	5	11	14	47	.196	.250	.314	.564	55	-12	-13	104	55	16	.481	1	0	0	-7	S	-1.9
1947	Chi-A	81	205	25	40	9	1	7	32	23	51	.195	.279	.351	.631	77	-8	-7	97	127	20	.570	2	2	-1	5	SO/3	-0.3
1948	Chi-A	33	48	2	9	0	0	1	3	1	12	.188	.204	.250	.454	21	-6	-5	95	68	2	.317	0	0	0	-0	/SO	-0.5
Total	5	219	584	56	120	17	4	15	61	46	138	.205	.267	.325	.592	64	-31	-30	99	96	52	.516	3	3	-1	-7	S/O3	-3.3
■ **NORM WALLEN**	Wallen, Norman Edward (born Norman Edward Walentoski) b: 2/13/17, Milwaukee, Wis. BR/TR, 5'11.5", 175 lbs. Deb: 4/20/45																											
1945	Bos-N	4	15	1	2	0	1	0	1	1	1	.133	.188	.267	.454	23	-2	-2	112	88	1	.385	0			-0	/3	-0.1
■ **TY WALLER**	Waller, Elliott Tyrone b: 3/14/57, Fresno, Cal. BR/TR, 6', 180 lbs. Deb: 9/06/80																											
1980	StL-N	5	12	3	1	0	0	0	0	1	5	.083	.154	.083	.237	-31	-2	-2	103	0	0	.182	0	0	0	0	/3	-0.1
1981	Chi-N	30	71	10	19	2	1	3	13	4	18	.268	.307	.451	.757	108	1	0	104	124	10	.731	2	0	1	-1	3/2O	0.0
1982	Chi-N	17	21	4	5	0	0	0	1	2	5	.238	.304	.238	.542	52	-1	-1	103	78	2	.438	0	0	0	-1	/O3	-0.2
1987	Hou-N	11	6	1	1	1	0	0	0	0	3	.167	.167	.333	.500	31	-1	-1	93	0	0	.400	0	0	0	-1	/O	0.0
Total	4	63	110	18	26	3	1	3	14	7	31	.236	.282	.364	.646	78	-3	-4	103	95	13	.583	2	0	1	-2	/3O2	-0.3
■ **DENNIS WALLING**	Walling, Dennis Martin b: 4/17/54, Neptune, N.J. BL/TR, 6', 180 lbs. Deb: 9/07/75																											
1975	Oak-A	6	8	0	1	1	0	0	2	0	4	.125	.125	.250	.375	4	-1	-1	93	384	0	.286	0	0	0	-1	/O	-0.1
1976	Oak-A	3	11	1	3	0	0	0	0	0	3	.273	.273	.273	.545	60	-1	-1	100	0	1	.375	0	0	0	0	/O	0.0
1977	Hou-N	6	21	1	6	0	1	0	6	2	4	.286	.348	.381	.729	103	-0	0	93	306	3	.625	0	1	-1	1	/O	0.0
1978	Hou-N	120	247	30	62	11	3	3	36	30	24	.251	.335	.356	.691	98	-2	-0	95	147	32	.677	9	2	2	-1	O	-0.2
1979	Hou-N	82	147	21	48	8	4	3	31	17	21	.327	.396	.497	.893	157	9	10	90	150	29	.903	3	2	-0	-4	O	0.5
1980	Hou-N	100	284	30	85	6	5	3	29	35	26	.299	.376	.387	.763	116	6	7	98	96	43	.730	4	3	-1	-4	1O	-0.1
1981	Hou-N	65	158	23	37	6	0	5	23	28	17	.234	.349	.367	.717	117	1	4	88	124	22	.704	2	1	0	-4	1O	-0.1
1982	Hou-N	85	146	22	30	4	1	1	14	23	19	.205	.314	.267	.581	65	-6	-6	99	131	12	.532	4	2	0	-4	O1	-1.1
1983	Hou-N	100	135	24	40	5	3	3	19	15	16	.296	.367	.444	.811	137	4	6	90	109	22	.786	2	2	-1	-4	13O	-0.1
1984	Hou-N	87	249	37	70	11	5	3	31	16	28	.281	.327	.402	.729	112	1	3	93	111	33	.674	7	1	2	2	31/O	0.5
1985	Hou-N	119	345	44	93	20	1	7	45	25	26	.270	.319	.394	.713	102	-1	0	96	114	42	.634	5	2	0	-5	31O	-0.6
1986	Hou-N	130	382	54	119	23	1	13	58	36	31	.312	.371	.479	.850	129	16	15	103	104	67	.809	1	1	-0	2	*3O/1	1.5
1987	Hou-N	110	325	45	92	21	4	5	33	39	37	.283	.360	.418	.778	114	3	6	93	87	50	.741	5	1	1	2	31/O	0.7
1988	Hou-N	65	176	19	43	10	2	1	20	15	18	.244	.304	.341	.645	91	-3	-2	93	127	19	.563	1	0	0	-1	3/1O	-0.2
	StL-N	19	58	3	13	3	0	0	1	2	7	.224	.250	.276	.526	49	-4	-4	104	25	4	.413	1	0	0	-2	O/31	-0.6
	Yr	84	234	22	56	13	2	1	21	17	25	.239	.291	.325	.616	80	-7	-6	96	105	23	.531	2	0	1	-3		-0.8
Total	14	1097	2692	354	742	129	30	47	348	283	281	.276	.345	.398	.743	111	22	38	95	114	380	.712	44	18	2	-22	3O1	0.1
■ **JOE WALLIS**	Wallis, Harold Joseph b: 1/9/52, E.St.Louis, Ill. BB/TR, 5'11", 180 lbs. Deb: 9/02/75																											
1975	Chi-N	16	56	9	16	2	2	1	4	5	14	.286	.344	.446	.791	114	1	1	104	55	9	.780	2	0	1	1	O	0.2
1976	Chi-N	121	338	51	86	11	5	5	21	33	62	.254	.323	.361	.684	86	-3	-7	109	59	39	.607	3	9	-5	8	O	-0.6
1977	Chi-N	56	80	14	20	3	0	2	8	16	25	.250	.375	.363	.738	87	0	-1	114	91	12	.726	0	1	-1	-6	O	-0.8
1978	Chi-N	28	55	7	17	2	1	1	6	5	13	.309	.367	.436	.803	112	2	1	110	88	8	.725	0	2	-1	-3	O	-0.3
	Oak-A	85	279	28	66	16	1	6	26	26	42	.237	.302	.366	.667	86	-5	-6	101	87	31	.589	1	4	-2	8	O/D	-0.1
1979	Oak-A	23	78	6	11	2	0	1	3	10	18	.141	.247	.205	.452	27	-8	-7	89	62	5	.412	1	0	0	-2	O	-0.8
Total	5	329	886	115	216	36	9	16	68	95	174	.244	.318	.359	.677	85	-13	-18	105	73	104	.614	7	16	-8	6	O/D	-2.4
■ **LEE WALLS**	Walls, Ray Lee b: 1/6/33, San Diego, Cal. BR/TR, 6'3", 205 lbs. Deb: 4/21/52 C																											
1952	Pit-N	32	80	6	15	0	1	2	5	8	22	.188	.261	.287	.549	52	-5	-5	100	67	6	.470	0	0	0	2	O	-0.3
1956	Pit-N	143	474	72	130	20	11	11	54	50	83	.274	.346	.432	.778	105	5	4	102	98	70	.722	3	5	-2	6	*O/3	0.3
1957	Pit-N	8	22	3	4	1	0	0	0	2	5	.182	.250	.227	.477	31	-2	-2	94	0	2	.444	1	0	0	0	/O	-0.1
	Chi-N	117	366	42	88	10	5	6	33	27	67	.240	.294	.344	.639	74	-15	-13	96	95	36	.548	5	3	-0	-0	O/3	-1.6
	Yr	125	388	45	92	11	5	6	33	29	72	.237	.292	.338	.629	71	-17	-15	96	89	38	.542	6	3	0	0		-1.7
1958	Chi-N	136	513	80	156	19	3	24	72	47	62	.304	.371	.493	.865	126	19	19	101	97	94	.841	4	4	-1	2	*O	1.6
1959	Chi-N	120	354	43	91	18	3	8	33	42	73	.257	.344	.393	.737	97	-2	-1	98	82	49	.686	0	2	-1	-11	*O	-1.4
1960	Cin-N	29	84	12	23	3	2	1	7	17	20	.274	.396	.393	.789	119	3	3	98	79	14	.800	2	0	1	0	O/1	0.3
	Phi-N	65	181	19	36	6	1	3	19	14	32	.199	.256	.293	.549	46	-13	-14	107	124	13	.464	3	2	-0	-4	3O/1	-2.0
	Yr	94	265	31	59	9	3	4	26	31	52	.223	.304	.325	.629	69	-10	-11	104	111	28	.575	5	2	0	-4		-1.7
1961	Phi-N	91	261	32	73	6	4	8	30	19	48	.280	.329	.425	.754	105	-1	1	94	90	34	.663	2	2	-1	-0	13O	-0.3
1962	LA-N	60	109	9	29	3	1	0	17	10	21	.266	.328	.312	.640	78	-4	-3	93	197	12	.549	1	0	0	-4	O1/3	-0.7
1963	LA-N	64	86	12	20	1	0	3	11	7	25	.233	.290	.349	.639	88	-2	-1	95	118	8	.529	0	0	0	-4	O/13	-0.7
1964	LA-N	37	28	1	5	1	0	0	3	2	12	.179	.233	.214	.448	29	-3	-2	92	205	1	.333	0	0	0	-2	/OC	-0.4
Total	10	902	2558	331	670	88	31	66	284	245	470	.262	.330	.398	.728	96	-19	-15	99	99	338	.682	21	18	-5	-15	O/31C	-5.3
■ **AUSTIN WALSH**	Walsh, Austin Edward b: 9/1/1891, Cambridge, Mass. d: 1/26/55, Glendale, Cal. BL/TL, 5'11", 175 lbs. Deb: 4/19/14																											
1914	Chi-F	57	121	14	29	6	1	1	10	4	25	.240	.264	.331	.595	77	-5	-4	91	84	11	.478	0			-3	O	-0.8
■ **JIMMY WALSH**	Walsh, James Charles b: 9/22/1885, Kallila, Ireland d: 7/3/62, Syracuse, N.Y. BL/TR, 5'10.5", 170 lbs. Deb: 8/26/12																											
1912	Phi-A	31	107	11	27	8	2	0	15	12		.252	.328	.364	.692	98	-0	-0	99	131	15	.725	7			0	O	-0.1
1913	Phi-A	97	303	56	77	16	5	0	27	38	40	.254	.341	.340	.681	103	0	2	97	93	39	.699	15			5	O	0.2
1914	NY-A	43	136	13	26	1	3	1	11	29	21	.191	.333	.265	.598	80	-2	-2	100	108	11	.597	6	9	-4	0	O	-0.8
	Phi-A	67	216	35	51	11	6	3	36	30	27	.236	.340	.384	.724	121	5	5	97	147	26	.695	6	12	-5	3	O/13S	0.0
	Yr	110	352	48	77	12	9	4	47	59	48	.219	.337	.338	.675	105	3	3	98	133	37	.655	12	21	-9	3		-0.8
1915	Phi-A	117	417	48	86	15	6	1	20	57	64	.206	.306	.278	.584	78	-12	-10	96	61	40	.577	22	12	-1	10	*O/31	-0.6
1916	Phi-A	114	390	42	91	13	6	1	27	54	36	.233	.330	.305	.635	93	-3	-2	98	84	45	.645	27	14	-0	-8	*O/1	-1.8
	Bos-A	14	17	5	3	1	0	0	2	4	2	.176	.333	.235	.569	76	-0	-0	94	179	2	.688	3	2	-0	-2	/O3	-0.2
	Yr	128	407	47	94	14	6	1	29	58	38	.231	.330	.302	.632	92	-4	-2	98	95	47	.647	30	16	-1	-11		-2.0
1917	Bos-A	57	185	25	49	6	3	0	12	25	14	.265	.352	.330	.682	100	2	1	108	72	22	.676	6			2	O	0.0
Total	6	540	1771	235	410	71	31	6	150	249	204	.232	.330	.317	.647	94	-11	-7	98	92	200	.648	92	49		9	O/31S	-3.3
■ **JOHN WALSH**	Walsh, John Thomas b: 5/16/1885, Wilkes-Barre, Pa. d: 7/6/38, Wilkes-Barre, Pa. TR , Deb: 03																											
1903	Phi-N	1	3	0	0	0	0	0	0	0		.000	.000	.000	.000	-99	-1	-1	92	0	0	.000	0			0	/3	0.0

YEAR	TM/L	G	AB	R	H	2B	3B	HR	RBI	BB	SO	AVG	OBP	SLG	PRO	/A	BR	/A	PF	CHI	RC	TA	SB	CS	SBR	FR	POS	TPR
■ JOE WALSH	Walsh, Joseph Francis b: 10/14/1886, Minersville, Pa. d: 1/6/67, Buffalo, N.Y. BR/TR, 6'2", 170 lbs. Deb: 10/08/10																											
1910	NY-A	1	4	0	2	1	0	0	2	0		.500	.500	.750	1.250	271	1	1	107	261	1	1.500	0			0	/C	0.1
1911	NY-A	4	9	2	2	1	0	0	0	0		.222	.222	.333	.556	49	-1	-1	111	0	1	.429	0			0	/C	0.0
Total	2	5	13	2	4	2	0	0	2	0		.308	.308	.462	.769	111	0	0	110	80	2	.667	0			0	/C	0.1
■ JOE WALSH	Walsh, Joseph Patrick "Tweet" b: 3/13/17, Roxbury, Mass. BR/TR, 5'10", 155 lbs. Deb: 7/01/38																											
1938	Bos-N	4	8	0	0	0	0	0	0	0	2	.000	.000	.000	.000	-99	-2	-2	88	0	0	.000	0			-0	/S	-0.1
■ JOE WALSH	Walsh, Joseph R. "Reddy" b: 11/5/1864, Chicago, Ill. d: 8/8/11, Omaha, Neb. BL/TR, Deb: 9/03/1891																											
1891	Bal-a	26	100	14	21	0	1	1	10	6	18	.210	.255	.260	.515	49	-7	-7	101	102	8	.456	4			0	S2	-0.5
■ DEE WALSH	Walsh, Leo Thomas b: 3/28/1890, St.Louis, Mo. d: 7/14/71, St.Louis, Mo. BB/TR, 5'9.5", 165 lbs. Deb: 4/10/13																											
1913	StL-A	23	53	8	9	0	1	0	5	6	11	.170	.302	.208	.509	52	-3	-3	95	162	4	.545	3			-2	S/3	-0.2
1914	StL-A	7	23	1	2	0	0	0	1	2	4	.087	.160	.087	.247	-26	-3	-3	98	191	0	.227	1	1	-0	-1	/S	-0.4
1915	StL-A	59	150	13	33	5	0	0	6	14	25	.220	.308	.253	.561	71	-5	-5	96	54	12	.512	6	6	-2	1	O/3P2S	-0.7
Total	3	89	226	22	44	5	1	0	12	22	40	.195	.292	.226	.517	57	-12	-11	96	93	17	.487	10	7		-2	/OS32P	-1.3
■ JIMMY WALSH	Walsh, Michael Timothy "Runt" b: 3/25/1886, Lima, Ohio d: 1/21/47, Baltimore, Md. BR/TR, 5'9", 174 lbs. Deb: 4/25/10																											
1910	Phi-N	88	242	28	60	8	3	3	31	25	38	.248	.323	.343	.666	98	-2	-1	96	117	29	.632	5			3	2O/S3	0.3
1911	Phi-N	94	289	29	78	20	3	1	31	21	30	.270	.324	.370	.694	87	-3	-6	108	95	36	.640	5			-7	O2/S3CP1	-1.3
1912	Phi-N	51	150	16	40	6	3	2	19	8	20	.267	.304	.387	.690	88	-3	-3	100	100	18	.627	3			0	23/C	-0.3
1913	Phi-N	26	30	3	10	4	0	0	5	1	5	.333	.355	.467	.822	119	1	1	112	130	5	.800	1			-0	/2S3O	0.1
1914	Bal-F	120	428	54	132	25	4	10	65	22	56	.308	.342	.456	.798	128	13	14	99	106	75	.794	18			-8	*3/2SO	0.7
1915	Bal-F	106	401	43	121	20	1	9	60	21	0	.302	.336	.424	.760	116	10	7	107	112	63	.725	12			-6	*3	0.4
	StL-F	17	31	5	6	1	0	0	1	3	0	.194	.265	.226	.491	44	-2	-2	105	51	2	.440	1			0	/3	-0.1
	Yr	123	432	48	127	21	1	9	61	24	0	.294	.331	.410	.741	111	8	5	107	104	64	.702	13			-6		0.3
Total	6	502	1571	178	447	84	14	25	212	101	149	.285	.329	.404	.733	107	14	9	103	106	229	.698	45			-18	3/O2SC1P	-0.2
■ TOM WALSH	Walsh, Thomas Joseph b: 2/28/1885, Davenport, Iowa d: 3/16/63, Naples, Fla. TR, 5'11", 170 lbs. Deb: 8/15/06																											
1906	Chi-N	2	1	0	0	0	0	0	0	0		.000	.000	.000	.000	-94	-0	-0	107	0	0	.000	0			0	/C	0.0
■ WALT WALSH	Walsh, Walter William b: 4/30/1897, Newark, N.J. d: 1/15/66, Avon By The Sea, N.J. BR/TR, 5'11", 170 lbs. Deb: 5/04/20																											
1920	Phi-N	2	0	0	0	0	0	0	0	0	0	—	—	—	—	—	0	0	109	—	—	—	0	0	0	0	R	0.0
■ ROXY WALTERS	Walters, Alfred John b: 11/5/1892, San Francisco, Cal. d: 6/3/56, Almeda, Cal. BR/TR, 5'8.5", 160 lbs. Deb: 9/16/15																											
1915	NY-A	2	3	0	1	0	0	0	0	0	0	.333	.333	.333	.667	101	-0	-0	98	0	0	.500	0			0	/C	0.0
1916	NY-A	66	203	13	54	9	3	0	23	14	42	.266	.320	.340	.660	97	-1	-1	101	119	24	.584	2			10	C	1.3
1917	NY-A	61	171	16	45	2	0	0	14	9	22	.263	.304	.275	.579	72	-5	-6	107	107	15	.468	2			2	C	0.1
1918	NY-A	64	191	18	38	5	1	0	12	9	18	.199	.239	.236	.474	46	-14	-12	95	97	11	.379	3			-1	C/O	-0.9
1919	Bos-A	48	135	7	26	2	0	0	9	7	15	.193	.259	.207	.466	35	-12	-11	91	117	8	.376	1			2	C	-0.6
1920	Bos-A	88	258	25	51	11	1	0	28	30	21	.198	.303	.248	.551	49	-19	-17	96	154	22	.502	2	2	-1	5	C/1	-0.5
1921	Bos-A	54	169	17	34	4	1	0	14	10	11	.201	.254	.237	.491	26	-19	-19	100	120	11	.407	3	0	1	3	C	-1.2
1922	Bos-A	38	98	4	19	2	0	0	6	6	8	.194	.240	.214	.455	20	-12	-11	96	102	6	.342	0	0	0	2	C	-0.7
1923	Bos-A	40	104	9	26	4	0	0	5	2	6	.250	.264	.288	.553	45	-8	-9	102	57	8	.400	0	2	-1	2	C/2	-0.4
1924	Cle-A	32	74	10	19	2	0	0	5	10	6	.257	.345	.284	.629	66	-4	-3	97	79	8	.554	0	1	-1	-1	C/2	-0.2
1925	Cle-A	5	20	0	4	0	0	0	0	0	2	.200	.200	.200	.400	2	-3	-3	106	0	1	.250	0	0	0	0	/C	-0.2
Total	11	498	1426	119	317	41	6	0	116	97	151	.222	.281	.259	.541	51	-96	-93	98	112	113	.449	13	5		25	C/O21	-3.3
■ FRED WALTERS	Walters, Fred James "Whale" b: 9/4/12, Laurel, Miss. d: 2/1/80, Laurel, Miss. BR/TR, 6'1", 210 lbs. Deb: 4/17/45																											
1945	Bos-A	40	93	2	16	2	0	0	5	10	9	.172	.252	.194	.446	32	-8	-8	95	100	4	.354	1	1	-0	-1	C	-0.5
■ KEN WALTERS	Walters, Kenneth Rogers b: 11/11/33, Fresno, Cal. BR/TR, 6'1", 180 lbs. Deb: 4/12/60																											
1960	Phi-N	124	426	42	102	10	0	8	37	16	50	.239	.269	.319	.588	56	-24	-27	107	94	34	.464	4	3	-1	6	*O	-2.6
1961	Phi-N	86	180	23	41	8	2	2	14	5	25	.228	.253	.328	.580	56	-12	-11	94	87	13	.456	2	2	-1	-6	O/13	-2.0
1963	Cin-N	49	75	6	14	2	0	1	7	4	14	.187	.237	.253	.491	40	-6	-6	104	134	4	.381	0	2	-1	-5	O/1	-1.4
Total	3	259	681	71	157	20	2	11	58	25	89	.231	.261	.314	.575	54	-42	-44	103	96	51	.467	6	7	-2	-5	O/13	-6.0
■ BUCKY WALTERS	Walters, William Henry b: 4/19/09, Philadelphia, Pa. BR/TR, 6'1", 180 lbs. Deb: 9/18/31 MC																											
1931	Bos-N	9	38	2	8	2	0	0	0	0	3	.211	.211	.263	.474	27	-4	-4	99	0	2	.333	0			0	/32	-0.2
1932	Bos-N	22	75	8	14	3	1	0	4	2	18	.187	.208	.253	.461	25	-8	-7	93	78	4	.344	0			-1	3	-0.5
1933	Bos-A	52	195	27	50	8	3	4	28	19	24	.256	.326	.390	.715	88	-3	-4	101	112	26	.664	1	1	-0	-0	3/2	0.0
1934	Bos-A	23	88	10	19	4	4	4	18	3	12	.216	.242	.489	.730	80	-3	-4	106	111	10	.667	0	0	0	6	3	0.2
	Phi-N	83	300	36	78	20	3	4	38	19	54	.260	.308	.387	.695	78	-7	-10	108	109	34	.592	1			-11	3/2P	-1.3
1935	Phi-N	49	96	14	24	2	1	0	6	9	12	.250	.314	.292	.606	56	-5	-6	114	77	9	.500	0			2	P/O23	0.0
1936	Phi-N	64	121	12	29	10	1	1	16	7	15	.240	.281	.364	.645	67	-5	-6	108	121	12	.537	0			8	P/23	0.0
1937	Phi-N	56	137	15	38	6	0	1	16	5	16	.277	.303	.343	.646	69	-5	-6	108	115	14	.520	1			4	P/3	0.0
1938	Phi-N	15	35	6	10	2	0	1	3	1	5	.286	.306	.429	.734	100	-0	-0	100	60	4	.654	1			0	P	0.0
	Cin-N	36	64	10	9	1	0	0	5	7	18	.141	.236	.156	.392	10	-8	-8	98	181	3	.321	0			3	P	0.0
	Yr	51	99	16	19	3	0	1	8	8	23	.192	.259	.253	.512	42	-8	-8	98	146	7	.432	1			3		0.0
1939	Cin-N	40	120	16	39	8	1	1	16	5	12	.325	.357	.433	.790	108	2	1	103	107	18	.711	1			4	P	0.0
1940	Cin-N	37	117	11	24	3	0	1	18	4	14	.205	.231	.256	.488	34	-11	-11	101	202	7	.383	2			-1	P	0.0
1941	Cin-N	39	106	6	20	6	0	0	9	7	13	.189	.239	.245	.484	37	-9	-9	99	125	6	.371	0			2	P	0.0
1942	Cin-N	40	99	13	24	6	1	2	13	3	13	.242	.265	.384	.649	88	-2	-2	101	109	10	.532	0			1	P/O	0.0
1943	Cin-N	37	90	11	24	7	1	1	12	6	15	.267	.313	.400	.712	106	0	0	99	111	12	.642	1			1	P	0.0
1944	Cin-N	37	107	9	30	4	0	0	13	8	18	.280	.330	.318	.648	87	-2	-2	95	137	12	.545	0			1	P	0.0
1945	Cin-N	24	61	11	14	3	0	3	8	3	14	.230	.266	.426	.692	96	-1	-1	94	79	6	.633	2			-0	P	0.0
1946	Cin-N	24	55	6	7	2	0	0	5	4	12	.127	.186	.164	.350	-0	-7	-8	104	207	2	.306	2			2	P	0.0
1947	Cin-N	20	45	3	12	2	0	0	4	2	13	.267	.298	.311	.609	68	-2	-2	91	106	4	.485	0			-1	P	0.0
1948	Cin-N	7	15	1	4	0	0	0	2	0	2	.267	.267	.267	.533	43	-1	-1	103	187	1	.333	0			1	/PM	0.0
1950	Bos-N	1	2	0	0	0	0	0	0	0	0	.000	.000	.000	.000	-99	-1	-1	86	0	0	.000	0			0	/P	0.0
Total	19	715	1966	227	477	99	16	23	234	114	303	.243	.286	.344	.630	69	-83	-90	103	118	198	.542	12	1		20	P3/2O	-1.8
■ DANNY WALTON	Walton, Daniel James "Mickey" b: 7/14/47, Los Angeles, Cal. BR/TR, 6', 195 lbs. Deb: 4/20/68																											
1968	Hou-N	2	2	0	0	0	0	0	0	0	1	.000	.000	.000	.000	-99	-0	-0	99	0	0	.000	0	0	0	0	H	0.0
1969	Sea-A	23	92	12	20	1	2	3	10	5	26	.217	.280	.370	.650	82	-3	-3	98	90	9	.571	2	0	1	-1	O	-0.3
1970	Mil-A	117	397	32	102	20	1	17	66	51	126	.257	.350	.441	.791	119	9	10	98	120	63	.770	2	3	-1	-10	*O	-0.5
1971	Mil-A	30	69	5	14	3	0	2	9	7	22	.203	.286	.333	.619	73	-2	-3	103	127	6	.534	0	0	0	-4	O/3	-0.7
	NY-A	5	14	1	2	0	0	1	2	0	7	.143	.143	.357	.500	39	-1	-1	97	102	1	.417	0	0	0	-1	/O	-0.2
	Yr	35	83	6	16	3	0	3	11	7	29	.193	.264	.337	.601	68	-4	-4	102	127	8	.537	0	0	0	-4		-0.9
1973	Min-A	37	96	13	17	1	1	4	8	17	28	.177	.301	.333	.634	76	-3	-3	104	71	10	.598	0	0	0	-4	OD/3	-0.7
1975	Min-A	42	63	4	11	2	0	1	8	4	18	.175	.224	.254	.478	32	-6	-6	107	162	3	.364	0	0	0	0	/1CD	-0.6
1976	LA-N	18	15	0	2	0	0	0	2	1	2	.133	.188	.133	.321	-8	-2	-2	100	385	0	.231	0	0	0	0	H	-0.1
1977	Hou-N	13	21	0	4	0	0	0	1	0	5	.190	.190	.190	.381	3	-3	-3	93	100	1	.235	0	0	0	0	/1	-0.2
1980	Tex-A	10	10	2	2	0	0	0	1	3	5	.200	.385	.200	.585	65	-0	-0	100	195	1	.625	0	0	0	0	/D	0.0
Total	9	297	779	69	174	27	4	28	107	88	240	.223	.310	.376	.686	90	-11	-11	100	119	94	.650	4	3	-1	-19	O/D1C3	-3.3
■ REGGIE WALTON	Walton, Reginald Sherard b: 10/24/52, Kansas City, Mo. BR/TR, 6'3", 205 lbs. Deb: 6/13/80																											
1980	Sea-A	31	83	8	23	6	0	2	9	3	10	.277	.310	.422	.732	96	-0	-1	103	86	10	.651	2	2	-1	-3	OD	-0.4
1981	Sea-A	12	6	1	0	0	0	0	0	1	2	.000	.143	.000	.143	-56	-1	-1	100	0	0	.167	0	0	0	-2	/OD	-0.2
1982	Pit-N	13	15	1	3	1	0	0	0	1	1	.200	.294	.267	.561	52	-1	-1	110	0	1	.500	0	0	0	-1	/O	-0.1

YEAR	TM/L	G	AB	R	H	2B	3B	HR	RBI	BB	SO	AVG	OBP	SLG	PRO	/A	BR	/A	PF	CHI	RC	TA	SB	CS	SBR	FR	POS	TPR
Total	3	56	104	10	26	7	0	2	9	5	13	.250	.297	.375	.672	81	-2	-3	104	67	12	.600	2	2	-1	-6	/OD	-0.7
■ **BILL WAMBSGANSS** Wambsganss, William Adolph b: 3/19/1894, Cleveland, Ohio d: 12/8/85, Lakewood, Ohio BR/TR, 5'11", 175 lbs. Deb: 8/04/14																												
1914	Cle-A	43	143	12	31	6	2	0	12	8	24	.217	.277	.287	.564	68	-6	-6	102	112	10	.462	2	7	-4	-3	S/2	-0.9
1915	Cle-A	121	375	30	73	4	4	0	21	36	50	.195	.272	.227	.499	48	-23	-25	104	84	24	.428	8	9	-3	-8	23	-3.6
1916	Cle-A	136	475	57	117	14	4	0	45	41	40	.246	.313	.293	.605	82	-10	-10	100	123	52	.553	13			-1	*S2/3	-0.1
1917	Cle-A	141	499	52	127	17	6	0	43	37	42	.255	.315	.313	.628	80	-5	-14	114	101	54	.581	16			17	*2/1	1.3
1918	Cle-A	87	315	34	93	15	2	0	40	21	21	.295	.345	.356	.701	103	4	1	108	138	44	.685	16			0	2	0.6
1919	Cle-A	139	526	60	146	17	6	2	60	32	24	.278	.323	.344	.667	82	-10	-14	107	123	63	.616	18			11	*2	1.0
1920	Cle-A	153	565	83	138	16	11	1	55	54	26	.244	.316	.317	.633	66	-26	-29	104	112	57	.555	9	18	-8	8	*2	-2.4
1921	Cle-A	107	410	80	117	28	5	2	47	44	27	.285	.359	.393	.752	92	-5	-4	99	93	61	.737	13	7	-0	-15	*2/3	-1.4
1922	Cle-A	142	538	89	141	22	6	0	47	60	26	.262	.341	.325	.666	73	-19	-20	102	92	64	.629	17	10	-1	-6	*2S	-1.5
1923	Cle-A	101	345	59	100	20	4	1	59	43	15	.290	.373	.380	.753	97	0	-0	101	153	51	.744	12	9	-2	9	2/3S	1.0
1924	Bos-A	156	632	93	174	41	5	0	49	54	33	.275	.336	.356	.692	76	-21	-24	104	64	79	.637	14	8	-1	15	*2	-0.4
1925	Bos-A	111	360	50	83	12	4	1	41	52	21	.231	.329	.294	.624	62	-22	-19	95	128	38	.574	3	5	-2	6	*2/1	-0.8
1926	Phi-A	54	54	11	19	3	0	0	1	8	8	.352	.444	.407	.852	105	2	1	118	15	10	.889	1	1	-0	-0	S/2	0.2
Total	13	1491	5237	710	1359	215	59	7	520	490	357	.259	.328	.327	.655	77	-139	-162	104	106	608	.605	142	74		34	*2S/31	-7.0
■ **LLOYD WANER** Waner, Lloyd James "Little Poison" b: 3/16/06, Harrah, Okla. d: 7/22/82, Oklahoma City, Okla. BL/TR, 5'9", 150 lbs. Deb: 4/12/27 H																												
1927	Pit-N	150	629	**133**	223	17	6	2	27	37	23	.355	.396	.410	.806	114	16	14	102	32	99	.776	14			-12	*O/2	-0.3
1928	Pit-N	152	659	121	221	22	14	5	61	40	13	.335	.377	.434	.811	104	11	5	107	64	104	.772	8			3	*O	0.2
1929	Pit-N	151	662	134	234	28	**20**	5	74	37	20	.353	.395	.479	.874	112	16	13	103	66	121	.862	6			11	*O	0.9
1930	Pit-N	68	260	32	94	8	3	1	36	5	5	.362	.376	.427	.803	96	-2	-1	97	111	39	.723	3			-3	O	-0.7
1931	Pit-N	154	681	90	**214**	25	13	4	57	39	16	.314	.352	.407	.759	103	3	3	101	61	99	.694	7			11	*O/2	0.6
1932	Pit-N	134	565	90	188	27	11	2	38	31	11	.333	.367	.430	.798	114	11	11	99	55	90	.743	6			6	*O	0.8
1933	Pit-N	121	500	59	138	14	5	0	26	22	8	.276	.307	.324	.631	84	-13	-10	95	64	52	.511	3			3	*O	-1.4
1934	Pit-N	140	611	95	173	27	6	1	48	38	12	.283	.326	.352	.678	78	-16	-20	105	70	73	.587	6			8	*O	-1.7
1935	Pit-N	122	537	83	166	22	14	0	46	22	10	.309	.336	.402	.739	91	-2	-7	107	68	73	.631	1			4	*O	-0.7
1936	Pit-N	106	414	67	133	13	8	1	31	31	5	.321	.369	.399	.767	109	4	6	98	67	62	.682	1			-3	O	-0.1
1937	Pit-N	129	537	80	177	23	4	1	45	34	12	.330	.370	.393	.762	105	6	4	102	73	81	.676	3			1	*O	0.0
1938	Pit-N	147	619	79	194	25	7	5	57	28	11	.313	.343	.401	.744	104	2	2	100	83	85	.643	5			-5	*O	-0.5
1939	Pit-N	112	379	49	108	15	3	0	24	17	13	.285	.321	.340	.661	78	-12	-12	100	68	42	.540	0			2	O/3	-1.1
1940	Pit-N	72	166	30	43	3	0	0	3	5	5	.259	.285	.277	.562	58	-10	-9	95	24	13	.435	2			1	O	-0.9
1941	Pit-N	3	4	2	1	0	0	0	1	2	0	.250	.500	.250	.750	112	0	0	103	361	1	1.000	0			0	/O	0.1
	Bos-N	19	51	7	21	1	0	0	4	2	0	.412	.434	.431	.865	155	3	3	93	66	10	.833	1			-1	O	0.2
	Cin-N	55	164	17	42	4	1	0	6	8	0	.256	.291	.293	.583	65	-8	-8	99	45	14	.448	0			-4	O	-1.3
	Yr	77	219	26	64	5	1	0	11	12	0	.292	.329	.324	.653	86	-4	-4	98	68	24	.532	1			-4		-1.0
1942	Phi-N	101	287	23	75	7	3	0	10	16	6	.261	.300	.307	.607	82	-8	-7	94	42	27	.488	1			-4	O	-1.2
1944	Bro-N	15	14	3	4	0	0	0	1	3	0	.286	.412	.286	.697	100	0	0	99	90	2	.636	0			-1	/O	-0.1
	Pit-N	19	14	2	5	0	0	0	2	2	0	.357	.438	.357	.795	119	1	1	105	143	2	.778	0			-2	/O	-0.1
	Yr	34	28	5	9	0	0	0	3	5	0	.321	.424	.321	.746	109	1	1	102	122	4	.737	0			-3		-0.2
1945	Pit-N	23	19	5	5	0	0	0	1	1	3	.263	.300	.263	.563	55	-1	-1	103	69	2	.429	0			-0	/O	-0.1
Total	18	1993	7772	1201	2459	281	118	27	598	420	173	.316	.353	.393	.747	99	1	-12	101	64	1092	.672	67			16	*O/23	-7.4
■ **PAUL WANER** Waner, Paul Glee "Big Poison" b: 4/16/03, Harrah, Okla. d: 8/29/65, Sarasota, Fla. BL/TL, 5'8.5", 153 lbs. Deb: 4/13/26 H																												
1926	Pit-N	144	536	101	180	35	**22**	8	79	66	19	**.336**	**.413**	.528	.941	135	**39**	30	112	94	**115**	1.022	11			7	*O	**3.1**
1927	Pit-N	155	623	113	**237**	40	**17**	9	**131**	60	14	**.380**	.437	.543	.980	158	54	53	102	111	144	1.052	5			9	*O1	5.3
1928	Pit-N	152	602	**142**	223	**50**	19	6	86	77	16	.370	.446	.547	.992	148	53	48	107	85	145	1.100	6			6	*O1	4.4
1929	Pit-N	151	596	131	200	43	15	15	100	89	24	.336	.424	.534	.958	131	35	32	103	91	135	1.073	15			7	*O/1	2.3
1930	Pit-N	145	589	117	217	32	18	8	77	57	18	.368	.428	.525	.952	133	29	32	97	77	129	1.043	18			6	*O	2.4
1931	Pit-N	150	559	88	180	35	10	6	70	73	21	.322	.404	.453	.857	129	26	26	101	98	108	.887	6			**20**	*O1	3.7
1932	Pit-N	154	630	107	215	**62**	10	8	82	56	24	.341	.397	.510	.906	143	37	38	99	78	130	.945	13			2	*O	2.8
1933	Pit-N	154	618	101	191	38	16	7	70	60	20	.309	.372	.456	.828	143	29	33	95	84	109	.794	3			3	*O	2.8
1934	Pit-N	146	599	**122**	**217**	32	16	14	90	68	24	**.362**	.429	.539	.968	150	50	46	105	78	142	1.010	8			6	*O	**4.3**
1935	Pit-N	139	549	98	176	29	12	11	78	61	22	.321	.392	.477	.869	124	26	21	107	92	105	.845	2			0	*O	1.5
1936	Pit-N	148	585	107	218	53	9	5	94	74	29	**.373**	.446	.520	.965	163	51	53	98	111	140	1.016	7			8	*O	5.2
1937	Pit-N	154	619	94	219	30	9	2	74	63	34	.354	.413	.441	.855	129	30	28	102	92	118	.827	4			-1	*O/1	1.9
1938	Pit-N	148	625	77	175	31	6	6	69	47	28	.280	.331	.378	.709	94	-5	-5	100	94	79	.614	2			-3	*O	-1.1
1939	Pit-N	125	461	62	151	30	6	3	45	35	18	.328	.375	.438	.813	118	11	12	100	80	74	.736	0			2	*O	1.1
1940	Pit-N	89	238	32	69	16	1	1	32	23	14	.290	.352	.378	.731	107	1	2	95	128	32	.653	0			-7	O/1	-0.6
1941	Bro-N	11	35	5	6	0	0	0	4	8	0	.171	.326	.171	.497	41	-2	-2	103	245	2	.452	0			-2	/O	-0.4
	Bos-N	95	294	40	82	10	2	2	46	47	14	.279	.378	.347	.725	113	4	7	93	154	41	.682	1			-5	O/1	-0.2
	Yr	106	329	45	88	10	2	2	50	55	14	.267	.372	.328	.701	104	2	4	94	166	43	.659	1			-7		-0.6
1942	Bos-N	114	333	43	86	17	1	1	39	62	20	.258	.376	.324	.701	111	6	7	95	130	45	.681	2			-8	O	-0.2
1943	Bro-N	82	225	29	70	16	0	1	26	35	9	.311	.406	.396	.802	132	11	11	100	102	37	.762	0			-2	O	0.7
1944	Bro-N	83	136	16	39	4	1	0	16	27	7	.287	.405	.331	.736	110	3	3	99	127	20	.720	0			-3	O	-0.1
	NY-A	9	7	1	1	0	0	0	1	2	1	.143	.333	.143	.476	36	-0	-1	106	361	1	.667	1	0	0	0	H	0.0
1945	NY-A	1	0	0	0	0	0	0	0	1	0	—	1.000	—	1.143	224	0	0	107	0	0	—	0	0	0	0	H	0.0
Total	20	2549	9459	1626	3152	603	190	113	1309	1091	376	.333	.404	.473	.877	133	490	473	101	97	1851	.905	104	0		43	*O/1	38.9
■ **JACK WANNER** Wanner, Clarence Curtis "Johnny" b: 11/29/1885, Geneseo, Ill. d: 5/28/19, Geneseo, Ill. BR/TR, 5'11.5", 190 lbs. Deb: 9/28/09																												
1909	NY-A	3	8	0	1	0	0	0	0	2		.125	.300	.125	.425	35	-0	-0	99	0	1	.571	1			0	/S	0.0
■ **PEE-WEE WANNINGER** Wanninger, Paul Louis b: 12/12/02, Birmingham, Ala. d: 3/7/81, N.Augusta, S.C. BL/TR, 5'7", 150 lbs. Deb: 4/22/25																												
1925	NY-A	117	403	35	95	13	6	1	22	11	34	.236	.256	.305	.561	44	-37	-35	96	58	30	.438	3	5	-2	-6	*S/32	-2.3
1927	Bos-A	18	60	4	12	0	0	0	1	6	2	.200	.284	.200	.484	29	-6	-6	95	28	4	.438	2	0	1	1	S	-0.3
	Cin-N	28	93	14	23	2	2	0	8	6	7	.247	.293	.312	.605	62	-5	-5	100	96	9	.500	0			-2	S	-0.3
Total	2	163	556	53	130	15	8	1	31	23	43	.234	.266	.295	.560	45	-48	-45	97	61	43	.448	5	5		-7	S/32	-2.9
■ **AARON WARD** Ward, Aaron Lee b: 8/28/1896, Booneville, Ark. d: 1/30/61, New Orleans, La. BR/TR, 5'10.5", 160 lbs. Deb: 8/14/17																												
1917	NY-A	8	26	0	3	0	0	0	1	1	5	.115	.148	.115	.264	-18	-4	-4	107	120	0	.174	0			0	/S	-0.3
1918	NY-A	20	32	2	4	1	0	0	1	2	7	.125	.176	.156	.333	0	-4	-4	95	73	1	.286	1			2	S/O2	0.0
1919	NY-A	27	34	5	7	2	0	0	2	5	6	.206	.308	.265	.572	58	-2	-2	106	81	3	.519	0			1	/13S2	0.0
1920	NY-A	127	496	62	127	18	7	11	54	33	84	.256	.304	.387	.691	80	-15	-16	102	89	58	.623	7	5	-1	4	*3S	-0.3
1921	NY-A	153	556	77	170	30	10	5	75	42	68	.306	.363	.423	.786	97	-0	-3	103	105	85	.739	6	8	-3	10	*23	1.0
1922	NY-A	154	558	69	149	19	5	7	68	45	64	.267	.328	.357	.685	77	-18	-19	102	113	68	.622	7	4	-0	4	*2/3	-0.4
1923	NY-A	152	567	79	161	26	11	10	82	56	65	.284	.351	.422	.773	99	1	-2	104	106	84	.739	8	8	-2	13	*2	1.3
1924	NY-A	120	400	42	101	13	10	8	66	40	45	.253	.324	.395	.719	85	-11	-10	99	122	52	.663	1	4	-2	9	*2/S	0.0
1925	NY-A	125	439	41	108	22	3	4	38	49	49	.246	.326	.337	.663	71	-21	-19	96	81	50	.600	1	4	-2	-14	*23	-2.6
1926	NY-A	22	31	5	10	2	0	0	3	2	6	.323	.364	.387	.751	96	-0	-0	99	85	4	.667	0	0	0	-1	/23	0.0
1927	Chi-A	145	463	75	125	25	8	5	56	63	56	.270	.360	.391	.751	93	-3	-4	102	95	67	.746	6	0	2	-25	*2/3	-2.1
1928	Cle-A	6	9	0	1	0	0	0	0	1	2	.111	.200	.111	.311	-15	-2	-2	106	0	0	.250	0	0	0	0	/3S2	0.0
Total	12	1059	3611	457	966	158	54	50	446	339	457	.268	.335	.383	.717	85	-77	-85	101	101	474	.666	37	33		2	23/S10	-3.4
■ **CHUCK WARD** Ward, Charles William b: 7/30/1894, St.Louis, Mo. d: 4/4/69, Indian Rocks, Fla. BR/TR, 5'11.5", 170 lbs. Deb: 4/11/17																												
1917	Pit-N	125	423	25	100	12	3	0	43	32	43	.236	.302	.279	.581	79	-10	-9	100	143	38	.505	5			-22	*S/23	-3.3
1918	Bro-N	2	6	0	2	0	0	0	3	0	0	.333	.333	.333	.667	102	0	-0	101	567	1	.500	0			0	/3	0.0
1919	Bro-N	45	150	7	35	1	2	0	8	7	11	.233	.277	.267	.543	68	-6	-5	94	78	11	.426	0			-5	3	-1.1

YEAR	TM/L	G	AB	R	H	2B	3B	HR	RBI	BB	SO	AVG	OBP	SLG	PRO	/A	BR	/A	PF	CHI	RC	TA	SB	CS	SBR	FR	POS	TPR
1920	Bro-N	19	71	7	11	1	0	0	4	3	3	.155	.200	.169	.369	6	-8	-9	111	137	3	.283	1	0	0	-2	S	-1.0
1921	Bro-N	12	28	1	2	1	0	0	0	4	2	.071	.188	.107	.295	-19	-5	-5	105	0	1	.269	0	0	0	1	S	-0.2
1922	Bro-N	33	91	12	25	5	1	0	14	5	8	.275	.320	.352	.671	77	-4	-3	95	153	10	.582	1	1	-0	-2	S/3	-0.2
Total	6	236	769	52	175	20	6	0	72	51	67	.228	.286	.269	.555	65	-33	-32	99	129	64	.466	7	1		-31	S/32	-5.8
■ CHRIS WARD	Ward, Chris Gilbert b: 5/18/49, Oakland, Cal. BL/TL, 6', 180 lbs. Deb: 9/10/72																											
1972	Chi-N	1	1	0	0	0	0	0	0	0	0	.000	.000	.000	.000	-88	-0	-0	114	0	0	.000	0	0	0	0	H	0.0
1974	Chi-N	92	137	8	28	4	0	1	15	18	13	.204	.297	.255	.552	55	-8	-8	100	152	10	.465	0	2	-1	0	O/1	-1.0
Total	2	93	138	8	28	4	0	1	15	18	13	.203	.295	.254	.548	54	-8	-8	100	151	10	.461	0	2	-1	0	/O1	-1.0
■ PIGGY WARD	Ward, Frank Gray b: 4/16/1867, Chambersburg, Pa. d: 10/24/12, Altoona, Pa. 5'9.5", 196 lbs. Deb: 6/12/1883																											
1883	Phi-N	1	5	0	0	0	0	0	0	0	2	.000	.000	.000	.000	-99	-1	-1	90	0	0	.000				0	/3	0.0
1889	Phi-N	7	25	0	4	1	0	0	4	0	7	.160	.160	.200	.360	1	-3	-3	104	239	1	.286	1			0	/2O	-0.2
1891	Pit-N	6	18	3	6	0	0	0	2	3	3	.333	.455	.333	.788	132	1	1	101	97	4	1.083	3			0	/O	0.1
1892	Bal-N	56	186	28	54	6	5	1	33	31	18	.290	.403	.392	.795	143	11	11	100	136	34	.894	10			4	O/2SC	1.2
1893	Bal-N	11	49	11	12	1	3	0	5	5	2	.245	.327	.388	.715	86	-1	-1	107	62	8	.784	4			-0	/O1	-0.1
	Cin-N	42	150	44	42	4	1	0	10	37	10	.280	.440	.320	.760	104	5	4	101	55	34	1.093	27			-2	O/1	0.1
	Yr	53	199	55	54	5	4	0	15	42	12	.271	.415	.337	.752	100	4	3	103	57	42	1.014	31			-2		0.0
1894	Was-N	98	347	86	105	11	7	0	36	80	31	.303	.447	.375	.822	104	7	9	98	81	78	1.083	41			-18	2O/S3	-0.3
Total	6	221	780	172	223	23	16	1	90	156	73	.286	.419	.360	.779	108	19	20	100	91	159	.980	86			-17	O/2S13C	0.8
■ GARY WARD	Ward, Gary Lamell b: 12/6/53, Los Angeles, Cal. BR/TR, 6'2", 195 lbs. Deb: 9/03/79																											
1979	Min-A	10	14	2	4	0	0	0	1	3	3	.286	.412	.286	.697	85	0	-0	109	96	2	.636	0	1	-1	-1	/O	-0.1
1980	Min-A	13	41	11	19	6	2	1	10	3	6	.463	.500	.780	1.280	226	8	7	109	111	16	1.591	0	0	0	-3	O	0.4
1981	Min-A	85	295	42	78	7	6	3	29	28	48	.264	.328	.359	.687	93	-1	-2	105	101	34	.607	5	2	0	7	O/D	0.3
1982	Min-A	152	570	85	165	33	7	28	91	37	105	.289	.334	.519	.853	130	21	21	100	98	95	.822	13	1	3	11	*O/D	3.0
1983	Min-A	157	623	76	173	34	5	19	88	44	98	.278	.328	.440	.768	104	7	3	105	110	85	.693	8	1	2	**23**	*O/D	2.5
1984	Tex-A	155	602	97	171	21	7	21	79	55	95	.284	.344	.447	.791	117	13	13	100	101	87	.723	7	5	-1	-5	*O/D	0.3
1985	Tex-A	154	593	77	170	28	7	15	70	39	97	.287	.332	.433	.765	99	5	-1	108	97	82	.719	26	7	4	0	*O/D	0.1
1986	Tex-A	105	380	54	120	15	2	5	51	31	72	.316	.373	.405	.779	119	8	10	96	123	56	.723	12	8	-1	-2	*O/D	0.4
1987	NY-A	146	529	65	131	22	1	16	78	33	101	.248	.293	.384	.677	80	-17	-15	98	127	55	.587	9	1	2	-1	OD1	-1.7
1988	NY-A	91	231	26	52	8	0	4	24	24	41	.225	.304	.312	.615	76	-8	-7	96	114	21	.521	0	1	-1	1	O1/3D	-0.8
Total	10	1068	3878	535	1083	174	37	112	521	297	666	.279	.332	.430	.762	106	37	29	102	108	532	.727	80	27	8	30	O/D13	4.4
■ JIM WARD	Ward, James H. b: 3/1855, Boston, Mass. d: 6/4/1886, Boston, Mass. Deb: 8/03/1876																											
1876	Phi-N	1	4	1	2	0	0	0	1	0	1	.500	.500	.500	1.000	236	1	1	99	169	1	1.000				0	/C	0.0
■ RUBE WARD	Ward, John Andrew b: 2/6/1879, New Lexington, Ohio d: 1/17/45, Akron, Ohio Deb: 4/28/02																											
1902	Bro-N	13	31	4	9	1	0	0	2	2		.290	.333	.323	.656	110	0	0	95	69	3	.545	0			1	O	0.0
■ JOHN WARD	Ward, John E. b: Washington, D.C. Deb: 5/23/1884																											
1884	Was-U	1	4	0	1	0	0	0		0		.250	.250	.250	.500	72	-0	-0	97	0	0	.333	0			0	/O	0.0
■ JAY WARD	Ward, John Francis b: 9/9/38, Brookfield, Mo. BR/TR, 6'1", 185 lbs. Deb: 5/06/63 C																											
1963	Min-A	9	15	0	1	1	0	0	2	1	5	.067	.125	.133	.258	-27	-3	-3	100	419	0	.214	0	0	0	-0	/3O	-0.2
1964	Min-A	12	31	4	7	2	0	0	2	6	13	.226	.351	.290	.642	80	-1	-1	101	94	4	.625	0	0	0	-1	/2O	0.0
1970	Cin-N	6	3	0	0	0	0	0	0	2	1	.000	.400	.000	.400	16	-0	-0	104	0	0	.667	0	0	0	0	/312	0.0
Total	3	27	49	4	8	3	0	0	4	9	19	.163	.293	.224	.518	46	-3	-3	101	175	4	.488	0	0	0	-1	/23O1	-0.2
■ MONTE WARD	Ward, John Montgomery b: 3/3/1860, Bellefonte, Pa. d: 3/4/25, Augusta, Ga. BL/TR, 5'9", 165 lbs. Deb: 7/15/1878 MH																											
1878	Pro-N	37	138	14	27	5	4	1	15	2	13	.196	.207	.312	.519	70	-5	-4	98	113	9	.405				2	P	0.0
1879	Pro-N	83	364	71	104	9	4	2	41	7	14	.286	.299	.349	.648	111	5	4	102	115	39	.515				4	*P3/O	0.0
1880	Pro-N	86	356	53	81	12	2	0	27	6	16	.228	.240	.272	.513	76	-10	-8	96	108	24	.375				14	*P3/OM	0.0
1881	Pro-N	85	357	56	87	18	6	0	53	5	10	.244	.254	.328	.582	87	-8	-4	93	167	30	.452				7	OPS	0.7
1882	Pro-N	83	355	58	87	10	3	1	39	13	22	.245	.272	.299	.570	78	-7	-10	106	116	30	.444				7	OP/S	0.0
1883	NY-N	88	380	76	97	18	7	7	54	8	25	.255	.271	.395	.665	99	-1	-1	100	97	42	.558				17	OP/3S2	2.0
1884	NY-N	113	482	98	122	11	8	2	51	28	47	.253	.294	.322	.616	95	-3	-2	98	96	47	.508				3	O2/PM	0.1
1885	NY-N	111	446	72	101	8	9	0	37	17	39	.226	.255	.285	.540	68	-13	-19	109	107	33	.417				2	*S	-0.9
1886	NY-N	122	491	82	134	17	5	2	81	19	46	.273	.300	.340	.640	107	-4	4	89	147	62	.622	36			-12	*S	-0.8
1887	NY-N	129	545	114	184	16	5	1	53	29	12	.338	.375	.391	.766	107	12	5	107	67	125	.989	**111**			27	*S	2.3
1888	NY-N	122	510	70	128	14	5	2	49	9	13	.251	.265	.310	.575	92	-9	-4	93	103	53	.539	38			-1	*S	0.0
1889	NY-N	114	479	87	143	13	4	1	67	27	7	.299	.339	.349	.687	89	-4	-8	105	125	79	.768	62			3	*S/2	0.0
1890	Bro-P	128	561	134	189	15	12	4	60	51	22	.337	.394	.428	.822	115	18	11	106	58	122	.957	63			14	*SM	2.6
1891	Bro-N	105	441	85	122	13	5	0	39	36	10	.277	.335	.329	.664	98	-2	0	97	69	69	.755	57			0	S2M	0.4
1892	Bro-N	148	614	109	163	13	3	1	47	82	19	.265	.355	.301	.656	99	4	3	101	66	99	.794	**88**			2	*2M	0.5
1893	NY-N	135	588	129	193	27	9	2	77	47	5	.328	.379	.415	.794	109	10	7	104	74	113	.856	46			6	*2M	0.9
1894	NY-N	136	540	100	143	12	5	0	77	34	6	.265	.310	.306	.615	50	-43	-43	100	136	65	.602	39			-1	*2M	-2.7
Total	17	1825	7647	1408	2105	231	96	26	867	420	326	.275	.314	.341	.655	93	-59	-67	100	100	1042	.647	540			93	S2PO/3	5.1
■ JOE WARD	Ward, Joseph A. b: 9/2/1884, Philadelphia, Pa. d: 8/11/34, Philadelphia, Pa. TR , Deb: 4/24/06																											
1906	Phi-N	35	129	12	38	8	6	0	11	5		.295	.321	.450	.771	155	5	6	92	73	20	.714	2			-4	3/2S	0.1
1909	NY-A	9	28	3	5	0	0	0	0	1		.179	.233	.179	.412	31	-2	-2	99	0	2	.391	2			-1	/21	-0.3
	Phi-N	74	184	21	49	8	2	0	23	9		.266	.304	.332	.636	93	-1	-2	106	137	20	.578	7			1	2/S1O	-0.1
1910	Phi-N	48	124	11	18	2	1	0	13	3	11	.145	.178	.177	.356	4	-15	-15	96	206	5	.264	1			-0	1/S3	-1.5
Total	3	166	465	47	110	18	9	0	47	18	11	.237	.271	.314	.585	80	-13	-13	99	129	46	.507	12			-4	/213SO	-1.8
■ HAP WARD	Ward, Joseph Nichols b: 11/15/1885, Leesburg, N.J. d: 9/13/79, Elmer, N.J. Deb: 5/18/12																											
1912	Det-A	1	2	0	0	0	0	0	0	0		.000	.000	.000	.000	-99	-1	-1	95	0	0	.000	0			0	/O	0.0
■ PETE WARD	Ward, Peter Thomas b: 7/26/39, Montreal, Que., Can BL/TR, 6'1", 185 lbs. Deb: 9/21/62 C																											
1962	Bal-A	8	21	1	3	2	0	0	2	4	5	.143	.280	.238	.518	43	-2	-2	95	159	2	.500	0	0	0	-0	/O	-0.1
1963	Chi-A	157	600	80	177	34	6	22	84	52	77	.295	.356	.482	.838	127	25	22	104	105	104	.811	7	6	-2	-8	*3/2S	1.4
1964	Chi-A	144	539	61	152	28	3	23	94	56	76	.282	.352	.473	.825	133	19	22	96	130	91	.795	1	1	-0	13	*3	3.9
1965	Chi-A	138	507	62	125	25	3	10	57	56	83	.247	.329	.367	.696	106	-1	4	92	116	61	.631	2	4	-2	7	*3/2	1.1
1966	Chi-A	84	251	22	55	7	1	3	28	24	49	.219	.295	.291	.586	73	-10	-8	94	143	23	.510	3	1	0	-3	O3/1	-1.4
1967	Chi-A	146	467	49	109	16	2	18	62	61	109	.233	.336	.392	.728	122	9	13	94	111	65	.707	3	2	-0	-10	O13	-0.3
1968	Chi-A	125	399	43	86	15	0	15	50	76	85	.216	.355	.366	.721	118	12	12	101	114	58	.740	4	3	-1	-0	31O	1.2
1969	Chi-A	105	199	22	49	7	0	6	32	33	38	.246	.362	.372	.734	97	2	0	108	140	30	.724	0	0	0	0	13/O	-0.1
1970	NY-A	66	77	5	20	2	2	1	18	9	17	.260	.337	.377	.714	105	-0	0	92	228	10	.655	0	0	0	0	1	0.0
Total	9	973	3060	345	776	136	17	98	427	371	539	.254	.342	.405	.747	115	56	64	98	122	443	.726	20	17	-4	-1	3O1/2S	5.7
■ PRESTON WARD	Ward, Preston Meyer b: 7/24/27, Columbia, Mo. BL/TR, 6'4", 190 lbs. Deb: 4/20/48																											
1948	Bro-N	42	146	9	38	9	2	1	21	15	23	.260	.329	.370	.699	85	-2	-3	104	138	19	.639	0			-1	1	-0.3
1950	Chi-N	80	285	31	72	11	2	6	33	27	42	.253	.317	.368	.686	76	-9	-10	105	106	34	.616	3			6	1	-0.7
1953	Chi-N	33	100	10	23	5	0	4	12	18	21	.230	.347	.400	.747	92	-1	-1	103	90	15	.753	3	1	0	-3	O/1	-0.4
	Pit-N	88	281	35	59	7	1	8	27	44	39	.210	.319	.327	.646	68	-12	-13	102	91	31	.597	1	3	-2	1	1	-1.4
	Yr	121	381	45	82	12	1	12	39	62	60	.215	.327	.346	.673	74	-13	-14	102	91	47	.644	4	4	-1	-2		-1.8
1954	Pit-N	117	360	37	97	16	2	7	48	39	61	.269	.341	.383	.724	91	-6	-4	97	119	49	.660	0	0	0	1	1O3	-0.5
1955	Pit-N	84	179	16	38	7	4	5	25	22	28	.212	.299	.380	.678	81	-6	-5	97	122	21	.625	0	0	0	2	1/O	-0.6
1956	Pit-N	16	30	3	10	0	1	1	11	6	4	.333	.444	.500	.944	150	3	2	102	258	7	1.050	0	0	0	-2	/3O	0.0

YEAR	TM/L	G	AB	R	H	2B	3B	HR	RBI	BB	SO	AVG	OBP	SLG	PRO	/A	BR	/A	PF	CHI	RC	TA	SB	CS	SBR	FR	POS	TPR
	Cle-A	87	150	18	38	10	0	6	21	16	20	.253	.325	.440	.765	99	-1	-1	101	93	23	.732	0	0	0	0	1O	-0.3
1957	Cle-A	10	11	2	2	1	0	0	0	0	2	.182	.182	.273	.455	22	-1	-1	102	0	1	.333	0	0	0	0	/1	0.0
1958	Cle-A	48	148	22	50	3	1	4	21	10	27	.338	.384	.453	.836	137	6	7	94	107	26	.780	0	1	-1	0	31	0.7
	KC-A	81	268	28	68	10	1	6	24	27	36	.254	.322	.366	.688	84	-4	-6	106	85	33	.613	0	1	-1	-2	13/O	-0.8
	Yr	129	416	50	118	13	2	10	45	37	63	.284	.344	.397	.740	102	2	1	101	94	58	.670	0	2	-1	-2		-0.1
1959	KC-A	58	109	8	27	4	1	2	19	7	12	.248	.293	.358	.651	77	-4	-4	101	166	11	.541	0	0	0	-1	1/O	-0.4
Total	9	744	2067	219	522	83	15	50	262	231	315	.253	.328	.380	.708	87	-36	-39	101	110	269	.660	7	6		1	1/O3	-4.7
■ BUZZY WARES Wares, Clyde Ellsworth b: 5/23/1886, Vandalia, Mich. d: 5/26/64, South Bend, Ind. BR/TR, 5'10", 150 lbs. Deb: 9/15/13 C																												
1913	StL-A	11	35	5	10	2	0	0	1	1	3	.286	.306	.343	.648	94	-1	-0	95	30	4	.600	2			0	/2	0.0
1914	StL-A	81	215	20	45	10	1	0	23	28	35	.209	.300	.265	.566	72	-7	-7	98	151	19	.528	10	10	-3	-11	S/2	-1.5
Total	2	92	250	25	55	12	1	0	24	29	38	.220	.301	.276	.577	75	-8	-7	97	136	23	.537	12	10		-11	/S2	-1.5
■ FRED WARNER Warner, Frederick John Rodney b: 1855, Philadelphia, Pa. d: 2/13/1886, Philadelphia, Pa. 5'7", 155 lbs. Deb: 4/30/1875																												
1875	Cen-n	14	59	11	14							.237															O	
1876	Phi-N	1	3	0	0	0	0	0	0	0	0	.000	.000	.000	.000	-99	-1	-1	99	0	0	.000				0	/O	0.0
1878	Ind-N	43	165	19	41	4	0	0	10	2	15	.248	.257	.273	.530	86	-4	-1	87	77	12	.379				-3	*S/O	-0.1
1879	Cle-N	76	316	32	77	11	4	0	22	2	20	.244	.248	.304	.552	81	-6	-6	99	85	24	.410				0	3O/1	-0.4
1883	Phi-N	39	141	13	32	6	1	0	13	5	21	.227	.253	.284	.537	70	-6	-4	90	115	10	.413				-11	3/O	-1.2
1884	Bro-a	84	352	40	78	4	0	1		17		.222	.259	.241	.501	69	-12	-11	98	0	23	.376				-7	*3/O	-1.5
Total	5	243	977	104	228	25	5	1	45	26	56	.233	.254	.272	.526	75	-30	-23	95	56	69	.391				-22	3/SO1	-3.2
■ HOOKS WARNER Warner, Hoke Hayden b: 5/22/1894, Del Rio, Tex. d: 2/19/47, San Francisco, Cal BL/TR, 5'10.5", 170 lbs. Deb: 8/21/16																												
1916	Pit-N	44	168	12	40	1	1	2	14	6	19	.238	.264	.292	.556	67	-6	-7	105	107	15	.477	6			-5	3/2	-1.3
1917	Pit-N	3	5	0	1	0	0	0	0	0	1	.200	.200	.200	.400	23	-0	-0	100	0	0	.250	0			-0	/3	0.0
1919	Pit-N	6	8	0	1	0	0	0	2	3	1	.125	.364	.125	.489	48	-0	-0	105	778	0	.571	0			-0	/3	0.0
1921	Chi-N	14	38	4	8	1	0	0	3	2	1	.211	.268	.237	.505	33	-3	-4	107	122	2	.419	1	1	-0	0	3	-0.3
Total	4	67	219	16	50	2	1	2	19	11	22	.228	.268	.274	.542	59	-10	-11	105	139	18	.465	7	1		-5	/32	-1.6
■ JOHN WARNER Warner, John Joseph b: 8/15/1872, New York, N.Y. d: 12/21/43, Far Rockaway, N.Y. BL/TR, 5'11", 165 lbs. Deb: 4/23/1895																												
1895	Bos-N	3	7	2	1	0	0	0	1	1	0	.143	.333	.143	.476	27	-1	-1	103	280	0	.500	0			-2	/C	-0.2
	Lou-N	67	232	20	62	4	2	1	20	11	16	.267	.320	.315	.635	69	-11	-9	95	74	27	.594	10			-5	C/12	-0.7
	Yr	70	239	22	63	4	2	1	21	12	16	.264	.320	.310	.630	68	-12	-10	95	86	28	.591	10			-8		-0.9
1896	Lou-N	33	110	9	25	1	1	0	10	10	10	.227	.303	.255	.558	50	-8	-7	98	103	10	.506	3			0	C/1	-0.5
	NY-N	19	54	9	14	1	0	0	3	3	7	.259	.310	.278	.588	58	-3	-3	99	58	5	.500	1			0	C	-0.2
	Yr	52	164	18	39	2	1	0	13	13	17	.238	.306	.262	.568	53	-11	-10	98	88	15	.504	4			0		-0.7
1897	NY-N	110	397	50	109	6	3	2	51	26		.275	.344	.320	.664	79	-11	-10	98	114	48	.615	8			10	*C	1.2
1898	NY-N	110	373	40	96	14	5	0	42	22		.257	.316	.322	.638	90	-7	-4	95	106	42	.581	9			13	*C/O	1.6
1899	NY-N	88	293	38	78	8	1	0	19	15		.266	.313	.300	.613	73	-11	-10	97	66	33	.572	15			11	C/1	0.6
1900	NY-N	34	108	15	27	4	0	0	13	8		.250	.302	.287	.589	67	-5	-4	97	131	10	.494	1			0	C	-0.3
1901	NY-N	87	291	19	70	6	1	0	20	3		.241	.248	.268	.516	56	-18	-15	91	86	21	.380	3			2	C	-0.1
1902	Bos-A	65	222	19	52	5	7	0	12	13		.234	.277	.320	.596	67	-10	-10	99	56	20	.494	0			5	C	0.0
1903	NY-N	89	285	38	81	8	5	0	34	7		.284	.301	.347	.649	81	-6	-8	106	110	32	.544	5			1	C	0.0
1904	NY-N	86	287	29	57	5	1	1	15	14		.199	.236	.233	.469	44	-18	-19	105	80	18	.383	7			-6	C	-1.8
1905	StL-N	41	137	9	35	2	2	1	12	6		.255	.287	.321	.608	91	-3	-2	91	89	14	.510	2			-2	C	0.1
	Det-A	36	119	12	24	2	3	0	7	8		.202	.252	.269	.521	68	-4	-4	98	80	9	.442	2			1	C	0.0
1906	Det-A	50	153	15	37	4	2	0	10	12		.242	.297	.294	.591	80	-2	-3	108	81	15	.526	4			6	C	0.7
	Was-A	32	103	5	21	4	1	1	9	2		.204	.219	.291	.510	67	-5	-4	91	99	7	.427	3			0	C	0.0
	Yr	82	256	20	58	8	3	1	19	14		.227	.267	.293	.560	76	-7	-7	102	89	22	.485	7			6		0.7
1907	Was-A	72	207	11	53	5	0	0	17	12		.256	.297	.280	.577	95	-3	-1	90	105	19	.474	3			-7	C	-0.1
1908	Was-A	51	116	8	28	2	1	0	8	8		.241	.290	.276	.566	90	-2	-1	95	94	11	.534	7			1	C/1	0.4
Total	14	1073	3494	348	870	81	35	6	303	181	33	.249	.294	.297	.591	73	-127	-116	98	92	339	.513	83			27	*C/1O2	0.7
■ JACKIE WARNER Warner, John Joseph b: 8/1/43, Monrovia, Cal. BR/TR, 6', 180 lbs. Deb: 4/12/66																												
1966	Cal-A	45	123	22	26	4	1	7	16	9	55	.211	.265	.431	.696	97	-1	-1	99	91	14	.626	0	0	0	-3	O	-0.5
■ JACK WARNER Warner, John Ralph b: 8/29/03, Evansville, Ind. d: 3/13/86, Mt.Vernon, Ill. BR/TR, 5'9.5", 165 lbs. Deb: 9/24/25																												
1925	Det-A	10	39	7	13	0	0	0	2	3	6	.333	.381	.333	.714	83	-1	-1	99	52	5	.615	0	0	0	0	3	0.0
1926	Det-A	100	311	41	78	8	6	0	34	38	24	.251	.342	.315	.657	74	-12	-10	97	118	37	.629	8	4	0	1	3/S	0.0
1927	Det-A	139	559	78	149	22	9	1	45	47	45	.267	.330	.343	.674	69	-21	-27	108	74	64	.634	15	0	5	-5	*3	-2.0
1928	Det-A	75	206	33	44	4	4	0	13	16	15	.214	.274	.272	.545	44	-17	-17	99	80	16	.464	4	4	-1	2	3/S	-1.3
1929	Bro-N	17	62	3	17	2	0	0	4	7	6	.274	.348	.306	.654	67	-3	-3	94	73	7	.644	3			-1	S	0.0
1930	Bro-N	21	25	4	8	1	0	0	0	2	7	.320	.370	.360	.730	77	-1	-1	101	0	3	.706	1			0	/3	0.0
1931	Bro-N	9	4	2	2	0	0	0	0	0	1	.500	.600	.500	1.100	196	1	1	101	0	1	1.500	0			0	/S3	0.1
1933	Phi-N	107	340	31	76	15	1	0	22	28	33	.224	.285	.274	.558	51	-17	-24	118	89	26	.444	1			1	23/S	-1.8
Total	8	478	1546	199	387	52	20	1	120	142	137	.250	.319	.312	.630	64	-71	-82	106	85	159	.567	32	8		-1	3/2S	-5.0
■ HAL WARNOCK Warnock, Harold Charles b: 1/6/12, New York, N.Y. BL/TR, 6'2", 180 lbs. Deb: 9/02/35																												
1935	StL-A	6	7	1	2	2	0	0	0	0	3	.286	.286	.571	.857	110	0	0	107	0	1	.800	0	0	0	-1	/O	0.0
■ BENNIE WARREN Warren, Bennie Louis b: 3/2/12, Elk City, Okla. BR/TR, 6'1", 184 lbs. Deb: 9/13/39																												
1939	Phi-N	18	56	4	13	0	0	1	7	7	7	.232	.317	.286	.603	67	-3	-2	94	135	6	.523	0			-0	C	-0.1
1940	Phi-N	106	289	33	71	6	1	12	34	40	46	.246	.339	.398	.737	106	1	2	97	84	39	.692	1			5	C/1	1.1
1941	Phi-N	121	345	34	74	13	2	9	35	44	66	.214	.309	.342	.651	86	-8	-6	97	87	36	.579	0			7	*C	1.1
1942	Phi-N	90	225	19	47	6	3	7	20	24	36	.209	.288	.356	.644	93	-4	-3	94	73	22	.561	0			1	C/1	0.0
1946	NY-N	39	69	7	11	1	1	4	8	14	21	.159	.301	.377	.678	90	-1	-1	102	79	9	.690	0			0	C	0.0
1947	NY-N	3	5	0	1	0	0	0	0	0	1	.200	.200	.200	.400	6	-1	-1	101	0	0	.200	0			0	/C	0.0
Total	6	377	989	97	217	26	7	33	104	129	177	.219	.313	.360	.673	92	-15	-10	97	85	111	.635	1			12	C/1	2.1
■ BILL WARREN Warren, William Hackney "Hack" b: 2/11/1883, Missouri d: 1/28/60, Whiteville, Tenn. BR/TR, 5'8", 165 lbs. Deb: 4/30/14																												
1914	Ind-F	26	50	5	12	2	0	0	5	5	7	.240	.309	.280	.589	63	-2	-3	111	129	5	.553	2			1	C	0.0
1915	New-F	5	3	0	1	0	0	0	1	0	0	.333	.333	.333	.667	104	-0	0	94	361	0	.500	0			0	/C1	0.0
Total	2	31	53	5	13	2	0	0	6	5	7	.245	.310	.283	.593	65	-2	-3	110	141	6	.550	2			1	/C1	0.0
■ RABBIT WARSTLER Warstler, Harold Burton b: 9/13/03, N.Canton, Ohio d: 5/31/64, N.Canton, Ohio BR/TR, 5'7.5", 150 lbs. Deb: 7/24/30																												
1930	Bos-A	54	162	16	30	2	3	1	13	20	21	.185	.275	.253	.528	37	-16	-14	93	98	12	.455	0	2	-1	-2	S	-1.0
1931	Bos-A	66	181	20	44	5	3	0	10	15	27	.243	.308	.304	.612	65	-10	-8	94	60	17	.529	2	3	-1	-0	2S/3	-0.4
1932	Bos-A	115	388	26	82	15	5	0	34	22	43	.211	.259	.276	.535	40	-36	-34	97	106	28	.452	9	6	-1	**20**	*S	-0.5
1933	Bos-A	92	322	44	70	13	1	1	17	42	36	.217	.308	.273	.581	54	-20	-21	101	63	29	.516	2	4	-2	-8	S	-2.1
1934	Phi-A	117	419	56	99	19	3	1	36	51	30	.236	.321	.303	.624	63	-23	-22	97	94	45	.582	9	3	1	11	*2/S	-0.3
1935	Phi-A	138	496	62	124	20	7	3	59	56	53	.250	.326	.337	.663	72	-21	-20	100	116	58	.614	8	4	0	1	*2/3	-1.3
1936	Phi-A	66	236	27	59	8	6	1	24	36	16	.250	.354	.347	.701	73	-9	-9	101	97	32	.678	0	0	0	4	2	0.0
	Bos-N	74	304	27	64	6	0	0	17	22	33	.211	.266	.230	.496	37	-27	-25	95	83	19	.386	2			-3	S	-2.3
1937	Bos-N	149	555	57	124	20	0	3	36	51	62	.223	.291	.276	.567	60	-34	-27	90	85	48	.474	4			-9	*S	-2.4
1938	Bos-N	142	467	37	108	10	4	0	40	48	38	.231	.303	.270	.573	67	-25	-18	88	115	39	.473	3			-9	*S/2	-1.6
1939	Bos-N	114	342	34	83	11	3	0	24	24	31	.243	.292	.292	.585	63	-20	-17	92	88	29	.474	2			3	S23	-0.7
1940	Bos-N	33	57	6	12	0	0	0	4	10	5	.211	.328	.211	.539	52	-3	-3	99	124	4	.449	0			0	2/3S	0.0
	Chi-N	45	159	19	36	4	1	1	18	8	19	.226	.263	.283	.546	51	-11	-11	100	139	12	.429	1			3	S2	-0.3
	Yr	78	216	25	48	4	1	1	22	18	24	.222	.282	.264	.546	52	-14	-14	99	134	17	.444	1			3		-0.3

YEAR	TM/L	G	AB	R	H	2B	3B	HR	RBI	BB	SO	AVG	OBP	SLG	PRO	/A	BR	/A	PF	CHI	RC	TA	SB	CS	SBR	FR	POS	TPR
Total	11	1205	4088	431	935	133	36	11	332	405	414	.229	.300	.287	.587	59	-256	-229	95	96	372	.513	42	<u>22</u>		12	S2/3	-12.9
■ **CARL WARWICK**	Warwick, Carl Wayne b: 2/27/37, Dallas, Tex. BR/TL, 5'10", 170 lbs. Deb: 4/11/61																											
1961	LA-N	19	11	2	1	0	0	0	1	2	3	.091	.231	.091	.322	-10	-2	-2	102	403	0	.273	0	0	0	-4	O	-0.6
	StL-N	55	152	27	38	6	2	4	16	18	33	.250	.329	.395	.724	81	-2	-5	113	90	21	.698	3	0	1	1	O	-0.5
	Yr	74	163	29	39	6	2	4	17	20	36	.239	.322	.374	.697	76	-4	-6	110	176	21	.667	3	0	1	-4		-1.1
1962	StL-N	13	23	4	8	0	0	1	4	2	2	.348	.400	.478	.878	124	1	1	109	113	4	.833	2	0	1	-1	O	0.0
	Hou-N	130	477	63	124	17	1	16	60	38	77	.260	.315	.400	.715	97	-7	-3	93	101	59	.635	2	3	-1	-2	*O	-1.3
	Yr	143	500	67	132	17	1	17	64	40	79	.264	.319	.404	.723	98	-6	-2	94	103	64	.649	4	3	-1	-3		-1.3
1963	Hou-N	150	528	49	134	19	5	7	47	49	70	.254	.320	.348	.668	100	-5	-0	92	98	58	.579	3	3	-1	1	*O/1	-0.8
1964	StL-N	88	158	14	41	7	1	3	15	11	30	.259	.308	.373	.681	81	-2	-4	112	90	19	.605	2	0	1	-6	O	-1.0
1965	StL-N	50	77	3	12	2	1	0	6	4	18	.156	.198	.208	.405	13	-9	-9	107	155	3	.313	1	0	0	-3	O/1	-1.3
	Bal-A	9	14	3	0	0	0	0	0	3	2	.000	.176	.000	.176	-45	-3	-3	100	0	0	.214	0	0	0	-1	/O	-0.3
1966	Chi-N	16	22	3	5	0	0	0	0	0	6	.227	.227	.227	.455	27	-2	-2	100	0	1	.294	0	0	0	-1	O	-0.3
Total	6	530	1462	168	363	51	10	31	149	127	241	.248	.309	.360	.670	87	-30	-27	98	101	165	.605	13	6	0	-17	O/1	-6.1
■ **BILL WARWICK**	Warwick, Firmin Newton b: 11/26/1897, Philadelphia, Pa. d: 12/19/84, San Antonio, Tex. BR/TR, 6'0.5", 180 lbs. Deb: 7/18/21																											
1921	Pit-N	1	1	0	0	0	0	0	0	0	0	.000	.000	.000	.000	-97	-0	-0	103	0	0	.000	0	0	0	0	/C	0.0
1925	StL-N	13	41	8	12	1	2	1	6	5	5	.293	.370	.488	.857	115	1	1	102	93	7	.833	0	1	-1	0	C	0.1
1926	StL-N	9	14	0	5	0	0	0	2	0	2	.357	.357	.357	.714	91	-0	-0	102	138	2	.556	0			0	/C	0.1
Total	3	23	56	8	17	1	2	1	8	5	7	.304	.361	.446	.807	105	1	0	102	102	9	.750	0	<u>1</u>		1	/C	0.2
■ **JIMMY WASDELL**	Wasdell, James Charles b: 5/15/14, Cleveland, Ohio d: 8/6/83, New Port Richey, Fla. BL/TL, 5'11", 185 lbs. Deb: 9/03/37																											
1937	Was-A	32	110	13	28	4	4	2	12	7	13	.255	.299	.418	.717	84	-4	-3	94	79	13	.639	0	1	-1	1	1/O	-0.5
1938	Was-A	53	140	19	33	2	1	2	16	12	12	.236	.296	.307	.603	54	-11	-10	95	110	13	.550	5	2	0	0	1/O	-1.1
1939	Was-A	29	109	12	33	5	1	0	13	9	16	.303	.361	.367	.728	96	-2	-0	90	112	15	.679	3	1	0	-1	1	-0.3
1940	Was-A	10	35	3	3	1	0	0	0	2	7	.086	.135	.114	.249	-37	-7	-7	93	0	1	.188	0	0	0	-0	/1	-0.6
	Bro-N	77	230	35	64	14	4	3	37	18	24	.278	.333	.413	.746	97	1	-1	108	132	32	.694	4			-6	O1	-1.0
1941	Bro-N	94	265	39	79	14	3	4	48	16	15	.298	.345	.419	.764	111	4	3	103	141	40	.706	2			-8	O1	-0.8
1942	Pit-N	122	409	44	106	11	2	3	38	47	22	.259	.337	.318	.655	91	-3	-3	101	101	46	.574	1			-4	O/1	-1.0
1943	Pit-N	4	2	0	1	0	0	0	1	2	0	.500	.750	.500	1.250	253	1	1	104	361	1	3.000	0			0	H	0.1
	Phi-N	141	522	54	136	19	6	4	67	46	22	.261	.323	.343	.666	99	-5	-1	94	129	58	.584	6			-5	1O	-1.2
	Yr	145	524	54	137	19	6	4	68	48	22	.261	.326	.344	.669	99	-5	-1	94	138	59	.590	6			-5		-1.1
1944	Phi-N	133	451	47	125	20	3	3	40	45	17	.277	.344	.355	.699	97	-1	-1	100	87	55	.606	0			-8	*O/1	-1.9
1945	Phi-N	134	500	65	150	19	8	7	60	32	11	.300	.346	.412	.758	114	6	8	96	97	72	.695	7			-0	O1	0.2
1946	Phi-N	26	51	7	13	0	2	1	5	3	2	.255	.309	.392	.701	104	-0	-0	95	81	6	.600	0			-3	O/1	-0.3
	Cle-A	32	41	1	11	0	0	0	4	4	4	.268	.333	.268	.602	78	-2	-1	89	138	4	.500	1	0	0	-1	/1O	-0.2
1947	Cle-A	1	1	0	0	0	0	0	0	0	0	.000	.000	.000	.000	-99	-0	-0	96	0	0	.000	0	0	0	0	H	0.0
Total	11	888	2866	339	782	109	34	29	341	243	165	.273	.332	.365	.697	96	-24	-16	98	109	355	.637	29	<u>4</u>		-36	O1	-8.6
■ **LINK WASEM**	Wasem, Lincoln William b: 1/30/11, Birmingham, Ohio d: 3/6/79, S.Laguna, Cal. BR/TR, 5'9.5", 180 lbs. Deb: 5/05/37																											
1937	Bos-N	2	1	0	0	0	0	0	0	0	0	.000	.000	.000	.000	-99	-0	-0	90	0	0	.000	0			0	/C	0.0
■ **LIBE WASHBURN**	Washburn, Libeus b: 6/16/1874, Lyme, N.H. d: 3/22/40, Malone, N.Y. BB/TL, 5'10", 180 lbs. Deb: 5/30/02																											
1902	NY-N	6	9	1	4	0	0	0	0	2		.444	.545	.444	.990	210	1	1	100	0	3	1.400	1			1	/O	0.2
1903	Phi-N	8	18	1	3	0	0	0	1	1		.167	.211	.167	.377	10	-2	-2	92	107	1	.267	0			-0	/PO	0.0
Total	2	14	27	2	7	0	0	0	1	3		.259	.333	.259	.593	80	-1	-1	95	68	3	.550	1			1	/OP	0.2
■ **CLAUDELL WASHINGTON**	Washington, Claudell b: 8/31/54, Los Angeles, Cal. BL/TL, 6', 190 lbs. Deb: 7/05/74																											
1974	Oak-A	73	221	16	63	10	5	0	19	13	44	.285	.328	.376	.703	101	0	0	100	90	24	.599	6	8	-3	-1	DO	-0.4
1975	Oak-A	148	590	86	182	24	7	10	77	32	80	.308	.349	.424	.773	126	12	17	93	112	85	.752	40	15	3	0	*O	1.7
1976	Oak-A	134	490	65	126	20	6	5	53	30	90	.257	.304	.353	.657	92	-6	-6	100	111	49	.612	37	20	-1	1	*O/D	-0.8
1977	Tex-A	129	521	63	148	31	2	12	68	25	112	.284	.321	.420	.741	96	-1	-4	105	112	68	.685	21	8	2	3	*O/D	-0.2
1978	Tex-A	12	42	1	7	0	0	0	2	1	12	.167	.186	.167	.353	-0	-6	-5	96	113	1	.216	0	1	-1	-1	/OD	-0.7
	Chi-A	86	314	33	83	16	5	6	31	12	57	.264	.294	.404	.698	94	-3	-4	101	86	34	.597	5	5	-2	-1	O/D	-0.8
	Yr	98	356	34	90	16	5	6	33	13	69	.253	.281	.376	.657	83	-9	-9	100	90	35	.548	5	6	-2	-3		-1.5
1979	Chi-A	131	471	79	132	33	5	13	66	28	93	.280	.325	.454	.779	105	4	2	102	102	65	.733	19	11	-1	1	*O	-0.1
1980	Chi-A	32	90	15	26	4	2	1	12	5	19	.289	.333	.411	.744	106	0	1	97	117	11	.662	4	2	0	-2	O/D	-0.1
	NY-N	79	284	38	78	16	4	10	42	20	63	.275	.325	.465	.789	123	6	7	96	105	42	.787	17	5	2	4	O	1.1
1981	Atl-N	85	320	37	93	22	3	5	37	15	47	.291	.330	.425	.755	114	4	5	100	102	44	.699	12	6	0	-4	O	-0.1
1982	Atl-N	150	563	94	150	24	6	16	80	50	107	.266	.333	.416	.748	101	6	1	107	118	80	.748	33	10	4	-9	*O	-0.6
1983	Atl-N	134	496	75	138	24	8	9	44	35	103	.278	.326	.413	.739	98	1	-2	106	77	67	.721	31	9	4	-3	*O	-0.3
1984	Atl-N	120	416	62	119	21	2	17	61	59	77	.286	.376	.469	.845	124	21	16	110	99	73	.871	21	9	1	-9	*O	0.4
1985	Atl-N	122	398	62	110	14	6	15	43	40	66	.276	.344	.455	.799	114	11	8	106	76	61	.779	14	4	2	-15	O	-0.8
1986	Atl-N	40	137	17	37	11	0	5	14	14	26	.270	.338	.460	.798	115	3	3	102	73	18	.730	4	7	-3	-6	O	-0.6
	NY-A	54	135	19	32	5	0	6	16	7	33	.237	.285	.407	.692	84	-3	-3	103	87	16	.654	6	1	1	-5	O	-0.7
1987	NY-A	102	312	42	87	17	0	9	44	27	54	.279	.336	.420	.756	102	0	1	98	111	46	.734	10	1	2	4	OD	0.5
1988	NY-A	126	455	62	140	22	3	11	64	24	74	.308	.345	.442	.787	124	10	13	96	109	68	.738	15	6	1	-2	*O	1.0
Total	15	1757	6255	866	1751	314	64	150	773	437	1157	.280	.330	.423	.753	107	60	48	102	101	852	.735	295	128	12	-43	*O/D	-1.5
■ **HERB WASHINGTON**	Washington, Herbert Lee b: 11/16/51, Belzonia, Miss. BR/TR, 6', 170 lbs. Deb: 4/04/74																											
1974	Oak-A	92	0	29	0	0	0	0	0	0	0	—	—	—	—	—	0	0	100	—	852	1.813	29	16	-1	0	R	0.0
1975	Oak-A	13	0	4	0	0	0	0	0	0	0	—	—	—	—	—	0	0	93	—	852	2.000	2	1	0	0	R	0.0
Total	2	105	0	33	0	0	0	0	0	0	0	—	—	—	—	—	0	0	93	—	1704	1.824	31	17	-1	0		0.0
■ **LaRUE WASHINGTON**	Washington, La Rue b: 9/7/53, Long Beach, Cal. BR/TR, 6', 170 lbs. Deb: 9/07/78																											
1978	Tex-A	3	3	0	0	0	0	0	0	0	1	.000	.000	.000	.000	-99	-1	-1	96	0	0	.000	0	0	0	0	/2D	0.0
1979	Tex-A	25	18	5	5	0	0	0	2	4	0	.278	.409	.278	.687	89	0	0	100	154	3	.786	2	1	0	-3	O/3	-0.2
Total	2	28	21	5	5	0	0	0	2	4	1	.238	.360	.238	.598	66	-1	-1	99	135	3	.647	2	1	0	-3	/O23D	-0.2
■ **RON WASHINGTON**	Washington, Ronald b: 4/29/52, New Orleans, La. BR/TR, 5'11", 155 lbs. Deb: 9/10/77																											
1977	LA-N	10	19	4	7	0	0	0	1	0	2	.368	.400	.368	.768	108	0	0	100	57	2	.643	1	1	-0	0	S	0.2
1981	Min-A	28	84	8	19	3	1	0	5	4	14	.226	.270	.286	.555	57	-4	-5	105	82	7	.493	4	1	1	-3	S/O	-0.5
1982	Min-A	119	451	48	122	17	6	5	39	14	79	.271	.292	.368	.661	80	-13	-13	100	88	45	.534	3	3	-1	-19	S2/3	-2.3
1983	Min-A	99	317	28	78	7	3	4	26	22	50	.246	.297	.325	.622	68	-12	-15	105	88	30	.542	10	5	0	-18	S2/3D	-2.7
1984	Min-A	88	197	25	58	11	5	3	23	4	31	.294	.312	.447	.759	102	1	-0	106	95	26	.653	1	1	-0	-8	S/23D	-0.1
1985	Min-A	70	135	24	37	6	4	1	14	8	15	.274	.315	.400	.715	91	-1	-2	103	97	17	.657	5	1	1	-3	S2/31D	0.0
1986	Min-A	48	74	15	19	3	0	4	11	3	21	.257	.286	.459	.745	92	-0	-1	108	95	9	.667	1	2	-1	0	2D/S3	0.0
1987	Bal-A	26	79	7	16	3	1	1	6	1	15	.203	.213	.304	.516	36	-7	-7	98	89	4	.379	0	1	-1	1	3/2OSD	-0.6
1988	Cle-A	69	223	30	57	14	2	2	21	9	35	.256	.300	.363	.663	83	-5	-5	102	96	24	.573	3	3	-1	-9	S/32D	-1.2
Total	9	557	1579	189	413	64	22	20	146	65	262	.262	.295	.368	.663	79	-42	-48	103	90	165	.576	28	18	-2	-59	S2/3D01	-7.2
■ **GEORGE WASHINGTON**	Washington, Sloan Vernon "Vern" b: 6/4/07, Linden, Tex. d: 2/17/85, Linden, Tex. BL/TR, 5'11.5", 190 lbs. Deb: 4/17/35																											
1935	Chi-A	108	339	40	96	22	3	8	47	10	18	.283	.310	.437	.746	84	-6	-10	109	93	45	.667	1	0	0	-4	O	-1.4
1936	Chi-A	20	49	6	8	2	0	1	5	1	4	.163	.180	.265	.445	9	-7	-7	99	101	2	.341	0	0	0	-2	O	-0.8
Total	2	128	388	46	104	24	3	9	52	11	22	.268	.294	.415	.708	75	-14	-18	108	94	48	.620	1	0	0	-7	/O	-2.2
■ **U. L. WASHINGTON**	Washington, U L b: 10/27/53, Stringtown, Okla. BB/TR, 5'11", 175 lbs. Deb: 9/06/77																											
1977	KC-A	10	20	0	4	1	1	0	1	5	4	.200	.360	.350	.710	94	0	0	100	57	3	.813	1	0	0	-1	/S	0.1
1978	KC-A	69	129	10	34	2	1	0	9	10	20	.264	.317	.295	.611	71	-4	-5	102	94	12	.583	12	6	0	-7	S2/D	-0.6

YEAR	TM/L	G	AB	R	H	2B	3B	HR	RBI	BB	SO	AVG	OBP	SLG	PRO	/A	BR	/A	PF	CHI	RC	TA	SB	CS	SBR	FR	POS	TPR
1979	KC-A	101	268	32	68	12	5	2	25	20	44	.254	.306	.358	.664	74	-8	-10	105	94	30	.606	10	7	-1	-11	S2/3	-1.3
1980	KC-A	153	549	79	150	16	11	6	53	53	78	.273	.337	.375	.712	96	-3	-2	98	94	70	.666	20	7	2	-23	*S	-1.0
1981	KC-A	98	339	40	77	19	1	2	29	41	43	.227	.311	.307	.617	79	-9	-8	99	105	32	.558	10	10	-3	-19	S	-2.3
1982	KC-A	119	437	64	125	19	3	10	60	38	48	.286	.343	.412	.755	106	4	4	100	116	65	.746	23	7	3	-5	*S/D	1.1
1983	KC-A	144	547	76	129	19	6	5	41	48	78	.236	.299	.320	.619	69	-22	-23	101	89	59	.617	40	7	8	-7	*S/D	-1.3
1984	KC-A	63	170	18	38	6	0	1	10	14	31	.224	.283	.276	.559	56	-10	-10	99	80	13	.468	4	6	-2	2	S	-0.5
1985	Mon-N	68	193	24	48	9	4	1	17	15	33	.249	.303	.352	.655	88	-5	-3	94	95	21	.593	6	3	0	-1	2/S3	-0.2
1986	Pit-N	72	135	14	27	0	4	0	10	15	27	.200	.280	.259	.539	50	-9	-9	100	114	12	.514	6	0	2	2	S/2	0.0
1987	Pit-N	10	10	1	3	0	0	0	0	2	3	.300	.417	.300	.717	90	0	-0	104	0	2	.714	0	0	0	0	/S3	0.0
Total	11	907	2797	358	703	103	36	27	255	261	409	.251	.315	.343	.658	82	-67	-67	100	98	320	.630	132	53	8	-68	S2/3D	-6.0

■ **MARK WASINGER** Wasinger, Mark Thomas b: 8/4/61, Monterey, Cal. BR/TR, 6', 165 lbs. Deb: 5/27/86

YEAR	TM/L	G	AB	R	H	2B	3B	HR	RBI	BB	SO	AVG	OBP	SLG	PRO	/A	BR	/A	PF	CHI	RC	TA	SB	CS	SBR	FR	POS	TPR
1986	SD-N	3	8	0	0	0	0	0	1	0	2	.000	.000	.000	.000	-99	-2	-2	95	0	0	.000	0	0	0	0	/32	-0.1
1987	SF-N	44	80	16	22	3	0	1	3	8	14	.275	.341	.350	.691	87	-2	-1	96	39	10	.623	2	0	1	1	32/S	0.0
1988	SF-N	3	2	1	0	0	0	0	0	0	0	.000	.000	.000	.000	-99	-1	-0	94	0	0	.000	0	0	0	0	/23	0.0
Total	3	50	90	17	22	3	0	1	4	8	16	.244	.306	.311	.617	68	-4	-4	96	35	10	.559	2	0	1	1	/32S	-0.1

■ **FRED WATERMAN** Waterman, Frederick A. b: 1846, New York, N.Y. d: 12/16/1899, Cincinnati, Ohio 5'7.5", 148 lbs. Deb: 5/05/1871

YEAR	TM/L	G	AB	R	H	2B	3B	HR	RBI	BB	SO	AVG	OBP	SLG	PRO	/A	BR	/A	PF	CHI	RC	TA	SB	CS	SBR	FR	POS	TPR
1871	Oly-n	32	167	46	51							.305															*3/C	
1872	Oly-n	9	45	13	18							.400															/3C	
1873	Nat-n	15	81	20	27							.333															/SO3	
1875	Chi-n	5	23	2	6							.261															/32	
Total	4 n	61	316	81	102							.323															/32	

■ **JOHN WATHAN** Wathan, John David b: 10/4/49, Cedar Rapids, Iowa BR/TR, 6'2", 205 lbs. Deb: 5/26/76 MC

YEAR	TM/L	G	AB	R	H	2B	3B	HR	RBI	BB	SO	AVG	OBP	SLG	PRO	/A	BR	/A	PF	CHI	RC	TA	SB	CS	SBR	FR	POS	TPR
1976	KC-A	27	42	5	12	1	0	0	5	2	5	.286	.333	.310	.643	89	-1	-1	100	148	4	.485	0	2	-1	-1	C/1	-0.1
1977	KC-A	55	119	18	39	5	3	2	21	5	8	.328	.355	.471	.825	122	3	3	100	134	20	.778	2	0	1	-1	C/1D	0.4
1978	KC-A	67	190	19	57	10	1	2	28	3	12	.300	.325	.395	.720	99	-0	-1	102	137	23	.604	2	1	0	-2	1C	-0.3
1979	KC-A	90	199	26	41	7	3	2	28	7	24	.206	.233	.302	.535	41	-16	-18	105	163	13	.416	2	1	0	-0	1CD/O	-1.9
1980	KC-A	126	453	57	138	14	7	6	58	50	42	.305	.377	.406	.784	117	11	12	98	114	69	.754	17	3	3	1	CO1	1.7
1981	KC-A	89	301	24	76	9	3	1	19	19	23	.252	.301	.312	.614	78	-9	-8	99	77	27	.525	11	6	-0	-6	CO/1	-1.1
1982	KC-A	121	448	79	121	11	3	3	51	48	46	.270	.343	.328	.671	85	-7	-7	100	138	49	.644	36	9	5	-10	*C/1	-0.5
1983	KC-A	128	437	49	107	18	3	2	32	27	56	.245	.290	.314	.604	65	-20	-21	101	87	40	.555	28	7	4	5	C1/O	-0.8
1984	KC-A	97	171	17	31	7	1	2	10	21	34	.181	.271	.269	.540	50	-11	-11	99	77	12	.480	6	6	-2	-1	C1/OD	-1.2
1985	KC-A	60	145	11	34	8	1	1	9	17	15	.234	.319	.324	.643	75	-4	-5	102	71	15	.569	1	1	-0	4	C/1D	0.1
Total	10	860	2505	305	656	90	25	21	261	199	265	.262	.320	.343	.663	83	-55	-57	100	111	271	.623	105	36	10	-11	C1/OD	-3.7

■ **DAVE WATKINS** Watkins, David Roger b: 3/15/44, Owensboro, Ky. BR/TR, 5'10", 185 lbs. Deb: 4/09/69

YEAR	TM/L	G	AB	R	H	2B	3B	HR	RBI	BB	SO	AVG	OBP	SLG	PRO	/A	BR	/A	PF	CHI	RC	TA	SB	CS	SBR	FR	POS	TPR
1969	Phi-N	69	148	17	26	2	1	4	12	22	53	.176	.291	.284	.574	63	-7	-7	98	89	13	.535	2	3	-1	-0	C/O3	-0.5

■ **GEORGE WATKINS** Watkins, George Archibald b: 6/4/1900, Freesrone Co., Tex d: 6/1/70, Houston, Tex. BL/TR, 6', 175 lbs. Deb: 4/15/30

YEAR	TM/L	G	AB	R	H	2B	3B	HR	RBI	BB	SO	AVG	OBP	SLG	PRO	/A	BR	/A	PF	CHI	RC	TA	SB	CS	SBR	FR	POS	TPR
1930	StL-N	119	391	85	146	32	7	17	87	24	49	.373	.415	.621	1.037	139	28	25	105	102	96	1.127	5			-1	O1/2	1.5
1931	StL-N	131	503	93	145	30	13	13	51	31	66	.288	.336	.477	.813	109	9	5	107	67	81	.813	15			-1	*O	-0.1
1932	StL-N	127	458	67	143	35	3	9	63	45	46	.312	.384	.461	.844	126	18	18	100	100	84	.895	18			-12	*O	-0.2
1933	StL-N	138	525	66	146	24	5	5	62	39	62	.278	.342	.371	.713	102	3	2	102	118	71	.666	11			-0	*O	-0.6
1934	NY-N	105	296	38	73	18	3	6	33	24	34	.247	.316	.389	.704	89	-5	-5	98	89	40	.659	2			-12	O	-2.0
1935	Phi-N	150	600	80	162	25	5	17	76	40	78	.270	.320	.413	.733	84	-5	-16	114	88	82	.661	3			5	*O	-1.6
1936	Phi-N	19	70	7	17	4	0	2	5	5	13	.243	.293	.386	.679	75	-2	-3	108	55	8	.630	2			-3	O	-0.6
	Bro-N	105	364	54	93	24	6	4	43	38	34	.255	.334	.387	.722	89	-3	-6	105	100	51	.690	5			-5	O	-1.4
	Yr	124	434	61	110	28	6	6	48	43	47	.253	.328	.387	.715	87	-5	-8	105	93	59	.682	7			-9		-2.0
Total	7	894	3207	490	925	192	42	73	420	246	382	.288	.347	.443	.790	105	43	21	105	94	513	.775	61			-30	O/12	-5.0

■ **ED WATKINS** Watkins, James Edward b: 6/21/1877, Philadelphia, Pa. d: 3/29/33, Kelvin, Ariz. Deb: 9/06/02

YEAR	TM/L	G	AB	R	H	2B	3B	HR	RBI	BB	SO	AVG	OBP	SLG	PRO	/A	BR	/A	PF	CHI	RC	TA	SB	CS	SBR	FR	POS	TPR
1902	Phi-N	1	3	0	0	0	0	0	0	1		.000	.250	.000	.250	-19	-0	-0	105	0	0	.333	0			-0	/O	0.0

■ **BILL WATKINS** Watkins, William Henry b: 5/5/1858, Brantford, Ont., Can d: 6/9/37, Port Huron, Mich. 5'10", 156 lbs. Deb: 8/01/1884 M

YEAR	TM/L	G	AB	R	H	2B	3B	HR	RBI	BB	SO	AVG	OBP	SLG	PRO	/A	BR	/A	PF	CHI	RC	TA	SB	CS	SBR	FR	POS	TPR
1884	Ind-a	34	127	16	26	4	0	0		5		.205	.241	.236	.477	61	-5	-5	96	0	7	.356				0	3/2SM	-0.3

■ **NEAL WATLINGTON** Watlington, Julius Neal b: 12/25/22, Yanceyville, N.C. BL/TR, 6', 195 lbs. Deb: 7/10/53

YEAR	TM/L	G	AB	R	H	2B	3B	HR	RBI	BB	SO	AVG	OBP	SLG	PRO	/A	BR	/A	PF	CHI	RC	TA	SB	CS	SBR	FR	POS	TPR
1953	Phi-A	21	44	4	7	1	0	0	3	3	8	.159	.213	.182	.395	7	-6	-6	102	139	2	.282	0	1	-1	2	/C	-0.4

■ **ART WATSON** Watson, Arthur Stanhope "Watty" b: 1/11/1884, Jeffersonville, Ind. d: 5/9/50, Buffalo, N.Y. BL/TR, 5'10", 175 lbs. Deb: 5/19/14

YEAR	TM/L	G	AB	R	H	2B	3B	HR	RBI	BB	SO	AVG	OBP	SLG	PRO	/A	BR	/A	PF	CHI	RC	TA	SB	CS	SBR	FR	POS	TPR
1914	Bro-F	22	46	7	13	4	1	1	3	1	6	.283	.298	.478	.776	119	1	1	101	43	7	.697	0			-0	C	0.1
1915	Bro-F	9	19	4	5	0	3	0	1	3	0	.263	.364	.579	.943	181	2	2	98	33	4	1.000	0			0	/C	0.2
	Buf-F	22	30	6	14	1	0	1	13	0	0	.467	.467	.600	1.067	215	4	4	100	223	9	1.125	0			0	/CO	0.4
	Yr	31	49	10	19	1	3	1	14	3	0	.388	.423	.592	1.015	200	6	6	99	169	13	1.067	0			0		0.6
Total	2	53	95	17	32	5	4	2	17	4	6	.337	.364	.537	.900	161	6	6	100	95	19	.873	0			-0	/CO	0.7

■ **JOHNNY WATSON** Watson, John Thomas b: 1/16/08, Tazewell, Va. d: 4/29/65, Huntington, W.Va. BL/TR, 6', 175 lbs. Deb: 9/26/30

YEAR	TM/L	G	AB	R	H	2B	3B	HR	RBI	BB	SO	AVG	OBP	SLG	PRO	/A	BR	/A	PF	CHI	RC	TA	SB	CS	SBR	FR	POS	TPR
1930	Det-A	4	12	1	3	2	0	0	3	1	2	.250	.308	.417	.724	78	-0	-0	105	199	2	.667	0	0	0	0	/S	0.0

■ **BOB WATSON** Watson, Robert Jose "Bull" b: 4/10/46, Los Angeles, Cal. BR/TR, 6'0.5", 201 lbs. Deb: 9/09/66 C

YEAR	TM/L	G	AB	R	H	2B	3B	HR	RBI	BB	SO	AVG	OBP	SLG	PRO	/A	BR	/A	PF	CHI	RC	TA	SB	CS	SBR	FR	POS	TPR
1966	Hou-N	1	1	0	0	0	0	0	0	0	0	.000	.000	.000	.000	-99	-0	-0	97	0	0	.000	0	0	0	0	H	0.0
1967	Hou-N	6	14	1	3	0	0	1	2	0	3	.214	.214	.429	.643	85	-0	-0	94	92	1	.500	0	0	0	0	/1	0.0
1968	Hou-N	45	140	13	32	7	0	2	8	13	32	.229	.299	.321	.620	87	-2	-2	99	66	13	.526	1	0	0	-7	O	-1.2
1969	Hou-N	20	40	3	11	3	0	0	3	6	5	.275	.396	.350	.746	109	1	1	102	86	6	.759	0	0	0	-0	/O1C	0.0
1970	Hou-N	97	327	48	89	19	2	11	61	24	59	.272	.330	.443	.773	112	1	4	94	133	46	.699	1	1	-0	-2	1/CO	-0.4
1971	Hou-N	129	468	49	135	17	3	9	67	41	56	.288	.348	.395	.744	119	6	10	93	131	62	.651	0	3	-2	-11	O1	-0.8
1972	Hou-N	147	548	74	171	27	4	16	86	53	83	.312	.381	.464	.844	131	28	24	106	119	100	.823	1	1	-0	-10	*O/1	0.7
1973	Hou-N	158	573	97	179	24	3	16	94	85	73	.312	.405	.449	.853	143	31	35	95	131	104	.834	1	4	-2	-3	*O1/C	2.3
1974	Hou-N	150	524	69	156	19	4	11	67	60	61	.298	.373	.412	.785	122	14	16	98	106	80	.731	3	4	-2	-13	*O1	-0.5
1975	Hou-N	132	485	67	157	27	1	18	85	40	50	.324	.379	.495	.874	149	25	29	94	114	87	.831	3	5	-2	-4	*1/O	1.6
1976	Hou-N	157	585	76	183	31	3	16	102	62	64	.313	.382	.458	.841	160	29	39	86	132	102	.808	3	3	-1	-4	*1	2.7
1977	Hou-N	151	554	77	160	38	6	22	110	57	69	.289	.362	.498	.861	139	21	27	93	131	102	.858	5	0	2	10	*1	3.1
1978	Hou-N	139	461	51	133	25	4	14	79	51	57	.289	.364	.451	.816	134	17	20	95	128	72	.767	3	1	0	5	*1	2.2
1979	Hou-N	49	163	15	39	4	0	3	18	16	23	.239	.307	.319	.626	79	-6	-4	90	119	16	.535	0	0	0	-1	1	-0.7
	Bos-A	84	312	48	105	19	4	13	53	29	33	.337	.402	.548	.950	143	23	20	107	99	66	.950	3	2	-0	3	1D	1.9
1980	NY-A	130	469	62	144	25	3	13	68	48	56	.307	.373	.456	.829	127	17	17	99	107	75	.766	2	1	0	0	*1D	1.1
1981	NY-A	59	156	15	33	3	3	6	12	24	17	.212	.317	.385	.701	101	0	0	100	60	17	.632	0	0	0	2	1/D	0.1
1982	NY-A	7	17	3	4	3	0	0	3	3	0	.235	.350	.412	.762	112	0	0	96	171	2	.714	0	0	0	-0	/1D	0.0
	Atl-N	57	114	16	28	3	1	5	22	14	20	.246	.328	.421	.749	101	1	0	107	137	15	.692	1	1	-0	1	1/O	0.0
1983	Atl-N	65	149	14	46	9	0	6	37	18	23	.309	.383	.490	.873	133	8	7	106	161	26	.827	0	2	-1	-0	1	0.4
1984	Atl-N	49	85	4	18	4	0	2	12	9	12	.212	.287	.329	.617	67	-3	-4	110	138	8	.536	0	0	0	-0	1	-0.4
Total	19	1832	6185	802	1826	307	41	184	989	653	796	.295	.367	.447	.814	130	213	239	97	120	1001	.796	27	28	-9	-35	*1O/DC	12.1

■ **ALLIE WATT** Watt, Albert Bailey b: 12/12/1899, Philadelphia, Pa. d: 3/15/68, Norfolk, Va. BR/TR, 5'8", 154 lbs. Deb: 10/03/20

YEAR	TM/L	G	AB	R	H	2B	3B	HR	RBI	BB	SO	AVG	OBP	SLG	PRO	/A	BR	/A	PF	CHI	RC	TA	SB	CS	SBR	FR	POS	TPR
1920	Was-A	1	1	0	1	1	0	0	1	0	0	1.000	1.000	2.000	3.000	717	1	1	95	176	2	—	0	0	0	0	/2	0.1

■ **JOHNNY WATWOOD** Watwood, John Clifford "Lefty" b: 8/17/05, Alexander City, Ala. d: 3/1/80, Goodwater, Ala. BL/TL, 6'1", 186 lbs. Deb: 4/16/29

YEAR	TM/L	G	AB	R	H	2B	3B	HR	RBI	BB	SO	AVG	OBP	SLG	PRO	/A	BR	/A	PF	CHI	RC	TA	SB	CS	SBR	FR	POS	TPR
1929	Chi-A	85	278	33	84	12	6	2	28	22	21	.302	.355	.410	.766	102	-1	1	95	80	41	.726	6	3	0	1	O	-0.1
1930	Chi-A	133	427	75	129	25	4	2	51	52	35	.302	.382	.393	.775	94	-0	-2	103	97	66	.748	5	7	-3	0	1O	-1.1

YEAR	TM/L	G	AB	R	H	2B	3B	HR	RBI	BB	SO	AVG	OBP	SLG	PRO	/A	BR	/A	PF	CHI	RC	TA	SB	CS	SBR	FR	POS	TPR
1931	Chi-A	128	367	51	104	16	6	1	47	56	30	.283	.380	.368	.748	105	1	5	92	112	56	.756	9	3	1	-3	*O/1	-0.3
1932	Chi-A	13	49	5	15	2	0	0	0	1	3	.306	.333	.347	.680	88	-2	-1	87	0	6	.559	0	0	0	-1	O	-0.2
	Bos-A	95	266	26	66	11	0	0	30	20	11	.248	.301	.289	.590	55	-18	-17	97	130	24	.510	7	4	-0	-1	O1	-2.0
	Yr	108	315	31	81	13	0	0	30	21	14	.257	.306	.298	.604	60	-20	-18	96	115	30	.517	7	4	-0	-3		-2.2
1933	Bos-A	13	30	2	4	0	0	0	2	3	3	.133	.212	.133	.345	-7	-5	-5	101	167	1	.269	0	0	0	-1	/O	-0.5
1939	Phi-N	2	6	0	1	0	0	0	0	0	0	.167	.167	.167	.333	-11	-1	-1	94	0	0	.200	0			0	/1	0.0
Total	6	469	1423	192	403	66	16	5	158	154	103	.283	.356	.363	.718	89	-26	-19	97	102	193	.678	27	17		-5	O/1	-4.2
■ **BOB WAY**	Way, Robert Clinton b: 4/2/06, Emlenton, Pa. d: 6/20/74, Pittsburgh, Pa. BR/TR, 5'10.5", 168 lbs. Deb: 4/12/27																											
1927	Chi-A	5	3	3	1	0	0	0	1	0	0	.333	.333	.333	.667	72	-0	-0	102	333	0	.500	0	0	0	0	/2	0.0
■ **ROY WEATHERLY**	Weatherly, Cyril Roy "Stormy" b: 2/25/15, Warren, Tex. BL/TR, 5'6.5", 170 lbs. Deb: 6/27/36																											
1936	Cle-A	84	349	64	117	28	6	8	53	16	29	.335	.364	.519	.883	110	7	4	106	89	61	.833	3	8	-4	5	O	0.2
1937	Cle-A	53	134	19	27	4	0	5	13	6	14	.201	.246	.343	.590	48	-12	-11	98	73	11	.509	1	1	-0	-4	O/3	-1.5
1938	Cle-A	83	210	32	55	14	3	2	18	14	14	.262	.308	.386	.694	74	-10	-9	99	70	24	.644	8	5	-1	2	O	-0.6
1939	Cle-A	95	323	43	100	16	6	1	32	19	23	.310	.348	.406	.754	94	-4	-3	98	81	47	.692	7	2	1	-7	O	-1.0
1940	Cle-A	135	578	90	175	35	11	12	59	27	26	.303	.335	.464	.799	112	2	7	93	62	88	.726	9	8	-2	3	*O	0.0
1941	Cle-A	102	363	59	105	21	5	3	37	32	20	.289	.350	.399	.750	97	-1	-2	101	87	52	.675	2	5	-2	-1	O	-0.9
1942	Cle-A	128	473	61	122	23	7	5	39	35	25	.258	.310	.368	.678	99	-7	-3	92	74	54	.594	8	13	-5	0	*O	-1.5
1943	NY-A	77	280	37	74	8	3	7	28	18	9	.264	.311	.389	.700	108	0	1	96	80	34	.614	4	7	-3	-4	O	-0.7
1946	NY-A	2	2	0	1	0	0	0	0	0	0	.500	.500	.500	1.000	179	0	0	100	0	1	1.000	0	0	0	0	H	0.0
1950	NY-N	52	69	10	18	3	3	0	11	13	10	.261	.378	.391	.769	105	1	1	98	157	10	.741	0			-1	O	0.0
Total	10	811	2781	415	794	152	44	43	290	180	170	.286	.331	.418	.749	99	-25	-14	97	78	382	.683	42	49		-6	O/3	-6.0
■ **ART WEAVER**	Weaver, Arthur Coggshall "Six O'Clock" b: 4/7/1879, Wichita, Kan. d: 3/23/17, Denver, Colo. TR , 6'1", Deb: 9/14/02																											
1902	StL-N	11	33	2	6	2	0	0	3	1		.182	.206	.242	.448	42	-2	-2	95	130	2	.333	0			0	C	0.0
1903	StL-N	16	49	4	12	0	0	0	5	4		.245	.302	.245	.547	60	-2	-2	96	134	4	.459	1			2	C	0.1
	Pit-N	16	48	8	11	0	1	0	3	2		.229	.260	.271	.531	50	-3	-3	105	74	3	.405	0			-1	C/1	-0.2
	Yr	32	97	12	23	0	1	0	8	6		.237	.282	.258	.539	55	-5	-5	101	108	8	.432	1			2		-0.1
1905	StL-A	28	92	5	11	2	1	0	3	1		.120	.129	.163	.292	-7	-11	-10	91	71	2	.198	0			3	C	-0.4
1908	Chi-A	15	35	1	7	1	0	0	1	1		.200	.222	.229	.451	51	-2	-2	94	47	2	.321	0			-1	C	-0.1
Total	4	86	257	20	47	5	2	0	15	9		.183	.211	.218	.428	33	-21	-19	96	88	13	.314	1			4	/C1	-0.6
■ **BUCK WEAVER**	Weaver, George Daniel b: 8/18/1890, Pottstown, Pa. d: 1/31/56, Chicago, Ill. BB/TR, 5'11", 170 lbs. Deb: 4/11/12																											
1912	Chi-A	147	523	55	117	21	8	1	43	9		.224	.245	.300	.546	56	-32	-32	99	92	41	.453	12			-3	*S	-2.0
1913	Chi-A	151	533	51	145	17	8	4	52	15	60	.272	.302	.356	.659	97	-8	-4	95	93	61	.601	20			**36**	*S	4.7
1914	Chi-A	136	541	64	133	20	9	2	28	20	40	.246	.279	.327	.606	80	-14	-16	103	55	47	.505	14	20	-8	5	*S	-0.7
1915	Chi-A	148	563	83	151	18	11	3	49	32	58	.268	.316	.355	.671	103	-2	-0	98	77	68	.609	24	20	-5	0	*S	0.8
1916	Chi-A	151	582	78	132	27	6	3	38	30	48	.227	.280	.309	.589	71	-18	-24	108	63	57	.529	22	13	-1	-6	3S	-2.2
1917	Chi-A	118	447	64	127	16	5	3	32	27	29	.284	.332	.362	.694	115	5	6	98	65	61	.666	19			-7	*3S	0.5
1918	Chi-A	112	420	37	126	12	5	0	29	11	24	.300	.323	.352	.675	103	-0	-0	101	73	53	.619	20			-2	S3/2	0.5
1919	Chi-A	140	571	89	169	33	9	3	75	11	21	.296	.315	.401	.716	96	-3	-6	105	110	77	.664	22			-4	3S	0.0
1920	Chi-A	151	630	104	210	35	8	2	75	28	23	.333	.367	.424	.791	114	7	11	96	93	94	.732	19	17	-5	-15	*3S	0.2
Total	9	1254	4810	625	1310	199	69	21	421	183	303	.272	.307	.356	.663	92	-65	-65	100	81	558	.595	172	70		4	S3/2	1.8
■ **JIM WEAVER**	Weaver, James Francis b: 10/10/59, Kingston, N.Y. BL/TL, 6'3", 190 lbs. Deb: 4/10/85																											
1985	Det-A	12	7	2	1	1	0	0	0	1	4	.143	.250	.286	.536	44	-1	-1	106	0	0	.429	0	1	-1	-2	/OD	-0.2
1987	Sea-A	7	4	2	0	0	0	0	0	2	3	.000	.333	.000	.333	0	-0	-1	103	0	0	.600	1	1	-0	0	/O	0.0
Total	2	19	11	4	1	1	0	0	0	3	7	.091	.286	.182	.468	29	-1	-1	105	0	0	.500	1	2	-1	-2	/OD	-0.2
■ **FARMER WEAVER**	Weaver, William B. b: 3/23/1865, Parkersburg, W.Va. d: 1/23/43, Akron, Ohio Deb: 1888																											
1888	Lou-a	26	112	12	28	1	1	0	8	3		.250	.276	.277	.553	88	-2	-1	91	68	12	.560	12			0	O	0.0
1889	Lou-a	124	499	62	145	17	6	0	60	40	22	.291	.352	.349	.700	106	2	6	96	95	70	.684	21			-3	*O/C32	-0.1
1890	Lou-a	130	557	101	161	27	9	3		29		.289	.332	.386	.718	106	8	1	107	0	89	.747	45			0	*O/S3	-0.4
1891	Lou-a	135	565	76	160	25	7	1	55	33	23	.283	.335	.358	.692	112	-0	9	90	69	80	.681	30			14	*O/C	1.5
1892	Lou-N	138	551	58	140	15	4	0	57	40	17	.254	.315	.296	.611	94	-8	-2	92	103	62	.589	30			-8	*OC1	-1.2
1893	Lou-N	106	439	79	128	17	7	2	49	27	12	.292	.348	.376	.724	98	-4	-1	96	83	65	.707	17			4	OC	0.0
1894	Lou-N	64	244	19	54	5	2	3	24	7	11	.221	.249	.295	.544	36	-28	-22	88	83	19	.442	3			2	OC1/2	-1.7
	Pit-N	30	115	16	40	7	2	0	24	6	1	.348	.405	.443	.848	113	1	3	94	132	23	.880	4			0	CS/3O	0.2
	Yr	94	359	35	94	12	4	3	48	13	12	.262	.301	.343	.643	62	-26	-19	90	100	40	.566	7			2		-1.5
Total	7	753	3082	423	856	114	38	9	277	185	86	.278	.330	.348	.678	98	-31	-7	95	72	420	.662	162			10	O/C1S32	-1.7
■ **SKEETER WEBB**	Webb, James Laverne b: 11/4/09, Meridian, Miss. d: 7/8/86, Meridian, Miss. BR/TR, 5'9.5", 150 lbs. Deb: 7/20/32																											
1932	StL-N	1	0	0	0	0	0	0	0	0	0	—	—	—	—	—	0	0	100	—	—	—	0			0	/S	0.0
1938	Cle-A	20	58	11	16	2	0	0	2	8	7	.276	.364	.310	.674	71	-2	-2	99	38	7	.643	1	0	0	-0	S/32	0.0
1939	Cle-A	81	269	28	71	14	1	2	26	15	24	.264	.305	.346	.651	68	-14	-13	98	89	28	.537	1	1	-0	-3	S	-0.7
1940	Chi-A	84	334	33	79	11	2	1	29	30	33	.237	.299	.290	.590	52	-23	-24	104	111	30	.491	3	6	-3	-12	2/S3	-3.3
1941	Chi-A	29	84	7	16	2	0	0	6	3	9	.190	.227	.214	.442	19	-10	-9	94	118	4	.333	1	0	0	-2	2/S3	-0.8
1942	Chi-A	32	94	5	16	2	1	0	4	4	13	.170	.204	.213	.417	17	-10	-10	99	70	4	.309	1	2	-1	-0	2	-1.0
1943	Chi-A	58	213	15	50	5	2	0	22	6	19	.235	.256	.277	.533	55	-12	-13	101	139	14	.409	5	4	-1	1	2	-1.0
1944	Chi-A	139	513	44	108	19	6	0	30	20	39	.211	.242	.271	.513	46	-37	-37	100	79	33	.400	7	3	0	-2	*S/2	-3.1
1945	Det-A	118	407	43	81	12	2	0	21	30	35	.199	.254	.238	.492	41	-30	-32	106	80	25	.395	8	7	-2	10	*S2	-2.0
1946	Det-A	64	169	12	37	1	1	0	17	9	18	.219	.258	.237	.495	36	-14	-15	108	162	10	.371	3	3	-1	0	2/S	-1.2
1947	Det-A	50	79	13	16	3	0	0	6	7	9	.203	.267	.241	.508	40	-6	-7	104	116	6	.460	3	0	1	-2	2/S	-0.5
1948	Phi-A	23	54	5	8	2	0	0	3	0	9	.148	.148	.185	.333	-12	-9	-9	102	101	1	.208	0	0	0	0	/2S	-0.7
Total	12	699	2274	216	498	73	15	3	166	132	215	.219	.263	.268	.531	46	-167	-172	102	98	583	.431	33	26		-9	S2/3	-14.3
■ **EARL WEBB**	Webb, William Earl b: 9/17/1898, Bon Air, Tenn. d: 5/23/65, Jamestown, Tenn. BL/TR, 6'1", 185 lbs. Deb: 8/13/25																											
1925	NY-N	4	3	0	0	0	0	0	0	1	1	.000	.250	.000	.250	-31	-1	-1	99	0	0	.333	0	0	0	0	H	0.0
1927	Chi-N	102	332	58	100	18	4	14	52	48	31	.301	.391	.506	.897	138	18	18	100	87	66	.948	3			2	O	1.6
1928	Chi-N	62	140	22	35	7	3	3	23	14	17	.250	.318	.407	.725	93	-3	-2	95	124	18	.676	0			1	O	-0.1
1930	Bos-A	127	449	61	145	30	6	16	66	44	56	.323	.385	.523	.908	137	18	23	93	79	91	.925	2	1	0	-8	*O	1.0
1931	Bos-A	151	589	96	196	**67**	3	14	103	70	51	.333	.404	.528	.932	153	37	42	94	93	127	.970	2	2	-1	-3	*O	2.7
1932	Bos-A	52	192	23	54	9	1	5	27	25	15	.281	.364	.417	.781	105	1	2	97	101	30	.761	0	0	0	-5	O/1	-0.4
	Det-A	88	338	49	97	19	8	3	51	39	18	.287	.361	.417	.778	99	1	-0	102	121	52	.748	1	1	-0	-2	O	-0.5
	Yr	140	530	72	151	28	9	8	78	64	33	.285	.362	.417	.779	101	1	1	100	114	82	.753	1	1	-0	-7		-0.9
1933	Det-A	6	11	1	3	0	0	0	3	3	0	.273	.429	.273	.701	84	0	-0	107	334	2	.750	0	0	0	-1	/O	0.0
	Chi-A	58	107	16	31	5	0	1	8	16	13	.290	.382	.364	.747	98	0	0	101	63	16	.724	0	0	0	-3	O1	-0.3
	Yr	64	118	17	34	5	0	1	11	19	13	.288	.387	.356	.743	97	0	0	101	94	18	.726	0	0	0	-3		-0.3
Total	7	650	2161	326	661	155	25	56	333	260	202	.306	.381	.478	.859	127	72	83	97	96	402	.867	8	4		-18	O/1	4.0
■ **BILL WEBB**	Webb, William Joseph b: 6/25/1895, Chicago, Ill. d: 1/12/43, Chicago, Ill. BR/TR, 5'10", 161 lbs. Deb: 9/17/17 C																											
1917	Pit-N	5	15	1	3	0	0	0	0	2	3	.200	.294	.200	.494	53	-1	-1	100	0	1	.417	0			-1	/2S	0.0
■ **JOE WEBBER**	Webber, Joseph Edward b: 1861, Hamilton, Ont., Canada d: 12/15/21, Hamilton, Ont., Can Deb: 7/22/1884																											
1884	Ind-a	3	8	0	0	0	0	0		0		.000	.111	.000	.111	-62	-1	-1	96	0	0	.125				0	/C	0.0
■ **HARRY WEBER**	Weber, Harry b: Indianapolis, Ind. Deb: 5/30/1884																											
1884	Det-N	2	8	0	0	0	0	0	0	0	2	.000	.000	.000	.000	-99	-2	-2	94	0	0	.000				0	/O	-0.1

YEAR	TM/L	G	AB	R	H	2B	3B	HR	RBI	BB	SO	AVG	OBP	SLG	PRO	/A	BR	/A	PF	CHI	RC	TA	SB	CS	SBR	FR	POS	TPR
■ **MITCH WEBSTER** Webster, Mitchell Dean b: 5/16/59, Larned, Kan. BB/TL, 6', 185 lbs. Deb: 9/02/83																												
1983	Tor-A	11	11	2	2	0	0	0	0	1	1	.182	.250	.182	.432	19	-1	-1	108	0	1	.333	0	0	0	-2	/OD	-0.3
1984	Tor-A	26	22	9	5	2	1	0	4	1	7	.227	.261	.409	.670	81	-1	-1	102	177	2	.556	0	0	0	-2	O/1D	-0.2
1985	Tor-A	4	1	0	0	0	0	0	0	0	0	.000	.000	.000	.000	-99	-0	-0	101	0	0	.000	0	1	-1	-1	/OD	-0.1
	Mon-N	74	212	32	58	8	2	11	30	20	33	.274	.336	.486	.822	136	7	9	94	88	33	.831	15	9	-1	2	O	0.9
1986	Mon-N	151	576	89	167	31	**13**	8	49	57	78	.290	.358	.431	.788	119	13	15	98	76	90	.797	36	15	2	5	*O	1.9
1987	Mon-N	156	588	101	165	30	8	15	63	70	95	.281	.363	.435	.798	104	10	5	106	89	99	.831	33	10	4	-3	*O	0.0
1988	Chi-N	70	264	36	70	11	6	4	26	19	50	.265	.322	.398	.719	101	2	0	104	94	35	.685	10	4	1	-1	O	-0.1
	Mon-N	81	259	33	66	5	2	2	13	36	37	.255	.357	.313	.669	89	-0	-2	106	61	31	.650	12	10	-2	2	O	-0.4
	Yr	151	523	69	136	16	8	6	39	55	87	.260	.340	.356	.695	95	1	-2	105	77	67	.671	22	14	-2	1		-0.5
Total	6	573	1933	302	533	87	32	40	185	204	301	.276	.350	.416	.766	108	29	24	102	82	291	.780	106	49	2	0	O/D1	1.7
■ **RAY WEBSTER** Webster, Ramon Alberto b: 8/31/42, Colon, Panama BL/TL, 6', 185 lbs. Deb: 4/11/67																												
1967	KC-A	122	360	41	92	15	4	11	51	32	44	.256	.320	.411	.731	115	6	6	100	118	46	.665	5	3	-0	-1	1O	-0.2
1968	Oak-A	66	196	17	42	11	1	3	23	12	24	.214	.260	.327	.586	78	-6	-6	98	135	16	.497	3	0	1	-1	1	-0.8
1969	Oak-A	64	77	5	20	0	1	1	13	12	8	.260	.367	.325	.691	103	-0	1	92	186	9	.633	0	0	0	0	1	0.0
1970	SD-N	95	116	12	30	3	0	2	11	11	12	.259	.323	.336	.659	81	-4	-3	95	95	13	.573	1	1	-0	-1	1/O	-0.5
1971	SD-N	10	8	0	1	0	0	0	0	2	1	.125	.300	.125	.425	25	-1	-1	96	0	0	.429	0	0	0	0	H	0.0
	Oak-A	7	5	0	0	0	0	0	0	0	2	.000	.000	.000	.000	-99	-1	-1	101	0	0	.000	0	0	0	0	/1	0.0
	Chi-N	16	16	1	5	2	0	0	0	1	3	.313	.353	.438	.790	112	0	0	110	0	3	.727	0	0	0	0	/1	0.0
Total	5	380	778	76	190	31	6	17	98	70	94	.244	.309	.365	.674	97	-5	-3	98	121	87	.618	9	4	0	-3	1/O	-1.5
■ **RAY WEBSTER** Webster, Raymond George b: 11/15/37, Grass Valley, Cal. BR/TR, 6', 175 lbs. Deb: 4/17/59																												
1959	Cle-A	40	74	10	15	2	1	2	10	5	7	.203	.253	.338	.591	63	-4	-4	97	127	6	.508	1	0	0	-2	2/3	-0.4
1960	Bos-A	7	3	1	0	0	0	0	1	1	0	.000	.250	.000	.250	-26	-1	-1	103	0	0	.333	0	0	0	0	/2	0.0
Total	2	47	77	11	15	2	1	2	11	6	7	.195	.253	.325	.578	59	-5	-4	97	121	6	.516	1	0	0	-2	/23	-0.4
■ **PETE WECKBECKER** Weckbecker, Peter b: 8/30/1864, Butler, Pa. d: 5/16/35, Hampton, Va. 5'7", 150 lbs. Deb: 10/05/1889																												
1889	Ind-N	1	1	0	0	0	0	0	2	0	0	.000	.000	.000	.000	-92	-0	-0	109	0	0	.000	0			0	/C	0.0
1890	Lou-a	32	101	17	24	1	0	0		8		.238	.300	.248	.548	59	-4	-5	107	0	10	.532	7			0	C	-0.4
Total	2	33	102	17	24	1	0	0	2	8	0	.235	.297	.245	.542	58	-5	-6	107	0	10	.526	7			0	/C	-0.4
■ **BERT WEEDEN** Weeden, Charles Albert b: 12/21/1882, Northwood, N.H. d: 1/7/39, Northwood, N.H. BL/TL, 6', 200 lbs. Deb: 6/04/11																												
1911	Bos-N	1	1	0	0	0	0	0	0	0	0	.000	.000	.000	.000	-97	-0	-0	103	0	0	.000	0			0	H	0.0
■ **JOHNNY WEEKLY** Weekly, Johnny b: 6/14/37, Waterproof, La. d: 11/24/74, Walnut Creek, Cal. BR/TR, 6' ", 200 lbs. Deb: 4/13/62																												
1962	Hou-N	13	26	3	5	1	0	2	2	7	4	.192	.364	.462	.825	129	1	1	93	44	5	.905	0	0	0	-1	/O	0.0
1963	Hou-N	34	80	4	18	3	0	3	14	7	14	.225	.295	.375	.670	99	-1	-0	92	151	9	.594	0	0	0	0	O	-0.1
1964	Hou-N	6	15	0	2	0	0	0	3	1	3	.133	.188	.133	.321	-8	-2	-2	96	615	0	.214	0	0	0	1	/O	-0.1
Total	3	53	121	7	25	4	0	5	19	15	21	.207	.299	.364	.663	93	-2	-1	93	179	14	.619	0	0	0	-0	/O	-0.2
■ **STUMP WEIDMAN** Weidman, George E. b: 2/17/1861, Rochester, N.Y. d: 3/2/05, New York, N.Y. BR/TR, Deb: 8/26/1880																												
1880	Buf-N	23	78	8	8	1	0	0	3	2	11	.103	.125	.115	.240	-20	-9	-8	91	122	1	.157				0	PO	0.0
1881	Det-N	13	47	8	12	1	0	0	5	2	2	.255	.286	.277	.562	73	-1	-2	106	136	4	.429				0	P	0.0
1882	Det-N	50	193	20	42	7	1	0	20	2	19	.218	.226	.264	.490	56	-9	-10	102	135	12	.351				1	P/OS	0.0
1883	Det-N	79	313	34	58	6	1	1	24	4	38	.185	.196	.220	.416	29	-27	-23	91	118	14	.286				-1	PO/2	0.0
1884	Det-N	81	300	24	49	6	0	0	26	13	41	.163	.198	.183	.381	22	-27	-24	94	166	11	.271				-3	OP/S2	-2.3
1885	Det-N	44	153	7	24	2	1	1	14	8	32	.157	.199	.203	.401	31	-12	-11	97	143	6	.302				-3	P/O2	0.0
1886	KC-N	51	179	13	30	2	0	0	7	5	46	.168	.190	.179	.369	12	-18	-20	107	71	7	.268	3			4	P/O	0.0
1887	Det-N	21	82	12	17	2	0	0	11	3	3	.207	.235	.232	.467	31	-7	-8	102	182	6	.431	6			0	P/O	0.0
	NY-a	14	46	5	7	1	1	0		4		.152	.220	.217	.437	27	-5	-4	88	0	3	.410	2			0	P/O	0.0
	NY-N	1	3	0	1	0	0	0	0	0	0	.333	.333	.333	.667	82	-0	-0	107	0	0	.500	0			0	/P	0.0
1888	NY-N	2	7	1	0	0	0	0	1	2	1	.000	.222	.000	.222	-24	-1	-1	93	0	0	.286	0			0	/P	0.0
Total	9	379	1401	132	248	28	4	2	111	45	193	.177	.203	.207	.410	28	-116	-109	97	127	64	.300	11			-3	PO/2S	-2.3
■ **RALPH WEIGEL** Weigel, Ralph Richard "Wig" b: 10/2/21, Coldwater, Ohio BR/TR, 6'1", 180 lbs. Deb: 9/18/46																												
1946	Cle-A	6	12	0	2	0	0	0	0	0	2	.167	.167	.167	.333	-8	-2	-2	89	0	0	.300	1	0	0	0	/C	0.0
1948	Chi-A	66	163	8	38	7	3	0	26	13	18	.233	.294	.313	.607	64	-9	-8	95	172	14	.500	1	2	-1	1	C/O	-0.4
1949	Was-A	34	60	4	14	2	0	0	4	8	6	.233	.324	.267	.590	62	-4	-3	91	86	5	.480	0	1	-1	-0	C	-0.2
Total	3	106	235	12	54	9	3	0	30	21	26	.230	.296	.294	.589	61	-15	-13	94	141	20	.497	2	3	-1	1	/CO	-0.6
■ **PODGE WEIHE** Weihe, John Garibaldi b: 11/13/1862, Cincinnati, Ohio d: 4/15/14, Cincinnati, Ohio BR/TR, 5'11", 175 lbs. Deb: 1883																												
1883	Cin-a	1	4	1	1	0	0	0		0		.250	.250	.250	.500	60	-0	-0	103	0	0	.333				0	/O	0.0
1884	Ind-a	63	256	29	65	13	2	4		9		.254	.279	.367	.646	116	3	4	96	0	27	.539				-1	O/21	0.3
Total	2	64	260	30	66	13	2	4		9		.254	.279	.365	.644	115	3	4	97	0	27	.536				-1	/O21	0.3
■ **ELMER WEINGARTNER** Weingartner, Elmer William "Dutch" b: 8/13/18, Cleveland, Ohio BR/TR, 5'11", 178 lbs. Deb: 4/19/45																												
1945	Cle-A	20	39	5	9	1	0	0	1	4	11	.231	.302	.256	.559	64	-2	-2	99	36	3	.467	0	0	0	-0	S	0.0
■ **PHIL WEINTRAUB** Weintraub, Philip "Mickey" b: 10/12/07, Chicago, Ill. d: 6/21/87, Palm Springs, Cal BL/TL, 6'1", 195 lbs. Deb: 9/05/33																												
1933	NY-N	8	15	3	3	0	0	1	1	3	2	.200	.333	.400	.733	110	0	0	99	42	2	.750	0			-3	/O	-0.2
1934	NY-N	31	74	13	26	2	0	0	15	15	10	.351	.461	.378	.839	130	4	4	98	193	15	.896	0			-4	O	0.0
1935	NY-N	64	112	18	27	3	3	1	6	17	13	.241	.341	.348	.689	89	-2	-1	96	51	14	.636	0			-2	1/O	-0.3
1937	Cin-N	49	177	27	48	10	4	3	20	19	25	.271	.345	.424	.769	118	2	4	91	91	25	.706	1			-4	O	-0.1
	NY-N	6	9	3	3	2	0	0	1	1	1	.333	.400	.556	.956	157	1	1	100	72	2	1.000	0			-0	/O	0.0
	Yr	55	186	30	51	12	4	3	21	20	26	.274	.348	.430	.778	120	3	5	92	90	30	.756	1			-4		-0.1
1938	Phi-N	100	351	51	109	23	2	4	45	64	43	.311	.422	.422	.844	132	19	19	100	108	68	.861	1			1	1	1.2
1944	NY-N	104	361	55	114	18	9	13	77	59	59	.316	.412	.524	.935	156	31	29	104	123	82	.984	0			-1	1	2.0
1945	NY-N	82	283	45	77	9	1	10	42	54	29	.272	.389	.417	.806	124	11	11	100	100	48	.806	2			3	1	1.1
Total	7	444	1382	215	407	67	19	32	207	232	182	.295	.398	.440	.838	132	66	67	99	107	256	.862	4			-9	1/O	3.7
■ **AL WEIS** Weis, Albert John b: 4/2/38, Franklin Square, N.Y BB/TR, 6' ", 160 lbs. Deb: 9/15/62																												
1962	Chi-A	7	12	2	1	0	0	0	0	2	3	.083	.267	.083	.350	-1	-2	-2	95	0	1	.455	1	0	0	0	/S23	0.0
1963	Chi-A	99	210	41	57	9	0	0	18	18	37	.271	.335	.314	.649	80	-4	-5	104	114	26	.652	15	1	4	4	2S/3	0.8
1964	Chi-A	133	328	36	81	4	4	2	23	22	41	.247	.300	.302	.602	71	-14	-12	96	93	32	.564	22	7	2	-2	*2/SO	0.1
1965	Chi-A	103	135	29	40	4	3	1	12	12	22	.296	.362	.393	.755	125	3	4	92	89	20	.724	4	1	1	6	2/S3O	1.5
1966	Chi-A	129	187	20	29	4	1	0	9	17	50	.155	.233	.187	.420	24	-18	-17	94	108	8	.343	3	5	-2	2	2S	-0.7
1967	Chi-A	50	53	9	13	2	0	0	4	1	7	.245	.273	.283	.556	69	-2	-2	94	111	3	.444	3	3	-1	0	2S	0.0
1968	NY-N	90	274	15	47	6	0	1	14	21	63	.172	.236	.204	.440	32	-22	-22	102	100	14	.355	3	1	0	-3	S2/3	-1.9
1969	NY-N	103	247	20	53	9	2	2	23	15	51	.215	.260	.291	.551	54	-15	-16	100	118	19	.450	3	3	-1	-3	S2/3	-1.0
1970	NY-N	75	121	20	25	7	1	1	11	7	21	.207	.256	.306	.562	48	-9	-9	104	107	8	.451	1	1	-0	-5	2S	-0.7
1971	NY-N	11	11	3	0	0	0	0	1	2	4	.000	.154	.000	.154	-55	-2	-2	96	0	0	.182	0	0	0	-0	/23	-0.1
Total	10	800	1578	195	346	45	11	7	115	117	299	.219	.279	.275	.554	59	-86	-84	99	102	132	.494	55	22	3	-1	2S/3O	-2.0
■ **BUTCH WEIS** Weis, Arthur John b: 3/2/03, St.Louis, Mo. BL/TL, 5'11", 180 lbs. Deb: 4/15/22																												
1922	Chi-N	2	2	2	1	0	0	0	0	0	0	.500	.500	.500	1.000	167	0	0	95	0	0	1.000	0	0	0	0	H	0.0
1923	Chi-N	22	26	2	6	1	0	0	2	5	8	.231	.355	.269	.624	64	-1	-1	104	101	3	.571	0	1	-1	-1	/O	-0.2
1924	Chi-N	37	133	19	37	8	1	0	23	15	14	.278	.356	.353	.709	90	-1	-1	101	189	17	.663	4	5	-2	5	O	0.1
1925	Chi-N	67	180	16	48	5	3	2	25	23	22	.267	.350	.361	.711	84	-4	-4	97	125	23	.662	2	4	-2	-7	O	-1.2
Total	4	128	341	39	92	14	4	2	50	43	44	.270	.353	.352	.705	85	-7	-6	99	147	43	.656	6	10	-4	-3	/O	-1.3

YEAR	TM/L	G	AB	R	H	2B	3B	HR	RBI	BB	SO	AVG	OBP	SLG	PRO	/A	BR	/A	PF	CHI	RC	TA	SB	CS	SBR	FR	POS	TPR
■ BUD WEISER	Weiser, Harry Budson b: 1/8/1891, Shamokin, Pa. d: 7/31/61, Shamokin, Pa. BR/TR, 5'11", 165 lbs. Deb: 4/29/15																											
1915	Phi-N	37	64	6	9	2	0	0	8	7	12	.141	.236	.172	.408	23	-6	-6	107	278	3	.368	2	2	-1	-4	O	-1.2
1916	Phi-N	4	10	1	3	1	0	0	1	0	3	.300	.300	.400	.700	119	0	0	96	99	1	.571	0			-1	/O	0.0
Total	2	41	74	7	12	3	0	0	9	7	15	.162	.244	.203	.447	34	-6	-6	106	256	5	.391	2	2		-5	/O	-1.2
■ GARY WEISS	Weiss, Gary Lee b: 12/27/55, Brenham, Tex. BB/TR, 5'10", 170 lbs. Deb: 9/13/80																											
1980	LA-N	8	0	2	0	0	0	0	0	0	0	—	—	—	—	—	0	0	97	—	—	—	0	0	0	0	/R	0.0
1981	LA-N	14	19	2	2	0	0	0	1	1	4	.105	.150	.105	.255	-27	-3	-3	98	196	0	.176	0	0	0	0	S	-0.1
Total	2	22	19	4	2	0	0	0	1	1	4	.105	.150	.105	.255	-27	-3	-3	98	196	5	.176	0	0	0	0	/S	-0.1
■ JOE WEISS	Weiss, Joseph Harold b: 1/27/1894, Chicago, Ill. d: 7/7/67, Cedar Rapids, Iowa BR/TR, 6', 165 lbs. Deb: 8/29/15																											
1915	Chi-F	29	85	6	19	1	2	0	11	3	24	.224	.250	.282	.532	59	-5	-4	97	165	6	.409	0			-1	1	-0.4
■ WALT WEISS	Weiss, Walter William b: 11/28/63, Tuxedo, N.Y. BB/TR, 6', 175 lbs. Deb: 7/12/87																											
1987	Oak-A	16	26	3	12	4	0	0	1	2	2	.462	.500	.615	1.115	214	4	4	91	25	7	1.188	1	2	-1	0	S/D	0.3
1988	Oak-A	147	452	44	113	17	3	3	39	35	56	.250	.317	.321	.637	83	-12	-9	95	101	47	.548	4	4	-1	8	*S	0.4
Total	2	163	478	47	125	21	3	3	40	37	58	.262	.326	.337	.663	90	-8	-5	95	97	54	.576	5	6	-2	8	S/D	0.7
■ JOHNNY WELAJ	Welaj, John Ludwig b: 5/27/14, Moss Creek, Pa. BR/TR, 6', 164 lbs. Deb: 5/02/39																											
1939	Was-A	63	201	23	55	11	2	1	33	13	20	.274	.318	.363	.681	82	-8	-5	90	147	25	.660	13	2	3	-4	O	-0.7
1940	Was-A	88	215	31	55	9	0	3	21	19	20	.256	.322	.340	.662	77	-9	-7	93	93	23	.596	8	7	-2	1	O	-1.0
1941	Was-A	49	96	16	20	4	0	0	5	6	16	.208	.255	.250	.505	35	-9	-9	98	74	6	.407	3	1	0	-0	O	-0.9
1943	Phi-A	93	281	45	68	16	1	0	15	15	17	.242	.280	.306	.586	71	-11	-11	101	64	24	.507	12	5	1	-4	O	-1.8
Total	4	293	793	115	198	40	3	4	74	53	73	.250	.298	.323	.621	70	-37	-32	96	94	79	.564	36	15	2	-8	O	-4.4
■ CURT WELCH	Welch, Curtis Benton b: 2/11/1862, E.Liverpool, Ohio d: 8/29/1896, E.Liverpool, Ohio BR , 5'10", 175 lbs. Deb: 5/01/1884																											
1884	Tol-a	109	425	61	95	24	5	0		10		.224	.248	.304	.552	79	-8	-11	104	0	33	.433				16	*O/2C1P	0.4
1885	StL-a	112	432	84	117	18	8	2		23		.271	.318	.363	.682	126	9	13	93	0	51	.594				13	*O	1.8
1886	StL-a	138	563	114	158	31	13	2		29		.281	.332	.393	.724	115	17	7	111	0	95	.798	59			13	*O/2	1.4
1887	StL-a	131	544	98	151	32	7	3		25		.278	.322	.379	.701	89	-3	-12	110	0	97	.842	89			17	*O/21	0.1
1888	Phi-a	136	549	125	155	22	8	1	61	33		.282	.355	.357	.712	131	21	21	101	81	106	.896	95			3	*O/2	1.7
1889	Phi-a	125	516	134	140	**39**	6	0	39	67	30	.271	.375	.370	.746	118	13	15	98	50	99	.912	66			6	*O	1.3
1890	Phi-a	103	396	100	106	21	4	2		49		.268	.391	.356	.747	127	15	17	97	0	82	.983	64			14	*O/P	2.2
	BB-a	19	68	16	9	4	0	0		9		.132	.244	.191	.435	30	-6	-6	100	0	5	.525	8			1	O/1	-0.4
	Yr	122	464	116	115	25	4	2	0	58		.248	.370	.332	.702	112	9	11	98	0	86	.905	72			14		1.8
1891	Bal-a	132	514	122	138	22	10	3	55	77	42	.268	.400	.368	.768	122	21	20	101	69	98	.936	50			9	*O2/S	2.0
1892	Bal-N	63	237	42	56	1	3	1	22	36	9	.236	.363	.278	.641	97	2	2	100	86	30	.702	14			-5	O	-0.4
	Cin-N	25	94	14	19	0	2	1	7	7	8	.202	.299	.277	.576	74	-2	-3	103	78	10	.613	7			-0	O	-0.3
	Yr	88	331	56	75	1	5	2	29	43	17	.227	.345	.278	.623	90	-1	-1	101	85	40	.676	21			-5		-0.7
1893	Lou-N	14	47	5	8	1	0	0	2	16	4	.170	.400	.191	.591	64	-1	-1	96	58	4	.718	1			0	O	0.0
Total	10	1107	4385	915	1152	215	66	15	186	381	93	.263	.345	.352	.697	110	78	63	102	32	711	.788	453			86	*O/21SPC	9.8
■ FRANK WELCH	Welch, Frank Tiguer "Bugger" b: 8/10/1897, Birmingham, Ala. d: 7/25/57, Birmingham, Ala. BR/TR, 5'9", 175 lbs. Deb: 9/09/19																											
1919	Phi-A	15	54	5	9	1	1	2	7	7	10	.167	.262	.333	.596	63	-3	-3	106	112	5	.556	0			1	O	-0.2
1920	Phi-A	100	360	43	93	17	5	4	40	26	41	.258	.312	.367	.679	84	-12	-8	94	99	39	.587	2	9	-5	3	O	-1.8
1921	Phi-A	115	403	48	115	18	6	7	45	34	43	.285	.347	.412	.759	90	-5	-7	103	84	60	.729	6	0	2	-3	*O	-1.5
1922	Phi-A	114	375	43	97	17	3	11	49	40	40	.259	.335	.408	.743	89	-5	-7	104	96	52	.706	3	4	-2	-6	*O	-2.1
1923	Phi-A	125	421	56	125	19	9	4	55	48	40	.297	.374	.413	.788	107	5	5	100	103	67	.757	1	4	-2	1	*O	-0.6
1924	Phi-A	94	293	47	85	13	2	5	31	35	27	.290	.372	.399	.771	99	-0	0	99	78	45	.744	2	3	-1	-2	O	-0.7
1925	Phi-A	85	202	40	56	5	4	4	41	29	14	.277	.373	.401	.774	94	-1	-2	103	148	33	.776	2	1	0	-6	O	-1.1
1926	Phi-A	75	174	26	49	8	1	4	23	26	9	.282	.381	.408	.789	90	2	-3	118	94	28	.777	2	5	-2	-6	O	-1.3
1927	Bos-A	15	28	2	5	2	0	0	4	5	1	.179	.303	.250	.553	47	-2	-2	95	190	2	.522	0	0	0	2	/O	0.0
Total	9	738	2310	310	634	100	31	41	295	250	225	.274	.350	.398	.748	92	-20	-27	102	99	330	.709	18	26		-17	O	-9.3
■ HERB WELCH	Welch, Herbert M. "Dutch" b: 10/19/1898, Ro Ellen, Tenn. d: 4/13/67, Memphis, Tenn. BL/TR, 5'6", 154 lbs. Deb: 9/15/25																											
1925	Bos-A	13	38	2	11	0	1	0	2	0	6	.289	.289	.342	.632	63	-2	-2	95	51	4	.481	0	0	0	0	S	0.0
■ MILT WELCH	Welch, Milton Edward b: 7/26/24, Farmersville, Ill BR/TR, 5'10", 175 lbs. Deb: 6/05/45																											
1945	Det-A	1	2	0	0	0	0	0	0	0	1	.000	.000	.000	.000	-94	-1	-1	106	0	0	.000	0	0	0	0	/C	0.0
■ HARRY WELCHONCE	Welchonce, Harry Monroe "Welch" b: 11/20/1883, North Point, Pa. d: 2/26/77, Arcadia, Cal. BL/TR, 6', 170 lbs. Deb: 4/17/11																											
1911	Phi-N	26	66	9	14	4	0	0	6	7	8	.212	.288	.273	.560	53	-4	-4	108	113	5	.481	0			-3	O	-0.7
■ MIKE WELDAY	Welday, Lyndon Earl b: 12/19/1879, Conway, Iowa d: 5/28/42, Leavenworth, Kan. BL/TL, Deb: 4/21/07																											
1907	Chi-A	24	35	2	8	1	1	0	0	6		.229	.341	.314	.656	107	1	1	104	0	4	.630	0			0	O	0.0
1909	Chi-A	29	74	3	14	0	0	0	5	4		.189	.231	.189	.420	34	-6	-5	97	138	3	.333	2			-4	O	-1.1
Total	2	53	109	5	22	1	1	0	5	10		.202	.269	.229	.498	59	-5	-5	99	90	7	.425	2			-4	/O	-1.1
■ OLLIE WELF	Welf, Oliver Henry b: 1/17/1889, Cleveland, Ohio d: 6/15/67, Cleveland, Ohio BR/TL, 5'9", 160 lbs. Deb: 8/30/16																											
1916	Cle-A	1	0	0	0	0	0	0	0	0	0	—	—	—	—	—	0	0	100	—	—	—	0			0	R	0.0
■ BRAD WELLMAN	Wellman, Brad Eugene b: 8/17/59, Lodi, Cal. BR/TR, 6', 170 lbs. Deb: 9/04/82																											
1982	SF-N	6	4	1	1	0	0	0	0	0	1	.250	.250	.250	.500	43	-0	-0	94	0	0	.333	0	0	0	0	/2	0.0
1983	SF-N	82	182	15	39	3	0	1	16	22	39	.214	.299	.247	.546	52	-11	-11	101	132	14	.477	5	3	-0	-8	2/S	-1.7
1984	SF-N	93	265	23	60	9	1	2	25	19	41	.226	.278	.291	.569	62	-14	-13	96	118	21	.486	10	5	0	3	2S/3	-0.4
1985	SF-N	71	174	16	41	11	1	0	16	4	33	.236	.269	.310	.580	66	-9	-8	93	118	14	.486	5	2	0	0	23/S	-0.6
1986	SF-N	12	13	0	2	0	0	0	1	1	2	.154	.214	.154	.368	3	-2	-2	96	199	0	.273	0	0	0	0	/S23	0.0
1987	LA-N	3	4	1	1	0	0	0	1	0	1	.250	.250	.250	.500	36	-0	-0	92	399	0	.333	0	0	0	0	/2S3	0.0
1988	KC-A	71	107	11	29	3	0	1	6	6	23	.271	.322	.327	.649	80	-2	-3	103	63	11	.543	1	2	-1	3	2S/3D	0.3
Total	7	338	749	67	173	26	2	4	65	52	140	.231	.286	.287	.573	62	-39	-37	98	116	61	.499	21	12	-1	-2	2/S3D	-2.4
■ BOB WELLMAN	Wellman, Robert Joseph b: 7/15/25, Norwood, Ohio BR/TR, 6'4", 210 lbs. Deb: 9/23/48																											
1948	Phi-A	4	10	1	2	0	1	0	0	3	2	.200	.385	.400	.785	107	0	0	102	0	2	.875	0	0	0	0	/1O	0.0
1950	Phi-A	11	15	1	5	0	0	1	1	0	3	.333	.333	.533	.867	133	0	0	90	31	3	.800	0	0	0	-0	/O	0.0
Total	2	15	25	2	7	0	1	1	1	3	5	.280	.357	.480	.837	122	0	1	95	17	5	.833	0	0	0	0	/O1	0.0
■ GREG WELLS	Wells, Gregory De Wayne b: 4/25/54, Mc Intosh, Ala. BR/TR, 6'5", 218 lbs. Deb: 8/10/81																											
1981	Tor-A	32	73	7	18	5	0	0	5	5	12	.247	.295	.315	.610	68	-2	-3	111	85	6	.475	0	2	-1	-1	1/D	-0.5
1982	Min-A	15	54	5	11	1	2	0	3	1	8	.204	.218	.296	.514	40	-5	-5	100	76	4	.395	0	0	0	-0	1/D	-0.4
Total	2	47	127	12	29	6	2	0	8	6	20	.228	.263	.307	.570	57	-7	-8	106	81	10	.450	0	2	-1	-1	/1D	-0.9
■ JAKE WELLS	Wells, Jacob b: 8/9/1863, Memphis, Tenn. d: 3/16/27, Hendersonville, N.C. BR/TR, Deb: 1888																											
1888	Det-N	16	57	5	9	1	0	0	2	0	5	.158	.158	.175	.333	7	-6	-6	98	72	2	.208	0			0	C	-0.5
1890	StL-a	30	105	17	25	3	0	0		10		.238	.333	.267	.600	68	-2	-5	116	0	10	.550	1			0	C/O	-0.3
Total	2	46	162	22	34	4	0	0	2	10	5	.210	.277	.235	.511	52	-8	-10	110	23	12	.422	1			0	/CO	-0.8
■ LEO WELLS	Wells, Leo Donald b: 7/18/17, Kansas City, Kan. BR/TR, 5'9", 170 lbs. Deb: 4/16/42																											
1942	Chi-A	35	62	8	12	2	0	1	4	4	5	.194	.242	.274	.517	46	-5	-5	99	70	4	.431	1	0	0	1	S/3	-0.2
1946	Chi-A	45	127	11	24	4	1	1	11	12	34	.189	.259	.260	.519	47	-9	-9	97	116	8	.436	3	4	-2	2	3/S	-0.5
Total	2	80	189	19	36	6	1	2	15	16	39	.190	.254	.265	.518	46	-14	-14	97	101	13	.438	4	4	-1	3	/3S	-0.7
■ JIMMY WELSH	Welsh, James Daniel b: 10/9/02, Denver, Colo. d: 10/30/70, Oakland, Cal. BL/TR, 6'1", 174 lbs. Deb: 4/14/25																											
1925	Bos-N	122	484	69	151	25	8	7	63	20	24	.312	.350	.440	.790	107	-0	4	94	101	74	.736	7	4	-0	6	*O/2	0.6

YEAR	TM/L	G	AB	R	H	2B	3B	HR	RBI	BB	SO	AVG	OBP	SLG	PRO	/A	BR	/A	PF	CHI	RC	TA	SB	CS	SBR	FR	POS	TPR
1926	Bos-N	134	490	69	136	18	11	3	57	33	28	.278	.333	.378	.711	105	-6	3	86	108	62	.655	6			10	*O	0.7
1927	Bos-N	131	497	72	143	26	7	9	54	23	27	.288	.330	.423	.752	107	-1	3	93	84	67	.712	11			10	*O/1	0.7
1928	NY-N	124	476	77	146	22	5	9	54	29	30	.307	.357	.431	.787	103	3	2	102	85	71	.745	4			-3	*O	-0.5
1929	NY-N	38	129	25	32	7	0	2	8	9	3	.248	.331	.349	.680	69	-6	-6	100	54	15	.660	3			-7	O	-1.4
	Bos-N	53	186	24	54	8	7	2	16	13	9	.290	.350	.441	.791	101	-2	-0	94	63	28	.758	1			13	O	0.7
	Yr	91	315	49	86	15	7	4	24	22	12	.273	.342	.403	.745	87	-8	-6	96	60	43	.716	4			6		-0.7
1930	Bos-N	113	422	51	116	21	9	3	36	29	23	.275	.327	.389	.716	74	-19	-17	97	73	53	.660	5			4	*O	-1.8
Total	6	715	2684	387	778	127	47	35	288	156	144	.290	.340	.411	.751	98	-33	-12	95	87	370	.704	37	4		32	O/21	-1.0
■ **TUB WELSH**	Welsh, James J. b: 7/3/1866, St.Louis, Mo. TR, 5'11", 230 lbs. Deb: 6/12/1890																											
1890	Tol-a	35	108	15	31	3	1	1		8		.287	.353	.361	.714	110	2	1	103	0	17	.740	7			0	C1	0.1
1895	Lou-N	47	153	18	37	4	1	1	8	13	7	.242	.310	.301	.610	62	-9	-8	95	46	15	.543	2			0	C1	-0.5
Total	2	82	261	33	68	7	2	2	8	21	7	.261	.328	.326	.653	81	-7	-6	98	27	32	.622	9			0	/C1	-0.4
■ **LEW WENDELL**	Wendell, Lewis Charles b: 3/22/1892, New York, N.Y. d: 7/11/53, Brooklyn, N.Y. BR/TR, 5'11", 178 lbs. Deb: 6/10/15																											
1915	NY-N	20	36	0	8	1	1	0	5	2	7	.222	.263	.306	.569	79	-1	-1	91	174	3	.464	0			-1	C	0.0
1916	NY-N	2	2	0	0	0	0	0	0	0	2	.000	.000	.000	.000	-99	-0	-0	96	0	0	.000	0			0	H	0.0
1924	Phi-N	21	32	3	8	1	0	0	2	3	5	.250	.314	.281	.596	56	-2	-2	108	81	3	.500	0	0	0	1	C	0.0
1925	Phi-N	18	26	0	2	0	0	0	3	1	3	.077	.111	.077	.188	-44	-6	-7	116	533	0	.125	0	0	0	0	/C	-0.5
1926	Phi-N	1	4	0	0	0	0	0	0	0	0	.000	.000	.000	.000	-97	-1	-1	103	0	0	.000	0			0	/C	0.0
Total	5	62	100	3	18	2	1	0	10	6	17	.180	.226	.220	.446	23	-10	-11	103	225	6	.341	0	0		-0	/C	-0.5
■ **JACK WENTZ**	Wentz, John George (born John George Wernz) b: 3/4/1863, Louisville, Ky. d: 9/14/07, Louisville, Ky. 5'10.5", 175 lbs. Deb: 4/15/1891																											
1891	Lou-a	1	4	0	1	0	0	0	0	0	0	.250	.250	.250	.500	50	-0	-0	90	0	0	.333	0			0	/2	0.0
■ **STAN WENTZEL**	Wentzel, Stanley Aaron b: 1/13/17, Lorane, Pa. BR/TR, 6'1", 200 lbs. Deb: 9/23/45																											
1945	Bos-N	4	19	3	4	0	1	0	6	0	3	.211	.211	.316	.526	40	-1	-2	112	300	1	.467	1			-0	/O	-0.2
■ **JULIE WERA**	Wera, Julian Valentine b: 2/9/02, Winona, Minn. d: 12/12/75, Rochester, Minn. BR/TR, 5'8", 164 lbs. Deb: 4/14/27																											
1927	NY-A	38	42	7	10	3	0	1	8	1	5	.238	.273	.381	.654	68	-2	-2	100	140	4	.563	0	0	0	-3	3	-0.2
1929	NY-A	5	12	1	5	0	0	0	2	1	1	.417	.462	.417	.878	129	1	1	99	137	2	.857	0	0	0	0	/3	0.1
Total	2	43	54	8	15	3	0	1	10	2	6	.278	.316	.389	.705	82	-2	-2	100	139	7	.615	0	0	0	-3	/3	-0.1
■ **BILLY WERBER**	Werber, William Murray b: 6/20/08, Berwyn, Md. BR/TR, 5'10", 170 lbs. Deb: 6/25/30																											
1930	NY-A	4	14	5	4	0	0	0	2	3	1	.286	.412	.286	.697	90	-0	0	90	169	2	.700	0	0	0	0	/S3	0.0
1933	NY-A	3	2	0	0	0	0	0	0	0	0	.000	.000	.000	.000	-99	-1	-1	91	0	0	.000	0	0	0	0	/3	0.0
	Bos-A	108	425	64	110	30	6	3	39	33	39	.259	.312	.379	.691	81	-12	-12	101	81	52	.653	15	5	2	-7	S3/2	-0.8
	Yr	111	427	64	110	30	6	3	39	33	39	.258	.311	.377	.688	81	-12	-13	101	79	52	.649	15	5	2	-7		-0.8
1934	Bos-A	152	623	129	200	41	10	11	67	77	37	.321	.397	.472	.868	116	22	17	106	60	121	.941	**40**	15	3	21	*3S	3.9
1935	Bos-A	124	462	84	118	30	3	14	61	69	41	.255	.357	.424	.781	94	1	-5	108	92	76	.849	**29**	7	5	16	*3	1.6
1936	Bos-A	145	535	89	147	29	6	10	67	89	37	.275	.382	.407	.790	90	-2	-8	106	93	89	.833	23	13	-1	-6	*3O/2	-1.2
1937	Phi-A	128	493	85	144	31	4	7	70	74	39	.292	.386	.414	.799	108	3	8	94	94	84	.867	**35**	13	3	-0	*3/O	1.1
1938	Phi-A	134	499	92	129	22	7	11	69	93	37	.259	.377	.397	.774	93	-3	-4	101	97	79	.810	19	15	-3	0	*3	-0.1
1939	Cin-N	147	599	**115**	173	35	5	5	57	91	46	.289	.388	.389	.777	106	12	9	103	73	96	.788	15			11	*3	2.4
1940	Cin-N	143	584	105	162	35	5	12	48	68	40	.277	.361	.416	.777	113	12	11	101	55	92	.781	16			7	*3	1.7
1941	Cin-N	109	418	56	100	9	2	4	46	53	24	.239	.328	.299	.627	78	-11	-11	99	116	43	.593	14			7	*3	-0.2
1942	NY-N	98	370	51	76	9	2	1	13	51	22	.205	.308	.249	.557	62	-15	-16	103	49	30	.511	9			11	3	-0.5
Total	11	1295	5024	875	1363	271	50	78	539	701	363	.271	.364	.392	.756	97	5	-12	102	81	765	.780	215	68		61	*3/SO2	7.9
■ **PERRY WERDEN**	Werden, Percival Wheritt b: 7/21/1865, St.Louis, Mo. d: 1/9/34, Minneapolis, Minn. BR/TR, 6'2", 220 lbs. Deb: 4/24/1884																											
1884	StL-U	18	76	7	18	2	0	0		2		.237	.256	.263	.520	73	-2	-2	104	0	5	.379	0			0	P/O	0.0
1888	Was-N	3	10	0	3	0	0	0	2	1	4	.300	.364	.300	.664	121	0	0	96	244	1	.571	0			0	/O	0.0
1890	Tol-a	128	498	113	147	22	**20**	6		78		.295	.403	.456	.859	152	37	34	103	0	118	1.071	59			1	*1/O	2.7
1891	Bal-a	139	552	102	160	20	18	6	104	52	59	.290	.363	.424	.787	127	19	18	101	126	104	.875	46			0	*1	0.9
1892	StL-N	149	598	73	154	22	6	8	84	59	52	.258	.328	.355	.683	114	6	10	95	105	78	.664	20			10	*1	0.8
1893	StL-N	125	500	73	138	22	**29**	1	94	49	25	.276	.349	.442	.791	112	6	7	99	122	83	.796	11			2	*1/O	0.7
1897	Lou-N	131	506	76	153	21	14	5	83	40		.302	.366	.429	.795	117	8	12	95	101	87	.799	14			17	*1	2.4
Total	7	693	2740	444	773	109	87	26	367	281	140	.282	.358	.414	.772	123	74	80	99	89	476	.819	150			31	1/PO	7.5
■ **JOHNNY WERHAS**	Werhas, John Charles "Peaches" b: 2/7/38, Highland Park, Mich. BR/TR, 6'2", 200 lbs. Deb: 4/14/64																											
1964	LA-N	29	83	6	16	2	1	0	8	13	12	.193	.302	.241	.543	60	-5	-4	92	164	6	.471	0	0	0	-4	3	-0.9
1965	LA-N	4	3	1	0	0	0	0	0	1	2	.000	.250	.000	.250	-25	-0	-0	91	0	0	.250	0	0	0	0	/1	0.0
1967	LA-N	7	7	0	1	0	0	0	0	0	3	.143	.143	.143	.286	-20	-1	-1	88	0	0	.167	0	0	0	0	H	0.0
	Cal-A	49	75	8	12	1	1	2	6	10	22	.160	.267	.280	.547	65	-3	-3	96	93	5	.478	0	0	0	0	3/1O	-0.2
Total	3	89	168	15	29	3	2	2	14	24	39	.173	.280	.250	.530	57	-10	-8	93	123	12	.469	0	0	0	-4	/31O	-1.1
■ **DON WERNER**	Werner, Donald Paul b: 3/8/53, Appleton, Wis. BR/TR, 6'1", 180 lbs. Deb: 9/02/75																											
1975	Cin-N	7	8	0	1	0	0	0	0	0	0	.125	.222	.125	.347	-2	-1	-1	104	0	0	.286	0	0	0	0	/C	0.0
1976	Cin-N	3	4	0	2	1	0	0	1	1	1	.500	.600	.750	1.350	273	1	1	103	128	2	2.000	0	0	0	0	/C	0.1
1977	Cin-N	10	23	3	4	0	0	2	4	2	3	.174	.240	.435	.675	77	-1	-1	100	100	2	.571	0	1	-1	-0	C	-0.1
1978	Cin-N	50	113	7	17	2	1	0	11	14	30	.150	.250	.186	.436	23	-11	-12	103	208	6	.381	1	0	0	-4	C	-1.4
1980	Cin-N	24	64	2	11	2	0	0	5	7	10	.172	.264	.203	.467	31	-6	-6	102	152	4	.400	1	0	0	-2	C	-0.6
1981	Tex-A	2	8	1	2	0	0	0	0	0	2	.250	.250	.250	.500	49	-1	-0	91	0	0	.286	0	1	-1	0	/D	0.0
1982	Tex-A	22	59	4	12	2	0	0	3	3	7	.203	.242	.237	.479	35	-5	-5	93	86	4	.354	0	0	0	3	C	0.0
Total	7	118	279	17	49	7	1	2	24	27	53	.176	.256	.229	.485	36	-24	-24	100	149	18	.412	2	2	-1	-3	C/D	-2.0
■ **JOE WERRICK**	Werrick, Joseph Abraham b: 10/25/1861, St.Paul, Minn. d: 5/10/43, St.Peter, Minn. TR , 5'9", 151 lbs. Deb: 9/27/1884																											
1884	StP-U	9	27	3	2	0	0	0		1		.074	.107	.074	.181	-38	-4	-4	100	0	0	.120	0			0	/S	-0.2
1886	Lou-a	136	561	75	140	20	14	3		33		.250	.294	.351	.645	96	1	-6	108	0	65	.596	19			-2	*3	-0.1
1887	Lou-a	136	533	90	152	21	13	7		38		.285	.336	.413	.749	103	6	-0	107	0	93	.814	49			-1	*3	-0.4
1888	Lou-a	111	413	49	89	12	7	0	51	30		.215	.274	.278	.552	88	-9	-3	91	135	36	.503	15			-15	3S/2O	-1.5
Total	4	392	1534	217	383	53	34	10	51	102		.250	.300	.348	.648	95	-5	-13	103	37	194	.632	83			-17	3/S2O	-2.2
■ **DON WERT**	Wert, Donald Ralph b: 7/29/38, Strasburg, Pa. BR/TR, 5'10", 162 lbs. Deb: 5/11/63																											
1963	Det-A	78	251	31	65	6	2	7	25	24	51	.259	.329	.382	.711	95	-0	-1	104	89	31	.641	3	3	-1	-0	32/S	0.0
1964	Det-A	148	525	63	135	18	5	9	55	50	74	.257	.329	.362	.691	96	-5	-2	96	110	63	.615	3	4	-2	1	*3/S	0.0
1965	Det-A	162	609	81	159	22	2	12	54	73	71	.261	.343	.363	.706	96	2	-2	105	84	76	.641	5	6	-2	5	*3/S2	0.2
1966	Det-A	150	559	56	150	20	2	11	70	64	69	.268	.346	.370	.716	104	5	4	102	130	71	.646	6	3	0	-18	*3	-1.8
1967	Det-A	142	534	60	137	23	2	6	40	44	59	.257	.321	.341	.662	96	-2	-2	99	88	58	.565	1	1	-0	-6	*3/S	-0.5
1968	Det-A	150	536	44	107	15	1	12	37	37	79	.200	.258	.299	.556	64	-21	-25	106	83	40	.455	0	3	-2	-7	*3/S	-3.2
1969	Det-A	132	423	46	95	11	1	14	50	49	60	.225	.307	.355	.661	82	-9	-11	103	105	45	.592	3	1	0	-4	*3	-1.2
1970	Det-A	128	363	34	79	13	0	6	33	44	56	.218	.309	.303	.612	67	-15	-16	103	104	33	.530	1	3	-2	-1	*3/2	-1.8
1971	Was-A	20	40	2	2	1	0	0	2	4	10	.050	.156	.075	.231	-36	-7	-7	92	272	0	.200	0	0	0	0	/S32	-0.6
Total	9	1110	3840	417	929	129	15	77	366	389	529	.242	.317	.343	.660	87	-52	-62	102	101	417	.600	22	24	-8	-29	*3/S2	-8.9
■ **DENNIS WERTH**	Werth, Dennis Dean b: 12/29/52, Lincoln, Ill. BR/TR, 6'1", 200 lbs. Deb: 9/17/79																											
1979	NY-A	3	4	1	1	0	0	0	0	0	0	.250	.250	.250	.500	37	-0	-0	96	0	0	.333	0	0	0	0	/1	0.0
1980	NY-A	39	65	15	20	3	0	3	12	12	19	.308	.416	.492	.908	149	5	5	99	114	13	.898	0	1	-1	-2	1/OC3D	0.2
1981	NY-A	34	55	7	6	1	0	0	1	12	12	.109	.269	.127	.396	17	-5	-6	100	56	2	.377	1	0	0	-1	1/OCD	-0.6
1982	KC-A	41	15	5	2	0	0	0	2	4	2	.133	.316	.133	.449	29	-1	-1	100	400	1	.429	0	0	0	0	1/C	-0.1

YEAR	TM/L	G	AB	R	H	2B	3B	HR	RBI	BB	SO	AVG	OBP	SLG	PRO	/A	BR	/A	PF	CHI	RC	TA	SB	CS	SBR	FR	POS	TPR
Total	4	117	139	28	29	4	0	3	15	28	33	.209	.341	.302	.643	82	-2	-2	100	120	16	.634	1	1	-0	-2	/1ODC3	-0.5
■ **DEL WERTS**	Werts, Dwight Lewis b: 1887, Ohio BR/TR, 5'6.5", 155 lbs. Deb: 5/23/14																											
1914	Buf-F	3	0	1	0	0	0	0	0	0	0	—	—	—	—	—	0	0	104	—	—	—	0			0	/S	0.0
■ **VIC WERTZ**	Wertz, Victor Woodrow b: 2/9/25, York, Pa. d: 7/7/83, Detroit, Mich. BL/TR, 6', 186 lbs. Deb: 4/15/47																											
1947	Det-A	102	333	60	96	22	4	6	44	47	66	.288	.376	.432	.809	119	11	10	104	100	56	.778	2	0	1	-5	O	0.2
1948	Det-A	119	391	49	97	19	9	7	67	48	70	.248	.335	.396	.731	97	-4	-2	96	129	56	.689	0	0	0	-1	O	-0.6
1949	Det-A	155	608	96	185	26	6	20	133	80	61	.304	.385	.465	.851	116	20	14	108	**141**	110	.820	2	3	-1	-5	*O	0.4
1950	Det-A	149	559	99	172	37	4	27	123	91	55	.308	.408	.533	.941	145	33	36	97	119	128	.980	0	1	-1	-12	*O	2.0
1951	Det-A	138	501	86	143	24	4	27	94	78	61	.285	.383	.511	.894	133	27	24	106	102	101	.896	0	3	-2	-4	*O	1.2
1952	Det-A	85	285	46	70	15	3	17	51	46	44	.246	.352	.498	.851	136	13	13	99	101	53	.860	1	0	0	-1	O	1.1
	StL-A	37	130	22	45	5	0	6	19	23	20	.346	.444	.523	.968	174	13	13	97	84	33	1.046	0	0	0	-5	O	0.7
	Yr	122	415	68	115	20	3	23	70	69	64	.277	.381	.506	.887	148	25	26	98	96	88	.930	1	0	0	-6		1.8
1953	StL-A	128	440	61	118	18	6	19	70	72	44	.268	.376	.466	.842	118	17	13	107	101	79	.832	1	4	-2	6	*O	1.3
1954	Bal-A	29	94	5	19	1	0	1	13	11	17	.202	.286	.245	.530	48	-7	-6	95	190	7	.447	0	0	0	1	O	-0.5
	Cle-A	94	295	33	81	14	2	14	48	34	40	.275	.350	.478	.828	118	9	7	106	99	50	.795	0	2	-1	3	1/O	0.6
	Yr	123	389	38	100	15	2	15	61	45	57	.257	.334	.422	.756	102	2	1	103	122	57	.708	0	2	-1	3		0.1
1955	Cle-A	74	257	30	65	11	2	14	55	32	33	.253	.338	.475	.813	112	5	4	104	128	41	.784	1	1	-0	0	1/O	0.0
1956	Cle-A	136	481	65	127	22	0	32	106	75	87	.264	.369	.509	.878	128	20	19	101	118	93	.898	0	0	0	3	*1	1.6
1957	Cle-A	144	515	84	145	21	0	28	105	78	88	.282	.378	.485	.864	132	25	24	102	132	97	.869	2	3	-1	-1	*1	2.1
1958	Cle-A	25	43	5	12	1	0	3	12	5	7	.279	.354	.512	.866	143	2	2	94	155	7	.818	0	0	0	0	/1	0.2
1959	Bos-A	94	247	38	68	13	0	7	49	22	32	.275	.339	.413	.752	100	2	-0	106	157	34	.685	0	0	0	3	1	0.2
1960	Bos-A	131	443	45	125	22	0	19	103	37	54	.282	.339	.460	.799	111	7	6	103	**155**	66	.727	0	2	-1	1	*1	-0.1
1961	Bos-A	99	317	33	83	16	2	11	60	38	43	.262	.345	.429	.774	104	2	2	102	139	46	.718	0	0	0	1	1	-0.5
	Det-A	8	6	0	1	0	0	0	1	0	1	.167	.167	.167	.333	-11	-1	-1	96	392	0	.200	0	0	0	0	H	0.0
	Yr	107	323	33	84	16	2	11	61	38	44	.260	.342	.424	.766	102	1	1	101	159	51	.741	0	0	0	1		-0.5
1962	Det-A	74	105	7	34	2	0	5	18	5	13	.324	.360	.486	.846	113	3	2	111	108	18	.792	0	0	0	0	1	0.1
1963	Det-A	6	5	0	0	0	0	0	0	0	1	.000	.000	.000	.000	-97	-1	-1	104	0	0	.000	0	0	0	0	H	0.0
	Min-A	35	44	3	6	0	0	3	7	6	5	.136	.240	.341	.581	60	-2	-2	100	122	4	.538	0	0	0	0	/1	-0.2
	Yr	41	49	3	6	0	0	3	7	6	6	.122	.218	.306	.524	45	-4	-4	101	104	3	.477	0	0	0	0		-0.2
Total	17	1862	6099	867	1692	289	42	266	1178	828	842	.277	.366	.469	.836	120	194	174	103	123	1079	.842	9	19	-9	-16	O1	9.8
■ **JIM WESSINGER**	Wessinger, James Michael b: 9/25/55, Utica, N.Y. BR/TR, 5'11", 170 lbs. Deb: 8/04/79																											
1979	Atl-N	10	7	2	0	0	0	0	0	1	4	.000	.125	.000	.125	-58	-2	-2	109	0	0	.143	0	0	0	0	/2	-0.1
■ **MAX WEST**	West, Max Edward b: 11/28/16, Dexter, Mo. BL/TR, 6'1.5", 182 lbs. Deb: 4/19/38																											
1938	Bos-N	123	418	47	98	16	5	10	63	38	38	.234	.300	.368	.668	94	-11	-4	88	124	46	.598	5			-5	*O/1	-1.2
1939	Bos-N	130	449	67	128	26	6	19	82	51	55	.285	.364	.497	.861	141	18	23	92	110	82	.848	1			-7	*O	1.4
1940	Bos-N	139	524	72	137	27	5	7	72	65	54	.261	.344	.372	.716	99	-1	0	99	131	72	.673	2			9	*O1	0.2
1941	Bos-N	138	484	63	134	28	4	12	68	72	68	.277	.373	.426	.798	134	17	21	93	104	80	.789	5			8	*O	2.4
1942	Bos-N	134	452	54	115	22	0	16	56	68	59	.254	.354	.409	.764	129	14	16	95	91	71	.760	4			-1	1O	0.8
1946	Bos-N	1	1	0	0	0	0	0	0	0	1	.000	.000	.000	.000	-99	-0	-0	95	0	0	.000	0			0	/1	0.0
	Cin-N	72	202	16	43	13	0	5	18	32	36	.213	.323	.351	.675	88	-2	-3	104	78	24	.640	1			-2	O	-0.5
	Yr	73	203	16	43	13	0	5	18	32	37	.212	.322	.350	.672	87	-2	-3	104	77	24	.636	1			-2		-0.5
1948	Pit-N	87	146	19	26	4	0	8	21	27	29	.178	.310	.370	.680	80	-4	-4	104	101	18	.669	1			-4	1O	-0.9
Total	7	824	2676	338	681	136	20	77	380	353	340	.254	.344	.407	.751	114	31	49	95	109	392	.737	19			-1	O1	2.2
■ **BUCK WEST**	West, Milton Douglas b: 8/29/1860, Spring Mill, Ohio d: 1/13/29, Mansfield, Ohio BL/TR, 5'10", 200 lbs. Deb: 8/24/1884																											
1884	Cin-a	33	131	20	32	2	9	0		2		.244	.256	.397	.653	106	1	0	106	0	14	.545				-6	O	-0.4
1890	Cle-N	37	151	20	37	6	1	2	29	7	11	.245	.283	.338	.621	88	-4	-2	94	163	16	.553	4			-1	O	-0.3
Total	2	70	282	40	69	8	10	2	29	9	11	.245	.271	.365	.636	96	-2	-2	99	89	30	.549	4			-7	/O	-0.7
■ **DICK WEST**	West, Richard Thomas b: 11/24/15, Louisville, Ky. BR/TR, 6'2", 180 lbs. Deb: 9/28/38																											
1938	Cin-N	1	1	0	0	0	0	0	0	0	0	.000	.000	.000	.000	-99	-0	-0	98	0	0	.000	0			0	H	0.0
1939	Cin-N	8	19	1	4	0	0	0	4	1	4	.211	.250	.211	.461	24	-2	-2	103	367	1	.333	0			-0	/OC	-0.2
1940	Cin-N	7	28	4	11	2	0	1	6	0	2	.393	.393	.571	.964	161	2	2	101	119	6	1.000	1			-0	/C	0.2
1941	Cin-N	67	172	15	37	5	2	1	17	6	23	.215	.246	.285	.531	50	-12	-12	99	118	12	.435	4			-4	C	-0.9
1942	Cin-N	33	79	9	14	3	0	1	8	5	13	.177	.226	.253	.479	40	-6	-6	101	129	5	.400	1			-1	C/O	-0.6
1943	Cin-N	3	0	1	0	0	0	0	0	0	0	—	—	—	—	—	0	0	99	—	—	—	0			0	R	0.0
Total	6	119	299	30	66	10	2	3	35	12	42	.221	.253	.298	.551	56	-18	-18	100	137	29	.464	6			-5	/CO	-1.5
■ **SAM WEST**	West, Samuel Filmore b: 10/5/04, Longview, Tex. d: 11/23/85, Lubbock, Tex. BL/TL, 5'11", 165 lbs. Deb: 4/17/27 C																											
1927	Was-A	38	67	9	16	4	1	0	6	8	8	.239	.320	.328	.648	71	-3	-3	97	91	7	.608	1	0	0	-1	O	-0.4
1928	Was-A	125	378	59	114	30	7	3	40	20	23	.302	.338	.442	.780	102	1	-0	102	78	54	.715	5	6	-2	-6	*O	-1.3
1929	Was-A	142	510	60	136	16	8	3	75	45	41	.267	.326	.347	.673	74	-20	-20	100	141	59	.605	9	8	-2	13	*O	-1.4
1930	Was-A	120	411	75	135	22	10	6	67	37	34	.328	.385	.474	.860	115	11	10	101	104	75	.847	5	5	-2	-3	*O	0.0
1931	Was-A	132	526	77	175	43	13	3	91	30	37	.333	.369	.481	.850	121	15	14	101	117	90	.805	6	8	-3	15	*O	1.7
1932	Was-A	146	554	88	159	27	12	6	83	48	57	.287	.345	.412	.756	95	-5	-4	100	115	79	.702	4	5	-2	14	*O	0.2
1933	StL-A	133	517	93	155	25	12	11	48	59	49	.300	.373	.458	.831	104	14	3	115	63	89	.830	10	8	-2	5	*O	0.2
1934	StL-A	122	482	90	157	22	10	9	55	62	55	.326	.403	.469	.871	119	18	15	104	64	92	.882	3	5	-2	5	*O	1.5
1935	StL-A	138	527	93	158	37	4	10	70	75	46	.300	.388	.442	.830	107	12	7	107	96	92	.827	1	6	-3	12	*O	1.4
1936	StL-A	152	533	78	148	26	4	7	70	94	70	.278	.386	.381	.767	87	-6	-9	103	103	85	.777	2	0	1	4	*O	-0.7
1937	StL-A	122	457	68	150	37	4	7	58	46	28	.328	.390	.473	.862	118	11	12	99	86	85	.854	1	1	-0	9	*O	1.5
1938	StL-A	44	165	17	51	8	2	1	27	14	9	.309	.363	.400	.763	91	-2	-2	100	135	25	.711	1	0	0	0	O	-0.1
	Was-A	92	344	51	104	19	5	5	47	33	21	.302	.363	.430	.794	103	-1	1	95	99	55	.755	1	1	-0	-5	O	-0.3
	Yr	136	509	68	155	27	7	6	74	47	30	.305	.363	.420	.784	99	-4	-1	96	112	79	.741	2	1	0	-5		-0.4
1939	Was-A	115	390	52	110	20	8	3	52	67	29	.282	.387	.397	.785	112	3	9	90	109	65	.780	1	1	-0	9	O1	1.2
1940	Was-A	57	99	7	25	6	1	1	18	16	13	.253	.357	.364	.720	94	-2	-0	93	167	14	.684	0	2	-1	-1	1/O	-0.3
1941	Was-A	26	37	3	10	0	0	0	6	11	2	.270	.438	.270	.708	93	0	1	98	213	6	.815	1	0	0	-0	/O	0.0
1942	Chi-A	49	151	14	35	5	0	0	25	31	18	.232	.363	.265	.628	79	-3	-3	99	225	18	.624	2	0	1	0	O	-0.4
Total	16	1753	6148	934	1838	347	101	75	838	696	540	.299	.371	.425	.796	103	44	32	101	104	991	.771	53	56	-18	70	*O/1	2.8
■ **MAX WEST**	West, Walter Maxwell b: 7/14/04, Sunset, Tex. d: 4/25/71, Houston, Tex. BR/TR, 5'11", 165 lbs. Deb: 9/18/28																											
1928	Bro-N	7	21	4	6	1	1	0	1	4	1	.286	.400	.429	.829	118	1	1	99	40	4	.867	0			2	/O	0.2
1929	Bro-N	5	8	1	2	1	0	0	1	1	0	.250	.333	.375	.708	80	-0	-0	94	114	1	.667	0			-1	/O	0.0
Total	2	12	29	5	8	2	1	0	2	5	1	.276	.382	.414	.796	107	0	0	98	59	5	.810	0			1	/O	0.2
■ **BILLY WEST**	West, William Nelson b: 8/21/1840, Philadelphia, Pa. d: 8/18/1891, Radnor, Pa. Deb: 5/22/1874																											
1874	Atl-n	10	43	4	8							.186															2	
1876	NY-N	1	4	0	0	0	0	0	0	0	0	.000	.000	.000	.000	-99	-1	-1	87	0	0	.000				0	/2	0.0
■ **OSCAR WESTERBERG**	Westerberg, Oscar William b: 7/8/1882, Alameda, Cal. d: 4/17/09, Alameda, Cal. BB/TR, Deb: 9/05/07																											
1907	Bos-N	2	6	0	2	0	0	0	1	1		.333	.429	.333	.762	149	0	0	95	189	1	.750	0			0	/S	0.1
■ **JIM WESTLAKE**	Westlake, James Patrick b: 7/3/30, Sacramento, Cal. BL/TL, 6'1", 190 lbs. Deb: 4/16/55																											
1955	Phi-N	1	1	0	0	0	0	0	0	0	1	.000	.000	.000	.000	-98	-0	-0	102	0	0	.000	0	0	0	0	H	0.0
■ **WALLY WESTLAKE**	Westlake, Waldon Thomas b: 11/8/20, Gridley, Cal. BR/TR, 6', 186 lbs. Deb: 4/15/47																											
1947	Pit-N	112	407	59	111	17	4	17	69	27	63	.273	.324	.459	.784	105	2	1	101	109	56	.715	5			1	*O	-0.2

YEAR	TM/L	G	AB	R	H	2B	3B	HR	RBI	BB	SO	AVG	OBP	SLG	PRO	/A	BR	/A	PF	CHI	RC	TA	SB	CS	SBR	FR	POS	TPR
1948	Pit-N	132	428	78	122	10	6	17	65	46	40	.285	.360	.456	.815	114	11	9	104	99	71	.782	2			1	*O	0.1
1949	Pit-N	147	525	77	148	24	8	23	104	45	69	.282	.345	.490	.835	120	14	13	101	123	86	.801	6			4	*O	0.9
1950	Pit-N	139	477	69	136	15	6	24	95	48	78	.285	.359	.493	.852	119	14	12	103	119	83	.817	1			-1	*O	0.7
1951	Pit-N	50	181	28	51	4	0	16	45	9	26	.282	.323	.569	.892	127	7	6	107	118	32	.844	0	1	-1	3	3O	0.8
	StL-N	73	267	36	68	8	5	6	39	24	42	.255	.325	.390	.715	91	-3	-4	101	126	34	.639	1	2	-1	2	O	-0.4
	Yr	123	448	64	119	12	5	22	84	33	68	.266	.324	.462	.786	106	4	2	103	124	68	.729	1	3	-2	5		0.4
1952	StL-N	21	74	7	16	3	0	0	10	8	11	.216	.293	.257	.549	55	-4	-4	98	209	5	.452	1	1	-0	8	O	0.3
	Cin-N	59	183	29	37	4	0	3	14	31	29	.202	.324	.273	.597	67	-7	-7	100	93	16	.525	0	2	-1	3	O	-0.6
	Yr	80	257	36	53	7	0	3	24	39	40	.206	.315	.268	.584	64	-12	-11	99	126	22	.512	1	3	-2	10		-0.3
	Cle-A	29	69	11	16	4	1	1	9	8	16	.232	.312	.362	.674	96	-1	-0	91	120	8	.618	1	0	0	-1	O	-0.1
1953	Cle-A	82	218	42	72	7	1	9	46	35	29	.330	.427	.495	.923	156	16	17	95	126	49	.967	2	0	1	-5	O	1.1
1954	Cle-A	85	240	36	63	9	2	11	42	26	37	.262	.340	.454	.794	109	4	3	106	112	36	.737	0	1	-1	-7	O	-0.7
1955	Cle-A	16	20	2	5	1	0	0	1	3	5	.250	.348	.300	.648	73	-1	-1	104	62	2	.563	0	0	0	-0	/O	0.0
	Bal-A	8	24	0	3	1	0	0	0	6	5	.125	.300	.167	.467	31	-2	-2	90	0	1	.455	0	0	0	-2	/O	-0.3
	Yr	24	44	2	8	2	0	0	1	9	10	.182	.321	.227	.548	50	-3	-3	99	44	4	.514	0	0	0	-2		-0.3
1956	Phi-N	5	4	0	0	0	0	0	0	1	3	.000	.200	.000	.200	-42	-1	-1	94	0	0	.250	0	0	0	0	H	0.0
Total	10	958	3117	474	848	107	33	127	539	317	453	.272	.346	.450	.795	111	48	43	101	115	480	.778	19	7		5	O/3	1.6
■ **AL WESTON**	Weston, Alfred John b: 12/11/05, Lynn, Mass. BR/TR, 6', 195 lbs. Deb: 7/07/29																											
1929	Bos-N	3	3	0	0	0	0	0	0	0	2	.000	.000	.000	.000	-99	-1	-1	94	0	0	.000	0			0	H	0.0
■ **WES WESTRUM**	Westrum, Wesley Noreen b: 11/28/22, Clearbrook, Minn. BR/TR, 5'11", 185 lbs. Deb: 9/17/47 MC																											
1947	NY-N	6	12	1	5	1	0	0	2	0	2	.417	.417	.500	.917	141	1	1	101	123	3	.857	0			0	/C	0.1
1948	NY-N	66	125	14	20	3	1	4	16	20	36	.160	.276	.296	.572	55	-8	-8	100	122	11	.566	3			-3	C	-0.6
1949	NY-N	64	169	23	41	4	1	7	28	37	39	.243	.385	.402	.787	110	4	4	102	119	28	.812	1			-1	C	0.4
1950	NY-N	140	437	68	103	13	3	23	71	92	73	.236	.371	.437	.808	114	9	10	98	105	74	.825	2			2	*C	1.6
1951	NY-N	124	361	59	79	12	0	20	70	104	93	.219	.400	.418	.818	118	15	14	102	128	70	.894	1	0	0	-7	*C	0.8
1952	NY-N	114	322	47	71	11	0	14	43	76	68	.220	.374	.385	.759	108	8	6	102	101	53	.791	1	2	-1	-4	*C	0.3
1953	NY-N	107	290	40	65	5	0	12	30	56	73	.224	.352	.366	.717	89	-4	-3	98	82	41	.708	2	0	1	-11	*C/3	-0.6
1954	NY-N	98	246	25	46	3	1	8	27	45	60	.187	.320	.305	.625	61	-13	-14	105	107	27	.606	0	1	-1	-14	C	-2.6
1955	NY-N	69	137	11	29	1	0	4	18	24	18	.212	.333	.307	.640	72	-5	-5	99	135	14	.573	0	1	-1	-14	C	-1.7
1956	NY-N	68	132	10	29	5	2	3	8	25	28	.220	.348	.356	.704	92	-1	-1	97	60	16	.670	0	0	0	-7	C	-0.5
1957	NY-N	63	91	4	15	1	0	1	2	10	24	.165	.255	.209	.464	26	-9	-10	102	38	5	.385	0	1	-1	-5	C	-1.2
Total	11	919	2322	302	503	59	8	96	315	489	514	.217	.357	.373	.730	95	-4	-6	101	105	342	.758	10	5		-64	C/3	-4.0
■ **DUTCH WETZEL**	Wetzel, Franklin Burton b: 7/7/1893, Columbus, Ind. d: 3/5/42, Hollywood, Cal. BR/TR, 5'9.5", 177 lbs. Deb: 9/15/20																											
1920	StL-A	7	21	4	9	1	1	0	5	4	1	.429	.520	.571	1.091	170	3	3	111	146	6	1.231	0	1	-1	0	/O	0.1
1921	StL-A	61	119	16	25	2	0	2	10	9	20	.210	.271	.277	.549	40	-11	-11	101	88	9	.457	0	0	0	-3	O	-1.4
Total	2	68	140	20	34	3	1	2	15	13	21	.243	.312	.321	.633	61	-8	-8	103	97	15	.551	0	1	-1	-3	/O	-1.3
■ **BILL WHALEY**	Whaley, William Carl b: 2/10/1899, Indianapolis, Ind. d: 3/3/43, Indianapolis, Ind. BR/TR, 5'11", 178 lbs. Deb: 4/18/23																											
1923	StL-A	23	50	5	12	2	1	0	1	4	2	.240	.309	.320	.629	63	-3	-3	104	21	5	.553	0	0	0	0	O	-0.3
■ **BERT WHALING**	Whaling, Albert James b: 6/22/1888, Los Angeles, Cal. d: 1/21/65, Sawtelle, Cal. BR/TR, 6', 185 lbs. Deb: 4/22/13																											
1913	Bos-N	79	211	22	51	8	2	0	25	10	32	.242	.283	.299	.581	70	-10	-8	95	144	19	.488	3			2	C	0.0
1914	Bos-N	60	172	18	36	7	0	0	12	21	28	.209	.303	.250	.553	62	-7	-8	104	101	13	.500	2			5	C	0.0
1915	Bos-N	72	190	10	42	6	2	0	13	8	38	.221	.264	.274	.537	64	-9	-8	98	95	14	.423	0	1	-1	-2	C	-0.7
Total	3	211	573	50	129	21	4	0	50	39	98	.225	.283	.276	.558	66	-25	-24	99	115	46	.470	5	1		6	C	-0.7
■ **MACK WHEAT**	Wheat, Mc Kinley Davis b: 6/9/1893, Polo, Mo. d: 8/14/79, Los Banos, Cal. BR/TR, 5'11.5", 167 lbs. Deb: 4/14/15																											
1915	Bro-N	8	14	0	1	0	0	0	0	0	5	.071	.071	.071	.143	-56	-3	-3	101	0	0	.077	0			0	/C	-0.1
1916	Bro-N	2	2	0	0	0	0	0	0	0	1	.000	.000	.000	.000	-97	-0	-0	103	0	0	.000	0			0	/C	0.0
1917	Bro-N	29	60	2	8	1	0	0	0	1	12	.133	.161	.150	.311	-4	-7	-8	104	0	1	.231	1			-2	C/O	-0.9
1918	Bro-N	57	157	11	34	7	1	1	3	8	24	.217	.255	.293	.548	66	-7	-7	101	23	12	.455	2			3	C/O	0.0
1919	Bro-N	41	112	5	23	3	0	0	8	2	22	.205	.246	.232	.478	47	-8	-7	94	120	7	.371	1			0	C	-0.3
1920	Phi-N	78	230	15	52	10	3	3	20	8	35	.226	.261	.335	.596	65	-9	-12	109	90	20	.508	3	1	0	2	C	-0.3
1921	Phi-N	10	27	1	5	2	1	0	4	0	3	.185	.241	.333	.575	50	-2	-2	102	163	2	.500	0	0	0	0	/C	0.0
Total	7	225	602	34	123	23	5	4	35	19	102	.204	.241	.279	.520	52	-36	-38	103	70	42	.425	7	1		5	C/O	-1.6
■ **ZACH WHEAT**	Wheat, Zachary Davis "Buck" b: 5/23/1888, Hamilton, Mo. d: 3/11/72, Sedalia, Mo. BL/TR, 5'10", 170 lbs. Deb: 09 H																											
1909	Bro-N	26	102	15	31	7	3	0	4	6		.304	.343	.431	.774	144	4	4	99	29	15	.718	1			-2	O	0.1
1910	Bro-N	156	606	78	172	36	15	2	55	47	80	.284	.341	.403	.744	123	11	14	95	74	87	.721	16			-5	*O	0.4
1911	Bro-N	140	534	55	153	26	13	5	76	29	58	.287	.332	.412	.744	111	3	5	97	116	79	.727	21			-2	*O	0.0
1912	Bro-N	123	453	70	138	28	7	8	65	39	40	.305	.367	.450	.818	129	13	16	95	98	79	.841	16			-2	*O	1.0
1913	Bro-N	138	535	64	161	28	10	7	58	25	45	.301	.335	.430	.764	112	10	7	104	89	79	.738	19			-0	*O	0.4
1914	Bro-N	145	533	66	170	26	9	9	89	47	50	.319	.377	.452	.830	145	29	29	101	128	95	.857	20			3	*O	2.9
1915	Bro-N	146	528	64	136	15	12	5	66	52	42	.258	.330	.360	.690	107	6	5	101	130	65	.660	21	14	-2	-1	*O	-0.2
1916	Bro-N	149	568	76	177	32	13	9	73	43	49	.312	.366	**.461**	.828	149	**34**	**33**	103	106	**103**	.844	19			8	*O	4.0
1917	Bro-N	109	362	38	113	15	11	1	41	20	18	.312	.352	.423	.774	132	15	13	104	101	53	.723	5			-3	O	0.8
1918	Bro-N	105	409	39	137	15	3	0	51	16	17	**.335**	.369	.386	.755	129	14	14	101	117	59	.695	9			2	*O	1.1
1919	Bro-N	137	536	70	159	23	11	5	62	33	27	.297	.344	.409	.753	134	16	20	94	109	76	.724	15			-1	*O	1.4
1920	Bro-N	148	583	89	191	26	13	9	73	48	21	.328	.385	.463	.848	128	32	24	111	101	102	.826	8	10	-4	-5	*O	0.7
1921	Bro-N	148	568	91	182	31	10	14	85	44	19	.320	.372	.484	.857	120	20	16	105	104	101	.845	11	8	-2	-5	*O	0.2
1922	Bro-N	152	600	92	201	29	12	16	112	45	22	.335	.388	.503	.891	135	24	29	95	119	116	.896	9	6	-1	-1	*O	1.9
1923	Bro-N	98	349	63	131	13	5	8	65	23	12	.375	.417	.510	.927	147	22	23	98	113	73	.932	3	3	-1	-16	O	0.3
1924	Bro-N	141	566	92	212	41	8	14	97	49	18	.375	.428	.549	.978	162	48	49	99	96	132	1.025	3	4	-2	5	*O	4.8
1925	Bro-N	150	616	125	221	42	14	14	103	45	22	.359	.403	.541	.944	148	35	41	94	103	134	.965	3	1	0	-9	*O	2.6
1926	Bro-N	111	411	68	119	31	2	5	35	21	14	.290	.326	.411	.737	98	-3	-2	99	67	53	.668	4			-3	*O	-0.9
1927	Phi-A	88	247	34	80	12	1	1	38	18	5	.324	.379	.393	.772	104	1	2	97	126	36	.725	2	0	1	-3	O	-0.4
Total	19	2410	9106	1289	2884	476	172	132	1248	650	559	.317	.367	.450	.817	130	334	341	100	104	1539	.803	205	46		-39	*O	21.1
■ **WOODY WHEATON**	Wheaton, Elwood Pierce b: 10/3/14, Philadelphia, Pa. BL/TL, 5'8.5", 160 lbs. Deb: 9/28/43																											
1943	Phi-A	7	30	2	6	2	0	0	2	3	2	.200	.294	.267	.561	64	-1	-1	101	79	2	.480	0	0	0	1	/O	0.0
1944	Phi-A	30	59	1	11	2	0	0	5	5	3	.186	.250	.220	.470	35	-5	-5	101	139	3	.358	1	2	-1	3	P/O	-0.1
Total	2	37	89	3	17	4	0	0	7	8	5	.191	.265	.236	.501	44	-6	-6	101	118	5	.403	1	2	-1	4	/OP	-0.1
■ **DON WHEELER**	Wheeler, Donald Wesley "Scott" b: 9/29/22, Minneapolis, Minn BR/TR, 5'10", 175 lbs. Deb: 4/23/49																											
1949	Chi-A	67	192	17	46	9	2	1	22	27	19	.240	.333	.323	.656	76	-7	-7	98	116	22	.603	2	0	1	5	C	0.2
■ **ED WHEELER**	Wheeler, Edward b: 6/15/1878, Sherman, Mich. d: 8/15/60, Ft.Worth, Tex. BB/TR, 5'10", 160 lbs. Deb: 5/10/02																											
1902	Bro-N	30	96	4	12	0	0	0	5	3		.125	.152	.125	.277	-14	-12	-12	95	144	2	.190	1			-3	32/S	-1.3
■ **ED WHEELER**	Wheeler, Edward Raymond b: 5/24/17, Los Angeles, Cal. BR/TR, 5'9", 160 lbs. Deb: 4/19/45																											
1945	Cle-A	46	72	12	14	2	0	0	1	8	13	.194	.275	.222	.497	46	-5	-5	99	23	5	.424	1	1	-0	-2	3S/2	-0.6
■ **GEORGE WHEELER**	Wheeler, George Harrison "Heavy" b: 11/10/1881, Shelburn, Ind. d: 6/14/18, Clinton, Ind. BL/TR, 5'9.5", 180 lbs. Deb: 7/27/10																											
1910	Cin-N	3	3	0	0	0	0	0	0	0	2	.000	.000	.000	.000	-99	-1	-1	101	0	0	.000	0			0	H	0.0
■ **HARRY WHEELER**	Wheeler, Harry Eugene b: 3/3/1858, Versailles, Ind. d: 10/9/1900, Cincinnati, Ohio BR/TR, 5'11", 165 lbs. Deb: 6/19/1878 M																											
1878	Pro-N	7	27	7	4	0	0	0	1	2	15	.148	.207	.148	.355	19	-2	-2	98	90	1	.261				0	/P	0.0
1879	Cin-N	1	3	0	0	0	0	0	0	0	2	.000	.000	.000	.000	-99	-1	-1	95	0	0	.000				0	/OP	0.0

YEAR	TM/L	G	AB	R	H	2B	3B	HR	RBI	BB	SO	AVG	OBP	SLG	PRO	/A	BR	/A	PF	CHI	RC	TA	SB	CS	SBR	FR	POS	TPR
1880	Cle-N	1	4	0	1	0	0	0	0	0	0	.250	.250	.250	.500	71	-0	-0	99	0	0	.333				0	/O	0.0
	Cin-N	17	65	1	6	2	0	0	2	0	15	.092	.092	.123	.215	-28	-8	-8	99	93	1	.136				0	O	-0.7
	Yr	18	69	1	7	2	0	0	2	0	15	.101	.101	.130	.232	-22	-8	-8	99	88	1	.145				0		-0.7
1882	Cin-a	76	344	59	86	11	11	1		7		.250	.265	.355	.620	99	2	-2	109	0	33	.500				-5	*O1/P	-0.6
1883	Col-a	82	371	42	84	6	6	1		6		.226	.239	.283	.522	77	-13	-6	87	0	26	.387				-1	*O/2P	-0.4
1884	StL-a	5	19	0	5	2	0	0		1		.263	.300	.368	.668	109	0	0	110	0	2	.571				0	/O	0.0
	KC-U	14	62	11	16	1	0	0		3		.258	.292	.274	.567	106	-0	1	87	0	5	.435	0			0	O/PM	0.1
	CP-U	37	158	29	36	5	3	1		4		.228	.247	.316	.563	90	-2	-2	99	0	13	.443	0			-5	O	-0.5
	Bal-U	17	69	3	18	2	0	0		0		.261	.261	.290	.551	78	-1	-2	110	0	5	.392	0			0	O	-0.1
	Yr	68	289	43	70	8	3	1		7		.242	.260	.301	.561	90	-3	-3	100	0	23	.429	0			-5		-0.5
Total	6	257	1122	152	256	29	20	3	3	23	32	.228	.244	.298	.541	80	-25	-22	98	8	86	.412	0			-10	O/P12	-2.2
■ **DICK WHEELER**	Wheeler, Richard (born Richard Wheeler Maynard) b: 1/14/1898, Keene, N.H. d: 2/12/62, Lexington, Mass. BR/TR, 5'11", 185 lbs. Deb: 6/17/18																											
1918	StL-N	3	6	0	0	0	0	0	0	0	3	.000	.000	.000	.000	-99	-1	-1	93	0	0	.000	0			-1	/O	-0.2
■ **BOBBY WHEELOCK**	Wheelock, Warren H. b: 8/6/1864, Charlestown, Mass. d: 3/13/28, Boston, Mass. BR/TR, 5'8", 160 lbs. Deb: 5/19/1887																											
1887	Bos-N	48	166	32	42	4	2	2	15	15	15	.253	.315	.337	.652	85	-4	-3	98	75	25	.734	20			0	OS/2	-0.1
1890	Col-a	52	190	24	45	6	1	1		25		.237	.326	.295	.620	86	-3	-3	99	0	30	.793	34			-2	S	-0.1
1891	Col-a	136	498	82	114	15	1	0	39	78	55	.229	.336	.263	.599	83	-13	-4	89	91	63	.685	52			17	*S	1.6
Total	3	236	854	138	201	25	4	3	54	118	70	.235	.330	.285	.614	84	-20	-9	93	68	118	.718	106			15	S/O2	1.4
■ **JIMMY WHELAN**	Whelan, James Francis b: 5/11/1890, Kansas City, Mo. d: 11/29/29, Dayton, Ohio BR/TR, 5'8.5", 165 lbs. Deb: 4/24/13																											
1913	StL-N	1	1	0	0	0	0	0	0	0	0	.000	.000	.000	.000	-99	-0	-0	93	0	0	.000	0			0	H	0.0
■ **TOM WHELAN**	Whelan, Thomas Joseph b: 1/3/1894, Lynn, Mass. d: 6/26/57, Boston, Mass. BR/TR, 5'10", 180 lbs. Deb: 8/13/20																											
1920	Bos-N	1	1	0	0	0	0	0	0	1	1	.000	.500	.000	.500	53	0	0	96	0	0	1.000	0	0	0	0	/1	0.0
■ **PETE WHISENANT**	Whisenant, Thomas Peter b: 12/14/29, Asheville, N.C. BR/TR, 6'2", 190 lbs. Deb: 4/16/52 C																											
1952	Bos-N	24	52	3	10	2	0	0	7	4	13	.192	.250	.231	.481	36	-5	-4	95	228	3	.378	1	1	-0	2	O	-0.2
1955	StL-N	58	115	10	22	5	1	2	9	5	29	.191	.225	.304	.529	39	-10	-10	101	89	8	.442	2	0	1	0	O	-1.0
1956	Chi-N	103	314	37	75	16	3	11	46	24	53	.239	.295	.414	.709	89	-6	-5	99	119	38	.660	8	2	1	0	O	-0.7
1957	Cin-N	67	90	18	19	3	2	5	11	5	24	.211	.253	.456	.708	81	-2	-3	105	81	10	.630	0	1	-1	-9	O	-1.3
1958	Cin-N	85	203	33	48	9	2	11	40	18	37	.236	.299	.463	.762	91	-1	-3	107	130	28	.723	3	0	1	-2	O/2	-0.5
1959	Cin-N	36	71	13	17	2	0	5	11	8	18	.239	.316	.479	.795	105	1	0	103	91	11	.764	0	0	0	-2	O	-0.2
1960	Cin-N	1	1	0	0	0	0	0	0	0	0	.000	.000	.000	.000	-99	-0	-0	98	0	0	.000	0	0	0	0	H	0.0
	Cle-A	7	6	0	1	0	0	0	0	0	2	.167	.167	.167	.333	-10	-1	-1	98	0	0	.200	0	0	0	-1	/O	-0.1
	Was-A	58	115	19	26	9	0	3	9	19	14	.226	.336	.383	.718	92	-1	-1	102	66	15	.699	2	1	0	-5	O	-0.7
	Yr	65	121	19	27	9	0	3	9	19	16	.223	.329	.372	.700	88	-2	-2	101	59	15	.673	2	1	0	-5		-0.8
1961	Min-A	10	6	1	0	0	0	0	0	1	2	.000	.143	.000	.143	-55	-1	-1	106	0	0	.167	0	0	0	-2	/O	-0.2
	Cin-N	26	15	6	3	0	0	0	1	2	4	.200	.294	.200	.494	33	-1	-1	104	134	1	.462	1	0	0	-4	O/C3	-0.5
Total	8	475	988	140	221	46	8	37	134	86	196	.224	.287	.399	.685	80	-29	-31	102	110	114	.644	17	5	2	-22	O/3C2	-5.4
■ **LARRY WHISENTON**	Whisenton, Larry b: 7/3/56, St.Louis, Mo. BL/TL, 6'1", 190 lbs. Deb: 9/17/77																											
1977	Atl-N	4	4	1	1	0	0	0	1	0	3	.250	.250	.250	.500	31	-0	-0	113	400	0	.333	0	0	0	0	H	0.0
1978	Atl-N	6	16	1	3	1	0	0	2	1	2	.188	.235	.250	.485	32	-1	-2	112	198	1	.385	0	0	0	-1	/O	-0.2
1979	Atl-N	13	37	3	9	2	1	0	1	3	3	.243	.300	.351	.651	71	-1	-2	109	30	4	.586	1	0	0	2	O	0.1
1981	Atl-N	9	5	1	1	0	0	0	0	2	1	.200	.429	.200	.629	83	0	0	100	0	1	.750	0	0	0	-1	/O	0.0
1982	Atl-N	84	143	21	34	7	2	4	17	23	33	.238	.343	.399	.742	100	2	0	107	97	20	.719	2	2	-1	-3	O	-0.3
Total	5	116	205	27	48	10	3	4	21	29	42	.234	.329	.371	.700	88	-1	-3	108	95	26	.667	3	2	-0	-3	/O	-0.4
■ **LEW WHISTLER**	Whistler, Lewis (born Lewis Wissler) b: 3/10/1868, St.Louis, Mo. d: 12/30/59, St.Louis, Mo. TR , Deb: 8/07/1890																											
1890	NY-N	45	170	27	49	9	7	2	29	20	37	.288	.366	.459	.825	150	9	10	95	110	32	.884	8			-1	1	0.5
1891	NY-N	72	265	39	65	8	7	4	38	24	45	.245	.315	.374	.689	109	0	3	94	102	33	.650	4			0	SO/123	0.3
1892	Bal-N	52	209	32	47	6	6	2	21	18	22	.225	.296	.340	.635	94	-2	-2	100	80	25	.642	12			-1	1/O	-0.6
	Lou-N	80	285	42	67	4	7	5	34	30	45	.235	.312	.351	.663	111	1	4	92	93	36	.670	14			-3	12	-0.3
	Yr	132	494	74	114	10	13	7	55	48	67	.231	.305	.346	.651	104	-1	2	95	88	62	.658	26			-4		-0.9
1893	Lou-N	13	47	5	10	1	1	0	9	5	5	.213	.302	.277	.578	58	-3	-3	96	193	4	.541	1			0	1	-0.1
	StL-N	10	38	5	9	1	0	0	2	3	2	.237	.293	.263	.556	50	-3	-3	99	56	3	.448	0			0	/O1	-0.1
	Yr	23	85	10	19	2	1	0	11	8	7	.224	.298	.271	.568	54	-6	-5	98	142	7	.500	1			0		-0.2
Total	4	272	1014	150	247	29	28	13	133	100	156	.244	.318	.366	.683	108	2	10	95	99	135	.678	39			-6	1/SO23	-0.3
■ **LOU WHITAKER**	Whitaker, Louis Rodman b: 5/12/57, Brooklyn, N.Y. BL/TR, 5'11", 160 lbs. Deb: 9/09/77																											
1977	Det-A	11	32	5	8	1	0	0	2	4	6	.250	.333	.281	.615	66	-1	-1	105	88	3	.577	2	2	-1	0	/2	0.0
1978	Det-A	139	484	71	138	12	7	3	58	61	65	.285	.366	.357	.724	97	5	-0	108	128	66	.669	7	7	-2	22	*2/D	2.7
1979	Det-A	127	423	75	121	14	8	3	42	78	66	.286	.398	.378	.777	115	10	12	96	101	69	.804	20	10	0	9	*2	2.6
1980	Det-A	145	477	68	111	19	1	1	45	73	79	.233	.335	.283	.618	67	-16	-20	105	127	50	.570	8	4	0	-1	*2	-1.2
1981	Det-A	109	335	48	88	14	4	5	36	40	42	.263	.343	.373	.716	101	3	1	105	101	45	.671	5	3	-0	5	*2	1.0
1982	Det-A	152	560	76	160	22	8	15	65	48	58	.286	.343	.434	.777	111	9	8	100	92	85	.737	11	3	2	15	*2/D	3.2
1983	Det-A	161	643	94	206	40	6	12	72	67	70	.320	.385	.457	.842	137	28	32	96	82	114	.829	17	10	-1	-7	*2	2.9
1984	Det-A	143	558	90	161	25	1	13	56	62	63	.289	.360	.407	.766	116	10	13	96	89	83	.718	6	5	-1	-1	*2	1.8
1985	Det-A	152	609	102	170	29	8	21	73	80	56	.279	.365	.456	.821	116	20	15	106	75	107	.821	6	4	-1	-7	*2	1.3
1986	Det-A	144	584	95	157	26	6	20	73	63	70	.269	.340	.437	.777	116	9	12	95	89	82	.727	13	8	-1	1	*2	1.9
1987	Det-A	149	604	110	160	38	6	16	59	71	108	.265	.343	.427	.770	107	4	6	97	74	93	.756	13	5	1	-4	*2	1.3
1988	Det-A	115	403	54	111	18	2	12	55	66	61	.275	.377	.419	.797	130	14	17	94	113	67	.790	2	0	1	-8	*2	1.7
Total	12	1547	5712	888	1591	258	57	121	636	713	744	.279	.359	.407	.767	111	94	96	100	95	865	.753	110	61	-4	26	*2/D	19.2
■ **STEVE WHITAKER**	Whitaker, Stephen Edward b: 5/7/43, Tacoma, Wash. BL/TR, 6', 180 lbs. Deb: 8/23/66																											
1966	NY-A	31	114	15	28	3	2	7	15	9	24	.246	.306	.491	.798	134	3	4	94	83	18	.767	0	0	0	2	O	0.5
1967	NY-A	122	441	37	107	12	3	11	50	23	89	.243	.285	.358	.643	94	-7	-4	94	111	43	.539	2	5	-2	6	*O	-0.4
1968	NY-A	28	60	3	7	2	0	0	3	8	18	.117	.221	.150	.371	14	-6	-6	101	143	2	.315	0	1	-1	-0	O	-0.8
1969	Sea-A	69	116	15	29	2	1	6	13	12	29	.250	.326	.440	.765	114	2	2	98	76	18	.750	2	0	1	-3	O	-0.1
1970	SF-N	16	27	3	3	1	0	0	4	2	14	.111	.172	.148	.321	-14	-4	-4	96	388	1	.240	0	0	0	-2	/O	-0.6
Total	5	266	758	73	174	20	6	24	85	54	174	.230	.285	.367	.652	93	-13	-9	95	114	82	.577	4	6	-2	2	O	-1.4
■ **FUZZ WHITE**	White, Albert Eugene b: 6/27/18, Springfield, Mo. BL/TR, 6', 175 lbs. Deb: 9/17/40																											
1940	StL-A	2	2	0	0	0	0	0	0	0	0	.000	.000	.000	.000	-95	-1	-1	106	0	0	.000	0	0	0	0	H	0.0
1947	NY-N	7	13	3	3	0	0	0	0	0	0	.231	.231	.231	.462	23	-1	-1	101	0	0	.273	0			-0	/O	-0.1
Total	2	9	15	3	3	0	0	0	0	0	0	.200	.200	.200	.400	6	-2	-2	101	0	0	.231	0	0		-0	/O	-0.1
■ **C.B. WHITE**	White, C. B. b: Wakeman, Ohio Deb: 6/01/1883																											
1883	Phi-N	1	1	0	0	0	0	0	0	0	0	.000	.000	.000	.000	-99	-0	-0	90	0	0	.000				0	/S3	0.0
■ **CHARLIE WHITE**	White, Charles b: 8/12/28, Kinston, N.C. BL/TR, 5'11", 192 lbs. Deb: 4/18/54																											
1954	Mil-N	50	93	14	22	4	0	1	8	9	8	.237	.304	.312	.616	65	-5	-4	93	98	8	.500	0	0	0	1	C	-0.2
1955	Mil-N	12	30	3	7	1	0	0	4	5	7	.233	.361	.267	.628	75	-1	-1	93	202	3	.583	0	0	0	1	C	0.0
Total	2	62	123	17	29	5	0	1	12	14	15	.236	.319	.301	.620	68	-6	-5	93	125	11	.547	0	0	0	1	/C	-0.2
■ **DEVON WHITE**	White, Devon Markes b: 12/29/62, Kingston, Jamaica BB/TR, 6'1", 170 lbs. Deb: 9/02/85																											
1985	Cal-A	21	7	7	1	0	0	0	0	1	3	.143	.333	.143	.476	36	-1	-1	101	0	1	.857	3	1	0	-5	O	-0.4
1986	Cal-A	29	51	8	12	1	1	1	3	6	8	.235	.316	.353	.669	86	-1	-1	96	57	7	.769	6	0	2	-3	O	-0.2
1987	Cal-A	159	639	103	168	33	5	24	87	39	135	.263	.307	.443	.750	97	-4	-4	99	104	87	.727	32	11	3	12	*O	0.6

YEAR	TM/L	G	AB	R	H	2B	3B	HR	RBI	BB	SO	AVG	OBP	SLG	PRO	/A	BR	/A	PF	CHI	RC	TA	SB	CS	SBR	FR	POS	TPR
1988	Cal-A	122	455	76	118	22	2	11	51	23	84	.259	.298	.389	.687	96	-7	-3	94	98	52	.626	17	8	0	10	*O	0.5
Total	4	331	1152	194	299	56	8	36	141	69	230	.260	.304	.416	.720	96	-13	-8	97	99	147	.696	58	20	5	14	O	0.5
■ DON WHITE	White, Donald William b: 1/8/19, Everett, Wash. d: 6/15/87, Carlsbad, Cal. BR/TR, 6'1", 195 lbs. Deb: 4/19/48																											
1948	Phi-A	86	253	29	62	14	2	1	28	19	16	.245	.303	.328	.631	67	-12	-13	102	110	25	.525	0	1	-1	-4	O3	-1.9
1949	Phi-A	57	169	12	36	6	0	0	10	14	12	.213	.273	.249	.522	39	-15	-15	99	82	12	.423	2	0	1	-3	O/3	-1.7
Total	2	143	422	41	98	20	2	1	38	33	28	.232	.291	.296	.587	56	-27	-28	100	99	38	.492	2	1	0	-7	O/3	-3.6
■ ED WHITE	White, Edward Perry b: 4/6/26, Anniston, Ala. d: 9/28/82, Lakeland, Fla. BR/TR, 6'2", 200 lbs. Deb: 9/16/55																											
1955	Chi-A	3	4	0	2	0	0	0	0	1	1	.500	.600	.500	1.100	197	1	1	101	0	1	1.500	0	0	0	-0	/O	0.0
■ ELDER WHITE	White, Elder Lafayette b: 12/23/34, Colerain, N.C. BR/TR, 5'11", 165 lbs. Deb: 4/10/62																											
1962	Chi-N	23	53	4	8	2	0	0	1	8	11	.151	.274	.189	.463	25	-5	-6	106	39	4	.468	3	0	1	1	S/3	-0.2
■ ELMER WHITE	White, Elmer b: 5/23/1850, Caton, N.Y. d: 3/17/1872, Caton, N.Y. Deb: 5/04/1871																											
1871	Cle-n	15	71	13	20							.282															O/C	
■ FRANK WHITE	White, Frank b: 9/4/50, Greenville, Miss. BR/TR, 5'11", 165 lbs. Deb: 6/12/73																											
1973	KC-A	51	139	20	31	6	1	0	5	8	23	.223	.265	.281	.546	49	-9	-10	109	50	11	.455	3	1	0	8	S2	0.4
1974	KC-A	99	204	19	45	6	3	1	18	5	33	.221	.239	.294	.533	50	-13	-14	106	112	13	.407	3	4	-2	-1	2S3/D	-1.2
1975	KC-A	111	304	43	76	10	2	7	36	20	39	.250	.298	.365	.664	85	-6	-7	102	105	34	.609	11	3	2	-1	2S/3CD	0.0
1976	KC-A	152	446	39	102	17	6	2	46	19	42	.229	.265	.307	.572	67	-19	-19	100	124	37	.499	20	11	-1	4	*2S	-0.6
1977	KC-A	152	474	59	116	21	5	5	50	25	67	.245	.285	.342	.627	70	-20	-20	100	112	49	.578	23	5	4	-2	*2/S	-0.5
1978	KC-A	143	461	66	127	24	6	7	50	26	59	.275	.318	.399	.717	98	-1	-2	102	96	59	.653	13	10	-2	-16	*2	-1.2
1979	KC-A	127	467	73	124	26	4	10	48	25	54	.266	.304	.403	.707	84	-8	-12	105	86	56	.669	28	8	4	-10	*2	-1.2
1980	KC-A	154	560	70	148	23	4	7	60	19	69	.264	.291	.357	.648	78	-19	-18	98	106	57	.559	19	6	2	-5	*2	-1.2
1981	KC-A	94	364	35	91	17	1	9	38	19	50	.250	.287	.376	.664	91	-6	-5	99	96	37	.561	4	2	0	-15	2	-1.8
1982	KC-A	145	524	71	156	45	6	11	56	16	65	.298	.321	.469	.790	114	8	8	100	82	73	.708	10	7	-1	-11	*2	0.3
1983	KC-A	146	549	52	143	35	6	11	77	20	51	.260	.286	.406	.693	87	-10	-11	101	120	58	.597	13	5	1	14	*2	0.8
1984	KC-A	129	479	58	130	22	5	17	56	27	72	.271	.313	.445	.758	108	3	4	99	86	63	.677	5	5	-2	16	*2	2.4
1985	KC-A	149	563	62	140	25	1	22	69	28	86	.249	.285	.414	.699	87	-10	-12	102	93	65	.625	10	4	1	15	*2	1.0
1986	KC-A	151	566	76	154	37	3	22	84	43	88	.272	.326	.465	.790	113	9	9	100	108	84	.732	4	4	-1	8	*2/S3	2.3
1987	KC-A	154	563	67	138	32	2	17	78	51	86	.245	.310	.400	.710	84	-11	-14	104	115	67	.628	1	3	-2	13	*2/D	0.8
1988	KC-A	150	537	48	126	25	1	8	58	21	67	.235	.269	.330	.598	65	-25	-27	103	117	44	.486	7	3	0	17	*2/D	0.0
Total	16	2107	7200	858	1847	371	56	156	829	372	951	.257	.295	.389	.684	86	-137	-150	101	103	805	.618	174	81	4	34	*2S/3DC	0.3
■ DOC WHITE	White, Guy Harris b: 4/9/1879, Washington, D.C. d: 2/19/69, Silver Spring, Md. BL/TL, 6'1", 150 lbs. Deb: 4/22/01																											
1901	Phi-N	31	98	15	27	3	1	1	10	2		.276	.290	.357	.647	87	-2	-2	103	88	11	.535	1			2	P/O	0.0
1902	Phi-N	61	179	17	47	3	1	1	15	11		.263	.305	.307	.613	86	-2	-3	105	89	19	.538	5			1	PO	0.0
1903	Chi-A	38	99	10	20	3	0	0	5	19		.202	.331	.232	.563	79	-2	-1	92	78	8	.544	1			3	P/O	0.0
1904	Chi-A	33	76	7	12	2	0	0	2	10		.158	.256	.184	.440	43	-4	-4	99	53	4	.422	3			0	P/O	0.0
1905	Chi-A	37	90	7	15	5	0	0	7	4		.167	.202	.222	.424	37	-6	-6	97	125	5	.360	3			-0	P/O	0.0
1906	Chi-A	29	65	11	12	1	1	0	3	13		.185	.321	.231	.551	82	-1	-0	92	73	6	.585	3			1	P/O	0.0
1907	Chi-A	48	90	12	20	1	0	0	2	12		.222	.314	.233	.547	74	-2	-2	104	34	7	.500	2			5	P/O2	0.0
1908	Chi-A	51	109	12	25	1	0	0	10	12		.229	.306	.239	.544	84	-2	-1	94	144	9	.500	4			7	P/O	0.0
1909	Chi-A	72	192	24	45	1	5	0	7	33		.234	.347	.292	.638	105	2	3	97	48	21	.653	7			-5	OP	0.1
1910	Chi-A	56	126	14	25	1	2	0	8	14		.198	.279	.238	.517	65	-5	-4	95	99	10	.455	2			2	PO	0.0
1911	Chi-A	39	78	12	20	1	1	0	6	7		.256	.318	.295	.613	74	-3	-3	97	88	8	.534	1			-1	P/1O	0.0
1912	Chi-A	32	56	5	7	1	1	0	0	7		.125	.222	.179	.401	15	-6	-6	99	0	2	.347	0			-1	P	0.0
1913	Chi-A	20	25	1	3	0	0	0	0	3	1	.120	.214	.120	.334	-2	-3	-3	95	67	1	.273	0			1	P/1	0.0
Total	13	547	1283	147	278	23	12	2	75	147	1	.217	.297	.258	.555	74	-37	-34	98	78	111	.507	32			16	P/O12	0.1
■ DEACON WHITE	White, James Laurie b: 12/7/1847, Caton, N.Y. d: 7/7/39, Aurora, Ill. BL/TR, 5'11", 175 lbs. Deb: 5/04/1871 M																											
1871	Cle-n	29	149	40	47							.315															*C/2	
1872	Cle-n	21	110	21	37							.336															C/2OM	
1873	Bos-n	60	325	76	124							.382															*C/O	
1874	Bos-n	69	349	73	112							.321															*CO/12	
1875	Bos-n	80	383	77	136							.355															*C/O1	
1876	Chi-N	66	303	66	104	18	1	1	**60**	7	3	.343	.358	.419	.777	126	18	6	125	**165**	47	.673				4	*C/O13P	1.2
1877	Bos-N	59	266	51	**103**	14	**11**	2	**49**	8	3	**.387**	.405	**.545**	**.950**	181	**28**	**25**	108	106	**60**	**.939**				2	1O/C	2.2
1878	Cin-N	61	258	41	81	4	1	0	29	10	5	.314	.340	.337	.677	129	6	8	95	109	30	.548				-6	*CO/3	0.2
1879	Cin-N	78	333	55	110	16	6	1	52	6	9	.330	.342	.423	.766	159	17	20	95	134	49	.659				0	*CO/1M	1.7
1880	Cin-N	35	141	21	42	4	2	0	7	9	7	.298	.340	.355	.695	137	5	6	99	45	17	.596				-3	O/12	0.1
1881	Buf-N	78	319	58	99	24	4	0	53	9	8	.310	.329	.411	.740	130	11	10	101	149	44	.636				-6	12O/3C	0.1
1882	Buf-N	83	337	51	95	17	0	1	33	15	16	.282	.313	.341	.654	105	4	2	104	100	37	.537				-15	*3C	-1.1
1883	Buf-N	94	391	62	114	14	5	0	47	23	18	.292	.331	.353	.684	108	4	4	100	125	47	.581				-13	*3C	-0.6
1884	Buf-N	110	452	82	147	16	11	5	74	32	13	.325	.370	.442	.812	145	28	23	107	125	76	.761				-9	*3/C	0.8
1885	Buf-N	98	404	54	118	6	6	0	57	12	11	.292	.313	.337	.649	111	4	4	99	140	44	.517				1	*3	0.6
1886	Det-N	124	491	65	142	19	5	1	76	31	35	.289	.331	.354	.686	100	5	-1	109	148	62	.613	9			-9	*3	-0.4
1887	Det-N	111	449	71	136	20	11	3	75	26	15	.303	.353	.416	.770	113	9	8	102	125	75	.773	20			-6	*3/O1	0.3
1888	Det-N	125	527	75	157	22	5	4	71	21	24	.298	.336	.381	.717	133	18	19	98	115	73	.657	12			-11	*3	1.2
1889	Pit-N	55	225	35	57	10	1	0	26	16	18	.253	.314	.307	.621	85	-7	-3	89	108	23	.542	2			-7	3/1	-0.5
1890	Buf-P	122	439	62	114	13	4	0	47	67	30	.260	.381	.308	.688	95	-4	4	92	97	54	.689	3			18	31/SP	1.6
Total	5 n	259	1316	287	456							.347															31/SP	
Total	15	1299	5335	849	1619	217	73	18	756	292	215	.303	.344	.382	.726	122	147	134	102	123	738	.650	46			-59	3C1O/2PS	7.4
■ JERRY WHITE	White, Jerome Cardell b: 8/23/52, Shirley, Mass. BB/TR, 5'10", 164 lbs. Deb: 9/16/74																											
1974	Mon-N	9	10	0	4	1	1	0	2	0	0	.400	.400	.700	1.100	195	1	1	104	110	3	1.667	3	0	1	-2	/O	0.0
1975	Mon-N	39	97	14	29	4	1	2	7	10	7	.299	.364	.423	.787	109	2	1	108	58	16	.800	5	2	0	4	O	0.4
1976	Mon-N	114	278	32	68	11	1	2	21	27	31	.245	.316	.313	.629	79	-7	-7	100	87	29	.593	15	7	0	-6	O	-1.7
1977	Mon-N	16	21	4	4	0	0	0	1	1	3	.190	.227	.190	.418	14	-3	-2	98	100	1	.333	1	0	0	-2	/O	-0.4
1978	Mon-N	18	10	2	2	0	0	0	0	1	3	.200	.273	.200	.473	35	-1	-1	96	0	1	.500	1	0	0	-1	/O	-0.1
	Chi-N	59	136	22	37	6	0	1	10	23	16	.272	.377	.338	.716	92	1	-1	110	81	18	.695	4	3	-1	0	O	-0.2
	Yr	77	146	24	39	6	0	1	10	24	19	.267	.371	.329	.699	91	0	-1	107	62	19	.681	5	3	-0	-1		-0.3
1979	Mon-N	88	138	30	41	7	1	3	18	21	23	.297	.394	.428	.821	121	5	5	102	105	25	.873	8	4	0	-6	O	-0.2
1980	Mon-N	110	214	22	56	9	3	7	23	30	37	.262	.355	.430	.785	119	6	6	99	81	34	.789	8	7	-2	-13	O	-1.2
1981	Mon-N	59	119	11	26	5	1	3	11	13	17	.218	.295	.353	.648	84	-3	-3	99	85	14	.632	5	2	0	-4	O	-0.7
1982	Mon-N	69	115	13	28	6	1	2	13	8	26	.243	.304	.365	.669	82	-2	-3	105	106	12	.598	3	3	-1	-3	O	-0.7
1983	Mon-N	40	34	4	5	1	0	0	0	12	8	.147	.383	.176	.559	59	-1	-1	102	0	4	.793	4	0	1	-3	O	-0.2
1986	StL-N	25	24	1	3	0	0	1	3	2	3	.125	.192	.250	.442	20	-3	-3	103	133	1	.364	0	0	0	-2	/O	-0.4
Total	11	646	1196	155	303	50	9	21	109	148	174	.253	.339	.363	.702	94	-4	-7	102	84	158	.701	57	28	0	-39	O	-5.4
■ JACK WHITE	White, John Peter b: 8/31/05, New York, N.Y. d: 6/19/71, Flushing, N.Y. BB/TR, 5'7.5", 150 lbs. Deb: 6/22/27																											
1927	Cin-N	5	4	1	0	0	0	0	0	0	0	.000	.000	.000	.000	-99	-1	-1	100	0	0	.000				0	/2S	0.0
1928	Cin-N	1	3	0	0	0	0	0	0	0	1	.000	.000	.000	.000	-99	-1	-1	96	0	0	.000				-0	/2	0.0
Total	2	6	7	1	0	0	0	0	0	0	1	.000	.000	.000	.000	-99	-2	-2	98	0	0	.000				-0	/2S	0.0
■ JACK WHITE	White, John Wallace b: 1/19/1878, Indianapolis, Ind. d: 9/30/63, Indianapolis, Ind BR/TR, 5'6", Deb: 6/26/04																											
1904	Bos-N	1	5	1	0	0	0	0	0	0		.000	.000	.000	.000	-99	-1	-1	97	0	0	.000	0			0	/O	0.0

YEAR	TM/L	G	AB	R	H	2B	3B	HR	RBI	BB	SO	AVG	OBP	SLG	PRO	/A	BR	/A	PF	CHI	RC	TA	SB	CS	SBR	FR	POS	TPR
■ JO-JO WHITE	White, Joyner Clifford b: 6/1/09, Red Oak, Ga. d: 10/9/86, Tacoma, Wash. BL/TR, 5'11", 165 lbs. Deb: 4/15/32 MC																											
1932	Det-A	80	208	25	54	6	3	2	21	22	19	.260	.330	.346	.677	74	-7	-8	102	90	23	.617	6	8	-3	1	O	-1.0
1933	Det-A	91	234	43	59	9	5	2	34	27	26	.252	.337	.359	.696	79	-5	-7	107	126	29	.661	5	5	-2	2	O	-0.8
1934	Det-A	115	384	97	120	18	5	0	44	69	39	.313	.419	.385	.804	111	9	10	98	99	71	.911	28	6	**5**	-3	*O	1.0
1935	Det-A	114	412	82	99	13	12	2	32	68	42	.240	.348	.345	.693	82	-11	-9	97	75	53	.709	19	10	-0	-5	O	-1.3
1936	Det-A	58	51	11	14	3	0	0	6	9	10	.275	.383	.333	.717	82	-1	-1	95	114	7	.757	2	0	1	-6	O	-0.5
1937	Det-A	94	305	50	75	5	7	0	21	50	40	.246	.354	.308	.662	63	-13	-18	109	77	37	.662	12	7	-1	-7	O	-2.6
1938	Det-A	78	206	40	54	6	1	0	15	30	15	.262	.359	.301	.660	67	-9	-10	100	82	24	.615	3	4	-2	2	O	-0.7
1943	Phi-A	139	500	69	124	17	7	1	30	61	51	.248	.335	.316	.651	90	-5	-5	101	72	59	.607	12	4	1	4	*O	-0.3
1944	Phi-A	85	267	30	59	4	2	1	21	40	27	.221	.329	.262	.591	69	-9	-9	101	104	27	.551	5	4	-1	1	O/S	-1.1
	Cin-N	24	85	9	20	2	0	0	5	10	7	.235	.316	.259	.575	66	-4	-3	95	83	8	.492	0			2	O	-0.2
Total	9	878	2652	456	678	83	42	8	229	386	276	.256	.353	.328	.681	81	-56	-60	101	88	337	.673	92	48		-9	O/S	-7.5
■ MIKE WHITE	White, Joyner Michael b: 12/18/38, Detroit, Mich. BR/TR, 5'8", 160 lbs. Deb: 9/21/63																											
1963	Hou-N	3	7	0	2	0	0	0	0	0	0	.286	.286	.286	.571	71	-0	-0	92	0	1	.400	0	0	0	-1	/2	0.0
1964	Hou-N	89	280	30	76	11	3	0	27	20	47	.271	.320	.332	.652	87	-6	-4	96	119	28	.533	1	1	-0	1	O2/3	-0.4
1965	Hou-N	8	9	0	0	0	0	0	0	1	2	.000	.100	.000	.100	-78	-2	-2	89	0	0	.111	0	0	0	0	/3	-0.1
Total	3	100	296	30	78	11	3	0	27	21	49	.264	.312	.321	.633	82	-8	-7	96	113	29	.534	1	1	-0	0	/O23	-0.5
■ MYRON WHITE	White, Myron Alan b: 8/1/57, Long Beach, Cal. BL/TL, 5'11", 180 lbs. Deb: 9/04/78																											
1978	LA-N	7	4	1	2	0	0	0	1	0	1	.500	.500	.500	1.000	182	0	0	99	198	1	.667	0	1	-1	-1	/O	-0.1
■ ROY WHITE	White, Roy Hilton b: 12/27/43, Los Angeles, Cal. BB/TR, 5'10", 160 lbs. Deb: 9/07/65 C																											
1965	NY-A	14	42	7	14	2	0	0	3	4	7	.333	.404	.381	.785	123	2	2	101	78	7	.793	2	1	0	-1	O/2	0.0
1966	NY-A	115	316	39	71	13	2	7	20	37	43	.225	.308	.345	.653	93	-5	-2	94	65	35	.629	14	7	0	0	O/2	-0.5
1967	NY-A	70	214	22	48	8	0	2	18	19	25	.224	.291	.290	.580	76	-7	-6	94	110	20	.538	10	4	1	-1	O3	-0.7
1968	NY-A	159	577	89	154	20	7	17	62	73	50	.267	.352	.414	.766	130	23	22	101	97	86	.755	20	11	-1	8	*O	2.7
1969	NY-A	130	448	55	130	30	5	7	74	81	51	.290	.400	.426	.826	137	22	24	95	**148**	81	.864	18	10	-1	-4	*O	1.7
1970	NY-A	162	609	109	180	30	6	22	94	95	66	.296	.391	.473	.864	148	33	39	92	103	116	.900	24	10	1	2	*O	3.5
1971	NY-A	147	524	86	153	22	7	19	84	86	66	.292	.399	.469	.868	150	34	36	97	120	103	.910	14	7	0	5	*O	3.8
1972	NY-A	155	556	76	150	29	0	10	54	**99**	59	.270	.385	.376	.761	137	23	28	92	91	88	.792	23	7	3	3	*O	3.3
1973	NY-A	162	639	88	157	22	3	18	60	78	81	.246	.330	.374	.704	97	-1	-2	101	71	80	.663	16	9	-1	0	*O	-0.6
1974	NY-A	136	473	68	130	19	8	7	43	67	44	.275	.369	.393	.763	125	14	16	96	83	73	.764	15	6	1	-1	OD	1.5
1975	NY-A	148	556	81	161	32	5	12	59	72	50	.290	.373	.430	.803	128	20	21	99	87	91	.793	16	15	-4	9	*O/1D	2.2
1976	NY-A	156	626	**104**	179	29	3	14	65	83	52	.286	.370	.409	.778	128	23	24	99	72	98	.782	31	13	2	6	*O	2.9
1977	NY-A	143	519	72	139	25	2	14	52	75	58	.268	.360	.405	.765	110	7	9	99	87	77	.754	18	11	-1	6	*O/D	0.8
1978	NY-A	103	346	44	93	13	3	8	43	42	35	.269	.351	.393	.744	110	5	5	99	108	48	.714	10	4	1	-7	OD	-0.2
1979	NY-A	81	205	24	44	6	0	3	27	23	21	.215	.294	.288	.582	60	-12	-11	96	153	17	.497	2	2	-1	-1	DO	-1.2
Total	15	1881	6650	964	1803	300	51	160	758	934	708	.271	.363	.404	.767	122	180	205	97	96	1020	.781	233	117	-0	24	*OD/312	19.2
■ SAM WHITE	White, Samuel Lambeth b: 8/23/1892, Greater Preston, Yorkshire, England d: 11/11/29, Philadelphia, Pa. BL/TR, 6', 185 lbs. Deb: 9/08/19																											
1919	Bos-N	1	1	0	0	0	0	0	0	0	0	.000	.000	.000	.000	-99	-0	-0	98	0	0	.000	0			0	/C	0.0
■ SAMMY WHITE	White, Samuel Charles b: 7/7/28, Wenatchee, Wash. BR/TR, 6'3", 195 lbs. Deb: 9/26/51																											
1951	Bos-A	4	11	0	2	0	0	0	0	0	3	.182	.182	.182	.364	-1	-2	-2	108	0	0	.222	0	0	0	-0	/C	-0.1
1952	Bos-A	115	381	35	107	20	2	10	49	16	43	.281	.310	.423	.732	96	-1	-4	107	96	46	.617	2	3	-1	4	*C	0.5
1953	Bos-A	136	476	59	130	34	2	13	64	29	48	.273	.318	.435	.752	93	-1	-6	109	96	63	.664	3	2	-0	1	*C	0.0
1954	Bos-A	137	493	46	139	25	2	14	75	21	50	.282	.311	.426	.737	100	-2	-2	100	113	60	.624	1	3	-2	-2	*C	0.0
1955	Bos-A	143	544	65	142	30	4	11	64	44	58	.261	.324	.392	.716	74	-8	-25	124	99	64	.621	1	2	-1	12	*C	-0.7
1956	Bos-A	114	392	28	96	15	2	5	44	35	40	.245	.307	.332	.638	67	-18	-20	103	113	37	.530	2	1	0	1	*C	-1.6
1957	Bos-A	111	340	24	73	10	1	3	31	25	38	.215	.268	.276	.545	45	-24	-28	110	119	22	.418	0	1	-1	-10	*C	-3.4
1958	Bos-A	102	328	25	85	15	3	6	35	21	37	.259	.306	.378	.684	83	-6	-8	105	99	37	.586	1	1	-0	-6	*C	-1.3
1959	Bos-A	119	377	34	107	13	4	1	42	23	39	.284	.327	.347	.674	81	-8	-10	106	123	40	.556	4	2	0	-0	*C	-0.3
1961	Mil-N	21	63	1	14	1	0	1	5	2	9	.222	.246	.286	.532	44	-5	-5	92	96	4	.400	0	0	0	4	C	0.0
1962	Phi-N	41	97	7	21	4	0	2	12	2	16	.216	.240	.320	.560	51	-7	-7	95	128	6	.415	0	0	0	1	C	-0.4
Total	11	1043	3502	324	916	167	20	66	421	218	381	.262	.307	.377	.684	79	-82	-117	108	107	379	.600	14	15	-5	4	*C	-7.3
■ BARNEY WHITE	White, William Barney b: 6/25/23, Paris, Tex. BR/TR, 5'10.5", 190 lbs. Deb: 6/05/45																											
1945	Bro-N	4	1	2	0	0	0	0	0	1	1	.000	.500	.000	.500	48	0	0	96	0	0	1.000	0			0	/S3	0.0
■ BILL WHITE	White, William De Kova b: 1/28/34, Lakewood, Fla. BL/TL, 6', 185 lbs. Deb: 5/07/56																											
1956	NY-N	138	508	63	130	23	7	22	59	47	72	.256	.324	.459	.782	110	4	6	97	88	76	.763	15	8	-0	1	*1/O	0.0
1958	SF-N	26	29	5	7	1	0	1	4	7	5	.241	.389	.379	.768	104	0	0	100	118	5	.864	1	0	0	-0	/1O	0.0
1959	StL-N	138	517	77	156	33	9	12	72	34	61	.302	.347	.470	.817	110	10	7	105	106	83	.782	15	10	-2	-10	O1	-1.0
1960	StL-N	144	554	81	157	27	10	16	79	42	83	.283	.336	.455	.791	105	10	4	108	113	84	.748	12	6	0	-2	*1O	-0.4
1961	StL-N	153	591	89	169	28	11	20	90	64	84	.286	.357	.472	.829	104	15	4	113	113	96	.789	8	11	-4	-4	*1	-1.2
1962	StL-N	159	614	93	199	31	3	20	102	58	69	.324	.388	.482	.870	122	28	21	109	120	114	.852	9	7	-2	2	*1O	1.6
1963	StL-N	162	658	106	200	26	8	27	109	59	100	.304	.361	.491	.852	133	35	30	107	109	117	.831	10	9	-2	-2	*1	2.5
1964	StL-N	160	631	92	191	37	4	21	102	52	103	.303	.357	.474	.831	117	26	17	112	122	107	.794	7	6	-2	-2	*1	0.9
1965	StL-N	148	543	82	157	26	3	24	73	63	86	.289	.367	.481	.848	128	27	22	107	96	97	.836	3	3	-1	2	*1	1.7
1966	Phi-N	159	577	85	159	23	6	22	103	68	109	.276	.355	.451	.806	121	18	17	101	**136**	96	.807	16	6	1	5	*1	1.5
1967	Phi-N	110	308	29	77	6	2	8	33	52	61	.250	.364	.360	.724	103	5	3	104	101	44	.729	6	1	1	1	1	0.1
1968	Phi-N	127	385	34	92	16	2	9	40	39	79	.239	.312	.361	.673	104	1	2	97	101	44	.598	0	1	-1	2	*1	0.0
1969	StL-N	49	57	7	12	1	0	0	4	11	15	.211	.338	.228	.566	62	-2	-2	100	123	5	.521	1	0	0	0	1	-0.3
Total	13	1673	5972	843	1706	278	65	202	870	596	927	.286	.353	.455	.809	115	177	132	106	111	968	.795	103	68	-10	-7	*1O	5.4
■ BILL WHITE	White, William Dighton b: 5/1/1860, Bridgeport, Ohio d: 12/29/24, Bellaire, Ohio TR , Deb: 5/03/1884																											
1884	Pit-a	74	291	25	66	7	10	0		13		.227	.262	.320	.582	94	-3	-1	97	0	25	.476				-11	S3/O	-1.1
1886	Lou-a	135	557	96	143	17	10	1		37		.257	.304	.329	.633	93	-0	-7	108	0	61	.568	14			15	*S/P	1.3
1887	Lou-a	132	512	85	129	7	9	2		47		.252	.315	.313	.627	72	-15	-21	107	0	65	.648	41			24	*S	0.0
1888	Lou-a	49	198	35	55	6	5	1	30	7		.278	.313	.374	.686	135	5	7	91	123	29	.692	15			-1	S3	0.8
	StL-a	76	275	31	48	2	3	2	30	21		.175	.238	.225	.464	46	-14	-19	111	135	17	.401	6			-9	S/2	-2.2
	Yr	125	473	66	103	8	8	3	60	28		.218	.269	.288	.556	79	-10	-12	103	131	43	.514	21			-10		-1.4
Total	4	466	1833	272	441	39	37	6	60	125		.241	.292	.312	.604	83	-27	-41	105	33	196	.560	76			19	S/3O2P	-1.2
■ BILL WHITE	White, William Edward b: Milner, Ga. Deb: 6/21/1879																											
1879	Pro-N	1	4	1	1	0	0	0	0	0	1	.250	.250	.250	.500	64	-0	-0	102	0	0	.333				0	/1	0.0
■ WILLIAM WHITE	White, William Warren (Also Played Under Name Of William Warren) d: 3/3/1898, Deb: 6/17/1871 M																											
1871	Oly-n	1	4	0	0							.000															/2	
1872	Nat-n	10	44	8	14							.318															3S	
1873	Nat-n	39	166	29	44							.265															*3/S	
1874	Bal-n	45	224	21	57							.254															*3M	
1875	Chi-n	70	304	37	72							.237															*3/SO2	
1884	Was-U	4	18	2	1	0	0	0		0		.056	.056	.056	.111	-64	-3	-3	97	0	0	.059	0			0	/3S2	-0.2
Total	5 n	165	742	95	187							.252															/3S2	
■ BURGESS WHITEHEAD	Whitehead, Burgess Urquhart "Whitey" b: 6/29/10, Tarboro, N.C. BR/TR, 5'10.5", 160 lbs. Deb: 4/30/33																											
1933	StL-N	12	7	2	2	0	0	0	1	0	1	.286	.286	.286	.571	62	-0	-0	102	188	0	.333	0			0	/S2	0.0
1934	StL-N	100	332	55	92	13	5	1	24	12	19	.277	.310	.355	.666	68	-11	-17	114	71	38	.572	5			1	2S3	-0.7

YEAR	TM/L	G	AB	R	H	2B	3B	HR	RBI	BB	SO	AVG	OBP	SLG	PRO	/A	BR	/A	PF	CHI	RC	TA	SB	CS	SBR	FR	POS	TPR
1935	StL-N	107	338	45	89	10	2	0	33	11	14	.263	.289	.305	.593	57	-19	-21	104	116	30	.472	5			-1	2/3S	-1.4
1936	NY-N	154	632	99	176	31	3	4	47	29	32	.278	.317	.356	.673	81	-17	-18	100	74	70	.580	14			28	*2	2.0
1937	NY-N	152	574	64	164	15	6	5	52	28	20	.286	.323	.359	.682	85	-12	-12	100	87	67	.582	7			26	*2	2.0
1939	NY-N	95	335	31	80	6	3	2	24	24	19	.239	.299	.293	.592	60	-19	-18	99	86	28	.474	1			18	2/S3	0.3
1940	NY-N	133	568	68	160	9	6	4	36	26	17	.282	.319	.340	.659	82	-14	-14	100	58	59	.550	9			10	32/S	0.0
1941	NY-N	116	403	41	92	15	4	1	23	14	10	.228	.258	.293	.551	53	-25	-26	103	69	27	.429	7			3	*2/3	-1.6
1946	Pit-N	55	127	10	28	1	2	0	5	6	6	.220	.261	.260	.521	47	-9	-9	103	56	8	.422	3			0	2/3S	-0.8
Total	9	924	3316	415	883	100	31	17	245	150	138	.266	.304	.331	.634	71	-126	-135	102	77	328	.544	51			85	23/S	-0.2
■ **MILT WHITEHEAD**	Whitehead, Milton P. b: 1862, Canada d: 8/15/01, Highland Township San Bernardino County, Cal. Deb: 4/20/1884																											
1884	StL-U	99	393	61	83	15	1	1		8		.211	.227	.262	.489	63	-14	-16	104	0	24	.358	0			-15	*S/OP23	-2.5
	KC-U	5	22	2	3	0	0	0		0		.136	.136	.136	.273	-9	-2	-2	87	0	0	.158	0			0	/2CS3	-0.1
	Yr	104	415	63	86	15	1	1		8		.207	.222	.255	.478	59	-16	-18	103	0	24	.347	0			-15		-2.6
Total	1	104	415	63	86	15	1	1		8		.207	.222	.255	.478	60	-16	-18	103	0	24	.347	0			-15	/S23OCP	-2.6
■ **GIL WHITEHOUSE**	Whitehouse, Gilbert Arthur b: 10/15/1893, Somerville, Mass. d: 2/14/26, Brewer, Me. BB/TR, 5'10", 170 lbs. Deb: 6/20/12																											
1912	Bos-N	2	3	0	0	0	0	0	0	0	3	.000	.000	.000	.000	-93	-1	-1	107	0	0	.000	0			0	/C	0.0
1915	New-F	35	120	16	27	6	2	0	9	6	16	.225	.262	.308	.570	73	-5	-4	94	88	11	.495	3			0	O/PC	-0.5
Total	2	37	123	16	27	6	2	0	9	6	19	.220	.256	.301	.557	68	-6	-5	94	86	11	.479	3			0	/OCP	-0.5
■ **GURDON WHITELEY**	Whiteley, Gurdon W. b: 10/5/1859, Ashaway, R.I. d: 11/24/24, Cranston, R.I. 5'11", 190 lbs. Deb: 8/07/1884																											
1884	Cle-N	8	34	4	5	0	0	0	0	1	8	.147	.171	.147	.318	1	-4	-4	102	0	1	.207				0	/O	-0.3
1885	Bos-N	33	135	14	25	2	2	1	7	1	25	.185	.191	.252	.443	45	-9	-7	94	70	7	.318				-1	O/C	-0.8
Total	2	41	169	18	30	2	2	1	7	2	33	.178	.187	.231	.418	35	-12	-11	95	55	8	.295				-1	/OC	-1.1
■ **GEORGE WHITEMAN**	Whiteman, George "Lucky" b: 12/23/1882, Peoria, Ill. d: 2/10/47, Houston, Tex. BR/TR, 5'7", 160 lbs. Deb: 9/13/07																											
1907	Bos-A	4	12	0	2	0	0	0	1	0		.167	.167	.167	.333	7	-1	-1	101	179	0	.200	0			0	/O	0.0
1913	NY-A	11	32	8	11	3	1	0	2	7	2	.344	.462	.500	.962	180	4	4	101	44	8	1.190	2			1	O	0.5
1918	Bos-A	71	214	24	57	14	0	1	28	20	9	.266	.335	.346	.681	110	1	2	95	133	28	.669	9			-13	O	-1.4
Total	3	86	258	32	70	17	1	1	31	27	11	.271	.345	.357	.702	116	4	5	96	122	36	.702	11			-11	/O	-0.9
■ **FRED WHITFIELD**	Whitfield, Fred Dwight b: 1/7/38, Vandiver, Ala. BL/TL, 6'1", 190 lbs. Deb: 5/27/62																											
1962	StL-N	73	158	20	42	7	1	8	34	7	30	.266	.301	.475	.776	96	0	-1	109	135	21	.689	1	0	0	0	1	-0.1
1963	Cle-A	109	346	44	87	17	3	21	54	24	61	.251	.307	.500	.807	126	9	10	97	96	54	.770	0	1	-1	-4	1	0.3
1964	Cle-A	101	293	29	79	13	1	10	29	12	58	.270	.303	.423	.726	97	-1	-2	103	80	34	.616	0	5	-3	-4	1	-1.2
1965	Cle-A	132	468	49	137	23	1	26	90	16	42	.293	.319	.513	.832	135	17	18	98	117	71	.754	2	2	-1	2	*1	1.4
1966	Cle-A	137	502	59	121	15	2	27	78	27	76	.241	.285	.440	.725	104	1	1	101	111	61	.649	1	2	-1	-5	*1	-1.0
1967	Cle-A	100	257	24	56	10	0	9	31	25	45	.218	.290	.362	.652	91	-3	-3	100	108	26	.587	3	3	-1	-1	1	-1.1
1968	Cin-N	87	171	15	44	8	0	6	32	9	29	.257	.302	.409	.712	101	2	0	111	153	20	.609	0	3	-2	-0	1	-0.3
1969	Cin-N	74	74	2	11	0	0	1	8	18	27	.149	.315	.189	.504	45	-5	-5	99	189	6	.508	0	0	0	0	1	-0.5
1970	Mon-N	4	15	0	1	0	0	0	0	1	3	.067	.125	.067	.192	-47	-3	-3	100	0	0	.133	0	0	0	0	/1	-0.2
Total	9	817	2284	242	578	93	8	108	356	139	371	.253	.301	.443	.743	107	17	14	101	113	293	.681	7	16	-8	-12	1	-2.7
■ **TERRY WHITFIELD**	Whitfield, Terry Bertland b: 1/12/53, Blythe, Cal. BL/TR, 6'1", 197 lbs. Deb: 9/29/74																											
1974	NY-A	2	5	0	1	0	0	0	0	0	1	.200	.200	.200	.400	16	-1	-1	96	0	0	.250	0	0	0	-0	/O	0.0
1975	NY-A	28	81	9	22	1	1	0	7	1	17	.272	.280	.309	.589	67	-4	-4	99	108	7	.443	1	0	0	-1	O/D	-0.4
1976	NY-A	1	0	0	0	0	0	0	0	0	0	—	—	—	—	—	0	0	99	—	—	—	0	0	0	-0	/O	0.0
1977	SF-N	114	326	41	93	21	3	7	36	20	46	.285	.330	.433	.763	99	1	-1	104	89	46	.688	2	3	-1	0	O	-0.4
1978	SF-N	149	488	70	141	20	2	10	32	33	69	.289	.337	.400	.736	115	3	8	92	56	62	.640	5	11	-5	-6	*O	-0.8
1979	SF-N	133	394	52	113	20	4	5	44	36	47	.287	.353	.396	.748	112	2	6	92	102	52	.670	5	4	-1	-4	*O	-0.1
1980	SF-N	118	321	38	95	16	2	4	26	20	44	.296	.339	.396	.735	109	2	3	96	74	42	.650	4	2	0	-4	O	-0.4
1984	LA-N	87	180	15	44	8	0	4	18	17	35	.244	.313	.356	.669	84	-3	-4	104	93	18	.572	1	4	-2	-5	O	-1.3
1985	LA-N	79	104	8	27	7	0	3	16	6	27	.260	.300	.413	.713	105	-1	0	93	123	12	.620	0	0	0	-5	O	-0.5
1986	LA-N	19	14	0	1	0	0	0	0	5	2	.071	.316	.071	.387	13	-1	-1	94	0	0	.429	0	0	0	-0	/O	-0.1
Total	10	730	1913	233	537	93	12	33	179	138	288	.281	.332	.394	.726	104	-2	7	96	83	248	.656	18	24	-9	-26	O/D	-4.0
■ **ED WHITING**	Whiting, Edward C. (Also Played Under Name Of Harry Zieber) b: 1860, Philadelphia, Pa. BL/TR, 188 lbs. Deb: 5/02/1882																											
1882	Bal-a	74	308	43	80	14	5	0		7		.260	.276	.338	.614	115	2	5	92	0	29	.487				2	*C/1O	0.7
1883	Lou-a	58	240	35	70	16	4	2		9		.292	.317	.417	.734	143	9	11	94	0	33	.641				-3	C/O231	1.0
1884	Lou-a	42	157	16	35	7	3	0		9		.223	.274	.306	.580	103	-1	1	89	0	13	.484				-12	C/O1	-0.6
1886	Was-N	6	21	0	0	0	0	0	0	1	12	.000	.045	.000	.045	-91	-5	-4	94	0	0	.048	0			0	/C	-0.3
Total	4	180	726	94	185	37	12	2	0	26	12	.255	.282	.347	.630	115	5	13	92	0	75	.518	0			-13	C/O123	0.8
■ **DICK WHITMAN**	Whitman, Dick Corwin b: 11/9/20, Woodburn, Ore. BL/TR, 5'11", 170 lbs. Deb: 4/16/46																											
1946	Bro-N	104	265	39	69	15	3	2	31	22	19	.260	.317	.362	.679	90	-3	-4	103	113	30	.609	5			-1	O	-0.6
1947	Bro-N	4	10	1	4	0	0	0	2	1	0	.400	.455	.400	.855	123	0	0	105	185	2	.833	0			0	/O	0.0
1948	Bro-N	60	165	24	48	13	0	0	20	14	12	.291	.346	.370	.716	90	-1	-2	104	123	22	.658	4			-2	O	-0.7
1949	Bro-N	23	49	8	9	2	0	0	2	4	4	.184	.245	.224	.470	26	-5	-5	102	69	2	.357	0			-1	O	-0.6
1950	Phi-N	75	132	21	33	7	0	0	12	10	10	.250	.317	.303	.620	66	-7	-6	97	116	13	.524	1			-2	O	-0.9
1951	Phi-N	19	17	0	2	0	0	0	0	0	1	.118	.118	.118	.235	-38	-3	-3	97	0	0	.133	0	0	0	-3	/O	-0.5
Total	6	285	638	93	165	37	3	2	67	51	46	.259	.316	.335	.652	77	-19	-20	102	111	69	.588	10	0		-10	O	-3.3
■ **FRANK WHITMAN**	Whitman, Walter Franklin "Hooker" b: 8/15/24, Marengo, Ind. BR/TR, 6'2", 175 lbs. Deb: 6/30/46																											
1946	Chi-A	17	16	7	1	0	0	0	1	2	6	.063	.211	.063	.273	-22	-3	-2	97	380	0	.250	0	1	-1	0	/S12	-0.2
1948	Chi-A	3	6	0	0	0	0	0	0	0	3	.000	.000	.000	.000	-99	-2	-2	95	0	0	.000	0	0	0	0	/S	-0.1
Total	2	20	22	7	1	0	0	0	1	2	9	.045	.160	.045	.205	-43	-4	-4	96	289	0	.182	0	1	-1	0	/S21	-0.3
■ **DAN WHITMER**	Whitmer, Daniel Charles b: 11/23/55, Redlands, Cal. BR/TR, 6'3", 195 lbs. Deb: 7/20/80																											
1980	Cal-A	48	87	8	21	3	0	0	7	4	21	.241	.275	.276	.551	54	-6	-5	96	114	7	.420	1	0	0	-9	C	-1.1
1981	Tor-A	7	9	0	1	1	0	0	0	1	2	.111	.200	.222	.422	19	-1	-1	111	0	0	.333	0	0	0	0	/C	0.0
Total	2	55	96	8	22	4	0	0	7	5	23	.229	.267	.271	.538	50	-7	-6	97	102	7	.427	1	0	0	-8	/C	-1.1
■ **PINKY WHITNEY**	Whitney, Arthur Carter b: 1/2/05, San Antonio, Tex. d: 9/1/87, Center, Tex. BR/TR, 5'10", 165 lbs. Deb: 4/11/28																											
1928	Phi-N	151	585	73	176	35	4	10	103	36	30	.301	.342	.426	.768	96	-2	-5	104	134	83	.707	3			4	*3	0.2
1929	Phi-N	154	612	89	200	43	14	8	115	61	35	.327	.390	.482	.872	105	14	5	110	131	113	.886	7			**21**	*3	3.4
1930	Phi-N	149	606	87	207	41	5	8	117	40	41	.342	.383	.465	.849	98	4	-1	106	140	104	.817	3			21	*3	1.9
1931	Phi-N	130	501	64	144	36	5	9	74	30	38	.287	.331	.433	.765	98	2	-2	106	115	73	.717	6			-6	*3	0.0
1932	Phi-N	154	624	93	186	33	11	13	124	35	66	.298	.335	.449	.784	97	6	-3	112	**153**	95	.733	6			2	*3/2	1.1
1933	Phi-N	31	121	12	32	4	0	3	19	8	8	.264	.310	.372	.682	80	-1	-4	118	140	12	.557	1			2	3	0.0
	Bos-N	100	382	42	94	17	2	8	49	25	23	.246	.296	.364	.660	91	-7	-5	96	120	40	.560	2			1	32	0.0
	Yr	131	503	54	126	21	2	11	68	33	31	.250	.299	.366	.665	88	-8	-9	101	125	55	.571	3			3		0.0
1934	Bos-N	146	563	58	146	26	2	12	79	25	54	.259	.294	.377	.671	91	-18	-8	86	117	61	.573	7			-1	*32/S	0.3
1935	Bos-N	126	458	41	125	23	4	4	60	24	36	.273	.312	.367	.679	86	-12	-9	96	123	51	.566	2			-4	32	-0.6
1936	Bos-N	10	40	1	7	0	0	0	5	2	4	.175	.233	.175	.408	12	-5	-5	95	268	1	.286	0			0	3	-0.3
	Phi-N	114	411	44	121	17	3	6	59	37	33	.294	.354	.394	.748	94	1	-4	108	118	58	.669	2			5	*3/2	1.0
	Yr	124	451	45	128	17	3	6	64	39	37	.284	.343	.375	.718	87	-4	-8	107	133	59	.633	2			5		0.7
1937	Phi-N	138	487	56	166	19	4	8	79	43	44	.341	.395	.446	.841	118	20	14	108	121	84	.785	6			1	*3	2.1
1938	Phi-N	102	300	27	83	9	1	3	38	27	22	.277	.336	.343	.680	87	-5	-5	100	123	34	.570	0			-3	3/12	-0.9
1939	Phi-N	34	75	9	14	0	1	1	6	7	4	.187	.256	.253	.509	40	-7	-6	94	100	5	.406	0			-0	1/23	-0.6
Total	12	1539	5765	696	1701	303	56	93	927	400	438	.295	.343	.415	.758	96	-9	-38	103	129	815	.702	45			42	*32/1S	7.6

YEAR	TM/L	G	AB	R	H	2B	3B	HR	RBI	BB	SO	AVG	OBP	SLG	PRO	/A	BR	/A	PF	CHI	RC	TA	SB	CS	SBR	FR	POS	TPR
■ **ART WHITNEY** Whitney, Arthur Wilson b: 1/16/1858, Brockton, Mass. d: 8/15/43, Lowell, Mass. BR/TR, 5'8", 155 lbs. Deb: 5/01/1880																												
1880	Wor-N	76	302	38	67	13	5	1	36	9	15	.222	.244	.308	.552	76	-4	-9	113	145	23	.434				0	*3	-0.9
1881	Det-N	58	214	23	39	7	5	0	9	7	15	.182	.208	.262	.470	44	-13	-15	106	57	12	.360				6	*3	-0.3
1882	Pro-N	11	40	2	3	0	0	0	1	2	11	.075	.119	.075	.194	-34	-6	-6	106	114	0	.135				0	S	-0.5
	Det-N	31	115	10	21	0	0	0	4	1	12	.183	.190	.183	.372	20	-10	-10	102	64	4	.234				0	3/SP	-0.8
	Yr	42	155	12	24	0	0	0	5	3	23	.155	.171	.155	.326	5	-16	-16	103	80	4	.206				0		-1.3
1884	Pit-a	23	94	10	28	4	0	0		1		.298	.305	.340	.646	117	1	2	97	0	10	.500				0	3/OS	0.1
1885	Pit-a	90	373	53	87	10	4	0		16		.233	.267	.282	.548	71	-10	-14	106	0	29	.427				-13	*S/32O	-2.2
1886	Pit-a	136	511	70	122	13	4	0		51		.239	.315	.280	.595	96	-5	2	93	0	51	.553	15			9	*3S/P	1.5
1887	Pit-N	119	431	57	112	11	4	0	51	55	18	.260	.346	.304	.650	90	-7	-2	93	122	50	.621	10			-8	*3	-0.6
1888	NY-N	90	328	28	72	1	4	1	28	8	22	.220	.240	.256	.496	65	-14	-11	93	118	22	.391	7			2	3	-0.5
1889	NY-N	129	473	71	103	12	2	1	59	56	39	.218	.303	.258	.561	56	-24	-28	105	144	44	.538	19			-3	*3/P	-1.9
1890	NY-P	119	442	71	97	12	3	0	45	64	19	.219	.322	.260	.582	53	-24	-32	109	109	41	.551	8			-5	3S	-2.4
1891	CM-a	93	347	42	69	6	1	3	33	31	20	.199	.270	.248	.518	45	-22	-29	112	102	26	.460	8			-6	3	-2.7
	StL-a	3	11	0	0	0	0	0	0	1	2	.000	.083	.000	.083	-66	-2	-3	114	0	0	.091	0			0	/3	-0.1
	Yr	96	358	42	69	6	1	3		32	22	.193	.265	.240	.505	42	-24	-31	112	100	25	.446	8			-6		-2.8
Total	11	978	3681	475	820	89	32	6	266	302	173	.223	.285	.269	.554	65	-140	-155	102	85	312	.482	67			-18	3S/P20	-11.3
■ **FRANK WHITNEY** Whitney, Frank Thomas "Jumbo" b: 2/18/1856, Brockton, Mass. d: 10/30/43, Baltimore, Md. BR/TR, 5'7.5", 152 lbs. Deb: 5/17/1876																												
1876	Bos-N	34	139	27	33	7	1	0	15	1	3	.237	.243	.302	.545	85	-3	-2	95	123	10	.406				3	O/2	0.1
■ **JIM WHITNEY** Whitney, James Evans "Grasshopper Jim" b: 11/10/1857, Conklin, N.Y. d: 5/21/1891, Binghamton, N.Y. BL/TR, 6'2", 172 lbs. Deb: 5/02/1881																												
1881	Bos-N	75	282	37	72	17	3	0	32	19	18	.255	.302	.337	.639	110	0	4	91	124	29	.543				-4	*PO/1	0.0
1882	Bos-N	61	251	49	81	18	7	5	48	24	13	.323	.382	.510	.892	178	24	22	103	100	50	.894				2	P/O1	0.0
1883	Bos-N	96	409	78	115	27	10	5	57	25	29	.281	.323	.433	.755	119	13	9	106	91	59	.687				-5	PO/1	0.0
1884	Bos-N	66	270	41	70	17	5	3	40	16	38	.259	.301	.393	.693	119	5	6	98	115	33	.610				4	PO1/3	0.0
1885	Bos-N	72	290	35	68	8	4	0	36	17	24	.234	.277	.290	.567	89	-5	-2	94	143	24	.455				5	PO/1	0.0
1886	KC-N	67	247	25	59	13	3	2	23	29	39	.239	.319	.340	.659	94	1	-2	107	88	29	.628	5			5	PO/3	0.0
1887	Was-N	54	201	29	53	9	6	2	22	18	24	.264	.324	.398	.722	106	0	2	95	83	30	.730	10			3	P/O	0.0
1888	Was-N	42	141	13	24	0	0	1	17	7	20	.170	.209	.191	.401	31	-11	-10	96	207	6	.316	3			-2	P/O1	0.0
1889	Ind-N	10	32	6	12	4	1	0	4	5	6	.375	.474	.563	1.036	176	4	4	109	66	10	1.300	2			0	/PO	0.0
1890	Phi-a	7	21	3	5	0	0	0		1		.238	.273	.238	.511	54	-1	-1	97	0	1	.375	0			0	/PO	0.0
Total	10	550	2144	316	559	113	39	18	279	161	211	.261	.313	.375	.688	112	30	31	99	111	271	.622	20			8	PO/13	0.0
■ **ERNIE WHITT** Whitt, Leo Ernest b: 6/13/52, Detroit, Mich. BL/TR, 6'2", 200 lbs. Deb: 9/12/76																												
1976	Bos-A	8	18	4	4	2	0	1	3	2	2	.222	.300	.500	.800	119	1	0	110	96	3	.786	0	0	0	1	/C	0.1
1977	Tor-A	23	41	4	7	3	0	0	6	2	12	.171	.209	.244	.453	22	-4	-5	103	238	2	.343	0	0	0	1	C	-0.2
1978	Tor-A	2	4	0	0	0	0	0	0	1	1	.000	.200	.000	.200	-39	-1	-1	100	0	0	.250	0	0	0	0	/C	0.0
1980	Tor-A	106	295	23	70	12	2	6	34	22	30	.237	.290	.353	.643	75	-10	-10	100	109	27	.531	1	3	-2	0	*C	-0.6
1981	Tor-A	74	195	16	46	9	0	1	16	20	30	.236	.307	.297	.604	67	-6	-9	111	103	19	.542	5	2	0	6	C	0.0
1982	Tor-A	105	284	28	74	14	2	11	42	26	34	.261	.323	.440	.763	99	2	-1	109	106	40	.713	3	1	0	-9	C/D	-0.4
1983	Tor-A	123	344	53	88	15	2	17	56	50	55	.256	.350	.459	.810	111	10	6	108	105	55	.786	1	1	-0	-11	*C	0.0
1984	Tor-A	124	315	35	75	12	1	15	46	43	49	.238	.331	.425	.757	106	3	3	102	102	44	.712	0	3	-2	-18	*C	-0.9
1985	Tor-A	139	412	55	101	21	2	19	64	47	59	.245	.324	.444	.768	107	4	3	101	106	58	.722	3	6	-3	-8	*C	-0.1
1986	Tor-A	131	395	48	106	19	2	16	56	35	39	.268	.328	.448	.776	104	5	2	105	99	56	.704	0	1	-1	-25	*C	-1.5
1987	Tor-A	135	446	57	120	24	1	19	75	44	50	.269	.336	.455	.791	107	5	4	101	115	64	.721	0	1	-1	-2	*C	1.1
1988	Tor-A	127	398	63	100	11	2	16	70	61	38	.251	.352	.410	.762	113	8	8	100	132	59	.741	4	2	0	-2	*C	1.1
Total	12	1097	3147	386	791	142	14	121	468	353	399	.251	.328	.421	.748	101	16	2	103	111	428	.712	17	20	-7	-68	*C/D	-1.4
■ **POSSUM WHITTED** Whitted, George Bostic b: 2/4/1890, Durham, N.C. d: 10/16/62, Wilmington, N.C. BR/TR, 5'8.5", 168 lbs. Deb: 9/16/12																												
1912	StL-N	12	46	7	12	3	0	0	7	3	5	.261	.306	.326	.632	73	-2	-2	100	166	5	.559	1			0	3	0.0
1913	StL-N	123	404	44	89	10	5	0	38	31	44	.220	.282	.270	.552	63	-22	-18	93	129	32	.486	9			3	OS3/21	-1.3
1914	StL-N	20	31	3	4	1	0	0	1	0	3	.129	.129	.161	.290	-13	-4	-5	104	72	1	.222	1			-2	/3O2	-0.6
	Bos-N	66	218	36	57	11	4	2	31	18	18	.261	.326	.376	.703	104	2	1	104	130	30	.702	10			3	O2/31S	0.3
	Yr	86	249	39	61	12	4	2	32	18	21	.245	.304	.349	.653	90	-2	-4	104	118	30	.633	11			1		-0.3
1915	Phi-N	128	448	46	126	17	3	1	43	29	47	.281	.328	.339	.667	95	1	-3	107	112	55	.614	24	15	-2	-6	*O/1	-1.5
1916	Phi-N	147	526	68	148	20	12	6	68	19	46	.281	.309	.399	.708	122	8	10	96	121	69	.658	29	17	-2	5	*O1	1.1
1917	Phi-N	149	553	69	155	24	9	3	70	30	56	.280	.317	.373	.690	103	6	1	108	133	68	.618	10			3	*O1/32	0.0
1918	Phi-N	24	86	7	21	4	0	0	3	4	10	.244	.278	.291	.568	67	-3	-4	109	46	7	.508	4			2	O	-0.2
1919	Phi-N	78	289	32	72	14	1	3	32	14	20	.249	.284	.336	.619	83	-6	-7	104	120	28	.535	5			2	O2/1	-0.6
	Pit-N	35	131	15	51	7	7	0	21	6	4	.389	.420	.550	.970	181	14	13	105	120	32	1.075	7			-2	1/3O	1.1
	Yr	113	420	47	123	21	8	3	53	20	24	.293	.327	.402	.729	114	8	6	104	121	57	.680	12			-0		0.5
1920	Pit-N	134	494	53	129	11	12	1	74	35	36	.261	.314	.338	.652	86	-8	-9	101	**178**	52	.574	11	11	-3	-3	*31/O	-0.9
1921	Pit-N	108	403	60	114	23	7	7	63	26	21	.283	.328	.427	.755	95	-2	-4	103	127	54	.682	5	10	-5	5	*O/1	-0.7
1922	Bro-N	1	1	0	0	0	0	0	0	0	0	.000	.000	.000	.000	-99	-0	-0	95	0	0	.000	0	0	0	0	H	0.0
Total	11	1025	3630	440	978	145	60	23	451	215	310	.269	.313	.361	.675	96	-16	-25	102	130	433	.613	116	53		11	O3/12S	-3.3
■ **FLOYD WICKER** Wicker, Floyd Euliss b: 9/12/43, Burlington, N.C. BL/TR, 6'2", 175 lbs. Deb: 6/23/68																												
1968	StL-N	5	4	2	2	0	0	0	0	0	0	.500	.500	.500	1.000	211	0	0	95	0	1	1.000	0	0	0	0	H	0.1
1969	Mon-N	41	39	2	4	0	0	0	2	2	20	.103	.146	.103	.249	-29	-7	-7	100	200	1	.171	0	0	0	-2	O	-0.9
1970	Mil-A	15	41	3	8	1	0	1	3	1	8	.195	.214	.293	.507	39	-4	-3	98	81	2	.371	0	0	0	-2	O	-0.5
1971	Mil-A	11	8	0	1	0	0	0	0	2	0	.125	.300	.125	.425	23	-1	-1	103	0	0	.333	0	0	0	0	H	0.0
	SF-N	9	21	3	3	0	0	0	1	2	5	.143	.250	.143	.393	14	-2	-2	100	136	1	.316	0	0	0	0	/O	-0.1
Total	4	81	113	10	18	1	0	1	6	7	33	.159	.215	.195	.410	15	-13	-13	100	123	5	.313	0	0	0	-3	/O	-1.4
■ **AL WICKLAND** Wickland, Albert b: 1/27/1888, Chicago, Ill. d: 3/14/80, Port Washington, Wis. BL/TL, 5'7", 155 lbs. Deb: 8/21/13																												
1913	Cin-N	26	79	7	17	5	5	0	8	6	19	.215	.279	.405	.684	92	-1	-1	102	91	9	.677	3			2	O	0.0
1914	Chi-F	157	536	74	148	31	10	6	68	**81**	58	.276	.371	.405	.776	134	17	24	91	111	92	.812	17			-4	*O	1.2
1915	Chi-F	30	86	11	21	2	2	1	5	13	0	.244	.343	.349	.692	108	1	1	97	55	12	.708	3			-1	O	-0.1
	Pit-F	110	389	63	117	12	8	1	30	52	0	.301	.383	.380	.764	122	14	13	104	76	67	.820	23			3	*O	1.1
	Yr	140	475	74	138	14	10	2	35	65	0	.291	.376	.375	.751	119	15	14	102	72	79	.798	26			2		1.0
1918	Bos-N	95	332	55	87	7	13	4	32	53	39	.262	.367	.398	.765	142	15	17	94	89	52	.812	12			-1	O	1.2
1919	NY-A	26	46	2	7	1	0	0	1	2	10	.152	.188	.174	.361	2	-6	-6	106	45	1	.256	0			-5	O	-1.2
Total	5	444	1468	212	397	58	38	12	144	207	126	.270	.362	.386	.748	124	40	48	96	90	234	.780	58			-7	O	2.2
■ **TOM WIEDENBAUER** Wiedenbauer, Thomas John b: 11/5/58, Menomonie, Wis. BR/TR, 6'1", 180 lbs. Deb: 9/14/79																												
1979	Hou-N	4	6	0	4	1	0	0	2	0	2	.667	.667	.833	1.500	339	2	2	90	158	3	2.500	0	0	0	-1	/O	0.1
■ **TOM WIEGHAUS** Wieghaus, Thomas Robert b: 2/1/57, Chicago Heights, Ill BR/TR, 6', 195 lbs. Deb: 10/04/81																												
1981	Mon-N	1	1	0	0	0	0	0	0	0	0	.000	.000	.000	.000	-99	-0	-0	99	0	0	.000	0	0	0	0	/C	0.0
1983	Mon-N	1	0	0	0	0	0	0	0	0	0	—	—	—	—	—	0	0	102	—	—	—	0	0	0	0	/C	0.0
1984	Hou-N	6	10	0	0	0	0	0	1	1	3	.000	.091	.000	.091	-78	-2	-2	93	0	0	.091	0	0	0	0	/C	-0.1
Total	3	8	11	0	0	0	0	0	1	1	3	.000	.083	.000	.083	-80	-3	-2	93	0	0	.083	0	0	0	0	/C	-0.1
■ **WHITEY WIETELMANN** Wietelmann, William Frederick b: 3/15/19, Zanesville, Ohio BB/TR, 6', 170 lbs. Deb: 9/06/39 C																												
1939	Bos-N	23	69	2	14	1	0	0	5	2	9	.203	.225	.217	.443	21	-8	-7	92	122	3	.305	1			1	S/2	-0.4
1940	Bos-N	35	41	3	8	1	0	0	1	5	5	.195	.283	.220	.502	41	-3	-3	99	41	3	.412	0			0	2/3S	-0.1
1941	Bos-N	16	33	1	3	0	0	0	0	1	2	.091	.118	.091	.209	-44	-6	-6	93	0	0	.133	0			0	2/S3	-0.4
1942	Bos-N	13	34	4	7	2	0	0	0	4	5	.206	.289	.265	.554	66	-2	-1	95	0	2	.448	0			0	S/2	0.0

YEAR	TM/L	G	AB	R	H	2B	3B	HR	RBI	BB	SO	AVG	OBP	SLG	PRO	/A	BR	/A	PF	CHI	RC	TA	SB	CS	SBR	FR	POS	TPR
1943	Bos-N	153	534	33	115	14	1	0	39	46	40	.215	.281	.245	.527	50	-32	-35	106	110	39	.442	9			19	*S	0.0
1944	Bos-N	125	417	46	100	18	1	2	32	33	25	.240	.300	.302	.602	74	-16	-14	95	87	40	.503	0			1	*S2/3	0.2
1945	Bos-N	123	428	53	116	15	3	4	33	39	27	.271	.335	.348	.683	80	-6	-12	112	71	53	.620	4			-8	2S/3P	-0.8
1946	Bos-N	44	78	7	16	0	0	0	5	14	8	.205	.326	.205	.531	55	-4	-4	95	117	6	.476	0			-1	S/32P	-0.2
1947	Pit-N	48	128	21	30	4	1	1	7	12	10	.234	.300	.305	.605	60	-7	-7	101	62	11	.490	0			-4	S2/31	-0.8
Total	9	580	1762	170	409	55	6	7	122	156	131	.232	.298	.282	.580	62	-84	-89	103	86	157	.497	14			8	S2/3P1	-2.5
■ AL WIGGINS	Wiggins, Alan Anthony b: 2/17/58, Los Angeles, Cal. BB/TR, 6'2", 160 lbs. Deb: 9/04/81																											
1981	SD-N	15	14	4	5	0	0	0	0	1	0	.357	.400	.357	.757	124	0	0	93	0	3	.889	2	0	1	-1	/O	0.0
1982	SD-N	72	254	40	65	3	3	1	15	13	19	.256	.295	.303	.598	74	-11	-9	92	75	25	.623	33	6	6	5	O/2	0.2
1983	SD-N	144	503	83	139	20	2	0	22	65	43	.276	.360	.324	.684	92	-4	-3	99	55	72	.776	66	13	12	-7	*O1	-0.1
1984	SD-N	158	596	106	154	19	7	3	34	75	57	.258	.344	.329	.673	91	-6	-5	99	63	79	.740	70	21	8	-29	*2	-2.1
1985	SD-N	10	37	3	2	1	0	0	0	2	4	.054	.103	.081	.184	-47	-7	-7	102	0	0	.135	0	1	-1	-1	/2	-0.9
	Bal-A	76	298	43	85	11	4	0	21	29	16	.285	.353	.349	.702	94	-2	-1	99	77	39	.724	30	13	1	-10	2	-0.6
1986	Bal-A	71	239	30	60	3	1	0	11	22	20	.251	.314	.272	.586	63	-12	-11	99	67	24	.581	21	7	2	-5	2/D	-1.0
1987	Bal-A	85	306	37	71	4	2	1	15	28	34	.232	.299	.268	.566	54	-20	-19	98	72	26	.528	20	7	2	-3	D2/O	-1.6
Total	7	631	2247	346	581	61	19	5	118	235	193	.259	.331	.309	.640	80	-61	-55	98	64	269	.678	242	68	32	-50	2O/D1	-6.1
■ DEL WILBER	Wilber, Delbert Quentin "Babe" b: 2/24/19, Lincoln Park, Mich BR/TR, 6'3", 200 lbs. Deb: 4/21/46 MC																											
1946	StL-N	4	4	0	0	0	0	0	0	1	0	.000	.200	.000	.200	-38	-1	-1	107	0	0	.250	0			-0	/C	0.0
1947	StL-N	51	99	7	23	8	1	0	12	5	13	.232	.269	.333	.603	56	-6	-7	106	135	8	.469	0			-4	C	-0.9
1948	StL-N	27	58	5	11	2	0	0	10	4	9	.190	.242	.224	.466	27	-6	-6	101	288	3	.340	0			0	C	-0.3
1949	StL-N	2	4	0	1	0	0	0	0	0	0	.250	.250	.250	.500	31	-0	-0	110	0	0	.333	0			0	/C	0.0
1951	Phi-N	84	245	30	68	7	3	8	34	17	26	.278	.324	.429	.753	104	-0	1	97	102	33	.663	0	1	-1	3	C	0.4
1952	Phi-N	2	2	0	0	0	0	0	0	0	1	.000	.000	.000	.000	-99	-1	-1	101	0	0	.000	0	0	0	0	H	0.0
	Bos-A	47	135	7	36	10	1	3	23	7	20	.267	.308	.422	.730	95	-0	-2	107	130	17	.641	1	0	0	1	C	0.2
1953	Bos-A	58	112	16	27	6	1	7	29	6	21	.241	.286	.500	.786	100	0	-1	109	139	14	.700	0	0	0	0	C/1	0.0
1954	Bos-A	24	61	2	8	2	1	1	7	4	6	.131	.185	.246	.431	17	-7	-7	100	147	3	.352	0	0	0	-0	C	-0.6
Total	8	299	720	67	174	35	7	19	115	44	96	.242	.287	.389	.676	80	-21	-24	103	135	78	.597	1	1		1	C/1	-1.2
■ CLAUDE WILBORN	Wilborn, Claude Edward b: 9/1/12, Woodsdale, N.C. BL/TR, 6'1", 180 lbs. Deb: 9/08/40																											
1940	Bos-N	5	7	0	0	0	0	0	0	0	1	.000	.000	.000	.000	-99	-2	-2	99	0	0	.000	0			-1	/O	-0.3
■ TED WILBORN	Wilborn, Thaddeaus Iglehart b: 12/16/58, Waco, Tex. BB/TR, 6', 165 lbs. Deb: 4/05/79																											
1979	Tor-A	22	12	3	0	0	0	0	0	1	7	.000	.077	.000	.077	-75	-3	-3	103	0	0	.077	0	1	-1	-2	/O	-0.5
1980	NY-A	8	8	2	2	0	0	0	1	0	1	.250	.250	.250	.500	38	-1	-1	99	195	1	.333	0	0	0	1	/O	0.0
Total	2	30	20	5	2	0	0	0	1	1	8	.100	.143	.100	.243	-32	-4	-4	102	74	1	.158	0	1	-1	-1	/O	-0.5
■ WILEY	Wiley Deb:6/23/1884																											
1884	Was-U	1	4	0	0	0	0	0		0		.000	.000	.000	.000	-99	-1	-1	97	0	0	.000	0			0	/3	0.0
■ ROB WILFONG	Wilfong, Robert Donald b: 9/1/53, Pasadena, Cal. BL/TR, 6'1", 180 lbs. Deb: 4/10/77																											
1977	Min-A	73	171	22	42	1	1	1	13	17	26	.246	.321	.281	.602	64	-8	-8	103	101	17	.575	10	4	1	3	2/D	0.1
1978	Min-A	92	199	23	53	8	0	1	11	19	27	.266	.336	.322	.658	91	-3	-2	94	65	24	.616	8	4	0	6	2/D	0.9
1979	Min-A	140	419	71	131	22	6	9	59	29	54	.313	.360	.458	.818	110	11	6	109	104	72	.796	11	4	1	19	*2/O	3.0
1980	Min-A	131	416	55	103	16	5	8	45	34	61	.248	.309	.368	.677	78	-9	-14	109	99	47	.612	10	6	-1	1	*2/O	-0.6
1981	Min-A	93	305	32	75	11	3	3	19	29	43	.246	.311	.331	.643	81	-6	-7	105	69	33	.562	2	4	-2	7	2	0.0
1982	Min-A	25	81	7	13	1	0	0	5	7	13	.160	.236	.173	.409	14	-9	-9	100	143	3	.297	0	2	-1	-2	2	-1.0
	Cal-A	55	102	17	25	4	2	1	11	7	17	.245	.294	.353	.647	76	-3	-3	100	113	11	.603	4	0	1	2	2/3OSD	0.1
	Yr	80	183	24	38	5	2	1	16	14	30	.208	.268	.273	.541	49	-13	-13	100	124	14	.466	4	2	0	0		-0.9
1983	Cal-A	65	177	17	45	7	1	2	17	10	25	.254	.294	.339	.633	77	-6	-5	96	101	17	.515	0	2	-1	10	23/SD	0.4
1984	Cal-A	108	307	31	76	13	2	6	33	20	53	.248	.298	.362	.659	80	-8	-9	101	102	34	.579	3	2	-0	5	2/SD	0.2
1985	Cal-A	83	217	16	41	3	0	4	13	16	32	.189	.245	.258	.503	38	-19	-19	101	76	15	.429	4	1	1	13	2/D	-0.2
1986	Cal-A	92	288	25	63	11	3	3	33	16	34	.219	.265	.309	.574	59	-17	-16	96	134	23	.464	1	4	-2	-0	2	-1.3
1987	SF-N	2	8	2	1	0	0	1	2	1	2	.125	.222	.500	.722	88	-0	-0	96	110	1	.857	1	0	0	0	/2	0.0
Total	11	959	2690	318	668	97	23	39	261	205	387	.248	.305	.345	.650	77	-78	-87	103	98	297	.584	54	33	-4	63	2/3SOD	1.6
■ SPIDER WILHELM	Wilhelm, Charles Ernest b: 5/23/29, Baltimore, Md. BR/TR, 5'9", 170 lbs. Deb: 9/06/53																											
1953	Phi-A	7	7	1	2	1	0	0	0	0	3	.286	.286	.429	.714	89	-0	-0	102	0	1	.600	0	0	0	-0	/S	0.0
■ JIM WILHELM	Wilhelm, James Webster b: 9/20/52, Greenbrae, Cal. BR/TR, 6'3", 190 lbs. Deb: 9/04/78																											
1978	SD-N	10	19	2	7	2	0	0	4	0	2	.368	.400	.474	.874	155	1	1	93	176	4	.917	1	0	0	-2	O	0.0
1979	SD-N	39	103	8	25	4	3	0	8	2	12	.243	.257	.340	.597	64	-6	-5	96	91	9	.481	1	1	-0	2	O	-0.4
Total	2	49	122	10	32	6	3	0	12	2	14	.262	.280	.361	.641	77	-5	-4	96	104	13	.538	2	1	0	-1	/O	-0.4
■ JOE WILHOIT	Wilhoit, Joseph William b: 12/20/1891, Hiawatha, Kan. d: 9/25/30, Santa Barbara, Cal. BL/TR, 6'2", 175 lbs. Deb: 4/12/16																											
1916	Bos-N	116	383	44	88	13	4	2	38	27	45	.230	.282	.300	.582	85	-10	-7	93	127	39	.546	18			-3	*O	-1.4
1917	Bos-N	54	186	20	51	5	0	1	10	17	15	.274	.335	.317	.652	105	1	1	96	63	21	.600	5			-6	O	-0.7
	Pit-N	9	10	0	2	0	0	0	0	1	1	.200	.273	.200	.473	46	-1	-1	100	0	1	.375	0			-0	/O1	0.0
	NY-N	34	50	9	17	2	2	0	8	8	5	.340	.431	.460	.891	179	5	5	97	134	10	.939	0			-2	O	0.3
	Yr	97	246	29	70	7	2	1	18	26	21	.285	.353	.341	.694	117	5	6	97	83	31	.653	5			-8		-0.4
1918	NY-N	64	135	13	37	3	3	0	15	17	14	.274	.355	.341	.696	115	3	3	98	123	17	.684	4			-7	O	-0.7
1919	Bos-A	6	18	7	6	0	0	0	2	5	2	.333	.478	.333	.812	142	1	1	91	123	3	1.000	1			-1	/O	0.0
Total	4	283	782	93	201	23	9	3	73	75	82	.257	.323	.321	.644	102	-1	3	95	110	91	.611	28			-19	O/1	-2.5
■ DENNEY WILIE	Wilie, Dennis Ernest b: 9/22/1890, Mt.Calm, Tex. d: 6/20/66, Hayward, Cal. BL/TL, 5'8", 155 lbs. Deb: 7/27/11																											
1911	StL-N	28	51	10	12	3	1	0	3	8	11	.235	.361	.333	.694	94	-0	-0	101	60	7	.769	3			-2	O	-0.2
1912	StL-N	30	48	2	11	0	1	0	6	7	9	.229	.351	.271	.622	72	-2	-1	100	155	5	.595	0			-4	O	-0.5
1915	Cle-A	45	131	14	33	4	1	2	10	26	18	.252	.384	.344	.727	114	4	3	104	67	17	.721	2	6	-3	-1	O	-0.2
Total	3	103	230	26	56	7	3	2	19	41	38	.243	.372	.326	.698	100	3	2	102	83	28	.706	5	6		-7	/O	-0.9
■ HARRY WILKE	Wilke, Henry Joseph b: 12/14/1900, Cincinnati, Ohio BR/TR, 5'10.5", 171 lbs. Deb: 5/12/27																											
1927	Chi-N	3	9	0	0	0	0	0	0	0	1	.000	.000	.000	.000	-99	-3	-3	100	0	0	.000	0			0	/3	-0.1
■ CURT WILKERSON	Wilkerson, Curtis Vernon b: 4/26/61, Petersburgh, Va. BB/TR, 5'9", 158 lbs. Deb: 9/10/83																											
1983	Tex-A	16	35	7	6	0	1	0	1	2	5	.171	.216	.229	.445	22	-4	-4	101	49	2	.448	3	0	1	-0	/S23	-0.2
1984	Tex-A	153	484	47	120	12	0	1	26	22	72	.248	.283	.279	.562	56	-28	-28	100	75	38	.449	12	10	-2	-14	*S2	-3.3
1985	Tex-A	129	360	35	88	11	6	0	22	22	63	.244	.295	.308	.604	61	-17	-21	108	79	33	.528	14	7	0	-6	*S2/D	-1.7
1986	Tex-A	110	236	27	56	10	3	0	15	11	42	.237	.274	.305	.579	61	-14	-12	96	83	19	.492	9	7	-2	-2	2S/D	-0.9
1987	Tex-A	85	138	28	37	5	3	2	14	6	16	.268	.308	.391	.700	82	-3	-4	104	93	16	.642	6	3	0	1	S23/D	0.0
1988	Tex-A	117	338	41	99	12	5	0	28	26	43	.293	.347	.358	.705	97	-0	-1	101	92	42	.632	9	4	0	-7	2S/3D	-0.1
Total	6	610	1591	185	406	50	18	3	106	89	241	.255	.299	.315	.614	68	-66	-70	102	82	150	.535	53	31	-3	-29	S2/3D	-6.2
■ BOBBY WILKINS	Wilkins, Robert Linwood b: 8/11/22, Denton, N.C. BR/TR, 5'9", 165 lbs. Deb: 4/18/44																											
1944	Phi-A	24	25	7	6	0	0	0	3	1	4	.240	.296	.240	.536	54	-1	-1	101	180	2	.400	0	0	0	-1	/S	-0.1
1945	Phi-A	62	154	22	40	6	0	0	4	10	17	.260	.305	.299	.604	81	-5	-4	94	31	13	.472	2	4	-2	-1	S/O	-0.4
Total	2	86	179	29	46	6	0	0	7	11	21	.257	.304	.291	.594	76	-6	-5	95	52	15	.465	2	4	-2	-1	/SO	-0.5
■ ED WILKINSON	Wilkinson, Edward Henry b: 6/20/1890, Jacksonville, Ore d: 4/9/18, Tucson, Ariz. BR/TR, 6', 170 lbs. Deb: 7/04/11																											
1911	NY-A	10	13	2	3	0	0	0	1	0		.231	.231	.231	.462	26	-1	-1	111	113	1	.300	0			-1	/O2	-0.1

YEAR	TM/L	G	AB	R	H	2B	3B	HR	RBI	BB	SO	AVG	OBP	SLG	PRO	/A	BR	/A	PF	CHI	RC	TA	SB	CS	SBR	FR	POS	TPR
■ **BOB WILL** Will, Robert Lee "Butch" b: 7/15/31, Berwyn, Ill. BL/TL, 5'10.5", 175 lbs. Deb: 4/16/57																												
1957	Chi-N	70	112	13	25	3	0	1	10	5	21	.223	.256	.277	.533	45	-9	-8	96	122	8	.416	1	0	0	-2	O	-1.1
1958	Chi-N	6	4	1	1	0	0	0	0	2	0	.250	.500	.250	.750	106	0	0	101	0	1	1.000	0	0	0	-0	/O	0.0
1960	Chi-N	138	475	58	121	20	9	6	53	47	54	.255	.323	.373	.696	92	-6	-5	98	113	56	.612	1	5	-3	1	*O	-1.1
1961	Chi-N	86	113	9	29	9	0	0	8	15	19	.257	.344	.336	.680	81	-3	-3	100	85	14	.616	0	1	-1	-6	O/1	-1.0
1962	Chi-N	87	92	6	22	3	0	2	15	13	22	.239	.333	.337	.670	76	-2	-3	106	160	11	.620	0	0	0	-1	/O	-0.3
1963	Chi-N	23	23	0	4	0	0	0	1	1	3	.174	.208	.174	.382	11	-3	-3	105	105	1	.263	0	0	0	0	/1	-0.2
Total	6	410	819	87	202	35	9	9	87	83	119	.247	.317	.344	.661	80	-23	-22	99	114	91	.591	2	6	-3	-9	O/1	-3.7
■ **JERRY WILLARD** Willard, Gerald Duane b: 3/14/60, Oxnard, Cal. BL/TR, 6'2", 195 lbs. Deb: 4/11/84																												
1984	Cle-A	87	246	21	55	8	1	10	37	26	55	.224	.298	.386	.684	83	-4	-6	106	118	28	.619	1	0	0	2	C/D	0.1
1985	Cle-A	104	300	39	81	13	0	7	36	28	59	.270	.334	.383	.718	102	-1	1	94	105	40	.649	0	0	0	9	C/D	1.4
1986	Oak-A	75	161	17	43	7	0	4	26	22	28	.267	.362	.385	.747	112	2	3	94	140	23	.699	0	1	-1	-5	C/D	0.1
1987	Oak-A	7	6	1	1	0	0	0	0	2	1	.167	.375	.167	.542	57	-0	-0	91	0	1	.600	0	0	0	0	/13D	0.0
Total	4	273	713	78	180	28	1	21	99	78	143	.252	.329	.383	.712	97	-4	-2	98	116	92	.665	1	1	-0	6	C/D31	1.6
■ **RIP WILLIAMS** Williams, Alva Mitchel "Buff" b: 1/31/1882, Carthage, Ill. d: 7/23/33, Keokuk, Iowa BR/TR, 5'11.5", 187 lbs. Deb: 4/12/11																												
1911	Bos-A	95	284	36	68	8	5	0	31	24		.239	.314	.303	.617	73	-10	-10	99	122	31	.583	9			-1	1C	-0.4
1912	Was-A	57	157	14	50	11	4	0	22	7		.318	.352	.439	.791	127	4	5	99	106	24	.738	2			5	C	1.4
1913	Was-A	66	106	9	30	6	2	1	12	9	16	.283	.339	.406	.745	111	2	1	106	93	16	.724	3			-2	C/1O	0.1
1914	Was-A	81	169	17	47	6	4	1	22	13	19	.278	.341	.379	.719	115	3	3	101	123	22	.661	2	2	-1	0	C/1O	0.6
1915	Was-A	91	197	14	48	8	4	0	31	18	20	.244	.320	.325	.645	92	-2	-2	101	165	23	.592	4	3	-1	2	C1/3	0.2
1916	Was-A	76	202	16	54	10	2	0	20	15	19	.267	.324	.337	.661	99	-1	-1	100	105	25	.608	5			-2	1C/3	-0.2
1918	Cle-A	28	71	5	17	2	2	0	7	9	6	.239	.325	.324	.649	89	-0	-1	108	111	9	.630	2			-1	1/C	-0.2
Total	7	494	1186	111	314	51	23	2	145	95	80	.265	.328	.352	.680	98	-4	-5	101	121	150	.634	27	5		2	C1/O3	1.5
■ **ART WILLIAMS** Williams, Arthur Franklin b: 8/26/1877, Somerville, Mass. d: 5/16/41, Arlington, Va. TR , Deb: 5/07/02																												
1902	Chi-N	47	160	17	37	3	0	0	14	15		.231	.297	.250	.547	74	-5	-4	96	123	15	.520	9			-0	O1	-0.7
■ **GUS WILLIAMS** Williams, August Joseph "Gloomy Gus" b: 5/7/1888, Omaha, Neb. d: 4/16/64, Sterling, Ill. BL/TL, 6', 185 lbs. Deb: 4/12/11																												
1911	StL-A	9	26	1	7	3	0	0	0	0		.269	.296	.385	.681	94	-1	-0	95	0	3	.579	0			-1	/O	-0.1
1912	StL-A	64	216	32	63	13	7	2	32	27		.292	.370	.444	.815	134	9	9	99	107	41	.922	18			-2	O	0.4
1913	StL-A	148	538	72	147	21	16	5	53	57	87	.273	.346	.400	.746	124	11	14	95	87	80	.783	31			-2	*O	0.5
1914	StL-A	143	499	51	126	19	6	4	47	36	120	.253	.308	.339	.647	97	-5	-3	98	99	56	.621	35	20	-2	-6	*O	-2.1
1915	StL-A	45	119	15	24	2	2	1	11	6	16	.202	.246	.277	.523	59	-7	-6	96	104	10	.531	11	1	3	-8	O	-1.3
Total	5	409	1398	171	367	58	31	12	143	126	223	.263	.327	.374	.702	110	8	14	97	94	191	.716	95	21		-18	O	-2.6
■ **BERNIE WILLIAMS** Williams, Bernard b: 10/8/48, Alameda, Cal. BR/TR, 6'1", 175 lbs. Deb: 9/07/70																												
1970	SF-N	7	16	2	5	2	0	0	1	2	1	.313	.389	.438	.826	126	1	1	96	55	2	.769	1	1	-0	1	/O	0.1
1971	SF-N	35	73	8	13	1	0	1	5	12	24	.178	.294	.233	.527	51	-4	-4	100	102	6	.484	1	1	-0	-6	O	-1.2
1972	SF-N	46	68	12	13	3	1	3	9	7	22	.191	.267	.397	.664	86	-2	-1	100	103	7	.596	0	0	0	1	O	0.0
1974	SD-N	14	15	1	2	0	0	0	0	0	6	.133	.133	.133	.267	-27	-2	-2	93	0	0	.154	0	0	0	-1	/O	-0.3
Total	4	102	172	23	33	6	1	4	15	21	53	.192	.280	.308	.588	66	-8	-8	99	90	15	.539	2	2	-1	-5	/O	-1.4
■ **BILLY WILLIAMS** Williams, Billy Leo b: 6/15/38, Whistler, Ala. BL/TR, 6'1", 175 lbs. Deb: 8/06/59 CH																												
1959	Chi-N	18	33	0	5	0	1	0	2	1	7	.152	.176	.212	.389	3	-5	-5	98	115	1	.267	0	0	0	-1	O	-0.4
1960	Chi-N	12	47	4	13	0	2	2	7	5	12	.277	.346	.489	.836	128	2	2	98	104	8	.800	0	0	0	-0	O	0.1
1961	Chi-N	146	529	75	147	20	7	25	86	45	70	.278	.340	.484	.824	115	11	11	100	107	87	.794	6	0	2	-6	*O	0.0
1962	Chi-N	159	618	94	184	22	8	22	91	70	72	.298	.373	.466	.839	117	21	16	106	97	107	.817	9	9	-3	4	*O	0.9
1963	Chi-N	161	612	87	175	36	9	25	95	68	78	.286	.359	.497	.856	137	34	30	105	101	108	.837	7	6	-2	8	*O	3.0
1964	Chi-N	162	645	100	201	39	2	33	98	59	84	.312	.371	.532	.903	143	42	38	105	87	125	.896	10	7	-1	-10	*O	2.4
1965	Chi-N	164	645	115	203	39	6	34	108	65	76	.315	.380	.552	.932	156	49	48	102	94	132	.937	10	1	2	2	*O	4.9
1966	Chi-N	162	648	100	179	23	5	29	91	69	61	.276	.350	.461	.811	123	20	20	100	88	104	.781	6	3	0	8	*O	2.5
1967	Chi-N	162	634	92	176	21	12	28	84	68	67	.278	.349	.481	.831	133	28	27	102	86	106	.804	6	3	0	-7	*O	1.3
1968	Chi-N	163	642	91	185	30	8	30	98	48	53	.288	.340	.500	.840	133	36	28	112	97	107	.796	4	1	1	-12	*O	1.0
1969	Chi-N	163	642	103	188	33	10	21	95	59	70	.293	.356	.474	.830	122	25	20	107	110	106	.786	3	2	-0	0	*O	1.1
1970	Chi-N	161	636	**137**	**205**	34	4	42	129	72	65	.322	.393	.586	.979	132	51	34	120	96	**147**	1.020	7	1	2	-1	*O	2.7
1971	Chi-N	157	594	86	179	27	5	28	93	77	44	.301	.384	.505	.889	137	39	33	110	104	112	.886	7	5	-1	-2	*O	2.5
1972	Chi-N	150	574	95	191	34	6	37	122	62	59	**.333**	.403	**.606**	**1.010**	161	**61**	**52**	114	116	**137**	**1.053**	3	1	0	-7	*O/1	4.0
1973	Chi-N	156	576	72	166	22	2	20	86	76	72	.288	.372	.438	.810	114	19	13	108	117	94	.782	4	3	-1	4	*O1	1.0
1974	Chi-N	117	404	55	113	22	0	16	68	67	44	.280	.383	.453	.836	133	19	19	100	116	71	.836	4	5	-2	5	1O	1.8
1975	Oak-A	155	520	68	127	20	1	23	81	76	68	.244	.343	.419	.762	123	10	15	93	111	78	.736	0	0	0	-0	*D/1	1.5
1976	Oak-A	120	351	36	74	12	0	11	41	58	44	.211	.323	.339	.662	94	-2	-1	100	104	41	.640	4	2	0	-0	*D/O	-0.1
Total	18	2488	9350	1410	2711	434	88	426	1475	1045	1046	.290	.364	.492	.856	131	463	401	105	101	1671	.863	90	49	-2	-15	*OD/1	30.2
■ **DALLAS WILLIAMS** Williams, Dallas Mc Kinley b: 2/28/58, Brooklyn, N.Y. BL/TL, 5'11", 165 lbs. Deb: 9/19/81																												
1981	Bal-A	2	2	0	1	0	0	0	0	0	0	.500	.500	.500	1.000	191	0	0	99	0	1	1.000	0	0	0	-0	/O	0.0
1983	Cin-N	18	36	2	2	0	0	0	1	3	6	.056	.128	.056	.184	-46	-7	-7	103	198	0	.147	0	0	0	-1	O	-0.8
Total	2	20	38	2	3	0	0	0	1	3	6	.079	.146	.079	.225	-35	-7	-7	103	188	1	.171	0	0	0	-1	/O	-0.8
■ **DAVEY WILLIAMS** Williams, David Carlous b: 11/2/27, Dallas, Tex. BR/TR, 5'10", 160 lbs. Deb: 9/16/49 C																												
1949	NY-N	13	50	7	12	1	1	1	5	7	4	.240	.333	.360	.693	85	-1	-1	102	86	7	.658	0			-0	2	0.0
1951	NY-N	30	64	17	17	1	0	2	8	5	8	.266	.319	.375	.694	85	-1	-1	102	103	7	.588	1	1	-0	0	2	0.0
1952	NY-N	138	540	70	137	26	3	13	55	48	63	.254	.324	.385	.709	94	-3	-5	102	84	71	.646	2	3	-1	-9	*2	-0.8
1953	NY-N	112	340	51	101	11	2	3	34	44	19	.297	.382	.368	.750	99	0	1	98	99	50	.696	2	5	-2	0	2	0.3
1954	NY-N	142	544	65	121	18	3	9	46	43	33	.222	.285	.316	.602	54	-35	-39	105	96	48	.503	1	1	-0	-2	*2	-3.2
1955	NY-N	82	247	25	62	4	1	4	15	17	17	.251	.305	.324	.628	68	-12	-11	99	66	24	.521	0	2	-1	5	2	-0.1
Total	6	517	1785	235	450	61	10	32	163	164	144	.252	.321	.351	.673	78	-52	-56	102	89	207	.604	6	12		-6	2	-3.8
■ **DEWEY WILLIAMS** Williams, Dewey Edgar "Dee" b: 2/5/16, Durham, N.C. BR/TR, 6', 160 lbs. Deb: 6/28/44																												
1944	Chi-N	79	262	23	63	7	2	0	27	23	18	.240	.302	.282	.584	65	-12	-12	101	131	22	.474	2			-3	C	-1.0
1945	Chi-N	59	100	16	28	2	2	2	5	13	13	.280	.363	.400	.763	113	2	2	99	38	14	.688	0			-3	C	0.0
1946	Chi-N	4	5	0	1	0	0	0	0	0	2	.200	.200	.200	.400	14	-1	-1	94	0	0	.250	0			0	/C	0.0
1947	Chi-N	3	2	0	0	0	0	0	0	0	1	.000	.000	.000	.000	-99	-1	-1	101	0	0	.000	0			0	/C	0.0
1948	Cin-N	48	95	9	16	2	0	1	5	10	18	.168	.248	.221	.469	27	-10	-10	103	78	6	.387	0			-1	C	-0.7
Total	5	193	464	48	108	11	4	3	37	46	52	.233	.302	.293	.595	66	-21	-21	101	97	41	.515	2			-7	C	-1.7
■ **EARL WILLIAMS** Williams, Earl Baxter b: 1/27/03, Cumberland Gap, Tenn. d: 3/10/58, Knoxville, Tn BR/TR, 6'0.5", 185 lbs. Deb: 5/27/28																												
1928	Bos-N	3	2	0	0	0	0	0	0	0	1	.000	.000	.000	.000	-99	-1	-1	97	0	0	.000	0			0	/C	0.0
■ **EARL WILLIAMS** Williams, Earl Craig b: 7/14/48, Newark, N.J. BR/TR, 6'3", 215 lbs. Deb: 9/13/70																												
1970	Atl-N	10	19	4	7	4	0	0	5	3	4	.368	.455	.579	1.033	168	2	2	104	176	5	1.077	0	0	0	0	/13	0.2
1971	Atl-N	145	497	64	129	14	1	33	87	42	80	.260	.326	.491	.817	117	17	11	110	105	78	.771	0	1	-1	0	C31	1.0
1972	Atl-N	151	565	72	146	24	2	28	87	62	118	.258	.338	.457	.795	118	17	14	105	111	85	.748	0	0	0	-1	*C31	1.9
1973	Bal-A	132	459	58	109	18	1	22	83	66	107	.237	.337	.425	.762	106	8	4	107	127	65	.723	0	2	-1	-6	C1/D	-0.3
1974	Bal-A	118	413	47	105	16	0	14	52	40	79	.254	.330	.395	.725	116	4	8	93	102	54	.656	0	2	-1	-3	C1/D	0.4
1975	Atl-N	111	383	42	92	13	0	11	50	34	63	.240	.307	.360	.667	89	-9	-6	95	115	40	.570	0	0	0	-3	1C	-1.3
1976	Atl-N	61	184	18	39	3	0	9	26	19	33	.212	.289	.375	.664	79	-4	-6	111	104	19	.582	0	0	0	0	C1	-0.4
	Mon-N	61	190	17	45	10	2	8	29	14	32	.237	.289	.437	.726	104	-0	-0	100	104	22	.634	0	0	0	4	1C	0.3
	Yr	122	374	35	84	13	2	17	55	33	65	.225	.289	.406	.696	91	-4	-6	106	105	43	.624	0	0	0	5		-0.1

YEAR	TM/L	G	AB	R	H	2B	3B	HR	RBI	BB	SO	AVG	OBP	SLG	PRO	/A	BR	/A	PF	CHI	RC	TA	SB	CS	SBR	FR	POS	TPR
1977	Oak-A	100	348	39	84	13	0	13	38	18	58	.241	.288	.391	.679	87	-9	-7	95	88	34	.569	2	0	1	-7	DC1	-1.3
Total	8	889	3058	361	756	115	6	138	457	298	574	.247	.321	.424	.745	106	27	19	102	109	401	.700	2	5	-2	-15	C1/3D	0.5

■ **EDDIE WILLIAMS** Williams, Edward Laquan b: 11/1/64, Shreveport, La. BR/TR, 6', 175 lbs. Deb: 4/18/86

YEAR	TM/L	G	AB	R	H	2B	3B	HR	RBI	BB	SO	AVG	OBP	SLG	PRO	/A	BR	/A	PF	CHI	RC	TA	SB	CS	SBR	FR	POS	TPR
1986	Cle-A	5	7	2	1	0	0	0	1	0	3	.143	.143	.143	.286	-22	-1	-1	98	398	0	.167	0	0	0	-2	/O	-0.2
1987	Cle-A	22	64	9	11	4	0	1	4	9	19	.172	.284	.281	.565	50	-4	-5	103	76	5	.509	0	0	0	-1	3	-0.5
1988	Cle-A	10	21	3	4	0	0	0	1	0	3	.190	.227	.190	.418	18	-2	-2	102	99	1	.278	0	0	0	0	3	-0.1
Total	3	37	92	14	16	4	0	1	6	9	25	.174	.262	.250	.512	39	-8	-8	102	103	6	.442	0	0	0	-2	/3O	-0.8

■ **DIB WILLIAMS** Williams, Edwin Dibrell b: 1/19/10, Greenbrier, Ark. BR/TR, 5'11.5", 175 lbs. Deb: 4/27/30

YEAR	TM/L	G	AB	R	H	2B	3B	HR	RBI	BB	SO	AVG	OBP	SLG	PRO	/A	BR	/A	PF	CHI	RC	TA	SB	CS	SBR	FR	POS	TPR
1930	Phi-A	67	191	24	50	10	3	3	22	15	19	.262	.322	.393	.715	81	-6	-6	99	87	25	.662	2	1	0	-2	2S/3	-0.4
1931	Phi-A	86	294	41	79	12	2	6	40	19	21	.269	.313	.384	.697	79	-8	-10	105	101	36	.623	2	0	1	-8	S2/O	-0.8
1932	Phi-A	62	215	30	54	10	1	4	24	22	23	.251	.329	.363	.692	69	-7	-11	114	89	26	.636	0	1	-1	-1	2/S	-0.8
1933	Phi-A	115	408	52	118	20	5	11	73	32	35	.289	.342	.444	.786	116	3	7	92	114	63	.741	1	0	0	-9	S2/1	0.4
1934	Phi-A	66	205	25	56	10	1	2	17	21	18	.273	.341	.361	.702	83	-6	-5	97	71	26	.633	0	1	-1	6	2/S	0.2
1935	Phi-A	4	10	0	1	0	0	0	0	0	1	.100	.100	.100	.200	-48	-2	-2	100	0	0	.111	0	0	0	0	/2	-0.1
	Bos-A	75	251	26	63	12	0	3	25	24	23	.251	.319	.335	.654	64	-11	-15	108	91	28	.590	2	0	1	2	32S/1	-0.8
	Yr	79	261	26	64	12	0	3	25	24	24	.245	.311	.326	.637	60	-14	-17	108	87	28	.569	2	0	1	2		-0.9
Total	6	475	1574	198	421	74	12	29	201	133	140	.267	.327	.385	.712	83	-37	-41	102	95	204	.651	7	3	0	-11	2S/310	-2.3

■ **DENNY WILLIAMS** Williams, Evon Daniel b: 12/13/1899, Portland, Ore. d: 3/24/29, Los Angeles, Cal. BL/TR, 5'8.5", 150 lbs. Deb: 4/15/21

YEAR	TM/L	G	AB	R	H	2B	3B	HR	RBI	BB	SO	AVG	OBP	SLG	PRO	/A	BR	/A	PF	CHI	RC	TA	SB	CS	SBR	FR	POS	TPR
1921	Cin-N	10	7	0	0	0	0	0	0	0	2	.000	.000	.000	.000	-99	-2	-2	101	0	0	.000	0	1	-1	-0	/O	-0.2
1924	Bos-A	25	85	17	31	3	0	0	4	10	5	.365	.438	.400	.837	113	3	2	104	39	15	.842	3	3	-1	-2	O	-0.1
1925	Bos-A	69	218	28	50	1	3	0	13	17	11	.229	.285	.261	.547	41	-20	-18	95	76	16	.437	2	6	-3	-1	O	-2.5
1928	Bos-A	16	18	1	4	0	0	0	1	1	1	.222	.263	.222	.485	29	-2	-2	98	86	1	.357	0	0	0	-2	/O	-0.3
Total	4	120	328	46	85	4	3	0	18	28	19	.259	.319	.290	.609	58	-21	-20	98	65	32	.510	5	10	-5	-5	/O	-3.1

■ **CY WILLIAMS** Williams, Fred b: 12/21/1887, Wadena, Ind. d: 4/23/74, Eagle River, Wis. BL/TL, 6'2", 180 lbs. Deb: 7/18/12

YEAR	TM/L	G	AB	R	H	2B	3B	HR	RBI	BB	SO	AVG	OBP	SLG	PRO	/A	BR	/A	PF	CHI	RC	TA	SB	CS	SBR	FR	POS	TPR
1912	Chi-N	28	62	3	15	1	1	0	1	6	14	.242	.309	.290	.599	62	-3	-3	104	19	6	.553	2			-2	O	-0.5
1913	Chi-N	49	156	17	35	3	3	4	32	5	26	.224	.262	.359	.621	77	-6	-5	99	171	15	.570	5			-3	O	-0.9
1914	Chi-N	55	94	12	19	2	2	0	5	13	13	.202	.312	.266	.578	74	-3	-3	98	72	8	.560	2			-2	O	-0.5
1915	Chi-N	151	518	59	133	22	6	13	64	26	49	.257	.305	.398	.703	110	5	4	102	102	64	.651	15	10	-2	-2	*O	-0.3
1916	Chi-N	118	405	55	113	19	9	**12**	66	51	64	.279	.372	.459	**.831**	132	27	19	117	125	74	**.863**	6			-9	*O	0.7
1917	Chi-N	138	468	53	113	22	4	5	42	38	78	.241	.308	.338	.646	94	-1	-3	105	96	52	.594	8			9	*O	0.2
1918	Phi-N	94	351	49	97	14	1	6	39	27	30	.276	.337	.373	.710	107	7	3	109	105	47	.681	10			-3	O	-0.4
1919	Phi-N	109	435	54	121	21	1	9	39	30	43	.278	.335	.393	.728	114	9	8	104	74	58	.691	9			-0	*O	0.3
1920	Phi-N	148	590	88	192	36	10	**15**	72	32	45	.325	.364	.497	.861	134	32	26	109	79	103	.846	18	12	-2	6	*O	2.4
1921	Phi-N	146	562	67	180	28	6	18	75	30	32	.320	.357	.488	.844	119	15	14	102	89	91	.783	5	15	-8	11	*O	1.1
1922	Phi-N	151	584	98	180	30	6	26	92	74	49	.308	.392	.514	.905	116	27	16	113	90	116	.935	11	14	-5	-4	*O	0.1
1923	Phi-N	136	535	98	157	22	3	**41**	114	59	57	.293	.371	.576	.947	129	33	23	114	99	112	.992	11	10	-3	-6	*O	0.9
1924	Phi-N	148	558	101	183	31	11	24	93	67	49	.328	.403	.552	.955	143	42	36	108	95	121	.995	7	12	-5	-6	*O	2.1
1925	Phi-N	107	314	78	104	11	5	13	60	53	34	.331	.435	.522	.958	124	23	15	116	105	72	1.032	4	9	-4	-6	O	0.2
1926	Phi-N	107	336	63	116	13	4	18	53	38	35	.345	.418	.568	.986	158	30	28	103	75	78	1.068	2			-8	O	1.6
1927	Phi-N	131	492	86	135	18	2	**30**	98	61	57	.274	.365	.502	.867	135	20	23	96	108	90	.888	0			2	*O	1.8
1928	Phi-N	99	238	31	61	9	0	12	37	54	34	.256	.400	.445	.845	116	9	8	104	93	45	.921	0			-4	O	0.1
1929	Phi-N	66	65	11	19	2	0	5	21	22	9	.292	.471	.554	1.025	140	7	5	110	141	18	1.261	0			0	O	0.4
1930	Phi-N	21	17	1	8	2	0	0	2	4	3	.471	.571	.588	1.160	171	3	3	106	69	6	1.556	0			-1	/O	0.1
Total	19	2002	6780	1024	1981	306	74	251	1005	690	721	.292	.365	.470	.835	123	278	216	107	96	1177	.836	115	82		-27	*O	9.4

■ **PAPA WILLIAMS** Williams, Fred b: 7/17/13, Meridian, Miss. BR/TR, 6'1", 200 lbs. Deb: 4/19/45

YEAR	TM/L	G	AB	R	H	2B	3B	HR	RBI	BB	SO	AVG	OBP	SLG	PRO	/A	BR	/A	PF	CHI	RC	TA	SB	CS	SBR	FR	POS	TPR
1945	Cle-A	16	19	0	4	0	0	0	0	1	2	.211	.250	.211	.461	35	-2	-2	99	0	1	.333	0	0	0	0	/1	-0.1

■ **GEORGE WILLIAMS** Williams, George b: 10/23/39, Detroit, Mich. BR/TR, 5'11", 165 lbs. Deb: 7/16/61

YEAR	TM/L	G	AB	R	H	2B	3B	HR	RBI	BB	SO	AVG	OBP	SLG	PRO	/A	BR	/A	PF	CHI	RC	TA	SB	CS	SBR	FR	POS	TPR
1961	Phi-N	17	36	4	9	0	0	0	1	4	4	.250	.325	.250	.575	59	-2	-2	94	45	3	.481	0	0	0	1	2	0.1
1962	Hou-N	5	8	1	3	1	0	0	2	0	1	.375	.375	.500	.875	143	0	0	93	197	2	.800	0	0	0	0	/2	0.1
1964	KC-A	37	91	10	19	6	0	0	2	6	12	.209	.265	.275	.540	48	-6	-7	105	34	7	.432	0	0	0	1	2/S3O	-0.3
Total	3	59	135	15	31	7	0	0	5	10	17	.230	.288	.281	.569	56	-8	-8	101	46	11	.462	0	0	0	2	/2O3S	-0.1

■ **HARRY WILLIAMS** Williams, Harry Peter b: 6/23/1890, Omaha, Neb. d: 12/21/63, Huntington Park, Cal. BR/TR, 6'1.5", 200 lbs. Deb: 8/07/13

YEAR	TM/L	G	AB	R	H	2B	3B	HR	RBI	BB	SO	AVG	OBP	SLG	PRO	/A	BR	/A	PF	CHI	RC	TA	SB	CS	SBR	FR	POS	TPR
1913	NY-A	27	82	18	21	3	1	1	12	15	10	.256	.378	.354	.731	113	2	2	101	136	12	.836	6			1	1	0.3

■ **JIM WILLIAMS** Williams, James Alfred b: 4/29/47, Zachary, La. BR/TR, 6'2", 190 lbs. Deb: 9/08/69

YEAR	TM/L	G	AB	R	H	2B	3B	HR	RBI	BB	SO	AVG	OBP	SLG	PRO	/A	BR	/A	PF	CHI	RC	TA	SB	CS	SBR	FR	POS	TPR
1969	SD-N	13	25	4	7	1	0	0	2	3	11	.280	.357	.320	.677	94	-0	-0	97	100	3	.611	0	0	0	-1	/O	0.0
1970	SD-N	11	14	4	4	0	0	0	0	1	3	.286	.333	.286	.619	71	-1	-1	95	0	2	.600	1	0	0	-1	/O	-0.1
Total	2	24	39	8	11	1	0	0	2	4	14	.282	.349	.308	.657	86	-1	-1	96	65	5	.607	1	0	0	-2	/O	-0.1

■ **JIMY WILLIAMS** Williams, James Francis b: 10/4/43, Santa Maria, Cal. BR/TR, 5'10", 170 lbs. Deb: 4/26/66 MC

YEAR	TM/L	G	AB	R	H	2B	3B	HR	RBI	BB	SO	AVG	OBP	SLG	PRO	/A	BR	/A	PF	CHI	RC	TA	SB	CS	SBR	FR	POS	TPR
1966	StL-N	13	11	1	3	0	0	0	1	1	5	.273	.333	.273	.606	71	-0	-0	100	140	1	.444	0	0	0	0	/S2	0.0
1967	StL-N	1	2	0	0	0	0	0	0	0	1	.000	.000	.000	.000	-99	-1	-1	101	0	0	.000	0	0	0	0	/S	0.0
Total	2	14	13	1	3	0	0	0	1	1	6	.231	.286	.231	.516	46	-1	-1	100	120	1	.364	0	0	0	0	/S2	0.0

■ **JIMMY WILLIAMS** Williams, James Thomas b: 12/20/1876, St.Louis, Mo. d: 1/16/65, St.Petersburg, Fla BR/TR, 5'9", 175 lbs. Deb: 4/15/1899

YEAR	TM/L	G	AB	R	H	2B	3B	HR	RBI	BB	SO	AVG	OBP	SLG	PRO	/A	BR	/A	PF	CHI	RC	TA	SB	CS	SBR	FR	POS	TPR
1899	Pit-N	152	617	126	219	28	**27**	9	116	60		.355	.416	.532	.947	164	51	52	99	89	151	1.050	26			5	*3	5.1
1900	Pit-N	106	416	73	110	15	11	5	68	32		.264	.317	.389	.706	94	-3	-5	103	115	58	.693	18			6	*3/S	0.2
1901	Bal-A	130	501	113	159	26	**21**	7	96	56		.317	.386	.495	.881	136	30	25	107	108	106	.950	21			-4	*2	1.4
1902	Bal-A	125	498	83	156	27	**21**	8	83	36		.313	.360	.500	.860	136	24	22	102	96	97	.874	14			-3	*23/1	2.1
1903	NY-A	132	502	60	134	30	12	3	82	39		.267	.320	.392	.712	115	9	9	100	152	68	.666	9			14	*2	2.6
1904	NY-A	146	559	62	147	31	7	2	74	38		.263	.310	.354	.664	100	7	0	112	130	67	.607	14			16	*2	1.8
1905	NY-A	129	470	54	107	20	8	6	62	50		.228	.302	.343	.644	105	4	3	102	119	54	.620	14			-0	*2	0.2
1906	NY-A	139	501	62	139	25	7	3	77	44		.277	.336	.373	.709	103	14	2	120	151	67	.660	8			12	*2	1.2
1907	NY-A	139	504	53	136	17	11	2	63	35		.270	.317	.359	.676	108	9	4	109	128	63	.625	14			-5	*2	-0.1
1908	StL-A	148	539	63	127	20	7	4	53	55		.236	.306	.321	.627	103	4	3	103	114	53	.570	7			3	*2	0.2
1909	StL-A	110	374	32	73	3	6	0	22	29		.195	.257	.235	.492	61	-19	-15	92	98	23	.415	6			-5	*2	-2.6
Total	11	1456	5481	781	1507	242	138	49	796	474		.275	.333	.396	.730	115	131	100	105	118	808	.705	151			40	*23/S1	12.1

■ **KEN WILLIAMS** Williams, Kenneth Roy b: 6/28/1890, Grants Pass, Ore. d: 1/22/59, Grants Pass, Ore. BL/TR, 6', 170 lbs. Deb: 7/14/15

YEAR	TM/L	G	AB	R	H	2B	3B	HR	RBI	BB	SO	AVG	OBP	SLG	PRO	/A	BR	/A	PF	CHI	RC	TA	SB	CS	SBR	FR	POS	TPR
1915	Cin-N	71	219	22	53	10	4	0	16	15	20	.242	.297	.324	.621	86	-3	-4	103	86	22	.544	4	3	-1	4	O	-0.2
1916	Cin-N	10	27	1	3	0	0	0	1	2	5	.111	.172	.111	.284	-12	-4	-3	98	132	1	.250	1			1	O	-0.2
1918	StL-A	2	1	0	0	0	0	0	0	1	0	.000	.500	.000	.500	51	0	0	99	0	0	1.000	0			0	H	0.0
1919	StL-A	65	227	32	68	10	5	6	35	26	25	.300	.376	.467	.843	140	11	12	97	104	42	.887	7			2	O	0.9
1920	StL-A	141	521	90	160	34	13	10	72	41	26	.307	.362	.480	.842	109	14	6	111	92	91	.848	18	8	1	13	*O	0.8
1921	StL-A	146	547	115	190	31	7	24	117	74	42	.347	.429	.561	.990	150	43	42	101	112	130	1.083	20	17	-4	10	*O	3.2
1922	StL-A	153	585	128	194	34	11	**39**	**155**	74	31	.332	.413	.627	1.040	159	56	51	106	121	150	1.183	37	19	-0	13	*O	5.0
1923	StL-A	147	555	106	198	37	12	29	91	79	32	.357	.439	.623	1.062	171	61	58	104	76	148	1.190	18	17	-5	12	*O	4.9
1924	StL-A	114	398	78	129	21	4	18	84	69	17	.324	.425	.533	.958	136	28	24	107	111	93	1.079	20	11	-1	6	*O	2.0
1925	StL-A	102	411	83	136	31	5	25	105	37	14	.331	.390	.613	1.003	141	29	24	108	103	97	1.079	10	5	0	6	*O	1.9
1926	StL-A	108	347	55	97	15	7	17	74	39	23	.280	.354	.510	.864	123	10	10	101	110	63	.874	5	4	-1	-0	O/2	0.1
1927	StL-A	131	423	70	136	23	6	17	74	57	30	.322	.403	.525	.928	132	24	21	106	92	89	1.007	9	0	3	9	*O	2.1
1928	Bos-A	133	462	59	140	25	1	8	67	37	15	.303	.356	.413	.769	103	1	2	98	109	66	.704	4	9	-4	-2	*O	-1.0
1929	Bos-A	74	139	21	48	14	2	3	21	15	7	.345	.409	.540	.949	140	9	8	102	86	29	.948	1	5	-3	-2	O/1	0.1

YEAR	TM/L	G	AB	R	H	2B	3B	HR	RBI	BB	SO	AVG	OBP	SLG	PRO	/A	BR	/A	PF	CHI	RC	TA	SB	CS	SBR	FR	POS	TPR
Total	14	1397	4862	860	1552	285	77	196	913	566	287	.319	.393	.530	.924	135	279	249	104	102	1020	.976	154	98		71	*O/12	19.6
■ KEN WILLIAMS	Williams, Kenneth Royal b: 4/6/64, Berkeley, Cal. BR/TR, 6'2", 187 lbs. Deb: 9/02/86																											
1986	Chi-A	15	31	2	4	0	0	1	1	1	11	.129	.182	.226	.408	11	-4	-4	101	40	1	.345	1	1	-0	0	O/D	-0.3
1987	Chi-A	116	391	48	110	18	2	11	50	10	83	.281	.315	.422	.737	87	-4	-8	109	101	50	.693	21	10	0	0	*O	-1.0
1988	Chi-A	73	220	18	35	4	2	8	28	10	64	.159	.223	.305	.527	47	-16	-16	97	122	15	.474	6	5	-1	-0	O3/D	-1.7
Total	3	204	642	68	149	22	4	20	79	21	158	.232	.276	.372	.648	71	-24	-28	104	105	66	.599	28	16	-1	0	O/3D	-3.0
■ MARK WILLIAMS	Williams, Mark Westley b: 7/28/53, Elmira, N.Y. BL/TL, 6', 180 lbs. Deb: 5/20/77																											
1977	Oak-A	3	2	0	0	0	0	0	1	1	1	.000	.333	.000	.333	0	-0	-0	95	0	0	.500	0	0	0	-0	/O	0.0
■ MATT WILLIAMS	Williams, Matthew Derrick b: 11/28/65, Bishop, Cal. BR/TR, 6'2", 205 lbs. Deb: 4/11/87																											
1987	SF-N	84	245	28	46	9	2	8	21	16	68	.188	.240	.339	.579	53	-18	-17	96	78	19	.502	4	3	-1	12	S3	0.2
1988	SF-N	52	156	17	32	6	1	8	19	8	41	.205	.253	.410	.663	93	-3	-2	94	86	14	.561	0	1	-1	5	3/S	0.2
Total	2	136	401	45	78	15	3	16	40	24	109	.195	.245	.367	.612	68	-21	-19	95	81	32	.533	4	4	-1	17	/S3	0.4
■ OTTO WILLIAMS	Williams, Otto George b: 11/2/1877, Newark, N.J. d: 3/19/37, Omaha, Neb. BR/TR, 5'6", Deb: 10/05/02 C																											
1902	StL-N	2	5	0	2	0	0	0	2	1		.400	.500	.400	.900	190	1	1	95	346	2	1.333	1			0	/S	0.1
1903	StL-N	53	187	10	38	4	2	0	9	9		.203	.240	.246	.486	41	-15	-14	96	64	13	.409	6			-1	S/2	-1.1
	Chi-N	38	130	14	29	5	0	0	13	4		.223	.246	.262	.508	48	-9	-8	95	123	11	.455	8			0	S/213	-0.5
	Yr	91	317	24	67	9	2	0	22	13		.211	.242	.252	.495	44	-24	-22	96	89	23	.428	14			-1		-1.6
1904	Chi-N	57	185	21	37	4	1	0	8	13		.200	.253	.232	.485	51	-10	-10	101	68	13	.439	9			1	O1S/23	-1.0
1906	Was-A	20	51	3	7	0	0	0	2	2		.137	.170	.137	.307	-3	-6	-5	91	104	1	.205	0			0	/S213	-0.5
Total	4	170	558	48	113	13	3	0	34	29		.203	.242	.237	.478	44	-39	-37	97	85	40	.416	24			-1	/SO213	-3.0
■ REGGIE WILLIAMS	Williams, Reginald Dewayne b: 8/29/60, Memphis, Tenn. BR/TR, 5'11", 185 lbs. Deb: 9/02/85																											
1985	LA-N	22	9	4	3	0	0	0	0	0	4	.333	.333	.333	.667	94	-0	-0	93	0	1	.667	1	0	0	-4	O	-0.3
1986	LA-N	128	303	35	84	14	2	4	32	23	57	.277	.332	.376	.709	101	-2	0	94	101	37	.643	9	3	1	-10	*O	-1.1
1987	LA-N	39	36	6	4	0	0	0	4	5	9	.111	.220	.111	.331	-10	-6	-5	92	399	1	.286	1	1	-0	-8	O	-1.4
1988	Cle-A	11	31	7	7	2	0	1	3	0	6	.226	.226	.387	.613	67	-1	-1	102	79	2	.462	0	0	0	-2	O	-0.2
Total	4	200	379	52	98	16	2	5	39	28	76	.259	.313	.351	.664	87	-9	-7	94	127	41	.606	11	4	1	-23	O	-3.0
■ DICK WILLIAMS	Williams, Richard Hirschfeld b: 5/7/28, St.Louis, Mo. BR/TR, 6', 190 lbs. Deb: 6/10/51 MC																											
1951	Bro-N	23	60	5	12	3	1	1	5	4	10	.200	.250	.333	.583	57	-4	-4	98	84	5	.500	0	0	0	-2	O	-0.6
1952	Bro-N	36	68	13	21	4	1	0	11	2	10	.309	.329	.397	.726	99	-0	-0	102	159	8	.569	0	0	0	-2	O/13	-0.2
1953	Bro-N	30	55	4	12	2	0	2	5	3	10	.218	.271	.364	.635	61	-3	-3	104	75	6	.545	0	0	0	-6	O	-1.0
1954	Bro-N	16	34	5	5	0	0	1	2	2	7	.147	.194	.235	.430	11	-5	-5	101	72	1	.333	0	0	0	-4	O	-0.8
1956	Bro-N	7	7	0	2	0	0	0	0	0	1	.286	.286	.286	.571	53	-0	-0	103	0	1	.400	0	0	0	0	H	0.0
	Bal-A	87	353	45	101	18	4	11	37	30	40	.286	.342	.453	.795	115	3	6	94	63	52	.730	5	5	-2	-4	O12/3	-0.2
1957	Bal-A	47	167	16	39	10	2	1	17	14	21	.234	.293	.335	.628	76	-7	-5	93	116	15	.519	0	1	-1	1	O31	-0.6
	Cle-A	67	205	33	58	7	0	6	17	12	19	.283	.326	.405	.731	97	-1	-1	102	66	24	.627	3	4	-2	-1	O3	-0.5
	Yr	114	372	49	97	17	2	7	34	26	40	.261	.311	.374	.684	88	-8	-7	98	88	42	.589	3	5	-2	-1		-1.1
1958	Bal-A	128	409	36	113	17	0	4	32	37	47	.276	.339	.347	.686	95	-5	-2	94	83	44	.567	0	6	-4	5	O31/2	-0.3
1959	KC-A	130	488	72	130	33	1	16	75	28	60	.266	.313	.436	.749	102	1	-0	101	120	64	.672	4	1	1	-5	31O/2	-0.6
1960	KC-A	127	420	47	121	31	0	12	65	39	68	.288	.350	.448	.798	116	8	8	99	114	62	.724	0	0	0	5	31O	1.1
1961	Bal-A	103	310	37	64	15	2	8	24	20	38	.206	.255	.345	.600	60	-19	-18	97	72	25	.494	0	4	-2	-11	O1/3	-3.6
1962	Bal-A	82	178	20	44	7	1	1	18	14	26	.247	.306	.315	.620	71	-8	-7	95	121	16	.500	0	0	0	-2	O1/3	-1.0
1963	Bos-A	79	136	15	35	8	0	2	12	15	25	.257	.331	.360	.691	89	-1	-2	106	91	17	.615	0	0	0	-2	31/O	-0.4
1964	Bos-A	61	69	10	11	2	0	5	11	7	10	.159	.247	.406	.653	77	-2	-3	102	108	6	.581	0	0	0	1	13/O	-0.2
Total	13	1023	2959	358	768	157	12	70	331	227	392	.260	.315	.392	.707	92	-44	-37	98	95	346	.636	12	21	-9	-29	O31/2	-8.9
■ RINALDO WILLIAMS	Williams, Rinaldo Lewis b: 12/18/1893, Santa Cruz, Cal. d: 4/24/66, Cottonwood, Ariz. BL/TR, Deb: 10/08/14																											
1914	Bro-F	4	15	1	4	2	0	0	0	0	0	.267	.267	.400	.667	89	-0	-0	101	0	2	.545	0			0	/3	0.0
■ BOB WILLIAMS	Williams, Robert Elias b: 4/27/1884, Monday, Ohio d: 8/6/62, Nelsonville, Ohio BR/TR, 6', 190 lbs. Deb: 7/03/11																											
1911	NY-A	20	47	3	9	2	0	0	8	5		.191	.269	.234	.503	37	-4	-4	111	246	3	.447	1			-1	C	-0.2
1912	NY-A	20	44	7	6	1	0	0	3	9		.136	.283	.159	.442	27	-4	-4	101	143	2	.421	0			1	C	0.0
1913	NY-A	6	19	0	3	0	0	0	0	1	3	.158	.200	.158	.358	5	-2	-2	101	0	1	.250	0			1	/C	0.0
1914	NY-A	59	178	9	29	5	2	1	17	26	26	.163	.287	.230	.517	56	-9	-9	100	145	12	.484	3	6	-3	-2	1	-1.4
Total	4	105	288	19	47	8	2	1	28	41	29	.163	.278	.215	.494	45	-19	-19	102	152	17	.453	4	6		-2	/1C	-1.6
■ TED WILLIAMS	Williams, Theodore Samuel "The Kid," "The Thumper" or "The Splendid Splinter" b: 8/30/18, San Diego, Cal. BL/TR, 6'3",205 lbs. Deb: 4/20/39 MH																											
1939	Bos-A	149	565	131	185	44	11	31	**145**	107	64	.327	.436	.609	1.045	152	56	49	108	108	**157**	1.164	2	1	0	-2	*O	3.8
1940	Bos-A	144	561	**134**	193	43	14	23	113	96	54	.344	**.442**	.594	1.036	165	57	57	101	98	154	1.132	4	4	-1	1	*O/P	4.3
1941	Bos-A	143	456	**135**	185	33	3	**37**	120	**145**	27	**.406**	**.551**	**.735**	**1.286**	**231**	**102**	**100**	103	97	**202**	**1.702**	2	4	-2	-4	*O	**8.0**
1942	Bos-A	150	522	**141**	186	34	5	**36**	**137**	**145**	51	**.356**	**.499**	**.648**	**1.147**	**213**	**93**	**90**	104	115	**185**	**1.400**	3	2	-0	4	*O	**8.3**
1946	Bos-A	150	514	**142**	176	37	8	38	123	**156**	44	.342	**.497**	**.667**	**1.164**	**195**	**94**	**84**	114	98	**188**	**1.431**	0	0	0	-0	*O	**7.7**
1947	Bos-A	156	528	**125**	181	40	9	**32**	**114**	**162**	47	**.343**	**.499**	**.634**	**1.133**	**198**	**91**	**85**	108	94	**186**	**1.394**	0	1	-1	3	*O	**8.1**
1948	Bos-A	137	509	124	188	**44**	3	25	127	**126**	41	**.369**	**.497**	**.615**	**1.112**	**194**	**76**	**75**	100	106	**172**	**1.347**	4	0	1	-1	*O	**6.6**
1949	Bos-A	155	566	**150**	194	**39**	3	**43**	**159**	**162**	48	.343	**.490**	**.650**	**1.141**	**187**	**89**	**83**	107	97	**193**	**1.349**	1	1	-0	1	*O	**7.5**
1950	Bos-A	89	334	82	106	24	1	28	97	82	21	.317	.452	.647	1.099	156	41	33	114	107	103	1.254	3	0	1	-4	O	2.6
1951	Bos-A	148	531	109	169	28	4	30	126	**144**	45	.318	**.464**	**.556**	**1.019**	162	**63**	**57**	108	124	**152**	**1.180**	1	1	-0	7	*O	**5.5**
1952	Bos-A	6	10	2	4	0	1	1	3	2	2	.400	.500	.900	1.400	266	2	2	107	93	5	1.833	0	0	0	0	/O	0.2
1953	Bos-A	37	91	17	37	6	0	13	34	19	10	.407	.509	.901	1.410	252	22	21	109	104	44	1.804	0	1	-1	-5	O	1.4
1954	Bos-A	117	386	93	133	23	1	29	89	**136**	32	**.345**	**.516**	**.635**	**1.151**	**213**	**71**	**71**	100	108	**139**	**1.452**	0	0	0	-7	*O	**6.1**
1955	Bos-A	98	320	77	114	21	3	28	83	91	24	.356	.501	.703	1.204	178	**59**	48	124	102	118	1.495	2	0	1	-4	O	3.9
1956	Bos-A	136	400	71	138	28	2	24	82	102	39	.345	**.479**	.605	1.084	180	54	53	103	98	121	1.255	0	0	0	-9	*O	3.7
1957	Bos-A	132	420	96	163	28	1	38	87	119	43	**.388**	**.528**	**.731**	**1.259**	219	**90**	84	110	83	167	**1.602**	0	1	-1	-9	*O	6.7
1958	Bos-A	129	411	81	135	23	2	26	85	98	49	**.328**	**.462**	.584	**1.046**	177	54	51	105	109	112	1.163	1	0	0	-17	*O	2.7
1959	Bos-A	103	272	32	69	15	0	10	43	52	27	.254	.377	.419	.796	112	8	6	106	118	45	.800	0	0	0	-11	O	-0.7
1960	Bos-A	113	310	56	98	15	0	29	72	75	41	.316	.454	.645	1.099	188	43	42	103	98	95	1.268	1	1	-0	-4	O	3.4
Total	19	2292	7706	1798	2654	525	71	521	1839	2019	709	.344	.483	.634	1.116	186	1166	1089	107	103	2538	1.372	24	17	-3	-63	*O/P	89.8
■ WALT WILLIAMS	Williams, Walter Allen "No-Neck" b: 12/19/43, Brownwood, Tex. BR/TR, 5'6", 165 lbs. Deb: 4/21/64 C																											
1964	Hou-N	10	9	1	0	0	0	0	0	0	2	.000	.000	.000	.000	-99	-2	-2	96	0	0	.111	1	0	0	-1	/O	-0.2
1967	Chi-A	104	275	35	66	16	3	3	15	17	20	.240	.289	.353	.642	95	-4	-2	94	59	27	.546	3	2	-0	-2	O	-0.7
1968	Chi-A	63	133	6	32	6	0	1	8	4	17	.241	.273	.308	.582	75	-4	-4	101	78	10	.443	0	1	-1	-3	O	-0.9
1969	Chi-A	135	471	59	143	22	1	3	32	26	33	.304	.344	.374	.718	93	0	-5	108	70	62	.630	6	2	1	2	*O	-0.4
1970	Chi-A	110	315	43	79	18	1	3	15	19	30	.251	.298	.343	.640	72	-11	-13	106	52	32	.541	3	3	-1	1	O	-1.6
1971	Chi-A	114	361	43	106	17	3	8	35	24	27	.294	.346	.424	.770	120	7	9	98	81	52	.703	5	5	-2	-1	O/3	0.3
1972	Chi-A	77	221	22	55	7	1	2	11	13	20	.249	.291	.317	.607	76	-6	-7	106	60	21	.524	6	1	1	1	O/3	-0.7
1973	Cle-A	104	350	43	101	15	1	8	38	14	29	.289	.318	.406	.724	105	0	1	97	90	43	.636	9	4	0	3	OD	0.3
1974	NY-A	43	53	5	6	0	0	0	3	1	10	.113	.130	.113	.243	-31	-9	-8	96	197	1	.160	1	0	0	-6	O/D	-1.5
1975	NY-A	82	185	27	52	5	1	5	16	8	23	.281	.321	.400	.721	104	0	0	99	69	23	.616	0	1	-1	-2	OD/2	-0.2
Total	10	842	2373	284	640	106	11	33	173	126	211	.270	.311	.365	.677	91	-28	-31	101	73	270	.595	34	19	-1	-8	O/D23	-5.6
■ WASH WILLIAMS	Williams, Washington J. b: Philadelphia, Pa. d: 1/1890, Philadelphia, Pa. 5'11", 180 lbs. Deb: 8/05/1884																											
1884	Ric-a	2	8	0	2	0	0	0		0		.250	.250	.250	.500	67	-0	-0	99	0	1	.333				0	/O	0.0
1885	Chi-N	1	4	0	1	0	0	0	0	0	0	.250	.250	.250	.500	55	-0	-0	114	0	0	.333				0	/OP	0.0
Total	2	3	12	0	3	0	0	0	0	0	0	.250	.250	.250	.500	62	-0	-1	104	0	1	.333				0	/OP	0.0

YEAR	TM/L	G	AB	R	H	2B	3B	HR	RBI	BB	SO	AVG	OBP	SLG	PRO	/A	BR	/A	PF	CHI	RC	TA	SB	CS	SBR	FR	POS	TPR
■ **BILLY WILLIAMS**	Williams, William b: 6/13/33, Newberry, S.C. BL/TR, 6'3", 195 lbs. Deb: 8/15/69																											
1969	Sea-A	4	10	1	0	0	0	0	0	1	3	.000	.167	.000	.167	-51	-2	-2	98	0	0	.182	0	0	0	1	/O	-0.1
■ **WOODY WILLIAMS**	Williams, Woodrow Wilson b: 8/22/12, Pamplin, Va. BR/TR, 5'11", 175 lbs. Deb: 9/05/38																											
1938	Bro-N	20	51	6	17	1	1	0	6	4	1	.333	.382	.392	.774	118	1	1	96	108	8	.735	1			-1	S/3	0.1
1943	Cin-N	30	69	8	26	2	1	0	11	1	3	.377	.386	.435	.820	138	3	3	99	132	11	.689	0			1	2/3S	0.5
1944	Cin-N	155	653	73	157	23	3	1	35	44	24	.240	.290	.289	.580	67	-31	-28	95	56	56	.479	7			14	*2	0.2
1945	Cin-N	133	482	46	114	14	0	0	27	39	24	.237	.296	.266	.562	60	-27	-24	94	75	40	.467	6			-5	*2	-1.7
Total	4	338	1255	133	314	40	5	1	79	88	52	.250	.301	.292	.594	70	-55	-47	95	70	115	.499	14			10	2/S3	-0.9
■ **NED WILLIAMSON**	Williamson, Edward Nagle b: 10/24/1857, Philadelphia, Pa. d: 3/3/1894, Willow Springs, Ark BR/TR, 5'11", 170 lbs. Deb: 5/01/1878																											
1878	Ind-N	63	250	31	58	10	2	1	19	5	15	.232	.247	.300	.547	91	-6	-1	87	84	19	.417				-3	*3	0.0
1879	Chi-N	80	320	66	94	20	13	1	36	24	31	.294	.343	.447	.790	151	20	18	105	92	50	.739				20	*3/1C	**3.6**
1880	Chi-N	75	311	65	78	20	2	0	31	15	26	.251	.285	.328	.613	102	3	0	105	107	30	.502				9	*3C/2	0.9
1881	Chi-N	82	343	56	92	12	6	1	48	19	19	.268	.307	.347	.654	97	2	-2	108	145	37	.550				17	*3/2PSC	2.0
1882	Chi-N	83	348	66	98	27	4	3	60	27	21	.282	.333	.408	.741	135	15	14	101	142	49	.676				9	*3/P	2.2
1883	Chi-N	98	402	83	111	**49**	5	2	59	22	48	.276	.314	.438	.751	115	12	6	109	119	57	.680				16	*3/CP	2.0
1884	Chi-N	107	417	84	116	18	8	**27**	84	42	56	.278	.344	.554	.898	165	37	31	108	94	82	.907				22	*3C/P	4.2
1885	Chi-N	113	407	87	97	16	5	3	65	**75**	60	.238	.357	.324	.681	107	14	5	114	**170**	48	.668				8	*3/PC	1.4
1886	Chi-N	121	430	69	93	17	8	6	58	80	71	.216	.339	.335	.674	91	6	-6	116	124	55	.703	13			-3	*S/CP	-0.9
1887	Chi-N	127	439	77	117	20	14	9	78	73	57	.267	.377	.437	.815	110	19	5	116	116	92	.978	45			-35	*S/P	-2.8
1888	Chi-N	132	452	75	113	9	14	8	73	65	71	.250	.352	.385	.737	128	21	17	107	140	72	.796	25			-10	*S	1.1
1889	Chi-N	47	173	16	41	3	1	1	30	23	22	.237	.340	.283	.623	77	-4	-4	99	176	18	.591	2			-21	S	-2.0
1890	Chi-P	73	261	34	51	7	4	1	26	36	35	.195	.311	.264	.576	54	-15	-17	104	101	23	.552	3			-13	3S	-2.1
Total	13	1201	4553	809	1159	228	86	63	667	506	532	.255	.332	.384	.716	112	123	67	108	124	630	.697	88			17	3S/CP21	9.6
■ **HOWIE WILLIAMSON**	Williamson, Nathaniel Howard b: 12/23/04, Little Rock, Ark. d: 8/15/69, Texarkana, Ark. BL/TL, 6', 170 lbs. Deb: 7/07/28																											
1928	StL-N	10	9	0	2	0	0	0	0	1	4	.222	.300	.222	.522	38	-1	-1	100	0	1	.429	0			0	H	0.0
■ **JULIUS WILLIGROD**	Willigrod, Julius b: 1870, Iowa d: 11/27/06, San Francisco, Cal BL , Deb: 7/15/1882																											
1882	Det-N	1	3	0	1	0	0	0	1	0	1	.333	.333	.333	.667	113	0	0	102	337	0	.500				0	/S	0.0
	Cle-N	9	36	5	5	1	1	0	2	3	7	.139	.205	.222	.427	41	-2	-2	90	81	2	.355				0	/O	-0.1
	Yr	10	39	5	6	1	1	0	3	3	8	.154	.214	.231	.445	47	-2	-2	91	140	2	.364				0		-0.1
Total	1	10	39	5	6	1	1	0	3	3	8	.154	.214	.231	.445	47	-2	-2	91	99	2	.364				0	/OS	-0.1
■ **HUGH WILLINGHAM**	Willingham, Thomas Hugh b: 5/30/06, Dalhart, Tex. d: 6/15/88, El Reno, Okla. BR/TR, 6', 180 lbs. Deb: 9/13/30																											
1930	Chi-A	3	4	2	1	0	0	0	0	2	1	.250	.500	.250	.750	94	0	0	103	0	1	1.000	0	0	0	0	/2	0.0
1931	Phi-N	23	35	5	9	2	1	1	3	2	9	.257	.297	.457	.754	94	-0	-0	106	56	5	.692	0			-1	/S3O	0.0
1932	Phi-N	4	2	0	0	0	0	0	0	0	0	.000	.000	.000	.000	-89	-1	-1	112	0	0	.000	0			0	H	0.0
1933	Phi-N	1	1	0	0	0	0	0	0	0	0	.000	.000	.000	.000	-85	-0	-0	118	0	0	.000	0			0	H	0.0
Total	4	31	42	7	10	2	1	1	3	4	10	.238	.304	.405	.709	83	-1	-1	106	45	6	.656	0	0		-1	/S3O2	0.0
■ **WILLS**	Wills Deb:5/14/1884																											
1884	Was-a	4	15	1	2	2	0	0		0		.133	.133	.267	.400	32	-1	-1	88	0	1	.308				0	/O	0.0
	KC-U	5	21	2	3	1	0	0		0		.143	.143	.190	.333	14	-2	-1	87	0	1	.222	0			0	/O	0.0
Total	1	9	36	3	5	3	0	0		0		.139	.139	.222	.361	22	-3	-2	88	0	1	.258	0			0	/O	0.0
■ **DAVE WILLS**	Wills, Davis Bowles b: 1/26/1877, Charlottesville, Va. d: 10/12/59, Washington, D.C. BL/TL, Deb: 6/08/1899																											
1899	Lou-N	24	94	15	21	3	1	0	12	2		.223	.240	.277	.516	42	-7	-8	103	144	7	.397	1			0	1	-0.6
■ **BUMP WILLS**	Wills, Elliott Taylor b: 7/27/52, Washington, D.C. BB/TR, 5'9", 172 lbs. Deb: 4/07/77																											
1977	Tex-A	152	541	87	155	28	6	9	62	65	96	.287	.363	.410	.773	105	9	6	105	101	83	.772	28	12	1	12	*2/S1D	3.0
1978	Tex-A	157	539	78	135	17	4	9	57	63	91	.250	.333	.347	.680	95	-5	-2	96	107	68	.713	52	14	7	24	*2	3.8
1979	Tex-A	146	543	90	148	21	3	5	46	53	58	.273	.342	.350	.692	87	-9	-9	100	91	68	.675	35	11	4	9	*2	1.0
1980	Tex-A	146	578	102	152	31	5	5	58	51	71	.263	.326	.360	.686	87	-9	-10	100	98	73	.668	34	9	5	16	*2	1.8
1981	Tex-A	102	410	51	103	13	2	2	41	32	49	.251	.307	.307	.614	85	-12	-7	91	107	38	.528	12	9	-2	24	*2/D	1.9
1982	Chi-N	128	419	64	114	18	4	6	38	46	76	.272	.351	.377	.728	100	3	1	103	85	61	.765	35	10	5	3	*2	1.4
Total	6	831	3030	472	807	128	24	36	302	310	441	.266	.338	.360	.698	94	-22	-21	99	98	390	.704	196	65	20	87	2/DS1	12.9
■ **MAURY WILLS**	Wills, Maurice Morning b: 10/2/32, Washington, D.C. BB/TR, 5'11", 170 lbs. Deb: 6/06/59 M																											
1959	LA-N	83	242	27	63	5	2	0	7	13	27	.260	.298	.298	.596	58	-14	-14	102	39	22	.497	7	3	0	5	S	-0.5
1960	LA-N	148	516	75	152	15	2	0	27	35	47	.295	.343	.331	.674	74	-9	-19	115	64	62	.669	**50**	12	**8**	24	*S	1.9
1961	LA-N	148	613	105	173	12	10	1	31	59	50	.282	.346	.339	.686	81	-13	-15	102	51	77	.657	**35**	15	2	11	*S	1.2
1962	LA-N	165	695	130	208	13	**10**	6	48	51	57	.299	.349	.373	.722	101	-5	1	93	60	106	.821	**104**	13	**23**	2	*S	4.1
1963	LA-N	134	527	83	159	19	3	0	34	44	48	.302	.357	.349	.706	110	4	7	95	75	69	.690	**40**	19	1	9	*S3	2.9
1964	LA-N	158	630	81	173	15	5	2	34	41	73	.275	.319	.324	.643	89	-15	-9	92	64	70	.621	**53**	17	**6**	-2	*S/3	0.5
1965	LA-N	158	650	92	186	14	7	0	33	40	64	.286	.331	.329	.661	95	-11	-4	91	56	77	.703	**94**	31	10	21	*S	4.6
1966	LA-N	143	594	60	162	14	2	1	39	34	60	.273	.314	.308	.622	76	-20	-18	97	76	57	.556	38	24	-3	7	*S/3	-0.2
1967	Pit-N	149	616	92	186	12	9	3	45	31	44	.302	.336	.365	.702	101	0	0	100	77	78	.641	29	10	3	14	*3/S	1.0
1968	Pit-N	153	627	76	174	12	6	0	31	45	57	.278	.327	.316	.643	93	-4	-5	101	58	67	.612	52	21	3	-9	*3S	-1.0
1969	Mon-N	47	189	23	42	3	0	0	8	20	21	.222	.297	.238	.535	51	-12	-12	100	63	15	.513	15	6	1	3	S/2	-0.1
	LA-N	104	434	57	129	7	8	4	39	39	40	.297	.357	.378	.734	107	4	5	99	77	59	.707	25	15	-1	-0	*S	1.6
	Yr	151	623	80	171	10	8	4	47	59	61	.274	.338	.335	.674	90	-8	-7	99	73	74	.648	40	21	-1	3		1.5
1970	LA-N	132	522	77	141	19	3	0	34	50	34	.270	.334	.318	.652	84	-17	-10	90	84	57	.604	28	13	1	-17	*S/3	-1.0
1971	LA-N	149	601	73	169	14	3	3	44	40	44	.281	.326	.329	.656	87	-11	-10	99	83	66	.565	15	8	-0	5	*S/3	1.5
1972	LA-N	71	132	16	17	3	1	0	4	10	18	.129	.190	.167	.357	2	-17	-16	94	75	5	.277	1	1	-0	2	S3	-1.1
Total	14	1942	7588	1067	2134	177	71	20	458	552	684	.281	.331	.331	.662	87	-139	-117	98	67	885	.647	586	208	51	75	*S3/2	15.4
■ **KID WILLSON**	Willson, Frank Hoxie b: 11/3/1895, Bloomington, Neb. d: 4/17/64, Union Gap, Wash. BL/TL, 6'1", 190 lbs. Deb: 7/02/18																											
1918	Chi-A	4	1	2	0	0	0	0	0	1	1	.000	.500	.000	.500	51	0	0	101	0	0	1.000	0			0	H	0.0
1927	Chi-A	7	10	1	1	0	0	0	1	0	2	.100	.100	.100	.200	-47	-2	-2	102	333	0	.111	0	0	0	0	/O	-0.1
Total	2	11	11	3	1	0	0	0	1	1	3	.091	.167	.091	.258	-30	-2	-2	102	277	0	.200	0	0		0	/O	-0.1
■ **WALT WILMOT**	Wilmot, Walter Robert b: 10/18/1863, Plover, Wis. d: 2/1/29, Chicago, Ill. BB/TR, Deb: 1888																											
1888	Was-N	119	473	61	106	16	9	4	43	23	55	.224	.263	.321	.584	91	-7	-4	96	83	53	.608	46			12	*O	0.7
1889	Was-N	108	432	88	125	19	**19**	9	57	51	32	.289	.367	.484	.851	151	21	27	92	69	94	.984	40			15	*O	3.2
1890	Chi-N	139	571	114	159	15	12	**13**	99	64	44	.278	.353	.415	.768	115	18	10	109	96	113	.920	76			9	*O	1.4
1891	Chi-N	121	498	102	139	14	10	11	71	55	21	.279	.357	.414	.770	119	16	11	106	83	91	.858	42			-2	*O	0.2
1892	Chi-N	92	380	47	82	7	7	2	35	40	20	.216	.297	.287	.584	85	-9	-5	92	81	43	.617	31			0	O	-0.7
1893	Chi-N	94	392	69	118	14	14	3	61	40	8	.301	.367	.431	.798	110	7	5	104	90	78	.909	39			-1	*O	0.0
1894	Chi-N	133	597	134	197	45	12	5	130	35	23	.330	.368	.471	.839	95	1	-8	108	107	134	.978	74			-8	*O	-1.8
1895	Chi-N	108	466	86	132	16	6	8	72	30	19	.283	.327	.395	.721	85	-10	-13	103	85	71	.725	28			3	*O	-1.5
1897	NY-N	11	34	8	9	2	0	1	4	2		.265	.306	.412	.717	92	-1	-1	98	69	5	.680	1			0	/O	0.0
1898	NY-N	35	138	16	33	4	2	2	22	9		.239	.286	.341	.626	86	-4	-3	95	133	15	.571	4			0	O	-0.1
Total	10	960	3981	725	1100	152	91	58	594	349	222	.276	.337	.404	.741	106	33	20	102	89	697	.817	381			28	O	1.4
■ **ARCHIE WILSON**	Wilson, Archie Clifton b: 11/25/23, Los Angeles, Cal. BR/TR, 5'11", 175 lbs. Deb: 9/18/51																											
1951	NY-A	4	4	0	0	0	0	0	0	0	0	.000	.200	.000	.200	-47	-1	-1	92	0	0	.200	0	0	0	-0	/O	0.0
1952	NY-A	3	2	0	1	0	0	0	1	0	0	.500	.500	.500	1.000	183	0	0	98	374	1	1.000	0	0	0	0	H	0.0
	Was-A	26	96	8	20	2	3	0	14	5	11	.208	.255	.292	.547	52	-6	-6	100	190	5	.405	0	0	0	1	O	-0.5

YEAR	TM/L	G	AB	R	H	2B	3B	HR	RBI	BB	SO	AVG	OBP	SLG	PRO	/A	BR	/A	PF	CHI	RC	TA	SB	CS	SBR	FR	POS	TPR
	Bos-A	18	38	1	10	3	0	0	2	2	3	.263	.300	.342	.642	73	-1	-2	107	57	4	.500	0	0	0	-2	O	-0.3
	Yr	47	136	9	31	5	3	0	17	7	14	.228	.271	.309	.580	59	-7	-8	103	163	12	.467	0	0	0	-0		-0.8
Total	2	51	140	9	31	5	3	0	17	7	14	.221	.268	.300	.568	57	-8	-9	102	151	9	.459	0	0	0	-1	/O	-0.8

■ ART WILSON Wilson, Arthur Earl "Dutch" b: 12/11/1885, Macon, Ill. d: 6/12/60, Chicago, Ill. BR/TR, 5'8", 170 lbs. Deb: 9/29/08

YEAR	TM/L	G	AB	R	H	2B	3B	HR	RBI	BB	SO	AVG	OBP	SLG	PRO	/A	BR	/A	PF	CHI	RC	TA	SB	CS	SBR	FR	POS	TPR
1908	NY-N	1	0	0	0	0	0	0	0	0		—	—	—	—	—	0	0	104	—	—	—	0			0	R	0.0
1909	NY-N	19	42	4	10	2	1	0	5	4		.238	.304	.333	.638	95	-0	-0	105	130	4	.563	0			-0	C	0.1
1910	NY-N	26	52	10	14	4	1	0	5	9	6	.269	.387	.385	.772	131	2	2	95	87	9	.842	2			-2	C/1	0.1
1911	NY-N	66	109	17	33	9	1	1	17	19	12	.303	.411	.431	.842	132	6	6	102	115	22	.961	6			-9	C	0.1
1912	NY-N	65	121	17	35	6	0	3	19	13	14	.289	.358	.413	.771	107	2	1	104	108	19	.756	2			-11	C	-0.6
1913	NY-N	54	79	5	15	0	1	0	8	11	11	.190	.289	.215	.504	44	-5	-6	103	171	5	.453	1			-3	C	-0.5
1914	Chi-F	137	440	78	128	31	8	10	64	70	80	.291	.388	.466	.854	158	26	32	91	100	89	.923	13			5	*C	4.4
1915	Chi-F	96	269	44	82	11	2	7	31	65	38	.305	.440	.439	.879	165	24	25	97	80	59	1.021	8			-10	C	1.9
1916	Pit-N	53	128	11	33	5	2	1	12	13	27	.258	.331	.352	.683	105	2	1	105	99	17	.663	4			3	C	0.7
	Chi-N	36	114	5	22	3	1	0	5	6	14	.193	.233	.237	.470	38	-7	-9	117	74	7	.370	1			-2	C	-1.0
	Yr	89	242	16	55	8	3	1	17	19	41	.227	.286	.298	.584	72	-6	-8	110	90	23	.519	5			1		-0.3
1917	Chi-N	81	211	17	45	9	2	2	25	32	36	.213	.322	.303	.626	88	-1	-2	105	138	22	.627	6			2	C	0.4
1918	Bos-N	89	280	15	69	8	2	0	19	24	31	.246	.310	.289	.600	89	-5	-3	94	89	26	.531	5			-7	C	-0.2
1919	Bos-N	71	191	14	49	8	1	0	16	25	19	.257	.346	.309	.655	100	1	1	98	105	22	.613	2			4	C/1	1.0
1920	Bos-N	16	19	0	1	0	0	0	0	1	1	.053	.143	.053	.195	-44	-3	-3	96	0	0	.167	0	0	0	0	/3C	-0.2
1921	Cle-A	2	1	0	0	0	0	0	0	0	0	.000	.000	.000	.000	-99	-0	-0	99	0	0	.000	0	0	0	0	/C	0.0
Total	14	812	2056	237	536	96	22	24	226	292	289	.261	.355	.364	.719	114	40	44	99	102	310	.723	50	0		-29	C/31	6.2

■ ARTIE WILSON Wilson, Arthur Lee b: 10/28/20, Springfield, Ala. BL/TR, 5'10", 162 lbs. Deb: 4/18/51

YEAR	TM/L	G	AB	R	H	2B	3B	HR	RBI	BB	SO	AVG	OBP	SLG	PRO	/A	BR	/A	PF	CHI	RC	TA	SB	CS	SBR	FR	POS	TPR
1951	NY-N	19	22	2	4	0	0	0	1	2	1	.182	.250	.182	.432	18	-2	-3	102	97	1	.444	2	0	1	0	/2S1	-0.1

■ CHARLIE WILSON Wilson, Charles Woodrow "Swamp Baby" b: 1/13/05, Clinton, S.C. d: 12/19/70, Rochester, N.Y. BB/TR, 5'10.5", 178 lbs. Deb: 4/14/31

YEAR	TM/L	G	AB	R	H	2B	3B	HR	RBI	BB	SO	AVG	OBP	SLG	PRO	/A	BR	/A	PF	CHI	RC	TA	SB	CS	SBR	FR	POS	TPR
1931	Bos-N	16	58	7	11	4	0	1	11	3	5	.190	.230	.310	.540	44	-5	-5	99	190	4	.447	0			0	3	-0.2
1932	StL-N	24	96	7	19	3	3	1	2	3	8	.198	.222	.323	.545	44	-8	-8	100	23	7	.442	0			-1	S	-0.6
1933	StL-N	1	1	0	0	0	0	0	0	0	1	.000	.000	.000	.000	-98	-0	-0	102	0	0	.000	0			0	/S	0.0
1935	StL-N	16	31	1	10	0	0	0	1	2	2	.323	.364	.323	.686	83	-0	-1	104	36	3	.522	0			-0	/3	0.0
Total	4	57	186	15	40	7	3	2	14	8	16	.215	.247	.317	.565	50	-13	-13	100	78	14	.453	0			-1	/S3	-0.8

■ EDDIE WILSON Wilson, Edward Francis b: 9/7/09, Hamden, Conn. d: 4/11/79, Hamden, Conn. BL/TL, 5'11", 165 lbs. Deb: 6/21/36

YEAR	TM/L	G	AB	R	H	2B	3B	HR	RBI	BB	SO	AVG	OBP	SLG	PRO	/A	BR	/A	PF	CHI	RC	TA	SB	CS	SBR	FR	POS	TPR
1936	Bro-N	52	173	28	60	8	1	3	25	14	25	.347	.402	.457	.859	125	8	7	105	101	34	.860	3			-7	O	-0.1
1937	Bro-N	36	54	11	12	4	1	1	8	17	14	.222	.408	.389	.797	113	2	2	104	120	11	.929	1			-4	O	-0.2
Total	2	88	227	39	72	12	2	4	33	31	39	.317	.404	.441	.844	122	10	8	105	106	44	.884	4			-11	/O	-0.3

■ FRANK WILSON Wilson, Francis Edward "Squash" b: 4/20/01, Malden, Mass. d: 11/25/74, Leicester, Mass. BL/TR, 6', 185 lbs. Deb: 6/20/24

YEAR	TM/L	G	AB	R	H	2B	3B	HR	RBI	BB	SO	AVG	OBP	SLG	PRO	/A	BR	/A	PF	CHI	RC	TA	SB	CS	SBR	FR	POS	TPR
1924	Bos-N	61	215	20	51	7	0	1	15	23	22	.237	.311	.284	.595	64	-11	-10	94	87	20	.518	3	4	-2	4	O	-0.8
1925	Bos-N	12	31	3	13	1	1	0	0	4	1	.419	.486	.516	1.002	167	3	3	94	0	8	1.158	2	1	0	0	O	0.3
1926	Bos-N	87	236	22	56	11	3	0	23	20	21	.237	.300	.309	.609	74	-12	-7	86	109	22	.539	3			-1	O	-1.0
1928	Cle-A	2	1	0	0	0	0	0	0	1	0	.000	.500	.000	.500	39	0	0	106	0	0	1.000	0	0	0	0	H	0.0
	StL-A	6	5	1	0	0	0	0	0	0	0	.000	.000	.000	.000	-97	-1	-1	104	0	0	.000	0	0	0	-0	/O	-0.1
	Yr	8	6	1	0	0	0	0	0	1	0	.000	.143	.000	.143	-57	-1	-1	104	0	0	.167	0	0	0	-0		-0.1
Total	4	168	488	46	120	19	4	1	38	48	44	.246	.315	.307	.622	74	-22	-15	90	91	50	.555	8	5		2	O	-1.6

■ TUG WILSON Wilson, George Archer b: 1860, Brooklyn, N.Y. d: 11/28/14, New York, N.Y. Deb: 5/09/1884

YEAR	TM/L	G	AB	R	H	2B	3B	HR	RBI	BB	SO	AVG	OBP	SLG	PRO	/A	BR	/A	PF	CHI	RC	TA	SB	CS	SBR	FR	POS	TPR
1884	Bro-a	24	82	13	19	4	0	0		5		.232	.276	.280	.556	87	-1	-1	98	0	7	.444				0	OC/12	0.0

■ SQUANTO WILSON Wilson, George Francis b: 3/29/1889, Old Town, Me. d: 3/26/67, Winthrop, Maine BB/TR, 5'9.5", 170 lbs. Deb: 10/02/11

YEAR	TM/L	G	AB	R	H	2B	3B	HR	RBI	BB	SO	AVG	OBP	SLG	PRO	/A	BR	/A	PF	CHI	RC	TA	SB	CS	SBR	FR	POS	TPR
1911	Det-A	5	16	2	3	0	0	0	0	2		.188	.278	.188	.465	28	-1	-2	108	0	1	.385	0			0	/C	0.0
1914	Bos-A	1	0	0	0	0	0	0	0	0	0	—	—	—	—	—	0	0	98	—	—	—	0			0	/1	0.0
Total	2	6	16	2	3	0	0	0	0	2	0	.188	.278	.188	.465	28	-1	-2	108	0	2	.385	0			0	/C1	0.0

■ ICEHOUSE WILSON Wilson, George Peacock b: 9/14/12, Maricopa, Cal. d: 10/13/73, Moraga, Cal. BR/TR, 6', 186 lbs. Deb: 5/31/34

YEAR	TM/L	G	AB	R	H	2B	3B	HR	RBI	BB	SO	AVG	OBP	SLG	PRO	/A	BR	/A	PF	CHI	RC	TA	SB	CS	SBR	FR	POS	TPR
1934	Det-A	1	1	0	0	0	0	0	0	0	0	.000	.000	.000	.000	-99	-0	-0	98	0	0	.000	0	0	0	0	H	0.0

■ GEORGE WILSON Wilson, George Washington "Teddy" b: 8/30/25, Cherryville, N.C. d: 10/29/74, Gastonia, N.C. BL/TR, 6'1.5", 185 lbs. Deb: 4/15/52

YEAR	TM/L	G	AB	R	H	2B	3B	HR	RBI	BB	SO	AVG	OBP	SLG	PRO	/A	BR	/A	PF	CHI	RC	TA	SB	CS	SBR	FR	POS	TPR
1952	Chi-A	8	9	0	1	0	0	0	1	1	2	.111	.200	.111	.311	-12	-1	-1	100	374	0	.250	0	0	0	0	/O	-0.1
	NY-N	62	112	9	27	7	0	2	16	3	14	.241	.261	.357	.618	68	-5	-5	102	136	11	.506	0	0	0	-3	O/1	-0.8
1953	NY-N	11	8	0	1	0	0	0	0	2	2	.125	.364	.125	.489	35	-1	-1	98	0	1	.571	0	0	0	0	H	0.0
1956	NY-N	53	68	5	9	1	0	1	2	5	14	.132	.192	.191	.383	3	-9	-9	97	53	3	.300	0	0	0	0	/O	-0.9
	NY-A	11	12	1	2	0	0	0	0	3	0	.167	.333	.167	.500	36	-1	-1	99	0	1	.500	0	0	0	-2	/O	-0.3
Total	3	145	209	15	40	8	0	3	19	14	32	.191	.246	.273	.518	41	-17	-17	100	103	15	.426	0	0	0	-5	/O1	-2.1

■ GLENN WILSON Wilson, Glenn Dwight b: 12/22/58, Baytown, Tex. BR/TR, 6'1", 190 lbs. Deb: 4/15/82

YEAR	TM/L	G	AB	R	H	2B	3B	HR	RBI	BB	SO	AVG	OBP	SLG	PRO	/A	BR	/A	PF	CHI	RC	TA	SB	CS	SBR	FR	POS	TPR
1982	Det-A	84	322	39	94	15	1	12	34	15	51	.292	.323	.457	.780	111	4	4	100	76	44	.686	2	3	-1	3	O/D	0.3
1983	Det-A	144	503	55	135	25	6	11	65	25	79	.268	.307	.408	.715	99	-5	-2	96	107	61	.619	1	1	-0	-11	*O	-1.4
1984	Phi-N	132	341	28	82	21	3	6	31	17	56	.240	.279	.372	.651	80	-9	-10	102	84	33	.559	7	1	2	-13	*O/3	-2.6
1985	Phi-N	161	608	73	167	39	5	14	102	35	117	.275	.314	.424	.738	103	2	0	102	138	73	.640	7	4	-0	16	*O	1.2
1986	Phi-N	155	584	70	158	30	4	15	84	42	91	.271	.324	.413	.736	98	0	-3	104	119	76	.661	5	1	1	18	*O	1.3
1987	Phi-N	154	569	55	150	21	2	14	54	38	82	.264	.311	.381	.692	79	-15	-18	104	85	62	.585	3	6	-3	12	*O/P	-1.4
1988	Sea-A	78	284	28	71	10	1	3	17	15	52	.250	.288	.324	.612	66	-11	-14	108	68	23	.476	1	1	-0	-1	O/D	-1.6
	Pit-N	37	126	11	34	8	0	2	15	3	18	.270	.292	.381	.673	94	-2	-1	98	111	13	.542	0	0	0	-1	O	-0.3
Total	7	945	3337	359	891	169	22	77	402	190	546	.267	.308	.400	.709	92	-36	-44	102	103	387	.633	26	17	-2	22	O/D3P	-4.5

■ GRADY WILSON Wilson, Grady Herbert b: 11/23/22, Columbus, Ga. BR/TR, 6'0.5", 170 lbs. Deb: 5/15/48

YEAR	TM/L	G	AB	R	H	2B	3B	HR	RBI	BB	SO	AVG	OBP	SLG	PRO	/A	BR	/A	PF	CHI	RC	TA	SB	CS	SBR	FR	POS	TPR
1948	Pit-N	12	10	1	1	1	0	0	1	0	3	.100	.100	.200	.300	-20	-2	-2	104	187	0	.222	0			-0	/S	0.0

■ HENRY WILSON Wilson, Henry C. b: Baltimore, Md. Deb: 10/12/1898

YEAR	TM/L	G	AB	R	H	2B	3B	HR	RBI	BB	SO	AVG	OBP	SLG	PRO	/A	BR	/A	PF	CHI	RC	TA	SB	CS	SBR	FR	POS	TPR
1898	Bal-N	1	2	0	0	0	0	0	0	1		.000	.333	.000	.333	0	-0	-0	103	0	0	.500	0			0	/C	0.0

■ JIMMY WILSON Wilson, James "Ace" b: 7/23/1900, Philadelphia, Pa. d: 5/31/47, Bradenton, Fla. BR/TR, 6'1.5", 200 lbs. Deb: 4/17/23 MC

YEAR	TM/L	G	AB	R	H	2B	3B	HR	RBI	BB	SO	AVG	OBP	SLG	PRO	/A	BR	/A	PF	CHI	RC	TA	SB	CS	SBR	FR	POS	TPR
1923	Phi-N	85	252	27	66	9	0	1	25	4	17	.262	.276	.310	.586	48	-17	-21	114	109	21	.463	4	2	0	-4	C/O	-2.0
1924	Phi-N	95	280	32	78	16	3	6	39	17	12	.279	.322	.421	.744	91	-2	-4	108	105	37	.684	5	4	-1	5	C/1O	0.0
1925	Phi-N	108	335	42	110	19	3	3	54	32	25	.328	.390	.430	.820	95	6	-2	116	125	57	.803	5	3	-0	-2	C/O	0.0
1926	Phi-N	90	279	40	85	10	2	4	32	25	20	.305	.362	.398	.760	101	2	1	103	90	40	.716	3			5	C	0.8
1927	Phi-N	128	443	50	122	15	2	2	45	34	15	.275	.330	.332	.662	80	-13	-11	96	103	48	.611	13			-4	*C	-0.6
1928	Phi-N	21	70	11	21	4	1	0	13	9	8	.300	.380	.386	.765	97	0	-0	104	171	10	.796	3			2	C	0.3
	StL-N	120	411	45	106	26	2	2	50	45	24	.258	.333	.345	.678	78	-13	-13	100	120	48	.646	9			1	*C	-0.3
	Yr	141	481	56	127	30	3	2	63	54	32	.264	.340	.351	.691	80	-13	-13	101	129	58	.667	12			4		0.0
1929	StL-N	120	394	59	128	27	8	4	71	43	19	.325	.394	.464	.859	114	8	9	98	125	71	.872	4			0	*C	1.7
1930	StL-N	107	362	54	115	25	7	1	58	28	17	.318	.368	.434	.802	89	-4	-7	105	125	57	.785	8			3	C	0.1
1931	StL-N	115	383	45	105	20	2	0	51	28	15	.274	.332	.337	.669	75	-10	-13	107	141	45	.601	5			3	*C	-0.5
1932	StL-N	92	274	36	68	16	2	2	28	15	18	.248	.290	.343	.633	69	-12	-12	100	104	28	.578	9			6	C/12	-0.3
1933	StL-N	113	369	34	94	17	0	1	45	23	33	.255	.300	.309	.609	73	-12	-13	102	145	34	.505	6			-0	*C	-0.9
1934	Phi-N	91	277	25	81	11	0	3	35	14	10	.292	.326	.365	.691	78	-6	-9	108	115	31	.560	1			6	C/12M	0.0
1935	Phi-N	93	290	38	81	20	0	1	37	19	19	.279	.326	.359	.684	74	-6	-12	114	125	35	.598	4			3	C/2M	-0.8
1936	Phi-N	85	230	25	64	12	0	1	27	12	21	.278	.314	.343	.658	71	-8	-10	108	117	24	.555	5			-2	C/1M	-0.9
1937	Phi-N	39	87	15	24	3	0	1	8	6	4	.276	.323	.345	.667	75	-2	-3	108	87	9	.552	1			-0	C/1M	-0.2

YEAR	TM/L	G	AB	R	H	2B	3B	HR	RBI	BB	SO	AVG	OBP	SLG	PRO	/A	BR	/A	PF	CHI	RC	TA	SB	CS	SBR	FR	POS	TPR
1938	Phi-N	3	2	0	0	0	0	0	0	0	1	.000	.000	.000	.000	-99	-1	-1	100	0	0	.000	0			0	/CM	0.0
1939	Cin-N	4	3	0	1	0	0	0	0	0	1	.333	.333	.333	.667	77	-0	-0	103	0	0	.500	0			0	/C	0.0
1940	Cin-N	16	37	2	9	2	0	0	3	2	1	.243	.282	.297	.579	59	-2	-2	101	101	3	.500	1			-1	C	-0.1
Total	18	1525	4778	580	1358	252	32	32	621	356	280	.284	.336	.370	.707	82	-92	-124	105	119	600	.650	86	9		20	*C/1O2	-3.7
■ **GARY WILSON** Wilson, James Garrett b: 1/12/1877, Baltimore, Md. d: 5/1/69, Randallstown, Md. BR/TR, 5'7", 168 lbs. Deb: 9/27/02																												
1902	Bos-A	2	8	0	1	0	0	0	1	0		.125	.125	.125	.250	-30	-1	-1	99	336	0	.143	0			1	/2	0.0
■ **JIM WILSON** Wilson, James George b: 12/29/60, Corvallis, Ore. BR/TR, 6'3", 230 lbs. Deb: 9/13/85																												
1985	Cle-A	4	14	2	5	0	0	0	4	1	3	.357	.400	.357	.757	116	0	0	94	317	2	.667	0	0	0	0	/1D	0.0
■ **CHIEF WILSON** Wilson, John Owen b: 8/21/1883, Austin, Tex. d: 2/22/54, Bertram, Tex. BL/TR, 6'2", 185 lbs. Deb: 4/15/08																												
1908	Pit-N	144	529	47	120	8	7	3	43	22		.227	.258	.285	.543	79	-15	-13	95	105	40	.452	12			4	*O	-1.0
1909	Pit-N	154	569	64	155	22	12	4	59	19		.272	.303	.374	.677	107	4	1	105	97	67	.616	17			13	*O	1.0
1910	Pit-N	146	536	59	148	14	13	4	50	21	68	.276	.312	.373	.685	89	-3	-10	112	84	64	.608	8			0	*O	-1.6
1911	Pit-N	148	544	72	163	34	12	12	**107**	41	55	.300	.353	.472	.826	129	19	18	101	126	93	.819	10			4	*O	1.7
1912	Pit-N	152	583	80	175	19	**36**	11	95	35	67	.300	.342	.513	.855	134	21	22	99	102	106	.863	16			4	*O	2.1
1913	Pit-N	155	580	71	154	12	14	10	73	32	62	.266	.307	.386	.694	101	-4	-1	96	107	68	.629	9			-2	*O	-0.6
1914	StL-N	154	580	64	150	27	12	9	73	32	66	.259	.302	.393	.695	102	1	-1	104	110	69	.647	14			17	*O	1.2
1915	StL-N	107	348	33	96	13	6	3	39	19	43	.276	.321	.374	.694	110	3	3	100	107	41	.603	8	15	-7	4	*O	-0.2
1916	StL-N	120	355	30	85	8	2	3	32	20	46	.239	.289	.299	.588	84	-8	-7	97	110	33	.500	4			-7	*O	-1.9
Total	9	1280	4624	520	1246	157	114	59	571	241	407	.269	.311	.391	.702	105	18	12	101	105	581	.643	98	15		38	*O	0.7
■ **LES WILSON** Wilson, Lester Wilbur "Tug" b: 7/15/1885, Gratiot County, Mich. d: 4/4/69, Edmonds, Wash. BL/TR, 5'11", 170 lbs. Deb: 7/15/11																												
1911	Bos-A	5	7	0	0	0	0	0	0	2		.000	.222	.000	.222	-36	-1	-1	99	0	0	.286	0			-1	/O	-0.1
■ **HACK WILSON** Wilson, Lewis Robert b: 4/26/1900, Ellwood City, Pa. d: 11/23/48, Baltimore, Md. BR/TR, 5'6", 190 lbs. Deb: 9/29/23 H																												
1923	NY-N	3	10	0	2	0	0	0	0	0	1	.200	.200	.200	.400	6	-1	-1	101	0	0	.250	0	0	0	-0	/O	-0.1
1924	NY-N	107	383	62	113	19	12	10	57	44	46	.295	.369	.486	.855	139	15	19	91	98	70	.861	4	3	-1	-10	*O	0.7
1925	NY-N	62	180	28	43	7	4	6	30	21	33	.239	.322	.422	.744	89	-4	-3	99	113	25	.741	5	2	0	-8	O	-1.1
1926	Chi-N	142	529	97	170	36	8	**21**	109	**69**	61	.321	.406	**.539**	**.944**	**144**	39	**35**	106	115	115	**1.031**	10			-1	*O	2.8
1927	Chi-N	146	551	119	175	30	12	**30**	129	71	70	.318	.401	.579	.980	160	46	46	100	117	126	1.088	13			-6	*O	3.3
1928	Chi-N	145	520	89	163	32	9	**31**	120	77	94	.313	.404	.588	.992	166	42	46	95	113	122	1.090	4			-13	*O	2.7
1929	Chi-N	150	574	135	198	30	5	39	**159**	78	83	.345	.425	.618	1.044	153	49	48	101	122	148	1.165	3			-7	*O	2.4
1930	Chi-N	155	585	146	208	35	6	**56**	**190**	**105**	84	.356	.454	**.723**	**1.177**	**170**	**75**	**70**	105	117	**189**	**1.411**	3			4	*O	5.4
1931	Chi-N	112	395	66	103	22	4	13	61	63	69	.261	.362	.435	.798	118	8	11	96	105	66	.808	1			-2	*O	0.4
1932	Bro-N	135	481	77	143	37	5	23	123	51	85	.297	.366	.538	.904	145	26	29	96	142	97	.926	2			-10	*O	1.0
1933	Bro-N	117	360	41	96	13	2	9	54	52	50	.267	.359	.389	.748	118	8	9	97	122	53	.732	7			-10	O/2	-0.5
1934	Bro-N	67	172	24	45	5	0	6	27	40	33	.262	.401	.395	.796	121	5	7	95	113	30	.818	0			-4	O	0.1
	Phi-N	7	20	0	2	0	0	0	3	3	4	.100	.217	.100	.317	-11	-3	-3	108	541	0	.250	0			-1	/O	-0.3
	Yr	74	192	24	47	5	0	6	30	43	37	.245	.383	.365	.748	106	2	3	96	155	31	.769	0			-4		-0.2
Total	12	1348	4760	884	1461	266	67	244	1062	674	713	.307	.395	.545	.940	145	305	311	99	119	1042	1.010	52	5		-67	*O/2	16.8
■ **TACK WILSON** Wilson, Michael b: 5/16/55, Shreveport, La. BR/TR, 5'10", 185 lbs. Deb: 4/09/83																												
1983	Min-A	5	4	4	1	1	0	0	1	0	0	.250	.250	.500	.750	96	-0	-0	105	195	1	.667	0	0	0	-0	/OD	0.0
1987	Cal-A	7	2	5	1	0	0	0	0	1	0	.500	.667	.500	1.167	220	1	1	99	0	1	2.000	0	0	0	-1	/OD	0.0
Total	2	12	6	9	2	1	0	0	1	1	0	.333	.429	.500	.929	148	0	0	103	112	1	1.000	0	0	0	-2	/OD	0.0
■ **PARKE WILSON** Wilson, Parke Asel b: 10/26/1867, Keithsburg, Ill. d: 12/20/34, Hermosa Beach, Cal BR/TR, 5'11", 166 lbs. Deb: 7/19/1893																												
1893	NY-N	31	114	16	28	4	1	2	21	7	9	.246	.289	.351	.640	69	-5	-6	104	125	13	.605	5			0	C	-0.4
1894	NY-N	49	175	35	58	5	5	1	32	14	5	.331	.387	.434	.822	100	0	0	100	114	33	.855	8			-15	C1	-0.8
1895	NY-N	67	238	32	56	9	0	0	30	14	16	.235	.281	.273	.554	47	-19	-17	95	129	22	.500	11			1	C1/3	-0.9
1896	NY-N	75	253	33	60	2	0	0	23	13	14	.237	.277	.245	.522	40	-21	-21	99	107	20	.440	9			-2	C/1	-1.3
1897	NY-N	46	154	29	46	9	3	0	22	15		.299	.365	.396	.761	105	1	1	98	105	25	.759	5			0	C1/O2	0.1
1898	NY-N	1	4	0	0	0	0	0	0	0		.000	.000	.000	.000	-99	-1	-1	95	0	0	.000	0			0	/O	0.0
1899	NY-N	97	328	49	88	8	6	0	42	43		.268	.360	.329	.689	95	-2	-0	97	122	46	.712	16			0	C1S3/O	0.0
Total	7	366	1266	194	336	37	15	3	170	106	44	.265	.327	.325	.652	74	-47	-43	98	117	159	.625	54			-17	C/1S3O2	-3.3
■ **BOB WILSON** Wilson, Robert b: 2/22/28, Dallas, Tex. BR/TR, 5'11", 197 lbs. Deb: 5/17/58																												
1958	LA-N	3	5	0	1	0	0	0	0	0	1	.200	.200	.200	.400	6	-1	-1	105	0	0	.250	0	0	0	-0	/O	0.0
■ **RED WILSON** Wilson, Robert James b: 3/7/29, Milwaukee, Wis. BR/TR, 5'10", 160 lbs. Deb: 9/22/51																												
1951	Chi-A	4	11	1	3	1	0	0	0	1	2	.273	.333	.364	.697	91	-0	-0	97	0	1	.500	0	0	0	0	/C	0.0
1952	Chi-A	2	3	0	0	0	0	0	0	0	1	.000	.000	.000	.000	-99	-1	-1	100	0	0	.000	0	0	0	-0	/C	0.0
1953	Chi-A	71	164	21	41	6	1	0	10	26	12	.250	.353	.299	.651	73	-4	-6	106	76	17	.575	2	3	-1	-3	C	-0.7
1954	Chi-A	8	20	2	4	0	0	1	1	1	2	.200	.238	.350	.588	57	-1	-1	104	38	2	.500	0	0	0	-0	/C	0.0
	Det-A	54	170	22	48	11	1	2	22	27	12	.282	.381	.394	.775	113	4	4	100	117	26	.740	3	1	0	2	C	0.9
	Yr	62	190	24	52	11	1	3	23	28	14	.274	.367	.389	.756	107	2	2	100	107	27	.714	3	1	0	2		0.9
1955	Det-A	78	241	26	53	9	0	2	17	26	23	.220	.296	.282	.578	58	-15	-14	97	86	18	.468	1	2	-1	2	C	-1.0
1956	Det-A	78	228	32	66	12	2	7	38	42	18	.289	.400	.452	.852	129	9	10	97	114	43	.870	2	1	0	1	C	1.2
1957	Det-A	60	180	21	43	8	1	3	13	25	19	.239	.341	.344	.686	82	-2	-4	107	72	22	.643	2	3	-1	4	C	0.1
1958	Det-A	103	298	31	89	13	1	3	29	35	30	.299	.376	.379	.755	104	5	3	104	95	45	.737	10	0	3	-4	*C	0.3
1959	Det-A	67	228	28	60	17	2	4	35	10	23	.263	.300	.408	.708	83	-3	-6	111	131	25	.601	2	2	-1	1	C	-0.1
1960	Det-A	45	134	17	29	4	0	1	14	16	14	.216	.300	.269	.569	54	-8	-8	102	141	12	.519	3	0	1	-3	C	-0.7
	Cle-A	32	88	5	19	3	0	1	10	6	7	.216	.274	.284	.558	52	-6	-6	98	140	7	.444	0	0	0	0	C	-0.3
	Yr	77	222	22	48	7	0	2	24	22	21	.216	.290	.275	.565	54	-14	-14	100	142	19	.492	3	0	1	-2		-1.0
Total	10	602	1765	206	455	84	8	24	189	215	163	.258	.341	.355	.696	87	-24	-29	102	103	217	.660	25	12	0	-1	C	-0.3
■ **MIKE WILSON** Wilson, Samuel Marshall b: 12/2/1896, Edge Hill, Pa. d: 5/16/78, Boynton Beach, Fla BR/TR, 5'10.5", 160 lbs. Deb: 6/04/21																												
1921	Pit-N	5	4	0	0	0	0	0	0	0	0	.000	.000	.000	.000	-97	-1	-1	103	0	0	.000	0	0	0	0	/C	0.0
■ **NEIL WILSON** Wilson, Samuel O'Neil b: 6/14/35, Lexington, Tenn. BL/TR, 6'1", 175 lbs. Deb: 4/17/60																												
1960	SF-N	6	10	0	0	0	0	0	0	1	2	.000	.091	.000	.091	-81	-2	-2	90	0	0	.091	0	0	0	0	/C	-0.1
■ **TOM WILSON** Wilson, Thomas G. "Slats" b: 6/3/1890, Fleming, Kan. d: 3/7/53, San Pedro, Cal. BR/TR, 6'1.5", 160 lbs. Deb: 9/08/14																												
1914	Was-A	1	1	0	0	0	0	0	0	0	0	.000	.000	.000	.000	-99	-0	-0	101	0	0	.000	0			0	/C	0.0
■ **BILL WILSON** Wilson, William Donald b: 11/6/28, Central City, Neb. BR/TR, 6'2", 200 lbs. Deb: 9/24/50																												
1950	Chi-A	3	6	0	0	0	0	0	0	2	2	.000	.250	.000	.250	-33	-1	-1	97	0	0	.333	0	0	0	-0	/O	-0.1
1953	Chi-A	9	17	1	1	0	0	0	1	0	7	.059	.111	.059	.170	-50	-4	-4	106	370	0	.118	0	0	0	-1	/O	-0.3
1954	Chi-A	20	35	4	6	1	0	2	5	5	7	.171	.310	.371	.681	83	-1	-1	104	100	3	.606	0	1	-1	-3	O	-0.4
	Phi-A	94	323	43	77	10	1	15	33	39	59	.238	.335	.415	.750	106	2	2	98	71	47	.722	1	2	-1	6	O	0.5
	Yr	114	358	47	83	11	1	17	38	46	64	.232	.333	.411	.743	103	1	1	99	77	51	.716	1	3	-2	3		0.1
1955	KC-A	98	273	39	61	12	0	15	38	24	63	.223	.289	.432	.721	91	-5	-6	101	87	32	.652	1	1	-0	2	O/P	-0.7
Total	4	224	654	87	145	23	1	32	77	72	136	.222	.308	.407	.715	93	-9	-9	100	86	83	.672	2	4	-2	5	O/P	-1.0
■ **BILL WILSON** Wilson, William G. b: 10/28/1867, Hannibal, Mo. d: 5/9/24, St.Paul, Minn. TR, Deb: 4/30/1890																												
1890	Pit-N	83	304	30	65	11	3	0	21	22	50	.214	.271	.270	.541	68	-16	-10	88	79	24	.464	5			8	CO1/S	0.1
1897	Lou-N	105	381	43	81	12	4	1	41	18		.213	.257	.273	.530	44	-32	-29	95	114	30	.453	9			1	*C/3	-1.1
1898	Lou-N	29	102	5	17	1	2	1	13	5		.167	.213	.245	.458	34	-9	-8	96	143	6	.400	3			0	C/1	-0.7
Total	3	217	787	78	163	24	9	2	75	45	50	.207	.257	.268	.525	51	-56	-47	92	104	60	.450	17			9	C/O13S	-1.7

YEAR	TM/L	G	AB	R	H	2B	3B	HR	RBI	BB	SO	AVG	OBP	SLG	PRO	/A	BR	/A	PF	CHI	RC	TA	SB	CS	SBR	FR	POS	TPR
■ **MOOKIE WILSON** Wilson, William Hayward b: 2/9/56, Bamberg, S.C. BB/TR, 5'10", 170 lbs. Deb: 9/02/80																												
1980	NY-N	27	105	16	26	5	3	0	4	12	19	.248	.325	.352	.677	93	-1	-1	96	41	12	.651	7	7	-2	4	O	0.0
1981	NY-N	92	328	49	89	8	8	3	14	20	59	.271	.317	.372	.689	94	-3	-3	101	43	38	.661	24	12	0	2	O	-0.3
1982	NY-N	159	639	90	178	25	9	5	55	32	102	.279	.315	.369	.684	92	-9	-8	99	91	78	.680	58	16	8	9	*O	0.8
1983	NY-N	152	638	91	176	25	6	7	51	18	103	.276	.300	.367	.667	85	-15	-14	99	70	71	.640	54	16	7	4	*O	-0.6
1984	NY-N	154	587	88	162	28	10	10	54	26	90	.276	.309	.409	.718	100	-2	-2	100	80	78	.715	46	9	8	11	*O	1.2
1985	NY-N	93	337	56	93	16	8	6	26	28	52	.276	.332	.424	.756	113	4	5	97	66	46	.744	24	9	2	-1	O	0.4
1986	NY-N	123	381	61	110	17	5	9	45	32	72	.289	.345	.430	.776	118	6	8	96	94	58	.784	25	7	3	4	*O	1.4
1987	NY-N	124	385	58	115	19	7	9	34	35	85	.299	.360	.455	.815	116	8	8	99	67	66	.838	21	6	3	0	*O	0.7
1988	NY-N	112	378	61	112	17	5	8	41	27	63	.296	.346	.431	.778	135	10	14	90	88	55	.734	15	4	2	1	*O	1.6
Total	9	1036	3778	570	1061	160	61	57	324	230	645	.281	.325	.401	.725	103	-2	8	98	75	501	.722	274	86	31	35	O	5.2
■ **WILLIE WILSON** Wilson, Willie James b: 7/9/55, Montgomery, Ala. BB/TR, 6'3", 190 lbs. Deb: 9/04/76																												
1976	KC-A	12	6	0	1	0	0	0	0	0	2	.167	.167	.167	.333	-2	-1	-1	100	0	0	.500	2	1	0	-1	/O	-0.1
1977	KC-A	13	34	10	11	2	0	0	1	1	8	.324	.343	.382	.725	97	-0	-0	100	30	4	.741	6	3	0	1	/OD	0.0
1978	KC-A	127	198	43	43	8	2	0	16	16	33	.217	.282	.278	.560	57	-11	-11	102	115	18	.704	46	12	7	-13	*O/D	-2.0
1979	KC-A	154	588	113	185	18	13	6	49	28	92	.315	.353	.420	.773	102	6	2	105	73	99	.877	**83**	12	**18**	14	*O	2.7
1980	KC-A	161	705	**133**	**230**	28	**15**	3	49	28	81	.326	.357	.421	.779	114	11	13	98	55	117	.838	79	10	**18**	5	*O	3.2
1981	KC-A	102	439	54	133	10	7	1	32	18	42	.303	.336	.364	.701	103	1	1	99	68	56	.677	34	8	5	22	*O	2.8
1982	KC-A	136	585	87	194	19	**15**	3	46	26	81	**.332**	.366	.431	.797	118	14	14	100	62	96	.791	37	11	5	-2	*O	1.3
1983	KC-A	137	576	90	159	22	8	2	33	33	75	.276	.316	.352	.669	83	-13	-14	101	55	72	.690	59	8	13	-10	*O	-1.2
1984	KC-A	128	541	81	163	24	9	2	44	39	56	.301	.352	.390	.742	106	4	5	99	70	82	.769	47	5	**11**	2	*O	1.4
1985	KC-A	141	605	87	168	25	**21**	4	43	29	94	.278	.316	.408	.724	95	-4	-5	102	57	80	.714	43	11	6	-4	*O	-0.4
1986	KC-A	156	631	77	170	20	7	9	44	31	97	.269	.313	.366	.679	85	-13	-13	100	65	76	.642	34	8	5	-3	*O	-1.5
1987	KC-A	146	610	97	170	18	**15**	4	30	32	88	.279	.321	.377	.698	82	-13	-16	104	44	78	.711	59	11	**11**	-4	*O/D	-1.2
1988	KC-A	147	591	81	155	17	**11**	1	37	22	106	.262	.291	.333	.624	72	-21	-23	103	78	61	.571	35	7	6	-6	*O	-2.4
Total	13	1560	6109	953	1782	211	123	35	424	303	855	.292	.330	.384	.714	94	-39	-49	101	64	839	.735	564	107	105	2	*O/D	2.6
■ **ED WINCENIAK** Winceniak, Edward Joseph b: 4/16/29, Chicago, Ill. BR/TR, 5'9", 165 lbs. Deb: 4/25/56																												
1956	Chi-N	15	17	1	2	0	0	0	0	1	3	.118	.167	.118	.284	-22	-3	-3	99	0	0	.188	0	0	0	-0	/32	-0.2
1957	Chi-N	17	50	5	12	3	0	1	8	2	9	.240	.269	.360	.629	70	-2	-2	96	158	4	.500	0	0	0	-1	/S32	-0.1
Total	2	32	67	6	14	3	0	1	8	3	12	.209	.243	.299	.541	46	-5	-5	97	117	5	.418	0	0	0	-1	/3S2	-0.3
■ **GORDIE WINDHORN** Windhorn, Gordon Ray b: 12/19/33, Watseka, Ill. BR/TR, 6'1", 185 lbs. Deb: 9/10/59																												
1959	NY-A	7	11	0	0	0	0	0	0	0	3	.000	.000	.000	.000	-99	-3	-3	93	0	0	.000	0	0	0	-1	/O	-0.3
1961	LA-N	34	33	10	8	2	1	2	6	4	3	.242	.324	.545	.870	123	1	1	102	101	5	.815	0	1	-1	-3	O	-0.2
1962	KC-A	14	19	1	3	1	0	0	1	0	3	.158	.158	.211	.368	-2	-3	-3	100	99	1	.250	0	0	0	-2	/O	-0.4
	LA-A	40	45	9	8	6	0	0	1	7	10	.178	.288	.311	.600	60	-2	-3	102	28	4	.564	1	1	-0	-6	O	-0.9
	Yr	54	64	10	11	7	0	0	2	7	13	.172	.254	.281	.535	43	-5	-5	102	49	5	.473	1	1	-0	-8		-1.3
Total	3	95	108	20	19	9	1	2	8	11	19	.176	.252	.333	.585	55	-7	-7	101	60	10	.522	1	2	-1	-11	/O	-1.8
■ **BILL WINDLE** Windle, Willis Brewer b: 12/13/04, Galena, Kan. d: 12/8/81, Corpus Christi, Tex BL/TL, 5'11.5", 170 lbs. Deb: 9/27/28																												
1928	Pit-N	1	1	1	1	1	0	0	0	0	0	1.000	1.000	2.000	3.000	624	1	1	107	0	2	—	0			0	/1	0.1
1929	Pit-N	2	1	0	0	0	0	0	0	0	1	.000	.000	.000	.000	-97	-0	-0	103	0	0	.000	0			0	/1	0.0
Total	2	3	2	1	1	1	0	0	0	0	1	.500	.500	1.000	1.500	259	0	0	105	0	2	2.000	0			0	/1	0.1
■ **ROBBIE WINE** Wine, Robert Paul Jr. b: 7/13/62, Norristown, Pa. BR/TR, 6'2", 190 lbs. Deb: 9/02/86																												
1986	Hou-N	9	12	2	3	1	0	0	0	1	4	.250	.308	.333	.641	75	-0	-0	103	0	1	.556	0	0	0	-1	/C	0.0
1987	Hou-N	14	29	1	3	1	0	0	0	1	10	.103	.133	.138	.271	-30	-5	-5	93	0	1	.192	0	0	0	-1	C	-0.4
Total	2	23	41	3	6	2	0	0	0	2	14	.146	.186	.195	.381	2	-6	-5	96	0	2	.286	0	0	0	-1	/C	-0.4
■ **BOBBY WINE** Wine, Robert Paul Sr. b: 9/17/38, New York, N.Y. BR/TR, 6'1", 187 lbs. Deb: 9/20/60 MC																												
1960	Phi-N	4	14	1	2	0	0	0	0	0	2	.143	.143	.143	.286	-20	-2	-2	107	0	0	.167	0	0	0	-1	/S	-0.2
1962	Phi-N	112	311	30	76	15	0	4	25	11	49	.244	.270	.331	.601	64	-18	-16	95	86	23	.458	2	0	1	3	S3	-0.2
1963	Phi-N	142	418	29	90	14	3	6	44	14	83	.215	.242	.306	.549	55	-24	-25	103	127	28	.421	1	3	-2	7	*S/3	-0.6
1964	Phi-N	126	283	28	60	8	3	4	34	25	37	.212	.276	.304	.580	64	-14	-13	99	142	23	.485	1	0	0	-1	*S3	-0.7
1965	Phi-N	139	394	31	90	8	1	5	33	31	69	.228	.285	.292	.577	66	-19	-17	95	105	30	.456	0	0	0	11	*S/1	1.0
1966	Phi-N	46	89	8	21	5	0	0	5	6	13	.236	.292	.292	.584	62	-4	-4	101	81	7	.465	0	1	-1	3	S/O	0.2
1967	Phi-N	135	363	27	69	12	5	2	28	29	77	.190	.250	.267	.517	46	-24	-26	104	113	23	.420	3	2	-0	10	*S/1	-0.1
1968	Phi-N	27	71	5	12	3	0	2	7	6	17	.169	.234	.296	.530	60	-4	-4	97	109	4	.429	0	0	0	1	S/3	0.0
1969	Mon-N	121	370	23	74	8	1	3	25	28	49	.200	.256	.251	.508	42	-28	-28	100	98	23	.394	0	0	0	9	*S/13	-0.5
1970	Mon-N	159	501	40	116	21	3	3	51	39	94	.232	.288	.303	.592	59	-29	-29	100	123	44	.485	0	1	-1	14	*S	0.4
1971	Mon-N	119	340	25	68	9	0	1	16	25	46	.200	.255	.235	.490	40	-27	-26	99	78	20	.371	0	0	0	-0	*S	-1.1
1972	Mon-N	34	18	2	4	1	0	0	0	0	2	.222	.222	.278	.500	40	-1	-1	102	0	1	.333	0	0	0	0	3/S2	0.0
Total	12	1164	3172	249	682	104	16	30	268	214	538	.215	.265	.286	.552	54	-195	-193	100	108	227	.453	7	7	-2	57	*S/3102	-1.8
■ **DAVE WINFIELD** Winfield, David Mark b: 10/3/51, St.Paul, Minn. BR/TR, 6'6", 220 lbs. Deb: 6/19/73																												
1973	SD-N	56	141	9	39	4	1	3	12	12	19	.277	.333	.383	.716	104	-0	1	94	76	17	.617	0	0	0	-2	O/1	-0.2
1974	SD-N	145	498	57	132	18	4	20	75	40	96	.265	.321	.438	.759	119	5	9	93	106	66	.693	9	7	-2	9	*O	1.2
1975	SD-N	143	509	74	136	20	2	15	76	69	82	.267	.358	.403	.761	111	8	9	100	125	77	.773	23	4	5	6	*O	1.4
1976	SD-N	137	492	81	139	26	4	13	69	65	78	.283	.370	.431	.801	143	18	25	89	112	80	.818	26	7	4	13	*O	3.8
1977	SD-N	157	615	104	169	29	7	25	92	58	75	.275	.337	.467	.804	129	10	20	88	108	95	.776	16	7	1	16	*O	3.1
1978	SD-N	158	587	88	181	30	5	24	97	55	81	.308	.370	.499	.869	152	31	36	93	112	105	.867	21	9	1	-13	*O/1	1.9
1979	SD-N	159	597	97	184	27	10	34	**118**	85	71	.308	.396	.558	.954	**163**	**47**	**50**	96	114	132	1.009	15	9	-1	11	*O	5.7
1980	SD-N	162	558	89	154	25	6	20	87	79	83	.276	.368	.450	.818	136	21	26	93	113	94	.837	23	7	3	-2	*O	2.1
1981	NY-A	105	388	52	114	25	1	13	68	43	41	.294	.366	.464	.830	137	19	19	100	129	66	.816	11	1	3	-6	*O/D	1.4
1982	NY-A	140	539	84	151	24	8	37	106	45	64	.280	.336	.560	.896	146	28	30	96	109	93	.856	5	3	-0	8	*O/D	3.3
1983	NY-A	152	598	99	169	26	8	32	116	58	77	.283	.348	.513	.861	135	26	27	99	119	97	.822	15	6	1	-4	*O	2.2
1984	NY-A	141	567	106	193	34	4	19	100	53	71	.340	.397	.515	.912	160	38	43	94	121	113	.895	6	4	-1	1	*O	3.9
1985	NY-A	155	633	105	174	34	6	26	114	52	96	.275	.330	.471	.801	121	13	16	96	116	94	.764	19	7	2	6	*O/D	2.1
1986	NY-A	154	565	90	148	31	5	24	104	77	106	.262	.352	.462	.814	117	17	14	103	132	89	.783	6	5	-1	1	*O/3D	0.9
1987	NY-A	156	575	83	158	22	1	27	97	76	96	.275	.359	.457	.817	119	14	16	98	119	91	.777	5	6	-2	-9	*O/D	0.1
1988	NY-A	149	559	96	180	37	2	25	107	69	88	.322	.398	.530	.928	164	43	47	96	121	115	.935	9	4	0	-7	*O/D	3.7
Total	16	2269	8421	1314	2421	412	74	357	1438	936	1224	.287	.360	.481	.841	136	337	386	95	116	1424	.855	209	86	11	29	*O/D13	36.6
■ **AL WINGO** Wingo, Absalom Holbrook "Red" b: 5/6/1898, Norcross, Ga. d: 10/9/64, Detroit, Mich. BL/TR, 5'11", 180 lbs. Deb: 9/09/19																												
1919	Phi-A	15	59	9	18	1	3	0	2	4	12	.305	.349	.424	.773	110	1	1	106	31	8	.707	0			-3	O	-0.3
1924	Det-A	78	150	21	43	12	2	1	26	21	13	.287	.374	.413	.788	103	1	1	100	132	23	.759	2	5	-2	-8	O	-1.1
1925	Det-A	130	440	104	163	34	10	5	68	69	31	.370	.456	.527	.983	150	35	36	99	94	106	1.086	14	13	-4	10	*O	2.9
1926	Det-A	108	298	45	84	19	0	1	45	52	32	.282	.389	.356	.744	98	-0	1	97	140	45	.750	4	2	0	3	O/3	-0.1
1927	Det-A	75	137	15	32	8	2	0	20	25	14	.234	.352	.321	.673	70	-4	-6	108	151	17	.667	1	0	0	-4	O	-1.1
1928	Det-A	87	242	30	69	13	2	2	30	40	17	.285	.389	.380	.769	103	3	3	99	105	38	.771	2	2	-1	-3	O	-0.4
Total	6	493	1326	224	409	87	19	9	191	211	119	.308	.404	.423	.827	114	35	36	100	114	237	.848	23	22		-6	O/3	-0.1
■ **ED WINGO** Wingo, Edmond Armand (born La Riviere) b: 10/8/1895, St.Anne De Bellevue, Que., Canada d: 12/5/64, Lachine, Que., Can. BR/TR, 5'6", 145 lbs. Deb: 10/02/20																												
1920	Phi-A	1	4	0	1	0	0	0	1	0	0	.250	.250	.250	.500	35	-0	-0	94	358	0	.333	0	0	0	0	/C	0.0
■ **IVEY WINGO** Wingo, Ivey Brown b: 7/8/1890, Gainesville, Ga. d: 5/6/45, Allentown, Pa. BL/TR, 5'10", 160 lbs. Deb: 4/20/11 MC																												
1911	StL-N	25	57	4	12	2	0	0	3	3	7	.211	.250	.246	.496	38	-5	-5	101	72	3	.378	0			0	C	-0.3

YEAR	TM/L	G	AB	R	H	2B	3B	HR	RBI	BB	SO	AVG	OBP	SLG	PRO	/A	BR	/A	PF	CHI	RC	TA	SB	CS	SBR	FR	POS	TPR
1912	StL-N	100	310	38	82	18	8	2	44	23	45	.265	.317	.394	.711	94	-4	-4	100	116	40	.675	8			10	C	1.1
1913	StL-N	112	307	25	78	5	8	2	35	17	41	.254	.295	.342	.637	88	-8	-5	93	115	34	.616	18			8	C/1O	0.9
1914	StL-N	80	237	24	71	8	5	4	26	18	17	.300	.352	.426	.778	126	8	7	104	83	38	.813	15			2	C	1.2
1915	Cin-N	119	339	26	75	11	6	3	29	13	33	.221	.250	.316	.566	69	-13	-14	103	95	27	.473	10	11	-4	1	C/O	-1.2
1916	Cin-N	119	347	30	85	8	11	2	40	25	27	.245	.298	.349	.646	100	-1	-1	98	125	40	.576	4			6	*CM	1.3
1917	Cin-N	121	399	37	106	16	11	2	39	25	13	.266	.311	.376	.687	119	4	7	92	96	47	.631	9			0	*C	1.4
1918	Cin-N	100	323	35	82	15	6	0	31	19	18	.254	.297	.337	.635	96	-3	-2	97	108	33	.560	6			5	C/O	1.2
1919	Cin-N	76	245	30	67	12	6	0	27	23	19	.273	.336	.371	.707	107	4	2	105	115	30	.663	4			1	C	0.9
1920	Cin-N	108	364	32	96	11	5	2	38	19	13	.264	.300	.338	.638	93	-8	-4	90	114	37	.544	6	4	-1	-4	*C/2	-0.1
1921	Cin-N	97	295	20	79	7	6	3	38	21	14	.268	.319	.363	.681	79	-9	-9	101	120	35	.606	3	2	-0	2	C/O	-0.1
1922	Cin-N	80	260	24	74	13	3	3	45	23	11	.285	.343	.392	.735	93	-4	-3	96	142	34	.663	1	4	-2	-2	C	-0.4
1923	Cin-N	61	171	10	45	9	2	1	24	9	11	.263	.304	.357	.661	75	-7	-6	98	132	18	.567	1	1	-0	-1	C	-0.3
1924	Cin-N	66	192	21	55	5	4	1	23	14	8	.286	.338	.370	.708	89	-3	-3	101	113	24	.630	1	1	-0	-3	C/1	-0.4
1925	Cin-N	55	146	6	30	7	0	0	12	11	8	.205	.261	.253	.515	33	-15	-14	97	115	10	.415	1	2	-1	-7	C	-1.8
1926	Cin-N	7	10	0	2	0	0	0	1	1	0	.200	.333	.200	.533	49	-1	-1	95	173	1	.500	0			-0	/C	0.0
1929	Cin-N	1	1	0	0	0	0	0	0	0	0	.000	.000	.000	.000	-99	-0	-0	99	0	0	.000	0			0	/C	0.0
Total	17	1327	4003	362	1039	147	81	25	455	264	285	.260	.307	.355	.662	91	-65	-54	98	112	452	.597	87	25		19	*C/O12	3.4
■ **GEORGE WINKELMAN**	Winkelman, George Edward b: 2/18/1865, Washington, D.C. d: 5/19/60, Washington, D.C. BL/TL, Deb: 8/04/1883																											
1883	Lou-a	4	13	2	0	0	0	0		1		.000	.071	.000	.071	-80	-2	-2	94	0	0	.077				0	/O	-0.1
1886	Was-N	1	5	0	1	0	0	0	0	0	1	.200	.200	.200	.400	23	-0	-0	94	0	0	.250	0			0	/OP	0.0
Total	2	5	18	2	1	0	0	0	0	1	1	.056	.105	.056	.161	-51	-3	-3	94	0	0	.118	0			0	/OP	-0.1
■ **HERM WINNINGHAM**	Winningham, Herman Son b: 12/1/61, Orangeburg, S.C. BL/TR, 6'1", 170 lbs. Deb: 9/01/84																											
1984	NY-N	14	27	5	11	1	1	0	5	1	7	.407	.429	.519	.947	165	2	2	100	140	6	1.000	2	1	0	-3	O	0.0
1985	Mon-N	125	312	30	74	6	5	3	21	28	72	.237	.300	.317	.617	78	-11	-9	94	77	32	.593	20	9	1	-10	*O	-2.2
1986	Mon-N	90	185	23	40	6	3	4	11	18	51	.216	.286	.346	.632	75	-7	-6	98	58	17	.603	12	7	-1	-5	O/S	-1.3
1987	Mon-N	137	347	34	83	20	3	4	41	34	68	.239	.307	.349	.656	69	-13	-16	106	123	37	.648	29	10	3	-5	*O	-2.3
1988	Mon-N	47	90	10	21	2	1	0	6	12	18	.233	.324	.278	.601	70	-3	-3	106	96	8	.539	4	5	-2	-2	O	-0.7
	Cin-N	53	113	6	26	1	3	0	15	5	27	.230	.263	.292	.555	56	-6	-7	105	182	9	.511	8	3	1	-2	O	-1.0
	Yr	100	203	16	47	3	4	0	21	17	45	.232	.291	.286	.577	63	-9	-10	105	142	18	.530	12	8	-1	-4		-1.7
Total	5	466	1074	108	255	36	16	11	99	98	243	.237	.301	.331	.633	74	-38	-39	101	102	108	.619	75	35	2	-26	O/S	-7.5
■ **TOM WINSETT**	Winsett, John Thomas "Long Tom" b: 11/24/09, Mc Kenzie, Tenn. BL/TR, 6'2", 190 lbs. Deb: 4/20/30																											
1930	Bos-A	1	1	0	0	0	0	0	0	0	1	.000	.000	.000	.000	-99	-0	-0	93	0	0	.000	0	0	0	0	H	0.0
1931	Bos-A	64	76	6	15	1	0	1	7	4	21	.197	.247	.250	.497	33	-8	-7	94	105	5	.393	0	0	0	-1	/O	-0.7
1933	Bos-A	6	12	1	1	0	0	0	0	1	6	.083	.154	.083	.237	-35	-2	-2	101	0	0	.182	0	0	0	-2	/O	-0.3
1935	StL-N	7	12	2	6	1	0	0	2	2	3	.500	.571	.583	1.155	203	2	2	104	103	4	1.500	0			-1	/O	0.1
1936	Bro-N	22	85	13	20	7	0	1	18	11	14	.235	.330	.353	.683	80	-2	-2	105	205	10	.627	0			1	O	-0.2
1937	Bro-N	118	350	32	83	15	5	5	42	45	64	.237	.329	.351	.681	81	-7	-9	104	110	44	.637	3			-1	*O/P	-1.3
1938	Bro-N	12	30	6	9	1	0	1	7	6	4	.300	.417	.433	.850	140	2	2	96	158	6	.864	0			-2	/O	0.0
Total	7	230	566	60	134	25	5	8	76	69	113	.237	.325	.341	.666	78	-15	-17	102	124	69	.624	3	0		-5	O/P	-2.4
■ **KETTLE WIRTS**	Wirts, Elwood Vernon b: 10/31/1897, Consumnes, Cal. d: 7/12/68, Sacramento, Cal. BR/TR, 5'11", 170 lbs. Deb: 7/20/21																											
1921	Chi-N	7	11	0	2	0	0	0	1	0	3	.182	.182	.182	.364	-3	-2	-2	107	183	0	.222	0	0	0	0	/C	0.0
1922	Chi-N	31	58	7	10	2	0	1	6	12	15	.172	.314	.259	.573	52	-4	-4	95	116	5	.563	0	0	0	2	C	-0.1
1923	Chi-N	5	5	2	1	0	0	0	1	2	0	.200	.429	.200	.629	68	-0	-0	104	352	1	.750	0	0	0	0	/C	0.0
1924	Chi-A	6	12	0	1	0	0	0	0	2	2	.083	.214	.083	.298	-22	-2	-2	97	0	0	.273	0	0	0	0	/C	0.0
Total	4	49	86	9	14	2	0	1	8	16	20	.163	.294	.221	.515	36	-8	-8	97	124	7	.486	0	0	0	2	/C	-0.1
■ **HUGHIE WISE**	Wise, Hugh Edward b: 3/9/06, Campbellsville, Ky. d: 7/21/87, Plantation, Fla. BB/TR, 6', 178 lbs. Deb: 9/26/30																											
1930	Det-A	2	6	0	2	0	0	0	0	0	0	.333	.333	.333	.667	66	-0	-0	105	0	1	.500	0	0	0	0	/C	0.0
■ **CASEY WISE**	Wise, Kendall Cole b: 9/8/32, Lafayette, Ind. BB/TR, 6', 170 lbs. Deb: 4/16/57																											
1957	Chi-N	43	106	12	19	3	1	0	7	11	14	.179	.256	.226	.483	32	-10	-10	96	121	6	.380	0	0	0	1	2/S	-0.5
1958	Mil-N	31	71	8	14	1	0	0	0	4	8	.197	.240	.211	.451	23	-8	-7	89	0	3	.328	1	1	-0	1	2/S3	-0.5
1959	Mil-N	22	76	11	13	2	0	1	5	10	5	.171	.267	.237	.504	38	-7	-6	95	98	5	.424	0	0	0	-2	2/S	-0.6
1960	Det-A	30	68	6	10	0	2	2	5	4	9	.147	.194	.294	.489	30	-7	-7	102	75	3	.410	1	0	0	0	2S/3	-0.4
Total	4	126	321	37	56	6	3	3	17	29	36	.174	.243	.240	.483	31	-32	-30	95	80	17	.401	2	1	0	-0	/2S3	-2.0
■ **NICK WISE**	Wise, Nicholas Joseph b: 6/15/1866, Boston, Mass. d: 1/15/23, Boston, Mass. BR/TR, 5'11", 194 lbs. Deb: 1888																											
1888	Bos-N	1	3	0	0	0	0	0	0	0	0	.000	.000	.000	.000	-95	-1	-1	106	0	0	.000	0			0	/OC	0.0
■ **SAM WISE**	Wise, Samuel Washington "Modoc" b: 8/18/1857, Akron, Ohio d: 1/22/10, Akron, Ohio TR, 5'10.5", 170 lbs. Deb: 7/30/1881																											
1881	Det-N	1	4	0	2	0	0	0	0	0	2	.500	.500	.500	1.000	202	0	0	106	0	1	1.000				0	/3	0.0
1882	Bos-N	78	298	44	66	11	4	4	34	5	45	.221	.234	.326	.560	75	-8	-9	103	107	23	.440				-12	*S/3	-1.2
1883	Bos-N	96	406	73	110	25	7	4	58	13	74	.271	.294	.397	.690	101	3	-1	106	123	48	.588				-6	*S	-0.1
1884	Bos-N	114	426	60	91	15	9	4	41	25	104	.214	.257	.319	.576	82	-10	-8	98	97	36	.481				1	*S/2	0.2
1885	Bos-N	107	424	71	120	20	10	4	46	25	61	.283	.323	.406	.729	144	15	19	94	84	57	.648				9	*S2/O	3.0
1886	Bos-N	96	387	71	112	19	12	4	72	33	61	.289	.345	.432	.777	139	16	18	97	126	70	.840	31			-3	12S	0.4
1887	Bos-N	113	467	103	156	27	17	9	92	36	44	.334	.390	.522	.913	157	33	35	98	101	115	1.061	43			-4	SO2	2.4
1888	Bos-N	105	417	66	100	19	12	4	40	34	66	.240	.306	.372	.678	111	9	5	106	83	59	.719	33			11	S/3102	1.8
1889	Was-N	121	472	79	118	15	8	4	62	61	62	.250	.341	.341	.682	101	-3	3	92	103	65	.706	24			-16	2S3O	-0.5
1890	Buf-P	119	505	95	148	29	11	6	102	46	45	.293	.359	.430	.789	122	8	16	92	114	87	.807	19			2	*2	1.9
1891	Bal-a	103	388	70	96	14	5	1	48	62	52	.247	.364	.317	.681	97	2	1	101	106	58	.777	33			-10	*2/S	0.0
1893	Was-N	122	521	102	162	27	17	5	77	49	27	.311	.375	.457	.831	137	15	25	90	80	99	.866	20			16	*23	3.3
Total	12	1175	4715	834	1281	221	112	49	672	389	643	.272	.332	.397	.729	117	81	105	97	101	718	.728	203			-12	S2/130	11.2
■ **PHIL WISNER**	Wisner, Philip N. b: 7/1869, Washington, D.C. d: 7/5/36, Washington, D.C. TR, Deb: 8/30/1895																											
1895	Was-N	1	0	0	0	0	0	0	0	0	0	—	—	—	—	—	0	0	103	—	—	—	0			0	/S	0.0
■ **DAVE WISSMAN**	Wissman, David Alvin b: 2/17/41, Greenfield, Mass. BL/TR, 6'2", 178 lbs. Deb: 9/15/64																											
1964	Pit-N	16	27	2	4	0	0	0	0	1	9	.148	.179	.148	.327	-7	-4	-4	101	0	1	.217	0	0	0	-1	O	-0.5
■ **TEX WISTERZIL**	Wisterzil, George John b: 3/7/1891, Detroit, Mich. d: 6/27/64, San Antonio, Tex. BR/TR, 5'9.5", 150 lbs. Deb: 4/14/14																											
1914	Bro-F	149	534	54	137	18	10	0	66	34	47	.257	.301	.328	.629	79	-14	-15	101	139	61	.569	17			13	*3	0.1
1915	Bro-F	36	106	13	33	3	3	0	21	21	0	.311	.425	.396	.821	147	7	7	98	180	22	.973	8			1	3	1.0
	Chi-F	7	20	3	4	1	0	0	0	3	0	.200	.304	.250	.554	67	-1	-1	97	149	2	.500	0			0	/3	-0.3
	StL-F	8	24	1	5	1	0	0	4	2	0	.208	.269	.250	.519	52	-1	-1	105	240	2	.526	2			0	/3	-0.1
	Chi-F	42	144	12	36	3	1	0	1	5	0	.250	.275	.285	.560	68	-6	-6	97	9	13	.444	2			1	3	-0.4
	Yr	93	294	29	78	8	4	0	26	31	0	.265	.335	.320	.655	96	-1	-1	98	112	37	.634	12			2		0.2
Total	2	242	828	83	215	26	14	0	92	65	47	.260	.314	.325	.638	85	-16	-15	100	126	99	.592	29			15	3	0.3
■ **MICKEY WITEK**	Witek, Nicholas Joseph b: 12/19/15, Luzerne, Pa. BR/TR, 5'10", 170 lbs. Deb: 4/16/40																											
1940	NY-N	119	433	34	111	7	0	3	31	24	17	.256	.295	.293	.589	63	-22	-22	100	86	36	.457	2			12	S2	0.1
1941	NY-N	26	94	11	34	5	0	1	16	4	2	.362	.388	.447	.835	131	4	4	103	131	16	.754	0			1	2	0.6
1942	NY-N	148	553	72	144	19	6	5	48	36	20	.260	.306	.344	.649	87	-8	-10	103	89	54	.528	2			5	*2	0.6
1943	NY-N	153	622	68	195	17	0	6	55	41	23	.314	.356	.370	.726	114	7	10	96	77	78	.607	1			14	*2	3.0
1946	NY-N	82	284	32	75	13	2	4	29	28	10	.264	.330	.366	.696	96	-1	-2	102	95	34	.616	1			0	23	0.0
1947	NY-N	51	160	22	35	4	1	3	17	15	12	.219	.286	.313	.598	58	-10	-10	101	107	15	.520	1			4	2/3	-0.1

YEAR	TM/L	G	AB	R	H	2B	3B	HR	RBI	BB	SO	AVG	OBP	SLG	PRO	/A	BR	/A	PF	CHI	RC	TA	SB	CS	SBR	FR	POS	TPR
1949	NY-A	1	1	0	1	0	0	0	0	0	0	1.000	1.000	1.000	2.000	428	0	0	100	0	1	—	0	0	0	0	H	0.0
Total	7	580	2147	239	595	65	9	22	196	148	84	.277	.324	.347	.670	90	-29	-29	100	89	235	.579	7	0		36	2/S3	4.2
■ **FRANK WITHROW** Withrow, Frank Blaine "Kid" b: 6/14/1891, Greenwood, Mo. d: 9/5/66, Omaha, Neb. BR/TR, 5'11.5", 187 lbs. Deb: 4/15/20																												
1920	Phi-N	48	132	8	24	4	1	0	12	8	26	.182	.239	.227	.467	32	-11	-12	109	155	8	.370	0	0	0	1	C	-0.7
1922	Phi-N	10	21	3	7	2	0	0	3	3	5	.333	.417	.429	.845	104	1	0	113	116	4	.857	0	0	0	0	/C	0.1
Total	2	58	153	11	31	6	1	0	15	11	31	.203	.265	.255	.520	43	-10	-12	109	149	12	.426	0	0	0	2	/C	-0.6
■ **CORKY WITHROW** Withrow, Raymond Wallace b: 11/28/37, High Coal, W.Va. BR/TR, 6'3.5", 197 lbs. Deb: 9/06/63																												
1963	StL-N	6	9	0	0	0	0	0	1	0	2	.000	.000	.000	.000	-93	-2	-2	107	0	0	.000	0	0	0	-0	/O	-0.2
■ **WHITEY WITT** Witt, Lawton Walter (born Ladislaw Waldemar Wittkowski) b: 9/28/1895, Orange, Mass. d: 7/14/88, Salem Co., N.J. BL/TR, 5'7", 150 lbs. Deb: 4/12/16																												
1916	Phi-A	143	563	64	138	16	15	2	36	55	71	.245	.315	.337	.652	98	-4	-3	98	57	66	.626	19			-4	*S	0.5
1917	Phi-A	128	452	62	114	13	4	0	28	65	45	.252	.346	.299	.645	103	1	4	94	79	50	.627	12			4	*S/O3	1.3
1919	Phi-A	122	460	56	123	15	6	0	33	46	26	.267	.334	.326	.660	81	-8	-11	106	85	52	.614	11			-9	O2/3	-1.9
1920	Phi-A	65	218	29	70	11	3	1	25	27	16	.321	.396	.413	.809	122	5	7	94	96	36	.788	2	3	-1	-9	O2/S	-0.5
1921	Phi-A	154	629	100	198	31	11	4	45	77	52	.315	.390	.418	.809	103	8	5	103	48	104	.800	16	15	-4	-10	*O	-2.0
1922	NY-A	140	528	98	157	11	6	4	40	**89**	29	.297	.400	.364	.763	99	5	3	102	67	81	.757	5	8	-3	-14	*O	-2.2
1923	NY-A	146	596	113	187	18	10	6	56	67	42	.314	.386	.408	.794	104	9	5	104	65	95	.757	2	7	-4	9	*O	-0.1
1924	NY-A	147	600	88	178	26	5	1	36	45	20	.297	.346	.362	.707	83	-16	-15	99	52	76	.632	9	7	-2	-5	*O	-2.9
1925	NY-A	31	40	9	8	2	1	0	0	6	2	.200	.304	.300	.604	56	-3	-3	96	0	4	.576	1	1	-0	-0	O	-0.3
1926	Bro-N	63	85	13	22	1	1	0	3	12	6	.259	.351	.294	.645	75	-2	-2	99	41	9	.603	1			-1	O	-0.3
Total	10	1139	4171	632	1195	144	62	18	302	489	309	.287	.362	.364	.726	97	-5	-9	100	64	574	.693	78	41		-37	OS/23	-8.4
■ **JERRY WITTE** Witte, Jerome Charles b: 7/30/15, St.Louis, Mo. BR/TR, 6'1", 190 lbs. Deb: 9/10/46																												
1946	StL-A	18	73	7	14	2	0	2	4	0	18	.192	.192	.301	.493	37	-7	-6	98	55	4	.373	0	0	0	0	1	-0.6
1947	StL-A	34	99	4	14	2	1	2	12	11	22	.141	.227	.242	.470	30	-10	-10	102	147	6	.398	0	0	0	-1	1	-1.2
Total	2	52	172	11	28	4	1	4	16	11	40	.163	.213	.267	.481	33	-16	-16	100	110	10	.388	0	0	0	-1	/1	-1.8
■ **JOHN WOCKENFUSS** Wockenfuss, Johnny Bilton b: 2/27/49, Welch, W.Va. BR/TR, 6', 190 lbs. Deb: 8/11/74																												
1974	Det-A	13	29	1	4	1	0	0	2	3	2	.138	.219	.172	.391	13	-3	-3	106	157	1	.320	0	0	0	-1	C	-0.3
1975	Det-A	35	118	15	27	6	3	4	13	10	15	.229	.289	.432	.721	98	-0	-1	104	81	13	.635	0	0	0	5	C	0.5
1976	Det-A	60	144	18	32	7	2	3	10	17	14	.222	.309	.361	.670	92	-1	-1	104	63	15	.593	0	3	-2	0	C	0.0
1977	Det-A	53	164	26	45	8	1	9	25	14	18	.274	.331	.500	.831	118	5	4	105	91	28	.800	0	0	0	2	C/OD	0.6
1978	Det-A	71	187	23	53	5	0	7	22	21	14	.283	.359	.422	.781	110	5	3	108	87	27	.711	0	1	-1	-9	O/D	-0.7
1979	Det-A	87	231	27	61	9	1	15	46	18	40	.264	.323	.506	.829	124	5	6	96	109	34	.768	2	2	-1	-1	1CD/O	0.4
1980	Det-A	126	372	56	102	13	2	16	65	68	64	.274	.391	.449	.839	123	17	14	105	118	68	.851	1	4	-2	1	1DCO	1.1
1981	Det-A	70	172	20	37	4	0	9	25	28	22	.215	.325	.395	.720	101	2	1	105	103	23	.686	0	0	0	-1	D1/CO	0.0
1982	Det-A	70	193	28	58	9	0	8	32	29	21	.301	.392	.472	.863	135	10	10	100	111	37	.870	0	0	0	1	C1DO/3	1.1
1983	Det-A	92	245	32	66	8	1	9	44	31	37	.269	.351	.420	.772	116	4	6	96	132	37	.730	1	1	-0	1	DC1/3O	0.7
1984	Phi-N	86	180	20	52	3	1	6	24	30	24	.289	.390	.417	.807	125	7	7	102	101	31	.803	1	0	0	-1	1C/3	0.6
1985	Phi-N	32	37	1	6	0	0	0	2	8	7	.162	.311	.162	.473	35	-3	-3	102	133	2	.412	0	0	0	0	/1C	-0.2
Total	12	795	2072	267	543	73	11	86	310	277	278	.262	.351	.432	.783	114	49	42	102	105	316	.768	5	11	-5	-2	C1DO/3	3.8
■ **ANDY WOEHR** Woehr, Andrew Emil b: 2/4/1896, Fort Wayne, Ind. BR/TR, 5'11", 165 lbs. Deb: 9/15/23																												
1923	Phi-N	13	41	3	14	2	0	0	3	1	1	.341	.357	.390	.747	85	-0	-1	114	66	6	.630	0	0	0	-0	3	0.0
1924	Phi-N	50	152	11	33	4	5	0	17	5	8	.217	.252	.309	.561	46	-11	-13	108	132	12	.463	2	2	-1	-3	3/2	-1.2
Total	2	63	193	14	47	6	5	0	20	6	9	.244	.274	.326	.600	55	-11	-14	109	118	17	.493	2	2	-1	-3	/32	-1.2
■ **JOE WOERLIN** Woerlin, Joseph b: 10/9/1864, France d: 6/22/19, St.Louis, Mo. Deb: 7/21/1895																												
1895	Was-N	1	3	1	1	0	0	0	0	0	0	.333	.333	.333	.667	72	-0	-0	103	0	0	.500	0			0	/S	0.0
■ **JIM WOHLFORD** Wohlford, James Eugene b: 2/28/51, Visalia, Cal. BR/TR, 5'11", 175 lbs. Deb: 9/01/72																												
1972	KC-A	15	25	3	6	1	0	0	0	2	6	.240	.321	.280	.601	80	-1	-1	100	0	3	.526	0	0	0	0	/2	0.0
1973	KC-A	45	109	21	29	1	3	2	10	11	12	.266	.333	.385	.719	93	0	-1	109	82	14	.651	1	1	-0	2	DO	0.1
1974	KC-A	143	501	55	136	16	7	2	44	39	74	.271	.328	.343	.671	88	-4	-8	106	97	55	.593	16	13	-3	-3	*O/D	-1.7
1975	KC-A	116	353	45	90	10	5	0	30	34	37	.255	.322	.312	.634	78	-9	-10	102	105	38	.575	12	7	-1	-6	*O/D	-1.8
1976	KC-A	107	293	47	73	10	2	1	24	29	24	.249	.319	.307	.626	84	-5	-5	100	99	27	.582	22	16	-3	-3	O/2D	-1.3
1977	Mil-A	129	391	41	97	16	3	2	36	21	49	.248	.288	.320	.608	69	-19	-16	95	109	32	.514	17	16	-5	-2	*O/2D	-2.7
1978	Mil-A	46	118	16	35	7	2	1	19	6	10	.297	.331	.415	.746	103	1	0	106	144	16	.667	3	2	-0	-5	O/D	-0.5
1979	Mil-A	63	175	19	46	13	1	1	17	8	28	.263	.295	.366	.661	77	-6	-6	100	97	19	.582	6	2	1	-2	O/D	-0.9
1980	SF-N	91	193	17	54	6	4	1	24	13	23	.280	.329	.368	.696	98	-2	-1	96	128	22	.589	1	4	-2	-2	O/3	-0.6
1981	SF-N	50	68	4	11	3	0	1	7	4	9	.162	.208	.250	.458	28	-6	-7	105	137	3	.339	0	0	0	-3	O	-1.0
1982	SF-N	97	250	37	64	12	1	2	25	30	36	.256	.336	.336	.672	94	-3	-1	94	109	28	.616	8	3	1	-3	O	-0.4
1983	Mon-N	83	141	7	39	8	0	1	14	5	14	.277	.301	.355	.656	80	-4	-4	102	104	14	.519	0	0	0	-8	O	-1.3
1984	Mon-N	95	213	20	64	13	2	5	29	14	19	.300	.344	.451	.794	133	5	8	91	102	34	.753	3	0	1	-5	O/3	0.1
1985	Mon-N	70	125	7	24	5	1	1	15	16	18	.192	.284	.272	.556	60	-7	-6	94	161	10	.481	0	2	-1	-5	O	-1.4
1986	Mon-N	70	94	10	25	4	2	1	11	9	17	.266	.330	.383	.713	98	-1	-0	98	112	11	.616	0	2	-1	-3	O/3	-0.5
Total	15	1220	3049	349	793	125	33	21	305	241	376	.260	.316	.343	.659	86	-59	-58	100	108	325	.595	89	68	-14	-48	O/D23	-13.9
■ **JOHN WOJCIK** Wojcik, John Joseph b: 4/6/42, Olean, N.Y. BL/TR, 6' ", 175 lbs. Deb: 9/09/62																												
1962	KC-A	16	43	8	13	4	0	0	9	13	4	.302	.474	.395	.869	137	3	3	100	210	11	1.133	3	0	1	0	O	0.4
1963	KC-A	19	59	7	11	0	0	0	2	8	8	.186	.284	.186	.470	32	-5	-5	108	76	4	.438	2	0	1	0	O	-0.4
1964	KC-A	6	22	1	3	0	0	0	0	2	8	.136	.208	.136	.345	-2	-3	-3	105	0	1	.263	0	0	0	-0	/O	-0.3
Total	3	41	124	16	27	4	0	0	11	23	20	.218	.345	.250	.595	64	-4	-5	104	115	15	.619	5	0	2	0	/O	-0.3
■ **RAY WOLF** Wolf, Raymond Bernard "Grandpa" b: 7/15/04, Chicago, Ill. d: 10/6/79, Fort Worth, Tex. BR/TR, 5'11", 175 lbs. Deb: 7/27/27																												
1927	Cin-N	1	1	0	0	0	0	0	0	0	0	.000	.000	.000	.000	-99	-0	-0	100	0	0	.000	0			0	/1	0.0
■ **CHICKEN WOLF** Wolf, William Van Winkle b: 5/12/1862, Louisville, Ky. d: 5/16/03, Louisville, Ky. BR, 5'9", 190 lbs. Deb: 5/02/1882 M																												
1882	Lou-a	78	318	46	95	11	8	0		9		.299	.318	.384	.702	145	11	14	94	0	40	.587				2	*O/S1P	1.3
1883	Lou-a	98	389	59	102	17	9	1		5		.262	.272	.360	.631	108	0	4	94	0	39	.505				15	*OC/S2	1.7
1884	Lou-a	110	486	79	146	24	11	3		4		.300	.310	.414	.724	154	18	26	89	0	64	.612				1	*OC/S31	2.3
1885	Lou-a	112	483	79	141	23	17	1		11		.292	.309	.416	.725	127	15	13	102	0	64	.623				-4	*O/C3P	0.3
1886	Lou-a	130	545	93	148	17	12	3		27		.272	.310	.363	.673	104	6	-0	108	0	70	.632	23			10	*O/1C2P	0.5
1887	Lou-a	137	569	103	160	28	13	1		34		.281	.331	.381	.712	94	-0	-7	107	0	89	.743	45			9	*O1	-0.1
1888	Lou-a	128	538	80	154	28	11	0	67	25		.286	.320	.379	.700	140	15	22	91	94	80	.708	41			3	OS/3C1	2.1
1889	Lou-a	130	546	72	159	20	9	3	57	29	34	.291	.333	.377	.710	109	2	6	96	67	76	.667	18			5	O12S/3M	0.6
1890	Lou-a	134	543	100	**197**	29	11	4		43		**.363**	.419	.479	.898	157	45	38	107	0	132	1.038	46			-3	*O3	2.6
1891	Lou-a	138	537	67	136	17	8	1	82	42	36	.253	.317	.320	.637	94	-10	-2	90	144	60	.586	13			1	*O/13	-0.5
1892	StL-N	3	14	1	2	0	0	0	1	0	1	.143	.143	.143	.286	-13	-2	-2	95	132	0	.167	0			0	/O	-0.1
Total	11	1198	4968	779	1440	214	109	17	207	229	71	.290	.326	.387	.713	121	99	111	98	34	714	.674	186			39	*O/S1C32P	10.7
■ **HARRY WOLFE** Wolfe, Harold "Whitey" b: 11/24/1890, Massachusetts d: 7/28/71, Fort Wayne, Ind. BR/TR, 5'8", 160 lbs. Deb: 4/15/17																												
1917	Chi-N	9	5	1	2	0	0	0	1	1	1	.400	.500	.400	.900	170	1	1	105	193	1	1.000	0			-1	/OS	0.0
	Pit-N	3	5	0	0	0	0	0	0	1	4	.000	.167	.000	.167	-47	-1	-1	100	0	0	.200	0			-0	/2S	0.0
	Yr	12	10	1	2	0	0	0	1	2	5	.200	.333	.200	.533	63	-0	-0	103	161	1	.500	0			-1		0.0
Total	1	12	10	1	2	0	0	0	1	2	5	.200	.333	.200	.533	64	-0	-0	102	96	1	.500	0			-1	/SO2	0.0
■ **LARRY WOLFE** Wolfe, Laurence Marcy b: 3/2/53, Melbourne, Fla. BR/TR, 5'11", 170 lbs. Deb: 9/16/77																												
1977	Min-A	8	25	3	6	1	0	0	6	1	0	.240	.269	.280	.549	49	-2	-2	103	340	2	.421	0	0	0	1	/3	0.0

YEAR	TM/L	G	AB	R	H	2B	3B	HR	RBI	BB	SO	AVG	OBP	SLG	PRO	/A	BR	/A	PF	CHI	RC	TA	SB	CS	SBR	FR	POS	TPR
1978	Min-A	88	235	25	55	10	1	3	25	36	27	.234	.336	.323	.659	91	-3	-2	94	116	26	.593	0	1	-1	4	3/S	0.1
1979	Bos-A	47	78	12	19	4	0	3	15	17	21	.244	.385	.410	.796	107	2	1	107	141	14	.833	0	0	0	-1	2/3SC1	0.1
1980	Bos-A	18	23	3	3	1	0	1	4	0	5	.130	.130	.304	.435	15	-3	-3	102	156	1	.333	0	0	0	-0	3/D	-0.2
Total	4	161	361	43	83	16	1	7	50	54	53	.230	.332	.338	.670	88	-6	-5	98	138	43	.632	0	1	-1	3	3/2SD1C	0.0
■ **POLLY WOLFE**	Wolfe, Roy Chamberlain b: 9/1/1888, Knoxville, Ill. d: 11/21/38, Morris, Ill. BL/TR, 5'10", 170 lbs. Deb: 9/22/12																											
1912	Chi-A	1	1	0	0	0	0	0	0	0		.000	.000	.000	.000	-99	-0	-0	99	0	0	.000	0			0	H	0.0
1914	Chi-A	8	28	0	6	0	0	0	0	3	6	.214	.290	.214	.505	50	-2	-2	103	0	2	.435	1	1	-0	-2	/O	-0.4
Total	2	9	29	0	6	0	0	0	0	3	6	.207	.281	.207	.488	45	-2	-2	103	0	2	.417	1	1		-2	/O	-0.4
■ **ABE WOLSTENHOLME**	Wolstenholme, Abraham Lincoln b: 3/4/1861, Philadelphia, Pa. d: 3/4/16, Philadelphia, Pa. Deb: 6/04/1883																											
1883	Phi-N	3	11	0	1	1	0	0	0	0	0	.091	.091	.182	.273	-22	-2	-1	90	0	0	.200				0	/CO	0.0
■ **HARRY WOLTER**	Wolter, Harry Meigs b: 7/11/1884, Monterey, Cal. d: 7/7/70, Palo Alto, Cal. BL/TL, 5'10", 175 lbs. Deb: 5/14/07																											
1907	Cin-N	4	15	1	2	0	0	0	1	0		.133	.133	.133	.267	-16	-2	-2	95	201	0	.154	0			0	/O	-0.1
	Pit-N	1	1	0	0	0	0	0	0	0		.000	.000	.000	.000	-95	-0	-0	105	0	0	.000	0			0	/P	0.0
	StL-N	16	47	4	16	0	0	0	6	3		.340	.380	.340	.720	134	2	2	96	142	7	.645	1			-2	O/P	0.0
	Yr	21	63	5	18	0	0	0	7	3		.286	.318	.286	.604	95	-1	-0	96	156	6	.489	1			-1		-0.1
1909	Bos-A	54	122	14	30	2	4	2	10	9		.246	.298	.377	.675	103	1	0	109	74	14	.620	2			-2	1P/O	-0.1
1910	NY-A	135	479	84	128	15	9	4	42	66		.267	.364	.361	.725	118	17	13	107	81	78	.812	39			-6	*O/1	0.1
1911	NY-A	122	434	78	132	17	15	4	36	62		.304	.396	.440	.836	120	21	14	111	64	86	.944	28			2	*O/1	0.7
1912	NY-A	12	32	8	11	2	1	0	1	10		.344	.512	.469	.980	178	4	4	101	22	10	1.476	5			-1	/O	0.2
1913	NY-A	127	425	53	108	18	6	2	43	80	50	.254	.377	.339	.716	109	9	9	101	108	58	.760	13			-12	*O	-1.0
1917	Chi-N	117	353	44	88	15	7	0	28	38	40	.249	.324	.331	.655	97	1	-1	105	92	39	.615	7			-8	O/1	-1.2
Total	7	588	1908	286	515	69	42	12	167	268	90	.270	.365	.369	.734	113	53	39	106	86	292	.778	95			-28	O/1P	-1.4
■ **HARRY WOLVERTON**	Wolverton, Harry Sterling "Fighting Harry" b: 12/6/1873, Mt.Vernon, Ohio d: 2/4/37, Oakland, Cal. BL/TR, 5'11", 205 lbs. Deb: 9/25/1898 M																											
1898	Chi-N	13	49	4	16	1	0	0	2	1		.327	.353	.347	.700	100	0	-0	103	36	7	.606	1			0	3	0.0
1899	Chi-N	99	389	50	111	14	11	1	49	30		.285	.350	.386	.736	108	3	5	96	87	59	.730	14			-6	3/S	-0.1
1900	Chi-N	3	11	2	2	0	0	0	0	2		.182	.308	.182	.490	42	-1	-1	93	0	1	.556	1			-1	/3	-0.1
	Phi-N	101	383	42	108	10	8	3	58	20		.282	.318	.373	.691	94	-5	-3	98	122	48	.607	4			-12	*3	-1.2
	Yr	104	394	44	110	10	8	3	58	22		.279	.317	.368	.685	93	-5	-4	98	118	49	.606	5			-13		-1.3
1901	Phi-N	93	379	42	117	15	4	0	43	22		.309	.347	.369	.716	107	5	3	103	99	54	.668	13			1	3	1.0
1902	Was-A	59	249	35	62	8	3	1	23	13		.249	.286	.317	.604	70	-11	-10	99	80	26	.535	8			2	3	-0.9
	Phi-N	34	136	12	40	3	2	0	16	9		.294	.338	.346	.684	107	2	1	105	104	17	.615	3			0	3	0.3
1903	Phi-N	123	494	72	152	13	12	0	53	18		.308	.332	.383	.715	114	2	7	92	96	68	.635	10			-4	*3	0.4
1904	Phi-N	102	398	43	106	15	5	0	49	26		.266	.311	.329	.640	108	-0	3	93	121	48	.599	18			-10	*3	-0.2
1905	Bos-N	122	463	38	104	15	7	2	55	23		.225	.261	.300	.562	71	-18	-16	97	140	40	.479	10			-0	*3	-0.8
1912	NY-A	33	50	6	15	1	1	0	4	2		.300	.340	.360	.700	99	-0	-0	101	74	6	.629	1			-1	/3M	0.0
Total	9	782	3001	346	833	95	53	7	352	166		.278	.318	.352	.669	98	-23	-11	97	106	373	.607	83			-31	3/S	-1.6
■ **SID WOMACK**	Womack, Sidney Kirk "Tex" b: 10/2/1896, Greensburg, La. d: 8/28/58, Jackson, Miss. BR/TR, 5'10.5", 185 lbs. Deb: 8/15/26																											
1926	Bos-N	1	3	0	0	0	0	0	1	0	0	.000	.000	.000	.000	-99	-1	-1	86	0	0	.000	0			0	/C	0.0
■ **WOOD**	Wood Deb:9/30/1874																											
1874	Bal-n	1	6	0	0							.000															/2	
■ **DOC WOOD**	Wood, Charles Spencer b: 2/28/1900, Batesville, Miss. d: 11/3/74, New Orleans, La. BR/TR, 5'10", 150 lbs. Deb: 7/21/23																											
1923	Phi-A	3	3	0	1	0	0	0	0	0	2	.333	.333	.333	.667	75	-0	-0	100	0	0	.500	0	0	0	-0	/S	0.0
■ **FRED WOOD**	Wood, Fred S. b: 1863, Hamilton, Ont., Canada d: 8/23/33, New York, N.Y. 5'5", 160 lbs. Deb: 5/14/1884																											
1884	Det-N	12	42	4	2	0	0	0	1	3	18	.048	.111	.048	.159	-52	-7	-7	94	175	0	.125				0	/COS	-0.5
1885	Buf-N	1	4	0	1	0	0	0	0	0	0	.250	.250	.250	.500	63	-0	-0	99	0	0	.333				0	/C	0.0
Total	2	13	46	4	3	0	0	0	1	3	18	.065	.122	.065	.188	-42	-7	-7	94	161	0	.140				0	/COS	-0.5
■ **GEORGE WOOD**	Wood, George A. "Dandy" b: 11/9/1858, Boston, Mass. d: 4/4/24, Harrisburg, Pa. BL/TR, 5'10.5", 175 lbs. Deb: 5/01/1880 M																											
1880	Wor-N	81	327	37	80	16	5	0	28	10	37	.245	.267	.324	.591	88	-0	-6	113	102	29	.470				-8	*O/31	-1.5
1881	Det-N	80	337	54	100	18	9	2	32	19	32	.297	.334	.421	.756	127	14	10	106	66	49	.679				-3	*O	0.6
1882	Det-N	84	375	69	101	12	12	**7**	29	14	30	.269	.296	.421	.717	125	11	10	102	47	48	.628				2	*O	0.9
1883	Det-N	99	441	81	133	26	11	5	47	25	37	.302	.339	.444	.784	149	19	25	91	67	68	.718				8	*O/P	3.0
1884	Det-N	114	473	79	119	16	10	8	29	39	75	.252	.309	.378	.687	123	8	13	94	42	57	.616				4	*O/3	1.4
1885	Det-N	82	362	62	105	19	8	5	28	13	19	.290	.315	.428	.743	142	14	15	97	49	50	.654				1	O3/SP	1.3
1886	Phi-N	106	450	81	123	18	15	4	50	23	75	.273	.309	.407	.715	118	8	9	98	72	61	.657	9			-4	*O/S3	0.6
1887	Phi-N	113	491	118	142	22	19	14	66	40	51	.289	.350	.497	.847	139	22	25	97	61	94	.885	19			-8	*O/S32	1.4
1888	Phi-N	106	433	67	99	19	6	6	15	39	44	.229	.303	.342	.645	94	5	-4	114	28	52	.641	20			3	*O/3P	-0.1
1889	Phi-N	97	422	77	106	21	4	5	53	53	33	.251	.336	.355	.692	91	-2	-5	104	83	58	.699	17			-3	O/SP	-0.9
	Bal-a	3	10	1	2	0	0	0	1	0	2	.200	.200	.200	.400	15	-1	-1	100	143	1	.375	1			0	/O	0.0
1890	Phi-P	132	539	115	156	20	14	9	102	51	35	.289	.360	.429	.788	109	8	6	102	115	92	.809	20			15	*O/3	1.2
1891	Phi-a	132	528	105	163	18	14	3	61	72	52	.309	.399	.413	.812	132	26	23	103	69	98	.874	22			9	*O/3SM	2.3
1892	Bal-N	21	76	9	17	1	1	0	10	10	8	.224	.330	.263	.593	82	-1	-1	100	163	7	.559	1			0	O	0.0
	Cin-N	30	107	10	21	2	4	0	14	10	17	.196	.271	.290	.561	69	-4	-4	103	141	10	.535	4			0	O	-0.3
	Yr	51	183	19	38	3	5	0	24	20	25	.208	.296	.279	.575	74	-5	-5	102	153	17	.545	5			0		-0.3
Total	13	1280	5371	965	1467	228	132	68	565	418	547	.273	.329	.403	.732	118	125	116	101	70	773	.698	113			14	*O/3SP21	9.9
■ **HARRY WOOD**	Wood, Harold Austin b: 2/10/1881, Waterville, Maine d: 5/18/55, Bethesda, Md. BL/TR, 5'10", 155 lbs. Deb: 4/19/03																											
1903	Cin-N	2	3	0	0	0	0	0	0	1		.000	.250	.000	.250	-23	-0	-0	109	0	0	.333	0			0	/O	0.0
■ **JOE WOOD**	Wood, Howard Ellsworth "Smokey Joe" b: 10/25/1889, Kansas City, Mo. d: 7/27/85, West Haven, Conn BR/TR, 5'11", 180 lbs. Deb: 8/24/08																											
1908	Bos-A	6	7	1	0	0	0	0	0	0		.000	.000	.000	.000	-99	-1	-1	98	0	0	.000	0			-0	/P	0.0
1909	Bos-A	24	55	4	9	0	1	0	3	2		.164	.207	.200	.407	26	-4	-5	109	105	2	.304	0			-4	P	0.0
1910	Bos-A	35	69	9	18	2	1	1	5	5		.261	.311	.362	.673	112	1	1	99	66	8	.588	0			2	P	0.0
1911	Bos-A	44	88	15	23	4	2	2	11	10		.261	.343	.420	.764	114	1	1	99	86	13	.754	1			2	P	0.0
1912	Bos-A	43	124	17	36	13	1	1	13	11		.290	.348	.435	.784	116	3	2	107	76	19	.739	0			8	P	0.0
1913	Bos-A	24	56	10	15	5	0	0	10	4	7	.268	.317	.357	.674	94	-0	-1	103	0	6	.610	1			0	P	0.0
1914	Bos-A	20	43	2	6	1	0	0	1	3	14	.140	.213	.163	.376	13	-5	-4	98	54	2	.324	1			0	P	0.0
1915	Bos-A	29	54	6	14	1	1	1	7	5	10	.259	.322	.370	.692	108	0	0	99	104	7	.634	1	1	-0	1	P	0.0
1917	Cle-A	10	6	1	0	0	0	0	0	0	3	.000	.000	.000	.000	-87	-1	-2	114	0	0	.000	0			0	/P	0.0
1918	Cle-A	119	422	41	125	22	4	5	66	36	38	.296	.356	.403	.759	119	14	10	108	133	63	.731	8			-3	O2/1	0.3
1919	Cle-A	72	192	30	49	10	5	1	27	32	21	.255	.367	.375	.742	102	3	1	107	131	28	.762	3			-10	O/P	-1.3
1920	Cle-A	61	137	25	37	11	2	1	30	25	16	.270	.390	.401	.792	106	3	2	104	182	24	.822	1	1	-0	-9	O/P	-1.1
1921	Cle-A	66	194	32	71	16	5	4	60	25	17	.366	.438	.562	1.000	155	16	16	99	170	49	1.106	2	0	1	-9	O	0.2
1922	Cle-A	142	505	74	150	33	8	8	92	50	63	.297	.367	.442	.809	108	7	6	102	136	85	.798	5	1	1	-3	*O	-0.6
Total	14	695	1952	267	553	118	30	24	325	208	189	.283	.357	.411	.768	110	36	27	104	125	305	.749	23	3		-26	OP/21	-2.5
■ **JAKE WOOD**	Wood, Jacob b: 6/22/37, Elizabeth, N.J. BR/TR, 6'1", 163 lbs. Deb: 4/11/61																											
1961	Det-A	162	663	96	171	17	**14**	11	69	58	141	.258	.321	.376	.697	89	-14	-10	96	92	84	.670	30	9	4	-24	*2	-1.0
1962	Det-A	111	367	68	83	10	5	8	30	33	59	.226	.292	.346	.638	64	-15	-21	111	79	40	.634	24	3	**5**	-21	2	-3.0
1963	Det-A	85	351	50	95	11	2	11	27	24	61	.271	.330	.407	.737	102	2	1	104	57	50	.730	18	5	2	-2	2/3	0.8
1964	Det-A	64	125	11	29	2	2	1	7	4	24	.232	.256	.304	.560	58	-8	-7	96	72	10	.438	0	0	0	-1	12/3O	-0.7
1965	Det-A	58	104	12	30	3	0	2	7	10	19	.288	.357	.375	.732	102	1	1	105	65	12	.631	3	3	-1	-2	2/1S3	0.0

YEAR	TM/L	G	AB	R	H	2B	3B	HR	RBI	BB	SO	AVG	OBP	SLG	PRO	/A	BR	/A	PF	CHI	RC	TA	SB	CS	SBR	FR	POS	TPR
1966	Det-A	98	230	39	58	9	3	2	27	28	48	.252	.336	.343	.679	94	-1	-1	102	133	27	.615	4	3	-1	-2	2/31	0.0
1967	Det-A	14	20	2	1	1	0	0	0	1	7	.050	.095	.100	.195	-43	-4	-4	99	0	0	.150	0	0	0	0	/12	-0.3
	Cin-N	16	17	1	2	0	0	0	1	1	3	.118	.167	.118	.284	-16	-3	-3	109	207	0	.200	0	0	0	-0	/O	-0.2
Total	7	608	1877	279	469	53	26	35	168	159	362	.250	.313	.362	.675	83	-40	-44	102	85	223	.651	79	23	10	-51	2/13OS	-4.4
■ JIMMY WOOD	Wood, James Leon b: 12/1/1844, Brooklyn, N.Y. d: 11/30/1886, 5'8.5", 150 lbs. Deb: 5/08/1871 M																											
1871	Chi-n	28	145	44	51							.352															*2M	
1872	Tro-n	25	118	40	38							.322															2M	
	Eck-n	7	34	9	6							.176															2M	
	Yr	32	152	49	44							.289																
1873	Phi-n	42	224	67	66							.295															*2M	
Total	3 n	102	521	160	161							.309															*2M	
■ JOE WOOD	Wood, Joseph Perry "Joe", "J.P." or "Little Joe" b: 10/3/19, Houston, Tex. d: 3/25/85, Houston, Tex. BR/TR, 5'9.5", 160 lbs. Deb: 5/02/43																											
1943	Det-A	60	164	22	53	4	4	1	17	6	13	.323	.347	.415	.762	116	4	3	106	87	21	.633	2	2	-1	-1	23	0.3
■ KEN WOOD	Wood, Kenneth Lanier b: 7/1/24, Lincolnton, N.C. BR/TR, 6', 200 lbs. Deb: 4/28/48																											
1948	StL-A	10	24	2	2	0	1	0	2	1	4	.083	.120	.167	.287	-23	-4	-5	106	169	0	.208	0	0	0	0	/O	-0.3
1949	StL-A	7	6	0	0	0	0	0	0	1	2	.000	.143	.000	.143	-61	-1	-1	100	0	0	.167	0	0	0	-1	/O	-0.2
1950	StL-A	128	369	42	83	24	0	13	62	38	58	.225	.299	.396	.695	72	-15	-19	107	116	40	.605	0	4	-2	-6	O	-2.6
1951	StL-A	109	333	40	79	19	0	15	44	27	49	.237	.296	.429	.726	90	-5	-7	105	84	40	.644	1	2	-1	-6	*O	-1.7
1952	Bos-A	15	20	0	2	0	0	0	0	3	4	.100	.217	.100	.317	-9	-3	-3	107	0	1	.278	0	0	0	-5	O	-0.8
	Was-A	61	210	26	50	8	6	6	32	30	21	.238	.333	.419	.752	108	2	2	100	115	30	.707	0	1	-1	8	O	0.8
	Yr	76	230	26	52	8	6	6	32	33	25	.226	.323	.391	.714	97	-1	-1	101	92	30	.665	0	1	-1	4		0.0
1953	Was-A	12	33	0	7	1	0	0	3	2	3	.212	.257	.242	.500	38	-3	-3	94	139	2	.370	0	0	0	0	/O	-0.2
Total	6	342	995	110	223	52	7	34	143	102	141	.224	.298	.393	.691	79	-30	-36	104	104	113	.636	1	7	-4	-9	O	-5.0
■ BOB WOOD	Wood, Robert Lynn b: 7/28/1865, Thorn Hill, Ohio d: 5/22/43, Churchill, Ohio BR/TR, Deb: 5/02/1898																											
1898	Cin-N	39	109	14	30	6	0	0	16	9		.275	.331	.330	.661	85	-1	-2	108	134	13	.582	1			0	C/O1	-0.1
1899	Cin-N	62	194	34	61	11	7	0	24	25		.314	.398	.443	.841	126	9	8	106	86	36	.872	3			-12	C/O31	0.0
1900	Cin-N	45	139	17	37	8	1	0	22	10		.266	.315	.338	.654	90	-3	-2	92	146	16	.588	3			0	C3/O	0.0
1901	Cle-A	98	346	45	101	23	3	1	49	12		.292	.316	.384	.700	101	-3	-0	95	114	45	.616	6			6	C/3O12S	1.2
1902	Cle-A	81	258	23	76	18	2	0	40	27		.295	.361	.380	.741	111	3	4	97	135	37	.692	1			-2	C1/O23	0.7
1904	Det-A	49	175	15	43	6	2	1	17	5		.246	.267	.320	.587	91	-3	-2	96	110	16	.470	1			2	C	0.5
1905	Det-A	8	24	1	2	1	0	0	0	1		.083	.120	.125	.245	-22	-3	-3	98	0	0	.182	0			0	/C	-0.2
Total	7	382	1245	149	350	73	15	2	168	89		.281	.330	.369	.699	102	-0	3	98	116	163	.631	15			-5	C/31O2S	2.1
■ ROY WOOD	Wood, Roy Winton "Woody" b: 8/29/1892, Monticello, Ark. d: 4/6/74, Fayetteville, Ark. BR/TR, 6', 175 lbs. Deb: 6/16/13																											
1913	Pit-N	14	35	4	10	4	0	0	2	1	8	.286	.306	.400	.706	105	-0	0	96	52	4	.600	0			2	/O1	0.1
1914	Cle-A	72	220	24	52	6	3	1	15	13	26	.236	.300	.305	.605	80	-5	-6	102	80	19	.525	6	9	-4	-2	O1	-1.4
1915	Cle-A	33	78	5	15	2	1	0	3	2	13	.192	.232	.244	.475	41	-6	-6	104	54	4	.369	1	2	-1	-1	1/O	-0.9
Total	3	119	333	33	77	12	4	1	20	16	47	.231	.285	.300	.585	73	-11	-12	102	71	27	.494	7	11		-1	/O1	-2.2
■ LARRY WOODALL	Woodall, Charles Lawrence b: 7/26/1894, Staunton, Va. d: 5/16/63, Cambridge, Mass. BR/TR, 5'9", 165 lbs. Deb: 5/20/20 C																											
1920	Det-A	18	49	4	12	1	0	0	5	2	6	.245	.275	.265	.540	42	-4	-4	103	135	4	.405	0	0	0	-1	C	-0.3
1921	Det-A	46	80	10	29	4	1	0	14	6	7	.363	.407	.438	.844	120	2	3	96	137	15	.824	1	0	0	-1	C	0.3
1922	Det-A	50	125	19	43	2	2	0	18	8	11	.344	.388	.392	.780	106	1	1	98	131	19	.699	0	1	-1	-2	C	0.0
1923	Det-A	71	148	20	41	12	2	1	19	22	9	.277	.371	.405	.776	108	1	2	97	103	24	.778	2	1	0	0	C	0.6
1924	Det-A	67	165	23	51	9	2	0	24	21	5	.309	.387	.388	.775	101	1	1	100	124	26	.746	0	0	0	-2	C	0.2
1925	Det-A	75	171	20	35	4	1	0	13	24	8	.205	.303	.240	.542	39	-16	-15	99	106	14	.485	1	0	0	-5	C	-1.3
1926	Det-A	67	146	18	34	5	0	0	15	15	2	.233	.304	.267	.571	51	-11	-10	97	131	13	.482	0	0	0	-2	C	-0.7
1927	Det-A	88	246	28	69	8	6	0	39	37	9	.280	.375	.362	.736	85	-2	-5	108	146	35	.763	9	0	3	1	C	0.0
1928	Det-A	65	186	19	39	7	1	0	13	24	10	.210	.300	.258	.558	48	-14	-13	99	93	16	.507	3	1	0	-1	C	-0.8
1929	Det-A	1	1	0	0	0	0	0	0	0	0	.000	.000	.000	.000	-99	-0	-0	97	0	0	.000	0	0	0	0	H	0.0
Total	10	548	1317	161	353	52	15	1	160	159	67	.268	.347	.333	.680	77	-41	-41	100	121	165	.635	16	3	3	-13	C	-2.0
■ DARRELL WOODARD	Woodard, Darrell Lee b: 12/10/56, Wilma, Ark. BR/TR, 5'11", 160 lbs. Deb: 8/06/78																											
1978	Oak-A	33	9	10	0	0	0	0	0	1	1	.000	.100	.000	.100	-69	-2	-2	101	0	-1	.308	3	4	-2	-1	2/3D	-0.3
■ MIKE WOODARD	Woodard, Michael Cary b: 3/2/60, Melrose Park, Ill. BL/TR, 5'9", 155 lbs. Deb: 9/11/85																											
1985	SF-N	24	82	12	20	1	0	0	9	5	3	.244	.287	.256	.543	57	-5	-4	93	171	7	.508	6	1	1	-0	2	-0.3
1986	SF-N	48	79	14	20	2	1	1	5	10	9	.253	.337	.342	.679	91	-1	-1	96	66	11	.721	7	2	1	0	2/S3	0.1
1987	SF-N	10	19	0	4	1	0	0	1	0	1	.211	.211	.263	.474	26	-2	-2	96	80	1	.333	0	0	0	0	/2	-0.1
1988	Chi-A	18	45	3	6	0	1	0	4	1	5	.133	.170	.178	.348	-3	-6	-6	97	199	1	.268	1	1	-0	0	2/D	-0.5
Total	4	100	225	29	50	4	2	1	19	16	18	.222	.277	.271	.548	55	-14	-13	95	131	20	.511	14	4	2	-0	/2D3S	-0.8
■ RED WOODHEAD	Woodhead, James b: 7/1851, Chelsea, Mass. d: 9/7/1881, Boston, Mass. 5'6", 160 lbs. Deb: 4/15/1873																											
1873	Mar-n	1	5	1	0							.000															/S	
1879	Syr-N	34	131	4	21	1	0	0	2	0	23	.160	.160	.168	.328	9	-12	-10	89	32	4	.200				-9	3	-1.6
■ GENE WOODLING	Woodling, Eugene Richard b: 8/16/22, Akron, Ohio BL/TR, 5'9.5", 195 lbs. Deb: 9/23/43 C																											
1943	Cle-A	8	25	5	8	2	1	1	5	1	5	.320	.346	.600	.946	194	2	2	90	101	5	.941	0	0	0	-1	/O	0.1
1946	Cle-A	61	133	8	25	1	4	0	9	16	13	.188	.280	.256	.536	57	-9	-7	89	101	11	.468	1	2	-1	-1	O	-1.0
1947	Pit-N	22	79	7	21	2	2	0	10	7	5	.266	.326	.342	.667	77	-3	-3	101	140	9	.576	0			2	O	0.0
1949	NY-A	112	296	60	80	13	7	5	44	52	21	.270	.381	.412	.793	109	5	5	100	110	50	.790	2	2	-1	-11	O	-0.8
1950	NY-A	122	449	81	127	20	10	6	60	70	31	.283	.381	.412	.793	104	3	3	99	104	75	.779	5	3	-0	11	*O	1.1
1951	NY-A	120	420	65	118	15	8	15	71	62	37	.281	.373	.462	.835	136	15	19	92	108	75	.815	0	4	-2	5	*O	1.7
1952	NY-A	122	408	58	126	19	6	12	63	59	31	.309	.397	.473	.870	145	24	25	98	103	81	.873	1	4	-2	7	*O	2.7
1953	NY-A	125	395	64	121	26	4	10	58	82	29	.306	**.429**	.468	.898	153	27	31	93	100	82	.922	2	7	-4	-1	*O	2.3
1954	NY-A	97	304	33	76	12	5	3	40	53	35	.250	.361	.352	.713	97	-0	0	99	131	42	.694	3	4	-2	-5	O	-0.8
1955	Bal-A	47	145	22	32	6	2	3	18	24	18	.221	.335	.352	.687	95	-3	-1	90	112	18	.664	1	1	-0	-4	O	-0.7
	Cle-A	79	259	33	72	15	1	5	35	36	15	.278	.372	.402	.774	104	4	2	104	110	38	.729	2	4	-2	-1	O	-0.4
	Yr	126	404	55	104	21	3	8	53	60	33	.257	.359	.384	.743	101	1	2	99	111	58	.709	3	5	-2	-5		-1.1
1956	Cle-A	100	317	56	83	17	0	8	38	69	29	.262	.398	.391	.790	108	7	6	101	98	53	.805	2	6	-3	-4	O	-0.3
1957	Cle-A	133	430	74	138	25	2	19	78	64	35	.321	.412	.521	.933	151	33	32	102	110	94	.960	0	5	-3	5	*O	2.8
1958	Bal-A	133	413	57	114	16	1	15	65	66	49	.276	.378	.429	.807	129	14	17	94	117	68	.790	4	2	0	-8	*O	0.2
1959	Bal-A	140	440	63	132	22	2	14	77	78	35	.300	.405	.455	.860	140	24	26	97	125	87	.889	1	1	-0	-10	*O	1.0
1960	Bal-A	140	435	68	123	18	3	11	62	84	40	.283	.403	.414	.817	119	17	16	102	114	80	.855	3	0	1	-5	*O	0.7
1961	Was-A	110	342	39	107	16	4	10	57	50	24	.313	.404	.471	.874	140	17	20	95	117	66	.873	1	0	0	-3	O	1.3
1962	Was-A	44	107	19	30	4	0	5	16	24	5	.280	.421	.458	.879	135	7	7	101	99	23	.974	1	0	0	-5	O	0.1
	NY-N	81	190	18	52	8	1	5	24	24	22	.274	.358	.405	.763	101	2	1	104	103	28	.713	0	0	0	-6	O	-0.7
Total	17	1796	5587	830	1585	257	63	147	830	921	479	.284	.388	.431	.819	123	185	203	98	111	986	.836	29	45	1	-34	*O	9.3
■ SAM WOODRUFF	Woodruff, Orville Francis b: 12/27/1876, Chilo, Ohio d: 7/22/37, Cincinnati, Ohio BR/TR, Deb: N/A.																											
1904	Cin-N	87	306	20	58	14	3	0	20	19		.190	.237	.255	.492	47	-17	-22	114	96	21	.427	9			-3	32/SO	-2.2
1910	Cin-N	21	61	6	9	1	0	0	2	7	8	.148	.235	.164	.399	17	-6	-6	101	70	3	.365	2			0	3/2	-0.5
Total	2	108	367	26	67	15	3	0	22	26	8	.183	.237	.240	.476	42	-23	-28	112	91	24	.417	11			-2	/32SO	-2.7
■ PETE WOODRUFF	Woodruff, Peter Frank b: Richmond, Va. BR/TR, Deb: 9/19/1899																											
1899	NY-N	20	61	11	15	1	1	2	7	9		.246	.343	.393	.736	107	0	1	97	72	9	.783	3			0	O/1	0.1

YEAR	TM/L	G	AB	R	H	2B	3B	HR	RBI	BB	SO	AVG	OBP	SLG	PRO	/A	BR	/A	PF	CHI	RC	TA	SB	CS	SBR	FR	POS	TPR
■ AL WOODS	Woods, Alvis b: 8/8/53, Oakland, Cal. BL/TL, 6'3", 190 lbs. Deb: 4/07/77																											
1977	Tor-A	122	440	58	125	17	4	6	35	36	38	.284	.338	.382	.720	93	-2	-4	103	76	55	.637	8	7	-2	-4	*O/D	-1.3
1978	Tor-A	62	220	19	53	12	3	3	25	11	23	.241	.280	.364	.644	80	-6	-7	100	113	21	.534	1	2	-1	0	O	-0.8
1979	Tor-A	132	436	57	121	24	4	5	36	40	28	.278	.340	.385	.725	92	-3	-5	103	77	58	.660	6	4	-1	-1	*O	-1.0
1980	Tor-A	109	373	54	112	18	2	15	47	37	35	.300	.365	.480	.845	130	15	15	100	83	66	.822	4	4	-1	-8	OD	0.4
1981	Tor-A	85	288	20	71	15	0	1	21	19	31	.247	.293	.309	.602	66	-10	-14	111	91	25	.487	3	4	-2	1	O/D	-1.6
1982	Tor-A	85	201	20	47	11	1	3	24	21	20	.234	.306	.343	.650	72	-6	-8	109	123	21	.569	1	3	-2	-9	OD	-2.0
1986	Min-A	23	28	5	9	1	0	2	8	3	5	.321	.387	.571	.959	146	2	2	108	145	6	1.000	0	0	0	0	/D	0.2
Total	7	618	1986	233	538	98	14	35	196	167	180	.271	.328	.387	.716	93	-10	-20	104	90	252	.654	23	24	-8	-21	O/D	-6.1
■ GARY WOODS	Woods, Gary Lee b: 7/20/54, Santa Barbara, Cal BR/TR, 6'2", 185 lbs. Deb: 9/14/76																											
1976	Oak-A	6	8	0	1	0	0	0	0	0	3	.125	.125	.125	.250	-27	-1	-1	100	0	0	.143	0	0	0	-1	/OD	-0.1
1977	Tor-A	60	227	21	49	9	1	0	17	7	38	.216	.246	.264	.510	38	-19	-20	103	114	14	.396	5	4	-1	-0	O	-2.3
1978	Tor-A	8	19	1	3	1	0	0	0	1	1	.158	.200	.211	.411	15	-2	-2	100	0	1	.375	1	0	0	-0	/O	-0.1
1980	Hou-N	19	53	8	20	5	0	2	15	2	9	.377	.400	.585	.985	176	5	5	98	160	12	1.000	1	0	0	-1	O	0.3
1981	Hou-N	54	110	10	23	4	1	0	12	11	22	.209	.281	.264	.545	62	-6	-5	88	162	8	.457	2	1	0	-4	O	-1.0
1982	Chi-N	117	245	28	66	15	1	4	30	21	48	.269	.327	.388	.715	96	-0	-1	103	110	31	.640	3	3	-1	-7	*O	-1.0
1983	Chi-N	93	190	25	46	9	0	4	22	15	27	.242	.298	.353	.650	79	-6	-6	101	110	18	.565	5	3	-0	-8	O/2	-1.5
1984	Chi-N	87	98	13	23	4	1	3	10	15	21	.235	.336	.388	.724	93	1	-1	110	83	13	.696	2	1	0	-13	O/2	-1.6
1985	Chi-N	81	82	11	20	3	0	0	4	14	18	.244	.354	.280	.635	69	-2	-3	116	69	9	.569	0	1	-1	-14	O	-1.9
Total	9	525	1032	117	251	50	4	13	110	86	187	.243	.303	.337	.640	76	-31	-34	103	110	106	.572	19	13	-2	-47	O/2D	-9.2
■ JIM WOODS	Woods, James Jerome "Woody" b: 9/17/39, Chicago, Ill. BR/TR, 6', 175 lbs. Deb: 9/27/57																											
1957	Chi-N	2	0	1	0	0	0	0	0	0	0	—	—	—	—	—	0	0	96	—	—	—	0	0	0	0	R	0.0
1960	Phi-N	11	34	4	6	0	0	1	3	3	13	.176	.243	.265	.508	36	-3	-3	107	101	2	.429	0	0	0	-1	3	-0.3
1961	Phi-N	23	48	6	11	3	0	2	9	4	15	.229	.302	.417	.719	94	-1	-1	94	140	5	.625	0	0	0	0	3	0.0
Total	3	36	82	11	17	3	0	3	12	7	28	.207	.278	.354	.631	69	-4	-4	99	124	113	.544	0	0	0	-1	/3	-0.3
■ RON WOODS	Woods, Ronald Lawrence b: 2/1/43, Hamilton, Ohio BR/TR, 5'10", 168 lbs. Deb: 4/22/69																											
1969	Det-A	17	15	3	4	0	0	1	3	2	3	.267	.353	.467	.820	123	1	0	103	120	3	.818	0	0	0	-1	/O	0.0
	NY-A	72	171	18	30	5	2	1	7	22	29	.175	.273	.246	.519	48	-12	-11	95	62	13	.462	2	0	1	-0	O	-1.2
	Yr	89	186	21	34	5	2	2	10	24	32	.183	.280	.263	.543	54	-12	-11	97	75	15	.487	2	0	1	-2	O	-1.2
1970	NY-A	95	225	30	51	5	3	8	27	33	35	.227	.326	.382	.708	102	-2	1	92	99	27	.661	4	2	0	-6	O	-0.8
1971	NY-A	25	32	4	8	1	0	1	2	4	2	.250	.333	.375	.708	103	0	0	97	54	4	.667	0	0	0	-2	/O	-0.1
	Mon-N	51	138	26	41	7	3	1	17	19	18	.297	.382	.413	.795	127	5	5	99	115	21	.731	0	2	-1	2	O	0.5
1972	Mon-N	97	221	21	57	5	1	10	31	22	33	.258	.325	.425	.750	109	3	2	102	103	30	.700	3	3	-1	-7	O	-0.9
1973	Mon-N	135	318	45	73	11	3	3	31	56	34	.230	.345	.311	.656	80	-5	-7	104	115	39	.657	12	6	0	-11	*O	-2.4
1974	Mon-N	90	127	15	26	0	0	1	12	17	17	.205	.303	.228	.532	48	-8	-9	104	145	9	.486	6	5	-1	-11	O	-2.3
Total	6	582	1247	162	290	34	12	26	130	175	171	.233	.328	.342	.670	88	-19	-18	100	105	146	.644	27	18	-3	-35	O	-7.2
■ TRACY WOODSON	Woodson, Tracy Michael b: 10/5/62, Richmond, Va. BR/TR, 6'3", 215 lbs. Deb: 4/07/87																											
1987	LA-N	53	136	14	31	8	1	1	11	9	21	.228	.286	.324	.609	67	-8	-6	92	93	12	.519	1	1	-0	3	3/1	-0.3
1988	LA-N	64	173	15	43	4	1	3	15	7	32	.249	.282	.335	.617	72	-6	-7	106	90	15	.493	1	2	-1	-2	31	-1.1
Total	2	117	309	29	74	12	2	4	26	16	53	.239	.284	.330	.614	69	-13	-13	100	91	28	.508	2	3	-1	1	/31	-1.4
■ WOODY WOODWARD	Woodward, William Frederick b: 9/23/42, Miami, Fla. BR/TR, 6'2", 180 lbs. Deb: 9/09/63																											
1963	Mil-N	10	2	1	0	0	0	0	0	0	0	.000	.000	.000	.000	-99	-1	-1	101	0	0	.000	0	0	0	0	/S	0.0
1964	Mil-N	77	115	18	24	2	1	0	11	6	28	.209	.260	.243	.504	44	-9	-8	97	161	7	.387	0	1	-1	-2	2S/31	-0.6
1965	Mil-N	112	265	17	55	7	4	0	11	10	50	.208	.236	.264	.501	39	-21	-22	104	65	16	.381	2	2	-1	1	*S/2	-0.9
1966	Atl-N	144	455	46	120	23	3	0	43	37	54	.264	.325	.327	.652	83	-10	-9	99	121	49	.555	2	2	-1	-16	2S	-1.5
1967	Atl-N	136	429	30	97	15	2	0	25	37	51	.226	.289	.270	.559	59	-21	-23	104	89	32	.441	0	6	-4	3	*2S	-1.4
1968	Atl-N	12	24	2	4	1	0	0	1	1	6	.167	.200	.208	.408	24	-2	-2	93	84	1	.333	1	0	0	-1	/S32	-0.1
	Cin-N	56	119	13	29	2	0	0	10	7	23	.244	.297	.261	.557	61	-4	-6	111	136	10	.451	1	0	0	-6	S/21	-0.6
	Yr	68	143	15	33	3	0	0	11	8	29	.231	.281	.252	.533	56	-7	-8	108	128	11	.432	2	0	1	-6		-0.7
1969	Cin-N	97	241	36	63	12	0	0	15	24	40	.261	.333	.311	.645	82	-5	-5	99	80	25	.556	3	2	-0	-10	S/2	-0.3
1970	Cin-N	100	264	23	59	8	3	1	14	20	21	.223	.283	.288	.571	51	-17	-19	104	69	21	.467	1	2	-1	-3	S32/1	-1.1
1971	Cin-N	136	273	22	66	9	1	0	18	27	28	.242	.310	.282	.592	71	-11	-9	96	95	25	.502	4	0	1	-2	S3/2	0.2
Total	9	880	2187	208	517	79	14	1	148	169	301	.236	.295	.287	.582	63	-101	-104	101	96	186	.486	14	15	-5	-34	S2/31	-6.3
■ JUNIOR WOOTEN	Wooten, Earl Hazwell b: 1/16/24, Pelzer, S.C. BR/TL, 5'11", 160 lbs. Deb: 9/16/47																											
1947	Was-A	6	24	0	2	0	0	0	1	0	4	.083	.083	.083	.167	-55	-5	-5	97	188	0	.130	1	0	0	0	/O	-0.4
1948	Was-A	88	258	34	66	8	3	1	23	24	21	.256	.324	.322	.646	70	-10	-11	103	90	29	.563	2	1	0	6	O/1P	-0.7
Total	2	94	282	34	68	8	3	1	24	24	25	.241	.305	.301	.607	61	-15	-16	103	98	29	.521	3	1	0	6	/O1P	-1.1
■ FAVEL WORDSWORTH	Wordsworth, Favel Perry b: 12/22/1850, New York, N.Y. d: 8/12/1888, New York, N.Y. Deb: 4/28/1873																											
1873	Res-n	11	45	6	10							.222															S	
■ CHUCK WORKMAN	Workman, Charles Thomas b: 1/6/15, Leeton, Mo. d: 1/3/53, Kansas City, Mo. BL/TR, 6', 175 lbs. Deb: 9/18/38																											
1938	Cle-A	2	5	1	2	0	0	0	0	0	0	.400	.400	.400	.800	102	0	0	99	0	1	.667	0	0	0	-0	/O	0.0
1941	Cle-A	9	4	2	0	0	0	0	0	1	1	.000	.200	.000	.200	-43	-1	-1	101	0	0	.250	0	0	0	0	H	0.0
1943	Bos-N	153	615	71	153	17	1	10	67	53	72	.249	.311	.328	.640	80	-12	-16	106	92	66	.576	12			5	*O/13	-1.7
1944	Bos-N	140	418	46	87	18	3	11	53	42	41	.208	.287	.344	.631	82	-14	-11	95	107	43	.565	1			-5	*O3	-2.3
1945	Bos-N	139	514	77	141	16	2	25	87	51	58	.274	.347	.459	.806	109	14	6	112	99	84	.793	9			-13	*3O	-0.9
1946	Bos-N	25	48	5	8	2	0	2	7	3	11	.167	.231	.333	.564	62	-3	-3	95	119	4	.488	0			-1	O	-0.3
	Pit-N	58	145	11	32	4	1	2	16	11	19	.221	.280	.303	.584	64	-7	-7	103	119	13	.500	2			6	O/3	-0.1
	Yr	83	193	16	40	6	1	4	23	14	30	.207	.268	.311	.579	64	-10	-10	101	121	17	.500	2			5		-0.4
Total	6	526	1749	213	423	57	7	50	230	161	202	.242	.311	.368	.679	88	-22	-32	104	100	209	.635	24	0		-8	O3/1	-5.3
■ HANK WORKMAN	Workman, Henry Kilgariff b: 2/5/26, Los Angeles, Cal. BL/TR, 6'1", 185 lbs. Deb: 9/04/50																											
1950	NY-A	2	5	1	1	0	0	0	0	0	1	.200	.200	.200	.400	3	-1	-1	99	0	0	.250	0	0	0	0	/1	0.0
■ HERB WORTH	Worth, Herbert b: 5/2/1847, d: 4/27/14, Brooklyn, N.Y. Deb: 7/29/1872																											
1872	Atl-n	1	6	1	1							.167															/O	
■ CRAIG WORTHINGTON	Worthington, Craig Richard b: 4/17/65, Los Angeles, Cal. BR/TR, 6', 160 lbs. Deb: 4/26/88																											
1988	Bal-A	26	81	5	15	2	0	2	4	9	24	.185	.267	.284	.551	57	-5	-4	95	55	6	.485	1	0	0	1	3	-0.3
■ RED WORTHINGTON	Worthington, Robert Lee b: 4/24/06, Alhambra, Cal. d: 12/8/63, Sepulveda, Cal. BR/TR, 5'11", 170 lbs. Deb: 4/14/31																											
1931	Bos-N	128	491	47	143	25	10	4	44	26	38	.291	.328	.407	.736	98	-3	-3	99	78	66	.655	1			-8	*O	-1.6
1932	Bos-N	105	435	62	132	35	8	8	61	15	24	.303	.330	.476	.806	122	7	11	93	104	68	.743	1			-5	*O	-0.1
1933	Bos-N	17	45	3	7	4	0	0	0	1	3	.156	.174	.244	.418	19	-5	-5	96	0	1	.293	0			-1	O	-0.6
1934	Bos-N	41	65	6	16	5	0	0	6	6	5	.246	.319	.323	.643	85	-2	-1	86	103	6	.538	0			-1	O	-0.2
	StL-N	1	1	0	0	0	0	0	0	0	1	.000	.000	.000	.000	-88	-0	-0	114	0	0	.000	0			0	H	0.0
	Yr	42	66	6	16	5	0	0	6	6	6	.242	.315	.318	.633	81	-3	-1	86	103	7	.560	0			-1		-0.2
Total	4	292	1037	118	298	69	18	12	111	48	71	.287	.321	.423	.745	103	-4	2	96	87	142	.667	2			-15	O	-2.5
■ CHUCK WORTMAN	Wortman, William Lewis b: 1/5/1892, Baltimore, Md. d: 8/19/77, Las Vegas, Nev. BR/TR, 5'7", 150 lbs. Deb: 7/20/16																											
1916	Chi-N	69	234	17	47	4	2	2	16	18	22	.201	.258	.261	.519	51	-11	-15	117	97	17	.444	4			-8	S	-2.1
1917	Chi-N	75	190	24	33	4	1	0	9	18	23	.174	.245	.205	.450	37	-13	-14	105	89	12	.401	6			-16	S/23	-3.4
1918	Chi-N	17	17	4	2	0	0	1	3	1	2	.118	.167	.294	.461	39	-1	-1	102	142	1	.600	3			-0	/2S	-0.1
Total	3	161	441	45	82	8	3	3	28	37	47	.186	.249	.238	.487	45	-26	-31	111	95	30	.432	13			-24	S/23	-5.6

YEAR	TM/L	G	AB	R	H	2B	3B	HR	RBI	BB	SO	AVG	OBP	SLG	PRO	/A	BR	/A	PF	CHI	RC	TA	SB	CS	SBR	FR	POS	TPR
■ RON WOTUS	Wotus, Ronald Allan b: 3/3/61, Colchester, Conn. BR/TR, 6'1", 164 lbs. Deb: 9/03/83																											
1983	Pit-N	5	3	0	0	0	0	0	0	0	1	.000	.000	.000	.000	-97	-1	-1	103	0	0	.000	0	0	0	0	/S2	0.0
1984	Pit-N	27	55	4	12	6	0	0	2	6	8	.218	.295	.327	.622	79	-2	-1	94	44	5	.511	0	0	0	0	S/2	0.1
Total	2	32	58	4	12	6	0	0	2	6	9	.207	.281	.310	.592	70	-3	-2	95	41	5	.480	0	0	0	1	/S2	0.1
■ JIMMY WOULFE	Woulfe, James Joseph b: 11/25/1859, New Orleans, La. d: 12/20/24, New Orleans, La. TR, 5'11", Deb: 5/16/1884																											
1884	Cin-a	8	34	3	5	0	1	0		1		.147	.171	.206	.377	23	-3	-3	106	0	1	.276				0	/O3	-0.2
	Pit-a	15	53	7	6	1	0	0		0		.113	.113	.132	.245	-20	-7	-6	97	0	1	.149				0	O	-0.5
	Yr	23	87	10	11	1	1	0		1		.126	.136	.161	.297	-2	-9	-9	100	0	2	.197				0		-0.7
Total	1	23	87	10	11	1	1	0		1		.126	.136	.161	.297	-2	-9	-9	100	0	2	.197				0	/O3	-0.7
■ AL WRIGHT	Wright, Albert Edgar "A-1" b: 11/11/12, San Francisco, Cal BR/TR, 6'1.5", 170 lbs. Deb: 4/25/33																											
1933	Bos-N	4	1	0	1	0	0	0	0	0	0	1.000	1.000	1.000	2.000	490	0	0	96	0	1	—	0			0	/2	0.1
■ AB WRIGHT	Wright, Albert Owen b: 11/16/05, Terlton, Okla. BR/TR, 6'1.5", 190 lbs. Deb: 4/20/35																											
1935	Cle-A	67	160	17	38	11	1	2	18	10	17	.237	.291	.356	.647	67	-8	-8	99	97	17	.577	2	1	0	-9	O	-1.6
1944	Bos-N	71	195	20	50	9	0	7	35	18	31	.256	.326	.410	.736	112	1	3	95	124	26	.667	0			-5	O	-0.6
Total	2	138	355	37	88	20	1	9	53	28	48	.248	.310	.386	.696	91	-7	-6	97	112	43	.626	2	1		-15	/O	-2.2
■ CY WRIGHT	Wright, Ceylon b: 8/16/1893, Minneapolis, Minn. d: 11/7/47, Hines, Ill. BL/TR, 5'9", 150 lbs. Deb: 6/30/16																											
1916	Chi-A	8	18	0	0	0	0	0	0	1	7	.000	.053	.000	.053	-78	-4	-4	108	0	0	.056	0			-0	/S	-0.3
■ GLENN WRIGHT	Wright, Forest Glenn "Buckshot" b: 2/6/01, Archie, Mo. d: 4/6/84, Olathe, Kan. BR/TR, 5'11", 170 lbs. Deb: 4/15/24																											
1924	Pit-N	153	616	80	177	28	18	7	111	27	52	.287	.318	.425	.744	92	-4	-9	106	152	82	.683	14	6	1	11	*S	1.5
1925	Pit-N	153	614	97	189	32	10	18	121	31	32	.308	.341	.480	.822	105	4	3	102	131	97	.762	3	7	-3	1	*S/3	1.3
1926	Pit-N	119	458	73	141	15	15	8	77	19	26	.308	.335	.459	.794	100	6	-2	112	121	67	.741	6			-6	*S	0.0
1927	Pit-N	143	570	78	160	26	4	9	105	39	46	.281	.328	.388	.716	89	-8	-10	102	**157**	71	.646	4			-19	*S	-1.4
1928	Pit-N	108	407	63	126	20	8	8	66	21	53	.310	.343	.457	.800	101	3	-1	107	114	61	.747	3			-17	*S/1O	-0.3
1929	Bro-N	24	25	4	5	0	0	1	6	3	6	.200	.286	.320	.606	53	-2	-2	94	187	2	.550	0			0	/S	0.0
1930	Bro-N	135	532	83	171	28	12	22	126	32	70	.321	.360	.543	.903	114	10	10	101	130	99	.895	2			8	*S	2.6
1931	Bro-N	77	268	36	76	9	4	9	32	14	35	.284	.324	.448	.772	104	1	1	101	78	39	.714	1			10	S	1.6
1932	Bro-N	127	446	50	122	31	5	11	60	12	57	.274	.293	.439	.732	98	-5	-3	96	97	57	.654	4			8	*S/1	1.4
1933	Bro-N	71	192	19	49	13	0	1	18	11	24	.255	.299	.339	.638	85	-5	-4	97	99	18	.513	1			-4	S/13	-0.4
1935	Chi-A	9	25	1	3	1	0	0	1	0	6	.120	.120	.160	.280	-26	-5	-5	109	85	1	.182	0	0	0	0	/2	-0.4
Total	11	1119	4153	584	1219	203	76	94	723	209	407	.294	.328	.447	.775	98	-5	-22	103	126	594	.715	38	13		-9	*S/1230	5.9
■ GEORGE WRIGHT	Wright, George b: 1/28/1847, Yonkers, N.Y. d: 8/21/37, Boston, Mass. BR/TR, 5'9.5", 150 lbs. Deb: 5/05/1871 MH																											
1871	Bos-n	17	88	35	36							.409															S/1	
1872	Bos-n	48	253	86	85							.336															*S	
1873	Bos-n	59	333	98	126							.378															*S	
1874	Bos-n	60	319	75	110							.345															*S	
1875	Bos-n	79	407	105	137							.337															*S	
1876	Bos-N	70	335	72	100	18	6	1	34	8	9	.299	.315	.397	.712	143	12	15	95	73	43	.600				15	*S/2P	2.5
1877	Bos-N	61	290	58	80	15	1	0	35	9	15	.276	.298	.334	.632	91	-0	-4	108	106	30	.505				8	*2/S	0.5
1878	Bos-N	59	267	35	60	5	1	0	12	6	22	.225	.242	.251	.493	58	-11	-13	108	52	17	.353				11	*S	0.1
1879	Pro-N	85	388	79	107	15	10	1	42	13	20	.276	.299	.374	.673	118	8	8	102	96	44	.562				20	*SM	2.9
1880	Bos-N	1	4	2	1	0	0	0	0	0	0	.250	.250	.250	.500	76	-0	-0	92	0	0	.333				0	/S	0.0
1881	Bos-N	7	25	4	5	0	0	0	0	3	1	.200	.286	.200	.486	60	-1	-1	91	0	1	.400				0	/S	0.0
1882	Pro-N	46	185	14	30	1	2	0	9	4	36	.162	.180	.189	.369	18	-16	-18	106	88	6	.252				-8	S	-1.9
Total	5 n	263	1400	399	494							.353															S	
Total	7	329	1494	264	383	54	20	2	132	43	103	.256	.277	.323	.600	92	-8	-14	103	82	142	.473				45	S/2P1	4.1
■ GEORGE WRIGHT	Wright, George De Witt b: 12/12/58, Oklahoma City, Okla BB/TR, 5'11", 180 lbs. Deb: 4/10/82																											
1982	Tex-A	150	557	69	147	20	5	11	50	30	78	.264	.305	.377	.682	93	-11	-6	93	84	61	.575	3	7	-3	4	*O	-0.9
1983	Tex-A	162	634	79	175	28	6	18	80	41	82	.276	.322	.424	.746	102	2	1	101	103	84	.674	8	7	-2	3	*O	0.0
1984	Tex-A	101	383	40	93	19	4	9	48	15	54	.243	.275	.384	.659	80	-11	-11	100	112	39	.550	0	2	-1	1	OD	-1.4
1985	Tex-A	109	363	21	69	13	0	2	18	25	49	.190	.242	.242	.485	31	-33	-37	108	76	19	.377	4	7	-3	4	*O/D	-3.7
1986	Tex-A	49	106	10	23	3	1	2	7	4	23	.217	.252	.321	.573	58	-7	-6	96	70	7	.467	3	5	-2	-5	O	-1.3
	Mon-N	56	117	12	22	5	2	0	5	11	28	.188	.264	.265	.529	47	-9	-8	98	64	8	.444	1	1	-0	-1	O	-1.0
Total	5	627	2160	231	529	88	18	42	208	126	314	.245	.289	.361	.650	78	-69	-68	100	91	218	.561	19	29	-12	6	O/D	-8.3
■ JOE WRIGHT	Wright, Joseph b: 1873, Pittsburgh, Pa. BL, 5'8", 175 lbs. Deb: 7/14/1895																											
1895	Lou-N	60	228	30	63	10	4	1	30	12	28	.276	.315	.368	.684	82	-8	-6	95	98	29	.630	7			-6	O/C	-1.3
1896	Lou-N	2	7	0	2	0	0	0	0	0	1	.286	.286	.286	.571	53	-0	-0	98	0	1	.400	0			0	/O	0.0
	Pit-N	15	52	5	16	2	1	0	6	1	2	.308	.321	.385	.705	94	-1	-1	93	86	7	.611	1			0	O/3	0.0
	Yr	17	59	5	18	2	1	0	6	1	3	.305	.317	.373	.690	89	-2	-1	94	76	7	.585	1			0		0.0
Total	2	77	287	35	81	12	5	1	36	13	31	.282	.316	.369	.685	83	-10	-7	95	94	37	.621	8			-6	/O3C	-1.3
■ PAT WRIGHT	Wright, Patrick Francis b: 7/5/1865, Pottsville, Pa. d: 5/29/43, Springfield, Ill. BB/TR, 6'2", 190 lbs. Deb: 7/11/1890																											
1890	Chi-N	1	2	0	0	0	0	0	0	1	0	.000	.333	.000	.333	1	-0	-0	109	0	0	.500	0			0	/2	0.0
■ SAM WRIGHT	Wright, Samuel b: 11/25/1848, New York, N.Y. d: 5/6/28, Boston, Mass. 5'7.5", 146 lbs. Deb: 4/21/1875																											
1875	NH-n	33	137	11	24							.175															S	
1876	Bos-N	2	8	0	1	0	0	0	0	0	0	.125	.125	.125	.250	-17	-1	-1	95	0	0	.143				0	/S	0.0
1880	Cin-N	9	34	0	3	0	0	0	0	0	5	.088	.088	.088	.176	-40	-5	-5	99	0	0	.097				0	/S	-0.4
1881	Bos-N	1	4	0	1	0	0	0	0	0	0	.250	.250	.250	.500	63	-0	-0	91	0	0	.333				0	/S	0.0
Total	3	12	46	0	5	0	0	0	0	0	5	.109	.109	.109	.217	-28	-6	-6	97	0	1	.122				0	/S	-0.4
■ TAFFY WRIGHT	Wright, Taft Shedron b: 8/10/11, Tabor City, N.C. d: 10/22/81, Orlando, Fla. BL/TR, 5'10", 180 lbs. Deb: 4/18/38																											
1938	Was-A	100	263	37	92	18	10	2	36	13	17	.350	.389	.517	.906	132	9	11	95	86	52	.890	1	2	-1	-6	O	0.4
1939	Was-A	129	499	77	154	29	11	4	93	38	19	.309	.359	.435	.794	113	1	8	90	**140**	78	.726	1	2	-1	-5	*O	-0.1
1940	Chi-A	147	581	79	196	31	9	5	88	43	25	.337	.385	.448	.832	111	13	10	104	123	101	.771	4	7	-3	-7	*O	-0.8
1941	Chi-A	136	513	71	165	35	5	10	97	60	27	.322	.399	.468	.867	137	22	27	94	135	101	.864	5	4	-1	-5	*O	1.1
1942	Chi-A	85	300	43	100	13	5	0	47	48	9	.333	.432	.410	.842	139	18	18	99	143	55	.826	1	8	-5	1	O	0.9
1946	Chi-A	115	422	46	116	19	4	7	52	42	17	.275	.342	.389	.731	107	2	4	97	109	55	.666	10	3	1	-4	*O	-0.5
1947	Chi-A	124	401	48	130	13	0	4	54	48	17	.324	.398	.387	.784	123	12	13	97	119	64	.741	8	6	-1	-5	*O	0.3
1948	Chi-A	134	455	50	127	15	6	4	61	39	18	.279	.341	.365	.706	92	-8	-6	95	116	57	.617	2	1	0	-4	*O	-1.2
1949	Phi-A	59	149	14	35	2	5	2	25	16	6	.235	.321	.356	.677	80	-5	-5	99	145	16	.590	0	0	0	-2	O	-0.6
Total	9	1029	3583	465	1115	175	55	38	553	347	155	.311	.376	.423	.799	116	64	81	96	124	580	.765	32	33	-10	-37	O	-0.5
■ TOM WRIGHT	Wright, Thomas Everette b: 9/22/23, Shelby, N.C. BL/TR, 5'11.5", 180 lbs. Deb: 9/15/48																											
1948	Bos-A	3	2	1	1	0	1	0	0	0	0	.500	.500	1.500	2.000	419	1	1	100	0	2	3.000	0	0	0	0	H	0.1
1949	Bos-A	5	4	1	1	1	0	0	1	1	1	.250	.400	.500	.900	128	0	0	107	171	1	1.000	0	0	0	0	H	0.0
1950	Bos-A	54	107	17	34	7	0	0	20	6	18	.318	.360	.383	.743	79	-2	-4	114	168	15	.640	0	0	0	-3	O	-0.6
1951	Bos-A	28	63	8	14	1	1	1	9	11	8	.222	.347	.317	.664	75	-1	-2	108	140	7	.604	0	0	0	-5	O	-0.7
1952	StL-A	29	66	6	16	0	0	1	6	12	20	.242	.359	.288	.647	84	-1	-1	97	102	7	.604	1	1	-0	0	O	0.0
	Chi-A	60	132	15	34	10	2	1	21	16	16	.258	.342	.386	.729	103	0	0	100	145	19	.683	1	0	0	-3	O	-0.2
	Yr	89	198	21	50	10	2	2	27	28	36	.253	.348	.354	.702	97	-1	-0	99	132	27	.664	2	1	0	-2		-0.2
1953	Chi-A	77	132	14	33	5	3	2	25	12	21	.250	.322	.379	.701	84	-2	-3	106	165	17	.640	0	0	0	-6	O	-1.0
1954	Was-A	76	171	13	42	4	4	1	17	18	38	.246	.325	.333	.658	82	-4	-4	98	107	20	.588	0	0	0	-4	O	-0.9

YEAR	TM/L	G	AB	R	H	2B	3B	HR	RBI	BB	SO	AVG	OBP	SLG	PRO	/A	BR	/A	PF	CHI	RC	TA	SB	CS	SBR	FR	POS	TPR
1955	Was-A	7	7	0	0	0	0	0	0	0	1	.000	.000	.000	.000	-99	-2	-2	91	0	0	.000	0	0	0	0	H	-0.1
1956	Was-A	2	1	0	0	0	0	0	0	0	0	.000	.000	.000	.000	-98	-0	-0	102	0	0	.000	0	0	0	0	H	0.0
Total	9	341	685	75	175	28	11	6	99	76	123	.255	.336	.355	.691	85	-12	-15	103	136	87	.642	2	1	0	-20	O	-3.4
■ **BILL WRIGHT** Wright, William H. Deb: 9/16/1887																												
1887	Was-N	1	3	0	2	0	0	0	0	0	0	.667	.667	.667	1.333	288	1	1	95	0	1	2.000	0			0	/C	0.1
■ **HARRY WRIGHT** Wright, William Henry b: 1/10/1835, Sheffield, England d: 10/3/1895, Atlantic City, N.J. BR/TR, 5'9.5", 157 lbs. Deb: 5/05/1871 MH																												
1871	Bos-n	31	161	42	43							.267															*O/PSM	
1872	Bos-n	48	214	38	56							.262															*O/PM	
1873	Bos-n	59	283	57	66							.233															*O/PM	
1874	Bos-n	41	189	44	58							.307															*O/CM	
1875	Bos-n	1	4	1	1							.250															/OM	
1876	Bos-N	1	3	0	0	0	0	0	0	0	1	.000	.000	.000	.000	-99	-1	-1	95	0	0	.000				0	/OM	0.0
1877	Bos-N	1	4	0	0	0	0	0	0	0	1	.000	.000	.000	.000	-92	-1	-1	108	0	0	.000				0	/OM	0.0
Total	5 n	180	851	182	224							.263															/OM	
Total	2	2	7	0	0	0	0	0	0	0	2	.000	.000	.000	.000	-97	-1	-2	103	0	0	.000				0	O/PCS	0.0
■ **DICK WRIGHT** Wright, William James b: 5/5/1890, Worcester, N.Y. d: 1/24/52, Bethlehem, Pa. TR , 5'10", 170 lbs. Deb: 6/30/15																												
1915	Bro-F	4	5	0	0	0	0	0	0	0	0	.000	.000	.000	.000	-99	-1	-1	98	0	0	.000	0			0	/C	0.0
■ **RASTY WRIGHT** Wright, William Smith b: 1/31/1863, Birmingham, Mich. d: 10/14/22, Duluth, Minn. 6'1", 258 lbs. Deb: 4/17/1890																												
1890	Syr-a	88	348	82	106	10	6	0		69		.305	.427	.368	.794	152	21	27	90	0	69	.959	30			3	O	2.2
	Cle-N	13	45	7	5	1	0	0	2	12	4	.111	.298	.133	.432	31	-3	-3	94	97	3	.525	3			0	O	-0.2
Total	1	101	393	89	111	11	6	0	2	81	4	.282	.411	.341	.752	137	17	24	91	12	72	.897	33			3	O	2.0
■ **RUSS WRIGHTSTONE** Wrightstone, Russell Guy b: 3/18/1893, Bowmansdale, Pa. d: 2/25/69, Harrisburg, Pa. BL/TR, 5'10.5", 176 lbs. Deb: 4/19/20																												
1920	Phi-N	76	206	23	54	6	1	3	17	10	25	.262	.303	.345	.647	79	-4	-6	109	82	21	.558	3	2	-0	4	3/S2	0.1
1921	Phi-N	109	372	59	110	13	4	9	51	18	20	.296	.332	.425	.756	97	-1	-2	102	101	51	.684	4	4	-1	2	3O/2	-0.2
1922	Phi-N	99	331	56	101	18	6	5	33	28	17	.305	.365	.441	.806	94	3	-3	113	72	53	.770	4	5	-2	5	3S/1	0.5
1923	Phi-N	119	392	59	107	21	7	7	57	21	19	.273	.315	.416	.731	80	-6	-14	114	109	51	.669	5	2	0	-1	3S/2	-1.0
1924	Phi-N	118	388	55	119	24	4	7	58	27	15	.307	.363	.443	.806	107	8	4	108	110	62	.773	5	4	-1	-6	3/2SO	0.4
1925	Phi-N	92	286	48	99	18	5	14	61	19	18	.346	.389	.591	.980	127	19	12	116	103	63	.995	0	3	-2	-9	OS32/1	0.1
1926	Phi-N	112	368	55	113	23	1	7	57	27	11	.307	.356	.432	.788	108	5	4	103	110	55	.753	5			2	132/O	0.4
1927	Phi-N	141	533	62	163	24	5	6	75	48	20	.306	.365	.403	.769	110	5	7	96	119	78	.741	9			0	*1/23	0.0
1928	Phi-N	33	91	7	19	5	1	1	11	14	5	.209	.321	.319	.639	65	-4	-5	104	122	10	.611	0			-4	O/1	-0.9
	NY-N	30	25	3	4	0	0	1	5	3	2	.160	.250	.280	.530	38	-2	-2	102	178	2	.476	0			0	/1	-0.2
	Yr	63	116	10	23	5	1	2	16	17	7	.198	.306	.310	.616	60	-6	-7	103	151	12	.581	0			-4		-1.1
Total	9	929	2992	427	889	152	34	60	425	215	152	.297	.349	.431	.780	100	22	-5	106	104	447	.735	35	20		-8	310/S2	-0.8
■ **ZEKE WRIGLEY** Wrigley, George Watson b: 1/18/1874, Philadelphia, Pa. d: 9/28/52, Philadelphia, Pa. 5'8.5", 150 lbs. Deb: 8/31/1896																												
1896	Was-N	5	9	1	1	0	0	0	2	1	1	.111	.200	.111	.311	-17	-1	-1	95	577	0	.250	0			0	/2S	0.0
1897	Was-N	104	388	65	110	14	8	3	64	21		.284	.320	.384	.704	86	-8	-9	101	121	51	.629	5			2	OS3/2	-0.6
1898	Was-N	111	400	50	98	9	10	2	39	20		.245	.283	.333	.615	77	-12	-13	102	86	41	.543	10			6	S2/O3	-0.2
1899	NY-N	4	15	1	3	0	0	0	1	1		.200	.250	.200	.450	27	-1	-1	97	108	1	.417	1			0	/3	0.0
	Bro-N	15	49	4	10	2	2	0	11	3		.204	.250	.327	.577	57	-3	-3	105	211	5	.538	2			0	S/3	-0.2
	Yr	19	64	5	13	2	2	0	12	4		.203	.250	.297	.547	50	-4	-5	103	195	6	.510	3			0		-0.2
Total	4	239	861	121	222	25	20	5	117	46	1	.258	.296	.351	.647	78	-26	-28	102	115	98	.574	18			8	S/O32	-1.0
■ **RICK WRONA** Wrona, Richard James b: 12/10/63, Tulsa, Okla. BR/TR, 6'1", 185 lbs. Deb: 9/03/88																												
1988	Chi-N	4	6	0	0	0	0	0	0	0	1	.000	.000	.000	.000	-96	-2	-2	104	0	0	.000	0	0	0	0	/C	-0.1
■ **YATS WUESTLING** Wuestling, George b: 10/18/03, St.Louis, Mo. d: 4/26/70, St.Louis, Mo. BR/TR, 5'11", 167 lbs. Deb: 6/15/29																												
1929	Det-A	54	150	13	30	4	1	0	16	9	24	.200	.250	.240	.490	27	-16	-16	97	152	9	.382	1	3	-2	-7	S/23	-1.7
1930	Det-A	4	9	0	0	0	0	0	0	2	3	.000	.182	.000	.182	-47	-2	-2	105	0	0	.222	0	0	0	0	/S	-0.1
	NY-A	25	58	5	11	0	1	0	3	4	14	.190	.242	.224	.466	21	-7	-6	90	77	3	.354	0	1	-1	0	S/3	-0.3
	Yr	29	67	5	11	0	1	0	3	6	17	.164	.233	.194	.427	10	-9	-8	92	66	3	.333	0	1	-1	0		-0.4
Total	2	83	217	18	41	4	2	0	19	15	41	.189	.245	.226	.470	22	-26	-24	96	125	12	.367	1	4	-2	-7	/S32	-2.1
■ **JOE WYATT** Wyatt, Loral John b: 4/6/1900, Petersburg, Ind. d: 12/5/70, Oblong, Ill. BR/TR, 6'1", 175 lbs. Deb: 9/11/24																												
1924	Cle-A	4	12	1	2	0	0	0	1	2	1	.167	.286	.167	.452	19	-1	-1	97	168	1	.400	0	0	0	-1	/O	-0.2
■ **REN WYLIE** Wylie, James Renwick b: 12/14/1861, Elizabeth, Pa. d: 8/17/51, Wilkinsburg, Pa. 5'11", 155 lbs. Deb: 8/11/1882																												
1882	Pit-a	1	3	0	0	0	0	0		0		.000	.000	.000	.000	-99	-1	-1	97	0	0	.000				0	/O	0.0
■ **FRANK WYMAN** Wyman, Frank H. b: 5/10/1862, Haverhill, Mass. d: 2/4/16, Everett, Mass. Deb: 6/24/1884																												
1884	KC-U	30	124	16	27	4	0	0		3		.218	.236	.250	.486	74	-4	-2	87	0	8	.351	0			4	O/P13	0.1
	CP-U	2	8	1	3	0	0	0		0		.375	.375	.375	.750	155	0	0	99	0	1	.600	0			0	/1	0.0
	Yr	32	132	17	30	4	0	0		3		.227	.244	.258	.502	80	-4	-2	88	0	9	.363	0			4		0.1
Total	1	32	132	17	30	4	0	0		3		.227	.244	.258	.502	80	-4	-2	88	0	9	.363	0			4	/O13P	0.1
■ **BUTCH WYNEGAR** Wynegar, Harold Delano b: 3/14/56, York, Pa. BB/TR, 6'1", 190 lbs. Deb: 4/09/76																												
1976	Min-A	149	534	58	139	21	2	10	69	79	63	.260	.358	.363	.721	113	10	11	98	121	72	.672	0	0	0	13	*CD	3.0
1977	Min-A	144	532	76	139	22	3	10	79	68	61	.261	.347	.370	.717	93	-2	-4	103	**141**	70	.661	2	3	-1	16	*C/3	1.4
1978	Min-A	135	454	36	104	22	1	4	45	47	42	.229	.310	.308	.618	79	-15	-11	94	117	46	.543	1	0	0	4	*C/3	-0.3
1979	Min-A	149	504	74	136	20	0	7	57	74	36	.270	.366	.351	.717	87	-1	-8	109	113	68	.666	2	2	-1	6	*C	0.4
1980	Min-A	146	486	61	124	18	3	5	57	63	36	.255	.343	.335	.678	80	-7	-13	109	127	59	.621	3	1	0	8	*C/D	0.2
1981	Min-A	47	150	11	37	5	0	0	10	17	9	.247	.327	.280	.607	73	-4	-5	105	95	13	.496	0	1	-1	2	C/D	-0.1
1982	Min-A	24	86	9	18	4	0	1	8	10	12	.209	.292	.291	.582	60	-5	-5	100	116	7	.500	0	0	0	1	C	-0.2
	NY-A	63	191	27	56	8	1	3	20	40	21	.293	.418	.393	.811	129	9	10	96	97	33	.811	0	1	-1	-1	C	1.1
	Yr	87	277	36	74	12	1	4	28	50	33	.267	.381	.361	.742	108	4	5	97	104	41	.716	0	1	-1	-0		0.9
1983	NY-A	94	301	40	89	18	2	6	42	52	29	.296	.401	.429	.830	130	14	15	99	112	54	.832	1	1	-0	-3	C	1.5
1984	NY-A	129	442	48	118	13	1	6	45	65	35	.267	.361	.342	.703	102	-0	3	94	108	53	.627	1	4	-2	5	*C	1.4
1985	NY-A	102	309	27	69	15	0	5	32	64	43	.223	.357	.320	.677	91	-3	-1	96	111	38	.649	0	0	0	5	C	0.8
1986	NY-A	61	194	19	40	4	1	7	29	30	21	.206	.313	.345	.658	78	-5	-6	103	131	20	.595	0	0	0	0	C	-0.2
1987	Cal-A	31	92	4	19	2	0	0	5	9	13	.207	.277	.228	.505	37	-8	-8	99	95	6	.400	0	0	0	-0	C/D	-0.5
1988	Cal-A	26	55	8	14	4	1	1	8	8	7	.255	.349	.418	.767	121	1	2	94	122	8	.721	0	0	0	-1	C	0.1
Total	13	1300	4330	498	1102	176	15	65	506	626	428	.255	.351	.347	.698	94	-16	-20	101	118	549	.665	10	13	-5	54	*C/D3	8.6
■ **EARLY WYNN** Wynn, Early "Gus" b: 1/6/20, Hartford, Ala. BB/TR, 6', 190 lbs. Deb: 9/13/39 CH																												
1939	Was-A	3	6	0	1	0	0	0	1	1	1	.167	.286	.167	.452	20	-1	-1	90	338	0	.400	0	0	0	-1	/P	0.0
1941	Was-A	5	15	1	2	1	0	0	0	0	5	.133	.133	.200	.333	-13	-2	-2	98	0	0	.214	0	0	0	0	/P	0.0
1942	Was-A	30	69	4	15	2	0	0	7	3	13	.217	.250	.246	.496	42	-6	-5	96	145	4	.364	0	0	0	-1	P	0.0
1943	Was-A	38	98	6	29	3	1	1	11	1	11	.296	.303	.378	.681	95	-1	-1	104	100	11	.543	0	0	0	-2	P	0.0
1944	Was-A	43	92	4	19	2	0	1	6	3	21	.207	.232	.261	.492	45	-7	-6	90	80	5	.360	0	0	0	-2	P	0.0
1946	Was-A	25	47	4	15	2	0	1	9	5	7	.319	.385	.426	.810	137	2	2	92	149	8	.781	0	0	0	0	P	0.0
1947	Was-A	54	120	6	33	6	0	2	13	1	19	.275	.281	.375	.656	84	-4	-3	97	94	13	.523	0	0	0	-1	P	0.0
1948	Was-A	73	106	9	23	3	1	0	16	14	22	.217	.308	.264	.572	51	-7	-7	103	193	9	.483	0	0	0	-2	P	-0.4
1949	Cle-A	35	70	3	10	1	0	1	7	4	10	.143	.189	.200	.389	3	-10	-10	98	141	2	.281	0	0	0	1	P	0.0
1950	Cle-A	39	77	12	18	5	1	2	10	10	12	.234	.322	.403	.724	86	-2	-2	98	93	11	.683	0	0	0	0	P	0.0
1951	Cle-A	41	108	8	20	8	1	1	13	7	9	.185	.235	.306	.540	48	-9	-8	95	129	7	.430	0	0	0	-1	P	0.0

YEAR	TM/L	G	AB	R	H	2B	3B	HR	RBI	BB	SO	AVG	OBP	SLG	PRO	/A	BR	/A	PF	CHI	RC	TA	SB	CS	SBR	FR	POS	TPR
1952	Cle-A	44	99	5	22	2	0	0	10	9	15	.222	.287	.242	.529	53	-7	-6	91	156	7	.412	0	0	0	-0	P	0.0
1953	Cle-A	37	91	11	25	2	0	3	10	7	17	.275	.327	.396	.722	99	-1	-0	95	82	13	.652	0	0	0	-1	P	0.0
1954	Cle-A	40	93	10	17	3	0	0	4	7	13	.183	.240	.215	.455	24	-10	-10	106	76	5	.346	0	0	0	-3	P	0.0
1955	Cle-A	34	84	8	15	3	0	1	7	6	17	.179	.233	.250	.483	29	-8	-9	104	109	5	.380	0	0	0	-3	P	0.0
1956	Cle-A	38	101	5	23	5	0	1	15	7	22	.228	.278	.307	.585	54	-7	-7	101	165	9	.494	1	0	0	1	P	0.0
1957	Cle-A	40	86	4	10	0	0	0	4	11	23	.116	.216	.116	.333	-7	-13	-13	102	158	3	.273	0	0	0	-0	P	0.0
1958	Chi-A	40	75	7	15	1	0	0	11	10	25	.200	.294	.213	.507	43	-6	-5	98	276	5	.419	0	0	0	-2	P	0.0
1959	Chi-A	37	90	11	22	7	0	2	8	9	18	.244	.320	.389	.709	97	-1	-0	97	77	12	.652	0	0	0	-1	P	0.0
1960	Chi-A	36	75	8	15	2	1	1	7	14	17	.200	.333	.293	.627	70	-3	-3	101	110	9	.617	0	0	0	-2	P	0.0
1961	Chi-A	17	37	4	6	0	0	0	2	3	11	.162	.225	.162	.387	5	-5	-5	99	131	1	.281	0	0	0	-2	P	0.0
1962	Chi-A	27	54	5	7	1	0	0	2	7	17	.130	.230	.148	.378	4	-7	-7	95	99	2	.319	0	0	0	-2	P	0.0
1963	Cle-A	20	11	1	3	0	0	0	0	2	5	.273	.385	.273	.657	91	-0	-0	97	0	1	.625	0	0	0	-0	P	0.0
Total	23	796	1704	136	365	59	5	17	173	141	330	.214	.275	.285	.560	54	-113	-109	98	126	145	.470	1	0	0	-23	P	-0.4
■ JIM WYNN	Wynn, James Sherman b: 3/12/42, Hamilton, Ohio BR/TR, 5'10", 160 lbs. Deb: 7/10/63																											
1963	Hou-N	70	250	31	61	10	5	4	27	30	53	.244	.325	.372	.697	109	0	3	92	114	32	.655	4	2	0	2	OS/3	0.4
1964	Hou-N	67	219	19	49	7	0	5	18	24	58	.224	.303	.324	.627	80	-6	-5	96	88	21	.564	5	5	-2	1	O	-0.7
1965	Hou-N	157	564	90	155	30	7	22	73	84	126	.275	.374	.470	.844	153	29	37	89	97	108	.934	43	4	**11**	10	*O	5.4
1966	Hou-N	105	418	62	107	21	1	18	62	41	81	.256	.324	.440	.764	113	5	7	97	97	58	.729	13	10	-2	6	*O	0.8
1967	Hou-N	158	594	102	148	29	3	37	107	74	137	.249	.334	.495	.829	144	25	30	94	116	102	.843	16	4	2	4	*O	3.1
1968	Hou-N	156	542	85	146	23	5	26	67	90	131	.269	.378	.474	.853	156	38	39	99	89	98	.866	11	17	-7	19	*O	4.8
1969	Hou-N	149	495	113	133	17	1	33	87	**148**	142	.269	.440	.507	.947	162	51	50	102	96	126	1.136	23	7	3	5	*O	5.1
1970	Hou-N	157	554	82	156	32	2	27	88	106	96	.282	.398	.493	.891	147	32	37	94	102	114	.964	24	5	4	9	*O	4.2
1971	Hou-N	123	404	38	82	16	0	7	45	56	63	.203	.303	.295	.598	75	-15	-11	93	133	36	.548	10	5	0	5	*O	-1.1
1972	Hou-N	145	542	117	148	29	3	24	90	103	99	.273	.391	.470	.862	135	34	30	106	109	107	.922	17	7	1	5	*O	3.1
1973	Hou-N	139	481	90	106	14	5	20	55	91	102	.220	.349	.395	.744	111	6	9	95	94	68	.753	14	11	-2	4	*O	0.4
1974	LA-N	150	535	104	145	17	4	32	108	108	104	.271	.393	.497	.891	160	36	42	93	122	109	.951	18	15	-4	2	*O	3.5
1975	LA-N	130	412	80	102	16	0	18	58	110	77	.248	.407	.417	.825	136	21	25	95	101	79	.903	7	3	0	-3	*O	1.8
1976	Atl-N	148	449	75	93	19	1	17	66	**127**	111	.207	.382	.367	.749	102	14	7	111	120	75	.835	16	6	1	10	*O	1.4
1977	NY-A	30	77	7	11	2	1	1	3	15	16	.143	.283	.234	.516	43	-6	-6	99	57	6	.515	1	0	0	1	D/O	-0.3
	Mil-A	36	117	10	23	3	1	0	10	17	31	.197	.299	.239	.538	51	-8	-7	95	144	10	.505	3	0	1	-2	OD	-0.8
	Yr	66	194	17	34	5	2	1	13	32	47	.175	.292	.237	.529	48	-14	-13	97	105	16	.509	4	0	1	-1		-1.1
Total	15	1920	6653	1105	1665	285	39	291	964	1224	1427	.250	.369	.436	.805	130	256	283	97	106	1148	.860	225	101	7	78	*O/DS3	31.1
■ MARVELL WYNNE	Wynne, Marvell b: 12/17/59, Chicago, Ill. BL/TL, 5'11", 175 lbs. Deb: 6/15/83																											
1983	Pit-N	103	366	66	89	16	2	7	26	38	52	.243	.319	.355	.675	84	-6	-8	103	69	43	.631	12	10	-2	-5	*O	-1.7
1984	Pit-N	154	653	77	174	24	11	0	39	42	81	.266	.311	.337	.648	87	-16	-12	94	60	67	.565	24	19	-4	-3	*O	-2.5
1985	Pit-N	103	337	21	69	6	3	2	18	18	48	.205	.247	.258	.505	40	-26	-27	103	77	21	.413	10	5	0	1	O	-3.0
1986	SD-N	137	288	34	76	19	2	7	37	15	45	.264	.303	.417	.719	101	-2	-1	95	105	32	.645	11	11	-3	-9	*O	-1.5
1987	SD-N	98	188	17	47	8	2	2	24	20	37	.250	.322	.346	.668	80	-6	-5	97	135	21	.632	11	6	-0	-7	O	-1.5
1988	SD-N	128	333	37	88	13	4	11	42	31	62	.264	.327	.426	.753	118	6	7	97	96	47	.698	3	4	-2	-1	*O	0.1
Total	6	723	2165	252	543	86	24	29	186	164	325	.251	.305	.353	.658	85	-51	-46	98	82	229	.598	71	55	-12	-24	O	-10.1
■ JOHNNY WYROSTEK	Wyrostek, John Barney b: 7/12/19, Fairmont City, Ill. d: 12/12/86, St.Louis, Mo. BL/TR, 6'2", 180 lbs. Deb: 9/10/42																											
1942	Pit-N	9	35	0	4	0	1	0	3	3	2	.114	.184	.171	.356	4	-4	-4	101	196	1	.290	0			1	/O	-0.3
1943	Pit-N	51	79	7	12	3	0	0	1	3	15	.152	.183	.190	.373	7	-9	-10	104	24	3	.265	0			-4	O/312	-1.5
1946	Phi-N	145	545	73	153	30	4	6	45	70	42	.281	.366	.383	.749	119	10	14	95	71	82	.726	7			11	*O	2.3
1947	Phi-N	128	454	68	124	24	7	5	51	61	45	.273	.364	.390	.754	100	1	1	100	104	67	.735	7			-1	*O	-0.4
1948	Cin-N	136	512	74	140	24	9	17	76	52	63	.273	.344	.455	.799	111	9	7	103	106	83	.782	7			-2	*O	-0.3
1949	Cin-N	134	474	54	118	20	4	9	46	58	63	.249	.333	.365	.698	91	-8	-5	96	88	60	.661	7			-0	*O	-1.2
1950	Cin-N	131	509	70	145	34	5	8	76	52	38	.285	.357	.418	.775	99	3	-0	105	131	76	.717	1			-3	*O/1	-0.7
1951	Cin-N	142	537	52	167	31	3	2	61	54	54	.311	.376	.391	.767	106	7	6	101	116	83	.703	2	1	0	-10	*O	-0.7
1952	Cin-N	30	106	12	25	1	3	1	10	18	7	.236	.347	.330	.677	89	-1	-1	100	109	12	.607	1	2	-1	5	O/1	0.2
	Phi-N	98	321	45	88	16	3	1	37	44	26	.274	.363	.352	.715	98	1	1	101	124	42	.646	1	7	-4	8	O	0.2
	Yr	128	427	57	113	17	6	2	47	62	33	.265	.359	.347	.706	96	-0	-0	101	122	56	.647	2	9	-5	13		0.4
1953	Phi-N	125	409	42	111	14	2	6	47	38	43	.271	.339	.359	.699	83	-10	-9	99	111	51	.610	0	3	-2	-2	*O	-1.6
1954	Phi-N	92	259	28	62	12	4	3	28	29	39	.239	.318	.351	.670	75	-10	-9	99	110	29	.593	0	0	0	-6	O1	-1.7
Total	11	1221	4240	525	1149	209	45	58	481	482	437	.271	.349	.383	.731	97	-12	-11	100	105	589	.695	33	13		-3	*O/132	-5.7
■ HENRY YAIK	Yaik, Henry b: 3/1/1864, Detroit, Mich. d: 9/21/35, Detroit, Mich. 5'11", 185 lbs. Deb: 1888																											
1888	Pit-N	2	6	0	2	0	0	0	1	1	0	.333	.429	.333	.762	157	0	0	95	179	1	.750	0			0	/OC	0.0
■ AD YALE	Yale, William M. b: 4/17/1870, Bristol, Conn. d: 4/27/48, Bridgeport, Conn. Deb: 9/18/05																											
1905	Bro-N	4	13	1	1	0	0	0	1	1		.077	.143	.077	.220	-34	-2	-2	96	355	0	.167	0			0	/1	-0.1
■ HUGH YANCY	Yancy, Hugh b: 10/16/49, Sarasota, Fla. BR/TR, 5'11", 170 lbs. Deb: 7/05/72																											
1972	Chi-A	3	9	0	1	0	0	0	0	0	0	.111	.111	.111	.222	-32	-1	-2	106	0	-0	.100	0	1	-1	0	/3	-0.1
1974	Chi-A	1	0	0	0	0	0	0	0	0	0	—	—	—	—	—	0	-0	102	—	0	—	0	0	0	0	/D	0.0
1976	Chi-A	3	10	0	1	1	0	0	0	0	3	.100	.100	.200	.300	-14	-1	-1	99	0	0	.222	0	0	0	0	/2	0.0
Total	3	7	19	0	2	1	0	0	0	0	3	.105	.105	.158	.263	-23	-3	-3	102	0	0	.167	0	1	-1	1	/23D	-0.1
■ GEORGE YANKOWSKI	Yankowski, George Edward b: 11/19/22, Cambridge, Mass. BR/TR, 6', 180 lbs. Deb: 8/17/42																											
1942	Phi-A	6	13	0	2	1	0	0	2	0	2	.154	.154	.231	.385	8	-2	-2	96	235	0	.250	0	0	0	0	/C	0.0
1949	Chi-A	12	18	0	3	1	0	0	2	0	2	.167	.167	.222	.389	2	-3	-3	98	171	0	.235	0	0	0	0	/C	-0.1
Total	2	18	31	0	5	2	0	0	4	0	4	.161	.161	.226	.387	5	-4	-4	97	198	0	.250	0	0	0	0	/C	-0.1
■ GEORGE YANTZ	Yantz, George Webb b: 7/27/1886, Louisville, Ky. d: 2/26/67, Louisville, Ky. BR/TR, 5'6.5", 168 lbs. Deb: 9/30/12																											
1912	Chi-N	1	1	0	1	0	0	0	0	0	0	1.000	1.000	1.000	2.000	432	0	0	104	0	1	—	0			0	/C	0.0
■ YAM YARYAN	Yaryan, Clarence Everett b: 11/5/1892, Knowlton, Iowa d: 11/16/64, Birmingham, Ala. BR/TR, 5'10.5", 180 lbs. Deb: 4/23/21																											
1921	Chi-A	45	102	11	31	8	2	0	15	9	16	.304	.366	.422	.788	101	0	0	99	120	16	.746	0	0	0	1	C	0.2
1922	Chi-A	36	71	9	14	2	0	2	9	6	10	.197	.269	.310	.579	50	-5	-5	101	115	6	.526	1	0	0	2	C	-0.2
Total	2	81	173	20	45	10	2	2	24	15	26	.260	.326	.376	.702	80	-5	-5	100	118	22	.648	1	0	0	3	/C	0.0
■ CARL YASTRZEMSKI	Yastrzemski, Carl Michael "Yaz" b: 8/22/39, Southampton, N.Y. BL/TR, 5'11", 175 lbs. Deb: 4/11/61																											
1961	Bos-A	148	583	71	155	31	6	11	80	50	96	.266	.327	.396	.723	91	-7	-8	102	126	72	.642	6	5	-1	-6	*O	-2.0
1962	Bos-A	160	646	99	191	43	6	19	94	66	82	.296	.364	.469	.833	120	20	18	102	100	103	.780	7	4	-0	12	*O	2.4
1963	Bos-A	151	570	91	**183**	**40**	3	14	68	**95**	72	**.321**	**.419**	.475	.894	142	**42**	38	106	87	**118**	.928	8	5	-1	9	*O	**4.2**
1964	Bos-A	151	567	77	164	29	9	15	67	75	90	.289	.374	.451	.826	126	23	22	102	100	89	.774	6	5	-1	17	*O/3	3.3
1965	Bos-A	133	494	78	154	**45**	3	20	72	70	58	.312	**.398**	**.536**	**.935**	**152**	**42**	**37**	107	97	102	**.948**	7	6	-2	5	*O	3.7
1966	Bos-A	160	594	81	165	**39**	2	16	80	84	60	.278	.368	.431	.799	118	24	17	109	117	92	.767	8	9	-3	-5	*O	0.3
1967	Bos-A	161	579	**112**	**189**	31	4	**44**	**121**	91	69	**.326**	**.421**	**.622**	**1.043**	179	**76**	**66**	115	109	**155**	**1.154**	10	8	-2	7	*O	**7.2**
1968	Bos-A	157	539	90	162	32	2	23	74	**119**	90	**.301**	**.429**	.495	**.924**	178	**58**	**57**	101	100	**121**	**1.015**	13	6	0	12	*O/1	**7.0**
1969	Bos-A	162	603	96	154	28	2	40	111	101	91	.255	.363	.507	.871	135	33	29	105	111	113	.900	15	7	0	5	*O1	3.0
1970	Bos-A	161	566	**125**	186	29	0	40	102	128	66	.329	**.453**	**.592**	**1.045**	168	**72**	**64**	111	96	**157**	**1.202**	23	13	-1	-0	1O	**5.6**
1971	Bos-A	148	508	75	129	21	2	15	70	106	60	.254	.384	.392	.775	114	18	14	106	124	80	.785	8	7	-2	10	*O	1.9
1972	Bos-A	125	455	70	120	18	2	12	68	67	44	.264	.363	.391	.754	118	16	13	105	141	66	.722	5	4	-1	4	O1	1.1
1973	Bos-A	152	540	82	160	25	4	19	95	105	58	.296	.411	.463	.874	138	37	32	106	129	103	.897	9	7	-2	-1	*13O	2.3
1974	Bos-A	148	515	**93**	155	25	2	15	79	104	48	.301	.421	.445	.866	140	38	34	107	120	102	.918	12	7	-1	-10	1O/D	1.8

YEAR	TM/L	G	AB	R	H	2B	3B	HR	RBI	BB	SO	AVG	OBP	SLG	PRO	/A	BR	/A	PF	CHI	RC	TA	SB	CS	SBR	FR	POS	TPR
1975	Bos-A	149	543	91	146	30	1	14	60	87	67	.269	.372	.405	.777	110	16	10	109	93	84	.764	8	4	0	-0	*1/OD	0.1
1976	Bos-A	155	546	71	146	23	2	21	102	80	67	.267	.362	.432	.794	119	23	16	110	134	86	.770	5	6	-2	-8	1OD	0.0
1977	Bos-A	150	558	99	165	27	3	28	102	73	40	.296	.378	.505	.884	118	30	17	117	117	110	.908	11	1	3	9	*O/1D	2.3
1978	Bos-A	144	523	70	145	21	2	17	81	76	44	.277	.372	.423	.795	114	18	13	107	125	85	.776	4	5	-2	-0	O1D	0.7
1979	Bos-A	147	518	69	140	28	1	21	87	62	46	.270	.351	.450	.800	106	10	5	107	115	81	.763	3	3	-1	-1	D1O	0.0
1980	Bos-A	105	364	49	100	21	1	15	50	44	38	.275	.353	.462	.814	119	11	10	102	93	58	.771	0	2	-1	-2	DO1	0.4
1981	Bos-A	91	338	36	83	14	1	7	53	49	28	.246	.341	.355	.696	95	1	-1	106	150	41	.635	0	1	-1	0	D1	-0.2
1982	Bos-A	131	459	53	126	22	1	16	72	59	50	.275	.360	.431	.791	105	11	5	110	119	72	.749	0	1	-1	1	*D1/O	0.4
1983	Bos-A	119	380	38	101	24	0	10	56	54	29	.266	.360	.408	.768	110	7	6	101	118	55	.723	0	0	0	-0	*D/1O	0.6
Total	23	3308	11988	1816	3419	646	59	452	1844	1845	1393	.285	.382	.462	.844	128	617	513	107	113	2147	.873	168	116	-19	56	*O1D/3	46.1
■ **AL YATES** Yates, Albert Arthur b: 5/26/45, Jersey City, N.J. BR/TR, 6'2", 210 lbs. Deb: 5/13/71																												
1971	Mil-A	24	47	5	13	2	0	1	4	3	7	.277	.320	.383	.703	95	-0	-0	103	78	5	.611	1	0	0	0	O	0.0
■ **BERT YEABSLEY** Yeabsley, Robert Watkins b: 12/17/1893, Philadelphia, Pa. d: 2/8/61, Philadelphia, Pa. TR, 5'9.5", 175 lbs. Deb: 5/28/19																												
1919	Phi-N	3	0	0	0	0	0	0	0	1	0	—	1.000	—	1.383	313	0	0	104	0	0	—	0			0	H	0.0
■ **GEORGE YEAGER** Yeager, George J. "Doc" b: 6/5/1874, Cincinnati, Ohio d: 7/5/40, Cincinnati, Ohio TR, 5'10", 190 lbs. Deb: 9/25/1896																												
1896	Bos-N	2	5	1	1	0	0	0	0	0	1	.200	.200	.200	.400	6	-1	-1	108	0	0	.250	0			0	/1	0.0
1897	Bos-N	30	95	20	23	2	3	2	15	7		.242	.294	.389	.684	76	-3	-4	107	102	12	.639	2			0	CO/23	-0.2
1898	Bos-N	68	221	37	59	13	1	3	24	16		.267	.325	.376	.701	99	1	-1	104	79	28	.636	1			0	C1/OS	0.0
1899	Bos-N	3	8	1	1	0	0	0	0	1		.125	.222	.125	.347	-2	-1	-1	105	0	0	.286	0			0	/OC	0.0
1901	Cle-A	39	139	13	31	5	0	0	14	4		.223	.245	.259	.504	43	-11	-10	95	123	10	.389	2			2	C/1O2	-0.4
	Pit-N	26	91	9	24	2	1	0	10	4		.264	.295	.308	.602	76	-3	-3	101	119	9	.493	1			-2	C/31	-0.1
1902	NY-N	38	108	6	22	2	1	0	9	11		.204	.277	.241	.518	62	-4	-4	100	120	8	.442	1			1	C/1O	0.0
	Bal-A	11	38	3	7	1	0	0	1	2		.184	.225	.211	.436	22	-4	-4	102	42	2	.323	0			-1	C	-0.3
Total	6	217	705	90	168	25	6	5	73	45	1	.238	.287	.312	.599	71	-26	-27	101	98	68	.512	7			-1	C/1O23S	-1.0
■ **JOE YEAGER** Yeager, Joseph F. "Little Joe" b: 8/28/1875, Philadelphia, Pa. d: 7/2/37, Detroit, Mich. BR/TR, Deb: 4/22/1898																												
1898	Bro-N	43	134	12	23	5	1	0	15	7		.172	.218	.224	.442	30	-12	-11	95	151	7	.351	1			5	P/OS2	0.0
1899	Bro-N	23	47	12	9	0	1	0	4	6		.191	.309	.234	.543	50	-3	-3	105	112	3	.500	0			0	SP/O3	-0.2
1900	Bro-N	3	9	0	3	0	0	0	0	0		.333	.333	.333	.667	80	-0	-0	108	0	1	.500	0			0	/P3	0.0
1901	Det-A	41	125	18	37	7	1	2	17	4		.296	.318	.416	.734	95	0	-2	110	92	18	.670	3			3	PS/2	0.0
1902	Det-A	50	161	17	39	6	5	1	23	5		.242	.265	.360	.625	74	-6	-6	99	124	16	.516	0			3	PO2/S3	0.2
1903	Det-A	109	402	36	103	15	6	0	43	18		.256	.288	.323	.611	88	-7	-6	97	126	41	.525	9			-13	*3/PS	-2.0
1905	NY-A	115	401	53	107	16	7	0	42	25		.267	.310	.342	.652	107	3	3	102	112	46	.578	8			-2	3S	0.6
1906	NY-A	57	123	20	37	6	1	0	12	13		.301	.368	.366	.734	110	5	2	120	97	18	.709	3			1	S2/3	0.3
1907	StL-A	123	436	32	104	21	7	1	44	31		.239	.289	.326	.615	100	-1	-0	98	111	45	.554	11			1	32S	0.6
1908	StL-A	10	15	3	5	1	0	0	1	1		.333	.375	.400	.775	150	1	1	103	63	3	.900	2			0	/2S	0.1
Total	10	574	1853	203	467	77	29	4	201	110		.252	.295	.331	.626	91	-21	-23	101	115	199	.551	37			-2	3/PS2O	-0.4
■ **STEVE YEAGER** Yeager, Stephen Wayne b: 11/24/48, Huntington, W.Va. BR/TR, 6', 190 lbs. Deb: 8/02/72																												
1972	LA-N	35	106	18	29	0	1	4	15	16	26	.274	.374	.406	.780	129	3	4	94	112	16	.750	0	0	0	-3	C	0.3
1973	LA-N	54	134	18	34	5	0	2	10	15	33	.254	.342	.336	.678	88	-2	-2	100	79	16	.615	1	0	0	-1	C	0.1
1974	LA-N	94	316	41	84	16	1	12	41	32	77	.266	.337	.437	.774	124	6	8	93	91	46	.722	2	2	-1	2	C	1.4
1975	LA-N	135	452	34	103	16	1	12	54	40	75	.228	.302	.347	.649	84	-13	-10	95	108	45	.561	2	5	-2	8	*C	0.0
1976	LA-N	117	359	42	77	11	3	11	35	30	84	.214	.288	.354	.642	82	-10	-9	100	84	38	.580	3	1	0	3	*C	0.0
1977	LA-N	125	387	53	99	21	2	16	55	43	84	.256	.336	.444	.781	107	4	4	100	100	57	.738	1	3	-2	0	*C	0.0
1978	LA-N	94	228	19	44	7	0	4	23	36	41	.193	.303	.276	.579	63	-11	-10	99	122	20	.529	0	0	0	-6	C	-1.5
1979	LA-N	105	310	33	67	9	2	13	41	29	68	.216	.283	.384	.667	80	-9	-9	100	103	31	.584	1	0	0	4	*C	-0.2
1980	LA-N	96	227	20	48	8	0	2	20	20	54	.211	.275	.273	.548	55	-14	-13	97	116	16	.444	2	3	-1	-13	C	-2.6
1981	LA-N	42	86	5	18	2	0	3	7	6	14	.209	.261	.337	.598	70	-4	-4	98	72	7	.500	0	0	0	-2	C	-0.5
1982	LA-N	82	196	13	48	5	2	2	18	13	28	.245	.295	.321	.617	77	-7	-6	95	102	19	.510	0	0	0	-9	C	-1.4
1983	LA-N	113	335	31	68	8	3	15	41	23	57	.203	.256	.379	.635	74	-13	-13	100	94	28	.537	1	1	-0	-9	*C	-1.9
1984	LA-N	74	197	16	45	4	0	4	29	20	38	.228	.300	.310	.609	69	-7	-8	104	156	19	.526	1	2	-1	-2	C	-0.9
1985	LA-N	53	121	4	25	4	1	0	9	7	24	.207	.250	.256	.506	45	-9	-8	93	116	7	.380	0	1	-1	-0	C	-0.7
1986	Sea-A	50	130	10	27	2	0	2	12	12	23	.208	.275	.269	.544	47	-9	-10	105	117	9	.435	0	0	0	-0	C	-0.6
Total	15	1269	3584	357	816	118	16	102	410	342	726	.228	.300	.355	.655	83	-95	-87	98	104	375	.593	14	18	-7	-28	*C	-8.5
■ **BILL YEATMAN** Yeatman, William Suter b: 1859, Alexandria, Va. d: 4/20/01, York, Pa. Deb: 4/20/1872																												
1872	Nat-n	1	3	0	0							.000															/O	
■ **ARCHIE YELLE** Yelle, Archie Joseph b: 6/11/1892, Saginaw, Mich. d: 5/2/83, Woodland, Cal. BR/TR, 5'10.5", 170 lbs. Deb: 5/12/17																												
1917	Det-A	25	51	4	7	1	0	0	0	5	4	.137	.214	.157	.371	14	-5	-5	98	0	2	.341	2			-1	C	-0.4
1918	Det-A	56	144	7	25	3	0	0	7	9	15	.174	.227	.194	.422	28	-13	-12	97	91	6	.319	0			-1	C	-0.9
1919	Det-A	6	4	1	0	0	0	0	0	1	0	.000	.200	.000	.200	-44	-1	-1	93	0	0	.250	0			0	/C	0.0
Total	3	87	199	12	32	4	0	0	7	15	19	.161	.223	.181	.404	23	-19	-18	97	65	8	.323	2			-2	/C	-1.3
■ **STEVE YERKES** Yerkes, Stephen Douglas b: 5/15/1888, Hatboro, Pa. d: 1/31/71, Lansdale, Pa. BR/TR, 5'9", 165 lbs. Deb: 9/29/09																												
1909	Bos-A	5	7	0	2	0	0	0	0	0		.286	.286	.286	.571	74	-0	-0	109	0	1	.400	0			0	/S	0.0
1911	Bos-A	142	502	70	140	24	3	1	57	52		.279	.354	.345	.698	96	-2	-1	99	116	68	.677	14			-13	*S23	-0.2
1912	Bos-A	131	523	73	132	22	6	0	42	41		.252	.312	.317	.629	75	-14	-19	107	75	54	.550	4			-18	*2	-3.8
1913	Bos-A	137	483	67	129	29	6	1	48	50	32	.267	.338	.358	.696	101	2	0	103	103	62	.667	11			-23	*2	-2.7
1914	Bos-A	92	293	23	64	17	2	1	23	14	23	.218	.259	.300	.559	70	-13	-12	98	95	24	.464	5	6	-2	-12	2	-2.8
	Pit-F	39	142	18	48	9	5	1	25	11	13	.338	.386	.493	.879	160	9	10	94	131	29	.883	2			-4	S	0.9
1915	Pit-F	121	434	44	125	17	8	1	49	30	27	.288	.334	.371	.705	104	4	2	104	114	63	.673	17			5	*2/S	0.9
1916	Chi-N	44	137	12	36	6	2	1	10	9	7	.263	.308	.358	.666	89	0	-2	117	76	16	.584	1			1	2	0.0
Total	7	711	2521	307	676	124	32	6	254	207	102	.268	.327	.350	.677	94	-13	-22	103	100	316	.625	54	6		-62	2S/3	-7.7
■ **TOM YEWCIC** Yewcic, Thomas J. "Kibby" b: 5/9/32, Conemaugh, Pa. BR/TR, 5'11", 180 lbs. Deb: 6/27/57																												
1957	Det-A	1	1	0	0	0	0	0	0	0	0	.000	.000	.000	.000	-93	-0	-0	107	0	0	.000	0	0	0	0	/C	0.0
■ **ED YEWELL** Yewell, Edwin Leonard b: 8/22/1862, Washington, D.C. d: 9/15/40, Washington, D.C. Deb: 5/12/1884																												
1884	Was-a	27	93	14	23	3	1	0		1		.247	.263	.301	.564	97	-1	0	88	0	8	.429				0	2/O3S	0.0
	Was-U	1	4	0	0	0	0	0		0		.000	.000	.000	.000	-99	-1	-1	97	0	0	.000	0			0	/3	0.0
Total	1	28	97	14	23	3	1	0		1		.237	.253	.289	.541	89	-2	-1	89	0	8	.405	0			0	/23OS	0.0
■ **JOE YINGLING** Yingling, Joseph Granville b: 7/23/1866, Westminster, Md. d: 10/24/46, Manchester, Md. BR/TL, 5'7.5", 145 lbs. Deb: 5/28/1886																												
1886	Was-N	1	2	0	0	0	0	0	0	0	1	.000	.000	.000	.000	-99	-0	-0	94	0	0	.000	0			0	/P	0.0
1894	Phi-N	1	4	0	1	0	0	0	0	0	1	.250	.250	.250	.500	23	-0	-0	95	0	0	.333	0			0	/S	0.0
Total	2	2	6	0	1	0	0	0	0	0	2	.167	.167	.167	.333	-14	-1	-1	95	0	0	.200	0			0	/SP	0.0
■ **BILL YOHE** Yohe, William Clyde b: 9/2/1878, Mt.Elere, Ill. d: 12/24/38, Bremerton, Wash. TR, 5'8", 180 lbs. Deb: 8/30/09																												
1909	Was-A	21	72	6	15	2	0	0	4	3		.208	.240	.236	.476	56	-4	-3	90	92	4	.386	2			1	3	-0.1
■ **TONY YORK** York, Anthony Batton b: 11/27/12, Irene, Tex. d: 4/18/70, Hillsboro, Tex. BR/TR, 5'10", 165 lbs. Deb: 4/18/44																												
1944	Chi-N	28	85	4	20	1	0	0	7	4	11	.235	.270	.247	.517	46	-6	-6	101	120	6	.373	0			2	S3	-0.1
■ **RUDY YORK** York, Preston Rudolph b: 8/17/13, Ragland, Ala. d: 2/5/70, Rome, Ga. BR/TR, 6'1", 209 lbs. Deb: 8/22/34 MC																												
1934	Det-A	3	6	0	1	0	0	0	0	1	3	.167	.286	.167	.452	20	-1	-1	98	0	0	.400	0	0	0	0	/C	0.0
1937	Det-A	104	375	72	115	18	3	35	103	41	52	.307	.375	.651	1.026	141	27	22	109	101	91	1.099	3	2	-0	-5	C3/1	2.0

YEAR	TM/L	G	AB	R	H	2B	3B	HR	RBI	BB	SO	AVG	OBP	SLG	PRO	/A	BR	/A	PF	CHI	RC	TA	SB	CS	SBR	FR	POS	TPR
1938	Det-A	135	463	85	138	27	2	33	127	92	74	.298	.417	.579	.995	146	34	34	100	119	116	1.110	1	2	-1	-5	*CO/1	2.7
1939	Det-A	102	329	66	101	16	1	20	68	41	50	.307	.387	.544	.931	122	17	11	111	96	70	.962	5	0	2	-2	C1	1.2
1940	Det-A	155	588	105	186	46	6	33	134	89	88	.316	.410	.583	.993	138	47	37	111	116	147	1.055	3	2	-0	5	*1	3.2
1941	Det-A	155	590	91	153	29	3	27	111	92	88	.259	.360	.456	.816	108	12	7	106	119	101	.804	3	1	0	-1	*1	0.1
1942	Det-A	153	577	81	150	26	4	21	90	73	71	.260	.343	.428	.771	103	11	2	113	108	86	.724	3	3	-1	16	*1	1.5
1943	Det-A	155	571	90	155	22	11	**34**	**118**	84	88	.271	.366	**.527**	.893	152	41	37	106	113	108	.883	5	5	-2	18	*1	5.3
1944	Det-A	151	583	77	161	27	7	18	98	68	73	.276	.353	.439	.792	119	18	15	105	121	91	.745	5	3	-0	5	*1	1.1
1945	Det-A	155	595	71	157	25	5	18	87	60	85	.264	.331	.413	.745	109	10	6	106	111	78	.668	6	6	-2	-2	*1	-0.2
1946	Bos-A	154	579	78	160	30	6	17	119	86	93	.276	.371	.437	.808	109	20	10	114	**158**	98	.785	3	2	-0	5	*1	0.7
1947	Bos-A	48	184	16	39	7	0	6	27	22	32	.212	.296	.348	.644	73	-6	-8	108	128	18	.555	0	0	0	-0	1	-0.8
	Chi-A	102	400	40	97	18	4	15	64	36	55	.243	.305	.420	.725	104	-2	-0	97	117	51	.651	1	0	0	-1	*1	-0.3
	Yr	150	584	56	136	25	4	21	91	58	87	.233	.302	.397	.699	93	-8	-8	100	121	72	.633	1	0	0	-1		-1.1
1948	Phi-A	31	51	4	8	0	0	0	6	7	15	.157	.259	.157	.415	12	-6	-6	102	253	2	.333	0	0	0	1	1	-0.4
Total	13	1603	5891	876	1621	291	52	277	1152	792	867	.275	.362	.483	.845	120	223	166	107	119	1057	.858	38	26	-4	34	*1C/3O	16.1
■ **TOM YORK** York, Thomas J. b: 7/13/1851, Brooklyn, N.Y. d: 2/17/36, New York, N.Y. BL , 5'9", 165 lbs. Deb: 5/09/1871 M																												
1871	Tro-n	29	156	37	34							.218															*O	
1872	Bal-n	49	249	60	67							.269															*O	
1873	Bal-n	56	279	68	79							.283															*O	
1874	Phi-n	50	241	37	60							.249															*O	
1875	Har-n	85	387	66	110							.284															*O	
1876	Har-N	67	263	47	68	12	7	1	39	10	4	.259	.286	.369	.655	108	5	1	108	134	28	.549				3	*O	0.3
1877	Har-N	56	237	43	67	16	7	1	37	3	11	.283	.292	.422	.714	137	5	9	89	124	30	.606				-0	*O	0.6
1878	Pro-N	62	269	56	83	19	**10**	1	26	8	19	.309	.329	.465	.793	162	16	17	98	61	42	.715				3	*OM	1.4
1879	Pro-N	81	342	69	106	25	5	1	50	19	28	.310	.346	.421	.767	149	19	18	102	126	51	.691				-4	*O	1.0
1880	Pro-N	53	203	21	43	9	2	0	18	8	29	.212	.242	.276	.518	78	-5	-4	96	120	14	.400				-4	O	-0.9
1881	Pro-N	85	316	57	96	23	5	2	47	29	26	.304	.362	.427	.790	158	18	21	93	118	50	.745				-3	*OM	1.5
1882	Pro-N	81	321	48	86	23	7	1	40	19	14	.268	.309	.393	.701	116	8	6	106	111	40	.617				-3	*O	0.1
1883	Cle-N	100	381	56	99	29	5	2	46	**37**	55	.260	.325	.378	.703	108	7	4	105	102	48	.642				-12	*O	-0.4
1884	Bal-a	83	314	64	70	14	7	1		34		.223	.318	.322	.640	114	6	6	99	0	33	.594				-5	*O	0.1
1885	Bal-a	22	87	6	23	4	2	0		8		.264	.326	.356	.683	112	2	1	106	0	10	.609				0	O	0.1
Total	5 n	269	1312	268	350							.267															O	
Total	10	690	2733	467	741	174	57	10	303	175	186	.271	.317	.387	.705	126	81	80	100	94	347	.624				-25	O	3.8
■ **NED YOST** Yost, Edgar Frederick b: 8/19/55, Eureka, Cal. BR/TR, 6'1", 190 lbs. Deb: 4/12/80																												
1980	Mil-A	15	31	0	5	0	0	0	0	0	6	.161	.161	.161	.323	-12	-5	-4	95	0	1	.185	0	0	0	0	C	-0.3
1981	Mil-A	18	27	4	6	0	0	3	3	3	6	.222	.300	.556	.856	148	1	1	96	49	5	.857	0	0	0	0	C	0.2
1982	Mil-A	40	98	13	27	6	3	1	8	7	20	.276	.324	.429	.752	111	0	1	94	71	14	.712	3	1	0	1	C/D	0.5
1983	Mil-A	61	196	21	44	5	1	6	28	5	36	.224	.244	.352	.596	67	-11	-9	92	126	15	.475	1	0	0	3	C	-0.1
1984	Tex-A	80	242	15	44	4	0	6	25	6	47	.182	.202	.273	.474	30	-23	-23	100	119	12	.356	1	2	-1	-4	C	-2.3
1985	Mon-N	5	11	1	2	0	0	0	0	0	2	.182	.182	.182	.364	2	-1	-1	94	0	0	.222	0	0	0	-1	/C	-0.1
Total	6	219	605	54	128	15	4	16	64	21	117	.212	.238	.329	.567	57	-38	-35	96	102	47	.469	5	3	-0	-0	C/D	-2.1
■ **EDDIE YOST** Yost, Edward Frederick Joseph "The Walking Man" b: 10/13/26, Brooklyn, N.Y. BR/TR, 5'10", 170 lbs. Deb: 8/16/44 MC																												
1944	Was-A	7	14	3	2	0	0	0	0	1	2	.143	.200	.143	.343	-1	-2	-2	90	0	1	.250	0	0	0	0	/3S	-0.1
1946	Was-A	8	25	2	2	1	0	0	1	5	5	.080	.233	.120	.353	1	-3	-3	92	129	1	.400	2	1	0	-0	/3	-0.2
1947	Was-A	115	428	52	102	17	3	0	14	45	57	.238	.314	.292	.606	71	-17	-16	97	44	41	.516	3	5	-2	-8	*3	-2.3
1948	Was-A	145	555	74	138	32	11	2	50	82	51	.249	.349	.357	.706	85	-9	-11	103	73	73	.662	4	3	-1	-13	*3	-2.9
1949	Was-A	124	435	57	110	19	7	9	45	91	41	.253	.383	.391	.774	115	5	11	91	83	71	.782	3	3	-1	1	*3	1.0
1950	Was-A	155	573	114	169	26	2	11	58	**141**	63	.295	.440	.405	.845	119	24	25	99	65	116	.915	6	6	-2	-2	*3	1.4
1951	Was-A	154	568	109	161	**36**	4	12	65	126	55	.283	.423	.424	.847	136	30	34	95	72	117	.919	6	4	-1	-26	*3/O	0.2
1952	Was-A	157	587	92	137	32	3	12	49	**129**	73	.233	.378	.359	.738	106	10	10	100	64	93	.762	4	3	-1	-35	*3	-2.6
1953	Was-A	152	577	107	157	30	7	9	45	**123**	59	.272	.403	.395	.799	123	19	24	94	56	103	.830	7	4	-0	-14	*3	0.2
1954	Was-A	155	539	101	138	26	4	11	47	131	71	.256	.406	.380	.786	118	19	20	98	72	97	.851	7	3	0	5	*3	1.8
1955	Was-A	122	375	64	91	17	5	7	48	95	54	.243	.410	.371	.780	122	11	16	91	114	66	.847	4	3	-1	2	*3	2.0
1956	Was-A	152	515	94	119	17	2	11	53	**151**	82	.231	.412	.336	.748	98	9	7	102	92	86	.831	8	5	-1	11	*3/O	1.9
1957	Was-A	110	414	47	104	13	5	9	38	73	49	.251	.370	.372	.742	105	4	6	98	80	58	.713	1	11	-6	-8	*3	-0.6
1958	Was-A	134	406	55	91	16	0	8	37	81	43	.224	.365	.323	.688	94	-1	0	97	98	52	.679	3	6	-3	-17	*3/O1	-1.5
1959	Det-A	148	521	**115**	145	19	0	21	61	**135**	77	.278	**.437**	.436	.873	127	38	29	111	73	115	.997	9	2	2	-9	*3/2	2.1
1960	Det-A	143	497	78	129	23	2	14	47	**125**	69	.260	**.416**	.398	.814	120	22	21	102	74	92	.877	5	4	-1	-18	*3	0.5
1961	LA-A	76	213	29	43	4	0	3	15	50	48	.202	.358	.263	.621	62	-7	-11	111	90	24	.624	0	1	-1	1	3	-0.5
1962	LA-A	52	104	22	25	9	1	0	10	30	21	.240	.415	.346	.761	105	3	3	102	110	17	.798	0	2	-1	-1	3/1	0.0
Total	18	2109	7346	1215	1863	337	56	139	683	1614	920	.254	.395	.371	.766	109	154	163	99	76	1225	.813	72	66	-18	-130	*3/O1S2	0.4
■ **ELMER YOTER** Yoter, Elmer Elsworth b: 6/26/1900, Plainfield, Pa. d: 7/26/66, Camp Hill, Pa. BR/TR, 5'7", 155 lbs. Deb: 9/09/21																												
1921	Phi-A	3	3	0	0	0	0	0	0	0	0	.000	.000	.000	.000	-97	-1	-1	103	0	0	.000	0	0	0	0	H	0.0
1924	Cle-A	19	66	3	18	1	1	0	7	5	8	.273	.324	.318	.642	68	-3	-3	97	110	7	.542	0	0	0	2	3	0.0
1927	Chi-N	13	27	2	6	1	1	0	5	4	4	.222	.323	.333	.656	76	-1	-1	100	194	3	.619	0			0	3	0.0
1928	Chi-N	1	0	0	0	0	0	0	0	0	0	—	—	—	—	—	0	0	95	—	—	—	0			0	/3	0.0
Total	4	36	96	5	24	2	2	0	12	9	12	.250	.314	.313	.627	65	-5	-5	98	132	13	.542	0	0		2	/3	0.0
■ **DEL YOUNG** Young, Delmer Edward b: 3/11/12, Cleveland, Ohio d: 12/8/79, San Francisco, Cal. BB/TR, 5'11", 168 lbs. Deb: 4/19/37																												
1937	Phi-N	109	360	36	70	9	2	0	24	18	55	.194	.235	.231	.465	25	-36	-40	108	104	20	.362	6			2	*2	-3.3
1938	Phi-N	108	340	27	78	13	2	0	31	20	35	.229	.276	.279	.556	53	-22	-22	100	118	27	.435	0			-4	S2	-1.8
1939	Phi-N	77	217	22	57	9	2	3	20	8	24	.263	.289	.364	.653	79	-8	-7	94	83	22	.533	1			-7	S2	-0.9
1940	Phi-N	15	33	2	8	0	1	0	1	2	1	.242	.286	.303	.589	64	-2	-2	97	37	3	.462	0			-0	/S2	0.0
Total	4	309	950	87	213	31	7	3	76	48	115	.224	.264	.281	.545	48	-68	-70	102	102	72	.440	7			-9	S2	-6.0
■ **DEL YOUNG** Young, Delmer John b: 12/24/1885, Macon City, Mo. d: 12/17/59, Cleveland, Ohio BL/TR, 5'11", 195 lbs. Deb: 09																												
1909	Cin-N	2	7	0	2	0	0	0	1	1		.286	.375	.286	.661	113	0	0	94	193	1	.600	0			0	/O	0.0
1914	Buf-F	80	174	17	48	5	5	4	22	3	13	.276	.288	.431	.719	100	-0	-1	104	91	22	.619	0			-7	O	-1.0
1915	Buf-F	12	15	0	2	0	0	0	0	1	0	.133	.188	.133	.321	-4	-2	-2	100	0	1	.308	1			0	/O	-0.1
Total	3	94	196	17	52	5	5	4	23	5	13	.265	.284	.403	.687	93	-2	-3	104	88	24	.590	1			-7	/O	-1.1
■ **DON YOUNG** Young, Donald Wayne b: 10/18/45, Houston, Tex. BR/TR, 6'2", 185 lbs. Deb: 9/09/65																												
1965	Chi-N	11	35	1	2	0	0	1	2	0	11	.057	.057	.143	.200	-45	-7	-7	102	104	0	.152	0	0	0	-2	O	-0.9
1969	Chi-N	101	272	36	65	12	3	6	27	38	74	.239	.343	.371	.714	94	1	-2	107	91	35	.671	1	5	-3	-7	*O	-1.7
Total	2	112	307	37	67	12	3	7	29	38	85	.218	.314	.345	.660	80	-6	-8	106	92	36	.602	1	5	-3	-9	O	-2.6
■ **GEORGE YOUNG** Young, George Joseph b: 4/1/1890, Brooklyn, N.Y. d: 3/13/50, Brightwaters, N.Y. BL/TR, 6', 185 lbs. Deb: 8/10/13																												
1913	Cle-A	2	2	0	0	0	0	0	0	0	0	.000	.000	.000	.000	-95	-0	-1	106	0	0	.000	0			0	H	0.0
■ **GERALD YOUNG** Young, Gerald Anthony b: 10/22/64, Tele, Honduras BB/TR, 6'2", 185 lbs. Deb: 7/08/87																												
1987	Hou-N	71	274	44	88	9	2	1	15	26	27	.321	.382	.380	.762	111	2	5	93	59	44	.801	26	9	2	7	O	1.1
1988	Hou-N	149	576	79	148	21	9	0	37	66	66	.257	.336	.325	.661	97	-5	-1	93	76	67	.690	65	27	3	5	*O	0.4
Total	2	220	850	123	236	30	11	1	52	92	93	.278	.351	.342	.693	102	-3	4	93	71	110	.724	91	36	6	12	O	1.5
■ **HERMAN YOUNG** Young, Herman John b: 4/14/1886, Boston, Mass. d: 12/13/66, Ipswich, Mass. BR/TR, 5'8", 155 lbs. Deb: 6/11/11																												
1911	Bos-N	9	25	2	6	0	0	0	0	0	3	.240	.269	.240	.509	42	-2	-2	103	0	2	.368	0			-0	/3S	-0.1

YEAR	TM/L	G	AB	R	H	2B	3B	HR	RBI	BB	SO	AVG	OBP	SLG	PRO	/A	BR	/A	PF	CHI	RC	TA	SB	CS	SBR	FR	POS	TPR
■ JOHN YOUNG	Young, John Thomas b: 2/9/49, Los Angeles, Cal. BL/TL, 6'3", 210 lbs. Deb: 9/09/71																											
1971	Det-A	2	4	1	2	1	0	0	1	0	0	.500	.500	.750	1.250	261	1	1	96	136	2	1.500	0	0	0	0	/1	0.1
■ PEP YOUNG	Young, Lemuel Floyd b: 8/29/07, Jamestown, N.C. d: 1/14/62, Jamestown, N.C. BR/TR, 5'9", 162 lbs. Deb: 4/25/33																											
1933	Pit-N	25	20	3	6	1	1	0	0	0	5	.300	.300	.450	.750	118	0	0	95	0	3	.643	0			0	/2S	0.0
1934	Pit-N	19	17	3	4	0	0	0	2	0	6	.235	.235	.235	.471	25	-2	-2	105	180	1	.308	0			-0	/2S	-0.1
1935	Pit-N	128	494	60	131	25	10	7	82	21	59	.265	.298	.399	.697	80	-11	-16	107	138	58	.594	2			-15	*2/3OS	-2.1
1936	Pit-N	125	475	47	118	23	10	6	77	29	52	.248	.293	.377	.670	81	-15	-14	98	141	53	.579	3			-19	*2	-2.3
1937	Pit-N	113	408	43	106	20	3	9	54	26	63	.260	.306	.390	.695	86	-8	-9	102	107	49	.613	4			3	S32	0.0
1938	Pit-N	149	562	58	156	36	5	4	79	40	64	.278	.329	.381	.710	94	-5	-5	100	129	70	.627	7			**32**	*2	3.7
1939	Pit-N	84	293	34	81	14	3	3	29	23	29	.276	.333	.375	.709	90	-4	-4	100	91	37	.621	1			1	2	0.0
1940	Pit-N	54	136	19	34	8	2	2	20	12	23	.250	.320	.382	.702	98	-1	-1	95	128	18	.657	1			-2	2/S3	0.0
1941	Cin-N	4	12	2	2	0	0	0	0	0	1	.167	.231	.167	.397	13	-1	-1	99	0	1	.300	0			0	/3	0.0
	StL-N	2	2	0	0	0	0	0	0	0	2	.000	.000	.000	.000	-91	-1	-1	110	0	0	.000	0			0	H	0.0
	Yr	6	14	2	2	0	0	0	0	0	3	.143	.200	.143	.343	-2	-2	-2	103	0	0	.250	0			0		0.0
1945	StL-N	27	47	5	7	1	0	1	4	1	8	.149	.167	.234	.401	11	-6	-6	100	99	2	.293	0			-1	S/32	-0.5
Total	10	730	2466	274	645	128	34	32	347	152	312	.262	.308	.380	.688	85	-54	-57	101	123	291	.614	18			-0	2/S3O	-1.3
■ MIKE YOUNG	Young, Michael Darren b: 3/20/60, Oakland, Cal. BB/TR, 6'2", 195 lbs. Deb: 9/14/82																											
1982	Bal-A	6	2	2	0	0	0	0	0	0	1	.000	.000	.000	.000	-99	-1	-1	100	0	0	.000	0	0	0	-0	/OD	0.0
1983	Bal-A	25	36	5	6	2	1	0	2	2	8	.167	.231	.278	.509	39	-3	-3	100	78	2	.452	1	0	0	-5	O/D	-0.7
1984	Bal-A	123	401	59	101	17	2	17	52	58	110	.252	.356	.431	.788	124	10	13	94	94	66	.795	6	2	1	-8	*O/D	0.2
1985	Bal-A	139	450	72	123	22	1	28	81	48	104	.273	.349	.513	.862	134	19	20	99	102	78	.833	1	5	-3	0	OD	1.6
1986	Bal-A	117	369	43	93	15	1	9	42	49	90	.252	.344	.371	.716	97	-1	-0	99	102	47	.662	3	1	0	-1	OD	-0.2
1987	Bal-A	110	363	46	87	10	1	16	39	46	91	.240	.328	.405	.733	96	-3	-2	98	80	48	.707	10	7	-1	-4	OD	-0.7
1988	Phi-N	75	146	13	33	14	0	1	14	26	43	.226	.347	.342	.689	97	1	0	101	106	19	.675	0	0	0	-3	O	-0.4
	Mil-A	8	14	2	0	0	0	0	0	2	5	.000	.176	.000	.176	-45	-3	-3	103	0	0	.214	0	0	0	-1	/OD	-0.3
Total	7	603	1781	242	443	80	6	71	230	231	452	.249	.341	.420	.761	110	20	25	98	95	262	.753	21	15	-3	-21	OD	-0.5
■ BABE YOUNG	Young, Norman Robert b: 7/1/15, Astoria, N.Y. d: 12/25/83, Everett, Mass. BL/TL, 6'2.5", 185 lbs. Deb: 9/26/36																											
1936	NY-N	1	1	0	0	0	0	0	0	0	0	.000	.000	.000	.000	-99	-0	-0	100	0	0	.000	0			0	H	0.0
1939	NY-N	22	75	8	23	4	0	3	14	5	6	.307	.373	.480	.853	129	3	3	99	116	14	.846	0			0	1	0.1
1940	NY-N	149	556	75	159	27	4	17	101	69	28	.286	.367	.441	.807	122	17	17	100	134	92	.784	4			-2	*1	0.2
1941	NY-N	152	574	90	152	28	5	25	104	66	39	.265	.346	.462	.807	122	18	16	103	117	93	.776	1			-3	*1	-0.7
1942	NY-N	101	287	37	80	17	1	11	59	34	22	.279	.365	.460	.825	137	14	14	103	133	50	.815	1			-2	O1	0.9
1946	NY-N	104	291	30	81	11	0	7	33	30	21	.278	.346	.388	.734	106	3	2	102	92	40	.679	3			-3	1O	-0.5
1947	NY-N	14	14	0	1	1	0	0	0	0	1	.071	.071	.143	.214	-44	-3	-3	101	0	0	.154	0			0	H	-0.2
	Cin-N	95	364	55	103	21	3	14	79	35	26	.283	.349	.473	.822	128	7	12	91	145	60	.777	0			-3	1	0.3
	Yr	109	378	55	104	22	3	14	79	35	27	.275	.340	.460	.800	120	4	8	92	126	59	.748	0			-3		0.1
1948	Cin-N	49	130	11	30	7	2	1	12	19	12	.231	.329	.338	.667	78	-3	-4	103	96	16	.630	0			-0	1/O	-0.3
	StL-N	41	111	14	27	5	2	1	13	16	6	.243	.339	.351	.690	86	-2	-2	101	116	14	.632	0			-2	1	-0.4
	Yr	90	241	25	57	12	4	2	25	35	18	.237	.333	.344	.678	82	-5	-6	102	106	30	.631	0			-2		-0.7
Total	8	728	2403	320	656	121	17	79	415	274	161	.273	.352	.436	.788	117	55	55	100	122	379	.770	9			-15	1/O	-0.6
■ RALPH YOUNG	Young, Ralph Stuart b: 9/19/1889, Philadelphia, Pa. d: 1/24/65, Philadelphia, Pa. BB/TR, 5'5", 165 lbs. Deb: 4/10/13																											
1913	NY-A	7	15	2	1	0	0	0	0	3	3	.067	.222	.067	.289	-15	-2	-2	101	0	1	.429	2			-1	/S	-0.1
1915	Det-A	123	378	44	92	6	5	0	31	53	31	.243	.339	.286	.625	80	-4	-8	108	98	41	.589	12	11	-3	-8	*2	-2.1
1916	Det-A	153	528	60	139	16	6	1	45	62	43	.263	.342	.322	.664	95	1	-2	105	95	61	.619	20	20	-6	-6	*2/S3	-0.2
1917	Det-A	141	503	64	116	18	2	1	35	61	35	.231	.317	.280	.598	84	-9	-8	98	92	49	.550	8			6	*2	0.8
1918	Det-A	91	298	31	56	7	1	0	21	54	17	.188	.313	.218	.531	62	-12	-11	97	120	26	.554	15			-11	2	-1.8
1919	Det-A	125	456	63	96	13	5	1	25	53	32	.211	.294	.268	.562	62	-25	-21	93	70	43	.511	8			9	*2/S	0.0
1920	Det-A	150	594	84	173	21	6	0	33	85	30	.291	.382	.347	.729	91	-1	-4	103	49	82	.694	8	13	-5	-11	*2	-1.6
1921	Det-A	107	401	70	120	8	3	0	29	69	23	.299	.406	.334	.740	94	-1	1	96	79	60	.748	11	9	-2	-16	*2	-1.2
1922	Phi-A	125	470	62	105	19	2	1	35	55	21	.223	.309	.279	.587	52	-31	-34	104	99	43	.531	8	6	-1	-4	*2	-2.9
Total	9	1022	3643	480	898	108	30	4	254	495	235	.247	.339	.296	.635	79	-85	-88	101	84	406	.599	92	59		-42	2/S3	-9.1
■ DICK YOUNG	Young, Richard Ennis b: 6/3/28, Seattle, Wash. BB/TR, 5'11", 175 lbs. Deb: 9/11/51																											
1951	Phi-N	15	68	7	16	5	0	0	2	3	6	.235	.268	.309	.576	56	-4	-4	97	32	5	.436	0	1	-1	-2	2	-0.6
1952	Phi-N	5	9	3	2	1	0	0	0	1	3	.222	.300	.333	.633	75	-0	-0	101	0	1	.714	1	0	0	0	/2	0.0
Total	2	20	77	10	18	6	0	0	2	4	9	.234	.272	.312	.583	59	-5	-4	97	28	6	.483	1	1	-0	-2	/2	-0.6
■ BOBBY YOUNG	Young, Robert George b: 1/22/25, Granite, Md. d: 1/28/85, Baltimore, Md. BL/TR, 6'1", 175 lbs. Deb: 7/28/48																											
1948	StL-N	3	1	0	0	0	0	0	0	0	1	.000	.000	.000	.000	-99	-0	-0	101	0	0	.000				0	/3	0.0
1951	StL-A	147	611	75	159	13	9	1	31	44	51	.260	.310	.316	.626	66	-26	-30	105	49	60	.518	8	7	-2	-0	*2	-2.5
1952	StL-A	149	575	59	142	15	9	4	39	56	48	.247	.314	.325	.639	80	-17	-15	97	78	62	.555	3	3	-1	-7	*2	-1.7
1953	StL-A	148	537	48	137	22	2	4	25	41	40	.255	.309	.326	.635	67	-22	-26	107	51	56	.530	2	1	0	-16	*2	-3.3
1954	Bal-A	130	432	43	106	13	6	4	24	54	42	.245	.331	.331	.662	86	-10	-8	95	60	49	.598	4	4	-1	-9	*2	-1.2
1955	Bal-A	59	186	5	37	3	0	1	8	11	23	.199	.244	.231	.475	31	-19	-17	90	65	10	.353	1	4	-2	-8	2	-2.2
	Cle-A	18	45	7	14	1	1	0	6	1	2	.311	.326	.378	.704	85	-1	-1	104	132	6	.581	0	0	0	0	2/3	0.0
	Yr	77	231	12	51	4	1	1	14	12	25	.221	.259	.260	.519	43	-20	-18	93	81	16	.397	1	4	-2	-7		-2.2
1956	Cle-A	1	0	0	0	0	0	0	0	0	0	—	—	—	—	—	0	0	101	—	—	—	0	0	0		R	0.0
1958	Phi-N	32	60	7	14	1	1	1	4	1	5	.233	.246	.333	.579	52	-4	-4	98	72	4	.412	0	0	0	-2	2	-0.4
Total	8	687	2447	244	609	68	28	15	137	208	212	.249	.308	.318	.626	71	-100	-101	100	61	262	.540	18	19		-42	2/3	-11.3
■ RUSS YOUNG	Young, Russell Charles b: 9/15/02, Bryan, Ohio d: 5/13/84, Roseville, Cal. BB/TR, 6', 175 lbs. Deb: 4/16/31																											
1931	StL-A	16	34	2	4	0	0	1	2	2	4	.118	.167	.206	.373	-3	-5	-5	102	66	1	.300	0	0	0	1	C	-0.2
■ JOEL YOUNGBLOOD	Youngblood, Joel Randolph b: 8/28/51, Houston, Tex. BR/TR, 6', 180 lbs. Deb: 4/13/76																											
1976	Cin-N	55	57	8	11	1	1	0	1	2	8	.193	.233	.246	.479	35	-5	-5	103	27	3	.383	1	0	0	-0	/O3C2	-0.5
1977	StL-N	25	27	1	5	2	0	0	1	3	5	.185	.267	.259	.526	44	-2	-2	96	57	1	.400	0	2	-1	-3	O/3	-0.6
	NY-N	70	182	16	46	11	1	0	11	13	40	.253	.303	.324	.627	71	-8	-7	96	75	16	.503	1	3	-2	-2	2O3	-0.9
	Yr	95	209	17	51	13	1	0	12	16	45	.244	.298	.316	.614	67	-10	-9	96	71	18	.491	1	5	-3	-5		-1.5
1978	NY-N	113	266	40	67	12	8	7	30	16	39	.252	.297	.436	.733	104	-0	0	98	87	35	.675	4	0	1	1	O2/3S	0.3
1979	NY-N	158	590	90	162	37	5	16	60	60	84	.275	.349	.436	.784	119	10	14	95	83	90	.763	18	13	-2	11	*O23	1.9
1980	NY-N	146	514	58	142	26	2	8	69	52	69	.276	.345	.381	.726	107	2	5	96	127	67	.672	14	11	-2	21	*O3/2	1.9
1981	NY-N	43	143	16	50	10	2	4	25	12	19	.350	.408	.531	.939	164	12	12	101	114	28	.902	2	5	-2	0	O	0.9
1982	NY-N	80	202	21	52	12	0	3	21	8	37	.257	.302	.361	.664	86	-4	-4	99	100	20	.544	0	4	-2	-5	O/2S3	-1.2
	Mon-N	40	90	16	18	2	0	0	8	9	21	.200	.294	.222	.516	44	-6	-7	105	157	6	.453	2	1	0	-4	O	-1.1
	Yr	120	292	37	70	14	0	3	29	17	58	.240	.300	.318	.618	72	-10	-11	101	120	28	.524	2	5	-2	-9		-2.3
1983	SF-N	124	373	59	109	20	3	17	53	33	59	.292	.358	.499	.856	134	17	16	101	88	64	.828	7	4	-0	-11	23O	0.6
1984	SF-N	134	469	50	119	17	1	10	51	48	86	.254	.328	.358	.686	96	-4	-2	96	103	56	.618	5	6	-2	-19	*3O/2	-2.4
1985	SF-N	95	230	24	62	6	0	4	24	30	37	.270	.356	.348	.704	105	0	2	93	104	29	.648	3	2	-0	1	O/3	0.1
1986	SF-N	97	184	20	47	12	0	5	28	18	34	.255	.325	.402	.727	104	-0	1	96	125	25	.671	1	1	-0	-6	O/132S	-0.6
1987	SF-N	69	91	9	23	3	0	3	11	5	13	.253	.299	.385	.684	83	-3	-2	96	100	10	.583	1	1	-0	-2	O/3	-0.5
1988	SF-N	83	123	12	31	4	0	0	16	10	17	.252	.313	.285	.598	77	-4	-3	94	183	11	.480	1	1	-0	-10	O	-1.5
Total	13	1332	3541	440	944	175	23	77	409	319	568	.267	.333	.394	.727	104	4	17	97	103	460	.681	60	54	-14	-28	O32/1SC	-3.6
■ HENRY YOUNGMAN	Youngman, Henry b: 1865, Indiana, Pa. d: 1/24/36, Pittsburgh, Pa. TR , Deb: 4/19/1890																											
1890	Pit-N	13	47	6	6	1	1	0	4	6	9	.128	.226	.191	.418	27	-4	-4	88	137	2	.390	1			0	/32	-0.2

■ ROSS YOUNGS Youngs, Ross Middlebrook "Pep" (born Royce Middlebrook Youngs) b: 4/10/1897, Shiner, Tex. d: 10/22/27, San Antonio, Tex. BL/TR, 5'8", 162 lbs. Deb: 9/25/17 H

YEAR	TM/L	G	AB	R	H	2B	3B	HR	RBI	BB	SO	AVG	OBP	SLG	PRO	/A	BR	/A	PF	CHI	RC	TA	SB	CS	SBR	FR	POS	TPR
1917	NY-N	7	26	5	9	2	3	0	1	1	5	.346	.370	.654	1.024	218	3	3	97	24	6	1.118	1			2	/O	0.5
1918	NY-N	121	474	70	143	16	8	1	25	44	49	.302	.368	.376	.744	130	16	18	98	46	67	.719	10			-9	*O/2	0.3
1919	NY-N	130	489	73	152	**31**	7	2	43	51	47	.311	.384	.415	.799	141	25	25	100	77	84	.846	24			0	*O	2.2
1920	NY-N	153	581	92	204	27	14	6	78	75	55	.351	.427	.477	.904	160	47	47	100	98	118	.942	18	18	-5	1	*O	3.6
1921	NY-N	141	504	90	165	24	16	3	102	71	47	.327	.411	.456	.868	133	24	26	98	**166**	96	.907	21	17	-4	-9	*O	0.6
1922	NY-N	149	559	105	185	34	10	7	86	55	50	.331	.398	.465	.863	118	19	16	104	113	105	.885	17	9	-0	2	*O	1.1
1923	NY-N	152	596	**121**	200	33	12	3	87	73	36	.336	.412	.446	.859	125	26	24	101	118	108	.860	13	19	-8	-1	*O	1.0
1924	NY-N	133	526	112	187	33	12	10	74	77	31	.356	.441	.521	.962	172	45	52	91	78	123	1.049	11	9	-2	-4	*O/2	4.1
1925	NY-N	130	500	82	132	24	6	6	53	66	51	.264	.354	.372	.726	87	-9	-8	99	89	69	.720	17	11	-2	-7	*O/2	-1.8
1926	NY-N	95	372	62	114	12	5	4	43	37	19	.306	.372	.398	.770	110	5	6	98	82	55	.806	21			2	O	0.4
Total	10	1211	4627	812	1491	236	93	42	592	550	390	.322	.399	.441	.839	131	201	209	99	98	831	.863	153	83		-23	*O/2	12.0

■ EDDIE YOUNT Yount, Floyd Edwin b: 12/19/16, Newton, N.C. d: 10/26/73, Newton, N.C. BR/TR, 6'1", 185 lbs. Deb: 9/09/37

YEAR	TM/L	G	AB	R	H	2B	3B	HR	RBI	BB	SO	AVG	OBP	SLG	PRO	/A	BR	/A	PF	CHI	RC	TA	SB	CS	SBR	FR	POS	TPR
1937	Phi-A	4	7	1	2	0	0	0	1	0	1	.286	.286	.286	.571	47	-1	-1	94	171	1	.400	0	0	0	-0	/O	0.0
1939	Pit-N	2	2	0	0	0	0	0	0	0	2	.000	.000	.000	.000	-99	-1	-1	100	0	0	.000	0			0	H	0.0
Total	2	6	9	1	2	0	0	0	1	0	3	.222	.222	.222	.444	15	-1	-1	95	133	1	.286	0	0		-0	/O	0.0

■ ROBIN YOUNT Yount, Robin R b: 9/16/55, Danville, Ill. BR/TR, 6', 165 lbs. Deb: 4/05/74

YEAR	TM/L	G	AB	R	H	2B	3B	HR	RBI	BB	SO	AVG	OBP	SLG	PRO	/A	BR	/A	PF	CHI	RC	TA	SB	CS	SBR	FR	POS	TPR
1974	Mil-A	107	344	48	86	14	5	3	26	12	46	.250	.277	.346	.623	77	-10	-11	102	80	31	.517	7	7	-2	-8	*S	-1.3
1975	Mil-A	147	558	67	149	28	2	8	52	33	69	.267	.309	.367	.677	90	-8	-8	100	92	64	.596	12	4	1	-16	*S	-0.8
1976	Mil-A	161	638	59	161	19	3	2	54	38	69	.252	.294	.301	.595	75	-21	-20	99	111	55	.491	16	11	-2	-5	*S/O	-1.8
1977	Mil-A	154	605	66	174	34	4	4	49	41	80	.288	.335	.377	.712	98	-5	-1	95	78	77	.639	16	7	1	-6	*S	1.1
1978	Mil-A	127	502	66	147	23	9	9	71	24	43	.293	.326	.428	.755	105	5	2	106	123	71	.701	16	5	2	21	*S	3.5
1979	Mil-A	149	577	72	154	26	5	8	51	35	52	.267	.310	.371	.681	83	-15	-15	100	87	63	.585	11	8	-2	3	*S	0.5
1980	Mil-A	143	611	121	179	**49**	10	23	87	26	67	.293	.323	.519	.842	134	19	23	95	78	101	.818	20	5	3	3	*S/D	3.8
1981	Mil-A	96	377	50	103	15	5	10	49	22	37	.273	.317	.419	.736	115	4	6	96	108	51	.667	4	1	1	25	S/D	3.9
1982	Mil-A	156	635	129	**210**	**46**	12	29	114	54	63	.331	.384	**.578**	**.962**	**170**	**50**	**55**	94	97	**136**	.975	14	3	2	-3	*S/D	**6.6**
1983	Mil-A	149	578	102	178	42	**10**	17	80	72	58	.308	.387	.503	.891	**156**	35	41	92	88	115	.909	12	5	1	-7	*S/D	4.2
1984	Mil-A	160	624	105	186	27	7	16	80	67	67	.298	.367	.441	.808	133	20	26	92	95	99	.769	14	4	2	5	*SD	4.2
1985	Mil-A	122	466	76	129	26	3	15	68	49	56	.277	.348	.442	.790	110	9	7	105	114	73	.765	10	4	1	-10	*OD/1	-0.4
1986	Mil-A	140	522	82	163	31	7	9	46	62	73	.312	.389	.450	.840	126	23	21	102	74	94	.845	14	5	1	6	*O/1D	2.3
1987	Mil-A	158	635	99	198	25	9	21	103	76	94	.312	.386	.479	.865	126	28	25	102	108	120	.879	19	9	0	1	*O/D	2.1
1988	Mil-A	162	621	92	190	38	**11**	13	91	63	63	.306	.373	.465	.838	129	28	25	103	106	106	.827	22	4	4	8	*O/D	3.5
Total	15	2131	8293	1234	2407	443	102	187	1021	674	937	.290	.345	.436	.781	117	162	177	99	96	1255	.755	207	82	13	18	*SO/D1	31.4

■ JEFF YURAK Yurak, Jeffrey Lynn b: 2/26/54, Pasadena, Cal. BB/TR, 6'3", 195 lbs. Deb: 9/15/78

YEAR	TM/L	G	AB	R	H	2B	3B	HR	RBI	BB	SO	AVG	OBP	SLG	PRO	/A	BR	/A	PF	CHI	RC	TA	SB	CS	SBR	FR	POS	TPR
1978	Mil-A	5	5	0	0	0	0	0	0	1	0	.000	.167	.000	.167	-47	-1	-1	106	0	0	.200	0	0	0	0	/O	0.0

■ SAL YVARS Yvars, Salvador Anthony b: 2/20/24, New York, N.Y. BR/TR, 5'10", 187 lbs. Deb: 9/27/47

YEAR	TM/L	G	AB	R	H	2B	3B	HR	RBI	BB	SO	AVG	OBP	SLG	PRO	/A	BR	/A	PF	CHI	RC	TA	SB	CS	SBR	FR	POS	TPR
1947	NY-N	1	5	0	1	0	0	0	0	0	2	.200	.200	.200	.400	6	-1	-1	101	0	0	.250	0			0	/C	0.0
1948	NY-N	15	38	4	8	1	0	1	6	3	1	.211	.286	.316	.602	63	-2	-2	100	150	3	.516	0			-1	C	-0.1
1949	NY-N	3	8	0	0	0	0	0	0	1	1	.000	.111	.000	.111	-67	-2	-2	102	0	0	.125	0			0	/C	-0.1
1950	NY-N	9	14	0	2	0	0	0	0	1	2	.143	.200	.143	.343	-8	-2	-2	98	0	0	.250	0			0	/C	-0.1
1951	NY-N	25	41	9	13	2	0	2	3	5	7	.317	.417	.512	.929	146	3	3	102	43	10	1.000	0	0	0	-1	C	0.2
1952	NY-N	66	151	15	37	3	0	4	18	10	16	.245	.296	.344	.641	75	-5	-5	102	110	14	.521	0	0	0	-2	C	-0.5
1953	NY-N	23	47	1	13	0	0	0	1	7	1	.277	.370	.277	.647	73	-2	-1	98	30	5	.541	0	0	0	-2	C	-0.1
	StL-N	30	57	4	14	2	0	1	6	4	6	.246	.306	.333	.640	66	-3	-3	102	106	5	.500	0	1	-1	-1	C	-0.2
	Yr	53	104	5	27	2	0	1	7	11	7	.260	.336	.308	.644	69	-4	-4	100	74	11	.537	0	1	-1	-3		-0.3
1954	StL-N	38	57	8	14	4	0	2	8	6	5	.246	.328	.421	.749	93	-1	-1	100	105	8	.727	1	0	0	-1	C	0.0
Total	8	210	418	41	102	12	0	10	42	37	41	.244	.315	.344	.659	76	-14	-14	101	89	46	.591	1	1		-6	C	-0.9

■ ELMER ZACHER Zacher, Elmer Henry "Silver" b: 9/17/1883, Buffalo, N.Y. d: 12/20/44, Buffalo, N.Y. BR/TR, 5'9", 190 lbs. Deb: 4/30/10

YEAR	TM/L	G	AB	R	H	2B	3B	HR	RBI	BB	SO	AVG	OBP	SLG	PRO	/A	BR	/A	PF	CHI	RC	TA	SB	CS	SBR	FR	POS	TPR
1910	NY-N	1	0	0	0	0	0	0	0	0	0	—	—	—	—	—	0	0	95	—	—	—	0			-0	/O	0.0
	StL-N	47	132	7	28	5	1	0	10	10	19	.212	.278	.265	.543	64	-7	-6	92	100	11	.481	3			3	O/2	-0.3
	Yr	48	132	7	28	5	1	0	10	10	19	.212	.278	.265	.543	64	-7	-6	92	97	11	.481	3			3		-0.3
Total	1	48	132	7	28	5	1	0	10	10	19	.212	.278	.265	.543	64	-7	-6	92	100	57	.481	3			3	/O2	-0.3

■ FRED ZAHNER Zahner, Frederick Joseph b: 6/5/1870, Louisville, Ky. d: 7/24/1900, Louisville, Ky. Deb: 7/23/1894

YEAR	TM/L	G	AB	R	H	2B	3B	HR	RBI	BB	SO	AVG	OBP	SLG	PRO	/A	BR	/A	PF	CHI	RC	TA	SB	CS	SBR	FR	POS	TPR
1894	Lou-N	13	45	7	9	0	1	0	3	3	5	.200	.250	.244	.494	23	-6	-5	88	75	3	.444	2			0	C/O1	-0.3
1895	Lou-N	21	49	7	11	1	1	0	6	6	4	.224	.321	.286	.607	62	-3	-2	95	120	5	.553	0			0	C	-0.1
Total	2	34	94	14	20	1	2	0	9	9	9	.213	.288	.266	.554	44	-9	-7	92	99	8	.500	2			0	/CO1	-0.4

■ FRANKIE ZAK Zak, Frank Thomas b: 2/22/22, Passaci, N.J. d: 2/6/72, Passaic, N.J. BR/TR, 5'10", 150 lbs. Deb: 4/21/44

YEAR	TM/L	G	AB	R	H	2B	3B	HR	RBI	BB	SO	AVG	OBP	SLG	PRO	/A	BR	/A	PF	CHI	RC	TA	SB	CS	SBR	FR	POS	TPR
1944	Pit-N	87	160	33	48	3	1	0	11	22	18	.300	.385	.331	.716	98	2	1	105	74	22	.711	6			-7	S	0.2
1945	Pit-N	15	28	2	4	2	0	0	3	3	5	.143	.226	.214	.440	22	-3	-3	103	174	2	.375	0			-0	S/2	-0.1
1946	Pit-N	21	20	8	4	0	0	0	0	1	0	.200	.238	.200	.438	24	-2	-2	103	0	1	.313	0			-0	S	-0.1
Total	3	123	208	43	56	5	1	0	14	26	23	.269	.350	.303	.653	81	-3	-4	105	81	25	.625	6			-8	/S2	0.0

■ JACK ZALUSKY Zalusky, John Francis b: 6/22/1879, Minneapolis, Minn d: 8/11/35, Minneapolis, Minn. BR/TR, 5'11.5", 172 lbs. Deb: 03

YEAR	TM/L	G	AB	R	H	2B	3B	HR	RBI	BB	SO	AVG	OBP	SLG	PRO	/A	BR	/A	PF	CHI	RC	TA	SB	CS	SBR	FR	POS	TPR
1903	NY-A	7	16	2	5	0	0	0	1	1		.313	.353	.313	.665	103	0	0	100	72	2	.545	0			-0	/C1	0.0

■ JOE ZAPUSTAS Zapustas, Joseph John b: 7/25/07, Boston, Mass. BR/TR, 6'1", 185 lbs. Deb: 9/28/33

YEAR	TM/L	G	AB	R	H	2B	3B	HR	RBI	BB	SO	AVG	OBP	SLG	PRO	/A	BR	/A	PF	CHI	RC	TA	SB	CS	SBR	FR	POS	TPR
1933	Phi-A	2	5	0	1	0	0	0	0	0	0	.200	.200	.200	.400	7	-1	-1	92	0	0	.250	0	0	0	-1	/O	0.0

■ JOSE ZARDON Zardon, Jose Antonio (Sanchez) "Guineo" b: 5/20/23, Havana, Cuba BR/TR, 6', 150 lbs. Deb: 4/18/45

YEAR	TM/L	G	AB	R	H	2B	3B	HR	RBI	BB	SO	AVG	OBP	SLG	PRO	/A	BR	/A	PF	CHI	RC	TA	SB	CS	SBR	FR	POS	TPR
1945	Was-A	54	131	13	38	5	3	0	13	7	11	.290	.326	.374	.700	111	0	1	93	96	15	.596	3	1	0	0	O	0.0

■ AL ZARILLA Zarilla, Allen Lee "Zeke" b: 5/1/19, Los Angeles, Cal. BL/TR, 5'11", 180 lbs. Deb: 6/30/43

YEAR	TM/L	G	AB	R	H	2B	3B	HR	RBI	BB	SO	AVG	OBP	SLG	PRO	/A	BR	/A	PF	CHI	RC	TA	SB	CS	SBR	FR	POS	TPR
1943	StL-A	70	228	27	58	7	1	2	17	17	20	.254	.309	.320	.629	84	-5	-5	100	79	23	.526	1	1	-0	-2	O	-0.9
1944	StL-A	100	288	43	86	13	6	6	45	29	33	.299	.375	.448	.823	132	13	12	102	110	52	.805	1	1	-0	-4	O	0.6
1946	StL-A	125	371	46	96	14	9	4	43	27	37	.259	.311	.377	.688	93	-5	-4	98	108	43	.596	3	5	-2	8	*O	-0.3
1947	StL-A	127	380	34	85	15	6	3	38	40	45	.224	.303	.318	.621	71	-14	-15	102	108	39	.548	3	6	-3	-6	*O	-2.9
1948	StL-A	144	529	77	174	39	3	12	74	48	48	.329	.389	.482	.871	123	22	18	106	88	103	.862	11	6	-0	-1	*O	1.1
1949	StL-A	15	56	10	14	1	0	1	6	8	2	.250	.354	.321	.675	79	-1	-1	100	94	7	.636	1	1	-0	-4	O	-0.5
	Bos-A	124	474	68	133	32	4	9	71	48	51	.281	.352	.422	.774	97	1	-3	107	109	70	.713	4	4	-1	-6	*O	-1.2
	Yr	139	530	78	147	33	4	10	77	56	53	.277	.352	.411	.763	96	-0	-5	106	108	77	.706	5	5	-2	-10		-1.7
1950	Bos-A	130	471	92	153	32	10	9	74	76	47	.325	.423	.493	.915	117	26	15	114	101	106	.963	2	3	-1	-7	*O	0.5
1951	Chi-A	120	382	56	98	21	2	10	60	60	57	.257	.363	.401	.764	110	4	6	97	117	58	.737	2	4	-2	-17	*O	-1.6
1952	Chi-A	39	99	14	23	4	1	2	7	14	6	.232	.333	.354	.687	91	-1	-1	100	64	13	.654	1	0	0	-6	O	-0.7
	StL-A	48	130	20	31	6	0	1	9	27	15	.238	.373	.308	.681	94	-0	0	97	78	17	.686	2	1	0	2	O	0.1
	Bos-A	21	60	9	11	0	1	2	8	7	8	.183	.269	.317	.585	58	-3	-4	107	119	6	.571	2	0	1	-1	O	-0.4
	Yr	108	289	43	65	10	2	5	24	48	29	.225	.339	.325	.664	85	-5	-5	100	82	38	.662	5	1	1	-6		-1.0
1953	Bos-A	57	67	11	13	2	0	0	4	14	13	.194	.333	.224	.557	49	-4	-5	109	99	5	.500	0	1	-1	-5	O	-1.0
Total	10	1120	3535	507	975	186	43	61	456	415	382	.276	.357	.405	.761	103	32	13	104	101	543	.735	33	33	-10	-48	O	-7.2

■ NORM ZAUCHIN Zauchin, Norbert Henry b: 11/17/29, Royal Oak, Mich. BR/TR, 6'4.5", 220 lbs. Deb: 9/23/51

YEAR	TM/L	G	AB	R	H	2B	3B	HR	RBI	BB	SO	AVG	OBP	SLG	PRO	/A	BR	/A	PF	CHI	RC	TA	SB	CS	SBR	FR	POS	TPR
1951	Bos-A	5	12	0	2	1	0	0	0	0	4	.167	.167	.250	.417	11	-2	-2	108	0	0	.250	0	1	-1	0	/1	-0.1
1955	Bos-A	130	477	65	114	10	0	27	93	69	105	.239	.339	.430	.769	85	3	-13	124	124	73	.755	3	0	1	2	*1	-1.6
1956	Bos-A	44	84	12	18	2	0	2	11	14	22	.214	.333	.310	.643	69	-3	-4	103	128	9	.586	0	0	0	0	1	-0.4

YEAR	TM/L	G	AB	R	H	2B	3B	HR	RBI	BB	SO	AVG	OBP	SLG	PRO	/A	BR	/A	PF	CHI	RC	TA	SB	CS	SBR	FR	POS	TPR
1957	Bos-A	52	91	11	24	3	0	3	14	9	13	.264	.343	.396	.739	92	0	-1	110	123	11	.644	0	0	0	1	1	0.0
1958	Was-A	96	303	35	69	8	2	15	37	38	68	.228	.316	.416	.732	103	-1	1	97	87	39	.676	0	0	0	4	1	0.2
1959	Was-A	19	71	11	15	4	0	3	4	7	14	.211	.291	.394	.686	86	-2	-2	100	45	7	.613	2	0	1	1	1	0.0
Total	6	346	1038	134	242	28	2	50	159	137	226	.233	.327	.408	.736	88	-4	-20	111	107	139	.715	5	1	1	7	1	-1.9
■ **JOE ZDEB** Zdeb, Joseph Edmund b: 6/27/53, Compton, Ill. BR/TR, 5'11", 185 lbs. Deb: 4/07/77																												
1977	KC-A	105	195	26	58	5	2	2	23	16	23	.297	.351	.374	.725	97	-0	-0	100	115	24	.646	6	5	-1	-20	O/3D	-2.4
1978	KC-A	60	127	18	32	2	3	0	11	7	18	.252	.291	.315	.606	69	-5	-5	102	109	12	.515	3	0	1	-10	O/23D	-1.6
1979	KC-A	15	23	3	4	1	1	0	0	2	4	.174	.240	.304	.544	43	-2	-2	105	0	2	.500	1	0	0	-2	/O	-0.3
Total	3	180	345	47	94	8	6	2	34	25	45	.272	.322	.348	.669	83	-7	-8	101	105	38	.603	10	5	0	-31	O/D32	-4.3
■ **DAVE ZEARFOSS** Zearfoss, David William Tilden b: 1/1/1868, Schenectady, N.Y. d: 9/12/45, Wilmington, Del. TR, Deb: 4/17/1896																												
1896	NY-N	19	60	5	13	1	1	0	6	5	5	.217	.288	.267	.555	49	-4	-4	99	108	5	.511	2			0	C	-0.3
1897	NY-N	5	10	1	3	0	1	0	0	0		.300	.300	.500	.800	113	0	0	98	0	2	.714	0			0	/C	0.0
1898	NY-N	1	1	0	1	0	0	0	0	0		1.000	1.000	1.000	2.000	508	0	0	95	0	1	—	0			0	/C	0.0
1904	StL-N	27	80	7	17	2	0	0	9	10		.213	.300	.237	.538	69	-3	-2	99	173	6	.460	0			-4	C	-0.3
1905	StL-N	20	51	2	8	0	1	0	2	4		.157	.218	.196	.414	28	-5	-4	91	70	2	.326	0			-1	C	-0.2
Total	5	72	202	15	42	3	3	0	17	19	5	.208	.279	.252	.532	58	-11	-10	97	120	16	.456	2			-4	/C	-0.8
■ **GEORGE ZEBER** Zeber, George William b: 8/29/50, Ellwood City, Pa. BB/TR, 5'11", 170 lbs. Deb: 5/07/77																												
1977	NY-A	25	65	8	21	3	0	3	10	9	11	.323	.405	.508	.913	149	4	5	99	94	14	.933	0	0	0	1	2/S3D	0.7
1978	NY-A	3	6	0	0	0	0	0	0	0	0	.000	.000	.000	.000	-99	-2	-2	99	0	0	.000	0	0	0	0	/2	-0.1
Total	2	28	71	8	21	3	0	3	10	9	11	.296	.375	.465	.840	130	3	3	99	87	14	.840	0	0	0	1	/23SD	0.6
■ **ROLLIE ZEIDER** Zeider, Rollie Hubert "Bunions" b: 11/16/1883, Auburn, Ind. d: 9/12/67, Garrett, Ind. BR/TR, 5'10", 162 lbs. Deb: 4/14/10																												
1910	Chi-A	136	498	57	108	9	2	0	31	62		.217	.305	.243	.548	76	-14	-11	95	84	52	.597	49			0	2S/3	-1.6
1911	Chi-A	73	217	39	55	3	0	2	21	29		.253	.347	.295	.642	82	-5	-4	97	101	32	.759	28			5	1S3/2	0.4
1912	Chi-A	129	420	57	103	12	10	1	42	50		.245	.330	.329	.658	89	-6	-5	99	101	62	.751	47			-2	13/S	-0.6
1913	Chi-A	16	20	4	7	0	0	0	2	4	1	.350	.458	.350	.808	144	1	1	95	102	4	1.077	3			-2	/312	0.0
	NY-A	50	159	15	37	2	0	0	12	25	9	.233	.341	.245	.586	71	-4	-4	101	111	13	.557	3			-2	S2/13	-0.4
	Yr	66	179	19	44	2	0	0	14	29	10	.246	.354	.257	.611	80	-3	-3	99	111	17	.607	6			-3		-0.4
1914	Chi-F	119	452	60	124	13	2	1	36	44	28	.274	.339	.319	.657	98	-5	0	91	78	64	.680	35			-2	*3/S	0.0
1915	Chi-F	129	494	65	112	22	2	0	34	43	24	.227	.289	.279	.568	70	-19	-17	97	85	47	.516	16			-2	23S	-1.6
1916	Chi-N	98	345	29	81	11	2	1	22	26	26	.235	.294	.287	.581	67	-8	-14	117	87	32	.519	9			6	32/OS1	-0.7
1917	Chi-N	108	354	36	86	14	2	0	27	28	30	.243	.302	.294	.596	79	-7	-8	105	100	35	.563	17			-13	S32/10	-2.2
1918	Chi-N	82	251	31	56	3	2	0	26	23	20	.223	.288	.251	.539	64	-10	-11	102	156	23	.523	16			-4	2/13	-1.0
Total	9	940	3210	393	769	89	22	5	253	334	138	.240	.314	.286	.599	79	-77	-74	100	96	366	.609	223			-14	23S1/O	-7.7
■ **BART ZELLER** Zeller, Barton Wallace b: 7/22/41, Chicago Heights, Ill. BR/TR, 6'1", 185 lbs. Deb: 5/21/70 C																												
1970	StL-N	1	0	0	0	0	0	0	0	0	0	—	—	—	—	—	0	0	106	—	—	—	0	0	0	0	/C	0.0
■ **GUS ZERNIAL** Zernial, Gus Edward "Ozark Ike" b: 6/27/23, Beaumont, Tex. BR/TR, 6'2.5", 210 lbs. Deb: 4/19/49																												
1949	Chi-A	73	198	29	63	17	2	5	38	15	26	.318	.366	.500	.866	131	7	7	98	114	37	.826	0	1	-1	-5	O	0.0
1950	Chi-A	143	543	75	152	16	4	29	93	38	110	.280	.330	.484	.815	110	1	3	97	94	84	.743	0	2	-1	1	*O	0.0
1951	Chi-A	4	19	2	2	0	0	0	4	2	2	.105	.190	.105	.296	-19	-3	-3	97	617	0	.235	0	0	0	1	/O	-0.1
	Phi-A	139	552	90	151	30	5	33	125	61	99	.274	.350	.525	.875	127	23	19	106	122	102	.854	2	2	-1	12	*O	2.4
	Yr	143	571	92	153	30	5	**33**	**129**	63	101	.268	.345	.511	.856	122	20	16	106	140	101	.830	2	2	-1	13		2.3
1952	Phi-A	145	549	76	144	15	1	29	100	70	87	.262	.347	.452	.799	109	14	7	111	118	89	.773	5	1	1	-1	*O	0.3
1953	Phi-A	147	556	85	158	21	3	42	108	57	79	.284	.355	.559	.914	141	30	29	102	97	113	.917	4	0	1	7	*O	3.3
1954	Phi-A	97	336	42	84	8	2	14	62	30	60	.250	.319	.411	.730	100	-2	-1	98	133	44	.662	0	0	0	-5	O/1	-0.8
1955	KC-A	120	413	62	105	9	3	30	84	30	90	.254	.309	.508	.818	115	6	5	101	104	59	.751	1	0	0	6	*O	0.7
1956	KC-A	109	272	36	61	12	0	16	44	33	66	.224	.317	.445	.762	98	-2	-2	101	97	40	.741	2	0	1	-2	O	-0.6
1957	KC-A	131	437	56	103	20	1	27	69	34	84	.236	.292	.471	.764	107	0	1	99	97	57	.697	1	1	-0	-5	*O/1	-1.0
1958	Det-A	66	124	8	40	7	1	5	23	6	25	.323	.354	.516	.870	131	6	5	104	117	22	.805	0	0	0	-3	O	0.0
1959	Det-A	60	132	11	30	4	0	7	26	7	27	.227	.266	.417	.683	76	-3	-5	111	135	14	.590	0	0	0	-0	1/O	-0.5
Total	11	1234	4131	572	1093	159	22	237	776	383	755	.265	.331	.486	.816	115	78	65	102	111	661	.797	15	7	0	6	*O/1	3.7
■ **CHARLIE ZIEGLER** Ziegler, Charles W. b: 2/2/1875, Canton, Ohio d: 3/16/04, Canton, Ohio Deb: 9/23/1899																												
1899	Cle-N	2	8	2	2	0	0	0	0	0	0	.250	.250	.250	.500	44	-1	-1	89	0	1	.333	0			0	/S2	0.0
1900	Phi-N	3	11	0	3	0	0	0	1	0		.273	.273	.273	.545	54	-1	-1	98	104	1	.375	0			0	/3	0.0
Total	2	5	19	2	5	0	0	0	1	0		.263	.263	.263	.526	50	-1	-1	94	60	1	.357	0			0	/32S	0.0
■ **BENNY ZIENTARA** Zientara, Benedict Joseph b: 2/14/20, Chicago, Ill. d: 4/16/85, Lake Elsinore, Cal. BR/TR, 5'8", 150 lbs. Deb: 9/11/41																												
1941	Cin-N	9	21	3	6	0	0	0	2	1	3	.286	.318	.286	.604	72	-1	-1	99	120	2	.467	0			0	/2	0.0
1946	Cin-N	78	280	26	81	10	2	0	16	14	11	.289	.323	.339	.662	85	-5	-6	104	64	30	.544	3			7	23	0.3
1947	Cin-N	117	418	60	108	18	1	2	24	23	23	.258	.297	.321	.618	70	-22	-17	91	65	39	.495	2			-2	*23	-0.7
1948	Cin-N	74	187	17	35	1	2	0	7	12	11	.187	.236	.214	.450	22	-20	-21	103	66	9	.325	0			-3	2/3S	-1.9
Total	4	278	906	106	230	29	5	2	49	50	48	.254	.293	.304	.596	64	-48	-45	98	66	80	.482	5			3	2/3S	-2.3
■ **BILL ZIES** Zies, William BL, Deb: 8/10/1891																												
1891	StL-a	2	3	0	1	0	0	0	0	0	0	.333	.333	.333	.667	82	-0	-0	114	0	0	.500	0			0	/C	0.0
■ **CHIEF ZIMMER** Zimmer, Charles Louis b: 11/23/1860, Marietta, Ohio d: 8/22/49, Cleveland, Ohio BR/TR, 6', 190 lbs. Deb: 7/18/1884 M																												
1884	Det-N	8	29	0	2	1	0	0	0	1	14	.069	.100	.103	.203	-38	-4	-4	94	0	0	.148				0	/CO	-0.3
1886	NY-a	6	19	1	3	0	0	0		1		.158	.238	.158	.396	25	-2	-2	104	0	1	.313	0			0	/C	0.0
1887	Cle-a	14	52	9	12	5	0	0		4		.231	.298	.327	.625	78	-2	-1	98	0	6	.575	1			0	C/1	0.0
1888	Cle-a	65	212	27	51	11	4	0	22	18		.241	.312	.330	.642	112	3	3	97	94	27	.665	15			7	C/O1S	1.5
1889	Cle-N	84	259	47	67	9	9	1	21	44	35	.259	.368	.375	.743	106	5	3	103	63	42	.813	14			2	C/1	0.6
1890	Cle-N	125	444	54	95	16	6	2	57	46	54	.214	.303	.291	.594	80	-13	-8	94	130	45	.576	15			19	*C	1.7
1891	Cle-N	116	440	55	112	21	4	3	69	33	49	.255	.312	.341	.653	88	-5	-8	105	129	53	.616	15			18	*C/3	1.7
1892	Cle-N	111	413	63	108	29	13	1	64	32	47	.262	.325	.402	.727	118	9	7	103	119	61	.731	18			5	*C	1.7
1893	Cle-N	57	227	27	70	13	7	2	41	16	15	.308	.357	.454	.810	112	4	3	104	105	39	.790	4			4	C/3	0.9
1894	Cle-N	90	341	55	97	20	5	4	65	17	31	.284	.328	.408	.735	70	-13	-21	111	119	51	.717	14			11	*C	-0.1
1895	Cle-N	88	315	60	107	21	2	5	56	33	30	.340	.417	.467	.884	134	15	17	97	98	69	.976	14			3	C/1	2.2
1896	Cle-N	91	336	46	93	18	3	3	46	31	48	.277	.354	.375	.729	86	-2	-8	110	100	47	.700	4			-1	*C/3	0.0
1897	Cle-N	80	294	50	93	22	3	0	40	25		.316	.378	.412	.789	100	5	-0	111	99	50	.786	8			5	C	1.3
1898	Cle-N	20	63	5	15	2	0	0	4	5		.238	.304	.270	.574	70	-2	-2	96	71	6	.521	2			0	C	-0.1
1899	Cle-N	20	73	9	25	2	1	2	14	5		.342	.400	.479	.879	161	4	5	89	111	15	.896	1			5	C	1.0
	Lou-N	75	262	43	78	11	3	2	29	22		.298	.370	.385	.755	106	4	3	103	85	42	.761	9			2	C1	0.7
	Yr	95	335	52	103	13	4	4	43	27		.307	.376	.406	.782	117	8	8	100	91	56	.789	10			6		1.7
1900	Pit-N	82	271	27	80	7	10	0	35	17		.295	.337	.395	.732	101	1	-0	103	102	38	.670	4			1	C/1	0.7
1901	Pit-N	69	236	17	52	7	3	0	21	20		.220	.281	.275	.557	63	-10	-11	101	108	20	.495	6			-9	C	-1.0
1902	Pit-N	42	142	13	38	4	2	0	17	11		.268	.320	.324	.644	96	0	-1	105	128	16	.587	4			-5	C/1	0.0
1903	Phi-N	37	118	9	26	3	1	1	19	9		.220	.276	.288	.564	68	-6	-4	92	165	10	.500	3			2	CM	0.0
Total	19	1280	4546	617	1224	222	76	26	620	390	323	.269	.336	.369	.705	96	-9	-29	102	106	639	.688	151			68	*C/103S	12.5
■ **DON ZIMMER** Zimmer, Donald William b: 1/17/31, Cincinnati, Ohio BR/TR, 5'9", 165 lbs. Deb: 7/02/54 MC																												
1954	Bro-N	24	33	3	6	0	1	0	0	3	8	.182	.270	.242	.513	34	-3	-3	101	0	2	.500	2	0	1	0	S	-0.1
1955	Bro-N	88	280	38	67	10	1	15	50	19	66	.239	.292	.443	.735	88	-4	-6	104	120	34	.673	5	3	-0	-1	2S/3	0.0
1956	Bro-N	17	20	4	6	1	0	0	2	0	7	.300	.333	.350	.683	82	-0	-0	103	121	2	.500	0	1	-1	0	/S32	0.0

YEAR	TM/L	G	AB	R	H	2B	3B	HR	RBI	BB	SO	AVG	OBP	SLG	PRO	/A	BR	/A	PF	CHI	RC	TA	SB	CS	SBR	FR	POS	TPR
1957	Bro-N	84	269	23	59	9	1	6	19	16	63	.219	.263	.327	.590	49	-16	-22	116	74	21	.475	1	3	-2	3	3S/2	-1.7
1958	LA-N	127	455	52	119	15	2	17	60	28	92	.262	.306	.415	.721	85	-9	-11	105	105	55	.654	14	2	3	20	*S3/2O	2.0
1959	LA-N	97	249	21	41	7	1	4	28	37	56	.165	.275	.249	.524	40	-21	-21	102	153	18	.475	3	1	0	5	S/32	-1.2
1960	Chi-N	132	368	37	95	16	7	6	35	27	56	.258	.309	.389	.697	91	-6	-5	98	88	42	.618	8	6	-1	-0	23/SO	0.0
1961	Chi-N	128	477	57	120	25	4	13	40	25	70	.252	.292	.403	.694	82	-14	-14	100	71	52	.599	5	1	1	2	*2/3O	0.3
1962	NY-N	14	52	3	4	1	0	0	1	3	10	.077	.127	.096	.223	-38	-10	-10	104	80	1	.160	0	1	-1	0	3	-1.0
	Cin-N	63	192	16	48	11	2	2	16	14	30	.250	.304	.359	.664	76	-6	-7	102	84	20	.563	1	2	-1	-3	32/S	-0.8
	Yr	77	244	19	52	12	2	2	17	17	40	.213	.267	.303	.570	52	-16	-17	102	84	19	.465	1	3	-2	-3		-1.8
1963	LA-N	22	23	4	5	1	0	1	2	3	10	.217	.308	.391	.699	105	-0	0	95	70	3	.632	0	0	0	0	3/2S	0.1
	Was-A	83	298	37	74	12	1	13	44	18	57	.248	.296	.426	.722	102	-1	-0	98	113	34	.636	3	2	-0	-1	3/2	0.0
1964	Was-A	121	341	38	84	16	2	12	38	27	94	.246	.302	.411	.712	95	-3	-3	101	91	40	.627	1	3	-2	-3	3/OC2	-0.5
1965	Was-A	95	226	20	45	6	0	2	17	26	59	.199	.287	.252	.540	55	-13	-13	100	112	17	.463	2	0	1	3	C32	-0.6
Total	12	1095	3283	353	773	130	22	91	352	246	678	.235	.291	.372	.663	76	-106	-116	102	98	340	.600	45	25	-2	26	32S/CO	-3.5
■ EDDIE ZIMMERMAN	Zimmerman, Edward Desmond b: 1/4/1883, Oceanic, N.J. d: 5/6/45, Emmaus, Pa. BR/TR, 5'9", 160 lbs. Deb: 9/29/06																											
1906	StL-N	5	14	0	3	0	0	0	1	0		.214	.214	.214	.429	35	-1	-1	101	122	1	.273	0			1	/3	0.0
1911	Bro-N	122	417	31	77	10	7	3	36	34	37	.185	.249	.264	.513	45	-33	-31	97	104	30	.456	9			1	*3	-2.5
Total	2	127	431	31	80	10	7	3	37	34	37	.186	.248	.262	.511	45	-34	-32	97	105	31	.450	9			1	3	-2.5
■ JERRY ZIMMERMAN	Zimmerman, Gerald Robert b: 9/21/34, Omaha, Neb. BR/TR, 6'2", 185 lbs. Deb: 4/14/61 C																											
1961	Cin-N	76	204	8	42	5	0	0	10	11	21	.206	.253	.230	.484	28	-20	-21	104	86	11	.353	1	1	-0	-2	C	-1.7
1962	Min-A	34	62	8	17	4	0	0	7	3	5	.274	.318	.339	.657	73	-2	-2	105	132	7	.543	0	0	0	-0	C	0.0
1963	Min-A	39	56	3	13	1	0	0	3	2	8	.232	.259	.250	.509	43	-4	-4	100	90	3	.348	0	0	0	-1	C	-0.4
1964	Min-A	63	120	6	24	3	0	0	12	10	15	.200	.278	.225	.503	42	-9	-9	101	188	7	.392	0	0	0	-8	C	-1.5
1965	Min-A	83	154	8	33	1	1	1	11	12	23	.214	.275	.253	.529	51	-10	-10	101	109	10	.409	0	0	0	-8	C	-1.2
1966	Min-A	60	119	11	30	4	1	1	15	15	23	.252	.341	.328	.668	84	-1	-2	111	150	13	.591	0	0	0	-5	C	-0.4
1967	Min-A	104	234	13	39	3	0	1	12	22	49	.167	.244	.192	.436	29	-20	-22	107	104	11	.338	0	1	-1	-27	*C	-4.7
1968	Min-A	24	45	3	5	1	0	0	2	3	10	.111	.184	.133	.317	-3	-6	-6	106	143	1	.250	0	0	0	-1	C	-0.6
Total	8	483	994	60	203	22	2	3	72	78	154	.204	.270	.239	.509	43	-71	-77	105	120	64	.414	1	2	-1	-51	C	-10.5
■ HEINIE ZIMMERMAN	Zimmerman, Henry b: 2/9/1887, New York, N.Y. d: 3/14/69, New York, N.Y. BR/TR, 5'11.5", 176 lbs. Deb: 9/08/07																											
1907	Chi-N	5	9	0	2	1	0	0	1	0		.222	.222	.333	.556	71	-0	-0	106	126	1	.429	0			1	/2SO	0.0
1908	Chi-N	46	113	17	33	4	1	0	9	1		.292	.298	.345	.643	101	0	-0	106	89	12	.525	2			-0	2/OS3	0.0
1909	Chi-N	65	183	23	50	9	2	0	21	3		.273	.285	.344	.629	96	-2	-2	101	121	19	.549	7			2	23S	0.0
1910	Chi-N	99	335	35	95	16	6	3	38	20	36	.284	.326	.394	.720	109	2	2	101	94	44	.667	7			-0	2S3/O1	0.4
1911	Chi-N	143	535	80	164	22	17	9	85	25	50	.307	.343	.462	.805	129	14	16	97	107	91	.809	23			0	*231	1.4
1912	Chi-N	145	557	95	**207**	**41**	14	**14**	99	38	60	**.372**	.418	**.571**	**.989**	**163**	**50**	**47**	104	98	**141**	**1.100**	23			0	*31	4.5
1913	Chi-N	127	447	69	140	28	12	9	95	41	40	.313	.379	.490	.868	149	26	27	99	**143**	87	.925	18			1	*3	2.7
1914	Chi-N	146	564	75	167	36	12	4	87	20	46	.296	.326	.424	.750	125	12	13	98	133	79	.708	17			-16	*3S2	0.2
1915	Chi-N	139	520	65	138	28	11	3	62	21	33	.265	.300	.379	.679	103	1	-0	102	122	61	.613	19	13	-2	-0	*23/S	0.0
1916	Chi-N	107	398	54	116	25	5	6	64	16	33	.291	.324	.425	.748	110	12	5	117	139	60	.720	15			10	32/S	1.8
	NY-N	40	151	22	41	4	0	0	19	7	10	.272	.304	.298	.602	89	-3	-2	96	178	16	.555	9			0	3/2	0.0
	Yr	147	549	76	157	29	5	6	**83**	23	43	.286	.318	.390	.708	105	9	3	111	150	76	.673	24			10		1.8
1917	NY-N	150	585	61	174	22	9	5	**102**	16	43	.297	.317	.391	.709	120	9	11	97	**171**	74	.630	13			15	*3/2	2.6
1918	NY-N	121	463	43	126	19	10	1	56	13	23	.272	.294	.363	.656	102	-2	-1	98	131	51	.582	14			-6	*31	-0.6
1919	NY-N	123	444	56	113	20	6	4	58	21	30	.255	.296	.354	.649	95	-4	-4	100	141	48	.577	8			1	*3	-0.1
Total	13	1456	5304	695	1566	275	105	58	796	242	404	.295	.331	.419	.750	120	116	112	101	129	784	.714	175	13		6	32/S10	12.9
■ ROY ZIMMERMAN	Zimmerman, Roy Franklin b: 9/13/16, Pine Grove, Pa. BL/TL, 6'2", 187 lbs. Deb: 9/02/45																											
1945	NY-N	27	98	14	27	1	0	5	15	5	16	.276	.330	.439	.769	113	1	1	100	92	14	.712	1			0	1/O	0.1
■ BILL ZIMMERMAN	Zimmerman, William H. b: 1/20/1889, Kengen, Germany d: 10/4/52, Newark, N.J. BR/TR, 5'8.5", 172 lbs. Deb: 4/14/15																											
1915	Bro-N	22	57	3	16	2	0	0	7	4	8	.281	.328	.316	.644	94	-0	-0	101	148	6	.561	1			-5	O	-0.6
■ FRANK ZINN	Zinn, Frank b: 12/21/1865, Phoenixville, Pa. d: 5/12/36, Manayunk, Pa. 5'8", 150 lbs. Deb: 1888																											
1888	Phi-a	2	7	0	0	0	0	0	0	1		.000	.125	.000	.125	-57	-1	-1	101	0	0	.143	0			0	/C	0.0
■ GUY ZINN	Zinn, Guy b: 2/13/1887, Hallbrook, W.Va. d: 10/6/49, Clarksburg, W.Va. BL/TR, 5'10.5", 170 lbs. Deb: 9/11/11																											
1911	NY-A	9	27	5	4	0	2	0	1	4		.148	.281	.296	.578	55	-1	-2	111	42	2	.565	0			-0	/O	-0.2
1912	NY-A	106	401	56	105	15	10	6	55	50		.262	.345	.394	.739	110	6	5	101	100	60	.764	17			-11	*O	-1.2
1913	Bos-N	36	138	15	41	8	2	1	15	4	23	.297	.322	.406	.727	113	1	2	95	94	18	.660	3			6	O	0.7
1914	Bal-F	61	225	30	63	10	6	3	25	16	26	.280	.328	.418	.746	114	3	3	99	93	34	.716	6			-5	O	-0.4
1915	Bal-F	102	312	30	84	18	3	5	43	35	28	.269	.343	.394	.737	110	7	4	107	112	45	.702	2			-3	O	-0.3
Total	5	314	1103	136	297	51	23	15	139	109	77	.269	.337	.398	.735	109	15	12	102	100	160	.718	28			-14	O	-1.4
■ BUD ZIPFEL	Zipfel, Marion Sylvester b: 11/18/38, Belleville, Ill. BL/TR, 6'3", 200 lbs. Deb: 7/26/61																											
1961	Was-A	50	170	17	34	7	5	4	18	15	49	.200	.265	.371	.635	71	-8	-7	95	96	17	.564	1	1	-0	-2	1	-1.3
1962	Was-A	68	184	21	44	4	1	6	21	17	43	.239	.307	.370	.676	81	-5	-5	101	97	21	.608	1	2	-1	-2	1O	-1.0
Total	2	118	354	38	78	11	6	10	39	32	92	.220	.287	.370	.657	76	-14	-13	98	96	38	.593	2	3	-1	-4	/1O	-2.3
■ RICHIE ZISK	Zisk, Richard Walter b: 2/6/49, Brooklyn, N.Y. BR/TR, 6'1", 200 lbs. Deb: 9/08/71																											
1971	Pit-N	7	15	2	3	1	0	1	2	4	7	.200	.368	.467	.835	136	1	1	99	81	3	.917	0	0	0	-1	/O	0.0
1972	Pit-N	17	37	4	7	3	0	0	4	7	10	.189	.318	.270	.588	67	-1	-1	103	164	3	.548	0	0	0	-2	O	-0.3
1973	Pit-N	103	333	44	108	23	7	10	54	21	63	.324	.364	.526	.890	156	18	21	92	106	62	.841	0	0	0	3	O	2.1
1974	Pit-N	149	536	75	168	30	3	17	100	65	91	.313	.388	.476	.863	144	29	31	98	129	99	.843	1	1	-0	9	*O	3.5
1975	Pit-N	147	504	69	146	27	3	20	75	68	109	.290	.376	.474	.851	136	24	24	99	99	90	.833	0	1	-1	-2	*O	1.7
1976	Pit-N	155	581	91	168	35	2	21	89	52	96	.289	.348	.465	.812	129	20	20	100	109	90	.746	1	0	0	0	*O	1.6
1977	Chi-A	141	531	78	154	17	6	30	101	55	98	.290	.360	.514	.874	136	25	25	99	117	94	.836	0	4	-2	2	*OD	2.1
1978	Tex-A	140	511	68	134	19	1	22	85	58	76	.262	.341	.432	.773	121	11	13	96	124	74	.723	3	3	-1	-6	OD	0.4
1979	Tex-A	144	503	69	132	21	1	18	64	57	75	.262	.338	.416	.753	102	1	1	100	95	69	.690	1	1	-0	-4	*O	-0.7
1980	Tex-A	135	448	48	130	17	1	19	77	39	72	.290	.347	.460	.807	119	11	11	100	114	66	.725	0	2	-1	-5	DO	0.4
1981	Sea-A	94	357	42	111	12	1	16	43	28	63	.311	.366	.485	.851	144	19	19	100	78	61	.797	0	2	-1	0	D	1.9
1982	Sea-A	131	503	61	147	28	1	21	62	49	89	.292	.356	.477	.833	116	18	12	109	87	86	.798	2	1	0	0	*D	1.2
1983	Sea-A	90	285	30	69	12	0	12	36	30	61	.242	.314	.411	.725	98	-1	-1	100	92	37	.662	0	0	0	0	D	0.0
Total	13	1453	5144	681	1477	245	26	207	792	533	910	.287	.355	.466	.821	126	174	176	100	106	834	.799	8	15	-7	-5	OD	13.9
■ BILLY ZITZMANN	Zitzmann, William Arthur b: 11/19/1895, Long Island City, N.Y. d: 5/29/85, Passaic, N.J. BR/TR, 5'10.5", 175 lbs. Deb: 4/17/19																											
1919	Pit-N	11	26	5	5	1	0	0	2	0	6	.192	.192	.231	.423	26	-2	-2	105	130	1	.381	2			-2	/O	-0.5
	Cin-N	2	1	0	0	0	0	0	0	0	0	.000	.000	.000	.000	-95	-0	-0	105	0	0	.000	0			-0	/O	0.0
	Yr	13	27	5	5	1	0	0	2	0	6	.185	.185	.222	.407	21	-3	-3	105	120	1	.364	2			-2		-0.5
1925	Cin-N	104	301	53	76	13	3	0	21	35	22	.252	.342	.316	.658	71	-13	-12	97	79	33	.623	11	11	-3	-17	O/S	-3.2
1926	Cin-N	53	94	21	23	2	1	0	3	6	7	.245	.304	.287	.591	63	-5	-5	95	38	8	.535	3			-5	O	-1.0
1927	Cin-N	88	232	47	66	10	4	0	24	20	18	.284	.352	.362	.714	91	-2	-2	100	100	30	.705	9			-5	O/S3	-0.8
1928	Cin-N	101	266	53	79	9	3	3	33	13	22	.297	.337	.387	.724	92	-5	-3	96	105	34	.706	13			-5	O/3	-1.0
1929	Cin-N	47	84	18	19	3	0	0	6	9	10	.226	.309	.262	.570	43	-7	-7	99	93	7	.554	4			-3	O/1	-1.0
Total	6	406	1004	197	268	38	11	3	89	83	85	.267	.333	.336	.668	77	-35	-32	98	89	114	.640	42	11		-37	O/S13	-7.5
■ FRANK ZUPO	Zupo, Frank Joseph "Noodles" b: 8/29/39, San Francisco, Cal BL/TR, 5'11", 182 lbs. Deb: 7/01/57																											
1957	Bal-A	10	12	2	1	0	0	0	0	1	4	.083	.154	.083	.237	-36	-2	-2	93	0	0	.182	0	0	0	-0	/C	-0.1
1958	Bal-A	1	2	0	0	0	0	0	0	0	1	.000	.000	.000	.000	-99	-1	-1	94	0	0	.000	0	0	0	0	/C	0.0

YEAR	TM/L	G	AB	R	H	2B	3B	HR	RBI	BB	SO	AVG	OBP	SLG	PRO	/A	BR	/A	PF	CHI	RC	TA	SB	CS	SBR	FR	POS	TPR
1961	Bal-A	5	4	1	2	1	0	0	0	1	1	.500	.600	.750	1.350	265	1	1	97	0	2	2.000	0	0	0	0	/C	0.1
Total	3	16	18	3	3	1	0	0	0	2	6	.167	.250	.222	.472	31	-2	-2	94	0	2	.400	0	0	0	-0	/C	0.0

■ **PAUL ZUVELLA** Zuvella, Paul b: 10/31/58, San Mateo, Cal. BR/TR, 6', 173 lbs. Deb: 9/04/82

YEAR	TM/L	G	AB	R	H	2B	3B	HR	RBI	BB	SO	AVG	OBP	SLG	PRO	/A	BR	/A	PF	CHI	RC	TA	SB	CS	SBR	FR	POS	TPR
1982	Atl-N	2	1	0	0	0	0	0	0	0	0	.000	.000	.000	.000	-93	-0	-0	107	0	0	.000	0	0	0	0	/S	0.0
1983	Atl-N	3	5	0	0	0	0	0	0	2	1	.000	.375	.000	.375	12	-0	-0	106	0	0	.600	0	0	0	0	/S	0.0
1984	Atl-N	11	25	2	5	1	0	0	1	2	3	.200	.259	.240	.499	37	-2	-2	110	65	2	.400	0	0	0	1	/2S	0.0
1985	Atl-N	81	190	16	48	8	1	0	4	16	14	.253	.311	.305	.616	69	-7	-8	106	27	19	.524	2	0	1	12	2S/3	0.8
1986	NY-A	21	48	2	4	1	0	0	2	5	4	.083	.170	.104	.274	-22	-8	-8	103	159	1	.222	0	0	0	1	S	-0.5
1987	NY-A	14	34	2	6	0	0	0	0	0	4	.176	.176	.176	.353	-6	-5	-5	98	0	1	.207	0	0	0	0	/2S3	-0.3
1988	Cle-A	51	130	9	30	5	1	0	7	8	13	.231	.275	.285	.560	56	-7	-8	102	75	10	.437	0	0	0	-8	S	-1.3
Total	7	183	433	31	93	15	2	0	14	33	39	.215	.272	.259	.531	46	-30	-32	104	56	33	.431	2	0	1	6	S/23	-1.3

■ **DUTCH ZWILLING** Zwilling, Edward Harrison b: 11/2/1888, St.Louis, Mo. d: 3/27/78, La Crescenta, Cal. BL/TL, 5'6.5", 160 lbs. Deb: 8/14/10

YEAR	TM/L	G	AB	R	H	2B	3B	HR	RBI	BB	SO	AVG	OBP	SLG	PRO	/A	BR	/A	PF	CHI	RC	TA	SB	CS	SBR	FR	POS	TPR
1910	Chi-A	27	87	7	16	5	0	0	5	11		.184	.283	.241	.524	68	-3	-3	95	90	6	.479	1			-1	O	-0.5
1914	Chi-F	154	592	91	185	38	8	**15**	95	46	68	.313	.362	.480	.842	154	28	35	91	100	114	.862	21			-4	*O	2.4
1915	Chi-F	150	548	65	157	32	7	13	**94**	67	65	.286	.364	.442	.806	142	26	28	97	128	101	.852	24			7	*O/1	2.9
1916	Chi-N	35	53	4	6	1	0	1	8	4	6	.113	.175	.189	.364	10	-6	-7	117	244	2	.298	0			-2	O	-1.0
Total	4	366	1280	167	364	76	15	29	202	128	<u>139</u>	.284	.350	.435	.785	136	45	53	95	117	223	.799	46			-0	O/1	3.8

The Pitcher Register

The Pitcher Register

The Pitcher Register consists of the central pitching statistics of every man who has pitched in major league play since 1871, *without exception.* Pitcher batting is expressed in Batting Wins in the Pitcher Batting column, and pitcher defense is expressed in Fielding Wins in the Pitcher Defense column.

The pitchers are listed alphabetically by surname and, when more than one pitcher bears the name, alphabetically by *given* name—not by "use name," by which we mean the name he may have had applied to him during his playing career. This is the standard method of alphabetizing used in other biographical reference works, and in the case of baseball it makes it easier to find a lesser-known player with a common surname like Smith or Johnson. This method also jibes with that employed in the Team Roster and Annual Record where, for example, Charles "Old Hoss" Radbourn is shown not as the puzzling O. Radbourn or H. Radbourn, as some reference books have it, but as C. Radbourn. On the whole, we have been conservative in ascribing nicknames, doing so only when the player was in fact known by that name during his playing days.

Each page of the Pitcher Register is topped at the corner by a finding aid: in capital letters, the surname of, first, the pitcher whose entry heads up the page and, second, the pitcher whose entry concludes it. Another finding aid is the use of boldface numerals indicating a league leading total in those categories in which a pitcher is truly attempting to excel. No boldface is given to the "leaders" in losses; in games started (innings pitched is the better category to highlight endurance); in hits allowed (the most would produce an absurd leader, while the fewest would tend to reward a man for pitching fewer innings—hits per nine innings is the better category in which to cite leaders); or (using the same reasoning as for hits allowed) in home runs allowed or bases on balls. Pitcher batting and pitcher defense, because the win-denominated numbers they produce are so small, are also not sorted for single-season leaders (although the all-time leaders in these categories, single season and lifetime, will be found in the separate section called "All-Time Leaders"). Condensed type will appear occasionally throughout this section; it has no special significance but is designed simply to accommodate unusually wide figures, such as the 108.00 ERA of Harry Heitmann, who allowed four earned runs in his career of one-third of an inning's work.

The record of a man who pitched in more than one season is given in one line for each season, plus a career total line. If he pitched for more than one team in a given year, his totals for each team are given on separate lines; and if the teams for which he pitched in his "traded year" are in the same league, then his full record is stated in both separate and combined fashion. (In the odd case of a man playing for three or more clubs in one year, with some of these clubs being in the same league, the combined total line will reflect only his play in that one league.) A man who pitched in only one year has no additional career total line since that would be identical to his seasonal listing.

While fractional innings are calculated for teams in the Annual Record, they are rounded off to the nearest whole inning for individuals, in accordance with baseball scoring practice from 1976 through 1981 (for the previous century, fractional innings pitched were simply lopped off). In 1981, this rounding-off procedure cost Sammy Stewart of Baltimore an ERA title, as Oakland's Steve McCatty won the crown despite having a higher ERA when fractional innings were counted; this singular occurrence led to a change in baseball scoring practice. In this book our database conforms to the 1976–1982 practice for all of pitching history, excepting those men who pitched only one-third of an inning in an entire season; rounding off their figures would produce an innings-pitched figure of zero, which in turn would produce a meaningless ERA. Accordingly, our policy regarding this relative handful of pitchers conforms to a 1978 ruling by the Baseball Playing Rules Committee that such fractional innings be stated. In a subsequent edition of *Total Baseball* we may well recalculate all fractional innings pitched.

Pitching records for the National Association are included in the Pitcher Register because the editors, like most baseball historians, regard it as a major league, inasmuch as it was the only professional league of its day and supplied the National League of 1876 with most of its personnel. However, until the SABR research project referred to in the Introduction to the Annual Record—which is expected to produce earned runs, strikeouts, hits allowed, bases on balls, and a fairly full range of traditional statistics heretofore unavailable—is completed we must continue the recent practice of carrying separate totals for the National Association rather than integrating them into the career marks of those pitchers whose major league tenures began before 1876 and concluded in that year or after it.

Gaps remain elsewhere in the official record of baseball and in the ongoing process of sabermetric reconstruction. The reader will note occasional blank elements in biographical lines; these are not typographical lapses but signs that the information does not exist or has not yet been found. However, unlike the case of batting records, there are no incomplete statistical columns for pitchers except in the National Association years of 1871–1875. Where official statistics did not exist or the raw data have not survived, as with batters facing pitchers before 1908 in the American League and before 1909 in the National, we have constructed figures from the available raw data. (For example, to obtain a pitcher's BFP—Batters Facing Pitchers—for calculating Op-

ponents' On Base Percentage or Batting Average, we have subtracted league base hits from league at-bats, divided by league innings pitched, multiplied by the pitcher's innings and added his hits and walks allowed and hit-by-pitch and sacrifices, if available. Research in this area continues, and by this book's next edition we hope to have eliminated the need for inferential data all the way back to 1871.)

For a key to the team and league abbreviations used in the Pitcher Register, flip to the last page of this volume. For a guide to the other procedures and abbreviations employed in the Pitcher Register, review the comments on the prodigiously extended pitching record below.

YEAR	TM/L	W	L	PCT	G	GS	CG	SHO	SV	IP	H	H/G	HR	BB	BB/G	SO	SO/G	ERA	/A	OAVG	OOBP	PR	/A	PF	CPI	WAT	PB	PD	TPI
■ RIP VAN WINKLE					Van Winkle, Rip "Half Moon" (Also Played in 1874 as Geoffrey Crayon)							b: 4/30/1820, Plattekill, N.Y.				d: 12/12/80, Hudson, N.Y.			BL/TL, 5'5", 145 lbs.				Deb: 5/7/1874 MUCH				
1874	Bos-n	27	30	.474	57																								
1875	Wes-n	29	22	.569	52																								
1883	Bal-a	5	18	.217	27	23	19	0	1	196	207	9.5	7	76	3.5	77	3.5	3.44	101	.274	.340	-3	1	106	106	-5.4	-0	0	-0.1
1884	Was-U	0	1	.000	1	1	1	0	0	8	10	11.3	0	2	2.3	3	3.4	4.50	110	.309	.349	-0	0	108	104	0.0	1	0	0.0
	KC-U	5	2	.714	8	6	5	0	0	52	66	11.4	0	9	1.6	14	2.4	4.33	104	.312	.340	3	1	94	94	1.4	2	0	0.1
	Yr	5	3	.625	7	7	6	0	0	60	76	11.4	0	11	1.7	17	2.6	4.35	104	.311	.341	3	1	95	94	1.0	2	0	0.1
1890	Cin-P	0	0	—	1	1	1	0	0	5	∞	2	2	∞	0	—	∞	-97	1.000	1.000	-2	-2	100	-98	0.0	0	0	-0.2
1907	NY-N	16	13	.552	35	34	18	0	2	251	224	8.0	19	78	2.8	170	6.1	2.76	126	.236	.293	17	20	103	116	1.5	1	2	2.2
1908	NY-N	16	12	.571	36	35	14	1	5	278	224	7.3	15	48	1.6	205	6.6	2.20	130	.215	.250	24	20	96	118	2.0	1	-3	2.2
1909	NY-N	25	7	.781	36	35	18	0	5	273	202	6.7	24	82	2.7	208	6.9	2.21	164	.201	.261	42	43	100	135	9.0	-1	1	4.2
1910	NY-N	18	12	.600	37	36	19	0	2	291	230	7.1	21	83	2.6	283	8.8	2.81	135	.211	.267	40	32	94	121	3.0	4	1	3.6
1911	NY-N	20	10	.667	36	35	21	0	4	286	210	6.6	18	61	1.9	289	9.1	1.76	188	.202	.246	54	49	96	147	5.0	4	-1	5.5
1912	NY-N	21	12	.636	35	35	13	0	3	262	215	7.4	23	77	2.6	249	8.6	2.92	116	.219	.275	16	14	98	111	4.5	3	1	1.7
1913	NY-N	19	10	.655	36	36	18	0	3	290	219	6.8	23	64	2.0	251	7.8	2.08	184	.202	.247	51	56	104	145	4.5	3	2	5.9
1914	Ind-F	11	11	.500	32	32	12	0	5	236	199	7.6	19	75	2.9	201	7.7	3.20	126	.226	.287	11	22	111	116	0.0	-1	1	2.2
1915	NY-N	22	9	.710	36	36	15	0	5	280	217	7.0	11	88	2.8	243	7.8	2.38	155	.211	.274	39	41	101	130	6.5	3	1	4.2
1916	NY-N	7	3	.700	13	13	5	0	3	96	79	7.4	7	28	2.6	72	6.8	3.00	140	.218	.274	10	13	107	123	2.0	1	3	1.5
	Bos-A	5	7	.417	16	16	1	0	0	104	114	9.9	8	29	2.5	72	6.2	3.81	112	.271	.318	4	5	102	109	-1.0	0	-2	0.7
1917	Bos-A	0	1	.000	1	1	0	0	0	⅓	5	135.0	2	1	27.0	1	27.0	108.00	1200	.833	.857	-2	-2	108	120	-1.0	0	0	-0.2
Total	2 n	56	52	.519	109																								
Total	14	190	128	.597	384	375	180	1	38	2903	2486	7.5	199	803	2.5	2338	7.2	2.76	134	.226	.285	304	313	101	118	31.6	23	6	33.6

Looking at the biographical line for any pitcher, we see first his use name in full capitals, then his given name and nickname (and any other name he may have used or been born with, such as the matronymic of a Latin American player). His date and place of birth follow "b" and his date and place of death follow "d"; years through 1900 are expressed fully, in four digits, and years after 1900 are expressed in only their last two digits. Then come his manner of batting and throwing, abbreviated for a lefthanded batter who throws right as BL/TR (a switch-hitter would be shown as BB for "bats both" and a switch thrower as TB for "throws both"). Next, and for most pitchers last, is the pitcher's debut date in the major leagues, if known at this point. While we, thanks to SABR research, are able to report most of these, for some individuals we have had to list only the two digits representing their rookie year.

Some pitchers continue in major league baseball after their pitching days are through, as managers, coaches, or even umpires. A pitcher whose biographical line concludes with an M can also be located in the Manager Roster; one whose line bears a C will be listed in the Coach Roster; and one with a U occupies a place in the Umpire Roster. (In the last case we have placed a U on the biographical line only for those pitchers who were employed as umpires by a league, for in the nineteenth century—and especially in the years of the National Association—there were literally hundreds of players who were pressed into service as umpires for a game or two; it would be misleading to accord such pitchers the same code we give to Bob Emslie or Bill Dinneen.) The select few who have been enshrined in the Baseball Hall of Fame are noted with an H. They are also listed in the Hall of Fame Roster found toward the end of Bill Deane's "Awards and Honors" essay in Part 1.

The explanations for the statistical column heads follow; for more technical information about formulas and calculations, see the Glossary. The vertical rules in the column-header line separate the stats into seven logical groupings: year, team, league; wins and losses; game-related counting stats; inning-related counting stats; basic calculated averages; sabermetric figures of more complex calculation; and win-denominated stats for batting, fielding, and Total Pitcher Index.

YEAR Year in which a man pitched (When a space in the column is blank, this indicates that the man pitched for two or more clubs in the last year stated in the column; if those clubs were in the same league, then the man will also have a combined total line, beginning with the abbreviation "Yr" placed in the TEAM/L column.)

Yr Year's totals for pitching with two or more clubs in same league; play in two leagues are not combined

TM/L Team and League (See comments for YEAR.)

W Wins

L Losses

PCT Win Percentage (Wins divided by decisions.)

G Games pitched

GS Games Started

CG Complete Games

SHO Shutouts (Complete-game shutouts only.)

SV Saves (Employing definition in force at the time, and 1969 definition for years prior to 1969.)

IP Innings Pitched (Fractional innings rounded off, as discussed above.)

H Hits allowed

H/G Hits allowed per Game (Game defined as nine innings.)

HR Home Runs allowed

BB Bases on Balls allowed

BB/G   Bases on Balls per Game (Game defined as nine innings; league leader calculated on basis of fewest bases on balls per nine innings.)

SO   Strikeouts

SO/G   Strikeouts per Game (Game defined as nine innings; league leader calculated on basis of most strikeouts per nine innings.)

ERA   Earned Run Average (In a handful of cases, a pitcher will have faced one or more batters for his full season's work yet failed to retire any of them [thus having an innings-pitched figure of zero]; if any of the men he put on base came around to score earned runs, these runs produced an infinite ERA, expressed in the pitcher's record as ∞.)

/A   Adjusted (This signifies that the stat to the immediate left is here normalized to league average and adjusted for home-park factor. A mark of 100 is a league-average performance, and superior marks exceed 100.)

OAVG   Opponents' Batting Average

OOBP   Opponents' On Base Percentage

PR   Pitching Runs (Linear Weights measure of runs saved *beyond* what a league-average pitcher might have saved, defined as zero. Occasionally the curious figure of −0 will appear in this column, or in the columns of other Linear Weights measures of batting, fielding, and the TPI. This "negative zero" figure signifies a run contribution that falls below the league average, but to so small a degree that it cannot be said to have cost the team a run. Also, this column and the Adjusted one to its right will each contain a pair of single-season leaders, the figures shown in boldface: the top mark in Starters' Runs and the top mark in Relievers' Runs. The former category is reserved for men who averaged more than three innings per game pitched, while the latter category is for those who averaged less than three innings per game pitched.)

PF   Park Factor (This is calculated separately for batters and pitchers; above 100 signifies a park favorable to hitters, below 100 signifies a park favorable to pitchers; see Home/Road section and Glossary for further data and technical information.)

CPI   Clutch Pitching Index (Expected runs over actual runs, with 100 being a league-average performance and marks over 100 being superior; see Glossary.)

WAT   Wins Above Team (How many wins a pitcher garnered beyond those expected of an average pitcher for that team; the formula is weighted so that a pitcher on a good team has a chance to compete with pitchers on poor teams, who otherwise would benefit from the larger potential spread between their team's won-lost percentage and their own; see Glossary for more information.)

PB   Pitcher Batting (Expressed in Batting Wins, which are park-adjusted Batting Runs—weighted, for those who played primarily at other positions, by the ratio of games pitched to games played—divided by the number of runs required to create an additional win beyond average. For more technical data about Runs Per Win and Batting Run formulas, see Glossary.)

PD   Pitcher Defense (Expressed in Fielding Wins, which are Fielding Runs divided by the number of runs required to create an additional win beyond average; see comment above on PB and also Glossary.)

TPI   Total Pitcher Index (The sum, expressed in wins beyond league average, of a pitcher's Pitching Runs, Batting Runs [in the AL since 1973, 0], and Fielding Runs, all divided by the Runs Per Win factor for that year—generally around 10, historically in the 9–11 range; see Glossary.)

Total   For players whose careers include play in the National Association as well as other major leagues, two totals are given, as described above and as illustrated in Rip Van Winkle's record, where the record of his years in the National Association is shown alongside the notation "Total 2 n," where *2* stands for the number of years totaled and *n* stands for National Association. For players whose careers began in 1876 or later, the lifetime record is shown alongside the notation "Total x," where *x* stands for the number of post-1875 years totaled.

YEAR	TM/L	W	L	PCT	G	GS	CG	SHO	SV	IP	H	H/G	HR	BB	BB/G	SO	SO/G	ERA	/A	OAVG	OOBP	PR	/A	PF	CPI	WAT	PB	PD	TPI
■ **DON AASE** Aase, Donald William b: 9/8/54, Orange, Cal. BR/TR, 6'3", 190 lbs. Deb: 7/26/77																													
1977	Bos-A	6	2	.750	13	13	4	2	0	92	85	8.3	6	19	1.9	49	4.8	3.13	151	.244	.282	10	16	116	87	1.5	0	-0	1.7
1978	Cal-A	11	8	.579	29	29	6	1	0	179	185	9.3	14	80	4.0	93	4.7	4.02	95	.270	.345	-5	-4	101	104	1.0	0	0	-0.3
1979	Cal-A	9	10	.474	37	28	7	1	2	185	200	9.7	19	77	3.7	96	4.7	4.82	80	.277	.340	-12	-19	92	93	-1.3	0	-2	-2.0
1980	Cal-A	8	13	.381	40	21	5	1	2	175	193	9.9	13	66	3.4	74	3.8	4.06	96	.287	.342	-0	-3	97	109	-0.6	0	-1	-0.3
1981	Cal-A	4	4	.500	39	0	0	0	11	65	56	7.8	4	24	3.3	38	5.3	2.35	161	.234	.302	9	10	104	127	0.3	0	-0	1.1
1982	Cal-A	3	3	.500	24	0	0	0	4	52	45	7.8	5	23	4.0	40	6.9	3.46	116	.243	.321	4	3	99	109	-0.3	0	-0	0.3
1984	Cal-A	4	1	.800	23	0	0	0	8	39	30	6.9	1	19	4.4	28	6.5	1.62	251	.221	.306	10	11	101	175	1.5	0	-0	1.1
1985	Bal-A	10	6	.625	54	0	0	0	14	88	83	8.5	6	35	3.6	67	6.9	3.78	108	.258	.325	4	3	98	103	2.0	0	0	0.3
1986	Bal-A	6	7	.462	66	0	0	0	34	82	71	7.8	6	28	3.1	67	7.4	2.96	140	.234	.294	11	11	99	101	0.1	0	0	1.1
1987	Bal-A	1	0	1.000	7	0	0	0	2	8	8	9.0	1	4	4.5	3	3.4	2.25	197	.276	.364	2	2	99	226	0.5	0	0	0.2
1988	Bal-A	0	0	—	35	0	0	0	0	47	40	7.7	4	37	7.1	28	5.4	4.02	96	.240	.368	-0	-1	97	115	0.0	0	-1	-0.1
Total	11	62	54	.534	367	91	22	5	77	1012	996	8.9	79	412	3.7	583	5.2	3.74	107	.261	.328	32	30	99	107	4.7	0	-4	3.1
■ **BERT ABBEY** Abbey, Bert Wood b: 11/29/1869, Essex, Vt. d: 6/11/62, Essex Junction, Vt. BR/TR, 5'11", 175 lbs. Deb: 6/14/1892																													
1892	Was-N	5	18	.217	27	23	19	0	1	196	207	9.5	7	76	3.5	77	3.5	3.44	101	.284	.352	-3	1	106	108	-5.4	-4	0	-0.1
1893	Chi-N	2	4	.333	7	7	5	0	0	56	74	11.9	1	20	3.2	6	1.0	5.46	89	.335	.390	-5	-4	104	93	-0.7	-0	0	-0.2
1894	Chi-N	2	7	.222	11	11	10	0	0	92	119	11.6	3	37	3.6	24	2.3	5.18	111	.336	.399	2	6	108	98	-2.2	-5	0	0.1
1895	Chi-N	0	1	.000	1	1	1	0	0	8	10	11.3	0	2	2.3	3	3.4	4.50	110	.327	.368	0	0	103	93	-0.4	0	0	0.0
	Bro-N	5	2	.714	8	6	5	0	0	52	66	11.4	0	9	1.6	14	2.4	4.33	104	.330	.359	3	3	94	94	1.4	1	0	0.1
	Yr	5	3	.625	9	7	6	0	0	60	76	11.4	0	11	1.7	17	2.6	4.35	104	.330	.360	3	1	95	94	1.0	0	0	0.1
1896	Bro-N	8	8	.500	25	18	12	0	0	164	210	11.5	7	48	2.6	37	2.0	5.16	74	.334	.382	-14	-24	88	91	0.9	0	0	-1.9
Total	5	22	40	.355	79	66	52	0	1	568	686	10.9	18	192	3.0	161	2.6	4.52	93	.317	.373	-18	-19	100	98	-6.4	-9	0	-2.0
■ **CHARLIE ABBEY** Abbey, Charles S. b: 10/1868, Falls City, Neb. BL, 5'8.5", 169 lbs. Deb: 8/16/1893																													
1896	Was-N	0	0	—	1	0	0	0	0	2	6	27.0	0	0	0.0	0	0.0	4.50	93	.541	.541	-0	-0	96	269	0.0	0	0	0.0
■ **DAN ABBOTT** Abbott, Leander Franklin "Big Dan" b: 3/16/1862, Portage, Ohio d: 2/13/30, Ottawa Lake, Mich. BR/TR, 5'11", 190 lbs. Deb: 4/19/1890																													
1890	Tol-a	0	2	.000	3	1	1	0	1	13	19	13.2	0	8	5.5	1	0.7	6.23	63	.358	.442	-3	-3	102	104	-0.9	0	0	-0.2
■ **GLENN ABBOTT** Abbott, William Glenn b: 2/16/51, Little Rock, Ark. BR/TR, 6'6", 200 lbs. Deb: 7/29/73																													
1973	Oak-A	1	0	1.000	5	3	1	0	0	19	16	7.6	3	7	3.3	6	2.8	3.79	86	.225	.291	0	-1	86	89	0.5	0	-0	0.0
1974	Oak-A	5	7	.417	19	17	3	0	0	96	89	8.3	4	34	3.2	38	3.6	3.00	119	.247	.314	7	6	99	102	-1.5	0	-0	0.6
1975	Oak-A	5	5	.500	30	15	3	1	0	114	109	8.6	12	50	3.9	51	4.0	4.26	81	.253	.325	-6	-10	91	92	-0.8	0	-0	-1.0
1976	Oak-A	2	4	.333	19	10	0	0	0	62	87	12.6	6	16	2.3	27	3.9	5.52	63	.333	.367	-14	-14	98	102	-1.1	0	0	-1.3
1977	Sea-A	12	13	.480	36	34	7	0	0	204	212	9.4	32	56	2.5	100	4.4	4.46	90	.270	.324	-9	-10	98	100	2.0	0	-0	-1.0
1978	Sea-A	7	15	.318	29	28	8	1	0	155	191	11.1	22	44	2.6	67	3.9	5.28	75	.303	.344	-26	-23	104	96	-1.0	0	0	-2.2
1979	Sea-A	4	10	.286	23	19	3	0	0	117	138	10.6	19	38	2.9	25	1.9	5.15	83	.301	.346	-12	-11	101	105	-2.2	0	-0	-1.0
1980	Sea-A	12	12	.500	31	31	7	2	0	215	228	9.5	27	49	2.1	78	3.3	4.10	103	.272	.310	-1	3	105	97	2.9	0	2	0.5
1981	Sea-A	4	9	.308	22	20	1	0	0	130	127	8.8	14	28	1.9	35	2.4	3.95	94	.258	.292	-4	-4	101	88	-1.6	0	0	-0.3
1983	Sea-A	5	3	.625	14	14	2	0	0	82	103	11.3	9	15	1.6	38	4.2	4.61	90	.311	.344	-5	-4	101	110	1.7	0	-1	-0.4
	Det-A	2	1	.667	7	7	1	1	0	47	43	8.2	5	7	1.3	11	2.1	1.91	201	.244	.269	11	10	95	156	0.3	0	-1	1.0
	Yr	7	4	.636	21	21	3	1	0	129	146	10.2	14	22	1.5	49	3.4	3.63	111	.285	.311	6	6	99	156	2.0	0	-1	0.6
1984	Det-A	3	4	.429	13	8	1	0	0	44	62	12.7	9	8	1.6	8	1.6	5.93	63	.326	.351	-9	-11	94	104	-1.1	0	0	-0.9
Total	11	62	83	.428	248	206	37	5	0	1285	1405	9.8	162	352	2.5	484	3.4	4.39	89	.280	.325	-68	-69	100	101	-1.9	0	0	-6.0
■ **AL ABER** Aber, Albert Julius "Lefty" b: 7/31/27, Cleveland, Ohio BL/TL, 6'2", 195 lbs. Deb: 9/15/50																													
1950	Cle-A	1	0	1.000	1	1	1	0	0	9	5	5.0	0	4	4.0	4	4.0	2.00	218	.167	.265	3	2	95	70	0.5	0	0	0.2
1953	Cle-A	1	1	.500	6	0	0	0	0	6	6	9.0	0	9	13.5	4	6.0	7.50	49	.240	.429	-2	-3	93	74	-0.1	1	0	-0.1
	Det-A	4	3	.571	17	10	2	0	0	67	63	8.5	3	41	5.5	34	4.6	4.43	91	.260	.359	-3	-3	102	97	1.1	-1	1	-0.2
	Yr	5	4	.556	23	10	2	0	0	73	69	8.5	3	50	6.2	38	4.7	4.68	86	.258	.366	-6	-5	101	97	1.0	1	1	-0.3
1954	Det-A	5	11	.313	32	18	4	0	3	125	121	8.7	8	40	2.9	54	3.9	3.96	95	.257	.311	-3	-3	101	86	-2.4	-2	1	-0.3
1955	Det-A	6	3	.667	39	1	0	0	3	80	86	9.7	9	28	3.1	37	4.2	3.37	111	.275	.329	5	3	95	126	1.5	-2	1	0.2
1956	Det-A	4	4	.500	42	0	0	0	7	63	65	9.3	1	25	3.6	21	3.0	3.43	115	.270	.327	5	4	95	106	-0.2	1	0	0.4
1957	Det-A	3	3	.500	28	0	0	0	1	37	46	11.2	6	11	2.7	15	3.6	6.81	60	.315	.347	-12	-11	107	84	0.0	-0	1	-1.0
	KC-A	0	0	—	3	0	0	0	0	3	6	18.0	2	2	6.0	0	0.0	12.00	32	.400	.471	-3	-3	102	113	0.0	0	0	-0.1
	Yr	3	3	.500	31	0	0	0	1	40	52	11.7	8	13	2.9	15	3.4	7.20	56	.317	.353	-15	-14	107	113	0.0	-0	1	-1.1
Total	6	24	25	.490	168	30	7	0	14	390	398	9.2	29	160	3.7	169	3.9	4.18	93	.269	.332	-11	-12	99	99	0.4	-3	3	-0.9
■ **BILL ABERNATHIE** Abernathie, William Edward b: 1/30/29, Torrance, Cal. BR/TR, 5'10", 190 lbs. Deb: 9/27/52																													
1952	Cle-A	0	0	—	1	0	0	0	1	2	4	18.0	1	1	4.5	0	0.0	13.50	24	.444	.500	-2	-2	88	96	0.0	-0	0	-0.1
■ **TED ABERNATHY** Abernathy, Talmadge Lafayette b: 10/30/21, Bynum, N.C. BR/TL, 6'2", 210 lbs. Deb: 9/19/42																													
1942	Phi-A	0	0	—	1	0	0	0	0	3	2	6.0	0	3	9.0	1	3.0	9.00	41	.222	.417	-2	-2	101	50	0.0	0	0	0.0
1943	Phi-A	0	3	.000	5	2	1	0	0	15	24	14.4	0	13	7.8	10	6.0	12.60	28	.353	.451	-16	-15	106	58	-1.4	0	0	-1.3
1944	Phi-A	0	0	—	1	0	0	0	0	3	5	15.0	0	1	3.0	2	6.0	3.00	117	.417	.462	0	0	102	247	0.0	-0	0	0.0
Total	3	0	3	.000	7	2	1	0	0	21	31	13.3	0	17	7.3	13	5.6	10.71	33	.348	.449	-17	-17	105	84	-1.4	0	0	-1.3
■ **TED ABERNATHY** Abernathy, Theodore Wade b: 3/6/33, Stanley, N.C. BR/TR, 6'4", 215 lbs. Deb: 4/13/55																													
1955	Was-A	5	9	.357	40	14	3	2	0	119	136	10.3	9	67	5.1	79	6.0	5.97	62	.294	.380	-27	-30	94	89	0.2	-1	1	-2.8
1956	Was-A	1	3	.250	5	4	2	0	0	30	35	10.5	2	10	3.0	18	5.4	4.20	105	.292	.348	-0	1	107	105	-0.6	-1	2	0.2
1957	Was-A	2	10	.167	26	16	2	0	0	85	100	10.6	9	65	6.9	50	5.3	6.78	57	.314	.425	-28	-28	102	98	-3.2	0	1	-2.5
1960	Was-A	0	0	—	2	0	0	0	0	3	4	12.0	0	4	12.0	1	3.0	12.00	33	.308	.471	-3	-3	102	58	0.0	0	0	-0.1
1963	Cle-A	7	2	.778	43	0	0	0	12	59	54	8.2	3	29	4.4	47	7.2	2.90	122	.251	.333	5	4	98	129	2.6	1	2	0.8
1964	Cle-A	2	6	.250	53	0	0	0	11	73	66	8.1	5	46	5.7	57	7.0	4.32	86	.247	.355	-6	-5	103	96	-1.9	-1	3	-0.2
1965	Chi-N	4	6	.400	**84**	0	0	0	**31**	136	113	7.5	7	56	3.7	104	6.9	2.58	142	.227	.304	14	16	103	116	-0.4	0	4	2.2
1966	Chi-N	1	3	.250	20	0	0	0	4	28	26	8.4	4	17	5.5	18	5.8	6.11	61	.255	.363	-8	-7	103	82	-0.5	-0	2	-0.6
	Atl-N	4	4	.500	38	0	0	0	4	65	58	8.0	5	36	5.0	42	5.8	3.88	90	.247	.335	-2	-3	97	101	-0.1	1	1	0.0
	Yr	5	7	.417	58	0	0	0	8	93	84	8.1	9	53	5.1	60	5.8	4.55	78	.248	.338	-10	-10	99	101	-0.6	-0	2	-0.6
1967	Cin-N	6	3	.667	**70**	0	0	0	**28**	106	63	5.3	1	41	3.5	88	7.5	1.27	288	.170	.255	**25**	**28**	109	100	1.3	-1	2	3.2
1968	Cin-N	10	7	.588	**78**	0	0	0	13	135	111	7.4	9	55	3.7	64	4.3	2.47	134	.228	.302	8	13	111	124	1.5	-1	3	1.8
1969	Chi-N	4	3	.571	56	0	0	0	3	85	75	7.9	8	42	4.4	55	5.8	3.18	119	.234	.316	4	6	105	112	0.0	1	2	0.9
1970	Chi-N	0	0	—	11	0	0	0	1	9	9	9.0	0	5	5.0	2	2.0	2.00	240	.281	.375	2	3	119	236	0.0	0	0	0.3
	StL-N	1	0	1.000	11	0	0	0	1	18	15	7.5	0	12	6.0	8	4.0	3.00	143	.246	.366	2	3	106	146	0.5	-0	1	0.3
	Yr	1	0	1.000	22	0	0	0	2	27	24	8.0	0	17	5.7	10	3.3	2.67	168	.255	.361	4	5	110	146	0.5	0	1	0.6
	KC-A	9	3	.750	36	0	0	0	12	56	41	6.6	3	38	6.1	49	7.9	2.57	144	.209	.328	7	7	100	127	3.6	0	0	0.8
1971	KC-A	4	6	.400	63	0	0	0	23	81	60	6.7	3	50	5.6	55	6.1	2.56	133	.210	.333	8	8	98	120	-1.2	-1	2	0.9
1972	KC-A	3	4	.429	45	0	0	0	5	58	44	6.8	2	19	2.9	28	4.3	1.71	179	.210	.276	9	9	100	124	-0.4	-1	1	1.0
Total	14	63	69	.477	681	34	7	2	148	1146	1010	7.9	70	592	4.6	765	6.0	3.46	105	.241	.332	11	23	103	111	1.4	-4	27	6.2
■ **WOODY ABERNATHY** Abernathy, Virgil Woodrow b: 2/1/15, Forest City, N.C. BL/TL, 6', 170 lbs. Deb: 7/28/46																													
1946	NY-N	1	1	.500	15	1	0	0	1	40	32	7.2	5	10	2.3	6	1.3	3.37	104	.232	.275	0	1	103	91	0.2	-1	-1	0.0
1947	NY-N	0	0	—	1	0	0	0	0	2	4	18.0	0	1	4.5	0	0.0	9.00	45	.400	.455	-1	-1	99	90	0.0	0	0	0.0
Total	2	1	1	.500	16	1	0	0	1	42	36	7.7	5	11	2.4	6	1.3	3.64	97	.243	.287	-1	-0	103	91	0.2	-1	-1	0.0
■ **HARRY ABLES** Ables, Harry Terrell "Hans" b: 10/4/1884, Terrell, Tex. d: 2/8/51, San Antonio, Tex. BR/TL, 6'2.5", 200 lbs. Deb: 9/04/05																													
1905	StL-A	0	3	.000	6	3	1	0	0	31	37	10.7	0	13	3.8	11	3.2	3.77	66	.322	.391	-4	-4	93	118	-1.4	-1	-1	-0.4
1909	Cle-A	1	1	.500	5	3	3	0	0	30	26	7.8	1	10	3.0	24	7.2	2.10	122	.226	.294	1	2	103	101	0.1	-2	-1	0.1
1911	NY-A	0	1	.000	3	2	0	0	0	11	16	13.1	0	7	5.7	6	4.9	9.82	38	.333	.418	-8	-7	111	58	-0.4	-1	-0	-0.6

YEAR	TM/L	W	L	PCT	G	GS	CG	SHO	SV	IP	H	H/G	HR	BB	BB/G	SO	SO/G	ERA	/A	OAVG	OOBP	PR	/A	PF	CPI	WAT	PB	PD	TPI
Total	3	1	5	.167	14	8	4	0	0	72	79	9.9	1	30	3.8	41	5.1	4.00	67	.284	.356	-11	-11	100	102	-1.7	-4	-2	-0.9
■ **GEORGE ABRAMS**	Abrams, George Allen b: 11/9/1899, Seattle, Wash. d: 12/5/86, Clearwater, Fla. BR/TR, 5'9", 170 lbs. Deb: 4/19/23																												
1923	Cin-N	0	0	—	3	0	0	0	0	5	10	18.0	0	3	5.4	1	1.8	9.00	43	.500	.583	-3	-3	96	125	0.0	0	0	-0.1
■ **JOHNNY ABREGO**	Abrego, Johnny Ray b: 7/4/62, Corpus Christi, Tex BR/TR, 6'1", 185 lbs. Deb: 9/04/85																												
1985	Chi-N	1	1	.500	6	5	0	0	0	24	32	12.0	3	12	4.5	13	4.9	6.38	66	.352	.404	-7	-6	117	109	0.0	-1	0	-0.5
■ **JIM ACKER**	Acker, James Justin b: 9/24/58, Freer, Tex. BR/TR, 6'2", 212 lbs. Deb: 4/07/83																												
1983	Tor-A	5	1	.833	38	5	0	0	1	98	103	9.5	7	38	3.5	44	4.0	4.32	102	.273	.350	-3	1	108	101	1.9	0	1	0.2
1984	Tor-A	3	5	.375	32	3	0	0	1	72	79	9.9	3	25	3.1	33	4.1	4.38	92	.286	.353	-3	-3	101	99	-1.2	0	-0	-0.2
1985	Tor-A	7	2	.778	61	0	0	0	10	86	86	9.0	7	43	4.5	42	4.4	3.24	127	.268	.357	9	8	99	141	2.0	0	1	1.0
1986	Tor-A	2	4	.333	23	5	0	0	0	60	63	9.4	6	22	3.3	32	4.8	4.35	100	.281	.336	-1	0	104	107	-1.0	0	1	0.1
	Atl-N	3	8	.273	21	14	0	0	0	95	100	9.5	7	26	2.5	37	3.5	3.79	102	.274	.316	-1	1	103	101	-2.1	-1	0	0.0
1987	Atl-N	4	9	.308	68	0	0	0	14	115	109	8.5	11	51	4.0	68	5.3	4.15	108	.253	.334	-1	4	109	98	-1.8	0	1	0.6
1988	Atl-N	0	4	.000	21	1	0	0	0	42	45	9.6	6	14	3.0	25	5.4	4.71	78	.280	.326	-6	-5	107	102	-1.9	1	0	-0.3
Total	6	24	33	.421	264	28	0	0	26	568	585	9.3	47	219	3.5	281	4.5	4.07	103	.272	.339	-5	6	105	107	-4.1	0	5	1.4
■ **TOM ACKER**	Acker, Thomas James b: 3/7/30, Paterson, N.J. BR/TR, 6'4", 215 lbs. Deb: 4/20/56																												
1956	Cin-N	4	3	.571	29	7	1	1	1	84	60	6.4	7	29	3.1	54	5.8	2.36	170	.201	.269	13	15	106	95	0.0	-1	1	1.6
1957	Cin-N	10	5	.667	49	6	1	0	4	109	122	10.1	16	41	3.4	67	5.5	4.95	83	.293	.352	-13	-10	106	108	2.5	-1	-0	-1.0
1958	Cin-N	4	3	.571	38	10	3	0	1	125	126	9.1	10	43	3.1	90	6.5	4.54	92	.266	.326	-8	-5	106	84	0.6	-1	-2	-0.7
1959	Cin-N	1	2	.333	37	0	0	0	2	63	57	8.1	10	37	5.3	45	6.4	4.14	98	.246	.354	-1	-1	103	116	-0.4	-0	-1	-0.1
Total	4	19	13	.594	153	23	5	1	8	381	365	8.6	43	150	3.5	256	6.0	4.11	100	.257	.327	-9	-0	105	99	2.7	-3	-2	-0.2
■ **FRITZ ACKLEY**	Ackley, Florian Frederick b: 4/10/37, Hayward, Wis. BL/TR, 6'1.5", 202 lbs. Deb: 9/21/63																												
1963	Chi-A	1	0	1.000	2	2	0	0	0	13	7	4.8	2	7	4.8	11	7.6	2.08	179	.167	.275	2	2	102	140	0.5	-0	0	0.3
1964	Chi-A	0	0	—	3	2	0	0	0	6	10	15.0	2	4	6.0	6	9.0	9.00	38	.345	.424	-4	-4	93	100	0.0	1	0	-0.1
Total	2	1	0	1.000	5	4	0	0	0	19	17	8.1	4	11	5.2	17	8.1	4.26	85	.239	.333	-1	-1	99	127	0.5	1	1	0.2
■ **CY ACOSTA**	Acosta, Cecilio (Miranda) b: 11/22/46, Sabino, Mexico BR/TR, 5'10", 165 lbs. Deb: 6/04/72																												
1972	Chi-A	3	0	1.000	26	0	0	0	5	35	25	6.4	2	17	4.4	28	7.2	1.54	211	.210	.304	6	7	106	177	1.5	-0	-0	0.7
1973	Chi-A	10	6	.625	48	0	0	0	18	97	66	6.1	8	39	3.6	60	5.6	2.23	177	.193	.283	17	18	103	108	2.5	0	-1	1.8
1974	Chi-A	0	3	.000	27	0	0	0	3	46	43	8.4	3	18	3.5	19	3.7	3.72	100	.256	.333	-0	-0	102	104	-1.4	0	0	0.0
1975	Phi-N	0	0	—	6	0	0	0	1	9		9.0	2	3	3.0	2	2.0	6.00	61	.273	.333	-2	-2	101	84	0.0	0	-0	-0.2
Total	4	13	9	.591	107	0	0	0	27	187	143	6.9	15	77	3.7	109	5.2	2.65	141	.216	.302	20	23	103	119	2.6	-0	-2	2.3
■ **ED ACOSTA**	Acosta, Eduardo Elixbet b: 3/9/44, Boquete, Panama BB/TR, 6'5", 215 lbs. Deb: 9/07/70																												
1970	Pit-N	0	0	—	3	0	0	0	1	3	5	15.0	1	2	6.0	1	3.0	12.00	32	.417	.500	-3	-3	96	100	0.0	0	0	-0.2
1971	SD-N	3	3	.500	8	6	3	1	0	46	43	8.4	4	7	1.4	16	3.1	2.74	124	.246	.272	4	3	98	100	0.6	-2	-0	0.1
1972	SD-N	3	6	.333	46	2	0	0	0	89	105	10.6	7	30	3.0	53	5.4	4.45	71	.302	.350	-10	-13	91	108	-0.5	-0	-1	-1.4
Total	3	6	9	.400	57	8	3	1	1	138	153	10.0	12	39	2.5	70	4.6	4.04	80	.286	.330	-9	-12	93	105	0.1	-2	-1	-1.5
■ **JOSE ACOSTA**	Acosta, Jose "Acostica" b: 3/4/1891, San Antonio Del Rio Blanco, Cuba BR/TR, 5'7", 140 lbs. Deb: 7/28/20																												
1920	Was-A	5	4	.556	17	5	4	1	1	83	92	10.0	1	26	2.8	9	1.0	4.01	91	.290	.344	-2	-3	96	91	0.9	1	-3	-0.4
1921	Was-A	5	4	.556	33	7	2	0	3	116	148	11.5	4	36	2.8	30	2.3	4.34	98	.317	.354	-1	-1	99	108	0.3	-2	-1	-0.3
1922	Chi-A	0	2	.000	5	1	0	0	0	15	25	15.0	4	6	3.6	6	3.6	8.40	49	.417	.443	-7	-7	101	115	-0.9	0	-0	-0.6
Total	3	10	10	.500	55	13	6	1	4	214	265	11.1	9	68	2.9	45	1.9	4.50	89	.314	.357	-10	-12	98	102	0.3	-1	-4	-1.3
■ **ACE ADAMS**	Adams, Ace Townsend b: 3/2/12, Willows, Cal. BR/TR, 5'10.5", 182 lbs. Deb: 4/15/41																												
1941	NY-N	4	1	.800	38	0	0	0	1	71	84	10.6	3	35	4.4	18	2.3	4.82	78	.304	.376	-9	-8	104	107	1.6	-1	-1	-1.0
1942	NY-N	7	4	.636	**61**	0	0	0	11	88	69	7.1	1	31	3.2	33	3.4	1.84	182	.223	.285	**14**	**15**	101	130	1.0	-1	0	1.6
1943	NY-N	11	7	.611	**70**	3	1	0	9	140	121	7.8	5	55	3.5	46	3.0	2.83	118	.236	.306	8	8	99	103	3.8	-1	-1	0.7
1944	NY-N	8	11	.421	**65**	4	1	0	**13**	138	149	9.7	8	58	3.8	32	2.1	4.24	90	.279	.343	-10	-7	105	103	-0.2	-2	-2	-0.9
1945	NY-N	11	9	.550	65	0	0	0	**15**	113	109	8.7	7	44	3.5	39	3.1	3.42	111	.252	.313	5	5	100	104	0.9	0	1	0.6
1946	NY-N	0	1	.000	3	0	0	0	0	3	9	27.0	2	1	3.0	3	9.0	15.00	23	.500	.526	-4	-4	103	117	-0.4	0	0	-0.3
Total	6	41	33	.554	302	7	2	0	49	553	541	8.8	26	224	3.6	171	2.8	3.47	104	.260	.325	5	9	102	108	6.7	-5	-2	0.7
■ **BABE ADAMS**	Adams, Charles Benjamin b: 5/18/1882, Tipton, Ind. d: 7/27/68, Silver Spring, Md BL/TR, 5'11.5", 185 lbs. Deb: 4/18/06																												
1906	StL-N	0	1	.000	1	1	0	0	0	4	9	20.3	0	2	4.5	0	0.0	13.50	20	.476	.527	-5	-5	104	71	-0.4	-0	0	-0.3
1907	Pit-N	0	2	.000	4	3	1	0	0	22	40	16.4	1	3	1.2	11	4.5	6.95	36	.439	.473	-11	-11	102	103	-0.9	0	0	-0.9
1909	Pit-N	12	3	.800	25	12	7	3	2	130	88	6.1	0	23	1.6	65	4.5	1.11	233	.196	.240	22	21	99	89	2.2	-3	-1	2.4
1910	Pit-N	18	9	.667	34	30	16	3	0	245	217	8.0	4	60	2.2	101	3.7	2.24	149	.240	.291	22	30	110	99	3.7	0	-5	2.9
1911	Pit-N	22	12	.647	40	37	24	6	0	293	253	7.8	5	42	1.3	133	4.1	2.33	142	.237	**.271**	35	32	97	87	4.4	5	-8	2.9
1912	Pit-N	11	8	.579	28	21	11	2	0	170	169	8.9	4	35	1.9	63	3.3	2.91	112	.254	.294	9	6	95	80	-0.5	4	-2	0.8
1913	Pit-N	21	10	.677	43	37	24	4	0	314	271	7.8	8	49	1.4	144	4.1	2.15	140	.235	**.261**	37	30	94	92	5.8	8	-1	4.0
1914	Pit-N	13	16	.448	40	35	19	3	1	283	253	8.0	5	39	1.2	91	2.9	2.51	103	.244	**.268**	9	2	93	80	0.0	1	-2	0.0
1915	Pit-N	14	14	.500	40	30	17	2	2	245	229	8.4	6	34	1.2	62	2.3	2.87	94	.252	.273	-3	-5	98	82	0.8	-2	-1	-0.8
1916	Pit-N	2	9	.182	16	10	4	1	0	72	91	11.4	2	12	1.5	22	2.8	5.75	49	.320	.338	-25	-24	107	76	-3.1	2	0	-2.2
1918	Pit-N	1	1	.500	3	3	2	0	0	23	15	5.9	0	4	1.6	6	2.3	1.17	246	.197	.232	4	4	105	93	0.0	1	-1	0.6
1919	Pit-N	17	10	.630	34	29	23	6	1	263	213	7.3	1	23	**0.8**	92	3.1	1.98	154	.220	**.235**	27	31	105	66	3.8	-0	-4	3.2
1920	Pit-N	17	13	.567	35	33	19	**8**	2	263	240	8.2	6	18	**0.6**	84	2.9	2.16	147	.244	**.250**	29	30	101	80	2.0	-5	-2	2.6
1921	Pit-N	14	5	.737	25	20	11	2	0	160	155	8.7	4	18	**1.0**	55	3.1	2.64	**145**	.251	**.268**	20	21	102	78	3.7	3	-2	2.4
1922	Pit-N	8	11	.421	27	19	12	4	0	171	191	10.1	1	15	**0.8**	39	2.1	3.58	116	.287	.297	10	11	101	84	-2.4	4	1	1.5
1923	Pit-N	13	7	.650	26	22	11	0	1	159	196	11.1	8	25	1.4	38	2.2	4.42	86	.309	.328	-7	-11	95	94	2.2	5	-2	-0.8
1924	Pit-N	3	1	.750	9	3	2	0	0	40	31	7.0	1	3	0.7	5	1.1	1.13	357	.209	.221	12	13	104	97	0.8	-0	-1	1.2
1925	Pit-N	6	5	.545	33	10	3	0	3	101	129	11.5	7	17	1.5	18	1.6	5.44	78	.306	.333	-13	-14	99	80	-0.6	1	-2	-1.3
1926	Pit-N	2	3	.400	19	0	0	0	3	37	51	12.4	5	8	1.9	7	1.7	6.08	70	.347	.360	-9	-8	111	101	-0.6	-0	-1	-0.7
Total	19	194	140	.581	482	355	206	44	15	2995	2841	8.5	68	430	1.3	1036	3.1	2.76	117	.253	.278	161	157	100	84	20.9	24	-32	17.5
■ **RED ADAMS**	Adams, Charles Dwight b: 10/7/21, Parlier, Cal. BR/TR, 6', 185 lbs. Deb: 5/05/46 C																												
1946	Chi-N	0	1	.000	8	0	0	0	0	12	18	13.5	1	7	5.3	8	6.0	8.25	39	.353	.424	-6	-7	93	84	-0.4	-0	1	-0.5
■ **DAN ADAMS**	Adams, Daniel Leslie "Rube" b: 6/19/1887, St.Louis, Mo. d: 10/6/64, St.Louis, Mo. BR/TR, 5'11.5", 165 lbs. Deb: 5/22/14																												
1914	KC-F	4	9	.308	36	14	6	0	3	136	141	9.3	3	52	3.4	38	2.5	3.51	88	.273	.347	-5	-7	96	105	-2.0	-1	0	-0.6
1915	KC-F	0	2	.000	11	2	0	0	0	35	41	10.5	2	13	3.3	16	4.1	4.63	63	.323	.385	-6	-7	97	99	-0.9	-0	0	-0.6
Total	2	4	11	.267	47	16	6	0	3	171	182	9.6	5	65	3.4	54	2.8	3.74	81	.283	.355	-11	-13	96	104	-2.9	-1	0	-1.2
■ **JOE ADAMS**	Adams, Joseph Edward b: 10/28/1877, Cowden, Ill. d: 10/8/52, Montgomery City, Mo TL, 6', 190 lbs. Deb: 4/26/02																												
1902	StL-N	0	0	—	1	0	0	0	0	4	9	20.3	0	2	4.5	0	0.0	9.00	31	.471	.521	-3	-3	99	104	0.0	-0	1	-0.1
■ **KARL ADAMS**	Adams, Karl Tutwiler "Rebel" b: 8/11/1891, Columbus, Ga. d: 9/17/67, Everett, Wash. BR/TR, 6'2", 170 lbs. Deb: 4/19/14																												
1914	Cin-N	0	0	—	4	0	0	0	0	8	14	15.8	0	5	5.6	5	5.6	9.00	33	.424	.463	-6	-5	107	92	0.0	0	0	-0.4
1915	Chi-N	1	9	.100	26	12	3	0	0	107	105	8.8	5	43	3.6	57	4.8	4.71	60	.267	.325	-23	-22	103	79	-3.9	-4	0	-2.6
Total	2	1	9	.100	30	12	3	0	0	115	119	9.3	5	48	3.8	62	4.9	5.01	57	.279	.336	-29	-28	103	79	-3.9	-4	0	-3.0
■ **RICK ADAMS**	Adams, Reuben Alexander b: 12/23/1878, Paris, Tex. d: 3/10/55, Paris, Tex. BL/TL, 6', 165 lbs. Deb: 7/13/05																												
1905	Was-A	2	5	.286	11	6	3	1	0	63	63	9.0	1	24	3.4	25	3.6	3.57	78	.285	.355	-6	-5	106	98	-1.1	0	0	-0.5
■ **BOB ADAMS**	Adams, Robert Andrew b: 1/20/07, Birmingham, Ala. d: 3/6/70, Jacksonville, Fla. BR/TR, 6'0.5", 165 lbs. Deb: 9/27/31																												
1931	Phi-N	0	1	.000	1	1	0	0	0	6	14	21.0	0	1	1.5	3	4.5	9.00	47	.424	.429	-3	-3	109	95	-0.4	-0	-0	-0.2
1932	Phi-N	0	0	—	4	0	0	0	0	6	7	10.5	0	2	3.0	2	3.0	1.50	288	.318	.360	2	2	111	317	0.0	0	0	0.2

YEAR	TM/L	W	L	PCT	G	GS	CG	SHO	SV	IP	H	H/G	HR	BB	BB/G	SO	SO/G	ERA	/A	OAVG	OOBP	PR	/A	PF	CPI	WAT	PB	PD	TPI
Total	2	0	1	.000	5	1	0	0	0	12	21	15.8	0	3	2.3	5	3.8	5.25	81	.382	.400	-2	-1	110	206	-0.4	-0	0	0.0

■ BOB ADAMS Adams, Robert Burdette b: 7/24/01, Holyoke, Mass. BR/TR, 5'11", 168 lbs. Deb: 9/22/25

YEAR	TM/L	W	L	PCT	G	GS	CG	SHO	SV	IP	H	H/G	HR	BB	BB/G	SO	SO/G	ERA	/A	OAVG	OOBP	PR	/A	PF	CPI	WAT	PB	PD	TPI
1925	Bos-A	0	0	—	2	0	0	0	0	6	10	15.0	1	3	4.5	1	1.5	7.50	58	.417	.464	-2	-2	99	124	0.0	0	1	0.0

■ WILLIE ADAMS Adams, William John Irvin b: 9/27/1890, Clearfield, Pa. d: 6/18/37, Albany, N.Y. BR/TR, 6'4", 180 lbs. Deb: 6/30/12

YEAR	TM/L	W	L	PCT	G	GS	CG	SHO	SV	IP	H	H/G	HR	BB	BB/G	SO	SO/G	ERA	/A	OAVG	OOBP	PR	/A	PF	CPI	WAT	PB	PD	TPI
1912	StL-A	2	3	.400	13	5	0	0	0	46	50	9.8	0	19	3.7	16	3.1	3.91	88	.284	.360	-3	-2	103	101	0.2	-2	-1	-0.3
1913	StL-A	0	0	—	4	0	0	0	0	9	12	12.0	1	4	4.0	5	5.0	10.00	29	.286	.388	-7	-7	98	55	0.0	0	-0	-0.6
1914	Pit-F	1	1	.500	15	2	1	0	2	55	70	11.5	4	22	3.6	14	2.3	3.76	82	.326	.391	-3	-4	96	146	0.1	-1	0	-0.4
1918	Phi-A	5	12	.294	32	14	7	0	0	169	164	8.7	2	97	5.2	39	2.1	4.42	67	.272	.372	-31	-27	108	91	-2.5	-3	1	-3.0
1919	Phi-A	0	0	—	1	0	0	0	0	5	7	12.6	1	2	3.6	0	0.0	3.60	100	.389	.476	-0	0	112	234	0.0	-0	0	0.0
Total	5	8	16	.333	65	21	8	0	2	284	303	9.6	8	144	4.6	74	2.3	4.37	71	.287	.376	-45	-40	104	104	-2.2	-7	-1	-4.3

■ MIKE ADAMSON Adamson, John Michael b: 9/13/47, San Diego, Cal. BR/TR, 6'2", 185 lbs. Deb: 7/01/67

YEAR	TM/L	W	L	PCT	G	GS	CG	SHO	SV	IP	H	H/G	HR	BB	BB/G	SO	SO/G	ERA	/A	OAVG	OOBP	PR	/A	PF	CPI	WAT	PB	PD	TPI
1967	Bal-A	0	1	.000	3	2	0	0	0	10	9	8.1	1	12	10.8	8	7.2	8.10	37	.257	.438	-5	-6	94	78	-0.4	1	-0	-0.4
1968	Bal-A	0	2	.000	2	2	0	0	0	8	9	10.1	2	4	4.5	4	4.5	9.00	33	.281	.361	-5	-5	101	66	-0.9	0	-0	-0.4
1969	Bal-A	0	1	.000	6	0	0	0	0	8	10	11.3	0	6	6.8	2	2.3	4.50	81	.357	.421	-1	-1	100	148	-0.4	-0	1	0.0
Total	3	0	4	.000	11	4	0	0	0	26	28	9.7	3	22	7.6	14	4.8	7.27	44	.295	.410	-12	-12	98	96	-1.7	1	0	-0.8

■ GRADY ADKINS Adkins, Grady Emmett "Butcher Boy" b: 6/29/1897, Jacksonville, Ark d: 3/31/66, Little Rock, Ark. BR/TR, 5'11", 175 lbs. Deb: 4/13/28

YEAR	TM/L	W	L	PCT	G	GS	CG	SHO	SV	IP	H	H/G	HR	BB	BB/G	SO	SO/G	ERA	/A	OAVG	OOBP	PR	/A	PF	CPI	WAT	PB	PD	TPI
1928	Chi-A	10	16	.385	36	27	14	0	1	225	235	9.4	12	89	3.6	54	2.2	3.72	109	.278	.341	8	8	100	113	-2.6	-3	-1	0.4
1929	Chi-A	2	11	.154	31	15	5	0	0	138	168	11.0	12	67	4.4	24	1.6	5.35	77	.303	.369	-17	-19	98	99	-4.0	3	2	-1.2
Total	2	12	27	.308	67	42	19	0	1	363	403	10.0	24	156	3.9	78	1.9	4.34	94	.288	.352	-9	-10	99	108	-6.6	-1	1	-0.8

■ DEWEY ADKINS Adkins, John Dewey b: 5/11/18, Norcatur, Kan. BR/TR, 6'2", 195 lbs. Deb: 9/19/42

YEAR	TM/L	W	L	PCT	G	GS	CG	SHO	SV	IP	H	H/G	HR	BB	BB/G	SO	SO/G	ERA	/A	OAVG	OOBP	PR	/A	PF	CPI	WAT	PB	PD	TPI
1942	Was-A	0	0	—	1	1	0	0	0	6	7	10.5	0	6	9.0	3	4.5	10.50	34	.259	.394	-5	-5	99	45	0.0	0	-0	-0.3
1943	Was-A	0	0	—	7	0	0	0	0	10	9	8.1	0	5	4.5	1	0.9	2.70	125	.250	.341	1	1	102	123	0.0	-0	-0	0.0
1949	Chi-N	2	4	.333	30	5	1	0	0	82	98	10.8	10	39	4.3	43	4.7	5.71	69	.298	.363	-15	-16	97	96	-0.4	1	1	-1.2
Total	3	2	4	.333	38	6	1	0	0	98	114	10.5	10	50	4.6	47	4.3	5.69	68	.291	.364	-19	-20	98	95	-0.4	1	1	-1.5

■ DOC ADKINS Adkins, Merle Theron b: 8/5/1872, Troy, Wis. d: 2/21/34, Durham, N.C. TR, 5'10.5", 220 lbs. Deb: 6/24/02

YEAR	TM/L	W	L	PCT	G	GS	CG	SHO	SV	IP	H	H/G	HR	BB	BB/G	SO	SO/G	ERA	/A	OAVG	OOBP	PR	/A	PF	CPI	WAT	PB	PD	TPI
1902	Bos-A	1	1	.500	4	2	1	0	0	20	30	13.5	2	7	3.1	3	1.3	4.05	87	.374	.424	-1	-1	98	159	0.0	-0	0	0.0
1903	NY-A	0	0	—	2	1	0	0	1	7	10	12.9	0	5	6.4	0	0.0	7.71	38	.360	.457	-4	-4	100	83	0.0	-0	-0	-0.3
Total	2	1	1	.500	6	3	1	0	1	27	40	13.3	2	12	4.0	3	1.0	5.00	67	.370	.433	-5	-5	99	139	0.0	-1	-0	-0.3

■ JUAN AGOSTO Agosto, Juan Roberto (Gonzalez) b: 2/23/58, Rio Piedras, P.R. BL/TL, 6', 175 lbs. Deb: 9/07/81

YEAR	TM/L	W	L	PCT	G	GS	CG	SHO	SV	IP	H	H/G	HR	BB	BB/G	SO	SO/G	ERA	/A	OAVG	OOBP	PR	/A	PF	CPI	WAT	PB	PD	TPI
1981	Chi-A	0	0	—	2	0	0	0	0	6	5	7.5	1	0	0.0	3	4.5	4.50	80	.238	.273	-1	-1	99	76	0.0	0	0	0.0
1982	Chi-A	0	0	—	1	0	0	0	0	2	7	31.5	0	0	0.0	1	4.5	18.00	22	.538	.538	-3	-3	97	78	0.0	0	0	-0.2
1983	Chi-A	2	2	.500	39	0	0	0	7	42	41	8.8	2	11	2.4	29	6.2	4.07	102	.283	.319	0	0	102	100	-0.3	0	0	0.1
1984	Chi-A	2	1	.667	49	0	0	0	7	55	54	8.8	2	34	5.6	26	4.3	3.11	143	.270	.374	5	8	111	148	0.6	0	2	1.1
1985	Chi-A	4	3	.571	54	0	0	0	1	60	45	6.8	3	23	3.5	39	5.8	3.60	115	.210	.289	4	4	100	73	0.4	0	2	0.5
1986	Chi-A	0	2	.000	9	0	0	0	0	5	6	10.8	0	4	7.2	3	5.4	7.20	59	.300	.417	-2	-2	101	76	-0.9	0	-0	-0.1
	Min-A	1	2	.333	17	1	0	0	1	20	43	19.3	1	14	6.3	9	4.0	9.00	51	.443	.513	-11	-10	109	120	-0.3	0	0	-0.8
	Yr	1	4	.200	26	1	0	0	1	25	49	17.6	1	18	6.5	12	4.3	8.64	52	.419	.496	-12	-11	108	120	-1.2	0	0	-0.9
1987	Hou-N	1	1	.500	27	0	0	0	2	27	26	8.7	1	10	3.3	6	2.0	2.67	142	.248	.305	4	3	93	115	0.1	-0	1	0.4
1988	Hou-N	10	2	.833	75	0	0	0	4	92	74	7.2	6	30	2.9	33	3.2	2.25	143	.226	.280	12	10	93	126	4.1	-0	4	1.5
Total	8	20	13	.606	273	1	0	0	22	309	301	8.8	16	126	3.7	149	4.3	3.61	108	.264	.332	10	10	100	113	3.7	-1	10	2.5

■ RICK AGUILERA Aguilera, Richard Warren b: 12/31/61, San Gabriel, Cal. BR/TR, 6'5", 195 lbs. Deb: 6/12/85

YEAR	TM/L	W	L	PCT	G	GS	CG	SHO	SV	IP	H	H/G	HR	BB	BB/G	SO	SO/G	ERA	/A	OAVG	OOBP	PR	/A	PF	CPI	WAT	PB	PD	TPI
1985	NY-N	10	7	.588	21	19	2	0	0	122	118	8.7	8	37	2.7	74	5.5	3.25	106	.258	.310	5	3	95	107	-0.2	3	-0	0.5
1986	NY-N	10	7	.588	28	20	2	0	0	142	145	9.2	15	36	2.3	104	6.6	3.87	90	.263	.311	-2	-6	93	99	-1.0	2	2	-0.2
1987	NY-N	11	3	.786	18	17	1	0	0	115	124	9.7	12	33	2.6	77	6.0	3.60	110	.276	.324	6	5	97	118	3.7	3	2	1.0
1988	NY-N	0	4	.000	11	3	0	0	0	25	29	10.4	2	10	3.6	16	5.8	6.84	44	.296	.360	-9	-11	88	73	-1.9	0	0	-0.9
Total	4	31	21	.596	78	59	5	0	0	404	416	9.3	37	116	2.6	271	6.0	3.79	94	.268	.317	-1	-10	95	105	0.6	8	4	0.4

■ HANK AGUIRRE Aguirre, Henry John b: 1/31/32, Azusa, Cal. BB/TL, 6'4", 205 lbs. Deb: 9/10/55 C

YEAR	TM/L	W	L	PCT	G	GS	CG	SHO	SV	IP	H	H/G	HR	BB	BB/G	SO	SO/G	ERA	/A	OAVG	OOBP	PR	/A	PF	CPI	WAT	PB	PD	TPI
1955	Cle-A	2	0	1.000	4	1	1	1	0	13	6	4.2	0	12	8.3	6	4.2	1.38	292	.143	.333	4	4	102	156	1.0	-1	-0	0.3
1956	Cle-A	3	5	.375	16	9	2	1	1	65	63	8.7	7	27	3.7	31	4.3	3.74	110	.253	.323	3	3	99	104	-1.3	-1	-1	0.0
1957	Cle-A	1	1	.500	10	1	0	0	0	20	26	11.7	0	13	5.8	9	4.0	5.85	66	.317	.390	-5	-4	102	93	0.0	-1	-0	-0.4
1958	Det-A	3	4	.429	44	3	0	0	5	70	67	8.6	5	27	3.5	38	4.9	3.73	104	.255	.318	0	1	103	97	-0.4	0	1	0.2
1959	Det-A	0	0	—	3	0	0	0	0	3	4	12.0	0	3	9.0	3	9.0	3.00	143	.364	.500	0	0	111	258	0.0	0	0	0.1
1960	Det-A	5	3	.625	37	6	1	0	10	95	75	7.1	7	30	2.8	80	7.6	2.84	139	.217	.280	11	12	102	89	1.3	-3	-2	0.7
1961	Det-A	4	4	.500	45	0	0	0	8	55	44	7.2	5	38	6.2	32	5.2	3.27	115	.224	.344	5	3	94	124	-0.7	-1	-1	0.1
1962	Det-A	16	8	.667	42	22	11	2	3	216	162	**6.8**	14	65	2.7	156	6.5	**2.21**	**198**	**.205**	**.265**	**42**	**52**	110	96	3.9	-9	-3	**4.4**
1963	Det-A	14	15	.483	38	33	14	3	0	226	222	8.8	25	68	2.7	134	5.3	3.66	103	.256	.312	-1	2	104	104	-0.1	-2	-3	-0.1
1964	Det-A	5	10	.333	32	27	3	0	1	162	134	7.4	15	59	3.3	88	4.9	3.78	91	.223	.296	-3	-6	95	80	-2.8	-4	-3	-1.2
1965	Det-A	14	10	.583	32	32	10	2	0	208	185	8.0	24	60	2.6	141	6.1	3.59	100	.236	.291	-3	0	104	92	1.0	-3	-1	-0.3
1966	Det-A	3	9	.250	30	14	2	0	0	104	104	9.0	14	26	2.3	50	4.3	3.81	92	.260	.305	-4	-4	102	105	-3.3	0	-2	-0.4
1967	Det-A	0	1	.000	31	1	0	0	0	41	34	7.5	2	17	3.7	33	7.2	2.41	131	.219	.293	4	3	98	109	-0.4	1	0	0.5
1968	LA-N	1	2	.333	25	0	0	0	3	39	32	7.4	0	13	3.0	25	5.8	0.69	393	.227	.287	10	9	91	350	-0.3	-0	-1	0.9
1969	Chi-N	1	0	1.000	41	0	0	0	1	45	45	9.0	2	12	2.4	19	3.8	2.60	146	.269	.317	5	6	105	138	0.5	1	1	0.8
1970	Chi-N	3	0	1.000	17	0	0	0	1	14	13	8.4	3	9	5.8	11	7.1	4.50	107	.250	.359	-1	0	119	124	1.5	-0	-0	0.0
Total	16	75	72	.510	447	149	44	9	33	1376	1216	8.0	123	479	3.1	856	5.6	3.24	116	.236	.301	67	82	103	107	-0.1	-21	-15	5.6

■ EDDIE AINSMITH Ainsmith, Edward Wilbur "Dorf" b: 2/4/1892, Cambridge, Mass. d: 9/6/81, Ft.Lauderdale, Fla BR/TR, 5'11", 180 lbs. Deb: 8/09/10

YEAR	TM/L	W	L	PCT	G	GS	CG	SHO	SV	IP	H	H/G	HR	BB	BB/G	SO	SO/G	ERA	/A	OAVG	OOBP	PR	/A	PF	CPI	WAT	PB	PD	TPI
1913	Was-A	0	0	—	1	0	0	0	0	⅓	2	54.0	0	0	0.0	0	0.0	54.00	—	.667	.667	-2	-2	105	43	0.0	0	0	-0.1

■ RALEIGH AITCHISON Aitchison, Raleigh Leonidas b: 12/5/1887, Tyndall, S.D. d: 9/26/58, Columbus, Kan. BR/TL, 5'11.5", 175 lbs. Deb: 4/19/11

YEAR	TM/L	W	L	PCT	G	GS	CG	SHO	SV	IP	H	H/G	HR	BB	BB/G	SO	SO/G	ERA	/A	OAVG	OOBP	PR	/A	PF	CPI	WAT	PB	PD	TPI
1911	Bro-N	0	1	.000	1	0	0	0	0	1	1	9.0	0	1	9.0	0	0.0	0.00	—	.200	.333	0	0	99	0	-0.4	0	0	0.0
1914	Bro-N	12	7	.632	26	17	8	3	0	172	156	8.2	4	60	3.1	87	4.6	2.67	105	.244	.304	2	3	101	98	2.9	1	-3	0.1
1915	Bro-N	0	4	.000	7	5	2	0	0	33	36	9.8	3	6	1.6	14	3.8	4.91	57	.267	.299	-8	-8	102	71	-1.9	-0	0	-0.7
Total	3	12	12	.500	34	22	10	3	0	206	193	8.4	7	67	2.9	101	4.4	3.01	93	.247	.304	-5	-5	101	93	0.6	1	-2	-0.6

■ JACK AKER Aker, Jackie Delane b: 7/13/40, Tulare, Cal. BR/TR, 6'2", 190 lbs. Deb: 5/03/64 C

YEAR	TM/L	W	L	PCT	G	GS	CG	SHO	SV	IP	H	H/G	HR	BB	BB/G	SO	SO/G	ERA	/A	OAVG	OOBP	PR	/A	PF	CPI	WAT	PB	PD	TPI
1964	KC-A	0	1	.000	9	0	0	0	0	16	17	9.6	6	10	5.6	7	3.9	9.00	43	.266	.412	-10	-9	108	87	-0.4	-0	1	-0.8
1965	KC-A	4	3	.571	34	0	0	0	3	51	45	7.9	3	18	3.2	26	4.6	3.18	108	.242	.314	2	1	100	104	1.2	-1	1	0.1
1966	KC-A	8	4	.667	66	0	0	0	**32**	113	81	6.5	7	28	2.2	68	5.4	1.99	165	.201	.253	**18**	**16**	95	102	2.4	-1	3	2.0
1967	KC-A	3	8	.273	57	0	0	0	12	88	87	8.9	9	32	3.3	65	6.6	4.30	76	.264	.327	-10	-10	102	97	-1.6	-0	2	-0.8
1968	Oak-A	4	4	.500	54	0	0	0	11	75	72	8.6	6	33	4.0	44	5.3	4.08	71	.258	.336	-9	-10	98	102	0.0	-0	0	-1.0
1969	Sea-A	0	2	.000	15	0	0	0	3	17	25	13.2	4	13	6.9	7	3.7	7.41	49	.357	.459	-7	-7	100	120	-0.9	0	1	-0.5
	NY-A	8	4	.667	38	0	0	0	11	66	51	7.0	4	22	3.0	40	5.5	2.05	170	.217	.293	12	10	96	129	2.1	-0	2	1.2
	Yr	8	6	.571	53	0	0	0	14	83	76	8.2	8	35	3.8	47	5.1	3.14	111	.248	.330	4	3	97	129	1.2	0	2	0.7
1970	NY-A	4	2	.667	41	0	0	0	16	70	57	7.3	3	20	2.6	36	4.6	2.06	165	.226	.285	13	10	91	124	0.7	-1	0	1.0
1971	NY-A	4	4	.500	41	0	0	0	4	56	48	7.7	3	26	4.2	24	3.9	2.57	131	.238	.312	6	5	97	125	0.0	-0	1	0.6
1972	NY-A	0	0	—	4	0	0	0	0	6	5	7.5	0	3	4.5	1	1.5	3.00	94	.238	.346	0	-0	92	114	0.0	-0	1	0.0
	Chi-N	6	6	.500	48	0	0	0	17	67	65	8.7	4	23	3.1	36	4.8	2.96	131	.259	.322	4	7	112	125	-0.5	-0	2	0.9
1973	Chi-N	4	5	.444	47	0	0	0	12	64	76	10.7	8	23	3.2	25	3.5	4.08	98	.308	.359	-3	-1	109	132	-0.2	-1	2	0.0
1974	Atl-N	0	1	.000	17	0	0	0	0	17	17	9.0	3	9	4.8	7	3.7	3.71	101	.298	.366	-0	0	104	161	-0.4	-0	0	0.0
	NY-N	2	1	.667	24	0	0	0	2	41	33	7.2	4	14	3.1	18	4.0	3.51	104	.213	.283	1	1	100	74	0.6	1	-1	0.0
	Yr	2	2	.500	41	0	0	0	2	58	50	7.8	7	23	3.6	25	3.9	3.57	103	.234	.307	0	1	101	74	0.2	-0	-0	0.0

YEAR	TM/L	W	L	PCT	G	GS	CG	SHO	SV	IP	H	H/G	HR	BB	BB/G	SO	SO/G	ERA	/A	OAVG	OOBP	PR	/A	PF	CPI	WAT	PB	PD	TPI
Total	11	47	45	.511	495	0	0	0	123	747	679	8.2	64	274	3.3	404	4.9	3.28	105	.247	.316	15	14	100	112	3.0	-5	13	2.7
■ DARREL AKERFELDS	Akerfelds, Darrel Wayne b: 6/12/62, Denver, Colo. BR/TR, 6'2", 210 lbs. Deb: 8/01/86																												
1986	Oak-A	0	0	—	2	0	0	0	0	5	7	12.6	2	3	5.4	5	9.0	7.20	55	.304	.385	-2	-2	94	111	0.0	0	0	-0.1
1987	Cle-A	2	6	.250	16	13	1	0	0	75	84	10.1	18	38	4.6	42	5.0	6.72	70	.284	.372	-19	-17	105	94	-1.3	0	-0	-1.5
Total	2	2	6	.250	18	13	1	0	0	80	91	10.2	20	41	4.6	47	5.3	6.75	69	.285	.373	-20	-19	104	95	-1.3	0	-0	-1.6
■ JERRY AKERS	Akers, Albert Earl b: 11/1/1887, Shelbyville, Ind. d: 5/15/79, Bay Pines, Fla. BR/TR, 5'11", 175 lbs. Deb: 5/04/12																												
1912	Was-A	1	1	.500	5	1	0	0	0	20	24	10.8	1	15	6.7	11	4.9	4.95	66	.300	.423	-4	-4	97	118	-0.1	0	-1	-0.4
■ GIBSON ALBA	Alba, Gibson Alberto (Rosado) b: 1/18/60, Santiago, D.R. BL/TL, 6'2", 160 lbs. Deb: 5/03/88																												
1988	StL-N	0	0	—	3	0	0	0	0	3	1	3.0	0	2	6.0	3	9.0	3.00	121	.091	.214	0	0	105	10	0.0	0	0	0.0
■ JOE ALBANESE	Albanese, Joseph Peter b: 6/26/33, New York, N.Y. BR/TR, 6'3", 215 lbs. Deb: 7/18/58																												
1958	Was-A	0	0	—	6	0	0	0	0	6	8	12.0	1	2	3.0	3	4.5	4.50	84	.348	.370	-0	-0	100	149	0.0	0	0	0.0
■ CY ALBERTS	Alberts, Frederick Joseph b: 1/14/1882, Grand Rapids, Mich d: 8/27/17, Fort Wayne, Ind. 6', 230 lbs. Deb: 9/17/10																												
1910	StL-N	1	2	.333	4	3	2	0	0	28	35	11.3	1	20	6.4	10	3.2	6.11	46	.330	.437	-10	-10	93	98	-0.2	-0	-1	-0.9
■ ED ALBOSTA	Albosta, Edward John "Rube" b: 10/27/18, Saginaw, Mich. BR/TR, 6'1", 175 lbs. Deb: 9/03/41																												
1941	Bro-N	0	2	.000	2	2	0	0	0	13	11	7.6	1	8	5.5	5	3.5	6.23	58	.239	.345	-4	-4	99	65	-0.9	-1	0	-0.3
1946	Pit-N	0	6	.000	17	6	0	0	0	40	41	9.2	3	35	7.9	19	4.3	6.07	59	.266	.395	-12	-11	106	86	-2.9	-1	0	-1.1
Total	2	0	8	.000	19	8	0	0	0	53	52	8.8	4	43	7.3	24	4.1	6.11	59	.260	.384	-16	-15	104	81	-3.8	-1	0	-1.4
■ ED ALBRECHT	Albrecht, Edward Arthur b: 2/28/29, Affton, Mo. d: 12/29/79, Cahokia, Ill. BR/TR, 5'10.5", 165 lbs. Deb: 10/02/49																												
1949	StL-A	1	0	1.000	1	1	1	0	0	5	1	1.8	0	4	7.2	1	1.8	5.40	81	.063	.250	-1	-1	104	0	0.5	-0	0	0.0
1950	StL-A	0	1	.000	2	1	0	0	0	7	6	7.7	0	7	9.0	1	1.3	5.14	99	.250	.406	-0	-0	111	96	-0.4	-0	0	0.0
Total	2	1	1	.500	3	2	1	0	0	12	7	5.3	0	11	8.3	2	1.5	5.25	91	.175	.346	-1	-1	108	56	0.1	-0	0	0.0
■ VIC ALBURY	Albury, Victor b: 5/12/47, Key West, Fla. BL/TL, 6', 190 lbs. Deb: 8/07/73																												
1973	Min-A	1	0	1.000	14	0	0	0	0	23	13	5.1	1	19	7.4	13	5.1	2.74	144	.169	.333	3	3	103	98	0.5	0	-1	0.2
1974	Min-A	8	9	.471	32	22	4	1	0	164	159	8.7	19	80	4.4	85	4.7	4.12	89	.259	.347	-9	-8	101	106	-0.6	0	-1	-0.9
1975	Min-A	6	7	.462	32	15	2	0	1	135	115	7.7	16	97	6.5	72	4.8	4.53	90	.237	.356	-11	-7	107	100	-0.1	0	1	-0.6
1976	Min-A	3	1	.750	23	0	0	0	0	50	51	9.2	0	24	4.3	23	4.1	3.60	96	.271	.348	-0	-1	98	107	1.0	0	0	0.0
Total	4	18	17	.514	101	37	6	1	1	372	338	8.2	36	220	5.3	193	4.7	4.11	92	.248	.350	-18	-13	103	103	0.8	0	-1	-1.3
■ SANTO ALCALA	Alcala, Santo (born Santo Anibal (Alcala)) b: 12/23/52, San Pedro De Macoris, D.R. BR/TR, 6'5", 195 lbs. Deb: 4/10/76																												
1976	Cin-N	11	4	.733	30	21	3	1	0	132	131	8.9	12	67	4.6	67	4.6	4.70	75	.261	.345	-18	-18	100	91	2.3	-0	-1	-1.8
1977	Cin-N	1	1	.500	7	2	0	0	0	16	22	12.4	1	7	3.9	9	5.1	5.63	69	.349	.411	-3	-3	99	115	0.0	-0	0	-0.2
	Mon-N	2	6	.250	31	10	0	0	2	102	104	9.2	12	47	4.1	64	5.6	4.68	83	.263	.342	-9	-9	99	93	-1.8	-1	-1	-1.0
	Yr	3	7	.300	38	12	0	0	2	118	126	9.6	13	54	4.1	73	5.6	4.81	81	.273	.350	-12	-12	99	93	-1.8	-0	-1	-1.2
Total	2	14	11	.560	68	33	3	1	2	250	257	9.3	25	121	4.4	140	5.0	4.75	78	.268	.348	-29	-30	100	93	0.5	-2	-2	-3.0
■ DALE ALDERSON	Alderson, Dale Leonard b: 3/8/18, Belden, Neb. d: 2/12/82, Garden Grove, Cal. BR/TR, 5'10", 190 lbs. Deb: 9/18/43																												
1943	Chi-N	0	1	.000	4	2	0	0	0	14	21	13.5	2	3	1.9	4	2.6	6.43	52	.356	.381	-5	-5	98	101	-0.4	-0	0	-0.4
1944	Chi-N	0	0	—	12	1	0	0	0	22	31	12.7	2	9	3.7	7	2.9	6.55	55	.344	.381	-7	-7	100	97	0.0	-1	1	-0.6
Total	2	0	1	.000	16	3	0	0	0	36	52	13.0	4	12	3.0	11	2.8	6.50	54	.349	.381	-12	-12	99	99	-0.4	-1	1	-1.0
■ JAY ALDRICH	Aldrich, Jay Robert b: 4/14/61, Alexandria, La. BR/TR, 6'3", 210 lbs. Deb: 6/05/87																												
1987	Mil-A	3	1	.750	31	0	0	0	0	58	71	11.0	8	13	2.0	22	3.4	4.97	92	.306	.340	-3	-3	102	105	0.9	0	-1	-0.2
■ VIC ALDRIDGE	Aldridge, Victor Eddington b: 10/25/1893, Indian Sprgs., Ind d: 4/17/73, Terre Haute, Ind. BR/TR, 5'9.5", 175 lbs. Deb: 4/15/17																												
1917	Chi-N	6	6	.500	30	5	1	1	2	107	100	8.4	1	37	3.1	44	3.7	3.11	91	.252	.312	-5	-3	105	93	0.2	-2	3	-0.2
1918	Chi-N	0	1	.000	3	0	0	0	0	12	11	8.3	0	6	4.5	10	7.5	1.50	181	.275	.354	2	2	98	252	-0.4	0	-0	0.2
1922	Chi-N	16	15	.516	36	34	20	2	0	258	287	10.0	14	56	2.0	66	2.3	3.52	111	.286	.323	17	11	96	107	0.0	4	1	1.5
1923	Chi-N	16	9	.640	30	30	15	2	0	217	209	8.7	17	67	2.8	64	2.7	3.48	119	.251	.303	12	16	103	91	3.1	3	-1	1.8
1924	Chi-N	15	12	.556	32	32	20	0	0	244	261	9.6	10	80	3.0	74	2.7	3.50	111	.279	.331	10	11	101	110	0.9	-3	-0	0.7
1925	Pit-N	15	7	.682	30	26	14	1	0	213	218	9.2	15	74	3.1	88	3.7	3.63	116	.269	.327	15	14	99	106	2.0	-0	-3	0.9
1926	Pit-N	10	13	.435	30	26	12	1	1	190	204	9.7	7	73	3.5	61	2.9	4.07	104	.279	.336	-5	4	111	97	-2.6	-2	-2	0.1
1927	Pit-N	15	10	.600	35	34	17	1	1	239	248	9.3	16	74	2.8	86	3.2	4.26	91	.270	.318	-9	-10	99	89	-0.2	1	-4	-1.2
1928	NY-N	4	7	.364	22	17	3	0	2	119	133	10.1	7	45	3.4	33	2.5	4.84	82	.285	.347	-11	-12	99	87	-2.2	2	-1	-0.9
Total	9	97	80	.548	248	204	102	8	6	1599	1671	9.4	87	512	2.9	526	3.0	3.76	105	.273	.324	25	33	101	100	0.8	3	-7	2.9
■ DOYLE ALEXANDER	Alexander, Doyle Lafayette b: 9/4/50, Cordova, Ala. BR/TR, 6'3", 190 lbs. Deb: 6/26/71																												
1971	LA-N	6	6	.500	17	12	4	0	0	92	105	10.3	6	18	1.8	30	2.9	3.82	89	.282	.314	-4	-4	98	96	-0.5	2	-1	-0.2
1972	Bal-A	6	8	.429	35	9	2	2	2	106	78	6.6	5	30	2.5	49	4.2	2.46	120	.203	.258	7	6	96	72	-1.2	-1	2	0.7
1973	Bal-A	12	8	.600	29	26	10	0	0	175	169	8.7	19	52	2.7	63	3.2	3.86	104	.258	.314	-1	3	105	98	0.0	0	1	0.4
1974	Bal-A	6	9	.400	30	12	2	0	0	114	127	10.0	7	43	3.4	40	3.2	4.03	83	.290	.350	-5	-9	92	110	-2.2	0	3	-0.5
1975	Bal-A	8	8	.500	32	11	3	1	1	133	127	8.6	7	47	3.2	46	3.1	3.05	111	.251	.312	11	5	89	105	-0.9	0	2	0.7
1976	Bal-A	3	4	.429	11	6	2	1	0	64	58	8.2	3	24	3.4	17	2.4	3.52	98	.247	.309	0	-1	97	91	-0.7	0	1	0.1
	NY-A	10	5	.667	19	19	5	2	0	137	114	7.5	9	39	2.6	41	2.7	3.28	104	.229	.285	4	2	97	83	1.2	0	-2	0.0
	Yr	13	9	.591	30	25	7	3	0	201	172	7.7	12	63	2.8	58	2.6	3.36	102	.234	.293	4	2	97	83	0.5	0	-1	0.1
1977	Tex-A	17	11	.607	34	34	12	1	0	237	221	8.4	24	82	3.1	82	3.1	3.65	116	.246	.307	11	15	104	95	1.1	0	1	1.6
1978	Tex-A	9	10	.474	31	28	7	1	0	191	198	9.3	18	71	3.3	81	3.8	3.86	94	.270	.328	-2	-5	96	105	-1.2	0	2	-0.3
1979	Tex-A	5	7	.417	23	18	0	0	0	113	114	9.1	3	69	5.5	50	4.0	4.46	94	.268	.362	-3	-3	99	95	-1.1	0	2	-0.1
1980	Atl-N	14	11	.560	35	35	7	1	0	232	227	8.8	20	74	2.9	114	4.4	4.19	87	.256	.311	-15	-14	101	85	1.7	1	3	-1.0
1981	SF-N	11	7	.611	24	24	1	1	0	152	156	9.2	11	44	2.6	77	4.6	2.90	126	.263	.313	10	13	105	122	2.2	1	-2	1.4
1982	NY-A	1	7	.125	16	11	0	0	0	67	81	10.9	14	14	1.9	26	3.5	6.04	65	.298	.324	-15	-16	97	88	-2.9	0	-0	-1.4
1983	NY-A	0	2	.000	8	5	0	0	0	28	31	10.0	6	7	2.3	17	5.5	6.43	62	.277	.314	-7	-8	98	76	-0.9	0	-0	-0.7
	Tor-A	7	6	.538	17	15	5	0	0	117	126	9.7	14	26	2.0	46	3.5	3.92	112	.279	.317	2	6	108	108	0.0	0	0	0.6
	Yr	7	8	.467	25	20	5	0	0	145	157	9.7	20	33	2.0	63	3.9	4.41	98	.278	.317	-5	-2	106	108	-0.9	0	0	-0.1
1984	Tor-A	17	6	**.739**	36	35	11	2	0	262	238	8.2	21	59	2.0	139	4.8	3.13	129	.242	.283	25	27	101	94	5.3	0	-0	2.7
1985	Tor-A	17	10	.630	36	36	6	1	0	261	268	9.2	28	67	2.3	142	4.9	3.45	119	.266	.313	20	19	99	115	0.6	0	0	2.0
1986	Tor-A	5	4	.556	17	17	3	0	0	111	120	9.7	18	20	1.6	65	5.3	4.46	98	.273	.306	-3	-1	104	96	0.3	0	-1	-0.1
	Atl-N	6	6	.500	17	17	2	0	0	117	135	10.4	9	17	1.3	74	5.7	3.85	100	.287	.306	-2	0	103	99	0.6	1	-1	0.0
1987	Atl-N	5	10	.333	16	16	3	0	0	118	115	8.8	21	27	2.1	64	4.9	4.12	108	.257	.299	-0	5	109	100	-1.7	-3	-2	0.0
	Det-A	9	0	1.000	11	11	3	3	0	88	63	6.4	3	26	2.7	44	4.5	1.53	279	.201	.262	29	27	96	122	4.5	0	0	2.9
1988	Det-A	14	11	.560	34	34	5	1	0	229	260	10.2	30	46	1.8	126	5.0	4.32	86	.282	.316	-9	-15	94	101	0.5	0	-3	-1.7
Total	18	188	156	.547	528	431	93	17	3	3144	3131	9.0	296	902	2.6	1433	4.1	3.71	104	.260	.310	54	51	100	99	4.7	1	7	7.1
■ PETE ALEXANDER	Alexander, Grover Cleveland b: 2/26/1887, Elba, Neb. d: 11/4/50, St.Paul, Neb. BR/TR, 6'1", 185 lbs. Deb: 4/15/11 H																												
1911	Phi-N	**28**	13	.683	48	37	**31**	**7**	3	**367**	285	**7.0**	5	129	3.2	227	5.6	2.57	142	**.219**	.293	34	44	108	83	**8.5**	-3	1	4.5
1912	Phi-N	19	17	.528	46	34	26	3	3	**310**	289	8.4	11	105	3.0	**195**	**5.7**	2.82	122	.245	.310	20	21	101	93	2.1	1	1	2.3
1913	Phi-N	22	8	.733	47	35	23	**9**	2	306	288	8.5	9	75	2.2	159	4.7	2.79	127	.254	.297	14	26	111	98	6.2	-5	2	2.5
1914	Phi-N	**27**	15	.643	46	39	**32**	6	1	**355**	327	8.3	8	76	1.9	**214**	**5.4**	2.38	118	.244	.284	16	17	101	94	8.1	3	4	2.7
1915	Phi-N	**31**	10	**.756**	49	42	**36**	**12**	3	**376**	253	**6.1**	3	64	1.5	**241**	**5.8**	**1.22**	**235**	**.191**	**.228**	**64**	**69**	104	75	**9.8**	-0	7	**9.3**
1916	Phi-N	**33**	12	.733	48	45	**38**	**16**	3	**389**	323	7.5	6	50	1.2	**167**	3.9	**1.55**	158	.230	.255	**46**	**39**	94	114	**9.5**	9	1	**5.9**
1917	Phi-N	**30**	13	.698	45	44	**34**	**8**	0	**388**	336	7.8	4	56	**1.3**	**200**	4.6	1.83	156	.234	.260	**38**	**45**	106	101	**7.9**	4	2	**6.3**
1918	Chi-N	2	1	.667	3	3	3	0	0	26	19	6.6	0	3	1.0	15	5.2	1.73	157	.207	.235	3	3	98	64	0.1	-1	0	0.3
1919	Chi-N	16	11	.593	30	27	20	**9**	1	235	180	**6.9**	3	38	1.5	121	4.6	**1.72**	**168**	**.211**	.241	31	30	99	79	2.0	1	5	**4.3**
1920	Chi-N	**27**	14	.659	46	40	**33**	7	5	**363**	335	8.3	8	69	1.7	**173**	4.3	**1.91**	**163**	.248	.280	**49**	**48**	99	112	**8.3**	5	2	**6.3**

YEAR	TM/L	W	L	PCT	G	GS	CG	SHO	SV	IP	H	H/G	HR	BB	BB/G	SO	SO/G	ERA	/A	OAVG	OOBP	PR	/A	PF	CPI	WAT	PB	PD	TPI
1921	Chi-N	15	13	.536	31	29	21	3	1	252	286	10.2	10	33	1.2	77	2.8	3.39	121	.296	.310	11	20	108	104	3.3	5	-1	2.6
1922	Chi-N	16	13	.552	33	31	20	1	1	246	283	10.4	8	34	1.2	48	1.8	3.62	108	.295	.316	13	8	96	98	1.2	-1	3	0.9
1923	Chi-N	22	12	.647	39	36	26	3	2	305	308	9.1	17	30	**0.9**	72	2.1	3.19	130	.259	**.271**	28	32	103	81	4.8	-0	4	3.6
1924	Chi-N	12	5	.706	21	20	12	0	0	169	183	9.7	9	25	1.3	33	1.8	3.04	129	.272	.295	16	16	101	103	3.4	1	2	1.9
1925	Chi-N	15	11	.577	32	30	20	1	0	236	270	10.3	14	29	**1.1**	63	2.4	3.39	124	.288	.309	23	21	98	106	3.6	3	-2	2.0
1926	Chi-N	3	3	.500	7	7	4	0	0	52	55	9.5	0	7	1.2	12	2.1	3.46	116	.270	.284	2	3	105	76	-0.1	3	1	0.7
	StL-N	9	7	.563	23	16	11	2	2	148	136	8.3	8	24	1.5	35	2.1	2.92	131	.242	.271	15	15	100	84	-0.1	-3	-0	1.1
	Yr	12	10	.545	30	23	15	2	2	200	191	8.6	8	31	1.4	47	2.1	3.06	126	.250	**.275**	17	18	101	84	-0.2	3	1	1.8
1927	StL-N	21	10	.677	37	30	22	2	3	268	261	8.8	11	38	**1.3**	48	1.6	2.52	**164**	.258	.277	**42**	**48**	106	109	3.5	3	1	**5.6**
1928	StL-N	16	9	.640	34	31	18	1	2	244	262	9.7	15	37	**1.4**	59	2.2	3.36	115	.277	.298	17	14	97	99	0.9	6	-1	1.9
1929	StL-N	9	8	.529	22	19	8	0	0	132	149	10.2	10	23	1.6	33	2.3	3.89	119	.285	.308	12	11	98	101	0.3	-4	2	0.8
1930	Phi-N	0	3	.000	9	3	0	0	0	22	40	16.4	5	6	2.5	6	2.5	9.00	60	.396	.422	-10	-9	109	99	-1.4	-0	-1	-0.7
Total	20	373	208	.642	696	598	438	90	32	5189	4868	8.4	164	951	1.6	2198	3.8	2.56	135	.250	.282	484	523	102	96	81.9	25	30	64.8
■ **BOB ALEXANDER**	Alexander, Robert Somerville b: 8/7/22, Vancouver, B.C., Can BR/TR, 6'2.5", 205 lbs. Deb: 4/11/55																												
1955	Bal-A	1	0	1.000	4	0	0	0	0	4	8	18.0	0	2	4.5	1	2.3	13.50	27	.444	.500	-4	-4	94	73	0.5	0	-0	-0.3
1957	Cle-A	0	1	.000	5	0	0	0	0	7	10	12.9	0	5	6.4	1	1.3	9.00	43	.357	.457	-4	-4	102	80	-0.4	-0	-0	-0.3
Total	2	1	1	.500	9	0	0	0	0	11	18	14.7	0	7	5.7	2	1.6	10.64	36	.391	.474	-8	-8	99	77	0.1	-0	-0	-0.6
■ **BRIAN ALLARD**	Allard, Brian Marshall b: 1/3/58, Spring Valley, Ill. BR/TR, 6'1", 175 lbs. Deb: 8/08/79																												
1979	Tex-A	1	3	.250	7	4	2	0	0	33	36	9.8	4	13	3.5	14	3.8	4.36	96	.283	.348	-0	-1	99	109	-0.9	0	0	0.0
1980	Tex-A	0	1	.000	5	2	0	0	0	14	13	8.4	0	10	6.4	10	6.4	5.79	70	.236	.358	-3	-3	100	60	-0.4	0	-0	-0.2
1981	Sea-A	3	2	.600	7	7	1	0	0	48	48	9.0	5	8	1.5	20	3.8	3.75	99	.265	.293	-0	-0	101	94	0.8	0	-0	0.0
Total	3	4	6	.400	19	13	3	0	0	95	97	9.2	9	31	2.9	44	4.2	4.26	92	.267	.323	-4	-4	100	94	-0.5	0	-0	-0.2
■ **FRANK ALLEN**	Allen, Frank Leon b: 8/26/1889, Newbern, Ala. d: 7/30/33, Gainesville, Ala. BR/TL, 5'9", 175 lbs. Deb: 5/18/12																												
1912	Bro-N	3	9	.250	20	15	5	1	0	109	119	9.8	1	57	4.7	58	4.8	3.63	91	.272	.358	-3	-4	97	99	-2.1	2	0	-0.1
1913	Bro-N	4	18	.182	34	25	11	0	2	175	144	7.4	6	81	4.2	82	4.2	2.83	119	.231	.319	7	10	105	106	-6.7	-1	-3	0.7
1914	Bro-N	8	14	.364	36	21	10	1	0	171	165	8.7	6	57	3.0	68	3.6	3.11	90	.265	.318	-6	-6	101	104	-3.0	0	-1	-0.6
	Pit-F	1	0	1.000	1	1	1	0	0	7	9	11.6	0	0	0.0	3	3.9	5.14	60	.344	.344	-2	-2	96	71	0.5	1	0	0.0
1915	Pit-F	23	13	.639	41	37	24	6	0	283	230	7.3	9	100	3.2	127	4.0	2.51	124	.227	.304	16	19	102	104	3.9	-5	3	1.8
1916	Bos-N	8	2	.800	19	14	7	2	1	113	102	8.1	1	31	2.5	63	5.0	2.07	115	.244	.295	7	4	91	119	2.7	3	-1	0.6
1917	Bos-N	3	11	.214	29	14	2	0	0	112	124	10.0	3	47	3.8	56	4.5	3.94	66	.297	.361	-15	-16	97	114	-3.9	1	-2	-1.8
Total	6	50	67	.427	180	127	60	10	3	970	893	8.3	26	373	3.5	457	4.2	2.93	101	.251	.322	5	5	100	106	-8.6	2	-4	0.6
■ **JOHN ALLEN**	Allen, John Marshall b: 10/27/1890, Berkeley Springs, W.Va. d: 9/24/67, Hagerstown, Md. BR/TR, 6'1", 170 lbs. Deb: 6/02/14																												
1914	Bal-F	0	0	—	1	0	0	0	0	2	2	9.0	0	2	9.0	2	9.0	18.00	18	.289	.449	-3	-3	99	28	0.0	0	0	-0.2
■ **JOHNNY ALLEN**	Allen, John Thomas b: 9/30/05, Lenoir, N.C. d: 3/29/59, St.Petersburg, Fla BR/TR, 6', 180 lbs. Deb: 4/19/32																												
1932	NY-A	17	4	**.810**	33	21	13	3	4	192	162	**7.6**	10	76	3.6	109	5.1	3.70	110	.228	.302	17	8	91	84	4.3	-1	-1	0.4
1933	NY-A	15	7	.682	25	24	10	1	1	185	171	8.3	9	87	4.2	119	5.8	4.38	86	.242	.326	-2	-12	88	82	2.4	1	-1	-1.2
1934	NY-A	5	2	.714	13	10	4	0	0	72	62	7.8	3	32	4.0	54	6.8	2.88	145	.227	.311	13	10	93	105	1.0	1	0	1.1
1935	NY-A	13	6	.684	23	23	12	2	0	167	149	**8.0**	11	58	3.1	113	**6.1**	3.61	111	**.238**	.305	16	7	90	90	2.3	1	1	0.9
1936	Cle-A	20	10	.667	36	31	19	4	1	243	234	8.7	5	97	3.6	165	**6.1**	3.44	153	.256	.322	43	50	105	106	5.3	-3	2	4.6
1937	Cle-A	15	1	**.938**	24	20	14	0	0	173	157	8.2	4	60	3.1	87	4.5	2.55	175	.244	.311	40	37	97	**120**	**7.0**	-6	1	3.1
1938	Cle-A	14	8	.636	30	27	13	0	0	200	189	8.5	15	81	3.6	112	5.0	4.18	112	.246	.319	13	11	98	87	2.0	4	2	1.6
1939	Cle-A	9	7	.563	28	26	9	2	0	175	199	10.2	9	56	2.9	79	4.1	4.58	97	.291	.338	1	-2	96	99	0.0	1	3	0.0
1940	Cle-A	9	8	.529	32	17	5	3	5	139	126	8.2	3	48	3.1	62	4.0	3.43	117	.243	.307	15	9	92	90	-0.7	1	-0	0.9
1941	StL-A	2	5	.286	20	9	2	0	1	67	89	12.0	4	29	3.9	27	3.6	6.58	64	.319	.379	-18	-18	101	86	-1.2	0	-0	-1.6
	Bro-N	3	0	1.000	11	4	1	0	0	57	38	6.0	6	12	1.9	21	3.3	2.53	143	.188	.229	7	7	99	74	1.5	-2	0	0.5
1942	Bro-N	10	6	.625	27	15	5	1	3	118	106	8.1	11	39	3.0	50	3.8	3.20	100	.238	.298	1	0	97	102	-0.6	0	0	0.0
1943	Bro-N	5	1	.833	17	1	0	0	1	38	42	9.9	3	25	5.9	15	3.6	4.26	78	.280	.383	-4	-4	99	122	2.0	2	-0	-0.1
	NY-N	1	3	.250	15	0	0	0	2	41	37	8.1	4	14	3.1	24	5.3	3.07	109	.245	.302	1	1	99	112	-0.5	-2	1	0.0
	Yr	6	4	.600	32	1	0	0	3	79	79	9.0	7	39	4.4	39	4.4	3.65	92	.261	.338	-2	-3	99	112	1.5	2	1	-0.1
1944	NY-N	4	7	.364	18	13	2	1	0	84	88	9.4	7	24	2.6	33	3.5	4.07	93	.260	.310	-4	-3	105	88	-0.9	-2	-1	-0.5
Total	13	142	75	.654	352	241	109	17	18	1951	1849	8.5	104	738	3.4	1070	4.9	3.75	112	.249	.317	139	101	96	95	23.9	-8	6	9.7
■ **LLOYD ALLEN**	Allen, Lloyd Cecil b: 5/8/50, Merced, Cal. BR/TR, 6'1", 185 lbs. Deb: 9/01/69																												
1969	Cal-A	0	1	.000	4	1	0	0	0	10	5	4.5	1	10	9.0	5	4.5	5.40	68	.147	.341	-2	-2	101	57	-0.4	1	1	0.0
1970	Cal-A	1	1	.500	8	2	0	0	0	24	23	8.6	0	11	4.1	12	4.5	2.63	130	.261	.343	3	2	92	134	0.0	-0	-0	0.1
1971	Cal-A	4	6	.400	54	1	0	0	15	94	75	7.2	4	40	3.8	72	6.9	2.49	138	.221	.297	10	10	99	105	-0.7	2	1	1.3
1972	Cal-A	3	7	.300	42	6	0	0	5	85	76	8.0	7	55	5.8	53	5.6	3.49	79	.240	.351	-4	-7	90	115	-1.9	-1	-1	-0.8
1973	Cal-A	0	0	—	5	0	0	0	1	9	15	15.0	0	5	5.0	4	4.0	10.00	37	.417	.465	-6	-6	96	80	0.0	0	0	-0.5
	Tex-A	0	6	.000	23	5	0	0	1	41	58	12.7	3	39	8.6	25	5.5	9.22	41	.326	.447	-25	-25	100	80	-2.9	0	1	-2.2
	Yr	0	6	.000	28	5	0	0	2	50	73	13.1	3	44	7.9	29	5.2	9.36	40	.338	.450	-31	-31	99	80	-2.9	0	1	-2.7
1974	Tex-A	0	1	.000	14	0	0	0	0	22	24	9.8	2	18	7.4	18	7.4	6.55	53	.276	.394	-7	-7	96	84	-0.4	0	-0	-0.7
	Chi-A	0	1	.000	6	2	0	0	0	7	7	9.0	0	12	15.4	3	3.9	10.29	36	.259	.500	-5	-5	102	69	-0.4	0	-0	-0.4
	Yr	0	2	.000	20	2	0	0	0	29	31	9.6	2	30	9.3	21	6.5	7.45	47	.265	.416	-12	-13	97	69	-0.8	0	-1	-1.1
1975	Chi-A	0	2	.000	3	2	0	0	0	5	8	14.4	2	6	10.8	2	3.6	12.60	31	.348	.452	-5	-5	104	87	-0.9	0	0	-0.3
Total	7	8	25	.242	159	19	0	0	22	297	291	8.8	19	196	5.9	194	5.9	4.70	71	.258	.365	-41	-46	96	102	-7.6	2	1	-3.5
■ **MYRON ALLEN**	Allen, Myron Smith "Zeke" b: 3/22/1854, Kingston, N.Y. d: 3/8/24, Kingston, N.Y. 5'8", 150 lbs. Deb: 7/19/1883																												
1883	NY-N	0	1	.000	1	1	1	0	0	8	8	9.0	0	3	3.4	0	0.0	1.13	281	.268	.335	2	2	101	277	-0.4	-1	0	0.1
1887	Cle-a	1	0	1.000	2	0	0	0	0	10	9	8.1	0	3	2.7	1	0.9	1.80	245	.253	.311	3	3	103	153	0.5	0	0	0.2
1888	KC-a	0	2	.000	2	2	2	0	0	18	17	8.5	0	1	0.5	2	1.0	2.50	137	.262	.273	1	2	112	89	-0.9	0	0	0.2
Total	3	1	3	.250	5	3	3	0	0	36	34	8.5	0	7	1.8	3	0.8	2.00	183	.261	.299	6	7	107	149	-0.8	-0	0	0.5
■ **NEIL ALLEN**	Allen, Neil Patrick b: 1/24/58, Kansas City, Kan. BR/TR, 6'3", 185 lbs. Deb: 4/15/79																												
1979	NY-N	6	10	.375	50	5	0	0	8	99	100	9.1	4	47	4.3	65	5.9	3.55	102	.268	.341	2	1	96	110	-0.2	-2	0	0.0
1980	NY-N	7	10	.412	59	0	0	0	22	97	87	8.1	7	40	3.7	79	7.3	3.71	94	.244	.312	-1	-2	97	92	0.0	-0	-1	-0.3
1981	NY-N	7	6	.538	43	0	0	0	18	67	64	8.6	4	26	3.5	50	6.7	2.96	121	.259	.315	4	5	103	124	1.7	1	1	0.7
1982	NY-N	3	7	.300	50	0	0	0	19	65	65	9.0	5	30	4.2	59	8.2	3.05	118	.266	.344	4	4	100	138	-1.2	1	-0	0.4
1983	NY-N	2	7	.222	21	4	1	1	2	54	57	9.5	6	36	6.0	32	5.3	4.50	81	.278	.378	-5	-5	100	117	-2.1	-1	-0	-0.6
	StL-N	10	6	.625	25	18	4	2	0	122	122	9.0	6	48	3.5	74	5.5	3.69	97	.265	.331	-1	-2	98	100	2.3	-1	-0	-0.2
	Yr	12	13	.480	46	22	5	3	2	176	179	9.2	12	84	4.3	106	5.4	3.94	91	.268	.346	-6	-7	99	100	0.2	-1	-1	-0.8
1984	StL-N	9	6	.600	57	1	0	0	3	119	105	7.9	6	49	3.7	66	5.0	3.55	100	.239	.311	1	-0	99	88	1.4	1	1	0.2
1985	StL-N	1	4	.200	23	1	0	0	2	29	32	9.9	3	17	5.3	10	3.1	5.59	60	.283	.370	-6	-7	93	94	-1.6	-0	0	-0.7
	NY-A	1	0	1.000	17	0	0	0	1	29	26	8.1	1	13	4.0	16	5.0	2.79	140	.234	.315	4	4	94	107	0.5	0	0	0.3
1986	Chi-A	7	2	.778	22	17	2	2	0	113	101	8.0	8	38	3.0	57	4.5	3.82	111	.244	.303	5	5	101	87	2.8	0	-0	0.5
1987	Chi-A	0	7	.000	15	10	0	0	0	50	74	13.3	6	26	4.7	26	4.7	7.02	69	.365	.432	-14	-12	109	110	-3.4	0	-0	-1.0
	NY-A	0	1	.000	8	1	0	0	0	25	23	8.3	2	10	3.6	16	5.8	3.60	121	.242	.311	2	2	97	95	-0.4	0	-0	0.2
	Yr	0	8	.000	23	11	0	0	0	75	97	11.6	8	36	4.3	42	5.0	5.88	80	.321	.389	-12	-10	105	95	-3.8	0	-0	-0.8
1988	NY-A	5	3	.625	41	2	0	1	0	117	121	9.3	14	37	2.8	61	4.7	3.85	99	.268	.317	2	-1	96	110	0.9	0	-2	-0.2
Total	10	58	69	.457	431	59	7	6	75	986	977	8.9	72	417	3.8	611	5.6	3.84	98	.263	.332	-4	-9	99	104	0.7	-1	-2	-0.7
■ **BOB ALLEN**	Allen, Robert Earl "Thin Man" b: 7/2/14, Smithville, Tenn. BR/TR, 6'1", 165 lbs. Deb: 9/19/37																												
1937	Phi-N	0	1	.000	3	1	0	0	0	12	18	13.5	2	8	6.0	8	6.0	6.75	64	.321	.406	-4	-3	111	104	-0.4	0	-1	-0.2

YEAR	TM/L	W	L	PCT	G	GS	CG	SHO	SV	IP	H	H/G	HR	BB	BB/G	SO	SO/G	ERA	/A	OAVG	OOBP	PR	/A	PF	CPI	WAT	PB	PD	TPI
■ **BOB ALLEN**	Allen, Robert Gray b: 10/23/37, Tatum, Tex. BL/TL, 6'2", 175 lbs. Deb: 4/14/61																												
1961	Cle-A	3	2	.600	48	0	0	0	3	82	96	10.5	7	40	4.4	42	4.6	3.73	104	.294	.367	3	1	97	136	0.6	0	0	0.1
1962	Cle-A	1	1	.500	30	0	0	0	4	31	29	8.4	5	25	7.3	23	6.7	5.81	67	.250	.372	-6	-7	99	93	0.0	-1	0	-0.6
1963	Cle-A	1	2	.333	43	0	0	0	2	56	58	9.3	5	29	4.7	51	8.2	4.66	76	.266	.345	-6	-7	98	96	-0.4	-0	0	-0.6
1966	Cle-A	2	2	.500	36	0	0	0	5	51	56	9.9	2	13	2.3	33	5.8	4.24	82	.273	.313	-5	-4	102	85	0.0	-0	1	-0.3
1967	Cle-A	0	5	.000	47	0	0	0	5	54	49	8.2	4	25	4.2	50	8.3	3.00	109	.243	.323	1	2	101	122	-2.4	0	1	0.2
Total	5	7	12	.368	204	0	0	0	19	274	288	9.5	23	132	4.3	199	6.5	4.11	88	.270	.345	-13	-15	99	111	-2.2	-1	2	-1.2
■ **DOUG ALLISON**	Allison, Douglas b: 1846, Philadelphia, Pa. d: 12/19/16, Washington, D.C. BR/TR, 5'10.5", 160 lbs. Deb: 5/05/1871																												
1878	Pro-N	0	0	—	1	0	0	0	0	5	11	19.8	0	1	1.8	0	0.0	1.80	124	.449	.470	0	0	97	443	0.0	0	0	0.0
■ **MACK ALLISON**	Allison, Mack Pendleton b: 1/23/1887, Owensboro, Ky. d: 3/13/64, St.Joseph, Mo. BR/TR, 6'1", 185 lbs. Deb: 9/13/11																												
1911	StL-A	2	1	.667	3	3	3	0	0	26	24	8.3	0	5	1.7	2	0.7	2.08	160	.253	.304	4	4	100	117	0.8	-0	-1	0.3
1912	StL-A	6	17	.261	31	20	11	1	1	169	171	9.1	4	49	2.6	43	2.3	3.62	95	.269	.327	-5	-3	103	93	-3.0	-4	-2	-0.4
1913	StL-A	1	3	.250	11	4	3	0	0	51	52	9.2	0	13	2.3	12	2.1	2.29	125	.287	.345	4	3	98	151	-0.6	-2	-2	0.2
Total	3	9	21	.300	45	27	17	1	1	246	247	9.0	4	67	2.5	57	2.1	3.18	104	.271	.328	2	3	101	107	-2.8	-6	-4	0.1
■ **LUIS ALOMA**	Aloma, Luis (Barba) "Witto" b: 7/23/23, Havana, Cuba BR/TR, 6'2", 195 lbs. Deb: 4/19/50																												
1950	Chi-A	7	2	.778	42	0	0	0	4	88	77	7.9	6	53	5.4	49	5.0	3.78	120	.234	.338	8	7	99	99	2.9	-2	-0	0.5
1951	Chi-A	6	0	1.000	25	1	1	1	3	69	52	6.8	3	24	3.1	25	3.3	1.83	216	.215	.286	18	16	96	141	3.0	2	-1	1.7
1952	Chi-A	3	1	.750	25	0	0	0	6	40	42	9.4	5	11	2.5	18	4.0	4.27	85	.278	.323	-3	-3	99	103	1.0	-1	0	-0.3
1953	Chi-A	2	0	1.000	24	0	0	0	2	38	41	9.7	7	23	5.4	23	5.4	4.74	87	.283	.370	-3	-3	104	124	1.0	-1	0	-0.2
Total	4	18	3	.857	116	1	1	1	15	235	212	8.1	21	111	4.3	115	4.4	3.45	120	.245	.327	20	18	99	116	7.9	-2	-2	1.7
■ **MATTY ALOU**	Alou, Mateo Rojas (born Mateo Rojas (Alou)) b: 12/22/38, Haina, D.R. BL/TL, 5'9", 160 lbs. Deb: 9/26/60																												
1965	SF-N	0	0	—	1	0	0	0	0	2	3	13.5	0	1	4.5	3	13.5	0.00	—	.333	.400	1	1	109	0	0.0	0	0	0.1
■ **PORFI ALTAMIRANO**	Altamirano, Porfirio (Ramirez) b: 5/17/52, Darillo, Nic. BR/TR, 6', 175 lbs. Deb: 5/09/82																												
1982	Phi-N	5	1	.833	29	0	0	0	2	39	41	9.5	2	14	3.2	26	6.0	4.15	81	.281	.331	-2	-3	94	99	1.9	0	0	-0.2
1983	Phi-N	2	3	.400	31	0	0	0	0	41	38	8.3	9	15	3.3	24	5.3	3.73	98	.255	.318	-0	-0	100	129	-0.6	-0	0	0.0
1984	Chi-N	0	0	—	5	0	0	0	0	11	8	6.5	2	1	0.8	7	5.7	4.91	80	.195	.209	-2	-1	109	42	0.0	-0	0	0.0
Total	3	7	4	.636	65	0	0	0	2	91	87	8.6	13	30	3.0	57	5.6	4.05	88	.259	.312	-4	-5	98	106	1.3	-0	1	-0.2
■ **ERNIE ALTEN**	Alten, Ernest Matthias "Lefty" b: 12/1/1894, Avon, Ohio d: 9/9/81, Napa, Cal. BR/TL, 6', 175 lbs. Deb: 4/17/20																												
1920	Det-A	0	1	.000	14	1	0	0	0	23	40	15.7	2	9	3.5	4	1.6	9.00	45	.392	.446	-13	-13	106	86	-0.4	-1	0	-1.1
■ **NICK ALTROCK**	Altrock, Nicholas b: 9/15/1876, Cincinnati, Ohio d: 1/20/65, Washington, D.C. BB/TL, 5'10", 197 lbs. Deb: 7/14/1898 C																												
1898	Lou-N	3	3	.500	11	7	6	0	0	70	89	11.4	2	21	2.7	13	1.7	4.50	78	.333	.381	-7	-8	98	100	0.2	0	0	-0.6
1902	Bos-A	0	2	.000	3	2	1	0	1	18	19	9.5	0	7	3.5	5	2.5	2.00	175	.296	.365	3	3	98	178	-0.9	-1	1	0.4
1903	Bos-A	0	1	.000	1	1	1	0	0	8	13	14.6	0	4	4.5	3	3.4	9.00	35	.390	.455	-5	-5	108	76	-0.4	1	1	-0.3
	Chi-A	4	3	.571	12	8	6	1	0	71	59	7.5	4	19	2.4	19	2.4	2.15	129	.246	.302	6	5	94	120	0.9	2	3	0.9
	Yr	4	4	.500	13	9	7	1	0	79	72	8.2	4	23	2.6	22	2.5	2.85	99	.264	.321	1	-0	95	120	0.5	1	4	0.6
1904	Chi-A	19	14	.576	38	36	31	6	1	307	274	8.0	2	48	1.4	87	2.6	2.96	85	.261	.293	-12	-16	97	74	0.0	0	4	-1.2
1905	Chi-A	23	12	.657	38	34	31	3	0	316	274	7.8	3	63	1.8	97	2.8	1.88	131	.257	.298	27	21	93	122	2.9	-4	9	3.4
1906	Chi-A	20	13	.606	38	30	25	4	0	288	269	8.4	0	42	1.3	99	3.1	2.06	116	.272	.302	20	11	89	113	-0.2	-0	4	1.6
1907	Chi-A	7	13	.350	30	21	15	1	2	214	210	8.8	3	31	1.3	61	2.6	2.57	100	.281	.309	-1	-0	101	100	-4.2	-0	5	0.6
1908	Chi-A	5	7	.417	23	13	8	1	2	136	127	8.4	2	18	1.2	21	1.4	2.71	81	.248	.276	-5	-8	93	86	-1.7	0	5	-0.2
1909	Chi-A	0	1	.000	1	1	1	0	0	9	16	16.0	0	1	1.0	2	2.0	5.00	48	.485	.500	-3	-3	97	154	-0.4	-0	0	-0.1
	Was-A	1	3	.250	9	5	2	0	0	38	55	13.0	0	5	1.2	9	2.1	5.45	44	.333	.357	-13	-13	96	78	-0.1	-1	0	-1.2
	Yr	1	4	.200	10	6	3	0	0	47	71	13.6	0	6	1.1	11	2.1	5.36	44	.359	.380	-15	-16	96	78	-0.5	-0	0	-1.3
1912	Was-A	0	1	.000	1	0	0	0	0	1	1	9.0	0	2	18.0	0	0.0	18.00	18	.200	.429	-2	-2	97	28	-0.4	-0	0	-0.1
1913	Was-A	0	0	—	4	0	0	0	0	9	7	7.0	0	4	4.0	2	2.0	5.00	61	.184	.279	-2	-2	105	20	0.0	-0	0	-0.1
1914	Was-A	0	0	—	1	0	0	0	0	1	3	27.0	0	0	0.0	0	0.0	0.00	—	.750	.750	0	0	100	0	0.0	0	0	0.0
1915	Was-A	0	0	—	1	0	0	0	1	3	7	21.0	0	1	3.0	2	6.0	9.00	33	.438	.471	-2	-2	99	102	0.0	-0	-0	-0.1
1918	Was-A	1	2	.333	5	3	1	0	0	24	24	9.0	1	6	2.3	5	1.9	3.00	95	.279	.313	-1	-0	103	114	-0.5	0	0	0.0
1919	Was-A	0	0	—	1	0	0	0	0	0	4	—	0	0	—	0	—	∞	—	1.000	1.000	-4	-4	99	55	0.0	0	0	-0.2
1924	Was-A	0	0	—	1	0	0	0	0	2	4	18.0	0	0	0.0	0	0.0	0.00	—	.500	.500	1	1	96	0	0.0	1	0	0.2
Total	16	83	75	.525	218	161	128	16	7	1515	1455	8.6	17	272	1.6	425	2.5	2.67	95	.273	.309	2	-21	95	102	-4.8	-1	32	3.0
■ **JOSE ALVAREZ**	Alvarez, Jose Lino b: 4/12/56, Tampa, Fla. BR/TR, 5'11", 175 lbs. Deb: 10/01/81																												
1981	Atl-N	0	0	—	1	0	0	0	0	2	0	0.0	0	0	0.0	2	9.0	0.00	—	.000	.000	1	1	100	0	0.0	0	0	0.1
1982	Atl-N	0	0	—	7	0	0	0	0	8	8	9.0	1	2	2.3	6	6.8	4.50	85	.308	.345	-1	-1	107	113	0.0	0	0	0.0
1988	Atl-N	5	6	.455	60	0	0	0	3	102	88	7.8	7	53	4.7	81	7.1	3.00	123	.240	.337	5	8	107	130	1.0	1	1	1.1
Total	3	5	6	.455	68	0	0	0	3	112	96	7.7	8	55	4.4	89	7.2	3.05	121	.241	.333	5	8	107	127	1.0	1	2	1.2
■ **RED AMES**	Ames, Leon Kessling b: 8/2/1882, Warren, Ohio d: 10/8/36, Warren, Ohio BB/TR, 5'10.5", 185 lbs. Deb: 03																												
1903	NY-N	2	0	1.000	2	2	2	1	0	14	5	3.2	0	8	5.1	14	9.0	1.29	263	.124	.269	3	3	103	37	1.0	-1	-1	0.3
1904	NY-N	4	6	.400	16	13	11	1	3	115	94	7.4	2	38	3.0	93	7.3	2.27	120	.247	.320	6	6	100	104	-2.1	-1	-0	0.6
1905	NY-N	22	8	.733	34	31	21	2	0	263	220	7.5	2	105	3.6	198	**6.8**	2.74	105	.253	.335	7	4	96	97	2.7	-0	1	0.5
1906	NY-N	12	10	.545	31	25	15	1	1	203	166	7.4	1	93	4.1	156	**6.9**	2.66	96	.250	.344	-1	-2	97	99	-1.6	-3	3	0.1
1907	NY-N	10	12	.455	39	26	17	2	1	233	184	7.1	4	108	4.2	146	**5.6**	2.16	118	.246	.349	8	10	104	119	-1.8	1	3	1.5
1908	NY-N	7	4	.636	18	15	5	0	1	114	96	7.6	0	27	2.1	81	6.4	1.82	129	.256	.308	7	7	100	112	0.0	0	1	0.9
1909	NY-N	15	10	.600	34	26	20	2	1	244	217	8.0	3	81	3.0	156	5.8	2.69	100	.241	.306	-3	-0	103	92	0.0	-5	7	0.7
1910	NY-N	12	11	.522	33	23	13	3	0	190	161	7.6	3	63	3.0	94	4.5	2.23	126	.237	.308	17	12	92	111	-1.5	-0	4	1.6
1911	NY-N	11	10	.524	34	23	13	1	2	205	170	7.5	0	54	2.4	118	5.2	2.68	125	.223	.277	17	15	99	66	-2.1	-3	3	1.5
1912	NY-N	11	5	.688	33	22	9	2	2	179	194	9.8	3	35	1.8	83	4.2	2.46	137	.275	.313	19	18	99	**117**	0.2	1	2	2.2
1913	NY-N	2	1	.667	8	5	2	0	1	42	35	7.5	0	8	1.7	30	6.4	2.14	149	.241	.280	5	5	100	102	0.0	-1	2	0.7
	Cin-N	11	13	.458	31	24	12	1	2	187	185	8.9	7	70	3.4	80	3.9	2.89	115	.265	.330	7	9	104	121	1.0	-5	-0	0.5
	Yr	13	14	.481	39	29	14	1	3	229	220	8.6	7	78	3.1	110	4.3	2.75	120	.261	.320	12	14	103	121	1.0	-1	2	1.2
1914	Cin-N	15	23	.395	47	36	18	3	**6**	297	274	8.3	8	94	2.8	128	3.9	2.64	113	.248	.301	5	12	107	102	0.2	-4	4	1.3
1915	Cin-N	2	4	.333	17	7	4	1	1	68	82	10.9	2	24	3.2	26	3.4	4.50	64	.311	.362	-13	-12	104	101	-0.8	-1	1	-1.2
	StL-N	9	3	.750	15	14	8	2	1	113	93	7.4	1	32	2.5	48	3.8	2.47	112	.226	.274	4	4	101	80	3.3	-2	1	0.3
	Yr	11	7	.611	32	21	12	3	2	181	175	8.7	3	56	2.8	74	3.7	3.23	87	.259	.308	-10	-9	102	80	2.5	-1	2	-0.9
1916	StL-N	11	16	.407	45	22	10	2	**8**	228	225	8.9	3	57	2.3	98	3.9	2.64	99	.263	.303	-1	-1	100	109	0.4	-0	-2	-0.2
1917	StL-N	15	10	.600	43	19	10	2	3	209	189	8.1	2	57	2.5	62	2.7	2.71	102	.249	.294	-0	1	102	97	1.9	2	4	0.8
1918	StL-N	9	14	.391	27	25	17	0	2	207	192	8.3	1	52	2.3	68	3.0	2.30	114	.252	.295	11	8	95	111	0.0	-0	-1	0.7
1919	StL-N	3	5	.375	23	7	1	0	1	70	88	11.3	1	25	3.2	19	2.4	4.89	58	.314	.363	-15	-16	97	94	-0.1	-0	-2	-1.8
	Phi-N	0	2	.000	3	2	1	0	1	16	26	14.6	0	3	1.7	4	2.3	6.19	51	.400	.408	-6	-5	109	104	-0.9	1	0	-0.3
	Yr	3	7	.300	26	9	2	0	2	86	114	11.9	1	28	2.9	23	2.4	5.13	56	.329	.369	-21	-22	99	104	-1.0	-0	-1	-2.1
Total	17	183	167	.523	533	367	209	26	36	3197	2896	8.2	43	1034	2.9	1702	4.8	2.63	108	.252	.314	76	78	100	102	-0.2	-21	30	10.7
■ **DOC AMOLE**	Amole, Morris George b: 7/5/1878, Coatesville, Pa. d: 3/7/12, Wilmington, Del. BR/TL, 5'9", 165 lbs. Deb: 8/19/1897																												
1897	Bal-N	4	4	.500	11	7	6	0	0	70	67	8.6	0	17	2.2	19	2.4	2.57	154	.273	.320	14	11	92	101	-1.1	-3	0	0.7
1898	Was-N	0	6	.000	7	5	4	0	0	49	83	15.2	0	22	4.0	11	2.0	7.90	48	.399	.457	-23	-22	105	86	-2.9	-2	0	-1.9
Total	2	4	10	.286	18	12	10	0	0	119	150	11.3	0	39	2.9	30	2.3	4.76	82	.331	.384	-10	-11	97	95	-4.0	-5	0	-1.2
■ **VICENTE AMOR**	Amor, Vicente (Alvarez) b: 8/8/32, Havana, Cuba BR/TR, 6'3", 182 lbs. Deb: 4/16/55																												
1955	Chi-N	0	1	.000	4	0	0	0	0	6	11	16.5	0	3	4.5	3	4.5	4.50	91	.407	.452	-0	-0	101	177	-0.4	0	1	0.0
1957	Cin-N	1	2	.333	9	4	1	0	0	27	39	13.0	2	10	3.3	9	3.0	6.00	69	.345	.392	-6	-6	106	105	-0.4	-0	-0	-0.5
Total	2	1	3	.250	13	4	1	0	0	33	50	13.6	2	13	3.5	12	3.3	5.73	72	.357	.404	-7	-6	105	118	-0.8	-0	-0	-0.5

YEAR	TM/L	W	L	PCT	G	GS	CG	SHO	SV	IP	H	H/G	HR	BB	BB/G	SO	SO/G	ERA	/A	OAVG	OOBP	PR	/A	PF	CPI	WAT	PB	PD	TPI
■ **WALTER ANCKER**	Ancker, Walter b: 4/10/1894, New York, N.Y. d: 2/13/54, Englewood, N.J. BR/TR, 6'1", 190 lbs. Deb: 9/03/15																												
1915	Phi-A	0	0	—	4	1	0	0	0	18	19	9.5	1	17	8.5	4	2.0	3.50	87	.279	.443	-1	-1	103	171	0.0	-1	0	-0.1
■ **LARRY ANDERSEN**	Andersen, Larry Eugene b: 5/6/53, Portland, Ore. BR/TR, 6'3", 200 lbs. Deb: 9/05/75																												
1975	Cle-A	0	0	—	3	0	0	0	0	6	4	6.0	0	2	3.0	4	6.0	4.50	84	.200	.261	-0	-0	100	39	0.0	0	0	0.0
1977	Cle-A	0	1	.000	11	0	0	0	0	14	10	6.4	1	9	5.8	8	5.1	3.21	124	.200	.306	1	1	98	92	-0.4	0	1	0.2
1979	Cle-A	0	0	—	8	0	0	0	0	17	25	13.2	3	4	2.1	7	3.7	7.41	61	.357	.377	-6	-6	106	93	0.0	0	0	-0.4
1981	Sea-A	3	3	.500	41	0	0	0	5	68	57	7.5	4	18	2.4	40	5.3	2.65	140	.228	.282	8	8	101	98	0.5	0	0	0.8
1982	Sea-A	0	0	—	40	1	0	0	1	80	100	11.2	16	23	2.6	32	3.6	5.96	75	.311	.359	-17	-13	110	100	0.0	0	1	-1.1
1983	Phi-N	1	0	1.000	17	0	0	0	0	26	19	6.6	0	9	3.1	14	4.8	2.42	150	.200	.264	4	4	100	62	0.5	-0	0	0.4
1984	Phi-N	3	7	.300	64	0	0	0	4	91	85	8.4	5	25	2.5	54	5.3	2.37	153	.248	.293	12	13	101	126	-2.0	-0	0	1.3
1985	Phi-N	3	3	.500	57	0	0	0	3	73	78	9.6	5	26	3.2	50	6.2	4.32	85	.274	.336	-6	-5	102	94	0.2	-0	2	-0.3
1986	Phi-N	0	0	—	10	0	0	0	0	13	19	13.2	0	3	2.1	9	6.2	4.15	93	.388	.400	-1	-0	104	150	0.0	0	0	0.0
	Hou-N	2	1	.667	38	0	0	0	1	65	64	8.9	2	23	3.2	33	4.6	2.77	137	.276	.328	7	7	102	140	0.3	-1	0	0.7
	Yr	2	1	.667	48	0	0	0	1	78	83	9.6	2	26	3.0	42	4.8	3.00	127	.294	.341	6	7	102	140	0.3	0	0	0.7
1987	Hou-N	9	5	.643	67	0	0	0	5	102	95	8.4	7	41	3.6	94	8.3	3.44	110	.246	.314	7	4	93	101	2.4	0	-0	0.4
1988	Hou-N	2	4	.333	53	0	0	0	5	83	82	8.9	3	20	2.2	66	7.2	2.93	110	.254	.294	5	3	93	102	-1.0	1	-0	0.3
Total	11	23	24	.489	409	1	0	0	24	638	638	9.0	46	203	2.9	411	5.8	3.57	106	.263	.316	14	15	100	106	0.5	-1	5	2.3
■ **ALLAN ANDERSON**	Anderson, Allan Lee b: 1/7/64, Lancaster, Ohio BL/TL, 5'11", 169 lbs. Deb: 6/11/86																												
1986	Min-A	3	6	.333	21	10	1	0	0	84	106	11.4	11	30	3.2	51	5.5	5.57	82	.316	.369	-13	-9	109	103	-1.0	0	0	-0.8
1987	Min-A	1	0	1.000	4	2	0	0	0	12	20	15.0	3	10	7.5	3	2.3	11.25	38	.392	.492	-9	-9	96	92	0.5	0	-0	-0.7
1988	Min-A	16	9	.640	30	30	3	1	0	202	199	8.9	14	37	**1.6**	83	3.7	**2.45**	**171**	.261	.298	34	39	105	**138**	2.6	0	0	4.3
Total	3	20	15	.571	55	42	4	1	0	298	325	9.8	28	77	2.3	137	4.1	3.68	117	.283	.329	12	20	106	126	2.1	0	1	2.8
■ **RED ANDERSON**	Anderson, Arnold Revola b: 6/19/12, Lawton, Iowa d: 8/7/72, Sioux City, Iowa BR/TR, 6'3", 210 lbs. Deb: 9/19/37																												
1937	Was-A	0	1	.000	2	1	0	0	0	11	11	9.0	0	11	9.0	3	2.5	6.55	67	.282	.442	-2	-3	96	93	-0.4	-0	0	-0.2
1940	Was-A	1	1	.500	2	2	2	0	0	14	12	7.7	0	5	3.2	3	1.9	3.86	108	.245	.309	1	0	95	80	0.1	1	0	0.2
1941	Was-A	4	6	.400	32	6	1	0	0	112	127	10.2	7	53	4.3	34	2.7	4.18	98	.296	.367	-0	-1	99	123	-0.5	2	-1	0.0
Total	3	5	8	.385	36	9	3	0	0	137	150	9.9	7	69	4.5	40	2.6	4.34	95	.290	.368	-2	-3	98	116	-0.8	3	-1	0.0
■ **DAVE ANDERSON**	Anderson, David S. b: 10/10/1868, Chester, Pa. d: 3/22/1897, Chester, Pa. TL , Deb: 8/24/1889																												
1889	Phi-N	0	1	.000	5	2	1	0	0	23	30	11.7	2	14	5.5	8	3.1	7.43	57	.332	.421	-9	-8	105	82	-0.4	-0	0	-0.6
1890	Phi-N	1	1	.500	3	2	1	0	0	19	31	14.7	0	11	5.2	7	3.3	7.58	50	.383	.457	-8	-8	107	91	-0.1	-1	0	-0.6
	Pit-N	2	11	.154	13	13	13	0	0	108	116	9.7	2	49	4.1	41	3.4	4.67	72	.290	.368	-13	-16	95	83	-0.5	-5	0	-1.6
	Yr	3	12	.200	16	15	14	0	0	127	147	10.4	2	60	4.3	48	3.4	5.10	67	.306	.383	-22	-23	97	83	-0.6	-1	0	-2.2
Total	2	3	13	.188	21	17	15	0	0	150	177	10.6	4	74	4.4	56	3.4	5.46	65	.310	.389	-30	-32	98	84	-1.0	-6	0	-2.8
■ **JOHN ANDERSON**	Anderson, John Charles b: 11/23/32, St.Paul, Minn. BR/TR, 6'1", 190 lbs. Deb: 8/17/58																												
1958	Phi-N	0	0	—	5	1	0	0	0	16	26	14.6	5	4	2.3	9	5.1	7.88	50	.361	.397	-7	-7	100	105	0.0	-0	-0	-0.6
1960	Bal-A	0	0	—	4	0	0	0	0	5	8	14.4	0	4	7.2	1	1.8	12.60	31	.444	.462	-5	-5	101	73	0.0	0	0	-0.3
1962	StL-N	0	0	—	5	0	0	0	1	6	4	6.0	0	3	4.5	3	4.5	1.50	281	.182	.269	2	2	107	97	0.0	0	-0	0.2
	Hou-N	0	0	—	10	0	0	0	0	18	26	13.0	1	3	1.5	6	3.0	5.00	75	.338	.358	-2	-3	95	103	0.0	-0	1	-0.1
	Yr	0	0	—	15	0	0	0	1	24	30	11.3	1	6	2.3	9	3.4	4.13	93	.300	.336	-0	-1	98	103	0.0	0	0	0.1
Total	3	0	0	—	24	1	0	0	1	45	64	12.8	6	14	2.8	19	3.8	6.40	61	.339	.374	-12	-13	99	99	0.0	-0	1	-0.8
■ **FRED ANDERSON**	Anderson, John Frederick b: 12/11/1885, Calahan, N.C. d: 11/8/57, Winston-Salem, N.C. BR/TR, 6'2", 180 lbs. Deb: 9/25/09																												
1909	Bos-A	0	0	—	1	1	0	0	0	8	3	3.4	0	1	1.1	5	5.6	1.13	238	.115	.148	1	1	108	91	0.0	-0	0	0.2
1913	Bos-A	0	6	.000	10	8	4	0	0	57	84	13.3	0	21	3.3	32	5.1	6.00	50	.350	.405	-19	-19	103	91	-2.9	-2	-0	-1.7
1914	Buf-F	13	15	.464	37	28	21	2	0	260	243	8.4	8	64	2.2	144	5.0	3.08	108	.249	.297	4	7	104	86	-2.0	-1	0	0.7
1915	Buf-F	19	13	.594	36	28	14	5	0	240	192	7.2	5	72	2.7	142	**5.3**	2.51	122	.222	.285	14	15	101	87	4.0	-3	2	1.5
1916	NY-N	9	13	.409	38	27	13	2	2	188	206	9.9	7	38	1.8	98	4.7	3.40	72	.277	.309	-16	-20	94	97	-3.3	-0	-2	-2.4
1917	NY-N	8	8	.500	38	18	8	1	3	162	122	6.8	1	34	1.9	69	3.8	**1.44**	**175**	.209	**.250**	23	19	93	87	-1.8	-3	-0	1.8
1918	NY-N	4	2	.667	18	4	2	1	**3**	71	62	7.9	1	17	2.2	24	3.0	2.66	100	.246	.283	1	-0	96	94	0.7	-3	3	0.0
Total	7	53	57	.482	178	114	62	11	8	986	912	8.3	22	247	2.3	514	4.7	2.86	101	.248	.294	7	3	99	91	-5.3	-13	2	0.1
■ **BUD ANDERSON**	Anderson, Karl Adam b: 5/27/56, Westbury, N.Y. BR/TR, 6'3", 210 lbs. Deb: 6/11/82																												
1982	Cle-A	3	4	.429	25	5	1	0	0	81	84	9.3	4	30	3.3	44	4.9	3.33	123	.268	.326	7	7	101	113	-0.3	0	-0	0.7
1983	Cle-A	1	6	.143	39	1	0	0	7	68	64	8.5	8	32	4.2	32	4.2	4.10	105	.255	.331	-0	2	106	105	-2.3	0	-1	0.0
Total	2	4	10	.286	64	6	1	0	7	149	148	8.9	12	62	3.7	76	4.6	3.68	114	.262	.328	7	9	103	109	-2.6	0	-1	0.7
■ **LARRY ANDERSON**	Anderson, Lawrence Dennis b: 12/3/52, Maywood, Cal. BR/TR, 6'3", 190 lbs. Deb: 9/25/74																												
1974	Mil-A	0	0	—	2	0	0	0	0	2	2	9.0	0	1	4.5	3	13.5	0.00	—	.250	.333	1	1	103	0	0.0	0	0	0.1
1975	Mil-A	1	0	1.000	8	1	1	1	0	30	36	10.8	3	6	1.8	13	3.9	5.10	75	.298	.328	-4	-4	101	85	0.5	0	0	-0.3
1977	Chi-A	1	3	.250	6	0	0	0	0	9	10	10.0	1	15	15.0	7	7.0	9.00	45	.286	.463	-5	-5	99	92	-1.0	0	-0	-0.4
Total	3	2	3	.400	16	1	1	1	0	41	48	10.5	4	22	4.8	23	5.0	5.71	68	.293	.366	-8	-8	101	82	-0.5	0	0	-0.6
■ **MIKE ANDERSON**	Anderson, Michael Allen b: 6/22/51, Florence, S.C. BR/TR, 6'2", 200 lbs. Deb: 9/02/71																												
1979	Phi-N	0	0	—	1	0	0	0	0	1	2	18.0	0	0	0.0	2	18.0	0.00	—	.400	.400	0	0	97	0	0.0	0	0	0.0
■ **CRAIG ANDERSON**	Anderson, Norman Craig b: 7/1/38, Washington, D.C. BR/TR, 6'2", 205 lbs. Deb: 6/23/61																												
1961	StL-N	4	3	.571	25	0	0	0	1	39	38	8.8	3	12	2.8	21	4.8	3.23	140	.255	.311	3	6	113	107	0.4	1	0	0.7
1962	NY-N	3	17	.150	50	14	2	0	4	131	150	10.3	18	63	4.3	62	4.3	5.36	80	.278	.353	-21	-16	108	93	-4.2	-2	3	-1.4
1963	NY-N	0	2	.000	3	2	0	0	0	9	17	17.0	0	3	3.0	6	6.0	9.00	38	.362	.392	-6	-6	104	70	-0.9	0	0	-0.4
1964	NY-N	0	1	.000	4	1	0	0	0	13	21	14.5	0	3	2.1	5	3.5	5.54	63	.382	.393	-3	-3	98	114	-0.4	-0	0	-0.2
Total	4	7	23	.233	82	17	2	0	5	192	226	10.6	21	81	3.8	94	4.4	5.11	83	.286	.351	-26	-19	108	96	-5.1	-1	3	-1.3
■ **RICK ANDERSON**	Anderson, Richard Arlen b: 11/29/56, Everett, Wash. BR/TR, 6', 175 lbs. Deb: 6/09/86																												
1986	NY-N	2	1	.667	15	5	0	0	1	50	45	8.1	3	11	2.0	21	3.8	2.70	128	.245	.279	6	4	93	105	0.0	-0	-0	0.3
1987	KC-A	0	2	.000	6	2	0	0	0	13	26	18.0	3	9	6.2	12	8.3	13.85	34	.394	.481	-14	-13	104	77	-0.9	0	0	-1.0
1988	KC-A	2	1	.667	7	3	0	0	0	34	41	10.9	3	9	2.4	9	2.4	4.24	96	.308	.347	-1	-1	103	118	0.5	0	-1	0.0
Total	3	4	4	.500	28	10	0	0	1	97	112	10.4	9	29	2.7	42	3.9	4.73	81	.292	.339	-9	-10	98	106	-0.4	-0	-1	-0.7
■ **RICK ANDERSON**	Anderson, Richard Lee b: 12/25/53, Inglewood, Cal. BR/TR, 6'2", 210 lbs. Deb: 9/18/79																												
1979	NY-A	0	0	—	1	0	0	0	0	2	1	4.5	0	4	18.0	0	0.0	4.50	89	.167	.500	-0	-0	95	134	0.0	0	1	0.0
1980	Sea-A	0	0	—	5	2	0	0	0	10	8	7.2	1	10	9.0	7	6.3	3.60	118	.229	.391	0	1	105	138	0.0	0	-0	0.0
Total	2	0	0	—	6	2	0	0	0	12	9	6.8	1	14	10.5	7	5.3	3.75	112	.220	.411	0	1	103	137	0.0	0	0	0.0
■ **BOB ANDERSON**	Anderson, Robert Carl b: 9/29/35, E. Chicago, Ind. BR/TR, 6'4.5", 210 lbs. Deb: 7/31/57																												
1957	Chi-N	0	1	.000	8	0	0	0	0	16	20	11.3	2	8	4.5	7	3.9	7.88	48	.317	.382	-7	-7	98	78	-0.4	-0	0	-0.6
1958	Chi-N	3	3	.500	17	8	2	0	0	66	61	8.3	3	29	4.0	51	7.0	3.95	101	.255	.331	-0	0	101	91	0.2	-1	0	0.0
1959	Chi-N	12	13	.480	37	36	7	1	0	235	245	9.4	21	77	2.9	113	4.3	4.14	94	.272	.326	-5	-6	99	98	0.0	-4	1	-0.9
1960	Chi-N	9	11	.450	38	30	5	0	1	204	201	8.9	26	68	3.0	115	5.1	4.10	92	.255	.318	-8	-7	101	97	1.1	-0	1	-0.5
1961	Chi-N	7	10	.412	57	12	1	0	8	152	162	9.6	14	56	3.3	96	5.7	4.26	96	.275	.334	-4	-3	102	100	0.0	0	3	0.1
1962	Chi-N	2	7	.222	57	4	0	0	4	108	111	9.3	9	60	5.0	82	6.8	5.00	86	.266	.358	-13	-9	109	90	-1.7	0	-0	-0.8
1963	Det-A	3	1	.750	32	3	0	0	0	60	58	8.7	5	21	3.2	38	5.7	3.30	114	.258	.327	2	3	104	121	1.0	2	-0	0.4
Total	7	36	46	.439	246	93	15	1	13	841	858	9.2	80	319	3.4	502	5.4	4.26	93	.266	.331	-34	-29	101	98	0.2	-4	5	-2.3
■ **SCOTT ANDERSON**	Anderson, Scott Richard b: 8/1/62, Corvallis, Ore. BR/TR, 6'6", 190 lbs. Deb: 4/08/87																												
1987	Tex-A	0	1	.000	8	0	0	0	0	11	17	13.9	0	8	6.5	6	4.9	9.82	47	.347	.441	-7	-6	104	71	-0.4	0	1	-0.4

YEAR	TM/L	W	L	PCT	G	GS	CG	SHO	SV	IP	H	H/G	HR	BB	BB/G	SO	SO/G	ERA	/A	OAVG	OOBP	PR	/A	PF	CPI	WAT	PB	PD	TPI
■ VARNEY ANDERSON	Anderson, Varney Samuel "Varn" b: 6/18/1866, Geneva, Ill. d: 11/5/41, Rockford, Ill. BR/TR, 5'10", 165 lbs. Deb: 8/01/1889																												
1889	Ind-N	0	1	.000	2	1	1	0	0	12	13	9.8	0	9	6.8	3	2.3	4.50	98	.292	.411	-1	-0	110	105	-0.4	-1	0	0.0
1894	Was-N	0	2	.000	2	2	2	0	0	14	15	9.6	0	6	3.9	3	1.9	7.07	75	.296	.370	-3	-3	100	54	-0.9	0	0	-0.1
1895	Was-N	9	16	.360	29	25	18	0	0	205	288	12.6	13	97	4.3	35	1.5	5.93	85	.353	.422	-26	-20	105	103	0.6	2	0	-1.2
1896	Was-N	0	1	.000	2	2	1	0	0	9	23	23.0	0	3	3.0	0	0.0	13.00	32	.501	.531	-9	-9	96	83	-0.4	1	0	-0.5
Total	4	9	20	.310	35	30	22	0	0	240	339	12.7	13	115	4.3	41	1.5	6.19	81	.354	.423	-38	-32	105	99	-1.1	3	0	-1.8
■ WALTER ANDERSON	Anderson, Walter Carl "Lefty" b: 9/25/1897, Grand Rapids, Mich BL/TL, 6'2", 160 lbs. Deb: 5/14/17																												
1917	Phi-A	0	0	—	14	2	0	0	0	39	32	7.4	0	21	4.8	10	2.3	3.00	86	.246	.355	-1	-2	97	105	0.0	1	-0	0.0
1919	Phi-A	1	0	1.000	3	0	0	0	0	14	13	8.4	0	8	5.1	10	6.4	3.86	94	.245	.355	-1	-0	112	82	0.5	-1	0	0.0
Total	2	1	0	1.000	17	2	0	0	0	53	45	7.6	0	29	4.9	20	3.4	3.23	88	.246	.355	-2	-2	101	99	0.5	0	-0	0.0
■ BILL ANDERSON	Anderson, William Edward "Lefty" b: 11/28/1895, Boston, Mass. d: 3/13/83, Medford, Mass. BR/TL, 6'1", 165 lbs. Deb: 9/10/25																												
1925	Bos-N	0	0	—	2	0	0	0	0	3	5	15.0	0	2	6.0	1	3.0	9.00	45	.500	.500	-2	-2	95	113	0.0	-0	-0	-0.1
■ WINGO ANDERSON	Anderson, Wingo Charlie b: 8/13/1886, Alvarado, Tex. d: 12/19/50, Fort Worth, Tex. BL/TL, 5'10.5", 150 lbs. Deb: 4/16/10																												
1910	Cin-N	0	0	—	7	2	0	0	0	17	16	8.5	0	17	9.0	11	5.8	4.76	65	.258	.425	-3	-3	102	101	0.0	-0	-1	-0.3
■ JOHN ANDRE	Andre, John Edward b: 1/3/23, Brockton, Mass. d: 11/25/76, Centerville, Mass. BL/TR, 6'4", 200 lbs. Deb: 4/16/55																												
1955	Chi-N	0	1	.000	22	3	0	0	1	45	45	9.0	7	28	5.6	19	3.8	5.80	71	.259	.357	-9	-9	101	86	-0.4	-1	-0	-0.8
■ ELBERT ANDREWS	Andrews, Elbert De Vore b: 12/11/01, Greenwood, S.C. d: 11/25/79, Greenwood, S.C. BL/TR, 6', 175 lbs. Deb: 5/01/25																												
1925	Phi-A	0	0	—	6	0	0	0	0	8	12	13.5	0	11	12.4	0	0.0	10.13	44	.375	.523	-5	-5	101	91	0.0	0	0	-0.4
■ HUB ANDREWS	Andrews, Herbert Carl b: 8/31/22, Burbank, Okla. BR/TR, 6', 170 lbs. Deb: 4/20/47																												
1947	NY-N	0	0	—	7	0	0	0	0	9	14	14.0	1	4	4.0	2	2.0	6.00	67	.368	.419	-2	-2	99	123	0.0	0	0	-0.1
1948	NY-N	0	0	—	1	0	0	0	0	3	3	9.0	0	0	0.0	0	0.0	0.00	—	.300	.300	1	1	98	0	0.0	0	0	0.2
Total	2	0	0	—	8	0	0	0	0	12	17	12.8	1	4	3.0	2	1.5	4.50	89	.354	.396	-1	-1	99	92	0.0	0	0	0.1
■ IVY ANDREWS	Andrews, Ivy Paul "Poison" b: 5/6/07, Dora, Ala. d: 11/24/70, Birmingham, Ala. BR/TR, 6'1", 200 lbs. Deb: 8/15/31																												
1931	NY-A	2	0	1.000	7	3	1	0	0	34	36	9.5	3	8	2.1	10	2.6	4.24	97	.273	.308	1	-1	94	96	1.0	0	0	0.0
1932	NY-A	2	1	.667	4	1	1	0	0	25	20	7.2	0	9	3.2	7	2.5	1.80	227	.215	.282	7	6	91	122	0.0	1	0	0.8
	Bos-A	8	6	.571	25	19	8	0	0	142	144	9.1	4	53	3.4	30	1.9	3.80	121	.262	.325	11	12	102	98	3.0	-3	-1	0.8
	Yr	10	7	.588	29	20	9	0	0	167	164	8.8	4	62	3.3	37	2.0	3.50	129	.255	.318	18	19	101	98	3.0	1	-0	1.6
1933	Bos-A	7	13	.350	34	17	5	0	1	140	157	10.1	8	61	3.9	37	2.4	4.95	88	.279	.343	-10	-9	102	91	-1.8	-0	-1	-0.8
1934	StL-A	4	11	.267	43	13	2	0	3	139	166	10.7	7	65	4.2	51	3.3	4.66	102	.301	.370	-3	2	106	110	-3.1	4	-2	0.3
1935	StL-A	13	7	.650	50	20	10	0	1	213	231	9.8	10	53	2.2	43	1.8	3.55	138	.273	.312	21	32	110	103	4.2	-6	-2	2.3
1936	StL-A	7	12	.368	36	25	11	0	1	191	221	10.4	19	50	2.4	33	1.6	4.85	111	.286	.325	4	11	107	95	-0.1	-1	-2	0.8
1937	Cle-A	3	4	.429	20	4	1	1	0	60	76	11.4	3	9	1.4	16	2.4	4.35	103	.311	.327	2	1	97	103	-0.6	1	-1	0.0
	NY-A	3	2	.600	11	5	3	1	1	49	49	9.0	2	17	3.1	17	3.1	3.12	144	.259	.319	8	7	97	111	-0.1	-1	0	0.6
	Yr	6	6	.500	31	9	4	2	1	109	125	10.3	5	26	2.1	33	2.7	3.80	118	.289	.323	10	8	97	111	-0.7	1	-0	0.6
1938	NY-A	1	3	.250	19	1	1	0	1	48	51	9.6	3	17	3.2	13	2.4	3.00	162	.268	.324	10	10	102	131	-1.1	-0	0	0.9
Total	8	50	59	.459	249	108	43	2	8	1041	1151	10.0	59	342	3.0	257	2.2	4.14	115	.279	.329	51	72	104	102	1.4	-7	-9	5.7
■ JOHN ANDREWS	Andrews, John Richard b: 2/9/49, Monterey Park, Cal. BL/TL, 5'10", 175 lbs. Deb: 4/08/73																												
1973	StL-N	1	1	.500	16	0	0	0	0	18	16	8.0	3	11	5.5	5	2.5	4.50	73	.235	.338	-2	-2	90	97	0.0	0	-0	-0.2
■ NATE ANDREWS	Andrews, Nathan Hardy b: 9/30/13, Pembroke, N.C. BR/TR, 6', 195 lbs. Deb: 5/01/37																												
1937	StL-N	0	0	—	4	0	0	0	0	9	12	12.0	1	3	3.0	6	6.0	4.00	97	.324	.375	-0	-0	100	145	0.0	0	0	0.1
1939	StL-N	1	2	.333	11	1	0	0	0	16	24	13.5	0	12	6.8	6	3.4	6.75	60	.343	.424	-5	-5	103	98	-0.6	-0	0	-0.4
1940	Cle-A	0	1	.000	6	0	0	0	0	12	16	12.0	1	6	4.5	3	2.3	6.00	67	.327	.400	-2	-3	92	104	-0.4	0	1	-0.1
1941	Cle-A	0	0	—	2	0	0	0	0	2	3	13.5	0	2	9.0	1	4.5	13.50	31	.300	.417	-2	-2	101	44	0.0	-0	0	-0.1
1943	Bos-N	14	20	.412	36	34	23	3	0	284	253	8.0	11	75	2.4	80	2.5	2.57	143	.238	.286	25	35	109	102	-1.5	-1	2	4.2
1944	Bos-N	16	15	.516	37	34	16	3	2	257	263	9.2	14	74	2.6	76	2.7	3.22	108	.261	.310	11	7	96	105	3.0	-3	1	0.5
1945	Bos-N	7	12	.368	21	19	8	0	0	138	160	10.4	9	52	3.4	26	1.7	4.57	94	.295	.348	-12	-4	113	102	-1.6	-0	0	-0.3
1946	Cin-N	2	4	.333	7	7	3	0	0	43	50	10.5	2	8	1.7	13	2.7	3.98	90	.281	.311	-3	-2	105	86	-0.6	-1	-0	-0.2
	NY-N	1	0	1.000	3	2	0	0	0	12	17	12.8	2	4	3.0	5	3.8	6.00	59	.362	.396	-3	-3	103	117	0.5	1	-0	-0.2
	Yr	3	4	.429	10	9	3	0	0	55	67	11.0	4	12	2.0	18	2.9	4.42	81	.296	.325	-6	-5	105	117	-0.1	-1	-0	-0.4
Total	8	41	54	.432	127	97	50	6	2	773	798	9.3	40	236	2.7	216	2.5	3.46	108	.265	.315	9	23	104	103	-1.2	-4	5	3.5
■ FRED ANDRUS	Andrus, Frederick Hotham b: 8/23/1850, Washington, Mich. d: 11/10/37, Detroit, Mich. BR/TR, 6'2", 185 lbs. Deb: 7/25/1876																												
1884	Chi-N	1	0	1.000	1	1	1	0	0	9	11	11.0	1	2	2.0	2	2.0	2.00	156	.311	.347	1	1	105	230	0.5	0	0	0.1
■ JOAQUIN ANDUJAR	Andujar, Joaquin b: 12/12/52, San Pedro De Macoris, D.R. BB/TR, 6', 170 lbs. Deb: 4/08/76																												
1976	Hou-N	9	10	.474	28	25	9	4	0	172	163	8.5	8	75	3.9	59	3.1	3.61	84	.255	.328	-2	-11	87	99	-0.3	-0	-1	-1.2
1977	Hou-N	11	8	.579	26	25	4	1	0	159	149	8.4	11	64	3.6	69	3.9	3.68	98	.251	.320	4	-1	92	97	1.7	1	2	0.2
1978	Hou-N	5	7	.417	35	13	2	0	1	111	88	7.1	3	58	4.7	55	4.5	3.41	100	.224	.319	2	-0	95	90	-0.5	-0	2	0.2
1979	Hou-N	12	12	.500	46	23	8	0	4	194	168	7.8	7	88	4.1	77	3.6	3.43	98	.233	.313	7	-1	90	85	-1.1	-0	4	0.2
1980	Hou-N	3	8	.273	35	14	0	0	2	122	132	9.7	8	43	3.2	75	5.5	3.91	90	.277	.331	-4	-6	97	102	-2.9	2	2	-0.1
1981	Hou-N	2	3	.400	9	3	0	0	0	24	29	10.9	2	12	4.5	18	6.8	4.88	62	.296	.363	-4	-5	87	104	-0.6	-0	-1	-0.5
	StL-N	6	1	.857	11	8	1	0	0	55	56	9.2	4	11	1.8	19	3.1	3.76	94	.265	.300	-2	-1	101	89	2.4	-2	0	-0.3
	Yr	8	4	.667	20	11	1	0	0	79	85	9.7	6	23	2.6	37	4.2	4.10	82	.273	.321	-5	-6	97	89	1.8	-0	-0	-0.8
1982	StL-N	15	10	.600	38	37	9	5	0	266	237	8.0	11	50	1.7	137	4.6	2.47	150	.240	.278	34	36	102	102	1.1	-1	2	4.1
1983	StL-N	6	16	.273	39	34	5	2	1	225	215	8.6	23	75	3.0	125	5.0	4.16	86	.253	.311	-13	-15	98	87	-5.1	-3	5	-1.2
1984	StL-N	**20**	14	.588	36	36	12	**4**	0	**261**	218	7.5	20	70	2.4	147	5.1	3.34	106	.229	.280	7	6	99	83	3.0	2	3	1.1
1985	StL-N	21	12	.636	38	38	10	2	0	270	265	8.8	15	82	2.7	112	3.7	3.40	99	.260	.318	6	-1	93	103	0.7	-1	-1	-0.3
1986	Oak-A	12	7	.632	28	26	7	1	1	155	139	8.1	23	56	3.3	72	4.2	3.83	102	.239	.308	6	2	94	99	3.2	0	0	0.2
1987	Oak-A	3	5	.375	13	13	1	0	0	61	63	9.3	11	26	3.8	32	4.7	6.05	67	.269	.347	-11	-13	91	85	-0.9	0	0	-1.1
1988	Hou-N	2	5	.286	23	10	0	0	0	79	94	10.7	9	21	2.4	35	4.0	3.99	81	.297	.342	-5	-7	93	124	-1.5	2	0	-0.4
Total	13	127	118	.518	405	305	68	19	9	2154	2016	8.4	155	731	3.1	1032	4.3	3.58	98	.250	.311	26	-17	95	95	-0.8	-1	19	0.9
■ NORM ANGELINI	Angelini, Norman Stanley b: 9/24/47, San Francisco, Cal. BL/TL, 5'11", 175 lbs. Deb: 7/22/72																												
1972	KC-A	2	1	.667	21	0	0	0	2	16	13	7.3	1	12	6.8	16	9.0	2.25	136	.228	.371	1	1	100	179	0.5	-0	0	0.1
1973	KC-A	0	0	—	7	0	0	0	1	4	2	4.5	0	7	15.8	3	6.8	4.50	93	.200	.474	-0	-0	109	143	0.0	0	0	0.0
Total	2	2	1	.667	28	0	0	0	3	20	15	6.7	1	19	8.5	19	8.5	2.70	121	.224	.393	1	1	102	172	0.5	-0	0	0.1
■ CAP ANSON	Anson, Adrian Constantine b: 4/11/1852, Marshalltown, Iowa d: 4/14/22, Chicago, Ill. BR/TR, 6', 227 lbs. Deb: 5/06/1871 MH																												
1883	Chi-N	0	0	—	2	0	0	0	1	3	1	3.0	0	1	3.0	0	0.0	0.00	—	.109	.196	1	1	107	0	0.0	1	0	0.1
1884	Chi-N	0	1	.000	1	0	0	0	0	1	3	27.0	2	1	9.0	1	9.0	18.00	17	.525	.596	-2	-2	105	167	-0.4	1	0	0.0
Total	2	0	1	.000	3	0	0	0	1	4	4	9.0	2	2	4.5	1	2.3	4.50	73	.268	.355	-1	-1	106	42	-0.4	1	0	0.1
■ JOHNNY ANTONELLI	Antonelli, John August b: 4/12/30, Rochester, N.Y. BL/TL, 6'1.5", 185 lbs. Deb: 7/04/48																												
1948	Bos-N	0	0	—	4	0	0	0	1	4	2	4.5	0	3	6.8	0	0.0	2.25	174	.143	.294	1	1	99	64	0.0	0	0	0.1
1949	Bos-N	3	7	.300	22	10	3	1	0	96	99	9.3	6	42	3.9	48	4.5	3.56	110	.273	.344	5	4	97	121	-1.9	-1	-1	0.2
1950	Bos-N	2	3	.400	20	6	2	1	0	58	81	12.6	2	22	3.4	33	5.1	5.90	60	.335	.389	-11	-15	85	98	-0.6	-1	0	-1.4
1953	Mil-N	12	12	.500	31	26	11	2	1	175	167	8.6	15	71	3.7	131	6.7	3.19	123	.242	.313	21	14	92	107	-2.2	0	1	1.5
1954	NY-N	21	7	**.750**	39	37	18	**6**	2	259	209	**7.3**	22	94	3.3	152	5.3	**2.29**	**181**	**.219**	.288	**51**	**53**	102	116	5.2	-0	2	**5.9**
1955	NY-N	14	16	.467	38	34	14	2	1	235	206	7.9	24	82	3.1	143	5.5	3.33	119	.234	.303	18	16	98	98	-1.7	3	1	2.1
1956	NY-N	20	13	.606	41	36	15	5	1	258	225	7.8	20	75	2.6	145	5.1	2.86	131	.234	.286	26	25	99	96	5.9	2	1	3.0
1957	NY-N	12	18	.400	40	30	8	3	0	212	228	9.7	19	67	2.8	114	4.8	3.78	106	.276	.326	2	5	103	108	-1.8	3	-2	0.7
1958	SF-N	16	13	.552	41	34	13	0	3	242	216	8.0	31	87	3.2	143	5.3	3.27	120	.239	.302	18	18	100	106	1.2	3	-3	1.9

YEAR	TM/L	W	L	PCT	G	GS	CG	SHO	SV	IP	H	H/G	HR	BB	BB/G	SO	SO/G	ERA	/A	OAVG	OOBP	PR	/A	PF	CPI	WAT	PB	PD	TPI
1959	SF-N	19	10	.655	40	38	17	**4**	1	282	247	7.9	29	76	2.4	165	5.3	3.10	119	.233	.283	27	19	94	94	4.3	2	-1	1.9
1960	SF-N	6	7	.462	41	10	1	1	11	112	106	8.5	7	47	3.8	57	4.6	3.78	88	.253	.323	-0	-5	89	97	-0.6	2	-1	-0.3
1961	Cle-A	0	4	.000	11	7	0	0	0	48	68	12.8	8	18	3.4	23	4.3	6.56	59	.338	.387	-14	-14	97	102	-1.9	1	1	-1.1
	Mil-N	1	0	1.000	9	0	0	0	0	11	16	13.1	2	3	2.5	8	6.5	7.36	50	.340	.373	-4	-5	91	89	0.5	-0	0	-0.4
Total	12	126	110	.534	377	268	102	25	21	1992	1870	8.4	185	687	3.1	1162	5.3	3.34	116	.247	.308	141	116	97	103	6.4	15	-0	14.1
■ **BOB APODACA**	Apodaca, Robert John b: 1/31/50, Los Angeles, Cal. BR/TR, 5'11", 170 lbs. Deb: 9/18/73																												
1973	NY-N	0	0	—	1	0	0	0	0	0	0	—	0	2	—	0	—	∞	—	—	1.000	-1	-1	100	62	0.0	0	0	0.0
1974	NY-N	6	6	.500	35	8	1	0	3	103	92	8.0	7	42	3.7	54	4.7	3.50	104	.241	.313	2	2	100	94	0.7	0	-0	0.1
1975	NY-N	3	4	.429	46	0	0	0	13	85	66	7.0	4	28	3.0	45	4.8	1.48	232	.222	.278	20	19	95	167	-0.5	1	2	2.4
1976	NY-N	3	7	.300	43	3	0	0	5	90	71	7.1	4	29	2.9	45	4.5	2.80	113	.223	.283	7	4	91	92	-2.2	0	1	0.5
1977	NY-N	4	8	.333	59	0	0	0	5	84	83	8.9	7	30	3.2	53	5.7	3.43	111	.255	.311	5	3	97	103	-0.9	-0	1	0.4
Total	5	16	25	.390	184	11	1	0	26	362	312	7.8	22	131	3.3	197	4.9	2.86	123	.236	.298	32	26	96	113	-2.9	2	4	3.4
■ **LUIS APONTE**	Aponte, Luis Eduardo (Yuripe) b: 6/14/53, El Tigre, Venez. BR/TR, 6', 180 lbs. Deb: 9/04/80																												
1980	Bos-A	0	0	—	4	0	0	0	0	7	6	7.7	0	2	2.6	1	1.3	1.29	321	.250	.286	2	2	102	217	0.0	0	0	0.2
1981	Bos-A	1	0	1.000	7	0	0	0	1	16	11	6.2	0	3	1.7	11	6.2	0.56	688	.208	.246	6	6	106	281	0.5	0	1	0.7
1982	Bos-A	2	2	.500	40	0	0	0	3	85	78	8.3	5	25	2.6	44	4.7	3.18	141	.246	.295	9	12	110	96	-0.1	0	2	1.4
1983	Bos-A	5	4	.556	34	0	0	0	3	62	74	10.7	7	23	3.3	32	4.6	3.63	114	.301	.359	3	4	102	145	0.7	0	1	0.4
1984	Cle-A	1	0	1.000	25	0	0	0	0	50	53	9.5	5	15	2.7	25	4.5	4.14	102	.269	.317	-1	1	106	96	0.5	0	-1	0.0
Total	5	9	6	.600	110	0	0	0	7	220	222	9.1	17	68	2.8	113	4.6	3.27	131	.265	.316	18	25	106	127	1.6	0	3	2.7
■ **FRED APPLEGATE**	Applegate, Frederick Romaine b: 5/9/1879, Williamsport, Pa. d: 4/21/68, Williamsport, Pa. BR/TR, 6'2", 180 lbs. Deb: 9/30/04																												
1904	Phi-A	1	2	.333	3	3	3	0	0	21	29	12.4	0	8	3.4	12	5.1	6.43	41	.353	.411	-9	-9	101	81	-0.5	0	0	-0.7
■ **ED APPLETON**	Appleton, Edward Samuel "Whitey" b: 2/29/1892, Arlington, Tex. d: 1/27/32, Arlington, Tex. BR/TR, 6'0.5", 173 lbs. Deb: 4/16/15																												
1915	Bro-N	4	10	.286	34	10	5	0	0	138	133	8.7	3	66	4.3	50	3.3	3.33	84	.263	.342	-9	-8	102	112	-3.3	-0	-1	-0.9
1916	Bro-N	1	2	.333	14	3	1	0	1	47	49	9.4	1	18	3.4	14	2.7	3.06	86	.278	.332	-2	-2	100	121	-0.6	-0	-1	-0.3
Total	2	5	12	.294	48	13	6	0	1	185	182	8.9	4	84	4.1	64	3.1	3.26	85	.267	.339	-11	-10	102	114	-3.9	-1	-1	-1.2
■ **PETE APPLETON**	Appleton, Peter William "Jake" (a.k.a. Jablonowski 1927-33) b: 5/20/04, Terryville, Conn. d: 1/18/74, Trenton, N.J. BR/TR, 5'11", 180 lbs. Deb: 9/14/27																												
1927	Cin-N	2	1	.667	6	2	2	1	0	30	29	8.7	0	17	5.1	3	0.9	1.80	218	.261	.359	7	7	100	207	0.5	2	1	1.1
1928	Cin-N	3	4	.429	31	1	0	0	0	83	101	11.0	7	22	2.4	20	2.2	4.66	83	.311	.346	-6	-7	97	103	-0.5	3	2	-0.2
1930	Cle-A	8	7	.533	39	7	2	0	1	119	122	9.2	8	53	4.0	45	3.4	4.01	122	.274	.342	9	12	105	116	0.1	-1	2	1.1
1931	Cle-A	4	4	.500	29	4	3	0	0	80	100	11.2	2	29	3.3	25	2.8	4.61	100	.293	.350	-2	0	106	97	0.0	0	-0	0.0
1932	Cle-A	0	0	—	4	0	0	0	0	5	11	19.8	1	3	5.4	1	1.8	16.20	30	.407	.467	-7	-6	107	66	0.0	0	0	-0.4
	Bos-A	0	3	.000	11	3	0	0	0	46	49	9.6	2	26	5.1	15	2.9	4.11	112	.265	.355	2	2	102	109	-1.4	-1	2	0.4
	Yr	0	3	.000	15	3	0	0	0	51	60	10.6	3	29	5.1	16	2.8	5.29	87	.283	.368	-5	-4	103	109	-1.4	0	2	0.0
1933	NY-A	0	0	—	1	0	0	0	0	2	3	13.5	0	1	4.5	0	0.0	0.00	—	.375	.444	1	1	88	0	0.0	0	0	0.1
1936	Was-A	14	9	.609	38	20	12	1	3	202	199	8.9	7	77	3.4	77	3.4	3.52	138	.254	.321	34	30	96	103	2.1	1	1	2.9
1937	Was-A	8	15	.348	35	18	7	4	2	168	167	8.9	16	72	3.9	62	3.3	4.39	100	.260	.333	4	0	96	97	-3.4	-1	3	0.1
1938	Was-A	7	9	.438	43	10	5	0	5	164	175	9.6	12	61	3.3	62	3.4	4.61	99	.270	.328	3	-0	96	90	-1.0	3	-0	0.1
1939	Was-A	5	10	.333	40	4	2	0	6	103	104	9.1	7	48	4.2	50	4.4	4.54	93	.265	.340	1	-4	91	97	-1.7	-0	0	-0.3
1940	Chi-A	4	0	1.000	25	0	0	0	5	58	54	8.4	8	28	4.3	21	3.3	5.59	81	.248	.327	-8	-7	103	79	2.0	-0	-0	-0.6
1941	Chi-A	0	3	.000	13	0	0	0	1	27	27	9.0	4	17	5.7	12	4.0	5.33	73	.257	.362	-4	-4	94	98	-1.4	0	-0	-0.3
1942	Chi-A	0	0	—	4	0	0	0	0	5	2	3.6	0	3	5.4	2	3.6	3.60	102	.133	.263	0	0	100	41	0.0	0	0	0.0
	StL-A	1	1	.500	14	0	0	0	2	27	25	8.3	1	11	3.7	12	4.0	3.00	125	.243	.316	2	2	102	106	0.0	1	1	0.4
	Yr	1	1	.500	18	0	0	0	2	32	27	7.6	1	14	3.9	14	3.9	3.09	120	.229	.308	2	2	102	106	0.0	0	1	0.4
1945	StL-A	0	0	—	2	0	0	0	0	2	3	13.5	0	7	31.5	1	4.5	18.00	21	.273	.556	-3	-3	114	65	0.0	0	0	-0.2
	Was-A	1	0	1.000	6	2	1	0	1	21	16	6.9	1	11	4.7	12	5.1	3.43	90	.211	.307	-0	-1	92	79	0.5	-0	-0	0.0
	Yr	1	0	1.000	8	2	1	0	1	23	19	7.4	1	18	7.0	13	5.1	4.70	67	.218	.349	-3	-4	94	79	0.5	0	0	-0.2
Total	14	57	66	.463	341	71	34	6	26	1142	1187	9.4	76	486	3.8	420	3.3	4.30	104	.268	.337	33	22	98	101	-4.2	6	12	4.2
■ **LUIS AQUINO**	Aquino, Luis Antonio (Colon) b: 5/19/64, Santurce, P.R. BR/TR, 6', 155 lbs. Deb: 8/08/86																												
1986	Tor-A	1	1	.500	7	0	0	0	0	11	14	11.5	2	3	2.5	5	4.1	6.55	67	.304	.340	-3	-3	104	84	0.0	0	0	-0.2
1988	KC-A	1	0	1.000	7	5	1	1	0	29	33	10.2	1	17	5.3	11	3.4	2.79	146	.282	.375	4	4	103	169	0.5	0	-0	0.4
Total	2	2	1	.667	14	5	1	1	0	40	47	10.6	3	20	4.5	16	3.6	3.82	109	.288	.366	1	1	103	146	0.5	0	-0	0.2
■ **FRED ARCHER**	Archer, Frederick Marvin "Lefty" b: 3/7/10, Johnson City, Tenn. d: 10/31/81, Charlotte, N.C. BL/TL, 6', 193 lbs. Deb: 9/05/36																												
1936	Phi-A	2	3	.400	6	5	2	0	0	37	41	10.0	3	15	3.6	9	2.2	6.32	84	.289	.360	-5	-4	105	83	0.2	0	-0	-0.2
1937	Phi-A	0	0	—	1	0	0	0	0	3	4	12.0	0	0	0.0	2	6.0	6.00	74	.333	.308	-0	-1	96	73	0.0	0	0	0.0
Total	2	2	3	.400	7	5	2	0	0	40	45	10.1	3	15	3.4	11	2.5	6.30	83	.292	.356	-6	-5	105	82	0.2	1	0	-0.2
■ **JIM ARCHER**	Archer, James William b: 5/25/32, Max Meadows, Va. BR/TL, 6', 190 lbs. Deb: 4/30/61																												
1961	KC-A	9	15	.375	39	27	9	2	5	205	204	9.0	11	60	2.6	110	4.8	3.20	131	.257	.306	19	23	104	103	0.0	-5	-0	1.8
1962	KC-A	0	1	.000	18	1	0	0	0	28	40	12.9	8	10	3.2	12	3.9	9.32	43	.342	.388	-17	-16	101	82	-0.4	0	-0	-1.5
Total	2	9	16	.360	57	28	9	2	5	233	244	9.4	19	70	2.7	122	4.7	3.94	106	.268	.316	2	6	104	100	-0.4	-4	-1	0.3
■ **RUGGER ARDIZOIA**	Ardizoia, Rinaldo Joseph b: 11/20/19, Oleggio, Italy BR/TR, 5'11", 180 lbs. Deb: 4/30/47																												
1947	NY-A	0	0	—	1	0	0	0	0	2	4	18.0	1	1	4.5	0	0.0	9.00	38	.500	.500	-1	-1	92	158	0.0	0	0	0.0
■ **FRANK ARELLANES**	Arellanes, Frank Julian b: 1/28/1882, Santa Cruz, Cal. d: 12/13/18, San Jose, Cal. BR/TR, 6', 180 lbs. Deb: 7/28/08																												
1908	Bos-A	4	3	.571	11	8	6	1	0	79	60	6.8	1	18	2.1	33	3.8	1.82	127	.213	.267	5	4	97	100	0.6	0	-1	0.3
1909	Bos-A	16	12	.571	45	28	17	1	**8**	231	192	7.5	3	43	1.7	82	3.2	2.18	123	.229	.270	8	13	108	76	-0.2	-2	0	1.5
1910	Bos-A	4	7	.364	18	13	2	0	0	100	106	9.5	1	24	2.2	33	3.0	2.88	85	.283	.332	-4	-5	97	114	-1.7	0	0	-0.4
Total	3	24	22	.522	74	49	25	2	8	410	358	7.9	5	85	1.9	148	3.2	2.28	112	.239	.285	9	12	103	90	-1.3	-1	-1	1.4
■ **RUDY ARIAS**	Arias, Rodolfo (Martinez) b: 6/6/31, Las Villas, Cuba BL/TL, 5'10", 165 lbs. Deb: 4/10/59																												
1959	Chi-A	2	0	1.000	34	0	0	0	2	44	49	10.0	7	20	4.1	28	5.7	4.09	90	.277	.350	-1	-2	95	125	1.0	-1	1	-0.1
■ **DON ARLICH**	Arlich, Donald Louis b: 2/15/43, Wayne, Mich. BL/TL, 6'2", 185 lbs. Deb: 10/02/65																												
1965	Hou-N	0	0	—	1	1	0	0	0	6	5	7.5	0	1	1.5	0	0.0	3.00	107	.227	.261	0	0	91	60	0.0	-0	0	0.0
1966	Hou-N	0	1	.000	7	0	0	0	0	4	11	24.8	0	4	9.0	1	2.3	15.75	23	.478	.571	-5	-5	99	87	-0.4	-0	-0	-0.5
Total	2	0	1	.000	8	1	0	0	0	10	16	14.4	0	5	4.5	1	0.9	8.10	41	.356	.431	-5	-5	94	71	-0.4	-0	-0	-0.5
■ **STEVE ARLIN**	Arlin, Stephen Ralph b: 9/25/45, Seattle, Wash. BR/TR, 6'3.5", 195 lbs. Deb: 6/17/69																												
1969	SD-N	0	1	.000	4	1	0	0	0	11	13	10.6	2	9	7.4	9	7.4	9.00	40	.289	.407	-7	-7	100	72	-0.4	-0	-0	-0.6
1970	SD-N	1	0	1.000	2	2	1	1	0	13	11	7.6	0	8	5.5	3	2.1	2.77	141	.244	.339	2	2	97	133	0.5	-1	0	0.1
1971	SD-N	9	19	.321	36	34	10	4	0	228	211	8.3	8	103	4.1	156	6.2	3.47	98	.244	.324	-0	-2	98	92	-2.4	-2	-1	-0.4
1972	SD-N	10	21	.323	38	37	12	3	0	250	217	7.8	19	122	4.4	159	5.7	3.60	87	.237	.325	-4	-13	91	99	-2.7	3	0	-1.1
1973	SD-N	11	14	.440	34	27	7	3	0	180	196	9.8	26	72	3.6	98	4.9	5.10	70	.278	.339	-29	-31	97	93	1.6	1	-1	-3.0
1974	SD-N	1	7	.125	16	12	1	0	1	64	85	12.0	5	37	5.2	18	2.5	5.91	59	.326	.400	-16	-17	97	104	-2.6	-1	-0	-1.7
	Cle-A	2	5	.286	11	10	1	0	0	44	59	12.1	1	22	4.5	20	4.1	6.55	56	.333	.405	-14	-14	101	85	-1.3	0	-1	-1.3
Total	6	34	67	.337	141	123	32	11	1	790	792	9.0	61	373	4.2	463	5.3	4.32	78	.263	.341	-68	-82	96	96	-7.3	1	-3	-8.0
■ **ORVILLE ARMBRUST**	Armbrust, Orville Martin b: 3/2/10, Beirne, Ark. d: 10/2/67, Mobile, Ala. BR/TR, 5'10", 195 lbs. Deb: 9/18/34																												
1934	Was-A	1	0	1.000	3	2	0	0	0	13	10	6.9	1	3	2.1	3	2.1	2.08	222	.208	.255	3	4	102	105	0.5	-1	1	0.4
■ **HOWARD ARMSTRONG**	Armstrong, Howard Elmer b: 12/2/1889, E.Claridon, Ohio d: 3/8/26, Canisteo, N.Y. TR, 5'9", 165 lbs. Deb: 9/30/11																												
1911	Phi-A	0	1	.000	1	0	0	0	0	3	3	9.0	0	1	3.0	0	0.0	0.00	—	.273	.333	1	1	88	0	-0.4	-0	0	0.1

YEAR	TM/L	W	L	PCT	G	GS	CG	SHO	SV	IP	H	H/G	HR	BB	BB/G	SO	SO/G	ERA	/A	OAVG	OOBP	PR	/A	PF	CPI	WAT	PB	PD	TPI
■ **JACK ARMSTRONG** Armstrong, Jack William b: 3/7/65, Englewood, N.J. BR/TR, 6'5", 220 lbs. Deb: 6/21/88																													
1988	Cin-N	4	7	.364	14	13	0	0	0	65	63	8.7	8	38	5.3	45	6.2	5.82	62	.256	.345	-17	-16	105	80	-1.8	-1	1	-1.5
■ **MIKE ARMSTRONG** Armstrong, Michael Dennis b: 3/7/54, Glen Cove, N.Y. BR/TR, 6'3", 193 lbs. Deb: 8/12/80																													
1980	SD-N	0	0	—	11	0	0	0	0	14	16	10.3	3	13	8.4	14	9.0	5.79	59	.296	.433	-3	-4	94	126	0.0	-0	-0	-0.4
1981	SD-N	0	2	.000	10	0	0	0	0	12	14	10.5	1	11	8.3	9	6.8	6.00	55	.311	.431	-3	-4	95	111	-0.9	0	-0	-0.3
1982	KC-A	5	5	.500	52	0	0	0	6	113	88	7.0	9	43	3.4	75	6.0	3.19	127	.215	.288	11	11	100	87	-0.4	0	-1	1.0
1983	KC-A	10	7	.588	58	0	0	0	3	103	86	7.5	11	45	3.9	52	4.5	3.84	108	.228	.310	3	4	102	91	1.8	0	-0	0.3
1984	NY-A	3	2	.600	36	0	0	0	1	54	47	7.8	6	26	4.3	43	7.2	3.50	106	.239	.319	3	1	93	109	0.3	0	0	0.1
1985	NY-A	0	0	—	9	0	0	0	0	15	9	5.4	4	2	1.2	11	6.6	3.00	130	.173	.204	2	2	94	86	0.0	0	-0	0.1
1986	NY-A	0	1	.000	7	1	0	0	0	9	13	13.0	4	5	5.0	8	8.0	9.00	48	.351	.429	-5	-5	103	108	-0.4	0	0	-0.4
1987	Cle-A	1	0	1.000	14	0	0	0	1	19	27	12.8	4	10	4.7	9	4.3	8.53	55	.333	.407	-9	-8	105	86	0.5	0	-0	-0.7
Total	8	19	17	.528	197	1	0	0	11	339	300	8.0	42	155	4.1	221	5.9	4.09	98	.240	.320	-1	-3	99	95	0.9	-0	-2	-0.3
■ **SCOTT ARNOLD** Arnold, Scott Gentry b: 8/18/62, Lexington, Ky. BR/TR, 6'2", 210 lbs. Deb: 4/07/88																													
1988	StL-N	0	0	—	6	0	0	0	0	7	9	11.6	0	4	5.1	8	10.3	5.14	70	.321	.406	-1	-1	105	106	0.0	0	0	0.0
■ **TONY ARNOLD** Arnold, Tony Dale b: 5/3/59, El Paso, Tex. BR/TR, 5'11", 170 lbs. Deb: 8/09/86																													
1986	Bal-A	0	2	.000	11	0	0	0	0	25	25	9.0	0	11	4.0	7	2.5	3.60	116	.278	.346	2	2	99	110	-0.9	0	1	0.3
1987	Bal-A	0	0	—	27	0	0	0	0	53	71	12.1	8	17	2.9	18	3.1	5.77	77	.330	.377	-8	-8	99	110	0.0	0	2	-0.5
Total	2	0	2	.000	38	0	0	0	0	78	96	11.1	8	28	3.2	25	2.9	5.08	86	.315	.367	-6	-6	99	110	-0.9	0	3	-0.2
■ **BRAD ARNSBERG** Arnsberg, Bradley James b: 8/20/63, Seattle, Wash. BR/TR, 6'4", 205 lbs. Deb: 9/06/86																													
1986	NY-A	0	0	—	2	1	0	0	0	8	13	14.6	1	1	1.1	3	3.4	3.38	127	.342	.359	1	1	103	173	0.0	0	-0	0.1
1987	NY-A	1	3	.250	6	2	0	0	0	19	22	10.4	5	13	6.2	14	6.6	5.68	77	.289	.385	-3	-3	97	121	-1.0	0	1	-0.1
Total	2	1	3	.250	8	3	0	0	0	27	35	11.7	6	14	4.7	17	5.7	5.00	87	.307	.377	-2	-2	99	136	-1.0	0	0	0.0
■ **ORIE ARNTZEN** Arntzen, Orie Edgar "Old Folks" b: 10/18/09, Beverly, Ill. d: 1/28/70, Cedar Rapids, Iowa BR/TR, 6'1", 200 lbs. Deb: 4/20/43																													
1943	Phi-A	4	13	.235	32	20	9	0	0	164	172	9.4	5	69	3.8	66	3.6	4.23	83	.277	.347	-17	-13	106	97	-2.3	-1	-3	-1.7
■ **GERRY ARRIGO** Arrigo, Gerald William b: 6/12/41, Chicago, Ill. BL/TL, 6'1", 185 lbs. Deb: 6/12/61																													
1961	Min-A	0	1	.000	7	2	0	0	0	10	9	8.1	0	10	9.0	6	5.4	9.90	44	.265	.412	-7	-6	107	58	-0.4	0	0	-0.5
1962	Min-A	0	0	—	1	0	0	0	0	1	3	27.0	0	1	9.0	1	9.0	18.00	23	.600	.667	-2	-2	104	93	0.0	0	0	0.0
1963	Min-A	1	2	.333	5	1	0	0	0	16	12	6.8	2	4	2.3	13	7.3	2.81	126	.211	.254	1	1	98	94	-0.5	-0	0	0.1
1964	Min-A	7	4	.636	41	12	2	1	1	105	97	8.3	11	45	3.9	96	8.2	3.86	94	.244	.317	-3	-3	100	96	1.7	0	0	-0.1
1965	Cin-N	2	4	.333	27	5	0	0	2	54	75	12.5	4	30	5.0	43	7.2	6.17	58	.342	.413	-16	-15	102	108	-1.1	1	-1	-1.5
1966	Cin-N	0	0	—	3	0	0	0	0	7	7	9.0	2	3	3.9	3	3.9	5.14	80	.250	.313	-1	-1	114	99	0.0	-0	-0	0.0
	NY-N	3	3	.500	17	5	0	0	0	43	47	9.8	5	16	3.3	28	5.9	3.77	93	.276	.325	-1	-1	97	117	0.5	3	1	0.2
	Yr	3	3	.500	20	5	0	0	0	50	54	9.7	7	19	3.4	31	5.6	3.96	90	.273	.323	-2	-2	99	117	0.5	-0	0	0.2
1967	Cin-N	6	6	.500	32	5	1	1	1	74	61	7.4	6	35	4.3	56	6.8	3.16	116	.232	.321	2	4	109	113	-0.3	1	-2	0.4
1968	Cin-N	12	10	.545	36	31	5	1	0	205	181	7.9	13	77	3.4	140	6.1	3.34	99	.237	.307	-8	-1	111	93	0.9	-3	2	0.0
1969	Cin-N	4	7	.364	20	16	1	0	0	91	89	8.8	9	61	6.0	35	3.5	4.15	85	.256	.374	-6	-6	99	117	-1.8	0	-2	-0.8
1970	Chi-A	0	3	.000	5	3	0	0	0	13	24	16.6	4	9	6.2	12	8.3	13.15	30	.393	.458	-14	-13	108	79	-1.4	-0	-0	-1.1
Total	10	35	40	.467	194	80	9	3	4	619	605	8.8	56	291	4.2	433	6.3	4.14	85	.258	.338	-53	-42	105	101	-2.4	2	-3	-3.3
■ **FERNANDO ARROYO** Arroyo, Fernando b: 3/21/52, Sacramento, Cal. BR/TR, 6'2", 180 lbs. Deb: 6/28/75																													
1975	Det-A	2	1	.667	14	2	1	0	0	53	56	9.5	5	22	3.7	25	4.2	4.58	88	.272	.341	-5	-3	106	93	0.7	0	1	-0.1
1977	Det-A	8	18	.308	38	28	8	1	0	209	227	9.8	23	52	2.2	60	2.6	4.18	102	.278	.317	-2	2	105	97	-4.7	0	6	0.8
1978	Det-A	0	0	—	2	0	0	0	0	4	8	18.0	1	0	0.0	1	2.3	9.00	45	.400	.429	-2	-2	107	102	0.0	0	0	-0.1
1979	Det-A	1	1	.500	6	0	0	0	0	12	17	12.8	3	4	3.0	7	5.3	8.25	49	.340	.368	-5	-6	96	87	0.0	0	0	-0.4
1980	Min-A	6	6	.500	21	11	1	1	0	92	97	9.5	7	32	3.1	27	2.6	4.70	94	.273	.331	-7	-3	109	85	0.3	0	-1	-0.3
1981	Min-A	7	10	.412	23	19	2	0	0	128	144	10.1	11	34	2.4	39	2.7	3.94	99	.290	.338	-4	-1	107	112	0.6	0	0	0.0
1982	Min-A	0	1	.000	6	0	0	0	0	14	17	10.9	2	6	3.9	4	2.6	5.14	81	.321	.377	-2	-2	102	119	-0.4	0	1	0.0
	Oak-A	0	0	—	10	0	0	0	0	22	23	9.4	4	7	2.9	9	3.7	5.32	74	.271	.330	-3	-3	96	90	0.0	0	0	-0.2
	Yr	0	1	.000	16	0	0	0	0	36	40	10.0	6	13	3.3	13	3.3	5.25	77	.288	.348	-5	-5	99	90	-0.4	0	1	-0.2
1986	Oak-A	0	0	—	1	0	0	0	0	0	0	—	0	3	—	0	—	—	—	—	1.000	0	0	94	0	0.0	0	0	0.0
Total	8	24	37	.393	121	60	12	2	0	534	589	9.9	56	160	2.7	172	2.9	4.45	94	.283	.332	-30	-17	106	98	-3.5	0	7	-0.3
■ **LUIS ARROYO** Arroyo, Luis Enrique b: 2/18/27, Penuelas, P.R. BL/TL, 5'8.5", 178 lbs. Deb: 4/20/55																													
1955	StL-N	11	8	.579	35	24	9	1	0	159	162	9.2	22	63	3.6	68	3.8	4.19	99	.261	.329	-3	-1	102	101	2.6	0	-2	-0.2
1956	Pit-N	3	3	.500	18	2	1	0	0	29	36	11.2	5	12	3.7	17	5.3	4.66	84	.298	.358	-3	-2	103	116	0.4	1	0	-0.1
1957	Pit-N	3	11	.214	54	10	0	0	1	131	151	10.4	19	31	2.1	101	6.9	4.67	80	.282	.323	-12	-14	96	96	-3.3	-1	-2	-1.6
1959	Cin-N	1	0	1.000	10	0	0	0	0	14	17	10.9	0	11	7.1	8	5.1	3.86	105	.321	.389	0	0	103	155	0.5	-0	0	0.0
1960	NY-A	5	1	.833	29	0	0	0	7	41	30	6.6	2	22	4.8	29	6.4	2.85	125	.207	.306	5	3	92	94	1.7	-0	0	0.3
1961	NY-A	15	5	.750	**65**	0	0	0	**29**	119	83	6.3	5	49	3.7	87	6.6	2.19	171	.199	.279	**24**	21	93	103	2.6	2	-1	2.1
1962	NY-A	1	3	.250	27	0	0	0	7	34	33	8.7	5	17	4.5	21	5.6	4.76	76	.262	.347	-3	-4	92	102	-1.1	1	-0	-0.3
1963	NY-A	1	1	.500	6	0	0	0	0	6	12	18.0	0	3	4.5	5	7.5	13.50	26	.444	.469	-7	-7	98	68	-0.1	0	-0	-0.6
Total	8	40	32	.556	244	36	10	1	44	533	524	8.8	58	208	3.5	336	5.7	3.92	98	.256	.322	2	-4	97	102	3.3	3	-5	-0.4
■ **RUDY ARROYO** Arroyo, Rudolph b: 6/19/50, New York, N.Y. BL/TL, 6'2", 195 lbs. Deb: 6/01/71																													
1971	StL-N	0	1	.000	9	0	0	0	0	12	18	13.5	2	5	3.8	5	3.8	5.25	66	.375	.418	-2	-2	100	146	-0.4	-0	-0	-0.2
■ **HARRY ARUNDEL** Arundel, Harry b: 1854, Philadelphia, Pa. d: 3/25/04, Cleveland, Ohio Deb: 7/19/1875																													
1882	Pit-a	4	10	.286	14	14	13	0	0	120	155	11.6	3	23	1.7	47	3.5	4.65	56	.318	.349	-26	-27	97	93	-3.2	0	0	-2.2
1884	Pro-N	1	0	1.000	1	1	1	0	0	9	8	8.0	0	4	4.0	4	4.0	1.00	285	.247	.330	2	2	96	271	0.5	0	0	0.2
Total	2	5	10	.333	15	15	14	0	0	129	163	11.4	3	27	1.9	51	3.6	4.40	59	.314	.348	-24	-26	97	105	-2.7	1	0	-2.0
■ **KEN ASH** Ash, Kenneth Lowther b: 9/16/01, Anmoore, W.Va. BR/TR, 5'11", 165 lbs. Deb: 4/17/25																													
1925	Chi-A	0	0	—	2	0	0	0	0	4	7	15.8	2	0	0.0	0	0.0	9.00	46	.389	.389	-2	-2	95	108	0.0	0	-0	-0.1
1928	Cin-N	3	3	.500	8	5	2	0	0	36	43	10.8	1	13	3.3	6	1.5	6.50	59	.314	.368	-10	-11	97	73	0.0	-1	0	-1.0
1929	Cin-N	1	5	.167	29	7	2	0	2	82	91	10.0	2	30	3.3	26	2.9	4.83	98	.292	.354	-1	-1	101	93	-1.8	-1	0	-0.1
1930	Cin-N	2	0	1.000	16	1	1	0	0	39	37	8.5	1	16	3.7	15	3.5	3.46	134	.268	.331	7	5	93	113	1.0	-1	1	0.5
Total	4	6	8	.429	55	13	5	0	2	161	178	10.0	6	59	3.3	47	2.6	4.98	90	.294	.353	-7	-8	98	93	-0.8	-3	1	-0.7
■ **PAUL ASSENMACHER** Assenmacher, Paul Andre b: 12/10/60, Detroit, Mich. BL/TL, 6'3", 195 lbs. Deb: 4/12/86																													
1986	Atl-N	7	3	.700	61	0	0	0	7	68	61	8.1	5	26	3.4	56	7.4	2.51	153	.241	.303	9	10	103	130	2.4	-0	1	1.2
1987	Atl-N	1	1	.500	52	0	0	0	2	55	58	9.5	8	24	3.9	39	6.4	5.07	88	.260	.331	-6	-4	109	87	0.1	-0	-1	-0.4
1988	Atl-N	8	7	.533	64	0	0	0	5	79	72	8.2	4	32	3.6	71	8.1	3.08	120	.251	.319	3	5	107	116	2.4	1	0	0.7
Total	3	16	11	.593	177	0	0	0	14	202	191	8.5	17	82	3.7	166	7.4	3.43	115	.250	.317	6	12	106	113	4.9	0	1	1.5
■ **KEITH ATHERTON** Atherton, Keith Rowe b: 2/19/59, Mathews, Va. BR/TR, 6'4", 200 lbs. Deb: 7/14/83																													
1983	Oak-A	2	5	.286	29	0	0	0	4	68	53	7.0	7	23	3.0	40	5.3	2.78	141	.215	.278	10	9	96	102	-1.2	0	-1	0.8
1984	Oak-A	7	6	.538	57	0	0	0	2	104	110	9.5	13	39	3.4	58	5.0	4.33	85	.274	.333	-4	-7	92	105	0.8	0	-2	-0.9
1985	Oak-A	4	7	.364	56	0	0	0	3	105	89	7.6	17	42	3.6	77	6.6	4.29	90	.231	.301	-2	-5	93	89	-1.3	0	-2	-0.6
1986	Oak-A	1	2	.333	13	0	0	0	0	15	18	10.8	2	11	6.6	8	4.8	6.00	65	.295	.387	-3	-3	94	102	-0.3	0	-0	-0.3
	Min-A	5	8	.385	47	0	0	0	10	82	82	9.0	9	35	3.8	59	6.5	3.73	123	.264	.331	4	8	109	116	-0.8	0	-0	0.7
	Yr	6	10	.375	60	0	0	0	10	97	100	9.3	11	46	4.3	67	6.2	4.08	110	.267	.341	1	4	107	116	-1.1	0	-0	0.4
1987	Min-A	7	5	.583	59	0	0	0	2	79	81	9.2	10	30	3.4	51	5.8	4.56	94	.262	.330	-1	-2	96	96	0.8	0	0	-0.1
1988	Min-A	7	5	.583	49	0	0	0	3	74	65	7.9	10	22	2.7	43	5.2	3.41	123	.235	.288	5	6	105	102	0.3	0	-0	0.6
Total	6	33	38	.465	310	0	0	0	24	527	498	8.5	68	202	3.4	336	5.7	3.98	102	.250	.315	9	5	98	101	-1.7	0	-5	0.2

YEAR	TM/L	W	L	PCT	G	GS	CG	SHO	SV	IP	H	H/G	HR	BB	BB/G	SO	SO/G	ERA	/A	OAVG	OOBP	PR	/A	PF	CPI	WAT	PB	PD	TPI
■ **TOMMY ATKINS**	Atkins, Francis Montgomery b: 12/9/1887, Ponca, Neb. d: 5/7/56, Cleveland, Ohio BL/TL, 5'10.5", 165 lbs. Deb: 10/02/09																												
1909	Phi-A	0	0	—	1	1	0	0	0	6	6	9.0	0	5	7.5	4	6.0	4.50	54	.261	.393	-1	-1	97	91	0.0	-0	0	0.0
1910	Phi-A	3	2	.600	15	3	2	0	2	57	53	8.4	0	23	3.6	29	4.6	2.68	91	.254	.330	-1	-2	97	108	-0.2	-1	0	-0.2
Total	2	3	2	.600	16	4	2	0	2	63	59	8.4	0	28	4.0	33	4.7	2.86	85	.254	.337	-2	-3	97	106	-0.2	-1	0	-0.2
■ **JAMES ATKINS**	Atkins, James Curtis b: 3/10/21, Birmingham, Ala. BL/TR, 6'3", 205 lbs. Deb: 9/29/50																												
1950	Bos-A	0	0	—	1	0	0	0	0	5	4	7.2	1	4	7.2	0	0.0	3.60	141	.235	.409	1	1	111	171	0.0	-0	0	0.0
1952	Bos-A	0	1	.000	3	1	0	0	0	10	11	9.9	0	7	6.3	2	1.8	3.60	109	.275	.375	0	0	107	122	-0.4	1	0	0.1
Total	2	0	1	.000	4	1	0	0	0	15	15	9.0	1	11	6.6	2	1.2	3.60	120	.263	.386	1	1	108	138	-0.4	0	0	0.1
■ **AL ATKINSON**	Atkinson, Albert Wright b: 3/9/1861, Clinton, Ill. d: 6/17/52, Elkhorn Township Mo. BR/TR, 5'11.5", 165 lbs. Deb: 5/01/1884																												
1884	Phi-a	11	11	.500	22	22	20	1	0	184	186	9.1	3	21	1.0	93	4.5	4.21	87	.271	.292	-20	-11	113	76	-1.6	-2	0	-0.9
	CP-U	6	10	.375	16	16	16	1	0	140	127	8.2	1	21	1.4	104	6.7	1.48	204	.247	.276	24	24	100	165	-1.5	-3	0	1.9
	Bal-U	3	5	.375	8	8	8	0	0	70	60	7.7	4	12	1.5	50	6.4	4.89	68	.237	.271	-15	-12	110	54	-1.3	-2	0	-1.1
	Yr	9	15	.375	24	24	24	1	0	210	187	8.0	5	33	1.4	154	6.6	2.61	119	.243	.275	9	12	103	54	-2.8	-3	0	0.8
1886	Phi-a	25	17	.595	45	45	44	1	0	397	414	9.4	11	101	2.3	154	3.5	3.97	89	.279	.325	-23	-19	103	91	6.6	-6	-1	-2.1
1887	Phi-a	6	8	.429	15	15	11	0	0	125	156	11.2	2	54	3.9	34	2.4	5.98	72	.320	.388	-23	-24	100	84	-0.7	-0	0	-1.7
Total	3	51	51	.500	106	106	99	3	0	916	943	9.3	21	209	2.1	435	4.3	3.98	90	.275	.317	-57	-41	104	95	1.5	-14	-1	-3.9
■ **BILL ATKINSON**	Atkinson, William Cecil Glenn b: 10/4/54, Chatham, Ont., Can. BL/TR, 5'7", 165 lbs. Deb: 9/18/76																												
1976	Mon-N	0	0	—	4	0	0	0	0	5	3	5.4	0	1	1.8	4	7.2	0.00	—	.176	.222	2	2	103	0	0.0	0	0	0.2
1977	Mon-N	7	2	.778	55	0	0	0	7	83	72	7.8	12	29	3.1	56	6.1	3.36	116	.234	.292	5	5	99	103	2.7	-0	1	0.6
1978	Mon-N	2	2	.500	29	0	0	0	3	45	45	9.0	5	28	5.6	32	6.4	4.40	78	.268	.363	-4	-5	96	113	0.1	1	0	-0.3
1979	Mon-N	2	0	1.000	10	0	0	0	1	14	9	5.8	0	4	2.6	7	4.5	1.93	196	.170	.228	3	3	101	19	1.0	-0	-0	0.2
Total	4	11	4	.733	98	0	0	0	11	147	129	7.9	17	62	3.8	99	6.1	3.43	108	.236	.307	6	5	98	95	3.8	1	1	0.7
■ **DON AUGUST**	August, Donald Glenn b: 7/3/63, Inglewood, Cal. BR/TR, 6'3", 190 lbs. Deb: 6/02/88																												
1988	Mil-A	13	7	.650	24	22	6	1	0	148	137	8.3	12	48	2.9	66	4.0	3.10	132	.245	.301	14	16	103	107	2.7	0	2	1.9
■ **JERRY AUGUSTINE**	Augustine, Gerald Lee b: 7/24/52, Kewaunee, Wis. BL/TL, 6', 183 lbs. Deb: 9/09/75																												
1975	Mil-A	2	0	1.000	5	3	1	0	0	27	26	8.7	2	12	4.0	8	2.7	3.00	128	.274	.351	2	3	101	147	1.0	0	-0	0.2
1976	Mil-A	9	12	.429	39	24	5	3	0	172	167	8.7	9	56	2.9	59	3.1	3.30	107	.261	.317	4	4	100	106	0.4	0	-2	0.2
1977	Mil-A	12	18	.400	33	33	10	1	0	209	222	9.6	23	72	3.1	68	2.9	4.48	88	.277	.331	-9	-13	97	98	-0.5	0	0	-1.2
1978	Mil-A	13	12	.520	35	30	9	2	0	188	204	9.8	14	61	2.9	59	2.8	4.55	87	.280	.332	-16	-13	104	90	-1.3	0	2	-1.0
1979	Mil-A	9	6	.600	43	2	0	0	5	86	95	9.9	6	30	3.1	41	4.3	3.45	122	.284	.336	7	7	99	124	0.2	0	-2	0.5
1980	Mil-A	4	3	.571	39	1	0	0	2	70	83	10.7	5	36	4.6	22	2.8	4.50	84	.301	.377	-4	-6	93	116	0.3	0	0	-0.4
1981	Mil-A	2	2	.500	27	2	0	0	2	61	75	11.1	4	18	2.7	26	3.8	4.28	82	.300	.346	-4	-5	95	106	-0.2	0	0	-0.5
1982	Mil-A	1	3	.250	20	2	1	0	0	62	63	9.1	13	26	3.8	22	3.2	5.08	74	.267	.337	-7	-9	92	102	-1.1	0	-1	-0.9
1983	Mil-A	3	3	.500	34	7	1	0	2	64	89	12.5	11	25	3.5	40	5.6	5.77	64	.328	.378	-12	-15	91	113	-0.1	0	-0	-1.4
1984	Mil-A	0	0	—	4	0	0	0	0	5	4	7.2	0	4	7.2	3	5.4	0.00	—	.211	.375	2	2	93	0	0.0	0	0	0.2
Total	10	55	59	.482	279	104	27	6	11	944	1028	9.8	87	340	3.2	348	3.3	4.23	90	.281	.338	-36	-44	98	104	-1.3	0	-3	-4.3
■ **ELDON AUKER**	Auker, Eldon LeRoy "Submarine" b: 9/21/10, Norcatur, Kan. BR/TR, 6'2", 194 lbs. Deb: 8/10/33																												
1933	Det-A	3	3	.500	15	6	2	1	0	55	63	10.3	3	25	4.1	17	2.8	5.24	87	.285	.359	-6	-4	107	92	0.1	-1	-1	-0.5
1934	Det-A	15	7	.682	43	18	10	2	1	205	234	10.3	9	56	2.5	86	3.8	3.42	123	.288	.333	24	18	94	123	1.0	-2	3	1.8
1935	Det-A	18	7	**.720**	36	25	13	2	0	195	213	9.8	13	61	2.8	63	2.9	3.83	108	.279	.337	14	6	93	112	3.9	1	1	0.7
1936	Det-A	13	16	.448	35	31	14	2	0	215	263	11.0	11	83	3.5	66	2.8	4.90	97	.302	.360	3	-3	95	105	-2.8	8	4	0.7
1937	Det-A	17	9	.654	39	32	19	1	1	253	250	8.9	13	97	3.5	73	2.6	3.88	128	.260	.327	21	31	108	97	2.7	4	5	3.9
1938	Det-A	11	10	.524	27	24	12	1	0	161	184	10.3	14	56	3.1	46	2.6	5.25	90	.284	.342	-8	-9	99	88	-0.4	-4	2	-0.8
1939	Bos-A	9	10	.474	31	25	6	1	0	151	183	10.9	13	61	3.6	43	2.6	5.36	92	.294	.352	-12	-7	107	94	-2.0	1	2	-0.3
1940	StL-A	16	11	.593	38	35	20	2	0	264	299	10.2	17	96	3.3	78	2.7	3.95	120	.281	.338	13	23	108	111	4.3	2	2	2.7
1941	StL-A	14	15	.483	34	31	13	0	0	216	268	11.2	20	85	3.5	60	2.5	5.50	76	.303	.362	-32	-31	101	95	0.9	-3	1	-2.9
1942	StL-A	14	13	.519	35	34	17	2	0	249	273	9.9	16	86	3.1	62	2.2	4.08	92	.277	.331	-12	-10	102	102	-0.6	-1	1	-0.9
Total	10	130	101	.563	333	261	126	14	2	1964	2230	10.2	129	706	3.2	594	2.7	4.42	101	.285	.342	4	14	101	103	7.1	5	20	4.4
■ **DENNIS AUST**	Aust, Dennis Kay b: 11/25/40, Tecumseh, Neb. BR/TR, 5'11", 180 lbs. Deb: 9/06/65																												
1965	StL-N	0	0	—	6	0	0	0	1	7	6	7.7	0	2	2.6	7	9.0	5.14	73	.214	.258	-1	-1	106	31	0.0	-0	0	0.0
1966	StL-N	0	1	.000	9	0	0	0	1	10	12	10.8	1	6	5.4	7	6.3	6.30	57	.308	.391	-3	-3	100	92	-0.4	-0	0	-0.2
Total	2	0	1	.000	15	0	0	0	2	17	18	9.5	1	8	4.2	14	7.4	5.82	63	.269	.338	-4	-4	102	67	-0.4	-0	0	-0.2
■ **RICK AUSTIN**	Austin, Rick Gerald b: 10/27/46, Seattle, Was. BR/TL, 6'4", 190 lbs. Deb: 6/21/70																												
1970	Cle-A	2	5	.286	31	8	1	1	3	68	74	9.8	10	26	3.4	53	7.0	4.76	90	.281	.346	-8	-4	115	103	-1.3	-0	1	-0.2
1971	Cle-A	0	0	—	23	0	0	0	1	23	25	9.8	3	20	7.8	20	7.8	5.09	74	.291	.417	-4	-3	108	130	0.0	-0	0	-0.2
1975	Mil-A	2	3	.400	32	0	0	0	2	40	32	7.2	3	32	7.2	30	6.7	4.05	95	.222	.363	-1	-1	101	99	0.0	0	-1	-0.1
1976	Mil-A	0	0	—	3	0	0	0	0	5	10	18.0	1	0	0.0	3	5.4	5.40	65	.435	.423	-1	-1	100	177	0.0	0	0	0.0
Total	4	4	8	.333	89	8	1	1	6	136	141	9.3	17	78	5.2	106	7.0	4.63	87	.273	.367	-14	-9	109	109	-1.3	-0	1	-0.5
■ **AL AUTRY**	Autry, Albert b: 2/29/52, Modesto, Cal. BR/TR, 6'5", 225 lbs. Deb: 9/14/76																												
1976	Atl-N	1	0	1.000	1	1	0	0	0	5	4	7.2	2	3	5.4	3	5.4	5.40	73	.222	.333	-1	-1	112	110	0.5	-0	-0	0.0
■ **JAY AVREA**	Avrea, James Epherium b: 7/6/20, Cleburne, Tex. BR/TR, 6'1.5", 175 lbs. Deb: 4/22/50																												
1950	Cin-N	0	0	—	2	0	0	0	0	5	6	10.8	0	3	5.4	2	3.6	3.60	122	.273	.360	0	0	106	109	0.0	-0	0	0.0
■ **JAKE AYDELOTT**	Aydelott, Jacob Stuart b: 7/6/1861, N.Manchester, Ind. d: 10/22/26, Detroit, Mich. 6', 180 lbs. Deb: 5/15/1884																												
1884	Ind-a	5	7	.417	12	12	11	0	0	106	129	11.0	0	29	2.5	30	2.5	4.92	66	.309	.354	-20	-20	100	92	1.3	-3	0	-1.8
1886	Phi-a	0	2	.000	2	2	2	0	0	18	21	10.5	0	12	6.0	5	2.5	4.00	89	.302	.405	-1	-1	103	130	-0.9	-1	0	0.0
Total	2	5	9	.357	14	14	13	0	0	124	150	10.9	0	41	3.0	35	2.5	4.79	69	.308	.362	-21	-21	101	98	0.4	-4	0	-1.8
■ **BILL AYERS**	Ayers, William Oscar b: 9/27/19, Newnan, Ga. d: 9/24/80, Newnan, Ga. BR/TR, 6'3", 185 lbs. Deb: 4/17/47																												
1947	NY-N	0	3	.000	13	4	0	0	1	35	46	11.8	7	14	3.6	22	5.7	8.23	49	.322	.379	-16	-16	99	80	-1.4	0	0	-1.3
■ **DOC AYERS**	Ayers, Yancy Wyatt b: 5/20/1890, Fancy Gap, Va. d: 5/26/68, Pulaski, Va. BR/TR, 6'1", 185 lbs. Deb: 9/09/13																												
1913	Was-A	1	1	.500	4	2	1	1	1	18	12	6.0	0	4	2.0	17	8.5	1.50	205	.182	.239	3	3	105	40	0.0	-1	1	0.4
1914	Was-A	12	15	.444	49	32	8	3	3	265	221	7.5	5	54	1.8	148	5.0	2.55	107	.238	.286	6	5	100	85	-2.4	0	-2	0.4
1915	Was-A	14	9	.609	40	16	8	2	3	211	178	7.6	1	38	1.6	96	4.1	2.22	132	.234	.276	17	17	99	88	1.6	-1	-4	1.1
1916	Was-A	5	9	.357	43	17	7	0	2	157	173	9.9	4	52	3.0	69	4.0	3.78	75	.285	.346	-17	-17	100	99	-2.0	-2	-4	-2.3
1917	Was-A	11	10	.524	40	15	12	3	1	208	192	8.3	3	59	2.6	78	3.4	2.16	114	.256	.317	12	7	93	128	0.9	0	-0	0.7
1918	Was-A	10	12	.455	40	24	11	4	3	220	215	8.8	2	63	2.6	67	2.7	2.82	101	.261	.312	-1	1	103	98	-2.4	-2	1	0.0
1919	Was-A	0	6	.000	11	5	0	0	1	44	52	10.6	0	17	3.5	12	2.5	2.86	111	.317	.395	2	2	99	163	-2.9	2	1	0.4
	Det-A	5	3	.625	24	5	3	1	0	94	88	8.4	2	31	3.0	32	3.1	2.68	111	.254	.320	6	3	92	105	0.5	-1	-0	0.2
	Yr	5	9	.357	35	10	3	1	1	138	140	9.1	2	48	3.1	44	2.9	2.74	111	.272	.337	7	5	94	105	-2.4	2	1	0.6
1920	Det-A	7	14	.333	46	23	8	3	1	209	217	9.3	6	62	2.7	103	**4.4**	3.88	104	.280	.340	-2	4	106	93	-1.8	-3	-0	0.1
1921	Det-A	0	0	—	2	1	0	0	0	4	9	20.3	0	2	4.5	0	0.0	9.00	46	.450	.478	-2	-2	96	110	0.0	0	-0	-0.1
Total	9	65	79	.451	299	140	58	17	15	1430	1357	8.5	23	382	2.4	622	3.9	2.84	105	.259	.314	23	21	100	100	-8.5	-8	-8	0.9
■ **BOB BABCOCK**	Babcock, Robert Ernest b: 8/25/49, New Castle, Pa. BR/TR, 6'5", 210 lbs. Deb: 7/22/79																												
1979	Tex-A	0	0	—	4	0	0	0	0	5	7	12.6	1	7	12.6	6	10.8	10.80	39	.318	.452	-4	-4	99	84	0.0	0	0	-0.2
1980	Tex-A	1	2	.333	19	0	0	0	0	23	20	7.8	3	8	3.1	15	5.9	4.70	86	.238	.306	-2	-2	100	80	-0.3	0	-0	-0.1
1981	Tex-A	1	1	.500	16	0	0	0	0	29	21	6.5	2	16	5.0	18	5.6	2.17	152	.219	.325	5	4	90	161	0.0	0	0	0.4
Total	3	2	3	.400	39	0	0	0	0	57	48	7.6	6	31	4.9	39	6.2	3.95	93	.238	.333	-1	-2	95	121	-0.3	0	0	0.1

YEAR	TM/L	W	L	PCT	G	GS	CG	SHO	SV	IP	H	H/G	HR	BB	BB/G	SO	SO/G	ERA	/A	OAVG	OOBP	PR	/A	PF	CPI	WAT	PB	PD	TPI
■ **JOHNNY BABICH**	Babich, John Charles b: 5/14/13, Albion, Cal. BR/TR, 6'1.5", 185 lbs. Deb: 6/19/34																												
1934	Bro-N	7	11	.389	25	19	7	0	1	135	148	9.9	5	51	3.4	62	4.1	4.20	92	.281	.341	-2	-5	95	99	-1.6	-3	2	-0.5
1935	Bro-N	7	14	.333	37	24	7	2	0	143	191	12.0	7	52	3.3	55	3.5	6.67	57	.317	.366	-42	-45	95	79	-3.1	-0	-0	-4.1
1936	Bos-N	0	0	—	3	0	0	0	0	6	11	16.5	1	6	9.0	1	1.5	10.50	37	.440	.545	-4	-4	96	115	0.0	-0	0	-0.3
1940	Phi-A	14	13	.519	31	30	16	1	0	229	222	8.7	16	80	3.1	94	3.7	3.73	116	.248	.307	17	15	99	92	4.0	-5	0	1.0
1941	Phi-A	2	7	.222	16	14	4	0	0	78	85	9.8	9	31	3.6	19	2.2	6.12	70	.281	.347	-17	-16	103	80	-2.1	4	1	-0.9
Total	5	30	45	.400	112	87	34	3	1	591	657	10.0	38	220	3.4	231	3.5	4.93	83	.279	.338	-49	-55	98	89	-2.8	-5	3	-4.8
■ **LES BACKMAN**	Backman, Lester John b: 3/20/1888, Cleves, Ohio d: 11/8/75, Cincinnati, Ohio TR, 6'0.5", 195 lbs. Deb: 09																												
1909	StL-N	3	11	.214	21	14	8	0	0	128	146	10.3	1	39	2.7	35	2.5	4.15	62	.302	.357	-22	-22	99	95	-2.8	-1	-0	-2.3
1910	StL-N	6	7	.462	26	11	4	0	2	116	117	9.1	4	53	4.1	41	3.2	3.03	93	.265	.346	0	-3	93	117	0.6	0	-1	-0.2
Total	2	9	18	.333	47	25	12	0	2	244	263	9.7	5	92	3.4	76	2.8	3.61	75	.284	.352	-22	-25	96	106	-2.2	-1	-1	-2.5
■ **EDDIE BACON**	Bacon, Edgar Suter b: 4/8/1895, Franklin Co., Ky. d: 10/2/63, Frankfurt, Ky. Deb: 8/13/17																												
1917	Phi-A	0	0	—	1	0	0	0	0	6	5	7.5	0	7	10.5	0	0.0	6.00	43	.238	.429	-2	-2	97	77	0.0	1	1	-0.1
■ **MIKE BACSIK**	Bacsik, Michael James b: 4/1/52, Dallas, Tex. BR/TR, 6'2", 180 lbs. Deb: 6/15/75																												
1975	Tex-A	1	2	.333	7	3	0	0	0	27	28	9.3	1	9	3.0	13	4.3	3.67	103	.275	.328	0	0	100	102	-0.4	0	-0	0.0
1976	Tex-A	3	2	.600	23	0	0	0	0	55	66	10.8	3	26	4.3	21	3.4	4.25	85	.308	.375	-4	-4	103	123	0.6	0	-1	-0.4
1977	Tex-A	0	0	—	2	0	0	0	0	2	9	40.5	1	0	0.0	1	4.5	22.50	19	.563	.563	-4	-4	104	96	0.0	0	0	-0.3
1979	Min-A	4	2	.667	31	0	0	0	0	66	61	8.3	6	29	4.0	33	4.5	4.36	105	.249	.318	-1	2	108	86	1.0	0	-0	0.1
1980	Min-A	0	0	—	10	0	0	0	0	23	26	10.2	1	11	4.3	9	3.5	4.30	103	.286	.356	-1	0	109	102	0.0	0	0	0.0
Total	5	8	6	.571	73	3	0	0	0	173	190	9.9	12	75	3.9	77	4.0	4.42	93	.284	.348	-10	-6	105	102	1.2	0	-1	-0.6
■ **FRED BACZEWSKI**	Baczewski, Frederic John "Lefty" b: 5/15/26, St.Paul, Minn. d: 11/14/76, Culver City, Cal. BL/TL, 6'2.5", 185 lbs. Deb: 4/26/53																												
1953	Chi-N	0	0	—	9	0	0	0	0	10	20	18.0	1	6	5.4	3	2.7	6.30	72	.435	.509	-2	-2	106	166	0.0	0	0	-0.1
	Cin-N	11	4	.733	24	18	10	1	1	138	125	8.2	13	52	3.4	58	3.8	3.46	124	.244	.310	13	13	100	104	4.1	-0	-3	1.0
	Yr	11	4	.733	33	18	10	1	1	148	145	8.8	14	58	3.5	61	3.7	3.65	118	.259	.325	10	11	101	104	4.1	0	-3	0.9
1954	Cin-N	6	6	.500	29	22	4	1	0	130	159	11.0	22	53	3.7	43	3.0	5.26	81	.305	.363	-17	-15	104	108	0.2	-4	-1	-1.7
1955	Cin-N	0	0	—	1	0	0	0	0	1	2	18.0	2	0	0.0	0	0.0	18.00	23	.400	.400	-2	-2	104	122	0.0	0	0	0.0
Total	3	17	10	.630	63	40	14	2	1	279	306	9.9	38	111	3.6	104	3.4	4.45	96	.282	.344	-8	-5	102	108	4.3	-3	-4	-0.8
■ **KING BADER**	Bader, Lore Verne "Lore" or "King" d: 6/2/73, Le Roy, Kan. BL/TR, 6', 175 lbs. Deb: 9/30/12 C																												
1912	NY-N	2	0	1.000	2	1	1	0	0	10	9	8.1	0	6	5.4	3	2.7	0.90	376	.231	.348	3	3	99	314	1.0	-0	0	0.3
1917	Bos-A	2	0	1.000	15	1	0	0	1	38	48	11.4	1	18	4.3	14	3.3	2.37	119	.306	.381	1	2	106	196	1.0	1	1	0.4
1918	Bos-A	1	3	.250	5	4	2	1	0	27	26	8.7	1	12	4.0	10	3.3	3.33	77	.271	.353	-2	-2	93	118	-1.1	-1	-1	-0.3
Total	3	5	3	.625	22	6	3	1	1	75	83	10.0	2	36	4.3	27	3.2	2.52	111	.284	.367	2	2	100	184	0.9	-1	-0	0.4
■ **ED BAECHT**	Baecht, Edward Joseph b: 5/15/07, Paden, Okla. d: 8/15/57, Grafton, Ill. BR/TR, 6'3", 195 lbs. Deb: 4/24/26																												
1926	Phi-N	2	0	1.000	28	1	1	0	0	56	73	11.7	4	28	4.5	14	2.3	6.11	67	.324	.378	-14	-13	107	95	1.0	-1	2	-1.0
1927	Phi-N	0	1	.000	1	1	0	0	0	6	12	18.0	0	2	3.0	0	0.0	12.00	33	.429	.452	-5	-5	100	70	-0.4	-0	0	-0.3
1928	Phi-N	1	1	.500	9	1	0	0	0	24	37	13.9	1	9	3.4	10	3.8	6.00	73	.385	.418	-5	-4	109	116	0.3	-0	0	-0.3
1931	Chi-N	2	4	.333	22	6	2	0	0	67	64	8.6	1	32	4.3	34	4.6	3.76	96	.250	.346	-1	-1	94	97	-1.1	1	1	0.1
1932	Chi-N	0	0	—	1	0	0	0	0	1	1	9.0	0	1	9.0	0	0.0	0.00	—	.333	.500	0	0	103	0	0.0	0	0	0.0
1937	StL-A	0	0	—	3	0	0	0	0	6	13	19.5	3	6	9.0	3	4.5	13.50	35	.419	.538	-6	-6	103	113	0.0	-0	0	-0.4
Total	6	5	6	.455	64	9	3	0	0	160	200	11.2	9	78	4.4	61	3.4	5.57	71	.313	.383	-30	-29	101	98	-0.2	-1	3	-1.9
■ **JIM BAGBY**	Bagby, James Charles Jacob Jr. b: 9/8/16, Cleveland, Ohio d: 9/2/88, Marietta, Ga. BR/TR, 6'2", 170 lbs. Deb: 4/18/38																												
1938	Bos-A	15	11	.577	43	25	10	1	2	199	218	9.9	9	90	4.1	73	3.3	4.21	114	.283	.356	13	13	100	110	-0.3	-0	2	1.3
1939	Bos-A	5	5	.500	21	11	3	0	0	80	119	13.4	7	36	4.0	35	3.9	7.09	70	.347	.405	-22	-19	107	97	-0.7	2	-0	-1.4
1940	Bos-A	10	16	.385	36	21	6	1	2	183	217	10.7	15	83	4.1	57	2.8	4.72	93	.296	.363	-7	-7	100	110	-4.0	-0	0	-0.6
1941	Cle-A	9	15	.375	33	27	12	0	2	201	214	9.6	10	76	3.4	53	2.4	4.03	103	.273	.338	3	3	101	102	-3.0	2	1	0.6
1942	Cle-A	17	9	.654	38	35	16	4	1	271	267	8.9	19	64	2.1	54	1.8	2.96	115	.258	.299	21	13	93	114	4.8	1	0	1.4
1943	Cle-A	17	14	.548	36	33	16	3	1	**273**	248	8.2	15	80	2.6	70	2.3	3.10	95	.240	.292	6	-5	90	92	0.5	5	3	0.3
1944	Cle-A	4	5	.444	13	10	2	0	0	79	101	11.5	2	34	3.9	12	1.4	4.33	80	.312	.378	-8	-8	101	116	-0.1	1	0	-0.6
1945	Cle-A	8	11	.421	25	19	11	3	1	159	171	9.7	3	59	3.3	38	2.2	3.74	89	.279	.337	-7	-8	98	102	-1.6	3	3	-0.1
1946	Bos-A	7	6	.538	21	11	6	1	0	107	117	9.8	4	49	4.1	16	1.3	3.70	105	.279	.351	2	2	111	111	-1.3	-2	-0	0.6
1947	Pit-N	5	4	.556	37	6	2	0	0	116	143	11.1	14	37	2.9	23	1.8	4.66	89	.304	.355	-8	-6	102	113	1.2	1	1	-0.4
Total	10	97	96	.503	303	198	84	13	9	1668	1815	9.8	98	608	3.3	431	2.3	3.96	97	.278	.337	-11	-24	98	106	-4.5	12	10	0.5
■ **JIM BAGBY**	Bagby, James Charles Jacob Sr. "Sarge" b: 10/5/1889, Barnett, Ga. d: 7/28/54, Marietta, Ga. BB/TR, 6', 170 lbs. Deb: 4/22/12																												
1912	Cin-N	2	1	.667	5	1	0	0	0	17	17	9.0	2	9	4.8	10	5.3	3.18	100	.266	.356	0	0	93	135	0.5	-1	0	0.0
1916	Cle-A	16	16	.500	48	27	14	3	5	273	253	8.3	2	67	2.2	88	2.9	2.60	108	.251	.303	7	6	99	96	0.0	-0	-2	0.4
1917	Cle-A	23	13	.639	49	37	26	8	7	321	277	7.8	6	73	2.0	83	2.3	1.96	154	.235	.283	25	38	113	103	3.5	2	-2	4.5
1918	Cle-A	17	16	.515	**45**	31	23	2	6	271	274	9.1	0	78	2.6	57	1.9	2.69	110	.276	.318	2	8	107	113	-2.1	0	-2	0.8
1919	Cle-A	17	11	.607	35	32	21	0	3	241	258	9.6	3	44	1.6	61	2.3	2.80	120	.275	.310	11	15	104	100	0.1	5	-0	2.1
1920	Cle-A	**31**	12	**.721**	**48**	38	**30**	3	0	**340**	338	8.9	9	79	2.1	73	1.9	2.89	132	.266	.311	34	34	100	101	**6.4**	6	-7	3.3
1921	Cle-A	14	12	.538	40	26	13	0	4	192	238	11.2	14	44	2.1	37	1.7	4.69	88	.308	.340	-9	-12	96	97	-1.7	-1	-2	-1.3
1922	Cle-A	4	5	.444	25	10	4	0	1	98	134	12.3	5	39	3.6	25	2.3	6.34	65	.340	.390	-25	-24	103	92	-0.5	2	1	-1.8
1923	Pit-N	3	2	.600	21	6	2	0	3	69	95	12.4	6	25	3.3	16	2.1	5.22	73	.336	.377	-9	-11	95	112	0.2	-2	-1	-1.2
Total	9	127	88	.591	316	208	133	16	29	1822	1884	9.3	47	458	2.3	450	2.2	3.11	109	.273	.317	37	59	103	102	6.4	11	-15	6.8
■ **STAN BAHNSEN**	Bahnsen, Stanley Raymond b: 12/15/44, Council Bluffs, Ia. BR/TR, 6'2", 185 lbs. Deb: 9/09/66																												
1966	NY-A	1	1	.500	4	3	1	0	1	23	15	5.9	3	7	2.7	16	6.3	3.52	91	.181	.244	-0	-1	94	59	0.1	-0	-0	0.0
1968	NY-A	17	12	.586	37	34	10	1	0	267	216	7.3	14	68	2.3	162	5.5	2.06	146	.221	.267	27	28	101	111	2.6	-4	-2	2.6
1969	NY-A	9	16	.360	40	33	5	2	1	221	222	9.0	28	90	3.7	130	5.3	3.83	91	.260	.326	-5	-9	96	109	-3.8	-3	1	-1.1
1970	NY-A	14	11	.560	36	35	6	2	0	233	227	8.8	23	75	2.9	116	4.5	3.32	102	.256	.311	10	2	91	109	-0.3	-0	1	0.2
1971	NY-A	14	12	.538	36	34	14	3	0	242	221	8.2	20	72	2.7	110	4.1	3.35	100	.248	.300	3	0	97	97	1.0	-0	3	0.3
1972	Chi-A	21	16	.568	43	41	5	1	0	252	263	9.4	22	73	2.6	157	5.6	3.61	90	.268	.318	-15	-10	106	104	0.1	-1	2	-0.9
1973	Chi-A	18	21	.462	42	42	14	4	0	282	290	9.3	20	117	3.7	120	3.8	3.57	110	.269	.338	8	11	103	112	-0.6	0	2	1.4
1974	Chi-A	12	15	.444	38	35	10	1	0	216	230	9.6	17	110	4.6	102	4.3	4.71	79	.277	.359	-26	-24	102	96	-1.7	0	1	-2.3
1975	Chi-A	4	6	.400	12	12	2	0	0	67	78	10.5	9	40	5.4	31	4.2	6.04	65	.291	.387	-17	-16	104	94	-0.6	0	-0	-1.4
	Oak-A	6	7	.462	21	16	2	0	0	100	88	7.9	2	37	3.3	49	4.4	3.24	107	.238	.304	6	2	91	86	-1.5	0	0	0.2
	Yr	10	13	.435	33	28	4	0	0	167	166	8.9	11	77	4.1	80	4.3	4.37	84	.259	.335	-11	-13	96	88	-2.1	0	0	-1.2
1976	Oak-A	8	7	.533	35	14	1	1	0	143	124	7.8	13	43	2.7	82	5.2	3.34	104	.232	.287	3	2	98	88	0.0	0	1	0.3
1977	Oak-A	1	2	.333	11	2	0	0	1	22	24	9.8	5	13	5.3	21	8.6	6.14	64	.286	.380	-5	-5	97	103	-0.1	0	-1	-0.5
	Mon-N	8	9	.471	23	22	3	1	0	127	142	10.1	14	38	2.7	58	4.1	4.82	81	.283	.329	-13	-13	99	90	0.1	-1	-0	-1.3
1978	Mon-N	1	5	.167	44	1	0	0	7	75	74	8.9	9	31	3.7	44	5.3	3.84	89	.261	.331	-2	-4	96	110	-1.9	-1	-0	-0.4
1979	Mon-N	3	1	.750	55	0	0	0	5	94	80	7.7	10	42	4.0	71	6.8	3.16	119	.236	.314	6	6	101	113	0.8	-0	-0	0.6
1980	Mon-N	7	6	.538	57	0	0	0	4	91	80	7.9	7	33	3.3	48	4.7	3.07	116	.235	.295	5	5	98	98	-0.1	1	-0	0.6
1981	Mon-N	2	1	.667	25	3	0	0	1	49	45	8.3	7	24	4.4	28	5.1	4.96	69	.247	.337	-8	-8	98	87	0.4	-0	-1	-1.0
1982	Cal-A	0	1	.000	7	0	0	0	0	10	13	11.7	0	8	7.2	5	4.5	4.50	90	.310	.420	-0	-1	99	126	-0.4	0	-0	0.0
	Phi-N	0	0	—	8	0	0	0	0	13	8	5.5	0	3	2.1	9	6.2	1.38	244	.182	.229	3	3	94	72	0.0	0	-0	0.3
Total	16	146	149	.495	574	327	73	16	20	2527	2440	8.7	223	924	3.3	1359	4.8	3.61	97	.255	.318	-19	-29	99	102	-5.9	-9	5	-2.4
■ **ED BAHR**	Bahr, Edson Garfield b: 10/16/19, Rouleau, Sask., Canada BR/TR, 6'1.5", 172 lbs. Deb: 5/01/46																												
1946	Pit-N	8	6	.571	27	14	7	0	0	137	128	8.4	8	52	3.4	44	2.9	2.63	137	.254	.321	12	15	106	133	2.1	-1	-0	1.5
1947	Pit-N	3	5	.375	19	11	1	0	0	82	82	9.0	5	43	4.7	25	2.7	4.61	90	.263	.356	-5	-4	102	92	-0.2	-2	-1	-0.6
Total	2	11	11	.500	46	25	8	0	0	219	210	8.6	13	95	3.9	69	2.8	3.37	113	.257	.334	7	11	104	117	1.9	-3	-1	0.9

YEAR	TM/L	W	L	PCT	G	GS	CG	SHO	SV	IP	H	H/G	HR	BB	BB/G	SO	SO/G	ERA	/A	OAVG	OOBP	PR	/A	PF	CPI	WAT	PB	PD	TPI
■ GROVER BAICHLEY	Baichley, Grover Cleveland b: 1/1890, Toledo, Ill. d: 6/30/56, San Jose, Cal. BR/TR, 5'9.5", 165 lbs. Deb: 8/24/14																												
1914	StL-A	0	0	—	4	0	0	0	0	7	9	11.6	0	3	3.9	3	3.9	5.14	53	.346	.414	-2	-2	100	103	0.0	-0	0	-0.1
■ SCOTT BAILES	Bailes, Scott Alan b: 12/18/61, Chillicothe, Ohio BL/TL, 6'2", 170 lbs. Deb: 4/09/86																												
1986	Cle-A	10	10	.500	62	10	0	0	7	113	123	9.8	12	43	3.4	60	4.8	4.94	83	.276	.334	-9	-11	98	90	-0.3	0	-1	-1.0
1987	Cle-A	7	8	.467	39	17	0	0	6	120	145	10.9	21	47	3.5	65	4.9	4.65	101	.296	.356	-2	0	105	122	1.2	0	0	0.0
1988	Cle-A	9	14	.391	37	21	5	2	0	145	149	9.2	22	46	2.9	53	3.3	4.90	83	.266	.319	-15	-14	102	90	-2.3	0	-0	-1.3
Total	3	26	32	.448	138	48	5	2	13	378	417	9.9	55	136	3.2	178	4.2	4.83	88	.279	.336	-27	-24	102	100	-1.4	0	-1	-2.3
■ SWEETBREADS BAILEY	Bailey, Abraham Lincoln b: 2/12/1895, Joliet, Ill. d: 9/27/39, Joliet, Ill. BR/TR, 6', 184 lbs. Deb: 5/23/19																												
1919	Chi-N	3	5	.375	21	5	0	0	0	71	75	9.5	2	20	2.5	19	2.4	3.17	91	.288	.336	-2	-2	99	122	-1.2	3	2	0.3
1920	Chi-N	1	2	.333	21	1	0	0	0	37	55	13.4	1	11	2.7	8	1.9	7.05	44	.359	.389	-16	-16	99	81	-0.4	-0	1	-1.6
1921	Chi-N	0	0	—	3	0	0	0	0	5	6	10.8	0	2	3.6	2	3.6	3.60	114	.300	.375	0	0	108	128	0.0	0	0	0.0
	Bro-N	0	0	—	7	0	0	0	0	24	35	13.1	1	7	2.6	6	2.3	5.25	76	.368	.402	-4	-3	105	118	0.0	-1	-0	-0.3
	Yr	0	0	—	10	0	0	0	0	29	41	12.7	1	9	2.8	8	2.5	4.97	80	.353	.389	-4	-3	105	118	0.0	0	0	-0.3
Total	3	4	7	.364	52	6	0	0	0	137	171	11.2	4	40	2.6	35	2.3	4.60	69	.324	.365	-22	-22	101	111	-1.6	2	2	-1.6
■ HARVEY BAILEY	Bailey, Harvey Francis b: 11/24/1876, Adrian, Mich. d: 7/10/22, Toledo, Ohio TL, 6', Deb: 6/30/1899																												
1899	Bos-N	6	4	.600	12	11	8	0	0	87	83	8.6	7	35	3.6	26	2.7	3.93	101	.274	.349	-1	0	103	92	-0.1	0	0	0.1
1900	Bos-N	0	0	—	4	1	0	0	0	20	24	10.8	0	11	4.9	9	4.0	4.95	90	.321	.408	-3	-1	120	94	0.0	0	0	0.0
Total	2	6	4	.600	16	12	8	0	0	107	107	9.0	7	46	3.9	35	2.9	4.12	98	.283	.361	-4	-1	106	92	-0.1	1	0	0.1
■ HOWARD BAILEY	Bailey, Howard L b: 7/31/57, Grand Haven, Mich. BR/TL, 6', 195 lbs. Deb: 4/12/81																												
1981	Det-A	1	4	.200	9	5	0	0	0	37	45	10.9	4	13	3.2	17	4.1	7.30	53	.308	.370	-15	-14	105	74	-1.5	0	1	-1.2
1982	Det-A	0	0	—	8	0	0	0	1	10	6	5.4	0	2	1.8	3	2.7	0.00	—	.182	.216	5	5	100	0	0.0	0	0	0.5
1983	Det-A	5	5	.500	33	3	0	0	0	72	69	8.6	11	25	3.1	21	2.6	4.88	79	.255	.318	-6	-8	95	87	-0.5	0	0	-0.7
Total	3	6	9	.400	50	8	0	0	1	119	120	9.1	15	40	3.0	41	3.1	5.22	74	.267	.327	-17	-18	98	76	-2.0	0	1	-1.4
■ JAMES BAILEY	Bailey, James Hopkins b: 12/16/34, Strawberry Plains, Tenn. BB/TL, 6'2.5", 210 lbs. Deb: 9/10/59																												
1959	Cin-N	0	1	.000	3	1	0	0	0	12	17	12.8	1	6	4.5	7	5.3	6.00	68	.333	.414	-3	-3	103	107	-0.4	-0	-0	-0.2
■ KING BAILEY	Bailey, Lemuel b: Cincinnati, Ohio BL/TL, 6' ", 185 lbs. Deb: 9/21/1895																												
1895	Cin-N	1	0	1.000	1	1	1	0	0	8	13	14.6	0	0	0.0	0	0.0	5.63	91	.387	.387	-1	-0	107	96	0.5	1	0	0.0
■ STEVE BAILEY	Bailey, Steven John b: 2/12/42, Bronx, N.Y. BR/TR, 6'1", 194 lbs. Deb: 4/14/67																												
1967	Cle-A	2	5	.286	32	1	0	0	2	65	62	8.6	5	42	5.8	46	6.4	3.88	84	.259	.368	-5	-4	101	122	-1.3	-1	0	-0.5
1968	Cle-A	0	1	.000	2	1	0	0	0	5	4	7.2	1	2	3.6	1	1.8	3.60	83	.235	.286	-0	-0	101	119	-0.4	0	-0	0.0
Total	2	2	6	.250	34	2	0	0	2	70	66	8.5	6	44	5.7	47	6.0	3.86	84	.258	.362	-5	-5	101	121	-1.7	-1	0	-0.5
■ BILL BAILEY	Bailey, William F. b: 4/12/1889, Ft.Smith, Ark. d: 11/2/26, Houston, Tex. BL/TL, 5'11", 165 lbs. Deb: 9/17/07																												
1907	StL-A	4	1	.800	6	5	3	0	0	48	39	7.3	0	15	2.8	17	3.2	2.44	102	.244	.309	1	0	98	86	1.6	-1	-1	0.0
1908	StL-A	3	5	.375	22	12	7	0	0	107	85	7.1	2	50	4.2	42	3.5	3.03	80	.220	.314	-8	-7	102	88	-1.2	-2	-2	-0.9
1909	StL-A	9	10	.474	32	20	17	1	0	199	174	7.9	2	75	3.4	114	5.2	2.44	96	.248	.325	1	-2	95	111	1.2	5	-1	0.2
1910	StL-A	3	18	.143	34	20	13	0	0	192	186	8.7	2	97	4.5	90	4.2	3.33	76	.262	.359	-17	-17	101	107	-5.9	0	-1	-1.9
1911	StL-A	0	3	.000	7	2	2	0	0	32	42	11.8	1	16	4.5	8	2.3	4.50	74	.339	.423	-4	-4	100	129	-1.4	-2	0	-0.3
1912	StL-A	0	1	.000	3	2	0	0	0	11	15	12.3	0	10	8.2	2	1.6	9.00	38	.341	.463	-7	-7	103	76	-0.4	1	-0	-0.6
1914	Bal-F	7	9	.438	19	18	10	1	0	129	106	7.4	2	68	4.7	131	9.1	3.07	103	.230	.338	2	1	99	98	-1.6	-0	3	0.5
1915	Bal-F	6	19	.240	36	23	11	2	0	190	179	8.5	8	115	5.4	98	4.6	4.64	73	.277	.386	-34	-27	111	86	-3.0	0	0	-2.5
	Chi-F	3	1	.750	5	5	3	3	0	33	23	6.3	1	10	2.7	24	6.5	2.18	132	.221	.289	3	3	95	84	0.9	0	0	0.3
	Yr	9	20	.310	41	28	14	5	0	223	202	8.2	9	125	5.0	122	4.9	4.28	77	.269	.373	-31	-24	109	84	-2.1	0	0	-2.2
1918	Det-A	1	2	.333	8	4	1	0	0	38	53	12.6	0	26	6.2	13	3.1	5.92	46	.368	.449	-13	-13	99	112	-0.3	-1	1	-1.3
1921	StL-N	2	5	.286	19	6	3	1	0	74	95	11.6	1	22	2.7	20	2.4	4.26	82	.330	.361	-4	-6	93	113	-1.7	-2	1	-0.6
1922	StL-N	0	2	.000	12	0	0	0	0	32	38	10.7	1	23	6.5	11	3.1	5.34	77	.325	.409	-4	-4	100	112	-0.9	0	1	-0.2
Total	11	38	76	.333	203	117	70	8	0	1085	1035	8.6	20	527	4.4	570	4.7	3.57	80	.266	.356	-85	-84	100	101	-12.7	-1	-0	-7.3
■ BOB BAILOR	Bailor, Robert Michael b: 3/10/51, Connellsville, Pa. BR/TR, 5'11", 170 lbs. Deb: 9/06/75																												
1980	Tor-A	0	0	—	3	0	0	0	0	2	4	18.0	0	1	4.5	0	0.0	9.00	45	.364	.417	-1	-1	101	75	0.0	2	0	0.0
■ LOREN BAIN	Bain, Herbert Loren b: 7/4/22, Staples, Minn. BR/TR, 6', 190 lbs. Deb: 6/23/45																												
1945	NY-N	0	0	—	3	0	0	0	0	8	10	11.3	1	4	4.5	1	1.1	7.88	48	.323	.395	-4	-4	100	84	0.0	0	-0	-0.2
■ DOUG BAIR	Bair, Charles Douglas b: 8/22/49, Defiance, Ohio BR/TR, 6', 170 lbs. Deb: 9/13/76																												
1976	Pit-N	0	0	—	4	0	0	0	0	6	4	6.0	0	5	7.5	4	6.0	6.00	58	.174	.321	-2	-2	99	34	0.0	0	0	-0.1
1977	Oak-A	4	6	.400	45	0	0	0	8	83	78	8.5	11	57	6.2	68	7.4	3.47	113	.253	.358	6	4	97	140	0.1	0	1	0.5
1978	Cin-N	7	6	.538	70	0	0	0	28	100	87	7.8	6	38	3.4	91	8.2	1.98	185	.236	.300	18	19	102	152	-0.3	-0	-1	1.9
1979	Cin-N	11	7	.611	65	0	0	0	16	94	93	8.9	7	51	4.9	86	8.2	4.31	84	.256	.342	-6	-7	96	95	1.2	-1	-0	-0.8
1980	Cin-N	3	6	.333	61	0	0	0	6	85	91	9.6	7	39	4.1	62	6.6	4.24	86	.277	.347	-6	-6	101	105	-1.7	-0	2	-0.3
1981	Cin-N	2	2	.500	24	0	0	0	0	39	42	9.7	5	17	3.9	16	3.7	5.77	61	.271	.339	-10	-10	101	79	-0.3	1	-1	-0.9
	StL-N	2	0	1.000	11	0	0	0	1	16	13	7.3	0	2	1.1	14	7.9	3.38	104	.224	.250	0	0	101	47	1.0	-0	0	0.0
	Yr	4	2	.667	35	0	0	0	1	55	55	9.0	5	19	3.1	30	4.9	5.07	69	.258	.316	-10	-10	101	47	0.7	1	-1	-0.9
1982	StL-N	5	3	.625	63	0	0	0	8	92	69	6.8	7	36	3.5	68	6.7	2.54	145	.211	.285	11	12	102	104	0.6	-1	0	1.2
1983	StL-N	1	1	.500	26	0	0	0	1	30	24	7.2	4	13	3.9	21	6.3	3.00	119	.224	.303	2	2	98	115	0.0	-0	-0	0.2
	Det-A	7	3	.700	27	1	0	0	4	56	51	8.2	8	19	3.1	39	6.3	3.86	100	.242	.305	1	-0	95	98	1.6	0	-0	0.0
1984	Det-A	5	3	.625	47	1	0	0	4	94	82	7.9	10	36	3.4	57	5.5	3.73	101	.238	.304	3	0	94	93	0.0	0	1	0.1
1985	Det-A	2	0	1.000	21	3	0	0	0	49	54	9.9	3	25	4.6	30	5.5	6.24	70	.281	.357	-11	-10	106	75	1.0	0	1	-0.8
	StL-N	0	0	—	2	0	0	0	0	2	1	4.5	0	2	9.0	0	0.0	0.00	—	.167	.375	1	1	93	0	0.0	0	0	0.1
1986	Oak-A	2	3	.400	31	0	0	0	4	45	37	7.4	5	18	3.6	40	8.0	3.00	131	.224	.291	6	5	94	107	-0.3	0	0	0.5
1987	Phi-N	2	0	1.000	11	0	0	0	0	14	17	10.9	4	5	3.2	10	6.4	5.79	74	.309	.361	-3	-2	105	116	1.0	-0	-0	-0.2
1988	Tor-A	0	0	—	10	0	0	0	0	13	14	9.7	2	3	2.1	8	5.5	4.15	95	.280	.309	-0	-0	99	110	0.0	0	0	0.0
Total	13	53	40	.570	518	5	0	0	80	818	757	8.3	79	366	4.0	614	6.8	3.71	102	.247	.322	10	6	99	107	3.9	-2	2	1.4
■ BOB BAIRD	Baird, Robert Allen b: 1/16/40, Knoxville, Tenn. d: 4/11/74, Chattanooga, Tenn. BL/TL, 6'4", 195 lbs. Deb: 9/03/62																												
1962	Was-A	0	1	.000	3	3	0	0	0	11	13	10.6	0	8	6.5	3	2.5	6.55	62	.310	.404	-3	-3	102	85	-0.4	-0	0	-0.2
1963	Was-A	0	3	.000	5	3	0	0	0	12	12	9.0	1	7	5.3	7	5.3	7.50	49	.261	.351	-5	-5	101	62	-1.4	0	-0	-0.4
Total	2	0	4	.000	8	6	0	0	0	23	25	9.8	1	15	5.9	10	3.9	7.04	55	.284	.376	-8	-8	102	73	-1.8	-0	-0	-0.6
■ JERSEY BAKELY	Bakely, Edward Enoch (born Edward Enoch Bakley) b: 4/17/1864, Blackwood, N.J. d: 2/17/15, Philadelphia, Pa. BR/TR, Deb: 5/11/1883																												
1883	Phi-a	5	3	.625	8	8	7	0	0	61	65	9.6	0	12	1.8	14	2.1	3.25	101	.278	.314	0	0	99	103	-0.2	1	0	0.1
1884	Phi-U	14	25	.359	39	38	38	1	0	345	390	10.2	0	76	2.0	204	5.3	4.49	64	.290	.328	-57	-62	95	82	2.8	-7	-2	-5.9
	WiL-U	0	2	.000	2	2	2	0	0	17	24	12.7	0	1	0.5	9	4.8	4.24	78	.338	.347	-2	-2	109	109	-0.9	-1	0	-0.1
	KC-U	2	3	.400	5	5	3	0	0	33	29	7.9	0	4	1.1	13	3.5	2.45	112	.241	.265	2	1	92	88	0.6	-1	0	0.0
	Yr	16	30	.348	46	45	43	1	0	395	443	10.1	0	81	1.8	226	5.1	4.31	67	.288	.324	-57	-63	95	88	2.5	-8	-2	-6.0
1888	Cle-a	25	33	.431	61	61	60	4	0	533	518	8.7	14	128	2.2	212	3.6	2.97	103	.268	.313	5	6	100	104	4.1	-5	-1	0.1
1889	Cle-N	12	22	.353	36	34	33	2	0	304	296	8.8	9	106	3.1	105	3.1	2.96	142	.270	.335	36	42	104	111	-4.8	-2	2	3.9
1890	Cle-P	13	25	.342	43	38	32	0	0	326	412	11.4	13	147	4.1	67	1.8	4.47	89	.321	.391	-9	-18	94	107	-4.7	-2	-1	-1.7
1891	Was-a	2	10	.167	13	12	11	0	0	104	127	11.0	7	60	5.2	32	2.8	5.37	70	.316	.405	-19	-19	101	98	-3.0	-0	0	-1.4
	Bal-a	4	2	.667	8	6	5	0	0	59	48	7.3	1	30	4.6	13	2.0	2.29	163	.236	.334	9	9	100	115	0.9	0	0	0.9
	Yr	6	12	.333	21	18	16	0	0	163	175	9.7	8	90	5.0	45	2.5	4.25	88	.289	.381	-10	-9	100	115	-2.1	-0	0	-0.5
Total	6	77	125	.381	215	204	191	7	0	1782	1909	9.6	44	564	2.8	669	3.4	3.67	94	.285	.341	-33	-42	99	101	-5.2	-16	-3	-4.1

YEAR	TM/L	W	L	PCT	G	GS	CG	SHO	SV	IP	H	H/G	HR	BB	BB/G	SO	SO/G	ERA	/A	OAVG	OOBP	PR	/A	PF	CPI	WAT	PB	PD	TPI
■ **DAVE BAKENHASTER**	Bakenhaster, David Lee b: 3/5/45, Columbus, O. BR/TR, 5'10", 168 lbs. Deb: 6/20/64																												
1964	StL-N	0	0	—	2	0	0	0	0	3	9	27.0	1	1	3.0	0	0.0	6.00	66	.474	.500	-1	-1	111	239	0.0	0	0	0.0
■ **AL BAKER**	Baker, Albert Jones b: 2/28/06, Batesville, Miss. d: 11/6/82, Kenedy, Tex. BR/TR, 5'11", 170 lbs. Deb: 8/20/38																												
1938	Bos-A	0	0	—	3	0	0	0	0	8	13	14.6	2	2	2.3	2	2.3	9.00	53	.371	.421	-4	-4	100	96	0.0	-1	0	-0.3
■ **BOCK BAKER**	Baker, Charles "Smiling Bock" b: 7/17/1878, Troy, N.Y. Deb: 4/28/01																												
1901	Cle-A	0	1	.000	1	1	1	0	0	8	23	25.9	0	6	6.8	0	0.0	5.63	63	.528	.585	-2	-2	97	242	-0.4	-1	0	-0.1
	Phi-A	0	1	.000	1	1	0	0	0	6	6	9.0	0	6	9.0	1	1.5	10.50	35	.280	.438	-5	-5	100	47	-0.4	0	-0	-0.3
	Yr	0	2	.000	2	2	1	0	0	14	29	18.6	0	12	7.7	1	0.6	7.71	47	.446	.533	-6	-6	98	47	-0.8	-1	-0	-0.4
■ **ERNIE BAKER**	Baker, Earnest Gould b: 8/8/1875, Concord, Mich. d: 10/25/45, Homer, Mich. 5'10", 160 lbs. Deb: 8/18/05																												
1905	Cin-N	0	0	—	1	0	0	0	0	4	7	15.8	1	0	0.0	1	2.3	4.50	68	.439	.472	-1	-1	103	190	0.0	-0	-0	0.0
■ **JESSE BAKER**	Baker, Jesse Ormond b: 6/3/1888, Anderson Island, Wash. d: 9/26/72, Tacoma, Wash. BL/TL, 5'11", 188 lbs. Deb: 4/23/11																												
1911	Chi-A	2	7	.222	22	8	3	0	1	94	101	9.7	3	30	2.9	51	4.9	3.93	81	.288	.351	-6	-8	95	98	-2.5	-2	1	-0.7
■ **KIRTLEY BAKER**	Baker, Kirtley "Whitey" b: 6/24/1869, Aurora, Ind. d: 4/15/27, Covington, Ky. BR/TR, 5'9", 160 lbs. Deb: 5/07/1890																												
1890	Pit-N	3	19	.136	25	21	19	2	0	178	209	10.6	11	86	4.3	76	3.8	5.61	60	.309	.387	-41	-44	95	85	-2.3	-2	0	-3.7
1893	Bal-N	3	8	.273	15	12	8	0	0	92	138	13.5	5	58	5.7	26	2.5	8.51	59	.363	.448	-39	-36	108	82	-2.3	2	0	-2.3
1894	Bal-N	0	1	.000	1	0	0	0	0	0	1	—	0	2	—	0	—	∞	—	1.000	1.000	-5	-5	96	24	-0.4	-0	0	-0.2
1898	Was-N	2	3	.400	6	5	4	0	0	47	56	10.7	1	18	3.4	7	1.3	3.06	123	.318	.382	3	4	105	140	0.2	2	0	0.5
1899	Was-N	1	7	.125	11	6	3	0	0	54	79	13.2	3	22	3.7	6	1.0	6.83	55	.366	.425	-18	-18	98	87	-2.5	-1	0	-1.5
Total	5	9	38	.191	58	44	34	2	0	371	483	11.7	20	186	4.5	115	2.8	6.31	61	.333	.409	-100	-100	100	92	-7.3	0	0	-7.2
■ **NEAL BAKER**	Baker, Neal Vernon b: 4/30/04, Laporte, Tex. d: 1/5/82, Houston, Tex. BR/TR, 6'1", 175 lbs. Deb: 6/26/27																												
1927	Phi-A	0	0	—	5	2	0	0	0	17	27	14.3	2	7	3.7	3	1.6	5.82	67	.365	.405	-3	-4	95	124	0.0	-0	0	-0.2
■ **NORM BAKER**	Baker, Norman Leslie b: 10/14/1863, Philadelphia, Pa. d: 2/20/49, Hurffville, N.J. Deb: 5/21/1883																												
1883	Pit-a	0	2	.000	3	3	2	0	0	19	24	11.4	0	11	5.2	5	2.4	3.32	97	.314	.400	-0	-0	98	163	-0.9	-1	0	-0.1
1885	Lou-a	13	12	.520	25	24	24	1	0	217	210	8.7	3	69	2.9	79	3.3	3.40	99	.266	.324	-4	-1	103	97	1.4	-2	0	-0.1
1890	BB-a	1	1	.500	2	2	2	0	0	17	16	8.5	0	6	3.2	10	5.3	3.71	107	.264	.330	0	0	103	85	0.3	-1	0	0.0
Total	3	14	15	.483	30	29	28	1	0	253	250	8.9	3	86	3.1	94	3.3	3.42	99	.269	.331	-3	-1	103	101	0.8	-4	0	-0.2
■ **STEVE BAKER**	Baker, Steven Byrne b: 8/30/56, Eugene, Ore. BR/TR, 6', 185 lbs. Deb: 5/25/78																												
1978	Det-A	2	4	.333	15	10	0	0	0	63	66	9.4	6	42	6.0	39	5.6	4.57	89	.276	.374	-6	-4	107	111	-1.0	0	-1	-0.4
1979	Det-A	1	7	.125	21	12	0	0	1	84	97	10.4	13	51	5.5	54	5.8	6.64	61	.296	.393	-23	-24	96	93	-3.0	0	-1	-2.2
1982	Oak-A	1	1	.500	5	3	0	0	0	26	30	10.4	3	4	1.4	14	4.8	4.50	87	.288	.309	-1	-2	96	93	0.1	0	-0	-0.1
1983	Oak-A	3	3	.500	35	1	0	0	5	54	59	9.8	4	26	4.3	23	3.8	4.33	91	.282	.357	-2	-2	96	110	0.2	0	-1	-0.2
	StL-N	0	1	.000	8	0	0	0	0	10	10	9.0	0	4	3.6	1	0.9	1.80	199	.286	.349	2	2	98	234	-0.4	0	0	0.2
Total	4	7	16	.304	84	26	0	0	6	237	262	9.9	26	127	4.8	131	5.0	5.13	78	.286	.369	-29	-30	99	107	-4.1	0	-2	-2.7
■ **TOM BAKER**	Baker, Thomas Calvin "Rattlesnake" b: 6/11/13, Nursery, Tex. BR/TR, 6'1.5", 180 lbs. Deb: 8/15/35																												
1935	Bro-N	1	0	1.000	11	1	1	0	0	42	48	10.3	2	20	4.3	10	2.1	4.29	89	.277	.351	-1	-2	95	101	0.5	4	-1	0.0
1936	Bro-N	1	8	.111	35	8	2	0	2	88	98	10.0	3	48	4.9	35	3.6	4.70	91	.288	.369	-7	-4	107	102	-3.3	1	0	-0.2
1937	Bro-N	0	1	.000	7	0	0	0	0	8	14	15.8	1	5	5.6	2	2.3	9.00	47	.378	.465	-5	-4	107	99	-0.4	0	0	-0.3
	NY-N	1	0	1.000	13	0	0	0	0	31	30	8.7	0	16	4.6	11	3.2	4.06	94	.268	.346	-1	-1	98	97	0.5	-0	-0	0.0
	Yr	1	1	.500	20	0	0	0	0	39	44	10.2	1	21	4.8	13	3.0	5.08	77	.293	.369	-5	-5	100	97	0.1	0	-0	-0.3
1938	NY-N	0	0	—	2	0	0	0	0	4	5	11.3	0	3	6.8	0	0.0	6.75	57	.313	.400	-1	-1	102	85	0.0	0	0	0.0
Total	4	3	9	.250	68	9	3	0	2	173	195	10.1	6	92	4.8	58	3.0	4.73	86	.288	.367	-14	-13	102	100	-2.7	5	-1	-0.5
■ **TOM BAKER**	Baker, Thomas Henry b: 5/6/34, Port Townsend, Wash. d: 3/9/80, Port Townsend, Wash BL/TL, 6', 195 lbs. Deb: 8/02/63																												
1963	Chi-N	0	1	.000	10	1	0	0	0	18	20	10.0	2	7	3.5	14	7.0	3.00	115	.282	.346	1	1	105	158	-0.4	-0	0	0.1
■ **MIKE BALAS**	Balas, Mitchell Francis (born Mitchell Francis Balaski) b: 5/17/10, Lowell, Mass. BR/TR, 6', 195 lbs. Deb: 4/27/38																												
1938	Bos-N	0	0	—	1	0	0	0	0	1	3	27.0	0	0	0.0	0	0.0	9.00	37	.375	.375	-1	-1	89	79	0.0	0	0	0.0
■ **JACK BALDSCHUN**	Baldschun, Jack Edward b: 10/16/36, Greenville, O. BR/TR, 6'1", 175 lbs. Deb: 4/28/61																												
1961	Phi-N	5	3	.625	**65**	0	0	0	3	100	90	8.1	7	49	4.4	59	5.3	3.87	102	.243	.331	2	1	98	96	1.9	-1	0	0.0
1962	Phi-N	12	7	.632	67	0	0	0	13	113	95	7.6	6	58	4.6	95	7.6	2.95	128	.231	.324	12	10	95	111	2.7	-1	0	1.0
1963	Phi-N	11	7	.611	65	0	0	0	16	114	99	7.8	7	42	3.3	89	7.0	2.29	146	.232	.302	13	13	102	129	1.6	-2	1	1.4
1964	Phi-N	6	9	.400	71	0	0	0	21	118	111	8.5	8	40	3.1	96	7.3	3.13	111	.246	.304	5	4	98	106	-2.3	1	1	0.8
1965	Phi-N	5	8	.385	65	0	0	0	6	99	102	9.3	4	42	3.8	81	7.4	3.82	88	.273	.339	-3	-5	95	108	-1.8	-1	1	-0.4
1966	Cin-N	1	5	.167	42	0	0	0	0	57	71	11.2	4	25	3.9	44	6.9	5.53	74	.318	.385	-12	-9	114	101	-1.9	0	0	-0.8
1967	Cin-N	0	0	—	9	0	0	0	0	13	15	10.4	0	9	6.2	12	8.3	4.15	88	.283	.387	-1	-1	109	111	0.0	-0	0	0.0
1969	SD-N	7	2	.778	61	0	0	0	1	77	80	9.4	7	29	3.4	67	7.8	4.79	75	.264	.326	-10	-10	100	83	3.1	0	-0	-0.9
1970	SD-N	1	0	1.000	12	0	0	0	0	13	24	16.6	2	4	2.8	12	8.3	10.38	38	.375	.400	-9	-9	97	75	0.5	0	-0	-0.8
Total	9	48	41	.539	457	0	0	0	60	704	687	8.8	45	298	3.8	555	7.1	3.69	98	.257	.329	-3	-5	99	106	3.8	-3	4	0.3
■ **LADY BALDWIN**	Baldwin, Charles Busted b: 4/8/1859, Ormel, N.Y. d: 3/7/37, Hastings, Mich. BL/TL, 5'11", 160 lbs. Deb: 9/30/1884																												
1884	Mil-U	1	1	.500	2	2	2	0	0	17	7	3.7	0	1	0.5	21	11.1	2.65	114	.130	.145	1	1	100	12	-0.2	0	0	0.1
1885	Det-N	11	9	.550	21	20	19	1	1	179	137	6.9	2	28	1.4	135	**6.8**	1.86	150	.222	**.255**	19	18	99	86	3.2	3	0	2.3
1886	Det-N	**42**	13	.764	56	56	55	**7**	0	487	371	**6.9**	11	100	1.8	**323**	6.0	2.24	152	**.223**	**.267**	58	**63**	103	82	8.3	2	3	6.7
1887	Det-N	13	10	.565	24	24	24	1	0	211	225	9.6	8	61	2.6	60	2.6	3.84	103	.288	.340	5	2	97	98	-1.5	3	0	0.5
1888	Det-N	3	3	.500	6	6	5	0	0	53	76	12.9	5	15	2.5	26	4.4	5.43	50	.351	.393	-15	-16	97	107	0.0	2	0	-1.2
1890	Bro-N	1	0	1.000	2	1	0	0	0	8	15	16.9	0	4	4.5	4	4.5	7.88	44	.417	.475	-4	-4	96	100	0.5	-0	0	-0.2
	Buf-P	2	5	.286	7	7	7	0	0	62	90	13.1	5	24	3.5	13	1.9	4.50	91	.352	.407	-2	-3	97	131	0.1	1	0	0.0
Total	6	73	41	.640	118	116	112	9	1	1017	921	8.2	31	233	2.1	582	5.2	2.86	119	.254	.299	61	63	100	89	10.4	11	3	8.2
■ **KID BALDWIN**	Baldwin, Clarence Geoghan b: 11/1/1864, Newport, Ky. d: 7/12/1897, Cincinnati, Ohio BR/TR, 5'6", 147 lbs. Deb: 7/27/1884																												
1885	Cin-a	0	0	—	2	1	0	0	0	4	5	11.3	0	6	13.5	1	2.3	9.00	37	.318	.507	-3	-3	103	88	0.0	-0	0	-0.1
■ **DAVE BALDWIN**	Baldwin, David George b: 3/30/38, Tucson, Ariz. BR/TR, 6'2", 200 lbs. Deb: 9/06/66																												
1966	Was-A	0	0	—	4	0	0	0	0	7	8	10.3	0	1	1.3	4	5.1	3.86	86	.267	.290	-0	-0	96	68	0.0	0	-0	0.0
1967	Was-A	2	4	.333	58	0	0	0	12	69	53	6.9	2	20	2.6	52	6.8	1.70	198	.215	.276	12	13	104	137	-0.8	-0	1	1.5
1968	Was-A	0	2	.000	40	0	0	0	5	42	40	8.6	7	12	2.6	30	6.4	4.07	69	.260	.301	-5	-6	94	104	-0.9	0	1	-0.5
1969	Was-A	2	4	.333	43	0	0	0	4	67	57	7.7	4	34	4.6	51	6.9	4.03	87	.236	.334	-3	-4	96	89	-1.0	-1	-0	-0.5
1970	Mil-A	2	1	.667	28	0	0	0	1	35	25	6.4	4	18	4.6	26	6.7	2.57	144	.205	.299	4	4	100	122	0.7	0	2	0.7
1973	Chi-A	0	0	—	3	0	0	0	0	5	7	12.6	0	4	7.2	1	1.8	3.60	109	.368	.478	0	0	103	200	0.0	0	0	0.0
Total	6	6	11	.353	176	0	0	0	22	225	190	7.6	17	89	3.6	164	6.6	3.08	109	.234	.307	8	7	99	113	-2.0	-1	4	1.2
■ **HARRY BALDWIN**	Baldwin, Howard Edward b: 6/3/1900, Baltimore, Md. d: 1/23/58, Baltimore, Md. BR/TR, 5'11", 160 lbs. Deb: 5/04/24																												
1924	NY-N	3	1	.750	10	2	1	0	0	34	42	11.1	5	11	2.9	5	1.3	4.24	80	.309	.353	-1	-3	88	127	0.7	1	-0	-0.2
1925	NY-N	0	0	—	1	0	0	0	0	1	3	27.0	0	1	9.0	0	0.0	9.00	47	.500	.571	-1	-1	98	160	0.0	0	0	0.0
Total	2	3	1	.750	11	2	1	0	0	35	45	11.6	5	12	3.1	5	1.3	4.37	78	.317	.363	-2	-4	88	128	0.7	1	-0	-0.2
■ **MARK BALDWIN**	Baldwin, Marcus Elmore "Fido" b: 10/29/1863, Pittsburgh, Pa. d: 11/10/29, Pittsburgh, Pa. BR/TR, 6', 190 lbs. Deb: 5/02/1887																												
1887	Chi-N	18	17	.514	40	39	35	1	1	334	329	8.9	23	122	3.3	164	**4.4**	3.40	137	.272	.339	24	47	115	111	-2.8	-5	-3	3.7
1888	Chi-N	13	15	.464	30	30	27	2	0	251	241	8.6	12	99	3.5	157	5.6	2.76	108	.266	.338	2	7	106	**125**	-3.0	-1	0	0.6
1889	Col-a	27	34	.443	**63**	59	54	6	1	**514**	458	8.0	9	274	4.8	**368**	6.4	3.61	99	.253	.351	14	-3	92	90	0.8	2	1	-0.1
1890	Chi-P	**34**	24	.586	**59**	57	**54**	1	0	**501**	498	8.9	10	249	4.5	**211**	3.8	3.31	131	.271	.358	52	58	103	103	4.1	-1	7	5.4
1891	Pit-N	22	28	.440	53	50	48	2	0	438	385	7.9	10	227	4.7	197	4.0	2.77	123	.249	.345	28	32	102	104	2.1	-4	2	2.7
1892	Pit-N	26	27	.491	56	53	45	0	0	440	447	9.1	11	194	4.0	157	3.2	3.48	89	.276	.354	-9	-20	94	103	-2.3	-10	-1	-2.8

YEAR	TM/L	W	L	PCT	G	GS	CG	SHO	SV	IP	H	H/G	HR	BB	BB/G	SO	SO/G	ERA	/A	OAVG	OOBP	PR	/A	PF	CPI	WAT	PB	PD	TPI
1893	Pit-N	0	0	—	1	1	0	0	0	2	6	27.0	0	1	4.5	0	0.0	13.50	36	.533	.571	-2	-2	105	102	0.0	-0	0	-0.1
	NY-N	16	20	.444	45	39	33	2	2	331	335	9.1	6	141	3.8	100	2.7	4.11	117	.278	.354	21	26	103	90	-3.1	-11	-2	1.1
	Yr	16	20	.444	46	40	33	2	**2**	333	341	9.2	6	142	3.8	100	2.7	4.16	116	.280	.356	19	24	103	90	-3.1	-0	-2	1.0
Total	7	156	165	.486	347	328	296	14	4	2811	2699	8.6	81	1307	4.2	1354	4.3	3.37	114	.266	.350	129	142	101	102	-4.2	-31	4	10.5
■ O. F. BALDWIN	Baldwin, O. F. b: Youngstown, Ohio Deb: 9/06/08																												
1908	StL-N	1	3	.250	4	4	0	0	0	15	16	9.6	0	11	6.6	5	3.0	6.00	39	.321	.470	-6	-6	100	84	-0.3	-1	0	-0.6
■ RICK BALDWIN	Baldwin, Rickey Alan b: 6/1/53, Fresno, Cal. BL/TR, 6'3", 180 lbs. Deb: 4/10/75																												
1975	NY-N	3	5	.375	54	0	0	0	6	97	97	9.0	4	34	3.2	54	5.0	3.34	103	.263	.323	3	1	95	105	-1.0	0	1	0.2
1976	NY-N	0	0	—	11	0	0	0	0	23	14	5.5	0	10	3.9	9	3.5	2.35	135	.189	.292	3	2	91	91	0.0	0	0	0.3
1977	NY-N	1	2	.333	40	0	0	0	1	63	62	8.9	6	31	4.4	23	3.3	4.43	86	.265	.358	-4	-4	97	103	-0.1	1	1	-0.2
Total	3	4	7	.364	105	0	0	0	7	183	173	8.5	10	75	3.7	86	4.2	3.59	98	.256	.332	3	-1	95	102	-1.1	1	1	0.3
■ JEFF BALLARD	Ballard, Jeffrey Scott b: 8/13/63, Billings, Mont. BL/TL, 6'3", 195 lbs. Deb: 5/09/87																												
1987	Bal-A	2	8	.200	14	14	0	0	0	70	100	12.9	15	35	4.5	27	3.5	6.56	68	.344	.413	-16	-16	99	116	-2.6	0	0	-1.4
1988	Bal-A	8	12	.400	25	25	6	1	0	153	167	9.8	15	42	2.5	41	2.4	4.41	88	.278	.329	-7	-9	97	97	1.1	0	-2	-1.0
Total	2	10	20	.333	39	39	6	1	0	223	267	10.8	30	77	3.1	68	2.7	5.09	80	.300	.357	-24	-26	98	103	-1.5	0	-2	-2.4
■ JAY BALLER	Baller, Jay Scot b: 10/6/50, Stayton, Ohio BR/TR, 6'6", 215 lbs. Deb: 9/19/82																												
1982	Phi-N	0	0	—	4	1	0	0	0	8	7	7.9	1	2	2.3	7	7.9	3.38	100	.226	.286	0	-0	94	92	0.0	0	0	0.0
1985	Chi-N	2	3	.400	20	4	0	0	1	52	52	9.0	8	17	2.9	31	5.4	3.46	121	.260	.314	1	4	117	122	-0.3	-1	-0	0.3
1986	Chi-N	2	4	.333	36	0	0	0	5	54	58	9.7	7	28	4.7	42	7.0	5.33	75	.275	.355	-10	-8	108	94	-0.6	-1	-1	-0.9
1987	Chi-N	0	1	.000	23	0	0	0	0	29	38	11.8	4	20	6.2	27	8.4	6.83	61	.325	.417	-9	-9	102	102	-0.4	0	-0	-0.7
Total	4	4	8	.333	83	5	0	0	6	143	155	9.8	20	67	4.2	107	6.7	4.85	84	.277	.350	-17	-12	109	106	-1.3	-1	-1	-1.3
■ MARK BALLINGER	Ballinger, Mark Alan b: 1/31/49, Glendale, Cal. BR/TR, 6'6", 205 lbs. Deb: 8/06/71																												
1971	Cle-A	1	2	.333	18	0	0	0	0	35	30	7.7	3	13	3.3	25	6.4	4.63	81	.233	.295	-5	-3	108	67	-0.1	-0	-0	-0.3
■ WIN BALLOU	Ballou, Noble Winfield b: 11/30/1897, Mount Morgan, Ky. d: 1/30/63, San Francisco, Cal BR/TL, 5'10.5", 170 lbs. Deb: 8/24/25																												
1925	Was-A	1	1	.500	10	1	1	0	0	28	38	12.2	1	13	4.2	13	4.2	4.50	93	.342	.408	-0	-1	95	132	-0.1	-0	0	0.0
1926	StL-A	11	10	.524	43	14	5	0	2	154	186	10.9	12	71	4.1	59	3.4	4.79	87	.311	.371	-13	-11	103	112	2.4	-3	3	-1.0
1927	StL-A	5	6	.455	21	11	4	0	0	90	105	10.5	4	46	4.6	17	1.7	4.80	94	.309	.384	-7	-3	109	109	0.7	-4	-0	-0.5
1929	Bro-N	2	3	.400	25	1	0	0	0	58	69	10.7	5	38	5.9	20	3.1	6.67	68	.304	.389	-13	-14	96	88	-0.2	-2	2	-1.1
Total	4	19	20	.487	99	27	10	0	2	330	398	10.9	22	168	4.6	109	3.0	5.10	85	.312	.381	-33	-28	103	109	2.8	-9	4	-2.6
■ TONY BALSAMO	Balsamo, Anthony Fred b: 11/21/37, Brooklyn, N.Y. BR/TR, 6'2", 185 lbs. Deb: 4/14/62																												
1962	Chi-N	0	1	.000	18	0	0	0	0	29	34	10.6	1	20	6.2	27	8.4	6.52	66	.293	.393	-8	-7	109	80	-0.4	0	1	-0.5
■ GEORGE BAMBERGER	Bamberger, George Irvin b: 8/1/25, Staten Island, N.Y. BR/TR, 6', 175 lbs. Deb: 4/19/51 MC																												
1951	NY-N	0	0	—	2	0	0	0	0	2	4	18.0	2	2	9.0	1	4.5	18.00	22	.444	.545	-3	-3	99	102	0.0	0	0	-0.2
1952	NY-N	0	0	—	5	0	0	0	0	4	6	13.5	1	6	13.5	0	0.0	9.00	42	.353	.522	-2	-2	101	122	0.0	0	0	-0.1
1959	Bal-A	0	0	—	3	1	0	0	1	8	15	16.9	1	2	2.3	2	2.3	7.88	48	.405	.436	-4	-4	98	105	0.0	-0	0	-0.2
Total	3	0	0	—	10	1	0	0	1	14	25	16.1	4	10	6.4	3	1.9	9.64	39	.397	.479	-9	-9	99	109	0.0	-0	0	-0.5
■ SAL BANDO	Bando, Salvatore Leonard b: 2/13/44, Cleveland, O. BR/TR, 6', 195 lbs. Deb: 9/03/66 C																												
1979	Mil-A	0	0	—	1	0	0	0	0	3	3	9.0	0	0	0.0	0	0.0	6.00	70	.231	.231	-1	-1	99	14	0.0	1	0	0.0
■ EDDIE BANE	Bane, Edward Norman b: 3/22/52, Chicago, Ill. BR/TL, 5'9", 160 lbs. Deb: 7/04/73																												
1973	Min-A	0	5	.000	23	6	0	0	2	60	62	9.3	5	30	4.5	42	6.3	4.95	80	.270	.351	-8	-7	103	89	-2.4	0	1	-0.5
1975	Min-A	3	1	.750	4	4	0	0	0	28	28	9.0	2	15	4.8	14	4.5	2.89	140	.262	.349	3	4	107	146	1.1	0	-1	0.3
1976	Min-A	4	7	.364	17	15	1	0	0	79	92	10.5	6	39	4.4	24	2.7	5.13	67	.290	.365	-14	-15	98	94	-1.7	0	-2	-1.6
Total	3	7	13	.350	44	25	1	0	2	167	182	9.8	13	84	4.5	80	4.3	4.69	79	.278	.357	-19	-18	101	101	-3.0	0	-1	-1.8
■ DICK BANEY	Baney, Richard Lee b: 11/1/46, Fullerton, Cal. BR/TR, 6', 185 lbs. Deb: 7/11/69																												
1969	Sea-A	1	0	1.000	9	1	0	0	0	19	21	9.9	2	7	3.3	9	4.3	3.79	96	.292	.346	-0	-0	100	125	0.5	-0	-0	0.0
1973	Cin-N	2	1	.667	11	1	0	0	2	31	26	7.5	1	6	1.7	17	4.9	2.90	116	.234	.295	3	2	92	90	0.2	1	-1	0.1
1974	Cin-N	1	0	1.000	22	1	0	0	1	41	51	11.2	4	17	3.7	12	2.6	5.49	64	.305	.362	-8	-9	96	94	0.5	-1	-1	-1.0
Total	3	4	1	.800	42	3	0	0	3	91	98	9.7	7	30	3.0	38	3.8	4.25	82	.280	.338	-6	-8	95	99	1.2	-0	-2	-0.9
■ DAN BANKHEAD	Bankhead, Daniel Robert b: 5/3/20, Empire, Ala. d: 5/2/76, Houston, Tex. BR/TR, 6'1", 184 lbs. Deb: 8/26/47																												
1947	Bro-N	0	0	—	4	0	0	0	1	10	15	13.5	1	8	7.2	6	5.4	7.20	58	.341	.444	-3	-3	103	107	0.0	1	-0	-0.1
1950	Bro-N	9	4	.692	41	12	2	1	3	129	119	8.3	16	88	6.1	96	6.7	5.51	78	.252	.365	-20	-17	104	89	1.9	1	-0	-1.5
1951	Bro-N	0	1	.000	7	1	0	0	0	14	27	17.4	5	14	9.0	9	5.8	15.43	24	.422	.512	-18	-18	95	82	-0.4	-0	0	-1.5
Total	3	9	5	.643	52	13	2	1	4	153	161	9.5	22	110	6.5	111	6.5	6.53	65	.277	.388	-41	-39	103	89	1.5	2	-0	-3.1
■ SCOTT BANKHEAD	Bankhead, Michael Scott b: 7/31/63, Raleigh, N.C. BR/TR, 5'10", 175 lbs. Deb: 5/25/86																												
1986	KC-A	8	9	.471	24	17	0	0	0	121	121	9.0	14	37	2.8	94	7.0	4.61	91	.259	.311	-6	-6	100	85	0.0	0	-0	-0.5
1987	Sea-A	9	8	.529	27	25	2	0	0	149	168	10.1	35	37	2.2	95	5.7	5.44	85	.283	.324	-16	-14	103	98	0.9	0	-2	-1.4
1988	Sea-A	7	9	.438	21	21	2	1	0	135	115	7.7	8	38	2.5	102	6.8	3.07	140	.224	.276	14	19	108	80	0.2	0	-1	1.8
Total	3	24	26	.480	72	63	4	1	0	405	404	9.0	57	112	2.5	291	6.5	4.40	100	.257	.305	-8	-1	104	88	1.1	0	-4	-0.1
■ BILL BANKS	Banks, William John (born William John Yerrick) b: 2/26/1874, Danville, Pa. d: 9/8/36, Danville, Pa. 5'11", 150 lbs. Deb: 9/27/1895																												
1895	Bos-N	1	0	1.000	1	1	0	0	0	7	7	9.0	0	4	5.1	4	5.1	0.00	—	.280	.379	4	4	102	0	0.5	-1	0	0.3
1896	Bos-N	0	3	.000	4	3	2	0	0	23	42	16.4	2	13	5.1	6	2.3	10.57	44	.417	.484	-16	-15	107	81	-1.4	0	0	-1.0
Total	2	1	3	.250	5	4	2	0	0	30	49	14.7	2	17	5.1	10	3.0	8.10	58	.390	.463	-12	-11	106	62	-0.9	-1	0	-0.7
■ FLOYD BANNISTER	Bannister, Floyd Franklin b: 6/10/55, Pierre, S.D. BL/TL, 6'1", 190 lbs. Deb: 4/19/77																												
1977	Hou-N	8	9	.471	24	23	4	1	0	143	138	8.7	11	68	4.3	112	7.0	4.03	90	.254	.338	-2	-7	92	96	-0.5	0	-1	-0.7
1978	Hou-N	3	9	.250	28	16	2	2	0	110	120	9.8	13	63	5.2	94	7.7	4.83	70	.280	.367	-15	-17	95	107	-2.7	0	-2	-1.9
1979	Sea-A	10	15	.400	30	30	6	2	0	182	185	9.1	25	68	3.4	115	5.7	4.05	105	.260	.324	4	5	101	103	-0.4	0	-2	0.2
1980	Sea-A	9	13	.409	32	32	8	0	0	218	200	8.3	24	66	2.7	155	6.4	3.47	122	.239	.292	14	19	105	91	0.9	0	-1	1.9
1981	Sea-A	9	9	.500	21	20	5	2	0	121	128	9.5	14	39	2.9	85	6.3	4.46	83	.268	.326	-11	-10	101	92	1.7	0	-1	-1.0
1982	Sea-A	12	13	.480	35	35	5	3	0	247	225	8.2	32	77	2.8	**209**	7.6	3.43	131	.243	.298	18	29	110	105	0.3	0	-1	3.0
1983	Chi-A	16	10	.615	34	34	5	2	0	217	191	7.9	19	71	2.9	193	**8.0**	3.36	123	.233	.293	17	19	102	90	0.2	0	-1	1.8
1984	Chi-A	14	11	.560	34	33	4	0	0	218	211	8.7	30	80	3.3	152	6.3	4.83	92	.252	.317	-20	-9	111	84	2.7	0	-2	-1.1
1985	Chi-A	10	14	.417	34	34	4	1	0	211	211	9.0	30	100	4.3	198	**8.4**	4.86	85	.261	.339	-17	-17	100	97	-2.7	0	-1	-1.7
1986	Chi-A	10	14	.417	28	27	6	1	0	165	162	8.8	17	48	2.6	92	5.0	3.55	120	.259	.308	12	13	101	106	-0.8	0	-1	1.2
1987	Chi-A	16	11	.593	34	34	11	2	0	229	216	8.5	38	49	1.9	124	4.9	3.58	136	.246	.282	23	32	109	102	3.5	0	-3	2.9
1988	KC-A	12	13	.480	31	31	2	0	0	189	182	8.7	22	68	3.2	113	5.4	4.33	94	.248	.313	-8	-5	103	88	-1.1	0	-0	-0.5
Total	12	129	141	.478	365	349	62	16	0	2250	2169	8.7	275	797	3.2	1642	6.6	4.01	105	.251	.313	15	49	103	96	1.1	1	-15	4.1
■ JIMMY BANNON	Bannon, James Henry "Foxy Grandpa" b: 5/5/1871, Amesbury, Mass. d: 3/24/48, Glen Rock, N.J. BR , 5'5", 160 lbs. Deb: 6/15/1893																												
1893	StL-N	0	1	.000	1	1	0	0	0	4	10	22.5	1	5	11.3	1	2.3	22.50	21	.488	.588	-8	-8	100	68	-0.4	0	0	-0.4
1894	Bos-N	0	0	—	1	0	0	0	0	2	4	18.0	1	1	4.5	0	0.0	0.00	—	.439	.495	1	1	111	0	0.0	0	0	0.1
1895	Bos-N	0	0	—	1	0	0	0	0	3	4	12.0	0	2	6.0	1	3.0	6.00	82	.341	.437	-0	-0	102	96	0.0	0	0	0.0
Total	3	0	1	.000	3	1	0	0	0	9	18	18.0	2	8	8.0	2	2.0	12.00	42	.435	.527	-7	-7	103	62	-0.4	1	0	-0.3
■ JACK BANTA	Banta, John Kay b: 6/24/25, Hutchinson, Kan. BL/TR, 6'2.5", 175 lbs. Deb: 9/18/47																												
1947	Bro-N	0	1	.000	3	1	0	0	0	8	7	7.9	1	4	4.5	3	3.4	6.75	62	.226	.316	-2	-2	103	57	-0.4	-0	1	-0.1
1948	Bro-N	0	1	.000	2	1	0	0	0	3	5	15.0	0	5	15.0	1	3.0	9.00	45	.385	.526	-2	-2	103	117	-0.4	-0	0	-0.1
1949	Bro-N	10	6	.625	48	12	2	1	3	152	125	7.4	12	68	4.0	97	5.7	3.38	117	.223	.309	11	10	98	95	0.0	-2	1	0.8
1950	Bro-N	4	4	.500	16	5	1	0	2	41	39	8.6	2	36	7.9	15	3.3	4.39	99	.252	.400	-1	-0	104	113	-0.5	-0	-1	0.0

YEAR	TM/L	W	L	PCT	G	GS	CG	SHO	SV	IP	H	H/G	HR	BB	BB/G	SO	SO/G	ERA	/A	OAVG	OOBP	PR	/A	PF	CPI	WAT	PB	PD	TPI
Total	4	14	12	.538	69	19	3	1	5	204	176	7.8	15	113	5.0	116	5.1	3.79	106	.232	.334	6	5	99	98	-1.3	-2	1	0.6
■ **STEVE BARBER**	Barber, Stephen David b: 2/22/39, Takoma Park, Md. BL/TL, 6', 195 lbs. Deb: 4/21/60																												
1960	Bal-A	10	7	.588	36	27	6	1	2	182	148	7.3	10	113	5.6	112	5.5	3.21	121	.226	.337	13	14	101	108	0.2	-4	0	1.0
1961	Bal-A	18	12	.600	37	34	14	**8**	1	248	194	7.0	13	130	4.7	150	5.4	3.34	116	.218	.313	19	14	96	90	0.6	2	4	2.1
1962	Bal-A	9	6	.600	28	19	5	2	0	140	145	9.3	9	61	3.9	89	5.7	3.47	109	.262	.331	8	5	95	111	1.9	-2	1	0.4
1963	Bal-A	20	13	.606	39	36	11	2	0	259	253	8.8	12	92	3.2	180	6.3	2.75	123	.258	.318	25	18	93	**127**	3.2	0	1	2.1
1964	Bal-A	9	13	.409	36	26	4	0	1	157	144	8.3	15	81	4.6	118	6.8	3.84	98	.248	.342	-4	-2	103	107	-3.7	1	3	0.2
1965	Bal-A	15	10	.600	37	32	7	2	0	221	177	7.2	16	81	3.3	130	5.3	2.69	127	.224	.290	19	18	99	107	0.7	-1	1	1.9
1966	Bal-A	10	5	.667	25	22	5	3	0	133	104	7.0	6	49	3.3	91	6.2	2.30	147	.218	.291	17	16	99	114	1.3	-3	1	1.6
1967	Bal-A	4	9	.308	15	15	1	1	0	75	47	5.6	5	61	7.3	48	5.8	4.08	74	.185	.341	-7	-9	94	85	-2.3	-0	0	-0.9
	NY-A	6	9	.400	17	17	3	1	0	98	103	9.5	4	54	5.0	70	6.4	4.04	77	.278	.363	-9	-10	96	114	-0.7	1	-1	-1.0
	Yr	10	18	.357	32	32	4	2	0	173	150	7.8	9	115	6.0	118	6.1	4.06	75	.238	.347	-16	-19	95	114	-3.0	-0	-1	-1.9
1968	NY-A	6	5	.545	20	19	3	1	0	128	127	8.9	7	64	4.5	87	6.1	3.23	93	.256	.337	-4	-3	101	120	0.4	-1	0	-0.4
1969	Sea-A	4	7	.364	25	16	0	0	0	86	99	10.4	9	48	5.0	69	7.2	4.81	76	.292	.377	-11	-11	100	110	-0.4	1	0	-0.9
1970	Chi-N	0	1	.000	5	0	0	0	0	6	10	15.0	0	6	9.0	3	4.5	9.00	53	.417	.516	-3	-3	119	105	-0.4	0	-0	-0.2
	Atl-N	0	1	.000	5	2	0	0	0	15	17	10.2	3	5	3.0	11	6.6	4.80	88	.288	.348	-1	-1	105	116	-0.4	0	0	0.0
	Yr	0	2	.000	10	2	0	0	0	21	27	11.6	3	11	4.7	14	6.0	6.00	73	.325	.402	-5	-4	109	116	-0.8	0	-0	-0.2
1971	Atl-N	3	1	.750	39	3	0	0	2	75	92	11.0	6	25	3.0	40	4.8	4.80	80	.301	.353	-11	-8	111	98	1.0	-0	0	-0.7
1972	Atl-N	0	0	—	5	0	0	0	0	16	18	10.1	1	6	3.4	6	3.4	5.63	65	.290	.352	-4	-3	106	81	0.0	-0	1	-0.2
	Cal-A	4	4	.500	34	3	0	0	2	58	37	5.7	4	30	4.7	34	5.3	2.02	136	.188	.288	7	5	90	121	0.1	1	-1	0.5
1973	Cal-A	3	2	.600	50	1	0	0	4	89	90	9.1	5	32	3.2	58	5.9	3.54	104	.265	.324	3	1	96	104	0.6	0	-1	0.1
1974	SF-N	0	1	.000	13	0	0	0	1	14	13	8.4	0	12	7.7	13	8.4	5.14	77	.255	.379	-2	-2	109	85	-0.4	0	-0	-0.1
Total	15	121	106	.533	466	272	59	21	13	2000	1818	8.2	125	950	4.3	1309	5.9	3.36	105	.245	.327	54	39	98	108	1.7	-6	11	5.5
■ **STEVE BARBER**	Barber, Steven Lee b: 3/13/48, Grand Rapids, Mich. BR/TR, 6'1", 190 lbs. Deb: 4/09/70																												
1970	Min-A	0	0	—	18	0	0	0	2	27	26	8.7	1	18	6.0	14	4.7	4.67	77	.263	.368	-3	-3	97	97	0.0	-0	-0	-0.3
1971	Min-A	1	0	1.000	4	2	0	0	0	12	8	6.0	2	13	9.8	4	3.0	6.00	60	.190	.375	-3	-3	104	79	0.5	-1	-0	-0.3
Total	2	1	0	1.000	22	2	0	0	2	39	34	7.8	3	31	7.2	18	4.2	5.08	71	.241	.370	-6	-6	99	91	0.5	-1	-0	-0.6
■ **FRANK BARBERICH**	Barberich, Frank Frederick b: 2/3/1882, New Town, N.Y. d: 5/1/65, Ocala, Fla. BB/TR, 5'10.5", 175 lbs. Deb: 9/17/07																												
1907	Bos-N	1	1	.500	2	2	1	0	0	12	19	14.3	0	5	3.8	1	0.8	6.00	41	.391	.448	-5	-5	99	101	0.2	-0	0	-0.4
1910	Bos-A	0	0	—	2	0	0	0	0	5	7	12.6	0	2	3.6	0	0.0	7.20	34	.350	.409	-3	-3	97	75	0.0	-0	0	-0.2
Total	2	1	1	.500	4	2	1	0	0	17	26	13.8	0	7	3.7	1	0.5	6.35	38	.379	.437	-7	-7	98	93	0.2	-1	0	-0.6
■ **CURT BARCLAY**	Barclay, Curtis Cordell b: 8/22/31, Chicago, Ill. d: 3/25/85, Missoula, Montana BR/TR, 6'3", 210 lbs. Deb: 4/21/57																												
1957	NY-N	9	9	.500	37	28	5	2	0	183	196	9.6	21	48	2.4	67	3.3	3.44	116	.274	.316	9	12	103	118	0.9	-0	3	1.5
1958	SF-N	1	0	1.000	6	1	0	0	0	16	16	9.0	3	5	2.8	6	3.4	2.81	140	.258	.343	2	2	100	169	0.5	2	0	0.4
1959	SF-N	0	0	—	1	0	0	0	0	⅓	2	54.0	0	2	54.0	0	0.0	54.00	—	.500	.667	-2	-2	94	59	0.0	0	0	-0.1
Total	3	10	9	.526	44	29	5	2	0	199	214	9.7	24	55	2.5	73	3.3	3.48	115	.274	.320	9	12	103	122	1.4	2	3	1.8
■ **RAY BARE**	Bare, Raymond Douglas b: 4/15/49, Miami, Fla. BR/TR, 6'2", 185 lbs. Deb: 7/30/72																												
1972	StL-N	0	1	.000	14	0	0	0	1	17	18	9.5	0	6	3.2	5	2.6	0.53	688	.281	.338	6	6	105	685	-0.4	0	-0	0.6
1974	StL-N	1	2	.333	10	3	0	0	0	24	25	9.4	2	9	3.4	6	2.3	6.00	62	.281	.333	-6	-6	103	72	-0.5	-0	1	-0.4
1975	Det-A	8	13	.381	29	21	6	1	0	151	174	10.4	10	47	2.8	71	4.2	4.47	90	.293	.339	-11	-7	106	96	0.4	0	1	-0.5
1976	Det-A	7	8	.467	30	21	3	2	0	134	157	10.5	13	51	3.4	59	4.0	4.63	80	.293	.350	-17	-14	105	102	0.1	0	1	-1.3
1977	Det-A	0	2	.000	5	4	0	0	0	14	24	15.4	3	7	4.5	4	2.6	12.86	33	.381	.437	-14	-13	105	68	-0.9	0	1	-1.0
Total	5	16	26	.381	88	49	9	3	1	340	398	10.5	28	120	3.2	145	3.8	4.79	81	.296	.348	-42	-35	105	125	-1.3	-0	4	-2.6
■ **CLYDE BARFOOT**	Barfoot, Clyde Raymond "Foots" b: 7/8/1891, Richmond, Va. d: 3/11/71, Highland Park, Cal BR/TR, 6', 170 lbs. Deb: 4/13/22																												
1922	StL-N	4	5	.444	42	2	1	0	2	118	139	10.6	2	30	2.3	19	1.4	4.19	98	.307	.344	-1	-1	100	103	-0.8	4	1	0.4
1923	StL-N	3	3	.500	33	2	1	1	1	101	112	10.0	7	27	2.4	23	2.0	3.74	96	.289	.327	3	-2	90	110	0.0	-0	0	-0.2
1926	Det-A	1	2	.333	11	1	0	0	2	31	42	12.2	4	9	2.6	7	2.0	4.94	79	.318	.354	-3	-3	98	109	-0.4	0	1	-0.2
Total	3	8	10	.444	86	5	2	1	5	250	293	10.5	13	66	2.4	49	1.8	4.10	95	.301	.339	-1	-6	96	106	-1.2	4	1	0.0
■ **GREG BARGAR**	Bargar, Greg Robert b: 1/27/59, Inglewood, Cal. BR/TR, 6'2", 185 lbs. Deb: 7/17/83																												
1983	Mon-N	2	0	1.000	8	3	0	0	0	20	23	10.3	6	8	3.6	9	4.0	6.75	55	.271	.340	-7	-7	101	85	1.0	-0	-0	-0.6
1984	Mon-N	0	1	.000	3	1	0	0	0	8	8	9.0	1	7	7.9	2	2.3	7.88	42	.286	.417	-4	-4	91	80	-0.4	-0	0	-0.3
1986	StL-N	0	2	.000	22	0	0	0	0	27	36	12.0	3	10	3.3	12	4.0	5.67	68	.330	.389	-6	-5	103	110	-0.9	-0	1	-0.4
Total	3	2	3	.400	33	4	0	0	0	55	67	11.0	10	25	4.1	23	3.8	6.38	58	.302	.375	-17	-16	101	97	-0.3	-0	0	-1.3
■ **CY BARGER**	Barger, Eros Bolivar b: 5/18/1885, Jamestown, Ky. d: 9/23/64, Columbia, Ky. BL/TR, 6', 160 lbs. Deb: 8/30/06																												
1906	NY-A	0	0	—	2	1	0	0	1	5	7	12.6	0	3	5.4	3	5.4	10.80	29	.359	.444	-5	-4	118	54	0.0	0	0	-0.3
1907	NY-A	0	0	—	1	0	0	0	0	6	10	15.0	0	1	1.5	0	0.0	3.00	93	.399	.422	-0	-0	110	194	0.0	-0	-1	0.0
1910	Bro-N	15	15	.500	35	30	25	2	1	272	267	8.8	2	107	3.5	87	2.9	2.88	103	.275	.351	5	3	98	122	2.6	4	2	0.8
1911	Bro-N	11	15	.423	30	30	21	1	0	217	224	9.3	4	71	2.9	60	2.5	3.53	96	.279	.342	-3	-4	99	104	0.0	1	1	0.0
1912	Bro-N	1	9	.100	16	11	6	0	0	94	120	11.5	4	42	4.0	30	2.9	5.46	61	.316	.390	-21	-22	97	92	-3.6	0	1	-1.9
1914	Pit-F	10	16	.385	33	26	18	1	1	228	252	9.9	7	63	2.5	70	2.8	4.34	71	.290	.342	-29	-32	96	89	-1.4	1	-1	-3.1
1915	Pit-F	9	8	.529	34	13	8	1	6	153	130	7.6	1	47	2.8	47	2.8	2.29	135	.238	.303	13	14	102	110	-0.5	2	2	2.0
Total	7	46	63	.422	151	111	78	5	9	975	1010	9.3	18	334	3.1	297	2.7	3.56	88	.279	.345	-41	-46	98	106	-2.9	8	4	-2.5
■ **LEN BARKER**	Barker, Leonard Harold b: 7/7/55, Fort Knox, Ky. BR/TR, 6'5", 225 lbs. Deb: 9/14/76																												
1976	Tex-A	1	0	1.000	2	2	1	1	0	15	7	4.2	0	6	3.6	7	4.2	2.40	150	.149	.268	2	2	103	56	0.5	0	0	0.2
1977	Tex-A	4	1	.800	15	3	0	0	1	47	36	6.9	1	24	4.6	51	9.8	2.68	157	.217	.311	7	8	104	102	1.3	0	1	0.9
1978	Tex-A	1	5	.167	29	0	0	0	4	52	63	10.9	6	29	5.0	33	5.7	4.85	75	.304	.387	-6	-7	96	119	-2.0	0	0	-0.6
1979	Cle-A	6	6	.500	29	19	2	0	0	137	146	9.6	6	70	4.6	93	6.1	4.93	91	.277	.358	-11	-7	106	88	0.0	0	-1	-0.7
1980	Cle-A	19	12	.613	36	36	8	1	0	246	237	8.7	17	92	3.4	**187**	**6.8**	4.17	100	.252	.316	-3	-0	103	82	4.3	0	-2	-0.1
1981	Cle-A	8	7	.533	22	22	9	3	0	154	150	8.8	7	46	2.7	**127**	**7.4**	3.92	87	.249	.298	-4	-8	93	75	0.5	0	0	-0.8
1982	Cle-A	15	11	.577	33	33	10	1	0	245	211	7.8	17	88	3.2	187	6.9	3.89	106	.232	.296	5	6	101	76	2.8	0	0	0.6
1983	Cle-A	8	13	.381	24	24	4	1	0	150	150	9.0	16	52	3.1	105	6.3	5.10	85	.266	.322	-17	-13	106	82	-1.3	0	-1	-1.3
	Atl-N	1	3	.250	6	6	0	0	0	33	31	8.5	0	14	3.8	21	5.7	3.82	99	.248	.315	-1	-0	104	76	-1.0	-0	1	0.0
1984	Atl-N	7	8	.467	21	20	1	0	0	126	120	8.6	10	38	2.7	95	6.8	3.86	102	.254	.303	-4	1	110	90	-0.4	-1	3	0.4
1985	Atl-N	2	9	.182	20	18	0	0	0	74	84	10.2	10	37	4.5	47	5.7	6.32	62	.288	.364	-22	-20	108	84	-3.0	-2	-1	-2.2
1987	Mil-A	2	1	.667	11	11	0	0	0	44	54	11.0	6	17	3.5	22	4.5	5.32	86	.303	.369	-4	-4	102	106	0.4	0	0	-0.3
Total	11	74	76	.493	248	194	35	7	5	1323	1289	8.8	96	513	3.5	975	6.6	4.35	93	.256	.321	-58	-42	103	84	2.1	-4	0	-3.9
■ **JEFF BARKLEY**	Barkley, Jeffrey Carver b: 11/21/59, Hickory, N.C. BB/TR, 6'3", 185 lbs. Deb: 9/16/84																												
1984	Cle-A	0	0	—	3	0	0	0	0	4	6	13.5	0	1	2.3	4	9.0	6.75	63	.353	.368	-1	-1	106	81	0.0	0	0	0.0
1985	Cle-A	0	3	.000	21	0	0	0	1	41	37	8.1	5	15	3.3	30	6.6	5.27	75	.243	.299	-5	-6	95	71	-1.4	0	0	-0.5
Total	2	0	3	.000	24	0	0	0	1	45	43	8.6	5	16	3.2	34	6.8	5.40	74	.254	.306	-6	-7	96	72	-1.4	0	0	-0.5
■ **MIKE BARLOW**	Barlow, Michael Roswell b: 4/30/48, Stamford, N.Y. BL/TR, 6'6", 210 lbs. Deb: 6/18/75																												
1975	StL-N	0	0	—	9	0	0	0	0	8	11	12.4	0	3	3.4	2	2.3	4.50	83	.355	.405	-1	-1	103	134	0.0	0	-0	0.0
1976	Hou-N	2	2	.500	16	0	0	0	0	22	27	11.0	0	17	7.0	11	4.5	4.50	67	.318	.411	-2	-4	87	129	0.0	-0	1	-0.2
1977	Cal-A	4	2	.667	20	1	0	0	1	59	53	8.1	3	27	4.1	25	3.8	4.58	84	.249	.336	-3	-5	95	81	1.2	0	0	-0.4
1978	Cal-A	0	0	—	1	0	0	0	0	2	3	13.5	0	0	0.0	1	4.5	4.50	85	.375	.375	-0	-0	101	117	0.0	0	0	0.0
1979	Cal-A	1	1	.500	35	0	0	0	0	86	106	11.1	8	30	3.1	33	3.5	5.13	76	.314	.370	-9	-12	92	105	0.0	0	-0	-1.1
1980	Tor-A	3	1	.750	40	1	0	0	5	55	57	9.3	4	21	3.4	19	3.1	4.09	100	.273	.338	-0	0	101	101	1.2	0	-0	0.0
1981	Tor-A	0	0	—	12	0	0	0	0	15	22	13.2	1	6	3.6	5	3.0	4.20	99	.338	.410	-1	-0	113	159	0.0	0	-0	0.0
Total	7	10	6	.625	133	2	0	0	6	247	279	10.2	16	104	3.8	96	3.5	4.63	83	.294	.363	-16	-21	96	105	2.4	-0	0	-1.7

YEAR	TM/L	W	L	PCT	G	GS	CG	SHO	SV	IP	H	H/G	HR	BB	BB/G	SO	SO/G	ERA	/A	OAVG	OOBP	PR	/A	PF	CPI	WAT	PB	PD	TPI
■ CHARLIE BARNABE	Barnabe, Charles Edward b: 6/12/1900, Russell Gulch, Colo. d: 8/16/77, Waco, Tex. BL/TL, 5'11.5", 164 lbs. Deb: 4/14/27																												
1927	Chi-A	0	5	.000	17	4	1	0	0	61	86	12.7	2	20	3.0	5	0.7	5.31	80	.351	.391	-8	-7	103	114	-2.4	1	1	-0.4
1928	Chi-A	0	2	.000	7	2	0	0	0	10	17	15.3	0	0	0.0	3	2.7	6.30	64	.395	.400	-3	-2	100	103	-0.9	2	1	0.1
Total	2	0	7	.000	24	6	1	0	0	71	103	13.1	2	20	2.5	8	1.0	5.45	78	.358	.392	-10	-10	102	113	-3.3	3	1	-0.3
■ FRANK BARNES	Barnes, Frank b: 8/26/28, Longwood, Miss. BR/TR, 6', 170 lbs. Deb: 9/22/57																												
1957	StL-N	0	1	.000	3	1	0	0	0	10	13	11.7	0	9	8.1	5	4.5	4.50	86	.317	.440	-1	-1	99	136	-0.4	-0	-0	0.0
1958	StL-N	1	1	.500	8	1	0	0	0	19	19	9.0	3	16	7.6	17	8.1	7.58	56	.260	.398	-8	-7	108	77	0.1	-0	0	-0.7
1960	StL-N	0	1	.000	4	1	0	0	1	8	8	9.0	1	9	10.1	8	9.0	3.38	120	.267	.439	0	1	108	201	-0.4	-0	-0	0.0
Total	3	1	3	.250	15	3	0	0	1	37	40	9.7	4	34	8.3	30	7.3	5.84	70	.278	.418	-8	-7	106	120	-0.7	-1	-1	-0.7
■ FRANK BARNES	Barnes, Frank Samuel "Lefty" b: 1/9/1900, Dallas, Tex. d: 9/27/67, Houston, Tex. BL/TL, 6'2.5", 195 lbs. Deb: 4/18/29																												
1929	Det-A	0	1	.000	4	1	0	0	0	5	10	18.0	0	3	5.4	0	0.0	7.20	57	.400	.483	-2	-2	97	124	-0.4	-0	0	-0.1
1930	NY-A	0	1	.000	2	2	0	0	0	12	13	9.8	0	13	9.8	2	1.5	8.25	49	.283	.435	-5	-6	87	76	-0.4	1	1	-0.2
Total	2	0	2	.000	6	3	0	0	0	17	23	12.2	0	16	8.5	2	1.1	7.94	52	.324	.451	-6	-7	90	90	-0.8	1	2	-0.3
■ JESS BARNES	Barnes, Jesse Lawrence "Nubby" b: 8/26/1892, Perkins, Okla. d: 9/9/61, Santa Rosa, N.Mex. BL/TR, 6', 170 lbs. Deb: 7/30/15																												
1915	Bos-N	3	0	1.000	9	3	2	0	0	45	41	8.2	1	10	2.0	16	3.2	1.40	191	.244	.299	7	6	97	186	1.5	-0	-1	0.7
1916	Bos-N	6	14	.300	33	18	9	3	1	163	154	8.5	3	37	2.0	55	3.0	2.37	100	.254	.294	4	0	91	111	-5.1	1	4	0.4
1917	Bos-N	13	21	.382	50	33	27	2	1	295	261	8.0	3	50	1.5	107	3.3	2.68	97	.241	.269	1	-2	97	79	-3.8	4	3	0.5
1918	NY-N	6	1	.857	9	9	4	2	0	55	53	8.7	0	13	2.1	12	2.0	1.80	147	.255	.295	6	5	96	137	2.4	-0	2	0.8
1919	NY-N	**25**	9	.735	38	34	23	4	1	296	263	8.0	8	35	1.1	92	2.8	2.40	117	.236	.255	17	13	96	80	**6.2**	5	3	2.4
1920	NY-N	20	15	.571	43	35	23	2	0	293	271	8.3	9	56	1.7	63	1.9	2.64	115	.250	.277	16	13	97	87	0.7	-2	3	1.3
1921	NY-N	15	9	.625	42	31	15	1	6	259	298	10.4	13	44	1.5	56	1.9	3.09	115	.299	.321	20	13	94	**124**	0.4	-0	1	1.3
1922	NY-N	13	8	.619	37	30	14	2	0	213	236	10.0	10	38	1.6	52	2.2	3.51	117	.278	.306	14	14	100	92	0.5	-1	3	1.6
1923	NY-N	3	1	.750	12	4	1	0	1	36	48	12.0	1	13	3.3	12	3.0	6.25	63	.329	.379	-9	-9	99	82	0.7	0	1	-0.6
	Bos-N	10	14	.417	31	23	12	5	2	195	204	9.4	8	43	2.0	41	1.9	2.77	148	.270	.304	27	29	102	114	1.4	-4	3	2.8
	Yr	13	15	.464	43	27	13	5	3	231	252	9.8	9	56	2.2	53	2.1	3.31	123	.280	.316	18	20	102	114	2.1	0	4	2.2
1924	Bos-N	15	20	.429	37	32	21	4	0	268	292	9.8	7	53	1.8	49	1.6	3.22	119	.284	.311	19	18	99	107	2.7	-1	1	1.7
1925	Bos-N	11	16	.407	32	28	17	0	0	216	255	10.6	14	63	2.6	55	2.3	4.54	89	.297	.334	-7	-11	95	96	-1.7	-1	-2	-1.3
1926	Bro-N	10	11	.476	31	24	10	1	1	158	204	11.6	6	35	2.0	29	1.7	5.24	73	.321	.348	-25	-24	101	89	0.3	-0	-1	-2.3
1927	Bro-N	2	10	.167	18	10	2	0	0	79	106	12.1	5	25	2.8	14	1.6	5.70	72	.331	.364	-16	-14	104	95	-3.7	-0	-0	-1.3
Total	13	152	149	.505	422	314	180	26	13	2571	2686	9.4	88	515	1.8	653	2.3	3.21	105	.273	.302	75	48	97	99	2.5	-0	20	8.0
■ JUNIE BARNES	Barnes, Junie Shoaf "Lefty" b: 12/1/11, Linwood, N.C. d: 12/31/63, Jacksonville, N.C. BL/TL, 5'11.5", 170 lbs. Deb: 9/12/34																												
1934	Cin-N	0	0	—	2	0	0	0	0	⅓	0	0/0	0	1	27.0	0	0.0	0.00	—	.000	.500	0	0	105	0	0.0	0	0	0.0
■ RICH BARNES	Barnes, Richard Monroe b: 7/21/59, Palm Beach, Fla. BR/TL, 6'4", 186 lbs. Deb: 7/18/82																												
1982	Chi-A	0	2	.000	6	2	0	0	1	17	21	11.1	1	4	2.1	6	3.2	4.76	83	.292	.342	-1	-2	97	91	-0.9	0	0	0.0
1983	Cle-A	1	1	.500	4	2	0	0	0	12	18	13.5	0	10	7.5	2	1.5	6.75	64	.375	.475	-4	-3	106	115	0.1	0	0	-0.2
Total	2	1	3	.250	10	4	0	0	1	29	39	12.1	1	14	4.3	8	2.5	5.59	73	.325	.399	-5	-5	101	101	-0.8	0	0	-0.2
■ BOB BARNES	Barnes, Robert Avery "Lefty" b: 1/6/02, Washburn, Ill. BL/TL, 5'11.5", 150 lbs. Deb: 7/08/24																												
1924	Chi-A	0	0	—	2	0	0	0	0	5	14	25.2	1	0	0.0	1	1.8	18.00	23	.519	.483	-8	-8	98	73	0.0	-0	0	-0.5
■ ROSS BARNES	Barnes, Roscoe Charles b: 5/8/1850, Mt.Morris, N.Y. d: 2/5/15, Chicago, Ill. BR/TR, 5'8.5", 145 lbs. Deb: 5/05/1871																												
1876	Chi-N	0	0	—	1	0	0	0	0	1	7	63.0	0	0	0.0	0	0.0	27.00	10	.716	.716	-3	-3	113	111	0.0	1	0	-0.1
■ VIRGIL BARNES	Barnes, Virgil Jennings "Zeke" b: 3/5/1897, Ontario, Kan. BR/TR, 6', 165 lbs. Deb: 9/25/19																												
1919	NY-N	0	0	—	1	0	0	0	0	2	6	27.0	0	1	4.5	1	4.5	18.00	16	.545	.583	-3	-3	96	77	0.0	0	0	-0.2
1920	NY-N	0	1	.000	1	1	0	0	0	7	9	11.6	0	1	1.3	2	2.6	3.86	78	.310	.333	-1	-1	97	91	-0.4	-0	0	0.0
1922	NY-N	1	0	1.000	22	3	1	0	2	52	46	8.0	1	11	1.9	16	2.8	3.46	119	.243	.277	4	4	100	66	0.5	-1	0	0.3
1923	NY-N	2	3	.400	22	2	0	0	1	53	59	10.0	2	19	3.2	6	1.0	3.91	101	.285	.336	1	0	99	101	-0.8	-2	0	-0.1
1924	NY-N	16	10	.615	35	29	15	1	3	229	239	9.4	10	57	2.2	59	2.3	3.07	110	.270	.309	20	8	88	108	0.3	-1	2	0.7
1925	NY-N	15	11	.577	32	27	17	1	2	222	242	9.8	9	53	2.1	53	2.1	3.53	119	.281	.317	18	17	98	102	0.4	-9	0	0.7
1926	NY-N	8	13	.381	31	25	9	2	1	185	183	8.9	4	56	2.7	54	2.6	2.87	130	.261	.311	20	18	98	109	-2.5	-7	-1	1.0
1927	NY-N	14	11	.560	35	29	12	2	2	229	251	9.9	14	51	2.0	66	2.6	3.97	97	.283	.318	-1	-3	98	97	-0.8	-7	-1	-1.0
1928	NY-N	3	3	.500	10	9	3	1	0	55	71	11.6	3	18	2.9	11	1.8	5.07	78	.330	.363	-7	-7	99	104	-0.4	-2	-1	-0.8
	Bos-N	2	7	.222	16	10	1	0	0	60	86	12.9	3	26	3.9	7	1.1	5.85	69	.344	.392	-12	-12	101	102	-1.4	-2	-1	-1.2
	Yr	5	10	.333	26	19	4	1	0	115	157	12.3	6	44	3.4	18	1.4	5.48	73	.338	.379	-19	-19	100	102	-1.8	-2	-1	-2.0
Total	9	61	59	.508	205	135	58	7	11	1094	1192	9.8	46	293	2.4	275	2.3	3.66	104	.282	.322	38	20	96	101	-5.1	-30	1	-0.6
■ REX BARNEY	Barney, Rex Edward b: 12/19/24, Omaha, Neb. BR/TR, 6'3", 185 lbs. Deb: 8/18/43																												
1943	Bro-N	2	2	.500	9	8	1	0	0	45	36	7.2	4	41	8.2	23	4.6	6.40	52	.217	.369	-15	-15	99	68	0.0	-2	-0	-1.5
1946	Bro-N	2	5	.286	16	9	1	0	0	54	46	7.7	2	51	8.5	36	6.0	5.83	59	.240	.390	-15	-15	100	77	-1.8	1	-0	-1.3
1947	Bro-N	5	2	.714	28	9	0	0	0	78	66	7.6	4	59	6.8	36	4.2	4.73	88	.240	.372	-6	-5	103	91	1.0	-1	-0	-0.6
1948	Bro-N	15	13	.536	44	34	12	4	0	247	193	7.0	17	122	4.4	138	5.0	3.10	131	.217	.312	24	27	103	101	-0.2	-2	-4	2.1
1949	Bro-N	9	8	.529	38	20	6	2	1	141	108	6.9	15	89	5.7	80	5.1	4.40	89	.216	.337	-6	-7	98	87	-1.4	1	-3	-0.9
1950	Bro-N	2	1	.667	20	1	0	0	0	34	25	6.6	6	48	12.7	23	6.1	6.35	68	.214	.449	-8	-8	104	104	0.3	0	-1	-0.7
Total	6	35	31	.530	155	81	20	6	1	599	474	7.1	48	410	6.2	336	5.0	4.30	92	.221	.347	-26	-23	101	92	-2.1	-4	-8	-2.9
■ EDGAR BARNHART	Barnhart, Edgar Vernon b: 9/16/04, Providence, Mo. BL/TR, 5'10", 160 lbs. Deb: 9/23/24																												
1924	StL-A	0	0	—	1	0	0	0	0	1	0	0.0	0	2	18.0	0	0.0	0.00	—	.000	.400	0	1	108	0	0.0	0	0	0.1
■ LES BARNHART	Barnhart, Leslie Earl "Barney" b: 2/23/05, Hoxie, Kan. d: 10/7/71, Scottsdale, Ariz. BR/TR, 6', 180 lbs. Deb: 9/22/28																												
1928	Cle-A	0	1	.000	2	1	0	0	0	9	13	13.0	1	4	4.0	1	1.0	7.00	63	.325	.386	-3	-3	108	86	-0.4	0	-0	-0.2
1930	Cle-A	1	0	1.000	1	1	0	0	0	8	12	13.5	0	4	4.5	1	1.1	6.75	73	.364	.400	-2	-2	105	101	0.5	-1	0	-0.1
Total	2	1	1	.500	3	2	0	0	0	17	25	13.2	1	8	4.2	2	1.1	6.88	67	.342	.393	-5	-4	107	93	0.1	-0	-0	-0.3
■ GEORGE BARNICLE	Barnicle, George Bernard "Barney" b: 8/26/17, Fitchburg, Mass. BR/TR, 6'2", 175 lbs. Deb: 9/06/39																												
1939	Bos-N	2	2	.500	6	1	0	0	0	18	16	8.0	1	8	4.0	15	7.5	5.00	73	.235	.304	-2	-3	93	62	0.3	-1	0	-0.2
1940	Bos-N	1	0	1.000	13	2	1	0	0	33	28	7.6	1	31	8.5	11	3.0	7.36	53	.233	.411	-13	-13	101	68	0.5	-1	1	-1.2
1941	Bos-N	0	1	.000	1	1	0	0	0	7	5	6.4	0	4	5.1	2	2.6	6.43	54	.238	.345	-2	-2	96	63	-0.4	-0	0	-0.1
Total	3	3	3	.500	20	4	1	0	0	58	49	7.6	2	43	6.7	28	4.3	6.52	58	.234	.372	-17	-18	98	66	0.4	-2	1	-1.5
■ ED BARNOWSKI	Barnowski, Edward Anthony b: 8/23/43, Scranton, Pa. BR/TR, 6'2", 195 lbs. Deb: 9/08/65																												
1965	Bal-A	0	0	—	4	0	0	0	0	4	3	6.8	0	7	15.8	6	13.5	2.25	152	.200	.455	1	1	99	240	0.0	0	0	0.0
1966	Bal-A	0	0	—	2	0	0	0	0	3	4	12.0	0	1	3.0	2	6.0	3.00	113	.364	.385	0	0	99	195	0.0	0	0	0.0
Total	2	0	0	—	6	0	0	0	0	7	7	9.0	0	8	10.3	8	10.3	2.57	132	.269	.429	1	1	99	221	0.0	0	0	0.0
■ SALOME BAROJAS	Barojas, Salome (Romero) b: 6/16/57, Cordoba, Mex. BR/TR, 5'9", 160 lbs. Deb: 4/11/82																												
1982	Chi-A	6	6	.500	61	0	0	0	21	107	96	8.1	9	46	3.9	56	4.7	3.53	112	.244	.321	7	5	97	102	-0.3	0	3	0.8
1983	Chi-A	3	3	.500	52	0	0	0	12	87	70	7.2	2	32	3.3	38	3.9	2.48	167	.224	.301	15	16	102	108	-0.5	0	0	1.6
1984	Chi-A	3	2	.600	24	0	0	0	1	39	48	11.1	3	19	4.4	18	4.2	4.62	96	.310	.379	-3	-1	111	117	0.7	0	1	0.0
	Sea-A	6	5	.545	19	14	0	0	1	95	88	8.3	12	41	3.9	37	3.5	3.98	104	.249	.330	0	2	103	104	1.0	0	1	0.2
	Yr	9	7	.563	43	14	0	0	2	134	136	9.1	15	60	4.0	55	3.7	4.16	101	.268	.345	-2	1	105	104	1.7	0	2	0.2
1985	Sea-A	0	5	.000	17	4	0	0	0	53	65	11.0	6	33	5.6	27	4.6	5.94	67	.305	.392	-11	-12	95	102	-2.4	0	0	-1.0
1988	Phi-N	0	0	—	6	0	0	0	0	9	7	7.0	1	8	8.0	1	1.0	8.00	44	.250	.385	-5	-4	103	69	0.0	0	0	-0.4
Total	5	18	21	.462	179	18	0	0	35	390	374	8.6	33	179	4.1	177	4.1	3.95	103	.257	.337	4	6	101	104	-1.5	0	5	1.2
■ JIM BARR	Barr, James Leland b: 2/10/48, Lynwood, Cal. BR/TR, 6'3", 205 lbs. Deb: 7/31/71																												
1971	SF-N	1	1	.500	17	0	0	0	0	35	33	8.5	3	5	1.3	16	4.1	3.60	95	.254	.275	-1	-1	99	85	0.0	-0	1	0.0

YEAR	TM/L	W	L	PCT	G	GS	CG	SHO	SV	IP	H	H/G	HR	BB	BB/G	SO	SO/G	ERA	/A	OAVG	OOBP	PR	/A	PF	CPI	WAT	PB	PD	TPI
1972	SF-N	8	10	.444	44	18	8	2	2	179	166	8.3	16	41	2.1	86	4.3	2.87	120	.246	.287	12	11	100	108	0.0	1	1	1.4
1973	SF-N	11	17	.393	41	33	8	3	2	231	240	9.4	24	49	1.9	88	3.4	3.82	100	.268	.304	-4	0	104	96	-4.3	-1	-0	0.0
1974	SF-N	13	9	.591	44	27	11	5	2	240	223	8.4	17	47	**1.8**	84	3.2	2.74	144	.251	.284	24	32	109	107	3.2	4	1	4.1
1975	SF-N	13	14	.481	35	33	12	2	0	244	244	9.0	17	58	2.1	77	2.8	3.06	121	.265	.304	15	17	102	110	-0.4	-2	3	1.9
1976	SF-N	15	12	.556	37	37	8	3	0	252	260	9.3	9	60	2.1	75	2.7	2.89	126	.266	.305	17	21	104	110	2.8	2	3	3.0
1977	SF-N	12	16	.429	38	38	6	2	0	234	286	11.0	18	56	2.2	97	3.7	4.77	86	.306	.341	-22	-17	105	96	-1.1	-2	3	-1.6
1978	SF-N	8	11	.421	32	25	5	2	1	163	180	9.9	7	35	1.9	44	2.4	3.53	92	.281	.312	1	-5	91	101	-2.3	-2	1	-0.6
1979	Cal-A	10	12	.455	36	25	5	0	0	197	217	9.9	22	55	2.5	69	3.2	4.20	92	.287	.333	1	-7	92	108	-1.9	0	2	-0.5
1980	Cal-A	1	4	.200	24	7	0	0	1	68	90	11.9	12	23	3.0	22	2.9	5.56	70	.323	.373	-11	-12	97	111	-1.2	0	-1	-1.2
1982	SF-N	4	3	.571	53	9	1	1	2	129	125	8.7	9	20	1.4	36	2.5	3.28	103	.262	.287	5	1	94	98	0.3	2	0	0.3
1983	SF-N	5	3	.625	53	0	0	0	2	93	106	10.3	7	20	1.9	47	4.5	3.97	92	.294	.322	-3	-3	101	105	1.1	-0	0	-0.2
Total	12	101	112	.474	454	252	64	20	12	2065	2170	9.5	161	469	2.0	741	3.2	3.56	105	.273	.310	33	39	101	104	-3.8	0	12	6.6

■ BOB BARR Barr, Robert Alexander b: 3/12/08, Newton, Mass. BR/TR, 6', 175 lbs. Deb: 9/11/35

YEAR	TM/L	W	L	PCT	G	GS	CG	SHO	SV	IP	H	H/G	HR	BB	BB/G	SO	SO/G	ERA	/A	OAVG	OOBP	PR	/A	PF	CPI	WAT	PB	PD	TPI
1935	Bro-N	0	0	—	2	0	0	0	0	2	5	22.5	0	2	9.0	0	0.0	4.50	85	.385	.467	-0	-0	95	216	0.0	0	0	0.0

■ BOB BARR Barr, Robert Mc Clelland b: 1856, Washington, D.C. d: 3/11/30, Washington, D.C. BR/TR, 6'1", 192 lbs. Deb: 1883

YEAR	TM/L	W	L	PCT	G	GS	CG	SHO	SV	IP	H	H/G	HR	BB	BB/G	SO	SO/G	ERA	/A	OAVG	OOBP	PR	/A	PF	CPI	WAT	PB	PD	TPI
1883	Pit-a	6	18	.250	26	23	19	0	**1**	203	263	11.7	5	28	1.2	81	3.6	4.39	74	.319	.342	-25	-26	98	103	-3.0	3	0	-1.8
1884	Was-a	9	23	.281	32	32	32	2	0	281	311	10.0	11	31	1.0	138	4.4	3.46	87	.289	.309	-7	-14	93	111	3.3	-2	-1	-1.5
	Ind-a	3	11	.214	16	16	15	0	0	132	160	10.9	2	19	1.3	69	4.7	4.98	65	.308	.333	-25	-25	100	86	-1.5	0	0	-2.0
	Yr	12	34	.261	48	48	47	2	0	413	471	10.3	13	50	1.1	207	4.5	3.94	79	.295	.317	-32	-39	96	86	1.8	-2	-1	-3.5
1886	Was-N	3	18	.143	22	22	21	1	0	191	216	10.2	7	54	2.5	80	3.8	4.34	76	.298	.347	-22	-22	100	92	-4.5	-2	0	-2.0
1890	Roc-a	28	24	.538	57	54	52	3	0	493	458	8.4	7	219	4.0	209	3.8	3.25	109	.261	.343	34	17	92	106	3.2	-1	4	1.6
1891	NY-N	0	4	.000	5	4	2	0	0	27	47	15.7	1	12	4.0	11	3.7	5.33	58	.396	.452	-6	-7	93	133	-1.9	-0	0	-0.5
Total	5	49	98	.333	158	151	141	6	1	1327	1455	9.9	33	363	2.5	588	4.0	3.84	87	.290	.338	-51	-75	95	103	-4.4	-3	3	-6.2

■ STEVE BARR Barr, Steven Charles b: 9/8/51, St.Louis, Mo. BL/TL, 6'4", 200 lbs. Deb: 10/01/74

YEAR	TM/L	W	L	PCT	G	GS	CG	SHO	SV	IP	H	H/G	HR	BB	BB/G	SO	SO/G	ERA	/A	OAVG	OOBP	PR	/A	PF	CPI	WAT	PB	PD	TPI
1974	Bos-A	1	0	1.000	1	1	1	0	0	9	7	7.0	0	6	6.0	3	3.0	4.00	96	.212	.333	-0	-0	106	67	0.5	0	0	0.0
1975	Bos-A	0	1	.000	3	2	0	0	0	7	11	14.1	1	7	9.0	2	2.6	2.57	159	.367	.474	1	1	108	350	-0.4	0	0	0.1
1976	Tex-A	2	6	.250	20	10	3	0	0	68	70	9.3	10	44	5.8	27	3.6	5.56	65	.269	.369	-15	-15	103	95	-1.8	0	0	-1.4
Total	3	3	7	.300	24	13	4	0	0	84	88	9.4	11	57	6.1	32	3.4	5.14	71	.272	.376	-15	-14	103	113	-1.7	0	0	-1.3

■ RED BARRETT Barrett, Charles Henry b: 2/14/15, Santa Barbara, Cal BR/TR, 5'11", 183 lbs. Deb: 9/15/37

YEAR	TM/L	W	L	PCT	G	GS	CG	SHO	SV	IP	H	H/G	HR	BB	BB/G	SO	SO/G	ERA	/A	OAVG	OOBP	PR	/A	PF	CPI	WAT	PB	PD	TPI
1937	Cin-N	0	0	—	1	0	0	0	0	6	5	7.5	0	2	3.0	1	1.5	1.50	243	.227	.292	2	1	93	155	0.0	-0	-0	0.1
1938	Cin-N	2	0	1.000	6	2	2	0	0	29	28	8.7	2	15	4.7	5	1.6	3.10	117	.257	.341	2	2	96	132	1.0	-0	-0	0.1
1939	Cin-N	0	0	—	2	0	0	0	0	5	5	9.0	0	1	1.8	1	1.8	1.80	217	.263	.273	1	1	100	154	0.0	-0	0	0.1
1940	Cin-N	1	0	1.000	3	0	0	0	0	3	5	15.0	0	1	3.0	0	0.0	6.00	63	.455	.500	-1	-1	98	141	0.5	0	0	0.0
1943	Bos-N	12	18	.400	38	31	14	3	0	255	240	8.5	11	63	2.2	64	2.3	3.18	115	.250	.290	6	14	109	91	-1.7	-5	1	1.2
1944	Bos-N	9	16	.360	42	30	11	1	2	230	257	10.1	13	63	2.5	54	2.1	4.07	85	.279	.321	-12	-15	96	95	-2.0	-1	2	-1.4
1945	Bos-N	2	3	.400	9	5	2	0	2	38	43	10.2	6	16	3.8	13	3.1	4.74	90	.281	.345	-4	-2	113	109	-0.1	-0	1	0.0
	StL-N	21	9	.700	36	29	22	3	0	247	244	8.9	12	38	1.4	63	2.3	2.73	135	.256	.283	29	26	97	105	3.8	-5	-1	2.1
	Yr	**23**	12	.657	45	34	**24**	3	2	**285**	287	9.1	18	54	1.7	76	2.4	3.00	126	.259	.291	25	24	99	105	3.7	-0	0	2.1
1946	StL-N	3	2	.600	23	9	1	1	2	67	75	10.1	5	24	3.2	22	3.0	4.03	87	.282	.339	-5	-4	103	104	0.0	-1	1	-0.4
1947	Bos-N	11	12	.478	36	30	12	3	1	211	200	8.5	16	53	2.3	53	2.3	3.54	110	.244	.289	12	8	95	83	-1.8	-2	-0	0.5
1948	Bos-N	7	8	.467	34	13	3	0	0	128	132	9.3	9	26	1.8	40	2.8	3.66	107	.268	.300	4	4	99	96	-1.6	-1	1	0.4
1949	Bos-N	1	1	.500	23	0	0	0	0	44	58	11.9	4	10	2.0	17	3.5	5.73	68	.326	.355	-8	-9	97	96	0.0	-0	1	-0.7
Total	11	69	69	.500	253	149	67	11	7	1263	1292	9.2	78	312	2.2	333	2.4	3.53	105	.264	.304	27	26	100	97	-1.9	-15	5	2.0

■ FRANK BARRETT Barrett, Francis Joseph "Red" b: 7/1/13, Ft.Lauderdale, Fla BR/TR, 6'2", 173 lbs. Deb: 10/01/39

YEAR	TM/L	W	L	PCT	G	GS	CG	SHO	SV	IP	H	H/G	HR	BB	BB/G	SO	SO/G	ERA	/A	OAVG	OOBP	PR	/A	PF	CPI	WAT	PB	PD	TPI
1939	StL-N	0	1	.000	1	0	0	0	0	2	1	4.5	0	1	4.5	3	13.5	4.50	89	.167	.286	-0	-0	103	41	-0.4	0	0	0.0
1944	Bos-A	8	7	.533	38	2	0	0	8	90	93	9.3	5	42	4.2	40	4.0	3.70	90	.271	.343	-3	-4	97	112	0.6	-1	0	-0.4
1945	Bos-A	4	3	.571	37	0	0	0	3	86	77	8.1	0	29	3.0	35	3.7	2.62	124	.249	.307	7	6	96	108	0.7	1	-1	0.7
1946	Bos-N	2	4	.333	23	0	0	0	1	35	35	9.0	2	17	4.4	12	3.1	5.14	62	.252	.331	-7	-8	94	69	-1.0	-1	1	-0.7
1950	Pit-N	1	2	.333	5	0	0	0	0	4	5	11.3	1	1	2.3	0	0.0	4.50	97	.357	.375	-0	-0	106	165	-0.1	0	0	0.0
Total	5	15	17	.469	104	2	0	0	12	217	211	8.8	8	90	3.7	90	3.7	3.53	93	.260	.328	-3	-6	96	104	-0.2	-1	1	-0.4

■ TIM BARRETT Barrett, Timothy Wayne b: 1/24/61, Huntingburg, Ind. BL/TR, 6'1", 185 lbs. Deb: 7/18/88

YEAR	TM/L	W	L	PCT	G	GS	CG	SHO	SV	IP	H	H/G	HR	BB	BB/G	SO	SO/G	ERA	/A	OAVG	OOBP	PR	/A	PF	CPI	WAT	PB	PD	TPI
1988	Mon-N	0	0	—	4	0	0	0	1	9	10	10.0	2	2	2.0	5	5.0	6.00	60	.270	.308	-3	-2	105	79	0.0	-0	0	-0.2

■ DICK BARRETT Barrett, Tracy Souter (a.k.a. Richard Oliver Barrett 1933-43) b: 9/28/06, Montoursville, Pa d: 10/30/66, Seattle, Wash. BR/TR, 5'9", 175 lbs. Deb: 6/27/33

YEAR	TM/L	W	L	PCT	G	GS	CG	SHO	SV	IP	H	H/G	HR	BB	BB/G	SO	SO/G	ERA	/A	OAVG	OOBP	PR	/A	PF	CPI	WAT	PB	PD	TPI
1933	Phi-A	4	4	.500	15	7	3	0	0	70	74	9.5	2	49	6.3	26	3.3	5.79	68	.272	.377	-12	-15	92	85	-0.1	2	0	-1.1
1934	Bos-N	1	3	.250	15	3	0	0	0	32	50	14.1	2	12	3.4	14	3.9	6.75	52	.365	.411	-10	-12	86	101	-0.9	-0	1	-0.9
1943	Chi-N	0	4	.000	15	4	0	0	0	45	52	10.4	2	28	5.6	20	4.0	4.80	69	.291	.384	-7	-7	98	105	-1.9	-1	0	-0.7
	Phi-N	10	9	.526	23	20	10	2	1	169	137	7.3	5	51	2.7	65	3.5	2.40	135	.221	.278	18	16	96	93	2.0	-0	0	1.7
	Yr	10	13	.435	38	24	10	2	1	214	189	7.9	7	79	3.3	85	3.6	2.90	112	.236	.302	11	8	96	93	0.1	-1	0	1.0
1944	Phi-N	12	18	.400	37	27	11	1	0	221	223	9.1	7	88	3.6	74	3.0	3.87	96	.262	.326	-6	-4	103	93	0.0	2	2	0.0
1945	Phi-N	8	20	.286	36	30	8	0	1	191	217	10.2	11	92	4.3	72	3.4	5.37	72	.281	.359	-33	-32	102	86	-0.6	-1	0	-3.0
Total	5	35	58	.376	141	91	32	3	2	728	753	9.3	29	320	4.0	271	3.4	4.29	85	.266	.338	-50	-53	99	91	-1.5	1	4	-4.0

■ BILL BARRETT Barrett, William Joseph "Whispering Bill" b: 5/28/1900, Cambridge, Mass. d: 1/26/51, Cambridge, Mass. BR/TR, 6', 175 lbs. Deb: 5/13/21

YEAR	TM/L	W	L	PCT	G	GS	CG	SHO	SV	IP	H	H/G	HR	BB	BB/G	SO	SO/G	ERA	/A	OAVG	OOBP	PR	/A	PF	CPI	WAT	PB	PD	TPI
1921	Phi-A	1	0	1.000	4	0	0	0	0	5	2	3.6	0	9	16.2	2	3.6	7.20	64	.133	.440	-2	-1	107	63	0.5	0	0	0.0

■ FRANCISCO BARRIOS Barrios, Francisco Javier (Jimenez) b: 6/10/53, Hermosillo, Mex. d: 4/9/82, Hermosillo, Mexico BR/TR, 5'11", 155 lbs. Deb: 8/18/74

YEAR	TM/L	W	L	PCT	G	GS	CG	SHO	SV	IP	H	H/G	HR	BB	BB/G	SO	SO/G	ERA	/A	OAVG	OOBP	PR	/A	PF	CPI	WAT	PB	PD	TPI
1974	Chi-A	0	0	—	2	0	0	0	0	2	7	31.5	0	2	9.0	2	9.0	27.00	14	.538	.600	-5	-5	102	61	0.0	0	0	-0.4
1976	Chi-A	5	9	.357	35	14	6	0	3	142	136	8.6	13	46	2.9	81	5.1	4.31	83	.255	.312	-12	-12	101	84	-0.7	0	-1	-1.2
1977	Chi-A	14	7	.667	33	31	9	0	0	231	241	9.4	22	58	2.3	119	4.6	4.13	97	.267	.310	-1	-3	99	90	2.9	0	-1	-0.3
1978	Chi-A	9	15	.375	33	32	9	2	0	196	180	8.3	13	85	3.9	79	3.6	4.04	95	.246	.323	-6	-4	102	87	-2.0	0	2	-0.1
1979	Chi-A	8	3	.727	15	15	2	0	0	95	88	8.3	9	33	3.1	28	2.7	3.60	120	.242	.310	7	8	103	95	2.8	0	-1	0.6
1980	Chi-A	1	1	.500	3	3	0	0	0	16	21	11.8	4	8	4.5	2	1.1	5.06	78	.323	.400	-2	-2	98	144	0.1	0	-0	-0.1
1981	Chi-A	1	3	.250	8	7	1	0	0	36	45	11.3	3	14	3.5	12	3.0	4.00	90	.292	.353	-1	-2	99	117	-0.9	0	-0	-0.1
Total	7	38	38	.500	129	102	27	2	3	718	718	9.0	64	246	3.1	323	4.0	4.15	94	.260	.320	-21	-19	101	91	2.2	0	-1	-1.6

■ FRANK BARRON Barron, Frank John b: 8/6/1890, St.Mary's, W.Va. d: 9/18/64, St.Mary's, W.Va. BL/TL, 6'1", 175 lbs. Deb: 8/19/14

YEAR	TM/L	W	L	PCT	G	GS	CG	SHO	SV	IP	H	H/G	HR	BB	BB/G	SO	SO/G	ERA	/A	OAVG	OOBP	PR	/A	PF	CPI	WAT	PB	PD	TPI
1914	Was-A	0	0	—	1	0	0	0	0	1	1	9.0	0	0	0.0	1	9.0	0.00	—	.333	.333	0	0	100	0	0.0	0	0	0.0

■ ED BARRY Barry, Edward "Jumbo" b: 10/2/1882, Madison, Wis. TL , Deb: 8/21/05

YEAR	TM/L	W	L	PCT	G	GS	CG	SHO	SV	IP	H	H/G	HR	BB	BB/G	SO	SO/G	ERA	/A	OAVG	OOBP	PR	/A	PF	CPI	WAT	PB	PD	TPI
1905	Bos-A	1	2	.333	7	5	2	0	0	41	38	8.3	2	15	3.3	18	4.0	2.85	93	.270	.340	-1	-1	100	118	-0.4	-0	-2	-0.2
1906	Bos-A	0	3	.000	3	3	3	0	0	21	23	9.9	2	5	2.1	10	4.3	6.00	46	.305	.348	-8	-7	104	68	-1.4	-0	-0	-0.6
1907	Bos-A	0	1	.000	2	2	1	0	0	17	13	6.9	1	5	2.6	6	3.2	2.12	124	.233	.296	1	1	103	107	-0.4	-0	-0	0.1
Total	3	1	6	.143	12	10	6	0	0	79	74	8.4	5	25	2.8	34	3.9	3.53	76	.272	.333	-8	-8	102	102	-2.2	-1	-2	-0.7

■ HARDIN BARRY Barry, Hardin "Finn" b: 3/26/1891, Susanville, Cal. d: 11/5/69, Carson City, Nev. BR/TR, 6', 185 lbs. Deb: 6/21/12

YEAR	TM/L	W	L	PCT	G	GS	CG	SHO	SV	IP	H	H/G	HR	BB	BB/G	SO	SO/G	ERA	/A	OAVG	OOBP	PR	/A	PF	CPI	WAT	PB	PD	TPI
1912	Phi-A	0	0	—	3	0	0	0	0	13	18	12.5	0	4	2.8	3	2.1	7.62	43	.360	.418	-6	-6	97	77	0.0	-0	-0	-0.5

■ TOM BARRY Barry, Thomas Arthur b: 4/10/1879, St.Louis, Mo. d: 6/4/46, St.Louis, Mo. Deb: 4/15/04

YEAR	TM/L	W	L	PCT	G	GS	CG	SHO	SV	IP	H	H/G	HR	BB	BB/G	SO	SO/G	ERA	/A	OAVG	OOBP	PR	/A	PF	CPI	WAT	PB	PD	TPI
1904	Phi-N	0	1	.000	1	1	0	0	0	1	6	54.0	0	1	9.0	1	9.0	27.00	10	.704	.735	-3	-3	97	109	-0.4	0	0	-0.2

■ BOB BARTHELSON Barthelson, Robert Edward b: 7/15/24, New Haven, Conn. BR/TR, 6', 185 lbs. Deb: 7/04/44

YEAR	TM/L	W	L	PCT	G	GS	CG	SHO	SV	IP	H	H/G	HR	BB	BB/G	SO	SO/G	ERA	/A	OAVG	OOBP	PR	/A	PF	CPI	WAT	PB	PD	TPI
1944	NY-N	1	1	.500	7	1	0	0	0	10	13	11.7	2	5	4.5	4	3.6	4.50	85	.310	.383	-1	-1	105	143	0.1	0	-0	0.0

■ JOHN BARTHOLD Barthold, John Francis "Hans" b: 4/14/1882, Philadelphia, Pa. d: 11/4/46, Fairview Village, Pa. BB/TR, 5'11", 180 lbs. Deb: 5/17/04

YEAR	TM/L	W	L	PCT	G	GS	CG	SHO	SV	IP	H	H/G	HR	BB	BB/G	SO	SO/G	ERA	/A	OAVG	OOBP	PR	/A	PF	CPI	WAT	PB	PD	TPI
1904	Phi-A	0	0	—	4	0	0	0	0	11	12	9.8	0	8	6.5	5	4.1	4.91	53	.302	.418	-3	-3	101	96	0.0	1	0	-0.2

YEAR	TM/L	W	L	PCT	G	GS	CG	SHO	SV	IP	H	H/G	HR	BB	BB/G	SO	SO/G	ERA	/A	OAVG	OOBP	PR	/A	PF	CPI	WAT	PB	PD	TPI
■ **LES BARTHOLOMEW** Bartholomew, Lester Justin b: 4/4/03, Madison, Wis. d: 9/19/72, Barrington, Ill. BR/TL, 5'11.5", 195 lbs. Deb: 4/11/28																													
1928	Pit-N	0	0	—	6	0	0	0	0	23	31	12.1	2	9	3.5	6	2.3	7.04	59	.356	.388	-8	-7	105	91	0.0	-0	-0	-0.6
1932	Chi-A	0	0	—	3	0	0	0	0	5	5	9.0	0	6	10.8	1	1.8	5.40	75	.250	.407	-1	-1	91	99	0.0	-0	0	0.0
Total	2	0	0	—	9	0	0	0	0	28	36	11.6	2	15	4.8	7	2.3	6.75	62	.336	.392	-8	-8	102	93	0.0	-0	-0	-0.6
■ **BILL BARTLEY** Bartley, William Jackson b: 1/8/1885, Cincinnati, Ohio d: 5/17/65, Cincinnati, Ohio BR/TR, 5'11.5", 190 lbs. Deb: 03																													
1903	NY-N	0	0	—	1	0	0	0	0	3	3	9.0	0	4	12.0	2	6.0	0.00	—	.284	.481	1	1	103	0	0.0	-0	0	0.1
1906	Phi-A	0	0	—	3	0	0	0	1	9	10	10.0	0	6	6.0	6	6.0	9.00	28	.308	.415	-6	-7	93	52	0.0	1	1	-0.5
1907	Phi-A	0	1	.000	15	3	2	0	1	56	44	7.1	0	19	3.1	16	2.6	2.25	118	.238	.309	2	2	104	91	-0.4	-2	-0	0.3
Total	3	0	1	.000	19	3	2	0	1	68	57	7.5	0	29	3.8	24	3.2	3.04	88	.250	.335	-3	-3	103	81	-0.4	-1	0	-0.1
■ **CHARLIE BARTSON** Bartson, Charles Franklin b: 3/13/1865, Peoria, Ill. d: 6/9/36, Peoria, Ill. 6', 170 lbs. Deb: 5/14/1890																													
1890	Chi-P	8	10	.444	25	19	16	0	1	188	222	10.6	8	66	3.2	47	2.3	4.26	102	.306	.364	-1	2	103	97	-1.8	-2	0	0.0
■ **JIM BASKETTE** Baskette, James Blaine "Big Jim" b: 12/10/1887, Athens, Tenn. d: 7/30/42, Athens, Tenn. BR/TR, 6'2", 185 lbs. Deb: 9/22/11																													
1911	Cle-A	1	2	.333	4	2	2	0	0	21	21	9.0	0	9	3.9	8	3.4	3.43	101	.273	.356	-0	0	103	103	-0.5	1	-0	0.0
1912	Cle-A	8	4	.667	29	11	7	1	1	116	109	8.5	2	46	3.6	51	4.0	3.18	107	.252	.334	2	3	101	102	2.2	-1	-3	0.0
1913	Cle-A	0	0	—	2	1	0	0	0	5	8	14.4	1	2	3.6	0	0.0	5.40	56	.400	.455	-1	-1	104	156	0.0	1	0	0.0
Total	3	9	6	.600	35	14	9	1	1	142	138	8.7	3	57	3.6	59	3.7	3.30	103	.261	.342	1	1	102	104	1.7	1	-3	0.0
■ **NORM BASS** Bass, Norman Delaney b: 1/21/39, Laurel, Miss. BR/TR, 6'3", 205 lbs. Deb: 4/23/61																													
1961	KC-A	11	11	.500	40	23	6	2	0	171	164	8.6	17	82	4.3	74	3.9	4.68	90	.255	.336	-13	-9	104	89	2.4	-2	-3	-1.3
1962	KC-A	2	6	.250	22	10	0	0	0	75	96	11.5	7	46	5.5	33	4.0	6.12	66	.317	.397	-18	-17	101	100	-1.7	-2	1	-1.6
1963	KC-A	0	0	—	3	1	0	0	0	8	11	12.4	2	9	10.1	4	4.5	11.25	35	.333	.455	-7	-6	109	82	0.0	-0	-0	-0.5
Total	3	13	17	.433	65	34	6	2	0	254	271	9.6	26	137	4.9	111	3.9	5.31	78	.277	.360	-37	-33	104	92	0.7	-4	-2	-3.4
■ **DICK BASS** Bass, Richard William b: 7/7/06, Rogersville, Tenn. BR/TR, 6'2", 175 lbs. Deb: 9/21/39																													
1939	Was-A	0	1	.000	1	1	0	0	0	8	7	7.9	0	6	6.8	1	1.1	6.75	63	.241	.378	-2	-2	91	65	-0.4	-0	0	-0.1
■ **CHARLIE BASTIAN** Bastian, Charles J. b: 7/4/1860, Philadelphia, Pa. d: 1/18/32, Pennsauken, N.J. BR/TR, 5'6.5", 145 lbs. Deb: 8/18/1884																													
1884	WiL-U	0	0	—	1	0	0	0	0	6	6	9.0	0	0	0.0	2	3.0	3.00	110	.265	.265	0	0	109	80	0.0	0	0	-0.1
■ **JOE BATCHELDER** Batchelder, Joseph Edmund "Win" b: 7/11/1898, Wenham, Mass. BR/TL, 5'7", 165 lbs. Deb: 9/29/23																													
1923	Bos-N	1	0	1.000	4	1	1	0	0	9	12	12.0	2	1	1.0	2	2.0	7.00	59	.353	.368	-3	-3	102	99	0.5	0	-0	-0.2
1924	Bos-N	0	0	—	3	0	0	0	0	5	4	7.2	0	2	3.6	2	3.6	3.60	106	.235	.316	0	0	99	75	0.0	-0	0	0.0
1925	Bos-N	0	0	—	4	0	0	0	0	7	10	12.9	0	1	1.3	2	2.6	5.14	79	.357	.324	-1	-1	95	102	0.0	-0	0	0.0
Total	3	1	0	1.000	11	1	1	0	0	21	26	11.1	2	4	1.7	6	2.6	5.57	72	.329	.341	-4	-4	99	94	0.5	-0	0	-0.2
■ **BUSH BATES** Bates, Bush Deb: 8/25/1889																													
1889	KC-a	0	1	.000	1	1	1	0	0	8	15	16.9	0	5	5.6	3	3.4	13.50	31	.416	.487	-9	-8	109	61	-0.4	-1	0	-0.5
■ **DICK BATES** Bates, Charles Richard b: 10/7/45, Mc Arthur, Ohio BL/TR, 6', 190 lbs. Deb: 4/27/69																													
1969	Sea-A	0	0	—	1	0	0	0	0	2	3	13.5	1	3	13.5	3	13.5	22.50	16	.375	.545	-4	-4	100	59	0.0	0	0	-0.3
■ **FRANK BATES** Bates, Creed Frank b: Chattanooga, Tenn. Deb: 10/07/1898																													
1898	Cle-N	2	1	.667	4	4	4	0	0	29	30	9.3	0	11	3.4	5	1.6	3.10	110	.289	.357	2	1	95	108	0.4	0	0	0.1
1899	StL-N	0	0	—	2	0	0	0	0	9	7	7.0	0	5	5.0	0	0.0	1.00	412	.235	.345	3	3	107	257	0.0	1	0	0.4
	Cle-N	1	18	.053	20	19	17	0	0	153	239	14.1	6	105	6.2	13	0.8	7.24	51	.382	.471	-57	-60	96	98	-5.8	1	0	-4.7
	Yr	1	18	.053	22	19	17	0	0	162	246	13.7	6	110	6.1	13	0.7	6.89	54	.375	.465	-55	-57	97	98	-5.8	1	0	-4.3
Total	2	3	19	.136	26	23	21	0	0	191	276	13.0	6	121	5.7	18	0.8	6.31	58	.363	.451	-53	-56	96	107	-5.4	1	0	-4.2
■ **JOE BATTIN** Battin, Joseph V. b: 11/11/1851, Philadelphia, Pa. d: 12/10/37, Akron, Ohio BR/TR, Deb: 8/11/1871 M																													
1877	StL-N	0	0	—	1	0	0	0	0	4	3	6.8	0	1	2.3	1	2.3	6.75	43	.216	.268	-2	-2	103	18	0.0	-0	0	0.0
1883	Pit-a	0	0	—	2	0	0	0	0	4	9	20.3	0	1	2.3	0	0.0	2.25	143	.449	.475	0	0	98	418	0.0	0	0	0.0
Total	2	0	0	—	3	0	0	0	0	8	12	13.5	0	2	2.3	1	1.1	4.50	68	.353	.389	-1	-1	101	218	0.0	-0	0	0.0
■ **CHRIS BATTON** Batton, Christopher Sean b: 8/24/54, Los Angeles, Cal. BR/TR, 6'4", 195 lbs. Deb: 9/19/76																													
1976	Oak-A	0	0	—	2	1	0	0	0	4	5	11.3	1	3	6.8	4	9.0	9.00	39	.313	.421	-2	-2	98	83	0.0	0	0	-0.2
■ **LOU BAUER** Bauer, Louis Walter b: 11/30/1898, Egg Harbor City, N.J. 6', 175 lbs. Deb: 8/13/18																													
1918	Phi-A	0	0	—	1	0	0	0	0	0	0	—	0	2	—	0	—	∞	—	—	1.000	-1	-1	108	62	0.0	0	0	0.0
■ **AL BAUERS** Bauers, Albert J. b: 1850, Columbus, Ohio d: 9/6/13, Wilkes-Barre, Pa. TL, Deb: 9/22/1884																													
1884	Col-a	1	2	.333	3	3	3	0	0	25	22	7.9	1	14	5.0	13	4.7	4.68	66	.244	.346	-4	-4	96	84	-0.6	0	0	-0.3
1886	StL-N	0	4	.000	4	4	3	0	0	29	31	9.6	1	27	8.4	13	4.0	6.21	52	.287	.429	-9	-10	98	88	-1.9	-1	0	-0.7
Total	2	1	6	.143	7	7	6	0	0	54	53	8.8	2	41	6.8	26	4.3	5.50	58	.267	.393	-13	-14	97	86	-2.5	-0	0	-1.0
■ **RUSS BAUERS** Bauers, Russell Lee b: 5/10/14, Townsend, Wis. BL/TR, 6'3", 195 lbs. Deb: 8/20/36																													
1936	Pit-N	0	0	—	1	1	0	0	0	1	2	18.0	0	4	36.0	0	0.0	45.00	9	.500	.636	-5	-5	96	51	0.0	0	0	-0.3
1937	Pit-N	13	6	.684	34	19	11	2	1	188	174	8.3	2	80	3.8	118	5.6	2.87	138	.245	.320	22	23	101	109	3.0	0	3	2.7
1938	Pit-N	13	14	.481	40	34	12	3	3	243	207	7.7	7	99	3.7	117	4.3	3.07	122	.233	.310	19	18	99	96	-2.4	4	-3	1.9
1939	Pit-N	2	4	.333	15	8	1	0	1	54	46	7.7	4	25	4.2	12	2.0	3.33	118	.240	.319	4	4	101	108	-0.7	-0	-1	0.3
1940	Pit-N	0	2	.000	15	2	0	0	0	31	42	12.2	2	18	5.2	11	3.2	7.55	48	.323	.405	-13	-13	95	84	-0.9	0	0	-1.2
1941	Pit-N	1	3	.250	8	5	1	0	0	37	40	9.7	1	25	6.1	20	4.9	5.59	66	.267	.369	-8	-8	102	78	-1.0	1	-1	-0.7
1946	Chi-N	2	1	.667	15	2	2	0	1	43	45	9.4	1	19	4.0	22	4.6	3.56	89	.273	.344	-1	-2	93	107	0.4	1	-0	0.0
1950	StL-A	0	0	—	1	0	0	0	0	2	6	27.0	0	1	4.5	0	0.0	4.50	113	.600	.636	0	0	111	347	0.0	0	0	0.0
Total	8	31	30	.508	129	71	27	5	6	599	562	8.4	17	271	4.1	300	4.5	3.53	107	.250	.329	19	17	99	101	-1.6	7	-2	2.7
■ **FRANK BAUMANN** Baumann, Frank Matt "The Beau" b: 7/1/33, St.Louis, Mo. BL/TL, 6', 205 lbs. Deb: 7/31/55																													
1955	Bos-A	2	1	.667	7	5	0	0	0	34	38	10.1	2	17	4.5	27	7.1	5.82	83	.281	.359	-7	-4	122	77	0.4	-0	0	-0.2
1956	Bos-A	2	1	.667	7	1	0	0	0	25	22	7.9	3	14	5.0	18	6.5	3.24	131	.234	.333	3	3	102	119	0.4	1	-1	0.3
1957	Bos-A	1	0	1.000	4	1	0	0	0	12	13	9.8	1	3	2.3	7	5.3	3.75	110	.277	.327	0	0	109	108	0.5	0	-0	0.1
1958	Bos-A	2	2	.500	10	7	2	0	0	52	56	9.7	4	27	4.7	31	5.4	4.50	88	.276	.369	-4	-3	105	105	0.0	1	-1	-0.2
1959	Bos-A	6	4	.600	26	10	2	0	1	96	96	9.0	11	55	5.2	48	4.5	4.03	101	.259	.352	-2	0	105	115	1.2	1	0	0.2
1960	Chi-A	13	6	.684	47	20	7	2	3	185	169	8.2	11	53	2.6	71	3.5	**2.68**	**143**	.247	.298	25	24	99	112	2.9	1	-2	2.3
1961	Chi-A	10	13	.435	53	23	5	1	3	188	249	11.9	22	59	2.8	75	3.6	5.60	71	.318	.360	-33	-34	99	99	-2.3	6	1	-2.5
1962	Chi-A	7	6	.538	40	10	3	1	4	120	117	8.8	10	36	2.7	55	4.1	3.38	111	.258	.311	8	5	94	108	0.2	4	0	1.0
1963	Chi-A	2	1	.667	24	1	0	0	1	50	52	9.4	2	17	3.1	31	5.6	3.06	121	.265	.321	3	4	102	114	0.3	-0	0	0.4
1964	Chi-A	0	3	.000	22	0	0	0	1	32	40	11.3	4	16	4.5	19	5.3	6.19	55	.320	.381	-9	-10	93	98	-1.4	-0	-0	-1.0
1965	Chi-N	0	1	.000	4	0	0	0	0	4	4	9.0	0	3	6.8	2	4.5	6.75	54	.286	.412	-1	-1	103	74	-0.4	0	0	0.0
Total	11	45	38	.542	244	78	19	4	13	798	856	9.7	70	300	3.4	384	4.3	4.11	95	.276	.337	-18	-16	101	106	1.8	14	-2	0.4
■ **GEORGE BAUMGARDNER** Baumgardner, George Washington b: 7/22/1891, Barboursville, W.Va. d: 12/13/70, Barboursville, W.Va. BL/TR, 5'11", 178 lbs. Deb: 4/14/12																													
1912	StL-A	11	14	.440	30	27	18	2	0	218	222	9.2	1	79	3.3	102	4.2	3.39	102	.274	.346	-1	1	103	106	2.1	-1	-0	0.1
1913	StL-A	10	19	.345	38	31	23	2	1	253	267	9.5	6	84	3.0	78	2.8	3.13	91	.283	.348	-6	-8	98	118	-1.2	3	-2	-0.9
1914	StL-A	14	13	.519	45	18	9	3	3	184	152	7.4	3	84	4.1	93	4.5	2.79	98	.229	.323	-1	-1	100	95	1.6	-1	-1	-0.2
1915	StL-A	0	2	.000	7	1	1	0	0	22	29	11.9	0	11	4.5	6	2.5	4.50	65	.358	.435	-4	-4	99	131	-0.9	-1	0	-0.3
1916	StL-A	1	0	1.000	4	2	0	0	0	8	12	13.5	0	5	5.6	4	4.5	7.88	34	.364	.447	-4	-5	94	83	0.5	0	-0	-0.4
Total	5	36	48	.429	124	79	51	7	4	685	682	9.0	10	263	3.5	283	3.7	3.22	93	.269	.345	-16	-16	100	108	2.1	-0	-3	-1.7
■ **ROSS BAUMGARTEN** Baumgarten, Ross b: 5/27/55, Highland Park, Ill. BL/TL, 6'1", 180 lbs. Deb: 8/16/78																													
1978	Chi-A	2	2	.500	7	4	1	1	0	23	29	11.3	3	9	3.5	15	5.9	5.87	66	.315	.368	-5	-5	102	98	0.2	0	-0	-0.4
1979	Chi-A	13	8	.619	28	28	4	3	0	191	175	8.2	18	83	3.9	72	3.4	3.53	123	.243	.317	15	17	103	102	3.5	0	-0	1.7

YEAR	TM/L	W	L	PCT	G	GS	CG	SHO	SV	IP	H	H/G	HR	BB	BB/G	SO	SO/G	ERA	/A	OAVG	OOBP	PR	/A	PF	CPI	WAT	PB	PD	TPI
1980	Chi-A	2	12	.143	24	23	3	1	0	136	127	8.4	10	52	3.4	66	4.4	3.44	115	.256	.318	9	8	98	106	-4.8	0	2	1.0
1981	Chi-A	5	9	.357	19	19	2	1	0	102	101	8.9	9	40	3.5	52	4.6	4.06	89	.260	.326	-4	-5	99	96	-2.2	0	0	-0.4
1982	Pit-N	0	5	.000	12	10	0	0	0	44	60	12.3	3	27	5.5	17	3.5	6.75	59	.349	.418	-15	-14	110	100	-2.4	-1	0	-1.3
Total	5	22	36	.379	90	84	10	6	0	496	492	8.9	43	211	3.8	222	4.0	4.01	101	.263	.331	-1	1	101	101	-5.7	-1	2	0.6
■ HARRY BAUMGARTNER	Baumgartner, Harry E. b: 10/8/1892, S.Pittsburg, Tenn. d: 12/3/30, Augusta, Ga. BL, 5'11", 175 lbs. Deb: 9/06/20																												
1920	Det-A	0	1	.000	9	0	0	0	0	18	18	9.0	1	6	3.0	7	3.5	4.00	101	.273	.333	-0	0	106	90	-0.4	0	0	0.0
■ STAN BAUMGARTNER	Baumgartner, Stanwood Fulton b: 12/14/1894, Houston, Tex. d: 10/4/55, Philadelphia, Pa. BL/TL, 6', 175 lbs. Deb: 6/26/14																												
1914	Phi-N	2	2	.500	15	3	2	1	0	60	60	9.0	0	16	2.4	24	3.6	3.30	85	.270	.315	-3	-3	101	89	0.1	-1	-1	-0.5
1915	Phi-N	0	2	.000	16	1	0	0	0	48	38	7.1	2	23	4.3	27	5.1	2.44	118	.226	.315	2	2	104	119	-0.9	-1	1	0.3
1916	Phi-N	0	0	—	1	0	0	0	0	4	5	11.3	0	1	2.3	0	0.0	2.25	109	.333	.353	0	0	94	202	0.0	-0	-0	0.0
1921	Phi-N	3	6	.333	22	7	2	0	0	67	103	13.8	8	22	3.0	13	1.7	6.99	58	.355	.386	-24	-22	107	94	0.0	1	-1	-1.9
1922	Phi-N	1	1	.500	6	1	0	0	0	10	18	16.2	1	5	4.5	2	1.8	6.30	76	.409	.451	-2	-2	117	137	0.2	0	0	0.0
1924	Phi-A	13	6	.684	36	16	12	1	4	181	181	9.0	6	73	3.6	45	2.2	2.88	148	.271	.332	27	28	101	**132**	4.2	-0	-2	2.5
1925	Phi-A	6	3	.667	37	11	2	1	3	113	120	9.6	2	35	2.8	18	1.4	3.58	124	.275	.327	10	11	101	99	1.0	0	-1	1.0
1926	Phi-A	1	1	.500	10	1	0	0	0	22	28	11.5	0	10	4.1	0	0.0	4.09	114	.326	.376	-0	1	116	125	0.0	0	1	0.2
Total	8	26	21	.553	143	40	18	3	7	505	553	9.9	19	185	3.3	129	2.3	3.71	107	.287	.341	9	16	103	114	4.6	-1	-3	1.6
■ GEORGE BAUSEWINE	Bausewine, George W. b: 3/22/1869, Philadelphia, Pa. d: 7/29/47, Norristown, Pa. 6'2", Deb: 9/14/1889																												
1889	Phi-a	1	4	.200	7	6	6	0	0	55	64	10.5	1	33	5.4	18	2.9	3.93	94	.306	.401	-0	-1	96	122	-1.5	-2	0	-0.2
■ ED BAUTA	Bauta, Eduardo (Galvez) b: 1/6/35, Florida Camaguey, Cuba BR/TR, 6'3", 200 lbs. Deb: 7/06/60																												
1960	StL-N	0	0	—	9	0	0	0	1	16	14	7.9	4	11	6.2	6	3.4	6.19	66	.237	.361	-4	-4	108	90	0.0	-0	-0	-0.3
1961	StL-N	2	0	1.000	13	0	0	0	5	19	12	5.7	2	5	2.4	12	5.7	1.42	319	.171	.224	6	7	113	91	1.0	1	-0	0.7
1962	StL-N	1	0	1.000	20	0	0	0	1	32	28	7.9	5	21	5.9	25	7.0	5.06	83	.239	.352	-4	-3	107	93	0.5	0	0	-0.2
1963	StL-N	3	4	.429	38	0	0	0	3	53	55	9.3	2	21	3.6	30	5.1	3.91	89	.279	.345	-4	-3	106	105	-0.8	-1	-1	-0.3
	NY-N	0	0	—	9	0	0	0	0	19	22	10.4	0	9	4.3	13	6.2	5.21	66	.289	.360	-4	-4	104	80	0.0	-0	0	-0.3
	Yr	3	4	.429	47	0	0	0	3	72	77	9.6	2	30	3.8	43	5.4	4.25	81	.278	.343	-8	-6	105	80	-0.8	-1	-1	-0.6
1964	NY-N	0	2	.000	8	0	0	0	1	10	17	15.3	1	3	2.7	3	2.7	5.40	64	.395	.426	-2	-2	98	143	-0.9	0	0	-0.1
Total	5	6	6	.500	97	0	0	0	11	149	148	8.9	14	70	4.2	89	5.4	4.35	88	.263	.342	-13	-9	106	98	-0.2	-0	-1	-0.5
■ JOSE BAUTISTA	Bautista, Jose Joaquin (Arias) b: 7/25/64, Bani, D.R. BR/TR, 6'1", 177 lbs. Deb: 4/09/88																												
1988	Bal-A	6	15	.286	33	25	3	0	0	172	171	8.9	21	45	2.4	76	4.0	4.29	90	.258	.309	-6	-8	97	91	-1.6	0	-1	-0.8
■ BILL BAYNE	Bayne, William Lear "Beverly" b: 4/18/1899, Pittsburgh, Pa. d: 5/22/81, St.Louis, Mo. BL/TL, 5'9", 160 lbs. Deb: 9/20/19																												
1919	StL-A	1	1	.500	2	2	1	0	0	12	16	12.0	0	6	4.5	0	0.0	5.25	60	.320	.393	-3	-3	98	92	0.0	0	0	-0.1
1920	StL-A	5	6	.455	18	13	6	1	0	100	102	9.2	3	41	3.7	38	3.4	3.69	114	.279	.363	1	6	111	108	-0.4	-2	-2	0.2
1921	StL-A	11	5	.688	47	14	6	1	3	164	167	9.2	8	80	4.4	82	4.5	4.72	92	.270	.347	-8	-7	101	86	2.9	5	-1	-0.2
1922	StL-A	4	5	.444	26	9	3	0	2	93	86	8.3	5	37	3.6	38	3.7	4.55	91	.249	.326	-5	-4	102	76	-1.1	-1	-2	-0.6
1923	StL-A	2	2	.500	19	2	0	0	0	46	49	9.6	4	31	6.1	15	2.9	4.50	93	.287	.397	-3	-2	105	121	0.1	-0	-1	-0.2
1924	StL-A	1	3	.250	22	3	0	0	0	51	47	8.3	4	29	5.1	20	3.5	4.41	103	.250	.356	-1	1	108	100	-0.9	2	-1	0.2
1928	Cle-A	2	5	.286	37	6	3	0	3	109	128	10.6	3	43	3.6	39	3.2	5.12	86	.309	.377	-13	-9	108	99	-0.9	3	2	-0.4
1929	Bos-A	5	5	.500	27	6	2	0	0	84	111	11.9	9	29	3.1	26	2.8	6.75	66	.326	.376	-23	-21	105	89	1.0	2	1	-1.6
1930	Bos-A	0	0	—	1	0	0	0	0	4	5	11.3	1	1	2.3	1	2.3	4.50	99	.294	.333	0	-0	96	128	0.0	0	0	0.0
Total	9	31	32	.492	199	55	21	2	8	663	711	9.7	37	297	4.0	259	3.5	4.83	89	.283	.360	-55	-40	105	94	0.7	10	-3	-2.7
■ WALTER BEALL	Beall, Walter Esau b: 7/29/1899, Washington, D.C. d: 1/28/59, Suitland, Md. BR/TR, 5'10", 178 lbs. Deb: 9/03/24																												
1924	NY-A	2	0	1.000	4	2	0	0	0	23	19	7.4	2	17	6.7	18	7.0	3.52	116	.237	.367	2	1	97	122	1.0	-1	-1	0.0
1925	NY-A	0	1	.000	8	1	0	0	0	11	11	9.0	0	19	15.5	8	6.5	13.09	33	.282	.524	-11	-11	97	63	-0.4	-1	0	-0.9
1926	NY-A	2	4	.333	20	9	1	0	1	82	71	7.8	2	68	7.5	56	6.1	3.51	111	.240	.378	5	4	97	120	-1.2	0	0	0.4
1927	NY-A	0	0	—	1	0	0	0	0	1	1	9.0	0	0	0.0	0	0.0	9.00	43	.333	.250	-1	-1	94	46	0.0	0	0	0.0
1929	Was-A	1	0	1.000	3	0	0	0	0	7	8	10.3	0	7	9.0	3	3.9	3.86	110	.348	.441	0	0	100	191	0.5	-1	0	0.0
Total	5	5	5	.500	36	12	1	0	1	124	110	8.0	4	111	8.1	85	6.2	4.43	90	.249	.395	-4	-6	97	119	-0.1	-1	0	-0.5
■ ALEX BEAM	Beam, Alexander Rodger b: 11/21/1870, Johnstown, Pa. d: 4/17/38, Nogales, Ariz. Deb: 5/25/1889																												
1889	Pit-N	1	1	.500	2	2	2	0	0	18	11	5.5	0	15	7.5	1	0.5	6.50	56	.189	.355	-5	-6	90	40	0.1	0	0	-0.3
■ ERNIE BEAM	Beam, Ernest Joseph b: 3/17/1867, Mansfield, Ohio d: 9/12/18, Mansfield, Ohio 185 lbs. Deb: 5/02/1895																												
1895	Phi-N	0	2	.000	9	1	1	0	**3**	25	33	11.9	1	25	9.0	3	1.1	11.52	41	.339	.474	-19	-19	98	60	-0.9	-1	0	-1.4
■ CHARLIE BEAMON	Beamon, Charles Alfonzo Sr. b: 12/25/34, Oakland, Cal. BR/TR, 5'11", 195 lbs. Deb: 9/26/56																												
1956	Bal-A	2	0	1.000	2	1	1	1	0	13	9	6.2	0	8	5.5	14	9.7	1.38	290	.191	.309	4	4	97	148	1.0	-1	0	0.4
1957	Bal-A	0	0	—	4	1	0	0	0	9	8	8.0	1	7	7.0	5	5.0	5.00	70	.229	.372	-1	-1	93	89	0.0	-0	0	-0.1
1958	Bal-A	1	3	.250	21	3	0	0	0	50	47	8.5	3	21	3.8	26	4.7	4.32	83	.266	.354	-3	-4	95	100	-0.9	-1	2	-0.2
Total	3	3	3	.500	27	5	1	1	0	72	64	8.0	4	36	4.5	45	5.6	3.88	94	.247	.349	-0	-2	95	107	0.1	-2	2	0.1
■ BELVE BEAN	Bean, Beveric Benton "Bill" b: 4/23/05, Mullin, Tex. d: 6/1/88, Comanche, Tex. BR/TR, 6'1.5", 197 lbs. Deb: 5/30/30																												
1930	Cle-A	3	3	.500	23	3	1	0	2	74	99	12.0	7	32	3.9	19	2.3	5.47	90	.331	.385	-7	-5	105	116	-0.1	2	0	-0.1
1931	Cle-A	0	1	.000	4	0	0	0	0	7	11	14.1	0	4	5.1	3	3.9	6.43	72	.379	.432	-2	-1	106	124	-0.4	-0	0	0.0
1933	Cle-A	1	2	.333	27	2	0	0	0	70	80	10.3	6	20	2.6	41	5.3	5.27	85	.300	.345	-8	-6	105	95	-0.4	-1	1	-0.5
1934	Cle-A	5	1	.833	21	1	0	0	0	51	53	9.4	2	21	3.7	20	3.5	3.88	115	.265	.341	3	3	100	103	1.9	0	1	0.4
1935	Cle-A	0	0	—	1	0	0	0	0	1	2	18.0	1	0	0.0	0	0.0	9.00	49	.400	.400	-1	-1	99	161	0.0	0	0	0.0
	Was-A	2	0	1.000	10	2	0	0	0	31	43	12.5	5	19	5.5	6	1.7	7.26	57	.339	.416	-10	-11	93	103	1.0	3	-1	-0.7
	Yr	2	0	1.000	11	2	0	0	0	32	45	12.7	6	19	5.3	6	1.7	7.31	57	.341	.416	-10	-11	93	103	1.0	0	-1	-0.7
Total	5	11	7	.611	86	8	1	0	2	234	288	11.1	21	96	3.7	89	3.4	5.35	86	.311	.370	-23	-20	102	105	2.0	4	1	-0.9
■ DAVE BEARD	Beard, Charles David b: 10/2/59, Atlanta, Ga. BL/TR, 6'5", 190 lbs. Deb: 7/16/80																												
1980	Oak-A	0	1	.000	13	0	0	0	1	16	12	6.8	0	7	3.9	12	6.8	3.38	113	.218	.313	1	1	94	76	-0.4	0	0	0.1
1981	Oak-A	1	1	.500	8	0	0	0	3	13	9	6.2	1	4	2.8	15	10.4	2.77	126	.191	.264	1	1	95	75	-0.1	0	0	0.1
1982	Oak-A	10	9	.526	54	2	0	0	11	92	85	8.3	9	35	3.4	73	7.1	3.42	115	.244	.305	7	5	96	104	1.9	0	-0	0.5
1983	Oak-A	5	5	.500	43	0	0	0	10	61	55	8.1	8	36	5.3	40	5.9	5.61	70	.246	.347	-10	-11	96	82	0.4	0	-1	-1.2
1984	Sea-A	3	2	.600	43	0	0	0	5	76	88	10.4	15	33	3.9	40	4.7	5.80	71	.291	.357	-15	-14	103	100	0.7	0	0	-1.3
1985	Chi-N	0	0	—	9	0	0	0	0	13	16	11.1	2	7	4.8	4	2.8	6.23	67	.314	.390	-4	-3	117	100	0.0	0	0	-0.2
Total	6	19	18	.514	170	2	0	0	30	271	265	8.8	35	122	4.1	184	6.1	4.68	85	.258	.332	-20	-21	99	95	2.5	0	-2	-2.0
■ MIKE BEARD	Beard, Michael Richard b: 6/21/50, Little Rock, Ark. BL/TL, 6'1", 185 lbs. Deb: 9/07/74																												
1974	Atl-N	0	0	—	6	0	0	0	0	9	5	5.0	1	1	1.0	7	7.0	3.00	125	.156	.206	1	1	104	32	0.0	0	0	0.1
1975	Atl-N	4	0	1.000	34	2	0	0	0	70	71	9.1	4	28	3.6	27	3.5	3.21	110	.265	.327	3	2	97	117	2.0	-0	0	0.2
1976	Atl-N	0	2	.000	30	0	0	0	1	34	38	10.1	1	14	3.7	8	2.1	4.24	93	.299	.347	-3	-1	112	107	-0.9	-0	1	0.0
1977	Atl-N	0	0	—	4	0	0	0	0	5	14	25.2	3	2	3.6	1	1.8	9.00	50	.452	.485	-3	-2	115	170	0.0	0	0	-0.1
Total	4	4	2	.667	74	2	0	0	1	118	128	9.8	9	45	3.4	43	3.3	3.74	99	.279	.335	-2	-0	103	110	1.1	-0	1	0.2
■ RALPH BEARD	Beard, Ralph William b: 2/11/29, Cincinnati, Ohio BR/TR, 6'5", 200 lbs. Deb: 6/29/54																												
1954	StL-N	0	4	.000	13	10	0	0	0	58	62	9.6	2	28	4.3	17	2.6	3.72	110	.278	.354	2	2	100	112	-1.9	-1	-1	0.0
■ GENE BEARDEN	Bearden, Henry Eugene b: 9/5/20, Lexa, Ark. BL/TL, 6'3", 198 lbs. Deb: 5/10/47																												
1947	Cle-A	0	0	—	1	0	0	0	0	⅓	2	54.0	0	1	27.0	0	0.0	81.00	—	.667	.750	-3	-3	94	38	0.0	0	0	-0.2
1948	Cle-A	20	7	.741	37	29	15	6	1	230	187	7.3	9	106	4.1	80	3.1	**2.43**	**166**	.229	.317	47	**41**	94	**133**	4.7	5	3	5.1
1949	Cle-A	8	8	.500	32	19	5	0	0	127	140	9.9	6	92	6.5	41	2.9	5.10	79	.286	.395	-13	-15	96	102	-1.1	-3	4	-1.3
1950	Cle-A	1	3	.250	14	3	0	0	0	45	57	11.4	5	32	6.4	10	2.0	6.20	70	.328	.422	-8	-9	95	112	-1.1	1	-1	-0.7
	Was-A	3	5	.375	12	9	4	0	0	69	81	10.6	1	33	4.3	20	2.6	4.17	111	.297	.374	3	3	101	113	-0.5	1	0	0.4

YEAR	TM/L	W	L	PCT	G	GS	CG	SHO	SV	IP	H	H/G	HR	BB	BB/G	SO	SO/G	ERA	/A	OAVG	OOBP	PR	/A	PF	CPI	WAT	PB	PD	TPI
	Yr	4	8	.333	26	12	4	0	0	114	138	10.9	6	65	5.1	30	2.4	4.97	91	.309	.393	-5	-6	99	113	-1.6	1	-0	-0.3
1951	Was-A	0	0	—	1	1	0	0	0	3	6	18.0	0	2	6.0	1	3.0	15.00	27	.429	.500	-4	-4	97	63	0.0	0	0	-0.2
	Det-A	3	4	.429	37	4	2	1	0	106	112	9.5	6	58	4.9	38	3.2	4.33	101	.275	.359	-2	1	107	106	-0.2	1	0	0.2
	Yr	3	4	.429	38	5	2	1	0	109	118	9.7	6	60	5.0	39	3.2	4.62	95	.280	.364	-6	-3	106	106	-0.2	0	0	0.0
1952	StL-A	7	8	.467	34	16	3	0	0	151	158	9.4	13	78	4.6	45	2.7	4.29	85	.270	.351	-10	-11	100	104	0.7	7	1	-0.2
1953	Chi-A	3	3	.500	25	3	0	0	0	58	48	7.4	8	33	5.1	24	3.7	2.95	140	.223	.324	7	8	104	130	-0.3	-1	0	0.7
Total	7	45	38	.542	193	84	29	7	1	789	791	9.0	48	435	5.0	259	3.0	3.96	103	.266	.356	17	11	98	115	2.2	10	8	3.8
■ **GARY BEARE**	Beare, Gary Ray b: 8/22/52, San Diego, Cal. BR/TR, 6'4", 205 lbs. Deb: 9/07/76																												
1976	Mil-A	2	3	.400	6	5	2	0	0	41	43	9.4	4	15	3.3	32	7.0	3.29	107	.274	.335	1	1	100	128	0.0	0	-0	0.1
1977	Mil-A	3	3	.500	17	6	0	0	0	59	63	9.6	6	38	5.8	32	4.9	6.41	61	.276	.374	-15	-16	97	80	0.5	0	2	-1.3
Total	2	5	6	.455	23	11	2	0	0	100	106	9.5	10	53	4.8	64	5.8	5.13	73	.275	.359	-14	-15	98	100	0.5	0	1	-1.2
■ **LARRY BEARNARTH**	Bearnarth, Lawrence Donald b: 9/11/41, New York, N.Y. BR/TR, 6'2", 203 lbs. Deb: 4/16/63 C																												
1963	NY-N	3	8	.273	58	2	0	0	4	126	127	9.1	7	47	3.4	48	3.4	3.43	100	.268	.329	-2	-0	104	113	-0.7	2	2	0.4
1964	NY-N	5	5	.500	44	1	0	0	3	78	79	9.1	6	38	4.4	31	3.6	4.15	84	.271	.347	-5	-6	98	108	1.3	-0	3	-0.3
1965	NY-N	3	5	.375	40	3	0	0	1	61	75	11.1	6	28	4.1	16	2.4	4.57	80	.304	.374	-7	-6	104	121	0.4	0	0	-0.5
1966	NY-N	2	3	.400	29	1	0	0	0	55	59	9.7	11	20	3.3	27	4.4	4.42	79	.281	.336	-5	-6	97	118	0.0	-0	1	-0.4
1971	Mil-A	0	0	—	2	0	0	0	0	3	10	30.0	1	2	6.0	2	6.0	18.00	20	.556	.600	-5	-5	104	101	0.0	0	0	-0.3
Total	5	13	21	.382	173	7	0	0	8	323	350	9.8	31	135	3.8	124	3.5	4.12	85	.282	.347	-24	-23	101	114	1.0	1	7	-1.1
■ **ED BEATIN**	Beatin, Ebenezer Ambrose b: 8/10/1866, Baltimore, Md. d: 5/9/25, Baltimore, Md. BR/TL, 5'9", 162 lbs. Deb: 8/02/1887																												
1887	Det-N	1	1	.500	2	2	2	0	0	18	13	6.5	2	8	4.0	6	3.0	4.00	99	.215	.307	0	-0	97	74	-0.1	-1	0	0.0
1888	Det-N	5	7	.417	12	12	12	0	0	107	111	9.3	6	16	1.3	44	3.7	2.86	96	.281	.309	-0	-1	97	112	-1.2	5	0	0.5
1889	Cle-N	20	15	.571	36	36	35	3	0	318	316	8.9	12	141	4.0	126	3.6	3.57	118	.274	.354	16	22	104	104	4.6	-6	-2	1.4
1890	Cle-N	22	31	.415	54	54	53	1	0	474	518	9.8	11	186	3.5	155	2.9	3.84	90	.294	.361	-14	-20	97	100	5.0	-8	3	-2.2
1891	Cle-N	0	3	.000	5	4	2	0	0	29	39	12.1	1	21	6.5	4	1.2	5.28	67	.336	.438	-6	-6	106	111	-1.4	-2	0	-0.5
Total	5	48	57	.457	109	108	104	4	0	946	997	9.5	32	372	3.5	335	3.2	3.68	99	.286	.355	-4	-5	100	103	6.9	-12	1	-0.8
■ **JIM BEATTIE**	Beattie, James Louis b: 7/4/54, Hampton, Va. BR/TR, 6'5", 210 lbs. Deb: 4/25/78																												
1978	NY-A	6	9	.400	25	22	0	0	0	128	123	8.6	8	51	3.6	65	4.6	3.73	98	.255	.329	1	-1	97	98	-2.7	0	1	0.0
1979	NY-A	3	6	.333	15	13	1	1	0	76	85	10.1	5	41	4.9	32	3.8	5.21	77	.294	.367	-8	-10	95	97	-1.8	0	1	-0.7
1980	Sea-A	5	15	.250	33	29	3	0	0	187	205	9.9	19	98	4.7	67	3.2	4.86	87	.286	.369	-17	-13	105	104	-3.3	0	0	-1.2
1981	Sea-A	3	2	.600	13	9	0	0	1	67	59	7.9	2	18	2.4	36	4.8	2.96	125	.232	.287	5	6	101	82	0.8	0	0	0.6
1982	Sea-A	8	12	.400	28	26	6	1	0	172	149	7.8	13	65	3.4	140	7.3	3.35	134	.233	.301	14	22	110	92	-1.5	0	1	2.3
1983	Sea-A	10	15	.400	30	29	8	2	0	197	197	9.0	12	66	3.0	132	6.0	3.84	108	.259	.319	5	6	101	93	0.7	0	3	0.9
1984	Sea-A	12	16	.429	32	32	12	2	0	211	206	8.8	13	75	3.2	119	5.1	3.41	121	.260	.324	14	17	103	107	-0.9	0	1	1.8
1985	Sea-A	5	6	.455	18	15	1	1	0	70	93	12.0	9	33	4.2	45	5.8	7.33	54	.316	.385	-25	-26	95	84	0.0	0	-1	-2.4
1986	Sea-A	0	6	.000	9	7	0	0	0	40	57	12.8	7	14	3.1	24	5.4	6.07	73	.341	.394	-8	-7	106	115	-2.9	0	0	-0.5
Total	9	52	87	.374	203	182	31	7	1	1148	1174	9.2	88	461	3.6	660	5.2	4.17	99	.267	.336	-19	-7	102	98	-11.6	0	7	0.8
■ **JOHNNY BEAZLEY**	Beazley, John Andrew "Nig" b: 5/25/18, Nashville, Tenn. BR/TR, 6'1.5", 190 lbs. Deb: 9/28/41																												
1941	StL-N	1	0	1.000	1	1	1	0	0	9	10	10.0	0	3	3.0	4	4.0	1.00	389	.294	.351	3	3	107	406	0.5	-0	-0	0.3
1942	StL-N	21	6	.778	43	23	13	3	3	215	181	7.6	4	73	3.1	91	3.8	2.13	159	.226	.289	28	30	103	114	4.4	-1	0	3.4
1946	StL-N	7	5	.583	19	18	5	0	0	103	109	9.5	6	55	4.8	36	3.1	4.46	79	.275	.365	-12	-11	103	99	-0.4	1	-0	-0.9
1947	Bos-N	2	0	1.000	9	2	2	0	0	29	30	9.3	1	19	5.9	12	3.7	4.34	89	.273	.368	-1	-2	95	106	1.0	-1	0	-0.1
1948	Bos-N	0	1	.000	3	2	0	0	0	16	19	10.7	2	7	3.9	4	2.3	4.50	87	.284	.347	-1	-1	99	109	-0.4	-1	-0	-0.1
1949	Bos-N	0	0	—	1	0	0	0	0	2	0	0.0	0	0	0.0	0	0.0	0.00	—	.000	.000	1	1	97	0	0.0	0	0	0.1
Total	6	31	12	.721	76	46	21	3	3	374	349	8.4	13	157	3.8	147	3.5	3.01	117	.247	.320	18	21	102	115	5.1	-1	-0	2.7
■ **BUCK BECANNON**	Becannon, James Melvin b: 8/22/1859, New York, N.Y. d: 11/5/23, New York, N.Y. 5'10", 165 lbs. Deb: 10/15/1884																												
1884	NY-a	1	0	1.000	1	1	1	0	0	6	2	3.0	0	2	3.0	2	3.0	1.50	208	.109	.197	1	1	96	16	0.5	-0	0	0.1
1885	NY-a	2	8	.200	10	10	10	0	0	85	108	11.4	5	24	2.5	13	1.4	6.25	45	.322	.367	-28	-33	86	81	-2.6	2	0	-2.4
Total	2	3	8	.273	11	11	11	0	0	91	110	10.9	5	26	2.6	15	1.5	5.93	47	.311	.358	-27	-32	87	77	-2.1	2	0	-2.3
■ **GEORGE BECHTEL**	Bechtel, George A. b: 1848, Philadelphia, Pa. 5'11", 165 lbs. Deb: 5/20/1871																												
1871	Ath-n	1	2	.333	3																								
1873	Phi-n	0	3	.000	3																								
1874	Phi-n	1	3	.250	4																								
1875	Cen-n	2	12	.143	14																								
	Ath-n	3	1	.750	4																								
	Yr	5	13	.278	18																								
Total	4 n	7	21	.250	28																								
■ **FRANK BECK**	Beck, Frank J. b: 1862, Poughkeepsie, N.Y. TR , Deb: 5/02/1884																												
1884	Pit-a	0	3	.000	3	3	3	0	0	25	33	11.9	0	6	2.2	11	4.0	6.12	54	.327	.364	-8	-8	101	81	-1.4	1	0	-0.5
	Bal-U	0	2	.000	2	2	1	0	0	9	17	17.0	0	4	4.0	7	7.0	8.00	41	.406	.457	-5	-5	110	100	-0.9	-1	0	-0.3
■ **GEORGE BECK**	Beck, George F. b: 1889, Moline, Ill. BR/TR, 5'11", 162 lbs. Deb: 5/15/14																												
1914	Cle-A	0	0	—	1	0	0	0	0	1	1	9.0	0	0	0.0	0	0.0	0.00	—	.250	.400	0	0	106	0	0.0	0	0	0.0
■ **RICH BECK**	Beck, Richard Henry b: 1/21/41, Pasco, Wash. BB/TR, 6'3", 190 lbs. Deb: 9/14/65																												
1965	NY-A	2	1	.667	3	3	1	1	0	21	22	9.4	1	7	3.0	10	4.3	2.14	163	.275	.330	3	3	101	178	0.6	-0	0	0.4
■ **BOOM-BOOM BECK**	Beck, Walter William b: 10/16/04, Decatur, Ill. d: 5/7/87, Champaign, Ill. BR/TR, 6'2", 200 lbs. Deb: 9/22/24 C																												
1924	StL-A	0	0	—	1	0	0	0	0	1	0	0.0	0	2	18.0	0	0.0	0.00	—	.000	.400	0	1	108	0	0.0	0	0	0.1
1927	StL-A	1	0	1.000	3	1	1	0	0	11	15	12.3	0	5	4.1	6	4.9	5.73	79	.333	.396	-2	-1	109	99	0.5	-0	-0	-0.1
1928	StL-A	2	3	.400	16	4	2	0	0	49	52	9.6	4	20	3.7	17	3.1	4.41	95	.289	.350	-2	-1	103	112	-0.5	1	0	0.0
1933	Bro-N	12	20	.375	43	35	15	3	1	257	270	9.5	9	69	2.4	89	3.1	3.54	93	.267	.314	-6	-7	98	95	-2.2	0	-1	-0.7
1934	Bro-N	2	6	.250	22	9	2	0	0	57	72	11.4	6	32	5.1	24	3.8	7.42	52	.301	.392	-21	-22	95	80	-1.8	1	1	-1.8
1939	Phi-N	7	14	.333	34	16	12	0	3	183	203	10.0	11	64	3.1	77	3.8	4.72	82	.284	.333	-16	-17	99	90	0.6	-3	-0	-1.8
1940	Phi-N	4	9	.308	29	15	4	0	0	129	147	10.3	13	41	2.9	38	2.7	4.33	91	.286	.343	-7	-6	102	112	-0.3	-3	1	-0.7
1941	Phi-N	1	9	.100	34	7	2	0	0	95	104	9.9	8	35	3.3	34	3.2	4.64	80	.276	.335	-11	-10	103	93	-3.2	-2	-3	-1.3
1942	Phi-N	0	1	.000	26	1	0	0	0	53	69	11.7	4	17	2.9	10	1.7	4.75	70	.325	.369	-8	-8	101	115	-0.4	1	-0	-0.7
1943	Phi-N	0	0	—	4	0	0	0	0	14	24	15.4	1	5	3.2	3	1.9	9.64	33	.393	.456	-10	-10	96	83	0.0	1	-0	-0.8
1944	Det-A	1	2	.333	28	2	0	0	1	74	67	8.1	5	27	3.3	25	3.0	3.89	91	.243	.305	-4	-3	104	85	-0.5	2	-2	-0.2
1945	Cin-N	2	4	.333	11	5	2	0	1	48	42	7.9	0	12	2.3	9	1.7	3.38	109	.236	.281	2	2	97	70	-0.4	-0	0	0.2
	Pit-N	6	1	.857	14	5	4	0	0	63	54	7.7	2	14	2.0	20	2.9	2.14	181	.234	.274	12	12	102	113	2.5	-1	-0	1.2
	Yr	8	5	.615	25	10	6	0	1	111	96	7.8	2	26	2.1	29	2.4	2.68	142	.234	.275	14	14	100	113	2.1	-0	-0	1.4
Total	12	38	69	.355	265	100	44	3	6	1034	1119	9.7	63	343	3.0	352	3.1	4.30	85	.277	.331	-72	-72	100	96	-5.7	-2	-4	-6.6
■ **CHARLIE BECKER**	Becker, Charles S. "Buck" b: 10/14/1888, Washington, D.C. d: 7/30/28, Washington, D, C. BL/TL, 6'2", 180 lbs. Deb: 8/02/11																												
1911	Was-A	3	5	.375	11	5	5	1	0	71	80	10.1	2	23	2.9	31	3.9	4.06	82	.268	.335	-6	-6	99	81	-0.3	-0	-0	-0.5
1912	Was-A	0	0	—	4	0	0	0	0	9	8	8.0	0	6	6.0	5	5.0	3.00	108	.258	.378	0	0	97	132	0.0	-0	-0	0.0
Total	2	3	5	.375	15	5	5	1	0	80	88	9.9	2	29	3.3	36	4.0	3.94	84	.267	.340	-5	-6	99	87	-0.3	0	-1	-0.5
■ **BOB BECKER**	Becker, Robert Charles b: 8/15/1875, Syracuse, N.Y. d: 10/11/51, Syracuse, N.Y. Deb: 9/06/1897																												
1897	Phi-N	0	2	.000	5	2	2	0	0	24	32	12.0	0	7	2.6	10	3.8	5.63	74	.343	.389	-3	-4	96	82	-0.9	-0	0	-0.3
1898	Phi-N	0	0	—	1	0	0	0	0	5	6	10.8	0	5	9.0	0	0.0	10.80	31	.320	.463	-4	-4	94	55	0.0	0	0	-0.2
Total	2	0	2	.000	6	2	2	0	0	29	38	11.8	0	12	3.7	10	3.1	6.52	62	.339	.403	-7	-8	96	77	-0.9	-0	0	-0.5

YEAR	TM/L	W	L	PCT	G	GS	CG	SHO	SV	IP	H	H/G	HR	BB	BB/G	SO	SO/G	ERA	/A	OAVG	OOBP	PR	/A	PF	CPI	WAT	PB	PD	TPI
■ **JAKE BECKLEY**	Beckley, Jacob Peter "Eagle Eye" b: 8/4/1867, Hannibal, Mo. d: 6/25/18, Kansas City, Mo. BL/TL, 5'10", 200 lbs. Deb: 1888 H																												
1902	Cin-N	0	1	.000	1	1	0	0	0	4	9	20.3	0	1	2.3	2	4.5	6.75	45	.471	.497	-2	-2	108	129	-0.4	0	1	-0.1
■ **JIM BECKMAN**	Beckman, James Joseph b: 3/1/05, Cincinnati, Ohio BR/TR, 5'10", 172 lbs. Deb: 7/27/27																												
1927	Cin-N	0	1	.000	4	1	0	0	0	12	18	13.5	2	6	4.5	0	0.0	6.00	65	.340	.403	-3	-3	100	121	-0.4	0	-1	-0.2
1928	Cin-N	0	1	.000	6	0	0	0	0	15	19	11.4	1	9	5.4	4	2.4	6.00	64	.306	.364	-3	-4	97	90	-0.4	-0	-0	-0.3
Total	2	0	2	.000	10	1	0	0	0	27	37	12.3	3	15	5.0	4	1.3	6.00	65	.322	.381	-6	-6	98	103	-0.8	-0	-1	-0.5
■ **BILL BECKMANN**	Beckmann, William Aloysius b: 12/8/07, Clayton, Mo. BR/TR, 6', 175 lbs. Deb: 5/02/39																												
1939	Phi-A	7	11	.389	27	19	7	2	0	155	198	11.5	15	41	2.4	20	1.2	5.40	87	.312	.347	-13	-12	102	98	0.4	0	-2	-1.1
1940	Phi-A	8	4	.667	34	9	6	2	1	127	132	9.4	11	35	2.5	47	3.3	4.18	104	.265	.309	3	2	99	92	3.0	-1	-2	0.0
1941	Phi-A	5	9	.357	22	15	4	0	1	130	141	9.8	11	33	2.3	28	1.9	4.57	93	.270	.314	-6	-4	103	84	-1.0	0	-3	-0.6
1942	Phi-A	0	1	.000	5	1	0	0	0	20	24	10.8	1	9	4.0	10	4.5	7.20	51	.289	.359	-8	-8	101	64	-0.4	1	-0	-0.6
	StL-N	1	0	1.000	2	0	0	0	0	7	4	5.1	0	1	1.3	3	3.9	0.00	—	.200	.227	3	3	103	0	0.5	-0	0	0.3
Total	4	21	25	.457	90	44	17	4	2	439	499	10.2	38	119	2.4	108	2.2	4.80	92	.284	.326	-22	-19	101	89	2.5	1	-7	-2.0
■ **JULIO BECQUER**	Becquer, Julio (Villegas) b: 12/20/31, Havana, Cuba BL/TL, 5'11.5", 178 lbs. Deb: 9/13/55																												
1960	Was-A	0	0	—	1	0	0	0	0	1	1	9.0	1	0	0.0	0	0.0	9.00	44	.250	.250	-1	-1	102	104	0.0	0	0	0.0
1961	Min-A	0	0	—	1	0	0	0	0	1	4	36.0	0	1	9.0	0	0.0	27.00	16	.500	.556	-3	-3	107	62	0.0	0	0	-0.2
Total	2	0	0	—	2	0	0	0	0	2	5	22.5	1	1	4.5	0	0.0	18.00	23	.417	.462	-3	-3	105	83	0.0	0	0	-0.2
■ **JOE BECKWITH**	Beckwith, Thomas Joseph b: 1/28/55, Opelika, Ala. BL/TR, 6'3", 200 lbs. Deb: 7/21/79																												
1979	LA-N	1	2	.333	17	0	0	0	2	37	42	10.2	4	15	3.6	28	6.8	4.38	85	.284	.339	-3	-3	99	105	-0.4	-1	0	-0.2
1980	LA-N	3	3	.500	38	0	0	0	0	60	60	9.0	1	23	3.5	40	6.0	1.95	177	.263	.326	11	10	96	175	-0.3	0	-1	1.0
1982	LA-N	2	1	.667	19	1	0	0	1	40	38	8.5	2	14	3.1	33	7.4	2.70	125	.252	.306	4	3	94	120	0.4	-1	-1	0.2
1983	LA-N	3	4	.429	42	3	0	0	1	71	73	9.3	5	35	4.4	50	6.3	3.55	102	.264	.340	1	1	100	114	-0.8	0	1	0.2
1984	KC-A	8	4	.667	49	1	0	0	2	101	92	8.2	13	25	2.2	75	6.7	3.39	117	.247	.290	7	7	99	105	1.9	0	0	0.7
1985	KC-A	1	5	.167	49	0	0	0	1	95	99	9.4	9	32	3.0	80	7.6	4.07	103	.269	.327	1	1	101	103	-2.0	0	0	0.1
1986	LA-N	0	0	—	15	0	0	0	0	18	28	14.0	5	6	3.0	13	6.5	7.00	50	.350	.395	-7	-7	95	111	0.0	0	-0	-0.7
Total	7	18	19	.486	229	5	0	0	7	422	432	9.2	39	150	3.2	319	6.8	3.54	107	.266	.323	14	12	99	117	-1.2	-1	-0	1.3
■ **PHIL BEDGOOD**	Bedgood, Phillip Burlette b: 3/8/1898, Harrison, Ga. d: 11/8/27, Fort Pierce, Fla. BR/TR, 6'3", 218 lbs. Deb: 9/20/22																												
1922	Cle-A	1	0	1.000	1	1	1	0	0	9	7	7.0	0	4	4.0	5	5.0	4.00	104	.233	.368	0	0	103	92	0.5	-0	0	0.0
1923	Cle-A	0	2	.000	9	2	0	0	0	19	16	7.6	0	14	6.6	7	3.3	5.21	75	.246	.381	-3	-3	99	79	-0.9	0	0	-0.1
Total	2	1	2	.333	10	3	1	0	0	28	23	7.4	0	18	5.8	12	3.9	4.82	83	.242	.377	-3	-3	100	83	-0.4	0	0	-0.1
■ **HUGH BEDIENT**	Bedient, Hugh Carpenter b: 10/23/1889, Gerry, N.Y. d: 7/21/65, Jamestown, N.Y. BR/TR, 6', 185 lbs. Deb: 4/26/12																												
1912	Bos-A	20	9	.690	41	28	19	0	2	231	206	8.0	6	55	2.1	122	4.8	2.92	117	.240	.288	11	13	102	82	0.0	1	0	1.3
1913	Bos-A	15	14	.517	43	28	15	1	5	259	255	8.9	0	67	2.3	122	4.2	2.78	108	.261	.312	4	7	103	95	-0.2	-3	-4	0.2
1914	Bos-A	8	12	.400	42	16	7	1	2	177	187	9.5	4	45	2.3	70	3.6	3.61	73	.281	.331	-17	-19	96	94	-3.5	-2	-1	-2.0
1915	Buf-F	16	18	.471	53	30	16	2	**10**	269	284	9.5	5	69	2.3	106	3.5	3.18	96	.274	.321	-4	-3	101	104	-0.6	-4	0	-0.6
Total	4	59	53	.527	179	102	57	4	19	936	932	9.0	15	236	2.3	420	4.0	3.09	99	.263	.312	-6	-4	101	94	-4.3	-8	-4	-1.1
■ **ANDY BEDNAR**	Bednar, Andrew Jackson b: 8/16/08, Streator, Ill. d: 11/26/37, Graham, Tex. BR/TR, 5'10.5", 180 lbs. Deb: 9/06/30																												
1930	Pit-N	0	0	—	2	0	0	0	0	1	4	36.0	0	1	9.0	1	9.0	36.00	13	.500	.500	-3	-3	98	47	0.0	0	0	-0.2
1931	Pit-N	0	0	—	3	0	0	0	0	4	10	22.5	1	0	0.0	2	4.5	11.25	35	.476	.455	-3	-3	102	105	0.0	0	0	-0.2
Total	2	0	0	—	5	0	0	0	0	5	14	25.2	1	1	1.8	3	5.4	16.20	25	.483	.469	-7	-7	101	93	0.0	0	0	-0.4
■ **STEVE BEDROSIAN**	Bedrosian, Stephen Wayne b: 12/6/57, Methuen, Mass. BR/TR, 6'3", 200 lbs. Deb: 8/14/81																												
1981	Atl-N	1	2	.333	15	1	0	0	0	24	15	5.6	2	15	5.6	9	3.4	4.50	78	.169	.292	-3	-3	100	49	-0.3	-0	-0	-0.2
1982	Atl-N	8	6	.571	64	3	0	0	11	138	102	6.7	7	57	3.7	123	8.0	2.41	159	.206	.287	18	22	107	100	0.4	-2	-0	2.1
1983	Atl-N	9	10	.474	70	1	0	0	19	120	100	7.5	11	51	3.8	114	8.6	3.60	105	.229	.308	0	3	104	91	-1.3	-1	0	0.2
1984	Atl-N	9	6	.600	40	4	0	0	11	84	65	7.0	5	33	3.5	81	8.7	2.36	167	.210	.287	12	15	110	104	1.7	-1	-1	1.4
1985	Atl-N	7	15	.318	37	37	0	0	0	207	198	8.6	17	111	4.8	134	5.8	3.83	102	.254	.346	-5	2	108	109	-2.6	-4	-2	-0.3
1986	Phi-N	8	6	.571	68	0	0	0	29	90	79	7.9	12	34	3.4	82	8.2	3.40	114	.232	.297	3	5	104	101	0.6	0	-1	0.5
1987	Phi-N	5	3	.625	65	0	0	0	**40**	89	79	8.0	11	28	2.8	74	7.5	2.83	151	.237	.295	12	14	105	119	1.1	-0	-1	1.3
1988	Phi-N	6	6	.500	57	0	0	0	28	74	75	9.1	6	27	3.3	61	7.4	3.77	94	.257	.317	-3	-2	103	98	1.0	-0	-0	-0.1
Total	8	53	54	.495	416	46	0	0	138	826	713	7.8	71	356	3.9	678	7.4	3.27	119	.232	.310	36	56	106	102	0.6	-9	-5	4.9
■ **FRED BEEBE**	Beebe, Frederick Leonard b: 12/31/1880, Lincoln, Neb. d: 10/30/57, Elgin, Ill. BR/TR, 6'1", 190 lbs. Deb: 4/17/06																												
1906	Chi-N	6	1	.857	14	6	4	0	1	70	56	7.2	1	32	4.1	55	7.1	2.70	97	.250	.356	-1	-1	99	102	1.4	-1	-1	-0.1
	StL-N	9	9	.500	20	19	16	1	0	161	115	6.4	1	68	3.8	116	6.5	3.02	91	.228	.330	-7	-5	104	71	2.3	-0	-0	-0.5
	Yr	15	10	.600	34	25	20	1	1	231	171	6.7	2	100	3.9	**171**	6.7	2.92	92	.233	.332	-7	-6	102	71	3.7	-1	-1	-0.6
1907	StL-N	7	19	.269	31	29	24	4	0	238	192	7.3	1	109	4.1	141	5.3	2.72	91	.250	.351	-7	-7	100	94	-3.0	-3	1	-0.6
1908	StL-N	5	13	.278	29	19	12	0	0	174	134	6.9	3	66	3.4	72	3.7	2.64	89	.240	.325	-6	-6	100	86	-1.2	-2	2	-0.4
1909	StL-N	15	21	.417	44	34	18	1	1	288	256	8.0	5	104	3.3	105	3.3	2.81	92	.229	.299	-7	-7	99	80	2.2	-2	0	-0.7
1910	Cin-N	12	14	.462	35	26	11	3	0	214	193	8.1	3	94	4.0	93	3.9	3.07	101	.246	.333	-1	1	102	96	-0.7	-3	3	0.1
1911	Phi-N	3	3	.500	9	8	3	0	0	48	52	9.8	2	24	4.5	20	3.8	4.50	81	.297	.391	-6	-4	108	109	0.0	2	1	-0.1
1916	Cle-A	5	3	.625	20	12	5	1	2	101	92	8.2	1	37	3.3	32	2.9	2.41	117	.251	.321	5	4	99	117	1.0	1	-0	0.5
Total	7	62	83	.428	202	153	93	10	4	1294	1090	7.6	17	534	3.7	634	4.4	2.87	94	.242	.329	-29	-25	101	90	2.0	-8	5	-1.8
■ **ED BEECHER**	Beecher, Edward H. b: 7/2/1860, Guilford, Conn. d: 9/12/35, Hartford, Conn. BL , 5'10", 185 lbs. Deb: 6/28/1887																												
1890	Buf-P	0	0	—	1	0	0	0	0	6	10	15.0	0	3	4.5	0	0.0	12.00	34	.384	.447	-5	-5	97	56	0.0	0	0	-0.3
■ **ROY BEECHER**	Beecher, Leroy "Colonel" b: 5/10/1884, Swanton, Ohio d: 10/11/52, Toledo, Ohio BL/TR, 6'2", 180 lbs. Deb: 9/29/07																												
1907	NY-N	0	2	.000	2	2	2	0	0	14	17	10.9	0	6	3.9	5	3.2	2.57	100	.330	.400	-0	-0	104	167	-0.9	-1	-0	0.0
1908	NY-N	0	0	—	2	0	0	0	1	6	11	16.5	0	3	4.5	0	0.0	7.50	31	.427	.487	-3	-3	100	101	0.0	1	0	-0.2
Total	2	0	2	.000	4	2	2	0	1	20	28	12.6	0	9	4.0	5	2.3	4.05	62	.363	.429	-4	-3	103	147	-0.9	-0	0	-0.2
■ **FRED BEENE**	Beene, Freddy Ray b: 11/24/42, Angleton, Tex. BB/TR, 5'9", 155 lbs. Deb: 9/18/68																												
1968	Bal-A	0	0	—	1	0	0	0	0	1	2	18.0	0	1	9.0	1	9.0	9.00	33	.500	.500	-1	-1	101	127	0.0	0	0	0.0
1969	Bal-A	0	0	—	2	0	0	0	0	3	2	6.0	0	1	3.0	0	0.0	0.00	—	.200	.273	1	1	100	0	0.0	0	0	0.1
1970	Bal-A	0	0	—	4	0	0	0	0	6	8	12.0	1	5	7.5	4	6.0	6.00	58	.320	.419	-2	-2	94	121	0.0	0	-0	-0.1
1972	NY-A	1	3	.250	29	1	0	0	3	58	55	8.5	3	24	3.7	37	5.7	2.33	121	.256	.331	5	3	92	151	-0.9	-1	0	0.2
1973	NY-A	6	0	1.000	19	4	0	0	1	91	67	6.6	5	27	2.7	49	4.8	1.68	228	.209	.269	22	22	100	128	3.0	0	1	2.5
1974	NY-A	0	0	—	6	0	0	0	1	10	9	8.1	1	2	1.8	10	9.0	2.70	128	.231	.286	1	1	95	102	0.0	0	0	0.1
	Cle-A	4	4	.500	32	0	0	0	2	73	68	8.4	7	26	3.2	35	4.3	4.93	74	.247	.310	-11	-10	101	70	0.2	0	1	-0.9
	Yr	4	4	.500	38	0	0	0	3	83	77	8.3	8	28	3.0	45	4.9	4.66	78	.244	.305	-10	-9	100	70	0.2	0	1	-0.8
1975	Cle-A	1	0	1.000	19	1	0	0	1	47	63	12.1	4	25	4.8	20	3.8	6.89	55	.323	.401	-16	-16	100	88	0.5	0	1	-1.5
Total	7	12	7	.632	112	6	0	0	8	289	274	8.5	21	111	3.5	156	4.9	3.61	98	.253	.322	-0	-2	98	109	2.8	-1	2	0.4
■ **ANDY BEENE**	Beene, Ramon Andrew b: 10/13/56, Freeport, Tex. BR/TR, 6'3", 205 lbs. Deb: 9/22/83																												
1983	Mil-A	0	0	—	1	0	0	0	0	2	3	13.5	0	1	4.5	0	0.0	4.50	82	.333	.400	-0	-0	91	125	0.0	0	0	0.0
1984	Mil-A	0	2	.000	5	3	0	0	0	19	28	13.3	1	9	4.3	11	5.2	10.89	34	.350	.424	-15	-15	93	61	-0.9	0	0	-1.2
Total	2	0	2	.000	6	3	0	0	0	21	31	13.3	1	10	4.3	11	4.7	10.29	36	.348	.422	-15	-15	92	67	-0.9	0	0	-1.2
■ **CLARENCE BEERS**	Beers, Clarence Scott b: 12/9/18, El Dorado, Kan. BR/TR, 6', 175 lbs. Deb: 5/02/48																												
1948	StL-N	0	0	—	1	0	0	0	0	1	3	27.0	0	1	9.0	0	0.0	9.00	43	.500	.571	-1	-1	99	161	0.0	0	0	0.0
■ **JOE BEGGS**	Beggs, Joseph Stanley "Fireman" b: 11/4/10, Rankin, Pa. d: 7/19/83, Indianapolis, Ind BR/TR, 6'1", 182 lbs. Deb: 4/19/38																												
1938	NY-A	3	2	.600	14	9	4	0	0	58	69	10.7	7	20	3.1	8	1.2	5.43	90	.299	.346	-4	-4	102	97	-0.1	1	2	0.0
1940	Cin-N	12	3	.800	37	1	0	0	**7**	77	68	7.9	1	21	2.5	25	2.9	1.99	189	.243	.295	**16**	**15**	98	142	3.4	-0	1	1.7

YEAR	TM/L	W	L	PCT	G	GS	CG	SHO	SV	IP	H	H/G	HR	BB	BB/G	SO	SO/G	ERA	/A	OAVG	OOBP	PR	/A	PF	CPI	WAT	PB	PD	TPI
1941	Cin-N	4	3	.571	37	0	0	0	5	57	57	9.0	2	27	4.3	19	3.0	3.79	94	.313	.385	-1	-1	98	138	0.0	1	0	0.0
1942	Cin-N	6	5	.545	38	0	0	0	8	89	65	6.6	4	33	3.3	24	2.4	2.12	158	.206	.274	12	12	102	108	0.5	-3	3	1.3
1943	Cin-N	7	6	.538	39	4	4	2	6	115	120	9.4	0	25	2.0	28	2.2	2.35	141	.274	.303	**13**	**12**	98	131	-0.2	-1	1	1.4
1944	Cin-N	1	0	1.000	1	1	1	0	0	9	8	8.0	0	0	0.0	2	2.0	2.00	171	.222	.222	2	1	95	51	0.5	-1	0	0.1
1946	Cin-N	12	10	.545	28	22	14	3	1	190	175	8.3	15	39	1.8	38	1.8	2.32	154	.247	.283	23	27	105	124	2.4	1	1	3.3
1947	Cin-N	0	3	.000	11	4	0	0	0	32	42	11.8	4	6	1.7	11	3.1	5.34	70	.316	.343	-5	-6	92	96	-1.4	-1	1	-0.5
	NY-N	3	3	.500	32	0	0	0	2	66	81	11.0	6	18	2.5	23	3.1	4.23	96	.300	.338	-1	-1	99	111	-0.1	-1	-0	-0.2
	Yr	3	6	.333	43	4	0	0	2	98	123	11.3	10	24	2.2	34	3.1	4.59	86	.305	.339	-6	-7	97	111	-1.5	-1	0	-0.7
1948	NY-N	0	0	—	1	0	0	0	0	⅓	2	54.0	0	0	0.0	0	0.0	0.00	—	.667	.667	0	0	98	0	0.0	0	0	0.0
Total	9	48	35	.578	238	41	23	5	29	693	687	8.9	39	189	2.5	178	2.3	2.96	124	.265	.308	55	56	100	120	5.0	-3	8	7.1
■ ED BEGLEY	Begley, Edward N. (born Edward N. Bagley) b: 1863, New York, N.Y. d: 7/24/19, Waterbury, Conn. Deb: 5/03/1884																												
1884	NY-N	12	18	.400	31	30	30	0	0	266	296	10.0	9	99	3.3	104	3.5	4.16	69	.291	.354	-35	-38	97	93	-5.1	-2	-2	-3.5
1885	NY-a	4	9	.308	15	14	10	0	0	115	131	10.3	5	48	3.8	44	3.4	4.93	57	.299	.368	-21	-27	86	95	-1.6	0	0	-2.3
Total	2	16	27	.372	46	44	40	0	0	381	427	10.1	14	147	3.5	148	3.5	4.39	65	.293	.358	-57	-65	93	94	-6.7	-2	-2	-5.8
■ PETIE BEHAN	Behan, Charles Frederick b: 12/11/1887, Dallas City, Pa. d: 1/22/57, Bradford, Pa. BR/TR, 5'10", 160 lbs. Deb: 9/16/21																												
1921	Phi-N	0	1	.000	2	2	1	0	0	11	17	13.9	0	1	0.8	3	2.5	5.73	71	.354	.360	-2	-2	107	85	-0.4	-1	-0	-0.2
1922	Phi-N	4	2	.667	7	5	3	1	0	47	49	9.4	3	14	2.7	13	2.5	2.49	192	.259	.309	8	12	117	126	1.4	-0	-1	1.2
1923	Phi-N	3	12	.200	31	17	5	0	2	131	182	12.5	11	57	3.9	27	1.9	5.50	86	.336	.393	-22	-11	118	110	-3.0	-3	-1	-1.2
Total	3	7	15	.318	40	24	9	1	2	189	248	11.8	14	72	3.4	43	2.0	4.76	98	.319	.371	-16	-2	117	112	-2.0	-3	-2	-0.2
■ RICK BEHENNA	Behenna, Richard Kipp b: 3/6/60, Miami, Fla. BR/TR, 6'2", 170 lbs. Deb: 4/12/83																												
1983	Atl-N	3	3	.500	14	6	0	0	0	37	37	9.0	7	12	2.9	17	4.1	4.62	82	.255	.313	-4	-3	104	93	-0.1	2	-0	-0.1
	Cle-A	0	2	.000	5	4	0	0	0	26	22	7.6	0	14	4.8	9	3.1	4.15	104	.232	.333	-0	0	106	74	-0.9	0	0	0.1
1984	Cle-A	0	3	.000	3	3	0	0	0	10	17	15.3	5	8	7.2	6	5.4	13.50	31	.386	.481	-11	-10	106	91	-1.4	0	0	-0.8
1985	Cle-A	0	2	.000	4	4	0	0	0	20	29	13.0	3	8	3.6	4	1.8	7.65	52	.354	.407	-8	-8	95	93	-0.9	0	-1	-0.7
Total	3	3	10	.231	26	17	0	0	0	93	105	10.2	15	42	4.1	36	3.5	6.10	66	.287	.361	-23	-21	103	88	-3.3	2	-1	-1.5
■ MEL BEHNEY	Behney, Melvin Brian b: 9/2/47, Newark, N.J. BL/TL, 6'2", 180 lbs. Deb: 8/14/70																												
1970	Cin-N	0	2	.000	5	1	0	0	0	10	15	13.5	1	8	7.2	2	1.8	4.50	93	.341	.442	-0	-0	103	167	-0.9	-0	-0	0.0
■ HANK BEHRMAN	Behrman, Henry Bernard b: 6/27/21, Brooklyn, N.Y. d: 1/20/87, New York, N.Y. BR/TR, 5'11", 174 lbs. Deb: 4/17/46																												
1946	Bro-N	11	5	.688	47	11	2	0	4	151	138	8.2	3	69	4.1	78	4.6	2.92	117	.241	.319	8	8	100	101	1.6	-3	-2	0.4
1947	Bro-N	0	0	—	2	0	0	0	0	4	3	6.8	1	4	9.0	2	4.5	9.00	46	.231	.389	-2	-2	103	71	0.0	0	0	-0.1
	Pit-N	0	2	.000	10	2	0	0	0	25	33	11.9	6	17	6.1	11	4.0	9.00	46	.347	.448	-14	-13	102	95	-0.9	-1	-1	-1.3
	Bro-N	5	3	.625	38	6	0	0	8	88	94	9.6	9	44	4.5	31	3.2	5.32	79	.274	.352	-12	-11	103	88	0.2	1	-1	-1.0
	Yr	5	5	.500	50	8	0	0	8	117	130	10.0	16	65	5.0	44	3.4	6.23	67	.287	.371	-28	-27	103	88	-0.7	-1	-2	-2.4
1948	Bro-N	5	4	.556	34	4	2	1	7	91	95	9.4	7	42	4.2	42	4.2	4.05	100	.268	.347	-1	0	103	107	0.1	-2	-0	-0.1
1949	NY-N	3	3	.500	43	4	1	1	0	71	64	8.1	5	52	6.6	25	3.2	4.94	82	.239	.357	-7	-7	101	85	0.2	-1	-0	-0.7
Total	4	24	17	.585	174	27	5	2	19	430	427	8.9	31	228	4.8	189	4.0	4.40	88	.259	.347	-28	-25	101	96	1.2	-5	-5	-2.8
■ TIM BELCHER	Belcher, Timothy Wayne b: 10/19/61, Mount Gilead, Ohio BR/TR, 6'3", 210 lbs. Deb: 9/06/87																												
1987	LA-N	4	2	.667	6	5	0	0	0	34	30	7.9	2	7	1.9	23	6.1	2.38	158	.240	.274	6	5	92	113	1.2	0	0	0.5
1988	LA-N	12	6	.667	36	27	4	1	4	180	143	7.2	8	51	2.6	152	7.6	2.90	125	.217	.273	11	15	105	79	2.0	-2	-1	1.3
Total	2	16	8	.667	42	32	4	1	4	214	173	7.3	10	58	2.4	175	7.4	2.82	130	.221	.273	18	20	103	84	3.2	-2	-1	1.8
■ BO BELINSKY	Belinsky, Robert b: 12/7/36, New York, N.Y. BL/TL, 6'2", 191 lbs. Deb: 4/18/62																												
1962	LA-A	10	11	.476	33	31	5	3	1	187	149	7.2	12	122	5.9	145	7.0	3.56	114	.216	.338	8	10	102	99	-1.1	1	-0	1.1
1963	LA-A	2	9	.182	13	13	2	0	0	77	78	9.1	12	35	4.1	60	7.0	5.73	59	.262	.343	-18	-20	92	83	-3.2	-2	1	-1.9
1964	LA-A	9	8	.529	23	22	4	1	0	135	120	8.0	8	49	3.3	91	6.1	2.87	112	.240	.313	11	5	89	110	0.4	-1	-1	0.3
1965	Phi-N	4	9	.308	30	14	3	0	1	110	103	8.4	13	48	3.9	71	5.8	4.83	70	.248	.326	-16	-18	95	85	-2.7	1	-1	-1.8
1966	Phi-N	0	2	.000	9	1	0	0	0	15	14	8.4	3	5	3.0	8	4.8	3.00	121	.250	.344	1	1	100	162	-0.9	0	0	0.1
1967	Hou-N	3	9	.250	27	18	0	0	0	115	112	8.8	12	54	4.2	80	6.3	4.70	68	.255	.341	-17	-19	95	91	-2.5	-1	-2	-2.2
1969	Pit-N	0	3	.000	8	3	0	0	0	18	17	8.5	1	14	7.0	15	7.5	4.50	75	.266	.398	-2	-2	94	116	-1.4	-0	0	-0.1
1970	Cin-N	0	0	—	3	0	0	0	0	8	10	11.3	0	6	6.8	6	6.8	4.50	93	.294	.400	-0	-0	103	114	0.0	1	-0	0.0
Total	8	28	51	.354	146	102	14	4	2	665	603	8.2	61	333	4.5	476	6.4	4.10	86	.241	.335	-32	-44	96	98	-11.4	-2	-3	-4.5
■ CHARLIE BELL	Bell, Charles C. b: 8/12/1868, Cincinnati, Ohio d: 2/7/37, Cincinnati, Ohio TR , Deb: 10/13/1889																												
1889	KC-a	1	0	1.000	1	1	1	0	0	9	4	4.0	0	3	3.0	3	3.0	1.00	418	.144	.228	3	3	109	33	0.5	0	0	0.3
1891	Lou-a	2	6	.250	10	9	8	0	0	77	93	10.9	4	20	2.3	16	1.9	4.68	74	.314	.357	-8	-11	92	89	-1.4	-2	0	-1.0
	CM-a	1	0	1.000	1	1	1	0	0	9	2	2.0	0	3	3.0	1	1.0	0.00	—	.078	.174	4	4	113	0	0.5	1	0	0.5
	Yr	3	6	.333	11	10	9	0	0	86	95	9.9	4	23	2.4	17	1.8	4.19	84	.295	.342	-4	-6	95	0	-0.9	-2	0	-0.5
Total	2	4	6	.400	12	11	10	0	0	95	99	9.4	4	26	2.5	20	1.9	3.88	92	.283	.333	-2	-3	96	75	-0.4	-1	0	-0.2
■ ERIC BELL	Bell, Eric Alvin b: 10/27/63, Modesto, Cal. BL/TL, 6'3", 195 lbs. Deb: 9/24/85																												
1985	Bal-A	0	0	—	4	0	0	0	0	6	4	6.0	1	4	6.0	4	6.0	4.50	91	.200	.333	-0	-0	98	91	0.0	0	0	0.0
1986	Bal-A	1	2	.333	4	4	0	0	0	23	23	9.0	4	14	5.5	18	7.0	5.09	82	.258	.352	-2	-2	99	100	-0.3	0	-1	-0.2
1987	Bal-A	10	13	.435	33	29	2	0	0	165	174	9.5	32	78	4.3	111	6.1	5.45	81	.271	.348	-18	-19	99	97	0.5	0	-1	-1.8
Total	3	11	15	.423	41	33	2	0	0	194	201	9.3	37	96	4.5	133	6.2	5.38	82	.267	.348	-21	-21	99	97	0.2	0	-2	-2.0
■ GARY BELL	Bell, Gary b: 11/17/36, San Antonio, Tex. BR/TR, 6'1", 196 lbs. Deb: 6/01/58																												
1958	Cle-A	12	10	.545	33	23	10	0	1	182	141	7.0	17	73	3.6	110	5.4	3.31	106	.213	.292	9	4	93	86	1.1	2	-2	0.3
1959	Cle-A	16	11	.593	44	28	12	1	5	234	208	8.0	28	105	4.0	136	5.2	4.04	91	.238	.316	-5	-10	95	95	0.6	3	-2	-0.8
1960	Cle-A	9	10	.474	28	23	6	2	1	155	139	8.1	15	82	4.8	109	6.3	4.12	92	.242	.338	-4	-5	98	96	-0.3	-0	1	-0.4
1961	Cle-A	12	16	.429	34	34	11	2	0	228	214	8.4	32	100	3.9	163	6.4	4.11	95	.245	.322	-2	-6	97	99	-1.8	1	-1	-0.5
1962	Cle-A	10	9	.526	57	6	1	0	12	108	104	8.7	14	52	4.3	80	6.7	4.25	92	.264	.343	-3	-4	99	111	0.7	1	-1	-0.3
1963	Cle-A	8	5	.615	58	7	0	0	5	119	91	6.9	13	52	3.9	98	7.4	2.95	120	.208	.293	9	8	98	101	1.7	-1	1	0.8
1964	Cle-A	8	6	.571	56	2	0	0	4	106	106	9.0	15	53	4.5	89	7.6	4.33	86	.260	.346	-8	-7	103	108	1.2	2	-0	-0.5
1965	Cle-A	6	5	.545	60	0	0	0	17	104	86	7.4	7	50	4.3	86	7.4	3.03	111	.226	.313	5	4	97	105	0.1	-0	-1	0.3
1966	Cle-A	14	15	.483	40	37	12	0	0	254	211	7.5	19	79	2.8	194	6.9	3.22	108	.228	.286	6	7	102	90	-0.5	-1	2	1.0
1967	Cle-A	1	5	.167	9	9	1	0	0	61	50	7.4	7	24	3.5	39	5.8	3.69	89	.234	.301	-3	-3	101	99	-1.8	-2	1	-0.3
	Bos-A	12	8	.600	29	24	8	0	3	165	143	7.8	16	47	2.6	115	6.3	3.16	115	.231	.284	1	9	113	97	0.8	1	-0	1.1
	Yr	13	13	.500	38	33	9	0	3	226	193	7.7	23	71	2.8	154	6.1	3.31	107	.231	.288	-2	6	110	97	-1.0	-2	1	0.8
1968	Bos-A	11	11	.500	35	27	9	3	1	199	177	8.0	7	68	3.1	103	4.7	3.12	96	.239	.302	-3	-3	101	93	-0.6	2	0	0.0
1969	Sea-A	2	6	.250	13	11	1	1	2	61	76	11.2	8	34	5.0	30	4.4	4.72	77	.305	.386	-7	-7	100	125	-1.4	1	0	-0.5
	Chi-A	0	0	—	23	2	0	0	0	39	48	11.1	8	23	5.3	26	6.0	6.23	64	.308	.397	-11	-10	110	108	0.0	-0	0	-0.9
	Yr	2	6	.250	36	13	1	1	2	100	124	11.2	16	57	5.1	56	5.0	5.31	71	.302	.386	-19	-17	104	108	-1.4	1	0	-1.4
Total	12	121	117	.508	519	233	71	9	51	2015	1794	8.0	206	842	3.8	1378	6.2	3.68	98	.239	.314	-17	-20	100	98	-0.2	9	-3	-0.7
■ GEORGE BELL	Bell, George Glenn "Farmer" b: 11/2/1874, Greenwood, N.Y. d: 12/25/41, New York, N.Y. BR/TR, 6', 195 lbs. Deb: 4/17/07																												
1907	Bro-N	8	16	.333	35	27	20	3	1	264	222	7.6	1	77	2.6	88	3.0	2.25	105	.256	.321	6	3	96	98	-3.2	-3	2	0.6
1908	Bro-N	4	15	.211	29	21	12	2	1	155	162	9.4	3	45	2.6	63	3.7	3.60	64	.300	.356	-22	-22	99	93	-3.9	1	1	-2.2
1909	Bro-N	16	15	.516	33	30	29	6	1	256	236	8.3	6	73	2.6	95	3.3	2.71	99	.251	.307	-3	-1	103	100	4.5	1	2	0.1
1910	Bro-N	10	27	.270	44	36	25	4	1	310	267	7.8	4	82	2.4	102	3.0	2.64	112	.241	.296	13	11	98	87	-7.6	-4	-3	0.4
1911	Bro-N	5	6	.455	19	12	6	2	0	101	123	11.0	2	28	2.5	28	2.5	4.28	79	.315	.364	-10	-10	99	105	0.3	-1	2	-0.9
Total	5	43	79	.352	160	126	92	17	4	1086	1010	8.4	16	305	2.5	376	3.1	2.85	95	.263	.320	-15	-19	99	95	-9.9	-6	3	-2.0
■ HI BELL	Bell, Herman S b: 7/16/1897, Mt.Sherman, Ky. d: 6/7/49, Glendale, Cal. BR/TR, 6', 185 lbs. Deb: 4/16/24																												
1924	StL-N	3	8	.273	28	11	5	0	1	113	124	9.9	5	29	2.3	29	2.3	4.94	80	.292	.333	-13	-12	103	83	-1.9	-3	0	-1.3

YEAR	TM/L	W	L	PCT	G	GS	CG	SHO	SV	IP	H	H/G	HR	BB	BB/G	SO	SO/G	ERA	/A	OAVG	OOBP	PR	/A	PF	CPI	WAT	PB	PD	TPI
1926	StL-N	6	6	.500	27	7	3	0	2	85	82	8.7	1	17	1.8	27	2.9	3.18	120	.255	.285	6	6	100	82	-0.8	-1	-1	0.3
1927	StL-N	1	3	.250	25	1	0	0	0	57	71	11.2	5	22	3.5	31	4.9	3.95	105	.317	.369	-0	1	106	138	-1.1	-1	0	0.0
1929	StL-N	0	2	.000	7	0	0	0	0	13	19	13.2	1	4	2.8	4	2.8	6.92	67	.339	.359	-3	-3	98	85	-0.9	-0	-0	-0.3
1930	StL-N	4	3	.571	39	9	2	0	**8**	115	143	11.2	4	23	1.8	42	3.3	3.91	129	.299	.328	**14**	**15**	102	103	-0.1	-3	1	1.1
1932	NY-N	8	4	.667	35	10	3	0	2	120	132	9.9	12	16	1.2	25	1.9	3.68	103	.280	.301	3	2	98	106	2.4	-2	-1	-0.1
1933	NY-N	6	5	.545	38	7	1	2	5	105	100	8.6	4	20	1.7	24	2.1	2.06	156	.246	.282	**15**	**13**	96	123	-0.4	-1	-1	1.2
1934	NY-N	4	3	.571	22	2	0	0	6	54	72	12.0	2	12	2.0	9	1.5	3.67	105	.319	.355	2	1	95	133	-0.1	-1	-1	0.0
Total	8	32	34	.485	221	47	14	2	24	662	743	10.1	34	143	1.9	191	2.6	3.70	108	.285	.319	23	22	100	106	-2.9	-12	-4	0.9
■ JERRY BELL	Bell, Jerry Houston b: 10/6/47, Madison, Tenn. BB/TR, 6'4", 190 lbs. Deb: 9/06/71																												
1971	Mil-A	2	1	.667	8	0	0	0	0	15	10	6.0	0	6	3.6	8	4.8	3.00	120	.200	.276	1	1	104	63	0.6	0	-0	0.1
1972	Mil-A	5	1	.833	25	3	0	0	0	71	50	6.3	1	33	4.2	20	2.5	1.65	180	.209	.306	11	10	97	149	2.2	-1	1	1.2
1973	Mil-A	9	9	.500	31	25	8	0	1	184	185	9.0	14	70	3.4	57	2.8	3.96	93	.263	.330	-3	-6	96	96	0.8	0	1	-0.4
1974	Mil-A	1	0	1.000	5	0	0	0	0	14	17	10.9	2	5	3.2	4	2.6	2.57	145	.315	.373	2	2	103	217	0.5	0	0	0.2
Total	4	17	11	.607	69	28	8	0	1	284	262	8.3	17	114	3.6	89	2.8	3.26	107	.250	.324	11	7	97	114	4.1	-1	1	1.1
■ RALPH BELL	Bell, Ralph Albert "Lefty" b: 11/6/1890, Kokoha, Mo. d: 10/18/59, Burlington, Iowa BL/TL, 5'11.5", 170 lbs. Deb: 7/16/12																												
1912	Chi-A	0	0	—	3	0	0	0	0	6	8	12.0	1	8	12.0	5	7.5	9.00	37	.333	.500	-4	-4	99	101	0.0	-0	0	-0.2
■ BILL BELL	Bell, William Samuel "Ding Dong" b: 10/24/33, Goldsboro, N.C. d: 10/11/62, Durham, N.C. BR/TR, 6'3", 200 lbs. Deb: 9/05/52																												
1952	Pit-N	0	1	.000	4	1	0	0	0	16	16	9.0	3	13	7.3	4	2.3	4.50	87	.254	.377	-1	-1	105	126	-0.4	-0	0	0.0
1955	Pit-N	0	0	—	1	0	0	0	0	1	0	0.0	0	1	9.0	0	0.0	0.00	—	.000	.250	0	0	101	0	0.0	0	0	0.0
Total	2	0	1	.000	5	1	0	0	0	17	16	8.5	3	14	7.4	4	2.1	4.24	93	.242	.370	-1	-1	105	118	-0.4	-0	0	0.0
■ CHIEF BENDER	Bender, Charles Albert b: 5/5/1884, Crow Wing Co., Minn d: 5/22/54, Philadelphia, Pa. BR/TR, 6'2", 185 lbs. Deb: 4/20/03 CH																												
1903	Phi-A	17	15	.531	36	33	29	2	0	270	239	8.0	6	65	2.2	127	4.2	3.07	98	.258	.307	-4	-2	102	83	-0.8	-1	-1	-0.2
1904	Phi-A	10	11	.476	29	20	18	4	0	204	167	7.4	1	59	2.6	149	6.6	2.87	91	.245	.305	-6	-6	101	77	-1.2	3	-2	-0.8
1905	Phi-A	18	11	.621	35	23	18	4	0	229	193	7.6	5	90	3.5	142	5.6	2.83	99	.251	.330	-5	-0	106	99	0.0	2	3	0.2
1906	Phi-A	15	10	.600	36	27	24	0	**3**	238	208	7.9	5	48	1.8	159	6.0	2.53	99	.259	.301	4	-1	93	93	2.0	7	-1	-0.2
1907	Phi-A	16	8	.667	33	24	20	4	3	219	185	7.6	1	34	1.4	112	4.6	2.05	129	.252	.285	12	15	104	90	2.1	3	-1	1.5
1908	Phi-A	8	9	.471	18	17	14	2	1	139	121	7.8	1	21	1.4	85	5.5	1.75	150	.236	.270	10	13	110	117	0.4	3	-2	1.4
1909	Phi-A	18	8	.692	34	29	24	5	1	250	196	7.1	1	45	1.6	161	5.8	1.66	145	.214	.254	23	21	97	71	2.8	4	2	2.7
1910	Phi-A	23	5	**.821**	30	25	25	3	0	250	182	6.6	1	47	1.7	155	5.6	1.58	154	.207	.255	26	24	97	81	6.9	7	2	4.0
1911	Phi-A	17	5	**.773**	31	24	16	2	3	216	198	8.3	2	58	2.4	114	4.8	2.17	136	.252	.307	28	19	88	117	3.8	-2	1	1.6
1912	Phi-A	13	8	.619	27	19	12	1	2	171	169	8.9	1	33	**1.7**	90	4.7	2.74	119	.277	.315	12	10	97	114	0.8	-1	-2	0.8
1913	Phi-A	21	10	.677	48	21	14	2	**13**	237	208	7.9	2	59	2.2	135	5.1	2.20	123	.228	.277	19	13	93	79	2.5	1	-2	1.2
1914	Phi-A	17	3	**.850**	28	23	14	7	2	179	159	8.0	4	55	2.8	107	5.4	2.26	112	.240	.299	9	5	93	106	6.0	1	-0	0.6
1915	Bal-F	4	16	.200	26	23	15	0	1	178	198	10.0	5	37	1.9	89	4.5	3.99	85	.298	.342	-19	-12	111	100	-3.7	4	1	-0.6
1916	Phi-N	7	7	.500	27	13	4	0	3	123	137	10.0	3	34	2.5	43	3.1	3.73	66	.287	.336	-15	-17	94	102	-1.1	4	1	-1.3
1917	Phi-N	8	2	.800	20	10	8	4	2	113	84	6.7	1	26	2.1	43	3.4	1.67	171	.215	.268	13	15	106	112	2.7	1	-2	1.7
1925	Chi-A	0	0	—	1	0	0	0	0	1	1	9.0	1	1	9.0	0	0.0	18.00	23	.333	.400	-2	-2	95	81	0.0	0	0	0.0
Total	16	212	128	.624	459	331	255	40	34	3017	2645	7.9	40	712	2.1	1711	5.1	2.46	112	.246	.296	106	97	99	94	23.2	34	-3	12.6
■ RAY BENGE	Benge, Raymond Adelphia b: 4/22/02, Jacksonville, Tex. BR/TR, 5'9.5", 160 lbs. Deb: 9/26/25																												
1925	Cle-A	1	0	1.000	2	2	1	1	0	12	9	6.8	0	3	2.3	3	2.3	1.50	313	.205	.250	4	4	107	81	0.5	0	-0	0.4
1926	Cle-A	1	0	1.000	8	0	0	0	0	12	15	11.3	0	4	3.0	3	2.3	3.75	104	.313	.345	0	0	97	117	0.5	0	0	0.1
1928	Phi-N	8	18	.308	40	28	12	1	1	202	219	9.8	15	88	3.9	68	3.0	4.54	96	.286	.348	-13	-4	109	100	0.5	-0	-2	-0.4
1929	Phi-N	11	15	.423	38	27	9	2	4	199	255	11.5	24	77	3.5	78	3.5	6.29	84	.322	.370	-35	-23	112	95	-1.3	-3	-3	-2.3
1930	Phi-N	11	15	.423	38	29	14	0	1	226	305	12.1	22	81	3.2	70	2.8	5.69	96	.328	.367	-18	-6	109	103	2.0	-3	-2	-0.8
1931	Phi-N	14	18	.438	38	31	16	2	2	247	251	9.1	12	61	2.2	117	4.3	3.17	133	.262	.304	19	28	109	104	0.3	-2	-2	2.6
1932	Phi-N	13	12	.520	41	28	13	2	6	222	247	10.0	15	58	2.4	89	3.6	4.05	106	.281	.324	-4	6	111	100	0.4	-3	-1	0.3
1933	Bro-N	10	17	.370	37	30	16	2	1	229	238	9.4	11	55	2.2	74	2.9	3.42	96	.268	.309	-2	-4	98	99	-1.9	0	-3	-0.6
1934	Bro-N	14	12	.538	36	32	14	1	0	227	252	10.0	11	61	2.4	64	2.5	4.32	90	.272	.317	-7	-11	95	84	2.0	-2	-1	-1.3
1935	Bro-N	9	9	.500	23	17	5	1	1	125	142	10.2	12	47	3.4	39	2.8	4.46	85	.289	.349	-6	-9	95	108	0.8	-1	-2	-1.0
1936	Bos-N	7	9	.438	21	19	2	0	0	115	161	12.6	6	38	3.0	32	2.5	5.79	67	.333	.380	-23	-25	96	96	-0.4	-3	-2	-2.6
	Phi-N	1	4	.200	15	6	0	0	1	46	70	13.7	3	19	3.7	13	2.5	4.70	95	.350	.403	-3	-1	111	137	-1.0	-2	-2	-0.3
	Yr	8	13	.381	36	25	2	0	1	161	231	12.9	9	57	3.2	45	2.5	5.48	74	.337	.385	-26	-26	100	137	-1.4	-3	-4	-2.9
1938	Cin-N	1	1	.500	9	0	0	0	2	15	13	7.8	1	6	3.6	5	3.0	4.20	87	.228	.302	-1	-1	96	70	0.0	0	-0	0.0
Total	12	101	130	.437	346	249	102	12	19	1877	2177	10.4	132	598	2.9	655	3.1	4.51	95	.292	.339	-88	-48	105	99	2.4	-17	-18	-5.9
■ HENRY BENN	Benn, Henry Omer b: 1/25/1890, Viola, Wis. d: 6/4/67, Madison, Wis. BR/TR, 6', 190 lbs. Deb: 9/24/14																												
1914	Cle-A	0	0	—	1	0	0	0	0	1	1	9.0	0	0	0.0	0	0.0	0.00	—	.250	.400	0	0	106	0	0.0	0	0	0.0
■ DAVE BENNETT	Bennett, David Hans b: 11/7/45, Berkeley, Cal. BR/TR, 6'5", 195 lbs. Deb: 6/12/64																												
1964	Phi-N	0	0	—	1	0	0	0	0	1	2	18.0	0	0	0.0	1	9.0	9.00	38	.400	.400	-1	-1	98	74	0.0	0	0	0.0
■ DENNIS BENNETT	Bennett, Dennis John b: 10/5/39, Oakland, Cal. BL/TL, 6'3", 192 lbs. Deb: 5/12/62																												
1962	Phi-N	9	9	.500	31	24	7	2	3	175	144	7.4	17	68	3.5	149	7.7	3.81	99	.224	.302	3	-1	95	82	0.0	-0	-1	-0.1
1963	Phi-N	9	5	.643	23	16	6	1	1	119	102	7.7	12	33	2.5	82	6.2	2.65	126	.231	.285	8	9	102	113	1.7	3	0	1.3
1964	Phi-N	12	14	.462	41	32	7	2	1	208	222	9.6	23	58	2.5	125	5.4	3.68	94	.280	.323	-3	-5	98	119	-2.7	3	-0	-0.2
1965	Bos-A	5	7	.417	34	18	3	0	0	142	152	9.6	15	53	3.4	85	5.4	4.37	86	.279	.340	-14	-9	109	105	0.4	2	-0	-0.7
1966	Bos-A	3	3	.500	16	13	0	0	0	75	75	9.0	9	23	2.8	47	5.6	3.24	117	.261	.313	2	5	110	125	0.3	1	-1	0.5
1967	Bos-A	4	3	.571	13	11	4	1	0	70	72	9.3	12	22	2.8	34	4.4	3.86	94	.268	.320	-5	-2	113	120	0.0	-0	-0	-0.1
	NY-N	1	1	.500	8	6	0	0	0	26	37	12.8	4	7	2.4	14	4.8	5.19	66	.336	.372	-5	-5	102	121	0.2	0	0	-0.4
1968	Cal-A	0	5	.000	16	7	1	0	1	48	46	8.6	6	17	3.2	36	6.8	3.56	80	.250	.316	-3	-4	96	113	-2.4	-1	0	-0.4
Total	7	43	47	.478	182	127	28	6	6	863	850	8.9	98	281	2.9	572	6.0	3.69	97	.260	.317	-18	-11	102	109	-2.5	7	-2	-0.1
■ FRANK BENNETT	Bennett, Francis Allen "Chip" b: 10/27/04, Mardela Springs, Md. d: 3/18/66, New Castle, Del. BR/TR, 5'10.5", 163 lbs. Deb: 9/17/27																												
1927	Bos-A	0	1	.000	4	1	0	0	0	12	15	11.3	0	6	4.5	1	0.8	3.00	136	.333	.404	2	1	99	184	-0.4	-1	0	0.1
1928	Bos-A	0	0	—	1	0	0	0	0	1	1	9.0	0	0	0.0	0	0.0	0.00	—	.250	.250	0	0	101	0	0.0	0	0	0.1
Total	2	0	1	.000	5	1	0	0	0	13	16	11.1	0	6	4.2	1	0.7	2.77	148	.327	.393	2	2	99	170	-0.4	-1	0	0.2
■ ALLEN BENSON	Benson, Allen Wilbert "Bullet Ben" b: 7/12/08, Hurley, S.Dak. BR/TR, 6'1", 185 lbs. Deb: 8/19/34																												
1934	Was-A	0	1	.000	2	2	0	0	0	10	19	17.1	0	5	4.5	4	3.6	11.70	39	.413	.491	-8	-8	102	78	-0.4	-0	-0	-0.6
■ CY BENTLEY	Bentley, Clytus G. b: 11/23/1850, East Haven, Conn. d: 2/26/1873, Middletown, Conn. Deb: 4/26/1872																												
1872	Man-n	2	14	.125	16																								
■ JACK BENTLEY	Bentley, John Needles b: 3/8/1895, Sandy Spring, Md. d: 10/24/69, Olney, Md. BL/TL, 5'11.5", 200 lbs. Deb: 9/06/13																												
1913	Was-A	1	0	1.000	3	1	0	0	1	11	5	4.1	0	2	1.6	5	4.1	0.00	—	.147	.194	4	4	105	0	0.5	-0	0	0.4
1914	Was-A	5	7	.417	30	11	3	2	**4**	125	110	7.9	3	53	3.8	55	4.0	2.38	115	.249	.334	5	5	100	130	-1.2	2	-1	0.7
1915	Was-A	0	2	.000	4	2	0	0	0	11	8	6.5	0	3	2.5	0	0.0	0.82	358	.200	.256	3	3	99	146	-0.9	-0	-0	0.2
1916	Was-A	0	0	—	2	0	0	0	0	1	0	0.0	0	1	9.0	1	9.0	0.00	—	.000	.250	0	0	100	0	0.0	0	0	0.1
1923	NY-N	13	8	.619	31	26	12	1	3	183	198	9.7	10	67	3.3	80	3.9	4.48	88	.277	.338	-10	-11	99	88	0.0	15	-1	0.3
1924	NY-N	16	5	.762	28	24	13	1	1	188	196	9.4	11	56	2.7	60	2.9	3.78	89	.273	.325	2	-8	88	99	4.5	5	-1	-0.5
1925	NY-N	11	9	.550	28	22	11	0	0	157	200	11.5	10	59	3.4	47	2.7	5.04	83	.323	.370	-14	-15	98	106	-0.2	5	-1	-1.3
1926	Phi-N	0	2	.000	7	3	0	0	0	25	37	13.3	2	10	3.6	7	2.5	8.28	49	.327	.376	-12	-12	107	68	-0.9	1	-0	-1.0
	NY-N	0	0	—	1	0	0	0	0	2	0	0.0	0	2	9.0	1	4.5	0.00	—	.000	.250	1	1	98	0	0.0	-0	0	0.1
	Yr	0	2	.000	8	3	0	0	0	27	37	12.3	2	12	4.0	8	2.7	7.67	53	.311	.368	-12	-11	106	0	-0.9	1	-0	-0.9
1927	NY-N	0	0	—	4	0	0	0	0	10	7	6.3	1	10	9.0	3	2.7	2.70	142	.206	.383	1	1	98	175	0.0	1	0	0.1

YEAR	TM/L	W	L	PCT	G	GS	CG	SHO	SV	IP	H	H/G	HR	BB	BB/G	SO	SO/G	ERA	/A	OAVG	OOBP	PR	/A	PF	CPI	WAT	PB	PD	TPI
Total	9	46	33	.582	138	89	39	4	9	713	761	9.6	37	263	3.3	259	3.3	4.01	90	.280	.340	-20	-31	96	102	1.8	27	-3	-0.9

■ AL BENTON Benton, John Alton b: 3/18/11, Noble, Okla. d: 4/14/68, Lynwood, Cal. BR/TR, 6'4", 215 lbs. Deb: 4/18/34

YEAR	TM/L	W	L	PCT	G	GS	CG	SHO	SV	IP	H	H/G	HR	BB	BB/G	SO	SO/G	ERA	/A	OAVG	OOBP	PR	/A	PF	CPI	WAT	PB	PD	TPI
1934	Phi-A	7	9	.438	32	21	7	0	1	155	145	8.4	7	88	5.1	58	3.4	4.88	91	.249	.345	-7	-8	98	82	-0.2	-4	0	-1.0
1935	Phi-A	3	4	.429	27	9	0	0	0	78	110	12.7	7	47	5.4	42	4.8	7.73	59	.328	.407	-28	-27	102	86	0.2	-3	-1	-2.7
1938	Det-A	5	3	.625	19	10	6	0	0	95	93	8.8	10	39	3.7	33	3.1	3.32	143	.259	.325	16	15	99	129	0.7	-2	1	1.3
1939	Det-A	6	8	.429	37	16	3	0	5	150	182	10.9	11	58	3.5	67	4.0	4.56	111	.294	.348	1	8	110	106	-1.3	-5	0	0.4
1940	Det-A	6	10	.375	42	0	0	0	**17**	79	93	10.6	5	36	4.1	50	5.7	4.44	107	.294	.357	-1	3	109	112	-3.0	-3	-0	0.0
1941	Det-A	15	6	.714	38	14	7	1	7	158	130	**7.4**	11	65	3.7	63	3.6	2.96	150	**.221**	.299	21	26	107	100	5.0	-5	-0	2.1
1942	Det-A	7	13	.350	35	30	9	1	2	227	210	8.3	9	84	3.3	110	4.4	2.89	143	.246	.308	19	31	113	111	-2.8	-6	-1	2.7
1945	Det-A	13	8	.619	31	27	12	5	3	192	175	8.2	7	63	3.0	76	3.6	2.02	175	.241	.296	29	32	105	**139**	1.2	-6	2	3.2
1946	Det-A	11	7	.611	28	15	6	1	1	141	132	8.4	9	58	3.7	60	3.8	3.64	102	.245	.315	-2	1	106	90	0.3	-1	1	0.1
1947	Det-A	6	7	.462	36	14	4	0	7	133	147	9.9	11	61	4.1	33	2.2	4.40	87	.288	.354	-10	-9	103	109	-1.0	-2	-0	-1.0
1948	Det-A	2	2	.500	30	0	0	0	3	44	45	9.2	4	36	7.4	18	3.7	5.73	72	.273	.390	-7	-8	97	99	0.0	-0	0	-0.7
1949	Cle-A	9	6	.600	40	11	4	2	10	136	116	7.7	7	51	3.4	41	2.7	2.12	190	.238	.307	31	29	96	146	0.4	-2	-2	2.5
1950	Cle-A	4	2	.667	36	0	0	0	4	63	57	8.1	7	30	4.3	26	3.7	3.57	122	.243	.327	7	6	95	111	0.5	-1	-1	0.4
1952	Bos-A	4	3	.571	24	0	0	0	6	38	37	8.8	1	17	4.0	20	4.7	2.37	166	.268	.342	6	7	107	162	0.6	-1	-0	0.5
Total	14	98	88	.527	455	167	58	10	66	1669	1672	8.9	106	733	3.9	697	3.7	3.66	116	.259	.330	74	108	104	112	0.6	-41	-1	7.8

■ RUBE BENTON Benton, John Clebon b: 6/27/1887, Clinton, N.C. d: 12/12/37, Dothan, Ala. BL/TL, 6'1", 190 lbs. Deb: 6/28/10

YEAR	TM/L	W	L	PCT	G	GS	CG	SHO	SV	IP	H	H/G	HR	BB	BB/G	SO	SO/G	ERA	/A	OAVG	OOBP	PR	/A	PF	CPI	WAT	PB	PD	TPI
1910	Cin-N	0	1	.000	12	2	0	0	0	38	44	10.4	1	23	5.4	15	3.6	4.74	66	.282	.378	-7	-7	102	92	-0.4	-1	1	-0.6
1911	Cin-N	3	3	.500	6	6	5	0	0	45	44	8.8	0	23	4.6	28	5.6	2.00	157	.270	.370	7	6	92	196	0.2	-0	-1	0.4
1912	Cin-N	18	20	.474	**50**	39	22	2	2	302	316	9.4	2	118	3.5	162	4.8	3.10	103	.271	.347	10	3	93	108	-0.7	-5	2	-0.1
1913	Cin-N	11	7	.611	23	22	9	1	0	144	140	8.8	4	60	3.8	68	4.3	3.50	95	.265	.338	-5	-3	104	105	3.2	1	-1	-0.2
1914	Cin-N	16	18	.471	41	31	16	5	2	271	223	7.4	3	95	3.2	121	4.0	2.96	101	.228	.295	-5	1	107	75	2.8	-3	0	-0.1
1915	Cin-N	6	13	.316	35	21	6	2	4	176	165	8.4	2	67	3.4	83	4.2	3.32	86	.257	.328	-11	-9	104	99	-3.2	-0	2	-0.7
	NY-N	3	5	.375	10	7	3	0	1	61	57	8.4	0	9	1.3	26	3.8	2.80	91	.253	.286	-0	-2	92	88	-0.6	1	-0	0.0
	Yr	9	18	.333	45	28	9	2	5	237	222	8.4	2	76	2.9	109	4.1	3.19	87	.252	.304	-12	-11	101	88	-3.8	-0	2	-0.7
1916	NY-N	16	8	.667	38	30	15	3	2	239	210	7.9	5	58	2.2	115	4.3	2.86	86	.241	.290	-6	-11	94	85	3.2	-4	-1	-1.7
1917	NY-N	15	9	.625	35	25	14	3	3	215	190	8.0	5	41	1.7	70	2.9	2.72	93	.238	.275	-0	-5	93	82	-0.2	-0	-2	-0.8
1918	NY-N	1	2	.333	3	3	2	0	0	24	17	6.4	0	3	1.1	9	3.4	1.88	141	.202	.222	2	2	96	50	-0.5	1	0	0.3
1919	NY-N	17	11	.607	35	28	11	1	2	209	181	7.8	5	52	2.2	53	2.3	2.63	107	.237	.279	7	4	96	91	-0.3	-1	-1	0.3
1920	NY-N	9	16	.360	33	25	12	4	2	193	222	10.4	8	31	1.4	52	2.4	3.03	100	.291	.312	2	-0	97	111	-4.9	-6	4	-0.1
1921	NY-N	5	2	.714	18	9	3	1	0	72	72	9.0	2	17	2.1	11	1.4	2.88	124	.266	.300	7	5	94	101	0.9	-1	-1	0.4
1923	Cin-N	14	10	.583	33	26	15	0	1	219	243	10.0	11	57	2.3	59	2.4	3.66	105	.284	.325	8	5	96	104	-0.1	4	1	0.8
1924	Cin-N	7	9	.438	32	15	6	1	1	163	166	9.2	2	24	**1.3**	42	2.3	2.76	139	.266	.289	20	19	99	99	-1.6	2	1	2.3
1925	Cin-N	9	10	.474	33	16	6	1	1	147	182	11.1	3	34	2.1	36	2.2	4.04	102	.301	.335	4	1	97	98	-0.9	0	-1	0.1
Total	15	150	144	.510	437	305	145	24	21	2518	2472	8.8	53	712	2.5	950	3.4	3.08	101	.260	.311	33	12	98	97	-3.1	-14	4	0.3

■ LARRY BENTON Benton, Lawrence James b: 11/20/1897, St.Louis, Mo. d: 4/3/53, Amberly Village, O. BR/TR, 5'11", 165 lbs. Deb: 4/25/23

YEAR	TM/L	W	L	PCT	G	GS	CG	SHO	SV	IP	H	H/G	HR	BB	BB/G	SO	SO/G	ERA	/A	OAVG	OOBP	PR	/A	PF	CPI	WAT	PB	PD	TPI
1923	Bos-N	5	9	.357	35	9	1	0	0	128	141	9.9	4	57	4.0	42	3.0	4.99	82	.293	.360	-14	-13	102	90	0.1	-1	1	-1.1
1924	Bos-N	5	7	.417	30	13	4	0	1	128	129	9.1	4	64	4.5	41	2.9	4.15	92	.274	.353	-4	-5	99	101	0.7	-3	-0	-0.7
1925	Bos-N	14	7	.667	31	21	16	2	1	183	170	8.4	6	70	3.4	49	2.4	3.10	131	.249	.313	24	20	95	99	4.4	1	-1	1.9
1926	Bos-N	14	14	.500	43	27	12	1	1	232	244	9.5	10	81	3.1	103	4.0	3.84	87	.280	.333	-0	-13	88	104	1.9	-3	-3	-1.8
1927	Bos-N	4	2	.667	11	10	3	0	0	60	72	10.8	3	27	4.1	25	3.8	4.50	83	.310	.375	-4	-5	95	115	1.4	0	-1	-0.4
	NY-N	13	5	.722	29	23	8	1	2	173	183	9.5	9	54	2.8	65	3.4	3.95	97	.275	.325	-1	-2	98	95	3.0	-2	-0	-0.4
	Yr	17	7	**.708**	40	33	11	1	2	233	255	9.8	12	81	3.1	90	3.5	4.09	93	.284	.336	-5	-7	97	95	4.4	0	-1	-0.8
1928	NY-N	**25**	9	**.735**	42	35	**28**	2	4	310	299	8.7	14	71	2.1	90	2.6	2.73	145	.258	.293	43	42	99	106	6.6	-3	0	4.0
1929	NY-N	11	17	.393	39	30	14	3	3	237	276	10.5	16	61	2.3	63	2.4	4.14	110	.297	.331	15	11	97	107	-4.6	-6	1	0.6
1930	NY-N	1	3	.250	8	4	1	0	1	30	42	12.6	8	14	4.2	16	4.8	7.80	61	.323	.381	-9	-10	96	92	-1.0	1	-0	-0.7
	Cin-N	7	12	.368	35	22	9	0	1	178	246	12.4	7	45	2.3	47	2.4	5.11	91	.337	.363	-3	-9	93	105	-0.3	-2	-3	-1.2
	Yr	8	15	.348	43	26	10	0	2	208	288	12.5	15	59	2.6	63	2.7	5.50	85	.334	.366	-12	-20	93	105	-1.3	1	-3	-1.9
1931	Cin-N	10	15	.400	38	23	12	2	2	204	240	10.6	6	53	2.3	35	1.5	3.35	113	.299	.335	12	10	98	**125**	0.6	-1	1	1.0
1932	Cin-N	6	13	.316	35	21	7	0	2	180	201	10.1	10	27	1.4	35	1.8	4.30	89	.285	.306	-8	-9	99	86	-1.9	0	-1	-0.9
1933	Cin-N	10	11	.476	34	19	7	2	2	153	160	9.4	5	36	2.1	33	1.9	3.71	92	.271	.309	-6	-5	102	89	1.8	-1	-2	-0.8
1934	Cin-N	0	1	.000	16	1	0	0	2	29	53	16.4	1	7	2.2	5	1.6	6.52	65	.393	.420	-8	-7	105	112	-0.4	0	0	-0.6
1935	Bos-N	2	3	.400	29	0	0	0	0	72	103	12.9	6	24	3.0	21	2.6	6.88	59	.338	.384	-23	-23	100	88	0.5	0	-1	-2.1
Total	13	127	128	.498	455	258	122	13	22	2297	2559	10.0	109	691	2.7	670	2.6	4.03	98	.288	.332	13	-18	97	102	12.8	-16	-9	-3.2

■ SID BENTON Benton, Sidney Wright b: 8/4/1895, Buckner, Ark. d: 3/8/77, Fayetteville, Ark. BR/TR, 6'1", 170 lbs. Deb: 4/18/22

YEAR	TM/L	W	L	PCT	G	GS	CG	SHO	SV	IP	H	H/G	HR	BB	BB/G	SO	SO/G	ERA	/A	OAVG	OOBP	PR	/A	PF	CPI	WAT	PB	PD	TPI
1922	StL-N	0	0	—	1	0	0	0	0	0	0	—	0	2	—	0	—	—	—	—	1.000	0	0	100	0	0.0	0	0	0.0

■ JOE BENZ Benz, Joseph Louis "Blitzen" or "Butcher Boy" b: 1/21/1886, New Alsace, Ind. d: 4/22/57, Chicago, Ill. BR/TR, 6'1.5", 196 lbs. Deb: 8/16/11

YEAR	TM/L	W	L	PCT	G	GS	CG	SHO	SV	IP	H	H/G	HR	BB	BB/G	SO	SO/G	ERA	/A	OAVG	OOBP	PR	/A	PF	CPI	WAT	PB	PD	TPI
1911	Chi-A	3	2	.600	12	6	2	0	0	56	52	8.4	0	13	2.1	28	4.5	2.25	141	.251	.302	7	6	95	105	0.5	-2	1	0.7
1912	Chi-A	13	17	.433	42	31	12	3	0	239	231	8.7	5	70	2.6	97	3.7	2.90	114	.259	.319	12	11	99	106	-2.5	-5	1	1.2
1913	Chi-A	7	10	.412	33	17	6	1	1	151	146	8.7	1	59	3.5	79	4.7	2.74	102	.254	.325	3	1	95	104	-1.7	-1	4	0.5
1914	Chi-A	14	19	.424	48	35	16	4	2	283	245	7.8	4	66	2.1	142	4.5	2.26	127	.236	.282	15	19	105	90	-1.3	-4	6	2.9
1915	Chi-A	15	11	.577	39	28	17	2	0	238	209	7.9	4	43	1.6	81	3.1	2.12	130	.238	.276	22	17	94	97	-0.6	-4	3	1.6
1916	Chi-A	9	5	.643	28	16	6	4	0	142	108	6.8	0	32	2.0	57	3.6	2.03	148	.214	.265	13	15	106	73	1.2	-4	1	1.4
1917	Chi-A	7	3	.700	19	13	7	2	0	95	76	7.2	1	23	2.2	25	2.4	2.46	101	.220	.272	2	0	93	66	0.8	-1	0	0.0
1918	Chi-A	8	8	.500	29	17	10	1	0	154	156	9.1	1	28	1.6	30	1.8	2.63	105	.269	.294	2	2	100	99	0.7	-1	3	0.6
1919	Chi-A	0	0	—	1	0	0	0	0	2	2	9.0	0	0	0.0	0	0.0	0.00	—	.250	.250	1	1	102	0	0.0	0	0	0.1
Total	9	76	75	.503	251	163	76	17	3	1360	1225	8.1	16	334	2.2	539	3.6	2.43	120	.243	.292	77	73	99	94	-2.9	-21	19	9.0

■ JUAN BERENGUER Berenguer, Juan Bautista b: 11/30/54, Aguadulce, Pan. BR/TR, 5'11", 186 lbs. Deb: 8/17/78

YEAR	TM/L	W	L	PCT	G	GS	CG	SHO	SV	IP	H	H/G	HR	BB	BB/G	SO	SO/G	ERA	/A	OAVG	OOBP	PR	/A	PF	CPI	WAT	PB	PD	TPI
1978	NY-N	0	2	.000	5	3	0	0	0	13	17	11.8	1	11	7.6	8	5.5	8.31	43	.327	.446	-7	-7	99	85	-0.9	-0	0	-0.6
1979	NY-N	1	1	.500	5	5	0	0	0	31	28	8.1	2	12	3.5	25	7.3	2.90	124	.252	.325	3	2	96	124	0.2	0	-1	0.2
1980	NY-N	0	1	.000	6	0	0	0	0	9	9	9.0	1	10	10.0	7	7.0	6.00	58	.250	.413	-2	-2	97	94	-0.4	0	0	-0.1
1981	KC-A	0	4	.000	8	3	0	0	0	20	22	9.9	4	16	7.2	20	9.0	8.55	42	.289	.412	-11	-11	99	81	-1.9	0	-1	-1.0
	Tor-A	2	9	.182	12	11	1	0	0	71	62	7.9	7	35	4.4	29	3.7	4.31	96	.235	.325	-5	-1	113	86	-2.7	0	-1	-0.1
	Yr	2	13	.133	20	14	1	0	0	91	84	8.3	11	51	5.0	49	4.8	5.24	77	.243	.341	-16	-12	110	86	-4.6	0	-1	-1.1
1982	Det-A	0	0	—	2	1	0	0	0	7	5	6.4	0	9	11.6	8	10.3	6.43	63	.200	.412	-2	-2	100	66	0.0	-0	-0	-0.1
1983	Det-A	9	5	.643	37	19	2	1	1	158	110	6.3	19	71	4.0	129	7.3	3.13	123	.193	.288	17	13	95	88	1.3	0	-2	1.1
1984	Det-A	11	10	.524	31	27	2	1	0	168	146	7.8	14	79	4.2	118	6.3	3.48	108	.232	.319	10	5	94	99	-2.1	0	-1	0.4
1985	Det-A	5	6	.455	31	13	0	0	0	95	96	9.1	12	48	4.5	82	7.8	5.59	79	.259	.342	-15	-13	106	81	-0.7	0	1	-1.1
1986	SF-N	2	3	.400	46	4	0	0	4	73	64	7.9	4	44	5.4	72	8.9	2.71	130	.242	.350	8	7	95	143	-0.5	-0	-1	0.6
1987	Min-A	8	1	.889	47	6	0	0	4	112	100	8.0	10	47	3.8	110	8.8	3.94	109	.239	.311	7	4	96	88	3.5	0	-1	0.3
1988	Min-A	8	4	.667	57	1	0	0	2	100	74	6.7	7	61	5.5	99	8.9	3.96	106	.207	.318	0	3	105	81	1.5	0	0	0.3
Total	11	46	46	.500	287	93	5	2	11	857	733	7.7	81	443	4.7	707	7.4	3.99	100	.231	.325	2	-2	99	94	-2.7	-0	-7	-0.1

■ BRUCE BERENYI Berenyi, Bruce Michael b: 8/21/54, Bryan, Ohio BR/TR, 6'3", 205 lbs. Deb: 7/05/80

YEAR	TM/L	W	L	PCT	G	GS	CG	SHO	SV	IP	H	H/G	HR	BB	BB/G	SO	SO/G	ERA	/A	OAVG	OOBP	PR	/A	PF	CPI	WAT	PB	PD	TPI
1980	Cin-N	2	2	.500	6	6	0	0	0	28	34	10.9	1	23	7.4	19	6.1	7.71	47	.318	.432	-13	-13	101	81	-0.1	-1	-0	-1.2
1981	Cin-N	9	6	.600	21	20	5	3	0	126	97	6.9	3	77	5.5	106	7.6	3.50	100	.211	.320	-0	0	101	79	-0.1	1	-1	0.1
1982	Cin-N	9	18	.333	34	34	4	1	0	222	208	8.4	8	96	3.9	157	6.4	3.36	111	.255	.326	6	9	104	104	-1.7	3	2	1.5
1983	Cin-N	9	14	.391	32	31	4	1	0	186	173	8.4	9	102	4.9	151	7.3	3.87	98	.247	.339	-5	-2	104	94	-1.8	2	3	0.2
1984	Cin-N	3	7	.300	13	11	0	0	0	51	63	11.1	0	42	7.4	53	9.4	6.00	64	.306	.418	-14	-12	107	94	-1.5	-1	0	-1.2
	NY-N	9	6	.600	19	19	0	0	0	115	100	7.8	6	53	4.1	81	6.3	3.76	96	.238	.317	-2	-2	100	88	0.8	1	-1	-0.1
	Yr	12	13	.480	32	30	0	0	0	166	163	8.8	6	95	5.2	134	7.3	4.45	83	.260	.351	-16	-14	102	88	-0.7	-1	-1	-1.3

YEAR	TM/L	W	L	PCT	G	GS	CG	SHO	SV	IP	H	H/G	HR	BB	BB/G	SO	SO/G	ERA	/A	OAVG	OOBP	PR	/A	PF	CPI	WAT	PB	PD	TPI
1985	NY-N	1	0	1.000	3	3	0	0	0	14	8	5.1	0	10	6.4	10	6.4	2.57	134	.170	.328	2	1	95	90	0.5	0	1	0.3
1986	NY-N	2	2	.500	14	7	0	0	0	40	47	10.6	5	22	4.9	30	6.7	6.30	55	.299	.380	-11	-13	93	91	-0.4	-1	0	-1.3
Total	7	44	55	.444	142	131	13	5	0	782	730	8.4	32	425	4.9	607	7.0	4.03	91	.251	.341	-37	-31	102	93	-4.3	5	3	-1.7
■ **HEINIE BERGER**	Berger, Charles b: 1/7/1882, Lasalle, Ill. d: 2/10/54, Lakewood, Ohio TR , 5'9", Deb: 5/06/07																												
1907	Cle-A	3	3	.500	14	7	5	1	0	87	74	7.7	0	20	2.1	50	5.2	3.00	79	.253	.301	-4	-6	93	68	-0.2	0	-1	-0.7
1908	Cle-A	13	8	.619	29	24	16	0	0	199	152	6.9	1	66	3.0	101	4.6	2.13	116	.219	.290	6	8	103	103	1.0	-4	-0	0.8
1909	Cle-A	13	14	.481	34	29	19	4	1	247	221	8.1	2	58	2.1	162	**5.9**	2.73	93	.256	.312	-7	-5	103	93	0.5	-1	-0	-0.5
1910	Cle-A	3	4	.429	13	8	2	0	0	65	57	7.9	0	32	4.4	24	3.3	3.05	84	.243	.341	-4	-3	102	97	-0.2	-1	-0	-0.5
Total	4	32	29	.525	90	68	42	5	1	598	504	7.6	3	176	2.6	337	5.1	2.60	96	.242	.306	-9	-7	102	93	1.1	-6	-2	-0.9
■ **JACK BERLY**	Berly, John Chambers b: 5/24/03, Natchitoches, La. d: 6/26/77, Houston, Tex. BR/TR, 5'11.5", 190 lbs. Deb: 4/22/24																												
1924	StL-N	0	0	—	4	0	0	0	0	8	8	9.0	1	4	4.5	2	2.3	5.63	71	.267	.353	-2	-1	103	81	0.0	-0	0	0.0
1931	NY-N	7	8	.467	27	11	4	1	0	111	114	9.2	6	51	4.1	45	3.6	3.89	93	.270	.346	-0	-3	93	108	-1.4	-1	1	-0.2
1932	Phi-N	1	2	.333	21	1	1	0	2	46	61	11.9	4	21	4.1	15	2.9	7.63	57	.333	.386	-19	-17	111	82	-0.4	-2	1	-1.6
1933	Phi-N	2	3	.400	13	6	1	1	0	50	62	11.2	5	22	4.0	4	0.7	5.04	80	.307	.372	-9	-6	121	108	0.0	0	1	-0.3
Total	4	10	13	.435	65	18	6	2	2	215	245	10.3	16	98	4.1	66	2.8	5.02	78	.292	.361	-31	-27	104	101	-1.8	-2	3	-2.1
■ **VICTOR BERNAL**	Bernal, Victor Hugo b: 10/6/53, Los Angeles, Cal. BR/TR, 6'1", 175 lbs. Deb: 4/06/77																												
1977	SD-N	1	1	.500	15	0	0	0	0	20	23	10.3	4	9	4.0	6	2.7	5.40	65	.287	.360	-3	-4	89	103	0.1	-0	-0	-0.4
■ **DWIGHT BERNARD**	Bernard, Dwight Vern b: 5/31/52, Mt.Vernon, Ill. BR/TR, 6'2", 170 lbs. Deb: 6/29/78																												
1978	NY-N	1	4	.200	30	1	0	0	0	48	54	10.1	4	27	5.1	26	4.9	4.31	82	.297	.380	-4	-4	99	123	-1.2	0	0	-0.3
1979	NY-N	0	3	.000	32	1	0	0	0	44	59	12.1	2	26	5.3	20	4.1	4.70	77	.331	.409	-5	-5	96	128	-1.4	0	0	-0.4
1981	Mil-A	0	0	—	6	0	0	0	0	5	5	9.0	0	6	10.8	1	1.8	3.60	97	.263	.407	0	-0	95	154	0.0	0	-0	0.0
1982	Mil-A	3	1	.750	47	0	0	0	6	79	78	8.9	4	27	3.1	45	5.1	3.76	100	.263	.316	3	0	92	96	0.8	0	-1	0.0
Total	4	4	8	.333	115	2	0	0	6	176	196	10.0	10	86	4.4	92	4.7	4.14	89	.290	.361	-6	-9	95	113	-1.8	1	-0	-0.7
■ **JOE BERNARD**	Bernard, Joseph Carl "J.C." b: 3/24/1882, Brighton, Ill. d: 9/22/60, Springfield, Ill BR/TR, 6'1", 175 lbs. Deb: 09																												
1909	StL-N	0	0	—	1	0	0	0	0	1	1	9.0	0	2	18.0	2	18.0	0.00	—	.250	.500	0	0	99	0	0.0	0	0	0.0
■ **BILL BERNHARD**	Bernhard, William Henry "Strawberry Bill" b: 3/16/1871, Clarence, N.Y. d: 3/30/49, San Diego, Cal. BB/TR, 6'1", 205 lbs. Deb: 4/24/1899																												
1899	Phi-N	6	6	.500	21	12	10	1	0	132	120	8.2	3	36	2.5	23	1.6	2.66	138	.264	.318	18	15	95	98	-1.1	0	0	1.4
1900	Phi-N	15	10	.600	32	27	20	0	2	219	284	11.7	3	74	3.0	49	2.0	4.77	76	.338	.392	-26	-28	98	98	1.8	-5	0	-2.8
1901	Phi-A	17	10	.630	31	27	26	1	0	257	328	11.5	6	50	1.8	58	2.0	4.52	81	.332	.364	-24	-25	100	94	3.0	-1	3	-1.8
1902	Phi-A	1	0	1.000	1	1	1	0	0	9	7	7.0	0	3	3.0	1	1.0	1.00	379	.236	.306	3	3	106	202	0.5	-1	-1	0.2
	Cle-A	17	5	.773	27	24	22	3	1	217	169	7.0	4	34	1.4	57	2.4	2.20	156	.236	.271	33	30	96	76	6.4	-1	1	3.1
	Yr	18	5	**.783**	28	25	23	3	1	226	176	**7.0**	4	37	1.5	58	2.3	2.15	160	**.236**	**.273**	36	32	96	76	6.9	-1	1	3.3
1903	Cle-A	14	6	.700	20	19	18	3	0	166	151	8.2	1	21	1.1	60	3.3	2.11	133	.264	.290	15	13	95	105	3.7	-0	1	1.5
1904	Cle-A	23	13	.639	38	37	35	4	0	321	323	9.1	3	55	1.5	137	3.8	2.13	119	.285	.318	17	15	98	133	3.6	-1	-2	1.5
1905	Cle-A	7	13	.350	22	19	17	0	0	174	185	9.6	5	34	1.8	56	2.9	3.36	79	.298	.334	-14	-14	100	101	-3.1	-6	-0	-1.4
1906	Cle-A	16	15	.516	31	30	23	2	0	255	235	8.3	1	47	1.7	85	3.0	2.54	105	.269	.307	4	4	99	94	-2.0	2	2	0.6
1907	Cle-A	0	4	.000	8	4	3	0	0	42	58	12.4	0	11	2.4	19	4.1	3.21	73	.355	.395	-3	-4	93	147	-1.9	0	0	-0.3
Total	9	116	82	.586	231	200	175	14	3	1792	1860	9.3	26	365	1.8	545	2.7	3.04	101	.291	.329	22	8	98	103	10.9	-11	4	2.0
■ **WALTER BERNHARDT**	Bernhardt, Walter Jacob b: 5/20/1893, Pleasant Village, Pa. d: 7/26/58, Watertown, N.Y. BR/TR, 6'2", 175 lbs. Deb: 7/16/18																												
1918	NY-A	0	0	—	1	0	0	0	0	1	0	0.0	0	0	0.0	0	0.0	0.00	—	.000	.000	0	0	94	0	0.0	0	0	0.0
■ **JOE BERRY**	Berry, Jonas Arthur "Jittery Joe" b: 12/16/04, Huntsville, Ark. d: 9/27/58, Anaheim, Cal. BL/TR, 5'10.5", 145 lbs. Deb: 9/06/42																												
1942	Chi-N	0	0	—	2	0	0	0	0	2	7	31.5	0	2	9.0	1	4.5	18.00	18	.538	.563	-3	-3	98	93	0.0	0	0	-0.2
1944	Phi-A	10	8	.556	53	0	0	0	**12**	111	78	6.3	4	23	1.9	44	3.6	1.95	180	.192	.231	18	19	102	65	1.6	-1	2	2.2
1945	Phi-A	8	7	.533	**52**	0	0	0	5	130	114	7.9	5	38	2.6	51	3.5	2.35	138	.232	.283	**15**	**13**	96	104	2.3	-1	1	1.4
1946	Phi-A	0	1	.000	5	0	0	0	0	13	15	10.4	1	3	2.1	5	3.5	2.77	136	.288	.333	1	1	107	153	-0.4	0	0	0.2
	Cle-A	3	6	.333	21	0	0	0	1	37	32	7.8	4	21	5.1	16	3.9	3.41	93	.235	.331	0	-1	90	113	-1.1	0	-1	-0.1
	Yr	3	7	.300	26	0	0	0	1	50	47	8.5	5	24	4.3	21	3.8	3.24	103	.249	.327	1	0	95	113	-1.5	0	-0	0.1
Total	4	21	22	.488	133	0	0	0	18	293	246	7.6	14	87	2.7	117	3.6	2.46	137	.224	.277	31	29	98	92	2.4	-1	3	3.5
■ **FRANK BERTAINA**	Bertaina, Frank Louis b: 4/14/44, San Francisco, Cal. BL/TL, 5'11", 177 lbs. Deb: 8/01/64																												
1964	Bal-A	1	0	1.000	6	4	1	1	0	26	18	6.2	3	13	4.5	18	6.2	2.77	135	.198	.287	2	3	103	106	0.5	-1	0	0.3
1965	Bal-A	0	0	—	2	1	0	0	0	6	9	13.5	0	4	6.0	5	7.5	6.00	57	.360	.419	-2	-2	99	113	0.0	-0	0	-0.1
1966	Bal-A	2	5	.286	16	9	0	0	0	63	52	7.4	3	36	5.1	46	6.6	3.14	108	.226	.335	2	2	99	111	-1.8	-1	-2	0.0
1967	Bal-A	1	1	.500	5	2	0	0	0	22	17	7.0	4	14	5.7	19	7.8	3.27	92	.224	.333	-0	-1	94	140	0.1	-0	0	0.0
	Was-A	6	5	.545	18	17	4	4	0	96	90	8.4	8	37	3.5	67	6.3	2.91	115	.251	.317	3	5	104	127	0.8	-3	-0	0.2
	Yr	7	6	.538	23	19	4	4	0	118	107	8.2	12	51	3.9	86	6.6	2.97	111	.246	.320	3	4	102	127	0.9	-0	-0	0.2
1968	Was-A	7	13	.350	27	23	1	0	0	127	133	9.4	15	69	4.9	81	5.7	4.68	60	.273	.362	-24	-27	94	107	-1.4	-0	0	-2.8
1969	Was-A	1	3	.250	14	5	0	0	0	36	43	10.8	8	23	5.8	25	6.3	6.50	54	.291	.382	-11	-12	96	97	-1.0	2	0	-0.9
	Bal-A	0	0	—	3	0	0	0	0	6	1	1.5	0	3	4.5	5	7.5	0.00	—	.063	.200	2	2	100	0	0.0	1	0	0.3
	Yr	1	3	.250	17	5	0	0	0	42	44	9.4	8	26	5.6	30	6.4	5.57	63	.267	.363	-9	-10	97	0	-1.0	2	0	-0.6
1970	StL-N	1	2	.333	8	5	0	0	0	31	36	10.5	1	15	4.4	14	4.1	3.19	135	.293	.359	3	4	106	146	-0.3	0	-0	0.4
Total	7	19	29	.396	99	66	6	5	0	413	399	8.7	42	214	4.7	280	6.1	3.84	85	.257	.343	-24	-26	99	114	-3.1	-1	-2	-2.6
■ **LEFTY BERTRAND**	Bertrand, Roman Mathias b: 2/28/09, Cobden, Minn. BR/TL, 6', 180 lbs. Deb: 4/15/36																												
1936	Phi-N	0	0	—	1	0	0	0	0	2	3	13.5	1	2	9.0	1	4.5	9.00	49	.333	.455	-1	-1	111	121	0.0	0	0	0.0
■ **FRED BESANA**	Besana, Frederick Cyril b: 4/5/31, Lincoln, Cal. BR/TL, 6'3.5", 200 lbs. Deb: 4/18/56																												
1956	Bal-A	1	0	1.000	7	2	0	0	0	18	22	11.0	0	14	7.0	7	3.5	5.50	73	.310	.409	-3	-3	97	107	0.5	-0	1	-0.2
■ **HERMAN BESSE**	Besse, Herman A. b: 8/16/11, St.Louis, Mo. d: 8/13/72, Los Angeles, Cal. BL/TL, 6'2", 190 lbs. Deb: 4/19/40																												
1940	Phi-A	0	3	.000	17	5	0	0	0	53	70	11.9	10	34	5.8	19	3.2	8.83	49	.315	.408	-26	-26	99	82	-1.4	2	-1	-2.2
1941	Phi-A	2	0	1.000	6	2	1	0	0	20	28	12.6	4	12	5.4	8	3.6	9.90	43	.329	.412	-13	-13	103	75	1.0	-0	0	-1.0
1942	Phi-A	2	9	.182	30	14	4	0	1	133	163	11.0	7	69	4.7	78	5.3	6.16	60	.300	.375	-37	-36	101	85	-2.7	2	-2	-3.4
1943	Phi-A	1	1	.500	5	1	0	0	0	16	18	10.1	2	4	2.3	3	1.7	3.38	103	.295	.338	-0	0	106	145	0.3	-1	0	0.0
1946	Phi-A	0	2	.000	7	3	0	0	1	21	19	8.1	1	9	3.9	10	4.3	5.14	73	.247	.315	-4	-3	107	64	-0.9	-0	-0	-0.3
Total	5	5	15	.250	65	25	5	0	2	243	298	11.0	24	128	4.7	118	4.4	6.78	57	.302	.379	-80	-78	102	86	-3.7	2	-3	-6.9
■ **DON BESSENT**	Bessent, Fred Donald b: 3/13/31, Jacksonville, Fla. BR/TR, 6', 175 lbs. Deb: 7/17/55																												
1955	Bro-N	8	1	.889	24	2	1	0	3	63	51	7.3	7	21	3.0	29	4.1	2.71	150	.220	.282	9	9	101	103	3.2	-2	-0	0.8
1956	Bro-N	4	3	.571	38	0	0	0	9	79	63	7.2	5	31	3.5	52	5.9	2.51	151	.221	.290	11	11	100	104	-0.1	-1	-1	0.9
1957	Bro-N	1	3	.250	27	0	0	0	0	44	58	11.9	5	19	3.9	24	4.9	5.73	77	.328	.377	-9	-6	114	105	-1.0	0	-0	-0.6
1958	LA-N	1	0	1.000	19	0	0	0	0	24	24	9.0	3	17	6.4	13	4.9	3.38	124	.270	.393	2	2	106	159	0.5	-0	1	0.3
Total	4	14	7	.667	108	2	1	0	12	210	196	8.4	20	88	3.8	118	5.1	3.34	121	.250	.320	13	17	104	110	2.6	-3	-1	1.4
■ **KARL BEST**	Best, Karl Jon b: 3/6/59, Aberdeen, Was. BR/TR, 6'4", 190 lbs. Deb: 8/19/83																												
1983	Sea-A	0	1	.000	4	0	0	0	0	5	14	25.2	2	5	9.0	3	5.4	14.40	29	.483	.583	-6	-6	101	122	-0.4	0	-0	-0.4
1984	Sea-A	1	1	.500	5	0	0	0	0	6	7	10.5	0	0	0.0	6	9.0	3.00	137	.292	.280	1	1	103	98	0.1	0	-0	0.1
1985	Sea-A	2	1	.667	15	0	0	0	4	32	25	7.0	1	6	1.7	32	9.0	1.97	201	.207	.250	8	7	95	80	0.6	0	-0	0.7
1986	Sea-A	2	3	.400	26	0	0	0	1	36	35	8.8	3	21	5.3	23	5.8	4.00	111	.255	.350	1	2	106	109	0.0	0	-0	0.1
1988	Min-A	0	0	—	11	0	0	0	0	12	15	11.3	1	7	5.3	9	6.8	6.00	70	.306	.373	-3	-2	105	95	0.0	0	-0	-0.2
Total	5	5	6	.455	61	0	0	0	5	91	96	9.5	7	39	3.9	73	7.2	4.05	104	.267	.338	1	2	102	97	0.3	0	-1	0.3
■ **JIM BETHKE**	Bethke, James Charles b: 11/5/46, Falls City, Neb. BR/TR, 6'3", 185 lbs. Deb: 4/12/65																												
1965	NY-N	2	0	1.000	25	0	0	0	0	40	41	9.2	3	22	4.9	19	4.3	4.27	86	.266	.375	-3	-3	104	113	1.0	-0	1	-0.1

YEAR TM/L	W	L	PCT	G	GS	CG	SHO	SV	IP	H	H/G	HR	BB	BB/G	SO	SO/G	ERA	/A	OAVG	OOBP	PR	/A	PF	CPI	WAT	PB	PD	TPI
■ **JEFF BETTENDORF** Bettendorf, Jeffrey Allen b: 12/10/60, Lompoc, Cal. BR/TR, 6'3", 180 lbs. Deb: 4/08/84																												
1984 Oak-A	0	0	—	3	0	0	0	1	10	9	8.1	3	5	4.5	5	4.5	4.50	82	.243	.333	-1	-1	92	120	0.0	0	-0	0.0
■ **HARRY BETTS** Betts, Harold Matthew "Chubby" or "Ginger" b: 6/19/1881, Alliance, Ohio d: 5/22/46, San Antonio, Tex. BR/TR, 5'10", 200 lbs. Deb: 9/22/03																												
1903 StL-N	0	1	.000	1	1	1	0	0	9	11	11.0	0	5	5.0	2	2.0	10.00	33	.347	.465	-7	-7	102	53	-0.4	-0	-0	-0.4
1913 Cin-N	0	0	—	1	0	0	0	0	3	1	3.0	0	3	9.0	0	0.0	3.00	111	.143	.417	0	0	104	139	0.0	-0	-0	0.0
Total 2	0	1	.000	2	1	1	0	0	12	12	9.0	0	8	6.0	2	1.5	8.25	40	.310	.454	-7	-7	102	75	-0.4	-1	-0	-0.4
■ **HUCK BETTS** Betts, Walter Martin b: 2/18/1897, Millsboro, Del. d: 6/13/87, Millsboro, Del. BR/TR, 5'11", 170 lbs. Deb: 4/26/20																												
1920 Phi-N	1	1	.500	27	4	1	0	0	88	86	8.8	3	33	3.4	18	1.8	3.58	98	.261	.322	-4	-1	112	88	0.2	-2	-1	-0.3
1921 Phi-N	3	7	.300	32	2	1	0	4	101	141	12.6	8	14	1.2	28	2.5	4.46	91	.337	.349	-8	-5	107	116	-0.4	1	0	-0.3
1922 Phi-N	1	0	1.000	7	0	0	0	0	15	23	13.8	3	8	4.8	4	2.4	9.60	50	.348	.408	-9	-8	117	78	0.5	-0	-0	-0.7
1923 Phi-N	2	4	.333	19	4	3	0	1	84	100	10.7	7	14	1.5	18	1.9	3.11	152	.314	.340	8	15	118	153	0.0	-4	0	1.2
1924 Phi-N	7	10	.412	37	9	2	0	2	144	160	10.0	8	42	2.6	46	2.9	4.31	99	.286	.332	-7	-1	111	94	0.7	-2	-2	-0.3
1925 Phi-N	4	5	.444	35	7	1	0	1	97	146	13.5	10	38	3.5	28	2.6	5.57	90	.342	.394	-14	-6	118	114	0.0	2	1	-0.1
1932 Bos-N	13	11	.542	31	27	16	3	1	222	229	9.3	9	35	1.4	32	1.3	2.80	129	.267	.289	27	20	93	111	1.2	2	-2	2.0
1933 Bos-N	11	11	.500	35	26	17	2	4	242	225	8.4	9	55	2.0	40	1.5	2.79	115	.248	.284	15	11	96	95	-0.8	2	4	1.8
1934 Bos-N	17	10	.630	40	27	10	2	3	213	258	10.9	17	42	1.8	69	2.9	4.06	86	.296	.326	0	-13	86	108	3.7	1	-2	-1.3
1935 Bos-N	2	9	.182	44	19	2	1	0	160	213	12.0	9	40	2.3	40	2.3	5.46	74	.321	.352	-26	-25	100	94	-1.5	-1	0	-2.3
Total 10	61	68	.473	307	125	53	8	16	1366	1581	10.4	83	321	2.1	323	2.1	3.93	98	.292	.326	-18	-12	101	105	3.6	-3	-0	-0.3
■ **BILL BEVENS** Bevens, Floyd Clifford b: 10/21/16, Hubbard, Ore. BR/TR, 6'3.5", 210 lbs. Deb: 5/12/44																												
1944 NY-A	4	1	.800	8	5	3	0	0	44	44	9.0	4	13	2.7	16	3.3	2.66	136	.273	.322	4	5	105	153	1.4	-2	-0	0.3
1945 NY-A	13	9	.591	29	25	14	2	0	184	174	8.5	12	68	3.3	76	3.7	3.67	97	.254	.314	-6	-2	106	96	1.6	-4	1	-0.5
1946 NY-A	16	13	.552	31	31	18	3	0	250	213	7.7	11	78	2.8	120	4.3	2.23	153	.232	.288	35	33	98	115	-0.3	-4	-4	2.7
1947 NY-A	7	13	.350	28	23	11	1	0	165	167	9.1	13	77	4.2	77	4.2	3.82	89	.264	.338	-2	-7	92	109	-4.7	-3	-0	-1.0
Total 4	40	36	.526	96	84	46	6	0	643	598	8.4	40	236	3.3	289	4.0	3.08	113	.250	.311	31	29	99	111	-2.0	-13	-4	1.5
■ **LOU BEVIL** Bevil, Louis Eugene (born Louis Eugene Bevilacqua) b: 11/27/22, Nelson, Ill. d: 2/1/73, Dixon, Ill. BB/TR, 5'11.5", 190 lbs. Deb: 9/02/42																												
1942 Was-A	0	1	.000	4	1	0	0	0	10	9	8.1	0	11	9.9	2	1.8	6.30	57	.265	.447	-3	-3	99	93	-0.4	-0	-0	-0.3
■ **BEN BEVILLE** Beville, Clarence Benjamin b: 8/28/1877, Colusa, Cal. d: 1/5/37, Yountville, Cal. 5'9", 190 lbs. Deb: 5/24/01																												
1901 Bos-A	0	2	.000	2	2	1	0	0	9	8	8.0	0	9	9.0	1	1.0	4.00	86	.257	.424	-0	-1	94	109	-0.9	1	-0	0.0
■ **JIM BIBBY** Bibby, James Blair b: 10/29/44, Franklinton, N.C. BR/TR, 6'5", 235 lbs. Deb: 9/04/72																												
1972 StL-N	1	3	.250	6	6	0	0	0	40	29	6.5	4	19	4.3	28	6.3	3.37	108	.206	.295	0	1	105	88	-0.9	0	0	0.2
1973 StL-N	0	2	.000	6	3	0	0	0	16	19	10.7	2	17	9.6	12	6.8	9.56	35	.306	.458	-10	-11	90	79	-0.9	0	0	-0.9
Tex-A	9	10	.474	26	23	11	2	1	180	121	**6.1**	14	106	5.3	155	7.8	3.25	117	**.192**	.309	11	11	100	86	2.0	0	-2	1.0
1974 Tex-A	19	19	.500	41	41	11	5	0	264	255	8.7	25	113	3.9	149	5.1	4.74	73	.255	.332	-33	-37	96	82	-1.1	0	0	-3.5
1975 Tex-A	2	6	.250	12	12	4	1	0	68	73	9.7	2	28	3.7	31	4.1	5.03	75	.274	.341	-9	-9	100	76	-1.9	0	-0	-0.9
Cle-A	5	9	.357	24	12	2	0	1	113	99	7.9	7	50	4.0	62	4.9	3.19	119	.235	.311	8	7	100	98	-2.0	0	1	0.8
Yr	7	15	.318	36	24	6	1	1	181	172	8.6	9	78	3.9	93	4.6	3.88	97	.248	.320	-2	-2	100	98	-3.9	0	0	-0.1
1976 Cle-A	13	7	.650	34	21	4	3	1	163	162	8.9	6	56	3.1	84	4.6	3.20	110	.266	.321	6	6	100	110	3.1	0	-1	0.5
1977 Cle-A	12	13	.480	37	30	9	2	2	207	197	8.6	17	73	3.2	141	6.1	3.57	112	.250	.313	12	10	98	97	1.0	0	-2	0.8
1978 Pit-N	8	7	.533	34	14	3	2	1	107	100	8.4	10	39	3.3	72	6.1	3.53	106	.246	.307	1	3	105	99	-0.1	1	0	0.4
1979 Pit-N	12	4	.750	34	17	4	1	0	138	110	7.2	9	47	3.1	103	6.7	2.80	139	.218	.286	14	17	104	90	3.1	2	-1	1.8
1980 Pit-N	19	6	**.760**	35	34	6	1	0	238	210	7.9	20	88	3.3	144	5.4	3.33	112	.238	.309	7	10	103	99	6.9	2	-2	1.1
1981 Pit-N	6	3	.667	14	14	2	2	0	94	79	7.6	4	26	2.5	48	4.6	2.49	135	.225	.278	10	9	96	94	1.9	1	-1	1.1
1983 Pit-N	5	12	.294	29	12	0	0	2	78	92	10.6	10	51	5.9	44	5.1	6.69	56	.297	.392	-26	-26	103	88	-3.8	-1	-0	-2.6
1984 Tex-A	0	0	—	8	0	0	0	0	16	19	10.7	1	10	5.6	6	3.4	4.50	89	.297	.387	-1	-1	101	118	0.0	0	0	0.0
Total 12	111	101	.524	340	239	56	19	8	1722	1565	8.2	131	723	3.8	1079	5.6	3.76	99	.243	.318	-10	-10	100	93	7.3	5	-7	-0.2
■ **VERN BICKFORD** Bickford, Vernon Edgell b: 8/17/20, Hellier, Ky. d: 5/6/60, Concord, Va. BR/TR, 6', 180 lbs. Deb: 4/24/48																												
1948 Bos-N	11	5	.688	33	22	10	1	1	146	125	7.7	9	63	3.9	60	3.7	3.27	120	.226	.306	11	10	99	92	2.0	1	-1	1.0
1949 Bos-N	16	11	.593	37	36	15	2	0	231	246	9.6	20	106	4.1	101	3.9	4.25	92	.273	.349	-5	-9	97	107	3.2	-1	2	-0.7
1950 Bos-N	19	14	.576	40	39	**27**	2	0	**312**	293	8.5	25	122	3.5	126	3.6	3.46	102	.248	.318	24	2	85	104	1.6	-3	-1	-0.3
1951 Bos-N	11	9	.550	25	20	12	3	0	165	146	8.0	7	76	4.1	76	4.1	3.11	123	.240	.327	16	13	97	108	1.3	-2	3	1.4
1952 Bos-N	7	12	.368	26	22	7	1	0	161	165	9.2	7	64	3.6	62	3.5	3.75	96	.269	.335	-0	-3	97	105	-1.2	-0	1	-0.1
1953 Mil-N	2	5	.286	20	9	2	0	1	58	60	9.3	8	35	5.4	25	3.9	5.28	74	.279	.376	-6	-9	92	106	-1.8	-1	1	-0.7
1954 Bal-A	0	1	.000	1	1	0	0	0	4	5	11.3	0	1	2.3	0	0.0	9.00	41	.333	.300	-2	-2	99	52	-0.4	-0	0	-0.1
Total 7	66	57	.537	182	149	73	9	2	1077	1040	8.7	76	467	3.9	450	3.8	3.71	101	.254	.330	36	4	93	103	4.7	-6	3	0.5
■ **DAN BICKHAM** Bickham, Daniel Denison b: 10/31/1864, Dayton, Ohio d: 3/3/51, Dayton, Ohio 5'10", 160 lbs. Deb: 8/13/1886																												
1886 Cin-a	1	0	1.000	1	1	1	0	0	9	13	13.0	0	3	3.0	6	6.0	3.00	110	.349	.397	0	0	96	188	0.5	0	0	0.1
■ **CHARLIE BICKNELL** Bicknell, Charles Stephen "Bud" b: 7/27/28, Plainfield, N.J. BR/TR, 5'11", 170 lbs. Deb: 4/22/48																												
1948 Phi-N	0	1	.000	17	1	0	0	0	26	29	10.0	5	17	5.9	5	1.7	5.88	65	.287	.383	-6	-6	97	106	-0.4	-1	-0	-0.6
1949 Phi-N	0	0	—	13	0	0	0	0	28	32	10.3	3	17	5.5	4	1.3	7.71	53	.291	.386	-11	-11	101	74	0.0	0	0	-0.9
Total 2	0	1	.000	30	1	0	0	0	54	61	10.2	8	34	5.7	9	1.5	6.83	58	.289	.385	-17	-17	99	89	-0.4	-0	-0	-1.5
■ **MIKE BIELECKI** Bielecki, Michael Joseph b: 7/31/59, Baltimore, Md. BR/TR, 6'3", 200 lbs. Deb: 9/14/84																												
1984 Pit-N	0	0	—	4	0	0	0	0	4	4	9.0	0	0	0.0	1	2.3	0.00	—	.250	.235	2	1	94	0	0.0	0	0	0.2
1985 Pit-N	2	3	.400	12	7	0	0	0	46	45	8.8	5	31	6.1	22	4.3	4.50	83	.257	.365	-5	-4	104	107	0.2	-1	1	-0.3
1986 Pit-N	6	11	.353	31	27	0	0	0	149	149	9.0	10	83	5.0	83	5.0	4.65	80	.262	.351	-15	-15	101	92	-0.9	-3	-1	-1.8
1987 Pit-N	2	3	.400	8	8	2	0	0	46	43	8.4	6	12	2.3	25	4.9	4.70	91	.250	.292	-3	-2	105	79	-0.4	-1	-0	-0.2
1988 Chi-N	2	2	.500	19	5	0	0	0	48	55	10.3	4	16	3.0	33	6.2	3.38	107	.284	.330	0	1	105	129	0.1	-0	-0	0.1
Total 5	12	19	.387	74	47	2	0	0	293	296	9.1	25	142	4.4	164	5.0	4.36	87	.263	.339	-21	-18	102	97	-1.0	-5	-0	-2.0
■ **HARRY BIEMILLER** Biemiller, Harry Lee b: 10/9/1897, Baltimore, Md. d: 5/25/65, Orlando, Fla. BR/TR, 6'1", 171 lbs. Deb: 8/26/20																												
1920 Was-A	1	0	1.000	5	2	1	0	0	17	21	11.1	1	13	6.9	10	5.3	4.76	77	.318	.430	-2	-2	96	127	0.5	-1	1	-0.1
1925 Cin-N	0	1	.000	23	1	0	0	2	47	45	8.6	2	21	4.0	9	1.7	4.02	102	.280	.371	1	1	97	118	-0.4	-0	2	0.1
Total 2	1	1	.500	28	3	1	0	2	64	66	9.3	3	34	4.8	19	2.7	4.22	95	.291	.388	-1	-2	96	120	0.1	-1	2	0.0
■ **LOU BIERBAUER** Bierbauer, Louis W. b: 9/23/1865, Erie, Pa. d: 1/31/26, Erie, Pa. BL/TR, 5'8", 140 lbs. Deb: 4/17/1886																												
1886 Phi-a	0	0	—	2	0	0	0	0	11	8	6.5	0	5	4.1	1	0.8	4.09	87	.212	.305	-1	-1	103	58	0.0	0	0	0.0
1887 Phi-a	0	0	—	1	0	0	0	1	1	0	0.0	0	0	0.0	1	9.0	0.00	—	.000	.000	0	0	100	0	0.0	0	0	0.0
1888 Phi-a	0	0	—	1	0	0	0	0	3	5	15.0	0	0	0.0	3	9.0	0.00	—	.385	.385	1	1	97	0	0.0	0	0	0.1
Total 3	0	0	—	4	0	0	0	1	15	13	7.8	0	5	3.0	5	3.0	3.00	116	.244	.309	1	1	101	43	0.0	0	0	0.1
■ **LYLE BIGBEE** Bigbee, Lyle Randolph "Al" b: 8/22/1893, Sweet Home, Ore. d: 8/5/42, Portland, Ore. BL/TR, 6', 180 lbs. Deb: 4/15/20																												
1920 Phi-A	0	3	.000	12	2	0	0	0	45	66	13.2	5	25	5.0	12	2.4	8.00	47	.369	.446	-21	-21	99	92	-1.4	0	0	-1.8
1921 Pit-N	0	0	—	5	0	0	0	0	8	4	4.5	0	4	4.5	1	1.1	1.13	341	.154	.267	2	2	102	86	0.0	-0	0	0.2
Total 2	0	3	.000	17	2	0	0	0	53	70	11.9	5	29	4.9	13	2.2	6.96	54	.341	.423	-19	-19	99	91	-1.4	0	0	-1.6
■ **CHARLIE BIGGS** Biggs, Charles Orval b: 9/15/06, French Lick, Ind. d: 5/24/54, French Lick, Ind. BR/TR, 6'1", 185 lbs. Deb: 9/03/32																												
1932 Chi-A	1	1	.500	6	4	0	0	0	25	32	11.5	2	12	4.3	1	0.4	6.84	59	.314	.402	-7	-8	91	91	0.3	-0	0	-0.6
■ **LARRY BIITTNER** Biittner, Lawrence David b: 7/27/45, Pocahontas, Ia. BL/TL, 6'2", 205 lbs. Deb: 7/17/70																												
1977 Chi-N	0	0	—	1	0	0	0	0	1	5	45.0	3	1	9.0	3	27.0	54.00	8	.556	.600	-6	-6	115	83	0.0	0	0	-0.3
■ **JIM BILBREY** Bilbrey, James Melvin b: 4/20/24, Rickman, Tenn. d: 12/26/85, Toledo, Ohio BR/TR, 6'2.5", 205 lbs. Deb: 5/17/49																												
1949 StL-A	0	0	—	1	0	0	0	0	1	1	9.0	0	3	27.0	0	0.0	18.00	24	.250	.571	-2	-2	104	56	0.0	0	0	0.0

YEAR	TM/L	W	L	PCT	G	GS	CG	SHO	SV	IP	H	H/G	HR	BB	BB/G	SO	SO/G	ERA	/A	OAVG	OOBP	PR	/A	PF	CPI	WAT	PB	PD	TPI
■ **EMIL BILDILLI** Bildilli, Emil "Hill Billy" b: 9/16/12, Diamond, Ind. d: 9/16/46, Hartford City, Ind. BR/TL, 5'10", 170 lbs. Deb: 8/24/37																													
1937	StL-A	0	1	.000	4	1	0	0	0	8	12	13.5	1	3	3.4	2	2.3	10.13	47	.353	.405	-5	-5	103	69	-0.4	-0	0	-0.3
1938	StL-A	1	2	.333	5	3	2	0	0	22	33	13.5	3	11	4.5	11	4.5	6.95	71	.359	.419	-5	-5	103	110	0.0	0	0	-0.3
1939	StL-A	1	1	.500	2	2	2	0	0	19	21	9.9	0	6	2.8	8	3.8	3.32	146	.266	.318	3	3	105	96	0.3	-1	0	0.3
1940	StL-A	2	4	.333	28	11	3	0	1	97	113	10.5	12	52	4.8	32	3.0	5.57	85	.298	.382	-13	-9	108	106	-0.6	-1	3	-0.5
1941	StL-A	0	0	—	2	0	0	0	0	2	5	22.5	0	3	13.5	2	9.0	13.50	31	.417	.533	-2	-2	101	92	0.0	0	0	-0.1
Total	5	4	8	.333	41	17	7	0	1	148	184	11.2	16	75	4.6	55	3.3	5.84	82	.309	.384	-22	-18	106	103	-0.7	-2	4	-0.9
■ **HARRY BILLIARD** Billiard, Harry Pree "Pree" b: 11/11/1883, Monroe, Ind. d: 6/3/23, Wooster, Ohio BR/TR, 6', 190 lbs. Deb: 7/31/08																													
1908	NY-A	0	0	—	6	0	0	0	0	17	15	7.9	1	14	7.4	10	5.3	2.65	91	.234	.410	-0	-0	101	190	0.0	-0	-1	0.0
1914	Ind-F	8	7	.533	32	16	5	0	2	126	117	8.4	4	63	4.5	45	3.2	3.71	93	.257	.356	-7	-3	108	100	-0.5	-1	-1	-0.4
1915	New-F	0	1	.000	14	2	0	0	1	28	32	10.3	0	28	9.0	7	2.3	5.79	49	.317	.466	-9	-9	94	100	-0.4	0	0	-0.8
Total	3	8	8	.500	52	18	5	0	3	171	164	8.6	5	105	5.5	62	3.3	3.95	82	.264	.381	-16	-13	105	109	-0.9	-0	-2	-1.2
■ **JACK BILLINGHAM** Billingham, John Eugene b: 2/21/43, Orlando, Fla. BR/TR, 6'4", 195 lbs. Deb: 4/11/68																													
1968	LA-N	3	0	1.000	50	1	0	0	8	71	54	6.8	0	30	3.8	46	5.8	2.15	126	.215	.294	7	4	91	106	1.5	0	1	0.6
1969	Hou-N	6	7	.462	52	4	1	0	2	83	92	10.0	12	29	3.1	71	7.7	4.23	86	.290	.352	-6	-5	101	122	-0.4	-0	-0	-0.5
1970	Hou-N	13	9	.591	46	24	8	2	0	188	190	9.1	10	63	3.0	134	6.4	3.97	96	.259	.322	2	-4	94	91	2.5	-2	1	-0.4
1971	Hou-N	10	16	.385	33	33	8	3	0	228	205	8.1	9	68	2.7	139	5.5	3.39	94	.243	.306	2	-5	92	87	-3.0	-2	0	-0.7
1972	Cin-N	12	12	.500	36	31	8	4	1	218	197	8.1	18	64	2.6	137	5.7	3.18	99	.241	.297	7	-1	91	98	-2.5	-3	-0	-0.5
1973	Cin-N	19	10	.655	40	40	16	**7**	0	**293**	257	7.9	20	95	2.9	155	4.8	3.04	111	.236	.300	20	10	92	97	2.0	-5	2	0.7
1974	Cin-N	19	11	.633	36	35	8	3	0	212	233	9.9	16	64	2.7	103	4.4	3.95	88	.288	.337	-7	-11	96	109	1.3	-5	1	-1.5
1975	Cin-N	15	10	.600	33	32	5	0	0	208	222	9.6	22	76	3.3	79	3.4	4.11	90	.279	.344	-11	-10	101	109	-1.4	-1	-2	-1.2
1976	Cin-N	12	10	.545	34	29	5	2	1	177	190	9.7	17	62	3.2	76	3.9	4.32	81	.279	.336	-16	-16	100	101	-1.6	3	-1	-1.3
1977	Cin-N	10	10	.500	36	23	3	2	0	162	195	10.8	16	56	3.1	76	4.2	5.22	74	.306	.360	-24	-24	99	100	-0.8	-1	2	-2.2
1978	Det-A	15	8	.652	30	30	10	4	0	202	218	9.7	16	65	2.9	59	2.6	3.88	104	.284	.340	-2	4	107	111	3.3	0	-1	0.2
1979	Det-A	10	7	.588	35	19	2	0	3	158	163	9.3	13	60	3.4	59	3.4	3.30	123	.275	.344	16	13	96	132	1.2	0	-1	1.2
1980	Det-A	0	0	—	8	0	0	0	0	7	11	14.1	1	6	7.7	3	3.9	7.71	55	.355	.447	-3	-3	105	107	0.0	0	0	-0.2
	Bos-A	1	3	.250	7	4	0	0	0	24	45	16.9	6	12	4.5	4	1.5	11.25	37	.413	.477	-19	-19	102	94	-0.9	0	-0	-1.6
	Yr	1	3	.250	15	4	0	0	0	31	56	16.3	7	18	5.2	7	2.0	10.45	40	.397	.470	-22	-22	103	94	-0.9	0	-0	-1.8
Total	13	145	113	.562	476	305	74	27	15	2231	2272	9.2	176	750	3.0	1141	4.6	3.83	93	.268	.329	-35	-66	97	103	1.2	-15	1	-7.4
■ **JOSH BILLINGS** Billings, Haskell Clark b: 9/27/07, New York, N.Y. d: 12/26/83, Greenbrae, Cal. BR/TR, 5'11", 180 lbs. Deb: 8/17/27																													
1927	Det-A	5	4	.556	10	9	5	0	0	67	64	8.6	3	39	5.2	18	2.4	4.84	92	.259	.361	-5	-3	107	88	0.2	0	-1	-0.2
1928	Det-A	5	10	.333	21	16	3	1	0	111	118	9.6	4	59	4.8	48	3.9	5.11	79	.276	.357	-13	-13	100	87	-1.9	3	-0	-0.9
1929	Det-A	0	1	.000	8	0	0	0	0	19	27	12.8	0	9	4.3	1	0.5	5.21	79	.365	.398	-2	-2	97	127	-0.4	-1	1	-0.1
Total	3	10	15	.400	39	25	8	1	0	197	209	9.5	7	107	4.9	67	3.1	5.03	83	.279	.362	-20	-18	102	91	-2.1	2	0	-1.2
■ **DOUG BIRD** Bird, James Douglas b: 3/5/50, Corona, Cal. BR/TR, 6'4", 180 lbs. Deb: 4/29/73																													
1973	KC-A	4	4	.500	54	0	0	0	20	102	81	7.1	10	30	2.6	83	7.3	3.00	139	.217	.273	9	13	109	86	-0.2	0	-2	1.2
1974	KC-A	7	6	.538	55	1	1	0	10	92	100	9.8	6	27	2.6	62	6.1	2.74	141	.286	.328	9	11	106	148	0.8	0	1	1.2
1975	KC-A	9	6	.600	51	4	0	0	11	105	100	8.6	7	40	3.4	81	6.9	3.26	118	.258	.320	6	7	101	113	0.7	0	-1	0.6
1976	KC-A	12	10	.545	39	27	2	1	2	198	191	8.7	17	31	**1.4**	107	4.9	3.36	103	.251	.278	4	2	99	88	-0.1	0	-1	0.1
1977	KC-A	11	4	.733	53	5	0	0	14	118	120	9.2	14	29	2.2	83	6.3	3.89	103	.270	.310	2	2	99	103	2.3	0	-1	0.1
1978	KC-A	6	6	.500	40	6	0	0	1	99	110	10.0	8	31	2.8	48	4.4	5.27	72	.284	.329	-16	-16	101	80	-0.7	0	-0	-1.6
1979	Phi-N	2	0	1.000	32	1	1	0	0	61	73	10.8	7	16	2.4	33	4.9	5.16	70	.305	.346	-10	-10	97	96	1.0	0	-1	-1.1
1980	NY-A	3	0	1.000	22	1	0	0	1	51	47	8.3	3	14	2.5	17	3.0	2.65	149	.257	.302	8	7	98	127	1.5	0	1	0.8
1981	NY-A	5	1	.833	17	4	0	0	0	53	58	9.8	5	16	2.7	28	4.8	2.72	133	.280	.323	6	5	99	154	1.9	0	0	0.6
	Chi-N	4	5	.444	12	12	2	1	0	75	72	8.6	5	16	1.9	34	4.1	3.60	103	.254	.292	-1	1	106	86	0.6	-1	-1	0.0
1982	Chi-N	9	14	.391	35	33	2	1	0	191	230	10.8	26	30	**1.4**	71	3.3	5.14	73	.297	.321	-32	-30	104	89	-1.6	-2	-2	-3.2
1983	Bos-A	1	4	.200	22	6	0	0	1	68	91	12.0	14	16	2.1	33	4.4	6.62	63	.324	.360	-19	-19	102	95	-1.4	0	0	-1.7
Total	11	73	60	.549	432	100	8	3	60	1213	1273	9.4	122	296	2.2	680	5.0	3.99	95	.272	.312	-35	-25	102	101	4.8	-2	-8	-3.0
■ **RED BIRD** Bird, James Edward b: 4/25/1890, Stephenville, Tex. d: 3/23/72, Murfreesboro, Ark. BL/TL, 5'11", 170 lbs. Deb: 9/17/21																													
1921	Was-A	0	0	—	1	0	0	0	0	5	5	9.0	0	1	1.8	2	3.6	5.40	79	.294	.333	-1	-1	99	78	0.0	-0	0	0.0
■ **MIKE BIRKBECK** Birkbeck, Michael Lawrence b: 3/10/61, Orrville, Ohio BR/TR, 6'1", 190 lbs. Deb: 8/17/86																													
1986	Mil-A	1	1	.500	7	4	0	0	0	22	24	9.8	0	12	4.9	13	5.3	4.50	96	.282	.371	-1	-0	103	95	0.0	0	-0	0.0
1987	Mil-A	1	4	.200	10	10	1	0	0	45	63	12.6	8	19	3.8	25	5.0	6.20	74	.335	.390	-9	-8	102	111	-1.5	0	1	-0.6
1988	Mil-A	10	8	.556	23	23	0	0	0	124	141	10.2	10	37	2.7	64	4.6	4.72	87	.285	.333	-10	-9	103	92	0.4	0	2	-0.6
Total	3	12	13	.480	40	37	1	0	0	191	228	10.7	18	68	3.2	102	4.8	5.04	84	.297	.351	-20	-17	103	96	-1.1	0	3	-1.2
■ **RALPH BIRKOFER** Birkofer, Ralph Joseph "Lefty" b: 11/5/08, Cincinnati, Ohio d: 3/16/71, Cincinnati, Ohio BL/TL, 5'11", 213 lbs. Deb: 4/25/33																													
1933	Pit-N	4	2	.667	9	8	3	1	0	51	43	7.6	1	17	3.0	20	3.5	2.29	136	.229	.295	6	5	94	105	0.7	1	-0	0.6
1934	Pit-N	11	12	.478	41	24	11	0	1	204	227	10.0	11	66	2.9	71	3.1	4.10	104	.277	.332	-1	4	105	98	-0.3	0	-2	0.3
1935	Pit-N	9	7	.563	37	18	8	1	1	150	173	10.4	5	42	2.5	80	4.8	4.08	104	.283	.327	-1	3	105	97	0.0	2	-3	0.2
1936	Pit-N	7	5	.583	34	13	2	0	0	109	130	10.7	4	41	3.4	44	3.6	4.71	82	.295	.356	-8	-10	96	97	0.5	0	-3	-1.2
1937	Bro-N	0	2	.000	11	1	0	0	0	30	45	13.5	3	9	2.7	9	2.7	6.60	64	.341	.372	-9	-8	107	93	-0.9	1	-0	-0.7
Total	5	31	28	.525	132	64	24	2	2	544	618	10.2	24	175	2.9	224	3.7	4.19	97	.282	.335	-13	-8	102	98	0.0	4	-8	-0.8
■ **BABE BIRRER** Birrer, Werner Joseph b: 7/4/28, Buffalo, N.Y. BR/TR, 6', 195 lbs. Deb: 6/05/55																													
1955	Det-A	4	3	.571	36	3	1	0	3	80	77	8.7	9	29	3.3	28	3.1	4.16	90	.248	.309	-2	-4	95	86	0.4	2	-1	-0.1
1956	Bal-A	0	0	—	4	0	0	0	0	5	9	16.2	0	1	1.8	1	1.8	7.20	56	.360	.385	-2	-2	97	78	0.0	-0	-0	-0.1
1958	LA-N	0	0	—	16	0	0	0	1	34	43	11.4	4	7	1.9	16	4.2	4.50	93	.309	.342	-2	-1	106	109	0.0	2	-1	0.0
Total	3	4	3	.571	56	3	1	0	4	119	129	9.8	13	37	2.8	45	3.4	4.39	89	.272	.322	-6	-7	98	92	0.4	4	-2	-0.2
■ **TIM BIRTSAS** Birtsas, Timothy Dean b: 9/5/60, Pontiac, Mich. BL/TL, 6'6", 235 lbs. Deb: 5/03/85																													
1985	Oak-A	10	6	.625	29	25	2	0	0	141	124	7.9	18	91	5.8	94	6.0	4.02	96	.238	.349	2	-2	93	112	2.5	0	-2	-0.4
1986	Oak-A	0	0	—	2	0	0	0	0	2	2	9.0	1	4	18.0	1	4.5	22.50	17	.286	.500	-4	-4	94	55	0.0	0	0	-0.3
1988	Cin-N	1	3	.250	36	4	0	0	0	64	61	8.6	6	24	3.4	38	5.3	4.22	86	.250	.318	-5	-4	105	91	-1.0	-1	-1	-0.5
Total	3	11	9	.550	67	29	2	0	0	207	187	8.1	25	119	5.2	133	5.8	4.26	89	.242	.342	-8	-10	97	105	1.5	-1	-3	-1.2
■ **FRANK BISCAN** Biscan, Frank Stephen "Porky" b: 3/13/20, Mt.Olive, Ill. d: 5/22/59, St.Louis, Mo. BL/TL, 5'11", 190 lbs. Deb: 5/03/42																													
1942	StL-A	0	1	.000	11	0	0	0	1	27	13	4.3	1	11	3.7	10	3.3	2.33	160	.143	.231	4	4	102	42	-0.4	-0	0	0.4
1946	StL-A	1	1	.500	16	0	0	0	1	23	28	11.0	0	22	8.6	9	3.5	5.09	69	.318	.446	-4	-4	100	124	0.1	-0	-0	-0.4
1948	StL-A	6	7	.462	47	4	1	0	2	99	129	11.7	3	71	6.5	45	4.1	6.09	77	.322	.423	-20	-16	109	107	0.9	0	0	-1.3
Total	3	7	9	.438	74	4	1	0	4	149	170	10.3	4	104	6.3	64	3.9	5.26	82	.294	.399	-20	-16	106	98	0.6	-0	0	-1.3
■ **CHARLIE BISHOP** Bishop, Charles Tuller b: 1/1/24, Atlanta, Ga. BR/TR, 6'2", 195 lbs. Deb: 8/22/52																													
1952	Phi-A	2	2	.500	6	5	1	0	0	31	29	8.4	2	24	7.0	17	4.9	6.39	64	.238	.358	-9	-8	112	64	0.0	-0	0	-0.6
1953	Phi-A	3	14	.176	39	20	1	1	2	161	174	9.7	15	86	4.8	66	3.7	5.65	74	.282	.368	-30	-26	105	89	-4.7	-4	2	-2.6
1954	Phi-A	4	6	.400	20	12	4	0	1	96	98	9.2	10	50	4.7	34	3.2	4.41	88	.275	.358	-7	-5	105	110	0.5	-2	-2	-0.8
1955	KC-A	1	0	1.000	4	0	0	0	0	7	6	7.7	1	8	10.3	4	5.1	5.14	82	.261	.472	-1	-1	106	152	0.5	0	0	0.0
Total	4	10	22	.313	69	37	6	1	3	295	307	9.4	28	168	5.1	121	3.7	5.31	77	.275	.367	-47	-40	106	95	-3.7	-6	1	-4.0
■ **JIM BISHOP** Bishop, James Morton b: 1/28/1898, Montgomery City, Mo. d: 9/20/73, Montgomery City, Mo. BR/TR, 6', 195 lbs. Deb: 4/26/23																													
1923	Phi-N	0	3	.000	15	0	0	0	1	33	48	13.1	2	11	3.0	5	1.4	6.27	75	.353	.405	-8	-6	118	100	-1.4	-2	1	-0.5
1924	Phi-N	0	1	.000	7	1	0	0	0	17	24	12.7	3	7	3.7	3	1.6	6.35	67	.348	.397	-5	-4	111	111	-0.4	-0	0	-0.3
Total	2	0	4	.000	22	1	0	0	1	50	72	13.0	5	18	3.2	8	1.4	6.30	72	.351	.403	-13	-10	115	104	-1.8	-2	1	-0.8

YEAR TM/L	W	L	PCT	G	GS	CG	SHO	SV	IP	H	H/G	HR	BB	BB/G	SO	SO/G	ERA	/A	OAVG	OOBP	PR	/A	PF	CPI	WAT	PB	PD	TPI
■ LLOYD BISHOP	Bishop, Lloyd Clifton b: 4/25/1890, Conway Springs, Kan. d: 6/18/68, Wichita, Kan. BR/TR, 6', 180 lbs. Deb: 9/05/14																											
1914 Cle-A	0	1	.000	3	1	0	0	0	8	14	15.8	0	3	3.4	1	1.1	5.63	52	.389	.436	-3	-2	106	121	-0.4	-0	-0	-0.2
■ BILL BISHOP	Bishop, William Henry "Lefty" b: 10/22/1900, Houtzdale, Pa. d: 2/14/56, St.Joseph, Mo. BL/TL, 5'8", 170 lbs. Deb: 9/15/21																											
1921 Phi-A	0	0	—	2	0	0	0	0	7	8	10.3	0	10	12.9	4	5.1	9.00	51	.267	.439	-4	-3	107	65	0.0	-1	0	-0.2
■ BILL BISHOP	Bishop, William Robinson b: 12/27/1869, Adamsburg, Pa. d: 12/15/32, Pittsburgh, Pa. Deb: 7/13/1886																											
1886 Pit-a	0	1	.000	2	2	2	0	0	17	17	9.0	0	11	5.8	4	2.1	3.18	98	.271	.379	1	-0	90	135	-0.4	-0	0	0.0
1887 Pit-N	0	3	.000	3	3	3	0	0	27	45	15.0	2	22	7.3	4	1.3	13.33	29	.388	.485	-28	-28	96	64	-1.4	-1	0	-1.8
1889 Chi-N	0	0	—	2	0	0	0	**2**	3	6	18.0	0	6	18.0	1	3.0	18.00	22	.432	.604	-5	-5	98	71	0.0	0	0	-0.3
Total 3	0	4	.000	7	5	5	0	2	47	68	13.0	2	39	7.5	9	1.7	9.96	36	.353	.462	-32	-33	94	90	-1.8	-2	0	-2.1
■ HI BITHORN	Bithorn, Hiram Gabriel (Sosa) b: 3/18/16, Santurce, P.R. d: 1/1/52, El Mante, Mex. BR/TR, 6'1", 200 lbs. Deb: 4/15/42																											
1942 Chi-N	9	14	.391	38	16	9	0	2	171	191	10.1	8	81	4.3	65	3.4	3.68	88	.296	.366	-7	-9	98	**130**	-1.4	-1	-1	-1.0
1943 Chi-N	18	12	.600	39	30	19	**7**	2	250	226	8.1	8	65	2.3	86	3.1	2.59	128	.242	.287	22	20	98	103	4.0	-0	1	2.3
1946 Chi-N	6	5	.545	26	7	2	1	1	87	97	10.0	5	25	2.6	34	3.5	3.83	83	.283	.324	-4	-6	93	100	0.1	-0	-0	-0.6
1947 Chi-A	1	0	1.000	2	0	0	0	0	2	2	9.0	0	0	0.0	0	0.0	0.00	—	.286	.286	1	1	99	0	0.5	0	0	0.1
Total 4	34	31	.523	105	53	30	8	5	510	516	9.1	21	171	3.0	185	3.3	3.16	103	.268	.321	12	6	97	111	3.2	-2	0	0.8
■ JEFF BITTIGER	Bittiger, Jeffrey Scott b: 4/13/62, Jersey City, N.J. BR/TR, 5'10", 175 lbs. Deb: 9/02/86																											
1986 Phi-N	1	1	.500	3	3	0	0	0	15	16	9.6	2	7	4.2	8	4.8	5.40	72	.271	.353	-3	-3	104	91	0.0	1	0	0.0
1987 Min-A	1	0	1.000	3	1	0	0	0	8	11	12.4	2	0	0.0	5	5.6	5.63	76	.314	.333	-1	-1	96	105	0.5	0	0	0.0
1988 Chi-A	2	4	.333	25	7	0	0	0	62	59	8.6	11	29	4.2	33	4.8	4.21	93	.255	.328	-2	-2	99	113	-0.7	0	-1	-0.2
Total 3	4	5	.444	31	11	0	0	0	85	86	9.1	15	36	3.8	46	4.9	4.55	87	.265	.333	-5	-6	99	108	-0.2	1	-1	-0.2
■ JIM BIVIN	Bivin, James Nathaniel b: 12/11/09, Jackson, Miss. d: 11/7/82, Pueblo, Colo. BR/TR, 6', 155 lbs. Deb: 4/16/35																											
1935 Phi-N	2	9	.182	47	14	0	0	1	162	220	12.2	20	65	3.6	54	3.0	5.78	81	.316	.373	-32	-19	117	102	-3.1	-1	-1	-1.8
■ DAVE BLACK	Black, David b: 4/19/1892, Chicago, Ill. d: 10/27/36, Pittsburgh, Pa. TR, 6'2", 175 lbs. Deb: 5/02/14																											
1914 Chi-F	1	0	1.000	8	1	1	0	0	25	28	10.1	1	4	1.4	19	6.8	6.12	47	.313	.343	-8	-9	89	58	0.5	1	0	-0.8
1915 Chi-F	6	7	.462	25	10	2	0	0	121	104	7.7	3	33	2.5	43	3.2	2.45	117	.259	.315	8	6	95	102	-1.2	-2	0	0.4
Bal-F	1	3	.250	8	4	1	0	0	34	32	8.5	2	15	4.0	10	2.6	3.71	91	.277	.360	-3	-1	111	99	-0.3	0	0	0.0
Yr	7	10	.412	33	14	3	0	0	155	136	7.9	5	48	2.8	53	3.1	2.73	110	.263	.325	5	4	99	99	-1.5	-2	0	0.4
1923 Bos-A	0	0	—	2	0	0	0	0	1	2	18.0	0	0	0.0	0	0.0	0.00	—	.500	.400	0	0	106	0	0.0	0	0	0.0
Total 3	8	10	.444	43	15	4	0	0	181	166	8.3	6	52	2.6	72	3.6	3.18	94	.272	.328	-2	-4	97	95	-1.0	-1	0	-0.4
■ DON BLACK	Black, Donald Paul b: 7/20/16, Salix, Iowa d: 4/21/59, Cuyahoga Falls, O. BR/TR, 6', 185 lbs. Deb: 4/24/43																											
1943 Phi-A	6	16	.273	33	26	12	1	1	208	193	8.4	8	110	4.8	65	2.8	4.20	83	.247	.337	-21	-16	106	87	-1.7	-1	0	-1.7
1944 Phi-A	10	12	.455	29	27	8	0	0	177	177	9.0	6	75	3.8	78	4.0	4.07	86	.259	.331	-13	-11	102	87	-0.3	-1	0	-1.1
1945 Phi-A	5	11	.313	26	18	8	0	0	125	154	11.1	5	69	5.0	47	3.4	5.18	63	.307	.383	-25	-27	96	100	-0.8	-1	-1	-2.9
1946 Cle-A	1	2	.333	18	4	0	0	0	44	45	9.2	5	21	4.3	15	3.1	4.50	70	.273	.351	-5	-7	90	104	-0.3	0	1	-0.5
1947 Cle-A	10	12	.455	30	28	8	3	0	191	177	8.3	17	85	4.0	72	3.4	3.91	89	.249	.326	-4	-9	94	97	-1.5	-1	1	-0.9
1948 Cle-A	2	2	.500	18	10	1	0	0	52	57	9.9	5	40	6.9	16	2.8	5.37	75	.282	.394	-6	-8	94	108	-0.3	-0	0	-0.6
Total 6	34	55	.382	154	113	37	4	1	797	803	9.1	46	400	4.5	293	3.3	4.35	80	.264	.346	-74	-77	99	94	-4.9	-4	0	-7.7
■ BUDDY BLACK	Black, Harry Ralston b: 6/30/57, San Mateo, Cal. BL/TL, 6'2", 180 lbs. Deb: 9/05/81																											
1981 Sea-A	0	0	—	2	0	0	0	0	1	2	18.0	0	3	27.0	0	0.0	0.00	—	.500	.714	0	0	101	0	0.0	0	0	0.1
1982 KC-A	4	6	.400	22	14	0	0	0	88	92	9.4	10	34	3.5	40	4.1	4.60	88	.269	.334	-5	-5	100	95	-1.4	0	0	-0.4
1983 KC-A	10	7	.588	24	24	3	0	0	161	159	8.9	19	43	2.4	58	3.2	3.80	109	.257	.304	5	6	102	99	1.8	0	2	0.8
1984 KC-A	17	12	.586	35	35	8	1	0	257	226	7.9	22	64	2.2	140	4.9	3.12	127	.233	**.281**	25	24	99	89	2.4	0	3	2.8
1985 KC-A	10	15	.400	33	33	5	2	0	206	216	9.4	17	59	2.6	122	5.3	4.33	97	.268	.320	-4	-3	101	91	-3.9	0	-1	-0.3
1986 KC-A	5	10	.333	56	4	0	0	9	121	100	7.4	14	43	3.2	68	5.1	3.20	131	.225	.298	13	13	100	103	-2.2	0	0	1.4
1987 KC-A	8	6	.571	29	18	0	0	1	122	126	9.3	16	35	2.6	61	4.5	3.61	128	.265	.319	12	14	104	116	0.9	0	-0	1.3
1988 KC-A	2	1	.667	17	0	0	0	0	22	23	9.4	2	11	4.5	19	7.8	4.91	83	.267	.347	-2	-2	103	91	0.5	0	-0	-0.2
Cle-A	2	3	.400	16	7	0	0	1	59	59	9.0	6	23	3.5	44	6.7	5.03	81	.262	.331	-7	-6	102	86	-0.3	0	1	-0.5
Yr	4	4	.500	33	7	0	0	1	81	82	9.1	8	34	3.8	63	7.0	5.00	81	.264	.335	-9	-8	102	86	0.2	0	1	-0.7
Total 8	58	60	.492	234	135	16	3	11	1037	1003	8.7	106	315	2.7	552	4.8	3.80	110	.253	.309	37	42	101	96	-2.2	0	5	5.0
■ JOE BLACK	Black, Joseph b: 2/8/24, Plainfield, N.J. BR/TR, 6'2", 220 lbs. Deb: 5/01/52																											
1952 Bro-N	15	4	.789	56	2	1	0	15	142	102	6.5	9	41	2.6	85	5.4	2.15	170	.201	.257	**25**	**24**	98	97	4.4	-1	-2	2.2
1953 Bro-N	6	3	.667	34	3	0	0	5	73	74	9.1	12	27	3.3	42	5.2	5.30	80	.259	.324	-8	-8	100	83	0.0	0	-0	-0.7
1954 Bro-N	0	0	—	5	0	0	0	0	7	11	14.1	3	5	6.4	3	3.9	11.57	35	.355	.432	-6	-6	101	87	0.0	0	0	-0.5
1955 Bro-N	1	0	1.000	6	0	0	0	0	15	15	9.0	1	5	3.0	9	5.4	3.00	136	.273	.323	2	2	101	130	0.5	0	-0	0.2
Cin-N	5	2	.714	32	11	1	0	3	102	106	9.4	13	25	2.2	54	4.8	4.24	99	.263	.298	-2	-0	104	88	1.6	-3	-0	-0.2
Yr	6	2	.750	38	11	1	0	3	117	121	9.3	14	30	2.3	63	4.8	4.08	103	.264	.301	-1	2	104	88	2.1	0	-1	0.0
1956 Cin-N	3	2	.600	32	0	0	0	2	62	61	8.9	11	25	3.6	27	3.9	4.50	89	.256	.326	-5	-3	106	96	0.1	-1	-0	-0.4
1957 Was-A	0	1	.000	7	0	0	0	0	13	22	15.2	4	1	0.7	2	1.4	6.92	56	.393	.383	-5	-4	102	123	-0.4	0	0	-0.3
Total 6	30	12	.714	172	16	2	0	25	414	391	8.5	53	129	2.8	222	4.8	3.91	102	.248	.301	1	3	101	94	6.2	-5	-3	0.3
■ BOB BLACK	Black, Robert Benjamin b: 12/10/1862, Cincinnati, Ohio d: 3/21/33, Sioux City, Iowa Deb: 8/17/1884																											
1884 KC-U	4	9	.308	16	15	13	0	0	123	127	9.3	1	17	1.2	93	6.8	3.22	86	.272	.297	-3	-6	92	94	1.0	4	0	-0.4
■ BUD BLACK	Black, William Carroll b: 7/9/32, St.Louis, Mo. BR/TR, 6'3", 197 lbs. Deb: 9/13/52																											
1952 Det-A	0	1	.000	2	2	0	0	0	8	14	15.8	0	5	5.6	0	0.0	10.13	37	.389	.452	-6	-6	103	76	-0.4	-0	-0	-0.5
1955 Det-A	1	1	.500	3	2	1	1	0	14	12	7.7	0	8	5.1	7	4.5	1.29	292	.231	.349	4	4	95	256	0.0	0	0	0.4
1956 Det-A	1	1	.500	5	1	0	0	0	10	10	9.0	2	5	4.5	7	6.3	3.60	110	.256	.333	1	0	95	134	0.0	-0	0	0.0
Total 3	2	3	.400	10	5	1	1	0	32	36	10.1	2	18	5.1	14	3.9	4.22	91	.283	.373	-1	-1	97	173	-0.4	-1	0	-0.1
■ CHARLIE BLACKBURN	Blackburn, Foster Edwin b: 1/6/1895, Chicago, Ill. d: 3/9/84, New Port Richey, Fla. 6'1", 165 lbs. Deb: 4/17/15																											
1915 KC-F	0	1	.000	7	2	0	0	0	16	19	10.7	2	13	7.3	7	3.9	8.44	35	.326	.448	-10	-10	97	76	-0.4	-1	0	-0.9
1921 Chi-A	0	0	—	1	0	0	0	0	1	0	0.0	0	1	9.0	0	0.0	0.00	—	.000	.333	0	0	102	0	0.0	0	0	0.0
Total 2	0	1	.000	8	2	0	0	0	17	19	10.1	2	14	7.4	7	3.7	7.94	38	.315	.444	-9	-9	97	72	-0.4	-1	0	-0.9
■ GEORGE BLACKBURN	Blackburn, George W. "Smiling George" b: 9/21/1871, Ozark, Mo. 5'11", 184 lbs. Deb: 7/06/1897																											
1897 Bal-N	2	2	.500	5	4	3	0	0	33	34	9.3	2	12	3.3	1	0.3	6.82	58	.288	.353	-9	-10	92	55	-0.5	-2	0	-0.9
■ JIM BLACKBURN	Blackburn, James Ray "Bones" b: 6/19/24, Warsaw, Ky. d: 10/26/69, Cincinnati, Ohio BR/TR, 6'4", 175 lbs. Deb: 7/24/48																											
1948 Cin-N	0	2	.000	16	0	0	0	0	32	38	10.7	1	14	3.9	10	2.8	4.22	100	.302	.361	-1	-0	106	114	-0.9	-1	-0	0.0
1951 Cin-N	0	0	—	2	0	0	0	0	4	8	18.0	3	2	4.5	1	2.3	15.75	26	.444	.545	-5	-5	103	104	0.0	0	0	-0.3
Total 2	0	2	.000	18	0	0	0	0	36	46	11.5	4	16	4.0	11	2.8	5.50	76	.319	.386	-6	-5	106	113	-0.9	-1	-0	-0.3
■ RON BLACKBURN	Blackburn, Ronald Hamilton b: 4/23/35, Mt.Airy, N.C. BR/TR, 6'0.5", 160 lbs. Deb: 4/15/58																											
1958 Pit-N	2	1	.667	38	2	0	0	3	64	61	8.6	7	27	3.8	31	4.4	3.38	110	.261	.327	4	2	94	126	0.4	1	1	0.4
1959 Pit-N	1	1	.500	26	0	0	0	1	44	50	10.2	5	15	3.1	19	3.9	3.68	111	.286	.337	1	2	104	128	0.0	1	-1	0.2
Total 2	3	2	.600	64	2	0	0	4	108	111	9.3	12	42	3.5	50	4.2	3.50	110	.271	.331	5	4	98	126	0.4	2	0	0.6
■ LENA BLACKBURNE	Blackburne, Russell Aubrey "Slats" b: 10/23/1886, Clifton Heights, Pa. d: 2/29/68, Riverside, N.J. BR/TR, 5'11", 160 lbs. Deb: 4/14/10 MC																											
1929 Chi-A	0	0	—	1	0	0	0	0	⅓	1	27.0	0	0	0.0	0	0.0	0.00	—	1.000	1.000	0	0	98	0	0.0	0	0	0.0
■ EWELL BLACKWELL	Blackwell, Ewell "The Whip" b: 10/23/22, Fresno, Cal. BR/TR, 6'6", 195 lbs. Deb: 4/21/42																											
1942 Cin-N	0	0	—	2	0	0	0	0	3	3	9.0	0	3	9.0	1	3.0	6.00	56	.231	.375	-1	-1	102	65	0.0	-0	0	0.0
1946 Cin-N	9	13	.409	33	25	10	**6**	0	194	160	7.4	1	79	3.7	100	4.6	2.46	146	.226	.303	21	24	105	97	-0.7	-4	4	2.8
1947 Cin-N	**22**	8	.733	33	33	**23**	6	0	273	227	7.5	10	95	3.1	**193**	**6.4**	2.47	152	.234	.300	48	39	92	116	8.2	-4	5	4.0

YEAR	TM/L	W	L	PCT	G	GS	CG	SHO	SV	IP	H	H/G	HR	BB	BB/G	SO	SO/G	ERA	/A	OAVG	OOBP	PR	/A	PF	CPI	WAT	PB	PD	TPI
1948	Cin-N	7	9	.438	22	20	4	1	1	139	134	8.7	12	52	3.4	114	7.4	4.53	93	.251	.317	-9	-5	106	82	0.3	1	4	0.0
1949	Cin-N	5	5	.500	30	4	0	0	1	77	80	9.4	7	34	4.0	55	6.4	4.21	94	.271	.349	-1	-2	98	108	0.9	-0	1	0.0
1950	Cin-N	17	15	.531	40	32	18	1	4	261	203	**7.0**	12	112	3.9	188	**6.5**	2.97	**148**	**.210**	.298	34	**41**	106	86	3.4	-3	2	**4.2**
1951	Cin-N	16	15	.516	38	32	11	2	2	233	204	7.9	16	97	3.7	120	4.6	3.44	118	.233	.311	13	16	103	93	2.5	8	0	2.5
1952	Cin-N	3	12	.200	23	17	3	0	0	102	107	9.4	6	60	5.3	48	4.2	5.38	70	.275	.373	-19	-19	100	90	-4.2	-0	-0	-1.8
	NY-A	1	0	1.000	5	2	0	0	1	16	12	6.8	0	12	6.8	7	3.9	0.56	618	.203	.333	6	5	95	488	0.5	-0	-0	0.5
1953	NY-A	2	0	1.000	8	4	0	0	1	20	17	7.6	2	13	5.8	11	4.9	3.60	98	.233	.352	1	-0	88	117	1.0	-1	0	0.0
1955	KC-A	0	1	.000	2	0	0	0	0	4	3	6.8	1	5	11.3	2	4.5	6.75	62	.250	.500	-1	-1	106	124	-0.4	0	-0	0.0
Total	10	82	78	.512	236	169	69	16	10	1322	1150	7.8	67	562	3.8	839	5.7	3.30	120	.235	.315	92	98	101	101	11.5	-3	15	12.2
■ GEORGE BLAEHOLDER Blaeholder, George Franklin b: 1/26/04, Orange, Cal. d: 12/29/47, Garden Grove, Cal. BR/TR, 5'11", 175 lbs. Deb: 4/20/25																													
1925	StL-A	0	0	—	2	0	0	0	0	2	6	27.0	3	1	4.5	1	4.5	31.50	15	.600	.615	-6	-6	108	90	0.0	0	0	-0.4
1927	StL-A	0	1	.000	1	1	1	0	0	9	8	8.0	1	4	4.0	2	2.0	5.00	90	.258	.351	-1	-0	109	91	-0.4	0	0	0.0
1928	StL-A	10	15	.400	38	26	9	1	3	214	235	9.9	23	52	2.2	87	3.7	4.37	95	.280	.314	-8	-5	103	95	-3.4	2	5	0.2
1929	StL-A	14	15	.483	42	24	13	**4**	2	222	237	9.6	18	61	2.5	72	2.9	4.18	101	.275	.312	2	1	100	92	-1.2	-3	6	0.3
1930	StL-A	11	13	.458	37	23	10	1	4	191	235	11.1	20	46	2.2	70	3.3	4.62	111	.303	.336	1	11	110	109	1.0	-2	-1	0.7
1931	StL-A	11	15	.423	35	32	13	1	0	226	280	11.2	15	56	2.2	79	3.1	4.54	101	.295	.332	-4	1	105	100	0.4	-3	3	0.2
1932	StL-A	14	14	.500	42	36	16	1	0	258	304	10.6	19	76	2.7	80	2.8	4.71	97	.290	.336	-7	-3	103	98	2.5	-3	0	-0.4
1933	StL-A	15	19	.441	38	36	14	3	0	256	283	9.9	24	69	2.4	63	2.2	4.71	107	.280	.323	-12	9	117	93	2.6	-2	3	1.2
1934	StL-A	14	18	.438	39	33	14	1	3	234	276	10.6	16	68	2.6	66	2.5	4.23	113	.296	.337	7	14	106	109	-0.1	-5	0	0.9
1935	StL-A	1	1	.500	6	2	0	0	0	18	25	12.5	3	6	3.0	0	0.0	7.00	70	.342	.373	-5	-4	110	98	0.1	-1	1	-0.3
	Phi-A	6	10	.375	23	22	10	1	0	149	173	10.4	10	49	3.0	22	1.3	3.99	114	.289	.336	8	10	102	112	-0.2	-6	2	0.5
	Yr	7	11	.389	29	24	10	1	0	167	198	10.7	13	55	3.0	22	1.2	4.31	107	.295	.340	3	5	103	112	-0.1	-1	2	0.2
1936	Cle-A	8	4	.667	35	16	6	1	0	134	158	10.6	21	47	3.2	30	2.0	5.10	103	.295	.350	-1	3	105	110	1.9	-3	1	0.1
Total	11	104	125	.454	338	251	106	14	12	1913	2220	10.4	173	535	2.5	572	2.7	4.54	103	.290	.331	-26	29	106	101	3.2	-26	19	3.0
■ DENNIS BLAIR Blair, Dennis Herman b: 6/5/54, Middletown, Ohio BR/TR, 6'5", 182 lbs. Deb: 5/26/74																													
1974	Mon-N	11	7	.611	22	22	4	1	0	146	113	7.0	7	72	4.4	76	4.7	3.27	116	.210	.305	6	8	104	79	2.3	-2	2	1.0
1975	Mon-N	8	15	.348	30	27	1	0	0	163	150	8.3	14	106	5.9	82	4.5	3.81	104	.251	.361	-3	3	109	114	-3.1	-1	-1	0.1
1976	Mon-N	0	2	.000	5	4	1	0	0	16	21	11.8	1	11	6.2	9	5.1	3.94	92	.300	.405	-1	-1	103	149	-0.9	-0	0	0.0
1980	SD-N	0	1	.000	5	1	0	0	0	14	18	11.6	3	3	1.9	11	7.1	6.43	53	.310	.344	-4	-5	94	88	-0.4	0	-0	-0.4
Total	4	19	25	.432	62	54	6	1	0	339	302	8.0	25	192	5.1	178	4.7	3.69	104	.239	.339	-2	6	106	100	-2.1	-4	1	0.7
■ BILL BLAIR Blair, William Ellsworth b: 9/17/1863, Pittsburgh, Pa. d: 2/22/1890, Pittsburgh, Pa. BL/TL, 5'8.5", 172 lbs. Deb: 1888																													
1888	Phi-a	1	3	.250	4	4	3	0	0	31	29	8.4	0	8	2.3	16	4.6	2.61	114	.260	.310	2	1	97	105	-1.1	1	0	0.2
■ DICK BLAISDELL Blaisdell, Howard Carleton b: 6/18/1862, Bradford, Mass. d: 8/20/1886, Malden, Mass. Deb: 7/09/1884																													
1884	KC-U	0	3	.000	3	3	3	0	0	26	49	17.0	0	4	1.4	8	2.8	8.65	32	.405	.424	-16	-17	92	83	-1.4	1	0	-1.1
■ ED BLAKE Blake, Edward James b: 12/23/25, E.St.Louis, Ill. BR/TR, 5'11", 175 lbs. Deb: 5/01/51																													
1951	Cin-N	0	0	—	3	0	0	0	0	4	10	22.5	3	1	2.3	1	2.3	11.25	36	.476	.458	-3	-3	103	144	0.0	0	0	-0.2
1952	Cin-N	0	0	—	2	0	0	0	0	3	3	9.0	0	0	0.0	0	0.0	0.00	—	.250	.250	1	1	100	0	0.0	0	0	0.2
1953	Cin-N	0	0	—	1	0	0	0	0	0	1	—	0	1	—	0	—	∞	—	1.000	1.000	-2	-2	100	43	0.0	0	0	-0.1
1957	KC-A	0	0	—	2	0	0	0	0	2	1	4.5	1	2	9.0	0	0.0	4.50	85	.167	.375	-0	-0	102	157	0.0	0	0	0.0
Total	4	0	0	—	8	0	0	0	0	9	15	15.0	4	4	4.0	1	1.0	8.00	49	.375	.413	-4	-4	102	99	0.0	0	1	-0.1
■ SHERIFF BLAKE Blake, John Frederick b: 9/17/1899, Ansted, W.Va. d: 10/31/82, Beckley, W.Va. BB/TR, 6', 180 lbs. Deb: 6/29/20																													
1920	Pit-N	0	0	—	6	0	0	0	0	13	21	14.5	0	6	4.2	17	11.8	8.31	38	.368	.431	-7	-7	101	77	0.0	-0	0	-0.6
1924	Chi-N	6	6	.500	29	11	4	0	1	106	123	10.4	3	44	3.7	42	3.6	4.58	85	.299	.360	-8	-8	101	99	-0.3	1	1	-0.5
1925	Chi-N	10	18	.357	36	31	14	0	2	231	260	10.1	17	114	4.4	93	3.6	4.87	86	.287	.362	-15	-17	98	97	-3.0	-4	0	-1.9
1926	Chi-N	11	12	.478	39	27	11	4	1	198	204	9.3	7	92	4.2	95	4.3	3.59	111	.280	.356	5	9	105	119	-1.3	-1	2	1.0
1927	Chi-N	13	14	.481	32	27	13	2	0	224	238	9.6	3	82	3.3	64	2.6	3.29	117	.282	.336	15	14	99	**117**	-2.0	-2	3	1.5
1928	Chi-N	17	11	.607	34	29	16	**4**	1	241	209	7.8	4	101	3.8	78	2.9	2.46	150	.240	.315	41	33	93	115	0.7	1	-2	3.1
1929	Chi-N	14	13	.519	35	30	13	1	1	218	244	10.1	8	103	4.3	70	2.9	4.29	108	.291	.363	10	8	98	109	-3.0	-2	-2	0.4
1930	Chi-N	10	14	.417	34	24	7	0	0	187	213	10.3	14	99	4.8	80	3.9	4.81	107	.291	.368	3	7	103	106	-3.8	-2	3	0.7
1931	Chi-N	0	4	.000	16	5	0	0	0	50	64	11.5	4	26	4.7	29	5.2	5.22	69	.312	.382	-8	-9	94	109	-1.9	3	1	-0.4
	Phi-N	4	5	.444	14	9	1	0	1	71	90	11.4	2	35	4.4	31	3.9	5.58	75	.305	.382	-14	-11	109	91	0.1	0	2	-0.7
	Yr	4	9	.308	30	14	1	0	1	121	154	11.5	6	61	4.5	60	4.5	5.43	73	.307	.380	-21	-20	103	91	-1.8	3	3	-1.1
1937	StL-A	2	2	.500	15	1	0	0	1	37	55	13.4	5	20	4.9	12	2.9	7.54	63	.350	.417	-12	-11	103	99	0.6	-1	0	-1.0
	StL-N	0	3	.000	14	2	2	0	0	44	45	9.2	1	18	3.7	20	4.1	3.68	106	.271	.328	1	1	100	104	-1.4	0	0	0.2
Total	10	87	102	.460	304	196	81	11	8	1620	1766	9.8	68	740	4.1	631	3.5	4.13	101	.284	.355	12	7	99	108	-15.3	-6	9	1.8
■ AL BLANCHE Blanche, Prosby Albert (born Prosper Belangio) b: 9/21/09, Somerville, Mass. BR/TR, 6', 178 lbs. Deb: 8/23/35																													
1935	Bos-N	0	0	—	6	0	0	0	0	17	14	7.4	0	5	2.6	4	2.1	1.59	254	.230	.275	5	5	100	149	0.0	-0	0	0.4
1936	Bos-N	0	1	.000	11	0	0	0	1	16	20	11.3	1	8	4.5	4	2.3	6.19	62	.303	.377	-4	-4	96	87	-0.4	0	1	-0.2
Total	2	0	1	.000	17	0	0	0	1	33	34	9.3	1	13	3.5	8	2.2	3.82	103	.268	.329	1	0	98	119	-0.4	-0	1	0.2
■ GIL BLANCO Blanco, Gilbert Henry b: 12/15/45, Phoenix, Ariz. BL/TL, 6'5", 205 lbs. Deb: 4/24/65																													
1965	NY-A	1	1	.500	17	1	0	0	0	20	16	7.2	1	12	5.4	14	6.3	4.05	86	.232	.333	-1	-1	101	92	0.0	0	-1	-0.1
1966	KC-A	2	4	.333	11	8	0	0	0	38	31	7.3	3	36	8.5	21	5.0	4.74	69	.237	.406	-5	-6	95	111	-0.8	-0	0	-0.5
Total	2	3	5	.375	28	9	0	0	0	58	47	7.3	4	48	7.4	35	5.4	4.50	74	.235	.382	-7	-7	97	105	-0.8	-0	-0	-0.6
■ FRED BLANDING Blanding, Frederick James "Fritz" b: 2/8/1888, Redlands, Cal. d: 7/16/50, Salem, Va. BR/TR, 6', 185 lbs. Deb: 9/15/10																													
1910	Cle-A	2	2	.500	6	5	4	1	0	45	43	8.6	0	12	2.4	25	5.0	2.80	92	.254	.319	-1	-1	102	97	0.1	-1	-0	-0.1
1911	Cle-A	7	11	.389	29	16	11	0	2	176	190	9.7	4	60	3.1	80	4.1	3.68	94	.283	.347	-7	-4	103	99	-2.4	2	0	-0.1
1912	Cle-A	18	14	.563	39	31	23	1	1	262	259	8.9	4	79	2.7	75	2.6	2.92	116	.267	.324	12	14	101	111	2.8	2	-0	1.3
1913	Cle-A	15	10	.600	41	22	14	3	0	215	234	9.8	6	72	3.0	63	2.6	2.55	119	.282	.341	9	12	104	**141**	1.2	4	-2	1.0
1914	Cle-A	3	9	.250	29	12	5	0	1	116	133	10.3	0	54	4.2	35	2.7	3.96	73	.301	.378	-16	-14	106	108	-1.5	-2	1	-1.3
Total	5	45	46	.495	144	86	57	5	4	814	859	9.5	14	277	3.1	278	3.1	3.13	102	.279	.341	-2	6	103	115	0.2	4	-2	0.8
■ FRED BLANK Blank, Frederick August b: 6/18/1874, Desoto, Mo. d: 2/5/36, St.Louis, Mo. BL/TL, 6'0.5", 175 lbs. Deb: 6/20/1894																													
1894	Cin-N	0	1	.000	1	1	1	0	0	8	5	5.6	0	9	10.1	1	1.1	4.50	120	.197	.407	1	1	102	77	-0.4	-1	0	0.0
■ HOMER BLANKENSHIP Blankenship, Homer "Si" b: 8/4/02, Bonham, Tex. d: 6/22/74, Longview, Tex. BR/TR, 6', 185 lbs. Deb: 9/06/22																													
1922	Chi-A	0	0	—	4	0	0	0	0	13	21	14.5	1	5	3.5	3	2.1	4.85	84	.389	.433	-1	-1	101	153	0.0	-1	-0	-0.1
1923	Chi-A	1	1	.500	4	0	0	0	1	5	9	16.2	0	1	1.8	1	1.8	3.60	110	.429	.417	0	0	99	210	0.1	0	0	0.0
1928	Pit-N	0	2	.000	5	2	1	0	0	22	27	11.0	1	9	3.7	6	2.5	5.73	73	.321	.367	-4	-4	105	90	-0.9	1	1	-0.1
Total	3	1	3	.250	13	2	1	0	1	40	57	12.8	2	15	3.4	10	2.3	5.17	80	.358	.396	-5	-5	103	126	-0.8	0	1	-0.2
■ KEVIN BLANKENSHIP Blankenship, Kevin De Wayne b: 1/26/63, Anaheim, Cal. BR/TR, 6', 175 lbs. Deb: 9/20/88																													
1988	Atl-N	0	1	.000	2	2	0	0	0	11	7	5.7	0	7	5.7	5	4.1	3.27	113	.194	.341	0	1	107	88	-0.4	-0	-0	0.0
	Chi-N	1	0	1.000	1	1	0	0	0	5	7	12.6	2	1	1.8	4	7.2	7.20	50	.318	.348	-2	-2	105	103	0.5	-0	-0	-0.1
	Yr	1	1	.500	3	3	0	0	0	16	14	7.9	2	8	4.5	9	5.1	4.50	82	.237	.328	-2	-1	106	103	0.1	-0	-0	-0.1
■ TED BLANKENSHIP Blankenship, Theodore b: 5/10/01, Bonham, Tex. d: 1/14/45, Atoka, Okla. BR/TR, 6'1", 170 lbs. Deb: 7/02/22																													
1922	Chi-A	8	10	.444	24	15	7	0	1	128	124	8.7	4	47	3.3	42	3.0	3.80	108	.266	.326	3	4	101	92	-1.0	-1	0	0.3
1923	Chi-A	9	14	.391	44	23	9	1	0	209	219	9.4	8	100	4.3	57	2.5	4.26	93	.287	.356	-7	-7	99	104	-1.6	2	-1	-0.5
1924	Chi-A	7	6	.538	25	11	7	0	1	129	167	11.7	1	38	2.7	36	2.5	5.02	83	.317	.354	-11	-13	98	89	1.3	5	-2	-0.8
1925	Chi-A	17	8	.680	40	23	16	3	1	232	218	8.5	11	69	2.7	81	3.1	3.03	138	.253	.301	35	30	95	100	4.8	2	-4	2.5
1926	Chi-A	13	10	.565	29	26	15	1	1	209	217	9.3	13	65	2.8	66	2.8	3.62	100	.273	.319	9	0	90	102	1.0	-1	-3	-0.3
1927	Chi-A	12	17	.414	37	34	11	3	0	237	280	10.6	14	74	2.8	51	1.9	5.05	84	.299	.342	-24	-21	103	88	-1.6	2	-3	-1.9

YEAR	TM/L	W	L	PCT	G	GS	CG	SHO	SV	IP	H	H/G	HR	BB	BB/G	SO	SO/G	ERA	/A	OAVG	OOBP	PR	/A	PF	CPI	WAT	PB	PD	TPI
1928	Chi-A	9	11	.450	27	22	8	0	0	158	186	10.6	9	80	4.6	36	2.1	4.61	88	.306	.377	-10	-10	100	114	-0.3	-2	-2	-1.2
1929	Chi-A	0	2	.000	8	1	0	0	0	18	28	14.0	3	9	4.5	7	3.5	9.00	46	.359	.411	-10	-10	98	85	-0.9	-0	-0	-0.8
1930	Chi-A	2	1	.667	7	1	0	0	0	15	23	13.8	0	7	4.2	2	1.2	9.00	54	.371	.419	-7	-7	105	80	0.7	-0	-0	-0.6
Total	9	77	79	.494	241	156	73	8	4	1335	1462	9.9	63	489	3.3	378	2.5	4.27	95	.287	.340	-20	-33	98	98	2.4	7	-15	-3.3
■ CY BLANTON	Blanton, Darrell Elijah b: 7/6/08, Waurika, Okla. d: 9/13/45, Norman, Okla. BL/TR, 5'11.5", 180 lbs. Deb: 9/23/34																												
1934	Pit-N	0	1	.000	1	1	0	0	0	8	5	5.6	1	4	4.5	5	5.6	3.38	126	.161	.278	1	1	105	62	-0.4	0	0	0.1
1935	Pit-N	18	13	.581	35	31	23	**4**	1	254	220	**7.8**	3	55	1.9	142	5.0	**2.59**	**164**	**.229**	**.266**	**40**	**46**	105	82	0.8	-5	2	**4.6**
1936	Pit-N	13	15	.464	44	32	15	4	3	236	235	9.0	9	55	2.1	127	4.8	3.51	110	.257	.295	13	9	96	87	-2.4	-3	1	0.7
1937	Pit-N	14	12	.538	36	34	14	4	0	243	250	9.3	13	76	2.8	143	5.3	3.30	120	.266	.320	17	18	101	112	-0.5	-1	-0	1.7
1938	Pit-N	11	7	.611	29	25	10	1	0	173	190	9.9	13	46	2.4	80	4.2	3.69	101	.281	.326	2	1	99	111	0.9	-1	2	0.2
1939	Pit-N	2	3	.400	10	6	1	0	0	42	45	9.6	4	10	2.1	11	2.4	4.29	92	.266	.302	-2	-2	101	84	-0.2	1	-0	0.0
1940	Phi-N	4	3	.571	13	10	5	0	0	77	82	9.6	7	21	2.5	24	2.8	4.32	91	.272	.315	-4	-3	102	95	1.3	-1	0	-0.4
1941	Phi-N	6	13	.316	28	25	7	1	0	164	186	10.2	11	57	3.1	64	3.5	4.50	83	.284	.339	-16	-14	103	96	0.5	-2	-3	-1.8
1942	Phi-N	0	4	.000	6	3	0	0	0	22	30	12.3	3	13	5.3	15	6.1	5.73	58	.345	.427	-6	-6	101	127	-1.9	-0	0	-0.5
Total	9	68	71	.489	202	167	75	14	4	1219	1243	9.2	64	337	2.5	611	4.5	3.55	111	.262	.309	46	51	101	96	-1.9	-12	2	4.6
■ WADE BLASINGAME	Blasingame, Wade Allen b: 11/22/43, Deming, N.Mex. BL/TL, 6'1", 185 lbs. Deb: 9/17/63																												
1963	Mil-N	0	0	—	2	0	0	0	0	3	7	21.0	0	2	6.0	6	18.0	12.00	27	.467	.500	-3	-3	100	90	0.0	0	0	-0.2
1964	Mil-N	9	5	.643	28	13	3	1	2	117	113	8.7	15	51	3.9	70	5.4	4.23	80	.257	.332	-9	-11	96	101	1.6	4	0	-0.6
1965	Mil-N	16	10	.615	38	36	10	1	1	225	200	8.0	17	116	4.6	117	4.7	3.76	97	.244	.336	-6	-3	103	103	2.7	3	1	0.2
1966	Atl-N	3	7	.300	16	12	0	0	0	68	71	9.4	5	25	3.3	34	4.5	5.29	66	.272	.338	-13	-14	97	76	-2.1	1	-0	-1.2
1967	Atl-N	1	0	1.000	10	4	0	0	0	25	27	9.7	1	21	7.6	20	7.2	4.68	75	.287	.412	-4	-3	105	120	0.5	0	0	-0.1
	Hou-N	4	7	.364	15	14	0	0	0	77	91	10.6	9	27	3.2	46	5.4	5.96	54	.298	.353	-22	-24	95	85	-0.8	2	-0	-2.1
	Yr	5	7	.417	25	18	0	0	0	102	118	10.4	10	48	4.2	66	5.8	5.65	58	.295	.366	-26	-27	98	85	-0.3	0	0	-2.2
1968	Hou-N	1	2	.333	22	2	0	0	1	36	45	11.3	3	10	2.5	22	5.5	4.75	63	.308	.344	-7	-7	100	100	-0.3	0	1	-0.6
1969	Hou-N	0	5	.000	26	5	0	0	1	52	66	11.4	4	33	5.7	33	5.7	5.37	68	.306	.391	-10	-10	101	108	-2.4	-1	0	-1.1
1970	Hou-N	3	3	.500	13	13	1	0	0	78	76	8.8	4	23	2.7	55	6.3	3.46	110	.261	.316	5	3	94	102	0.1	-0	0	0.3
1971	Hou-N	9	11	.450	30	28	2	0	0	158	177	10.1	11	45	2.6	93	5.3	4.61	69	.285	.338	-20	-25	92	92	-0.8	5	1	-1.9
1972	Hou-N	0	0	—	10	0	0	0	0	8	4	4.5	1	8	9.0	9	10.1	9.00	40	.148	.350	-5	-5	105	44	0.0	0	0	-0.4
	NY-A	0	1	.000	12	1	0	0	0	17	14	7.4	5	11	5.8	7	3.7	4.24	67	.250	.361	-2	-3	92	146	-0.4	0	1	-0.1
Total	10	46	51	.474	222	128	16	2	5	864	891	9.3	75	372	3.9	512	5.3	4.52	76	.271	.344	-95	-103	98	98	-1.9	14	4	-7.8
■ STEVE BLASS	Blass, Stephen Robert b: 4/18/42, Canaan, Conn. BR/TR, 6', 165 lbs. Deb: 5/10/64																												
1964	Pit-N	5	8	.385	24	13	3	1	0	105	107	9.2	9	45	3.9	67	5.7	4.03	88	.266	.334	-6	-5	101	104	-1.4	-1	0	-0.6
1966	Pit-N	11	7	.611	34	25	1	0	0	156	173	10.0	12	46	2.7	76	4.4	3.87	92	.284	.334	-4	-5	99	107	1.0	1	-3	-0.6
1967	Pit-N	6	8	.429	32	16	2	0	0	127	126	8.9	12	47	3.3	72	5.1	3.54	95	.261	.323	-2	-2	100	111	-1.0	-1	0	-0.2
1968	Pit-N	18	6	**.750**	33	31	12	7	0	220	191	7.8	13	57	2.3	132	5.4	2.13	140	.234	.285	21	21	100	**125**	6.6	-1	-1	2.3
1969	Pit-N	16	10	.615	38	32	9	0	2	210	207	8.9	21	86	3.7	147	6.3	4.46	76	.258	.330	-20	-25	94	91	2.4	6	3	-1.7
1970	Pit-N	10	12	.455	31	31	6	1	0	197	187	8.5	14	73	3.3	120	5.5	3.52	111	.254	.322	12	8	96	106	-2.0	-2	0	0.6
1971	Pit-N	15	8	.652	33	33	12	**5**	0	240	226	8.5	16	68	2.6	136	5.1	2.85	118	.249	.297	17	13	97	109	1.7	-3	1	1.3
1972	Pit-N	19	8	.704	33	32	11	2	0	250	227	8.2	18	84	3.0	117	4.2	2.48	139	.246	.308	27	27	100	**132**	3.5	1	2	3.4
1973	Pit-N	3	9	.250	23	18	1	0	0	89	109	11.0	11	84	8.5	27	2.7	9.81	34	.313	.451	-61	-64	92	76	-3.0	4	1	-5.3
1974	Pit-N	0	0	—	1	0	0	0	0	5	5	9.0	2	7	12.6	2	3.6	9.00	39	.238	.429	-3	-3	97	91	0.0	-0	0	-0.2
Total	10	103	76	.575	282	231	57	16	2	1599	1558	8.8	128	597	3.4	896	5.0	3.62	95	.258	.323	-20	-34	98	110	7.8	4	4	-1.0
■ STEVE BLATERIC	Blateric, Stephen Lawrence b: 3/20/44, Denver, Colo. BR/TR, 6'3", 200 lbs. Deb: 9/17/71																												
1971	Cin-N	0	0	—	2	0	0	0	0	3	5	15.0	2	0	0.0	4	12.0	12.00	28	.385	.429	-3	-3	96	98	0.0	0	0	-0.2
1972	NY-A	0	0	—	1	0	0	0	0	4	2	4.5	0	0	0.0	4	9.0	0.00	—	.143	.143	1	1	92	0	0.0	-0	0	0.2
1975	Cal-A	0	0	—	2	0	0	0	0	4	9	20.3	0	1	2.3	5	11.3	6.75	54	.429	.417	-1	-1	96	125	0.0	0	0	0.0
Total	3	0	0	—	5	0	0	0	0	11	16	13.1	2	1	0.8	13	10.6	5.73	57	.333	.346	-3	-3	94	72	0.0	-0	0	0.0
■ HENRY BLAUVELT	Blauvelt, Henry Russell b: 4/8/1873, Nyack, N.Y. d: 12/28/26, Portland, Ore. Deb: 6/22/1890																												
1890	Roc-a	0	0	—	2	0	0	0	0	12	19	14.3	0	8	6.0	5	3.8	10.50	34	.376	.461	-9	-9	92	69	0.0	1	0	-0.5
■ GARY BLAYLOCK	Blaylock, Gary Nelson b: 10/11/31, Clarkton, Mo. BR/TR, 6', 196 lbs. Deb: 4/10/59 C																												
1959	StL-N	4	5	.444	26	12	3	0	0	100	117	10.5	14	43	3.9	61	5.5	5.13	82	.298	.361	-13	-10	106	106	-0.1	0	0	-0.8
	NY-A	0	1	.000	15	1	0	0	0	26	30	10.4	0	15	5.2	20	6.9	3.46	103	.306	.390	1	0	92	148	-0.4	1	-0	0.1
■ BOB BLAYLOCK	Blaylock, Robert Edward b: 6/28/35, Chattanooga, Okla BR/TR, 6'1", 185 lbs. Deb: 7/22/56																												
1956	StL-N	1	6	.143	14	6	0	0	0	41	45	9.9	7	24	5.3	39	8.6	6.37	59	.276	.365	-12	-12	99	83	-2.4	-1	0	-1.1
1959	StL-N	0	1	.000	3	1	0	0	0	9	8	8.0	1	3	3.0	3	3.0	4.00	105	.229	.289	-0	0	106	73	-0.4	-0	0	0.0
Total	2	1	7	.125	17	7	0	0	0	50	53	9.5	8	27	4.9	42	7.6	5.94	64	.268	.352	-12	-12	101	81	-2.8	-1	0	-1.1
■ RAY BLEMKER	Blemker, Ray b: 8/9/37, Huntingburg, Ind. BR/TL, 5'11", 190 lbs. Deb: 7/03/60																												
1960	KC-A	0	0	—	1	0	0	0	0	2	3	13.5	1	2	9.0	0	0.0	22.50	17	.375	.545	-4	-4	101	59	0.0	0	0	-0.3
■ CLARENCE BLETHEN	Blethen, Clarence Waldo "Climax" b: 7/11/1893, Dover-Foxcroft, Maine d: 4/11/73, Frederick, Md. BL/TR, 5'11", 165 lbs. Deb: 9/17/23																												
1923	Bos-A	0	0	—	5	0	0	0	0	18	29	14.5	0	7	3.5	2	1.0	7.00	60	.382	.414	-6	-6	106	95	0.0	-1	-1	-0.6
1929	Bro-N	0	0	—	2	0	0	0	0	2	4	18.0	0	3	13.5	0	0.0	9.00	50	.444	.538	-1	-1	96	136	0.0	0	0	0.0
Total	2	0	0	—	7	0	0	0	0	20	33	14.8	0	10	4.5	2	0.9	7.20	59	.388	.430	-7	-7	105	99	0.0	-1	-0	-0.6
■ BOB BLEWETT	Blewett, Robert Lawrence b: 6/28/1877, Fond Du Lac, Wis. d: 3/17/58, Sedro Woolley, Wash. BL/TL, 5'11", 170 lbs. Deb: 6/17/02																												
1902	NY-N	0	2	.000	5	3	2	0	0	28	39	12.5	0	7	2.3	8	2.6	4.82	60	.355	.394	-6	-6	104	95	-0.9	-1	-1	-0.6
■ ELMER BLISS	Bliss, Elmer Ward b: 3/9/1875, Penfield, Pa. d: 3/18/62, Bradford, Pa. BL/TR, 6', 180 lbs. Deb: 03																												
1903	NY-A	1	0	1.000	1	0	0	0	0	5	4	7.2	0	0	0.0	2	3.6	0.00	—	.239	.239	2	2	100	0	0.5	-0	-0	0.1
■ JOE BLONG	Blong, Joseph Myles b: 9/17/1853, St.Louis, Mo. d: 9/22/1892, St.Louis, Mo. BR/TR, Deb: 5/04/1875																												
1875	RS-n	3	11	.214	14																								
1876	StL-N	0	0	—	1	0	0	0	0	4	2	4.5	0	1	2.3	0	0.0	0.00	—	.152	.213	1	1	82	0	0.0	0	0	0.1
1877	StL-N	10	9	.526	25	21	17	0	0	187	203	9.8	0	38	1.8	51	2.5	2.74	106	.285	.321	1	3	103	100	1.5	-1	-1	0.3
Total	2	10	9	.526	26	21	17	0	0	191	205	9.7	0	39	1.8	51	2.4	2.69	107	.282	.319	2	4	103	98	1.5	-1	-1	0.4
■ VIDA BLUE	Blue, Vida Rochelle b: 7/28/49, Mansfield, La. BB/TL, 6', 189 lbs. Deb: 7/20/69																												
1969	Oak-A	1	1	.500	12	4	0	0	1	42	49	10.5	13	18	3.9	24	5.1	6.64	50	.290	.351	-14	-16	91	96	0.0	-0	-1	-1.5
1970	Oak-A	2	0	1.000	6	6	2	2	0	39	20	4.6	0	12	2.8	35	8.1	2.08	171	.152	.224	7	6	96	25	1.0	2	0	0.9
1971	Oak-A	24	8	.750	39	39	24	**8**	0	312	209	**6.0**	19	88	2.5	301	**8.7**	**1.82**	**189**	**.189**	**.249**	57	**56**	99	90	6.1	-2	-4	5.7
1972	Oak-A	6	10	.375	25	23	5	4	0	151	117	7.0	11	48	2.9	111	6.6	2.80	104	.215	.274	5	2	95	86	-3.1	-2	-2	-0.2
1973	Oak-A	20	9	.690	37	37	13	4	0	264	214	7.3	26	105	3.6	158	5.4	3.27	100	.224	.298	16	-0	86	94	4.4	0	-2	-0.2
1974	Oak-A	17	15	.531	40	40	12	1	0	282	246	7.9	17	98	3.1	174	5.6	3.26	110	.236	.298	12	10	99	88	-0.8	0	-6	0.4
1975	Oak-A	22	11	.667	39	38	13	2	1	278	243	7.9	21	99	3.2	189	6.1	3.01	115	.236	.301	24	14	91	102	3.1	0	-2	1.2
1976	Oak-A	18	13	.581	37	37	20	6	0	298	268	8.1	9	63	1.9	166	5.0	2.36	147	.239	.276	**39**	37	98	100	1.6	0	-3	3.8
1977	Oak-A	14	19	.424	38	38	16	1	0	280	284	9.1	23	86	2.8	157	5.0	3.83	103	.264	.313	8	3	97	95	1.1	0	-1	0.1
1978	SF-N	18	10	.643	35	35	9	4	0	258	233	8.1	12	70	2.4	171	6.0	2.79	117	.246	.291	23	14	91	103	3.4	2	-2	1.4
1979	SF-N	14	14	.500	34	34	10	0	0	237	246	9.3	23	111	4.2	138	5.2	5.01	70	.272	.344	-33	-40	93	88	1.8	0	2	-3.7
1980	SF-N	14	10	.583	31	31	10	3	0	224	202	8.1	14	61	2.5	129	5.2	2.97	117	.242	.288	16	13	96	97	3.0	-4	2	1.1
1981	SF-N	8	6	.571	18	18	1	0	0	125	97	7.0	7	54	3.9	63	4.5	2.45	150	.217	.296	15	17	105	113	1.1	1	2	2.4
1982	KC-A	13	12	.520	31	31	6	2	0	181	163	8.1	20	80	4.0	103	5.1	3.78	107	.238	.314	6	6	100	96	-0.8	0	-0	0.5
1983	KC-A	0	5	.000	19	14	1	0	0	85	96	10.2	12	35	3.7	53	5.6	6.04	69	.286	.348	-19	-18	102	85	-2.4	0	-0	-1.6
1985	SF-N	8	8	.500	33	20	1	0	0	131	115	7.9	17	80	5.5	103	7.1	4.47	76	.240	.341	-13	-15	95	98	1.7	1	0	-1.4

YEAR	TM/L	W	L	PCT	G	GS	CG	SHO	SV	IP	H	H/G	HR	BB	BB/G	SO	SO/G	ERA	/A	OAVG	OOBP	PR	/A	PF	CPI	WAT	PB	PD	TPI
1986	SF-N	10	10	.500	28	28	0	0	0	157	137	7.9	19	77	4.4	100	5.7	3.27	108	.239	.323	8	5	95	120	-0.2	1	-1	0.5
Total	17	209	161	.565	502	473	143	37	2	3344	2939	7.9	263	1185	3.2	2175	5.9	3.26	108	.237	.300	155	92	95	96	21.0	-1	-16	9.4

■ JIM BLUEJACKET Bluejacket, James (born James Smith) b: 7/8/1887, Adair, Okla. d: 3/26/47, Pekin, Ill. BR/TR, 6'2.5", 200 lbs. Deb: 8/06/14

YEAR	TM/L	W	L	PCT	G	GS	CG	SHO	SV	IP	H	H/G	HR	BB	BB/G	SO	SO/G	ERA	/A	OAVG	OOBP	PR	/A	PF	CPI	WAT	PB	PD	TPI
1914	Bro-F	4	5	.444	17	7	3	1	1	67	77	10.3	2	19	2.6	29	3.9	3.76	86	.302	.350	-4	-4	101	110	-0.4	-0	0	-0.3
1915	Bro-F	10	11	.476	24	21	10	2	0	163	155	8.6	2	75	4.1	48	2.7	3.15	95	.258	.340	-2	-3	98	108	0.4	-3	-2	-0.8
1916	Cin-N	0	1	.000	3	2	0	0	0	7	12	15.4	0	3	3.9	1	1.3	7.71	34	.400	.455	-4	-4	101	94	-0.4	-0	-0	-0.4
Total	3	14	17	.452	44	30	13	3	1	237	244	9.3	4	97	3.7	78	3.0	3.46	88	.275	.347	-10	-11	99	108	-0.4	-4	-2	-1.5

■ CLINT BLUME Blume, Clinton Willis b: 10/17/1898, Brooklyn, N.Y. d: 6/12/73, Islip, L.I., N.Y. BR/TR, 5'11", 175 lbs. Deb: 9/30/22

YEAR	TM/L	W	L	PCT	G	GS	CG	SHO	SV	IP	H	H/G	HR	BB	BB/G	SO	SO/G	ERA	/A	OAVG	OOBP	PR	/A	PF	CPI	WAT	PB	PD	TPI
1922	NY-N	1	0	1.000	1	1	1	0	0	9	7	7.0	0	1	1.0	2	2.0	1.00	412	.212	.229	3	3	100	97	0.5	1	-1	0.4
1923	NY-N	2	0	1.000	12	1	0	0	0	24	22	8.3	0	20	7.5	2	0.8	3.75	105	.265	.400	1	1	99	129	1.0	-0	-0	0.0
Total	2	3	0	1.000	13	2	1	0	0	33	29	7.9	0	21	5.7	4	1.1	3.00	133	.250	.359	4	4	99	120	1.5	1	-1	0.4

■ BERT BLYLEVEN Blyleven, Rik Aalbert b: 4/6/51, Zeist, Holland BR/TR, 6'3", 200 lbs. Deb: 6/05/70

YEAR	TM/L	W	L	PCT	G	GS	CG	SHO	SV	IP	H	H/G	HR	BB	BB/G	SO	SO/G	ERA	/A	OAVG	OOBP	PR	/A	PF	CPI	WAT	PB	PD	TPI
1970	Min-A	10	9	.526	27	25	5	1	0	164	143	7.8	17	47	2.6	135	7.4	3.18	113	.232	.284	10	7	97	93	-1.3	-1	-2	0.5
1971	Min-A	16	15	.516	38	38	17	5	0	278	267	8.6	21	59	1.9	224	7.3	2.82	128	.255	.294	20	25	104	111	1.9	-3	-0	2.4
1972	Min-A	17	17	.500	39	38	11	3	0	287	247	7.7	22	69	2.2	228	7.1	2.73	121	.233	.282	11	18	107	99	0.0	-1	1	2.2
1973	Min-A	20	17	.541	40	40	25	**9**	0	325	296	8.2	16	67	1.9	258	7.1	2.52	156	.242	.282	**47**	51	103	103	1.9	0	-2	5.5
1974	Min-A	17	17	.500	37	37	19	3	0	281	244	7.8	14	77	2.5	249	8.0	2.66	138	.233	.287	30	31	101	97	-0.2	0	0	3.4
1975	Min-A	15	10	.600	35	35	20	3	0	276	219	7.1	24	84	2.7	233	7.6	3.00	135	.219	.278	24	33	107	87	3.3	0	3	3.8
1976	Min-A	4	5	.444	12	12	4	0	0	95	101	9.6	3	35	3.3	75	7.1	3.13	110	.283	.345	4	3	98	131	-0.6	0	0	0.4
	Tex-A	9	11	.450	24	24	14	6	0	202	182	8.1	11	46	2.0	144	6.4	2.76	131	.242	.288	17	19	103	102	-0.4	0	2	2.3
	Yr	13	16	.448	36	36	18	6	0	297	283	8.6	14	81	2.5	219	6.6	2.88	124	.254	.304	21	22	101	102	-1.0	0	2	2.7
1977	Tex-A	14	12	.538	30	30	15	5	0	235	181	6.9	20	69	2.6	182	7.0	2.72	**155**	.214	.275	35	**39**	104	93	-1.0	0	0	**4.2**
1978	Pit-N	14	10	.583	34	34	11	4	0	244	217	8.0	17	66	2.4	182	6.7	3.02	124	.235	.286	15	20	105	92	1.1	-3	1	2.0
1979	Pit-N	12	5	.706	37	37	4	0	0	237	238	9.0	21	92	3.5	172	6.5	3.61	108	.265	.330	4	7	104	112	2.4	-3	-2	0.3
1980	Pit-N	8	13	.381	34	32	5	2	0	217	219	9.1	20	59	2.4	168	7.0	3.82	97	.262	.307	-5	-2	103	94	-2.9	-4	-0	-0.6
1981	Cle-A	11	7	.611	20	20	9	1	0	159	145	8.2	9	40	2.3	107	6.1	2.89	119	.245	.295	14	9	93	102	2.2	0	-1	0.8
1982	Cle-A	2	2	.500	4	4	0	0	0	20	16	7.2	2	11	4.9	19	8.5	4.95	83	.211	.303	-2	-2	101	62	0.1	0	0	-0.1
1983	Cle-A	7	10	.412	24	24	5	0	0	156	160	9.2	8	44	2.5	123	7.1	3.92	110	.267	.324	3	7	106	95	-0.3	0	1	0.8
1984	Cle-A	19	7	.731	33	32	12	4	0	245	204	7.5	19	74	2.7	170	6.2	2.87	**148**	.224	.283	31	**37**	106	94	**7.0**	0	0	**4.0**
1985	Cle-A	9	11	.450	23	23	15	4	0	180	163	8.1	14	49	2.5	129	6.4	3.25	122	.240	.295	18	14	95	96	1.4	0	-1	1.3
	Min-A	8	5	.615	14	14	9	1	0	114	101	8.0	9	26	2.1	77	6.1	3.00	144	.237	.280	15	17	104	96	1.8	0	-0	1.7
	Yr	17	16	.515	37	37	**24**	**5**	0	**294**	264	8.1	23	75	2.3	**206**	6.3	3.15	130	.236	.283	33	31	99	96	3.2	0	-1	3.0
1986	Min-A	17	14	.548	36	36	16	3	0	**272**	262	8.7	50	58	1.9	215	7.1	4.00	114	.250	.293	6	17	109	98	3.6	0	-1	1.6
1987	Min-A	15	12	.556	37	37	8	1	0	267	249	8.4	46	101	3.4	196	6.6	4.01	107	.249	.320	14	8	96	109	1.0	0	1	0.9
1988	Min-A	10	17	.370	33	33	7	0	0	207	240	10.4	21	51	2.2	145	6.3	5.43	77	.294	.343	-34	-29	105	88	-5.1	0	-1	-2.8
Total	19	254	226	.529	611	605	231	55	0	4461	4094	8.3	384	1224	2.5	3431	6.9	3.25	121	.244	.297	276	332	103	99	15.9	-14	1	34.6

■ MIKE BLYZKA Blyzka, Michael John b: 12/25/28, Hamtramck, Mich. BR/TR, 5'11.5", 190 lbs. Deb: 4/21/53

YEAR	TM/L	W	L	PCT	G	GS	CG	SHO	SV	IP	H	H/G	HR	BB	BB/G	SO	SO/G	ERA	/A	OAVG	OOBP	PR	/A	PF	CPI	WAT	PB	PD	TPI
1953	StL-A	2	6	.250	33	9	2	0	0	94	110	10.5	6	56	5.4	23	2.2	6.41	69	.292	.377	-25	-21	111	80	-1.1	-3	-1	-2.3
1954	Bal-A	1	5	.167	37	0	0	0	1	86	83	8.7	2	51	5.3	35	3.7	4.71	78	.254	.347	-9	-10	99	78	-1.5	-1	0	-1.0
Total	2	3	11	.214	70	9	2	0	1	180	193	9.6	8	107	5.3	58	2.9	5.60	72	.274	.363	-35	-31	105	79	-2.6	-4	-0	-3.3

■ CHARLIE BOARDMAN Boardman, Charles Louis b: 4/27/1893, Seneca Falls, N.Y. d: 8/10/68, Sacramento, Cal. BL/TL, 6'2.5", 194 lbs. Deb: 9/26/13

YEAR	TM/L	W	L	PCT	G	GS	CG	SHO	SV	IP	H	H/G	HR	BB	BB/G	SO	SO/G	ERA	/A	OAVG	OOBP	PR	/A	PF	CPI	WAT	PB	PD	TPI
1913	Phi-A	0	2	.000	2	2	1	0	0	9	10	10.0	0	6	6.0	4	4.0	2.00	135	.294	.400	1	1	93	231	-0.9	-0	-0	0.0
1914	Phi-A	0	0	—	2	0	0	0	0	7	10	12.9	0	4	5.1	2	2.6	5.14	49	.357	.438	-2	-2	93	119	0.0	-0	0	-0.1
1915	StL-N	1	0	1.000	3	1	1	0	0	19	12	5.7	0	15	7.1	7	3.3	2.84	97	.188	.333	-0	-0	101	89	0.5	0	-0	0.0
Total	3	1	2	.333	7	3	2	0	0	35	32	8.2	0	25	6.4	13	3.3	3.09	88	.254	.373	-1	-1	97	132	-0.4	-0	-1	-0.1

■ RANDY BOCKUS Bockus, Randy Walter b: 10/5/60, Canton, Ohio BL/TR, 6'2", 190 lbs. Deb: 9/10/86

YEAR	TM/L	W	L	PCT	G	GS	CG	SHO	SV	IP	H	H/G	HR	BB	BB/G	SO	SO/G	ERA	/A	OAVG	OOBP	PR	/A	PF	CPI	WAT	PB	PD	TPI
1986	SF-N	0	0	—	5	0	0	0	0	7	7	9.0	1	6	7.7	4	5.1	2.57	137	.241	.361	1	1	95	191	0.0	-0	1	0.1
1987	SF-N	1	0	1.000	12	0	0	0	0	17	17	9.0	2	4	2.1	9	4.8	3.71	104	.266	.309	1	0	95	105	0.5	-0	0	0.0
1988	SF-N	1	1	.500	20	0	0	0	0	32	35	9.8	2	13	3.7	18	5.1	4.78	67	.297	.355	-5	-6	93	102	0.0	0	0	-0.5
Total	3	2	1	.667	37	0	0	0	0	56	59	9.5	5	23	3.7	31	5.0	4.18	83	.280	.343	-3	-5	94	114	0.5	-0	1	-0.4

■ MIKE BODDICKER Boddicker, Michael James b: 8/23/57, Cedar Rapids, Iowa BR/TR, 5'11", 172 lbs. Deb: 10/04/80

YEAR	TM/L	W	L	PCT	G	GS	CG	SHO	SV	IP	H	H/G	HR	BB	BB/G	SO	SO/G	ERA	/A	OAVG	OOBP	PR	/A	PF	CPI	WAT	PB	PD	TPI
1980	Bal-A	0	1	.000	1	1	0	0	0	7	6	7.7	1	5	6.4	4	5.1	6.43	62	.207	.324	-2	-2	99	52	-0.4	0	-0	-0.1
1981	Bal-A	0	0	—	2	0	0	0	0	6	6	9.0	1	2	3.0	2	3.0	4.50	81	.261	.320	-1	-1	99	96	0.0	0	-0	0.0
1982	Bal-A	1	0	1.000	7	0	0	0	0	26	25	8.7	2	12	4.2	20	6.9	3.46	117	.258	.336	2	2	99	115	0.5	0	0	0.2
1983	Bal-A	16	8	.667	27	26	10	**5**	0	179	141	**7.1**	13	52	2.6	120	6.0	2.77	146	**.216**	.271	26	25	99	88	2.1	0	3	3.0
1984	Bal-A	**20**	11	.645	34	34	16	4	0	261	218	7.5	23	81	2.8	128	4.4	**2.79**	135	.228	.289	**35**	28	94	105	4.6	0	6	3.6
1985	Bal-A	12	17	.414	32	32	9	2	0	203	227	10.1	13	89	3.9	135	6.0	4.08	100	.286	.357	2	-0	98	115	-3.2	0	6	0.5
1986	Bal-A	14	12	.538	33	33	7	0	0	218	214	8.8	30	74	3.1	175	7.2	4.71	88	.255	.320	-13	-13	99	88	2.4	0	3	-0.9
1987	Bal-A	10	12	.455	33	33	7	2	0	226	212	8.4	29	78	3.1	152	6.1	4.18	106	.248	.313	7	7	99	94	0.9	0	4	0.9
1988	Bal-A	6	12	.333	21	21	4	0	0	147	149	9.1	14	51	3.1	100	6.1	3.86	100	.265	.332	2	0	97	109	0.0	0	-1	0.0
	Bos-A	7	3	.700	15	14	1	1	0	89	85	8.6	3	26	2.6	56	5.7	2.63	163	.257	.312	13	16	108	126	1.7	0	2	2.0
	Yr	13	15	.464	36	35	5	1	0	236	234	8.9	17	77	2.9	156	5.9	3.39	119	.256	.314	15	17	101	126	1.7	0	1	2.0
Total	9	86	76	.531	205	194	54	14	0	1362	1283	8.5	129	470	3.1	892	5.9	3.66	111	.250	.314	72	62	98	101	8.6	0	22	9.2

■ GEORGE BOEHLER Boehler, George Henry b: 1/2/1892, Lawrenceburg, Ind. d: 6/23/58, Lawrenceburg, Ind BR/TR, 6'2", 180 lbs. Deb: 9/13/12

YEAR	TM/L	W	L	PCT	G	GS	CG	SHO	SV	IP	H	H/G	HR	BB	BB/G	SO	SO/G	ERA	/A	OAVG	OOBP	PR	/A	PF	CPI	WAT	PB	PD	TPI
1912	Det-A	0	2	.000	5	4	2	0	0	32	50	14.1	0	14	3.9	15	4.2	6.47	50	.365	.431	-11	-12	96	100	-0.9	-1	1	-0.8
1913	Det-A	0	1	.000	1	1	1	0	0	8	11	12.4	0	6	6.8	2	2.3	6.75	44	.355	.487	-3	-3	101	107	-0.4	1	1	-0.2
1914	Det-A	2	3	.400	18	6	2	0	0	63	54	7.7	1	48	6.9	37	5.3	3.57	78	.242	.394	-6	-5	102	114	-0.5	1	-0	-0.5
1915	Det-A	1	1	.500	8	0	0	0	0	15	19	11.4	0	4	2.4	7	4.2	1.80	171	.328	.381	2	2	105	261	-0.1	2	-0	0.4
1916	Det-A	1	1	.500	5	2	1	0	0	13	12	8.3	0	9	6.2	8	5.5	4.85	60	.261	.404	-3	-3	103	89	0.0	0	1	-0.1
1920	StL-A	0	1	.000	3	1	0	0	0	7	10	12.9	1	4	5.1	2	2.6	7.71	55	.303	.378	-3	-3	111	72	-0.4	0	0	-0.1
1921	StL-A	0	0	—	1	0	0	0	0	1	1	9.0	0	0	0.0	0	0.0	0.00	—	.500	.333	0	0	101	0	0.0	0	0	0.0
1923	Pit-N	1	3	.250	10	3	1	0	0	28	33	10.6	1	26	8.4	12	3.9	6.11	62	.314	.438	-7	-7	95	106	-1.0	1	-0	-0.5
1926	Bro-N	1	0	1.000	10	1	0	0	0	35	42	10.8	1	23	5.9	10	2.6	4.37	88	.302	.395	-2	-2	101	125	0.5	0	-1	-0.1
Total	9	6	12	.333	61	18	7	0	0	202	232	10.3	4	134	6.0	93	4.1	4.72	70	.300	.410	-33	-32	100	120	-2.8	3	1	-1.9

■ JOE BOEHLING Boehling, John Joseph b: 3/20/1891, Richmond, Va. d: 9/8/41, Richmond, Va. BL/TL, 5'11", 168 lbs. Deb: 6/20/12

YEAR	TM/L	W	L	PCT	G	GS	CG	SHO	SV	IP	H	H/G	HR	BB	BB/G	SO	SO/G	ERA	/A	OAVG	OOBP	PR	/A	PF	CPI	WAT	PB	PD	TPI
1912	Was-A	0	0	—	3	0	0	0	0	5	4	7.2	0	6	10.8	2	3.6	7.20	45	.235	.480	-2	-2	97	83	0.0	0	0	-0.1
1913	Was-A	17	7	.708	38	25	18	3	4	235	197	7.5	3	82	3.1	110	4.2	2.14	143	.229	.303	20	24	105	104	4.0	0	2	2.9
1914	Was-A	12	8	.600	27	24	14	2	1	196	180	8.3	3	76	3.5	91	4.2	3.03	90	.258	.339	-6	-6	100	105	1.8	4	2	-0.4
1915	Was-A	14	13	.519	40	32	14	2	0	229	217	8.5	5	119	4.7	108	4.2	3.22	91	.255	.352	-7	-8	99	110	-1.0	0	2	-0.4
1916	Was-A	9	11	.450	27	19	7	2	0	140	134	8.6	1	54	3.5	52	3.3	3.09	92	.260	.333	-4	-4	100	100	-1.0	0	4	0.0
	Cle-A	2	4	.333	12	9	3	0	0	61	63	9.3	0	23	3.4	18	2.7	2.66	106	.281	.353	1	1	99	136	-0.9	1	1	0.3
	Yr	11	15	.423	39	28	10	2	0	201	197	8.8	1	77	3.4	70	3.1	2.96	96	.265	.336	-3	-3	100	136	-1.9	0	4	0.3
1917	Cle-A	1	6	.143	12	7	1	0	0	46	50	9.8	1	16	3.1	11	2.2	4.70	64	.291	.361	-10	-9	113	84	-2.6	-0	-0	-0.8
1920	Cle-A	0	1	.000	3	2	0	0	0	13	16	11.1	0	10	6.9	4	2.8	4.85	78	.333	.448	-2	-2	100	125	-0.4	1	0	0.0
Total	7	55	50	.524	162	118	57	9	5	925	861	8.4	13	386	3.8	396	3.9	2.97	98	.254	.337	-10	-5	102	107	-0.1	7	11	1.5

■ LARRY BOERNER Boerner, Lawrence Hyer b: 1/21/05, Staunton, Va. d: 10/16/69, Staunton, Va. BR/TR, 6'4.5", 175 lbs. Deb: 6/30/32

YEAR	TM/L	W	L	PCT	G	GS	CG	SHO	SV	IP	H	H/G	HR	BB	BB/G	SO	SO/G	ERA	/A	OAVG	OOBP	PR	/A	PF	CPI	WAT	PB	PD	TPI
1932	Bos-A	0	4	.000	21	5	0	0	0	61	71	10.5	2	37	5.5	19	2.8	5.02	91	.302	.391	-4	-3	102	114	-1.9	-3	0	-0.4

■ JOE BOEVER Boever, Joseph Martin b: 10/4/60, Kirkwood, Mo. BR/TR, 6'1", 200 lbs. Deb: 7/19/85

YEAR	TM/L	W	L	PCT	G	GS	CG	SHO	SV	IP	H	H/G	HR	BB	BB/G	SO	SO/G	ERA	/A	OAVG	OOBP	PR	/A	PF	CPI	WAT	PB	PD	TPI
1985	StL-N	0	0	—	13	0	0	0	0	16	17	9.6	3	4	2.3	20	11.3	4.50	75	.270	.304	-2	-2	93	99	0.0	0	-0	-0.2

YEAR	TM/L	W	L	PCT	G	GS	CG	SHO	SV	IP	H	H/G	HR	BB	BB/G	SO	SO/G	ERA	/A	OAVG	OOBP	PR	/A	PF	CPI	WAT	PB	PD	TPI
1986	StL-N	0	1	.000	11	0	0	0	0	22	19	7.8	2	11	4.5	8	3.3	1.64	235	.232	.323	5	5	103	213	-0.4	0	-0	0.6
1987	Atl-N	1	0	1.000	14	0	0	0	0	18	29	14.5	4	12	6.0	18	9.0	7.50	59	.367	.441	-7	-6	109	118	0.5	0	-0	-0.5
1988	Atl-N	0	2	.000	16	0	0	0	1	20	12	5.4	1	1	0.4	7	3.1	1.80	205	.182	.200	4	4	107	66	-0.9	0	0	0.5
Total	4	1	3	.250	54	0	0	0	1	76	77	9.1	10	28	3.3	53	6.3	3.67	105	.266	.326	0	1	104	128	-0.8	0	-1	0.4

■ JOHN BOGART Bogart, John Renzie "Big John" b: 9/21/1900, Bloomsburg, Pa. d: 12/7/86, Clarence, N.Y. BR/TR, 6'2", 195 lbs. Deb: 9/17/20

YEAR	TM/L	W	L	PCT	G	GS	CG	SHO	SV	IP	H	H/G	HR	BB	BB/G	SO	SO/G	ERA	/A	OAVG	OOBP	PR	/A	PF	CPI	WAT	PB	PD	TPI
1920	Det-A	2	1	.667	4	3	0	0	0	24	16	6.0	0	18	6.8	5	1.9	3.00	134	.195	.340	2	3	106	82	0.7	-0	-1	0.2

■ RAY BOGGS Boggs, Raymond Joseph "Lefty" b: 12/12/04, Reamsville, Kan. BL/TL, 6'0.5", 170 lbs. Deb: 9/01/28

YEAR	TM/L	W	L	PCT	G	GS	CG	SHO	SV	IP	H	H/G	HR	BB	BB/G	SO	SO/G	ERA	/A	OAVG	OOBP	PR	/A	PF	CPI	WAT	PB	PD	TPI
1928	Bos-N	0	0	—	4	0	0	0	0	5	2	3.6	0	7	12.6	0	0.0	5.40	75	.167	.522	-1	-1	101	122	0.0	0	0	0.0

■ TOMMY BOGGS Boggs, Thomas Winton b: 10/25/55, Poughkeepsie, N.Y. BR/TR, 6'2", 195 lbs. Deb: 7/19/76

YEAR	TM/L	W	L	PCT	G	GS	CG	SHO	SV	IP	H	H/G	HR	BB	BB/G	SO	SO/G	ERA	/A	OAVG	OOBP	PR	/A	PF	CPI	WAT	PB	PD	TPI
1976	Tex-A	1	7	.125	13	13	3	0	0	90	87	8.7	7	34	3.4	36	3.6	3.50	103	.257	.319	0	1	103	105	-2.9	0	-1	0.1
1977	Tex-A	0	3	.000	6	6	0	0	0	27	40	13.3	1	12	4.0	15	5.0	6.00	70	.351	.408	-6	-5	104	105	-1.4	0	-0	-0.4
1978	Atl-N	2	8	.200	16	12	1	1	0	59	80	12.2	8	26	4.0	21	3.2	6.71	61	.323	.378	-21	-17	114	91	-2.6	0	-2	-1.7
1979	Atl-N	0	2	.000	3	3	0	0	0	13	21	14.5	0	4	2.8	1	0.7	6.23	66	.362	.406	-4	-3	110	98	-0.9	0	0	-0.2
1980	Atl-N	12	9	.571	32	26	4	3	0	192	180	8.4	14	46	2.2	84	3.9	3.42	107	.249	.290	4	5	101	90	1.6	-2	-2	0.1
1981	Atl-N	3	13	.188	25	24	2	0	0	143	140	8.8	11	54	3.4	81	5.1	4.09	85	.265	.325	-10	-10	100	97	-5.0	-1	-0	-1.1
1982	Atl-N	2	2	.500	10	10	0	0	0	46	43	8.4	2	22	4.3	29	5.7	3.33	116	.253	.340	1	3	107	112	-0.1	0	-0	0.3
1983	Atl-N	0	0	—	5	0	0	0	0	6	8	12.0	1	1	1.5	5	7.5	6.00	63	.320	.333	-2	-1	104	91	0.0	0	-0	0.0
1985	Tex-A	0	0	—	4	0	0	0	0	7	13	16.7	3	2	2.6	6	7.7	11.57	39	.382	.417	-6	-5	110	87	0.0	0	0	-0.4
Total	9	20	44	.313	114	94	10	4	0	583	612	9.4	47	201	3.1	278	4.3	4.23	88	.273	.328	-41	-33	103	97	-11.3	-1	-5	-3.3

■ WARREN BOGLE Bogle, Warren Frederick b: 10/19/46, Passaic, N.J. BL/TL, 6'4", 220 lbs. Deb: 7/31/68

YEAR	TM/L	W	L	PCT	G	GS	CG	SHO	SV	IP	H	H/G	HR	BB	BB/G	SO	SO/G	ERA	/A	OAVG	OOBP	PR	/A	PF	CPI	WAT	PB	PD	TPI
1968	Oak-A	0	0	—	16	1	0	0	0	23	26	10.2	3	8	3.1	26	10.2	4.30	68	.283	.330	-3	-4	98	108	0.0	-0	1	-0.3

■ PAT BOHEN Bohen, Leo Ignatius b: 9/30/1891, Oakland, Iowa d: 4/8/42, Napa, Cal. BR/TR, 5'10.5", 155 lbs. Deb: 10/01/13

YEAR	TM/L	W	L	PCT	G	GS	CG	SHO	SV	IP	H	H/G	HR	BB	BB/G	SO	SO/G	ERA	/A	OAVG	OOBP	PR	/A	PF	CPI	WAT	PB	PD	TPI
1913	Phi-A	0	1	.000	1	1	1	0	0	8	3	3.4	0	2	2.3	5	5.6	1.13	241	.115	.179	2	1	93	59	-0.4	-0	0	0.2
1914	Pit-N	0	0	—	1	0	0	0	0	1	2	18.0	0	2	18.0	0	0.0	18.00	14	.500	.714	-2	-2	93	94	0.0	-0	0	-0.1
Total	2	0	1	.000	2	1	1	0	0	9	5	5.0	0	4	4.0	5	5.0	3.00	90	.167	.286	-0	-0	93	62	-0.4	-1	0	0.1

■ CHARLIE BOHN Bohn, Charles b: 1857, Cleveland, Ohio d: 8/1/03, Cleveland, Ohio Deb: 6/20/1882

YEAR	TM/L	W	L	PCT	G	GS	CG	SHO	SV	IP	H	H/G	HR	BB	BB/G	SO	SO/G	ERA	/A	OAVG	OOBP	PR	/A	PF	CPI	WAT	PB	PD	TPI
1882	Lou-a	1	1	.500	2	2	2	0	0	18	21	10.5	0	3	1.5	1	0.5	3.00	80	.297	.325	-1	-1	90	115	0.0	-0	0	0.0

■ JOHN BOHNET Bohnet, John Kelly b: 1/18/61, Pasadena, Cal. BB/TL, 6', 175 lbs. Deb: 5/10/82

YEAR	TM/L	W	L	PCT	G	GS	CG	SHO	SV	IP	H	H/G	HR	BB	BB/G	SO	SO/G	ERA	/A	OAVG	OOBP	PR	/A	PF	CPI	WAT	PB	PD	TPI
1982	Cle-A	0	0	—	3	3	0	0	0	12	11	8.3	4	7	5.3	4	3.0	6.75	61	.250	.358	-4	-4	101	94	0.0	0	0	-0.2

■ DAN BOITANO Boitano, Danny Jon b: 3/22/53, Sacramento, Cal. BR/TR, 6', 185 lbs. Deb: 10/01/78

YEAR	TM/L	W	L	PCT	G	GS	CG	SHO	SV	IP	H	H/G	HR	BB	BB/G	SO	SO/G	ERA	/A	OAVG	OOBP	PR	/A	PF	CPI	WAT	PB	PD	TPI
1978	Phi-N	0	0	—	1	0	0	0	0	1	0	0.0	0	1	9.0	0	0.0	0.00	—	.000	.250	0	0	104	0	0.0	0	0	0.0
1979	Mil-A	0	0	—	5	0	0	0	0	6	6	9.0	1	3	4.5	5	7.5	1.50	280	.273	.346	2	2	99	346	0.0	0	0	0.2
1980	Mil-A	0	1	.000	11	0	0	0	0	18	26	13.0	7	6	3.0	11	5.5	8.00	47	.342	.388	-8	-8	93	106	-0.4	0	0	-0.7
1981	NY-N	2	1	.667	15	0	0	0	0	16	21	11.8	2	5	2.8	8	4.5	5.63	64	.309	.368	-4	-4	103	99	0.7	0	0	-0.3
1982	Tex-A	0	0	—	19	0	0	0	0	30	33	9.9	5	13	3.9	28	8.4	5.40	71	.280	.353	-4	-5	94	98	0.0	0	-0	-0.4
Total	5	2	2	.500	51	0	0	0	0	71	86	10.9	15	28	3.5	52	6.6	5.70	67	.300	.364	-14	-15	96	120	0.3	0	-0	-1.2

■ DICK BOKELMANN Bokelmann, Richard Werner b: 10/26/26, Arlington Heights, Ill. BR/TR, 6'0.5", 180 lbs. Deb: 8/03/51

YEAR	TM/L	W	L	PCT	G	GS	CG	SHO	SV	IP	H	H/G	HR	BB	BB/G	SO	SO/G	ERA	/A	OAVG	OOBP	PR	/A	PF	CPI	WAT	PB	PD	TPI
1951	StL-N	3	3	.500	20	1	0	0	3	52	49	8.5	2	31	5.4	22	3.8	3.81	105	.245	.345	1	1	101	97	-0.1	-2	-1	-0.1
1952	StL-N	0	1	.000	11	0	0	0	0	13	20	13.8	0	7	4.8	5	3.5	9.00	40	.357	.415	-8	-8	97	72	-0.4	0	1	-0.6
1953	StL-N	0	0	—	3	0	0	0	0	3	4	12.0	0	0	0.0	0	0.0	6.00	72	.308	.308	-1	-1	101	57	0.0	0	0	0.0
Total	3	3	4	.429	34	1	0	0	3	68	73	9.7	2	38	5.0	27	3.6	4.90	80	.271	.358	-7	-7	100	91	-0.5	-2	0	-0.7

■ JOE BOKINA Bokina, Joseph b: 4/4/10, Northampton, Mass. BR/TR, 6', 184 lbs. Deb: 4/16/36

YEAR	TM/L	W	L	PCT	G	GS	CG	SHO	SV	IP	H	H/G	HR	BB	BB/G	SO	SO/G	ERA	/A	OAVG	OOBP	PR	/A	PF	CPI	WAT	PB	PD	TPI
1936	Was-A	0	2	.000	5	1	0	0	0	8	15	16.9	0	6	6.8	5	5.6	9.00	54	.395	.477	-4	-4	96	98	-0.9	-0	0	-0.2

■ BERNIE BOLAND Boland, Bernard Anthony b: 1/21/1892, Rochester, N.Y. d: 9/12/73, Detroit, Mich. BR/TR, 5'8.5", 168 lbs. Deb: 4/14/15

YEAR	TM/L	W	L	PCT	G	GS	CG	SHO	SV	IP	H	H/G	HR	BB	BB/G	SO	SO/G	ERA	/A	OAVG	OOBP	PR	/A	PF	CPI	WAT	PB	PD	TPI
1915	Det-A	13	7	.650	45	18	8	1	2	203	167	7.4	2	75	3.3	72	3.2	3.10	99	.230	.307	-4	-0	105	78	0.0	-1	0	0.0
1916	Det-A	10	3	.769	46	9	5	1	3	130	111	7.7	1	73	5.1	59	4.1	3.95	74	.240	.349	-16	-15	103	80	3.2	2	-3	-1.6
1917	Det-A	16	11	.593	43	28	13	3	6	238	192	7.3	0	95	3.6	89	3.4	2.68	96	.226	.308	-1	-3	96	81	2.7	-5	0	-0.8
1918	Det-A	14	10	.583	29	25	14	4	0	204	176	7.8	1	67	3.0	63	2.8	2.65	103	.236	.299	3	2	99	84	3.6	-0	-1	0.1
1919	Det-A	14	16	.467	35	30	18	1	1	243	222	8.2	7	80	3.0	71	2.6	3.04	98	.253	.318	5	-2	92	93	-3.2	-2	-2	-0.6
1920	Det-A	0	2	.000	4	3	1	0	0	17	23	12.2	0	14	7.4	4	2.1	7.94	51	.348	.476	-8	-7	106	88	-0.9	-0	0	-0.6
1921	StL-A	1	4	.200	7	6	0	0	0	27	34	11.3	2	28	9.3	6	2.0	9.33	46	.309	.438	-15	-15	101	74	-1.5	-1	0	-1.3
Total	7	68	53	.562	209	119	59	10	12	1062	925	7.8	13	432	3.7	364	3.1	3.25	89	.241	.321	-35	-40	99	84	3.9	-8	-5	-4.8

■ BILL BOLDEN Bolden, William Horace "Big Bill" b: 5/9/1893, Dandridge, Tenn. d: 12/8/66, Jefferson City, Tenn. BR/TR, 6'4", 200 lbs. Deb: 6/27/19

YEAR	TM/L	W	L	PCT	G	GS	CG	SHO	SV	IP	H	H/G	HR	BB	BB/G	SO	SO/G	ERA	/A	OAVG	OOBP	PR	/A	PF	CPI	WAT	PB	PD	TPI
1919	StL-N	0	1	.000	3	1	0	0	0	12	17	12.8	0	4	3.0	4	3.0	5.25	54	.340	.393	-3	-3	97	103	-0.4	0	0	-0.2

■ STEW BOLEN Bolen, Stewart O'Neal b: 10/12/02, Jackson, Ala. d: 8/30/69, Mobile, Ala. BL/TL, 5'11", 180 lbs. Deb: 4/15/26

YEAR	TM/L	W	L	PCT	G	GS	CG	SHO	SV	IP	H	H/G	HR	BB	BB/G	SO	SO/G	ERA	/A	OAVG	OOBP	PR	/A	PF	CPI	WAT	PB	PD	TPI
1926	StL-A	0	0	—	5	0	0	0	0	15	21	12.6	2	6	3.6	7	4.2	6.00	69	.356	.409	-3	-3	103	115	0.0	1	-0	-0.1
1927	StL-A	0	1	.000	3	1	1	0	0	10	14	12.6	0	5	4.5	7	6.3	8.10	56	.368	.432	-4	-4	109	81	-0.4	0	0	-0.2
1931	Phi-N	3	12	.200	28	16	2	0	0	99	117	10.6	5	63	5.7	55	5.0	6.36	66	.297	.391	-27	-24	109	85	-4.1	-1	0	-2.2
1932	Phi-N	0	0	—	5	0	0	0	0	16	18	10.1	0	10	5.6	3	1.7	2.81	154	.281	.395	2	3	111	171	0.0	-0	-0	0.2
Total	4	3	13	.188	41	17	3	0	0	140	170	10.9	7	84	5.4	72	4.6	6.04	70	.306	.396	-33	-28	109	98	-4.5	-0	0	-2.3

■ BOBBY BOLIN Bolin, Bobby Donald b: 1/29/39, Hickory Grove, S.C. BR/TR, 6'4", 185 lbs. Deb: 4/18/61

YEAR	TM/L	W	L	PCT	G	GS	CG	SHO	SV	IP	H	H/G	HR	BB	BB/G	SO	SO/G	ERA	/A	OAVG	OOBP	PR	/A	PF	CPI	WAT	PB	PD	TPI
1961	SF-N	2	2	.500	37	1	0	0	5	48	37	6.9	6	37	6.9	48	9.0	3.19	122	.210	.344	4	4	96	128	-0.1	0	-1	0.3
1962	SF-N	7	3	.700	41	5	2	0	5	92	84	8.2	10	35	3.4	74	7.2	3.62	107	.243	.315	3	3	99	102	1.1	2	-1	0.3
1963	SF-N	10	6	.625	47	12	2	0	7	137	128	8.4	13	57	3.7	134	8.8	3.28	94	.242	.318	0	-3	94	110	1.6	2	-2	-0.3
1964	SF-N	6	9	.400	38	23	5	3	1	175	143	7.4	16	77	4.0	146	7.5	3.24	108	.220	.310	6	5	99	100	-2.2	0	-1	0.5
1965	SF-N	14	6	.700	45	13	2	0	2	163	125	6.9	17	56	3.1	135	7.5	2.76	140	.214	.282	14	20	109	105	3.0	1	-2	2.1
1966	SF-N	11	10	.524	36	34	10	4	1	224	174	7.0	25	70	2.8	143	5.7	2.89	121	.211	.276	18	15	97	93	-1.0	4	-2	1.8
1967	SF-N	6	8	.429	37	15	0	0	0	120	120	9.0	16	50	3.8	69	5.2	4.88	69	.258	.329	-20	-20	99	88	-1.7	2	-1	-1.9
1968	SF-N	10	5	.667	34	19	6	3	0	177	128	6.5	9	46	2.3	126	6.4	1.98	145	.200	.256	20	18	96	90	2.2	-1	-1	1.9
1969	SF-N	7	7	.500	30	22	2	0	0	146	149	9.2	17	49	3.0	102	6.3	4.44	81	.260	.321	-14	-14	100	90	-0.7	3	-1	-1.1
1970	Mil-A	5	11	.313	32	20	3	0	1	132	131	8.9	20	67	4.6	81	5.5	4.91	76	.256	.339	-17	-18	100	93	-1.8	2	-1	-1.6
	Bos-A	2	0	1.000	6	0	0	0	2	8	2	2.3	0	5	5.6	8	9.0	0.00	—	.080	.250	3	4	110	0	1.0	-0	0	0.4
	Yr	7	11	.389	38	20	3	0	3	140	133	8.6	20	72	4.6	89	5.7	4.63	81	.243	.329	-14	-14	100	0	-0.8	2	-1	-1.2
1971	Bos-A	5	3	.625	52	0	0	0	6	70	74	9.5	7	24	3.1	51	6.6	4.24	86	.273	.322	-6	-5	105	96	0.9	0	-1	-0.5
1972	Bos-A	0	1	.000	21	0	0	0	5	31	24	7.0	3	11	3.2	27	7.8	2.90	111	.209	.281	1	1	105	87	-0.4	-0	-0	0.1
1973	Bos-A	3	4	.429	39	0	0	0	15	53	45	7.6	5	13	2.2	31	5.3	2.72	147	.232	.278	7	8	105	103	-0.7	0	1	0.9
Total	13	88	75	.540	495	164	32	10	50	1576	1364	7.8	164	597	3.4	1175	6.7	3.40	103	.231	.303	18	17	100	97	1.2	15	-11	2.9

■ GREG BOLLO Bollo, Gregory Gene b: 11/16/43, Detroit, Mich. BR/TR, 6'4", 183 lbs. Deb: 5/09/65

YEAR	TM/L	W	L	PCT	G	GS	CG	SHO	SV	IP	H	H/G	HR	BB	BB/G	SO	SO/G	ERA	/A	OAVG	OOBP	PR	/A	PF	CPI	WAT	PB	PD	TPI
1965	Chi-A	0	0	—	15	0	0	0	0	23	12	4.7	5	9	3.5	16	6.3	3.52	89	.152	.256	-0	-1	91	74	0.0	0	0	0.0
1966	Chi-A	0	1	.000	3	1	0	0	0	7	7	9.0	0	3	3.9	4	5.1	2.57	124	.269	.367	1	0	93	158	-0.4	-0	0	0.0
Total	2	0	1	.000	18	1	0	0	0	30	19	5.7	5	12	3.6	20	6.0	3.30	95	.181	.283	1	-1	91	94	-0.4	-0	0	0.0

■ TOM BOLTON Bolton, Thomas Edward b: 5/6/62, Nashville, Tenn. BL/TL, 6'2", 172 lbs. Deb: 5/17/87

YEAR	TM/L	W	L	PCT	G	GS	CG	SHO	SV	IP	H	H/G	HR	BB	BB/G	SO	SO/G	ERA	/A	OAVG	OOBP	PR	/A	PF	CPI	WAT	PB	PD	TPI
1987	Bos-A	1	0	1.000	29	0	0	0	0	62	83	12.0	5	27	3.9	49	7.1	4.35	102	.329	.390	1	0	99	139	0.5	0	0	0.1
1988	Bos-A	1	3	.250	28	0	0	0	1	30	35	10.5	1	14	4.2	21	6.3	4.80	89	.285	.350	-3	-2	108	90	-1.0	0	1	0.0
Total	2	2	3	.400	57	0	0	0	1	92	118	11.5	6	41	4.0	70	6.8	4.50	98	.315	.377	-2	-1	102	123	-0.5	0	1	0.1

YEAR	TM/L	W	L	PCT	G	GS	CG	SHO	SV	IP	H	H/G	HR	BB	BB/G	SO	SO/G	ERA	/A	OAVG	OOBP	PR	/A	PF	CPI	WAT	PB	PD	TPI
■ MARK BOMBACK	Bomback, Mark Vincent b: 4/14/53, Portsmouth, Va. BR/TR, 5'11", 170 lbs. Deb: 9/12/78																												
1978	Mil-A	0	0	—	2	1	0	0	0	2	5	22.5	1	1	4.5	1	4.5	13.50	29	.500	.545	-2	-2	104	114	0.0	0	0	-0.1
1980	NY-N	10	8	.556	36	25	2	1	0	163	191	10.5	17	49	2.7	68	3.8	4.09	86	.297	.344	-9	-11	97	117	2.4	3	2	-0.5
1981	Tor-A	5	5	.500	20	11	0	0	0	90	84	8.4	6	35	3.5	33	3.3	3.90	106	.251	.318	-2	2	113	90	1.2	0	0	0.3
1982	Tor-A	1	5	.167	16	8	0	0	0	60	87	13.1	10	25	3.8	22	3.3	6.00	74	.343	.401	-13	-10	109	118	-1.9	0	0	-0.9
Total	4	16	18	.471	74	45	2	1	0	315	367	10.5	34	110	3.1	124	3.5	4.46	87	.295	.350	-26	-21	104	109	1.7	3	3	-1.2
■ TOMMY BOND	Bond, Thomas Henry b: 4/2/1856, Granard, Ireland d: 1/24/41, Boston, Mass. BR/TR, 5'7.5", 160 lbs. Deb: 5/05/1874 M																												
1874	Atl-n	22	32	.407	55																								
1875	Har-n	19	16	.543	39																								
1876	Har-N	31	13	.705	45	45	45	6	0	408	355	7.8	2	13	0.3	88	**1.9**	1.68	142	.238	.245	29	32	103	57	2.5	1	6	3.6
1877	Bos-N	**40**	17	**.702**	58	58	58	**6**	0	521	530	**9.2**	5	36	**0.6**	**170**	2.9	**2.11**	135	**.272**	**.285**	**41**	43	101	100	3.0	-4	4	4.0
1878	Bos-N	**40**	19	**.678**	**59**	59	**57**	**9**	0	**533**	571	9.6	5	33	0.6	**182**	3.1	2.06	117	.284	.296	14	21	105	108	-9.4	-5	3	1.9
1879	Bos-N	43	19	.694	64	64	59	**12**	0	555	543	8.8	8	24	**0.4**	155	2.5	**1.96**	**129**	.262	**.270**	33	35	101	101	12.0	1	8	4.2
1880	Bos-N	26	29	.473	63	57	49	3	0	493	559	10.2	1	45	0.8	118	2.2	2.67	83	.295	.311	-16	-25	93	111	-0.5	-1	10	-1.8
1881	Bos-N	0	3	.000	3	3	2	0	0	25	40	14.4	3	2	0.7	2	0.7	4.32	60	.374	.386	-4	-5	93	140	-1.4	-0	0	-0.4
1882	Wor-N	0	1	.000	2	2	0	0	0	12	12	9.0	0	7	5.3	2	1.5	4.50	69	.268	.367	-2	-2	107	83	-0.4	-1	0	-0.1
1884	Bos-U	13	9	.591	23	21	19	0	0	189	185	8.8	3	14	0.7	128	6.1	3.00	98	.261	.276	0	-1	98	88	1.7	4	0	0.4
	Ind-a	0	5	.000	5	5	5	0	0	43	62	13.0	5	4	0.8	15	3.1	5.65	58	.346	.361	-12	-11	100	107	-2.4	-1	0	-0.9
Total	2 n	41	48	.461	94																								
Total	8	193	115	.627	322	314	294	36	0	2779	2857	9.3	32	178	0.6	860	2.8	2.25	112	.273	.285	83	86	100	97	5.1	-6	30	10.9
■ JULIO BONETTI	Bonetti, Julio Giacomo b: 7/14/11, Genoa, Italy d: 6/17/52, Belmont, Cal. BR/TR, 6', 180 lbs. Deb: 4/22/37																												
1937	StL-A	4	11	.267	28	16	7	0	1	143	190	12.0	13	60	3.8	43	2.7	5.85	82	.321	.380	-20	-17	103	100	-0.8	-2	2	-1.4
1938	StL-A	2	3	.400	17	0	0	0	0	28	41	13.2	1	13	4.2	7	2.3	6.43	77	.350	.412	-5	-5	103	102	0.2	-1	0	-0.4
1940	Chi-N	0	0	—	1	0	0	0	0	1	3	27.0	0	4	36.0	0	0.0	27.00	14	.429	.636	-3	-3	99	77	0.0	0	0	-0.1
Total	3	6	14	.300	46	16	7	0	1	172	234	12.2	14	77	4.0	50	2.6	6.07	79	.327	.389	-27	-24	103	100	-0.6	-3	2	-1.9
■ HANK BONEY	Boney, Henry Tate "Haney" b: 10/28/03, Wallace, N.C. BR/TR, 5'11", 176 lbs. Deb: 6/28/27																												
1927	NY-N	0	0	—	3	0	0	0	0	4	4	9.0	0	2	4.5	0	0.0	2.25	171	.267	.353	1	1	98	163	0.0	0	-0	0.0
■ TINY BONHAM	Bonham, Ernest Edward b: 8/16/13, Ione, Cal. d: 9/15/49, Pittsburgh, Pa. BR/TR, 6'2", 215 lbs. Deb: 8/08/40																												
1940	NY-A	9	3	.750	12	12	10	3	0	99	83	7.5	4	13	1.2	37	3.4	1.91	220	.224	.249	27	25	96	104	2.6	-0	-2	2.4
1941	NY-A	9	6	.600	23	14	7	1	2	127	118	8.4	12	31	2.2	43	3.0	2.98	132	.246	.290	17	13	95	111	-0.6	-1	-3	0.9
1942	NY-A	21	5	**.808**	28	27	**22**	**6**	0	226	199	7.9	11	24	**1.0**	71	2.8	2.27	151	.237	**.257**	**35**	29	94	103	6.0	-2	-4	2.4
1943	NY-A	15	8	.652	28	26	17	4	1	226	197	7.8	13	52	2.1	71	2.8	2.27	136	.236	.277	26	21	94	116	0.6	1	-5	1.8
1944	NY-A	12	9	.571	26	25	17	1	0	214	228	9.6	14	41	1.7	54	2.3	2.99	121	.273	.303	11	15	105	116	0.8	-3	-3	1.0
1945	NY-A	8	11	.421	23	23	12	0	0	181	186	9.2	11	22	**1.1**	42	2.1	3.28	108	.265	.284	2	6	106	92	-2.1	2	-3	0.6
1946	NY-A	5	8	.385	18	14	6	2	3	105	97	8.3	6	23	2.0	30	2.6	3.69	93	.243	.279	-2	-3	98	70	-2.1	-0	-2	-0.4
1947	Pit-N	11	8	.579	33	18	7	3	3	150	167	10.0	17	35	2.1	63	3.8	3.84	108	.277	.318	4	5	102	107	3.1	-0	-3	0.1
1948	Pit-N	6	10	.375	22	20	7	0	0	136	145	9.6	18	23	1.5	42	2.8	4.30	96	.276	.308	-5	-3	104	97	-2.5	-2	-4	-0.7
1949	Pit-N	7	4	.636	18	14	5	1	0	89	81	8.2	11	23	2.3	25	2.5	4.25	97	.246	.293	-2	-1	102	83	1.9	-1	-2	-0.3
Total	10	103	72	.589	231	193	110	21	9	1553	1501	8.7	117	287	1.7	478	2.8	3.06	120	.254	.286	111	107	99	102	7.7	-7	-29	7.8
■ BILL BONHAM	Bonham, William Gordon b: 10/1/48, Glendale, Cal. BR/TR, 6'3", 190 lbs. Deb: 4/07/71																												
1971	Chi-N	2	1	.667	33	2	0	0	0	60	63	9.4	6	36	5.4	41	6.2	4.65	82	.281	.382	-8	-6	110	114	0.5	-0	1	-0.4
1972	Chi-N	1	1	.500	19	4	0	0	4	58	56	8.7	4	25	3.9	49	7.6	3.10	125	.260	.335	2	5	112	125	0.0	1	0	0.7
1973	Chi-N	7	5	.583	44	15	3	0	6	152	126	7.5	10	64	3.8	121	7.2	3.02	132	.230	.309	11	16	109	102	1.3	-3	4	1.9
1974	Chi-N	11	22	.333	44	36	10	2	1	243	246	9.1	13	109	4.0	191	7.1	3.85	96	.263	.335	-6	-4	102	99	-3.5	-3	5	-0.1
1975	Chi-N	13	15	.464	38	36	7	2	0	229	254	10.0	15	109	4.3	165	6.5	4.72	81	.281	.356	-28	-23	105	94	0.0	0	1	-2.0
1976	Chi-N	9	13	.409	32	31	3	0	0	196	215	9.9	11	96	4.4	110	5.1	4.27	91	.283	.356	-17	-8	111	106	-1.4	1	0	-0.6
1977	Chi-N	10	13	.435	34	34	1	0	0	215	207	8.7	15	82	3.4	134	5.6	4.35	103	.254	.319	-10	3	115	81	-1.6	1	3	0.8
1978	Cin-N	11	5	.688	23	23	1	0	0	140	151	9.7	9	50	3.2	83	5.3	3.54	104	.276	.331	1	2	102	113	2.3	2	3	0.8
1979	Cin-N	9	7	.563	29	29	2	0	0	176	173	8.8	14	60	3.1	78	4.0	3.78	95	.261	.325	-1	-4	96	100	0.1	-1	0	-0.4
1980	Cin-N	2	1	.667	4	4	0	0	0	19	21	9.9	1	5	2.4	13	6.2	4.74	77	.276	.321	-2	-2	101	76	0.4	-0	-0	-0.2
Total	10	75	83	.475	300	214	27	4	11	1488	1512	9.1	98	636	3.8	985	6.0	4.00	97	.266	.337	-58	-20	106	100	-1.9	-2	18	0.5
■ JOE BONIKOWSKI	Bonikowski, Joseph Peter b: 1/16/41, Philadelphia, Pa. BR/TR, 6', 175 lbs. Deb: 4/12/62																												
1962	Min-A	5	7	.417	30	13	3	0	2	100	95	8.6	6	38	3.4	45	4.1	3.87	106	.255	.321	1	3	104	93	-1.5	-1	1	0.3
■ BILL BONNESS	Bonness, William John "Lefty" b: 12/15/23, Cleveland, Ohio BR/TL, 6'4", 200 lbs. Deb: 9/26/44																												
1944	Cle-A	0	1	.000	2	1	0	0	0	7	11	14.1	0	5	6.4	1	1.3	7.71	45	.367	.474	-3	-3	101	103	-0.4	-0	0	-0.2
■ GUS BONO	Bono, Adlai Wendell b: 8/29/1894, Doe Run, Mo. d: 12/3/48, Dearborn, Mich. BR/TR, 5'11", 175 lbs. Deb: 9/13/20																												
1920	Was-A	0	2	.000	4	1	0	0	0	12	17	12.8	0	6	4.5	4	3.0	9.00	41	.315	.383	-7	-7	96	52	-0.9	-0	0	-0.5
■ GREG BOOKER	Booker, Gregory Scott b: 6/22/60, Lynchburg, Va. BR/TR, 6'6", 230 lbs. Deb: 9/11/83																												
1983	SD-N	0	1	.000	6	1	0	0	0	12	18	13.5	2	9	6.8	5	3.8	7.50	48	.375	.466	-5	-5	99	115	-0.4	-0	0	-0.4
1984	SD-N	1	1	.500	32	1	0	0	0	57	67	10.6	4	27	4.3	28	4.4	3.32	106	.295	.359	2	1	98	148	0.0	1	0	0.2
1985	SD-N	0	1	.000	17	0	0	0	0	22	20	8.2	3	17	7.0	7	2.9	6.95	52	.247	.373	-8	-8	101	74	-0.4	-0	-0	-0.8
1986	SD-N	1	0	1.000	9	0	0	0	0	11	10	8.2	0	4	3.3	7	5.7	1.64	218	.233	.298	3	2	96	141	0.5	0	-0	0.2
1987	SD-N	1	1	.500	44	0	0	0	1	68	62	8.2	5	30	4.0	17	2.3	3.18	126	.246	.330	7	6	98	118	0.2	-1	-0	0.5
1988	SD-N	2	2	.500	34	2	0	0	0	64	68	9.6	5	19	2.7	43	6.0	3.38	99	.278	.324	1	-0	97	122	0.0	1	1	0.1
Total	6	5	6	.455	142	4	0	0	1	234	245	9.4	19	106	4.1	107	4.1	3.77	96	.273	.346	-2	-4	98	123	-0.1	1	0	-0.2
■ RED BOOLES	Booles, Seabron Jesse b: 7/14/1880, Bernice, La. d: 3/16/55, Monroe, La. BL/TL, 5'10", 150 lbs. Deb: 7/30/09																												
1909	Cle-A	0	1	.000	4	1	0	0	0	23	20	7.8	0	8	3.1	6	2.3	1.96	130	.235	.309	1	2	103	114	-0.4	0	-0	0.2
■ DANNY BOONE	Boone, Daniel Hugh b: 1/14/54, Long Beach, Cal. BL/TL, 5'8", 150 lbs. Deb: 4/11/81																												
1981	SD-N	1	0	1.000	37	0	0	0	2	63	63	9.0	2	21	3.0	43	6.1	2.86	116	.267	.324	4	3	95	123	0.5	1	1	0.6
1982	SD-N	1	0	1.000	10	0	0	0	1	16	21	11.8	2	3	1.7	8	4.5	5.63	59	.323	.348	-4	-4	92	94	0.5	0	0	-0.3
	Hou-N	0	1	.000	10	0	0	0	1	13	7	4.8	1	4	2.8	4	2.8	3.46	104	.171	.234	0	0	100	51	-0.4	-0	0	0.0
	Yr	1	1	.500	20	0	0	0	2	29	28	8.7	3	7	2.2	12	3.7	4.66	74	.264	.302	-3	-4	95	51	0.1	0	0	-0.3
Total	2	2	1	.667	57	0	0	0	4	92	91	8.9	5	28	2.7	55	5.4	3.42	98	.266	.317	1	-1	95	108	0.6	1	2	0.3
■ GEORGE BOONE	Boone, George Morris b: 3/1/1871, Louisville, Ky. d: 9/24/10, Louisville, Ky. Deb: 4/23/1891																												
1891	Lou-a	0	0	—	4	1	0	0	1	15	15	9.0	0	9	5.4	4	2.4	7.80	44	.275	.377	-7	-7	92	47	0.0	0	0	-0.5
■ DAN BOONE	Boone, James Albert b: 1/19/1895, Samantha, Ala. d: 5/11/68, Tuscaloosa, Ala. BR/TR, 6'2", 190 lbs. Deb: 9/10/19																												
1919	Phi-A	0	1	.000	3	2	0	0	0	15	24	14.4	0	10	6.0	1	0.6	6.60	55	.375	.459	-6	-5	112	106	-0.4	-1	1	-0.4
1921	Det-A	0	0	—	1	0	0	0	0	2	1	4.5	0	2	9.0	0	0.0	4.50	91	.143	.333	-0	-0	96	40	0.0	-0	0	0.0
1922	Cle-A	4	6	.400	11	10	4	2	0	75	87	10.4	3	19	2.3	9	1.1	4.08	102	.298	.334	-0	1	103	99	-1.0	-1	1	0.1
1923	Cle-A	4	6	.400	27	4	2	0	0	70	93	12.0	3	31	4.0	15	1.9	6.04	65	.322	.379	-16	-16	99	88	-1.2	0	3	-1.2
Total	4	8	13	.381	42	16	6	2	0	162	205	11.4	6	62	3.4	25	1.4	5.17	78	.314	.367	-22	-21	102	94	-2.6	-1	4	-1.5
■ AMOS BOOTH	Booth, Amos Smith "Darling" b: 9/14/1853, Cincinnati, O. d: 7/1/21, Miamisburg, Ohio BR/TR, Deb: 4/25/1876																												
1876	Cin-N	0	1	.000	3	1	0	0	0	10	22	19.8	0	0	0.0	0	0.0	9.90	23	.442	.442	-8	-8	100	72	-0.4	-0	0	-0.6
1877	Cin-N	1	7	.125	12	8	6	0	0	86	114	11.9	1	13	1.4	18	1.9	3.56	71	.327	.351	-7	-10	90	108	-2.2	-1	0	-0.7
Total	2	1	8	.111	15	9	6	0	0	96	136	12.8	1	13	1.2	18	1.7	4.22	60	.341	.362	-16	-18	91	105	-2.6	-1	0	-1.3
■ EDDIE BOOTH	Booth, Edward H. b: Brooklyn, N.Y. Deb: 4/26/1872																												
1876	NY-N	0	0	—	1	0	0	0	0	5	16	28.8	0	0	0.0	0	0.0	10.80	20	.535	.535	-5	-5	93	110	0.0	-0	0	-0.3

YEAR	TM/L	W	L	PCT	G	GS	CG	SHO	SV	IP	H	H/G	HR	BB	BB/G	SO	SO/G	ERA	/A	OAVG	OOBP	PR	/A	PF	CPI	WAT	PB	PD	TPI
■ JOHN BOOZER	Boozer, John Morgan b: 7/6/38, Columbia, S.C. d: 1/24/86, Lexington, S.C. BR/TR, 6'3", 205 lbs. Deb: 7/22/62																												
1962	Phi-N	0	0	—	9	0	0	0	0	20	22	9.9	3	10	4.5	13	5.8	5.85	64	.282	.364	-4	-5	95	89	0.0	-0	0	-0.4
1963	Phi-N	3	4	.429	26	8	2	0	1	83	67	7.3	11	33	3.6	69	7.5	2.93	114	.227	.301	3	4	102	120	-0.6	-0	-2	0.2
1964	Phi-N	3	4	.429	22	3	0	0	2	60	64	9.6	6	18	2.7	51	7.7	5.10	68	.271	.326	-10	-11	98	81	-0.8	-1	1	-1.0
1966	Phi-N	0	0	—	2	2	0	0	0	5	8	14.4	1	3	5.4	5	9.0	7.20	50	.348	.407	-2	-2	100	109	0.0	-0	0	-0.1
1967	Phi-N	5	4	.556	28	7	1	0	1	75	86	10.3	6	24	2.9	48	5.8	4.08	86	.292	.343	-6	-5	104	110	0.5	1	0	-0.3
1968	Phi-N	2	2	.500	38	0	0	0	5	69	76	9.9	3	15	2.0	49	6.4	3.65	81	.279	.315	-5	-5	99	98	0.1	-0	0	-0.5
1969	Phi-N	1	2	.333	46	2	0	0	6	82	91	10.0	12	36	4.0	47	5.2	4.28	84	.283	.351	-6	-6	100	118	-0.1	1	-1	-0.6
Total	7	14	16	.467	171	22	3	0	15	394	414	9.5	42	139	3.2	282	6.4	4.09	83	.272	.331	-31	-30	100	106	-0.9	-0	-1	-2.7
■ PEDRO BORBON	Borbon, Pedro (Rodriguez) b: 12/2/46, Valverde, Mao, D.R. BR/TR, 6'2", 185 lbs. Deb: 4/09/69																												
1969	Cal-A	2	3	.400	22	0	0	0	0	41	55	12.1	5	11	2.4	20	4.4	6.15	60	.324	.370	-11	-11	101	93	-0.1	-0	-0	-1.1
1970	Cin-N	0	2	.000	12	1	0	0	0	17	21	11.1	2	6	3.2	6	3.2	6.88	61	.309	.380	-5	-5	103	86	-0.9	-0	2	-0.3
1971	Cin-N	0	0	—	3	0	0	0	0	4	3	6.8	1	1	2.3	4	9.0	4.50	74	.200	.250	-0	-1	96	69	0.0	0	0	0.0
1972	Cin-N	8	3	.727	62	2	0	0	11	122	115	8.5	5	32	2.4	48	3.5	3.17	99	.254	.299	4	-0	91	96	1.7	-1	-1	-0.1
1973	Cin-N	11	4	.733	80	0	0	0	14	121	137	10.2	4	35	2.6	60	4.5	2.16	156	.298	.335	**20**	16	92	193	2.5	1	0	1.9
1974	Cin-N	10	7	.588	73	0	0	0	14	139	133	8.6	11	32	2.1	53	3.4	3.24	108	.255	.296	6	4	96	100	-0.2	-0	-1	0.3
1975	Cin-N	9	5	.643	67	0	0	0	5	125	145	10.4	6	21	1.5	29	2.1	2.95	125	.301	.323	9	10	101	136	-0.2	2	-1	1.2
1976	Cin-N	4	3	.571	69	1	0	0	8	121	135	10.0	4	31	2.3	53	3.9	3.35	105	.292	.330	2	2	100	120	-0.2	0	-0	0.2
1977	Cin-N	10	5	.667	73	0	0	0	18	127	131	9.3	7	24	1.7	48	3.4	3.19	122	.268	.301	10	10	99	103	2.2	-0	-2	0.8
1978	Cin-N	8	2	.800	62	0	0	0	4	99	102	9.3	6	27	2.5	35	3.2	5.00	73	.274	.316	-16	-15	102	76	2.7	-0	-0	-1.5
1979	Cin-N	2	2	.500	30	0	0	0	2	45	48	9.6	2	8	1.6	23	4.6	3.40	106	.277	.298	2	1	96	98	-0.1	1	0	0.2
	SF-N	4	3	.571	30	0	0	0	3	46	56	11.0	7	13	2.5	26	5.1	4.89	71	.303	.342	-6	-7	93	105	0.9	0	-1	-0.7
	Yr	6	5	.545	60	0	0	0	5	91	104	10.3	9	21	2.1	49	4.8	4.15	85	.287	.321	-4	-6	95	105	0.8	1	-1	-0.5
1980	StL-N	1	0	1.000	10	0	0	0	1	19	17	8.1	3	10	4.7	4	1.9	3.79	98	.250	.321	-0	-0	102	121	0.5	0	-0	0.0
Total	12	69	39	.639	593	4	0	0	80	1026	1098	9.6	63	251	2.2	409	3.6	3.52	101	.280	.318	15	4	97	115	8.8	2	-3	0.9
■ GEORGE BORCHERS	Borchers, George Benard "Chief" b: 4/18/1869, Sacramento, Cal. d: 10/24/38, Sacramento, Cal. BB/TR, 5'10", 180 lbs. Deb: 1888																												
1888	Chi-N	4	4	.500	10	10	7	1	0	67	67	9.0	2	29	3.9	26	3.5	3.49	86	.274	.351	-5	-4	106	104	-0.4	-3	0	-0.5
1895	Lou-N	0	1	.000	1	1	0	0	0	1	1	9.0	0	3	27.0	0	0.0	45.00	10	.280	.608	-4	-4	99	24	-0.4	0	0	-0.2
Total	2	4	5	.444	11	11	7	1	0	68	68	9.0	2	32	4.2	26	3.4	4.10	74	.274	.357	-9	-8	106	102	-0.8	-3	0	-0.7
■ JOE BORDEN	Borden, Joseph Emley (a.k.a. Joseph Emley Josephs in 1875) b: 5/9/1854, Jacobstown, N.J. d: 10/14/29, Yeadon, Pa. BR/TR, 5'9", 140 lbs. Deb:7/24/1875																												
1875	Phi-n	2	4	.333	7																								
1876	Bos-N	11	12	.478	29	24	16	2	1	218	257	10.6	4	51	2.1	34	1.4	2.89	75	.298	.337	-14	-17	94	107	-2.2	-3	-1	-1.8
■ RICH BORDI	Bordi, Richard Albert b: 4/18/59, San Francisco, Cal. BR/TR, 6'7", 210 lbs. Deb: 7/16/80																												
1980	Oak-A	0	0	—	1	0	0	0	0	2	4	18.0	0	0	0.0	0	0.0	4.50	84	.400	.400	-0	-0	94	146	0.0	0	0	0.0
1981	Oak-A	0	0	—	2	0	0	0	0	2	1	4.5	0	1	4.5	0	0.0	0.00	—	.143	.250	1	1	95	0	0.0	0	0	0.1
1982	Sea-A	0	2	.000	7	2	0	0	0	13	18	12.5	4	1	0.7	10	6.9	8.31	54	.310	.333	-6	-6	110	75	-0.9	0	0	-0.4
1983	Chi-N	0	2	.000	11	1	0	0	1	25	34	12.2	2	12	4.3	20	7.2	5.04	73	.321	.387	-4	-4	101	112	-0.9	-0	0	-0.3
1984	Chi-N	5	2	.714	31	7	0	0	4	83	78	8.5	11	20	2.2	41	4.4	3.47	113	.242	.282	1	4	109	95	1.1	-1	-1	0.2
1985	NY-A	6	8	.429	51	3	0	0	2	98	95	8.7	5	29	2.7	64	5.9	3.21	121	.253	.301	10	7	94	100	-2.1	0	-1	0.7
1986	Bal-A	6	4	.600	52	1	0	0	3	107	105	8.8	13	41	3.4	83	7.0	4.46	93	.254	.323	-3	-4	99	91	1.4	0	0	-0.2
1987	NY-A	3	1	.750	16	1	0	0	0	33	42	11.5	7	12	3.3	23	6.3	7.64	57	.309	.362	-12	-12	97	81	0.9	0	-1	-1.1
1988	Oak-A	0	1	.000	2	2	0	0	0	8	6	6.8	0	5	5.6	6	6.8	4.50	82	.214	.324	-0	-1	93	65	-0.4	0	-0	0.0
Total	9	20	20	.500	173	17	0	0	10	371	383	9.3	42	121	2.9	247	6.0	4.34	93	.263	.318	-13	-13	100	93	-0.9	-2	-2	-1.0
■ BILL BORDLEY	Bordley, William Clarke b: 1/9/58, Los Angeles, Cal. BR/TL, 6'3", 185 lbs. Deb: 6/30/80																												
1980	SF-N	2	3	.400	8	6	0	0	0	31	34	9.9	3	21	6.1	11	3.2	4.65	75	.288	.390	-4	-4	96	118	-0.3	0	1	-0.2
■ PAUL BORIS	Boris, Paul Stanley b: 12/13/55, Irvington, N.J. BR/TR, 6'2", 200 lbs. Deb: 5/21/82																												
1982	Min-A	1	2	.333	23	0	0	0	0	50	46	8.3	8	19	3.4	30	5.4	3.96	105	.246	.312	1	1	102	105	-0.1	0	-1	0.0
■ FRANK BORK	Bork, Frank Bernard b: 7/13/40, Buffalo, N.Y. BR/TL, 6'2", 175 lbs. Deb: 4/15/64																												
1964	Pit-N	2	2	.500	33	2	0	0	2	42	51	10.9	6	11	2.4	31	6.6	4.07	87	.295	.341	-2	-2	101	122	0.0	0	0	-0.1
■ TOM BORLAND	Borland, Thomas Bruce "Spike" b: 2/14/33, El Dorado, Kan. BL/TL, 6'3", 172 lbs. Deb: 5/15/60																												
1960	Bos-A	0	4	.000	26	4	0	0	3	51	67	11.8	4	23	4.1	32	5.6	6.53	63	.322	.381	-15	-14	105	86	-1.9	-2	0	-1.4
1961	Bos-A	0	0	—	1	0	0	0	0	1	3	27.0	0	0	0.0	0	0.0	18.00	23	.500	.500	-2	-2	103	64	0.0	0	0	0.0
Total	2	0	4	.000	27	4	0	0	3	52	70	12.1	4	23	4.0	32	5.5	6.75	60	.327	.384	-17	-15	105	85	-1.9	-2	0	-1.4
■ HANK BOROWY	Borowy, Henry Ludwig b: 5/12/16, Bloomfield, N.J. BR/TR, 6', 175 lbs. Deb: 4/18/42																												
1942	NY-A	15	4	.789	25	21	13	4	1	178	157	7.9	6	66	3.3	85	4.3	2.53	136	.233	.299	22	18	94	110	3.8	-1	1	1.9
1943	NY-A	14	9	.609	29	27	14	3	0	217	195	8.1	11	72	3.0	113	4.7	2.82	110	.241	.300	11	6	94	106	-0.5	3	1	1.1
1944	NY-A	17	12	.586	35	30	19	3	2	253	224	8.0	15	88	3.1	107	3.8	2.63	137	.236	.299	22	28	105	110	1.8	-3	1	2.8
1945	NY-A	10	5	.667	18	18	7	1	0	132	107	7.3	6	58	4.0	35	2.4	3.14	114	.221	.300	3	6	106	86	2.3	1	1	0.9
	Chi-N	11	2	.846	15	14	11	1	1	122	105	7.7	2	47	3.5	47	3.5	2.14	169	.231	.300	23	20	95	124	3.9	0	-1	2.1
1946	Chi-N	12	10	.545	32	28	8	1	0	201	220	9.9	9	61	2.7	95	4.3	3.76	85	.274	.320	-8	-13	93	93	0.3	1	0	-1.2
1947	Chi-N	8	12	.400	40	25	7	1	2	183	190	9.3	19	63	3.1	75	3.7	4.38	96	.267	.324	-6	-3	104	93	-1.1	-1	0	-0.3
1948	Chi-N	5	10	.333	39	17	2	1	1	127	156	11.1	9	49	3.5	50	3.5	4.89	77	.308	.363	-13	-16	95	105	-1.5	2	2	-1.1
1949	Phi-N	12	12	.500	28	28	12	2	0	193	188	8.8	19	63	2.9	43	2.0	4.20	97	.259	.315	-3	-3	101	92	-0.6	3	-1	0.0
1950	Phi-N	0	0	—	3	0	0	0	0	6	5	7.5	0	4	6.0	3	4.5	6.00	66	.250	.360	-1	-1	96	67	0.0	0	0	0.0
	Pit-N	1	3	.250	11	3	0	0	0	25	32	11.5	6	9	3.2	9	3.2	6.48	68	.311	.365	-6	-6	106	100	-0.6	-0	0	-0.5
	Yr	1	3	.250	14	3	0	0	0	31	37	10.7	6	13	3.8	12	3.5	6.39	67	.301	.364	-8	-7	104	100	-0.6	0	0	-0.5
	Det-A	1	1	.500	13	2	1	0	0	33	23	6.3	3	16	4.4	12	3.3	3.27	132	.205	.291	5	4	95	95	-0.1	-0	0	0.3
1951	Det-A	2	2	.500	26	1	0	0	0	45	58	11.6	3	27	5.4	16	3.2	7.00	63	.314	.393	-14	-13	107	84	0.1	-1	1	-1.2
Total	10	108	82	.568	314	214	94	17	7	1715	1660	8.7	108	623	3.3	690	3.6	3.51	104	.254	.315	34	26	99	101	7.8	2	6	4.8
■ CHRIS BOSIO	Bosio, Christopher Louis b: 4/3/63, Carmichael, Cal. BR/TR, 6'3", 220 lbs. Deb: 8/03/86																												
1986	Mil-A	0	4	.000	10	4	0	0	0	35	41	10.5	9	13	3.3	29	7.5	6.94	62	.293	.351	-11	-10	103	87	-1.9	0	0	-0.8
1987	Mil-A	11	8	.579	46	19	2	1	2	170	187	9.9	18	50	2.6	150	7.9	5.24	87	.276	.324	-15	-13	102	81	0.4	0	1	-1.0
1988	Mil-A	7	15	.318	38	22	9	1	6	182	190	9.4	13	38	1.9	84	4.2	3.36	121	.268	.300	12	15	103	105	-4.8	0	3	1.8
Total	3	18	27	.400	94	45	11	2	8	387	418	9.7	40	101	2.3	263	6.1	4.51	96	.274	.316	-13	-9	102	93	-6.3	0	4	0.0
■ DICK BOSMAN	Bosman, Richard Allen b: 2/17/44, Kenosha, Wis. BR/TR, 6'2", 195 lbs. Deb: 6/01/66 C																												
1966	Was-A	2	6	.250	13	7	0	0	0	39	60	13.8	4	12	2.8	20	4.6	7.62	43	.361	.391	-18	-19	96	89	-1.7	0	-1	-1.8
1967	Was-A	3	1	.750	7	7	2	1	0	51	38	6.7	3	10	1.8	25	4.4	1.76	190	.204	.242	8	9	104	102	1.1	0	-1	1.1
1968	Was-A	2	9	.182	46	10	0	0	1	139	139	9.0	9	35	2.3	63	4.1	3.69	76	.262	.306	-11	-14	94	93	-3.0	1	-0	-1.3
1969	Was-A	14	5	.737	31	26	5	2	1	193	156	7.3	11	39	1.8	99	4.6	**2.19**	**159**	.220	.259	31	28	96	95	4.5	-1	1	3.0
1970	Was-A	16	12	.571	36	34	7	3	0	231	212	8.3	16	71	2.8	134	5.2	3.00	120	.245	.300	18	16	97	103	4.0	-2	0	1.4
1971	Was-A	12	16	.429	35	35	7	1	0	237	245	9.3	29	71	2.7	113	4.3	3.72	88	.272	.323	-7	-12	94	112	0.9	-1	-2	-1.6
1972	Tex-A	8	10	.444	29	29	1	1	0	173	183	9.5	11	48	2.5	105	5.5	3.64	82	.273	.322	-11	-13	97	101	1.4	-2	1	-1.5
1973	Tex-A	2	5	.286	7	7	1	1	0	40	42	9.4	6	17	3.8	14	3.1	4.27	89	.268	.341	-2	-2	100	107	-0.6	0	-0	-0.2
	Cle-A	1	8	.111	22	17	2	0	0	97	130	12.1	19	29	2.7	41	3.8	6.22	61	.320	.370	-26	-26	99	99	-3.3	0	-1	-2.5
	Yr	3	13	.188	29	24	3	1	0	137	172	11.3	25	46	3.0	55	3.6	5.65	67	.304	.360	-28	-28	99	99	-3.9	0	-1	-2.7
1974	Cle-A	7	5	.583	25	18	2	1	0	127	126	8.9	13	29	2.1	56	4.0	4.11	89	.255	.295	-7	-6	101	80	1.3	0	-2	-0.8
1975	Cle-A	0	2	.000	6	3	0	0	0	29	33	10.2	3	8	2.5	11	3.4	4.03	94	.292	.346	-1	-1	100	118	-0.9	0	0	0.0
	Oak-A	11	4	.733	22	21	2	0	0	123	112	8.2	12	24	1.8	42	3.1	3.51	98	.240	.278	4	-1	91	81	2.6	0	-1	-0.1
	Yr	11	6	.647	28	24	2	0	0	152	145	8.6	15	32	1.9	53	3.1	3.61	97	.248	.287	3	-2	93	81	1.7	0	-1	-0.1

YEAR	TM/L	W	L	PCT	G	GS	CG	SHO	SV	IP	H	H/G	HR	BB	BB/G	SO	SO/G	ERA	/A	OAVG	OOBP	PR	/A	PF	CPI	WAT	PB	PD	TPI
1976	Oak-A	4	2	.667	27	15	0	0	0	112	118	9.5	13	19	1.5	34	2.7	4.10	85	.274	.301	-7	-8	98	93	0.8	0	1	-0.7
Total	11	82	85	.491	306	229	29	10	2	1591	1594	9.0	149	412	2.3	757	4.3	3.67	92	.261	.307	-28	-49	97	98	7.1	-4	-5	-5.0
■ MEL BOSSER	Bosser, Melvin Edward b: 2/8/20, Johnstown, Pa. BR/TR, 6', 173 lbs. Deb: 4/29/45																												
1945	Cin-N	2	0	1.000	7	2	0	0	0	16	9	5.1	0	17	9.6	3	1.7	3.38	109	.158	.351	1	1	97	79	1.0	-1	-0	0.0
■ ANDY BOSWELL	Boswell, Andrew Cottrell b: 9/5/1874, New Gretna, N.J. d: 2/3/36, Ocean City, N.J. Deb: 5/10/1895																												
1895	NY-N	2	2	.500	5	4	3	0	0	34	41	10.9	1	22	5.8	18	4.8	5.82	78	.319	.418	-4	-5	94	91	0.0	-1	0	-0.4
	Was-N	1	2	.333	6	3	3	0	0	30	44	13.2	1	19	5.7	12	3.6	6.00	84	.363	.449	-4	-3	105	110	0.0	-0	0	-0.1
	Yr	3	4	.429	11	7	6	0	0	64	85	12.0	2	41	5.8	30	4.2	5.91	81	.340	.433	-8	-8	100	110	0.0	-1	0	-0.5
■ DAVE BOSWELL	Boswell, David Wilson b: 1/20/45, Baltimore, Md. BR/TR, 6'3", 185 lbs. Deb: 9/18/64																												
1964	Min-A	2	0	1.000	4	4	0	0	0	23	21	8.2	4	12	4.7	25	9.8	4.30	84	.236	.327	-2	-2	100	97	1.0	0	1	0.0
1965	Min-A	6	5	.545	27	12	1	0	0	106	77	6.5	20	46	3.9	85	7.2	3.40	100	.204	.294	1	0	98	105	-0.7	4	-1	0.3
1966	Min-A	12	5	.706	28	21	8	1	0	169	120	6.4	19	65	3.5	173	9.2	3.14	120	.197	.275	6	12	110	85	3.2	-2	1	1.3
1967	Min-A	14	12	.538	37	32	11	3	0	223	162	6.5	14	107	4.3	204	8.2	3.27	104	.202	.299	-1	3	106	83	-0.5	4	-1	0.7
1968	Min-A	10	13	.435	34	28	7	2	0	190	148	7.0	19	87	4.1	143	6.8	3.32	95	.213	.303	-7	-3	106	94	-1.3	5	-2	0.0
1969	Min-A	20	12	.625	39	38	10	0	0	256	215	7.6	18	99	3.5	190	6.7	3.23	112	.226	.301	11	11	100	90	1.3	3	-2	1.3
1970	Min-A	3	7	.300	18	15	0	0	0	69	80	10.4	12	44	5.7	45	5.9	6.39	56	.292	.388	-20	-21	97	95	-2.5	-0	-1	-2.1
1971	Det-A	0	0	—	3	0	0	0	0	4	3	6.8	0	6	13.5	3	6.8	6.75	49	.200	.409	-1	-2	95	68	0.0	0	0	0.0
	Bal-A	1	2	.333	15	1	0	0	0	25	32	11.5	4	15	5.4	14	5.0	4.32	80	.305	.388	-2	-2	100	141	-0.6	0	0	-0.1
	Yr	1	2	.333	18	1	0	0	0	29	35	10.9	4	21	6.5	17	5.3	4.66	74	.289	.392	-4	-4	99	141	-0.6	0	0	-0.1
Total	8	68	56	.548	205	151	37	6	0	1065	858	7.3	110	481	4.1	882	7.5	3.52	99	.219	.306	-17	-3	103	91	-0.1	14	-4	1.4
■ DEREK BOTELHO	Botelho, Derek Wayne b: 8/2/56, Long Beach, Cal. BR/TR, 6'2", 180 lbs. Deb: 7/18/82																												
1982	KC-A	2	1	.667	8	4	0	0	0	24	25	9.4	4	8	3.0	12	4.5	4.13	98	.275	.330	-0	-0	100	115	0.4	0	-0	0.0
1985	Chi-N	1	3	.250	11	7	1	0	0	44	52	10.6	8	23	4.7	23	4.7	5.32	79	.299	.379	-8	-5	117	115	-0.9	-0	-0	-0.5
Total	2	3	4	.429	19	11	1	0	0	68	77	10.2	12	31	4.1	35	4.6	4.90	85	.291	.363	-9	-5	111	115	-0.5	-0	-1	-0.5
■ RALPH BOTTING	Botting, Ralph Wayne b: 5/12/55, Houlton, Maine BL/TL, 6', 195 lbs. Deb: 6/28/79																												
1979	Cal-A	2	0	1.000	12	1	0	0	0	30	46	13.8	6	15	4.5	22	6.6	8.70	45	.362	.425	-15	-16	92	93	1.0	0	0	-1.4
1980	Cal-A	0	3	.000	6	6	0	0	0	26	40	13.8	1	13	4.5	12	4.2	5.88	67	.348	.408	-5	-6	97	106	-1.4	0	-0	-0.5
Total	2	2	3	.400	18	7	0	0	0	56	86	13.8	7	28	4.5	34	5.5	7.39	53	.355	.417	-20	-22	94	99	-0.4	0	-0	-1.9
■ BOB BOTZ	Botz, Robert Allen b: 4/28/35, Milwaukee, Wis. BR/TR, 5'11", 170 lbs. Deb: 5/08/62																												
1962	LA-A	2	1	.667	35	0	0	0	2	63	71	10.1	7	11	1.6	24	3.4	3.43	118	.285	.313	4	4	102	123	0.4	-1	-1	0.2
■ CARL BOULDIN	Bouldin, Carl Edward b: 9/17/39, Germantown, Ky. BB/TR, 6'2", 180 lbs. Deb: 9/02/61																												
1961	Was-A	0	1	.000	2	1	0	0	0	3	9	27.0	0	2	6.0	2	6.0	18.00	22	.500	.550	-5	-5	97	74	-0.4	-0	0	-0.3
1962	Was-A	1	2	.333	6	3	1	0	0	20	26	11.7	0	9	4.0	12	5.4	5.85	69	.321	.387	-4	-4	102	89	-0.1	-1	-0	-0.4
1963	Was-A	2	2	.500	10	3	0	0	0	23	31	12.1	3	8	3.1	10	3.9	5.87	63	.307	.351	-6	-6	101	91	0.5	-1	0	-0.5
1964	Was-A	0	3	.000	9	3	0	0	0	25	30	10.8	2	11	4.0	12	4.3	5.40	69	.294	.364	-5	-5	103	93	-1.4	-0	0	-0.5
Total	4	3	8	.273	27	10	1	0	0	71	96	12.2	5	30	3.8	36	4.6	6.21	61	.318	.377	-19	-19	102	90	-1.4	-2	0	-1.7
■ JAKE BOULTES	Boultes, Jacob John b: 8/6/1884, St.Louis, Mo. d: 12/24/55, St.Louis, Mo. TR , 6'3", Deb: 4/18/07																												
1907	Bos-N	5	9	.357	24	12	11	0	0	140	140	9.0	1	50	3.2	49	3.2	2.70	90	.294	.370	-4	-4	99	121	-0.6	-1	4	0.0
1908	Bos-N	3	5	.375	17	5	1	0	0	75	80	9.6	7	8	1.0	28	3.4	3.00	83	.304	.327	-5	-4	106	117	-0.3	-1	-0	-0.4
1909	Bos-N	0	0	—	1	0	0	0	0	8	9	10.1	2	0	0.0	1	1.1	6.75	39	.290	.313	-4	-4	102	73	0.0	1	0	-0.2
Total	3	8	14	.364	42	17	12	0	0	223	229	9.2	10	58	2.3	78	3.1	2.95	83	.297	.354	-13	-12	101	118	-0.9	-1	3	-0.6
■ JIM BOUTON	Bouton, James Alan b: 3/8/39, Newark, N.J. BR/TR, 6', 170 lbs. Deb: 4/22/62																												
1962	NY-A	7	7	.500	36	16	3	1	2	133	124	8.4	9	59	4.0	71	4.8	3.99	91	.254	.327	-0	-5	92	95	-1.1	-1	0	-0.6
1963	NY-A	21	7	.750	40	30	12	6	1	249	191	6.9	18	87	3.1	148	5.3	2.53	141	.212	.280	30	29	98	101	4.7	-6	-1	2.4
1964	NY-A	18	13	.581	38	37	11	4	0	271	227	7.5	32	60	2.0	125	4.2	3.02	121	.225	.270	18	19	101	92	-0.8	-3	-3	1.4
1965	NY-A	4	15	.211	30	25	2	0	0	151	158	9.4	23	60	3.6	97	5.8	4.83	72	.269	.335	-23	-22	101	97	-5.5	-0	-0	-2.2
1966	NY-A	3	8	.273	24	19	3	0	1	120	117	8.8	13	38	2.9	65	4.9	2.70	119	.257	.307	10	7	94	142	-2.1	-1	1	0.7
1967	NY-A	1	0	1.000	17	1	0	0	0	44	47	9.6	5	18	3.7	31	6.3	4.70	66	.275	.338	-7	-8	96	98	0.5	-0	0	-0.8
1968	NY-A	1	1	.500	12	3	1	0	0	44	49	10.0	5	9	1.8	24	4.9	3.68	82	.287	.321	-3	-3	101	119	0.0	-0	1	-0.2
1969	Sea-A	2	1	.667	57	1	0	0	1	92	77	7.5	12	38	3.7	68	6.7	3.91	93	.219	.296	-3	-3	100	81	0.7	-1	1	-0.2
	Hou-N	0	2	.000	16	1	1	0	1	31	32	9.3	1	12	3.5	32	9.3	4.06	90	.267	.341	-2	-1	101	92	-0.9	-0	0	-0.1
1970	Hou-N	4	6	.400	29	6	1	0	0	73	84	10.4	5	33	4.1	49	6.0	5.42	70	.285	.351	-11	-13	94	85	-0.8	2	-0	-1.0
1978	Atl-N	1	3	.250	5	5	0	0	0	29	25	7.8	4	21	6.5	10	3.1	4.97	82	.234	.357	-4	-3	114	91	-0.7	-1	-0	-0.3
Total	10	62	63	.496	304	144	34	11	6	1237	1131	8.2	127	435	3.2	720	5.2	3.58	99	.243	.306	4	-4	98	99	-6.0	-13	-0	-0.9
■ CY BOWEN	Bowen, Sutherland Mc Coy b: 2/17/1871, Kingston, Ind. d: 1/25/25, Greensburg, Ind. BR/TR, 6', 175 lbs. Deb: 4/28/1896																												
1896	NY-N	0	1	.000	2	1	1	0	0	12	12	9.0	0	9	6.8	3	2.3	6.00	72	.282	.407	-2	-2	99	71	-0.4	0	0	-0.1
■ FRANK BOWERMAN	Bowerman, Frank Eugene "Mike" b: 12/5/1868, Romeo, Mich. d: 11/30/48, Romeo, Mich. BR/TR, 6'2", 190 lbs. Deb: 8/24/1895 M																												
1904	NY-N	0	0	—	1	0	0	0	0	1	3	27.0	0	1	9.0	0	0.0	9.00	30	.544	.614	-1	-1	100	164	0.0	0	0	0.0
■ STEW BOWERS	Bowers, Stewart Cole "Doc" b: 2/26/15, New Freedom, Pa. BB/TR, 6', 170 lbs. Deb: 8/05/35																												
1935	Bos-A	2	1	.667	10	2	1	0	0	24	26	9.8	1	17	6.4	5	1.9	3.38	143	.283	.377	3	4	108	154	0.5	0	0	0.4
1936	Bos-A	0	0	—	5	0	0	0	0	6	10	15.0	1	2	3.0	0	0.0	9.00	59	.370	.414	-3	-2	106	89	0.0	0	-0	-0.1
Total	2	2	1	.667	15	2	1	0	0	30	36	10.8	2	19	5.7	5	1.5	4.50	110	.303	.385	0	1	108	141	0.5	0	0	0.3
■ GRANT BOWLER	Bowler, Grant Tierney "Moose" b: 10/24/07, Denver, Col. d: 6/25/68, Denver, Colo. BR/TR, 6', 190 lbs. Deb: 8/21/31																												
1931	Chi-A	0	1	.000	13	3	1	0	0	35	40	10.3	1	24	6.2	15	3.9	5.40	78	.288	.388	-4	-5	96	98	-0.4	-0	-1	-0.4
1932	Chi-A	0	0	—	4	0	0	0	0	6	15	22.5	1	3	4.5	2	3.0	16.50	25	.484	.514	-8	-8	91	79	0.0	-0	0	-0.6
Total	2	0	1	.000	17	3	1	0	0	41	55	12.1	2	27	5.9	17	3.7	7.02	59	.324	.410	-12	-13	95	95	-0.4	-1	-1	-1.0
■ CHARLIE BOWLES	Bowles, Charles James b: 3/15/17, Norwood, Mass. BR/TR, 6'3", 180 lbs. Deb: 9/25/43																												
1943	Phi-A	1	1	.500	2	2	2	0	0	18	17	8.5	0	4	2.0	6	3.0	3.00	116	.258	.292	1	1	106	91	0.3	-1	0	0.1
1945	Phi-A	0	3	.000	8	4	1	0	0	33	35	9.5	3	23	6.3	11	3.0	5.18	63	.273	.377	-7	-7	96	98	-1.4	0	0	-0.6
Total	2	1	4	.200	10	6	3	0	0	51	52	9.2	3	27	4.8	17	3.0	4.41	76	.268	.350	-6	-6	100	95	-1.1	-0	0	-0.5
■ EMMETT BOWLES	Bowles, Emmett Jerome "Chief" b: 8/2/1898, Wanette, Okla. d: 9/3/59, Flagstaff, Ariz. BR/TR, 6', 180 lbs. Deb: 9/12/22																												
1922	Chi-A	0	0	—	1	0	0	0	0	1	2	18.0	0	1	9.0	0	0.0	27.00	15	.500	.500	-3	-3	101	44	0.0	0	0	-0.1
■ ABE BOWMAN	Bowman, Alvah Edson b: 1/25/1893, Greenup, Ill. d: 10/11/79, Longview, Tex. BR/TR, 6'1", 190 lbs. Deb: 5/19/14																												
1914	Cle-A	2	7	.222	22	10	2	1	0	73	74	9.1	0	45	5.5	27	3.3	4.44	65	.277	.389	-14	-12	106	95	-1.5	-2	-0	-1.3
1915	Cle-A	0	1	.000	2	1	0	0	0	1	1	9.0	0	3	27.0	0	0.0	27.00	12	.250	.571	-3	-3	106	37	-0.4	0	1	-0.1
Total	2	2	8	.200	24	11	2	1	0	74	75	9.1	0	48	5.8	27	3.3	4.74	61	.277	.393	-16	-15	106	94	-1.9	-2	0	-1.4
■ JOE BOWMAN	Bowman, Joseph Emil b: 6/17/10, Argentine, Kan. BL/TR, 6'2", 190 lbs. Deb: 4/18/32																												
1932	Phi-A	0	1	.000	7	0	0	0	0	11	14	11.5	2	6	4.9	4	3.3	8.18	60	.318	.418	-5	-4	111	94	-0.4	0	1	-0.2
1934	NY-N	5	4	.556	30	10	3	0	3	107	119	10.0	9	36	3.0	36	3.0	3.62	106	.279	.335	5	3	95	120	-0.3	0	-0	0.2
1935	Phi-N	7	10	.412	33	17	6	1	1	148	157	9.5	13	56	3.4	58	3.5	4.26	111	.269	.333	-4	7	117	100	0.0	0	-0	0.8
1936	Phi-N	9	20	.310	40	28	12	0	1	204	243	10.7	14	53	2.3	80	3.5	5.03	88	.289	.334	-23	-13	111	85	-1.9	-1	-3	-1.4
1937	Pit-N	8	8	.500	30	19	7	0	1	128	161	11.3	11	35	2.5	38	2.7	4.57	87	.306	.347	-9	-9	101	107	-0.8	1	0	-0.6
1938	Pit-N	3	4	.429	17	1	0	0	1	60	68	10.2	2	20	3.0	25	3.8	4.65	80	.285	.332	-6	-6	99	86	-0.8	2	-1	-0.4
1939	Pit-N	10	14	.417	37	27	10	1	1	185	217	10.6	15	43	2.1	58	2.8	4.48	88	.292	.328	-11	-11	101	97	-0.8	12	0	0.1
1940	Pit-N	9	10	.474	32	24	10	0	2	188	209	10.0	10	66	3.2	57	2.7	4.45	82	.274	.334	-13	-17	95	92	-0.6	10	0	-0.7
1941	Pit-N	3	2	.600	18	7	1	1	1	69	77	10.0	3	28	3.7	22	2.9	3.00	123	.278	.342	5	5	102	138	0.4	1	-0	0.7

YEAR	TM/L	W	L	PCT	G	GS	CG	SHO	SV	IP	H	H/G	HR	BB	BB/G	SO	SO/G	ERA	/A	OAVG	OOBP	PR	/A	PF	CPI	WAT	PB	PD	TPI
1944	Bos-A	12	8	.600	26	24	10	1	0	168	175	9.4	14	64	3.4	53	2.8	4.82	69	.269	.333	-26	-28	97	84	2.2	3	-2	-2.7
1945	Bos-A	0	2	.000	3	3	0	0	0	12	18	13.5	1	9	6.8	0	0.0	9.00	36	.360	.443	-8	-8	96	85	-0.9	0	-0	-0.6
	Cin-N	11	13	.458	25	24	15	1	0	186	198	9.6	8	68	3.3	71	3.4	3.58	103	.270	.330	5	2	97	108	1.4	-4	-2	-0.3
Total	11	77	96	.445	298	184	74	5	11	1466	1656	10.2	102	484	3.0	502	3.1	4.40	89	.282	.336	-89	-79	102	99	-2.5	25	-7	-5.1
■ **BOB BOWMAN**	Bowman, Robert James b: 10/3/10, Keystone, W.Va. d: 9/4/72, Bluefield, W.Va. BR/TR, 5'10.5", 160 lbs. Deb: 4/21/39																												
1939	StL-N	13	5	.722	51	15	4	2	**9**	169	141	7.5	8	60	3.2	78	4.2	2.61	154	.232	.292	25	26	103	109	3.0	-3	-1	2.3
1940	StL-N	7	5	.583	28	17	7	0	0	114	118	9.3	9	43	3.4	43	3.4	4.34	90	.267	.331	-6	-6	101	97	0.5	-2	-0	-0.7
1941	NY-N	6	7	.462	29	6	2	0	1	80	100	11.2	10	36	4.0	25	2.8	5.74	66	.302	.368	-19	-17	104	97	-0.2	-1	1	-1.6
1942	Chi-N	0	0	—	1	0	0	0	0	1	1	9.0	0	0	0.0	0	0.0	0.00	—	.250	.250	0	0	98	0	0.0	0	0	0.0
Total	4	26	17	.605	109	38	13	2	10	364	360	8.9	27	139	3.4	146	3.6	3.83	102	.260	.322	-0	4	102	102	3.3	-5	-1	-0.0
■ **BOB BOWMAN**	Bowman, Robert Leroy b: 5/10/31, Laytonville, Cal. BR/TR, 6'1", 195 lbs. Deb: 4/16/55																												
1959	Phi-N	0	1	.000	5	0	0	0	0	6	5	7.5	1	5	7.5	0	0.0	6.00	67	.227	.370	-1	-1	102	81	-0.4	0	0	0.0
■ **ROGER BOWMAN**	Bowman, Roger Clinton b: 8/18/27, Amsterdam, N.Y. BR/TL, 6', 175 lbs. Deb: 9/22/49																												
1949	NY-N	0	0	—	2	2	0	0	0	6	6	9.0	1	7	10.5	4	6.0	4.50	90	.261	.419	-0	-0	101	150	0.0	-0	1	0.0
1951	NY-N	2	4	.333	9	5	0	0	0	26	35	12.1	2	22	7.6	24	8.3	6.23	63	.297	.408	-7	-7	99	97	-1.3	-0	-0	-0.6
1952	NY-N	0	0	—	2	1	0	0	0	3	6	18.0	0	3	9.0	3	9.0	12.00	31	.429	.556	-3	-3	101	93	0.0	-0	0	-0.2
1953	Pit-N	0	4	.000	30	2	0	0	0	65	65	9.0	9	29	4.0	36	5.0	4.85	94	.261	.330	-4	-2	106	94	-1.9	1	0	0.0
1955	Pit-N	0	3	.000	7	2	0	0	0	17	25	13.2	2	10	5.3	8	4.2	8.47	48	.347	.424	-8	-8	101	86	-1.4	0	0	-0.6
Total	5	2	11	.154	50	12	0	0	0	117	137	10.5	14	71	5.5	75	5.8	5.85	73	.288	.376	-22	-20	103	96	-4.6	-0	1	-1.4
■ **SUMNER BOWMAN**	Bowman, Sumner Sallade b: 2/9/1867, Millersburg, Pa. d: 1/11/54, Millersburg, Pa. BL/TL, 6', 160 lbs. Deb: 6/11/1890																												
1890	Phi-N	0	0	—	1	1	0	0	0	8	11	12.4	0	2	2.3	2	2.3	7.88	48	.344	.382	-4	-4	107	59	0.0	1	0	-0.1
	Pit-N	2	5	.286	9	7	6	0	0	71	100	12.7	1	50	6.3	22	2.8	6.59	51	.349	.446	-24	-25	95	94	0.5	2	0	-1.8
	Yr	2	5	.286	10	8	6	0	0	79	111	12.6	1	52	5.9	24	2.7	6.72	51	.349	.440	-28	-29	96	94	0.5	1	0	-1.9
1891	Phi-a	2	5	.286	8	8	8	0	0	68	73	9.7	0	37	4.9	22	2.9	3.44	111	.289	.380	2	3	103	113	-1.5	0	0	0.3
Total	2	4	10	.286	18	16	14	0	0	147	184	11.3	1	89	5.4	46	2.8	5.20	69	.322	.414	-26	-26	99	101	-1.0	3	0	-1.6
■ **TED BOWSFIELD**	Bowsfield, Edward Oliver b: 1/10/35, Vernon, B.C., Canada BR/TL, 6'1", 190 lbs. Deb: 7/20/58																												
1958	Bos-A	4	2	.667	16	10	2	0	0	66	58	7.9	3	36	4.9	38	5.2	3.82	103	.233	.328	-0	1	105	86	1.0	-1	1	0.1
1959	Bos-A	0	1	.000	5	2	0	0	0	9	16	16.0	2	9	9.0	4	4.0	15.00	27	.390	.500	-11	-11	105	71	-0.4	-0	-0	-0.9
1960	Bos-A	1	2	.333	17	2	0	0	2	21	20	8.6	1	13	5.6	18	7.7	5.14	79	.260	.362	-3	-2	105	84	-0.2	0	1	-0.1
	Cle-A	3	4	.429	11	6	1	1	0	41	47	10.3	1	20	4.4	14	3.1	5.05	75	.296	.368	-5	-6	98	90	-0.4	-0	1	-0.4
	Yr	4	6	.400	28	8	1	1	2	62	67	9.7	2	33	4.8	32	4.6	5.08	77	.280	.362	-8	-8	101	90	-0.6	0	1	-0.5
1961	LA-A	11	8	.579	41	21	4	1	0	157	154	8.8	18	63	3.6	88	5.0	3.73	121	.255	.319	5	14	112	107	2.7	-1	-1	1.2
1962	LA-A	9	8	.529	34	25	1	0	1	139	154	10.0	12	40	2.6	52	3.4	4.40	92	.277	.321	-7	-6	102	92	0.0	1	-3	-0.6
1963	KC-A	5	7	.417	41	11	2	1	3	111	115	9.3	14	47	3.8	67	5.4	4.46	89	.269	.338	-10	-6	109	103	-0.4	-1	2	-0.4
1964	KC-A	4	7	.364	50	9	2	1	0	119	135	10.2	12	31	2.3	45	3.4	4.08	96	.285	.325	-6	-2	108	105	0.1	-1	0	-0.2
Total	7	37	39	.487	215	86	12	4	6	663	699	9.5	63	259	3.5	326	4.4	4.34	94	.270	.332	-38	-19	107	98	2.4	-4	1	-1.3
■ **OIL CAN BOYD**	Boyd, Dennis Ray b: 10/6/59, Meridian, Miss. BR/TR, 6'1", 155 lbs. Deb: 9/13/82																												
1982	Bos-A	0	1	.000	3	1	0	0	0	8	11	12.4	2	2	2.3	2	2.3	5.63	80	.314	.351	-1	-1	110	110	-0.4	0	0	0.0
1983	Bos-A	4	8	.333	15	13	5	0	0	99	103	9.4	9	23	2.1	43	3.9	3.27	127	.269	.308	9	10	102	115	-1.8	0	-1	0.9
1984	Bos-A	12	12	.500	29	26	10	3	0	198	207	9.4	18	53	2.4	134	6.1	4.36	101	.269	.313	-8	1	110	87	-0.7	0	2	0.3
1985	Bos-A	15	13	.536	35	35	13	3	0	272	273	9.0	26	67	2.2	154	5.1	3.71	114	.261	.304	13	15	102	99	1.2	0	3	1.9
1986	Bos-A	16	10	.615	30	30	10	0	0	214	222	9.3	32	45	1.9	129	5.4	3.79	109	.265	.301	10	8	99	106	0.9	0	1	0.9
1987	Bos-A	1	3	.250	7	7	0	0	0	37	47	11.4	6	9	2.2	12	2.9	5.84	76	.315	.347	-6	-6	99	99	-0.9	0	1	-0.3
1988	Bos-A	9	7	.563	23	23	1	0	0	130	147	10.2	25	41	2.8	71	4.9	5.33	80	.289	.339	-20	-15	108	101	0.3	0	-1	-1.5
Total	7	57	54	.514	142	135	39	6	0	958	1010	9.5	118	240	2.3	545	5.1	4.13	103	.271	.313	-3	12	103	100	-1.4	0	5	2.2
■ **JAKE BOYD**	Boyd, Jacob Henry b: 1/19/1874, Martinsburg, W.Va. d: 8/12/32, Gettysburg, Pa. TL , 160 lbs. Deb: 9/20/1894																												
1894	Was-N	0	3	.000	3	3	3	0	0	19	37	17.5	1	14	6.6	3	1.4	8.53	62	.433	.513	-7	-7	100	112	-1.4	-1	0	-0.4
1895	Was-N	2	11	.154	14	12	8	0	0	85	126	13.3	1	35	3.7	16	1.7	7.09	71	.365	.424	-22	-19	105	83	-3.6	1	0	-1.4
1896	Was-N	1	2	.333	4	2	2	0	0	32	45	12.7	0	15	4.2	6	1.7	6.75	62	.356	.424	-8	-9	96	81	-0.3	-1	0	-0.7
Total	3	3	16	.158	21	17	13	0	0	136	208	13.8	2	64	4.2	25	1.7	7.21	68	.373	.438	-37	-35	102	87	-5.3	-2	0	-2.5
■ **GARY BOYD**	Boyd, Gary Lee b: 8/22/46, Pasadena, Cal. BR/TR, 6'4", 200 lbs. Deb: 8/01/69																												
1969	Cle-A	0	2	.000	8	3	0	0	0	11	8	6.5	1	14	11.5	9	7.4	9.00	39	.205	.400	-7	-7	96	56	-0.9	-0	-0	-0.6
■ **RAY BOYD**	Boyd, Raymond C. b: 2/11/1887, Hortonville, Ind. d: 2/11/20, Hortonville, Ind. BR/TR, 5'10", 160 lbs. Deb: 9/24/10																												
1910	StL-A	0	2	.000	3	2	1	0	0	14	16	10.3	0	5	3.2	6	3.9	4.50	56	.286	.355	-3	-3	101	83	-0.9	-0	-1	-0.3
1911	Cin-N	2	2	.500	7	4	3	0	1	44	34	7.0	0	19	3.9	20	4.1	2.66	118	.206	.296	4	2	92	70	0.2	-0	-0	0.2
Total	2	2	4	.333	10	6	4	0	1	58	50	7.8	0	24	3.7	26	4.0	3.10	97	.226	.310	1	-1	94	73	-0.7	-0	-1	-0.1
■ **CLOYD BOYER**	Boyer, Cloyd Victor "Junior" b: 9/1/27, Alba, Mo. BR/TR, 6'1", 188 lbs. Deb: 4/23/49 C																												
1949	StL-N	0	0	—	4	1	0	0	0	3	5	15.0	0	7	21.0	0	0.0	12.00	36	.357	.571	-3	-3	108	97	0.0	0	0	-0.1
1950	StL-N	7	7	.500	36	14	6	2	1	120	105	7.9	15	49	3.7	82	6.2	3.53	121	.233	.309	8	10	103	102	0.0	0	0	1.0
1951	StL-N	2	5	.286	19	8	1	0	1	63	68	9.7	9	46	6.6	40	5.7	5.29	75	.286	.406	-9	-9	101	116	-1.5	0	-2	-0.9
1952	StL-N	6	6	.500	23	14	4	2	0	110	108	8.8	11	47	3.8	44	3.6	4.25	85	.258	.334	-6	-8	97	98	-0.7	2	-2	-0.7
1955	KC-A	5	5	.500	30	11	2	0	0	98	107	9.8	21	69	6.3	32	2.9	6.24	67	.282	.393	-25	-22	106	103	0.8	-2	-1	-2.3
Total	5	20	23	.465	112	48	13	4	2	394	393	9.0	56	218	5.0	198	4.5	4.75	85	.262	.357	-35	-32	102	103	-1.4	0	-4	-3.0
■ **HENRY BOYLE**	Boyle, Henry J. "Handsome Henry" b: 9/20/1860, Philadelphia, Pa. d: 5/25/32, Philadelphia, Pa. TR , Deb: 7/09/1884																												
1884	StL-U	15	3	.833	19	16	16	2	1	150	118	7.1	3	10	0.6	88	5.3	1.74	170	.221	.236	21	20	98	98	0.1	3	0	1.9
1885	StL-N	16	24	.400	42	39	39	1	0	367	346	8.5	2	100	2.5	133	3.3	2.75	100	.260	.311	3	-0	97	101	3.0	1	1	0.0
1886	StL-N	9	15	.375	25	24	23	2	0	165	183	10.0	5	46	2.5	101	5.5	2.24	144	.294	.343	20	18	98	**171**	0.5	4	0	2.1
1887	Ind-N	13	24	.351	38	38	37	0	0	328	356	9.8	11	69	1.9	85	2.3	3.65	113	.292	.330	15	17	101	99	2.1	-1	-4	1.0
1888	Ind-N	15	22	.405	37	37	36	3	0	323	315	8.8	11	58	1.6	98	2.7	3.26	85	.269	.303	-15	-18	98	87	1.4	-2	2	-1.6
1889	Ind-N	21	23	.477	46	45	38	2	0	379	422	10.0	14	95	2.3	97	2.3	3.92	113	.298	.342	5	22	110	96	2.1	4	-5	2.0
Total	6	89	111	.445	207	199	189	10	1	1712	1740	9.1	46	378	2.0	602	3.2	3.14	109	.276	.317	48	54	101	103	9.2	8	-7	5.4
■ **HARRY BOYLES**	Boyles, Harry "Stretch" b: 11/29/11, Granite City, Ill. BR/TR, 6'5", 185 lbs. Deb: 8/03/38																												
1938	Chi-A	0	4	.000	9	2	1	0	1	29	31	9.6	2	25	7.8	18	5.6	5.28	89	.263	.395	-2	-2	98	102	-1.9	-1	1	0.0
1939	Chi-A	0	0	—	2	0	0	0	0	3	4	12.0	0	6	18.0	1	3.0	12.00	41	.308	.526	-2	-2	106	76	0.0	-0	0	-0.1
Total	2	0	4	.000	11	2	1	0	1	32	35	9.8	2	31	8.7	19	5.3	5.91	80	.267	.410	-4	-4	99	99	-1.9	-1	1	-0.1
■ **GENE BRABENDER**	Brabender, Eugene Mathew b: 8/16/41, Madison, Wis. BR/TR, 6'5.5", 225 lbs. Deb: 5/11/66																												
1966	Bal-A	4	3	.571	31	1	0	0	2	71	57	7.2	4	29	3.7	62	7.9	3.55	95	.229	.303	-1	-1	99	88	-0.1	-1	1	-0.1
1967	Bal-A	6	4	.600	14	14	3	1	0	94	77	7.4	6	23	2.2	71	6.8	3.35	90	.220	.267	-1	-3	94	70	1.3	-1	-0	-0.4
1968	Bal-A	6	7	.462	37	15	3	2	3	125	116	8.4	9	48	3.5	92	6.6	3.31	91	.248	.315	-5	-4	101	106	-1.1	-0	-1	-0.5
1969	Sea-A	13	14	.481	40	29	7	1	0	202	193	8.6	26	103	4.6	139	6.2	4.37	83	.254	.347	-17	-16	100	103	2.3	-1	-3	-2.0
1970	Mil-A	6	15	.286	29	21	2	0	1	129	127	8.9	7	79	5.5	76	5.3	6.00	62	.255	.355	-33	-33	100	68	-3.2	-2	0	-3.3
Total	5	35	43	.449	151	80	15	4	6	621	570	8.3	53	282	4.1	440	6.4	4.25	80	.245	.326	-56	-58	99	90	-0.8	-5	-3	-6.3
■ **JACK BRACKEN**	Bracken, John James b: 4/14/1881, Cleveland, Ohio d: 7/16/54, Highland Park, Mich. BR/TR, 5'11", 175 lbs. Deb: 8/07/01																												
1901	Cle-A	4	8	.333	12	12	12	0	0	100	137	12.3	4	31	2.8	18	1.6	6.21	57	.348	.395	-28	-29	97	83	-1.0	0	-1	-2.4
■ **JOHN BRACKENRIDGE**	Brackenridge, John Givler b: 12/24/1880, Harrisburg, Pa. d: 3/20/53, Harrisburg, Pa. BR/TR, 6', Deb: 4/15/04																												
1904	Phi-N	0	1	.000	7	1	0	0	0	34	37	9.8	4	16	4.2	11	2.9	5.56	48	.312	.411	-11	-11	97	92	-0.4	-0	2	-0.8

YEAR	TM/L	W	L	PCT	G	GS	CG	SHO	SV	IP	H	H/G	HR	BB	BB/G	SO	SO/G	ERA	/A	OAVG	OOBP	PR	/A	PF	CPI	WAT	PB	PD	TPI
■ DON BRADEY	Bradey, Donald Eugene b: 10/4/34, Charlotte, N.C. BR/TR, 5'9", 180 lbs. Deb: 9/25/64																												
1964	Hou-N	0	2	.000	3	1	0	0	0	2	6	27.0	0	3	13.5	2	9.0	22.50	15	.429	.500	-4	-4	98	60	-0.9	0	0	-0.3
■ LARRY BRADFORD	Bradford, Larry b: 12/21/49, Chicago, Ill. BR/TL, 6'1", 200 lbs. Deb: 9/24/77																												
1977	Atl-N	0	0	—	2	0	0	0	0	3	3	9.0	1	0	0.0	1	3.0	3.00	151	.273	.273	0	1	115	167	0.0	0	0	0.1
1979	Atl-N	1	0	1.000	21	0	0	0	2	19	11	5.2	0	10	4.7	11	5.2	0.95	436	.172	.275	6	7	110	178	0.5	-0	0	0.7
1980	Atl-N	3	4	.429	56	0	0	0	4	55	49	8.0	3	22	3.6	32	5.2	2.45	149	.243	.310	7	7	101	132	-0.4	-0	0	0.7
1981	Atl-N	2	0	1.000	25	0	0	0	1	27	26	8.7	1	12	4.0	14	4.7	3.67	95	.268	.336	-1	-1	100	106	1.0	0	0	0.0
Total	4	6	4	.600	104	0	0	0	7	104	89	7.7	5	44	3.8	58	5.0	2.51	148	.238	.310	13	14	103	135	1.1	-0	1	1.5
■ BILL BRADFORD	Bradford, William D b: 8/28/21, Choctaw, Ark. BR/TR, 6'2", 180 lbs. Deb: 4/24/56																												
1956	KC-A	0	0	—	1	0	0	0	0	2	2	9.0	2	1	4.5	0	0.0	9.00	48	.250	.333	-1	-1	105	119	0.0	0	0	0.0
■ FRED BRADLEY	Bradley, Fred Langdon b: 7/31/20, Parsons, Kan. BR/TR, 6'1", 180 lbs. Deb: 5/01/48																												
1948	Chi-A	0	0	—	8	0	0	0	0	16	11	6.2	2	4	2.3	2	1.1	4.50	95	.190	.242	-0	-0	100	51	0.0	-0	0	0.0
1949	Chi-A	0	0	—	1	1	0	0	0	2	4	18.0	0	3	13.5	0	0.0	13.50	31	.444	.583	-2	-2	99	89	0.0	-0	0	-0.1
Total	2	0	0	—	9	1	0	0	0	18	15	7.5	2	7	3.5	2	1.0	5.50	77	.224	.295	-2	-2	100	55	0.0	-0	0	-0.1
■ FOGHORN BRADLEY	Bradley, George H. b: 7/1/1855, Milford, Mass. d: 4/3/1900, Philadelphia, Pa. BR/TR, Deb: 8/23/1876																												
1876	Bos-N	9	10	.474	22	21	16	1	1	173	201	10.5	1	16	0.8	16	0.8	2.50	87	.295	.311	-4	-6	94	101	-1.8	-0	-0	-0.5
■ GEORGE BRADLEY	Bradley, George Washington "Grin" b: 7/13/1852, Reading, Pa. d: 10/2/31, Philadelphia, Pa. BR/TR, 5'10.5", 175 lbs. Deb: 5/04/1875																												
1875	StL-n	33	26	.559	60																								
1876	StL-N	45	19	.703	64	64	63	**16**	0	573	470	**7.4**	3	38	0.6	103	1.6	**1.23**	154	**.228**	**.242**	**69**	42	82	67	**22.5**	9	3	4.1
1877	Chi-N	18	23	.439	50	44	35	2	0	394	452	10.3	4	39	0.9	59	1.3	3.31	84	.296	.314	-22	-24	99	86	-0.2	2	1	-1.7
1879	Tro-N	13	40	.245	54	54	53	3	0	487	590	10.9	12	26	0.5	133	2.5	2.85	88	.305	.314	-19	-19	100	114	-2.6	4	5	-0.7
1880	Pro-N	13	8	.619	28	20	16	4	1	196	158	7.3	2	6	**0.3**	54	2.5	1.38	159	.229	**.236**	22	18	92	88	0.0	1	0	1.8
1881	Cle-N	2	4	.333	6	6	5	0	0	51	70	12.4	2	3	0.5	6	1.1	3.88	69	.339	.349	-6	-7	96	109	-0.5	0	0	-1.7
1882	Cle-N	6	9	.400	18	16	15	0	0	147	164	10.0	5	22	1.3	32	2.0	3.73	69	.290	.316	-14	-19	90	91	-1.8	-2	0	-1.9
1883	Phi-a	16	7	.696	26	23	22	0	0	214	215	9.0	8	22	0.9	56	2.4	3.15	104	.267	.286	3	3	99	98	1.0	1	0	0.2
1884	Cin-U	25	15	.625	41	38	36	3	0	342	350	9.2	7	23	0.6	168	4.4	2.71	117	.270	.283	11	17	105	106	-1.4	-5	3	1.3
Total	8	138	125	.525	287	265	245	28	1	2404	2469	9.2	43	179	0.7	611	2.3	2.50	101	.272	.286	45	7	95	92	17.0	11	11	1.4
■ HERB BRADLEY	Bradley, Herbert Theodore b: 1/3/03, Agenda, Kan. d: 10/16/59, Clay Center, Kan. BR/TR, 6', 170 lbs. Deb: 5/09/27																												
1927	Bos-A	1	1	.500	6	2	2	0	0	23	16	6.3	0	7	2.7	6	2.3	3.13	131	.198	.272	3	2	99	51	0.3	1	-0	0.3
1928	Bos-A	0	3	.000	15	5	1	1	0	47	64	12.3	2	16	3.1	14	2.7	7.28	56	.339	.381	-17	-17	101	79	-1.4	-1	1	-1.4
1929	Bos-A	0	0	—	3	0	0	0	0	4	7	15.8	1	2	4.5	0	0.0	6.75	66	.438	.450	-1	-1	105	158	0.0	-0	0	0.0
Total	3	1	4	.200	24	7	3	1	0	74	87	10.6	3	25	3.0	20	2.4	5.96	69	.304	.355	-15	-15	101	74	-1.1	-0	1	-1.1
■ BERT BRADLEY	Bradley, Steven Bert b: 12/23/56, Athens, Ga. BR/TR, 6'1", 190 lbs. Deb: 9/03/83																												
1983	Oak-A	0	0	—	6	0	0	0	0	8	14	15.8	1	4	4.5	3	3.4	6.75	58	.400	.450	-2	-3	96	129	0.0	0	1	-0.1
■ TOM BRADLEY	Bradley, Thomas William b: 3/16/47, Asheville, N.C. BR/TR, 6'2.5", 180 lbs. Deb: 9/09/69																												
1969	Cal-A	0	1	.000	3	0	0	0	0	2	9	40.5	1	0	0.0	2	9.0	27.00	14	.600	.600	-5	-5	101	83	-0.4	0	0	-0.4
1970	Cal-A	2	5	.286	17	11	1	1	0	70	71	9.1	3	33	4.2	53	6.8	4.11	83	.270	.347	-3	-6	92	97	-1.6	0	0	-0.4
1971	Chi-A	15	15	.500	45	39	7	6	2	286	273	8.6	16	74	2.3	206	6.5	2.96	114	.248	.291	16	13	97	96	0.4	-1	-2	1.1
1972	Chi-A	15	14	.517	40	40	11	2	0	260	225	7.8	19	65	2.3	209	7.2	2.98	109	.231	.277	3	8	106	86	-1.4	-3	-0	0.6
1973	SF-N	13	12	.520	35	34	6	1	0	224	212	8.5	26	69	2.8	136	5.5	3.90	98	.246	.301	-6	-2	104	88	-0.5	1	-2	-0.2
1974	SF-N	8	11	.421	30	21	2	0	0	134	152	10.2	15	52	3.5	72	4.8	5.17	76	.282	.337	-23	-18	109	88	-0.5	-3	-1	-2.1
1975	SF-N	2	3	.400	13	6	0	0	0	42	57	12.2	6	18	3.9	13	2.8	6.21	59	.326	.382	-12	-12	102	99	-0.4	-1	0	-1.1
Total	7	55	61	.474	183	151	27	10	2	1018	999	8.8	86	311	2.7	691	6.1	3.72	95	.254	.305	-30	-21	102	91	-4.4	-5	-5	-2.5
■ BILL BRADLEY	Bradley, William Joseph b: 2/13/1878, Cleveland, Ohio d: 3/11/54, Cleveland, Ohio BR/TR, 6', 185 lbs. Deb: 8/26/1899 M																												
1901	Cle-A	0	0	—	1	0	0	0	0	1	4	36.0	0	0	0.0	0	0.0	0.00	—	.609	.609	0	0	97	0	0.0	0	0	0.0
■ JOE BRADSHAW	Bradshaw, Joe Siah b: 8/17/1897, Roellen, Tenn. d: 1/30/85, Tavares, Fla. BR/TR, 6'2.5", 200 lbs. Deb: 5/09/29																												
1929	Bro-N	0	0	—	2	0	0	0	0	4	3	6.8	0	4	9.0	1	2.3	4.50	101	.231	.450	0	0	96	133	0.0	0	0	0.0
■ NEAL BRADY	Brady, Cornelius Joseph b: 3/4/1897, Covington, Ky. d: 6/19/47, Fort Mitchell, Ky BR/TR, 6'0.5", 197 lbs. Deb: 9/25/15																												
1915	NY-A	0	0	—	2	1	0	0	0	9	9	9.0	0	7	7.0	6	6.0	3.00	97	.281	.410	-0	-0	99	157	0.0	-1	0	0.0
1917	NY-A	1	0	1.000	2	1	0	0	0	9	6	6.0	0	5	5.0	4	4.0	2.00	143	.188	.297	1	1	107	81	0.5	0	1	0.2
1925	Cin-N	1	3	.250	20	3	2	0	1	64	73	10.3	4	20	2.8	12	1.7	4.64	89	.289	.338	-3	-4	97	93	-1.0	1	0	-0.2
Total	3	2	3	.400	24	5	2	0	1	82	88	9.7	4	32	3.5	22	2.4	4.17	93	.278	.342	-2	-3	98	98	-0.5	1	1	0.0
■ JIM BRADY	Brady, James Joseph "Diamond Jim" b: 3/2/36, Jersey City, N.J. BL/TL, 6'2", 185 lbs. Deb: 5/12/56																												
1956	Det-A	0	0	—	6	0	0	0	0	6	15	22.5	3	11	16.5	3	4.5	30.00	13	.484	.605	-17	-17	95	63	0.0	0	0	-1.4
■ KING BRADY	Brady, James Ward b: 5/28/1881, Elmer, N.J. d: 8/21/47, Albany, N.Y. BR/TR, 6', 190 lbs. Deb: 9/21/05																												
1905	Phi-N	1	1	.500	2	2	2	0	0	13	19	13.2	0	2	1.4	3	2.1	3.46	88	.370	.394	-1	-1	102	143	0.0	-0	0	0.0
1906	Pit-N	1	1	.500	3	2	1	0	0	23	30	11.7	0	4	1.6	14	5.5	2.35	113	.345	.374	1	1	101	176	-0.1	-1	-1	0.0
1907	Pit-N	0	0	—	1	0	0	0	0	2	2	9.0	0	1	4.5	0	0.0	0.00	—	.289	.379	1	1	102	0	0.0	0	-0	0.0
1908	Bos-A	1	0	1.000	1	1	1	1	0	9	8	8.0	0	0	0.0	3	3.0	0.00	—	.242	.242	2	2	97	0	0.5	-0	-0	0.3
1912	Bos-N	0	0	—	1	0	0	0	0	3	5	15.0	0	3	9.0	0	0.0	18.00	21	.313	.421	-5	-5	110	33	0.0	-0	0	-0.3
Total	5	3	2	.600	8	5	4	1	0	50	64	11.5	0	10	1.8	20	3.6	3.06	90	.330	.363	-2	-2	101	120	0.4	-1	-1	0.0
■ BILL BRADY	Brady, William A. "King" b: 1888, TR , Deb: 4/13/12																												
1912	Bos-N	0	0	—	1	0	0	0	0	1	2	18.0	0	0	0.0	0	0.0	0.00	—	.500	.500	0	0	110	0	0.0	0	0	0.0
■ DICK BRAGGINS	Braggins, Richard Realf b: 12/25/1879, Mercer, Pa. d: 8/16/63, Lake Wales, Fla. BR/TR, 5'11", 170 lbs. Deb: 5/16/01																												
1901	Cle-A	1	2	.333	4	3	2	0	0	32	44	12.4	1	15	4.2	1	0.3	4.78	75	.348	.418	-4	-4	97	116	-0.2	-1	0	-0.3
■ ASA BRAINARD	Brainard, Asa "Count" b: 1841, Albany, N.Y. d: 12/29/1888, Denver, Colo. TR , 5'8.5", 150 lbs. Deb: 5/05/1871																												
1871	Oly-n	13	15	.464	30																								
1872	Oly-n	2	7	.222	9																								
	Man-n	0	3	.000	3																								
	Yr	2	10	.167	12																								
1873	Bal-n	4	7	.364	13																								
1874	Bal-n	5	24	.172	29																								
Total	4 n	24	56	.300	84																								
■ AL BRAITHWOOD	Braithwood, Alfred b: 2/15/1892, Braceville, Ill. d: 11/24/60, Rowlesburg, W.Va. 6'1.5", 145 lbs. Deb: 9/01/15																												
1915	Pit-F	0	0	—	2	0	0	0	0	3	0	0.0	0	0	0.0	2	6.0	0.00	—	.000	.000	1	1	102	0	0.0	0	0	0.1
■ ERV BRAME	Brame, Ervin Beckham b: 10/12/01, Big Rock, Tenn. d: 11/22/49, Hopkinsville, Ky. BL/TR, 6'2", 190 lbs. Deb: 4/14/28																												
1928	Pit-N	7	4	.636	24	11	6	0	0	96	110	10.3	5	44	4.1	22	2.1	5.06	82	.291	.356	-11	-10	105	89	1.0	4	-1	-0.5
1929	Pit-N	16	11	.593	37	28	19	1	0	230	250	9.8	17	71	2.8	68	2.7	4.54	105	.278	.323	4	6	102	89	0.7	12	-4	1.3
1930	Pit-N	17	8	.680	32	29	**22**	0	1	236	291	11.1	21	56	2.1	55	2.1	4.69	103	.305	.337	7	4	98	102	4.7	11	-3	1.0
1931	Pit-N	9	13	.409	26	21	15	2	0	180	211	10.6	14	45	2.3	33	1.6	4.20	93	.295	.328	-7	-6	102	104	-1.9	5	-2	-0.1
1932	Pit-N	3	1	.750	23	3	0	0	0	51	84	14.8	6	16	2.8	10	1.8	7.41	52	.365	.403	-20	-20	100	96	0.9	1	-1	-1.8
Total	5	52	37	.584	142	92	62	3	1	793	946	10.7	63	232	2.6	188	2.1	4.76	94	.298	.338	-26	-24	101	97	5.4	33	-10	-0.1
■ RALPH BRANCA	Branca, Ralph Theodore Joseph "Hawk" b: 1/6/26, Mt.Vernon, N.Y. BR/TR, 6'3", 220 lbs. Deb: 6/12/44																												
1944	Bro-N	0	2	.000	21	1	0	0	1	45	46	9.2	2	32	6.4	16	3.2	7.00	53	.274	.388	-17	-17	102	74	-0.9	-1	0	-1.6
1945	Bro-N	5	6	.455	16	15	7	1	1	110	73	6.0	4	79	6.5	69	5.6	3.03	119	.189	.319	9	7	95	93	-1.0	-2	0	0.5

YEAR	TM/L	W	L	PCT	G	GS	CG	SHO	SV	IP	H	H/G	HR	BB	BB/G	SO	SO/G	ERA	/A	OAVG	OOBP	PR	/A	PF	CPI	WAT	PB	PD	TPI
1946	Bro-N	3	1	.750	24	10	2	2	3	67	62	8.3	4	41	5.5	42	5.6	3.90	88	.246	.347	-4	-4	100	97	0.7	0	-1	-0.4
1947	Bro-N	21	12	.636	43	36	15	4	1	280	251	8.1	22	98	3.2	148	4.8	2.67	157	.240	.307	44	47	103	122	1.4	-3	-4	4.2
1948	Bro-N	14	9	.609	36	28	11	1	1	216	189	7.9	24	80	3.3	122	5.1	3.50	116	.232	.302	11	14	103	97	1.8	1	-4	1.1
1949	Bro-N	13	5	.722	34	27	9	2	1	187	181	8.7	21	91	4.4	109	5.2	4.38	90	.253	.337	-7	-9	98	97	2.5	-2	-4	-1.4
1950	Bro-N	7	9	.438	43	15	5	0	7	142	152	9.6	24	55	3.5	100	6.3	4.69	92	.271	.333	-9	-6	104	102	-2.0	1	-1	-0.4
1951	Bro-N	13	12	.520	42	27	13	3	3	204	180	7.9	19	85	3.8	118	5.2	3.26	115	.237	.313	16	11	95	106	-2.2	-0	-3	0.8
1952	Bro-N	4	2	.667	16	7	2	0	0	61	52	7.7	8	21	3.1	26	3.8	3.84	96	.232	.307	-1	-1	98	95	0.3	-0	-1	-0.1
1953	Bro-N	0	0	—	7	0	0	0	0	11	15	12.3	4	5	4.1	5	4.1	9.82	43	.341	.431	-7	-7	100	92	0.0	0	0	-0.5
	Det-A	4	7	.364	17	14	7	0	1	102	98	8.6	7	31	2.7	50	4.4	4.15	98	.253	.302	-2	-1	102	81	-0.3	-1	-1	-0.2
1954	Det-A	3	3	.500	17	5	0	0	0	45	63	12.6	10	30	6.0	15	3.0	5.80	65	.330	.419	-10	-10	101	132	0.3	2	-0	-0.8
	NY-A	1	0	1.000	5	3	0	0	0	13	9	6.2	0	13	9.0	7	4.8	2.77	127	.209	.377	1	1	94	145	0.5	1	0	0.2
	Yr	4	3	.571	22	8	0	0	0	58	72	11.2	10	43	6.7	22	3.4	5.12	73	.305	.403	-9	-9	100	145	0.8	2	-0	-0.6
1956	Bro-N	0	0	—	1	0	0	0	0	2	1	4.5	0	2	9.0	2	9.0	0.00	—	.143	.333	1	1	100	0	0.0	0	0	0.1
Total	12	88	68	.564	322	188	71	13	19	1485	1372	8.3	149	663	4.0	829	5.0	3.79	104	.245	.324	26	26	100	103	1.1	-6	-18	1.5

■ **HARVEY BRANCH** Branch, Harvey Alfred b: 2/8/39, Memphis, Tenn. BR/TL, 6', 175 lbs. Deb: 9/18/62

YEAR	TM/L	W	L	PCT	G	GS	CG	SHO	SV	IP	H	H/G	HR	BB	BB/G	SO	SO/G	ERA	/A	OAVG	OOBP	PR	/A	PF	CPI	WAT	PB	PD	TPI
1962	StL-N	0	1	.000	1	1	0	0	0	5	5	9.0	1	5	9.0	2	3.6	5.40	78	.263	.417	-1	-1	107	120	-0.4	-0	0	0.0

■ **NORM BRANCH** Branch, Norman Downs "Red" b: 3/22/15, Spokane, Wash. d: 11/21/71, Navasota, Tex. BR/TR, 6'3", 200 lbs. Deb: 5/05/41

YEAR	TM/L	W	L	PCT	G	GS	CG	SHO	SV	IP	H	H/G	HR	BB	BB/G	SO	SO/G	ERA	/A	OAVG	OOBP	PR	/A	PF	CPI	WAT	PB	PD	TPI
1941	NY-A	5	1	.833	27	0	0	0	2	47	37	7.1	2	26	5.0	28	5.4	2.87	137	.224	.323	7	6	95	116	1.6	-1	1	0.5
1942	NY-A	0	1	.000	10	0	0	0	2	16	18	10.1	3	16	9.0	13	7.3	6.19	55	.290	.425	-4	-5	94	118	-0.4	0	0	-0.3
Total	2	5	2	.714	37	0	0	0	4	63	55	7.9	5	42	6.0	41	5.9	3.71	102	.242	.353	2	1	94	117	1.2	-1	1	0.2

■ **ROY BRANCH** Branch, Roy b: 7/12/53, St.Louis, Mo. BR/TR, 6', 175 lbs. Deb: 9/11/79

YEAR	TM/L	W	L	PCT	G	GS	CG	SHO	SV	IP	H	H/G	HR	BB	BB/G	SO	SO/G	ERA	/A	OAVG	OOBP	PR	/A	PF	CPI	WAT	PB	PD	TPI
1979	Sea-A	0	1	.000	2	2	0	0	0	11	12	9.8	2	7	5.7	6	4.9	8.18	52	.273	.365	-5	-5	101	68	-0.4	0	-0	-0.3

■ **CHICK BRANDOM** Brandom, Chester Milton b: 3/31/1887, Coldwater, Kan. d: 10/7/58, Santa Ana, Cal. TR , 5'8", 161 lbs. Deb: 9/03/08

YEAR	TM/L	W	L	PCT	G	GS	CG	SHO	SV	IP	H	H/G	HR	BB	BB/G	SO	SO/G	ERA	/A	OAVG	OOBP	PR	/A	PF	CPI	WAT	PB	PD	TPI
1908	Pit-N	1	0	1.000	3	1	1	0	1	17	13	6.9	0	4	2.1	8	4.2	0.53	409	.242	.306	3	3	92	340	0.5	-0	0	0.4
1909	Pit-N	1	0	1.000	13	2	0	0	2	41	33	7.2	0	10	2.2	21	4.6	1.10	235	.239	.295	7	7	99	203	0.5	-1	1	0.9
1915	New-F	1	1	.500	16	1	1	0	0	50	55	9.9	0	15	2.7	15	2.7	3.42	83	.293	.348	-2	-3	94	112	0.0	1	0	-0.2
Total	3	3	1	.750	32	4	2	0	3	108	101	8.4	0	29	2.4	44	3.7	2.08	127	.266	.323	8	7	96	182	1.0	-0	1	1.1

■ **BUCKY BRANDON** Brandon, Darrell G b: 7/8/40, Nacogdoches, Tex. BR/TR, 6'2", 200 lbs. Deb: 4/19/66

YEAR	TM/L	W	L	PCT	G	GS	CG	SHO	SV	IP	H	H/G	HR	BB	BB/G	SO	SO/G	ERA	/A	OAVG	OOBP	PR	/A	PF	CPI	WAT	PB	PD	TPI
1966	Bos-A	8	8	.500	40	17	5	2	2	158	129	7.3	13	70	4.0	101	5.8	3.30	115	.222	.308	2	9	110	96	0.9	2	0	1.2
1967	Bos-A	5	11	.313	39	19	2	0	3	158	147	8.4	21	59	3.4	96	5.5	4.16	88	.245	.312	-16	-9	113	95	-3.7	1	-0	-0.8
1968	Bos-A	0	0	—	8	0	0	0	0	13	19	13.2	1	9	6.2	10	6.9	6.23	48	.333	.433	-5	-5	101	111	0.0	-0	0	-0.4
1969	Sea-A	0	1	.000	8	1	0	0	0	15	15	9.0	4	16	9.6	10	6.0	8.40	43	.250	.423	-8	-8	100	84	-0.4	0	0	-0.7
	Min-A	0	0	—	3	0	0	0	0	3	5	15.0	1	3	9.0	1	3.0	3.00	121	.357	.400	0	0	100	343	0.0	0	-0	0.0
	Yr	0	1	.000	11	1	0	0	0	18	20	10.0	5	19	9.5	11	5.5	7.50	48	.263	.398	-8	-8	100	343	-0.4	0	-0	-0.7
1971	Phi-N	6	6	.500	52	0	0	0	4	83	81	8.8	5	47	5.1	44	4.8	3.90	93	.264	.352	-4	-3	105	108	0.9	-0	-0	-0.3
1972	Phi-N	7	7	.500	42	6	0	0	2	104	106	9.2	9	46	4.0	67	5.8	3.46	99	.268	.348	-0	-1	99	126	1.5	-1	-2	-0.3
1973	Phi-N	2	4	.333	36	0	0	0	2	56	54	8.7	5	25	4.0	25	4.0	5.46	73	.261	.337	-11	-9	109	76	-0.6	0	0	-0.8
Total	7	28	37	.431	228	43	7	2	13	590	556	8.5	59	275	4.2	354	5.4	4.04	91	.250	.332	-42	-25	107	102	-1.4	1	-2	-2.1

■ **ED BRANDT** Brandt, Edward Arthur "Big Ed" b: 2/17/05, Spokane, Wash. d: 11/1/44, Spokane, Wash. BL/TL, 6'1", 190 lbs. Deb: 4/26/28

YEAR	TM/L	W	L	PCT	G	GS	CG	SHO	SV	IP	H	H/G	HR	BB	BB/G	SO	SO/G	ERA	/A	OAVG	OOBP	PR	/A	PF	CPI	WAT	PB	PD	TPI
1928	Bos-N	9	21	.300	38	31	12	1	0	225	234	9.4	22	109	4.4	84	3.4	5.08	80	.273	.350	-27	-26	101	88	-1.4	4	2	-1.8
1929	Bos-N	8	13	.381	26	21	13	0	0	168	196	10.5	12	83	4.4	50	2.7	5.52	83	.302	.373	-15	-17	97	98	0.3	2	2	-1.1
1930	Bos-N	4	11	.267	41	13	4	1	1	147	168	10.3	15	59	3.6	65	4.0	5.02	98	.291	.346	-1	-2	99	97	-3.2	1	1	0.1
1931	Bos-N	18	11	.621	33	29	23	3	2	250	228	8.2	11	77	2.8	112	4.0	2.92	135	.244	.299	26	28	102	102	**5.8**	5	3	**3.8**
1932	Bos-N	16	16	.500	35	31	19	2	1	254	271	9.6	11	57	2.0	79	2.8	3.97	91	.275	.313	-3	-10	93	90	0.0	0	2	-0.8
1933	Bos-N	18	14	.563	41	32	23	3	4	288	256	8.0	10	77	2.4	104	3.3	2.59	123	.245	.289	24	19	96	106	1.0	8	-0	3.0
1934	Bos-N	16	14	.533	40	28	20	3	5	255	249	8.8	13	83	2.9	106	3.7	3.53	99	.254	.311	15	-1	86	96	0.6	5	-3	0.0
1935	Bos-N	5	19	.208	29	25	12	0	0	175	224	11.5	12	66	3.4	61	3.1	4.99	81	.319	.367	-19	-19	100	110	-2.1	-0	1	-1.6
1936	Bro-N	11	13	.458	38	29	12	1	2	234	246	9.5	14	65	2.5	104	4.0	3.50	122	.268	.313	13	20	107	104	0.6	-0	-2	1.8
1937	Pit-N	11	10	.524	33	25	7	3	2	176	177	9.1	11	67	3.4	74	3.8	3.12	127	.263	.328	16	17	101	124	-0.6	1	1	1.8
1938	Pit-N	5	4	.556	24	14	5	1	0	96	93	8.7	3	35	3.3	38	3.6	3.47	108	.250	.310	3	3	99	91	0.0	3	-0	0.5
Total	11	121	146	.453	378	278	150	18	17	2268	2342	9.3	134	778	3.1	877	3.5	3.87	101	.269	.325	33	13	98	101	1.0	28	5	5.7

■ **BILL BRANDT** Brandt, William George b: 3/21/15, Aurora, Ind. d: 5/16/68, Fort Wayne, Ind. BR/TR, 5'8.5", 170 lbs. Deb: 9/20/41

YEAR	TM/L	W	L	PCT	G	GS	CG	SHO	SV	IP	H	H/G	HR	BB	BB/G	SO	SO/G	ERA	/A	OAVG	OOBP	PR	/A	PF	CPI	WAT	PB	PD	TPI
1941	Pit-N	0	1	.000	2	1	0	0	0	7	5	6.4	0	3	3.9	0	0.0	3.86	96	.200	.286	-0	-0	102	50	-0.4	-0	-0	0.0
1942	Pit-N	1	1	.500	3	3	1	0	0	16	23	12.9	1	5	2.8	4	2.3	5.06	67	.343	.384	-3	-3	102	115	0.1	-0	-0	-0.3
1943	Pit-N	4	1	.800	29	3	0	0	0	57	57	9.0	3	19	3.0	17	2.7	3.16	110	.248	.303	1	2	103	97	1.5	-0	-0	0.2
Total	3	5	3	.625	34	7	1	0	0	80	85	9.6	4	27	3.0	21	2.4	3.60	96	.264	.318	-2	-1	103	96	1.2	-1	-1	-0.1

■ **JEFF BRANTLEY** Brantley, Jeffrey Hoke b: 9/5/63, Florence, Ala. BR/TR, 5'11", 180 lbs. Deb: 8/05/88

YEAR	TM/L	W	L	PCT	G	GS	CG	SHO	SV	IP	H	H/G	HR	BB	BB/G	SO	SO/G	ERA	/A	OAVG	OOBP	PR	/A	PF	CPI	WAT	PB	PD	TPI
1988	SF-N	0	1	.000	9	1	0	0	1	21	22	9.4	2	6	2.6	11	4.7	5.57	58	.275	.330	-5	-5	93	76	-0.4	0	1	-0.4

■ **ROY BRASHEAR** Brashear, Roy Parks b: 1/3/1874, Ashtabula, Ohio d: 4/20/51, Los Angeles, Cal. TR , Deb: 6/25/1899

YEAR	TM/L	W	L	PCT	G	GS	CG	SHO	SV	IP	H	H/G	HR	BB	BB/G	SO	SO/G	ERA	/A	OAVG	OOBP	PR	/A	PF	CPI	WAT	PB	PD	TPI
1899	Lou-N	1	0	1.000	3	0	0	0	0	8	8	9.0	0	2	2.3	5	5.6	4.50	88	.283	.331	-1	-0	103	62	0.5	0	0	0.0

■ **JOHN BRAUN** Braun, John Paul b: 12/26/39, Madison, Wis. BR/TR, 6'5", 218 lbs. Deb: 10/02/64

YEAR	TM/L	W	L	PCT	G	GS	CG	SHO	SV	IP	H	H/G	HR	BB	BB/G	SO	SO/G	ERA	/A	OAVG	OOBP	PR	/A	PF	CPI	WAT	PB	PD	TPI
1964	Mil-N	0	0	—	1	0	0	0	0	2	2	9.0	0	1	4.5	1	4.5	0.00	—	.286	.333	1	1	96	0	0.0	0	0	0.1

■ **GARLAND BRAXTON** Braxton, Edgar Garland b: 6/10/1900, Snow Camp, N.C. d: 2/25/66, Norfolk, Va. BB/TL, 5'11", 152 lbs. Deb: 5/27/21

YEAR	TM/L	W	L	PCT	G	GS	CG	SHO	SV	IP	H	H/G	HR	BB	BB/G	SO	SO/G	ERA	/A	OAVG	OOBP	PR	/A	PF	CPI	WAT	PB	PD	TPI
1921	Bos-N	1	3	.250	17	2	0	0	0	37	44	10.7	0	17	4.1	16	3.9	4.86	72	.310	.382	-4	-6	92	96	-0.9	-1	1	-0.5
1922	Bos-N	1	2	.333	25	4	2	0	0	67	75	10.1	3	24	3.2	15	2.0	3.36	119	.286	.347	6	5	98	123	0.0	-2	-1	0.2
1925	NY-A	1	1	.500	3	2	0	0	0	19	26	12.3	1	5	2.4	11	5.2	6.63	64	.338	.376	-5	-5	97	83	0.1	0	0	-0.3
1926	NY-A	5	1	.833	37	1	0	0	2	67	71	9.5	1	19	2.6	30	4.0	2.69	145	.275	.317	10	9	97	122	1.8	1	0	1.0
1927	Was-A	10	9	.526	**58**	2	0	0	**13**	155	144	8.4	5	33	1.9	96	5.6	2.96	134	.246	**.281**	**20**	**17**	96	85	-0.4	1	-2	1.5
1928	Was-A	13	11	.542	38	24	15	2	6	218	177	**7.3**	7	44	1.8	94	3.9	**2.52**	**163**	**.222**	**.258**	37	38	101	79	1.5	-4	0	3.5
1929	Was-A	12	10	.545	37	20	9	0	4	182	219	10.8	6	51	2.5	59	2.9	4.85	88	.299	.335	-12	-12	100	87	1.8	-1	-1	-1.2
1930	Was-A	3	2	.600	15	0	0	0	5	27	22	7.3	3	9	3.0	7	2.3	3.33	137	.222	.277	4	4	98	94	0.0	-1	-1	0.2
	Chi-A	4	10	.286	19	10	2	0	1	91	127	12.6	9	33	3.3	44	4.4	6.43	76	.333	.382	-18	-16	105	98	-2.1	-2	-1	-1.5
	Yr	7	12	.368	34	10	2	0	6	118	149	11.4	12	42	3.2	51	3.9	5.72	84	.310	.360	-14	-12	103	98	-2.1	-1	-2	-1.3
1931	Chi-A	0	3	.000	17	3	0	0	1	47	71	13.6	1	23	4.4	28	5.4	6.89	61	.338	.400	-13	-14	96	92	-1.4	-1	1	-1.2
	StL-A	0	0	—	11	1	0	0	0	18	27	13.5	2	10	5.0	7	3.5	10.50	44	.370	.442	-12	-12	105	78	0.0	1	-0	-0.9
	Yr	0	3	.000	28	4	0	0	1	65	98	13.6	3	33	4.6	35	4.8	7.89	55	.344	.405	-25	-26	98	78	-1.4	-1	0	-2.1
1933	StL-A	0	1	.000	5	1	0	0	0	8	11	12.4	0	8	9.0	5	5.6	10.13	50	.289	.417	-5	-5	117	60	-0.4	-0	0	-0.3
Total	10	50	53	.485	282	70	28	2	32	936	1014	9.8	38	276	2.7	412	4.0	4.13	101	.278	.323	7	4	99	91	-0.0	-8	-5	0.5

■ **AL BRAZLE** Brazle, Alpha Eugene "Cotton" b: 10/19/13, Loyal, Okla. d: 10/24/73, Grand Junction, Colo. BL/TL, 6'2", 185 lbs. Deb: 7/25/43

YEAR	TM/L	W	L	PCT	G	GS	CG	SHO	SV	IP	H	H/G	HR	BB	BB/G	SO	SO/G	ERA	/A	OAVG	OOBP	PR	/A	PF	CPI	WAT	PB	PD	TPI
1943	StL-N	8	2	.800	13	9	8	1	0	88	74	7.6	0	29	3.0	26	2.7	1.53	221	.231	.293	18	18	100	152	1.9	2	0	2.4
1946	StL-N	11	10	.524	37	15	6	2	0	153	152	8.9	1	55	3.2	58	3.4	3.29	107	.261	.321	2	4	103	94	-1.9	-1	0	0.4
1947	StL-N	14	8	.636	44	19	7	0	4	168	186	10.0	7	48	2.6	85	4.6	2.84	148	.284	.331	23	26	104	**139**	1.7	0	3	3.0
1948	StL-N	10	6	.625	42	23	6	3	1	156	171	9.9	8	50	2.9	55	3.2	3.81	103	.281	.328	3	2	99	106	1.4	-2	3	0.3
1949	StL-N	14	8	.636	39	25	9	1	0	206	208	9.1	18	61	2.7	75	3.3	3.19	136	.263	.316	19	27	108	121	0.4	-5	-0	2.2
1950	StL-N	11	9	.550	46	12	3	0	6	165	188	10.3	12	80	4.4	47	2.6	4.09	104	.296	.372	1	3	103	**125**	0.9	-0	-1	0.2
1951	StL-N	6	5	.545	56	8	5	0	7	154	139	8.1	13	60	3.5	66	3.9	3.10	129	.245	.314	**15**	15	101	116	0.2	-3	-2	1.0
1952	StL-N	12	5	.706	46	6	3	2	**16**	109	75	6.2	7	42	3.5	55	4.5	2.72	133	.198	.273	12	11	97	87	2.9	-1	-2	0.9
1953	StL-N	6	7	.462	60	0	0	0	**18**	92	101	9.9	8	43	4.2	57	5.6	4.21	103	.280	.350	1	1	101	112	-0.9	1	2	0.4

YEAR	TM/L	W	L	PCT	G	GS	CG	SHO	SV	IP	H	H/G	HR	BB	BB/G	SO	SO/G	ERA	/A	OAVG	OOBP	PR	/A	PF	CPI	WAT	PB	PD	TPI
1954	StL-N	5	4	.556	58	0	0	0	8	84	93	10.0	10	24	2.6	30	3.2	4.18	98	.288	.331	-1	-1	100	109	0.8	-2	-0	-0.2
Total	10	97	64	.602	441	117	47	9	60	1375	1387	9.1	84	492	3.2	554	3.6	3.31	121	.266	.325	93	105	102	116	7.4	-10	3	10.6
■ **HARRY BRECHEEN**	Brecheen, Harry David "Harry The Cat" b: 10/14/14, Broken Bow, Okla. BL/TL, 5'10", 160 lbs. Deb: 4/22/40 C																												
1940	StL-N	0	0	—	3	0	0	0	0	3	2	6.0	0	2	6.0	4	12.0	0.00	—	.167	.286	1	1	101	0	0.0	0	0	0.2
1943	StL-N	9	6	.600	29	13	8	1	4	135	98	6.5	4	39	2.6	68	4.5	2.27	149	.206	.266	17	17	100	86	-0.9	1	1	2.1
1944	StL-N	16	5	.762	30	22	13	3	0	189	174	8.3	8	46	2.2	88	4.2	2.86	120	.242	.288	16	12	95	96	2.9	1	0	1.4
1945	StL-N	15	4	**.789**	24	18	13	3	2	157	136	7.8	5	44	2.5	63	3.6	2.52	146	.238	.294	22	20	97	111	**4.6**	-1	-1	1.9
1946	StL-N	15	15	.500	36	30	14	5	3	231	212	8.3	8	67	2.6	117	4.6	2.49	141	.244	.297	24	26	103	108	-3.5	-4	2	2.7
1947	StL-N	16	11	.593	29	28	18	1	1	223	220	8.9	20	66	2.7	89	3.6	3.31	127	.260	.312	19	22	104	111	0.6	5	1	2.9
1948	StL-N	20	7	**.741**	33	30	21	**7**	1	233	193	7.5	6	49	1.9	**149**	**5.8**	**2.24**	**175**	.222	**.262**	44	43	99	90	**6.3**	-0	1	4.7
1949	StL-N	14	11	.560	32	31	14	2	1	215	207	8.7	18	65	2.7	88	3.7	3.35	130	.252	.308	17	24	108	105	-1.4	4	-1	2.9
1950	StL-N	8	11	.421	27	23	12	2	1	163	151	8.3	18	45	2.5	80	4.4	3.81	112	.244	.295	6	8	103	88	-1.7	4	-0	1.1
1951	StL-N	8	4	.667	24	16	5	0	2	139	134	8.7	11	54	3.5	57	3.7	3.24	123	.256	.325	11	12	101	116	1.9	2	-0	1.4
1952	StL-N	7	5	.583	25	13	4	1	2	100	82	7.4	12	28	2.5	54	4.9	3.33	109	.223	.277	4	3	97	91	0.2	2	2	0.7
1953	StL-A	5	13	.278	26	16	3	0	1	117	122	9.4	7	31	2.4	44	3.4	3.08	144	.269	.316	12	17	111	118	-2.0	-2	2	1.9
Total	12	133	92	.591	318	240	125	25	18	1905	1731	8.2	117	536	2.5	901	4.3	2.92	133	.242	.295	193	206	102	102	7.0	11	6	23.9
■ **BILL BRECKINRIDGE**	Breckinridge, William Robertson b: 10/16/07, Tulsa, Okla. d: 8/23/58, Tulsa, Okla. BR/TR, 5'11", 175 lbs. Deb: 6/30/29																												
1929	Phi-A	0	0	—	3	1	0	0	0	10	10	9.0	0	16	14.4	2	1.8	8.10	55	.270	.473	-4	-4	104	85	0.0	-1	-0	-0.4
■ **FRED BREINING**	Breining, Fred Lawrence b: 11/15/55, San Francisco, Cal. BR/TR, 6'4", 185 lbs. Deb: 9/04/80																												
1980	SF-N	0	0	—	5	0	0	0	0	7	8	10.3	0	4	5.1	3	3.9	5.14	68	.333	.433	-1	-1	96	117	0.0	0	0	0.0
1981	SF-N	5	2	.714	45	1	0	0	1	78	66	7.6	4	38	4.4	37	4.3	2.54	144	.243	.325	8	10	105	142	1.5	-1	-0	0.9
1982	SF-N	11	6	.647	54	9	2	0	0	143	146	9.2	6	52	3.3	98	6.2	3.08	110	.269	.325	8	5	94	120	2.2	2	1	0.7
1983	SF-N	11	12	.478	32	32	6	0	0	203	202	9.0	15	60	2.7	117	5.2	3.81	96	.259	.308	-4	-3	101	91	-0.2	1	-1	-0.3
1984	Mon-N	0	0	—	4	0	0	0	0	7	4	5.1	0	5	6.4	5	6.4	1.29	255	.190	.333	2	2	91	228	0.0	-0	-0	0.1
Total	5	27	20	.574	140	42	8	0	1	438	426	8.8	25	159	3.3	260	5.3	3.33	107	.260	.319	13	12	99	112	3.5	1	-0	1.4
■ **ALONZO BREITENSTEIN**	Breitenstein, Alonzo b: 11/9/1857, Utica, N.Y. d: 6/19/32, Utica, N.Y. Deb: 7/07/1883																												
1883	Phi-N	0	1	.000	1	1	0	0	0	5	8	14.4	0	2	3.6	0	0.0	9.00	35	.369	.423	-3	-3	99	70	-0.4	-0	0	-0.2
■ **TED BREITENSTEIN**	Breitenstein, Theodore P. "Theo" b: 6/1/1869, St.Louis, Mo. d: 5/3/35, St.Louis, Mo. BL/TL, 5'9", 167 lbs. Deb: 4/28/1891																												
1891	StL-a	2	0	1.000	6	1	1	1	1	29	15	4.7	2	14	4.3	13	4.0	2.17	191	.164	.275	5	6	112	68	1.0	-2	0	0.4
1892	StL-N	9	19	.321	39	32	28	1	0	282	280	8.9	8	148	4.7	126	4.0	4.69	68	.272	.363	-44	-47	97	79	-2.2	-4	0	-4.4
1893	StL-N	19	24	.442	48	42	38	1	1	383	359	8.4	8	156	3.7	102	2.4	**3.20**	146	.263	.338	63	63	100	103	0.6	-5	4	5.3
1894	StL-N	27	23	.540	**56**	50	**46**	1	0	**447**	497	10.0	21	191	3.8	140	2.8	4.79	114	.303	.376	27	34	103	91	7.2	-2	4	3.0
1895	StL-N	19	30	.388	54	50	**46**	1	1	430	458	9.6	16	178	3.7	127	2.7	4.44	111	.293	.365	17	22	102	91	4.7	-7	4	1.5
1896	StL-N	18	26	.409	44	43	37	1	1	340	376	10.0	12	138	3.7	114	3.0	4.50	95	.303	.372	-5	-8	98	91	4.5	3	4	0.0
1897	Cin-N	23	12	.657	40	39	32	2	0	320	345	9.7	3	91	2.6	98	2.8	3.63	127	.297	.348	24	35	107	93	4.3	3	1	3.6
1898	Cin-N	20	14	.588	39	37	32	3	0	316	313	8.9	2	123	3.5	68	1.9	3.42	113	.280	.351	7	15	107	94	-0.5	1	4	2.0
1899	Cin-N	13	9	.591	26	24	21	0	0	211	219	9.3	2	71	3.0	59	2.5	3.58	113	.291	.352	6	11	105	92	1.1	8	0	2.1
1900	Cin-N	10	10	.500	24	20	18	1	0	192	205	9.6	4	79	3.7	39	1.8	3.66	94	.296	.368	1	-5	93	104	1.1	1	0	-0.4
1901	StL-N	0	3	.000	3	3	1	0	0	15	24	14.4	1	14	8.4	3	1.8	6.60	48	.386	.498	-5	-6	95	125	-1.4	0	1	-0.3
Total	11	160	170	.485	379	341	300	12	3	2965	3091	9.4	79	1203	3.7	889	2.7	4.04	109	.288	.360	96	121	102	93	20.4	-3	21	12.8
■ **AD BRENNAN**	Brennan, Addison Foster b: 7/18/1881, Laharpe, Kan. d: 1/7/62, Kansas City, Mo. BL/TL, 5'11", 170 lbs. Deb: 5/19/10																												
1910	Phi-N	2	0	1.000	19	5	2	0	0	73	72	8.9	2	28	3.5	28	3.5	2.34	123	.264	.339	6	4	95	143	1.0	2	-1	0.5
1911	Phi-N	2	1	.667	5	3	1	0	0	23	22	8.6	0	12	4.7	12	4.7	3.52	104	.259	.357	-0	0	108	101	0.5	-0	0	0.1
1912	Phi-N	11	9	.550	27	19	13	1	2	174	185	9.6	4	49	2.5	78	4.0	3.57	96	.268	.319	-3	-3	101	82	1.5	4	2	0.4
1913	Phi-N	14	12	.538	40	25	12	1	1	207	204	8.9	5	46	2.0	94	4.1	2.39	148	.268	.304	19	27	111	**129**	-1.1	-3	1	2.7
1914	Chi-F	5	5	.500	16	11	5	1	0	86	84	8.8	6	21	2.2	31	3.2	3.56	80	.256	.305	-3	-7	89	88	-0.5	2	-0	-0.5
1915	Chi-F	3	9	.250	19	13	7	2	0	106	117	9.9	4	30	2.5	40	3.4	3.74	77	.230	.283	-8	-10	95	55	-3.4	1	-1	-1.0
1918	Was-A	0	0	—	2	1	0	0	0	5	7	12.6	0	5	9.0	0	0.0	5.40	53	.241	.371	-1	-1	103	71	0.0	-0	0	-0.1
	Cle-A	0	0	—	1	0	0	0	0	3	3	9.0	0	3	9.0	0	0.0	3.00	98	.333	.500	-0	-0	107	210	0.0	-0	-0	0.0
	Yr	0	0	—	3	1	0	0	0	8	10	11.3	0	8	9.0	0	0.0	4.50	64	.256	.383	-2	-1	104	210	0.0	-0	0	-0.1
Total	7	37	36	.507	129	77	40	5	3	677	694	9.2	21	194	2.6	283	3.8	3.11	104	.258	.311	8	10	101	100	-2.0	5	1	2.1
■ **DON BRENNAN**	Brennan, James Donald b: 12/2/03, Augusta, Maine d: 4/26/53, Boston, Mass. BR/TR, 6', 210 lbs. Deb: 4/16/33																												
1933	NY-A	5	1	.833	18	10	3	0	3	85	92	9.7	4	47	5.0	46	4.9	4.98	76	.275	.355	-7	-11	88	94	1.8	2	1	-0.7
1934	Cin-N	4	3	.571	28	7	2	0	2	78	89	10.3	3	35	4.0	31	3.6	3.81	112	.290	.358	2	4	105	121	1.3	0	-1	0.4
1935	Cin-N	5	5	.500	38	5	2	1	5	114	101	8.0	4	44	3.5	48	3.8	3.16	121	.242	.312	11	9	95	104	0.5	-1	-2	0.5
1936	Cin-N	5	2	.714	41	4	0	0	9	94	117	11.2	2	35	3.4	40	3.8	4.40	89	.305	.361	-4	-5	97	105	1.6	-2	-0	-0.7
1937	Cin-N	1	1	.500	10	0	0	0	0	16	25	14.1	1	10	5.6	6	3.4	6.75	54	.347	.427	-5	-6	93	103	0.2	-1	0	-0.5
	NY-N	1	0	1.000	6	0	0	0	0	9	12	12.0	0	9	9.0	1	1.0	7.00	55	.316	.440	-3	-3	98	98	0.5	0	-0	-0.2
	Yr	2	1	.667	16	0	0	0	0	25	37	13.3	1	19	6.8	7	2.5	6.84	54	.336	.432	-8	-9	95	98	0.7	-1	-0	-0.7
Total	5	21	12	.636	141	26	7	1	19	396	436	9.9	14	180	4.1	172	3.9	4.20	93	.281	.351	-6	-13	96	105	5.9	-2	-2	-1.2
■ **TOM BRENNAN**	Brennan, Thomas Martin b: 10/30/52, Chicago, Ill. BR/TR, 6'1", 180 lbs. Deb: 9/05/81																												
1981	Cle-A	2	2	.500	7	6	1	0	0	48	49	9.2	5	14	2.6	15	2.8	3.19	107	.259	.307	3	1	93	114	0.0	0	1	0.2
1982	Cle-A	4	2	.667	30	4	0	0	2	93	112	10.8	9	10	1.0	46	4.5	4.26	97	.300	.316	-2	-1	101	101	1.1	0	1	0.0
1983	Cle-A	2	2	.500	11	5	1	1	0	40	45	10.1	3	8	1.8	21	4.7	3.82	113	.288	.323	1	2	106	108	0.2	0	-0	0.2
1984	Chi-A	0	1	.000	4	1	0	0	0	7	8	10.3	1	3	3.9	3	3.9	3.86	115	.308	.367	0	0	111	149	-0.4	0	0	0.1
1985	LA-N	1	3	.250	12	4	0	0	0	32	41	11.5	2	11	3.1	17	4.8	7.31	45	.333	.361	-13	-14	92	76	-1.1	-0	1	-1.2
Total	5	9	10	.474	64	20	2	1	2	220	255	10.4	20	46	1.9	102	4.2	4.38	89	.294	.324	-11	-12	99	103	-0.2	-0	3	-0.7
■ **BILL BRENNAN**	Brennan, William Raymond b: 1/15/63, Tampa, Fla. BR/TR, 6'3", 194 lbs. Deb: 7/19/88																												
1988	LA-N	0	1	.000	4	2	0	0	0	9	13	13.0	0	6	6.0	7	7.0	7.00	52	.342	.432	-4	-3	105	91	-0.4	-0	0	-0.2
■ **JIM BRENNEMAN**	Brenneman, James Leroy b: 2/13/41, San Diego, Cal. BR/TR, 6'2", 180 lbs. Deb: 7/09/65																												
1965	NY-A	0	0	—	3	0	0	0	0	2	5	22.5	1	3	13.5	2	9.0	18.00	19	.455	.571	-3	-3	101	95	0.0	0	0	-0.2
■ **BERT BRENNER**	Brenner, Delbert Henry "Dutch" b: 7/18/1887, Minneapolis, Minn d: 4/11/71, St.Louis Park, Minn. BR/TR, 6', 175 lbs. Deb: 9/21/12																												
1912	Cle-A	1	0	1.000	2	1	1	0	0	13	14	9.7	0	4	2.8	3	2.1	2.77	122	.286	.340	1	1	101	129	0.5	-1	0	0.1
■ **LYNN BRENTON**	Brenton, Lynn Davis "Buck" or "Herb" b: 10/7/1890, Peoria, Ill. d: 10/14/68, Los Angeles, Cal. BR/TR, 5'10", 165 lbs. Deb: 8/09/13																												
1913	Cle-A	0	0	—	1	0	0	0	0	2	4	18.0	0	0	0.0	2	9.0	9.00	34	.400	.400	-1	-1	104	72	0.0	0	0	0.0
1915	Cle-A	2	3	.400	11	5	1	1	0	51	60	10.6	1	20	3.5	18	3.2	3.35	93	.308	.378	-2	-1	106	136	0.1	-1	-1	-0.3
1920	Cin-N	2	1	.667	5	1	1	0	1	18	17	8.5	0	4	2.0	13	6.5	5.00	55	.236	.273	-4	-4	88	32	0.4	0	2	-0.2
1921	Cin-N	1	8	.111	17	9	2	0	1	60	80	12.0	0	17	2.6	19	2.9	4.05	95	.342	.370	-2	-1	101	123	-3.4	-0	2	0.0
Total	4	5	12	.294	34	15	4	1	2	131	161	11.1	1	41	2.8	52	3.6	3.98	86	.315	.360	-9	-8	102	115	-2.9	-2	3	-0.5
■ **ROGER BRESNAHAN**	Bresnahan, Roger Philip "The Duke Of Tralee" b: 6/11/1879, Toledo, Ohio d: 12/4/44, Toledo, Ohio BR/TR, 5'9", 200 lbs. Deb: 8/27/1897 MCH																												
1897	Was-N	4	0	1.000	6	5	3	1	0	41	52	11.4	1	10	2.2	12	2.6	3.95	111	.332	.372	2	2	102	110	2.0	1	0	0.3
1901	Bal-A	0	1	.000	2	1	0	0	0	6	10	15.0	0	4	6.0	3	4.5	6.00	65	.393	.476	-2	-1	107	122	-0.4	0	0	0.0
1910	StL-N	0	0	—	1	0	0	0	0	3	6	18.0	0	1	3.0	0	0.0	0.00	—	.400	.438	1	1	93	0	0.0	0	1	0.1
Total	3	4	1	.800	9	6	3	1	0	50	68	12.2	1	15	2.7	15	2.7	3.96	107	.345	.391	1	1	102	104	1.6	2	1	0.4
■ **RUBE BRESSLER**	Bressler, Raymond Bloom b: 10/23/1894, Coder, Pa. d: 11/7/66, Cincinnati, Ohio BR/TL, 6', 187 lbs. Deb: 4/24/14																												
1914	Phi-A	10	4	.714	29	10	8	1	2	148	112	6.8	1	56	3.4	96	5.8	1.76	144	.220	.302	16	13	93	122	1.4	4	-2	1.5
1915	Phi-A	4	17	.190	32	20	7	1	0	178	183	9.3	3	118	6.0	69	3.5	5.21	58	.283	.399	-45	-43	103	90	-3.7	1	0	-4.0

YEAR	TM/L	W	L	PCT	G	GS	CG	SHO	SV	IP	H	H/G	HR	BB	BB/G	SO	SO/G	ERA	/A	OAVG	OOBP	PR	/A	PF	CPI	WAT	PB	PD	TPI
1916	Phi-A	0	2	.000	4	2	0	0	0	15	16	9.6	0	14	8.4	8	4.8	6.60	45	.296	.457	-6	-6	105	88	-0.9	1	-0	-0.5
1917	Cin-N	0	0	—	2	1	0	0	0	9	15	15.0	0	5	5.0	2	2.0	6.00	42	.429	.455	-3	-3	93	135	0.0	-0	-0	-0.3
1918	Cin-N	8	5	.615	17	13	10	0	0	128	124	8.7	3	39	2.7	37	2.6	2.46	108	.261	.308	4	3	96	**123**	1.3	4	3	1.2
1919	Cin-N	2	4	.333	13	4	1	0	0	42	37	7.9	1	8	1.7	13	2.8	3.43	86	.248	.276	-2	-2	101	72	-1.5	2	1	-0.1
1920	Cin-N	2	0	1.000	10	2	1	1	0	20	24	10.8	0	2	0.9	4	1.8	1.80	154	.300	.302	3	2	88	171	1.0	1	0	0.2
Total	7	26	32	.448	107	52	27	3	2	540	511	8.5	8	242	4.0	229	3.8	3.40	82	.262	.343	-33	-37	98	109	-2.4	11	0	-2.0
■ **DUKE BRETT**	Brett, Herbert James "Herb" b: 5/23/1900, Lawrenceville, Va. d: 11/25/74, St.Petersburg, Fla BR/TR, 6', 175 lbs. Deb: 8/08/24																												
1924	Chi-N	0	0	—	1	1	0	0	0	5	6	10.8	0	7	12.6	1	1.8	5.40	72	.300	.448	-1	-1	101	130	0.0	-0	-0	0.0
1925	Chi-N	1	1	.500	10	1	0	0	0	17	12	6.4	0	3	1.6	6	3.2	3.71	113	.194	.232	1	1	98	25	0.1	-0	0	0.1
Total	2	1	1	.500	11	2	0	0	0	22	18	7.4	0	10	4.1	7	2.9	4.09	101	.220	.296	0	0	99	49	0.1	-0	0	0.1
■ **KEN BRETT**	Brett, Kenneth Alven b: 9/18/48, Brooklyn, N.Y. BL/TL, 6', 190 lbs. Deb: 9/27/67																												
1967	Bos-A	0	0	—	1	0	0	0	0	2	3	13.5	0	0	0.0	2	9.0	4.50	81	.375	.375	-0	-0	113	118	0.0	0	0	0.0
1969	Bos-A	2	3	.400	8	8	0	0	0	39	41	9.5	6	22	5.1	23	5.3	5.31	72	.275	.371	-7	-7	105	102	-0.6	2	0	-0.3
1970	Bos-A	8	9	.471	41	14	1	0	2	139	118	7.6	17	79	5.1	155	10.0	4.08	100	.223	.325	-6	0	110	88	-1.1	6	1	0.8
1971	Bos-A	0	3	.000	29	2	0	0	1	59	57	8.7	7	35	5.3	57	8.7	5.34	68	.253	.352	-12	-11	105	83	-1.4	-0	-0	-1.1
1972	Mil-A	7	12	.368	26	22	2	1	0	133	121	8.2	13	49	3.3	74	5.0	4.53	65	.242	.306	-22	-23	97	74	-1.1	2	-1	-2.4
1973	Phi-N	13	9	.591	31	25	10	1	0	212	206	8.7	19	74	3.1	111	4.7	3.44	116	.259	.317	5	13	109	107	3.3	8	2	2.6
1974	Pit-N	13	9	.591	27	27	10	3	0	191	192	9.0	9	52	2.5	96	4.5	3.30	106	.257	.305	7	4	97	93	1.3	10	0	1.5
1975	Pit-N	9	5	.643	23	16	4	1	0	118	110	8.4	10	43	3.3	47	3.6	3.36	106	.250	.315	4	2	98	104	1.3	4	0	0.7
1976	NY-A	0	0	—	2	0	0	0	1	2	2	9.0	0	0	0.0	1	4.5	0.00	—	.222	.222	1	1	97	0	0.0	0	0	0.1
	Chi-A	10	12	.455	27	26	16	1	1	201	171	7.7	5	76	3.4	91	4.1	3.31	108	.234	.303	5	6	101	83	1.2	2	1	0.6
	Yr	10	12	.455	29	26	16	1	2	203	173	7.7	5	76	3.4	92	4.1	3.28	109	.233	.302	5	6	101	83	1.2	0	1	0.7
1977	Chi-A	6	4	.600	13	13	2	0	0	83	101	11.0	10	15	1.6	39	4.2	4.99	81	.305	.332	-8	-9	99	95	0.5	0	-0	-0.8
	Cal-A	7	10	.412	21	21	5	0	0	142	157	10.0	15	38	2.4	41	2.6	4.25	91	.287	.331	-3	-6	95	104	-0.8	0	2	-0.3
	Yr	13	14	.481	34	34	7	0	0	225	258	10.3	25	53	2.1	80	3.2	4.52	87	.293	.331	-11	-15	96	104	-0.3	0	2	-1.1
1978	Cal-A	3	5	.375	31	10	1	1	1	100	100	9.0	12	42	3.8	43	3.9	4.95	77	.262	.334	-13	-12	101	84	-1.2	0	2	-1.0
1979	Min-A	0	0	—	9	0	0	0	0	13	16	11.1	1	6	4.2	3	2.1	4.85	94	.320	.379	-1	-0	108	117	0.0	0	0	0.0
	LA-N	4	3	.571	30	0	0	0	2	47	52	10.0	1	12	2.3	13	2.5	3.45	108	.277	.322	2	1	99	98	0.6	1	2	0.4
1980	KC-A	0	0	—	8	0	0	0	1	13	8	5.5	0	5	3.5	4	2.8	0.00	—	.174	.259	6	6	97	0	0.0	0	0	0.6
1981	KC-A	1	1	.500	22	0	0	0	2	32	35	9.8	2	14	3.9	7	2.0	4.22	86	.282	.347	-2	-2	99	106	0.0	0	0	-0.1
Total	14	83	85	.494	349	184	51	8	11	1526	1490	8.8	127	562	3.3	807	4.8	3.93	94	.257	.320	-45	-37	101	93	2.0	35	8	1.3
■ **MARV BREUER**	Breuer, Marvin Howard "Baby Face" b: 4/29/14, Rolla, Mo. BR/TR, 6'2", 185 lbs. Deb: 5/04/39																												
1939	NY-A	0	0	—	1	0	0	0	0	1	2	18.0	0	1	9.0	0	0.0	9.00	44	.667	.500	-0	-1	85	165	0.0	0	0	0.0
1940	NY-A	8	9	.471	27	22	10	0	0	164	175	9.6	20	61	3.3	71	3.9	4.55	92	.267	.327	-3	-6	96	96	-1.5	-5	-1	-1.0
1941	NY-A	9	7	.563	26	18	7	1	2	141	131	8.4	10	49	3.1	77	4.9	4.09	96	.243	.306	1	-2	95	81	-1.2	-3	-1	-0.5
1942	NY-A	8	9	.471	27	19	6	0	1	164	157	8.6	11	37	2.0	72	4.0	3.07	112	.252	.292	11	7	94	103	-2.6	-3	-2	0.1
1943	NY-A	0	1	.000	5	1	0	0	0	14	22	14.1	0	6	3.9	6	3.9	8.36	37	.349	.400	-8	-8	94	71	-0.4	0	0	-0.7
Total	5	25	26	.490	86	60	23	1	3	484	487	9.1	41	154	2.9	226	4.2	4.04	95	.258	.312	0	-11	95	93	-5.7	-10	-3	-2.1
■ **JIM BREWER**	Brewer, James Thomas b: 11/17/37, Merced, Cal. d: 11/16/87, Tyler, Tex. BL/TL, 6'1", 186 lbs. Deb: 7/17/60 C																												
1960	Chi-N	0	3	.000	5	4	0	0	0	22	25	10.2	2	6	2.5	7	2.9	5.73	66	.272	.323	-5	-5	101	68	-1.4	0	0	-0.3
1961	Chi-N	1	7	.125	36	11	0	0	0	87	116	12.0	17	21	2.2	57	5.9	5.79	71	.321	.356	-17	-16	102	103	-2.7	0	-2	-1.6
1962	Chi-N	0	1	.000	6	1	0	0	0	6	10	15.0	2	3	4.5	1	1.5	9.00	48	.435	.481	-3	-3	109	121	-0.4	0	0	-0.2
1963	Chi-N	3	2	.600	29	1	0	0	0	50	59	10.6	10	15	2.7	35	6.3	4.86	71	.294	.332	-9	-8	105	110	0.5	0	-1	-0.8
1964	LA-N	4	3	.571	34	5	1	1	1	93	79	7.6	5	25	2.4	63	6.1	3.00	108	.232	.278	6	2	91	88	0.6	2	-1	0.3
1965	LA-N	3	2	.600	19	2	0	0	2	49	33	6.1	1	28	5.1	31	5.7	1.84	173	.196	.308	9	7	90	136	0.0	-1	0	0.8
1966	LA-N	0	2	.000	13	0	0	0	2	22	17	7.0	0	11	4.5	8	3.3	3.68	93	.221	.301	-0	-1	95	71	-0.9	0	0	0.0
1967	LA-N	5	4	.556	30	11	0	0	1	101	78	7.0	8	31	2.8	74	6.6	2.67	113	.218	.277	8	4	89	100	0.9	-1	-1	0.2
1968	LA-N	8	3	.727	54	0	0	0	14	76	59	7.0	5	33	3.9	75	8.9	2.49	110	.219	.296	4	2	91	114	2.8	0	0	0.3
1969	LA-N	7	6	.538	59	0	0	0	20	88	71	7.3	5	41	4.2	92	9.4	2.56	137	.221	.312	10	9	97	118	0.2	0	0	1.0
1970	LA-N	7	6	.538	58	0	0	0	24	89	66	6.7	10	33	3.3	91	9.2	3.13	115	.207	.274	9	5	89	89	0.0	-0	0	0.4
1971	LA-N	6	5	.545	55	0	0	0	22	81	55	6.1	4	24	2.7	66	7.3	1.89	179	.194	.249	14	14	98	92	0.0	1	0	1.6
1972	LA-N	8	7	.533	51	0	0	0	17	78	41	4.7	6	25	2.9	69	8.0	1.27	253	.157	.224	19	17	93	107	-0.1	0	0	1.9
1973	LA-N	6	8	.429	56	0	0	0	20	72	58	7.3	8	25	3.1	56	7.0	3.00	121	.229	.284	5	5	99	107	-1.9	1	0	0.6
1974	LA-N	4	4	.500	24	0	0	0	0	39	29	6.7	5	10	2.3	26	6.0	2.54	128	.207	.250	5	3	90	97	-0.8	-0	-0	0.2
1975	LA-N	3	1	.750	21	0	0	0	2	33	44	12.0	2	12	3.3	21	5.7	5.18	65	.333	.375	-6	-7	93	108	0.9	-0	0	-0.6
	Cal-A	1	0	1.000	21	0	0	0	5	35	38	9.8	2	11	2.8	22	5.7	1.80	202	.281	.327	8	7	96	218	0.5	0	-0	0.7
1976	Cal-A	3	1	.750	13	0	0	0	2	20	20	9.0	0	6	2.7	16	7.2	2.70	121	.256	.306	2	1	93	103	1.1	0	0	0.1
Total	17	69	65	.515	584	35	1	1	132	1041	898	7.8	92	360	3.1	810	7.0	3.07	110	.236	.295	59	37	95	106	-0.7	2	-3	4.6
■ **JACK BREWER**	Brewer, John Herndon "Buddy" b: 7/21/19, Los Angeles, Cal. BR/TR, 6'2", 170 lbs. Deb: 7/15/44																												
1944	NY-N	1	4	.200	14	7	2	0	0	55	66	10.8	8	16	2.6	21	3.4	5.56	68	.288	.337	-12	-11	105	89	-1.3	0	-1	-1.0
1945	NY-N	8	6	.571	28	21	8	0	0	160	162	9.1	14	58	3.3	49	2.8	3.82	100	.260	.324	-0	-0	100	102	0.9	-1	-3	-0.3
1946	NY-N	0	0	—	1	0	0	0	0	2	3	13.5	0	2	9.0	3	13.5	13.50	26	.333	.455	-2	-2	103	51	0.0	0	0	-0.1
Total	3	9	10	.474	43	28	10	0	0	217	231	9.6	22	76	3.2	73	3.0	4.35	87	.268	.329	-15	-13	102	98	-0.4	-1	-3	-1.4
■ **TOM BREWER**	Brewer, Thomas Austin b: 9/3/31, Wadesboro, S.C. BR/TR, 6'1", 175 lbs. Deb: 4/18/54																												
1954	Bos-A	10	9	.526	33	23	7	0	0	163	152	8.4	15	95	5.2	69	3.8	4.64	81	.249	.349	-17	-16	101	90	1.5	4	-2	-1.4
1955	Bos-A	11	10	.524	31	28	9	2	0	193	198	9.2	21	87	4.1	91	4.2	4.20	115	.263	.342	-5	14	122	103	-0.4	-4	3	1.6
1956	Bos-A	19	9	.679	32	32	15	4	0	244	200	7.4	14	112	4.1	127	4.7	3.50	121	.220	.305	18	20	102	80	4.7	6	4	3.1
1957	Bos-A	16	13	.552	32	32	15	2	0	238	225	8.5	24	93	3.5	128	4.8	3.86	107	.250	.321	-2	7	109	97	0.7	-1	6	1.3
1958	Bos-A	12	12	.500	33	32	10	1	0	227	227	9.0	21	93	3.7	124	4.9	3.73	106	.259	.331	1	6	105	107	-0.3	-0	4	1.1
1959	Bos-A	10	12	.455	36	32	11	3	2	215	219	9.2	14	88	3.7	121	5.1	3.77	108	.265	.333	2	7	105	105	-0.7	-4	4	0.8
1960	Bos-A	10	15	.400	34	29	8	1	1	187	220	10.6	13	72	3.5	60	2.9	4.81	85	.301	.359	-20	-15	105	101	-0.7	0	3	-1.1
1961	Bos-A	3	2	.600	10	9	0	0	0	42	37	7.9	4	29	6.2	13	2.8	3.43	120	.242	.349	3	3	103	128	0.6	2	1	0.6
Total	8	91	82	.526	241	217	75	13	3	1509	1478	8.8	126	669	4.0	733	4.4	4.00	104	.257	.333	-19	26	107	98	5.4	2	22	6.0
■ **ALAN BRICE**	Brice, Alan Healey b: 10/1/37, New York, N.Y. BR/TR, 6'5", 215 lbs. Deb: 9/22/61																												
1961	Chi-A	0	1	.000	3	0	0	0	0	3	4	12.0	0	3	9.0	3	9.0	0.00	—	.308	.438	1	1	99	0	-0.4	0	0	0.1
■ **RALPH BRICKNER**	Brickner, Ralph Harold "Brick" b: 5/2/25, Cincinnati, Ohio BR/TR, 6'3.5", 215 lbs. Deb: 5/04/52																												
1952	Bos-A	3	1	.750	14	1	0	0	1	33	32	8.7	1	11	3.0	9	2.5	2.18	180	.264	.319	5	6	107	158	1.0	0	-1	0.7
■ **MARSHALL BRIDGES**	Bridges, Marshall "Sheriff" b: 6/2/31, Jackson, Miss. BB/TL, 6'1", 165 lbs. Deb: 6/17/59																												
1959	StL-N	6	3	.667	27	4	1	0	1	76	67	7.9	10	37	4.4	76	9.0	4.26	98	.240	.317	-3	-1	106	93	1.8	2	-2	0.0
1960	StL-N	2	2	.500	20	1	0	0	1	31	33	9.6	2	16	4.6	27	7.8	3.48	116	.266	.347	1	2	108	122	-0.1	-0	-0	0.1
	Cin-N	4	0	1.000	14	0	0	0	2	25	14	5.0	1	7	2.5	26	9.4	1.08	346	.161	.223	7	7	99	80	2.0	0	-0	0.8
	Yr	6	2	.750	34	1	0	0	3	56	47	7.6	3	23	3.7	53	8.5	2.41	162	.220	.294	8	9	104	80	1.9	-0	-1	0.9
1961	Cin-N	0	1	.000	13	0	0	0	0	21	26	11.1	4	11	4.7	17	7.3	7.71	54	.317	.388	-9	-8	103	87	-0.4	-0	-0	-0.7
1962	NY-A	8	4	.667	52	0	0	0	18	72	49	6.1	4	48	6.0	66	8.3	3.13	116	.194	.316	7	4	92	93	1.2	-2	2	0.4
1963	NY-A	2	0	1.000	23	0	0	0	1	33	27	7.4	2	30	8.2	35	9.5	3.82	93	.237	.382	-1	-1	98	126	1.0	0	2	0.1
1964	Was-A	0	3	.000	17	0	0	0	2	30	37	11.1	3	17	5.1	16	4.8	5.70	66	.303	.383	-7	-7	103	98	-1.4	-0	0	-0.6
1965	Was-A	1	2	.333	40	0	0	0	0	57	62	9.8	3	25	3.9	39	6.2	2.68	131	.268	.336	5	5	102	145	-0.2	0	-0	0.6
Total	7	23	15	.605	206	5	1	0	25	345	315	8.2	29	191	5.0	302	7.9	3.76	102	.244	.334	1	3	101	106	3.9	0	1	0.7

YEAR	TM/L	W	L	PCT	G	GS	CG	SHO	SV	IP	H	H/G	HR	BB	BB/G	SO	SO/G	ERA	/A	OAVG	OOBP	PR	/A	PF	CPI	WAT	PB	PD	TPI
■ **TOMMY BRIDGES**	Bridges, Thomas Jefferson Davis b: 12/28/06, Gordonsville, Tenn d: 4/19/68, Nashville, Tenn. BR/TR, 5'10.5", 155 lbs. Deb: 8/13/30 C																												
1930	Det-A	3	2	.600	8	5	2	0	0	38	28	6.6	4	23	5.4	17	4.0	4.03	122	.215	.323	3	4	106	96	0.6	1	-0	0.4
1931	Det-A	8	16	.333	35	23	8	2	0	173	182	9.5	13	108	5.6	105	5.5	4.99	94	.263	.358	-12	-6	107	95	-2.1	-3	-1	-0.8
1932	Det-A	14	12	.538	34	26	10	**4**	1	201	174	7.8	14	119	5.3	108	4.8	3.36	136	.233	.334	25	27	102	116	1.1	-1	-1	2.4
1933	Det-A	14	12	.538	33	28	17	2	2	233	192	**7.4**	8	110	4.2	120	4.6	3.09	148	**.226**	.313	31	38	107	103	1.5	2	1	4.2
1934	Det-A	22	11	.667	36	35	23	3	1	275	249	8.1	16	104	3.4	151	4.9	3.67	115	.241	.309	25	17	94	91	0.7	-3	-2	1.0
1935	Det-A	21	10	.677	36	34	23	4	1	274	277	9.1	22	113	3.7	**163**	5.4	3.51	117	.259	.329	29	18	93	113	3.0	3	-1	1.9
1936	Det-A	**23**	11	.676	39	38	26	5	0	295	289	8.8	21	115	3.5	**175**	5.3	3.60	133	.255	.322	47	38	95	109	6.0	1	1	3.7
1937	Det-A	15	12	.556	34	31	18	3	0	245	267	9.8	15	91	3.3	138	5.1	4.08	122	.274	.336	15	24	108	101	-0.5	1	1	2.6
1938	Det-A	13	9	.591	25	20	13	0	1	151	171	10.2	14	58	3.5	101	6.0	4.59	104	.287	.347	3	3	99	106	1.3	-1	-1	0.0
1939	Det-A	17	7	.708	29	26	16	2	2	198	186	8.5	11	61	2.8	129	5.9	3.50	145	.243	.301	25	34	110	91	5.1	-0	-1	3.4
1940	Det-A	12	9	.571	29	28	12	2	0	198	171	7.8	11	88	4.0	133	6.0	3.36	142	.229	.307	22	31	109	93	-0.2	-2	-1	2.8
1941	Det-A	9	12	.429	25	22	10	1	0	148	128	7.8	10	70	4.3	90	5.5	3.41	131	.233	.316	12	17	107	100	-1.3	-3	2	1.7
1942	Det-A	9	7	.563	23	22	11	2	1	174	164	8.5	6	61	3.2	97	5.0	2.74	150	.246	.309	18	27	113	115	1.5	-3	1	2.8
1943	Det-A	12	7	.632	25	22	11	3	0	192	159	7.5	9	61	2.9	124	5.8	2.39	143	.226	.284	19	22	104	105	2.7	2	-0	2.8
1945	Det-A	1	0	1.000	4	1	0	0	0	11	14	11.5	2	2	1.6	6	4.9	3.27	108	.311	.333	0	0	105	164	0.5	-0	1	0.0
1946	Det-A	1	1	.500	9	1	0	0	1	21	24	10.3	5	8	3.4	17	7.3	6.00	62	.279	.347	-6	-5	106	92	-0.1	0	0	-0.4
Total	16	194	138	.584	424	362	200	33	10	2827	2675	8.5	181	1192	3.8	1674	5.3	3.57	126	.248	.321	257	293	103	103	19.8	-6	-3	28.5
■ **BUTTONS BRIGGS**	Briggs, Herbert Theodore b: 7/8/1875, Poughkeepsie, N.Y. d: 2/18/11, Cleveland, Ohio BR/TR, 6'1", 180 lbs. Deb: 4/23/1896																												
1896	Chi-N	12	8	.600	26	21	19	0	1	194	202	9.4	6	108	5.0	84	**3.9**	4.31	110	.290	.385	1	9	108	97	1.2	-6	0	0.3
1897	Chi-N	4	17	.190	22	22	21	0	0	187	246	11.8	6	85	4.1	60	2.9	5.29	82	.340	.410	-20	-20	101	98	-6.4	-6	0	-2.0
1898	Chi-N	1	3	.250	4	4	3	0	0	30	38	11.4	0	10	3.0	14	4.2	5.70	64	.332	.385	-7	-7	102	77	-1.0	2	0	-0.3
1904	Chi-N	19	11	.633	34	30	28	3	3	277	252	8.2	2	77	2.5	112	3.6	2.05	132	.268	.328	21	20	99	127	1.2	-0	-4	1.7
1905	Chi-N	8	8	.500	20	20	13	5	0	168	141	7.6	1	52	2.8	68	3.6	2.14	140	.255	.326	16	16	100	115	-1.4	-4	-2	1.5
Total	5	44	47	.484	106	97	84	8	4	856	879	9.2	15	332	3.5	338	3.6	3.42	105	.290	.363	11	16	102	110	-6.4	-15	-6	1.2
■ **JOHN BRIGGS**	Briggs, Jonathan Tift b: 1/24/34, Natoma, Cal. BR/TR, 5'10", 175 lbs. Deb: 4/17/56																												
1956	Chi-N	0	0	—	3	0	0	0	0	5	5	9.0	1	4	7.2	1	1.8	1.80	211	.238	.429	1	1	101	364	0.0	0	0	0.1
1957	Chi-N	0	1	.000	3	0	0	0	0	4	7	15.8	2	3	6.8	1	2.3	13.50	28	.368	.435	-4	-4	98	84	-0.4	0	-0	-0.3
1958	Chi-N	5	5	.500	20	17	3	1	0	96	99	9.3	12	45	4.2	46	4.3	4.50	89	.270	.347	-6	-6	101	102	0.3	2	-1	-0.4
1959	Cle-A	0	1	.000	4	1	0	0	0	13	12	8.3	1	3	2.1	5	3.5	2.08	176	.245	.283	3	2	95	144	-0.4	-0	-0	0.2
1960	Cle-A	4	2	.667	21	2	0	0	1	36	32	8.0	4	15	3.8	19	4.8	4.50	85	.250	.322	-3	-3	98	89	1.1	-0	-1	-0.3
	KC-A	0	2	.000	8	1	0	0	0	11	19	15.5	3	12	9.8	8	6.5	13.09	30	.380	.492	-11	-11	101	82	-0.9	-0	-0	-1.0
	Yr	4	4	.500	29	3	0	0	1	47	51	9.8	7	27	5.2	27	5.2	6.51	59	.282	.368	-14	-14	99	82	0.2	-0	-1	-1.3
Total	5	9	11	.450	59	21	3	1	1	165	174	9.5	23	82	4.5	80	4.4	5.02	78	.275	.356	-20	-20	100	108	-0.3	1	-2	-1.7
■ **NELSON BRILES**	Briles, Nelson Kelley b: 8/5/43, Dorris, Cal. BR/TR, 5'11", 195 lbs. Deb: 4/19/65																												
1965	StL-N	3	3	.500	37	2	0	0	4	82	79	8.7	4	26	2.9	52	5.7	3.51	107	.258	.326	0	2	106	102	0.0	-0	-1	0.1
1966	StL-N	4	15	.211	49	17	0	0	6	154	162	9.5	14	54	3.2	100	5.8	3.21	112	.279	.341	7	7	100	137	-5.8	-2	1	0.6
1967	StL-N	14	5	.737	49	14	4	2	6	155	139	8.1	8	40	2.3	94	5.5	2.44	137	.236	.287	16	16	99	110	3.0	0	-2	1.6
1968	StL-N	19	11	.633	33	33	13	4	0	244	251	9.3	18	55	2.0	141	5.2	2.80	99	.266	.306	5	-1	93	124	1.6	1	-2	-0.2
1969	StL-N	15	13	.536	36	33	10	3	0	228	218	8.6	17	63	2.5	126	5.0	3.51	101	.251	.297	2	1	99	92	0.0	-1	-1	0.0
1970	StL-N	6	7	.462	30	19	1	1	0	107	129	10.9	14	36	3.0	59	5.0	6.22	69	.297	.345	-26	-23	106	83	0.0	1	-2	-2.1
1971	Pit-N	8	4	.667	37	14	4	2	1	136	131	8.7	12	35	2.3	76	5.0	3.04	110	.250	.299	6	5	97	106	1.1	4	-1	0.8
1972	Pit-N	14	11	.560	28	27	9	2	0	196	185	8.5	14	43	2.0	120	5.5	3.08	113	.249	.286	8	8	100	96	-1.3	-1	-0	0.8
1973	Pit-N	14	13	.519	33	33	7	1	0	219	201	8.3	19	51	2.1	94	3.9	2.84	119	.244	.283	20	13	92	104	0.8	3	0	1.6
1974	KC-A	5	7	.417	18	17	3	0	0	103	118	10.3	9	21	1.8	41	3.6	4.02	96	.293	.326	-5	-2	106	104	-0.7	0	-1	-0.2
1975	KC-A	6	6	.500	24	16	3	0	2	112	127	10.2	19	25	2.0	73	5.9	4.26	90	.285	.328	-6	-5	101	111	-0.6	0	0	-0.4
1976	Tex-A	11	9	.550	32	31	7	1	1	210	224	9.6	17	47	2.0	98	4.2	3.26	111	.273	.311	6	8	103	113	1.7	0	-3	0.5
1977	Tex-A	6	4	.600	28	15	2	1	1	108	114	9.5	13	30	2.5	57	4.8	4.25	99	.275	.329	-2	-0	104	102	0.3	0	-1	-0.1
	Bal-A	0	0	—	2	0	0	0	1	4	5	11.3	2	0	0.0	2	4.5	6.75	56	.294	.294	-1	-1	92	100	0.0	0	-0	0.0
	Yr	6	4	.600	30	15	2	1	2	112	119	9.6	15	30	2.4	59	4.7	4.34	97	.271	.315	-3	-2	103	100	0.3	0	-1	-0.1
1978	Bal-A	4	4	.500	16	8	1	0	0	54	58	9.7	6	21	3.5	30	5.0	4.67	73	.279	.343	-5	-7	91	98	-0.3	0	-1	-0.8
Total	14	129	112	.535	452	279	64	17	22	2112	2141	9.1	186	547	2.3	1163	5.0	3.44	102	.264	.309	27	19	99	107	-0.2	5	-12	2.2
■ **FRANK BRILL**	Brill, Francis Hasbrouck (born Francis Hasbrouck Briell) b: 3/30/1864, Astoria, L.I., N.Y. d: 11/19/44, Flushing, N.Y. BR/TR, 5'8", 155 lbs. Deb: 6/23/1884																												
1884	Det-N	2	10	.167	12	12	12	1	0	103	148	12.9	7	26	2.3	18	1.6	5.50	54	.346	.384	-29	-29	99	98	-2.1	-3	0	-2.5
■ **JIM BRILLHEART**	Brillheart, James Benson b: 9/28/03, Dublin, Va. d: 9/2/72, Radford, Va. BR/TL, 5'11", 170 lbs. Deb: 4/17/22																												
1922	Was-A	4	6	.400	31	10	3	0	1	120	120	9.0	3	72	5.4	47	3.5	3.60	104	.275	.373	6	2	93	125	-0.5	-3	-2	-0.3
1923	Was-A	0	1	.000	12	0	0	0	0	18	27	13.5	1	12	6.0	8	4.0	7.00	54	.360	.449	-6	-6	95	104	-0.4	-0	0	-0.5
1927	Chi-N	4	2	.667	32	12	4	0	0	129	140	9.8	4	38	2.7	36	2.5	4.12	94	.286	.327	-3	-4	99	96	0.8	-5	-1	-0.9
1931	Bos-A	0	0	—	11	1	0	0	0	20	27	12.1	2	15	6.7	7	3.1	5.40	78	.325	.420	-2	-3	97	132	0.0	2	1	0.0
Total	4	8	9	.471	86	23	7	0	1	287	314	9.8	10	137	4.3	98	3.1	4.17	92	.290	.362	-5	-11	96	111	-0.1	-7	-2	-1.7
■ **LOU BRISSIE**	Brissie, Leland Victor b: 6/5/24, Anderson, S.C. BL/TL, 6'4.5", 210 lbs. Deb: 9/28/47																												
1947	Phi-A	0	1	.000	1	1	0	0	0	7	9	11.6	1	5	6.4	4	5.1	6.43	58	.310	.412	-2	-2	100	102	-0.4	-0	0	-0.1
1948	Phi-A	14	10	.583	39	25	11	0	5	194	202	9.4	6	95	4.4	127	**5.9**	4.13	105	.269	.347	3	5	102	100	1.2	-0	-2	0.3
1949	Phi-A	16	11	.593	34	29	18	0	3	229	220	8.6	20	118	4.6	118	4.6	4.28	97	.251	.341	-2	-4	99	94	2.2	3	-4	-0.4
1950	Phi-A	7	19	.269	46	31	15	2	8	246	237	8.7	22	117	4.3	101	3.7	4.02	106	.253	.331	15	7	93	100	-2.9	-2	-1	0.3
1951	Phi-A	0	2	.000	2	2	0	0	0	13	20	13.8	0	8	5.5	3	2.1	6.92	63	.357	.438	-4	-4	106	97	-0.9	-0	-0	-0.3
	Cle-A	4	3	.571	54	4	1	0	9	112	90	7.2	5	61	4.9	50	4.0	3.21	119	.223	.322	11	7	93	101	-0.1	0	-2	0.6
	Yr	4	5	.444	56	6	1	0	9	125	110	7.9	5	69	5.0	53	3.8	3.60	108	.239	.336	7	4	94	101	-1.0	-0	-2	0.3
1952	Cle-A	3	2	.600	42	1	0	0	2	83	68	7.4	5	34	3.7	28	3.0	3.47	93	.221	.289	2	-2	88	79	0.0	1	1	0.0
1953	Cle-A	0	0	—	16	0	0	0	2	13	21	14.5	2	13	9.0	5	3.5	7.62	49	.389	.493	-5	-6	93	129	0.0	0	0	-0.5
Total	7	44	48	.478	234	93	45	2	29	897	867	8.7	61	451	4.5	436	4.4	4.07	100	.254	.337	18	2	96	97	-0.9	1	-7	-0.1
■ **JIM BRITT**	Britt, James Edward b: 2/25/1856, Brooklyn, N.Y. d: 2/28/23, San Francisco, Cal Deb: 5/02/1872																												
1872	Atl-n	8	27	.229	35																								
1873	Atl-n	17	36	.321	54																								
Total	2 n	25	63	.284	89																								
■ **JACK BRITTIN**	Brittin, John Albert b: 3/4/24, Athens, Ill. BR/TR, 5'11", 175 lbs. Deb: 9/15/50																												
1950	Phi-N	0	0	—	3	0	0	0	0	4	2	4.5	0	3	6.8	3	6.8	4.50	88	.143	.294	-0	-0	96	30	0.0	0	0	0.0
1951	Phi-N	0	0	—	3	0	0	0	0	4	5	11.3	0	6	13.5	3	6.8	9.00	43	.294	.478	-2	-2	97	79	0.0	0	0	-0.1
Total	2	0	0	—	6	0	0	0	0	8	7	7.9	0	9	10.1	6	6.8	6.75	58	.226	.400	-2	-3	96	55	0.0	0	0	-0.1
■ **JIM BRITTON**	Britton, James Allan b: 3/25/44, N.Tonawanda, N.Y. BR/TR, 6'5", 225 lbs. Deb: 9/20/67																												
1967	Atl-N	0	2	.000	2	2	0	0	0	13	15	10.4	2	2	1.4	4	2.8	6.23	57	.278	.304	-4	-4	105	66	-0.9	-0	-0	-0.3
1968	Atl-N	4	6	.400	34	9	2	2	3	90	81	8.1	1	34	3.4	61	6.1	3.10	90	.245	.310	-1	-3	94	94	-1.0	-0	0	-0.3
1969	Atl-N	7	5	.583	24	13	2	1	1	88	69	7.1	10	49	5.0	60	6.1	3.78	98	.218	.313	-2	-1	103	94	0.1	0	-1	-0.1
1971	Mon-N	2	3	.400	16	6	0	0	0	46	49	9.6	10	27	5.3	23	4.5	5.67	61	.274	.371	-11	-11	100	103	-0.1	-1	-1	-1.2
Total	4	13	16	.448	76	30	4	3	4	237	214	8.1	23	112	4.3	148	5.6	4.03	82	.243	.324	-18	-19	99	94	-1.9	-1	-2	-1.9
■ **TONY BRIZZOLARA**	Brizzolara, Anthony John b: 1/14/57, Santa Monica, Cal. BR/TR, 6'5", 215 lbs. Deb: 5/19/79																												
1979	Atl-N	6	9	.400	20	19	2	0	0	107	133	11.2	6	33	2.8	64	5.4	5.30	78	.303	.347	-19	-14	110	86	-0.2	-3	0	-1.6
1983	Atl-N	1	0	1.000	14	0	0	0	1	20	22	9.9	2	6	2.7	17	7.6	3.60	105	.278	.318	0	0	104	114	0.5	0	-0	0.0
1984	Atl-N	1	2	.333	10	4	0	0	0	29	33	10.2	4	13	4.0	17	5.3	5.28	75	.284	.348	-5	-4	110	96	-0.4	-1	0	-0.4

YEAR	TM/L	W	L	PCT	G	GS	CG	SHO	SV	IP	H	H/G	HR	BB	BB/G	SO	SO/G	ERA	/A	OAVG	OOBP	PR	/A	PF	CPI	WAT	PB	PD	TPI
Total	3	8	11	.421	44	23	2	0	1	156	188	10.8	12	52	3.0	98	5.7	5.08	80	.297	.344	-24	-18	109	91	-0.1	-4	-0	-2.0
■ **JOHNNY BROACA**	Broaca, John Joseph b: 10/3/09, Lawrence, Mass. d: 5/16/85, Lawrence, Mass. BR/TR, 5'11", 190 lbs. Deb: 6/02/34																												
1934	NY-A	12	9	.571	26	24	13	1	0	177	203	10.3	9	65	3.3	74	3.8	4.17	100	.284	.340	6	-0	93	104	-0.7	-7	-2	-0.8
1935	NY-A	15	7	.682	29	27	14	2	0	201	199	8.9	16	79	3.5	78	3.5	3.58	112	.254	.318	19	10	90	105	2.6	-4	-3	0.2
1936	NY-A	12	7	.632	37	27	12	1	3	206	235	10.3	16	66	2.9	84	3.7	4.24	107	.284	.333	18	7	90	107	-0.5	-6	-2	-0.1
1937	NY-A	1	4	.200	7	6	3	0	0	44	58	11.9	5	17	3.5	9	1.8	4.70	95	.324	.373	-0	-1	97	128	-1.7	-2	-1	-0.3
1939	Cle-A	4	2	.667	22	2	0	0	0	46	53	10.4	5	28	5.5	13	2.5	4.70	95	.288	.375	-0	-1	96	119	0.7	-2	0	-0.2
Total	5	44	29	.603	121	86	42	4	3	674	748	10.0	51	255	3.4	258	3.4	4.09	105	.278	.336	43	14	92	108	0.4	-19	-8	-1.2
■ **PETE BROBERG**	Broberg, Peter Sven b: 3/2/50, W.Palm Beach, Fla. BR/TR, 6'3", 205 lbs. Deb: 6/20/71																												
1971	Was-A	5	9	.357	18	18	7	1	0	125	104	7.5	10	53	3.8	89	6.4	3.46	94	.228	.317	0	-3	94	95	-0.6	0	-1	-0.3
1972	Tex-A	5	12	.294	39	25	3	2	1	176	153	7.8	14	85	4.3	133	6.8	4.30	69	.237	.330	-24	-26	97	85	-1.4	-2	1	-2.9
1973	Tex-A	5	9	.357	22	20	6	1	0	119	130	9.8	8	66	5.0	57	4.3	5.60	68	.283	.371	-23	-24	100	86	0.1	0	-0	-2.2
1974	Tex-A	0	4	.000	12	2	0	0	0	29	29	9.0	7	13	4.0	15	4.7	8.07	43	.264	.336	-14	-15	96	66	-1.9	0	0	-1.4
1975	Mil-A	14	16	.467	38	32	7	2	0	220	219	9.0	17	106	4.3	100	4.1	4.13	93	.263	.353	-8	-7	101	103	1.5	0	-0	-0.7
1976	Mil-A	1	7	.125	20	11	1	0	0	92	99	9.7	5	72	7.0	28	2.7	4.99	71	.281	.400	-15	-15	100	107	-2.7	0	-1	-1.5
1977	Chi-N	1	2	.333	22	0	0	0	0	36	34	8.5	8	18	4.5	20	5.0	4.75	94	.256	.329	-3	-1	115	107	-0.4	-1	0	-0.1
1978	Oak-A	10	12	.455	35	26	2	0	0	166	174	9.4	16	65	3.5	94	5.1	4.61	84	.269	.332	-15	-14	103	89	0.6	0	1	-1.2
Total	8	41	71	.366	206	134	26	6	1	963	942	8.8	85	478	4.5	536	5.0	4.56	79	.259	.346	-104	-104	100	94	-4.8	-3	-0	-10.3
■ **LEW BROCKETT**	Brockett, Lewis Albert "King" b: 7/23/1880, Brownsville, Ill. d: 9/19/60, Norris City, Ill. TR, 5'10.5", 168 lbs. Deb: 4/25/07																												
1907	NY-A	1	2	.333	8	4	1	0	0	46	58	11.3	1	26	5.1	13	2.5	6.26	45	.334	.421	-19	-18	110	82	-0.3	-0	-1	-1.7
1909	NY-A	10	8	.556	26	18	10	3	1	170	148	7.8	3	59	3.1	70	3.7	2.12	116	.245	.318	7	6	99	124	1.3	3	4	1.2
1911	NY-A	2	4	.333	16	8	2	0	0	75	73	8.8	3	39	4.7	25	3.0	4.68	79	.256	.356	-11	-8	111	78	-0.9	2	1	-0.6
Total	3	13	14	.481	50	30	13	3	1	291	279	8.6	7	124	3.8	108	3.3	3.43	82	.263	.346	-23	-20	104	105	0.1	5	3	-1.1
■ **DICK BRODOWSKI**	Brodowski, Richard Stanley b: 7/26/32, Bayonne, N.J. BR/TR, 6'1", 182 lbs. Deb: 6/15/52																												
1952	Bos-A	5	5	.500	20	12	4	0	0	115	111	8.7	12	50	3.9	42	3.3	4.38	90	.252	.328	-9	-6	107	91	0.1	1	0	-0.3
1955	Bos-A	1	0	1.000	16	0	0	0	0	32	36	10.1	5	25	7.0	10	2.8	5.63	86	.295	.405	-6	-3	122	115	0.5	3	1	0.1
1956	Was-A	0	3	.000	7	3	1	0	0	18	31	15.5	5	12	6.0	8	4.0	9.00	49	.397	.457	-10	-9	107	113	-1.4	-1	0	-0.8
1957	Was-A	0	1	.000	6	0	0	0	0	11	12	9.8	2	10	8.2	4	3.3	11.45	34	.261	.404	-9	-9	102	53	-0.4	-0	0	-0.8
1958	Cle-A	1	0	1.000	5	0	0	0	0	10	3	2.7	0	6	5.4	12	10.8	0.00	—	.100	.243	4	4	93	0	0.5	-0	0	0.4
1959	Cle-A	2	2	.500	18	0	0	0	5	30	19	5.7	3	21	6.3	9	2.7	1.80	203	.181	.323	7	6	95	183	-0.2	0	-0	0.6
Total	6	9	11	.450	72	15	5	0	5	216	212	8.8	27	124	5.2	85	3.5	4.75	85	.258	.353	-23	-17	107	103	-0.9	3	1	-0.8
■ **ERNIE BROGLIO**	Broglio, Ernest Gilbert b: 8/27/35, Berkeley, Cal. BR/TR, 6'2", 200 lbs. Deb: 4/11/59																												
1959	StL-N	7	12	.368	35	25	6	3	0	181	174	8.7	20	89	4.4	133	6.6	4.72	89	.250	.332	-16	-11	106	85	-2.0	-3	1	-1.1
1960	StL-N	**21**	9	**.700**	52	24	9	3	0	226	172	6.8	18	100	4.0	188	7.5	2.75	148	.213	.297	25	33	108	105	**5.5**	3	1	4.0
1961	StL-N	9	12	.429	29	26	7	2	0	175	166	8.5	19	75	3.9	113	5.8	4.11	110	.248	.318	-2	8	113	92	-2.0	-3	-1	0.6
1962	StL-N	12	9	.571	34	30	11	4	0	222	193	7.8	22	93	3.8	132	5.4	3.00	140	.237	.312	23	30	107	116	1.3	-2	1	3.1
1963	StL-N	18	8	.692	39	35	11	5	0	250	202	7.3	24	90	3.2	145	5.2	2.99	116	.216	.284	8	13	106	91	4.1	-3	0	1.3
1964	StL-N	3	5	.375	11	11	3	1	0	69	65	8.5	7	26	3.4	36	4.7	3.52	112	.247	.314	0	3	111	104	-1.3	-0	-0	0.3
	Chi-N	4	7	.364	18	16	3	0	1	100	111	10.0	12	30	2.7	46	4.1	4.05	93	.281	.329	-6	-3	106	110	-1.2	3	-1	-0.1
	Yr	7	12	.368	29	27	6	1	1	169	176	9.4	19	56	3.0	82	4.4	3.83	100	.267	.321	-6	-0	108	110	-2.5	-0	-1	0.2
1965	Chi-N	1	6	.143	26	6	0	0	0	51	63	11.1	7	46	8.1	22	3.9	6.88	53	.313	.434	-19	-18	103	104	-2.3	-0	-1	-1.9
1966	Chi-N	2	6	.250	15	11	2	0	1	62	70	10.2	14	38	5.5	34	4.9	6.39	58	.290	.383	-19	-19	103	99	-1.2	3	2	-1.3
Total	8	77	74	.510	259	184	52	18	2	1336	1216	8.2	143	587	4.0	849	5.7	3.75	107	.242	.318	-4	36	107	100	0.9	-2	1	4.9
■ **KEN BRONDELL**	Brondell, Kenneth Leroy b: 10/17/21, Bradshaw, Neb. BR/TR, 6'1", 195 lbs. Deb: 5/03/44																												
1944	NY-N	0	1	.000	7	2	1	0	0	19	27	12.8	3	8	3.8	1	0.5	8.53	45	.329	.380	-10	-10	105	76	-0.4	-1	-0	-0.9
■ **JIM BRONSTAD**	Bronstad, James Warren b: 6/22/36, Ft.Worth, Tex. BR/TR, 6'3", 196 lbs. Deb: 6/07/59																												
1959	NY-A	0	3	.000	16	3	0	0	2	29	34	10.6	2	13	4.0	14	4.3	5.28	67	.288	.361	-5	-6	92	90	-1.4	-0	0	-0.5
1963	Was-A	1	3	.250	25	0	0	0	1	57	66	10.4	9	22	3.5	22	3.5	5.68	65	.297	.357	-13	-13	101	96	-0.5	-1	1	-1.2
1964	Was-A	0	1	.000	4	0	0	0	0	7	10	12.9	0	2	2.6	9	11.6	5.14	73	.345	.387	-1	-1	103	102	-0.4	0	-0	0.0
Total	3	1	7	.125	45	3	0	0	3	93	110	10.6	11	37	3.6	45	4.4	5.52	66	.298	.361	-19	-19	98	95	-2.3	-2	1	-1.7
■ **IKE BROOKENS**	Brookens, Edward Dwain b: 1/3/49, Chambersburg, Pa. BR/TR, 6'5", 170 lbs. Deb: 6/17/75																												
1975	Det-A	0	0	—	3	0	0	0	0	10	11	9.9	3	5	4.5	8	7.2	5.40	75	.282	.370	-2	-2	106	122	0.0	0	0	0.0
■ **HARRY BROOKS**	Brooks, Harry Frank b: 11/30/1865, Philadelphia d: 12/5/45, Philadelphia, Pa. Deb: 7/24/1886																												
1886	NY-a	0	1	.000	1	1	0	0	0	2	9	40.5	0	2	9.0	0	0.0	36.00	10	.625	.671	-7	-7	106	63	-0.4	-0	0	-0.4
■ **JIM BROSNAN**	Brosnan, James Patrick b: 10/24/29, Cincinnati, O. BR/TR, 6'4", 197 lbs. Deb: 4/15/54																												
1954	Chi-N	1	0	1.000	18	0	0	0	0	33	44	12.0	9	18	4.9	17	4.6	9.55	43	.331	.399	-20	-20	102	80	0.5	-0	1	-1.7
1956	Chi-N	5	9	.357	30	10	1	1	1	95	95	9.0	9	45	4.3	51	4.8	3.79	100	.270	.341	-0	0	101	114	-0.5	-0	-1	0.0
1957	Chi-N	5	5	.500	41	5	1	0	0	99	79	7.2	11	46	4.2	73	6.6	3.36	113	.219	.305	6	5	98	96	0.9	2	1	0.8
1958	Chi-N	3	4	.429	8	8	2	0	0	52	41	7.1	3	29	5.0	24	4.2	3.12	128	.225	.326	5	5	101	105	-0.2	-1	1	0.5
	StL-N	8	4	.667	33	12	2	0	7	115	107	8.4	10	50	3.9	65	5.1	3.44	124	.250	.324	6	11	108	107	2.4	-1	0	1.0
	Yr	11	8	.579	41	20	4	0	7	167	148	8.0	13	79	4.3	89	4.8	3.34	125	.241	.325	11	16	106	107	2.2	-1	1	1.5
1959	StL-N	1	3	.250	20	1	0	0	2	33	34	9.3	5	15	4.1	18	4.9	4.91	85	.276	.352	-4	-3	106	104	-0.8	1	1	0.0
	Cin-N	8	3	.727	26	9	1	1	2	83	79	8.6	7	26	2.8	56	6.1	3.36	121	.248	.307	5	6	103	101	2.7	-2	1	0.5
	Yr	9	6	.600	46	10	1	1	4	116	113	8.8	12	41	3.2	74	5.7	3.80	108	.255	.318	2	4	104	101	1.9	1	1	0.5
1960	Cin-N	7	2	.778	57	2	0	0	12	99	79	7.2	4	22	2.0	62	5.6	2.36	158	.225	.264	15	15	99	97	2.8	2	-0	1.7
1961	Cin-N	10	4	.714	53	0	0	0	16	80	77	8.7	7	18	2.0	40	4.5	3.04	136	.249	.284	9	10	103	100	2.1	-0	1	1.0
1962	Cin-N	4	4	.500	48	0	0	0	13	65	76	10.5	6	18	2.5	51	7.1	3.32	119	.292	.331	4	5	100	132	-0.6	-1	-0	0.3
1963	Cin-N	0	1	.000	6	0	0	0	0	5	8	14.4	2	3	5.4	4	7.2	7.20	47	.421	.440	-2	-2	103	155	-0.4	0	-0	-0.1
	Chi-A	3	8	.273	45	0	0	0	14	73	71	8.8	7	22	2.7	46	5.7	2.84	131	.263	.311	6	7	102	135	-2.9	1	-0	0.8
Total	9	55	47	.539	385	47	7	2	67	832	790	8.5	80	312	3.4	507	5.5	3.54	112	.254	.317	32	39	102	107	6.0	0	4	4.8
■ **FRANK BROSSEAU**	Brosseau, Franklin Lee b: 7/31/44, Drayton, N.D. BR/TR, 6'1", 180 lbs. Deb: 9/10/69																												
1969	Pit-N	0	0	—	2	0	0	0	0	2	2	9.0	0	2	9.0	2	9.0	9.00	38	.286	.444	-1	-1	94	63	0.0	0	0	0.0
1971	Pit-N	0	0	—	1	0	0	0	0	2	1	4.5	0	0	0.0	0	0.0	0.00	—	.200	.200	1	1	97	0	0.0	0	0	0.1
Total	2	0	0	—	3	0	0	0	0	4	3	6.8	0	2	4.5	2	4.5	4.50	75	.250	.357	-0	-1	95	31	0.0	0	0	0.1
■ **DAN BROUTHERS**	Brouthers, Dennis Joseph "Big Dan" b: 5/8/1858, Sylvan Lake, N.Y. d: 8/3/32, E.Orange, N.J. BL/TL, 6'2", 207 lbs. Deb: 6/23/1879 H																												
1879	Tro-N	0	2	.000	3	2	2	0	0	21	35	15.0	0	8	3.4	6	2.6	5.57	45	.376	.426	-7	-7	100	112	-0.9	1	0	-0.5
1883	Buf-N	0	0	—	1	0	0	0	0	2	9	40.5	0	3	13.5	2	9.0	31.50	10	.622	.687	-6	-6	99	77	0.0	1	0	-0.3
Total	2	0	2	.000	4	2	2	0	0	23	44	17.2	0	11	4.3	8	3.1	7.83	33	.409	.464	-13	-13	100	109	-0.9	1	0	-0.8
■ **FRANK BROWER**	Brower, Frank Willard "Turkeyfoot" b: 3/26/1893, Gainesville, Va. d: 11/20/60, Baltimore, Md. BL/TR, 6'2", 180 lbs. Deb: 8/14/20																												
1924	Cle-A	0	0	—	4	0	0	0	0	10	7	6.3	0	4	3.6	0	0.0	0.90	458	.212	.316	4	4	97	276	0.0	1	-0	0.4
■ **ALTON BROWN**	Brown, Alton Leo "Deacon" b: 4/16/25, Norfolk, Va. BR/TR, 6'2", 195 lbs. Deb: 4/21/51																												
1951	Was-A	0	0	—	7	0	0	0	0	12	14	10.5	1	12	9.0	7	5.3	9.00	44	.298	.450	-7	-7	97	77	0.0	-0	-0	-0.6
■ **BOARDWALK BROWN**	Brown, Carroll William b: 2/20/1887, Woodbury, N.J. d: 2/8/77, Burlington, N.J. BR/TR, 6'1.5", 178 lbs. Deb: 9/27/11																												
1911	Phi-A	0	1	.000	2	1	1	0	0	12	12	9.0	0	2	1.5	6	4.5	4.50	66	.267	.298	-2	-2	88	55	-0.4	-1	0	-0.1
1912	Phi-A	13	11	.542	34	24	15	3	0	199	204	9.2	2	87	3.9	64	2.9	3.66	89	.283	.367	-7	-9	97	112	-1.1	-3	3	-0.6
1913	Phi-A	17	11	.607	43	35	11	3	1	235	200	7.7	6	87	3.3	70	2.7	2.95	92	.219	.294	-1	-6	93	69	-0.5	-1	-2	-0.8
1914	Phi-A	1	6	.143	15	8	2	0	0	66	64	8.7	1	26	3.5	20	2.7	4.09	62	.268	.340	-10	-11	93	81	-2.7	-2	0	-1.1

YEAR	TM/L	W	L	PCT	G	GS	CG	SHO	SV	IP	H	H/G	HR	BB	BB/G	SO	SO/G	ERA	/A	OAVG	OOBP	PR	/A	PF	CPI	WAT	PB	PD	TPI
	NY-A	5	5	.500	20	14	8	0	1	122	123	9.1	2	42	3.1	57	4.2	3.25	85	.271	.334	-7	-7	100	100	0.4	1	3	-0.3
	Yr	6	11	.353	35	22	10	0	1	188	187	9.0	3	68	3.3	77	3.7	3.54	75	.270	.336	-17	-18	98	100	-2.3	-2	3	-1.4
1915	NY-A	2	6	.250	19	11	5	0	1	97	95	8.8	4	47	4.4	34	3.2	4.08	71	.275	.370	-12	-13	99	103	-1.8	-1	-0	-1.3
Total	5	38	40	.487	133	93	42	6	3	731	698	8.6	15	291	3.6	251	3.1	3.47	83	.257	.334	-38	-48	96	91	-6.1	-6	3	-4.2
■ CHARLIE BROWN	Brown, Charles E. b: 1878, Baltimore, Md. TL , 6', 180 lbs. Deb: 8/04/1897																												
1897	Cle-N	1	2	.333	4	4	2	0	0	24	30	11.3	2	17	6.4	8	3.0	7.88	60	.329	.434	-9	-8	110	76	-0.5	0	0	-0.6
■ BUSTER BROWN	Brown, Charles Edward "Yank" b: 8/31/1881, Boone, Iowa d: 2/9/14, Sioux City, Iowa BR/TR, Deb: 6/22/05																												
1905	StL-N	8	11	.421	23	21	17	3	0	179	172	8.6	5	62	3.1	57	2.9	2.97	96	.283	.359	0	-2	95	114	0.8	-2	2	0.0
1906	StL-N	8	16	.333	32	27	21	0	0	238	208	7.9	2	112	4.2	109	4.1	2.65	103	.265	.364	-0	2	104	115	-0.4	0	1	0.4
1907	StL-N	1	6	.143	9	8	6	0	0	64	57	8.0	2	45	6.3	17	2.4	3.38	73	.272	.412	-6	-6	100	117	-2.0	2	2	-0.4
	Phi-N	9	6	.600	21	16	13	4	0	130	118	8.2	3	56	3.9	38	2.6	2.42	105	.273	.364	1	2	103	129	0.7	1	-1	0.1
	Yr	10	12	.455	30	24	19	4	0	194	175	8.1	5	101	4.7	55	2.6	2.74	92	.271	.374	-6	-5	102	129	-1.3	2	1	-0.3
1908	Phi-N	0	0	—	3	0	0	0	0	7	9	11.6	0	5	6.4	3	3.9	2.57	90	.357	.481	-0	-0	98	230	0.0	0	1	0.1
1909	Phi-N	0	0	—	7	1	0	0	0	25	22	7.9	1	16	5.8	10	3.6	3.24	85	.259	.382	-2	-1	106	128	0.0	-1	0	0.0
	Bos-N	4	8	.333	18	17	8	2	0	123	108	7.9	1	56	4.1	32	2.3	3.15	84	.244	.339	-7	-7	102	96	0.4	-1	0	-0.6
	Yr	4	8	.333	25	18	8	2	0	148	130	7.9	2	72	4.4	42	2.6	3.16	84	.246	.344	-9	-8	102	96	0.4	-1	1	-0.6
1910	Bos-N	9	23	.281	46	29	16	1	2	263	251	8.6	4	94	3.2	88	3.0	2.67	134	.268	.337	11	27	118	122	-3.5	-0	1	3.1
1911	Bos-N	8	18	.308	42	25	13	0	2	241	259	9.7	11	116	4.3	76	2.8	4.29	86	.285	.372	-24	-16	109	104	0.4	4	-0	-1.0
1912	Bos-N	4	15	.211	31	21	13	1	0	168	146	7.8	7	66	3.5	68	3.6	4.02	93	.228	.302	-11	-5	110	57	-3.8	1	0	-0.3
1913	Bos-N	0	0	—	2	0	0	0	0	13	19	13.2	0	3	2.1	3	2.1	4.85	63	.396	.436	-2	-3	96	137	0.0	-0	-0	-0.2
Total	9	51	103	.331	234	165	107	11	4	1451	1369	8.5	36	631	3.9	501	3.1	3.21	98	.267	.354	-42	-11	107	108	-7.4	3	7	1.2
■ CURLY BROWN	Brown, Charles Roy "Lefty" b: 12/9/1888, Spring Hill, Kan. d: 6/10/68, Spring Hill, Kan. BL/TL, 5'10.5", 165 lbs. Deb: 9/08/11																												
1911	StL-A	1	2	.333	3	2	2	0	0	23	22	8.6	0	5	2.0	8	3.1	2.74	122	.247	.295	2	2	100	78	0.1	-1	0	0.2
1912	StL-A	1	3	.250	16	4	2	1	0	65	69	9.6	0	35	4.8	28	3.9	4.85	71	.277	.373	-11	-10	103	85	-0.5	-0	-3	-1.1
1913	StL-A	1	1	.500	2	2	2	0	0	14	12	7.7	0	4	2.6	3	1.9	2.57	111	.245	.302	1	0	98	91	0.2	0	0	0.0
1915	Cin-N	0	2	.000	7	3	0	0	0	27	26	8.7	2	6	2.0	13	4.3	4.67	61	.245	.293	-6	-5	104	63	-0.9	1	-1	-0.5
Total	4	3	8	.273	28	11	6	1	0	129	129	9.0	2	50	3.5	52	3.6	4.19	77	.262	.336	-14	-14	102	80	-1.1	0	-4	-1.4
■ CLINT BROWN	Brown, Clinton Harold b: 7/8/03, Blackash, Pa. d: 12/31/55, Rocky River, Ohio BL/TR, 6'1", 190 lbs. Deb: 9/27/28																												
1928	Cle-A	0	1	.000	2	1	1	0	0	11	14	11.5	0	2	1.6	2	1.6	4.91	89	.304	.327	-1	-1	108	77	-0.4	-0	0	0.0
1929	Cle-A	0	2	.000	3	1	1	0	0	16	18	10.1	0	6	3.4	1	0.6	3.38	126	.286	.338	2	2	101	113	-0.9	-1	1	0.1
1930	Cle-A	11	13	.458	35	31	16	**3**	1	214	271	11.4	14	51	2.1	54	2.3	4.96	99	.314	.344	-7	-1	105	103	-1.7	2	2	0.3
1931	Cle-A	11	15	.423	39	33	12	2	0	233	284	11.0	10	55	2.1	50	1.9	4.71	98	.295	.331	-9	-2	106	92	-2.4	-2	4	0.0
1932	Cle-A	15	12	.556	37	32	21	1	1	263	298	10.2	14	50	**1.7**	59	2.0	4.07	118	.279	.310	12	21	107	94	-0.4	6	2	2.9
1933	Cle-A	11	12	.478	33	23	10	2	1	185	202	9.8	10	34	**1.7**	47	2.3	3.41	132	.276	.304	18	22	105	110	-0.4	-3	3	2.2
1934	Cle-A	4	3	.571	17	2	0	0	1	50	83	14.9	3	14	2.5	15	2.7	5.94	75	.359	.390	-8	-8	100	110	0.2	2	-0	-0.5
1935	Cle-A	4	3	.571	23	5	1	0	2	49	61	11.2	3	14	2.6	20	3.7	5.14	85	.300	.338	-4	-4	99	91	0.3	0	1	-0.2
1936	Chi-A	6	2	.750	38	2	0	0	5	83	106	11.5	5	24	2.6	19	2.1	4.99	100	.315	.360	0	-0	99	108	1.9	-0	0	0.0
1937	Chi-A	7	7	.500	**53**	0	0	0	**18**	100	92	8.3	7	36	3.2	51	4.6	3.42	138	.242	.302	**13**	**14**	102	96	-0.7	1	1	1.6
1938	Chi-A	1	3	.250	8	0	0	0	2	14	16	10.3	0	9	5.8	2	1.3	4.50	105	.333	.403	0	0	98	140	-0.8	1	1	0.2
1939	Chi-A	11	10	.524	**61**	0	0	0	18	118	127	9.7	8	27	2.1	41	3.1	3.89	126	.281	.309	10	13	106	105	-0.5	1	2	1.5
1940	Chi-A	4	6	.400	37	0	0	0	10	66	75	10.2	5	16	2.2	23	3.1	3.68	122	.284	.320	5	6	103	116	-1.2	-1	0	0.5
1941	Cle-A	3	3	.500	41	0	0	0	5	74	77	9.4	3	28	3.4	22	2.7	3.28	127	.279	.341	7	7	101	129	0.1	0	3	1.0
1942	Cle-A	1	1	.500	7	0	0	0	0	9	16	16.0	2	2	2.0	4	4.0	6.00	57	.356	.396	-2	-3	93	131	0.0	-0	-0	-0.2
Total	15	89	93	.489	434	130	62	8	64	1485	1740	10.5	84	368	2.2	410	2.5	4.27	110	.291	.328	36	67	104	103	-6.9	5	19	9.4
■ CURT BROWN	Brown, Curtis Steven b: 1/15/60, Ft.Lauderdale, Fla. BR/TR, 6'5", 200 lbs. Deb: 6/10/83																												
1983	Cal-A	1	1	.500	10	0	0	0	0	16	25	14.1	1	4	2.3	7	3.9	7.31	54	.368	.397	-6	-6	96	89	0.1	0	-0	-0.5
1984	NY-A	1	1	.500	13	0	0	0	0	17	18	9.5	1	4	2.1	10	5.3	2.65	141	.281	.310	3	2	93	144	0.0	0	0	0.2
1986	Mon-N	0	1	.000	6	0	0	0	0	12	15	11.3	0	2	1.5	4	3.0	3.00	122	.319	.321	1	1	98	140	-0.4	-0	0	0.1
1987	Mon-N	0	1	.000	5	0	0	0	0	7	10	12.9	2	4	5.1	6	7.7	7.71	56	.333	.400	-3	-3	106	104	-0.4	0	0	-0.1
Total	4	2	4	.333	34	0	0	0	0	52	68	11.8	4	14	2.4	27	4.7	4.85	79	.325	.353	-5	-6	97	121	-0.7	-0	0	-0.3
■ ED BROWN	Brown, Edward P. b: Chicago, Ill. TR , Deb: 8/19/1882																												
1882	StL-a	0	0	—	1	0	0	0	0	2	2	9.0	0	0	0.0	1	4.5	0.00	—	.266	.266	1	1	104	0	0.0	-0	0	0.1
1884	Tol-a	0	1	.000	1	1	1	0	0	9	19	19.0	0	4	4.0	1	1.0	9.00	38	.437	.484	-6	-6	105	106	-0.4	-0	0	-0.3
Total	2	0	1	.000	2	1	1	0	0	11	21	17.2	0	4	3.3	2	1.6	7.36	45	.412	.454	-5	-5	105	87	-0.4	-0	0	-0.2
■ ELMER BROWN	Brown, Elmer Young "Shook" b: 3/25/1883, Southport, Ind. d: 1/23/55, Indianapolis, Ind. BL/TR, 5'11.5", 172 lbs. Deb: 9/16/11																												
1911	StL-A	1	1	.500	5	3	1	1	0	17	16	8.5	0	14	7.4	5	2.6	6.35	52	.242	.375	-6	-6	100	56	0.3	-1	0	-0.4
1912	StL-A	5	8	.385	23	13	2	1	0	120	122	9.2	2	42	3.2	45	3.4	3.00	115	.280	.359	5	6	103	133	0.4	-1	-1	0.5
1913	Bro-N	0	0	—	3	1	0	0	0	13	6	4.2	0	10	6.9	6	4.2	2.08	162	.158	.333	2	2	105	118	0.0	-1	0	0.1
1914	Bro-N	1	2	.333	11	4	1	0	0	37	33	8.0	2	23	5.6	22	5.4	3.89	72	.402	.525	-5	-4	101	183	-0.4	-1	1	-0.4
1915	Bro-N	0	0	—	1	0	0	0	0	2	4	18.0	0	3	13.5	1	4.5	9.00	31	.500	.636	-1	-1	102	143	0.0	0	0	0.0
Total	5	7	11	.389	43	21	4	2	0	189	181	8.6	4	92	4.4	79	3.8	3.48	95	.287	.390	-5	-4	102	135	0.3	-3	0	-0.2
■ HAL BROWN	Brown, Hector Harold "Skinny" b: 12/11/24, Greensboro, N.C. BR/TR, 6'2", 180 lbs. Deb: 4/19/51																												
1951	Chi-A	0	0	—	3	0	0	0	1	9	15	15.0	3	4	4.0	4	4.0	9.00	44	.385	.432	-5	-5	96	108	0.0	1	0	-0.2
1952	Chi-A	2	3	.400	24	8	1	0	0	72	82	10.3	8	21	2.6	31	3.9	4.25	86	.284	.328	-5	-5	99	103	-0.5	1	-0	-0.4
1953	Bos-A	11	6	.647	30	25	6	1	0	166	177	9.6	16	57	3.1	62	3.4	4.66	93	.269	.324	-12	-6	108	86	2.0	5	-0	-0.1
1954	Bos-A	1	8	.111	40	5	1	0	0	118	126	9.6	6	41	3.1	66	5.0	4.12	91	.269	.324	-5	-5	101	88	-3.3	-0	1	-0.3
1955	Bos-A	1	0	1.000	2	0	0	0	0	4	2	4.5	0	2	4.5	2	4.5	2.25	215	.143	.250	1	1	122	27	0.5	0	-0	0.2
	Bal-A	0	4	.000	15	5	1	0	0	57	51	8.1	5	26	4.1	26	4.1	4.11	90	.241	.313	-1	-3	94	85	-1.9	-1	-1	-0.4
	Yr	1	4	.200	17	5	1	0	0	61	53	7.8	5	28	4.1	28	4.1	3.98	95	.235	.309	-0	-1	95	85	-1.4	0	-1	-0.2
1956	Bal-A	9	7	.563	35	14	4	1	2	152	142	8.4	18	37	2.2	57	3.4	4.03	100	.247	.290	2	-0	97	83	1.8	1	0	0.1
1957	Bal-A	7	8	.467	25	20	7	2	1	150	132	7.9	17	37	2.2	62	3.7	3.90	90	.236	.281	-2	-6	93	78	-0.5	2	-1	-0.5
1958	Bal-A	7	5	.583	19	17	4	2	1	97	96	8.9	9	20	1.9	44	4.1	3.06	117	.259	.293	8	6	95	110	1.2	-0	-0	0.5
1959	Bal-A	11	9	.550	31	21	2	0	3	164	158	8.7	16	32	**1.8**	81	4.4	3.79	100	.252	.283	1	0	98	86	1.5	-3	-1	-0.2
1960	Bal-A	12	5	.706	30	20	6	1	0	159	155	8.8	14	22	**1.2**	66	3.7	3.06	127	.258	**.280**	14	15	101	101	2.8	3	-1	1.7
1961	Bal-A	10	6	.625	27	23	6	3	1	167	153	8.2	14	33	1.8	61	3.3	3.18	121	.247	.280	16	13	96	95	0.8	-0	-0	1.2
1962	Bal-A	6	4	.600	22	11	0	0	1	86	88	9.2	12	21	2.2	25	2.6	4.08	92	.268	.312	-1	-3	95	103	1.2	1	-1	-0.2
	NY-A	0	1	1.000	2	1	0	0	0	7	9	11.6	3	2	2.6	2	2.6	6.43	57	.333	.333	-2	-2	92	129	-0.4	-0	0	-0.1
	Yr	6	5	.545	24	12	0	0	1	93	97	9.4	15	23	2.2	27	2.6	4.26	88	.270	.306	-3	-5	95	129	0.8	1	-1	-0.3
1963	Hou-N	5	11	.313	26	20	6	3	0	141	137	8.7	14	8	0.5	68	4.3	3.32	94	.255	.258	-0	-3	95	86	-1.9	-1	-3	-0.7
1964	Hou-N	3	15	.167	27	21	3	1	1	132	154	10.5	18	26	1.8	53	3.6	3.95	88	.292	.320	-6	-7	98	117	-5.5	-1	-2	-0.9
Total	14	85	92	.480	358	211	47	13	11	1681	1677	9.0	173	389	2.1	710	3.8	3.81	98	.260	.298	3	-12	98	93	-2.2	8	-9	-0.3
■ JACKIE BROWN	Brown, Jackie Gene b: 5/31/43, Holdenville, Okla. BR/TR, 6'1", 195 lbs. Deb: 7/02/70 C																												
1970	Was-A	2	2	.500	24	5	1	0	0	57	49	7.7	8	37	5.8	47	7.4	3.95	91	.231	.344	-1	-2	97	107	0.2	-0	-1	-0.3
1971	Was-A	3	4	.429	14	9	0	0	0	47	60	11.5	9	27	5.2	21	4.0	5.94	55	.316	.395	-13	-14	94	112	0.2	-0	1	-1.3
1973	Tex-A	5	5	.500	25	3	2	1	2	67	82	11.0	7	25	3.4	45	6.0	3.90	98	.309	.371	-1	-1	100	136	1.2	0	-1	-0.1
1974	Tex-A	13	12	.520	35	26	9	2	0	217	219	9.1	13	74	3.1	134	5.6	3.57	98	.265	.325	1	-2	96	101	0.0	0	-1	-0.2
1975	Tex-A	5	5	.500	17	7	2	1	0	70	70	9.0	7	35	4.5	35	4.5	4.24	89	.266	.351	-4	-4	100	105	0.1	0	-2	-0.4
	Cle-A	1	2	.333	25	3	1	0	1	69	72	9.4	9	29	3.8	41	5.3	4.30	88	.276	.339	-4	-4	100	108	-0.4	0	-0	-0.3
	Yr	6	7	.462	42	10	3	1	1	139	142	9.2	16	64	4.1	76	4.9	4.27	88	.269	.342	-7	-8	100	108	-0.3	0	-2	-0.7
1976	Cle-A	9	11	.450	32	27	5	2	0	180	193	9.6	14	55	2.8	104	5.2	4.25	83	.276	.328	-15	-15	100	95	-1.2	0	-1	-1.5

YEAR	TM/L	W	L	PCT	G	GS	CG	SHO	SV	IP	H	H/G	HR	BB	BB/G	SO	SO/G	ERA	/A	OAVG	OOBP	PR	/A	PF	CPI	WAT	PB	PD	TPI
1977	Mon-N	9	12	.429	42	25	6	2	0	186	189	9.1	15	71	3.4	89	4.3	4.50	86	.264	.328	-12	-13	99	87	-0.8	-2	-2	-1.6
Total	7	47	53	.470	214	105	26	8	3	893	934	9.4	82	353	3.6	516	5.2	4.18	87	.272	.338	-48	-54	98	101	-0.7	-3	-6	-5.7
■ KEVIN BROWN	Brown, James Kevin b: 3/14/65, Milledgeville, Ga. BR/TR, 6'4", 195 lbs. Deb: 9/30/86																												
1986	Tex-A	1	0	1.000	1	1	0	0	0	5	6	10.8	0	0	0.0	4	7.2	3.60	111	.316	.316	0	0	95	103	0.5	0	0	0.0
1988	Tex-A	1	1	.500	4	4	1	0	0	23	33	12.9	2	8	3.1	12	4.7	4.30	94	.330	.382	-1	-1	102	137	0.1	0	-0	0.0
Total	2	2	1	.667	5	5	1	0	0	28	39	12.5	2	8	2.6	16	5.1	4.18	97	.328	.372	-1	-0	101	131	0.6	0	-0	0.0
■ JIM BROWN	Brown, James W. H. b: 12/12/1860, Clinton Co., Pa. d: 4/6/08, Williamsport, Pa. Deb: 4/17/1884																												
1884	Alt-U	1	9	.100	11	11	7	0	0	74	99	12.0	0	36	4.4	39	4.7	5.35	61	.326	.397	-19	-17	109	102	-3.4	0	0	-1.2
	NY-N	0	1	.000	1	1	1	0	0	9	10	10.0	0	8	8.0	2	2.0	5.00	57	.291	.424	-2	-2	97	101	-0.4	-0	0	-0.1
	StP-U	1	4	.200	6	6	4	1	0	36	43	10.8	1	14	3.5	20	5.0	3.75	80	.302	.364	-3	-3	100	124	-0.9	2	0	0.0
1886	Phi-a	0	1	.000	1	1	1	0	0	8	9	10.1	0	3	3.4	4	4.5	3.38	105	.294	.357	0	0	103	123	-0.4	-1	0	0.0
Total	2	2	15	.118	19	19	13	1	0	127	161	11.4	1	61	4.3	65	4.6	4.75	67	.315	.388	-24	-22	105	109	-5.1	1	0	-1.3
■ JOHN BROWN	Brown, John J. "Ad" b: Trenton, N.J. Deb: 8/11/1897																												
1897	Bro-N	0	1	.000	1	1	0	0	0	5	7	12.6	0	4	7.2	0	0.0	7.20	61	.354	.463	-2	-2	102	88	-0.4	0	0	0.0
■ JOPHERY BROWN	Brown, Jophery Clifford b: 1/22/45, Grambling, La. BL/TR, 6'2", 190 lbs. Deb: 9/21/68																												
1968	Chi-N	0	0	—	1	0	0	0	0	2	2	9.0	0	1	4.5	0	0.0	4.50	75	.286	.333	-0	-0	112	92	0.0	0	0	0.0
■ JOE BROWN	Brown, Joseph E. b: 4/4/1859, Warren, Pa. d: 6/28/1888, Warren, Pa. Deb: 8/16/1884																												
1884	Chi-N	4	2	.667	7	6	5	0	0	50	56	10.1	4	7	1.3	27	4.9	4.68	66	.292	.317	-9	-9	105	77	0.8	-1	0	-0.6
1885	Bal-a	0	4	.000	4	4	4	0	0	38	52	12.3	0	4	0.9	9	2.1	5.68	62	.338	.355	-10	-9	109	81	-1.9	-1	0	-0.7
Total	2	4	6	.400	11	10	9	0	0	88	108	11.0	4	11	1.1	36	3.7	5.11	64	.313	.334	-20	-18	107	79	-1.1	-2	0	-1.3
■ JOE BROWN	Brown, Joseph Henry b: 7/3/1900, Little Rock, Ark. d: 3/7/50, Los Angeles, Cal. BR/TR, 6', 176 lbs. Deb: 5/17/27																												
1927	Chi-A	0	0	—	1	1	0	0	0	0	2	—	0	1	—	0	—	∞	—	1.000	1.000	-3	-3	103	48	0.0	0	0	-0.1
■ KEITH BROWN	Brown, Keith Edward b: 2/14/64, Flagstaff, Ariz. BR/TR, 6'4", 205 lbs. Deb: 8/25/88																												
1988	Cin-N	2	1	.667	4	3	0	0	0	16	14	7.9	1	4	2.3	6	3.4	2.81	129	.237	.286	1	1	105	100	0.4	-0	0	0.1
■ LEW BROWN	Brown, Lewis J. "Blower" b: 2/1/1858, Leominster, Mass. d: 1/16/1889, Boston, Mass. BR/TR, 5'10.5", 185 lbs. Deb: 6/17/1876 M																												
1878	Pro-N	0	0	—	1	0	0	0	0	1	0	0.0	0	4	36.0	0	0.0	18.00	12	.000	.597	-2	-2	97	44	0.0	0	0	-0.1
1884	Bos-U	0	0	—	1	0	0	0	1	1	6	54.0	0	1	9.0	0	0.0	36.00	8	.684	.717	-4	-4	98	83	0.0	0	0	-0.2
Total	2	0	0	—	2	0	0	0	1	2	6	27.0	0	5	22.5	0	0.0	27.00	10	.523	.668	-5	-5	97	63	0.0	0	0	-0.3
■ LLOYD BROWN	Brown, Lloyd Andrew "Gimpy" b: 12/25/04, Beeville, Tex. d: 1/14/74, Opalocka, Fla. BL/TL, 5'9", 170 lbs. Deb: 7/17/25																												
1925	Bro-N	0	3	.000	17	5	1	0	0	63	79	11.3	1	25	3.6	23	3.3	4.14	98	.319	.379	1	-1	95	121	-1.4	-2	0	-0.2
1928	Was-A	4	4	.500	27	10	2	0	1	107	112	9.4	7	40	3.4	38	3.2	4.04	101	.273	.330	0	1	101	100	0.1	0	3	0.4
1929	Was-A	8	7	.533	40	15	7	1	0	168	186	10.0	7	69	3.7	48	2.6	4.18	102	.297	.352	1	1	100	111	1.0	3	2	0.6
1930	Was-A	16	12	.571	38	22	10	1	0	197	220	10.1	6	65	3.0	59	2.7	4.25	107	.293	.343	9	7	98	107	-1.0	2	3	1.1
1931	Was-A	15	14	.517	42	32	15	1	0	259	256	8.9	13	79	2.7	79	2.7	3.20	135	.257	.307	34	32	98	110	-2.2	3	1	3.4
1932	Was-A	15	12	.556	46	24	10	2	5	203	239	10.6	11	55	2.4	53	2.3	4.43	99	.296	.338	1	-1	98	104	-1.2	-5	1	-0.4
1933	StL-A	1	6	.143	8	6	0	0	0	39	57	13.2	1	17	3.9	7	1.6	7.15	70	.350	.396	-12	-9	117	90	-2.1	1	1	-0.6
	Bos-A	8	11	.421	33	21	9	2	1	163	180	9.9	4	64	3.5	37	2.0	4.03	108	.281	.338	5	6	102	105	0.0	6	4	1.6
	Yr	9	17	.346	41	27	9	2	1	202	237	10.6	5	81	3.6	44	2.0	4.63	97	.295	.350	-8	-3	105	105	-2.1	1	5	1.0
1934	Cle-A	5	10	.333	38	15	5	0	6	117	116	8.9	7	51	3.9	39	3.0	3.85	117	.263	.336	8	8	100	108	-3.1	1	0	0.9
1935	Cle-A	8	7	.533	42	8	4	2	4	122	123	9.1	6	37	2.7	45	3.3	3.61	122	.265	.316	**11**	**11**	99	103	0.0	-2	1	0.9
1936	Cle-A	8	10	.444	24	16	12	1	1	140	166	10.7	13	45	2.9	34	2.2	4.18	126	.294	.344	13	17	105	120	-1.3	2	1	1.8
1937	Cle-A	2	6	.250	31	5	2	0	0	77	107	12.5	4	27	3.2	32	3.7	6.55	68	.329	.382	-16	-18	97	87	-2.1	-1	0	-1.5
1940	Phi-N	1	3	.250	18	2	0	0	3	38	58	13.7	3	16	3.8	16	3.8	6.16	64	.354	.400	-10	-9	102	110	-0.4	-1	0	-0.9
Total	12	91	105	.464	404	181	77	10	21	1693	1899	10.1	83	590	3.1	510	2.7	4.20	106	.288	.340	45	45	100	107	-13.7	6	18	7.1
■ MACE BROWN	Brown, Mace Stanley b: 5/21/09, North English, Ia. BR/TR, 6'1", 190 lbs. Deb: 5/21/35 C																												
1935	Pit-N	4	1	.800	18	5	2	0	0	73	84	10.4	5	22	2.7	28	3.5	3.58	118	.287	.333	4	5	105	120	1.4	-0	2	0.7
1936	Pit-N	10	11	.476	47	10	3	0	3	165	178	9.7	8	55	3.0	56	3.1	3.87	100	.275	.326	3	-0	96	100	-1.4	-2	1	0.0
1937	Pit-N	7	2	.778	50	2	0	1	**7**	108	109	9.1	2	45	3.8	60	5.0	4.17	95	.261	.330	-3	-2	101	85	2.3	2	-1	-0.1
1938	Pit-N	15	9	.625	**51**	2	0	0	5	133	155	10.5	5	44	3.0	55	3.7	3.79	99	.294	.340	-0	-1	99	114	1.7	-2	0	-0.2
1939	Pit-N	9	13	.409	47	19	8	1	7	200	232	10.4	8	52	2.3	71	3.2	3.38	117	.293	.328	12	13	101	**120**	-0.9	-4	0	0.9
1940	Pit-N	10	9	.526	48	17	5	2	**7**	173	181	9.4	5	49	2.5	73	3.8	3.49	105	.267	.315	7	3	95	100	0.4	-1	1	0.3
1941	Pit-N	0	0	—	1	0	0	0	0	1	2	18.0	0	0	0.0	0	0.0	0.00	—	.333	.333	0	0	102	0	0.0	0	0	0.1
	Bro-N	3	2	.600	24	0	0	0	3	43	31	6.5	3	26	5.4	22	4.6	3.14	115	.208	.320	2	2	99	106	-0.1	-1	1	0.2
	Yr	3	2	.600	25	0	0	0	3	44	33	6.8	3	26	5.3	22	4.5	3.07	118	.213	.321	3	3	99	106	-0.1	0	1	0.3
1942	Bos-A	9	3	.750	34	0	0	0	6	60	56	8.4	4	28	4.2	20	3.0	3.45	106	.255	.333	1	1	100	115	2.2	-1	1	0.2
1943	Bos-A	6	6	.500	**49**	0	0	0	9	93	71	6.9	2	51	4.9	40	3.9	2.13	162	.222	.319	**12**	**14**	104	141	0.6	-2	0	1.4
1946	Bos-A	3	1	.750	18	0	0	0	1	26	26	9.0	2	16	5.5	10	3.5	2.08	187	.268	.362	4	5	111	221	0.5	-1	1	0.6
Total	10	76	57	.571	387	55	18	4	48	1075	1125	9.4	44	388	3.2	435	3.6	3.47	110	.271	.328	43	41	100	113	6.7	-11	6	4.1
■ MARK BROWN	Brown, Mark Anthony b: 7/13/59, Bellows Falls, Vt. BB/TR, 6'2", 190 lbs. Deb: 8/09/84																												
1984	Bal-A	1	2	.333	9	0	0	0	0	23	22	8.6	2	7	2.7	10	3.9	3.91	96	.256	.319	0	-0	94	94	-0.5	0	-0	0.0
1985	Min-A	0	0	—	6	0	0	0	0	16	21	11.8	1	7	3.9	5	2.8	6.75	64	.333	.384	-5	-4	104	88	0.0	0	-0	-0.3
Total	2	1	2	.333	15	0	0	0	0	39	43	9.9	3	14	3.2	15	3.5	5.08	78	.289	.347	-4	-5	98	91	-0.5	0	-1	-0.3
■ MIKE BROWN	Brown, Michael Gary b: 3/4/59, Haddon Twshp., N.J. BR/TR, 6'2", 195 lbs. Deb: 9/16/82																												
1982	Bos-A	1	0	1.000	3	0	0	0	0	6	7	10.5	0	1	1.5	4	6.0	0.00	—	.304	.333	-3	3	110	0	0.5	0	-0	0.3
1983	Bos-A	6	6	.500	19	18	3	1	0	104	110	9.5	12	43	3.7	35	3.0	4.67	89	.276	.341	-7	-6	102	101	0.2	0	-1	-0.6
1984	Bos-A	1	8	.111	15	11	0	0	0	67	104	14.0	9	19	2.6	32	4.3	6.85	64	.347	.387	-21	-18	110	96	-3.5	0	0	-1.6
1985	Bos-A	0	0	—	2	1	0	0	0	3	9	27.0	0	3	9.0	3	9.0	24.00	18	.500	.545	-7	-7	102	60	0.0	0	0	-0.5
1986	Bos-A	4	4	.500	15	10	0	0	0	57	72	11.4	10	25	3.9	32	5.1	5.37	77	.316	.377	-7	-8	99	117	-0.5	0	0	-0.6
	Sea-A	0	2	.000	6	2	0	0	0	16	19	10.7	4	11	6.2	9	5.1	7.31	61	.302	.405	-6	-5	106	97	-0.9	0	0	-0.4
	Yr	4	6	.400	21	12	0	0	0	73	91	11.2	14	36	4.4	41	5.1	5.79	72	.308	.380	-13	-13	100	97	-1.4	0	1	-1.0
1987	Sea-A	0	0	—	1	0	0	0	0	⅓	3	81.0	0	0	0.0	0	0.0	54.00	—	.750	.750	-2	-2	103	68	0.0	0	-0	-0.1
Total	6	12	20	.375	61	42	3	1	0	253	324	11.5	35	102	3.6	115	4.1	5.76	74	.313	.371	-47	-43	104	100	-4.2	0	0	-3.5
■ MORDECAI BROWN	Brown, Mordecai Peter Centennial "Three Finger" or "Miner" b: 10/19/1876, Nyesville, Ind. d: 2/14/48, Terre Haute, Ind. BB/TR, 5'10", 175 lbs. Deb: 4/19/03 MH																												
1903	StL-N	9	13	.409	26	24	19	1	0	201	231	10.3	7	59	2.6	83	3.7	2.60	128	.316	.372	15	16	102	**153**	1.8	-1	1	1.8
1904	Chi-N	15	10	.600	26	23	21	4	1	212	155	**6.6**	1	50	2.1	81	3.4	1.87	144	**.227**	.286	20	19	99	85	-0.1	1	-1	2.0
1905	Chi-N	18	12	.600	30	24	24	4	0	249	219	7.9	3	44	1.6	89	3.2	2.17	138	.262	.299	23	23	100	104	0.0	-1	-0	2.4
1906	Chi-N	26	6	.813	36	32	27	**9**	3	277	198	6.4	1	61	2.0	144	4.7	**1.04**	**251**	.225	**.279**	**49**	**48**	99	139	4.0	2	2	**6.1**
1907	Chi-N	20	6	.769	34	27	20	6	3	233	180	7.0	2	40	1.5	107	4.1	1.39	181	.241	.285	28	29	102	113	3.3	-0	4	**4.0**
1908	Chi-N	29	9	.763	44	31	27	9	**5**	312	214	**6.2**	1	49	1.4	123	3.5	1.47	163	**.219**	.260	30	32	102	75	7.7	1	-1	3.8
1909	Chi-N	**27**	9	.750	**50**	34	**32**	8	**7**	**343**	246	6.5	1	53	1.4	172	4.5	1.31	188	.202	.239	**49**	44	95	77	4.8	1	-0	5.1
1910	Chi-N	25	14	.641	46	31	**27**	8	**7**	295	256	7.8	3	64	2.0	143	4.4	1.86	157	.232	**.277**	38	**35**	96	99	-1.2	-0	3	4.0
1911	Chi-N	21	11	.656	**53**	27	21	0	**13**	270	267	8.9	5	55	1.8	129	4.3	2.80	114	.262	.303	18	12	94	100	2.8	6	-4	1.3
1912	Chi-N	5	6	.455	15	8	5	2	0	89	92	9.3	2	20	2.0	34	3.4	2.63	132	.267	.309	8	8	102	104	-1.4	2	-2	0.8
1913	Cin-N	11	12	.478	39	16	11	1	6	173	174	9.1	7	44	2.3	41	2.1	2.91	114	.277	.312	6	8	104	119	1.4	-0	-2	0.6
1914	StL-F	12	6	.667	26	18	13	2	0	175	172	8.8	7	43	2.2	81	4.2	3.29	105	.286	.334	-2	3	108	95	4.2	2	0	0.6
	Bro-F	2	5	.286	9	8	5	0	0	58	63	9.8	1	18	2.8	32	5.0	4.19	77	.307	.363	-6	-6	101	87	-1.4	-0	0	-0.5
	Yr	14	11	.560	35	26	18	2	0	233	235	9.1	8	61	2.4	113	4.4	3.52	97	.291	.341	-8	-3	106	87	2.8	2	0	0.1
1915	Chi-F	17	8	.680	35	25	17	3	4	236	189	7.2	2	64	2.4	95	3.6	2.10	137	.220	.279	25	21	95	93	3.7	5	5	3.5

YEAR	TM/L	W	L	PCT	G	GS	CG	SHO	SV	IP	H	H/G	HR	BB	BB/G	SO	SO/G	ERA	/A	OAVG	OOBP	PR	/A	PF	CPI	WAT	PB	PD	TPI
1916	Chi-N	2	3	.400	12	4	2	0	0	48	52	9.8	0	9	1.7	21	3.9	3.94	78	.289	.320	-7	-5	117	88	-0.1	0	-0	-0.4
Total	14	239	130	.648	481	332	271	57	49	3171	2708	7.7	43	673	1.9	1375	3.9	2.06	140	.246	.292	293	288	100	102	29.5	17	5	35.1
■ **MYRL BROWN**	Brown, Myrl Lincoln b: 10/10/1894, Waynesboro, Pa. d: 2/23/81, Harrisburg, Pa. BR/TR, 5'11", 172 lbs. Deb: 8/19/22																												
1922	Pit-N	3	1	.750	7	5	2	0	0	35	42	10.8	2	13	3.3	9	2.3	5.91	70	.296	.353	-7	-7	101	73	0.9	1	0	-0.4
■ **NORM BROWN**	Brown, Norman b: 2/1/19, Evergreen, N.C. BB/TR, 6'3", 180 lbs. Deb: 10/03/43																												
1943	Phi-A	0	0	—	1	1	0	0	0	7	5	6.4	0	0	0.0	1	1.3	0.00	—	.185	.185	3	3	106	0	0.0	-0	0	0.4
1946	Phi-A	0	1	.000	4	0	0	0	0	7	8	10.3	2	6	7.7	3	3.9	6.43	59	.267	.378	-2	-2	107	103	-0.4	0	0	-0.1
Total	2	0	1	.000	5	1	0	0	0	14	13	8.4	2	6	3.9	4	2.6	3.21	113	.228	.297	0	1	107	52	-0.4	-0	0	0.3
■ **PAUL BROWN**	Brown, Paul Dwayne b: 6/18/41, Ft.Smith, Ark. BR/TR, 6'1", 190 lbs. Deb: 7/23/61																												
1961	Phi-N	0	1	.000	5	1	0	0	0	10	13	11.7	3	8	7.2	1	0.9	8.10	49	.325	.440	-5	-5	98	107	-0.4	0	0	-0.3
1962	Phi-N	0	6	.000	23	9	0	0	1	64	74	10.4	9	33	4.6	29	4.1	5.91	64	.298	.377	-14	-15	95	98	-2.9	0	-0	-1.4
1963	Phi-N	0	1	.000	6	2	0	0	0	15	15	9.0	2	5	3.0	11	6.6	4.20	80	.238	.310	-2	-1	102	87	-0.4	0	0	0.0
1968	Phi-N	0	0	—	2	0	0	0	0	4	6	13.5	0	1	2.3	4	9.0	9.00	33	.353	.368	-3	-3	99	59	0.0	0	0	-0.2
Total	4	0	8	.000	36	12	0	0	1	93	108	10.5	14	47	4.5	45	4.4	6.00	61	.293	.373	-23	-24	97	95	-3.7	1	0	-1.9
■ **RAY BROWN**	Brown, Paul Percival b: 1/31/1889, Chicago, Ill. d: 5/29/55, Los Angeles, Cal. Deb: 09																												
1909	Chi-N	1	0	1.000	1	1	1	0	0	9	5	5.0	0	4	4.0	2	2.0	2.00	123	.172	.273	1	0	95	65	0.5	-1	-0	0.0
■ **STUB BROWN**	Brown, Richard P. b: 8/3/1870, Baltimore, Md. d: 3/11/48, Baltimore, Md. TL, 6'2", 220 lbs. Deb: 8/15/1893																												
1893	Bal-N	0	0	—	2	0	0	0	0	9	13	13.0	0	5	5.0	0	0.0	6.00	84	.355	.432	-1	-1	108	102	0.0	-0	0	0.0
1894	Bal-N	4	0	1.000	9	6	3	0	0	50	59	10.6	3	24	4.3	8	1.4	5.04	102	.316	.394	2	1	96	98	2.0	-4	0	-0.2
1897	Cin-N	0	1	.000	2	1	1	0	0	13	17	11.8	1	8	5.5	2	1.4	4.15	111	.339	.430	0	1	107	144	-0.4	-1	0	0.0
Total	3	4	1	.800	13	7	4	0	0	72	89	11.1	4	37	4.6	10	1.3	5.00	101	.325	.406	1	0	100	107	1.6	-5	0	-0.2
■ **BOB BROWN**	Brown, Robert M. b: 1891, BR/TR, 5'6", 165 lbs. Deb: 5/02/14																												
1914	Buf-F	0	0	—	15	1	0	0	3	37	39	9.5	3	16	3.9	13	3.2	3.41	98	.300	.377	-1	-0	104	126	0.0	0	0	0.0
■ **BOB BROWN**	Brown, Robert Murray b: 4/1/11, Dorchester, Mass. BR/TR, 6'0.5", 190 lbs. Deb: 4/21/30																												
1930	Bos-N	0	0	—	3	0	0	0	0	6	10	15.0	0	8	12.0	1	1.5	10.50	47	.417	.529	-4	-4	99	101	0.0	-0	0	-0.2
1931	Bos-N	0	1	.000	3	1	0	0	0	6	9	13.5	0	3	4.5	2	3.0	9.00	44	.375	.387	-3	-3	102	76	-0.4	0	0	-0.2
1932	Bos-N	14	7	.667	35	28	9	0	1	213	187	7.9	6	104	4.4	110	4.6	3.30	110	.238	.323	14	8	93	99	3.9	0	-1	0.7
1933	Bos-N	0	0	—	5	0	0	0	0	7	6	7.7	0	3	3.9	3	3.9	2.57	124	.250	.321	1	0	96	122	0.0	-0	0	0.0
1934	Bos-N	1	3	.250	16	8	2	1	0	58	59	9.2	2	36	5.6	21	3.3	5.74	61	.262	.363	-11	-14	86	77	-0.9	1	-1	-1.3
1935	Bos-N	1	8	.111	15	10	2	1	0	65	79	10.9	2	36	5.0	17	2.4	6.37	63	.302	.378	-17	-17	100	81	-2.5	-1	-1	-1.7
1936	Bos-N	0	2	.000	2	2	0	0	0	8	10	11.3	1	3	3.4	5	5.6	5.63	69	.278	.333	-1	-2	96	79	-0.9	-0	0	-0.1
Total	7	16	21	.432	79	49	13	2	1	363	360	8.9	11	193	4.8	159	3.9	4.49	82	.261	.346	-22	-32	94	92	-0.8	-1	-2	-2.8
■ **SCOTT BROWN**	Brown, Scott Edward b: 8/31/56, De Quincy, La. BR/TR, 6'2", 220 lbs. Deb: 8/11/81																												
1981	Cin-N	1	0	1.000	10	0	0	0	0	13	16	11.1	0	1	0.7	7	4.8	2.77	127	.314	.321	1	1	101	136	0.5	-0	0	0.1
■ **STEVE BROWN**	Brown, Steven Elbert b: 2/12/57, San Francisco, Cal. BR/TR, 6'5", 200 lbs. Deb: 8/01/83																												
1983	Cal-A	2	3	.400	12	4	2	1	0	46	45	8.8	4	16	3.1	23	4.5	3.52	111	.256	.313	3	2	96	104	-0.1	0	0	0.2
1984	Cal-A	0	1	.000	3	3	0	0	0	11	16	13.1	0	9	7.4	5	4.1	9.00	45	.340	.439	-6	-6	101	74	-0.4	0	-0	-0.5
Total	2	2	4	.333	15	7	2	1	0	57	61	9.6	4	25	3.9	28	4.4	4.58	86	.274	.341	-3	-4	97	98	-0.5	0	-0	-0.3
■ **TOM BROWN**	Brown, Thomas Dale b: 8/10/49, Lafayette, La. BR/TR, 6'1", 170 lbs. Deb: 9/14/78																												
1978	Sea-A	0	0	—	6	0	0	0	0	13	14	9.7	2	4	2.8	8	5.5	4.15	95	.286	.340	-1	-0	104	115	0.0	0	0	0.0
■ **TOM BROWN**	Brown, Thomas T. b: 9/21/1860, Liverpool, England d: 10/27/27, Washington, D.C. BL/TR, 5'10", 168 lbs. Deb: 1882 M																												
1882	Bal-a	0	0	—	2	0	0	0	0	8	13	14.6	0	6	6.8	2	2.3	1.13	245	.370	.462	1	1	102	650	0.0	1	0	0.1
1883	Col-a	0	1	.000	3	1	1	0	0	14	14	9.0	0	10	6.4	6	3.9	5.79	52	.266	.383	-4	-4	91	77	-0.4	1	0	-0.3
1884	Col-a	2	1	.667	4	0	0	0	0	19	27	12.8	0	7	3.3	5	2.4	7.11	44	.343	.397	-8	-8	96	82	0.1	1	0	-0.6
1885	Pit-a	0	0	—	2	0	0	0	0	6	0	0.0	0	3	4.5	2	3.0	3.00	115	.000	.157	0	0	107	38	0.0	1	0	0.0
1886	Pit-a	0	0	—	1	0	0	0	0	2	2	9.0	0	5	22.5	1	4.5	9.00	34	.271	.565	-1	-1	90	105	0.0	0	0	0.0
Total	5	2	2	.500	12	1	1	0	0	49	56	10.3	0	31	5.7	16	2.9	5.33	58	.295	.394	-12	-12	97	169	-0.3	4	0	-0.8
■ **JUMBO BROWN**	Brown, Walter George b: 4/30/07, Greene, R.I. d: 10/2/66, Freeport, N.Y. BR/TR, 6'4", 295 lbs. Deb: 8/26/25																												
1925	Chi-N	0	0	—	2	0	0	0	0	6	5	7.5	0	4	6.0	0	0.0	3.00	140	.217	.321	1	1	98	87	0.0	-0	0	0.1
1927	Cle-A	0	2	.000	8	0	0	0	0	19	19	9.0	3	26	12.3	8	3.8	6.16	66	.284	.469	-4	-4	99	129	-0.9	1	0	-0.2
1928	Cle-A	0	1	.000	5	0	0	0	0	15	19	11.4	0	15	9.0	12	7.2	6.60	66	.365	.479	-4	-4	108	118	-0.4	1	-0	-0.1
1932	NY-A	5	2	.714	19	3	3	1	1	56	58	9.3	1	30	4.8	31	5.0	4.50	91	.270	.360	-0	-3	91	98	0.2	-1	1	-0.1
1933	NY-A	7	5	.583	21	8	1	0	0	74	78	9.5	3	52	6.3	55	6.7	5.23	72	.269	.372	-8	-12	88	93	-0.1	-0	-0	-1.1
1935	NY-A	6	5	.545	20	8	3	1	0	87	94	9.7	2	37	3.8	41	4.2	3.62	111	.279	.344	8	4	90	115	-0.4	3	0	0.6
1936	NY-A	1	4	.200	20	3	0	0	1	64	93	13.1	4	29	4.1	19	2.7	5.91	77	.352	.404	-6	-10	90	117	-1.7	-3	1	-0.9
1937	Cin-N	1	0	1.000	4	1	0	0	0	10	16	14.4	0	3	2.7	4	3.6	8.10	45	.390	.432	-5	-5	93	84	0.5	-0	-0	-0.4
	NY-N	1	0	1.000	4	0	0	0	0	9	5	5.0	0	5	5.0	4	4.0	1.00	382	.172	.286	3	3	98	196	0.5	0	1	0.4
	Yr	2	0	1.000	8	1	0	0	0	19	21	9.9	0	8	3.8	8	3.8	4.74	79	.300	.367	-2	-2	95	196	1.0	0	0	0.0
1938	NY-N	5	3	.625	43	0	0	0	5	90	65	6.5	5	28	2.8	42	4.2	1.80	215	.204	.263	**20**	**21**	102	122	0.7	1	-1	2.0
1939	NY-N	4	0	1.000	31	0	0	0	7	56	69	11.1	1	25	4.0	24	3.9	4.18	92	.304	.365	-2	-2	99	114	2.0	1	0	0.0
1940	NY-N	2	4	.333	41	0	0	0	**7**	55	49	8.0	5	25	4.1	31	5.1	3.44	112	.232	.308	3	3	100	101	-0.8	-1	-1	0.1
1941	NY-N	1	5	.167	31	0	0	0	**8**	57	49	7.7	2	21	3.3	30	4.7	3.32	114	.238	.297	2	**3**	104	90	-1.9	-1	-1	0.1
Total	12	33	31	.516	249	23	7	2	29	598	619	9.3	26	300	4.5	301	4.5	4.06	98	.271	.349	7	-4	96	109	-2.3	2	0	0.5
■ **WALTER BROWN**	Brown, Walter Irving b: 4/23/15, Jamestown, N.Y. BR/TR, 5'11", 175 lbs. Deb: 5/16/47																												
1947	StL-A	1	0	1.000	19	0	0	0	0	46	50	9.8	3	28	5.5	10	2.0	4.89	80	.294	.386	-6	-5	106	108	0.5	-1	0	-0.5
■ **CAL BROWNING**	Browning, Calvin Duane b: 3/16/38, Burns Flat, Okla. BL/TL, 5'11", 190 lbs. Deb: 6/12/60																												
1960	StL-N	0	0	—	1	0	0	0	0	1	5	45.0	1	1	9.0	0	0.0	27.00	15	.714	.750	-3	-3	108	127	0.0	0	0	-0.1
■ **FRANK BROWNING**	Browning, Frank "Dutch" b: 10/29/1882, Falmouth, Ky. d: 5/19/48, San Antonio, Tex. BR/TR, 5'5", 145 lbs. Deb: 4/16/10																												
1910	Det-A	2	2	.500	11	6	2	0	3	49	51	9.4	0	10	1.8	16	2.9	2.57	98	.262	.298	-0	-0	100	95	-0.1	-2	1	0.1
■ **PETE BROWNING**	Browning, Louis Rogers "The Gladiator" b: 7/17/1861, Louisville, Ky. d: 9/10/05, Louisville, Ky. BR/TR, 6', 180 lbs. Deb: 5/02/1882																												
1884	Lou-a	0	1	.000	1	1	0	0	0	⅓	2	54.0	0	2	54.0	0	0.0	54.00	—	1.000	1.000	-2	-2	87	87	-0.4	1	0	-0.1
■ **TOM BROWNING**	Browning, Thomas Leo b: 4/28/60, Casper, Wyoming BL/TL, 6'1", 185 lbs. Deb: 9/09/84																												
1984	Cin-N	1	0	1.000	3	3	0	0	0	23	27	10.6	0	5	2.0	14	5.5	1.57	246	.303	.337	5	6	107	248	0.5	-0	0	0.7
1985	Cin-N	20	9	.690	38	38	6	4	0	261	242	8.3	29	73	2.5	155	5.3	3.55	106	.245	.294	1	7	105	95	5.1	2	-2	0.8
1986	Cin-N	14	13	.519	39	39	4	2	0	243	225	8.3	26	70	2.6	147	5.4	3.81	102	.245	.291	-2	2	104	88	-0.3	-1	-3	-0.1
1987	Cin-N	10	13	.435	32	31	2	0	0	183	201	9.9	27	61	3.0	117	5.8	5.02	84	.284	.338	-19	-16	103	98	-2.0	1	-2	-1.6
1988	Cin-N	18	5	.783	36	36	5	2	0	251	205	7.4	36	64	2.3	124	4.4	3.41	106	.224	.276	1	6	105	94	6.5	0	-3	0.5
Total	5	63	40	.612	148	147	17	8	0	961	900	8.4	118	273	2.6	557	5.2	3.81	101	.249	.298	-13	4	104	97	9.8	2	-9	0.3
■ **BRUCE BRUBAKER**	Brubaker, Bruce Ellsworth b: 12/29/41, Harrisburg, Pa. BR/TR, 6'1", 198 lbs. Deb: 4/15/67																												
1967	LA-N	0	0	—	1	0	0	0	0	1	3	27.0	1	0	0.0	2	18.0	27.00	11	.429	.429	-3	-3	89	63	0.0	0	0	-0.1
1970	Mil-A	0	0	—	1	0	0	0	0	2	2	9.0	1	1	4.5	0	0.0	9.00	41	.250	.333	-1	-1	100	77	0.0	0	0	0.0
Total	2	0	0	—	2	0	0	0	0	3	5	15.0	2	1	3.0	2	6.0	15.00	23	.333	.375	-4	-4	96	72	0.0	0	0	-0.1
■ **LOU BRUCE**	Bruce, Louis R. b: 1/16/1877, St.Regis, N.Y. d: 2/9/68, Ilion, N.Y. BL/TR, 5'5", 145 lbs. Deb: 6/22/04																												
1904	Phi-A	0	0	—	2	0	0	0	0	11	11	9.0	1	2	1.6	2	1.6	4.91	53	.284	.319	-3	-3	101	70	0.0	0	0	-0.2

YEAR	TM/L	W	L	PCT	G	GS	CG	SHO	SV	IP	H	H/G	HR	BB	BB/G	SO	SO/G	ERA	/A	OAVG	OOBP	PR	/A	PF	CPI	WAT	PB	PD	TPI
■ BOB BRUCE	Bruce, Robert James b: 5/16/33, Detroit, Mich. BR/TR, 6'3", 200 lbs. Deb: 9/14/59																												
1959	Det-A	0	1	.000	2	1	0	0	0	2	2	9.0	1	3	13.5	1	4.5	9.00	48	.250	.417	-1	-1	111	109	-0.4	0	0	0.0
1960	Det-A	4	7	.364	34	15	1	0	0	130	127	8.8	16	56	3.9	76	5.3	3.74	105	.250	.329	2	3	102	106	-1.1	0	1	0.4
1961	Det-A	1	2	.333	14	6	0	0	0	45	57	11.4	6	24	4.8	25	5.0	4.40	86	.320	.395	-2	-3	94	146	-0.6	0	-1	-0.3
1962	Hou-N	10	9	.526	32	27	6	0	0	175	164	8.4	16	82	4.2	135	6.9	4.06	92	.248	.337	-2	-7	95	98	2.2	5	0	-0.1
1963	Hou-N	5	9	.357	30	25	1	1	0	170	162	8.6	7	60	3.2	123	6.5	3.60	87	.250	.317	-6	-9	95	90	-0.8	2	-1	-0.8
1964	Hou-N	15	9	.625	35	29	9	4	0	202	191	8.5	8	33	1.5	135	6.0	2.76	126	.246	.273	17	16	98	92	4.9	2	-0	1.9
1965	Hou-N	9	18	.333	35	34	7	1	0	230	241	9.4	22	38	1.5	145	5.7	3.72	87	.270	.301	-5	-13	91	100	-2.6	-1	0	-1.3
1966	Hou-N	3	13	.188	25	23	1	0	0	130	160	11.1	16	29	2.0	71	4.9	5.33	67	.301	.343	-25	-26	99	91	-4.7	-2	0	-2.7
1967	Atl-N	2	3	.400	12	7	1	0	1	39	42	9.7	3	15	3.5	22	5.1	4.85	73	.269	.335	-6	-6	105	84	-0.3	0	-0	-0.5
Total	9	49	71	.408	219	167	26	6	1	1123	1146	9.2	95	340	2.7	733	5.9	3.85	91	.263	.318	-28	-45	96	98	-3.4	6	-1	-3.4
■ FRED BRUCKBAUER	Bruckbauer, Frederick John b: 5/27/38, New Ulm, Minn. BR/TR, 6'1", 185 lbs. Deb: 4/25/61																												
1961	Min-A	0	0	—	1	0	0	0	0	0	3	—	0	1	—	0	—	∞	—	1.000	1.000	-3	-3	107	65	0.0	0	0	-0.2
■ ANDY BRUCKMILLER	Bruckmiller, Andrew b: 1/1/1882, Mc Keesport, Pa. d: 1/12/70, Mc Keesport, Pa. BR/TR, 5'11", 175 lbs. Deb: 6/26/05																												
1905	Det-A	0	0	—	1	0	0	0	0	1	4	36.0	0	1	9.0	1	9.0	27.00	10	.615	.666	-3	-3	100	74	0.0	-0	0	-0.2
■ MIKE BRUHERT	Bruhert, Michael Edwin b: 6/24/51, Jamaica, N.Y. BR/TR, 6'6", 220 lbs. Deb: 4/09/78																												
1978	NY-N	4	11	.267	27	22	1	1	0	134	171	11.5	6	34	2.3	56	3.8	4.77	75	.317	.352	-18	-18	99	99	-2.7	-3	0	-2.0
■ JACK BRUNER	Bruner, Jack Raymond b: 7/1/24, Waterloo, Iowa BL/TL, 6'1", 185 lbs. Deb: 9/16/49																												
1949	Chi-A	1	2	.333	4	2	0	0	0	8	10	11.3	0	8	9.0	4	4.5	7.88	53	.357	.500	-3	-3	99	96	-0.2	-0	-0	-0.2
1950	Chi-A	0	0	—	9	0	0	0	0	12	7	5.3	0	14	10.5	8	6.0	3.75	121	.184	.400	1	1	99	114	0.0	0	-0	0.1
	StL-A	1	2	.333	13	1	0	0	1	35	36	9.3	4	23	5.9	16	4.1	4.63	110	.267	.377	-0	2	111	113	-0.1	-1	-1	0.0
	Yr	1	2	.333	22	1	0	0	1	47	43	8.2	4	37	7.1	24	4.6	4.40	112	.247	.378	1	3	108	113	-0.1	0	-1	0.1
Total	2	2	4	.333	26	3	0	0	1	55	53	8.7	4	45	7.4	28	4.6	4.91	98	.264	.399	-2	-1	107	111	-0.3	-1	-1	-0.1
■ ROY BRUNER	Bruner, Walter Roy b: 2/10/17, Cecilia, Ky. d: 11/30/86, St.Matthews, Ky. BR/TR, 6', 165 lbs. Deb: 9/14/39																												
1939	Phi-N	0	4	.000	4	4	2	0	0	27	38	12.7	3	13	4.3	11	3.7	6.67	58	.339	.402	-8	-8	99	98	-1.9	-1	-0	-0.7
1940	Phi-N	0	0	—	2	0	0	0	0	6	5	7.5	2	6	9.0	4	6.0	6.00	65	.227	.379	-1	-1	102	114	0.0	0	0	0.0
1941	Phi-N	0	3	.000	13	1	0	0	0	29	37	11.5	1	25	7.8	13	4.0	4.97	75	.336	.440	-4	-4	103	140	-1.4	-1	-0	-0.4
Total	3	0	7	.000	19	5	2	0	0	62	80	11.6	6	44	6.4	28	4.1	5.81	66	.328	.418	-14	-14	101	119	-3.3	-1	-1	-1.1
■ GEORGE BRUNET	Brunet, George Stuart "Lefty" b: 6/8/35, Houghton, Mich. BR/TL, 6'1", 195 lbs. Deb: 9/14/56																												
1956	KC-A	0	0	—	6	1	0	0	0	9	10	10.0	1	11	11.0	5	5.0	7.00	62	.286	.447	-3	-3	105	100	0.0	-0	0	-0.2
1957	KC-A	0	1	.000	4	2	0	0	0	11	13	10.6	2	4	3.3	3	2.5	5.73	67	.277	.333	-2	-2	102	83	-0.4	-0	0	-0.2
1959	KC-A	0	0	—	2	0	0	0	0	5	10	18.0	2	7	12.6	7	12.6	10.80	37	.435	.563	-4	-4	103	140	0.0	0	1	-0.2
1960	KC-A	0	2	.000	3	2	0	0	0	10	12	10.8	0	10	9.0	4	3.6	4.50	87	.308	.442	-1	-1	101	142	-0.9	-0	1	0.0
	Mil-N	2	0	1.000	17	6	0	0	0	50	53	9.5	6	22	4.0	39	7.0	5.04	67	.275	.344	-7	-9	89	94	1.0	-1	0	-0.9
1961	Mil-N	0	0	—	5	0	0	0	0	5	7	12.6	1	2	3.6	0	0.0	5.40	68	.412	.391	-1	-1	91	162	0.0	0	0	0.0
1962	Hou-N	2	4	.333	17	11	2	0	0	54	62	10.3	2	21	3.5	36	6.0	4.50	83	.291	.349	-3	-5	95	95	-0.4	-1	1	-0.4
1963	Hou-N	0	3	.000	5	2	0	0	0	13	24	16.6	2	6	4.2	11	7.6	6.92	45	.393	.448	-5	-5	95	125	-1.4	-0	0	-0.5
	Bal-A	0	1	.000	16	0	0	0	1	20	25	11.2	3	9	4.0	13	5.8	5.40	63	.301	.372	-4	-4	93	107	-0.4	-0	0	-0.4
1964	LA-A	2	2	.500	10	7	0	0	0	42	38	8.1	2	25	5.4	36	7.7	3.64	88	.237	.335	-0	-2	89	96	0.0	0	0	-0.1
1965	Cal-A	9	11	.450	41	26	8	3	2	197	149	6.8	9	69	3.2	141	6.4	2.56	133	.209	.277	20	18	98	87	-0.2	-2	-1	1.5
1966	Cal-A	13	13	.500	41	32	8	2	0	212	183	7.8	21	106	4.5	148	6.3	3.31	103	.234	.322	3	3	100	114	0.2	-2	0	0.1
1967	Cal-A	11	19	.367	40	37	7	2	1	250	203	7.3	19	90	3.2	165	5.9	3.31	94	.223	.289	-2	-6	96	88	-5.0	-4	-2	-1.2
1968	Cal-A	13	17	.433	39	36	8	5	0	245	191	7.0	23	68	2.5	132	4.8	2.87	100	.215	.268	3	-0	96	89	0.6	-3	-3	-0.6
1969	Cal-A	6	7	.462	23	19	2	2	0	101	98	8.7	15	39	3.5	56	5.0	3.83	96	.255	.318	-2	-2	101	109	0.3	-1	-1	-0.3
	Sea-A	2	5	.286	12	11	2	0	0	64	70	9.8	11	28	3.9	37	5.2	5.34	68	.280	.349	-12	-12	100	96	-0.9	1	1	-1.0
	Yr	8	12	.400	35	30	4	2	0	165	168	9.2	26	67	3.7	93	5.1	4.42	83	.264	.329	-14	-14	101	96	-0.6	-1	0	-1.3
1970	Was-A	8	6	.571	24	20	2	1	0	118	124	9.5	10	48	3.7	67	5.1	4.42	82	.275	.340	-9	-11	97	96	1.8	1	-1	-1.0
	Pit-N	1	1	.500	12	1	0	0	0	17	19	10.1	1	9	4.8	17	9.0	2.65	147	.311	.387	3	2	96	217	0.0	-0	0	0.2
1971	StL-N	0	1	.000	7	0	0	0	0	9	12	12.0	3	7	7.0	4	4.0	6.00	58	.316	.413	-3	-3	100	138	-0.4	0	-0	-0.2
Total	15	69	93	.426	324	213	39	15	4	1432	1303	8.2	133	581	3.7	921	5.8	3.62	92	.244	.314	-30	-46	97	98	-6.1	-13	-3	-5.4
■ TOM BRUNO	Bruno, Thomas Michael b: 1/26/53, Chicago, Ill. BR/TR, 6'5", 210 lbs. Deb: 8/01/76																												
1976	KC-A	1	0	1.000	12	0	0	0	0	17	20	10.6	3	9	4.8	11	5.8	6.88	50	.290	.363	-6	-6	99	82	0.5	0	-0	-0.6
1977	Tor-A	0	1	.000	12	0	0	0	0	18	30	15.0	4	13	6.5	9	4.5	8.00	53	.366	.440	-8	-7	105	114	-0.4	0	0	-0.6
1978	StL-N	4	3	.571	18	3	0	0	1	50	38	6.8	3	17	3.1	33	5.9	1.98	173	.209	.274	9	8	96	112	0.9	-1	-1	0.7
1979	StL-N	2	3	.400	27	1	0	0	0	38	37	8.8	1	22	5.2	27	6.4	4.26	91	.253	.351	-2	-2	104	89	-0.5	-0	0	-0.1
Total	4	7	7	.500	69	4	0	0	1	123	125	9.1	11	61	4.5	80	5.9	4.24	87	.261	.341	-8	-7	100	101	0.5	-1	-1	-0.6
■ WARREN BRUSSTAR	Brusstar, Warren Scott b: 2/2/52, Oakland, Cal. BR/TR, 6'3", 200 lbs. Deb: 5/06/77																												
1977	Phi-N	7	2	.778	46	0	0	0	3	71	64	8.1	7	24	3.0	46	5.8	2.66	145	.250	.312	10	9	98	136	1.9	-1	1	1.0
1978	Phi-N	6	3	.667	58	0	0	0	0	89	74	7.5	0	30	3.0	60	6.1	2.33	160	.239	.307	12	14	104	117	1.2	0	2	1.7
1979	Phi-N	1	0	1.000	13	0	0	0	1	14	23	14.8	1	4	2.6	3	1.9	7.07	51	.383	.409	-5	-5	97	99	0.5	0	0	-0.4
1980	Phi-N	2	2	.500	26	0	0	0	0	39	42	9.7	3	13	3.0	21	4.8	3.69	104	.286	.333	-0	1	106	117	-0.1	0	0	0.1
1981	Phi-N	0	1	.000	14	0	0	0	0	12	12	9.0	0	10	7.5	8	6.0	4.50	87	.250	.383	-1	-1	112	95	-0.4	0	0	0.0
1982	Phi-N	2	3	.400	22	0	0	0	2	23	31	12.1	2	5	2.0	11	4.3	4.70	72	.348	.363	-3	-3	94	125	-0.6	-0	0	-0.3
	Chi-A	2	0	1.000	10	0	0	0	0	18	19	9.5	2	3	1.5	8	4.0	3.50	113	.257	.295	1	1	97	96	1.0	-1	0	0.1
1983	Chi-N	3	1	.750	59	0	0	0	1	80	67	7.5	1	37	4.2	46	5.2	2.36	156	.234	.316	11	12	101	124	1.1	-0	0	1.2
1984	Chi-N	1	1	.500	41	0	0	0	3	64	57	8.0	4	21	3.0	36	5.1	3.09	126	.247	.304	4	6	109	106	-0.1	1	0	0.7
1985	Chi-N	4	3	.571	51	0	0	0	4	74	87	10.6	8	36	4.4	34	4.1	6.08	69	.292	.364	-20	-15	117	86	0.6	-0	-2	-1.7
Total	9	28	16	.636	340	0	0	0	14	484	476	8.9	28	183	3.4	273	5.1	3.51	109	.265	.329	8	17	105	113	5.1	-1	3	2.4
■ CLAY BRYANT	Bryant, Claiborne Henry b: 11/16/11, Madison Heights, Va. BR/TR, 6'2.5", 195 lbs. Deb: 4/19/35 C																												
1935	Chi-N	1	2	.333	9	1	0	0	2	23	34	13.3	1	7	2.7	13	5.1	5.09	75	.358	.390	-3	-3	95	123	-0.6	2	-0	0.0
1936	Chi-N	1	2	.333	26	0	0	0	3	57	57	9.0	0	24	3.8	35	5.5	3.32	124	.259	.331	**4**	**5**	102	103	-0.5	1	1	0.7
1937	Chi-N	9	3	.750	38	10	4	1	3	135	117	7.8	1	78	5.2	75	5.0	4.27	92	.232	.334	-5	-5	100	74	2.3	5	-3	-0.2
1938	Chi-N	19	11	.633	44	30	17	3	2	270	235	7.8	6	125	4.2	**135**	4.5	3.10	126	.235	.315	21	24	103	98	2.1	4	-3	2.6
1939	Chi-N	2	1	.667	4	4	2	0	0	31	42	12.2	3	14	4.1	9	2.6	5.81	67	.307	.370	-7	-7	100	94	0.4	0	-1	-0.5
1940	Chi-N	0	1	.000	8	0	0	0	0	26	26	9.0	2	14	4.8	5	1.7	4.85	78	.265	.345	-3	-3	99	94	-0.4	1	0	-0.2
Total	6	32	20	.615	129	45	23	4	7	542	511	8.5	13	262	4.4	272	4.5	3.74	105	.249	.330	8	11	101	93	3.3	13	-6	2.4
■ RON BRYANT	Bryant, Ronald Raymond b: 11/12/47, Redlands, Cal. BB/TL, 6', 190 lbs. Deb: 9/29/67																												
1967	SF-N	0	0	—	1	0	0	0	0	4	3	6.8	0	0	0.0	2	4.5	4.50	74	.200	.250	-0	-1	99	28	0.0	-0	-0	0.0
1969	SF-N	4	3	.571	16	8	0	0	1	58	60	9.3	8	25	3.9	30	4.7	4.34	83	.271	.345	-5	-5	100	110	0.1	1	0	-0.3
1970	SF-N	5	8	.385	34	11	1	0	0	96	103	9.7	7	38	3.6	66	6.2	4.78	81	.274	.336	-8	-10	96	89	-1.8	-1	1	-0.9
1971	SF-N	7	10	.412	27	22	3	2	0	140	146	9.4	9	49	3.2	79	5.1	3.79	90	.272	.328	-5	-6	99	102	-2.3	1	0	-0.4
1972	SF-N	14	7	.667	35	28	11	4	0	214	176	7.4	20	77	3.2	107	4.5	2.90	119	.224	.290	13	13	100	102	4.6	1	-4	1.0
1973	SF-N	**24**	12	.667	41	39	8	0	0	270	240	8.0	23	115	3.8	143	4.8	3.53	108	.234	.312	4	9	104	92	**5.8**	1	0	1.1
1974	SF-N	3	15	.167	41	23	0	0	0	127	142	10.1	11	68	4.8	75	5.3	5.60	71	.286	.361	-28	-23	109	88	-5.8	-2	-0	-2.4
1975	StL-N	0	1	.000	10	1	0	0	0	9	20	20.0	2	7	7.0	7	7.0	16.00	23	.444	.491	-12	-12	103	75	-0.4	-0	0	-1.1
Total	8	57	56	.504	205	132	23	6	1	918	890	8.7	80	379	3.7	509	5.0	4.02	92	.254	.324	-41	-34	102	96	0.2	0	-3	-3.0
■ T. R. BRYDEN	Bryden, Thomas Ray b: 1/17/59, Moses Lake, Wash. BR/TR, 6'4", 190 lbs. Deb: 4/10/86																												
1986	Cal-A	2	1	.667	16	0	0	0	0	34	38	10.1	4	21	5.6	25	6.6	6.62	60	.290	.384	-9	-10	95	87	0.3	0	0	-0.8

YEAR	TM/L	W	L	PCT	G	GS	CG	SHO	SV	IP	H	H/G	HR	BB	BB/G	SO	SO/G	ERA	/A	OAVG	OOBP	PR	/A	PF	CPI	WAT	PB	PD	TPI
■ **TOD BRYNAN**	Brynan, Charles Ruley b: 7/1863, Philadelphia, Pa. d: 5/10/25, Philadelphia, Pa. BR/TR, Deb: 1888																												
1888	Chi-N	2	1	.667	3	3	2	0	0	25	29	10.4	1	7	2.5	11	4.0	6.48	46	.304	.352	-10	-10	106	63	0.3	0	0	-0.7
1891	Bos-N	0	1	.000	1	1	0	0	0	1	4	36.0	0	3	27.0	0	0.0	54.00	7	.601	.725	-6	-6	109	47	-0.4	0	0	-0.3
Total	2	2	2	.500	4	4	2	0	0	26	33	11.4	1	10	3.5	11	3.8	8.31	36	.324	.384	-16	-15	106	62	-0.1	0	0	-1.0
■ **JIM BUCHANAN**	Buchanan, James Forrest b: 7/1/1876, Chatham Hill, Va. d: 6/15/49, Norfolk, Neb. BL/TR, 5'10", 165 lbs. Deb: 4/16/05																												
1905	StL-A	5	9	.357	22	15	12	1	**2**	141	149	9.5	2	27	1.7	54	3.4	3.51	70	.296	.332	-14	-16	93	93	0.1	0	0	-1.6
■ **BOB BUCHANAN**	Buchanan, Robert Gordon b: 5/3/61, Ridley Park, Pa. BL/TL, 6'1", 185 lbs. Deb: 7/13/85																												
1985	Cin-N	1	0	1.000	14	0	0	0	0	16	25	14.1	4	9	5.1	3	1.7	8.44	45	.368	.442	-9	-8	105	103	0.5	-0	0	-0.8
■ **GARLAND BUCKEYE**	Buckeye, Garland Maiers "Gob" b: 10/16/1897, Heron Lake, Minn. d: 11/14/75, Stone Lake, Wis. BB/TL, 6', 260 lbs. Deb: 6/19/18																												
1918	Was-A	0	0	—	1	0	0	0	0	2	3	13.5	0	6	27.0	2	9.0	18.00	16	.333	.600	-3	-3	103	68	0.0	0	0	-0.2
1925	Cle-A	13	8	.619	30	18	11	1	0	153	161	9.5	3	58	3.4	49	2.9	3.65	129	.267	.329	13	18	107	94	3.5	2	-1	1.8
1926	Cle-A	6	9	.400	32	18	5	1	0	166	160	8.7	3	69	3.7	36	2.0	3.09	127	.264	.329	17	15	97	115	-2.3	2	-1	1.5
1927	Cle-A	10	17	.370	35	25	13	2	1	205	231	10.1	6	74	3.2	38	1.7	3.95	103	.296	.345	4	3	99	110	-2.2	3	-1	0.5
1928	Cle-A	1	5	.167	9	6	0	0	0	35	58	14.9	2	5	1.3	6	1.5	6.69	66	.389	.396	-10	-9	108	105	-1.7	-1	-0	-0.8
	NY-N	0	0	—	1	0	0	0	0	4	9	20.3	1	2	4.5	3	6.8	13.50	29	.409	.458	-4	-4	99	77	0.0	1	0	-0.2
Total	5	30	39	.435	108	67	29	4	1	565	622	9.9	15	214	3.4	134	2.1	3.90	108	.287	.342	16	19	101	106	-2.7	7	-3	2.6
■ **ED BUCKINGHAM**	Buckingham, Edward Taylor b: 5/12/1874, Metuchen, N.J. d: 7/30/42, Bridgeport, Conn. Deb: 8/30/1895																												
1895	Was-N	0	0	—	1	1	0	0	0	3	6	18.0	0	2	6.0	1	3.0	6.00	84	.437	.509	-0	-0	105	152	0.0	-0	0	0.0
■ **JESS BUCKLES**	Buckles, Jesse Robert "Jim" b: 5/20/1890, La Verne, Cal. d: 8/2/75, Westminster, Cal. BL/TL, 6'2.5", 205 lbs. Deb: 9/17/16																												
1916	NY-A	0	0	—	2	0	0	0	0	4	3	6.8	0	1	2.3	2	4.5	2.25	127	.188	.235	0	0	101	22	0.0	-0	0	0.0
■ **JOHN BUCKLEY**	Buckley, John Edward b: 1869, Marlboro, Mass. d: 5/3/42, Westborough, Mass. TR , 6'1", 200 lbs. Deb: 7/15/1890																												
1890	Buf-P	1	3	.250	4	4	4	0	0	34	49	13.0	5	16	4.2	4	1.1	7.68	53	.350	.417	-13	-14	97	85	-0.1	-2	0	-1.0
■ **MIKE BUDNICK**	Budnick, Michael Joe b: 9/15/19, Astoria, Ore. BR/TR, 6'1", 200 lbs. Deb: 4/18/46																												
1946	NY-N	2	3	.400	35	7	1	1	3	88	75	7.7	13	48	4.9	36	3.7	3.17	111	.231	.324	2	3	103	123	0.0	3	1	0.7
1947	NY-N	0	0	—	7	1	0	0	0	12	16	12.0	0	10	7.5	6	4.5	10.50	39	.314	.419	-9	-9	99	56	0.0	0	0	-0.7
Total	2	2	3	.400	42	8	1	1	3	100	91	8.2	13	58	5.2	42	3.8	4.05	89	.242	.337	-6	-5	103	115	0.0	3	1	0.0
■ **CHARLIE BUFFINTON**	Buffinton, Charles G. b: 6/14/1861, Fall River, Mass. d: 9/23/07, Fall River, Mass. BR/TR, 6'1", 180 lbs. Deb: 5/17/1882 M																												
1882	Bos-N	2	3	.400	5	5	4	1	0	42	53	11.4	2	14	3.0	17	3.6	4.07	72	.316	.368	-6	-5	102	117	-0.6	-0	0	-0.4
1883	Bos-N	25	14	.641	43	41	34	4	1	333	346	9.4	4	51	1.4	188	5.1	3.03	105	.276	.304	4	6	102	92	0.0	-1	-0	0.5
1884	Bos-N	48	16	.750	67	67	63	8	0	587	506	7.8	15	76	1.2	417	6.4	2.15	130	.241	.268	54	41	93	88	14.9	13	4	5.5
1885	Bos-N	22	27	.449	51	50	49	6	0	434	425	8.8	10	112	2.3	242	5.0	2.88	93	.267	.315	-3	-10	95	106	2.7	5	5	0.0
1886	Bos-N	7	10	.412	18	17	16	0	0	151	203	12.1	4	39	2.3	47	2.8	4.59	70	.336	.376	-22	-23	97	107	-1.3	4	0	-1.9
1887	Phi-N	21	17	.553	40	38	35	1	0	332	352	9.5	16	92	2.5	160	4.3	3.66	104	.287	.337	14	5	94	103	-2.4	5	7	1.5
1888	Phi-N	28	17	.622	46	46	43	3	0	400	324	7.3	6	59	1.3	199	4.5	1.91	168	.234	.265	41	**58**	113	92	6.1	-3	9	**7.1**
1889	Phi-N	28	16	.636	47	43	37	2	0	380	390	9.2	10	121	2.9	153	3.6	3.24	130	.281	.338	33	41	105	106	8.2	-2	2	3.8
1890	Phi-P	19	15	.559	36	33	28	0	1	283	312	9.9	8	126	4.0	89	2.8	3.82	112	.292	.366	13	14	101	102	1.8	4	2	1.8
1891	Bos-a	29	9	**.763**	48	43	33	2	**3**	364	303	7.5	8	120	3.0	158	3.9	2.55	137	.240	**.306**	47	38	94	89	5.8	0	6	3.8
1892	Bal-N	3	8	.273	13	13	9	0	0	97	130	12.1	4	46	4.3	30	2.8	4.92	68	.335	.405	-18	-17	102	110	-0.7	4	0	-1.0
Total	11	232	152	.604	414	396	351	27	5	3403	3344	8.8	87	856	2.3	1700	4.5	2.96	113	.269	.316	160	150	99	98	34.5	29	34	20.7
■ **BOB BUHL**	Buhl, Robert Ray b: 8/12/28, Saginaw, Mich. BR/TR, 6'2", 180 lbs. Deb: 4/17/53																												
1953	Mil-N	13	8	.619	30	18	8	3	0	154	133	7.8	9	73	4.3	83	4.9	2.98	132	.235	.323	22	16	92	114	0.6	-2	1	1.4
1954	Mil-N	2	7	.222	31	14	2	1	3	110	117	9.6	5	65	5.3	57	4.7	4.01	93	.277	.364	1	-4	91	112	-2.7	-2	-0	-0.6
1955	Mil-N	13	11	.542	38	27	11	1	1	202	168	7.5	13	109	4.9	117	5.2	3.21	115	.227	.321	19	11	92	102	-0.2	-3	-0	0.6
1956	Mil-N	18	8	.692	38	33	13	2	0	217	190	7.9	18	105	4.4	86	3.6	3.32	109	.236	.321	11	7	96	102	3.5	-4	0	0.3
1957	Mil-N	18	7	**.720**	34	31	14	2	0	217	191	7.9	15	121	5.0	117	4.9	2.74	124	.241	.337	28	16	88	**135**	3.8	-3	-2	1.0
1958	Mil-N	5	2	.714	11	10	3	0	1	73	74	9.1	5	30	3.7	27	3.3	3.45	99	.260	.329	4	-0	87	106	1.1	0	1	0.1
1959	Mil-N	15	9	.625	31	25	12	**4**	0	198	181	8.2	19	74	3.4	105	4.8	2.86	128	.243	.309	24	18	93	120	2.3	-4	3	1.7
1960	Mil-N	16	9	.640	36	33	11	2	0	239	202	7.6	23	103	3.9	121	4.6	3.09	109	.229	.306	18	7	89	108	2.3	-1	3	0.8
1961	Mil-N	9	10	.474	32	28	9	1	0	188	180	8.6	23	98	4.7	77	3.7	4.12	89	.256	.345	-2	-9	91	109	-1.2	-3	1	-1.2
1962	Mil-N	0	1	.000	1	1	0	0	0	2	6	27.0	0	4	18.0	1	4.5	22.50	17	.545	.625	-4	-4	98	81	-0.4	-0	0	-0.3
	Chi-N	12	13	.480	34	30	8	1	0	212	204	8.7	23	94	4.0	109	4.6	3.69	116	.255	.332	6	14	109	111	2.6	-7	-2	0.6
	Yr	12	14	.462	35	31	8	1	0	214	210	8.8	23	98	4.1	110	4.6	3.87	110	.259	.337	2	10	108	111	2.2	-0	-2	0.3
1963	Chi-N	11	14	.440	37	34	6	0	0	226	219	8.7	24	62	2.5	108	4.3	3.38	102	.259	.309	-2	2	105	109	-1.8	-3	1	0.0
1964	Chi-N	15	14	.517	36	35	11	3	0	228	208	8.2	22	68	2.7	107	4.2	3.83	98	.244	.298	-7	-2	106	88	1.6	-2	2	0.0
1965	Chi-N	13	11	.542	32	31	2	0	0	184	207	10.1	26	57	2.8	92	4.5	4.40	83	.284	.329	-18	-15	103	107	2.4	-4	0	-1.9
1966	Chi-N	0	0	—	1	1	0	0	0	2	4	18.0	1	1	4.5	1	4.5	18.00	21	.400	.417	-3	-3	103	66	0.0	-0	0	-0.2
	Phi-N	6	8	.429	32	18	1	0	1	132	156	10.6	10	39	2.7	59	4.0	4.77	76	.298	.347	-17	-17	100	95	-1.4	-2	1	-1.7
	Yr	6	8	.429	33	19	1	0	1	134	160	10.7	11	40	2.7	60	4.0	4.97	73	.299	.349	-20	-20	100	95	-1.4	-0	1	-1.9
1967	Phi-N	0	0	—	3	0	0	0	0	3	6	18.0	2	2	6.0	1	3.0	12.00	29	.462	.533	-3	-3	104	126	0.0	0	0	-0.2
Total	15	166	132	.557	457	369	111	20	6	2587	2446	8.5	238	1105	3.8	1268	4.4	3.55	104	.251	.325	75	37	97	109	12.5	-41	8	0.4
■ **DE WAYNE BUICE**	Buice, De Wayne Allison b: 8/20/57, Lynwood, Cal. BR/TR, 6', 170 lbs. Deb: 4/25/87																												
1987	Cal-A	6	7	.462	57	0	0	0	17	114	87	6.9	12	40	3.2	109	8.6	3.39	131	.213	.282	14	13	100	86	0.0	0	0	1.3
1988	Cal-A	2	4	.333	32	0	0	0	3	41	45	9.9	5	19	4.2	38	8.3	5.93	63	.287	.350	-9	-10	95	87	-0.8	0	0	-0.8
Total	2	8	11	.421	89	0	0	0	20	155	132	7.7	17	59	3.4	147	8.5	4.06	105	.234	.302	5	3	98	86	-0.8	0	0	0.5
■ **CY BUKER**	Buker, Cyril Owen b: 2/5/19, Greenwood, Wis. BL/TR, 5'11", 190 lbs. Deb: 5/17/45																												
1945	Bro-N	7	2	.778	42	4	0	0	5	87	90	9.3	2	45	4.7	48	5.0	3.31	109	.268	.349	5	3	95	122	2.3	0	-1	0.2
■ **RED BULLOCK**	Bullock, Malton Joseph b: 10/12/12, Biloxi, Miss. BL/TL, 6'1", 192 lbs. Deb: 5/19/36																												
1936	Phi-A	0	2	.000	12	2	0	0	0	17	19	10.1	0	37	19.6	7	3.7	13.76	38	.271	.519	-16	-16	105	63	-0.9	-1	0	-1.3
■ **WALLY BUNKER**	Bunker, Wallace Edward b: 1/25/45, Seattle, Wash. BR/TR, 6'2", 197 lbs. Deb: 9/29/63																												
1963	Bal-A	0	1	.000	1	1	0	0	0	4	10	22.5	1	3	6.8	1	2.3	13.50	25	.476	.520	-4	-4	93	101	-0.4	0	-0	-0.3
1964	Bal-A	19	5	**.792**	29	29	12	1	0	214	161	6.8	17	62	2.6	96	4.0	2.69	139	.207	.266	22	25	103	84	**6.3**	-2	0	2.6
1965	Bal-A	10	8	.556	34	27	4	1	2	189	170	8.1	16	58	2.8	84	4.0	3.38	101	.242	.298	2	1	99	95	-0.3	-1	-1	-0.1
1966	Bal-A	10	6	.625	29	24	3	0	0	143	151	9.5	16	48	3.0	89	5.6	4.28	79	.269	.327	-13	-14	99	99	0.4	-0	-1	-1.5
1967	Bal-A	3	7	.300	29	9	1	0	1	88	83	8.5	7	31	3.2	51	5.2	4.09	74	.254	.318	-8	-10	94	90	-1.8	-1	1	-1.1
1968	Bal-A	2	0	1.000	18	10	2	1	0	71	59	7.5	4	14	1.8	44	5.6	2.41	125	.225	.262	5	5	101	94	1.0	-0	-0	0.5
1969	KC-A	12	11	.522	35	31	10	1	2	223	198	8.0	29	62	2.5	130	5.2	3.23	117	.238	.291	10	13	104	103	2.2	0	3	1.8
1970	KC-A	2	11	.154	24	15	2	1	0	122	109	8.0	16	50	3.7	59	4.4	4.20	88	.238	.309	-7	-7	100	86	-4.0	0	-1	-0.7
1971	KC-A	2	3	.400	7	6	0	0	0	32	35	9.8	7	6	1.7	15	4.2	5.06	67	.271	.301	-6	-6	98	88	-0.5	-1	-0	-0.6
Total	9	60	52	.536	206	152	34	5	5	1086	976	8.1	113	334	2.8	569	4.7	3.51	100	.240	.297	-0	2	100	93	2.9	-6	2	0.6
■ **JIM BUNNING**	Bunning, James Paul David b: 10/23/31, Southgate, Ky. BR/TR, 6'3", 190 lbs. Deb: 7/20/55																												
1955	Det-A	3	5	.375	15	8	0	0	1	51	59	10.4	8	32	5.6	37	6.5	6.35	59	.291	.390	-14	-15	95	94	-1.0	-0	0	-1.3
1956	Det-A	5	1	.833	15	3	0	0	1	53	55	9.3	6	28	4.8	34	5.8	3.74	106	.257	.339	2	1	95	112	2.0	2	-0	0.2
1957	Det-A	**20**	8	.714	45	30	14	1	1	**267**	214	7.2	33	72	2.4	182	6.1	2.70	151	.218	.275	**32**	**41**	107	105	**6.6**	2	-5	4.2
1958	Det-A	14	12	.538	35	34	10	3	0	220	188	7.7	28	79	3.2	177	7.2	3.52	110	.228	.292	6	9	103	92	1.2	-0	-3	0.5
1959	Det-A	17	13	.567	40	35	14	1	1	250	220	7.9	37	75	2.7	**201**	7.2	3.89	110	.234	.295	-1	11	111	92	2.6	0	-5	0.8
1960	Det-A	11	14	.440	36	34	10	3	0	252	217	7.8	20	64	2.3	**201**	**7.2**	2.79	141	.236	.285	**30**	**32**	102	105	-0.6	-2	-1	**3.0**
1961	Det-A	17	11	.607	38	37	12	4	1	268	232	7.8	25	71	2.4	194	6.5	3.19	118	.229	.281	25	17	94	89	-0.3	-3	-2	1.2

YEAR	TM/L	W	L	PCT	G	GS	CG	SHO	SV	IP	H	H/G	HR	BB	BB/G	SO	SO/G	ERA	/A	OAVG	OOBP	PR	/A	PF	CPI	WAT	PB	PD	TPI
1962	Det-A	19	10	.655	41	35	12	2	6	258	262	9.1	28	74	2.6	184	6.4	3.59	122	.261	.316	11	23	110	109	4.5	4	-5	2.3
1963	Det-A	12	13	.480	39	35	6	2	1	248	245	8.9	38	69	2.5	196	7.1	3.88	97	.254	.304	-7	-3	104	102	-0.1	-1	-2	-0.5
1964	Phi-N	19	8	.704	41	39	13	5	2	284	248	7.9	23	46	**1.5**	219	6.9	2.63	132	.233	.269	29	26	98	102	4.8	-2	-4	2.2
1965	Phi-N	19	9	.679	39	39	15	7	0	291	253	7.8	23	62	1.9	268	8.3	2.60	129	.232	.275	30	24	95	106	5.1	4	1	3.2
1966	Phi-N	19	14	.576	43	41	16	**5**	1	314	260	7.5	26	55	1.6	252	7.2	2.41	150	.223	.266	42	42	100	101	1.7	1	-3	4.4
1967	Phi-N	17	15	.531	40	40	16	**6**	0	**302**	241	7.2	18	73	2.2	**253**	7.5	2.29	153	.217	.269	**36**	**41**	104	99	1.0	2	-3	**4.7**
1968	Pit-N	4	14	.222	27	26	3	1	0	160	168	9.4	14	48	2.7	95	5.3	3.88	77	.272	.327	-16	-16	100	104	-5.1	-2	-2	-2.1
1969	Pit-N	10	9	.526	25	25	4	0	0	156	147	8.5	10	49	2.8	124	7.2	3.81	89	.249	.309	-4	-7	94	86	-0.2	-3	-3	-1.3
	LA-N	3	1	.750	9	9	1	0	0	56	65	10.4	5	10	1.6	33	5.3	3.38	104	.288	.319	1	1	97	119	1.0	-1	-1	0.0
	Yr	13	10	.565	34	34	5	0	0	212	212	9.0	15	59	2.5	157	6.7	3.69	92	.257	.305	-2	-7	95	119	0.8	-3	-4	-1.3
1970	Phi-N	10	15	.400	34	33	4	0	0	219	233	9.6	19	56	2.3	147	6.0	4.11	96	.274	.317	-1	-4	98	98	-1.6	-2	-1	-0.6
1971	Phi-N	5	12	.294	29	16	1	0	1	110	126	10.3	11	37	3.0	58	4.7	5.48	66	.297	.349	-25	-23	105	89	-2.6	-0	-0	-2.2
Total	17	224	184	.549	591	519	151	40	16	3759	3433	8.2	372	1000	2.4	2855	6.8	3.27	115	.242	.294	179	200	101	100	19.0	-1	-40	18.7

■ **BILL BURBACH** Burbach, William David b: 8/22/47, Dickeyville, Wis. BR/TR, 6'4", 215 lbs. Deb: 4/11/69

YEAR	TM/L	W	L	PCT	G	GS	CG	SHO	SV	IP	H	H/G	HR	BB	BB/G	SO	SO/G	ERA	/A	OAVG	OOBP	PR	/A	PF	CPI	WAT	PB	PD	TPI
1969	NY-A	6	8	.429	31	24	2	1	0	141	112	7.1	15	102	6.5	82	5.2	3.64	95	.219	.346	-0	-3	96	109	-0.9	-1	-1	-0.4
1970	NY-A	0	2	.000	4	4	0	0	0	17	23	12.2	2	9	4.8	10	5.3	10.06	34	.324	.398	-12	-13	91	63	-0.9	-1	-0	-1.1
1971	NY-A	0	1	.000	2	0	0	0	0	3	6	18.0	0	5	15.0	3	9.0	12.00	28	.400	.500	-3	-3	97	93	-0.4	-0	-0	-0.2
Total	3	6	11	.353	37	28	2	1	0	161	141	7.9	17	116	6.5	95	5.3	4.47	77	.236	.357	-15	-18	95	104	-2.2	-2	-1	-1.7

■ **LARRY BURCHART** Burchart, Larry Wayne b: 2/8/46, Tulsa, Okla. BR/TR, 6'3", 205 lbs. Deb: 4/10/69

YEAR	TM/L	W	L	PCT	G	GS	CG	SHO	SV	IP	H	H/G	HR	BB	BB/G	SO	SO/G	ERA	/A	OAVG	OOBP	PR	/A	PF	CPI	WAT	PB	PD	TPI
1969	Cle-A	0	2	.000	29	0	0	0	0	42	42	9.0	2	24	5.1	26	5.6	4.29	81	.266	.349	-3	-4	96	99	-0.9	0	-1	-0.4

■ **FRED BURCHELL** Burchell, Frederick Duff b: 7/14/1879, Perth Amboy, N.J. d: 11/20/51, Jordan, N.Y. BR/TL, 5'11", 190 lbs. Deb: 4/17/03

YEAR	TM/L	W	L	PCT	G	GS	CG	SHO	SV	IP	H	H/G	HR	BB	BB/G	SO	SO/G	ERA	/A	OAVG	OOBP	PR	/A	PF	CPI	WAT	PB	PD	TPI
1903	Phi-N	0	3	.000	6	3	2	0	0	44	48	9.8	0	14	2.9	12	2.5	2.86	108	.306	.370	2	1	94	123	-1.4	-0	-0	0.1
1907	Bos-A	0	1	.000	2	1	0	0	0	10	8	7.2	0	2	1.8	6	5.4	2.70	97	.241	.285	-0	-0	103	64	-0.4	-0	-0	0.0
1908	Bos-A	10	8	.556	31	19	9	0	0	180	161	8.1	2	65	3.3	94	4.7	2.95	79	.247	.326	-11	-13	97	104	1.3	1	-2	-1.5
1909	Bos-A	3	3	.500	10	5	1	0	0	52	51	8.8	1	11	1.9	12	2.1	2.94	91	.271	.318	-3	-2	108	98	-0.3	-0	1	0.0
Total	4	13	15	.464	49	28	12	0	0	286	268	8.4	3	92	2.9	124	3.9	2.93	86	.260	.330	-12	-13	99	105	-0.8	0	-2	-1.4

■ **FREDDIE BURDETTE** Burdette, Freddie Thomason b: 9/15/36, Moultrie, Ga. BR/TR, 6'1", 170 lbs. Deb: 9/05/62

YEAR	TM/L	W	L	PCT	G	GS	CG	SHO	SV	IP	H	H/G	HR	BB	BB/G	SO	SO/G	ERA	/A	OAVG	OOBP	PR	/A	PF	CPI	WAT	PB	PD	TPI
1962	Chi-N	0	0	—	8	0	0	0	1	10	5	4.5	2	8	7.2	5	4.5	3.60	119	.161	.325	0	1	109	111	0.0	-0	0	0.1
1963	Chi-N	0	0	—	4	0	0	0	0	5	5	9.0	1	2	3.6	1	1.8	3.60	96	.313	.368	-0	-0	105	170	0.0	0	0	0.0
1964	Chi-N	1	0	1.000	18	0	0	0	0	20	17	7.6	2	10	4.5	4	1.8	3.15	119	.243	.326	1	1	106	132	0.5	0	-0	0.2
Total	3	1	0	1.000	30	0	0	0	1	35	27	6.9	5	20	5.1	10	2.6	3.34	116	.231	.331	1	2	107	131	0.5	0	0	0.3

■ **LEW BURDETTE** Burdette, Selva Lewis b: 11/22/26, Nitro, W.Va. BR/TR, 6'2", 180 lbs. Deb: 9/26/50 C

YEAR	TM/L	W	L	PCT	G	GS	CG	SHO	SV	IP	H	H/G	HR	BB	BB/G	SO	SO/G	ERA	/A	OAVG	OOBP	PR	/A	PF	CPI	WAT	PB	PD	TPI
1950	NY-A	0	0	—	2	0	0	0	0	1	3	27.0	0	0	0.0	0	0.0	9.00	49	.500	.500	-0	-1	96	129	0.0	0	0	0.0
1951	Bos-N	0	0	—	3	0	0	0	0	4	6	13.5	0	5	11.3	1	2.3	6.75	57	.375	.522	-1	-1	97	142	0.0	-0	0	0.0
1952	Bos-N	6	11	.353	45	9	5	0	7	137	138	9.1	8	47	3.1	47	3.1	3.61	100	.265	.323	2	-0	97	104	-1.4	-0	1	0.0
1953	Mil-N	15	5	.750	46	13	6	1	8	175	177	9.1	7	56	2.9	58	3.0	3.24	121	.264	.321	20	13	92	110	4.1	-1	2	1.3
1954	Mil-N	15	14	.517	38	32	13	4	0	238	224	8.5	17	62	2.3	79	3.0	2.76	135	.251	.298	35	25	91	111	-1.7	-4	1	2.2
1955	Mil-N	13	8	.619	42	33	11	2	0	230	253	9.9	25	73	2.9	70	2.7	4.03	92	.280	.332	0	-9	92	108	1.8	3	2	-0.4
1956	Mil-N	19	10	.655	39	35	16	**6**	1	256	234	8.2	22	52	1.8	110	3.9	**2.71**	**134**	.241	.279	30	26	96	100	2.5	0	1	2.9
1957	Mil-N	17	9	.654	37	33	14	1	0	257	260	9.1	25	59	2.1	78	2.7	3.71	92	.264	.301	5	-9	88	96	1.5	2	2	-0.6
1958	Mil-N	20	10	**.667**	40	36	19	3	0	275	279	9.1	18	50	**1.6**	113	3.7	2.91	118	.264	.298	**32**	16	87	109	3.1	8	3	2.6
1959	Mil-N	**21**	15	.583	41	39	20	**4**	1	290	312	9.7	38	38	1.2	105	3.3	4.07	90	.273	.294	-4	-13	93	93	1.6	5	0	-0.7
1960	Mil-N	19	13	.594	45	32	**18**	4	4	276	277	9.0	19	35	**1.1**	83	2.7	3.36	100	.260	.284	12	0	89	91	1.0	5	5	0.9
1961	Mil-N	18	11	.621	40	36	14	3	0	**272**	295	9.8	31	33	**1.1**	92	3.0	4.00	92	.273	.294	1	-10	91	90	3.0	5	2	-0.3
1962	Mil-N	10	9	.526	37	19	6	1	2	144	172	10.8	26	23	1.4	59	3.7	4.88	79	.298	.322	-15	-16	98	101	0.0	0	1	-1.4
1963	Mil-N	6	5	.545	15	13	4	1	0	84	71	7.6	15	24	2.6	28	3.0	3.64	90	.228	.281	-3	-3	100	95	0.3	-0	-0	-0.3
	StL-N	3	8	.273	21	14	3	0	2	98	106	9.7	6	16	1.5	45	4.1	3.77	92	.278	.310	-5	-3	106	98	-2.9	-1	-1	-0.5
	Yr	9	13	.409	36	27	7	1	2	182	177	8.8	21	40	2.0	73	3.6	3.71	91	.255	.296	-9	-7	103	98	-2.6	-0	-2	-0.8
1964	StL-N	1	0	1.000	8	0	0	0	0	10	10	9.0	1	3	2.7	3	2.7	1.80	218	.256	.302	2	2	111	201	0.5	-0	0	0.2
	Chi-N	9	9	.500	28	17	8	2	0	131	152	10.4	15	19	1.3	40	2.7	4.88	77	.292	.313	-20	-16	106	88	0.6	6	2	-0.7
	Yr	10	9	.526	36	17	8	2	0	141	162	10.3	16	22	1.4	43	2.7	4.66	81	.289	.313	-18	-14	107	88	1.1	-0	2	-0.5
1965	Chi-N	0	2	.000	7	3	0	0	0	20	26	11.7	3	4	1.8	5	2.3	5.40	68	.299	.333	-4	-4	103	93	-0.9	1	0	-0.2
	Phi-N	3	3	.500	19	9	1	1	0	71	95	12.0	5	17	2.2	23	2.9	5.45	62	.329	.367	-15	-17	95	100	-0.1	1	0	-1.4
	Yr	3	5	.375	26	12	1	1	0	91	121	12.0	8	21	2.1	28	2.8	5.44	63	.321	.357	-19	-20	97	100	-1.0	1	0	-1.6
1966	Cal-A	7	2	.778	54	0	0	0	5	80	80	9.0	4	12	1.3	27	3.0	3.37	101	.268	.293	1	0	100	96	2.6	-0	-1	0.0
1967	Cal-A	1	0	1.000	19	0	0	0	1	18	16	8.0	4	0	0.0	8	4.0	5.00	62	.232	.239	-4	-4	96	66	0.5	0	0	-0.3
Total	18	203	144	.585	626	373	158	33	31	3067	3186	9.3	289	628	1.8	1074	3.2	3.66	98	.268	.304	68	-19	93	100	16.1	29	19	3.3

■ **BILL BURDICK** Burdick, William Byron b: 10/11/1859, Austin, Minn. d: 10/23/49, Spokane, Wash. BR/TR, Deb: 1888

YEAR	TM/L	W	L	PCT	G	GS	CG	SHO	SV	IP	H	H/G	HR	BB	BB/G	SO	SO/G	ERA	/A	OAVG	OOBP	PR	/A	PF	CPI	WAT	PB	PD	TPI
1888	Ind-N	10	10	.500	20	20	20	0	0	176	168	8.6	12	43	2.2	55	2.8	2.81	98	.265	.311	0	-1	98	112	2.3	-2	0	-0.2
1889	Ind-N	2	4	.333	10	4	2	0	1	46	58	11.3	7	13	2.5	16	3.1	4.50	98	.324	.370	-2	-0	110	121	-0.7	-1	0	0.0
Total	2	12	14	.462	30	24	22	0	1	222	226	9.2	19	56	2.3	71	2.9	3.16	98	.278	.324	-2	-2	100	114	1.6	-3	0	-0.2

■ **TOM BURGMEIER** Burgmeier, Thomas Henry b: 8/2/43, St.Paul, Minn. BL/TL, 5'11", 185 lbs. Deb: 4/10/68

YEAR	TM/L	W	L	PCT	G	GS	CG	SHO	SV	IP	H	H/G	HR	BB	BB/G	SO	SO/G	ERA	/A	OAVG	OOBP	PR	/A	PF	CPI	WAT	PB	PD	TPI
1968	Cal-A	1	4	.200	56	2	0	0	5	73	65	8.0	5	24	3.0	33	4.1	4.32	66	.250	.302	-11	-12	96	78	-1.2	0	3	-0.8
1969	KC-A	3	1	.750	31	0	0	0	0	54	67	11.2	5	21	3.5	23	3.8	4.17	91	.316	.365	-3	-2	104	130	1.1	-0	2	0.0
1970	KC-A	6	6	.500	41	0	0	0	1	68	59	7.8	6	23	3.0	43	5.7	3.18	116	.236	.290	4	4	100	97	1.1	-0	2	0.6
1971	KC-A	9	7	.563	67	0	0	0	17	88	71	7.3	3	30	3.1	44	4.5	1.74	196	.223	.297	17	16	98	147	0.6	2	3	2.3
1972	KC-A	6	2	.750	51	0	0	0	9	55	67	11.0	0	33	5.4	18	2.9	4.25	72	.313	.388	-7	-7	100	120	2.1	1	1	-0.5
1973	KC-A	0	0	—	6	0	0	0	1	10	13	11.7	2	4	3.6	4	3.6	5.40	77	.310	.383	-2	-1	109	116	0.0	0	-0	-0.1
1974	Min-A	5	3	.625	50	0	0	0	4	92	92	9.0	7	26	2.5	34	3.3	4.50	81	.270	.315	-9	-9	101	83	1.0	0	3	-0.5
1975	Min-A	5	8	.385	46	0	0	0	11	76	76	9.0	7	23	2.7	41	4.9	3.08	132	.264	.314	6	8	107	121	-1.3	0	0	0.9
1976	Min-A	8	1	.889	57	0	0	0	1	115	95	7.4	11	29	2.3	45	3.5	2.50	138	.226	.276	13	12	98	109	3.5	0	2	1.5
1977	Min-A	6	4	.600	61	0	0	0	7	97	113	10.5	15	33	3.1	35	3.2	5.10	81	.299	.350	-11	-10	102	104	0.9	0	1	-0.8
1978	Bos-A	2	1	.667	35	1	0	0	4	61	74	10.9	7	23	3.4	24	3.5	4.43	91	.302	.362	-4	-3	106	118	0.2	0	1	-0.1
1979	Bos-A	3	2	.600	44	0	0	0	4	89	89	9.0	8	16	1.6	60	6.1	2.73	164	.263	.296	15	17	106	129	0.2	0	1	1.8
1980	Bos-A	5	4	.556	62	0	0	0	24	99	87	7.9	3	20	1.8	54	4.9	2.00	206	.241	.279	22	23	102	124	0.4	0	3	2.7
1981	Bos-A	4	5	.444	32	0	0	0	6	60	61	9.2	5	17	2.6	35	5.3	2.85	136	.268	.322	5	7	106	138	-0.8	0	1	0.9
1982	Bos-A	7	0	1.000	40	0	0	0	2	102	98	8.6	6	22	1.9	44	3.9	2.29	196	.259	.295	20	**25**	110	141	3.5	0	2	2.8
1983	Oak-A	6	7	.462	49	0	0	0	4	96	89	8.3	2	32	3.0	39	3.7	2.81	140	.244	.296	13	12	96	100	0.1	0	2	1.4
1984	Oak-A	3	0	1.000	17	0	0	0	2	23	15	5.9	2	8	3.1	8	3.1	2.35	157	.190	.258	4	3	92	93	1.5	0	0	0.4
Total	17	79	55	.590	745	3	0	0	102	1258	1231	8.8	94	384	2.7	584	4.2	3.23	118	.261	.312	73	83	102	115	12.9	2	27	12.5

■ **SANDY BURK** Burk, Charles Sanford b: 4/22/1887, Columbus, Ohio d: 10/11/34, Brooklyn, N.Y. BR/TR, 5'8", 155 lbs. Deb: 9/12/10

YEAR	TM/L	W	L	PCT	G	GS	CG	SHO	SV	IP	H	H/G	HR	BB	BB/G	SO	SO/G	ERA	/A	OAVG	OOBP	PR	/A	PF	CPI	WAT	PB	PD	TPI
1910	Bro-N	0	3	.000	4	3	1	0	0	19	17	8.1	0	27	12.8	14	6.6	6.16	48	.258	.484	-7	-7	98	100	-1.4	-1	0	-0.6
1911	Bro-N	1	3	.250	13	7	1	0	0	58	54	8.4	1	47	7.3	15	2.3	5.12	66	.261	.405	-11	-11	99	90	-0.7	-1	0	-1.1
1912	Bro-N	0	0	—	2	0	0	0	0	8	9	10.1	0	3	3.4	2	2.3	3.38	98	.273	.333	0	-0	97	90	0.0	0	0	0.0
	StL-N	1	3	.250	12	4	2	0	1	45	37	7.4	0	12	2.4	17	3.4	2.40	146	.226	.282	5	5	103	71	-0.7	-2	-1	0.3
	Yr	1	3	.250	14	4	2	0	1	53	46	7.8	0	15	2.5	19	3.2	2.55	136	.234	.291	5	5	102	71	-0.7	0	-1	0.3
1913	StL-N	0	2	.000	19	5	0	0	1	70	81	10.4	1	33	4.2	29	3.7	5.14	60	.290	.366	-15	-16	97	86	-0.9	-2	-0	-1.7
1915	Pit-F	2	0	1.000	2	2	1	0	0	18	8	4.0	0	11	5.5	9	4.5	1.00	310	.153	.300	4	4	102	120	1.0	-0	0	0.5
Total	5	4	11	.267	52	21	5	0	2	218	206	8.5	2	133	5.5	86	3.6	4.25	77	.257	.367	-24	-24	99	88	-2.7	-5	-1	-2.6

YEAR	TM/L	W	L	PCT	G	GS	CG	SHO	SV	IP	H	H/G	HR	BB	BB/G	SO	SO/G	ERA	/A	OAVG	OOBP	PR	/A	PF	CPI	WAT	PB	PD	TPI
■ ELMER BURKART	Burkart, Elmer Robert "Swede" b: 2/1/17, Torresdale, Pa. BR/TR, 6'2", 190 lbs. Deb: 9/14/36																												
1936	Phi-N	0	0	—	2	2	0	0	0	8	4	4.5	0	12	13.5	2	2.3	3.38	132	.160	.432	1	1	111	131	0.0	-0	0	0.1
1937	Phi-N	0	0	—	7	0	0	0	0	16	20	11.3	0	9	5.1	4	2.3	6.19	70	.323	.397	-4	-3	111	89	0.0	-1	0	-0.3
1938	Phi-N	0	1	.000	2	1	1	0	0	10	12	10.8	0	3	2.7	1	0.9	4.50	89	.286	.348	-1	-1	106	87	-0.4	-0	-0	0.0
1939	Phi-N	1	0	1.000	5	0	0	0	0	8	11	12.4	0	2	2.3	2	2.3	4.50	87	.344	.371	-1	-1	99	115	0.5	1	-0	0.0
Total	4	1	1	.500	16	3	1	0	0	42	47	10.1	0	26	5.6	9	1.9	4.93	85	.292	.387	-5	-3	107	102	0.1	-1	-0	-0.2
■ JOHN BURKE	Burke, John Patrick b: 1/27/1877, Hazelton, Pa. d: 8/4/50, Jersey City, N.J. BR/TR, Deb: 6/27/02																												
1902	NY-N	0	1	.000	2	1	1	0	0	14	21	13.5	0	3	1.9	3	1.9	5.79	50	.372	.404	-5	-4	104	86	-0.4	-0	0	-0.3
■ BOBBY BURKE	Burke, Robert James "Lefty" b: 1/23/07, Joliet, Ill. d: 2/8/71, Joliet, Ill. BL/TL, 6'0.5", 150 lbs. Deb: 4/16/27																												
1927	Was-A	3	2	.600	36	6	1	0	0	100	91	8.2	6	32	2.9	20	1.8	3.96	100	.245	.312	2	0	96	80	0.3	-2	0	-0.1
1928	Was-A	2	4	.333	26	7	2	1	0	85	87	9.2	1	18	1.9	27	2.9	3.92	105	.277	.307	1	2	101	86	-0.9	1	0	0.2
1929	Was-A	6	8	.429	37	17	4	0	0	141	154	9.8	6	55	3.5	51	3.3	4.79	89	.279	.340	-8	-8	100	85	-0.5	-3	-2	-1.1
1930	Was-A	3	4	.429	24	4	2	0	3	74	62	7.5	2	29	3.5	35	4.3	3.65	125	.229	.301	8	8	98	81	-1.0	-1	-1	0.5
1931	Was-A	8	3	.727	30	13	3	1	2	129	124	8.7	6	50	3.5	38	2.7	4.26	101	.255	.321	2	1	98	88	1.9	-0	0	0.1
1932	Was-A	3	6	.333	22	10	2	0	0	91	98	9.7	4	44	4.4	32	3.2	5.14	85	.272	.350	-7	-8	98	86	-2.0	0	-1	-0.7
1933	Was-A	4	3	.571	25	6	4	1	0	64	64	9.0	1	31	4.4	28	3.9	3.23	123	.256	.338	7	5	93	117	-0.3	0	0	0.6
1934	Was-A	8	8	.500	37	15	7	1	0	168	155	8.3	2	72	3.9	52	2.8	3.21	143	.245	.316	24	26	102	100	1.0	1	0	2.7
1935	Was-A	1	8	.111	15	10	2	0	0	66	90	12.3	7	27	3.7	16	2.2	7.50	55	.327	.384	-22	-25	93	83	-3.3	-0	1	-2.0
1937	Phi-N	0	0	—	2	0	0	0	0	0	1	—	0	2	—	0	—	∞	—	.500	.750	-1	-1	111	91	0.0	0	0	0.0
Total	10	38	46	.452	254	88	27	4	5	918	926	9.1	35	360	3.5	299	2.9	4.29	100	.263	.329	6	-1	99	89	-4.8	-3	-3	0.2
■ STEVE BURKE	Burke, Steven Michael b: 3/5/55, Stockton, Cal. BB/TR, 6'2", 200 lbs. Deb: 9/10/77																												
1977	Sea-A	0	1	.000	6	0	0	0	0	16	12	6.8	0	7	3.9	6	3.4	2.81	143	.226	.297	2	2	98	97	-0.4	0	0	0.2
1978	Sea-A	0	1	.000	18	0	0	0	0	49	46	8.4	2	24	4.4	16	2.9	3.49	113	.258	.343	2	2	104	109	-0.4	0	0	0.2
Total	2	0	2	.000	24	0	0	0	0	65	58	8.0	2	31	4.3	22	3.0	3.32	119	.251	.332	4	5	103	106	-0.8	0	0	0.4
■ TIM BURKE	Burke, Timothy Philip b: 2/19/59, Omaha, Neb. BR/TR, 6'3", 205 lbs. Deb: 4/08/85																												
1985	Mon-N	9	4	.692	**78**	0	0	0	8	120	86	6.5	9	44	3.3	87	6.5	2.40	141	.204	.284	**16**	13	94	107	2.4	-0	1	1.4
1986	Mon-N	9	7	.563	68	2	0	0	4	101	103	9.2	7	46	4.1	82	7.3	2.94	124	.262	.339	9	8	98	138	1.3	-0	1	0.9
1987	Mon-N	7	0	1.000	55	0	0	0	18	91	64	6.3	3	17	1.7	58	5.7	1.19	364	.196	.229	**29**	**32**	106	112	3.5	-1	1	**3.2**
1988	Mon-N	3	5	.375	61	0	0	0	18	82	84	9.2	7	25	2.7	42	4.6	3.40	107	.272	.320	0	2	105	121	-0.9	-0	0	0.2
Total	4	28	16	.636	262	2	0	0	48	394	337	7.7	26	132	3.0	269	6.1	2.47	151	.232	.295	55	55	100	119	6.3	-2	3	5.7
■ WALTER BURKE	Burke, Walter R. b: California d: 3/3/11, Memphis, Tenn. 6', 200 lbs. Deb: 6/10/1882																												
1882	Buf-N	0	1	.000	1	1	0	0	0	4	10	22.5	0	0	0.0	0	0.0	11.25	26	.478	.478	-4	-4	103	87	-0.4	-1	0	-0.2
1883	Buf-N	0	0	—	1	1	0	0	0	8	9	10.1	0	3	3.4	1	1.1	5.63	55	.292	.354	-2	-2	99	67	0.0	-0	0	-0.1
1884	Bos-U	19	15	.559	38	36	34	0	0	322	326	9.1	10	31	0.9	255	7.1	2.85	103	.268	.286	6	3	98	105	1.4	1	-4	0.0
1887	Det-N	0	1	.000	2	2	1	0	0	15	21	12.6	0	5	3.0	3	1.8	6.00	66	.347	.397	-3	-3	97	88	-0.4	-0	0	-0.2
Total	4	19	17	.528	42	40	35	0	0	349	366	9.4	10	39	1.0	259	6.7	3.15	95	.275	.296	-3	-6	98	103	0.6	-1	-4	-0.5
■ BILLY BURKE	Burke, William Ignatius b: 7/11/1889, Clinton, Mass. d: 2/9/67, Worcester, Mass. BL/TL, 5'10", 165 lbs. Deb: 4/30/10																												
1910	Bos-N	1	0	1.000	19	1	1	0	0	64	68	9.6	1	29	4.1	22	3.1	4.08	88	.302	.387	-7	-3	118	109	0.5	-1	-1	-0.4
1911	Bos-N	0	1	.000	2	1	0	0	0	3	6	18.0	0	5	15.0	1	3.0	21.00	18	.429	.579	-6	-6	109	57	-0.4	0	-0	-0.4
Total	2	1	1	.500	21	2	1	0	0	67	74	9.9	1	34	4.6	23	3.1	4.84	74	.310	.400	-13	-9	118	107	0.1	-0	-1	-0.8
■ JESSE BURKETT	Burkett, Jesse Cail "Crab" b: 12/4/1868, Wheeling, W.Va. d: 5/27/53, Worcester, Mass. BL/TL, 5'8", 155 lbs. Deb: 4/22/1890 H																												
1890	NY-N	3	10	.231	21	12	6	0	0	118	134	10.2	3	92	7.0	82	6.3	5.57	60	.302	.422	-26	-29	94	92	-3.4	9	0	-2.3
1894	Cle-N	0	0	—	1	0	0	0	0	4	6	13.5	0	1	2.3	0	0.0	4.50	131	.370	.407	0	1	111	122	0.0	0	0	0.0
1902	StL-A	0	1	.000	1	0	0	0	0	1	4	36.0	0	1	9.0	2	18.0	9.00	40	.614	.665	-1	-1	102	222	-0.4	0	0	0.0
Total	3	3	11	.214	23	12	6	0	0	123	144	10.5	3	94	6.9	84	6.1	5.56	62	.309	.425	-27	-29	95	94	-3.8	10	0	-2.3
■ JOHN BURKETT	Burkett, John David b: 11/28/64, New Brighton, Pa. BR/TR, 6'2", 175 lbs. Deb: 9/15/87																												
1987	SF-N	0	0	—	3	0	0	0	0	6	7	10.5	2	3	4.5	5	7.5	4.50	86	.304	.393	-0	-0	95	173	0.0	-0	0	0.0
■ KEN BURKHART	Burkhart, Kenneth William (born Kenneth William Burkhardt) b: 11/18/16, Knoxville, Tenn. BR/TR, 6'1", 190 lbs. Deb: 4/21/45 U																												
1945	StL-N	18	8	.692	42	22	12	4	2	217	206	8.5	9	66	2.7	67	2.8	2.90	127	.251	.305	22	19	97	109	3.0	1	-1	1.9
1946	StL-N	6	3	.667	25	13	5	2	2	100	111	10.0	4	36	3.2	32	2.9	2.88	122	.282	.343	6	7	103	137	0.5	-0	-2	0.5
1947	StL-N	3	6	.333	34	6	1	0	1	95	108	10.2	13	23	2.2	44	4.2	5.21	81	.292	.334	-12	-11	104	93	-1.9	-1	1	-1.0
1948	StL-N	0	0	—	20	0	0	0	1	37	50	12.2	4	14	3.4	16	3.9	5.59	70	.331	.386	-7	-7	99	111	0.0	0	0	-0.5
	Cin-N	0	3	.000	16	0	0	0	0	42	42	9.0	3	16	3.4	14	3.0	6.86	61	.255	.324	-14	-12	106	53	-1.4	2	-0	-0.9
	Yr	0	3	.000	36	0	0	0	1	79	92	10.5	7	30	3.4	30	3.4	6.27	65	.289	.348	-20	-19	103	53	-1.4	0	0	-1.4
1949	Cin-N	0	0	—	11	0	0	0	1	28	29	9.3	2	10	3.2	8	2.6	3.21	123	.282	.339	3	2	98	136	0.0	0	0	0.3
Total	5	27	20	.574	148	41	18	6	7	519	546	9.5	35	165	2.9	181	3.1	3.85	99	.273	.328	-2	-1	100	109	0.2	1	-1	0.3
■ WALLY BURNETTE	Burnette, Wallace Harper b: 6/20/29, Blairs, Va. BR/TR, 6'0.5", 178 lbs. Deb: 7/15/56																												
1956	KC-A	6	8	.429	18	14	4	1	0	121	115	8.6	13	39	2.9	54	4.0	2.90	150	.252	.308	17	19	105	125	1.0	-5	-1	1.5
1957	KC-A	7	12	.368	38	9	1	0	1	113	115	9.2	8	44	3.5	57	4.5	4.30	89	.268	.329	-6	-6	102	91	-0.4	1	2	-0.2
1958	KC-A	1	1	.500	12	4	0	0	0	28	29	9.3	2	14	4.5	11	3.5	3.54	114	.264	.344	1	2	107	115	0.0	0	-0	0.1
Total	3	14	21	.400	68	27	5	1	1	262	259	8.9	23	97	3.3	122	4.2	3.57	115	.260	.321	11	15	104	110	0.6	-4	1	1.4
■ DENNIS BURNS	Burns, Dennis b: 5/24/1898, Tiff City, Mo. d: 5/21/69, Tulsa, Okla. BR/TR, 5'10", 180 lbs. Deb: 9/22/23																												
1923	Phi-A	2	1	.667	4	3	2	0	0	27	21	7.0	1	7	2.3	8	2.7	2.00	203	.210	.252	6	6	102	80	0.6	-1	0	0.5
1924	Phi-A	6	8	.429	37	17	7	0	1	154	191	11.2	3	68	4.0	26	1.5	5.08	84	.314	.370	-15	-14	101	97	-0.5	-2	-0	-1.4
Total	2	8	9	.471	41	20	9	0	1	181	212	10.5	4	75	3.7	34	1.7	4.62	92	.299	.354	-9	-8	101	94	0.1	-3	-0	-0.9
■ FARMER BURNS	Burns, James "Slab" b: Ashtabula, Ohio TR, 5'7", 168 lbs. Deb: 7/06/01																												
1901	StL-N	0	0	—	1	0	0	0	0	1	2	18.0	0	1	9.0	0	0.0	9.00	35	.563	.721	-1	-1	95	141	0.0	0	0	0.0
■ DICK BURNS	Burns, Richard Simon b: 12/26/1863, Holyoke, Mass. d: 11/11/37, Holyoke, Mass. BL, 140 lbs. Deb: 5/03/1883																												
1883	Det-N	2	12	.143	17	13	13	0	0	128	172	12.1	8	33	2.3	30	2.1	4.50	65	.330	.370	-19	-22	94	112	-4.7	-1	0	-1.7
1884	Cin-U	23	15	.605	40	40	34	1	0	330	298	8.1	7	47	1.3	167	4.6	2.45	129	.246	.274	20	26	105	102	-2.2	11	1	4.8
1885	StL-N	0	0	—	1	0	0	0	0	3	3	9.0	0	0	0.0	2	6.0	9.00	30	.271	.271	-2	-2	97	25	0.0	0	0	-0.1
Total	3	25	27	.481	58	53	47	1	0	461	473	9.2	15	80	1.6	199	3.9	3.07	101	.271	.303	-1	2	102	104	-6.9	10	1	3.0
■ BRITT BURNS	Burns, Robert Britt b: 6/8/59, Houston, Tex. BL/TL, 6'5", 215 lbs. Deb: 8/05/78																												
1978	Chi-A	0	2	.000	2	2	0	0	0	8	14	15.8	2	3	3.4	3	3.4	12.38	31	.378	.415	-8	-8	102	69	-0.9	0	0	-0.5
1979	Chi-A	0	0	—	6	0	0	0	0	5	10	18.0	1	1	1.8	2	3.6	5.40	80	.435	.423	-1	-1	103	180	0.0	0	-0	0.0
1980	Chi-A	15	13	.536	34	32	11	1	0	238	213	8.1	17	63	2.4	133	5.0	2.84	140	.241	.289	32	30	98	103	2.9	0	-1	3.0
1981	Chi-A	10	6	.625	24	23	5	1	0	157	139	8.0	14	49	2.8	108	6.2	2.64	137	.238	.298	18	17	99	121	2.1	0	-4	1.4
1982	Chi-A	13	5	.722	28	28	5	1	0	169	168	8.9	12	67	3.6	116	6.2	4.05	98	.257	.323	1	-2	97	92	3.9	0	-3	-0.4
1983	Chi-A	10	11	.476	29	26	8	4	0	174	165	8.5	14	55	2.8	115	5.9	3.57	116	.249	.307	10	11	102	96	-2.5	0	2	0.8
1984	Chi-A	4	12	.250	34	16	2	0	3	117	130	10.0	7	45	3.5	85	6.5	5.00	89	.280	.345	-13	-7	111	85	-3.7	0	-0	-0.7
1985	Chi-A	18	11	.621	36	34	8	4	0	227	206	8.2	26	79	3.1	172	6.8	3.96	104	.242	.304	5	4	100	91	3.4	0	-1	0.3
Total	8	70	60	.538	193	161	39	11	3	1095	1045	8.6	93	362	3.0	734	6.0	3.66	110	.251	.310	44	45	100	98	5.2	0	-11	3.9
■ TOM BURNS	Burns, Thomas Everett b: 3/30/1857, Honesdale, Pa. d: 3/19/02, Jersey City, N.J. BR/TR, 5'7", 152 lbs. Deb: 5/01/1880 M																												
1880	Chi-N	0	0	—	1	0	0	0	0	1	2	18.0	0	2	18.0	1	9.0	0.00	—	.424	.596	0	0	98	0	0.0	0	0	0.0
■ OYSTER BURNS	Burns, Thomas P. b: 9/6/1864, Philadelphia, Pa. d: 11/11/28, Brooklyn, N.Y. BR/TR, 5'8", 183 lbs. Deb: 8/18/1884																												
1884	Bal-a	0	0	—	2	0	0	0	**1**	9	12	12.0	0	2	2.0	6	6.0	3.00	105	.329	.364	0	0	98	166	0.0	1	0	0.0

YEAR	TM/L	W	L	PCT	G	GS	CG	SHO	SV	IP	H	H/G	HR	BB	BB/G	SO	SO/G	ERA	/A	OAVG	OOBP	PR	/A	PF	CPI	WAT	PB	PD	TPI
1885	Bal-a	7	4	.636	15	11	10	1	**3**	106	112	9.5	3	21	1.8	30	2.5	3.57	100	.283	.319	-4	-0	109	99	2.4	2	0	0.0
1887	Bal-a	1	0	1.000	3	0	0	0	0	11	16	13.1	0	4	3.3	2	1.6	9.82	41	.354	.407	-7	-7	94	58	0.5	2	0	-0.4
1888	Bal-a	0	1	.000	5	0	0	0	0	13	12	8.3	0	3	2.1	2	1.4	4.15	72	.258	.303	-2	-2	98	63	-0.3	2	0	-0.4
Total	4	8	5	.615	25	11	10	1	4	139	152	9.8	3	30	1.9	40	2.6	4.08	86	.290	.329	-12	-9	106	97	2.6	6	0	-0.8
■ **TODD BURNS** Burns, Todd Edward b: 7/6/63, Maywood, Cal. BR/TR, 6'2", 186 lbs. Deb: 5/31/88																													
1988	Oak-A	8	2	.800	17	14	2	0	1	103	93	8.1	8	34	3.0	57	5.0	3.15	118	.241	.301	9	6	93	103	2.3	0	-1	0.6
■ **BILL BURNS** Burns, William Thomas "Sleepy Bill" b: 1/29/1880, San Saba, Tex. d: 6/6/53, Ramona, Cal. , BB/TL, 6'2", 195 lbs. Deb: 4/18/08																													
1908	Was-A	6	11	.353	23	19	11	2	0	165	135	7.4	3	18	1.0	55	3.0	1.69	137	.229	.257	13	11	97	112	-1.8	-1	2	1.6
1909	Was-A	1	1	.500	6	4	1	0	0	29	25	7.8	0	7	2.2	13	4.0	1.24	191	.229	.294	4	4	96	154	0.3	-0	0	0.5
	Chi-A	7	13	.350	23	19	10	3	0	168	161	8.6	2	34	1.8	50	2.7	2.04	117	.264	.312	8	7	97	131	-3.4	1	1	0.8
	Yr	8	14	.364	29	23	11	3	0	197	186	8.5	2	41	1.9	63	2.9	1.92	125	.258	.305	12	10	96	**131**	-3.1	-0	1	1.3
1910	Chi-A	0	0	—	1	0	0	0	0	⅓	0	0.0	0	1	27.0	0	0.0	0.00	—	.000	.500	0	0	95	0	0.0	0	0	0.0
	Cin-N	8	13	.381	31	21	13	2	0	179	183	9.2	3	49	2.5	57	2.9	3.47	89	.273	.333	-9	-7	102	95	-2.5	2	1	-0.6
1911	Cin-N	1	0	1.000	6	3	0	0	1	18	17	8.5	1	3	1.5	5	2.5	3.00	104	.254	.315	1	0	92	106	0.5	2	1	0.3
	Phi-N	6	10	.375	21	14	8	3	1	121	132	9.8	5	26	1.9	47	3.5	3.42	107	.287	.333	-0	3	108	110	-2.3	-1	2	0.5
	Yr	7	10	.412	27	17	8	3	2	139	149	9.6	6	29	1.9	52	3.4	3.37	107	.281	.326	1	4	106	110	-1.8	2	3	0.8
1912	Det-A	1	4	.200	6	5	2	0	0	39	52	12.0	0	9	2.1	6	1.4	5.31	60	.338	.382	-8	-9	96	94	-1.3	1	-0	-0.8
Total	5	30	52	.366	117	85	45	10	2	719	705	8.8	14	147	1.8	233	2.9	2.72	104	.265	.313	8	8	100	112	-10.5	4	6	2.3
■ **PETE BURNSIDE** Burnside, Peter Willits b: 7/2/30, Evanston, Ill. BR/TL, 6'2", 180 lbs. Deb: 9/20/55																													
1955	NY-N	1	0	1.000	2	2	1	0	0	13	10	6.9	1	9	6.2	2	1.4	2.77	143	.204	.328	2	2	98	110	0.5	0	0	0.2
1957	NY-N	1	4	.200	10	9	1	1	0	31	47	13.6	5	13	3.8	18	5.2	8.71	46	.356	.407	-17	-16	103	84	-1.3	-1	-0	-1.5
1958	SF-N	0	0	—	6	1	0	0	0	11	20	16.4	3	5	4.1	4	3.3	6.55	60	.400	.455	-3	-3	100	148	0.0	0	0	-0.2
1959	Det-A	1	3	.250	30	0	0	0	1	62	55	8.0	7	25	3.6	49	7.1	3.77	114	.237	.311	1	4	111	97	-0.9	-1	0	0.3
1960	Det-A	7	7	.500	31	15	2	0	2	114	122	9.6	14	50	3.9	71	5.6	4.26	92	.277	.348	-5	-4	102	111	0.6	-1	-1	-0.5
1961	Was-A	4	9	.308	33	16	4	2	2	113	106	8.4	11	51	4.1	56	4.5	4.54	86	.251	.325	-6	-8	97	88	-1.2	-3	-1	-1.0
1962	Was-A	5	11	.313	40	20	6	0	2	150	152	9.1	20	51	3.1	74	4.4	4.44	91	.263	.318	-8	-6	102	95	-1.3	-3	-2	-1.0
1963	Bal-A	0	1	.000	6	0	0	0	0	7	11	14.1	0	2	2.6	6	7.7	5.14	66	.344	.400	-1	-1	93	112	-0.4	-0	-0	-0.1
	Was-A	0	1	.000	38	1	0	0	0	67	84	11.3	12	24	3.2	23	3.1	6.18	59	.308	.353	-19	-19	101	94	-0.4	-0	-1	-2.0
	Yr	0	2	.000	44	1	0	0	0	74	95	11.6	12	26	3.2	29	3.5	6.08	60	.310	.355	-20	-20	100	94	-0.8	-0	-1	-2.1
Total	8	19	36	.345	196	64	14	3	7	568	607	9.6	73	230	3.6	303	4.8	4.80	83	.275	.339	-57	-52	102	98	-4.4	-8	-5	-5.8
■ **SHELDON BURNSIDE** Burnside, Sheldon John b: 12/22/54, South Bend, Ind. BR/TL, 6'5", 200 lbs. Deb: 9/04/78																													
1978	Det-A	0	0	—	2	0	0	0	0	4	4	9.0	0	2	4.5	3	6.8	9.00	45	.250	.333	-2	-2	107	34	0.0	0	0	-0.1
1979	Det-A	1	1	.500	10	0	0	0	0	21	28	12.0	2	8	3.4	13	5.6	6.43	63	.333	.385	-5	-6	96	95	0.0	0	0	-0.4
1980	Cin-N	1	0	1.000	7	0	0	0	0	5	6	10.8	1	1	1.8	2	3.6	1.80	203	.333	.368	1	1	101	341	0.5	-0	1	0.2
Total	3	2	1	.667	19	0	0	0	0	30	38	11.4	3	11	3.3	18	5.4	6.00	67	.322	.376	-6	-7	98	128	0.5	-0	1	-0.3
■ **GEORGE BURPO** Burpo, George Harvie b: 6/19/22, Jenkins, Ky. BR/TL, 6', 195 lbs. Deb: 6/09/46																													
1946	Cin-N	0	0	—	2	0	0	0	0	2	4	18.0	0	5	22.5	1	4.5	18.00	20	.400	.600	-3	-3	105	75	0.0	0	0	-0.2
■ **HARRY BURRELL** Burrell, Harry J. b: 1866, Vermont d: 12/11/14, Omaha, Neb. Deb: 9/13/1891																													
1891	StL-a	4	2	.667	7	4	3	0	0	43	51	10.7	4	21	4.4	19	4.0	4.81	86	.310	.388	-5	-3	112	104	0.3	-0	0	-0.1
■ **AL BURRIS** Burris, Alva Burton b: 1/28/1874, Warwick, Md. d: 3/24/38, Salisbury, Md. BR/TR, Deb: 6/22/1894																													
1894	Phi-N	0	0	—	1	0	0	0	0	5	14	25.2	0	2	3.6	0	0.0	18.00	28	.523	.556	-7	-7	94	70	0.0	1	0	-0.3
■ **RAY BURRIS** Burris, Bertram Ray b: 8/22/50, Idabel, Okla. BR/TR, 6'5", 200 lbs. Deb: 4/08/73																													
1973	Chi-N	1	1	.500	31	1	0	0	0	65	65	9.0	2	27	3.7	57	7.9	2.91	137	.261	.326	6	8	109	118	0.0	0	1	0.9
1974	Chi-N	3	5	.375	40	5	0	0	1	75	91	10.9	8	26	3.1	40	4.8	6.60	56	.300	.352	-25	-24	102	76	-0.2	-0	-0	-2.5
1975	Chi-N	15	10	.600	36	35	8	2	0	238	259	9.8	25	73	2.8	108	4.1	4.12	93	.281	.329	-13	-8	105	104	3.6	2	-4	-1.0
1976	Chi-N	15	13	.536	37	36	10	4	0	249	251	9.1	22	70	2.5	112	4.0	3.11	125	.263	.310	11	22	111	118	2.2	-5	1	2.0
1977	Chi-N	14	16	.467	39	39	5	1	0	221	270	11.0	29	67	2.7	105	4.3	4.72	95	.305	.351	-20	-6	115	110	-1.1	1	3	0.0
1978	Chi-N	7	13	.350	40	32	4	1	1	199	210	9.5	15	79	3.6	94	4.3	4.75	84	.274	.344	-26	-17	111	90	-3.0	-1	2	-1.5
1979	Chi-N	0	0	—	14	0	0	0	0	22	23	9.4	0	15	6.1	14	5.7	6.14	68	.284	.398	-6	-5	112	77	0.0	0	0	-0.3
	NY-A	1	3	.250	15	0	0	0	0	28	40	12.9	5	10	3.2	19	6.1	6.11	66	.342	.379	-6	-7	95	111	-1.0	0	0	-0.5
	NY-N	0	2	.000	4	4	0	0	0	22	21	8.6	2	6	2.5	10	4.1	3.27	110	.247	.301	1	1	96	99	-0.9	-0	0	0.1
1980	NY-N	7	13	.350	29	29	1	0	0	170	181	9.6	20	54	2.9	83	4.4	4.02	87	.277	.329	-8	-10	97	109	-1.6	-2	-1	-1.3
1981	Mon-N	9	7	.563	22	21	4	0	0	136	117	7.7	9	41	2.7	52	3.4	3.04	112	.235	.291	7	6	98	95	0.1	1	-1	0.6
1982	Mon-N	4	14	.222	37	15	2	0	2	124	143	10.4	14	53	3.8	55	4.0	4.72	80	.297	.360	-15	-13	104	110	-5.4	1	-1	-1.2
1983	Mon-N	4	7	.364	40	17	2	1	0	154	139	8.1	13	56	3.3	100	5.8	3.68	100	.244	.307	-1	-0	101	92	-1.5	3	1	0.3
1984	Oak-A	13	10	.565	34	28	5	1	0	212	193	8.2	15	90	3.8	93	3.9	3.14	117	.244	.323	20	13	92	113	2.2	0	-3	0.9
1985	Mil-A	9	13	.409	29	28	6	0	0	170	182	9.6	25	53	2.8	81	4.3	4.82	91	.272	.322	-13	-8	106	94	-0.8	0	-1	-0.8
1986	StL-N	4	5	.444	23	10	0	0	0	82	92	10.1	13	32	3.5	34	3.7	5.60	69	.287	.355	-17	-16	103	94	-0.3	0	-1	-1.6
1987	Mil-A	2	2	.500	10	2	0	0	0	23	33	12.9	4	12	4.7	8	3.1	5.87	78	.351	.413	-4	-3	102	129	-0.1	0	0	-0.2
Total	15	108	134	.446	480	302	47	10	4	2190	2310	9.5	221	764	3.1	1065	4.4	4.17	93	.274	.331	-108	-68	104	103	-7.8	-1	-5	-6.1
■ **JOHN BURROWS** Burrows, John b: 10/30/13, Winnfield, La. d: 4/27/87, Coal Run, Ohio BR/TL, 5'10", 200 lbs. Deb: 4/25/43																													
1943	Phi-A	0	1	.000	4	1	0	0	0	8	8	9.0	0	9	10.1	3	3.4	7.88	44	.276	.450	-4	-4	106	77	-0.4	-0	0	-0.3
	Chi-N	0	2	.000	23	1	0	0	2	33	25	6.8	0	16	4.4	18	4.9	3.82	87	.205	.307	-2	-2	98	58	-0.9	1	0	0.0
1944	Chi-N	0	0	—	3	0	0	0	0	3	7	21.0	0	3	9.0	1	3.0	18.00	20	.467	.526	-5	-5	100	66	0.0	0	0	-0.4
Total	2	0	3	.000	30	2	0	0	2	44	40	8.2	0	28	5.7	22	4.5	5.52	61	.241	.357	-10	-11	100	62	-1.3	1	0	-0.7
■ **JIM BURTON** Burton, Jim Scott b: 10/27/49, Royal Oak, Mich. BR/TL, 6'3", 195 lbs. Deb: 6/10/75																													
1975	Bos-A	1	2	.333	29	4	0	0	1	53	58	9.8	6	19	3.2	39	6.6	2.89	141	.276	.332	5	7	108	149	-0.6	0	0	0.7
1977	Bos-A	0	0	—	1	0	0	0	0	3	2	6.0	0	1	3.0	3	9.0	0.00	—	.200	.273	1	2	116	0	0.0	0	0	0.2
Total	2	1	2	.333	30	4	0	0	1	56	60	9.6	6	20	3.2	42	6.8	2.73	150	.273	.329	7	9	108	141	-0.6	0	0	0.9
■ **MOE BURTSCHY** Burtschy, Edward Frank b: 4/18/22, Cincinnati, Ohio BR/TR, 6'3", 208 lbs. Deb: 6/17/50																													
1950	Phi-A	0	1	.000	9	1	0	0	0	19	22	10.4	2	21	9.9	12	5.7	7.11	60	.289	.440	-5	-6	93	98	-0.4	-0	0	-0.5
1951	Phi-A	0	0	—	7	0	0	0	0	17	18	9.5	0	12	6.4	4	2.1	5.29	83	.277	.392	-2	-2	106	91	0.0	0	0	-0.1
1954	Phi-A	5	4	.556	46	0	0	0	4	95	80	7.6	7	53	5.0	54	5.1	3.79	103	.234	.341	-1	1	105	100	1.6	-1	0	0.0
1955	KC-A	2	0	1.000	7	0	0	0	0	11	17	13.9	0	10	8.2	9	7.4	10.64	40	.354	.467	-8	-8	106	71	1.0	0	-0	-0.7
1956	KC-A	3	1	.750	21	0	0	0	0	43	41	8.6	6	30	6.3	18	3.8	3.98	109	.263	.379	1	2	105	137	1.3	-1	2	0.3
Total	5	10	6	.625	90	1	0	0	4	185	178	8.7	15	126	6.1	97	4.7	4.72	87	.259	.375	-16	-13	104	106	3.5	-1	1	-1.0
■ **DENNIS BURTT** Burtt, Dennis Allen b: 11/29/57, San Diego, Cal. BB/TR, 6', 180 lbs. Deb: 9/04/85																													
1985	Min-A	2	2	.500	5	2	0	0	0	28	20	6.4	2	7	2.3	9	2.9	3.86	112	.200	.248	1	1	104	52	0.1	0	0	0.2
1986	Min-A	0	0	—	3	0	0	0	0	2	7	31.5	1	3	13.5	1	4.5	31.50	15	.538	.625	-6	-6	109	70	0.0	0	0	-0.4
Total	2	2	2	.500	8	2	0	0	0	30	27	8.1	3	10	3.0	10	3.0	5.70	76	.239	.296	-5	-5	104	53	0.1	0	0	-0.2
■ **DICK BURWELL** Burwell, Richard Matthew b: 1/23/40, Alton, Ill. BR/TR, 6'1", 190 lbs. Deb: 9/13/60																													
1960	Chi-N	0	0	—	3	1	0	0	0	10	11	9.9	2	7	6.3	1	0.9	5.40	70	.306	.432	-2	-2	101	133	0.0	0	0	-0.1
1961	Chi-N	0	0	—	2	0	0	0	0	4	6	13.5	0	4	9.0	0	0.0	9.00	46	.375	.476	-2	-2	102	91	0.0	-0	0	-0.1
Total	2	0	0	—	5	1	0	0	0	14	17	10.9	2	11	7.1	1	0.6	6.43	60	.327	.446	-4	-4	101	121	0.0	0	0	-0.2
■ **BILL BURWELL** Burwell, William Edwin b: 3/27/1895, Jarbalo, Kan. d: 6/11/73, Ormond Beach, Fla BL/TR, 5'11", 175 lbs. Deb: 5/01/20 MC																													
1920	StL-A	6	4	.600	33	2	0	0	4	113	133	10.6	5	42	3.3	30	2.4	3.66	115	.303	.369	2	7	111	123	1.1	-2	-0	0.5
1921	StL-A	2	4	.333	33	3	1	0	2	84	102	10.9	2	29	3.1	17	1.8	5.14	84	.309	.352	-8	-8	101	89	-1.0	-0	-1	-0.7

YEAR	TM/L	W	L	PCT	G	GS	CG	SHO	SV	IP	H	H/G	HR	BB	BB/G	SO	SO/G	ERA	/A	OAVG	OOBP	PR	/A	PF	CPI	WAT	PB	PD	TPI
1928	Pit-N	1	0	1.000	4	1	0	0	0	21	18	7.7	2	8	3.4	2	0.9	5.14	81	.234	.299	-3	-2	105	60	0.5	-0	1	-0.1
Total	3	9	8	.529	70	6	1	0	6	218	253	10.4	9	79	3.3	49	2.0	4.38	97	.299	.356	-9	-3	106	104	0.6	-3	-1	-0.3
■ **STEVE BUSBY**	Busby, Steven Lee b: 9/29/49, Burbank, Cal. BR/TR, 6'2", 205 lbs. Deb: 9/08/72																												
1972	KC-A	3	1	.750	5	5	3	0	0	40	28	6.3	1	8	1.8	31	7.0	1.57	194	.200	.235	7	7	100	88	1.0	0	-0	0.8
1973	KC-A	16	15	.516	37	37	7	1	0	238	246	9.3	18	105	4.0	174	6.6	4.24	98	.271	.344	-11	-2	109	99	-0.8	0	2	0.0
1974	KC-A	22	14	.611	38	38	20	3	0	292	284	8.8	14	92	2.8	198	6.1	3.39	114	.258	.316	8	15	106	97	5.6	0	3	1.9
1975	KC-A	18	12	.600	34	34	18	3	0	260	233	8.1	18	81	2.8	160	5.5	3.08	124	.242	.298	20	22	101	98	1.6	0	4	2.7
1976	KC-A	3	3	.500	13	13	1	0	0	72	58	7.3	7	49	6.1	29	3.6	4.38	79	.218	.341	-7	-7	99	86	-0.2	0	-0	-0.7
1978	KC-A	1	0	1.000	7	5	0	0	0	21	24	10.3	2	15	6.4	10	4.3	7.71	49	.282	.394	-9	-9	101	72	0.5	0	0	-0.8
1979	KC-A	6	6	.500	22	12	4	0	0	94	71	6.8	10	64	6.1	45	4.3	3.64	122	.220	.333	6	8	105	110	-0.2	0	2	1.0
1980	KC-A	1	3	.250	11	6	0	0	0	42	59	12.6	3	19	4.1	12	2.6	6.21	63	.335	.402	-10	-11	97	98	-1.1	0	-0	-1.0
Total	8	70	54	.565	167	150	53	7	0	1059	1003	8.5	73	433	3.7	659	5.6	3.72	105	.253	.324	4	23	104	97	6.4	0	10	3.9
■ **DON BUSCHHORN**	Buschhorn, Donald Lee b: 4/29/46, Independence, Mo. BR/TR, 6', 170 lbs. Deb: 5/15/65																												
1965	KC-A	0	1	.000	12	3	0	0	0	31	36	10.5	7	8	2.3	9	2.6	4.35	79	.295	.338	-3	-3	100	128	-0.4	1	-0	-0.2
■ **GUY BUSH**	Bush, Guy Terrell "The Mississippi Mudcat" b: 8/23/01, Aberdeen, Miss. d: 7/2/85, Shannon, Miss. BR/TR, 6', 175 lbs. Deb: 9/17/23																												
1923	Chi-N	0	0	—	1	0	0	0	0	1	1	9.0	0	0	0.0	2	18.0	0.00	—	.250	.250	0	0	103	0	0.0	0	0	0.0
1924	Chi-N	2	5	.286	16	8	4	0	0	81	91	10.1	7	24	2.7	36	4.0	4.00	98	.285	.335	-1	-1	101	106	-1.6	-1	-2	-0.3
1925	Chi-N	6	13	.316	42	15	5	0	**4**	182	213	10.5	15	52	2.6	76	3.8	4.30	97	.300	.339	-1	-2	98	107	-2.9	-2	3	0.0
1926	Chi-N	13	9	.591	35	16	7	2	2	157	149	8.5	3	42	2.4	32	1.8	2.87	140	.258	.303	17	20	105	104	1.6	-3	-1	1.7
1927	Chi-N	10	10	.500	36	22	9	1	2	193	177	8.3	3	79	3.7	62	2.9	3.03	127	.250	.322	19	18	99	106	-1.0	-4	0	1.4
1928	Chi-N	15	6	.714	42	24	9	2	2	204	229	10.1	10	86	3.8	61	2.7	3.84	96	.293	.357	3	-3	93	117	3.5	-6	-1	-0.9
1929	Chi-N	18	7	.720	**50**	29	18	2	**8**	271	277	9.2	16	107	3.6	82	2.7	3.65	126	.265	.330	32	29	98	106	3.0	-4	0	2.3
1930	Chi-N	15	10	.600	46	25	11	0	3	225	291	11.6	22	86	3.4	75	3.0	6.20	83	.316	.368	-31	-27	103	90	0.6	3	1	-1.8
1931	Chi-N	16	8	.667	39	24	14	1	2	180	190	9.5	9	66	3.3	54	2.7	4.50	80	.268	.327	-13	-18	94	83	3.6	-1	4	-1.4
1932	Chi-N	19	11	.633	40	30	15	1	0	239	262	9.9	13	70	2.6	73	2.7	3.20	124	.278	.328	18	21	103	**123**	2.1	-1	1	2.2
1933	Chi-N	20	12	.625	41	32	20	4	2	264	261	8.9	9	68	2.3	84	2.9	2.69	118	.257	.300	19	14	95	109	2.9	-1	4	1.7
1934	Chi-N	18	10	.643	40	27	15	1	2	209	213	9.2	15	54	2.3	75	3.2	3.83	102	.262	.304	5	2	97	92	2.8	1	1	0.3
1935	Pit-N	11	11	.500	41	25	8	1	2	204	237	10.5	16	40	1.8	42	1.9	4.32	98	.285	.317	-7	-2	105	94	-1.3	-1	-1	-0.3
1936	Pit-N	1	3	.250	16	0	0	0	2	35	49	12.6	3	11	2.8	10	2.6	5.91	65	.336	.373	-7	-8	96	99	-1.0	1	1	-0.5
	Bos-N	4	5	.444	15	11	5	0	0	90	98	9.8	2	20	2.0	28	2.8	3.40	114	.281	.315	6	5	96	104	-0.1	-1	1	0.4
	Yr	5	8	.385	31	11	5	0	2	125	147	10.6	5	31	2.2	38	2.7	4.10	94	.297	.332	-1	-3	96	104	-1.1	1	1	-0.1
1937	Bos-N	8	15	.348	32	20	11	1	1	181	201	10.0	8	48	2.4	56	2.8	3.53	100	.282	.322	8	-0	90	110	-4.1	-2	1	-0.1
1938	StL-N	0	1	.000	6	0	0	0	1	6	6	9.0	1	3	4.5	1	1.5	4.50	94	.286	.375	-0	-0	111	125	-0.4	0	-0	0.0
1945	Cin-N	0	0	—	4	0	0	0	1	4	5	11.3	0	3	6.8	1	2.3	9.00	41	.278	.381	-2	-2	97	51	0.0	0	-0	-0.1
Total	17	176	136	.564	542	308	151	16	34	2726	2950	9.7	152	859	2.8	850	2.8	3.85	104	.277	.328	65	43	98	104	7.7	-21	12	4.6
■ **JOE BUSH**	Bush, Leslie Ambrose "Bullet Joe" b: 11/27/1892, Brainerd, Minn. d: 11/1/74, Ft.Lauderdale, Fla. BR/TR, 5'9", 173 lbs. Deb: 9/30/12																												
1912	Phi-A	0	0	—	1	1	0	0	0	8	14	15.8	0	4	4.5	3	3.4	7.88	41	.368	.429	-4	-4	97	86	0.0	1	-0	-0.3
1913	Phi-A	15	6	.714	39	16	6	1	3	200	199	9.0	3	66	3.0	81	3.6	3.83	71	.248	.310	-20	-25	93	67	2.7	-0	4	-2.0
1914	Phi-A	16	12	.571	38	22	14	2	3	206	184	8.0	2	81	3.5	109	4.8	3.06	83	.242	.322	-7	-12	93	88	-1.9	2	-0	-1.3
1915	Phi-A	5	15	.250	25	18	8	0	0	146	137	8.4	3	89	5.5	89	5.5	4.13	73	.263	.375	-19	-18	103	97	-1.2	-3	0	-2.0
1916	Phi-A	15	24	.385	40	33	25	8	0	287	222	7.0	3	130	4.1	157	4.9	2.57	116	.219	.310	8	13	105	91	4.8	-5	4	1.5
1917	Phi-A	11	17	.393	37	31	17	4	2	233	207	8.0	3	111	4.3	121	4.7	2.47	104	.241	.328	5	3	97	112	0.9	1	0	0.4
1918	Bos-A	15	15	.500	36	31	26	7	2	273	241	7.9	3	91	3.0	125	4.1	2.11	122	.242	.299	20	14	93	113	-2.9	7	3	2.7
1919	Bos-A	0	0	—	3	2	0	0	0	9	11	11.0	0	4	4.0	3	3.0	5.00	59	.324	.395	-2	-2	91	95	0.0	1	0	-0.1
1920	Bos-A	15	15	.500	35	32	18	0	1	244	287	10.6	3	94	3.5	88	3.2	4.24	87	.300	.369	-12	-15	97	99	1.0	2	3	-1.1
1921	Bos-A	16	9	.640	37	32	21	3	1	254	244	8.6	10	93	3.3	96	3.4	3.51	122	.260	.322	22	22	100	97	4.2	6	0	3.0
1922	NY-A	26	7	**.788**	39	30	20	0	3	255	240	8.5	16	85	3.0	92	3.2	3.32	121	.252	.307	21	19	99	96	8.5	8	1	2.8
1923	NY-A	19	15	.559	37	30	22	3	0	276	263	8.6	7	117	3.8	125	4.1	3.42	117	.260	.328	17	18	101	100	-2.7	7	2	2.7
1924	NY-A	17	16	.515	39	31	19	3	1	252	262	9.4	9	109	3.9	80	2.9	3.57	115	.273	.342	19	15	97	110	-2.4	14	2	2.9
1925	StL-A	14	14	.500	33	28	15	2	0	209	230	9.9	18	91	3.9	63	2.7	5.08	93	.284	.345	-16	-8	108	89	-1.0	3	2	0.0
1926	Was-A	1	8	.111	12	11	3	0	0	71	83	10.5	6	35	4.4	27	3.4	6.72	58	.292	.372	-21	-22	97	75	-3.5	1	0	-1.8
	Pit-N	6	6	.500	19	11	9	2	3	111	97	7.9	7	35	2.8	38	3.1	3.00	141	.236	.292	10	15	111	94	-0.5	2	-1	1.8
1927	Pit-N	1	2	.333	5	3	0	0	0	7	14	18.0	1	5	6.4	1	1.3	12.86	30	.412	.452	-7	-7	99	78	-0.6	1	0	-0.4
	NY-N	1	1	.500	3	2	1	0	0	12	18	13.5	1	5	3.8	6	4.5	7.50	51	.340	.397	-5	-5	98	82	-0.1	1	0	-0.3
	Yr	2	3	.400	8	5	1	0	0	19	32	15.2	2	10	4.7	7	3.3	9.47	41	.368	.420	-12	-12	98	82	-0.7	1	0	-0.7
1928	Phi-A	2	1	.667	11	2	1	0	1	35	39	10.0	1	18	4.6	15	3.9	5.14	78	.300	.369	-4	-4	99	97	0.1	-1	1	-0.4
Total	17	195	183	.516	489	366	225	35	20	3088	2992	8.7	96	1263	3.7	1319	3.8	3.51	99	.259	.330	4	-7	99	97	5.4	48	20	8.1
■ **JACK BUSHELMAN**	Bushelman, John Francis b: 8/29/1885, Cincinnati, Ohio d: 10/26/55, Roanoke, Va. BR/TR, 6'2", 175 lbs. Deb: 09																												
1909	Cin-N	0	1	.000	1	1	1	0	0	7	7	9.0	1	4	5.1	3	3.9	2.57	95	.241	.333	0	-0	94	155	-0.4	-0	-0	0.0
1911	Bos-A	0	1	.000	3	1	1	0	0	12	8	6.0	0	10	7.5	5	3.8	3.00	110	.186	.352	0	0	99	84	-0.4	-0	-0	0.0
1912	Bos-A	1	0	1.000	3	0	0	0	0	8	9	10.1	0	5	5.6	5	5.6	4.50	76	.310	.412	-1	-1	102	114	0.5	-0	0	0.0
Total	3	1	2	.333	7	2	2	0	0	27	24	8.0	1	19	6.3	13	4.3	3.33	93	.238	.364	-1	-1	98	111	-0.3	-1	-0	0.0
■ **FRANK BUSHEY**	Bushey, Francis Clyde b: 8/1/06, Wheaton, Kan. d: 3/18/72, Topeka, Kan. BR/TR, 6', 180 lbs. Deb: 9/17/27																												
1927	Bos-A	0	0	—	1	0	0	0	0	1	2	18.0	0	2	18.0	0	0.0	9.00	45	.500	.667	-1	-1	99	164	0.0	0	0	0.0
1930	Bos-A	0	1	.000	11	0	0	0	0	30	34	10.2	1	15	4.5	4	1.2	6.30	71	.306	.375	-5	-6	96	88	-0.4	-1	0	-0.5
Total	2	0	1	.000	12	0	0	0	0	31	36	10.5	1	17	4.9	4	1.2	6.39	70	.313	.387	-6	-7	96	91	-0.4	-1	0	-0.5
■ **TOM BUSKEY**	Buskey, Thomas William b: 2/20/47, Harrisburg, Pa. BR/TR, 6'3", 200 lbs. Deb: 8/05/73																												
1973	NY-A	0	1	.000	8	0	0	0	1	17	18	9.5	2	4	2.1	8	4.2	5.29	72	.286	.319	-3	-3	100	85	-0.4	0	0	-0.2
1974	NY-A	0	1	.000	4	0	0	0	1	6	10	15.0	1	3	4.5	3	4.5	6.00	58	.400	.467	-2	-2	95	152	-0.4	0	-0	-0.1
	Cle-A	2	6	.250	51	0	0	0	17	93	93	9.0	10	33	3.2	40	3.9	3.19	115	.263	.318	4	5	101	123	-1.8	0	1	0.6
	Yr	2	7	.222	55	0	0	0	18	99	103	9.4	11	36	3.3	43	3.9	3.36	109	.271	.326	3	3	101	123	-2.2	0	1	0.5
1975	Cle-A	5	3	.625	50	0	0	0	7	77	69	8.1	7	29	3.4	29	3.4	2.57	147	.252	.313	10	10	100	145	1.1	0	2	1.3
1976	Cle-A	5	4	.556	39	0	0	0	1	94	88	8.4	9	34	3.3	32	3.1	3.64	96	.256	.320	-1	-1	100	106	0.4	0	1	0.0
1977	Cle-A	0	0	—	21	0	0	0	0	34	45	11.9	6	8	2.1	15	4.0	5.29	76	.313	.344	-5	-5	98	105	0.0	0	-0	-0.4
1978	Tor-A	0	1	.000	8	0	0	0	0	13	14	9.7	1	5	3.5	7	4.8	3.46	111	.275	.322	0	1	102	117	-0.4	0	1	0.1
1979	Tor-A	6	10	.375	44	0	0	0	7	79	74	8.4	10	25	2.8	44	5.0	3.42	131	.249	.304	7	9	106	109	0.6	0	2	1.0
1980	Tor-A	3	1	.750	33	0	0	0	0	67	68	9.1	11	26	3.5	34	4.6	4.43	92	.278	.337	-3	-3	101	111	1.2	0	0	-0.1
Total	8	21	27	.438	258	0	0	0	34	480	479	9.0	57	167	3.1	212	4.0	3.66	106	.267	.322	9	12	101	117	0.3	0	5	2.2
■ **MAX BUTCHER**	Butcher, Albert Maxwell b: 9/21/10, Holden, W.Va. d: 9/15/57, Man, W.Va. BR/TR, 6'2", 220 lbs. Deb: 4/20/36																												
1936	Bro-N	6	6	.500	38	15	5	0	2	148	154	9.4	11	59	3.6	55	3.3	3.95	108	.268	.333	1	5	107	103	0.7	-3	-2	0.1
1937	Bro-N	11	15	.423	39	24	8	1	0	192	203	9.5	12	75	3.5	57	2.7	4.27	98	.280	.346	-8	-2	107	105	0.5	-2	3	0.0
1938	Bro-N	5	4	.556	24	8	3	1	2	73	104	12.8	9	39	4.8	21	2.6	6.53	56	.334	.406	-22	-24	96	104	0.8	0	1	-2.0
	Phi-N	4	8	.333	12	12	11	0	0	98	94	8.6	6	31	2.8	29	2.7	2.94	136	.253	.307	9	12	106	117	0.3	1	0	1.3
	Yr	9	12	.429	36	20	14	1	2	171	198	10.4	15	70	3.7	50	2.6	4.47	86	.290	.351	-13	-12	101	117	1.1	0	1	-0.7
1939	Phi-N	2	13	.133	19	16	3	0	0	104	131	11.3	10	51	4.4	27	2.3	5.63	69	.308	.373	-20	-20	99	98	-4.2	-1	-2	-2.1
	Pit-N	4	4	.500	14	12	5	2	0	87	104	10.8	2	23	2.4	21	2.2	3.41	116	.297	.332	5	5	101	118	0.4	-2	2	0.5
	Yr	6	17	.261	33	28	8	2	0	191	235	11.1	12	74	3.5	48	2.3	4.62	85	.302	.354	-15	-15	100	118	-3.8	-1	-0	-1.6
1940	Pit-N	8	9	.471	35	24	6	2	2	136	161	10.7	13	46	3.0	40	2.6	6.02	61	.290	.342	-33	-36	95	79	-0.6	4	1	-2.9
1941	Pit-N	17	12	.586	33	32	19	0	0	236	249	9.5	11	66	2.5	61	2.3	3.05	121	.265	.311	15	17	102	112	2.2	-1	0	1.7
1942	Pit-N	5	8	.385	24	18	9	0	1	151	144	8.6	7	44	2.6	49	2.9	2.92	116	.247	.296	7	8	102	103	-0.9	-2	0	0.6

YEAR	TM/L	W	L	PCT	G	GS	CG	SHO	SV	IP	H	H/G	HR	BB	BB/G	SO	SO/G	ERA	/A	OAVG	OOBP	PR	/A	PF	CPI	WAT	PB	PD	TPI
1943	Pit-N	10	8	.556	33	21	10	2	1	194	191	8.9	4	57	2.6	45	2.1	2.60	134	.262	.311	17	19	103	122	0.8	-1	0	2.0
1944	Pit-N	13	11	.542	35	27	13	5	1	199	216	9.8	8	46	2.1	43	1.9	3.12	120	.273	.308	11	14	104	111	-1.0	-0	3	1.7
1945	Pit-N	10	8	.556	28	20	12	2	0	169	184	9.8	7	46	2.4	37	2.0	3.04	128	.277	.321	14	16	102	124	0.5	0	1	1.8
Total	10	95	106	.473	334	229	104	15	9	1787	1935	9.7	100	583	2.9	485	2.4	3.73	102	.276	.327	-3	14	102	109	-0.5	-7	7	2.7
■ **JOHN BUTCHER**	Butcher, John Daniel b: 3/8/57, Glendale, Cal. BB/TR, 6'4", 185 lbs. Deb: 9/08/80																												
1980	Tex-A	3	3	.500	6	6	1	0	0	35	34	8.7	2	13	3.3	27	6.9	4.11	99	.248	.309	-0	-0	100	76	0.2	0	0	0.0
1981	Tex-A	1	2	.333	5	3	1	1	0	28	18	5.8	0	8	2.6	19	6.1	1.61	205	.186	.245	6	5	90	74	-0.5	0	0	0.6
1982	Tex-A	1	5	.167	18	13	2	0	1	94	102	9.8	10	34	3.3	39	3.7	4.88	79	.280	.340	-8	-11	94	93	-1.7	0	1	-0.8
1983	Tex-A	6	6	.500	38	6	1	1	5	123	128	9.4	8	41	3.0	58	4.2	3.51	117	.270	.326	8	8	101	110	0.3	0	0	0.8
1984	Min-A	13	11	.542	34	34	8	1	0	225	242	9.7	18	53	2.1	83	3.3	3.44	123	.276	.317	14	20	106	112	1.2	0	-1	1.9
1985	Min-A	11	14	.440	34	33	8	2	0	208	239	10.3	24	43	1.9	92	4.0	4.98	87	.289	.323	-19	-15	104	90	-1.0	0	0	-1.4
1986	Min-A	0	3	.000	16	10	1	0	0	70	82	10.5	11	24	3.1	29	3.7	6.30	73	.294	.347	-16	-13	109	83	-1.4	0	0	-1.2
	Cle-A	1	5	.167	13	8	1	1	0	51	86	15.2	6	13	2.3	16	2.8	6.88	59	.381	.415	-15	-16	98	109	-2.0	0	-1	-1.4
	Yr	1	8	.111	29	18	2	1	0	121	168	12.5	17	37	2.8	45	3.3	6.55	67	.330	.375	-32	-29	104	109	-3.4	0	-1	-2.6
Total	7	36	49	.424	164	113	23	6	6	834	931	10.0	79	229	2.5	363	3.9	4.41	94	.284	.329	-31	-23	102	99	-4.9	0	1	-1.5
■ **SAL BUTERA**	Butera, Salvatore Philip b: 9/25/52, Richmond Hill, N.Y BR/TR, 6', 190 lbs. Deb: 4/10/80																												
1985	Mon-N	0	0	—	1	0	0	0	0	1	0	0.0	0	0	0.0	0	0.0	0.00	—	.000	.000	0	0	94	0	0.0	0	0	0.0
1986	Cin-N	0	0	—	1	0	0	0	0	1	0	0.0	0	1	9.0	1	9.0	0.00	—	.000	.250	0	0	104	0	0.0	0	0	0.0
Total	2	0	0	—	2	0	0	0	0	2	0	0.0	0	1	4.5	1	4.5	0.00	—	.000	.143	1	1	99	0	0.0	0	0	0.0
■ **BILL BUTLAND**	Butland, Wilburn Rue b: 3/22/18, Terre Haute, Ind. BR/TL, 6'5", 185 lbs. Deb: 5/29/40																												
1940	Bos-A	1	2	.333	3	3	1	0	0	21	27	11.6	0	10	4.3	5	2.1	5.57	79	.307	.374	-3	-3	100	88	-0.5	-1	1	-0.2
1942	Bos-A	7	1	.875	23	10	6	2	1	111	85	6.9	8	33	2.7	46	3.7	2.51	146	.206	.267	14	14	100	91	2.8	-1	0	1.5
1946	Bos-A	1	0	1.000	5	2	0	0	0	16	23	12.9	3	13	7.3	10	5.6	11.25	34	.343	.444	-14	-13	111	72	0.5	0	0	-1.1
1947	Bos-A	0	0	—	1	0	0	0	0	2	3	13.5	0	0	0.0	1	4.5	4.50	88	.333	.333	-0	-0	107	94	0.0	0	0	0.0
Total	4	9	3	.750	32	15	7	2	1	150	138	8.3	11	56	3.4	62	3.7	3.90	97	.240	.307	-3	-2	102	89	2.8	-2	1	0.2
■ **CECIL BUTLER**	Butler, Cecil Dean "Slewfoot" b: 10/23/37, Dallas, Ga. BR/TR, 6'4", 195 lbs. Deb: 4/23/62																												
1962	Mil-N	2	0	1.000	9	2	1	0	0	31	26	7.5	4	9	2.6	22	6.4	2.61	148	.217	.269	5	4	98	101	1.0	-1	0	0.4
1964	Mil-N	0	0	—	2	0	0	0	0	4	7	15.8	2	0	0.0	2	4.5	9.00	38	.368	.368	-2	-2	96	104	0.0	0	0	-0.1
Total	2	2	0	1.000	11	2	1	0	0	35	33	8.5	6	9	2.3	24	6.2	3.34	114	.237	.282	2	2	98	101	1.0	-1	0	0.3
■ **CHARLIE BUTLER**	Butler, Charles Thomas b: 5/12/06, Green Cove Springs, Fla. d: 5/10/64, Brunswick, Ga. BR/TL, 6'1.5", 210 lbs. Deb: 5/01/33																												
1933	Phi-N	0	0	—	1	0	0	0	0	1	1	9.0	0	2	18.0	0	0.0	9.00	45	.250	.500	-1	-1	121	81	0.0	0	0	0.0
■ **IKE BUTLER**	Butler, Isaac Burr b: 8/22/1873, Langston, Mich. d: 3/17/48, Oakland, Cal. TR , 6', 175 lbs. Deb: 8/05/02																												
1902	Bal-A	1	10	.091	16	14	12	0	0	116	168	13.0	1	45	3.5	13	1.0	5.35	70	.365	.422	-23	-21	104	104	-4.1	-3	-1	-1.9
■ **BILL BUTLER**	Butler, William Franklin b: 3/12/47, Hyattsville, Md. BL/TL, 6'2", 210 lbs. Deb: 4/09/69																												
1969	KC-A	9	10	.474	34	29	5	4	0	194	174	8.1	15	91	4.2	156	7.2	3.90	97	.240	.321	-6	-3	104	90	0.9	-4	-3	-0.8
1970	KC-A	4	12	.250	25	25	2	1	0	141	117	7.5	17	87	5.6	75	4.8	3.77	98	.229	.336	-1	-1	100	106	-3.1	-3	-2	-0.5
1971	KC-A	1	2	.333	14	6	0	0	0	44	45	9.2	6	18	3.7	32	6.5	3.48	98	.268	.332	-0	-0	98	127	-0.5	-1	-0	-0.1
1972	Cle-A	0	0	—	6	2	0	0	0	12	9	6.8	1	10	7.5	6	4.5	1.50	221	.220	.365	2	2	108	275	0.0	-0	-0	0.2
1974	Min-A	4	6	.400	26	12	2	0	1	99	91	8.3	9	56	5.1	79	7.2	4.09	89	.251	.347	-5	-5	101	101	-1.0	0	-2	-0.6
1975	Min-A	5	4	.556	23	8	1	0	0	82	100	11.0	12	35	3.8	55	6.0	5.93	69	.301	.358	-19	-17	107	92	0.7	0	-0	-1.6
1977	Min-A	0	1	.000	6	4	0	0	0	21	19	8.1	5	15	6.4	5	2.1	6.86	61	.244	.372	-6	-6	102	82	-0.4	0	-1	-0.6
Total	7	23	35	.397	134	86	10	5	1	593	555	8.4	65	312	4.7	408	6.2	4.20	89	.250	.338	-36	-30	102	102	-3.4	-7	-8	-4.0
■ **TOM BUTTERS**	Butters, Thomas Arden b: 4/8/38, Delaware, O. BR/TR, 6'2", 195 lbs. Deb: 9/08/62																												
1962	Pit-N	0	0	—	4	0	0	0	0	6	5	7.5	0	6	9.0	10	15.0	1.50	266	.238	.414	2	2	101	328	0.0	0	0	0.2
1963	Pit-N	0	0	—	6	1	0	0	0	16	15	8.4	1	8	4.5	11	6.2	4.50	72	.259	.347	-2	-2	99	96	0.0	0	-0	-0.1
1964	Pit-N	2	2	.500	28	4	0	0	0	64	52	7.3	3	37	5.2	58	8.2	2.39	149	.221	.320	8	8	101	132	0.0	0	-1	0.8
1965	Pit-N	0	1	.000	5	0	0	0	0	9	9	9.0	2	5	5.0	6	6.0	7.00	50	.250	.341	-3	-4	98	72	-0.4	-0	0	-0.3
Total	4	2	3	.400	43	5	0	0	0	95	81	7.7	6	56	5.3	85	8.1	3.13	113	.231	.333	4	4	100	133	-0.4	0	-0	0.6
■ **FRANK BUTTERY**	Buttery, Frank b: 5/13/1851, Silver Mine, Conn. d: 12/16/02, Silver Mine, Conn. Deb: 4/26/1872																												
1872	Man-n	3	2	.600	6																								
■ **RALPH BUXTON**	Buxton, Ralph Stanley "Buck" b: 6/7/11, Weyburn, Sask., Can BR/TR, 5'11.5", 163 lbs. Deb: 9/11/38																												
1938	Phi-A	0	1	.000	5	0	0	0	0	9	12	12.0	1	5	5.0	9	9.0	5.00	100	.324	.395	-0	0	105	131	-0.4	-0	0	0.0
1949	NY-A	0	1	.000	14	0	0	0	2	27	22	7.3	3	16	5.3	14	4.7	4.00	102	.229	.336	1	0	97	98	-0.4	-0	-0	0.0
Total	2	0	2	.000	19	0	0	0	2	36	34	8.5	4	21	5.3	23	5.8	4.25	101	.256	.353	0	0	99	106	-0.8	-1	-0	0.0
■ **JOHN BUZHARDT**	Buzhardt, John William b: 8/17/36, Prosperity, S.C. BR/TR, 6'2.5", 195 lbs. Deb: 9/10/58																												
1958	Chi-N	3	0	1.000	6	2	1	0	0	24	16	6.0	2	7	2.6	9	3.4	1.88	212	.184	.242	6	6	101	81	1.5	-0	1	0.6
1959	Chi-N	4	5	.444	31	10	1	1	0	101	107	9.5	12	29	2.6	33	2.9	4.99	78	.271	.312	-12	-12	99	82	-0.3	-1	-1	-1.2
1960	Phi-N	5	16	.238	30	29	5	0	0	200	198	8.9	14	68	3.1	73	3.3	3.87	107	.259	.316	-2	6	110	94	-4.2	-1	-1	0.5
1961	Phi-N	6	18	.250	41	27	6	1	0	202	200	8.9	28	65	2.9	92	4.1	4.50	87	.263	.320	-11	-13	98	94	-2.4	-2	0	-1.3
1962	Chi-A	8	12	.400	28	25	8	2	0	152	156	9.2	16	59	3.5	64	3.8	4.20	89	.264	.330	-4	-8	94	100	-2.5	-1	2	-0.7
1963	Chi-A	9	4	.692	19	18	6	3	0	126	100	7.1	8	31	2.2	59	4.2	2.43	153	.216	.270	17	18	102	96	1.8	-3	1	1.8
1964	Chi-A	10	8	.556	31	25	8	3	0	160	150	8.4	13	35	2.0	97	5.5	2.98	113	.250	.290	11	7	93	105	-0.7	2	1	1.0
1965	Chi-A	13	8	.619	32	30	4	1	1	189	167	8.0	12	56	2.7	108	5.1	3.00	104	.242	.302	10	3	91	103	0.9	0	-1	0.2
1966	Chi-A	6	11	.353	33	22	5	4	1	150	144	8.6	13	30	1.8	66	4.0	3.84	83	.248	.284	-7	-11	93	82	-2.8	-1	3	-0.9
1967	Chi-A	3	9	.250	28	7	0	0	0	89	100	10.1	11	37	3.7	33	3.3	3.94	76	.294	.366	-7	-9	93	136	-3.3	0	0	-0.9
	Bal-A	0	1	.000	7	1	0	0	0	12	14	10.5	1	5	3.8	7	5.3	4.50	67	.298	.358	-2	-2	94	111	-0.4	-0	0	-0.1
	Yr	3	10	.231	35	8	0	0	0	101	114	10.2	12	42	3.7	40	3.6	4.01	75	.288	.351	-9	-11	93	111	-3.7	0	1	-1.0
	Hou-N	0	0	—	1	0	0	0	0	1	0	0.0	0	0	0.0	0	0.0	0.00	—	.000	.000	0	0	95	0	0.0	0	0	0.1
1968	Hou-N	4	4	.500	39	4	0	0	5	84	73	7.8	0	35	3.8	37	4.0	3.11	96	.239	.315	-1	-1	100	92	0.4	1	1	0.1
Total	11	71	96	.425	326	200	44	15	7	1490	1425	8.6	130	457	2.8	678	4.1	3.67	97	.253	.309	-1	-16	98	97	-12.0	-7	7	-0.8
■ **BUD BYERLY**	Byerly, Eldred William b: 10/26/20, Webster Groves, Mo BR/TR, 6'2.5", 185 lbs. Deb: 9/26/43																												
1943	StL-N	1	0	1.000	2	2	0	0	0	13	14	9.7	0	5	3.5	6	4.2	3.46	98	.280	.339	-0	-0	100	107	0.5	-0	-0	0.0
1944	StL-N	2	2	.500	9	4	2	0	0	42	37	7.9	2	20	4.3	13	2.8	3.43	100	.228	.310	1	0	95	87	-0.4	-0	1	0.0
1945	StL-N	4	5	.444	33	8	2	0	0	95	111	10.5	3	41	3.9	39	3.7	4.74	78	.288	.355	-10	-11	97	93	-1.2	1	2	-0.7
1950	Cin-N	0	1	.000	4	1	0	0	0	15	12	7.2	1	4	2.4	5	3.0	2.40	183	.218	.271	3	3	106	98	-0.4	-0	-0	0.3
1951	Cin-N	2	1	.667	40	0	0	0	0	66	69	9.4	6	25	3.4	28	3.8	3.27	124	.267	.332	5	6	103	126	0.6	-0	1	0.6
1952	Cin-N	0	1	.000	12	2	0	0	1	25	29	10.4	0	7	2.5	14	5.0	5.04	74	.309	.350	-4	-4	100	85	-0.4	0	0	-0.3
1956	Was-A	2	4	.333	25	0	0	0	4	52	45	7.8	6	14	2.4	19	3.3	2.94	151	.243	.295	7	9	107	119	-0.3	-1	0	0.8
1957	Was-A	6	6	.500	47	0	0	0	6	95	94	8.9	6	22	2.1	39	3.7	3.13	123	.264	.294	7	8	102	107	1.4	-1	1	0.8
1958	Was-A	2	0	1.000	17	0	0	0	1	24	34	12.8	4	11	4.1	13	4.9	6.75	56	.347	.404	-8	-8	100	107	1.0	-0	0	-0.7
	Bos-A	1	2	.333	18	0	0	0	0	30	31	9.3	1	7	2.1	16	4.8	1.80	219	.272	.305	7	7	105	190	-0.4	-1	0	0.7
	Yr	3	2	.600	35	0	0	0	1	54	65	10.8	5	18	3.0	29	4.8	4.00	97	.302	.347	-1	-1	103	190	0.6	-0	0	0.0
1959	SF-N	1	0	1.000	11	0	0	0	0	13	11	7.6	2	5	3.5	4	2.8	1.38	267	.234	.308	4	3	94	271	0.5	0	1	0.4
1960	SF-N	1	0	1.000	19	0	0	0	2	22	32	13.1	3	6	2.5	13	5.3	5.32	63	.340	.368	-4	-5	89	120	0.5	-0	-0	-0.4
Total	11	22	22	.500	237	17	4	0	14	492	519	9.5	34	167	3.1	209	3.8	3.70	104	.273	.327	8	8	100	115	1.4	-4	4	1.5
■ **HARRY BYRD**	Byrd, Harry Gladwin b: 2/3/25, Darlington, S.C. d: 5/14/85, Darlington, S.C. BR/TR, 6'1", 188 lbs. Deb: 4/21/50																												
1950	Phi-A	0	0	—	6	0	0	0	0	11	25	20.5	3	9	7.4	2	1.6	16.36	26	.481	.554	-14	-15	93	88	0.0	-0	0	-1.2
1952	Phi-A	15	15	.500	37	28	15	3	2	228	244	9.6	12	98	3.9	116	4.6	3.32	124	.274	.346	9	20	112	126	-0.4	-3	0	1.9

YEAR	TM/L	W	L	PCT	G	GS	CG	SHO	SV	IP	H	H/G	HR	BB	BB/G	SO	SO/G	ERA	/A	OAVG	OOBP	PR	/A	PF	CPI	WAT	PB	PD	TPI
1953	Phi-A	11	20	.355	40	37	11	2	0	237	279	10.6	23	115	4.4	122	4.6	5.51	76	.294	.374	-40	-34	105	96	-1.3	-1	-1	-3.4
1954	NY-A	9	7	.563	25	21	5	1	0	132	131	8.9	10	43	2.9	52	3.5	3.00	117	.258	.319	11	8	94	119	-1.3	1	-1	0.7
1955	Bal-A	3	2	.600	14	8	1	1	1	65	64	8.9	7	28	3.9	25	3.5	4.57	81	.261	.345	-4	-6	94	97	0.9	-0	-1	-0.6
	Chi-A	4	6	.400	25	12	1	1	1	91	85	8.4	10	30	3.0	44	4.4	4.65	83	.251	.308	-7	-8	98	79	-1.6	-3	0	-0.9
	Yr	7	8	.467	39	20	2	2	2	156	149	8.6	17	58	3.3	69	4.0	4.62	82	.251	.313	-11	-14	96	79	-0.7	-0	-1	-1.5
1956	Chi-A	0	1	.000	3	1	0	0	0	4	9	20.3	0	4	9.0	0	0.0	11.25	38	.474	.500	-3	-3	102	105	-0.4	-0	0	-0.2
1957	Det-A	4	3	.571	37	1	0	0	5	59	53	8.1	6	28	4.3	20	3.1	3.36	121	.249	.329	3	5	107	121	0.5	-1	-0	0.3
Total	7	46	54	.460	187	108	33	8	9	827	890	9.7	71	355	3.9	381	4.1	4.35	92	.277	.350	-46	-34	104	108	-3.6	-8	-3	-3.4

■ **JEFF BYRD** Byrd, Jeffrey Alan b: 11/11/56, La Mesa, Cal. BR/TR, 6'3", 195 lbs. Deb: 6/20/77

YEAR	TM/L	W	L	PCT	G	GS	CG	SHO	SV	IP	H	H/G	HR	BB	BB/G	SO	SO/G	ERA	/A	OAVG	OOBP	PR	/A	PF	CPI	WAT	PB	PD	TPI
1977	Tor-A	2	13	.133	17	17	1	0	0	87	98	10.1	5	68	7.0	40	4.1	6.21	69	.286	.398	-21	-19	105	86	-4.6	0	1	-1.6

■ **JERRY BYRNE** Byrne, Gerald Wilford b: 2/2/07, Parnell, Mich. d: 8/11/55, Lansing, Mich. BR/TR, 6', 170 lbs. Deb: 8/31/29

YEAR	TM/L	W	L	PCT	G	GS	CG	SHO	SV	IP	H	H/G	HR	BB	BB/G	SO	SO/G	ERA	/A	OAVG	OOBP	PR	/A	PF	CPI	WAT	PB	PD	TPI
1929	Chi-A	0	1	.000	3	1	0	0	0	7	11	14.1	0	6	7.7	1	1.3	7.71	54	.379	.447	-3	-3	98	104	-0.4	-0	-0	-0.2

■ **TOMMY BYRNE** Byrne, Thomas Joseph b: 12/31/19, Baltimore, Md. BL/TL, 6'1", 182 lbs. Deb: 4/27/43

YEAR	TM/L	W	L	PCT	G	GS	CG	SHO	SV	IP	H	H/G	HR	BB	BB/G	SO	SO/G	ERA	/A	OAVG	OOBP	PR	/A	PF	CPI	WAT	PB	PD	TPI
1943	NY-A	2	1	.667	11	2	0	0	0	32	28	7.9	1	35	9.8	22	6.2	6.47	48	.248	.420	-11	-12	94	84	0.1	-0	0	-1.1
1946	NY-A	0	1	.000	4	1	0	0	0	9	7	7.0	1	8	8.0	5	5.0	6.00	57	.194	.356	-2	-3	98	62	-0.4	0	0	-0.2
1947	NY-A	0	0	—	4	1	0	0	0	4	5	11.3	0	6	13.5	2	4.5	4.50	76	.294	.478	-0	-0	92	159	0.0	0	0	0.0
1948	NY-A	8	5	.615	31	11	5	1	2	134	79	5.3	8	101	6.8	93	6.2	3.29	125	.172	.326	15	12	96	91	0.1	5	-1	1.7
1949	NY-A	15	7	.682	32	30	12	3	0	196	125	**5.7**	11	179	8.2	129	**5.9**	3.72	110	**.183**	.360	10	8	97	93	1.8	1	-3	0.5
1950	NY-A	15	9	.625	31	31	10	2	0	203	188	8.3	23	160	7.1	118	5.2	4.74	93	.245	.384	-4	-8	96	107	-0.2	7	-2	-0.2
1951	NY-A	2	1	.667	9	3	0	0	0	21	16	6.9	0	36	15.4	14	6.0	6.86	53	.213	.478	-6	-8	88	92	0.1	1	-0	-0.6
	StL-A	4	10	.286	19	17	7	2	0	123	104	7.6	5	114	8.3	57	4.2	3.80	118	.235	.399	4	10	109	126	-1.1	3	-1	1.3
	Yr	6	11	.353	28	20	7	2	0	144	120	7.5	5	150	9.4	71	4.4	4.25	103	.230	.408	-2	2	106	126	-1.0	1	-1	0.7
1952	StL-A	7	14	.333	29	24	14	0	0	196	182	8.4	16	112	5.1	91	4.2	4.68	78	.247	.347	-22	-22	100	89	-2.2	6	-4	-1.9
1953	Chi-A	2	0	1.000	6	6	0	0	0	16	18	10.1	0	26	14.6	4	2.3	10.13	41	.295	.494	-11	-11	104	75	1.0	1	0	-0.9
	Was-A	0	5	.000	6	5	2	0	0	34	35	9.3	3	22	5.8	22	5.8	4.24	88	.276	.374	-1	-2	93	122	-2.4	-1	0	-0.1
	Yr	2	5	.286	12	11	2	0	0	50	53	9.5	3	48	8.6	26	4.7	6.12	63	.282	.418	-12	-13	96	122	-1.4	1	1	-1.0
1954	NY-A	3	2	.600	5	5	4	1	0	40	36	8.1	1	19	4.3	24	5.4	2.70	130	.240	.325	5	4	94	111	-0.2	4	0	0.8
1955	NY-A	16	5	**.762**	27	22	9	3	2	160	137	7.7	12	87	4.9	76	4.3	3.15	119	.237	.335	14	10	94	119	4.2	4	-1	1.3
1956	NY-A	7	3	.700	37	8	1	0	6	110	108	8.8	9	72	5.9	52	4.3	3.35	118	.262	.369	10	7	95	138	1.0	5	0	1.3
1957	NY-A	4	6	.400	30	4	1	0	2	85	70	7.4	8	60	6.4	57	6.0	4.34	79	.227	.358	-5	-9	90	96	-1.8	4	-1	-0.5
Total	13	85	69	.552	281	170	65	12	12	1363	1138	7.5	98	1037	6.8	766	5.1	4.11	96	.229	.366	-5	-23	97	105	-0.0	40	-11	1.4

■ **MARTY BYSTROM** Bystrom, Martin Eugene b: 7/26/58, Coral Gables, Fla. BR/TR, 6'5", 200 lbs. Deb: 9/07/80

YEAR	TM/L	W	L	PCT	G	GS	CG	SHO	SV	IP	H	H/G	HR	BB	BB/G	SO	SO/G	ERA	/A	OAVG	OOBP	PR	/A	PF	CPI	WAT	PB	PD	TPI
1980	Phi-N	5	0	1.000	6	5	1	1	0	36	26	6.5	1	9	2.3	21	5.3	1.50	256	.195	.246	8	9	106	88	2.5	-1	1	1.2
1981	Phi-N	4	3	.571	9	9	1	0	0	54	55	9.2	3	16	2.7	24	4.0	3.33	117	.264	.317	1	3	112	105	0.2	-1	1	0.3
1982	Phi-N	5	6	.455	19	16	1	0	0	89	93	9.4	2	35	3.5	50	5.1	4.85	70	.277	.344	-12	-15	94	82	-0.9	-0	-1	-1.5
1983	Phi-N	6	9	.400	24	23	1	1	0	119	136	10.3	6	44	3.3	87	6.6	4.61	79	.285	.346	-13	-13	100	92	-2.2	2	-1	-1.1
1984	Phi-N	4	4	.500	11	11	0	0	0	57	66	10.4	5	22	3.5	36	5.7	5.05	72	.283	.341	-9	-9	101	88	0.0	-0	-0	-0.8
	NY-A	2	2	.500	7	7	0	0	0	39	34	7.8	3	13	3.0	24	5.5	3.00	124	.230	.293	4	3	93	96	0.0	0	-0	0.3
1985	NY-A	3	2	.600	8	8	0	0	0	41	44	9.7	8	19	4.2	16	3.5	5.71	68	.280	.356	-7	-8	94	98	0.0	0	0	-0.6
Total	6	29	26	.527	84	79	4	2	0	435	454	9.4	28	158	3.3	258	5.3	4.26	86	.268	.330	-28	-28	100	91	-0.4	-0	-1	-2.2

■ **GREG CADARET** Cadaret, Gregory James b: 2/27/62, Detroit, Mich. BL/TL, 6'3", 200 lbs. Deb: 7/05/87

YEAR	TM/L	W	L	PCT	G	GS	CG	SHO	SV	IP	H	H/G	HR	BB	BB/G	SO	SO/G	ERA	/A	OAVG	OOBP	PR	/A	PF	CPI	WAT	PB	PD	TPI
1987	Oak-A	6	2	.750	29	0	0	0	0	40	37	8.3	6	24	5.4	30	6.7	4.50	90	.252	.352	-0	-2	91	110	2.1	0	1	0.0
1988	Oak-A	5	2	.714	58	0	0	0	3	72	60	7.5	2	36	4.5	65	8.1	2.88	129	.226	.312	9	7	93	103	0.7	0	0	0.7
Total	2	11	4	.733	87	0	0	0	3	112	97	7.8	8	60	4.8	95	7.6	3.46	111	.235	.326	9	5	92	105	2.8	0	1	0.7

■ **LEON CADORE** Cadore, Leon Joseph "Caddy" b: 11/20/1890, Chicago, Ill. d: 3/16/58, Spokane, Wash. BR/TR, 6'1", 190 lbs. Deb: 4/28/15

YEAR	TM/L	W	L	PCT	G	GS	CG	SHO	SV	IP	H	H/G	HR	BB	BB/G	SO	SO/G	ERA	/A	OAVG	OOBP	PR	/A	PF	CPI	WAT	PB	PD	TPI
1915	Bro-N	0	2	.000	7	2	1	0	0	21	28	12.0	0	8	3.4	12	5.1	5.57	50	.337	.404	-7	-6	102	97	-0.9	-1	0	-0.7
1916	Bro-N	0	0	—	1	0	0	0	0	6	10	15.0	0	0	0.0	2	3.0	4.50	58	.370	.370	-1	-1	100	117	0.0	-0	1	0.0
1917	Bro-N	13	13	.500	37	30	21	1	3	264	231	7.9	3	63	2.1	115	3.9	2.45	116	.241	.282	8	11	105	96	1.1	5	-2	1.7
1918	Bro-N	1	0	1.000	2	2	1	1	0	17	6	3.2	0	2	1.1	5	2.6	0.53	543	.115	.158	4	4	104	91	0.5	-0	0	0.6
1919	Bro-N	14	12	.538	35	27	16	3	0	251	228	8.2	5	39	1.4	94	3.4	2.37	115	.245	.274	15	10	94	97	1.4	-2	-3	0.4
1920	Bro-N	15	14	.517	35	30	16	4	0	254	256	9.1	4	56	2.0	79	2.8	2.62	130	.270	.304	14	22	108	107	-2.4	2	2	2.9
1921	Bro-N	13	14	.481	35	30	12	2	0	212	243	10.3	17	46	2.0	79	3.4	4.16	95	.292	.325	-9	-5	105	97	-0.7	-1	-1	-0.6
1922	Bro-N	8	15	.348	29	21	13	0	0	190	224	10.6	13	57	2.7	49	2.3	4.36	90	.299	.336	-5	-10	95	100	-3.7	5	-3	-0.7
1923	Bro-N	4	1	.800	8	4	3	0	0	36	39	9.8	2	13	3.3	5	1.3	3.25	120	.291	.342	3	3	98	133	1.5	-1	-1	0.0
	Chi-A	0	1	.000	1	1	0	0	0	2	6	27.0	0	2	9.0	3	13.5	27.00	15	.500	.533	-5	-5	99	53	-0.4	0	0	-0.3
1924	NY-N	0	0	—	2	0	0	0	0	4	2	4.5	0	3	6.8	2	4.5	0.00	—	.154	.313	2	2	88	0	0.0	0	0	0.2
Total	10	68	72	.486	192	147	83	11	3	1257	1273	9.1	44	289	2.1	445	3.2	3.14	106	.269	.305	19	26	101	100	-3.6	5	-7	3.5

■ **CHARLIE CADY** Cady, Charles B. b: 12/1865, Chicago, Ill. d: 6/7/09, Kankakee, Ill. 5'11", 180 lbs. Deb: 9/05/1883

YEAR	TM/L	W	L	PCT	G	GS	CG	SHO	SV	IP	H	H/G	HR	BB	BB/G	SO	SO/G	ERA	/A	OAVG	OOBP	PR	/A	PF	CPI	WAT	PB	PD	TPI
1883	Cle-N	0	1	.000	1	1	1	0	0	8	13	14.6	0	4	4.5	5	5.6	7.88	41	.373	.438	-4	-4	104	85	-0.4	-1	0	-0.2
1884	CP-U	3	1	.750	4	4	4	0	0	35	37	9.5	0	13	3.3	15	3.9	2.83	106	.276	.340	1	1	100	132	1.1	-1	0	-0.8
Total	2	3	2	.600	5	5	5	0	0	43	50	10.5	0	17	3.6	20	4.2	3.77	81	.296	.361	-4	-3	101	123	0.7	-1	0	-1.0

■ **JOHN CAHILL** Cahill, John Patrick Francis "Patsy" b: 1864, San Francisco, Cal. d: 11/1/01, Pleasanton, Cal. BR/TR, 5'7.5", 168 lbs. Deb: 5/31/1884

YEAR	TM/L	W	L	PCT	G	GS	CG	SHO	SV	IP	H	H/G	HR	BB	BB/G	SO	SO/G	ERA	/A	OAVG	OOBP	PR	/A	PF	CPI	WAT	PB	PD	TPI
1884	Col-a	1	0	1.000	2	1	1	0	0	16	15	8.4	0	4	2.3	1	0.6	5.06	61	.256	.304	-3	-3	96	60	0.5	0	0	-0.2
1886	StL-N	1	0	1.000	2	0	0	0	0	12	11	8.3	0	3	2.3	2	1.5	3.00	108	.256	.305	0	0	98	85	0.5	-0	0	0.0
1887	Ind-N	0	2	.000	6	1	1	0	0	22	40	16.4	2	19	7.8	5	2.0	14.32	29	.408	.505	-25	-25	101	67	-0.9	-1	0	-1.7
Total	3	2	2	.500	10	2	2	0	0	50	66	11.9	2	26	4.7	8	1.4	8.64	41	.331	.408	-28	-28	99	69	0.1	-1	0	-1.9

■ **LES CAIN** Cain, Leslie b: 1/13/48, San Luis Obispo, Cal. BL/TL, 6'1", 200 lbs. Deb: 4/28/68

YEAR	TM/L	W	L	PCT	G	GS	CG	SHO	SV	IP	H	H/G	HR	BB	BB/G	SO	SO/G	ERA	/A	OAVG	OOBP	PR	/A	PF	CPI	WAT	PB	PD	TPI
1968	Det-A	1	0	1.000	8	4	0	0	0	24	25	9.4	1	20	7.5	13	4.9	3.00	102	.269	.395	-0	0	103	166	0.5	0	0	0.1
1970	Det-A	12	7	.632	29	29	5	0	0	181	167	8.3	15	98	4.9	156	7.8	3.83	101	.247	.343	-2	1	104	104	2.9	-0	-0	0.0
1971	Det-A	10	9	.526	26	26	3	1	0	145	121	7.5	14	91	5.6	118	7.3	4.34	76	.228	.343	-14	-17	95	89	-0.6	0	-1	-1.7
1972	Det-A	0	3	.000	5	5	0	0	0	24	18	6.8	2	16	6.0	16	6.0	3.75	92	.209	.330	-2	-1	112	88	-1.4	-0	-0	-0.1
Total	4	23	19	.548	68	64	8	1	0	374	331	8.0	32	225	5.4	303	7.3	3.97	90	.239	.346	-18	-17	101	101	1.4	0	-1	-1.7

■ **SUGAR CAIN** Cain, Merritt Patrick b: 4/5/07, Macon, Ga. d: 4/3/75, Atlanta, Ga. BL/TR, 5'11", 190 lbs. Deb: 4/15/32

YEAR	TM/L	W	L	PCT	G	GS	CG	SHO	SV	IP	H	H/G	HR	BB	BB/G	SO	SO/G	ERA	/A	OAVG	OOBP	PR	/A	PF	CPI	WAT	PB	PD	TPI
1932	Phi-A	3	4	.429	10	6	3	0	0	45	42	8.4	1	28	5.6	24	4.8	5.00	99	.256	.355	-3	-0	111	86	-1.0	0	-0	0.0
1933	Phi-A	13	12	.520	38	32	16	1	1	218	244	10.1	18	137	5.7	43	1.8	4.25	92	.280	.373	1	-8	92	**125**	0.0	0	-1	-0.8
1934	Phi-A	9	17	.346	36	32	15	0	0	231	235	9.2	15	128	5.0	66	2.6	4.40	101	.266	.354	2	1	98	103	-3.4	-3	-1	-0.2
1935	Phi-A	0	5	.000	6	5	0	0	0	26	39	13.5	1	19	6.6	5	1.7	6.58	69	.382	.457	-6	-6	102	124	-2.4	-1	0	-0.5
	StL-A	9	8	.529	31	24	8	0	0	168	197	10.6	7	104	5.6	68	3.6	5.25	93	.290	.384	-15	-7	110	99	1.7	-3	-3	-1.0
	Yr	9	13	.409	37	29	8	0	0	194	236	10.9	8	123	5.7	73	3.4	5.43	89	.302	.394	-21	-13	109	99	-0.7	-1	-3	-1.5
1936	StL-A	1	1	.500	4	3	1	0	0	16	20	11.3	0	9	5.1	8	4.5	6.75	80	.286	.367	-3	-2	107	67	0.2	-0	-0	-0.1
	Chi-A	14	10	.583	30	26	14	1	0	195	228	10.5	18	75	3.5	42	1.9	4.75	104	.293	.356	6	5	99	109	1.4	-4	-3	-0.1
	Yr	15	11	.577	34	29	15	1	0	211	248	10.6	18	84	3.6	50	2.1	4.91	102	.292	.357	3	2	99	109	1.6	0	-3	-0.2
1937	Chi-A	4	2	.667	18	6	1	0	0	69	88	11.5	7	51	6.7	17	2.2	6.13	77	.325	.424	-12	-11	102	113	0.8	-1	0	-1.0
1938	Chi-A	0	1	.000	5	3	0	0	0	20	26	11.7	0	18	8.1	6	2.7	4.50	105	.321	.436	1	0	98	146	-0.4	-1	-1	0.0
Total	7	53	60	.469	178	137	58	2	1	988	1119	10.2	67	569	5.2	279	2.5	4.83	95	.287	.374	-28	-29	100	109	-3.1	-12	-8	-3.7

■ **BOB CAIN** Cain, Robert Max "Sugar" b: 10/16/24, Longford, Kan. BL/TL, 6', 165 lbs. Deb: 9/18/49

YEAR	TM/L	W	L	PCT	G	GS	CG	SHO	SV	IP	H	H/G	HR	BB	BB/G	SO	SO/G	ERA	/A	OAVG	OOBP	PR	/A	PF	CPI	WAT	PB	PD	TPI
1949	Chi-A	0	0	—	6	0	0	0	1	11	7	5.7	0	5	4.1	5	4.1	2.45	170	.179	.273	2	2	99	57	0.0	-0	-0	0.1
1950	Chi-A	9	12	.429	34	23	11	1	2	172	153	8.0	12	109	5.7	77	4.0	3.92	116	.244	.355	12	12	99	109	0.8	-1	0	1.1
1951	Chi-A	1	2	.333	4	4	1	0	0	26	25	8.7	3	13	4.5	3	1.0	3.81	103	.248	.345	1	0	96	116	-0.5	1	-0	0.1

YEAR	TM/L	W	L	PCT	G	GS	CG	SHO	SV	IP	H	H/G	HR	BB	BB/G	SO	SO/G	ERA	/A	OAVG	OOBP	PR	/A	PF	CPI	WAT	PB	PD	TPI
	Det-A	11	10	.524	35	22	6	1	2	149	135	8.2	12	82	5.0	58	3.5	4.71	93	.239	.344	-10	-5	107	85	1.1	2	0	-0.2
	Yr	12	12	.500	39	26	7	1	2	175	160	8.2	15	95	4.9	61	3.1	4.58	94	.240	.340	-9	-5	105	85	0.6	1	-0	-0.1
1952	StL-A	12	10	.545	29	27	8	1	2	170	169	8.9	15	62	3.3	70	3.7	4.13	89	.264	.325	-9	-9	100	96	2.8	-1	-2	-1.1
1953	StL-A	4	10	.286	32	13	1	0	1	100	129	11.6	8	45	4.1	36	3.2	6.21	71	.310	.376	-25	-20	111	87	-1.3	-0	-2	-2.0
Total	5	37	44	.457	140	89	27	3	8	628	618	8.9	50	316	4.5	249	3.6	4.50	94	.259	.346	-27	-20	103	95	2.9	0	-4	-2.0

■ CHARLIE CALDWELL Caldwell, Charles William "Chuck" b: 8/2/01, Bristol, Va. d: 11/1/57, Princeton, N.J. BR/TR, 5'10", 180 lbs. Deb: 7/07/25

YEAR	TM/L	W	L	PCT	G	GS	CG	SHO	SV	IP	H	H/G	HR	BB	BB/G	SO	SO/G	ERA	/A	OAVG	OOBP	PR	/A	PF	CPI	WAT	PB	PD	TPI
1925	NY-A	0	0	—	3	0	0	0	0	3	7	21.0	0	3	9.0	1	3.0	15.00	28	.467	.556	-4	-4	97	79	0.0	-0	-0	-0.2

■ EARL CALDWELL Caldwell, Earl Welton "Teach" b: 4/9/05, Sparks, Tex. d: 9/15/81, Mission, Tex. BR/TR, 6'1", 178 lbs. Deb: 9/08/28

YEAR	TM/L	W	L	PCT	G	GS	CG	SHO	SV	IP	H	H/G	HR	BB	BB/G	SO	SO/G	ERA	/A	OAVG	OOBP	PR	/A	PF	CPI	WAT	PB	PD	TPI
1928	Phi-N	1	4	.200	5	5	1	1	0	35	46	11.8	5	17	4.4	6	1.5	5.66	77	.348	.409	-6	-5	109	122	-0.7	-0	0	-0.4
1935	StL-A	3	2	.600	6	5	2	1	0	37	34	8.3	2	17	4.1	5	1.2	3.65	134	.245	.325	3	5	110	97	0.8	-0	1	0.6
1936	StL-A	7	16	.304	41	25	10	2	2	189	252	12.0	15	83	4.0	59	2.8	6.00	90	.319	.389	-20	-13	107	102	-2.4	-1	-1	-1.2
1937	StL-A	0	0	—	9	2	0	0	0	29	39	12.1	3	13	4.0	8	2.5	6.83	70	.317	.391	-7	-7	103	89	0.0	0	0	-0.5
1945	Chi-A	6	7	.462	27	11	5	1	4	105	108	9.3	8	37	3.2	45	3.9	3.60	90	.265	.325	-3	-4	96	107	-0.1	-0	3	-0.1
1946	Chi-A	13	4	.765	39	0	0	0	8	91	60	5.9	2	29	2.9	42	4.2	2.08	164	.186	.251	**14**	**13**	97	63	4.9	1	1	1.6
1947	Chi-A	1	4	.200	40	0	0	0	8	54	53	8.8	4	30	5.0	22	3.7	3.67	100	.261	.351	0	-0	99	118	-1.3	-1	-1	-0.1
1948	Chi-A	1	5	.167	25	1	0	0	3	39	53	12.2	3	22	5.1	10	2.3	5.31	80	.335	.416	-4	-5	100	126	-1.4	-0	-0	-0.4
	Bos-A	1	1	.500	8	0	0	0	0	9	11	11.0	2	11	11.0	5	5.0	13.00	32	.333	.500	-9	-9	97	75	-0.1	0	-0	-0.7
	Yr	2	6	.250	33	1	0	0	3	48	64	12.0	5	33	6.2	15	2.8	6.75	63	.332	.424	-13	-13	99	75	-1.5	-0	-1	-1.1
Total	8	33	43	.434	200	49	18	5	25	588	656	10.0	44	259	4.0	202	3.1	4.68	92	.284	.357	-32	-25	102	100	-0.3	-2	3	-1.2

■ RALPH CALDWELL Caldwell, Ralph Grant "Lefty" b: 1/18/1884, Philadelphia, Pa. d: 8/5/69, W.Trenton, N.J. BL/TL, 5'9", 155 lbs. Deb: 9/10/04

YEAR	TM/L	W	L	PCT	G	GS	CG	SHO	SV	IP	H	H/G	HR	BB	BB/G	SO	SO/G	ERA	/A	OAVG	OOBP	PR	/A	PF	CPI	WAT	PB	PD	TPI
1904	Phi-N	2	2	.500	6	5	5	0	0	41	40	8.8	1	15	3.3	30	6.6	4.17	63	.283	.360	-7	-7	97	81	0.5	3	0	-0.6
1905	Phi-N	1	3	.250	7	2	1	0	1	34	44	11.6	1	7	1.9	29	7.7	4.24	72	.351	.398	-5	-4	102	112	-1.0	-2	-1	-0.4
Total	2	3	5	.375	13	7	6	0	1	75	84	10.1	2	22	2.6	59	7.1	4.20	67	.315	.378	-11	-11	99	95	-0.5	1	-1	-1.0

■ MIKE CALDWELL Caldwell, Ralph Michael b: 1/22/49, Tarboro, N.C. BR/TL, 6', 185 lbs. Deb: 9/04/71

YEAR	TM/L	W	L	PCT	G	GS	CG	SHO	SV	IP	H	H/G	HR	BB	BB/G	SO	SO/G	ERA	/A	OAVG	OOBP	PR	/A	PF	CPI	WAT	PB	PD	TPI
1971	SD-N	1	0	1.000	6	0	0	0	0	7	4	5.1	0	3	3.9	5	6.4	0.00	—	.174	.269	3	3	98	0	0.5	1	0	0.4
1972	SD-N	7	11	.389	42	20	4	2	2	164	183	10.0	10	49	2.7	102	5.6	4.01	78	.282	.331	-10	-16	91	100	0.2	-1	5	-1.2
1973	SD-N	5	14	.263	55	13	3	1	10	149	146	8.8	8	53	3.2	86	5.2	3.74	95	.260	.318	-1	-3	97	93	-2.9	-1	2	-0.2
1974	SF-N	14	5	.737	31	27	6	2	0	189	176	8.4	17	63	3.0	83	4.0	2.95	134	.249	.308	14	21	109	117	5.3	-3	4	2.5
1975	SF-N	7	13	.350	38	21	4	0	1	163	194	10.7	16	48	2.7	57	3.1	4.80	77	.296	.342	-21	-20	102	96	-3.1	-0	2	-1.8
1976	SF-N	1	7	.125	50	9	0	0	2	107	145	12.2	5	20	1.7	55	4.6	4.88	75	.324	.348	-16	-15	104	98	-2.8	-0	1	-1.3
1977	Cin-N	0	0	—	14	0	0	0	1	25	25	9.0	1	8	2.9	11	4.0	3.96	98	.260	.314	-0	-0	99	82	0.0	2	0	0.1
	Mil-A	5	8	.385	21	12	2	0	0	94	101	9.7	6	36	3.4	38	3.6	4.60	86	.271	.333	-5	-7	97	85	-0.4	0	3	-0.3
1978	Mil-A	22	9	.710	37	34	**23**	6	1	293	258	7.9	14	54	1.7	131	4.0	2.37	166	.234	.271	46	51	104	96	5.7	0	1	5.8
1979	Mil-A	16	6	**.727**	30	30	16	4	0	235	252	9.7	18	39	1.5	89	3.4	3.29	127	.278	.305	24	24	99	112	4.1	0	5	2.9
1980	Mil-A	13	11	.542	34	33	11	2	1	225	248	9.9	29	56	2.2	74	3.0	4.04	93	.285	.326	0	-7	93	110	0.3	0	0	-0.6
1981	Mil-A	11	9	.550	24	23	3	0	0	144	151	9.4	18	38	2.4	41	2.6	3.94	89	.272	.312	-4	-7	95	104	-0.3	0	-0	-0.7
1982	Mil-A	17	13	.567	35	34	12	3	0	258	269	9.4	30	58	2.0	75	2.6	3.91	96	.271	.307	5	-4	92	101	-0.5	0	2	-0.2
1983	Mil-A	12	11	.522	32	32	10	2	0	228	269	10.6	35	51	2.0	58	2.3	4.54	82	.296	.331	-12	-21	91	109	-0.3	0	-0	-2.0
1984	Mil-A	6	13	.316	26	19	4	1	0	126	160	11.4	11	21	1.5	34	2.4	4.64	80	.314	.334	-9	-13	93	102	-2.4	0	1	-1.1
Total	14	137	130	.513	475	307	98	23	18	2407	2581	9.7	218	597	2.2	939	3.5	3.81	99	.276	.316	13	-13	97	102	3.4	-2	24	2.3

■ RAY CALDWELL Caldwell, Raymond Benjamin "Rube" or "Sum" b: 4/26/1888, Corydon, Pa. d: 8/17/67, Salamanca, N.Y. BL/TR, 6'2", 190 lbs. Deb: 9/09/10

YEAR	TM/L	W	L	PCT	G	GS	CG	SHO	SV	IP	H	H/G	HR	BB	BB/G	SO	SO/G	ERA	/A	OAVG	OOBP	PR	/A	PF	CPI	WAT	PB	PD	TPI
1910	NY-A	1	0	1.000	6	2	1	0	1	19	19	9.0	1	9	4.3	17	8.1	3.79	70	.260	.341	-3	-2	106	94	0.5	-1	-0	-0.3
1911	NY-A	14	14	.500	41	27	19	1	1	255	240	8.5	7	79	2.8	145	5.1	3.35	111	.260	.327	-0	10	111	92	0.0	3	-3	1.4
1912	NY-A	8	16	.333	30	26	13	3	0	183	196	9.6	1	67	3.3	95	4.7	4.48	79	.277	.344	-23	-19	105	81	0.1	2	1	-1.5
1913	NY-A	9	8	.529	27	16	15	2	1	164	131	7.2	5	60	3.3	87	4.8	2.41	126	.219	.299	9	11	104	91	2.3	3	-1	1.2
1914	NY-A	17	9	.654	31	23	22	5	1	213	153	6.5	5	51	2.2	92	3.9	1.94	141	.205	.260	19	19	100	76	5.3	1	-3	2.2
1915	NY-A	19	16	.543	36	35	31	3	0	305	266	7.8	6	107	3.2	130	3.8	2.89	100	.244	.315	2	0	99	96	3.5	8	-3	0.0
1916	NY-A	5	12	.294	21	18	14	1	0	166	142	7.7	6	65	3.5	76	4.1	2.98	96	.243	.327	-3	-2	101	102	-3.8	-0	-1	-0.2
1917	NY-A	13	16	.448	32	29	21	1	0	236	199	7.6	8	76	2.9	102	3.9	2.86	100	.234	.302	-5	-0	107	85	-0.5	5	-1	1.1
1918	NY-A	9	8	.529	24	21	14	1	1	177	173	8.8	2	62	3.2	59	3.0	3.05	85	.261	.318	-6	-9	94	94	0.8	5	-2	-0.9
1919	Bos-A	7	4	.636	18	12	6	1	0	86	92	9.6	1	31	3.2	23	2.4	3.98	74	.279	.346	-7	-10	91	87	1.7	1	-1	-0.9
	Cle-A	5	1	.833	6	6	4	1	0	53	33	5.6	1	19	3.2	24	4.1	1.70	198	.181	.266	9	10	104	71	1.8	3	-1	1.3
	Yr	12	5	.706	24	18	10	2	0	139	125	8.1	2	50	3.2	47	3.0	3.11	100	.243	.312	2	-0	96	71	3.5	1	-3	0.4
1920	Cle-A	20	10	.667	34	33	20	1	0	238	286	10.8	9	63	2.4	80	3.0	3.86	98	.303	.350	-2	-2	100	106	1.5	1	-3	-0.4
1921	Cle-A	6	6	.500	37	12	4	1	4	147	159	9.7	7	49	3.0	76	4.7	4.90	84	.275	.326	-10	-13	96	74	-1.1	1	-0	-1.1
Total	12	133	120	.526	343	260	184	21	9	2242	2089	8.4	59	738	3.0	1006	4.0	3.22	99	.253	.318	-19	-6	102	90	12.1	32	-18	1.9

■ JEFF CALHOUN Calhoun, Jeffrey Wilton b: 4/11/58, La Grange, Ga. BL/TL, 6'2", 190 lbs. Deb: 9/02/84

YEAR	TM/L	W	L	PCT	G	GS	CG	SHO	SV	IP	H	H/G	HR	BB	BB/G	SO	SO/G	ERA	/A	OAVG	OOBP	PR	/A	PF	CPI	WAT	PB	PD	TPI
1984	Hou-N	0	1	.000	9	0	0	0	0	15	5	3.0	0	2	1.2	11	6.6	1.20	275	.100	.130	4	3	92	95	-0.4	0	-0	0.4
1985	Hou-N	2	5	.286	44	0	0	0	4	64	56	7.9	2	24	3.4	47	6.6	2.53	136	.243	.309	8	7	96	120	-1.5	-0	0	0.7
1986	Hou-N	1	0	1.000	20	0	0	0	0	27	28	9.3	3	12	4.0	14	4.7	3.67	103	.264	.336	0	0	102	117	0.5	0	-1	0.0
1987	Phi-N	3	1	.750	42	0	0	0	1	43	25	5.2	1	26	5.4	31	6.5	1.47	292	.168	.284	13	13	105	129	1.0	-0	1	1.4
1988	Phi-N	0	0	—	3	0	0	0	0	2	6	27.0	2	1	4.5	1	4.5	18.00	20	.462	.500	-3	-3	103	109	0.0	0	0	-0.2
Total	5	6	7	.462	118	0	0	0	5	151	120	7.2	8	65	3.9	104	6.2	2.50	149	.219	.296	21	20	99	119	-0.4	-0	0	2.3

■ FRED CALIGIURI Caligiuri, Frederick John b: 10/22/18, W.Hickory, Pa. BR/TR, 6', 190 lbs. Deb: 9/03/41

YEAR	TM/L	W	L	PCT	G	GS	CG	SHO	SV	IP	H	H/G	HR	BB	BB/G	SO	SO/G	ERA	/A	OAVG	OOBP	PR	/A	PF	CPI	WAT	PB	PD	TPI
1941	Phi-A	2	2	.500	5	5	4	0	0	43	45	9.4	2	14	2.9	7	1.5	2.93	146	.257	.307	6	6	103	113	0.3	1	-1	0.6
1942	Phi-A	0	3	.000	13	2	0	0	1	37	45	10.9	2	18	4.4	20	4.9	6.32	58	.300	.378	-11	-11	101	83	-1.4	-0	0	-1.0
Total	2	2	5	.286	18	7	4	0	1	80	90	10.1	4	32	3.6	27	3.0	4.50	89	.277	.341	-5	-4	102	99	-1.1	1	-1	-0.4

■ WILL CALIHAN Calihan, William T. b: 1867, Oswego, N.Y. d: 12/20/17, Rochester, N.Y. 5'8", 150 lbs. Deb: 4/17/1890

YEAR	TM/L	W	L	PCT	G	GS	CG	SHO	SV	IP	H	H/G	HR	BB	BB/G	SO	SO/G	ERA	/A	OAVG	OOBP	PR	/A	PF	CPI	WAT	PB	PD	TPI
1890	Roc-a	18	15	.545	37	36	31	0	0	296	276	8.4	4	125	3.8	127	3.9	3.28	108	.262	.340	19	9	92	104	2.0	-3	0	0.3
1891	Phi-a	6	6	.500	13	11	11	0	0	112	151	12.1	7	47	3.8	28	2.3	6.43	59	.338	.401	-34	-32	103	84	-0.2	-1	0	-2.5
Total	2	24	21	.533	50	47	42	0	0	408	427	9.4	11	172	3.8	155	3.4	4.15	88	.285	.358	-15	-23	95	98	1.8	-4	0	-2.2

■ BEN CALLAHAN Callahan, Benjamin Franklin b: 5/19/57, Mt.Airy, N.C. BR/TR, 6'7", 230 lbs. Deb: 6/22/83

YEAR	TM/L	W	L	PCT	G	GS	CG	SHO	SV	IP	H	H/G	HR	BB	BB/G	SO	SO/G	ERA	/A	OAVG	OOBP	PR	/A	PF	CPI	WAT	PB	PD	TPI
1983	Oak-A	1	2	.333	4	2	0	0	0	9	18	18.0	0	5	5.0	2	2.0	13.00	30	.400	.442	-9	-9	96	64	-0.3	0	0	-0.7

■ NIXEY CALLAHAN Callahan, James Joseph b: 3/18/1874, Fitchburg, Mass. d: 10/4/34, Boston, Mass. BR/TR, 5'10.5", 180 lbs. Deb: 5/12/1894 M

YEAR	TM/L	W	L	PCT	G	GS	CG	SHO	SV	IP	H	H/G	HR	BB	BB/G	SO	SO/G	ERA	/A	OAVG	OOBP	PR	/A	PF	CPI	WAT	PB	PD	TPI
1894	Phi-N	1	2	.333	9	2	1	0	2	34	64	16.9	3	17	4.5	9	2.4	10.06	50	.424	.483	-18	-19	94	87	-0.5	-1	0	-1.4
1897	Chi-N	12	9	.571	23	22	21	1	0	190	221	10.5	6	55	2.6	52	2.5	4.03	108	.313	.363	6	7	101	99	2.7	4	0	0.6
1898	Chi-N	20	10	.667	31	31	30	2	0	274	267	8.8	2	71	2.3	73	2.4	2.46	149	.276	.326	35	37	102	113	4.1	4	2	4.4
1899	Chi-N	21	12	.636	35	34	33	3	0	294	327	10.0	5	76	2.3	77	2.4	3.06	120	.305	.351	26	20	96	115	5.2	4	5	2.9
1900	Chi-N	13	16	.448	32	32	32	2	0	285	347	11.0	5	74	2.3	77	2.4	3.82	91	.324	.368	-4	-10	94	107	-0.5	3	7	-0.1
1901	Chi-A	15	8	.652	27	22	20	1	0	215	195	8.2	4	50	2.1	70	2.9	2.43	145	.261	.307	29	26	96	102	1.5	8	5	4.3
1902	Chi-A	16	14	.533	35	31	29	2	0	282	287	9.2	8	89	2.8	75	2.4	3.61	93	.288	.346	-1	-8	94	94	-0.6	3	6	-0.7
1903	Chi-A	1	2	.333	3	3	3	0	0	28	40	12.9	0	5	1.6	12	3.9	4.50	62	.360	.387	-5	-5	94	110	-0.3	1	1	-0.4
Total	8	99	73	.576	195	177	169	11	2	1602	1748	9.8	33	437	2.5	445	2.5	3.39	108	.300	.349	69	47	97	105	11.6	25	25	9.6

■ JIM CALLAHAN Callahan, James W. b: Moberly, Mo. Deb: 9/03/1898

YEAR	TM/L	W	L	PCT	G	GS	CG	SHO	SV	IP	H	H/G	HR	BB	BB/G	SO	SO/G	ERA	/A	OAVG	OOBP	PR	/A	PF	CPI	WAT	PB	PD	TPI
1898	StL-N	0	2	.000	2	2	1	0	0	8	18	20.3	2	7	7.9	2	2.3	16.88	23	.469	.551	-12	-11	110	75	-0.9	-1	0	-0.8

■ JOE CALLAHAN Callahan, Joseph Thomas b: 10/8/16, E.Boston, Mass. d: 5/24/49, S.Boston, Mass. BR/TR, 6'2", 170 lbs. Deb: 9/13/39

YEAR	TM/L	W	L	PCT	G	GS	CG	SHO	SV	IP	H	H/G	HR	BB	BB/G	SO	SO/G	ERA	/A	OAVG	OOBP	PR	/A	PF	CPI	WAT	PB	PD	TPI
1939	Bos-N	1	0	1.000	4	1	1	0	0	17	17	9.0	0	3	1.6	8	4.2	3.18	115	.250	.288	1	1	93	75	0.5	-0	0	0.1
1940	Bos-N	0	2	.000	6	2	0	0	0	15	20	12.0	1	13	7.8	3	1.8	10.20	38	.351	.458	-11	-11	101	76	-0.9	-1	1	-0.9

YEAR	TM/L	W	L	PCT	G	GS	CG	SHO	SV	IP	H	H/G	HR	BB	BB/G	SO	SO/G	ERA	/A	OAVG	OOBP	PR	/A	PF	CPI	WAT	PB	PD	TPI
Total	2	1	2	.333	10	3	1	0	0	32	37	10.4	1	16	4.5	11	3.1	6.47	58	.296	.372	-9	-10	97	75	-0.4	-1	1	-0.8
■ RAY CALLAHAN	Callahan, Raymond James "Pat" b: 8/29/1891, Ashland, Wis. d: 1/23/73, Olympia, Wash. BL/TL, 5'10.5", 170 lbs. Deb: 9/12/15																												
1915	Cin-N	0	0	—	3	0	0	0	0	6	12	18.0	1	1	1.5	4	6.0	9.00	32	.364	.382	-4	-4	104	82	0.0	0	-0	-0.3
■ DICK CALMUS	Calmus, Richard Lee b: 1/7/44, Los Angeles, Cal. BR/TR, 6'4", 187 lbs. Deb: 4/22/63																												
1963	LA-N	3	1	.750	21	1	0	0	0	44	32	6.5	3	16	3.3	25	5.1	2.66	116	.204	.277	3	2	94	86	0.7	-1	-0	0.1
1967	Chi-N	0	0	—	1	1	0	0	0	4	5	11.3	2	0	0.0	1	2.3	9.00	38	.278	.278	-2	-2	100	70	0.0	0	0	-0.1
Total	2	3	1	.750	22	2	0	0	0	48	37	6.9	5	16	3.0	26	4.9	3.19	97	.211	.277	1	-0	94	85	0.7	-0	-0	0.0
■ MARK CALVERT	Calvert, Mark b: 9/29/56, Tulsa, Okla. BR/TR, 6'1", 195 lbs. Deb: 4/17/83																												
1983	SF-N	1	4	.200	18	4	0	0	0	37	46	11.2	2	34	8.3	14	3.4	6.32	58	.307	.437	-11	-11	101	103	-1.4	-1	0	-1.0
1984	SF-N	2	4	.333	10	5	1	0	0	32	40	11.3	4	9	2.5	5	1.4	5.06	69	.303	.342	-5	-6	98	100	-0.5	-1	0	-0.5
Total	2	3	8	.273	28	9	1	0	0	69	86	11.2	6	43	5.6	19	2.5	5.74	63	.305	.396	-16	-16	99	102	-1.9	-1	1	-1.5
■ PAUL CALVERT	Calvert, Paul Leo Emile b: 10/6/17, Montreal, Que., Can. BR/TR, 6', 175 lbs. Deb: 9/24/42																												
1942	Cle-A	0	0	—	1	0	0	0	0	2	0	0.0	0	2	9.0	2	9.0	0.00	—	.000	.286	1	1	93	0	0.0	0	0	0.1
1943	Cle-A	0	0	—	5	0	0	0	0	8	6	6.8	0	6	6.8	2	2.3	4.50	66	.200	.351	-1	-1	90	66	0.0	-0	0	-0.1
1944	Cle-A	1	3	.250	35	4	0	0	0	77	89	10.4	4	38	4.4	31	3.6	4.56	76	.289	.360	-10	-9	101	101	-0.8	1	2	-0.6
1945	Cle-A	0	0	—	1	0	0	0	0	1	3	27.0	0	1	9.0	1	9.0	18.00	18	.429	.500	-2	-2	98	67	0.0	0	0	-0.1
1949	Was-A	6	17	.261	34	23	5	0	1	161	175	9.8	11	86	4.8	52	2.9	5.42	75	.279	.358	-22	-25	96	86	-2.5	-2	3	-2.2
1950	Det-A	2	2	.500	32	0	0	0	4	51	71	12.5	7	25	4.4	14	2.5	6.35	68	.324	.392	-10	-11	95	102	-0.3	-0	1	-0.9
1951	Det-A	0	0	—	1	0	0	0	0	1	1	9.0	0	0	0.0	0	0.0	0.00	—	.250	.250	0	0	107	0	0.0	0	0	0.1
Total	7	9	22	.290	109	27	5	0	5	301	345	10.3	22	158	4.7	102	3.0	5.32	74	.287	.364	-43	-47	97	91	-3.6	-2	5	-3.7
■ ERNIE CAMACHO	Camacho, Ernest Carlos b: 2/1/55, Salinas, Cal. BR/TR, 6'1", 180 lbs. Deb: 5/22/80																												
1980	Oak-A	0	0	—	5	0	0	0	0	12	20	15.0	2	5	3.8	9	6.8	6.75	56	.364	.426	-4	-4	94	116	0.0	0	-0	-0.3
1981	Pit-N	0	1	.000	7	3	0	0	0	22	23	9.4	0	15	6.1	11	4.5	4.91	68	.295	.396	-3	-4	96	101	-0.4	-0	0	-0.4
1983	Cle-A	0	1	.000	4	0	0	0	0	5	5	9.0	1	2	3.6	2	3.6	5.40	80	.250	.348	-1	-1	106	92	-0.4	0	-0	0.0
1984	Cle-A	5	9	.357	69	0	0	0	23	100	83	7.5	6	37	3.3	48	4.3	2.43	174	.229	.294	17	20	106	120	-1.6	0	-0	2.0
1985	Cle-A	0	1	.000	2	0	0	0	0	3	4	12.0	0	1	3.0	2	6.0	9.00	44	.333	.333	-2	-2	95	58	-0.4	0	0	-0.1
1986	Cle-A	2	4	.333	51	0	0	0	20	57	60	9.5	1	31	4.9	36	5.7	4.11	100	.269	.348	1	-0	98	100	-1.0	0	1	0.1
1987	Cle-A	0	1	.000	15	0	0	0	1	14	21	13.5	1	5	3.2	9	5.8	9.00	52	.350	.420	-7	-7	105	77	-0.4	0	1	-0.5
1988	Hou-N	0	3	.000	13	0	0	0	1	18	25	12.5	1	12	6.0	13	6.5	7.50	43	.352	.435	-8	-9	93	93	-1.4	-0	0	-0.8
Total	8	7	20	.259	166	3	0	0	45	231	241	9.4	12	108	4.2	130	5.1	4.25	95	.274	.348	-7	-5	101	107	-5.6	-1	1	-0.0
■ FRED CAMBRIA	Cambria, Frederick Dennis b: 1/22/48, Cambria Heights, N.Y. BR/TR, 6'2", 195 lbs. Deb: 8/26/70																												
1970	Pit-N	1	2	.333	6	5	0	0	0	33	37	10.1	2	12	3.3	14	3.8	3.55	110	.272	.333	2	1	96	112	-0.5	1	0	0.2
■ JACK CAMERON	Cameron, John William "Happy Jack" b: 1885, Canada d: 8/17/51, Boston, Mass. Deb: 9/13/06																												
1906	Bos-N	0	0	—	2	1	0	0	0	6	4	6.0	0	6	9.0	2	3.0	0.00	—	.212	.403	2	2	106	0	0.0	-0	0	0.2
■ HARRY CAMNITZ	Camnitz, Henry Richardson b: 10/26/1884, Mc Kinney, Ky. d: 1/6/51, Louisville, Ky. BR/TR, 6'1", 168 lbs. Deb: 09																												
1909	Pit-N	0	0	—	1	0	0	0	0	4	6	13.5	0	1	2.3	1	2.3	4.50	57	.353	.389	-1	-1	99	116	0.0	-0	0	0.0
1911	StL-N	1	0	1.000	2	0	0	0	0	2	0	0.0	0	1	4.5	2	9.0	0.00	—	.000	.143	1	1	102	0	0.5	0	0	0.1
Total	2	1	0	1.000	3	0	0	0	0	6	6	9.0	0	2	3.0	3	4.5	3.00	96	.261	.320	-0	-0	100	77	0.5	-0	0	0.1
■ HOWIE CAMNITZ	Camnitz, Samuel Howard "Red" b: 8/22/1881, Covington, Ky. d: 3/2/60, Louisville, Ky. BR/TR, 5'9", 169 lbs. Deb: 4/22/04																												
1904	Pit-N	1	4	.200	10	2	2	0	0	49	48	8.8	0	20	3.7	21	3.9	4.22	63	.285	.371	-8	-8	98	79	-1.5	-1	-1	-0.8
1906	Pit-N	1	0	1.000	2	1	1	1	0	9	6	6.0	0	5	5.0	5	5.0	2.00	132	.212	.331	1	1	101	104	0.5	-0	-0	0.0
1907	Pit-N	13	8	.619	31	19	15	4	1	180	135	6.8	0	59	3.0	85	4.3	2.15	117	.235	.309	6	7	102	84	0.8	-5	-0	0.8
1908	Pit-N	16	9	.640	38	26	17	3	2	237	182	6.9	6	69	2.6	118	4.5	1.56	139	.240	.307	21	16	92	132	0.1	-2	-1	1.8
1909	Pit-N	25	6	**.806**	41	30	20	5	3	283	207	6.6	1	68	2.2	133	4.2	1.62	159	.211	.267	31	30	99	95	5.4	0	-2	3.2
1910	Pit-N	12	13	.480	38	31	16	1	2	260	246	8.5	1	61	2.1	120	4.2	3.22	104	.256	.308	-5	3	110	80	-2.0	-4	-2	-0.1
1911	Pit-N	20	15	.571	40	33	18	1	1	268	245	8.2	8	84	2.8	139	4.7	3.12	106	.248	.309	8	6	97	91	1.0	-3	-3	0.0
1912	Pit-N	22	12	.647	41	32	22	2	2	277	256	8.3	9	82	2.7	121	3.9	2.83	115	.245	.307	18	13	95	90	1.7	1	-3	1.0
1913	Pit-N	6	17	.261	36	22	5	1	2	192	203	9.5	7	84	3.9	64	3.0	3.75	80	.282	.352	-12	-16	94	111	-6.2	-1	1	-1.6
	Phi-N	3	3	.500	9	5	1	0	1	49	49	9.0	1	23	4.2	21	3.9	3.67	97	.268	.347	-3	-1	111	102	-0.3	-2	-1	-0.2
	Yr	9	20	.310	45	27	6	1	3	241	252	9.4	8	107	4.0	85	3.2	3.73	84	.277	.344	-14	-16	98	102	-6.5	-1	-0	-1.8
1914	Pit-F	14	19	.424	36	34	20	1	1	262	256	8.8	8	90	3.1	82	2.8	3.23	95	.258	.324	-1	-4	96	99	0.0	-3	-3	-1.0
1915	Pit-F	0	0	—	4	2	0	0	0	20	19	8.5	1	11	4.9	6	2.7	4.50	69	.279	.379	-3	-3	102	87	0.0	-1	0	-0.3
Total	11	133	106	.556	326	237	137	19	15	2086	1852	8.0	42	656	2.8	915	3.9	2.75	107	.248	.313	53	44	99	97	-0.5	-22	-15	2.8
■ RICK CAMP	Camp, Rick Lamar b: 6/10/53, Trion, Ga. BR/TR, 6'1", 185 lbs. Deb: 9/15/76																												
1976	Atl-N	0	1	.000	5	1	0	0	0	11	13	10.6	0	2	1.6	6	4.9	6.55	60	.302	.326	-4	-3	112	57	-0.4	-0	1	-0.2
1977	Atl-N	6	3	.667	54	0	0	0	10	79	89	10.1	6	47	5.4	51	5.8	3.99	113	.283	.366	-1	5	115	123	2.2	-1	-0	0.3
1978	Atl-N	2	4	.333	42	4	0	0	0	74	99	12.0	5	32	3.9	23	2.8	3.77	108	.329	.390	-2	3	114	155	-0.6	-1	0	0.2
1980	Atl-N	6	4	.600	77	0	0	0	22	108	92	7.7	3	29	2.4	33	2.8	1.92	191	.235	.284	20	21	101	133	1.0	-0	4	2.6
1981	Atl-N	9	3	.750	48	0	0	0	17	76	68	8.1	5	12	1.4	47	5.6	1.78	196	.239	.266	14	**14**	100	142	3.3	-1	0	1.5
1982	Atl-N	11	13	.458	51	21	3	0	5	177	199	10.1	18	52	2.6	68	3.5	3.66	105	.291	.331	-1	4	107	**124**	-2.2	-3	1	0.1
1983	Atl-N	10	9	.526	40	16	1	0	0	140	146	9.4	16	38	2.4	61	3.9	3.79	100	.270	.319	-2	0	104	106	-0.2	-2	0	-0.1
1984	Atl-N	8	6	.571	31	21	1	0	0	149	134	8.1	11	63	3.8	69	4.2	3.26	121	.245	.320	5	11	110	109	1.2	-2	0	1.1
1985	Atl-N	4	6	.400	66	2	0	0	3	128	130	9.1	8	61	4.3	49	3.4	3.94	99	.263	.344	-5	-1	108	103	0.0	1	-2	0.0
Total	9	56	49	.533	414	65	5	0	57	942	970	9.3	72	336	3.2	407	3.9	3.37	115	.269	.328	26	53	107	120	4.3	-9	3	5.5
■ KID CAMP	Camp, Winfield Scott b: 1870, Columbus, Ohio d: 3/2/1895, Omaha, Neb. 6', 160 lbs. Deb: 5/03/1892																												
1892	Pit-N	0	1	.000	4	1	1	0	0	23	31	12.1	4	9	3.5	6	2.3	6.26	49	.336	.395	-8	-8	94	99	-0.4	-1	0	-0.7
1894	Chi-N	0	1	.000	3	2	2	0	0	22	34	13.9	0	12	4.9	6	2.5	6.55	88	.377	.450	-3	-2	108	100	-0.4	-3	0	-0.2
Total	2	0	2	.000	7	3	3	0	0	45	65	13.0	4	21	4.2	12	2.4	6.40	67	.356	.423	-11	-10	101	99	-0.8	-4	0	-0.9
■ BERT CAMPANERIS	Campaneris, Dagoberto (Blanco) "Campy" (born Dagoberto Campaneria (Blanco)) b: 3/9/42, Pueblo Nuevo, Cuba BR/TR, 5'10", 160 lbs. Deb: 7/23/64																												
1965	KC-A	0	0	—	1	0	0	0	0	1	1	9.0	0	2	18.0	1	9.0	9.00	38	.333	.600	-1	-1	100	106	0.0	0	0	0.0
■ ARCHIE CAMPBELL	Campbell, Archibald Stewart "Iron Man" b: 10/20/03, Maplewood, N.J. BR/TR, 6', 180 lbs. Deb: 4/21/28																												
1928	NY-A	0	1	.000	13	1	0	0	2	24	30	11.3	0	11	4.1	9	3.4	5.25	68	.288	.350	-3	-4	89	77	-0.4	0	-0	-0.4
1929	Was-A	0	1	.000	4	0	0	0	0	4	10	22.5	1	5	11.3	1	2.3	15.75	27	.500	.600	-5	-5	100	101	-0.4	0	0	-0.3
1930	Cin-N	2	4	.333	23	3	1	0	4	58	71	11.0	2	31	4.8	19	2.9	5.43	85	.311	.380	-3	-5	93	100	-0.3	0	2	-0.2
Total	3	2	6	.250	40	4	1	0	6	86	111	11.6	3	47	4.9	29	3.0	5.86	74	.315	.385	-11	-15	92	93	-1.1	0	2	-0.9
■ DAVE CAMPBELL	Campbell, David Alan b: 9/3/51, Princeton, Ind. BR/TR, 6'3", 210 lbs. Deb: 5/06/77																												
1977	Atl-N	0	6	.000	65	0	0	0	13	89	78	7.9	7	33	3.3	42	4.2	3.03	149	.239	.304	9	15	115	109	-2.9	-1	-2	1.2
1978	Atl-N	4	4	.500	53	0	0	0	1	69	67	8.7	10	49	6.4	45	5.9	4.83	85	.258	.376	-10	-6	114	110	0.5	0	0	-0.5
Total	2	4	10	.286	118	0	0	0	14	158	145	8.3	17	82	4.7	87	5.0	3.82	113	.247	.337	-1	9	115	109	-2.4	-1	-2	0.7
■ HUGH CAMPBELL	Campbell, Hugh F. d: 1881, Elizabeth, N.J. Deb: 4/28/1873																												
1873	Res-n	2	16	.111	18																								
■ JOHN CAMPBELL	Campbell, John Millard b: 9/13/07, Washington, D.C. BR/TR, 6'1.5", 184 lbs. Deb: 7/23/33																												
1933	Was-A	0	0	—	1	0	0	0	0	1	1	9.0	0	1	9.0	0	0.0	0.00	—	.200	.333	0	0	93	0	0.0	0	0	0.0
■ MIKE CAMPBELL	Campbell, Michael Thomas b: 2/17/64, Seattle, Wash. BR/TR, 6'3", 210 lbs. Deb: 7/04/87																												
1987	Sea-A	1	4	.200	9	9	1	0	0	49	41	7.5	9	25	4.6	35	6.4	4.78	96	.224	.316	-2	-1	103	87	-1.4	0	0	0.0
1988	Sea-A	6	10	.375	20	20	2	0	0	115	128	10.0	18	43	3.4	63	4.9	5.87	73	.280	.337	-24	-20	108	84	-0.9	0	-1	-1.9

YEAR	TM/L	W	L	PCT	G	GS	CG	SHO	SV	IP	H	H/G	HR	BB	BB/G	SO	SO/G	ERA	/A	OAVG	OOBP	PR	/A	PF	CPI	WAT	PB	PD	TPI
Total	2	7	14	.333	29	29	3	0	0	164	169	9.3	27	68	3.7	98	5.4	5.54	79	.264	.331	-26	-21	107	85	-2.3	0	-1	-1.9
■ **BILLY CAMPBELL**	Campbell, William James b: 11/5/1873, Pittsburgh, Pa. d: 10/6/57, Cincinnati, Ohio BL/TL, 5'10", 165 lbs. Deb: 4/17/05																												
1905	StL-N	1	1	.500	2	2	2	0	0	17	27	14.3	0	7	3.7	2	1.1	7.41	38	.390	.446	-8	-9	95	85	0.2	-0	1	-0.6
1907	Cin-N	3	0	1.000	3	3	3	0	0	21	19	8.1	0	3	1.3	4	1.7	2.14	109	.269	.298	1	0	95	93	1.5	0	0	0.1
1908	Cin-N	12	13	.480	35	24	19	2	2	221	203	8.3	3	44	1.8	73	3.0	2.61	93	.276	.325	-6	-4	104	97	0.2	-4	4	0.0
1909	Cin-N	7	11	.389	30	15	7	0	2	148	162	9.9	0	39	2.4	37	2.3	2.68	91	.288	.344	-1	-4	94	132	-2.1	-0	2	-0.1
Total	4	23	25	.479	70	44	31	2	4	407	411	9.1	3	93	2.1	116	2.6	2.81	87	.286	.337	-15	-16	99	109	-0.2	-4	8	-0.6
■ **BILL CAMPBELL**	Campbell, William Richard b: 8/9/48, Highland Park, Mich. BL/TR, 6'3", 185 lbs. Deb: 7/14/73																												
1973	Min-A	3	3	.500	28	2	0	0	7	52	44	7.6	5	20	3.5	42	7.3	3.12	127	.226	.298	4	5	103	96	0.0	0	0	0.5
1974	Min-A	8	7	.533	63	0	0	0	19	120	109	8.2	4	55	4.1	89	6.7	2.63	139	.242	.323	13	14	101	118	0.5	0	1	1.5
1975	Min-A	4	6	.400	47	7	2	1	5	121	119	8.9	13	46	3.4	76	5.7	3.79	107	.262	.326	-0	4	107	107	-0.8	0	1	0.4
1976	Min-A	17	5	**.773**	**78**	0	0	0	20	168	145	7.8	9	62	3.3	115	6.2	3.00	115	.234	.302	10	8	98	99	6.1	0	-0	0.8
1977	Bos-A	13	9	.591	69	0	0	0	**31**	140	112	7.2	13	60	3.9	114	7.3	2.96	160	.224	.304	17	**27**	116	109	-0.1	0	1	2.9
1978	Bos-A	7	5	.583	29	0	0	0	4	51	62	10.9	3	17	3.0	47	8.3	3.88	103	.308	.350	-1	1	106	121	-0.2	0	1	0.1
1979	Bos-A	3	4	.429	41	0	0	0	9	55	55	9.0	5	23	3.8	25	4.1	4.25	105	.262	.331	-0	1	106	95	-0.8	0	1	0.3
1980	Bos-A	4	0	1.000	23	0	0	0	0	41	44	9.7	1	22	4.8	17	3.7	4.83	85	.284	.367	-4	-3	102	91	2.0	0	-1	-0.3
1981	Bos-A	1	1	.500	30	0	0	0	7	48	45	8.4	5	20	3.8	37	6.9	3.19	121	.245	.313	3	4	106	114	0.0	0	0	0.4
1982	Chi-N	3	6	.333	62	0	0	0	8	100	89	8.0	6	40	3.6	71	6.4	3.69	101	.245	.306	-1	1	104	90	-1.1	-0	2	0.3
1983	Chi-N	6	8	.429	**82**	0	0	0	8	122	128	9.4	4	49	3.6	97	7.2	4.50	82	.275	.336	-12	-11	101	86	-0.1	-1	2	-0.9
1984	Phi-N	6	5	.545	57	0	0	0	1	81	68	7.6	2	35	3.9	52	5.8	3.44	106	.222	.293	1	2	101	73	0.5	-0	-1	0.0
1985	StL-N	5	3	.625	50	0	0	0	4	64	55	7.7	5	21	3.0	41	5.8	3.52	96	.230	.289	1	-1	93	83	0.0	2	-1	-0.1
1986	Det-A	3	6	.333	34	0	0	0	3	56	46	7.4	5	21	3.4	37	5.9	3.86	103	.230	.297	2	1	95	85	-1.7	0	-1	0.0
1987	Mon-N	0	0	—	7	0	0	0	0	10	18	16.2	2	4	3.6	4	3.6	8.10	53	.360	.400	-4	-4	106	97	0.0	0	0	-0.3
Total	15	83	68	.550	700	9	2	1	126	1229	1139	8.3	82	495	3.6	864	6.3	3.54	110	.248	.316	30	46	103	98	4.3	1	5	5.6
■ **CARDELL CAMPER**	Camper, Cardell b: 7/6/52, Boley, Okla. BR/TR, 6'3", 208 lbs. Deb: 9/11/77																												
1977	Cle-A	1	0	1.000	3	1	0	0	0	9	7	7.0	0	4	4.0	9	9.0	4.00	100	.200	.275	0	-0	98	38	0.5	0	-0	0.0
■ **SAL CAMPFIELD**	Campfield, William Holton b: 2/19/1868, Meadville, Pa. d: 5/16/52, Meadville, Pa. BR/TR, 6'0.5", Deb: 5/15/1896																												
1896	NY-N	1	1	.500	6	2	2	0	0	27	31	10.3	1	6	2.0	6	2.0	4.00	108	.311	.350	1	1	99	95	0.0	-0	0	0.0
■ **SAL CAMPISI**	Campisi, Salvatore John b: 8/11/42, Brooklyn, N.Y. BR/TR, 6'2", 210 lbs. Deb: 8/15/69																												
1969	StL-N	1	0	1.000	7	0	0	0	0	10	4	3.6	0	6	5.4	7	6.3	0.90	395	.121	.250	3	3	99	79	0.5	0	0	0.3
1970	StL-N	2	2	.500	37	0	0	0	4	49	53	9.7	2	37	6.8	26	4.8	2.94	146	.282	.401	6	7	106	183	0.1	-0	0	0.7
1971	Min-A	0	0	—	6	0	0	0	0	4	5	11.3	1	4	9.0	2	4.5	4.50	80	.294	.429	-0	-0	104	169	0.0	0	0	0.0
Total	3	3	2	.600	50	0	0	0	4	63	62	8.9	3	47	6.7	35	5.0	2.71	152	.261	.382	9	10	105	166	0.6	-0	0	1.0
■ **HUGH CANAVAN**	Canavan, Hugh Edward "Hugo" b: 5/13/1897, Worcester, Mass. d: 9/4/67, Boston, Mass. BL/TL, 5'8", 160 lbs. Deb: 4/23/18																												
1918	Bos-N	0	4	.000	11	3	3	0	0	47	70	13.4	0	15	2.9	18	3.4	6.32	42	.366	.409	-19	-19	95	96	-1.9	-0	1	-1.8
■ **JOHN CANDELARIA**	Candelaria, John Robert "Candy Man" b: 11/6/53, New York, N.Y. BL/TL, 6'7", 205 lbs. Deb: 6/08/75																												
1975	Pit-N	8	6	.571	18	18	4	1	0	121	95	7.1	8	36	2.7	95	7.1	2.75	129	.212	.268	12	11	98	78	0.0	-0	-1	0.9
1976	Pit-N	16	7	.696	32	31	11	4	1	220	173	7.1	22	60	2.5	138	5.6	3.15	111	.216	.267	9	8	99	82	3.8	3	-1	1.1
1977	Pit-N	20	5	**.800**	33	33	6	1	0	231	197	7.7	29	50	**1.9**	133	5.2	**2.34**	**170**	.232	.272	**40**	42	102	**126**	6.9	4	-1	4.9
1978	Pit-N	12	11	.522	30	29	3	1	1	189	191	9.1	15	49	2.3	94	4.5	3.24	116	.261	.308	7	11	105	108	-0.5	3	-2	1.4
1979	Pit-N	14	9	.609	33	30	8	0	0	207	201	8.7	25	41	1.8	101	4.4	3.22	121	.253	.288	12	15	104	104	0.1	-1	0	1.6
1980	Pit-N	11	14	.440	35	34	7	0	1	233	246	9.5	14	50	1.9	97	3.7	4.02	93	.276	.309	-11	-8	103	90	-1.9	2	-0	-0.6
1981	Pit-N	2	2	.500	6	6	0	0	0	41	42	9.2	3	11	2.4	14	3.1	3.51	96	.271	.315	-0	-1	96	106	0.2	0	0	0.0
1982	Pit-N	12	7	.632	31	30	1	1	1	175	166	8.5	13	37	1.9	133	6.8	2.93	135	.255	.294	13	20	110	109	2.5	3	-1	2.4
1983	Pit-N	15	8	.652	33	32	2	0	0	198	191	8.7	15	45	2.0	157	7.1	3.23	116	.257	.299	9	11	103	101	3.6	-0	-2	1.0
1984	Pit-N	12	11	.522	33	28	3	1	2	185	179	8.7	19	34	1.7	133	6.5	2.72	124	.256	.285	18	13	94	122	1.4	1	-2	1.2
1985	Pit-N	2	4	.333	37	0	0	0	9	54	57	9.5	7	14	2.3	47	7.8	3.67	102	.275	.314	-0	1	104	117	-0.1	-0	-0	0.0
	Cal-A	7	3	.700	13	13	1	1	0	71	70	8.9	7	24	3.0	53	6.7	3.80	110	.262	.322	3	3	101	108	1.7	0	-1	0.2
1986	Cal-A	10	2	.833	16	16	1	1	0	92	68	6.7	4	26	2.5	81	7.9	2.54	157	.206	.266	17	15	95	81	3.8	0	-0	1.5
1987	Cal-A	8	6	.571	20	20	0	0	0	117	127	9.8	17	20	1.5	74	5.7	4.69	95	.279	.304	-3	-3	100	92	1.5	0	1	-0.1
	NY-N	2	0	1.000	3	3	0	0	0	12	17	12.8	1	3	2.3	10	7.5	6.00	66	.333	.351	-3	-3	97	93	1.0	0	0	-0.2
1988	NY-A	13	7	.650	25	24	6	2	1	157	150	8.6	18	23	1.3	121	6.9	3.38	112	.248	.273	10	7	96	93	2.8	0	0	0.7
Total	14	164	102	.617	398	347	53	13	16	2303	2170	8.5	217	523	2.0	1481	5.8	3.23	117	.250	.290	134	144	101	101	26.8	14	-10	16.0
■ **MILO CANDINI**	Candini, Mario Cain b: 8/3/17, Manteca, Cal. BR/TR, 6', 187 lbs. Deb: 5/01/43																												
1943	Was-A	11	7	.611	28	21	8	3	1	166	144	7.8	3	65	3.5	67	3.6	2.49	135	.238	.308	15	16	102	115	1.4	-1	1	1.8
1944	Was-A	6	7	.462	28	10	4	2	1	103	110	9.6	3	49	4.3	31	2.7	4.11	76	.276	.350	-8	-11	91	100	0.6	3	-0	-0.8
1946	Was-A	2	0	1.000	9	0	0	0	1	22	15	6.1	1	4	1.6	6	2.5	2.05	161	.192	.232	4	3	94	61	1.0	1	-0	0.4
1947	Was-A	3	4	.429	38	2	0	0	1	87	96	9.9	5	35	3.6	31	3.2	5.17	72	.273	.332	-14	-14	101	76	0.1	-0	0	-1.3
1948	Was-A	2	3	.400	35	4	1	0	3	94	96	9.2	1	63	6.0	23	2.2	5.17	89	.267	.372	-9	-6	107	86	0.1	3	0	-0.2
1949	Was-A	0	0	—	3	0	0	0	1	6	4	6.0	0	1	1.5	1	1.5	4.50	90	.200	.238	-0	-0	96	30	0.0	0	-0	0.0
1950	Phi-N	1	0	1.000	18	0	0	0	0	30	32	9.6	2	15	4.5	10	3.0	2.70	147	.281	.362	5	4	96	172	0.5	-0	1	0.4
1951	Phi-N	1	0	1.000	15	0	0	0	0	30	33	9.9	3	18	5.4	14	4.2	6.00	64	.275	.367	-7	-7	97	82	0.5	1	0	-0.5
Total	8	26	21	.553	174	37	13	5	8	538	530	8.9	18	250	4.2	183	3.1	3.91	93	.259	.335	-15	-16	100	99	4.2	6	1	-0.2
■ **TOM CANDIOTTI**	Candiotti, Thomas Caesar b: 8/31/57, Walnut Creek, Cal. BR/TR, 6'3", 205 lbs. Deb: 8/08/83																												
1983	Mil-A	4	4	.500	10	8	2	1	0	56	62	10.0	4	16	2.6	21	3.4	3.21	115	.291	.343	5	3	91	139	-0.2	0	-0	0.3
1984	Mil-A	2	2	.500	8	6	0	0	0	32	38	10.7	5	10	2.8	23	6.5	5.34	69	.277	.327	-5	-6	93	84	0.3	0	-0	-0.5
1986	Cle-A	16	12	.571	36	34	**17**	3	0	252	234	8.4	18	106	3.8	167	6.0	3.57	115	.246	.323	17	15	98	100	1.8	0	3	1.7
1987	Cle-A	7	18	.280	32	32	7	2	0	202	193	8.6	28	93	4.1	111	4.9	4.77	98	.250	.327	-7	-2	105	90	-3.5	0	0	-0.1
1988	Cle-A	14	8	.636	31	31	11	1	0	217	225	9.3	15	53	2.2	137	5.7	3.28	124	.272	.315	17	19	102	116	3.6	0	2	2.2
Total	5	43	44	.494	117	111	37	7	0	759	752	8.9	70	278	3.3	459	5.4	3.85	109	.259	.323	28	28	100	104	2.0	0	5	3.6
■ **JOHN CANEIRA**	Caneira, John Cascaes b: 10/7/52, Waterbury, Conn. BR/TR, 6'3", 180 lbs. Deb: 9/10/77																												
1977	Cal-A	2	2	.500	6	4	0	0	0	29	27	8.4	5	16	5.0	17	5.3	4.03	96	.252	.344	0	-1	95	118	0.2	0	-1	0.0
1978	Cal-A	0	0	—	2	2	0	0	0	8	8	9.0	2	3	3.4	0	0.0	6.75	57	.286	.344	-3	-3	101	86	0.0	0	-0	-0.2
Total	2	2	2	.500	8	6	0	0	0	37	35	8.5	7	19	4.6	17	4.1	4.62	83	.259	.344	-3	-3	96	111	0.2	0	-1	-0.2
■ **JOHN CANGELOSI**	Cangelosi, John Anthony b: 3/10/63, Brooklyn, N.Y. BB/TL, 5'8", 150 lbs. Deb: 6/30/85																												
1988	Pit-N	0	0	—	1	0	0	0	0	2	1	4.5	0	0	0.0	0	0.0	0.00	—	.143	.143	1	1	97	0	0.0	0	0	0.1
■ **GUY CANTRELL**	Cantrell, Guy Dewey "Gunner" b: 4/9/04, Clarita, Okla. d: 1/31/61, Mc Alester, Okla. BR/TR, 6', 190 lbs. Deb: 8/18/25																												
1925	Bro-N	1	0	1.000	14	3	1	0	0	36	42	10.5	0	14	3.5	13	3.3	3.00	135	.294	.354	5	4	95	136	0.5	-1	1	0.4
1927	Bro-N	0	0	—	6	0	0	0	0	10	10	9.0	0	6	5.4	5	4.5	2.70	151	.250	.340	1	2	104	124	0.0	0	0	0.2
	Phi-A	0	2	.000	2	2	2	0	0	18	25	12.5	0	7	3.5	7	3.5	5.00	78	.338	.390	-2	-2	95	107	-0.9	0	0	-0.1
1930	Det-A	1	5	.167	16	2	1	0	0	35	38	9.8	5	20	5.1	20	5.1	5.66	87	.271	.351	-4	-3	106	94	-1.9	-2	1	-0.2
Total	3	2	7	.222	38	7	4	0	0	99	115	10.5	5	47	4.3	45	4.1	4.27	101	.290	.358	1	1	100	115	-2.3	-3	2	0.3
■ **BEN CANTWELL**	Cantwell, Benjamin Caldwell b: 4/13/02, Milan, Tenn. d: 12/4/62, Salem, Mo. BR/TR, 6'1", 168 lbs. Deb: 8/19/27																												
1927	NY-N	1	1	.500	5	2	1	0	0	20	26	11.7	1	2	0.9	6	2.7	4.05	95	.313	.333	-0	-0	98	107	-0.1	0	-0	0.0
1928	NY-N	1	0	1.000	7	1	0	0	1	18	20	10.0	1	4	2.0	0	0.0	4.50	88	.282	.316	-1	-1	99	82	0.5	1	1	0.0
	Bos-N	3	3	.500	22	9	3	0	0	90	112	11.2	7	36	3.6	18	1.8	5.10	79	.304	.363	-11	-11	101	96	0.8	-1	1	-0.9
	Yr	4	3	.571	29	10	3	0	1	108	132	11.0	8	40	3.3	18	1.5	5.00	81	.300	.354	-12	-12	101	96	1.3	1	2	-0.9
1929	Bos-N	4	13	.235	27	20	8	0	2	157	171	9.8	11	52	3.0	25	1.4	4.47	102	.280	.329	4	2	97	94	-3.1	0	4	0.5

YEAR	TM/L	W	L	PCT	G	GS	CG	SHO	SV	IP	H	H/G	HR	BB	BB/G	SO	SO/G	ERA	/A	OAVG	OOBP	PR	/A	PF	CPI	WAT	PB	PD	TPI
1930	Bos-N	9	15	.375	31	21	10	0	2	173	213	11.1	15	45	2.3	43	2.2	4.89	101	.312	.344	2	1	99	103	-2.3	2	4	0.6
1931	Bos-N	7	9	.438	33	16	9	2	2	156	160	9.2	4	34	2.0	32	1.8	3.63	108	.262	.294	4	5	102	81	0.3	0	3	0.8
1932	Bos-N	13	11	.542	37	9	3	1	5	146	133	8.2	6	33	2.0	33	2.0	2.96	122	.247	.290	15	11	93	98	1.2	2	3	1.6
1933	Bos-N	20	10	**.667**	40	29	18	2	2	255	242	8.5	12	54	1.9	57	2.0	2.61	122	.249	.286	21	17	96	105	**4.8**	-1	4	2.1
1934	Bos-N	5	11	.313	27	19	6	1	5	143	163	10.3	8	34	2.1	45	2.8	4.34	81	.285	.321	-4	-13	86	92	-3.3	2	2	-0.9
1935	Bos-N	4	25	.138	39	24	13	0	0	211	235	10.0	15	44	1.9	34	1.5	4.61	87	.282	.313	-14	-14	100	86	-7.1	3	2	-0.7
1936	Bos-N	9	9	.500	34	12	4	0	2	133	127	8.6	8	35	2.4	42	2.8	3.05	127	.252	.299	14	12	96	107	0.7	-1	3	1.4
1937	NY-N	0	1	.000	1	1	0	0	0	4	6	13.5	1	1	2.3	1	2.3	9.00	42	.375	.389	-2	-2	98	90	-0.4	0	0	-0.1
	Bro-N	0	0	—	13	0	0	0	0	27	32	10.7	1	8	2.7	12	4.0	4.67	90	.288	.317	-2	-1	107	86	0.0	-0	2	0.0
	Yr	0	1	.000	14	1	0	0	0	31	38	11.0	2	9	2.6	13	3.8	5.23	79	.299	.326	-5	-4	106	86	-0.4	0	2	-0.1
Total	11	76	108	.413	316	163	75	6	21	1533	1640	9.6	90	382	2.2	348	2.0	3.91	101	.275	.313	25	4	97	96	-8.0	7	28	4.4

■ MIKE CANTWELL Cantwell, Michael Joseph b: 1/15/1896, Washington, D.C. d: 1/5/53, Oteen, N.C. BL/TL, 5'10", 155 lbs. Deb: 9/17/16

YEAR	TM/L	W	L	PCT	G	GS	CG	SHO	SV	IP	H	H/G	HR	BB	BB/G	SO	SO/G	ERA	/A	OAVG	OOBP	PR	/A	PF	CPI	WAT	PB	PD	TPI
1916	NY-A	0	0	—	1	0	0	0	0	2	0	0.0	0	2	9.0	0	0.0	0.00	—	.000	.333	1	1	101	0	0.0	0	0	0.1
1919	Phi-N	1	3	.250	5	3	2	0	0	27	36	12.0	1	9	3.0	6	2.0	5.67	56	.343	.395	-8	-8	109	100	-0.5	-0	-1	-0.7
1920	Phi-N	0	3	.000	5	1	0	0	0	23	25	9.8	1	15	5.9	8	3.1	3.91	90	.284	.387	-2	-1	112	125	-1.4	-1	0	0.0
Total	3	1	6	.143	11	4	2	0	0	52	61	10.6	2	26	4.5	14	2.4	4.67	71	.310	.390	-10	-8	110	107	-1.9	-1	-0	-0.6

■ TOM CANTWELL Cantwell, Thomas Aloysius b: 12/23/1888, Washington, D.C. d: 4/1/68, Washington, D.C. BL/TR, 6', 170 lbs. Deb: 09

YEAR	TM/L	W	L	PCT	G	GS	CG	SHO	SV	IP	H	H/G	HR	BB	BB/G	SO	SO/G	ERA	/A	OAVG	OOBP	PR	/A	PF	CPI	WAT	PB	PD	TPI
1909	Cin-N	1	0	1.000	6	1	1	0	0	22	16	6.5	0	7	2.9	7	2.9	1.64	149	.205	.279	2	2	94	98	0.5	1	-0	0.2
1910	Cin-N	0	0	—	2	0	0	0	0	1	2	18.0	0	3	27.0	0	0.0	18.00	17	.400	.625	-2	-2	102	82	0.0	0	0	-0.1
Total	2	1	0	1.000	8	1	1	0	0	23	18	7.0	0	10	3.9	7	2.7	2.35	105	.217	.309	1	0	94	98	0.5	1	-0	0.1

■ MIKE CAPEL Capel, Michael Lee b: 10/13/61, Marshall, Tex. BR/TR, 6'1", 175 lbs. Deb: 5/07/88

YEAR	TM/L	W	L	PCT	G	GS	CG	SHO	SV	IP	H	H/G	HR	BB	BB/G	SO	SO/G	ERA	/A	OAVG	OOBP	PR	/A	PF	CPI	WAT	PB	PD	TPI
1988	Chi-N	2	1	.667	22	0	0	0	0	29	34	10.6	5	13	4.0	19	5.9	4.97	73	.293	.373	-5	-4	105	119	0.6	-0	-0	-0.4

■ DOUG CAPILLA Capilla, Douglas Edmund b: 1/7/52, Honolulu, Hawaii BL/TL, 5'11", 160 lbs. Deb: 9/12/76

YEAR	TM/L	W	L	PCT	G	GS	CG	SHO	SV	IP	H	H/G	HR	BB	BB/G	SO	SO/G	ERA	/A	OAVG	OOBP	PR	/A	PF	CPI	WAT	PB	PD	TPI
1976	StL-N	1	0	1.000	7	0	0	0	0	8	8	9.0	0	4	4.5	5	5.6	5.63	65	.242	.324	-2	-2	105	50	0.5	0	0	-0.1
1977	StL-N	0	0	—	2	0	0	0	0	2	2	9.0	0	2	9.0	1	4.5	18.00	21	.222	.364	-3	-3	95	18	0.0	0	0	-0.2
	Cin-N	7	8	.467	22	16	1	0	0	106	94	8.0	10	59	5.0	74	6.3	4.25	91	.237	.336	-4	-4	99	89	-1.0	-3	-1	-0.7
	Yr	7	8	.467	24	16	1	0	0	108	96	8.0	10	61	5.1	75	6.3	4.50	86	.236	.337	-7	-8	99	89	-1.0	0	-1	-0.9
1978	Cin-N	0	1	.000	6	3	0	0	0	11	14	11.5	1	11	9.0	9	7.4	9.82	37	.318	.439	-8	-8	102	73	-0.4	-0	-0	-0.7
1979	Cin-N	1	0	1.000	5	0	0	0	0	6	7	10.5	1	5	7.5	0	0.0	9.00	40	.269	.406	-4	-4	96	68	0.5	0	0	-0.2
	Chi-N	0	1	.000	13	1	0	0	0	17	14	7.4	1	7	3.7	10	5.3	2.65	159	.206	.273	2	3	112	75	-0.4	0	0	0.3
	Yr	1	1	.500	18	1	0	0	0	23	21	8.2	2	12	4.7	10	3.9	4.30	94	.221	.303	-1	-1	108	75	0.1	0	0	0.1
1980	Chi-N	2	8	.200	39	11	0	0	0	90	82	8.2	7	51	5.1	51	5.1	4.10	95	.253	.351	-5	-2	108	104	-2.4	0	1	0.0
1981	Chi-N	1	0	1.000	42	0	0	0	0	51	52	9.2	1	34	6.0	28	4.9	3.18	117	.284	.391	2	3	106	155	0.5	-0	0	0.3
Total	6	12	18	.400	136	31	1	0	0	291	273	8.4	21	173	5.4	178	5.5	4.36	88	.252	.353	-21	-16	104	102	-2.7	-2	0	-1.3

■ GEORGE CAPPUZZELLO Cappuzzello, George Angelo b: 1/15/54, Youngstown, Ohio BR/TL, 6', 175 lbs. Deb: 5/31/81

YEAR	TM/L	W	L	PCT	G	GS	CG	SHO	SV	IP	H	H/G	HR	BB	BB/G	SO	SO/G	ERA	/A	OAVG	OOBP	PR	/A	PF	CPI	WAT	PB	PD	TPI
1981	Det-A	1	1	.500	18	3	0	0	1	34	28	7.4	2	18	4.8	19	5.0	3.44	112	.222	.329	1	2	105	94	0.0	0	-0	0.1
1982	Hou-N	0	1	.000	17	0	0	0	0	19	16	7.6	2	7	3.3	13	6.2	2.84	126	.232	.321	2	2	100	130	-0.4	-0	0	0.2
Total	2	1	2	.333	35	3	0	0	1	53	44	7.5	4	25	4.2	32	5.4	3.23	116	.226	.326	2	3	103	107	-0.4	-0	0	0.3

■ BUZZ CAPRA Capra, Lee William b: 10/1/47, Chicago, Ill. BR/TR, 5'10", 168 lbs. Deb: 9/15/71

YEAR	TM/L	W	L	PCT	G	GS	CG	SHO	SV	IP	H	H/G	HR	BB	BB/G	SO	SO/G	ERA	/A	OAVG	OOBP	PR	/A	PF	CPI	WAT	PB	PD	TPI
1971	NY-N	0	1	.000	3	0	0	0	0	5	3	5.4	0	5	9.0	6	10.8	9.00	37	.167	.333	-3	-3	96	28	-0.4	-0	0	-0.2
1972	NY-N	3	2	.600	14	6	0	0	0	53	50	8.5	7	27	4.6	45	7.6	4.58	72	.253	.339	-7	-7	96	94	0.4	1	1	-0.4
1973	NY-N	2	7	.222	24	0	0	0	4	42	35	7.5	4	28	6.0	35	7.5	3.86	95	.233	.346	-1	-1	100	108	-2.5	0	0	0.0
1974	Atl-N	16	8	.667	39	27	11	5	1	217	163	**6.8**	13	84	3.5	137	5.7	**2.28**	**165**	**.208**	.282	33	36	104	103	3.6	0	-3	3.6
1975	Atl-N	4	7	.364	12	12	5	0	0	78	77	8.9	8	28	3.2	35	4.0	4.27	83	.257	.315	-6	-6	97	87	-0.6	-2	0	-0.7
1976	Atl-N	0	1	.000	5	0	0	0	0	9	9	9.0	0	6	6.0	4	4.0	9.00	44	.265	.341	-5	-5	112	45	-0.4	0	0	-0.4
1977	Atl-N	6	11	.353	45	16	0	0	0	139	142	9.2	28	80	5.2	100	6.5	5.37	84	.263	.357	-23	-13	115	99	-0.5	-2	-0	-1.4
Total	7	31	37	.456	142	61	16	5	5	543	479	7.9	60	258	4.3	362	6.0	3.88	99	.237	.320	-12	-1	105	98	-0.4	-2	-1	0.5

■ PAT CARAWAY Caraway, Cecil Bradford Patrick b: 9/26/05, Erath Co., Tex. d: 6/9/74, El Paso, Tex. BL/TL, 6'4", 175 lbs. Deb: 4/19/30

YEAR	TM/L	W	L	PCT	G	GS	CG	SHO	SV	IP	H	H/G	HR	BB	BB/G	SO	SO/G	ERA	/A	OAVG	OOBP	PR	/A	PF	CPI	WAT	PB	PD	TPI
1930	Chi-A	10	10	.500	38	21	9	1	1	193	194	9.0	11	57	2.7	83	3.9	3.87	126	.267	.313	17	22	105	100	1.8	-2	3	2.1
1931	Chi-A	10	24	.294	51	32	11	1	2	220	268	11.0	17	101	4.1	55	2.3	6.22	67	.295	.363	-45	-49	96	85	-4.0	-0	-1	-4.5
1932	Chi-A	2	6	.250	19	9	1	0	0	65	80	11.1	6	37	5.1	13	1.8	6.78	60	.304	.391	-17	-20	91	89	-0.9	-1	0	-1.7
Total	3	22	40	.355	108	62	21	2	3	478	542	10.2	34	195	3.7	151	2.8	5.35	83	.286	.348	-45	-48	99	92	-3.1	-3	2	-4.1

■ JOHN CARDEN Carden, John Bruton b: 5/19/21, Killeen, Tex. d: 2/8/49, Mexia, Tex. BR/TR, 6'5", 210 lbs. Deb: 5/18/46

YEAR	TM/L	W	L	PCT	G	GS	CG	SHO	SV	IP	H	H/G	HR	BB	BB/G	SO	SO/G	ERA	/A	OAVG	OOBP	PR	/A	PF	CPI	WAT	PB	PD	TPI
1946	NY-N	0	0	—	1	0	0	0	0	2	4	18.0	0	4	18.0	1	4.5	22.50	16	.400	.600	-4	-4	103	60	0.0	0	-0	-0.3

■ CONRAD CARDINAL Cardinal, Conrad Seth b: 3/30/42, Brooklyn, N.Y. BR/TR, 6'1", 190 lbs. Deb: 4/11/63

YEAR	TM/L	W	L	PCT	G	GS	CG	SHO	SV	IP	H	H/G	HR	BB	BB/G	SO	SO/G	ERA	/A	OAVG	OOBP	PR	/A	PF	CPI	WAT	PB	PD	TPI
1963	Hou-N	0	1	.000	6	1	0	0	0	13	15	10.4	0	7	4.8	7	4.8	6.23	50	.283	.349	-4	-4	95	67	-0.4	-0	0	-0.4

■ BEN CARDONI Cardoni, Armand Joseph "Big Ben" b: 8/21/20, Jessup, Pa. d: 4/2/69, Jessup, Pa. BR/TR, 6'3", 195 lbs. Deb: 8/22/43

YEAR	TM/L	W	L	PCT	G	GS	CG	SHO	SV	IP	H	H/G	HR	BB	BB/G	SO	SO/G	ERA	/A	OAVG	OOBP	PR	/A	PF	CPI	WAT	PB	PD	TPI
1943	Bos-N	0	0	—	11	0	0	0	1	28	38	12.2	1	14	4.5	5	1.6	6.43	57	.336	.405	-10	-9	109	93	0.0	-1	0	-0.9
1944	Bos-N	0	6	.000	22	5	1	0	0	76	83	9.8	5	37	4.4	24	2.8	3.91	89	.284	.355	-2	-4	96	121	-2.9	0	-1	-0.4
1945	Bos-N	0	0	—	3	0	0	0	0	4	6	13.5	0	3	6.8	5	11.3	9.00	48	.300	.417	-2	-2	113	66	0.0	0	0	-0.1
Total	3	0	6	.000	36	5	1	0	1	108	127	10.6	6	54	4.5	34	2.8	4.75	75	.299	.371	-14	-14	100	111	-2.9	-1	-1	-1.4

■ DON CARDWELL Cardwell, Donald Eugene b: 12/7/35, Winston-Salem, N.C. BR/TR, 6'4", 210 lbs. Deb: 4/21/57

YEAR	TM/L	W	L	PCT	G	GS	CG	SHO	SV	IP	H	H/G	HR	BB	BB/G	SO	SO/G	ERA	/A	OAVG	OOBP	PR	/A	PF	CPI	WAT	PB	PD	TPI
1957	Phi-N	4	8	.333	30	19	5	1	1	128	122	8.6	17	42	3.0	92	6.5	4.92	78	.251	.311	-15	-15	99	78	-2.0	1	0	-1.3
1958	Phi-N	3	6	.333	16	14	3	0	0	108	99	8.3	16	37	3.1	77	6.4	4.50	88	.241	.305	-7	-7	100	81	-1.1	1	0	-0.5
1959	Phi-N	9	10	.474	25	22	5	1	0	153	135	7.9	22	65	3.8	106	6.2	4.06	99	.238	.314	-2	-1	102	96	1.1	-3	-3	-0.5
1960	Phi-N	1	2	.333	5	4	0	0	0	28	28	9.0	4	11	3.5	21	6.8	4.50	92	.262	.333	-2	-1	110	99	-0.1	2	-0	0.1
	Chi-N	8	14	.364	31	26	6	1	0	177	166	8.4	19	68	3.5	129	6.6	4.37	87	.249	.317	-12	-12	101	88	-0.7	3	-1	-0.9
	Yr	9	16	.360	36	30	6	1	0	205	194	8.5	23	79	3.5	150	6.6	4.39	87	.250	.318	-14	-13	102	88	-0.8	2	-2	-0.8
1961	Chi-N	15	14	.517	39	38	13	3	0	259	243	8.4	22	88	3.1	156	5.4	3.82	107	.246	.308	6	8	102	89	3.0	-1	2	0.9
1962	Chi-N	7	16	.304	41	29	6	1	4	196	205	9.4	27	60	2.8	104	4.8	4.91	87	.267	.323	-21	-14	109	87	-2.0	-1	1	-1.2
1963	Pit-N	13	15	.464	33	32	7	2	0	214	195	8.2	21	52	2.2	112	4.7	3.07	106	.245	.298	5	4	99	110	0.2	-2	-1	0.2
1964	Pit-N	1	2	.333	4	4	1	1	0	19	15	7.1	1	7	3.3	10	4.7	2.84	125	.217	.305	1	2	101	105	-0.4	-0	0	0.2
1965	Pit-N	13	10	.565	37	34	12	2	0	240	214	8.0	21	59	2.2	107	4.0	3.19	109	.239	.291	9	8	98	98	0.3	3	2	1.4
1966	Pit-N	6	6	.500	32	14	1	0	1	102	112	9.9	15	27	2.4	60	5.3	4.59	78	.282	.333	-11	-12	99	102	-0.7	-1	2	-0.9
1967	NY-N	5	9	.357	26	16	3	3	0	118	112	8.5	8	39	3.0	71	5.4	3.58	96	.249	.317	-3	-2	102	96	-0.3	2	2	0.2
1968	NY-N	7	13	.350	29	25	5	1	1	180	156	7.8	9	50	2.5	82	4.1	2.95	104	.233	.289	1	2	103	92	-2.4	-4	2	0.1
1969	NY-N	8	10	.444	30	21	4	0	0	152	145	8.6	15	47	2.8	60	3.6	3.02	118	.252	.310	10	9	99	119	-2.6	1	2	1.3
1970	NY-N	0	2	.000	16	1	0	0	0	25	31	11.2	3	6	2.2	8	2.9	6.48	65	.316	.357	-7	-6	103	88	-0.9	-1	0	-0.6
	Atl-N	2	1	.667	16	2	1	1	0	23	31	12.1	5	13	5.1	16	6.3	9.00	47	.326	.405	-13	-12	105	81	0.6	1	1	-1.0
	Yr	2	3	.400	32	3	1	1	0	48	62	11.6	8	19	3.6	24	4.5	7.69	55	.312	.368	-19	-19	104	82	-0.3	-1	1	-1.6
Total	14	102	138	.425	410	301	72	17	7	2122	2009	8.5	225	671	2.8	1211	5.1	3.92	95	.250	.310	-60	-48	101	95	-8.0	2	10	-2.5

■ TEX CARLETON Carleton, James Otto b: 8/19/06, Comanche, Tex. d: 1/11/77, Fort Worth, Tex. BB/TR, 6'1.5", 180 lbs. Deb: 4/17/32

YEAR	TM/L	W	L	PCT	G	GS	CG	SHO	SV	IP	H	H/G	HR	BB	BB/G	SO	SO/G	ERA	/A	OAVG	OOBP	PR	/A	PF	CPI	WAT	PB	PD	TPI
1932	StL-N	10	13	.435	44	22	9	3	0	196	198	9.1	12	70	3.2	113	5.2	4.09	96	.261	.321	-5	-4	101	90	-0.8	-2	2	-0.2
1933	StL-N	17	11	.607	44	33	15	4	3	277	263	8.5	15	97	3.2	147	4.8	3.38	99	.249	.312	-1	-1	100	95	2.5	2	-1	0.0
1934	StL-N	16	11	.593	40	31	16	0	2	241	260	9.7	14	52	1.9	103	3.8	4.26	106	.271	.311	-5	7	111	85	-0.6	0	0	0.8
1935	Chi-N	11	8	.579	31	22	8	0	1	171	169	8.9	17	60	3.2	84	4.4	3.89	98	.257	.316	2	-1	95	101	-1.1	-3	2	-0.1
1936	Chi-N	14	10	.583	35	26	12	4	1	197	204	9.3	14	67	3.1	88	4.0	3.65	112	.268	.327	8	10	102	108	0.6	6	2	1.8
1937	Chi-N	16	8	.667	32	27	18	4	0	208	183	7.9	10	94	4.1	105	4.5	3.16	124	.236	.316	17	18	100	103	2.2	1	1	2.0

YEAR	TM/L	W	L	PCT	G	GS	CG	SHO	SV	IP	H	H/G	HR	BB	BB/G	SO	SO/G	ERA	/A	OAVG	OOBP	PR	/A	PF	CPI	WAT	PB	PD	TPI
1938	Chi-N	10	9	.526	33	24	9	0	0	168	213	11.4	11	74	4.0	80	4.3	5.41	72	.307	.376	-30	-28	103	99	-1.0	3	0	-2.4
1940	Bro-N	6	6	.500	34	17	4	1	2	149	140	8.5	12	47	2.8	88	5.3	3.81	108	.245	.304	1	5	106	90	-0.7	-0	-1	0.4
Total	8	100	76	.568	293	202	91	16	9	1607	1630	9.1	105	561	3.1	808	4.5	3.91	101	.261	.322	-13	4	102	96	1.1	6	6	2.3
■ **CISCO CARLOS**	Carlos, Francisco Manuel b: 9/17/40, Monrovia, Cal. BR/TR, 6'3", 205 lbs. Deb: 8/25/67																												
1967	Chi-A	2	0	1.000	8	7	1	1	0	42	23	4.9	0	9	1.9	27	5.8	0.86	351	.161	.209	11	10	93	69	1.0	-1	0	1.1
1968	Chi-A	4	14	.222	29	21	0	0	0	122	121	8.9	13	37	2.7	57	4.2	3.91	78	.258	.321	-13	-12	102	101	-4.3	-1	2	-1.1
1969	Chi-A	4	3	.571	25	4	0	0	0	49	52	9.6	4	23	4.2	28	5.1	5.69	70	.274	.362	-11	-9	110	81	0.9	-1	1	-0.9
	Was-A	1	1	.500	6	4	0	0	0	18	23	11.5	2	6	3.0	5	2.5	4.50	78	.348	.377	-2	-2	96	138	0.0	1	0	0.0
	Yr	5	4	.556	31	8	0	0	0	67	75	10.1	6	29	3.9	33	4.4	5.37	72	.287	.349	-13	-11	106	138	0.9	-1	1	-0.9
1970	Was-A	0	0	—	5	0	0	0	0	6	3	4.5	0	4	6.0	2	3.0	1.50	240	.150	.280	1	1	97	99	0.0	0	0	0.2
Total	4	11	18	.379	73	36	1	1	0	237	222	8.4	19	79	3.0	119	4.5	3.72	88	.250	.315	-13	-12	101	94	-2.4	-3	4	-0.7
■ **DON CARLSEN**	Carlsen, Donald Herbert b: 10/15/26, Chicago, Ill. BR/TR, 6'1", 175 lbs. Deb: 4/28/48																												
1948	Chi-N	0	0	—	1	0	0	0	0	1	5	45.0	0	2	18.0	1	9.0	36.00	10	.625	.700	-4	-4	95	75	0.0	0	0	-0.2
1951	Pit-N	2	3	.400	7	6	2	0	0	43	50	10.5	4	14	2.9	20	4.2	4.19	104	.292	.344	-1	1	110	112	0.0	0	-1	0.0
1952	Pit-N	0	1	.000	5	1	0	0	0	10	20	18.0	1	5	4.5	2	1.8	10.80	36	.417	.472	-8	-8	105	86	-0.4	0	1	-0.5
Total	3	2	4	.333	13	7	2	0	0	54	75	12.5	5	21	3.5	23	3.8	6.00	71	.330	.385	-13	-11	108	106	-0.4	0	0	-0.7
■ **HAL CARLSON**	Carlson, Harold Gust b: 5/17/1892, Rockford, Ill. d: 5/28/30, Chicago, Ill. BR/TR, 6', 180 lbs. Deb: 4/13/17																												
1917	Pit-N	7	11	.389	34	17	9	1	1	161	140	7.8	0	49	2.7	68	3.8	2.91	96	.241	.294	-3	-2	103	85	0.9	-2	2	-0.2
1918	Pit-N	0	1	.000	3	2	0	0	0	12	12	9.0	1	5	3.8	5	3.8	3.75	77	.286	.347	-1	-1	105	118	-0.4	-0	-0	-0.1
1919	Pit-N	8	10	.444	22	14	7	1	0	141	114	7.3	0	39	2.5	49	3.1	2.23	137	.243	.292	11	13	105	113	-1.2	-1	1	1.5
1920	Pit-N	14	13	.519	39	31	16	3	3	247	262	9.5	4	63	2.3	62	2.3	3.35	95	.281	.322	-6	-5	101	96	0.2	3	-5	-0.6
1921	Pit-N	4	8	.333	31	10	3	0	4	110	121	9.9	6	23	1.9	37	3.0	4.25	90	.290	.317	-6	-5	102	88	-2.6	1	1	-0.2
1922	Pit-N	9	12	.429	39	18	6	0	2	145	193	12.0	10	58	3.6	64	4.0	5.71	73	.323	.373	-26	-25	101	94	-2.5	3	2	-1.7
1923	Pit-N	0	0	—	4	0	0	0	0	13	19	13.2	2	2	1.4	4	2.8	4.85	79	.358	.373	-1	-1	95	137	0.0	-0	0	-0.1
1924	Phi-N	8	17	.320	38	24	12	1	2	204	267	11.8	9	55	2.4	66	2.9	4.85	88	.329	.363	-22	-13	111	105	-1.7	2	0	-0.8
1925	Phi-N	13	14	.481	35	32	18	**4**	0	234	281	10.8	19	52	2.0	80	3.1	4.23	119	.298	.331	1	21	118	103	1.1	-3	-1	1.7
1926	Phi-N	17	12	.586	35	34	20	3	0	267	293	9.9	9	47	1.6	55	1.9	3.24	127	.281	.308	17	25	107	104	5.5	3	-4	2.6
1927	Phi-N	4	5	.444	11	9	4	0	1	64	80	11.3	7	18	2.5	13	1.8	5.20	75	.316	.350	-9	-9	100	101	0.8	0	-1	-0.8
	Chi-N	12	8	.600	27	22	15	2	0	184	201	9.8	9	27	1.3	27	1.3	3.18	121	.280	.301	15	14	99	107	1.1	-3	0	1.1
	Yr	16	13	.552	38	31	19	2	1	248	281	10.2	16	45	1.6	40	1.5	3.70	105	.289	.314	6	5	99	107	1.9	0	-1	0.3
1928	Chi-N	3	2	.600	20	5	2	0	4	56	74	11.9	4	15	2.4	11	1.8	5.95	62	.329	.357	-12	-14	93	87	0.1	0	0	-1.2
1929	Chi-N	11	5	.688	31	14	6	2	2	112	131	10.5	8	31	2.5	35	2.8	5.14	90	.292	.331	-5	-7	98	85	1.1	1	2	-0.3
1930	Chi-N	4	2	.667	8	6	3	0	0	52	68	11.8	5	14	2.4	14	2.4	5.02	102	.313	.353	-0	1	103	102	0.6	-0	1	0.2
Total	14	114	120	.487	377	238	121	17	19	2002	2256	10.1	93	498	2.2	590	2.7	3.97	99	.291	.327	-49	-10	105	99	3.0	4	-0	1.1
■ **LEON CARLSON**	Carlson, Leon Alton "Swede" b: 2/17/1895, Jamestown, N.Y. d: 9/15/61, Jamestown, N.Y. BR/TR, 6'3", 195 lbs. Deb: 5/31/20 C																												
1920	Was-A	0	0	—	3	0	0	0	0	12	14	10.5	1	2	1.5	3	2.3	3.75	98	.292	.320	0	-0	96	100	0.0	-0	-0	0.0
■ **STEVE CARLTON**	Carlton, Steven Norman "Lefty" b: 12/22/44, Miami, Fla. BL/TL, 6'4", 210 lbs. Deb: 4/12/65																												
1965	StL-N	0	0	—	15	2	0	0	0	25	27	9.7	3	8	2.9	21	7.6	2.52	149	.287	.346	3	3	106	191	0.0	-0	1	0.4
1966	StL-N	3	3	.500	9	9	2	1	0	52	56	9.7	2	18	3.1	25	4.3	3.12	116	.280	.332	3	3	100	124	0.0	1	0	0.4
1967	StL-N	14	9	.609	30	28	11	2	1	193	173	8.1	10	62	2.9	168	7.8	2.98	112	.238	.296	8	8	99	97	-0.3	1	0	0.9
1968	StL-N	13	11	.542	34	33	10	5	0	232	214	8.3	11	61	2.4	162	6.3	2.99	93	.246	.291	-0	-5	93	95	-1.2	2	-1	-0.4
1969	StL-N	17	11	.607	31	31	12	2	0	236	185	7.1	15	93	3.5	210	8.0	2.17	164	.216	.291	37	36	99	**122**	2.5	5	-1	4.5
1970	StL-N	10	19	.345	34	33	13	2	0	254	239	8.5	25	109	3.9	193	6.8	3.72	116	.251	.322	9	16	106	106	-4.3	2	-1	1.8
1971	StL-N	20	9	.690	37	36	18	4	0	273	275	9.1	23	98	3.2	172	5.7	3.56	98	.262	.323	-3	-3	100	106	5.0	1	-0	-0.1
1972	Phi-N	**27**	10	.730	41	41	**30**	8	0	**346**	257	6.7	17	87	2.3	**310**	8.1	**1.98**	**173**	.206	.255	**57**	**55**	99	94	**11.7**	5	-2	**6.8**
1973	Phi-N	13	20	.394	40	40	**18**	3	0	**293**	293	9.0	29	113	3.5	223	6.8	3.90	102	.260	.324	-8	3	109	100	-1.9	-0	-1	0.3
1974	Phi-N	16	13	.552	39	39	17	1	0	291	249	7.7	21	136	4.2	**240**	7.4	3.22	117	.234	.318	13	18	104	103	2.0	2	-1	2.0
1975	Phi-N	15	14	.517	37	37	14	3	0	255	217	7.7	24	104	3.7	192	6.8	3.56	103	.233	.304	2	3	101	92	-0.4	-0	-1	0.2
1976	Phi-N	20	7	**.741**	35	35	13	2	0	253	224	8.0	19	72	2.6	195	6.9	3.13	117	.237	.288	11	15	105	92	4.7	2	-4	1.5
1977	Phi-N	**23**	10	.697	36	36	17	2	0	283	229	7.3	25	89	2.8	198	6.3	2.64	146	.223	.284	40	38	98	104	3.9	9	1	5.2
1978	Phi-N	16	13	.552	34	34	12	3	0	247	228	8.3	30	63	2.3	161	5.9	2.84	131	.246	.292	20	24	104	121	0.0	7	1	3.6
1979	Phi-N	18	11	.621	35	35	13	4	0	251	202	7.2	25	89	3.2	213	7.6	3.62	101	.219	.288	3	1	97	78	3.6	4	-1	0.3
1980	Phi-N	**24**	9	.727	38	38	13	3	0	**304**	243	7.2	15	90	2.7	**286**	8.5	2.34	**164**	.218	.273	**43**	**51**	106	96	**7.1**	-1	-1	**5.7**
1981	Phi-N	13	4	.765	24	24	10	1	0	190	152	7.2	9	62	2.9	179	**8.5**	2.42	162	.222	.282	23	**31**	112	103	4.4	-1	-1	**3.5**
1982	Phi-N	**23**	11	.676	38	38	**19**	**6**	0	**296**	253	7.7	17	86	2.6	**286**	8.7	3.10	109	.232	.285	17	9	94	86	5.6	5	-1	1.3
1983	Phi-N	15	16	.484	37	37	8	3	0	**284**	277	8.8	20	84	2.7	**275**	**8.7**	3.11	117	.258	.308	17	17	100	110	-2.3	3	-1	1.9
1984	Phi-N	13	7	.650	33	33	1	0	0	229	214	8.4	14	79	3.1	163	6.4	3.58	102	.246	.304	0	2	101	89	3.3	2	-3	0.1
1985	Phi-N	1	8	.111	16	16	0	0	0	92	84	8.2	6	53	5.2	48	4.7	3.33	111	.249	.342	3	4	102	119	-3.4	0	1	0.5
1986	Phi-N	4	8	.333	16	16	0	0	0	83	102	11.1	15	45	4.9	62	6.7	6.18	63	.297	.374	-23	-21	104	97	-2.3	1	-1	-2.0
	SF-N	1	3	.250	6	6	0	0	0	30	36	10.8	4	16	4.8	18	5.4	5.10	69	.303	.379	-5	-5	95	115	-0.9	1	1	-0.3
	Yr	5	11	.313	22	22	0	0	0	113	138	11.0	19	61	4.9	80	6.4	5.89	64	.297	.375	-27	-27	102	115	-3.2	1	-0	-2.3
	Chi-A	4	3	.571	10	10	0	0	0	63	58	8.3	6	25	3.6	40	5.7	3.71	114	.252	.320	3	4	101	104	0.8	0	-0	0.3
1987	Cle-A	5	9	.357	23	14	3	0	1	109	111	9.2	17	63	5.2	71	5.9	5.37	87	.266	.357	-11	-8	105	97	-0.3	0	-0	-0.8
	Min-A	1	5	.167	9	7	0	0	0	43	54	11.3	7	23	4.8	20	4.2	6.70	64	.310	.395	-11	-11	96	96	-2.0	0	0	-0.9
	Yr	6	14	.300	32	21	3	0	1	152	165	9.8	24	86	5.1	91	5.4	5.74	80	.276	.365	-21	-20	102	96	-2.3	0	-0	-1.7
1988	Min-A	0	1	.000	4	1	0	0	0	10	20	18.0	5	5	4.5	5	4.5	16.20	26	.408	.463	-14	-13	105	75	-0.4	0	0	-1.1
Total	24	329	244	.574	741	709	254	55	2	5217	4672	8.1	414	1833	3.2	4136	7.1	3.22	115	.240	.302	240	271	101	100	34.9	51	-16	35.6
■ **DON CARMAN**	Carman, Donald Wayne b: 8/14/59, Oklahoma City, Okla BL/TL, 6'3", 195 lbs. Deb: 10/01/83																												
1983	Phi-N	0	0	—	1	0	0	0	1	1	0	0.0	0	0	0.0	0	0.0	0.00	—	.000	.000	0	0	100	0	0.0	0	0	0.0
1984	Phi-N	0	1	.000	11	0	0	0	0	13	14	9.7	2	6	4.2	16	11.1	5.54	66	.255	.328	-3	-3	101	77	-0.4	-0	-0	-0.2
1985	Phi-N	9	4	.692	71	0	0	0	7	86	52	5.4	6	38	4.0	87	9.1	2.09	176	.178	.269	14	15	102	100	2.9	-0	0	1.6
1986	Phi-N	10	5	.667	50	14	2	1	1	134	113	7.6	11	52	3.5	98	6.6	3.22	120	.234	.308	7	10	104	103	2.3	-3	2	0.9
1987	Phi-N	13	11	.542	35	35	3	2	0	211	194	8.3	34	69	2.9	125	5.3	4.22	101	.244	.302	-3	1	105	93	1.3	-3	-3	-0.4
1988	Phi-N	10	14	.417	36	32	2	0	0	201	211	9.4	20	70	3.1	116	5.2	4.30	83	.270	.326	-19	-17	103	98	0.3	-5	-3	-2.4
Total	6	42	35	.545	204	81	7	3	9	646	584	8.1	73	235	3.3	442	6.2	3.78	103	.242	.307	-3	7	104	97	6.4	-12	-4	-0.5
■ **CHET CARMICHAEL**	Carmichael, Chester Keller b: 1/9/1888, Muncie, Ind. d: 8/22/60, Rochester, N.Y. BR/TR, 5'11.5", 200 lbs. Deb: 09																												
1909	Cin-N	0	0	—	2	0	0	0	0	7	9	11.6	0	3	3.9	2	2.6	0.00	—	.321	.424	2	2	94	0	0.0	-0	-0	0.2
■ **EDDIE CARNETT**	Carnett, Edwin Elliott "Lefty" b: 10/21/16, Springfield, Mo. BL/TL, 6', 185 lbs. Deb: 4/19/41																												
1941	Bos-N	0	0	—	2	0	0	0	0	1	4	36.0	0	3	27.0	2	18.0	27.00	13	.500	.636	-3	-3	96	84	0.0	0	0	-0.2
1944	Chi-A	0	0	—	2	0	0	0	0	2	3	13.5	1	0	0.0	1	4.5	9.00	39	.333	.333	-1	-1	102	89	0.0	1	0	0.0
1945	Cle-A	0	0	—	2	0	0	0	0	2	0	0.0	0	0	0.0	1	4.5	0.00	—	.000	.000	1	1	98	0	0.0	0	0	0.1
Total	3	0	0	—	6	0	0	0	0	5	7	12.6	1	3	5.4	4	7.2	9.00	38	.304	.385	-3	-3	99	53	0.0	1	0	-0.1
■ **PAT CARNEY**	Carney, Patrick Joseph "Doc" b: 8/7/1876, Holyoke, Mass. d: 1/9/53, Worcester, Mass. BL/TL, 6', 200 lbs. Deb: 9/20/01																												
1902	Bos-N	0	1	.000	2	1	0	0	0	5	6	10.8	1	3	5.4	3	5.4	9.00	29	.322	.416	-3	-4	94	69	-0.4	1	-0	-0.2
1903	Bos-N	4	5	.444	10	9	9	0	0	78	93	10.7	2	31	3.6	29	3.3	4.04	80	.323	.393	-7	-7	98	108	0.2	2	-0	-0.6
1904	Bos-N	0	4	.000	4	2	1	0	0	26	40	13.8	1	12	4.2	5	1.7	5.88	47	.383	.451	-9	-9	102	110	-1.9	0	-0	-0.7
Total	3	4	10	.286	16	12	10	0	0	109	139	11.5	4	46	3.8	37	3.1	4.71	66	.338	.409	-19	-20	99	107	-2.1	2	-1	-1.5
■ **CRIS CARPENTER**	Carpenter, Cris Howell b: 4/5/65, St.Augustine, Fla. BR/TR, 6'1", 185 lbs. Deb: 5/14/88																												
1988	StL-N	2	3	.400	8	8	1	0	0	48	56	10.5	3	9	1.7	24	4.5	4.69	77	.298	.325	-7	-6	105	91	-0.3	-0	-0	-0.6

YEAR	TM/L	W	L	PCT	G	GS	CG	SHO	SV	IP	H	H/G	HR	BB	BB/G	SO	SO/G	ERA	/A	OAVG	OOBP	PR	/A	PF	CPI	WAT	PB	PD	TPI
■ **LEW CARPENTER**	Carpenter, Lewis Emmett b: 8/16/13, Woodstock, Ga. d: 4/25/79, Marietta, Ga. BR/TR, 6'2", 195 lbs. Deb: 5/01/43																												
1943	Was-A	0	0	—	4	0	0	0	0	3	1	3.0	0	4	12.0	1	3.0	0.00	—	.125	.462	1	1	102	0	0.0	0	0	0.1
■ **PAUL CARPENTER**	Carpenter, Paul Calvin b: 8/12/1894, Granville, Ohio d: 3/14/68, Newark, Ohio BR/TR, 5'11", 165 lbs. Deb: 7/26/16																												
1916	Pit-N	0	0	—	5	0	0	0	0	8	8	9.0	0	4	4.5	5	5.6	1.13	249	.258	.333	1	1	107	290	0.0	-0	0	0.1
■ **BOB CARPENTER**	Carpenter, Robert Louis b: 12/12/17, Chicago, Ill. BR/TR, 6'3", 195 lbs. Deb: 9/12/40																												
1940	NY-N	2	0	1.000	5	3	2	0	0	33	29	7.9	2	14	3.8	25	6.8	2.73	141	.238	.314	4	4	100	124	1.0	-0	0	0.4
1941	NY-N	11	6	.647	29	19	8	1	2	132	138	9.4	15	42	2.9	42	2.9	3.82	99	.265	.321	-3	-1	104	107	2.9	-0	-2	-0.2
1942	NY-N	11	10	.524	28	25	12	2	0	186	192	9.3	13	51	2.5	53	2.6	3.15	107	.263	.309	3	4	101	112	-0.7	-1	-3	0.1
1946	NY-N	1	3	.250	12	6	1	1	0	39	37	8.5	7	18	4.2	13	3.0	4.85	73	.245	.322	-6	-6	103	87	-0.7	-0	-0	-0.6
1947	NY-N	0	0	—	2	0	0	0	0	3	5	15.0	0	3	9.0	0	0.0	12.00	34	.385	.471	-3	-3	99	72	0.0	0	0	-0.1
	Chi-N	0	1	.000	4	1	0	0	0	7	10	12.9	1	4	5.1	1	1.3	5.14	82	.323	.400	-1	-1	104	127	-0.4	0	0	0.0
	Yr	0	1	.000	6	1	0	0	0	10	15	13.5	1	7	6.3	1	0.9	7.20	58	.341	.423	-3	-3	102	127	-0.4	0	0	-0.1
Total	5	25	20	.556	80	54	23	4	2	400	411	9.2	38	132	3.0	134	3.0	3.60	99	.262	.318	-5	-1	102	109	2.1	-1	-6	-0.4
■ **FRANK CARPIN**	Carpin, Frank Dominic b: 9/14/38, Brooklyn, N.Y. BL/TL, 5'10", 172 lbs. Deb: 5/25/65																												
1965	Pit-N	3	1	.750	39	0	0	0	4	40	35	7.9	0	24	5.4	27	6.1	3.15	110	.243	.352	2	1	98	117	0.9	-0	1	0.3
1966	Hou-N	1	0	1.000	10	0	0	0	0	6	9	13.5	0	6	9.0	2	3.0	7.50	47	.346	.455	-3	-3	99	97	0.5	0	-0	-0.2
Total	2	4	1	.800	49	0	0	0	4	46	44	8.6	0	30	5.9	29	5.7	3.72	94	.259	.368	-1	-1	98	114	1.4	-0	1	0.1
■ **ALEX CARRASQUEL**	Carrasquel, Alejandro Eloy (Aparicio) b: 7/24/12, Caracas, Venez. d: 8/19/69, Caracas, Venez. BR/TR, 6'1", 182 lbs. Deb: 4/23/39																												
1939	Was-A	5	9	.357	40	17	7	0	2	159	165	9.3	7	68	3.8	41	2.3	4.70	90	.266	.333	-1	-8	91	86	-1.1	1	0	-0.6
1940	Was-A	6	2	.750	28	0	0	0	0	48	42	7.9	4	29	5.4	19	3.6	4.88	86	.240	.341	-3	-4	95	85	2.3	-1	0	-0.3
1941	Was-A	6	2	.750	35	5	4	0	2	97	103	9.6	7	49	4.5	30	2.8	3.43	119	.278	.362	8	7	99	139	2.2	0	4	1.1
1942	Was-A	7	7	.500	35	15	7	1	4	152	161	9.5	7	53	3.1	40	2.4	3.43	105	.267	.322	4	3	99	108	1.2	-0	1	0.4
1943	Was-A	11	7	.611	39	13	4	1	5	144	160	10.0	3	54	3.4	48	3.0	3.69	91	.279	.335	-6	-5	102	104	1.4	1	1	-0.3
1944	Was-A	8	7	.533	43	7	3	0	2	134	143	9.6	8	50	3.4	35	2.4	3.43	91	.273	.332	0	-5	91	116	1.6	1	1	-0.2
1945	Was-A	7	5	.583	35	7	5	2	1	123	105	7.7	5	40	2.9	38	2.8	2.71	114	.228	.286	9	5	92	91	0.3	-1	0	0.4
1949	Chi-A	0	0	—	3	0	0	0	0	4	8	18.0	1	4	9.0	1	2.3	13.50	31	.421	.522	-4	-4	99	88	0.0	0	0	-0.3
Total	8	50	39	.562	258	64	30	4	16	861	887	9.3	42	347	3.6	252	2.6	3.73	97	.265	.330	6	-10	96	104	7.9	0	7	0.2
■ **BILL CARRICK**	Carrick, William Martin "Doughnut Bill" b: 9/5/1873, Erie, Pa. d: 3/7/32, Philadelphia, Pa. TR, Deb: 7/30/1898																												
1898	NY-N	3	1	.750	5	4	4	0	0	40	39	8.8	0	21	4.7	10	2.3	3.37	101	.277	.370	1	0	94	103	1.0	-0	0	0.0
1899	NY-N	16	27	.372	44	43	**40**	3	0	362	485	12.1	4	122	3.0	60	1.5	4.65	82	.346	.399	-32	-34	99	103	-1.9	-6	2	-3.2
1900	NY-N	19	22	.463	**45**	41	32	1	0	342	415	10.9	7	92	2.4	63	1.7	3.53	104	.324	.369	7	6	99	117	1.4	-3	0	0.3
1901	Was-A	14	23	.378	42	37	34	0	0	324	367	10.2	12	93	2.6	70	1.9	3.75	98	.306	.356	-3	-3	100	104	-4.0	-5	-1	-0.2
1902	Was-A	11	17	.393	31	30	28	0	0	258	344	12.0	10	72	2.5	36	1.3	4.85	74	.346	.391	-37	-37	100	102	-2.0	-1	-3	-3.5
Total	5	63	90	.412	167	155	138	4	0	1326	1650	11.2	33	400	2.7	239	1.6	4.14	89	.329	.378	-64	-68	99	107	-5.5	-15	-2	-6.6
■ **DON CARRITHERS**	Carrithers, Donald George b: 9/15/49, Lynwood, Cal. BR/TR, 6'2", 180 lbs. Deb: 8/01/70																												
1970	SF-N	2	1	.667	11	2	0	0	0	22	31	12.7	5	14	5.7	14	5.7	7.36	53	.333	.417	-8	-9	96	106	0.4	-0	0	-0.8
1971	SF-N	5	3	.625	22	12	2	1	1	80	77	8.7	6	37	4.2	41	4.6	4.05	85	.254	.329	-5	-6	99	94	0.7	0	-0	-0.5
1972	SF-N	4	8	.333	25	14	2	0	1	90	108	10.8	10	42	4.2	42	4.2	5.80	59	.296	.372	-23	-24	100	92	-1.5	1	0	-2.2
1973	SF-N	1	2	.333	25	3	0	0	0	58	64	9.9	2	35	5.4	36	5.6	4.81	80	.278	.377	-7	-6	104	96	-0.5	0	1	-0.4
1974	Mon-N	5	2	.714	22	3	0	0	1	60	56	8.4	6	17	2.6	31	4.7	3.00	126	.249	.302	4	5	104	115	1.6	1	1	0.7
1975	Mon-N	5	3	.625	19	14	5	2	0	101	90	8.0	7	38	3.4	37	3.3	3.30	120	.240	.311	4	8	109	97	1.2	0	2	1.1
1976	Mon-N	6	12	.333	34	19	2	0	0	140	153	9.8	9	78	5.0	71	4.6	4.44	81	.286	.371	-14	-13	103	112	-0.1	-1	1	-1.2
1977	Min-A	0	1	.000	7	0	0	0	0	14	16	10.3	2	6	3.9	3	1.9	7.07	59	.271	.338	-5	-5	102	66	-0.4	0	0	-0.3
Total	8	28	32	.467	165	67	11	3	3	565	595	9.5	47	267	4.3	275	4.4	4.46	83	.272	.350	-55	-49	103	101	1.4	0	5	-3.6
■ **CLAY CARROLL**	Carroll, Clay Palmer "Hawk" b: 5/2/41, Clanton, Ala. BR/TR, 6'1", 178 lbs. Deb: 9/02/64																												
1964	Mil-N	2	0	1.000	11	1	0	0	1	20	15	6.7	1	3	1.3	17	7.6	1.80	189	.200	.228	4	4	96	77	1.0	-0	1	0.5
1965	Mil-N	0	1	.000	19	1	0	0	1	35	35	9.0	3	13	3.3	16	4.1	4.37	83	.269	.331	-3	-3	103	96	-0.4	-1	-0	-0.3
1966	Atl-N	8	7	.533	**73**	3	0	0	11	144	127	7.9	8	29	1.8	67	4.2	2.38	148	.236	.274	20	18	97	106	0.1	-2	1	1.9
1967	Atl-N	6	12	.333	42	7	1	0	0	93	111	10.7	6	29	2.8	35	3.4	5.52	64	.304	.348	-22	-21	105	86	-2.8	-1	1	-2.0
1968	Atl-N	0	1	.000	10	0	0	0	0	22	26	10.6	1	6	2.5	10	4.1	4.91	57	.310	.333	-5	-5	94	91	-0.4	-0	0	-0.5
	Cin-N	7	7	.500	58	1	0	0	17	122	102	7.5	3	32	2.4	61	4.5	2.29	145	.230	.286	9	14	111	105	-0.1	1	2	2.0
	Yr	7	8	.467	68	1	0	0	17	144	128	8.0	4	38	2.4	71	4.4	2.69	120	.242	.294	5	9	108	105	-0.5	-0	2	1.5
1969	Cin-N	12	6	.667	71	4	0	0	7	151	149	8.9	9	78	4.6	90	5.4	3.52	101	.262	.347	1	0	99	119	2.6	3	3	0.6
1970	Cin-N	9	4	.692	65	0	0	0	16	104	104	9.0	4	27	2.3	63	5.5	2.60	161	.259	.304	17	**18**	103	123	1.2	-1	1	1.9
1971	Cin-N	10	4	.714	61	0	0	0	15	94	78	7.5	5	42	4.0	64	6.1	2.49	134	.234	.315	10	9	96	129	3.3	-1	4	1.3
1972	Cin-N	6	4	.600	**65**	0	0	0	**37**	96	89	8.3	5	32	3.0	51	4.8	2.25	140	.256	.311	13	10	91	151	0.0	0	1	1.2
1973	Cin-N	8	8	.500	53	5	0	0	14	93	111	10.7	5	34	3.3	41	4.0	3.68	91	.307	.361	-0	-3	92	132	-1.5	0	1	-0.2
1974	Cin-N	12	5	.706	57	3	0	0	6	101	96	8.6	3	30	2.7	46	4.1	2.14	163	.256	.301	17	15	96	141	2.4	-0	2	1.7
1975	Cin-N	7	5	.583	56	2	0	0	7	96	93	8.7	2	32	3.0	44	4.1	2.63	140	.255	.314	11	11	101	116	-0.7	-2	-0	0.9
1976	Chi-A	4	4	.500	29	0	0	0	6	77	67	7.8	1	24	2.8	38	4.4	2.57	139	.242	.299	8	9	101	106	0.7	0	0	1.0
1977	StL-N	4	2	.667	51	1	0	0	4	90	77	7.7	8	24	2.4	34	3.4	2.50	149	.238	.286	14	12	95	122	1.0	-1	1	1.3
	Chi-A	1	3	.250	8	0	0	0	1	11	14	11.5	3	4	3.3	4	3.3	4.91	82	.311	.367	-1	-1	99	134	-1.0	0	0	0.0
1978	Pit-N	0	0	—	2	0	0	0	0	4	2	4.5	0	3	6.8	0	0.0	2.25	167	.143	.294	1	1	105	60	0.0	0	0	0.1
Total	15	96	73	.568	731	28	1	0	143	1353	1296	8.6	67	442	2.9	681	4.5	2.94	120	.257	.313	94	89	99	117	5.4	-4	18	11.4
■ **ED CARROLL**	Carroll, Edgar Fleischer b: 7/27/07, Baltimore, Md. d: 10/13/84, Rossville, Md. BR/TR, 6'3", 185 lbs. Deb: 5/01/29																												
1929	Bos-A	1	0	1.000	24	3	0	0	0	67	77	10.3	6	20	2.7	13	1.7	5.64	79	.291	.344	-10	-9	105	81	0.5	-2	0	-0.9
■ **OWNIE CARROLL**	Carroll, Owen Thomas b: 11/11/02, Kearny, N.J. d: 6/8/75, Orange, N.J. BR/TR, 5'10.5", 165 lbs. Deb: 6/20/25																												
1925	Det-A	2	2	.500	10	4	1	0	0	41	46	10.1	1	28	6.1	12	2.6	3.73	115	.293	.398	3	3	98	138	0.0	1	-2	0.2
1927	Det-A	10	6	.625	31	15	8	0	0	172	186	9.7	5	73	3.8	41	2.1	3.98	112	.281	.348	3	9	107	103	1.7	-3	2	0.8
1928	Det-A	16	12	.571	34	28	19	2	2	231	219	8.5	6	87	3.4	51	2.0	3.27	124	.262	.324	20	20	100	109	3.8	-0	1	2.0
1929	Det-A	9	17	.346	34	26	12	0	1	202	249	11.1	10	86	3.8	54	2.4	4.63	89	.310	.370	-9	-11	97	112	-3.5	2	2	-0.6
1930	Det-A	0	5	.000	6	3	0	0	0	20	30	13.5	3	9	4.0	4	1.8	10.80	46	.333	.394	-14	-13	106	63	-2.4	-1	0	-1.0
	NY-A	0	1	.000	10	1	0	0	0	33	49	13.4	2	18	4.9	8	2.2	6.55	62	.374	.438	-7	-9	87	123	-0.4	0	1	-0.6
	Yr	0	6	.000	16	4	0	0	0	53	79	13.4	5	27	4.6	12	2.0	8.15	54	.357	.421	-21	-22	94	123	-2.8	-1	1	-1.6
	Cin-N	0	1	.000	3	2	1	0	0	14	17	10.9	3	3	1.9	0	0.0	4.50	103	.309	.339	1	0	93	128	-0.4	-0	0	0.0
1931	Cin-N	3	9	.250	29	12	4	0	0	107	135	11.4	6	51	4.3	24	2.0	5.55	68	.314	.381	-20	-21	98	99	-2.0	0	1	-1.8
1932	Cin-N	10	19	.345	32	26	15	0	1	210	245	10.5	7	44	1.9	55	2.4	4.50	85	.286	.325	-14	-16	99	85	-1.9	2	-1	-1.3
1933	Bro-N	13	15	.464	33	31	11	0	0	226	248	9.9	9	54	2.2	45	1.8	3.78	87	.281	.320	-11	-13	98	97	1.2	-1	3	-1.0
1934	Bro-N	1	3	.250	26	5	0	0	1	74	108	13.1	9	33	4.0	17	2.1	6.45	60	.342	.402	-20	-21	95	105	-0.8	1	3	-1.5
Total	9	64	90	.416	248	153	71	2	5	1330	1532	10.4	61	486	3.3	311	2.1	4.43	89	.294	.350	-68	-72	99	103	-4.7	2	10	-4.8
■ **DICK CARROLL**	Carroll, Richard Thomas "Shadow" b: 7/21/1884, Cleveland, Ohio d: 11/22/45, Cleveland, Ohio BR/TR, 6'2", Deb: 9/25/09																												
1909	NY-A	0	0	—	2	1	0	0	0	5	7	12.6	1	1	1.8	1	1.8	3.60	68	.292	.320	-1	-1	99	130	0.0	0	-0	0.0
■ **TOM CARROLL**	Carroll, Thomas Michael b: 11/5/52, Utica, N.Y. BL/TR, 6'3", 190 lbs. Deb: 7/07/74																												
1974	Cin-N	4	3	.571	16	13	0	0	0	78	68	7.8	11	44	5.1	37	4.3	3.69	95	.231	.326	-1	-2	96	106	-0.1	-1	-1	-0.3
1975	Cin-N	4	1	.800	12	7	0	0	0	47	52	10.0	1	26	5.0	14	2.7	4.98	74	.284	.377	-7	-7	101	90	1.0	-2	-1	-0.8
Total	2	8	4	.667	28	20	0	0	0	125	120	8.6	12	70	5.0	51	3.7	4.18	85	.252	.345	-8	-9	98	100	0.9	-2	-2	-1.1
■ **KID CARSEY**	Carsey, Wilfred b: 10/22/1870, New York, N.Y. d: 3/29/60, Miami, Fla. BL/TR, 5'7", 168 lbs. Deb: 4/08/1891																												
1891	Was-a	14	37	.275	54	53	46	1	0	415	513	11.1	18	161	3.5	174	3.8	4.99	75	.319	.381	-58	-58	101	92	-5.8	-6	5	-4.7

YEAR	TM/L	W	L	PCT	G	GS	CG	SHO	SV	IP	H	H/G	HR	BB	BB/G	SO	SO/G	ERA	/A	OAVG	OOBP	PR	/A	PF	CPI	WAT	PB	PD	TPI
1892	Phi-N	19	16	.543	43	36	30	1	1	318	320	9.1	6	104	2.9	76	2.2	3.11	108	.274	.334	6	9	103	101	-0.9	-4	3	0.8
1893	Phi-N	20	15	.571	39	35	30	1	0	318	375	10.6	7	124	3.5	50	1.4	4.81	95	.310	.374	-5	-8	98	93	0.7	-8	3	-0.9
1894	Phi-N	18	12	.600	35	31	26	0	0	277	349	11.3	22	102	3.3	41	1.3	5.56	90	.330	.389	-7	-17	94	93	1.9	3	3	-0.9
1895	Phi-N	24	16	.600	44	40	35	0	1	342	460	12.1	14	118	3.1	64	1.7	4.92	96	.343	.396	-5	-8	98	107	0.3	3	-0	-0.3
1896	Phi-N	11	11	.500	27	21	18	1	1	187	273	13.1	4	72	3.5	36	1.7	5.63	79	.364	.420	-26	-24	102	101	0.6	1	0	-1.8
1897	Phi-N	2	1	.667	4	4	2	0	0	28	35	11.3	0	16	5.1	1	0.3	5.14	81	.329	.417	-3	-3	96	97	0.7	-0	0	-0.2
	StL-N	3	8	.273	12	11	11	0	0	99	133	12.1	5	31	2.8	14	1.3	6.00	71	.345	.394	-19	-19	99	85	0.4	3	0	-1.3
	Yr	5	9	.357	16	15	13	0	0	127	168	11.9	5	47	3.3	15	1.1	5.81	73	.341	.399	-21	-22	98	85	1.1	-0	0	-1.5
1898	StL-N	2	12	.143	20	13	10	0	0	124	177	12.8	2	37	2.7	10	0.7	6.39	62	.359	.404	-38	-34	110	81	-3.2	-1	0	-2.8
1899	Cle-N	1	8	.111	10	9	8	0	0	78	109	12.6	2	24	2.8	11	1.3	5.77	64	.356	.403	-17	-18	96	89	-0.6	1	0	-1.3
	Was-N	1	2	.333	4	3	2	0	0	29	27	8.4	0	4	1.2	3	0.9	3.72	102	.269	.297	0	0	98	58	0.0	-2	0	-0.9
	Yr	2	10	.167	14	12	10	0	0	107	136	11.4	2	28	2.4	14	1.2	5.21	71	.334	.377	-16	-18	97	58	-0.6	1	0	-2.2
1901	Bro-N	1	0	1.000	2	0	0	0	0	7	9	11.6	1	3	3.9	4	5.1	10.29	33	.348	.436	-5	-5	103	61	0.5	-0	-0	-0.4
Total	10	116	138	.457	294	256	218	4	3	2222	2780	11.3	81	796	3.2	484	2.0	4.96	85	.325	.383	-176	-181	100	95	-5.4	-9	13	-14.7
■ AL CARSON	Carson, Albert James "Soldier" b: 8/22/1882, Chicago, Ill. d: 11/26/62, San Diego, Cal. TR , Deb: 5/06/10																												
1910	Chi-N	0	0	—	2	0	0	0	0	7	6	7.7	0	1	1.3	2	2.6	3.86	76	.240	.269	-1	-1	96	47	0.0	0	0	0.0
■ ARNOLD CARTER	Carter, Arnold Lee "Hook" or "Lefty" b: 3/14/18, Rainelle, W.Va. BL/TL, 5'10", 170 lbs. Deb: 4/29/44																												
1944	Cin-N	11	7	.611	33	18	9	3	3	149	143	8.6	1	40	2.4	33	2.0	2.60	132	.256	.301	17	14	95	114	0.8	5	1	2.1
1945	Cin-N	2	4	.333	13	6	2	1	0	47	54	10.3	2	13	2.5	4	0.8	3.06	120	.286	.330	4	3	97	132	-0.4	0	0	0.4
Total	2	13	11	.542	46	24	11	4	3	196	197	9.0	3	53	2.4	37	1.7	2.71	129	.264	.309	21	17	95	118	0.4	5	1	2.5
■ NICK CARTER	Carter, Conrad Powell b: 5/19/1879, Oatlands, Va. d: 11/23/61, Grasonville, Md. TR , 5'8", 126 lbs. Deb: 4/14/08																												
1908	Phi-A	2	5	.286	14	5	2	0	0	61	58	8.6	1	17	2.5	17	2.5	2.95	89	.270	.329	-4	-2	110	114	-1.2	-2	1	-0.1
■ PAUL CARTER	Carter, Paul Warren "Nick" b: 5/1/1894, Lake Park, Ga. d: 9/11/84, Lake Park, Ga. BL/TR, 6'3", 175 lbs. Deb: 9/15/14																												
1914	Cle-A	1	3	.250	5	4	1	0	0	25	35	12.6	0	5	1.8	9	3.2	2.88	101	.340	.370	-0	0	106	161	-0.4	-1	-0	0.0
1915	Cle-A	1	1	.500	11	2	2	0	0	42	44	9.4	1	18	3.9	14	3.0	3.21	97	.272	.344	-1	-0	106	112	0.2	1	1	0.1
1916	Chi-N	2	2	.500	8	5	2	0	0	36	26	6.5	1	17	4.3	14	3.5	2.75	112	.203	.289	-1	1	117	76	0.2	-1	1	0.3
1917	Chi-N	5	8	.385	23	13	6	0	2	113	115	9.2	2	19	1.5	34	2.7	3.27	87	.276	.302	-7	-5	105	95	-1.3	-0	-1	-0.6
1918	Chi-N	3	2	.600	21	4	1	0	2	73	78	9.6	2	19	2.3	13	1.6	2.71	100	.290	.320	0	0	98	136	-0.1	0	2	0.2
1919	Chi-N	5	4	.556	28	7	2	0	1	85	81	8.6	1	28	3.0	17	1.8	2.65	109	.252	.309	3	2	99	109	0.2	1	0	0.3
1920	Chi-N	3	6	.333	31	8	2	0	2	106	131	11.1	3	36	3.1	14	1.2	4.67	67	.324	.369	-18	-18	99	102	-1.4	-0	-2	-2.0
Total	7	20	26	.435	127	43	16	0	7	480	510	9.6	10	142	2.7	115	2.2	3.32	89	.283	.328	-24	-20	103	109	-2.6	-1	1	-1.7
■ SOL CARTER	Carter, Solomon Mobley "Buck" b: 12/23/08, Picayune, Miss. BR/TR, 6', 178 lbs. Deb: 4/15/31																												
1931	Phi-A	0	0	—	2	0	0	0	0	2	1	4.5	0	4	18.0	1	4.5	22.50	20	.143	.455	-4	-4	101	23	0.0	0	1	-0.2
■ BOB CARUTHERS	Caruthers, Robert Lee "Parisian Bob" b: 1/5/1864, Memphis, Tenn. d: 8/5/11, Peoria, Ill. BL/TR, 5'7", 138 lbs. Deb: 9/07/1884 MU																												
1884	StL-a	7	2	.778	13	7	7	0	0	83	61	6.6	1	15	1.6	58	6.3	2.60	135	.213	.252	6	8	109	74	1.9	2	0	1.2
1885	StL-a	**40**	13	**.755**	53	53	53	**6**	0	482	430	8.0	3	57	1.1	190	3.5	**2.07**	139	.250	.274	**63**	43	89	112	7.3	11	0	4.8
1886	StL-a	30	14	.682	44	43	42	2	0	387	323	7.5	2	86	2.0	166	3.9	2.33	157	.236	.282	48	57	106	100	1.2	24	-2	**10.5**
1887	StL-a	29	9	**.763**	39	39	39	2	0	341	337	8.9	6	61	1.6	74	2.0	3.30	136	.271	**.305**	38	45	105	91	4.9	21	6	3.8
1888	Bro-a	29	15	.659	44	43	42	4	0	392	337	7.7	4	53	1.2	140	3.2	2.39	131	.244	.272	29	32	102	88	2.5	9	2	3.0
1889	Bro-a	**40**	11	**.784**	56	50	46	**7**	1	445	444	9.0	15	104	**2.1**	118	2.4	3.13	113	.275	.319	35	19	92	98	**11.2**	18	2	3.3
1890	Bro-N	23	11	.676	37	33	30	1	0	300	292	8.8	9	87	2.6	64	1.9	3.09	111	.271	.325	16	11	96	97	0.7	11	3	3.2
1891	Bro-N	18	14	.563	38	32	29	2	1	297	323	9.8	7	107	3.2	69	2.1	3.12	105	.291	.353	7	5	98	112	4.1	11	0	1.9
1892	StL-N	2	10	.167	16	10	10	0	1	102	131	11.6	10	27	2.4	21	1.9	5.91	54	.326	.368	-30	-31	97	84	-3.3	5	0	-2.5
Total	9	218	99	.688	340	310	298	24	3	2829	2678	8.5	57	597	1.9	900	2.9	2.84	121	.262	.303	213	190	98	99	30.5	112	12	29.2
■ CHUCK CARY	Cary, Charles Douglas b: 3/3/60, Whittier, Cal. BL/TL, 6'4", 210 lbs. Deb: 8/22/85																												
1985	Det-A	0	1	.000	16	0	0	0	2	24	16	6.0	2	8	3.0	22	8.3	3.38	130	.190	.274	2	3	106	70	-0.4	0	-0	0.2
1986	Det-A	1	2	.333	22	0	0	0	0	32	33	9.3	3	15	4.2	21	5.9	3.38	117	.273	.343	3	2	95	135	-0.5	0	-0	0.2
1987	Atl-N	1	1	.500	13	0	0	0	1	17	17	9.0	3	4	2.1	15	7.9	3.71	120	.266	.314	1	1	109	121	0.1	-0	0	0.1
1988	Atl-N	0	0	—	7	0	0	0	0	8	8	9.0	1	4	4.5	7	7.9	6.75	55	.250	.333	-3	-3	107	67	0.0	0	0	-0.2
Total	4	2	4	.333	58	0	0	0	3	81	74	8.2	9	31	3.4	65	7.2	3.78	110	.246	.317	3	4	102	106	-0.8	-0	-1	0.3
■ SCOTT CARY	Cary, Scott Russell "Red" b: 4/11/23, Kendallville, Ind. BL/TL, 5'11.5", 168 lbs. Deb: 5/01/47																												
1947	Was-A	3	1	.750	23	3	1	0	0	55	73	11.9	5	20	3.3	25	4.1	5.89	63	.312	.363	-13	-13	101	90	1.2	-1	-1	-1.3
■ JERRY CASALE	Casale, Jerry Joseph b: 9/27/33, Brooklyn, N.Y. BR/TR, 6'2", 200 lbs. Deb: 9/14/58																												
1958	Bos-A	0	0	—	2	0	0	0	0	3	1	3.0	0	2	6.0	3	9.0	0.00	—	.111	.273	1	1	105	0	0.0	0	0	0.1
1959	Bos-A	13	8	.619	31	26	9	3	0	180	162	8.1	20	89	4.4	93	4.7	4.30	94	.238	.329	-9	-5	105	91	3.0	3	-4	-0.5
1960	Bos-A	2	9	.182	29	14	1	0	0	96	113	10.6	14	67	6.3	54	5.1	6.19	66	.294	.386	-25	-22	105	98	-3.1	3	-0	-1.8
1961	LA-A	1	5	.167	13	7	0	0	1	43	52	10.9	9	25	5.2	35	7.3	6.49	70	.297	.386	-12	-9	112	98	-1.8	4	-0	-0.5
	Det-A	0	0	—	3	1	0	0	0	12	15	11.3	3	3	2.3	6	4.5	5.25	72	.313	.353	-2	-2	94	118	0.0	-0	0	-0.1
	Yr	1	5	.167	16	8	0	0	1	55	67	11.0	12	28	4.6	41	6.7	6.22	70	.298	.375	-13	-11	108	118	-1.8	4	-0	-0.6
1962	Det-A	1	2	.333	18	1	0	0	0	37	33	8.0	5	18	4.4	16	3.9	4.62	95	.236	.315	-3	-1	110	84	-0.5	-1	0	-0.1
Total	5	17	24	.415	96	49	10	3	1	371	376	9.1	51	204	4.9	207	5.0	5.07	82	.262	.351	-48	-38	106	93	-2.4	8	-5	-2.9
■ JOE CASCARELLA	Cascarella, Joseph Thomas "Crooning Joe" b: 6/28/07, Philadelphia, Pa. BR/TR, 5'10.5", 175 lbs. Deb: 4/17/34																												
1934	Phi-A	12	15	.444	42	22	9	2	1	194	214	9.9	8	104	4.8	71	3.3	4.69	94	.288	.369	-4	-6	98	106	-0.2	-4	2	-0.7
1935	Phi-A	1	6	.143	9	3	1	0	0	32	29	8.2	1	22	6.2	15	4.2	5.34	85	.252	.352	-3	-3	102	81	-2.2	-1	2	-0.1
	Bos-A	0	3	.000	6	4	0	0	0	17	25	13.2	3	11	5.8	9	4.8	6.88	70	.329	.409	-5	-4	108	107	-1.4	-0	0	-0.3
	Yr	1	9	.100	15	7	1	0	0	49	54	9.9	4	33	6.1	24	4.4	5.88	79	.283	.373	-8	-7	104	107	-3.6	-1	2	-0.4
1936	Bos-A	0	2	.000	10	1	0	0	0	21	27	11.6	0	9	3.9	7	3.0	6.86	78	.329	.396	-4	-4	106	83	-0.9	-1	0	-0.3
	Was-A	9	8	.529	22	16	7	1	1	139	147	9.5	7	54	3.5	34	2.2	4.08	119	.276	.343	15	12	96	110	0.0	-2	-2	0.6
	Yr	9	10	.474	32	17	7	1	1	160	174	9.8	7	63	3.5	41	2.3	4.44	110	.283	.350	11	8	97	110	-0.9	-1	-2	0.3
1937	Was-A	0	5	.000	10	4	1	0	1	32	50	14.1	3	23	6.5	10	2.8	8.16	54	.347	.435	-13	-13	96	94	-2.4	-0	0	-1.0
	Cin-N	1	2	.333	11	3	2	0	1	44	44	9.0	1	22	4.5	16	3.3	3.89	94	.263	.342	0	-1	93	100	0.0	-1	-0	-0.1
1938	Cin-N	4	7	.364	33	1	0	0	4	61	66	9.7	2	22	3.2	30	4.4	4.57	79	.275	.327	-5	-6	96	84	-1.8	-1	-0	-0.6
Total	5	27	48	.360	143	54	20	3	8	540	602	10.0	25	267	4.4	192	3.2	4.85	91	.287	.362	-19	-25	98	101	-8.9	-9	1	-2.5
■ CHARLIE CASE	Case, Charles Emmett b: 9/7/1879, Smith Landing, O. d: 4/16/64, Clairmont, Ohio BR/TR, 6', 170 lbs. Deb: 7/05/01																												
1901	Cin-N	1	2	.333	3	3	3	0	0	27	34	11.3	0	6	2.0	5	1.7	4.67	71	.331	.367	-4	-4	100	87	-0.1	-1	0	-0.3
1904	Pit-N	10	5	.667	18	17	14	3	0	141	129	8.2	0	31	2.0	49	3.1	2.94	91	.269	.318	-3	-4	98	82	1.8	1	0	-0.3
1905	Pit-N	11	11	.500	31	24	18	3	1	217	202	8.4	2	66	2.7	57	2.4	2.57	118	.278	.350	10	11	102	117	-2.4	-2	-3	0.8
1906	Pit-N	1	1	.500	2	2	1	0	0	11	8	6.5	0	5	4.1	3	2.5	5.73	46	.234	.348	-4	-4	101	41	-0.1	1	0	-0.2
Total	4	23	19	.548	54	46	36	6	1	396	373	8.5	2	108	2.5	114	2.6	2.93	99	.278	.340	-1	-1	100	101	-0.8	-2	-3	-0.0
■ DAN CASEY	Casey, Daniel Maurice b: 11/20/1862, Binghamton, N.Y. d: 2/8/43, Washington, D.C. BR/TL, Deb: 8/18/1884																												
1884	Wil-U	1	1	.500	2	2	2	0	0	18	23	11.5	0	4	2.0	10	5.0	1.00	329	.316	.352	4	5	109	440	0.5	-1	0	0.4
1885	Det-N	4	8	.333	12	12	12	1	0	104	105	9.1	1	35	3.0	79	6.8	3.29	85	.273	.334	-5	-6	99	101	-0.7	-3	0	-0.7
1886	Phi-N	24	18	.571	44	44	39	4	0	369	326	8.0	8	104	2.5	193	4.7	2.41	131	.249	.305	36	31	96	109	-2.5	-4	-1	2.3
1887	Phi-N	28	13	.683	45	45	43	**4**	0	390	377	8.7	15	115	2.7	119	2.7	**2.86**	133	.269	.324	52	41	94	**114**	5.3	-8	-2	2.5
1888	Phi-N	14	18	.438	33	33	31	1	0	286	298	9.4	6	48	1.5	108	3.4	3.15	102	.282	.313	-10	2	113	96	-3.4	-5	0	0.0
1889	Phi-N	6	10	.375	20	20	15	1	0	153	170	10.0	4	72	4.2	65	3.8	3.76	112	.297	.376	4	8	105	**114**	-2.1	-1	0	0.6
1890	Syr-a	19	22	.463	45	42	40	2	0	361	365	9.1	8	165	4.1	169	4.2	4.14	86	.278	.359	-11	-23	92	96	1.6	-3	3	-2.1
Total	7	96	90	.516	201	198	182	13	0	1681	1664	8.9	42	543	2.9	743	4.0	3.17	110	.272	.332	70	61	99	109	-1.3	-24	-1	3.0

YEAR	TM/L	W	L	PCT	G	GS	CG	SHO	SV	IP	H	H/G	HR	BB	BB/G	SO	SO/G	ERA	/A	OAVG	OOBP	PR	/A	PF	CPI	WAT	PB	PD	TPI
■ HUGH CASEY	Casey, Hugh Thomas b: 10/14/13, Atlanta, Ga. d: 7/3/51, Atlanta, Ga. BR/TR, 6'1", 207 lbs. Deb: 4/29/35																												
1935	Chi-N	0	0	—	13	0	0	0	0	26	29	10.0	2	14	4.8	10	3.5	3.81	100	.279	.361	1	0	95	126	0.0	-0	0	0.0
1939	Bro-N	15	10	.600	40	25	15	0	1	227	228	9.0	13	54	2.1	79	3.1	2.93	142	.260	.305	25	31	106	113	1.7	0	2	3.5
1940	Bro-N	11	8	.579	44	10	5	2	2	154	136	7.9	13	51	3.0	53	3.1	3.62	113	.237	.298	4	8	106	94	0.1	2	2	1.2
1941	Bro-N	14	11	.560	45	18	4	1	7	162	155	8.6	8	57	3.2	61	3.4	3.89	93	.251	.312	-5	-5	99	86	-1.9	-1	2	-0.3
1942	Bro-N	6	3	.667	50	2	0	1	**13**	112	91	7.3	3	44	3.5	54	4.3	2.25	143	.221	.298	13	12	97	114	0.0	-0	-1	1.2
1946	Bro-N	11	5	.688	46	1	0	0	5	100	101	9.1	2	33	3.0	31	2.8	1.98	172	.267	.318	**16**	**16**	100	168	1.6	-1	3	2.0
1947	Bro-N	10	4	.714	46	0	0	0	**18**	77	75	8.8	7	29	3.4	40	4.7	3.97	105	.260	.326	1	2	103	100	2.0	-1	0	0.0
1948	Bro-N	3	0	1.000	22	0	0	0	4	36	59	14.8	6	17	4.3	7	1.8	8.00	51	.391	.453	-16	-16	103	110	1.5	-1	0	-1.5
1949	Pit-N	4	1	.800	33	0	0	0	5	39	50	11.5	4	14	3.2	9	2.1	4.62	89	.314	.369	-2	-2	102	120	1.6	1	-2	-0.2
	NY-A	1	0	1.000	4	0	0	0	0	8	11	12.4	0	8	9.0	5	5.6	7.88	52	.324	.452	-3	-3	97	84	0.5	-0	0	-0.2
Total	9	75	42	.641	343	56	24	4	55	941	935	8.9	58	321	3.1	349	3.3	3.44	112	.260	.320	33	42	102	110	7.1	-3	7	5.7
■ BILL CASEY	Casey, William B. b: St.Louis, Mo. Deb: 8/17/1887																												
1887	Phi-a	0	0	—	1	0	0	0	0	1	4	36.0	0	1	9.0	0	0.0	18.00	24	.601	.653	-2	-2	100	113	0.0	0	0	0.0
■ CARL CASHION	Cashion, Jay Carl b: 6/6/1891, Mecklenburg, N.C. d: 11/17/35, Lake Millicent, Wis. BL/TR, 6'2", 200 lbs. Deb: 8/04/11																												
1911	Was-A	1	5	.167	11	9	5	0	0	71	67	8.5	4	47	6.0	26	3.3	4.18	79	.220	.338	-7	-7	99	70	-1.7	2	0	-0.3
1912	Was-A	10	6	.625	26	17	13	1	1	170	150	7.9	4	103	5.5	84	4.4	3.18	102	.250	.365	3	1	97	120	0.6	2	-1	0.1
1913	Was-A	1	1	.500	4	3	0	0	0	9	7	7.0	0	14	14.0	3	3.0	6.00	51	.269	.558	-3	-3	105	126	0.0	0	0	-0.1
1914	Was-A	0	1	.000	2	1	0	0	0	5	4	7.2	0	6	10.8	1	1.8	10.80	25	.250	.478	-4	-4	100	52	-0.4	-0	0	-0.3
Total	4	12	13	.480	43	30	18	1	1	255	228	8.0	8	170	6.0	114	4.0	3.71	88	.241	.366	-11	-13	98	105	-1.5	5	1	-0.6
■ CRAIG CASKEY	Caskey, Craig Douglas b: 12/11/49, Visalia, Cal. BB/TL, 5'11", 185 lbs. Deb: 7/19/73																												
1973	Mon-N	0	0	—	9	1	0	0	0	14	15	9.6	3	4	2.6	6	3.9	5.79	66	.278	.328	-3	-3	105	89	0.0	-0	0	-0.2
■ ED CASSIAN	Cassian, Edwin b: Connecticut 5'8", 160 lbs. Deb: 6/26/1891																												
1891	Phi-N	1	3	.250	6	4	3	0	0	38	40	9.5	0	16	3.8	10	2.4	2.84	112	.284	.357	2	1	95	116	-0.9	-1	0	0.0
	Was-a	2	4	.333	7	5	5	0	0	53	73	12.4	4	35	5.9	14	2.4	5.60	67	.343	.436	-11	-11	101	113	0.0	2	0	-0.6
■ JOHN CASSIDY	Cassidy, John P. b: 1857, Brooklyn, N.Y. d: 7/2/1891, Brooklyn, N.Y. TL, 5'8", 168 lbs. Deb: 4/24/1875																												
1875	Atl-n	1	25	.038	27																								
1877	Har-N	1	1	.500	2	2	2	0	0	18	24	12.0	0	1	0.5	2	1.0	5.00	49	.328	.337	-4	-5	87	71	0.0	1	0	-0.3
■ GEORGE CASTER	Caster, George Jasper "Ug" b: 8/4/07, Colton, Cal. d: 12/18/55, Lakewood, Cal. BR/TR, 6'1.5", 180 lbs. Deb: 9/10/34																												
1934	Phi-A	3	2	.600	5	3	2	0	0	37	32	7.8	3	14	3.4	15	3.6	3.41	130	.235	.316	4	4	98	106	0.7	0	1	0.5
1935	Phi-A	1	4	.200	25	1	0	0	1	63	86	12.3	8	37	5.3	24	3.4	6.29	73	.322	.401	-13	-12	102	107	-1.1	0	2	-0.9
1937	Phi-A	12	19	.387	34	33	19	3	0	232	227	8.8	23	107	4.2	100	3.9	4.42	101	.258	.334	5	1	96	96	0.9	0	-0	0.0
1938	Phi-A	16	20	.444	42	40	20	2	1	281	310	9.9	25	117	3.7	112	3.6	4.36	115	.277	.344	14	20	105	106	3.3	1	-2	1.8
1939	Phi-A	9	9	.500	28	17	7	1	0	136	144	9.5	16	45	3.0	59	3.9	4.90	96	.276	.329	-4	-3	102	96	2.1	-1	0	-0.2
1940	Phi-A	4	19	.174	36	24	11	0	2	178	234	11.8	18	69	3.5	75	3.8	6.57	66	.312	.366	-43	-44	99	86	-6.2	-3	-1	-4.2
1941	StL-A	3	7	.300	32	9	3	0	3	104	105	9.1	12	37	3.2	36	3.1	5.02	83	.259	.319	-10	-10	101	82	-1.7	-2	1	-0.9
1942	StL-A	8	2	.800	39	0	0	0	5	80	62	7.0	3	39	4.4	34	3.8	2.81	133	.217	.310	8	8	102	105	2.9	-1	1	0.8
1943	StL-A	6	8	.429	35	0	0	0	8	76	69	8.2	4	41	4.9	43	5.1	2.13	156	.246	.335	10	10	101	176	-0.6	-1	0	1.1
1944	StL-A	6	6	.500	42	0	0	0	**12**	81	91	10.1	5	33	3.7	46	5.1	2.44	140	.264	.346	9	9	100	177	-0.8	1	-0	1.0
1945	StL-A	1	2	.333	10	0	0	0	1	16	20	11.3	0	7	3.9	9	5.1	6.75	57	.308	.370	-6	-5	114	68	-0.5	0	-0	-0.4
	Det-A	5	1	.833	22	0	0	0	2	51	47	8.3	3	27	4.8	23	4.1	3.88	91	.250	.342	-3	-2	105	101	1.9	0	0	-0.1
	Yr	6	3	.667	32	0	0	0	3	67	67	9.0	3	34	4.6	32	4.3	4.57	79	.265	.349	-9	-7	107	101	1.4	0	-0	-0.5
1946	Det-A	2	1	.667	26	0	0	0	4	41	42	9.2	1	24	5.3	19	4.2	5.71	65	.264	.362	-10	-9	106	70	0.3	-0	1	-0.8
Total	12	76	100	.432	376	127	62	6	39	1376	1469	9.6	121	597	3.9	595	3.9	4.55	95	.273	.343	-40	-32	101	105	1.2	-6	1	-2.3
■ TONY CASTILLO	Castillo, Antonio b: 3/1/63, Quibor, Venez. BL/TL, 6', 170 lbs. Deb: 8/14/88																												
1988	Tor-A	1	0	1.000	14	0	0	0	0	15	10	6.0	2	2	1.2	14	8.4	3.00	131	.200	.222	2	2	99	79	0.5	0	0	0.2
■ MANNY CASTILLO	Castillo, Esteban Manuel Antonio (Cabrera) b: 4/1/57, Santo Domingo, D.R. BB/TR, 5'9", 160 lbs. Deb: 9/01/80																												
1983	Sea-A	0	0	—	1	0	0	0	0	3	8	24.0	3	3	9.0	2	6.0	21.00	20	.533	.632	-6	-6	101	109	0.0	1	0	-0.3
■ ROBERT CASTILLO	Castillo, Robert Ernie b: 4/18/55, Los Angeles, Cal. BR/TR, 5'10", 170 lbs. Deb: 9/10/77																												
1977	LA-N	1	0	1.000	6	1	0	0	0	11	12	9.8	2	2	1.6	7	5.7	4.09	94	.279	.304	-0	-0	98	109	0.5	-0	0	0.0
1978	LA-N	0	4	.000	18	0	0	0	1	34	28	7.4	2	33	8.7	30	7.9	3.97	87	.239	.381	-1	-2	97	123	-1.9	-1	0	-0.2
1979	LA-N	2	0	1.000	19	0	0	0	7	24	26	9.8	0	13	4.9	25	9.4	1.13	331	.277	.364	7	7	99	363	1.0	-0	0	0.7
1980	LA-N	8	6	.571	61	0	0	0	5	98	70	6.4	4	45	4.1	60	5.5	2.76	125	.206	.294	9	8	96	90	0.1	-0	1	0.8
1981	LA-N	2	4	.333	34	1	0	0	5	51	50	8.8	5	24	4.2	35	6.2	5.29	63	.262	.336	-10	-11	96	80	-1.2	2	-1	-0.9
1982	Min-A	13	11	.542	40	25	6	1	0	219	194	8.0	26	85	3.5	123	5.1	3.66	114	.241	.309	10	12	102	101	3.7	0	-2	1.0
1983	Min-A	8	12	.400	27	25	3	0	0	158	170	9.7	17	65	3.7	90	5.1	4.78	91	.278	.344	-12	-8	106	97	-0.7	0	0	-0.7
1984	Min-A	2	1	.667	10	2	0	0	0	25	14	5.0	2	19	6.8	7	2.5	1.80	235	.177	.327	6	7	106	181	0.5	0	-0	0.7
1985	LA-N	2	2	.500	35	5	0	0	0	68	59	7.8	9	41	5.4	57	7.5	5.43	61	.230	.336	-14	-16	92	75	-0.2	-0	1	-1.5
Total	9	38	40	.487	250	59	9	1	18	688	623	8.1	67	327	4.3	434	5.7	3.95	98	.246	.326	-5	-5	100	107	1.8	0	-0	-0.1
■ SLICK CASTLEMAN	Castleman, Clydell b: 9/8/13, Donelson, Tenn. BR/TR, 6', 185 lbs. Deb: 5/09/34																												
1934	NY-N	1	0	1.000	7	1	0	0	0	17	18	9.5	1	10	5.3	5	2.6	5.29	73	.277	.364	-2	-3	95	90	0.5	1	1	-0.1
1935	NY-N	15	6	.714	29	25	9	1	0	174	186	9.6	14	64	3.3	64	3.3	4.09	93	.268	.325	-1	-5	95	99	3.4	-0	1	-0.3
1936	NY-N	4	7	.364	29	12	2	1	1	112	148	11.9	6	56	4.5	54	4.3	5.63	70	.323	.395	-20	-21	98	104	-2.1	-1	1	-1.9
1937	NY-N	11	6	.647	23	23	10	2	0	160	148	8.3	19	33	1.9	78	4.4	3.32	115	.247	.283	11	9	98	102	0.6	-4	-3	0.2
1938	NY-N	4	5	.444	21	14	4	0	0	91	108	10.7	4	37	3.7	18	1.8	4.15	93	.296	.360	-4	-3	102	114	-0.8	-2	-1	-0.4
1939	NY-N	1	2	.333	12	4	0	0	0	34	36	9.5	1	23	6.1	6	1.6	4.50	86	.286	.388	-2	-2	99	111	-0.4	1	-1	-0.1
Total	6	36	26	.581	121	79	25	4	1	588	644	9.9	45	223	3.4	225	3.4	4.24	91	.279	.340	-19	-25	98	103	1.2	-6	-1	-2.6
■ ROY CASTLETON	Castleton, Royal Eugene b: 7/26/1885, Salt Lake City, Utah d: 6/24/67, Los Angeles, Cal. BR/TL, 5'11", 167 lbs. Deb: 4/16/07																												
1907	NY-A	1	1	.500	3	2	1	0	0	16	11	6.2	1	3	1.7	3	1.7	2.81	99	.215	.258	-0	-0	110	58	0.1	-1	-0	0.0
1909	Cin-N	1	1	.500	4	1	1	0	0	14	14	9.0	0	6	3.9	5	3.2	1.93	126	.275	.373	1	1	94	201	0.0	1	0	0.1
1910	Cin-N	1	2	.333	4	2	1	0	0	14	15	9.6	0	6	3.9	5	3.2	3.21	97	.288	.373	-0	-0	102	125	-0.4	-1	0	0.0
Total	3	3	4	.429	11	5	3	0	0	44	40	8.2	1	15	3.1	13	2.7	2.66	105	.259	.337	0	1	102	125	-0.3	-0	0	0.1
■ PAUL CASTNER	Castner, Paul Henry "Lefty" b: 2/16/1897, St.Paul, Minn. d: 3/3/86, St.Paul, Minn. BL/TL, 5'11", 187 lbs. Deb: 8/06/23																												
1923	Chi-A	0	0	—	6	0	0	0	0	10	14	12.6	0	5	4.5	0	0.0	6.30	63	.326	.373	-3	-3	99	82	0.0	-0	0	-0.2
■ BILL CASTRO	Castro, William Radhames (Checo) b: 12/13/53, Santiago, D.R. BR/TR, 5'11", 170 lbs. Deb: 8/20/74																												
1974	Mil-A	0	0	—	8	0	0	0	0	18	19	9.5	2	5	2.5	10	5.0	4.50	83	.264	.308	-2	-2	103	81	0.0	0	0	-0.1
1975	Mil-A	3	2	.600	18	5	0	0	1	75	78	9.4	3	17	2.0	25	3.0	2.52	152	.272	.309	11	11	101	133	0.8	0	0	1.2
1976	Mil-A	4	6	.400	39	0	0	0	8	70	70	9.0	4	19	2.4	23	3.0	3.47	102	.265	.316	0	0	100	102	0.0	0	-0	0.0
1977	Mil-A	8	6	.571	51	0	0	0	13	69	76	9.9	7	23	3.0	28	3.7	4.17	94	.293	.340	-1	-2	97	115	2.0	0	1	0.0
1978	Mil-A	5	4	.556	42	0	0	0	8	50	43	7.7	2	14	2.5	17	3.1	1.80	219	.234	.299	11	12	104	155	-0.1	0	0	1.3
1979	Mil-A	3	1	.750	39	0	0	0	6	44	40	8.2	2	13	2.7	10	2.0	2.05	205	.244	.293	11	11	99	140	0.8	0	-0	1.0
1980	Mil-A	2	4	.333	56	0	0	0	8	84	89	9.5	2	17	1.8	32	3.4	2.79	135	.274	.309	12	9	93	116	-1.0	0	1	1.0
1981	NY-A	1	1	.500	11	0	0	0	0	19	26	12.3	2	5	2.4	4	1.9	3.79	96	.329	.360	-0	-0	99	146	0.0	0	-0	0.0
1982	KC-A	3	2	.600	21	4	0	0	1	76	72	8.5	8	20	2.4	37	4.4	3.43	118	.243	.292	5	5	100	94	0.3	0	-1	0.4
1983	KC-A	2	0	1.000	18	0	0	0	0	41	51	11.2	4	12	2.6	17	3.7	6.59	63	.300	.358	-11	-11	102	78	1.0	0	0	-1.0
Total	10	31	26	.544	303	9	0	0	45	546	564	9.3	36	145	2.4	203	3.3	3.33	117	.269	.315	36	34	99	116	3.8	0	0	3.8

YEAR	TM/L	W	L	PCT	G	GS	CG	SHO	SV	IP	H	H/G	HR	BB	BB/G	SO	SO/G	ERA	/A	OAVG	OOBP	PR	/A	PF	CPI	WAT	PB	PD	TPI
■ **ELI CATES**	Cates, Eli Eldo b: 1/26/1877, Greensfork, Ind. d: 5/29/64, Richmond, Ind. BR/TR, 5'9.5", 175 lbs. Deb: 4/20/08																												
1908	Was-A	4	8	.333	19	10	7	0	0	115	112	8.8	3	32	2.5	33	2.6	2.50	92	.261	.314	-1	-2	97	125	-1.5	1	1	-0.2
■ **TED CATHER**	Cather, Theodore P b: 5/20/1889, Chester, Pa. d: 4/9/45, Elkton, Md. BR/TR, 5'10.5", 178 lbs. Deb: 9/23/12																												
1913	StL-N	0	0	—	1	0	0	0	0	⅓	1	27.0	0	2	54.0	0	0.0	54.00	—	.500	.800	-2	-2	97	62	0.0	0	0	-0.1
■ **HARDIN CATHEY**	Cathey, Hardin "Lil Abner" b: 7/6/19, Burns, Tenn. BR/TR, 6'4", 190 lbs. Deb: 4/16/42																												
1942	Was-A	1	1	.500	12	2	0	0	0	30	44	13.2	1	16	4.8	8	2.4	7.50	48	.341	.408	-13	-13	99	84	0.2	1	-0	-1.1
■ **KEEFE CATO**	Cato, John Keefe b: 5/6/58, Yonkers, N.Y. BR/TR, 6'1", 185 lbs. Deb: 6/13/83																												
1983	Cin-N	1	0	1.000	4	0	0	0	0	4	2	4.5	0	1	2.3	3	6.8	2.25	168	.154	.214	1	1	104	22	0.5	0	0	0.1
1984	Cin-N	0	1	.000	8	0	0	0	1	16	22	12.4	5	4	2.3	12	6.8	7.88	49	.344	.361	-8	-7	107	96	-0.4	1	0	-0.5
Total	2	1	1	.500	12	0	0	0	1	20	24	10.8	5	5	2.3	15	6.7	6.75	57	.312	.337	-7	-6	107	81	0.1	1	0	-0.4
■ **JOHN CATTANACH**	Cattanach, John Leckie b: 5/10/1863, Providence, R.I. d: 11/10/26, Providence, R.I. 5'10", Deb: 6/05/1884																												
1884	Pro-N	0	0	—	1	1	0	0	0	5	2	3.6	0	4	7.2	2	3.6	9.00	32	.128	.307	-3	-3	96	14	0.0	-1	0	-0.2
	StL-U	1	1	.500	2	2	2	0	0	17	12	6.4	0	4	2.1	13	6.9	2.12	139	.203	.254	2	2	98	77	-0.3	-1	0	0.0
■ **BILL CAUDILL**	Caudill, William Holland b: 7/13/56, Santa Monica, Cal. BR/TR, 6'1", 190 lbs. Deb: 5/12/79																												
1979	Chi-N	1	7	.125	29	12	0	0	0	90	89	8.9	16	41	4.1	104	10.4	4.80	88	.255	.333	-11	-6	112	96	-2.9	-2	1	-0.6
1980	Chi-N	4	6	.400	72	2	0	0	1	128	100	7.0	10	59	4.1	112	7.9	2.18	178	.223	.303	20	24	108	145	0.0	0	-1	2.5
1981	Chi-N	1	5	.167	30	10	0	0	0	71	87	11.0	9	31	3.9	45	5.7	5.83	64	.301	.363	-18	-17	106	94	-1.6	0	-1	-1.7
1982	Sea-A	12	9	.571	70	0	0	0	26	96	65	6.1	9	35	3.3	111	10.4	2.34	191	.192	.266	19	23	110	98	2.3	0	-1	2.2
1983	Sea-A	2	8	.200	63	0	0	0	26	73	70	8.6	10	38	4.7	73	9.0	4.68	88	.257	.347	-5	-5	101	101	-2.3	0	-1	-0.5
1984	Oak-A	9	7	.563	68	0	0	0	36	96	77	7.2	9	31	2.9	89	8.3	2.72	135	.218	.274	14	10	92	98	1.4	0	-1	0.9
1985	Tor-A	4	6	.400	67	0	0	0	14	69	53	6.9	9	35	4.6	46	6.0	3.00	137	.209	.303	9	9	99	114	-1.7	0	-1	0.8
1986	Tor-A	2	4	.333	40	0	0	0	2	36	36	9.0	6	17	4.3	32	8.0	6.25	70	.254	.337	-8	-8	104	74	-1.0	0	-1	-0.7
1987	Oak-A	0	0	—	6	0	0	0	1	8	10	11.3	3	1	1.1	8	9.0	9.00	45	.294	.314	-4	-4	91	69	0.0	0	-0	-0.3
Total	9	35	52	.402	445	24	0	0	106	667	587	7.9	81	288	3.9	620	8.4	3.68	110	.237	.312	15	27	104	107	-5.8	-1	-6	2.6
■ **RED CAUSEY**	Causey, Cecil Algernon b: 8/11/1893, Georgetown, Fla. d: 11/11/60, Avon Park, Fla. BR/TR, 6'1", 160 lbs. Deb: 4/26/18																												
1918	NY-N	11	6	.647	29	18	10	2	2	158	143	8.1	2	42	2.4	48	2.7	2.79	95	.245	.296	-0	-2	96	91	1.7	-3	-1	-0.6
1919	NY-N	9	3	.750	19	16	6	0	0	105	99	8.5	5	38	3.3	25	2.1	3.69	76	.251	.313	-9	-10	96	87	2.2	-1	-1	-1.2
	Bos-N	4	5	.444	10	10	3	0	0	69	81	10.6	1	20	2.6	14	1.8	4.57	64	.308	.351	-13	-13	100	93	0.3	-2	0	-1.4
	Yr	13	8	.619	29	26	9	0	0	174	180	9.3	6	58	3.0	39	2.0	4.03	71	.273	.325	-22	-23	98	93	2.5	-1	-2	-2.6
1920	Phi-N	7	14	.333	35	26	11	1	3	181	203	10.1	4	79	3.9	30	1.5	4.33	81	.299	.360	-24	-16	112	98	-2.0	-3	-2	-2.0
1921	Phi-N	3	3	.500	7	7	4	0	0	51	58	10.2	4	11	1.9	8	1.4	2.82	143	.294	.327	5	7	107	144	0.8	-1	-0	0.6
	NY-N	1	1	.500	7	1	0	0	0	15	13	7.8	0	6	3.6	1	0.6	2.40	148	.228	.292	2	2	94	86	-0.1	0	-0	0.2
	Yr	4	4	.500	14	8	4	0	0	66	71	9.7	4	17	2.3	9	1.2	2.73	144	.278	.315	8	9	104	86	0.7	-1	-0	0.8
1922	NY-N	4	3	.571	24	2	1	0	1	71	69	8.7	2	34	4.3	13	1.6	3.17	130	.262	.330	7	7	100	113	-0.1	-0	1	0.8
Total	5	39	35	.527	131	80	35	3	6	650	666	9.2	18	230	3.2	139	1.9	3.59	90	.273	.329	-31	-26	102	99	2.8	-9	-2	-3.6
■ **PUG CAVET**	Cavet, Tiller H. b: 12/26/1889, Mcgregor, Tex. d: 8/4/66 San Luis Obispo, Cal. TL , 6'3", 176 lbs. Deb: 4/25/11																												
1911	Det-A	0	0	—	1	1	0	0	0	4	6	13.5	0	1	2.3	1	2.3	4.50	80	.316	.350	-1	-0	107	90	0.0	-0	0	0.0
1914	Det-A	7	7	.500	31	14	6	1	2	151	129	7.7	2	44	2.6	51	3.0	2.44	114	.238	.306	5	6	102	100	-0.2	-2	1	0.7
1915	Det-A	4	2	.667	17	7	2	0	1	71	83	10.5	1	22	2.8	26	3.3	4.06	76	.300	.355	-9	-8	105	100	0.2	1	0	-0.5
Total	3	11	9	.550	49	22	8	1	3	226	218	8.7	3	67	2.7	78	3.1	2.99	97	.260	.323	-4	-2	103	100	0.0	-0	1	0.2
■ **JOSE CECENA**	Cecena, Jose Isabel (Lugo) b: 8/20/63, Ciudad Obregon, Mexico BR/TR, 5'11", 180 lbs. Deb: 4/06/88																												
1988	Tex-A	0	0	—	22	0	0	0	1	26	20	6.9	2	23	8.0	27	9.3	4.85	84	.213	.372	-3	-2	102	89	0.0	0	-0	-0.1
■ **ART CECCARELLI**	Ceccarelli, Arthur Edward "Chic" b: 4/2/30, New Haven, Conn. BR/TL, 6', 190 lbs. Deb: 5/03/55																												
1955	KC-A	4	7	.364	31	16	3	1	0	124	123	8.9	20	71	5.2	68	4.9	5.30	79	.258	.348	-18	-15	106	91	-0.6	-3	-2	-1.8
1956	KC-A	0	1	.000	3	2	0	0	0	10	13	11.7	3	4	3.6	2	1.8	7.20	60	.317	.367	-3	-3	105	102	-0.4	-0	1	-0.2
1957	Bal-A	0	5	.000	20	8	1	0	0	58	62	9.6	3	31	4.8	30	4.7	4.50	78	.278	.361	-5	-6	93	100	-2.4	-1	-1	-0.8
1959	Chi-N	5	5	.500	18	15	4	2	0	102	95	8.4	19	37	3.3	56	4.9	4.76	82	.245	.308	-9	-10	99	87	0.2	-1	-1	-1.0
1960	Chi-N	0	0	—	7	1	0	0	0	13	16	11.1	1	4	2.8	10	6.9	5.54	68	.296	.339	-3	-3	101	82	0.0	0	-0	-0.2
Total	5	9	18	.333	79	42	8	3	0	307	309	9.1	46	147	4.3	166	4.9	5.04	78	.261	.338	-38	-37	101	91	-3.2	-6	-2	-4.0
■ **REX CECIL**	Cecil, Rex Rolston b: 10/8/16, Lindsay, Okla. d: 10/30/66, Long Beach, Cal. BL/TR, 6'3", 195 lbs. Deb: 8/13/44																												
1944	Bos-A	4	5	.444	11	9	4	0	0	61	72	10.6	5	33	4.9	33	4.9	5.16	64	.286	.364	-12	-13	97	95	-0.4	2	-0	-1.0
1945	Bos-A	2	5	.286	7	7	1	0	0	45	46	9.2	4	27	5.4	30	6.0	5.20	62	.261	.353	-9	-10	96	85	-1.3	1	1	-0.7
Total	2	6	10	.375	18	16	5	0	0	106	118	10.0	9	60	5.1	63	5.3	5.18	63	.276	.359	-21	-22	96	91	-1.7	2	1	-1.7
■ **PETE CENTER**	Center, Marvin Earl b: 4/22/12, Hazel Green, Ky. BR/TR, 6'4", 190 lbs. Deb: 9/11/42																												
1942	Cle-A	0	0	—	1	0	0	0	0	3	7	21.0	0	4	12.0	0	0.0	18.00	19	.438	.545	-5	-5	93	73	0.0	-0	-0	-0.3
1943	Cle-A	1	2	.333	24	1	0	0	1	42	29	6.2	3	18	3.9	10	2.1	2.79	106	.201	.281	2	1	90	92	-0.5	-1	-0	0.0
1945	Cle-A	6	3	.667	31	8	2	0	1	86	89	9.3	2	28	2.9	34	3.6	3.98	83	.270	.320	-6	-6	98	87	1.5	-2	-2	-1.0
1946	Cle-A	0	2	.000	21	0	0	0	1	29	29	9.0	2	20	6.2	6	1.9	4.97	64	.269	.382	-5	-6	90	97	-0.9	-0	-0	-0.6
Total	4	7	7	.500	77	9	2	0	3	160	154	8.7	7	70	3.9	50	2.8	4.11	78	.258	.329	-13	-16	94	90	0.1	-3	-2	-1.9
■ **RICK CERONE**	Cerone, Richard Aldo b: 5/19/54, Newark, N.J. BR/TR, 5'11", 192 lbs. Deb: 8/17/75																												
1987	NY-A	0	0	—	2	0	0	0	0	2	0	0.0	0	1	4.5	1	4.5	0.00	—	.000	.143	1	1	97	0	0.0	1	0	0.1
■ **JOHN CERUTTI**	Cerutti, John Joseph b: 4/28/60, Albany, N.Y. BL/TL, 6'2", 195 lbs. Deb: 9/01/85																												
1985	Tor-A	0	2	.000	4	1	0	0	0	7	10	12.9	1	4	5.1	5	6.4	5.14	80	.323	.417	-1	-1	99	136	-0.9	0	0	0.0
1986	Tor-A	9	4	.692	34	20	2	1	1	145	150	9.3	25	47	2.9	89	5.5	4.16	105	.268	.321	0	3	104	111	2.4	0	0	0.3
1987	Tor-A	11	4	.733	44	21	2	0	0	151	144	8.6	30	59	3.5	92	5.5	4.41	101	.251	.320	1	1	99	104	2.8	0	-2	0.0
1988	Tor-A	6	7	.462	46	12	0	0	1	124	120	8.7	12	42	3.0	65	4.7	3.12	126	.256	.315	12	11	99	124	-0.9	0	3	1.4
Total	4	26	17	.605	128	54	4	1	2	427	424	8.9	68	152	3.2	251	5.3	3.96	108	.260	.321	12	14	101	112	3.4	0	1	1.7
■ **RAY CHADWICK**	Chadwick, Ray Charles b: 11/17/62, Durham, N.C. BB/TR, 6'2", 180 lbs. Deb: 7/29/86																												
1986	Cal-A	0	5	.000	7	7	0	0	0	27	39	13.0	5	15	5.0	9	3.0	7.33	54	.336	.414	-9	-10	95	101	-2.4	0	0	-0.8
■ **LEON CHAGNON**	Chagnon, Leon Wilbur "Shag" b: 9/28/02, Pittsfield, N.H. d: 7/30/53, Amesbury, Mass. BR/TR, 6', 182 lbs. Deb: 10/05/29																												
1929	Pit-N	0	0	—	1	1	0	0	0	7	11	14.1	1	1	1.3	4	5.1	9.00	53	.333	.353	-3	-3	102	63	0.0	-0	0	-0.2
1930	Pit-N	0	3	.000	18	4	3	0	0	62	92	13.4	9	23	3.3	27	3.9	6.82	71	.355	.400	-13	-14	98	107	-1.4	-1	0	-1.1
1932	Pit-N	9	6	.600	30	10	4	1	0	128	140	9.8	10	34	2.4	52	3.7	3.94	98	.276	.316	-1	-1	100	101	0.8	2	-1	0.0
1933	Pit-N	6	4	.600	39	5	1	0	1	100	100	9.0	2	17	1.5	35	3.2	3.69	85	.259	.288	-4	-6	94	74	0.4	-2	-1	-0.8
1934	Pit-N	4	1	.800	33	1	0	0	1	58	68	10.6	5	24	3.7	19	2.9	4.81	89	.288	.343	-5	-4	105	100	1.5	0	1	-0.1
1935	NY-N	0	2	.000	14	1	0	0	1	38	32	7.6	7	5	1.2	16	3.8	3.55	107	.232	.250	2	1	95	94	-0.9	-1	0	0.0
Total	6	19	16	.543	135	22	8	1	3	393	443	10.1	34	104	2.4	153	3.5	4.51	86	.284	.323	-24	-27	98	93	0.4	-2	-0	-2.2
■ **BOB CHAKALES**	Chakales, Robert Edward "Chick" b: 8/10/27, Asheville, N.C. BR/TR, 6'1", 185 lbs. Deb: 4/21/51																												
1951	Cle-A	3	4	.429	17	10	2	1	0	68	80	10.6	3	43	5.7	32	4.2	4.76	80	.292	.383	-5	-7	93	108	-1.0	2	-0	-0.4
1952	Cle-A	1	2	.333	5	1	0	0	0	12	19	14.3	2	8	6.0	7	5.3	9.75	33	.388	.466	-8	-9	88	91	-0.6	1	-0	-0.7
1953	Cle-A	0	2	.000	7	3	1	0	0	27	28	9.3	2	10	3.3	6	2.0	2.67	139	.283	.336	4	3	93	169	-0.9	0	0	0.4
1954	Cle-A	2	0	1.000	3	0	0	0	0	10	4	3.6	0	12	10.8	3	2.7	0.90	419	.114	.340	3	3	101	200	1.0	1	-0	0.4
	Bal-A	3	7	.300	38	6	0	0	3	89	81	8.2	8	43	4.3	44	4.4	3.74	98	.245	.324	-0	-1	99	99	-0.7	2	0	0.2
	Yr	5	7	.417	41	6	0	0	3	99	85	7.7	8	55	5.0	47	4.3	3.45	107	.232	.326	3	3	99	99	0.3	1	-0	0.6
1955	Chi-A	0	0	—	7	0	0	0	0	12	11	8.3	2	6	4.5	6	4.5	1.50	258	.256	.340	3	3	98	315	0.0	-0	0	0.3
	Was-A	2	3	.400	29	0	0	0	0	55	55	9.0	4	25	4.1	28	4.6	5.24	71	.263	.335	-8	-9	94	77	0.2	-1	1	-0.9

YEAR	TM/L	W	L	PCT	G	GS	CG	SHO	SV	IP	H	H/G	HR	BB	BB/G	SO	SO/G	ERA	/A	OAVG	OOBP	PR	/A	PF	CPI	WAT	PB	PD	TPI
	Yr	2	3	.400	36	0	0	0	0	67	66	8.9	6	31	4.2	34	4.6	4.57	82	.262	.336	-4	-6	95	77	0.2	-0	1	-0.6
1956	Was-A	4	4	.500	43	1	0	0	4	96	94	8.8	3	57	5.3	33	3.1	4.03	110	.268	.364	1	4	107	108	0.8	-1	1	0.4
1957	Was-A	0	1	.000	4	2	0	0	0	18	20	10.0	2	10	5.0	12	6.0	5.50	70	.274	.353	-3	-3	102	86	-0.4	0	0	-0.2
	Bos-A	0	2	.000	18	0	0	0	3	32	53	14.9	5	11	3.1	16	4.5	8.16	51	.379	.419	-16	-14	109	95	-0.9	1	-1	-1.3
	Yr	0	3	.000	22	2	0	0	3	50	73	13.1	7	21	3.8	28	5.0	7.20	56	.341	.396	-19	-18	106	95	-1.3	0	-0	-1.5
Total	7	15	25	.375	171	23	3	1	10	419	445	9.6	31	225	4.8	187	4.0	4.55	86	.277	.360	-28	-30	99	111	-2.5	4	1	-1.8

■ GEORGE CHALMERS Chalmers, George W. "Dut" b: 6/7/1888, Edinburgh, Scot. d: 8/5/40, Bronx, N.Y. BR/TR, 6'1", 189 lbs. Deb: 9/21/10

YEAR	TM/L	W	L	PCT	G	GS	CG	SHO	SV	IP	H	H/G	HR	BB	BB/G	SO	SO/G	ERA	/A	OAVG	OOBP	PR	/A	PF	CPI	WAT	PB	PD	TPI
1910	Phi-N	1	1	.500	4	3	2	0	0	22	21	8.6	0	11	4.5	12	4.9	5.32	54	.280	.379	-6	-6	95	75	0.0	-0	1	-0.4
1911	Phi-N	13	10	.565	38	22	11	3	4	209	196	8.4	5	101	4.3	101	4.3	3.10	118	.256	.346	7	13	108	113	1.3	-2	-1	1.1
1912	Phi-N	3	4	.429	12	8	3	0	0	58	64	9.9	4	37	5.7	22	3.4	3.26	105	.288	.395	1	1	101	152	-0.3	0	-2	0.0
1913	Phi-N	3	10	.231	26	13	4	0	1	116	133	10.3	3	51	4.0	46	3.6	4.81	74	.296	.368	-21	-16	111	93	-4.0	-1	1	-1.5
1914	Phi-N	0	3	.000	3	2	1	0	0	18	23	11.5	0	15	7.5	6	3.0	5.50	51	.324	.443	-5	-5	101	110	-1.4	-1	0	-0.5
1915	Phi-N	8	9	.471	26	20	13	1	1	170	159	8.4	3	45	2.4	82	4.3	2.49	115	.255	.297	5	7	104	110	-1.8	-1	1	0.8
1916	Phi-N	1	4	.200	12	8	2	0	0	54	49	8.2	2	19	3.2	21	3.5	3.17	78	.244	.302	-3	-4	94	91	-1.6	-2	0	-0.6
Total	7	29	41	.414	121	76	36	4	6	647	645	9.0	17	279	3.9	290	4.0	3.41	96	.268	.343	-22	-11	105	109	-7.8	-6	1	-1.1

■ CRAIG CHAMBERLAIN Chamberlain, Craig Philip b: 2/2/57, Hollywood, Cal. BR/TR, 6'1", 190 lbs. Deb: 8/12/79

YEAR	TM/L	W	L	PCT	G	GS	CG	SHO	SV	IP	H	H/G	HR	BB	BB/G	SO	SO/G	ERA	/A	OAVG	OOBP	PR	/A	PF	CPI	WAT	PB	PD	TPI
1979	KC-A	4	4	.500	10	10	4	0	0	70	68	8.7	7	18	2.3	30	3.9	3.73	119	.261	.303	4	6	105	99	-0.1	0	-2	0.4
1980	KC-A	0	1	.000	5	0	0	0	0	9	10	10.0	3	5	5.0	3	3.0	7.00	56	.270	.349	-3	-3	97	90	-0.4	0	0	-0.2
Total	2	4	5	.444	15	10	4	0	0	79	78	8.9	10	23	2.6	33	3.8	4.10	107	.262	.309	1	2	104	98	-0.5	0	-2	0.2

■ BILL CHAMBERLAIN Chamberlain, William Vincent b: 4/21/09, Stoughton, Mass. BR/TL, 5'10.5", 173 lbs. Deb: 8/02/32

YEAR	TM/L	W	L	PCT	G	GS	CG	SHO	SV	IP	H	H/G	HR	BB	BB/G	SO	SO/G	ERA	/A	OAVG	OOBP	PR	/A	PF	CPI	WAT	PB	PD	TPI
1932	Chi-A	0	5	.000	12	5	0	0	0	41	39	8.6	3	25	5.5	11	2.4	4.61	88	.250	.344	-1	-2	91	95	-2.4	-0	-1	-0.3

■ ICEBOX CHAMBERLIN Chamberlin, Elton P. b: 11/5/1867, Buffalo, N.Y. d: 9/22/29, Baltimore, Md. BR/TB, Deb: 1886

YEAR	TM/L	W	L	PCT	G	GS	CG	SHO	SV	IP	H	H/G	HR	BB	BB/G	SO	SO/G	ERA	/A	OAVG	OOBP	PR	/A	PF	CPI	WAT	PB	PD	TPI
1886	Lou-a	0	3	.000	4	4	4	0	0	31	39	11.3	0	17	4.9	18	5.2	6.68	56	.318	.401	-11	-10	108	80	-1.4	-0	0	-0.7
1887	Lou-a	18	16	.529	36	36	35	1	0	309	340	9.9	8	117	3.4	118	3.4	3.79	120	.293	.358	18	26	106	111	-1.1	-4	0	1.9
1888	Lou-a	14	9	.609	24	24	21	1	0	196	177	8.1	2	59	2.7	119	5.5	2.53	113	.254	.312	12	7	93	110	5.0	1	0	0.7
	StL-a	11	2	.846	14	14	13	1	0	112	61	4.9	1	27	2.2	57	4.6	1.61	202	.170	.228	18	20	106	51	3.5	-3	0	1.8
	Yr	25	11	.694	38	38	34	2	0	308	238	7.0	3	86	2.5	176	5.1	2.19	137	.225	.283	30	28	98	51	**8.5**	1	0	2.5
1889	StL-a	32	15	.681	53	51	44	2	1	422	376	8.0	18	165	3.5	202	4.3	2.96	141	.253	.327	41	57	109	103	1.5	-1	-3	4.8
1890	StL-a	3	1	.750	5	5	3	0	0	35	47	12.1	0	26	6.7	14	3.6	5.91	75	.338	.443	-8	-6	115	105	0.8	-2	0	-0.5
	Col-a	12	6	.667	25	21	19	6	0	175	128	6.6	3	70	3.6	114	5.9	2.21	168	.218	.301	32	29	96	108	1.9	2	0	2.9
	Yr	15	7	.682	30	26	22	**6**	0	210	175	7.5	3	96	4.1	128	5.5	2.83	135	.241	.329	24	23	99	108	2.7	-2	0	2.4
1891	Phi-a	22	23	.489	49	46	44	0	0	406	397	8.8	10	206	4.6	204	4.5	4.23	90	.270	.360	-23	-19	103	83	-2.1	2	0	-1.2
1892	Cin-N	19	23	.452	52	49	43	2	0	406	391	8.7	8	170	3.8	169	3.7	3.39	100	.266	.342	-5	-0	103	95	-4.6	2	-4	0.0
1893	Cin-N	16	12	.571	34	27	19	1	0	241	248	9.3	3	112	4.2	59	2.2	3.73	128	.281	.362	25	28	102	103	2.2	-3	-1	2.0
1894	Cin-N	10	9	.526	23	22	18	1	0	178	220	11.1	10	91	4.6	57	2.9	5.81	93	.326	.406	-10	-8	102	91	1.9	5	0	-0.1
1896	Cle-N	0	1	.000	2	2	1	0	0	11	21	17.2	0	5	4.1	2	1.6	7.36	64	.428	.481	-4	-3	108	108	-0.4	-0	0	-0.2
Total	10	157	120	.567	321	301	264	15	1	2522	2445	8.7	63	1065	3.8	1133	4.0	3.57	112	.269	.345	86	120	103	97	7.2	-2	-8	11.4

■ CLIFF CHAMBERS Chambers, Clifford Day "Lefty" b: 1/10/22, Portland, Ore. BL/TL, 6'3", 208 lbs. Deb: 4/24/48

YEAR	TM/L	W	L	PCT	G	GS	CG	SHO	SV	IP	H	H/G	HR	BB	BB/G	SO	SO/G	ERA	/A	OAVG	OOBP	PR	/A	PF	CPI	WAT	PB	PD	TPI
1948	Chi-N	2	9	.182	29	12	3	1	0	104	100	8.7	4	48	4.2	51	4.4	4.41	85	.254	.334	-5	-8	95	84	-3.1	-1	0	-0.7
1949	Pit-N	13	7	.650	34	21	10	1	0	177	186	9.5	15	58	2.9	93	4.7	3.97	104	.268	.325	1	3	102	101	3.8	3	1	0.7
1950	Pit-N	12	15	.444	37	33	11	2	0	249	262	9.5	18	92	3.3	93	3.4	4.30	102	.265	.328	-4	2	106	90	1.8	7	-3	0.7
1951	Pit-N	3	6	.333	10	10	2	1	0	60	64	9.6	5	31	4.7	19	2.9	5.55	78	.276	.364	-11	-8	110	87	-0.8	2	-2	-0.6
	StL-N	11	6	.647	21	16	9	1	0	129	120	8.4	13	56	3.9	45	3.1	3.84	104	.251	.324	2	2	101	102	2.4	-0	-1	0.1
	Yr	14	12	.538	31	26	11	2	0	189	184	8.8	18	87	4.1	64	3.0	4.38	94	.257	.333	-9	-6	104	102	1.6	2	-3	-0.5
1952	StL-N	4	4	.500	26	13	2	1	1	98	110	10.1	8	33	3.0	47	4.3	4.13	88	.285	.339	-4	-6	97	108	-0.4	4	0	-0.1
1953	StL-N	3	6	.333	32	8	0	0	0	80	82	9.2	7	43	4.8	26	2.9	4.84	89	.266	.348	-5	-5	101	94	-1.7	-1	0	-0.4
Total	6	48	53	.475	189	113	37	7	1	897	924	9.3	70	361	3.6	374	3.8	4.29	96	.266	.333	-26	-19	102	95	2.0	14	-4	-0.3

■ ROME CHAMBERS Chambers, Jerome b: 8/1874, Weaverville, N.C. BL/TL, 6'2", 173 lbs. Deb: 5/07/00

YEAR	TM/L	W	L	PCT	G	GS	CG	SHO	SV	IP	H	H/G	HR	BB	BB/G	SO	SO/G	ERA	/A	OAVG	OOBP	PR	/A	PF	CPI	WAT	PB	PD	TPI
1900	Bos-N	0	0	—	1	0	0	0	1	4	5	11.3	0	5	11.3	2	4.5	11.25	39	.330	.496	-3	-3	120	61	0.0	-0	0	-0.2

■ JOHNNIE CHAMBERS Chambers, Johnnie Monroe b: 9/10/11, Copper Hill, Tenn d: 5/11/77, Palatka, Fla. BL/TR, 6', 185 lbs. Deb: 5/04/37

YEAR	TM/L	W	L	PCT	G	GS	CG	SHO	SV	IP	H	H/G	HR	BB	BB/G	SO	SO/G	ERA	/A	OAVG	OOBP	PR	/A	PF	CPI	WAT	PB	PD	TPI
1937	StL-N	0	0	—	2	0	0	0	0	2	5	22.5	0	2	9.0	1	4.5	18.00	22	.455	.538	-3	-3	100	67	0.0	0	0	-0.2

■ BILL CHAMBERS Chambers, William Christopher b: 9/13/1889, Cameron, W.Va. d: 3/27/62, Fort Wayne, Ind. 5'9", 185 lbs. Deb: 7/11/10

YEAR	TM/L	W	L	PCT	G	GS	CG	SHO	SV	IP	H	H/G	HR	BB	BB/G	SO	SO/G	ERA	/A	OAVG	OOBP	PR	/A	PF	CPI	WAT	PB	PD	TPI
1910	StL-N	0	0	—	1	0	0	0	0	1	1	9.0	0	0	0.0	0	0.0	0.00	—	.250	.250	0	0	93	0	0.0	0	0	0.0

■ BILL CHAMPION Champion, Buford Billy b: 9/18/47, Shelby, N.C. BR/TR, 6'4", 188 lbs. Deb: 6/04/69

YEAR	TM/L	W	L	PCT	G	GS	CG	SHO	SV	IP	H	H/G	HR	BB	BB/G	SO	SO/G	ERA	/A	OAVG	OOBP	PR	/A	PF	CPI	WAT	PB	PD	TPI
1969	Phi-N	5	10	.333	23	20	4	2	1	117	130	10.0	7	63	4.8	70	5.4	5.00	72	.286	.366	-18	-18	100	96	-1.1	0	1	-1.6
1970	Phi-N	0	2	.000	7	1	0	0	0	14	21	13.5	3	10	6.4	12	7.7	9.00	44	.375	.457	-8	-8	98	103	-0.9	-0	0	-0.7
1971	Phi-N	3	5	.375	37	9	0	0	0	109	100	8.3	10	48	4.0	49	4.0	4.38	83	.249	.324	-11	-9	105	87	-0.3	-1	1	-0.9
1972	Phi-N	4	14	.222	30	22	2	0	0	133	155	10.5	11	54	3.7	54	3.7	5.08	67	.301	.360	-24	-25	99	98	-3.9	0	1	-2.3
1973	Mil-A	5	8	.385	37	11	2	0	1	136	139	9.2	10	62	4.1	67	4.4	3.71	99	.267	.346	2	-0	96	111	-1.0	0	2	0.1
1974	Mil-A	11	4	.733	31	23	2	0	0	162	168	9.3	12	49	2.7	60	3.3	3.61	103	.270	.319	0	2	103	101	3.9	0	-1	0.1
1975	Mil-A	6	6	.500	27	13	3	1	0	110	125	10.2	11	55	4.5	40	3.3	5.89	65	.290	.363	-26	-25	101	85	0.9	0	0	-2.3
1976	Mil-A	0	1	.000	10	3	0	0	0	24	35	13.1	0	13	4.9	8	3.0	7.13	49	.361	.426	-10	-10	100	91	-0.4	0	1	-0.8
Total	8	34	50	.405	202	102	13	3	2	805	873	9.8	64	354	4.0	360	4.0	4.68	78	.282	.350	-94	-93	100	97	-2.8	-1	4	-8.4

■ DEAN CHANCE Chance, Wilmer Dean b: 6/1/41, Wayne, O. BR/TR, 6'3", 200 lbs. Deb: 9/11/61

YEAR	TM/L	W	L	PCT	G	GS	CG	SHO	SV	IP	H	H/G	HR	BB	BB/G	SO	SO/G	ERA	/A	OAVG	OOBP	PR	/A	PF	CPI	WAT	PB	PD	TPI
1961	LA-A	0	2	.000	5	4	0	0	0	18	33	16.5	0	5	2.5	11	5.5	7.00	64	.412	.443	-6	-5	112	110	-0.9	-1	1	-0.4
1962	LA-A	14	10	.583	50	24	6	2	8	207	195	8.5	14	66	2.9	127	5.5	2.96	137	.250	.308	23	25	102	**114**	1.5	-5	1	2.2
1963	LA-A	13	18	.419	45	35	6	2	3	248	229	8.3	10	90	3.3	168	6.1	3.19	105	.243	.311	12	4	92	98	-0.6	-1	1	0.4
1964	LA-A	**20**	9	.690	46	35	**15**	**11**	4	**278**	194	6.3	7	86	2.8	207	6.7	**1.65**	**195**	.195	.258	**61**	**48**	89	96	6.1	-4	-2	4.5
1965	Cal-A	15	10	.600	36	33	10	4	0	226	197	7.8	12	101	4.0	164	6.5	3.15	108	.238	.323	8	6	98	107	3.6	-2	3	0.8
1966	Cal-A	12	17	.414	41	37	11	2	1	260	206	7.1	18	114	3.9	180	6.2	3.08	111	.222	.306	10	10	100	102	-2.7	-6	2	0.6
1967	Min-A	20	14	.588	41	39	**18**	5	1	**284**	244	7.7	17	68	2.2	220	7.0	2.73	125	.229	.275	16	22	106	94	1.3	-6	1	2.0
1968	Min-A	16	16	.500	43	39	15	6	1	292	224	6.9	15	63	1.9	234	7.2	2.53	125	.211	.256	15	20	106	79	0.5	-6	3	2.1
1969	Min-A	5	4	.556	20	15	1	0	0	88	76	7.8	6	35	3.6	50	5.1	2.97	122	.233	.310	6	6	100	106	-0.2	-1	-1	0.4
1970	Cle-A	9	8	.529	45	19	1	1	4	155	172	10.0	18	59	3.4	109	6.3	4.24	101	.287	.350	-9	1	115	114	1.1	-3	-1	-0.2
	NY-N	0	1	.000	3	0	0	0	1	2	3	13.5	0	2	9.0	0	0.0	13.50	31	.500	.500	-2	-2	103	79	-0.4	0	0	-0.1
1971	Det-A	4	6	.400	31	14	0	0	0	90	91	9.1	5	50	5.0	64	6.4	3.50	94	.265	.358	-0	-2	95	121	-1.4	-2	0	-0.4
Total	11	128	115	.527	406	294	83	33	23	2148	1864	7.8	122	739	3.1	1534	6.4	2.92	119	.234	.300	134	135	100	100	7.9	-37	8	11.9

■ ED CHANDLER Chandler, Edward Oliver b: 2/17/22, Pinson, Ala. BR/TR, 6'2", 190 lbs. Deb: 4/18/47

YEAR	TM/L	W	L	PCT	G	GS	CG	SHO	SV	IP	H	H/G	HR	BB	BB/G	SO	SO/G	ERA	/A	OAVG	OOBP	PR	/A	PF	CPI	WAT	PB	PD	TPI
1947	Bro-N	0	1	.000	15	1	0	0	1	30	31	9.3	7	12	3.6	8	2.4	6.30	66	.263	.328	-7	-7	103	80	-0.4	0	0	-0.6

■ SPUD CHANDLER Chandler, Spurgeon Ferdinand b: 9/12/07, Commerce, Ga. BR/TR, 6', 181 lbs. Deb: 5/06/37 C

YEAR	TM/L	W	L	PCT	G	GS	CG	SHO	SV	IP	H	H/G	HR	BB	BB/G	SO	SO/G	ERA	/A	OAVG	OOBP	PR	/A	PF	CPI	WAT	PB	PD	TPI
1937	NY-A	7	4	.636	12	10	6	2	0	82	79	8.7	8	20	2.2	31	3.4	2.85	157	.253	.298	16	15	97	123	-0.1	-2	2	1.4
1938	NY-A	14	5	.737	23	23	14	2	0	172	183	9.6	7	47	2.5	36	1.9	4.03	121	.271	.315	15	16	102	91	2.6	2	4	2.1
1939	NY-A	3	0	1.000	11	0	0	0	0	19	26	12.3	0	9	4.3	4	1.9	2.84	139	.329	.389	4	2	85	198	1.5	1	1	0.4
1940	NY-A	8	7	.533	27	24	6	1	0	172	184	9.6	12	60	3.1	56	2.9	4.60	91	.275	.337	-4	-8	96	94	-0.4	1	3	-0.3
1941	NY-A	10	4	.714	28	20	11	4	4	164	146	8.0	5	60	3.3	60	3.3	3.18	123	.239	.302	18	14	95	93	1.3	-1	3	1.5
1942	NY-A	16	5	.762	24	24	17	3	0	201	176	7.9	13	74	3.3	74	3.3	2.37	145	.237	.306	29	24	94	**136**	3.3	4	3	3.3
1943	NY-A	**20**	4	**.833**	30	30	**20**	**5**	0	253	197	7.0	5	54	1.9	134	4.8	**1.64**	**189**	.215	**.258**	**47**	**41**	94	110	**7.0**	7	3	**6.1**
1944	NY-A	0	0	—	1	1	0	0	0	6	6	9.0	1	1	1.5	1	1.5	4.50	80	.300	.333	-1	-1	105	120	0.0	-0	0	0.0

YEAR	TM/L	W	L	PCT	G	GS	CG	SHO	SV	IP	H	H/G	HR	BB	BB/G	SO	SO/G	ERA	/A	OAVG	OOBP	PR	/A	PF	CPI	WAT	PB	PD	TPI
1945	NY-A	2	1	.667	4	4	2	1	0	31	30	8.7	2	7	2.0	12	3.5	4.65	77	.250	.291	-4	-4	106	63	0.4	1	0	-0.2
1946	NY-A	20	8	.714	34	32	20	6	2	257	200	7.0	7	90	3.2	138	4.8	2.10	163	.218	.283	40	38	98	106	5.5	-0	4	4.7
1947	NY-A	9	5	.643	17	16	13	2	0	128	100	7.0	4	41	2.9	68	4.8	2.46	139	.214	.272	18	14	92	85	0.3	4	3	2.3
Total	11	109	43	.717	211	184	109	26	6	1485	1327	8.0	64	463	2.8	614	3.7	2.84	132	.240	.296	176	149	96	106	21.4	16	27	21.3
■ ESTY CHANEY	Chaney, Esty Clyon b: 1/29/1891, Hadley, Pa. d: 2/5/52, Cleveland, Ohio BR/TR, 5'11", 170 lbs. Deb: 8/02/13																												
1913	Bos-A	0	0	—	1	0	0	0	0	1	1	9.0	0	2	18.0	0	0.0	9.00	33	.200	.429	-1	-1	103	55	0.0	0	0	0.0
1914	Bro-F	0	0	—	1	0	0	0	0	4	7	15.8	0	2	4.5	1	2.3	6.75	48	.416	.478	-2	-2	101	109	0.0	-0	0	-0.1
Total	2	0	0	—	2	0	0	0	0	5	8	14.4	0	4	7.2	1	1.8	7.20	44	.367	.465	-2	-2	101	98	0.0	-0	0	-0.1
■ TINY CHAPLIN	Chaplin, James Bailey b: 7/13/05, Los Angeles, Cal. d: 3/25/39, National City, Cal BR/TR, 6'1", 195 lbs. Deb: 4/13/28																												
1928	NY-N	0	2	.000	12	1	0	0	0	24	27	10.1	0	8	3.0	5	1.9	4.50	88	.284	.330	-1	-1	99	78	-0.9	-1	-0	-0.2
1930	NY-N	2	6	.250	19	8	3	0	1	73	89	11.0	8	16	2.0	20	2.5	5.18	92	.305	.343	-2	-3	96	96	-2.2	-0	0	-0.2
1931	NY-N	3	0	1.000	16	3	1	0	1	42	39	8.4	2	16	3.4	7	1.5	3.21	112	.242	.315	3	2	93	99	1.5	0	-1	0.1
1936	Bos-N	10	15	.400	40	31	14	0	2	232	273	10.6	21	62	2.4	86	3.3	4.11	94	.294	.337	-2	-6	96	111	-1.8	-0	2	-0.4
Total	4	15	23	.395	87	43	18	0	4	371	428	10.4	31	102	2.5	118	2.9	4.25	95	.290	.335	-2	-9	96	105	-3.4	-1	1	-0.7
■ ED CHAPMAN	Chapman, Edwin Volney b: 11/28/05, Courtland, Miss. BB/TR, 6'1", 185 lbs. Deb: 8/06/33																												
1933	Was-A	0	0	—	6	1	0	0	0	9	10	10.0	2	2	2.0	4	4.0	8.00	50	.270	.308	-4	-4	93	61	0.0	-0	-0	-0.3
■ FRED CHAPMAN	Chapman, Frederick Joseph b: 11/24/1872, Little Cooley, Pa. d: 12/14/57, Union City, Pa. BR/TR, 5'8", 165 lbs. Deb: 7/22/1887																												
1887	Phi-a	0	0	—	1	1	1	0	0	5	8	14.4	0	2	3.6	4	7.2	7.20	59	.376	.430	-2	-2	100	91	0.0	-0	0	-0.1
■ BEN CHAPMAN	Chapman, William Benjamin b: 12/25/08, Nashville, Tenn. BR/TR, 6', 190 lbs. Deb: 4/15/30 MC																												
1944	Bro-N	5	3	.625	11	9	6	0	0	79	75	8.5	4	33	3.8	37	4.2	3.42	108	.242	.318	2	2	102	96	1.5	6	-2	0.7
1945	Bro-N	3	3	.500	10	7	2	0	0	54	64	10.7	3	32	5.3	23	3.8	5.50	65	.296	.390	-10	-11	95	98	-0.3	-0	1	-1.0
	Phi-N	0	0	—	3	0	0	0	0	7	7	9.0	0	6	7.7	4	5.1	7.71	50	.259	.382	-3	-3	102	59	0.0	0	0	-0.2
	Yr	3	3	.500	13	7	2	0	0	61	71	10.5	3	38	5.6	27	4.0	5.75	63	.289	.378	-13	-14	95	59	-0.3	-0	1	-1.2
1946	Phi-N	0	0	—	1	0	0	0	0	1	1	9.0	0	0	0.0	1	9.0	0.00	—	.200	.200	0	0	98	0	0.0	-0	0	0.0
Total	3	8	6	.571	25	16	8	0	0	141	147	9.4	7	71	4.5	65	4.1	4.40	83	.263	.349	-11	-12	99	94	1.2	6	-1	-0.5
■ BILL CHAPPELLE	Chappelle, William Hogan "Big Bill" b: 3/22/1884, Waterloo, N.Y. d: 12/31/44, Mineola, N.Y. BR/TR, 6'2", 206 lbs. Deb: 8/20/08																												
1908	Bos-N	2	4	.333	13	7	3	1	0	70	60	7.7	0	17	2.2	23	3.0	1.80	138	.263	.325	4	5	106	126	-0.5	-1	1	0.7
1909	Bos-N	1	1	.500	5	3	2	0	0	29	31	9.6	0	11	3.4	8	2.5	1.86	142	.279	.350	2	3	102	190	0.3	2	1	0.4
	Cin-N	0	0	—	1	0	0	0	1	4	5	11.3	0	2	4.5	0	0.0	2.25	108	.278	.381	0	0	94	196	0.0	-0	0	0.0
	Yr	1	1	.500	6	3	2	0	1	33	36	9.8	0	13	3.5	8	2.2	1.91	137	.277	.347	3	3	101	196	0.3	2	1	0.4
1914	Bro-F	4	2	.667	16	6	4	0	0	74	71	8.6	1	29	3.5	31	3.8	3.16	102	.255	.332	0	1	101	100	1.0	-3	0	-0.2
Total	3	7	7	.500	35	16	9	1	1	177	167	8.5	1	59	3.0	62	3.2	2.39	118	.263	.334	7	9	103	127	0.8	-3	2	0.9
■ NORM CHARLTON	Charlton, Norman Wood b: 1/6/63, Fort Polk, La. BB/TR, 6'3", 195 lbs. Deb: 8/19/88																												
1988	Cin-N	4	5	.444	10	10	0	0	0	61	60	8.9	6	20	3.0	39	5.8	3.98	91	.256	.317	-4	-2	105	97	-0.7	-1	-0	-0.3
■ PETE CHARTON	Charton, Frank Lane b: 12/21/42, Jackson, Tenn. BL/TR, 6'2", 190 lbs. Deb: 4/19/64																												
1964	Bos-A	0	2	.000	25	5	0	0	0	65	67	9.3	12	24	3.3	37	5.1	5.26	71	.275	.338	-12	-11	103	95	-0.9	-0	2	-0.9
■ KEN CHASE	Chase, Kendall Fay "Lefty" b: 10/6/13, Oneonta, N.Y. d: 1/16/85, Oneonta, N.Y. BL/TL, 6'2", 210 lbs. Deb: 4/23/36																												
1936	Was-A	0	0	—	1	0	0	0	0	2	2	9.0	0	4	18.0	1	4.5	13.50	36	.250	.500	-2	-2	96	56	0.0	0	0	0.0
1937	Was-A	4	3	.571	14	9	4	0	0	76	74	8.8	4	60	7.1	43	5.1	4.14	106	.257	.381	4	2	96	115	0.7	-4	-0	-0.1
1938	Was-A	9	10	.474	32	21	7	0	1	150	151	9.1	4	113	6.8	64	3.8	5.58	82	.268	.389	-13	-17	96	89	-0.4	1	1	-1.3
1939	Was-A	10	19	.345	32	31	15	1	0	232	215	8.3	10	114	4.4	118	4.6	3.80	111	.243	.324	21	11	91	94	-3.2	-2	0	0.7
1940	Was-A	15	17	.469	35	34	20	1	0	262	260	8.9	14	143	4.9	129	4.4	3.23	129	.261	.350	34	27	95	**134**	1.8	-1	-1	2.5
1941	Was-A	6	18	.250	33	30	8	1	0	206	228	10.0	11	115	5.0	98	4.3	5.07	81	.280	.364	-21	-22	99	94	-5.8	-2	1	-2.1
1942	Bos-A	5	1	.833	13	10	4	0	0	80	82	9.2	5	41	4.6	34	3.8	3.82	96	.263	.346	-1	-1	100	109	1.7	1	-1	-0.1
1943	Bos-A	0	4	.000	7	5	0	0	0	27	36	12.0	0	30	10.0	9	3.0	7.00	49	.316	.452	-11	-11	104	96	-1.9	-1	0	-1.0
	NY-N	4	12	.250	21	20	4	1	0	129	140	9.8	7	74	5.2	86	6.0	4.12	81	.275	.364	-11	-11	99	110	-2.5	0	-1	-1.1
Total	8	53	84	.387	188	160	62	4	1	1164	1188	9.2	55	694	5.4	582	4.5	4.28	96	.265	.359	-1	-22	96	107	-9.6	-7	-1	-2.5
■ JIM CHATTERTON	Chatterton, James M. b: 10/14/1864, Brooklyn, N.Y. d: 12/15/44, Tewksbury, Mass. Deb: 6/07/1884																												
1884	KC-U	0	1	.000	1	1	0	0	0	5	11	19.8	0	2	3.6	2	3.6	3.60	77	.443	.484	-0	-0	92	262	-0.4	-0	0	0.0
■ NESTOR CHAVEZ	Chavez, Nestor Isais (Silva) b: 7/6/47, Chacao, Venez. d: 3/16/69, Maracaibo, Venez. BR/TR, 6', 170 lbs. Deb: 9/09/67																												
1967	SF-N	1	0	1.000	2	0	0	0	0	5	4	7.2	0	3	5.4	3	5.4	0.00	—	.211	.318	2	2	99	0	0.5	-0	0	0.2
■ DAVE CHEADLE	Cheadle, David Baird b: 2/19/52, Greensboro, N.C. BL/TL, 6'2", 203 lbs. Deb: 9/16/73																												
1973	Atl-N	0	1	.000	2	0	0	0	0	2	2	9.0	1	3	13.5	2	9.0	18.00	23	.250	.455	-3	-3	113	54	-0.4	0	0	-0.2
■ CHARLIE CHECH	Chech, Charles William b: 4/27/1878, Madison, Wis. d: 1/31/38, Los Angeles, Cal. BR/TR, 5'11.5", 190 lbs. Deb: 4/14/05																												
1905	Cin-N	14	14	.500	39	25	20	1	0	268	300	10.1	4	77	2.6	79	2.7	2.89	106	.314	.372	3	5	103	**134**	-0.4	2	-1	0.5
1906	Cin-N	1	4	.200	11	5	5	0	3	66	59	8.0	1	24	3.3	17	2.3	2.32	132	.273	.361	2	5	116	130	-1.2	1	-0	0.6
1908	Cle-A	11	7	.611	27	20	14	4	0	166	136	7.4	2	34	1.8	51	2.8	1.73	142	.229	.279	12	14	103	125	0.6	-1	1	1.8
1909	Bos-A	7	5	.583	17	13	6	1	0	107	107	9.0	3	27	2.3	40	3.4	2.94	91	.260	.314	-6	-3	108	95	0.0	-3	-0	-0.3
Total	4	33	30	.524	94	63	45	6	3	607	602	8.9	10	162	2.4	187	2.8	2.52	113	.277	.335	12	22	105	124	-1.0	-1	0	2.6
■ VIRGIL CHEEVES	Cheeves, Virgil Earl "Chief" b: 2/12/01, Oklahoma City, Okla. d: 5/5/79, Dallas, Tex. BR/TR, 6', 195 lbs. Deb: 9/07/20																												
1920	Chi-N	0	0	—	5	2	0	0	0	18	16	8.0	0	7	3.5	3	1.5	3.50	89	.250	.315	-1	-1	99	76	0.0	-0	-1	-0.1
1921	Chi-N	11	12	.478	37	22	9	2	0	163	192	10.6	8	47	2.6	39	2.2	4.64	88	.309	.350	-15	-10	108	98	1.4	-2	-3	-1.3
1922	Chi-N	12	11	.522	39	23	9	1	2	183	195	9.6	9	76	3.7	40	2.0	4.08	96	.281	.350	0	-3	96	102	0.1	2	-1	-0.2
1923	Chi-N	3	4	.429	19	8	0	0	0	71	89	11.3	8	37	4.7	13	1.6	6.21	67	.314	.389	-17	-16	103	95	-0.6	-1	-1	-1.6
1924	Cle-A	0	0	—	8	1	0	0	0	17	26	13.8	2	17	9.0	2	1.1	7.94	52	.388	.489	-7	-7	97	120	0.0	0	0	-0.5
1927	NY-N	0	0	—	3	0	0	0	0	6	8	12.0	1	4	6.0	1	1.5	4.50	85	.333	.400	-0	-0	98	161	0.0	0	0	0.0
Total	6	26	27	.491	111	56	18	3	2	458	526	10.3	28	188	3.7	98	1.9	4.74	84	.300	.362	-41	-37	102	100	0.9	-1	-5	-3.7
■ ITALO CHELINI	Chelini, Italo Vincent "Chilly" or "Lefty" b: 10/10/14, San Francisco, Cal d: 8/25/72, San Francisco, Cal BL/TL, 5'10.5", 175 lbs. Deb: 9/12/35																												
1935	Chi-A	0	0	—	2	0	0	0	0	5	7	12.6	1	4	7.2	1	1.8	12.60	39	.350	.480	-5	-4	109	73	0.0	0	0	-0.2
1936	Chi-A	4	3	.571	18	6	5	0	0	84	100	10.7	8	30	3.2	16	1.7	4.93	101	.291	.344	1	0	99	100	0.3	-1	-1	-0.1
1937	Chi-A	0	1	.000	4	0	0	0	0	9	15	15.0	2	0	0.0	3	3.0	10.00	47	.405	.410	-5	-5	102	86	-0.4	0	-0	-0.4
Total	3	4	4	.500	24	6	5	0	0	98	122	11.2	11	34	3.1	20	1.8	5.79	85	.304	.357	-9	-9	99	98	-0.1	-1	-1	-0.7
■ LARRY CHENEY	Cheney, Laurance Russell b: 5/2/1886, Belleville, Kan. d: 1/6/69, Daytona Beach, Fla. BR/TR, 6'1.5", 185 lbs. Deb: 9/09/11																												
1911	Chi-N	1	0	1.000	3	1	0	0	0	10	8	7.2	0	3	2.7	11	9.9	0.00	—	.229	.289	4	4	94	0	0.5	0	1	0.5
1912	Chi-N	**26**	10	.722	42	37	**28**	4	0	303	262	7.8	5	111	3.3	140	4.2	2.85	122	.228	.300	19	21	102	73	**6.4**	4	-2	2.3
1913	Chi-N	21	14	.600	**54**	36	25	2	**11**	305	271	8.0	7	98	2.9	136	4.0	2.57	121	.241	.300	22	18	97	102	1.3	2	-0	2.1
1914	Chi-N	20	18	.526	**50**	40	21	6	5	311	239	6.9	9	140	4.1	157	4.5	2.55	108	.215	.300	8	7	99	91	1.0	3	1	1.1
1915	Chi-N	8	9	.471	25	18	6	2	0	131	120	8.2	1	55	3.8	68	4.7	3.57	79	.246	.318	-12	-11	103	82	0.0	-1	2	-1.1
	Bro-N	0	2	.000	5	4	1	0	0	27	16	5.3	0	17	5.7	11	3.7	1.67	168	.174	.304	3	3	102	117	-0.9	-0	0	0.4
	Yr	8	11	.421	30	22	7	2	0	158	136	7.7	1	72	4.1	79	4.5	3.25	87	.233	.310	-9	-7	103	117	-0.9	-1	2	-0.7
1916	Bro-N	18	12	.600	41	32	15	5	0	253	178	**6.3**	5	105	3.7	166	**5.9**	1.92	137	**.198**	.281	20	20	100	97	-0.2	-3	-0	2.0
1917	Bro-N	8	12	.400	35	24	14	1	2	210	185	7.9	4	73	3.1	102	4.4	2.36	121	.239	.303	8	11	105	113	-1.4	2	-1	1.4
1918	Bro-N	11	13	.458	32	21	15	0	1	201	177	7.9	2	74	3.3	83	3.7	3.00	96	.241	.307	-5	-3	104	91	0.2	2	1	0.1
1919	Bro-N	1	3	.250	9	4	2	0	0	39	45	10.4	1	14	3.2	14	3.2	4.15	66	.300	.353	-5	-6	94	106	-0.9	-0	0	-0.6
	Bos-N	0	2	.000	8	2	0	0	0	33	35	9.5	0	15	4.1	13	3.5	3.55	82	.294	.368	-2	-2	100	118	-0.9	0	0	-0.1
	Phi-N	2	5	.286	9	6	5	0	0	57	69	10.9	2	28	4.4	25	3.9	4.58	69	.315	.375	-11	-9	109	113	-0.5	-2	-1	-1.1

YEAR	TM/L	W	L	PCT	G	GS	CG	SHO	SV	IP	H	H/G	HR	BB	BB/G	SO	SO/G	ERA	/A	OAVG	OOBP	PR	/A	PF	CPI	WAT	PB	PD	TPI
	Yr	3	10	.231	26	12	7	0	0	129	149	10.4	3	57	4.0	52	3.6	4.19	71	.304	.363	-18	-18	102	113	-2.3	-0	-1	-1.8
Total	9	116	100	.537	313	225	132	20	19	1880	1605	7.7	36	733	3.5	926	4.4	2.70	110	.233	.305	48	54	101	94	4.6	8	0	7.0
■ TOM CHENEY	Cheney, Thomas Edgar b: 10/14/34, Morgan, Ga. BR/TR, 5'11", 170 lbs. Deb: 4/21/57																												
1957	StL-N	0	1	.000	4	3	0	0	0	9	6	6.0	0	15	15.0	10	10.0	5.00	77	.207	.477	-1	-1	99	115	-0.4	-0	0	0.0
1959	StL-N	0	1	.000	11	2	0	0	0	12	17	12.8	2	11	8.3	8	6.0	6.75	62	.354	.476	-4	-3	106	134	-0.4	0	0	-0.2
1960	Pit-N	2	2	.500	11	8	1	1	0	52	44	7.6	5	33	5.7	35	6.1	3.98	91	.238	.348	-1	-2	97	105	-0.3	0	-1	-0.2
1961	Pit-N	0	0	—	1	0	0	0	0	0	1	—	1	4	—	0	—	∞	—	.500	.833	-4	-4	99	59	0.0	0	0	-0.2
	Was-A	1	3	.250	10	7	0	0	0	30	32	9.6	8	26	7.8	20	6.0	8.70	45	.283	.406	-16	-16	97	83	-0.6	2	-0	-1.3
1962	Was-A	7	9	.438	37	23	4	3	1	173	134	7.0	12	97	5.0	147	7.6	3.17	128	.213	.316	15	17	102	98	0.9	-3	0	1.4
1963	Was-A	8	9	.471	23	21	7	4	0	136	99	6.6	14	40	2.6	97	6.4	2.71	135	.202	.258	14	14	101	88	1.8	-3	-2	1.0
1964	Was-A	1	3	.250	15	6	1	0	1	49	45	8.3	10	13	2.4	25	4.6	3.67	102	.245	.291	-0	0	103	109	-0.6	0	-0	0.0
1966	Was-A	0	1	.000	3	1	0	0	0	5	4	7.2	1	6	10.8	3	5.4	5.40	61	.222	.440	-1	-1	96	125	-0.4	0	0	0.0
Total	8	19	29	.396	115	71	13	8	2	466	382	7.4	53	245	4.7	345	6.7	3.77	102	.225	.320	2	4	101	97	-0.0	-3	-3	0.5
■ JACK CHESBRO	Chesbro, John Dwight "Happy Jack" b: 6/5/1874, N.Adams, Mass. d: 11/6/31, Conway, Mass. BR/TR, 5'9", 180 lbs. Deb: 7/12/1899 CH																												
1899	Pit-N	6	9	.400	19	17	15	0	0	149	165	10.0	3	59	3.6	28	1.7	4.11	92	.304	.373	-4	-5	98	95	-1.7	-3	0	-0.7
1900	Pit-N	15	13	.536	32	26	20	3	1	216	220	9.2	4	79	3.3	56	2.3	3.67	102	.286	.353	1	2	101	93	-0.9	-1	0	0.0
1901	Pit-N	21	10	**.677**	36	28	26	**6**	1	288	261	8.2	4	52	1.6	129	4.0	2.38	134	.265	.310	30	26	96	103	1.7	3	-3	2.3
1902	Pit-N	**28**	6	**.824**	35	33	31	**8**	1	286	242	7.6	1	62	2.0	136	4.3	2.17	126	.256	.316	19	18	98	97	6.5	-2	-2	1.7
1903	NY-A	21	15	.583	40	36	33	1	0	325	300	8.3	7	74	2.0	147	4.1	2.77	107	.266	.312	7	7	100	97	2.4	0	1	0.8
1904	NY-A	**41**	12	**.774**	**55**	51	**48**	6	0	**455**	338	**6.7**	4	88	1.7	239	4.7	1.82	158	**.227**	**.270**	39	**53**	111	87	**14.0**	5	4	**7.0**
1905	NY-A	19	15	.559	41	38	24	3	0	303	262	7.8	5	71	2.1	156	4.6	2.20	123	.256	.305	15	17	103	111	3.3	1	1	2.1
1906	NY-A	23	17	.575	**49**	42	24	4	1	325	314	8.7	2	75	2.1	152	4.2	2.96	107	.279	.324	-10	8	118	93	-0.8	-2	-1	0.8
1907	NY-A	10	10	.500	30	25	17	1	0	206	192	8.4	0	46	2.0	78	3.4	2.53	110	.271	.315	0	6	110	96	0.6	-1	-1	0.6
1908	NY-A	14	20	.412	45	31	21	3	1	289	271	8.4	6	67	2.1	124	3.9	2.93	83	.250	.303	-17	-16	101	96	2.5	-2	0	-1.7
1909	NY-A	0	4	.000	9	4	2	0	0	50	70	12.6	2	13	2.3	17	3.1	6.30	39	.347	.394	-21	-21	99	84	-1.9	-0	1	-1.9
	Bos-A	0	1	.000	1	1	0	0	0	6	7	10.5	1	4	6.0	3	4.5	4.50	60	.318	.423	-1	-1	108	141	-0.4	0	-0	-0.1
	Yr	0	5	.000	10	5	2	0	0	56	77	12.4	3	17	2.7	20	3.2	6.11	41	.339	.385	-23	-23	100	141	-2.3	-0	1	-2.0
Total	11	198	132	.600	392	332	261	35	5	2898	2642	8.2	39	690	2.1	1265	3.9	2.68	111	.264	.314	57	96	104	96	25.3	0	1	10.9
■ BOB CHESNES	Chesnes, Robert Vincent b: 5/6/21, Oakland, Cal. d: 5/23/79, Everett, Wash. BB/TR, 6', 180 lbs. Deb: 5/06/48																												
1948	Pit-N	14	6	.700	25	23	15	0	0	194	180	8.4	13	90	4.2	69	3.2	3.57	116	.247	.331	8	12	104	104	3.8	7	3	2.3
1949	Pit-N	7	13	.350	27	25	8	1	1	145	153	9.5	15	82	5.1	49	3.0	5.90	70	.276	.371	-30	-28	102	86	-2.6	6	2	-1.8
1950	Pit-N	3	3	.500	9	7	2	0	0	39	44	10.2	7	17	3.9	12	2.8	5.54	79	.293	.368	-6	-5	106	106	0.6	-0	2	-0.2
Total	3	24	22	.522	61	55	25	1	1	378	377	9.0	35	189	4.5	130	3.1	4.67	89	.263	.350	-28	-22	104	98	1.8	13	7	0.3
■ MITCH CHETKOVICH	Chetkovich, Mitchell b: 7/21/17, Fairpoint, Ohio d: 8/24/71, Grass Valley, Cal. BR/TR, 6'3.5", 208 lbs. Deb: 4/19/45																												
1945	Phi-N	0	0	—	4	0	0	0	0	3	2	6.0	0	3	9.0	0	0.0	0.00	—	.182	.333	1	1	102	0	0.0	0	-0	0.1
■ TONY CHEVEZ	Chevez, Silvio Antonio (born Aguilera (Chevez)) b: 6/20/54, Telica, Nicaragua BR/TR, 5'11", 177 lbs. Deb: 5/31/77																												
1977	Bal-A	0	0	—	4	0	0	0	0	8	10	11.3	3	8	9.0	7	7.9	12.38	30	.294	.435	-7	-8	92	75	0.0	0	-0	-0.6
■ FLOYD CHIFFER	Chiffer, Floyd John b: 4/20/56, Glen Cove, N.Y. BR/TR, 6'2", 185 lbs. Deb: 4/07/82																												
1982	SD-N	4	3	.571	51	0	0	0	4	79	73	8.3	9	34	3.9	48	5.5	2.96	111	.247	.326	6	3	92	135	0.5	-1	-0	0.2
1983	SD-N	0	2	.000	15	0	0	0	1	23	17	6.7	0	10	3.9	15	5.9	3.13	115	.210	.287	1	1	99	67	-0.9	-0	0	0.1
1984	SD-N	1	0	1.000	15	1	0	0	0	28	42	13.5	1	16	5.1	20	6.4	7.71	46	.347	.417	-13	-13	98	84	0.5	-0	-1	-1.3
Total	3	5	5	.500	81	1	0	0	5	130	132	9.1	10	60	4.2	83	5.7	4.02	85	.266	.342	-6	-9	94	112	0.1	-1	-1	-1.0
■ HARRY CHILD	Child, Harry Stephen Patrick (born Harry Stephen Patrick Chesley) b: 5/23/05, Baltimore, Md. d: 11/8/72, Alexandria, Va. BB/TR, 5'11", 187 lbs. Deb: 7/16/30																												
1930	Was-A	0	0	—	5	0	0	0	0	10	10	9.0	1	5	4.5	5	4.5	6.30	72	.263	.341	-2	-2	98	73	0.0	-0	0	-0.1
■ CHILDERS	Childers b:St.Louis, Mo. Deb: 7/27/1895																												
1895	Lou-N	0	0	—	1	0	0	0	0	0	2	—	0	6	—	0	—	∞	—	1.000	1.000	-5	-5	99	59	0.0	0	0	-0.2
■ ROCKY CHILDRESS	Childress, Rodney Osborne b: 2/18/62, Santa Rosa, Cal. BR/TR, 6'2", 195 lbs. Deb: 5/17/85																												
1985	Phi-N	0	1	.000	16	1	0	0	0	33	45	12.3	3	9	2.5	14	3.8	6.27	59	.326	.358	-10	-10	102	86	-0.4	-0	-0	-0.9
1986	Phi-N	0	0	—	2	0	0	0	0	3	4	12.0	0	1	3.0	1	3.0	6.00	65	.364	.417	-1	-1	104	97	0.0	0	0	0.0
1987	Hou-N	1	2	.333	32	0	0	0	0	48	46	8.6	4	18	3.4	26	4.9	3.00	127	.260	.318	6	4	93	130	-0.3	-0	-0	0.4
1988	Hou-N	1	0	1.000	11	0	0	0	0	23	26	10.2	3	9	3.5	24	9.4	6.26	52	.280	.350	-7	-8	93	78	0.5	0	-0	-0.7
Total	4	2	3	.400	61	1	0	0	0	107	121	10.2	10	37	3.1	65	5.5	4.79	76	.289	.340	-12	-14	96	104	-0.2	-0	-1	-1.2
■ BOB CHIPMAN	Chipman, Robert Howard "Mr. Chips" b: 10/11/18, Brooklyn, N.Y. d: 11/8/73, Huntington, N.Y. BL/TL, 6'2", 190 lbs. Deb: 9/28/41																												
1941	Bro-N	1	0	1.000	1	0	0	0	0	5	3	5.4	0	1	1.8	3	5.4	0.00	—	.150	.190	2	2	99	0	0.5	-0	0	0.2
1942	Bro-N	0	0	—	2	0	0	0	0	1	1	9.0	0	2	18.0	1	9.0	0.00	—	.250	.500	0	0	97	0	0.0	0	0	0.0
1943	Bro-N	0	0	—	1	0	0	0	0	2	2	9.0	0	2	9.0	0	0.0	0.00	—	.400	.571	1	1	99	0	0.0	0	0	0.1
1944	Bro-N	3	1	.750	11	3	1	0	0	36	38	9.5	1	24	6.0	20	5.0	4.25	87	.270	.365	-3	-2	102	105	1.2	-0	0	-0.1
	Chi-N	9	9	.500	26	21	8	1	2	129	147	10.3	9	40	2.8	41	2.9	3.49	104	.288	.333	2	2	100	124	0.3	-3	-0	0.0
	Yr	12	10	.545	37	24	9	1	2	165	185	10.1	10	64	3.5	61	3.3	3.65	99	.284	.341	-1	-0	100	124	1.5	-0	0	-0.1
1945	Chi-N	4	5	.444	25	10	3	1	0	72	63	7.9	4	34	4.3	29	3.6	3.50	103	.230	.313	2	1	95	90	-1.3	1	1	0.2
1946	Chi-N	6	5	.545	34	10	5	3	2	109	103	8.5	8	54	4.5	42	3.5	3.14	101	.255	.338	3	1	93	123	0.1	-3	-1	-0.2
1947	Chi-N	7	6	.538	32	17	5	1	0	135	135	9.0	6	66	4.4	51	3.4	3.67	115	.264	.346	6	8	104	108	1.1	-3	1	0.6
1948	Chi-N	2	1	.667	34	3	0	0	4	60	73	10.9	5	24	3.6	16	2.4	3.60	104	.293	.348	2	1	95	133	0.7	1	1	0.3
1949	Chi-N	7	8	.467	38	11	3	1	1	113	110	8.8	7	63	5.0	46	3.7	3.98	99	.248	.342	1	-1	97	97	1.0	-0	-1	-0.1
1950	Bos-N	7	7	.500	27	12	4	0	1	124	127	9.2	10	37	2.7	40	2.9	4.43	80	.262	.315	-4	-12	85	83	-0.5	-0	-3	-1.4
1951	Bos-N	4	3	.571	33	0	0	0	4	52	59	10.2	5	19	3.3	17	2.9	4.85	79	.284	.343	-5	-6	97	95	0.6	-1	-0	-0.6
1952	Bos-N	1	1	.500	29	0	0	0	0	42	28	6.0	5	20	4.3	16	3.4	2.79	129	.188	.279	4	4	97	97	0.1	1	0	0.5
Total	12	51	46	.526	293	87	29	7	14	880	889	9.1	60	386	3.9	322	3.3	3.72	100	.261	.333	13	-1	96	105	3.8	-8	-2	-0.5
■ NELSON CHITTUM	Chittum, Nelson Boyd b: 3/25/33, Harrisonburg, Va. BR/TR, 6'1", 180 lbs. Deb: 8/17/58																												
1958	StL-N	0	1	.000	13	2	0	0	0	29	31	9.6	5	7	2.2	13	4.0	6.52	65	.265	.307	-8	-7	108	63	-0.4	0	0	-0.6
1959	Bos-A	3	0	1.000	21	0	0	0	0	30	29	8.7	0	11	3.3	12	3.6	1.20	338	.266	.323	9	10	105	284	1.5	0	1	1.1
1960	Bos-A	0	0	—	6	0	0	0	0	8	8	9.0	0	6	6.8	5	5.6	4.50	91	.242	.350	-1	-0	105	77	0.0	-0	0	0.0
Total	3	3	1	.750	40	2	0	0	0	67	68	9.1	5	24	3.2	30	4.0	3.90	107	.263	.320	0	2	106	164	1.1	0	1	0.5
■ BOB CHLUPSA	Chlupsa, Robert Joseph b: 9/16/45, New York, N.Y. BR/TR, 6'7", 215 lbs. Deb: 7/16/70																												
1970	StL-N	0	2	.000	14	0	0	0	0	16	26	14.6	2	9	5.1	10	5.6	9.00	48	.366	.422	-9	-8	106	87	-0.9	0	1	-0.6
1971	StL-N	0	0	—	1	0	0	0	0	2	3	13.5	0	0	0.0	1	4.5	9.00	39	.333	.333	-1	-1	100	46	0.0	0	0	0.0
Total	2	0	2	.000	15	0	0	0	0	18	29	14.5	2	9	4.5	11	5.5	9.00	47	.363	.413	-10	-10	105	83	-0.9	0	1	-0.6
■ DON CHOATE	Choate, Donald Leon b: 7/2/38, Potosi, Mo. BR/TR, 6', 185 lbs. Deb: 9/12/60																												
1960	SF-N	0	0	—	4	0	0	0	0	8	7	7.9	0	4	4.5	7	7.9	2.25	148	.233	.324	1	1	89	126	0.0	0	0	0.1
■ CHIEF CHOUNEAU	Chouneau, William (born William Cadreau) b: 9/2/1889, Cloquet, Minn. d: 9/17/48, Cloquet, Minn. TR , 5'9", 150 lbs. Deb: 10/09/10																												
1910	Chi-A	0	1	.000	1	1	0	0	0	5	7	12.6	0	0	0.0	1	1.8	3.60	67	.292	.292	-1	-1	95	76	-0.4	0	-0	0.0
■ MIKE CHRIS	Chris, Michael b: 10/8/57, Santa Monica, Cal. BL/TL, 6'3", 180 lbs. Deb: 7/31/79																												
1979	Det-A	3	3	.500	13	8	0	0	0	39	46	10.6	3	21	4.8	31	7.2	6.92	59	.297	.374	-12	-12	96	75	-0.1	0	0	-1.0
1982	SF-N	0	2	.000	9	6	0	0	0	26	23	8.0	2	26	9.0	10	3.5	4.85	70	.245	.403	-4	-4	94	108	-0.9	-0	1	-0.2
1983	SF-N	0	0	—	7	0	0	0	0	13	16	11.1	1	16	11.1	5	3.5	8.31	44	.308	.472	-7	-7	101	94	0.0	-0	-0	-0.6
Total	3	3	5	.375	29	14	0	0	0	78	85	9.8	6	63	7.3	46	5.3	6.46	58	.282	.403	-22	-23	96	89	-1.0	-0	1	-1.8

YEAR	TM/L	W	L	PCT	G	GS	CG	SHO	SV	IP	H	H/G	HR	BB	BB/G	SO	SO/G	ERA	/A	OAVG	OOBP	PR	/A	PF	CPI	WAT	PB	PD	TPI
■ **GARY CHRISTENSON** Christenson, Gary Richard b: 5/5/53, Mineola, N.Y. BL/TL, 6'5", 200 lbs. Deb: 9/01/79																													
1979	KC-A	0	0	—	6	0	0	0	0	11	10	8.2	1	2	1.6	4	3.3	3.27	136	.250	.279	1	1	105	95	0.0	0	0	0.1
1980	KC-A	3	0	1.000	24	0	0	0	1	31	35	10.2	4	18	5.2	16	4.6	5.23	75	.278	.372	-4	-4	97	100	1.5	0	1	-0.3
Total	2	3	0	1.000	30	0	0	0	1	42	45	9.6	5	20	4.3	20	4.3	4.71	86	.271	.351	-3	-3	99	99	1.5	0	1	-0.2
■ **LARRY CHRISTENSON** Christenson, Larry Richard b: 11/10/53, Everett, Wash. BR/TR, 6'4", 215 lbs. Deb: 4/13/73																													
1973	Phi-N	1	4	.200	10	9	1	0	0	34	53	14.0	3	20	5.3	11	2.9	6.62	60	.366	.443	-11	-10	109	112	-1.3	-1	-0	-0.9
1974	Phi-N	1	1	.500	10	1	0	0	2	23	20	7.8	2	15	5.9	18	7.0	4.30	87	.241	.354	-2	-1	104	95	0.0	-1	-0	-0.1
1975	Phi-N	11	6	.647	29	26	5	2	1	172	149	7.8	12	45	2.4	88	4.6	3.66	100	.236	.283	-1	0	101	74	2.3	6	-2	0.3
1976	Phi-N	13	8	.619	32	29	2	0	0	169	199	10.6	8	42	2.2	54	2.9	3.67	100	.297	.333	-3	-0	105	112	0.0	4	-3	0.1
1977	Phi-N	19	6	.760	34	34	5	1	0	219	229	9.4	21	69	2.8	118	4.8	4.07	95	.268	.323	-4	-5	98	97	5.0	1	-2	-0.5
1978	Phi-N	13	14	.481	33	33	9	3	0	228	209	8.3	16	47	**1.9**	131	5.2	3.24	115	.244	.278	9	12	104	86	-2.0	-2	-0	1.0
1979	Phi-N	5	10	.333	19	17	2	0	0	106	118	10.0	9	30	2.5	53	4.5	4.50	81	.291	.336	-9	-10	97	97	-2.7	5	-0	-0.5
1980	Phi-N	5	1	.833	14	14	0	0	0	74	62	7.5	4	27	3.3	49	6.0	4.01	96	.227	.299	-3	-1	106	70	1.9	4	1	0.3
1981	Phi-N	4	7	.364	20	15	0	0	1	107	108	9.1	8	30	2.5	70	5.9	3.53	111	.267	.312	-0	4	112	104	-1.9	-2	-1	0.3
1982	Phi-N	9	10	.474	33	33	3	0	0	223	212	8.6	15	53	2.1	145	5.9	3.47	97	.253	.296	3	-2	94	90	-1.4	-2	-1	-0.5
1983	Phi-N	2	4	.333	9	9	0	0	0	48	42	7.9	2	17	3.2	44	8.3	3.94	92	.233	.296	-2	-2	100	69	-1.1	-1	1	-0.1
Total	11	83	71	.539	243	220	27	6	4	1403	1401	9.0	100	395	2.5	781	5.0	3.79	97	.262	.310	-23	-15	101	92	-1.2	11	-8	-0.6
■ **CLAY CHRISTIANSEN** Christiansen, Clay C. b: 6/28/58, Wichita, Kan. BR/TR, 6'5", 205 lbs. Deb: 5/10/84																													
1984	NY-A	2	4	.333	24	1	0	0	2	39	50	11.5	4	12	2.8	27	6.2	6.00	62	.309	.354	-9	-10	93	86	-1.1	0	-0	-0.9
■ **RUSS CHRISTOPHER** Christopher, Russell Ormand b: 9/12/07, Richmond, Cal. d: 12/5/54, Richmond, Cal. BR/TR, 6'3.5", 170 lbs. Deb: 4/14/42																													
1942	Phi-A	4	13	.235	30	18	10	0	1	165	154	8.4	8	99	5.4	58	3.2	3.82	97	.254	.357	-3	-2	101	111	-3.0	-3	6	0.0
1943	Phi-A	5	8	.385	24	15	5	0	2	133	120	8.1	3	58	3.9	56	3.8	3.45	101	.242	.318	-2	1	106	90	0.7	-1	8	0.8
1944	Phi-A	14	14	.500	35	24	13	1	1	215	200	8.4	6	63	2.6	84	3.5	2.97	118	.245	.301	11	13	102	96	1.0	3	5	2.4
1945	Phi-A	13	13	.500	33	27	17	2	2	227	213	8.4	9	75	3.0	100	4.0	3.17	102	.251	.313	5	2	96	101	3.5	-0	7	0.9
1946	Phi-A	5	7	.417	30	13	1	0	0	119	119	9.0	5	44	3.3	79	6.0	4.31	87	.254	.319	-11	-7	107	75	0.9	-1	4	-0.3
1947	Phi-A	10	7	.588	44	0	0	0	12	81	70	7.8	4	33	3.7	33	3.7	2.89	128	.236	.309	7	7	100	106	1.6	-0	0	0.8
1948	Cle-A	3	2	.600	45	0	0	0	**17**	59	55	8.4	3	27	4.1	14	2.1	2.90	139	.247	.322	9	7	94	123	0.0	-0	0	0.7
Total	7	54	64	.458	241	97	46	3	35	999	931	8.4	38	399	3.6	424	3.8	3.37	106	.248	.320	16	21	101	99	4.7	-3	30	5.3
■ **BUBBA CHURCH** Church, Emory Nicholas b: 9/12/24, Birmingham, Ala. BR/TR, 6', 180 lbs. Deb: 4/30/50																													
1950	Phi-N	8	6	.571	31	18	8	2	1	142	113	7.2	12	56	3.5	50	3.2	2.73	145	.225	.301	22	19	96	115	-0.2	0	-0	1.9
1951	Phi-N	15	11	.577	38	33	15	4	1	247	246	9.0	17	90	3.3	104	3.8	3.53	109	.261	.322	12	8	97	105	2.9	5	-2	1.1
1952	Phi-N	0	0	—	2	1	0	0	0	5	11	19.8	0	1	1.8	3	5.4	10.80	34	.440	.464	-4	-4	99	86	0.0	-0	-0	-0.3
	Cin-N	5	9	.357	29	22	5	1	0	153	173	10.2	21	48	2.8	47	2.8	4.35	86	.301	.354	-11	-10	100	122	-1.4	3	-1	-0.7
	Yr	5	9	.357	31	23	5	1	0	158	184	10.5	21	49	2.8	50	2.8	4.56	82	.306	.357	-15	-14	100	122	-1.4	-0	-1	-1.0
1953	Cin-N	3	3	.500	11	7	2	0	0	44	55	11.3	9	19	3.9	12	2.5	5.93	72	.318	.388	-8	-8	100	113	0.3	1	-0	-0.6
	Chi-N	4	5	.444	27	11	1	0	1	104	115	10.0	16	49	4.2	47	4.1	5.02	91	.276	.350	-8	-5	106	102	0.2	1	-1	-0.4
	Yr	7	8	.467	38	18	3	0	1	148	170	10.3	25	68	4.1	59	3.6	5.29	85	.288	.358	-17	-13	105	102	0.5	1	-1	-1.0
1954	Chi-N	1	3	.250	7	3	1	0	0	15	21	12.6	8	13	7.8	8	4.8	9.60	43	.350	.447	-9	-9	102	115	-0.7	-1	0	-0.8
1955	Chi-N	0	0	—	2	0	0	0	1	3	4	12.0	1	1	3.0	3	9.0	6.00	68	.286	.333	-1	-1	101	100	0.0	-0	0	0.0
Total	6	36	37	.493	147	95	32	7	4	713	738	9.3	84	277	3.5	274	3.5	4.10	97	.272	.338	-7	-10	99	110	1.1	9	-4	0.2
■ **LEN CHURCH** Church, Leonard b: 3/21/42, Chicago, Ill. d: 4/22/88, Richardson, Tex. BB/TR, 6', 190 lbs. Deb: 8/27/66																													
1966	Chi-N	0	1	.000	4	0	0	0	0	6	10	15.0	1	7	10.5	3	4.5	7.50	49	.400	.486	-3	-3	103	141	-0.4	-0	0	-0.2
■ **CHUCK CHURN** Churn, Clarence Nottingham b: 2/1/30, Bridgetown, Va. BR/TR, 6'3", 205 lbs. Deb: 4/18/57																													
1957	Pit-N	0	0	—	5	0	0	0	0	8	9	10.1	1	4	4.5	4	4.5	4.50	83	.333	.382	-1	-1	96	143	0.0	-0	1	0.0
1958	Cle-A	0	0	—	6	0	0	0	0	9	12	12.0	1	5	5.0	4	4.0	6.00	59	.343	.415	-2	-2	93	113	0.0	0	0	-0.2
1959	LA-N	3	2	.600	14	0	0	0	1	31	28	8.1	2	10	2.9	24	7.0	4.94	81	.255	.312	-3	-3	101	72	0.2	0	0	-0.2
Total	3	3	2	.600	25	0	0	0	1	48	49	9.2	4	19	3.6	32	6.0	5.06	76	.285	.345	-6	-6	99	91	0.2	0	1	-0.4
■ **MARK CIARDI** Ciardi, Mark Thomas b: 8/19/61, New Brunswick, N.J. BR/TR, 6' ", 180 lbs. Deb: 4/09/87																													
1987	Mil-A	1	1	.500	4	3	0	0	0	16	26	14.6	5	9	5.1	8	4.5	9.56	48	.361	.432	-9	-9	102	96	0.0	0	0	-0.7
■ **AL CICOTTE** Cicotte, Alva Warren "Bozo" b: 12/23/29, Melvindale, Mich. d: 11/29/82, Westland, Mich. BR/TR, 6'3", 185 lbs. Deb: 4/22/57																													
1957	NY-A	2	2	.500	20	2	0	0	2	65	57	7.9	5	30	4.2	36	5.0	3.05	112	.237	.320	5	3	90	113	-0.3	-0	0	0.2
1958	Was-A	0	3	.000	8	4	0	0	0	28	36	11.6	3	14	4.5	14	4.5	4.82	78	.316	.385	-3	-3	100	121	-1.4	-0	-1	-0.3
	Det-A	3	1	.750	14	2	0	0	0	43	50	10.5	1	15	3.1	21	4.4	3.56	109	.307	.351	1	2	103	127	1.0	-1	1	0.2
	Yr	3	4	.429	22	6	0	0	0	71	86	10.9	4	29	3.7	35	4.4	4.06	95	.309	.365	-2	-2	102	127	-0.4	-0	1	-0.1
1959	Cle-A	3	1	.750	26	1	0	0	1	44	46	9.4	4	25	5.1	23	4.7	5.32	69	.299	.378	-7	-8	95	107	0.8	1	0	-0.6
1961	StL-N	2	6	.250	29	7	0	0	1	75	83	10.0	16	34	4.1	51	6.1	5.28	86	.283	.357	-10	-6	113	107	-2.0	1	0	-0.4
1962	Hou-N	0	0	—	5	0	0	0	0	5	8	14.4	1	1	1.8	4	7.2	3.60	104	.381	.409	0	0	95	213	0.0	0	0	0.0
Total	5	10	13	.435	102	16	0	0	4	260	280	9.7	30	119	4.1	149	5.2	4.36	89	.284	.355	-14	-14	101	115	-1.9	0	1	-0.9
■ **EDDIE CICOTTE** Cicotte, Edward Victor "Knuckles" b: 6/19/1884, Detroit, Mich. d: 5/5/69, Detroit, Mich. BB/TR, 5'9", 175 lbs. Deb: 9/03/05																													
1905	Det-A	1	1	.500	3	1	1	0	0	18	25	12.5	0	5	2.5	6	3.0	3.50	76	.356	.399	-2	-2	100	144	0.0	1	-1	-0.2
1908	Bos-A	11	12	.478	39	24	17	2	2	207	198	8.6	0	59	2.6	95	4.1	2.43	95	.260	.320	-1	-3	97	124	-0.1	3	0	-0.2
1909	Bos-A	13	5	.722	27	17	10	1	2	160	117	6.6	3	56	3.1	82	4.6	1.97	136	.210	.283	9	13	108	89	3.3	2	-0	1.4
1910	Bos-A	15	11	.577	36	30	20	3	0	250	213	7.7	4	86	3.1	104	3.7	2.74	90	.233	.308	-6	-8	97	89	1.5	-1	3	-0.6
1911	Bos-A	11	15	.423	35	25	16	1	0	220	236	9.7	2	73	3.0	106	4.3	2.82	117	.282	.342	13	11	99	122	-2.5	-2	0	0.9
1912	Bos-A	1	3	.250	9	6	2	0	0	46	58	11.3	0	15	2.9	20	3.9	5.67	60	.319	.374	-12	-12	102	81	-1.2	0	1	-0.9
	Chi-A	9	7	.563	20	18	13	1	0	152	159	9.4	3	37	2.2	70	4.1	2.84	117	.277	.320	9	8	99	116	1.0	1	2	1.0
	Yr	10	10	.500	29	24	15	1	0	198	217	9.9	3	52	2.4	90	4.1	3.50	95	.286	.332	-3	-4	100	116	-0.2	0	3	0.1
1913	Chi-A	18	12	.600	41	30	18	3	1	268	224	7.5	2	73	2.5	121	4.1	1.58	177	.226	.281	40	36	95	114	3.2	-2	7	4.9
1914	Chi-A	11	16	.407	45	30	15	4	3	269	220	7.4	0	72	2.4	122	4.1	2.04	141	.232	.288	21	25	105	98	-1.6	-1	6	3.6
1915	Chi-A	13	12	.520	39	26	15	1	3	223	216	8.7	2	48	1.9	106	4.3	3.03	91	.261	.306	-2	-7	94	90	-1.9	1	0	-0.5
1916	Chi-A	15	7	**.682**	44	19	11	2	5	187	138	6.6	1	70	3.4	91	4.4	1.78	**168**	.218	.296	22	25	106	**117**	3.0	1	1	3.2
1917	Chi-A	**28**	12	.700	49	35	29	7	4	**347**	246	6.4	2	70	1.8	150	3.9	**1.53**	163	.203	**.248**	**44**	37	93	72	3.7	2	-1	4.3
1918	Chi-A	12	19	.387	38	30	24	1	2	266	275	9.3	2	40	**1.4**	104	3.5	2.77	100	.271	.291	-0	-0	100	93	-3.0	1	-0	0.1
1919	Chi-A	**29**	7	**.806**	40	35	**30**	5	1	**307**	256	7.5	5	49	**1.4**	110	3.2	1.82	181	.228	.261	48	50	102	85	**9.9**	0	-4	5.2
1920	Chi-A	21	10	.677	37	35	28	4	2	303	316	9.4	6	74	2.2	87	2.6	3.27	109	.275	.320	18	10	94	95	2.7	-2	0	0.8
Total	14	208	149	.583	502	361	249	35	25	3223	2897	8.1	32	827	2.3	1374	3.8	2.38	122	.246	.297	200	186	99	98	18.0	5	15	23.0
■ **PETE CIMINO** Cimino, Peter William b: 10/17/42, Philadelphia, Pa. BR/TR, 6'2", 195 lbs. Deb: 9/22/65																													
1965	Min-A	0	0	—	1	0	0	0	0	1	0	0.0	0	0	0.0	0	0.0	0.00	—	.000	.000	0	0	98	0	0.0	0	0	0.0
1966	Min-A	2	5	.286	35	0	0	0	4	65	53	7.3	4	30	4.2	57	7.9	2.91	130	.222	.304	4	6	110	105	-1.6	-0	-1	0.6
1967	Cal-A	3	3	.500	46	1	0	0	1	88	73	7.5	12	31	3.2	80	8.2	3.27	95	.229	.292	-0	-2	96	108	0.0	2	-1	-0.1
1968	Cal-A	0	0	—	4	0	0	0	0	7	7	9.0	0	4	5.1	2	2.6	2.57	111	.259	.344	0	0	96	143	0.0	0	-0	0.0
Total	4	5	8	.385	86	1	0	0	5	161	133	7.4	16	65	3.6	139	7.8	3.07	109	.226	.298	4	5	102	107	-1.6	1	-2	0.5
■ **LOU CIOLA** Ciola, Louis Alexander b: 9/6/22, Norfolk, Va. BR/TR, 5'9", 165 lbs. Deb: 7/25/43																													
1943	Phi-A	1	3	.250	12	3	2	0	0	44	48	9.8	2	22	4.5	7	1.4	5.52	63	.273	.350	-11	-10	106	77	-0.3	-1	-0	-1.0
■ **GALEN CISCO** Cisco, Galen Bernard b: 3/7/36, St. Mary's, Ohio BR/TR, 6', 200 lbs. Deb: 6/11/61 C																													
1961	Bos-A	2	4	.333	17	8	0	0	0	52	67	11.6	5	28	4.8	26	4.5	6.75	61	.325	.393	-16	-15	103	91	-0.8	-0	-0	-1.4
1962	Bos-A	4	7	.364	23	9	1	0	0	83	95	10.3	11	50	5.4	43	4.7	6.72	61	.292	.383	-25	-24	103	86	-1.3	-1	1	-2.2
	NY-N	1	1	.500	4	2	1	0	0	19	15	7.1	0	11	5.2	13	6.2	3.32	129	.208	.333	1	2	108	82	0.3	-1	0	0.1

YEAR	TM/L	W	L	PCT	G	GS	CG	SHO	SV	IP	H	H/G	HR	BB	BB/G	SO	SO/G	ERA	/A	OAVG	OOBP	PR	/A	PF	CPI	WAT	PB	PD	TPI
1963	NY-N	7	15	.318	51	17	1	0	0	156	165	9.5	15	64	3.7	81	4.7	4.33	79	.273	.343	-18	-16	104	102	0.1	0	-1	-1.6
1964	NY-N	6	19	.240	36	25	5	2	0	192	182	8.5	17	54	2.5	78	3.7	3.61	96	.256	.307	-2	-3	98	101	-3.7	0	2	-0.1
1965	NY-N	4	8	.333	35	17	1	1	0	112	119	9.6	12	51	4.1	58	4.7	4.50	82	.272	.343	-12	-10	104	101	0.2	2	-2	-0.9
1967	Bos-A	0	1	.000	11	0	0	0	1	22	21	8.6	4	8	3.3	8	3.3	3.68	99	.266	.322	-1	-0	113	130	-0.4	-0	0	0.0
1969	KC-A	1	1	.500	15	0	0	0	1	22	17	7.0	4	15	6.1	18	7.4	3.68	102	.215	.327	-0	0	104	117	0.1	0	0	0.1
Total	7	25	56	.309	192	78	9	3	2	658	681	9.3	68	281	3.8	325	4.4	4.57	80	.271	.341	-73	-66	102	99	-5.5	0	1	-6.0
■ **RALPH CITARELLA**	Citarella, Ralph Alexander b: 2/7/58, East Orange, N.J. BR/TR, 6', 180 lbs. Deb: 9/13/83																												
1983	StL-N	0	0	—	6	0	0	0	0	11	8	6.5	0	3	2.5	4	3.3	1.64	218	.205	.262	2	2	98	93	0.0	-0	0	0.2
1984	StL-N	0	1	.000	10	2	0	0	0	22	20	8.2	0	7	2.9	15	6.1	3.68	96	.238	.316	-0	-0	99	75	-0.4	0	0	0.0
1987	Chi-A	0	0	—	5	0	0	0	0	11	13	10.6	4	4	3.3	9	7.4	7.36	66	.302	.388	-4	-3	109	104	0.0	0	-0	-0.2
Total	3	0	1	.000	21	2	0	0	0	44	41	8.4	4	14	2.9	28	5.7	4.09	94	.247	.323	-1	-1	101	87	-0.4	0	0	0.0
■ **BOBBY CLACK**	Clack, Robert S. "Gentlemanly Bob" (born Robert S. Clark) b: 1851, Brooklyn, N.Y. d: 10/22/33, Danvers, Mass. BR/TR, 5'9", 153 lbs. Deb: 5/15/1874																												
1876	Cin-N	0	0	—	1	0	0	0	0	2	2	9.0	0	0	0.0	0	0.0	4.50	51	.265	.265	-0	-0	100	32	0.0	-0	0	0.0
■ **JIM CLANCY**	Clancy, James b: 12/18/55, Chicago, Ill. BR/TR, 6'2", 185 lbs. Deb: 7/26/77																												
1977	Tor-A	4	9	.308	13	13	4	1	0	77	80	9.4	7	47	5.5	44	5.1	5.03	85	.280	.367	-8	-7	105	100	-0.5	0	1	-0.5
1978	Tor-A	10	12	.455	31	30	7	0	0	194	199	9.2	10	91	4.2	106	4.9	4.08	95	.270	.344	-7	-5	102	99	1.7	0	1	-0.4
1979	Tor-A	2	7	.222	12	11	2	0	0	64	65	9.1	8	31	4.4	33	4.6	5.48	82	.272	.345	-9	-7	106	87	-1.4	0	0	-0.6
1980	Tor-A	13	16	.448	34	34	15	2	0	251	217	7.8	19	128	4.6	152	5.5	3.30	124	.233	.323	21	22	101	103	1.0	0	0	2.2
1981	Tor-A	6	12	.333	22	22	2	0	0	125	126	9.1	12	64	4.6	56	4.0	4.90	85	.262	.351	-17	-11	113	90	-0.4	0	-3	-1.2
1982	Tor-A	16	14	.533	40	40	11	3	0	267	251	8.5	26	77	2.6	139	4.7	3.71	120	.248	.300	11	22	109	91	1.8	0	-2	2.0
1983	Tor-A	15	11	.577	34	34	11	1	0	223	238	9.6	23	61	2.5	99	4.0	3.91	112	.271	.314	4	12	108	102	0.9	0	-2	0.9
1984	Tor-A	13	15	.464	36	36	5	0	0	220	249	10.2	25	88	3.6	118	4.8	5.11	79	.287	.352	-27	-26	101	95	-2.4	0	0	-2.4
1985	Tor-A	9	6	.600	23	23	1	0	0	129	117	8.2	15	37	2.6	66	4.6	3.77	109	.241	.292	5	5	99	90	-0.1	0	-1	0.4
1986	Tor-A	14	14	.500	34	34	6	3	0	219	202	8.3	24	63	2.6	126	5.2	3.95	111	.243	.295	6	10	104	85	-0.9	0	1	1.1
1987	Tor-A	15	11	.577	37	37	5	1	0	241	234	8.7	24	80	3.0	180	6.7	3.55	125	.255	.313	25	24	99	106	-0.3	0	2	2.5
1988	Tor-A	11	13	.458	36	31	4	0	1	196	207	9.5	26	47	2.2	118	5.4	4.50	87	.272	.318	-11	-12	99	96	-1.9	0	-1	-1.2
Total	12	128	140	.478	352	345	73	11	1	2206	2185	8.9	219	814	3.3	1237	5.0	4.10	103	.259	.322	-8	28	104	96	-2.5	0	-4	2.8
■ **BRYAN CLARK**	Clark, Bryan Donald b: 7/12/56, Madera, Cal. BL/TL, 6'2", 185 lbs. Deb: 4/11/81																												
1981	Sea-A	2	5	.286	29	9	1	0	2	93	92	8.9	3	55	5.3	52	5.0	4.35	85	.261	.352	-7	-7	101	93	-1.0	0	1	-0.5
1982	Sea-A	5	2	.714	37	5	1	1	0	115	104	8.1	6	58	4.5	70	5.5	2.74	164	.241	.330	17	22	110	126	1.7	0	1	2.4
1983	Sea-A	7	10	.412	41	17	2	0	0	162	160	8.9	14	72	4.0	76	4.2	3.94	105	.261	.337	2	3	101	106	0.6	0	3	0.6
1984	Tor-A	1	2	.333	20	3	0	0	0	46	66	12.9	6	22	4.3	21	4.1	5.87	69	.342	.403	-10	-9	101	116	-0.5	0	1	-0.7
1985	Cle-A	3	4	.429	31	3	0	0	2	63	78	11.1	8	34	4.9	24	3.4	6.29	63	.311	.386	-15	-16	95	97	0.3	0	1	-1.4
1986	Chi-A	0	0	—	5	0	0	0	0	8	8	9.0	0	2	2.3	5	5.6	4.50	94	.276	.323	-0	-0	101	75	0.0	0	0	0.0
1987	Chi-A	0	0	—	11	0	0	0	0	19	19	9.0	1	8	3.8	8	3.8	2.37	205	.297	.351	4	5	109	209	0.0	0	-0	0.5
Total	7	18	23	.439	174	37	4	1	4	506	527	9.4	38	251	4.5	256	4.6	4.16	99	.273	.351	-8	-2	103	111	1.1	0	7	0.9
■ **ED CLARK**	Clark, Edward C. b: Cincinnati, Ohio Deb: 7/04/1886																												
1886	Phi-a	0	1	.000	1	1	1	0	0	8	10	11.3	2	2	2.3	2	2.3	6.75	53	.317	.357	-3	-3	103	94	-0.4	-0	0	-0.1
1891	Col-a	0	0	—	1	0	0	0	0	2	2	9.0	0	0	0.0	1	4.5	0.00	—	.275	.275	1	1	90	0	0.0	-0	0	0.1
Total	2	0	1	.000	2	1	1	0	0	10	12	10.8	2	2	1.8	3	2.7	5.40	65	.309	.343	-2	-2	100	75	-0.4	-0	0	0.0
■ **GEORGE CLARK**	Clark, George Myron b: 5/19/1891, Smithland, Iowa d: 11/14/40, Sioux City, Iowa BR/TL, 6', 190 lbs. Deb: 5/16/13																												
1913	NY-A	0	1	.000	11	1	0	0	0	19	22	10.4	1	19	9.0	5	2.4	9.00	34	.272	.427	-13	-13	104	63	-0.4	1	-0	-1.2
■ **GINGER CLARK**	Clark, Harvey Daniel b: 3/7/1879, Wooster, Ohio d: 5/10/43, Lake Charles, La. BR/TR, 5'11", 165 lbs. Deb: 8/11/02																												
1902	Cle-A	1	0	1.000	1	1	0	0	0	6	10	15.0	0	3	4.5	1	1.5	6.00	57	.399	.463	-2	-2	96	115	0.5	1	0	0.0
■ **MIKE CLARK**	Clark, Michael John b: 2/12/22, Camden, N.J. BR/TR, 6'4", 190 lbs. Deb: 7/27/52																												
1952	StL-N	2	0	1.000	12	4	0	0	0	25	32	11.5	2	14	5.0	10	3.6	6.12	59	.311	.380	-7	-7	97	94	1.0	-1	0	-0.6
1953	StL-N	1	0	1.000	23	2	0	0	1	36	46	11.5	2	21	5.3	17	4.3	4.75	91	.315	.404	-2	2	101	125	0.5	-1	0	-0.1
Total	2	3	0	1.000	35	6	0	0	1	61	78	11.5	4	35	5.2	27	4.0	5.31	76	.313	.394	-8	-9	99	112	1.5	-1	1	-0.7
■ **SPIDER CLARK**	Clark, Owen F. b: 9/16/1867, Brooklyn, N.Y. d: 2/8/1892, Brooklyn, N.Y. TR, 5'10", 150 lbs. Deb: 5/02/1889																												
1890	Buf-P	0	0	—	1	0	0	0	0	4	8	18.0	0	2	4.5	2	4.5	6.75	61	.428	.483	-1	-1	97	124	0.0	0	0	0.0
■ **PHIL CLARK**	Clark, Philip James b: 10/3/32, Albany, Ga. BR/TR, 6'3", 210 lbs. Deb: 4/15/58																												
1958	StL-N	0	1	.000	7	0	0	0	1	8	11	12.4	2	3	3.4	1	1.1	3.38	126	.355	.400	1	1	108	226	-0.4	-0	-0	0.0
1959	StL-N	0	1	.000	7	0	0	0	0	7	8	10.3	0	8	10.3	5	6.4	12.86	33	.286	.444	-7	-7	106	46	-0.4	0	0	-0.5
Total	2	0	2	.000	14	0	0	0	1	15	19	11.4	2	11	6.6	6	3.6	7.80	54	.322	.423	-6	-6	107	142	-0.8	-0	0	-0.5
■ **RICKEY CLARK**	Clark, Rickey Charles b: 3/21/46, Mt.Clemens, Mich. BR/TR, 6'2", 170 lbs. Deb: 4/22/67																												
1967	Cal-A	12	11	.522	32	30	1	1	0	174	144	7.4	15	69	3.6	81	4.2	2.59	120	.224	.300	12	10	96	**121**	0.0	-4	1	0.8
1968	Cal-A	1	11	.083	21	17	0	0	0	94	74	7.1	4	54	5.2	60	5.7	3.54	81	.217	.317	-6	-7	96	86	-4.8	-1	1	-0.8
1969	Cal-A	0	0	—	6	1	0	0	0	10	12	10.8	2	7	6.3	6	5.4	5.40	68	.300	.396	-2	-2	101	122	0.0	0	-0	-0.1
1971	Cal-A	2	1	.667	11	7	1	1	1	44	36	7.4	6	28	5.7	28	5.7	2.86	120	.220	.337	3	3	99	137	0.6	1	-0	0.3
1972	Cal-A	4	9	.308	26	15	2	0	1	110	105	8.6	10	55	4.5	61	5.0	4.50	61	.261	.339	-17	-21	90	93	-2.4	-1	1	-2.3
Total	5	19	32	.373	96	70	4	2	2	432	371	7.7	37	213	4.4	236	4.9	3.38	89	.233	.320	-10	-18	95	108	-6.6	-5	1	-2.1
■ **BOB CLARK**	Clark, Robert William b: 8/22/1897, Newport, Pa. d: 5/18/44, Carlsbad, N.Mex. BR/TR, 6'3", 188 lbs. Deb: 5/26/20																												
1920	Cle-A	1	2	.333	11	2	2	1	0	42	59	12.6	0	13	2.8	8	1.7	3.43	111	.383	.435	2	2	100	181	-0.6	-0	-0	0.1
1921	Cle-A	0	0	—	5	0	0	0	0	9	23	23.0	2	6	6.0	2	2.0	15.00	27	.511	.566	-11	-11	96	98	0.0	-1	0	-0.9
Total	2	1	2	.333	16	2	2	1	0	51	82	14.5	2	19	3.4	10	1.8	5.47	70	.412	.466	-9	-9	99	166	-0.6	-1	-0	-0.8
■ **TERRY CLARK**	Clark, Terry Lee b: 10/18/60, Los Angeles, Cal. BR/TR, 6'2", 190 lbs. Deb: 7/07/88																												
1988	Cal-A	6	6	.500	15	15	2	1	0	94	120	11.5	8	31	3.0	39	3.7	5.07	74	.323	.368	-11	-14	95	108	0.4	0	0	-1.2
■ **OTIE CLARK**	Clark, William Otis b: 5/22/18, Boscobel, Wis. BR/TR, 6'1.5", 190 lbs. Deb: 4/17/45																												
1945	Bos-A	4	4	.500	12	9	4	1	0	82	86	9.4	6	19	2.1	20	2.2	3.07	105	.268	.307	3	1	96	114	0.3	0	-2	0.0
■ **WATTY CLARK**	Clark, William Watson "Lefty" b: 5/16/02, St.Joseph, La. d: 3/4/72, Clearwater, Fla. BL/TL, 6'0.5", 175 lbs. Deb: 5/28/24																												
1924	Cle-A	1	3	.250	12	1	0	0	0	26	38	13.2	0	14	4.8	6	2.1	6.92	60	.345	.409	-8	-8	97	89	-0.8	1	-0	-0.6
1927	Bro-N	7	2	.778	27	3	1	0	2	74	74	9.0	2	19	2.3	32	3.9	2.31	176	.265	.305	**13**	**14**	104	136	2.8	-1	0	1.4
1928	Bro-N	12	9	.571	40	19	10	2	3	195	193	8.9	4	50	2.3	85	3.9	2.68	147	.259	.294	28	27	99	104	1.6	-2	1	2.6
1929	Bro-N	16	19	.457	41	36	19	3	1	**279**	295	9.5	14	71	2.3	140	4.5	3.74	121	.270	.310	30	25	96	94	0.0	-3	-0	1.9
1930	Bro-N	13	13	.500	44	24	9	1	6	200	209	9.4	20	38	**1.7**	81	3.6	4.18	117	.271	.299	17	16	99	89	-1.5	0	0	1.5
1931	Bro-N	14	10	.583	34	28	16	3	1	233	243	9.4	4	52	2.0	96	3.7	3.21	122	.267	.302	17	18	101	96	1.8	4	-3	2.0
1932	Bro-N	20	12	.625	40	36	19	2	0	273	282	9.3	10	49	1.6	99	3.3	3.49	106	.264	.295	12	7	96	88	4.0	2	1	0.9
1933	Bro-N	2	4	.333	11	8	4	1	1	51	61	10.8	2	6	1.1	14	2.5	4.76	69	.303	.326	-8	-8	98	84	-0.6	-0	-0	-0.8
	NY-N	3	4	.429	16	5	0	0	0	44	58	11.9	3	11	2.3	11	2.3	4.70	68	.317	.352	-7	-7	96	104	-0.9	1	1	-0.5
	Yr	5	8	.385	27	13	4	1	1	95	119	11.3	5	17	1.6	25	2.4	4.74	68	.307	.331	-15	-16	97	104	-1.5	-0	0	-1.3
1934	NY-N	1	2	.333	5	4	1	0	0	19	23	10.9	5	5	2.4	6	2.8	6.63	58	.295	.337	-5	-6	95	89	-0.6	0	0	-0.4
	Bro-N	2	0	1.000	17	1	0	0	0	25	40	14.4	0	9	3.2	10	3.6	5.40	72	.345	.394	-4	-4	95	108	1.0	-1	-0	-0.4
	Yr	3	2	.600	22	5	1	0	0	44	63	12.9	5	14	2.9	16	3.3	5.93	65	.325	.371	-9	-10	95	108	0.4	0	0	-0.8
1935	Bro-N	13	8	.619	33	25	11	1	0	207	215	9.3	11	28	**1.2**	35	1.5	3.30	115	.264	.286	16	12	95	94	3.5	0	2	1.3
1936	Bro-N	7	11	.389	33	16	1	1	2	120	162	12.2	11	28	2.1	28	2.1	4.43	97	.316	.347	-5	-2	107	114	-1.0	0	0	-0.1
1937	Bro-N	0	0	—	2	0	0	0	0	2	4	18.0	0	3	13.5	0	0.0	9.00	47	.308	.438	-1	-1	107	83	0.0	0	0	0.0
Total	12	111	97	.534	355	206	91	14	16	1748	1897	9.8	86	383	2.0	643	3.3	3.66	112	.275	.309	96	82	98	97	9.3	1	1	8.8

YEAR	TM/L	W	L	PCT	G	GS	CG	SHO	SV	IP	H	H/G	HR	BB	BB/G	SO	SO/G	ERA	/A	OAVG	OOBP	PR	/A	PF	CPI	WAT	PB	PD	TPI
■ BILL CLARK	Clark, William Winfield b: 4/11/1875, Circleville, Ohio d: 4/15/59, Los Angeles, Cal. BR/TR, 5'10", 175 lbs. Deb: 7/12/1897																												
1897	Lou-N	1	1	.500	3	2	2	0	0	22	30	12.3	0	1	0.4	1	0.4	4.09	103	.348	.356	1	0	97	99	0.2	-0	0	0.0
■ LEFTY CLARKE	Clarke, Alan Thomas b: 3/8/1896, Clarksville, Md. d: 3/11/75, Cheverly, Md. BB/TL, 5'11", 180 lbs. Deb: 10/02/21																												
1921	Cin-N	0	1	.000	1	1	1	0	0	5	7	12.6	0	2	3.6	1	1.8	5.40	71	.304	.360	-1	-1	101	75	-0.4	-0	-0	0.0
■ HENRY CLARKE	Clarke, Henry Tefft b: 8/28/1875, Bellevue, Neb. d: 3/28/50, Colorado Springs, Colo. BR/TR, Deb: 6/26/1897																												
1897	Cle-N	0	4	.000	5	4	3	0	0	31	32	9.3	4	12	3.5	3	0.9	6.10	78	.288	.357	-6	-5	110	71	-1.9	0	0	-0.3
1898	Chi-N	1	0	1.000	1	1	1	0	0	9	8	8.0	0	5	5.0	1	1.0	2.00	183	.258	.362	2	2	102	157	0.5	0	0	0.2
Total	2	1	4	.200	6	5	4	0	0	40	40	9.0	4	17	3.8	4	0.9	5.17	87	.282	.358	-5	-3	108	91	-1.4	0	0	-0.1
■ RUFE CLARKE	Clarke, Rufus Rivers b: 4/13/1900, Estill, S.C. d: 2/8/83, Columbia, S.C. BR/TR, 6'1", 203 lbs. Deb: 9/03/23																												
1923	Det-A	1	1	.500	5	0	0	0	0	6	6	9.0	0	6	9.0	2	3.0	4.50	84	.300	.481	-0	-0	95	143	0.0	0	0	0.0
1924	Det-A	0	0	—	2	0	0	0	0	5	3	5.4	0	5	9.0	1	1.8	3.60	116	.158	.360	0	0	99	67	0.0	-0	0	0.0
Total	2	1	1	.500	7	0	0	0	0	11	9	7.4	0	11	9.0	3	2.5	4.09	97	.231	.423	0	-0	97	108	0.0	-0	0	0.0
■ STAN CLARKE	Clarke, Stanley Martin b: 8/9/60, Toledo, Ohio BL/TL, 6'1", 180 lbs. Deb: 6/07/83																												
1983	Tor-A	1	1	.500	10	0	0	0	0	11	10	8.2	2	5	4.1	7	5.7	3.27	134	.256	.326	1	1	108	149	0.0	0	0	0.1
1985	Tor-A	0	0	—	4	0	0	0	0	4	3	6.8	1	2	4.5	2	4.5	4.50	91	.214	.313	-0	-0	99	100	0.0	0	0	0.0
1986	Tor-A	0	1	.000	10	0	0	0	0	13	18	12.5	4	10	6.9	9	6.2	9.00	49	.375	.452	-7	-7	104	109	-0.4	0	0	-0.5
1987	Sea-A	2	2	.500	22	0	0	0	0	23	31	12.1	7	10	3.9	13	5.1	5.48	84	.333	.383	-3	-2	103	143	0.1	0	-0	-0.1
Total	4	3	4	.429	46	0	0	0	0	51	62	10.9	14	27	4.8	31	5.5	5.82	77	.320	.385	-9	-8	104	132	-0.3	0	0	-0.5
■ WEBBO CLARKE	Clarke, Vibert Ernesto b: 6/8/28, Colon, Panama d: 6/14/70, Cristobal, C.Z. BL/TL, 6', 165 lbs. Deb: 9/04/55																												
1955	Was-A	0	0	—	7	2	0	0	0	21	17	7.3	2	14	6.0	9	3.9	4.71	79	.221	.333	-2	-2	94	78	0.0	-0	0	-0.1
■ DAD CLARKE	Clarke, William H. b: 1/7/1865, Oswego, N.Y. d: 6/3/11, Lorain, Ohio BB/TR, Deb: N/A.																												
1888	Chi-N	1	0	1.000	2	2	1	0	0	16	23	12.9	2	6	3.4	6	3.4	5.06	59	.352	.406	-4	-4	106	125	0.5	2	0	0.0
1891	Col-a	1	2	.333	4	3	2	0	0	21	30	12.9	0	16	6.9	2	0.9	6.86	49	.351	.453	-7	-8	90	91	-0.3	0	0	-0.6
1894	NY-N	3	4	.429	15	6	5	0	1	84	114	12.2	3	26	2.8	15	1.6	4.93	106	.347	.395	4	3	98	105	-1.2	-0	0	0.2
1895	NY-N	18	15	.545	37	30	27	1	1	282	336	10.7	5	60	1.9	67	2.1	3.38	134	.316	.353	44	36	94	117	1.8	-1	-2	2.7
1896	NY-N	17	24	.415	48	40	33	1	1	351	431	11.1	9	60	1.5	66	1.7	4.26	101	.325	.354	4	2	99	94	-4.1	-4	-3	-0.4
1897	NY-N	2	1	.667	6	4	2	0	0	31	43	12.5	1	11	3.2	10	2.9	6.10	68	.352	.406	-6	-7	96	87	0.1	-1	0	-0.5
	Lou-N	1	3	.250	4	4	4	0	0	33	44	12.0	3	9	2.5	6	1.6	3.82	110	.343	.386	2	1	97	137	-0.7	-1	0	0.0
	Yr	3	4	.429	10	8	6	0	0	64	87	12.2	4	20	2.8	16	2.3	4.92	85	.348	.396	-4	-5	97	137	-0.6	-1	0	-0.5
1898	Lou-N	0	1	.000	1	1	1	0	0	9	10	10.0	1	2	2.0	1	1.0	5.00	70	.303	.343	-1	-1	98	83	-0.4	-1	0	-0.1
Total	7	43	50	.462	117	90	75	2	3	827	1031	11.2	24	190	2.1	173	1.9	4.17	106	.327	.366	35	22	97	104	-4.3	-6	-5	1.3
■ DAD CLARKSON	Clarkson, Arthur Hamilton b: 8/31/1866, Cambridge, Mass. d: 2/6/11, Cambridge, Mass. 5'10", 165 lbs. Deb: 8/20/1891																												
1891	NY-N	1	2	.333	5	2	1	0	0	28	24	7.7	0	18	5.8	11	3.5	2.89	107	.244	.361	1	1	93	102	-0.5	2	0	0.2
1892	Bos-N	1	0	1.000	1	1	1	0	0	7	5	6.4	0	3	3.9	0	0.0	1.29	283	.212	.300	2	2	111	143	0.5	-1	0	0.1
1893	StL-N	12	9	.571	24	21	17	1	0	186	194	9.4	4	79	3.8	37	1.8	3.48	134	.284	.358	25	25	100	112	2.9	-5	0	1.6
1894	StL-N	8	17	.320	32	32	24	1	0	233	318	12.3	9	117	4.5	46	1.8	6.37	86	.348	.422	-27	-23	103	91	-3.5	-4	0	-1.9
1895	StL-N	1	6	.143	7	7	7	0	0	61	91	13.4	7	26	3.8	9	1.3	7.38	66	.367	.427	-18	-17	102	92	-1.8	-3	0	-1.4
	Bal-N	12	3	.800	20	14	10	0	0	142	169	10.7	5	64	4.1	23	1.5	3.87	128	.316	.389	15	17	104	123	3.2	-4	0	1.1
	Yr	13	9	.591	27	21	17	0	0	203	260	11.5	12	90	4.0	32	1.4	4.92	101	.332	.401	-3	1	103	123	1.4	-3	0	-0.3
1896	Bal-N	4	2	.667	7	4	3	0	0	47	72	13.8	1	18	3.4	7	1.3	4.98	86	.375	.429	-3	-4	99	121	0.0	0	0	-0.2
Total	6	39	39	.500	96	81	63	2	0	704	873	11.2	26	325	4.2	133	1.7	4.91	100	.324	.397	-5	1	102	106	0.8	-15	0	-0.5
■ JOHN CLARKSON	Clarkson, John Gibson b: 7/1/1861, Cambridge, Mass. d: 2/4/09, Belmont, Mass. BR/TR, 5'10", 155 lbs. Deb: 5/02/1882 H																												
1882	Wor-N	1	2	.333	3	3	2	0	0	24	49	18.4	0	2	0.8	3	1.1	4.50	69	.428	.437	-4	-4	107	170	0.2	1	0	-0.1
1884	Chi-N	10	3	.769	14	13	12	0	0	118	94	7.2	10	25	1.9	102	**7.8**	2.14	146	.227	.271	11	13	105	106	3.3	4	0	1.8
1885	Chi-N	**53**	16	.768	**70**	70	**68**	**10**	0	**623**	497	7.2	21	97	1.4	**308**	4.4	1.85	161	.229	.262	**67**	**78**	106	105	-0.9	3	8	**9.1**
1886	Chi-N	36	17	.679	55	55	50	3	0	467	419	8.1	20	86	1.7	313	6.0	2.41	151	.252	.289	46	63	110	108	-2.7	1	4	6.8
1887	Chi-N	**38**	21	.644	**60**	59	**56**	2	0	**523**	513	8.8	20	92	1.6	**237**	4.1	3.08	**152**	.271	**.305**	**56**	**92**	115	98	7.1	2	8	**9.8**
1888	Bos-N	33	20	.623	54	54	53	3	0	**483**	448	8.3	17	119	2.2	223	4.2	2.76	108	.259	.307	4	12	105	101	8.1	2	2	1.7
1889	Bos-N	**49**	19	**.721**	**73**	72	**68**	**8**	1	**620**	589	8.6	16	203	2.9	**284**	4.1	**2.73**	**145**	.266	.327	**89**	**85**	98	113	**12.1**	3	11	**9.0**
1890	Bos-N	25	18	.581	44	44	43	2	0	383	370	8.7	14	140	3.3	138	3.2	3.27	118	.269	.337	13	24	108	99	0.7	3	-1	2.6
1891	Bos-N	33	19	.635	55	51	47	3	**3**	461	435	8.5	18	154	3.0	141	2.8	2.79	131	.262	.325	28	44	109	101	0.5	4	5	5.2
1892	Bos-N	8	6	.571	16	16	15	4	0	146	115	7.1	4	60	3.7	48	3.0	2.34	156	.228	.311	15	21	111	101	-1.1	1	0	2.3
	Cle-N	17	10	.630	29	28	27	1	1	243	235	8.7	4	72	2.7	91	3.4	2.56	130	.267	.322	20	20	101	112	0.2	-5	0	1.5
	Yr	25	16	.610	45	44	42	5	1	389	350	8.1	8	132	3.1	139	3.2	2.48	139	.253	.318	35	42	105	112	-0.9	1	0	3.8
1893	Cle-N	16	17	.485	36	35	31	0	0	295	358	10.9	11	95	2.9	62	1.9	4.45	108	.316	.369	7	11	103	103	-3.1	-3	4	1.1
1894	Cle-N	8	10	.444	22	18	13	1	0	151	173	10.3	6	46	2.7	28	1.7	4.41	134	.310	.362	15	25	111	93	-1.5	-3	0	1.8
Total	12	327	178	.648	531	518	485	37	5	4537	4295	8.5	161	1191	2.4	1978	3.9	2.81	134	.263	.313	369	485	106	104	22.9	12	41	52.6
■ WALTER CLARKSON	Clarkson, Walter Hamilton b: 11/3/1878, Cambridge, Mass. d: 10/10/46, Cambridge, Mass. TR, 5'10", 150 lbs. Deb: 7/02/04																												
1904	NY-A	1	2	.333	13	4	2	0	1	66	63	8.6	3	25	3.4	43	5.9	5.05	57	.274	.345	-18	-16	111	68	-0.6	2	-1	-1.7
1905	NY-A	3	3	.500	9	4	3	0	0	46	40	7.8	1	13	2.5	35	6.8	3.91	69	.257	.315	-6	-6	103	67	0.1	-2	-0	-0.6
1906	NY-A	9	4	.692	32	16	9	3	0	151	135	8.0	6	55	3.3	64	3.8	2.32	137	.263	.335	6	14	118	131	1.7	-1	-2	1.4
1907	NY-A	1	1	.500	5	2	0	0	0	17	19	10.1	1	8	4.2	3	1.6	6.35	44	.308	.387	-7	-7	110	70	0.1	0	0	-0.6
	Cle-A	4	6	.400	17	10	9	1	0	91	77	7.6	1	29	2.9	32	3.2	1.98	119	.252	.317	6	4	93	119	-1.4	-3	-1	0.4
	Yr	5	7	.417	22	12	9	1	0	108	96	8.0	2	37	3.1	35	2.9	2.67	91	.261	.329	-2	-3	96	119	-1.3	0	-0	-0.2
1908	Cle-A	0	0	—	2	1	0	0	0	3	6	18.0	0	2	6.0	1	3.0	12.00	21	.400	.526	-3	-3	103	87	0.0	0	-0	-0.2
Total	5	18	16	.529	78	37	23	4	1	374	340	8.2	12	132	3.2	178	4.3	3.18	89	.266	.335	-23	-14	108	106	-0.1	-4	-4	-1.3
■ BILL CLARKSON	Clarkson, William Henry "Blackie" b: 9/27/1898, Portsmouth, Va. d: 8/27/71, Raleigh, N.C. BR/TR, 5'11", 160 lbs. Deb: 5/02/27																												
1927	NY-N	3	9	.250	26	7	2	0	2	87	92	9.5	3	52	5.4	28	2.9	4.34	88	.280	.365	-4	-5	98	105	-3.5	-1	0	-0.5
1928	NY-N	0	0	—	4	0	0	0	0	6	10	15.0	0	1	1.5	3	4.5	7.50	53	.455	.440	-2	-2	99	104	0.0	0	0	-0.1
	Bos-N	0	2	.000	19	1	0	0	0	35	53	13.6	2	22	5.7	8	2.1	6.69	60	.349	.409	-10	-10	101	102	-0.9	-0	1	-0.8
	Yr	0	2	.000	23	1	0	0	0	41	63	13.8	2	23	5.0	11	2.4	6.80	59	.362	.412	-13	-13	101	102	-0.9	0	1	-0.9
1929	Bos-N	0	1	.000	2	1	0	0	0	7	16	20.6	0	4	5.1	0	0.0	10.29	45	.485	.500	-4	-4	97	110	-0.4	0	0	-0.2
Total	3	3	12	.200	51	9	2	0	2	135	171	11.4	5	79	5.3	39	2.6	5.40	73	.319	.389	-21	-22	99	105	-4.8	-1	1	-1.6
■ MARTY CLARY	Clary, Martin Keith b: 4/3/62, Detroit, Mich. BR/TR, 6'4", 190 lbs. Deb: 9/05/87																												
1987	Atl-N	0	1	.000	7	1	0	0	0	15	20	12.0	2	4	2.4	7	4.2	6.00	74	.328	.368	-3	-3	109	100	-0.4	-0	-0	-0.2
■ GOWELL CLASET	Claset, Gowell Sylvester "Lefty" b: 11/26/07, Battle Creek, Mich d: 3/8/81, St.Petersburg, Fla. BB/TL, 6'3.5", 210 lbs. Deb: 4/12/33																												
1933	Phi-A	2	0	1.000	8	1	0	0	0	11	23	18.8	1	11	9.0	1	0.8	9.82	40	.426	.507	-7	-7	92	116	1.0	1	0	-0.4
■ FRITZ CLAUSEN	Clausen, Frederick William b: 4/26/1869, New York, N.Y. d: 2/11/60, Memphis, Tenn. BR/TL, 5'11", 190 lbs. Deb: 7/23/1892																												
1892	Lou-N	9	13	.409	24	24	24	2	0	200	181	8.1	3	87	3.9	94	4.2	3.06	100	.254	.335	5	0	93	96	-0.1	-3	0	-0.2
1893	Lou-N	1	4	.200	5	5	3	0	0	33	41	11.2	2	22	6.0	4	1.1	6.00	76	.321	.421	-5	-5	98	98	-1.2	-1	0	-0.4
	Chi-N	6	2	.750	10	9	8	0	1	76	71	8.4	1	39	4.6	31	3.7	3.08	158	.262	.355	14	15	104	114	2.3	-4	0	1.0
	Yr	7	6	.538	15	14	11	0	1	109	112	9.2	3	61	5.0	35	2.9	3.96	121	.281	.377	9	10	102	114	1.1	-1	0	0.6
1894	Chi-N	0	1	.000	1	1	0	0	0	4	5	11.3	0	3	6.8	1	2.3	11.25	51	.329	.439	-3	-2	108	50	-0.4	-0	0	-0.1
1896	Lou-N	0	2	.000	2	2	1	0	0	11	17	13.9	1	6	4.9	4	3.3	6.55	68	.377	.451	-3	-3	102	108	-0.9	-1	0	-0.2
Total	4	16	22	.421	42	41	36	2	1	324	315	8.8	7	157	4.4	134	3.7	3.58	103	.269	.355	8	4	97	100	-0.3	-8	0	0.1
■ AL CLAUSS	Clauss, Albert Stanley "Lefty" b: 6/24/1891, New Haven, Conn. d: 9/13/52, New Haven, Conn. BR/TL, 5'10.5", 178 lbs. Deb: 4/22/13																												
1913	Det-A	0	1	.000	5	1	0	0	0	13	11	7.6	0	12	8.3	1	0.7	4.85	61	.220	.391	-3	-3	101	77	-0.4	-1	-0	-0.2

YEAR	TM/L	W	L	PCT	G	GS	CG	SHO	SV	IP	H	H/G	HR	BB	BB/G	SO	SO/G	ERA	/A	OAVG	OOBP	PR	/A	PF	CPI	WAT	PB	PD	TPI
■ DANNY CLAY	Clay, Danny Bruce b: 10/24/61, Sun Walley, Cal. BR/TR, 6'1", 190 lbs. Deb: 5/01/88																												
1988	Phi-N	0	1	.000	17	0	0	0	0	24	27	10.1	5	21	7.9	12	4.5	6.00	59	.303	.421	-7	-7	103	123	-0.4	-0	-0	-0.7
■ KEN CLAY	Clay, Kenneth Earl b: 4/6/54, Lynchburg, Va. BR/TR, 6'3", 185 lbs. Deb: 6/07/77																												
1977	NY-A	2	3	.400	21	3	0	0	1	56	53	8.5	6	24	3.9	20	3.2	4.34	91	.251	.326	-2	-2	97	90	-0.8	0	0	-0.2
1978	NY-A	3	4	.429	28	6	0	0	0	76	89	10.5	3	21	2.5	32	3.8	4.26	86	.291	.333	-4	-5	97	93	-1.0	0	-0	-0.5
1979	NY-A	1	7	.125	32	5	0	0	2	78	88	10.2	12	25	2.9	28	3.2	5.42	74	.291	.340	-10	-12	95	94	-3.0	0	0	-1.1
1980	Tex-A	2	3	.400	8	8	0	0	0	43	43	9.0	4	29	6.1	17	3.6	4.60	88	.256	.371	-3	-3	100	101	-0.3	0	-1	-0.2
1981	Sea-A	2	7	.222	22	14	0	0	0	101	116	10.3	10	42	3.7	32	2.9	4.63	80	.294	.362	-11	-10	101	108	-2.0	0	-1	-1.1
Total	5	10	24	.294	111	36	0	0	3	354	389	9.9	35	141	3.6	129	3.3	4.68	82	.281	.347	-30	-33	98	98	-7.1	0	-2	-3.1
■ MARK CLEAR	Clear, Mark Alan b: 5/27/56, Los Angeles, Cal. BR/TR, 6'4", 200 lbs. Deb: 4/04/79																												
1979	Cal-A	11	5	.688	52	0	0	0	14	109	87	7.2	6	68	5.6	98	8.1	3.63	107	.219	.328	7	3	92	91	2.7	0	-1	0.2
1980	Cal-A	11	11	.500	58	0	0	0	9	106	82	7.0	2	65	5.5	105	8.9	3.31	118	.216	.330	9	7	97	90	2.0	0	-1	0.6
1981	Bos-A	8	3	.727	34	0	0	0	9	77	69	8.1	11	51	6.0	82	9.6	4.09	95	.239	.353	-4	-2	106	112	2.3	0	-1	-0.2
1982	Bos-A	14	9	.609	55	0	0	0	14	105	92	7.9	11	61	5.2	109	9.3	3.00	150	.238	.343	13	17	110	140	1.7	0	-0	1.7
1983	Bos-A	4	5	.444	48	0	0	0	4	96	101	9.5	10	68	6.4	81	7.6	6.28	66	.273	.384	-24	-23	102	85	-0.3	0	-1	-2.2
1984	Bos-A	8	3	.727	47	0	0	0	8	67	47	6.3	2	70	9.4	76	10.2	4.03	109	.198	.374	-0	3	110	96	2.4	0	0	0.3
1985	Bos-A	1	3	.250	41	0	0	0	3	56	45	7.2	1	50	8.0	55	8.8	3.70	114	.225	.386	3	3	102	116	-0.9	0	1	0.4
1986	Mil-A	5	5	.500	59	0	0	0	16	74	53	6.4	4	36	4.4	85	10.3	2.19	197	.201	.294	16	17	103	115	0.2	0	-0	1.7
1987	Mil-A	8	5	.615	58	1	0	0	6	78	70	8.1	9	55	6.3	81	9.3	4.50	101	.239	.361	-0	1	102	104	0.9	0	1	0.1
1988	Mil-A	1	0	1.000	25	0	0	0	0	29	23	7.1	4	21	6.5	26	8.1	2.79	146	.215	.338	4	4	103	147	0.5	0	-0	0.4
Total	10	71	49	.592	477	1	0	0	83	797	669	7.6	60	545	6.2	798	9.0	3.83	109	.229	.349	24	31	102	106	11.5	0	-2	3.0
■ JOE CLEARY	Cleary, Joseph Christopher "Fire" b: 12/3/18, Cork, Ireland BR/TR, 5'9", 150 lbs. Deb: 8/04/45																												
1945	Was-A	0	0	—	1	0	0	0	0	⅓	5	135.0	0	3	81.0	1	27.0	189.00	—	.833	.889	-7	-7	92	49	0.0	0	0	-0.4
■ ROGER CLEMENS	Clemens, William Roger b: 8/4/62, Dayton, Ohio BR/TR, 6'4", 205 lbs. Deb: 5/15/84																												
1984	Bos-A	9	4	.692	21	20	5	1	0	133	146	9.9	13	29	2.0	126	8.5	4.33	101	.271	.308	-5	1	110	86	2.4	0	0	0.1
1985	Bos-A	7	5	.583	15	15	3	1	0	98	83	7.6	5	37	3.4	74	6.8	3.31	127	.228	.302	9	10	102	88	1.1	0	0	1.0
1986	Bos-A	**24**	4	**.857**	33	33	10	1	0	254	179	**6.3**	21	67	2.4	238	8.4	**2.48**	**166**	**.195**	**.251**	**48**	**46**	99	79	**9.7**	0	-1	4.8
1987	Bos-A	**20**	9	**.690**	36	36	**18**	**7**	0	282	248	7.9	19	83	2.6	256	8.2	2.97	149	.235	.294	47	46	99	100	**6.5**	0	-2	4.4
1988	Bos-A	18	12	.600	35	35	**14**	**8**	0	264	217	7.4	17	62	2.1	**291**	**9.9**	2.93	146	.220	.268	31	40	108	80	2.0	0	-2	4.1
Total	5	78	34	.696	140	139	50	18	0	1031	873	7.6	75	278	2.4	985	8.6	3.05	141	.226	.280	130	143	103	87	21.7	0	-4	14.4
■ BILL CLEMENSEN	Clemensen, William Melville b: 6/20/19, New Brunswick, N.J. BR/TR, 6'1", 193 lbs. Deb: 5/22/39																												
1939	Pit-N	0	1	.000	12	1	0	0	0	27	32	10.7	0	20	6.7	13	4.3	7.33	54	.311	.414	-10	-10	101	81	-0.4	1	1	-0.7
1941	Pit-N	1	0	1.000	2	1	1	0	0	13	7	4.8	0	7	4.8	4	2.8	2.77	133	.159	.264	1	1	102	51	0.5	-1	-0	0.0
1946	Pit-N	0	0	—	1	0	0	0	0	2	0	0.0	0	0	0.0	2	9.0	0.00	—	.000	.000	1	1	106	0	0.0	0	0	0.1
Total	3	1	1	.500	15	2	1	0	0	42	39	8.4	0	27	5.8	19	4.1	5.57	69	.255	.359	-8	-8	101	67	0.1	0	1	-0.6
■ PAT CLEMENTS	Clements, Patrick Brian b: 2/2/62, Mc Cloud, Cal. BR/TL, 6', 175 lbs. Deb: 4/09/85																												
1985	Cal-A	5	0	1.000	41	0	0	0	1	62	47	6.8	4	25	3.6	19	2.8	3.34	125	.218	.300	6	6	101	90	2.5	0	1	0.7
	Pit-N	0	2	.000	27	0	0	0	2	34	39	10.3	2	15	4.0	17	4.5	3.71	101	.289	.353	-0	0	104	122	-0.9	0	-1	0.0
1986	Pit-N	0	4	.000	65	0	0	0	2	61	53	7.8	1	32	4.7	31	4.6	2.80	134	.251	.340	6	6	101	133	-1.9	-1	1	0.7
1987	NY-A	3	3	.500	55	0	0	0	7	80	91	10.2	4	30	3.4	36	4.0	4.95	88	.299	.357	-4	-5	97	98	-0.2	0	1	-0.4
1988	NY-A	0	0	—	6	1	0	0	0	8	12	13.5	1	4	4.5	3	3.4	6.75	56	.343	.390	-2	-3	96	102	0.0	0	-0	-0.2
Total	4	8	9	.471	194	1	0	0	12	245	242	8.9	12	106	3.9	106	3.9	3.89	104	.269	.340	5	5	100	108	-0.5	-0	1	0.8
■ LANCE CLEMONS	Clemons, Lance Levis b: 7/6/47, Philadelphia, Pa. BL/TL, 6'2", 205 lbs. Deb: 8/12/71																												
1971	KC-A	1	0	1.000	10	3	0	0	0	24	26	9.8	2	12	4.5	20	7.5	4.13	83	.263	.342	-2	-2	98	100	0.5	2	0	0.0
1972	StL-N	0	1	.000	3	1	0	0	0	5	8	14.4	1	5	9.0	2	3.6	10.80	34	.364	.500	-4	-4	105	92	-0.4	-0	0	-0.3
1974	Bos-A	1	0	1.000	6	0	0	0	0	6	8	12.0	1	4	6.0	1	1.5	10.50	37	.296	.406	-5	-4	106	62	0.5	0	0	-0.3
Total	3	2	1	.667	19	4	0	0	0	35	42	10.8	4	21	5.4	23	5.9	6.17	57	.284	.379	-10	-10	101	92	0.6	2	0	-0.6
■ REGGIE CLEVELAND	Cleveland, Reginald Leslie b: 5/23/48, Swift Current, Sask., Canada BR/TR, 6'1", 195 lbs. Deb: 10/01/69																												
1969	StL-N	0	0	—	1	1	0	0	0	4	7	15.8	0	1	2.3	3	6.8	9.00	40	.368	.400	-2	-2	99	67	0.0	-0	0	-0.1
1970	StL-N	0	4	.000	16	1	0	0	0	26	31	10.7	3	18	6.2	22	7.6	7.62	56	.298	.380	-10	-10	106	79	-1.9	0	-1	-0.9
1971	StL-N	12	12	.500	34	34	10	2	0	222	238	9.6	20	53	2.1	148	6.0	4.01	87	.271	.312	-13	-13	100	93	-1.3	-0	-0	-1.4
1972	StL-N	14	15	.483	33	33	11	3	0	231	229	8.9	21	60	2.3	153	6.0	3.94	93	.258	.303	-12	-7	105	88	0.1	2	-1	-0.6
1973	StL-N	14	10	.583	32	32	6	3	0	224	211	8.5	13	61	2.5	122	4.9	3.01	110	.246	.294	16	7	90	97	2.3	5	-2	0.9
1974	Bos-A	12	14	.462	41	27	10	0	0	221	234	9.5	25	69	2.8	103	4.2	4.32	89	.271	.325	-17	-12	106	96	-1.6	0	1	-1.0
1975	Bos-A	13	9	.591	31	20	3	1	0	171	173	9.1	19	52	2.7	78	4.1	4.42	92	.263	.315	-12	-7	108	87	0.0	0	-0	-0.6
1976	Bos-A	10	9	.526	41	14	3	0	2	170	159	8.4	3	61	3.2	76	4.0	3.07	126	.246	.312	9	15	110	95	0.3	0	-0	1.6
1977	Bos-A	11	8	.579	36	27	9	1	2	190	211	10.0	20	43	2.0	85	4.0	4.26	111	.281	.319	-4	10	116	96	-0.3	0	-1	0.8
1978	Bos-A	0	1	.000	1	0	0	0	0	⅓	1	27.0	0	0	0.0	0	0.0	0.00	—	.333	.333	0	0	106	0	-0.4	0	0	0.0
	Tex-A	5	7	.417	53	0	0	0	12	76	65	7.7	5	23	2.7	46	5.4	3.08	117	.236	.289	6	5	96	94	-1.3	0	0	0.5
	Yr	5	8	.385	54	0	0	0	12	76	66	7.8	5	23	2.7	46	5.4	3.08	117	.237	.289	6	5	96	94	-1.7	0	0	0.5
1979	Mil-A	1	5	.167	29	1	0	0	4	55	77	12.6	9	23	3.8	22	3.6	6.71	63	.344	.388	-15	-15	99	103	-2.1	0	-1	-1.5
1980	Mil-A	11	9	.550	45	13	5	2	4	154	150	8.8	9	49	2.9	54	3.2	3.74	101	.254	.311	5	0	93	88	0.5	0	-1	0.0
1981	Mil-A	2	3	.400	35	0	0	0	1	65	57	7.9	5	30	4.2	18	2.5	5.12	68	.239	.321	-11	-12	95	69	-0.7	0	-1	-1.3
Total	13	105	106	.498	428	203	57	12	25	1809	1843	9.2	152	543	2.7	930	4.6	4.01	95	.264	.314	-61	-41	103	92	-6.4	6	-8	-3.6
■ TEX CLEVENGER	Clevenger, Truman Eugene b: 7/9/32, Visalia, Cal. BR/TR, 6'1", 180 lbs. Deb: 4/18/54																												
1954	Bos-A	2	4	.333	23	8	1	0	0	68	67	8.9	9	29	3.8	43	5.7	4.76	79	.262	.329	-8	-8	101	92	-0.7	0	0	-0.6
1956	Was-A	0	0	—	20	1	0	0	0	32	33	9.3	4	21	5.9	17	4.8	5.34	83	.264	.362	-4	-3	107	92	0.0	-0	0	-0.2
1957	Was-A	7	6	.538	52	9	2	0	8	140	139	8.9	11	47	3.0	75	4.8	4.18	92	.261	.317	-6	-5	102	89	2.0	1	1	-0.2
1958	Was-A	9	9	.500	**55**	4	0	0	6	124	119	8.6	12	50	3.6	70	5.1	4.35	87	.251	.318	-8	-8	100	86	1.7	0	3	-0.4
1959	Was-A	8	5	.615	50	7	2	2	8	117	114	8.8	9	51	3.9	71	5.5	3.92	100	.256	.328	-1	-0	102	100	2.4	1	4	0.5
1960	Was-A	5	11	.313	53	11	1	0	7	129	150	10.5	10	49	3.4	49	3.4	4.19	95	.298	.353	-5	-3	102	114	-2.8	-1	-0	-0.4
1961	LA-A	2	1	.667	12	0	0	0	1	16	13	7.3	1	13	7.3	11	6.2	1.69	267	.220	.361	4	5	112	229	0.6	-0	1	0.5
	NY-A	1	1	.500	21	0	0	0	0	32	35	9.8	3	21	5.9	14	3.9	4.78	79	.287	.390	-3	-4	93	115	-0.2	0	1	-0.2
	Yr	3	2	.600	33	0	0	0	1	48	48	9.0	4	34	6.4	25	4.7	3.75	107	.265	.381	1	1	100	115	0.4	-0	1	0.3
1962	NY-A	2	0	1.000	21	0	0	0	0	38	36	8.5	3	17	4.0	11	2.6	2.84	128	.248	.329	5	3	92	132	1.0	-0	0	0.3
Total	8	36	37	.493	307	40	6	2	30	696	706	9.1	62	298	3.9	361	4.7	4.18	93	.265	.334	-25	-22	101	102	4.0	1	8	-0.7
■ STEW CLIBURN	Cliburn, Stewart Walker b: 12/19/56, Jackson, Miss. BR/TR, 6', 195 lbs. Deb: 9/17/84																												
1984	Cal-A	0	0	—	1	0	0	0	0	2	3	13.5	0	1	4.5	1	4.5	13.50	30	.333	.400	-2	-2	101	41	0.0	0	0	-0.1
1985	Cal-A	9	3	.750	44	0	0	0	6	99	87	7.9	5	26	2.4	48	4.4	2.09	199	.241	.289	23	23	101	140	2.7	0	1	2.4
1988	Cal-A	4	2	.667	40	1	0	0	0	84	83	8.9	11	32	3.4	42	4.5	4.07	92	.266	.335	-1	-3	95	115	1.2	0	0	-0.2
Total	3	13	5	.722	85	1	0	0	6	185	173	8.4	16	59	2.9	91	4.4	3.11	128	.254	.312	20	18	98	127	3.9	0	2	2.1
■ JIM CLINTON	Clinton, James Lawrence "Big Jim" b: 8/10/1850, New York, N.Y. d: 9/3/21, Brooklyn, N.Y. BR/TR, 5'8.5", 174 lbs. Deb: 5/21/1872 M																												
1875	Atl-n	1	12	.077	14																								
1876	Lou-N	0	1	.000	1	1	1	0	0	9	12	12.0	0	0	0.0	1	1.0	6.00	41	.324	.324	-4	-4	106	50	-0.4	0	0	-0.2
■ TONY CLONINGER	Cloninger, Tony Lee b: 8/13/40, Lincoln, N.C. BR/TR, 6', 210 lbs. Deb: 6/15/61																												
1961	Mil-N	7	2	.778	19	10	3	0	0	84	84	9.0	16	33	3.5	51	5.5	5.25	70	.258	.325	-11	-15	91	87	2.4	-0	1	-1.3
1962	Mil-N	8	3	.727	24	15	4	1	0	111	113	9.2	10	46	3.7	69	5.6	4.30	90	.264	.331	-4	-5	98	94	2.4	-2	0	-0.6
1963	Mil-N	9	11	.450	41	18	4	2	1	145	131	8.1	17	63	3.9	100	6.2	3.79	87	.239	.315	-8	-8	100	98	-1.4	-1	-2	-1.0

YEAR	TM/L	W	L	PCT	G	GS	CG	SHO	SV	IP	H	H/G	HR	BB	BB/G	SO	SO/G	ERA	/A	OAVG	OOBP	PR	/A	PF	CPI	WAT	PB	PD	TPI
1964	Mil-N	19	14	.576	38	34	15	3	2	243	206	7.6	20	82	3.0	163	6.0	3.56	95	.231	.292	-1	-4	96	86	1.4	4	-0	-0.1
1965	Mil-N	24	11	.686	40	38	16	1	1	279	247	8.0	20	119	3.8	211	6.8	3.29	111	.236	.313	8	11	103	101	6.8	2	-1	1.3
1966	Atl-N	14	11	.560	39	38	11	1	1	258	253	8.8	29	116	4.0	178	6.2	4.12	85	.258	.331	-15	-17	97	102	1.1	10	-0	-0.8
1967	Atl-N	4	7	.364	16	16	1	0	0	77	85	9.9	13	31	3.6	55	6.4	5.14	69	.285	.344	-15	-14	105	101	-1.3	1	-0	-1.3
1968	Atl-N	1	3	.250	8	1	0	0	0	19	15	7.1	0	11	5.2	7	3.3	4.26	65	.227	.325	-3	-3	94	70	-0.9	-0	0	-0.3
	Cin-N	4	3	.571	17	17	2	2	0	91	81	8.0	7	48	4.7	65	6.4	4.05	82	.233	.324	-11	-8	111	86	0.4	3	-0	-0.4
	Yr	5	6	.455	25	18	2	2	0	110	96	7.9	7	59	4.8	72	5.9	4.09	79	.231	.324	-14	-11	108	86	-0.5	-0	0	-0.7
1969	Cin-N	11	17	.393	35	34	6	2	0	190	184	8.7	24	103	4.9	103	4.9	5.02	71	.250	.342	-30	-31	99	87	-4.5	1	-2	-3.1
1970	Cin-N	9	7	.563	30	18	0	0	1	148	136	8.3	10	78	4.7	56	3.4	3.83	109	.249	.342	4	6	103	105	-0.8	3	2	1.1
1971	Cin-N	3	6	.333	28	8	1	1	0	97	79	7.3	12	49	4.5	51	4.7	3.90	86	.230	.322	-5	-6	96	99	-1.4	1	0	-0.4
1972	StL-N	0	2	.000	17	0	0	0	0	26	29	10.0	2	19	6.6	11	3.8	5.19	70	.293	.402	-5	-4	105	110	-0.9	-0	1	-0.3
Total	12	113	97	.538	352	247	63	13	6	1768	1643	8.4	180	798	4.1	1120	5.7	4.07	88	.247	.325	-96	-99	100	95	3.3	21	-2	-7.2
■ AL CLOSTER	Closter, Alan Edward b: 6/15/43, Creighton, Neb. BL/TL, 6'2", 190 lbs. Deb: 4/19/66																												
1966	Was-A	0	0	—	1	0	0	0	0	⅓	1	27.0	0	2	54.0	0	0.0	0.00	—	.500	.750	0	0	96	0	0.0	0	0	0.0
1971	NY-A	2	2	.500	14	1	0	0	0	28	33	10.6	4	13	4.2	22	7.1	5.14	65	.289	.356	-5	-6	97	104	0.0	-1	1	-0.5
1972	NY-A	0	0	—	2	0	0	0	0	2	2	9.0	1	4	18.0	2	9.0	13.50	21	.250	.500	-2	-2	92	82	0.0	-0	0	-0.1
1973	Atl-N	0	0	—	4	0	0	0	0	4	7	15.8	1	4	9.0	2	4.5	15.75	26	.389	.478	-5	-5	113	67	0.0	0	0	-0.4
Total	4	2	2	.500	21	1	0	0	0	34	43	11.4	6	23	6.1	26	6.9	6.88	50	.303	.391	-13	-13	98	98	0.0	-1	1	-1.0
■ ED CLOUGH	Clough, Edgar George "Big Ed" or "Spec" b: 10/28/06, Wiconisco, Pa. d: 1/30/44, Harrisburg, Pa. BL/TL, 6', 188 lbs. Deb: 8/28/24																												
1925	StL-N	0	1	.000	3	1	0	0	0	10	11	9.9	1	5	4.5	3	2.7	8.10	53	.289	.378	-4	-4	101	65	-0.4	-0	-0	-0.3
1926	StL-N	0	0	—	1	0	0	0	0	2	5	22.5	0	3	13.5	0	0.0	22.50	17	.556	.600	-4	-4	100	76	0.0	-0	0	-0.3
Total	2	0	1	.000	4	1	0	0	0	12	16	12.0	1	8	6.0	3	2.3	10.50	40	.340	.433	-8	-8	101	67	-0.4	-0	-0	-0.6
■ BILL CLOWERS	Clowers, William Perry b: 8/14/1898, San Marcos, Tex. d: 1/13/78, Sweeny, Tex. BL/TL, 5'11", 175 lbs. Deb: 7/20/26																												
1926	Bos-A	0	0	—	2	0	0	0	0	2	2	9.0	0	0	0.0	0	0.0	0.00	—	.333	.250	1	1	106	0	0.0	0	0	0.1
■ BRYAN CLUTTERBUCK	Clutterbuck, Bryan Richard b: 12/17/59, Detroit, Mich. BR/TR, 6'4", 223 lbs. Deb: 7/18/86																												
1986	Mil-A	0	1	.000	20	0	0	0	0	57	68	10.7	8	16	2.5	38	6.0	4.26	101	.296	.344	-0	0	103	118	-0.4	0	-0	0.0
■ DAVID CLYDE	Clyde, David Eugene b: 4/22/55, Kansas City, Kan. BL/TL, 6'1.5", 180 lbs. Deb: 6/27/73																												
1973	Tex-A	4	8	.333	18	18	0	0	0	93	106	10.3	8	54	5.2	74	7.2	5.03	76	.293	.385	-12	-13	100	105	-0.2	0	-0	-1.2
1974	Tex-A	3	9	.250	28	21	4	0	0	117	129	9.9	14	47	3.6	52	4.0	4.38	79	.286	.352	-10	-12	96	110	-3.2	0	-2	-1.3
1975	Tex-A	0	1	.000	1	1	0	0	0	7	6	7.7	0	6	7.7	2	2.6	2.57	147	.273	.414	1	1	100	195	-0.4	0	-0	0.1
1978	Cle-A	8	11	.421	28	25	5	0	0	153	166	9.8	4	60	3.5	83	4.9	4.29	82	.280	.342	-9	-13	94	91	-0.2	0	-1	-1.3
1979	Cle-A	3	4	.429	9	8	1	0	0	46	50	9.8	7	13	2.5	17	3.3	5.87	77	.279	.328	-8	-7	106	79	-0.4	0	-0	-0.6
Total	5	18	33	.353	84	73	10	0	0	416	457	9.9	33	180	3.9	228	4.9	4.63	80	.285	.354	-39	-44	97	100	-4.4	0	-3	-4.3
■ TOM CLYDE	Clyde, Thomas Knox b: 8/17/23, Wachapreague, Va. BR/TR, 6'3", 195 lbs. Deb: 5/31/43																												
1943	Phi-A	0	0	—	4	0	0	0	0	6	7	10.5	1	4	6.0	0	0.0	9.00	39	.304	.375	-4	-4	106	77	0.0	-0	-0	-0.3
■ ANDY COAKLEY	Coakley, Andrew James (played under name of Jack Mc Allister In 1902) b: 11/20/1882, Providence, R.I. d: 9/27/63, New York, N.Y. BL/TR, 6', 165 lbs. Deb: 9/17/02																												
1902	Phi-A	2	1	.667	3	3	3	0	0	27	25	8.3	0	9	3.0	9	3.0	2.67	142	.269	.334	3	3	106	103	0.2	1	0	0.4
1903	Phi-A	0	3	.000	6	3	2	0	0	38	48	11.4	2	11	2.6	20	4.7	5.45	55	.332	.379	-11	-10	102	88	-1.4	-0	-0	-0.9
1904	Phi-A	4	4	.500	8	8	8	2	0	62	50	7.3	1	23	3.3	33	4.8	2.03	129	.242	.318	4	4	101	120	-0.2	-2	-0	0.4
1905	Phi-A	18	8	.692	35	31	21	3	0	255	227	8.0	2	73	2.6	145	5.1	1.84	153	.262	.319	23	28	106	**144**	2.8	-4	-2	3.0
1906	Phi-A	7	8	.467	22	16	10	0	0	149	144	8.7	0	44	2.7	59	3.6	3.14	80	.279	.335	-7	-11	93	92	-1.0	-1	-3	-1.3
1907	Cin-N	17	16	.515	37	30	21	1	1	265	269	9.1	1	79	2.7	89	3.0	2.34	100	.294	.355	4	0	95	131	3.0	-5	-3	-0.3
1908	Cin-N	8	18	.308	32	28	20	4	2	242	219	8.1	3	64	2.4	61	2.3	1.86	131	.271	.327	13	16	104	137	-5.0	-4	-5	1.3
	Chi-N	2	0	1.000	4	3	2	1	0	20	14	6.3	0	6	2.7	7	3.1	0.90	266	.222	.289	3	3	102	167	1.0	-1	-0	0.4
	Yr	10	18	.357	36	31	22	5	2	262	233	8.0	3	70	2.4	68	2.3	1.79	136	.266	.320	16	19	104	167	-4.0	-4	-5	1.7
1909	Chi-N	0	1	.000	1	1	0	0	0	2	7	31.5	0	3	13.5	1	4.5	18.00	14	.583	.667	-3	-3	95	106	-0.4	0	0	-0.2
1911	NY-A	0	1	.000	2	1	1	0	0	12	20	15.0	0	2	1.5	4	3.0	5.25	71	.377	.400	-3	-2	111	110	-0.4	0	0	-0.1
Total	9	58	60	.492	150	124	88	11	3	1072	1023	8.6	9	314	2.6	428	3.6	2.36	110	.278	.337	25	27	101	128	-1.4	-15	-13	2.7
■ JIM COATES	Coates, James Alton b: 8/4/32, Farnham, Va. BR/TR, 6'4", 192 lbs. Deb: 9/21/56																												
1956	NY-A	0	0	—	2	0	0	0	0	2	1	4.5	0	4	18.0	0	0.0	13.50	29	.167	.500	-2	-2	95	55	0.0	0	0	-0.1
1959	NY-A	6	1	.857	37	4	2	0	0	100	89	8.0	10	36	3.2	64	5.8	2.88	123	.234	.301	11	7	92	115	2.5	-1	0	0.6
1960	NY-A	13	3	.813	35	18	6	2	1	149	139	8.4	16	66	4.0	73	4.4	4.29	83	.248	.323	-7	-12	92	90	4.2	4	-2	-1.0
1961	NY-A	11	5	.688	43	11	4	1	5	141	128	8.2	15	53	3.4	80	5.1	3.45	109	.243	.316	9	5	93	108	0.4	-3	-0	0.1
1962	NY-A	7	6	.538	50	6	0	0	6	118	119	9.1	9	50	3.8	67	5.1	4.42	82	.263	.337	-6	-10	92	93	-0.5	-1	-2	-1.2
1963	Was-A	2	4	.333	20	2	0	0	0	44	51	10.4	4	21	4.3	31	6.3	5.32	69	.297	.373	-8	-8	101	100	0.0	-1	0	-0.8
	Cin-N	0	0	—	9	0	0	0	0	16	21	11.8	2	7	3.9	11	6.2	5.63	60	.313	.373	-4	-4	103	102	0.0	-0	0	-0.3
1965	Cal-A	2	0	1.000	17	0	0	0	3	28	23	7.4	1	16	5.1	15	4.8	3.54	96	.228	.315	-0	-0	98	91	1.0	-0	0	0.0
1966	Cal-A	1	1	.500	9	4	1	1	0	32	32	9.0	3	10	2.8	16	4.5	3.94	87	.258	.311	-2	-2	100	94	0.0	-1	-0	-0.2
1967	Cal-A	1	2	.333	25	1	0	0	0	52	47	8.1	5	23	4.0	39	6.8	4.33	72	.244	.333	-6	-7	96	92	-0.4	1	0	-0.6
Total	9	43	22	.662	247	46	13	4	15	682	650	8.6	65	286	3.8	396	5.2	4.01	89	.252	.326	-16	-33	94	99	7.2	-2	-4	-3.5
■ GEORGE COBB	Cobb, George Washington b: San Francisco, Cal. Deb: 4/15/1892																												
1892	Bal-N	10	37	.213	53	47	42	0	0	394	495	11.3	21	140	3.2	159	3.6	4.87	69	.321	.377	-69	-66	102	97	-9.5	6	2	-4.9
■ HERB COBB	Cobb, Herbert Edward b: 8/6/04, Pinetops, N.C. d: 1/8/80, Tarboro, N.C. BR/TR, 5'11", 150 lbs. Deb: 4/21/29																												
1929	StL-A	0	0	—	1	0	0	0	0	1	3	27.0	1	1	9.0	0	0.0	36.00	12	.600	.571	-4	-4	100	68	0.0	0	0	-0.2
■ TY COBB	Cobb, Tyrus Raymond "The Georgia Peach" b: 12/18/1886, Narrows, Ga. d: 7/17/61, Atlanta, Ga. BL/TR, 6'1", 175 lbs. Deb: 8/30/05 MH																												
1918	Det-A	0	0	—	2	0	0	0	0	4	6	13.5	0	2	4.5	0	0.0	4.50	61	.400	.471	-1	-1	99	152	0.0	1	0	0.0
1925	Det-A	0	0	—	1	0	0	0	1	1	0	0.0	0	0	0.0	0	0.0	0.00	—	.000	.000	0	0	98	0	0.0	1	0	0.0
Total	2	0	0	—	3	0	0	0	1	5	6	10.8	0	2	3.6	0	0.0	3.60	85	.333	.400	-0	-0	99	121	0.0	2	0	0.0
■ JAIME COCANOWER	Cocanower, James Stanley b: 2/14/57, San Juan, P.R. BR/TR, 6'4", 200 lbs. Deb: 9/07/83																												
1983	Mil-A	2	0	1.000	5	3	1	0	0	30	21	6.3	1	12	3.6	8	2.4	1.80	206	.200	.288	8	6	91	124	1.0	0	0	0.7
1984	Mil-A	8	16	.333	33	27	1	0	0	175	188	9.7	13	78	4.0	65	3.3	4.01	92	.279	.357	-0	-6	93	115	-2.6	0	1	-0.4
1985	Mil-A	6	8	.429	24	15	3	1	0	116	122	9.5	6	73	5.7	44	3.4	4.34	101	.274	.380	-3	1	106	114	-0.1	0	0	0.1
1986	Mil-A	0	1	.000	17	2	0	0	0	45	40	8.0	1	38	7.6	22	4.4	4.40	98	.248	.390	-1	-0	103	105	-0.4	0	1	0.1
Total	4	16	25	.390	79	47	5	1	0	366	371	9.1	21	201	4.9	139	3.4	3.98	100	.268	.364	4	0	98	114	-2.1	0	3	0.5
■ GOAT COCHRAN	Cochran, Alvah Jackson "Al" or "Goat" b: 1/31/1891, Concord, Ga. d: 5/23/47, Atlanta, Ga. BR/TR, 5'10", 175 lbs. Deb: 8/25/15																												
1915	Cin-N	0	0	—	1	0	0	0	0	2	5	22.5	0	0	0.0	1	4.5	9.00	32	.455	.455	-1	-1	104	101	0.0	0	0	0.0
■ GENE COCREHAM	Cocreham, Eugene b: 11/14/1884, Luling, Tex. d: 12/27/45, Luling, Tex. BR/TR, 6'3.5", 192 lbs. Deb: 9/25/13																												
1913	Bos-N	0	1	.000	1	1	0	0	0	8	13	14.6	0	4	4.5	3	3.4	7.88	39	.371	.439	-4	-4	96	89	-0.4	-1	0	-0.3
1914	Bos-N	3	4	.429	15	3	1	0	0	45	48	9.6	2	27	5.4	15	3.0	4.80	59	.296	.385	-10	-10	102	100	-1.0	-0	-1	-1.1
1915	Bos-N	0	0	—	1	0	0	0	0	2	3	13.5	0	0	0.0	0	0.0	4.50	60	.429	.429	-0	-0	97	137	0.0	0	0	0.0
Total	3	3	5	.375	17	4	1	0	0	55	64	10.5	2	31	5.1	18	2.9	5.24	55	.314	.395	-15	-14	101	100	-1.4	-1	-1	-1.4
■ CHRIS CODIROLI	Codiroli, Christopher Allen b: 3/26/58, Oxnard, Cal. BR/TR, 6'1", 160 lbs. Deb: 9/11/82																												
1982	Oak-A	1	2	.333	3	3	0	0	0	17	16	8.5	1	4	2.1	5	2.6	4.24	93	.246	.286	-0	-1	96	67	-0.2	0	0	0.0
1983	Oak-A	12	12	.500	37	31	7	2	1	206	208	9.1	17	72	3.1	85	3.7	4.46	88	.264	.325	-9	-12	96	89	1.1	0	-2	-1.3
1984	Oak-A	6	4	.600	28	14	1	0	1	89	111	11.2	16	34	3.4	44	4.4	5.87	63	.304	.365	-18	-22	92	99	1.2	0	-0	-2.0
1985	Oak-A	14	14	.500	37	37	4	0	0	226	228	9.1	23	78	3.1	111	4.4	4.46	87	.259	.317	-8	-15	93	87	0.8	0	-1	-1.5
1986	Oak-A	5	8	.385	16	16	1	0	0	92	91	8.9	15	38	3.7	43	4.2	4.01	98	.250	.323	2	-1	94	106	-1.2	0	1	0.0

YEAR	TM/L	W	L	PCT	G	GS	CG	SHO	SV	IP	H	H/G	HR	BB	BB/G	SO	SO/G	ERA	/A	OAVG	OOBP	PR	/A	PF	CPI	WAT	PB	PD	TPI
1987	Oak-A	0	2	.000	3	3	0	0	0	11	12	9.8	1	8	6.5	4	3.3	9.00	45	.273	.389	-6	-6	91	60	-0.9	0	0	-0.4
1988	Cle-A	0	4	.000	14	2	0	0	1	19	32	15.2	2	10	4.7	12	5.7	9.47	43	.372	.446	-12	-11	102	87	-1.9	0	0	-1.0
Total	7	38	46	.452	138	106	13	2	3	660	698	9.5	75	244	3.3	304	4.1	4.80	81	.269	.332	-51	-68	94	91	-1.1	0	-2	-6.2

■ SLICK COFFMAN Coffman, George David b: 12/11/10, Veto, Ala. BR/TR, 6', 155 lbs. Deb: 5/21/37

YEAR	TM/L	W	L	PCT	G	GS	CG	SHO	SV	IP	H	H/G	HR	BB	BB/G	SO	SO/G	ERA	/A	OAVG	OOBP	PR	/A	PF	CPI	WAT	PB	PD	TPI
1937	Det-A	7	5	.583	28	5	1	0	0	101	121	10.8	8	39	3.5	22	2.0	4.37	114	.295	.357	3	7	108	113	0.1	0	-1	0.6
1938	Det-A	4	4	.500	39	6	1	0	2	96	120	11.3	6	48	4.5	31	2.9	6.00	79	.310	.378	-13	-13	99	93	-0.2	0	-1	-1.2
1939	Det-A	2	1	.667	23	1	0	0	0	42	51	10.9	4	22	4.7	10	2.1	6.43	79	.295	.368	-8	-6	110	85	0.5	-1	0	-0.5
1940	StL-A	2	2	.500	31	4	1	0	1	75	108	13.0	5	23	2.8	26	3.1	6.24	76	.334	.372	-15	-13	108	93	0.2	-0	1	-1.0
Total	4	15	12	.556	121	16	3	0	3	314	400	11.5	23	132	3.8	89	2.6	5.59	87	.309	.369	-34	-25	105	99	0.6	-1	-1	-2.1

■ KEVIN COFFMAN Coffman, Kevin Reese b: 1/19/65, Austin, Tex. BR/TR, 6'2", 175 lbs. Deb: 9/05/87

YEAR	TM/L	W	L	PCT	G	GS	CG	SHO	SV	IP	H	H/G	HR	BB	BB/G	SO	SO/G	ERA	/A	OAVG	OOBP	PR	/A	PF	CPI	WAT	PB	PD	TPI
1987	Atl-N	2	3	.400	5	5	0	0	0	25	31	11.2	2	22	7.9	14	5.0	4.68	95	.313	.444	-2	-1	109	150	-0.1	-0	1	0.0
1988	Atl-N	2	6	.250	18	11	0	0	0	67	62	8.3	3	54	7.3	24	3.2	5.78	64	.251	.386	-17	-16	107	82	-1.0	2	0	-1.3
Total	2	4	9	.308	23	16	0	0	0	92	93	9.1	5	76	7.4	38	3.7	5.48	71	.269	.403	-19	-16	108	101	-1.1	1	2	-1.3

■ DICK COFFMAN Coffman, Samuel Richard b: 12/18/06, Veto, Ala. d: 3/24/72, Athens, Ala. BR/TR, 6'2", 195 lbs. Deb: 4/28/27

YEAR	TM/L	W	L	PCT	G	GS	CG	SHO	SV	IP	H	H/G	HR	BB	BB/G	SO	SO/G	ERA	/A	OAVG	OOBP	PR	/A	PF	CPI	WAT	PB	PD	TPI
1927	Was-A	0	1	.000	5	2	0	0	0	16	20	11.3	0	2	1.1	5	2.8	3.38	118	.313	.338	1	1	96	124	-0.4	0	0	0.2
1928	StL-A	4	5	.444	29	7	3	0	1	86	122	12.8	7	37	3.9	25	2.6	6.07	69	.359	.405	-19	-18	103	112	-0.7	-3	0	-1.8
1929	StL-A	1	1	.500	27	3	1	1	1	53	61	10.4	3	14	2.4	11	1.9	5.94	71	.295	.331	-10	-10	100	74	0.0	-1	0	-0.9
1930	StL-A	8	18	.308	38	30	12	1	1	196	250	11.5	14	69	3.2	54	2.5	5.14	100	.311	.363	-11	-0	110	105	-3.8	-6	0	-0.4
1931	StL-A	9	13	.409	32	17	11	2	1	169	159	8.5	10	51	2.7	39	2.1	3.89	118	.241	.294	9	13	105	81	0.0	-5	-2	0.7
1932	StL-A	5	3	.625	9	6	3	0	0	61	66	9.7	3	21	3.1	14	2.1	3.10	148	.277	.338	9	10	103	139	1.5	-2	-1	0.7
	Was-A	1	6	.143	22	9	2	1	0	76	92	10.9	2	31	3.7	17	2.0	4.86	90	.307	.368	-3	-4	98	105	-2.6	-1	-1	-0.4
	Yr	6	9	.400	31	15	5	1	0	137	158	10.4	5	52	3.4	31	2.0	4.07	110	.293	.352	6	6	100	105	-1.1	-2	-1	0.3
1933	StL-A	3	7	.300	21	13	3	1	1	81	114	12.7	9	39	4.3	19	2.1	5.89	85	.329	.394	-14	-8	117	112	-0.8	-3	0	-0.8
1934	StL-A	9	10	.474	40	21	6	1	3	173	212	11.0	11	59	3.1	55	2.9	4.53	105	.303	.352	-1	5	106	109	0.6	-0	0	0.4
1935	StL-A	5	11	.313	41	18	5	0	2	144	206	12.9	14	46	2.9	34	2.1	6.13	80	.335	.372	-27	-20	110	100	-2.2	-1	-1	-1.9
1936	NY-N	7	5	.583	42	2	0	0	7	102	119	10.5	7	23	2.0	26	2.3	3.88	102	.296	.330	2	1	98	113	-0.1	-0	1	0.2
1937	NY-N	8	3	.727	42	1	0	0	3	80	93	10.5	4	31	3.5	30	3.4	3.04	126	.289	.353	**8**	**7**	98	150	1.6	2	0	1.0
1938	NY-N	8	4	.667	**51**	3	1	1	**12**	111	116	9.4	3	21	1.7	21	1.7	3.49	111	.268	.302	4	5	102	91	1.6	-3	-2	0.0
1939	NY-N	1	2	.333	28	0	0	0	3	38	50	11.8	1	6	1.4	9	2.1	3.08	125	.316	.343	4	3	99	147	-0.4	-1	-0	0.2
1940	Bos-N	1	5	.167	31	0	0	0	3	48	63	11.8	4	11	2.1	11	2.1	5.44	71	.323	.357	-8	-8	101	100	-1.8	-1	-0	-0.8
1945	Phi-N	2	1	.667	14	0	0	0	0	26	39	13.5	0	2	0.7	2	0.7	5.19	75	.351	.353	-4	-4	102	96	0.8	0	1	-0.1
Total	15	72	95	.431	472	132	47	8	38	1460	1782	11.0	92	463	2.9	372	2.3	4.65	96	.302	.349	-61	-29	105	106	-6.7	-23	-3	-3.7

■ DICK COGAN Cogan, Richard Henry b: 12/5/1871, Paterson, N.J. d: 5/2/48, Paterson, N.J. 5'7", 150 lbs. Deb: 5/10/1897

YEAR	TM/L	W	L	PCT	G	GS	CG	SHO	SV	IP	H	H/G	HR	BB	BB/G	SO	SO/G	ERA	/A	OAVG	OOBP	PR	/A	PF	CPI	WAT	PB	PD	TPI
1897	Bal-N	0	0	—	1	0	0	0	0	2	4	18.0	0	2	9.0	0	0.0	13.50	29	.439	.540	-2	-2	92	73	0.0	-0	0	-0.1
1899	Chi-N	2	3	.400	5	5	5	0	0	44	54	11.0	1	24	4.9	9	1.8	4.30	86	.327	.412	-2	-3	96	114	-0.4	1	0	0.0
1900	NY-N	0	0	—	2	0	0	0	0	8	10	11.3	0	6	6.8	1	1.1	6.75	54	.330	.441	-3	-3	99	81	0.0	-0	0	-0.2
Total	3	2	3	.400	8	5	5	0	0	54	68	11.3	1	32	5.3	10	1.7	5.00	74	.332	.422	-7	-8	96	108	-0.4	0	0	-0.3

■ HY COHEN Cohen, Hyman b: 1/29/31, Brooklyn, N.Y. BR/TR, 6'5", 220 lbs. Deb: 4/17/55

YEAR	TM/L	W	L	PCT	G	GS	CG	SHO	SV	IP	H	H/G	HR	BB	BB/G	SO	SO/G	ERA	/A	OAVG	OOBP	PR	/A	PF	CPI	WAT	PB	PD	TPI
1955	Chi-N	0	0	—	7	1	0	0	0	17	28	14.8	2	10	5.3	4	2.1	7.94	52	.378	.453	-7	-7	101	104	0.0	-0	-0	-0.6

■ SYD COHEN Cohen, Sydney Harry b: 5/7/08, Baltimore, Md. d: 4/9/88, El Paso, Tex. BB/TL, 5'11", 180 lbs. Deb: 9/18/34

YEAR	TM/L	W	L	PCT	G	GS	CG	SHO	SV	IP	H	H/G	HR	BB	BB/G	SO	SO/G	ERA	/A	OAVG	OOBP	PR	/A	PF	CPI	WAT	PB	PD	TPI
1934	Was-A	1	1	.500	3	2	2	0	0	18	25	12.5	2	6	3.0	6	3.0	7.50	61	.333	.373	-6	-6	102	82	0.1	0	1	-0.3
1936	Was-A	0	2	.000	19	1	0	0	1	36	44	11.0	4	14	3.5	21	5.3	5.25	92	.303	.370	-1	-2	96	111	-0.9	-1	2	0.0
1937	Was-A	2	4	.333	33	0	0	0	4	55	64	10.5	1	17	2.8	22	3.6	3.11	142	.299	.345	9	8	96	140	-0.8	-1	2	0.8
Total	3	3	7	.300	55	3	2	0	5	109	133	11.0	7	37	3.1	49	4.0	4.54	101	.306	.358	2	1	97	121	-1.6	-2	5	0.5

■ ROCKY COLAVITO Colavito, Rocco Domenico b: 8/10/33, New York, N.Y. BR/TR, 6'3", 190 lbs. Deb: 9/10/55 C

YEAR	TM/L	W	L	PCT	G	GS	CG	SHO	SV	IP	H	H/G	HR	BB	BB/G	SO	SO/G	ERA	/A	OAVG	OOBP	PR	/A	PF	CPI	WAT	PB	PD	TPI
1958	Cle-A	0	0	—	1	0	0	0	0	3	0	0.0	0	3	9.0	1	3.0	0.00	—	.000	.250	1	1	93	0	0.0	1	0	0.1
1968	NY-A	1	0	1.000	1	0	0	0	0	3	1	3.0	0	2	6.0	1	3.0	0.00	—	.111	.273	1	1	101	0	0.5	0	0	0.1
Total	2	1	0	1.000	2	0	0	0	0	6	1	1.5	0	5	7.5	2	3.0	0.00	—	.059	.261	2	2	97	0	0.5	1	0	0.2

■ VINCE COLBERT Colbert, Vincent Norman b: 12/20/45, Washington, D.C. BR/TR, 6'4", 200 lbs. Deb: 5/19/70

YEAR	TM/L	W	L	PCT	G	GS	CG	SHO	SV	IP	H	H/G	HR	BB	BB/G	SO	SO/G	ERA	/A	OAVG	OOBP	PR	/A	PF	CPI	WAT	PB	PD	TPI
1970	Cle-A	1	1	.500	23	0	0	0	2	31	37	10.7	4	16	4.6	17	4.9	7.26	59	.298	.380	-12	-10	115	77	0.1	-0	0	-0.9
1971	Cle-A	7	6	.538	50	10	2	0	2	143	140	8.8	11	71	4.5	74	4.7	3.97	95	.265	.347	-8	-3	108	107	1.8	-0	0	-0.2
1972	Cle-A	1	7	.125	22	11	1	1	0	75	74	8.9	8	38	4.6	36	4.3	4.56	73	.267	.361	-12	-10	108	103	-2.9	1	0	-0.9
Total	3	9	14	.391	95	21	3	1	4	249	251	9.1	23	125	4.5	127	4.6	4.55	81	.270	.356	-32	-24	109	102	-1.0	0	1	-2.0

■ JIM COLBORN Colborn, James William b: 5/22/46, Santa Paula, Cal. BR/TR, 6', 185 lbs. Deb: 7/13/69

YEAR	TM/L	W	L	PCT	G	GS	CG	SHO	SV	IP	H	H/G	HR	BB	BB/G	SO	SO/G	ERA	/A	OAVG	OOBP	PR	/A	PF	CPI	WAT	PB	PD	TPI
1969	Chi-N	1	0	1.000	6	2	0	0	0	15	15	9.0	2	9	5.4	4	2.4	3.00	126	.283	.385	1	1	105	189	0.5	-0	0	0.1
1970	Chi-N	3	1	.750	34	5	0	0	4	73	88	10.8	3	23	2.8	50	6.2	3.58	134	.298	.343	4	10	119	124	1.0	-1	1	1.0
1971	Chi-N	0	1	.000	14	0	0	0	0	10	18	16.2	1	3	2.7	2	1.8	7.20	53	.383	.420	-4	-4	110	103	-0.4	0	0	-0.3
1972	Mil-A	7	7	.500	39	12	4	1	0	148	135	8.2	14	43	2.6	97	5.9	3.10	96	.245	.296	-0	-2	97	104	1.1	-1	-1	-0.4
1973	Mil-A	20	12	.625	43	36	22	4	1	314	297	8.5	21	87	2.5	135	3.9	3.18	115	.251	.301	22	17	96	98	5.7	0	1	1.9
1974	Mil-A	10	13	.435	33	31	10	1	0	224	230	9.2	27	60	2.4	83	3.3	4.06	92	.268	.316	-11	-8	103	97	-0.9	0	0	-0.8
1975	Mil-A	11	13	.458	36	29	8	1	2	206	215	9.4	18	65	2.8	79	3.5	4.28	90	.270	.324	-11	-10	101	91	0.9	0	1	-0.8
1976	Mil-A	9	15	.375	32	32	7	0	0	226	232	9.2	20	54	2.2	101	4.0	3.70	95	.268	.307	-5	-4	100	99	-1.1	0	-0	-0.4
1977	KC-A	18	14	.563	36	35	6	1	0	239	233	8.8	22	81	3.1	103	3.9	3.62	111	.255	.320	12	11	99	103	-2.0	0	1	1.2
1978	KC-A	1	2	.333	8	3	0	0	0	28	31	10.0	4	12	3.9	8	2.6	4.82	79	.282	.352	-3	-3	101	105	-0.5	0	1	-0.2
	Sea-A	3	10	.231	20	19	3	0	0	114	125	9.9	21	38	3.0	26	2.1	5.37	73	.279	.337	-20	-18	104	93	-2.2	0	2	-1.5
	Yr	4	12	.250	28	22	3	0	0	142	156	9.9	25	50	3.2	34	2.2	5.26	74	.279	.337	-23	-21	104	93	-2.7	0	3	-1.7
Total	10	83	88	.485	301	204	60	8	7	1597	1619	9.1	153	475	2.7	688	3.9	3.80	98	.265	.317	-15	-11	101	100	2.1	-3	6	-0.2

■ TOM COLCOLOUGH Colcolough, Thomas Bernard b: 10/8/1870, Charleston, S.C. d: 12/10/19, Charleston, S.C. BR/TR, 5'10.5", 180 lbs. Deb: 8/01/1893

YEAR	TM/L	W	L	PCT	G	GS	CG	SHO	SV	IP	H	H/G	HR	BB	BB/G	SO	SO/G	ERA	/A	OAVG	OOBP	PR	/A	PF	CPI	WAT	PB	PD	TPI
1893	Pit-N	2	0	1.000	8	3	1	0	1	44	45	9.2	1	32	6.5	7	1.4	4.09	120	.280	.400	3	4	105	113	1.0	-0	0	0.3
1894	Pit-N	8	5	.615	22	14	11	0	0	149	207	12.5	5	70	4.2	29	1.8	7.13	71	.352	.421	-30	-35	95	81	1.6	-2	0	-2.6
1895	Pit-N	1	1	.500	6	5	2	0	0	35	38	9.8	1	21	5.4	15	3.9	5.66	81	.297	.396	-3	-4	96	81	0.0	2	0	0.0
1899	NY-N	4	5	.444	11	8	7	0	0	82	85	9.3	1	41	4.5	14	1.5	3.95	96	.291	.378	-1	-1	99	96	0.4	1	0	0.0
Total	4	15	11	.577	47	30	21	0	1	310	375	10.9	8	164	4.8	65	1.9	5.69	82	.321	.404	-31	-36	97	89	3.0	1	0	-2.3

■ BERT COLE Cole, Albert George b: 7/1/1896, San Francisco, Cal d: 5/30/75, San Mateo, Cal. BL/TL, 6'1", 180 lbs. Deb: 4/19/21

YEAR	TM/L	W	L	PCT	G	GS	CG	SHO	SV	IP	H	H/G	HR	BB	BB/G	SO	SO/G	ERA	/A	OAVG	OOBP	PR	/A	PF	CPI	WAT	PB	PD	TPI
1921	Det-A	7	4	.636	20	11	7	1	1	110	134	11.0	3	36	2.9	22	1.8	4.25	96	.305	.352	0	-2	96	104	1.9	3	-0	0.0
1922	Det-A	1	6	.143	23	5	2	1	0	79	105	12.0	4	39	4.4	21	2.4	4.90	80	.313	.379	-8	-9	97	106	-2.5	-1	0	-0.8
1923	Det-A	13	5	.722	52	13	6	1	5	163	183	10.1	9	61	3.4	32	1.8	4.14	91	.284	.340	-3	-6	95	99	3.8	2	-1	-0.4
1924	Det-A	3	9	.250	28	11	2	1	2	109	135	11.1	4	35	2.9	16	1.3	4.71	89	.314	.358	-6	-6	99	102	-3.3	1	1	-0.4
1925	Det-A	2	3	.400	14	2	1	0	1	34	44	11.6	2	15	4.0	7	1.9	5.82	74	.336	.382	-5	-6	98	102	-0.5	0	1	-0.3
	Cle-A	1	1	.500	13	2	0	0	1	44	55	11.3	1	25	5.1	9	1.8	6.14	76	.322	.403	-9	-7	107	91	0.1	-0	-0	-0.6
	Yr	3	4	.429	27	4	1	0	2	78	99	11.4	3	40	4.6	16	1.8	6.00	75	.327	.391	-14	-13	103	91	-0.4	0	1	-0.9
1927	Chi-A	1	4	.200	27	2	0	0	0	67	79	10.6	3	19	2.6	12	1.6	4.70	91	.309	.346	-4	-3	103	99	-1.3	-1	2	-0.2
Total	6	28	32	.467	177	46	18	4	10	606	735	10.9	26	230	3.4	119	1.8	4.66	87	.305	.358	-34	-40	98	101	-1.8	5	2	-2.7

■ DAVE COLE Cole, David Bruce b: 8/29/30, Williamsport, Md. BR/TR, 6'2", 175 lbs. Deb: 9/09/50

YEAR	TM/L	W	L	PCT	G	GS	CG	SHO	SV	IP	H	H/G	HR	BB	BB/G	SO	SO/G	ERA	/A	OAVG	OOBP	PR	/A	PF	CPI	WAT	PB	PD	TPI
1950	Bos-N	0	1	.000	4	0	0	0	0	8	7	7.9	0	3	3.4	8	9.0	1.13	313	.259	.344	3	2	85	334	-0.4	-0	-0	0.2
1951	Bos-N	2	4	.333	23	7	1	0	0	68	64	8.5	3	64	8.5	33	4.4	4.24	91	.254	.406	-2	-3	97	119	-0.9	3	0	0.1
1952	Bos-N	1	1	.500	22	3	0	0	0	45	38	7.6	2	42	8.4	22	4.4	4.00	90	.241	.401	-1	-2	97	124	0.1	-1	0	-0.2
1953	Mil-N	0	1	.000	10	0	0	0	0	15	17	10.2	1	14	8.4	13	7.8	8.40	47	.279	.413	-7	-7	92	68	-0.4	1	0	-0.4

YEAR	TM/L	W	L	PCT	G	GS	CG	SHO	SV	IP	H	H/G	HR	BB	BB/G	SO	SO/G	ERA	/A	OAVG	OOBP	PR	/A	PF	CPI	WAT	PB	PD	TPI
1954	Chi-N	3	8	.273	18	14	2	1	0	84	74	7.9	7	62	6.6	37	4.0	5.36	77	.241	.361	-12	-11	102	80	-1.9	1	-0	-0.9
1955	Phi-N	0	3	.000	7	3	0	0	0	18	21	10.5	3	14	7.0	6	3.0	6.50	63	.304	.398	-5	-5	102	104	-1.4	-0	0	-0.3
Total	6	6	18	.250	84	27	3	1	0	238	221	8.4	16	199	7.5	119	4.5	4.92	80	.253	.388	-25	-26	98	109	-4.9	5	1	-1.5
■ ED COLE	Cole, Edward William (born Edward William Kisleauskas) b: 3/22/09, Wilkes-Barre, Pa. BR/TR, 5'11", 170 lbs. Deb: 4/22/38																												
1938	StL-A	1	5	.167	36	6	1	0	3	89	116	11.7	8	48	4.9	26	2.6	5.16	96	.313	.391	-4	-2	103	118	-1.5	-1	-1	-0.3
1939	StL-A	0	2	.000	6	0	0	0	0	6	8	12.0	1	6	9.0	5	7.5	7.50	65	.308	.412	-2	-2	105	102	-0.9	-0	0	-0.1
Total	2	1	7	.125	42	6	1	0	3	95	124	11.7	9	54	5.1	31	2.9	5.31	93	.312	.393	-6	-4	103	117	-2.4	-2	-1	-0.4
■ KING COLE	Cole, Leonard Leslie b: 4/15/1886, Toledo, Iowa d: 1/6/16, Bay City, Mich. BR/TR, 6'1", 170 lbs. Deb: 09																												
1909	Chi-N	1	0	1.000	1	1	1	1	0	9	6	6.0	0	3	3.0	1	1.0	0.00	—	.194	.265	3	2	95	0	0.5	2	-0	0.3
1910	Chi-N	20	4	**.833**	33	29	21	4	1	240	174	**6.5**	2	130	4.9	114	4.3	**1.80**	**162**	**.211**	.325	33	30	96	**136**	6.3	2	-1	3.4
1911	Chi-N	18	7	.720	32	27	13	2	0	221	188	7.7	3	99	4.0	101	4.1	3.14	102	.236	.328	7	1	94	93	4.3	-1	-2	-0.2
1912	Chi-N	1	2	.333	8	3	0	0	0	19	36	17.1	2	8	3.8	9	4.3	10.89	32	.400	.460	-16	-16	102	78	-0.6	1	0	-1.2
	Pit-N	2	2	.500	12	4	2	0	0	49	61	11.2	1	18	3.3	11	2.0	6.43	51	.308	.372	-16	-17	95	68	-0.3	-1	-0	-1.6
	Yr	3	4	.429	20	7	2	0	0	68	97	12.8	3	26	3.4	20	2.6	7.68	43	.334	.393	-32	-33	97	68	-0.9	1	0	-2.8
1914	NY-A	11	9	.550	33	15	8	2	0	142	151	9.6	3	51	3.2	43	2.7	3.30	83	.288	.352	-9	-9	100	115	2.0	-3	-3	-1.2
1915	NY-A	3	3	.500	10	6	2	0	1	51	41	7.2	2	22	3.9	19	3.4	3.18	91	.224	.317	-1	-2	99	86	0.3	-1	-0	-0.2
Total	6	56	27	.675	129	85	47	9	2	731	657	8.1	13	331	4.1	298	3.7	3.11	96	.248	.338	-0	-9	97	108	12.5	-2	-5	-0.7
■ JOHN COLEMAN	Coleman, John b: Bristol, Pa. TR , Deb: 6/23/1890																												
1890	Phi-N	0	1	.000	1	1	0	0	0	2	4	18.0	0	3	13.5	2	9.0	27.00	14	.433	.572	-5	-5	107	42	-0.4	0	0	-0.3
■ JOHN COLEMAN	Coleman, John b: Jefferson City, Mo. TL , Deb: 9/25/1895																												
1895	StL-N	0	1	.000	1	1	1	0	0	8	12	13.5	1	8	9.0	5	5.6	13.50	36	.368	.493	-8	-8	102	63	-0.4	-0	0	-0.4
■ JOHN COLEMAN	Coleman, John Francis b: 3/6/1863, Saratoga Spgs., N.Y d: 5/31/22, Detroit, Mich. BL/TR, 5'9.5", 170 lbs. Deb: 5/01/1883																												
1883	Phi-N	12	48	.200	65	61	59	3	0	538	772	12.9	17	48	0.8	159	2.7	4.87	64	.344	.358	-103	-104	99	99	2.4	4	2	-7.9
1884	Phi-N	5	15	.250	21	19	14	1	0	154	216	12.6	9	22	1.3	37	2.2	4.91	59	.341	.363	-33	-34	97	99	-3.1	2	0	-2.8
	Phi-a	0	2	.000	3	2	2	0	0	21	28	12.0	0	2	0.9	5	2.1	3.43	107	.329	.344	-0	1	113	135	-0.9	0	0	0.0
1885	Phi-a	2	2	.500	8	3	3	0	0	60	82	12.3	0	5	0.8	12	1.8	3.45	96	.338	.351	-1	-1	102	132	0.0	3	0	0.0
1886	Phi-a	1	1	.500	3	1	1	0	0	21	18	7.7	1	5	2.1	2	0.9	2.57	138	.241	.289	2	2	103	109	0.1	0	0	-0.4
1889	Phi-a	3	2	.600	5	5	4	0	0	34	38	10.1	2	14	3.7	6	1.6	2.91	127	.298	.367	4	3	96	150	0.2	-2	0	0.0
1890	Pit-N	0	2	.000	2	2	1	0	0	14	28	18.0	1	6	3.9	3	1.9	9.64	35	.433	.481	-9	-10	95	92	-0.9	0	0	-0.6
Total	6	23	72	.242	107	93	84	4	0	842	1182	12.6	30	102	1.1	224	2.4	4.68	67	.341	.359	-142	-144	99	104	-2.2	7	2	-11.7
■ JOE COLEMAN	Coleman, Joseph Howard b: 2/3/47, Boston, Mass. BR/TR, 6'3", 175 lbs. Deb: 9/28/65 C																												
1965	Was-A	2	0	1.000	2	2	2	0	0	18	9	4.5	0	8	4.0	7	3.5	1.50	235	.153	.246	4	4	102	69	1.0	-1	1	0.5
1966	Was-A	1	0	1.000	1	1	1	0	0	9	6	6.0	0	2	2.0	4	4.0	2.00	165	.188	.229	1	1	96	53	0.5	-0	0	0.2
1967	Was-A	8	9	.471	28	22	3	0	0	134	154	10.3	6	47	3.2	77	5.2	4.63	72	.291	.352	-21	-19	104	97	0.0	-2	-2	-2.2
1968	Was-A	12	16	.429	33	33	12	2	0	223	212	8.6	19	51	2.1	139	5.6	3.27	85	.250	.296	-7	-12	94	101	0.7	-0	-1	-1.5
1969	Was-A	12	13	.480	40	36	12	4	1	248	222	8.1	26	100	3.6	182	6.6	3.27	107	.243	.315	10	6	96	112	-1.3	-2	1	0.4
1970	Was-A	8	12	.400	39	29	6	1	0	219	190	7.8	25	89	3.7	152	6.2	3.58	101	.233	.308	3	1	97	96	-0.7	2	0	0.2
1971	Det-A	20	9	.690	39	38	16	3	0	286	241	7.6	17	96	3.0	236	7.4	3.15	105	.229	.293	10	5	95	87	4.8	-3	-2	0.0
1972	Det-A	19	14	.576	40	39	9	3	0	280	216	6.9	23	110	3.5	222	7.1	2.80	123	.214	.293	9	20	112	98	1.1	-3	-1	1.9
1973	Det-A	23	15	.605	40	40	13	2	0	288	283	8.8	32	93	2.9	202	6.3	3.53	110	.258	.317	9	11	101	108	4.0	0	0	1.1
1974	Det-A	14	12	.538	41	41	11	2	0	286	272	8.6	30	158	5.0	177	5.6	4.31	91	.254	.350	-22	-13	108	101	2.5	0	2	-1.1
1975	Det-A	10	18	.357	31	31	6	1	0	201	234	10.5	27	85	3.8	125	5.6	5.55	73	.291	.358	-39	-34	106	93	0.0	0	0	-3.2
1976	Det-A	2	5	.286	12	12	1	0	0	67	80	10.7	1	34	4.6	38	5.1	4.84	76	.308	.385	-10	-9	105	105	-1.3	0	2	-0.6
	Chi-N	2	8	.200	39	4	0	0	4	79	72	8.2	9	35	4.0	66	7.5	4.10	95	.246	.322	-5	-2	111	96	-2.8	-0	0	-0.1
1977	Oak-A	4	4	.500	43	12	2	0	2	128	114	8.0	11	49	3.4	55	3.9	2.95	133	.241	.310	16	14	97	113	0.7	0	-0	1.3
1978	Oak-A	3	0	1.000	10	0	0	0	0	20	12	5.4	1	5	2.3	4	1.8	1.35	287	.185	.236	5	6	103	117	1.5	0	0	0.6
	Tor-A	2	0	1.000	31	0	0	0	0	61	67	9.9	6	30	4.4	28	4.1	4.57	84	.286	.360	-5	-5	102	107	1.0	0	-1	-0.5
	Yr	5	0	1.000	41	0	0	0	0	81	79	8.8	7	35	3.9	32	3.6	3.78	102	.263	.334	0	1	102	107	2.5	0	-1	0.1
1979	SF-N	0	0	—	5	0	0	0	0	4	3	6.8	0	2	4.5	0	0.0	0.00	—	.231	.333	2	2	93	0	0.0	0	-0	0.1
	Pit-N	0	0	—	10	0	0	0	0	21	29	12.4	1	9	3.9	14	6.0	6.00	65	.326	.386	-5	-5	104	93	0.0	0	-1	-0.4
	Yr	0	0	—	15	0	0	0	0	25	32	11.5	1	11	4.0	14	5.0	5.04	76	.308	.370	-4	-3	102	93	0.0	0	-1	-0.3
Total	15	142	135	.513	484	340	94	18	7	2572	2416	8.5	234	1003	3.5	1728	6.0	3.69	97	.250	.321	-45	-28	102	100	11.7	-10	-1	-3.3
■ JOE COLEMAN	Coleman, Joseph Patrick b: 7/30/22, Medford, Mass. BR/TR, 6'2.5", 200 lbs. Deb: 9/19/42																												
1942	Phi-A	0	1	.000	1	0	0	0	0	6	8	12.0	0	1	1.5	0	0.0	3.00	123	.308	.321	0	0	101	133	-0.4	-1	0	0.0
1946	Phi-A	0	2	.000	4	2	0	0	0	13	19	13.2	1	8	5.5	8	5.5	5.54	68	.345	.422	-3	-3	107	122	-0.9	1	-0	-0.1
1947	Phi-A	6	12	.333	32	21	9	2	1	160	171	9.6	17	62	3.5	65	3.7	4.33	85	.275	.338	-11	-11	100	102	-3.2	-1	-2	-1.3
1948	Phi-A	14	13	.519	33	29	13	3	0	216	224	9.3	11	90	3.8	86	3.6	4.08	106	.269	.334	5	6	102	99	-0.7	-4	-1	0.1
1949	Phi-A	13	14	.481	33	30	18	1	1	240	249	9.3	12	127	4.8	109	4.1	3.86	107	.271	.357	9	7	99	111	-1.3	0	-5	0.3
1950	Phi-A	0	5	.000	15	6	2	0	0	54	74	12.3	9	50	8.3	12	2.0	8.50	50	.332	.446	-24	-25	93	95	-2.4	-0	-2	-2.3
1951	Phi-A	1	6	.143	28	9	1	0	1	96	117	11.0	12	59	5.5	34	3.2	6.00	73	.305	.396	-20	-17	106	103	-2.3	1	-1	-1.6
1953	Phi-A	3	4	.429	21	9	2	1	0	90	85	8.5	8	49	4.9	18	1.8	4.00	105	.254	.348	-0	2	105	107	0.3	2	-2	0.2
1954	Bal-A	13	17	.433	33	32	15	4	0	221	184	7.5	16	96	3.9	103	4.2	3.50	105	.232	.310	5	4	99	91	2.3	2	1	0.8
1955	Bal-A	0	1	.000	6	2	0	0	0	12	19	14.3	5	10	7.5	4	3.0	10.50	35	.373	.455	-9	-9	94	105	-0.4	1	0	-0.7
	Det-A	2	1	.667	17	0	0	0	3	25	22	7.9	1	14	5.0	5	1.8	3.24	116	.239	.339	2	1	95	109	0.5	1	0	0.3
	Yr	2	2	.500	23	2	0	0	3	37	41	10.0	6	24	5.8	9	2.2	5.59	67	.281	.377	-7	-8	94	109	0.1	1	0	-0.4
Total	10	52	76	.406	223	140	60	11	6	1133	1172	9.3	92	566	4.5	444	3.5	4.38	92	.271	.351	-45	-43	100	102	-8.5	2	-11	-4.3
■ PERCY COLEMAN	Coleman, Pierce D. b: 10/15/1876, Mason, Ohio d: 2/16/48, Van Nuys, Cal. Deb: 7/02/1897																												
1897	StL-N	1	2	.333	12	4	2	0	0	57	99	15.6	0	32	5.1	10	1.6	8.21	52	.405	.474	-25	-25	99	90	0.2	-1	0	-1.9
1898	Cin-N	0	1	.000	1	1	1	0	0	9	13	13.0	0	3	3.0	2	2.0	3.00	129	.362	.411	1	1	107	174	-0.4	-1	0	0.0
Total	2	1	3	.250	13	5	3	0	0	66	112	15.3	0	35	4.8	12	1.6	7.50	56	.399	.466	-24	-24	100	101	-0.2	-2	0	-1.9
■ RIP COLEMAN	Coleman, Walter Gary b: 7/31/31, Troy, N.Y. BL/TL, 6'2", 185 lbs. Deb: 8/15/55																												
1955	NY-A	2	1	.667	10	6	0	0	1	29	40	12.4	2	16	5.0	15	4.7	5.28	71	.331	.410	-4	-5	94	117	0.2	1	0	-0.3
1956	NY-A	3	5	.375	29	9	0	0	2	88	97	9.9	6	42	4.3	42	4.3	3.68	107	.285	.357	5	3	95	126	-1.6	-3	0	0.0
1957	KC-A	0	7	.000	19	6	1	1	0	41	53	11.6	5	25	5.5	15	3.3	5.93	65	.325	.402	-10	-9	102	109	-3.4	-1	0	-0.9
1959	KC-A	2	10	.167	29	11	2	0	2	81	85	9.4	8	34	3.8	54	6.0	4.56	87	.273	.336	-6	-5	103	98	-3.7	-2	-0	-0.7
	Bal-A	0	0	—	3	0	0	0	0	4	4	9.0	0	2	4.5	4	9.0	0.00	—	.267	.353	2	2	98	0	0.0	0	1	0.3
	Yr	2	10	.167	32	11	2	0	2	85	89	9.4	8	36	3.8	58	6.1	4.34	91	.271	.334	-5	-4	102	0	-3.7	-2	1	-0.4
1960	Bal-A	0	2	.000	5	1	0	0	0	4	8	18.0	0	5	11.3	0	0.0	11.25	35	.444	.583	-3	-3	101	106	-0.9	-0	0	-0.2
Total	5	7	25	.219	95	33	3	1	5	247	287	10.5	21	124	4.5	130	4.7	4.59	85	.296	.370	-17	-19	99	111	-9.4	-5	2	-1.8
■ ALLAN COLLAMORE	Collamore, Allan Edward b: 6/5/1887, Worcester, Mass. d: 8/8/80, Battle Creek, Mich. BR/TR, 6', 170 lbs. Deb: 4/15/11																												
1911	Phi-A	0	1	.000	2	0	0	0	0	2	6	27.0	0	3	13.5	1	4.5	36.00	8	.600	.733	-7	-7	88	57	-0.4	0	0	-0.5
1914	Cle-A	3	7	.300	27	8	3	0	0	105	100	8.6	3	49	4.2	32	2.7	3.26	89	.264	.357	-6	-4	106	113	-0.4	-2	-1	-0.4
1915	Cle-A	2	5	.286	11	6	5	2	0	64	52	7.3	1	22	3.1	15	2.1	2.39	131	.235	.305	4	5	106	105	-0.8	0	1	0.7
Total	3	5	13	.278	40	14	8	2	0	171	158	8.3	4	74	3.9	48	2.5	3.32	90	.259	.347	-9	-6	106	109	-1.6	-2	-0	-0.2
■ HAP COLLARD	Collard, Earl Clinton b: 8/29/1898, Williams, Ariz. d: 7/9/68, Jamestown, Cal. BR/TR, 6', 170 lbs. Deb: 4/23/27																												
1927	Cle-A	0	0	—	4	0	0	0	0	5	8	14.4	0	3	5.4	2	3.6	5.40	76	.333	.379	-1	-1	99	108	0.0	0	0	0.0
1928	Cle-A	0	0	—	1	0	0	0	0	4	4	9.0	0	4	9.0	1	2.3	2.25	195	.250	.400	1	1	108	199	0.0	0	-0	0.1
1930	Phi-N	6	12	.333	30	15	4	0	0	127	188	13.3	15	39	2.8	25	1.8	6.80	80	.350	.385	-26	-19	109	97	0.0	-2	1	-1.6
Total	3	6	12	.333	35	15	4	0	0	136	200	13.2	15	46	3.0	28	1.9	6.62	81	.347	.385	-26	-19	109	101	0.0	-1	1	-1.5

YEAR	TM/L	W	L	PCT	G	GS	CG	SHO	SV	IP	H	H/G	HR	BB	BB/G	SO	SO/G	ERA	/A	OAVG	OOBP	PR	/A	PF	CPI	WAT	PB	PD	TPI
■ **ORLIN COLLIER**	Collier, Orlin Edward b: 2/17/07, E.Prairie, Mo. d: 9/9/44, Memphis, Tenn. BR/TR, 5'11.5", 180 lbs. Deb: 9/11/31																												
1931	Det-A	0	1	.000	2	2	0	0	0	10	17	15.3	0	7	6.3	3	2.7	8.10	58	.362	.436	-4	-4	107	93	-0.4	-1	-0	-0.3
■ **HARRY COLLIFLOWER**	Colliflower, James Harry "Collie" b: 3/11/1869, Petersville, Md. d: 8/14/61, Washington, D.C. BL/TL, 5'11.5", 175 lbs. Deb: 7/21/1899																												
1899	Cle-N	1	11	.083	14	12	11	0	0	98	152	14.0	6	41	3.8	8	0.7	8.17	45	.380	.438	-47	-49	96	79	-2.2	2	0	-3.5
■ **DAN COLLINS**	Collins, Daniel Thomas b: 7/12/1854, St.Louis, Mo. d: 9/21/1883, New Orleans, La. Deb: 6/08/1874																												
1874	Chi-n	1	1	.500	2																								
■ **DON COLLINS**	Collins, Donald Edward b: 9/15/52, Lyons, Ga. BR/TL, 6'2", 195 lbs. Deb: 5/04/77																												
1977	Atl-N	3	9	.250	40	6	0	0	2	71	82	10.4	8	41	5.2	27	3.4	5.07	89	.299	.383	-9	-4	115	112	-2.0	-2	-1	-0.6
1980	Cle-A	0	0	—	4	0	0	0	0	6	9	13.5	0	7	10.5	0	0.0	7.50	56	.346	.485	-2	-2	103	103	0.0	0	0	-0.1
Total	2	3	9	.250	44	6	0	0	2	77	91	10.6	8	48	5.6	27	3.2	5.26	85	.303	.392	-11	-7	114	111	-2.0	-2	-1	-0.7
■ **RIP COLLINS**	Collins, Harry Warren b: 2/26/1896, Weatherford, Tex. d: 5/27/68, Bryan, Tex. BB/TR, 6'1", 205 lbs. Deb: 4/19/20																												
1920	NY-A	14	8	.636	36	18	10	2	1	187	171	8.2	6	79	3.8	66	3.2	3.22	116	.247	.337	12	11	99	98	0.6	-4	-1	0.6
1921	NY-A	11	5	.688	28	16	7	2	0	137	158	10.4	6	78	5.1	64	4.2	5.45	78	.293	.384	-18	-18	99	92	1.2	-1	-1	-1.8
1922	Bos-A	14	11	.560	32	29	15	3	0	211	219	9.3	4	103	4.4	69	2.9	3.75	107	.274	.354	7	6	99	107	3.8	-3	-1	0.2
1923	Det-A	3	7	.300	17	14	3	1	0	92	104	10.2	3	22	2.2	25	2.4	4.89	77	.284	.328	-9	-11	95	77	-2.2	-1	0	-1.1
1924	Det-A	14	7	.667	34	30	11	1	0	216	199	8.3	6	63	2.6	75	3.1	3.21	130	.249	.298	25	23	99	87	2.9	-5	0	1.8
1925	Det-A	6	11	.353	26	20	5	0	0	140	149	9.6	7	52	3.3	33	2.1	4.56	94	.281	.339	-3	-4	98	91	-2.9	-4	3	-0.3
1926	Det-A	8	8	.500	30	13	5	3	1	122	128	9.4	4	44	3.2	44	3.2	2.73	144	.278	.340	18	16	98	144	-0.1	-1	1	1.6
1927	Det-A	13	7	.650	30	25	10	1	0	173	207	10.8	5	59	3.1	37	1.9	4.68	95	.312	.357	-10	-5	107	103	2.7	0	5	0.1
1929	StL-A	11	6	.647	26	20	10	1	1	155	162	9.4	16	73	4.2	47	2.7	4.01	105	.270	.348	4	4	100	113	2.5	4	0	0.8
1930	StL-A	9	7	.563	35	20	6	1	2	172	168	8.8	11	63	3.3	75	3.9	4.34	118	.259	.320	6	15	110	91	2.2	-3	-0	1.2
1931	StL-A	5	5	.500	17	14	2	0	0	107	130	10.9	5	38	3.2	34	2.9	3.79	121	.307	.363	7	10	105	135	0.8	-1	1	1.0
Total	11	108	82	.568	311	219	84	15	5	1712	1795	9.4	73	674	3.5	569	3.0	4.00	106	.275	.341	38	45	101	102	11.5	-18	8	4.1
■ **ORTH COLLINS**	Collins, Orth Stein "Buck" b: 4/27/1880, Lafayette, Ind. d: 12/13/49, Ft.Lauderdale, Fla BL/TR, 6', 150 lbs. Deb: 6/01/04																												
1909	Was-A	0	0	—	1	0	0	0	0	1	0	0.0	0	0	0.0	1	9.0	0.00	—	.000	.000	0	0	96	0	0.0	-0	0	0.0
■ **PHIL COLLINS**	Collins, Philip Eugene "Fidgety Phil" b: 8/27/01, Chicago, Ill. d: 8/14/48, Chicago, Ill. BR/TR, 5'11", 175 lbs. Deb: 10/07/23																												
1923	Chi-N	1	0	1.000	1	1	0	0	0	5	8	14.4	0	1	1.8	2	3.6	3.60	115	.400	.409	0	0	103	183	0.5	-0	1	0.0
1929	Phi-N	9	7	.563	43	11	3	0	5	153	172	10.1	18	83	4.9	61	3.6	5.76	91	.284	.367	-18	-9	112	92	1.6	-1	-1	-0.8
1930	Phi-N	16	11	.593	47	25	17	1	3	239	287	10.8	22	86	3.2	87	3.3	4.78	114	.299	.352	5	17	109	105	**5.8**	3	-2	1.8
1931	Phi-N	12	16	.429	42	27	16	2	4	240	268	10.1	14	83	3.1	73	2.7	3.86	109	.283	.337	0	9	109	109	0.0	-4	0	0.7
1932	Phi-N	14	12	.538	43	21	6	0	3	184	231	11.3	21	65	3.2	66	3.2	5.28	82	.314	.368	-29	-20	111	107	1.0	3	-0	-1.5
1933	Phi-N	8	13	.381	42	13	5	1	**6**	151	178	10.6	9	57	3.4	40	2.4	4.11	98	.293	.355	-13	-1	121	111	-0.3	-3	-2	-0.4
1934	Phi-N	13	18	.419	45	32	15	0	1	254	277	9.8	30	87	3.1	72	2.6	4.18	108	.273	.327	-3	9	111	106	1.3	-5	-4	0.2
1935	Phi-N	0	2	.000	3	3	0	0	0	15	24	14.4	5	9	5.4	4	2.4	11.40	41	.348	.423	-12	-11	117	79	-0.9	-1	0	-0.9
	StL-N	7	6	.538	26	8	2	0	2	83	96	10.4	6	26	2.8	18	2.0	4.55	89	.290	.343	-5	-5	100	100	-0.9	-1	-1	-0.5
	Yr	7	8	.467	29	11	2	0	2	98	120	11.0	11	35	3.2	22	2.0	5.60	74	.300	.357	-17	-16	103	100	-1.8	-1	-1	-1.4
Total	8	80	85	.485	292	141	64	4	24	1324	1541	10.5	125	497	3.4	423	2.9	4.66	99	.291	.350	-75	-8	111	105	8.1	-8	-8	-1.4
■ **RAY COLLINS**	Collins, Raymond Williston b: 2/11/1887, Colchester, Vt. d: 1/9/70, Burlington, Vt. BL/TL, 6'1", 185 lbs. Deb: 7/19/09																												
1909	Bos-A	4	3	.571	12	8	4	2	0	74	70	8.5	2	18	2.2	31	3.8	2.80	96	.269	.317	-3	-1	108	104	0.0	-0	1	0.0
1910	Bos-A	13	11	.542	35	26	18	4	1	245	205	7.5	1	41	1.5	109	4.0	1.62	152	.229	.264	25	23	97	100	0.4	-0	-4	2.1
1911	Bos-A	11	12	.478	31	24	14	0	1	195	184	8.5	1	44	2.0	86	4.0	2.40	137	.256	.302	20	19	99	103	-0.7	0	-3	1.6
1912	Bos-A	13	8	.619	27	24	17	4	0	199	192	8.7	4	42	1.9	82	3.7	2.53	135	.256	.297	18	20	102	106	-1.1	0	-3	1.7
1913	Bos-A	19	8	.704	30	30	19	3	0	247	242	8.8	3	37	1.3	88	3.2	2.62	115	.263	.293	8	11	103	94	5.7	2	-4	0.7
1914	Bos-A	20	13	.606	39	30	16	6	0	272	252	8.3	3	56	1.9	72	2.4	2.51	105	.258	.298	7	3	96	100	0.6	-0	-6	-0.2
1915	Bos-A	4	7	.364	25	9	2	0	2	105	101	8.7	1	31	2.7	43	3.7	4.29	66	.261	.317	-16	-17	96	68	-2.5	4	-3	-1.5
Total	7	84	62	.575	199	151	90	19	4	1337	1246	8.4	15	269	1.8	511	3.4	2.51	115	.254	.294	60	57	99	98	2.4	6	-22	4.4
■ **JACKIE COLLUM**	Collum, Jack Dean b: 6/21/27, Victor, Ia. BL/TL, 5'7.5", 160 lbs. Deb: 9/21/51																												
1951	StL-N	2	1	.667	3	2	1	1	0	17	11	5.8	0	10	5.3	5	2.6	1.59	251	.204	.318	4	5	101	174	0.5	1	0	0.6
1952	StL-N	0	0	—	2	0	0	0	0	3	2	6.0	0	1	3.0	0	0.0	0.00	—	.200	.250	1	1	97	0	0.0	0	0	0.2
1953	StL-N	0	0	—	7	0	0	0	0	11	15	12.3	1	4	3.3	5	4.1	6.55	66	.326	.365	-3	-3	101	88	0.0	-0	1	-0.1
	Cin-N	7	11	.389	30	12	4	1	3	125	123	8.9	8	39	2.8	51	3.7	3.74	115	.263	.326	8	8	100	102	-1.1	3	1	1.1
	Yr	7	11	.389	37	12	4	1	3	136	138	9.1	9	43	2.8	56	3.7	3.97	108	.269	.330	5	5	100	102	-1.1	-0	2	1.0
1954	Cin-N	7	3	.700	36	2	1	0	0	79	86	9.8	8	32	3.6	28	3.2	3.76	113	.283	.352	3	4	104	125	2.2	2	3	0.9
1955	Cin-N	9	8	.529	32	17	5	0	1	134	128	8.6	17	37	2.5	49	3.3	3.63	116	.254	.306	6	9	104	102	0.8	2	-0	1.1
1956	StL-N	6	2	.750	38	1	0	0	7	60	63	9.4	6	27	4.1	17	2.6	4.20	89	.281	.354	-3	-3	99	112	2.1	1	1	-0.1
1957	Chi-N	1	1	.500	9	0	0	0	1	11	8	6.5	0	9	7.4	7	5.7	6.55	58	.211	.353	-3	-3	98	54	0.2	0	0	-0.2
	Bro-N	0	0	—	3	0	0	0	0	4	7	15.8	1	1	2.3	3	6.8	9.00	49	.368	.381	-2	-2	114	89	0.0	0	0	-0.1
	Yr	1	1	.500	12	0	0	0	1	15	15	9.0	1	10	6.0	10	6.0	7.20	55	.254	.347	-6	-5	102	89	0.2	0	0	-0.3
1958	LA-N	0	0	—	2	0	0	0	0	3	4	12.0	2	2	6.0	0	0.0	9.00	47	.308	.400	-2	-2	106	114	0.0	-0	0	-0.1
1962	Min-A	0	2	.000	8	3	0	0	0	15	29	17.4	1	11	6.6	5	3.0	11.40	36	.414	.482	-12	-12	104	84	-0.9	-1	0	-1.1
	Cle-A	0	0	—	1	0	0	0	0	1	4	36.0	0	0	0.0	1	9.0	18.00	22	.571	.571	-2	-2	99	91	0.0	0	0	0.0
	Yr	0	2	.000	9	3	0	0	0	16	33	18.6	1	11	6.2	6	3.4	11.81	35	.418	.489	-14	-14	103	91	-0.9	-1	0	-1.1
Total	9	32	28	.533	171	37	11	2	12	463	480	9.3	44	173	3.4	171	3.3	4.16	100	.273	.338	-5	-0	102	107	3.8	8	5	2.2
■ **DICK COLPAERT**	Colpaert, Richard Charles b: 1/44, Fraser, Mich. BR/TR, 5'10", 182 lbs. Deb: 7/21/70																												
1970	Pit-N	1	0	1.000	8	0	0	0	0	11	9	7.4	3	8	6.5	6	4.9	5.73	68	.237	.362	-2	-2	96	103	0.5	0	-0	-0.1
■ **LOYD COLSON**	Colson, Loyd Albert b: 11/4/47, Wellington, Tex. BR/TR, 6'1", 190 lbs. Deb: 9/25/70																												
1970	NY-A	0	0	—	1	0	0	0	0	2	3	13.5	0	0	0.0	3	13.5	4.50	76	.333	.333	-0	-0	91	91	0.0	0	0	0.0
■ **LARRY COLTON**	Colton, Lawrence Robert b: 6/8/42, Los Angeles, Cal. BL/TR, 6'3", 200 lbs. Deb: 5/06/68																												
1968	Phi-N	0	0	—	1	0	0	0	0	2	3	13.5	0	0	0.0	2	9.0	4.50	65	.333	.333	-0	-0	99	92	0.0	0	0	0.0
■ **GEOFF COMBE**	Combe, Geoffrey Wade b: 2/1/56, Melrose, Mass. BR/TR, 6'2", 185 lbs. Deb: 9/02/80																												
1980	Cin-N	0	0	—	4	0	0	0	0	7	9	11.6	0	4	5.1	10	12.9	10.29	36	.346	.419	-5	-5	101	58	0.0	0	0	-0.4
1981	Cin-N	1	0	1.000	14	0	0	0	0	18	27	13.5	3	10	5.0	9	4.5	7.50	47	.370	.435	-8	-8	101	107	0.5	0	-0	-0.8
Total	2	1	0	1.000	18	0	0	0	0	25	36	13.0	3	14	5.0	19	6.8	8.28	43	.364	.431	-13	-13	101	93	0.5	0	-0	-1.2
■ **JORGE COMELLAS**	Comellas, Jorge (Pous) "Pancho" b: 12/7/16, Havana, Cuba BR/TR, 6', 190 lbs. Deb: 4/19/45																												
1945	Chi-N	0	2	.000	7	1	0	0	0	12	11	8.3	1	6	4.5	6	4.5	4.50	80	.244	.333	-1	-1	95	85	-0.9	-0	1	0.0
■ **STEVE COMER**	Comer, Steven Michael b: 1/13/54, Minneapolis, Minn. BB/TR, 6'3", 195 lbs. Deb: 4/15/78																												
1978	Tex-A	11	5	.688	30	11	3	2	1	117	107	8.2	5	37	2.8	65	5.0	2.31	157	.249	.303	19	17	96	130	2.8	0	1	1.9
1979	Tex-A	17	12	.586	36	36	6	1	0	242	230	8.6	24	84	3.1	86	3.2	3.68	114	.252	.315	15	14	99	101	2.6	0	-0	1.3
1980	Tex-A	2	4	.333	12	11	0	0	0	42	65	13.9	5	22	4.7	9	1.9	7.93	51	.367	.434	-18	-18	100	97	-0.8	0	0	-1.6
1981	Tex-A	8	2	.800	36	1	0	0	6	77	70	8.2	1	31	3.6	22	2.6	2.57	128	.241	.309	9	6	90	112	2.9	0	1	0.8
1982	Tex-A	1	6	.143	37	3	1	0	6	97	133	12.3	11	36	3.3	23	2.1	5.10	75	.342	.388	-11	-14	94	125	-2.2	0	-0	-1.3
1983	Phi-N	1	0	1.000	3	1	0	0	0	9	11	11.0	0	3	3.0	1	1.0	5.00	73	.314	.368	-1	-1	100	89	0.5	-0	-0	-0.1
1984	Cle-A	4	8	.333	22	20	1	0	0	117	146	11.2	11	39	3.0	39	3.0	5.69	74	.309	.357	-22	-19	106	91	-1.7	0	0	-1.7
Total	7	44	37	.543	176	83	11	3	13	701	762	9.8	57	252	3.2	245	3.1	4.13	95	.281	.339	-9	-15	98	108	4.1	-0	2	-0.7
■ **CHARLIE COMISKEY**	Comiskey, Charles Albert "Commy" or "The Old Roman" b: 8/15/1859, Chicago, Ill. d: 10/26/31, Eagle River, Wis. BR/TR, 6', 180 lbs. Deb: 5/02/1882 MH																												
1882	StL-a	0	1	.000	2	1	1	0	0	8	12	13.5	0	3	3.4	2	2.3	0.00	—	.352	.404	2	2	104	0	-0.4	0	0	0.2
1884	StL-a	0	0	—	1	0	0	0	0	4	1	2.3	0	0	0.0	4	9.0	2.25	156	.084	.084	0	1	109	50	0.0	0	0	0.1

YEAR	TM/L	W	L	PCT	G	GS	CG	SHO	SV	IP	H	H/G	HR	BB	BB/G	SO	SO/G	ERA	/A	OAVG	OOBP	PR	/A	PF	CPI	WAT	PB	PD	TPI
1889	StL-a	0	0	—	1	0	0	0	0	⅓	0	0.0	0	0	0.0	0	0.0	0.00	—	—	—	0	0	109	0	0.0	0	0	0.0
Total	3	0	1	.000	4	1	1	0	0	12	13	9.8	0	3	2.3	6	4.5	0.75	404	.283	.327	3	3	106	17	-0.4	0	0	0.3
■ JACK COMPTON	Compton, Harry Leroy b: 3/9/1882, Lancaster, Ohio d: 7/4/74, Lancaster, Ohio BR/TR, 5'9", 157 lbs. Deb: 9/07/11																												
1911	Cin-N	0	1	.000	8	3	0	0	1	25	19	6.8	0	15	5.4	6	2.2	3.96	79	.204	.321	-2	-2	92	57	-0.4	0	-0	-0.1
■ CLINT COMPTON	Compton, Robert Clinton b: 11/1/50, Montgomery, Ala. BL/TL, 5'11", 185 lbs. Deb: 10/03/72																												
1972	Chi-N	0	0	—	1	0	0	0	0	2	2	9.0	0	2	9.0	0	0.0	9.00	43	.286	.444	-1	-1	112	62	0.0	0	0	0.0
■ KEITH COMSTOCK	Comstock, Keith Martin b: 12/23/55, San Francisco, Cal. BL/TL, 6', 174 lbs. Deb: 4/03/84																												
1984	Min-A	0	0	—	4	0	0	0	0	6	6	9.0	2	4	6.0	2	3.0	9.00	47	.261	.357	-3	-3	106	73	0.0	0	0	-0.2
1987	SF-N	2	0	1.000	15	0	0	0	1	21	19	8.1	1	10	4.3	21	9.0	3.00	129	.253	.333	3	2	95	126	1.0	-0	0	0.2
	SD-N	0	1	.000	26	0	0	0	0	36	33	8.3	4	21	5.3	38	9.5	5.50	73	.252	.344	-6	-6	98	82	-0.4	-0	-1	-0.6
	Yr	2	1	.667	41	0	0	0	1	57	52	8.2	5	31	4.9	59	9.3	4.58	86	.251	.340	-3	-4	97	82	0.6	-0	-1	-0.4
1988	SD-N	0	0	—	7	0	0	0	0	8	8	9.0	1	3	3.4	9	10.1	6.75	50	.250	.314	-3	-3	97	57	0.0	0	0	-0.2
Total	3	2	1	.667	52	0	0	0	1	71	66	8.4	8	38	4.8	70	8.9	5.20	75	.253	.339	-9	-10	97	91	0.6	-0	-0	-0.8
■ RALPH COMSTOCK	Comstock, Ralph Remick "Commy" b: 11/24/1890, Sylvania, Ohio d: 9/13/66, Toledo, Ohio BR/TR, 5'10", 168 lbs. Deb: 8/26/13																												
1913	Det-A	2	5	.286	10	7	1	0	1	60	90	13.5	0	16	2.4	37	5.6	5.40	55	.344	.384	-16	-16	101	94	-1.1	1	0	-1.5
1915	Bos-A	1	0	1.000	3	0	0	0	0	9	10	10.0	2	2	2.0	1	1.0	2.00	141	.294	.333	1	1	96	258	0.5	0	0	0.1
	Pit-F	3	3	.500	12	7	3	0	2	53	44	7.5	3	7	1.2	18	3.1	3.23	96	.237	.268	-1	-1	102	74	-0.2	-2	0	-0.2
1918	Pit-N	5	6	.455	15	8	6	0	1	81	78	8.7	0	14	1.6	44	4.9	3.00	96	.259	.286	-2	-1	105	83	-0.7	-0	0	0.0
Total	3	11	14	.440	40	22	10	0	4	203	222	9.8	5	39	1.7	100	4.4	3.72	80	.284	.316	-19	-17	102	91	-1.5	-1	0	-1.6
■ DAVE CONCEPCION	Concepcion, David Ismael (Benitez) b: 6/17/48, Aragua, Venez. BR/TR, 6'2", 155 lbs. Deb: 4/06/70																												
1988	Cin-N	0	0	—	1	0	0	0	0	1	2	18.0	0	0	0.0	1	9.0	0.00	—	.333	.333	0	0	105	0	0.0	0	0	0.0
■ DAVID CONE	Cone, David Bryan b: 1/2/63, Kansas City, Mo. BL/TR, 6'1", 180 lbs. Deb: 6/08/86																												
1986	KC-A	0	0	—	11	0	0	0	0	23	29	11.3	2	13	5.1	21	8.2	5.48	77	.309	.398	-3	-3	100	106	0.0	0	-0	-0.2
1987	NY-N	5	6	.455	21	13	1	0	1	99	87	7.9	11	44	4.0	68	6.2	3.73	106	.239	.324	4	3	97	104	-1.1	-1	-0	0.1
1988	NY-N	20	3	**.870**	35	28	8	4	0	231	178	6.9	10	80	3.1	213	8.3	2.22	137	.213	.280	32	21	88	108	**7.9**	2	-1	2.2
Total	3	25	9	.735	67	41	9	4	1	353	294	7.5	23	137	3.5	302	7.7	2.86	118	.227	.301	32	20	91	107	6.8	1	-2	2.1
■ BOB CONE	Cone, Robert Earl b: 2/27/1894, Galveston, Tex. d: 5/24/55, Galveston, Tex. 6'2", 172 lbs. Deb: 7/25/15																												
1915	Phi-A	0	0	—	1	1	0	0	0	1	5	45.0	0	0	0.0	0	0.0	27.00	11	.714	.714	-3	-3	103	87	0.0	0	0	-0.2
■ DICK CONGER	Conger, Richard b: 4/3/21, Los Angeles, Cal. d: 2/16/70, Los Angeles, Cal. BR/TR, 6', 185 lbs. Deb: 4/22/40																												
1940	Det-A	1	0	1.000	2	0	0	0	0	3	2	6.0	0	3	9.0	1	3.0	3.00	159	.200	.357	0	1	109	128	0.5	0	0	0.0
1941	Pit-N	0	0	—	2	1	0	0	0	4	3	6.8	0	3	6.8	2	4.5	0.00	—	.214	.353	2	2	102	0	0.0	0	-0	0.2
1942	Pit-N	0	0	—	2	1	0	0	0	8	9	10.1	0	5	5.6	3	3.4	2.25	150	.290	.368	1	1	102	209	0.0	-0	1	0.1
1943	Phi-N	2	7	.222	13	10	2	0	0	55	72	11.8	3	24	3.9	18	2.9	6.05	53	.327	.396	-16	-17	96	96	-2.1	-1	-0	-1.7
Total	4	3	7	.300	19	12	2	0	0	70	86	11.1	3	35	4.5	24	3.1	5.14	65	.313	.389	-13	-14	97	105	-1.6	-1	0	-1.4
■ ALLEN CONKWRIGHT	Conkwright, Allen Howard "Red" b: 12/4/1896, Sedalia, Mo. BR/TR, 5'10", 170 lbs. Deb: 9/16/20																												
1920	Det-A	2	1	.667	5	2	0	0	1	19	29	13.7	0	16	7.6	4	1.9	7.11	57	.397	.506	-7	-6	106	114	0.7	1	0	-0.4
■ GENE CONLEY	Conley, Donald Eugene b: 11/10/30, Muskogee, Okla. BR/TR, 6'8", 225 lbs. Deb: 4/17/52																												
1952	Bos-N	0	3	.000	4	3	0	0	0	13	23	15.9	4	9	6.2	6	4.2	7.62	47	.397	.472	-6	-6	97	145	-1.4	1	0	-0.4
1954	Mil-N	14	9	.609	28	27	12	2	0	194	171	7.9	17	79	3.7	113	5.2	2.97	125	.240	.316	24	16	91	115	1.0	-2	-0	1.3
1955	Mil-N	11	7	.611	22	21	10	0	0	158	152	8.7	23	52	3.0	107	6.1	4.16	89	.254	.306	-2	-8	92	95	1.3	-0	-0	-0.8
1956	Mil-N	8	9	.471	31	19	5	1	3	158	169	9.6	13	52	3.0	68	3.9	3.13	116	.276	.327	11	9	96	**127**	-1.9	-1	-1	0.7
1957	Mil-N	9	9	.500	35	18	6	1	1	148	133	8.1	9	64	3.9	61	3.7	3.16	108	.244	.316	12	4	88	107	-1.8	1	0	0.5
1958	Mil-N	0	6	.000	26	7	0	0	2	72	89	11.1	8	17	2.1	53	6.6	4.88	70	.309	.347	-7	-12	87	103	-2.9	1	0	-1.0
1959	Phi-N	12	7	.632	25	22	12	3	1	180	159	7.9	13	42	2.1	102	5.1	3.00	134	.235	.278	19	20	102	88	3.8	3	-0	2.4
1960	Phi-N	8	14	.364	29	25	9	2	0	183	192	9.4	10	42	2.1	117	5.8	3.69	112	.272	.306	2	9	110	96	-0.5	-2	-2	0.7
1961	Bos-A	11	14	.440	33	30	6	2	1	200	229	10.3	33	65	2.9	113	5.1	4.91	84	.287	.339	-20	-17	103	103	-0.8	4	-1	-1.3
1962	Bos-A	15	14	.517	34	33	9	2	1	242	238	8.9	28	68	2.5	134	5.0	3.94	104	.256	.306	1	4	103	95	1.4	4	-1	0.7
1963	Bos-A	3	4	.429	9	9	0	0	0	41	51	11.2	4	21	4.6	14	3.1	6.59	59	.305	.382	-13	-12	107	85	-0.2	0	-1	-1.2
Total	11	91	96	.487	276	214	69	13	9	1589	1606	9.1	162	511	2.9	888	5.0	3.82	101	.264	.317	20	8	98	103	-2.0	8	-6	1.6
■ ED CONLEY	Conley, Edward J. b: 7/10/1864, Sandwich, Mass. d: 10/16/1894, Cumberland, R.I. 5'11.5", Deb: 7/20/1884																												
1884	Pro-N	4	4	.500	8	8	8	1	0	71	63	8.0	4	22	2.8	33	4.2	2.15	132	.246	.306	6	5	96	128	-1.3	-2	0	0.3
■ SNIPE CONLEY	Conley, James Patrick b: 4/25/1894, Cressona, Pa. d: 1/7/78, De Soto, Tex. BR/TR, 5'11.5", 179 lbs. Deb: 5/20/14																												
1914	Bal-F	4	6	.400	35	11	4	2	1	125	112	8.1	2	47	3.4	86	6.2	2.52	126	.259	.340	10	9	99	133	-1.3	-2	-0	0.7
1915	Bal-F	1	4	.200	25	6	4	0	0	86	97	10.2	5	32	3.3	40	4.2	4.29	79	.314	.386	-12	-9	111	118	-0.8	1	1	-0.6
1918	Cin-N	2	0	1.000	5	0	0	0	1	14	17	10.9	2	5	3.2	2	1.3	5.14	52	.321	.367	-4	-4	96	109	1.0	0	0	-0.3
Total	3	7	10	.412	65	17	8	2	2	225	226	9.0	9	84	3.4	128	5.1	3.36	96	.284	.359	-6	-4	103	126	-1.1	-1	1	-0.2
■ BOB CONLEY	Conley, Robert Burns b: 2/1/34, Knott County, Va. BR/TR, 6'1", 188 lbs. Deb: 9/11/58																												
1958	Phi-N	0	0	—	2	2	0	0	0	8	9	10.1	0	1	1.1	0	0.0	7.88	50	.273	.278	-3	-3	100	33	0.0	-0	-0	-0.2
■ BERT CONN	Conn, Albert Thomas b: 9/22/1879, Philadelphia, Pa. d: 11/2/44, Philadelphia, Pa. TR , Deb: 9/16/1898																												
1898	Phi-N	0	1	.000	1	1	0	0	0	7	13	16.7	1	2	2.6	3	3.9	6.43	53	.421	.457	-2	-2	94	128	-0.4	1	0	0.0
1900	Phi-N	0	2	.000	4	1	1	0	0	17	29	15.4	0	16	8.5	2	1.1	8.47	43	.402	.511	-9	-9	98	97	-0.9	1	0	-0.6
Total	2	0	3	.000	5	2	1	0	0	24	42	15.8	1	18	6.8	5	1.9	7.88	45	.408	.496	-11	-12	97	106	-1.3	2	0	-0.6
■ SARGE CONNALLY	Connally, George Walter b: 8/31/1898, Mcgregor, Tex. d: 1/27/78, Temple, Tex. BR/TR, 5'11", 170 lbs. Deb: 9/10/21																												
1921	Chi-A	0	1	.000	5	2	0	0	0	22	29	11.9	0	10	4.1	6	2.5	6.55	67	.330	.400	-6	-5	102	82	-0.4	2	0	-0.2
1923	Chi-A	0	0	—	3	0	0	0	0	9	7	7.0	0	12	12.0	3	3.0	6.00	66	.241	.444	-2	-2	99	97	0.0	0	0	-0.1
1924	Chi-A	7	13	.350	44	13	6	0	6	160	177	10.0	4	68	3.8	55	3.1	4.05	102	.290	.359	3	2	98	108	-2.0	-1	3	0.3
1925	Chi-A	6	7	.462	40	2	0	0	8	105	122	10.5	2	58	5.0	45	3.9	4.63	90	.310	.388	-3	-5	95	112	-0.6	1	3	-0.1
1926	Chi-A	6	5	.545	31	8	5	0	3	108	128	10.7	0	35	2.9	47	3.9	3.17	115	.300	.349	10	6	90	127	0.2	-1	2	0.6
1927	Chi-A	10	15	.400	43	18	11	1	5	198	217	9.9	8	83	3.8	58	2.6	4.09	104	.292	.358	1	4	103	111	-1.7	3	1	0.7
1928	Chi-A	2	5	.286	28	5	1	0	2	74	89	10.8	1	29	3.5	28	3.4	4.86	83	.313	.369	-7	-7	100	102	-1.3	-1	-0	-0.7
1929	Chi-A	0	0	—	11	0	0	0	1	11	13	10.6	0	8	6.5	3	2.5	4.91	84	.317	.404	-1	-1	98	117	0.0	0	-0	0.0
1931	Cle-A	5	5	.500	17	9	5	0	1	86	87	9.1	7	50	5.2	37	3.9	4.19	111	.256	.353	2	4	106	111	0.0	0	-0	0.4
1932	Cle-A	8	6	.571	35	7	4	1	3	112	119	9.6	6	42	3.4	32	2.6	4.34	110	.266	.329	2	6	107	93	0.0	-0	0	0.5
1933	Cle-A	5	3	.625	41	3	1	0	1	103	112	9.8	4	49	4.3	30	2.6	4.89	92	.271	.350	-7	-5	105	88	1.1	1	-2	-0.5
1934	Cle-A	0	0	—	5	0	0	0	1	5	4	7.2	0	5	9.0	1	1.8	5.40	83	.222	.391	-1	-1	100	78	0.0	-0	0	0.0
Total	12	49	60	.450	303	67	33	2	31	993	1104	10.0	32	449	4.1	345	3.1	4.31	99	.288	.359	-7	-5	100	106	-4.7	4	5	0.9
■ BILL CONNELLY	Connelly, William Wirt "Wild Bill" b: 6/29/25, Alberta, Va. d: 11/27/80, Richmond, Va. BL/TR, 6', 175 lbs. Deb: 8/22/45																												
1945	Phi-A	1	1	.500	2	1	0	0	0	8	7	7.9	0	8	9.0	0	0.0	4.50	72	.259	.429	-1	-1	96	111	0.2	0	-0	0.0
1950	Chi-A	0	0	—	2	0	0	0	0	2	5	22.5	1	1	4.5	0	0.0	13.50	34	.455	.462	-2	-2	99	107	0.0	0	0	-0.1
	Det-A	0	0	—	2	0	0	0	0	4	4	9.0	1	2	4.5	1	2.3	6.75	64	.250	.333	-1	-1	95	75	0.0	0	0	0.0
	Yr	0	0	—	4	0	0	0	0	6	9	13.5	2	3	4.5	1	1.5	9.00	49	.333	.387	-3	-3	96	75	0.0	0	0	-0.1
1952	NY-N	5	0	1.000	11	4	0	0	0	32	22	6.2	4	25	7.0	22	6.2	4.50	84	.208	.351	-3	-3	101	95	2.5	3	0	0.0
1953	NY-N	0	1	.000	8	2	0	0	0	20	33	14.8	4	17	7.6	11	4.9	11.25	37	.371	.472	-15	-16	98	84	-0.4	-1	-0	-1.4
Total	4	6	2	.750	25	7	0	0	0	66	71	9.7	10	53	7.2	34	4.6	6.95	56	.285	.405	-22	-22	99	93	2.3	3	-0	-1.5
■ ED CONNOLLY	Connolly, Edward Joseph Jr. b: 12/3/39, Brooklyn, N.Y. BL/TL, 6'1", 190 lbs. Deb: 4/19/64																												
1964	Bos-A	4	11	.267	27	15	1	1	0	81	80	8.9	3	64	7.1	73	8.1	4.89	77	.261	.389	-11	-10	103	98	-3.1	0	-1	-1.1

YEAR	TM/L	W	L	PCT	G	GS	CG	SHO	SV	IP	H	H/G	HR	BB	BB/G	SO	SO/G	ERA	/A	OAVG	OOBP	PR	/A	PF	CPI	WAT	PB	PD	TPI
1967	Cle-A	2	1	.667	15	4	0	0	0	49	63	11.6	6	34	6.2	45	8.3	7.53	43	.315	.407	-23	-23	101	88	0.6	0	-0	-2.2
Total	2	6	12	.333	42	19	1	1	0	130	143	9.9	9	98	6.8	118	8.2	5.88	61	.282	.396	-35	-33	103	94	-2.5	0	-1	-3.3
■ JOHN CONNOR	Connor, John b: 1853, Scotland d: 10/13/32, Boston, Mass. Deb: 7/26/1884																												
1884	Bos-N	1	4	.200	7	7	7	0	0	60	70	10.5	1	18	2.7	29	4.3	3.15	88	.301	.351	-1	-2	93	121	-1.7	-2	0	-0.3
1885	Buf-N	0	1	.000	1	1	1	0	0	9	14	14.0	0	2	2.0	0	0.0	4.00	74	.367	.398	-1	-1	105	141	-0.4	-0	0	0.0
	Lou-a	1	3	.250	4	4	4	0	0	35	43	11.1	0	12	3.1	19	4.9	4.89	69	.315	.370	-6	-6	103	94	-0.9	-1	0	-0.5
Total	2	2	8	.200	12	12	12	0	0	104	127	11.0	1	32	2.8	48	4.2	3.81	78	.312	.362	-9	-10	98	114	-3.0	-4	0	-0.8
■ JOE CONNORS	Connors, Joseph P. b: Paterson, N.J. Deb: 5/03/1884																												
1884	Alt-U	0	1	.000	1	1	1	0	0	9	18	18.0	0	5	5.0	0	0.0	7.00	47	.420	.480	-4	-4	109	127	-0.4	-0	0	-0.2
	KC-U	0	1	.000	2	1	1	0	0	12	24	18.0	1	0	0.0	1	0.8	4.50	61	.420	.420	-2	-2	92	177	-0.4	-1	0	-0.2
	Yr	0	2	.000	3	2	2	0	0	21	42	18.0	1	5	2.1	1	0.4	5.57	53	.420	.447	-6	-6	99	177	-0.8	-0	0	-0.4
■ BILL CONNORS	Connors, William Joseph b: 11/2/41, Schenectady, N.Y. BR/TR, 6'1", 180 lbs. Deb: 5/03/66 C																												
1966	Chi-N	0	1	.000	11	0	0	0	0	16	20	11.3	4	7	3.9	3	1.7	7.31	51	.308	.360	-7	-6	103	89	-0.4	0	0	-0.5
1967	NY-N	0	0	—	6	1	0	0	0	13	8	5.5	3	5	3.5	13	9.0	6.23	55	.170	.259	-4	-4	102	47	0.0	-0	-0	-0.4
1968	NY-N	0	1	.000	9	0	0	0	0	14	21	13.5	0	7	4.5	8	5.1	9.00	34	.339	.403	-9	-9	103	65	-0.4	1	0	-0.8
Total	3	0	2	.000	26	1	0	0	0	43	49	10.3	7	19	4.0	24	5.0	7.53	45	.282	.348	-20	-20	102	69	-0.8	1	-0	-1.7
■ TED CONOVAR	Conovar, Theodore "Huck" b: 3/10/1868, Lexington, Ky. d: 7/27/10, Paris, Ky. 5'10.5", 165 lbs. Deb: 5/26/1889																												
1889	Cin-a	0	0	—	1	0	0	0	1	2	4	18.0	0	2	9.0	1	4.5	13.50	29	.432	.532	-2	-2	103	74	0.0	0	0	-0.1
■ TIM CONROY	Conroy, Timothy James b: 4/3/60, Mc Keesport, Pa. BL/TL, 6', 178 lbs. Deb: 6/23/78																												
1978	Oak-A	0	0	—	2	2	0	0	0	5	3	5.4	0	9	16.2	0	0.0	7.20	54	.188	.464	-2	-2	103	86	0.0	0	-0	-0.1
1982	Oak-A	2	2	.500	5	5	1	0	0	25	20	7.2	1	18	6.5	17	6.1	3.60	109	.222	.345	1	1	96	99	0.3	0	-0	0.1
1983	Oak-A	7	10	.412	39	18	3	1	0	162	141	7.8	17	98	5.4	112	6.2	3.94	100	.232	.337	2	-0	96	100	-0.8	0	-2	-0.2
1984	Oak-A	1	6	.143	38	14	0	0	0	93	82	7.9	11	63	6.1	69	6.7	5.32	69	.236	.353	-14	-17	92	81	-2.4	0	-1	-1.7
1985	Oak-A	0	1	.000	16	2	0	0	0	25	22	7.9	3	15	5.4	8	2.9	4.32	89	.237	.345	-0	-1	93	100	-0.4	0	-0	-0.1
1986	StL-N	5	11	.313	25	21	1	0	0	115	122	9.5	15	56	4.4	79	6.2	5.24	73	.275	.353	-19	-18	103	94	-3.0	1	-1	-1.7
1987	StL-N	3	2	.600	10	9	0	0	0	41	48	10.5	0	25	5.5	22	4.8	5.49	72	.306	.394	-6	-7	97	95	0.1	-2	-0	-0.7
Total	7	18	32	.360	135	71	5	1	0	466	438	8.5	47	284	5.5	307	5.9	4.71	82	.249	.352	-38	-44	97	94	-6.2	-1	-6	-4.4
■ JIM CONSTABLE	Constable, Jimmy Lee "Sheriff" b: 6/14/33, Jonesboro, Tenn. BB/TL, 6'1", 185 lbs. Deb: 6/24/56																												
1956	NY-N	0	0	—	3	0	0	0	0	4	9	20.3	0	7	15.8	1	2.3	15.75	24	.429	.567	-5	-5	99	85	0.0	0	0	-0.4
1957	NY-N	1	1	.500	16	0	0	0	0	28	27	8.7	2	7	2.3	13	4.2	2.89	139	.262	.330	3	3	103	132	0.1	-0	-0	0.3
1958	SF-N	1	0	1.000	9	0	0	0	1	8	10	11.3	1	3	3.4	4	4.5	5.63	70	.323	.371	-1	-2	100	102	0.5	1	1	0.0
	Cle-A	0	1	.000	6	2	0	0	0	9	17	17.0	1	4	4.0	3	3.0	12.00	29	.415	.468	-8	-8	93	77	-0.4	1	-0	-0.7
	Was-A	0	1	.000	15	2	0	0	0	28	29	9.3	3	15	4.8	25	8.0	4.82	78	.271	.360	-3	-3	100	100	-0.4	0	0	-0.2
	Yr	0	2	.000	21	4	0	0	0	37	46	11.2	4	19	4.6	28	6.8	6.57	57	.309	.384	-12	-12	99	100	-0.8	1	-0	-0.9
1962	Mil-N	1	1	.500	3	2	1	1	1	18	14	7.0	1	4	2.0	12	6.0	2.00	193	.222	.261	4	4	98	116	0.0	-0	-0	0.3
1963	SF-N	0	0	—	4	0	0	0	0	2	3	13.5	0	1	4.5	1	4.5	4.50	69	.333	.364	-0	-0	94	124	0.0	0	0	0.0
Total	5	3	4	.429	56	6	1	1	2	97	109	10.1	8	41	3.8	59	5.5	4.92	78	.291	.363	-12	-12	100	110	-0.2	2	-0	-0.7
■ SANDY CONSUEGRA	Consuegra, Sandalio Simeon (Castello) b: 9/3/20, Potrerillos, Cuba BR/TR, 5'10", 165 lbs. Deb: 6/10/50																												
1950	Was-A	7	8	.467	21	18	8	2	2	125	132	9.5	6	57	4.1	38	2.7	4.39	105	.270	.344	3	3	101	93	0.5	-1	0	0.2
1951	Was-A	7	8	.467	40	12	5	0	3	146	140	8.6	10	63	3.9	31	1.9	4.01	100	.251	.324	2	-0	97	92	0.9	-0	1	0.0
1952	Was-A	6	0	1.000	30	2	0	0	5	74	80	9.7	2	27	3.3	19	2.3	3.04	121	.276	.334	5	5	100	123	3.0	-0	-1	0.5
1953	Was-A	0	0	—	4	0	0	0	0	5	9	16.2	0	4	7.2	0	0.0	10.80	34	.391	.481	-4	-4	93	78	0.0	0	0	-0.3
	Chi-A	7	5	.583	29	13	5	1	3	124	122	8.9	9	28	2.0	30	2.2	2.54	163	.258	.299	20	22	104	130	0.1	-4	3	2.2
	Yr	7	5	.583	33	13	5	1	3	129	131	9.1	9	32	2.2	30	2.1	2.86	144	.264	.308	16	18	103	130	0.1	0	3	1.9
1954	Chi-A	16	3	**.842**	39	17	3	2	3	154	142	8.3	9	35	2.0	31	1.8	2.69	138	.248	.285	18	18	100	105	**5.9**	1	1	2.1
1955	Chi-A	6	5	.545	44	7	3	0	7	126	120	8.6	4	18	1.3	35	2.5	2.64	147	.256	.279	**18**	17	98	101	-0.4	-2	-0	1.5
1956	Chi-A	1	2	.333	28	1	0	0	3	38	45	10.7	0	11	2.6	7	1.7	5.21	81	.296	.339	-4	-4	102	75	-0.5	-1	0	-0.4
	Bal-A	1	1	.500	4	1	0	0	0	9	10	10.0	2	2	2.0	1	1.0	4.00	100	.294	.324	0	0	97	134	0.1	0	-0	0.0
	Yr	2	3	.400	32	2	0	0	3	47	55	10.5	2	13	2.5	8	1.5	4.98	84	.293	.332	-4	-4	101	134	-0.4	-1	-0	-0.4
1957	Bal-A	0	0	—	5	0	0	0	0	5	4	7.2	0	0	0.0	0	0.0	1.80	195	.211	.200	1	1	93	39	0.0	0	0	0.1
	NY-N	0	0	—	4	0	0	0	0	4	7	15.8	1	1	2.3	1	2.3	2.25	178	.389	.400	1	1	103	381	0.0	0	0	0.1
Total	8	51	32	.614	248	71	24	5	26	810	811	9.0	43	246	2.7	193	2.1	3.37	119	.262	.313	60	59	100	105	9.6	-6	4	6.0
■ NARDI CONTRERAS	Contreras, Arnaldo Juan b: 9/19/51, Tampa, Fla. BB/TR, 6'2", 193 lbs. Deb: 5/23/80																												
1980	Chi-A	0	0	—	8	0	0	0	0	14	18	11.6	1	7	4.5	8	5.1	5.79	68	.333	.415	-3	-3	98	111	0.0	0	0	-0.1
■ JIM CONWAY	Conway, James P. b: Clifton, Pa. TR , Deb: 5/05/1884																												
1884	Bro-a	3	9	.250	13	13	10	0	0	105	132	11.3	4	15	1.3	25	2.1	4.46	72	.316	.340	-14	-14	100	105	-2.2	-3	0	-1.4
1885	Phi-a	0	1	.000	2	2	1	0	0	12	19	14.3	0	2	1.5	0	0.0	7.50	44	.372	.395	-6	-6	102	78	-0.4	-1	0	-0.4
1889	KC-a	19	19	.500	41	37	33	0	0	335	334	9.0	12	90	2.4	115	3.1	3.25	129	.275	.325	22	35	109	98	4.1	-6	3	2.9
Total	3	22	29	.431	56	52	44	0	0	452	485	9.7	16	107	2.1	140	2.8	3.64	108	.288	.330	2	14	106	99	1.5	-11	3	1.1
■ JERRY CONWAY	Conway, Jerome Patrick b: 6/7/01, Holyoke, Mass. d: 4/16/80, Holyoke, Mass. BL/TL, 6'2", 190 lbs. Deb: 8/31/20																												
1920	Was-A	0	0	—	1	0	0	0	0	2	1	4.5	0	1	4.5	0	0.0	0.00	—	.167	.286	1	1	96	0	0.0	0	0	0.1
■ PETE CONWAY	Conway, Peter J. b: 10/30/1866, Burmont, Pa. d: 1/13/03, Clifton Heights, N.J. BR/TR, 5'10.5", Deb: 1885																												
1885	Buf-N	10	17	.370	27	27	26	0	0	210	256	11.0	10	44	1.9	94	4.0	4.67	63	.312	.347	-43	-40	105	92	0.8	-4	0	-3.7
1886	KC-N	5	15	.250	23	20	19	0	0	180	236	11.8	6	61	3.1	81	4.1	5.75	65	.330	.383	-49	-40	114	88	0.0	1	0	-3.2
	Det-N	6	5	.545	11	11	11	0	0	91	93	9.2	1	25	2.5	35	3.5	3.36	101	.278	.328	-1	0	103	96	-1.3	0	0	0.1
	Yr	11	20	.355	34	31	30	0	0	271	329	10.9	7	86	2.9	116	3.9	4.95	74	.313	.365	-50	-39	110	96	-1.3	1	0	-3.1
1887	Det-N	8	9	.471	17	17	16	0	0	146	132	**8.1**	3	47	2.9	40	2.5	2.90	136	**.256**	.318	19	17	97	100	-2.4	0	0	1.5
1888	Det-N	30	14	.682	45	45	43	4	0	391	315	7.3	11	57	1.3	176	4.1	2.26	121	.233	.264	25	21	97	82	**9.6**	14	2	3.8
1889	Pit-N	2	1	.667	3	3	2	0	0	22	26	10.6	1	16	6.5	2	0.8	4.91	74	.310	.421	-2	-3	90	112	0.6	0	0	-0.1
Total	5	61	61	.500	126	123	117	4	0	1040	1058	9.2	32	250	2.2	428	3.7	3.59	89	.277	.321	-51	-44	102	89	7.3	12	2	-1.6
■ DICK CONWAY	Conway, Richard Butler b: 4/25/1865, Lowell, Mass. d: 9/9/26, Lowell, Mass. BL/TR, 5'7.5", 140 lbs. Deb: 7/22/1886																												
1886	Bal-a	2	7	.222	9	9	8	0	0	77	106	12.4	6	43	5.0	64	7.5	6.90	47	.338	.418	-29	-31	94	95	-1.7	0	0	-2.3
1887	Bos-N	9	15	.375	26	26	25	0	0	222	249	10.1	10	86	3.5	45	1.8	4.66	84	.299	.364	-15	-18	97	94	-3.5	2	0	-1.1
1888	Bos-N	4	2	.667	6	6	6	0	0	53	49	8.3	2	8	1.4	12	2.0	2.38	125	.259	.289	3	4	105	106	0.9	-1	0	0.3
Total	3	15	24	.385	41	41	39	0	0	352	404	10.3	18	137	3.5	121	3.1	4.81	76	.302	.367	-42	-45	98	96	-4.3	2	0	-3.1
■ JOE CONZELMAN	Conzelman, Joseph Harrison b: 7/14/1885, Bristol, Conn. d: 4/17/79, Mountain Brook, Ala. BR/TR, 6', 170 lbs. Deb: 5/01/13																												
1913	Pit-N	0	1	.000	3	2	1	0	0	15	13	7.8	0	5	3.0	9	5.4	1.20	252	.245	.317	3	3	94	231	-0.4	-1	0	0.3
1914	Pit-N	5	6	.455	33	9	4	1	2	101	88	7.8	2	40	3.6	39	3.5	2.94	88	.254	.320	-2	-4	93	106	0.1	-2	1	-0.4
1915	Pit-N	1	1	.500	18	1	0	0	0	47	41	7.9	0	20	3.8	22	4.2	3.45	78	.248	.330	-4	-4	98	90	0.0	-1	1	-0.4
Total	3	6	8	.429	54	12	5	1	2	163	142	7.8	2	65	3.6	70	3.9	2.93	91	.252	.323	-2	-5	94	113	-0.3	-3	2	-0.5
■ DENNIS COOK	Cook, Dennis Bryan b: 10/4/62, La Marque, Tex. BL/TL, 6'3", 185 lbs. Deb: 9/12/88																												
1988	SF-N	2	1	.667	4	4	1	1	0	22	9	3.7	1	11	4.5	13	5.3	2.86	113	.125	.233	1	1	93	34	0.5	1	-1	0.1
■ EARL COOK	Cook, Earl Davis b: 12/10/08, Stouffville, Ont., BR/TR, 6', 195 lbs. Deb: 9/12/41																												
1941	Det-A	0	0	—	1	0	0	0	0	2	4	18.0	0	0	0.0	1	4.5	4.50	99	.400	.400	-0	-0	107	153	0.0	0	0	0.0
■ GLEN COOK	Cook, Glen Patrick b: 9/8/59, Buffalo, N.Y. BR/TR, 5'11", 180 lbs. Deb: 6/23/85																												
1985	Tex-A	2	3	.400	9	7	0	0	0	40	53	11.9	12	18	4.0	19	4.3	9.45	48	.327	.396	-24	-22	110	83	0.1	0	-1	-1.9

YEAR	TM/L	W	L	PCT	G	GS	CG	SHO	SV	IP	H	H/G	HR	BB	BB/G	SO	SO/G	ERA	/A	OAVG	OOBP	PR	/A	PF	CPI	WAT	PB	PD	TPI
■ **MIKE COOK**	Cook, Michael Horace b: 8/14/63, Charleston, S.C. BR/TR, 6'3", 200 lbs. Deb: 7/01/86																												
1986	Cal-A	0	2	.000	5	1	0	0	0	9	13	13.0	3	7	7.0	6	6.0	9.00	44	.333	.435	-5	-5	95	99	-0.9	0	0	-0.4
1987	Cal-A	1	2	.333	16	1	0	0	0	34	34	9.0	7	18	4.8	27	7.1	5.56	80	.264	.351	-4	-4	100	96	-0.3	0	1	-0.2
1988	Cal-A	0	1	.000	3	0	0	0	0	4	4	9.0	0	1	2.3	2	4.5	4.50	84	.308	.400	-0	-0	95	110	-0.4	0	0	0.0
Total	3	1	5	.167	24	2	0	0	0	47	51	9.8	10	26	5.0	35	6.7	6.13	70	.282	.373	-9	-10	98	98	-1.6	0	1	-0.6
■ **ROLLIN COOK**	Cook, Rollin Edward b: 10/5/1890, Toledo, Ohio d: 8/11/75, Toledo, Ohio BR/TR, 5'9", 152 lbs. Deb: 7/06/15																												
1915	StL-A	0	0	—	5	0	0	0	0	14	16	10.3	0	9	5.8	7	4.5	7.07	41	.276	.382	-6	-6	99	61	0.0	0	0	-0.5
■ **RON COOK**	Cook, Ronald Wayne b: 7/11/47, Jefferson, Tex. BL/TL, 6'1", 175 lbs. Deb: 4/10/70																												
1970	Hou-N	4	4	.500	41	7	0	0	2	82	80	8.8	4	42	4.6	50	5.5	3.73	102	.274	.357	3	1	94	123	0.1	2	0	0.2
1971	Hou-N	0	4	.000	5	4	0	0	0	26	23	8.0	2	8	2.8	10	3.5	4.85	66	.237	.291	-4	-5	92	62	-1.9	0	0	-0.4
Total	2	4	8	.333	46	11	0	0	2	108	103	8.6	6	50	4.2	60	5.0	4.00	91	.265	.341	-1	-4	93	108	-1.8	2	0	-0.2
■ **DANNY COOMBS**	Coombs, Daniel Bernard b: 3/23/42, Lincoln, Me. BR/TL, 6'4", 200 lbs. Deb: 9/27/63																												
1963	Hou-N	0	0	—	1	0	0	0	0	⅓	3	81.0	0	0	0.0	0	0.0	27.00	—	.750	.750	-1	-1	95	139	0.0	0	0	0.0
1964	Hou-N	1	1	.500	7	1	0	0	0	18	21	10.5	1	10	5.0	14	7.0	5.00	70	.300	.390	-3	-3	98	107	0.2	-0	-0	-0.3
1965	Hou-N	0	2	.000	26	3	0	0	0	47	54	10.3	3	23	4.4	35	6.7	4.79	67	.292	.367	-7	-8	91	105	-0.9	0	1	-0.7
1966	Hou-N	0	0	—	2	0	0	0	0	3	4	12.0	0	0	0.0	3	9.0	3.00	119	.333	.333	0	0	99	136	0.0	-0	0	0.0
1967	Hou-N	3	0	1.000	6	2	0	0	0	24	21	7.9	0	9	3.4	23	8.6	3.38	95	.233	.297	0	-0	95	73	1.5	0	0	0.0
1968	Hou-N	4	3	.571	40	2	0	0	2	47	52	10.0	0	17	3.3	29	5.6	3.26	92	.286	.338	-1	-1	100	116	0.8	1	1	0.1
1969	Hou-N	0	1	.000	8	0	0	0	0	8	12	13.5	0	2	2.3	3	3.4	6.75	54	.364	.417	-3	-3	101	90	-0.4	-0	-0	-0.2
1970	SD-N	10	14	.417	35	27	5	1	0	188	185	8.9	12	76	3.6	105	5.0	3.30	118	.256	.322	16	13	97	113	0.6	-1	-2	0.9
1971	SD-N	1	6	.143	19	7	0	0	0	58	81	12.6	10	25	3.9	37	5.7	6.21	55	.327	.383	-18	-18	98	103	-2.1	1	1	-1.5
Total	9	19	27	.413	144	42	5	1	2	393	433	9.9	26	162	3.7	249	5.7	4.08	88	.280	.344	-16	-22	97	108	-0.3	0	0	-1.7
■ **JACK COOMBS**	Coombs, John Wesley "Colby Jack" b: 11/18/1882, Le Grand, Iowa d: 4/15/57, Palestine, Tex. BB/TR, 6', 185 lbs. Deb: 7/05/06 M																												
1906	Phi-A	10	10	.500	23	18	13	1	0	173	144	7.5	0	68	3.5	90	4.7	2.50	100	.250	.329	4	0	93	101	-0.7	2	-0	0.1
1907	Phi-A	6	9	.400	23	17	10	2	2	133	109	7.4	2	64	4.3	73	4.9	3.11	85	.246	.341	-8	-7	104	87	-2.6	-1	0	-0.7
1908	Phi-A	7	5	.583	26	18	10	4	0	153	130	7.6	1	64	3.8	80	4.7	2.00	131	.233	.316	7	10	110	137	1.6	4	-0	1.2
1909	Phi-A	12	11	.522	30	25	18	6	1	206	156	6.8	1	73	3.2	97	4.2	2.32	104	.213	.289	4	2	97	75	-2.0	1	0	0.3
1910	Phi-A	**31**	9	.775	**45**	38	35	**13**	1	353	248	6.3	0	115	2.9	224	5.7	1.30	188	.201	.273	48	45	97	113	7.3	3	-5	5.0
1911	Phi-A	**28**	12	.700	47	40	26	1	2	337	360	9.6	8	119	3.2	185	4.9	3.53	84	.280	.348	-7	-21	88	103	2.5	15	-3	-1.0
1912	Phi-A	21	10	.677	40	32	23	1	2	262	227	7.8	5	94	3.2	120	4.1	3.30	99	.241	.316	1	-1	97	86	3.9	5	-1	0.3
1913	Phi-A	0	0	—	2	2	0	0	0	5	5	9.0	0	6	10.8	0	0.0	10.80	25	.250	.444	-4	-4	93	50	0.0	1	-0	-0.3
1914	Phi-A	0	1	.000	2	2	0	0	0	8	8	9.0	0	3	3.4	1	1.1	4.50	56	.267	.353	-2	-2	93	76	-0.4	0	-0	-0.1
1915	Bro-N	15	10	.600	29	24	17	2	0	196	166	7.6	1	91	4.2	56	2.6	2.57	109	.236	.326	4	5	102	116	2.3	4	-4	0.6
1916	Bro-N	13	8	.619	27	21	10	3	0	159	136	7.7	3	44	2.5	47	2.7	2.66	99	.239	.287	-1	-1	100	91	0.3	-0	-5	-0.6
1917	Bro-N	7	11	.389	31	14	9	0	0	141	147	9.4	7	49	3.1	34	2.2	3.96	72	.284	.340	-20	-17	105	105	-1.5	2	-3	-1.9
1918	Bro-N	8	14	.364	27	22	16	2	0	189	191	9.1	10	49	2.3	44	2.1	3.81	75	.266	.306	-22	-20	104	85	-2.4	-0	-3	-2.3
1920	Det-A	0	0	—	2	0	0	0	0	6	7	10.5	0	2	3.0	1	1.5	3.00	134	.318	.375	1	1	106	147	0.0	-0	-0	0.0
Total	14	158	110	.590	354	273	187	35	8	2321	2034	7.9	38	841	3.3	1052	4.1	2.78	99	.244	.315	4	-7	98	100	8.3	35	-24	0.6
■ **BOBBY COOMBS**	Coombs, Raymond Franklin b: 2/2/08, Goodwins Mills, Me. BR/TR, 5'9.5", 160 lbs. Deb: 6/08/33																												
1933	Phi-A	0	1	.000	21	0	0	0	2	31	47	13.6	4	20	5.8	8	2.3	7.55	52	.348	.421	-11	-13	92	103	-0.4	1	-0	-1.0
1943	NY-N	0	1	.000	9	0	0	0	0	16	33	18.6	1	8	4.5	5	2.8	12.94	26	.423	.461	-17	-17	99	71	-0.4	0	0	-1.5
Total	2	0	2	.000	30	0	0	0	2	47	80	15.3	5	28	5.4	13	2.5	9.38	40	.376	.435	-28	-29	94	92	-0.8	1	0	-2.5
■ **WILLIAM COON**	Coon, William K. b: 3/21/1855, Pennsylvania d: 8/30/15, Burlington, N.J. Deb: 9/04/1875																												
1876	Phi-N	0	0	—	2	0	0	0	0	7	9	11.6	0	0	0.0	0	0.0	5.14	47	.316	.316	-2	-2	105	54	0.0	-0	0	-0.1
■ **JOHNNY COONEY**	Cooney, John Walter b: 3/18/01, Cranston, R.I. d: 7/8/86, Sarasota, Fla. BR/TL, 5'10", 165 lbs. Deb: 4/19/21 MC																												
1921	Bos-N	0	1	.000	8	1	0	0	0	21	19	8.1	3	10	4.3	9	3.9	3.86	91	.241	.322	-0	-1	92	97	-0.4	-0	0	0.0
1922	Bos-N	1	2	.333	4	3	1	0	0	25	19	6.8	0	6	2.2	7	2.5	2.16	185	.224	.263	5	5	98	92	0.0	-1	0	0.4
1923	Bos-N	3	5	.375	23	8	5	2	0	98	92	8.4	3	22	2.0	23	2.1	3.31	124	.246	.288	8	9	102	76	0.2	4	-2	1.3
1924	Bos-N	8	9	.471	34	19	12	2	2	181	176	8.8	4	50	2.5	67	3.3	3.18	120	.260	.305	14	13	99	95	1.8	2	-1	1.3
1925	Bos-N	14	14	.500	31	29	20	2	0	246	267	9.8	18	50	1.8	65	2.4	3.48	117	.274	.306	22	16	95	101	1.3	5	1	2.4
1926	Bos-N	3	3	.500	19	8	3	1	0	83	106	11.5	0	29	3.1	23	2.5	4.01	83	.320	.368	-2	-6	88	123	0.4	3	0	-0.5
1928	Bos-N	3	7	.300	24	6	2	0	1	90	106	10.6	7	31	3.1	18	1.8	4.30	94	.303	.352	-3	-3	101	109	-0.3	-0	3	0.0
1929	Bos-N	2	3	.400	14	2	1	0	3	45	57	11.4	4	22	4.4	11	2.2	5.00	92	.315	.376	-1	-2	97	115	0.1	2	1	-0.1
1930	Bos-N	0	0	—	2	0	0	0	0	7	16	20.6	2	3	3.9	1	1.3	18.00	27	.471	.488	-10	-10	99	73	0.0	-1	1	-0.6
Total	9	34	44	.436	159	76	44	7	6	796	858	9.7	41	223	2.5	224	2.5	3.72	106	.278	.322	32	21	97	100	3.1	14	4	4.2
■ **BOB COONEY**	Cooney, Robert Daniel b: 7/12/07, Glens Falls, N.Y. d: 5/4/76, Glens Falls, N.Y. BR/TR, 5'11", 160 lbs. Deb: 9/06/31																												
1931	StL-A	0	3	.000	5	4	1	0	0	39	46	10.6	1	20	4.6	13	3.0	4.15	111	.291	.372	1	2	105	119	-1.4	1	-0	0.3
1932	StL-A	1	2	.333	23	3	1	0	1	71	94	11.9	8	36	4.6	23	2.9	6.97	66	.324	.396	-20	-19	103	95	-0.2	-3	-2	-2.0
Total	2	1	5	.167	28	7	2	0	1	110	140	11.5	9	56	4.6	36	2.9	5.97	77	.313	.388	-19	-17	103	103	-1.6	-2	-2	-1.7
■ **BILL COONEY**	Cooney, William A. "Cush" b: 4/4/1887, Boston, Mass. d: 11/6/28, Roxbury, Mass. TR , Deb: 09																												
1909	Bos-N	0	0	—	3	0	0	0	0	6	4	6.0	0	2	3.0	3	4.5	1.50	176	.182	.250	1	1	102	58	0.0	0	-0	0.1
■ **WILBUR COOPER**	Cooper, Arley Wilbur b: 2/24/1892, Bearsville, W.Va. d: 8/7/73, Encino, Cal. BR/TL, 5'11", 175 lbs. Deb: 8/29/12																												
1912	Pit-N	3	0	1.000	6	4	3	2	0	38	32	7.6	1	15	3.6	30	7.1	1.66	196	.224	.297	7	7	95	125	1.5	-0	0	0.6
1913	Pit-N	5	3	.625	30	9	3	1	0	93	98	9.5	0	45	4.4	39	3.8	3.29	92	.276	.350	-1	-3	94	115	0.9	-1	-1	-0.5
1914	Pit-N	16	15	.516	40	34	19	0	0	267	246	8.3	4	79	2.7	102	3.4	2.12	122	.254	.301	20	14	93	**126**	2.3	2	0	1.6
1915	Pit-N	5	16	.238	38	21	11	1	4	186	180	8.7	4	52	2.5	71	3.4	3.29	82	.262	.310	-11	-12	98	95	-5.5	-3	1	-1.5
1916	Pit-N	12	11	.522	42	23	16	2	2	246	189	6.9	4	74	2.7	111	4.1	1.87	150	.215	.271	21	26	107	100	2.3	0	-1	3.0
1917	Pit-N	17	11	.607	40	34	23	7	1	298	276	8.3	4	54	1.6	99	3.0	2.36	118	.258	.288	12	14	103	112	6.5	2	-3	1.6
1918	Pit-N	19	14	.576	38	29	26	3	**3**	273	219	7.2	2	65	2.1	117	3.9	2.11	137	.223	.273	20	24	105	90	2.5	3	-2	2.9
1919	Pit-N	19	13	.594	35	32	**27**	4	1	287	229	7.2	10	74	2.3	106	3.3	2.67	115	.225	.277	8	13	105	87	3.4	6	-5	1.6
1920	Pit-N	24	15	.615	44	37	28	3	2	327	307	8.4	4	52	1.4	114	3.1	2.39	133	.253	.282	27	28	101	92	5.1	1	-3	2.8
1921	Pit-N	**22**	14	.611	38	38	29	2	0	**327**	341	9.4	9	80	2.2	134	3.7	3.25	118	.272	.313	19	22	102	97	1.3	4	-3	2.3
1922	Pit-N	23	14	.622	41	37	**27**	4	0	295	330	10.1	13	61	1.9	129	3.9	3.17	131	.286	.318	**30**	**32**	101	113	3.6	9	-2	**3.9**
1923	Pit-N	17	19	.472	39	38	26	1	0	295	331	10.1	11	71	2.2	77	2.3	3.57	107	.288	.328	14	8	95	106	-3.6	4	-1	0.9
1924	Pit-N	20	14	.588	38	35	25	4	1	269	296	9.9	13	40	1.3	62	2.1	3.28	122	.283	.307	18	22	104	106	0.0	9	-4	2.8
1925	Chi-N	12	14	.462	32	26	13	0	0	212	249	10.6	18	61	2.6	41	1.7	4.29	98	.291	.335	-0	-2	98	101	0.6	1	-2	-0.3
1926	Chi-N	2	1	.667	8	8	3	2	0	55	65	10.6	6	21	3.4	18	2.9	4.42	91	.311	.358	-4	-3	105	121	0.4	3	-1	0.0
	Det-A	0	4	.000	8	3	0	0	0	14	27	17.4	0	9	5.8	2	1.3	10.93	36	.443	.500	-11	-11	98	92	-1.9	-1	0	-0.9
Total	15	216	178	.548	517	408	279	36	14	3482	3415	8.8	103	853	2.2	1252	3.2	2.89	116	.262	.304	169	180	101	103	19.4	40	-25	20.8
■ **CAL COOPER**	Cooper, Calvin Asa b: 8/11/22, Great Falls, S.C. BR/TR, 6'2.5", 180 lbs. Deb: 9/14/48																												
1948	Was-A	0	0	—	1	0	0	0	0	1	5	45.0	1	1	9.0	0	0.0	45.00	10	.625	.667	-5	-4	107	71	0.0	0	0	-0.3
■ **DON COOPER**	Cooper, Donald James b: 1/15/57, New York, N.Y. BR/TR, 6'1", 185 lbs. Deb: 4/09/81																												
1981	Min-A	1	5	.167	27	2	0	0	0	59	61	9.3	9	32	4.9	33	5.0	4.27	91	.274	.359	-4	-2	107	122	-1.6	0	-1	-0.3
1982	Min-A	0	1	.000	6	1	0	0	0	11	14	11.5	0	11	9.0	5	4.1	9.82	42	.311	.439	-7	-7	102	64	-0.4	0	0	-0.6
1983	Tor-A	0	0	—	4	0	0	0	0	5	8	14.4	3	0	0.0	5	9.0	7.20	61	.348	.348	-2	-2	108	130	0.0	0	0	-0.1
1985	NY-A	0	0	—	7	0	0	0	0	10	12	10.8	2	3	2.7	4	3.6	5.40	72	.300	.341	-1	-2	94	105	0.0	0	-0	-0.1
Total	4	1	6	.143	44	3	0	0	0	85	95	10.1	14	46	4.9	47	5.0	5.29	75	.287	.368	-14	-13	104	113	-2.0	0	-1	-1.1

YEAR	TM/L	W	L	PCT	G	GS	CG	SHO	SV	IP	H	H/G	HR	BB	BB/G	SO	SO/G	ERA	/A	OAVG	OOBP	PR	/A	PF	CPI	WAT	PB	PD	TPI
■ **GUY COOPER**	Cooper, Guy Evans "Rebel" b: 1/28/1893, Rome, Ga. d: 8/2/51, Santa Monica, Cal. BB/TR, 6'1", 185 lbs. Deb: 5/02/14																												
1914	NY-A	0	0	—	1	0	0	0	0	3	3	9.0	0	2	6.0	3	9.0	9.00	30	.273	.385	-2	-2	100	45	0.0	-0	0	-0.1
	Bos-A	1	1	.500	9	1	0	0	0	22	23	9.4	1	9	3.7	5	2.0	5.32	49	.299	.393	-6	-7	96	89	-0.1	-1	-1	-0.7
	Yr	1	1	.500	10	1	0	0	0	25	26	9.4	1	11	4.0	8	2.9	5.76	46	.295	.392	-8	-9	97	89	-0.1	-0	-1	-0.8
1915	Bos-A	0	0	—	1	0	0	0	0	2	0	0.0	0	2	9.0	0	0.0	0.00	—	.000	.286	1	1	96	0	0.0	0	0	0.1
Total	2	1	1	.500	11	1	0	0	0	27	26	8.7	1	13	4.3	8	2.7	5.33	50	.280	.385	-8	-8	96	78	-0.1	-1	-1	-0.7
■ **MORT COOPER**	Cooper, Morton Cecil b: 3/2/13, Atherton, Mo. d: 11/17/58, Little Rock, Ark. BR/TR, 6'2", 210 lbs. Deb: 9/14/38																												
1938	StL-N	2	1	.667	4	3	1	0	1	24	17	6.4	1	12	4.5	11	4.1	3.00	140	.195	.294	2	3	111	80	0.6	0	1	0.4
1939	StL-N	12	6	.667	45	26	7	2	4	211	208	8.9	6	97	4.1	130	**5.5**	3.24	124	.260	.334	16	18	103	113	1.6	3	-3	1.9
1940	StL-N	11	12	.478	38	29	16	3	3	231	225	8.8	12	86	3.4	95	3.7	3.62	108	.253	.317	6	7	101	98	-1.6	-2	-2	0.3
1941	StL-N	13	9	.591	29	25	12	0	0	187	175	8.4	15	69	3.3	118	5.7	3.90	100	.244	.309	-5	-0	107	88	-0.8	-1	-1	0.0
1942	StL-N	**22**	7	.759	37	35	22	**10**	0	279	207	**6.7**	9	68	2.2	152	4.9	**1.77**	**191**	**.204**	**.255**	**48**	**50**	103	100	3.8	-1	-3	**5.5**
1943	StL-N	**21**	8	**.724**	37	32	24	6	3	274	228	7.5	5	79	2.6	141	4.6	2.30	147	.226	.281	33	33	100	98	2.3	-1	-2	3.4
1944	StL-N	22	7	.759	34	33	22	**7**	1	252	227	8.1	6	60	2.1	97	3.5	2.46	140	.239	.285	32	27	95	103	4.1	2	-5	2.6
1945	StL-N	2	0	1.000	4	3	1	0	0	24	20	7.5	1	7	2.6	14	5.3	1.50	246	.227	.289	6	6	97	176	1.0	1	-0	0.7
	Bos-N	7	4	.636	20	11	4	1	1	78	77	8.9	4	27	3.1	45	5.2	3.35	128	.257	.319	4	8	113	104	2.0	1	0	1.0
	Yr	9	4	.692	24	14	5	1	1	102	97	8.6	5	34	3.0	59	5.2	2.91	142	.249	.310	10	14	109	104	3.0	1	-0	1.7
1946	Bos-N	13	11	.542	28	27	15	3	1	199	181	8.2	16	39	**1.8**	83	3.8	3.12	103	.239	**.273**	7	2	94	83	0.4	2	-3	0.0
1947	Bos-N	2	5	.286	10	7	2	0	0	47	48	9.2	2	13	2.5	15	2.9	4.02	96	.271	.318	0	-1	95	91	-1.7	-1	-1	-0.2
	NY-N	1	5	.167	8	8	2	0	0	37	51	12.4	7	13	3.2	12	2.9	7.05	57	.323	.374	-12	-12	99	89	-2.0	4	-1	-0.8
	Yr	3	10	.231	18	15	4	0	0	84	99	10.6	9	26	2.8	27	2.9	5.36	74	.294	.339	-12	-13	97	89	-3.7	-1	-2	-1.0
1949	Chi-N	0	0	—	1	0	0	0	0	0	2	—	1	1	—	0	—	∞	—	1.000	1.000	-3	-3	97	75	0.0	0	0	-0.2
Total	11	128	75	.631	295	239	128	32	14	1843	1666	8.1	85	571	2.8	913	4.5	2.96	123	.240	.296	132	138	101	99	9.7	6	-19	14.6
■ **PAT COOPER**	Cooper, Orge Patterson b: 11/26/17, Albemarle, N.C. BR/TR, 6'3", 180 lbs. Deb: 5/11/46																												
1946	Phi-A	0	0	—	1	0	0	0	0	1	1	9.0	0	1	9.0	0	0.0	0.00	—	.250	.400	0	0	107	0	0.0	0	0	0.0
■ **MAYS COPELAND**	Copeland, Mays b: 8/31/13, Mountain View, Ark d: 11/29/82, Indio, Cal. BR/TR, 6', 180 lbs. Deb: 4/27/35																												
1935	StL-N	0	0	—	1	0	0	0	0	1	2	18.0	0	0	0.0	0	0.0	9.00	45	.667	.500	-1	-1	100	128	0.0	0	0	0.0
■ **HENRY COPPOLA**	Coppola, Henry Peter b: 8/6/12, E.Douglas, Mass. BR/TR, 5'11", 175 lbs. Deb: 4/19/35																												
1935	Was-A	3	4	.429	19	5	2	1	0	59	72	11.0	6	29	4.4	19	2.9	5.95	69	.300	.368	-10	-12	93	93	0.0	-0	-0	-1.1
1936	Was-A	0	0	—	6	0	0	0	1	14	17	10.9	1	12	7.7	2	1.3	4.50	108	.315	.420	1	1	96	155	0.0	0	0	0.1
Total	2	3	4	.429	25	5	2	1	1	73	89	11.0	7	41	5.1	21	2.6	5.67	75	.303	.379	-9	-11	93	105	0.0	0	0	-1.0
■ **DOUG CORBETT**	Corbett, Douglas Mitchell b: 11/4/52, Sarasota, Fla. BR/TR, 6'1", 185 lbs. Deb: 4/10/80																												
1980	Min-A	8	6	.571	73	0	0	0	23	136	102	6.8	7	42	2.8	89	5.9	1.99	223	.213	.273	**31**	**37**	109	114	1.3	0	3	4.1
1981	Min-A	2	6	.250	**54**	0	0	0	17	88	80	8.2	5	34	3.5	60	6.1	2.56	153	.239	.302	11	13	107	119	-1.3	0	2	1.6
1982	Min-A	0	2	.000	10	0	0	0	3	22	27	11.0	3	10	4.1	15	6.1	5.32	78	.300	.370	-3	-3	102	103	-0.9	0	1	-0.1
	Cal-A	1	7	.125	33	0	0	0	8	57	46	7.3	8	25	3.9	37	5.8	5.05	80	.223	.303	-6	-6	99	70	-3.1	0	0	-0.5
	Yr	1	9	.100	43	0	0	0	11	79	73	8.3	11	35	4.0	52	5.9	5.13	79	.247	.323	-9	-9	100	70	-4.0	0	1	-0.6
1983	Cal-A	1	1	.500	11	0	0	0	0	17	26	13.8	1	4	2.1	18	9.5	3.71	106	.351	.387	1	0	96	164	0.1	0	-0	0.0
1984	Cal-A	5	1	.833	45	1	0	0	4	85	76	8.0	2	30	3.2	48	5.1	2.12	191	.244	.306	18	18	101	140	2.0	0	0	1.9
1985	Cal-A	3	3	.500	30	0	0	0	0	46	49	9.6	7	20	3.9	24	4.7	4.89	85	.274	.345	-4	-4	101	102	-0.2	0	0	-0.2
1986	Cal-A	4	2	.667	46	0	0	0	10	79	66	7.5	11	22	2.5	36	4.1	3.65	109	.231	.285	5	3	95	92	0.7	0	1	0.4
1987	Bal-A	0	2	.000	11	0	0	0	1	23	25	9.8	5	13	5.1	16	6.3	7.83	57	.281	.365	-9	-9	99	77	-0.9	0	1	-0.6
Total	8	24	30	.444	313	1	0	0	66	553	497	8.1	49	200	3.3	343	5.6	3.32	125	.242	.306	44	50	103	110	-2.3	0	8	6.6
■ **JOE CORBETT**	Corbett, Joseph A. b: 12/4/1875, San Francisco, Cal. d: 5/2/45, San Francisco, Cal. BR/TR, 5'10", Deb: 8/23/1895																												
1895	Was-N	0	2	.000	3	3	3	0	0	19	26	12.3	3	9	4.3	3	1.4	5.68	89	.347	.417	-2	-1	105	116	-0.9	-1	0	0.0
1896	Bal-N	3	0	1.000	8	3	3	0	1	41	31	6.8	0	17	3.7	28	6.1	2.20	196	.229	.315	10	10	99	96	1.5	1	0	0.9
1897	Bal-N	24	8	.750	37	37	34	1	0	313	330	9.5	2	115	3.3	149	4.3	3.11	128	.292	.358	42	30	92	112	3.8	1	3	2.9
1904	StL-N	5	8	.385	14	14	12	0	0	109	110	9.1	2	51	4.2	68	5.6	4.38	62	.292	.388	-20	-20	99	88	-1.4	1	0	-1.9
Total	4	32	18	.640	62	57	52	1	1	482	497	9.3	7	192	3.6	248	4.6	3.42	110	.290	.364	30	19	95	105	3.0	2	3	1.9
■ **SHERM CORBETT**	Corbett, Sherman Stanley b: 11/3/62, New Braunfels, Tex. BL/TL, 6'4", 210 lbs. Deb: 5/29/88																												
1988	Cal-A	2	1	.667	34	0	0	0	1	46	47	9.2	2	23	4.5	28	5.5	4.11	92	.273	.343	-1	-2	95	105	0.6	0	0	-0.1
■ **RAY CORBIN**	Corbin, Alton Ray b: 2/12/49, Live Oak, Fla. BR/TR, 6'2", 200 lbs. Deb: 4/06/71																												
1971	Min-A	8	11	.421	52	11	2	0	3	140	141	9.1	19	70	4.5	83	5.3	4.11	88	.265	.345	-10	-8	104	113	-0.9	1	1	-0.5
1972	Min-A	8	9	.471	31	19	5	3	0	162	135	7.5	12	53	2.9	83	4.6	2.61	126	.230	.295	8	12	107	111	-0.5	-3	-2	0.9
1973	Min-A	8	5	.615	51	7	1	0	14	148	124	7.5	7	60	3.6	83	5.0	3.04	130	.229	.304	13	15	103	94	1.6	0	-1	1.4
1974	Min-A	7	6	.538	29	15	1	0	0	112	133	10.7	8	40	3.2	50	4.0	5.30	69	.294	.346	-21	-20	101	85	0.5	0	1	-1.9
1975	Min-A	5	7	.417	18	11	3	0	0	90	105	10.5	13	38	3.8	49	4.9	5.10	80	.295	.357	-13	-10	107	104	-0.7	0	1	-0.9
Total	5	36	38	.486	181	63	12	3	17	652	638	8.8	59	261	3.6	348	4.8	3.84	96	.258	.326	-23	-11	105	102	0.0	-2	0	-1.0
■ **JACK CORCORAN**	Corcoran, John H. b: 1860, Lowell, Mass. Deb: 5/01/1884																												
1884	Bro-a	0	0	—	1	0	0	0	0	1	0	0.0	0	1	9.0	0	0.0	0.00	—	.000	.269	0	0	100	0	0.0	0	0	0.0
■ **LARRY CORCORAN**	Corcoran, Lawrence J. b: 8/10/1859, Brooklyn, N.Y. d: 10/14/1891, Newark, N.J. TB, 120 lbs. Deb: 5/01/1880																												
1880	Chi-N	43	14	.754	63	60	57	5	2	536	404	6.8	6	99	1.7	**268**	**4.5**	1.95	120	.217	.257	25	23	98	72	-4.2	1	7	3.0
1881	Chi-N	**31**	14	.689	45	44	43	4	0	397	380	8.6	10	78	1.8	150	3.4	2.31	124	.264	.301	20	25	103	105	3.0	-3	-2	2.0
1882	Chi-N	27	12	**.692**	39	39	38	3	0	356	281	**7.1**	5	63	1.6	170	4.3	**1.95**	140	**.224**	**.261**	37	31	95	85	3.6	-1	1	2.9
1883	Chi-N	34	20	.630	56	53	51	3	0	474	483	9.2	7	82	1.6	216	4.1	2.49	134	.272	.304	34	45	107	111	3.8	-3	2	4.2
1884	Chi-N	35	23	.603	60	59	57	7	0	517	473	8.2	35	116	2.0	272	4.7	2.40	129	.252	.296	33	41	105	114	6.0	2	7	4.8
1885	Chi-N	5	2	.714	7	7	6	1	0	59	63	9.6	2	24	3.7	10	1.5	3.66	81	.284	.354	-6	-5	106	109	-0.2	2	0	-0.1
	NY-N	2	1	.667	3	3	2	0	0	25	24	8.6	1	11	4.0	10	3.6	2.88	100	.263	.342	-0	-0	102	124	-0.1	1	0	0.1
	Yr	7	3	.700	10	10	8	1	0	84	87	9.3	3	35	3.8	20	2.1	3.43	86	.278	.351	-6	-5	104	124	-0.3	2	0	0.0
1886	Was-N	0	1	.000	2	1	1	0	0	14	16	10.3	0	4	2.6	3	1.9	5.79	57	.301	.349	-4	-4	100	65	-0.3	0	0	-0.6
1887	Ind-N	0	2	.000	2	2	1	0	0	15	23	13.8	3	19	11.4	4	2.4	12.60	33	.368	.515	-14	-14	101	80	-0.9	0	0	-0.9
Total	8	177	89	.665	277	268	256	23	2	2393	2147	8.1	69	496	1.9	1103	4.1	2.35	122	.249	.289	127	140	102	98	10.7	0	16	15.4
■ **MIKE CORCORAN**	Corcoran, Michael b: Brooklyn, N.Y. Deb: 7/15/1884																												
1884	Chi-N	0	1	.000	1	1	1	0	0	9	16	16.0	1	7	7.0	2	2.0	4.00	78	.396	.485	-1	-1	105	223	-0.4	-0	0	0.0
■ **ED COREY**	Corey, Edward Norman "Ike" (born Abraham Simon Cohen) b: 7/13/1899, Chicago, Ill. d: 9/17/70, Kenosha, Wis. BR/TR, 6', 170 lbs. Deb: 7/02/18																												
1918	Chi-A	0	0	—	1	0	0	0	0	2	2	9.0	0	1	4.5	0	0.0	4.50	62	.333	.429	-0	-0	100	109	0.0	-0	0	0.0
■ **FRED COREY**	Corey, Frederick Harrison b: 1857, S.Kingston, R.I. d: 11/27/12, Providence, R.I. BR/TR, Deb: 5/01/1878																												
1878	Pro-N	1	2	.333	5	5	2	0	0	23	22	8.6	0	7	2.7	7	2.7	2.35	95	.262	.318	-0	-0	97	97	-0.5	-1	0	-0.1
1880	Wor-N	8	9	.471	25	17	9	2	2	148	131	8.0	6	16	1.0	47	2.9	2.43	109	.246	.268	-1	3	111	85	-0.2	-4	0	0.0
1881	Wor-N	6	15	.286	23	21	20	1	0	189	231	11.0	3	31	1.5	33	1.6	3.71	80	.314	.342	-20	-15	107	97	-3.4	-1	0	-1.3
1882	Wor-N	1	13	.071	21	14	12	0	0	139	180	11.7	5	19	1.2	36	2.3	3.56	87	.321	.344	-10	-7	107	120	-4.8	1	0	-0.5
1883	Phi-a	10	7	.588	18	16	15	0	0	148	182	11.1	2	24	1.5	42	2.6	3.41	96	.308	.335	-2	-2	99	123	-1.2	3	0	-0.1
1885	Phi-a	1	0	1.000	1	1	1	0	0	9	18	18.0	2	1	1.0	3	3.0	7.00	47	.428	.441	-4	-4	102	135	0.5	0	0	-0.2
Total	6	27	46	.370	93	74	59	3	2	656	764	10.5	18	98	1.3	168	2.3	3.32	90	.300	.326	-37	-25	106	105	-9.6	-2	0	-2.2
■ **POP CORKHILL**	Corkhill, John Stewart b: 4/11/1858, Parkesburg, Pa. d: 4/4/21, Pennsauken, N.J. BL/TR, 5'10", 180 lbs. Deb: 5/01/1883																												
1884	Cin-a	1	0	1.000	1	0	0	0	0	5	1	1.8	0	2	3.6	4	7.2	1.80	185	.068	.181	1	1	103	14	0.5	0	0	0.1
1885	Cin-a	1	4	.200	8	1	0	0	1	37	36	8.8	2	10	2.4	12	2.9	3.65	91	.267	.317	-2	-1	103	96	-1.5	1	0	0.0

YEAR TM/L	W	L	PCT	G	GS	CG	SHO	SV	IP	H	H/G	HR	BB	BB/G	SO	SO/G	ERA	/A	OAVG	OOBP	PR	/A	PF	CPI	WAT	PB	PD	TPI
1886 Cin-a	0	0	—	1	0	0	0	0	1	1	9.0	0	0	0.0	1	9.0	18.00	18	.271	.271	-2	-2	96	14	0.0	0	0	0.0
1887 Cin-a	1	0	1.000	5	0	0	0	0	15	22	13.2	0	5	3.0	3	1.8	6.00	76	.356	.404	-3	-2	106	95	0.5	1	0	-0.1
1888 Cin-a	0	0	—	2	0	0	0	1	5	8	14.4	1	0	0.0	1	1.8	10.80	28	.376	.376	-4	-4	99	63	0.0	0	0	-0.4
Total 5	3	4	.429	17	1	0	0	2	63	68	9.7	3	17	2.4	21	3.0	4.86	74	.288	.335	-10	-9	103	85	-0.5	2	0	-0.4
■ **MIKE CORKINS** Corkins, Michael Patrick b: 5/25/46, Riverside, Cal. BR/TR, 6'1", 190 lbs. Deb: 9/08/69																												
1969 SD-N	1	3	.250	6	4	0	0	0	17	27	14.3	3	8	4.2	13	6.9	8.47	43	.370	.407	-9	-9	100	94	-0.4	0	0	-0.8
1970 SD-N	5	6	.455	24	18	1	0	0	111	109	8.8	11	79	6.4	75	6.1	4.62	85	.258	.371	-7	-9	97	108	0.6	2	-1	-0.7
1971 SD-N	0	0	—	8	0	0	0	0	13	14	9.7	1	6	4.2	16	11.1	3.46	98	.280	.357	0	-0	98	128	0.0	0	0	0.0
1972 SD-N	6	9	.400	47	9	2	1	6	140	125	8.0	14	62	4.0	108	6.9	3.54	89	.240	.317	-1	-6	91	103	0.3	3	1	-0.3
1973 SD-N	5	8	.385	47	11	2	0	3	122	130	9.6	12	61	4.5	82	6.0	4.50	79	.274	.362	-11	-13	97	106	0.2	4	-2	-1.0
1974 SD-N	2	2	.500	25	2	0	0	0	56	53	8.5	5	32	5.1	41	6.6	4.82	73	.255	.350	-7	-8	97	88	0.4	-0	-1	-0.8
Total 6	19	28	.404	157	44	5	1	9	459	458	9.0	46	248	4.9	335	6.6	4.39	80	.262	.351	-36	-45	95	104	1.1	9	-3	-3.6
■ **MARDIE CORNEJO** Cornejo, Nieves Mardie b: 8/5/51, Wellington, Kan. BR/TR, 6'3", 200 lbs. Deb: 4/08/78																												
1978 NY-N	4	2	.667	25	0	0	0	3	37	37	9.0	1	14	3.4	17	4.1	2.43	146	.285	.348	5	5	99	177	1.3	0	-0	0.4
■ **JEFF CORNELL** Cornell, Jeffery Ray b: 5/10/57, Kansas City, Mo. BB/TR, 5'11", 170 lbs. Deb: 6/02/84																												
1984 SF-N	1	3	.250	23	0	0	0	0	38	51	12.1	4	22	5.2	19	4.5	6.16	57	.340	.409	-11	-11	98	111	-0.7	-0	-0	-1.1
■ **TERRY CORNUTT** Cornutt, Terry Stanton b: 10/2/52, Roseburg, Ore. BR/TR, 6'2", 195 lbs. Deb: 4/09/77																												
1977 SF-N	1	2	.333	28	1	0	0	0	44	38	7.8	4	22	4.5	23	4.7	3.89	106	.229	.314	0	1	105	85	-0.3	-0	-1	0.0
1978 SF-N	0	0	—	1	0	0	0	0	3	1	3.0	0	0	0.0	0	0.0	0.00	—	.100	.100	1	1	91	0	0.0	0	0	0.1
Total 2	1	2	.333	29	1	0	0	0	47	39	7.5	4	22	4.2	23	4.4	3.64	111	.222	.303	1	2	104	79	-0.3	-0	-1	0.1
■ **ED CORREA** Correa, Edwin Josue (Andino) b: 4/29/66, Hato Rey, P.R. BR/TR, 6'2", 192 lbs. Deb: 9/18/85																												
1985 Chi-A	1	0	1.000	5	1	0	0	0	10	11	9.9	2	11	9.9	10	9.0	7.20	58	.275	.431	-3	-3	100	99	0.5	0	-0	-0.3
1986 Tex-A	12	14	.462	32	32	4	2	0	202	167	7.4	15	126	5.6	189	8.4	4.23	94	.223	.334	-1	-6	95	83	-2.0	0	3	-0.2
1987 Tex-A	3	5	.375	15	15	0	0	0	70	83	10.7	17	52	6.7	61	7.8	7.59	61	.296	.410	-24	-23	104	96	-0.7	0	-0	-1.9
Total 3	16	19	.457	52	48	4	2	0	282	261	8.3	34	189	6.0	260	8.3	5.17	80	.244	.358	-29	-32	97	87	-2.2	0	2	-2.4
■ **FRANK CORRIDON** Corridon, Frank J. "Fiddler" b: 11/25/1880, Newport, R.I. d: 2/21/41, Syracuse, N.Y. BR/TR, 6', 170 lbs. Deb: 4/15/04																												
1904 Chi-N	5	5	.500	12	10	9	0	0	100	88	7.9	2	37	3.3	34	3.1	3.06	88	.264	.350	-4	-4	99	96	-0.8	0	3	0.0
Phi-N	6	5	.545	12	11	11	1	0	94	88	8.4	2	28	2.7	44	4.2	2.20	120	.278	.351	6	5	97	139	1.8	-0	2	0.8
Yr	11	10	.524	24	21	20	1	0	194	176	8.2	4	65	3.0	78	3.6	2.64	101	.268	.341	2	1	98	139	1.0	0	5	0.8
1905 Phi-N	10	12	.455	35	26	18	1	1	212	203	8.6	2	57	2.4	79	3.4	3.48	88	.284	.351	-12	-10	102	88	-2.0	4	2	-0.7
1907 Phi-N	18	14	.563	37	32	23	3	2	274	228	7.5	0	89	2.9	131	4.3	2.46	103	.255	.329	0	2	103	91	0.0	-1	5	0.8
1908 Phi-N	14	10	.583	27	24	18	2	1	208	178	7.7	0	48	2.1	50	2.2	2.51	92	.261	.315	-4	-5	98	86	1.3	-1	3	-0.1
1909 Phi-N	11	7	.611	27	19	11	3	0	171	147	7.7	0	61	3.2	69	3.6	2.11	131	.242	.318	9	13	106	123	2.4	-0	5	1.9
1910 StL-N	6	14	.300	30	18	9	0	3	156	168	9.7	1	55	3.2	51	2.9	3.81	74	.283	.353	-13	-17	93	96	-2.9	0	3	-1.4
Total 6	70	67	.511	180	140	99	10	7	1215	1100	8.1	7	375	2.8	458	3.4	2.80	96	.266	.336	-18	-16	100	99	-0.2	2	22	1.3
■ **JIM CORSI** Corsi, James Bernard b: 9/9/61, Newton, Mass. BR/TR, 6'1", 210 lbs. Deb: 6/28/88																												
1988 Oak-A	0	1	.000	11	1	0	0	0	21	20	8.6	1	6	2.6	10	4.3	3.86	96	.260	.292	0	-0	93	88	-0.4	0	-0	0.0
■ **BARRY CORT** Cort, Barry Lee b: 4/15/56, Toronto, Ont., Can. BR/TR, 6'5", 210 lbs. Deb: 4/22/77																												
1977 Mil-A	1	1	.500	7	3	1	0	0	24	25	9.4	1	9	3.4	17	6.4	3.38	116	.281	.343	2	1	97	123	0.1	0	0	0.2
■ **AL CORWIN** Corwin, Elmer Nathan b: 12/3/26, Newburgh, N.Y. BR/TR, 6'1", 170 lbs. Deb: 7/25/51																												
1951 NY-N	5	1	.833	15	8	3	1	1	59	49	7.5	7	21	3.2	30	4.6	3.66	107	.222	.287	2	2	99	82	1.7	-2	-2	-0.1
1952 NY-N	6	1	.857	21	7	1	0	2	68	58	7.7	5	36	4.8	36	4.8	2.65	142	.237	.326	8	8	101	140	2.3	-1	-1	0.7
1953 NY-N	6	4	.600	48	7	2	1	2	107	122	10.3	17	68	5.7	49	4.1	4.96	84	.290	.390	-8	-9	98	123	1.4	4	-1	-0.5
1954 NY-N	1	3	.250	20	0	0	0	0	31	35	10.2	4	14	4.1	14	4.1	4.06	102	.297	.355	0	0	102	130	-1.1	-0	-1	0.0
1955 NY-N	0	1	.000	13	0	0	0	0	25	25	9.0	3	17	6.1	13	4.7	3.96	100	.263	.362	0	-0	98	125	-0.4	-0	-0	0.0
Total 5	18	10	.643	117	22	6	2	5	290	289	9.0	36	156	4.8	142	4.4	3.97	101	.263	.350	2	1	99	119	3.9	1	-5	0.1
■ **MIKE COSGROVE** Cosgrove, Michael John b: 2/17/51, Phoenix, Ariz. BL/TL, 6'1", 170 lbs. Deb: 9/10/72																												
1972 Hou-N	0	1	.000	7	1	0	0	1	14	16	10.3	2	3	1.9	7	4.5	4.50	81	.286	.317	-2	-1	105	98	-0.4	-0	-0	-0.1
1973 Hou-N	1	1	.500	13	0	0	0	0	10	11	9.9	1	8	7.2	2	1.8	1.80	193	.282	.388	2	2	95	311	0.0	0	-0	0.2
1974 Hou-N	7	3	.700	45	0	0	0	2	90	76	7.6	2	39	3.9	47	4.7	3.50	101	.232	.311	1	0	98	80	2.1	-1	-0	0.0
1975 Hou-N	1	2	.333	32	3	1	0	5	71	62	7.9	2	37	4.7	32	4.1	3.04	113	.245	.330	5	3	95	112	-0.1	0	0	0.3
1976 Hou-N	3	4	.429	22	16	1	1	0	90	106	10.6	6	58	5.8	34	3.4	5.50	55	.303	.391	-20	-25	87	102	-0.4	-0	-0	-2.5
Total 5	12	11	.522	119	20	2	1	8	275	271	8.9	13	145	4.7	122	4.0	4.03	83	.264	.347	-14	-21	94	105	1.2	-2	-1	-2.1
■ **JIM COSMAN** Cosman, James Henry b: 2/19/43, Brockport, N.Y. BR/TR, 6'4.5", 211 lbs. Deb: 10/02/66																												
1966 StL-N	1	0	1.000	1	1	1	1	0	9	2	2.0	0	2	2.0	5	5.0	0.00	—	.074	.167	4	4	100	0	0.5	-0	-0	0.4
1967 StL-N	1	0	1.000	10	5	0	0	0	31	21	6.1	2	24	7.0	11	3.2	3.19	105	.198	.360	1	1	99	121	0.5	-0	-0	0.0
1970 Chi-N	0	0	—	1	0	0	0	0	1	3	27.0	1	1	9.0	0	0.0	27.00	18	.600	.667	-3	-2	119	91	0.0	0	0	-0.1
Total 3	2	0	1.000	12	6	1	1	0	41	26	5.7	3	27	5.9	16	3.5	3.07	112	.188	.337	2	2	100	93	1.0	-1	-1	0.3
■ **JOHN COSTELLO** Costello, John Reilly b: 12/24/60, New York, N.Y. BR/TR, 6'1", 180 lbs. Deb: 6/02/88																												
1988 StL-N	5	2	.714	36	0	0	0	1	50	44	7.9	3	25	4.5	38	6.8	1.80	201	.235	.322	9	10	105	190	1.7	-1	-1	1.0
■ **DAN COTTER** Cotter, Daniel Joseph b: 4/14/1867, Boston, Mass. d: 9/4/35, Boston, Mass. TR, Deb: 7/16/1890																												
1890 Buf-P	0	1	.000	1	1	1	0	0	9	18	18.0	1	7	7.0	0	0.0	14.00	29	.428	.509	-10	-10	97	71	-0.4	-1	0	-0.5
■ **ENSIGN COTTRELL** Cottrell, Ensign Stover b: 8/29/1888, Hoosick Falls, N.Y d: 2/27/47, Syracuse, N.Y. BL/TL, 5'9.5", 173 lbs. Deb: 6/21/11																												
1911 Pit-N	0	0	—	1	0	0	0	0	1	4	36.0	0	1	9.0	0	0.0	9.00	37	.667	.714	-1	-1	97	242	0.0	0	0	0.0
1912 Chi-N	0	0	—	1	0	0	0	0	4	8	18.0	0	1	2.3	1	2.3	9.00	39	.444	.474	-2	-2	102	92	0.0	-0	-0	-0.1
1913 Phi-A	1	0	1.000	2	1	1	0	0	10	15	13.5	0	2	1.8	3	2.7	5.40	50	.326	.354	-3	-3	93	80	0.5	1	-0	-0.2
1914 Bos-N	0	1	.000	1	1	0	0	0	1	2	18.0	0	3	27.0	1	9.0	9.00	32	.333	.500	-1	-1	102	141	-0.4	0	0	0.0
1915 NY-A	0	1	.000	7	0	0	0	0	21	29	12.4	2	7	3.0	7	3.0	3.43	85	.330	.385	-1	-1	99	166	-0.4	-1	0	-0.1
Total 5	1	2	.333	12	2	1	0	0	37	58	14.1	2	14	3.4	12	2.9	4.86	60	.354	.406	-8	-8	97	136	-0.3	-0	0	-0.4
■ **JOHNNY COUCH** Couch, John Daniel b: 3/31/1891, Vaughn, Mont. d: 12/8/75, San Mateo, Cal. BL/TR, 6', 180 lbs. Deb: 4/11/17																												
1917 Det-A	0	0	—	3	0	0	0	0	13	13	9.0	0	1	0.7	1	0.7	2.77	93	.255	.269	-0	-0	96	67	0.0	-0	0	0.0
1922 Cin-N	16	9	.640	43	34	18	2	1	264	301	10.3	13	56	1.9	45	1.5	3.89	99	.289	.321	6	-1	94	95	2.7	-2	1	-0.2
1923 Cin-N	2	7	.222	19	8	1	0	0	69	98	12.8	2	15	2.0	14	1.8	6.00	64	.344	.365	-15	-16	96	87	-2.8	-1	-1	-1.6
Phi-N	2	4	.333	11	7	2	0	0	65	91	12.6	4	21	2.9	18	2.5	5.26	90	.335	.380	-9	-4	118	106	0.0	-0	-0	-0.3
Yr	4	11	.267	30	15	3	0	0	134	189	12.7	6	36	2.4	32	2.1	5.64	76	.339	.372	-24	-20	107	106	-2.8	-1	-1	-1.9
1924 Phi-N	4	8	.333	37	6	3	0	3	137	170	11.2	13	39	2.6	23	1.5	4.73	90	.306	.342	-13	-7	111	102	-0.4	-0	1	-0.5
1925 Phi-N	5	6	.455	34	7	2	1	2	94	112	10.7	9	39	3.7	11	1.1	5.46	92	.298	.354	-12	-5	118	91	0.1	-2	1	-0.3
Total 5	29	34	.460	147	62	26	3	6	642	785	11.0	41	171	2.4	112	1.6	4.64	90	.304	.341	-44	-33	104	95	-0.4	-5	2	-2.9
■ **MIKE COUCHEE** Couchee, Michael Eugene b: 12/4/57, San Jose, Cal. BR/TR, 6', 190 lbs. Deb: 4/05/83																												
1983 SD-N	0	1	.000	8	0	0	0	0	14	12	7.7	1	6	3.9	5	3.2	5.14	70	.214	.286	-2	-2	99	47	-0.4	0	-0	-0.1
■ **ED COUGHLIN** Coughlin, Edward E. b: 8/5/1861, Hartford, Conn. d: 12/25/52, Hartford, Conn. Deb: 5/15/1884																												
1884 Buf-N	0	0	—	1	0	0	0	0	0	3	—	0	0	—	0	—	∞	—	1.000	1.000	-3	-3	105	55	0.0	-0	0	-0.1
■ **ROSCOE COUGHLIN** Coughlin, William Edward b: 3/15/1868, Walpole, Mass. d: 3/20/51, Chelsea, Mass. TR, 5'10", 160 lbs. Deb: 4/22/1890																												
1890 Chi-N	4	6	.400	11	10	10	0	0	95	102	9.7	3	40	3.8	29	2.7	4.26	89	.290	.363	-7	-5	107	91	-1.7	1	0	-0.2
1891 NY-N	3	4	.429	8	7	6	0	0	61	74	10.9	5	23	3.4	22	3.2	3.84	81	.314	.375	-3	-5	93	120	-0.6	1	0	-0.2

YEAR	TM/L	W	L	PCT	G	GS	CG	SHO	SV	IP	H	H/G	HR	BB	BB/G	SO	SO/G	ERA	/A	OAVG	OOBP	PR	/A	PF	CPI	WAT	PB	PD	TPI
Total	2	7	10	.412	19	17	16	0	0	156	176	10.2	8	63	3.6	51	2.9	4.10	86	.300	.368	-11	-10	101	102	-2.3	2	0	-0.4

■ **FRITZ COUMBE** Coumbe, Frederick Nicholas b: 12/13/1889, Antrim, Pa. d: 3/21/78, Paradise, Cal. BL/TL, 6', 152 lbs. Deb: 4/22/14

YEAR	TM/L	W	L	PCT	G	GS	CG	SHO	SV	IP	H	H/G	HR	BB	BB/G	SO	SO/G	ERA	/A	OAVG	OOBP	PR	/A	PF	CPI	WAT	PB	PD	TPI
1914	Bos-A	1	2	.333	17	5	1	0	1	62	49	7.1	0	16	2.3	17	2.5	1.45	181	.222	.274	9	8	96	115	-0.6	-1	0	1.0
	Cle-A	1	5	.167	14	5	2	0	0	55	59	9.7	0	16	2.6	22	3.6	3.27	89	.288	.351	-3	-2	106	110	-1.4	1	1	-0.1
	Yr	2	7	.222	31	10	3	0	1	117	108	8.3	0	32	2.5	39	3.0	2.31	119	.254	.312	6	6	101	110	-2.0	-1	1	0.9
1915	Cle-A	4	7	.364	30	12	4	1	2	114	123	9.7	1	37	2.9	37	2.9	3.47	90	.294	.355	-7	-4	106	112	-0.1	1	3	0.0
1916	Cle-A	7	5	.583	29	13	7	2	0	120	121	9.1	1	27	2.0	39	2.9	2.03	139	.279	.323	11	10	99	154	1.1	-3	5	1.4
1917	Cle-A	8	6	.571	34	10	4	1	5	134	119	8.0	0	35	2.4	30	2.0	2.15	140	.251	.307	8	13	113	113	0.0	-2	3	1.7
1918	Cle-A	13	7	.650	30	17	9	0	3	150	164	9.8	4	52	3.1	41	2.5	3.06	96	.286	.340	-5	-2	107	119	2.0	-1	5	0.3
1919	Cle-A	1	1	.500	8	2	0	0	1	24	32	12.0	2	9	3.4	7	2.6	5.25	64	.348	.406	-5	-5	104	112	-0.1	1	0	-0.3
1920	Cin-N	0	1	.000	3	0	0	0	0	15	17	10.2	0	4	2.4	7	4.2	4.80	58	.304	.328	-3	-3	88	76	-0.4	1	0	-0.1
1921	Cin-N	3	4	.429	28	6	3	0	1	87	89	9.2	2	21	2.2	12	1.2	3.21	120	.280	.314	6	6	101	104	-0.1	1	2	1.0
Total	8	38	38	.500	193	70	30	4	13	761	773	9.1	10	217	2.6	212	2.5	2.80	109	.277	.329	10	21	105	119	0.4	-1	19	4.9

■ **HARRY COURTNEY** Courtney, Henry Seymour b: 11/19/1898, Asheville, N.C. d: 12/11/54, Lyme, Conn. BB/TL, 6'4", 185 lbs. Deb: 9/13/19

YEAR	TM/L	W	L	PCT	G	GS	CG	SHO	SV	IP	H	H/G	HR	BB	BB/G	SO	SO/G	ERA	/A	OAVG	OOBP	PR	/A	PF	CPI	WAT	PB	PD	TPI
1919	Was-A	3	0	1.000	4	3	2	1	0	26	25	8.7	0	19	6.6	6	2.1	2.77	115	.269	.393	1	1	99	149	1.5	-0	-1	0.0
1920	Was-A	8	11	.421	37	24	10	1	0	188	223	10.7	6	77	3.7	48	2.3	4.74	77	.298	.371	-20	-23	96	93	-0.5	4	-3	-2.0
1921	Was-A	6	9	.400	30	15	3	0	1	133	159	10.8	7	71	4.8	26	1.8	5.62	76	.305	.381	-20	-20	99	94	-1.8	2	-0	-1.6
1922	Was-A	0	1	.000	5	0	0	0	0	10	11	9.9	0	9	8.1	4	3.6	3.60	104	.306	.417	0	0	93	161	-0.4	-1	0	0.0
	Chi-A	5	6	.455	18	11	5	0	0	87	100	10.3	5	37	3.8	28	2.9	4.97	82	.299	.363	-9	-9	101	95	-0.4	3	-0	-0.5
	Yr	5	7	.417	23	11	5	0	0	97	111	10.3	5	46	4.3	32	3.0	4.82	84	.300	.369	-8	-8	100	95	-0.8	-1	-0	-0.5
Total	4	22	27	.449	94	53	20	2	1	444	518	10.5	18	213	4.3	112	2.3	4.91	79	.299	.375	-47	-50	98	98	-1.6	7	-5	-4.1

■ **HARRY COVELESKI** Coveleski, Harry Frank "The Giant Killer" (born Harry Frank Kowalewski) b: 4/23/1886, Shamokin, Pa. d: 8/4/50, Shamokin, Pa. BB/TL, 6', 180 lbs. Deb: 9/10/07

YEAR	TM/L	W	L	PCT	G	GS	CG	SHO	SV	IP	H	H/G	HR	BB	BB/G	SO	SO/G	ERA	/A	OAVG	OOBP	PR	/A	PF	CPI	WAT	PB	PD	TPI
1907	Phi-N	1	0	1.000	4	0	0	0	0	20	10	4.5	0	3	1.3	6	2.7	0.00	—	.172	.225	5	6	103	0	0.5	-0	0	0.7
1908	Phi-N	4	1	.800	6	5	5	2	0	44	29	5.9	0	12	2.5	22	4.5	1.23	188	.215	.288	5	5	98	110	1.4	0	1	0.8
1909	Phi-N	6	10	.375	24	17	8	2	1	122	109	8.0	0	49	3.6	56	4.1	2.73	101	.247	.329	-2	1	106	103	-1.9	-3	1	0.2
1910	Cin-N	1	1	.500	7	4	2	0	0	39	35	8.1	1	42	9.7	27	6.2	5.31	58	.246	.431	-10	-10	102	95	0.0	-1	1	-0.9
1914	Det-A	22	12	.647	44	36	23	5	2	303	251	7.5	4	100	3.0	124	3.7	2.50	112	.227	.298	8	10	102	87	5.3	5	7	1.9
1915	Det-A	22	13	.629	**50**	38	20	1	4	313	271	7.8	2	87	2.5	150	4.3	2.44	126	.233	.298	18	22	105	92	-0.6	-2	4	2.6
1916	Det-A	21	11	.656	44	39	22	3	2	324	278	7.7	6	63	1.8	108	3.0	1.97	147	.237	.282	31	34	103	108	4.0	1	4	4.6
1917	Det-A	4	6	.400	16	11	2	0	0	69	70	9.1	0	14	1.8	15	2.0	2.61	98	.265	.307	0	-0	96	99	-1.0	-0	2	0.1
1918	Det-A	0	1	.000	3	1	1	0	0	14	17	10.9	0	6	3.9	3	1.9	3.86	71	.315	.371	-2	-2	99	115	-0.4	0	1	0.0
Total	9	81	55	.596	198	151	83	13	9	1248	1070	7.7	13	376	2.7	511	3.7	2.39	120	.236	.302	55	66	103	96	7.3	-1	20	10.0

■ **STAN COVELESKI** Coveleski, Stanley Anthony (born Stanislaus Kowalewski) b: 7/13/1889, Shamokin, Pa. d: 3/20/84, South Bend, Ind. BR/TR, 5'11", 166 lbs. Deb: 9/10/12 H

YEAR	TM/L	W	L	PCT	G	GS	CG	SHO	SV	IP	H	H/G	HR	BB	BB/G	SO	SO/G	ERA	/A	OAVG	OOBP	PR	/A	PF	CPI	WAT	PB	PD	TPI
1912	Phi-A	2	1	.667	5	2	2	1	0	21	18	7.7	0	4	1.7	9	3.9	3.43	95	.231	.277	-0	-0	97	56	0.3	-0	-0	0.0
1916	Cle-A	15	13	.536	45	27	11	1	3	232	247	9.6	6	58	2.3	76	2.9	3.41	82	.278	.323	-15	-16	99	96	1.2	0	2	-1.4
1917	Cle-A	19	14	.576	45	36	24	**9**	4	298	202	**6.1**	3	94	2.8	133	4.0	1.81	**167**	**.194**	.261	28	**40**	113	68	0.2	-5	-4	3.8
1918	Cle-A	22	13	.629	38	33	25	2	1	311	261	7.6	2	76	2.2	87	2.5	1.82	162	.229	.272	33	39	107	97	2.9	-3	-0	4.4
1919	Cle-A	24	12	.667	43	34	24	4	4	286	286	9.0	2	60	1.9	118	3.7	2.61	129	.267	.308	19	24	104	102	3.6	4	3	3.3
1920	Cle-A	24	14	.632	41	38	26	3	2	315	284	**8.1**	6	65	1.9	**133**	3.8	2.49	153	**.243**	**.285**	**46**	**46**	100	87	-0.1	3	3	**5.4**
1921	Cle-A	23	13	.639	43	40	28	2	2	315	341	9.7	6	84	2.4	99	2.8	3.37	122	.280	.316	32	26	96	102	1.7	-5	7	2.5
1922	Cle-A	17	14	.548	35	33	21	3	2	277	292	9.5	14	64	2.1	98	3.2	3.31	125	.274	.308	22	26	103	102	1.6	-7	1	1.9
1923	Cle-A	13	14	.481	33	31	17	**5**	2	228	251	9.9	8	42	1.7	54	2.1	**2.76**	**142**	.282	.308	**31**	30	99	121	-1.5	-8	3	2.5
1924	Cle-A	15	16	.484	37	33	18	2	0	240	286	10.7	6	73	2.7	58	2.2	4.05	102	.294	.337	5	2	97	98	1.6	-4	-1	-0.2
1925	Was-A	20	5	**.800**	32	32	15	3	0	241	230	8.6	7	73	2.7	58	2.2	**2.84**	**147**	.255	.307	42	36	95	104	**6.2**	-7	0	2.7
1926	Was-A	14	11	.560	36	34	11	3	1	245	272	10.0	1	81	3.0	50	1.8	3.12	125	.286	.331	24	22	97	117	0.6	1	1	2.3
1927	Was-A	2	1	.667	5	4	0	0	0	14	13	8.4	0	8	5.1	3	1.9	3.21	124	.250	.333	1	1	96	105	0.4	0	-0	0.1
1928	NY-A	5	1	.833	12	8	2	0	0	58	72	11.2	5	20	3.1	5	0.8	5.74	62	.323	.358	-11	-14	89	96	1.6	-2	1	-1.3
Total	14	215	142	.602	450	385	224	38	21	3081	3055	8.9	66	802	2.3	981	2.9	2.89	127	.262	.305	257	270	101	98	20.3	-33	15	26.0

■ **CHET COVINGTON** Covington, Chester Rogers "Chesty" b: 11/6/10, Cairo, Ill. d: 6/11/76, Pembroke Park, Fla. BB/TL, 6'2", 195 lbs. Deb: 4/23/44

YEAR	TM/L	W	L	PCT	G	GS	CG	SHO	SV	IP	H	H/G	HR	BB	BB/G	SO	SO/G	ERA	/A	OAVG	OOBP	PR	/A	PF	CPI	WAT	PB	PD	TPI
1944	Phi-N	1	1	.500	19	0	0	0	0	39	46	10.6	2	8	1.8	13	3.0	4.62	80	.297	.321	-4	-4	103	89	0.2	-1	-0	-0.4

■ **TEX COVINGTON** Covington, William Wilkes b: 3/19/1887, Henryville, Tenn. d: 12/10/31, Denison, Tex. BL/TR, 6'1", 175 lbs. Deb: 4/25/11

YEAR	TM/L	W	L	PCT	G	GS	CG	SHO	SV	IP	H	H/G	HR	BB	BB/G	SO	SO/G	ERA	/A	OAVG	OOBP	PR	/A	PF	CPI	WAT	PB	PD	TPI
1911	Det-A	7	1	.875	17	6	5	0	0	84	94	10.1	2	33	3.5	29	3.1	4.07	88	.297	.381	-7	-5	107	109	2.9	-1	-1	-0.5
1912	Det-A	3	4	.429	14	9	2	1	0	63	58	8.3	0	30	4.3	19	2.7	4.14	77	.253	.347	-6	-7	96	81	-0.1	0	-0	-0.6
Total	2	10	5	.667	31	15	7	1	0	147	152	9.3	2	63	3.9	48	2.9	4.10	83	.278	.367	-12	-11	102	97	2.8	-1	-2	-1.1

■ **JOE COWLEY** Cowley, Joseph Alan b: 8/15/58, Lexington, Ky. BR/TR, 6'5", 210 lbs. Deb: 4/13/82

YEAR	TM/L	W	L	PCT	G	GS	CG	SHO	SV	IP	H	H/G	HR	BB	BB/G	SO	SO/G	ERA	/A	OAVG	OOBP	PR	/A	PF	CPI	WAT	PB	PD	TPI
1982	Atl-N	1	2	.333	17	8	0	0	0	52	53	9.2	6	16	2.8	27	4.7	4.50	85	.265	.317	-5	-4	107	89	-0.5	-0	0	-0.3
1984	NY-A	9	2	.818	16	11	3	1	0	83	75	8.1	12	31	3.4	71	7.7	3.58	104	.234	.303	4	1	93	99	3.4	0	1	0.2
1985	NY-A	12	6	.667	30	26	1	0	0	160	132	7.4	29	85	4.8	97	5.5	3.94	99	.224	.326	4	-1	94	109	1.6	0	-1	0.0
1986	Chi-A	11	11	.500	27	27	4	0	0	162	133	7.4	20	83	4.6	132	7.3	3.89	109	.223	.316	5	6	101	94	1.3	0	-1	0.6
1987	Phi-N	0	4	.000	5	4	0	0	0	12	21	15.8	2	17	12.8	5	3.8	15.00	28	.389	.548	-15	-14	105	78	-1.9	1	-0	-1.1
Total	5	33	25	.569	95	76	8	1	0	469	414	7.9	69	232	4.5	332	6.4	4.20	95	.235	.326	-7	-11	98	99	3.9	0	-1	-0.6

■ **DANNY COX** Cox, Danny Bradford b: 9/21/59, Northampton, England BR/TR, 6'4", 235 lbs. Deb: 8/06/83

YEAR	TM/L	W	L	PCT	G	GS	CG	SHO	SV	IP	H	H/G	HR	BB	BB/G	SO	SO/G	ERA	/A	OAVG	OOBP	PR	/A	PF	CPI	WAT	PB	PD	TPI
1983	StL-N	3	6	.333	12	12	0	0	0	83	92	10.0	6	23	2.5	36	3.9	3.25	110	.286	.327	4	3	98	125	-1.4	-2	1	0.2
1984	StL-N	9	11	.450	29	27	1	1	0	156	171	9.9	9	54	3.1	70	4.0	4.04	88	.289	.347	-8	-9	99	110	-1.4	-0	1	-0.7
1985	StL-N	18	9	.667	35	35	10	4	0	241	226	8.4	19	64	2.4	131	4.9	2.88	117	.251	.296	19	13	93	113	1.8	1	-1	1.3
1986	StL-N	12	13	.480	32	32	8	0	0	220	189	7.7	14	60	2.5	108	4.4	2.90	132	.234	.285	20	23	103	95	-0.2	-3	-5	1.6
1987	StL-N	11	9	.550	31	31	2	0	0	199	224	10.1	17	71	3.2	101	4.6	3.89	102	.290	.345	4	2	97	120	-0.6	-1	-1	0.0
1988	StL-N	3	8	.273	13	13	0	0	0	86	89	9.3	6	25	2.6	47	4.9	3.98	91	.272	.319	-5	-3	105	98	-2.3	-2	0	-0.4
Total	6	56	56	.500	152	150	21	5	0	985	991	9.1	71	297	2.7	493	4.5	3.40	108	.266	.317	35	29	99	110	-4.1	-7	-4	2.0

■ **ERNIE COX** Cox, Ernest Thompson b: 2/19/1894, Birmingham, Ala. d: 4/29/74, Birmingham, Ala. BL/TR, 6'1", 180 lbs. Deb: 5/05/22

YEAR	TM/L	W	L	PCT	G	GS	CG	SHO	SV	IP	H	H/G	HR	BB	BB/G	SO	SO/G	ERA	/A	OAVG	OOBP	PR	/A	PF	CPI	WAT	PB	PD	TPI
1922	Chi-A	0	0	—	1	0	0	0	0	1	1	9.0	0	2	18.0	0	0.0	18.00	23	.250	.500	-2	-2	101	39	0.0	0	0	0.0

■ **GEORGE COX** Cox, George Melvin b: 11/15/04, Sherman, Tex. BR/TR, 6'1", 170 lbs. Deb: 4/12/28

YEAR	TM/L	W	L	PCT	G	GS	CG	SHO	SV	IP	H	H/G	HR	BB	BB/G	SO	SO/G	ERA	/A	OAVG	OOBP	PR	/A	PF	CPI	WAT	PB	PD	TPI
1928	Chi-A	1	2	.333	26	2	0	0	0	89	110	11.1	6	39	3.9	22	2.2	5.26	77	.313	.375	-12	-12	100	103	-0.3	-2	1	-1.1

■ **GLENN COX** Cox, Glenn Melvin b: 2/3/31, Montebello, Cal. BR/TR, 6'2", 210 lbs. Deb: 9/20/55

YEAR	TM/L	W	L	PCT	G	GS	CG	SHO	SV	IP	H	H/G	HR	BB	BB/G	SO	SO/G	ERA	/A	OAVG	OOBP	PR	/A	PF	CPI	WAT	PB	PD	TPI
1955	KC-A	0	2	.000	2	2	0	0	0	2	11	49.5	0	1	4.5	2	9.0	36.00	12	.611	.632	-7	-7	106	66	-0.9	-0	0	-0.5
1956	KC-A	0	2	.000	3	3	1	0	0	23	15	5.9	2	22	8.6	6	2.3	4.30	101	.203	.366	-0	0	105	101	-0.9	-1	-1	-0.1
1957	KC-A	1	0	1.000	10	0	0	0	0	14	18	11.6	1	9	5.8	8	5.1	5.14	75	.321	.409	-2	-2	102	118	0.5	0	0	-0.1
1958	KC-A	0	0	—	2	0	0	0	0	4	6	13.5	1	3	6.8	1	2.3	9.00	45	.400	.474	-2	-2	107	110	0.0	0	-0	-0.1
Total	4	1	4	.200	17	5	1	0	0	43	50	10.5	4	35	7.3	17	3.6	6.49	64	.307	.415	-12	-11	104	106	-1.3	-1	-1	-0.8

■ **CASEY COX** Cox, Joseph Casey b: 7/3/41, Long Beach, Cal. BR/TR, 6'5", 200 lbs. Deb: 4/15/66

YEAR	TM/L	W	L	PCT	G	GS	CG	SHO	SV	IP	H	H/G	HR	BB	BB/G	SO	SO/G	ERA	/A	OAVG	OOBP	PR	/A	PF	CPI	WAT	PB	PD	TPI
1966	Was-A	4	5	.444	66	0	0	0	7	113	104	8.3	6	35	2.8	46	3.7	3.50	94	.250	.304	-1	-2	96	95	0.0	-1	0	-0.2
1967	Was-A	7	4	.636	54	0	0	0	1	73	67	8.3	2	21	2.6	32	3.9	2.96	113	.250	.306	2	3	104	105	1.8	-0	0	0.3
1968	Was-A	0	1	.000	4	0	0	0	0	8	7	7.9	0	0	0.0	4	4.5	2.25	124	.250	.241	1	0	94	86	-0.4	0	-0	0.0
1969	Was-A	12	7	.632	52	13	4	0	0	172	161	8.4	15	64	3.3	73	3.8	2.77	126	.251	.314	16	14	96	**129**	2.2	-2	-1	1.1
1970	Was-A	8	12	.400	37	30	1	0	1	192	211	9.9	27	44	2.1	68	3.2	4.45	81	.285	.320	-16	-18	97	101	-0.7	-2	-2	-2.1
1971	Was-A	5	7	.417	54	11	0	0	7	124	131	9.5	9	40	2.9	43	3.1	3.99	82	.273	.328	-7	-10	94	99	0.2	-1	-1	-1.2
1972	Tex-A	3	5	.375	35	4	0	0	4	65	73	10.1	7	26	3.6	27	3.7	4.43	67	.277	.338	-10	-11	97	99	0.2	1	0	-1.0
	NY-A	0	1	.000	5	1	0	0	0	12	13	9.8	0	3	2.3	4	3.0	4.50	63	.289	.346	-2	-2	92	87	-0.4	0	-0	-0.2

YEAR	TM/L	W	L	PCT	G	GS	CG	SHO	SV	IP	H	H/G	HR	BB	BB/G	SO	SO/G	ERA	/A	OAVG	OOBP	PR	/A	PF	CPI	WAT	PB	PD	TPI
	Yr	3	6	.333	40	5	0	0	4	77	86	10.1	7	29	3.4	31	3.6	4.44	66	.276	.336	-12	-13	96	87	-0.2	1	-0	-1.2
1973	NY-A	0	0	—	1	0	0	0	0	3	5	15.0	0	1	3.0	0	0.0	6.00	64	.357	.444	-1	-1	100	127	0.0	0	0	0.0
Total	8	39	42	.481	308	59	5	0	20	762	772	9.1	66	234	2.8	297	3.5	3.70	91	.266	.318	-17	-27	97	106	2.9	-6	-3	-3.3
■ **LES COX**	Cox, Leslie Warren b: 8/14/05, Junction, Tex. d: 10/14/34, San Angelo, Tex. BR/TR, 6', 164 lbs. Deb: 9/11/26																												
1926	Chi-A	0	1	.000	2	0	0	0	0	5	6	10.8	2	5	9.0	3	5.4	5.40	67	.261	.393	-1	-1	90	137	-0.4	0	0	0.0
■ **RED COX**	Cox, Plateau Rex b: 2/16/1895, Laurel Springs, N.C. d: 10/15/84, Roanoke, Va. BL/TR, 6'2", 190 lbs. Deb: 4/17/20																												
1920	Det-A	0	0	—	3	0	0	0	0	5	9	16.2	0	3	5.4	1	1.8	5.40	75	.375	.444	-1	-1	106	132	0.0	-0	0	0.0
■ **TERRY COX**	Cox, Terry Lee b: 3/30/49, Odessa, Tex. BR/TR, 6'5", 215 lbs. Deb: 9/07/70																												
1970	Cal-A	0	0	—	3	0	0	0	0	2	4	18.0	0	0	0.0	3	13.5	4.50	76	.400	.400	-0	-0	92	145	0.0	0	0	0.0
■ **BILL COX**	Cox, William Donald b: 6/23/13, Ashmore, Ill. BR/TR, 6'1", 185 lbs. Deb: 6/06/36																												
1936	StL-N	0	0	—	2	0	0	0	0	3	4	12.0	0	1	3.0	1	3.0	6.00	63	.333	.333	-1	-1	95	86	0.0	0	-0	0.0
1937	Chi-A	1	0	1.000	3	2	1	1	0	13	9	6.2	0	5	3.5	8	5.5	0.69	679	.200	.280	6	6	102	282	0.5	0	-0	0.6
1938	Chi-A	0	2	.000	7	1	0	0	0	12	11	8.3	0	13	9.8	5	3.8	6.75	70	.244	.414	-3	-3	98	73	-0.9	-0	0	-0.2
	StL-A	1	4	.200	22	7	1	0	0	63	81	11.6	8	35	5.0	16	2.3	7.00	71	.315	.392	-15	-14	103	91	-1.0	-1	0	-1.3
	Yr	1	6	.143	29	8	1	0	0	75	92	11.0	8	48	5.8	21	2.5	6.96	70	.305	.395	-18	-17	102	91	-1.9	-0	0	-1.5
1939	StL-A	0	2	.000	4	2	1	0	0	9	10	10.0	0	8	8.0	8	8.0	10.00	48	.256	.383	-5	-5	105	44	-0.9	-0	1	-0.3
1940	StL-A	0	1	.000	12	0	0	0	0	17	23	12.2	3	12	6.4	7	3.7	7.41	64	.333	.417	-6	-5	108	104	-0.4	-0	0	-0.4
Total	5	2	9	.182	50	12	3	1	0	117	138	10.6	11	74	5.7	45	3.5	6.54	74	.296	.385	-24	-22	103	109	-2.7	-2	1	-1.6
■ **BILL COYLE**	Coyle, William Claude b: Pittsburgh, Pa. TR , Deb: 7/07/1893																												
1893	Bos-N	0	1	.000	2	1	0	0	0	8	14	15.8	1	3	3.4	2	2.3	9.00	52	.400	.447	-4	-4	101	90	-0.4	-1	0	-0.2
■ **CHARLIE COZART**	Cozart, Charles Rhubin b: 10/17/19, Lenoir, N.C. BR/TL, 6', 190 lbs. Deb: 4/17/45																												
1945	Bos-N	1	0	1.000	5	0	0	0	0	8	10	11.3	2	15	16.9	4	4.5	10.13	42	.303	.510	-6	-5	113	104	0.5	-0	1	-0.3
■ **ROY CRABB**	Crabb, James Roy b: 8/23/1890, Monticello, Iowa d: 3/30/40, Lewiston, Mont. BR/TR, 5'11", 160 lbs. Deb: 8/10/12																												
1912	Chi-A	0	1	.000	2	1	0	0	0	9	6	6.0	0	4	4.0	3	3.0	1.00	332	.214	.313	2	2	99	247	-0.4	-0	0	0.3
	Phi-A	2	4	.333	7	7	3	0	0	43	48	10.0	0	17	3.6	12	2.5	3.77	86	.287	.367	-2	-2	97	109	-1.2	-3	0	-0.1
	Yr	2	5	.286	9	8	3	0	0	52	54	9.3	0	21	3.6	15	2.6	3.29	99	.277	.359	0	-0	98	109	-1.6	-0	0	0.2
■ **GEORGE CRABLE**	Crable, George E. b: 1885, Nebraska BL/TL, 6'1", 190 lbs. Deb: 8/03/10																												
1910	Bro-N	0	0	—	2	1	1	0	0	7	5	6.4	0	5	6.4	3	3.9	5.14	58	.217	.400	-2	-2	98	74	0.0	0	0	-0.1
■ **WALT CRADDOCK**	Craddock, Walter Anderson b: 3/25/32, Pax, W.Va. d: 7/6/80, Parma Heights, O. BR/TL, 5'11.5", 176 lbs. Deb: 9/03/55																												
1955	KC-A	0	2	.000	4	2	0	0	0	15	18	10.8	3	10	6.0	9	5.4	7.80	54	.300	.384	-6	-6	106	83	-0.9	-1	-0	-0.5
1956	KC-A	0	2	.000	2	2	0	0	0	9	9	9.0	1	10	10.0	8	8.0	7.00	62	.265	.422	-3	-3	105	88	-0.9	-0	0	-0.2
1958	KC-A	0	3	.000	23	1	0	0	0	37	41	10.0	4	20	4.9	22	5.4	5.84	69	.289	.369	-9	-7	107	90	-1.4	-0	0	-0.6
Total	3	0	7	.000	29	5	0	0	0	61	68	10.0	8	40	5.9	39	5.8	6.49	64	.288	.381	-18	-16	106	88	-3.2	-1	0	-1.3
■ **MOLLY CRAFT**	Craft, Maurice Montague b: 11/28/1895, Portsmouth, Va. d: 10/25/78, Los Angeles, Cal. BR/TR, 6'2", 165 lbs. Deb: 8/08/16																												
1916	Was-A	0	1	.000	2	1	1	0	0	11	12	9.8	0	6	4.9	9	7.4	3.27	87	.316	.409	-1	-1	100	148	-0.4	-0	0	0.0
1917	Was-A	0	0	—	8	0	0	0	1	14	17	10.9	0	8	5.1	2	1.3	3.86	64	.315	.403	-2	-2	93	126	0.0	0	0	-0.1
1918	Was-A	0	0	—	3	0	0	0	0	7	5	6.4	0	1	1.3	5	6.4	1.29	222	.208	.240	1	1	103	80	0.0	-0	0	0.1
1919	Was-A	0	3	.000	16	2	0	0	1	49	59	10.8	2	18	3.3	17	3.1	3.86	83	.309	.374	-3	-4	99	118	-1.4	-2	0	-0.5
Total	4	0	4	.000	29	3	1	0	2	81	93	10.3	2	33	3.7	33	3.7	3.56	84	.303	.374	-5	-5	98	120	-1.8	-2	1	-0.5
■ **HOWARD CRAGHEAD**	Craghead, Howard Oliver "Judge" b: 5/25/08, Selma, Cal. d: 7/15/62, San Zieloe, Cal. BR/TR, 6'2", 200 lbs. Deb: 4/30/31																												
1931	Cle-A	0	0	—	4	0	0	0	0	6	8	12.0	0	2	3.0	2	3.0	6.00	77	.320	.370	-1	-1	106	84	0.0	0	0	0.0
1933	Cle-A	0	0	—	11	0	0	0	0	17	19	10.1	1	10	5.3	2	1.1	6.35	71	.292	.380	-4	-4	105	87	0.0	-0	0	-0.3
Total	2	0	0	—	15	0	0	0	0	23	27	10.6	1	12	4.7	4	1.6	6.26	72	.300	.377	-5	-4	105	86	0.0	-0	0	-0.3
■ **GEORGE CRAIG**	Craig, George Mc Carthy "Lefty" b: 11/15/1887, Philadelphia, Pa. d: 4/23/11, Indianapolis, Ind. TL , Deb: 7/12/07																												
1907	Phi-A	0	0	—	2	0	0	0	0	2	2	9.0	0	3	13.5	0	0.0	9.00	29	.285	.499	-1	-1	104	70	0.0	-0	-0	-0.1
■ **PETE CRAIG**	Craig, Peter Joel b: 7/10/40, Lasalle, Ont., Can. BL/TR, 6'5", 220 lbs. Deb: 9/06/64																												
1964	Was-A	0	0	—	2	1	0	0	0	2	8	36.0	1	4	18.0	0	0.0	40.50	9	.667	.750	-8	-8	103	69	0.0	0	0	-0.6
1965	Was-A	0	3	.000	3	3	0	0	0	14	18	11.6	1	8	5.1	2	1.3	8.36	42	.321	.388	-8	-8	102	71	-1.4	1	1	-0.5
1966	Was-A	0	0	—	1	0	0	0	0	2	2	9.0	0	1	4.5	1	4.5	4.50	74	.250	.300	-0	-0	96	72	0.0	0	-0	0.0
Total	3	0	3	.000	6	4	0	0	0	18	28	14.0	2	13	6.5	3	1.5	11.50	31	.368	.441	-16	-16	102	71	-1.4	1	0	-1.1
■ **ROGER CRAIG**	Craig, Roger Lee b: 2/17/30, Durham, N.C. BR/TR, 6'4", 185 lbs. Deb: 7/17/55 MC																												
1955	Bro-N	5	3	.625	21	10	3	0	2	91	81	8.0	8	43	4.3	48	4.7	2.77	147	.238	.322	13	13	101	126	0.0	-2	-1	1.0
1956	Bro-N	12	11	.522	35	32	8	2	1	199	169	7.6	25	87	3.9	109	4.9	3.71	102	.231	.310	1	2	100	94	-1.7	-5	-2	-0.5
1957	Bro-N	6	9	.400	32	13	1	0	0	111	102	8.3	18	47	3.8	69	5.6	4.62	96	.249	.325	-9	-2	114	93	-2.1	-1	1	-0.1
1958	LA-N	2	1	.667	9	2	1	0	0	32	30	8.4	3	12	3.4	16	4.5	4.50	93	.242	.309	-2	-1	106	71	0.6	-1	-1	-0.2
1959	LA-N	11	5	.688	29	17	7	**4**	0	153	122	7.2	13	45	2.6	76	4.5	2.06	194	.217	.275	32	33	101	120	2.4	-4	-0	3.0
1960	LA-N	8	3	.727	21	15	6	1	0	116	99	7.7	8	43	3.3	69	5.4	3.26	131	.230	.303	7	13	114	93	2.4	-3	-0	1.2
1961	LA-N	5	6	.455	40	14	2	0	2	113	130	10.4	22	52	4.1	63	5.0	6.13	67	.288	.363	-26	-26	102	93	-1.1	0	-1	-2.5
1962	NY-N	10	24	.294	42	33	13	0	3	233	261	10.1	35	70	2.7	118	4.6	4.52	95	.288	.339	-15	-6	108	108	1.3	-6	3	-0.7
1963	NY-N	5	22	.185	46	31	14	0	2	236	249	9.5	28	58	2.2	108	4.1	3.78	90	.267	.309	-13	-10	104	103	-6.1	-2	3	-0.9
1964	StL-N	7	9	.438	39	19	3	0	5	166	180	9.8	16	35	1.9	84	4.6	3.25	121	.276	.310	5	13	111	**122**	-2.0	2	2	1.8
1965	Cin-N	1	4	.200	40	0	0	0	3	64	74	10.4	6	25	3.5	30	4.2	3.66	99	.289	.349	-1	-0	102	133	-1.5	-0	0	0.0
1966	Phi-N	2	1	.667	14	0	0	0	1	23	31	12.1	4	5	2.0	13	5.1	5.48	66	.326	.350	-5	-5	100	106	0.4	-0	1	-0.4
Total	12	74	98	.430	368	186	58	7	19	1537	1528	8.9	186	522	3.1	803	4.7	3.82	104	.259	.319	-13	23	106	106	-7.4	-23	5	1.7
■ **GERALD CRAM**	Cram, Gerald Allen b: 12/9/47, Los Angeles, Cal. BR/TR, 6', 180 lbs. Deb: 9/03/69																												
1969	KC-A	0	1	.000	5	2	0	0	0	17	15	7.9	0	6	3.2	10	5.3	3.18	119	.231	.296	1	1	104	70	-0.4	-0	-0	0.1
1974	NY-N	0	1	.000	10	0	0	0	0	22	22	9.0	1	4	1.6	8	3.3	1.64	223	.275	.310	5	5	100	204	-0.4	0	0	0.6
1975	NY-N	0	1	.000	4	0	0	0	0	5	7	12.6	2	2	3.6	2	3.6	5.40	64	.333	.391	-1	-1	95	153	-0.4	0	0	0.0
1976	KC-A	0	0	—	4	0	0	0	0	4	8	18.0	0	1	2.3	2	4.5	6.75	51	.421	.429	-1	-1	99	116	0.0	0	0	0.0
Total	4	0	3	.000	23	2	0	0	0	48	52	9.8	3	13	2.4	22	4.1	3.00	122	.281	.327	3	3	101	144	-1.2	-0	0	0.7
■ **DOC CRAMER**	Cramer, Roger Maxwell "Flit" b: 7/22/05, Beach Haven, N.J. BL/TR, 6'2", 185 lbs. Deb: 9/18/29 C																												
1938	Bos-A	0	0	—	1	0	0	0	0	4	3	6.8	0	3	6.8	1	2.3	4.50	107	.214	.353	0	0	100	75	0.0	0	0	0.0
■ **BILL CRAMER**	Cramer, William Wendell b: 5/21/1891, Bedford, Ind. d: 9/11/66, Fort Wayne, Ind. BR/TR, 6', 175 lbs. Deb: 6/25/12																												
1912	Cin-N	0	0	—	1	0	0	0	0	2	6	27.0	0	0	0.0	2	9.0	0.00	—	.400	.400	1	1	93	0	0.0	-0	-0	0.0
■ **DOC CRANDALL**	Crandall, James Otis b: 10/8/1887, Wadena, Ind. d: 8/17/51, Bell, Cal. BR/TR, 5'10.5", 180 lbs. Deb: 4/24/08																												
1908	NY-N	12	12	.500	32	24	13	0	0	215	198	8.3	3	59	2.5	77	3.2	2.93	80	.276	.339	-14	-14	100	93	-2.8	5	-1	-1.1
1909	NY-N	6	4	.600	30	7	4	0	6	122	117	8.6	5	33	2.4	55	4.1	2.88	93	.252	.305	-4	-3	103	97	0.0	2	2	0.2
1910	NY-N	17	4	.810	42	18	13	2	5	208	194	8.4	10	43	1.9	73	3.2	2.55	110	.246	.289	11	6	92	97	6.0	10	-1	1.6
1911	NY-N	15	5	.750	41	15	9	2	5	199	199	9.0	11	51	2.3	94	4.3	2.62	128	.256	.307	17	16	99	116	3.2	5	1	2.6
1912	NY-N	13	7	.650	37	10	7	1	2	162	181	10.1	7	35	1.9	60	3.3	3.61	94	.278	.317	-4	-4	99	88	-0.4	6	-0	0.4
1913	NY-N	2	4	.333	24	0	1	0	0	55	61	10.0	0	13	2.1	28	4.6	3.11	103	.293	.323	1	0	100	115	-1.3	2	1	-1.5
	NY-N	2	0	1.000	11	0	1	0	0	43	41	8.6	0	11	2.3	14	2.9	2.51	127	.248	.287	3	3	100	93	1.0	3	0	-0.8
	Yr	4	4	.500	35	0	2	0	0	98	102	9.4	0	24	2.2	42	3.9	2.85	112	.273	.305	4	4	100	93	-0.3	2	1	-2.3
1914	StL-F	13	9	.591	27	21	18	1	0	196	194	8.9	8	52	2.4	84	3.9	3.54	98	.259	.318	-7	-1	108	90	3.7	8	0	0.0
1915	StL-F	21	15	.583	51	33	22	4	1	313	307	8.8	5	77	2.2	117	3.4	2.59	120	.263	.314	15	18	102	117	1.0	15	3	**4.1**

YEAR	TM/L	W	L	PCT	G	GS	CG	SHO	SV	IP	H	H/G	HR	BB	BB/G	SO	SO/G	ERA	/A	OAVG	OOBP	PR	/A	PF	CPI	WAT	PB	PD	TPI
1916	StL-A	0	0	—	2	0	0	0	0	1	7	63.0	0	1	9.0	0	0.0	36.00	7	.636	.692	-4	-4	94	96	0.0	-0	-0	-0.3
1918	Bos-N	1	2	.333	5	3	3	0	0	34	39	10.3	1	4	1.1	4	1.1	2.38	110	.307	.324	1	1	95	160	-0.2	1	0	0.1
Total	10	102	62	.622	302	131	91	10	19	1548	1538	8.9	50	379	2.2	606	3.5	2.92	104	.264	.313	17	18	100	103	10.2	58	5	5.3
■ **ED CRANE**	Crane, Edward Nicholas "Cannon-Ball" b: 5/1862, Boston, Mass. d: 9/19/1896, Rochester, N.Y. BR/TR, 5'10.5", 204 lbs. Deb: 4/17/1884																												
1884	Bos-U	0	2	.000	4	2	1	0	0	18	17	8.5	1	6	3.0	13	6.5	4.00	73	.254	.316	-2	-2	98	87	-0.9	1	0	-0.1
1886	Was-N	1	7	.125	10	8	7	1	0	70	91	11.7	5	53	6.8	39	5.0	7.20	46	.328	.436	-30	-30	100	89	-1.8	-1	0	-2.3
1888	NY-N	5	6	.455	12	11	11	1	1	93	70	6.8	3	40	3.9	58	5.6	2.42	104	.221	.309	4	1	89	99	-1.6	2	0	0.2
1889	NY-N	14	10	.583	29	25	23	0	0	230	221	8.6	10	136	5.3	130	5.1	3.68	111	.268	.371	9	10	101	109	-1.6	3	0	1.2
1890	NY-P	16	19	.457	43	35	28	0	0	330	323	8.8	12	210	5.7	117	3.2	4.64	98	.268	.376	-15	-3	107	83	-4.2	8	-1	0.4
1891	CM-a	14	14	.500	32	31	25	1	0	250	216	7.8	3	139	5.0	122	4.4	**2.45**	**171**	.247	.350	35	48	113	**122**	1.0	-7	0	4.0
	Cin-N	4	8	.333	15	13	11	1	0	117	134	10.3	3	64	4.9	51	3.9	4.08	77	.302	.389	-9	-12	93	106	-1.1	-3	0	-1.2
1892	NY-N	16	24	.400	47	43	35	2	1	364	350	8.7	10	189	4.7	174	4.3	3.81	85	.265	.358	-21	-23	98	93	-3.8	4	0	-1.7
1893	NY-N	2	4	.333	10	7	4	0	0	68	84	11.1	2	41	5.4	11	1.5	5.96	81	.320	.412	-10	-9	103	91	-1.0	4	0	-0.2
	Bro-N	0	2	.000	2	2	1	0	0	10	19	17.1	2	9	8.1	5	4.5	13.50	32	.420	.516	-10	-10	91	80	-0.9	0	0	-0.6
	Yr	2	6	.250	12	9	5	0	0	78	103	11.9	4	50	5.8	16	1.8	6.92	68	.334	.427	-19	-19	101	80	-1.9	4	0	-0.8
Total	8	72	96	.429	204	177	146	6	2	1550	1525	8.9	51	887	5.2	720	4.2	3.99	95	.270	.370	-48	-34	102	99	-15.9	12	-1	-0.3
■ **LARRY CRAWFORD**	Crawford, Charles Lowrie b: 4/27/14, Swissvale, Pa. BL/TL, 6'1", 165 lbs. Deb: 7/21/37																												
1937	Phi-N	0	0	—	6	0	0	0	0	6	12	18.0	2	1	1.5	2	3.0	15.00	29	.387	.406	-7	-7	111	63	0.0	0	-0	-0.6
■ **JIM CRAWFORD**	Crawford, James Frederick "Catfish" b: 9/29/50, Chicago, Ill. BL/TL, 6'3", 200 lbs. Deb: 4/06/73																												
1973	Hou-N	2	4	.333	48	0	0	0	6	70	69	8.9	7	33	4.2	56	7.2	4.50	77	.256	.331	-6	-8	95	90	-1.0	1	1	-0.6
1975	Hou-N	3	5	.375	44	2	0	0	4	87	92	9.5	0	37	3.8	37	3.8	3.62	95	.280	.347	0	-2	95	105	-0.1	2	0	0.0
1976	Det-A	1	8	.111	32	5	1	0	2	109	115	9.5	4	43	3.6	68	5.6	4.54	81	.275	.331	-12	-10	105	85	-3.4	0	5	-0.5
1977	Det-A	7	8	.467	37	7	0	0	1	126	156	11.1	13	50	3.6	91	6.5	4.79	89	.310	.361	-10	-7	105	112	0.1	0	1	-0.6
1978	Det-A	2	3	.400	20	0	0	0	0	39	45	10.4	3	19	4.4	24	5.5	4.38	92	.292	.367	-3	-1	107	113	-0.5	0	-0	-0.1
Total	5	15	28	.349	181	14	1	0	13	431	477	10.0	27	182	3.8	276	5.8	4.41	86	.285	.346	-31	-29	101	100	-4.9	3	6	-1.8
■ **STEVE CRAWFORD**	Crawford, Steven Ray b: 4/29/58, Pryor, Okla. BR/TR, 6'5", 225 lbs. Deb: 9/02/80																												
1980	Bos-A	2	0	1.000	6	4	2	0	0	32	41	11.5	3	8	2.3	10	2.8	3.66	113	.306	.345	1	2	102	128	1.0	0	-0	0.1
1981	Bos-A	0	5	.000	14	11	0	0	0	58	69	10.7	10	18	2.8	29	4.5	4.97	78	.301	.350	-8	-7	106	112	-2.4	0	0	-0.6
1982	Bos-A	1	0	1.000	5	0	0	0	0	9	14	14.0	0	0	0.0	2	2.0	2.00	224	.341	.341	2	2	110	223	0.5	0	0	0.2
1984	Bos-A	5	0	1.000	35	0	0	0	1	62	69	10.0	6	21	3.0	21	3.0	3.34	132	.286	.340	5	7	110	136	2.5	0	-0	0.7
1985	Bos-A	6	5	.545	44	1	0	0	12	91	103	10.2	5	28	2.8	58	5.7	3.76	112	.289	.332	4	5	102	113	0.5	0	1	0.5
1986	Bos-A	0	2	.000	40	0	0	0	4	57	69	10.9	5	19	3.0	32	5.1	3.95	105	.308	.355	2	1	99	129	-0.9	0	0	0.1
1987	Bos-A	5	4	.556	29	0	0	0	0	73	91	11.2	13	32	3.9	43	5.3	5.30	83	.314	.386	-7	-7	99	120	0.7	0	0	-0.5
Total	7	19	16	.543	173	16	2	0	17	382	456	10.7	42	126	3.0	195	4.6	4.15	102	.301	.351	-2	3	103	124	1.9	0	1	0.5
■ **JACK CREEL**	Creel, Jack Dalton "Tex" b: 4/23/16, Kyle, Tex. BR/TR, 6', 165 lbs. Deb: 4/22/45																												
1945	StL-N	5	4	.556	26	8	2	0	2	87	78	8.1	5	45	4.7	34	3.5	4.14	89	.245	.345	-3	-4	97	95	-0.4	-2	0	-0.5
■ **KEITH CREEL**	Creel, Steven Keith b: 2/4/59, Dallas, Tex. BR/TR, 6'2", 180 lbs. Deb: 5/25/82																												
1982	KC-A	1	4	.200	9	6	0	0	0	42	43	9.2	8	25	5.4	13	2.8	5.36	76	.267	.358	-6	-6	100	101	-1.5	0	0	-0.5
1983	KC-A	2	5	.286	25	10	1	0	0	89	116	11.7	17	35	3.5	31	3.1	6.37	65	.320	.379	-23	-22	102	101	-1.4	0	-1	-2.1
1985	Cle-A	2	5	.286	15	8	0	0	0	62	73	10.6	7	23	3.3	31	4.5	4.79	83	.296	.354	-4	-6	95	107	-0.7	0	-1	-0.6
1987	Tex-A	0	0	—	6	0	0	0	0	10	12	10.8	2	5	4.5	5	4.5	4.50	103	.293	.370	-0	0	104	132	0.0	0	0	0.0
Total	4	5	14	.263	55	24	1	0	0	203	244	10.8	34	88	3.9	80	3.5	5.59	73	.300	.366	-33	-33	100	105	-3.6	0	-2	-3.2
■ **BOB CREMINS**	Cremins, Robert Anthony "Lefty" or "Crooked Arm" b: 2/15/06, Pelham Manor, N.Y. BL/TL, 5'11", 178 lbs. Deb: 8/17/27																												
1927	Bos-A	0	0	—	4	0	0	0	0	5	5	9.0	0	3	5.4	0	0.0	5.40	76	.250	.333	-1	-1	99	61	0.0	0	0	0.0
■ **WALKER CRESS**	Cress, Walker James "Foots" b: 3/6/17, Ben Hur, Va. BR/TR, 6'5", 205 lbs. Deb: 4/27/48																												
1948	Cin-N	0	1	.000	30	2	1	0	0	60	60	9.0	2	42	6.3	33	5.0	4.50	93	.271	.387	-4	-2	106	107	-0.4	2	-1	0.0
1949	Cin-N	0	0	—	3	0	0	0	0	2	2	9.0	0	3	13.5	0	0.0	0.00	—	.286	.500	1	1	98	0	0.0	0	-0	0.1
Total	2	0	1	.000	33	2	1	0	0	62	62	9.0	2	45	6.5	33	4.8	4.35	96	.272	.391	-3	-1	106	104	-0.4	2	-1	0.1
■ **TIM CREWS**	Crews, Stanley Timothy b: 4/3/61, Tampa, Fla. BR/TR, 6' ", 180 lbs. Deb: 7/27/87																												
1987	LA-N	1	1	.500	20	0	0	0	3	29	30	9.3	2	8	2.5	20	6.2	2.48	152	.268	.323	5	4	92	154	0.1	-0	0	0.4
1988	LA-N	4	0	1.000	42	0	0	0	0	72	77	9.6	3	16	2.0	45	5.6	3.13	116	.278	.309	3	4	105	116	2.0	0	-1	0.3
Total	2	5	1	.833	62	0	0	0	3	101	107	9.5	5	24	2.1	65	5.8	2.94	125	.275	.313	8	8	101	127	2.1	-0	-1	0.7
■ **JERRY CRIDER**	Crider, Jerry Stephen b: 9/2/41, Sioux Falls, S.D. BR/TR, 6'2", 200 lbs. Deb: 5/21/69																												
1969	Min-A	1	0	1.000	21	1	0	0	1	29	31	9.6	3	15	4.7	16	5.0	4.66	78	.284	.369	-3	-3	100	111	0.5	2	0	0.0
1970	Chi-A	4	7	.364	32	8	0	0	4	91	101	10.0	13	34	3.4	40	4.0	4.45	90	.288	.348	-7	-4	108	112	0.2	-1	-2	-0.7
Total	2	5	7	.417	53	9	0	0	5	120	132	9.9	16	49	3.7	56	4.2	4.50	87	.287	.353	-11	-8	106	112	0.7	0	-2	-0.7
■ **CHUCK CRIM**	Crim, Charles Robert b: 7/23/61, Van Nuys, Cal. BR/TR, 6' ", 175 lbs. Deb: 4/08/87																												
1987	Mil-A	6	8	.429	53	5	0	0	12	130	133	9.2	15	39	2.7	56	3.9	3.67	124	.266	.319	12	13	102	112	-1.7	0	-0	1.2
1988	Mil-A	7	6	.538	**70**	0	0	0	9	105	95	8.1	11	28	2.4	58	5.0	2.91	140	.247	.294	12	14	103	121	0.0	0	0	1.4
Total	2	13	14	.481	123	5	0	0	21	235	228	8.7	26	67	2.6	114	4.4	3.33	130	.258	.308	24	27	102	116	-1.7	0	0	2.6
■ **JACK CRIMIAN**	Crimian, John Melvin b: 2/17/26, Philadelphia, Pa. BR/TR, 5'10", 180 lbs. Deb: 7/03/51																												
1951	StL-N	1	0	1.000	11	0	0	0	1	17	24	12.7	3	8	4.2	5	2.6	9.00	44	.338	.400	-10	-9	101	78	0.5	0	-0	-0.8
1952	StL-N	0	0	—	5	0	0	0	0	8	15	16.9	4	4	4.5	4	4.5	10.13	36	.417	.463	-6	-6	97	121	0.0	0	0	-0.5
1956	KC-A	4	8	.333	54	7	0	0	3	129	129	9.0	19	49	3.4	59	4.1	5.51	79	.265	.329	-19	-17	105	82	0.0	1	-0	-1.5
1957	Det-A	0	1	.000	4	0	0	0	0	6	9	13.5	1	4	6.0	1	1.5	12.00	34	.375	.448	-5	-5	107	70	-0.4	0	0	-0.4
Total	4	5	9	.357	74	7	0	0	4	160	177	10.0	27	65	3.7	69	3.9	6.36	67	.287	.350	-40	-37	104	83	0.1	1	-1	-3.2
■ **DODE CRISS**	Criss, Dode b: 3/12/1885, Sherman, Miss. d: 9/8/55, Sherman, Miss. BL/TR, 6'2", 200 lbs. Deb: 4/20/08																												
1908	StL-A	0	1	.000	9	1	0	0	0	18	15	7.5	1	13	6.5	9	4.5	6.50	37	.250	.408	-8	-8	102	74	-0.4	1	-1	-0.8
1909	StL-A	1	5	.167	11	6	3	0	0	55	53	8.7	0	32	5.2	43	7.0	3.44	68	.262	.369	-6	-7	95	103	-1.7	5	-1	-0.6
1910	StL-A	2	1	.667	6	0	0	0	0	19	12	5.7	0	9	4.3	9	4.3	1.42	178	.176	.309	2	2	101	123	0.8	1	0	0.3
1911	StL-A	0	2	.000	4	2	0	0	0	18	24	12.0	0	10	5.0	9	4.5	8.50	39	.333	.429	-10	-10	100	67	-0.9	0	0	-0.8
Total	4	3	9	.250	30	9	3	0	0	110	104	8.5	1	64	5.2	70	5.7	4.42	58	.259	.375	-22	-23	98	96	-2.2	8	-1	-1.9
■ **BILL CRISTALL**	Cristall, William Arthur "Lefty" b: 9/12/1878, Odessa, Russia d: 1/28/39, Buffalo, N.Y. BL/TL, 5'7", 145 lbs. Deb: 9/03/01																												
1901	Cle-A	1	5	.167	6	6	5	1	0	48	54	10.1	1	30	5.6	12	2.3	4.88	73	.304	.405	-6	-7	97	96	-1.7	2	1	-0.4
■ **LEO CRISTANTE**	Cristante, Leo Dante b: 12/10/26, Detroit, Mich. d: 8/24/77, Dearborn, Mich. BR/TR, 6'1", 205 lbs. Deb: 4/21/51																												
1951	Phi-N	1	1	.500	10	1	0	0	0	22	28	11.5	3	9	3.7	6	2.5	4.91	78	.318	.380	-2	-3	97	123	0.0	-0	0	-0.2
1955	Det-A	0	1	.000	20	1	0	0	0	37	37	9.0	1	14	3.4	9	2.2	3.16	119	.261	.321	3	2	95	104	-0.4	-1	-1	0.0
Total	2	1	2	.333	30	2	0	0	0	59	65	9.9	4	23	3.5	15	2.3	3.81	99	.283	.344	1	-0	96	111	-0.4	-1	-1	-0.2
■ **MORRIE CRITCHLEY**	Critchley, Morris Arthur b: 3/26/1850, New London, Conn. d: 3/6/10, Pittsburgh, Pa. 6'1", 190 lbs. Deb: 5/08/1882																												
1882	Pit-a	1	0	1.000	1	1	1	1	0	9	7	7.0	0	1	1.0	3	3.0	0.00	—	.220	.243	3	3	97	0	0.5	-1	0	0.2
	StL-a	0	4	.000	4	4	4	0	0	34	43	11.4	3	7	1.9	2	0.5	4.24	66	.314	.347	-6	-5	104	111	-1.9	-0	0	-0.4
	Yr	1	4	.200	5	5	5	1	0	43	50	10.5	3	8	1.7	5	1.0	3.35	82	.296	.328	-3	-3	102	111	-1.4	-1	0	-0.2
■ **CLAUDE CROCKER**	Crocker, Claude Arthur b: 7/20/24, Caroleen, N.C. BR/TR, 6'2", 185 lbs. Deb: 8/01/44																												
1944	Bro-N	0	0	—	2	0	0	0	0	3	6	18.0	0	5	15.0	1	3.0	12.00	31	.400	.550	-3	-3	102	95	0.0	0	0	-0.1
1945	Bro-N	0	0	—	1	0	0	0	1	2	2	9.0	0	1	4.5	1	4.5	0.00	—	.286	.375	1	1	95	0	0.0	0	0	0.1
Total	2	0	0	—	3	0	0	0	1	5	8	14.4	0	6	10.8	2	3.6	7.20	51	.364	.500	-2	-2	99	57	0.0	0	0	0.0

YEAR TM/L	W	L	PCT	G	GS	CG	SHO	SV	IP	H	H/G	HR	BB	BB/G	SO	SO/G	ERA	/A	OAVG	OOBP	PR	/A	PF	CPI	WAT	PB	PD	TPI
■ **RAY CRONE**	Crone, Raymond Hayes b: 8/7/31, Memphis, Tenn. BR/TR, 6'2", 165 lbs. Deb: 4/13/54																											
1954 Mil-N	1	0	1.000	19	2	1	0	1	49	44	8.1	6	19	3.5	33	6.1	2.02	184	.247	.320	11	9	91	188	0.5	-0	-0	0.9
1955 Mil-N	10	9	.526	33	15	6	1	0	140	117	7.5	11	42	2.7	76	4.9	3.47	106	.227	.280	9	3	92	77	-0.4	-1	0	0.2
1956 Mil-N	11	10	.524	35	21	6	0	2	170	173	9.2	19	44	2.3	73	3.9	3.86	94	.263	.304	-2	-5	96	94	-1.4	0	-1	-0.4
1957 Mil-N	3	1	.750	11	5	2	0	0	42	54	11.6	8	15	3.2	15	3.2	4.50	76	.312	.365	-3	-5	88	132	0.7	1	1	-0.3
NY-N	4	8	.333	25	17	2	0	1	121	131	9.7	11	40	3.0	56	4.2	4.31	93	.272	.328	-6	-4	103	93	-1.5	-4	3	-0.4
Yr	7	9	.438	36	22	4	0	1	163	185	10.2	19	55	3.0	71	3.9	4.36	88	.282	.338	-9	-9	99	93	-0.8	1	3	-0.7
1958 SF-N	1	2	.333	14	1	0	0	0	24	35	13.1	5	13	4.9	7	2.6	6.75	58	.354	.414	-7	-8	100	115	-0.4	-0	-0	-0.7
Total 5	30	30	.500	137	61	17	1	4	546	554	9.1	60	173	2.9	260	4.3	3.87	96	.263	.316	2	-8	96	102	-2.5	-3	2	-0.7
■ **JACK CRONIN**	Cronin, John J. b: 5/26/1874, W.New Brighton, S.I., N.Y. d: 7/12/29, Middletown, N.Y. BR/TR, 6' ", 200 lbs. Deb: 8/24/1895																											
1895 Bro-N	0	0	—	2	0	0	0	2	5	10	18.0	0	3	5.4	1	1.8	10.80	41	.437	.502	-3	-4	94	83	0.0	1	0	-0.1
1898 Pit-N	2	2	.500	4	4	2	1	0	28	35	11.3	0	8	2.6	9	2.9	3.54	100	.329	.376	0	0	98	117	0.1	-0	0	0.0
1899 Cin-N	2	2	.500	5	5	5	0	0	41	56	12.3	2	16	3.5	9	2.0	5.49	74	.351	.410	-7	-7	105	98	-0.1	-1	0	-0.5
1901 Det-A	13	15	.464	30	28	21	1	0	220	261	10.7	6	42	1.7	62	2.5	3.89	103	.316	.349	-5	3	109	98	-2.5	1	-3	0.0
1902 Det-A	0	0	—	4	0	0	0	0	17	26	13.8	1	8	4.2	5	2.6	9.53	38	.378	.443	-11	-11	101	69	0.0	-1	0	-0.8
Bal-A	3	5	.375	10	8	8	0	0	76	66	7.8	1	24	2.8	20	2.4	2.61	143	.257	.320	8	9	104	97	0.1	-2	2	1.2
Yr	3	5	.375	14	8	8	0	0	93	92	8.9	2	32	3.1	25	2.4	3.87	96	.282	.346	-3	-2	104	97	0.1	-1	3	0.4
NY-N	5	6	.455	13	12	11	0	0	114	105	8.3	3	18	1.4	52	4.1	2.45	118	.267	.299	4	6	104	93	0.9	-1	0	0.6
1903 NY-N	6	4	.600	20	11	8	0	1	116	130	10.1	5	37	2.9	50	3.9	3.80	89	.312	.377	-7	-5	103	106	0.0	-0	0	-0.4
1904 Bro-N	12	23	.343	40	34	33	4	0	307	284	8.3	10	79	2.3	110	3.2	2.70	99	.272	.330	1	-1	98	106	-1.3	-2	-1	-0.1
Total 7	43	57	.430	128	102	88	6	3	924	973	9.5	28	235	2.3	318	3.1	3.40	97	.295	.345	-21	-11	103	101	-2.8	-6	-1	-0.1
■ **GEORGE CROSBY**	Crosby, George W. b: 1860, Iowa d: 1/9/13, San Francisco, Cal. Deb: 5/22/1884																											
1884 Chi-N	1	2	.333	3	3	3	0	0	28	27	8.7	3	12	3.9	11	3.5	3.54	88	.262	.339	-2	-1	105	109	-0.5	1	0	0.0
■ **KEN CROSBY**	Crosby, Kenneth Stewart b: 12/15/47, New Denver, B.C., Canada BR/TR, 6'2", 179 lbs. Deb: 8/05/75																											
1975 Chi-N	1	0	1.000	9	0	0	0	0	8	10	11.3	0	7	7.9	6	6.8	3.38	113	.294	.405	0	0	105	157	0.5	0	0	0.1
1976 Chi-N	0	0	—	7	1	0	0	0	12	20	15.0	3	8	6.0	5	3.8	12.00	32	.377	.438	-11	-11	111	78	0.0	0	0	-0.9
Total 2	1	0	1.000	16	1	0	0	0	20	30	13.5	3	15	6.7	11	4.9	8.55	45	.345	.425	-11	-10	109	109	0.5	1	0	-0.8
■ **LEM CROSS**	Cross, George Lewis b: 1/9/1872, Sanbornton, N.H. d: 10/9/30, Manchester, N.H. 5'9", 155 lbs. Deb: 8/06/1893																											
1893 Cin-N	0	2	.000	3	3	2	0	0	21	24	10.3	3	9	3.9	7	3.0	5.57	86	.303	.374	-2	-2	102	95	-0.9	1	0	0.0
1894 Cin-N	3	4	.429	8	7	3	0	0	53	94	16.0	8	21	3.6	11	1.9	8.49	64	.410	.459	-19	-18	102	99	0.0	-1	0	-1.2
Total 2	3	6	.333	11	10	5	0	0	74	118	14.4	11	30	3.6	18	2.2	7.66	68	.382	.437	-21	-20	102	98	-0.9	0	0	-1.2
■ **DOUG CROTHERS**	Crothers, Douglas b: 11/16/1859, Natchez, Miss. d: 3/29/07, St.Louis, Mo. BR/TR, Deb: 8/07/1884																											
1884 KC-U	1	2	.333	3	3	3	0	0	25	26	9.4	0	6	2.2	11	4.0	1.80	153	.273	.316	3	3	92	182	0.3	-1	0	0.1
1885 NY-a	7	11	.389	18	18	18	1	0	154	192	11.2	4	49	2.9	40	2.3	5.08	55	.318	.369	-31	-39	86	95	-0.4	1	0	-3.1
Total 2	8	13	.381	21	21	21	1	0	179	218	11.0	4	55	2.8	51	2.6	4.63	60	.312	.362	-28	-36	87	107	-0.1	-0	0	-3.0
■ **BILL CROUCH**	Crouch, William Elmer b: 8/20/10, Wilmington, Del. d: 12/26/80, Howell, Mich. BB/TR, 6'1", 180 lbs. Deb: 5/09/39																											
1939 Bro-N	4	0	1.000	6	3	3	0	0	38	37	8.8	3	14	3.3	10	2.4	2.61	160	.255	.315	6	7	106	139	2.0	-1	-1	0.6
1941 Phi-N	2	3	.400	20	5	1	0	1	59	65	9.9	4	17	2.6	26	4.0	4.42	84	.286	.329	-5	-5	103	96	0.4	-0	1	-0.2
StL-N	1	2	.333	18	4	0	0	6	45	45	9.0	2	14	2.8	15	3.0	3.00	130	.271	.317	3	4	107	125	-0.6	-2	-1	0.2
Yr	3	5	.375	38	9	1	0	7	104	110	9.5	6	31	2.7	41	3.5	3.81	100	.280	.324	-2	-0	105	125	-0.2	-0	1	0.0
1945 StL-N	1	0	1.000	6	0	0	0	0	13	12	8.3	1	7	4.8	4	2.8	3.46	107	.255	.351	0	0	97	129	0.5	-0	0	0.0
Total 3	8	5	.615	50	12	4	0	7	155	159	9.2	10	52	3.0	55	3.2	3.48	111	.272	.324	4	7	104	117	2.3	-3	0	0.6
■ **BILL CROUCH**	Crouch, William Henry "Skip" b: 12/3/1886, Marshallton, Del. d: 12/22/45, Highland Park, Mich. BL/TL, 6'1", 210 lbs. Deb: 7/12/10																											
1910 StL-A	0	0	—	1	1	1	0	0	8	6	6.8	0	7	7.9	2	2.3	3.38	75	.231	.394	-1	-1	101	111	0.0	-0	-0	0.0
■ **ZACH CROUCH**	Crouch, Zachary Quinn b: 10/26/65, Folsom, Cal. BL/TL, 6'3", 190 lbs. Deb: 6/04/88																											
1988 Bos-A	0	0	—	3	0	0	0	0	1	4	36.0	0	2	18.0	0	0.0	9.00	48	.571	.667	-1	-1	108	246	0.0	0	0	0.0
■ **GENERAL CROWDER**	Crowder, Alvin Floyd b: 1/11/1899, Winston-Salem, N.C d: 4/3/72, Winston-Salem, N.C. BL/TR, 5'10", 170 lbs. Deb: 7/24/26																											
1926 Was-A	7	4	.636	19	12	6	0	1	100	97	8.7	3	60	5.4	26	2.3	3.96	99	.261	.353	1	-1	97	101	1.2	1	1	0.1
1927 Was-A	4	7	.364	15	11	4	2	0	67	58	7.8	3	42	5.6	22	3.0	4.57	87	.232	.339	-3	-4	96	75	-1.9	-1	-1	-0.5
StL-A	3	5	.375	21	8	2	1	3	74	71	8.6	3	42	5.1	30	3.6	4.99	91	.260	.355	-7	-4	109	80	0.0	0	-1	-0.3
Yr	7	12	.368	36	19	6	3	3	141	129	8.2	6	84	5.4	52	3.3	4.79	89	.246	.344	-10	-8	103	80	-1.9	-1	-2	-0.8
1928 StL-A	21	5	**.808**	41	31	19	1	2	244	238	8.8	11	91	3.4	99	3.7	3.69	113	.258	.319	10	13	103	93	**8.2**	-2	-5	0.6
1929 StL-A	17	15	.531	40	34	19	**4**	4	267	272	9.2	22	93	3.1	79	2.7	3.91	108	.271	.324	10	9	100	102	0.5	-3	-2	0.4
1930 StL-A	3	7	.300	13	10	5	1	1	77	85	9.9	11	27	3.2	42	4.9	4.68	110	.283	.331	-0	4	110	109	-1.4	-2	1	0.3
Was-A	15	9	.625	27	25	20	0	1	202	191	8.5	6	69	3.1	65	2.9	3.61	127	.249	.308	23	21	98	90	0.5	-2	-4	1.4
Yr	18	16	.529	40	35	25	1	2	279	276	8.9	17	96	3.1	107	3.5	3.90	121	.259	.314	23	25	101	90	-0.9	-2	-3	1.7
1931 Was-A	18	11	.621	44	26	13	1	2	234	255	9.8	13	72	2.8	85	3.3	3.88	111	.275	.325	13	11	98	105	1.0	-1	-3	0.6
1932 Was-A	**26**	13	.667	50	39	21	3	1	**327**	319	8.8	17	77	2.1	103	2.8	3.33	131	.252	.292	42	38	98	96	3.9	1	-2	3.4
1933 Was-A	**24**	15	.615	**52**	35	17	0	4	299	311	9.4	14	81	2.4	110	3.3	3.97	100	.267	.312	10	1	93	93	-1.3	1	-3	-0.1
1934 Was-A	4	10	.286	29	13	4	0	3	101	142	12.7	9	38	3.4	39	3.5	6.77	68	.326	.373	-26	-24	102	87	-2.4	0	-1	-2.1
Det-A	5	1	.833	9	9	3	1	0	67	81	10.9	3	20	2.7	30	4.0	4.16	101	.295	.341	2	0	94	105	1.6	-2	-1	-0.2
Yr	9	11	.450	38	22	7	1	3	168	223	11.9	12	58	3.1	69	3.7	5.73	78	.314	.361	-23	-24	99	105	-0.8	0	-2	-2.3
1935 Det-A	16	10	.615	33	32	16	2	0	241	269	10.0	16	67	2.5	59	2.2	4.26	97	.285	.331	5	-4	93	100	0.0	-2	-3	-0.8
1936 Det-A	4	3	.571	9	7	1	0	0	44	64	13.1	5	21	4.3	10	2.0	8.39	57	.342	.403	-16	-18	95	84	0.3	-0	-0	-1.4
Total 11	167	115	.592	402	292	150	16	22	2344	2453	9.4	136	800	3.1	799	3.1	4.12	104	.270	.325	64	43	98	96	10.2	-11	-24	1.4
■ **CAP CROWELL**	Crowell, Minot Joy b: 9/5/1892, Roxbury, Mass. d: 9/30/62, Central Falls, R.I. BR/TR, 6'1", 178 lbs. Deb: 6/23/15																											
1915 Phi-A	2	6	.250	10	8	4	0	0	54	56	9.3	1	47	7.8	15	2.5	5.50	55	.292	.443	-15	-15	103	102	-0.4	-0	-0	-1.4
1916 Phi-A	0	5	.000	9	6	1	0	0	40	43	9.7	0	34	7.6	15	3.4	4.95	60	.289	.427	-9	-9	105	104	-2.4	-2	-1	-1.0
Total 2	2	11	.154	19	14	5	0	0	94	99	9.5	1	81	7.8	30	2.9	5.27	57	.290	.436	-25	-24	104	103	-2.8	-2	-1	-2.4
■ **BILLY CROWELL**	Crowell, William Theodore b: 11/6/1865, Cincinnati, Ohio d: 7/24/35, Ft.Worth, Tex. BR/TR, 5'8.5", 160 lbs. Deb: 4/20/1887																											
1887 Cle-a	14	31	.311	45	45	45	1	0	389	541	12.5	9	138	3.2	72	1.7	4.88	90	.344	.397	-25	-20	103	114	0.6	-13	-5	-2.8
1888 Cle-a	5	13	.278	18	18	16	0	0	151	212	12.6	8	61	3.6	61	3.6	5.84	53	.346	.405	-47	-46	100	101	-2.6	-5	0	-4.1
Lou-a	0	1	.000	1	1	1	0	0	9	12	12.0	1	6	6.0	5	5.0	6.00	48	.334	.429	-3	-3	93	112	-0.4	-0	0	-0.2
Yr	5	14	.263	19	19	17	0	0	160	224	12.6	9	67	3.8	66	3.7	5.85	52	.345	.406	-50	-50	100	112	-3.0	-5	0	-4.3
Total 2	19	45	.297	64	64	62	1	0	549	765	12.5	18	205	3.4	138	2.3	5.16	78	.344	.400	-75	-70	102	110	-2.4	-18	-5	-7.1
■ **WOODY CROWSON**	Crowson, Thomas Woodrow b: 9/9/18, Fuquay Sprgs., N.C d: 8/14/47, Mayodan, N.C. BR/TR, 6'2", 185 lbs. Deb: 4/17/45																											
1945 Phi-A	0	0	—	1	0	0	0	0	3	2	6.0	0	3	9.0	2	6.0	6.00	54	.200	.357	-1	-1	96	60	0.0	-0	0	0.0
■ **CAL CRUM**	Crum, Calvin N. b: 7/27/1890, Cooks Mills, Ill. d: 12/7/45, Tulsa, Okla. BR/TR, 6'1", 175 lbs. Deb: 4/17/17																											
1917 Bos-N	0	0	—	1	0	0	0	0	1	1	9.0	0	1	9.0	0	0.0	0.00	—	.250	.400	0	0	97	0	0.0	0	0	0.1
1918 Bos-N	0	1	.000	1	1	0	0	0	2	6	27.0	0	3	13.5	0	0.0	18.00	15	.600	.667	-3	-3	95	106	-0.4	-0	0	-0.2
Total 2	0	1	.000	2	1	0	0	0	3	7	21.0	0	4	12.0	0	0.0	12.00	22	.500	.600	-3	-3	96	70	-0.4	-0	1	-0.1
■ **ROY CRUMPLER**	Crumpler, Roy Maxton b: 7/8/1896, Clinton, N.C. BL/TL, 6'1", 195 lbs. Deb: 9/16/20																											
1920 Det-A	1	0	1.000	2	2	1	0	0	13	17	11.8	2	11	7.6	2	1.4	5.54	73	.315	.439	-3	-2	106	128	0.5	1	-0	-0.1
1925 Phi-N	0	0	—	3	1	0	0	0	5	8	14.4	0	2	3.6	1	1.8	7.20	70	.381	.435	-2	-1	118	94	0.0	-0	0	0.0
Total 2	1	0	1.000	5	3	1	0	0	18	25	12.5	2	13	6.5	3	1.5	6.00	72	.333	.438	-4	-3	109	118	0.5	1	-0	-0.1
■ **DICK CRUTCHER**	Crutcher, Richard Louis b: 11/25/1889, Frankfort, Ky. d: 6/19/52, Frankfort, Ky. BR/TR, 5'9", 148 lbs. Deb: 4/14/14																											
1914 Bos-N	5	6	.455	33	15	5	1	0	159	169	9.6	4	66	3.7	48	2.7	3.45	82	.293	.361	-12	-11	102	120	-1.4	-1	1	-1.1

YEAR	TM/L	W	L	PCT	G	GS	CG	SHO	SV	IP	H	H/G	HR	BB	BB/G	SO	SO/G	ERA	/A	OAVG	OOBP	PR	/A	PF	CPI	WAT	PB	PD	TPI
1915	Bos-N	2	2	.500	14	4	1	0	2	44	50	10.2	1	16	3.3	17	3.5	4.30	62	.309	.368	-8	-8	97	106	-0.1	0	0	-0.7
Total	2	7	8	.467	47	19	6	1	2	203	219	9.7	5	82	3.6	65	2.9	3.64	77	.296	.362	-19	-19	101	117	-1.5	-0	1	-1.8
■ TODD CRUZ	Cruz, Todd Ruben b: 11/23/55, Highland Park, Mich BR/TR, 6', 175 lbs. Deb: 9/04/78																												
1984	Bal-A	0	0	—	1	0	0	0	0	1	0	0.0	0	0	0.0	0	0.0	0.00	—	.000	.000	0	0	94	0	0.0	0	0	0.0
■ VICTOR CRUZ	Cruz, Victor Manuel (born b: 12/24/57, Rancho Viejo La Vega, D.R. BR/TR, 5'9", 174 lbs. Deb: 6/24/78																												
1978	Tor-A	7	3	.700	32	0	0	0	9	47	28	5.4	0	35	6.7	51	9.8	1.72	224	.179	.322	11	11	102	141	2.7	0	-0	1.1
1979	Cle-A	3	9	.250	61	0	0	0	10	79	70	8.0	10	44	5.0	63	7.2	4.22	107	.244	.335	0	2	106	102	-3.0	0	-2	0.0
1980	Cle-A	6	7	.462	55	0	0	0	12	86	71	7.4	10	27	2.8	88	9.2	3.45	121	.229	.285	6	7	103	93	-0.4	0	-1	0.5
1981	Pit-N	1	1	.500	22	0	0	0	1	34	33	8.7	6	15	4.0	28	7.4	2.65	127	.264	.340	3	3	96	186	0.1	-0	0	0.2
1983	Tex-A	1	3	.250	17	0	0	0	5	25	16	5.8	2	10	3.6	18	6.5	1.44	286	.184	.262	7	7	101	154	-0.9	0	-0	0.7
Total	5	18	23	.439	187	0	0	0	37	271	218	7.2	28	131	4.4	248	8.2	3.09	133	.226	.311	27	30	103	121	-1.5	-0	-3	2.5
■ COOKIE CUCCURULLO	Cuccurullo, Arthur Joseph b: 2/8/18, Asbury Park, N.J. d: 1/23/83, W.Orange, N.J. BL/TL, 5'10", 168 lbs. Deb: 10/03/43																												
1943	Pit-N	0	1	.000	1	1	0	0	0	7	10	12.9	0	3	3.9	3	3.9	6.43	54	.357	.382	-2	-2	103	93	-0.4	1	0	0.0
1944	Pit-N	2	1	.667	32	4	0	0	4	106	110	9.3	5	44	3.7	31	2.6	4.08	92	.270	.339	-5	-4	104	99	0.3	5	1	0.2
1945	Pit-N	1	3	.250	29	4	0	0	1	57	68	10.7	2	34	5.4	17	2.7	5.21	75	.305	.392	-9	-8	102	103	-1.0	-0	0	-0.7
Total	3	3	5	.375	62	9	0	0	5	170	188	10.0	7	81	4.3	51	2.7	4.55	83	.286	.359	-17	-15	103	100	-1.1	5	1	-0.5
■ JIM CUDWORTH	Cudworth, James Alaric "Cuddy" b: 8/22/1858, Fairhaven, Mass. d: 12/21/43, Middleboro, Mass. BR/TR, 6', 165 lbs. Deb: 7/27/1884																												
1884	KC-U	0	0	—	2	1	1	0	0	17	19	10.1	1	3	1.6	6	3.2	4.24	65	.288	.319	-2	-3	92	93	0.0	-0	0	-0.1
■ CHARLIE CUELLAR	Cuellar, Jesus Patracis b: 9/24/17, Ybor City, Fla. BR/TR, 5'11", 183 lbs. Deb: 7/02/50																												
1950	Chi-A	0	0	—	2	0	0	0	0	1	6	54.0	0	3	27.0	1	9.0	45.00	10	.600	.692	-4	-4	99	72	0.0	0	0	-0.3
■ MIKE CUELLAR	Cuellar, Miguel Angel (Santana) b: 5/8/37, Las Villas, Cuba BL/TL, 6', 165 lbs. Deb: 4/18/59																												
1959	Cin-N	0	0	—	2	0	0	0	0	4	7	15.8	1	4	9.0	5	11.3	15.75	26	.368	.458	-5	-5	103	64	0.0	-0	0	-0.4
1964	StL-N	5	5	.500	32	7	1	0	4	72	80	10.0	8	33	4.1	56	7.0	4.50	87	.288	.356	-8	-5	111	113	-0.6	-2	1	-0.5
1965	Hou-N	1	4	.200	25	4	0	0	2	56	55	8.8	3	21	3.4	46	7.4	3.54	91	.262	.324	0	-2	91	105	-1.2	-1	0	-0.2
1966	Hou-N	12	10	.545	38	28	11	1	2	227	193	7.7	10	52	2.1	175	6.9	2.22	160	.229	.268	35	34	99	102	2.3	-2	0	3.6
1967	Hou-N	16	11	.593	36	32	16	3	1	246	233	8.5	16	63	2.3	203	7.4	3.04	106	.248	.291	9	5	95	99	4.4	1	-0	0.6
1968	Hou-N	8	11	.421	28	24	11	2	1	171	152	8.0	8	45	2.4	133	7.0	2.74	110	.237	.283	5	5	100	95	-0.5	2	-0	0.8
1969	Bal-A	23	11	.676	39	39	18	5	0	291	213	6.6	18	79	2.4	182	5.6	2.38	153	.204	.258	**40**	**41**	100	82	0.2	-3	0	**4.2**
1970	Bal-A	**24**	8	**.750**	40	40	**21**	4	0	298	273	8.2	34	69	2.1	190	5.7	3.47	101	.242	.283	8	1	94	89	4.7	-3	-3	-0.6
1971	Bal-A	20	9	.690	38	38	21	4	0	292	250	7.7	30	78	2.4	124	3.8	3.08	113	.234	.282	13	13	100	96	2.4	-4	0	1.0
1972	Bal-A	18	12	.600	35	35	17	4	0	248	197	7.1	21	71	2.6	132	4.8	2.58	115	.220	.271	14	10	96	97	3.0	-1	0	1.0
1973	Bal-A	18	13	.581	38	38	17	2	0	267	265	8.9	29	84	2.8	140	4.7	3.27	123	.258	.310	16	22	105	112	-0.5	0	1	2.4
1974	Bal-A	22	10	**.688**	38	38	20	5	0	269	253	8.5	17	86	2.9	106	3.5	3.11	107	.252	.307	15	7	92	104	5.3	0	-2	0.5
1975	Bal-A	14	12	.538	36	36	17	5	0	256	229	8.1	17	84	3.0	105	3.7	3.66	92	.249	.304	4	-8	89	90	-0.6	0	2	-0.5
1976	Bal-A	4	13	.235	26	19	2	1	1	107	129	10.9	8	50	4.2	32	2.7	4.96	69	.307	.369	-17	-18	97	106	-4.9	0	-0	-1.8
1977	Cal-A	0	1	.000	2	1	0	0	0	3	9	27.0	2	3	9.0	3	9.0	21.00	18	.500	.571	-6	-6	95	92	-0.4	0	0	-0.4
Total	15	185	130	.587	453	379	172	36	11	2807	2538	8.1	222	822	2.6	1632	5.2	3.14	110	.243	.293	123	94	97	97	13.6	-13	-1	9.7
■ BOBBY CUELLAR	Cuellar, Robert b: 8/20/52, Alice, Tex. BR/TR, 5'11", 188 lbs. Deb: 9/09/77																												
1977	Tex-A	0	0	—	4	0	0	0	0	7	4	5.1	1	2	2.6	3	3.9	1.29	328	.182	.250	2	2	104	193	0.0	0	-0	0.2
■ BERT CUETO	Cueto, Dagoberto (Concepcion) b: 8/14/37, San Luis, Pinar, Cuba BR/TR, 6'4", 170 lbs. Deb: 6/18/61																												
1961	Min-A	1	3	.250	7	5	0	0	0	21	27	11.6	7	10	4.3	5	2.1	7.29	59	.300	.373	-8	-7	107	98	-0.8	-0	0	-0.6
■ JACK CULLEN	Cullen, John Patrick b: 10/6/39, Newark, N.J. BR/TR, 5'11", 170 lbs. Deb: 9/09/62																												
1962	NY-A	0	0	—	2	0	0	0	1	3	2	6.0	0	2	6.0	2	6.0	0.00	—	.182	.308	1	1	92	0	0.0	0	0	0.1
1965	NY-A	3	4	.429	12	9	2	1	0	59	59	9.0	2	21	3.2	25	3.8	3.05	114	.262	.320	3	3	101	112	-0.3	-0	1	0.3
1966	NY-A	1	0	1.000	5	0	0	0	0	11	11	9.0	0	5	4.1	7	5.7	4.09	79	.256	.320	-1	-1	94	81	0.5	-0	-0	-0.1
Total	3	4	4	.500	19	9	2	1	1	73	72	8.9	2	28	3.5	34	4.2	3.08	112	.258	.319	3	3	100	103	0.2	-1	0	0.3
■ NICK CULLOP	Cullop, Henry Nicholas "Tomato Face" b: 10/16/1900, St.Louis, Mo. d: 12/8/78, Westerville, Ohio BR/TR, 6', 200 lbs. Deb: 4/14/26																												
1927	Cle-A	0	0	—	1	0	0	0	0	1	3	27.0	0	0	0.0	0	0.0	9.00	45	.600	.600	-1	-1	99	158	0.0	0	0	0.0
■ NICK CULLOP	Cullop, Norman Andrew b: 9/17/1887, Chilhowie, Va. d: 4/15/61, Tazewell, Va. BL/TL, 5'11.5", 172 lbs. Deb: 5/20/13																												
1913	Cle-A	3	7	.300	23	8	4	0	0	98	105	9.6	3	35	3.2	30	2.8	4.41	69	.291	.358	-16	-15	104	91	-2.3	-1	1	-1.4
1914	Cle-A	0	1	.000	1	0	0	0	0	3	4	12.0	0	1	3.0	3	9.0	3.00	97	.364	.417	-0	-0	106	183	-0.4	-0	0	0.0
	KC-F	14	19	.424	44	36	22	4	1	296	256	7.8	6	87	2.6	149	4.5	2.34	131	.215	.275	28	24	96	72	-0.8	-3	2	2.4
1915	KC-F	22	11	.667	44	36	22	3	2	302	278	8.3	8	67	2.0	111	3.3	2.44	120	.249	.297	20	16	97	110	5.7	1	9	2.9
1916	NY-A	13	6	.684	28	22	9	0	1	167	151	8.1	4	32	1.7	77	4.1	2.05	140	.243	.284	14	15	101	109	3.5	-3	-4	0.9
1917	NY-A	5	9	.357	30	18	5	2	1	146	161	9.9	2	31	1.9	27	1.7	3.33	86	.307	.348	-11	-8	107	113	-1.6	-1	-0	-0.8
1921	StL-A	0	2	.000	4	1	0	0	0	12	18	13.5	1	6	4.5	3	2.3	8.25	52	.340	.393	-5	-5	101	76	-0.9	-1	0	-0.4
Total	6	57	55	.509	174	121	62	9	5	1024	973	8.6	24	259	2.3	400	3.5	2.73	109	.251	.303	30	28	99	97	3.2	-9	8	3.6
■ BUD CULLOTON	Culloton, Bernard Aloysius b: 1897, Kingston, N.Y. d: 11/9/76, Kingston, N.Y. BR/TR, 5'11", 180 lbs. Deb: 4/16/25																												
1925	Pit-N	0	1	.000	9	1	0	0	0	21	19	8.1	1	1	0.4	3	1.3	2.57	164	.241	.247	4	4	99	77	-0.4	-0	-0	0.3
1926	Pit-N	0	0	—	4	0	0	0	0	4	3	6.8	0	6	13.5	1	2.3	6.75	63	.214	.429	-1	-1	111	77	0.0	0	0	0.0
Total	2	0	1	.000	13	1	0	0	0	25	22	7.9	1	7	2.5	4	1.4	3.24	130	.237	.284	3	3	101	77	-0.4	-0	-0	0.3
■ RAY CULP	Culp, Raymond Leonard b: 8/6/41, Elgin, Tex. BR/TR, 6', 200 lbs. Deb: 4/10/63																												
1963	Phi-N	14	11	.560	34	30	10	5	0	203	148	6.6	15	102	4.5	176	7.8	2.97	113	.206	.305	7	8	102	96	0.7	-0	-0	0.9
1964	Phi-N	8	7	.533	30	19	3	1	0	135	139	9.3	15	56	3.7	96	6.4	4.13	84	.263	.333	-9	-10	98	105	-0.4	-1	-1	-1.1
1965	Phi-N	14	10	.583	33	30	11	2	0	204	188	8.3	14	78	3.4	134	5.9	3.22	104	.243	.317	7	3	95	108	1.6	-2	-1	0.0
1966	Phi-N	7	4	.636	34	12	1	0	1	111	106	8.6	19	53	4.3	100	8.1	5.03	72	.246	.335	-18	-17	100	89	1.2	-2	-1	-1.9
1967	Chi-N	8	11	.421	30	22	4	1	0	153	138	8.1	22	59	3.5	111	6.5	3.88	87	.239	.307	-9	-8	100	97	-2.2	-1	-1	-1.0
1968	Bos-A	16	6	.727	35	30	11	6	0	216	166	6.9	18	82	3.4	190	7.9	2.92	103	.210	.289	1	2	101	93	5.0	-1	-1	0.0
1969	Bos-A	17	8	.680	32	32	9	2	0	227	195	7.7	25	79	3.1	172	6.8	3.81	100	.231	.297	-4	-0	105	85	4.3	1	-0	0.0
1970	Bos-A	17	14	.548	33	33	15	1	0	251	211	7.6	22	91	3.3	197	7.1	3.05	134	.224	.296	19	29	110	95	0.5	-4	-1	2.7
1971	Bos-A	14	16	.467	35	35	12	3	0	242	236	8.8	21	67	2.5	151	5.6	3.61	101	.253	.301	-4	1	105	92	-1.9	-2	-2	-0.1
1972	Bos-A	5	8	.385	16	16	4	1	0	105	104	8.9	8	53	4.5	52	4.5	4.46	72	.260	.343	-16	-14	105	91	-2.0	1	0	-1.4
1973	Bos-A	2	6	.250	10	9	0	0	0	50	46	8.3	9	32	5.8	32	5.8	4.50	89	.247	.366	-4	-3	105	114	-2.1	0	0	-0.2
Total	11	122	101	.547	322	268	80	22	1	1897	1677	8.0	188	752	3.6	1411	6.7	3.58	99	.235	.310	-29	-10	103	95	4.7	-11	-7	-2.1
■ BILL CULP	Culp, William Edward b: 6/11/1887, Bellaire, Ohio d: 9/3/69, Arnold, Pa. BB/TR, 6'1.5", 165 lbs. Deb: 9/08/10																												
1910	Phi-N	0	0	—	4	0	0	0	1	7	8	10.3	0	4	5.1	4	5.1	7.71	37	.333	.429	-4	-4	95	69	0.0	-0	1	-0.2
■ GEORGE CULVER	Culver, George Raymond b: 7/8/43, Salinas, Cal. BR/TR, 6'2", 185 lbs. Deb: 9/07/66																												
1966	Cle-A	0	2	.000	5	1	0	0	0	10	15	13.5	1	7	6.3	6	5.4	8.10	43	.357	.451	-5	-5	102	98	-0.9	-0	0	-0.4
1967	Cle-A	7	3	.700	53	1	0	0	3	75	71	8.5	2	31	3.7	41	4.9	3.96	83	.258	.335	-6	-6	101	95	2.3	0	1	-0.4
1968	Cin-N	11	16	.407	42	35	5	2	2	226	229	9.1	8	84	3.3	114	4.5	3.23	103	.264	.334	-6	2	111	113	-3.1	-1	2	0.4
1969	Cin-N	5	7	.417	32	13	0	0	4	101	117	10.4	8	52	4.6	58	5.2	4.28	83	.291	.379	-8	-8	99	121	-1.4	-2	2	-0.8
1970	StL-N	3	3	.500	11	7	2	0	0	57	64	10.1	6	24	3.8	23	3.6	4.58	94	.284	.353	-3	-2	106	106	0.2	0	2	0.0
	Hou-N	3	3	.500	32	0	0	0	3	45	44	8.8	1	21	4.2	31	6.2	3.20	119	.254	.340	4	3	94	115	0.1	0	-1	0.2
	Yr	6	6	.500	43	7	2	0	3	102	108	9.5	7	45	4.0	54	4.8	3.97	103	.270	.345	1	1	101	115	0.3	0	1	0.2
1971	Hou-N	5	8	.385	59	0	0	0	7	95	89	8.4	4	38	3.6	57	5.4	2.65	121	.257	.324	9	6	92	133	-1.4	-1	1	0.6
1972	Hou-N	6	2	.750	45	0	0	0	2	97	73	6.8	7	43	4.0	82	7.6	3.06	119	.212	.302	4	6	105	95	1.8	0	0	0.7
1973	LA-N	4	4	.500	28	0	0	0	2	42	45	9.6	4	21	4.5	23	4.9	3.00	121	.292	.362	3	3	99	171	-0.5	-0	2	0.4

YEAR	TM/L	W	L	PCT	G	GS	CG	SHO	SV	IP	H	H/G	HR	BB	BB/G	SO	SO/G	ERA	/A	OAVG	OOBP	PR	/A	PF	CPI	WAT	PB	PD	TPI
	Phi-N	3	1	.750	14	0	0	0	0	19	26	12.3	0	15	7.1	7	3.3	4.74	84	.342	.436	-2	-2	109	137	1.1	0	1	0.0
	Yr	7	5	.583	42	0	0	0	2	61	71	10.5	4	36	5.3	30	4.4	3.54	106	.305	.384	1	1	102	137	0.6	-0	2	0.4
1974	Phi-N	1	0	1.000	14	0	0	0	0	22	20	8.2	1	16	6.5	9	3.7	6.55	57	.267	.378	-7	-7	104	74	0.5	-0	-0	-0.7
Total	9	48	49	.495	335	57	7	2	23	789	793	9.0	42	352	4.0	451	5.1	3.62	97	.266	.344	-17	-8	103	114	-1.3	-4	8	0.0
■ **JOHN CUMBERLAND**	Cumberland, John Sheldon b: 5/10/47, Westbrook, Me. BR/TL, 6', 185 lbs. Deb: 9/27/68																												
1968	NY-A	0	0	—	1	0	0	0	0	2	3	13.5	1	1	4.5	1	4.5	9.00	33	.333	.400	-1	-1	101	105	0.0	0	0	0.0
1969	NY-A	0	0	—	2	0	0	0	0	4	3	6.8	0	4	9.0	0	0.0	4.50	77	.231	.389	-0	-0	96	98	0.0	0	0	0.0
1970	NY-A	3	4	.429	15	8	1	0	0	64	62	8.7	9	15	2.1	38	5.3	3.94	86	.252	.289	-2	-4	91	90	-0.8	-1	-1	-0.5
	SF-N	2	0	1.000	7	0	0	0	0	11	6	4.9	0	4	3.3	6	4.9	0.82	474	.158	.227	4	4	96	98	1.0	-0	0	0.4
1971	SF-N	9	6	.600	45	21	5	2	2	185	153	7.4	22	55	2.7	65	3.2	2.92	117	.223	.277	11	10	99	98	0.8	-2	-3	0.5
1972	SF-N	0	4	.000	9	6	0	0	0	25	38	13.7	6	7	2.5	8	2.9	8.64	40	.336	.363	-14	-14	100	80	-1.9	-0	-1	-1.4
	StL-N	1	1	.500	14	1	0	0	0	22	23	9.4	6	7	2.9	7	2.9	6.55	56	.291	.330	-8	-7	105	91	0.0	-1	-1	-0.8
	Yr	1	5	.167	23	7	0	0	0	47	61	11.7	12	14	2.7	15	2.9	7.66	46	.316	.349	-22	-22	102	91	-1.9	-0	-2	-2.2
1974	Cal-A	0	1	.000	17	0	0	0	0	22	24	9.8	2	10	4.1	12	4.9	3.68	91	.289	.362	-0	-1	93	129	-0.4	0	-0	0.0
Total	6	15	16	.484	110	36	6	2	2	335	312	8.4	46	103	2.8	137	3.7	3.81	90	.246	.297	-10	-14	97	97	-1.3	-5	-5	-1.8
■ **CANDY CUMMINGS**	Cummings, William Arthur b: 10/18/1848, Ware, Mass. d: 5/16/24, Toledo, Ohio BR/TR, 5'9", 120 lbs. Deb: 4/22/1872 H																												
1872	Mut-n	33	20	.623	55																								
1873	Bal-n	28	14	.667	42																								
1874	Phi-n	28	26	.519	54																								
1875	Har-n	35	12	.745	47																								
1876	Har-N	16	8	.667	24	24	24	5	0	216	215	9.0	0	14	0.6	26	1.1	1.67	142	.264	.276	15	17	103	96	-0.5	-8	-1	0.8
1877	Cin-N	5	14	.263	19	19	16	0	0	156	219	12.6	2	13	0.8	11	0.6	4.38	58	.340	.353	-27	-32	90	93	0.0	1	0	-2.6
Total	4 n	124	72	.633	198																								
Total	2	21	22	.488	43	43	40	5	0	372	434	10.5	2	27	0.7	37	0.9	2.81	88	.297	.310	-12	-14	98	95	-0.5	-7	-1	-1.8
■ **BRUCE CUNNINGHAM**	Cunningham, Bruce Lee b: 9/29/05, San Francisco, Cal. d: 3/8/84, Hayward, Cal. BR/TR, 5'10.5", 165 lbs. Deb: 5/07/29																												
1929	Bos-N	4	6	.400	17	8	4	0	1	92	100	9.8	7	32	3.1	22	2.2	4.50	102	.282	.333	2	1	97	97	0.3	-0	1	0.1
1930	Bos-N	5	6	.455	36	6	2	0	0	107	121	10.2	7	41	3.4	28	2.4	5.47	90	.289	.342	-6	-6	99	82	0.0	0	3	-0.2
1931	Bos-N	3	12	.200	33	16	6	1	1	137	157	10.3	7	54	3.5	32	2.1	4.47	88	.296	.353	-9	-8	102	104	-4.0	-4	4	-0.7
1932	Bos-N	1	0	1.000	18	3	0	0	0	47	50	9.6	1	19	3.6	21	4.0	3.45	105	.281	.358	2	1	93	125	0.5	2	1	0.3
Total	4	13	24	.351	104	33	12	1	2	383	428	10.1	22	146	3.4	103	2.4	4.63	94	.289	.346	-11	-13	99	99	-3.2	-2	9	-0.5
■ **BERT CUNNINGHAM**	Cunningham, Ellsworth Elmer b: 11/25/1865, Wilmington, Del. d: 5/14/52, Cragmere, Del. BR/TR, Deb: 9/15/1887																												
1887	Bro-a	0	2	.000	3	3	3	0	0	23	26	10.2	0	13	5.1	8	3.1	5.09	83	.299	.390	-2	-2	99	92	-0.9	-1	0	-0.1
1888	Bal-a	22	29	.431	51	51	50	0	0	453	412	8.2	9	157	3.1	186	3.7	3.40	88	.255	.321	-17	-20	98	89	1.0	-2	1	-1.9
1889	Bal-a	16	19	.457	39	33	29	0	1	279	306	9.9	11	141	4.5	140	4.5	4.87	79	.294	.378	-32	-32	99	90	-2.6	-2	0	-2.7
1890	Phi-P	3	9	.250	14	11	11	0	0	109	133	11.0	0	67	5.5	33	2.7	5.28	81	.313	.407	-13	-12	101	90	-3.2	-4	0	-1.2
	Buf-P	9	15	.375	25	25	24	2	0	211	251	10.7	8	134	5.7	78	3.3	5.84	70	.308	.405	-38	-41	97	84	2.0	1	0	-3.0
	Yr	12	24	.333	39	36	35	2	0	320	384	10.8	8	201	5.7	111	3.1	5.65	74	.310	.406	-50	-53	98	84	-1.2	-4	0	-4.2
1891	Bal-a	12	14	.462	30	25	21	0	0	238	241	9.1	8	138	5.2	59	2.2	4.01	93	.277	.376	-8	-7	100	99	-1.8	-1	0	-0.6
1895	Lou-N	11	16	.407	31	28	24	1	0	231	299	11.6	6	104	4.1	49	1.9	4.75	99	.335	.404	1	-1	99	109	3.1	6	0	0.4
1896	Lou-N	7	14	.333	27	20	17	0	1	189	242	11.5	6	74	3.5	37	1.8	5.10	87	.334	.396	-15	-14	102	96	0.8	3	0	-0.8
1897	Lou-N	14	13	.519	29	27	25	0	0	235	286	11.0	3	72	2.8	49	1.9	4.14	102	.323	.374	5	2	97	101	3.2	-0	0	0.1
1898	Lou-N	28	15	.651	44	42	41	0	0	362	387	9.6	8	65	1.6	34	0.8	3.16	111	.295	.329	18	14	98	100	**9.2**	3	-1	1.5
1899	Lou-N	17	17	.500	39	37	33	1	0	324	385	10.7	2	75	2.1	36	1.0	3.86	102	.320	.359	-0	3	103	97	0.3	2	6	1.2
1900	Chi-N	4	3	.571	8	7	7	0	0	64	84	11.8	0	21	3.0	7	1.0	4.36	80	.341	.393	-5	-6	94	106	0.7	-1	0	-0.6
1901	Chi-N	0	1	.000	1	1	1	0	0	9	11	11.0	0	3	3.0	2	2.0	5.00	68	.324	.379	-2	-2	103	84	-0.4	0	1	0.0
Total	12	143	167	.461	341	310	286	4	2	2727	3063	10.1	61	1064	3.5	718	2.4	4.23	91	.302	.368	-107	-119	99	95	11.4	2	7	-7.7
■ **GEORGE CUNNINGHAM**	Cunningham, George Harold b: 7/13/1894, Sturgeon Lake, Minn. d: 3/10/72, Chattanooga, Tenn. BR/TR, 5'11", 185 lbs. Deb: 4/14/16																												
1916	Det-A	7	10	.412	35	14	5	0	2	150	146	8.8	0	74	4.4	68	4.1	2.76	105	.269	.360	1	2	103	131	-2.4	5	1	1.0
1917	Det-A	2	7	.222	44	8	4	0	4	139	113	7.3	2	51	3.3	49	3.2	2.91	88	.227	.304	-4	-5	96	77	-2.5	1	0	-0.4
1918	Det-A	6	7	.462	27	14	10	0	1	140	131	8.4	0	38	2.4	39	2.5	3.15	87	.255	.301	-6	-6	99	80	0.3	3	1	-0.6
1919	Det-A	1	1	.500	17	0	0	0	1	48	54	10.1	0	15	2.8	11	2.1	4.88	61	.292	.361	-9	-10	92	78	0.0	3	0	-0.7
Total	4	16	25	.390	123	36	19	0	8	477	444	8.4	2	178	3.4	167	3.2	3.13	88	.255	.327	-17	-19	99	95	-4.6	11	2	-0.7
■ **MIKE CUNNINGHAM**	Cunningham, Mody b: 6/14/1882, Lancaster, S.C. d: 12/10/69, Lancaster, S.C. BR/TR, 5'10.5", 175 lbs. Deb: 8/31/06																												
1906	Phi-A	1	0	1.000	5	1	1	0	0	28	29	9.3	1	9	2.9	15	4.8	3.21	78	.293	.352	-2	-2	93	111	0.5	1	-0	-0.2
■ **NIG CUPPY**	Cuppy, George Joseph (born George Koppe) b: 7/3/1869, Logansport, Ind. d: 7/27/22, Elkhart, Ind. TR , 5'7", 160 lbs. Deb: 4/16/1892																												
1892	Cle-N	28	13	.683	47	42	38	1	1	376	333	8.0	9	121	2.9	103	2.5	2.51	132	.250	.312	32	33	101	103	4.2	1	4	3.8
1893	Cle-N	17	10	.630	31	30	24	0	0	244	316	11.7	6	75	2.8	39	1.4	4.50	107	.330	.379	5	8	103	108	2.3	1	-0	0.8
1894	Cle-N	24	15	.615	43	33	29	**3**	0	316	381	10.9	11	128	3.6	65	1.9	4.56	129	.321	.387	27	47	111	103	4.8	-1	2	4.1
1895	Cle-N	26	14	.650	47	40	36	1	2	353	384	9.8	9	95	2.4	91	2.3	3.54	128	.297	.345	49	39	95	103	0.3	10	5	4.4
1896	Cle-N	25	14	.641	46	40	35	1	1	358	388	9.8	8	75	1.9	86	2.2	3.12	151	.298	.337	50	63	108	107	1.2	6	4	6.8
1897	Cle-N	10	6	.625	19	17	13	1	0	139	150	9.7	3	26	1.7	23	1.5	3.17	149	.297	.332	18	24	110	101	1.8	-4	0	1.9
1898	Cle-N	9	8	.529	18	15	13	1	0	128	147	10.3	4	25	1.8	27	1.9	3.30	103	.310	.345	4	2	95	110	-0.1	-4	0	-0.1
1899	StL-N	11	8	.579	21	21	18	1	0	172	203	10.6	3	26	1.4	25	1.3	3.14	131	.318	.345	14	19	107	113	0.6	-3	0	1.6
1900	Bos-N	8	4	.667	17	13	9	0	1	105	107	9.2	8	24	2.1	23	2.0	3.09	144	.287	.330	7	16	120	112	2.3	1	0	1.7
1901	Bos-A	4	6	.400	13	11	9	0	0	93	111	10.7	1	14	1.4	22	2.1	4.16	83	.317	.343	-5	-7	94	87	-1.5	0	-2	-0.7
Total	10	162	98	.623	302	262	224	9	5	2284	2520	9.9	62	609	2.4	504	2.0	3.49	127	.300	.347	201	242	104	105	15.9	7	13	24.3
■ **SAMMY CURRAN**	Curran, Simon Francis b: 10/30/1874, Dorchester, Mass. d: 5/19/36, Dorchester, Mass. Deb: 8/01/02																												
1902	Bos-N	0	0	—	1	0	0	0	0	7	6	7.7	0	0	0.0	3	3.9	1.29	203	.253	.253	1	1	94	103	0.0	-0	-0	0.1
■ **LAFAYETTE CURRENCE**	Currence, Delancy Lafayette b: 12/3/51, Rock Hill, S.C. BB/TL, 5'11", 175 lbs. Deb: 7/24/75																												
1975	Mil-A	0	2	.000	8	1	0	0	0	19	25	11.8	5	14	6.6	7	3.3	7.58	51	.316	.415	-8	-8	101	101	-0.9	0	-0	-0.7
■ **CLARENCE CURRIE**	Currie, Clarence Ffranklin b: 12/30/1878, Glencoe, Ont., Can. d: 7/15/41, Little Chute, Wis BR/TR, Deb: 4/25/02																												
1902	Cin-N	3	4	.429	10	7	6	1	0	65	70	9.7	1	17	2.4	20	2.8	3.74	80	.298	.346	-7	-5	108	86	-0.4	-2	1	-0.4
	StL-N	7	5	.583	15	12	10	2	0	125	125	9.0	0	35	2.5	30	2.2	2.59	106	.283	.336	3	2	99	107	1.8	-0	2	0.4
	Yr	10	9	.526	25	19	16	3	0	190	195	9.2	1	52	2.5	50	2.4	2.98	95	.288	.339	-4	-3	102	107	1.4	-2	3	0.0
1903	StL-N	4	12	.250	22	16	13	1	1	148	155	9.4	7	60	3.6	52	3.2	4.01	83	.299	.383	-12	-11	102	99	-1.7	-3	4	-0.6
	Chi-N	1	2	.333	6	3	2	0	1	33	35	9.5	1	9	2.5	9	2.5	3.00	102	.304	.370	1	0	94	120	-0.6	2	1	0.1
	Yr	5	14	.263	28	19	15	1	2	181	190	9.4	8	69	3.4	61	3.0	3.83	86	.296	.366	-11	-11	100	120	-2.3	-3	5	-0.5
Total	2	15	23	.395	53	38	31	4	2	371	385	9.3	9	121	2.9	111	2.7	3.40	90	.294	.360	-16	-14	101	101	-0.9	-4	7	-0.5
■ **MURPHY CURRIE**	Currie, Murphy Archibald b: 8/31/1893, Fayetteville, N.C. d: 6/22/39, Asheboro, N.C. BR/TR, 5'11.5", 185 lbs. Deb: 8/31/16																												
1916	StL-N	0	0	—	6	0	0	0	0	14	7	4.5	1	9	5.8	8	5.1	1.93	136	.149	.271	1	1	100	91	0.0	-0	-1	0.0
■ **BILL CURRIE**	Currie, William Cleveland b: 11/29/28, Leary, Ga. BR/TR, 6', 175 lbs. Deb: 4/13/55																												
1955	Was-A	0	0	—	3	0	0	0	0	4	7	15.8	3	2	4.5	2	4.5	13.50	28	.350	.417	-4	-4	94	93	0.0	0	0	-0.3
■ **GEORGE CURRY**	Curry, George James "Soldier Boy" b: 12/21/1888, Bridgeport, Conn. d: 10/5/63, Stratford, Conn. BR/TR, 6', 185 lbs. Deb: 7/16/11																												
1911	StL-A	0	3	.000	3	3	0	0	0	16	19	10.7	0	24	13.5	2	1.1	7.31	46	.339	.538	-7	-7	100	111	-1.4	-1	-0	-0.5
■ **STEVE CURRY**	Curry, Stephen T. b: 9/13/65, Winter Park, Fla. BR/TR, 6'6", 217 lbs. Deb: 7/10/88																												
1988	Bos-A	0	1	.000	3	3	0	0	0	11	15	12.3	0	14	11.5	4	3.3	8.18	52	.357	.492	-5	-5	108	103	-0.4	0	0	-0.3

YEAR	TM/L	W	L	PCT	G	GS	CG	SHO	SV	IP	H	H/G	HR	BB	BB/G	SO	SO/G	ERA	/A	OAVG	OOBP	PR	/A	PF	CPI	WAT	PB	PD	TPI
■ **WES CURRY**	Curry, Wesley b: 4/1/1860, Wilmington, Del. d: 5/19/33, Philadelphia, Pa. Deb: 8/06/1884																												
1884	Ric-a	0	2	.000	2	2	2	0	0	16	15	8.4	1	3	1.7	1	0.6	5.06	65	.256	.292	-3	-3	102	66	-0.9	-0	0	-0.2
■ **CLIFF CURTIS**	Curtis, Clifton Garfield b: 7/3/1883, Delaware, Ohio d: 4/23/43, Newark, Ohio BR/TR, 6'2", 180 lbs. Deb: 09																												
1909	Bos-N	4	5	.444	10	9	8	2	0	83	53	5.7	1	30	3.3	22	2.4	1.41	187	.191	.275	11	11	102	111	1.0	-3	0	1.4
1910	Bos-N	6	24	.200	43	37	12	2	2	251	251	9.0	9	124	4.4	75	2.7	3.55	101	.277	.371	-14	1	118	116	-7.0	-5	6	0.3
1911	Bos-N	1	8	.111	12	9	5	0	1	77	79	9.2	4	34	4.0	23	2.7	4.44	84	.265	.344	-9	-6	109	85	-2.7	-0	1	-0.4
	Chi-N	1	2	.333	4	1	0	0	0	7	7	9.0	0	5	6.4	4	5.1	3.86	83	.241	.405	-0	-1	94	116	-0.6	0	0	0.0
	Phi-N	2	1	.667	8	5	3	1	0	45	45	9.0	0	15	3.0	13	2.6	2.60	141	.260	.323	4	5	108	114	0.5	0	-0	0.5
	Yr	4	11	.267	24	15	8	1	1	129	131	9.1	4	54	3.8	40	2.8	3.77	97	.259	.332	-5	-1	108	114	-2.8	0	0	0.1
1912	Phi-N	2	5	.286	10	8	2	0	0	50	55	9.9	3	17	3.1	20	3.6	3.24	106	.271	.339	1	1	101	111	-1.4	-2	1	0.0
	Bro-N	4	7	.364	19	9	3	0	1	80	72	8.1	4	37	4.2	22	2.5	3.94	84	.238	.332	-5	-6	97	77	-0.1	1	-0	-0.4
	Yr	6	12	.333	29	17	5	0	1	130	127	8.8	7	54	3.7	42	2.9	3.67	91	.249	.328	-4	-5	98	77	-1.5	-2	0	-0.4
1913	Bro-N	8	9	.471	30	16	5	0	2	152	145	8.6	1	55	3.3	57	3.4	3.26	103	.255	.321	-1	2	105	92	0.6	-3	1	0.0
Total	5	28	61	.315	136	94	38	5	6	745	707	8.5	22	317	3.8	236	2.9	3.31	103	.256	.339	-13	9	108	103	-9.7	-11	8	1.4
■ **JACK CURTIS**	Curtis, Jack Patrick b: 1/11/37, Rhodhiss, N.C. BL/TL, 5'10", 175 lbs. Deb: 4/22/61																												
1961	Chi-N	10	13	.435	31	27	6	0	0	180	220	11.0	23	51	2.6	57	2.8	4.90	84	.303	.339	-17	-16	102	103	0.4	3	0	-1.1
1962	Chi-N	0	2	.000	4	3	0	0	0	18	18	9.0	2	6	3.0	8	4.0	3.50	122	.277	.333	1	2	109	126	-0.9	0	-0	0.2
	Mil-N	4	4	.500	30	5	0	0	1	76	82	9.7	8	27	3.2	40	4.7	4.14	93	.282	.344	-2	-2	98	110	-0.1	2	-1	-0.1
	Yr	4	6	.400	34	8	0	0	1	94	100	9.6	10	33	3.2	48	4.6	4.02	98	.280	.342	-1	-1	100	110	-1.0	0	-1	0.1
1963	Cle-A	0	0	—	4	0	0	0	0	5	8	14.4	0	5	9.0	3	5.4	18.00	20	.348	.467	-8	-8	98	45	0.0	0	0	-0.6
Total	3	14	19	.424	69	35	6	0	1	279	328	10.6	33	89	2.9	108	3.5	4.84	84	.297	.343	-26	-25	101	105	-0.6	5	-1	-1.6
■ **JACK CURTIS**	Curtis, John Duffield b: 3/9/48, Newton, Mass. BL/TL, 6'1", 175 lbs. Deb: 8/13/70																												
1970	Bos-A	0	0	—	1	0	0	0	0	2	4	18.0	1	1	4.5	1	4.5	13.50	30	.333	.385	-2	-2	110	70	0.0	0	0	-0.1
1971	Bos-A	2	2	.500	5	3	1	0	0	26	30	10.4	3	6	2.1	19	6.6	3.12	117	.291	.327	1	2	105	140	0.0	-0	-1	0.0
1972	Bos-A	11	8	.579	26	21	8	3	0	154	161	9.4	8	50	2.9	106	6.2	3.74	86	.271	.324	-11	-9	105	96	0.7	-3	-0	-1.2
1973	Bos-A	13	13	.500	35	30	10	4	0	221	225	9.2	24	83	3.4	101	4.1	3.58	112	.264	.328	6	10	105	112	-1.3	0	-1	1.0
1974	StL-N	10	14	.417	33	29	5	2	1	195	199	9.2	15	83	3.8	89	4.1	3.78	99	.267	.335	-3	-1	103	106	-2.9	-1	0	-0.1
1975	StL-N	8	9	.471	39	18	4	0	1	147	151	9.2	13	65	4.0	67	4.1	3.43	110	.268	.338	3	5	103	122	-0.6	2	2	0.9
1976	StL-N	6	11	.353	37	15	3	1	1	134	139	9.3	11	65	4.4	52	3.5	4.50	81	.276	.352	-15	-12	105	100	-1.8	1	0	-1.0
1977	SF-N	3	3	.500	43	9	1	1	1	77	95	11.1	5	48	5.6	47	5.5	5.49	75	.314	.400	-14	-12	105	106	0.2	1	1	-0.9
1978	SF-N	4	3	.571	46	0	0	0	1	63	60	8.6	1	29	4.1	38	5.4	3.71	88	.262	.330	-1	-3	91	97	0.2	-0	0	-0.3
1979	SF-N	10	9	.526	27	18	3	2	0	121	121	9.0	15	42	3.1	85	6.3	4.17	84	.257	.313	-6	-9	93	92	1.7	1	-1	-0.9
1980	SD-N	10	8	.556	30	27	6	0	0	187	184	8.9	9	67	3.2	71	3.4	3.51	96	.262	.321	2	-3	94	101	1.9	1	1	-0.1
1981	SD-N	2	6	.250	28	8	0	0	0	67	70	9.4	11	30	4.0	31	4.2	5.10	65	.275	.345	-12	-13	95	99	-1.3	-1	-0	-1.4
1982	SD-N	8	6	.571	26	18	1	1	0	116	121	9.4	15	46	3.6	54	4.2	4.11	80	.271	.335	-6	-10	92	109	1.1	3	-1	-0.8
	Cal-A	0	1	.000	8	0	0	0	1	12	16	12.0	0	3	2.3	10	7.5	6.00	67	.320	.352	-3	-3	99	75	-0.4	0	-0	-0.2
1983	Cal-A	1	2	.333	37	3	0	0	5	90	89	8.9	5	40	4.0	36	3.6	3.80	103	.258	.332	3	1	96	101	-0.2	0	-1	0.0
1984	Cal-A	1	2	.333	17	0	0	0	0	29	30	9.3	4	11	3.4	18	5.6	4.34	93	.263	.323	-1	-1	101	98	-0.4	0	0	0.0
Total	15	89	97	.478	438	199	42	14	11	1641	1695	9.3	140	669	3.7	825	4.5	3.96	92	.270	.335	-59	-60	100	105	-3.1	4	-0	-5.1
■ **VERN CURTIS**	Curtis, Vernon Eugene "Turk" b: 5/24/20, Cairo, Ill. BR/TR, 6', 170 lbs. Deb: 9/06/43																												
1943	Was-A	0	0	—	2	0	0	0	0	4	3	6.8	0	6	13.5	1	2.3	6.75	50	.200	.429	-2	-2	102	70	0.0	0	0	-0.1
1944	Was-A	0	1	.000	3	1	0	0	0	10	8	7.2	0	3	2.7	2	1.8	2.70	115	.235	.297	1	0	91	92	-0.4	-0	0	0.0
1946	Was-A	0	0	—	11	0	0	0	0	16	19	10.7	1	10	5.6	7	3.9	7.31	45	.297	.363	-7	-7	94	72	0.0	-0	0	-0.6
Total	3	0	1	.000	16	1	0	0	0	30	30	9.0	1	19	5.7	10	3.0	5.70	57	.265	.355	-7	-8	94	78	-0.4	-1	0	-0.7
■ **ED CUSHMAN**	Cushman, Edgar Leander b: 3/27/1852, Eaglesville, Ohio d: 9/26/15, Erie, Pa. BR/TL, Deb: 7/06/1883																												
1883	Buf-N	3	3	.500	7	7	5	0	0	50	61	11.0	0	17	3.1	34	6.1	3.96	79	.309	.363	-5	-5	99	105	-0.1	-0	0	-0.3
1884	Mil-U	4	0	1.000	4	4	4	2	0	36	10	2.5	0	3	0.8	47	11.8	1.00	301	.091	.115	8	8	100	90	2.0	-1	0	0.7
1885	Phi-a	3	7	.300	10	10	10	0	0	87	101	10.4	1	17	1.8	37	3.8	3.52	94	.302	.336	-3	-2	102	111	-2.0	-1	0	-0.1
	NY-a	8	14	.364	22	22	22	0	0	191	158	7.4	2	33	1.6	133	6.3	2.78	101	.236	.272	10	0	86	78	-1.3	0	0	0.0
	Yr	11	21	.344	32	32	32	0	0	278	259	8.4	3	50	1.6	170	5.5	3.01	98	.258	.293	7	-2	91	78	-3.3	-1	0	-0.1
1886	NY-a	17	20	.459	38	37	37	2	0	326	278	7.7	6	99	2.7	167	4.6	3.12	117	.240	.300	12	19	106	88	2.7	-8	0	1.1
1887	NY-a	10	15	.400	26	26	25	0	0	220	310	12.7	9	83	3.4	64	2.6	5.97	66	.347	.402	-41	-49	92	98	1.6	4	0	-3.4
1890	Tol-a	17	21	.447	40	38	34	0	1	316	346	9.9	5	107	3.0	125	3.6	4.19	94	.294	.353	-11	-8	102	96	-3.2	-9	-4	-1.7
Total	6	62	80	.437	147	144	137	4	1	1226	1264	9.3	23	359	2.6	607	4.5	3.85	93	.279	.331	-29	-36	99	93	-0.3	-15	-4	-3.7
■ **HARVEY CUSHMAN**	Cushman, Harvey Barnes b: 7/10/1877, Rockland, Me. d: 12/27/20, Emsworth, Pa. Deb: 8/24/02																												
1902	Pit-N	0	4	.000	4	4	3	0	0	26	30	10.4	0	31	10.7	12	4.2	7.27	37	.313	.481	-13	-13	98	83	-1.9	-0	-1	-1.1
■ **MIKE CVENGROS**	Cvengros, Michael John b: 12/1/01, Pana, Ill. d: 8/2/70, Hot Springs, Ark. BL/TL, 5'8", 159 lbs. Deb: 9/30/22																												
1922	NY-N	0	1	.000	1	1	1	0	0	9	6	6.0	1	3	3.0	3	3.0	4.00	103	.194	.278	0	0	100	62	-0.4	-0	0	0.0
1923	Chi-A	12	13	.480	40	26	14	0	3	214	216	9.1	6	107	4.5	86	3.6	4.42	89	.269	.353	-10	-11	99	90	0.9	-1	0	-1.1
1924	Chi-A	3	12	.200	26	15	2	0	0	106	119	10.1	5	67	5.7	36	3.1	5.86	71	.300	.384	-19	-20	98	91	-4.1	2	0	-1.6
1925	Chi-A	3	9	.250	22	11	4	0	0	105	109	9.3	7	55	4.7	32	2.7	4.29	97	.278	.359	1	-1	95	107	-3.1	-1	-0	-0.2
1927	Pit-N	2	1	.667	23	4	0	0	1	54	55	9.2	3	24	4.0	21	3.5	3.33	116	.271	.339	4	3	99	123	0.2	-0	1	0.4
1929	Chi-N	5	4	.556	32	2	0	0	2	64	82	11.5	2	29	4.1	23	3.2	4.64	99	.319	.381	1	-0	98	116	-0.6	2	0	0.2
Total	6	25	40	.385	144	59	21	0	6	552	587	9.6	24	285	4.6	201	3.3	4.58	90	.282	.361	-24	-29	98	99	-7.1	1	1	-2.3
■ **JOHN D'ACQUISTO**	D'Acquisto, John Francis b: 12/24/51, San Diego, Cal. BR/TR, 6'2", 205 lbs. Deb: 9/02/73																												
1973	SF-N	1	1	.500	7	3	1	0	0	28	23	7.4	4	19	6.1	29	9.3	3.54	108	.219	.336	0	1	104	112	0.0	-1	-0	0.0
1974	SF-N	12	14	.462	38	36	5	1	0	215	182	7.6	13	124	5.2	167	7.0	3.77	105	.227	.333	-3	4	109	88	0.5	-1	-4	0.0
1975	SF-N	2	4	.333	10	6	0	0	0	28	29	9.3	5	34	10.9	22	7.1	10.29	36	.264	.439	-21	-21	102	68	-0.9	-0	-0	-1.9
1976	SF-N	3	8	.273	28	19	0	0	0	106	93	7.9	5	102	8.7	53	4.5	5.35	68	.243	.394	-22	-20	104	90	-2.2	2	0	-1.8
1977	StL-N	0	0	—	3	2	0	0	0	8	5	5.6	0	10	11.3	9	10.1	4.50	83	.185	.410	-1	-1	95	94	0.0	-0	-0	0.0
	SD-N	1	2	.333	17	12	0	0	0	44	49	10.0	3	47	9.6	45	9.2	6.95	50	.297	.441	-15	-17	89	96	-0.2	-0	0	-1.5
	Yr	1	2	.333	20	14	0	0	0	52	54	9.3	3	57	9.9	54	9.3	6.58	54	.278	.432	-15	-18	90	96	-0.2	-0	0	-1.5
1978	SD-N	4	3	.571	45	3	0	0	10	93	60	5.8	2	56	5.4	104	10.1	2.13	156	.185	.300	15	12	93	104	0.4	1	-1	1.3
1979	SD-N	9	13	.409	51	11	1	1	2	134	140	9.4	15	86	5.8	97	6.5	4.90	74	.275	.375	-17	-19	97	105	-0.3	1	-2	-2.0
1980	SD-N	2	3	.400	39	0	0	0	1	67	67	9.0	2	36	4.8	44	5.9	3.76	90	.270	.354	-1	-3	94	110	-0.2	-1	-0	-0.3
	Mon-N	0	2	.000	11	0	0	0	2	21	14	6.0	0	9	3.9	15	6.4	2.14	166	.206	.291	3	3	98	104	-0.9	0	0	0.3
	Yr	2	5	.286	50	0	0	0	3	88	81	8.3	2	45	4.6	59	6.0	3.38	101	.252	.338	2	0	95	104	-1.1	-1	-0	0.0
1981	Cal-A	0	0	—	6	0	0	0	0	19	26	12.3	2	12	5.7	8	3.8	10.89	35	.338	.411	-15	-15	104	64	0.0	0	-0	-1.3
1982	Oak-A	0	1	.000	11	0	0	0	0	17	20	10.6	1	9	4.8	7	3.7	5.29	74	.290	.372	-2	-3	96	91	-0.4	0	0	-0.2
Total	10	34	51	.400	266	92	7	2	15	780	708	8.2	52	544	6.3	600	6.9	4.56	81	.245	.361	-78	-76	101	96	-4.2	0	-8	-7.4
■ **JOHN DAGENHARD**	Dagenhard, John Douglas b: 4/25/17, Magnolia, Ohio BR/TR, 6'2", 195 lbs. Deb: 9/28/43																												
1943	Bos-N	1	0	1.000	2	1	1	0	0	11	9	7.4	0	4	3.3	2	1.6	0.00	—	.225	.326	4	4	109	0	0.5	-0	1	0.6
■ **PETE DAGLIA**	Daglia, Peter George b: 2/28/06, Napa, Cal. d: 3/11/52, Willits, Cal. BR/TR, 6'1", 200 lbs. Deb: 6/08/32																												
1932	Chi-A	2	4	.333	12	5	2	0	0	50	67	12.1	4	20	3.6	16	2.9	5.76	71	.324	.389	-7	-9	91	107	0.0	-1	-1	-0.9
■ **JAY DAHL**	Dahl, Jay Steven b: 12/6/45, San Bernardino, Cal. d: 6/20/65, Salisbury, N.C. BB/TL, 5'10", 183 lbs. Deb: 9/27/63																												
1963	Hou-N	0	1	.000	1	1	0	0	0	3	7	21.0	0	0	0.0	0	0.0	15.00	21	.438	.438	-4	-4	95	55	-0.4	0	-0	-0.3
■ **JERRY DAHLKE**	Dahlke, Jerome Alexander "Joe" b: 6/8/30, Marathon, Wis. BR/TR, 6', 180 lbs. Deb: 5/06/56																												
1956	Chi-A	0	0	—	5	0	0	0	0	2	5	22.5	0	6	27.0	1	4.5	22.50	19	.455	.611	-4	-4	102	77	0.0	0	0	-0.3

YEAR	TM/L	W	L	PCT	G	GS	CG	SHO	SV	IP	H	H/G	HR	BB	BB/G	SO	SO/G	ERA	/A	OAVG	OOBP	PR	/A	PF	CPI	WAT	PB	PD	TPI
■ SAM DAILEY	Dailey, Samuel Laurence b: 3/31/04, Oakford, Ill. d: 12/2/79, Columbia, Mo. BL/TR, 5'11", 168 lbs. Deb: 7/04/29																												
1929	Phi-N	2	2	.500	20	5	0	0	0	51	74	13.1	5	23	4.1	18	3.2	7.59	69	.349	.400	-16	-13	112	90	0.1	-2	-1	-1.4
■ VINCE DAILEY	Dailey, Vincent Perry b: 12/25/1864, Osceola, Pa. d: 11/14/19, Hornell, N.Y. 6', 200 lbs. Deb: 4/21/1890																												
1890	Cle-N	0	1	.000	2	1	0	0	0	7	12	15.4	0	7	9.0	0	0.0	7.71	45	.395	.508	-3	-3	97	110	-0.4	1	0	-0.2
■ BILL DAILEY	Dailey, William Garland b: 5/13/35, Arlington, Va. BR/TR, 6'3", 185 lbs. Deb: 8/17/61																												
1961	Cle-A	1	0	1.000	12	0	0	0	0	19	16	7.6	0	6	2.8	7	3.3	0.95	410	.232	.289	6	6	97	248	0.5	-0	0	0.6
1962	Cle-A	2	2	.500	27	0	0	0	1	43	43	9.0	0	17	3.6	24	5.0	3.56	110	.270	.333	2	2	99	104	0.0	-0	-0	0.1
1963	Min-A	6	3	.667	66	0	0	0	21	109	80	6.6	9	19	1.6	72	5.9	1.98	179	.208	.239	20	19	98	105	1.1	2	2	2.5
1964	Min-A	1	2	.333	14	0	0	0	0	15	23	13.8	3	17	10.2	6	3.6	8.40	43	.377	.524	-8	-8	100	129	-0.4	0	0	-0.7
Total	4	10	7	.588	119	0	0	0	22	186	162	7.8	12	59	2.9	109	5.3	2.76	133	.241	.299	20	19	98	121	1.2	1	3	2.5
■ ED DAILY	Daily, Edward M. b: 9/7/1862, Providence, R.I. d: 10/21/1891, Washington, D.C. BR/TR, Deb: 1885																												
1885	Phi-N	26	23	.531	50	50	49	4	0	440	370	7.6	12	90	1.8	140	2.9	2.21	132	.238	.280	30	35	104	101	1.9	-1	-4	2.9
1886	Phi-N	16	9	.640	27	23	22	1	0	218	211	8.7	7	59	2.4	95	3.9	3.06	104	.267	.318	6	3	96	102	0.7	3	0	0.2
1887	Phi-N	0	4	.000	6	5	4	0	0	41	52	11.4	2	25	5.5	7	1.5	7.24	52	.325	.416	-15	-16	94	79	-1.9	2	0	-1.1
	Was-N	0	1	.000	1	1	1	0	0	7	5	6.4	0	6	7.7	3	3.9	7.71	52	.213	.374	-3	-3	99	42	-0.4	0	0	-0.1
	Yr	0	5	.000	7	6	5	0	0	48	57	10.7	2	31	5.8	10	1.9	7.31	52	.311	.410	-17	-19	94	42	-2.3	2	0	-1.2
1888	Was-N	2	7	.222	9	8	8	0	0	74	88	10.7	6	19	2.3	20	2.4	4.99	57	.310	.353	-18	-18	101	89	-1.7	1	0	-1.5
1889	Col-a	0	0	—	2	0	0	0	1	2	1	4.5	0	4	18.0	2	9.0	27.00	13	.160	.487	-5	-5	92	19	0.0	0	0	-0.3
1890	BB-a	10	15	.400	27	27	27	0	0	236	252	9.6	3	93	3.5	82	3.1	4.04	98	.289	.358	-5	-2	103	99	2.0	3	0	-0.1
	NY-N	2	0	1.000	2	1	1	0	0	16	6	3.4	0	6	3.4	0	0.0	2.25	149	.125	.222	2	2	94	1	1.0	-0	0	0.2
	Lou-a	6	3	.667	12	10	9	1	0	93	83	8.0	1	30	2.9	31	3.0	1.94	208	.254	.316	20	22	104	150	0.0	2	0	2.6
1891	Lou-a	4	8	.333	15	14	11	0	0	111	149	12.1	6	48	3.9	27	2.2	5.76	60	.337	.402	-25	-29	92	93	-0.8	2	0	-5.1
Total	7	66	70	.485	151	139	132	6	1	1238	1217	8.8	37	380	2.8	407	3.0	3.41	98	.270	.327	-12	-10	100	101	0.8	12	-4	-2.3
■ HUGH DAILY	Daily, Hugh Ignatius "One Arm" (born Harry Criss) b: 1857, Baltimore, Md. BR/TR, 6'2", 180 lbs. Deb: 5/01/1882																												
1882	Buf-N	15	14	.517	29	29	29	0	0	256	246	8.6	6	70	2.5	116	4.1	2.99	100	.260	.311	-3	-0	103	96	-0.7	-6	-5	-0.9
1883	Cle-N	23	19	.548	45	43	40	4	1	379	360	8.5	5	99	2.4	171	4.1	2.42	134	.258	.307	30	35	104	109	-1.1	-11	-0	2.2
1884	CP-U	27	27	.500	56	56	54	4	0	485	430	8.0	11	71	1.3	469	8.7	1.91	158	.243	.272	59	59	100	128	5.3	-2	2	5.4
	Was-U	1	1	.500	2	2	2	0	0	16	16	9.0	0	1	0.6	14	7.9	2.25	132	.265	.277	1	1	98	115	0.1	-1	0	0.1
	Yr	28	28	.500	58	58	56	4	0	501	446	8.0	11	72	1.3	**483**	8.7	1.92	157	.243	.272	**61**	**61**	100	115	5.4	-2	2	5.5
1885	StL-N	3	8	.273	11	11	10	1	0	91	92	9.1	5	44	4.4	31	3.1	3.96	69	.273	.357	-11	-12	97	103	-1.0	-3	0	-1.3
1886	Was-N	0	6	.000	6	6	6	0	0	49	69	12.7	2	40	7.3	15	2.8	7.35	45	.346	.455	-22	-22	100	94	-2.9	-1	0	-1.7
1887	Cle-a	4	12	.250	16	16	16	0	0	140	181	11.6	1	44	2.8	30	1.9	3.66	120	.328	.377	10	12	103	**132**	-1.3	-8	0	0.3
Total	6	73	87	.456	165	163	157	9	1	1416	1394	8.9	30	369	2.3	846	5.4	2.74	117	.265	.313	64	72	102	114	-1.6	-31	-3	4.1
■ BRUCE DAL CANTON	Dal Canton, John Bruce b: 6/15/42, California, Pa. BR/TR, 6'2", 205 lbs. Deb: 9/03/67 C																												
1967	Pit-N	2	1	.667	8	2	1	0	0	24	19	7.1	1	10	3.8	13	4.9	1.88	180	.211	.297	4	4	100	130	0.5	1	-0	0.5
1968	Pit-N	1	1	.500	7	0	0	0	2	17	7	3.7	0	6	3.2	8	4.2	2.12	141	.127	.227	2	2	100	26	0.0	-0	-0	0.1
1969	Pit-N	8	2	.800	57	0	0	0	5	86	79	8.3	3	49	5.1	56	5.9	3.35	101	.252	.344	2	0	94	113	2.9	2	-0	0.2
1970	Pit-N	9	4	.692	41	6	1	0	1	85	94	10.0	7	39	4.1	53	5.6	4.55	85	.282	.354	-5	-6	96	104	2.2	-1	-0	-0.7
1971	KC-A	8	6	.571	25	22	2	0	0	141	144	9.2	8	44	2.8	58	3.7	3.45	99	.262	.312	0	-1	98	97	0.7	-2	-2	-0.4
1972	KC-A	6	6	.500	35	16	1	0	2	132	135	9.2	7	29	2.0	75	5.1	3.41	90	.265	.299	-5	-5	100	92	0.1	-2	-2	-0.8
1973	KC-A	4	3	.571	32	3	1	0	3	97	108	10.0	8	46	4.3	38	3.5	4.82	86	.284	.359	-11	-7	109	98	0.2	0	0	-0.6
1974	KC-A	8	10	.444	31	22	9	2	0	175	135	6.9	5	82	4.2	96	4.9	3.14	123	.211	.302	9	14	106	77	-0.6	0	1	1.5
1975	KC-A	0	2	.000	4	2	0	0	0	9	23	23.0	0	7	7.0	5	5.0	15.00	26	.479	.554	-11	-11	101	81	-0.9	0	0	-0.9
	Atl-N	2	7	.222	26	9	0	0	3	67	63	8.5	2	24	3.2	38	5.1	3.36	105	.248	.313	2	1	97	94	-2.1	-1	1	0.1
1976	Atl-N	3	5	.375	42	1	0	0	1	73	67	8.3	6	42	5.2	36	4.4	3.58	110	.244	.338	-1	3	112	111	-0.5	0	1	0.5
1977	Chi-A	0	2	.000	8	0	0	0	2	24	20	7.5	1	13	4.9	9	3.4	3.75	107	.230	.327	1	1	99	85	-0.9	0	-1	0.0
Total	11	51	49	.510	316	83	15	2	19	930	894	8.7	48	391	3.8	485	4.7	3.68	99	.253	.325	-11	-6	102	95	1.6	-3	-3	-0.5
■ GENE DALE	Dale, Emmett Eugene b: 6/16/1889, St.Louis, Mo. d: 3/20/58, St. Louis, Mo. BR/TR 6'3", 179 lbs. Deb: 9/19/11																												
1911	StL-N	0	2	.000	5	2	0	0	0	15	13	7.8	0	16	9.6	13	7.8	6.60	53	.250	.443	-5	-5	102	79	-0.9	0	0	-0.3
1912	StL-N	0	5	.000	19	3	1	0	0	62	76	11.0	4	51	7.4	37	5.4	6.53	54	.292	.414	-22	-21	103	84	-2.4	1	-1	-1.9
1915	Cin-N	18	17	.514	49	35	20	4	3	297	256	7.8	6	107	3.2	104	3.2	2.45	117	.243	.306	10	14	104	114	2.2	2	-2	1.6
1916	Cin-N	3	4	.429	17	5	2	0	0	70	80	10.3	3	33	4.2	23	3.0	5.14	51	.304	.372	-20	-19	101	94	0.2	-0	1	-1.9
Total	4	21	28	.429	90	45	23	4	3	444	425	8.6	13	207	4.2	177	3.6	3.59	82	.261	.339	-37	-32	103	105	-0.9	3	-1	-2.5
■ BUD DALEY	Daley, Leavitt Leo b: 10/7/32, Orange, Cal. BL/TL, 6'1", 185 lbs. Deb: 9/10/55																												
1955	Cle-A	0	1	.000	2	1	0	0	0	7	10	12.9	1	1	1.3	2	2.6	6.43	63	.333	.344	-2	-2	102	87	-0.4	-0	0	-0.1
1956	Cle-A	1	0	1.000	14	0	0	0	0	20	21	9.4	2	14	6.3	13	5.8	6.30	65	.273	.396	-5	-5	99	92	0.5	-0	1	-0.3
1957	Cle-A	2	8	.200	34	10	1	0	2	87	99	10.2	7	40	4.1	54	5.6	4.45	87	.279	.364	-6	-6	102	106	-3.0	-0	1	-0.3
1958	KC-A	3	2	.600	26	5	1	0	0	71	67	8.5	5	19	2.4	39	4.9	3.30	122	.249	.310	4	6	107	101	0.6	-1	1	0.6
1959	KC-A	16	13	.552	39	29	12	2	1	216	212	8.8	24	62	2.6	125	5.2	3.17	125	.257	.313	17	19	103	122	3.7	5	-0	2.5
1960	KC-A	16	16	.500	37	35	13	1	0	231	234	9.1	27	96	3.7	126	4.9	4.56	86	.263	.335	-18	-16	101	94	3.8	1	1	-1.3
1961	KC-A	4	8	.333	16	10	2	0	1	64	84	11.8	6	22	3.1	36	5.1	4.92	85	.319	.375	-6	-5	104	115	-0.7	-1	0	-0.4
	NY-A	8	9	.471	23	17	7	0	0	130	127	8.8	17	51	3.5	83	5.7	3.95	95	.257	.326	1	-3	93	107	-2.7	-1	-1	-0.4
	Yr	12	17	.414	39	27	9	0	1	194	211	9.8	23	73	3.4	119	5.5	4.27	91	.275	.337	-5	-8	97	107	-3.4	-1	-0	-0.8
1962	NY-A	7	5	.583	43	6	0	0	4	105	105	9.0	8	21	1.8	55	4.7	3.60	101	.258	.296	4	0	92	92	0.0	-0	0	0.0
1963	NY-A	0	0	—	1	0	0	0	1	1	2	18.0	0	0	0.0	0	0.0	0.00	—	.667	.500	0	0	98	0	0.0	0	0	0.0
1964	NY-A	3	2	.600	13	3	0	0	1	35	37	9.5	3	25	6.4	16	4.1	4.63	79	.274	.395	-4	-4	101	117	0.0	1	1	-0.2
Total	10	60	64	.484	248	116	36	3	10	967	998	9.3	100	351	3.3	549	5.1	4.03	97	.266	.333	-15	-14	100	105	1.8	3	4	0.1
■ BILL DALEY	Daley, William b: 6/27/1868, Poughkeepsie, N.Y d: 5/4/22, Poughkeepsie, N.Y. TL , Deb: 7/17/1889																												
1889	Bos-N	3	3	.500	9	7	4	0	0	48	34	6.4	1	43	8.1	40	7.5	4.31	92	.212	.379	-2	-2	98	80	-0.6	-1	0	-0.1
1890	Bos-P	18	7	**.720**	34	25	19	2	2	235	246	9.4	7	167	6.4	110	4.2	3.60	122	.281	.396	17	21	104	**121**	3.6	-5	0	1.4
1891	Bos-a	8	6	.571	19	11	10	0	2	127	119	8.4	7	81	5.7	68	4.8	2.98	117	.262	.374	11	7	94	131	-1.2	-2	0	0.4
Total	3	29	16	.644	62	43	33	2	4	410	399	8.8	15	291	6.4	218	4.8	3.49	116	.268	.388	26	26	100	119	1.8	-8	0	1.7
■ GEORGE DALY	Daly, George Josephs "Pecks" b: 7/28/1887, Buffalo, N.Y. d: 12/12/57, Buffalo, N.Y. BR/TR, 5'10.5", 175 lbs. Deb: 09																												
1909	NY-N	0	3	.000	3	3	3	0	0	21	31	13.3	0	8	3.4	8	3.4	6.00	45	.341	.400	-8	-8	103	90	-1.4	-1	-1	-0.7
■ BILL DAMMAN	Damman, William Henry "Wee Willie" b: 8/9/1872, Chicago, Ill. d: 12/6/48, Lynnhaven, Va. BL/TL, 5'7", 155 lbs. Deb: 4/24/1897																												
1897	Cin-N	6	4	.600	16	11	7	1	0	95	122	11.6	2	37	3.5	21	2.0	4.74	97	.335	.396	-4	-1	107	101	0.3	-1	0	0.0
1898	Cin-N	16	10	.615	35	22	16	2	2	225	277	11.1	3	67	2.7	51	2.0	3.64	106	.326	.375	-1	5	107	115	0.4	1	0	0.7
1899	Cin-N	2	1	.667	9	5	3	1	1	48	74	13.9	0	11	2.1	2	0.4	4.88	83	.379	.412	-5	-4	105	111	0.4	-2	0	-0.4
Total	3	24	15	.615	60	38	26	4	3	368	473	11.6	5	115	2.8	74	1.8	4.08	100	.335	.385	-11	-0	107	111	1.1	-2	0	0.3
■ ART DANEY	Daney, Arthur Lee b: 7/9/04, Talihina, Okla. d: 3/11/88, Phoenix, Ariz. BR/TR, 5'11", 165 lbs. Deb: 5/25/28																												
1928	Phi-A	0	0	—	1	0	0	0	0	1	1	9.0	0	0	0.0	0	0.0	0.00	—	.250	.250	0	0	99	0	0.0	0	0	0.1
■ DAVE DANFORTH	Danforth, David Charles "Dauntless Dave" b: 3/7/1890, Granger, Tex. d: 9/19/70, Baltimore, Md. BL/TL, 6', 167 lbs. Deb: 8/01/11																												
1911	Phi-A	4	1	.800	14	2	1	0	1	34	29	7.7	1	17	4.5	21	5.6	3.71	80	.240	.348	-1	-3	88	88	1.0	0	-0	-0.2
1912	Phi-A	0	0	—	3	0	0	0	0	20	26	11.7	0	12	5.4	8	3.6	4.05	80	.338	.427	-2	-2	97	144	0.0	-0	0	-0.1
1916	Chi-A	6	5	.545	28	8	1	0	2	94	87	8.3	1	37	3.5	49	4.7	3.26	92	.259	.338	-4	-3	106	98	-0.2	-1	1	-0.2
1917	Chi-A	11	6	.647	**50**	9	1	1	**9**	173	155	8.1	1	74	3.8	79	4.1	2.65	94	.244	.325	0	-3	93	102	0.0	1	-2	-0.5
1918	Chi-A	6	15	.286	39	11	5	0	2	139	148	9.6	1	40	2.6	48	3.1	3.43	81	.288	.339	-10	-10	100	101	-4.3	-2	0	-1.2
1919	Chi-A	1	2	.333	15	1	0	0	1	42	58	12.4	1	20	4.3	17	3.6	7.71	43	.333	.405	-21	-21	102	70	-0.6	0	-0	-1.9

YEAR	TM/L	W	L	PCT	G	GS	CG	SHO	SV	IP	H	H/G	HR	BB	BB/G	SO	SO/G	ERA	/A	OAVG	OOBP	PR	/A	PF	CPI	WAT	PB	PD	TPI
1922	StL-A	5	2	.714	20	10	3	0	1	80	93	10.5	1	38	4.3	48	5.4	3.26	126	.304	.369	7	8	102	142	1.0	-2	-1	0.4
1923	StL-A	16	14	.533	38	26	16	0	1	226	221	8.8	4	87	3.5	96	3.8	3.94	106	.262	.331	1	6	105	86	1.7	3	-1	0.8
1924	StL-A	15	12	.556	41	27	11	1	4	220	246	10.1	16	69	2.8	65	2.7	4.50	101	.292	.336	-7	1	108	97	2.1	-2	-3	-0.2
1925	StL-A	7	9	.438	38	15	5	0	2	159	172	9.7	19	61	3.5	53	3.0	4.36	109	.284	.339	1	7	108	108	-1.5	-2	-4	0.1
Total	10	71	66	.518	286	109	43	2	23	1187	1235	9.4	45	455	3.4	484	3.7	3.88	95	.277	.341	-36	-24	103	100	-0.8	-6	-9	-3.0
■ CHUCK DANIEL	Daniel, Charles Edward b: 9/17/33, Bluffton, Ark. BR/TR, 6'2", 195 lbs. Deb: 9/21/57																												
1957	Det-A	0	0	—	1	0	0	0	0	2	3	13.5	1	0	0.0	2	9.0	9.00	45	.333	.333	-1	-1	107	89	0.0	0	0	0.0
■ BENNIE DANIELS	Daniels, Bennie b: 6/17/32, Tuscaloosa, Ala. BL/TR, 6'1.5", 193 lbs. Deb: 9/24/57																												
1957	Pit-N	0	1	.000	1	1	0	0	0	7	5	6.4	0	3	3.9	2	2.6	1.29	289	.208	.286	2	2	96	167	-0.4	-0	1	0.3
1958	Pit-N	0	3	.000	8	5	1	0	0	28	31	10.0	3	15	4.8	7	2.3	5.46	68	.290	.370	-5	-5	94	96	-1.4	-0	1	-0.4
1959	Pit-N	7	9	.438	34	12	0	0	1	101	115	10.2	9	39	3.5	67	6.0	5.44	75	.287	.345	-17	-15	104	85	-1.1	6	-0	-0.9
1960	Pit-N	1	3	.250	10	6	0	0	0	40	52	11.7	4	17	3.8	16	3.6	7.87	46	.311	.365	-18	-19	97	70	-1.1	-0	1	-1.6
1961	Was-A	12	11	.522	32	28	12	1	0	212	184	7.8	14	80	3.4	110	4.7	3.44	114	.237	.305	14	11	97	93	3.0	3	1	1.5
1962	Was-A	7	16	.304	44	21	3	1	2	161	172	9.6	14	68	3.8	66	3.7	4.86	84	.280	.346	-16	-14	102	94	-2.3	-1	5	-0.9
1963	Was-A	5	10	.333	35	24	6	1	1	169	163	8.7	19	58	3.1	88	4.7	4.37	84	.250	.307	-14	-13	101	84	-0.2	1	3	-0.8
1964	Was-A	8	10	.444	33	24	3	2	0	163	147	8.1	20	64	3.5	73	4.0	3.70	101	.245	.311	-1	1	103	102	1.0	-0	2	0.4
1965	Was-A	5	13	.278	33	18	1	0	1	116	135	10.5	16	39	3.0	42	3.3	4.73	75	.290	.339	-16	-16	102	103	-3.4	0	-0	-1.5
Total	9	45	76	.372	230	139	26	5	5	997	1004	9.1	99	383	3.5	471	4.3	4.44	86	.264	.326	-71	-68	101	93	-5.9	9	12	-3.9
■ CHARLIE DANIELS	Daniels, Charles L. b: 7/1/1861, Roxbury, Mass. d: 2/9/38, Boston, Mass. Deb: 4/18/1884																												
1884	Bos-U	0	2	.000	2	2	2	0	0	17	20	10.6	0	2	1.1	12	6.4	4.24	69	.298	.319	-2	-2	98	85	-0.9	0	0	-0.1
■ PETE DANIELS	Daniels, Peter J. "Smiling Pete" b: 4/8/1864, County Cavan, Ireland d: 2/13/28, Indianapolis, Ind. BL/TL, Deb: 4/19/1890																												
1890	Pit-N	1	2	.333	4	4	3	0	0	28	40	12.9	1	12	3.9	8	2.6	7.07	48	.353	.414	-11	-12	95	81	0.3	1	0	-0.7
1898	StL-N	1	6	.143	10	6	3	0	0	55	62	10.1	0	14	2.3	13	2.1	3.60	110	.306	.351	0	2	110	96	-1.5	-0	0	0.2
Total	2	2	8	.200	14	10	6	0	0	83	102	11.1	1	26	2.8	21	2.3	4.77	79	.323	.375	-11	-9	105	91	-1.2	1	0	-0.5
■ GEORGE DARBY	Darby, George William "Deacon" b: 2/6/1869, Kansas City, Mo. d: 2/25/37, Sacramento, Cal. BR/TR, 5'10.5", 160 lbs. Deb: 4/28/1893																												
1893	Cin-N	1	1	.500	4	3	2	0	0	29	41	12.7	2	18	5.6	6	1.9	7.76	61	.350	.436	-10	-10	102	86	0.0	0	0	-0.6
■ PAT DARCY	Darcy, Patrick Leonard b: 5/12/50, Troy, Ohio BL/TR, 6'3", 175 lbs. Deb: 9/12/74																												
1974	Cin-N	1	0	1.000	6	2	0	0	0	17	17	9.0	2	8	4.2	14	7.4	3.71	94	.262	.342	-0	-0	96	115	0.5	0	0	0.0
1975	Cin-N	11	5	.688	27	22	1	0	1	131	134	9.2	4	59	4.1	46	3.2	3.57	103	.269	.337	1	2	101	105	0.6	-3	-0	-0.1
1976	Cin-N	2	3	.400	11	4	0	0	2	39	41	9.5	2	22	5.1	15	3.5	6.23	56	.279	.364	-12	-12	100	73	-0.8	1	-0	-1.1
Total	3	14	8	.636	44	28	1	0	3	187	192	9.2	8	89	4.3	75	3.6	4.14	88	.270	.344	-11	-11	101	99	0.3	-2	-1	-1.2
■ AL DARK	Dark, Alvin Ralph "Blackie" b: 1/7/22, Comanche, Okla. BR/TR, 5'11", 185 lbs. Deb: 7/14/46 MC																												
1953	NY-N	0	0	—	1	1	0	0	0	1	1	9.0	1	1	9.0	0	0.0	18.00	23	.250	.400	-2	-2	98	68	0.0	1	0	0.0
■ RON DARLING	Darling, Ronald Maurice b: 8/19/60, Honolulu, Hawaii BR/TR, 6'3", 195 lbs. Deb: 9/06/83																												
1983	NY-N	1	3	.250	5	5	1	0	0	35	31	8.0	0	17	4.4	23	5.9	2.83	128	.248	.345	3	3	100	121	-0.7	-1	0	0.3
1984	NY-N	12	9	.571	33	33	2	2	0	206	179	7.8	17	104	4.5	136	5.9	3.80	95	.235	.326	-5	-5	100	95	0.4	-1	2	-0.3
1985	NY-N	16	6	.727	36	35	4	2	0	248	214	7.8	21	114	4.1	167	6.1	2.90	118	.235	.317	19	15	95	**120**	3.8	2	3	2.2
1986	NY-N	15	6	.714	34	34	4	2	0	237	203	7.7	21	81	3.1	184	7.0	2.81	123	.234	.297	24	17	93	113	1.7	-2	4	2.0
1987	NY-N	12	8	.600	32	32	2	0	0	208	183	7.9	24	96	4.2	167	7.2	4.28	93	.233	.316	-5	-7	97	85	0.8	0	3	-0.3
1988	NY-N	17	9	.654	34	34	7	4	0	241	218	8.1	24	60	2.2	161	6.0	3.25	93	.245	.291	5	-6	88	104	1.2	6	0	0.0
Total	6	73	41	.640	174	173	20	10	0	1175	1028	7.9	107	472	3.6	838	6.4	3.35	104	.237	.310	43	17	95	105	7.2	5	13	3.9
■ BOB DARNELL	Darnell, Robert Jack b: 11/6/30, Wewoka, Okla. BR/TR, 5'10", 175 lbs. Deb: 8/10/54																												
1954	Bro-N	0	0	—	6	1	0	0	0	14	15	9.6	2	7	4.5	5	3.2	3.21	127	.278	.355	1	1	101	154	0.0	-0	0	0.2
1956	Bro-N	0	0	—	1	0	0	0	0	1	1	9.0	0	0	0.0	0	0.0	0.00	—	.200	.200	0	0	100	0	0.0	0	0	0.0
Total	2	0	0	—	7	1	0	0	0	15	16	9.6	2	7	4.2	5	3.0	3.00	136	.271	.343	2	2	100	144	0.0	-0	0	0.2
■ MIKE DARR	Darr, Michael Edward b: 3/23/56, Pomona, Cal. BR/TR, 6'4", 190 lbs. Deb: 9/06/77																												
1977	Tor-A	0	1	.000	1	1	0	0	0	1	3	27.0	1	4	36.0	1	9.0	45.00	9	.429	.667	-5	-5	105	68	-0.4	0	0	-0.3
■ GEORGE DARROW	Darrow, George Oliver b: 7/12/03, Beloit, Kan. d: 3/24/83, Sun City, Ariz. BL/TL, 6', 180 lbs. Deb: 4/22/34																												
1934	Phi-N	2	6	.250	17	8	2	0	1	49	57	10.5	4	28	5.1	14	2.6	5.51	82	.302	.394	-8	-6	111	106	-1.3	1	0	-0.3
■ BOBBY DARWIN	Darwin, Arthur Bobby Lee b: 2/16/43, Los Angeles, Cal. BR/TR, 6'2", 190 lbs. Deb: 9/30/62																												
1962	LA-A	0	1	.000	1	1	0	0	0	3	8	24.0	0	4	12.0	6	18.0	12.00	34	.421	.522	-3	-3	102	101	-0.4	-0	0	-0.2
1969	LA-N	0	0	—	3	0	0	0	0	4	4	9.0	0	5	11.3	0	0.0	9.00	39	.333	.524	-2	-2	97	98	0.0	-0	-0	-0.1
Total	2	0	1	.000	4	1	0	0	0	7	12	15.4	0	9	11.6	6	7.7	10.29	36	.387	.523	-5	-5	99	99	-0.4	-0	-0	-0.3
■ DANNY DARWIN	Darwin, Danny Wayne b: 10/25/55, Bonham, Tex. BR/TR, 6'3", 185 lbs. Deb: 9/08/78																												
1978	Tex-A	1	0	1.000	3	1	0	0	0	9	11	11.0	0	1	1.0	8	8.0	4.00	90	.324	.333	-0	-0	96	102	0.5	0	-0	0.0
1979	Tex-A	4	4	.500	20	6	1	0	0	78	50	5.8	5	30	3.5	58	6.7	4.04	104	.186	.272	2	1	99	53	0.0	0	-1	0.0
1980	Tex-A	13	4	.765	53	2	0	0	8	110	98	8.0	4	50	4.1	104	8.5	2.62	155	.243	.321	17	18	100	124	4.9	0	-0	1.8
1981	Tex-A	9	9	.500	22	22	6	2	0	146	115	7.1	12	57	3.5	98	6.0	3.64	91	.218	.296	0	-6	90	81	-0.7	0	-1	-0.6
1982	Tex-A	10	8	.556	56	1	0	0	7	89	95	9.6	6	37	3.7	61	6.2	3.44	112	.279	.340	6	4	94	128	2.6	0	1	0.5
1983	Tex-A	8	13	.381	28	26	9	2	0	183	175	8.6	9	62	3.0	92	4.5	3.49	118	.250	.308	12	13	101	93	-2.2	0	-1	1.2
1984	Tex-A	8	12	.400	35	32	5	1	0	224	249	10.0	19	54	2.2	123	4.9	3.94	102	.279	.321	2	2	101	101	-0.7	0	-2	0.0
1985	Mil-A	8	18	.308	39	29	11	1	2	218	212	8.8	34	65	2.7	125	5.2	3.80	115	.254	.306	8	14	106	108	-4.3	0	-3	1.1
1986	Mil-A	6	8	.429	27	14	5	1	0	130	120	8.3	13	35	2.4	80	5.5	3.53	122	.246	.294	9	11	103	95	-0.7	0	1	1.2
	Hou-N	5	2	.714	12	8	1	0	0	54	50	8.3	3	9	1.5	40	6.7	2.33	162	.239	.266	8	9	102	103	1.1	-1	-0	0.8
1987	Hou-N	9	10	.474	33	30	3	1	0	196	184	8.4	17	69	3.2	134	6.2	3.58	106	.246	.310	11	5	93	97	0.1	2	-2	0.5
1988	Hou-N	8	13	.381	44	20	3	0	3	192	189	8.9	20	48	2.3	129	6.0	3.84	84	.259	.303	-8	-13	93	98	-2.8	-1	2	-1.2
Total	11	89	101	.468	372	191	44	8	20	1629	1548	8.6	142	517	2.9	1052	5.8	3.59	109	.251	.307	68	56	98	99	-2.2	0	-6	5.3
■ LEE DASHNER	Dashner, Lee Claire "Lefty" b: 4/25/1887, Renault, Ill. d: 12/16/59, El Dorado, Kan. BB/TL, 5'11.5", 192 lbs. Deb: 8/04/13																												
1913	Cle-A	0	0	—	1	0	0	0	0	2	0	0.0	0	0	0.0	2	9.0	4.50	68	.000	.000	-0	-0	104	54	0.0	0	0	0.0
■ FRANK DASSO	Dasso, Francis Joseph Nicholas b: 8/31/17, Chicago, Ill. BR/TR, 5'11.5", 185 lbs. Deb: 4/22/45																												
1945	Cin-N	4	5	.444	16	12	6	0	0	96	89	8.3	9	53	5.0	39	3.7	3.66	101	.253	.340	2	0	97	118	0.4	-0	0	0.0
1946	Cin-N	0	0	—	2	0	0	0	0	1	2	18.0	0	2	18.0	1	9.0	27.00	13	.400	.571	-3	-3	105	45	0.0	0	0	-0.2
Total	2	4	5	.444	18	12	6	0	0	97	91	8.4	9	55	5.1	40	3.7	3.90	95	.255	.344	-1	-2	97	117	0.4	-0	0	-0.2
■ DAN DAUB	Daub, Daniel William "Mickey" b: 1/12/1868, Middletown, Ohio d: 3/25/51, Bradenton, Fla. 5'10", 160 lbs. Deb: 8/31/1892																												
1892	Cin-N	1	2	.333	4	3	2	0	0	25	23	8.3	0	13	4.7	7	2.5	2.88	118	.257	.351	1	1	103	108	-0.5	-1	0	0.1
1893	Bro-N	6	6	.500	12	12	12	0	0	103	104	9.1	3	61	5.3	25	2.2	3.84	111	.278	.379	10	5	91	110	0.0	-1	0	0.2
1894	Bro-N	9	12	.429	33	26	14	0	0	215	283	11.8	7	90	3.8	45	1.9	6.32	79	.340	.405	-24	-31	94	83	-2.3	-6	0	-2.7
1895	Bro-N	10	10	.500	25	21	16	0	0	185	212	10.3	4	51	2.5	36	1.8	4.33	103	.308	.356	9	3	94	91	-0.8	-2	0	0.0
1896	Bro-N	12	11	.522	32	24	18	0	0	225	255	10.2	4	63	2.5	53	2.1	3.60	107	.308	.357	19	6	88	104	1.9	3	0	0.6
1897	Bro-N	6	11	.353	19	16	11	0	0	138	180	11.7	8	48	3.1	19	1.2	6.13	72	.338	.393	-28	-26	102	83	-2.1	1	0	-1.9
Total	6	44	52	.458	125	102	73	0	0	891	1057	10.7	26	326	3.3	185	1.9	4.81	91	.316	.377	-12	-42	94	94	-3.8	-7	0	-3.7
■ HOOKS DAUSS	Dauss, George August (born George August Daus) b: 9/22/1889, Indianapolis, Ind d: 7/27/63, St.Louis, Mo. BR/TR, 5'10.5", 168 lbs. Deb: 9/28/12																												
1912	Det-A	1	1	.500	2	2	2	0	0	17	11	5.8	0	9	4.8	7	3.7	3.18	101	.186	.324	0	0	96	71	0.1	1	1	0.1
1913	Det-A	13	12	.520	33	29	22	2	1	225	188	7.5	4	82	3.3	107	4.3	2.48	119	.228	.308	10	12	101	95	2.3	3	-1	1.2
1914	Det-A	18	15	.545	45	35	22	3	**4**	302	286	8.5	3	87	2.6	150	4.5	2.86	98	.257	.321	-4	-2	102	99	1.0	6	0	-0.1
1915	Det-A	24	13	.649	46	35	27	1	2	310	261	7.6	1	115	3.3	132	3.8	2.50	124	.235	.313	16	20	105	100	0.0	0	9	3.4

YEAR	TM/L	W	L	PCT	G	GS	CG	SHO	SV	IP	H	H/G	HR	BB	BB/G	SO	SO/G	ERA	/A	OAVG	OOBP	PR	/A	PF	CPI	WAT	PB	PD	TPI
1916	Det-A	19	12	.613	39	29	18	1	4	239	220	8.3	2	90	3.4	95	3.6	3.20	91	.257	.339	-10	-8	103	99	2.1	8	3	0.3
1917	Det-A	17	14	.548	37	31	22	6	2	271	243	8.1	3	87	2.9	102	3.4	2.42	106	.245	.311	7	4	96	104	1.5	-0	4	0.8
1918	Det-A	12	16	.429	33	26	21	1	3	250	243	8.7	3	58	2.1	73	2.6	2.99	91	.263	.302	-6	-7	99	90	-0.2	3	1	-0.2
1919	Det-A	21	9	.700	34	32	22	2	0	256	262	9.2	9	63	2.2	73	2.6	3.55	84	.267	.315	-9	-16	92	84	5.3	-2	6	-1.3
1920	Det-A	13	21	.382	38	32	18	0	0	270	308	10.3	11	84	2.8	82	2.7	3.57	113	.289	.345	7	14	106	108	-0.6	0	8	2.3
1921	Det-A	10	15	.400	32	28	16	0	1	233	275	10.6	11	81	3.1	68	2.6	4.33	95	.297	.352	-1	-6	96	103	-1.9	3	5	0.1
1922	Det-A	13	13	.500	39	25	12	1	4	219	251	10.3	7	59	2.4	78	3.2	4.19	94	.289	.327	-4	-6	97	90	-0.3	3	1	-0.2
1923	Det-A	21	13	.618	50	39	22	4	3	316	331	9.4	10	78	2.2	105	3.0	3.62	105	.272	.310	13	6	95	89	3.6	6	1	1.1
1924	Det-A	12	11	.522	40	10	5	0	6	131	155	10.6	6	40	2.7	44	3.0	4.60	91	.302	.339	-5	-6	99	95	-0.8	-2	0	-0.6
1925	Det-A	16	11	.593	35	30	16	1	1	228	238	9.4	11	85	3.4	58	2.3	3.16	136	.272	.330	31	29	98	**119**	2.2	1	-1	2.8
1926	Det-A	12	6	.667	35	5	0	0	9	124	135	9.8	6	49	3.6	27	2.0	4.21	93	.287	.343	-3	-4	98	100	3.1	4	-0	0.0
Total	15	222	182	.550	538	388	245	22	40	3391	3407	9.0	87	1067	2.8	1201	3.2	3.30	103	.266	.324	43	32	99	98	17.4	32	37	9.7
■ **VIC DAVALILLO**	Davalillo, Victor Jose (Romero) b: 7/31/36, Cabimas, Venez. BL/TL, 5'7", 150 lbs. Deb: 4/09/63																												
1969	StL-N	0	0	—	2	0	0	0	0	0	2	—	0	2	—	0	—	∞	—	1.000	1.000	-1	-1	99	170	0.0	0	0	0.0
■ **CLAUDE DAVENPORT**	Davenport, Claude Edwin "Big Dave" b: 5/28/1898, Runge, Tex. d: 6/13/76, Corpus Christi, Tex. BR/TR, 6'6", 193 lbs. Deb: 10/02/20																												
1920	NY-N	0	0	—	1	0	0	0	0	2	2	9.0	1	1	4.5	0	0.0	4.50	67	.250	.333	-0	-0	97	146	0.0	-0	0	0.0
■ **DAVE DAVENPORT**	Davenport, David W. b: 2/20/1890, De Ridder, La. d: 10/16/54, El Dorado, Ark. BR/TR, 6'6", 220 lbs. Deb: 4/17/14																												
1914	Cin-N	2	2	.500	10	6	3	1	2	54	38	6.3	1	30	5.0	22	3.7	2.50	120	.202	.311	2	3	107	93	0.4	-1	-0	0.2
	StL-F	8	13	.381	33	26	13	2	4	216	204	8.5	3	80	3.3	142	**5.9**	3.46	100	.251	.324	-6	0	108	86	-0.8	-6	2	-0.2
1915	StL-F	22	18	.550	**55**	46	**30**	**10**	1	**393**	300	**6.9**	5	96	2.2	**229**	5.2	2.20	141	**.215**	.268	**36**	**40**	102	81	-0.6	-9	-3	3.1
1916	StL-A	12	11	.522	**59**	31	13	1	2	291	267	8.3	4	100	3.1	129	4.0	2.85	94	.256	.326	-1	-6	94	105	0.2	3	-3	-0.6
1917	StL-A	17	17	.500	47	39	20	2	2	281	273	8.7	5	105	3.4	100	3.2	3.07	85	.260	.331	-13	-14	98	100	4.2	-6	-1	-2.2
1918	StL-A	10	11	.476	31	22	12	2	1	180	182	9.1	0	69	3.5	60	3.0	3.25	85	.273	.340	-10	-10	100	102	0.0	1	2	-0.7
1919	StL-A	2	11	.154	24	16	5	0	0	123	135	9.9	4	41	3.0	37	2.7	3.95	80	.280	.339	-10	-11	98	89	-4.5	-3	1	-1.3
Total	6	73	83	.468	259	186	96	18	12	1538	1399	8.2	22	521	3.0	719	4.2	2.93	100	.248	.315	-1	1	100	93	-1.1	-21	-3	-1.7
■ **LUM DAVENPORT**	Davenport, Joubert Lum b: 6/27/1900, Tucson, Ariz. d: 4/21/61, Dallas, Tex. BL/TL, 6'1", 165 lbs. Deb: 5/02/21																												
1921	Chi-A	0	3	.000	13	2	0	0	0	35	41	10.5	1	32	8.2	9	2.3	6.94	63	.318	.433	-10	-10	102	94	-1.4	2	-0	-0.7
1922	Chi-A	1	1	.500	9	1	0	0	0	16	14	7.9	2	13	7.3	9	5.1	11.25	36	.233	.370	-13	-13	101	39	0.0	-0	0	-1.0
1923	Chi-A	0	0	—	2	0	0	0	0	4	7	15.8	0	4	9.0	1	2.3	6.75	58	.438	.550	-1	-1	99	147	0.0	0	0	0.0
1924	Chi-A	0	0	—	1	0	0	0	0	2	1	4.5	0	2	9.0	1	4.5	0.00	—	.125	.300	1	1	98	0	0.0	0	-0	0.1
Total	4	1	4	.200	25	3	0	0	0	57	63	9.9	3	51	8.1	20	3.2	7.89	54	.296	.420	-23	-23	101	79	-1.4	2	0	-1.6
■ **MIKE DAVEY**	Davey, Michael Gerard b: 6/2/52, Spokane, Wash. BR/TL, 6'2", 190 lbs. Deb: 8/13/77																												
1977	Atl-N	0	0	—	16	0	0	0	2	16	19	10.7	1	9	5.1	7	3.9	5.06	89	.302	.373	-2	-1	115	104	0.0	-0	0	0.0
1978	Atl-N	0	0	—	3	0	0	0	0	3	1	3.0	0	1	3.0	0	0.0	0.00	—	.125	.222	1	1	114	0	0.0	0	0	0.1
Total	2	0	0	—	19	0	0	0	2	19	20	9.5	1	10	4.7	7	3.3	4.26	104	.282	.357	-1	0	115	87	0.0	-0	0	0.1
■ **RAY DAVIAULT**	Daviault, Raymond Joseph Robert b: 5/27/34, Montreal, Que., Can BR/TR, 6'1", 170 lbs. Deb: 4/13/62																												
1962	NY-N	1	5	.167	36	3	0	0	0	81	92	10.2	14	48	5.3	51	5.7	6.22	69	.288	.382	-21	-18	108	96	-0.9	-1	-1	-1.8
■ **TED DAVIDSON**	Davidson, Thomas Eugene b: 10/4/39, Las Vegas, Nev. BR/TL, 6', 192 lbs. Deb: 7/24/65																												
1965	Cin-N	4	3	.571	24	1	0	0	1	69	57	7.4	5	17	2.2	54	7.0	2.22	163	.233	.278	10	11	102	130	0.2	-2	0	1.0
1966	Cin-N	5	4	.556	54	0	0	0	4	85	82	8.7	11	23	2.4	54	5.7	3.92	105	.253	.299	-3	2	114	93	0.7	-2	-0	0.0
1967	Cin-N	1	0	1.000	9	0	0	0	0	13	13	9.0	0	3	2.1	6	4.2	4.15	88	.250	.291	-1	-1	109	58	0.5	0	0	0.0
1968	Cin-N	1	0	1.000	23	0	0	0	0	22	27	11.0	3	7	2.9	7	2.9	6.14	54	.307	.351	-8	-7	111	85	0.5	-0	0	-0.7
	Atl-N	0	0	—	4	0	0	0	0	7	10	12.9	2	4	5.1	3	3.9	6.43	43	.345	.424	-3	-3	94	127	0.0	0	0	-0.2
	Yr	1	0	1.000	27	0	0	0	0	29	37	11.5	5	11	3.4	10	3.1	6.21	51	.316	.369	-10	-10	107	127	0.5	-0	0	-0.9
Total	4	11	7	.611	114	1	0	0	5	196	189	8.7	21	54	2.5	124	5.7	3.67	103	.256	.303	-4	2	108	104	1.9	-3	1	0.1
■ **JERRY DAVIE**	Davie, Gerald Lee b: 2/10/33, Detroit, Mich. BR/TR, 6', 180 lbs. Deb: 4/14/59																												
1959	Det-A	2	2	.500	11	5	1	0	0	37	40	9.7	8	17	4.1	20	4.9	4.14	104	.265	.351	-1	1	111	131	0.0	2	1	0.3
■ **GEORGE DAVIES**	Davies, George Washington b: 2/22/1868, Portage, Wis. d: 9/22/06, Waterloo, Wis. 180 lbs. Deb: 8/18/1891																												
1891	CM-a	7	5	.583	12	12	12	1	0	102	94	8.3	2	35	3.1	61	5.4	2.65	158	.259	.324	12	17	113	103	1.4	1	0	1.8
1892	Cle-N	10	16	.385	26	26	23	0	0	216	201	8.4	4	69	2.9	95	4.0	2.58	128	.259	.320	17	18	101	107	-5.5	-5	0	1.2
1893	Cle-N	0	2	.000	3	3	1	0	0	15	28	16.8	1	10	6.0	3	1.8	11.40	42	.415	.491	-11	-11	103	79	-0.9	0	0	-0.7
	NY-N	1	1	.500	5	1	1	0	0	36	41	10.3	1	13	3.3	7	1.8	6.25	77	.302	.363	-6	-6	103	68	0.0	2	0	-0.2
	Yr	1	3	.250	8	4	2	0	0	51	69	12.2	2	23	4.1	10	1.8	7.76	62	.340	.407	-17	-17	103	68	-0.9	0	0	-0.9
Total	3	18	24	.429	46	42	37	1	0	369	364	8.9	8	127	3.1	166	4.0	3.32	113	.271	.334	12	18	104	101	-5.0	-2	0	2.1
■ **CHICK DAVIES**	Davies, Lloyd Garrison b: 3/6/1892, Peabody, Mass. d: 9/5/73, Middletown, Conn. BL/TL, 5'8", 145 lbs. Deb: 7/11/14																												
1914	Phi-A	1	0	1.000	1	1	1	0	0	9	8	8.0	0	3	3.0	4	4.0	1.00	254	.258	.324	2	2	93	282	0.5	0	0	0.2
1915	Phi-A	1	2	.333	4	2	0	0	0	15	20	12.0	0	12	7.2	2	1.2	9.00	34	.339	.458	-10	-10	103	72	0.1	0	1	-0.8
1925	NY-N	0	0	—	2	1	0	0	0	7	13	16.7	0	4	5.1	5	6.4	6.43	65	.361	.415	-2	-2	98	105	0.0	-0	0	-0.1
1926	NY-N	2	4	.333	38	1	0	0	**6**	89	96	9.7	3	35	3.5	27	2.7	3.94	95	.277	.332	-1	-2	98	97	-0.9	1	1	0.0
Total	4	4	6	.400	45	5	1	0	6	120	137	10.3	3	54	4.1	38	2.9	4.50	80	.290	.354	-11	-12	98	109	-0.3	1	2	-0.7
■ **CURT DAVIS**	Davis, Curtis Benton "Coonskin" b: 9/7/03, Greenfield, Mo. d: 10/13/65, Covina, Cal. BR/TR, 6'2", 185 lbs. Deb: 4/21/34																												
1934	Phi-N	19	17	.528	**51**	31	18	3	5	274	283	9.3	14	60	2.0	99	3.3	2.96	152	.269	.309	34	47	111	120	5.4	-1	9	5.8
1935	Phi-N	16	14	.533	44	27	19	3	2	231	264	10.3	14	47	1.8	74	2.9	3.66	129	.285	.322	9	27	117	109	3.5	-1	1	2.9
1936	Phi-N	2	4	.333	10	8	3	0	0	60	71	10.7	6	19	2.9	18	2.7	4.65	96	.291	.340	-4	-1	111	101	-0.1	-1	0	-0.1
	Chi-N	11	9	.550	24	20	10	0	1	153	146	8.6	11	31	1.8	52	3.1	3.00	137	.251	.288	17	19	102	103	-0.2	-2	3	2.0
	Yr	13	13	.500	34	28	13	0	1	213	217	9.2	17	50	2.1	70	3.0	3.46	121	.263	.302	13	17	105	103	-0.3	-1	3	1.9
1937	Chi-N	10	5	.667	28	14	8	0	1	124	138	10.0	7	30	2.2	32	2.3	4.06	96	.286	.328	-2	-2	100	101	1.3	4	2	0.3
1938	StL-N	12	8	.600	40	21	8	2	3	173	187	9.7	9	27	**1.4**	36	1.9	3.64	116	.272	.297	3	11	111	91	2.7	2	0	1.4
1939	StL-N	22	16	.579	49	31	13	3	7	248	279	10.1	18	48	1.7	70	2.5	3.63	111	.280	.312	8	11	103	103	-0.8	13	1	2.6
1940	StL-N	0	4	.000	14	7	0	0	1	54	73	12.2	4	19	3.2	12	2.0	5.17	75	.327	.381	-8	-8	101	112	-1.9	-3	1	-0.8
	Bro-N	8	7	.533	22	18	9	0	2	137	135	8.9	13	19	1.2	46	3.0	3.81	107	.256	.280	1	4	106	86	-0.5	-1	1	0.5
	Yr	8	11	.421	36	25	9	0	3	191	208	9.8	17	38	1.8	58	2.7	4.19	96	.277	.310	-7	-3	105	86	-2.4	-3	2	-0.3
1941	Bro-N	13	7	.650	28	16	10	5	2	154	141	8.2	6	27	1.6	50	2.9	2.98	121	.244	.276	11	11	99	87	0.0	2	4	1.7
1942	Bro-N	15	6	.714	32	26	13	5	2	206	179	7.8	10	51	2.2	60	2.6	2.36	136	.233	.282	22	20	97	112	1.4	-0	3	2.5
1943	Bro-N	10	13	.435	31	21	8	2	3	164	182	10.0	8	39	2.1	47	2.6	3.79	88	.281	.316	-8	-8	99	98	-2.2	-1	2	-0.6
1944	Bro-N	10	11	.476	31	23	12	1	4	194	207	9.6	12	39	1.8	49	2.3	3.34	110	.270	.305	6	7	102	105	1.4	-2	2	0.7
1945	Bro-N	10	10	.500	24	18	10	0	0	150	171	10.3	9	21	1.3	39	2.3	3.24	111	.280	.304	9	6	95	111	-1.2	-1	0	0.5
1946	Bro-N	0	0	—	1	0	0	0	0	2	3	13.5	1	2	9.0	0	0.0	13.50	25	.375	.500	-2	-2	100	98	0.0	0	0	-0.1
Total	13	158	131	.547	429	281	141	24	33	2324	2459	9.5	142	479	1.9	684	2.6	3.42	116	.270	.306	96	138	104	104	8.8	7	30	19.3
■ **DIXIE DAVIS**	Davis, Frank Talmadge b: 10/12/1890, Wilson Mills, N.C. d: 2/4/44, Raleigh, N.C. BR/TR, 5'11", 155 lbs. Deb: 7/12/12																												
1912	Cin-N	0	1	.000	7	0	0	0	0	27	25	8.3	0	16	5.3	12	4.0	2.67	119	.243	.350	2	2	93	113	-0.4	-0	-1	0.1
1915	Chi-A	0	0	—	2	0	0	0	0	3	2	6.0	0	2	6.0	2	6.0	0.00	—	.250	.455	1	1	94	0	0.0	0	0	0.1
1918	Phi-N	0	2	.000	17	2	1	0	0	47	43	8.2	1	30	5.7	18	3.4	3.06	100	.247	.341	-2	**0**	111	116	-0.9	-1	-1	-0.1
1920	StL-A	18	12	.600	38	31	22	0	0	269	250	8.4	10	149	5.0	85	2.8	3.18	133	.256	.359	18	31	111	117	3.6	2	-4	3.0
1921	StL-A	16	16	.500	40	36	20	2	0	265	279	9.5	12	123	4.2	100	3.4	4.45	97	.281	.356	-5	-4	101	98	-0.9	-2	-1	-0.6
1922	StL-A	11	6	.647	25	25	7	2	0	174	162	**8.4**	10	87	4.5	65	3.4	4.09	101	**.250**	.337	-1	1	102	89	1.0	-3	-0	-0.2
1923	StL-A	4	6	.400	19	17	5	1	0	109	106	8.8	4	63	5.2	36	3.0	3.63	115	.259	.353	4	6	105	109	-0.8	0	-2	0.5
1924	StL-A	11	13	.458	29	24	11	5	0	160	159	8.9	9	72	4.0	45	2.5	4.11	111	.263	.337	2	8	108	94	-0.7	-2	-1	0.5

YEAR	TM/L	W	L	PCT	G	GS	CG	SHO	SV	IP	H	H/G	HR	BB	BB/G	SO	SO/G	ERA	/A	OAVG	OOBP	PR	/A	PF	CPI	WAT	PB	PD	TPI
1925	StL-A	12	7	.632	35	23	9	0	1	180	192	9.6	10	106	5.3	58	2.9	4.60	103	.279	.365	-4	3	108	102	2.2	-4	1	0.0
1926	StL-A	3	8	.273	27	7	2	0	1	83	93	10.1	7	40	4.3	39	4.2	4.66	89	.292	.357	-6	-5	103	105	-1.8	-0	-0	-0.4
Total	10	75	71	.514	239	165	77	10	2	1317	1311	9.0	63	688	4.7	460	3.1	3.97	107	.266	.352	11	43	106	103	1.3	-11	-9	2.9

■ **IRON DAVIS** Davis, George Allen b: 3/9/1890, Lancaster, N.Y. d: 6/4/61, Buffalo, N.Y. BB/TR, 5'10.5", 175 lbs. Deb: 7/16/12

YEAR	TM/L	W	L	PCT	G	GS	CG	SHO	SV	IP	H	H/G	HR	BB	BB/G	SO	SO/G	ERA	/A	OAVG	OOBP	PR	/A	PF	CPI	WAT	PB	PD	TPI
1912	NY-A	1	4	.200	10	7	5	0	0	54	61	10.2	3	28	4.7	22	3.7	6.50	54	.293	.385	-19	-18	105	76	-0.9	-1	-1	-1.7
1913	Bos-N	0	0	—	2	0	0	0	0	8	7	7.9	1	5	5.6	3	3.4	4.50	68	.241	.343	-1	-1	96	94	0.0	-0	-0	-0.1
1914	Bos-N	3	3	.500	9	6	4	1	0	56	42	6.8	1	26	4.2	26	4.2	3.38	84	.215	.311	-4	-3	102	71	-0.5	0	-1	-0.4
1915	Bos-N	3	3	.500	15	9	4	0	0	73	85	10.5	2	19	2.3	26	3.2	3.82	70	.304	.343	-9	-9	97	110	-0.2	1	0	-0.8
Total	4	7	10	.412	36	22	13	1	0	191	195	9.2	7	78	3.7	77	3.6	4.48	66	.274	.346	-32	-32	101	88	-1.6	-0	-3	-3.0

■ **STORM DAVIS** Davis, George Earl b: 12/26/61, Dallas, Tex. BR/TR, 6'4", 207 lbs. Deb: 4/29/82

YEAR	TM/L	W	L	PCT	G	GS	CG	SHO	SV	IP	H	H/G	HR	BB	BB/G	SO	SO/G	ERA	/A	OAVG	OOBP	PR	/A	PF	CPI	WAT	PB	PD	TPI
1982	Bal-A	8	4	.667	29	8	1	0	0	101	96	8.6	8	28	2.5	67	6.0	3.48	116	.257	.301	7	6	99	100	1.3	0	-0	0.6
1983	Bal-A	13	7	.650	34	29	6	1	0	200	180	8.1	14	64	2.9	125	5.6	3.60	112	.238	.296	11	9	99	84	1.3	0	-1	0.8
1984	Bal-A	14	9	.609	35	31	10	2	1	225	205	8.2	7	71	2.8	105	4.2	3.12	121	.247	.304	22	16	94	96	2.3	0	-3	1.3
1985	Bal-A	10	8	.556	31	28	8	1	0	175	172	8.8	11	70	3.6	93	4.8	4.53	90	.256	.324	-7	-9	98	81	0.8	0	-1	-0.8
1986	Bal-A	9	12	.429	25	25	2	0	0	154	166	9.7	16	49	2.9	96	5.6	3.62	115	.275	.327	10	9	99	116	-0.5	0	1	1.0
1987	SD-N	2	7	.222	21	10	0	0	0	63	70	10.0	5	36	5.1	37	5.3	6.14	65	.280	.370	-14	-15	98	80	-2.0	-1	0	-1.4
	Oak-A	1	1	.500	5	5	0	0	0	30	28	8.4	3	11	3.3	28	8.4	3.30	123	.241	.305	4	3	91	103	0.0	0	-1	0.2
1988	Oak-A	16	7	.696	33	33	1	0	0	202	211	9.4	16	91	4.1	127	5.7	3.70	100	.274	.347	6	0	93	121	2.0	0	-2	-0.1
Total	7	73	55	.570	213	169	28	4	1	1150	1128	8.8	80	420	3.3	678	5.3	3.79	104	.258	.320	37	20	97	98	5.2	-1	-6	1.6

■ **GEORGE DAVIS** Davis, George Stacey b: 8/23/1870, Cohoes, N.Y. d: 10/17/40, Philadelphia, Pa. BB/TR, 5'9", 180 lbs. Deb: 4/19/1890 M

YEAR	TM/L	W	L	PCT	G	GS	CG	SHO	SV	IP	H	H/G	HR	BB	BB/G	SO	SO/G	ERA	/A	OAVG	OOBP	PR	/A	PF	CPI	WAT	PB	PD	TPI
1891	Cle-N	0	1	.000	3	0	0	0	1	4	8	18.0	0	3	6.8	4	9.0	15.75	23	.430	.509	-6	-5	106	57	-0.4	1	0	-0.3

■ **JIM DAVIS** Davis, James Bennett b: 9/15/24, Red Bluff, Cal. BB/TL, 6', 180 lbs. Deb: 4/18/54

YEAR	TM/L	W	L	PCT	G	GS	CG	SHO	SV	IP	H	H/G	HR	BB	BB/G	SO	SO/G	ERA	/A	OAVG	OOBP	PR	/A	PF	CPI	WAT	PB	PD	TPI
1954	Chi-N	11	7	.611	46	12	2	0	4	128	114	8.0	12	51	3.6	58	4.1	3.52	118	.247	.312	8	9	102	103	3.3	-1	1	0.9
1955	Chi-N	7	11	.389	42	16	0	0	3	134	122	8.2	16	58	3.9	62	4.2	4.43	92	.246	.320	-6	-5	101	88	-1.6	-4	-0	-0.8
1956	Chi-N	5	7	.417	46	11	2	1	2	120	116	8.7	11	59	4.4	66	5.0	3.68	103	.256	.345	1	2	101	111	0.3	-0	0	0.2
1957	StL-N	0	1	.000	10	0	0	0	1	14	18	11.6	1	6	3.9	5	3.2	5.14	75	.340	.393	-2	-2	99	117	-0.4	-0	0	-0.1
	NY-N	1	0	1.000	10	0	0	0	0	11	13	10.6	2	5	4.1	6	4.9	6.55	61	.283	.346	-3	-3	103	80	0.5	0	0	-0.2
	Yr	1	1	.500	20	0	0	0	1	25	31	11.2	3	11	4.0	11	4.0	5.76	68	.310	.372	-5	-5	101	80	0.1	-0	0	-0.3
Total	4	24	26	.480	154	39	4	1	10	407	383	8.5	42	179	4.0	197	4.4	4.00	100	.253	.329	-2	0	101	100	2.1	-5	1	-0.0

■ **JOEL DAVIS** Davis, Joel Clark b: 1/30/65, Jacksonville, Fla. BL/TR, 6'5", 205 lbs. Deb: 8/11/85

YEAR	TM/L	W	L	PCT	G	GS	CG	SHO	SV	IP	H	H/G	HR	BB	BB/G	SO	SO/G	ERA	/A	OAVG	OOBP	PR	/A	PF	CPI	WAT	PB	PD	TPI
1985	Chi-A	3	3	.500	12	11	1	0	0	71	71	9.0	6	26	3.3	37	4.7	4.18	99	.256	.319	-0	-0	100	90	0.0	0	-1	-0.1
1986	Chi-A	4	5	.444	19	19	1	0	0	105	115	9.9	9	51	4.4	54	4.6	4.71	90	.280	.357	-6	-5	101	100	0.0	0	1	-0.4
1987	Chi-A	1	5	.167	13	9	1	0	0	55	56	9.2	7	29	4.7	25	4.1	5.73	85	.264	.350	-8	-5	109	83	-1.9	0	-1	-0.5
1988	Chi-A	0	1	.000	5	2	0	0	0	16	21	11.8	4	5	2.8	10	5.6	6.75	58	.328	.371	-5	-5	99	102	-0.4	0	-0	-0.4
Total	4	8	14	.364	49	41	3	0	0	247	263	9.6	26	111	4.0	126	4.6	4.92	88	.273	.346	-19	-16	102	93	-2.3	0	-2	-1.4

■ **DAISY DAVIS** Davis, John A. b: 5/17/1858, Boston, Mass. Deb: 5/06/1884

YEAR	TM/L	W	L	PCT	G	GS	CG	SHO	SV	IP	H	H/G	HR	BB	BB/G	SO	SO/G	ERA	/A	OAVG	OOBP	PR	/A	PF	CPI	WAT	PB	PD	TPI
1884	StL-a	10	12	.455	25	24	20	1	0	198	196	8.9	1	35	1.6	143	6.5	2.91	121	.267	.300	7	13	109	109	-3.4	-3	0	1.0
	Bos-N	1	3	.250	4	4	3	0	0	31	50	14.5	2	8	2.3	13	3.8	7.84	35	.373	.408	-17	-17	93	80	-1.2	-3	0	-1.4
1885	Bos-N	5	6	.455	11	11	10	1	0	94	110	10.5	2	28	2.7	30	2.9	4.31	62	.303	.353	-16	-17	95	95	0.5	-0	0	-1.4
Total	2	16	21	.432	40	39	33	2	0	323	356	9.9	5	71	2.0	186	5.2	3.79	84	.289	.328	-25	-21	103	102	-4.1	-6	0	-1.8

■ **JOHN DAVIS** Davis, John Kirk b: 1/5/63, Chicago, Ill. BR/TR, 6'7", 215 lbs. Deb: 7/24/87

YEAR	TM/L	W	L	PCT	G	GS	CG	SHO	SV	IP	H	H/G	HR	BB	BB/G	SO	SO/G	ERA	/A	OAVG	OOBP	PR	/A	PF	CPI	WAT	PB	PD	TPI
1987	KC-A	5	2	.714	27	0	0	0	2	44	29	5.9	0	26	5.3	24	4.9	2.25	206	.195	.315	11	12	104	114	1.5	0	0	1.2
1988	Chi-A	2	5	.286	34	1	0	0	1	64	77	10.8	5	50	7.0	37	5.2	6.61	59	.297	.411	-19	-19	99	93	-1.2	0	-0	-1.8
Total	2	7	7	.500	61	1	0	0	3	108	106	8.8	5	76	6.3	61	5.1	4.83	87	.260	.376	-8	-8	101	101	0.3	0	0	-0.6

■ **BUD DAVIS** Davis, John Wilbur "Country" b: 12/7/1896, Merry Point, Va. d: 5/26/67, Williamsburg, Va. BL/TR, 6', 207 lbs. Deb: 4/19/15

YEAR	TM/L	W	L	PCT	G	GS	CG	SHO	SV	IP	H	H/G	HR	BB	BB/G	SO	SO/G	ERA	/A	OAVG	OOBP	PR	/A	PF	CPI	WAT	PB	PD	TPI
1915	Phi-A	0	2	.000	18	2	2	0	0	67	65	8.7	1	59	7.9	18	2.4	4.03	75	.273	.429	-8	-7	103	128	-0.9	2	-1	-0.5

■ **MARK DAVIS** Davis, Mark William b: 10/19/60, Livermore, Cal. BL/TL, 6'3", 180 lbs. Deb: 9/12/80

YEAR	TM/L	W	L	PCT	G	GS	CG	SHO	SV	IP	H	H/G	HR	BB	BB/G	SO	SO/G	ERA	/A	OAVG	OOBP	PR	/A	PF	CPI	WAT	PB	PD	TPI
1980	Phi-N	0	0	—	2	1	0	0	0	7	4	5.1	0	5	6.4	5	6.4	2.57	149	.160	.300	1	1	106	62	0.0	0	-0	0.1
1981	Phi-N	1	4	.200	9	9	0	0	0	43	49	10.3	7	24	5.0	29	6.1	7.74	50	.299	.376	-20	-18	112	77	-1.5	-0	-0	-1.7
1983	SF-N	6	4	.600	20	20	2	2	0	111	93	7.5	14	50	4.1	83	6.7	3.49	105	.227	.311	2	2	101	101	1.2	0	-1	0.2
1984	SF-N	5	17	.227	46	27	1	0	0	175	201	10.3	25	54	2.8	124	6.4	5.35	66	.293	.339	-34	-36	98	94	-5.2	0	-2	-3.6
1985	SF-N	5	12	.294	77	1	0	0	7	114	89	7.0	13	41	3.2	131	10.3	3.55	96	.219	.286	1	-2	95	87	-2.0	1	-1	-0.1
1986	SF-N	5	7	.417	67	2	0	0	4	84	63	6.8	6	34	3.6	90	9.6	3.00	118	.212	.287	7	5	95	91	-1.1	0	-0	0.5
1987	SF-N	4	5	.444	20	11	1	0	0	71	72	9.1	9	28	3.5	51	6.5	4.69	83	.273	.346	-5	-6	95	102	-0.8	2	-0	-0.5
	SD-N	5	3	.625	43	0	0	0	2	62	51	7.4	5	31	4.5	47	6.8	3.19	125	.224	.317	6	6	98	104	1.5	0	0	0.6
	Yr	9	8	.529	63	11	1	0	2	133	123	8.3	14	59	4.0	98	6.6	3.99	98	.247	.325	1	-1	96	104	0.7	2	0	0.1
1988	SD-N	5	10	.333	62	0	0	0	28	98	70	6.4	2	42	3.9	102	9.4	2.02	166	.199	.279	16	15	97	102	-2.7	1	2	2.0
Total	8	36	62	.367	346	71	4	2	41	765	692	8.1	81	309	3.6	662	7.8	4.00	90	.244	.315	-27	-34	98	95	-10.6	6	-1	-2.5

■ **PEACHES DAVIS** Davis, Ray Thomas b: 5/31/05, Glen Rose, Tex. BL/TR, 6'3.5", 190 lbs. Deb: 7/11/36

YEAR	TM/L	W	L	PCT	G	GS	CG	SHO	SV	IP	H	H/G	HR	BB	BB/G	SO	SO/G	ERA	/A	OAVG	OOBP	PR	/A	PF	CPI	WAT	PB	PD	TPI
1936	Cin-N	8	8	.500	26	15	5	0	5	126	139	9.9	7	36	2.6	32	2.3	3.57	109	.280	.325	6	5	97	111	0.3	-1	0	0.3
1937	Cin-N	11	13	.458	42	24	11	1	3	218	252	10.4	5	51	2.1	59	2.4	3.59	101	.295	.332	8	1	93	112	2.1	-3	-3	-0.5
1938	Cin-N	7	12	.368	29	19	11	1	1	168	193	10.3	9	40	2.1	28	1.5	3.96	92	.290	.325	-3	-6	96	103	-3.3	1	-3	-0.8
1939	Cin-N	1	0	1.000	20	0	0	0	2	31	43	12.5	5	11	3.2	4	1.2	6.39	61	.341	.387	-9	-9	100	105	0.5	0	0	-0.7
Total	4	27	33	.450	117	58	27	2	11	543	627	10.4	26	138	2.3	123	2.0	3.86	96	.293	.332	2	-9	95	109	-0.4	-3	-6	-1.7

■ **BOB DAVIS** Davis, Robert Edward b: 9/11/33, New York, N.Y. BR/TR, 6', 170 lbs. Deb: 7/26/58

YEAR	TM/L	W	L	PCT	G	GS	CG	SHO	SV	IP	H	H/G	HR	BB	BB/G	SO	SO/G	ERA	/A	OAVG	OOBP	PR	/A	PF	CPI	WAT	PB	PD	TPI
1958	KC-A	0	4	.000	8	4	0	0	0	31	45	13.1	5	12	3.5	22	6.4	7.84	51	.346	.407	-14	-13	107	89	-1.9	-0	0	-1.1
1960	KC-A	0	0	—	21	0	0	0	1	32	31	8.7	1	22	6.2	28	7.9	3.66	107	.263	.370	1	1	101	121	0.0	0	1	0.2
Total	2	0	4	.000	29	4	0	0	1	63	76	10.9	6	34	4.9	50	7.1	5.71	70	.306	.388	-13	-12	104	105	-1.9	-0	2	-0.9

■ **RON DAVIS** Davis, Ronald Gene b: 8/6/55, Houston, Tex. BR/TR, 6'4", 205 lbs. Deb: 7/29/78

YEAR	TM/L	W	L	PCT	G	GS	CG	SHO	SV	IP	H	H/G	HR	BB	BB/G	SO	SO/G	ERA	/A	OAVG	OOBP	PR	/A	PF	CPI	WAT	PB	PD	TPI
1978	NY-A	0	0	—	4	0	0	0	0	2	3	13.5	0	3	13.5	0	0.0	13.50	27	.333	.500	-2	-2	97	61	0.0	0	0	-0.1
1979	NY-A	14	2	.875	44	0	0	0	9	85	84	8.9	5	28	3.0	43	4.6	2.86	140	.262	.317	13	11	95	125	**5.9**	0	1	1.1
1980	NY-A	9	3	.750	53	0	0	0	7	131	121	8.3	9	32	2.2	65	4.5	2.95	134	.246	.290	16	14	98	102	2.0	0	0	1.5
1981	NY-A	4	5	.444	43	0	0	0	6	73	47	5.8	6	25	3.1	83	10.2	2.71	134	.186	.253	8	7	99	73	-0.8	0	-1	0.7
1982	Min-A	3	9	.250	63	0	0	0	22	106	106	9.0	16	47	4.0	89	7.6	4.42	94	.261	.336	-4	-3	102	103	-2.0	0	-0	-0.3
1983	Min-A	5	8	.385	66	0	0	0	30	89	89	9.0	6	33	3.3	84	8.5	3.34	130	.266	.327	7	10	106	120	-0.7	0	-2	0.8
1984	Min-A	7	11	.389	64	0	0	0	29	83	79	8.6	11	41	4.4	74	8.0	4.55	93	.253	.335	-5	-3	106	97	-2.1	0	-0	-0.3
1985	Min-A	2	6	.250	57	0	0	0	25	65	55	7.6	7	35	4.8	72	10.0	3.46	125	.230	.330	5	6	104	114	-1.8	0	-0	0.6
1986	Min-A	2	6	.250	36	0	0	0	2	39	55	12.7	7	29	6.7	30	6.9	9.00	51	.340	.444	-21	-19	109	90	-1.7	0	-0	-1.7
	Chi-N	0	2	.000	17	0	0	0	0	20	31	13.9	3	3	1.3	10	4.5	7.65	53	.356	.374	-9	-8	108	85	-0.9	-0	-1	-0.8
1987	Chi-N	0	0	—	21	0	0	0	0	32	43	12.1	8	12	3.4	31	8.7	5.91	70	.328	.382	-6	-6	102	119	0.0	0	-1	-0.6
	LA-N	0	0	—	4	0	0	0	0	4	7	15.8	0	6	13.5	1	2.3	6.75	56	.412	.560	-1	-1	92	171	0.0	0	0	0.0
	Yr	0	0	—	25	0	0	0	0	36	50	12.5	8	18	4.5	32	8.0	6.00	68	.336	.408	-8	-8	101	171	0.0	0	-0	-0.6
1988	SF-N	1	1	.500	9	0	0	0	0	17	15	7.9	4	6	3.2	15	7.9	4.76	68	.234	.306	-2	-3	93	94	0.0	-0	0	-0.2
Total	11	47	53	.470	481	0	0	0	130	746	735	8.9	82	300	3.6	597	7.2	4.05	101	.260	.329	-2	3	101	104	-2.1	-0	-3	0.7

■ **STEVE DAVIS** Davis, Steven Kennon b: 8/4/60, San Antonio, Tex. BL/TL, 6'1", 195 lbs. Deb: 8/25/85

YEAR	TM/L	W	L	PCT	G	GS	CG	SHO	SV	IP	H	H/G	HR	BB	BB/G	SO	SO/G	ERA	/A	OAVG	OOBP	PR	/A	PF	CPI	WAT	PB	PD	TPI
1985	Tor-A	2	1	.667	10	5	0	0	0	28	23	7.4	5	13	4.2	22	7.1	3.54	116	.223	.308	2	2	99	111	0.2	0	0	0.2
1986	Tor-A	0	0	—	3	0	0	0	0	4	8	18.0	2	5	11.3	5	11.3	15.75	28	.471	.591	-5	-5	104	100	0.0	0	0	-0.4
Total	2	2	1	.667	13	5	0	0	0	32	31	8.7	7	18	5.1	27	7.6	5.06	82	.258	.353	-3	-3	100	110	0.2	0	0	-0.2

YEAR	TM/L	W	L	PCT	G	GS	CG	SHO	SV	IP	H	H/G	HR	BB	BB/G	SO	SO/G	ERA	/A	OAVG	OOBP	PR	/A	PF	CPI	WAT	PB	PD	TPI
■ WILEY DAVIS	Davis, Wiley Anderson b: 8/1/1875, Seymour, Tenn. d: 9/22/42, Detroit, Mich. BR/TR, 5'10", 165 lbs. Deb: 4/18/1896																												
1896	Cin-N	1	1	.500	2	0	0	0	0	4	8	18.0	0	2	4.5	1	2.3	9.00	50	.440	.495	-2	-2	103	95	-0.1	-0	0	-0.1
■ WOODY DAVIS	Davis, Woodrow Wilson "Babe" b: 4/25/13, Nicholls, Ga. BL/TR, 6'1", 200 lbs. Deb: 5/02/38																												
1938	Det-A	0	0	—	2	0	0	0	0	6	3	4.5	0	4	6.0	1	1.5	1.50	317	.158	.304	2	2	99	142	0.0	-0	-0	0.2
■ MIKE DAVISON	Davison, Michael Lynn b: 8/4/45, Galesburg, Ill. BL/TL, 6'1", 170 lbs. Deb: 10/01/69																												
1969	SF-N	0	0	—	1	0	0	0	0	2	2	9.0	0	0	0.0	2	9.0	4.50	80	.250	.250	-0	-0	100	38	0.0	0	0	0.0
1970	SF-N	3	5	.375	31	0	0	0	1	36	46	11.5	4	22	5.5	21	5.3	6.50	60	.324	.398	-10	-10	96	100	-1.1	0	1	-0.8
Total	2	3	5	.375	32	0	0	0	1	38	48	11.4	4	22	5.2	23	5.4	6.39	60	.320	.391	-10	-11	96	97	-1.1	0	1	-0.8
■ BILL DAWLEY	Dawley, William Chester b: 2/6/58, Norwich, Conn. BR/TR, 6'5", 235 lbs. Deb: 4/15/83																												
1983	Hou-N	6	6	.500	48	0	0	0	14	80	51	5.7	9	22	2.5	60	6.7	2.81	116	.185	.243	7	4	90	71	-0.2	0	-1	0.3
1984	Hou-N	11	4	.733	60	0	0	0	5	98	82	7.5	5	35	3.2	47	4.3	1.93	171	.234	.291	18	15	92	151	3.7	1	-1	1.6
1985	Hou-N	5	3	.625	49	0	0	0	2	81	76	8.4	7	37	4.1	48	5.3	3.56	97	.259	.326	0	-1	96	114	1.0	0	0	0.0
1986	Chi-A	0	7	.000	46	0	0	0	2	98	91	8.4	10	28	2.6	66	6.1	3.31	128	.247	.296	10	10	101	104	-3.4	0	-1	0.9
1987	StL-N	5	8	.385	60	0	0	0	2	97	93	8.6	15	38	3.5	65	6.0	4.45	89	.259	.325	-4	-5	97	101	-2.3	1	1	-0.3
1988	Phi-N	0	2	.000	8	0	0	0	0	9	16	16.0	3	4	4.0	3	3.0	13.00	27	.381	.426	-10	-9	103	75	-0.9	0	-0	-0.9
Total	6	27	30	.474	271	0	0	0	25	463	409	8.0	49	164	3.2	289	5.6	3.40	108	.242	.301	22	13	96	109	-2.1	3	-2	1.6
■ JOE DAWSON	Dawson, Ralph Fenton b: 3/9/1897, Bow, Wash. d: 1/4/78, Longview, Tex. BR/TR, 5'11", 182 lbs. Deb: 7/04/24																												
1924	Cle-A	1	2	.333	4	4	0	0	0	20	24	10.8	0	21	9.4	7	3.1	6.75	61	.300	.447	-6	-6	97	91	-0.3	0	1	-0.4
1927	Pit-N	3	7	.300	20	7	4	0	0	81	80	8.9	2	32	3.6	17	1.9	4.44	87	.268	.321	-5	-5	99	81	-2.5	-1	-0	-0.5
1928	Pit-N	7	7	.500	31	7	1	0	3	129	116	8.1	6	56	3.9	36	2.5	3.28	127	.242	.316	10	13	105	93	-0.7	3	-3	1.3
1929	Pit-N	0	1	.000	4	0	0	0	0	9	13	13.0	2	3	3.0	2	2.0	8.00	60	.342	.390	-3	-3	102	90	-0.4	1	0	-0.1
Total	4	11	17	.393	59	18	5	0	3	239	233	8.8	10	112	4.2	62	2.3	4.14	99	.260	.333	-3	-1	102	89	-3.9	3	-3	0.3
■ REX DAWSON	Dawson, Rexford Paul b: 2/10/1889, Skagit Co., Wash. d: 10/20/58, Indianapolis, Ind. BL/TR, 6', 185 lbs. Deb: 10/03/13																												
1913	Was-A	0	0	—	1	0	0	0	0	1	1	9.0	0	0	0.0	1	9.0	0.00	—	.250	.250	0	0	105	0	0.0	0	0	0.0
■ PEA RIDGE DAY	Day, Clyde Henry b: 8/26/1899, Pea Ridge, Ark. d: 3/22/34, Kansas City, Mo. BR/TR, 6', 190 lbs. Deb: 9/19/24																												
1924	StL-N	1	1	.500	3	3	1	0	0	18	22	11.0	0	6	3.0	3	1.5	4.50	88	.306	.341	-1	-1	103	93	0.1	-1	-0	-0.1
1925	StL-N	2	4	.333	17	4	1	0	1	40	53	11.9	5	7	1.6	13	2.9	6.30	68	.325	.360	-9	-9	101	87	-0.9	-1	-1	-0.9
1926	Cin-N	0	0	—	4	0	0	0	0	7	13	16.7	1	2	2.6	2	2.6	7.71	46	.406	.405	-3	-3	93	110	0.0	-0	-0	-0.3
1931	Bro-N	2	2	.500	22	2	1	0	1	57	75	11.8	5	13	2.1	30	4.7	4.58	85	.315	.346	-5	-4	101	109	0.0	0	-1	-0.4
Total	4	5	7	.417	46	9	3	0	2	122	163	12.0	11	28	2.1	48	3.5	5.31	76	.323	.354	-18	-17	101	100	-0.8	-2	-2	-1.7
■ BILL DAY	Day, William b: 7/28/1867, Wilmington, Del. d: 8/6/23, Wilmington, Del. TR , 5'8", 150 lbs. Deb: 8/20/1889																												
1889	Phi-N	0	3	.000	4	3	2	0	0	19	16	7.6	0	23	10.9	20	9.5	5.21	81	.243	.439	-2	-2	105	92	-1.4	-2	0	-0.2
1890	Phi-N	1	1	.500	4	2	2	0	0	24	26	9.8	0	12	4.5	9	3.4	3.00	127	.292	.376	2	2	107	130	-0.1	-1	0	0.1
	Pit-N	0	6	.000	6	6	6	0	0	50	66	11.9	1	24	4.3	10	1.8	5.22	65	.335	.407	-9	-10	95	99	-2.9	-3	0	-1.0
	Yr	1	7	.125	10	8	8	0	0	74	92	11.2	1	36	4.4	19	2.3	4.50	78	.321	.397	-8	-8	99	99	-3.0	-1	0	-0.9
Total	2	1	10	.091	14	11	10	0	0	93	108	10.5	1	59	5.7	39	3.8	4.65	79	.307	.406	-10	-10	100	106	-4.4	-6	0	-1.1
■ KEN DAYLEY	Dayley, Kenneth Grant b: 2/25/59, Jerome, Idaho BL/TL, 6', 171 lbs. Deb: 5/13/82																												
1982	Atl-N	5	6	.455	20	11	0	0	0	71	79	10.0	9	25	3.2	34	4.3	4.56	84	.286	.332	-8	-6	107	104	-0.9	1	-1	-0.6
1983	Atl-N	5	8	.385	24	16	0	0	0	105	100	8.6	12	39	3.3	70	6.0	4.29	89	.257	.323	-8	-6	104	93	-1.9	2	-2	-0.6
1984	Atl-N	0	3	.000	4	4	0	0	0	19	28	13.3	5	6	2.8	10	4.7	5.21	76	.341	.380	-3	-3	110	143	-1.4	1	0	-0.1
	StL-N	0	2	.000	3	2	0	0	0	5	16	28.8	1	5	9.0	0	0.0	18.00	20	.615	.656	-8	-8	99	106	-0.9	0	-0	-0.7
	Yr	0	5	.000	7	6	0	0	0	24	44	16.5	6	11	4.1	10	3.8	7.88	49	.404	.444	-11	-11	107	106	-2.3	1	0	-0.8
1985	StL-N	4	4	.500	57	0	0	0	11	65	65	9.0	2	18	2.5	62	8.6	2.77	121	.263	.306	6	4	93	115	-0.7	1	2	0.7
1986	StL-N	0	3	.000	31	0	0	0	5	39	42	9.7	1	11	2.5	33	7.6	3.23	119	.275	.318	2	3	103	109	-1.4	0	0	0.3
1987	StL-N	9	5	.643	53	0	0	0	4	61	52	7.7	2	33	4.9	63	9.3	2.66	150	.234	.335	10	9	97	128	1.0	0	-1	0.8
1988	StL-N	2	7	.222	54	0	0	0	5	55	48	7.9	2	19	3.1	38	6.2	2.78	130	.239	.301	4	5	105	107	-2.3	-0	-0	0.5
Total	7	25	38	.397	246	33	0	0	25	420	430	9.2	34	156	3.3	310	6.6	3.77	99	.269	.329	-5	-1	102	109	-8.5	4	-3	0.3
■ REN DEAGLE	Deagle, Lorenzo Burroughs b: 6/26/1858, New York, N.Y. d: 12/24/36, Kansas City, Mo. BR/TR, 5'9", 190 lbs. Deb: 5/17/1883																												
1883	Cin-a	10	8	.556	18	18	17	1	0	148	136	8.3	0	34	2.1	48	2.9	2.31	140	.250	.294	16	15	98	118	-1.1	-5	0	0.9
1884	Cin-a	3	1	.750	4	4	4	1	0	34	39	10.3	0	9	2.4	12	3.2	5.03	66	.296	.342	-7	-6	103	83	0.7	-2	0	-0.6
	Lou-a	4	6	.400	12	12	8	0	0	87	80	8.3	0	13	1.3	23	2.4	2.59	109	.253	.282	6	2	87	104	-1.8	-2	0	0.0
	Yr	7	7	.500	16	16	12	1	0	121	119	8.9	0	22	1.6	35	2.6	3.27	90	.265	.300	-0	-4	91	104	-1.1	-2	0	-0.6
Total	2	17	15	.531	34	34	29	2	0	269	255	8.5	0	56	1.9	83	2.8	2.74	113	.257	.296	16	11	95	109	-2.2	-9	0	0.3
■ COT DEAL	Deal, Ellis Fergason b: 1/23/23, Arapaho, Okla. BB/TR, 5'10.5", 185 lbs. Deb: 9/11/47 C																												
1947	Bos-A	0	1	.000	5	2	0	0	0	13	20	13.8	0	7	4.8	6	4.2	9.00	44	.364	.429	-8	-7	107	73	-0.4	1	0	-0.5
1948	Bos-A	1	0	1.000	4	0	0	0	0	4	3	6.8	0	3	6.8	2	4.5	0.00	—	.200	.333	2	2	97	0	0.5	0	0	0.2
1950	StL-N	0	0	—	3	0	0	0	0	1	3	27.0	0	2	18.0	1	9.0	18.00	24	.500	.556	-2	-2	103	96	0.0	0	0	-0.1
1954	StL-N	2	3	.400	33	0	0	0	1	72	85	10.6	14	36	4.5	25	3.1	6.25	65	.297	.370	-17	-17	100	96	-0.3	0	0	-1.5
Total	4	3	4	.429	45	2	0	0	1	90	111	11.1	14	48	4.8	34	3.4	6.50	63	.307	.381	-25	-24	101	89	-0.2	1	0	-1.9
■ CHUBBY DEAN	Dean, Alfred Lovill b: 8/24/16, Mt.Airy, N.C. d: 12/21/70, Riverside, Cal. BL/TL, 5'11", 181 lbs. Deb: 4/14/36																												
1937	Phi-A	1	0	1.000	2	1	0	0	0	9	7	7.0	0	6	6.0	4	4.0	4.00	111	.219	.325	1	0	96	79	0.5	0	0	0.0
1938	Phi-A	2	1	.667	6	1	0	0	0	23	22	8.6	3	15	5.9	3	1.2	3.52	142	.250	.359	3	4	105	137	0.7	2	1	0.4
1939	Phi-A	5	8	.385	54	1	0	0	7	117	132	10.2	8	80	6.2	39	3.0	5.23	90	.289	.381	-8	-7	102	106	0.3	8	1	0.3
1940	Phi-A	6	13	.316	30	19	8	1	1	159	220	12.5	21	63	3.6	38	2.2	6.62	66	.324	.375	-40	-40	99	94	-1.0	4	1	-3.5
1941	Phi-A	2	4	.333	18	7	2	0	0	76	90	10.7	9	35	4.1	22	2.6	6.16	69	.294	.362	-17	-16	103	87	-0.5	1	0	-1.2
	Cle-A	1	4	.200	8	8	2	0	0	53	57	9.7	3	24	4.1	14	2.4	4.42	94	.282	.357	-2	-1	101	104	-1.4	0	1	0.0
	Yr	3	8	.273	26	15	4	0	0	129	147	10.3	12	59	4.1	36	2.5	5.44	78	.289	.360	-19	-17	102	104	-1.9	1	1	-1.2
1942	Cle-A	8	11	.421	27	22	8	0	1	173	170	8.8	7	66	3.4	46	2.4	3.80	89	.261	.322	-3	-8	93	96	-1.3	8	-3	-0.7
1943	Cle-A	5	5	.500	17	9	3	0	0	76	83	9.8	1	34	4.0	29	3.4	4.50	66	.281	.351	-10	-13	90	90	-0.3	2	-1	-1.3
Total	7	30	46	.395	162	68	23	1	9	686	781	10.2	52	323	4.2	195	2.6	5.08	79	.288	.357	-75	-83	98	97	-3.0	25	-1	-6.0
■ DORY DEAN	Dean, Charles Wilson b: 11/6/1852, Cincinnati, Ohio d: 5/4/35, Nashville, Tenn. BR/TR, Deb: N/A.																												
1876	Cin-N	4	26	.133	30	30	26	0	0	263	397	13.6	1	24	0.8	22	0.8	3.73	62	.352	.365	-41	-41	100	111	-0.9	0	-0	-3.4
■ HARRY DEAN	Dean, James Harry b: 5/12/15, Rockmart, Ga. d: 6/1/60, Rockmart, Ga. BR/TR, 6'4", 185 lbs. Deb: 4/16/41																												
1941	Was-A	0	0	—	2	0	0	0	0	2	2	9.0	0	3	13.5	0	0.0	4.50	91	.250	.500	-0	-0	99	166	0.0	0	-0	0.0
■ DIZZY DEAN	Dean, Jay Hanna b: 1/16/11, Lucas, Ark. d: 7/17/74, Reno, Nevada BR/TR, 6'2", 182 lbs. Deb: 9/28/30 H																												
1930	StL-N	1	0	1.000	1	1	1	0	0	9	3	3.0	0	3	3.0	5	5.0	1.00	506	.103	.182	4	4	102	44	0.5	0	1	0.5
1932	StL-N	18	15	.545	46	33	16	**4**	2	**286**	280	8.8	14	102	3.2	**191**	**6.0**	3.30	118	.260	.322	18	19	101	109	3.0	5	-1	2.3
1933	StL-N	20	18	.526	**48**	34	**26**	3	4	293	279	8.6	11	64	2.0	**199**	**6.1**	3.04	110	.250	.290	10	10	100	89	-0.4	1	-5	0.7
1934	StL-N	**30**	7	**.811**	50	33	24	**7**	7	312	288	8.3	14	75	2.2	**195**	5.6	2.65	**170**	.241	.286	49	**64**	111	104	**10.5**	3	-2	**7.0**
1935	StL-N	**28**	12	.700	50	36	**29**	3	5	**324**	326	9.1	16	82	2.3	**182**	5.1	3.11	130	.258	.302	33	33	100	105	5.1	4	-4	3.3
1936	StL-N	24	13	.649	**51**	34	**28**	2	**11**	**315**	310	8.9	21	53	1.5	195	5.6	3.17	120	.253	.281	30	22	95	93	4.4	2	-3	1.9
1937	StL-N	13	10	.565	27	25	17	4	1	197	200	9.1	9	33	**1.5**	120	5.5	2.70	144	.259	.287	27	26	100	111	1.1	2	-3	2.6
1938	Chi-N	7	1	.875	13	10	3	1	0	75	63	7.6	2	8	1.0	22	2.6	1.80	216	.226	.250	17	17	103	102	2.8	-0	-1	1.7
1939	Chi-N	6	4	.600	19	13	7	2	0	96	98	9.2	4	17	1.6	27	2.5	3.38	116	.261	.288	6	6	100	87	0.6	-1	-1	0.4
1940	Chi-N	3	3	.500	10	9	3	0	0	54	68	11.3	4	20	3.3	18	3.0	5.17	74	.306	.356	-8	-8	99	100	0.1	0	1	-0.6
1941	Chi-N	0	0	—	1	1	0	0	0	1	3	27.0	0	0	0.0	1	9.0	18.00	19	.429	.429	-2	-2	94	52	0.0	0	0	-0.1
1947	StL-A	0	0	—	1	1	0	0	0	4	3	6.8	0	1	2.3	0	0.0	0.00	—	.231	.286	2	2	106	0	0.0	0	-0	0.2

YEAR	TM/L	W	L	PCT	G	GS	CG	SHO	SV	IP	H	H/G	HR	BB	BB/G	SO	SO/G	ERA	/A	OAVG	OOBP	PR	/A	PF	CPI	WAT	PB	PD	TPI
Total	12	150	83	.644	317	230	154	26	30	1966	1921	8.8	95	458	2.1	1155	5.3	3.04	129	.253	.294	184	194	101	100	27.7	16	-19	19.9
■ PAUL DEAN	Dean, Paul Dee "Daffy" b: 8/14/13, Lucas, Ark. d: 3/17/81, Springdale, Ark. BR/TR, 6', 175 lbs. Deb: 4/18/34																												
1934	StL-N	19	11	.633	39	26	16	5	2	233	225	8.7	19	52	2.0	150	**5.8**	3.44	131	.248	.290	16	28	111	91	0.6	1	-6	2.4
1935	StL-N	19	12	.613	46	33	19	2	5	270	261	8.7	16	55	1.8	143	4.8	3.37	120	.249	.289	20	20	100	89	-0.2	-5	-6	0.9
1936	StL-N	5	5	.500	17	14	5	0	1	92	113	11.1	3	20	2.0	28	2.7	4.60	83	.300	.330	-6	-8	95	90	-0.5	-4	-3	-1.3
1937	StL-N	0	0	—	1	0	0	0	0	0	1	—	0	2	—	0	—	∞	—	1.000	1.000	-3	-3	100	39	0.0	0	0	-0.2
1938	StL-N	3	1	.750	5	4	2	1	0	31	37	10.7	3	5	1.5	14	4.1	2.61	161	.298	.321	4	5	111	169	1.1	-0	-1	0.5
1939	StL-N	0	1	.000	16	2	0	0	0	43	54	11.3	4	10	2.1	16	3.3	6.07	66	.310	.335	-10	-10	103	81	-0.4	-1	-0	-1.0
1940	NY-N	4	4	.500	27	7	2	0	0	99	110	10.0	8	29	2.6	32	2.9	3.91	99	.281	.326	-1	-1	100	109	0.2	-2	-1	-0.3
1941	NY-N	0	0	—	5	0	0	0	0	6	8	12.0	0	3	4.5	3	4.5	3.00	126	.320	.393	0	1	104	175	0.0	0	0	0.0
1943	StL-A	0	0	—	3	1	0	0	0	13	16	11.1	0	3	2.1	1	0.7	3.46	96	.296	.345	-0	-0	101	114	0.0	-0	-0	0.0
Total	9	50	34	.595	159	87	44	8	8	787	825	9.4	53	179	2.0	387	4.4	3.75	110	.266	.305	20	32	103	96	0.8	-11	-17	1.0
■ WAYLAND DEAN	Dean, Wayland Ogden b: 6/20/02, Richmond, W.Va. d: 4/10/30, Huntington, W.Va. BB/TR, 6'1", 178 lbs. Deb: 4/17/24																												
1924	NY-N	6	12	.333	26	20	6	0	0	126	139	9.9	9	45	3.2	39	2.8	5.00	68	.280	.339	-16	-23	88	84	-4.2	1	3	-1.8
1925	NY-N	10	7	.588	33	14	6	1	1	151	169	10.1	13	50	3.0	53	3.2	4.65	90	.282	.334	-6	-8	98	91	0.5	3	0	-0.4
1926	Phi-N	8	16	.333	33	26	15	1	0	204	245	10.8	9	89	3.9	52	2.3	4.90	84	.307	.365	-24	-18	107	101	-1.7	5	-2	-1.2
1927	Phi-N	0	1	.000	2	0	0	0	0	3	6	18.0	0	2	6.0	1	3.0	12.00	33	.500	.533	-3	-3	100	91	-0.4	1	0	0.0
	Chi-N	0	0	—	2	0	0	0	0	2	0	0.0	0	2	9.0	2	9.0	0.00	—	.000	.333	1	1	99	0	0.0	0	0	0.1
	Yr	0	1	.000	4	0	0	0	0	5	6	10.8	0	4	7.2	3	5.4	7.20	54	.375	.458	-2	-2	100	0	-0.4	0	0	0.1
Total	4	24	36	.400	96	60	27	2	1	486	559	10.4	31	188	3.5	147	2.7	4.87	81	.293	.350	-48	-50	99	93	-5.8	10	2	-3.3
■ DENNIS DeBARR	DeBarr, Dennis Lee b: 1/16/53, Cheyenne, Wyo. BL/TL, 6'2", 190 lbs. Deb: 5/14/77																												
1977	Tor-A	0	1	.000	14	0	0	0	0	21	29	12.4	1	8	3.4	10	4.3	6.00	71	.337	.378	-4	-4	105	94	-0.4	0	0	-0.3
■ JOE DeBERRY	DeBerry, Joseph Gaddy b: 11/29/1896, Mt.Gilead, N.C. d: 10/9/44, Southern Pines, N.C BL/TR, 6'1", 175 lbs. Deb: 8/24/20																												
1920	StL-A	2	4	.333	10	7	3	1	0	55	65	10.6	2	20	3.3	12	2.0	4.91	86	.307	.372	-7	-4	111	92	-0.9	-1	0	-0.3
1921	StL-A	0	1	.000	10	1	0	0	0	12	15	11.3	0	10	7.5	1	0.8	6.75	64	.300	.410	-3	-3	101	79	-0.4	-0	0	-0.2
Total	2	2	5	.286	20	8	3	1	0	67	80	10.7	2	30	4.0	13	1.7	5.24	81	.305	.380	-10	-7	109	90	-1.3	-1	0	-0.5
■ DAVE DeBUSSCHERE	DeBusschere, David Albert b: 10/16/40, Detroit, Mich. BR/TR, 6'6", 225 lbs. Deb: 4/22/62																												
1962	Chi-A	0	0	—	12	0	0	0	0	18	5	2.5	1	23	11.5	8	4.0	2.00	187	.089	.354	4	3	94	138	0.0	0	0	0.4
1963	Chi-A	3	4	.429	24	10	1	1	0	84	80	8.6	9	34	3.6	53	5.7	3.11	119	.249	.323	5	6	102	126	-0.8	-2	0	0.4
Total	2	3	4	.429	36	10	1	1	0	102	85	7.5	10	57	5.0	61	5.4	2.91	128	.225	.329	9	9	101	128	-0.8	-2	0	0.8
■ ART DECATUR	Decatur, Arthur Rue b: 1/14/1894, Cleveland, Ohio d: 4/25/66, Talladega, Ala. BR/TR, 6'1", 190 lbs. Deb: 4/15/22																												
1922	Bro-N	3	4	.429	29	2	1	0	1	88	87	8.9	3	29	3.0	31	3.2	2.76	141	.265	.313	13	11	95	120	-0.4	-2	-1	0.7
1923	Bro-N	3	3	.500	36	5	2	0	3	98	101	9.3	3	32	2.9	25	2.3	2.57	152	.264	.319	**16**	**14**	98	127	0.0	-3	-1	0.9
1924	Bro-N	10	9	.526	31	10	3	0	1	126	156	11.1	12	27	1.9	38	2.7	4.14	92	.308	.343	-4	-5	98	115	-1.2	-3	-2	-0.9
1925	Bro-N	0	0	—	1	0	0	0	0	1	3	27.0	0	0	0.0	0	0.0	18.00	23	.600	.500	-2	-2	95	79	0.0	0	0	0.0
	Phi-N	4	13	.235	25	15	4	0	2	128	170	12.0	13	35	2.5	31	2.2	5.27	95	.316	.353	-14	-4	118	97	-4.2	-6	-2	-0.8
	Yr	4	13	.235	26	15	4	0	2	129	173	12.1	13	35	2.4	31	2.2	5.37	93	.319	.355	-16	-5	117	97	-4.2	0	-2	-0.8
1926	Phi-N	0	0	—	2	1	0	0	0	3	6	18.0	0	2	6.0	0	0.0	6.00	68	.375	.444	-1	-1	107	128	0.0	-0	-0	0.0
1927	Phi-N	3	5	.375	29	3	0	0	0	95	130	12.3	11	20	1.9	27	2.6	7.39	53	.334	.356	-37	-37	100	78	0.3	0	-2	-3.5
Total	6	23	34	.404	153	36	10	0	7	539	653	10.9	42	145	2.4	152	2.5	4.51	92	.302	.340	-28	-22	103	107	-5.5	-14	-9	-3.6
■ MARTY DECKER	Decker, Dee Martin b: 6/7/57, Upland, Cal. BR/TR, 5'10", 168 lbs. Deb: 9/20/83																												
1983	SD-N	0	0	—	4	0	0	0	0	9	5	5.0	1	3	3.0	9	9.0	2.00	180	.167	.265	2	2	99	105	0.0	0	0	0.2
■ JOE DECKER	Decker, George Henry b: 6/16/47, Storm Lake, Ia. BR/TR, 6', 180 lbs. Deb: 9/18/69																												
1969	Chi-N	1	0	1.000	4	1	0	0	0	12	10	7.5	0	6	4.5	13	9.8	3.00	126	.222	.314	1	1	105	83	0.5	-0	-0	0.1
1970	Chi-N	2	7	.222	24	17	1	0	0	109	108	8.9	12	56	4.6	79	6.5	4.62	104	.263	.349	-7	2	119	101	-2.5	1	-1	0.3
1971	Chi-N	3	2	.600	21	4	0	0	0	46	62	12.1	2	25	4.9	37	7.2	4.70	81	.343	.405	-6	-5	110	131	0.5	1	1	-0.2
1972	Chi-N	1	0	1.000	5	1	0	0	0	13	9	6.2	1	4	2.8	7	4.8	2.08	187	.188	.250	2	3	112	80	0.5	-0	-0	0.2
1973	Min-A	10	10	.500	29	24	6	3	0	170	167	8.8	12	88	4.7	109	5.8	4.18	94	.260	.349	-7	-5	103	97	0.0	0	0	-0.4
1974	Min-A	16	14	.533	37	37	11	1	0	249	234	8.5	24	97	3.5	158	5.7	3.29	111	.252	.318	9	10	101	111	1.0	0	-2	0.8
1975	Min-A	1	3	.250	10	7	1	0	0	26	25	8.7	2	36	12.5	8	2.8	8.65	47	.260	.452	-14	-13	107	76	-0.9	0	-0	-1.2
1976	Min-A	2	7	.222	13	12	0	0	0	58	60	9.3	3	51	7.9	35	5.4	5.28	65	.273	.401	-11	-12	98	101	-2.6	0	1	-1.0
1979	Sea-A	0	1	.000	9	2	0	0	0	27	27	9.0	2	14	4.7	12	4.0	4.33	99	.255	.339	-0	-0	101	90	-0.4	0	1	0.0
Total	9	36	44	.450	152	105	19	4	0	710	702	8.9	58	377	4.8	458	5.8	4.17	94	.262	.349	-34	-19	105	104	-3.9	1	-1	-1.4
■ JEFF DEDMON	Dedmon, Jeffrey Linden b: 3/4/60, Torrance, Cal. BL/TR, 6'2", 200 lbs. Deb: 9/02/83																												
1983	Atl-N	0	0	—	5	0	0	0	0	4	10	22.5	1	0	0.0	3	6.8	13.50	28	.455	.435	-4	-4	104	81	0.0	0	0	-0.3
1984	Atl-N	4	3	.571	54	0	0	0	4	81	86	9.6	5	35	3.9	51	5.7	3.78	104	.277	.347	-2	1	110	115	0.6	-1	2	0.3
1985	Atl-N	6	3	.667	60	0	0	0	0	86	84	8.8	5	49	5.1	41	4.3	4.08	95	.264	.355	-5	-2	108	106	2.0	-0	3	0.1
1986	Atl-N	6	6	.500	57	0	0	0	3	100	90	8.1	8	39	3.5	58	5.2	2.97	130	.242	.314	8	10	103	117	0.6	-1	1	1.1
1987	Atl-N	3	4	.429	53	3	0	0	4	90	82	8.2	8	42	4.2	40	4.0	3.90	114	.246	.326	2	6	109	98	0.0	1	1	0.8
1988	Cle-A	1	0	1.000	21	0	0	0	1	34	35	9.3	3	21	5.6	17	4.5	4.50	90	.276	.376	-2	-2	102	118	0.5	0	1	0.0
Total	6	20	16	.556	250	3	0	0	12	395	387	8.8	30	186	4.2	210	4.8	3.83	105	.261	.340	-2	9	107	109	3.7	-0	9	2.0
■ DUMMY DEEGAN	Deegan, W. John b: New York, N.Y. Deb: 8/03/01																												
1901	NY-N	0	1	.000	2	1	1	0	0	17	27	14.3	0	6	3.2	8	4.2	6.35	50	.384	.432	-6	-6	95	95	-0.4	-1	0	-0.4
■ JOHN DEERING	Deering, John Thomas b: 6/25/1879, Lynn, Mass. d: 2/15/43, Beverly, Mass. TR , Deb: 03																												
1903	Det-A	3	4	.429	10	8	5	0	0	61	77	11.4	3	24	3.5	14	2.1	3.84	74	.332	.395	-6	-7	96	132	-0.3	3	-1	-0.7
	NY-A	4	3	.571	9	7	6	1	0	60	59	8.9	0	18	2.7	14	2.1	3.75	79	.279	.336	-5	-5	100	81	0.3	-3	-1	-0.5
	Yr	7	7	.500	19	15	11	1	0	121	136	10.1	3	42	3.1	28	2.1	3.79	76	.307	.367	-11	-12	98	81	0.0	3	-2	-1.2
■ MIKE DEGERICK	Degerick, Michael Arthur b: 4/1/43, New York, N.Y. BR/TR, 6'2", 178 lbs. Deb: 9/04/61																												
1961	Chi-A	0	0	—	1	0	0	0	0	2	2	9.0	0	1	4.5	0	0.0	4.50	88	.400	.429	-0	-0	99	149	0.0	0	0	0.0
1962	Chi-A	0	0	—	1	0	0	0	0	1	1	9.0	0	1	9.0	0	0.0	0.00	—	.250	.400	0	0	94	0	0.0	0	0	0.1
Total	2	0	0	—	2	0	0	0	0	3	3	9.0	0	2	6.0	0	0.0	3.00	130	.333	.417	0	0	97	100	0.0	0	0	0.1
■ PEP DEININGER	Deininger, Otto Charles b: 10/10/1877, Wasseralfingen, Germany d: 9/25/50, Boston, Mass. BL/TL, 5'8.5", 180 lbs. Deb: 4/26/02																												
1902	Bos-A	0	0	—	2	1	0	0	0	12	19	14.3	3	9	6.8	2	1.5	9.75	36	.386	.481	-8	-8	98	93	0.0	1	-0	-0.5
■ JOSE DeJESUS	DeJesus. Jose Luis b: 1/6/65, Brooklyn, N.Y. BR/TR, 6'5", 175 lbs. Deb: 9/09/88																												
1988	KC-A	0	1	.000	2	1	0	0	0	3	6	18.0	0	5	15.0	2	6.0	24.00	17	.429	.579	-7	-7	103	51	-0.4	0	0	-0.5
■ TOM de la CRUZ	de la Cruz, Tomas (Rivero) b: 9/18/14, Marianao, Cuba d: 9/6/58, Havana, Cuba BR/TR, 6'2", 168 lbs. Deb: 4/20/44																												
1944	Cin-N	9	9	.500	34	20	9	0	1	191	170	8.0	9	45	2.1	65	3.1	3.25	105	.238	.281	8	4	95	81	-1.3	-0	-0	0.3
■ JIM DELAHANTY	Delahanty, James Christopher b: 6/20/1879, Cleveland, Ohio d: 10/17/53, Cleveland, Ohio BR/TR, 5'10.5", 170 lbs. Deb: 4/19/01																												
1904	Bos-N	0	0	—	1	1	0	0	0	3	5	15.0	0	1	3.0	0	0.0	0.00	—	.398	.443	1	1	102	0	0.0	0	0	0.1
1905	Bos-N	0	0	—	1	0	0	0	0	2	5	22.5	1	0	0.0	0	0.0	4.50	68	.501	.501	-0	-0	102	300	0.0	0	0	0.0
Total	2	0	0	—	2	1	0	0	0	5	10	18.0	1	1	1.8	0	0.0	1.80	160	.444	.468	1	1	102	120	0.0	1	0	0.1
■ ART DELANEY	Delaney, Arthur Dewey "Swede" (born Arthur Dewey Helenius) b: 11/28/01, Greensboro, N.C. d: 5/2/70, Hayward, Cal. BR/TR, 5'10.5", 178 lbs. Deb: 4/16/24																												
1924	StL-N	1	0	1.000	8	1	1	0	0	20	19	8.5	0	6	2.7	2	0.9	1.80	221	.250	.305	5	5	103	143	0.5	0	0	0.5
1928	Bos-N	9	17	.346	39	22	8	0	2	192	197	9.2	11	56	2.6	45	2.1	3.80	106	.267	.308	4	5	101	89	0.4	-3	1	0.3
1929	Bos-N	3	5	.375	20	8	3	1	0	75	103	12.4	6	35	4.2	17	2.0	6.12	75	.336	.390	-12	-13	97	103	0.1	1	-1	-1.1
Total	3	13	22	.371	67	31	12	1	2	287	319	10.0	17	97	3.0	64	2.0	4.26	98	.285	.331	-3	-3	100	97	1.0	-2	0	-0.3

YEAR	TM/L	W	L	PCT	G	GS	CG	SHO	SV	IP	H	H/G	HR	BB	BB/G	SO	SO/G	ERA	/A	OAVG	OOBP	PR	/A	PF	CPI	WAT	PB	PD	TPI
■ JOSE DeLEON	DeLeon, Jose (Chestaro) b: 12/20/60, La Vega, D.R. BR/TR, 6'3", 210 lbs. Deb: 7/23/83																												
1983	Pit-N	7	3	.700	15	15	3	2	0	108	75	6.3	5	47	3.9	118	9.8	2.83	132	.196	.281	10	11	103	75	2.0	-1	-1	1.0
1984	Pit-N	7	13	.350	30	28	5	1	0	192	147	6.9	10	92	4.3	153	7.2	3.75	90	.214	.304	-3	-8	94	75	-2.6	-3	-3	-1.4
1985	Pit-N	2	19	.095	31	25	1	0	3	163	138	7.6	15	89	4.9	149	8.2	4.69	80	.231	.329	-20	-17	104	78	-7.9	-2	-1	-1.9
1986	Pit-N	1	3	.250	9	1	0	0	1	16	17	9.6	2	17	9.6	11	6.2	8.44	44	.266	.422	-8	-8	101	75	-0.6	0	0	-0.7
	Chi-A	4	5	.444	13	13	1	0	0	79	49	5.6	7	42	4.8	68	7.7	2.96	143	.179	.292	11	11	101	86	0.0	0	0	1.2
1987	Chi-A	11	12	.478	33	31	2	0	0	206	177	7.7	24	97	4.2	153	6.7	4.02	121	.230	.319	10	19	109	93	0.1	0	-3	1.5
1988	StL-N	13	10	.565	34	34	3	1	0	225	198	7.9	13	86	3.4	208	8.3	3.68	98	.237	.304	-6	-2	105	86	2.4	-1	-2	-0.4
Total	6	45	65	.409	165	147	15	4	4	989	801	7.3	76	470	4.3	860	7.8	3.86	101	.222	.311	-6	5	103	83	-6.6	-6	-9	-0.7
■ LUIS DeLEON	DeLeon, Luis Antonio (Tricoche) b: 8/19/57, Ponce, P.R. BR/TR, 6'1", 153 lbs. Deb: 9/06/81																												
1981	StL-N	0	1	.000	10	0	0	0	0	15	11	6.6	1	3	1.8	8	4.8	2.40	147	.200	.237	2	2	101	68	-0.4	-0	-0	0.2
1982	SD-N	9	5	.643	61	0	0	0	15	102	77	6.8	10	16	1.4	60	5.3	2.03	163	.212	.241	18	14	92	106	2.1	0	1	1.6
1983	SD-N	6	6	.500	63	0	0	0	13	111	89	7.2	8	27	2.2	90	7.3	2.68	135	.224	.265	12	11	99	92	0.0	-0	-2	1.0
1984	SD-N	2	2	.500	32	0	0	0	0	43	44	9.2	12	12	2.5	44	9.2	5.44	65	.256	.314	-9	-9	98	94	-0.1	-0	0	-0.9
1985	SD-N	0	3	.000	29	0	0	0	3	39	39	9.0	6	10	2.3	31	7.2	4.15	88	.267	.319	-2	-2	101	107	-1.4	0	-0	-0.2
1987	Bal-A	0	2	.000	11	0	0	0	1	21	19	8.1	1	8	3.4	13	5.6	4.71	94	.253	.326	-1	-1	99	82	-0.9	0	-0	0.0
Total	6	17	19	.472	206	0	0	0	32	331	279	7.6	38	76	2.1	246	6.7	3.13	114	.231	.274	20	16	97	97	-0.7	-0	-1	1.7
■ FLAME DELHI	Delhi, Lee William b: 11/5/1892, Harqua Hala, Ariz. d: 5/9/66, San Rafael, Cal. BR/TR, 6'2.5", 198 lbs. Deb: 4/16/12																												
1912	Chi-A	0	0	—	1	0	0	0	0	3	7	21.0	0	3	9.0	2	6.0	9.00	37	.412	.500	-2	-2	99	115	0.0	0	0	0.0
■ WHEEZER DELL	Dell, William George b: 6/11/1887, Tuscarora, Nev. d: 8/24/66, Independence, Cal. BR/TR, 6'4", 210 lbs. Deb: 4/22/12																												
1912	StL-N	0	0	—	3	0	0	0	0	2	3	13.5	0	3	13.5	0	0.0	13.50	26	.188	.316	-2	-2	103	1	0.0	0	0	-0.1
1915	Bro-N	11	10	.524	40	24	12	4	1	215	166	6.9	5	100	4.2	94	3.9	2.34	120	.218	.306	10	11	102	109	0.0	-1	0	1.2
1916	Bro-N	8	9	.471	32	16	9	2	1	155	143	8.3	2	43	2.5	76	4.4	2.26	116	.256	.305	6	6	100	**124**	-2.0	-2	-1	0.3
1917	Bro-N	0	4	.000	17	4	0	0	1	58	55	8.5	3	25	3.9	28	4.3	3.72	76	.263	.333	-7	-6	105	102	-1.9	-2	-1	-0.8
Total	4	19	23	.452	92	44	21	6	3	430	367	7.7	10	171	3.6	198	4.1	2.55	108	.237	.310	7	9	102	113	-3.9	-5	-2	0.6
■ IKE DELOCK	Delock, Ivan Martin b: 11/11/29, Highland Park, Mich BR/TR, 5'11", 175 lbs. Deb: 4/17/52																												
1952	Bos-A	4	9	.308	39	7	1	1	5	95	88	8.3	9	50	4.7	46	4.4	4.26	92	.245	.335	-6	-3	107	93	-2.5	-1	-0	-0.4
1953	Bos-A	3	1	.750	23	1	0	0	1	49	60	11.0	2	20	3.7	22	4.0	4.41	98	.308	.368	-2	-0	108	113	0.9	-1	-1	-0.1
1955	Bos-A	9	7	.563	29	18	6	0	3	144	136	8.5	16	61	3.8	88	5.5	3.75	129	.247	.323	3	18	122	101	0.3	-2	-1	1.7
1956	Bos-A	13	7	.650	48	8	1	0	9	128	122	8.6	12	80	5.6	105	7.4	4.22	101	.252	.354	-1	0	102	104	2.6	-2	0	0.0
1957	Bos-A	9	8	.529	49	2	0	0	11	94	80	7.7	11	45	4.3	62	5.9	3.83	108	.230	.318	-0	3	109	95	0.0	-1	-1	0.1
1958	Bos-A	14	8	.636	31	19	9	1	2	160	155	8.7	13	56	3.1	82	4.6	3.37	117	.252	.310	7	10	105	103	3.1	-4	-1	0.6
1959	Bos-A	11	6	.647	28	17	4	0	0	134	120	8.1	12	62	4.2	55	3.7	2.96	137	.236	.315	13	16	105	120	2.9	-3	-2	1.2
1960	Bos-A	9	10	.474	24	23	3	1	0	129	145	10.1	21	52	3.6	49	3.4	4.74	86	.283	.349	-13	-10	105	107	1.0	-3	-1	-1.2
1961	Bos-A	6	9	.400	28	28	3	1	0	156	185	10.7	24	52	3.0	80	4.6	4.90	84	.293	.342	-15	-13	105	105	-1.1	-2	-2	-1.5
1962	Bos-A	4	5	.444	17	13	4	2	0	86	89	9.3	10	24	2.5	49	5.1	3.77	108	.268	.311	2	3	103	107	-0.2	-1	-1	0.1
1963	Bos-A	1	2	.333	6	6	1	0	0	32	31	8.7	4	12	3.4	23	6.5	4.50	86	.246	.309	-3	-2	107	82	-0.3	-2	0	-0.3
	Bal-A	1	3	.250	7	5	0	0	0	30	25	7.5	7	16	4.8	11	3.3	5.10	66	.236	.328	-5	-6	93	97	-1.0	-1	0	-0.6
	Yr	2	5	.286	13	11	1	0	0	62	56	8.1	11	28	4.1	34	4.9	4.79	76	.240	.318	-8	-8	100	97	-1.3	-2	0	-0.9
Total	11	84	75	.528	329	147	32	6	31	1237	1236	9.0	141	530	3.9	672	4.9	4.04	103	.259	.331	-20	16	107	104	5.7	-22	-8	-0.4
■ RAMON de los SANTOS	de los Santos, Ramon (Genero) b: 1/19/49, Santo Domingo, D.R. BL/TL, 6'1", 175 lbs. Deb: 8/21/74																												
1974	Hou-N	1	1	.500	12	0	0	0	0	12	11	8.3	0	9	6.8	7	5.3	2.25	157	.234	.351	2	2	98	148	0.0	0	0	0.2
■ AL DEMAREE	Demaree, Albert Wentworth b: 9/8/1884, Quincy, Ill. d: 4/30/62, Los Angeles, Cal. BL/TR, 6', 170 lbs. Deb: 9/26/12																												
1912	NY-N	1	0	1.000	2	2	1	1	0	16	17	9.6	0	2	1.1	11	6.2	1.69	200	.270	.292	3	3	99	138	0.5	-1	0	0.2
1913	NY-N	13	4	.765	31	24	11	2	2	200	176	7.9	4	38	1.7	76	3.4	2.21	145	.243	.279	22	22	100	106	2.8	-4	-3	1.6
1914	NY-N	10	17	.370	38	30	13	2	0	224	219	8.8	3	77	3.1	89	3.6	3.09	84	.263	.321	-8	-12	94	99	-4.8	-2	-1	-1.5
1915	Phi-N	14	11	.560	32	26	13	3	1	210	201	8.6	4	58	2.5	69	3.0	3.04	94	.260	.307	-7	-4	104	97	-0.7	-0	-5	-0.9
1916	Phi-N	19	14	.576	39	35	25	3	1	285	252	8.0	4	48	1.5	130	4.1	2.62	94	.242	.273	-0	-5	94	82	-0.6	-3	-6	-1.7
1917	Chi-N	5	9	.357	24	18	6	1	1	141	125	8.0	5	37	2.4	43	2.7	2.55	111	.244	.288	2	5	105	104	-1.8	-1	1	0.4
	NY-N	4	5	.444	15	11	1	0	0	78	70	8.1	1	17	2.0	23	2.7	2.65	95	.239	.274	1	-1	93	82	-1.3	-1	0	-0.1
	Yr	9	14	.391	39	29	7	1	1	219	195	8.0	6	54	2.2	66	2.7	2.59	105	.241	.281	3	3	101	82	-3.1	-1	1	0.3
1918	NY-N	8	6	.571	26	14	8	2	1	142	143	9.1	5	25	1.6	39	2.5	2.47	107	.262	.291	5	3	96	112	0.0	-3	-0	0.0
1919	Bos-N	6	6	.500	25	13	6	0	3	128	147	10.3	8	35	2.5	34	2.4	3.80	77	.300	.336	-13	-13	100	114	1.0	-5	-2	-1.9
Total	8	80	72	.526	232	173	84	14	9	1424	1350	8.5	34	337	2.1	514	3.2	2.77	99	.256	.296	6	-3	98	99	-4.9	-20	-16	-3.9
■ FRED DEMARRIS	Demarris, Fred b: 1865, Nashua, N.H. TR , Deb: 7/26/1890																												
1890	Chi-N	0	0	—	1	0	0	0	0	2	1	4.5	0	1	4.5	1	4.5	0.00	—	.160	.276	1	1	107	0	0.0	-0	0	0.0
■ LARRY DEMERY	Demery, Lawrence Calvin b: 6/4/53, Bakersfield, Cal. BR/TR, 6', 170 lbs. Deb: 6/02/74																												
1974	Pit-N	6	6	.500	19	15	2	0	0	95	95	9.0	12	51	4.8	51	4.8	4.26	82	.262	.348	-7	-8	97	107	-0.4	0	-1	-0.8
1975	Pit-N	7	5	.583	45	8	1	0	4	115	95	7.4	7	43	3.4	59	4.6	2.90	122	.230	.301	9	8	98	101	0.2	1	-1	0.9
1976	Pit-N	10	7	.588	36	15	4	1	2	145	123	7.6	8	58	3.6	72	4.5	3.17	110	.234	.303	5	5	99	97	0.4	-1	-0	0.4
1977	Pit-N	6	5	.545	39	8	0	0	1	90	100	10.0	13	47	4.7	35	3.5	5.10	78	.279	.359	-12	-11	102	100	-0.4	-0	-0	-1.1
Total	4	29	23	.558	139	46	7	1	7	445	413	8.4	40	199	4.0	217	4.4	3.72	97	.249	.325	-4	-6	99	101	-0.2	0	-2	-0.6
■ HARRY DeMILLER	DeMiller, Harry b: 11/12/1867, Wooster, Ohio d: 10/19/28, Santa Ana, Cal. TL , Deb: 8/20/1892																												
1892	Chi-N	1	1	.500	4	2	2	0	0	24	29	10.9	1	16	6.0	15	5.6	6.38	48	.312	.413	-8	-9	93	83	0.0	1	0	-0.6
■ DON DeMOLA	DeMola, Donald John b: 7/5/52, Glen Cove, N.Y. BR/TR, 6'2", 185 lbs. Deb: 4/13/74																												
1974	Mon-N	1	0	1.000	25	1	0	0	0	58	46	7.1	7	21	3.3	47	7.3	3.10	122	.223	.289	3	4	104	101	0.5	-1	-1	0.3
1975	Mon-N	4	7	.364	60	0	0	0	1	98	92	8.4	8	42	3.9	63	5.8	4.13	96	.251	.325	-5	-2	109	91	-1.1	-1	-3	-0.5
Total	2	5	7	.417	85	1	0	0	1	156	138	8.0	15	63	3.6	110	6.3	3.75	104	.241	.313	-2	3	107	95	-0.6	-2	-3	-0.2
■ BEN DeMOTT	DeMott, Benjamin Harrison b: 4/2/1889, Green Village, N.J. d: 7/5/63, Somerville, N.J. BR/TR, 6', 192 lbs. Deb: 8/15/10																												
1910	Cle-A	0	3	.000	6	4	1	0	0	28	45	14.5	0	8	2.6	13	4.2	5.46	47	.388	.432	-9	-9	102	116	-1.4	0	0	-0.8
1911	Cle-A	0	1	.000	1	1	0	0	0	4	10	22.5	0	2	4.5	2	4.5	11.25	31	.588	.632	-4	-3	103	117	-0.4	-0	0	-0.2
Total	2	0	4	.000	7	5	1	0	0	32	55	15.5	0	10	2.8	15	4.2	6.19	43	.414	.458	-13	-12	102	116	-1.8	-0	1	-1.0
■ CON DEMPSEY	Dempsey, Cornelius Francis b: 9/16/23, San Francisco, Cal BR/TR, 6'4", 190 lbs. Deb: 4/28/51																												
1951	Pit-N	0	2	.000	3	2	0	0	0	7	11	14.1	2	4	5.1	3	3.9	9.00	48	.393	.455	-4	-4	110	108	-0.9	-0	0	-0.2
■ MARK DEMPSEY	Dempsey, Mark Steven b: 12/17/57, Dayton, Ohio BR/TR, 6'6", 225 lbs. Deb: 9/04/82																												
1982	SF-N	0	0	—	3	1	0	0	0	6	11	16.5	1	2	3.0	4	6.0	7.50	45	.440	.464	-3	-3	94	127	0.0	-0	0	-0.2
■ BILL DENEHY	Denehy, William Francis b: 3/31/46, Middletown, Conn. BB/TR, 6'3", 200 lbs. Deb: 4/16/67																												
1967	NY-N	1	7	.125	15	8	0	0	0	54	51	8.5	8	29	4.8	35	5.8	4.67	74	.248	.333	-8	-7	102	95	-2.6	-1	-0	-0.8
1968	Was-A	0	0	—	3	0	0	0	0	2	4	18.0	0	4	18.0	1	4.5	9.00	31	.444	.615	-1	-1	94	147	0.0	0	0	-0.1
1971	Det-A	0	3	.000	31	1	0	0	1	49	47	8.6	4	28	5.1	27	5.0	4.22	78	.250	.353	-4	-5	95	99	-1.4	1	-0	-0.4
Total	3	1	10	.091	49	9	0	0	1	105	102	8.7	12	61	5.2	63	5.4	4.54	74	.253	.350	-13	-14	98	98	-4.0	0	-1	-1.3
■ BRIAN DENMAN	Denman, Brian John b: 2/12/56, Minneapolis, Minn. BR/TR, 6'4", 205 lbs. Deb: 8/22/82																												
1982	Bos-A	3	4	.429	9	9	2	1	0	49	55	10.1	6	9	1.7	9	1.7	4.78	94	.282	.311	-4	-2	110	87	-0.7	0	-0	-0.1
■ DON DENNIS	Dennis, Donald Ray b: 3/3/42, Uniontown, Kan. BR/TR, 6'2", 190 lbs. Deb: 6/18/65																												
1965	StL-N	2	3	.400	41	0	0	0	6	55	47	7.7	3	16	2.6	29	4.7	2.29	164	.236	.290	8	9	106	126	-0.4	1	2	1.2
1966	StL-N	4	2	.667	38	1	0	0	2	60	73	10.9	8	17	2.6	25	3.8	4.95	73	.302	.343	-9	-9	100	102	1.0	-1	3	-0.6

YEAR	TM/L	W	L	PCT	G	GS	CG	SHO	SV	IP	H	H/G	HR	BB	BB/G	SO	SO/G	ERA	/A	OAVG	OOBP	PR	/A	PF	CPI	WAT	PB	PD	TPI
Total	2	6	5	.545	79	1	0	0	8	115	120	9.4	11	33	2.6	54	4.2	3.68	100	.272	.319	-1	-0	103	113	0.6	-0	4	0.6
■ **JERRY DENNY**	Denny, Jeremiah Dennis (born Jeremiah Dennis Eldridge) b: 3/16/1859, New York, N.Y. d: 8/16/27, Houston, Tex. BR/TR, 5'11.5", 180 lbs. Deb: 5/02/1881																												
1888	Ind-N	0	0	—	1	0	0	0	0	4	5	11.3	1	4	9.0	1	2.3	9.00	31	.320	.459	-3	-3	98	90	0.0	0	0	-0.1
■ **JOHN DENNY**	Denny, John Allen b: 11/8/52, Prescott, Ariz. BR/TR, 6'3", 185 lbs. Deb: 9/12/74																												
1974	StL-N	0	0	—	2	0	0	0	0	2	3	13.5	0	0	0.0	1	4.5	0.00	—	.273	.273	1	1	103	0	0.0	0	0	0.1
1975	StL-N	10	7	.588	25	24	3	2	0	136	149	9.9	5	51	3.4	72	4.8	3.97	95	.280	.343	-5	-3	103	98	1.5	1	2	0.0
1976	StL-N	11	9	.550	30	30	8	3	0	207	189	8.2	11	74	3.2	74	3.2	**2.52**	**145**	.246	.315	23	**26**	105	129	2.1	2	1	**3.4**
1977	StL-N	8	8	.500	26	26	3	1	0	150	165	9.9	9	62	3.7	60	3.6	4.50	83	.281	.349	-10	-13	95	96	-0.1	-2	3	-1.2
1978	StL-N	14	11	.560	33	33	11	2	0	234	200	7.7	13	74	2.8	103	4.0	2.96	116	.238	.299	16	12	96	101	3.3	3	8	2.4
1979	StL-N	8	11	.421	31	31	5	2	0	206	206	9.0	24	100	4.4	99	4.3	4.85	80	.264	.343	-25	-22	104	92	-2.1	-1	2	-2.1
1980	Cle-A	8	6	.571	16	16	4	1	0	109	116	9.6	4	47	3.9	59	4.9	4.38	95	.284	.362	-4	-3	103	100	1.2	0	1	-0.1
1981	Cle-A	10	6	.625	19	19	6	3	0	146	139	8.6	9	66	4.1	94	5.8	3.14	109	.254	.334	8	5	93	120	2.2	0	5	1.0
1982	Cle-A	6	11	.353	21	21	5	0	0	138	126	8.2	11	73	4.8	94	6.1	5.02	82	.240	.337	-14	-14	101	76	-2.4	0	1	-1.2
	Phi-N	0	2	.000	4	4	0	0	0	22	18	7.4	1	10	4.1	19	7.8	4.09	82	.217	.298	-1	-2	94	62	-0.9	1	1	0.0
1983	Phi-N	**19**	6	**.760**	36	36	7	1	0	243	229	8.5	9	53	2.0	139	5.1	2.37	154	.250	.291	**34**	**34**	100	116	**6.3**	0	1	**4.0**
1984	Phi-N	7	7	.500	22	22	2	0	0	154	122	7.1	11	29	1.7	94	5.5	2.45	148	.214	.253	19	20	101	85	0.0	0	4	2.8
1985	Phi-N	11	14	.440	33	33	6	2	0	231	252	9.8	15	83	3.2	123	4.8	3.82	96	.282	.339	-6	-4	102	111	-0.6	-2	1	-0.3
1986	Cin-N	11	10	.524	27	27	2	1	0	171	179	9.4	15	56	2.9	115	6.1	4.21	92	.272	.327	-9	-6	104	97	-0.1	2	3	-0.1
Total	13	123	108	.532	325	322	62	18	0	2149	2093	8.8	137	778	3.3	1146	4.8	3.58	104	.258	.322	27	32	101	103	10.4	2	31	8.7
■ **EDDIE DENT**	Dent, Elliott Estill b: 12/8/1887, Baltimore, Md. d: 11/25/74, Birmingham, Ala. BR/TR, 6'1", 190 lbs. Deb: 09																												
1909	Bro-N	2	4	.333	6	5	4	0	0	42	47	10.1	2	15	3.2	17	3.6	4.29	62	.307	.369	-8	-8	103	104	-0.1	-1	-1	-0.7
1911	Bro-N	2	1	.667	5	3	1	0	0	32	30	8.4	0	10	2.8	3	0.8	3.66	92	.256	.326	-1	-1	99	82	0.6	-0	0	0.0
1912	Bro-N	0	0	—	1	0	0	0	0	1	4	36.0	0	1	9.0	1	9.0	36.00	9	.571	.625	-4	-4	97	53	0.0	-0	0	-0.2
Total	3	4	5	.444	12	8	5	0	0	75	81	9.7	2	26	3.1	21	2.5	4.44	67	.292	.357	-12	-12	101	94	0.5	-2	-0	-0.9
■ **ROGER DENZER**	Denzer, Roger "Peaceful Valley" b: 10/5/1871, Leseur, Minn. d: 9/18/49, Leseur, Minn. TR, 6', 180 lbs. Deb: 4/24/1897																												
1897	Chi-N	2	8	.200	12	10	8	0	0	95	125	11.8	4	34	3.2	17	1.6	5.21	83	.340	.396	-9	-9	101	96	-2.8	-3	0	-0.9
1901	NY-N	2	6	.250	11	9	3	1	0	62	69	10.0	2	5	0.7	22	3.2	3.34	95	.304	.319	-0	-1	95	96	-1.3	-1	-2	-0.2
Total	2	4	14	.222	23	19	11	1	0	157	194	11.1	6	39	2.2	39	2.2	4.47	86	.326	.368	-10	-11	99	96	-4.1	-4	-2	-1.1
■ **GEORGE DERBY**	Derby, George H. "Jonah" b: 7/6/1857, Webster, Mass. d: 7/4/25, Philadelphia, Pa. BL/TR, 6', 175 lbs. Deb: 5/02/1881																												
1881	Det-N	29	26	.527	56	55	55	**9**	0	495	505	9.2	3	86	1.6	**212**	**3.9**	2.20	134	.276	.309	**32**	**41**	106	115	5.3	-11	2	**3.2**
1882	Det-N	17	20	.459	40	39	38	3	0	362	386	9.6	8	81	2.0	182	4.5	3.26	92	.281	.321	-15	-10	104	100	-2.8	-7	2	-1.2
1883	Buf-N	2	10	.167	14	13	12	0	1	108	173	14.4	3	15	1.3	34	2.8	5.92	53	.370	.389	-33	-34	99	97	-4.2	-1	0	-2.6
Total	3	48	56	.462	110	107	105	12	1	965	1064	9.9	14	182	1.7	428	4.0	3.01	99	.290	.323	-17	-2	105	108	-1.7	-19	3	-0.6
■ **PAUL DERRINGER**	Derringer, Samuel Paul "Duke" b: 10/17/06, Springfield, Ky. d: 11/17/87, Sarasota, Fla. BR/TR, 6'3.5", 205 lbs. Deb: 4/16/31																												
1931	StL-N	18	8	**.692**	35	23	15	4	2	212	225	9.6	9	65	2.8	134	5.7	3.35	119	.274	.326	12	15	103	112	1.6	-6	0	0.9
1932	StL-N	11	14	.440	39	30	14	1	0	233	296	11.4	6	67	2.6	78	3.0	4.06	96	.310	.350	-5	-4	101	113	-0.8	-0	-2	-0.5
1933	StL-N	0	2	.000	3	2	1	0	0	17	24	12.7	0	9	4.8	3	1.6	4.24	79	.353	.405	-2	-2	100	148	-0.9	-1	0	-0.1
	Cin-N	7	25	.219	33	31	16	2	1	231	240	9.4	4	51	2.0	86	3.4	3.23	105	.271	.308	3	4	102	98	-7.7	-1	1	0.4
	Yr	7	27	.206	36	33	17	2	1	248	264	9.6	4	60	2.2	89	3.2	3.30	103	.277	.315	1	2	102	98	-8.6	-1	1	0.3
1934	Cin-N	15	21	.417	47	31	18	1	4	261	297	10.2	8	59	2.0	122	4.2	3.59	119	.283	.319	14	19	105	103	2.5	-0	-2	1.8
1935	Cin-N	22	13	.629	45	33	20	3	2	277	295	9.6	13	49	1.6	120	3.9	3.51	109	.271	.302	16	10	95	97	**6.8**	-4	3	0.7
1936	Cin-N	19	19	.500	**51**	37	13	2	5	282	331	10.6	11	42	1.3	121	3.9	4.02	97	.289	.312	-0	-4	97	91	0.9	-1	-0	-0.4
1937	Cin-N	10	14	.417	43	26	12	1	1	223	240	9.7	7	55	2.2	94	3.8	4.04	90	.271	.306	-3	-10	93	84	1.2	1	1	-0.8
1938	Cin-N	21	14	.600	41	37	**26**	4	3	**307**	315	9.2	20	49	1.4	132	3.9	2.93	124	.262	.288	29	24	96	107	2.6	-0	-2	2.2
1939	Cin-N	25	7	**.781**	38	35	28	5	0	301	321	9.6	15	35	**1.0**	128	3.8	2.93	134	.272	.288	33	33	100	108	**7.5**	-0	-3	3.1
1940	Cin-N	20	12	.625	37	37	26	3	0	297	280	8.5	17	48	**1.5**	115	3.5	3.06	123	.246	**.272**	26	23	98	91	-0.8	-2	-3	1.8
1941	Cin-N	12	14	.462	29	28	17	2	1	228	233	9.2	16	54	2.1	76	3.0	3.32	107	.266	.302	8	6	98	107	-2.8	-3	-1	0.2
1942	Cin-N	10	11	.476	29	27	13	1	0	209	203	8.7	4	49	2.1	68	2.9	3.06	110	.250	.294	6	7	102	89	-0.5	-2	-4	0.2
1943	Chi-N	10	14	.417	32	22	10	2	3	174	184	9.5	7	39	2.0	75	3.9	3.57	93	.264	.300	-4	-5	98	87	-1.8	1	-4	-0.7
1944	Chi-N	7	13	.350	42	16	7	0	3	180	205	10.3	13	39	2.0	69	3.5	4.15	87	.284	.316	-11	-11	100	95	-3.0	-2	-1	-1.2
1945	Chi-N	16	11	.593	35	30	15	1	4	214	223	9.4	8	51	2.1	86	3.6	3.45	105	.265	.305	8	4	95	95	-1.0	0	-2	0.2
Total	15	223	212	.513	579	445	251	32	29	3646	3912	9.7	158	761	1.9	1507	3.7	3.46	108	.272	.306	131	111	99	99	3.8	-20	-17	7.8
■ **JIM DERRINGTON**	Derrington, Charles James "Blackie" b: 11/29/39, Compton, Cal. BL/TL, 6'3", 190 lbs. Deb: 9/30/56																												
1956	Chi-A	0	1	.000	1	1	0	0	0	6	9	13.5	2	6	9.0	3	4.5	7.50	56	.375	.484	-2	-2	102	143	-0.4	0	-0	-0.1
1957	Chi-A	0	1	.000	20	5	0	0	0	37	29	7.1	4	29	7.1	14	3.4	4.86	75	.216	.355	-4	-5	97	84	-0.4	-0	-1	-0.5
Total	2	0	2	.000	21	6	0	0	0	43	38	8.0	6	35	7.3	17	3.6	5.23	71	.241	.376	-7	-7	97	92	-0.8	0	-1	-0.6
■ **JIM DESHAIES**	Deshaies, James Joseph b: 6/23/60, Massena, N.Y. BL/TL, 6'4", 222 lbs. Deb: 8/07/84																												
1984	NY-A	0	1	.000	2	2	0	0	0	7	14	18.0	1	7	9.0	5	6.4	11.57	32	.438	.525	-6	-6	93	100	-0.4	0	0	-0.4
1985	Hou-N	0	0	—	2	0	0	0	0	3	1	3.0	0	0	0.0	2	6.0	0.00	—	.100	.100	1	1	96	0	0.0	0	0	0.1
1986	Hou-N	12	5	.706	26	26	1	1	0	144	124	7.8	16	59	3.7	128	8.0	3.25	116	.234	.309	8	9	102	107	2.6	-2	-1	0.6
1987	Hou-N	11	6	.647	26	25	1	0	0	152	149	8.8	22	57	3.4	104	6.2	4.62	82	.257	.318	-9	-14	93	91	3.1	0	-1	-1.4
1988	Hou-N	11	14	.440	31	31	3	2	0	207	164	7.1	20	72	3.1	127	5.5	3.00	108	.218	.281	10	5	93	97	-1.8	-3	-2	-0.1
Total	5	34	26	.567	87	84	5	3	0	513	452	7.9	59	195	3.4	366	6.4	3.65	98	.237	.304	4	-5	96	98	3.5	-5	-4	-1.2
■ **JIMMIE DeSHONG**	DeShong, James Brooklyn b: 11/30/09, Harrisburg, Pa. BR/TR, 5'11", 165 lbs. Deb: 4/12/32																												
1932	Phi-A	0	0	—	6	0	0	0	0	10	17	15.3	3	9	8.1	5	4.5	11.70	42	.378	.482	-8	-8	111	95	0.0	-1	0	-0.6
1934	NY-A	6	7	.462	31	12	6	0	3	134	126	8.5	6	56	3.8	40	2.7	4.10	102	.243	.317	6	1	93	82	-1.6	2	0	0.2
1935	NY-A	4	1	.800	29	3	0	0	3	69	64	8.3	6	33	4.3	30	3.9	3.26	123	.242	.324	9	6	90	117	1.3	-1	2	0.6
1936	Was-A	18	10	.643	34	31	16	2	2	224	255	10.2	11	96	3.9	59	2.4	4.62	105	.285	.353	10	6	96	101	3.8	2	-2	0.5
1937	Was-A	14	15	.483	37	34	20	0	1	264	290	9.9	15	124	4.2	86	2.9	4.91	90	.280	.354	-8	-15	96	93	0.2	2	1	-1.1
1938	Was-A	5	8	.385	31	14	1	0	0	131	160	11.0	11	83	5.7	41	2.8	6.60	69	.310	.398	-26	-29	96	94	-1.5	2	0	-2.2
1939	Was-A	0	3	.000	7	6	1	0	0	41	56	12.3	7	31	6.8	12	2.6	8.56	49	.337	.422	-18	-20	91	93	-1.4	0	1	-1.4
Total	7	47	44	.516	175	100	44	2	9	873	968	10.0	59	432	4.5	273	2.8	5.08	88	.281	.358	-35	-59	95	95	0.8	6	3	-4.0
■ **SHORTY DesJARDIEN**	DesJardien, Paul Raymond b: 8/24/1893, Coffeyville, Kan. d: 3/7/56, Monrovia, Cal. BR/TR, 6'4.5", 205 lbs. Deb: 5/20/16																												
1916	Cle-A	0	0	—	1	0	0	0	0	1	1	9.0	0	1	9.0	0	0.0	18.00	16	.200	.333	-2	-2	99	13	0.0	0	0	-0.1
■ **RUBE DESSAU**	Dessau, Frank Rolland b: 3/29/1883, New Galilee, Pa. d: 5/6/52, York, Pa. BB/TR, 5'11", 175 lbs. Deb: 9/22/07																												
1907	Bos-N	0	1	.000	2	2	1	0	0	9	13	13.0	0	10	10.0	1	1.0	11.00	22	.380	.531	-9	-9	99	69	-0.4	-0	-0	-0.7
1910	Bro-N	2	3	.400	19	0	0	0	1	51	67	11.8	0	29	5.1	24	4.2	5.82	51	.328	.424	-16	-16	98	96	0.0	-1	-1	-1.7
Total	2	2	4	.333	21	2	1	0	1	60	80	12.0	0	39	5.8	25	3.8	6.60	44	.336	.441	-24	-25	98	92	-0.4	-1	-1	-2.4
■ **TOM DETTORE**	Dettore, Thomas Anthony b: 11/17/47, Canonsburg, Pa. BL/TR, 6'4", 200 lbs. Deb: 6/11/73																												
1973	Pit-N	0	1	.000	12	1	0	0	0	23	33	12.9	1	14	5.5	13	5.1	5.87	57	.340	.435	-6	-6	92	113	-0.4	-0	-0	-0.6
1974	Chi-N	3	5	.375	16	9	0	0	0	65	64	8.9	4	31	4.3	43	6.0	4.15	89	.255	.345	-4	-3	102	94	-0.2	2	1	0.0
1975	Chi-N	5	4	.556	36	5	0	0	0	85	88	9.3	8	31	3.3	46	4.9	5.40	71	.270	.343	-17	-15	105	80	0.8	1	0	-1.3
1976	Chi-N	0	1	.000	4	0	0	0	0	7	11	14.1	3	2	2.6	4	5.1	10.29	38	.355	.394	-5	-5	111	87	-0.4	0	0	-0.4
Total	4	8	11	.421	68	15	0	0	0	180	196	9.8	16	78	3.9	106	5.3	5.20	72	.278	.359	-31	-29	103	90	-0.2	2	1	-2.3
■ **MEL DEUTSCH**	Deutsch, Melvin Elliott b: 7/26/15, Caldwell, Tex. BR/TR, 6'4", 215 lbs. Deb: 4/21/46																												
1946	Bos-A	0	0	—	3	0	0	0	0	6	7	10.5	1	3	4.5	2	3.0	6.00	65	.280	.357	-2	-1	111	86	0.0	-0	-0	-0.1

YEAR	TM/L	W	L	PCT	G	GS	CG	SHO	SV	IP	H	H/G	HR	BB	BB/G	SO	SO/G	ERA	/A	OAVG	OOBP	PR	/A	PF	CPI	WAT	PB	PD	TPI
■ **CHARLIE DEVENS**	Devens, Charles b: 1/1/10, Milton, Mass. BR/TR, 6'1", 180 lbs. Deb: 9/24/32																												
1932	NY-A	1	0	1.000	1	1	1	0	0	9	6	6.0	0	7	7.0	4	4.0	2.00	204	.200	.342	2	2	91	166	0.5	0	-0	0.2
1933	NY-A	3	3	.500	14	8	2	0	0	62	59	8.6	1	50	7.3	23	3.3	4.35	87	.250	.375	-1	-4	88	103	-0.4	-1	-1	-0.4
1934	NY-A	1	0	1.000	1	1	1	0	0	11	9	7.4	0	5	4.1	4	3.3	1.64	255	.225	.304	3	3	93	167	0.5	1	0	0.6
Total	3	5	3	.625	16	10	4	0	0	82	74	8.1	1	62	6.8	31	3.4	3.73	104	.242	.363	5	1	89	118	0.6	0	-1	0.4
■ **ADRIAN DEVINE**	Devine, Paul Adrian b: 12/2/51, Galveston, Tex. BR/TR, 6'4", 185 lbs. Deb: 6/27/73																												
1973	Atl-N	2	3	.400	24	1	0	0	4	32	45	12.7	6	12	3.4	15	4.2	6.47	64	.338	.388	-10	-8	113	106	-0.3	0	-1	-0.8
1975	Atl-N	1	0	1.000	5	2	0	0	0	16	19	10.7	2	7	3.9	8	4.5	4.50	78	.284	.355	-2	-2	97	109	0.5	-1	-0	-0.2
1976	Atl-N	5	6	.455	48	1	0	0	9	73	72	8.9	3	26	3.2	48	5.9	3.21	123	.255	.310	2	6	112	102	0.2	-2	-1	0.4
1977	Tex-A	11	6	.647	56	2	0	0	15	106	102	8.7	8	31	2.6	67	5.7	3.57	118	.259	.309	6	8	104	100	1.5	0	2	1.0
1978	Atl-N	5	4	.556	31	6	0	0	3	65	84	11.6	3	25	3.5	26	3.6	5.95	69	.323	.371	-17	-14	114	88	1.1	-1	0	-1.3
1979	Atl-N	1	2	.333	40	0	0	0	0	67	84	11.3	8	25	3.4	22	3.0	3.22	128	.311	.368	4	7	110	170	-0.2	-1	-0	0.6
1980	Tex-A	1	1	.500	13	0	0	0	0	28	49	15.8	4	9	2.9	8	2.6	4.82	84	.377	.415	-2	-2	100	159	0.1	0	-0	-0.2
Total	7	26	22	.542	217	12	0	0	31	387	455	10.6	34	135	3.1	194	4.5	4.21	97	.296	.348	-19	-5	108	116	2.9	-4	1	-0.5
■ **JIM DEVINE**	Devine, Walter James b: 10/5/1858, Brooklyn, N.Y. d: 1/11/05, Syracuse, N.Y. TL , Deb: 5/08/1883																												
1883	Bal-a	1	1	.500	2	2	1	0	0	11	15	12.3	0	1	0.8	3	2.5	7.36	51	.331	.345	-5	-4	113	62	0.3	-0	0	-0.3
■ **HAL DEVINEY**	Deviney, Harold John b: 4/11/1893, Newton, Mass. d: 1/4/33, Westwood, Mass. BR/TR, Deb: 7/30/20																												
1920	Bos-A	0	0	—	1	0	0	0	0	3	7	21.0	0	2	6.0	0	0.0	15.00	24	.500	.563	-4	-4	97	77	0.0	2	-0	-0.1
■ **JIM DEVLIN**	Devlin, James Alexander b: 1849, Philadelphia, Pa. d: 10/10/1883, Philadelphia, Pa. BR/TR, 5'11", 175 lbs. Deb: 4/21/1873																												
1875	Chi-n	6	16	.273	26																								
1876	Lou-N	30	35	.462	**68**	68	**66**	5	0	**622**	566	8.2	3	37	0.5	**122**	1.8	1.56	**157**	.247	.259	52	**61**	106	78	15.0	9	3	**7.1**
1877	Lou-N	35	25	.583	**61**	61	**61**	4	0	**559**	617	9.9	4	41	0.7	141	2.3	2.25	**162**	.288	.302	35	**86**	130	112	**17.5**	-5	3	**9.2**
Total	2	65	60	.520	129	129	127	9	0	1181	1183	9.0	7	78	0.6	263	2.0	1.89	158	.267	.279	86	144	117	94	32.5	4	6	16.3
■ **JIM DEVLIN**	Devlin, James H. b: 4/16/1866, Troy, N.Y. d: 12/14/1900, Troy, N.Y. TL , Deb: 6/28/1886																												
1886	NY-N	0	0	—	1	0	0	0	1	2	3	13.5	0	4	18.0	2	9.0	18.00	16	.361	.568	-3	-3	85	58	0.0	-0	0	-0.2
1887	Phi-N	0	2	.000	2	2	2	0	0	18	20	10.0	0	10	5.0	6	3.0	6.00	63	.297	.388	-4	-4	94	74	-0.9	1	0	-0.2
1888	StL-a	6	5	.545	11	11	10	0	0	90	82	8.2	3	20	2.0	45	4.5	3.20	102	.255	.299	-1	1	106	87	-1.1	2	0	0.3
1889	StL-a	5	3	.625	9	8	5	0	0	60	56	8.4	1	24	3.6	37	5.6	2.40	174	.262	.336	10	12	109	129	-0.2	-2	0	0.9
Total	4	11	10	.524	23	21	17	0	1	170	161	8.5	4	58	3.1	90	4.8	3.39	107	.263	.327	1	5	105	100	-2.2	1	0	0.8
■ **CHARLIE DEWALD**	Dewald, Charles H. b: 1867, Newark, N.J. d: 8/22/04, Cleveland, Ohio TL , Deb: 9/02/1890																												
1890	Cle-P	2	0	1.000	2	2	2	0	0	14	13	8.4	0	5	3.2	6	3.9	0.64	618	.258	.325	6	5	94	396	1.0	1	0	0.5
■ **CARLOS DIAZ**	Diaz, Carlos Antonio b: 1/7/58, Kapotte, Hawaii BR/TL, 6', 161 lbs. Deb: 6/30/82																												
1982	Atl-N	3	2	.600	19	0	0	0	1	25	31	11.2	3	9	3.2	16	5.8	4.68	82	.307	.354	-3	-2	107	113	0.3	-0	0	-0.2
	NY-N	0	0	—	4	0	0	0	0	4	6	13.5	0	4	9.0	0	0.0	0.00	—	.353	.476	2	2	100	0	0.0	0	0	0.2
	Yr	3	2	.600	23	0	0	0	1	29	37	11.5	3	13	4.0	16	5.0	4.03	95	.311	.373	-1	-1	106	0	0.3	-0	0	0.0
1983	NY-N	3	1	.750	54	0	0	0	2	83	62	6.7	1	35	3.8	64	6.9	2.06	176	.211	.289	15	15	100	107	1.2	-0	1	1.6
1984	LA-N	1	0	1.000	37	0	0	0	1	41	47	10.3	4	24	5.3	36	7.9	5.49	68	.285	.372	-9	-8	104	93	0.5	-0	-1	-0.8
1985	LA-N	6	3	.667	46	0	0	0	0	79	70	8.0	7	18	2.1	73	8.3	2.62	126	.230	.270	9	6	92	98	0.9	-0	-1	0.5
1986	LA-N	0	0	—	19	0	0	0	0	25	33	11.9	2	7	2.5	18	6.5	4.32	82	.317	.354	-2	-2	95	118	0.0	-0	0	-0.1
Total	5	13	6	.684	179	0	0	0	4	257	249	8.7	17	97	3.4	207	7.2	3.22	110	.253	.315	11	10	98	102	2.9	-1	0	1.2
■ **ROB DIBBLE**	Dibble, Robert Keith b: 1/24/64, Bridgeport, Conn. BR/TL, 6'4", 230 lbs. Deb: 6/29/88																												
1988	Cin-N	1	1	.500	37	0	0	0	0	59	43	6.6	2	21	3.2	59	9.0	1.83	198	.207	.277	11	12	105	123	0.0	-0	-1	1.1
■ **PEDRO DIBUT**	Dibut, Pedro (Villafana) b: 11/18/1892, Cienfuegos, Cuba d: 12/4/79, Hialeah, Fla. BR/TR, 5'8", 190 lbs. Deb: 5/01/24																												
1924	Cin-N	3	0	1.000	7	2	2	0	0	37	24	5.8	1	12	2.9	15	3.6	2.19	175	.188	.254	7	7	99	66	1.5	1	1	0.9
1925	Cin-N	0	0	—	1	0	0	0	0	0	3	—	0	0	—	0	—	∞	—	1.000	1.000	-2	-2	97	84	0.0	0	0	-0.1
Total	2	3	0	1.000	8	2	2	0	0	37	27	6.6	1	12	2.9	15	3.6	2.68	143	.206	.269	5	5	99	66	1.5	1	1	0.8
■ **LEO DICKERMAN**	Dickerman, Leo Louis b: 10/31/1896, De Soto, Mo. d: 4/30/82, Atkins, Ark. BR/TR, 6'4", 192 lbs. Deb: 4/21/23																												
1923	Bro-N	8	12	.400	35	20	7	1	0	160	180	10.1	4	72	4.0	58	3.3	3.71	105	.283	.352	5	3	98	109	-2.0	3	2	0.8
1924	Bro-N	0	0	—	7	2	0	0	0	20	20	9.0	0	16	7.2	9	4.0	5.40	70	.263	.396	-3	-4	98	86	0.0	-0	0	-0.2
	StL-N	7	4	.636	18	13	8	1	0	120	108	8.1	6	51	3.8	28	2.1	2.40	165	.249	.324	20	21	103	141	2.1	1	0	2.3
	Yr	7	4	.636	25	15	8	1	0	140	128	8.2	6	67	4.3	37	2.4	2.83	140	.250	.333	16	17	102	141	2.1	-0	0	2.1
1925	StL-N	4	11	.267	29	20	7	2	1	131	135	9.3	10	79	5.4	40	2.7	5.56	77	.273	.370	-19	-18	101	85	-3.6	-3	3	-1.5
Total	3	19	27	.413	89	55	22	4	1	431	443	9.3	20	218	4.6	135	2.8	3.99	101	.270	.353	2	3	100	109	-3.5	0	6	1.4
■ **GEORGE DICKERSON**	Dickerson, George Clark b: 12/1/1892, Renner, Tex. d: 7/9/38, Los Angeles, Cal. BR/TR, 6'1", 170 lbs. Deb: 8/02/17																												
1917	Cle-A	0	0	—	1	0	0	0	0	1	0	0.0	0	0	0.0	0	0.0	0.00	—	.000	.000	0	0	113	0	0.0	0	0	0.0
■ **EMERSON DICKMAN**	Dickman, George Emerson b: 11/12/14, Buffalo, N.Y. d: 4/27/81, New York, N.Y. BR/TR, 6'2", 175 lbs. Deb: 6/27/36																												
1936	Bos-A	0	0	—	1	0	0	0	0	1	2	18.0	0	1	9.0	2	18.0	9.00	59	.400	.500	-0	-0	106	109	0.0	0	0	0.0
1938	Bos-A	5	5	.500	32	11	3	1	0	104	117	10.1	9	54	4.7	22	1.9	5.28	91	.288	.372	-6	-6	100	101	-0.7	4	-0	-0.1
1939	Bos-A	8	3	.727	48	1	0	0	5	114	126	9.9	10	43	3.4	46	3.6	4.42	112	.282	.339	3	6	107	107	1.9	-4	3	0.5
1940	Bos-A	8	6	.571	35	9	2	0	3	100	121	10.9	15	38	3.4	40	3.6	6.03	73	.291	.354	-18	-18	100	90	0.6	-2	2	-1.6
1941	Bos-A	1	1	.500	9	3	1	0	0	31	37	10.7	4	17	4.9	16	4.6	6.39	66	.301	.380	-8	-8	101	92	0.0	-1	-1	-0.7
Total	5	22	15	.595	125	24	6	1	8	350	403	10.4	38	153	3.9	126	3.2	5.32	88	.288	.358	-30	-25	102	99	1.8	-2	4	-1.9
■ **JIM DICKSON**	Dickson, James Edward b: 4/20/38, Portland, Ore. BL/TR, 6'1", 185 lbs. Deb: 7/02/63																												
1963	Hou-N	0	1	.000	13	0	0	0	2	15	22	13.2	0	2	1.2	6	3.6	6.00	52	.344	.348	-5	-5	95	80	-0.4	-0	-0	-0.4
1964	Cin-N	1	0	1.000	4	0	0	0	0	5	8	14.4	0	5	9.0	6	10.8	7.20	50	.444	.520	-2	-2	102	135	0.5	0	0	-0.1
1965	KC-A	3	2	.600	68	0	0	0	0	86	68	7.1	6	47	4.9	54	5.7	3.45	100	.220	.318	0	-0	100	95	0.9	-0	-1	0.0
1966	KC-A	1	0	1.000	24	1	0	0	1	37	37	9.0	4	23	5.6	20	4.9	5.35	61	.264	.357	-8	-9	95	91	0.5	0	-0	-0.8
Total	4	5	3	.625	109	1	0	0	3	143	135	8.5	10	77	4.8	86	5.4	4.34	78	.254	.340	-14	-15	98	94	1.5	-0	-1	-1.3
■ **MURRY DICKSON**	Dickson, Murry Monroe b: 8/21/16, Tracy, Mo. BR/TR, 5'10.5", 157 lbs. Deb: 9/30/39																												
1939	StL-N	0	0	—	1	0	0	0	0	4	1	2.3	0	1	2.3	2	4.5	0.00	—	.091	.167	2	2	103	0	0.0	-0	0	0.2
1940	StL-N	0	0	—	1	1	0	0	0	2	5	22.5	0	1	4.5	0	0.0	13.50	29	.500	.545	-2	-2	101	88	0.0	0	-0	-0.1
1942	StL-N	6	3	.667	36	7	2	0	2	121	91	6.8	1	61	4.5	66	4.9	2.90	117	.216	.314	6	7	103	92	0.0	-0	1	0.9
1943	StL-N	8	2	.800	31	7	2	0	0	116	114	8.8	4	49	3.8	44	3.4	3.57	95	.257	.331	-3	-2	100	98	1.9	1	-0	0.0
1946	StL-N	15	6	**.714**	47	19	12	2	1	184	160	7.8	8	56	2.7	82	4.0	2.89	122	.234	.291	11	13	103	89	2.7	4	4	2.3
1947	StL-N	13	16	.448	47	25	11	4	3	232	211	8.2	16	88	3.4	111	4.3	3.06	138	.243	.310	26	30	104	108	-3.7	0	1	3.2
1948	StL-N	12	16	.429	42	29	11	1	1	252	257	9.2	39	85	3.0	113	4.0	4.14	94	.265	.321	-5	-7	99	108	-3.5	5	1	0.0
1949	Pit-N	12	14	.462	44	20	11	2	0	224	216	8.7	17	80	3.2	89	3.6	3.29	125	.255	.319	19	21	102	113	0.0	1	4	2.7
1950	Pit-N	10	15	.400	51	22	8	0	3	225	227	9.1	20	83	3.3	76	3.0	3.80	115	.260	.324	9	14	106	101	0.6	3	2	1.9
1951	Pit-N	20	16	.556	45	35	19	3	2	289	294	9.2	32	101	3.1	112	3.5	4.02	108	.262	.323	-2	10	110	101	5.2	5	4	2.1
1952	Pit-N	14	21	.400	43	34	21	2	2	278	278	9.0	26	76	2.5	112	3.6	3.56	110	.261	.307	5	11	105	104	3.8	3	3	1.9
1953	Pit-N	10	19	.345	45	26	10	1	4	201	240	10.7	27	58	2.6	88	3.9	4.52	101	.298	.343	-5	1	106	113	0.5	-4	-0	-0.2
1954	Phi-N	10	20	.333	40	31	12	4	3	226	256	10.2	31	73	2.9	64	2.5	3.78	105	.286	.336	7	5	98	123	-5.4	0	2	0.7
1955	Phi-N	12	11	.522	36	28	12	4	0	216	190	7.9	27	82	3.4	92	3.8	3.50	118	.238	.305	13	15	102	102	0.6	0	1	1.7
1956	Phi-N	0	3	.000	3	3	0	0	0	23	20	7.8	1	12	4.7	1	0.4	5.09	71	.241	.330	-3	-4	95	66	-1.4	1	0	-0.2
	StL-N	13	8	.619	28	27	12	3	0	196	175	8.0	20	57	2.6	109	5.0	3.08	122	.240	.292	15	15	99	100	2.9	4	4	2.4
	Yr	13	11	.542	31	30	12	3	0	219	195	8.0	21	69	2.8	110	4.5	3.29	113	.240	.296	12	11	99	100	1.5	1	4	2.2
1957	StL-N	5	3	.625	14	13	3	1	0	74	87	10.6	8	25	3.0	29	3.5	4.14	93	.296	.347	-2	-2	99	117	0.6	1	2	0.0

YEAR	TM/L	W	L	PCT	G	GS	CG	SHO	SV	IP	H	H/G	HR	BB	BB/G	SO	SO/G	ERA	/A	OAVG	OOBP	PR	/A	PF	CPI	WAT	PB	PD	TPI
1958	KC-A	9	5	.643	27	9	3	0	1	99	99	9.0	12	31	2.8	46	4.2	3.27	123	.258	.311	5	8	107	119	2.4	2	2	1.3
	NY-A	1	2	.333	6	2	0	0	1	20	18	8.1	4	12	5.4	9	4.0	5.85	64	.237	.344	-5	-5	99	82	-0.6	0	0	-0.3
	Yr	10	7	.588	33	11	3	0	2	119	117	8.8	16	43	3.3	55	4.2	3.71	107	.253	.313	1	4	106	82	1.8	2	2	1.0
1959	KC-A	2	1	.667	38	0	0	0	0	71	85	10.8	9	27	3.4	36	4.6	4.94	80	.290	.344	-9	-8	103	100	0.6	-1	-0	-0.7
Total	18	172	181	.487	625	338	149	27	23	3053	3024	8.9	302	1058	3.1	1281	3.8	3.66	110	.259	.318	81	121	103	105	7.2	25	31	19.8
■ **WALT DICKSON**	Dickson, Walter R. "Hickory" b: 12/3/1878, New Summerfield, Tex. d: 12/9/18, Ardmore, Okla. BR/TR, 5'11.5", 175 lbs. Deb: 4/26/10																												
1910	NY-N	1	0	1.000	12	1	0	0	0	30	31	9.3	1	9	2.7	9	2.7	5.40	52	.272	.325	-8	-9	92	60	0.5	0	-1	-0.8
1912	Bos-N	3	19	.136	36	20	9	1	1	189	233	11.1	2	61	2.9	47	2.2	3.86	97	.306	.360	-9	-2	110	105	-6.9	-2	2	-0.1
1913	Bos-N	6	7	.462	19	15	8	0	0	128	118	8.3	4	45	3.2	47	3.3	3.23	95	.249	.308	-0	-2	96	91	0.1	-1	-1	-0.4
1914	Pit-F	9	19	.321	40	32	19	3	1	257	262	9.2	5	74	2.6	63	2.2	3.15	98	.305	.361	2	-2	96	**133**	-3.9	-7	1	-0.7
1915	Pit-F	7	5	.583	27	11	4	0	0	97	115	10.7	5	33	3.1	36	3.3	4.18	74	.316	.376	-12	-12	102	118	0.3	-1	2	-1.0
Total	5	26	50	.342	134	79	40	4	2	701	759	9.7	17	222	2.9	202	2.6	3.59	90	.295	.351	-29	-27	100	112	-9.9	-10	3	-3.0
■ **GEORGE DIEHL**	Diehl, George Krause b: 2/25/18, Emmaus, Pa. d: 8/24/86, Kingsport, Tenn. BR/TR, 6'2", 196 lbs. Deb: 4/19/42																												
1942	Bos-N	0	0	—	1	0	0	0	0	4	2	4.5	0	2	4.5	0	0.0	2.25	144	.167	.333	0	0	98	112	0.0	-0	0	0.0
1943	Bos-N	0	0	—	1	0	0	0	0	4	4	9.0	0	3	6.8	1	2.3	4.50	82	.267	.368	-1	-0	109	97	0.0	-0	1	0.0
Total	2	0	0	—	2	0	0	0	0	8	6	6.8	0	5	5.6	1	1.1	3.38	102	.222	.353	-0	0	103	105	0.0	-0	1	0.0
■ **LARRY DIERKER**	Dierker, Lawrence Edward b: 9/22/46, Hollywood, Cal. BR/TR, 6'4", 190 lbs. Deb: 9/22/64																												
1964	Hou-N	0	1	.000	3	1	0	0	0	9	7	7.0	1	3	3.0	5	5.0	2.00	174	.219	.278	2	1	98	149	-0.4	-0	-0	0.1
1965	Hou-N	7	8	.467	26	19	1	0	0	147	135	8.3	16	37	2.3	109	6.7	3.49	92	.240	.286	1	-4	91	91	0.9	-1	-2	-0.6
1966	Hou-N	10	8	.556	29	28	8	2	0	187	173	8.3	17	45	2.2	108	5.2	3.18	112	.240	.282	9	8	99	90	2.0	0	-1	0.8
1967	Hou-N	6	5	.545	15	15	4	0	0	99	95	8.6	4	25	2.3	68	6.2	3.36	96	.252	.295	0	-2	95	87	1.2	2	-1	0.0
1968	Hou-N	12	15	.444	32	32	10	1	0	234	206	7.9	14	89	3.4	161	6.2	3.31	91	.240	.309	-8	-8	100	96	0.0	-4	-2	-1.4
1969	Hou-N	20	13	.606	39	37	20	4	0	305	240	7.1	18	72	2.1	232	6.8	2.33	157	.214	.259	43	45	101	88	4.2	-1	-1	4.8
1970	Hou-N	16	12	.571	37	36	17	2	1	270	263	8.8	31	82	2.7	191	6.4	3.87	98	.254	.310	6	-2	94	98	2.7	0	-1	-0.3
1971	Hou-N	12	6	.667	24	23	6	2	0	159	150	8.5	8	33	1.9	91	5.2	2.72	118	.248	.286	13	9	92	100	3.4	-3	0	0.6
1972	Hou-N	15	8	.652	31	31	12	5	0	215	209	8.7	14	51	2.1	115	4.8	3.39	107	.256	.299	2	6	105	94	3.0	-1	-2	0.3
1973	Hou-N	1	1	.500	14	3	0	0	0	27	27	9.0	3	13	4.3	18	6.0	4.33	80	.265	.350	-2	-3	95	106	0.0	-0	-0	-0.2
1974	Hou-N	11	10	.524	33	33	7	3	0	224	189	7.6	18	82	3.3	150	6.0	2.89	122	.232	.303	18	16	98	107	0.6	1	0	1.8
1975	Hou-N	14	16	.467	34	34	14	2	0	232	225	8.7	24	91	3.5	127	4.9	4.00	86	.260	.329	-9	-14	95	100	2.1	-4	-1	-1.9
1976	Hou-N	13	14	.481	28	28	7	4	0	188	171	8.2	9	72	3.4	112	5.4	3.69	82	.243	.315	-4	-14	87	87	-0.3	-0	-1	-1.5
1977	StL-N	2	6	.250	11	9	0	0	0	39	40	9.2	7	16	3.7	6	1.4	4.62	81	.267	.343	-3	-4	95	106	-2.0	-1	-0	-0.4
Total	14	139	123	.531	356	329	106	25	1	2335	2130	8.2	184	711	2.7	1493	5.8	3.30	104	.243	.299	67	35	97	95	17.4	-12	-12	2.1
■ **BILL DIETRICH**	Dietrich, William John "Bullfrog" b: 3/29/10, Philadelphia, Pa. d: 6/20/78, Philadelphia, Pa. BR/TR, 6', 185 lbs. Deb: 4/13/33																												
1933	Phi-A	0	1	.000	8	1	0	0	0	17	13	6.9	1	19	10.1	4	2.1	5.82	67	.236	.416	-3	-4	92	97	-0.4	1	0	-0.1
1934	Phi-A	11	12	.478	39	23	14	4	3	208	201	8.7	12	114	4.9	88	3.8	4.67	95	.255	.344	-4	-6	98	90	0.6	3	-2	-0.3
1935	Phi-A	7	13	.350	43	15	8	1	3	185	203	9.9	7	101	4.9	59	2.9	5.40	84	.276	.359	-19	-17	102	83	-1.0	-6	-1	-2.1
1936	Phi-A	4	6	.400	21	4	0	0	3	72	91	11.4	4	40	5.0	34	4.3	6.50	82	.305	.381	-12	-10	105	87	0.4	-2	1	-0.8
	Was-A	0	1	.000	5	0	0	0	0	8	13	14.6	0	6	6.8	4	4.5	10.13	48	.351	.432	-5	-5	96	72	-0.4	0	0	-0.3
	Chi-A	4	4	.500	14	11	6	1	0	83	93	10.1	8	36	3.9	39	4.2	4.66	107	.284	.353	3	3	99	108	-0.2	1	-0	0.3
	Yr	8	11	.421	40	15	6	1	3	163	197	10.9	12	82	4.5	77	4.3	5.74	89	.297	.370	-13	-11	101	108	-0.2	-2	1	-0.8
1937	Chi-A	8	10	.444	29	20	7	1	1	143	162	10.2	15	72	4.5	62	3.9	4.91	96	.285	.358	-5	-3	102	104	-1.9	1	1	-0.1
1938	Chi-A	2	4	.333	8	7	1	0	0	48	49	9.2	7	31	5.8	11	2.1	5.44	87	.259	.357	-3	-4	98	94	-0.6	-1	-0	-0.4
1939	Chi-A	7	8	.467	25	19	2	0	0	128	134	9.4	14	56	3.9	43	3.0	5.20	94	.272	.343	-8	-4	106	92	-1.2	2	-1	-0.1
1940	Chi-A	10	6	.625	23	17	6	1	0	150	154	9.2	10	65	3.9	43	2.6	4.02	112	.266	.336	6	8	103	104	1.7	3	-2	0.9
1941	Chi-A	5	8	.385	19	15	4	1	0	109	114	9.4	7	50	4.1	26	2.1	5.37	72	.263	.338	-15	-18	94	77	-1.5	0	-1	-1.7
1942	Chi-A	6	11	.353	26	23	6	0	0	160	173	9.7	16	70	3.9	39	2.2	4.89	75	.277	.348	-22	-22	100	97	-1.8	-1	-0	-2.2
1943	Chi-A	12	10	.545	26	26	12	2	0	187	180	8.7	4	53	2.6	52	2.5	2.79	120	.253	.301	10	11	101	105	0.4	0	1	1.5
1944	Chi-A	16	17	.485	36	36	15	2	0	246	269	9.8	15	68	2.5	70	2.6	3.62	97	.279	.320	-5	-3	102	106	0.9	-3	-1	-0.6
1945	Chi-A	7	10	.412	18	16	6	3	0	122	136	10.0	4	36	2.7	43	3.2	4.20	77	.279	.324	-11	-13	96	87	-1.2	1	0	-1.2
1946	Chi-A	3	3	.500	11	9	3	0	1	62	63	9.1	4	24	3.5	20	2.9	2.61	131	.267	.327	6	6	97	145	0.1	-2	1	0.5
1947	Phi-A	5	2	.714	11	9	2	1	0	61	48	7.1	0	40	5.9	18	2.7	3.10	119	.223	.347	4	4	100	104	1.5	-2	-1	0.2
1948	Phi-A	1	2	.333	4	2	0	0	0	15	21	12.6	0	9	5.4	5	3.0	6.00	72	.356	.429	-3	-3	102	111	-0.5	-0	0	-0.2
Total	16	108	128	.458	366	253	92	17	11	2004	2117	9.5	128	890	4.0	660	3.0	4.48	92	.271	.341	-85	-80	101	98	-5.1	-5	-3	-6.7
■ **DUTCH DIETZ**	Dietz, Lloyd Arthur b: 2/9/12, Cincinnati, Ohio d: 10/29/72, Beaumont, Tex. BR/TR, 5'11.5", 180 lbs. Deb: 4/26/40																												
1940	Pit-N	0	1	.000	4	2	0	0	0	15	22	13.2	2	4	2.4	8	4.8	6.00	61	.355	.394	-4	-4	95	113	-0.4	-0	-0	-0.3
1941	Pit-N	7	2	.778	33	6	4	1	1	100	88	7.9	6	33	3.0	22	2.0	2.34	158	.233	.296	14	15	102	124	2.5	-1	0	1.5
1942	Pit-N	6	9	.400	40	13	3	0	3	134	139	9.3	8	57	3.8	35	2.4	3.96	85	.268	.334	-10	-9	102	102	-0.8	1	-2	-1.0
1943	Pit-N	0	3	.000	8	0	0	0	0	9	12	12.0	0	4	4.0	4	4.0	6.00	58	.324	.386	-3	-3	103	90	-1.4	0	1	-0.1
	Phi-N	1	1	.500	21	0	0	0	2	36	42	10.5	2	15	3.8	10	2.5	6.50	50	.292	.352	-13	-13	96	70	0.1	0	-0	-1.3
	Yr	1	4	.200	29	0	0	0	2	45	54	10.8	2	19	3.8	14	2.8	6.40	51	.297	.354	-15	-16	97	70	-1.3	0	1	-1.4
Total	4	14	16	.467	106	21	7	1	6	294	303	9.3	18	113	3.5	79	2.4	3.89	90	.266	.329	-14	-13	101	106	-0.0	-0	-1	-1.2
■ **REESE DIGGS**	Diggs, Reese Wilson "Diggsy" b: 9/22/15, Mathews, Va. d: 10/30/78, Baltimore, Md. BB/TR, 6'2", 180 lbs. Deb: 9/15/34																												
1934	Was-A	1	2	.333	4	3	2	0	0	21	26	11.1	3	15	6.4	2	0.9	6.86	67	.313	.418	-6	-5	102	101	-0.3	0	-0	-0.4
■ **JACK DiLAURO**	DiLauro, Jack Edward b: 5/3/43, Akron, Ohio BB/TL, 6'2", 185 lbs. Deb: 5/15/69																												
1969	NY-N	1	4	.200	23	4	0	0	1	64	50	7.0	4	18	2.5	27	3.8	2.39	149	.216	.266	9	8	99	96	-1.6	-1	0	0.7
1970	Hou-N	1	3	.250	42	0	0	0	3	34	34	9.0	4	17	4.5	23	6.1	4.24	90	.262	.336	-1	-2	94	107	-0.9	-0	-0	-0.1
Total	2	2	7	.222	65	4	0	0	4	98	84	7.7	8	35	3.2	50	4.6	3.03	121	.232	.292	8	7	97	99	-2.5	-2	-0	0.6
■ **GORDON DILLARD**	Dillard, Gordon Lee b: 5/20/64, Salinas, Cal. BL/TL, 6'1", 180 lbs. Deb: 8/12/88																												
1988	Bal-A	0	0	—	2	1	0	0	0	3	3	9.0	1	4	12.0	2	6.0	6.00	65	.273	.467	-1	-1	97	148	0.0	0	0	0.0
■ **HARLEY DILLINGER**	Dillinger, Harley Hugh "Hoke" or "Lefty" b: 10/30/1894, Pomeroy, Ohio d: 1/8/59, Cleveland, Ohio BR/TL, 5'11", 175 lbs. Deb: 8/16/14																												
1914	Cle-A	0	1	.000	11	2	1	0	0	34	41	10.9	0	25	6.6	11	2.9	4.50	64	.325	.441	-7	-6	106	127	-0.4	-1	-1	-0.6
■ **BILL DILLMAN**	Dillman, William Howard b: 5/25/45, Trenton, N.J. BR/TR, 6'2", 180 lbs. Deb: 4/14/67																												
1967	Bal-A	5	9	.357	32	15	2	1	3	124	115	8.3	13	33	2.4	69	5.0	4.35	69	.249	.300	-15	-18	94	81	-1.7	-0	-1	-2.0
1970	Mon-N	2	3	.400	18	0	0	0	0	31	28	8.1	4	18	5.2	17	4.9	5.23	79	.255	.351	-4	-4	102	93	-0.2	-0	0	-0.3
Total	2	7	12	.368	50	15	2	1	3	155	143	8.3	17	51	3.0	86	5.0	4.53	71	.250	.311	-20	-22	95	83	-1.9	-0	-1	-2.3
■ **STEVE DILLON**	Dillon, Stephen Edward b: 3/20/43, Yonkers, N.Y. BL/TL, 5'10", 160 lbs. Deb: 9/05/63																												
1963	NY-N	0	0	—	1	0	0	0	0	2	3	13.5	0	0	0.0	1	4.5	9.00	38	.429	.429	-1	-1	104	70	0.0	0	0	0.0
1964	NY-N	0	0	—	2	0	0	0	0	3	4	12.0	1	2	6.0	2	6.0	9.00	39	.333	.400	-2	-2	98	95	0.0	0	0	-0.1
Total	2	0	0	—	3	0	0	0	0	5	7	12.6	1	2	3.6	3	5.4	9.00	38	.368	.409	-3	-3	101	85	0.0	0	0	-0.1
■ **FRANK DIMICHELE**	Dimichele, Frank Lawrence b: 2/16/65, Philadelphia, Pa. BL/TR, 6'3", 205 lbs. Deb: 4/08/88																												
1988	Cal-A	0	0	—	4	0	0	0	0	5	5	9.0	2	2	3.6	1	1.8	9.00	42	.263	.333	-3	-3	95	72	0.0	0	-0	-0.2
■ **BILL DINNEEN**	Dinneen, William Henry "Big Bill" b: 4/5/1876, Syracuse, N.Y. d: 1/13/55, Syracuse, N.Y. BR/TR, 6'1", 190 lbs. Deb: 4/22/1898 U																												
1898	Was-N	9	16	.360	29	27	22	0	0	218	238	9.8	6	88	3.6	83	3.4	4.00	94	.300	.370	-10	-6	105	98	0.5	-5	0	-0.8
1899	Was-N	14	20	.412	37	35	30	0	0	291	350	10.8	6	106	3.3	91	2.8	3.93	96	.322	.382	-2	-5	98	109	1.9	6	4	0.4
1900	Bos-N	20	14	.588	40	37	33	1	0	321	304	8.5	11	105	2.9	107	3.0	3.14	141	.272	.334	20	**46**	120	98	4.4	1	3	**5.2**
1901	Bos-N	16	19	.457	37	34	31	0	0	309	295	8.6	8	77	2.2	141	4.1	2.94	127	.274	.326	13	27	112	99	-1.9	-0	-1	2.6
1902	Bos-A	21	21	.500	42	42	39	2	0	371	348	8.4	9	99	2.4	136	3.3	2.94	119	.272	.324	26	23	98	96	-3.1	-6	-6	1.6
1903	Bos-A	21	13	.618	37	34	32	6	**2**	299	255	7.7	6	66	2.0	148	4.5	2.26	140	.251	.297	23	30	108	102	-1.3	-1	-2	3.1

YEAR	TM/L	W	L	PCT	G	GS	CG	SHO	SV	IP	H	H/G	HR	BB	BB/G	SO	SO/G	ERA	/A	OAVG	OOBP	PR	/A	PF	CPI	WAT	PB	PD	TPI
1904	Bos-A	23	14	.622	37	37	37	5	0	336	283	7.6	8	63	1.7	153	4.1	2.20	120	.250	.290	15	16	101	99	0.3	-1	-2	1.6
1905	Bos-A	12	15	.444	31	29	23	2	1	244	235	8.7	7	50	1.8	97	3.6	3.73	71	.277	.318	-29	-29	100	79	-2.0	-3	0	-2.9
1906	Bos-A	8	19	.296	28	27	22	1	0	219	209	8.6	4	52	2.1	60	2.5	2.92	95	.276	.323	-6	-3	104	97	-1.0	-2	-3	-0.6
1907	Bos-A	0	4	.000	5	5	3	0	0	33	42	11.5	5	8	2.2	8	2.2	5.18	51	.336	.376	-10	-9	103	102	-1.9	-1	-1	-0.9
	StL-A	7	10	.412	24	16	15	2	4	155	153	8.9	3	33	1.9	38	2.2	2.44	102	.282	.323	2	1	98	115	-0.8	2	-3	-0.1
	Yr	7	14	.333	29	21	18	2	**4**	188	195	9.3	8	41	2.0	46	2.2	2.92	86	.292	.333	-8	-8	99	115	-2.7	-1	-4	-1.0
1908	StL-A	14	7	.667	27	16	11	1	0	167	133	7.2	2	53	2.9	39	2.1	2.10	116	.231	.300	5	6	102	119	3.1	0	-3	0.4
1909	StL-A	6	7	.462	17	13	8	3	0	112	112	9.0	3	29	2.3	26	2.1	3.46	68	.267	.316	-12	-14	95	84	0.7	2	-0	-1.4
Total	12	171	179	.489	391	352	306	23	7	3075	2957	8.7	78	829	2.4	1127	3.3	3.01	108	.275	.327	35	80	104	99	-1.1	-9	-15	8.2
■ MIKE DIORIO Diorio, Ronald Michael b: 7/15/46, Waterbury, Conn. BR/TR, 6'6", 212 lbs. Deb: 8/09/73																													
1973	Phi-N	0	0	—	23	0	0	0	1	19	18	8.5	1	6	2.8	11	5.2	2.37	169	.257	.304	3	3	109	139	0.0	0	-0	0.3
1974	Phi-N	0	0	—	2	0	0	0	0	1	2	18.0	1	1	9.0	0	0.0	18.00	21	.400	.500	-2	-2	104	95	0.0	0	0	0.0
Total	2	0	0	—	25	0	0	0	1	20	20	9.0	2	7	3.1	11	4.9	3.15	126	.267	.318	1	2	109	137	0.0	0	0	0.3
■ FRANK DiPINO DiPino, Frank Michael b: 10/22/56, Syracuse, N.Y. BL/TL, 5'10", 175 lbs. Deb: 9/14/81																													
1981	Mil-A	0	0	—	2	0	0	0	0	2	0	0.0	0	3	13.5	3	13.5	0.00	—	.000	.300	1	1	95	0	0.0	0	0	0.1
1982	Hou-N	2	2	.500	6	6	0	0	0	28	32	10.3	1	11	3.5	25	8.0	6.11	59	.302	.352	-8	-8	100	75	0.1	-1	-0	-0.8
1983	Hou-N	3	4	.429	53	0	0	0	20	71	52	6.6	2	20	2.5	67	8.5	2.66	123	.205	.262	8	5	90	66	-0.6	1	1	0.6
1984	Hou-N	4	9	.308	57	0	0	0	14	75	74	8.9	3	36	4.3	65	7.8	3.36	98	.260	.337	2	-1	92	113	-2.5	-1	0	0.0
1985	Hou-N	3	7	.300	54	0	0	0	6	76	69	8.2	7	43	5.1	49	5.8	4.03	86	.248	.347	-4	-5	96	104	-2.1	-0	-1	-0.6
1986	Hou-N	1	3	.250	31	0	0	0	3	40	27	6.1	5	16	3.6	27	6.1	3.60	105	.189	.269	1	1	102	72	-1.1	0	0	0.1
	Chi-N	2	4	.333	30	0	0	0	0	40	47	10.6	6	14	3.1	43	9.7	5.17	78	.297	.343	-6	-5	108	101	-0.6	-0	1	-0.3
	Yr	3	7	.300	61	0	0	0	3	80	74	8.3	11	30	3.4	70	7.9	4.39	89	.243	.301	-6	-4	105	101	-1.7	0	2	-0.2
1987	Chi-N	3	3	.500	69	0	0	0	4	80	75	8.4	7	34	3.8	61	6.9	3.15	132	.252	.321	8	9	102	122	0.2	0	1	1.0
1988	Chi-N	2	3	.400	63	0	0	0	6	90	102	10.2	6	32	3.2	69	6.9	5.00	72	.285	.337	-15	-14	105	87	-0.3	-0	-0	-1.5
Total	8	20	35	.364	365	6	0	0	53	502	478	8.6	37	209	3.7	409	7.3	3.93	92	.253	.322	-14	-17	99	95	-6.9	-2	1	-1.4
■ GEORGE DISCH Disch, George Charles b: 3/15/1879, Lincoln, Mo. d: 8/25/50, Rapid City, S.D. 5'11", Deb: 8/08/05																													
1905	Det-A	0	2	.000	8	3	1	0	0	48	43	8.1	1	8	1.5	14	2.6	2.63	101	.263	.297	0	0	100	93	-0.9	-1	0	0.0
■ ALEC DISTASO Distaso, Alec John b: 12/23/48, Los Angeles, Cal. BR/TR, 6'2", 200 lbs. Deb: 4/20/69																													
1969	Chi-N	0	0	—	2	0	0	0	0	5	6	10.8	0	1	1.8	1	1.8	3.60	105	.316	.333	-0	0	105	115	0.0	0	0	0.0
■ ART DITMAR Ditmar, Arthur John b: 4/3/29, Winthrop, Mass. BR/TR, 6'2", 185 lbs. Deb: 4/19/54																													
1954	Phi-A	1	4	.200	14	5	0	0	0	39	50	11.5	4	36	8.3	14	3.2	6.46	60	.314	.437	-12	-11	105	107	-0.9	0	-0	-1.0
1955	KC-A	12	12	.500	35	22	7	1	1	175	180	9.3	23	86	4.4	79	4.1	5.04	83	.270	.353	-21	-16	106	96	2.1	-1	1	-1.4
1956	KC-A	12	22	.353	44	34	14	2	1	254	254	9.0	30	108	3.8	126	4.5	4.43	98	.262	.335	-8	-2	105	97	0.5	-4	-1	-0.7
1957	NY-A	8	3	.727	46	11	0	0	6	127	128	9.1	9	35	2.5	64	4.5	3.26	105	.261	.310	7	2	90	104	1.5	-0	-1	0.1
1958	NY-A	9	8	.529	38	13	4	0	4	140	124	8.0	14	38	2.4	52	3.3	3.41	110	.237	.290	6	5	99	91	-1.0	1	-2	0.5
1959	NY-A	13	9	.591	38	25	7	1	1	202	156	7.0	17	52	2.3	96	4.3	2.90	123	.211	**.267**	22	15	92	82	2.0	2	-1	1.5
1960	NY-A	15	9	.625	34	28	8	1	0	200	195	8.8	25	56	2.5	65	2.9	3.06	117	.256	.305	18	11	92	**121**	0.0	0	-1	1.0
1961	NY-A	2	3	.400	12	8	1	0	0	54	59	9.8	9	14	2.3	24	4.0	4.67	80	.285	.325	-4	-5	93	105	-0.9	-2	1	-0.5
	KC-A	0	5	.000	20	5	0	0	1	54	60	10.0	6	23	3.8	19	3.2	5.67	74	.286	.351	-10	-9	104	87	-2.4	-0	-0	-0.8
	Yr	2	8	.200	32	13	1	0	1	108	119	9.9	15	37	3.1	43	3.6	5.17	77	.281	.334	-14	-14	99	87	-3.3	-2	0	-1.3
1962	KC-A	2	2	.000	6	5	0	0	0	22	31	12.7	1	13	5.3	13	5.3	6.55	61	.323	.407	-6	-6	101	94	-0.9	-0	0	-0.5
Total	9	72	77	.483	287	156	41	5	14	1267	1237	8.8	138	461	3.3	552	3.9	3.99	97	.256	.321	-8	-17	98	98	-0.0	-4	-6	-1.8
■ SONNY DIXON Dixon, John Craig b: 11/5/24, Charlotte, N.C. BB/TR, 6'2.5", 205 lbs. Deb: 4/20/53																													
1953	Was-A	5	8	.385	43	6	3	0	3	120	123	9.2	13	31	2.3	40	3.0	3.75	99	.267	.310	3	-0	93	104	-1.5	0	2	0.2
1954	Was-A	1	2	.333	16	0	0	0	1	30	26	7.8	3	12	3.6	7	2.1	3.00	123	.236	.304	2	2	99	111	-0.2	-1	1	0.2
	Phi-A	5	7	.417	38	6	1	0	4	107	136	11.4	8	27	2.3	42	3.5	4.88	80	.308	.344	-14	-12	105	95	0.8	2	3	-0.6
	Yr	6	9	.400	**54**	6	1	0	5	137	162	10.6	11	39	2.6	49	3.2	4.47	86	.293	.336	-11	-9	103	95	0.6	-1	3	-0.4
1955	KC-A	0	0	—	2	0	0	0	0	2	6	27.0	1	0	0.0	0	0.0	13.50	31	.545	.545	-2	-2	106	122	0.0	0	0	-0.1
1956	NY-A	0	1	.000	3	0	0	0	1	4	5	11.3	0	5	11.3	1	2.3	2.25	175	.294	.435	1	1	95	283	-0.4	-0	0	0.1
Total	4	11	18	.379	102	12	4	0	9	263	296	10.1	25	75	2.6	90	3.1	4.17	91	.284	.328	-9	-11	99	104	-1.3	1	6	-0.2
■ KEN DIXON Dixon, Kenneth John b: 10/17/60, Monroe, Va. BB/TR, 5'11", 166 lbs. Deb: 9/22/84																													
1984	Bal-A	0	1	.000	2	2	0	0	0	13	14	9.7	1	4	2.8	8	5.5	4.15	91	.269	.321	-0	-1	94	90	-0.4	0	0	0.0
1985	Bal-A	8	4	.667	34	18	3	1	1	162	144	8.0	20	64	3.6	108	6.0	3.67	111	.237	.307	9	7	98	101	2.1	0	-1	0.6
1986	Bal-A	11	13	.458	35	33	2	0	0	202	194	8.6	33	83	3.7	170	7.6	4.59	91	.249	.318	-9	-10	99	92	0.2	0	-1	-0.9
1987	Bal-A	7	10	.412	34	15	0	0	5	105	128	11.0	31	27	2.3	91	7.8	6.43	69	.292	.332	-23	-23	99	93	0.0	0	-0	-2.1
Total	4	26	28	.481	105	68	5	1	6	482	480	9.0	85	178	3.3	377	7.0	4.67	90	.256	.318	-23	-26	99	95	1.8	0	-2	-2.4
■ TOM DIXON Dixon, Thomas Earl b: 4/23/55, Orlando, Fla. BR/TR, 5'11", 175 lbs. Deb: 7/30/77																													
1977	Hou-N	1	0	1.000	9	4	1	0	0	30	40	12.0	0	7	2.1	15	4.5	3.30	109	.320	.356	2	1	92	135	0.5	-1	0	0.0
1978	Hou-N	7	11	.389	30	19	3	2	1	140	140	9.0	8	40	2.6	66	4.2	3.99	85	.265	.306	-6	-9	95	87	-1.4	-2	-1	-1.1
1979	Hou-N	1	2	.333	19	1	0	0	0	26	39	13.5	2	15	5.2	9	3.1	6.58	51	.348	.415	-8	-9	90	103	-0.5	0	1	-0.7
1983	Mon-N	0	1	.000	4	0	0	0	0	4	6	13.5	1	1	2.3	4	9.0	9.00	41	.375	.421	-2	-2	101	95	-0.4	0	0	-0.2
Total	4	9	14	.391	62	24	4	2	1	200	225	10.1	11	63	2.8	94	4.2	4.32	80	.288	.332	-15	-20	94	97	-1.8	-2	-0	-2.0
■ BILL DOAK Doak, William Leopold "Spittin' Bill" b: 1/28/1891, Pittsburgh, Pa. d: 11/26/54, Bradenton, Fla. BR/TR, 6'0.5", 165 lbs. Deb: 9/01/12																													
1912	Cin-N	0	0	—	1	1	0	0	0	2	4	18.0	0	1	4.5	0	0.0	4.50	71	.444	.500	-0	-0	93	199	0.0	0	0	0.0
1913	StL-N	2	8	.200	15	12	5	1	1	93	79	7.6	4	39	3.8	51	4.9	3.10	100	.236	.317	1	0	97	98	-2.0	-3	1	-0.1
1914	StL-N	19	6	.760	36	33	16	7	1	256	193	6.8	2	87	3.1	118	4.1	**1.72**	**167**	.216	.282	30	33	104	110	6.7	-4	5	4.0
1915	StL-N	16	18	.471	38	36	19	3	1	276	263	8.6	4	85	2.8	124	4.0	2.64	105	.261	.310	3	4	101	116	0.0	1	7	1.3
1916	StL-N	12	8	.600	29	26	11	3	0	192	177	8.3	5	55	2.6	82	3.8	2.63	100	.251	.298	-0	-0	100	106	3.7	-2	2	0.0
1917	StL-N	16	20	.444	44	37	16	3	2	281	257	8.2	6	85	2.7	111	3.6	3.11	89	.250	.305	-12	-10	102	92	-3.8	-5	5	-1.1
1918	StL-N	9	15	.375	31	23	16	1	1	211	191	8.1	3	60	2.6	74	3.2	2.43	108	.249	.295	8	5	95	108	-0.7	1	5	1.2
1919	StL-N	13	14	.481	31	29	13	3	0	203	182	8.1	5	55	2.4	69	3.1	3.10	91	.246	.291	-4	-7	97	85	2.3	-4	4	-0.6
1920	StL-N	20	12	.625	39	37	20	5	1	270	256	8.5	7	80	2.7	90	3.0	2.53	121	.253	.306	18	16	98	105	5.1	-6	0	1.1
1921	StL-N	15	6	**.714**	32	28	13	2	1	209	224	9.6	3	37	1.6	83	3.6	**2.58**	135	.278	.307	28	21	93	116	3.9	-3	2	2.0
1922	StL-N	11	13	.458	37	29	8	2	2	180	222	11.1	12	69	3.5	73	3.7	5.55	74	.311	.368	-29	-29	100	89	-2.2	-3	0	-2.8
1923	StL-N	8	13	.381	30	26	7	3	0	185	199	9.7	4	69	3.4	53	2.6	3.26	110	.279	.338	15	7	90	115	-3.0	-8	3	0.1
1924	StL-N	2	1	.667	11	1	0	0	3	22	25	10.2	0	14	5.7	7	2.9	3.27	121	.313	.398	1	2	103	162	0.6	-0	1	0.2
	Bro-N	11	5	.688	21	16	8	2	0	149	130	7.9	8	35	2.1	32	1.9	3.08	123	.239	.281	13	12	98	86	1.9	-0	3	1.4
	Yr	13	6	.684	32	17	8	2	3	171	155	8.2	8	49	2.6	39	2.1	3.11	123	.249	.298	14	14	99	86	2.5	-0	3	1.6
1927	Bro-N	11	8	.579	27	20	6	1	0	145	153	9.5	6	40	2.5	32	2.0	3.48	117	.271	.315	7	10	104	100	2.8	-3	1	0.8
1928	Bro-N	3	8	.273	28	12	4	1	3	99	104	9.5	1	35	3.2	12	1.1	3.27	120	.271	.324	8	7	99	104	-2.5	-2	3	0.8
1929	StL-N	1	2	.333	3	2	0	0	0	9	17	17.0	1	5	5.0	3	3.0	12.00	39	.415	.449	-7	-7	98	79	-0.4	0	-0	-0.5
Total	16	169	157	.518	453	368	162	37	16	2782	2676	8.7	71	851	2.8	1014	3.3	2.98	107	.259	.310	80	65	99	103	12.4	-41	42	7.8
■ WALT DOAN Doan, Walter Rudolph b: 3/12/1887, Bellevue, Idaho d: 10/19/35, W.Brandywine, Pa. BL/TR, 6', 165 lbs. Deb: 9/20/09																													
1909	Cle-A	0	1	.000	1	1	0	0	0	5	10	18.0	0	1	1.8	2	3.6	5.40	47	.400	.423	-2	-2	103	127	-0.4	-0	0	-0.1
1910	Cle-A	0	0	—	6	0	0	0	0	18	31	15.5	1	8	4.0	7	3.5	5.50	47	.413	.476	-6	-6	102	146	0.0	1	-1	-0.6
Total	2	0	1	.000	7	1	0	0	0	23	41	16.0	1	9	3.5	9	3.5	5.48	47	.410	.464	-8	-7	102	142	-0.4	1	-1	-0.7
■ JOHN DOBB Dobb, John Kenneth "Lefty" b: 11/15/01, Muskegon, Mich. TL , 6'2", 180 lbs. Deb: 8/13/24																													
1924	Chi-A	0	0	—	2	0	0	0	0	2	4	18.0	0	1	4.5	2	9.0	9.00	46	.400	.455	-1	-1	98	88	0.0	0	0	0.0

YEAR	TM/L	W	L	PCT	G	GS	CG	SHO	SV	IP	H	H/G	HR	BB	BB/G	SO	SO/G	ERA	/A	OAVG	OOBP	PR	/A	PF	CPI	WAT	PB	PD	TPI
■ RAY DOBENS	Dobens, Raymond Joseph "Lefty" b: 7/28/06, Nashua, N.H. d: 4/21/80, Stuart, Fla. BL/TL, 5'8", 175 lbs. Deb: 7/07/29																												
1929	Bos-A	0	0	—	11	2	0	0	0	28	32	10.3	0	9	2.9	4	1.3	3.86	116	.302	.347	1	2	105	111	0.0	1	-1	0.1
■ JESS DOBERNIC	Dobernic, Andrew Joseph b: 11/20/17, Mt.Olive, Ill. BR/TR, 5'1", 170 lbs. Deb: 7/02/39																												
1939	Chi-A	0	1	.000	4	0	0	0	0	3	3	9.0	0	6	18.0	1	3.0	15.00	33	.231	.476	-3	-3	106	50	-0.4	-0	0	-0.2
1948	Chi-N	7	2	.778	54	0	0	0	1	86	67	7.0	8	40	4.2	48	5.0	3.14	120	.213	.296	8	6	95	97	2.9	-0	-2	0.4
1949	Chi-N	0	0	—	4	0	0	0	0	4	9	20.3	2	4	9.0	0	0.0	20.25	19	.450	.520	-7	-7	97	75	0.0	0	-0	-0.6
	Cin-N	0	0	—	14	0	0	0	0	19	28	13.3	7	16	7.6	6	2.8	9.95	40	.329	.436	-12	-13	98	94	0.0	0	0	-1.1
	Yr	0	0	—	18	0	0	0	0	23	37	14.5	9	20	7.8	6	2.3	11.74	34	.352	.452	-20	-20	98	94	0.0	0	-0	-1.7
Total	3	7	3	.700	76	0	0	0	1	112	107	8.6	17	66	5.3	55	4.4	5.22	73	.247	.342	-15	-17	96	94	2.5	-0	-2	-1.5
■ CHUCK DOBSON	Dobson, Charles Thomas b: 1/10/44, Kansas City, Mo. BR/TR, 6'4", 200 lbs. Deb: 4/19/66																												
1966	KC-A	4	6	.400	14	14	1	0	0	84	71	7.6	7	50	5.4	61	6.5	4.07	80	.234	.343	-6	-7	95	97	-0.6	-1	1	-0.7
1967	KC-A	10	10	.500	32	29	4	1	0	198	172	7.8	17	75	3.4	110	5.0	3.68	89	.233	.303	-10	-9	102	88	2.1	0	-0	-0.8
1968	Oak-A	12	14	.462	35	34	11	3	0	225	197	7.9	20	80	3.2	168	6.7	3.00	97	.234	.299	-1	-2	98	106	-1.2	2	2	0.1
1969	Oak-A	15	13	.536	35	35	11	1	0	235	244	9.3	16	80	3.1	137	5.2	3.87	86	.270	.326	-6	-14	91	98	-0.1	-3	-2	-1.9
1970	Oak-A	16	15	.516	41	40	13	**5**	0	267	230	7.8	32	92	3.1	149	5.0	3.74	95	.229	.294	-1	-6	96	85	-1.0	-3	-2	-1.1
1971	Oak-A	15	5	.750	30	30	7	1	0	189	185	8.8	24	71	3.4	100	4.8	3.81	90	.259	.323	-7	-8	99	106	3.6	3	0	-0.5
1973	Oak-A	0	1	.000	1	1	0	0	0	2	6	27.0	1	2	9.0	3	13.5	9.00	36	.429	.500	-1	-1	86	174	-0.4	0	0	0.0
1974	Cal-A	2	3	.400	5	5	2	0	0	30	39	11.7	3	13	3.9	16	4.8	5.70	59	.315	.380	-7	-8	93	95	0.0	0	0	-0.7
1975	Cal-A	0	2	.000	9	2	0	0	0	28	30	9.6	5	13	4.2	14	4.5	6.75	54	.275	.349	-9	-10	96	78	-0.9	0	-1	-0.9
Total	9	74	69	.517	202	190	49	11	0	1258	1174	8.4	125	476	3.4	758	5.4	3.78	88	.247	.314	-48	-64	97	96	1.5	-2	-1	-6.5
■ JOE DOBSON	Dobson, Joseph Gordon "Burrhead" b: 1/20/17, Durant, Okla. BR/TR, 6'2", 197 lbs. Deb: 4/26/39 C																												
1939	Cle-A	2	3	.400	35	3	0	0	1	78	87	10.0	3	51	5.9	27	3.1	5.88	76	.290	.384	-11	-12	96	91	-0.6	-2	0	-1.2
1940	Cle-A	3	7	.300	40	7	2	1	3	100	101	9.1	8	48	4.3	57	5.1	4.95	81	.268	.345	-6	-10	92	91	-2.4	-1	-0	-0.9
1941	Bos-A	12	5	.706	27	18	7	1	0	134	136	9.1	8	67	4.5	69	4.6	4.50	93	.262	.345	-5	-5	101	93	3.2	0	-2	-0.5
1942	Bos-A	11	9	.550	30	23	10	3	0	183	155	7.6	9	68	3.3	72	3.5	3.30	111	.231	.300	7	8	100	90	-1.0	-1	2	0.9
1943	Bos-A	7	11	.389	25	20	9	3	0	164	144	7.9	4	57	3.1	63	3.5	3.13	110	.239	.299	3	6	104	89	-1.2	-3	-2	0.1
1946	Bos-A	13	7	.650	32	24	9	1	0	167	148	8.0	11	68	3.7	91	4.9	3.23	120	.234	.306	5	12	111	92	-0.3	-3	2	1.3
1947	Bos-A	18	8	.692	33	31	15	1	1	229	203	8.0	15	73	2.9	110	4.3	2.95	134	.238	**.296**	19	26	107	101	4.9	1	-2	2.8
1948	Bos-A	16	10	.615	38	32	16	5	2	245	237	8.7	14	92	3.4	116	4.3	3.56	117	.253	.316	20	16	97	99	0.0	2	-1	1.6
1949	Bos-A	14	12	.538	33	27	12	2	2	213	219	9.3	12	97	4.1	87	3.7	3.85	113	.269	.345	8	12	103	106	-2.0	-1	-2	0.9
1950	Bos-A	15	10	.600	39	27	12	1	4	207	217	9.4	15	81	3.5	81	3.5	4.17	122	.275	.338	9	21	111	103	-0.2	1	1	2.4
1951	Chi-A	7	6	.538	28	21	6	0	3	147	136	8.3	17	51	3.1	67	4.1	3.61	109	.248	.307	8	5	96	104	0.2	-5	0	0.0
1952	Chi-A	14	10	.583	29	25	11	3	1	201	164	7.3	11	60	2.7	101	4.5	2.51	145	.222	.278	26	25	99	96	1.7	0	-2	2.5
1953	Chi-A	5	5	.500	23	15	3	1	1	101	96	8.6	10	37	3.3	50	4.5	3.65	113	.249	.313	4	5	104	98	-0.6	-3	-1	0.2
1954	Bos-A	0	0	—	2	0	0	0	0	3	5	15.0	0	1	3.0	1	3.0	6.00	62	.385	.429	-1	-1	101	110	0.0	0	0	0.0
Total	14	137	103	.571	414	273	112	22	18	2172	2048	8.5	137	851	3.5	992	4.1	3.62	112	.250	.318	87	109	102	97	1.7	-15	-5	10.1
■ PAT DOBSON	Dobson, Patrick Edward b: 2/12/42, Depew, N.Y. BR/TR, 6'3", 190 lbs. Deb: 5/31/67 C																												
1967	Det-A	1	2	.333	28	1	0	0	0	49	38	7.0	6	27	5.0	34	6.2	2.94	108	.216	.319	2	1	98	127	-0.5	-1	-1	0.0
1968	Det-A	5	8	.385	47	10	2	1	7	125	89	6.4	13	48	3.5	93	6.7	2.66	115	.200	.277	4	6	103	99	-2.6	-0	1	0.8
1969	Det-A	5	10	.333	49	9	1	0	9	105	100	8.6	10	39	3.3	64	5.5	3.60	103	.253	.310	0	1	102	102	-3.1	-1	0	0.0
1970	SD-N	14	15	.483	40	34	8	1	1	251	257	9.2	28	78	2.8	185	6.6	3.76	104	.265	.316	8	4	97	108	2.6	0	-0	0.3
1971	Bal-A	20	8	.714	38	37	18	4	1	282	248	7.9	24	63	2.0	187	6.0	2.90	120	.235	.276	18	18	100	92	3.4	-4	-1	1.4
1972	Bal-A	16	18	.471	38	36	13	3	0	268	220	7.4	13	69	2.3	161	5.4	2.65	111	.224	.275	12	9	96	86	-1.9	-1	-2	0.6
1973	Atl-N	3	7	.300	12	10	1	0	0	58	73	11.3	1	19	2.9	23	3.6	4.97	83	.315	.356	-8	-5	113	92	-1.8	-1	0	-0.5
	NY-A	9	8	.529	22	21	6	1	0	142	150	9.5	22	34	2.2	70	4.4	4.18	92	.266	.307	-6	-6	100	96	0.7	0	0	-0.5
1974	NY-A	19	15	.559	39	39	12	2	0	281	282	9.0	23	75	2.4	157	5.0	3.07	112	.262	.309	17	12	95	112	0.4	0	-1	1.1
1975	NY-A	11	14	.440	33	30	7	1	0	208	205	8.9	21	83	3.6	129	5.6	4.07	91	.261	.326	-6	-9	98	98	-2.1	0	-0	-0.8
1976	Cle-A	16	12	.571	35	35	6	0	0	217	226	9.4	13	65	2.7	117	4.9	3.48	101	.272	.319	1	1	100	107	2.1	0	-1	0.0
1977	Cle-A	3	12	.200	33	17	0	0	1	133	155	10.5	23	65	4.4	81	5.5	6.16	65	.299	.371	-31	-32	98	95	-4.2	0	0	-2.9
Total	11	122	129	.486	414	279	74	14	19	2119	2043	8.7	197	665	2.8	1301	5.5	3.54	100	.255	.308	11	0	99	100	-7.0	-8	-3	-0.5
■ GEORGE DOCKINS	Dockins, George Woodrow "Lefty" b: 5/5/17, Clyde, Kan. BL/TL, 6', 175 lbs. Deb: 5/05/45																												
1945	StL-N	8	6	.571	31	12	5	2	0	126	132	9.4	4	38	2.7	33	2.4	3.21	115	.269	.311	8	7	97	108	-0.5	1	-0	0.7
1947	Bro-N	0	0	—	4	0	0	0	0	5	10	18.0	2	2	3.6	1	1.8	12.60	33	.400	.429	-5	-5	103	86	0.0	-0	0	-0.3
Total	2	8	6	.571	35	12	5	2	0	131	142	9.8	6	40	2.7	34	2.3	3.57	104	.275	.317	3	2	97	108	-0.5	1	-0	0.4
■ SAM DODGE	Dodge, Samuel Edward b: 12/19/1889, Philadelphia, Pa. BR/TR, 6'1", 170 lbs. Deb: 9/24/21																												
1921	Bos-A	0	0	—	1	0	0	0	0	1	1	9.0	0	1	9.0	0	0.0	9.00	48	.500	.500	-1	-1	100	106	0.0	0	0	0.0
1922	Bos-A	0	0	—	3	0	0	0	0	6	11	16.5	0	3	4.5	3	4.5	4.50	89	.379	.424	-0	-0	99	158	0.0	-0	0	0.0
Total	2	0	0	—	4	0	0	0	0	7	12	15.4	0	4	5.1	3	3.9	5.14	79	.387	.432	-1	-1	99	150	0.0	-0	0	0.0
■ FRED DOE	Doe, Alfred George "Count" b: 4/18/1864, Rockport, Mass. d: 10/4/38, Quincy, Mass. BR/TR, 5'10", 165 lbs. Deb: 8/23/1890																												
1890	Buf-P	0	1	.000	1	1	1	0	0	6	10	15.0	0	7	10.5	2	3.0	12.00	34	.384	.514	-5	-5	97	71	-0.4	-0	0	-0.3
	Pit-P	0	0	—	1	0	0	0	0	4	4	9.0	0	2	4.5	2	4.5	4.50	87	.272	.359	-0	-0	92	73	0.0	0	0	0.0
	Yr	0	1	.000	2	1	1	0	0	10	14	12.6	0	9	8.1	4	3.6	9.00	45	.343	.462	-5	-6	95	73	-0.4	-0	0	-0.3
■ ED DOHENY	Doheny, Edward R. b: 11/24/1874, Northfield, Vt. d: 12/29/16, Medfield, Mass. BL/TL, 5'10.5", 165 lbs. Deb: 9/16/1895																												
1895	NY-N	0	3	.000	3	3	3	0	0	26	37	12.8	2	19	6.6	9	3.1	6.92	65	.356	.455	-6	-7	94	101	-1.4	-0	0	-0.5
1896	NY-N	6	7	.462	17	15	9	0	0	108	112	9.3	3	59	4.9	39	3.3	4.50	96	.289	.383	-2	-2	99	91	-0.3	-2	0	-0.3
1897	NY-N	4	4	.500	10	10	10	0	0	85	69	7.3	0	45	4.8	37	3.9	2.12	196	.241	.345	21	19	96	126	-0.8	-1	0	1.6
1898	NY-N	7	19	.269	28	27	23	0	0	213	238	10.1	1	101	4.3	96	4.1	3.68	92	.305	.384	-2	-7	94	111	-6.7	-1	0	-0.6
1899	NY-N	14	17	.452	35	33	30	1	0	265	282	9.6	2	156	5.3	115	3.9	4.52	84	.296	.395	-20	-21	99	91	1.6	0	5	-1.3
1900	NY-N	4	14	.222	20	18	12	0	0	134	148	9.9	2	96	6.4	44	3.0	5.51	67	.303	.418	-27	-27	99	87	-4.6	-0	0	-2.3
1901	NY-N	2	5	.286	10	6	6	0	0	74	88	10.7	1	17	2.1	36	4.4	4.50	70	.325	.378	-10	-11	95	91	-0.8	3	0	-0.9
	Pit-N	6	2	.750	11	10	6	1	0	77	68	7.9	1	22	2.6	28	3.3	1.99	160	.262	.332	11	10	96	135	1.2	1	-1	0.9
	Yr	8	7	.533	21	16	12	1	0	151	156	9.3	2	39	2.3	64	3.8	3.22	99	.291	.345	2	-1	96	135	0.4	3	-1	0.0
1902	Pit-N	16	4	.800	22	21	19	2	0	188	161	7.7	0	61	2.9	88	4.2	2.54	107	.258	.338	5	4	98	96	2.6	-2	-1	0.3
1903	Pit-N	16	8	.667	27	25	22	2	2	223	209	8.4	1	89	3.6	75	3.0	3.19	104	.278	.369	2	3	101	98	0.7	-1	5	0.8
Total	9	75	83	.475	183	168	140	6	2	1393	1412	9.1	13	665	4.3	567	3.7	3.76	93	.288	.378	-26	-38	98	100	-8.5	-3	8	-2.3
■ JOHN DOLAN	Dolan, John b: 9/12/1867, Newport, Ky. d: 5/8/48, Springfield, Ohio TR, 5'10", 170 lbs. Deb: 9/05/1890																												
1890	Cin-N	1	1	.500	2	2	2	0	0	18	17	8.5	3	10	5.0	9	4.5	4.50	84	.265	.364	-2	-1	106	103	0.0	-1	0	-0.1
1891	Col-a	12	11	.522	27	24	19	0	2	203	216	9.6	8	84	3.7	68	3.0	4.17	80	.287	.359	-10	-19	90	91	1.9	-3	0	-1.8
1892	Was-N	2	2	.500	5	4	3	0	0	37	39	9.5	0	15	3.6	8	1.9	4.38	80	.284	.354	-4	-4	106	79	0.4	0	0	-0.2
1893	StL-N	0	1	.000	3	1	1	0	1	17	26	13.8	1	7	3.7	1	0.5	4.24	110	.368	.425	1	1	100	155	-0.4	0	0	0.1
1895	Chi-N	0	1	.000	2	2	1	0	0	11	16	13.1	0	6	4.9	1	0.8	6.55	75	.361	.437	-2	-2	103	92	-0.4	-0	0	-0.1
Total	5	15	16	.484	39	33	26	0	1	286	314	9.9	12	122	3.8	87	2.7	4.31	82	.294	.366	-18	-25	94	94	1.5	-4	0	-2.1
■ COZY DOLAN	Dolan, Patrick Henry b: 12/3/1872, Cambridge, Mass. d: 3/29/07, Louisville, Ky. BL/TL, Deb: N/A.																												
1895	Bos-N	11	7	.611	25	21	18	3	1	198	215	9.8	11	67	3.0	47	2.1	4.27	114	.297	.356	11	14	102	95	1.5	-1	0	1.1
1896	Bos-N	1	4	.200	6	5	3	0	0	41	55	12.1	1	27	5.9	14	3.1	4.83	97	.345	.440	-2	-1	107	122	-1.5	-2	0	-0.1
1905	Bos-N	0	1	.000	2	0	0	0	0	4	7	15.8	2	1	2.3	1	2.3	9.00	34	.413	.446	-3	-3	102	116	-0.3	1	0	-0.3
1906	Bos-N	0	1	.000	2	0	0	0	0	12	12	9.0	1	6	4.5	7	5.3	4.50	62	.288	.378	-2	-2	106	93	-0.4	0	-1	-0.1
Total	4	12	13	.480	35	26	21	3	1	255	289	10.2	15	101	3.6	69	2.4	4.45	106	.306	.374	4	8	103	100	-0.7	-1	-1	0.6

YEAR	TM/L	W	L	PCT	G	GS	CG	SHO	SV	IP	H	H/G	HR	BB	BB/G	SO	SO/G	ERA	/A	OAVG	OOBP	PR	/A	PF	CPI	WAT	PB	PD	TPI
■ **TOM DOLAN**	Dolan, Thomas J. b: 1/10/1859, New York, N.Y. d: 1/16/13, St.Louis, Mo. BR/TR, Deb: 9/30/1879																												
1883	StL-a	0	0	—	1	0	0	0	0	4	4	9.0	0	0	0.0	0	0.0	4.50	77	.266	.266	-1	-0	105	55	0.0	-0	0	0.0
■ **ART DOLL**	Doll, Arthur James "Moose" b: 5/7/13, Chicago, Ill. d: 4/28/78, Calumet City, Ill. BR/TR, 6'1", 190 lbs. Deb: 9/21/35																												
1936	Bos-N	0	1	.000	1	1	0	0	0	8	11	12.4	1	2	2.3	2	2.3	3.38	115	.355	.400	1	0	96	203	-0.4	-0	0	0.0
1938	Bos-N	0	0	—	3	0	0	0	0	4	4	9.0	0	3	6.8	1	2.3	2.25	150	.286	.412	1	0	89	225	0.0	0	0	0.1
Total	2	0	1	.000	4	1	0	0	0	12	15	11.3	1	5	3.8	3	2.3	3.00	123	.333	.404	1	1	94	210	-0.4	0	0	0.1
■ **RED DONAHUE**	Donahue, Francis Rostell b: 1/23/1873, Waterbury, Conn. d: 8/25/13, Philadelphia, Pa. BR/TR, Deb: 5/06/1893																												
1893	NY-N	0	0	—	2	0	0	0	1	5	8	14.4	1	3	5.4	1	1.8	9.00	53	.378	.456	-2	-2	103	95	0.0	-0	0	-0.1
1895	StL-N	0	1	.000	1	1	1	0	0	8	9	10.1	2	3	3.4	2	2.3	6.75	73	.304	.368	-2	-2	102	86	-0.4	-1	0	-0.1
1896	StL-N	7	24	.226	32	32	28	0	0	267	376	12.7	6	98	3.3	70	2.4	5.80	74	.356	.411	-42	-45	98	93	-4.9	-7	-1	-4.2
1897	StL-N	10	35	.222	**46**	42	**38**	1	1	348	484	12.5	16	106	2.7	64	1.7	6.13	69	.353	.399	-70	-73	99	86	0.0	-2	6	-5.5
1898	Phi-N	16	17	.485	35	35	33	1	0	284	327	10.4	7	80	2.5	57	1.8	3.55	96	.311	.360	2	-5	94	108	-1.4	-6	4	-0.7
1899	Phi-N	21	8	.724	35	31	27	4	0	279	292	9.4	6	63	2.0	51	1.6	3.39	108	.293	.335	14	9	95	93	4.7	-5	3	0.6
1900	Phi-N	15	10	.600	32	24	21	2	0	240	299	11.2	6	50	1.9	41	1.5	3.60	100	.329	.364	3	0	98	115	1.8	-1	0	0.0
1901	Phi-N	21	13	.618	35	34	34	1	1	304	307	9.1	2	60	1.8	89	2.6	2.61	128	.286	.328	24	24	100	111	1.3	-9	-2	2.3
1902	StL-A	22	11	.667	35	34	33	2	0	316	322	9.2	7	65	1.9	63	1.8	2.76	132	.288	.327	28	31	102	110	4.4	-10	7	3.8
1903	StL-A	8	7	.533	16	15	14	0	0	131	145	10.0	0	22	1.5	51	3.5	2.75	103	.303	.334	3	1	96	120	1.0	-2	0	0.1
	Cle-A	7	9	.438	16	15	14	4	0	137	142	9.3	3	12	0.8	45	3.0	2.43	116	.290	.307	8	6	95	118	-1.7	-1	1	0.7
	Yr	15	16	.484	32	30	28	4	0	268	287	9.6	3	34	1.1	96	3.2	2.59	109	.296	.320	11	7	95	118	-0.7	-2	1	0.8
1904	Cle-A	19	14	.576	35	32	30	6	0	277	281	9.1	2	49	1.6	127	4.1	2.40	106	.286	.320	6	4	98	120	0.3	-1	2	0.6
1905	Cle-A	6	12	.333	20	18	14	1	0	138	132	8.6	2	25	1.6	45	2.9	3.39	78	.276	.312	-11	-11	100	80	-3.1	-5	1	-1.0
1906	Det-A	13	14	.481	28	28	26	3	0	241	260	9.7	1	54	2.0	82	3.1	2.73	109	.301	.343	-1	6	110	120	0.2	-5	-0	0.7
Total	13	165	175	.485	368	341	313	25	3	2975	3384	10.2	61	690	2.1	788	2.4	3.61	96	.310	.351	-41	-53	99	105	2.2	-55	20	-2.8
■ **DEACON DONAHUE**	Donahue, John Stephen Michael b: 6/23/20, Chicago, Ill. BR/TR, 6', 180 lbs. Deb: 9/16/43																												
1943	Phi-N	0	0	—	2	0	0	0	0	4	4	9.0	0	1	2.3	1	2.3	4.50	72	.235	.316	-1	-1	96	58	0.0	0	0	0.0
1944	Phi-N	0	2	.000	6	0	0	0	0	9	18	18.0	0	2	2.0	2	2.0	8.00	46	.429	.444	-4	-4	103	101	-0.9	-0	0	-0.3
Total	2	0	2	.000	8	0	0	0	0	13	22	15.2	0	3	2.1	3	2.1	6.92	51	.373	.406	-5	-5	100	88	-0.9	-0	0	-0.3
■ **ATLEY DONALD**	Donald, Richard Atley "Swampy" b: 8/19/10, Morton, Miss. BL/TR, 6'1", 186 lbs. Deb: 4/21/38																												
1938	NY-A	0	1	.000	2	2	0	0	0	12	7	5.3	0	14	10.5	6	4.5	5.25	93	.175	.400	-1	-1	102	75	-0.4	-0	0	0.0
1939	NY-A	13	3	.813	24	20	11	2	1	153	144	8.5	12	60	3.5	55	3.2	3.71	106	.247	.311	16	4	85	99	3.2	3	-1	0.4
1940	NY-A	8	3	.727	24	11	6	1	0	119	113	8.5	11	59	4.5	60	4.5	3.03	139	.249	.335	18	16	96	137	2.1	-2	-2	1.1
1941	NY-A	9	5	.643	22	20	10	0	0	159	141	8.0	11	69	3.9	71	4.0	3.57	110	.237	.316	10	6	95	97	-0.1	-4	-0	0.2
1942	NY-A	11	3	.786	20	19	10	1	0	148	132	8.0	6	45	2.7	53	3.2	3.10	111	.237	.292	9	5	94	90	2.6	-1	-2	0.2
1943	NY-A	6	4	.600	22	15	2	0	0	119	134	10.1	10	38	2.9	57	4.3	4.61	67	.276	.326	-17	-20	94	88	-0.2	-2	-2	-2.4
1944	NY-A	13	10	.565	30	19	9	0	0	159	173	9.8	13	59	3.3	48	2.7	3.34	108	.280	.338	2	5	105	**129**	0.8	-0	-1	0.4
1945	NY-A	5	4	.556	9	9	6	2	0	64	62	8.7	3	25	3.5	19	2.7	2.95	121	.248	.314	3	4	106	107	0.2	0	-2	0.3
Total	8	65	33	.663	153	115	54	6	1	933	906	8.7	66	369	3.6	369	3.6	3.52	106	.253	.320	39	22	96	106	8.2	-6	-10	0.2
■ **ED DONALDS**	Donalds, Edward Alexander "Erston" b: 6/22/1885, Bidwell, Ohio d: 7/3/50, Columbus, Ohio BR/TR, 5'11", 180 lbs. Deb: 9/01/12																												
1912	Cin-N	1	0	1.000	1	0	0	0	0	4	7	15.8	0	0	0.0	1	2.3	4.50	71	.412	.412	-0	-1	93	141	0.5	-0	0	0.0
■ **MIKE DONLIN**	Donlin, Michael Joseph "Turkey Mike" b: 5/30/1878, Peoria, Ill. d: 9/24/33, Hollywood, Cal. BL/TL, 5'9", 170 lbs. Deb: 7/19/1899																												
1899	StL-N	0	1	.000	3	1	0	0	0	15	15	9.0	0	14	8.4	6	3.6	7.80	53	.283	.433	-7	-6	107	67	-0.4	1	0	-0.4
1902	Cin-N	0	0	—	1	0	0	0	0	1	1	9.0	0	0	0.0	0	0.0	0.00	—	.283	.283	0	0	108	0	0.0	0	0	0.0
Total	2	0	1	.000	4	1	0	0	0	16	16	9.0	0	14	7.9	6	3.4	7.31	55	.283	.426	-6	-6	107	63	-0.4	1	0	-0.4
■ **ED DONNELLY**	Donnelly, Edward "Big Ed" or "Ned" (born Edward O'Donnell) b: 7/29/1880, Hampton, N.Y. d: 11/28/57, Rutland, Vt. BR/TR, 6'1", 205 lbs. Deb: 9/19/11																												
1911	Bos-N	3	2	.600	5	4	4	1	0	37	33	8.0	0	9	2.2	16	3.9	2.43	153	.236	.291	4	5	109	88	1.1	-2	0	0.4
1912	Bos-N	5	10	.333	37	18	10	0	0	184	225	11.0	10	72	3.5	67	3.3	4.35	86	.296	.360	-19	-12	110	98	-0.1	2	1	-0.7
Total	2	8	12	.400	42	22	14	1	0	221	258	10.5	10	81	3.3	83	3.4	4.03	93	.286	.350	-15	-7	110	97	1.0	1	1	-0.3
■ **ED DONNELLY**	Donnelly, Edward Vincent b: 12/10/34, Allen, Mich. BR/TR, 6', 175 lbs. Deb: 8/01/59																												
1959	Chi-N	1	1	.500	9	0	0	0	0	14	18	11.6	1	9	5.8	6	3.9	3.21	121	.305	.391	1	1	99	175	0.0	0	0	0.1
■ **FRANK DONNELLY**	Donnelly, Franklin Marion b: 10/7/1869, Tamaroa, Ill. d: 2/3/53, Canton, Ill. 180 lbs. Deb: 8/15/1893																												
1893	Chi-N	3	1	.750	7	5	3	0	**2**	42	51	10.9	1	17	3.6	6	1.3	5.36	91	.316	.381	-3	-2	104	88	1.1	4	0	0.1
■ **BLIX DONNELLY**	Donnelly, Sylvester Urban b: 1/21/14, Olivia, Minn. d: 6/20/76, Olivia, Minn. BR/TR, 5'10", 166 lbs. Deb: 5/06/44																												
1944	StL-N	2	1	.667	27	4	2	1	2	76	61	7.2	2	34	4.0	45	5.3	2.13	161	.218	.301	13	11	95	123	0.0	-1	1	1.2
1945	StL-N	8	10	.444	31	23	9	4	2	166	157	8.5	10	87	4.7	76	4.1	3.52	105	.250	.342	5	3	97	112	-2.6	-2	-3	-0.2
1946	StL-N	1	2	.333	13	0	0	0	0	14	17	10.9	1	10	6.4	11	7.1	3.86	91	.347	.444	-1	-1	103	182	-0.6	0	-0	0.0
	Phi-N	3	4	.429	12	8	2	0	1	76	64	7.6	7	24	2.8	38	4.5	2.96	113	.220	.282	4	3	98	86	-0.1	2	-1	0.4
	Yr	4	6	.400	25	8	2	0	1	90	81	8.1	8	34	3.4	49	4.9	3.10	109	.238	.306	3	3	99	86	-0.7	0	-1	0.4
1947	Phi-N	4	6	.400	38	10	5	1	5	121	113	8.4	6	46	3.4	31	2.3	2.98	139	.265	.333	15	16	102	131	0.0	-2	-0	1.3
1948	Phi-N	5	7	.417	26	19	8	1	2	132	125	8.5	13	49	3.3	46	3.1	3.68	104	.261	.325	4	2	97	111	-0.1	2	-3	0.1
1949	Phi-N	2	1	.667	23	10	1	0	0	78	84	9.7	7	40	4.6	36	4.2	5.08	80	.294	.373	-9	-9	101	105	0.5	-1	-2	-1.0
1950	Phi-N	2	4	.333	14	1	0	0	0	21	30	12.9	5	10	4.3	10	4.3	4.29	92	.330	.392	-0	-1	96	170	-1.2	-0	0	0.0
1951	Bos-N	0	1	.000	6	0	0	0	0	7	8	10.3	1	6	7.7	3	3.9	7.71	50	.286	.395	-3	-3	97	86	-0.4	-0	0	-0.2
Total	8	27	36	.429	190	75	27	7	12	691	659	8.6	52	306	4.0	296	3.9	3.49	108	.257	.334	27	22	98	116	-4.5	-1	-8	1.6
■ **JIM DONOHUE**	Donohue, James Thomas b: 10/31/38, St.Louis, Mo. BR/TR, 6'4", 190 lbs. Deb: 4/11/61																												
1961	Det-A	1	1	.500	14	0	0	0	1	20	23	10.3	2	15	6.7	20	9.0	3.60	105	.287	.388	1	0	94	158	-0.1	-0	0	0.0
	LA-A	4	6	.400	38	7	0	0	5	100	93	8.4	16	50	4.5	79	7.1	4.32	104	.246	.329	-3	2	112	101	-0.3	-1	-0	0.1
	Yr	5	7	.417	52	7	0	0	6	120	116	8.7	18	65	4.9	99	7.4	4.20	104	.253	.340	-2	3	109	101	-0.4	-0	-0	0.1
1962	LA-A	1	0	1.000	12	1	0	0	0	24	24	9.0	4	11	4.1	14	5.3	3.75	108	.258	.346	1	1	102	129	0.5	0	-1	0.0
	Min-A	0	1	.000	6	1	0	0	1	10	12	10.8	2	6	5.4	3	2.7	7.20	57	.324	.391	-4	-3	104	99	-0.4	-0	1	-0.2
	Yr	1	1	.500	18	2	0	0	1	34	36	9.5	6	17	4.5	17	4.5	4.76	85	.273	.346	-3	-3	102	99	0.1	0	-0	-0.2
Total	2	6	8	.429	70	9	0	0	7	154	152	8.9	24	82	4.8	116	6.8	4.32	100	.259	.344	-5	-0	108	113	-0.3	-1	-1	-0.1
■ **PETE DONOHUE**	Donohue, Peter Joseph b: 11/5/1900, Athens, Tex. d: 8/23/88, Ft.Worth, Tex. BR/TR, 6'2", 185 lbs. Deb: 7/01/21																												
1921	Cin-N	7	6	.538	21	11	7	0	1	118	117	8.9	5	26	2.0	44	3.4	3.36	114	.263	.295	6	6	101	86	1.0	0	2	0.9
1922	Cin-N	18	9	**.667**	33	30	18	2	1	242	257	9.6	7	43	1.6	66	2.5	3.12	124	.276	.304	26	20	94	100	3.8	-2	1	1.7
1923	Cin-N	21	15	.583	42	36	19	2	3	274	304	10.0	3	68	2.2	84	2.8	3.38	114	.278	.318	19	14	96	97	-0.2	3	1	1.6
1924	Cin-N	16	9	.640	35	32	16	3	0	222	248	10.1	9	36	1.5	72	2.9	3.61	106	.285	.314	6	6	99	99	3.1	-0	-1	0.4
1925	Cin-N	21	14	.600	42	38	**27**	3	2	**301**	310	9.3	3	49	1.5	78	2.3	3.08	134	.268	.293	40	35	97	91	3.5	7	-3	3.8
1926	Cin-N	**20**	14	.588	47	38	17	**5**	2	**286**	298	9.4	6	39	**1.2**	73	2.3	3.37	106	.268	.291	15	6	93	85	1.2	9	-3	1.1
1927	Cin-N	6	16	.273	33	24	12	1	1	191	253	11.9	3	32	1.5	48	2.3	4.10	96	.328	.340	-4	-4	100	112	-5.2	1	0	-0.2
1928	Cin-N	7	11	.389	23	18	8	0	0	150	180	10.8	10	32	1.9	37	2.2	4.74	81	.309	.331	-13	-15	97	95	-2.3	-0	1	-1.2
1929	Cin-N	10	13	.435	32	24	7	0	0	178	243	12.3	12	51	2.6	30	1.5	5.41	88	.331	.366	-14	-13	101	103	0.1	4	0	-0.7
1930	Cin-N	1	3	.250	8	5	2	0	1	34	53	14.0	0	13	3.4	4	1.1	6.35	73	.363	.414	-5	-7	93	101	-0.6	-1	1	-0.5
	NY-N	7	6	.538	18	11	4	0	1	87	135	14.0	6	18	1.9	26	2.7	6.10	78	.360	.387	-11	-13	96	103	-0.2	1	-2	-1.1
	Yr	8	9	.471	26	16	6	0	2	121	188	14.0	6	31	2.3	30	2.2	6.17	76	.360	.393	-16	-20	95	103	-0.8	-1	-1	-1.6
1931	NY-N	0	1	.000	4	1	0	0	0	11	14	11.5	1	4	3.3	4	3.3	5.73	63	.311	.353	-2	-3	93	92	-0.4	-0	0	-0.2
	Cle-A	0	0	—	2	0	0	0	0	5	9	16.2	1	5	9.0	4	7.2	9.00	51	.429	.538	-3	-2	106	132	0.0	-0	-0	-0.2
1932	Bos-A	0	1	.000	4	2	0	0	0	13	18	12.5	2	6	4.2	1	0.7	7.62	60	.340	.400	-5	-4	102	94	-0.4	-0	0	-0.3
Total	12	134	118	.532	344	270	137	16	12	2112	2439	10.4	68	422	1.8	571	2.4	3.87	103	.293	.321	56	26	97	96	3.4	21	-2	5.1

YEAR	TM/L	W	L	PCT	G	GS	CG	SHO	SV	IP	H	H/G	HR	BB	BB/G	SO	SO/G	ERA	/A	OAVG	OOBP	PR	/A	PF	CPI	WAT	PB	PD	TPI
LINO DONOSO	Donoso, Lino (Galeta) b: 9/23/22, Havana, Cuba BL/TL, 5'11", 160 lbs. Deb: 6/18/55																												
1955	Pit-N	4	6	.400	25	9	3	0	1	95	106	10.0	16	35	3.3	38	3.6	5.31	77	.287	.340	-13	-13	101	97	0.1	-1	0	-1.2
1956	Pit-N	0	0	—	3	0	0	0	0	2	2	9.0	0	1	4.5	1	4.5	0.00	—	.250	.333	1	1	103	0	0.0	0	0	0.1
Total	2	4	6	.400	28	9	3	0	1	97	108	10.0	16	36	3.3	39	3.6	5.20	78	.286	.340	-13	-12	101	95	0.1	-1	0	-1.1
DICK DONOVAN	Donovan, Richard Edward b: 12/7/27, Boston, Mass. BL/TR, 6'3", 190 lbs. Deb: 4/24/50																												
1950	Bos-N	0	2	.000	10	3	0	0	0	30	28	8.4	4	34	10.2	9	2.7	8.10	44	.255	.435	-13	-15	85	80	-0.9	1	0	-1.2
1951	Bos-N	0	0	—	8	2	0	0	0	14	17	10.9	0	11	7.1	4	2.6	5.14	75	.298	.406	-2	-2	97	104	0.0	1	0	0.0
1952	Bos-N	0	2	.000	7	2	0	0	1	13	18	12.5	1	12	8.3	6	4.2	5.54	65	.346	.457	-3	-3	97	148	-0.9	-0	1	-0.2
1954	Det-A	0	0	—	2	0	0	0	0	6	9	13.5	1	5	7.5	2	3.0	10.50	36	.360	.438	-5	-4	101	81	0.0	-0	0	-0.3
1955	Chi-A	15	9	.625	29	24	11	5	0	187	186	9.0	17	48	2.3	88	4.2	3.32	117	.261	.306	13	11	98	107	1.2	5	1	1.7
1956	Chi-A	12	10	.545	34	31	14	3	0	235	212	8.1	22	59	2.3	120	4.6	3.64	116	.240	.287	14	15	102	83	-0.1	7	2	2.5
1957	Chi-A	16	6	**.727**	28	28	**16**	2	0	221	203	8.3	17	45	1.8	88	3.6	2.77	132	.247	.287	25	22	97	109	4.2	2	0	2.6
1958	Chi-A	15	14	.517	34	34	16	4	0	248	240	8.7	23	53	**1.9**	127	4.6	3.01	122	.251	.291	21	18	98	106	-0.4	-1	-1	1.7
1959	Chi-A	9	10	.474	31	29	5	1	0	180	171	8.6	15	58	2.9	71	3.6	3.65	101	.247	.305	4	1	95	93	-2.3	1	-2	0.0
1960	Chi-A	6	1	.857	33	8	0	0	3	79	87	9.9	13	25	2.8	30	3.4	5.35	72	.283	.329	-13	-13	99	90	2.4	-0	1	-1.1
1961	Was-A	10	10	.500	23	22	11	2	0	169	138	7.3	10	35	1.9	62	3.3	**2.40**	**163**	.224	**.262**	31	**29**	97	97	2.2	2	-1	**3.2**
1962	Cle-A	20	10	.667	34	34	16	**5**	0	251	255	9.1	23	47	**1.7**	94	3.4	3.59	109	.263	.295	11	9	99	96	**5.8**	6	-1	1.4
1963	Cle-A	11	13	.458	30	30	7	3	0	206	211	9.2	27	28	**1.2**	84	3.7	4.24	84	.265	.290	-14	-16	98	88	-0.7	-1	-1	-1.7
1964	Cle-A	7	9	.438	30	23	5	0	1	158	181	10.3	19	29	1.7	83	4.7	4.56	82	.290	.316	-16	-15	103	95	-0.8	3	1	-1.0
1965	Cle-A	1	3	.250	12	3	0	0	0	23	32	12.5	6	6	2.3	12	4.7	5.87	57	.333	.373	-6	-6	97	117	-1.0	-1	0	-0.6
Total	15	122	99	.552	345	273	101	25	5	2020	1988	8.9	198	495	2.2	880	3.9	3.66	104	.258	.301	47	31	98	97	8.7	24	1	7.0
TOM DONOVAN	Donovan, Thomas Joseph BR/TR, 6'2", 168 lbs. Deb: 9/10/01																												
1901	Cle-A	0	0	—	1	0	0	0	0	7	16	20.6	0	3	3.9	0	0.0	5.14	69	.471	.514	-1	-1	97	190	0.0	0	0	0.0
BILL DONOVAN	Donovan, Willard Earl b: 7/6/16, Maywood, Ill. BR/TL, 6'2", 198 lbs. Deb: 4/19/42																												
1942	Bos-N	3	6	.333	31	10	2	1	0	89	97	9.8	2	32	3.2	23	2.3	3.44	94	.283	.337	-1	-2	98	114	-0.7	1	2	0.1
1943	Bos-N	1	0	1.000	7	0	0	0	0	15	17	10.2	0	9	5.4	1	0.6	1.80	204	.304	.377	3	3	109	275	0.5	0	1	0.5
Total	2	4	6	.400	38	10	2	1	0	104	114	9.9	2	41	3.5	24	2.1	3.20	103	.286	.343	1	1	100	137	-0.2	1	3	0.6
BILL DONOVAN	Donovan, William Edward "Wild Bill" b: 10/13/1876, Lawrence, Mass. d: 12/9/23, Forsyth, N.Y. BR/TR, 5'11", 190 lbs. Deb: 4/22/1898 M																												
1898	Was-N	1	6	.143	17	7	6	0	0	88	88	9.0	0	69	7.1	36	3.7	4.30	88	.282	.412	-7	-5	105	101	-1.9	-1	0	-0.4
1899	Bro-N	1	2	.333	5	2	2	0	1	25	35	12.6	0	13	4.7	11	4.0	4.32	91	.356	.431	-1	-1	102	128	-0.7	-0	0	0.0
1900	Bro-N	1	2	.333	5	4	2	0	0	31	36	10.5	0	18	5.2	13	3.8	6.68	59	.314	.407	-10	-9	106	68	-0.6	-2	0	-0.9
1901	Bro-N	**25**	15	.625	**45**	38	36	2	**3**	351	324	8.3	1	152	3.9	226	5.8	2.77	124	.267	.352	22	26	103	112	2.9	-1	-1	2.4
1902	Bro-N	17	15	.531	35	33	30	4	1	298	250	7.6	1	111	3.4	170	5.1	2.78	94	.251	.331	-0	-6	94	85	-0.4	0	1	-0.4
1903	Det-A	17	16	.515	35	34	**34**	4	0	307	247	7.2	3	95	2.8	187	5.5	2.29	124	.240	.305	23	19	96	98	1.5	4	-3	1.7
1904	Det-A	17	16	.515	34	34	30	3	0	293	251	7.7	5	94	2.9	137	4.2	2.46	104	.253	.318	5	3	98	104	3.6	5	0	0.3
1905	Det-A	18	15	.545	34	32	27	5	0	281	236	7.6	2	101	3.2	105	3.4	2.59	102	.251	.323	2	2	100	100	1.2	2	-4	-0.2
1906	Det-A	9	15	.375	25	25	22	0	0	212	221	9.4	4	72	3.1	85	3.6	3.14	94	.294	.356	-11	-4	110	113	-2.8	-6	-1	-0.4
1907	Det-A	25	4	**.862**	32	28	27	3	1	271	222	7.4	3	82	2.7	123	4.1	2.19	114	.246	.309	10	9	98	100	**10.0**	8	-6	0.4
1908	Det-A	18	7	.720	29	28	25	6	0	243	210	7.8	2	53	2.0	141	5.2	2.07	114	.231	.278	8	8	99	103	4.5	0	-6	0.2
1909	Det-A	8	7	.533	21	17	13	4	2	140	121	7.8	0	60	3.9	76	4.9	2.31	114	.235	.322	3	5	106	106	-1.3	0	-2	0.3
1910	Det-A	17	7	.708	26	23	20	3	0	207	184	8.0	4	61	2.7	107	4.7	2.43	103	.243	.305	2	2	100	103	4.5	-2	-6	-0.6
1911	Det-A	10	9	.526	20	19	15	1	0	168	160	8.6	4	64	3.4	81	4.3	3.32	108	.250	.321	0	5	107	85	-0.9	3	-4	0.4
1912	Det-A	1	0	1.000	3	1	0	0	0	10	5	4.5	0	2	1.8	6	5.4	0.90	356	.147	.216	3	3	96	24	0.5	-1	-0	0.2
1915	NY-A	0	3	.000	9	1	0	0	0	34	35	9.3	1	10	2.6	17	4.5	4.76	61	.278	.336	-7	-7	99	75	-1.4	-1	-1	-0.8
1916	NY-A	0	0	—	1	0	0	0	0	1	1	9.0	0	1	9.0	0	0.0	0.00	—	.250	.400	0	0	101	0	0.0	0	0	0.0
1918	Det-A	1	0	1.000	2	1	0	0	0	6	5	7.5	0	1	1.5	1	1.5	1.50	182	.227	.261	1	1	99	95	0.5	0	-0	0.1
Total	18	186	139	.572	378	327	289	35	8	2966	2631	8.0	30	1059	3.2	1522	4.6	2.69	105	.254	.326	42	47	100	100	19.2	10	-33	2.3
JOHN DOPSON	Dopson, John Robert b: 7/14/63, Baltimore, Md. BL/TR, 6'4", 205 lbs. Deb: 9/04/85																												
1985	Mon-N	0	2	.000	4	3	0	0	0	13	25	17.3	4	4	2.8	4	2.8	11.08	30	.379	.414	-11	-11	94	83	-0.9	0	0	-0.9
1988	Mon-N	3	11	.214	26	26	1	0	0	169	150	8.0	15	58	3.1	101	5.4	3.04	119	.235	.297	8	11	105	105	-4.1	-3	-2	0.7
Total	2	3	13	.188	30	29	1	0	0	182	175	8.7	19	62	3.1	105	5.2	3.61	100	.249	.307	-3	-0	104	104	-5.0	-3	-2	-0.2
JOHN DORAN	Doran, John F. b: 1869, New Jersey TL, 5'11", 175 lbs. Deb: 4/11/1891																												
1891	Lou-a	5	10	.333	15	14	12	1	0	126	160	11.4	3	75	5.4	55	3.9	5.43	63	.325	.414	-24	-28	92	96	-1.2	-1	0	-2.3
MIKE DORGAN	Dorgan, Michael Cornelius b: 10/2/1853, Middletown, Conn. d: 4/26/09, Syracuse, N.Y. BR/TR, 5'9", 180 lbs. Deb: 5/08/1877 M																												
1879	Syr-N	0	0	—	2	0	0	0	0	12	13	9.8	0	2	1.5	8	6.0	2.25	105	.282	.312	0	0	95	121	0.0	0	0	0.0
1880	Pro-N	0	0	—	1	0	0	0	0	8	4	4.5	0	0	0.0	2	2.3	1.13	194	.155	.155	1	1	92	43	0.0	0	0	0.1
1883	NY-N	0	1	.000	1	1	1	0	0	7	8	10.3	0	6	7.7	3	3.9	3.86	82	.295	.423	-1	-1	101	135	-0.4	-0	0	0.0
1884	NY-N	8	6	.571	14	14	12	0	0	113	98	7.8	5	51	4.1	90	7.2	3.50	82	.242	.327	-7	-8	97	84	0.3	3	0	-0.6
Total	4	8	7	.533	18	15	13	0	0	140	123	7.9	5	59	3.8	103	6.6	3.28	85	.244	.324	-6	-7	96	88	-0.1	3	0	-0.5
FRITZ DORISH	Dorish, Harry b: 7/13/21, Swoyersville, Pa. BR/TR, 5'11", 204 lbs. Deb: 4/15/47 C																												
1947	Bos-A	7	8	.467	41	9	2	0	2	136	149	9.9	6	54	3.6	50	3.3	4.70	84	.283	.346	-15	-11	107	90	-1.0	-1	1	-1.1
1948	Bos-A	0	1	.000	9	0	0	0	0	14	18	11.6	1	6	3.9	5	3.2	5.79	72	.281	.338	-2	-3	97	75	-0.4	0	0	-0.1
1949	Bos-A	0	0	—	5	0	0	0	0	8	7	7.9	1	1	1.1	5	5.6	2.25	193	.241	.267	2	2	103	133	0.0	0	0	0.2
1950	StL-A	4	9	.308	29	13	4	0	0	109	162	13.4	13	36	3.0	36	3.0	6.44	79	.337	.391	-23	-17	111	100	-1.2	0	-1	-1.4
1951	Chi-A	5	6	.455	32	4	2	1	0	97	101	9.4	6	31	2.9	29	2.7	3.53	112	.272	.325	6	4	96	110	-0.7	1	0	0.5
1952	Chi-A	8	4	.667	39	1	1	0	**11**	91	66	6.5	4	42	4.2	47	4.6	2.47	147	.208	.293	**12**	**12**	99	105	1.9	-1	2	1.3
1953	Chi-A	10	6	.625	55	6	2	0	18	146	140	8.6	9	52	3.2	69	4.3	3.39	122	.254	.318	10	12	104	105	1.0	-2	2	1.3
1954	Chi-A	6	4	.600	37	6	2	1	6	109	88	7.3	9	29	2.4	48	4.0	2.72	136	.228	.278	12	12	100	99	0.0	-2	-1	1.0
1955	Chi-A	2	0	1.000	13	0	0	0	1	17	16	8.5	0	9	4.8	6	3.2	1.59	244	.258	.342	4	4	98	223	1.0	0	1	0.5
	Bal-A	3	3	.500	35	1	0	0	6	66	58	7.9	4	28	3.8	22	3.0	3.14	118	.238	.311	6	4	94	102	0.6	-1	1	0.4
	Yr	5	3	.625	48	1	0	0	7	83	74	8.0	4	37	4.0	28	3.0	2.82	133	.242	.317	11	8	94	102	1.6	0	1	0.9
1956	Bal-A	0	0	—	13	0	0	0	0	20	22	9.9	3	3	1.3	4	1.8	4.05	99	.297	.305	0	-0	97	116	0.0	0	1	0.1
	Bos-A	0	2	.000	15	0	0	0	0	23	23	9.0	1	10	3.9	11	4.3	3.52	120	.277	.333	2	2	102	118	-0.9	0	1	0.3
	Yr	0	2	.000	28	0	0	0	0	43	45	9.4	4	13	2.7	15	3.1	3.77	110	.283	.320	2	2	99	118	-0.9	0	2	0.4
Total	10	45	43	.511	323	40	13	2	44	836	850	9.2	57	301	3.2	332	3.6	3.82	106	.267	.327	15	22	102	104	0.3	-6	7	3.0
GUS DORNER	Dorner, Augustus b: 8/18/1876, Chambersburg, Pa. d: 5/4/56, Chambersburg, Pa. BR/TR, 5'10", 176 lbs. Deb: 9/17/02																												
1902	Cle-A	3	1	.750	4	4	4	1	0	36	33	8.3	1	13	3.3	5	1.3	1.25	274	.267	.337	9	9	96	240	1.0	2	0	0.9
1903	Cle-A	4	5	.444	12	8	4	2	0	74	83	10.1	4	24	2.9	28	3.4	4.50	62	.306	.363	-13	-14	95	93	-0.8	-2	0	-1.2
1906	Cin-N	0	1	.000	2	1	1	0	0	15	16	9.6	0	4	2.4	5	3.0	1.20	255	.307	.368	2	3	116	284	-0.4	-1	-0	0.3
	Bos-N	8	25	.242	34	32	29	0	0	257	264	9.2	5	103	3.6	104	3.6	3.89	72	.299	.382	-36	-32	106	96	-4.9	-4	3	-2.9
	Yr	8	26	.235	36	33	30	0	0	272	280	9.3	5	107	3.5	109	3.6	3.74	75	.299	.380	-33	-28	106	96	-5.3	-1	3	-2.6
1907	Bos-N	12	16	.429	36	31	24	2	0	271	253	8.4	4	92	3.1	85	2.8	3.12	78	.279	.356	-20	-21	99	95	1.0	-3	-3	-2.5
1908	Bos-N	8	19	.296	38	28	14	3	0	216	176	7.3	3	77	3.2	41	1.7	3.54	70	.255	.342	-29	-26	106	71	-4.2	-1	2	-2.5
1909	Bos-N	1	2	.333	5	2	0	0	1	25	17	6.1	1	17	6.1	7	2.5	2.52	105	.198	.343	0	0	102	115	0.1	-0	-0	0.0
Total	6	36	69	.343	131	106	76	8	1	894	842	8.5	18	330	3.3	275	2.8	3.43	77	.279	.360	-85	-79	102	99	-8.2	-10	1	-7.9
BERT DORR	Dorr, Charles Albert b: 2/2/1862, New York d: 6/16/14, Dickinson Town, N.Y. Deb: 8/24/1882																												
1882	StL-a	2	6	.250	8	8	8	0	0	66	53	7.2	0	1	0.1	34	4.6	2.59	108	.225	.228	1	2	104	48	-1.8	-2	0	0.0
CAL DORSETT	Dorsett, Calvin Leavelle "Preacher" b: 6/10/13, Lone Oak, Tex. d: 10/22/70, Elk City, Okla. BR/TR, 6', 180 lbs. Deb: 8/19/40																												
1940	Cle-A	0	0	—	1	0	0	0	0	1	1	9.0	1	0	0.0	0	0.0	9.00	45	.250	.250	-1	-1	92	105	0.0	0	0	0.0

YEAR	TM/L	W	L	PCT	G	GS	CG	SHO	SV	IP	H	H/G	HR	BB	BB/G	SO	SO/G	ERA	/A	OAVG	OOBP	PR	/A	PF	CPI	WAT	PB	PD	TPI
1941	Cle-A	0	1	.000	5	2	0	0	0	11	21	17.2	0	10	8.2	5	4.1	10.64	39	.382	.477	-8	-8	101	82	-0.4	-0	0	-0.6
1947	Cle-A	0	0	—	2	0	0	0	0	1	3	27.0	1	3	27.0	1	9.0	36.00	10	.500	.667	-4	-4	94	77	0.0	0	0	-0.2
Total	3	0	1	.000	8	2	0	0	0	13	25	17.3	2	13	9.0	6	4.2	12.46	33	.385	.487	-12	-12	99	84	-0.4	-0	0	-0.8
■ **JIM DORSEY**	Dorsey, James Edward b: 8/2/55, Oak Park, Ill. BR/TR, 6'7", 190 lbs. Deb: 9/02/80																												
1980	Cal-A	1	2	.333	4	4	0	0	0	16	25	14.1	2	8	4.5	8	4.5	9.00	43	.368	.436	-9	-9	97	86	-0.2	0	0	-0.7
1984	Bos-A	0	0	—	2	0	0	0	0	3	6	18.0	0	2	6.0	4	12.0	9.00	49	.462	.533	-2	-2	110	112	0.0	0	0	0.0
1985	Bos-A	0	1	.000	2	1	0	0	0	5	12	21.6	2	10	18.0	2	3.6	21.60	19	.444	.595	-10	-10	102	80	-0.4	0	-0	-0.7
Total	3	1	3	.250	8	5	0	0	0	24	43	16.1	4	20	7.5	14	5.3	11.63	35	.398	.492	-20	-20	99	88	-0.6	0	-0	-1.4
■ **JERRY DORSEY**	Dorsey, Michael Jeremiah b: 1854, Canada d: 11/3/38, Auburn, N.Y. Deb: 7/09/1884																												
1884	Bal-U	0	1	.000	1	1	0	0	0	4	7	15.8	1	0	0.0	3	6.8	9.00	37	.387	.387	-3	-3	110	89	-0.4	-1	0	-0.1
■ **JACK DOSCHER**	Doscher, John Henry Jr. b: 7/27/1880, Troy, N.Y. d: 5/27/71, Park Ridge, N.J. BL/TL, 6'1", Deb: 03																												
1903	Chi-N	0	1	.000	1	1	0	0	0	3	6	18.0	0	2	6.0	5	15.0	12.00	25	.478	.579	-3	-3	94	81	-0.4	-0	0	-0.1
	Bro-N	0	0	—	3	0	0	0	0	7	8	10.3	1	9	11.6	4	5.1	7.71	43	.325	.520	-3	-3	102	102	0.0	-0	0	-0.2
	Yr	0	1	.000	4	1	0	0	0	10	14	12.6	1	11	9.9	9	8.1	9.00	36	.367	.518	-6	-6	99	102	-0.4	-0	-0	-0.3
1904	Bro-N	0	0	—	2	0	0	0	0	6	1	1.5	0	1	1.5	2	3.0	0.00	—	.062	.117	2	2	98	0	0.0	-0	-0	0.2
1905	Bro-N	1	5	.167	12	7	6	0	0	71	60	7.6	1	30	3.8	33	4.2	3.17	96	.257	.349	-1	-1	102	91	-1.3	-2	-2	-0.2
1906	Bro-N	0	1	.000	2	1	1	0	0	14	12	7.7	0	4	2.6	10	6.4	1.29	183	.257	.316	2	2	90	175	-0.4	-1	-0	0.2
1908	Cin-N	1	3	.250	7	4	3	0	0	44	31	6.3	1	22	4.5	7	1.4	1.84	132	.228	.348	2	3	104	133	-0.9	-0	-0	0.3
Total	5	2	10	.167	27	13	10	0	0	145	118	7.3	3	68	4.2	61	3.8	2.86	98	.251	.356	-1	-1	101	108	-3.0	-3	-2	0.2
■ **RICHARD DOTSON**	Dotson, Richard Elliott b: 1/10/59, Cincinnati, Ohio BR/TR, 6'1", 190 lbs. Deb: 9/04/79																												
1979	Chi-A	2	0	1.000	5	5	1	1	0	24	28	10.5	0	6	2.3	13	4.9	3.75	116	.286	.318	1	2	103	91	1.0	0	0	0.2
1980	Chi-A	12	10	.545	33	32	8	0	0	198	185	8.4	20	87	4.0	109	5.0	4.27	93	.247	.322	-5	-7	98	89	2.4	0	1	-0.5
1981	Chi-A	9	8	.529	24	24	5	**4**	0	141	145	9.3	13	49	3.1	73	4.7	3.77	96	.270	.331	-2	-2	99	110	0.4	0	-0	-0.2
1982	Chi-A	11	15	.423	34	31	3	1	0	197	219	10.0	19	73	3.3	109	5.0	3.84	103	.282	.343	5	2	97	119	-3.1	0	-1	0.2
1983	Chi-A	22	7	**.759**	35	35	8	1	0	240	209	7.8	19	106	4.0	137	5.1	3.23	128	.240	.324	23	24	102	113	**6.2**	0	4	3.0
1984	Chi-A	14	15	.483	32	32	14	1	0	246	216	7.9	24	103	3.8	120	4.4	3.59	124	.238	.315	11	23	111	100	0.8	0	-0	2.4
1985	Chi-A	3	4	.429	9	9	0	0	0	52	53	9.2	5	17	2.9	33	5.7	4.50	92	.261	.323	-2	-2	100	89	-0.6	0	-0	-0.1
1986	Chi-A	10	17	.370	34	34	3	1	0	197	226	10.3	24	69	3.2	110	5.0	5.48	77	.289	.345	-28	-27	101	88	-2.5	0	-1	-2.6
1987	Chi-A	11	12	.478	31	31	7	2	0	211	201	8.6	24	86	3.7	114	4.9	4.18	116	.249	.319	7	16	109	93	0.1	0	2	1.7
1988	NY-A	12	9	.571	32	29	4	0	0	171	178	9.4	27	72	3.8	77	4.1	5.00	76	.266	.336	-19	-23	96	95	1.1	0	-1	-2.3
Total	10	106	97	.522	269	262	53	11	0	1677	1660	8.9	175	668	3.6	895	4.8	4.13	101	.259	.328	-9	6	102	100	5.8	0	3	1.8
■ **GARY DOTTER**	Dotter, Gary Richard b: 8/7/42, St.Louis, Mo. BL/TL, 6'1", 180 lbs. Deb: 9/10/61																												
1961	Min-A	0	0	—	2	0	0	0	0	6	6	9.0	0	4	6.0	2	3.0	9.00	48	.273	.357	-3	-3	107	49	0.0	-0	0	-0.2
1963	Min-A	0	0	—	2	0	0	0	0	2	0	0.0	0	0	0.0	2	9.0	0.00	—	.000	.000	1	1	98	0	0.0	0	0	0.1
1964	Min-A	0	0	—	3	0	0	0	0	4	3	6.8	1	3	6.8	6	13.5	2.25	161	.188	.300	1	1	100	175	0.0	0	0	0.1
Total	3	0	0	—	7	0	0	0	0	12	9	6.8	1	7	5.3	10	7.5	5.25	75	.205	.296	-2	-2	103	83	0.0	-0	0	0.0
■ **BABE DOTY**	Doty, Elmer L. b: 12/17/1867, Genoa, Ohio d: 11/20/29, Toledo, Ohio BL/TR, 6', 160 lbs. Deb: 8/18/1890																												
1890	Tol-a	1	0	1.000	1	1	1	0	0	9	9	9.0	0	1	1.0	4	4.0	1.00	395	.276	.297	3	3	102	277	0.5	-0	0	0.3
■ **TOM DOUGHERTY**	Dougherty, Thomas James "Sugar Boy" b: 5/30/1881, Chicago, Ill. d: 11/6/53, Milwaukee, Wis. BL/TR, Deb: 4/24/04																												
1904	Chi-A	1	0	1.000	1	0	0	0	0	2	0	0.0	0	0	0.0	0	0.0	0.00	—	.000	.000	1	1	97	0	0.5	-0	0	0.1
■ **WHAMMY DOUGLAS**	Douglas, Charles William b: 2/17/35, Carrboro, N.C. BR/TR, 6'2", 185 lbs. Deb: 7/29/57																												
1957	Pit-N	3	3	.500	11	8	0	0	0	47	48	9.2	5	30	5.7	28	5.4	3.26	114	.270	.380	3	2	96	157	0.5	-1	-0	0.1
■ **LARRY DOUGLAS**	Douglas, Lawrence Howard b: 6/5/1890, Jellico, Tenn. d: 11/4/49, Jellico, Tenn. 6'3", 175 lbs. Deb: 6/17/15																												
1915	Bal-F	1	0	1.000	2	0	0	0	0	3	3	9.0	0	2	6.0	1	3.0	3.00	113	.289	.404	0	0	111	138	0.5	0	0	0.0
■ **PHIL DOUGLAS**	Douglas, Phillip Brooks "Shufflin' Phil" b: 6/17/1890, Cedartown, Ga. d: 8/1/52, Sequatchie Valley, Tenn. BR/TR, 6'3", 190 lbs. Deb: 8/30/12																												
1912	Chi-A	0	1	.000	3	1	0	0	0	12	21	15.8	0	6	4.5	7	5.3	7.50	44	.382	.443	-6	-6	99	96	-0.4	-0	0	-0.4
1914	Cin-N	11	18	.379	45	25	13	0	1	239	186	7.0	7	92	3.5	121	4.6	2.56	117	.223	.297	6	11	107	94	-0.4	-3	-2	0.8
1915	Cin-N	1	5	.167	8	7	0	0	0	47	53	10.1	0	23	4.4	29	5.6	5.36	53	.299	.357	-14	-13	104	82	-1.8	-1	0	-1.3
	Bro-N	5	5	.500	20	13	5	1	0	117	104	8.0	1	17	1.3	63	4.8	2.62	107	.241	.269	2	2	102	79	-0.2	-1	0	0.2
	Chi-N	1	1	.500	4	4	2	1	0	25	17	6.1	0	7	2.5	18	6.5	2.16	131	.187	.245	2	2	103	47	0.0	-1	0	0.1
	Yr	7	11	.389	32	24	7	2	0	189	174	8.3	1	47	2.2	110	5.2	3.24	87	.247	.284	-10	-9	103	47	-2.0	-2	0	-1.0
1917	Chi-N	14	20	.412	**51**	37	20	5	1	293	269	8.3	13	50	1.5	151	4.6	2.55	111	.250	.280	5	10	105	103	-2.9	-4	4	1.1
1918	Chi-N	10	9	.526	25	19	11	2	2	157	145	8.3	2	31	1.8	51	2.9	2.12	128	.246	.276	11	10	98	105	-2.0	1	3	1.7
1919	Chi-N	10	6	.625	25	19	8	4	0	162	133	7.4	0	34	1.9	63	3.5	2.00	144	.230	.264	16	16	99	96	1.7	-2	5	2.2
	NY-N	2	4	.333	8	6	4	0	0	51	53	9.4	0	6	1.1	21	3.7	2.12	133	.264	.278	5	4	96	116	-1.3	-2	0	0.2
	Yr	12	10	.545	33	25	12	4	0	213	186	7.9	0	40	1.7	84	3.5	2.03	141	.238	.265	21	20	99	116	0.4	-2	5	2.4
1920	NY-N	14	10	.583	46	21	10	3	2	226	225	9.0	6	55	2.2	71	2.8	2.71	112	.263	.302	11	8	97	100	0.8	-4	1	0.5
1921	NY-N	15	10	.600	40	27	13	3	2	222	266	10.8	17	55	2.2	55	2.2	4.22	84	.308	.338	-11	-16	94	106	-0.2	0	1	-1.4
1922	NY-N	11	4	.733	24	21	9	1	0	158	154	**8.8**	6	35	2.0	33	1.9	**2.62**	**157**	**.257**	**.296**	26	26	100	107	2.6	0	0	2.7
Total	9	94	93	.503	299	200	95	20	8	1709	1626	8.6	52	411	2.2	683	3.6	2.80	111	.256	.295	54	57	101	99	-4.1	-16	12	6.4
■ **KIP DOWD**	Dowd, James Joseph b: 2/16/1889, Holyoke, Mass. d: 12/20/60, Holyoke, Mass. BR/TR, 5'10.5", 160 lbs. Deb: 7/05/10																												
1910	Pit-N	0	0	—	1	0	0	0	0	2	4	18.0	0	2	9.0	1	4.5	0.00	—	.400	.538	1	1	110	0	0.0	0	0	0.1
■ **DAVE DOWLING**	Dowling, David Barclay b: 8/23/42, Baton Rouge, La. BR/TL, 6'2", 181 lbs. Deb: 10/03/64																												
1964	StL-N	0	0	—	1	0	0	0	0	1	2	18.0	0	0	0.0	0	0.0	0.00	—	.400	.400	0	0	111	0	0.0	0	0	0.0
1966	Chi-N	1	0	1.000	1	1	1	0	0	9	10	10.0	0	0	0.0	3	3.0	2.00	185	.270	.270	2	2	103	112	0.5	-0	-0	0.1
Total	2	1	0	1.000	2	1	1	0	0	10	12	10.8	0	0	0.0	3	2.7	1.80	207	.286	.286	2	2	103	100	0.5	-0	-0	0.1
■ **PETE DOWLING**	Dowling, Henry Peter b: St.Louis, Mo. d: 6/30/05, Hot Lake, Ore. TL, 5'11", Deb: 7/17/1897																												
1897	Lou-N	1	2	.333	4	4	2	0	0	26	39	13.5	0	8	2.8	3	1.0	5.88	71	.370	.415	-5	-5	97	93	-0.2	-0	0	-0.3
1898	Lou-N	13	20	.394	36	32	30	0	0	286	284	8.9	7	120	3.8	84	2.6	4.19	84	.280	.356	-18	-21	98	83	-2.9	1	-0	-1.7
1899	Lou-N	13	17	.433	34	32	29	0	0	290	321	10.0	6	93	2.9	88	2.7	3.10	127	.304	.361	24	27	103	119	-2.1	-1	0	2.5
1901	Mil-A	1	4	.200	10	4	3	0	1	50	71	12.8	1	14	2.5	25	4.5	5.58	64	.356	.398	-11	-11	98	93	-1.0	1	0	-0.8
	Cle-A	11	22	.333	33	30	28	2	0	256	269	9.5	1	104	3.7	99	3.5	3.87	92	.290	.362	-6	-9	97	92	-3.4	-5	-1	-0.7
	Yr	12	26	.316	43	34	31	2	1	306	340	10.0	2	118	3.5	124	3.6	4.15	86	.302	.368	-16	-20	98	92	-4.4	1	-0	-1.5
Total	4	39	65	.375	117	102	92	2	1	908	984	9.8	15	339	3.4	299	3.0	3.88	95	.298	.364	-15	-19	99	98	-9.6	-4	-1	-1.0
■ **AL DOWNING**	Downing, Alphonso Erwin b: 6/28/41, Trenton, N.J. BR/TL, 5'11", 175 lbs. Deb: 7/19/61																												
1961	NY-A	0	1	.000	5	1	0	0	0	9	7	7.0	0	12	12.0	12	12.0	8.00	47	.212	.426	-4	-4	93	62	-0.4	-0	0	-0.3
1962	NY-A	0	0	—	1	0	0	0	0	1	0	0.0	0	0	0.0	1	9.0	0.00	—	.000	.000	0	0	92	0	0.0	0	0	0.0
1963	NY-A	13	5	.722	24	22	10	4	0	176	114	**5.8**	7	80	4.1	171	**8.7**	2.56	139	**.184**	.274	21	20	98	75	2.1	-2	-1	1.8
1964	NY-A	13	8	.619	37	35	11	1	2	244	201	7.4	18	120	4.4	**217**	8.0	3.47	105	.223	.308	4	5	101	89	0.2	1	0	0.7
1965	NY-A	12	14	.462	35	32	8	2	0	212	185	7.9	16	105	4.5	179	7.6	3.40	103	.237	.324	1	2	101	104	-0.3	-1	0	0.2
1966	NY-A	10	11	.476	30	30	1	0	0	200	178	8.0	23	79	3.6	152	6.8	3.56	90	.235	.305	-3	-8	94	100	0.8	-1	-4	-1.3
1967	NY-A	14	10	.583	31	28	10	4	0	202	158	7.0	13	61	2.7	171	7.6	2.63	118	.217	.279	14	10	96	98	3.4	1	-1	1.1
1968	NY-A	3	3	.500	15	12	1	0	0	61	54	8.0	7	20	3.0	40	5.9	3.54	85	.237	.293	-4	-4	101	95	0.0	0	-0	-0.3
1969	NY-A	7	5	.583	30	15	5	1	0	131	117	8.0	12	49	3.4	85	5.8	3.37	103	.240	.302	4	1	96	98	1.1	-0	-2	0.0
1970	Oak-A	3	3	.500	10	6	1	0	0	41	39	8.6	5	22	4.8	26	5.7	3.95	90	.252	.344	-1	-2	96	110	-0.2	-0	2	0.0
	Mil-A	2	10	.167	17	16	1	0	0	94	79	7.6	8	59	5.6	53	5.1	3.35	111	.232	.340	4	4	100	116	-3.5	-2	0	0.2
	Yr	5	13	.278	27	22	2	0	0	135	118	7.9	13	81	5.4	79	5.3	3.53	104	.237	.339	3	2	99	116	-3.7	-0	2	0.2

YEAR	TM/L	W	L	PCT	G	GS	CG	SHO	SV	IP	H	H/G	HR	BB	BB/G	SO	SO/G	ERA	/A	OAVG	OOBP	PR	/A	PF	CPI	WAT	PB	PD	TPI
1971	LA-N	20	9	.690	37	36	12	**5**	0	262	245	8.4	16	84	2.9	136	4.7	2.68	127	.247	.303	23	21	98	115	5.1	1	-1	2.3
1972	LA-N	9	9	.500	31	30	7	4	0	203	196	8.7	13	67	3.0	117	5.2	2.97	108	.254	.311	11	5	93	115	-0.8	-1	5	0.9
1973	LA-N	9	9	.500	30	28	5	2	0	193	155	7.2	19	68	3.2	124	5.8	3.31	110	.219	.284	8	7	99	84	-1.4	-1	1	0.6
1974	LA-N	5	6	.455	21	16	1	1	0	98	94	8.6	7	45	4.1	63	5.8	3.67	89	.255	.333	-0	-5	90	104	-1.5	-0	1	-0.3
1975	LA-N	2	1	.667	22	6	0	0	1	75	59	7.1	6	28	3.4	39	4.7	2.88	118	.215	.286	6	4	93	91	0.4	-1	1	0.4
1976	LA-N	1	2	.333	17	3	0	0	0	47	43	8.2	3	18	3.4	30	5.7	3.83	90	.250	.311	-2	-2	99	90	-0.5	-1	0	-0.1
1977	LA-N	0	1	.000	12	1	0	0	0	20	22	9.9	4	16	7.2	23	10.3	6.75	57	.278	.384	-6	-6	98	93	-0.4	-0	0	-0.6
Total	17	123	107	.535	405	317	73	24	3	2269	1946	7.7	177	933	3.7	1639	6.5	3.22	106	.232	.305	76	50	97	99	4.1	-7	3	5.3
■ **DAVE DOWNS**	Downs, David Ralph b: 6/21/52, Logan, Utah BR/TR, 6'5", 220 lbs. Deb: 9/02/72																												
1972	Phi-N	1	1	.500	4	4	1	1	0	23	25	9.8	1	3	1.2	5	2.0	2.74	125	.294	.326	2	2	99	139	0.2	0	0	0.2
■ **KELLY DOWNS**	Downs, Kelly Robert b: 10/25/60, Ogden, Utah BR/TR, 6'4", 195 lbs. Deb: 7/29/86																												
1986	SF-N	4	4	.500	14	14	1	0	0	88	78	8.0	5	30	3.1	64	6.5	2.76	128	.236	.298	9	7	95	107	0.0	0	0	0.7
1987	SF-N	12	9	.571	41	28	4	3	1	186	185	9.0	14	67	3.2	137	6.6	3.63	107	.258	.321	9	5	95	102	0.4	-0	-4	0.0
1988	SF-N	13	9	.591	27	26	6	3	0	168	140	7.5	11	47	2.5	118	6.3	3.32	97	.225	.277	2	-2	93	80	2.0	2	0	0.0
Total	3	29	22	.569	82	68	11	6	1	442	403	8.2	30	144	2.9	319	6.5	3.34	106	.241	.300	21	11	94	94	2.4	2	-4	0.7
■ **TOM DOWSE**	Dowse, Thomas Joseph b: 8/12/1866, Ireland d: 12/14/46, Riverside, Cal. BR/TR, 5'11", 175 lbs. Deb: 4/21/1890																												
1890	Cle-N	0	0	—	1	0	0	0	0	5	6	10.8	0	1	1.8	0	0.0	5.40	64	.314	.348	-1	-1	97	68	0.0	-0	0	0.0
■ **JESS DOYLE**	Doyle, Jesse Herbert b: 4/14/1898, Knoxville, Tenn. d: 4/15/61, Belleville, Ill. BR/TR, 5'11", 175 lbs. Deb: 4/14/25																												
1925	Det-A	4	7	.364	45	3	0	0	8	118	158	12.1	6	50	3.8	31	2.4	5.95	72	.340	.392	-20	-22	98	100	-1.7	3	-1	-1.7
1926	Det-A	0	0	—	2	0	0	0	1	4	6	13.5	0	1	2.3	2	4.5	4.50	87	.316	.350	-0	-0	98	92	0.0	0	0	0.0
1927	Det-A	0	0	—	7	0	0	0	0	12	16	12.0	0	5	3.8	5	3.8	8.25	54	.314	.368	-5	-5	107	56	0.0	0	0	-0.3
1931	StL-A	0	0	—	1	0	0	0	0	1	3	27.0	0	1	9.0	0	0.0	27.00	17	.500	.571	-3	-2	105	55	0.0	0	0	-0.1
Total	4	4	7	.364	55	3	0	0	9	135	183	12.2	6	57	3.8	38	2.5	6.27	69	.338	.390	-29	-29	99	96	-1.7	3	-1	-2.1
■ **JOHN DOYLE**	Doyle, John Aloysius b: 1858, Nova Scotia, Canada d: 12/24/15, Providence, R.I. Deb: 7/26/1882																												
1882	StL-a	0	3	.000	3	3	3	0	0	24	41	15.4	0	3	1.1	5	1.9	2.63	106	.382	.399	0	0	104	228	-1.4	-0	0	0.0
■ **SLOW JOE DOYLE**	Doyle, Judd Bruce b: 9/15/1881, Clay Center, Kan. d: 11/21/47, Tannersville, N.Y. BR/TR, 5'8", 150 lbs. Deb: 8/25/06																												
1906	NY-A	2	1	.667	9	6	3	2	0	45	34	6.8	1	13	2.6	28	5.6	2.40	132	.232	.295	1	4	118	84	0.3	-0	0	0.5
1907	NY-A	11	11	.500	29	23	15	1	1	194	169	7.8	2	67	3.1	94	4.4	2.64	106	.257	.326	-2	3	110	96	0.7	-1	-3	0.0
1908	NY-A	1	1	.500	12	4	2	1	0	48	42	7.9	1	14	2.6	20	3.8	2.63	92	.235	.297	-1	-1	101	98	0.3	1	-2	-0.2
1909	NY-A	8	6	.571	17	15	8	3	0	126	103	7.4	3	37	2.6	57	4.1	2.57	96	.232	.294	-1	-2	99	84	1.2	1	-4	-0.5
1910	NY-A	0	2	.000	3	2	1	0	0	12	19	14.3	0	5	3.8	6	4.5	8.25	32	.365	.431	-8	-7	106	76	-0.9	0	1	-0.6
	Cin-N	0	0	—	5	0	0	0	0	11	16	13.1	0	11	9.0	4	3.3	6.55	47	.327	.450	-4	-4	102	100	0.0	-0	-1	-0.4
Total	5	22	21	.512	75	50	29	7	1	436	383	7.9	7	147	3.0	209	4.3	2.85	95	.251	.319	-15	-7	106	91	1.6	-1	-8	-1.2
■ **PAUL DOYLE**	Doyle, Paul Sinnott b: 10/2/39, Philadelphia, Pa. BL/TL, 5'11", 172 lbs. Deb: 5/28/69																												
1969	Atl-N	2	0	1.000	36	0	0	0	4	39	31	7.2	4	16	3.7	25	5.8	2.08	178	.231	.305	7	7	103	167	1.0	-0	1	0.8
1970	Cal-A	3	1	.750	40	0	0	0	5	42	43	9.2	7	21	4.5	34	7.3	5.14	66	.267	.353	-7	-8	92	97	0.9	-0	1	-0.7
	SD-N	0	2	.000	9	0	0	0	2	7	9	11.6	0	6	7.7	2	2.6	6.43	61	.360	.469	-2	-2	97	114	-0.9	-0	1	0.0
1972	Cal-A	0	0	—	2	0	0	0	0	2	2	9.0	0	3	13.5	4	18.0	0.00	—	.250	.417	1	1	90	0	0.0	0	0	0.1
Total	3	5	3	.625	87	0	0	0	11	90	85	8.5	11	46	4.6	65	6.5	3.80	94	.259	.346	-1	-2	97	126	1.0	-1	3	0.2
■ **CARL DOYLE**	Doyle, William Carl b: 7/30/12, Knoxville, Tenn. d: 9/4/51, Knoxville, Tenn. BR/TR, 6'1", 185 lbs. Deb: 8/05/35																												
1935	Phi-A	2	7	.222	14	9	3	0	0	80	86	9.7	3	72	8.1	34	3.8	5.96	77	.282	.415	-13	-12	102	97	-1.9	-2	1	-1.1
1936	Phi-A	0	3	.000	8	6	1	0	0	39	66	15.2	4	29	6.7	12	2.8	10.85	49	.369	.467	-25	-24	105	83	-1.4	1	-1	-1.8
1939	Bro-N	1	2	.333	5	1	1	1	1	18	8	4.0	1	7	3.5	7	3.5	1.00	416	.136	.224	6	6	106	88	-0.5	0	0	0.7
1940	Bro-N	0	0	—	3	0	0	0	1	6	18	27.0	3	6	9.0	4	6.0	25.50	16	.545	.636	-14	-14	106	84	0.0	1	0	-1.0
	StL-N	3	3	.500	21	5	1	0	0	81	99	11.0	7	41	4.6	44	4.9	5.89	66	.294	.376	-18	-18	101	93	-0.2	2	0	-1.5
	Yr	3	3	.500	24	5	1	0	1	87	117	12.1	10	47	4.9	48	5.0	7.24	54	.313	.394	-33	-32	102	93	-0.2	1	0	-2.5
Total	4	6	15	.286	51	21	6	1	2	224	277	11.1	18	155	6.2	101	4.1	6.91	64	.303	.409	-66	-62	103	92	-4.0	1	0	-4.7
■ **TOM DOZIER**	Dozier, Thomas Dean b: 9/5/61, San Pablo, Cal. BR/TR, 6'2", 190 lbs. Deb: 5/17/86																												
1986	Oak-A	0	0	—	4	0	0	0	0	6	6	9.0	1	5	7.5	4	6.0	6.00	65	.261	.367	-1	-1	94	96	0.0	0	0	0.0
■ **BUZZ DOZIER**	Dozier, William Joseph b: 8/31/27, Waco, Tex. BR/TR, 6'3", 185 lbs. Deb: 9/12/47																												
1947	Was-A	0	0	—	2	0	0	0	0	5	2	3.6	0	1	1.8	2	3.6	0.00	—	.133	.188	2	2	101	0	0.0	-0	0	0.2
1949	Was-A	0	0	—	2	0	0	0	0	6	12	18.0	0	6	9.0	1	1.5	12.00	34	.429	.529	-5	-5	96	85	0.0	-0	-0	-0.4
Total	2	0	0	—	4	0	0	0	0	11	14	11.5	0	7	5.7	3	2.5	6.55	60	.326	.420	-3	-3	98	46	0.0	-0	-0	-0.2
■ **DOUG DRABEK**	Drabek, Douglas Dean b: 7/25/62, Victoria, Tex. BR/TR, 6'1", 185 lbs. Deb: 5/30/86																												
1986	NY-A	7	8	.467	27	21	0	0	0	132	126	8.6	13	50	3.4	76	5.2	4.09	105	.251	.319	1	3	103	93	-1.2	0	-1	0.1
1987	Pit-N	11	12	.478	29	28	1	1	0	176	165	8.4	22	46	2.4	120	6.1	3.89	110	.247	.293	4	7	105	90	-0.3	-1	1	0.7
1988	Pit-N	15	7	.682	33	32	3	1	0	219	194	8.0	21	50	2.1	127	5.2	3.08	109	.239	.284	9	7	97	101	3.9	3	-1	0.9
Total	3	33	27	.550	89	81	4	2	0	527	485	8.3	56	146	2.5	323	5.5	3.60	108	.245	.296	14	17	101	95	2.4	2	-2	1.7
■ **MOE DRABOWSKY**	Drabowsky, Myron Walter b: 7/21/35, Ozanna, Poland BR/TR, 6'3", 190 lbs. Deb: 8/07/56 C																												
1956	Chi-N	2	4	.333	9	7	3	0	0	51	37	6.5	1	39	6.9	36	6.4	2.47	154	.207	.347	7	7	101	127	-0.3	0	-0	0.8
1957	Chi-N	13	15	.464	36	33	12	2	0	240	214	8.0	22	94	3.5	170	6.4	3.53	108	.242	.315	9	7	98	100	1.7	2	0	1.0
1958	Chi-N	9	11	.450	22	20	4	1	0	126	118	8.4	19	73	5.2	77	5.5	4.50	89	.245	.344	-8	-7	101	99	-0.3	-1	-0	-0.8
1959	Chi-N	5	10	.333	31	23	3	1	0	142	138	8.7	21	75	4.8	70	4.4	4.12	95	.251	.342	-3	-4	99	109	-2.4	-1	-0	-0.4
1960	Chi-N	3	1	.750	32	7	0	0	1	50	71	12.8	3	23	4.1	26	4.7	6.48	58	.338	.391	-15	-15	101	95	1.2	-1	-1	-1.5
1961	Mil-N	0	2	.000	16	0	0	0	2	25	26	9.4	4	18	6.5	5	1.8	4.68	78	.277	.381	-2	-3	91	126	-0.9	0	0	-0.1
1962	Cin-N	2	6	.250	23	10	1	0	1	83	84	9.1	13	31	3.4	56	6.1	4.99	79	.267	.332	-10	-10	100	95	-2.3	-2	-1	-1.1
	KC-A	1	1	.500	10	3	0	0	0	28	29	9.3	8	10	3.2	19	6.1	5.14	78	.266	.320	-4	-3	101	108	0.1	-0	0	-0.3
1963	KC-A	7	13	.350	26	22	9	2	0	174	135	7.0	16	64	3.3	109	5.6	3.05	129	.214	.293	11	17	109	95	-2.4	0	-2	1.9
1964	KC-A	5	13	.278	53	21	1	0	1	168	176	9.4	24	72	3.9	119	6.4	5.30	74	.273	.346	-31	-26	108	91	-2.0	-5	1	-2.9
1965	KC-A	1	5	.167	14	5	0	0	0	39	44	10.2	5	18	4.2	25	5.8	4.38	78	.291	.363	-4	-4	100	124	-1.6	-1	-0	-0.4
1966	Bal-A	6	0	1.000	44	3	0	0	7	96	62	5.8	10	29	2.7	98	9.2	2.81	120	.181	.244	7	6	99	69	3.0	3	-1	1.0
1967	Bal-A	7	5	.583	43	0	0	0	12	95	66	6.3	7	25	2.4	96	9.1	1.61	188	.194	.250	17	15	94	120	1.3	2	1	2.0
1968	Bal-A	4	4	.500	45	0	0	0	7	61	35	5.2	3	25	3.7	46	6.8	1.92	156	.166	.264	7	7	101	86	-0.4	0	-0	0.9
1969	KC-A	11	9	.550	52	0	0	0	11	98	68	6.2	10	30	2.8	76	7.0	2.94	128	.190	.251	8	9	104	68	2.4	1	1	1.2
1970	KC-A	1	2	.333	24	0	0	0	2	36	28	7.0	3	12	3.0	38	9.5	3.25	114	.217	.282	2	2	100	85	-0.2	0	0	0.2
	Bal-A	4	2	.667	21	0	0	0	1	33	30	8.2	7	15	4.1	21	5.7	3.82	92	.233	.315	-0	-1	94	111	0.0	-1	-0	-0.1
	Yr	5	4	.556	45	0	0	0	3	69	58	7.6	10	27	3.5	59	7.7	3.52	102	.221	.292	2	1	97	111	-0.2	0	-0	0.1
1971	StL-N	6	1	.857	51	0	0	0	8	60	45	6.8	2	33	5.0	49	7.4	3.45	101	.207	.313	0	0	100	77	2.4	-0	-1	0.0
1972	StL-N	1	1	.500	30	0	0	0	2	28	29	9.3	4	14	4.5	22	7.1	2.57	142	.259	.344	3	3	105	177	0.0	-0	-1	0.3
	Chi-A	0	0	—	7	0	0	0	0	7	6	7.7	0	2	2.6	4	5.1	2.57	126	.240	.296	0	1	106	92	0.0	-0	-0	0.0
Total	17	88	105	.456	589	154	33	6	55	1640	1441	7.9	182	702	3.9	1162	6.4	3.71	100	.236	.315	-5	3	101	98	-0.7	-0	-4	1.7
■ **DICK DRAGO**	Drago, Richard Anthony b: 6/25/45, Toledo, Ohio BR/TR, 6'1", 190 lbs. Deb: 4/11/69																												
1969	KC-A	11	13	.458	41	26	10	2	1	201	190	8.5	19	65	2.9	108	4.8	3.76	100	.248	.303	-3	0	104	90	0.8	-3	2	0.0
1970	KC-A	9	15	.375	35	34	7	1	0	240	239	9.0	20	72	2.7	127	4.8	3.75	99	.266	.317	-1	-1	100	101	-0.8	-6	-1	-0.7
1971	KC-A	17	11	.607	35	34	15	4	0	241	251	9.4	14	46	1.7	109	4.1	2.99	114	.276	.313	13	11	98	**119**	2.7	1	0	1.3
1972	KC-A	12	17	.414	34	33	11	2	0	239	230	8.7	22	51	1.9	135	5.1	3.01	102	.254	.295	2	1	100	107	-2.7	-2	-2	-0.3
1973	KC-A	12	14	.462	37	33	10	1	0	213	252	10.6	16	76	3.2	98	4.1	4.23	99	.300	.358	-10	-1	109	112	-2.2	0	1	0.0
1974	Bos-A	7	10	.412	33	18	8	0	3	176	165	8.4	17	56	2.9	90	4.6	3.48	111	.251	.310	3	7	106	101	-1.8	0	-2	0.6

YEAR	TM/L	W	L	PCT	G	GS	CG	SHO	SV	IP	H	H/G	HR	BB	BB/G	SO	SO/G	ERA	/A	OAVG	OOBP	PR	/A	PF	CPI	WAT	PB	PD	TPI
1975	Bos-A	2	2	.500	40	2	0	0	15	73	69	8.5	5	31	3.8	43	5.3	3.82	107	.247	.319	-0	2	108	89	-0.2	0	0	0.2
1976	Cal-A	7	8	.467	43	0	0	0	6	79	80	9.1	7	31	3.5	43	4.9	4.44	74	.264	.335	-8	-10	93	93	0.0	0	-2	-1.2
1977	Cal-A	0	1	.000	13	0	0	0	2	21	22	9.4	3	3	1.3	15	6.4	3.00	129	.272	.287	3	2	95	129	-0.4	0	-0	0.2
	Bal-A	6	3	.667	36	0	0	0	3	40	49	11.0	2	15	3.4	20	4.5	3.60	105	.308	.357	2	1	92	136	0.8	0	-0	0.0
	Yr	6	4	.600	49	0	0	0	5	61	71	10.5	5	18	2.7	35	5.2	3.39	112	.293	.335	5	3	93	136	0.4	0	-0	0.2
1978	Bos-A	4	4	.500	37	1	0	0	7	77	71	8.3	5	32	3.7	42	4.9	3.04	132	.246	.321	6	8	106	114	-0.6	0	-1	0.8
1979	Bos-A	10	6	.625	53	1	0	0	13	89	85	8.6	6	21	2.1	67	6.8	3.03	148	.254	.297	12	14	106	107	1.1	0	0	1.4
1980	Bos-A	7	7	.500	43	7	1	0	3	133	127	8.6	17	44	3.0	63	4.3	4.13	100	.251	.312	-1	-0	102	92	-0.2	0	-1	0.0
1981	Sea-A	4	6	.400	39	0	0	0	5	54	71	11.8	4	15	2.5	27	4.5	5.50	67	.324	.358	-11	-11	101	94	0.0	0	0	-1.0
Total	13	108	117	.480	519	189	62	10	58	1876	1901	9.1	157	558	2.7	987	4.7	3.62	103	.266	.318	6	23	102	104	-3.5	-10	-4	1.3
■ **LOGAN DRAKE**	Drake, Logan Gaffney "L.G." b: 12/26/1900, Spartanburg, S.C. d: 6/1/40, Columbia, S.C. BR/TR, 5'10.5", 165 lbs. Deb: 9/21/22																												
1922	Cle-A	0	0	—	1	0	0	0	0	3	4	12.0	0	2	6.0	1	3.0	3.00	138	.364	.429	0	0	103	224	0.0	-0	-0	0.0
1923	Cle-A	0	0	—	4	0	0	0	0	4	2	4.5	0	4	9.0	2	4.5	4.50	87	.133	.333	-0	-0	99	42	0.0	-0	-0	0.0
1924	Cle-A	0	1	.000	5	1	0	0	0	11	18	14.7	0	10	8.2	8	6.5	10.64	39	.400	.492	-8	-8	97	84	-0.4	-0	-0	-0.6
Total	3	0	1	.000	10	1	0	0	0	18	24	12.0	0	16	8.0	11	5.5	8.00	51	.338	.447	-8	-8	99	98	-0.4	-0	-0	-0.6
■ **TOM DRAKE**	Drake, Thomas Kendall b: 8/7/14, Birmingham, Ala. d: 7/2/88, Birmingham, Ala. BR/TR, 6'1", 185 lbs. Deb: 4/24/39																												
1939	Cle-A	0	1	.000	8	1	0	0	0	15	23	13.8	2	19	11.4	1	0.6	9.00	49	.377	.512	-7	-8	96	119	-0.4	-0	0	-0.6
1941	Bro-N	1	1	.500	10	2	0	0	0	25	26	9.4	2	9	3.2	12	4.3	4.32	83	.280	.337	-2	-2	99	101	-0.1	0	-0	-0.1
Total	2	1	2	.333	18	3	0	0	0	40	49	11.0	4	28	6.3	13	2.9	6.07	65	.318	.416	-9	-10	98	108	-0.5	0	0	-0.7
■ **DAVE DRAVECKY**	Dravecky, David Francis b: 2/14/56, Youngstown, Ohio BR/TL, 6'1", 195 lbs. Deb: 6/15/82																												
1982	SD-N	5	3	.625	31	10	0	0	2	105	86	7.4	8	33	2.8	59	5.1	2.57	128	.225	.282	12	9	92	105	1.0	-0	2	1.0
1983	SD-N	14	10	.583	28	28	9	1	0	184	181	8.9	18	44	2.2	74	3.6	3.57	101	.262	.302	1	1	99	100	2.3	-2	1	0.0
1984	SD-N	9	8	.529	50	14	3	2	8	157	125	7.2	12	51	2.9	71	4.1	2.92	120	.222	.285	12	10	98	95	-0.5	-0	-2	0.8
1985	SD-N	13	11	.542	34	31	7	2	0	215	200	8.4	18	57	2.4	105	4.4	2.93	125	.249	.295	16	17	101	111	0.8	-1	-1	1.7
1986	SD-N	9	11	.450	26	26	3	1	0	161	149	8.3	17	54	3.0	87	4.9	3.07	116	.246	.301	12	9	96	**115**	-0.1	0	0	1.0
1987	SD-N	3	7	.300	30	10	1	0	0	79	71	8.1	10	31	3.5	60	6.8	3.76	106	.240	.313	3	2	98	101	-1.2	0	0	0.2
	SF-N	7	5	.583	18	18	4	3	0	112	115	9.2	8	33	2.7	78	6.3	3.21	120	.272	.322	11	8	95	122	0.4	0	1	1.0
	Yr	10	12	.455	48	28	5	3	0	191	186	8.8	18	64	3.0	138	6.5	3.44	114	.257	.315	14	10	96	122	-0.8	0	1	1.2
1988	SF-N	2	2	.500	7	7	1	0	0	37	33	8.0	4	8	1.9	19	4.6	3.16	102	.243	.272	1	0	93	102	0.0	-0	0	0.0
Total	7	62	57	.521	224	144	28	9	10	1050	960	8.2	95	311	2.7	553	4.7	3.13	115	.246	.298	68	56	97	107	2.7	-2	1	5.7
■ **CLEM DREISEWERD**	Dreisewerd, Clement John "Steamboat" b: 1/24/16, Old Monroe, Mo. BL/TL, 6'1.5", 195 lbs. Deb: 8/29/44																												
1944	Bos-A	2	4	.333	7	7	3	0	0	49	52	9.6	2	9	1.7	9	1.7	4.04	82	.268	.295	-3	-4	97	76	-0.9	0	-1	-0.4
1945	Bos-A	0	1	.000	2	2	0	0	0	10	13	11.7	0	2	1.8	3	2.7	4.50	72	.325	.372	-1	-1	96	104	-0.4	-0	-0	-0.1
1946	Bos-A	4	1	.800	20	1	0	0	0	47	50	9.6	3	15	2.9	19	3.6	4.21	92	.276	.322	-4	-2	111	91	1.0	-1	1	-0.1
1948	StL-A	0	2	.000	13	0	0	0	1	22	28	11.5	6	8	3.3	6	2.5	5.73	81	.318	.371	-4	-3	109	122	-0.9	-1	0	-0.2
	NY-N	0	0	—	4	0	0	0	1	13	17	11.8	3	5	3.5	2	1.4	5.54	70	.321	.379	-2	-2	98	121	0.0	1	-0	-0.1
Total	4	6	8	.429	46	10	3	0	2	141	160	10.2	14	39	2.5	39	2.5	4.53	83	.288	.329	-14	-12	103	95	-1.2	-1	-0	-0.9
■ **BOB DRESSER**	Dresser, Robert Nicholson b: 10/4/1878, Newton, Mass. d: 7/27/24, Duxbury, Mass. TL , Deb: 8/13/02																												
1902	Bos-N	0	1	.000	1	1	1	0	0	9	12	12.0	0	0	0.0	8	8.0	3.00	87	.345	.345	-0	-0	94	120	-0.4	0	-0	0.0
■ **ROB DRESSLER**	Dressler, Robert Anthony b: 2/2/54, Portland, Ore. BR/TR, 6'3", 180 lbs. Deb: 9/07/75																												
1975	SF-N	1	0	1.000	3	2	1	0	0	16	17	9.6	0	4	2.3	6	3.4	1.13	328	.274	.313	4	5	102	273	0.5	-0	0	0.6
1976	SF-N	3	10	.231	25	19	0	0	0	108	125	10.4	8	35	2.9	33	2.8	4.42	83	.291	.338	-11	-9	104	100	-3.3	-1	1	-0.9
1978	StL-N	0	1	.000	3	2	0	0	0	13	12	8.3	0	4	2.8	4	2.8	2.08	165	.267	.327	2	2	96	156	-0.4	-0	0	0.2
1979	Sea-A	3	2	.600	21	11	2	0	0	104	134	11.6	11	22	1.9	36	3.1	4.93	87	.312	.341	-8	-8	101	99	0.8	0	-0	-0.7
1980	Sea-A	4	10	.286	30	14	3	0	0	149	161	9.7	14	33	2.0	50	3.0	3.99	106	.280	.316	1	4	105	99	-1.5	0	1	0.5
Total	5	11	23	.324	82	48	6	0	0	390	449	10.4	33	98	2.3	129	3.0	4.18	97	.291	.329	-11	-6	103	108	-3.9	-1	2	-0.3
■ **DAVE DREW**	Drew, David Deb: 5/14/1884																												
1884	Phi-U	0	1	.000	1	0	0	0	0	7	7	9.0	0	0	0.0	2	2.6	3.86	74	.265	.265	-1	-1	95	63	-0.3	1	0	-0.1
■ **KARL DREWS**	Drews, Karl August b: 2/22/20, Staten Island, N.Y d: 8/15/63, Dania, Fla. BR/TR, 6'4.5", 192 lbs. Deb: 9/08/46																												
1946	NY-A	0	1	.000	3	1	0	0	0	6	6	9.0	0	6	9.0	4	6.0	9.00	38	.250	.419	-4	-4	98	55	-0.4	-0	0	-0.3
1947	NY-A	6	6	.500	30	10	0	0	1	92	92	9.0	6	55	5.4	45	4.4	4.89	70	.264	.365	-12	-15	92	93	-1.2	-2	0	-1.6
1948	NY-A	2	3	.400	19	2	0	0	1	38	35	8.3	3	31	7.3	11	2.6	3.79	109	.248	.375	2	1	96	129	-0.8	-1	1	0.1
	StL-A	3	2	.600	20	2	0	0	2	38	43	10.2	3	38	9.0	11	2.6	8.05	58	.289	.429	-16	-14	109	80	0.9	-0	0	-1.2
	Yr	5	5	.500	39	4	0	0	3	76	78	9.2	6	69	8.2	22	2.6	5.92	74	.269	.403	-14	-13	103	80	0.1	-1	1	-1.1
1949	StL-A	4	12	.250	31	23	3	1	0	140	180	11.6	11	66	4.2	35	2.3	6.62	66	.317	.389	-38	-35	104	87	-2.3	-5	-1	-3.6
1951	Phi-N	1	0	1.000	5	3	1	0	0	23	29	11.3	2	7	2.7	13	5.1	6.26	61	.296	.364	-6	-6	97	80	0.5	1	0	-0.4
1952	Phi-N	14	15	.483	33	30	15	5	0	229	213	8.4	13	52	2.0	96	3.8	2.71	136	.252	.293	26	25	99	116	-2.4	-2	0	2.5
1953	Phi-N	9	10	.474	47	27	6	0	3	185	218	10.6	26	50	2.4	72	3.5	4.52	93	.293	.341	-5	-7	98	111	-1.2	-2	1	-0.7
1954	Phi-N	1	0	1.000	8	0	0	0	0	16	18	10.1	2	8	4.5	6	3.4	5.63	71	.300	.366	-3	-3	98	97	0.5	-1	0	-0.2
	Cin-N	4	4	.500	22	9	1	1	0	60	79	11.9	6	19	2.9	29	4.3	6.00	71	.326	.369	-13	-12	104	93	0.2	1	0	-0.9
	Yr	5	4	.556	30	9	1	1	0	76	97	11.5	8	27	3.2	35	4.1	5.92	71	.320	.368	-16	-15	103	93	0.7	-1	0	-1.1
Total	8	44	53	.454	218	107	26	7	7	827	913	9.9	72	332	3.6	322	3.5	4.76	84	.284	.350	-68	-70	99	103	-6.2	-12	3	-6.3
■ **DENNY DRISCOLL**	Driscoll, John F. b: 11/19/1855, Lowell, Mass. d: 7/11/1886, Lowell, Mass. BL , 5'10.5", 160 lbs. Deb: 7/01/1880																												
1880	Buf-N	1	3	.250	6	4	4	0	0	42	48	10.3	1	9	1.9	17	3.6	3.86	59	.296	.333	-7	-7	96	91	-0.2	-1	0	-0.6
1882	Pit-a	13	9	.591	23	23	23	0	0	201	162	7.3	0	12	0.5	59	2.6	**1.21**	**215**	.226	.238	33	31	97	113	2.6	-2	-4	2.3
1883	Pit-a	18	21	.462	41	40	35	1	0	336	427	11.4	3	39	1.0	79	2.1	3.99	81	.315	.334	-26	-28	98	106	6.0	-5	6	-2.3
1884	Lou-a	6	6	.500	13	13	10	0	0	102	110	9.7	3	7	**0.6**	16	1.4	3.44	82	.284	.296	-2	-7	87	102	-1.3	-0	0	-0.6
Total	4	38	39	.494	83	80	72	1	0	681	747	9.9	7	67	0.9	171	2.3	3.08	95	.285	.303	-2	-12	96	106	7.1	-8	2	-1.2
■ **MICHAEL DRISCOLL**	Driscoll, Michael Columbus b: 10/19/1892, Rockland, Mass. d: 3/22/53, Foxboro, Mass. BR/TR, 6'1", 160 lbs. Deb: 7/06/16																												
1916	Phi-A	0	1	.000	1	0	0	0	0	5	6	10.8	0	2	3.6	0	0.0	5.40	55	.273	.333	-1	-1	105	60	-0.4	-0	0	0.0
■ **TOM DROHAN**	Drohan, Thomas F b: 8/26/1887, Fall River, Mass. d: 9/17/26, Kewanee, Ill. BR/TR, 5'10", 175 lbs. Deb: 5/01/13																												
1913	Was-A	0	0	—	2	0	0	0	0	2	5	22.5	1	0	0.0	2	9.0	9.00	34	.500	.500	-1	-1	105	154	0.0	0	0	0.0
■ **DICK DROTT**	Drott, Richard Fred "Hummer" b: 7/1/36, Cincinnati, Ohio d: 8/16/85, Glendale Heights, Ill. BR/TR, 6', 185 lbs. Deb: 4/16/57																												
1957	Chi-N	15	11	.577	38	32	7	3	0	229	200	7.9	22	129	5.1	170	6.7	3.58	106	.234	.334	8	6	98	106	4.3	-4	-1	0.0
1958	Chi-N	7	11	.389	39	31	4	0	0	167	156	8.4	23	99	5.3	127	6.8	5.44	73	.245	.342	-28	-27	101	81	-1.6	3	0	-2.2
1959	Chi-N	1	2	.333	8	6	1	1	0	27	25	8.3	5	26	8.7	15	5.0	6.00	65	.245	.395	-6	-6	99	97	-0.4	-0	-0	-0.6
1960	Chi-N	0	6	.000	23	9	0	0	0	55	63	10.3	7	42	6.9	32	5.2	7.20	53	.296	.401	-21	-21	101	88	-2.9	-1	-0	-2.0
1961	Chi-N	1	4	.200	35	8	0	0	0	98	75	6.9	13	51	4.7	48	4.4	4.22	97	.215	.307	-2	-1	102	83	-1.2	2	-2	-0.1
1962	Hou-N	1	0	1.000	6	1	0	0	0	13	12	8.3	1	9	6.2	10	6.9	7.62	49	.240	.350	-5	-6	95	53	0.5	-0	-0	-0.5
1963	Hou-N	2	12	.143	27	14	2	1	0	98	95	8.7	13	49	4.5	58	5.3	4.96	63	.257	.344	-18	-20	95	93	-4.6	-0	-1	-2.2
Total	7	27	46	.370	176	101	14	5	0	687	626	8.2	84	405	5.3	460	6.0	4.78	79	.243	.342	-73	-76	99	92	-5.9	-2	-4	-7.6
■ **LOUIS DRUCKE**	Drucke, Louis Frank b: 12/3/1888, Waco, Tex. d: 9/22/55, Waco, Tex. TR , 6'1", 188 lbs. Deb: 09																												
1909	NY-N	2	1	.667	3	3	2	0	0	24	20	7.5	0	13	4.9	8	3.0	2.25	119	.227	.327	1	1	103	115	0.3	-0	-0	0.1
1910	NY-N	12	10	.545	34	27	15	0	0	215	174	7.3	3	82	3.4	151	**6.3**	2.47	113	.228	.312	13	8	92	98	-0.9	4	2	1.4
1911	NY-N	4	4	.500	15	10	4	0	0	76	83	9.8	1	41	4.9	42	5.0	4.03	83	.281	.384	-5	-6	99	111	-0.8	-1	1	-0.5
1912	NY-N	0	0	—	1	0	0	0	1	2	5	22.5	0	1	4.5	0	0.0	13.50	25	.417	.462	-2	-2	99	68	0.0	0	-0	-0.1
Total	4	18	15	.545	53	40	21	0	1	317	282	8.0	4	137	3.9	201	5.7	2.90	101	.243	.333	7	1	95	102	-1.4	3	2	0.9

YEAR	TM/L	W	L	PCT	G	GS	CG	SHO	SV	IP	H	H/G	HR	BB	BB/G	SO	SO/G	ERA	/A	OAVG	OOBP	PR	/A	PF	CPI	WAT	PB	PD	TPI
■ CARL DRUHOT	Druhot, Carl A. "Collie" b: 9/1/1882, Ohio d: 2/11/18, Portland, Ore. BL/TL, 5'7", 150 lbs. Deb: 4/18/06																												
1906	Cin-N	2	2	.500	4	3	1	0	0	25	27	9.7	0	7	2.5	14	5.0	4.32	71	.311	.376	-5	-4	116	82	0.3	-0	-1	-0.4
	StL-N	6	7	.462	15	13	12	1	0	130	117	8.1	1	46	3.2	45	3.1	2.63	104	.270	.347	0	1	104	107	1.2	1	0	0.2
	Yr	8	9	.471	19	16	13	1	0	155	144	8.4	1	53	3.1	59	3.4	2.90	96	.276	.348	-5	-2	106	107	1.5	-0	-1	-0.2
1907	StL-N	0	1	.000	1	1	0	0	0	2	3	13.5	0	4	18.0	1	4.5	18.00	14	.433	.671	-3	-3	100	64	-0.4	0	0	-0.2
Total	2	8	10	.444	20	17	13	1	0	157	147	8.4	1	57	3.3	60	3.4	3.10	90	.279	.358	-8	-5	106	102	1.1	1	-1	-0.4
■ TIM DRUMMOND	Drummond, Timothy Darnell b: 12/24/64, La Plata, Md. BR/TR, 6'3", 170 lbs. Deb: 9/12/87																												
1987	Pit-N	0	0	—	6	0	0	0	0	6	5	7.5	0	3	4.5	5	7.5	4.50	95	.227	.308	-0	-0	105	61	0.0	-0	0	0.0
■ DON DRYSDALE	Drysdale, Donald Scott b: 7/23/36, Van Nuys, Cal. BR/TR, 6'5", 190 lbs. Deb: 4/17/56 H																												
1956	Bro-N	5	5	.500	25	12	2	0	0	99	95	8.6	9	31	2.8	55	5.0	2.64	144	.255	.312	12	13	100	133	-0.8	1	1	1.6
1957	Bro-N	17	9	.654	34	29	9	4	0	221	197	8.0	17	61	2.5	148	6.0	2.69	165	.236	.291	29	**43**	114	107	3.6	-1	5	**5.4**
1958	LA-N	12	13	.480	44	29	6	1	0	212	214	9.1	21	72	3.1	131	5.6	4.16	101	.263	.329	-5	1	106	95	0.5	8	3	1.3
1959	LA-N	17	13	.567	44	36	15	**4**	2	271	237	7.9	26	93	3.1	**242**	**8.0**	3.45	116	.233	.305	15	16	101	94	0.1	4	2	2.3
1960	LA-N	15	14	.517	41	36	15	5	2	269	214	7.2	27	72	2.4	**246**	8.2	2.84	**151**	.215	**.273**	27	**43**	114	91	-0.4	1	4	**5.5**
1961	LA-N	13	10	.565	40	37	10	3	0	244	236	8.7	29	83	3.1	182	6.7	3.69	111	.254	.324	9	11	102	109	-0.2	5	-1	1.5
1962	LA-N	**25**	9	.735	43	41	19	2	1	**314**	272	7.8	21	78	2.2	**232**	6.6	2.84	126	.230	.280	**38**	26	91	90	6.1	5	1	3.1
1963	LA-N	19	17	.528	42	42	17	3	0	315	287	8.2	25	57	1.6	251	7.2	2.63	117	.242	.280	23	16	94	108	-2.9	4	3	2.5
1964	LA-N	18	16	.529	40	40	21	5	0	**321**	242	6.8	15	68	1.9	237	6.6	2.19	148	.207	.253	**48**	**37**	91	85	1.5	4	2	**4.8**
1965	LA-N	23	12	.657	44	42	20	7	1	308	270	7.9	30	66	1.9	210	6.1	2.78	115	.232	.276	26	14	90	103	3.1	21	1	3.7
1966	LA-N	13	16	.448	40	40	11	3	0	274	279	9.2	21	45	1.5	177	5.8	3.42	100	.265	.300	6	0	95	100	-3.9	3	-1	0.2
1967	LA-N	13	16	.448	38	38	9	3	0	282	269	8.6	19	60	1.9	196	6.3	2.74	110	.251	.293	20	8	89	112	0.0	0	3	1.1
1968	LA-N	14	12	.538	31	31	12	8	0	239	201	7.6	11	56	2.1	155	5.8	2.15	127	.231	.282	22	15	91	117	2.0	1	2	2.2
1969	LA-N	5	4	.556	12	12	1	1	0	63	71	10.1	9	13	1.9	24	3.4	4.43	79	.291	.322	-6	-6	97	106	0.3	0	0	-0.5
Total	14	209	166	.557	518	465	167	49	6	3432	3084	8.1	280	855	2.2	2486	6.5	2.95	121	.239	.290	266	232	98	102	9.0	59	26	34.7
■ MONK DUBIEL	Dubiel, Walter John b: 2/12/19, Hartford, Conn. d: 10/23/69, Hartford, Conn. BR/TR, 6', 190 lbs. Deb: 4/19/44																												
1944	NY-A	13	13	.500	30	28	19	3	0	232	217	8.4	12	86	3.3	79	3.1	3.38	107	.248	.309	1	6	105	95	-1.0	-2	0	0.5
1945	NY-A	10	9	.526	26	20	9	1	0	151	157	9.4	9	62	3.7	45	2.7	4.65	77	.266	.329	-22	-18	106	82	0.0	4	-2	-1.6
1948	Phi-N	8	10	.444	37	17	6	2	4	150	139	8.3	13	58	3.5	42	2.5	3.90	98	.248	.315	1	-1	97	94	0.3	1	-2	-0.2
1949	Chi-N	6	9	.400	32	20	3	1	4	148	142	8.6	16	54	3.3	52	3.2	4.14	95	.250	.314	-2	-3	97	91	0.1	3	1	0.1
1950	Chi-N	6	10	.375	39	12	4	2	2	143	152	9.6	12	67	4.2	51	3.2	4.15	107	.270	.346	-0	5	107	104	-0.8	0	2	0.7
1951	Chi-N	2	2	.500	22	0	0	0	1	55	46	7.5	3	22	3.6	19	3.1	2.29	172	.232	.308	10	10	100	132	0.3	-1	0	0.9
1952	Chi-N	0	0	—	1	0	0	0	0	1	1	9.0	0	0	0.0	1	9.0	0.00	—	.333	.333	0	0	103	0	0.0	0	0	0.0
Total	7	45	53	.459	187	97	41	9	11	880	854	8.7	65	349	3.6	289	3.0	3.87	100	.254	.321	-10	-1	103	96	-1.1	5	-0	0.4
■ JEAN DUBUC	Dubuc, Jean Joseph Octave Arthur "Chauncey" b: 9/15/1888, St.Johnsbury, Vt. d: 8/28/58, Fort Myers, Fla. BR/TR, 5'10.5", 185 lbs. Deb: 6/25/08 C																												
1908	Cin-N	5	6	.455	15	9	7	1	0	85	62	6.6	2	41	4.3	32	3.4	2.75	89	.233	.346	-4	-3	104	91	-0.1	-1	1	-0.3
1909	Cin-N	2	5	.286	19	5	2	0	1	71	72	9.1	0	46	5.8	19	2.4	3.68	66	.269	.384	-8	-10	94	111	-1.5	0	0	-0.9
1912	Det-A	17	10	.630	37	26	23	2	3	250	217	7.8	2	109	3.9	97	3.5	2.77	116	.235	.321	16	12	96	99	5.0	6	4	2.3
1913	Det-A	15	14	.517	36	28	22	1	2	243	228	8.4	1	91	3.4	73	2.7	2.89	102	.252	.325	1	2	101	97	2.6	5	7	2.0
1914	Det-A	13	14	.481	36	27	15	2	1	224	216	8.7	3	76	3.1	70	2.8	3.46	81	.257	.324	-18	-16	102	85	-1.2	7	3	-0.5
1915	Det-A	17	12	.586	39	33	22	5	2	258	231	8.1	6	88	3.1	74	2.6	3.21	96	.245	.316	-7	-4	105	88	-1.6	0	1	-0.1
1916	Det-A	10	10	.500	36	16	8	1	1	170	134	7.1	1	84	4.4	40	2.1	2.96	98	.233	.336	-3	-1	103	97	-1.2	5	4	0.9
1918	Bos-A	0	1	.000	2	1	1	0	0	11	11	9.0	1	5	4.1	1	0.8	4.09	63	.268	.348	-2	-2	93	97	-0.4	0	0	-0.1
1919	NY-N	6	4	.600	36	5	1	0	3	132	119	8.1	4	37	2.5	32	2.2	2.66	106	.246	.292	4	2	96	103	-0.1	-1	2	0.2
Total	9	85	76	.528	256	150	101	12	13	1444	1290	8.0	20	577	3.6	438	2.7	3.04	96	.246	.325	-21	-19	100	95	1.5	21	23	3.5
■ JIM DUCKWORTH	Duckworth, James Raymond b: 5/24/39, National City, Cal. BR/TR, 6'4", 194 lbs. Deb: 4/13/63																												
1963	Was-A	4	12	.250	37	15	2	0	0	121	131	9.7	13	67	5.0	66	4.9	6.02	61	.278	.369	-32	-32	101	86	-2.3	-3	-1	-3.4
1964	Was-A	1	6	.143	30	2	0	0	3	56	52	8.4	9	25	4.0	56	9.0	4.34	86	.244	.327	-4	-4	103	99	-2.1	0	0	-0.2
1965	Was-A	2	2	.500	17	8	0	0	0	64	45	6.3	11	36	5.1	74	10.4	3.94	90	.202	.307	-3	-3	102	96	0.2	-2	-1	-0.5
1966	Was-A	0	3	.000	5	4	0	0	0	14	14	9.0	2	10	6.4	14	9.0	5.14	64	.259	.379	-3	-3	96	106	-1.4	-0	-0	-0.3
	KC-A	0	2	.000	8	0	0	0	1	12	14	10.5	2	10	7.5	10	7.5	9.00	36	.292	.424	-7	-8	95	76	-0.9	-0	-0	-0.7
	Yr	0	5	.000	13	4	0	0	1	26	28	9.7	4	20	6.9	24	8.3	6.92	48	.269	.392	-10	-10	96	76	-2.3	-0	-1	-1.0
Total	4	7	25	.219	97	29	2	0	4	267	256	8.6	37	148	5.0	220	7.4	5.26	69	.253	.350	-50	-49	101	92	-6.5	-5	-2	-5.1
■ CLISE DUDLEY	Dudley, Elzie Clise b: 8/8/03, Graham, N.C. BL/TR, 6'1", 195 lbs. Deb: 4/18/29																												
1929	Bro-N	6	14	.300	35	21	8	1	0	157	202	11.6	9	64	3.7	33	1.9	5.68	80	.315	.370	-17	-20	96	96	-3.7	-1	2	-1.6
1930	Bro-N	2	4	.333	21	7	2	0	1	67	103	13.8	3	27	3.6	18	2.4	6.31	78	.371	.409	-10	-11	99	111	-1.1	0	1	-0.8
1931	Phi-N	8	14	.364	30	24	8	0	0	179	206	10.4	10	56	2.8	50	2.5	3.52	120	.287	.338	7	14	109	120	-1.8	0	1	1.6
1932	Phi-N	1	1	.500	13	0	0	0	1	18	23	11.5	3	8	4.0	5	2.5	7.00	62	.329	.387	-6	-5	111	95	0.0	3	0	-0.1
1933	Pit-N	0	0	—	1	0	0	0	0	⅓	6	162.0	0	1	27.0	0	0.0	135.00	—	.857	.875	-5	-5	94	67	0.0	0	0	-0.3
Total	5	17	33	.340	100	52	18	1	2	421	540	11.5	25	156	3.3	106	2.3	5.02	89	.315	.366	-31	-26	103	109	-6.6	2	4	-1.2
■ HAL DUES	Dues, Hal Joseph b: 9/22/54, La Marque, Tex. BR/TR, 6'3", 180 lbs. Deb: 9/09/77																												
1977	Mon-N	1	1	.500	6	4	0	0	0	23	26	10.2	2	9	3.5	9	3.5	4.30	90	.265	.324	-1	-1	99	87	0.1	-1	0	0.0
1978	Mon-N	5	6	.455	25	12	1	0	1	99	85	7.7	5	42	3.8	36	3.3	2.36	145	.240	.322	13	12	96	142	-0.1	0	-0	1.2
1980	Mon-N	0	1	.000	6	1	0	0	0	12	17	12.8	1	4	3.0	2	1.5	6.75	53	.333	.368	-4	-4	98	84	-0.4	-0	0	-0.3
Total	3	6	8	.429	37	17	1	0	1	134	128	8.6	8	55	3.7	47	3.2	3.09	114	.254	.327	8	6	96	127	-0.4	-1	0	0.9
■ LARRY DUFF	Duff, Cecil Elba b: 11/30/1897, Radersburg, Mont. d: 11/10/69, Bend, Ore. BL/TR, 6'1", 175 lbs. Deb: 9/05/22																												
1922	Chi-A	1	1	.500	3	1	0	0	0	13	16	11.1	1	3	2.1	7	4.8	4.85	84	.340	.358	-1	-1	101	112	0.0	0	-0	0.0
■ JIM DUFFALO	Duffalo, James Francis b: 11/25/35, Helvetia, Pa. BR/TR, 6'1", 175 lbs. Deb: 4/12/61																												
1961	SF-N	5	1	.833	24	4	1	0	1	62	59	8.6	9	32	4.6	37	5.4	4.21	92	.257	.343	-1	-2	96	111	1.9	3	-1	0.0
1962	SF-N	1	2	.333	24	2	0	0	0	42	42	9.0	3	23	4.9	29	6.2	3.64	107	.256	.340	1	1	99	110	-0.6	-0	-0	0.0
1963	SF-N	4	2	.667	34	5	0	0	2	75	56	6.7	3	37	4.4	55	6.6	2.88	108	.209	.303	3	2	94	91	0.8	-1	1	0.2
1964	SF-N	5	1	.833	35	3	1	0	3	74	57	6.9	9	31	3.8	55	6.7	2.92	120	.209	.289	5	5	99	104	1.9	-0	-1	0.4
1965	SF-N	0	1	.000	2	0	0	0	0	⅓	1	27.0	0	2	54.0	0	0.0	27.00	—	.500	.750	-1	-1	109	92	-0.4	0	0	0.0
	Cin-N	0	1	.000	22	0	0	0	0	44	33	6.8	3	30	6.1	34	7.0	3.48	104	.212	.345	0	1	102	108	-0.4	-1	1	0.0
	Yr	0	2	.000	24	0	0	0	0	44	34	7.0	3	32	6.5	34	7.0	3.68	98	.215	.353	-1	-0	102	108	-0.8	0	1	0.0
Total	5	15	8	.652	141	14	2	0	6	297	248	7.5	27	155	4.7	210	6.4	3.39	105	.227	.321	8	5	98	104	3.2	0	-0	0.6
■ JOHN DUFFIE	Duffie, John Brown b: 10/4/45, Greenwood, S.C. BR/TR, 6'7", 210 lbs. Deb: 9/18/67																												
1967	LA-N	0	2	.000	2	2	0	0	0	10	11	9.9	1	4	3.6	6	5.4	2.70	111	.282	.341	1	0	89	170	-0.9	-0	0	0.0
■ BERNIE DUFFY	Duffy, Bernard Allen b: 8/18/1893, Vinson, Okla. d: 2/9/62, Abilene, Tex. BR/TR, 5'11", 180 lbs. Deb: 9/20/13																												
1913	Pit-N	0	0	—	3	2	0	0	0	11	18	14.7	0	3	2.5	8	6.5	5.73	53	.360	.389	-3	-3	94	100	0.0	0	0	-0.2
■ DAN DUGAN	Dugan, Daniel Phillip b: 2/22/07, Plainfield, N.J. d: 6/25/68, Green Brook, N.J. BL/TL, 6'1.5", 187 lbs. Deb: 9/05/28																												
1928	Chi-A	0	0	—	1	0	0	0	0	⅓	0	0.0	0	0	0.0	0	0.0	0.00	—	.000	.000	0	0	100	0	0.0	0	0	0.0
1929	Chi-A	1	4	.200	19	2	0	0	1	65	77	10.7	8	19	2.6	15	2.1	6.65	62	.300	.336	-17	-18	98	75	-1.1	-1	-2	-1.8
Total	2	1	4	.200	20	2	0	0	1	65	77	10.7	8	19	2.6	15	2.1	6.65	62	.298	.334	-17	-18	98	75	-1.1	-1	-2	-1.8
■ ED DUGAN	Dugan, Edward J. b: 1864, Brooklyn, N.Y. Deb: 8/05/1884																												
1884	Ric-a	5	14	.263	20	20	20	0	0	166	196	10.6	5	15	0.8	60	3.3	4.50	74	.303	.318	-23	-22	102	91	-1.2	-4	0	-2.2
■ BILL DUGGLEBY	Duggleby, William James "Frosty Bill" b: 3/16/1874, Utica, N.Y. d: 8/30/44, Redfield, N.Y. TR , Deb: 4/21/1898																												
1898	Phi-N	3	3	.500	9	5	4	0	0	54	70	11.7	4	18	3.0	12	2.0	5.50	62	.337	.390	-11	-13	94	92	0.0	2	0	-0.8

YEAR	TM/L	W	L	PCT	G	GS	CG	SHO	SV	IP	H	H/G	HR	BB	BB/G	SO	SO/G	ERA	/A	OAVG	OOBP	PR	/A	PF	CPI	WAT	PB	PD	TPI
1901	Phi-N	19	12	.613	34	28	25	5	0	276	294	9.6	9	40	1.3	94	3.1	2.87	116	.297	.329	14	14	100	112	1.0	-3	5	1.9
1902	Phi-A	1	1	.500	2	2	2	0	0	17	19	10.1	0	4	2.1	4	2.1	3.18	119	.308	.350	1	1	106	108	-0.1	-1	1	0.2
	Phi-N	11	17	.393	33	28	25	0	1	259	282	9.8	2	57	2.0	60	2.1	3.37	90	.305	.353	-17	-10	109	96	-0.6	-2	2	-0.7
1903	Phi-N	13	16	.448	36	30	28	3	2	264	318	10.8	4	79	2.7	57	1.9	3.75	82	.327	.385	-14	-19	94	111	2.4	3	0	-1.7
1904	Phi-N	12	13	.480	32	27	22	2	1	224	265	10.6	3	53	2.1	55	2.2	3.78	70	.324	.373	-26	-28	97	104	3.0	1	-0	-2.8
1905	Phi-N	18	17	.514	38	36	27	1	0	289	270	8.4	10	83	2.6	75	2.3	2.46	124	.277	.342	17	19	102	127	-1.2	-2	-2	1.8
1906	Phi-N	13	19	.406	42	30	22	5	2	280	241	7.7	5	66	2.1	83	2.7	2.25	109	.262	.319	12	6	93	106	-2.3	-1	0	0.7
1907	Phi-N	0	2	.000	5	2	2	0	0	29	43	13.3	2	11	3.4	8	2.5	7.45	34	.393	.470	-16	-16	103	87	-0.9	0	1	-1.3
	Pit-N	2	2	.500	9	3	1	1	0	40	34	7.6	0	12	2.7	4	0.9	2.70	93	.260	.332	-1	-1	102	85	-0.2	-0	1	0.0
	Yr	2	4	.333	14	5	3	1	0	69	77	10.0	2	23	3.0	12	1.6	4.70	54	.314	.378	-17	-17	103	85	-1.1	0	2	-1.3
Total	8	92	102	.474	240	191	158	17	6	1732	1836	9.5	39	423	2.2	452	2.3	3.19	92	.300	.353	-42	-46	99	108	1.1	-3	8	-2.7
■ MARTIN DUKE	Duke, Martin F. "Duck" (born Martin F. Duck) b: Columbus, Ohio d: 12/31/1898, Minneapolis, Minn. TL , Deb: 8/24/1891																												
1891	Was-a	0	3	.000	4	3	2	0	0	23	36	14.1	0	19	7.4	5	2.0	7.43	50	.372	.475	-9	-9	101	96	-1.4	-1	0	-0.7
■ JAN DUKES	Dukes, Noble Jan b: 8/16/45, Cheyenne, Wyo. BL/TL, 5'11", 175 lbs. Deb: 9/06/69																												
1969	Was-A	0	2	.000	8	0	0	0	0	11	8	6.5	0	4	3.3	3	2.5	2.45	142	.216	.286	1	1	96	90	-0.9	0	-0	0.1
1970	Was-A	0	0	—	5	0	0	0	0	7	6	7.7	0	1	1.3	4	5.1	2.57	140	.240	.286	1	1	97	94	0.0	-0	0	0.1
1972	Tex-A	0	0	—	3	0	0	0	0	2	1	4.5	0	5	22.5	0	0.0	4.50	66	.167	.462	-0	-0	97	161	0.0	0	0	0.0
Total	3	0	2	.000	16	0	0	0	0	20	15	6.7	0	10	4.5	7	3.1	2.70	129	.221	.313	2	2	97	98	-0.9	0	-0	0.2
■ TOM DUKES	Dukes, Thomas Earl b: 8/31/42, Knoxville, Tenn. BR/TR, 6'2", 185 lbs. Deb: 8/15/67																												
1967	Hou-N	0	2	.000	17	0	0	0	1	24	25	9.4	2	11	4.1	23	8.6	5.25	61	.275	.355	-5	-5	95	89	-0.9	0	-0	-0.5
1968	Hou-N	2	2	.500	43	0	0	0	4	53	62	10.5	3	28	4.8	37	6.3	4.25	71	.291	.367	-7	-7	100	115	0.2	-0	0	-0.7
1969	SD-N	1	0	1.000	13	0	0	0	1	22	26	10.6	2	10	4.1	15	6.1	7.36	49	.295	.356	-9	-9	100	68	0.5	-0	0	-0.8
1970	SD-N	1	6	.143	53	0	0	0	10	69	62	8.1	7	25	3.3	56	7.3	4.04	97	.246	.309	0	-1	97	93	-2.1	-1	-0	-0.1
1971	Bal-A	1	5	.167	28	0	0	0	4	38	40	9.5	4	8	1.9	30	7.1	3.55	98	.263	.297	-0	-0	100	98	-2.1	0	-1	0.0
1972	Cal-A	0	1	.000	7	0	0	0	1	11	11	9.0	1	0	0.0	8	6.5	1.64	168	.262	.279	2	1	90	183	-0.4	0	-0	0.1
Total	6	5	16	.238	161	0	0	0	21	217	226	9.4	19	82	3.4	169	7.0	4.35	79	.270	.331	-20	-22	98	101	-4.8	-1	-1	-2.0
■ BOB DULIBA	Duliba, Robert John b: 1/9/35, Glen Lyon, Pa. BR/TR, 5'10", 180 lbs. Deb: 8/11/59																												
1959	StL-N	0	1	.000	11	0	0	0	1	23	19	7.4	2	12	4.7	14	5.5	2.74	153	.237	.330	3	4	106	139	-0.4	-0	1	0.4
1960	StL-N	4	4	.500	27	0	0	0	0	41	49	10.8	6	16	3.5	23	5.0	4.17	97	.310	.365	-2	-1	108	137	-0.3	-0	-0	0.0
1962	StL-N	2	0	1.000	28	0	0	0	2	39	33	7.6	3	17	3.9	22	5.1	2.08	203	.239	.313	8	9	107	168	1.0	-0	0	0.9
1963	LA-A	1	1	.500	6	0	0	0	1	8	3	3.4	0	6	6.8	4	4.5	1.13	298	.125	.290	2	2	92	148	0.1	-0	-0	0.2
1964	LA-A	6	4	.600	58	0	0	0	9	73	80	9.9	5	22	2.7	33	4.1	3.58	90	.287	.336	0	-3	89	117	1.0	-1	1	-0.2
1965	Bos-A	4	2	.667	39	0	0	0	1	64	60	8.4	6	22	3.1	27	3.8	3.80	99	.248	.298	-2	-0	109	91	1.4	-1	-0	0.0
1967	KC-A	0	0	—	7	0	0	0	0	10	13	11.7	3	1	0.9	6	5.4	6.30	52	.342	.350	-3	-3	102	110	0.0	0	-0	-0.3
Total	7	17	12	.586	176	0	0	0	14	258	257	9.0	25	96	3.3	129	4.5	3.45	108	.268	.326	6	8	102	124	2.8	-2	1	1.0
■ GEORGE DUMONT	Dumont, George Henry "Pea Soup" b: 11/13/1895, Minneapolis, Minn. d: 10/13/56, Minneapolis, Minn. BR/TR, 5'11", 163 lbs. Deb: 9/14/15																												
1915	Was-A	2	1	.667	6	4	3	2	0	40	23	5.2	0	12	2.7	18	4.0	2.02	145	.169	.247	4	4	99	41	0.4	-0	-1	0.3
1916	Was-A	2	3	.400	17	5	2	0	1	53	37	6.3	0	17	2.9	21	3.6	3.06	93	.194	.263	-1	-1	100	40	-0.4	-0	-1	-0.2
1917	Was-A	5	14	.263	37	23	8	2	2	205	171	7.5	3	76	3.3	65	2.9	2.55	97	.227	.303	3	-2	93	87	-4.5	-4	-3	-1.0
1918	Was-A	1	1	.500	4	1	1	0	0	14	18	11.6	0	6	3.9	12	7.7	5.14	55	.295	.353	-4	-4	103	75	0.0	1	0	-0.2
1919	Bos-A	0	4	.000	13	2	0	0	0	35	45	11.6	1	19	4.9	12	3.1	4.37	67	.326	.411	-4	-6	91	124	-1.9	-0	0	-0.5
Total	5	10	23	.303	77	35	14	4	3	347	294	7.6	4	130	3.4	128	3.3	2.85	92	.230	.305	-3	-8	95	78	-6.4	-4	-4	-1.6
■ DAN DUMOULIN	Dumoulin, Daniel Lynn b: 8/20/53, Kokomo, Ind. BR/TR, 6', 175 lbs. Deb: 9/05/77																												
1977	Cin-N	0	0	—	5	0	0	0	0	5	12	21.6	0	3	5.4	5	9.0	14.40	27	.462	.469	-6	-6	99	75	0.0	0	0	-0.4
1978	Cin-N	1	0	1.000	3	0	0	0	0	5	7	12.6	0	3	5.4	2	3.6	1.80	204	.368	.478	1	1	102	405	0.5	0	0	0.1
Total	2	1	0	1.000	8	0	0	0	0	10	19	17.1	0	6	5.4	7	6.3	8.10	47	.422	.473	-5	-5	101	240	0.5	0	0	-0.3
■ NICK DUMOVICH	Dumovich, Nicholas b: 1/2/02, Sacramento, Cal. d: 12/12/78, Laguna Hills, Cal. BL/TL, 6', 170 lbs. Deb: 4/20/23																												
1923	Chi-N	3	5	.375	28	8	1	0	1	94	118	11.3	4	45	4.3	23	2.2	4.60	90	.319	.382	-6	-5	103	117	-1.2	1	1	-0.2
■ ED DUNDON	Dundon, Edward Joseph "Dummy" b: 7/10/1859, Columbus, Ohio d: 8/18/1893, Columbus, Ohio TR , Deb: 6/02/1883																												
1883	Col-a	3	16	.158	20	19	16	0	0	167	213	11.5	7	38	2.0	31	1.7	4.47	67	.316	.352	-22	-27	91	108	-5.4	-3	0	-2.5
1884	Col-a	6	4	.600	11	9	7	0	0	81	85	9.4	9	15	1.7	37	4.1	3.78	82	.278	.312	-5	-6	96	113	-0.2	-1	0	-0.4
Total	2	9	20	.310	31	28	23	0	0	248	298	10.8	16	53	1.9	68	2.5	4.25	72	.304	.340	-27	-33	93	109	-5.6	-4	0	-2.9
■ JIM DUNEGAN	Dunegan, James William b: 8/6/47, Burlington, Iowa BR/TR, 6'1", 205 lbs. Deb: 5/28/70																												
1970	Chi-N	0	2	.000	7	0	0	0	0	13	13	9.0	2	12	8.3	3	2.1	4.85	99	.277	.397	-1	-0	119	134	-0.9	0	0	0.1
■ WILEY DUNHAM	Dunham, Henry Huston b: 1/30/1877, Piketown, Ohio d: 1/16/34, Cleveland, Ohio 6'1", 180 lbs. Deb: 5/24/02																												
1902	StL-N	2	3	.400	7	5	3	0	1	38	47	11.1	1	13	3.1	15	3.6	5.68	48	.328	.384	-12	-12	99	76	0.0	-1	-0	-1.1
■ DAVEY DUNKLE	Dunkle, Edward Perks b: 8/30/1872, Phillipsburg, Pa. d: 11/19/41, Lock Haven, Pa. BB/TR, 6'2", 220 lbs. Deb: 8/28/1897																												
1897	Phi-N	5	2	.714	7	7	7	0	0	62	72	10.5	0	23	3.3	9	1.3	3.48	119	.313	.375	6	5	96	114	1.8	-1	0	0.3
1898	Phi-N	1	4	.200	12	7	4	0	0	68	83	11.0	1	38	5.0	21	2.8	7.01	48	.324	.411	-26	-27	94	70	-1.5	-0	0	-2.2
1899	Was-N	0	2	.000	4	2	2	0	0	26	46	15.9	3	14	4.8	9	3.1	10.04	38	.412	.477	-18	-18	98	82	-0.9	0	0	-1.3
1903	Chi-A	4	4	.500	12	7	6	0	1	82	96	10.5	1	31	3.4	26	2.9	4.06	68	.315	.379	-10	-12	94	106	0.5	2	-2	-1.2
	Was-A	5	9	.357	14	13	10	0	0	108	111	9.3	4	33	2.8	51	4.3	4.25	77	.288	.344	-16	-12	111	84	0.5	-4	-2	-1.3
	Yr	9	13	.409	26	20	16	0	1	190	207	9.8	5	64	3.0	77	3.6	4.17	73	.300	.360	-26	-23	104	84	1.0	2	-4	-2.5
1904	Was-A	2	9	.182	12	11	7	0	0	74	95	11.6	1	23	2.8	23	2.8	4.99	52	.337	.387	-20	-20	99	93	-1.5	-2	-1	-2.0
Total	5	17	30	.362	61	47	36	0	1	420	503	10.8	10	162	3.5	139	3.0	5.04	65	.320	.384	-83	-83	100	92	-1.1	-4	-5	-7.7
■ FRED DUNLAP	Dunlap, Frederick C. "Sure Shot" b: 5/21/1859, Philadelphia, Pa. d: 12/1/02, Philadelphia, Pa. BR/TR, 5'8", 165 lbs. Deb: 5/01/1880 M																												
1884	StL-U	0	0	—	1	0	0	0	0	1	2	18.0	0	0	0.0	1	9.0	18.00	16	.420	.420	-2	-2	98	41	0.0	1	0	0.0
1887	Det-N	0	0	—	1	0	0	0	1	2	4	18.0	0	0	0.0	1	4.5	4.50	88	.432	.432	-0	-0	97	165	0.0	0	0	0.0
Total	2	0	0	—	2	0	0	0	1	3	6	18.0	0	0	0.0	2	6.0	9.00	40	.428	.428	-2	-2	98	123	0.0	1	0	0.0
■ JACK DUNLEAVY	Dunleavy, John Francis b: 9/14/1879, Harrison, N.J. d: 4/12/44, S.Norwalk, Conn. TL , 5'6", 167 lbs. Deb: 03																												
1903	StL-N	6	8	.429	14	13	9	0	0	102	101	8.9	2	57	5.0	51	4.5	4.06	82	.289	.400	-9	-8	102	97	1.3	2	1	-0.7
1904	StL-N	1	4	.200	7	5	5	0	0	55	63	10.3	4	23	3.8	28	4.6	4.42	61	.314	.387	-10	-11	99	105	-1.4	1	0	-0.9
Total	2	7	12	.368	21	18	14	0	0	157	164	9.4	6	80	4.6	79	4.5	4.18	74	.298	.396	-19	-19	101	100	-0.1	3	1	-1.6
■ JIM DUNN	Dunn, James William "Bill" b: 2/25/31, Valdosta, Ga. BR/TR, 6'0.5", 185 lbs. Deb: 8/26/52																												
1952	Pit-N	0	0	—	3	0	0	0	0	5	4	7.2	0	3	5.4	2	3.6	3.60	109	.190	.292	0	0	105	45	0.0	-0	0	0.0
■ JACK DUNN	Dunn, John Joseph b: 10/6/1872, Meadville, Pa. d: 10/22/28, Towson, Md. BR/TR, 5'9", Deb: 5/06/1897																												
1897	Bro-N	14	9	.609	25	21	21	0	0	217	251	10.4	6	66	2.7	26	1.1	4.60	96	.312	.364	-7	-5	102	86	3.6	-3	0	-0.6
1898	Bro-N	16	21	.432	41	37	31	0	0	323	352	9.8	11	82	2.3	66	1.8	3.59	97	.299	.345	0	-4	96	99	2.3	1	-1	-0.3
1899	Bro-N	23	13	.639	41	34	29	2	2	299	323	9.7	8	86	2.6	48	1.4	3.70	106	.299	.351	5	8	102	95	-1.4	0	3	1.1
1900	Bro-N	3	4	.429	10	7	5	0	0	63	88	12.6	1	28	4.0	6	0.9	5.57	70	.355	.421	-13	-12	106	98	-1.0	-0	0	-0.9
	Phi-N	5	5	.500	10	9	9	1	0	80	87	9.8	2	29	3.3	12	1.3	4.84	75	.300	.364	-10	-11	98	78	-0.3	1	0	-0.8
	Yr	8	9	.471	20	16	14	1	0	143	175	11.0	3	57	3.6	18	1.1	5.16	73	.325	.390	-23	-22	101	78	-1.3	-0	0	-1.7
1901	Phi-N	0	1	.000	2	2	0	0	0	5	11	19.8	0	7	12.6	1	1.8	19.80	17	.506	.650	-9	-9	100	66	-0.4	1	0	-0.6
	Bal-A	3	3	.500	9	6	6	0	0	60	74	11.1	2	21	3.2	5	0.8	3.60	108	.324	.381	0	2	107	126	0.0	0	0	0.2
1902	NY-N	0	3	.000	3	2	2	0	0	27	28	9.3	0	12	4.0	6	2.0	3.67	79	.291	.369	-3	-2	104	93	-1.4	0	1	-0.1
1904	NY-N	0	0	—	1	0	0	0	1	4	3	6.8	1	3	6.8	1	2.3	4.50	80	.229	.373	-1	-1	100	109	0.0	0	0	0.0
Total	7	64	59	.520	142	118	103	3	3	1078	1217	10.2	31	334	2.8	171	1.4	4.12	93	.308	.362	-37	-34	101	95	1.4	0	3	-2.0

YEAR	TM/L	W	L	PCT	G	GS	CG	SHO	SV	IP	H	H/G	HR	BB	BB/G	SO	SO/G	ERA	/A	OAVG	OOBP	PR	/A	PF	CPI	WAT	PB	PD	TPI
■ MIKE DUNNE	Dunne, Michael Dennis b: 10/27/62, South Bend, Ind. BR/TR, 6'4", 190 lbs. Deb: 6/05/87																												
1987	Pit-N	13	6	.684	23	23	5	1	0	163	143	7.9	10	68	3.8	72	4.0	3.04	**141**	.240	.312	19	22	105	110	3.9	-1	2	2.5
1988	Pit-N	7	11	.389	30	28	1	0	0	170	163	8.6	15	88	4.7	70	3.7	3.92	86	.255	.340	-9	-11	97	109	-2.5	-1	0	-1.1
Total	2	20	17	.541	53	51	6	1	0	333	306	8.3	25	156	4.2	142	3.8	3.49	109	.248	.327	10	11	101	109	1.4	-1	2	1.4
■ ANDY DUNNING	Dunning, Andrew Jackson b: 8/12/1871, New York, N.Y. d: 6/21/52, New York, N.Y. BR/TR, 6', 175 lbs. Deb: 5/23/1889																												
1889	Pit-N	0	2	.000	2	2	2	0	0	18	20	10.0	1	16	8.0	4	2.0	7.00	52	.297	.432	-6	-7	90	81	-0.9	-1	0	-0.5
1891	NY-N	0	1	.000	1	1	0	0	0	2	3	13.5	1	3	13.5	2	9.0	4.50	69	.361	.531	-0	-0	93	275	-0.4	0	0	0.0
Total	2	0	3	.000	3	3	2	0	0	20	23	10.3	2	19	8.5	6	2.7	6.75	53	.304	.444	-6	-7	90	100	-1.3	-1	0	-0.5
■ STEVE DUNNING	Dunning, Steven John b: 5/15/49, Denver, Colo. BR/TR, 6'2", 205 lbs. Deb: 6/14/70																												
1970	Cle-A	4	9	.308	19	17	0	0	0	94	93	8.9	16	54	5.2	77	7.4	4.98	86	.261	.359	-13	-7	115	102	-2.3	-1	1	-0.6
1971	Cle-A	8	14	.364	31	29	3	1	1	184	173	8.5	25	109	5.3	132	6.5	4.50	84	.254	.354	-21	-15	108	104	-0.1	2	2	-1.1
1972	Cle-A	6	4	.600	16	16	1	0	0	105	98	8.4	16	43	3.7	52	4.5	3.26	102	.248	.320	-2	1	108	123	1.4	5	-1	0.6
1973	Cle-A	0	2	.000	4	3	0	0	0	18	17	8.5	2	13	6.5	10	5.0	6.50	58	.250	.361	-5	-5	99	71	-0.9	0	0	-0.4
	Tex-A	2	6	.250	23	12	2	0	0	94	101	9.7	11	52	5.0	38	3.6	5.36	71	.275	.362	-16	-16	100	91	-1.1	0	-0	-1.5
	Yr	2	8	.200	27	15	2	0	0	112	118	9.5	13	65	5.2	48	3.9	5.54	69	.271	.361	-21	-22	100	91	-2.0	0	-0	-1.9
1974	Tex-A	0	0	—	1	0	0	0	0	2	3	13.5	2	3	13.5	1	4.5	22.50	15	.333	.500	-4	-4	96	71	0.0	0	0	-0.3
1976	Cal-A	0	0	—	4	0	0	0	0	6	9	13.5	2	6	9.0	4	6.0	7.50	44	.310	.405	-3	-3	93	117	0.0	0	0	-0.2
	Mon-N	2	6	.250	32	7	1	0	0	91	93	9.2	6	33	3.3	72	7.1	4.15	87	.274	.328	-7	-5	103	98	-1.0	0	0	-0.4
1977	Oak-A	1	0	1.000	6	0	0	0	0	18	17	8.5	2	10	5.0	4	2.0	4.00	98	.254	.346	0	-0	97	108	0.5	0	0	0.0
Total	7	23	41	.359	136	84	7	1	1	612	604	8.9	82	323	4.8	390	5.7	4.57	82	.261	.348	-71	-56	106	103	-3.5	6	3	-3.9
■ FRANK DUPEE	Dupee, Frank Oliver b: 4/29/1877, Monkton, Vt. d: 8/14/56, Portland, Me. TL, 6'1", 200 lbs. Deb: 8/24/01																												
1901	Chi-A	0	1	.000	1	1	0	0	0	0	0	—	0	3	—	0	—	∞	—	—	1.000	-3	-3	96	31	-0.4	0	0	-0.1
■ MIKE DUPREE	Dupree, Michael Dennis b: 5/29/53, Kansas City, Kan. BR/TR, 6'1", 185 lbs. Deb: 4/13/76																												
1976	SD-N	0	0	—	12	0	0	0	0	16	18	10.1	4	7	3.9	5	2.8	9.00	35	.286	.352	-10	-10	90	66	0.0	0	0	-0.9
■ KID DURBIN	Durbin, Blaine Alphonsus b: 9/10/1886, Kansas d: 9/11/43, Kirkwood, Mo. BL/TL, 5'8", 155 lbs. Deb: 4/24/07																												
1907	Chi-N	0	1	.000	5	1	1	0	1	17	14	7.4	0	10	5.3	5	2.6	5.29	47	.255	.380	-5	-5	102	57	-0.4	1	0	-0.5
■ RYNE DUREN	Duren, Rinold George b: 2/22/29, Cazenovia, Wis. BR/TR, 6'2", 190 lbs. Deb: 9/25/54																												
1954	Bal-A	0	0	—	1	0	0	0	0	2	3	13.5	0	1	4.5	2	9.0	9.00	41	.333	.364	-1	-1	99	61	0.0	0	0	0.0
1957	KC-A	0	3	.000	14	6	0	0	1	43	37	7.7	4	30	6.3	37	7.7	5.23	73	.236	.358	-7	-7	102	82	-1.4	-1	0	-0.6
1958	NY-A	6	4	.600	44	1	0	0	**20**	76	40	4.7	4	43	5.1	87	10.3	2.01	186	.157	.293	15	15	99	103	0.0	0	0	1.6
1959	NY-A	3	6	.333	41	0	0	0	14	77	49	5.7	6	43	5.0	96	11.2	1.87	190	.181	.295	17	14	92	138	-1.5	-1	0	1.4
1960	NY-A	3	4	.429	42	1	0	0	9	49	27	5.0	3	49	9.0	67	12.3	4.96	72	.160	.362	-6	-8	92	68	-1.1	-1	1	-0.7
1961	NY-A	0	1	.000	4	0	0	0	0	5	2	3.6	2	4	7.2	7	12.6	5.40	70	.125	.286	-1	-1	93	85	-0.4	0	0	0.0
	LA-A	6	12	.333	40	14	1	1	2	99	87	7.9	13	75	6.8	108	9.8	5.18	87	.233	.359	-13	-7	112	89	-2.2	-2	-1	-0.9
	Yr	6	13	.316	44	14	1	1	2	104	89	7.7	15	79	6.8	115	10.0	5.19	86	.229	.356	-14	-8	111	89	-2.6	0	-1	-0.9
1962	LA-A	2	9	.182	42	3	0	0	8	71	53	6.7	1	57	7.2	74	9.4	4.44	91	.206	.355	-4	-3	102	77	-3.6	-1	-1	-0.4
1963	Phi-N	6	2	.750	33	7	1	0	2	87	65	6.7	6	52	5.4	84	8.7	3.31	101	.210	.328	-0	0	102	98	1.9	0	-1	0.0
1964	Phi-N	0	0	—	2	0	0	0	0	3	5	15.0	0	1	3.0	5	15.0	6.00	58	.357	.412	-1	-1	98	115	0.0	0	-0	0.0
	Cin-N	0	2	.000	26	0	0	0	1	44	41	8.4	1	15	3.1	39	8.0	2.86	125	.248	.314	3	4	102	111	-0.9	-0	-1	0.3
	Yr	0	2	.000	28	0	0	0	1	47	46	8.8	1	16	3.1	44	8.4	3.06	117	.256	.317	2	3	101	111	-0.9	0	-1	0.3
1965	Phi-N	0	0	—	6	0	0	0	0	11	10	8.2	0	4	3.3	6	4.9	3.27	103	.270	.341	0	0	95	117	0.0	-0	0	0.0
	Was-A	1	1	.500	16	0	0	0	0	23	24	9.4	0	18	7.0	18	7.0	6.65	53	.286	.409	-8	-8	102	81	0.1	0	-0	-0.8
Total	10	27	44	.380	311	32	2	1	57	590	443	6.8	40	392	6.0	630	9.6	3.83	99	.209	.337	-5	-3	101	96	-9.1	-6	-3	-0.1
■ DON DURHAM	Durham, Donald Gary b: 3/21/49, Yosemite, Ky. BR/TR, 6', 170 lbs. Deb: 7/16/72																												
1972	StL-N	2	7	.222	10	8	1	0	0	48	42	7.9	1	22	4.1	35	6.6	4.31	84	.240	.309	-5	-4	105	71	-2.4	4	-1	0.0
1973	Tex-A	0	4	.000	15	4	0	0	1	40	49	11.0	7	23	5.2	23	5.2	7.65	50	.304	.386	-17	-17	100	81	-1.9	0	-0	-1.6
Total	2	2	11	.154	25	12	1	0	1	88	91	9.3	8	45	4.6	58	5.9	5.83	64	.271	.346	-22	-21	103	75	-4.3	4	-1	-1.6
■ ED DURHAM	Durham, Edward Fant "Bull" b: 8/17/08, Chester, S.C. d: 4/27/76, Chester, S.C. BL/TR, 5'11", 170 lbs. Deb: 4/19/29																												
1929	Bos-A	1	0	1.000	14	1	0	0	0	22	34	13.9	2	14	5.7	6	2.5	9.41	47	.374	.444	-13	-12	105	84	0.5	-0	-0	-1.0
1930	Bos-A	4	15	.211	33	12	6	1	1	140	144	9.3	9	43	2.8	28	1.8	4.69	95	.270	.316	-1	-4	96	85	-3.8	-4	-0	-0.7
1931	Bos-A	8	10	.444	38	15	7	2	0	165	175	9.5	9	50	2.7	53	2.9	4.25	99	.266	.320	2	-0	97	90	0.6	-6	-2	-0.7
1932	Bos-A	6	13	.316	34	22	4	0	0	175	187	9.6	13	49	2.5	52	2.7	3.81	121	.274	.320	13	15	102	110	0.5	-3	1	1.2
1933	Chi-A	10	6	.625	24	21	6	0	0	139	137	8.9	12	46	3.0	65	4.2	4.47	99	.256	.315	-3	-1	103	88	2.8	-0	-1	-0.1
Total	5	29	44	.397	143	71	23	3	1	641	677	9.5	45	202	2.8	204	2.9	4.45	99	.271	.323	-1	-2	100	94	0.6	-14	-3	-1.3
■ JOHN DURHAM	Durham, John Garfield b: 10/7/1881, Douglass, Kan. d: 5/7/49, Coffeyville, Kan. 6', 175 lbs. Deb: 9/15/02																												
1902	Chi-A	1	1	.500	3	3	3	0	0	20	21	9.4	0	16	7.2	3	1.3	5.85	57	.295	.424	-5	-6	94	80	0.0	-1	0	-0.4
■ BULL DURHAM	Durham, Louis Raphael (born Louis Raphael Staub) b: 6/27/1877, New Oxford, Pa. d: 6/28/60, Bentley, Kan. TR, 5'10", Deb: 9/15/04																												
1904	Bro-N	2	0	1.000	2	2	1	0	0	11	10	8.2	0	5	4.1	1	0.8	3.27	81	.265	.351	-1	-1	98	90	1.0	0	-0	0.0
1907	Was-A	0	0	—	2	0	0	0	0	5	10	18.0	0	4	7.2	1	1.8	12.60	19	.443	.527	-6	-6	94	73	0.0	-0	-0	-0.4
1908	NY-N	0	0	—	1	0	0	0	0	2	2	9.0	0	1	4.5	2	9.0	9.00	26	.289	.379	-1	-1	100	39	0.0	0	0	-0.1
1909	NY-N	0	0	—	4	0	0	0	1	11	15	12.3	0	2	1.6	2	1.6	3.27	82	.326	.354	-1	-1	103	129	0.0	-0	-0	0.0
Total	4	2	0	1.000	9	2	1	0	1	29	37	11.5	0	12	3.7	6	1.9	5.28	49	.327	.391	-9	-9	99	99	1.0	-0	-1	-0.5
■ RICH DURNING	Durning, Richard Knott b: 10/10/1892, Louisville, Ky. d: 9/23/48, Castle Point, N.Y BL/TL, 6'2", 178 lbs. Deb: 4/16/17																												
1917	Bro-N	0	0	—	1	0	0	0	0	1	0	0.0	0	0	0.0	0	0.0	0.00	—	.000	.000	0	0	105	0	0.0	0	0	0.0
1918	Bro-N	0	0	—	1	0	0	0	0	2	3	13.5	0	4	18.0	0	0.0	13.50	21	.375	.538	-2	-2	104	79	0.0	0	0	-0.1
Total	2	0	0	—	2	0	0	0	0	3	3	9.0	0	4	12.0	0	0.0	9.00	32	.273	.438	-2	-2	104	53	0.0	0	0	-0.1
■ JESSE DURYEA	Duryea, James Whitney "Cyclone Jim" b: 9/7/1862, Osage, Iowa d: 8/7/42, Algona, Iowa BR/TR, 5'10", 175 lbs. Deb: 4/20/1889																												
1889	Cin-a	32	19	.627	53	48	38	2	1	401	372	8.3	9	127	2.9	183	4.1	2.56	155	.260	.321	**57**	**63**	103	112	6.5	5	-0	6.3
1890	Cin-N	16	12	.571	33	32	29	2	0	274	270	8.9	11	60	2.0	108	3.5	2.92	129	.273	.315	19	26	106	101	-0.3	-1	0	2.5
1891	Cin-N	1	9	.100	10	10	8	0	0	77	101	11.8	4	25	2.9	23	2.7	5.38	58	.331	.381	-17	-19	93	88	-3.7	-4	0	-1.8
	StL-a	1	1	.500	3	3	2	0	0	24	19	7.1	0	10	3.8	13	4.9	3.38	123	.231	.314	1	2	112	63	-0.1	1	0	0.3
1892	Cin-N	2	5	.286	9	7	5	0	0	68	55	7.3	3	26	3.4	21	2.8	3.57	95	.233	.309	-2	-1	103	71	-1.6	-1	0	-0.1
	Was-N	3	10	.231	18	15	13	1	2	127	102	7.2	6	45	3.2	48	3.4	2.41	145	.232	.303	12	15	106	101	-2.6	-4	0	1.2
	Yr	5	15	.250	27	22	18	1	2	195	157	7.2	9	71	3.3	69	3.2	2.82	123	.232	.305	10	14	105	101	-4.2	-1	0	1.1
1893	Was-N	4	10	.286	17	15	9	0	0	117	182	14.0	8	56	4.3	20	1.5	7.54	57	.372	.436	-37	-42	92	92	-0.5	2	0	-3.0
Total	5	59	66	.472	143	130	104	5	3	1088	1101	9.1	41	349	2.9	416	3.4	3.45	111	.277	.336	33	45	103	100	-2.3	-1	-0	5.4
■ ERV DUSAK	Dusak, Ervin Frank "Four Sack" b: 7/29/20, Chicago, Ill. BR/TR, 6'2", 185 lbs. Deb: 9/18/41																												
1948	StL-N	0	0	—	1	0	0	0	0	1	0	0.0	0	1	9.0	0	0.0	0.00	—	.000	.250	0	0	99	0	0.0	0	0	0.0
1950	StL-N	0	2	.000	14	2	0	0	1	36	27	6.8	2	27	6.8	16	4.0	3.75	113	.211	.342	2	2	103	96	-0.9	-0	0	0.1
1951	StL-N	0	0	—	5	0	0	0	0	10	14	12.6	0	7	6.3	8	7.2	7.20	55	.333	.429	-4	-4	101	85	0.0	1	0	-0.1
	Pit-N	0	1	.000	3	1	0	0	0	7	10	12.9	2	9	11.6	2	2.6	11.57	37	.357	.526	-6	-6	110	95	-0.4	1	-0	-0.4
	Yr	0	1	.000	8	1	0	0	0	17	24	12.7	2	16	8.5	10	5.3	9.00	46	.343	.471	-10	-9	104	95	-0.4	1	0	-0.5
Total	3	0	3	.000	23	3	0	0	1	54	51	8.5	4	44	7.3	26	4.3	5.33	79	.254	.385	-8	-7	103	92	-1.3	2	0	-0.4
■ CARL DUSER	Duser, Carl Robert b: 7/22/32, Hazleton, Pa. BL/TL, 6'1", 175 lbs. Deb: 9/15/56																												
1956	KC-A	1	1	.500	2	2	0	0	0	6	14	21.0	0	2	3.0	5	7.5	9.00	48	.452	.485	-3	-3	105	106	0.2	-0	0	-0.2
1958	KC-A	0	0	—	1	0	0	0	0	2	5	22.5	0	1	4.5	0	0.0	4.50	90	.500	.500	-0	-0	107	257	0.0	0	0	0.0
Total	2	1	1	.500	3	2	0	0	0	8	19	21.4	0	3	3.4	5	5.6	7.88	54	.463	.489	-3	-3	105	144	0.2	-0	0	-0.2

YEAR	TM/L	W	L	PCT	G	GS	CG	SHO	SV	IP	H	H/G	HR	BB	BB/G	SO	SO/G	ERA	/A	OAVG	OOBP	PR	/A	PF	CPI	WAT	PB	PD	TPI
■ **BOB DUSTAL**	Dustal, Robert Andrew b: 9/28/35, Sayreville, N.J. BR/TR, 6', 172 lbs. Deb: 4/09/63																												
1963	Det-A	0	1	.000	7	0	0	0	0	6	10	15.0	0	5	7.5	4	6.0	9.00	42	.357	.429	-4	-3	104	82	-0.4	0	1	-0.2
■ **BILL DUZEN**	Duzen, William George b: 2/21/1870, Buffalo, N.Y. d: 3/11/44, Buffalo, N.Y. BR/TR, 5'11", 165 lbs. Deb: 9/21/1890																												
1890	Buf-P	0	2	.000	2	2	2	0	0	13	20	13.8	2	14	9.7	5	3.5	13.85	30	.365	.494	-14	-14	97	64	-0.9	1	0	-0.8
■ **FRANK DWYER**	Dwyer, John Francis b: 3/25/1868, Lee, Mass. d: 2/4/43, Pittsfield, Mass. BR/TR, 5'8", 145 lbs. Deb: 1888 M																												
1888	Chi-N	4	1	.800	5	5	5	1	0	42	32	6.9	1	9	1.9	17	3.6	1.07	280	.223	.269	8	9	106	166	1.4	-0	0	1.0
1889	Chi-N	16	13	.552	32	30	27	0	0	276	307	10.0	14	72	2.3	63	2.1	3.59	110	.297	.343	14	11	98	109	1.6	-1	0	0.9
1890	Chi-P	3	6	.333	12	6	6	0	1	69	98	12.8	4	25	3.3	17	2.2	6.26	69	.347	.400	-16	-15	103	88	-1.7	-0	0	-1.0
1891	CM-a	19	23	.452	45	41	39	1	0	375	424	10.2	12	145	3.5	128	3.1	3.98	105	.300	.365	-11	8	113	100	-1.1	1	1	1.3
1892	StL-N	2	8	.200	10	10	6	0	0	64	90	12.7	1	24	3.4	16	2.3	5.63	57	.346	.401	-17	-17	97	93	-2.3	-1	0	-1.5
	Cin-N	19	10	.655	33	27	24	3	1	259	251	8.7	6	49	1.7	45	1.6	2.33	146	.267	.303	28	31	103	113	4.1	-5	0	2.5
	Yr	21	18	.538	43	37	30	3	1	323	341	9.5	7	73	2.0	61	1.7	2.98	112	.284	.325	11	13	102	113	1.8	-1	0	1.0
1893	Cin-N	18	15	.545	37	30	28	1	**2**	287	332	10.4	17	93	2.9	53	1.7	4.14	115	.306	.360	17	20	102	108	1.7	-3	4	1.8
1894	Cin-N	19	22	.463	45	40	34	1	1	348	471	12.2	27	106	2.7	49	1.3	5.07	107	.346	.394	10	13	102	108	2.0	2	2	1.4
1895	Cin-N	18	15	.545	37	31	23	2	0	280	355	11.4	10	74	2.4	46	1.5	4.24	121	.330	.373	17	28	107	109	1.7	1	1	2.6
1896	Cin-N	24	11	.686	36	34	30	3	1	289	321	10.0	8	60	1.9	57	1.8	3.15	143	.303	.341	39	44	103	112	4.5	4	-2	4.2
1897	Cin-N	18	13	.581	37	31	22	0	0	247	315	11.5	5	56	2.0	41	1.5	3.79	122	.333	.371	14	22	107	113	0.2	-0	-2	1.9
1898	Cin-N	16	10	.615	31	28	24	0	0	240	257	9.6	3	42	1.6	29	1.1	3.04	127	.296	.328	15	22	107	101	0.4	-5	-1	1.6
1899	Cin-N	0	5	.000	5	5	2	0	0	33	48	13.1	1	9	2.5	2	0.5	5.73	71	.365	.406	-7	-6	105	93	-2.4	1	0	-0.4
Total	12	176	152	.537	365	318	270	12	6	2809	3301	10.6	109	764	2.4	563	1.8	3.85	114	.311	.358	113	172	105	108	10.1	-5	2	16.3
■ **BEN DYER**	Dyer, Benjamin Franklin b: 2/13/1893, Chicago, Ill. d: 8/7/59, Kenosha, Wis. BR/TR, 5'10", 170 lbs. Deb: 5/23/14																												
1918	Det-A	0	0	—	2	0	0	0	0	2	0	0.0	0	0	0.0	0	0.0	0.00	—	.000	.000	1	1	99	0	0.0	0	0	0.1
■ **EDDIE DYER**	Dyer, Edwin Hawley b: 10/11/1900, Morgan City, La. d: 4/20/64, Houston, Tex. BL/TL, 5'11.5", 168 lbs. Deb: 7/08/22 M																												
1922	StL-N	0	0	—	2	0	0	0	0	4	7	15.8	0	0	0.0	3	6.8	2.25	183	.412	.412	1	1	100	288	0.0	0	0	0.1
1923	StL-N	2	1	.667	4	3	2	1	0	22	30	12.3	0	5	2.0	7	2.9	4.09	88	.333	.371	-0	-1	90	118	0.5	1	-0	0.0
1924	StL-N	8	11	.421	29	15	7	1	0	137	174	11.4	6	51	3.4	23	1.5	4.60	86	.331	.382	-11	-10	103	119	0.0	1	1	-0.5
1925	StL-N	4	3	.571	27	5	1	0	3	82	93	10.2	4	24	2.6	25	2.7	4.17	103	.278	.334	1	1	101	92	0.5	-2	0	0.0
1926	StL-N	1	0	1.000	6	0	0	0	0	9	7	7.0	0	14	14.0	4	4.0	12.00	32	.219	.449	-8	-8	100	48	0.5	0	0	-0.6
1927	StL-N	0	0	—	1	0	0	0	0	2	5	22.5	1	2	9.0	1	4.5	18.00	23	.500	.583	-3	-3	106	94	0.0	0	0	-0.1
Total	6	15	15	.500	69	23	10	2	3	256	316	11.1	11	96	3.4	63	2.2	4.75	85	.313	.371	-21	-20	101	110	1.5	1	1	-1.1
■ **JIMMY DYGERT**	Dygert, James Henry "Sunny Jim" b: 7/5/1884, Utica, N.Y. d: 2/8/36, New Orleans, La. TR, 5'10", 185 lbs. Deb: 9/08/05																												
1905	Phi-A	1	4	.200	6	3	2	0	0	35	41	10.5	2	11	2.8	24	6.2	4.37	64	.318	.372	-7	-6	106	103	-1.6	0	2	-0.4
1906	Phi-A	11	13	.458	35	25	15	4	0	214	175	7.4	1	91	3.8	106	4.5	2.69	93	.246	.332	-0	-5	93	95	-2.0	1	0	-0.4
1907	Phi-A	21	8	.724	42	28	18	5	1	262	200	**6.9**	2	85	2.9	151	5.2	2.34	114	**.233**	.302	6	9	104	83	5.0	-4	-1	0.9
1908	Phi-A	11	15	.423	41	27	15	5	1	239	184	6.9	3	97	3.7	164	6.2	2.86	91	.220	.309	-13	-7	110	89	-0.6	-7	2	-0.4
1909	Phi-A	9	5	.643	32	12	6	1	0	137	117	7.7	1	50	3.3	79	5.2	2.43	99	.242	.327	1	-0	97	109	0.4	1	-2	-0.1
1910	Phi-A	4	4	.500	19	8	6	1	0	99	81	7.4	0	49	4.5	59	5.4	2.55	96	.231	.331	-0	-1	97	105	-1.0	-2	-2	-0.5
Total	6	57	49	.538	175	103	62	16	2	986	798	7.3	9	383	3.5	583	5.3	2.65	97	.237	.319	-13	-9	101	94	0.2	-11	-0	-0.9
■ **JIMMY DYKES**	Dykes, James Joseph b: 11/10/1896, Philadelphia, Pa. d: 6/15/76, Philadelphia, Pa. BR/TR, 5'9", 185 lbs. Deb: 5/06/18 MC																												
1927	Phi-A	0	0	—	2	0	0	0	1	2	2	9.0	0	1	4.5	0	0.0	4.50	87	.333	.375	-0	-0	95	123	0.0	1	0	0.0
■ **ARNOLD EARLEY**	Earley, Arnold Carl b: 6/4/33, Lincoln Park, Mich. BL/TL, 6'1", 195 lbs. Deb: 9/27/60																												
1960	Bos-A	0	1	.000	2	0	0	0	0	4	9	20.3	1	4	9.0	5	11.3	15.75	26	.429	.520	-5	-5	105	79	-0.4	0	0	-0.4
1961	Bos-A	2	4	.333	33	0	0	0	7	50	42	7.6	3	34	6.1	44	7.9	3.96	104	.226	.341	0	1	103	91	-0.8	-1	0	0.0
1962	Bos-A	4	5	.444	38	3	0	0	5	68	76	10.1	8	46	6.1	59	7.8	5.82	70	.281	.372	-14	-13	103	95	-0.2	0	1	-1.1
1963	Bos-A	3	7	.300	53	4	0	0	1	116	124	9.6	13	43	3.3	97	7.5	4.73	82	.270	.335	-14	-11	107	94	-1.8	1	0	-0.9
1964	Bos-A	1	1	.500	25	3	1	0	1	50	51	9.2	3	18	3.2	45	8.1	2.70	139	.266	.321	5	6	103	138	0.1	0	1	0.7
1965	Bos-A	0	1	.000	57	0	0	0	0	74	79	9.6	5	29	3.5	47	5.7	3.65	103	.271	.334	-2	1	109	113	-0.4	-0	0	0.1
1966	Chi-N	2	1	.667	13	0	0	0	0	18	14	7.0	1	9	4.5	12	6.0	3.50	106	.226	.311	0	0	103	91	0.7	-0	-1	0.0
1967	Hou-N	0	0	—	2	0	0	0	0	1	5	45.0	1	1	9.0	1	9.0	36.00	9	.625	.667	-4	-4	95	88	0.0	0	0	-0.2
Total	8	12	20	.375	223	10	1	0	14	381	400	9.4	35	184	4.3	310	7.3	4.49	87	.269	.344	-33	-25	105	103	-2.8	0	1	-1.8
■ **THOMAS EARLEY**	Earley, Thomas Francis Aloysius b: 2/19/17, Roxbury, Mass. d: 4/5/88, Nantucket, Mass. BR/TR, 6', 180 lbs. Deb: 9/27/38																												
1938	Bos-N	1	0	1.000	2	1	1	0	0	11	8	6.5	2	1	0.8	4	3.3	3.27	103	.186	.217	1	0	89	59	0.5	-0	0	0.0
1939	Bos-N	1	4	.200	14	2	0	0	1	40	49	11.0	1	19	4.3	9	2.0	4.72	77	.304	.370	-4	-5	93	105	-1.2	1	1	-0.3
1940	Bos-N	2	0	1.000	4	1	1	1	0	16	16	9.0	1	3	1.7	5	2.8	3.94	99	.267	.323	-0	-0	101	98	1.0	1	-0	0.1
1941	Bos-N	6	8	.429	33	13	6	1	3	139	120	7.8	9	46	3.0	54	3.5	2.53	137	.233	.296	17	15	96	119	0.3	1	-1	1.5
1942	Bos-N	6	11	.353	27	18	6	0	1	113	120	9.6	10	55	4.4	28	2.2	4.70	69	.276	.353	-17	-18	98	99	-1.0	-1	0	-1.8
1945	Bos-N	2	1	.667	11	2	1	0	0	41	36	7.9	4	19	4.2	4	0.9	4.61	93	.235	.309	-4	-2	113	78	0.6	0	0	0.0
Total	6	18	24	.429	91	37	15	2	5	360	349	8.7	27	143	3.6	104	2.6	3.78	93	.256	.324	-7	-10	98	104	0.2	2	0	-0.5
■ **BILL EARLEY**	Earley, William Albert b: 1/30/56, Cincinnati, Ohio BR/TR, 6'4", 200 lbs. Deb: 9/22/86																												
1986	StL-N	0	0	—	3	0	0	0	0	3	0	0.0	0	2	6.0	2	6.0	0.00	—	.000	.182	1	1	103	0	0.0	0	0	0.1
■ **GEORGE EARNSHAW**	Earnshaw, George Livingston "Moose" b: 2/15/1900, New York, N.Y. d: 12/1/76, Little Rock, Ark. BR/TR, 6'4", 210 lbs. Deb: 6/03/28 C																												
1928	Phi-A	7	7	.500	26	22	7	3	1	158	143	8.1	7	100	5.7	117	**6.7**	3.82	105	.240	.342	4	3	99	96	-1.6	1	-1	0.3
1929	Phi-A	**24**	8	.750	44	33	13	3	1	255	233	**8.2**	8	125	4.4	149	5.3	3.28	135	**.241**	.326	27	32	104	97	3.6	-3	-3	2.6
1930	Phi-A	22	13	.629	49	39	20	**3**	2	296	299	9.1	20	139	4.2	193	5.9	4.44	101	.266	.338	7	1	96	98	-1.0	1	-1	0.1
1931	Phi-A	21	7	.750	43	30	23	3	6	282	255	8.1	16	75	2.4	152	4.9	3.67	121	.236	.284	22	24	101	80	2.6	7	0	3.0
1932	Phi-A	19	13	.594	36	33	21	1	0	245	262	9.6	28	94	3.5	109	4.0	4.78	104	.270	.333	-8	5	111	96	-0.4	3	1	0.9
1933	Phi-A	5	10	.333	21	18	4	0	0	118	153	11.7	8	58	4.4	37	2.8	5.95	66	.311	.379	-22	-27	92	96	-2.8	0	1	-2.2
1934	Chi-A	14	11	.560	33	30	16	2	0	227	242	9.6	28	104	4.1	97	3.8	4.52	103	.270	.343	-1	3	103	106	4.6	0	-1	0.3
1935	Chi-A	1	2	.333	3	3	0	0	0	18	26	13.0	2	11	5.5	8	4.0	9.00	54	.342	.420	-9	-8	109	80	-0.4	0	0	-0.6
	Bro-N	8	12	.400	25	22	6	2	0	166	175	9.5	14	53	2.9	72	3.9	4.12	93	.270	.318	-2	-6	95	97	-1.3	1	0	-0.4
1936	Bro-N	4	9	.308	19	13	4	1	1	93	113	10.9	7	30	2.9	40	3.9	5.32	80	.297	.349	-13	-11	107	89	-1.9	0	-0	-0.9
	StL-N	2	1	.667	20	6	1	0	1	58	80	12.4	4	20	3.1	28	4.3	6.36	60	.333	.386	-15	-17	95	92	0.4	-0	1	-1.4
	Yr	6	10	.375	39	19	5	1	2	151	193	11.5	11	50	3.0	68	4.1	5.72	72	.310	.359	-29	-27	102	92	-1.5	0	1	-2.3
Total	9	127	93	.577	319	249	115	18	12	1916	1981	9.3	142	809	3.8	1002	4.7	4.38	100	.265	.333	-9	-0	101	95	1.8	10	-2	1.7
■ **LOGAN EASLEY**	Easley, Kenneth Logan b: 11/4/61, Salt Lake City, Utah BR/TR, 6'1", 185 lbs. Deb: 4/09/87																												
1987	Pit-N	1	1	.500	17	0	0	0	1	26	23	8.0	5	17	5.9	21	7.3	5.54	77	.242	.347	-4	-4	105	93	0.0	-0	1	-0.2
■ **MAL EASON**	Eason, Malcolm Wayne "Kid" b: 3/13/1879, Brookville, Pa. d: 4/16/70, Douglas, Ariz. TR, Deb: 10/01/00 U																												
1900	Chi-N	1	0	1.000	1	1	1	0	0	9	9	9.0	0	3	3.0	2	2.0	1.00	349	.283	.345	3	2	94	308	0.5	-0	0	0.2
1901	Chi-N	8	17	.320	27	25	23	1	0	221	246	10.0	9	60	2.4	68	2.8	3.58	95	.309	.367	-6	-4	103	111	-2.3	-5	-2	-0.5
1902	Chi-N	1	1	.500	2	2	2	0	0	18	21	10.5	0	2	1.0	4	2.0	1.00	265	.315	.335	4	3	95	311	0.0	0	0	0.4
	Bos-N	9	14	.391	27	26	20	2	0	206	237	10.4	4	59	2.6	50	2.2	2.75	95	.312	.362	1	-3	94	134	-3.4	-6	-1	-0.3
	Yr	10	15	.400	29	28	22	2	0	224	258	10.4	4	61	2.5	54	2.2	2.61	100	.313	.360	4	0	94	134	-3.4	0	-0	0.1
1903	Det-A	2	5	.286	7	6	6	1	0	56	60	9.6	1	19	3.1	21	3.4	3.38	84	.297	.357	-3	-3	96	110	-1.4	-2	1	-0.1
1905	Bro-N	5	21	.192	27	27	20	3	0	207	230	10.0	5	72	3.1	64	2.8	4.30	71	.311	.376	-30	-29	102	93	-5.6	-1	1	-2.7
1906	Bro-N	10	17	.370	34	26	18	3	1	227	212	8.4	1	74	2.9	64	2.5	3.25	73	.277	.348	-16	-23	90	89	-2.2	-3	1	-2.2
Total	6	36	75	.324	125	113	90	10	1	944	1015	9.7	20	289	2.8	273	2.6	3.39	84	.302	.362	-48	-58	97	112	-14.4	-18	1	-5.2
■ **CARL EAST**	East, Carlton William b: 8/27/1894, Marietta, Ga. d: 1/15/53, Whitesburg, Ga. BL/TR, 6'2", 178 lbs. Deb: 8/24/15																												
1915	StL-A	0	0	—	1	1	0	0	0	3	6	18.0	0	2	6.0	1	3.0	18.00	16	.400	.471	-5	-5	99	47	0.0	-0	-0	-0.3

YEAR	TM/L	W	L	PCT	G	GS	CG	SHO	SV	IP	H	H/G	HR	BB	BB/G	SO	SO/G	ERA	/A	OAVG	OOBP	PR	/A	PF	CPI	WAT	PB	PD	TPI
■ **HUGH EAST**	East, Gordon Hugh b: 7/7/19, Birmingham, Ala. d: 11/2/81, Charleston, S.C. BR/TR, 6'2", 185 lbs. Deb: 9/13/41																												
1941	NY-N	1	1	.500	2	2	0	0	0	16	19	10.7	0	9	5.1	4	2.3	3.38	112	.297	.378	0	1	104	141	0.0	0	0	0.1
1942	NY-N	0	2	.000	4	1	0	0	0	7	15	19.3	1	7	9.0	2	2.6	10.29	33	.429	.489	-5	-5	101	113	-0.9	2	0	-0.3
1943	NY-N	1	3	.250	13	5	1	0	0	40	51	11.5	4	25	5.6	21	4.7	5.40	62	.298	.388	-9	-9	99	104	-0.5	-1	-1	-1.0
Total	3	2	6	.250	19	8	1	0	0	63	85	12.1	5	41	5.9	27	3.9	5.43	64	.315	.400	-14	-14	100	114	-1.4	1	-1	-1.2
■ **JAMIE EASTERLY**	Easterly, James Morris b: 2/17/53, Houston, Tex. BB/TL, 5'9", 180 lbs. Deb: 4/06/74																												
1974	Atl-N	0	0	—	3	0	0	0	0	3	6	18.0	0	4	12.0	0	0.0	15.00	25	.400	.526	-4	-4	104	68	0.0	0	0	-0.3
1975	Atl-N	2	9	.182	21	13	0	0	0	69	73	9.5	5	42	5.5	34	4.4	4.96	71	.275	.367	-10	-11	97	96	-3.1	-1	-0	-1.2
1976	Atl-N	1	1	.500	4	4	0	0	0	22	23	9.4	0	13	5.3	11	4.5	4.91	80	.280	.375	-3	-2	112	88	0.1	-1	0	-0.2
1977	Atl-N	2	4	.333	22	5	0	0	1	59	72	11.0	5	30	4.6	37	5.6	6.10	74	.303	.382	-14	-10	115	89	-0.3	1	-1	-1.0
1978	Atl-N	3	6	.333	37	6	0	0	1	78	91	10.5	9	45	5.2	42	4.8	5.65	72	.299	.389	-18	-14	114	101	-0.9	1	0	-1.2
1979	Atl-N	0	0	—	4	0	0	0	0	3	7	21.0	0	3	9.0	3	9.0	12.00	34	.467	.556	-3	-3	110	98	0.0	0	0	-0.2
1981	Mil-A	3	3	.500	44	0	0	0	4	62	46	6.7	0	34	4.9	31	4.5	3.19	109	.219	.316	3	2	95	88	-0.3	0	0	0.2
1982	Mil-A	0	2	.000	28	0	0	0	2	31	39	11.3	6	15	4.4	16	4.6	4.65	81	.312	.380	-2	-3	92	137	-0.9	0	1	-0.1
1983	Mil-A	0	1	.000	12	0	0	0	1	12	14	10.5	0	10	7.5	6	4.5	3.75	99	.350	.464	0	-0	91	197	-0.4	0	0	0.0
	Cle-A	4	2	.667	41	0	0	0	3	57	69	10.9	4	22	3.5	39	6.2	3.63	119	.309	.372	3	4	106	144	1.3	0	0	0.5
	Yr	4	3	.571	53	0	0	0	4	69	83	10.8	4	32	4.2	45	5.9	3.65	115	.312	.382	3	4	103	144	0.9	0	0	0.5
1984	Cle-A	3	1	.750	26	1	0	0	2	69	74	9.7	3	23	3.0	42	5.5	3.39	125	.273	.327	5	6	106	110	1.1	0	0	0.7
1985	Cle-A	4	1	.800	50	7	0	0	0	99	96	8.7	9	53	4.8	58	5.3	3.91	101	.264	.352	3	0	95	120	1.7	0	-0	0.0
1986	Cle-A	0	2	.000	13	0	0	0	0	18	27	13.5	3	12	6.0	9	4.5	7.50	55	.365	.438	-7	-7	98	111	-0.9	0	-0	-0.6
1987	Cle-A	1	1	.500	16	0	0	0	0	32	26	7.3	4	13	3.7	22	6.2	4.50	104	.218	.292	-0	1	105	73	0.2	0	0	0.1
Total	13	23	33	.411	321	36	0	0	14	614	663	9.7	48	319	4.7	350	5.1	4.60	87	.283	.364	-47	-39	103	108	-2.4	-0	0	-3.3
■ **JACK EASTON**	Easton, John S. b: 2/28/1867, Bridgeport, Ohio d: 11/28/03, Steubenville, Ohio Deb: 9/23/1889																												
1889	Col-a	1	0	1.000	4	1	1	0	1	18	13	6.5	0	21	10.5	7	3.5	3.50	102	.215	.418	1	0	92	116	0.5	-1	0	0.0
1890	Col-a	15	14	.517	37	29	23	0	1	256	213	7.5	4	125	4.4	147	5.2	3.52	105	.241	.335	10	5	96	89	-2.1	-0	0	0.4
1891	Col-a	5	10	.333	18	16	13	0	0	135	145	9.7	6	59	3.9	52	3.5	4.53	74	.289	.364	-12	-18	90	87	-2.0	2	0	-1.3
	StL-a	3	2	.600	7	6	4	0	0	48	48	9.0	2	23	4.3	22	4.1	5.06	82	.275	.359	-7	-5	112	72	0.0	-1	0	-0.4
	Col-a	0	2	.000	2	2	2	0	0	15	15	9.0	0	4	2.4	13	7.8	3.60	93	.275	.324	0	-0	90	77	-0.9	-1	0	0.0
	Yr	8	14	.364	27	24	19	0	0	198	208	9.5	8	86	3.9	87	4.0	4.59	77	.285	.360	-19	-23	95	77	-2.9	1	0	-1.7
1892	StL-N	2	0	1.000	5	2	2	0	0	31	38	11.0	2	26	7.5	4	1.2	6.39	50	.315	.437	-11	-11	97	94	1.0	-0	0	-0.9
1894	Pit-N	0	1	.000	3	1	1	0	0	20	26	11.7	0	4	1.8	1	0.4	4.05	124	.337	.370	3	2	95	107	-0.4	-1	0	0.1
Total	5	26	29	.473	76	57	46	0	2	523	498	8.6	14	262	4.5	246	4.2	4.11	89	.266	.356	-16	-26	96	88	-3.9	-3	0	-2.1
■ **RAWLY EASTWICK**	Eastwick, Rawlins Jackson b: 10/24/50, Camden, N.J. BR/TR, 6'3", 180 lbs. Deb: 9/12/74																												
1974	Cin-N	0	0	—	8	0	0	0	2	18	12	6.0	1	5	2.5	14	7.0	2.00	175	.188	.239	3	3	96	75	0.0	-0	-0	0.3
1975	Cin-N	5	3	.625	58	0	0	0	**22**	90	77	7.7	6	25	2.5	61	6.1	2.60	142	.229	.283	10	11	101	99	-0.2	-1	-1	0.9
1976	Cin-N	11	5	.688	71	0	0	0	**26**	108	93	7.8	3	27	2.3	70	5.8	2.08	168	.232	.278	17	17	100	112	1.4	-2	-2	1.5
1977	Cin-N	2	2	.500	23	0	0	0	7	43	40	8.4	3	8	1.7	17	3.6	2.93	132	.244	.279	5	5	99	91	-0.1	-0	-1	0.3
	StL-N	3	7	.300	41	1	0	0	4	54	74	12.3	6	21	3.5	30	5.0	4.67	80	.332	.383	-5	-6	95	129	-2.1	1	-1	-0.4
	Yr	5	9	.357	64	1	0	0	11	97	114	10.6	9	29	2.7	47	4.4	3.90	97	.295	.340	0	-1	97	129	-2.2	-0	-2	-0.1
1978	NY-A	2	1	.667	8	0	0	0	0	25	22	7.9	2	4	1.4	13	4.7	3.24	113	.232	.267	1	1	97	74	0.2	0	0	0.1
	Phi-N	2	1	.667	22	0	0	0	0	40	31	7.0	5	18	4.0	14	3.1	4.05	92	.209	.288	-2	-1	104	74	0.4	-0	-1	-0.2
1979	Phi-N	3	6	.333	51	0	0	0	6	83	90	9.8	8	25	2.7	47	5.1	4.88	75	.284	.332	-10	-11	97	88	-1.6	-1	-2	-1.3
1980	KC-A	0	1	.000	14	0	0	0	0	22	37	15.1	2	8	3.3	5	2.0	5.32	74	.363	.412	-3	-3	97	133	-0.4	0	1	-0.2
1981	Chi-N	0	1	.000	30	0	0	0	1	43	43	9.0	2	15	3.1	24	5.0	2.30	161	.264	.317	6	7	106	153	-0.4	-0	0	0.7
Total	8	28	27	.509	326	1	0	0	68	526	519	8.9	38	156	2.7	295	5.0	3.30	111	.258	.308	22	22	100	104	-2.8	-3	-6	1.7
■ **CRAIG EATON**	Eaton, Craig b: 9/7/54, Glendale, Ohio BR/TR, 5'11", 175 lbs. Deb: 9/05/79																												
1979	KC-A	0	0	—	5	0	0	0	0	10	8	7.2	0	3	2.7	4	3.6	2.70	165	.222	.268	2	2	105	76	0.0	0	0	0.2
■ **ZEB EATON**	Eaton, Zebulon Vance "Red" b: 2/2/20, Cooleemee, N.C. BR/TR, 5'10", 185 lbs. Deb: 4/18/44																												
1944	Det-A	0	0	—	6	0	0	0	0	16	19	10.7	2	8	4.5	4	2.3	5.63	63	.322	.397	-4	-4	104	109	0.0	-1	-0	-0.3
1945	Det-A	4	2	.667	17	3	0	0	0	53	48	8.2	0	40	6.8	15	2.5	4.08	86	.247	.382	-4	-3	105	100	0.7	2	0	0.0
Total	2	4	2	.667	23	3	0	0	0	69	67	8.7	2	48	6.3	19	2.5	4.43	80	.265	.386	-8	-7	104	102	0.7	2	-0	-0.3
■ **GARY EAVE**	Eave, Gary Louis b: 7/22/63, Monroe, La. BR/TR, 6'4", 190 lbs. Deb: 4/12/88																												
1988	Atl-N	0	0	—	5	0	0	0	0	5	7	12.6	0	3	5.4	0	0.0	9.00	41	.333	.417	-3	-3	107	66	0.0	0	-0	-0.2
■ **VALLIE EAVES**	Eaves, Vallie Ennis "Chief" "Tom" b: 9/6/11, Allen, Okla. d: 4/19/60, Norman, Okla. BR/TR, 6'2.5", 180 lbs. Deb: 9/12/35																												
1935	Phi-A	1	2	.333	3	3	1	0	0	14	12	7.7	0	15	9.6	6	3.9	5.14	89	.240	.397	-1	-1	102	94	-0.1	-1	-0	-0.1
1939	Chi-A	0	1	.000	2	1	1	0	0	12	11	8.3	1	8	6.0	5	3.8	4.50	109	.250	.370	0	1	106	108	-0.4	0	0	0.1
1940	Chi-A	0	2	.000	5	3	0	0	0	19	22	10.4	2	24	11.4	11	5.2	6.63	68	.301	.480	-5	-5	103	120	-0.9	-1	-1	-0.4
1941	Chi-N	3	3	.500	12	7	4	0	0	59	56	8.5	4	21	3.2	24	3.7	3.51	97	.253	.325	1	-1	94	105	0.3	-1	-1	-0.3
1942	Chi-N	0	0	—	2	0	0	0	0	3	4	12.0	0	2	6.0	0	0.0	9.00	36	.308	.438	-2	-2	98	69	0.0	0	-0	-0.1
Total	5	4	8	.333	24	14	6	0	0	107	105	8.8	7	70	5.9	46	3.9	4.54	86	.262	.376	-7	-8	98	106	-1.1	-2	-2	-0.8
■ **EDDIE EAYRS**	Eayrs, Edwin b: 11/10/1890, Blackstone, Mass. d: 11/30/69, Warwick, R.I. BL/TL, 5'7", 160 lbs. Deb: 6/30/13																												
1913	Pit-N	0	0	—	2	0	0	0	0	8	8	9.0	0	6	6.8	5	5.6	2.25	134	.267	.389	1	1	94	188	0.0	-0	0	0.1
1920	Bos-N	1	2	.333	7	3	0	0	0	26	36	12.5	1	12	4.2	7	2.4	5.54	56	.346	.413	-7	-7	99	107	-0.2	2	1	-0.6
1921	Bos-N	0	0	—	2	0	0	0	0	5	9	16.2	0	9	16.2	1	1.8	16.20	22	.391	.563	-7	-7	92	68	0.0	-2	-0	-0.6
Total	3	1	2	.333	11	3	0	0	0	39	53	12.2	1	27	6.2	13	3.0	6.23	51	.338	.434	-13	-13	97	118	-0.2	0	1	-1.1
■ **HARRY ECCLES**	Eccles, Harry Josiah "Bugs" b: 7/9/1893, Kennedy, N.Y. d: 6/2/55, Jamestown, N.Y. BL/TL, 6'2", 170 lbs. Deb: 9/13/15																												
1915	Phi-A	0	1	.000	5	1	0	0	1	21	18	7.7	2	6	2.6	13	5.6	4.71	64	.240	.296	-4	-4	103	64	-0.4	-0	-1	-0.4
■ **DENNIS ECKERSLEY**	Eckersley, Dennis Lee b: 10/3/54, Oakland, Cal. BR/TR, 6'2", 190 lbs. Deb: 4/12/75																												
1975	Cle-A	13	7	.650	34	24	6	2	2	187	147	7.1	16	90	4.3	152	7.3	2.60	145	.215	.307	25	24	100	116	3.3	0	-3	2.3
1976	Cle-A	13	12	.520	36	30	9	3	1	199	155	7.0	13	78	3.5	200	9.0	3.44	102	.214	.290	2	2	100	76	0.3	0	-1	0.1
1977	Cle-A	14	13	.519	33	33	12	3	0	247	214	7.8	31	54	2.0	191	7.0	3.53	113	.231	**.273**	15	13	98	83	2.2	0	-3	0.9
1978	Bos-A	20	8	.714	35	35	16	3	0	268	258	8.7	30	71	2.4	162	5.4	2.99	134	.251	.300	24	30	106	115	4.4	0	-1	3.1
1979	Bos-A	17	10	.630	33	33	17	2	0	247	234	8.5	29	59	2.1	150	5.5	2.99	**150**	.250	.294	34	**41**	106	**116**	2.2	0	1	**4.3**
1980	Bos-A	12	14	.462	30	30	8	0	0	198	188	8.5	25	44	2.0	121	5.5	4.27	97	.248	.286	-5	-3	102	78	-1.6	0	-1	-0.4
1981	Bos-A	9	8	.529	23	23	8	2	0	154	160	9.4	9	35	2.0	79	4.6	4.27	91	.267	.305	-10	-7	106	79	-0.2	0	-1	-0.7
1982	Bos-A	13	13	.500	33	33	11	3	0	224	228	9.2	31	43	1.7	127	5.1	3.74	120	.261	.295	9	19	110	100	-1.3	0	-1	1.8
1983	Bos-A	9	13	.409	28	28	2	0	0	176	223	11.4	27	39	2.0	77	3.9	5.63	74	.303	.341	-30	-29	102	92	-1.8	0	-1	-2.7
1984	Bos-A	4	4	.500	9	9	2	0	0	65	71	9.8	10	13	1.8	33	4.6	4.98	88	.284	.315	-7	-4	110	91	-0.1	0	1	-0.2
	Chi-N	10	8	.556	24	24	2	0	0	160	152	8.5	11	36	2.0	81	4.6	3.04	129	.250	.290	10	15	109	101	-0.6	-3	1	1.5
1985	Chi-N	11	7	.611	25	25	6	2	0	169	145	7.7	15	19	1.0	117	6.2	3.09	136	.229	.252	10	21	117	75	2.5	0	0	2.4
1986	Chi-N	6	11	.353	33	32	1	0	0	201	226	10.1	21	43	**1.9**	137	6.1	4.57	88	.285	.316	-19	-12	108	92	-1.7	2	0	-1.0
1987	Oak-A	6	8	.429	54	2	0	0	16	116	99	7.7	11	17	1.3	113	8.8	3.03	134	.228	.259	19	13	91	84	-1.0	0	-0	1.2
1988	Oak-A	4	2	.667	60	0	0	0	**45**	73	52	6.4	5	11	1.4	70	8.6	2.34	158	.198	.229	13	11	93	70	0.2	0	-1	1.0
Total	14	161	138	.538	490	361	100	20	64	2684	2552	8.6	284	652	2.2	1810	6.1	3.61	113	.249	.293	87	136	104	94	6.8	-1	-10	13.6
■ **AL ECKERT**	Eckert, Albert George "Obbie" b: 5/17/06, Milwaukee, Wis. d: 4/20/74, Milwaukee, Wis. BL/TL, 5'10", 174 lbs. Deb: 4/21/30																												
1930	Cin-N	0	1	.000	2	1	0	0	0	5	7	12.6	0	4	7.2	1	1.8	7.20	64	.304	.407	-1	-1	93	75	-0.4	-0	0	0.0
1931	Cin-N	0	1	.000	14	1	0	0	0	19	26	12.3	3	9	4.3	5	2.4	9.00	42	.325	.389	-11	-11	98	72	-0.4	0	0	-0.9
1935	StL-N	0	0	—	2	0	0	0	0	3	7	21.0	0	1	3.0	1	3.0	12.00	34	.467	.471	-3	-3	100	85	0.0	0	0	-0.2
Total	3	0	2	.000	18	2	0	0	0	27	40	13.3	3	14	4.7	7	2.3	9.00	44	.339	.403	-15	-15	97	74	-0.8	0	0	-1.1

YEAR	TM/L	W	L	PCT	G	GS	CG	SHO	SV	IP	H	H/G	HR	BB	BB/G	SO	SO/G	ERA	/A	OAVG	OOBP	PR	/A	PF	CPI	WAT	PB	PD	TPI
■ CHARLIE ECKERT	Eckert, Charles William "Buzz" b: 8/8/1897, Philadelphia, Pa. d: 8/22/86, Trevose, Pa. BR/TR, 5'10.5", 165 lbs. Deb: 9/18/19																												
1919	Phi-A	0	1	.000	2	1	1	0	0	16	17	9.6	1	3	1.7	6	3.4	3.94	92	.270	.303	-1	-1	112	76	-0.4	-0	0	0.0
1920	Phi-A	0	0	—	2	0	0	0	0	6	8	12.0	0	1	1.5	1	1.5	4.50	83	.421	.476	-0	-1	99	153	0.0	-0	-0	0.0
1922	Phi-A	0	2	.000	21	0	0	0	0	50	61	11.0	7	23	4.1	15	2.7	4.68	92	.319	.376	-4	-2	106	129	-0.9	-1	1	-0.1
Total	3	0	3	.000	25	1	1	0	0	72	86	10.8	8	27	3.4	22	2.8	4.50	91	.315	.367	-5	-3	107	119	-1.3	-2	1	-0.1
■ DON EDDY	Eddy, Donald Eugene b: 10/25/46, Mason City, Iowa BR/TL, 5'11", 170 lbs. Deb: 9/07/70																												
1970	Chi-A	0	0	—	7	0	0	0	0	12	10	7.5	0	6	4.5	9	6.8	2.25	178	.244	.333	2	2	108	143	0.0	0	0	0.2
1971	Chi-A	0	2	.000	22	0	0	0	0	23	19	7.4	3	19	7.4	14	5.5	2.35	144	.232	.369	3	3	97	200	-0.9	1	-0	0.3
Total	2	0	2	.000	29	0	0	0	0	35	29	7.5	3	25	6.4	23	5.9	2.31	155	.236	.358	5	5	101	180	-0.9	1	-0	0.5
■ STEVE EDDY	Eddy, Steven Allen b: 8/21/57, Sterling, Ill. BR/TR, 6'2", 185 lbs. Deb: 6/13/79																												
1979	Cal-A	1	1	.500	7	4	0	0	0	32	36	10.1	1	20	5.6	7	2.0	4.78	81	.290	.382	-2	-3	92	106	0.0	0	0	-0.2
■ JOE EDELEN	Edelen, Benny Joe b: 9/16/55, Durant, Okla. BR/TR, 6', 165 lbs. Deb: 4/18/81																												
1981	StL-N	1	0	1.000	13	0	0	0	0	17	29	15.4	2	3	1.6	10	5.3	9.53	37	.367	.388	-11	-11	101	72	0.5	0	0	-1.0
	Cin-N	1	0	1.000	5	0	0	0	0	13	5	3.5	1	0	0.0	5	3.5	0.69	507	.128	.125	4	4	101	22	0.5	-0	-0	0.4
	Yr	2	0	1.000	18	0	0	0	0	30	34	10.2	3	3	0.9	15	4.5	5.70	62	.283	.296	-7	-7	101	22	1.0	0	-0	-0.6
1982	Cin-N	0	0	—	9	0	0	0	0	15	22	13.2	2	8	4.8	11	6.6	9.00	42	.344	.405	-9	-9	104	77	0.0	0	0	-0.7
Total	2	2	0	1.000	27	0	0	0	0	45	56	11.2	5	11	2.2	26	5.2	6.80	53	.308	.342	-16	-16	102	60	1.0	0	-0	-1.3
■ ED EDELEN	Edelen, Edward Joseph "Doc" b: 3/16/12, Bryantown, Md. d: 2/1/82, La Plata, Md. BR/TR, 6', 191 lbs. Deb: 8/20/32																												
1932	Was-A	0	0	—	2	0	0	0	0	1	0	0.0	0	6	54.0	0	0.0	27.00	16	.000	.600	-3	-3	98	41	0.0	0	0	-0.1
■ JOHN EDELMAN	Edelman, John Rogers b: 7/27/35, Philadelphia, Pa. BR/TR, 6'3", 185 lbs. Deb: 6/02/55																												
1955	Mil-N	0	0	—	5	0	0	0	0	6	7	10.5	0	8	12.0	3	4.5	10.50	35	.304	.484	-4	-5	92	67	0.0	0	0	-0.3
■ CHARLIE EDEN	Eden, Charles M. b: 1/18/1855, Lexington, Ky. d: 9/17/20, Cincinnati, Ohio BR/TR, Deb: 8/17/1877																												
1884	Pit-a	0	1	.000	2	1	1	0	0	12	12	9.0	1	3	2.3	3	2.3	6.00	55	.269	.315	-4	-4	101	67	-0.4	1	0	-0.2
1885	Pit-a	1	2	.333	4	1	0	0	0	16	22	12.4	0	3	1.7	5	2.8	5.63	61	.339	.369	-4	-4	107	87	-0.4	0	0	-0.2
Total	2	1	3	.250	6	2	1	0	0	28	34	10.9	1	6	1.9	8	2.6	5.79	58	.311	.346	-8	-7	104	78	-0.8	1	0	-0.4
■ TOM EDENS	Edens, Thomas Patrick b: 6/9/61, Ontario, Ore. BR/TR, 6'3", 185 lbs. Deb: 6/02/87																												
1987	NY-N	0	0	—	2	2	0	0	0	8	15	16.9	2	4	4.5	4	4.5	6.75	59	.417	.452	-2	-2	97	153	0.0	-0	0	-0.1
■ BUTCH EDGE	Edge, Claude Lee b: 7/18/56, Houston, Tex. BR/TR, 6'3", 203 lbs. Deb: 8/13/79																												
1979	Tor-A	3	4	.429	9	9	1	0	0	52	60	10.4	6	24	4.2	19	3.3	5.19	86	.283	.354	-6	-4	106	94	0.5	0	-0	-0.4
■ BILL EDGERTON	Edgerton, William Albert b: 8/16/41, South Bend, Ind. BL/TL, 6'2", 185 lbs. Deb: 9/03/66																												
1966	KC-A	0	1	.000	6	1	0	0	0	8	10	11.3	0	7	7.9	3	3.4	3.38	97	.303	.415	0	-0	95	171	-0.4	0	0	0.0
1967	KC-A	1	0	1.000	7	0	0	0	0	8	11	12.4	1	3	3.4	6	6.8	2.25	146	.324	.385	1	1	102	279	0.5	0	0	0.1
1969	Sea-A	0	1	.000	4	0	0	0	0	4	10	22.5	1	0	0.0	2	4.5	13.50	27	.455	.478	-4	-4	100	86	-0.4	0	0	-0.3
Total	3	1	2	.333	17	1	0	0	0	20	31	13.9	2	10	4.5	11	4.9	4.95	68	.348	.417	-3	-4	99	197	-0.3	0	1	-0.2
■ GEORGE EDMONDSON	Edmondson, George Henderson "Big Ed" b: 5/18/1896, Waxahachie, Tex. d: 7/11/73, Waco, Tex. BR/TR, 6'1", 179 lbs. Deb: 8/15/22																												
1922	Cle-A	0	0	—	2	0	0	0	0	2	4	18.0	0	0	0.0	0	0.0	9.00	46	.444	.444	-1	-1	103	86	0.0	0	0	0.0
1923	Cle-A	0	0	—	1	0	0	0	0	4	8	18.0	0	3	6.8	0	0.0	11.25	35	.444	.545	-3	-3	99	94	0.0	-0	0	-0.2
1924	Cle-A	0	0	—	5	1	0	0	0	8	10	11.3	1	5	5.6	3	3.4	9.00	46	.294	.385	-4	-4	97	61	0.0	0	-0	-0.3
Total	3	0	0	—	8	1	0	0	0	14	22	14.1	1	8	5.1	3	1.9	9.64	42	.361	.443	-9	-9	99	74	0.0	-0	0	-0.5
■ PAUL EDMONDSON	Edmondson, Paul Michael b: 2/12/43, Kansas City, Kan. d: 2/13/70, Santa Barbara, Cal. BR/TR, 6'5", 195 lbs. Deb: 6/20/69																												
1969	Chi-A	1	6	.143	14	13	1	0	0	88	72	7.4	5	39	4.0	46	4.7	3.68	108	.227	.312	-1	3	110	84	-2.2	-1	3	0.6
■ BOB EDMONDSON	Edmondson, Robert E. b: 4/30/1879, Paris, Ky. d: 8/14/31, Lawrence, Kan. BR/TR, 5'11", 185 lbs. Deb: 9/15/06																												
1906	Was-A	0	1	.000	2	1	1	0	0	10	10	9.0	0	2	1.8	0	0.0	4.50	56	.286	.324	-2	-2	94	62	-0.4	0	0	-0.1
■ SAM EDMONSTON	Edmonston, Samuel Sherwood "Big Sam" b: 8/30/1883, Washington, D.C. d: 4/12/79, Corpus Christi, Tex. BL/TL, 5'11.5", 185 lbs. Deb: 6/24/07																												
1907	Was-A	0	0	—	1	0	0	0	0	3	8	24.0	0	1	3.0	0	0.0	9.00	27	.515	.544	-2	-2	94	124	0.0	-0	0	-0.1
■ EDWARDS	Edwards Deb:9/13/1875																												
1875	Atl-n	0	0	—	1																								
■ FOSTER EDWARDS	Edwards, Foster Hamilton "Eddie" b: 9/1/03, Holstein, Iowa d: 1/4/80, Orleans, Mass. BR/TR, 6'3", 175 lbs. Deb: 7/02/25																												
1925	Bos-N	0	0	—	1	0	0	0	0	2	6	27.0	0	1	4.5	1	4.5	9.00	45	.545	.500	-1	-1	95	159	0.0	0	0	0.0
1926	Bos-N	2	0	1.000	3	3	1	0	0	25	20	7.2	0	13	4.7	4	1.4	0.72	465	.230	.320	9	7	88	397	1.0	-1	0	0.6
1927	Bos-N	2	8	.200	29	11	1	0	0	92	95	9.3	2	45	4.4	37	3.6	4.99	75	.274	.346	-11	-13	95	82	-2.4	-2	-1	-1.4
1928	Bos-N	2	1	.667	21	3	2	0	0	49	67	12.3	2	23	4.2	17	3.1	5.69	71	.327	.382	-9	-9	101	98	0.8	-1	0	-0.9
1930	NY-A	0	0	—	2	0	0	0	0	2	5	22.5	0	2	9.0	1	4.5	18.00	23	.500	.583	-3	-3	87	76	0.0	0	0	-0.2
Total	5	6	9	.400	56	17	4	0	0	170	193	10.2	4	84	4.4	60	3.2	4.76	79	.292	.360	-16	-19	96	133	-0.6	-4	-1	-1.9
■ JIM JOE EDWARDS	Edwards, James Corbette "Little Joe" b: 12/14/1894, Banner, Miss. d: 1/19/65, Sarepta, Miss. BR/TL, 6'2", 185 lbs. Deb: 5/14/22																												
1922	Cle-A	3	8	.273	25	7	0	0	0	93	113	10.9	1	40	3.9	44	4.3	4.45	93	.313	.365	-4	-3	103	109	-2.5	-2	-1	-0.5
1923	Cle-A	10	10	.500	38	21	8	1	1	179	200	10.1	5	75	3.8	68	3.4	3.72	106	.286	.347	5	4	99	110	-0.7	-5	-1	0.0
1924	Cle-A	4	3	.571	10	7	5	1	0	57	64	10.1	3	34	5.4	15	2.4	2.84	145	.305	.380	9	8	97	189	0.9	-1	0	0.7
1925	Cle-A	0	3	.000	13	3	1	0	0	36	60	15.0	0	23	5.8	12	3.0	8.25	57	.382	.438	-15	-14	107	91	-1.4	-1	1	-1.2
	Chi-A	1	2	.333	9	4	1	1	0	45	46	9.2	4	23	4.6	20	4.0	4.00	104	.263	.345	2	1	95	104	-0.4	-1	1	0.1
	Yr	1	5	.167	22	7	2	1	0	81	106	11.8	4	46	5.1	32	3.6	5.89	75	.318	.387	-13	-13	100	104	-1.8	-1	2	-1.1
1926	Chi-A	6	9	.400	32	16	8	3	1	142	140	8.9	4	63	4.0	41	2.6	4.18	87	.264	.332	-3	-9	90	86	-1.9	-3	-1	-1.2
1928	Cin-N	2	2	.500	18	1	0	0	2	32	43	12.1	1	20	5.6	11	3.1	7.59	51	.347	.409	-13	-13	97	84	0.0	0	-1	-1.2
Total	6	26	37	.413	145	59	23	6	4	584	666	10.3	18	278	4.3	211	3.3	4.38	91	.295	.359	-19	-26	97	109	-6.0	-13	-1	-3.3
■ SHERMAN EDWARDS	Edwards, Sherman Stanley b: 7/25/09, Mt.Ida, Ark. BR/TR, 6', 165 lbs. Deb: 9/21/34																												
1934	Cin-N	0	0	—	1	0	0	0	0	3	4	12.0	0	1	3.0	1	3.0	3.00	142	.333	.385	0	0	105	174	0.0	-0	0	0.0
■ HARRY EELLS	Eells, Harry Archibald "Slippery" b: 2/14/1881, Ida Grove, Iowa d: 10/15/40, Los Angeles, Cal. BR/TR, 6'1", 195 lbs. Deb: 4/22/06																												
1906	Cle-A	4	5	.444	14	8	6	1	0	86	77	8.1	1	48	5.0	35	3.7	2.62	102	.264	.368	1	0	99	129	-1.0	0	1	0.1
■ WISH EGAN	Egan, Aloysius Jerome b: 6/16/1881, Evart, Mich. d: 4/13/51, Detroit, Mich. 6'3", 185 lbs. Deb: 9/03/02																												
1902	Det-A	0	2	.000	3	3	2	0	0	22	23	9.4	0	6	2.5	0	0.0	2.86	125	.294	.344	2	2	101	111	-0.9	0	1	0.2
1905	StL-N	6	15	.286	23	19	18	0	0	171	189	9.9	2	39	2.1	29	1.5	3.58	79	.312	.363	-11	-14	95	102	-2.7	-3	5	-0.9
1906	StL-N	2	9	.182	16	12	7	0	0	86	97	10.2	3	27	2.8	23	2.4	4.60	59	.315	.374	-19	-18	104	87	-2.6	-2	1	-1.7
Total	3	8	26	.235	42	34	27	0	0	279	309	10.0	5	72	2.3	52	1.7	3.84	75	.312	.365	-28	-30	98	98	-6.2	-5	6	-2.4
■ JIM EGAN	Egan, James K. "Troy Terrier" b: 1858, Ansonia, Conn. d: 9/26/1884, New Haven, Conn. TL, Deb: 5/15/1882																												
1882	Tro-N	4	6	.400	12	10	10	0	0	100	133	12.0	2	24	2.2	20	1.8	4.14	68	.327	.365	-14	-15	98	112	-0.2	-2	0	-1.2
■ RIP EGAN	Egan, John Joseph b: 7/9/1871, Philadelphia, Pa. d: 12/22/50, Cranston, R.I. 5'11", 168 lbs. Deb: 4/30/1894																												
1894	Was-N	0	0	—	1	0	0	0	0	5	8	14.4	1	2	3.6	2	3.6	10.80	49	.385	.439	-3	-3	100	73	0.0	-0	0	-0.1
■ DICK EGAN	Egan, Richard Wallis b: 3/24/37, Berkeley, Cal. BL/TL, 6'4", 193 lbs. Deb: 4/09/63 C																												
1963	Det-A	0	1	.000	20	0	0	0	0	21	25	10.7	4	3	1.3	16	6.9	5.14	73	.287	.304	-4	-3	104	91	-0.4	0	0	-0.2
1964	Det-A	0	0	—	23	0	0	0	2	34	33	8.7	4	17	4.5	21	5.6	4.50	77	.246	.325	-3	-4	95	89	0.0	-0	1	-0.3
1966	Cal-A	0	0	—	11	0	0	0	0	14	17	10.9	2	6	3.9	11	7.1	4.50	76	.309	.365	-2	-2	100	129	0.0	-0	0	-0.1
1967	LA-N	1	1	.500	20	0	0	0	0	32	34	9.6	3	15	4.2	20	5.6	6.19	49	.272	.358	-10	-11	89	77	0.1	-0	-0	-1.1
Total	4	1	2	.333	74	0	0	0	2	101	109	9.7	13	41	3.7	68	6.1	5.17	65	.272	.337	-18	-20	96	91	-0.3	-1	0	-1.7

■ HOWARD EHMKE Ehmke, Howard Jonathan "Bob" b: 4/24/1894, Silver Creek, N.Y. d: 3/17/59, Philadelphia, Pa. BR/TR, 6'3", 190 lbs. Deb: 4/12/15

YEAR	TM/L	W	L	PCT	G	GS	CG	SHO	SV	IP	H	H/G	HR	BB	BB/G	SO	SO/G	ERA	/A	OAVG	OOBP	PR	/A	PF	CPI	WAT	PB	PD	TPI
1915	Buf-F	0	2	.000	18	2	0	0	0	54	69	11.5	2	25	4.2	18	3.0	5.50	56	.325	.409	-15	-15	101	103	-0.9	-2	2	-1.3
1916	Det-A	3	1	.750	5	4	4	0	0	37	34	8.3	0	15	3.6	15	3.6	3.16	92	.252	.327	-1	-1	103	90	0.9	-1	1	0.0
1917	Det-A	10	15	.400	35	25	13	4	2	206	174	7.6	3	88	3.8	90	3.9	2.97	86	.243	.330	-7	-9	96	96	-3.0	3	2	-0.4
1919	Det-A	17	10	.630	33	31	20	2	0	249	255	9.2	5	107	3.9	79	2.9	3.18	94	.274	.353	1	-6	92	113	2.2	4	4	0.0
1920	Det-A	15	18	.455	38	33	23	2	3	268	250	8.4	8	124	4.2	98	3.3	3.26	124	.253	.344	16	23	106	103	2.0	1	6	3.0
1921	Det-A	13	14	.481	30	22	13	1	0	196	220	10.1	15	81	3.7	68	3.1	4.55	90	.286	.354	-6	-10	96	101	0.5	2	1	-0.5
1922	Det-A	17	17	.500	45	30	16	1	1	280	299	9.6	12	101	3.2	108	3.5	4.21	93	.281	.343	-5	-9	97	97	-0.4	-4	1	-1.0
1923	Bos-A	20	17	.541	43	39	28	2	3	317	318	9.0	12	119	3.4	121	3.4	3.78	111	.272	.339	7	15	106	101	**5.3**	-2	5	1.9
1924	Bos-A	19	17	.528	45	36	26	4	4	**315**	324	9.3	9	81	2.3	119	3.4	3.46	128	.265	.308	27	34	105	90	3.7	-3	1	3.3
1925	Bos-A	9	20	.310	34	31	**22**	0	1	261	285	9.8	8	85	2.9	95	3.3	3.72	117	.285	.336	19	19	99	106	0.0	-5	4	1.7
1926	Bos-A	3	10	.231	14	14	7	1	0	97	115	10.7	3	45	4.2	38	3.5	5.47	78	.303	.360	-16	-13	106	88	-1.5	-1	1	-1.1
	Phi-A	12	4	.750	20	18	10	1	0	147	125	7.7	1	50	3.1	55	3.4	2.82	165	.232	.292	20	30	116	84	3.7	-3	0	3.0
	Yr	15	14	.517	34	32	17	2	0	244	240	8.9	4	95	3.5	93	3.4	3.87	116	.260	.317	4	17	112	84	2.2	-1	1	1.9
1927	Phi-A	12	10	.545	30	27	10	1	0	190	200	9.5	13	60	2.8	68	3.2	4.22	93	.281	.336	-2	-6	95	101	-0.9	-1	2	-0.4
1928	Phi-A	9	8	.529	23	18	5	1	0	139	135	8.7	6	44	2.8	34	2.2	3.63	110	.254	.309	6	6	99	88	-1.5	1	0	0.7
1929	Phi-A	7	2	.778	11	8	2	0	0	55	48	7.9	2	15	2.5	20	3.3	3.27	135	.233	.279	6	7	104	74	1.3	-2	0	0.5
1930	Phi-A	0	1	.000	3	1	0	0	0	10	22	19.8	4	2	1.8	4	3.6	11.70	38	.458	.491	-8	-8	96	115	-0.4	0	0	-0.5
Total	15	166	166	.500	427	339	199	20	14	2821	2873	9.2	103	1042	3.3	1030	3.3	3.75	105	.271	.335	44	55	101	98	11.0	-11	32	8.9

■ RED EHRET Ehret, Philip Sydney b: 8/31/1868, Louisville, Ky. d: 7/28/40, Cincinnati, Ohio BR/TR, 6', 175 lbs. Deb: 1888

YEAR	TM/L	W	L	PCT	G	GS	CG	SHO	SV	IP	H	H/G	HR	BB	BB/G	SO	SO/G	ERA	/A	OAVG	OOBP	PR	/A	PF	CPI	WAT	PB	PD	TPI
1888	KC-a	3	2	.600	7	6	5	0	0	52	58	10.0	1	22	3.8	12	2.1	3.98	86	.296	.367	-5	-3	112	107	1.0	-1	0	-0.2
1889	Lou-a	10	29	.256	45	38	35	1	0	364	441	10.9	12	115	2.8	135	3.3	4.80	82	.315	.367	-38	-35	102	91	2.0	2	2	-2.4
1890	Lou-a	25	14	.641	43	38	35	4	2	359	351	8.8	5	79	2.0	174	4.4	2.53	159	.271	.313	53	59	104	**121**	-0.9	-4	-1	5.2
1891	Lou-a	13	13	.500	26	24	23	2	0	221	225	9.2	2	70	2.9	76	3.1	3.46	99	.278	.336	6	-1	92	88	2.7	2	0	0.0
1892	Pit-N	16	20	.444	39	36	32	0	0	316	290	8.3	7	83	2.4	101	2.9	2.65	116	.256	.307	22	15	94	97	-3.3	4	-3	1.4
1893	Pit-N	18	18	.500	39	35	32	**4**	0	314	322	9.2	3	115	3.3	70	2.0	3.44	142	.281	.346	43	51	105	103	-4.6	-7	2	4.0
1894	Pit-N	19	21	.475	46	38	31	1	0	347	441	11.4	12	128	3.3	102	2.6	5.16	98	.332	.391	7	-5	95	95	-1.3	-9	-0	-1.1
1895	StL-N	6	19	.240	37	32	18	0	0	232	360	14.0	11	88	3.4	55	2.1	6.05	81	.376	.429	-33	-30	102	106	-2.8	-3	0	-2.4
1896	Cin-N	18	14	.563	34	33	29	2	0	277	298	9.7	5	74	2.4	60	1.9	3.44	131	.297	.345	28	33	103	100	-1.4	-3	1	2.8
1897	Cin-N	8	10	.444	34	19	11	0	2	184	256	12.5	3	47	2.3	43	2.1	4.79	96	.353	.392	-10	-4	107	103	-2.2	-3	0	-0.4
1898	Lou-N	3	7	.300	12	10	9	0	0	89	130	13.1	3	20	2.0	20	2.0	5.76	61	.364	.398	-21	-22	98	91	-1.7	1	0	-1.7
Total	11	139	167	.454	362	309	260	14	4	2755	3172	10.4	64	841	2.7	848	2.8	4.02	105	.307	.359	53	58	100	101	-12.5	-20	1	5.2

■ RUBE EHRHARDT Ehrhardt, Welton Claude b: 11/20/1894, Beecher, Ill. d: 4/27/80, Chicago Heights, Ill. BR/TR, 6'2", 190 lbs. Deb: 7/18/24

YEAR	TM/L	W	L	PCT	G	GS	CG	SHO	SV	IP	H	H/G	HR	BB	BB/G	SO	SO/G	ERA	/A	OAVG	OOBP	PR	/A	PF	CPI	WAT	PB	PD	TPI
1924	Bro-N	5	3	.625	15	9	6	2	0	84	71	7.6	5	17	1.8	13	1.4	2.25	169	.232	.273	15	14	98	106	0.3	-2	-2	1.1
1925	Bro-N	10	14	.417	36	24	12	0	1	208	239	10.3	10	62	2.7	47	2.0	5.02	81	.293	.333	-17	-22	95	83	-0.8	2	4	-1.5
1926	Bro-N	2	5	.286	44	1	0	0	4	97	101	9.4	5	35	3.2	25	2.3	3.90	99	.275	.319	-1	-0	101	99	-1.3	0	-2	-0.1
1927	Bro-N	3	7	.300	46	3	2	0	2	96	90	8.4	3	37	3.5	22	2.1	3.56	114	.264	.322	4	5	104	103	-1.4	1	3	0.9
1928	Bro-N	1	3	.250	28	2	1	0	2	54	74	12.3	1	27	4.5	12	2.0	4.67	84	.352	.397	-4	-4	99	132	-0.9	0	1	-0.2
1929	Cin-N	1	2	.333	24	1	1	1	1	49	58	10.7	2	22	4.0	9	1.7	4.78	99	.305	.368	-0	-0	101	107	-0.2	-0	1	0.0
Total	6	22	34	.393	193	40	22	3	10	588	633	9.7	26	200	3.1	128	2.0	4.15	97	.284	.331	-4	-7	99	99	-4.3	1	4	0.2

■ HACK EIBEL Eibel, Henry Hack b: 12/6/1893, Brooklyn, N.Y. d: 10/16/45, Macon, Ga. BL/TL, 5'11", 220 lbs. Deb: 6/13/12

YEAR	TM/L	W	L	PCT	G	GS	CG	SHO	SV	IP	H	H/G	HR	BB	BB/G	SO	SO/G	ERA	/A	OAVG	OOBP	PR	/A	PF	CPI	WAT	PB	PD	TPI
1920	Bos-A	0	0	—	3	0	0	0	0	10	10	9.0	0	3	2.7	5	4.5	3.60	102	.270	.325	0	0	97	83	0.0	-0	0	0.0

■ JUAN EICHELBERGER Eichelberger, Juan Tyrone b: 10/21/53, St.Louis, Mo. BR/TR, 6'2", 195 lbs. Deb: 9/07/78

YEAR	TM/L	W	L	PCT	G	GS	CG	SHO	SV	IP	H	H/G	HR	BB	BB/G	SO	SO/G	ERA	/A	OAVG	OOBP	PR	/A	PF	CPI	WAT	PB	PD	TPI
1978	SD-N	0	0	—	3	0	0	0	0	3	4	12.0	0	2	6.0	2	6.0	12.00	28	.267	.353	-3	-3	93	31	0.0	0	0	-0.2
1979	SD-N	1	1	.500	3	3	1	0	0	21	15	6.4	1	11	4.7	12	5.1	3.43	106	.211	.313	1	0	97	83	0.1	1	-0	0.1
1980	SD-N	4	2	.667	15	13	0	0	0	89	73	7.4	8	55	5.6	43	4.3	3.64	93	.233	.342	-0	-3	94	109	1.2	-1	-1	-0.4
1981	SD-N	8	8	.500	25	24	3	1	0	141	136	8.7	5	74	4.7	81	5.2	3.51	94	.259	.346	-0	-3	95	111	1.8	-3	1	-0.4
1982	SD-N	7	14	.333	31	24	8	0	0	178	171	8.6	23	72	3.6	74	3.7	4.20	79	.251	.318	-12	-18	92	95	-3.7	-2	-1	-2.0
1983	Cle-A	4	11	.267	28	15	2	0	0	134	132	8.9	10	59	4.0	56	3.8	4.90	88	.259	.334	-12	-9	106	81	-2.9	0	-1	-0.8
1988	Atl-N	2	0	1.000	20	0	0	0	0	37	44	10.7	3	10	2.4	13	3.2	3.89	95	.297	.327	-2	-1	107	117	1.0	-0	1	0.0
Total	7	26	36	.419	125	79	14	1	0	603	575	8.6	50	283	4.2	281	4.2	4.10	87	.254	.332	-28	-36	97	98	-2.5	-4	-2	-3.7

■ MARK EICHHORN Eichhorn, Mark Anthony b: 11/21/60, San Jose, Cal. BR/TR, 6'4", 200 lbs. Deb: 8/30/82

YEAR	TM/L	W	L	PCT	G	GS	CG	SHO	SV	IP	H	H/G	HR	BB	BB/G	SO	SO/G	ERA	/A	OAVG	OOBP	PR	/A	PF	CPI	WAT	PB	PD	TPI
1982	Tor-A	0	3	.000	7	7	0	0	0	38	40	9.5	4	14	3.3	16	3.8	5.45	82	.260	.316	-6	-4	109	70	-1.4	0	-1	-0.4
1986	Tor-A	14	6	.700	69	0	0	0	10	157	105	6.0	8	45	2.6	166	9.5	1.72	254	.191	.257	**43**	**46**	104	108	3.9	0	2	**4.9**
1987	Tor-A	10	6	.625	**89**	0	0	0	4	128	110	7.7	14	52	3.7	96	6.8	3.16	140	.234	.311	19	18	99	115	0.7	0	2	1.9
1988	Tor-A	0	3	.000	37	0	0	0	1	67	79	10.6	3	27	3.6	28	3.8	4.16	94	.304	.371	-1	-2	99	123	-1.4	0	1	0.0
Total	4	24	18	.571	202	7	0	0	15	390	334	7.7	29	138	3.2	306	7.1	2.98	145	.233	.302	54	59	102	109	1.8	0	4	6.4

■ DAVE EILAND Eiland, David William b: 7/5/66, Dade City, Fla. BR/TR, 6'3", 210 lbs. Deb: 8/03/88

YEAR	TM/L	W	L	PCT	G	GS	CG	SHO	SV	IP	H	H/G	HR	BB	BB/G	SO	SO/G	ERA	/A	OAVG	OOBP	PR	/A	PF	CPI	WAT	PB	PD	TPI
1988	NY-A	0	0	—	3	3	0	0	0	13	15	10.4	6	4	2.8	7	4.8	6.23	61	.294	.368	-3	-4	96	128	0.0	0	0	-0.2

■ DAVE EILERS Eilers, David Louis b: 12/3/36, Oldenburg, Tex. BR/TR, 5'11", 188 lbs. Deb: 7/27/64

YEAR	TM/L	W	L	PCT	G	GS	CG	SHO	SV	IP	H	H/G	HR	BB	BB/G	SO	SO/G	ERA	/A	OAVG	OOBP	PR	/A	PF	CPI	WAT	PB	PD	TPI
1964	Mil-N	0	0	—	6	0	0	0	0	8	11	12.4	1	1	1.1	1	1.1	4.50	75	.333	.351	-1	-1	96	130	0.0	0	-0	0.0
1965	Mil-N	0	0	—	6	0	0	0	0	4	8	18.0	1	0	0.0	1	2.3	11.25	32	.421	.400	-3	-3	103	81	0.0	0	0	-0.2
	NY-N	1	1	.500	11	0	0	0	2	18	20	10.0	2	4	2.0	9	4.5	4.00	92	.274	.325	-1	-1	104	106	0.3	0	-0	0.0
	Yr	1	1	.500	17	0	0	0	2	22	28	11.5	3	4	1.6	10	4.1	5.32	69	.304	.340	-4	-4	104	106	0.3	0	-0	-0.2
1966	NY-N	1	1	.500	23	0	0	0	0	35	39	10.0	7	7	1.8	14	3.6	4.63	75	.287	.320	-4	-4	97	107	0.2	-0	1	-0.3
1967	Hou-N	6	4	.600	35	0	0	0	1	59	68	10.4	3	17	2.6	27	4.1	3.97	81	.296	.342	-4	-5	95	111	1.6	-1	0	-0.5
Total	4	8	6	.571	81	0	0	0	3	124	146	10.6	14	29	2.1	52	3.8	4.43	76	.297	.336	-13	-14	97	109	2.1	-0	0	-1.0

■ JAKE EISENHARDT Eisenhardt, Jacob Henry b: 10/3/22, Perkasie, Pa. BL/TL, 6'3.5", 195 lbs. Deb: 6/10/44

YEAR	TM/L	W	L	PCT	G	GS	CG	SHO	SV	IP	H	H/G	HR	BB	BB/G	SO	SO/G	ERA	/A	OAVG	OOBP	PR	/A	PF	CPI	WAT	PB	PD	TPI
1944	Cin-N	0	0	—	1	0	0	0	0	1	0	0.0	0	1	9.0	0	0.0	0.00	—	.000	.500	0	0	95	0	0.0	0	0	0.0

■ HARRY EISENSTAT Eisenstat, Harry b: 10/10/15, Brooklyn, N.Y. BL/TL, 5'11", 185 lbs. Deb: 5/19/35

YEAR	TM/L	W	L	PCT	G	GS	CG	SHO	SV	IP	H	H/G	HR	BB	BB/G	SO	SO/G	ERA	/A	OAVG	OOBP	PR	/A	PF	CPI	WAT	PB	PD	TPI
1935	Bro-N	0	1	.000	2	0	0	0	0	5	9	16.2	0	2	3.6	2	3.6	12.60	30	.429	.440	-5	-5	95	66	-0.4	-0	1	-0.3
1936	Bro-N	1	2	.333	5	2	1	0	0	14	22	14.1	1	6	3.9	5	3.2	5.79	74	.344	.394	-3	-2	107	110	-0.3	0	0	-0.1
1937	Bro-N	3	3	.500	13	4	0	0	0	48	61	11.4	2	11	2.1	12	2.3	3.94	106	.308	.341	-0	1	107	115	0.5	-1	1	0.1
1938	Det-A	9	6	.600	32	9	5	0	4	125	131	9.4	7	29	2.1	37	2.7	3.74	127	.266	.306	15	14	99	94	1.0	-1	1	1.2
1939	Det-A	2	2	.500	10	2	1	0	0	30	39	11.7	3	9	2.7	6	1.8	6.90	73	.315	.356	-8	-6	110	79	0.0	1	1	-0.3
	Cle-A	6	7	.462	26	11	4	1	2	104	109	9.4	8	23	2.0	38	3.3	3.29	135	.265	.300	15	13	96	110	-1.2	0	-1	1.2
	Yr	8	9	.471	36	13	5	1	2	134	148	9.9	11	32	2.1	44	3.0	4.10	112	.277	.313	8	7	99	110	-1.2	1	-0	0.9
1940	Cle-A	1	4	.200	27	3	0	0	4	72	78	9.8	6	12	1.5	27	3.4	3.13	129	.282	.309	**10**	7	92	129	-1.6	1	-0	0.7
1941	Cle-A	1	1	.500	21	0	0	0	2	34	43	11.4	2	16	4.2	11	2.9	4.24	98	.312	.389	-0	-0	101	133	0.0	1	-1	0.0
1942	Cle-A	2	1	.667	29	1	0	0	2	48	58	10.9	1	6	1.1	19	3.6	2.44	139	.304	.322	7	5	93	161	0.5	0	-0	0.5
Total	8	25	27	.481	165	32	11	1	14	480	550	10.3	30	114	2.1	157	2.9	3.83	113	.287	.324	31	27	99	113	-1.5	1	1	3.0

■ ED EITELJORG Eiteljorg, Edward Henry b: 10/14/1871, Berlin, Germany d: 12/7/42, Greencastle, Ind. 6'2", 190 lbs. Deb: 5/02/1890

YEAR	TM/L	W	L	PCT	G	GS	CG	SHO	SV	IP	H	H/G	HR	BB	BB/G	SO	SO/G	ERA	/A	OAVG	OOBP	PR	/A	PF	CPI	WAT	PB	PD	TPI
1890	Chi-N	0	1	.000	1	1	0	0	0	2	5	22.5	0	1	4.5	1	4.5	22.50	17	.488	.533	-4	-4	107	49	-0.4	-0	0	-0.2
1891	Was-a	1	5	.167	8	7	6	0	0	61	79	11.7	4	41	6.0	23	3.4	6.20	60	.329	.427	-17	-17	101	95	-1.4	-1	0	-1.3
Total	2	1	6	.143	9	8	6	0	0	63	84	12.0	4	42	6.0	24	3.4	6.71	56	.336	.431	-21	-21	101	93	-1.8	-1	0	-1.5

■ HEINIE ELDER Elder, Henry Knox b: 8/23/1890, Seattle, Wash. d: 11/13/58, Long Beach, Cal. BL/TL, 6'2", 200 lbs. Deb: 7/07/13

YEAR	TM/L	W	L	PCT	G	GS	CG	SHO	SV	IP	H	H/G	HR	BB	BB/G	SO	SO/G	ERA	/A	OAVG	OOBP	PR	/A	PF	CPI	WAT	PB	PD	TPI
1913	Det-A	0	0	—	1	0	0	0	0	3	4	12.0	0	5	15.0	0	0.0	9.00	33	.286	.474	-2	-2	101	79	0.0	-0	-0	-0.1

YEAR	TM/L	W	L	PCT	G	GS	CG	SHO	SV	IP	H	H/G	HR	BB	BB/G	SO	SO/G	ERA	/A	OAVG	OOBP	PR	/A	PF	CPI	WAT	PB	PD	TPI
■ **HOD ELLER**	Eller, Horace Owen b: 7/5/1894, Muncie, Ind. d: 7/18/61, Indianapolis, Ind BR/TR, 5'11.5", 185 lbs. Deb: 4/16/17																												
1917	Cin-N	10	5	.667	37	11	7	1	1	152	131	7.8	2	37	2.2	77	4.6	2.37	106	.239	.279	6	2	93	98	2.6	-2	-2	-0.1
1918	Cin-N	16	12	.571	37	22	14	0	1	218	205	8.5	1	59	2.4	84	3.5	2.35	113	.253	.300	10	7	96	113	1.5	-2	-4	0.1
1919	Cin-N	19	9	.679	38	30	16	7	2	248	216	7.8	7	50	1.8	137	**5.0**	2.40	123	.238	.274	14	15	101	96	-0.1	6	-3	2.1
1920	Cin-N	13	12	.520	35	22	15	2	0	210	208	8.9	6	52	2.2	76	3.3	2.96	94	.266	.307	4	-4	88	98	-0.3	2	-1	-0.4
1921	Cin-N	2	2	.500	13	3	0	0	1	34	46	12.2	3	15	4.0	7	1.9	5.03	76	.322	.384	-5	-5	101	109	0.2	0	-1	-0.4
Total	5	60	40	.600	160	88	52	10	5	862	806	8.4	19	213	2.2	381	4.0	2.62	106	.253	.294	29	16	95	101	3.9	5	-11	1.3
■ **JOE ELLICK**	Ellick, Joseph J. b: 4/3/1854, Cincinnati, Ohio d: 4/21/23, Kansas City, Kan. 5'10", 162 lbs. Deb: 5/13/1875 M																												
1878	Mil-N	0	1	.000	1	0	0	0	0	3	1	3.0	0	1	3.0	0	0.0	3.00	87	.110	.198	-0	-0	114	22	-0.4	-0	0	0.0
■ **BRUCE ELLINGSEN**	Ellingsen, Harold Bruce b: 4/26/49, Pocatello, Idaho BL/TL, 6', 180 lbs. Deb: 7/04/74																												
1974	Cle-A	1	1	.500	16	2	0	0	0	42	45	9.6	5	17	3.6	16	3.4	3.21	114	.278	.335	2	2	101	140	0.0	0	0	0.2
■ **CLAUDE ELLIOTT**	Elliott, Claude Judson "Chaucer" or "Old Pardee" b: 11/17/1879, Pardeeville, Wis. d: 6/21/23, Pardeeville, Wis. BR/TR, 6', 190 lbs. Deb: 04																												
1904	Cin-N	3	1	.750	9	6	4	1	0	58	53	8.2	1	23	3.6	19	2.9	2.95	103	.272	.360	-1	1	111	107	0.8	1	0	0.1
	NY-N	0	1	.000	3	1	1	0	0	15	21	12.6	2	3	1.8	8	4.8	3.00	91	.357	.388	-0	-0	100	189	-0.4	0	-1	0.0
	Yr	3	2	.600	12	7	5	1	0	73	74	9.1	3	26	3.2	27	3.3	2.96	101	.287	.352	-2	0	109	189	0.4	1	-1	0.1
1905	NY-N	0	1	.000	10	2	2	0	**6**	38	41	9.7	3	12	2.8	20	4.7	4.03	71	.305	.366	-4	-5	96	104	-0.4	-0	0	-0.4
Total	2	3	3	.500	22	9	7	1	6	111	115	9.3	6	38	3.1	47	3.8	3.32	89	.296	.366	-6	-5	104	117	0.0	1	-0	-0.3
■ **HAL ELLIOTT**	Elliott, Harold William b: 5/29/1899, Mt.Clemens, Mich. d: 4/25/63, Honolulu, Hawaii BR/TR, 6'1.5", 170 lbs. Deb: 4/19/29																												
1929	Phi-N	3	7	.300	40	8	2	0	2	114	146	11.5	5	59	4.7	32	2.5	6.08	87	.398	.468	-17	-10	112	127	-1.7	-1	1	-0.8
1930	Phi-N	6	11	.353	**48**	11	2	0	0	117	191	14.7	7	58	4.5	37	2.8	7.69	71	.382	.431	-35	-29	109	100	0.2	-3	1	-2.5
1931	Phi-N	0	2	.000	16	4	0	0	2	33	46	12.5	5	19	5.2	8	2.2	9.55	44	.338	.420	-21	-20	109	76	-0.9	-0	0	-1.7
1932	Phi-N	2	4	.333	16	7	0	0	0	58	70	10.9	5	38	5.9	13	2.0	5.74	75	.297	.393	-12	-9	111	98	-1.0	-0	-1	-0.9
Total	4	11	24	.314	120	30	4	0	4	322	453	12.7	22	174	4.9	90	2.5	6.96	73	.366	.434	-85	-68	110	107	-3.4	-5	2	-5.9
■ **GLENN ELLIOTT**	Elliott, Herbert Glenn "Lefty" b: 11/11/19, Sapulpa, Okla d: 7/27/69, Portland, Ore. BB/TL, 5'10", 170 lbs. Deb: 4/17/47																												
1947	Bos-N	0	1	.000	11	0	0	0	1	19	18	8.5	4	11	5.2	8	3.8	4.74	82	.269	.363	-1	-2	95	121	-0.4	0	0	0.0
1948	Bos-N	1	0	1.000	1	1	0	0	0	3	5	15.0	0	1	3.0	2	6.0	3.00	130	.357	.400	0	0	99	202	0.5	-0	0	0.0
1949	Bos-N	3	4	.429	22	6	1	0	0	68	70	9.3	7	27	3.6	15	2.0	3.97	98	.269	.333	1	-0	97	109	-0.3	-1	1	0.0
Total	3	4	5	.444	34	7	1	0	1	90	93	9.3	11	39	3.9	25	2.5	4.10	95	.273	.342	-1	-2	97	115	-0.2	-1	1	0.0
■ **JUMBO ELLIOTT**	Elliott, James Thomas b: 10/22/1900, St.Louis, Mo. d: 1/7/70, Terre Haute, Ind. BR/TL, 6'3", 235 lbs. Deb: 4/21/23																												
1923	StL-A	0	0	—	1	0	0	0	0	1	1	9.0	0	3	27.0	0	0.0	27.00	15	.333	.571	-3	-3	105	46	0.0	0	0	-0.1
1925	Bro-N	0	2	.000	3	1	0	0	0	11	17	13.9	0	9	7.4	3	2.5	8.18	50	.362	.474	-5	-5	95	92	-0.9	-1	-0	-0.4
1927	Bro-N	6	13	.316	30	21	12	2	3	188	188	9.0	5	60	2.9	99	4.7	3.30	123	.269	.316	13	16	104	104	-2.6	-2	-4	1.1
1928	Bro-N	9	14	.391	41	21	7	2	1	192	194	9.1	8	64	3.0	74	3.5	3.89	101	.268	.324	2	1	99	91	-2.8	2	-3	0.0
1929	Bro-N	1	2	.333	6	3	0	0	0	19	21	9.9	2	16	7.6	7	3.3	6.63	68	.280	.404	-4	-4	96	90	-0.3	0	-0	-0.3
1930	Bro-N	10	7	.588	35	21	6	2	1	198	204	9.3	16	70	3.2	59	2.7	3.95	124	.271	.329	22	21	99	104	0.6	-2	-3	1.5
1931	Phi-N	**19**	14	.576	**52**	30	12	2	5	249	288	10.4	15	83	3.0	99	3.6	4.27	99	.287	.342	-11	-2	109	101	5.1	-7	-5	-1.1
1932	Phi-N	11	10	.524	39	22	8	0	0	166	210	11.4	14	47	2.5	62	3.4	5.42	80	.300	.343	-28	-20	111	87	0.4	-1	-2	-2.0
1933	Phi-N	6	10	.375	35	21	6	0	2	162	188	10.4	8	49	2.7	43	2.4	3.83	105	.295	.340	-9	4	121	111	-0.3	-0	-4	0.1
1934	Phi-N	0	1	.000	3	1	0	0	0	5	8	14.4	0	4	7.2	1	1.8	10.80	42	.333	.448	-4	-4	111	66	-0.4	-0	-0	-0.3
	Bos-N	1	1	.500	7	3	0	0	0	15	19	11.4	2	9	5.4	6	3.6	6.00	58	.284	.377	-3	-4	86	93	0.0	0	-0	-0.3
	Yr	1	2	.333	10	4	0	0	0	20	27	12.1	2	13	5.8	7	3.1	7.20	52	.293	.387	-7	-8	92	93	-0.4	-0	-0	-0.6
Total	10	63	74	.460	252	144	51	8	12	1206	1338	10.0	70	414	3.1	453	3.4	4.25	101	.283	.337	-30	3	106	99	-1.2	-9	-21	-1.8
■ **DOCK ELLIS**	Ellis, Dock Phillip b: 3/11/45, Los Angeles, Cal. BB/TR, 6'3", 205 lbs. Deb: 6/18/68																												
1968	Pit-N	6	5	.545	26	10	2	0	0	104	82	7.1	4	38	3.3	52	4.5	2.51	119	.213	.284	6	6	100	89	0.6	-1	0	0.5
1969	Pit-N	11	17	.393	35	33	8	2	0	219	206	8.5	14	76	3.1	173	7.1	3.58	94	.250	.312	1	-5	94	94	-4.3	-3	1	-0.7
1970	Pit-N	13	10	.565	30	30	9	4	0	202	194	8.6	9	87	3.9	128	5.7	3.21	121	.257	.337	19	15	96	**119**	0.5	-3	2	1.4
1971	Pit-N	19	9	.679	31	31	11	2	0	227	207	8.2	15	63	2.5	137	5.4	3.05	110	.239	.288	11	8	97	91	3.2	2	0	1.2
1972	Pit-N	15	7	.682	25	25	4	1	0	163	156	8.6	6	33	1.8	96	5.3	2.71	128	.253	.290	14	14	100	103	2.0	-1	-1	1.3
1973	Pit-N	12	14	.462	28	28	3	1	0	192	176	8.3	7	55	2.6	122	5.7	3.05	110	.240	.295	13	7	92	87	-0.9	-2	1	0.5
1974	Pit-N	12	9	.571	26	26	9	0	0	177	163	8.3	13	41	2.1	91	4.6	3.15	111	.242	.289	9	7	97	91	0.7	3	-1	0.9
1975	Pit-N	8	9	.471	27	24	5	2	0	140	163	10.5	9	43	2.8	69	4.4	3.79	93	.292	.337	-2	-4	98	112	-1.5	0	-1	-0.4
1976	NY-A	17	8	.680	32	32	8	1	0	212	195	8.3	14	76	3.2	65	2.8	3.18	108	.247	.310	8	6	97	104	2.6	0	-3	0.3
1977	NY-A	1	1	.500	3	3	1	0	0	20	18	8.1	1	8	3.6	5	2.3	1.80	219	.237	.306	5	5	97	162	-0.1	0	-0	0.5
	Oak-A	1	5	.167	7	7	0	0	0	26	35	12.1	5	14	4.8	11	3.8	9.69	41	.315	.391	-16	-17	97	69	-1.6	0	-0	-1.4
	Tex-A	10	6	.625	23	22	7	1	1	167	158	8.5	13	42	2.3	90	4.9	2.91	145	.254	.292	22	24	104	111	0.9	0	-1	2.4
	Yr	12	12	.500	33	32	8	1	1	213	211	8.9	19	64	2.7	106	4.5	3.63	114	.260	.306	10	12	102	111	-0.8	0	-2	1.5
1978	Tex-A	9	7	.563	22	22	3	0	0	141	131	8.4	15	46	2.9	45	2.9	4.21	86	.245	.302	-7	-9	96	80	0.5	0	0	-0.9
1979	Tex-A	1	5	.167	10	9	0	0	0	47	64	12.3	5	16	3.1	10	1.9	5.94	71	.323	.372	-9	-9	99	94	-1.9	0	-0	-0.8
	NY-N	3	7	.300	17	14	1	0	0	85	110	11.6	9	34	3.6	41	4.3	6.04	60	.320	.371	-22	-23	96	93	-1.1	-1	0	-2.2
	Pit-N	0	0	—	3	1	0	0	0	7	9	11.6	1	2	2.6	1	1.3	2.57	151	.346	.379	1	1	104	245	0.0	-0	0	0.1
	Yr	3	7	.300	20	15	1	0	0	92	119	11.6	10	36	3.5	42	4.1	5.77	63	.316	.369	-21	-22	97	245	-1.1	-1	0	-2.1
Total	12	138	119	.537	345	317	71	14	1	2129	2067	8.7	140	674	2.8	1136	4.8	3.45	103	.255	.310	51	25	97	99	-0.4	-6	-2	2.7
■ **JIM ELLIS**	Ellis, James Russell b: 3/25/45, Tulare, Cal. BR/TL, 6'2", 185 lbs. Deb: 8/11/67																												
1967	Chi-N	1	1	.500	8	1	0	0	0	17	20	10.6	1	9	4.8	8	4.2	3.18	106	.313	.387	0	0	100	172	0.0	0	-0	0.0
1969	StL-N	0	0	—	2	1	0	0	0	5	7	12.6	0	3	5.4	0	0.0	1.80	198	.318	.400	1	1	99	297	0.0	0	-0	0.1
Total	2	1	1	.500	10	2	0	0	0	22	27	11.0	1	12	4.9	8	3.3	2.86	120	.314	.390	1	1	100	200	0.0	0	-0	0.1
■ **SAMMY ELLIS**	Ellis, Samuel Joseph b: 2/11/41, Youngstown, Ohio BL/TR, 6'1", 175 lbs. Deb: 4/14/62 C																												
1962	Cin-N	2	2	.500	8	4	0	0	0	28	29	9.3	6	29	9.3	27	8.7	6.75	59	.269	.421	-9	-9	100	103	-0.3	0	-0	-0.8
1964	Cin-N	10	3	.769	52	5	2	0	14	122	101	7.5	9	28	2.1	125	9.2	2.58	139	.223	.266	13	14	102	95	3.2	-0	0	1.5
1965	Cin-N	22	10	.688	44	39	15	2	2	264	222	7.6	22	104	3.5	183	6.2	3.78	95	.226	.302	-7	-5	102	82	5.7	-1	-3	-0.8
1966	Cin-N	12	19	.387	41	36	7	0	0	221	226	9.2	35	78	3.2	154	6.3	5.29	78	.264	.320	-41	-29	114	83	-3.3	-3	-3	-3.3
1967	Cin-N	8	11	.421	32	27	8	1	0	176	197	10.1	18	67	3.4	80	4.1	3.84	96	.286	.349	-9	-3	109	**123**	-2.2	-2	-1	-0.6
1968	Cal-A	9	10	.474	42	24	3	0	2	164	150	8.2	22	56	3.1	93	5.1	3.95	72	.244	.305	-18	-20	96	96	1.1	-3	-2	-2.6
1969	Chi-A	0	3	.000	10	5	0	0	0	29	42	13.0	6	16	5.0	15	4.7	5.90	67	.336	.410	-7	-6	110	126	-1.4	0	-0	-0.5
Total	7	63	58	.521	229	140	35	3	18	1004	967	8.7	118	378	3.4	677	6.1	4.15	87	.253	.318	-78	-59	105	95	2.8	-9	-8	-7.1
■ **GEORGE ELLISON**	Ellison, George Russell b: 1/24/1895, California d: 1/20/78, San Francisco, Cal BR/TR, 6'3", 185 lbs. Deb: 8/21/20																												
1920	Cle-A	0	0	—	1	0	0	0	0	1	0	0.0	0	2	18.0	1	9.0	0.00	—	.000	.400	0	0	100	0	0.0	0	0	0.1
■ **DICK ELLSWORTH**	Ellsworth, Richard Clark b: 3/22/40, Lusk, Wyo. BL/TL, 6'3.5", 180 lbs. Deb: 6/22/58																												
1958	Chi-N	0	1	.000	1	1	0	0	0	2	4	18.0	0	3	13.5	0	0.0	18.00	22	.364	.533	-3	-3	101	61	-0.4	-0	0	-0.2
1960	Chi-N	7	13	.350	31	27	6	0	0	177	170	8.6	12	72	3.7	94	4.8	3.71	102	.257	.328	1	1	101	102	-1.1	-3	-0	-0.1
1961	Chi-N	10	11	.476	37	31	7	1	0	187	213	10.3	23	48	2.3	91	4.4	3.85	107	.292	.330	4	5	102	121	1.2	-5	3	0.4
1962	Chi-N	9	20	.310	37	33	6	0	1	209	241	10.4	23	77	3.3	113	4.9	5.08	84	.291	.351	-26	-19	109	95	-2.4	1	0	-1.5
1963	Chi-N	22	10	.688	37	37	19	4	0	291	223	6.9	14	75	2.3	185	5.7	2.10	**165**	.210	.259	38	**44**	105	93	6.7	-2	2	**5.2**
1964	Chi-N	14	18	.438	37	36	16	1	0	257	267	9.4	34	71	2.5	148	5.2	3.75	100	.266	.312	-6	0	106	110	-1.2	-6	2	-0.2
1965	Chi-N	14	15	.483	36	34	8	0	1	222	227	9.2	22	57	2.3	130	5.3	3.81	96	.265	.309	-7	-4	103	99	1.2	-2	2	-0.3
1966	Chi-N	8	22	.267	38	37	9	0	0	269	321	10.7	28	51	1.7	144	4.8	3.98	93	.294	.322	-11	-8	103	108	-4.5	-0	2	-0.6
1967	Phi-N	6	7	.462	32	21	3	1	0	125	152	10.9	6	36	2.6	45	3.2	4.39	80	.306	.352	-14	-12	104	105	-0.5	-1	1	-1.2
1968	Bos-A	16	7	.696	31	28	10	1	0	196	196	9.0	16	37	1.7	106	4.9	3.03	99	.260	.297	-1	-1	101	111	4.4	-4	-0	-0.5
1969	Bos-A	0	0	—	2	2	0	0	0	12	16	12.0	1	4	3.0	4	3.0	3.75	101	.320	.370	-0	0	105	140	0.0	-0	0	0.0

YEAR	TM/L	W	L	PCT	G	GS	CG	SHO	SV	IP	H	H/G	HR	BB	BB/G	SO	SO/G	ERA	/A	OAVG	OOBP	PR	/A	PF	CPI	WAT	PB	PD	TPI
	Cle-A	6	9	.400	34	22	3	1	0	135	162	10.8	10	40	2.7	48	3.2	4.13	84	.301	.349	-8	-10	96	112	0.2	-1	0	-1.0
	Yr	6	9	.400	36	24	3	1	0	147	178	10.9	11	44	2.7	52	3.2	4.10	86	.302	.351	-8	-10	97	112	0.2	-0	0	-1.0
1970	Cle-A	3	3	.500	29	1	0	0	2	44	49	10.0	4	14	2.9	13	2.7	4.50	95	.299	.346	-4	-1	115	106	0.2	-1	1	0.0
	Mil-A	0	0	—	14	0	0	0	1	16	11	6.2	0	3	1.7	9	5.1	1.69	220	.196	.246	4	4	100	76	0.0	0	0	0.4
	Yr	3	3	.500	43	1	0	0	3	60	60	9.0	4	17	2.6	22	3.3	3.75	110	.269	.317	-0	3	111	76	0.2	-1	1	0.4
1971	Mil-A	0	1	.000	11	0	0	0	0	15	22	13.2	1	7	4.2	10	6.0	4.80	75	.361	.417	-2	-2	104	141	-0.4	-0	-0	-0.2
Total	13	115	137	.456	407	310	87	9	5	2157	2274	9.5	194	595	2.5	1140	4.8	3.71	99	.272	.318	-36	-5	104	105	3.4	-25	12	0.2
■ STEVE ELLSWORTH	Ellsworth, Steven Clark b: 7/30/60, Chicago, Ill. BR/TR, 6'8", 220 lbs. Deb: 4/07/88																												
1988	Bos-A	1	6	.143	8	7	0	0	0	36	47	11.8	7	16	4.0	16	4.0	6.75	64	.315	.381	-11	-10	108	97	-2.5	0	-0	-0.9
■ DON ELSTON	Elston, Donald Ray b: 4/6/29, Campbellstown, Ohio BR/TR, 6', 165 lbs. Deb: 9/17/53																												
1953	Chi-N	0	1	.000	2	1	0	0	0	5	11	19.8	1	0	0.0	2	3.6	14.40	32	.458	.440	-6	-5	106	71	-0.4	-0	0	-0.4
1957	Bro-N	0	0	—	1	0	0	0	0	1	1	9.0	0	0	0.0	1	9.0	0.00	—	.250	.250	0	0	114	0	0.0	0	0	0.1
	Chi-N	6	7	.462	39	14	2	0	8	144	139	8.7	15	55	3.4	102	6.4	3.56	107	.259	.328	5	4	98	113	0.7	-2	0	0.2
	Yr	6	7	.462	40	14	2	0	8	145	140	8.7	15	55	3.4	103	6.4	3.54	107	.259	.327	5	4	98	113	0.7	0	0	0.3
1958	Chi-N	9	8	.529	**69**	0	0	0	10	97	75	7.0	9	39	3.6	84	7.8	2.88	138	.214	.287	**12**	**12**	101	95	1.1	1	1	1.5
1959	Chi-N	10	8	.556	**65**	0	0	0	13	98	77	7.1	11	46	4.2	82	7.5	3.31	118	.218	.305	7	6	99	101	1.4	0	-0	0.6
1960	Chi-N	8	9	.471	60	0	0	0	11	127	109	7.7	17	55	3.9	85	6.0	3.40	111	.231	.307	5	5	101	109	1.2	-1	-2	0.3
1961	Chi-N	6	7	.462	58	0	0	0	8	93	108	10.5	11	45	4.4	59	5.7	5.61	73	.297	.378	-16	-16	102	98	0.6	-0	0	-1.4
1962	Chi-N	4	8	.333	57	0	0	0	8	66	57	7.8	6	32	4.4	37	5.0	2.45	174	.247	.327	11	13	109	162	-0.4	-1	1	1.4
1963	Chi-N	4	1	.800	51	0	0	0	4	70	57	7.3	6	21	2.7	41	5.3	2.83	122	.226	.286	4	5	105	101	1.5	-0	-1	0.4
1964	Chi-N	2	5	.286	48	0	0	0	1	54	68	11.3	4	34	5.7	26	4.3	5.33	71	.330	.404	-11	-9	106	122	-1.3	-0	1	-0.8
Total	9	49	54	.476	450	15	2	0	63	755	702	8.4	80	327	3.9	519	6.2	3.70	105	.251	.326	11	16	102	110	4.4	-4	2	1.9
■ BONES ELY	Ely, Frederick William b: 6/7/1863, N.Girard, Pa. d: 1/10/52, Berkeley, Cal. BR/TR, 6'1", 155 lbs. Deb: 6/19/1884																												
1884	Buf-N	0	1	.000	1	1	0	0	0	5	17	30.6	1	5	9.0	4	7.2	14.40	22	.556	.619	-6	-6	105	127	-0.4	-1	0	-0.4
1886	Lou-a	0	4	.000	6	4	4	0	**1**	44	53	10.8	0	26	5.3	28	5.7	5.32	70	.309	.400	-9	-8	108	97	-1.9	-1	0	-0.7
1890	Syr-a	0	0	—	1	0	0	0	0	2	7	31.5	0	0	0.0	0	0.0	22.50	16	.571	.571	-4	-4	92	66	0.0	0	0	-0.2
1894	StL-N	0	0	—	1	0	0	0	0	1	0	0.0	0	3	27.0	0	0.0	0.00	—	.000	.540	1	1	103	0	0.0	0	0	0.0
Total	4	0	5	.000	9	5	4	0	1	52	77	13.3	1	34	5.9	32	5.5	6.75	55	.355	.442	-19	-18	107	97	-2.3	-2	0	-1.3
■ HARRY ELY	Ely, Harry Deb: 9/24/1892																												
1892	Bal-N	0	1	.000	1	1	1	0	0	7	14	18.0	0	7	9.0	0	0.0	7.71	44	.429	.530	-3	-3	102	127	-0.4	-0	0	-0.2
■ RED EMBREE	Embree, Charles Willard b: 8/30/17, El Monte, Cal. BR/TR, 6', 165 lbs. Deb: 9/10/41																												
1941	Cle-A	0	1	.000	1	1	0	0	0	4	7	15.8	0	3	6.8	4	9.0	6.75	62	.438	.524	-1	-1	101	152	-0.4	-0	0	0.0
1942	Cle-A	3	4	.429	19	6	2	0	0	63	58	8.3	0	31	4.4	44	6.3	3.86	88	.242	.330	-1	-3	93	83	-0.3	-0	-0	-0.3
1944	Cle-A	0	1	.000	3	1	0	0	0	3	2	6.0	0	5	15.0	4	12.0	15.00	23	.167	.412	-4	-4	101	27	-0.4	0	0	-0.3
1945	Cle-A	4	4	.500	8	8	5	1	0	70	56	7.2	3	26	3.3	42	5.4	1.93	172	.215	.281	11	11	98	120	0.0	-1	1	1.3
1946	Cle-A	8	12	.400	28	26	8	0	0	200	170	7.7	15	79	3.6	87	3.9	3.47	91	.227	.297	1	-7	90	83	-1.0	1	-1	-0.7
1947	Cle-A	8	10	.444	27	21	6	0	0	163	137	7.6	13	67	3.7	56	3.1	3.15	111	.233	.306	10	6	94	105	-1.3	-1	1	0.5
1948	NY-A	5	3	.625	20	8	4	0	0	77	77	9.0	6	30	3.5	25	2.9	3.74	110	.261	.328	5	3	96	107	0.2	-1	-1	0.1
1949	StL-A	3	13	.188	35	19	4	0	1	127	146	10.3	13	89	6.3	24	1.7	5.39	81	.294	.395	-17	-14	104	108	-3.8	-1	-1	-1.4
Total	8	31	48	.392	141	90	29	1	1	707	653	8.3	50	330	4.2	286	3.6	3.72	97	.246	.325	4	-10	95	99	-7.0	-3	-2	-0.8
■ SLIM EMBREY	Embrey, Charles Akin b: 8/17/01, Columbia, Tenn. d: 10/10/47, Nashville, Tenn. BR/TR, 6'2", 184 lbs. Deb: 10/01/23																												
1923	Chi-A	0	0	—	1	0	0	0	0	3	7	21.0	0	2	6.0	1	3.0	9.00	44	.500	.500	-2	-2	99	130	0.0	0	0	0.0
■ CHARLIE EMIG	Emig, Charles H. b: Bellevue, Ky. Deb: 9/04/1896																												
1896	Lou-N	0	1	.000	1	1	1	0	0	8	12	13.5	1	7	7.9	1	1.1	7.88	56	.370	.482	-3	-3	102	102	-0.4	-1	0	-0.2
■ SLIM EMMERICH	Emmerich, William Peter b: 9/29/19, Allentown, Pa. BR/TR, 6'1", 170 lbs. Deb: 5/14/45																												
1945	NY-N	4	4	.500	31	7	1	0	0	100	111	10.0	8	33	3.0	27	2.4	4.86	78	.278	.328	-12	-12	100	86	0.0	-2	-0	-1.2
1946	NY-N	0	0	—	2	0	0	0	0	4	6	13.5	1	0	0.0	1	2.3	4.50	78	.400	.375	-0	-0	103	171	0.0	0	0	0.0
Total	2	4	4	.500	33	7	1	0	0	104	117	10.1	9	33	2.9	28	2.4	4.85	78	.282	.330	-12	-12	100	89	0.0	-2	-0	-1.2
■ BOB EMSLIE	Emslie, Robert Daniel b: 1/27/1859, Guelph, Ont., Can. d: 4/26/43, St.Thomas, Ont., Canada BR/TR, 5'11", Deb: 1883 U																												
1883	Bal-a	9	13	.409	24	23	21	1	0	201	188	8.4	3	41	1.8	62	2.8	3.18	118	.253	.292	3	12	113	89	2.3	-4	0	0.9
1884	Bal-a	32	17	.653	50	50	50	4	0	455	419	8.3	6	88	1.7	264	5.2	2.75	115	.253	.290	25	21	98	106	5.9	-3	-1	1.6
1885	Bal-a	3	10	.231	13	13	11	0	0	107	131	11.0	2	30	2.5	27	2.3	4.29	83	.314	.360	-12	-9	109	106	-2.6	-0	0	-0.6
	Phi-a	0	4	.000	4	4	3	0	0	29	37	11.5	0	6	1.9	9	2.8	6.52	51	.323	.356	-11	-10	102	68	-1.9	-1	0	-0.8
	Yr	3	14	.176	17	17	14	0	0	136	168	11.1	2	36	2.4	36	2.4	4.76	73	.316	.359	-23	-19	108	68	-4.5	-0	0	-1.4
Total	3	44	44	.500	91	90	85	5	0	792	775	8.8	11	165	1.9	362	4.1	3.20	105	.264	.303	5	14	103	100	3.7	-8	-1	1.1
■ JOE ENGEL	Engel, Joseph William b: 3/12/1893, Washington, D.C. d: 6/12/69, Chattanooga, Tenn BR/TL, 6'1.5", 183 lbs. Deb: 5/30/12																												
1912	Was-A	2	5	.286	17	10	2	0	1	75	70	8.4	2	50	6.0	29	3.5	3.96	82	.253	.375	-5	-6	97	103	-1.8	-1	1	-0.4
1913	Was-A	8	9	.471	36	24	6	2	0	165	124	6.8	2	85	4.6	70	3.8	3.05	101	.207	.317	-2	0	105	73	-1.7	-5	-1	0.0
1914	Was-A	7	5	.583	35	15	1	0	3	124	108	7.8	2	75	5.4	41	3.0	2.98	92	.254	.372	-3	-3	100	125	0.8	1	-0	-0.3
1915	Was-A	0	3	.000	11	3	0	0	0	34	30	7.9	0	19	5.0	9	2.4	3.18	92	.261	.380	-1	-1	99	122	-1.4	-1	1	0.0
1917	Cin-N	0	1	.000	1	1	1	0	0	8	12	13.5	0	6	6.8	2	2.3	5.63	45	.353	.429	-3	-3	93	120	-0.4	-0	0	-0.2
1919	Cle-A	0	0	—	1	0	0	0	0	0	0	—	0	3	—	0	—	∞	—	—	1.000	-2	-2	104	46	0.0	0	0	-0.1
1920	Was-A	0	0	—	1	0	0	0	0	2	0	0.0	0	4	18.0	0	0.0	18.00	20	.000	.556	-3	-3	96	32	0.0	-0	0	-0.2
Total	7	17	23	.425	102	53	10	2	4	408	344	7.6	6	242	5.3	151	3.3	3.38	88	.237	.354	-19	-18	101	99	-4.5	-6	0	-1.2
■ STEVE ENGEL	Engel, Steven Michael b: 12/31/61, Cincinnati, Ohio BR/TL, 6'3", 216 lbs. Deb: 7/30/85																												
1985	Chi-N	1	5	.167	11	8	1	0	1	52	61	10.6	10	26	4.5	29	5.0	5.54	76	.298	.367	-11	-8	117	108	-1.9	2	0	-0.5
■ RICK ENGLE	Engle, Richard Douglas b: 4/7/57, Corbin, Ky. BR/TL, 5'11.5", 181 lbs. Deb: 9/02/81																												
1981	Mon-N	0	0	—	1	0	0	0	0	2	6	27.0	0	1	4.5	2	9.0	18.00	19	.500	.538	-3	-3	98	72	0.0	0	0	-0.2
■ JACK ENRIGHT	Enright, Jackson Percy b: 11/29/1895, Fort Worth, Tex. d: 8/18/75, Pompano Beach, Fla BR/TR, 5'11", 177 lbs. Deb: 9/26/17																												
1917	NY-A	0	1	.000	1	1	0	0	0	5	5	9.0	0	3	5.4	1	1.8	5.40	53	.294	.400	-2	-1	107	81	-0.4	-0	1	0.0
■ TERRY ENYART	Enyart, Terry Gene b: 10/10/50, Ironton, Ohio BR/TL, 6'2", 190 lbs. Deb: 6/17/74																												
1974	Mon-N	0	0	—	2	0	0	0	0	2	4	18.0	0	4	18.0	2	9.0	13.50	28	.444	.615	-2	-2	104	98	0.0	0	-0	-0.1
■ JOHNNY ENZMANN	Enzmann, John "Gentleman John" b: 3/4/1890, Brooklyn, N.Y. d: 3/14/84, Riverhead, N.Y. BR/TR, 5'10", 165 lbs. Deb: 7/10/14																												
1914	Bro-N	1	0	1.000	7	1	0	0	0	19	21	9.9	1	8	3.8	5	2.4	4.74	59	.300	.381	-4	-4	101	103	0.5	-1	1	-0.3
1918	Cle-A	5	7	.417	30	14	8	0	2	137	130	8.5	2	29	1.9	38	2.5	2.36	125	.263	.301	6	9	107	114	-1.7	-3	0	0.8
1919	Cle-A	3	2	.600	14	4	2	0	0	55	67	11.0	0	8	1.3	13	2.1	2.29	147	.312	.342	6	7	104	161	0.0	-0	-1	0.5
1920	Phi-N	2	3	.400	16	1	1	0	0	59	79	12.1	1	16	2.4	35	5.3	3.81	92	.320	.370	-4	-2	112	118	0.0	1	0	0.0
Total	4	11	12	.478	67	20	11	0	2	270	297	9.9	4	61	2.0	91	3.0	2.83	111	.289	.332	3	9	107	124	-1.2	-3	-0	1.0
■ AL EPPERLY	Epperly, Albert Paul "Tub" or "Pard" b: 5/7/18, Glidden, Iowa BL/TR, 6'2", 194 lbs. Deb: 4/25/38																												
1938	Chi-N	2	0	1.000	9	4	1	0	0	27	28	9.3	1	15	5.0	10	3.3	3.67	106	.264	.352	0	1	103	112	1.0	1	0	0.2
1950	Bro-N	0	0	—	5	0	0	0	0	9	14	14.0	1	5	5.0	3	3.0	5.00	87	.378	.432	-1	-1	104	160	0.0	0	-0	0.0
Total	2	2	0	1.000	14	4	1	0	0	36	42	10.5	2	20	5.0	13	3.3	4.00	100	.294	.373	-0	-0	103	124	1.0	1	0	0.2
■ GREG ERARDI	Erardi, Joseph Gregory b: 5/31/54, Syracuse, N.Y. BR/TR, 6'1", 190 lbs. Deb: 9/06/77																												
1977	Sea-A	0	1	.000	5	0	0	0	0	9	12	12.0	3	6	6.0	5	5.0	6.00	67	.300	.391	-2	-2	98	124	-0.4	0	0	-0.1

■ **EDDIE ERAUTT** Erautt, Edward Lorenz Sebastian b: 9/26/24, Portland, Ore. BR/TR, 5'11.5", 185 lbs. Deb: 4/16/47

YEAR	TM/L	W	L	PCT	G	GS	CG	SHO	SV	IP	H	H/G	HR	BB	BB/G	SO	SO/G	ERA	/A	OAVG	OOBP	PR	/A	PF	CPI	WAT	PB	PD	TPI
1947	Cin-N	4	9	.308	36	10	2	0	0	119	146	11.0	5	53	4.0	43	3.3	5.07	74	.307	.375	-13	-17	92	99	-2.3	-1	1	-1.6
1948	Cin-N	0	0	—	2	0	0	0	0	3	3	9.0	0	1	3.0	0	0.0	6.00	70	.250	.308	-1	-1	106	46	0.0	0	0	0.0
1949	Cin-N	4	11	.267	39	9	1	0	1	113	99	7.9	9	61	4.9	43	3.4	3.35	118	.247	.339	**9**	8	98	124	-2.6	1	-1	0.8
1950	Cin-N	4	2	.667	33	2	1	0	1	65	82	11.4	9	22	3.0	35	4.8	5.68	77	.307	.369	-11	-9	106	100	1.3	0	-0	-0.8
1951	Cin-N	0	0	—	30	0	0	0	0	39	50	11.5	4	23	5.3	20	4.6	5.77	70	.314	.404	-8	-7	103	109	0.0	-0	1	-0.6
1953	Cin-N	0	0	—	4	0	0	0	0	5	11	19.8	1	3	5.4	1	1.8	5.40	80	.500	.560	-1	-1	100	239	0.0	-0	0	0.0
	StL-N	3	1	.750	20	1	0	0	0	36	43	10.8	6	16	4.0	15	3.8	6.25	69	.299	.377	-8	-8	101	94	0.9	-0	0	-0.6
	Yr	3	1	.750	24	1	0	0	0	41	54	11.9	7	19	4.2	16	3.5	6.15	70	.325	.401	-8	-8	101	94	0.9	-0	0	-0.6
Total	6	15	23	.395	164	22	4	0	2	380	434	10.3	34	179	4.2	157	3.7	4.86	83	.293	.369	-33	-35	98	109	-2.7	-1	1	-2.8

■ **DON ERICKSON** Erickson, Don Lee b: 12/13/31, Springfield, Ill. BR/TR, 6', 175 lbs. Deb: 9/01/58

YEAR	TM/L	W	L	PCT	G	GS	CG	SHO	SV	IP	H	H/G	HR	BB	BB/G	SO	SO/G	ERA	/A	OAVG	OOBP	PR	/A	PF	CPI	WAT	PB	PD	TPI
1958	Phi-N	0	1	.000	9	0	0	0	1	12	11	8.3	3	9	6.8	9	6.8	4.50	88	.244	.364	-1	-1	100	125	-0.4	-0	-0	0.0

■ **ERIC ERICKSON** Erickson, Eric George Adolph b: 3/13/1895, Goteborg, Sweden d: 5/19/65, Jamestown, N.Y. BR/TR, 6'2", 190 lbs. Deb: 10/06/14

YEAR	TM/L	W	L	PCT	G	GS	CG	SHO	SV	IP	H	H/G	HR	BB	BB/G	SO	SO/G	ERA	/A	OAVG	OOBP	PR	/A	PF	CPI	WAT	PB	PD	TPI
1914	NY-N	0	1	.000	1	1	0	0	0	5	8	14.4	0	3	5.4	3	5.4	0.00	—	.364	.407	2	1	94	0	-0.4	-0	-0	0.1
1916	Det-A	0	0	—	8	0	0	0	0	16	13	7.3	0	8	4.5	7	3.9	2.81	103	.220	.324	0	0	103	87	0.0	-1	-1	0.0
1918	Det-A	4	5	.444	12	9	8	0	1	94	81	7.8	2	29	2.8	48	4.6	2.49	110	.240	.301	3	3	99	98	0.1	-3	-3	-0.2
1919	Det-A	0	2	.000	3	2	0	0	0	15	17	10.2	0	10	6.0	4	2.4	6.60	45	.293	.406	-6	-6	92	71	-0.9	-0	0	-0.5
	Was-A	6	11	.353	20	15	7	1	0	132	130	8.9	7	63	4.3	86	5.9	3.95	81	.254	.344	-11	-11	99	88	-1.0	-1	-3	-1.5
	Yr	6	13	.316	23	17	7	1	0	147	147	9.0	7	73	4.5	90	**5.5**	4.22	75	.258	.349	-16	-17	98	88	-1.9	-0	-2	-2.0
1920	Was-A	12	16	.429	39	27	12	0	1	239	231	8.7	13	128	4.8	87	3.3	3.84	95	.264	.365	-1	-5	96	105	-0.6	4	-4	-0.4
1921	Was-A	8	10	.444	32	22	9	3	0	179	181	9.1	7	65	3.3	71	3.6	3.62	117	.269	.330	13	12	99	102	-1.4	-4	-3	0.5
1922	Was-A	4	12	.250	30	17	6	2	2	142	144	9.1	8	73	4.6	61	3.9	4.94	76	.279	.354	-14	-19	93	90	-3.7	-2	-2	-2.1
Total	7	34	57	.374	145	93	42	6	4	822	805	8.8	37	379	4.1	367	4.0	3.85	93	.264	.345	-14	-24	97	97	-7.9	-6	-15	-4.1

■ **HAL ERICKSON** Erickson, Harold James b: 7/17/19, Portland, Ore. BR/TR, 6'5", 230 lbs. Deb: 4/14/53

YEAR	TM/L	W	L	PCT	G	GS	CG	SHO	SV	IP	H	H/G	HR	BB	BB/G	SO	SO/G	ERA	/A	OAVG	OOBP	PR	/A	PF	CPI	WAT	PB	PD	TPI
1953	Det-A	0	1	.000	18	0	0	0	1	32	43	12.1	4	10	2.8	19	5.3	4.78	85	.323	.372	-3	-3	102	123	-0.4	-1	-0	-0.2

■ **PAUL ERICKSON** Erickson, Paul Walford "Li'L Abner" b: 12/14/15, Zion, Ohio BR/TR, 6'2", 200 lbs. Deb: 6/29/41

YEAR	TM/L	W	L	PCT	G	GS	CG	SHO	SV	IP	H	H/G	HR	BB	BB/G	SO	SO/G	ERA	/A	OAVG	OOBP	PR	/A	PF	CPI	WAT	PB	PD	TPI
1941	Chi-N	5	7	.417	32	15	7	1	1	141	126	8.0	2	64	4.1	85	5.4	3.70	92	.234	.312	-1	-5	94	78	-0.4	1	-1	-0.5
1942	Chi-N	1	6	.143	18	7	1	0	0	63	70	10.0	4	41	5.9	26	3.7	5.43	60	.288	.384	-15	-15	98	96	-2.3	-1	0	-1.5
1943	Chi-N	1	3	.250	15	4	0	0	0	43	47	9.8	4	22	4.6	24	5.0	6.07	55	.280	.364	-13	-13	98	80	-0.9	0	-0	-1.3
1944	Chi-N	5	9	.357	33	15	5	3	1	124	113	8.2	5	67	4.9	82	6.0	3.56	102	.243	.329	1	1	100	100	-1.9	-1	2	0.1
1945	Chi-N	7	4	.636	28	9	3	0	3	108	94	7.8	5	48	4.0	53	4.4	3.33	108	.233	.319	6	3	95	99	0.0	0	-0	0.3
1946	Chi-N	9	7	.563	32	14	5	1	0	137	119	7.8	2	65	4.3	70	4.6	2.43	131	.232	.314	15	11	93	113	0.5	-4	-1	0.7
1947	Chi-N	7	12	.368	40	20	6	0	1	174	179	9.3	17	93	4.8	82	4.2	4.34	97	.268	.356	-5	-2	104	107	-1.8	3	0	0.1
1948	Chi-N	0	0	—	3	0	0	0	0	6	7	10.5	0	6	9.0	4	6.0	6.00	63	.292	.419	-1	-1	95	97	0.0	-0	0	-0.1
	Phi-N	2	0	1.000	4	2	0	0	0	17	19	10.1	2	17	9.0	5	2.6	5.29	72	.292	.434	-3	-3	97	128	1.0	-0	0	-0.2
	NY-N	0	0	—	2	0	0	0	0	1	0	0.0	0	2	18.0	1	9.0	0.00	—	.000	.400	0	0	98	0	0.0	0	0	0.0
	Yr	2	0	1.000	9	2	0	0	0	24	26	9.8	2	25	9.4	10	3.8	5.25	73	.283	.429	-3	-4	96	0	1.0	-0	0	-0.3
Total	8	37	48	.435	207	86	27	5	6	814	774	8.6	41	425	4.7	432	4.8	3.86	93	.250	.338	-16	-24	98	99	-5.8	-2	-0	-2.4

■ **RALPH ERICKSON** Erickson, Ralph Lief b: 6/25/04, Dubois, Idaho BL/TL, 6'1", 175 lbs. Deb: 9/11/29

YEAR	TM/L	W	L	PCT	G	GS	CG	SHO	SV	IP	H	H/G	HR	BB	BB/G	SO	SO/G	ERA	/A	OAVG	OOBP	PR	/A	PF	CPI	WAT	PB	PD	TPI
1929	Pit-N	0	0	—	1	0	0	0	0	1	2	18.0	0	2	18.0	0	0.0	27.00	18	.500	.667	-2	-2	102	56	0.0	0	0	-0.1
1930	Pit-N	1	0	1.000	7	0	0	0	0	14	21	13.5	1	10	6.4	2	1.3	7.07	69	.375	.437	-3	-3	98	115	0.5	-0	0	-0.2
Total	2	1	0	1.000	8	0	0	0	0	15	23	13.8	1	12	7.2	2	1.2	8.40	58	.383	.455	-6	-6	98	111	0.5	-0	0	-0.3

■ **ROGER ERICKSON** Erickson, Roger Farrell b: 8/30/56, Springfield, Ill. BR/TR, 6'3", 180 lbs. Deb: 4/06/78

YEAR	TM/L	W	L	PCT	G	GS	CG	SHO	SV	IP	H	H/G	HR	BB	BB/G	SO	SO/G	ERA	/A	OAVG	OOBP	PR	/A	PF	CPI	WAT	PB	PD	TPI
1978	Min-A	14	13	.519	37	37	14	0	0	266	268	9.1	19	79	2.7	121	4.1	3.96	90	.263	.317	-5	-12	94	90	2.0	0	0	-1.1
1979	Min-A	3	10	.231	24	21	0	0	0	123	154	11.3	17	48	3.5	47	3.4	5.63	81	.310	.365	-19	-14	108	100	-3.6	0	-0	-1.3
1980	Min-A	7	13	.350	32	27	7	0	0	191	198	9.3	13	56	2.6	97	4.6	3.25	136	.268	.318	17	25	109	112	-2.9	0	0	2.6
1981	Min-A	3	8	.273	14	14	1	0	0	91	93	9.2	7	31	3.1	44	4.4	3.86	101	.262	.311	-2	0	107	95	-1.5	0	-0	0.0
1982	Min-A	4	3	.571	7	7	2	0	0	41	56	12.3	6	12	2.6	12	2.6	4.83	86	.326	.367	-3	-3	102	123	1.2	0	1	-0.2
	NY-A	4	5	.444	16	11	0	0	1	71	86	10.9	5	17	2.2	37	4.7	4.44	89	.301	.334	-3	-4	97	100	-0.3	0	-1	-0.4
	Yr	8	8	.500	23	18	2	0	1	112	142	11.4	11	29	2.3	49	3.9	4.58	88	.308	.345	-6	-7	98	100	0.9	0	-1	-0.6
1983	NY-A	0	1	.000	5	0	0	0	0	17	13	6.9	1	8	4.2	7	3.7	4.24	94	.213	.304	-0	-0	98	66	-0.4	0	0	0.0
Total	6	35	53	.398	135	117	24	0	1	800	868	9.8	68	251	2.8	365	4.1	4.13	98	.277	.328	-16	-9	102	99	-5.5	0	-1	-0.4

■ **DICK ERRICKSON** Errickson, Richard Merriwell "Lief" b: 3/5/14, Vineland, N.J. BL/TR, 6'1", 175 lbs. Deb: 4/27/38

YEAR	TM/L	W	L	PCT	G	GS	CG	SHO	SV	IP	H	H/G	HR	BB	BB/G	SO	SO/G	ERA	/A	OAVG	OOBP	PR	/A	PF	CPI	WAT	PB	PD	TPI
1938	Bos-N	9	7	.563	34	10	6	1	6	123	113	8.3	1	56	4.1	40	2.9	3.15	107	.246	.326	9	3	89	102	1.0	-1	2	0.3
1939	Bos-N	6	9	.400	28	11	3	0	1	128	143	10.1	6	54	3.8	33	2.3	4.01	91	.293	.354	-1	-5	93	115	-0.2	1	2	-0.2
1940	Bos-N	12	13	.480	34	29	17	3	4	236	241	9.2	8	90	3.4	34	1.3	3.17	123	.270	.333	18	19	101	**124**	1.3	-3	1	1.8
1941	Bos-N	6	12	.333	38	23	5	2	1	166	192	10.4	12	62	3.4	45	2.4	4.77	73	.287	.348	-21	-24	96	96	-1.6	-0	0	-2.3
1942	Bos-N	2	5	.286	21	4	0	0	1	59	76	11.6	8	20	3.1	15	2.3	5.03	65	.309	.361	-11	-12	98	109	-0.9	-1	-1	-1.3
	Chi-N	1	1	.500	13	0	0	0	0	24	39	14.6	1	8	3.0	9	3.4	4.13	78	.411	.436	-2	-2	98	186	0.1	-1	1	-0.1
	Yr	3	6	.333	34	4	0	0	1	83	115	12.5	9	28	3.0	24	2.6	4.77	68	.337	.383	-13	-14	98	186	-0.8	-1	-0	-1.4
Total	5	36	47	.434	168	77	31	6	13	736	804	9.8	36	290	3.5	176	2.2	3.85	93	.282	.345	-9	-21	96	113	-0.3	-5	5	-1.8

■ **CARL ERSKINE** Erskine, Carl Daniel "Oisk" b: 12/13/26, Anderson, Ind. BR/TR, 5'10", 165 lbs. Deb: 7/25/48

YEAR	TM/L	W	L	PCT	G	GS	CG	SHO	SV	IP	H	H/G	HR	BB	BB/G	SO	SO/G	ERA	/A	OAVG	OOBP	PR	/A	PF	CPI	WAT	PB	PD	TPI
1948	Bro-N	6	3	.667	17	9	3	0	0	64	51	7.2	5	35	4.9	29	4.1	3.23	126	.231	.331	5	6	103	117	1.3	-2	-1	0.3
1949	Bro-N	8	1	.889	22	3	2	0	0	80	68	7.6	6	51	5.7	49	5.5	4.61	85	.235	.348	-5	-6	98	88	3.2	-2	0	-0.6
1950	Bro-N	7	6	.538	22	13	3	0	1	103	109	9.5	15	35	3.1	50	4.4	4.72	92	.273	.329	-7	-4	104	97	-0.4	1	-1	-0.3
1951	Bro-N	16	12	.571	46	19	7	0	4	190	206	9.8	23	78	3.7	95	4.5	4.45	84	.280	.345	-10	-15	95	107	-1.2	-2	-0	-1.6
1952	Bro-N	14	6	.700	33	26	10	4	2	207	167	7.3	17	71	3.1	131	5.7	2.70	136	.220	.287	24	22	98	105	2.2	-0	2	2.6
1953	Bro-N	20	6	**.769**	39	33	16	4	3	247	213	7.8	21	95	3.5	187	6.8	3.53	121	.230	.302	21	20	100	89	4.1	0	-2	1.8
1954	Bro-N	18	15	.545	38	37	12	2	1	260	239	8.3	31	92	3.2	166	5.7	4.15	99	.243	.305	-2	-2	101	84	-1.7	-1	-0	-0.2
1955	Bro-N	11	8	.579	31	29	7	2	1	195	185	8.5	29	64	3.0	84	3.9	3.78	108	.253	.308	5	6	101	104	-0.9	-0	-2	0.4
1956	Bro-N	13	11	.542	31	28	8	1	0	186	189	9.1	25	57	2.8	95	4.6	4.26	89	.264	.313	-10	-10	100	93	-1.3	-3	0	-1.2
1957	Bro-N	5	3	.625	15	7	1	0	0	66	62	8.5	8	20	2.7	26	3.5	3.55	125	.248	.299	2	7	114	99	0.7	-2	-1	0.4
1958	LA-N	4	4	.500	31	9	2	1	0	98	115	10.6	14	35	3.2	54	5.0	5.14	82	.297	.344	-13	-10	106	99	0.3	-3	1	-1.1
1959	LA-N	0	3	.000	10	3	0	0	1	23	33	12.9	5	13	5.1	15	5.9	7.83	51	.320	.393	-10	-10	101	89	-1.4	-1	-0	-0.9
Total	12	122	78	.610	335	216	71	14	13	1719	1637	8.6	199	646	3.4	981	5.1	3.99	101	.252	.316	0	4	101	97	4.9	-13	-4	-0.4

■ **CHICO ESCARREGA** Escarrega, Ernesto (Acosta) b: 12/27/49, Los Mochis, Mex. BR/TR, 5'11", 185 lbs. Deb: 4/26/82

YEAR	TM/L	W	L	PCT	G	GS	CG	SHO	SV	IP	H	H/G	HR	BB	BB/G	SO	SO/G	ERA	/A	OAVG	OOBP	PR	/A	PF	CPI	WAT	PB	PD	TPI
1982	Chi-A	1	3	.250	38	2	0	0	1	74	73	8.9	3	16	1.9	33	4.0	3.65	108	.263	.297	4	2	97	86	-1.0	0	-0	0.2

■ **DUKE ESPER** Esper, Charles H. b: 7/28/1868, Salem, N.J. d: 8/31/10, Philadelphia, Pa. TL, 5'11.5", 185 lbs. Deb: 4/18/1890

YEAR	TM/L	W	L	PCT	G	GS	CG	SHO	SV	IP	H	H/G	HR	BB	BB/G	SO	SO/G	ERA	/A	OAVG	OOBP	PR	/A	PF	CPI	WAT	PB	PD	TPI
1890	Phi-a	8	9	.471	18	16	14	1	0	144	176	11.0	1	67	4.2	61	3.8	4.94	79	.318	.391	-17	-16	101	100	1.0	4	0	-1.0
	Pit-N	0	2	.000	2	2	2	0	0	17	18	9.5	0	9	4.8	12	6.4	5.29	64	.288	.377	-3	-4	95	73	-0.9	-1	0	-0.2
	Phi-N	5	0	1.000	5	5	4	0	0	41	40	8.8	1	17	3.7	15	3.3	3.07	124	.271	.346	2	3	107	108	2.5	-1	0	0.2
	Yr	5	2	.714	7	7	6	0	0	58	58	9.0	1	26	4.0	27	4.2	3.72	99	.276	.356	-1	-0	103	108	1.6	-1	0	0.0
1891	Phi-N	20	15	.571	39	36	25	1	1	296	302	9.2	8	121	3.7	108	3.3	3.56	90	.278	.350	-7	-12	95	93	3.3	2	0	-0.8
1892	Phi-N	11	6	.647	21	18	14	0	1	160	171	9.6	2	58	3.3	45	2.5	3.43	98	.287	.350	-3	-1	103	103	1.7	1	0	0.1
	Pit-N	2	0	1.000	3	3	1	0	0	18	18	9.0	0	12	6.0	5	2.5	5.50	56	.273	.385	-4	-5	94	71	1.0	-1	0	-0.4
	Yr	13	6	.684	24	21	15	0	1	178	189	9.6	2	70	3.5	50	2.5	3.64	92	.285	.354	-7	-6	102	71	2.7	1	0	-0.3
1893	Was-N	12	28	.300	42	36	34	0	0	334	442	11.9	14	156	4.2	78	2.1	4.72	91	.335	.405	-1	-16	92	**118**	-0.8	9	2	-0.5
1894	Was-N	5	10	.333	19	15	7	0	0	122	191	14.1	8	40	3.0	27	2.0	7.52	71	.380	.426	-30	-30	100	87	-0.1	2	0	-2.0
	Bal-N	10	2	.833	16	9	8	0	2	102	107	9.4	1	36	3.2	25	2.2	3.88	132	.291	.354	16	14	96	91	2.9	-0	0	1.1

YEAR	TM/L	W	L	PCT	G	GS	CG	SHO	SV	IP	H	H/G	HR	BB	BB/G	SO	SO/G	ERA	/A	OAVG	OOBP	PR	/A	PF	CPI	WAT	PB	PD	TPI
	Yr	15	12	.556	35	24	15	0	2	224	298	12.0	9	76	3.1	52	2.1	5.87	89	.343	.395	-13	-16	98	91	2.8	2	0	-0.9
1895	Bal-N	10	12	.455	34	25	16	1	1	218	248	10.2	2	79	3.3	39	1.6	3.92	127	.306	.368	21	25	104	103	-3.9	-7	0	1.6
1896	Bal-N	14	5	.737	20	18	14	1	0	156	168	9.7	3	39	2.3	19	1.1	3.58	120	.297	.342	14	13	99	95	1.4	-2	0	0.9
1897	StL-N	1	6	.143	8	8	7	0	0	61	95	14.0	4	12	1.8	8	1.2	5.31	80	.379	.407	-7	-7	99	112	-1.2	1	0	-0.4
1898	StL-N	3	5	.375	10	8	6	0	0	65	86	11.9	1	22	3.0	14	1.9	6.09	65	.342	.394	-18	-15	110	78	0.7	2	0	-1.1
Total	9	101	100	.502	237	199	152	4	5	1734	2062	10.7	45	668	3.5	456	2.4	4.41	94	.313	.377	-37	-49	98	100	7.6	8	2	-2.5
■ **NINO ESPINOSA**	Espinosa, Arnulfo Acevedo (born Arnulfo Acevedo (Espinosa)) b: 8/15/53, Villa Altagracia, D.R. d: 12/24/87, Santo Domingo, D.R. BR/TR, 6'1", 192 lbs. Deb: 9/13/74																												
1974	NY-N	0	0	—	2	1	0	0	0	9	12	12.0	1	0	0.0	2	2.0	5.00	73	.324	.308	-1	-1	100	93	0.0	0	0	0.0
1975	NY-N	0	1	.000	2	0	0	0	0	3	8	24.0	0	1	3.0	2	6.0	18.00	19	.471	.500	-5	-5	95	59	-0.4	0	0	-0.4
1976	NY-N	4	4	.500	12	5	0	0	0	42	41	8.8	3	13	2.8	30	6.4	3.64	87	.265	.309	-1	-2	91	100	-0.1	-1	-1	-0.3
1977	NY-N	10	13	.435	32	29	7	1	0	200	188	8.5	17	55	2.5	105	4.7	3.42	111	.249	.301	11	8	97	95	0.9	-1	-0	0.6
1978	NY-N	11	15	.423	32	32	6	1	0	204	230	10.1	24	75	3.3	76	3.4	4.72	75	.292	.347	-26	-26	99	104	0.4	2	2	-2.2
1979	Phi-N	14	12	.538	33	33	8	3	0	212	211	9.0	20	65	2.8	88	3.7	3.65	100	.262	.317	2	-0	97	101	0.6	2	0	0.1
1980	Phi-N	3	5	.375	12	12	1	0	0	76	73	8.6	9	19	2.3	13	1.5	3.79	101	.250	.297	-2	0	106	91	-1.3	-1	-0	0.0
1981	Phi-N	2	5	.286	14	14	2	0	0	74	98	11.9	11	24	2.9	22	2.7	6.08	64	.333	.376	-21	-18	112	102	-1.6	-0	-1	-1.8
	Tor-A	0	0	—	1	0	0	0	0	1	4	36.0	0	0	0.0	0	0.0	9.00	46	.667	.667	-1	-1	113	207	0.0	0	0	0.0
Total	8	44	55	.444	140	126	24	5	0	821	865	9.5	85	252	2.8	338	3.7	4.17	88	.275	.325	-43	-45	100	99	-1.5	1	0	-4.0
■ **MARK ESSER**	Esser, Mark Gerald b: 4/1/56, Erie, Pa. BR/TL, 6'1", 190 lbs. Deb: 4/22/79																												
1979	Chi-A	0	0	—	2	0	0	0	0	2	2	9.0	0	4	18.0	1	4.5	13.50	32	.286	.545	-2	-2	103	63	0.0	0	0	-0.1
■ **BILL ESSICK**	Essick, William Earl "Vinegar Bill" b: 12/18/1881, Grand Ridge, Ill. d: 10/12/51, Los Angeles, Cal. TR, Deb: 9/12/06																												
1906	Cin-N	2	2	.500	6	4	3	0	0	39	39	9.0	1	16	3.7	16	3.7	3.00	102	.292	.376	-2	0	116	121	0.3	-1	-1	0.0
1907	Cin-N	0	2	.000	3	2	2	0	0	22	23	9.4	0	8	3.3	7	2.9	2.86	82	.302	.376	-1	-1	95	120	-0.9	-1	1	0.0
Total	2	2	4	.333	9	6	5	0	0	61	62	9.1	1	24	3.5	23	3.4	2.95	95	.296	.376	-3	-1	109	121	-0.6	-2	-0	0.0
■ **DICK ESTELLE**	Estelle, Richard Henry b: 1/18/42, Lakewood, N.J. BB/TL, 6'2", 170 lbs. Deb: 9/04/64																												
1964	SF-N	1	2	.333	6	6	0	0	0	42	39	8.4	3	23	4.9	23	4.9	3.00	117	.247	.335	3	2	99	130	-0.5	-1	-1	0.1
1965	SF-N	0	0	—	6	1	0	0	0	11	12	9.8	0	8	6.5	6	4.9	4.09	94	.261	.375	-1	-0	109	106	0.0	0	0	0.0
Total	2	1	2	.333	12	7	0	0	0	53	51	8.7	3	31	5.3	29	4.9	3.23	111	.250	.344	2	2	101	125	-0.5	-0	-1	0.1
■ **GEORGE ESTOCK**	Estock, George John b: 11/2/24, Stirling, N.J. BR/TR, 6', 185 lbs. Deb: 4/21/51																												
1951	Bos-N	0	1	.000	37	1	0	0	3	60	56	8.4	2	37	5.6	11	1.7	4.35	88	.258	.354	-3	-3	97	95	-0.4	1	0	-0.2
■ **CHUCK ESTRADA**	Estrada, Charles Leonard b: 2/15/38, San Luis Obispo, Cal. BR/TR, 6'1", 185 lbs. Deb: 4/21/60 C																												
1960	Bal-A	**18**	11	.621	36	25	12	1	2	209	162	**7.0**	18	101	4.3	144	6.2	3.57	109	**.218**	.315	7	7	101	92	1.8	-0	-0	0.7
1961	Bal-A	15	9	.625	33	31	6	1	0	212	159	**6.8**	19	132	5.6	160	6.8	3.69	104	**.207**	.326	8	4	96	91	1.3	-3	-2	-0.1
1962	Bal-A	9	17	.346	34	33	6	0	0	223	199	8.0	24	121	4.9	165	6.7	3.83	98	.240	.339	3	-2	95	107	-3.9	-0	-3	-0.4
1963	Bal-A	3	2	.600	8	7	0	0	0	31	26	7.5	2	19	5.5	16	4.6	4.65	73	.226	.333	-3	-4	93	77	0.4	-1	-0	-0.5
1964	Bal-A	3	2	.600	17	6	0	0	0	55	62	10.1	8	21	3.4	32	5.2	5.24	72	.282	.344	-10	-9	103	94	0.0	-1	-1	-1.0
1966	Chi-N	1	1	.500	9	1	0	0	0	12	16	12.0	2	5	3.8	3	2.3	7.50	49	.314	.373	-5	-5	103	82	0.2	-0	-0	-0.5
1967	NY-N	1	2	.333	9	2	0	0	0	22	28	11.5	5	17	7.0	15	6.1	9.41	37	.326	.434	-15	-15	102	84	-0.1	-1	-0	-1.4
Total	7	50	44	.532	146	105	24	2	2	764	652	7.7	78	416	4.9	535	6.3	4.08	93	.232	.333	-15	-23	98	95	-0.3	-5	-7	-3.2
■ **OSCAR ESTRADA**	Estrada, Oscar b: 2/15/04, Havana, Cuba d: 1/2/78, Havana, Cuba BL/TL, 5'8", 160 lbs. Deb: 4/21/29																												
1929	StL-A	0	0	—	1	0	0	0	0	1	1	9.0	0	1	9.0	0	0.0	0.00	—	.250	.400	0	0	100	0	0.0	0	0	0.1
■ **JOHN EUBANK**	Eubank, John Franklin "Honest John" b: 9/9/1872, Servia, Ind. d: 11/3/58, Bellevue, Mich. BR/TR, 6'2", 215 lbs. Deb: 9/19/05																												
1905	Det-A	1	0	1.000	3	2	0	0	0	17	13	6.9	0	3	1.6	1	0.5	2.12	125	.234	.273	1	1	100	78	0.5	1	-1	0.0
1906	Det-A	4	10	.286	24	12	7	1	2	135	147	9.8	0	35	2.3	38	2.5	3.53	84	.303	.350	-13	-8	110	96	-2.9	-1	1	-0.7
1907	Det-A	3	3	.500	15	8	4	1	0	81	88	9.8	0	20	2.2	17	1.9	2.67	93	.302	.347	-1	-2	98	121	-0.5	-1	1	0.0
Total	3	8	13	.381	42	22	11	2	2	233	248	9.6	0	58	2.2	56	2.2	3.13	89	.298	.344	-13	-9	105	104	-2.9	-1	1	-0.7
■ **UEL EUBANKS**	Eubanks, Uel Melvin "Poss" b: 2/14/03, Quinlan, Tex. d: 11/21/54, Dallas, Tex. BR/TR, 6'3", 175 lbs. Deb: 7/20/22																												
1922	Chi-N	0	0	—	2	0	0	0	0	2	5	22.5	0	4	18.0	1	4.5	22.50	17	.556	.563	-4	-4	96	76	0.0	1	0	-0.2
■ **FRANK EUFEMIA**	Eufemia, Frank Anthony b: 12/23/59, Bronx, N.Y. BR/TR, 5'11", 185 lbs. Deb: 5/21/85																												
1985	Min-A	4	2	.667	39	0	0	0	2	62	56	8.1	7	21	3.0	30	4.4	3.77	114	.250	.308	3	4	104	102	1.1	0	1	0.4
■ **CHICK EVANS**	Evans, Charles Franklin b: 10/15/1889, Arlington, Vt. d: 9/2/16, Schenectady, N.Y. BR/TR, Deb: 09																												
1909	Bos-N	0	3	.000	4	3	1	0	0	22	25	10.2	0	14	5.7	11	4.5	4.50	59	.305	.406	-5	-5	102	107	-1.4	-1	0	-0.4
1910	Bos-N	1	1	.500	13	1	0	0	2	31	28	8.1	1	27	7.8	12	3.5	5.23	69	.275	.439	-8	-6	118	101	0.2	-1	0	-0.5
Total	2	1	4	.200	17	4	1	0	2	53	53	9.0	1	41	7.0	23	3.9	4.92	65	.288	.425	-12	-10	111	104	-1.2	-2	0	-0.9
■ **JAKE EVANS**	Evans, Jacob "Bloody Jake" b: Baltimore, Md. d: 2/3/07, Baltimore, Md. TR, 5'8", 154 lbs. Deb: 1879																												
1880	Tro-N	0	0	—	1	0	0	0	0	4	11	24.8	0	0	0.0	0	0.0	13.50	20	.503	.503	-5	-5	112	80	0.0	0	0	-0.3
1882	Wor-N	0	1	.000	1	1	1	0	0	8	13	14.6	1	0	0.0	2	2.3	5.63	55	.373	.373	-2	-2	107	111	-0.4	-0	0	-0.1
1883	Cle-N	0	0	—	1	0	0	0	0	3	0	0.0	0	0	0.0	1	3.0	0.00		.000	.000	1	1	104	0	0.0	-0	0	0.1
Total	3	0	1	.000	3	1	1	0	0	15	24	14.4	1	0	0.0	3	1.8	6.60	46	.370	.370	-6	-6	108	80	-0.4	-0	0	-0.3
■ **ROY EVANS**	Evans, Roy b: 3/19/1874, Knoxville, Tenn. d: 8/15/15, Galveston, Tex. BR/TR, 6', 180 lbs. Deb: 5/15/1897																												
1897	StL-N	0	0	—	3	0	0	0	0	13	33	22.8	1	13	9.0	4	2.8	9.69	44	.499	.581	-8	-8	99	136	0.0	0	0	-0.5
	Lou-N	5	4	.556	9	8	6	0	0	59	66	10.1	4	24	3.7	20	3.1	4.12	102	.305	.374	1	1	97	106	1.2	-2	0	0.0
	Yr	5	4	.556	12	8	6	0	0	72	99	12.4	5	37	4.6	24	3.0	5.13	82	.350	.425	-6	-7	98	106	1.2	0	0	-0.5
1898	Was-N	3	3	.500	7	6	4	0	0	51	50	8.8	0	25	4.4	11	1.9	3.35	112	.278	.366	1	2	105	101	0.8	-2	0	0.0
1899	Was-N	3	4	.429	7	7	6	0	0	54	60	10.0	1	25	4.2	27	4.5	5.67	67	.305	.384	-11	-11	98	72	0.4	-1	0	-0.9
1902	NY-N	8	11	.421	23	17	17	0	0	176	186	9.5	2	58	3.0	48	2.5	3.17	91	.294	.354	-8	-5	104	104	1.1	-2	2	-0.3
	Bro-N	5	6	.455	13	11	11	2	0	97	91	8.4	0	33	3.1	35	3.2	2.69	97	.270	.335	1	-1	94	99	-0.9	3	-3	-0.3
	Yr	13	17	.433	36	28	28	2	0	273	277	9.1	2	91	3.0	83	2.7	3.00	93	.286	.347	-7	-6	100	99	0.2	-2	-2	-0.6
1903	Bro-N	5	9	.357	15	12	9	0	0	110	121	9.9	1	41	3.4	42	3.4	3.27	102	.309	.385	-0	1	102	117	-2.2	-0	-2	0.0
	StL-A	0	4	.000	7	7	4	0	0	54	66	11.0	1	14	2.3	24	4.0	4.17	68	.325	.368	-7	-8	96	102	-1.9	-1	0	-0.7
Total	5	29	41	.414	84	68	57	2	0	614	673	9.9	10	233	3.4	211	3.1	3.66	88	.303	.371	-30	-30	100	103	-1.5	-4	-3	-2.7
■ **RED EVANS**	Evans, Russell Edison b: 11/12/06, Chicago, Ill. d: 6/14/82, Lakeview, Ark. BR/TR, 5'11", 168 lbs. Deb: 4/24/36																												
1936	Chi-A	0	3	.000	17	0	0	0	1	47	70	13.4	4	22	4.2	19	3.6	7.66	65	.338	.387	-14	-14	99	87	-1.4	-1	1	-1.1
1939	Bro-N	1	8	.111	24	6	0	0	1	64	74	10.4	4	26	3.7	28	3.9	5.20	80	.284	.338	-9	-7	106	83	-3.5	1	1	-0.4
Total	2	1	11	.083	41	6	0	0	2	111	144	11.7	8	48	3.9	47	3.8	6.24	72	.308	.360	-23	-21	103	84	-4.9	-0	3	-1.5
■ **ART EVANS**	Evans, William Arthur b: 8/3/11, Elvins, Mo. d: 1/8/52, Wichita, Kan. BB/TL, 6'1.5", 181 lbs. Deb: 6/20/32																												
1932	Chi-A	0	0	—	7	0	0	0	0	18	19	9.5	1	10	5.0	6	3.0	3.00	136	.257	.345	3	2	91	137	0.0	-0	1	0.2
■ **BILL EVANS**	Evans, William James b: 2/10/1894, Reidsville, N.C. d: 12/21/46, Burlington, N.C. BR/TR, 6', 175 lbs. Deb: 8/13/16																												
1916	Pit-N	2	5	.286	13	6	3	0	0	63	57	8.1	2	16	2.3	21	3.0	3.00	94	.249	.300	-3	-1	107	92	-1.1	-1	2	0.0
1917	Pit-N	0	4	.000	8	2	1	0	0	27	24	8.0	0	14	4.7	5	1.7	3.33	83	.231	.317	-2	-2	103	82	-1.9	-0	-0	-0.1
1919	Pit-N	0	4	.000	7	3	2	0	0	37	41	10.0	1	18	4.4	15	3.6	5.59	55	.297	.355	-11	-10	105	81	-1.9	-1	1	-1.0
Total	3	2	13	.133	28	11	6	0	0	127	122	8.6	3	48	3.4	41	2.9	3.83	75	.259	.321	-16	-13	106	87	-4.9	-2	2	-1.1
■ **BILL EVANS**	Evans, William Lawrence b: 3/25/19, Quanah, Texas d: 11/30/83, Grand Junction, Colo. BR/TR, 6'2", 180 lbs. Deb: 4/21/49																												
1949	Chi-A	0	1	.000	4	0	0	0	0	6	6	9.0	0	8	12.0	1	1.5	7.50	56	.261	.452	-2	-2	99	78	-0.4	-0	-0	-0.1
1951	Bos-A	0	0	—	9	0	0	0	0	15	15	9.0	0	8	4.8	3	1.8	4.20	104	.268	.348	-0	0	106	94	0.0	-1	-0	0.0
Total	2	0	1	.000	13	0	0	0	0	21	21	9.0	0	16	6.9	4	1.7	5.14	84	.266	.381	-2	-2	104	89	-0.4	-1	-0	-0.1

YEAR	TM/L	W	L	PCT	G	GS	CG	SHO	SV	IP	H	H/G	HR	BB	BB/G	SO	SO/G	ERA	/A	OAVG	OOBP	PR	/A	PF	CPI	WAT	PB	PD	TPI
■ **LEON EVERITT**	Everitt, Edward Leon b: 1/12/47, Marshall, Tex. BL/TR, 6'1.5", 195 lbs. Deb: 4/21/69																												
1969	SD-N	0	1	.000	5	0	0	0	0	16	18	10.1	4	12	6.8	11	6.2	7.88	46	.300	.413	-8	-8	100	94	-0.4	-0	0	-0.6
■ **BOB EWING**	Ewing, George Lemuel "Long Bob" b: 4/24/1873, New Hampshire, O. d: 6/20/47, Wapakoneta, Ohio BR/TR, 6'1.5", 170 lbs. Deb: 4/19/02																												
1902	Cin-N	5	6	.455	15	12	10	0	0	118	126	9.6	1	47	3.6	44	3.4	2.97	101	.297	.367	-3	0	108	118	-0.4	-1	-1	0.0
1903	Cin-N	14	13	.519	29	28	27	1	1	247	254	9.3	3	64	2.3	104	3.8	2.77	126	.293	.349	14	20	107	113	-0.3	5	3	2.3
1904	Cin-N	11	13	.458	26	24	22	0	0	212	198	8.4	3	58	2.5	99	4.2	2.46	123	.272	.329	6	14	111	111	-2.7	5	-1	1.3
1905	Cin-N	20	11	.645	40	34	30	4	0	312	284	8.2	5	79	2.3	164	4.7	2.51	122	.271	.328	17	19	103	109	4.8	5	-3	1.7
1906	Cin-N	13	14	.481	33	32	26	2	0	288	248	7.8	4	60	1.9	145	4.5	2.38	129	.259	.304	8	22	116	92	1.6	-4	0	2.5
1907	Cin-N	17	19	.472	41	37	32	2	0	333	279	7.5	2	85	2.3	147	4.0	1.73	136	.255	.313	27	23	95	121	1.7	0	-6	1.9
1908	Cin-N	17	15	.531	37	32	23	4	3	294	247	7.6	5	57	1.7	95	2.9	2.20	111	.256	.301	5	8	104	94	2.1	-2	-4	0.4
1909	Cin-N	11	12	.478	31	29	14	2	0	218	195	8.1	1	63	2.6	86	3.6	2.44	100	.238	.298	4	0	94	93	-0.6	-3	-4	-0.4
1910	Phi-N	16	14	.533	34	32	20	4	0	255	235	8.3	5	86	3.0	102	3.6	3.00	96	.251	.318	1	-3	95	93	0.9	3	-2	-0.2
1911	Phi-N	0	1	.000	4	3	1	0	0	24	29	10.9	2	14	5.3	12	4.5	7.88	47	.309	.398	-12	-11	108	71	-0.4	0	-0	-0.9
1912	StL-N	0	0	—	1	1	0	0	0	1	2	18.0	0	1	9.0	0	0.0	0.00	—	.333	.429	0	0	103	0	0.0	0	0	0.0
Total	11	124	118	.512	291	264	205	19	4	2302	2097	8.2	31	614	2.4	998	3.9	2.49	114	.264	.321	68	91	103	104	6.7	8	-19	8.6
■ **JOHN EWING**	Ewing, John "Long John" b: 6/1/1863, Cincinnati, Ohio d: 4/23/1895, Denver, Colo. TR , Deb: 1883																												
1888	Lou-a	8	13	.381	21	21	21	2	0	191	175	8.2	3	34	1.6	87	4.1	2.83	101	.256	.292	5	1	93	90	0.5	-1	0	0.0
1889	Lou-a	6	30	.167	40	39	37	1	0	331	407	11.1	6	147	4.0	155	4.2	4.87	81	.318	.389	-38	-34	102	97	-3.3	-6	1	-3.0
1890	NY-P	18	12	.600	35	31	27	1	2	267	293	9.9	6	104	3.5	145	**4.9**	4.25	107	.291	.357	-0	9	107	86	1.5	-2	0	0.6
1891	NY-N	21	8	**.724**	33	30	28	5	0	269	237	7.9	2	105	3.5	138	4.6	**2.28**	137	.249	.324	32	25	93	107	6.7	-1	0	2.1
Total	4	53	63	.457	129	121	113	9	2	1058	1112	9.5	17	390	3.3	525	4.5	3.68	99	.284	.349	-1	-3	99	95	5.4	-10	1	-0.3
■ **BUCK EWING**	Ewing, William b: 10/17/1859, Hoaglands, Ohio d: 10/20/06, Cincinnati, Ohio BR/TR, 5'10", 188 lbs. Deb: 9/09/1880 MH																												
1882	Tro-N	0	0	—	1	0	0	0	0	1	2	18.0	0	1	9.0	0	0.0	9.00	31	.422	.523	-1	-1	98	111	0.0	0	0	0.0
1884	NY-N	0	1	.000	1	1	1	0	0	8	7	7.9	0	4	4.5	3	3.4	1.13	255	.244	.336	2	2	97	249	-0.4	0	0	0.1
1885	NY-N	0	1	.000	1	0	0	0	0	2	4	18.0	0	3	13.5	0	0.0	4.50	64	.427	.566	-0	-0	102	254	-0.4	0	0	0.0
1888	NY-N	0	0	—	2	0	0	0	0	7	8	10.3	1	4	5.1	6	7.7	2.57	98	.301	.393	0	-0	89	217	0.0	1	0	0.0
1889	NY-N	2	0	1.000	3	2	2	0	0	20	23	10.3	0	8	3.6	12	5.4	4.05	101	.304	.371	-0	0	101	101	1.0	1	0	0.0
1890	NY-P	0	1	.000	1	1	1	0	0	9	11	11.0	1	3	3.0	2	2.0	4.00	114	.314	.368	0	1	107	120	-0.4	1	0	0.0
Total	6	2	3	.400	9	4	4	0	0	47	55	10.5	2	23	4.4	23	4.4	3.45	105	.306	.384	1	1	100	154	-0.2	4	0	0.1
■ **GEORGE EYRICH**	Eyrich, George Lincoln b: 3/3/25, Reading, Pa. BR/TR, 5'11", 175 lbs. Deb: 6/13/43																												
1943	Phi-N	0	0	—	9	0	0	0	0	19	23	10.9	1	9	4.3	5	2.4	3.32	97	.291	.356	0	-0	96	139	0.0	-0	-0	0.0
■ **RED FABER**	Faber, Urban Charles b: 9/6/1888, Cascade, Iowa d: 9/25/76, Chicago, Ill. BB/TR, 6'2", 180 lbs. Deb: 4/17/14 CH																												
1914	Chi-A	10	9	.526	40	19	11	2	**4**	181	154	7.7	3	64	3.2	88	4.4	2.69	107	.239	.319	1	4	105	100	1.4	1	2	0.6
1915	Chi-A	24	14	.632	**50**	32	21	2	2	300	264	7.9	3	99	3.0	182	5.5	2.55	108	.240	.309	13	7	94	100	1.7	3	0	1.1
1916	Chi-A	17	9	.654	35	25	15	3	1	205	167	7.3	1	61	2.7	87	3.8	2.02	148	.228	.292	18	22	106	103	2.7	-4	2	2.4
1917	Chi-A	16	13	.552	41	29	16	3	3	248	224	8.1	1	85	3.1	84	3.0	1.92	129	.247	.319	20	16	93	**136**	-2.5	-4	2	1.5
1918	Chi-A	4	1	.800	11	9	5	1	1	81	70	7.8	3	23	2.6	26	2.9	1.22	227	.245	.292	14	14	100	208	1.6	-2	1	1.6
1919	Chi-A	11	9	.550	25	20	9	0	0	162	185	10.3	7	45	2.5	45	2.5	3.83	86	.287	.341	-11	-10	102	97	-1.3	-0	0	-0.9
1920	Chi-A	23	13	.639	40	39	28	2	1	319	332	9.4	8	88	2.5	108	3.0	2.99	119	.277	.328	29	20	94	111	1.0	-3	-1	1.5
1921	Chi-A	25	15	.625	43	39	**32**	4	1	331	293	**8.0**	10	87	2.4	124	3.4	**2.47**	**177**	**.242**	**.287**	**66**	**70**	102	103	**8.9**	-4	1	**6.8**
1922	Chi-A	21	17	.553	43	38	**31**	4	2	**352**	334	8.5	10	83	2.1	148	3.8	**2.81**	**145**	.252	**.289**	**48**	**50**	101	95	2.6	-2	1	**4.9**
1923	Chi-A	14	11	.560	32	31	15	2	0	232	233	9.0	6	62	2.4	91	3.5	3.41	116	.259	.301	15	14	99	85	2.9	3	2	1.9
1924	Chi-A	9	11	.450	21	20	9	0	0	161	173	9.7	5	58	3.2	47	2.6	3.86	108	.282	.334	7	5	98	101	0.4	-2	-2	0.1
1925	Chi-A	12	11	.522	34	32	16	1	0	238	266	10.1	8	59	2.2	71	2.7	3.78	110	.289	.324	16	10	95	99	0.2	-4	1	0.7
1926	Chi-A	15	9	.625	27	25	13	1	0	185	203	9.9	3	57	2.8	65	3.2	3.55	102	.281	.328	10	2	90	100	2.8	0	-3	-0.1
1927	Chi-A	4	7	.364	18	15	6	0	0	111	131	10.6	2	41	3.3	39	3.2	4.54	94	.312	.363	-5	-3	103	106	-1.1	2	2	0.0
1928	Chi-A	13	9	.591	27	27	16	2	0	201	223	10.0	11	68	3.0	43	1.9	3.76	108	.286	.337	6	7	100	113	2.9	-3	1	0.4
1929	Chi-A	13	13	.500	31	31	15	1	0	234	241	9.3	10	61	2.3	68	2.6	3.88	107	.273	.316	9	7	98	94	2.8	-2	2	0.5
1930	Chi-A	8	13	.381	29	26	10	0	1	169	188	10.0	7	49	2.6	62	3.3	4.21	116	.283	.326	8	13	105	99	-0.5	-5	2	0.9
1931	Chi-A	10	14	.417	44	19	5	1	1	184	210	10.3	11	57	2.8	49	2.4	3.82	110	.285	.335	12	8	96	116	1.1	-3	-2	0.3
1932	Chi-A	2	11	.154	42	5	0	0	6	106	123	10.4	0	38	3.2	26	2.2	3.74	109	.290	.343	**9**	4	91	114	-3.5	3	-0	0.5
1933	Chi-A	3	4	.429	36	2	0	0	5	86	92	9.6	2	28	2.9	18	1.9	3.45	128	.275	.322	8	9	103	112	0.0	-3	-0	0.6
Total	20	254	213	.544	669	483	273	29	28	4086	4106	9.0	111	1213	2.7	1471	3.2	3.15	119	.266	.317	294	266	98	106	24.1	-30	11	25.3
■ **ROY FACE**	Face, Elroy Leon b: 2/20/28, Stephentown, N.Y. BB/TR, 5'8", 155 lbs. Deb: 4/16/53																												
1953	Pit-N	6	8	.429	41	13	2	0	0	119	145	11.0	19	30	2.3	56	4.2	6.58	69	.297	.338	-30	-27	106	78	1.2	-2	-1	-2.6
1955	Pit-N	5	7	.417	42	10	4	0	5	126	128	9.1	10	40	2.9	84	6.0	3.57	114	.268	.321	7	7	101	106	0.3	-1	-1	0.5
1956	Pit-N	12	13	.480	**68**	3	0	0	6	135	131	8.7	16	42	2.8	96	6.4	3.53	110	.256	.306	4	5	103	103	1.3	-0	1	0.6
1957	Pit-N	4	6	.400	59	1	0	0	10	94	97	9.3	9	24	2.3	53	5.1	3.06	121	.270	.309	9	7	96	124	0.0	-1	-1	0.5
1958	Pit-N	5	2	.714	57	0	0	0	**20**	84	77	8.3	6	22	2.4	47	5.0	2.89	128	.244	.290	10	8	94	98	1.3	-1	1	0.8
1959	Pit-N	18	1	**.947**	57	0	0	0	10	93	91	8.8	5	25	2.4	69	6.7	2.71	151	.266	.308	13	14	104	129	**8.6**	0	-0	1.4
1960	Pit-N	10	8	.556	**68**	0	0	0	24	115	93	7.3	11	29	2.3	72	5.6	2.90	126	.226	.269	11	9	97	96	-0.9	2	1	1.3
1961	Pit-N	6	12	.333	62	0	0	0	**17**	92	94	9.2	12	10	1.0	55	5.4	3.82	105	.267	.282	2	2	99	94	-3.0	0	2	0.4
1962	Pit-N	8	7	.533	63	0	0	0	**28**	91	74	7.3	7	18	1.8	45	4.5	1.88	212	.231	.267	**21**	**21**	101	142	-0.5	-1	-1	2.0
1963	Pit-N	3	9	.250	56	0	0	0	16	70	75	9.6	6	19	2.4	41	5.3	3.21	101	.285	.326	1	0	99	134	-2.7	0	1	0.2
1964	Pit-N	3	3	.500	55	0	0	0	4	80	82	9.2	11	27	3.0	63	7.1	5.17	69	.269	.321	-15	-14	101	85	0.0	-0	0	-1.4
1965	Pit-N	5	2	.714	16	0	0	0	0	20	20	9.0	1	7	3.1	19	8.5	2.70	129	.263	.318	2	2	98	133	1.3	-0	-0	0.1
1966	Pit-N	6	6	.500	54	0	0	0	18	70	68	8.7	9	24	3.1	67	8.6	2.70	132	.262	.315	7	7	99	153	-0.7	-1	1	0.7
1967	Pit-N	7	5	.583	61	0	0	0	17	74	62	7.5	5	22	2.7	41	5.0	2.43	139	.230	.282	8	8	100	112	1.1	-1	-1	0.7
1968	Pit-N	2	4	.333	43	0	0	0	13	52	46	8.0	3	7	1.2	34	5.9	2.60	115	.238	.267	2	2	100	94	-0.9	-0	-0	0.2
	Det-A	0	0	—	2	0	0	0	0	1	2	18.0	0	1	9.0	1	9.0	0.00	—	.500	.600	0	0	103	0	0.0	0	0	0.0
1969	Mon-N	4	2	.667	44	0	0	0	5	59	62	9.5	11	15	2.3	34	5.2	3.97	94	.263	.304	-2	-2	103	107	1.6	0	-1	-0.1
Total	16	104	95	.523	848	27	6	0	193	1375	1347	8.8	141	362	2.4	877	5.7	3.48	109	.260	.303	48	50	100	109	8.0	-5	1	5.3
■ **TONY FAETH**	Faeth, Anthony Joseph b: 7/9/1893, Aberdeen, S.D. d: 12/22/82, St.Paul, Minn. BR/TR, 6', 180 lbs. Deb: 8/10/19																												
1919	Cle-A	0	0	—	6	0	0	0	0	18	13	6.5	0	10	5.0	7	3.5	0.50	673	.224	.338	5	6	104	540	0.0	-1	-0	0.5
1920	Cle-A	0	0	—	13	0	0	0	0	25	31	11.2	0	20	7.2	14	5.0	4.32	88	.333	.456	-1	-1	100	145	0.0	-1	0	-0.1
Total	2	0	0	—	19	0	0	0	0	43	44	9.2	0	30	6.3	21	4.4	2.72	133	.291	.412	4	4	102	310	0.0	-1	-0	0.4
■ **EVERETT FAGAN**	Fagan, Everett Joseph b: 1/13/18, Pottersville, N.J. d: 2/16/83, Morristown, N.J. BR/TR, 6', 195 lbs. Deb: 4/24/43																												
1943	Phi-A	2	6	.250	18	2	0	0	3	37	41	10.0	4	14	3.4	9	2.2	6.32	55	.283	.345	-12	-12	106	75	-0.8	-0	0	-1.1
1946	Phi-A	0	1	.000	20	0	0	0	0	45	47	9.4	2	24	4.8	12	2.4	4.80	78	.264	.354	-6	-5	107	85	-0.4	1	-0	-0.4
Total	2	2	7	.222	38	2	0	0	3	82	88	9.7	6	38	4.2	21	2.3	5.49	66	.272	.350	-19	-17	107	81	-1.2	1	0	-1.5
■ **BILL FAGAN**	Fagan, William A. "Clinkers" b: 2/15/1869, Troy, N.Y. d: 3/21/30, Troy, N.Y. 5'11", 165 lbs. Deb: 9/15/1887																												
1887	NY-a	1	4	.200	6	6	6	0	0	45	55	11.0	1	24	4.8	12	2.4	4.00	99	.315	.398	1	-0	92	130	-0.9	-2	0	-0.1
1888	KC-a	5	11	.313	17	17	15	0	0	142	179	11.3	4	75	4.8	49	3.1	5.70	60	.322	.402	-42	-36	112	93	-0.3	-1	0	-2.9
Total	2	6	15	.286	23	23	21	0	0	187	234	11.3	5	99	4.8	61	2.9	5.29	68	.320	.401	-40	-35	107	102	-1.2	-3	0	-3.0
■ **FRANK FAHEY**	Fahey, Francis Raymond b: 1/22/1896, Milford, Mass. d: 3/19/54, Boston, Mass. BB/TR, 6'1", 190 lbs. Deb: 4/25/18																												
1918	Phi-A	0	0	—	3	0	0	0	0	9	5	5.0	0	14	14.0	1	1.0	6.00	50	.200	.500	-3	-3	108	92	0.0	-0	-1	-0.2
■ **JERRY FAHR**	Fahr, Gerald Warren b: 12/9/24, Marmaduke, Ark. BR/TR, 6'5", 185 lbs. Deb: 4/29/51																												
1951	Cle-A	0	0	—	5	0	0	0	0	6	11	16.5	0	2	3.0	0	0.0	4.50	85	.500	.520	-0	-0	93	214	0.0	0	0	0.0

YEAR	TM/L	W	L	PCT	G	GS	CG	SHO	SV	IP	H	H/G	HR	BB	BB/G	SO	SO/G	ERA	/A	OAVG	OOBP	PR	/A	PF	CPI	WAT	PB	PD	TPI
■ PETE FAHRER	Fahrer, Clarence Willie b: 3/10/1890, Holgate, Ohio d: 6/10/67, Fremont, Mich. TR , 6', 190 lbs. Deb: 8/17/14																												
1914	Cin-N	0	0	—	5	0	0	0	0	8	8	9.0	0	4	4.5	2	2.3	1.13	266	.308	.364	1	2	107	395	0.0	-0	0	0.2
■ JIM FAIRBANK	Fairbank, James Lee "Lee" or "Smoky" b: 3/17/1881, Deansboro, N.Y. d: 12/27/55, Utica, N.Y. 5'10", 185 lbs. Deb: 03																												
1903	Phi-A	1	1	.500	4	1	1	0	0	24	33	12.4	1	12	4.5	10	3.8	4.88	62	.351	.425	-5	-5	102	121	0.0	-1	1	-0.3
1904	Phi-A	0	1	.000	3	1	1	0	0	17	19	10.1	0	13	6.9	6	3.2	6.35	41	.307	.427	-7	-7	101	78	-0.4	-1	1	-0.5
Total	2	1	2	.333	7	2	2	0	0	41	52	11.4	1	25	5.5	16	3.5	5.49	52	.333	.426	-12	-12	101	103	-0.4	-1	2	-0.8
■ RAGS FAIRCLOTH	Faircloth, James Lamar b: 8/19/1892, Kenton, Tenn. d: 10/5/53, Tucson, Ariz. BR/TR, 5'11", 160 lbs. Deb: 5/06/19																												
1919	Phi-N	0	0	—	2	0	0	0	0	2	5	22.5	0	0	0.0	0	0.0	9.00	35	.625	.500	-1	-1	109	135	0.0	0	0	0.0
■ PETE FALCONE	Falcone, Peter Frank b: 10/1/53, Brooklyn, N.Y. BL/TL, 6'2", 185 lbs. Deb: 4/13/75																												
1975	SF-N	12	11	.522	34	32	3	1	0	190	171	8.1	16	111	5.3	131	6.2	4.17	89	.244	.342	-11	-10	102	95	0.7	-5	-0	-1.5
1976	StL-N	12	16	.429	32	32	9	2	0	212	173	7.3	12	93	3.9	138	5.9	3.23	114	.222	.300	7	10	105	87	-0.5	-2	-4	0.5
1977	StL-N	4	8	.333	27	22	1	1	1	124	130	9.4	19	61	4.4	75	5.4	5.44	68	.273	.351	-21	-24	95	92	-2.1	2	-1	-2.1
1978	StL-N	2	7	.222	19	14	0	0	0	75	94	11.3	9	48	5.8	28	3.4	5.76	59	.319	.409	-18	-19	96	112	-2.1	1	-2	-1.9
1979	NY-N	6	14	.300	33	31	1	1	0	184	194	9.5	24	76	3.7	113	5.5	4.16	87	.276	.340	-9	-11	96	111	-2.4	0	-3	-1.4
1980	NY-N	7	10	.412	37	23	1	0	1	157	163	9.3	16	58	3.3	109	6.2	4.53	77	.269	.326	-16	-18	97	92	0.0	-1	-3	-2.1
1981	NY-N	5	3	.625	35	9	1	1	1	95	84	8.0	3	36	3.4	56	5.3	2.56	140	.241	.302	10	11	103	115	1.6	1	-2	1.1
1982	NY-N	8	10	.444	40	23	3	0	2	171	159	8.4	24	71	3.7	101	5.3	3.84	94	.252	.322	-4	-4	100	109	0.7	-2	-3	-0.9
1983	Atl-N	9	4	.692	33	15	2	0	0	107	102	8.6	14	60	5.0	59	5.0	3.62	105	.256	.349	0	2	104	127	2.2	-1	-2	0.0
1984	Atl-N	5	7	.417	35	16	2	1	2	120	115	8.6	15	57	4.3	55	4.1	4.13	96	.252	.329	-7	-2	110	102	-0.9	1	-1	-0.2
Total	10	70	90	.438	325	217	25	7	7	1435	1385	8.7	152	671	4.2	865	5.4	4.07	90	.257	.333	-70	-66	101	102	-2.8	-6	-20	-8.5
■ CHET FALK	Falk, Chester Emanuel "Spot" b: 5/15/05, Austin, Tex. d: 1/7/82, Austin, Tex. BL/TL, 6'2", 170 lbs. Deb: 4/20/25																												
1925	StL-A	0	0	—	13	0	0	0	0	25	38	13.7	2	17	6.1	7	2.5	8.28	57	.362	.430	-11	-10	108	90	0.0	2	0	-0.5
1926	StL-A	4	4	.500	18	8	3	0	0	74	95	11.6	1	27	3.3	7	0.9	5.35	78	.338	.396	-11	-10	103	104	0.7	-1	-1	-0.9
1927	StL-A	1	0	1.000	9	0	0	0	0	16	25	14.1	1	10	5.6	2	1.1	5.63	80	.352	.422	-3	-2	109	124	0.5	-0	0	-0.1
Total	3	5	4	.556	40	8	3	0	0	115	158	12.4	4	54	4.2	16	1.3	6.03	72	.346	.408	-24	-22	105	104	1.2	1	0	-1.5
■ CY FALKENBERG	Falkenberg, Frederick Peter b: 12/17/1880, Chicago, Ill. d: 4/14/61, San Francisco, Cal BR/TR, 6'5", 180 lbs. Deb: 4/21/03																												
1903	Pit-N	1	5	.167	10	6	3	0	0	56	65	10.4	0	32	5.1	24	3.9	3.86	86	.319	.416	-4	-3	101	118	-2.2	-0	1	-0.1
1905	Was-A	7	2	.778	12	10	6	2	0	75	71	8.5	1	31	3.7	35	4.2	3.84	73	.274	.352	-10	-9	106	86	2.8	-2	-1	-0.9
1906	Was-A	14	20	.412	40	36	30	2	1	299	277	8.3	1	108	3.3	178	5.4	2.86	89	.270	.340	-6	-11	94	102	1.5	2	1	-1.0
1907	Was-A	6	17	.261	32	24	17	1	1	234	195	7.5	0	77	3.0	108	4.2	2.35	102	.249	.316	5	1	94	96	-2.5	-3	2	0.3
1908	Was-A	6	2	.750	17	8	5	1	0	83	70	7.6	2	21	2.3	34	3.7	1.95	118	.236	.291	4	3	97	128	2.3	0	1	0.4
	Cle-A	2	4	.333	8	7	2	0	0	46	52	10.2	1	10	2.0	17	3.3	3.91	63	.284	.328	-8	-7	103	93	-1.2	-1	-0	-0.7
	Yr	8	6	.571	25	15	7	1	0	129	122	8.5	3	31	2.2	51	3.6	2.65	89	.253	.301	-4	-4	99	93	1.1	0	0	-0.3
1909	Cle-A	10	9	.526	24	18	13	2	0	165	135	7.4	0	50	2.7	82	4.5	2.40	106	.231	.297	1	3	103	84	1.2	-1	3	0.6
1910	Cle-A	14	13	.519	37	29	18	3	1	257	246	8.6	3	75	2.6	107	3.7	2.94	87	.261	.320	-12	-11	102	98	1.6	-0	3	-0.8
1911	Cle-A	8	5	.615	15	13	7	0	1	107	117	9.8	0	24	2.0	46	3.9	3.28	105	.282	.326	1	2	103	94	1.4	-2	1	0.1
1913	Cle-A	23	10	.697	39	36	23	6	0	276	238	7.8	2	88	2.9	166	5.4	2.22	137	.235	.299	22	25	104	100	5.9	-2	-3	2.5
1914	Ind-F	25	16	.610	**49**	43	33	**9**	3	**377**	332	7.9	5	89	2.1	**236**	5.6	2.22	156	.236	.284	41	**52**	108	97	2.2	-3	5	6.2
1915	New-F	9	11	.450	25	21	14	0	1	172	175	9.2	6	47	2.5	76	4.0	3.24	88	.293	.344	-4	-8	94	104	-1.5	-6	0	-1.3
	Bro-F	3	3	.500	7	7	5	1	0	48	31	5.8	1	12	2.3	20	3.8	1.50	198	.208	.267	8	8	98	90	0.2	-1	0	0.8
	Yr	12	14	.462	32	28	19	1	1	220	206	8.4	7	59	2.4	96	3.9	2.86	100	.276	.329	4	0	95	90	-1.3	-6	0	-0.5
1917	Phi-A	2	6	.250	15	8	4	0	0	81	86	9.6	1	26	2.9	35	3.9	3.33	77	.293	.350	-6	-7	97	110	-1.2	1	1	-0.4
Total	12	130	123	.514	330	266	180	27	8	2276	2090	8.3	23	690	2.7	1164	4.6	2.68	105	.256	.317	33	37	101	99	10.5	-19	13	5.7
■ ED FALLENSTEIN	Fallenstein, Edward Joseph "Jack" (born Edward Joseph Valestin) b: 12/22/08, Newark, N.J. d: 11/24/71, Orange, N.J. BR/TR, 6'3", 180 lbs. Deb: 4/16/31																												
1931	Phi-N	0	0	—	24	0	0	0	0	42	56	12.0	2	26	5.6	15	3.2	7.07	59	.333	.408	-15	-13	109	89	0.0	0	0	-1.2
1933	Bos-N	2	1	.667	9	4	1	1	0	35	43	11.1	1	13	3.3	5	1.3	3.60	89	.305	.363	-1	-2	96	128	0.4	1	-0	0.0
Total	2	2	1	.667	33	4	1	1	0	77	99	11.6	3	39	4.6	20	2.3	5.49	68	.320	.388	-16	-15	107	107	0.4	1	-0	-1.2
■ BOB FALLON	Fallon, Robert Joseph b: 2/18/60, Bronx, N.Y. BL/TL, 6'3", 200 lbs. Deb: 4/26/84																												
1984	Chi-A	0	0	—	3	3	0	0	0	15	12	7.2	0	11	6.6	10	6.0	3.60	123	.235	.371	1	1	111	104	0.0	0	0	0.2
1985	Chi-A	0	0	—	10	0	0	0	0	16	25	14.1	5	9	5.1	17	9.6	6.19	67	.362	.430	-4	-4	100	148	0.0	0	1	-0.2
Total	2	0	0	—	13	3	0	0	0	31	37	10.7	5	20	5.8	27	7.8	4.94	87	.308	.404	-3	-2	105	127	0.0	0	1	0.0
■ CLIFF FANNIN	Fannin, Clifford Bryson "Mule" b: 5/13/24, Louisa, Ky. d: 12/11/66, Sandusky, Ohio BL/TR, 6', 170 lbs. Deb: 9/02/45																												
1945	StL-A	0	0	—	5	0	0	0	0	10	8	7.2	0	5	4.5	5	4.5	2.70	142	.222	.317	1	1	114	96	0.0	-0	0	0.1
1946	StL-A	5	2	.714	27	7	4	1	2	87	76	7.9	4	42	4.3	52	5.4	3.00	116	.236	.319	5	5	100	105	1.8	-1	-0	0.4
1947	StL-A	6	8	.429	26	18	6	2	1	146	134	8.3	10	77	4.7	77	4.7	3.58	109	.245	.333	2	5	106	105	0.6	-0	0	0.6
1948	StL-A	10	14	.417	34	29	10	3	1	214	198	8.3	14	104	4.4	102	4.3	4.16	112	.245	.329	3	12	109	90	0.7	-1	-2	1.0
1949	StL-A	8	14	.364	30	25	5	0	1	143	177	11.1	15	93	5.9	57	3.6	6.17	71	.308	.397	-31	-29	104	98	0.4	-2	-3	-2.9
1950	StL-A	5	9	.357	25	16	3	0	1	102	116	10.2	18	58	5.1	42	3.7	6.53	78	.280	.366	-22	-17	111	86	-0.3	-2	-0	-1.6
1951	StL-A	0	2	.000	7	1	0	0	0	15	20	12.0	6	5	3.0	11	6.6	6.60	68	.317	.357	-4	-3	109	118	-0.9	-0	0	-0.2
1952	StL-A	0	2	.000	10	2	0	0	0	16	34	19.1	5	9	5.1	6	3.4	12.94	28	.453	.506	-16	-16	100	94	-0.9	0	-0	-1.5
Total	8	34	51	.400	164	98	28	6	6	733	763	9.4	72	393	4.8	352	4.3	4.85	89	.269	.353	-64	-42	106	96	1.4	-6	-6	-4.1
■ JACK FANNING	Fanning, John Jacob b: 1863, S.Orange, N.J. d: 6/10/17, Aberdeen, Wash. 5'9", 163 lbs. Deb: 9/20/1889																												
1889	Ind-N	0	1	.000	1	1	0	0	0	1	3	27.0	0	2	18.0	0	0.0	18.00	25	.533	.655	-2	-2	110	98	-0.4	-0	0	0.0
1894	Phi-N	1	3	.250	5	4	2	0	0	32	45	12.7	4	20	5.6	7	2.0	8.16	61	.355	.443	-10	-11	94	86	-1.0	-1	0	-0.8
Total	2	1	4	.200	6	5	2	0	0	33	48	13.1	4	22	6.0	7	1.9	8.45	59	.363	.454	-12	-13	94	86	-1.4	-1	0	-0.8
■ HARRY FANOK	Fanok, Harry Michael "The Flame Thrower" b: 5/11/40, Whippany, N.J. BB/TR, 6', 180 lbs. Deb: 4/16/63																												
1963	StL-N	2	1	.667	12	0	0	0	1	26	24	8.3	3	21	7.3	25	8.7	5.19	67	.255	.380	-6	-5	106	101	0.3	1	-0	-0.3
1964	StL-N	0	0	—	4	0	0	0	0	8	5	5.6	0	3	3.4	10	11.3	5.63	70	.179	.242	-2	-2	111	23	0.0	-0	0	-0.1
Total	2	2	1	.667	16	0	0	0	1	34	29	7.7	3	24	6.4	35	9.3	5.29	68	.238	.351	-7	-6	107	83	0.3	1	-0	-0.4
■ FRANK FANOVICH	Fanovich, Frank Joseph "Lefty" b: 1/11/22, New York, N.Y. BL/TL, 5'11", 180 lbs. Deb: 4/25/49																												
1949	Cin-N	0	2	.000	29	1	0	0	0	43	44	9.2	2	28	5.9	27	5.7	5.44	73	.257	.365	-7	-7	98	80	-0.9	-0	0	-0.6
1953	Phi-A	0	3	.000	26	3	0	0	0	62	62	9.0	5	37	5.4	37	5.4	5.52	76	.273	.372	-10	-9	105	93	-1.4	-0	-1	-0.9
Total	2	0	5	.000	55	4	0	0	0	105	106	9.1	7	65	5.6	64	5.5	5.49	75	.266	.369	-17	-16	102	87	-2.3	-1	-0	-1.5
■ STAN FANSLER	Fansler, Stanley Robert b: 2/12/65, Elkins, W.V.A BR/TR, 5'11", 180 lbs. Deb: 9/06/86																												
1986	Pit-N	0	3	.000	5	5	0	0	0	24	20	7.5	2	15	5.6	13	4.9	3.75	100	.247	.354	-0	-0	101	116	-1.4	-0	0	0.0
■ HARRY FANWELL	Fanwell, Harry Clayton b: 10/16/1886, Patapsco, Md. d: 7/15/65, Baltimore, Md. BB/TR, 6', 175 lbs. Deb: 7/23/10																												
1910	Cle-A	2	9	.182	17	11	5	1	0	92	87	8.5	0	38	3.7	30	2.9	3.62	71	.163	.227	-11	-11	102	29	-3.4	-3	1	-1.3
■ ED FARMER	Farmer, Edward Joseph b: 10/18/49, Evergreen Park, Ill BR/TR, 6'5", 200 lbs. Deb: 6/09/71																												
1971	Cle-A	5	4	.556	43	4	0	0	4	79	77	8.8	9	41	4.7	48	5.5	4.33	87	.263	.350	-8	-5	108	105	1.4	-1	-0	-0.5
1972	Cle-A	2	5	.286	46	1	0	0	7	61	51	7.5	10	27	4.0	33	4.9	4.43	75	.231	.307	-9	-8	108	87	-1.3	-0	0	-0.7
1973	Cle-A	0	2	.000	16	0	0	0	1	17	25	13.2	4	5	2.6	10	5.3	4.76	79	.325	.357	-2	-2	99	135	-0.9	0	-0	-0.1
	Det-A	3	0	1.000	24	0	0	0	2	45	52	10.4	3	27	5.4	28	5.6	5.00	77	.292	.388	-6	-6	101	103	1.5	0	-1	-0.5
	Yr	3	2	.600	40	0	0	0	3	62	77	11.2	7	32	4.6	38	5.5	4.94	78	.301	.379	-8	-7	101	103	0.6	0	-1	-0.6
1974	Phi-N	2	1	.667	14	3	0	0	0	31	41	11.9	5	27	7.8	20	5.8	8.42	45	.323	.428	-16	-16	104	88	0.5	-1	-0	-1.6
1977	Bal-A	0	0	—	1	0	0	0	0	0	1	—	0	1	—	0	—	∞	—	1.000	1.000	-1	-1	92	86	0.0	0	0	0.0
1978	Mil-A	1	0	1.000	3	0	0	0	0	11	7	5.7	1	4	3.3	6	4.9	0.82	481	.175	.244	4	4	104	191	0.5	0	0	0.4
1979	Tex-A	2	0	1.000	11	2	0	0	0	33	30	8.2	2	19	5.2	25	6.8	4.36	96	.252	.354	-0	-1	99	97	1.0	0	0	0.0

YEAR	TM/L	W	L	PCT	G	GS	CG	SHO	SV	IP	H	H/G	HR	BB	BB/G	SO	SO/G	ERA	/A	OAVG	OOBP	PR	/A	PF	CPI	WAT	PB	PD	TPI
	Chi-A	3	7	.300	42	3	0	0	14	81	66	7.3	2	34	3.8	48	5.3	2.44	177	.219	.291	16	17	103	99	-1.7	0	0	1.7
	Yr	5	7	.417	53	5	0	0	14	114	96	7.6	4	53	4.2	73	5.8	3.00	143	.226	.305	16	16	102	99	-0.7	0	0	1.7
1980	Chi-A	7	9	.438	64	0	0	0	30	100	92	8.3	6	56	5.0	54	4.9	3.33	119	.244	.340	8	7	98	110	0.0	0	1	0.8
1981	Chi-A	3	3	.500	42	0	0	0	10	53	53	9.0	5	34	5.8	42	7.1	4.58	79	.262	.362	-5	-6	99	103	0.0	0	1	-0.4
1982	Phi-N	2	6	.250	47	4	0	0	6	76	66	7.8	2	50	5.9	58	6.9	4.86	70	.234	.345	-11	-13	94	71	-2.1	-1	0	-1.3
1983	Phi-N	0	6	.000	12	3	0	0	0	27	35	11.7	2	20	6.7	16	5.3	6.00	61	.307	.409	-7	-7	100	101	-2.9	-0	0	-0.6
	Oak-A	0	0	—	5	1	0	0	0	10	15	13.5	1	0	0.0	7	6.3	3.60	109	.366	.357	1	0	96	166	0.0	0	-0	0.0
Total	11	30	43	.411	370	21	0	0	75	624	611	8.8	52	345	5.0	395	5.7	4.30	89	.257	.347	-37	-34	101	101	-4.0	-3	1	-2.8
■ **JIM FARR**	Farr, James Alfred b: 5/18/56, Waverly, N.Y. BR/TR, 6'1", 195 lbs. Deb: 9/07/82																												
1982	Tex-A	0	0	—	5	0	0	0	0	18	20	10.0	0	7	3.5	6	3.0	2.50	154	.278	.338	3	3	94	145	0.0	0	-0	0.2
■ **STEVE FARR**	Farr, Steven Michael b: 12/12/56, La Plata, Md. BR/TR, 5'10", 198 lbs. Deb: 5/16/84																												
1984	Cle-A	3	11	.214	31	16	0	0	1	116	106	8.2	14	46	3.6	83	6.4	4.58	93	.245	.322	-7	-4	106	85	-3.8	0	1	-0.3
1985	KC-A	2	1	.667	16	3	0	0	1	38	34	8.1	2	20	4.7	36	8.5	3.08	137	.245	.341	5	5	101	126	0.4	0	0	0.5
1986	KC-A	8	4	.667	56	0	0	0	8	109	90	7.4	10	39	3.2	83	6.9	3.14	134	.228	.300	13	13	100	102	2.3	0	1	1.3
1987	KC-A	4	3	.571	47	0	0	0	1	91	97	9.6	9	44	4.4	88	8.7	4.15	112	.270	.350	3	5	104	110	0.4	0	-1	0.3
1988	KC-A	5	4	.556	62	1	0	0	20	83	74	8.0	5	30	3.3	72	7.8	2.49	163	.240	.308	14	15	103	130	0.3	0	-1	1.4
Total	5	22	23	.489	212	20	0	0	31	437	401	8.3	40	179	3.7	362	7.5	3.60	119	.246	.322	27	33	103	107	-0.4	0	-0	3.2
■ **JOHN FARRELL**	Farrell, John Edward b: 8/4/62, Monmouth Beach, N.J. BR/TR, 6'4", 210 lbs. Deb: 8/18/87																												
1987	Cle-A	5	1	.833	10	9	1	0	0	69	68	8.9	7	22	2.9	28	3.7	3.39	138	.256	.320	8	10	105	115	2.2	0	-0	0.9
1988	Cle-A	14	10	.583	31	30	4	0	0	210	216	9.3	15	67	2.9	92	3.9	4.24	96	.269	.326	-6	-4	102	94	2.7	0	-0	-0.4
Total	2	19	11	.633	41	39	5	0	0	279	284	9.2	22	89	2.9	120	3.9	4.03	104	.265	.325	2	6	103	99	4.9	0	-1	0.5
■ **KERBY FARRELL**	Farrell, Major Kerby b: 9/3/13, Leapwood, Tenn. d: 12/17/75, Nashville, Tenn. BL/TL, 5'11", 172 lbs. Deb: 4/24/43 MC																												
1943	Bos-N	0	1	.000	5	0	0	0	0	23	24	9.4	1	9	3.5	4	1.6	4.30	85	.276	.340	-2	-2	109	92	-0.4	1	0	-0.1
■ **TURK FARRELL**	Farrell, Richard Joseph b: 4/8/34, Boston, Mass. d: 6/10/77, Great Yarmouth, England BR/TR, 6'4", 215 lbs. Deb: 9/21/56																												
1956	Phi-N	0	1	.000	1	1	0	0	0	4	6	13.5	0	3	6.8	0	0.0	13.50	27	.353	.476	-4	-4	95	55	-0.4	-0	0	-0.2
1957	Phi-N	10	2	.833	52	0	0	0	10	83	74	8.0	2	36	3.9	54	5.9	2.39	161	.242	.317	**14**	13	99	129	4.1	0	0	1.5
1958	Phi-N	8	9	.471	54	0	0	0	11	94	84	8.0	7	40	3.8	73	7.0	3.35	118	.244	.310	6	6	100	102	0.4	0	-2	0.5
1959	Phi-N	1	6	.143	38	0	0	0	6	57	61	9.6	9	25	3.9	31	4.9	4.74	85	.288	.341	-5	-5	102	112	-2.2	-0	-0	-0.4
1960	Phi-N	10	6	.625	59	0	0	0	11	103	88	7.7	3	29	2.5	70	6.1	2.71	153	.239	.292	12	16	110	104	3.3	0	-1	1.7
1961	Phi-N	2	1	.667	5	0	0	0	0	10	10	9.0	3	6	5.4	10	9.0	6.30	62	.270	.370	-3	-3	98	106	0.8	0	-0	-0.2
	LA-N	6	6	.500	50	0	0	0	10	89	107	10.8	12	43	4.3	80	8.1	5.06	81	.296	.365	-10	-10	102	108	-0.8	-2	-2	-1.2
	Yr	8	7	.533	55	0	0	0	10	99	117	10.6	15	49	4.5	90	8.2	5.18	79	.293	.363	-13	-12	101	108	0.0	0	-2	-1.4
1962	Hou-N	10	20	.333	43	29	11	2	4	242	210	7.8	21	55	2.0	203	7.5	3.01	124	.233	.275	25	19	95	91	-2.9	2	-2	1.9
1963	Hou-N	14	13	.519	34	26	12	0	1	202	161	7.2	12	35	1.6	141	6.3	3.03	103	.219	.250	6	2	95	68	2.9	1	-1	0.2
1964	Hou-N	11	10	.524	32	27	7	0	0	198	196	8.9	21	52	2.4	117	5.3	3.27	106	.261	.305	6	4	98	115	2.3	-3	-1	0.0
1965	Hou-N	11	11	.500	33	29	8	3	1	208	202	8.7	18	35	1.5	122	5.3	3.50	92	.252	.281	1	-7	91	88	2.0	-1	-2	-0.9
1966	Hou-N	6	10	.375	32	21	3	0	2	153	167	9.8	23	28	1.6	101	5.9	4.59	78	.278	.302	-17	-18	99	91	-1.3	-0	-2	-1.9
1967	Hou-N	1	0	1.000	7	0	0	0	0	12	11	8.3	0	7	5.3	10	7.5	4.50	71	.244	.358	-1	-2	95	80	0.5	-0	0	-0.1
	Phi-N	9	6	.600	50	1	0	0	12	92	76	7.4	6	15	1.5	68	6.7	2.05	171	.228	.256	14	15	104	113	1.5	-0	-1	1.5
	Yr	10	6	.625	57	1	0	0	12	104	87	7.5	6	22	1.9	78	6.8	2.34	149	.229	.266	12	13	103	113	2.0	-0	-1	1.4
1968	Phi-N	4	6	.400	54	0	0	0	12	83	83	9.0	7	32	3.5	57	6.2	3.47	85	.271	.328	-4	-5	99	120	-0.7	-0	-0	-0.5
1969	Phi-N	3	4	.429	46	0	0	0	3	74	92	11.2	8	27	3.3	40	4.9	4.01	89	.307	.360	-3	-4	100	130	0.2	-0	-2	-0.5
Total	14	106	111	.488	590	134	41	5	83	1704	1628	8.6	152	468	2.5	1177	6.2	3.45	103	.254	.299	35	21	98	100	9.7	-3	-16	1.4
■ **FAST**	Fast b:Milwaukee, Wis. Deb: 7/11/1887																												
1887	Ind-N	0	1	.000	4	2	1	0	1	16	25	14.1	1	8	4.5	0	0.0	10.69	38	.372	.439	-12	-12	101	66	-0.4	-1	0	-0.8
■ **DARCY FAST**	Fast, Darcy Rae b: 3/10/47, Dallas, Ore. BL/TL, 6'3", 195 lbs. Deb: 6/15/68																												
1968	Chi-N	0	1	.000	8	1	0	0	0	10	8	7.2	1	8	7.2	10	9.0	5.40	62	.216	.348	-3	-2	112	74	-0.4	-0	0	-0.2
■ **JACK FASZHOLZ**	Faszholz, John Edward "Preacher" b: 4/11/27, St.Louis, Mo. BR/TR, 6'3", 205 lbs. Deb: 4/25/53																												
1953	StL-N	0	0	—	4	1	0	0	0	12	16	12.0	3	1	0.8	7	5.3	6.75	64	.327	.353	-3	-3	101	95	0.0	-0	-0	-0.3
■ **BILL FAUL**	Faul, William Alvan b: 4/21/40, Cincinnati, Ohio BR/TR, 5'10", 184 lbs. Deb: 9/19/62																												
1962	Det-A	0	0	—	1	0	0	0	0	2	4	18.0	1	3	13.5	2	9.0	27.00	16	.444	.615	-5	-5	110	64	0.0	0	0	-0.3
1963	Det-A	5	6	.455	28	10	2	0	1	97	93	8.6	14	48	4.5	64	5.9	4.64	81	.251	.336	-11	-9	104	97	-0.3	0	-2	-1.1
1964	Det-A	0	0	—	1	1	0	0	0	5	5	9.0	2	2	3.6	1	1.8	10.80	32	.250	.318	-4	-4	95	55	0.0	-0	-0	-0.3
1965	Chi-N	6	6	.500	17	16	5	3	0	97	83	7.7	12	18	1.7	59	5.5	3.53	104	.232	.272	0	1	103	86	0.6	-1	-2	0.0
1966	Chi-N	1	4	.200	17	6	1	0	0	51	47	8.3	12	18	3.2	32	5.6	5.12	72	.242	.314	-9	-8	103	90	-1.0	-2	-1	-0.9
1970	SF-N	0	0	—	7	0	0	0	1	10	15	13.5	1	6	5.4	6	5.4	7.20	54	.357	.429	-3	-4	96	103	0.0	0	-0	-0.3
Total	6	12	16	.429	71	33	8	3	2	262	247	8.5	42	95	3.3	164	5.6	4.71	79	.249	.317	-32	-29	103	91	-0.7	-2	-5	-2.9
■ **JIM FAULKNER**	Faulkner, James Leroy "Lefty" b: 7/27/1899, Beatrice, Neb. d: 6/1/62, W.Palm Beach, Fla. BB/TL, 6'3", 190 lbs. Deb: 9/15/27																												
1927	NY-N	1	0	1.000	3	1	0	0	0	10	13	11.7	0	5	4.5	2	1.8	3.60	107	.317	.404	0	0	98	147	0.5	1	-0	0.1
1928	NY-N	9	8	.529	38	8	3	0	2	117	131	10.1	5	41	3.2	32	2.5	3.54	112	.289	.339	6	5	99	116	-1.1	1	1	0.7
1930	Bro-N	0	0	—	2	1	0	0	1	⅓	2	54.0	1	1	27.0	0	0.0	81.00	—	.667	.750	-3	-3	99	65	0.0	0	0	-0.1
Total	3	10	8	.556	43	10	3	0	3	127	146	10.3	6	47	3.3	34	2.4	3.76	105	.293	.347	3	3	99	118	-0.6	1	1	0.7
■ **BUCK FAUSETT**	Fausett, Robert Shaw "Leaky" b: 4/8/08, Sheridan, Ark. BL/TR, 5'10", 170 lbs. Deb: 4/18/44																												
1944	Cin-N	0	0	—	2	0	0	0	0	11	13	10.6	0	7	5.7	3	2.5	5.73	60	.295	.407	-3	-3	95	94	0.0	-0	0	-0.2
■ **CHARLIE FAUST**	Faust, Charles Victor "Victory" b: 10/9/1880, Marion, Kan. d: 6/18/15, Fort Steilacoom, Wash. BR/TR, 6'2", Deb: 10/07/11																												
1911	NY-N	0	0	—	2	0	0	0	0	2	2	9.0	0	0	0.0	0	0.0	4.50	74	.250	.250	-0	-0	99	36	0.0	0	0	0.0
■ **CLAY FAUVER**	Fauver, Clayton King "Cayt" b: 8/1/1872, N.Eaton, Ohio d: 3/3/42, Chatsworth, Ga. BB/TR, 5'10", Deb: 9/07/1899																												
1899	Lou-N	1	0	1.000	1	1	1	0	0	9	11	11.0	0	2	2.0	1	1.0	0.00	—	.326	.363	4	4	103	0	0.5	-1	0	0.4
■ **VERN FEAR**	Fear, Luvern Carl b: 8/21/24, Everly, Iowa d: 9/6/76, Spencer, Iowa BB/TR, 6', 170 lbs. Deb: 8/03/52																												
1952	Chi-N	0	0	—	4	0	0	0	0	8	9	10.1	1	3	3.4	4	4.5	7.88	49	.290	.361	-4	-4	103	68	0.0	-0	0	-0.3
■ **JACK FEE**	Fee, John b: 1870, Carbondale, Pa. d: 3/3/13, Carbondale, Pa. Deb: 9/14/1889																												
1889	Ind-N	2	2	.500	7	3	2	0	0	40	39	8.8	2	31	7.0	10	2.3	4.27	104	.271	.400	-1	1	110	109	0.2	-2	0	0.0
■ **HARRY FELDMAN**	Feldman, Harry b: 11/10/19, New York, N.Y. d: 3/16/62, Fort Smith, Ark. BR/TR, 6', 175 lbs. Deb: 9/10/41																												
1941	NY-N	1	1	.500	3	3	1	1	0	20	21	9.4	0	6	2.7	9	4.0	4.05	93	.280	.318	-1	-1	104	89	0.0	0	-0	0.0
1942	NY-N	7	1	.875	31	6	2	1	0	114	100	7.9	5	73	5.8	49	3.9	3.16	106	.236	.345	2	2	101	118	2.9	3	-0	0.6
1943	NY-N	4	5	.444	31	10	1	0	0	105	114	9.8	7	58	5.0	49	4.2	4.29	78	.279	.369	-11	-11	99	111	0.6	-1	0	-1.1
1944	NY-N	11	13	.458	40	27	8	1	2	205	214	9.4	18	91	4.0	70	3.1	4.17	91	.266	.336	-13	-8	105	102	0.6	-0	-3	-1.0
1945	NY-N	12	13	.480	35	30	10	3	1	218	213	8.8	14	69	2.8	74	3.1	3.26	117	.251	.303	13	13	100	101	-0.9	-3	-2	0.8
1946	NY-N	0	2	.000	3	2	0	0	0	4	9	20.3	1	3	6.8	3	6.8	18.00	20	.474	.500	-6	-6	103	72	-0.9	-0	-0	-0.5
Total	6	35	35	.500	143	78	22	6	3	666	671	9.1	45	300	4.1	254	3.4	3.80	96	.260	.333	-16	-11	102	105	2.3	-1	-5	-1.2
■ **HARRY FELIX**	Felix, Harry b: 1870, Brooklyn, N.Y. d: 10/17/61, Miami, Fla. TR , 5'7.5", 160 lbs. Deb: 10/05/01																												
1901	NY-N	0	0	—	1	0	0	0	0	2	3	13.5	0	0	0.0	0	0.0	0.00	—	.370	.370	1	1	95	0	0.0	-0	0	0.1
1902	Phi-N	1	3	.250	9	5	3	0	0	45	61	12.2	1	11	2.2	10	2.0	5.60	54	.349	.387	-14	-13	109	81	-0.7	-1	-1	-1.2
Total	2	1	3	.250	10	5	3	0	0	47	64	12.3	1	11	2.1	10	1.9	5.36	57	.350	.387	-13	-12	109	78	-0.7	-1	-1	-1.1

YEAR	TM/L	W	L	PCT	G	GS	CG	SHO	SV	IP	H	H/G	HR	BB	BB/G	SO	SO/G	ERA	/A	OAVG	OOBP	PR	/A	PF	CPI	WAT	PB	PD	TPI
■ **BOB FELLER**	Feller, Robert William Andrew "Rapid Robert" b: 11/3/18, Van Meter, Iowa BR/TR, 6', 185 lbs. Deb: 7/19/36 H																												
1936	Cle-A	5	3	.625	14	8	5	0	1	62	52	7.5	1	47	6.8	76	11.0	3.34	158	.229	.369	12	13	105	122	0.9	-2	-1	1.0
1937	Cle-A	9	7	.563	26	19	9	0	1	149	116	7.0	4	106	6.4	150	9.1	3.38	132	.218	.344	21	18	97	103	0.5	-1	1	1.7
1938	Cle-A	17	11	.607	39	36	20	2	1	278	225	**7.3**	13	208	6.7	**240**	**7.8**	4.08	115	**.220**	.353	22	19	98	93	1.6	2	-2	1.6
1939	Cle-A	**24**	9	.727	39	35	**24**	4	1	**297**	227	**6.9**	13	142	4.3	**246**	**7.5**	2.85	156	**.210**	.299	**58**	**53**	96	97	7.1	5	0	**5.7**
1940	Cle-A	**27**	11	.711	**43**	37	**31**	**4**	4	**320**	245	**6.9**	13	118	3.3	**261**	**7.3**	**2.62**	154	**.210**	**.282**	**63**	50	92	92	7.2	2	-4	4.7
1941	Cle-A	**25**	13	.658	**44**	40	28	**6**	2	**343**	284	7.5	15	194	5.1	**260**	**6.8**	3.15	132	.226	.329	38	39	101	107	**7.6**	1	-1	3.9
1945	Cle-A	5	3	.625	9	9	7	1	0	72	50	6.3	1	35	4.4	59	7.4	2.50	132	.192	.290	7	6	98	78	1.0	-0	-1	0.5
1946	Cle-A	**26**	15	.634	**48**	42	**36**	**10**	4	**371**	277	6.7	11	153	3.7	**348**	8.4	2.18	145	.208	.286	**54**	41	90	100	**8.6**	-1	-1	4.0
1947	Cle-A	**20**	11	.645	42	37	20	**5**	3	**299**	230	6.9	17	127	3.8	**196**	**5.9**	2.68	130	.215	.296	**34**	27	94	101	4.8	2	2	3.2
1948	Cle-A	19	15	.559	44	38	18	2	3	280	255	8.2	20	116	3.7	**164**	5.3	3.57	113	.241	.315	22	14	94	98	-2.2	-8	-1	0.5
1949	Cle-A	15	14	.517	36	28	15	0	0	211	198	8.4	18	84	3.6	108	4.6	3.75	107	.248	.317	10	6	96	94	-1.7	4	-3	0.6
1950	Cle-A	16	11	.593	35	34	16	3	0	247	230	8.4	20	103	3.8	119	4.3	3.43	127	.247	.320	32	26	95	107	0.0	-2	-4	1.8
1951	Cle-A	**22**	8	**.733**	33	32	16	4	0	250	239	8.6	22	95	3.4	111	4.0	3.49	109	.253	.321	17	9	93	110	5.6	-4	-3	0.1
1952	Cle-A	9	13	.409	30	30	11	0	0	192	219	10.3	13	83	3.9	81	3.8	4.73	68	.288	.351	-23	-32	88	97	-3.8	1	0	-3.0
1953	Cle-A	10	7	.588	25	25	10	1	0	176	163	8.3	16	60	3.1	60	3.1	3.58	103	.251	.313	8	2	93	102	0.0	-2	1	0.1
1954	Cle-A	13	3	.813	19	19	9	1	0	140	127	8.2	13	39	2.5	59	3.8	3.09	122	.239	.291	10	11	101	96	2.8	1	-2	1.0
1955	Cle-A	4	4	.500	25	11	2	1	0	83	71	7.7	7	31	3.4	25	2.7	3.47	117	.235	.303	5	5	102	92	-0.6	-2	-1	0.2
1956	Cle-A	0	4	.000	19	4	2	0	1	58	63	9.8	7	23	3.6	18	2.8	4.97	83	.280	.340	-5	-5	99	93	-1.9	-2	-1	-0.7
Total	18	266	162	.621	570	484	279	44	21	3828	3271	7.7	224	1764	4.1	2581	6.1	3.25	122	.231	.315	385	299	95	99	37.5	-6	-21	26.9
■ **TERRY FELTON**	Felton, Terry Lane b: 10/29/57, Texarkana, Ark. BR/TR, 6'1", 180 lbs. Deb: 9/28/79																												
1979	Min-A	0	0	—	1	0	0	0	0	2	0	0.0	0	0	0.0	1	4.5	0.00	—	.000	.000	1	1	108	0	0.0	0	0	0.1
1980	Min-A	0	3	.000	5	4	0	0	0	18	20	10.0	2	9	4.5	14	7.0	7.00	63	.286	.361	-6	-5	109	73	-1.4	0	-0	-0.4
1981	Min-A	0	0	—	1	0	0	0	0	1	4	36.0	1	2	18.0	1	9.0	54.00	7	.500	.600	-6	-6	107	51	0.0	0	0	-0.4
1982	Min-A	0	13	.000	48	6	0	0	3	117	99	7.6	18	76	5.8	92	7.1	5.00	83	.230	.346	-12	-11	102	90	-6.4	0	-2	-1.2
Total	4	0	16	.000	55	10	0	0	3	138	123	8.0	21	87	5.7	108	7.0	5.54	76	.240	.349	-23	-21	103	86	-7.8	0	-2	-1.9
■ **HOD FENNER**	Fenner, Horace Alfred b: 7/12/1897, Martin, Mich. d: 11/20/54, Detroit, Mich. BR/TR, 5'10.5", 165 lbs. Deb: 9/09/21																												
1921	Chi-A	0	0	—	2	1	0	0	0	7	14	18.0	0	3	3.9	1	1.3	7.71	57	.452	.500	-3	-3	102	120	0.0	-0	-0	-0.2
■ **STAN FERENS**	Ferens, Stanley "Lefty" b: 3/5/15, Wendell, Pa. BB/TL, 5'11", 170 lbs. Deb: 6/10/42																												
1942	StL-A	3	4	.429	19	3	1	0	0	69	76	9.9	2	21	2.7	23	3.0	3.78	99	.279	.324	-1	-0	102	100	-0.7	-1	0	0.0
1946	StL-A	2	9	.182	34	6	1	0	0	88	100	10.2	3	38	3.9	28	2.9	4.50	78	.293	.354	-10	-10	100	100	-3.2	-0	-1	-1.0
Total	2	5	13	.278	53	9	2	0	0	157	176	10.1	5	59	3.4	51	2.9	4.18	86	.287	.341	-11	-10	101	100	-3.9	-1	-1	-1.0
■ **CHARLIE FERGUSON**	Ferguson, Charles Augustus b: 5/10/1875, Okemos, Mich. d: 5/17/31, Sault Ste.Marie, Mich. TR, 5'11", Deb: 9/20/01																												
1901	Chi-N	0	0	—	1	0	0	0	0	2	1	4.5	0	2	9.0	0	0.0	0.00	—	.164	.370	1	1	103	0	0.0	-0	0	0.1
■ **CHARLIE FERGUSON**	Ferguson, Charles J. b: 4/17/1863, Charlottesville, Va. d: 4/29/1888, Philadelphia, Pa. BB/TR, 6', 165 lbs. Deb: 5/01/1884																												
1884	Phi-N	21	25	.457	50	47	46	2	1	417	443	9.6	13	93	2.0	194	4.2	3.54	82	.281	.321	-26	-30	97	90	5.8	8	-2	-2.1
1885	Phi-N	26	20	.565	48	45	45	5	0	405	345	7.7	5	81	1.8	197	4.4	2.22	131	.241	.281	27	31	104	97	4.2	15	1	5.3
1886	Phi-N	30	9	.769	48	45	43	4	**2**	396	317	7.2	11	69	1.6	212	4.8	**1.98**	160	.231	.268	**58**	52	96	100	**9.6**	13	5	**7.2**
1887	Phi-N	22	10	.688	37	33	31	2	1	297	297	9.0	13	47	1.4	125	3.8	3.00	127	.275	.306	35	26	94	103	4.0	17	0	5.1
Total	4	99	64	.607	183	170	165	13	4	1515	1402	8.3	42	290	1.7	728	4.3	2.67	118	.257	.294	94	82	98	97	23.6	52	4	15.5
■ **GEORGE FERGUSON**	Ferguson, George Cecil "Cecil" b: 8/19/1886, Ellsworth, Kan. d: 9/5/43, Orlando, Fla. BR/TR, 5'10", 165 lbs. Deb: 4/19/06																												
1906	NY-N	2	0	1.000	22	1	1	1	**7**	52	43	7.4	1	24	4.2	32	5.5	2.60	99	.254	.353	**0**	-0	97	110	1.0	2	1	0.1
1907	NY-N	3	2	.600	15	5	4	0	1	64	63	8.9	2	20	2.8	37	5.2	2.11	121	.292	.366	3	3	104	157	0.4	-1	-0	0.3
1908	Bos-N	11	11	.500	37	20	13	3	0	208	168	7.3	1	84	3.6	98	4.2	2.47	100	.250	.341	-3	0	106	100	1.9	1	-3	-0.2
1909	Bos-N	5	23	.179	36	30	19	3	0	227	235	9.3	2	83	3.3	87	3.4	3.73	71	.282	.355	-28	-27	102	99	-6.1	2	0	-2.8
1910	Bos-N	7	7	.500	26	14	10	1	0	123	110	8.0	3	58	4.2	40	2.9	3.80	94	.254	.351	-11	-3	118	90	1.8	-1	-0	-0.3
1911	Bos-N	1	3	.250	6	3	0	0	0	24	40	15.0	3	12	4.5	4	1.5	9.75	38	.388	.452	-17	-16	109	84	-0.2	1	0	-1.3
Total	6	29	46	.387	142	73	47	8	8	698	659	8.5	12	281	3.6	298	3.8	3.34	83	.272	.355	-56	-44	106	103	-1.2	3	-3	-4.2
■ **ALEX FERGUSON**	Ferguson, James Alexander b: 2/16/1897, Montclair, N.J. d: 4/26/76, Sepulveda, Cal. BR/TR, 6', 180 lbs. Deb: 8/16/18																												
1918	NY-A	0	0	—	1	0	0	0	0	2	2	9.0	0	2	9.0	1	4.5	0.00	—	.333	.500	1	1	94	0	0.0	-0	0	0.0
1921	NY-A	3	1	.750	17	4	1	0	1	56	64	10.3	4	27	4.3	9	1.4	5.95	71	.296	.368	-10	-11	99	85	0.6	-1	-0	-1.0
1922	Bos-A	9	16	.360	39	27	10	1	2	198	201	9.1	5	62	2.8	44	2.0	4.32	93	.265	.316	-6	-7	99	75	-1.2	-6	-1	-1.3
1923	Bos-A	9	13	.409	34	27	11	0	0	198	229	10.4	5	67	3.0	72	3.3	4.05	104	.297	.350	-1	3	106	104	0.2	-6	-1	-0.3
1924	Bos-A	14	17	.452	41	32	15	0	2	238	259	9.8	6	108	4.1	78	2.9	3.78	117	.286	.351	12	17	105	113	0.6	-7	1	1.2
1925	Bos-A	0	2	.000	5	4	0	0	1	16	22	12.4	6	5	2.8	5	2.8	10.69	41	.314	.364	-11	-11	99	68	-0.9	-0	-0	-0.9
	NY-A	4	2	.667	21	5	0	0	1	54	83	13.8	3	42	7.0	20	3.3	7.83	54	.358	.454	-21	-21	97	97	1.2	-1	1	-1.8
	Was-A	5	1	.833	7	6	3	0	0	55	52	8.5	2	23	3.8	24	3.9	3.27	128	.256	.329	7	6	95	106	1.7	-2	-1	0.2
	Yr	9	5	.643	33	15	3	0	2	125	157	11.3	11	70	5.0	49	3.5	6.19	68	.309	.387	-25	-27	97	106	2.0	-1	-1	-2.5
1926	Was-A	3	4	.429	19	4	0	0	1	48	69	12.9	4	18	3.4	16	3.0	7.69	51	.343	.386	-20	-20	97	81	-0.7	-0	1	-1.8
1927	Phi-N	8	16	.333	31	31	16	0	0	227	280	11.1	15	65	2.6	73	2.9	4.84	81	.313	.351	-23	-23	100	101	0.0	-5	0	-2.5
1928	Phi-N	5	10	.333	34	19	5	1	2	132	162	11.0	14	48	3.3	50	3.4	5.66	77	.312	.362	-25	-19	109	94	0.6	-5	1	-2.0
1929	Phi-N	1	2	.333	5	4	1	0	0	13	19	13.2	2	10	6.9	3	2.1	11.77	45	.345	.433	-10	-9	112	68	-0.3	-1	0	-0.7
	Bro-N	0	1	.000	3	3	0	0	0	2	7	31.5	2	1	4.5	1	4.5	22.50	20	.583	.533	-4	-4	96	109	-0.4	0	0	-0.2
	Yr	1	3	.250	8	7	1	0	0	15	26	15.6	4	11	6.6	4	2.4	13.20	39	.388	.451	-14	-13	110	109	-0.7	-1	1	-0.9
Total	10	61	85	.418	257	166	62	2	10	1239	1449	10.5	68	478	3.5	396	2.9	4.90	85	.299	.355	-112	-99	102	96	1.4	-33	0	-11.1
■ **BOB FERGUSON**	Ferguson, Robert Lester b: 4/18/19, Birmingham, Ala. BR/TR, 6'1.5", 180 lbs. Deb: 4/29/44																												
1944	Cin-N	0	3	.000	9	2	0	0	1	16	24	13.5	3	10	5.6	9	5.1	9.00	38	.358	.439	-10	-10	95	94	-1.4	0	0	-0.8
■ **BOB FERGUSON**	Ferguson, Robert V. "Death To Flying Things" b: 1/31/1845, Brooklyn, N.Y. d: 5/3/1894, Brooklyn, N.Y. BB/TR, 5'9.5", 149 lbs. Deb: 5/18/1871 M																												
1873	Atl-n	0	1	.000	1																								
1874	Atl-n	0	1	.000	1																								
1877	Har-N	1	1	.500	3	2	2	0	0	25	38	13.7	0	2	0.7	1	0.4	3.96	62	.358	.370	-3	-4	87	114	0.0	0	0	-0.3
1883	Phi-N	0	0	—	1	0	0	0	0	1	2	18.0	0	0	0.0	0	0.0	9.00	35	.423	.423	-1	-1	99	80	0.0	0	0	0.0
Total	2 n	0	2	.000	2																								
Total	2	1	1	.500	4	2	2	0	0	26	40	13.8	0	2	0.7	1	0.3	4.15	59	.361	.372	-4	-5	87	113	0.0	0	0	-0.3
■ **SID FERNANDEZ**	Fernandez, Charles Sidney b: 10/12/62, Honolulu, Hawaii BL/TL, 6'1", 220 lbs. Deb: 9/20/83																												
1983	LA-N	0	1	.000	2	1	0	0	0	6	7	10.5	0	7	10.5	9	13.5	6.00	60	.280	.455	-2	-2	100	104	-0.4	0	0	0.0
1984	NY-N	6	6	.500	15	15	0	0	0	90	74	7.4	8	34	3.4	62	6.2	3.50	103	.226	.291	1	1	100	87	-0.5	-0	-2	0.0
1985	NY-N	9	9	.500	26	26	3	0	0	170	108	**5.7**	14	80	4.2	180	**9.5**	2.81	122	**.181**	.277	15	12	95	79	-1.6	2	-0	1.4
1986	NY-N	16	6	.727	32	31	2	1	1	204	161	7.1	13	91	4.0	200	8.8	3.53	98	.216	.297	4	-1	93	79	2.3	2	-3	-0.2
1987	NY-N	12	8	.600	28	27	3	1	0	156	130	7.5	16	67	3.9	134	7.7	3.81	104	.224	.308	5	3	97	87	0.8	1	-2	0.1
1988	NY-N	12	10	.545	31	31	1	1	0	187	127	**6.1**	15	70	3.4	189	9.1	3.03	100	**.191**	.270	9	0	88	75	-1.5	6	-3	0.2
Total	6	55	40	.579	134	131	9	3	1	813	607	6.7	66	349	3.9	774	8.6	3.33	104	.206	.290	32	12	94	81	-0.9	10	-10	1.5
■ **DON FERRARESE**	Ferrarese, Donald Hugh b: 6/19/29, Oakland, Cal. BR/TL, 5'9", 170 lbs. Deb: 4/11/55																												
1955	Bal-A	0	0	—	6	0	0	0	0	9	8	8.0	0	11	11.0	5	5.0	3.00	124	.276	.442	1	1	94	204	0.0	-0	0	0.0
1956	Bal-A	4	10	.286	36	14	3	1	2	102	86	7.6	8	64	5.6	81	7.1	5.03	80	.229	.340	-10	-12	97	74	-2.6	-3	1	-1.3
1957	Bal-A	1	1	.500	8	2	0	0	0	19	14	6.6	1	12	5.7	13	6.2	4.74	74	.200	.313	-2	-3	93	57	0.0	-0	0	-0.2
1958	Cle-A	3	4	.429	28	10	2	0	1	95	91	8.6	5	46	4.4	62	5.9	3.69	95	.254	.334	1	-2	93	101	-0.4	-1	-1	-0.4
1959	Cle-A	5	3	.625	15	10	4	0	0	76	58	6.9	6	51	6.0	45	5.3	3.20	114	.219	.342	6	4	95	118	0.5	2	0	0.6
1960	Chi-A	0	1	.000	5	0	0	0	0	4	8	18.0	2	9	20.3	4	9.0	18.00	21	.400	.586	-6	-6	99	93	-0.4	0	0	-0.5

YEAR	TM/L	W	L	PCT	G	GS	CG	SHO	SV	IP	H	H/G	HR	BB	BB/G	SO	SO/G	ERA	/A	OAVG	OOBP	PR	/A	PF	CPI	WAT	PB	PD	TPI
1961	Phi-N	5	12	.294	42	14	3	1	1	139	120	7.8	14	68	4.4	89	5.8	3.76	105	.234	.322	4	3	98	96	-0.2	-1	-2	0.0
1962	Phi-N	0	1	.000	5	0	0	0	0	7	9	11.6	1	3	3.9	6	7.7	7.71	49	.310	.364	-3	-3	95	74	-0.4	0	0	-0.1
	StL-N	1	4	.200	38	0	0	0	1	57	55	8.7	2	31	4.9	45	7.1	2.68	157	.270	.355	8	10	107	159	-1.5	1	1	1.2
	Yr	1	5	.167	43	0	0	0	1	64	64	9.0	3	34	4.8	51	7.2	3.23	129	.274	.356	5	7	106	159	-1.9	0	1	1.1
Total	8	19	36	.345	183	50	12	2	5	508	449	8.0	39	295	5.2	350	6.2	3.99	96	.241	.341	-2	-8	97	103	-5.0	-1	-1	-0.7
■ **BILL FERRAZZI**	Ferrazzi, William Joseph b: 4/19/07, W.Quincy, Mass. BR/TR, 6'2.5", 200 lbs. Deb: 9/07/35																												
1935	Phi-A	1	2	.333	3	2	0	0	0	7	7	9.0	0	5	6.4	0	0.0	5.14	89	.269	.364	-1	-0	102	89	-0.1	0	0	0.0
■ **TONY FERREIRA**	Ferreira, Anthony Ross b: 10/4/62, Riverside, Cal. BL/TL, 6'1", 160 lbs. Deb: 9/17/85																												
1985	KC-A	0	0	—	2	0	0	0	0	6	6	9.0	0	2	3.0	5	7.5	7.50	56	.273	.333	-2	-2	101	47	0.0	0	0	-0.1
■ **WES FERRELL**	Ferrell, Wesley Cheek b: 2/2/08, Greensboro, N.C. d: 12/9/76, Sarasota, Fla. BR/TR, 6'2", 195 lbs. Deb: 9/09/27																												
1927	Cle-A	0	0	—	1	0	0	0	0	1	3	27.0	0	2	18.0	0	0.0	27.00	15	.600	.625	-3	-3	99	73	0.0	0	0	-0.1
1928	Cle-A	0	2	.000	2	2	1	0	0	16	15	8.4	0	5	2.8	4	2.3	2.25	195	.242	.299	3	4	108	106	-0.9	1	0	0.5
1929	Cle-A	21	10	.677	43	25	18	1	5	243	256	9.5	7	109	4.0	100	3.7	3.59	119	.279	.347	18	18	101	116	5.6	5	3	2.5
1930	Cle-A	25	13	.658	43	35	25	1	3	297	299	9.1	14	106	3.2	143	4.3	3.30	148	.262	.318	45	53	105	113	6.4	8	-3	5.7
1931	Cle-A	22	12	.647	40	35	**27**	2	3	276	276	9.0	9	130	4.2	123	4.0	3.75	123	.255	.333	19	27	106	101	5.8	18	5	5.0
1932	Cle-A	23	13	.639	38	34	26	3	1	288	299	9.3	17	104	3.3	105	3.3	3.66	131	.264	.324	26	36	107	108	3.5	5	1	4.2
1933	Cle-A	11	12	.478	28	26	16	1	0	201	225	10.1	8	70	3.1	41	1.8	4.21	107	.282	.335	2	6	105	101	-0.4	8	1	0.6
1934	Bos-A	14	5	.737	26	23	17	3	1	181	205	10.2	4	49	**2.4**	67	3.3	3.63	130	.282	.324	17	22	105	104	4.8	9	-2	2.9
1935	Bos-A	**25**	14	.641	41	38	**31**	3	0	**322**	336	9.4	16	108	3.0	110	3.1	3.52	137	.267	.321	33	47	108	107	**6.4**	21	2	**7.4**
1936	Bos-A	20	15	.571	39	38	**28**	3	0	**301**	330	9.9	11	119	3.6	106	3.2	4.19	127	.274	.339	28	38	106	100	3.8	12	-3	4.5
1937	Bos-A	3	6	.333	12	11	5	0	0	73	111	13.7	14	34	4.2	31	3.8	7.64	62	.348	.409	-25	-24	102	100	-1.6	6	2	-1.2
	Was-A	11	13	.458	25	24	21	0	0	208	214	9.3	11	88	3.8	92	4.0	3.94	112	.265	.334	16	11	96	101	-0.5	5	-1	1.0
	Yr	14	19	.424	37	35	**26**	0	0	**281**	325	10.4	25	122	3.9	123	3.9	4.90	92	.288	.355	-9	-13	97	101	-2.1	6	1	-0.2
1938	Was-A	13	8	.619	23	22	9	0	0	149	193	11.7	12	68	4.1	36	2.2	5.92	77	.311	.378	-19	-22	96	95	2.9	6	1	-1.3
	NY-A	2	2	.500	5	4	1	0	0	30	52	15.6	6	18	5.4	7	2.1	8.10	60	.388	.455	-11	-11	102	117	-0.4	0	1	-0.7
	Yr	15	10	.600	28	26	10	0	0	179	245	12.3	18	86	4.3	43	2.2	6.28	74	.324	.390	-30	-33	97	117	2.5	6	2	-2.0
1939	NY-A	1	2	.333	3	3	1	0	0	19	14	6.6	2	17	8.1	6	2.8	4.74	83	.219	.365	-0	-2	85	102	-0.7	-0	0	-0.1
1940	Bro-N	0	0	—	1	0	0	0	0	4	4	9.0	0	4	9.0	4	9.0	6.75	61	.250	.429	-1	-1	106	80	0.0	-0	1	0.0
1941	Bos-N	2	1	.667	4	3	1	0	0	14	13	8.4	1	9	5.8	10	6.4	5.14	67	.241	.359	-2	-3	96	81	0.7	2	-0	0.0
Total	15	193	128	.601	374	323	227	17	13	2623	2845	9.8	132	1040	3.6	985	3.4	4.04	117	.275	.338	147	198	104	105	35.4	104	5	30.9
■ **TOM FERRICK**	Ferrick, Thomas Jerome b: 1/6/15, New York, N.Y. BR/TR, 6'2.5", 220 lbs. Deb: 4/19/41 C																												
1941	Phi-A	8	10	.444	36	4	2	1	7	119	130	9.8	8	33	2.5	30	2.3	3.78	113	.275	.319	5	6	103	103	0.5	1	2	1.0
1942	Cle-A	3	2	.600	31	2	2	0	3	81	56	6.2	3	32	3.6	28	3.1	2.00	170	.200	.278	**15**	**13**	93	113	0.6	0	2	1.6
1946	Cle-A	0	0	—	9	0	0	0	1	18	25	12.5	3	4	2.0	9	4.5	5.00	63	.321	.349	-3	-4	90	112	0.0	1	0	-0.2
	StL-A	4	1	.800	25	1	0	0	5	32	26	7.3	1	5	1.4	13	3.7	2.81	124	.224	.248	2	2	100	65	1.6	-1	0	0.2
	Yr	4	1	.800	34	1	0	0	6	50	51	9.2	4	9	1.6	22	4.0	3.60	94	.263	.288	-1	-1	96	65	1.6	1	0	0.0
1947	Was-A	1	7	.125	31	0	0	0	9	60	57	8.6	1	20	3.0	23	3.5	3.15	118	.256	.306	4	4	101	98	-2.7	-1	2	0.5
1948	Was-A	2	5	.286	37	0	0	0	10	74	75	9.1	3	38	4.6	34	4.1	4.14	111	.261	.342	1	4	107	97	-0.7	-1	1	0.4
1949	StL-A	6	4	.600	50	0	0	0	6	104	102	8.8	9	41	3.5	34	2.9	3.89	112	.258	.322	4	5	104	98	2.0	-1	1	0.6
1950	StL-A	1	3	.250	16	0	0	0	2	24	24	9.0	2	7	2.6	6	2.3	4.13	123	.267	.304	1	3	111	94	-0.6	-0	1	0.3
	NY-A	8	4	.667	30	0	0	0	9	57	49	7.7	5	22	3.5	20	3.2	3.63	121	.233	.303	6	5	96	90	0.5	0	1	0.5
	Yr	9	7	.563	46	0	0	0	11	81	73	8.1	7	29	3.2	26	2.9	3.78	122	.243	.304	7	7	100	90	-0.1	-0	1	0.8
1951	NY-A	1	1	.500	9	0	0	0	1	12	21	15.8	4	7	5.3	3	2.3	7.50	49	.389	.444	-5	-5	88	137	-0.1	0	0	-0.4
	Was-A	2	0	1.000	22	0	0	0	2	42	36	7.7	3	7	1.5	17	3.6	2.36	169	.234	.264	8	8	97	109	1.0	0	0	0.8
	Yr	3	1	.750	31	-0	0	0	3	54	57	9.5	7	14	2.3	20	3.3	3.50	112	.274	.314	4	2	95	109	0.9	0	0	0.4
1952	Was-A	4	3	.571	27	0	0	0	1	51	53	9.4	2	11	1.9	28	4.9	3.00	123	.273	.309	4	4	100	112	0.5	1	1	0.6
Total	9	40	40	.500	323	7	4	1	56	674	654	8.7	44	227	3.0	245	3.3	3.47	117	.256	.311	42	44	100	101	2.6	1	11	5.9
■ **BOB FERRIS**	Ferris, Robert Eugene b: 5/7/55, Arlington, Va. BR/TR, 6'6", 225 lbs. Deb: 9/12/79																												
1979	Cal-A	0	0	—	2	0	0	0	0	6	5	7.5	1	3	4.5	2	3.0	1.50	258	.217	.296	2	2	92	236	0.0	0	0	0.2
1980	Cal-A	0	2	.000	5	3	0	0	0	15	23	13.8	2	9	5.4	4	2.4	6.00	65	.354	.432	-3	-3	97	124	-0.9	0	0	-0.2
Total	2	0	2	.000	7	3	0	0	0	21	28	12.0	3	12	5.1	6	2.6	4.71	83	.318	.396	-1	-2	95	156	-0.9	0	0	0.0
■ **DAVE FERRISS**	Ferriss, David Meadow "Boo" b: 12/5/21, Shaw, Miss. BL/TR, 6'2", 208 lbs. Deb: 4/29/45 C																												
1945	Bos-A	21	10	.677	35	31	26	5	2	265	263	8.9	6	85	2.9	94	3.2	2.95	110	.264	.322	12	8	96	114	7.1	12	5	2.7
1946	Bos-A	25	6	**.806**	40	35	26	6	3	274	274	9.0	14	71	2.3	106	3.5	3.25	119	.259	.305	8	19	111	97	7.1	2	0	2.4
1947	Bos-A	12	11	.522	33	28	14	1	0	218	241	9.9	14	92	3.8	64	2.6	4.05	98	.287	.356	-8	-2	107	114	-0.3	7	-1	0.5
1948	Bos-A	7	3	.700	31	9	1	0	3	115	127	9.9	7	61	4.8	30	2.3	5.24	79	.286	.376	-12	-14	97	97	1.1	2	0	-1.0
1949	Bos-A	0	0	—	4	0	0	0	0	7	7	9.0	1	4	5.1	1	1.3	3.86	112	.292	.414	0	0	103	161	0.0	1	-0	0.1
1950	Bos-A	0	0	—	1	0	0	0	0	1	2	18.0	0	1	9.0	1	9.0	18.00	28	.500	.500	-1	-1	111	67	0.0	0	0	0.0
Total	6	65	30	.684	144	103	67	12	8	880	914	9.3	42	314	3.2	296	3.0	3.64	103	.272	.334	-2	11	104	107	15.0	23	5	4.7
■ **CY FERRY**	Ferry, Alfred Joseph b: 9/27/1878, Hudson, N.Y. d: 9/27/38, Pittsfield, Mass. BR/TR, 6'1", 170 lbs. Deb: 5/12/04																												
1904	Det-A	0	1	.000	3	1	1	0	0	13	12	8.3	0	11	7.6	4	2.8	6.23	41	.268	.412	-5	-5	98	68	-0.4	1	0	-0.4
1905	Cle-A	0	0	—	1	1	0	0	0	2	3	13.5	1	0	0.0	2	9.0	13.50	20	.374	.374	-2	-2	100	64	0.0	-0	0	-0.1
Total	2	0	1	.000	4	2	1	0	0	15	15	9.0	1	11	6.6	6	3.6	7.20	36	.284	.407	-8	-8	98	67	-0.4	1	0	-0.5
■ **JACK FERRY**	Ferry, John Francis b: 4/7/1887, Pittsfield, Mass. d: 8/29/54, Pittsfield, Mass. BR/TR, 5'11", 175 lbs. Deb: 9/04/10																												
1910	Pit-N	1	2	.333	6	3	2	0	0	31	26	7.5	0	8	2.3	12	3.5	2.32	144	.230	.287	2	3	110	83	-0.5	1	0	0.5
1911	Pit-N	6	4	.600	26	8	4	1	3	86	83	8.7	3	27	2.8	32	3.3	3.14	105	.260	.322	3	2	97	103	0.6	3	-2	0.3
1912	Pit-N	2	0	1.000	11	3	1	1	1	39	33	7.6	1	23	5.3	10	2.3	3.00	108	.226	.335	2	1	95	92	1.0	-1	1	0.1
1913	Pit-N	1	0	1.000	4	0	0	0	0	5	4	7.2	0	2	3.6	2	3.6	5.40	56	.286	.300	-1	-1	94	72	0.5	0	0	0.0
Total	4	10	6	.625	47	14	7	2	4	161	146	8.2	4	60	3.4	56	3.1	3.02	109	.247	.318	6	5	99	95	1.6	3	-1	0.9
■ **ALEX FERSON**	Ferson, Alexander "Colonel" b: 7/14/1866, Philadelphia, Pa. d: 12/5/57, Boston, Mass. BR/TR, 5'9", 165 lbs. Deb: 5/04/1889																												
1889	Was-N	17	17	.500	36	34	28	1	0	288	319	10.0	9	105	3.3	85	2.7	3.91	98	.297	.359	4	-2	96	103	5.4	-5	0	-0.5
1890	Buf-P	1	7	.125	10	10	7	0	0	71	88	11.2	5	40	5.1	13	1.6	5.45	75	.317	.403	-10	-11	97	96	-2.1	1	0	-0.7
1892	Bal-N	0	1	.000	2	1	1	0	0	9	17	17.0	1	6	6.0	8	8.0	11.00	31	.415	.490	-8	-8	102	84	-0.4	-1	0	-0.5
Total	3	18	25	.419	48	45	36	1	0	368	424	10.4	15	151	3.7	106	2.6	4.38	89	.304	.372	-13	-20	96	101	2.9	-5	0	-1.7
■ **LOU FETTE**	Fette, Louis Henry William b: 3/15/07, Alma, Mo. d: 1/3/81, Warrensburg, Mo. BR/TR, 6'1.5", 200 lbs. Deb: 4/26/37																												
1937	Bos-N	20	10	.667	35	33	23	**5**	0	259	243	8.4	5	81	2.8	70	2.4	2.88	122	.251	.305	30	18	90	106	**5.3**	3	0	2.1
1938	Bos-N	11	13	.458	33	32	17	3	1	240	235	8.8	11	79	3.0	83	3.1	3.15	107	.258	.315	17	6	89	110	-1.2	0	2	0.7
1939	Bos-N	10	10	.500	27	26	11	**6**	0	146	123	7.6	7	61	3.8	35	2.2	2.96	123	.229	.304	16	11	93	98	1.6	-4	3	1.0
1940	Bos-N	0	5	.000	7	5	0	0	0	32	38	10.7	0	18	5.1	2	0.6	5.63	69	.302	.390	-6	-6	101	90	-2.4	1	-1	-0.5
	Bro-N	0	0	—	2	0	0	0	0	3	3	9.0	0	2	6.0	0	0.0	0.00	—	.300	.417	1	1	106	0	0.0	0	-0	0.1
	Yr	0	5	.000	9	5	0	0	0	35	41	10.5	0	20	5.1	2	0.5	5.14	76	.299	.386	-5	-5	101	0	-2.4	1	-1	-0.4
1945	Bos-N	0	2	.000	5	1	0	0	0	11	16	13.1	1	7	5.7	4	3.3	5.73	75	.356	.453	-2	-2	113	133	-0.9	-0	0	-0.1
Total	5	41	40	.506	109	97	51	14	1	691	658	8.6	24	248	3.2	194	2.5	3.15	112	.253	.316	55	29	91	105	2.4	0	4	3.3
■ **JOHN FICK**	Fick, John Ralph b: 5/18/21, Baltimore, Md. d: 6/9/58, Somers Point, N.J. BL/TL, 5'10", 150 lbs. Deb: 7/29/44																												
1944	Phi-N	0	0	—	4	0	0	0	0	5	3	5.4	0	3	5.4	2	3.6	3.60	103	.150	.292	0	0	103	32	0.0	0	0	0.0
■ **MARK FIDRYCH**	Fidrych, Mark Steven "The Bird" b: 8/14/54, Worcester, Mass. BR/TR, 6'3", 175 lbs. Deb: 4/20/76																												
1976	Det-A	19	9	.679	31	29	**24**	4	0	250	217	7.8	12	53	1.9	97	3.5	**2.34**	**158**	.235	.274	33	**37**	105	105	6.3	0	5	**4.9**
1977	Det-A	6	4	.600	11	11	7	1	0	81	82	9.1	2	12	1.3	42	4.7	2.89	148	.269	.291	11	12	105	103	1.4	0	-1	1.2

YEAR	TM/L	W	L	PCT	G	GS	CG	SHO	SV	IP	H	H/G	HR	BB	BB/G	SO	SO/G	ERA	/A	OAVG	OOBP	PR	/A	PF	CPI	WAT	PB	PD	TPI
1978	Det-A	2	0	1.000	3	3	2	0	0	22	17	7.0	1	5	2.0	10	4.1	2.45	165	.213	.259	3	4	107	74	1.0	0	1	0.6
1979	Det-A	0	3	.000	4	4	0	0	0	15	23	13.8	3	9	5.4	5	3.0	10.20	40	.371	.452	-10	-10	96	85	-1.4	0	-0	-0.8
1980	Det-A	2	3	.400	9	9	1	0	0	44	58	11.9	5	20	4.1	16	3.3	5.73	74	.309	.367	-8	-7	105	96	-0.5	0	1	-0.5
Total	5	29	19	.604	58	56	34	5	0	412	397	8.7	23	99	2.2	170	3.7	3.10	126	.255	.296	29	36	105	101	6.8	0	5	5.4
■ **CLARENCE FIEBER**	Fieber, Clarence Thomas "Lefty" b: 9/4/13, San Francisco, Cal d: 8/20/85, Redwood City, Cal BL/TL, 6'4", 187 lbs. Deb: 5/18/32																												
1932	Chi-A	1	0	1.000	3	0	0	0	0	5	6	10.8	0	3	5.4	1	1.8	1.80	226	.273	.360	1	1	91	233	0.5	0	0	0.1
■ **JIM FIELD**	Field, James C. b: 4/24/1863, Philadelphia, Pa. d: 5/13/53, Atlantic City, N.J Deb: 1883																												
1890	Roc-a	1	0	1.000	2	1	1	0	1	10	7	6.3	0	4	3.6	2	1.8	2.70	132	.210	.295	1	1	92	77	0.5	0	0	0.1
■ **JOCKO FIELDS**	Fields, John Joseph b: 10/20/1864, Cork, Ireland d: 10/14/50, Jersey City, N.J. BR/TR, 5'10", 160 lbs. Deb: 5/31/1887																												
1887	Pit-N	0	0	—	1	0	0	0	0	1	0	0.0	0	2	18.0	0	0.0	0.00	—	.000	.432	0	0	96	0	0.0	0	0	0.0
■ **LOU FIENE**	Fiene, Louis Henry "Big Finn" b: 12/29/1884, Ft.Dodge, Iowa d: 12/22/64, Chicago, Ill. BR/TR, 6', 175 lbs. Deb: 5/07/06																												
1906	Chi-A	1	1	.500	6	2	1	0	0	31	35	10.2	0	9	2.6	12	3.5	2.90	83	.311	.362	-1	-2	89	127	-0.1	0	0	-0.1
1907	Chi-A	0	1	.000	6	1	1	0	1	26	30	10.4	0	7	2.4	15	5.2	4.15	62	.315	.362	-5	-5	101	87	-0.4	-0	0	-0.4
1908	Chi-A	0	1	.000	1	1	1	0	0	9	9	9.0	0	1	1.0	3	3.0	4.00	55	.257	.278	-2	-2	93	58	-0.4	-0	0	0.0
1909	Chi-A	2	5	.286	13	6	4	0	0	75	75	9.4	1	18	2.3	24	3.0	4.13	58	.284	.341	-13	-14	97	82	-1.5	-2	1	-1.3
Total	4	3	8	.273	26	10	7	0	1	138	149	9.7	1	35	2.3	54	3.5	3.85	63	.294	.346	-20	-22	95	91	-2.4	-2	2	-1.8
■ **DANNY FIFE**	Fife, Danny Wayne b: 10/5/49, Harrisburg, Ill. BR/TR, 6'3", 175 lbs. Deb: 8/18/73																												
1973	Min-A	3	2	.600	10	7	1	0	0	52	54	9.3	2	29	5.0	18	3.1	4.33	91	.270	.366	-3	-2	103	99	0.5	0	-0	-0.2
1974	Min-A	0	0	—	4	0	0	0	0	5	10	18.0	0	4	7.2	3	5.4	16.20	23	.417	.517	-7	-7	101	60	0.0	0	-0	-0.6
Total	2	3	2	.600	14	7	1	0	0	57	64	10.1	2	33	5.2	21	3.3	5.37	73	.286	.383	-10	-9	103	95	0.5	0	-0	-0.8
■ **JACK FIFIELD**	Fifield, John Proctor b: 10/5/1871, Enfield, N.H. d: 10/12/08, Wareham, Mass. 5'11", 160 lbs. Deb: 4/28/1897																												
1897	Phi-N	5	18	.217	27	26	21	0	0	211	263	11.2	7	80	3.4	38	1.6	5.55	75	.328	.389	-29	-33	96	84	-6.0	3	0	-2.4
1898	Phi-N	11	9	.550	21	21	18	2	0	171	170	8.9	2	60	3.2	31	1.6	3.32	102	.280	.345	6	1	94	96	0.6	-3	0	-0.1
1899	Phi-N	3	8	.273	14	11	9	1	1	93	110	10.6	0	36	3.5	8	0.8	4.06	90	.319	.383	-2	-4	95	100	-3.1	1	0	-0.2
	Was-N	2	4	.333	6	6	6	0	0	47	73	14.0	1	17	3.3	12	2.3	6.13	62	.380	.431	-12	-12	98	98	-0.1	0	0	-0.9
	Yr	5	12	.294	20	17	15	1	1	140	183	11.8	1	53	3.4	20	1.3	4.76	78	.341	.400	-14	-16	96	98	-3.2	1	0	-1.1
Total	3	21	39	.350	68	64	54	3	1	522	616	10.6	10	193	3.3	89	1.5	4.60	82	.317	.378	-37	-48	95	92	-8.6	1	0	-3.6
■ **FRANK FIGGEMEIER**	Figgemeier, Frank Y. b: 4/22/1874, St.Louis, Mo. d: 4/15/15, St.Louis, Mo. Deb: 9/25/1894																												
1894	Phi-N	0	1	.000	1	1	1	0	0	8	12	13.5	1	4	4.5	2	2.3	11.25	44	.370	.439	-5	-6	94	63	-0.4	0	0	-0.3
■ **ED FIGUEROA**	Figueroa, Eduardo (Padilla) b: 10/14/48, Ciales, P.R. BR/TR, 6'1", 190 lbs. Deb: 4/09/74																												
1974	Cal-A	2	8	.200	25	12	5	1	0	105	119	10.2	3	36	3.1	49	4.2	3.69	91	.294	.349	-1	-4	93	114	-2.6	0	0	-0.3
1975	Cal-A	16	13	.552	33	32	16	2	0	245	213	7.8	14	84	3.1	139	5.1	2.90	125	.233	.298	24	20	96	96	3.2	0	1	2.2
1976	NY-A	19	10	.655	34	34	14	4	0	257	237	8.3	13	94	3.3	119	4.2	3.01	114	.246	.309	15	12	97	106	2.0	0	-3	0.9
1977	NY-A	16	11	.593	32	32	12	2	0	239	228	8.6	19	75	2.8	104	3.9	3.58	110	.252	.306	13	10	97	94	-0.5	0	-2	0.8
1978	NY-A	20	9	.690	35	35	12	2	0	253	233	8.3	22	77	2.7	92	3.3	2.99	123	.248	.302	22	19	97	110	3.3	0	-0	1.9
1979	NY-A	4	6	.400	16	16	4	1	0	105	109	9.3	6	35	3.0	42	3.6	4.11	98	.275	.330	1	-1	95	94	-1.4	0	0	0.0
1980	NY-A	3	3	.500	15	9	0	0	1	58	90	14.0	3	24	3.7	16	2.5	6.98	57	.363	.417	-19	-20	98	95	-0.6	0	1	-1.7
	Tex-A	0	7	.000	8	8	0	0	0	40	62	13.9	9	12	2.7	9	2.0	5.85	69	.365	.398	-8	-8	100	131	-3.4	0	1	-0.6
	Yr	3	10	.231	23	17	0	0	1	98	152	14.0	12	36	3.3	25	2.3	6.52	61	.360	.407	-27	-28	99	131	-4.0	0	1	-2.3
1981	Oak-A	0	0	—	2	1	0	0	0	8	8	9.0	1	6	6.8	1	1.1	5.63	62	.258	.378	-2	-2	95	90	0.0	0	0	-0.1
Total	8	80	67	.544	200	179	63	12	1	1310	1299	8.9	90	443	3.0	571	3.9	3.51	105	.261	.319	46	26	96	103	0.0	0	-3	3.1
■ **TOM FILER**	Filer, Thomas Carson b: 12/1/56, Philadelphia, Pa. BR/TR, 6'1", 195 lbs. Deb: 6/08/82																												
1982	Chi-N	1	2	.333	8	8	0	0	0	41	50	11.0	5	18	4.0	15	3.3	5.49	68	.301	.364	-9	-8	104	97	-0.3	-1	2	-0.6
1985	Tor-A	7	0	1.000	11	9	0	0	0	49	38	7.0	6	18	3.3	24	4.4	3.86	107	.222	.292	2	1	99	87	3.5	0	-0	0.1
1988	Mil-A	5	8	.385	19	16	2	1	0	102	108	9.5	8	33	2.9	39	3.4	4.41	93	.281	.329	-5	-4	103	98	-1.9	0	3	0.0
Total	3	13	10	.565	38	33	2	1	0	192	196	9.2	19	69	3.2	78	3.7	4.50	89	.271	.328	-12	-10	102	95	1.3	-1	4	-0.5
■ **EDDIE FILES**	Files, Charles Edward b: 5/19/1883, Portland, Me. d: 5/10/54, Cornish, Maine BR/TR, Deb: 10/03/08																												
1908	Phi-A	0	0	—	2	0	0	0	0	9	8	8.0	0	3	3.0	6	6.0	6.00	44	.286	.394	-4	-3	110	71	0.0	-0	-0	-0.3
■ **MARC FILLEY**	Filley, Marcus Lucius b: 2/28/12, Troy, N.Y. BR/TR, 5'11", 172 lbs. Deb: 4/19/34																												
1934	Was-A	0	0	—	1	0	0	0	0	⅓	2	54.0	0	0	0.0	0	0.0	27.00	—	.667	.667	-1	-1	102	83	0.0	0	0	0.0
■ **DANA FILLINGIM**	Fillingim, Dana b: 11/6/1893, Columbus, Ga. d: 2/3/61, Tuskegee, Ala. BL/TR, 5'10", 175 lbs. Deb: 8/02/15																												
1915	Phi-A	0	5	.000	8	4	1	0	0	39	42	9.7	0	32	7.4	17	3.9	3.46	88	.313	.449	-2	-2	103	164	-2.4	-0	-0	-0.2
1918	Bos-N	7	6	.538	14	13	10	4	0	113	99	7.9	0	28	2.2	29	2.3	2.23	118	.243	.291	7	5	95	106	1.4	0	0	0.6
1919	Bos-N	6	13	.316	32	19	9	0	2	186	185	9.0	2	39	1.9	50	2.4	3.39	86	.270	.297	-10	-10	100	89	-2.3	1	2	-0.6
1920	Bos-N	12	21	.364	37	30	22	2	0	272	292	9.7	8	79	2.6	66	2.2	3.11	100	.287	.327	1	0	99	114	-2.1	-2	6	0.3
1921	Bos-N	15	10	.600	44	22	11	3	1	240	249	9.3	10	56	2.1	54	2.0	3.45	101	.272	.306	9	1	92	92	2.5	5	-1	0.4
1922	Bos-N	5	9	.357	25	12	5	1	2	117	143	11.0	6	37	2.8	25	1.9	4.54	88	.311	.347	-6	-7	98	102	0.1	-2	-1	-0.8
1923	Bos-N	1	9	.100	35	12	1	0	0	100	141	12.7	6	36	3.2	27	2.4	5.22	79	.345	.384	-14	-12	102	113	-3.5	1	0	-1.0
1925	Phi-N	1	0	1.000	5	1	0	0	0	9	19	19.0	0	6	6.0	2	2.0	10.00	50	.432	.500	-6	-5	118	96	0.5	0	0	-0.3
Total	8	47	73	.392	200	113	59	10	5	1076	1170	9.8	32	313	2.6	270	2.3	3.56	93	.287	.328	-21	-29	98	104	-5.8	3	6	-1.6
■ **PETE FILSON**	Filson, William Peter b: 9/28/58, Darby, Pa. BB/TL, 6'2", 195 lbs. Deb: 5/15/82																												
1982	Min-A	0	2	.000	5	3	0	0	0	12	17	12.8	2	8	6.0	10	7.5	9.00	46	.321	.397	-7	-6	102	77	-0.9	0	-0	-0.5
1983	Min-A	4	1	.800	26	8	0	0	1	90	87	8.7	9	29	2.9	49	4.9	3.40	127	.252	.310	7	9	106	107	1.6	0	-2	0.8
1984	Min-A	6	5	.545	55	7	0	0	1	119	106	8.0	14	54	4.1	59	4.5	4.08	103	.238	.317	-1	2	106	93	0.5	0	-1	0.0
1985	Min-A	4	5	.444	40	6	1	0	2	96	93	8.7	13	30	2.8	42	3.9	3.66	118	.251	.303	5	7	104	104	-0.2	0	-1	0.6
1986	Min-A	0	0	—	4	0	0	0	0	6	13	19.5	1	2	3.0	4	6.0	6.00	76	.406	.457	-1	-1	109	163	0.0	0	-0	0.0
	Chi-A	0	1	.000	3	1	0	0	0	12	14	10.5	4	5	3.8	4	3.0	6.00	71	.286	.352	-2	-2	101	108	-0.4	0	-0	-0.2
	Yr	0	1	.000	7	1	0	0	0	18	27	13.5	5	7	3.5	8	4.0	6.00	73	.329	.382	-4	-3	104	108	-0.4	0	-0	-0.2
1987	NY-A	1	0	1.000	7	2	0	0	0	22	26	10.6	2	9	3.7	10	4.1	3.27	133	.299	.364	3	3	97	159	0.5	0	1	0.3
Total	6	15	14	.517	140	27	1	0	4	357	356	9.0	45	137	3.5	178	4.5	4.01	107	.258	.322	4	11	105	105	1.1	0	-4	1.0
■ **JOEL FINCH**	Finch, Joel D b: 8/20/56, South Bend, Ind. BR/TR, 6'2", 175 lbs. Deb: 9/27/79																												
1979	Bos-A	0	3	.000	15	7	0	0	0	57	65	10.3	5	25	3.9	25	3.9	4.89	92	.289	.360	-4	-3	106	98	-1.4	0	1	-0.1
■ **BILL FINCHER**	Fincher, William Allen b: 5/26/1894, Atlanta, Ga. d: 5/7/46, Shreveport, La. BR/TR, 6'1", 180 lbs. Deb: 4/23/16																												
1916	StL-A	0	1	.000	12	1	0	0	0	21	22	9.4	0	7	3.0	5	2.1	2.14	124	.282	.341	2	1	94	159	-0.4	0	1	0.3
■ **TOMMY FINE**	Fine, Thomas Morgan b: 10/10/14, Cleburne, Tex. BB/TR, 6', 180 lbs. Deb: 4/26/47																												
1947	Bos-A	1	2	.333	9	7	1	0	0	36	41	10.3	0	19	4.8	10	2.5	5.50	72	.285	.363	-7	-6	107	78	-0.5	1	2	-0.3
1950	StL-A	0	1	.000	14	0	0	0	0	37	53	12.9	6	25	6.1	6	1.5	8.03	63	.342	.431	-14	-12	111	95	-0.4	1	0	-0.9
Total	2	1	3	.250	23	7	1	0	0	73	94	11.6	6	44	5.4	16	2.0	6.78	67	.314	.398	-21	-18	109	87	-0.9	2	2	-1.2
■ **ROLLIE FINGERS**	Fingers, Roland Glen b: 8/25/46, Steubenville, Ohio BR/TR, 6'4", 190 lbs. Deb: 9/15/68																												
1968	Oak-A	0	0	—	1	0	0	0	0	1	4	36.0	1	1	9.0	0	0.0	36.00	8	.571	.667	-4	-4	98	82	0.0	0	0	-0.2
1969	Oak-A	6	7	.462	60	8	1	1	12	119	116	8.8	13	41	3.1	61	4.6	3.71	89	.257	.320	-1	-5	91	105	-0.9	0	2	-0.2
1970	Oak-A	7	9	.438	45	19	1	0	2	148	137	8.3	13	48	2.9	79	4.8	3.65	97	.250	.308	1	-2	96	94	-1.7	-0	1	-0.1
1971	Oak-A	4	6	.400	48	8	2	1	17	129	94	6.6	14	30	2.1	98	6.8	3.00	114	.207	.262	7	6	99	81	-1.8	1	2	0.9
1972	Oak-A	11	9	.550	65	0	0	0	21	111	85	6.9	8	32	2.6	113	9.2	2.51	115	.212	.270	7	5	95	89	-0.8	2	-0	0.8
1973	Oak-A	7	8	.467	62	2	0	0	22	127	107	7.6	5	39	2.8	110	7.8	1.91	171	.226	.288	27	19	86	124	-1.5	0	-1	1.9
1974	Oak-A	9	5	.643	**76**	0	0	0	18	119	104	7.9	5	29	2.2	95	7.2	2.65	135	.240	.277	13	12	99	98	1.5	0	2	1.5

YEAR	TM/L	W	L	PCT	G	GS	CG	SHO	SV	IP	H	H/G	HR	BB	BB/G	SO	SO/G	ERA	/A	OAVG	OOBP	PR	/A	PF	CPI	WAT	PB	PD	TPI
1975	Oak-A	10	6	.625	**75**	0	0	0	24	127	95	6.7	13	33	2.3	115	8.1	2.98	116	.213	.272	11	7	91	88	0.4	0	0	0.7
1976	Oak-A	13	11	.542	70	0	0	0	20	135	118	7.9	3	40	2.7	113	7.5	2.47	141	.243	.295	16	15	98	116	0.0	0	2	1.8
1977	SD-N	8	9	.471	**78**	0	0	0	**35**	132	123	8.4	12	36	2.5	113	7.7	3.00	117	.248	.295	13	7	89	108	0.7	-2	-0	0.5
1978	SD-N	6	13	.316	67	0	0	0	**37**	107	84	7.1	4	29	2.4	72	6.1	2.52	131	.212	.263	13	9	93	75	-3.9	-0	0	1.0
1979	SD-N	9	9	.500	54	0	0	0	13	84	91	9.8	7	37	4.0	65	7.0	4.50	81	.281	.347	-7	-8	97	100	1.3	-1	-1	-0.9
1980	SD-N	11	9	.550	66	0	0	0	23	103	101	8.8	3	32	2.8	69	6.0	2.80	121	.263	.311	9	7	94	117	2.0	2	-1	0.8
1981	Mil-A	6	3	.667	47	0	0	0	**28**	78	55	6.3	3	13	1.5	61	7.0	1.04	336	.198	.232	**23**	**21**	95	136	1.1	0	0	2.3
1982	Mil-A	5	6	.455	50	0	0	0	29	80	63	7.1	5	20	2.3	71	8.0	2.59	146	.220	.264	13	10	92	92	-1.2	0	0	1.1
1984	Mil-A	1	2	.333	33	0	0	0	23	46	38	7.4	5	13	2.5	40	7.8	1.96	189	.213	.264	10	9	93	122	-0.2	0	-0	0.9
1985	Mil-A	1	6	.143	47	0	0	0	17	55	59	9.7	9	19	3.1	24	3.9	5.07	86	.272	.324	-6	-4	106	93	-2.3	0	1	-0.2
Total	17	114	118	.491	944	37	4	2	341	1701	1474	7.8	123	492	2.6	1299	6.9	2.90	119	.235	.289	146	106	94	101	-7.3	3	7	12.6
■ HERMAN FINK	Fink, Herman Adam b: 8/22/11, Concord, N.C. d: 8/24/80, Salisbury, N.C. BR/TR, 6'2", 198 lbs. Deb: 9/16/35																												
1935	Phi-A	0	3	.000	5	3	0	0	0	16	18	10.1	0	10	5.6	2	1.1	9.00	51	.290	.392	-8	-8	102	56	-1.4	-0	0	-0.6
1936	Phi-A	8	16	.333	34	24	9	0	3	189	222	10.6	18	78	3.7	53	2.5	5.38	98	.294	.353	-7	-2	105	98	-0.4	-4	-2	-0.6
1937	Phi-A	2	1	.667	28	3	1	0	1	80	82	9.2	6	35	3.9	18	2.0	4.05	110	.263	.335	5	4	96	101	0.7	-1	-0	0.2
Total	3	10	20	.333	67	30	10	0	4	285	322	10.2	24	123	3.9	73	2.3	5.21	96	.285	.351	-10	-6	103	96	-1.1	-5	-2	-1.0
■ PEMBROKE FINLAYSON	Finlayson, Pembroke b: 7/31/1888, Cheraw, S.C. d: 3/6/12, Brooklyn, N.Y. BR/TR, Deb: 6/06/08																												
1908	Bro-N	0	0	—	1	0	0	0	0	⅓	0	0.0	0	4	108.0	0	0.0	135.00	—	—	1.000	-5	-5	99	25	0.0	0	0	-0.3
1909	Bro-N	0	0	—	1	0	0	0	0	7	7	9.0	0	4	5.1	2	2.6	5.14	52	.212	.297	-2	-2	103	34	0.0	-0	-0	-0.1
Total	2	0	0	—	2	0	0	0	0	7	7	9.0	0	8	10.3	2	2.6	11.57	23	.212	.366	-7	-7	103	34	0.0	-0	-0	-0.4
■ CHUCK FINLEY	Finley, Charles Edward b: 11/26/62, Monroe, La. BL/TL, 6'6", 220 lbs. Deb: 5/29/86																												
1986	Cal-A	3	1	.750	25	0	0	0	0	46	40	7.8	2	23	4.5	37	7.2	3.33	120	.235	.323	4	3	95	100	0.9	0	1	0.4
1987	Cal-A	2	7	.222	35	3	0	0	0	91	102	10.1	7	43	4.3	63	6.2	4.65	96	.287	.365	-2	-2	100	106	-2.3	0	-0	-0.1
1988	Cal-A	9	15	.375	31	31	2	0	0	194	191	8.9	15	82	3.8	111	5.1	4.18	90	.263	.336	-4	-9	95	100	-2.5	0	-1	-0.9
Total	3	14	23	.378	91	34	2	0	0	331	333	9.1	24	148	4.0	211	5.7	4.19	95	.266	.342	-2	-8	96	102	-3.9	0	-0	-0.6
■ HAPPY FINNERAN	Finneran, Joseph Ignatius "Smokey Joe" b: 10/29/1891, E.Orange, N.J. d: 2/3/42, Orange, N.J. BR/TR, 5'10.5", 169 lbs. Deb: 8/20/12																												
1912	Phi-N	0	2	.000	14	4	0	0	1	46	50	9.8	2	10	2.0	10	2.0	2.54	135	.273	.314	4	5	101	121	-0.9	0	0	0.5
1913	Phi-N	0	0	—	3	0	0	0	0	5	12	21.6	0	2	3.6	0	0.0	7.20	49	.462	.500	-2	-2	111	141	0.0	1	-0	0.0
1914	Bro-F	12	11	.522	27	23	13	2	1	175	153	7.9	6	60	3.1	54	2.8	3.19	102	.237	.308	0	1	101	85	0.6	-4	1	-0.1
1915	Bro-F	10	12	.455	37	24	12	1	2	215	197	8.2	2	87	3.6	68	2.8	2.80	106	.249	.331	5	4	98	111	-0.1	-3	2	0.3
1918	Det-A	0	2	.000	5	2	0	0	1	14	22	14.1	0	8	5.1	2	1.3	9.64	28	.393	.469	-11	-11	99	73	-0.9	-0	1	-0.9
	NY-A	3	6	.333	23	13	4	0	0	114	134	10.6	7	35	2.8	34	2.7	3.79	69	.305	.354	-13	-15	94	115	-1.4	1	-1	-1.5
	Yr	3	8	.273	28	15	4	0	1	128	156	11.0	7	43	3.0	36	2.5	4.43	59	.315	.367	-24	-26	95	115	-2.3	-0	0	-2.4
Total	5	25	33	.431	109	66	29	3	5	569	568	9.0	17	202	3.2	168	2.7	3.31	91	.266	.333	-16	-19	99	104	-2.7	-5	3	-1.7
■ STEVE FIREOVID	Fireovid, Stephen John b: 6/6/57, Bryan, Ohio BB/TR, 6'2", 195 lbs. Deb: 9/06/81																												
1981	SD-N	0	1	.000	5	4	0	0	0	26	30	10.4	2	7	2.4	11	3.8	2.77	119	.294	.336	2	2	95	157	-0.4	-0	0	0.1
1983	SD-N	0	0	—	3	0	0	0	0	5	4	7.2	0	2	3.6	1	1.8	1.80	200	.235	.300	1	1	99	151	0.0	0	0	0.1
1984	Phi-N	0	0	—	6	0	0	0	0	6	4	6.0	0	0	0.0	3	4.5	1.50	243	.200	.200	1	1	101	58	0.0	0	0	0.2
1985	Chi-A	0	0	—	4	0	0	0	0	7	17	21.9	0	2	2.6	2	2.6	5.14	81	.472	.500	-1	-1	100	202	0.0	0	-0	0.0
1986	Sea-A	2	0	1.000	10	1	0	0	0	21	28	12.0	1	4	1.7	10	4.3	4.29	104	.333	.371	-0	0	106	122	1.0	0	-0	0.0
Total	5	2	1	.667	28	5	0	0	0	65	83	11.5	3	15	2.1	27	3.7	3.32	115	.320	.357	3	3	100	141	0.6	-0	0	0.4
■ TED FIRTH	Firth, John E. b: 1856, Massachusetts d: 6/23/02, Tewksbury, Mass. Deb: 8/15/1884																												
1884	Ric-a	0	1	.000	1	1	1	0	0	9	14	14.0	0	5	5.0	0	0.0	8.00	41	.364	.437	-5	-5	102	88	-0.4	0	0	-0.2
■ CARL FISCHER	Fischer, Charles William b: 11/5/05, Medina, N.Y. d: 12/10/63, Medina, N.Y. BR/TL, 6', 180 lbs. Deb: 7/19/30																												
1930	Was-A	1	1	.500	8	4	1	0	1	33	37	10.1	0	18	4.9	21	5.7	4.91	93	.285	.363	-1	-1	98	96	-0.1	-1	1	-0.1
1931	Was-A	13	9	.591	46	23	7	0	3	191	207	9.8	12	80	3.8	96	4.5	4.38	98	.273	.341	-0	-2	98	100	0.0	-5	-4	-0.8
1932	Was-A	3	2	.600	12	7	1	1	1	51	57	10.1	4	31	5.5	23	4.1	4.94	88	.282	.374	-3	-3	98	107	0.0	1	-2	-0.3
	StL-A	3	7	.300	24	11	4	0	0	97	122	11.3	12	45	4.2	35	3.2	5.57	82	.310	.375	-12	-11	103	108	-1.3	1	-1	-0.9
	Yr	6	9	.400	36	18	5	1	1	148	179	10.9	16	76	4.6	58	3.5	5.35	84	.300	.375	-14	-14	101	108	-1.3	1	-3	-1.2
1933	Det-A	11	15	.423	35	22	9	0	3	183	176	8.7	5	84	4.1	93	4.6	3.54	129	.251	.329	15	21	107	103	-1.9	-4	-2	1.5
1934	Det-A	6	4	.600	20	15	4	1	1	95	107	10.1	5	38	3.6	39	3.7	4.36	97	.288	.348	1	-2	94	107	-0.4	-3	-2	-0.5
1935	Det-A	0	1	.000	3	1	0	0	0	12	16	12.0	2	5	3.8	7	5.3	6.00	69	.320	.393	-2	-3	93	110	-0.4	-0	-0	-0.2
	Chi-A	5	5	.500	24	11	3	1	0	89	102	10.3	7	39	3.9	31	3.1	6.17	79	.283	.352	-17	-13	109	76	0.1	-1	-1	-1.2
	Yr	5	6	.455	27	12	3	1	0	101	118	10.5	9	44	3.9	38	3.4	6.15	78	.286	.355	-19	-15	107	76	-0.3	-0	-1	-1.4
1937	Cle-A	0	1	.000	2	0	0	0	0	1	2	18.0	0	1	9.0	1	9.0	18.00	25	.667	.600	-1	-2	97	83	-0.4	0	0	0.0
	Was-A	4	5	.444	17	11	2	0	2	72	74	9.3	6	31	3.9	30	3.8	4.38	101	.270	.342	2	0	96	100	-0.2	-1	-2	-0.1
	Yr	4	6	.400	19	11	2	0	2	73	76	9.4	6	32	3.9	31	3.8	4.56	97	.274	.346	0	-1	96	100	-0.6	0	-2	-0.1
Total	7	46	50	.479	191	105	31	3	11	824	900	9.8	53	372	4.1	376	4.1	4.62	97	.277	.349	-17	-14	101	100	-4.6	-12	-13	-2.6
■ HANK FISCHER	Fischer, Henry William "Bulldog" b: 1/11/40, Yonkers, N.Y. BR/TR, 6', 190 lbs. Deb: 4/16/62																												
1962	Mil-N	2	3	.400	29	0	0	0	4	37	43	10.5	4	20	4.9	29	7.1	5.35	72	.291	.364	-6	-6	98	97	-0.5	-0	0	-0.5
1963	Mil-N	4	3	.571	31	6	1	0	0	74	74	9.0	8	28	3.4	72	8.8	4.99	66	.262	.331	-14	-14	100	85	0.4	-0	-0	-1.5
1964	Mil-N	11	10	.524	37	28	9	5	2	168	177	9.5	17	39	2.1	99	5.3	4.02	84	.265	.305	-9	-12	96	93	-0.3	1	-1	-1.1
1965	Mil-N	8	9	.471	31	19	2	0	0	123	126	9.2	18	39	2.9	79	5.8	3.88	94	.270	.324	-5	-3	103	116	-1.0	-1	-2	-0.6
1966	Atl-N	2	3	.400	14	8	0	0	0	48	55	10.3	3	14	2.6	22	4.1	3.94	89	.296	.341	-2	-2	97	111	-0.5	-1	-1	-0.4
	Cin-N	0	6	.000	11	9	0	0	0	38	53	12.6	3	15	3.6	24	5.7	6.63	62	.331	.394	-13	-11	114	90	-2.9	-1	-0	-1.1
	Yr	2	9	.182	25	17	0	0	0	86	108	11.3	6	29	3.0	46	4.8	5.13	74	.309	.364	-15	-13	105	90	-3.4	-1	-1	-1.5
	Bos-A	2	3	.400	6	5	1	0	0	31	35	10.2	4	11	3.2	26	7.5	2.90	131	.287	.348	2	3	110	171	-0.2	0	0	0.4
1967	Bos-A	1	2	.333	9	2	1	0	1	27	24	8.0	3	8	2.7	18	6.0	2.33	156	.229	.289	3	4	113	132	-0.5	-0	0	0.4
Total	6	30	39	.435	168	77	14	5	7	546	587	9.7	60	174	2.9	369	6.1	4.24	84	.275	.329	-43	-41	101	105	-5.5	-3	-5	-4.4
■ JEFF FISCHER	Fischer, Jeffrey Thomas b: 8/17/63, W.Palm Beach, Fla. BR/TR, 6'3", 185 lbs. Deb: 6/19/87																												
1987	Mon-N	0	1	.000	4	2	0	0	0	14	21	13.5	3	5	3.2	6	3.9	8.36	52	.362	.394	-7	-6	106	92	-0.4	0	0	-0.5
■ RUBE FISCHER	Fischer, Reuben Walter b: 9/19/16, Carlock, S.D. BR/TR, 6'4", 190 lbs. Deb: 9/12/41																												
1941	NY-N	1	0	1.000	2	1	1	0	0	11	10	8.2	0	6	4.9	9	7.4	2.45	154	.238	.327	1	2	104	127	0.5	0	0	0.2
1943	NY-N	5	10	.333	22	17	4	0	1	131	140	9.6	4	59	4.1	47	3.2	4.60	73	.281	.354	-18	-18	99	91	-0.5	4	-2	-1.6
1944	NY-N	6	14	.300	38	18	2	1	2	129	128	8.9	7	87	6.1	39	2.7	5.16	74	.266	.374	-22	-19	105	92	-3.3	-2	-2	-2.2
1945	NY-N	3	8	.273	31	4	0	0	1	77	90	10.5	6	49	5.7	27	3.2	5.61	68	.288	.378	-15	-15	100	95	-2.6	2	-1	-1.3
1946	NY-N	1	2	.333	15	1	0	0	0	36	48	12.0	3	21	5.3	14	3.5	6.25	56	.316	.392	-11	-11	103	92	-0.1	-1	0	-1.1
Total	5	16	34	.320	108	41	7	1	4	384	416	9.8	20	222	5.2	136	3.2	5.09	71	.280	.369	-65	-63	102	94	-6.0	2	-5	-6.0
■ TODD FISCHER	Fischer, Todd Richard b: 9/15/60, Columbus, Ohio BR/TR, 5'10", 170 lbs. Deb: 5/29/86																												
1986	Cal-A	0	0	—	9	0	0	0	0	17	18	9.5	4	8	4.2	7	3.7	4.24	94	.286	.356	-0	-0	95	142	0.0	0	0	0.0
■ BILL FISCHER	Fischer, William Charles b: 10/11/30, Wausau, Wis. BR/TR, 6', 190 lbs. Deb: 4/21/56 C																												
1956	Chi-A	0	0	—	3	0	0	0	0	2	6	27.0	0	1	4.5	2	9.0	18.00	23	.545	.583	-3	-3	102	78	0.0	0	0	-0.2
1957	Chi-A	7	8	.467	33	11	3	1	1	124	139	10.1	1	35	2.5	48	3.5	3.48	105	.291	.337	4	2	97	110	-1.5	-2	-1	0.0
1958	Chi-A	2	3	.400	17	3	0	0	0	36	43	10.8	6	13	3.3	16	4.0	6.75	55	.301	.348	-12	-12	98	81	-0.5	-0	1	-1.0
	Det-A	2	4	.333	22	0	0	0	2	31	46	13.4	6	13	3.8	16	4.6	7.55	51	.362	.404	-13	-13	103	101	-0.9	0	0	-1.1
	Was-A	0	3	.000	3	3	0	0	0	21	24	10.3	1	5	2.1	10	4.3	3.86	98	.320	.349	-0	-0	100	127	-1.4	0	0	0.0
	Yr	4	10	.286	42	6	0	0	2	88	113	11.6	13	31	3.2	42	4.3	6.34	60	.325	.369	-25	-25	100	127	-2.8	0	2	-2.1
1959	Was-A	9	11	.450	34	29	6	1	0	187	211	10.2	16	43	2.1	62	3.0	4.28	92	.281	.317	-9	-7	102	94	0.8	-2	4	-0.5

YEAR	TM/L	W	L	PCT	G	GS	CG	SHO	SV	IP	H	H/G	HR	BB	BB/G	SO	SO/G	ERA	/A	OAVG	OOBP	PR	/A	PF	CPI	WAT	PB	PD	TPI
1960	Was-A	3	5	.375	20	7	1	0	0	77	85	9.9	7	17	2.0	31	3.6	4.91	81	.281	.314	-9	-8	102	80	-0.8	1	1	-0.5
	Det-A	5	3	.625	20	6	1	0	0	55	50	8.2	6	18	2.9	24	3.9	3.44	115	.244	.298	3	3	102	99	1.3	2	0	0.6
	Yr	8	8	.500	40	13	2	0	0	132	135	9.2	13	35	2.4	55	3.8	4.30	92	.265	.307	-6	-5	102	99	0.5	1	2	0.1
1961	Det-A	3	2	.600	26	1	0	0	3	47	54	10.3	10	17	3.3	18	3.4	4.98	76	.292	.346	-5	-6	94	113	0.0	-1	-0	-0.6
	KC-A	1	0	1.000	15	0	0	0	2	21	26	11.1	2	6	2.6	12	5.1	3.86	109	.321	.360	0	1	104	139	0.5	-0	0	0.1
	Yr	4	2	.667	41	1	0	0	5	68	80	10.6	12	23	3.0	30	4.0	4.63	84	.301	.350	-5	-6	97	139	0.5	-1	-0	-0.5
1962	KC-A	4	12	.250	34	16	5	0	2	128	150	10.5	16	8	0.6	38	2.7	3.94	102	.293	.298	0	1	101	106	-3.6	-2	-1	-0.1
1963	KC-A	9	6	.600	45	2	0	0	3	96	86	8.1	13	29	2.7	34	3.2	3.56	111	.242	.296	1	4	109	104	2.2	-0	-1	0.3
1964	Min-A	0	1	.000	9	0	0	0	0	7	16	20.6	2	5	6.4	2	2.6	7.71	47	.471	.512	-3	-3	100	170	-0.4	0	0	-0.2
Total	9	45	58	.437	281	78	16	2	13	832	936	10.1	86	210	2.3	313	3.4	4.34	90	.287	.325	-46	-42	101	102	-4.3	-4	5	-3.2
■ LEO FISHEL	Fishel, Leo b: 12/13/1877, Babylon, N.Y. d: 5/19/60, Hempstead, N.Y. 6', 175 lbs. Deb: 5/03/1899																												
1899	NY-N	0	1	.000	1	1	1	0	0	9	9	9.0	0	6	6.0	6	6.0	6.00	63	.283	.397	-2	-2	99	66	-0.4	-0	0	-0.1
■ FISHER	Fisher b:Johnstown, Pa. Deb: 7/17/1884																												
1884	Phi-U	1	7	.125	8	8	8	0	0	71	76	9.6	0	13	1.6	42	5.3	3.55	81	.279	.312	-4	-5	95	92	-2.3	0	0	-2.1
1885	Buf-N	0	1	.000	1	1	1	0	0	9	10	10.0	0	2	2.0	4	4.0	5.00	59	.292	.332	-2	-2	105	68	-0.4	-1	0	-0.1
Total	2	1	8	.111	9	9	9	0	0	80	86	9.7	0	15	1.7	46	5.2	3.71	77	.280	.314	-6	-7	96	90	-2.7	-0	0	-2.2
■ BRIAN FISHER	Fisher, Brian Kevin b: 3/18/62, Honolulu, Hawaii BR/TR, 6'4", 210 lbs. Deb: 5/07/85																												
1985	NY-A	4	4	.500	55	0	0	0	14	98	77	7.1	4	29	2.7	85	7.8	2.39	163	.216	.271	19	16	94	94	-0.6	0	0	1.7
1986	NY-A	9	5	.643	62	0	0	0	6	97	105	9.7	14	37	3.4	67	6.2	4.92	87	.277	.337	-8	-7	103	97	1.5	0	-1	-0.7
1987	Pit-N	11	9	.550	37	26	6	3	0	185	185	9.0	27	72	3.5	117	5.7	4.52	94	.262	.330	-9	-5	105	99	1.2	4	-1	-0.2
1988	Pit-N	8	10	.444	33	22	1	1	1	146	157	9.7	13	57	3.5	66	4.1	4.62	73	.277	.340	-19	-21	97	97	-1.5	-2	-2	-2.5
Total	4	32	28	.533	187	48	7	4	21	526	524	9.0	58	195	3.3	335	5.7	4.23	93	.261	.324	-17	-16	100	97	0.6	3	-5	-1.7
■ CHAUNCEY FISHER	Fisher, Chauncey Burr "Peach" or "Whoa Bill" b: 1/8/1872, Anderson, Ind. d: 4/27/39, Los Angeles, Cal. BR/TR, 5'11", 175 lbs. Deb: 9/20/1893																												
1893	Cle-N	0	2	.000	2	2	2	0	0	18	26	13.0	0	9	4.5	9	4.5	5.50	87	.355	.425	-2	-1	103	108	-0.9	-0	0	0.0
1894	Cle-N	0	2	.000	3	2	0	0	0	11	22	18.0	0	5	4.1	0	0.0	11.45	51	.439	.490	-7	-7	111	75	-0.9	-1	0	-0.4
	Cin-N	2	8	.200	11	11	10	0	0	91	134	13.3	4	44	4.4	14	1.4	7.32	74	.366	.434	-20	-19	102	86	-2.6	-1	0	-1.3
	Yr	2	10	.167	14	13	10	0	0	102	156	13.8	4	49	4.3	14	1.2	7.76	70	.375	.440	-28	-26	102	86	-3.5	-1	0	-1.7
1896	Cin-N	10	7	.588	27	15	13	2	2	160	199	11.2	9	36	2.0	25	1.4	4.44	101	.328	.366	-1	1	103	100	-0.2	1	0	0.2
1897	Bro-N	9	7	.563	20	13	11	1	1	149	184	11.1	5	43	2.6	31	1.9	4.23	104	.326	.374	1	3	102	103	1.7	-1	0	0.2
1901	NY-N	0	0	—	1	1	0	0	0	4	11	24.8	0	2	4.5	1	2.3	15.75	20	.519	.560	-6	-6	95	77	0.0	-0	-0	-0.3
	StL-N	0	0	—	1	0	0	0	0	3	7	21.0	0	1	3.0	0	0.0	15.00	21	.478	.511	-4	-4	95	64	0.0	-0	0	-0.2
	Yr	0	0	—	2	1	0	0	0	7	18	23.1	0	3	3.9	1	1.3	15.43	20	.502	.541	-9	-10	95	64	0.0	-0	0	-0.5
Total	5	21	26	.447	65	44	36	3	3	436	583	12.0	18	140	2.9	80	1.7	5.37	87	.344	.394	-39	-33	103	97	-2.9	-3	0	-1.8
■ CLARENCE FISHER	Fisher, Clarence Henry b: 8/27/1898, Letart, W.Va. d: 11/2/65, Point Pleasant, W.Va. BR/TR, 6', 174 lbs. Deb: 9/14/19																												
1919	Was-A	0	0	—	2	0	0	0	0	4	8	18.0	0	3	6.8	1	2.3	13.50	24	.421	.500	-5	-5	99	67	0.0	0	0	-0.3
1920	Was-A	0	1	.000	2	0	0	0	0	4	5	11.3	0	5	11.3	0	0.0	9.00	41	.714	.833	-2	-2	96	137	-0.4	-0	1	-0.1
Total	2	0	1	.000	4	0	0	0	0	8	13	14.6	0	8	9.0	1	1.1	11.25	30	.500	.618	-7	-7	98	102	-0.4	-0	1	-0.4
■ DON FISHER	Fisher, Donald Raymond b: 2/6/16, Cleveland, Ohio d: 7/29/73, Mayfield Heights Ohio BR/TR, 6', 210 lbs. Deb: 8/25/45																												
1945	NY-N	1	0	1.000	2	1	1	1	0	18	12	6.0	0	7	3.5	4	2.0	2.00	190	.190	.284	4	4	100	99	0.5	-0	0	0.4
■ EDDIE FISHER	Fisher, Eddie Gene b: 7/16/36, Shreveport, La. BR/TR, 6'2.5", 200 lbs. Deb: 6/22/59																												
1959	SF-N	2	6	.250	17	5	0	0	1	40	57	12.8	8	8	1.8	15	3.4	7.87	47	.339	.365	-17	-19	94	82	-2.1	-1	-1	-1.8
1960	SF-N	1	0	1.000	3	1	1	0	0	13	11	7.6	2	2	1.4	7	4.8	3.46	96	.244	.260	0	-0	89	101	0.5	1	0	0.1
1961	SF-N	0	2	.000	15	1	0	0	1	34	36	9.5	7	9	2.4	16	4.2	5.29	73	.267	.308	-5	-5	96	85	-0.9	0	0	-0.4
1962	Chi-A	9	5	.643	57	12	2	1	5	183	169	8.3	17	45	2.2	88	4.3	3.10	121	.245	.288	18	13	94	102	1.9	0	0	1.3
1963	Chi-A	9	8	.529	33	15	2	1	0	121	114	8.5	14	28	2.1	67	5.0	3.94	94	.244	.286	-4	-3	102	83	-0.7	-1	1	-0.2
1964	Chi-A	6	3	.667	59	2	0	0	9	125	86	6.2	13	32	2.3	74	5.3	3.02	112	.192	.246	8	5	93	66	0.7	-0	0	0.5
1965	Chi-A	15	7	.682	**82**	0	0	0	24	165	118	6.4	13	43	2.3	90	4.9	2.40	130	.205	**.252**	19	13	91	93	2.8	0	1	1.6
1966	Chi-A	1	3	.250	23	0	0	0	6	35	27	6.9	1	17	4.4	18	4.6	2.31	138	.214	.306	4	3	93	119	-0.9	-0	0	0.4
	Bal-A	5	3	.625	44	0	0	0	13	72	60	7.5	4	19	2.4	39	4.9	2.63	129	.226	.278	6	6	99	98	0.2	0	0	0.7
	Yr	6	6	.500	**67**	0	0	0	19	107	87	7.3	5	36	3.0	57	4.8	2.52	132	.221	.285	11	10	97	98	-0.7	-0	1	1.1
1967	Bal-A	4	3	.571	46	0	0	0	1	90	82	8.2	7	26	2.6	53	5.3	3.60	84	.245	.302	-4	-6	94	92	0.7	0	-1	-0.6
1968	Cle-A	4	2	.667	54	0	0	0	4	95	87	8.2	8	17	1.6	42	4.0	2.84	105	.248	.279	1	2	101	107	0.9	-1	1	0.2
1969	Cal-A	3	2	.600	52	1	0	0	2	97	100	9.3	9	28	2.6	47	4.4	3.62	101	.272	.320	0	0	101	109	0.7	-1	0	0.0
1970	Cal-A	4	4	.500	67	2	0	0	8	130	117	8.1	15	35	2.4	74	5.1	3.05	112	.239	.289	10	5	92	104	-0.1	-1	1	0.6
1971	Cal-A	10	8	.556	57	3	0	0	3	119	92	7.0	11	50	3.8	82	6.2	2.72	127	.211	.293	10	10	99	100	1.6	-1	-0	0.9
1972	Cal-A	4	5	.444	43	1	0	0	4	81	73	8.1	6	31	3.4	32	3.6	3.78	73	.247	.309	-6	-9	90	89	-0.3	-1	-0	-1.1
	Chi-A	0	1	.000	6	4	0	0	0	22	31	12.7	1	9	3.7	10	4.1	4.50	72	.348	.392	-3	-3	106	131	-0.4	-1	0	-0.3
	Yr	4	6	.400	49	5	0	0	4	103	104	9.1	7	40	3.5	42	3.7	3.93	73	.267	.328	-10	-12	93	131	-0.7	-1	0	-1.4
1973	Chi-A	6	7	.462	26	16	2	0	0	111	135	10.9	12	38	3.1	57	4.6	4.86	81	.301	.356	-13	-11	103	102	-0.1	0	0	-1.0
	StL-N	2	1	.667	6	0	0	0	0	7	3	3.9	1	1	1.3	1	1.3	1.29	257	.125	.192	2	2	90	62	0.5	0	-0	0.2
Total	15	85	70	.548	690	63	7	2	81	1540	1398	8.2	149	438	2.6	812	4.7	3.41	100	.243	.294	27	3	96	96	5.0	-4	4	1.1
■ ED FISHER	Fisher, Edward Fredrick b: 10/31/1876, Wayne, Mich. d: 7/24/51, Spokane, Wash. BR/TR, 6'2", 200 lbs. Deb: 9/05/02																												
1902	Det-A	0	0	—	1	0	0	0	0	4	4	9.0	0	1	2.3	0	0.0	0.00	—	.284	.332	2	2	101	0	0.0	-0	-0	0.1
■ FRITZ FISHER	Fisher, Frederick Brown b: 11/28/41, Adrian, Mich. BL/TL, 6'1", 180 lbs. Deb: 4/19/64																												
1964	Det-A	0	0	—	1	0	0	0	0	⅓0	2	54.0	0	2	54.0	1	27.0	108.00	—	.667	.800	-4	-4	95	36	0.0	0	0	-0.2
■ HARRY FISHER	Fisher, Harry Devereux b: 1/3/26, Newbury, Ont., Can. d: 9/20/81, Waterloo, Ont., Ca BL/TR, 6', 180 lbs. Deb: 9/16/51																												
1952	Pit-N	1	2	.333	8	3	0	0	0	18	17	8.5	4	13	6.5	5	2.5	7.00	56	.266	.386	-7	-6	105	92	0.1	1	-0	-0.4
■ JACK FISHER	Fisher, John Howard "Fat Jack" b: 3/4/39, Frostburg, Md. BR/TR, 6'2", 215 lbs. Deb: 4/14/59																												
1959	Bal-A	1	6	.143	27	7	1	1	2	89	76	7.7	7	38	3.8	52	5.3	3.03	125	.230	.307	8	8	98	106	-2.4	-1	-1	0.6
1960	Bal-A	12	11	.522	40	20	8	3	2	198	174	7.9	13	78	3.5	99	4.5	3.41	114	.241	.308	10	11	101	95	-1.2	2	0	1.3
1961	Bal-A	10	13	.435	36	25	10	1	1	196	205	9.4	17	75	3.4	118	5.4	3.90	99	.270	.333	3	-1	96	107	-3.2	-2	-2	-0.5
1962	Bal-A	7	9	.438	32	25	4	0	1	152	173	10.2	23	56	3.3	81	4.8	5.09	74	.284	.343	-19	-22	95	97	-0.6	-1	-1	-2.2
1963	SF-N	6	10	.375	36	12	2	0	1	116	132	10.2	12	38	2.9	57	4.4	4.58	68	.284	.338	-17	-19	94	99	-2.6	1	-0	-1.9
1964	NY-N	10	17	.370	40	34	8	1	0	228	256	10.1	23	56	2.2	115	4.5	4.22	82	.283	.327	-17	-19	98	102	1.0	1	-1	-1.9
1965	NY-N	8	24	.250	43	36	10	0	1	254	252	8.9	22	68	2.4	116	4.1	3.93	94	.259	.307	-11	-7	104	91	-3.5	0	2	-0.5
1966	NY-N	11	14	.440	38	33	10	2	0	230	229	9.0	26	54	2.1	127	5.0	3.68	95	.260	.303	-2	-5	97	100	0.7	-1	3	-0.3
1967	NY-N	9	18	.333	39	30	7	1	0	220	251	10.3	21	64	2.6	117	4.8	4.70	73	.287	.333	-32	-31	102	94	-1.7	-2	1	-3.2
1968	Chi-A	8	13	.381	35	28	2	0	0	181	176	8.8	14	48	2.4	80	4.0	2.98	102	.257	.308	-0	1	102	117	-0.8	-1	-0	0.0
1969	Cin-N	4	4	.500	34	15	0	0	1	113	137	10.9	15	30	2.4	55	4.4	5.50	64	.295	.343	-24	-25	99	89	-0.3	-1	-2	-2.6
Total	11	86	139	.382	400	265	62	9	9	1977	2061	9.4	193	605	2.8	1017	4.6	4.06	88	.269	.322	-101	-109	99	99	-14.6	-6	-1	-11.2
■ MAURICE FISHER	Fisher, Maurice Wayne b: 2/16/31, Uniondale, Ind. BR/TR, 6'5", 210 lbs. Deb: 4/16/55																												
1955	Cin-N	0	0	—	1	0	0	0	0	3	5	15.0	1	2	6.0	1	3.0	6.00	70	.385	.467	-1	-1	104	170	0.0	-0	0	0.0
■ RAY FISHER	Fisher, Raymond Lyle "Chic" b: 10/4/1887, Middlebury, Vt. d: 11/3/82, Ann Arbor, Mich. BR/TR, 5'11.5", 180 lbs. Deb: 7/02/10																												
1910	NY-A	5	3	.625	17	7	3	0	1	92	95	9.3	0	18	1.8	42	4.1	2.93	91	.274	.315	-4	-3	106	97	0.4	-2	1	-0.1
1911	NY-A	10	11	.476	29	22	8	2	0	172	178	9.3	3	55	2.9	99	5.2	3.24	115	.269	.330	2	9	111	97	-0.5	-4	4	1.0
1912	NY-A	2	8	.200	17	13	5	0	0	90	107	10.7	2	32	3.2	47	4.7	5.90	60	.312	.374	-26	-24	105	79	-1.9	-4	3	-1.9
1913	NY-A	12	16	.429	43	31	14	1	1	246	244	8.9	3	71	2.6	92	3.4	3.18	95	.261	.319	-7	-4	104	90	1.4	3	2	0.1
1914	NY-A	10	12	.455	29	26	17	2	1	209	177	7.6	2	61	2.6	86	3.7	2.28	120	.241	.303	11	11	100	105	0.0	-2	3	1.6

YEAR	TM/L	W	L	PCT	G	GS	CG	SHO	SV	IP	H	H/G	HR	BB	BB/G	SO	SO/G	ERA	/A	OAVG	OOBP	PR	/A	PF	CPI	WAT	PB	PD	TPI
1915	NY-A	18	11	.621	30	28	20	4	0	248	219	7.9	7	62	2.3	97	3.5	2.10	138	.243	.295	23	22	99	119	5.1	-5	0	1.9
1916	NY-A	11	8	.579	31	21	9	1	2	179	191	9.6	4	51	2.6	56	2.8	3.17	90	.285	.339	-7	-6	101	113	1.3	1	-1	-0.6
1917	NY-A	8	9	.471	23	18	12	3	0	144	126	7.9	3	43	2.7	64	4.0	2.19	131	.243	.304	8	11	107	113	0.1	-0	1	1.4
1919	Cin-N	14	5	.737	26	20	12	5	1	174	141	7.3	5	38	2.0	41	2.1	2.17	136	.226	.264	14	15	101	94	1.7	3	3	2.5
1920	Cin-N	10	11	.476	33	22	10	1	1	201	189	8.5	5	50	2.2	56	2.5	2.73	101	.249	.292	9	1	88	89	-1.2	1	2	0.4
Total	10	100	94	.515	278	208	110	19	7	1755	1667	8.5	34	481	2.5	680	3.5	2.82	106	.257	.310	23	32	101	101	6.4	-9	19	6.3

■ TOM FISHER Fisher, Thomas Chalmers "Red" b: 11/1/1880, Anderson, Ind. d: 9/3/72, Anderson, Ind. BR/TR, 5'10.5", 185 lbs. Deb: 4/17/04

YEAR	TM/L	W	L	PCT	G	GS	CG	SHO	SV	IP	H	H/G	HR	BB	BB/G	SO	SO/G	ERA	/A	OAVG	OOBP	PR	/A	PF	CPI	WAT	PB	PD	TPI
1904	Bos-N	6	16	.273	31	21	19	2	0	214	257	10.8	5	82	3.4	84	3.5	4.25	65	.327	.397	-36	-35	102	106	-2.9	3	-5	-3.8

■ TOM FISHER Fisher, Thomas Gene b: 4/4/42, Cleveland, Ohio BR/TR, 6', 180 lbs. Deb: 9/20/67

YEAR	TM/L	W	L	PCT	G	GS	CG	SHO	SV	IP	H	H/G	HR	BB	BB/G	SO	SO/G	ERA	/A	OAVG	OOBP	PR	/A	PF	CPI	WAT	PB	PD	TPI
1967	Bal-A	0	0	—	2	0	0	0	0	3	2	6.0	0	2	6.0	1	3.0	0.00	—	.182	.308	1	1	94	0	0.0	0	0	0.1

■ CHEROKEE FISHER Fisher, William Charles b: 12/1845, Philadelphia, Pa. d: 9/26/12, New York, N.Y. BR/TR, 5'9", 164 lbs. Deb: 5/06/1871

YEAR	TM/L	W	L	PCT	G	GS	CG	SHO	SV	IP	H	H/G	HR	BB	BB/G	SO	SO/G	ERA	/A	OAVG	OOBP	PR	/A	PF	CPI	WAT	PB	PD	TPI
1871	Rok-n	4	20	.167	24																								
1872	Bal-n	9	3	.750	13																								
1873	Ath-n	2	2	.500	7																								
1874	Har-n	14	21	.400	35																								
1875	Phi-n	22	18	.550	40																								
1876	Cin-N	4	20	.167	28	24	22	0	0	229	294	11.6	6	6	0.2	29	1.1	3.03	76	.316	.320	-18	-18	100	102	0.6	-2	-2	-1.8
1878	Pro-N	0	1	.000	1	1	1	0	0	9	14	14.0	0	0	0.0	2	2.0	4.00	56	.365	.365	-2	-2	97	108	-0.4	-0	0	-0.1
Total	5 n	51	64	.443	119																								
Total	2	4	21	.160	29	25	23	0	0	238	308	11.6	6	6	0.2	31	1.2	3.06	75	.318	.322	-20	-20	100	102	0.2	-3	-2	-1.9

■ MAX FISKE Fiske, Maximilian Patrick "Ski" b: 10/12/1888, Chicago, Ill. d: 5/15/28, Chicago, Ill. BR/TR, 5'11", 185 lbs. Deb: 4/19/14

YEAR	TM/L	W	L	PCT	G	GS	CG	SHO	SV	IP	H	H/G	HR	BB	BB/G	SO	SO/G	ERA	/A	OAVG	OOBP	PR	/A	PF	CPI	WAT	PB	PD	TPI
1914	Chi-F	12	12	.500	38	22	7	0	0	198	161	7.3	7	59	2.7	87	4.0	3.14	91	.231	.298	2	-6	89	81	-1.5	2	2	-0.3

■ PAUL FITTERY Fittery, Paul Clarence b: 10/10/1887, Lebanon, Pa. d: 1/28/74, Cartersville, Ga. BB/TL, 5'8.5", 156 lbs. Deb: 9/05/14

YEAR	TM/L	W	L	PCT	G	GS	CG	SHO	SV	IP	H	H/G	HR	BB	BB/G	SO	SO/G	ERA	/A	OAVG	OOBP	PR	/A	PF	CPI	WAT	PB	PD	TPI
1914	Cin-N	0	2	.000	8	4	2	0	0	44	41	8.4	0	12	2.5	21	4.3	3.07	97	.246	.295	-1	-0	107	73	-0.9	-1	0	-0.1
1917	Phi-N	1	1	.500	17	2	1	0	0	56	69	11.1	1	27	4.3	13	2.1	4.50	64	.317	.395	-11	-10	106	116	0.0	-1	1	-0.9
Total	2	1	3	.250	25	6	3	0	0	100	110	9.9	1	39	3.5	34	3.1	3.87	75	.286	.353	-13	-11	106	97	-0.9	-2	2	-1.0

■ JOHN FITZGERALD Fitzgerald, John Francis b: 9/15/33, Brooklyn, N.Y. BL/TL, 6'3", 190 lbs. Deb: 9/28/58

YEAR	TM/L	W	L	PCT	G	GS	CG	SHO	SV	IP	H	H/G	HR	BB	BB/G	SO	SO/G	ERA	/A	OAVG	OOBP	PR	/A	PF	CPI	WAT	PB	PD	TPI
1958	SF-N	0	0	—	1	1	0	0	0	3	1	3.0	1	1	3.0	3	9.0	3.00	131	.111	.200	0	0	100	87	0.0	-0	0	0.0

■ JOHN FITZGERALD Fitzgerald, John H. b: 5/30/1870, Natick, Mass. d: 3/31/21, Boston, Mass. Deb: 7/18/1891

YEAR	TM/L	W	L	PCT	G	GS	CG	SHO	SV	IP	H	H/G	HR	BB	BB/G	SO	SO/G	ERA	/A	OAVG	OOBP	PR	/A	PF	CPI	WAT	PB	PD	TPI
1891	Bos-a	1	1	.500	6	3	2	0	1	32	49	13.8	2	11	3.1	16	4.5	5.63	62	.367	.415	-7	-8	94	108	-0.2	-1	0	-0.6

■ JOHN FITZGERALD Fitzgerald, John J. Deb: 4/18/1890

YEAR	TM/L	W	L	PCT	G	GS	CG	SHO	SV	IP	H	H/G	HR	BB	BB/G	SO	SO/G	ERA	/A	OAVG	OOBP	PR	/A	PF	CPI	WAT	PB	PD	TPI
1890	Roc-a	3	8	.273	11	11	8	1	0	78	77	8.9	0	45	5.2	35	4.0	4.04	88	.273	.373	-1	-4	92	99	-2.5	-0	0	-0.3

■ JOHN FITZGERALD Fitzgerald, John T. b: Leadville, Col. Deb: 6/04/1891

YEAR	TM/L	W	L	PCT	G	GS	CG	SHO	SV	IP	H	H/G	HR	BB	BB/G	SO	SO/G	ERA	/A	OAVG	OOBP	PR	/A	PF	CPI	WAT	PB	PD	TPI
1891	Lou-a	14	18	.438	33	32	29	3	0	276	280	9.1	6	95	3.1	111	3.6	3.59	96	.278	.340	4	-5	92	90	1.5	1	0	-0.3
1892	Lou-N	1	3	.250	4	4	4	0	0	34	45	11.9	2	11	2.9	3	0.8	4.24	72	.332	.382	-4	-4	93	119	-0.7	-0	0	-0.3
Total	2	15	21	.417	37	36	33	3	0	310	325	9.4	8	106	3.1	114	3.3	3.66	93	.284	.345	1	-9	92	93	0.8	1	0	-0.6

■ PAUL FITZKE Fitzke, Paul Frederick Herman "Bob" b: 7/30/1900, Lacrosse, Wis. d: 6/30/50, Sacramento, Cal. BR/TR, 5'11.5", 185 lbs. Deb: 9/01/24

YEAR	TM/L	W	L	PCT	G	GS	CG	SHO	SV	IP	H	H/G	HR	BB	BB/G	SO	SO/G	ERA	/A	OAVG	OOBP	PR	/A	PF	CPI	WAT	PB	PD	TPI
1924	Cle-A	0	0	—	1	0	0	0	0	4	5	11.3	0	3	6.8	1	2.3	4.50	92	.313	.421	-0	-0	97	123	0.0	-0	-0	0.0

■ AL FITZMORRIS Fitzmorris, Alan James b: 3/21/46, Buffalo, N.Y. BB/TR, 6'2", 190 lbs. Deb: 9/08/69

YEAR	TM/L	W	L	PCT	G	GS	CG	SHO	SV	IP	H	H/G	HR	BB	BB/G	SO	SO/G	ERA	/A	OAVG	OOBP	PR	/A	PF	CPI	WAT	PB	PD	TPI
1969	KC-A	1	1	.500	7	0	0	0	2	11	9	7.4	1	4	3.3	3	2.5	4.09	92	.237	.289	-1	-0	104	82	0.1	-0	-0	0.0
1970	KC-A	8	5	.615	43	11	2	0	1	118	112	8.5	14	52	4.0	47	3.6	4.42	84	.254	.326	-9	-9	100	92	2.5	4	1	-0.4
1971	KC-A	7	5	.583	36	15	2	1	0	127	112	7.9	6	55	3.9	53	3.8	4.18	81	.245	.319	-10	-11	98	78	0.8	2	2	-0.7
1972	KC-A	2	5	.286	38	2	0	0	3	101	99	8.8	10	28	2.5	51	4.5	3.74	82	.252	.300	-8	-8	100	89	-1.4	1	2	-0.5
1973	KC-A	8	3	.727	15	13	3	1	0	89	88	8.9	5	25	2.5	26	2.6	2.83	147	.259	.309	10	13	109	113	2.3	0	2	1.6
1974	KC-A	13	6	.684	34	27	9	4	1	190	189	9.0	8	63	3.0	53	2.5	2.79	138	.260	.313	18	22	106	116	4.1	0	3	2.7
1975	KC-A	16	12	.571	35	35	11	3	0	242	239	8.9	16	76	2.8	78	2.9	3.57	107	.262	.317	6	7	101	99	0.4	0	1	0.8
1976	KC-A	15	11	.577	35	33	8	2	0	220	227	9.3	6	56	2.3	80	3.3	3.07	113	.273	.314	11	10	99	110	0.7	0	4	1.4
1977	Cle-A	6	10	.375	29	21	1	0	0	133	164	11.1	12	53	3.6	54	3.7	5.41	74	.306	.363	-20	-21	98	95	-1.2	0	0	-1.9
1978	Cle-A	0	1	.000	7	0	0	0	0	14	19	12.2	3	7	4.5	5	3.2	6.43	55	.333	.415	-4	-4	94	113	-0.4	0	0	-0.4
	Cal-A	1	0	1.000	9	2	0	0	0	32	26	7.3	2	14	3.9	8	2.3	1.69	227	.236	.313	7	8	101	195	0.5	0	-0	0.8
	Yr	1	1	.500	16	2	0	0	0	46	45	8.8	5	21	4.1	13	2.5	3.13	119	.268	.342	3	3	99	195	0.1	0	-0	0.4
Total	10	77	59	.566	288	159	36	11	7	1277	1284	9.0	83	433	3.1	458	3.2	3.65	101	.265	.321	0	6	101	103	8.4	7	12	3.4

■ FREDDIE FITZSIMMONS Fitzsimmons, Frederick Landis "Fat Freddie" b: 7/28/01, Mishawaka, Ind. d: 11/18/79, Yucca Valley, Cal. BR/TR, 5'11", 185 lbs. Deb: 8/12/25 MC

YEAR	TM/L	W	L	PCT	G	GS	CG	SHO	SV	IP	H	H/G	HR	BB	BB/G	SO	SO/G	ERA	/A	OAVG	OOBP	PR	/A	PF	CPI	WAT	PB	PD	TPI
1925	NY-N	6	3	.667	10	8	6	1	0	75	70	8.4	4	18	2.2	17	2.0	2.64	159	.248	.289	14	13	98	105	1.1	2	2	1.7
1926	NY-N	14	10	.583	37	26	12	0	0	219	224	9.2	7	58	2.4	48	2.0	2.88	130	.272	.315	23	21	98	118	2.5	-6	3	1.8
1927	NY-N	17	10	.630	42	31	14	1	3	245	260	9.6	15	67	2.5	78	2.9	3.71	103	.275	.317	6	3	98	101	1.3	-0	2	0.5
1928	NY-N	20	9	.690	40	32	16	1	1	261	264	9.1	13	65	2.2	67	2.3	3.69	107	.268	.307	9	8	99	90	3.7	1	2	1.0
1929	NY-N	15	11	.577	37	31	14	4	1	222	242	9.8	14	66	2.7	55	2.2	4.09	111	.285	.326	15	12	97	103	0.7	-1	4	1.3
1930	NY-N	19	7	**.731**	41	29	17	1	1	224	230	9.2	26	59	2.4	76	3.1	4.26	112	.266	.307	18	12	96	92	5.5	5	6	2.1
1931	NY-N	18	11	.621	35	33	19	4	0	254	242	8.6	16	62	2.2	78	2.8	3.05	118	.251	.291	23	16	93	100	2.0	9	8	3.3
1932	NY-N	11	11	.500	35	31	11	0	0	238	287	10.9	18	83	3.1	65	2.5	4.42	86	.299	.352	-14	-17	98	109	0.8	3	7	-0.6
1933	NY-N	16	11	.593	36	35	13	1	0	252	243	8.7	14	72	2.6	65	2.3	2.89	111	.301	.354	12	9	96	**154**	-0.1	3	6	1.8
1934	NY-N	18	14	.563	38	37	14	3	1	263	266	9.1	12	51	1.7	73	2.5	3.05	126	.261	.294	30	24	95	103	-1.4	5	5	3.3
1935	NY-N	4	8	.333	18	15	6	**4**	0	94	104	10.0	7	22	2.1	23	2.2	4.02	95	.281	.318	-0	-2	95	100	-2.7	1	1	0.0
1936	NY-N	10	7	.588	28	17	7	0	2	141	147	9.4	6	39	2.5	35	2.2	3.32	119	.274	.317	11	10	98	111	0.0	-2	1	0.8
1937	NY-N	2	2	.500	6	4	1	1	0	27	28	9.3	3	8	2.7	13	4.3	4.67	82	.272	.324	-2	-3	98	90	-0.3	2	-0	0.0
	Bro-N	4	8	.333	13	13	4	0	0	91	91	9.0	2	32	3.2	29	2.9	4.25	99	.263	.318	-3	-1	107	82	-1.0	-1	1	0.0
	Yr	6	10	.375	19	17	5	1	0	118	119	9.1	5	40	3.1	42	3.2	4.35	94	.265	.319	-6	-3	105	82	-1.3	2	0	0.0
1938	Bro-N	11	8	.579	27	26	12	3	0	203	205	9.1	8	43	1.9	38	1.7	3.01	120	.261	.298	17	14	96	104	2.3	-0	5	1.9
1939	Bro-N	7	9	.438	27	20	5	0	3	151	178	10.6	6	28	1.7	44	2.6	3.87	107	.293	.320	1	5	106	100	-1.7	3	5	1.3
1940	Bro-N	16	2	**.889**	20	18	11	4	1	134	120	8.1	5	25	1.7	35	2.4	2.82	145	.233	.269	15	19	106	83	**6.9**	-2	1	1.9
1941	Bro-N	6	1	.857	13	12	3	1	0	83	78	8.5	3	26	2.8	19	2.1	2.06	175	.245	.302	15	14	99	144	2.1	-0	2	1.8
1942	Bro-N	0	0	—	1	1	0	0	0	3	6	18.0	1	1	3.0	0	0.0	15.00	21	.400	.438	-4	-4	97	68	0.0	0	0	-0.2
1943	Bro-N	3	4	.429	9	7	1	1	0	45	50	10.0	6	21	4.2	12	2.4	5.40	62	.281	.358	-10	-10	99	93	-0.6	-1	0	-1.0
Total	19	217	146	.598	513	426	186	30	13	3225	3335	9.3	186	846	2.4	870	2.4	3.51	111	.272	.314	174	144	98	106	21.1	20	59	22.7

■ PATSY FLAHERTY Flaherty, Patrick Joseph b: 6/29/1876, Mansfield, Pa. d: 1/23/68, Alexandria, La. BL/TL, 5'8", 165 lbs. Deb: 9/08/1899

YEAR	TM/L	W	L	PCT	G	GS	CG	SHO	SV	IP	H	H/G	HR	BB	BB/G	SO	SO/G	ERA	/A	OAVG	OOBP	PR	/A	PF	CPI	WAT	PB	PD	TPI
1899	Lou-N	2	3	.400	5	4	4	0	0	39	41	9.5	0	5	1.2	5	1.2	2.31	171	.294	.318	7	7	103	118	-0.4	1	0	0.8
1900	Pit-N	0	0	—	4	1	0	0	0	22	30	12.3	0	9	3.7	5	2.0	6.14	61	.350	.411	-6	-6	101	83	0.0	-1	0	-0.4
1903	Chi-A	11	25	.306	40	34	29	2	1	294	338	10.3	9	50	1.5	65	2.0	3.73	74	.312	.342	-26	-31	94	100	-6.6	-2	2	-2.8
1904	Chi-A	1	2	.333	5	5	4	0	0	43	36	7.5	1	10	2.1	14	2.9	2.09	120	.249	.297	2	2	97	108	-0.5	2	1	0.3
	Pit-N	19	9	.679	29	28	28	5	0	242	210	7.8	3	59	2.2	54	2.0	2.05	130	.260	.319	18	17	98	117	4.1	6	4	2.3
1905	Pit-N	10	10	.500	27	20	15	0	1	188	197	9.4	2	49	2.3	44	2.1	3.49	87	.299	.353	-11	-10	102	97	-2.2	2	2	-0.7
1907	Bos-N	12	15	.444	27	25	23	0	0	217	197	8.2	4	59	2.4	34	1.4	2.70	90	.272	.333	-6	-6	99	97	1.4	2	2	-0.4
1908	Bos-N	12	18	.400	31	31	21	0	0	244	221	8.2	6	81	3.0	50	1.8	3.25	76	.272	.344	-24	-21	106	89	-0.3	-1	2	-2.0
1910	Phi-N	0	0	—	1	0	0	0	0	⅓	1	27.0	0	1	27.0	0	0.0	0.00	—	.333	.500	0	0	95	0	0.0	0	0	0.0
1911	Bos-N	0	2	.000	4	2	1	0	0	14	21	13.5	0	8	5.1	0	0.0	7.07	53	.350	.451	-6	-5	109	96	-0.9	1	-0	-0.4
Total	9	67	84	.444	173	150	125	7	2	1303	1292	8.9	25	331	2.3	271	1.9	3.10	88	.286	.339	-50	-53	99	100	-5.4	11	12	-3.3

YEAR	TM/L	W	L	PCT	G	GS	CG	SHO	SV	IP	H	H/G	HR	BB	BB/G	SO	SO/G	ERA	/A	OAVG	OOBP	PR	/A	PF	CPI	WAT	PB	PD	TPI
■ **MIKE FLANAGAN**	Flanagan, Michael Kendall b: 12/16/51, Manchester, N.H. BL/TL, 6', 185 lbs. Deb: 9/05/75																												
1975	Bal-A	0	1	.000	2	1	0	0	0	10	9	8.1	0	6	5.4	7	6.3	2.70	125	.250	.357	1	1	89	131	-0.4	0	0	0.1
1976	Bal-A	3	5	.375	20	10	4	0	0	85	83	8.8	7	33	3.5	56	5.9	4.13	83	.260	.324	-6	-7	97	92	-1.2	0	0	-0.6
1977	Bal-A	15	10	.600	36	33	15	2	1	235	235	9.0	17	70	2.7	149	5.7	3.64	103	.266	.315	11	3	92	100	0.0	0	-0	0.3
1978	Bal-A	19	15	.559	40	40	17	2	0	281	271	8.7	22	87	2.8	167	5.3	4.04	85	.257	.311	-8	-19	91	86	0.0	0	-2	-2.0
1979	Bal-A	**23**	9	.719	39	38	16	**5**	0	266	245	8.3	23	70	2.4	190	6.4	3.08	132	.245	.293	34	29	96	102	4.1	0	-0	2.8
1980	Bal-A	16	13	.552	37	37	12	2	0	251	278	10.0	27	71	2.5	128	4.6	4.12	97	.287	.330	-2	-3	99	107	-1.7	0	0	-0.2
1981	Bal-A	9	6	.600	20	20	3	2	0	116	108	8.4	11	37	2.9	72	5.6	4.19	87	.244	.305	-7	-7	99	79	0.8	0	1	-0.5
1982	Bal-A	15	11	.577	36	35	11	1	0	236	233	8.9	24	76	2.9	103	3.9	3.97	102	.259	.316	3	2	99	96	0.0	0	0	0.2
1983	Bal-A	12	4	.750	20	20	3	1	0	125	135	9.7	10	31	2.2	50	3.6	3.31	122	.278	.318	11	10	99	121	3.1	0	-1	0.9
1984	Bal-A	13	13	.500	34	34	10	2	0	227	213	8.4	24	81	3.2	115	4.6	3.53	107	.250	.312	12	6	94	105	-0.6	0	-1	0.5
1985	Bal-A	4	5	.444	15	15	1	0	0	86	101	10.6	14	28	2.9	42	4.4	5.13	79	.297	.346	-9	-10	98	106	-0.6	0	-0	-0.9
1986	Bal-A	7	11	.389	29	28	2	0	0	172	179	9.4	15	66	3.5	96	5.0	4.24	98	.270	.329	-1	-1	99	98	-1.3	0	-2	-0.3
1987	Bal-A	3	6	.333	16	16	4	0	0	95	102	9.7	9	36	3.4	50	4.7	4.93	90	.278	.337	-5	-5	99	91	-0.8	0	-0	-0.4
	Tor-A	3	2	.600	7	7	0	0	0	49	46	8.4	3	15	2.8	43	7.9	2.39	186	.237	.292	11	11	99	115	0.0	0	-0	1.1
	Yr	6	8	.429	23	23	4	0	0	144	148	9.3	12	51	3.2	93	5.8	4.06	109	.263	.321	7	6	99	115	-0.8	0	-0	0.7
1988	Tor-A	13	13	.500	34	34	2	1	0	211	220	9.4	23	80	3.4	99	4.2	4.18	94	.271	.334	-5	-6	99	107	-1.0	0	1	-0.5
Total	14	155	124	.556	385	368	100	18	1	2445	2458	9.0	229	787	2.9	1367	5.0	3.88	100	.264	.318	41	2	96	100	0.4	0	-4	0.5
■ **RAY FLANIGAN**	Flanigan, Raymond Arthur b: 1/8/23, Morgantown, W.Va. BR/TR, 6', 190 lbs. Deb: 9/20/46																												
1946	Cle-A	0	1	.000	3	1	0	0	0	9	11	11.0	1	8	8.0	2	2.0	11.00	29	.289	.396	-7	-8	90	55	-0.4	1	0	-0.5
■ **TOM FLANIGAN**	Flanigan, Thomas Anthony b: 9/6/34, Cincinnati, Ohio BR/TL, 6'3", 175 lbs. Deb: 4/14/54																												
1954	Chi-A	0	0	—	2	0	0	0	0	2	1	4.5	0	1	4.5	0	0.0	0.00	—	.200	.286	1	1	100	0	0.0	0	0	0.1
1958	StL-N	0	0	—	1	0	0	0	0	1	2	18.0	1	1	9.0	0	0.0	9.00	47	.500	.600	-1	-1	108	216	0.0	0	0	0.0
Total	2	0	0	—	3	0	0	0	0	3	3	9.0	1	2	6.0	0	0.0	3.00	130	.333	.417	0	0	102	72	0.0	0	0	0.1
■ **JACK FLATER**	Flater, John William b: 9/22/1880, Sandymount, Md. d: 3/20/70, Westminster, Md. TR , 5'10", 175 lbs. Deb: 9/18/08																												
1908	Phi-A	1	3	.250	5	3	3	0	0	39	35	8.1	0	12	2.8	8	1.8	2.08	126	.252	.320	1	2	110	141	-0.8	-0	2	0.5
■ **JOHN FLAVIN**	Flavin, John Thomas b: 5/7/42, Albany, Cal. BL/TL, 6'2", 208 lbs. Deb: 8/25/64																												
1964	Chi-N	0	1	.000	5	1	0	0	0	5	11	19.8	0	3	5.4	5	9.0	12.60	30	.500	.519	-5	-5	106	88	-0.4	-0	-0	-0.4
■ **FRANK FLEET**	Fleet, Frank H. b: 1848, New York, N.Y. d: 6/13/1900, New York, N.Y. Deb: 10/18/1871																												
1871	Mut-n	0	1	.000	1																								
1873	Res-n	0	3	.000	3																								
1875	StL-n	2	1	.667	3																								
	Atl-n	0	1	.000	1																								
	Yr	2	2	.500	4																								
Total	3 n	2	6	.250	8																								
■ **BILL FLEMING**	Fleming, Leslie Fletchard b: 7/31/13, Rowland, Cal. BR/TR, 6', 190 lbs. Deb: 8/21/40																												
1940	Bos-A	1	2	.333	10	6	1	0	0	46	53	10.4	4	20	3.9	24	4.7	4.89	90	.290	.364	-3	-3	100	104	-0.5	-2	-1	-0.4
1941	Bos-A	1	1	.500	16	1	0	0	1	41	32	7.0	4	24	5.3	20	4.4	3.95	106	.212	.311	1	1	101	85	0.0	1	1	0.2
1942	Chi-N	5	6	.455	33	14	4	2	2	134	117	7.9	9	63	4.2	59	4.0	3.02	107	.230	.315	4	3	98	107	0.1	-4	-1	-0.1
1943	Chi-N	0	1	.000	11	0	0	0	0	32	40	11.3	2	12	3.4	12	3.4	6.47	51	.303	.367	-11	-11	98	78	-0.4	-1	1	-1.0
1944	Chi-N	9	10	.474	39	18	9	1	0	158	163	9.3	6	62	3.5	42	2.4	3.13	115	.269	.328	8	8	100	**121**	-0.2	-1	1	0.9
1946	Chi-N	0	1	.000	14	1	0	0	0	29	37	11.5	2	12	3.7	10	3.1	6.21	51	.301	.355	-9	-10	93	78	-0.4	-0	0	-0.9
Total	6	16	21	.432	123	40	14	3	3	440	442	9.0	27	193	3.9	167	3.4	3.80	94	.259	.331	-9	-11	99	106	-1.4	-7	1	-1.3
■ **VAN FLETCHER**	Fletcher, Alfred Vanoide b: 8/6/24, East Bend, N.C. BR/TR, 6'2", 185 lbs. Deb: 4/12/55																												
1955	Det-A	0	0	—	9	0	0	0	0	12	13	9.8	1	2	1.5	4	3.0	3.00	125	.260	.278	1	1	95	99	0.0	0	-0	0.1
■ **SAM FLETCHER**	Fletcher, Samuel S. b: Altoona, Pa. TR , 6'2", 210 lbs. Deb: 09																												
1909	Bro-N	0	1	.000	1	1	1	0	0	9	13	13.0	0	2	2.0	5	5.0	8.00	33	.351	.385	-5	-5	103	63	-0.4	-0	0	-0.4
1912	Cin-N	0	0	—	2	0	0	0	0	10	15	13.5	1	11	9.9	3	2.7	11.70	27	.357	.491	-9	-9	93	72	0.0	1	0	-0.6
Total	2	0	1	.000	3	1	1	0	0	19	28	13.3	1	13	6.2	8	3.8	9.95	30	.354	.446	-15	-15	98	68	-0.4	0	0	-1.0
■ **TOM FLETCHER**	Fletcher, Thomas Wayne b: 6/28/42, Elmira, N.Y. BB/TL, 6', 170 lbs. Deb: 9/12/62																												
1962	Det-A	0	0	—	1	0	0	0	0	2	4	18.0	1	3	13.5	2	9.0	27.00	16	.444	.615	-5	-5	110	64	0.0	0	0	-0.3
■ **JOHN FLINN**	Flinn, John Richard b: 9/2/54, Merced, Cal. BR/TR, 6', 175 lbs. Deb: 5/06/78																												
1978	Bal-A	1	1	.500	13	0	0	0	0	16	24	13.5	3	13	7.3	8	4.5	7.88	43	.348	.440	-7	-8	91	105	0.0	0	0	-0.7
1979	Bal-A	0	0	—	4	0	0	0	0	3	2	6.0	0	1	3.0	0	0.0	0.00	—	.222	.273	1	1	96	0	0.0	0	0	0.1
1980	Mil-A	2	1	.667	20	1	0	0	2	37	31	7.5	3	20	4.9	15	3.6	3.89	97	.220	.311	1	-1	93	78	0.4	0	-0	0.0
1982	Bal-A	2	0	1.000	5	0	0	0	0	14	13	8.4	1	3	1.9	13	8.4	1.29	314	.260	.302	4	4	99	264	1.0	0	-0	0.4
Total	4	5	2	.714	42	1	0	0	2	70	70	9.0	7	37	4.8	36	4.6	4.11	91	.260	.343	-1	-3	94	118	1.4	0	-0	-0.2
■ **HILLY FLITCRAFT**	Flitcraft, Hildreth Milton b: 8/21/23, Woodstown, N.J. BL/TL, 6'2", 180 lbs. Deb: 8/31/42																												
1942	Phi-N	0	0	—	3	0	0	0	0	3	6	18.0	0	2	6.0	1	3.0	9.00	37	.429	.471	-2	-2	101	103	0.0	0	0	-0.1
■ **MORT FLOHR**	Flohr, Moritz Herman "Dutch" b: 8/15/11, Canisteo, N.Y. BL/TL, 6', 173 lbs. Deb: 6/08/34																												
1934	Phi-A	0	2	.000	14	3	0	0	0	31	34	9.9	3	33	9.6	6	1.7	5.81	76	.296	.444	-5	-5	98	123	-0.9	1	1	-0.2
■ **JESSE FLORES**	Flores, Jesse Sandoval b: 11/2/14, Guadalajara, Mexico BR/TR, 5'10", 175 lbs. Deb: 4/16/42																												
1942	Chi-N	0	1	.000	4	0	0	0	0	5	5	9.0	1	2	3.6	6	10.8	3.60	90	.227	.292	-0	-0	98	101	-0.4	0	0	0.0
1943	Phi-A	12	14	.462	31	27	13	0	0	231	208	8.1	13	70	2.7	113	4.4	3.12	112	.240	.295	5	10	106	95	3.2	-1	1	1.2
1944	Phi-A	9	11	.450	27	25	11	2	0	186	172	8.3	8	49	2.4	65	3.1	3.39	103	.245	.292	1	2	102	84	-0.3	-1	-1	0.2
1945	Phi-A	7	10	.412	29	24	9	4	1	191	180	8.5	6	63	3.0	52	2.5	3.44	94	.250	.309	-2	-4	96	89	0.9	-2	-3	-0.8
1946	Phi-A	9	7	.563	29	15	8	4	1	155	147	8.5	8	38	2.2	48	2.8	2.32	162	.249	.292	20	25	107	121	3.1	3	-2	2.9
1947	Phi-A	4	13	.235	28	20	4	0	0	151	139	8.3	10	59	3.5	41	2.4	3.40	109	.244	.313	5	5	100	97	-4.7	1	-1	0.5
1950	Cle-A	3	3	.500	28	2	1	1	4	53	53	9.0	3	25	4.2	27	4.6	3.74	117	.261	.342	5	4	95	107	-0.4	-2	-2	0.0
Total	7	44	59	.427	176	113	46	11	6	972	904	8.4	49	306	2.8	352	3.3	3.19	112	.246	.302	34	42	102	97	1.4	-0	-7	4.0
■ **BEN FLOWERS**	Flowers, Bennett b: 6/15/27, Wilson, N.C. BR/TR, 6'4", 195 lbs. Deb: 9/29/51																												
1951	Bos-A	0	0	—	1	0	0	0	0	3	2	6.0	0	1	3.0	2	6.0	0.00	—	.200	.273	1	1	106	0	0.0	-0	0	0.1
1953	Bos-A	1	4	.200	32	6	1	1	3	79	87	9.9	6	24	2.7	36	4.1	3.87	112	.280	.325	1	4	108	106	-1.5	-0	1	0.4
1955	Det-A	0	0	—	4	0	0	0	0	6	5	7.5	1	2	3.0	2	3.0	6.00	63	.238	.292	-1	-1	95	64	0.0	-0	0	0.0
	StL-N	1	0	1.000	4	4	0	0	0	27	27	9.0	1	12	4.0	19	6.3	3.67	113	.255	.325	1	1	102	92	0.5	-1	-0	0.0
1956	StL-N	1	1	.500	3	3	0	0	0	12	15	11.3	1	5	3.8	5	3.8	6.75	55	.341	.377	-4	-4	99	89	0.0	-0	0	-0.3
	Phi-N	0	2	.000	32	0	0	0	0	41	54	11.9	9	10	2.2	22	4.8	5.71	63	.331	.357	-9	-10	95	112	-0.9	0	1	-0.8
	Yr	1	3	.250	35	3	0	0	0	53	69	11.7	10	15	2.5	27	4.6	5.94	61	.330	.362	-13	-14	96	112	-0.9	-0	1	-1.1
Total	4	3	7	.300	76	13	1	1	3	168	190	10.2	18	54	2.9	86	4.6	4.50	90	.290	.335	-11	-8	103	100	-1.9	-2	1	-0.6
■ **WES FLOWERS**	Flowers, Charles Wesley b: 8/13/13, Vanndale, Ark. BL/TL, 6'1.5", 190 lbs. Deb: 8/08/40																												
1940	Bro-N	1	1	.500	5	2	0	0	0	21	23	9.9	2	10	4.3	8	3.4	3.43	119	.299	.375	1	2	106	170	0.0	-0	0	0.2
1944	Bro-N	1	1	.500	9	1	0	0	0	17	26	13.8	3	13	6.9	3	1.6	7.94	46	.333	.430	-8	-8	102	100	0.2	1	0	-0.6
Total	2	2	2	.500	14	3	0	0	0	38	49	11.6	5	23	5.4	11	2.6	5.45	72	.316	.402	-7	-7	104	139	0.2	1	0	-0.4
■ **CARNEY FLYNN**	Flynn, Cornelius Francis Xavier b: 1/23/1875, Cincinnati, Ohio d: 2/10/47, Cincinnati, Ohio BL/TL, 5'11", 165 lbs. Deb: 7/17/1894																												
1894	Cin-N	0	2	.000	2	1	0	0	0	8	16	18.0	4	10	11.3	4	4.5	19.13	28	.439	.560	-12	-12	102	76	-0.9	-1	0	-0.7
1896	NY-N	0	2	.000	3	2	1	0	0	11	18	14.7	0	8	6.5	4	3.3	12.27	35	.391	.481	-10	-10	99	60	-0.9	1	0	-0.5

YEAR TM/L	W	L	PCT	G	GS	CG	SHO	SV	IP	H	H/G	HR	BB	BB/G	SO	SO/G	ERA	/A	OAVG	OOBP	PR	/A	PF	CPI	WAT	PB	PD	TPI
Was-N	0	1	.000	4	1	1	0	0	20	43	19.3	0	10	4.5	3	1.3	8.55	49	.458	.510	-9	-10	96	109	-0.4	-0	0	-0.7
Yr	0	3	.000	7	3	2	0	0	31	61	17.7	0	18	5.2	7	2.0	9.87	43	.436	.500	-19	-19	97	109	-1.3	1	0	-1.2
Total 2	0	5	.000	9	4	2	0	0	39	77	17.8	4	28	6.5	11	2.5	11.77	38	.436	.514	-31	-32	98	88	-2.2	1	0	-1.9
■ JOCKO FLYNN	Flynn, John A. b: 6/30/1864, Lawrence, Mass. d: 12/30/07, Lawrence, Mass. 5'6.5", 143 lbs. Deb: 5/01/1886																											
1886 Chi-N	23	6	**.793**	32	29	28	2	1	257	207	7.2	9	63	2.2	146	5.1	2.24	**162**	.232	.283	30	40	110	100	4.3	2	0	4.4
■ STU FLYTHE	Flythe, Stuart Mcguire b: 12/5/11, Conway, N.C. d: 10/18/63, Durham, N.C. BR/TR, 6'2", 175 lbs. Deb: 5/31/36																											
1936 Phi-A	0	0	—	17	3	0	0	0	39	49	11.3	4	61	14.1	14	3.2	13.15	40	.302	.493	-35	-34	105	68	0.0	0	0	-2.6
■ GENE FODGE	Fodge, Eugene Arlan "Suds" b: 7/9/31, South Bend, Ind. BR/TR, 6', 175 lbs. Deb: 4/20/58																											
1958 Chi-N	1	1	.500	16	4	1	0	0	40	47	10.6	5	11	2.5	15	3.4	4.72	84	.296	.331	-3	-3	101	99	0.1	-1	0	-0.3
■ JIM FOGARTY	Fogarty, James G. b: 2/12/1864, San Francisco, Cal d: 5/20/1891, Philadelphia, Pa. BR, 5'10.5", 180 lbs. Deb: 5/01/1884 M																											
1884 Phi-N	0	0	—	1	0	0	0	0	1	2	18.0	0	0	0.0	1	9.0	0.00	—	.424	.424	0	0	97	0	0.0	0	0	0.0
1886 Phi-N	0	1	.000	1	0	0	0	0	6	7	10.5	1	0	0.0	4	6.0	0.00	—	.305	.305	2	2	96	0	-0.4	0	0	0.2
1887 Phi-N	0	0	—	1	0	0	0	0	3	3	9.0	0	1	3.0	0	0.0	9.00	42	.275	.336	-2	-2	94	36	0.0	0	0	0.0
1889 Phi-N	0	0	—	4	0	0	0	0	4	4	9.0	0	2	4.5	0	0.0	9.00	47	.276	.363	-2	-2	105	40	0.0	1	0	-0.1
Total 4	0	1	.000	7	0	0	0	0	14	16	10.3	1	3	1.9	5	3.2	4.50	79	.301	.339	-1	-1	98	19	-0.4	2	0	0.1
■ CURRY FOLEY	Foley, Charles Joseph b: 1/14/1856, Milltown, Ireland d: 10/20/1898, Boston, Mass. TL, 180 lbs. Deb: 5/13/1879																											
1879 Bos-N	9	9	.500	21	16	16	0	**1**	162	175	9.7	1	15	0.8	57	3.2	2.50	101	.281	.298	-0	1	101	102	-2.3	5	0	0.8
1880 Bos-N	14	14	.500	36	28	21	0	0	238	264	10.0	1	40	1.5	68	2.6	3.89	57	.290	.320	-40	-45	93	79	0.9	8	0	-4.0
1881 Buf-N	2	4	.333	10	6	2	0	0	41	70	15.4	1	5	1.1	2	0.4	5.27	53	.390	.406	-11	-11	101	113	-1.1	1	0	-0.9
1882 Buf-N	0	0	—	1	0	0	0	0	1	2	18.0	0	0	0.0	0	0.0	18.00	17	.422	.422	-2	-2	103	40	0.0	0	0	0.0
1883 Buf-N	1	0	1.000	1	0	0	0	0	1	0	0.0	0	4	36.0	0	0.0	0.00	—	.000	.594	0	0	99	0	0.5	0	0	0.0
Total 5	26	27	.491	69	50	39	0	1	443	511	10.4	3	64	1.3	127	2.6	3.53	67	.297	.322	-53	-57	97	90	-2.0	14	0	-4.1
■ JOHN FOLEY	Foley, John J b: Hannibal, Mo. TL, Deb: 1885																											
1885 Pro-N	0	1	.000	1	1	1	0	0	8	6	6.8	0	5	5.6	2	2.3	4.50	58	.218	.338	-1	-2	93	61	-0.4	0	0	0.0
■ RICH FOLKERS	Folkers, Richard Nevin b: 10/17/46, Waterloo, Iowa BL/TL, 6'2", 180 lbs. Deb: 6/10/70																											
1970 NY-N	0	2	.000	16	1	0	0	2	29	36	11.2	6	25	7.8	15	4.7	6.52	64	.313	.421	-8	-8	103	117	-0.9	0	1	-0.5
1972 StL-N	1	0	1.000	9	0	0	0	0	13	12	8.3	0	5	3.5	7	4.8	3.46	105	.240	.304	-0	0	105	74	0.5	-0	0	0.0
1973 StL-N	4	4	.500	34	9	1	0	3	82	74	8.1	10	34	3.7	44	4.8	3.62	91	.239	.317	0	-3	90	102	0.0	-1	-0	-0.4
1974 StL-N	6	2	.750	55	0	0	0	2	90	65	6.5	4	38	3.8	57	5.7	3.00	125	.207	.289	6	7	103	81	1.9	-1	-1	0.6
1975 SD-N	6	11	.353	45	15	4	0	0	142	155	9.8	8	39	2.5	87	5.5	4.18	88	.278	.318	-9	-8	101	88	-1.7	1	-0	-0.7
1976 SD-N	2	3	.400	33	3	0	0	0	60	67	10.1	10	25	3.8	26	3.9	5.25	60	.279	.344	-12	-14	90	97	-0.2	-0	-0	-1.4
1977 Mil-A	0	1	.000	3	0	0	0	0	6	7	10.5	2	4	6.0	6	9.0	4.50	87	.269	.355	-0	-0	97	144	-0.4	0	0	0.0
Total 7	19	23	.452	195	28	5	0	7	422	416	8.9	40	170	3.6	242	5.2	4.12	87	.258	.324	-22	-25	98	93	-0.8	-1	-1	-2.4
■ LEW FONSECA	Fonseca, Lewis Albert b: 1/21/1899, Oakland, Cal. BR/TR, 5'10.5", 180 lbs. Deb: 4/13/21 M																											
1932 Chi-A	0	0	—	1	0	0	0	0	1	0	0.0	0	0	0.0	0	0.0	0.00	—	.000	.000	0	0	91	0	0.0	-0	0	0.0
■ RAY FONTENOT	Fontenot, Silton Ray b: 8/8/57, Lake Charles, La. BL/TL, 6', 175 lbs. Deb: 6/30/83																											
1983 NY-A	8	2	.800	15	15	3	1	0	97	101	9.4	3	25	2.3	27	2.5	3.34	119	.266	.311	8	7	98	98	2.8	0	1	0.8
1984 NY-A	8	9	.471	35	24	0	0	0	169	189	10.1	8	58	3.1	85	4.5	3.62	103	.290	.347	7	2	93	119	-1.1	0	-0	0.2
1985 Chi-N	6	10	.375	38	23	0	0	0	155	177	10.3	23	45	2.6	70	4.1	4.35	96	.294	.336	-13	-3	117	114	-1.8	-4	2	-0.3
1986 Chi-N	3	5	.375	42	0	0	0	2	56	57	9.2	5	21	3.4	24	3.9	3.86	104	.266	.324	-1	1	108	104	-0.5	-0	-1	0.0
Min-A	0	0	—	15	0	0	0	0	16	27	15.2	3	4	2.3	10	5.6	10.13	45	.360	.407	-11	-10	109	75	0.0	0	0	-0.8
Total 4	25	26	.490	145	62	3	1	2	493	551	10.1	42	153	2.8	216	3.9	4.03	99	.287	.336	-9	-2	104	110	-0.6	-4	2	-0.1
■ JIM FOOR	Foor, James Emerson b: 1/13/49, St.Louis, Mo. BL/TL, 6'2", 170 lbs. Deb: 4/09/71																											
1971 Det-A	0	0	—	3	0	0	0	0	1	2	18.0	0	4	36.0	2	18.0	18.00	18	.400	.667	-2	-2	95	98	0.0	0	0	-0.1
1972 Det-A	1	0	1.000	7	0	0	0	0	4	6	13.5	1	6	13.5	2	4.5	13.50	26	.353	.522	-5	-4	112	79	0.5	0	0	-0.4
1973 Pit-N	0	0	—	3	0	0	0	0	1	2	18.0	0	1	9.0	1	9.0	0.00	—	.286	.375	0	0	92	0	0.0	0	0	0.1
Total 3	1	0	1.000	13	0	0	0	0	6	10	15.0	1	11	16.5	5	7.5	12.00	29	.345	.525	-6	-6	106	69	0.5	0	0	-0.4
■ DAVY FORCE	Force, David W. "Wee Davy" or "Tom Thumb" b: 7/27/1849, New York, N.Y. d: 6/21/18, Englewood, N.J. BR/TR, 5'4", 130 lbs. Deb: 5/05/1871																											
1873 Bal-n	1	1	.500	2																								
■ DAVE FORD	Ford, David Alan b: 12/29/56, Cleveland, Ohio BR/TR, 6'4", 190 lbs. Deb: 9/02/78																											
1978 Bal-A	1	0	1.000	2	1	0	0	0	15	10	6.0	0	2	1.2	5	3.0	0.00	—	.196	.226	6	6	91	0	0.5	0	-0	0.7
1979 Bal-A	2	1	.667	9	2	0	0	2	30	23	6.9	2	7	2.1	7	2.1	2.10	193	.219	.259	7	6	96	113	0.1	0	0	0.7
1980 Bal-A	1	3	.250	25	3	1	0	1	70	66	8.5	11	13	1.7	22	2.8	4.24	94	.251	.288	-2	-2	99	86	-1.1	0	-1	-0.2
1981 Bal-A	1	2	.333	15	2	0	0	0	40	61	13.7	2	10	2.3	12	2.7	6.52	56	.359	.384	-13	-13	99	92	-0.5	0	-0	-1.2
Total 4	5	6	.455	51	8	1	0	3	155	160	9.3	15	32	1.9	46	2.7	4.01	96	.272	.306	-1	-3	98	84	-1.0	0	-1	-0.0
■ WHITEY FORD	Ford, Edward Charles "Chairman Of The Board" b: 10/21/28, New York, N.Y. BL/TL, 5'10", 178 lbs. Deb: 7/01/50 CH																											
1950 NY-A	9	1	.900	20	12	7	2	1	112	87	7.0	7	52	4.2	59	4.7	2.81	156	.216	.303	22	20	96	105	3.7	0	0	1.9
1953 NY-A	18	6	.750	32	30	11	3	0	207	187	8.1	13	110	4.8	110	4.8	3.00	117	.245	.341	23	12	88	**127**	3.7	6	0	1.8
1954 NY-A	16	8	.667	34	28	11	3	1	211	170	7.3	10	101	4.3	125	5.3	2.82	125	.227	.312	21	16	94	106	0.0	1	1	1.9
1955 NY-A	**18**	7	.720	39	33	**18**	5	2	254	188	6.7	20	113	4.0	137	4.9	2.62	142	.208	.294	38	31	94	102	3.6	2	-0	3.4
1956 NY-A	19	6	**.760**	31	30	18	2	1	226	187	7.4	13	84	3.3	141	5.6	**2.47**	160	.228	.299	42	37	95	115	4.9	3	5	4.6
1957 NY-A	11	5	.688	24	17	5	0	0	129	114	8.0	10	53	3.7	84	5.9	2.58	132	.237	.312	17	12	90	125	1.2	-1	2	1.3
1958 NY-A	14	7	.667	30	29	15	**7**	1	219	174	7.2	14	62	2.5	145	6.0	**2.01**	**186**	.217	**.274**	**43**	**42**	99	117	2.0	1	1	**5.1**
1959 NY-A	16	10	.615	35	29	9	2	1	204	194	8.6	13	89	3.9	114	5.0	3.04	117	.250	.324	19	11	92	119	3.2	7	4	2.2
1960 NY-A	12	9	.571	33	29	8	**4**	0	193	168	7.8	15	65	3.0	85	4.0	3.08	116	.235	.294	17	11	92	96	-1.0	2	1	1.4
1961 NY-A	**25**	4	**.862**	39	39	11	3	0	**283**	242	7.7	23	92	2.9	209	6.6	3.21	117	.229	.289	26	17	93	89	**9.1**	3	0	1.9
1962 NY-A	17	8	.680	38	37	7	0	0	258	243	8.5	22	69	2.4	160	5.6	2.90	126	.246	.295	31	21	92	110	3.1	-0	4	2.6
1963 NY-A	**24**	7	**.774**	38	37	13	3	1	**269**	240	8.0	26	56	1.9	189	6.3	2.74	130	.241	.279	26	24	98	110	**6.4**	0	-0	2.6
1964 NY-A	17	6	.739	39	36	12	8	1	245	212	7.8	10	57	2.1	172	6.3	2.13	171	.230	.272	41	41	101	107	4.2	0	2	**5.0**
1965 NY-A	16	13	.552	37	36	9	2	1	244	241	8.9	22	50	1.8	162	6.0	3.25	108	.258	.292	6	7	101	103	2.5	2	2	1.1
1966 NY-A	2	5	.286	22	9	0	0	0	73	79	9.7	8	24	3.0	43	5.3	2.47	130	.277	.324	8	6	94	178	-1.2	-2	3	0.8
1967 NY-A	2	4	.333	7	7	2	1	0	44	40	8.2	2	9	1.8	21	4.3	1.64	189	.247	.283	8	7	96	171	-0.7	-0	2	1.0
Total 16	236	106	.690	498	438	156	45	10	3171	2766	7.9	228	1086	3.1	1956	5.6	2.74	133	.235	.298	387	318	95	111	44.7	25	26	38.6
■ GENE FORD	Ford, Eugene Matthew b: 6/23/12, Ft.Dodge, Iowa d: 9/7/70, Emmetsburg, Iowa BR/TR, 6'2", 195 lbs. Deb: 6/17/36																											
1936 Bos-N	0	0	—	2	1	0	0	0	2	2	9.0	0	3	13.5	0	0.0	13.50	29	.250	.455	-2	-2	96	44	0.0	0	0	-0.1
1938 Chi-A	0	0	—	4	0	0	0	0	14	21	13.5	1	12	7.7	2	1.3	10.29	46	.350	.446	-9	-9	98	77	0.0	-0	0	-0.6
Total 2	0	0	—	6	1	0	0	0	16	23	12.9	1	15	8.4	2	1.1	10.69	43	.338	.447	-11	-11	98	73	0.0	-0	0	-0.7
■ GENE FORD	Ford, Eugene Wyman b: 4/16/1881, Milton, N.S., Can. d: 8/23/73, Dunedin, Fla. BR/TR, 6', 170 lbs. Deb: 5/05/05																											
1905 Det-A	0	1	.000	7	1	1	0	0	35	51	13.1	0	14	3.6	20	5.1	5.66	47	.367	.425	-12	-12	100	101	-0.4	-1	0	-1.1
■ WENTY FORD	Ford, Percival Edmund Wentworth b: 11/25/46, Nassau, Bahamas d: 7/8/80, Nassau, Bahamas BR/TR, 5'11", 165 lbs. Deb: 9/10/73																											
1973 Atl-N	1	2	.333	4	2	1	0	0	16	17	9.6	3	8	4.5	4	2.3	5.63	74	.279	.361	-3	-3	113	99	-0.3	1	0	-0.1
■ RUSS FORD	Ford, Russell William b: 4/25/1883, Brandon, Man., Can. d: 1/24/60, Rockingham, N.C. BR/TR, 5'11", 175 lbs. Deb: 4/28/09																											
1909 NY-A	0	0	—	1	0	0	0	0	3	4	12.0	0	4	12.0	2	6.0	9.00	27	.333	.579	-2	-2	99	113	0.0	-0	0	-0.1
1910 NY-A	26	6	.813	36	33	29	8	1	300	194	**5.8**	4	70	2.1	209	6.3	1.65	162	.188	.245	29	34	106	62	**9.7**	4	-3	4.2
1911 NY-A	22	11	.667	37	33	26	1	0	281	251	8.0	3	76	2.4	158	5.1	2.27	163	.237	.291	33	45	111	91	6.4	-3	-1	4.5
1912 NY-A	13	21	.382	36	35	30	0	0	292	317	9.8	10	79	2.4	112	3.5	3.54	99	.280	.329	-6	-1	105	102	1.7	6	1	0.7

YEAR	TM/L	W	L	PCT	G	GS	CG	SHO	SV	IP	H	H/G	HR	BB	BB/G	SO	SO/G	ERA	/A	OAVG	OOBP	PR	/A	PF	CPI	WAT	PB	PD	TPI
1913	NY-A	12	18	.400	33	28	15	1	2	237	244	9.3	9	58	2.2	72	2.7	2.66	114	.275	.322	7	10	104	123	0.7	0	-4	0.7
1914	Buf-F	21	6	**.778**	35	26	19	5	**6**	247	190	6.9	11	41	**1.5**	123	4.5	1.82	**183**	.214	.254	38	41	104	95	7.8	-3	3	4.7
1915	Buf-F	5	9	.357	21	15	7	0	0	127	140	9.9	7	48	3.4	34	2.4	4.54	68	.285	.352	-21	-21	101	94	-1.9	3	3	-1.4
Total	7	99	71	.582	199	170	126	15	9	1487	1340	8.1	44	376	2.3	710	4.3	2.59	125	.243	.296	78	106	106	93	24.4	8	0	13.3

■ TOM FORD Ford, Thomas Walter b: 1866, Chattanooga, Tenn. 5'10.5", 155 lbs. Deb: 5/06/1890

YEAR	TM/L	W	L	PCT	G	GS	CG	SHO	SV	IP	H	H/G	HR	BB	BB/G	SO	SO/G	ERA	/A	OAVG	OOBP	PR	/A	PF	CPI	WAT	PB	PD	TPI
1890	Col-a	0	0	—	1	0	0	0	0	2	0	0.0	0	3	13.5	0	0.0	0.00	—	.000	.364	1	1	96	0	0.0	-0	0	0.1
	BB-a	0	6	.000	7	6	6	0	0	49	70	12.9	2	32	5.9	12	2.2	5.14	77	.352	.442	-7	-6	103	131	-2.9	-3	0	-0.8
	Yr	0	6	.000	8	6	6	0	0	51	70	12.4	2	35	6.2	12	2.1	4.94	80	.343	.439	-6	-6	102	131	-2.9	-0	0	-0.7

■ HAPPY FOREMAN Foreman, August b: 7/20/1897, Memphis, Tenn. d: 2/13/53, New York, N.Y. BL/TL, 5'7", 160 lbs. Deb: 9/03/24

YEAR	TM/L	W	L	PCT	G	GS	CG	SHO	SV	IP	H	H/G	HR	BB	BB/G	SO	SO/G	ERA	/A	OAVG	OOBP	PR	/A	PF	CPI	WAT	PB	PD	TPI
1924	Chi-A	0	0	—	3	0	0	0	0	4	7	15.8	0	4	9.0	1	2.3	2.25	184	.467	.550	1	1	98	474	0.0	-0	-0	0.0
1926	Bos-A	0	0	—	3	0	0	0	0	7	3	3.9	0	5	6.4	3	3.9	3.86	110	.130	.276	0	0	106	27	0.0	-0	1	0.1
Total	2	0	0	—	6	0	0	0	0	11	10	8.2	0	9	7.4	4	3.3	3.27	129	.263	.388	1	1	103	189	0.0	-1	1	0.1

■ FRANK FOREMAN Foreman, Francis Isaiah "Monkey" b: 5/1/1863, Baltimore, Md. d: 11/19/57, Baltimore, Md. BL/TL, 6', 160 lbs. Deb: 5/15/1884

YEAR	TM/L	W	L	PCT	G	GS	CG	SHO	SV	IP	H	H/G	HR	BB	BB/G	SO	SO/G	ERA	/A	OAVG	OOBP	PR	/A	PF	CPI	WAT	PB	PD	TPI
1884	CP-U	1	2	.333	3	3	1	0	0	18	23	11.5	0	2	1.0	10	5.0	4.00	75	.316	.334	-2	-2	100	102	-0.3	-1	0	-0.2
	KC-U	0	1	.000	1	1	1	0	0	8	17	19.1	0	2	2.3	5	5.6	5.63	49	.434	.462	-2	-3	92	153	-0.4	-0	0	-0.1
	Yr	1	3	.250	4	4	2	0	0	26	40	13.8	0	4	1.4	15	5.2	4.50	65	.357	.380	-4	-5	97	153	-0.7	-1	0	-0.3
1885	Bal-a	2	1	.667	3	3	2	0	0	27	33	11.0	0	9	3.0	11	3.7	6.00	59	.313	.368	-8	-7	109	75	0.7	1	0	-0.4
1889	Bal-a	23	21	.523	51	48	43	5	0	414	364	7.9	8	137	3.0	180	3.9	3.52	109	.250	.315	15	14	99	75	0.3	-9	-4	0.0
1890	Cin-N	13	10	.565	25	24	20	0	0	198	201	9.1	6	89	4.0	57	2.6	3.95	96	.279	.358	-9	-4	106	93	-0.3	-1	0	-0.2
1891	Was-a	18	21	.462	43	41	39	1	1	345	381	9.9	8	142	3.7	170	4.4	3.73	100	.295	.365	-0	0	101	104	5.1	9	-2	0.9
1892	Was-N	2	4	.333	11	7	4	0	0	60	53	8.0	6	37	5.6	16	2.4	3.30	106	.249	.360	-0	1	106	120	-0.3	7	0	0.8
	Bal-N	0	3	.000	4	3	2	0	0	25	40	14.4	1	11	4.0	5	1.8	6.84	49	.375	.434	-10	-10	102	96	-1.4	0	0	-0.7
	Yr	2	7	.222	15	10	6	0	0	85	93	9.8	7	48	5.1	21	2.2	4.34	80	.291	.384	-10	-8	105	96	-1.7	7	0	0.1
1893	NY-N	0	1	.000	2	1	0	0	0	6	19	28.5	1	10	15.0	0	0.0	30.00	16	.546	.648	-17	-17	103	64	-0.4	-1	0	-1.0
1895	Cin-N	11	14	.440	32	27	19	0	1	219	253	10.4	11	92	3.8	55	2.3	4.11	125	.310	.380	17	25	107	112	-1.9	4	0	2.6
1896	Cin-N	15	6	.714	27	23	18	1	1	191	214	10.1	2	62	2.9	38	1.8	3.68	123	.305	.362	15	18	103	102	3.3	-1	0	1.5
1901	Bos-A	0	1	.000	1	1	1	0	0	8	8	9.0	1	2	2.3	1	1.1	9.00	38	.280	.327	-5	-5	94	42	-0.4	-1	0	-0.3
	Bal-A	12	6	.667	24	22	18	1	1	191	225	10.6	2	58	2.7	41	1.9	3.68	106	.314	.366	-0	5	107	108	3.2	5	-3	0.1
	Yr	12	7	.632	25	23	19	1	1	199	233	10.5	3	60	2.7	42	1.9	3.89	100	.313	.364	-5	-0	106	108	2.8	-1	-3	-0.2
1902	Bal-A	0	2	.000	2	2	2	0	0	16	28	15.8	0	6	3.4	2	1.1	6.19	60	.410	.458	-5	-4	104	113	-0.9	1	1	-0.2
Total	11	97	93	.511	229	206	170	8	4	1726	1859	9.7	46	659	3.4	591	3.1	3.96	101	.292	.358	-12	11	103	97	6.3	12	-8	2.8

■ BROWNIE FOREMAN Foreman, John Davis b: 8/6/1875, Baltimore, Md. d: 10/10/26, Baltimore, Md. BL/TL, 5'8", 150 lbs. Deb: 7/18/1895

YEAR	TM/L	W	L	PCT	G	GS	CG	SHO	SV	IP	H	H/G	HR	BB	BB/G	SO	SO/G	ERA	/A	OAVG	OOBP	PR	/A	PF	CPI	WAT	PB	PD	TPI
1895	Pit-N	8	6	.571	19	16	12	0	2	140	131	**8.4**	0	64	4.1	54	3.5	3.21	143	**.267**	.351	25	22	96	100	0.6	-5	0	1.3
1896	Pit-N	3	3	.500	9	9	5	0	0	62	73	10.6	4	35	5.1	18	2.6	6.68	61	.316	.406	-16	-18	93	77	0.0	1	0	-1.3
	Cin-N	0	4	.000	4	3	2	0	0	18	39	19.5	2	16	8.0	4	2.0	16.50	27	.459	.545	-24	-24	103	68	-1.9	-1	0	-1.6
	Yr	3	7	.300	13	12	7	0	0	80	112	12.6	6	51	5.7	22	2.5	8.89	47	.355	.444	-40	-42	95	68	-1.9	1	0	-2.9
Total	2	11	13	.458	32	28	19	0	2	220	243	9.9	6	115	4.7	76	3.1	5.28	84	.301	.388	-16	-20	96	91	-1.3	-5	0	-1.6

■ BILL FORMAN Forman, William Orange b: 10/10/1886, Venango, Pa. d: 10/3/58, Uniontown, Pa. BB/TR, 5'11", 180 lbs. Deb: 9/20/09

YEAR	TM/L	W	L	PCT	G	GS	CG	SHO	SV	IP	H	H/G	HR	BB	BB/G	SO	SO/G	ERA	/A	OAVG	OOBP	PR	/A	PF	CPI	WAT	PB	PD	TPI
1909	Was-A	0	2	.000	2	2	1	0	0	11	8	6.5	0	7	5.7	2	1.6	4.91	48	.211	.362	-3	-3	96	59	-0.9	0	1	-0.2
1910	Was-A	0	0	—	1	0	0	0	0	1	1	9.0	0	0	0.0	0	0.0	9.00	28	.333	.333	-1	-1	102	39	0.0	0	0	0.0
Total	2	0	2	.000	3	2	1	0	0	12	9	6.8	0	7	5.3	2	1.5	5.25	46	.220	.360	-4	-4	96	58	-0.9	1	1	-0.2

■ MIKE FORNIELES Fornieles, Jose Miguel (Torres) b: 1/18/32, Havana, Cuba BR/TR, 5'11", 155 lbs. Deb: 9/02/52

YEAR	TM/L	W	L	PCT	G	GS	CG	SHO	SV	IP	H	H/G	HR	BB	BB/G	SO	SO/G	ERA	/A	OAVG	OOBP	PR	/A	PF	CPI	WAT	PB	PD	TPI
1952	Was-A	2	2	.500	4	2	2	1	0	26	13	4.5	1	11	3.8	12	4.2	1.38	266	.143	.231	7	7	100	55	0.0	-1	-0	0.6
1953	Chi-A	8	7	.533	39	16	5	0	3	153	160	9.4	8	61	3.6	72	4.2	3.59	115	.270	.336	7	9	104	110	-0.5	-3	2	0.8
1954	Chi-A	1	2	.333	15	6	0	0	1	42	41	8.8	4	14	3.0	18	3.9	4.29	87	.252	.307	-3	-3	100	79	-0.6	0	1	-0.1
1955	Chi-A	6	3	.667	26	9	2	0	2	86	84	8.8	12	29	3.0	23	2.4	3.87	100	.255	.315	1	-0	98	103	0.9	-2	0	-0.1
1956	Chi-A	0	1	.000	6	0	0	0	0	16	22	12.4	1	6	3.4	6	3.4	4.50	94	.306	.354	-1	-0	102	105	-0.4	0	0	0.0
	Bal-A	4	7	.364	30	11	1	1	1	111	109	8.8	7	25	2.0	53	4.3	3.97	101	.266	.302	2	0	97	85	-1.0	-1	2	0.1
	Yr	4	8	.333	36	11	1	1	1	127	131	9.3	8	31	2.2	59	4.2	4.04	100	.271	.310	2	0	97	85	-1.4	0	2	0.1
1957	Bal-A	2	6	.250	15	4	1	1	0	57	57	9.0	4	17	2.7	43	6.8	4.26	82	.257	.308	-3	-5	93	77	-2.0	1	1	-0.3
	Bos-A	8	7	.533	25	18	7	1	2	125	136	9.8	7	38	2.7	64	4.6	3.53	117	.271	.318	4	8	109	103	0.0	-2	-1	0.6
	Yr	10	13	.435	40	22	8	2	2	182	193	9.5	11	55	2.7	107	5.3	3.76	105	.267	.315	1	4	104	103	-2.0	1	-1	0.3
1958	Bos-A	4	6	.400	37	7	1	0	1	111	123	10.0	10	33	2.7	49	4.0	4.95	80	.284	.337	-15	-12	105	89	-1.1	-0	-0	-1.2
1959	Bos-A	5	3	.625	46	0	0	0	11	82	77	8.5	6	29	3.2	54	5.9	3.07	132	.254	.313	7	9	105	118	1.1	-1	0	0.9
1960	Bos-A	10	5	.667	**70**	0	0	0	**14**	109	86	7.1	6	49	4.0	64	5.3	2.64	154	.219	.306	15	17	105	110	3.4	2	0	2.0
1961	Bos-A	9	8	.529	57	2	1	0	15	119	121	9.2	18	54	4.1	70	5.3	4.69	88	.265	.337	-9	-7	103	101	1.1	0	2	-0.4
1962	Bos-A	3	6	.333	42	1	0	0	5	82	96	10.5	14	37	4.1	36	4.0	5.38	76	.303	.378	-13	-12	103	115	-1.3	-0	0	-1.1
1963	Bos-A	0	0	—	9	0	0	0	0	14	16	10.3	0	5	3.2	5	3.2	6.43	60	.286	.333	-4	-4	107	59	0.0	1	-0	-0.3
	Min-A	1	1	.500	11	0	0	0	0	23	24	9.4	0	13	5.1	7	2.7	4.70	76	.273	.368	-3	-3	98	91	0.0	1	-1	-0.2
	Yr	1	1	.500	20	0	0	0	0	37	40	9.7	0	18	4.4	12	2.9	5.35	69	.276	.355	-7	-7	101	91	0.0	1	-1	-0.5
Total	12	63	64	.496	432	76	20	4	55	1156	1165	9.1	98	421	3.3	576	4.5	3.96	101	.263	.325	-7	5	102	99	-0.4	-7	5	1.3

■ KEN FORSCH Forsch, Kenneth Roth b: 9/8/46, Sacramento, Cal. BR/TR, 6'4", 195 lbs. Deb: 9/07/70

YEAR	TM/L	W	L	PCT	G	GS	CG	SHO	SV	IP	H	H/G	HR	BB	BB/G	SO	SO/G	ERA	/A	OAVG	OOBP	PR	/A	PF	CPI	WAT	PB	PD	TPI
1970	Hou-N	1	2	.333	4	4	1	0	0	24	28	10.5	1	5	1.9	13	4.9	5.63	68	.298	.333	-4	-5	94	73	-0.4	-1	-0	-0.4
1971	Hou-N	8	8	.500	33	23	7	2	0	188	162	7.8	8	53	2.5	131	6.3	2.54	126	.230	.284	19	14	92	96	0.2	-1	-2	1.1
1972	Hou-N	6	8	.429	30	24	1	0	0	156	163	9.4	19	62	3.6	113	6.5	3.92	93	.273	.335	-8	-5	105	113	-1.6	-1	-2	-0.8
1973	Hou-N	9	12	.429	46	26	5	0	4	201	197	8.8	18	74	3.3	149	6.7	4.21	83	.257	.319	-12	-16	95	88	-1.7	-4	-2	-2.2
1974	Hou-N	8	7	.533	70	0	0	0	10	103	98	8.6	3	37	3.2	48	4.2	2.80	127	.255	.320	10	9	98	116	0.5	-1	-0	0.8
1975	Hou-N	4	8	.333	34	9	2	0	2	109	114	9.4	9	30	2.5	54	4.5	3.22	107	.277	.324	5	3	95	123	-0.9	-1	-0	0.1
1976	Hou-N	4	3	.571	52	0	0	0	19	92	76	7.4	5	26	2.5	49	4.8	2.15	141	.226	.280	14	9	87	118	0.6	-0	1	1.0
1977	Hou-N	5	8	.385	42	5	0	0	8	86	80	8.4	2	28	2.9	45	4.7	2.72	133	.246	.302	11	8	92	104	-1.5	-1	1	0.9
1978	Hou-N	10	6	.625	52	6	4	2	7	133	136	9.2	2	37	2.5	71	4.8	2.71	126	.268	.309	13	10	95	118	2.7	0	1	1.1
1979	Hou-N	11	6	.647	26	24	10	2	0	178	155	7.8	14	35	**1.8**	58	2.9	3.03	111	.236	**.271**	14	7	90	85	2.0	0	2	0.9
1980	Hou-N	12	13	.480	32	32	6	3	0	222	230	9.3	15	41	1.7	84	3.4	3.20	109	.266	.300	10	7	97	104	-2.2	3	1	1.2
1981	Cal-A	11	7	.611	20	20	10	**4**	0	153	143	8.4	7	27	1.6	55	3.2	2.88	132	.250	.282	13	16	104	96	2.8	0	0	1.8
1982	Cal-A	13	11	.542	37	35	12	4	0	228	225	8.9	25	57	2.3	73	2.9	3.87	104	.258	.307	5	4	99	96	-0.7	0	-2	0.2
1983	Cal-A	11	12	.478	31	31	11	1	0	219	226	9.3	21	61	2.5	81	3.3	4.07	96	.266	.316	0	-4	96	95	1.1	0	-1	-0.4
1984	Cal-A	1	1	.500	2	2	1	0	0	16	14	7.9	2	3	1.7	10	5.6	2.25	180	.237	.274	3	3	101	135	0.0	0	1	0.5
1986	Cal-A	0	1	.000	10	0	0	0	1	17	24	12.7	4	10	5.3	13	6.9	9.53	42	.343	.424	-10	-10	95	87	-0.4	0	0	-0.9
Total	16	114	113	.502	521	241	70	18	51	2125	2071	8.8	155	586	2.5	1047	4.4	3.37	106	.257	.305	84	50	96	101	0.5	-5	-3	4.9

■ BOB FORSCH Forsch, Robert Herbert b: 1/13/50, Sacramento, Cal. BR/TR, 6'4", 200 lbs. Deb: 7/07/74

YEAR	TM/L	W	L	PCT	G	GS	CG	SHO	SV	IP	H	H/G	HR	BB	BB/G	SO	SO/G	ERA	/A	OAVG	OOBP	PR	/A	PF	CPI	WAT	PB	PD	TPI
1974	StL-N	7	4	.636	19	14	5	2	0	100	84	7.6	5	34	3.1	39	3.5	2.97	126	.230	.292	7	9	103	90	1.3	1	-0	1.1
1975	StL-N	15	10	.600	34	34	7	4	0	230	213	8.3	14	70	2.7	108	4.2	2.86	132	.244	.299	20	23	103	103	2.7	10	1	3.8
1976	StL-N	8	10	.444	33	32	2	0	0	194	209	9.7	17	71	3.3	76	3.5	3.94	93	.277	.335	-9	-6	105	108	0.0	1	0	-0.4
1977	StL-N	20	7	.741	35	35	8	2	0	217	210	8.7	20	69	2.9	95	3.9	3.48	107	.251	.308	10	6	95	99	6.9	0	-1	0.5
1978	StL-N	11	17	.393	34	34	7	3	0	234	205	7.9	15	97	3.7	114	4.4	3.69	93	.238	.313	-3	-7	96	88	-1.2	3	1	-0.3
1979	StL-N	11	11	.500	33	32	7	1	0	219	215	8.8	16	52	2.1	92	3.8	3.82	102	.262	.302	-2	2	104	89	-0.6	-1	1	0.2
1980	StL-N	11	10	.524	31	31	8	0	0	215	225	9.4	12	33	**1.4**	87	3.6	3.77	98	.273	.298	-4	-2	102	88	1.5	9	2	1.0
1981	StL-N	10	5	.667	20	20	1	0	0	124	106	7.7	7	29	2.1	41	3.0	3.19	110	.232	.277	4	5	101	81	1.8	-1	0	0.4
1982	StL-N	15	9	.625	36	34	6	2	1	233	238	9.2	16	54	2.1	69	2.7	3.48	106	.268	.308	3	6	102	101	1.8	3	-2	0.7
1983	StL-N	10	12	.455	34	30	6	2	0	187	190	9.1	23	54	2.6	56	2.7	4.28	83	.266	.313	-13	-15	98	94	-0.8	5	-0	-1.1

YEAR	TM/L	W	L	PCT	G	GS	CG	SHO	SV	IP	H	H/G	HR	BB	BB/G	SO	SO/G	ERA	/A	OAVG	OOBP	PR	/A	PF	CPI	WAT	PB	PD	TPI
1984	StL-N	2	5	.286	16	11	1	0	0	52	64	11.1	6	19	3.3	21	3.6	6.06	58	.303	.356	-14	-15	99	85	-1.5	1	0	-1.2
1985	StL-N	9	6	.600	34	19	3	1	2	136	132	8.7	11	47	3.1	48	3.2	3.90	86	.258	.319	-5	-8	93	94	-0.2	4	-0	-0.4
1986	StL-N	14	10	.583	33	33	3	0	0	230	211	8.3	19	68	2.7	104	4.1	3.25	118	.247	.299	12	15	103	101	2.5	3	-1	1.9
1987	StL-N	11	7	.611	33	30	2	1	0	179	189	9.5	15	45	2.3	89	4.5	4.32	92	.273	.315	-5	-7	97	90	0.6	9	-1	0.1
1988	StL-N	9	4	.692	30	12	1	1	0	109	111	9.2	8	38	3.1	40	3.3	3.72	97	.270	.324	-3	-1	105	109	2.9	2	-2	0.0
	Hou-N	1	4	.200	6	6	0	0	0	28	42	13.5	2	6	1.9	14	4.5	6.43	50	.359	.376	-9	-10	93	99	-1.4	0	-0	-0.9
	Yr	10	8	.556	36	18	1	1	0	137	153	10.1	10	44	2.9	54	3.5	4.27	83	.287	.334	-12	-11	102	99	1.5	2	-2	-0.9
Total	15	164	131	.556	461	407	67	19	3	2687	2644	8.9	206	786	2.6	1093	3.7	3.70	100	.259	.310	-10	-5	100	95	16.3	49	-1	5.4
■ TERRY FORSTER	Forster, Terry Jay b: 1/14/52, Sioux Falls, S.D. BL/TL, 6'3", 200 lbs. Deb: 4/11/71																												
1971	Chi-A	2	3	.400	45	3	0	0	1	50	46	8.3	5	23	4.1	48	8.6	3.96	85	.241	.320	-3	-3	97	91	-0.4	1	0	-0.2
1972	Chi-A	6	5	.545	62	0	0	0	29	100	75	6.8	0	44	4.0	104	9.4	2.25	145	.208	.291	9	11	106	92	-0.1	4	1	1.9
1973	Chi-A	6	11	.353	51	12	4	0	16	173	174	9.1	7	78	4.1	120	6.2	3.23	122	.266	.339	11	14	103	117	-2.3	0	5	1.9
1974	Chi-A	7	8	.467	59	1	0	0	**24**	134	120	8.1	6	48	3.2	105	7.1	3.63	102	.245	.314	-0	1	102	88	-0.4	0	3	0.5
1975	Chi-A	3	3	.500	17	1	0	0	4	37	30	7.3	0	24	5.8	32	7.8	2.19	180	.236	.348	7	7	104	156	0.2	0	2	0.9
1976	Chi-A	2	12	.143	29	16	1	0	1	111	126	10.2	7	41	3.3	70	5.7	4.38	82	.288	.346	-11	-10	101	99	-4.5	0	2	-0.8
1977	Pit-N	6	4	.600	33	6	0	0	1	87	90	9.3	7	32	3.3	58	6.0	4.45	90	.269	.328	-5	-4	102	90	0.1	3	0	0.0
1978	LA-N	5	4	.556	47	0	0	0	22	65	56	7.8	2	23	3.2	46	6.4	1.94	179	.233	.297	12	11	97	137	-0.1	2	-0	1.3
1979	LA-N	1	2	.333	17	0	0	0	2	16	18	10.1	0	11	6.2	8	4.5	5.63	66	.295	.397	-3	-3	99	87	-0.4	0	1	-0.2
1980	LA-N	0	0	—	9	0	0	0	0	12	10	7.5	0	4	3.0	2	1.5	3.00	115	.222	.286	1	1	96	67	0.0	0	0	0.1
1981	LA-N	0	1	.000	21	0	0	0	0	31	37	10.7	1	15	4.4	17	4.9	4.06	82	.308	.380	-2	-2	96	123	-0.4	-0	1	-0.1
1982	LA-N	5	6	.455	56	0	0	0	3	83	66	7.2	3	31	3.4	52	5.6	3.04	111	.221	.289	5	3	94	86	-0.9	-0	1	0.4
1983	Atl-N	3	2	.600	56	0	0	0	13	79	60	6.8	3	31	3.5	54	6.2	2.16	175	.217	.294	13	14	104	118	0.3	2	1	1.8
1984	Atl-N	2	0	1.000	25	0	0	0	5	27	30	10.0	1	7	2.3	10	3.3	2.67	148	.297	.327	3	4	110	155	1.0	1	0	0.5
1985	Atl-N	2	3	.400	46	0	0	0	1	59	49	7.5	7	28	4.3	37	5.6	2.29	170	.222	.304	9	11	108	145	0.0	-0	-1	1.0
1986	Cal-A	4	1	.800	41	0	0	0	5	41	47	10.3	2	17	3.7	28	6.1	3.51	114	.297	.368	3	2	95	140	1.4	0	1	0.3
Total	16	54	65	.454	614	39	5	0	127	1105	1034	8.4	51	457	3.7	791	6.4	3.23	114	.251	.322	49	56	102	109	-6.5	11	16	9.3
■ GARY FORTUNE	Fortune, Garrett Reese b: 10/11/1894, High Point, N.C. d: 9/23/55, Washington, D.C. BB/TR, 5'11.5", 176 lbs. Deb: 10/05/16																												
1916	Phi-N	0	1	.000	1	1	0	0	0	5	2	3.6	0	4	7.2	3	5.4	3.60	68	.118	.286	-1	-1	94	24	-0.4	-0	-0	0.0
1918	Phi-N	0	2	.000	5	2	1	0	0	31	41	11.9	2	19	5.5	10	2.9	8.13	38	.333	.404	-18	-17	111	76	-0.9	0	-0	-1.5
1920	Bos-A	0	2	.000	14	3	1	0	0	42	46	9.9	0	23	4.9	10	2.1	5.79	63	.282	.371	-9	-10	97	68	-0.9	-0	-0	-0.9
Total	3	0	5	.000	20	6	2	0	0	78	89	10.3	2	46	5.3	23	2.7	6.58	52	.294	.380	-28	-28	102	69	-2.2	-0	-1	-2.4
■ JERRY FOSNOW	Fosnow, Gerald Eugene b: 9/21/40, Deshler, Ohio BR/TL, 6'4", 195 lbs. Deb: 6/29/64																												
1964	Min-A	0	1	.000	7	0	0	0	0	11	13	10.6	3	8	6.5	9	7.4	10.64	34	.302	.389	-9	-9	100	69	-0.4	0	-0	-0.8
1965	Min-A	3	3	.500	29	0	0	0	2	47	33	6.3	7	25	4.8	35	6.7	4.40	77	.193	.292	-5	-5	98	71	-0.5	-1	0	-0.5
Total	2	3	4	.429	36	0	0	0	2	58	46	7.1	10	33	5.1	44	6.8	5.59	62	.215	.313	-14	-14	99	71	-0.9	-1	0	-1.3
■ LARRY FOSS	Foss, Larry Curtis b: 4/18/36, Castleton, Kan. BR/TR, 6'2", 187 lbs. Deb: 9/18/61																												
1961	Pit-N	1	1	.500	3	3	0	0	0	15	15	9.0	3	11	6.6	9	5.4	6.00	67	.273	.400	-3	-3	99	107	0.0	-0	-0	-0.3
1962	NY-N	0	1	.000	5	1	0	0	0	12	17	12.8	2	7	5.3	3	2.3	4.50	95	.362	.439	-1	-0	108	179	-0.4	-0	-0	0.0
Total	2	1	2	.333	8	4	0	0	0	27	32	10.7	5	18	6.0	12	4.0	5.33	77	.314	.417	-4	-4	103	139	-0.4	-0	-0	-0.3
■ TONY FOSSAS	Fossas, Emilio Antonio b: 9/23/57, Havana, Cuba BL/TL, 6', 195 lbs. Deb: 5/15/88																												
1988	Tex-A	0	0	—	5	0	0	0	0	6	11	16.5	0	2	3.0	0	0.0	4.50	90	.423	.464	-0	-0	102	178	0.0	0	0	0.0
■ ALAN FOSTER	Foster, Alan Benton b: 12/8/46, Pasadena, Cal. BR/TR, 6', 180 lbs. Deb: 4/25/67																												
1967	LA-N	0	1	.000	4	2	0	0	0	17	10	5.3	0	3	1.6	15	7.9	2.12	142	.169	.210	2	2	89	24	-0.4	-0	0	0.2
1968	LA-N	1	1	.500	3	3	0	0	0	16	11	6.2	1	2	1.1	10	5.6	1.69	161	.200	.228	2	2	91	92	0.1	0	-0	0.2
1969	LA-N	3	9	.250	24	15	2	2	0	103	119	10.4	11	29	2.5	59	5.2	4.37	80	.290	.337	-9	-10	97	105	-3.2	-1	-0	-1.0
1970	LA-N	10	13	.435	33	33	7	1	0	199	200	9.0	22	81	3.7	83	3.8	4.25	85	.264	.330	-4	-14	89	102	-2.4	-1	-1	-1.6
1971	Cle-A	8	12	.400	36	26	3	0	0	182	158	7.8	19	82	4.1	97	4.8	4.15	91	.232	.315	-14	-8	108	82	0.5	-4	-4	-1.6
1972	Cal-A	0	1	.000	8	0	0	0	0	13	12	8.3	3	6	4.2	11	7.6	4.85	57	.245	.345	-3	-3	90	106	-0.4	0	0	-0.2
1973	StL-N	13	9	.591	35	29	6	2	0	204	195	8.6	17	63	2.8	106	4.7	3.13	105	.254	.308	12	4	90	111	2.2	1	-2	0.3
1974	StL-N	7	10	.412	31	25	5	1	0	162	167	9.3	16	61	3.4	78	4.3	3.89	96	.268	.331	-5	-3	103	105	-2.0	-1	-1	-0.4
1975	SD-N	3	1	.750	17	4	1	0	0	45	41	8.2	1	21	4.2	20	4.0	2.40	153	.244	.321	6	6	101	129	1.1	-1	0	0.6
1976	SD-N	3	6	.333	26	11	2	0	0	87	75	7.8	9	35	3.6	22	2.3	3.21	98	.235	.308	3	-1	90	107	-1.1	-0	-1	-0.1
Total	10	48	63	.432	217	148	26	6	0	1028	988	8.6	99	383	3.4	501	4.4	3.73	94	.254	.319	-8	-24	96	101	-5.6	-7	-8	-3.6
■ ED FOSTER	Foster, Eddy Lee "Slim" b: Birmingham, Ala. d: 3/1/29, Montgomery, Ala. BR/TR, 6'1", Deb: 7/31/08																												
1908	Cle-A	1	0	1.000	6	1	1	0	2	21	16	6.9	1	12	5.1	11	4.7	2.14	115	.229	.357	1	1	103	171	0.5	-1	-1	0.0
■ RUBE FOSTER	Foster, George b: 1/5/1888, Lehigh, Okla d: 3/1/76, Bokoshe, Okla. BR/TR, 5'7.5", 170 lbs. Deb: 4/10/13																												
1913	Bos-A	3	4	.429	19	8	4	1	0	68	64	8.5	1	28	3.7	36	4.8	3.18	95	.249	.332	-2	-1	103	93	-0.6	-1	-0	-0.1
1914	Bos-A	14	8	.636	32	27	17	5	0	212	164	7.0	2	52	2.2	89	3.8	1.70	155	.218	.274	24	22	96	100	1.3	1	-0	2.5
1915	Bos-A	19	8	.704	37	33	21	5	1	255	217	7.7	3	86	3.0	82	2.9	2.12	133	.237	.310	24	20	96	121	1.7	7	1	3.0
1916	Bos-A	14	7	.667	33	19	9	3	2	182	173	8.6	0	86	4.3	53	2.6	3.07	85	.263	.352	-5	-9	92	111	2.2	0	2	-0.7
1917	Bos-A	8	7	.533	17	16	9	1	0	125	108	7.8	0	53	3.8	34	2.4	2.52	112	.243	.329	2	4	106	107	-0.7	2	1	0.8
Total	5	58	34	.630	138	103	60	15	3	842	726	7.8	6	305	3.3	294	3.1	2.36	116	.240	.315	43	36	97	109	3.9	8	3	5.5
■ LARRY FOSTER	Foster, Larry Lynn b: 12/24/37, Lansing, Mich. BL/TR, 6', 185 lbs. Deb: 9/18/63																												
1963	Det-A	0	0	—	1	0	0	0	0	2	4	18.0	0	1	4.5	1	4.5	13.50	28	.364	.417	-2	-2	104	51	0.0	0	0	-0.1
■ STEVE FOUCAULT	Foucault, Steven Raymond b: 10/3/49, Duluth, Minn. BL/TR, 6', 205 lbs. Deb: 4/07/73																												
1973	Tex-A	2	4	.333	32	0	0	0	8	56	54	8.7	6	31	5.0	28	4.5	3.86	99	.262	.361	-0	-0	100	121	-0.1	0	0	0.0
1974	Tex-A	8	9	.471	69	0	0	0	12	144	123	7.7	8	40	2.5	106	6.6	2.25	155	.234	.288	22	20	96	120	-0.9	0	0	2.1
1975	Tex-A	8	4	.667	59	0	0	0	10	107	96	8.1	10	55	4.6	56	4.7	4.12	92	.249	.335	-4	-4	100	100	2.2	0	-0	-0.4
1976	Tex-A	8	8	.500	46	0	0	0	5	76	68	8.1	9	25	3.0	41	4.9	3.32	109	.249	.306	2	2	103	116	0.5	0	2	0.5
1977	Det-A	7	7	.500	44	0	0	0	13	74	64	7.8	7	17	2.1	58	7.1	3.16	135	.226	.267	7	9	105	78	0.6	0	-1	0.8
1978	Det-A	2	4	.333	24	0	0	0	4	37	48	11.7	1	21	5.1	18	4.4	3.16	128	.324	.395	3	4	107	179	-1.0	0	-0	0.3
	KC-A	0	0	—	3	0	0	0	0	2	5	22.5	0	1	4.5	0	0.0	4.50	85	.417	.462	-0	-0	101	205	0.0	0	0	0.0
	Yr	2	4	.333	27	0	0	0	4	39	53	12.2	1	22	5.1	18	4.2	3.23	125	.323	.395	2	3	107	205	-1.0	0	-0	0.3
Total	6	35	36	.493	277	0	0	0	52	496	458	8.3	41	190	3.4	307	5.6	3.21	117	.250	.317	29	30	100	114	1.3	0	2	3.3
■ JACK FOURNIER	Fournier, Jacques Frank b: 9/29/1892, Au Sable, Mich. d: 9/5/73, Tacoma, Wash. BL/TR, 6', 195 lbs. Deb: 4/13/12																												
1922	StL-N	0	0	—	1	0	0	0	0	1	0	0.0	0	0	0.0	0	0.0	0.00	—	.000	.000	0	0	100	0	0.0	0	0	0.0
■ HENRY FOURNIER	Fournier, Julius Henry "Frenchy" b: 8/8/1865, Syracuse, N.Y. d: 12/8/45, Detroit, Mich. TL , Deb: 8/22/1894																												
1894	Cin-N	1	3	.250	6	4	4	0	0	45	71	14.2	4	20	4.0	5	1.0	5.40	100	.382	.442	-0	0	102	131	-0.7	-3	0	-0.1
■ DAVE FOUTZ	Foutz, David Luther "Scissors" b: 9/7/1856, Carroll Co., Md. d: 3/5/1897, Waverly, Ind. BR/TR, 6'2", 161 lbs. Deb: 7/29/1884 M																												
1884	StL-a	15	6	.714	25	25	19	2	0	207	167	7.3	7	36	1.6	95	4.1	2.17	**162**	.229	.265	25	31	109	113	2.9	0	0	3.2
1885	StL-a	33	14	.702	47	46	46	2	0	408	351	7.7	9	92	2.0	147	3.2	2.63	110	.243	.289	28	11	89	98	-0.1	8	7	2.3
1886	StL-a	**41**	16	**.719**	59	57	55	11	**1**	504	418	7.5	5	144	2.6	283	5.1	**2.11**	**173**	.235	.293	**75**	**87**	106	119	6.6	8	3	10.3
1887	StL-a	25	12	.676	40	38	36	1	0	339	369	9.8	7	90	2.4	94	2.5	3.88	116	.291	.338	16	23	105	97	-0.9	16	-0	1.9
1888	Bro-a	12	7	.632	23	19	19	0	0	176	146	7.5	3	35	1.8	73	3.7	2.51	124	.238	.279	11	12	102	87	0.1	5	0	1.1
1889	Bro-a	3	0	1.000	12	4	3	0	0	60	70	10.5	2	19	2.9	21	3.2	4.35	81	.307	.360	-3	-5	92	95	1.5	4	0	-0.4
1890	Bro-N	2	1	.667	5	2	2	0	**2**	29	29	9.0	0	6	1.9	4	1.2	1.86	184	.276	.315	5	5	96	144	0.0	2	0	0.5
1891	Bro-N	3	2	.600	6	5	5	0	0	52	51	8.8	1	16	2.8	14	2.4	3.29	100	.270	.327	0	-0	98	85	0.7	1	0	0.0
1892	Bro-N	13	8	.619	27	20	17	0	1	203	210	9.3	3	63	2.8	56	2.5	3.41	96	.280	.336	-3	-3	99	94	0.1	-0	0	-0.2

YEAR	TM/L	W	L	PCT	G	GS	CG	SHO	SV	IP	H	H/G	HR	BB	BB/G	SO	SO/G	ERA	/A	OAVG	OOBP	PR	/A	PF	CPI	WAT	PB	PD	TPI
1893	Bro-N	0	0	—	6	0	0	0	0	18	28	14.0	2	8	4.0	3	1.5	7.50	57	.372	.432	-6	-6	91	96	0.0	1	0	-0.4
1894	Bro-N	0	0	—	1	0	0	0	0	2	4	18.0	0	1	4.5	0	0.0	13.50	37	.439	.495	-2	-2	94	65	0.0	0	0	0.0
Total	11	147	66	.690	251	216	202	16	4	1998	1843	8.3	39	510	2.3	790	3.6	2.84	124	.256	.306	147	151	100	104	10.9	46	9	18.3
■ **JESSE FOWLER**	Fowler, Jesse Peter "Pete" b: 10/30/1898, Spartanburg, S.C. d: 9/23/73, Columbia, S.C. BR/TL, 5'10.5", 158 lbs. Deb: 7/29/24																												
1924	StL-N	1	1	.500	13	3	0	0	0	33	28	7.6	0	18	4.9	5	1.4	4.36	91	.226	.327	-2	-1	103	64	0.1	0	-1	-0.1
■ **ART FOWLER**	Fowler, John Arthur b: 7/3/22, Converse, S.C. BR/TR, 5'11", 180 lbs. Deb: 4/17/54 C																												
1954	Cin-N	12	10	.545	40	29	8	1	0	228	256	10.1	20	85	3.4	93	3.7	3.83	111	.286	.346	6	11	104	116	1.6	-2	-1	0.8
1955	Cin-N	11	10	.524	46	28	8	3	2	208	198	8.6	20	63	2.7	94	4.1	3.89	108	.250	.302	3	7	104	86	0.9	-0	-1	0.6
1956	Cin-N	11	11	.500	45	23	8	0	1	178	191	9.7	15	35	1.8	86	4.3	4.04	99	.278	.306	-5	-1	106	91	-1.8	-0	1	0.0
1957	Cin-N	3	0	1.000	33	7	1	0	0	88	111	11.4	11	24	2.5	45	4.6	6.44	64	.310	.349	-25	-23	106	81	1.5	0	0	-2.1
1959	LA-N	3	4	.429	36	0	0	0	2	61	70	10.3	8	23	3.4	47	6.9	5.31	75	.294	.343	-9	-9	101	95	-0.8	-1	0	-0.8
1961	LA-A	5	8	.385	53	3	0	0	11	89	68	6.9	12	29	2.9	78	7.9	3.64	124	.209	.269	4	9	112	77	-0.7	-1	-1	0.6
1962	LA-A	4	3	.571	48	0	0	0	5	77	67	7.8	6	25	2.9	38	4.4	2.81	144	.234	.292	10	11	102	108	0.3	1	-0	1.1
1963	LA-A	5	3	.625	57	0	0	0	10	89	70	7.1	5	19	1.9	53	5.4	2.43	138	.219	.258	12	9	92	91	1.4	0	-1	0.9
1964	LA-A	0	2	.000	4	0	0	0	1	7	8	10.3	2	5	6.4	5	6.4	10.29	31	.296	.412	-5	-5	89	74	-0.9	-0	0	-0.4
Total	9	54	51	.514	362	90	25	4	32	1025	1039	9.1	99	308	2.7	539	4.7	4.02	102	.265	.314	-10	8	104	95	1.5	-3	-3	0.7
■ **DICK FOWLER**	Fowler, Richard John b: 3/30/21, Toronto, Ont., Can. d: 5/22/72, Oneonta, N.Y. BR/TR, 6'4.5", 215 lbs. Deb: 9/13/41																												
1941	Phi-A	1	2	.333	4	3	1	0	0	24	26	9.8	4	8	3.0	8	3.0	3.38	127	.289	.337	2	2	103	157	-0.2	-1	0	0.1
1942	Phi-A	6	11	.353	31	17	4	0	1	140	159	10.2	13	45	2.9	38	2.4	4.95	75	.287	.337	-20	-19	101	92	0.0	-1	-2	-2.2
1945	Phi-A	1	2	.333	7	3	2	1	0	37	41	10.0	1	18	4.4	21	5.1	4.86	67	.283	.353	-6	-7	96	87	0.0	4	-1	-0.3
1946	Phi-A	9	16	.360	32	28	14	1	0	206	213	9.3	16	75	3.3	89	3.9	3.28	115	.263	.322	5	11	107	113	0.9	-2	-1	0.9
1947	Phi-A	12	11	.522	36	31	16	3	0	227	210	8.3	12	85	3.4	75	3.0	2.81	131	.249	.316	22	22	100	118	0.4	-3	-2	1.9
1948	Phi-A	15	8	.652	29	26	16	2	2	205	221	9.7	15	76	3.3	50	2.2	3.78	115	.281	.342	12	13	102	119	3.0	-2	-1	0.9
1949	Phi-A	15	11	.577	31	28	15	4	1	214	210	8.8	13	115	4.8	43	1.8	3.74	111	.262	.352	11	10	99	112	1.6	2	1	1.2
1950	Phi-A	1	5	.167	11	9	2	0	0	67	75	10.1	7	56	7.5	15	2.0	6.45	66	.300	.425	-14	-16	93	103	-1.4	-1	0	-1.4
1951	Phi-A	5	11	.313	22	22	4	0	0	125	141	10.2	11	72	5.2	29	2.1	5.62	78	.291	.377	-21	-17	106	95	-2.6	-0	-1	-1.6
1952	Phi-A	1	2	.333	18	3	1	0	0	59	71	10.8	4	28	4.3	14	2.1	6.41	64	.302	.377	-18	-15	112	82	-0.4	-2	1	-1.5
Total	10	66	79	.455	221	170	75	11	4	1304	1367	9.4	96	578	4.0	382	2.6	4.11	97	.273	.346	-27	-15	102	109	1.3	-6	-6	-2.0
■ **ALAN FOWLKES**	Fowlkes, Alan Kim b: 8/8/58, Brawley, Cal. BR/TR, 6'2", 190 lbs. Deb: 4/07/82																												
1982	SF-N	4	2	.667	21	15	1	0	0	85	111	11.8	12	24	2.5	50	5.3	5.19	65	.321	.362	-15	-17	94	111	0.9	-1	-0	-1.7
1985	Cal-A	0	0	—	2	0	0	0	0	7	8	10.3	4	4	5.1	5	6.4	9.00	46	.276	.364	-4	-4	101	94	0.0	0	0	-0.2
Total	2	4	2	.667	23	15	1	0	0	92	119	11.6	16	28	2.7	55	5.4	5.48	63	.317	.362	-19	-21	94	110	0.9	-1	-0	-1.9
■ **HENRY FOX**	Fox, Henry (born Henry Fuchs) b: 11/18/1874, Scranton, Pa. d: 6/6/27, Scranton, Pa. Deb: 9/04/02																												
1902	Phi-N	0	0	—	1	0	0	0	1	1	2	18.0	0	1	9.0	1	9.0	18.00	17	.441	.542	-2	-2	109	53	0.0	0	0	-0.1
■ **HOWIE FOX**	Fox, Howard Francis b: 3/1/21, Coburg, Ore. d: 10/9/55, San Antonio, Tex. BR/TR, 6'3", 210 lbs. Deb: 9/28/44																												
1944	Cin-N	0	0	—	2	0	0	0	0	2	2	9.0	0	0	0.0	0	0.0	0.00	—	.222	.222	1	1	95	0	0.0	-0	0	0.1
1945	Cin-N	8	13	.381	45	15	7	0	0	164	169	9.3	6	77	4.2	54	3.0	4.94	75	.268	.345	-21	-23	97	83	-0.4	3	4	-1.5
1946	Cin-N	0	0	—	4	0	0	0	0	5	12	21.6	2	5	9.0	1	1.8	18.00	20	.462	.548	-8	-8	105	82	0.0	0	0	-0.7
1948	Cin-N	6	9	.400	34	24	5	0	1	171	185	9.7	11	62	3.3	63	3.3	4.53	93	.280	.336	-11	-6	106	94	-0.3	1	1	-0.3
1949	Cin-N	6	19	.240	38	30	9	0	0	215	221	9.3	13	77	3.2	60	2.5	3.98	100	.265	.325	2	-0	98	96	-5.5	2	6	0.7
1950	Cin-N	11	8	.579	34	22	10	1	1	187	196	9.4	14	85	4.1	64	3.1	4.33	101	.269	.344	-4	1	106	98	2.7	-0	3	0.4
1951	Cin-N	9	14	.391	40	30	9	4	2	228	239	9.4	15	69	2.7	57	2.3	3.83	106	.272	.324	3	6	103	100	-1.4	-2	1	0.4
1952	Phi-N	2	7	.222	13	11	2	0	0	62	70	10.2	8	26	3.8	16	2.3	5.08	73	.287	.349	-9	-10	99	99	-2.7	-2	1	-0.9
1954	Bal-A	1	2	.333	38	0	0	0	2	74	80	9.7	2	34	4.1	27	3.3	3.65	101	.289	.363	1	0	99	120	0.0	1	1	0.2
Total	9	43	72	.374	248	132	42	5	6	1108	1174	9.5	71	435	3.5	342	2.8	4.33	93	.274	.338	-47	-39	102	96	-7.6	2	17	-1.6
■ **JOHN FOX**	Fox, John Joseph b: 2/7/1859, Roxbury, Mass. d: 4/18/1893, Boston, Mass. Deb: 6/02/1881																												
1881	Bos-N	6	8	.429	17	16	12	0	0	124	144	10.5	0	39	2.8	30	2.2	3.34	77	.303	.356	-8	-10	93	107	-0.4	-3	0	-1.4
1883	Bal-a	6	13	.316	20	19	18	0	0	165	209	11.4	2	32	1.7	49	2.7	4.04	93	.314	.346	-13	-5	113	110	0.4	-5	0	-0.7
1884	Pit-a	1	6	.143	7	7	7	0	0	59	76	11.6	2	16	2.4	22	3.4	5.64	58	.321	.364	-16	-16	101	91	-1.7	0	0	-1.2
1886	Was-N	0	1	.000	1	1	1	0	0	8	11	12.4	0	11	12.4	3	3.4	9.00	37	.341	.508	-5	-5	100	89	-0.4	0	0	-0.3
Total	4	13	28	.317	45	43	38	0	0	356	440	11.1	4	98	2.5	104	2.6	4.17	77	.312	.357	-42	-37	104	106	-2.1	-8	0	-3.6
■ **TERRY FOX**	Fox, Terrence Edward b: 7/31/35, Chicago, Ill. BR/TR, 6', 175 lbs. Deb: 9/04/60																												
1960	Mil-N	0	0	—	5	0	0	0	0	8	6	6.8	0	6	6.8	5	5.6	4.50	75	.200	.333	-1	-1	89	58	0.0	-0	0	0.0
1961	Det-A	5	2	.714	39	0	0	0	12	57	42	6.6	6	16	2.5	32	5.1	1.42	265	.200	.264	16	15	94	162	0.9	0	1	1.6
1962	Det-A	3	1	.750	44	0	0	0	16	58	48	7.4	2	16	2.5	23	3.6	1.71	257	.227	.279	15	17	110	143	1.0	2	0	2.0
1963	Det-A	8	6	.571	46	0	0	0	11	80	81	9.1	9	20	2.3	35	3.9	3.60	104	.263	.307	0	1	104	107	1.2	-0	0	0.2
1964	Det-A	4	3	.571	32	0	0	0	5	61	77	11.4	4	16	2.4	28	4.1	3.39	102	.316	.348	2	0	95	143	0.4	1	1	0.2
1965	Det-A	6	4	.600	42	0	0	0	10	78	59	6.8	7	31	3.6	34	3.9	2.77	130	.214	.293	6	7	104	106	0.6	-1	2	0.8
1966	Det-A	0	1	.000	4	0	0	0	1	10	9	8.1	3	2	1.8	6	5.4	6.30	56	.243	.268	-3	-3	102	74	-0.4	-0	0	-0.2
	Phi-N	3	2	.600	36	0	0	0	4	44	57	11.7	3	17	3.5	22	4.5	4.50	80	.322	.378	-4	-4	100	122	0.3	-0	-0	-0.4
Total	7	29	19	.604	248	0	0	0	59	396	379	8.6	34	124	2.8	185	4.2	3.00	125	.254	.309	31	33	101	125	4.0	1	4	4.2
■ **BILL FOXEN**	Foxen, William Aloysius b: 5/31/1884, Tenafly, N.J. d: 4/17/37, Brooklyn, N.Y. BL/TL, 5'11.5", 165 lbs. Deb: 5/05/08																												
1908	Phi-N	7	7	.500	22	16	10	2	0	147	126	7.7	2	53	3.2	52	3.2	1.96	118	.263	.346	6	6	98	137	-0.5	-2	2	0.9
1909	Phi-N	3	7	.300	18	7	5	1	0	83	65	7.0	0	32	3.5	37	4.0	3.36	82	.219	.303	-7	-5	106	63	-1.9	3	4	0.0
1910	Phi-N	5	5	.500	16	9	5	0	0	78	73	8.4	2	40	4.6	33	3.8	2.54	114	.268	.368	4	3	95	153	0.0	-0	2	0.4
	Chi-N	0	0	—	2	0	0	0	0	5	7	12.6	0	3	5.4	2	3.6	9.00	32	.350	.435	-3	-3	96	67	0.0	-0	0	-0.3
	Yr	5	5	.500	18	9	5	0	0	83	80	8.7	2	43	4.7	35	3.8	2.93	99	.271	.364	1	-0	95	67	0.0	-0	2	0.1
1911	Chi-N	1	1	.500	3	1	0	0	0	13	12	8.3	0	12	8.3	6	4.2	2.08	154	.255	.407	2	2	94	217	-0.1	1	1	0.3
Total	4	16	20	.444	61	33	20	3	0	326	283	7.8	4	140	3.9	130	3.6	2.57	102	.254	.345	2	2	99	124	-2.5	1	8	1.3
■ **JIMMIE FOXX**	Foxx, James Emory "Beast" or "Double X" b: 10/22/07, Sudlersville, Md. d: 7/21/67, Miami, Fla. BR/TR, 6', 195 lbs. Deb: 5/01/25 H																												
1939	Bos-A	0	0	—	1	0	0	0	0	1	0	0.0	0	0	0.0	1	9.0	0.00	—	.000	.000	1	1	107	0	0.0	1	0	0.1
1945	Phi-N	1	0	1.000	9	2	0	0	0	23	13	5.1	0	14	5.5	10	3.9	1.57	248	.171	.298	6	6	102	135	0.5	2	-1	0.6
Total	2	1	0	1.000	10	2	0	0	0	24	13	4.9	0	14	5.3	11	4.1	1.50	262	.165	.289	6	6	102	130	0.5	3	-1	0.7
■ **PAUL FOYTACK**	Foytack, Paul Eugene b: 11/16/30, Scranton, Pa. BR/TR, 5'11", 175 lbs. Deb: 4/21/53																												
1953	Det-A	0	0	—	6	0	0	0	0	10	15	13.5	1	9	8.1	7	6.3	10.80	38	.375	.490	-8	-7	102	83	0.0	-0	0	-0.6
1955	Det-A	0	1	.000	22	1	0	0	0	50	48	8.6	4	36	6.5	38	6.8	5.22	72	.259	.370	-7	-8	95	90	-0.4	-1	0	-0.8
1956	Det-A	15	13	.536	43	33	16	1	1	256	211	7.4	24	142	5.0	184	6.5	3.59	110	.226	.323	16	11	95	98	0.1	-5	-1	0.4
1957	Det-A	14	11	.560	38	27	8	1	1	212	175	7.4	19	104	4.4	118	5.0	3.14	129	.226	.313	15	22	107	107	1.6	1	-2	2.1
1958	Det-A	15	13	.536	39	33	16	2	1	230	198	7.7	23	77	3.0	135	5.3	3.44	113	.233	.294	8	11	103	92	1.2	3	-2	1.3
1959	Det-A	14	14	.500	39	37	11	2	1	240	239	9.0	34	64	2.4	110	4.1	4.65	92	.259	.305	-21	-10	111	85	0.2	-4	-2	-1.4
1960	Det-A	2	11	.154	28	13	1	0	2	97	108	10.0	11	49	4.5	38	3.5	6.12	64	.286	.361	-24	-24	102	82	-4.4	2	-2	-2.1
1961	Det-A	11	10	.524	32	20	6	0	0	170	152	8.0	27	56	3.0	89	4.7	3.92	96	.238	.299	2	-3	94	95	-1.8	2	-3	-0.3
1962	Det-A	10	7	.588	29	21	5	1	0	144	145	9.1	18	86	5.4	63	3.9	4.38	100	.259	.355	-6	0	110	108	1.2	-2	0	0.0
1963	Det-A	0	1	.000	9	0	0	0	1	18	18	9.0	4	8	4.0	7	3.5	8.50	44	.265	.333	-10	-9	104	62	-0.4	-0	-0	-0.9
	LA-A	5	5	.500	25	8	0	0	0	70	68	8.7	9	29	3.7	37	4.8	3.73	90	.255	.323	-1	-3	92	111	0.6	1	-0	-0.2
	Yr	5	6	.455	34	8	0	0	1	88	86	8.8	13	37	3.8	44	4.5	4.70	73	.256	.325	-11	-12	95	111	0.2	-0	-1	-1.1
1964	LA-A	0	1	.000	2	0	0	0	0	2	4	18.0	2	2	9.0	1	4.5	18.00	18	.364	.462	-3	-3	89	89	-0.4	0	0	-0.2
Total	11	86	87	.497	312	193	63	7	7	1499	1381	8.3	176	662	4.0	827	5.0	4.14	97	.246	.321	-38	-23	102	96	-2.5	-3	-12	-2.7

YEAR TM/L	W	L	PCT	G	GS	CG	SHO	SV	IP	H	H/G	HR	BB	BB/G	SO	SO/G	ERA	/A	OAVG	OOBP	PR	/A	PF	CPI	WAT	PB	PD	TPI
■ KEN FRAILING Frailing, Kenneth Douglas b: 1/19/48, Marion, Wis. BL/TL, 6', 190 lbs. Deb: 9/01/72																												
1972 Chi-A	1	0	1.000	4	0	0	0	0	3	3	9.0	1	1	3.0	1	3.0	3.00	108	.250	.308	0	0	106	173	0.5	0	0	0.0
1973 Chi-A	0	0	—	10	0	0	0	0	18	18	9.0	1	7	3.5	15	7.5	2.00	197	.254	.325	4	4	103	172	0.0	0	0	0.4
1974 Chi-N	6	9	.400	55	16	1	0	1	125	150	10.8	11	43	3.1	71	5.1	3.89	95	.296	.349	-4	-3	102	119	-0.1	1	0	-0.1
1975 Chi-N	2	5	.286	41	0	0	0	1	53	61	10.4	6	26	4.4	39	6.6	5.43	70	.293	.365	-11	-9	105	96	-1.3	0	2	-0.7
1976 Chi-N	1	2	.333	6	3	0	0	0	19	20	9.5	0	5	2.4	10	4.7	2.37	164	.274	.316	2	3	111	134	-0.3	-0	0	0.3
Total 5	10	16	.385	116	19	1	0	2	218	252	10.4	19	82	3.4	136	5.6	3.96	95	.290	.348	-8	-5	104	120	-1.2	1	2	-0.1
■ OSSIE FRANCE France, Osman Beverly "O. B." b: 10/4/1858, Greensburg, Ohio d: 5/2/47, Akron, Ohio BL/TL, 5'8", 155 lbs. Deb: 7/14/1890																												
1890 Chi-N	0	0	—	1	0	0	0	0	2	3	13.5	0	2	9.0	0	0.0	13.50	28	.364	.488	-2	-2	107	55	0.0	-0	0	-0.1
■ EARL FRANCIS Francis, Earl Coleman b: 7/14/35, Slab Fork, W.Va. BR/TR, 6'2", 210 lbs. Deb: 6/30/60																												
1960 Pit-N	1	0	1.000	7	0	0	0	0	18	14	7.0	0	4	2.0	8	4.0	2.00	182	.222	.275	4	3	97	104	0.5	-1	-0	0.3
1961 Pit-N	2	8	.200	23	15	0	0	0	103	110	9.6	4	47	4.1	53	4.6	4.19	95	.274	.345	-2	-2	99	96	-2.9	-1	0	-0.2
1962 Pit-N	9	8	.529	36	23	5	1	0	176	153	7.8	8	83	4.2	121	6.2	3.07	130	.235	.320	17	18	101	103	-0.7	1	1	2.1
1963 Pit-N	4	6	.400	33	13	0	0	0	97	107	9.9	6	43	4.0	72	6.7	4.55	72	.284	.356	-14	-14	99	100	-0.6	3	0	-1.0
1964 Pit-N	0	1	.000	2	1	0	0	0	6	7	10.5	2	1	1.5	6	9.0	9.00	40	.269	.321	-4	-4	101	64	-0.4	-0	-0	-0.3
1965 StL-N	0	0	—	2	0	0	0	0	5	7	12.6	1	3	5.4	3	5.4	5.40	69	.318	.385	-1	-1	106	129	0.0	-0	-0	0.0
Total 6	16	23	.410	103	52	5	1	0	405	398	8.8	21	181	4.0	263	5.8	3.78	100	.258	.335	0	0	100	100	-4.1	2	2	0.9
■ RAY FRANCIS Francis, Ray James b: 3/8/1893, Sherman, Tex. d: 7/6/34, Atlanta, Ga. BL/TL, 6'1.5", 182 lbs. Deb: 4/18/22																												
1922 Was-A	7	18	.280	39	26	15	2	2	225	265	10.6	7	66	2.6	64	2.6	4.28	87	.303	.343	-6	-13	93	100	-5.1	-1	-1	-1.5
1923 Det-A	5	8	.385	33	6	0	0	1	79	95	10.8	2	28	3.2	27	3.1	4.44	85	.308	.357	-4	-6	95	104	-1.9	-1	-0	-0.6
1925 NY-A	0	0	—	4	0	0	0	0	5	5	9.0	0	3	5.4	1	1.8	7.20	59	.278	.391	-2	-2	97	67	0.0	0	-0	-0.1
Bos-A	0	2	.000	6	4	0	0	0	28	44	14.1	3	13	4.2	4	1.3	7.71	57	.373	.414	-10	-10	99	98	-0.9	-0	0	-0.8
Yr	0	2	.000	10	4	0	0	0	33	49	13.4	3	16	4.4	5	1.4	7.64	57	.358	.405	-12	-12	99	98	-0.9	0	0	-0.9
Total 3	12	28	.300	82	36	15	2	3	337	409	10.9	12	110	2.9	96	2.6	4.65	82	.310	.354	-22	-31	94	100	-7.9	-3	-1	-3.0
■ JOHNNY FRANCO Franco, John Anthony b: 9/17/60, Brooklyn, N.Y. BL/TL, 5'10", 170 lbs. Deb: 4/24/84																												
1984 Cin-N	6	2	.750	54	0	0	0	4	79	74	8.4	3	36	4.1	55	6.3	2.62	147	.256	.334	9	11	107	141	2.3	-0	1	1.2
1985 Cin-N	12	3	.800	67	0	0	0	12	99	83	7.5	5	40	3.6	61	5.5	2.18	173	.234	.305	16	**18**	105	141	4.3	0	2	2.1
1986 Cin-N	6	6	.500	74	0	0	0	29	101	90	8.0	7	44	3.9	84	7.5	2.94	132	.242	.317	9	11	104	119	-0.3	-0	1	1.2
1987 Cin-N	8	5	.615	68	0	0	0	32	82	76	8.3	6	27	3.0	61	6.7	2.52	167	.245	.299	14	15	103	128	1.4	-0	-1	1.4
1988 Cin-N	6	6	.500	70	0	0	0	**39**	86	60	6.3	3	27	2.8	46	4.8	1.57	231	.198	.259	**18**	**20**	105	120	-0.4	-0	1	2.2
Total 5	38	22	.633	333	0	0	0	116	447	383	7.7	24	174	3.5	307	6.2	2.38	163	.235	.304	65	74	105	129	7.3	-1	3	8.1
■ CHARLIE FRANK Frank, Charles b: 5/30/1870, Mobile, Ala. d: 5/24/22, Memphis, Tenn. Deb: 8/18/1893																												
1894 StL-N	0	0	—	2	0	0	0	0	3	6	18.0	1	7	21.0	1	3.0	15.00	37	.439	.629	-3	-3	103	109	0.0	0	0	-0.1
■ FRED FRANKHOUSE Frankhouse, Frederick Meloy b: 4/9/04, Port Royal, Pa. BR/TR, 5'11", 175 lbs. Deb: 9/11/27																												
1927 StL-N	5	1	.833	6	6	5	1	0	50	41	7.4	2	16	2.9	20	3.6	2.70	153	.218	.274	7	8	106	81	1.8	0	-1	0.8
1928 StL-N	3	2	.600	21	10	1	0	1	84	91	9.8	6	36	3.9	29	3.1	3.96	98	.277	.353	0	-1	97	108	0.0	1	1	0.1
1929 StL-N	7	2	.778	30	12	6	0	1	133	149	10.1	9	43	2.9	37	2.5	4.13	112	.289	.341	9	7	98	109	2.5	4	3	1.2
1930 StL-N	2	3	.400	8	1	0	0	0	20	31	13.9	1	11	4.9	4	1.8	7.20	70	.373	.442	-5	-5	102	104	-0.7	-1	0	-0.4
Bos-N	7	6	.538	27	11	3	1	0	111	138	11.2	13	43	3.5	30	2.4	5.59	88	.313	.371	-8	-8	99	101	1.1	4	-0	-0.3
Yr	9	9	.500	35	12	3	1	0	131	169	11.6	14	54	3.7	34	2.3	5.84	85	.323	.383	-13	-13	99	101	0.4	-1	-0	-0.7
1931 Bos-N	8	8	.500	26	15	6	0	1	127	125	8.9	4	43	3.0	50	3.5	4.04	97	.252	.314	-2	-2	102	77	1.3	-0	1	0.0
1932 Bos-N	4	6	.400	37	6	3	0	0	109	113	9.3	7	45	3.7	35	2.9	3.55	102	.278	.340	4	1	93	125	-1.0	-1	4	0.3
1933 Bos-N	16	15	.516	43	30	14	2	2	245	249	9.1	12	77	2.8	83	3.0	3.16	101	.267	.318	5	1	96	112	-0.7	3	4	0.9
1934 Bos-N	17	9	.654	37	31	13	2	1	234	239	9.2	10	77	3.0	78	3.0	3.19	110	.262	.319	23	8	86	111	4.2	2	-0	0.8
1935 Bos-N	11	15	.423	40	29	10	1	0	231	278	10.8	12	81	3.2	64	2.5	4.75	85	.293	.347	-19	-19	100	95	3.5	6	3	-0.9
1936 Bro-N	13	10	.565	41	31	9	1	2	234	236	9.1	18	89	3.4	84	3.2	3.65	117	.257	.320	9	16	107	102	3.0	-5	1	1.3
1937 Bro-N	10	13	.435	33	26	9	1	0	179	214	10.8	8	78	3.9	64	3.2	4.27	98	.297	.361	-7	-2	107	113	0.7	-0	3	0.1
1938 Bro-N	3	5	.375	30	8	2	1	0	94	92	8.8	6	44	4.2	32	3.1	4.02	90	.256	.337	-2	-4	96	99	-0.7	-1	1	-0.3
1939 Bos-N	0	2	.000	23	0	0	0	4	38	37	8.8	3	18	4.3	12	2.8	2.61	140	.253	.337	6	4	93	150	-0.9	-1	-1	0.3
Total 13	106	97	.522	402	216	81	10	12	1889	2033	9.7	111	701	3.3	622	3.0	3.92	101	.275	.335	19	6	98	105	14.1	11	17	3.9
■ JACK FRANKLIN Franklin, James Wilford b: 10/20/19, Paris, Ill. BR/TR, 5'11.5", 170 lbs. Deb: 6/12/44																												
1944 Bro-N	0	0	—	1	0	0	0	0	2	2	9.0	1	4	18.0	0	0.0	13.50	27	.250	.571	-2	-2	102	104	0.0	0	0	-0.1
■ JAY FRANKLIN Franklin, John William b: 3/16/53, Arlington, Va. BR/TR, 6'2", 180 lbs. Deb: 9/04/71																												
1971 SD-N	0	1	.000	3	1	0	0	0	6	5	7.5	3	4	6.0	4	6.0	6.00	57	.250	.333	-2	-2	98	128	-0.4	-0	0	-0.1
■ CHICK FRASER Fraser, Charles Carrolton b: 3/17/1871, Chicago, Ill. d: 5/8/40, Wendell, Idaho BR/TR, 5'10.5", 188 lbs. Deb: 4/19/1896 C																												
1896 Lou-N	12	27	.308	43	38	36	0	1	349	396	10.2	9	166	4.3	91	2.3	4.87	91	.308	.387	-20	-17	102	90	0.7	-9	3	-1.8
1897 Lou-N	15	19	.441	35	34	32	0	0	286	332	10.4	11	133	4.2	70	2.2	4.09	103	.313	.389	7	3	97	111	1.5	-4	7	0.5
1898 Lou-N	7	17	.292	26	26	20	1	0	203	230	10.2	5	100	4.4	58	2.6	5.32	66	.308	.389	-39	-41	98	82	-4.8	-2	0	-3.6
Cle-N	2	3	.400	6	6	6	0	0	42	49	10.5	2	12	2.6	19	4.1	5.57	61	.314	.363	-9	-10	95	74	-0.6	0	0	-0.8
Yr	9	20	.310	32	32	26	1	0	245	279	10.2	7	112	4.1	77	2.8	5.36	65	.309	.385	-48	-51	97	74	-5.4	-2	0	-4.4
1899 Phi-N	21	12	.636	35	33	29	4	0	271	278	9.2	1	85	2.8	68	2.3	3.35	109	.288	.346	15	10	95	94	1.0	-2	3	0.9
1900 Phi-N	15	9	.625	29	26	22	1	0	223	250	10.1	7	93	3.8	58	2.3	3.15	115	.306	.377	14	12	98	**132**	2.5	3	0	1.4
1901 Phi-A	22	16	.579	40	37	35	2	0	331	344	9.4	6	132	3.6	110	3.0	3.81	96	.288	.359	-5	-6	100	94	2.0	-3	2	-0.3
1902 Phi-N	12	13	.480	27	26	24	3	0	224	238	9.6	2	74	3.0	97	3.9	3.42	89	.301	.372	-16	-10	109	102	1.8	-0	-1	-0.9
1903 Phi-N	12	17	.414	31	29	26	1	1	250	260	9.4	8	97	3.5	104	3.7	4.50	69	.298	.378	-34	-39	94	84	1.4	5	1	-3.3
1904 Phi-N	14	24	.368	42	36	32	2	1	302	287	8.6	5	100	3.0	127	3.8	3.25	81	.277	.347	-17	-20	97	94	1.0	-1	2	-1.8
1905 Bos-N	14	21	.400	39	38	35	2	0	334	320	8.6	8	149	4.0	130	3.5	3.29	93	.282	.373	-11	-9	102	109	2.3	4	-1	-0.9
1906 Cin-N	10	20	.333	31	28	25	2	0	236	221	8.4	1	80	3.1	58	2.2	2.67	114	.277	.349	-1	10	116	109	-3.7	-2	1	1.2
1907 Chi-N	8	5	.615	22	15	9	2	1	138	112	7.3	1	46	3.0	41	2.7	2.28	110	.250	.323	3	4	102	96	-0.8	-3	0	0.4
1908 Chi-N	11	9	.550	26	17	11	2	2	163	141	7.8	4	61	3.4	66	3.6	2.26	106	.263	.345	1	2	102	124	-1.5	-2	4	0.7
1909 Chi-N	0	0	—	1	0	0	0	0	3	2	6.0	0	4	12.0	1	3.0	0.00	—	.222	.462	1	1	95	0	0.0	-0	-0	0.1
Total 14	175	212	.452	433	389	342	22	6	3355	3460	9.3	70	1332	3.6	1098	2.9	3.68	92	.292	.367	-111	-104	101	100	2.8	-14	19	-8.2
■ WILLIE FRASER Fraser, William Patrick b: 5/26/64, New York, N.Y. BR/TR, 6'3", 200 lbs. Deb: 9/10/86																												
1986 Cal-A	0	0	—	1	1	0	0	0	4	6	13.5	0	1	2.3	2	4.5	9.00	44	.353	.350	-2	-2	95	61	0.0	0	0	-0.1
1987 Cal-A	10	10	.500	36	23	5	1	1	177	160	8.1	26	63	3.2	106	5.4	3.92	114	.240	.308	11	11	100	99	0.8	0	-3	0.7
1988 Cal-A	12	13	.480	34	32	2	0	0	195	203	9.4	33	80	3.7	86	4.0	5.40	70	.267	.339	-31	-35	95	91	0.5	0	-1	-3.4
Total 3	22	23	.489	71	56	7	1	1	376	369	8.8	59	144	3.4	194	4.6	4.74	86	.256	.325	-22	-27	97	94	1.3	0	-3	-2.8
■ VIC FRASIER Frasier, Victor Patrick b: 8/5/04, Ruston, La. d: 1/10/77, Jacksonville, Tex. BR/TR, 6', 182 lbs. Deb: 4/18/31																												
1931 Chi-A	13	15	.464	46	29	13	2	4	254	258	9.1	11	127	4.5	87	3.1	4.46	94	.259	.341	-2	-8	96	92	2.6	-1	-1	-0.7
1932 Chi-A	3	13	.188	29	21	4	0	0	146	180	11.1	14	70	4.3	33	2.0	6.23	65	.297	.368	-28	-35	91	89	-3.5	-3	2	-3.1
1933 Chi-A	1	1	.500	10	1	0	0	0	20	32	14.4	2	11	4.9	4	1.8	9.00	49	.438	.494	-10	-10	103	107	0.1	-1	1	-0.8
Det-A	5	5	.500	20	14	4	0	0	104	129	11.2	9	59	5.1	26	2.3	6.66	69	.377	.457	-28	-24	107	117	0.1	-1	0	-2.1
Yr	6	6	.500	30	15	4	0	0	124	161	11.7	11	70	5.1	30	2.2	7.04	65	.388	.463	-38	-34	106	117	0.2	-1	2	-2.9
1934 Det-A	1	3	.250	8	2	0	0	0	23	30	11.7	0	12	4.7	11	4.3	5.87	72	.313	.387	-4	-4	94	91	-1.2	0	2	-0.1
1937 Bos-N	0	0	—	3	0	0	0	0	8	12	13.5	1	1	1.1	2	2.3	5.63	63	.364	.351	-2	-2	90	115	0.0	-0	0	-0.1
1939 Chi-A	0	1	.000	10	1	0	0	0	24	45	16.9	0	11	4.1	7	2.6	10.13	49	.405	.452	-15	-14	106	81	-0.4	0	0	-1.1
Total 6	23	38	.377	126	68	21	2	4	579	686	10.7	37	291	4.5	170	2.6	5.77	74	.304	.379	-88	-97	97	96	-2.3	-3	4	-8.0

YEAR	TM/L	W	L	PCT	G	GS	CG	SHO	SV	IP	H	H/G	HR	BB	BB/G	SO	SO/G	ERA	/A	OAVG	OOBP	PR	/A	PF	CPI	WAT	PB	PD	TPI
■ **GEORGE FRAZIER**	Frazier, George Allen b: 10/13/54, Oklahoma City, Okla BR/TR, 6'5", 205 lbs. Deb: 5/25/78																												
1978	StL-N	0	3	.000	14	0	0	0	0	22	22	9.0	2	6	2.5	8	3.3	4.09	84	.250	.292	-1	-2	96	78	-1.4	0	0	0.0
1979	StL-N	2	4	.333	25	0	0	0	0	32	35	9.8	3	12	3.4	14	3.9	4.50	87	.278	.336	-3	-2	104	96	-1.0	-0	0	-0.1
1980	StL-N	1	4	.200	22	0	0	0	3	23	24	9.4	2	7	2.7	11	4.3	2.74	135	.273	.323	2	2	102	144	-1.3	0	0	0.3
1981	NY-A	0	1	.000	16	0	0	0	3	28	26	8.4	1	11	3.5	17	5.5	1.61	225	.245	.316	6	6	99	191	-0.4	0	-0	0.6
1982	NY-A	4	4	.500	63	0	0	0	1	112	103	8.3	7	39	3.1	69	5.5	3.46	114	.252	.315	8	6	97	104	0.1	0	0	0.6
1983	NY-A	4	4	.500	61	0	0	0	8	115	94	7.4	5	45	3.5	78	6.1	3.44	116	.227	.296	8	7	98	83	-0.4	0	0	0.7
1984	Cle-A	3	2	.600	22	0	0	0	1	44	45	9.2	3	14	2.9	24	4.9	3.68	115	.259	.311	2	3	106	93	0.7	0	-1	0.2
	Chi-N	6	3	.667	37	0	0	0	3	64	53	7.5	4	26	3.7	58	8.2	4.08	96	.221	.293	-3	-1	109	67	0.8	0	-1	-0.1
1985	Chi-N	7	8	.467	51	0	0	0	2	76	88	10.4	11	52	6.2	46	5.4	6.39	66	.299	.401	-24	-19	117	98	-0.1	-1	-0	-1.9
1986	Chi-N	2	4	.333	35	0	0	0	0	52	63	10.9	5	34	5.9	41	7.1	5.37	75	.310	.403	-9	-8	108	114	-0.6	-0	-1	-0.9
	Min-A	1	1	.500	15	0	0	0	6	27	23	7.7	2	16	5.3	25	8.3	4.33	106	.232	.328	-0	1	109	85	0.1	0	0	0.1
1987	Min-A	5	5	.500	54	0	0	0	2	81	77	8.6	9	51	5.7	58	6.4	5.00	86	.258	.358	-5	-6	96	97	-0.2	0	-1	-0.6
Total	10	35	43	.449	415	0	0	0	29	676	653	8.7	54	313	4.2	449	6.0	4.19	96	.257	.334	-20	-11	103	99	-3.7	-1	-3	-1.1
■ **BUCK FREEMAN**	Freeman, Alexander Vernon b: 7/5/1893, Mart, Tex. d: 2/21/53, Fort Sam Houston, Tex. BB/TR, 5'10", 167 lbs. Deb: 4/13/21																												
1921	Chi-N	9	10	.474	38	20	6	0	3	177	189	9.6	12	70	3.6	42	2.1	4.12	100	.281	.346	-7	-0	108	102	1.0	-0	-1	-0.1
1922	Chi-N	0	1	.000	11	1	0	0	1	26	47	16.3	0	10	3.5	10	3.5	8.65	45	.412	.450	-13	-14	96	91	-0.4	-0	1	-1.1
Total	2	9	11	.450	49	21	6	0	4	203	236	10.5	12	80	3.5	52	2.3	4.70	87	.300	.361	-20	-14	107	100	0.6	-1	-0	-1.2
■ **HARVEY FREEMAN**	Freeman, Harvey Bayard "Buck" b: 12/22/1897, Nottville, Mich. d: 1/10/70, Kalamazoo, Mich. BR/TR, 5'10", 160 lbs. Deb: 7/10/21																												
1921	Phi-A	1	4	.200	18	4	2	0	0	48	65	12.2	2	35	6.6	5	0.9	7.69	60	.346	.447	-18	-17	107	92	-1.0	-2	1	-1.4
■ **HERSH FREEMAN**	Freeman, Hershell Baskin "Buster" b: 7/1/28, Gadsden, Ala. BR/TR, 6'3", 220 lbs. Deb: 9/10/52																												
1952	Bos-A	1	0	1.000	4	1	1	0	0	14	13	8.4	1	5	3.2	5	3.2	3.21	122	.260	.339	1	1	107	123	0.5	1	0	0.2
1953	Bos-A	1	4	.200	18	2	0	0	0	39	50	11.5	2	17	3.9	15	3.5	5.54	78	.316	.374	-7	-5	108	95	-1.5	-1	0	-0.5
1955	Bos-A	0	0	—	2	0	0	0	0	2	1	4.5	0	1	4.5	1	4.5	0.00	—	.200	.333	1	1	122	0	0.0	0	0	0.1
	Cin-N	7	4	.636	52	0	0	0	11	92	94	9.2	3	30	2.9	37	3.6	2.15	196	.276	.326	**19**	**21**	104	174	1.7	1	1	2.3
1956	Cin-N	14	5	.737	64	0	0	0	18	109	112	9.2	2	34	2.8	50	4.1	3.39	118	.274	.321	5	7	106	101	3.7	-1	-0	0.7
1957	Cin-N	7	2	.778	52	0	0	0	8	84	90	9.6	14	14	1.5	36	3.9	4.50	91	.277	.303	-6	-4	106	97	2.5	0	-0	-0.3
1958	Cin-N	0	0	—	3	0	0	0	0	8	4	4.5	0	5	5.6	7	7.9	3.38	124	.154	.281	1	1	106	44	0.0	-0	0	0.1
	Chi-N	0	1	.000	9	0	0	0	0	13	23	15.9	3	3	2.1	7	4.8	8.31	48	.354	.377	-6	-6	101	87	-0.4	-0	-0	-0.5
	Yr	0	1	.000	12	0	0	0	0	21	27	11.6	3	8	3.4	14	6.0	6.43	63	.293	.347	-6	-6	103	87	-0.4	-0	0	-0.4
Total	6	30	16	.652	204	3	1	0	37	361	387	9.6	25	109	2.7	158	3.9	3.71	111	.281	.327	7	16	106	116	6.5	-0	1	2.1
■ **JIMMY FREEMAN**	Freeman, Jimmy Lee b: 6/29/51, Carlsbad, N.Mex. BL/TL, 6'4", 180 lbs. Deb: 9/01/72																												
1972	Atl-N	2	2	.500	6	6	1	0	0	36	40	10.0	5	22	5.5	18	4.5	6.00	61	.278	.371	-10	-9	106	88	0.2	-0	-1	-0.9
1973	Atl-N	0	2	.000	13	5	0	0	1	37	50	12.2	7	25	6.1	20	4.9	7.78	53	.327	.412	-17	-15	113	93	-0.9	-1	-1	-1.5
Total	2	2	4	.333	19	11	1	0	1	73	90	11.1	12	47	5.8	38	4.7	6.90	57	.303	.393	-27	-24	109	90	-0.7	-1	-1	-2.4
■ **BUCK FREEMAN**	Freeman, John Frank b: 10/30/1871, Catasauqua, Pa. d: 6/25/49, Wilkes-Barre, Pa. BL/TL, 5'9", 169 lbs. Deb: 6/27/1891																												
1891	Was-a	3	2	.600	5	4	4	0	0	44	35	7.2	0	33	6.8	28	5.7	3.89	96	.232	.369	-1	-1	101	79	1.0	0	0	0.0
1899	Was-N	0	0	—	2	0	0	0	0	7	15	19.3	3	3	3.9	0	0.0	7.71	49	.459	.504	-3	-3	98	158	0.0	1	0	-0.2
Total	2	3	2	.600	7	4	4	0	0	51	50	8.8	3	36	6.4	28	4.9	4.41	85	.272	.391	-4	-4	100	90	1.0	1	0	-0.2
■ **JULIE FREEMAN**	Freeman, Julius Benjamin b: 11/7/1868, Missouri d: 6/10/21, St.Louis, Mo. Deb: 1888																												
1888	StL-a	0	1	.000	1	1	0	0	0	6	7	10.5	0	4	6.0	1	1.5	4.50	72	.305	.408	-1	-1	106	112	-0.4	0	0	0.0
■ **MARK FREEMAN**	Freeman, Mark Price b: 12/7/30, Memphis, Tenn. BR/TR, 6'4", 220 lbs. Deb: 4/18/59																												
1959	KC-A	0	0	—	3	0	0	0	0	4	6	13.5	0	3	6.8	1	2.3	9.00	44	.375	.450	-2	-2	103	83	0.0	0	-0	-0.1
	NY-A	0	0	—	1	1	0	0	0	7	6	7.7	0	2	2.6	4	5.1	2.57	138	.240	.310	1	1	92	114	0.0	-0	0	0.0
	Yr	0	0	—	4	1	0	0	0	11	12	9.8	0	5	4.1	5	4.1	4.91	75	.286	.367	-1	-1	96	114	0.0	0	-0	-0.1
1960	Chi-N	3	3	.500	30	8	1	0	1	77	70	8.2	10	33	3.9	50	5.8	5.61	67	.240	.323	-16	-16	101	71	0.6	-0	-2	-1.7
Total	2	3	3	.500	34	9	1	0	1	88	82	8.4	10	38	3.9	55	5.6	5.52	68	.246	.329	-17	-17	100	75	0.6	-1	-2	-1.8
■ **MARVIN FREEMAN**	Freeman, Marvin b: 4/10/63, Chicago, Ill. BR/TR, 6'7", 200 lbs. Deb: 9/16/86																												
1986	Phi-N	2	0	1.000	3	3	0	0	0	16	6	3.4	0	10	5.6	8	4.5	2.25	172	.120	.262	3	3	104	44	1.0	-1	-0	0.2
1988	Phi-N	2	3	.400	11	11	0	0	0	52	55	9.5	2	43	7.4	37	6.4	6.06	59	.276	.398	-15	-14	103	87	0.0	0	0	-1.3
Total	2	4	3	.571	14	14	0	0	0	68	61	8.1	2	53	7.0	45	6.0	5.16	70	.245	.371	-12	-12	103	77	1.0	-0	-0	-1.1
■ **JAKE FREEZE**	Freeze, Carl Alexander b: 4/25/1900, Huntington, Ark. d: 4/9/83, San Angelo, Tex. BR/TR, 5'8", 150 lbs. Deb: 7/01/25																												
1925	Chi-A	0	0	—	2	0	0	0	0	4	3	6.8	1	3	6.8	1	2.3	2.25	185	.200	.316	1	1	95	190	0.0	-0	-0	0.0
■ **DAVE FREISLEBEN**	Freisleben, David James b: 10/31/51, Coraopolis, Pa. BR/TR, 5'11", 195 lbs. Deb: 4/26/74																												
1974	SD-N	9	14	.391	33	31	6	2	0	212	194	8.2	13	112	4.8	130	5.5	3.65	96	.241	.336	-0	-3	97	98	0.4	2	-0	-0.1
1975	SD-N	5	14	.263	36	27	4	1	0	181	206	10.2	11	82	4.1	77	3.8	4.28	86	.289	.358	-13	-12	101	108	-4.0	-1	0	-1.3
1976	SD-N	10	13	.435	34	24	6	3	1	172	163	8.5	10	66	3.5	81	4.2	3.51	90	.248	.318	0	-7	90	95	-0.4	2	2	-0.3
1977	SD-N	7	9	.438	33	23	1	0	0	139	140	9.1	21	71	4.6	72	4.7	4.60	76	.266	.350	-11	-17	89	106	0.2	0	-2	-1.8
1978	SD-N	0	3	.000	12	4	0	0	0	27	41	13.7	3	15	5.0	16	5.3	6.00	55	.363	.427	-7	-8	93	124	-1.4	-1	0	-0.8
	Cle-A	1	4	.200	12	10	0	0	0	44	52	10.6	4	31	6.3	19	3.9	7.16	49	.299	.401	-17	-18	94	82	-1.3	0	-0	-1.6
1979	Tor-A	2	3	.400	42	2	0	0	3	91	101	10.0	5	53	5.2	35	3.5	4.95	90	.294	.383	-7	-5	106	104	0.3	0	-1	-0.4
Total	6	34	60	.362	202	121	17	6	4	866	897	9.3	67	430	4.5	430	4.5	4.29	83	.269	.351	-55	-70	96	101	-6.2	2	-1	-6.3
■ **TONY FREITAS**	Freitas, Antonio b: 5/5/08, Mill Valley, Cal. BR/TL, 5'8", 161 lbs. Deb: 5/31/32																												
1932	Phi-A	12	5	.706	23	18	10	1	0	150	150	9.0	11	48	2.9	31	1.9	3.84	129	.263	.322	11	18	111	105	2.3	-2	1	1.8
1933	Phi-A	2	4	.333	19	9	2	0	1	64	90	12.7	8	24	3.4	15	2.1	7.31	54	.337	.391	-22	-24	92	91	-1.0	-1	0	-2.1
1934	Cin-N	6	12	.333	30	18	5	0	1	153	194	11.4	6	25	1.5	37	2.2	4.00	106	.311	.335	1	4	105	111	-0.2	0	2	0.7
1935	Cin-N	5	10	.333	31	18	5	0	2	144	174	10.9	6	38	2.4	51	3.2	4.56	84	.295	.332	-9	-12	95	93	-1.9	-0	1	-1.0
1936	Cin-N	0	2	.000	4	0	0	0	0	7	6	7.7	0	2	2.6	1	1.3	1.29	304	.240	.286	2	2	97	200	-0.9	-0	0	0.2
Total	5	25	33	.431	107	63	22	1	4	518	614	10.7	31	137	2.4	135	2.3	4.48	96	.296	.337	-16	-12	102	103	-1.7	-2	4	-0.4
■ **LARRY FRENCH**	French, Lawrence Herbert b: 11/1/07, Visalia, Cal. d: 2/9/87, San Diego, Cal. BB/TL, 6'1", 195 lbs. Deb: 4/18/29																												
1929	Pit-N	7	5	.583	30	13	6	0	1	123	130	9.5	10	62	4.5	49	3.6	4.90	98	.276	.353	-3	-2	102	96	0.1	-1	1	0.0
1930	Pit-N	17	18	.486	42	35	21	3	1	275	325	10.6	20	89	2.9	90	2.9	4.35	111	.295	.341	19	15	98	105	-1.3	1	-1	1.3
1931	Pit-N	15	13	.536	39	33	20	1	1	276	301	9.8	9	70	2.3	73	2.4	3.26	120	.278	.318	19	20	102	110	1.6	-1	-1	1.9
1932	Pit-N	18	16	.529	**47**	33	19	3	4	274	301	9.9	17	62	2.0	72	2.4	3.02	128	.276	.312	26	26	100	123	-1.0	0	-4	2.3
1933	Pit-N	18	13	.581	47	35	21	5	1	291	290	9.0	9	55	1.7	88	2.7	2.72	115	.257	.289	20	13	94	101	0.7	-1	-4	0.8
1934	Pit-N	12	18	.400	49	35	16	3	1	264	299	10.2	8	59	2.0	103	3.5	3.58	119	.281	.316	14	20	105	102	-3.3	-1	-3	1.7
1935	Chi-N	17	10	.630	42	30	16	**4**	2	246	279	10.2	10	44	1.6	90	3.3	2.96	129	.286	.313	29	23	95	**126**	-0.4	-3	1	2.1
1936	Chi-N	18	9	.667	43	28	16	4	3	252	262	9.4	16	54	1.9	104	3.7	3.39	121	.266	.305	18	20	102	102	3.6	0	-3	1.7
1937	Chi-N	16	10	.615	42	28	11	4	0	208	229	9.9	17	65	2.8	100	4.3	3.98	99	.274	.324	-2	-1	100	101	0.5	-4	2	-0.2
1938	Chi-N	10	19	.345	43	27	10	3	0	201	210	9.4	17	62	2.8	83	3.7	3.81	102	.271	.320	-0	2	103	105	-6.6	2	1	0.5
1939	Chi-N	15	8	.652	36	21	10	2	1	194	205	9.5	7	50	2.3	98	4.5	3.29	119	.269	.309	13	13	100	101	3.0	1	2	1.7
1940	Chi-N	14	14	.500	40	33	18	3	2	246	240	8.8	12	64	2.3	107	3.9	3.29	115	.256	.301	15	14	99	101	0.4	1	2	1.8
1941	Chi-N	5	14	.263	26	18	6	1	0	138	161	10.5	10	43	2.8	60	3.9	4.63	73	.285	.332	-15	-19	94	93	-4.2	1	-1	-1.8
	Bro-N	0	0	—	6	1	0	0	0	16	16	9.0	1	4	2.3	8	4.5	3.38	107	.267	.313	0	0	99	111	0.0	0	0	0.1
	Yr	5	14	.263	32	19	6	1	0	154	177	10.3	11	47	2.7	68	4.0	4.50	76	.282	.327	-15	-18	94	111	-4.2	1	-1	-1.7
1942	Bro-N	15	4	**.789**	38	14	8	4	0	148	127	7.7	1	36	2.2	62	3.8	1.82	176	.233	.282	24	23	97	127	3.6	4	-1	2.9
Total	14	197	171	.535	570	384	198	40	17	3152	3375	9.6	164	819	2.3	1187	3.4	3.44	114	.272	.315	178	167	99	107	-3.3	1	-7	16.8

YEAR	TM/L	W	L	PCT	G	GS	CG	SHO	SV	IP	H	H/G	HR	BB	BB/G	SO	SO/G	ERA	/A	OAVG	OOBP	PR	/A	PF	CPI	WAT	PB	PD	TPI
■ **BILL FRENCH**	French, William b: Baltimore, Md. Deb: 4/14/1873																												
1873	Mar-n	0	1	.000	1																								
■ **BENNY FREY**	Frey, Benjamin Rudolph b: 4/6/06, Dexter, Mich. d: 11/1/37, Jackson, Mich. BR/TR, 5'10", 165 lbs. Deb: 9/18/29																												
1929	Cin-N	1	2	.333	3	3	2	0	0	24	29	10.9	2	8	3.0	1	0.4	4.13	115	.302	.352	2	2	101	119	-0.2	1	1	0.3
1930	Cin-N	11	18	.379	44	28	14	2	1	245	295	10.8	15	62	2.3	43	1.6	4.70	98	.305	.340	7	-2	93	99	-0.1	5	6	0.7
1931	Cin-N	8	12	.400	34	17	7	1	2	134	166	11.1	2	36	2.4	19	1.3	4.90	77	.319	.359	-15	-17	98	96	0.4	4	4	-0.8
1932	StL-N	0	2	.000	2	0	0	0	0	3	6	18.0	0	2	6.0	0	0.0	12.00	33	.600	.667	-3	-3	101	105	-0.9	-0	-0	-0.2
	Cin-N	4	10	.286	28	15	5	0	0	131	159	10.9	10	30	2.1	27	1.9	4.33	89	.299	.333	-7	-7	99	104	-1.9	-0	3	-0.4
	Yr	4	12	.250	30	15	5	0	0	134	165	11.1	10	32	2.1	27	1.8	4.50	85	.305	.340	-9	-10	99	104	-2.8	-0	3	-0.6
1933	Cin-N	6	4	.600	37	9	1	1	0	132	144	9.8	4	21	1.4	12	0.8	3.82	89	.281	.301	-7	-6	102	86	1.8	3	1	0.0
1934	Cin-N	11	16	.407	39	30	12	2	2	245	288	10.6	10	42	1.5	33	1.2	3.53	121	.289	.314	15	20	105	108	1.5	-1	4	2.3
1935	Cin-N	6	10	.375	38	13	3	1	3	114	164	12.9	6	32	2.5	24	1.9	6.87	56	.335	.373	-36	-38	95	83	-1.3	4	2	-3.0
1936	Cin-N	10	8	.556	31	12	5	0	0	131	164	11.3	5	30	2.1	20	1.4	4.26	92	.296	.329	-4	-5	97	95	1.4	2	0	-0.3
Total	8	57	82	.410	256	127	49	7	8	1159	1415	11.0	54	263	2.0	179	1.4	4.50	90	.303	.335	-48	-56	99	98	0.7	17	20	-1.4
■ **BERNIE FRIBERG**	Friberg, Bernard Albert (born Gustaf Bernhard Friberg) b: 8/18/1899, Manchester, N.H. d: 12/8/58, Lynn, Mass. BR/TR, 5'11. ", 178 lbs. Deb: 8/20/19																												
1925	Phi-N	0	0	—	1	0	0	0	0	4	4	9.0	0	3	6.8	1	2.3	4.50	112	.286	.412	-0	0	118	110	0.0	0	0	0.0
■ **MARION FRICANO**	Fricano, Marion John b: 7/15/23, Brant, N.Y. d: 5/18/76, Tijuana, Mex. BR/TR, 6', 170 lbs. Deb: 9/06/52																												
1952	Phi-A	1	0	1.000	2	0	0	0	0	5	5	9.0	0	1	1.8	0	0.0	1.80	229	.238	.261	1	1	112	102	0.5	0	0	0.1
1953	Phi-A	9	12	.429	39	23	10	0	0	211	206	8.8	21	90	3.8	67	2.9	3.88	108	.257	.332	3	7	105	106	0.9	-3	-2	0.4
1954	Phi-A	5	11	.313	37	20	4	0	1	152	163	9.7	17	64	3.8	43	2.5	5.15	76	.275	.344	-24	-21	105	87	-0.4	-3	-2	-2.5
1955	KC-A	0	0	—	10	0	0	0	0	20	19	8.5	2	9	4.0	5	2.3	3.15	133	.253	.333	2	2	106	124	0.0	1	0	0.4
Total	4	15	23	.395	88	43	14	0	1	388	393	9.1	40	164	3.8	115	2.7	4.31	95	.264	.336	-19	-10	105	99	1.0	-5	-3	-1.6
■ **SKIPPER FRIDAY**	Friday, Grier William b: 10/26/1897, Gastonia, N.C. d: 8/25/62, Gastonia, N.C. BR/TR, 5'11", 170 lbs. Deb: 6/17/23																												
1923	Was-A	0	1	.000	7	2	1	0	0	30	35	10.5	2	22	6.6	9	2.7	6.90	55	.313	.418	-10	-10	95	89	-0.4	0	1	-0.8
■ **CY FRIED**	Fried, Arthur Edwin b: 7/23/1897, San Antonio, Tex. d: 10/10/70, San Antonio, Tex. BL/TL, 5'11.5", 150 lbs. Deb: 9/17/20																												
1920	Det-A	0	0	—	2	0	0	0	0	2	3	13.5	0	4	18.0	0	0.0	13.50	30	.500	.700	-2	-2	106	98	0.0	0	0	-0.1
■ **BOB FRIEDRICH**	Friedrich, Robert George b: 8/30/06, Cincinnati, Ohio BR/TR, 5'11.5", 165 lbs. Deb: 5/17/32																												
1932	Was-A	0	0	—	2	0	0	0	0	4	4	9.0	0	7	15.8	2	4.5	11.25	39	.250	.500	-3	-3	98	67	0.0	-0	-0	-0.2
■ **BILL FRIEL**	Friel, William Edward b: 4/1/1876, Renovo, Pa. d: 12/24/59, St.Louis, Mo. BL/TR, 5'10", 215 lbs. Deb: 5/03/01																												
1902	StL-A	0	0	—	1	0	0	0	0	4	4	9.0	0	0	0.0	0	0.0	4.50	81	.284	.284	-0	-0	102	49	0.0	0	-0	0.0
■ **DANNY FRIEND**	Friend, Daniel Sebastian b: 4/18/1873, Cincinnati, Ohio d: 6/1/42, Chillicothe, Ohio TL , 5'9", 175 lbs. Deb: 9/10/1895																												
1895	Chi-N	2	2	.500	5	5	5	0	0	41	50	11.0	5	14	3.1	10	2.2	5.27	94	.321	.377	-2	-2	103	99	-0.1	-1	0	-0.1
1896	Chi-N	18	14	.563	36	33	28	1	0	291	298	9.2	11	139	4.3	86	2.7	4.76	99	.287	.371	-13	-1	108	82	0.4	-2	-2	-0.1
1897	Chi-N	12	11	.522	24	24	23	0	0	203	244	10.8	5	86	3.8	58	2.6	4.52	96	.320	.389	-5	-4	101	100	1.8	2	0	0.0
1898	Chi-N	0	2	.000	2	2	2	0	0	17	20	10.6	1	10	5.3	4	2.1	5.29	69	.316	.409	-3	-3	102	96	-0.9	0	0	-0.1
Total	4	32	29	.525	67	64	58	1	0	552	612	10.0	22	249	4.1	158	2.6	4.73	97	.303	.379	-23	-10	105	90	1.2	0	-2	-0.3
■ **BOB FRIEND**	Friend, Robert Bartmess "Warrior" b: 11/24/30, Lafayette, Ind. BR/TR, 6', 190 lbs. Deb: 4/28/51																												
1951	Pit-N	6	10	.375	34	22	3	1	0	150	173	10.4	12	68	4.1	41	2.5	4.26	102	.293	.362	-5	1	110	115	-0.8	-3	0	0.0
1952	Pit-N	7	17	.292	35	23	6	1	0	185	186	9.0	15	84	4.1	75	3.6	4.18	94	.258	.333	-9	-5	105	97	0.4	-4	0	-0.8
1953	Pit-N	8	11	.421	32	24	8	0	0	171	193	10.2	18	57	3.0	66	3.5	4.89	93	.286	.339	-12	-6	106	95	1.5	-3	1	-0.7
1954	Pit-N	7	12	.368	35	20	4	2	2	170	204	10.8	16	58	3.1	73	3.9	5.08	81	.302	.347	-19	-18	102	95	0.4	5	-1	-1.2
1955	Pit-N	14	9	.609	44	20	9	2	2	200	178	8.0	18	52	2.3	98	4.4	**2.84**	**143**	.242	.285	**27**	27	101	109	4.6	-2	3	3.0
1956	Pit-N	17	17	.500	49	42	19	4	3	**314**	310	8.9	25	85	2.4	166	4.8	3.47	112	.258	.302	11	15	103	95	2.6	-1	-1	1.3
1957	Pit-N	14	18	.438	40	38	17	3	0	**277**	273	8.9	28	68	2.2	143	4.6	3.38	110	.257	.298	15	10	96	102	1.2	2	-1	1.0
1958	Pit-N	**22**	14	.611	38	38	16	1	0	274	299	9.8	25	61	2.0	135	4.4	3.68	101	.281	.318	8	1	94	106	3.3	-4	0	-0.3
1959	Pit-N	8	19	.296	35	35	7	2	0	235	267	10.2	19	52	2.0	104	4.0	4.02	102	.283	.321	-2	2	104	99	-6.1	-0	0	0.2
1960	Pit-N	18	12	.600	38	37	16	4	1	276	266	8.7	18	45	1.5	183	6.0	3.00	121	.251	.278	23	19	97	94	-0.4	-5	0	1.5
1961	Pit-N	14	19	.424	41	35	10	1	1	236	271	10.3	16	45	1.7	108	4.1	3.85	104	.289	.319	5	4	99	102	-2.5	-3	-1	0.0
1962	Pit-N	18	14	.563	39	36	13	**5**	1	262	280	9.6	23	53	1.8	144	4.9	3.06	130	.273	.306	26	27	101	119	-0.4	-4	0	2.4
1963	Pit-N	17	16	.515	39	38	12	4	0	269	236	7.9	13	44	**1.5**	144	4.8	2.34	139	.233	.264	28	27	99	97	2.2	-3	-1	2.6
1964	Pit-N	13	18	.419	35	35	13	3	0	240	253	9.5	10	50	1.9	128	4.8	3.34	107	.271	.306	5	6	101	101	-2.7	-3	2	0.5
1965	Pit-N	8	12	.400	34	34	8	2	0	222	221	9.0	17	47	1.9	74	3.0	3.24	107	.260	.301	7	6	98	106	-3.0	-5	0	0.1
1966	NY-A	1	4	.200	12	8	0	0	0	45	61	12.2	2	9	1.8	22	4.4	4.80	67	.330	.355	-7	-8	94	105	-1.3	-1	1	-0.7
	NY-N	5	8	.385	22	12	2	1	1	86	101	10.6	11	16	1.7	30	3.1	4.40	79	.289	.316	-8	-9	97	98	-0.3	-3	-2	-1.2
Total	16	197	230	.461	602	497	163	36	11	3612	3772	9.4	286	894	2.2	1734	4.3	3.58	107	.269	.310	94	99	100	102	-1.3	-36	1	7.7
■ **PETE FRIES**	Fries, Peter Martin b: 10/30/1857, Scranton, Pa. d: 7/30/37, Chicago, Ill. BL/TL, 5'8", 160 lbs. Deb: 1883																												
1883	Col-a	0	3	.000	3	3	3	0	0	25	34	12.2	1	14	5.0	7	2.5	6.48	47	.330	.410	-9	-10	91	95	-1.4	1	0	-0.6
■ **JOHN FRILL**	Frill, John Edmond b: 4/3/1879, Reading, Pa. d: 9/28/18, Westerly, R.I. BR/TL, 5'10.5", 170 lbs. Deb: 4/16/10																												
1910	NY-A	2	2	.500	10	5	3	1	1	48	55	10.3	1	5	0.9	27	5.1	4.50	59	.289	.311	-11	-10	106	70	-0.2	-1	0	-1.0
1912	StL-A	0	1	.000	3	3	0	0	0	4	16	36.0	1	1	2.3	2	4.5	22.50	15	.571	.600	-9	-8	103	89	-0.4	0	0	-0.6
	Cin-N	1	0	1.000	3	2	0	0	0	15	19	11.4	0	1	0.6	4	2.4	6.00	53	.311	.344	-4	-5	93	62	0.5	0	0	-0.3
Total	2	3	3	.500	16	10	3	1	1	67	90	12.1	2	7	0.9	33	4.4	5.91	48	.323	.348	-23	-23	103	69	-0.1	-1	0	-1.9
■ **DANNY FRISELLA**	Frisella, Daniel Vincent "Bear" b: 3/4/46, San Francisco, Cal. d: 1/1/77, Phoenix, Ariz. BL/TR, 6', 185 lbs. Deb: 7/27/67																												
1967	NY-N	1	6	.143	14	11	0	0	0	74	68	8.3	6	33	4.0	51	6.2	3.41	101	.249	.320	-0	0	102	110	-2.1	-1	-0	0.0
1968	NY-N	2	4	.333	19	4	0	0	2	51	53	9.4	5	17	3.0	47	8.3	3.88	79	.270	.324	-5	-5	103	103	-0.7	-1	0	-0.4
1969	NY-N	0	0	—	3	0	0	0	0	5	8	14.4	1	3	5.4	5	9.0	7.20	50	.381	.458	-2	-2	99	122	0.0	-0	-0	-0.1
1970	NY-N	8	3	.727	30	1	0	0	1	66	49	6.7	4	34	4.6	54	7.4	3.00	139	.204	.297	8	9	103	90	2.5	1	0	1.0
1971	NY-N	8	5	.615	53	0	0	0	12	91	76	7.5	6	30	3.0	93	9.2	1.98	168	.227	.290	15	14	96	138	1.5	1	1	1.6
1972	NY-N	5	8	.385	39	0	0	0	9	67	63	8.5	8	20	2.7	46	6.2	3.36	99	.243	.292	1	-0	96	99	-1.8	0	1	0.1
1973	Atl-N	1	2	.333	42	0	0	0	8	45	40	8.0	5	23	4.6	27	5.4	4.20	98	.241	.323	-3	-0	113	93	-0.3	0	0	0.0
1974	Atl-N	3	4	.429	36	1	0	0	6	42	37	7.9	4	28	6.0	27	5.8	5.14	73	.240	.348	-7	-6	104	81	-0.7	0	-0	-0.6
1975	SD-N	1	6	.143	65	0	0	0	9	98	86	7.9	7	51	4.7	67	6.2	3.12	118	.242	.330	6	6	101	117	-2.3	0	-0	0.6
1976	StL-N	0	0	—	18	0	0	0	1	23	19	7.4	3	13	5.1	11	4.3	3.91	94	.232	.330	-1	-1	105	103	0.0	-0	0	0.0
	Mil-A	5	2	.714	32	0	0	0	9	49	30	5.5	4	34	6.2	43	7.9	2.76	128	.175	.310	4	4	100	99	1.8	0	0	0.4
Total	10	34	40	.459	351	17	0	0	57	611	529	7.8	53	286	4.2	471	6.9	3.31	108	.235	.315	15	18	101	107	-2.1	1	1	2.6
■ **EMIL FRISK**	Frisk, John Emil b: 10/15/1874, Kalkaska, Mich. d: 1/27/22, Seattle, Wash. BL/TR, 6'1", 190 lbs. Deb: 9/02/1899																												
1899	Cin-N	3	6	.333	9	9	9	0	0	68	81	10.7	1	17	2.3	17	2.3	3.97	102	.320	.363	-1	1	105	97	-1.8	1	0	0.2
1901	Det-A	5	4	.556	11	7	6	0	0	75	94	11.3	1	26	3.1	22	2.6	4.32	93	.328	.384	-5	-3	109	104	0.1	2	2	0.4
Total	2	8	10	.444	20	16	15	0	0	143	175	11.0	2	43	2.7	39	2.5	4.15	97	.324	.374	-6	-2	107	101	-1.7	3	2	0.6
■ **CHARLIE FRITZ**	Fritz, Charles Cornelius b: 6/18/1882, Mobile, Ala. d: 7/30/43, Mobile, Ala. TL , Deb: 10/05/07																												
1907	Phi-A	0	0	—	1	1	0	0	0	3	0	0.0	0	3	9.0	1	3.0	3.00	88	.000	.285	-0	-0	104	2	0.0	-0	-0	0.0
■ **BILL FROATS**	Froats, William John b: 10/20/30, New York, N.Y. BL/TL, 6', 180 lbs. Deb: 4/22/55																												
1955	Det-A	0	0	—	1	0	0	0	0	2	0	0.0	0	2	9.0	0	0.0	0.00	—	.000	.286	1	1	95	0	0.0	0	0	0.1
■ **SAM FROCK**	Frock, Samuel William b: 12/23/1882, Baltimore, Md. d: 11/3/25, Baltimore, Md. BR/TR, 6', 168 lbs. Deb: 9/21/07																												
1907	Bos-N	1	2	.333	5	3	3	1	0	33	28	7.6	1	11	3.0	12	3.3	3.00	81	.261	.341	-2	-2	99	89	-0.1	-1	-2	-0.3
1909	Pit-N	2	1	.667	8	4	3	0	1	36	44	11.0	0	4	1.0	11	2.8	2.50	103	.299	.331	0	0	99	139	0.0	-1	0	0.1

YEAR	TM/L	W	L	PCT	G	GS	CG	SHO	SV	IP	H	H/G	HR	BB	BB/G	SO	SO/G	ERA	/A	OAVG	OOBP	PR	/A	PF	CPI	WAT	PB	PD	TPI
1910	Pit-N	0	0	—	1	0	0	0	0	2	2	9.0	0	2	9.0	1	4.5	4.50	74	.400	.625	-0	-0	110	198	0.0	0	0	0.0
	Bos-N	12	19	.387	45	29	13	2	2	255	245	8.6	8	91	3.2	170	6.0	3.21	112	.262	.330	-5	11	118	100	1.2	-4	1	1.0
	Yr	12	19	.387	46	29	13	2	2	257	247	8.6	8	93	3.3	171	6.0	3.22	111	.263	.332	-5	10	118	100	1.2	0	2	1.0
1911	Bos-N	0	1	.000	4	1	1	0	0	16	29	16.3	0	5	2.8	8	4.5	5.63	66	.426	.473	-4	-3	109	143	-0.4	-0	0	-0.2
Total	4	15	23	.395	63	37	20	3	3	342	348	9.2	9	113	3.0	202	5.3	3.24	104	.276	.341	-11	5	114	106	0.7	-6	0	0.6
■ **TODD FROHWIRTH**	Frohwirth, Todd Gerard b: 9/28/62, Milwaukee, Wis. BR/TR, 6'4", 190 lbs. Deb: 8/10/87																												
1987	Phi-N	1	0	1.000	10	0	0	0	0	11	12	9.8	0	2	1.6	9	7.4	0.00	—	.293	.326	5	5	105	0	0.5	-0	0	0.5
1988	Phi-N	1	2	.333	12	0	0	0	0	12	16	12.0	2	11	8.3	11	8.3	8.25	43	.327	.435	-6	-6	103	95	-0.2	0	1	-0.5
Total	2	2	2	.500	22	0	0	0	0	23	28	11.0	2	13	5.1	20	7.8	4.30	91	.311	.390	-1	-1	104	50	0.3	-0	1	0.0
■ **ART FROMME**	Fromme, Arthur Henry b: 9/3/1883, Quincy, Ill. d: 8/24/56, Los Angeles, Cal. BR/TR, 6', 178 lbs. Deb: 9/14/06																												
1906	StL-N	1	2	.333	3	3	3	1	0	25	19	6.8	0	10	3.6	11	4.0	1.44	190	.238	.330	3	4	104	153	0.0	0	1	0.5
1907	StL-N	5	13	.278	23	16	13	2	0	146	138	8.5	3	67	4.1	67	4.1	2.90	85	.280	.370	-7	-7	100	114	-1.7	0	0	-0.7
1908	StL-N	5	13	.278	20	14	9	2	0	116	102	7.9	1	50	3.9	62	4.8	2.72	86	.265	.352	-5	-5	100	105	-1.2	-1	-0	-0.5
1909	Cin-N	19	13	.594	37	34	22	4	2	279	195	6.3	2	101	3.3	126	4.1	1.90	128	.201	.278	22	17	94	85	3.5	3	2	2.1
1910	Cin-N	3	4	.429	11	5	1	0	0	49	44	8.1	2	39	7.2	10	1.8	2.94	106	.260	.402	1	1	102	155	-0.3	-1	0	0.0
1911	Cin-N	10	11	.476	38	26	11	1	0	208	190	8.2	8	79	3.4	107	4.6	3.46	91	.248	.331	-1	-8	92	94	0.4	-1	1	-0.8
1912	Cin-N	16	18	.471	43	37	23	3	0	296	285	8.7	7	88	2.7	120	3.6	2.74	116	.251	.311	22	15	93	96	-0.8	-8	-0	0.5
1913	Cin-N	1	4	.200	9	7	2	0	0	56	55	8.8	1	21	3.4	24	3.9	4.18	80	.274	.336	-6	-5	104	88	-1.2	-0	-1	-0.5
	NY-N	11	6	.647	26	12	3	0	0	112	112	9.0	5	29	2.3	50	4.0	4.02	79	.260	.304	-10	-10	100	76	-0.1	-0	1	-0.9
	Yr	12	10	.545	35	19	5	0	0	168	167	8.9	6	50	2.7	74	4.0	4.07	79	.263	.310	-16	-16	101	76	-1.3	-0	1	-1.4
1914	NY-N	9	5	.643	38	12	3	1	2	138	142	9.3	7	44	2.9	57	3.7	3.20	82	.283	.339	-6	-9	94	121	1.6	1	3	-0.4
1915	NY-N	0	1	.000	4	1	0	0	0	12	15	11.3	1	2	1.5	4	3.0	6.00	42	.306	.315	-4	-5	92	72	-0.4	1	0	-0.3
Total	10	80	90	.471	252	167	90	14	4	1437	1297	8.1	37	530	3.3	638	4.0	2.91	97	.250	.324	8	-12	96	99	-0.2	-6	7	-1.0
■ **DAVE FROST**	Frost, Carl David b: 11/17/52, Long Beach, Cal. BR/TR, 6'6", 235 lbs. Deb: 9/11/77																												
1977	Chi-A	1	1	.500	4	3	0	0	0	24	30	11.3	0	3	1.1	15	5.6	3.00	134	.323	.337	3	3	99	143	0.0	0	0	0.3
1978	Cal-A	5	4	.556	11	10	2	1	0	80	71	8.0	6	24	2.7	30	3.4	2.59	148	.240	.294	11	11	101	116	0.2	0	1	1.3
1979	Cal-A	16	10	.615	36	33	12	2	1	239	226	8.5	17	77	2.9	107	4.0	3.58	108	.251	.308	17	8	92	94	2.4	0	-1	0.6
1980	Cal-A	4	8	.333	15	15	2	0	0	78	97	11.2	8	21	2.4	28	3.2	5.31	74	.308	.350	-11	-12	97	93	-1.0	0	-1	-1.2
1981	Cal-A	1	8	.111	12	9	0	0	0	47	44	8.4	3	19	3.6	16	3.1	5.55	68	.250	.320	-10	-9	104	64	-3.4	0	0	-0.8
1982	KC-A	6	6	.500	21	14	0	0	1	82	103	11.3	7	30	3.3	26	2.9	5.49	74	.313	.370	-13	-13	100	98	-0.5	0	-1	-1.3
Total	6	33	37	.471	99	84	16	3	1	550	571	9.3	41	174	2.8	222	3.6	4.11	95	.271	.324	-3	-12	96	97	-2.3	0	-3	-1.1
■ **JOHNSON FRY**	Fry, Johnson "Jay" b: 11/21/01, Huntington, W.Va. d: 4/7/59, Carmi, Ill. BR/TR, 6'1", 150 lbs. Deb: 8/24/23																												
1923	Cle-A	0	0	—	1	0	0	0	0	4	6	13.5	0	4	9.0	0	0.0	11.25	35	.353	.476	-3	-3	99	66	0.0	1	0	-0.1
■ **CHARLIE FRYE**	Frye, Charles Andrew b: 7/17/14, Hickory, N.C. d: 5/25/45, Hickory, N.C. BR/TR, 6'1", 175 lbs. Deb: 7/28/40																												
1940	Phi-N	0	6	.000	15	5	1	0	0	50	58	10.4	3	26	4.7	18	3.2	4.68	84	.291	.368	-5	-4	102	108	-2.9	1	-1	-0.3
■ **WOODIE FRYMAN**	Fryman, Woodrow Thompson b: 4/15/40, Ewing, Ky. BR/TL, 6'3", 197 lbs. Deb: 4/15/66																												
1966	Pit-N	12	9	.571	36	28	9	3	1	182	182	9.0	13	47	2.3	105	5.2	3.81	94	.261	.306	-4	-5	99	88	0.1	-1	-2	-0.7
1967	Pit-N	3	8	.273	28	18	3	1	1	113	121	9.6	12	44	3.5	74	5.9	4.06	83	.276	.340	-9	-9	100	112	-2.5	-1	2	-0.7
1968	Phi-N	12	14	.462	34	32	10	5	0	214	198	8.3	12	64	2.7	151	6.4	2.78	106	.246	.300	5	4	99	110	-0.1	-2	-1	0.0
1969	Phi-N	12	15	.444	36	35	10	1	0	228	243	9.6	15	89	3.5	150	5.9	4.42	81	.270	.340	-21	-21	100	92	1.4	-2	-1	-2.3
1970	Phi-N	8	6	.571	27	20	4	3	0	128	122	8.6	11	43	3.0	97	6.8	4.08	97	.253	.312	-0	-2	98	89	1.6	-2	-0	-0.3
1971	Phi-N	10	7	.588	37	17	3	2	2	149	133	8.0	7	46	2.8	104	6.3	3.38	107	.242	.295	1	4	105	85	2.7	-0	3	0.7
1972	Phi-N	4	10	.286	23	17	3	2	1	120	131	9.8	15	39	2.9	69	5.2	4.35	78	.279	.332	-12	-13	99	102	-1.7	1	1	-1.1
	Det-A	10	3	.769	16	14	6	1	0	114	93	7.3	6	31	2.4	72	5.7	2.05	168	.220	.280	13	18	112	114	3.3	-2	-1	1.8
1973	Det-A	6	13	.316	34	29	1	0	0	170	200	10.6	23	64	3.4	119	6.3	5.35	72	.294	.355	-29	-28	101	94	-4.0	0	1	-2.5
1974	Det-A	6	9	.400	27	22	4	1	0	142	120	7.6	16	67	4.2	92	5.8	4.31	91	.233	.319	-11	-6	108	85	-0.7	0	-1	-0.7
1975	Mon-N	9	12	.429	38	20	7	3	3	157	141	8.1	10	68	3.9	118	6.8	3.32	119	.239	.319	5	11	109	98	-0.8	1	1	1.5
1976	Mon-N	13	13	.500	34	32	4	2	2	216	218	9.1	14	76	3.2	123	5.1	3.38	107	.263	.325	3	6	103	111	3.6	-3	-0	0.3
1977	Cin-N	5	5	.500	17	12	0	0	1	75	83	10.0	13	45	5.4	57	6.8	5.40	72	.292	.379	-12	-13	99	112	-0.3	2	1	-0.9
1978	Chi-N	2	4	.333	13	9	0	0	0	56	64	10.3	6	37	5.9	28	4.5	5.14	77	.309	.396	-10	-7	111	119	-0.9	-1	1	-0.6
	Mon-N	5	7	.417	19	17	4	3	1	95	93	8.8	4	37	3.5	53	5.0	3.60	95	.260	.331	-0	-2	96	100	-0.6	-2	-0	-0.4
	Yr	7	11	.389	32	26	4	3	1	151	157	9.4	10	74	4.4	81	4.8	4.17	87	.276	.356	-10	-9	101	100	-1.5	-1	1	-1.0
1979	Mon-N	3	6	.333	44	0	0	0	10	58	52	8.1	4	22	3.4	44	6.8	2.79	135	.248	.321	6	6	101	126	-1.9	-1	1	0.6
1980	Mon-N	7	4	.636	61	0	0	0	17	80	61	6.9	1	30	3.4	59	6.6	2.25	158	.209	.281	12	12	98	89	1.1	-0	-1	1.1
1981	Mon-N	5	3	.625	35	0	0	0	7	43	38	8.0	1	14	2.9	25	5.2	1.88	181	.247	.308	8	7	98	159	0.7	1	0	0.9
1982	Mon-N	9	4	.692	60	0	0	0	12	70	66	8.5	3	26	3.3	46	5.9	3.73	101	.259	.318	-1	0	104	94	2.4	0	1	0.2
1983	Mon-N	0	3	.000	6	0	0	0	0	3	8	24.0	1	1	3.0	1	3.0	21.00	18	.571	.563	-6	-6	101	74	-1.4	0	0	-0.4
Total	18	141	155	.476	625	322	68	27	58	2413	2367	8.8	187	890	3.3	1587	5.9	3.77	96	.259	.323	-61	-42	102	101	2.0	-12	5	-3.5
■ **CHARLIE FUCHS**	Fuchs, Charles Thomas b: 11/18/13, Union City, N.J. d: 6/10/69, Weehawken, N.J. BB/TR, 5'8", 168 lbs. Deb: 4/17/42																												
1942	Det-A	3	3	.500	9	4	1	1	0	37	43	10.5	5	19	4.6	15	3.6	6.57	63	.285	.362	-12	-10	113	82	0.2	-1	1	-0.9
1943	Phi-N	2	7	.222	17	9	4	1	1	78	76	8.8	4	34	3.9	12	1.4	4.27	76	.266	.337	-8	-9	96	94	-2.1	-2	-1	-1.1
	StL-A	0	0	—	13	0	0	0	0	36	42	10.5	4	11	2.8	9	2.3	4.00	83	.294	.344	-3	-3	101	120	0.0	-1	-0	-0.3
1944	Bro-N	1	0	1.000	8	0	0	0	0	16	25	14.1	2	9	5.1	5	2.8	5.63	65	.347	.417	-4	-3	102	132	0.5	0	1	-0.2
Total	3	6	10	.375	47	13	5	2	1	167	186	10.0	15	73	3.9	41	2.2	4.85	72	.285	.353	-26	-25	101	101	-1.4	-4	1	-2.5
■ **MIGUEL FUENTES**	Fuentes, Miguel (Pinet) b: 5/10/46, Loiza, P.R. d: 1/29/70, Loiza, P.R. BR/TR, 6', 160 lbs. Deb: 9/01/69																												
1969	Sea-A	1	3	.250	8	4	1	0	0	26	29	10.0	1	16	5.5	14	4.8	5.19	70	.284	.381	-5	-4	100	90	-0.6	0	-1	-0.4
■ **OSCAR FUHR**	Fuhr, Oscar Lawrence b: 8/22/1893, Defiance, Mo. d: 3/27/75, Dallas, Tex. BL/TL, 6'0.5", 176 lbs. Deb: 4/19/21																												
1921	Chi-N	0	0	—	1	0	0	0	0	4	11	24.8	1	0	0.0	2	4.5	9.00	46	.500	.500	-2	-2	108	141	0.0	-0	0	-0.1
1924	Bos-A	3	6	.333	23	10	4	1	0	80	100	11.2	1	39	4.4	30	3.4	5.96	74	.310	.378	-15	-14	105	84	-1.0	-1	1	-1.1
1925	Bos-A	0	6	.000	39	6	0	0	0	91	138	13.6	7	30	3.0	27	2.7	6.63	66	.364	.394	-23	-23	99	100	-2.9	0	1	-1.9
Total	3	3	12	.200	63	16	4	1	0	175	249	12.8	9	69	3.5	59	3.0	6.38	69	.344	.389	-40	-39	102	94	-3.9	-1	2	-3.1
■ **JOHN FULGHAM**	Fulgham, John Thomas b: 6/9/56, St.Louis, Mo. BR/TR, 6'2", 205 lbs. Deb: 6/19/79																												
1979	StL-N	10	6	.625	20	19	10	2	0	146	123	7.6	10	26	1.6	75	4.6	2.53	154	.227	.264	20	22	104	90	1.7	1	-2	2.3
1980	StL-N	4	6	.400	15	14	4	1	0	85	66	7.0	7	32	3.4	48	5.1	3.39	109	.219	.293	2	3	102	84	-0.6	-3	-0	0.0
Total	2	14	12	.538	35	33	14	3	0	231	189	7.4	17	58	2.3	123	4.8	2.84	134	.224	.275	22	25	104	88	1.1	-2	-2	2.3
■ **ED FULLER**	Fuller, Edward Ashton b: 3/22/1868, Washington, D.C. d: 3/16/35, Hyattsville, Md. BR/TR, 6', 158 lbs. Deb: 7/11/1886																												
1886	Was-N	0	1	.000	2	1	1	0	0	13	15	10.4	0	5	3.5	3	2.1	6.92	48	.303	.366	-5	-5	100	60	-0.4	-0	0	-0.4
■ **CURT FULLERTON**	Fullerton, Curtis Hooper b: 9/13/1898, Ellsworth, Me. d: 1/2/75, Winthrop, Mass. BL/TR, 6', 162 lbs. Deb: 4/14/21																												
1921	Bos-A	0	1	.000	4	1	1	0	0	15	22	13.2	3	10	6.0	4	2.4	9.00	48	.355	.434	-8	-8	100	92	-0.4	-0	-0	-0.6
1922	Bos-A	1	4	.200	31	3	0	0	0	64	70	9.8	4	35	4.9	17	2.4	5.48	73	.290	.375	-10	-11	99	92	-1.2	2	1	-0.7
1923	Bos-A	2	15	.118	37	15	6	0	1	143	167	10.5	9	71	4.5	37	2.3	5.10	82	.300	.371	-18	-14	106	99	-6.1	2	-2	-1.2
1924	Bos-A	7	12	.368	33	20	9	0	2	152	166	9.8	1	73	4.3	33	2.0	4.32	103	.283	.356	-2	2	105	95	-1.5	-4	-0	-0.1
1925	Bos-A	0	3	.000	4	2	0	0	0	23	22	8.6	1	9	3.5	3	1.2	3.13	139	.259	.330	3	3	99	117	-1.4	-0	1	0.3
1933	Bos-A	0	2	.000	6	2	2	0	0	25	36	13.0	1	13	4.7	10	3.6	8.64	51	.364	.431	-12	-12	102	84	-0.9	0	-1	-0.9
Total	6	10	37	.213	115	43	18	0	3	422	483	10.3	19	211	4.5	104	2.2	5.12	84	.296	.370	-46	-39	104	96	-11.5	-1	-1	-3.2
■ **CHRISTOPHER FULMER**	Fulmer, Christopher b: 7/4/1858, Tamaqua, Pa. d: 11/9/31, Tamaqua, Pa. BR/TR, 5'8", 165 lbs. Deb: 8/04/1884																												
1886	Bal-a	0	0	—	1	0	0	0	0	2	2	9.0	0	1	4.5	0	0.0	4.50	72	.271	.357	-0	-0	94	86	0.0	0	0	0.0

YEAR	TM/L	W	L	PCT	G	GS	CG	SHO	SV	IP	H	H/G	HR	BB	BB/G	SO	SO/G	ERA	/A	OAVG	OOBP	PR	/A	PF	CPI	WAT	PB	PD	TPI
■ BILL FULTON	Fulton, William David b: 10/22/63, Pittsburgh, Pa. BR/TR, 6'3", 195 lbs. Deb: 9/12/87																												
1987	NY-A	1	0	1.000	3	0	0	0	0	5	9	16.2	4	1	1.8	2	3.6	10.80	40	.409	.458	-4	-4	97	130	0.5	0	0	-0.2
■ FRANK FUNK	Funk, Franklin Ray b: 8/30/35, Washington, D.C. BR/TR, 6', 175 lbs. Deb: 9/03/60 C																												
1960	Cle-A	4	2	.667	9	0	0	0	1	32	27	7.6	3	9	2.5	18	5.1	1.97	193	.248	.295	7	7	98	174	1.1	-0	0	0.7
1961	Cle-A	11	11	.500	56	0	0	0	11	92	79	7.7	9	31	3.0	64	6.3	3.33	117	.234	.298	7	6	97	99	0.4	-1	0	0.4
1962	Cle-A	2	1	.667	47	0	0	0	6	81	62	6.9	11	32	3.6	49	5.4	3.22	121	.212	.292	7	6	99	101	0.5	-1	-0	0.5
1963	Mil-N	3	3	.500	25	0	0	0	0	44	42	8.6	3	13	2.7	19	3.9	2.66	123	.258	.313	3	3	100	130	0.0	-0	-1	0.2
Total	4	20	17	.541	137	0	0	0	18	249	210	7.6	26	85	3.1	150	5.4	3.00	126	.233	.298	24	22	98	115	2.0	-3	-1	1.8
■ TOM FUNK	Funk, Thomas James b: 3/13/62, Kansas City, Mo. BL/TL, 6'2", 210 lbs. Deb: 7/24/86																												
1986	Hou-N	0	0	—	8	0	0	0	0	8	10	11.3	1	6	6.8	2	2.3	6.75	56	.286	.390	-3	-3	102	85	0.0	-0	0	-0.2
■ EDDIE FUSSELBACK	Fusselback, Edward L. b: 7/17/1856, Philadelphia, Pa. d: 4/14/26, Philadelphia, Pa. 5'6", 156 lbs. Deb: 5/03/1882																												
1882	StL-a	1	2	.333	4	2	2	0	**1**	23	34	13.3	0	2	0.8	3	1.2	4.70	60	.348	.362	-5	-5	104	101	-0.3	0	0	-0.3
■ FRED FUSSELL	Fussell, Frederick Morris "Moonlight Ace" b: 10/7/1895, Sheridan, Mo. d: 10/23/66, Syracuse, N.Y. BL/TL, 5'10", 155 lbs. Deb: 9/23/22																												
1922	Chi-N	1	1	.500	3	2	1	0	0	19	24	11.4	0	8	3.8	4	1.9	4.74	83	.333	.395	-1	-2	96	109	0.0	-1	0	-0.1
1923	Chi-N	3	5	.375	28	2	1	0	3	76	90	10.7	2	31	3.7	38	4.5	5.57	74	.298	.356	-13	-12	103	80	-1.2	-0	0	-1.0
1928	Pit-N	8	9	.471	28	20	9	2	1	160	183	10.3	6	41	2.3	43	2.4	3.60	116	.295	.327	7	10	105	109	-1.4	-4	-3	0.4
1929	Pit-N	2	2	.500	21	3	0	0	1	40	68	15.3	8	8	1.8	18	4.0	8.55	56	.389	.407	-17	-17	102	97	-0.2	2	0	-1.2
Total	4	14	17	.452	80	27	11	2	5	295	365	11.1	16	88	2.7	103	3.1	4.85	87	.312	.350	-25	-20	103	100	-2.8	-2	-2	-1.9
■ FRANK GABLER	Gabler, Frank Harold "The Great Gabbo" b: 11/6/11, E.Highlands, Cal. d: 11/1/67, Long Beach, Cal. BR/TR, 6'1", 175 lbs. Deb: 4/19/35																												
1935	NY-N	2	1	.667	26	1	0	0	0	60	79	11.9	6	20	3.0	24	3.6	5.70	67	.315	.359	-11	-13	95	95	0.3	-1	0	-1.2
1936	NY-N	9	8	.529	43	14	5	0	6	162	170	9.4	11	34	1.9	46	2.6	3.11	127	.274	.310	16	15	98	120	-1.0	2	-1	1.5
1937	NY-N	0	0	—	6	0	0	0	0	9	20	20.0	1	2	2.0	3	3.0	10.00	38	.455	.458	-6	-6	98	101	0.0	0	0	-0.5
	Bos-N	4	7	.364	19	9	2	1	2	76	84	9.9	7	16	1.9	19	2.3	5.09	69	.283	.315	-10	-13	90	81	-1.6	0	-0	-1.2
	Yr	4	7	.364	25	9	2	1	2	85	104	11.0	8	18	1.9	22	2.3	5.61	63	.305	.334	-16	-19	91	81	-1.6	0	-0	-1.7
1938	Bos-N	0	0	—	1	0	0	0	0	⅓	3	81.0	0	1	27.0	0	0.0	81.00	—	1.000	1.000	-3	-3	89	65	0.0	0	-0	-0.2
	Chi-A	1	7	.125	18	7	3	0	0	69	101	13.2	12	34	4.4	17	2.2	9.13	52	.348	.411	-33	-34	98	84	-2.8	0	-1	-2.8
Total	4	16	23	.410	113	31	10	1	8	376	457	10.9	37	107	2.6	109	2.6	5.27	75	.303	.345	-47	-54	96	101	-5.1	2	-2	-4.4
■ JOHN GABLER	Gabler, John Richard "Gabe" b: 10/2/30, Kansas City, Mo. BB/TR, 6'2", 165 lbs. Deb: 9/18/59																												
1959	NY-A	1	1	.500	3	1	0	0	0	19	21	9.9	1	10	4.7	11	5.2	2.84	125	.284	.376	2	1	92	169	0.0	-1	0	0.1
1960	NY-A	3	3	.500	21	4	0	0	1	52	46	8.0	2	32	5.5	19	3.3	4.15	86	.242	.342	-2	-3	92	88	-0.5	-0	0	-0.3
1961	Was-A	3	8	.273	29	9	0	0	4	93	104	10.1	5	37	3.6	33	3.2	4.84	81	.283	.345	-8	-10	97	88	-1.5	1	1	-0.6
Total	3	7	12	.368	53	14	0	0	5	164	171	9.4	8	79	4.3	63	3.5	4.39	86	.271	.348	-8	-11	95	98	-2.0	-0	1	-0.8
■ KEN GABLES	Gables, Kenneth Harlin "Coral" b: 1/31/19, Walnut Grove, Mo. d: 1/2/60, Walnut Grove, Mo. BR/TR, 5'11", 210 lbs. Deb: 4/18/45																												
1945	Pit-N	11	7	.611	29	16	6	0	1	139	139	9.0	5	46	3.0	49	3.2	4.14	94	.256	.316	-5	-4	102	80	1.7	-3	-2	-0.8
1946	Pit-N	2	4	.333	32	7	0	0	1	101	113	10.1	3	52	4.6	39	3.5	5.26	69	.281	.359	-21	-19	106	80	-0.5	1	-2	-1.8
1947	Pit-N	0	0	—	1	0	0	0	0	⅓	3	81.0	1	0	0.0	0	0.0	54.00	—	.750	.750	-2	-2	102	111	0.0	0	0	-0.1
Total	3	13	11	.542	62	23	6	0	2	240	255	9.6	9	98	3.7	88	3.3	4.69	80	.269	.336	-28	-24	104	80	1.2	-1	-4	-2.7
■ JOHN GADDY	Gaddy, John Wilson "Sheriff" b: 2/5/14, Wadesboro, N.C. d: 5/3/66, Albemarle, N.C. BR/TR, 6'0.5", 182 lbs. Deb: 9/27/38																												
1938	Bro-N	2	0	1.000	2	2	1	0	0	13	13	9.0	0	4	2.8	3	2.1	0.69	524	.255	.316	4	4	96	444	1.0	-0	-0	0.4
■ BRENT GAFF	Gaff, Brent Allen b: 10/5/58, Fort Wayne, Ind. BR/TR, 6'2", 200 lbs. Deb: 7/07/82																												
1982	NY-N	0	3	.000	7	5	0	0	0	32	41	11.5	3	10	2.8	14	3.9	4.50	80	.323	.366	-3	-3	100	122	-1.4	-0	-0	-0.3
1983	NY-N	1	0	1.000	4	0	0	0	0	10	18	16.2	0	1	0.9	4	3.6	6.30	58	.360	.358	-3	-3	100	86	0.5	-0	0	-0.2
1984	NY-N	3	2	.600	47	0	0	0	1	84	77	8.3	4	36	3.9	42	4.5	3.64	99	.247	.318	-0	-0	100	93	0.3	-1	0	0.0
Total	3	4	5	.444	58	5	0	0	1	126	136	9.7	7	47	3.4	60	4.3	4.07	89	.278	.335	-7	-7	100	100	-0.6	-1	0	-0.5
■ NEMO GAINES	Gaines, Willard Roland b: 12/23/1897, Alexandria, Va. d: 1/26/79, Warrenton, Va. BL/TL, 6', 180 lbs. Deb: 6/26/21																												
1921	Was-A	0	0	—	4	0	0	0	0	5	5	9.0	0	2	3.6	1	1.8	0.00	—	.294	.368	2	2	99	0	0.0	-0	-0	0.2
■ FRED GAISER	Gaiser, Frederick Jacob b: 8/31/1885, Stuttgart, Germany d: 10/9/18, Trenton, N.J. Deb: 9/03/08																												
1908	StL-N	0	0	—	1	0	0	0	0	2	4	18.0	0	3	13.5	2	9.0	9.00	26	.449	.588	-1	-1	100	125	0.0	-0	0	0.0
■ BOB GALASSO	Galasso, Robert Joseph b: 1/13/52, Connellsville, Pa. BL/TR, 6'1", 205 lbs. Deb: 7/24/77																												
1977	Sea-A	0	6	.000	11	7	0	0	0	35	57	14.7	8	8	2.1	21	5.4	9.00	45	.365	.400	-19	-19	98	87	-2.9	0	-0	-1.7
1979	Mil-A	3	1	.750	31	0	0	0	3	51	64	11.3	5	26	4.6	28	4.9	4.41	95	.299	.370	-1	-1	99	119	0.8	0	-0	-0.1
1981	Sea-A	1	1	.500	13	1	0	0	1	32	32	9.0	2	13	3.7	14	3.9	4.78	77	.264	.331	-4	-4	101	80	0.2	0	-0	-0.3
Total	3	4	8	.333	55	8	0	0	4	118	153	11.7	15	47	3.6	63	4.8	5.87	68	.312	.370	-24	-24	99	99	-1.9	0	-1	-2.1
■ MILT GALATZER	Galatzer, Milton b: 5/4/07, Chicago, Il.. d: 1/29/76, San Francisco, Cal BL/TL, 5'10", 168 lbs. Deb: 6/25/33																												
1936	Cle-A	0	0	—	1	0	0	0	0	6	7	10.5	0	5	7.5	3	4.5	4.50	117	.292	.414	0	1	105	125	0.0	0	0	0.0
■ RICH GALE	Gale, Richard Blackwell b: 1/19/54, Littleton, N.H. BR/TR, 6'7", 225 lbs. Deb: 4/30/78																												
1978	KC-A	14	8	.636	31	30	9	3	0	192	171	8.0	10	100	4.7	88	4.1	3.09	123	.244	.334	15	15	101	115	2.0	0	-2	1.4
1979	KC-A	9	10	.474	34	31	2	1	0	182	197	9.7	19	99	4.9	103	5.1	5.64	79	.278	.361	-28	-24	105	88	-0.9	0	-1	-2.3
1980	KC-A	13	9	.591	32	28	6	1	1	191	169	8.0	16	78	3.7	97	4.6	3.91	101	.239	.312	3	0	97	85	-0.1	0	-1	0.0
1981	KC-A	6	6	.500	19	15	2	0	0	102	107	9.4	14	38	3.4	47	4.1	5.38	67	.270	.334	-19	-20	99	83	0.2	0	-2	-2.0
1982	SF-N	7	14	.333	33	29	2	0	0	170	193	10.2	9	81	4.3	102	5.4	4.24	80	.294	.365	-12	-16	94	114	-4.2	1	1	-1.4
1983	Cin-N	4	6	.400	33	7	0	0	1	90	103	10.3	8	43	4.3	53	5.3	5.80	65	.286	.360	-22	-20	104	82	-0.6	1	-1	-1.9
1984	Bos-A	2	3	.400	13	4	0	0	0	43	57	11.9	6	18	3.8	28	5.9	5.65	78	.315	.380	-8	-6	110	104	-0.5	0	-0	-0.5
Total	7	55	56	.495	195	144	21	5	2	970	997	9.3	82	457	4.2	518	4.8	4.54	85	.269	.345	-72	-71	100	97	-4.1	3	-5	-6.7
■ DENNY GALEHOUSE	Galehouse, Dennis Ward b: 12/7/11, Marshallville, Ohio BR/TR, 6'1", 195 lbs. Deb: 4/30/34																												
1934	Cle-A	0	0	—	1	0	0	0	0	1	2	18.0	0	1	9.0	0	0.0	18.00	25	.500	.429	-2	-2	100	68	0.0	0	-0	0.0
1935	Cle-A	1	0	1.000	5	1	1	0	0	13	16	11.1	1	9	6.2	8	5.5	9.00	49	.314	.413	-7	-7	99	73	0.5	-0	0	-0.5
1936	Cle-A	8	7	.533	36	15	5	0	1	148	161	9.8	5	68	4.1	71	4.3	4.86	109	.280	.353	3	7	105	94	0.2	-0	-2	0.4
1937	Cle-A	9	14	.391	36	29	7	0	3	201	238	10.7	11	83	3.7	78	3.5	4.57	98	.302	.363	1	-2	97	110	-3.4	-1	1	-0.2
1938	Cle-A	7	8	.467	36	12	5	1	3	114	119	9.4	12	65	5.1	66	5.2	4.34	108	.275	.366	6	4	98	119	-1.3	-1	0	0.3
1939	Bos-A	9	10	.474	30	18	6	1	0	147	160	9.8	6	52	3.2	68	4.2	4.53	109	.276	.333	1	7	107	90	-2.0	-3	0	0.4
1940	Bos-A	6	6	.500	25	20	5	0	0	120	155	11.6	10	41	3.1	53	4.0	5.18	85	.313	.361	-11	-11	100	104	-0.3	-4	1	-1.1
1941	StL-A	9	10	.474	30	24	11	2	0	190	183	8.7	10	68	3.2	61	2.9	3.65	115	.253	.318	11	11	101	96	0.4	-0	1	1.2
1942	StL-A	12	12	.500	32	28	12	3	1	192	193	9.0	5	79	3.7	75	3.5	3.61	104	.262	.335	1	3	102	102	-1.0	1	1	0.5
1943	StL-A	11	11	.500	31	28	14	2	1	224	217	8.7	8	74	3.0	114	4.6	2.77	120	.255	.308	13	14	101	115	0.6	-3	-3	0.8
1944	StL-A	9	10	.474	24	19	6	2	0	153	162	9.5	6	44	2.6	80	4.7	3.12	110	.266	.312	5	5	100	106	-1.8	-4	-2	0.0
1946	StL-A	8	12	.400	30	24	11	2	0	180	194	9.7	9	52	2.6	90	4.5	3.65	96	.273	.319	-3	-3	100	97	-0.7	-3	-2	-0.8
1947	StL-A	1	3	.250	9	4	0	0	1	32	42	11.8	3	16	4.5	11	3.1	6.19	63	.311	.374	-9	-8	106	91	-0.6	-1	0	-0.8
	Bos-A	11	7	.611	21	21	11	3	0	149	150	9.1	7	34	2.1	38	2.3	3.32	119	.260	.297	6	11	107	92	1.6	-4	-1	0.6
	Yr	12	10	.545	30	25	11	3	1	181	192	9.5	10	50	**2.5**	49	2.4	3.83	103	.269	.313	-2	2	107	92	1.0	-1	-1	-0.2
1948	Bos-A	8	8	.500	27	15	6	1	3	137	152	10.0	10	46	3.0	38	2.5	4.01	104	.282	.336	4	2	97	109	-1.6	0	-2	0.1
1949	Bos-A	0	0	—	2	0	0	0	0	2	4	18.0	1	3	13.5	0	0.0	13.50	32	.400	.538	-2	-2	103	108	0.0	0	0	-0.1
Total	15	109	118	.480	375	258	100	17	13	2003	2148	9.7	104	735	3.3	851	3.8	3.98	103	.275	.334	19	29	101	103	-9.4	-25	-8	0.8
■ DOUG GALLAGHER	Gallagher, Douglas Eugene b: 2/21/40, Fremont, Ohio BR/TL, 6'3.5", 195 lbs. Deb: 4/09/62																												
1962	Det-A	0	4	.000	9	2	0	0	1	25	31	11.2	2	15	5.4	14	5.0	4.68	94	.290	.368	-2	-1	110	110	-1.9	1	0	0.0

YEAR	TM/L	W	L	PCT	G	GS	CG	SHO	SV	IP	H	H/G	HR	BB	BB/G	SO	SO/G	ERA	/A	OAVG	OOBP	PR	/A	PF	CPI	WAT	PB	PD	TPI
■ **ED GALLAGHER**	Gallagher, Edward Michael "Lefty" b: 11/28/10, Dorchester, Mass. d: 12/22/81, Hyannis, Mass. BB/TL, 6'2", 197 lbs. Deb: 7/08/32																												
1932	Bos-A	0	3	.000	9	3	0	0	0	24	30	11.3	3	28	10.5	6	2.3	12.38	37	.323	.468	-21	-21	102	68	-1.4	-1	0	-1.7
■ **WILLIAM GALLAGHER**	Gallagher, William John b: Philadelphia, Pa. TL , Deb: 5/02/1883																												
1883	Bal-a	0	5	.000	7	5	4	0	0	52	79	13.7	0	6	1.0	19	3.3	5.54	67	.355	.372	-13	-10	113	97	-2.4	-1	0	-0.8
1884	Phi-U	1	2	.333	3	3	3	0	0	25	32	11.5	3	4	1.4	12	4.3	3.24	88	.316	.342	-1	-1	95	159	0.0	-1	0	-0.1
Total	2	1	7	.125	10	8	7	0	0	77	111	13.0	3	10	1.2	31	3.6	4.79	72	.343	.362	-14	-12	107	117	-2.4	-2	0	-0.9
■ **BERT GALLIA**	Gallia, Melvin Allys b: 10/14/1891, Beeville, Tex. d: 3/19/76, Devine, Tex. BR/TR, 6', 165 lbs. Deb: 9/04/12																												
1912	Was-A	0	0	—	2	0	0	0	0	2	0	0.0	0	3	13.5	0	0.0	0.00	—	.000	.333	1	1	97	0	0.0	0	0	0.1
1913	Was-A	1	5	.167	31	4	0	0	3	96	85	8.0	2	46	4.3	46	4.3	4.13	74	.222	.317	-13	-11	105	58	-2.1	-2	2	-0.8
1914	Was-A	0	0	—	2	0	0	0	0	6	3	4.5	0	4	6.0	4	6.0	4.50	61	.120	.241	-1	-1	100	11	0.0	-0	-0	-0.1
1915	Was-A	17	11	.607	43	29	14	3	1	260	220	7.6	2	64	2.2	130	4.5	2.28	128	.234	.286	19	19	99	92	1.9	-2	-1	1.7
1916	Was-A	17	12	.586	49	31	13	1	2	284	278	8.8	3	99	3.1	120	3.8	2.76	103	.266	.334	2	2	100	117	3.1	1	-3	0.0
1917	Was-A	9	13	.409	42	23	9	1	1	208	191	8.3	1	93	4.0	84	3.6	2.99	83	.258	.344	-7	-12	93	106	-1.8	3	-1	-1.1
1918	StL-A	8	6	.571	19	17	10	1	0	124	126	9.1	1	61	4.4	48	3.5	3.48	79	.268	.350	-10	-10	100	101	1.4	-3	0	-1.3
1919	StL-A	12	14	.462	34	25	14	1	1	222	220	8.9	10	92	3.7	83	3.4	3.61	87	.264	.343	-9	-11	98	97	-0.6	-1	2	-1.1
1920	StL-A	0	1	.000	2	1	0	0	0	4	8	18.0	0	3	6.8	0	0.0	6.75	62	.400	.478	-1	-1	111	126	-0.4	-0	-0	0.0
	Phi-N	2	6	.250	18	5	1	0	2	72	79	9.9	2	29	3.6	35	4.4	4.50	78	.287	.348	-11	-8	112	87	-1.5	-1	-0	-0.9
Total	9	66	68	.493	242	135	61	7	10	1278	1210	8.5	21	494	3.5	550	3.9	3.13	92	.256	.329	-31	-34	99	98	0.0	-6	-2	-3.5
■ **BILL GALLIVAN**	Gallivan, Philip Joseph b: 5/29/07, Seattle, Wash. d: 11/24/69, St.Paul, Minn. BR/TR, 6', 170 lbs. Deb: 4/21/31																												
1931	Bro-N	0	1	.000	6	1	0	0	0	15	23	13.8	2	7	4.2	1	0.6	5.40	72	.354	.405	-3	-2	101	134	-0.4	-0	1	-0.1
1932	Chi-A	1	3	.250	13	3	1	0	0	33	49	13.4	4	24	6.5	12	3.3	7.64	53	.338	.428	-12	-13	91	101	-0.4	1	-0	-1.0
1934	Chi-A	4	7	.364	35	7	3	0	1	127	155	11.0	14	64	4.5	55	3.9	5.60	83	.295	.367	-16	-14	103	98	0.1	1	-1	-1.2
Total	3	5	11	.313	54	11	4	0	1	175	227	11.7	20	95	4.9	68	3.5	5.97	75	.309	.383	-30	-29	101	102	-0.7	1	-0	-2.3
■ **BALVINO GALVEZ**	Galvez, Balvino (Jerez) b: 3/31/64, San Pedro De Macoris, D.R. BR/TR, 6', 170 lbs. Deb: 5/07/86																												
1986	LA-N	0	1	.000	10	0	0	0	0	21	19	8.1	3	12	5.1	11	4.7	3.86	91	.241	.341	-0	-1	95	111	-0.4	-0	0	0.0
■ **JIM GALVIN**	Galvin, James Francis "Pud', "Gentle Jeems" or "The Little Steam Engine" b: 12/25/1856, St.Louis, Mo. d: 3/7/02, Pittsburgh, Pa. BR/TR, 5'8", 190 lbs. Deb: 5/22/1875 MH																												
1875	StL-n	4	2	.667	8																								
1879	Buf-N	37	27	.578	66	66	65	6	0	593	585	8.9	3	31	0.5	136	2.1	2.28	124	.263	.273	14	**37**	114	87	-3.1	2	3	**4.5**
1880	Buf-N	20	35	.364	58	54	46	5	0	459	528	10.4	5	32	0.6	128	2.5	2.71	84	.298	.310	-17	-22	96	113	7.0	-2	2	-2.1
1881	Buf-N	29	24	.547	56	53	48	5	0	474	546	10.4	4	46	**0.9**	136	2.6	2.37	118	.301	.318	21	23	101	**126**	0.8	-2	7	2.7
1882	Buf-N	28	23	.549	52	51	48	3	0	445	476	9.6	8	40	0.8	162	3.3	3.18	94	.281	.298	-14	-10	103	90	1.8	-6	1	-1.2
1883	Buf-N	46	29	.613	**76**	75	**72**	**5**	0	**656**	676	9.3	9	50	0.7	279	3.8	2.72	115	.274	.288	31	29	99	94	**17.6**	-3	1	2.3
1884	Buf-N	46	22	.676	72	72	71	**12**	0	636	566	8.0	23	63	0.9	369	5.2	2.00	157	.247	.267	69	81	105	102	15.1	-14	7	7.1
1885	Buf-N	13	19	.406	33	32	31	3	1	284	356	11.3	8	37	1.2	93	2.9	4.09	72	.318	.340	-40	-36	105	100	2.2	-2	3	-2.9
	Pit-a	3	7	.300	11	11	9	0	0	88	97	9.9	2	7	0.7	27	2.8	3.68	94	.292	.306	-4	-2	107	92	-2.0	-4	0	-0.4
1886	Pit-a	29	21	.580	50	50	49	2	0	435	457	9.5	3	75	**1.6**	72	1.5	2.67	116	.280	.312	38	21	90	**123**	-0.2	5	4	2.4
1887	Pit-N	28	21	.571	49	48	47	2	0	441	490	10.0	12	67	1.4	76	1.6	3.29	118	.297	.324	38	29	96	107	8.1	-2	7	2.9
1888	Pit-N	23	25	.479	50	50	49	6	0	437	446	9.2	9	53	1.1	107	2.2	2.64	102	.278	.301	10	3	95	105	-0.9	-5	3	0.0
1889	Pit-N	23	16	.590	41	40	38	4	0	341	392	10.3	19	78	**2.1**	77	2.0	4.17	87	.304	.344	-5	-21	90	97	6.0	0	1	-1.8
1890	Pit-P	12	13	.480	26	25	23	1	0	217	275	11.4	3	49	2.0	35	1.5	4.35	90	.321	.358	-3	-11	92	92	0.3	-1	0	-0.9
1891	Pit-N	14	13	.519	33	31	23	2	0	247	256	9.3	10	62	2.3	46	1.7	2.88	119	.281	.327	13	15	102	106	3.0	-5	0	1.0
1892	Pit-N	5	6	.455	12	12	10	0	0	96	104	9.8	0	28	2.6	29	2.7	2.63	117	.289	.341	7	5	94	126	-0.7	-2	0	0.2
	StL-N	5	6	.455	12	12	10	0	0	92	102	10.0	4	26	2.5	27	2.6	3.23	99	.294	.343	1	-0	97	115	0.8	-5	0	-0.4
	Yr	10	12	.455	24	24	20	0	0	188	206	9.9	4	54	2.6	56	2.7	2.92	107	.292	.342	8	4	95	115	0.1	-2	0	-0.2
Total	14	361	307	.540	697	682	639	56	1	5941	6352	9.6	122	744	1.1	1799	2.7	2.87	108	.284	.307	157	154	100	103	55.8	-45	39	13.4
■ **LOU GALVIN**	Galvin, Louis J. b: 4/1862, St.Paul, Minn. d: 6/17/1895, Deb: 10/01/1884																												
1884	StP-U	0	2	.000	3	3	3	0	0	25	21	7.6	0	10	3.6	17	6.1	2.88	105	.233	.309	0	0	100	95	-0.9	-0	0	0.0
■ **BOB GAMBLE**	Gamble, Robert J. b: 2/1867, Hazelton, Pa. 5'10", 155 lbs. Deb: 1888																												
1888	Phi-a	0	1	.000	1	1	1	0	0	9	10	10.0	0	3	3.0	2	2.0	8.00	37	.295	.352	-5	-5	97	48	-0.4	0	0	-0.3
■ **GUSSIE GANNON**	Gannon, James Edward b: 11/26/1873, Erie, Pa. d: 4/12/66, Erie, Pa. 5'11", 154 lbs. Deb: 6/15/1895																												
1895	Pit-N	0	0	—	1	0	0	0	0	5	7	12.6	0	2	3.6	0	0.0	1.80	256	.352	.411	2	2	96	298	0.0	-0	0	0.1
■ **BILL GANNON**	Gannon, William G. b: 1876, New Haven, Conn. d: 4/26/27, Fort Worth, Tex. Deb: 8/28/1898																												
1898	StL-N	0	1	.000	1	1	1	0	0	9	13	13.0	0	5	5.0	2	2.0	11.00	36	.362	.439	-7	-7	110	53	-0.4	-1	0	-0.4
■ **JIM GANTNER**	Gantner, James Elmer b: 1/5/53, Fond Du Lac, Wis. BL/TR, 6', 180 lbs. Deb: 9/03/76																												
1979	Mil-A	0	0	—	1	0	0	0	0	1	2	18.0	0	0	0.0	0	0.0	0.00	—	.400	.400	0	0	99	0	0.0	1	0	0.0
■ **GENE GARBER**	Garber, Henry Eugene b: 11/13/47, Lancaster, Pa. BR/TR, 5'10", 175 lbs. Deb: 6/17/69																												
1969	Pit-N	0	0	—	2	1	0	0	0	5	6	10.8	3	1	1.8	3	5.4	5.40	63	.333	.350	-1	-1	94	171	0.0	-0	-0	0.0
1970	Pit-N	0	3	.000	14	0	0	0	0	22	22	9.0	4	10	4.1	7	2.9	5.32	73	.275	.362	-3	-3	96	105	-1.4	1	1	-0.1
1972	Pit-N	0	0	—	4	0	0	0	0	6	7	10.5	3	3	4.5	3	4.5	7.50	46	.269	.345	-3	-3	100	99	0.0	-0	0	-0.2
1973	KC-A	9	9	.500	48	8	4	0	11	153	164	9.6	14	49	2.9	60	3.5	4.24	98	.283	.334	-7	-1	109	101	-0.7	0	1	0.0
1974	KC-A	1	2	.333	17	0	0	0	1	28	35	11.3	3	13	4.2	14	4.5	4.82	80	.313	.371	-4	-3	106	117	-0.4	0	-0	-0.2
	Phi-N	4	0	1.000	34	0	0	0	4	48	39	7.3	1	31	5.8	27	5.1	2.06	182	.236	.346	8	9	104	175	2.0	-0	0	1.0
1975	Phi-N	10	12	.455	**71**	0	0	0	14	110	104	8.5	13	27	2.2	69	5.6	3.60	102	.254	.297	0	1	101	98	-1.7	-0	0	0.0
1976	Phi-N	9	3	.750	59	0	0	0	11	93	78	7.5	4	30	2.9	92	8.9	2.81	131	.228	.292	7	9	105	94	2.1	1	1	1.2
1977	Phi-N	8	6	.571	64	0	0	0	19	103	82	7.2	6	23	2.0	78	6.8	2.36	163	.220	.264	18	17	98	94	-0.5	-1	2	1.8
1978	Phi-N	2	1	.667	22	0	0	0	3	39	26	6.0	1	11	2.5	24	5.5	1.38	269	.191	.263	10	10	104	122	0.4	-0	0	1.1
	Atl-N	4	4	.500	43	0	0	0	22	78	58	6.7	11	13	1.5	61	7.0	2.54	161	.204	.242	9	13	114	91	0.5	-1	1	1.5
	Yr	6	5	.545	65	0	0	0	25	117	84	6.5	12	24	1.8	85	6.5	2.15	184	.199	.242	19	**23**	111	91	0.9	-0	1	2.6
1979	Atl-N	6	16	.273	68	0	0	0	25	106	121	10.3	10	24	2.0	56	4.8	4.33	95	.283	.325	-7	-2	110	94	-4.0	1	1	0.0
1980	Atl-N	5	5	.500	68	0	0	0	7	82	95	10.4	6	24	2.6	51	5.6	3.84	95	.288	.331	-2	-2	101	109	0.0	0	2	0.0
1981	Atl-N	4	6	.400	35	0	0	0	2	59	49	7.5	2	20	3.1	34	5.2	2.59	135	.214	.275	6	6	100	77	-0.7	-1	2	0.8
1982	Atl-N	8	10	.444	69	0	0	0	30	119	100	7.6	4	32	2.4	68	5.1	2.34	164	.231	.279	17	20	107	105	-1.8	-0	2	2.4
1983	Atl-N	4	5	.444	43	0	0	0	9	61	72	10.6	8	23	3.4	45	6.6	4.57	83	.301	.351	-6	-5	104	116	-0.8	0	2	-0.2
1984	Atl-N	3	6	.333	62	0	0	0	11	106	103	8.7	7	24	2.0	55	4.7	3.06	129	.254	.291	6	10	110	102	-1.4	-1	1	1.1
1985	Atl-N	6	6	.500	59	0	0	0	1	97	98	9.1	8	25	2.3	66	6.1	3.62	108	.263	.306	-0	3	108	99	1.0	-0	1	0.4
1986	Atl-N	5	5	.500	61	0	0	0	24	78	76	8.8	3	20	2.3	56	6.5	2.54	152	.260	.304	10	11	103	126	0.5	0	1	1.3
1987	Atl-N	8	10	.444	49	0	0	0	10	69	87	11.3	7	28	3.7	48	6.3	4.43	101	.311	.363	-3	0	109	124	0.3	-0	2	0.2
	KC-A	0	0	—	13	0	0	0	8	14	13	8.4	1	1	0.6	3	1.9	2.57	181	.245	.273	3	3	104	106	0.0	0	0	0.3
1988	KC-A	0	4	.000	26	0	0	0	6	33	29	7.9	4	13	3.5	20	5.5	3.55	115	.238	.319	2	2	103	108	-1.9	0	0	0.2
Total	19	96	113	.459	931	9	4	0	218	1509	1464	8.7	123	445	2.7	940	5.6	3.34	117	.257	.308	60	94	106	105	-8.5	-0	20	12.6
■ **BOB GARBER**	Garber, Robert Mitchell b: 9/10/28, Hunker, Pa. BR/TR, 6'1", 190 lbs. Deb: 5/13/56																												
1956	Pit-N	0	0	—	2	0	0	0	0	4	3	6.8	1	3	6.8	3	6.8	2.25	173	.200	.333	1	1	103	194	0.0	0	-0	0.1
■ **MIKE GARCIA**	Garcia, Edward Miguel "The Big Bear" b: 11/17/23, San Gabriel, Cal. d: 1/13/86, Fairview Park, O. BR/TR, 6'1", 195 lbs. Deb: 10/03/48																												
1948	Cle-A	0	0	—	1	0	0	0	0	2	3	13.5	0	0	0.0	1	4.5	0.00	—	.333	.333	1	1	94	0	0.0	0	0	0.1
1949	Cle-A	14	5	.737	41	20	8	5	2	176	154	7.9	6	60	3.1	94	4.8	**2.35**	**171**	.241	.301	36	33	96	**124**	3.9	3	1	3.7
1950	Cle-A	11	11	.500	33	29	11	0	0	184	191	9.3	15	74	3.6	76	3.7	3.86	113	.266	.330	15	10	95	105	-1.9	-1	2	1.1
1951	Cle-A	20	13	.606	47	30	15	1	6	254	239	8.5	10	82	2.9	118	4.2	3.15	121	.246	.304	27	19	93	97	0.1	1	1	2.0
1952	Cle-A	22	11	.667	46	36	19	**6**	4	292	284	8.8	9	87	2.7	143	4.4	2.37	136	.253	.306	42	28	88	**127**	3.2	-1	2	2.9

YEAR	TM/L	W	L	PCT	G	GS	CG	SHO	SV	IP	H	H/G	HR	BB	BB/G	SO	SO/G	ERA	/A	OAVG	OOBP	PR	/A	PF	CPI	WAT	PB	PD	TPI
1953	Cle-A	18	9	.667	38	35	21	3	0	272	260	8.6	18	81	2.7	134	4.4	3.24	114	.250	.304	23	14	93	100	2.7	4	-1	1.7
1954	Cle-A	19	8	.704	45	34	13	**5**	5	259	220	7.6	6	71	2.5	129	4.5	**2.64**	**143**	.229	**.278**	**31**	**32**	101	83	-0.3	-2	0	3.3
1955	Cle-A	11	13	.458	38	31	6	2	3	211	230	9.8	17	56	2.4	120	5.1	4.01	101	.278	.323	-1	1	102	98	-3.2	2	-1	0.1
1956	Cle-A	11	12	.478	35	30	8	4	0	198	213	9.7	18	74	3.4	119	5.4	3.77	109	.272	.334	8	7	99	110	-2.0	-3	-0	0.4
1957	Cle-A	12	8	.600	38	27	9	1	0	211	221	9.4	14	73	3.1	110	4.7	3.75	103	.269	.328	1	3	102	102	2.3	-1	-2	0.0
1958	Cle-A	1	0	1.000	6	1	0	0	0	8	15	16.9	2	7	7.9	2	2.3	9.00	39	.395	.500	-5	-5	93	122	0.5	-0	0	-0.4
1959	Cle-A	3	6	.333	29	8	1	0	1	72	72	9.0	4	31	3.9	49	6.1	4.00	92	.265	.332	-1	-3	95	98	-1.9	-1	0	-0.3
1960	Chi-A	0	0	—	15	0	0	0	2	18	23	11.5	2	10	5.0	8	4.0	4.50	85	.338	.402	-1	-1	99	147	0.0	0	0	0.0
1961	Was-A	0	1	.000	16	0	0	0	0	19	23	10.9	1	13	6.2	14	6.6	4.74	83	.287	.381	-2	-2	97	110	-0.4	0	-1	-0.1
Total	14	142	97	.594	428	281	111	27	23	2176	2148	8.9	122	719	3.0	1117	4.6	3.26	117	.257	.314	175	137	96	105	3.0	0	2	14.5
■ **MIGUEL GARCIA**	Garcia, Miguel Angel (Silfontes) b: 4/3/67, Caracas, Venez. BL/TL, 5'11", 173 lbs. Deb: 4/30/87																												
1987	Cal-A	0	0	—	1	0	0	0	0	2	3	13.5	0	3	13.5	0	0.0	13.50	33	.375	.545	-2	-2	100	72	0.0	0	0	-0.1
	Pit-N	0	0	—	1	0	0	0	0	1	0	0.0	0	0	0.0	0	0.0	0.00	—	.000	.000	0	0	105	0	0.0	0	0	0.0
1988	Pit-N	0	0	—	1	0	0	0	0	2	3	13.5	1	2	9.0	2	9.0	4.50	75	.375	.500	-0	-0	97	298	0.0	0	0	0.0
Total	2	0	0	—	3	0	0	0	0	5	6	10.8	1	5	9.0	2	3.6	7.20	55	.333	.480	-2	-2	100	148	0.0	0	0	-0.1
■ **RALPH GARCIA**	Garcia, Ralph b: 12/14/48, Los Angeles, Cal. BR/TR, 6', 195 lbs. Deb: 9/26/72																												
1972	SD-N	0	0	—	3	0	0	0	0	5	4	7.2	0	3	5.4	3	5.4	1.80	174	.211	.318	1	1	91	134	0.0	0	0	0.1
1974	SD-N	0	0	—	8	0	0	0	0	10	15	13.5	1	7	6.3	9	8.1	6.30	56	.357	.415	-3	-3	97	119	0.0	0	0	-0.2
Total	2	0	0	—	11	0	0	0	0	15	19	11.4	1	10	6.0	12	7.2	4.80	71	.311	.387	-2	-2	95	124	0.0	0	0	-0.1
■ **RAMON GARCIA**	Garcia, Ramon (Garcia) b: 3/5/24, La Esperanza, Cuba BR/TR, 5'10", 170 lbs. Deb: 4/19/48																												
1948	Was-A	0	0	—	4	0	0	0	0	4	11	24.8	0	4	9.0	2	4.5	15.75	29	.524	.615	-5	-5	107	97	0.0	0	0	-0.3
■ **ART GARDINER**	Gardiner, Arthur Cecil b: 12/26/1899, Brooklyn, N.Y. d: 10/21/54, Copiaque, N.Y. BR/TR, Deb: 9/25/23																												
1923	Phi-N	0	0	—	1	0	0	0	0	0	1	—	0	1	—	0	—	—	—	1.000	1.000	0	0	118	0	0.0	0	0	0.0
■ **GID GARDNER**	Gardner, Frank Washington b: 1859, E.Cambridge, Mass. d: 8/1/14, Cambridge, Mass. Deb: 8/23/1879																												
1879	Tro-N	0	2	.000	2	2	2	0	0	14	27	17.4	0	0	0.0	3	1.9	5.79	43	.411	.411	-5	-5	100	112	-0.9	-0	0	-0.3
1880	Cle-N	1	8	.111	9	9	9	0	0	77	80	9.4	2	20	2.3	21	2.5	2.57	90	.277	.323	-2	-2	97	122	-3.6	0	0	-0.1
1883	Bal-a	1	0	1.000	2	0	0	0	0	7	9	11.6	1	1	1.3	2	2.6	5.14	73	.318	.341	-1	-1	113	105	0.5	0	0	0.0
1884	CP-U	0	1	.000	1	1	0	0	0	6	10	15.0	0	1	1.5	4	6.0	6.00	50	.376	.399	-2	-2	100	102	-0.3	0	0	-0.2
1885	Bal-a	0	1	.000	1	1	1	0	0	9	16	16.0	2	6	6.0	3	3.0	10.00	36	.399	.477	-7	-6	109	99	-0.4	0	0	-0.4
Total	5	2	12	.143	15	13	12	0	0	113	142	11.3	5	28	2.2	33	2.6	3.90	65	.316	.356	-17	-17	100	117	-4.7	0	0	-1.0
■ **FRED GARDNER**	Gardner, Frederick b: Palmer, Mass. Deb: 8/09/1887																												
1887	Bal-a	0	1	.000	3	2	1	0	0	13	23	15.9	0	10	6.9	3	2.1	11.08	37	.400	.489	-10	-10	94	76	-0.4	0	0	-0.6
■ **HARRY GARDNER**	Gardner, Harry Ray b: 6/1/1887, Quincy, Mich. d: 8/2/61, Canby, Ore. TR, 6'2", 180 lbs. Deb: 4/17/11																												
1911	Pit-N	1	1	.500	13	3	2	0	2	42	39	8.4	2	20	4.3	24	5.1	4.50	74	.244	.335	-5	-6	97	74	0.0	0	-1	-0.5
1912	Pit-N	0	0	—	1	0	0	0	0	0	3	—	0	1	—	0	—	—	—	.500	.571	0	0	95	0	0.0	0	0	0.0
Total	2	1	1	.500	14	3	2	0	2	42	42	9.0	2	21	4.5	24	5.1	4.50	74	.253	.344	-5	-6	97	74	0.0	0	-1	-0.5
■ **JIM GARDNER**	Gardner, James Anderson b: 10/4/1874, Pittsburgh, Pa. d: 4/24/05, Pittsburgh, Pa. TR, Deb: 6/20/1895																												
1895	Pit-N	8	2	.800	11	10	8	0	0	85	99	10.5	1	27	2.9	31	3.3	2.65	174	.311	.365	20	19	96	153	2.9	1	0	1.6
1897	Pit-N	5	5	.500	14	11	8	0	0	95	115	10.9	4	32	3.0	35	3.3	5.21	83	.322	.378	-9	-9	100	85	0.4	-1	0	-0.8
1898	Pit-N	10	13	.435	25	22	19	1	0	185	179	8.7	3	48	2.3	41	2.0	3.21	110	.275	.325	8	7	98	88	-1.3	-1	0	0.4
1899	Pit-N	1	0	1.000	6	3	0	0	0	32	52	14.6	1	13	3.7	2	0.6	7.59	50	.391	.445	-13	-14	98	86	0.5	0	0	-1.0
1902	Chi-N	1	2	.333	3	3	2	0	0	25	23	8.3	0	10	3.6	6	2.2	2.88	92	.267	.343	-0	-1	95	95	-0.4	0	0	0.0
Total	5	25	22	.532	59	49	37	1	0	422	468	10.0	9	130	2.8	115	2.5	3.86	101	.303	.357	5	2	98	101	2.1	-1	0	0.2
■ **GLENN GARDNER**	Gardner, Miles Glenn b: 1/25/16, Burnsville, N.C. d: 7/7/64, Rochester, N.Y. BR/TR, 5'11", 180 lbs. Deb: 7/21/45																												
1945	StL-N	3	1	.750	17	4	2	1	1	55	50	8.2	2	27	4.4	20	3.3	3.27	113	.242	.325	3	3	97	103	0.7	2	-0	0.4
■ **ROB GARDNER**	Gardner, Richard Frank b: 12/19/44, Binghamton, N.Y. BR/TL, 6'1", 176 lbs. Deb: 9/01/65																												
1965	NY-N	0	2	.000	5	4	0	0	0	28	23	7.4	4	7	2.3	19	6.1	3.21	115	.217	.261	1	1	104	87	-0.9	-1	0	0.1
1966	NY-N	4	8	.333	41	17	3	0	1	134	147	9.9	15	64	4.3	74	5.0	5.10	68	.285	.358	-22	-24	97	98	-1.1	-0	0	-2.4
1967	Chi-N	0	2	.000	18	5	0	0	0	32	33	9.3	2	6	1.7	16	4.5	3.94	86	.260	.289	-2	-2	100	78	-0.9	-0	0	-0.1
1968	Cle-A	0	0	—	5	0	0	0	0	3	5	15.0	0	2	6.0	6	18.0	6.00	50	.417	.467	-1	-1	101	137	0.0	0	0	0.0
1970	NY-A	1	0	1.000	1	1	0	0	0	7	8	10.3	2	4	5.1	6	7.7	5.14	66	.276	.364	-1	-1	91	120	0.5	1	0	0.0
1971	Oak-A	0	0	—	4	1	0	0	0	8	8	9.0	1	3	3.4	5	5.6	2.25	152	.267	.324	1	1	99	187	0.0	0	0	0.2
	NY-A	0	0	—	2	0	0	0	0	3	3	9.0	0	2	6.0	2	6.0	3.00	112	.273	.385	0	0	97	141	0.0	0	0	0.0
	Yr	0	0	—	6	1	0	0	0	11	11	9.0	1	5	4.1	7	5.7	2.45	139	.268	.340	1	1	98	141	0.0	0	0	0.2
1972	NY-A	8	5	.615	20	14	1	0	0	97	91	8.4	9	28	2.6	58	5.4	3.06	92	.243	.292	0	-3	92	100	1.5	-1	-1	-0.4
1973	Oak-A	0	0	—	3	0	0	0	0	7	10	12.9	2	4	5.1	2	2.6	5.14	64	.370	.438	-1	-1	86	172	0.0	-0	-0	-0.1
	Mil-A	1	1	.500	10	0	0	0	1	13	17	11.8	0	13	9.0	5	3.5	9.69	38	.327	.463	-8	-9	96	71	0.1	0	0	-0.7
	Yr	1	1	.500	13	0	0	0	1	20	27	12.1	2	17	7.6	7	3.1	8.10	44	.342	.455	-10	-10	92	71	0.1	0	0	-0.8
Total	8	14	18	.438	109	42	4	0	2	332	345	9.4	35	133	3.6	193	5.2	4.34	76	.269	.333	-34	-39	96	99	-0.8	-1	0	-3.4
■ **WES GARDNER**	Gardner, Wesley Brian b: 4/29/61, Benton, Ark. BR/TR, 6'4", 197 lbs. Deb: 7/29/84																												
1984	NY-N	1	1	.500	21	0	0	0	1	25	34	12.2	0	8	2.9	19	6.8	6.48	56	.321	.362	-8	-8	100	72	0.0	-0	0	-0.7
1985	NY-N	0	2	.000	9	0	0	0	0	12	18	13.5	1	8	6.0	11	8.3	5.25	65	.375	.426	-2	-2	95	149	-0.9	0	0	-0.1
1986	Bos-A	0	0	—	1	0	0	0	0	1	1	9.0	0	0	0.0	1	9.0	9.00	46	.333	.250	-1	-1	99	47	0.0	0	0	0.0
1987	Bos-A	3	6	.333	49	1	0	0	10	90	98	9.8	17	42	4.2	70	7.0	5.40	82	.279	.354	-9	-10	99	102	-1.3	0	-1	-1.0
1988	Bos-A	8	6	.571	36	18	1	0	2	149	119	7.2	17	64	3.9	106	6.4	3.50	122	.220	.300	8	13	108	95	0.4	0	-0	1.3
Total	5	12	15	.444	116	19	1	0	13	277	270	8.8	35	122	4.0	207	6.7	4.48	95	.257	.330	-12	-8	104	97	-1.8	-0	-1	-0.5
■ **BILL GARFIELD**	Garfield, William Milton b: 10/26/1867, Sheffield, Ohio d: 12/16/41, Danville, Ill. BR/TR, 5'11.5", 160 lbs. Deb: 7/10/1889																												
1889	Pit-N	0	2	.000	4	2	2	0	0	29	45	14.0	2	17	5.3	4	1.2	7.76	47	.371	.449	-12	-13	90	92	-0.9	-2	0	-1.1
1890	Cle-N	1	7	.125	9	8	7	0	0	70	91	11.7	3	35	4.5	16	2.1	4.89	71	.331	.407	-10	-11	97	109	-2.5	-1	0	-0.9
Total	2	1	9	.100	13	10	9	0	0	99	136	12.4	5	52	4.7	20	1.8	5.73	61	.344	.420	-22	-24	95	104	-3.4	-3	0	-2.0
■ **BOB GARIBALDI**	Garibaldi, Robert Roy b: 3/3/42, Stockton, Cal. BL/TR, 6'4", 210 lbs. Deb: 7/15/62																												
1962	SF-N	0	0	—	9	0	0	0	1	12	13	9.8	1	5	3.8	9	6.8	5.25	74	.265	.327	-2	-2	99	74	0.0	-0	0	-0.1
1963	SF-N	0	1	.000	4	0	0	0	1	8	8	9.0	0	4	4.5	4	4.5	1.13	275	.276	.382	2	2	94	381	-0.4	-0	0	0.2
1966	SF-N	0	0	—	1	0	0	0	0	1	1	9.0	0	0	0.0	0	0.0	0.00	—	.250	.250	0	0	97	0	0.0	0	0	0.0
1969	SF-N	0	1	.000	1	1	0	0	0	5	6	10.8	0	2	3.6	1	1.8	1.80	200	.316	.364	1	1	100	262	-0.4	-0	0	0.1
Total	4	0	2	.000	15	1	0	0	2	26	28	9.7	1	11	3.8	14	4.8	3.12	115	.277	.348	2	1	97	202	-0.8	-0	0	0.2
■ **LOU GARLAND**	Garland, Louis Lyman b: 7/16/05, Archie, Mo. BR/TR, 6'2.5", 200 lbs. Deb: 8/31/31																												
1931	Chi-A	0	2	.000	7	2	0	0	0	17	30	15.9	2	14	7.4	4	2.1	10.06	42	.400	.489	-11	-11	96	100	-0.9	-0	1	-0.9
■ **WAYNE GARLAND**	Garland, Marcus Wayne b: 10/26/50, Nashville, Tenn. BR/TR, 6', 195 lbs. Deb: 9/13/73																												
1973	Bal-A	0	1	.000	4	1	0	0	0	16	14	7.9	1	7	3.9	10	5.6	3.94	102	.233	.309	-0	0	105	77	-0.4	0	-0	0.0
1974	Bal-A	5	5	.500	20	6	0	0	1	91	68	6.7	5	26	2.6	40	4.0	2.97	113	.211	.269	7	4	92	74	-0.5	0	-1	0.3
1975	Bal-A	2	5	.286	29	1	0	0	4	87	80	8.3	7	31	3.2	46	4.8	3.72	91	.252	.312	1	-3	89	95	-1.7	0	-0	-0.3
1976	Bal-A	20	7	.741	38	25	14	4	1	232	224	8.7	10	64	2.5	113	4.4	2.68	128	.255	.301	22	19	97	116	**6.4**	0	2	2.3
1977	Cle-A	13	19	.406	38	38	21	1	0	283	281	8.9	23	88	2.8	118	3.8	3.59	111	.261	.313	15	13	98	100	-1.4	0	-0	1.2
1978	Cle-A	2	3	.400	6	6	0	0	0	30	43	12.9	6	16	4.8	13	3.9	7.80	45	.347	.417	-13	-14	94	97	-0.1	0	0	-1.2
1979	Cle-A	4	10	.286	18	14	2	0	0	95	120	11.4	11	34	3.2	40	3.8	5.21	86	.318	.364	-10	-8	106	109	-3.1	0	-1	-0.7
1980	Cle-A	6	9	.400	25	20	4	1	0	150	163	9.8	18	48	2.9	55	3.3	4.62	90	.276	.330	-10	-8	103	95	-1.4	0	-1	-0.8

YEAR	TM/L	W	L	PCT	G	GS	CG	SHO	SV	IP	H	H/G	HR	BB	BB/G	SO	SO/G	ERA	/A	OAVG	OOBP	PR	/A	PF	CPI	WAT	PB	PD	TPI
1981	Cle-A	3	7	.300	12	10	2	1	0	56	89	14.3	8	14	2.3	15	2.4	5.79	59	.374	.390	-13	-15	93	124	-2.1	0	0	-1.3
Total	9	55	66	.455	190	121	43	7	6	1040	1082	9.4	89	328	2.8	450	3.9	3.89	97	.272	.322	-3	-12	98	102	-4.3	0	-1	-0.5
■ **MIKE GARMAN**	Garman, Michael Douglas b: 9/16/49, Caldwell, Idaho BR/TR, 6'3", 195 lbs. Deb: 9/22/69																												
1969	Bos-A	1	0	1.000	2	2	0	0	0	12	13	9.8	0	10	7.5	10	7.5	4.50	84	.277	.404	-1	-1	105	106	0.5	1	0	0.0
1971	Bos-A	1	1	.500	3	3	0	0	0	19	15	7.1	3	9	4.3	6	2.8	3.79	96	.217	.313	-1	-0	105	97	0.0	0	-1	0.0
1972	Bos-A	0	1	.000	3	1	0	0	0	3	4	12.0	1	2	6.0	1	3.0	12.00	27	.286	.375	-3	-3	105	59	-0.4	0	0	-0.2
1973	Bos-A	0	0	—	12	0	0	0	0	22	32	13.1	1	15	6.1	9	3.7	5.32	75	.352	.431	-4	-3	105	128	0.0	0	-0	-0.2
1974	StL-N	7	2	.778	64	0	0	0	6	82	66	7.2	4	27	3.0	45	4.9	2.63	142	.227	.290	9	10	103	101	2.4	-1	0	1.0
1975	StL-N	3	8	.273	66	0	0	0	10	79	73	8.3	3	48	5.5	48	5.5	2.39	157	.245	.341	11	12	103	152	-2.5	-0	-1	1.1
1976	Chi-N	2	4	.333	47	2	0	0	1	76	79	9.4	7	35	4.1	37	4.4	4.97	78	.273	.345	-12	-9	111	91	-0.8	-1	0	-0.9
1977	LA-N	4	4	.500	49	0	0	0	12	63	60	8.6	7	22	3.1	29	4.1	2.71	141	.254	.318	8	8	98	142	-0.6	-1	-0	0.7
1978	LA-N	0	1	.000	10	0	0	0	0	16	15	8.4	3	3	1.7	5	2.8	4.50	77	.259	.286	-2	-2	97	91	-0.4	0	-0	-0.1
	Mon-N	4	6	.400	47	0	0	0	13	61	54	8.0	5	31	4.6	23	3.4	4.43	77	.238	.323	-6	-7	96	81	-0.7	-1	-0	-0.7
	Yr	4	7	.364	57	0	0	0	13	77	69	8.1	8	34	4.0	28	3.3	4.44	77	.242	.316	-7	-9	96	81	-1.1	0	-0	-0.8
Total	9	22	27	.449	303	8	0	0	42	433	411	8.5	34	202	4.2	213	4.4	3.64	103	.254	.331	0	5	103	112	-2.5	-2	-2	0.7
■ **WILLIE GARONI**	Garoni, William b: 7/28/1877, Ft.Lee, N.J. d: 9/9/14, Ft.Lee, N.J. 6'1", 165 lbs. Deb: 9/07/1899																												
1899	NY-N	0	1	.000	3	1	1	0	0	10	12	10.8	0	2	1.8	2	1.8	4.50	85	.322	.356	-1	-1	99	81	-0.4	-1	0	0.0
■ **SCOTT GARRELTS**	Garrelts, Scott William b: 10/30/61, Urbana, Ill. BR/TR, 6'4", 195 lbs. Deb: 10/02/82																												
1982	SF-N	0	0	—	1	0	0	0	0	2	3	13.5	0	2	9.0	4	18.0	13.50	25	.333	.455	-2	-2	94	51	0.0	0	0	-0.1
1983	SF-N	2	2	.500	5	5	1	1	0	36	33	8.3	4	19	4.8	16	4.0	2.50	147	.254	.351	5	5	101	178	0.0	0	0	0.6
1984	SF-N	2	3	.400	21	3	0	0	0	43	45	9.4	6	34	7.1	32	6.7	5.65	62	.274	.388	-10	-10	98	103	0.0	-0	-0	-1.0
1985	SF-N	9	6	.600	74	0	0	0	13	106	76	6.5	2	58	4.9	106	9.0	2.29	149	.198	.302	15	13	95	101	2.8	1	2	1.7
1986	SF-N	13	9	.591	53	18	2	0	10	174	144	7.4	17	74	3.8	125	6.5	3.10	114	.231	.307	12	8	95	110	2.0	2	2	1.2
1987	SF-N	11	7	.611	64	0	0	0	12	106	70	5.9	10	55	4.7	127	10.8	3.23	120	.192	.292	10	8	95	87	1.2	0	-0	0.7
1988	SF-N	5	9	.357	65	0	0	0	13	98	80	7.3	3	46	4.2	86	7.9	3.58	90	.226	.310	-1	-4	93	83	-2.2	-1	-0	-0.5
Total	7	42	36	.538	283	26	3	1	48	565	451	7.2	42	288	4.6	496	7.9	3.25	108	.222	.314	29	17	95	103	3.8	2	3	2.6
■ **CLARENCE GARRETT**	Garrett, Clarence Raymond "Laz" b: 3/6/1891, Reader, W.Va. d: 2/11/77, Moundsville, W.Va. BR/TR, 6'5.5", 185 lbs. Deb: 9/13/15																												
1915	Cle-A	2	2	.500	4	4	2	0	0	23	19	7.4	1	6	2.3	5	2.0	2.35	133	.224	.283	2	2	106	93	0.4	-0	1	0.3
■ **GREG GARRETT**	Garrett, Gregory b: 3/12/48, Atascadero, Cal. BB/TL, 6', 200 lbs. Deb: 4/24/70																												
1970	Cal-A	5	6	.455	32	7	0	0	0	75	48	5.8	6	44	5.3	53	6.4	2.64	129	.190	.306	9	6	92	107	-0.7	-1	-0	0.6
1971	Cin-N	0	1	.000	2	1	0	0	0	9	7	7.0	0	10	10.0	2	2.0	1.00	334	.250	.436	2	2	96	517	-0.4	0	0	0.3
Total	2	5	7	.417	34	8	0	0	0	84	55	5.9	6	54	5.8	55	5.9	2.46	138	.196	.321	11	9	92	151	-1.1	-0	-0	0.9
■ **CLIFF GARRISON**	Garrison, Clifford William b: 8/13/05, Belmont, Okla. BR/TR, 6', 180 lbs. Deb: 4/16/28																												
1928	Bos-A	0	0	—	6	0	0	0	0	16	22	12.4	2	6	3.4	0	0.0	7.88	52	.361	.384	-7	-7	101	88	0.0	-0	1	-0.5
■ **JIM GARRY**	Garry, James Thomas b: 9/21/1869, Great Barrington, Mass d: 1/15/17, Pittsfield, Mass. Deb: 5/02/1893																												
1893	Bos-N	0	1	.000	1	0	0	0	0	1	5	45.0	0	4	36.0	2	18.0	63.00	7	.655	.774	-6	-6	101	53	-0.4	-0	0	-0.3
■ **NED GARVER**	Garver, Ned Franklin b: 12/25/25, Ney, Ohio BR/TR, 5'10.5", 180 lbs. Deb: 4/28/48																												
1948	StL-A	7	11	.389	38	24	7	0	5	198	200	9.1	14	95	4.3	75	3.4	3.41	137	.268	.349	19	28	109	129	0.1	4	1	3.4
1949	StL-A	12	17	.414	41	32	16	1	3	224	245	9.8	14	102	4.1	70	2.8	3.98	110	.277	.347	5	10	104	108	1.9	2	-0	1.2
1950	StL-A	13	18	.419	37	31	**22**	2	0	260	264	9.1	18	108	3.7	85	2.9	3.39	**149**	.264	.335	**34**	**49**	111	**119**	1.3	4	2	**5.8**
1951	StL-A	20	12	.625	33	30	**24**	1	0	246	237	8.7	17	96	3.5	84	3.1	3.73	121	.255	.324	11	21	109	100	**7.9**	7	1	3.2
1952	StL-A	7	10	.412	21	21	7	2	0	149	130	7.9	14	55	3.3	60	3.6	3.68	99	.235	.308	-0	-0	100	90	0.0	1	0	0.0
	Det-A	1	0	1.000	1	1	1	0	0	9	9	9.0	1	3	3.0	3	3.0	2.00	189	.265	.324	2	2	103	201	0.5	0	0	0.3
	Yr	8	10	.444	22	22	8	2	0	158	139	7.9	15	58	3.3	63	3.6	3.59	102	.235	.303	2	1	100	201	0.5	1	0	0.3
1953	Det-A	11	11	.500	30	26	13	0	1	198	228	10.4	16	66	3.0	69	3.1	4.45	91	.290	.341	-10	-9	102	101	2.3	-1	1	-0.7
1954	Det-A	14	11	.560	35	32	16	3	1	246	216	7.9	20	62	2.3	93	3.4	2.82	134	.236	.281	25	26	101	98	3.0	-0	2	2.9
1955	Det-A	12	16	.429	33	32	16	1	0	231	251	9.8	21	67	2.6	83	3.2	3.97	94	.279	.326	-0	-6	95	104	-2.6	5	0	0.0
1956	Det-A	0	2	.000	6	3	1	0	0	18	15	7.5	2	13	6.5	6	3.0	4.00	99	.234	.363	0	-0	95	114	-0.9	-0	1	0.0
1957	KC-A	6	13	.316	24	23	6	1	0	145	120	7.4	13	55	3.4	61	3.8	3.85	100	.223	.296	-1	-0	102	76	-1.8	0	-0	0.0
1958	KC-A	12	11	.522	31	28	10	3	1	201	192	8.6	24	66	3.0	72	3.2	4.03	100	.244	.301	-6	0	107	86	1.2	0	5	0.6
1959	KC-A	10	13	.435	32	30	9	2	1	201	214	9.6	22	42	1.9	61	2.7	3.72	107	.270	.305	3	6	103	103	0.1	7	-1	1.2
1960	KC-A	4	9	.308	28	15	5	2	0	122	110	8.1	15	35	2.6	50	3.7	3.84	102	.240	.288	0	1	101	86	-1.2	-1	-0	0.0
1961	LA-A	0	3	.000	12	2	0	0	0	29	40	12.4	2	16	5.0	9	2.8	5.59	81	.348	.418	-5	-3	112	119	-1.4	-1	1	-0.2
Total	14	129	157	.451	402	330	153	18	12	2477	2471	9.0	213	881	3.2	881	3.2	3.73	112	.260	.321	78	121	104	102	10.4	26	13	17.7
■ **JERRY GARVIN**	Garvin, Theodore Jared b: 10/21/55, Oakland, Cal. BL/TL, 6'3", 195 lbs. Deb: 4/10/77																												
1977	Tor-A	10	18	.357	34	34	12	1	0	245	247	9.1	33	85	3.1	127	4.7	4.19	102	.264	.321	-3	2	105	101	0.6	0	5	0.7
1978	Tor-A	4	12	.250	26	22	3	0	0	145	189	11.7	20	48	3.0	67	4.2	5.52	70	.319	.367	-28	-27	102	103	-2.6	0	1	-2.4
1979	Tor-A	0	1	.000	8	1	0	0	0	23	15	5.9	2	10	3.9	14	5.5	2.74	163	.197	.297	4	4	106	108	-0.4	0	-0	0.4
1980	Tor-A	4	7	.364	61	0	0	0	8	83	70	7.6	6	27	2.9	52	5.6	2.28	180	.233	.289	16	17	101	126	-0.6	0	1	1.7
1981	Tor-A	1	2	.333	35	4	0	0	0	53	46	7.8	3	23	3.9	25	4.2	3.40	122	.240	.312	2	4	113	97	0.0	0	0	0.5
1982	Tor-A	1	1	.500	32	4	0	0	0	58	81	12.6	10	26	4.0	35	5.4	7.29	61	.335	.394	-21	-18	109	94	0.0	0	2	-1.5
Total	6	20	41	.328	196	65	15	1	8	607	648	9.6	74	219	3.2	320	4.7	4.42	94	.277	.335	-30	-17	105	104	-3.0	0	9	-0.6
■ **NED GARVIN**	Garvin, Virgil Lee b: 1/1/1874, Navasota, Tex. d: 6/16/08, Fresno, Cal. TR , 6'3.5", 160 lbs. Deb: 7/13/1896																												
1896	Phi-N	0	1	.000	2	1	1	0	0	13	19	13.2	0	7	4.8	4	2.8	7.62	59	.364	.440	-5	-5	102	78	-0.4	-1	0	-0.3
1899	Chi-N	9	13	.409	24	23	22	4	0	199	202	9.1	1	42	1.9	69	3.1	2.85	129	.286	.326	22	18	96	99	-2.3	-4	0	1.3
1900	Chi-N	10	18	.357	30	28	25	1	0	246	225	8.2	4	63	2.3	107	3.9	2.41	145	.265	.316	**35**	29	94	106	-3.7	-4	4	2.7
1901	Mil-A	7	20	.259	37	27	22	1	2	257	258	9.0	4	90	3.2	122	**4.3**	3.47	104	.281	.345	6	4	98	94	-4.0	-9	3	0.6
1902	Chi-A	10	10	.500	23	19	16	2	0	175	169	8.7	3	43	2.2	55	2.8	2.21	152	.277	.325	26	22	94	**128**	-1.0	-2	3	2.5
	Bro-N	1	1	.500	2	2	2	1	0	18	15	7.5	0	4	2.0	7	3.5	1.00	260	.248	.294	4	3	94	182	0.0	-0	0	0.4
1903	Bro-N	15	18	.455	38	34	30	2	2	298	277	8.4	2	84	2.5	154	4.7	3.08	108	.273	.336	6	8	102	87	-2.4	-8	7	1.5
1904	Bro-N	5	15	.250	23	22	16	2	0	182	141	7.0	6	78	3.9	86	4.3	1.68	159	.238	.332	21	20	98	**153**	-3.4	-3	3	2.6
	NY-A	0	1	.000	2	2	0	0	0	12	14	10.5	0	2	1.5	8	6.0	2.25	128	.316	.345	0	1	111	158	-0.4	-1	1	0.2
Total	7	57	97	.370	181	158	134	13	4	1400	1320	8.5	20	413	2.7	612	3.9	2.72	124	.272	.332	116	102	97	109	-17.6	-34	22	11.5
■ **HARRY GASPAR**	Gaspar, Harry Lambert b: 4/28/1883, Kingsley, Iowa d: 5/14/40, Orange, Cal. BR/TR, 6', 180 lbs. Deb: 09																												
1909	Cin-N	19	11	.633	44	29	19	4	2	260	228	7.9	0	57	2.0	65	2.3	2.01	121	.242	.291	17	12	94	108	4.6	-3	-5	0.8
1910	Cin-N	15	17	.469	48	31	16	4	**7**	275	257	8.4	6	75	2.5	74	2.4	2.59	120	.255	.317	14	16	102	110	-0.7	-3	-2	1.1
1911	Cin-N	11	17	.393	44	32	11	2	4	254	272	9.6	9	69	2.4	76	2.7	3.30	95	.283	.340	3	-5	92	115	-2.2	-2	-1	-0.8
1912	Cin-N	1	3	.250	7	6	2	0	0	37	38	9.2	0	16	3.9	13	3.2	4.14	77	.266	.344	-3	-4	93	77	-0.9	0	-0	-0.3
Total	4	46	48	.489	143	98	48	10	13	826	795	8.7	15	217	2.4	228	2.5	2.69	108	.260	.318	31	20	96	110	0.8	-8	-8	0.8
■ **CHARLIE GASSAWAY**	Gassaway, Charles Cason "Sheriff" b: 8/12/18, Gassaway, Tenn. BL/TL, 6'2.5", 210 lbs. Deb: 9/25/44																												
1944	Chi-N	0	1	.000	2	2	0	0	0	12	20	15.0	3	10	7.5	7	5.3	7.50	48	.385	.484	-5	-5	100	134	-0.4	0	-0	-0.4
1945	Phi-A	4	7	.364	24	11	4	0	0	118	114	8.7	4	55	4.2	50	3.8	3.74	87	.252	.333	-5	-6	96	93	0.2	-2	-1	-0.9
1946	Cle-A	1	1	.500	13	6	0	0	0	51	54	9.5	2	26	4.6	23	4.1	3.88	82	.273	.359	-2	-4	90	111	0.1	-1	0	-0.4
Total	3	5	9	.357	39	19	4	0	0	181	188	9.3	9	91	4.5	80	4.0	4.03	81	.268	.352	-12	-16	95	101	-0.1	-2	-2	-1.7
■ **MILT GASTON**	Gaston, Nathaniel Milton b: 1/27/1896, Ridgefield Park, N.J. BR/TR, 6'1", 185 lbs. Deb: 4/20/24																												
1924	NY-A	5	3	.625	29	2	0	0	1	86	92	9.6	3	44	4.6	24	2.5	4.50	91	.286	.364	-3	-4	97	103	0.4	-1	-1	-0.5
1925	StL-A	15	14	.517	42	30	16	0	1	239	284	10.7	8	101	3.8	84	3.2	4.41	107	.305	.366	-0	9	108	108	-0.5	2	-2	0.9
1926	StL-A	10	18	.357	32	28	14	1	0	214	227	9.5	13	101	4.2	39	1.6	4.33	96	.283	.351	-7	-4	103	104	-1.8	-2	-1	-0.5

YEAR	TM/L	W	L	PCT	G	GS	CG	SHO	SV	IP	H	H/G	HR	BB	BB/G	SO	SO/G	ERA	/A	OAVG	OOBP	PR	/A	PF	CPI	WAT	PB	PD	TPI
1927	StL-A	13	17	.433	37	30	21	0	1	254	275	9.7	18	100	3.5	77	2.7	5.00	90	.281	.338	-24	-13	109	86	1.4	5	0	-0.6
1928	Was-A	6	12	.333	28	22	8	3	0	149	179	10.8	3	53	3.2	45	2.7	5.50	75	.302	.349	-24	-23	101	80	-3.0	-3	1	-2.2
1929	Bos-A	12	19	.387	39	29	20	1	2	244	265	9.8	15	81	3.0	83	3.1	3.73	120	.289	.339	14	20	105	117	0.3	0	-2	1.8
1930	Bos-A	13	20	.394	38	34	20	2	2	273	272	9.0	15	98	3.2	99	3.3	3.92	114	.259	.315	22	16	96	95	1.7	-3	1	1.2
1931	Bos-A	2	13	.133	23	18	4	0	0	119	137	10.4	4	41	3.1	33	2.5	4.46	95	.291	.338	-1	-3	97	101	-5.1	-2	-0	-0.4
1932	Chi-A	7	17	.292	28	25	7	1	1	167	183	9.9	10	73	3.9	44	2.4	3.99	102	.279	.346	9	1	91	115	-1.3	2	1	0.4
1933	Chi-A	8	12	.400	30	25	7	1	0	167	177	9.5	9	60	3.2	39	2.1	4.85	91	.272	.329	-11	-8	103	85	-1.1	-1	-1	-0.8
1934	Chi-A	6	19	.240	29	28	10	1	0	194	247	11.5	16	84	3.9	48	2.2	5.85	79	.313	.371	-29	-26	103	96	-4.3	-3	3	-2.2
Total	11	97	164	.372	355	271	127	10	8	2106	2338	10.0	114	836	3.6	615	2.6	4.55	97	.287	.345	-54	-34	102	99	-13.3	-4	-1	-2.9
■ **WELCOME GASTON** Gaston, Welcome Thornburg b: 12/19/1872, Guernsey Co., Ohio d: 12/13/44, Columbus, Ohio TL , Deb: 10/06/1898																													
1898	Bro-N	1	1	.500	2	2	2	0	0	16	17	9.6	0	9	5.1	0	0.0	2.81	124	.294	.389	1	1	96	142	0.2	-0	0	0.1
1899	Bro-N	0	0	—	1	0	0	0	0	3	3	9.0	0	4	12.0	0	0.0	3.00	131	.283	.480	0	0	102	194	0.0	1	0	0.1
Total	2	1	1	.500	3	2	2	0	0	19	20	9.5	0	13	6.2	0	0.0	2.84	125	.292	.405	2	1	97	151	0.2	1	0	0.2
■ **HANK GASTRIGHT** Gastright, Henry Carl (born Henry Carl Gastreich) b: 3/29/1865, Covington, Ky. d: 10/9/37, Cold Springs, Ky. BR/TR, 6'2", 190 lbs. Deb: 4/19/1889																													
1889	Col-a	10	16	.385	32	26	21	0	0	223	255	10.3	8	104	4.2	115	4.6	4.60	77	.303	.379	-19	-26	92	97	-1.7	-3	0	-2.4
1890	Col-a	30	14	.682	48	45	41	4	0	401	312	7.0	8	135	3.0	199	4.5	2.94	126	.229	.298	41	34	96	84	6.6	2	-4	2.9
1891	Col-a	12	19	.387	35	33	28	1	0	284	280	8.9	7	136	4.3	109	3.5	3.80	88	.272	.357	-3	-14	90	91	-2.4	3	0	-1.0
1892	Was-N	3	3	.500	11	7	6	0	0	80	94	10.6	3	38	4.3	32	3.6	5.17	67	.306	.383	-17	-15	106	88	0.6	0	0	-1.2
1893	Pit-N	3	1	.750	9	5	3	0	0	59	74	11.3	3	39	5.9	12	1.8	6.25	78	.323	.422	-10	-9	105	93	0.7	-4	0	-0.9
	Bos-N	12	4	.750	19	18	16	0	0	156	179	10.3	9	76	4.4	27	1.6	5.13	92	.304	.383	-8	-7	101	95	2.2	-2	0	-0.7
	Yr	15	5	**.750**	28	23	19	0	0	215	253	10.6	12	115	4.8	39	1.6	5.44	87	.309	.394	-18	-16	102	95	2.9	-4	0	-1.6
1894	Bro-N	2	6	.250	16	8	6	1	2	93	135	13.1	1	55	5.3	20	1.9	6.39	79	.362	.445	-11	-14	94	98	-2.1	-3	0	-1.2
1896	Cin-N	0	0	—	1	0	0	0	0	6	8	12.0	0	1	1.5	0	0.0	4.50	100	.343	.370	-0	0	103	95	0.0	-0	0	0.0
Total	7	72	63	.533	171	142	121	6	2	1302	1337	9.2	39	584	4.0	514	3.6	4.22	91	.281	.360	-26	-52	95	91	3.9	-7	-4	-4.5
■ **AUBREY GATEWOOD** Gatewood, Aubrey Lee b: 11/17/38, Little Rock, Ark. BR/TR, 6'1", 170 lbs. Deb: 9/11/63																													
1963	LA-A	1	1	.500	4	3	1	0	0	24	12	4.5	0	16	6.0	13	4.9	1.50	224	.148	.280	6	5	92	99	0.1	-1	0	0.4
1964	LA-A	3	3	.500	15	7	0	0	0	60	59	8.9	4	12	1.8	25	3.8	2.25	143	.258	.294	9	6	89	139	0.0	-1	-0	0.5
1965	Cal-A	4	5	.444	46	3	0	0	0	92	91	8.9	5	37	3.6	37	3.6	3.42	99	.266	.328	0	-0	98	113	-0.1	1	-0	0.0
1970	Atl-N	0	0	—	3	0	0	0	0	2	4	18.0	0	2	9.0	0	0.0	4.50	94	.364	.500	-0	-0	105	216	0.0	0	0	0.0
Total	4	8	9	.471	68	13	1	0	0	178	166	8.4	9	67	3.4	75	3.8	2.78	120	.250	.314	15	11	94	121	0.0	-1	-1	0.9
■ **CHIPPY GAW** Gaw, George Joseph b: 3/13/1892, W.Newton, Mass. d: 5/26/68, Boston, Mass. BR/TR, 5'11", 180 lbs. Deb: 4/20/20																													
1920	Chi-N	1	1	.500	6	1	0	0	0	13	16	11.1	1	3	2.1	4	2.8	4.85	64	.320	.345	-2	-3	99	99	0.0	-0	-0	-0.2
■ **DALE GEAR** Gear, Dale Dudley b: 2/2/1872, Lone Elm, Kan. d: 9/23/51, Topeka, Kan. 5'11", 165 lbs. Deb: 8/15/1896																													
1896	Cle-N	0	2	.000	3	2	2	0	0	23	35	13.7	1	6	2.3	6	2.3	5.48	86	.374	.412	-3	-2	108	106	-0.9	2	0	0.0
1901	Was-A	4	11	.267	24	16	14	1	1	163	199	11.0	9	22	1.2	35	1.9	4.03	91	.322	.345	-7	-6	100	100	-3.2	0	1	-0.5
Total	2	4	13	.235	27	18	16	1	1	186	234	11.3	10	28	1.4	41	2.0	4.21	90	.329	.354	-10	-9	101	101	-4.1	2	1	-0.5
■ **DINTY GEARIN** Gearin, Dennis John b: 10/15/1897, Providence, R.I. d: 3/11/59, Providence, R.I. BL/TL, 5'4", 148 lbs. Deb: 8/06/23																													
1923	NY-N	1	1	.500	6	2	1	0	0	24	23	8.6	1	10	3.8	9	3.4	3.38	117	.264	.327	2	2	99	109	-0.1	0	-0	0.1
1924	NY-N	1	2	.333	6	3	2	0	0	29	30	9.3	3	16	5.0	4	1.2	2.48	136	.275	.357	4	3	88	193	-0.6	1	-0	0.3
	Bos-N	0	1	.000	1	1	0	0	0	⅓	3	81.0	0	2	54.0	0	0.0	135.00	—	1.000	1.000	-5	-5	99	46	-0.4	0	0	-0.3
	Yr	1	3	.250	7	4	2	0	0	29	33	10.2	3	18	5.6	4	1.2	4.03	84	.295	.381	-1	-2	88	46	-1.0	1	-0	0.0
Total	2	2	4	.333	13	6	3	0	0	53	56	9.5	4	28	4.8	13	2.2	3.74	97	.281	.357	1	-1	92	155	-1.1	1	-0	0.1
■ **BOB GEARY** Geary, Robert Norton "Speed" b: 5/10/1891, Cincinnati, Ohio d: 1/3/80, Cincinnati, Ohio BR/TR, 5'11", 168 lbs. Deb: 4/25/18																													
1918	Phi-A	2	5	.286	16	7	6	2	4	87	94	9.7	0	31	3.2	22	2.3	2.69	111	.289	.348	1	3	108	135	-1.0	-1	-1	0.2
1919	Phi-A	0	3	.000	9	2	1	0	0	32	32	9.0	1	18	5.1	9	2.5	4.78	76	.264	.360	-6	-4	112	78	-1.4	2	0	-0.1
1921	Cin-N	1	1	.500	10	1	0	0	0	29	38	11.8	1	2	0.6	10	3.1	4.34	88	.333	.323	-2	-2	101	101	0.1	-0	-0	-0.1
Total	3	3	9	.250	35	10	7	2	4	148	164	10.0	2	51	3.1	41	2.5	3.47	95	.293	.345	-7	-3	107	116	-2.3	1	-1	0.0
■ **BOB GEBHARD** Gebhard, Robert Henry b: 1/3/43, Lamberton, Minn. BR/TR, 6'2", 210 lbs. Deb: 8/02/71 C																													
1971	Min-A	1	2	.333	17	0	0	0	0	18	17	8.5	0	11	5.5	13	6.5	3.00	120	.243	.341	1	1	104	112	-0.3	0	1	0.2
1972	Min-A	0	1	.000	13	0	0	0	1	21	36	15.4	3	13	5.6	13	5.6	8.57	38	.371	.440	-13	-12	107	98	-0.4	0	1	-1.1
1974	Mon-N	0	0	—	1	0	0	0	0	2	5	22.5	1	0	0.0	0	0.0	4.50	84	.500	.455	-0	-0	104	310	0.0	0	0	0.0
Total	3	1	3	.250	31	0	0	0	1	41	58	12.7	4	24	5.3	26	5.7	5.93	58	.328	.401	-12	-11	106	114	-0.7	0	1	-0.9
■ **PETE GEBRIAN** Gebrian, Peter "Gabe" b: 8/10/23, Bayonne, N.J. BR/TR, 6', 170 lbs. Deb: 5/06/47																													
1947	Chi-A	2	3	.400	27	4	0	0	5	66	61	8.3	7	33	4.5	17	2.3	4.50	81	.247	.333	-6	-6	99	91	-0.2	-2	-1	-0.8
■ **JIM GEDDES** Geddes, James Lee b: 3/23/49, Columbus, Ohio BR/TR, 6'2", 200 lbs. Deb: 4/28/72																													
1972	Chi-A	0	0	—	5	1	0	0	0	10	12	10.8	1	10	9.0	3	2.7	7.20	45	.293	.442	-5	-4	106	93	0.0	-0	-0	-0.4
1973	Chi-A	0	0	—	6	1	0	0	0	16	14	7.9	0	14	7.9	7	3.9	2.81	140	.255	.425	2	2	103	178	0.0	0	0	0.2
Total	2	0	0	—	11	2	0	0	0	26	26	9.0	1	24	8.3	10	3.5	4.50	82	.271	.432	-3	-2	104	145	0.0	-0	0	-0.2
■ **JOE GEDEON** Gedeon, Elmer Joseph b: 12/5/1893, Sacramento, Cal. d: 5/19/41, San Francisco, Cal BR/TR, 6', 167 lbs. Deb: 5/13/13																													
1913	Was-A	0	0	—	1	0	0	0	1	0	0	—	0	0	—	0	—	—	—	.000	.000	0	0	105	0	0.0	0	0	0.0
■ **COUNT GEDNEY** Gedney, Alfred W., b: 5/10/1849, Brooklyn, N.Y. d: 3/26/22, Hackensack, N.J. 5'9", 140 lbs. Deb: 4/27/1872																													
1875	Mut-n	1	0	1.000	1																								
■ **JOHNNY GEE** Gee, John Alexander "Whiz" b: 12/7/15, Syracuse, N.Y. d: 1/23/88, Cortland, N.Y. BL/TL, 6'9", 225 lbs. Deb: 9/17/39																													
1939	Pit-N	1	2	.333	3	3	1	0	0	20	20	9.0	0	10	4.5	16	7.2	4.05	97	.253	.319	-0	-0	101	80	-0.3	-1	0	0.0
1941	Pit-N	0	2	.000	3	2	0	0	0	7	10	12.9	0	5	6.4	2	2.6	6.43	57	.294	.366	-2	-2	102	77	-0.9	0	0	-0.1
1943	Pit-N	4	4	.500	15	10	2	0	0	82	89	9.8	5	27	3.0	18	2.0	4.28	81	.280	.330	-8	-7	103	94	-0.1	-1	-3	-1.0
1944	Pit-N	0	0	—	4	0	0	0	0	11	20	16.4	0	5	4.1	3	2.5	7.36	51	.377	.424	-5	-4	104	97	0.0	0	0	-0.3
	NY-N	0	0	—	4	0	0	0	0	5	5	9.0	0	0	0.0	3	5.4	0.00	—	.263	.263	2	2	105	0	0.0	0	0	0.3
	Yr	0	0	—	8	0	0	0	0	16	25	14.1	0	5	2.8	6	3.4	5.06	74	.347	.385	-3	-2	104	0	0.0	0	0	0.0
1945	NY-N	0	0	—	2	0	0	0	1	3	5	15.0	0	2	6.0	1	3.0	9.00	42	.385	.467	-2	-2	100	85	0.0	-0	0	-0.1
1946	NY-N	2	4	.333	13	6	1	0	0	47	60	11.5	3	15	2.9	22	4.2	4.02	88	.308	.356	-3	-3	103	119	-0.4	0	-1	-0.2
Total	6	7	12	.368	44	21	4	0	1	175	209	10.7	8	64	3.3	65	3.3	4.42	81	.294	.346	-18	-16	103	95	-1.7	-1	-3	-1.4
■ **BILLY GEER** Geer, William Henry Harrison (born George Harrison Geer) b: 8/13/1849, Syracuse, N.Y. TR , 5'8", 160 lbs. Deb: 10/15/1874																													
1884	Bro-a	0	0	—	2	0	0	0	0	5	14	25.2	0	3	5.4	1	1.8	12.60	26	.507	.555	-5	-5	100	107	0.0	0	0	-0.3
■ **CHARLIE GEGGUS** Geggus, Charles Frederick b: 3/25/1862, San Francisco, Cal d: 1/16/17, San Francisco, Cal Deb: 8/07/1884																													
1884	Was-U	10	9	.526	23	21	19	0	0	177	143	7.3	2	38	1.9	156	7.9	2.54	116	.226	.270	9	8	98	85	2.0	1	0	0.8
■ **HENRY GEHRING** Gehring, Henry b: 1/24/1881, St.Paul, Minn. d: 4/18/12, Kansas City, Mo. BR/TR, Deb: 7/16/07																													
1907	Was-A	3	7	.300	15	9	8	2	0	87	92	9.5	1	14	1.4	31	3.2	3.31	72	.296	.327	-7	-9	94	89	-0.3	3	-2	-1.0
1908	Was-A	0	1	.000	3	1	0	0	0	5	9	16.2	0	2	3.6	0	0.0	14.40	16	.450	.542	-7	-7	97	65	-0.4	2	0	-0.6
Total	2	3	8	.273	18	10	8	2	0	92	101	9.9	1	16	1.6	31	3.0	3.91	61	.305	.341	-14	-16	94	88	-0.7	5	-2	-1.6
■ **PAUL GEHRMAN** Gehrman, Paul Arthur "Dutch" b: 5/3/12, Marquam, Ore. d: 10/23/86, Bend, Ore. BR/TR, 6', 195 lbs. Deb: 9/15/37																													
1937	Cin-N	0	1	.000	2	1	0	0	0	9	11	11.0	0	5	5.0	1	1.0	3.00	121	.282	.364	1	1	93	141	-0.4	-0	0	0.0
■ **GARY GEIGER** Geiger, Gary Merle b: 4/4/37, Sand Ridge, Ill. BL/TR, 6', 168 lbs. Deb: 4/15/58																													
1958	Cle-A	0	0	—	1	0	0	0	0	2	2	9.0	0	1	4.5	2	9.0	9.00	39	.286	.333	-1	-1	93	47	0.0	0	0	0.0

YEAR	TM/L	W	L	PCT	G	GS	CG	SHO	SV	IP	H	H/G	HR	BB	BB/G	SO	SO/G	ERA	/A	OAVG	OOBP	PR	/A	PF	CPI	WAT	PB	PD	TPI
■ **EMIL GEIS**	Geis, Emil Michael b: 3/1861, Villmar, Germany 5'11", 170 lbs. Deb: 7/19/1882																												
1882	Bal-a	4	9	.308	13	13	10	1	0	96	84	7.9	2	22	2.1	10	0.9	4.88	56	.240	.285	-23	-23	102	48	0.5	-2	0	-1.9
■ **BILL GEIS**	Geis, William J. (born William J. Geiss) b: 7/15/1858, Chicago, Ill. d: 9/18/24, Chicago, Ill. 5'10", 164 lbs. Deb: 5/01/1884																												
1884	Det-N	0	0	—	1	0	0	0	0	5	14	25.2	0	2	3.6	1	1.8	14.40	21	.508	.541	-6	-6	99	84	0.0	-0	0	-0.4
■ **DAVE GEISEL**	Geisel, John David b: 1/18/55, Windber, Pa. BL/TL, 6'3", 210 lbs. Deb: 6/13/78																												
1978	Chi-N	1	0	1.000	18	1	0	0	0	23	27	10.6	0	11	4.3	15	5.9	4.30	92	.278	.349	-2	-1	111	89	0.5	-0	-0	-0.1
1979	Chi-N	0	0	—	7	0	0	0	0	15	10	6.0	0	4	2.4	5	3.0	0.60	700	.189	.259	5	6	112	209	0.0	-0	-0	0.6
1981	Chi-N	2	0	1.000	11	2	0	0	0	16	11	6.2	0	10	5.6	7	3.9	0.56	661	.204	.318	5	6	106	469	1.0	-0	-0	0.6
1982	Tor-A	1	1	.500	16	2	0	0	0	32	32	9.0	6	17	4.8	22	6.2	3.94	113	.260	.359	1	2	109	132	0.0	0	-0	0.1
1983	Tor-A	0	3	.000	47	0	0	0	5	52	47	8.1	4	31	5.4	50	8.7	4.67	94	.240	.348	-3	-2	108	85	-1.4	0	-1	-0.1
1984	Sea-A	1	1	.500	20	3	0	0	3	43	47	9.8	2	9	1.9	28	5.9	4.19	98	.273	.314	-1	-0	103	83	0.1	0	-1	0.0
1985	Sea-A	0	0	—	12	0	0	0	0	27	35	11.7	3	15	5.0	17	5.7	6.33	62	.310	.391	-7	-7	95	94	0.0	0	-0	-0.6
Total	7	5	5	.500	131	8	0	0	8	208	209	9.0	15	97	4.2	144	6.2	4.02	104	.259	.341	-2	4	106	132	0.2	-1	-2	0.5
■ **VERN GEISHERT**	Geishert, Vernon William b: 1/10/46, Madison, Wis. BR/TR, 6'1", 215 lbs. Deb: 8/26/69																												
1969	Cal-A	1	1	.500	11	3	0	0	1	31	32	9.3	4	7	2.0	18	5.2	4.65	79	.267	.308	-4	-3	101	84	0.1	-1	0	-0.3
■ **EMIL GEISS**	Geiss, Emil August b: 3/20/1867, Chicago, Ill. d: 10/4/11, Chicago, Ill. Deb: 5/18/1887																												
1887	Chi-N	0	1	.000	1	1	1	0	0	9	17	17.0	0	3	3.0	4	4.0	8.00	58	.418	.458	-4	-3	115	97	-0.4	-1	0	-0.2
■ **CHARLIE GELBERT**	Gelbert, Charles Magnus b: 1/26/06, Scranton, Pa. d: 1/13/67, Easton, Pa. BR/TR, 5'11", 170 lbs. Deb: 4/16/29																												
1940	Was-A	0	0	—	2	0	0	0	0	4	5	11.3	2	3	6.8	1	2.3	9.00	46	.278	.381	-2	-2	95	93	0.0	1	0	-0.2
■ **JOHN GELNAR**	Gelnar, John Richard b: 6/25/43, Granite, Okla BR/TR, 6'2", 185 lbs. Deb: 8/04/64																												
1964	Pit-N	0	0	—	7	0	0	0	0	9	11	11.0	2	1	1.0	4	4.0	5.00	71	.314	.316	-1	-1	101	113	0.0	0	-0	-0.1
1967	Pit-N	0	1	.000	10	1	0	0	0	19	30	14.2	4	11	5.2	5	2.4	8.05	42	.375	.430	-10	-10	100	111	-0.4	0	0	-0.9
1969	Sea-A	3	10	.231	39	10	0	0	3	109	103	8.5	7	26	2.1	69	5.7	3.30	110	.250	.295	4	4	100	93	-2.7	-2	-0	0.2
1970	Mil-A	4	3	.571	53	0	0	0	4	92	98	9.6	7	23	2.3	48	4.7	4.21	88	.277	.320	-5	-5	100	93	1.0	-0	1	-0.3
1971	Mil-A	0	0	—	2	0	0	0	0	1	3	27.0	0	1	9.0	0	0.0	18.00	20	.429	.500	-2	-2	104	66	0.0	0	0	0.0
Total	5	7	14	.333	111	11	0	0	7	230	245	9.6	20	62	2.4	126	4.9	4.19	87	.276	.321	-14	-14	100	95	-2.1	-2	1	-1.1
■ **JOE GENEWICH**	Genewich, Joseph Edward b: 1/15/1897, Elmira, N.Y. d: 12/21/85, Lockport, N.Y. BR/TR, 6', 174 lbs. Deb: 9/13/22																												
1922	Bos-N	0	2	.000	6	2	1	0	0	23	29	11.3	2	11	4.3	4	1.6	7.04	57	.319	.370	-8	-8	98	79	-0.9	-0	-0	-0.6
1923	Bos-N	13	14	.481	43	24	12	1	1	227	272	10.8	15	46	1.8	54	2.1	3.73	110	.303	.334	7	9	102	115	3.2	2	2	1.2
1924	Bos-N	10	19	.345	34	27	11	2	1	200	258	11.6	4	65	2.9	43	1.9	5.22	73	.329	.373	-30	-31	99	98	0.0	-2	-0	-3.1
1925	Bos-N	12	10	.545	34	21	10	0	0	169	185	9.9	4	41	2.2	34	1.8	3.99	102	.279	.319	5	1	95	87	2.0	1	-1	0.1
1926	Bos-N	8	16	.333	37	26	12	2	2	216	239	10.0	6	63	2.6	59	2.5	3.88	86	.288	.327	-1	-13	88	101	-3.1	-1	1	-1.2
1927	Bos-N	11	8	.579	40	19	7	1	1	181	199	9.9	7	54	2.7	38	1.9	3.83	97	.279	.321	2	-2	95	97	3.2	-1	0	-0.2
1928	Bos-N	3	7	.300	13	11	4	0	0	81	88	9.8	14	18	2.0	15	1.7	4.11	98	.280	.317	-1	-1	101	110	-0.3	-3	1	-0.2
	NY-N	11	4	.733	26	18	10	2	3	158	136	7.7	10	54	3.1	37	2.1	3.19	124	.232	.292	14	14	99	84	2.6	-1	1	1.3
	Yr	14	11	.560	39	29	14	2	3	239	224	8.4	24	72	2.7	52	2.0	3.50	114	.248	.297	13	13	100	84	2.3	-3	2	1.1
1929	NY-N	3	7	.300	21	9	1	0	1	85	133	14.1	9	30	3.2	19	2.0	6.78	67	.359	.397	-19	-21	97	103	-2.3	3	0	-1.5
1930	NY-N	2	5	.286	18	9	3	0	3	61	71	10.5	6	20	3.0	13	1.9	5.61	85	.297	.342	-4	-6	96	87	-1.7	-1	2	-0.3
Total	9	73	92	.442	272	166	71	8	12	1401	1610	10.3	77	402	2.6	316	2.0	4.29	92	.293	.335	-36	-57	97	98	2.7	-4	5	-4.5
■ **GARY GENTRY**	Gentry, Gary Edward b: 10/6/46, Phoenix, Ariz. BR/TR, 6', 170 lbs. Deb: 4/10/69																												
1969	NY-N	13	12	.520	35	35	6	3	0	234	192	7.4	24	81	3.1	154	5.9	3.42	104	.222	.289	5	4	99	87	-2.2	-4	1	0.1
1970	NY-N	9	9	.500	32	29	5	2	1	188	155	7.4	19	86	4.1	134	6.4	3.69	113	.224	.313	8	10	103	95	-0.1	-3	-1	0.6
1971	NY-N	12	11	.522	32	31	8	3	0	203	167	7.4	16	82	3.6	155	6.9	3.24	103	.224	.300	5	2	96	91	0.3	-5	-1	-0.3
1972	NY-N	7	10	.412	32	26	3	0	0	164	153	8.4	20	75	4.1	120	6.6	4.01	83	.250	.329	-10	-13	96	104	-2.0	-1	2	-1.1
1973	Atl-N	4	6	.400	16	14	3	0	1	87	74	7.7	7	35	3.6	42	4.3	3.41	121	.231	.305	2	7	113	90	-0.7	0	-1	0.7
1974	Atl-N	0	0	—	3	1	0	0	0	7	4	5.1	1	2	2.6	0	0.0	1.29	292	.167	.259	2	2	104	171	0.0	-0	0	0.2
1975	Atl-N	1	1	.500	7	2	0	0	0	20	25	11.2	3	8	3.6	10	4.5	4.95	71	.313	.367	-3	-3	97	115	0.1	-1	0	-0.3
Total	7	46	49	.484	157	138	25	8	2	903	770	7.7	90	369	3.7	615	6.1	3.56	102	.231	.307	9	9	100	94	-4.6	-12	-0	-0.1
■ **RUFE GENTRY**	Gentry, James Ruffus b: 5/18/18, Winston-Salem, N.C BR/TR, 6'1", 180 lbs. Deb: 9/10/43																												
1943	Det-A	1	3	.250	4	4	2	0	0	29	30	9.3	2	12	3.7	8	2.5	3.72	92	.268	.349	-1	-1	104	113	-0.9	-1	0	-0.1
1944	Det-A	12	14	.462	37	30	10	3	0	204	211	9.3	9	108	4.8	68	3.0	4.24	84	.273	.358	-18	-16	104	102	-2.8	-1	1	-1.5
1946	Det-A	0	0	—	2	0	0	0	0	3	4	12.0	0	7	21.0	1	3.0	15.00	25	.333	.579	-4	-4	106	71	0.0	0	0	-0.3
1947	Det-A	0	0	—	1	0	0	0	0	⅓	1	27.0	0	2	54.0	0	0.0	81.00	—	.500	.750	-3	-3	103	30	0.0	0	0	-0.2
1948	Det-A	0	0	—	4	0	0	0	0	7	5	6.4	0	5	6.4	1	1.3	2.57	161	.208	.367	1	1	97	138	0.0	0	0	0.2
Total	5	13	17	.433	48	34	12	3	0	243	251	9.3	11	134	5.0	78	2.9	4.37	81	.272	.363	-25	-22	103	104	-3.7	-1	1	-1.9
■ **LEFTY GEORGE**	George, Thomas Edward b: 8/13/1886, Pittsburgh, Pa. d: 5/13/55, York, Pa. BL/TL, 6', 155 lbs. Deb: 4/14/11																												
1911	StL-A	4	9	.308	27	13	6	1	0	116	136	10.6	4	51	4.0	23	1.8	4.19	79	.256	.332	-11	-11	100	73	0.1	-3	-1	-1.4
1912	Cle-A	0	5	.000	11	5	2	0	0	44	69	14.1	1	18	3.7	18	3.7	4.91	69	.373	.434	-8	-7	101	137	-2.4	1	0	-0.6
1915	Cin-N	2	2	.500	5	3	2	1	0	28	24	7.7	1	8	2.6	11	3.5	3.86	74	.242	.319	-3	-3	104	82	0.1	2	1	0.0
1918	Bos-N	1	5	.167	9	5	4	0	0	54	56	9.3	0	21	3.5	22	3.7	2.33	113	.281	.343	3	2	95	160	-1.8	-2	2	0.2
Total	4	7	21	.250	52	26	14	2	0	242	285	10.6	6	98	3.6	74	2.8	3.87	81	.281	.351	-19	-20	99	105	-4.0	-2	1	-1.8
■ **BILL GEORGE**	George, William M. b: 1/27/1865, Bellaire, Ohio d: 8/23/16, Wheeling, W.Va. BR/TL, 5'8", 165 lbs. Deb: 5/11/1887																												
1887	NY-N	3	9	.250	13	13	11	0	0	108	126	10.5	1	89	7.4	49	4.1	5.25	81	.307	.431	-14	-12	106	105	-3.3	-4	0	-1.2
1888	NY-N	2	1	.667	4	3	3	1	0	34	18	4.8	0	11	2.9	26	6.9	1.32	190	.166	.243	6	4	89	57	0.1	1	0	0.5
1889	Col-a	0	0	—	2	0	0	0	0	8	11	12.4	1	3	3.4	3	3.4	7.88	45	.343	.399	-4	-4	92	77	0.0	0	0	-0.2
Total	3	5	10	.333	19	16	14	1	0	150	155	9.3	2	103	6.2	78	4.7	4.50	84	.282	.395	-12	-12	101	93	-3.2	-3	0	-0.9
■ **OSCAR GEORGY**	Georgy, Oscar John b: 11/25/16, New Orleans, La. BR/TR, 6'3.5", 180 lbs. Deb: 6/04/38																												
1938	NY-N	0	0	—	1	0	0	0	0	1	2	18.0	0	1	9.0	0	0.0	18.00	21	.400	.500	-2	-2	102	53	0.0	0	0	-0.1
■ **DAVE GERARD**	Gerard, David Frederick b: 8/6/36, New York, N.Y. BR/TR, 6'2", 205 lbs. Deb: 4/10/62																												
1962	Chi-N	2	3	.400	39	0	0	0	3	59	67	10.2	10	28	4.3	30	4.6	4.88	88	.289	.361	-6	-4	109	113	0.1	1	-0	-0.2
■ **GEORGE GERBERMAN**	Gerberman, George Alois b: 3/8/42, El Campo, Tex. BR/TR, 6', 180 lbs. Deb: 9/23/62																												
1962	Chi-N	0	0	—	1	1	0	0	0	5	3	5.4	1	5	9.0	1	1.8	1.80	238	.158	.333	1	1	109	200	0.0	0	0	0.2
■ **RUSTY GERHARDT**	Gerhardt, Allen Russell b: 8/13/50, Baltimore, Md. BB/TL, 5'9", 175 lbs. Deb: 7/27/74																												
1974	SD-N	2	1	.667	23	1	0	0	1	36	44	11.0	1	17	4.3	22	5.5	7.00	50	.308	.382	-13	-14	97	71	0.7	-0	-0	-1.4
■ **AL GERHEAUSER**	Gerheauser, Albert "Lefty" b: 6/24/17, St.Louis, Mo. d: 5/28/72, Springfield, Mo. BL/TL, 6'3", 190 lbs. Deb: 4/24/43																												
1943	Phi-N	10	19	.345	38	31	11	2	0	215	222	9.3	10	70	2.9	92	3.9	3.60	90	.263	.314	-5	-9	96	96	-2.8	-2	-1	-1.2
1944	Phi-N	8	16	.333	30	29	10	2	0	183	210	10.3	8	65	3.2	66	3.2	4.57	81	.285	.340	-20	-18	103	91	-2.2	3	-1	-1.5
1945	Pit-N	5	10	.333	32	14	5	0	1	140	170	10.9	5	54	3.5	55	3.5	3.92	99	.304	.358	-2	-1	102	121	-2.9	3	2	0.4
1946	Pit-N	2	2	.500	35	3	1	0	0	82	92	10.1	2	25	2.7	32	3.5	3.95	91	.286	.331	-5	-3	106	94	0.3	2	1	0.0
1948	StL-A	0	3	.000	14	2	0	0	0	23	32	12.5	0	10	3.9	10	3.9	7.43	63	.317	.374	-8	-7	109	69	-1.4	0	-0	-0.6
Total	5	25	50	.333	149	79	27	4	1	643	726	10.2	25	224	3.1	255	3.6	4.13	87	.283	.336	-40	-38	101	98	-9.0	6	-0	-2.9
■ **STEVE GERKIN**	Gerkin, Stephen Paul "Splinter" b: 11/19/15, Grafton, W.Va. d: 11/9/78, Bay Pines, Fla. BR/TR, 6'1", 162 lbs. Deb: 5/13/45																												
1945	Phi-A	0	12	.000	21	12	3	0	0	102	112	9.9	4	27	2.4	25	2.2	3.62	90	.285	.328	-3	-4	96	107	-5.9	-4	0	-0.7
■ **LES GERMAN**	German, Lester Stanley b: 6/1/1869, Baltimore, Md. d: 6/10/34, Germantown, Md. BR/TR, 5'8", 165 lbs. Deb: 8/27/1890																												
1890	BB-a	5	11	.313	17	16	15	0	0	132	147	10.0	2	54	3.7	37	2.5	4.84	82	.298	.367	-14	-13	103	88	0.1	-2	0	-1.1

YEAR	TM/L	W	L	PCT	G	GS	CG	SHO	SV	IP	H	H/G	HR	BB	BB/G	SO	SO/G	ERA	/A	OAVG	OOBP	PR	/A	PF	CPI	WAT	PB	PD	TPI
1893	NY-N	8	8	.500	20	18	14	0	0	152	162	9.6	6	70	4.1	35	2.1	4.14	116	.289	.367	9	11	103	102	-0.2	2	0	1.2
1894	NY-N	9	8	.529	23	15	10	0	1	134	178	12.0	7	66	4.4	17	1.1	5.78	91	.342	.416	-7	-8	98	98	-1.8	1	0	-0.5
1895	NY-N	7	11	.389	25	18	16	0	0	178	243	12.3	7	78	3.9	36	1.8	5.97	76	.346	.412	-23	-29	94	94	-2.2	3	0	-1.9
1896	NY-N	0	0	—	1	0	0	0	0	3	9	27.0	0	1	3.0	0	0.0	15.00	29	.541	.567	-4	-4	99	87	0.0	-0	0	-0.2
	Was-N	2	20	.091	28	20	14	0	1	167	240	12.9	6	74	4.0	20	1.1	6.36	66	.361	.425	-37	-40	96	92	-9.0	0	0	-3.1
	Yr	2	20	.091	29	20	14	0	1	170	249	13.2	6	75	4.0	20	1.1	6.51	64	.365	.428	-41	-44	96	92	-9.0	-0	0	-3.3
1897	Was-N	3	5	.375	15	5	4	0	0	84	117	12.5	2	33	3.5	2	0.2	5.68	77	.353	.412	-13	-12	102	94	-0.7	2	0	-0.7
Total	6	34	63	.351	129	92	73	0	2	850	1096	11.6	30	376	4.0	147	1.6	5.52	82	.333	.402	-88	-93	99	95	-13.8	6	0	-6.3
■ ED GERNER	Gerner, Edwin Frederick "Lefty" b: 7/22/1897, Philadelphia, Pa. d: 5/15/70, Philadelphia, Pa. BL/TL, 5'8.5", 175 lbs. Deb: 5/14/19																												
1919	Cin-N	1	0	1.000	5	1	0	0	0	17	22	11.6	0	3	1.6	2	1.1	3.18	93	.333	.365	-0	-0	101	151	0.5	0	1	0.0
■ LEFTY GERVAIS	Gervais, Lucien Edward b: 7/6/1890, Grover, Wis. d: 10/19/50, Los Angeles, Cal. BL/TL, 5'10", 165 lbs. Deb: 4/17/13																												
1913	Bos-N	0	1	.000	5	2	1	0	0	16	18	10.1	0	4	2.3	1	0.6	5.63	54	.383	.386	-4	-5	96	98	-0.4	-0	-0	-0.4
■ CHARLIE GESSNER	Gessner, Charles J. b: Philadelphia, Pa. Deb: 7/19/1886																												
1886	Phi-a	0	1	.000	1	1	1	0	0	8	13	14.6	0	5	5.6	0	0.0	9.00	39	.376	.455	-5	-5	103	82	-0.4	-0	0	-0.3
■ AL GETTEL	Gettel, Allen Jones b: 9/17/17, Norfolk, Va. BR/TR, 6'3.5", 200 lbs. Deb: 4/20/45																												
1945	NY-A	9	8	.529	27	17	9	0	3	155	141	8.2	11	53	3.1	67	3.9	3.89	92	.243	.308	-9	-6	106	84	0.0	2	-1	-0.4
1946	NY-A	6	7	.462	26	11	5	2	0	103	89	7.8	6	40	3.5	54	4.7	2.97	115	.229	.301	6	5	98	94	-1.2	-2	0	0.4
1947	Cle-A	11	10	.524	31	21	9	2	0	149	122	7.4	12	62	3.7	64	3.9	3.20	109	.229	.306	8	5	94	101	0.1	4	1	0.9
1948	Cle-A	0	1	.000	5	2	0	0	0	8	15	16.9	2	10	11.3	4	4.5	16.88	24	.385	.520	-11	-11	94	71	-0.4	-0	-0	-1.0
	Chi-A	8	10	.444	22	19	7	0	1	148	154	9.4	7	60	3.6	49	3.0	4.01	106	.268	.337	4	4	100	101	1.6	0	-1	0.4
	Yr	8	11	.421	27	21	7	0	1	156	169	9.8	9	70	4.0	53	3.1	4.67	91	.275	.349	-7	-7	99	101	1.2	-0	-1	-0.6
1949	Chi-A	2	5	.286	19	7	1	1	1	63	69	9.9	12	26	3.7	22	3.1	6.43	65	.283	.353	-16	-16	99	84	-1.0	-0	-1	-1.5
	Was-A	0	2	.000	16	1	0	0	1	35	43	11.1	4	24	6.2	7	1.8	5.40	75	.314	.404	-5	-5	96	118	-0.9	-1	1	-0.4
	Yr	2	7	.222	35	8	1	1	2	98	112	10.3	16	50	4.6	29	2.7	6.06	68	.292	.367	-20	-21	98	118	-1.9	-0	0	-1.9
1951	NY-N	1	2	.333	30	1	0	0	0	57	52	8.2	12	25	3.9	36	5.7	4.89	80	.240	.313	-6	-6	99	90	-0.6	-1	1	-0.5
1955	StL-N	1	0	1.000	8	0	0	0	0	17	26	13.8	6	10	5.3	7	3.7	9.00	46	.361	.419	-9	-9	102	104	0.5	1	-1	-0.7
Total	7	38	45	.458	184	79	31	5	6	735	711	8.7	72	310	3.8	310	3.8	4.27	89	.255	.328	-37	-39	99	95	-1.9	3	-1	-2.8
■ CHARLIE GETTIG	Gettig, Charles Henry b: 1871, Baltimore, Md. d: 4/11/35, Baltimore, Md. 5'10", 172 lbs. Deb: 8/05/1896																												
1896	NY-N	1	0	1.000	4	1	1	0	1	14	20	12.9	0	8	5.1	5	3.2	9.64	45	.359	.440	-8	-8	99	61	0.5	1	0	-0.5
1897	NY-N	1	1	.500	3	2	2	0	0	19	23	10.9	0	9	4.3	7	3.3	5.21	80	.322	.398	-2	-2	96	86	-0.1	-0	0	-0.1
1898	NY-N	6	3	.667	17	8	7	0	0	115	141	11.0	1	39	3.1	14	1.1	3.83	89	.325	.380	-3	-6	94	111	1.5	2	0	-0.4
1899	NY-N	7	8	.467	18	15	12	0	0	128	161	11.3	3	54	3.8	25	1.8	4.43	86	.332	.399	-8	-9	99	107	0.9	1	0	-0.5
Total	4	15	12	.556	42	26	22	0	1	276	345	11.3	4	110	3.6	51	1.7	4.50	82	.330	.393	-21	-25	97	105	2.8	4	0	-1.5
■ TOM GETTINGER	Gettinger, Thomas L. b: 1870, Mobile, Ala. BL/TL, 5'10", 180 lbs. Deb: 9/21/1889																												
1895	Lou-N	0	0	—	2	0	0	0	0	6	13	19.5	1	1	1.5	0	0.0	7.50	63	.457	.475	-2	-2	99	131	0.0	0	0	0.0
■ PRETZELS GETZIEN	Getzien, Charles H. "Charlie" b: 2/14/1864, Germany d: 6/19/32, Chicago, Ill. BR/TR, 5' 10", 172 lbs. Deb: 8/13/1884																												
1884	Det-N	5	12	.294	17	17	17	1	0	147	118	7.2	2	25	1.5	107	6.6	1.96	151	.228	.264	17	16	99	83	0.6	-4	0	1.1
1885	Det-N	12	25	.324	37	37	37	1	0	330	360	9.8	8	92	2.5	110	3.0	3.03	92	.289	.338	-8	-9	99	**121**	-3.7	-1	-2	-1.0
1886	Det-N	30	11	.732	43	43	42	1	0	387	388	9.0	6	85	2.0	172	4.0	3.05	112	.274	.315	11	16	103	99	2.5	-4	-3	0.9
1887	Det-N	29	13	**.690**	43	42	41	2	0	367	373	9.1	24	106	2.6	135	3.3	3.73	106	.279	.331	13	9	97	99	4.3	-1	-1	0.5
1888	Det-N	19	25	.432	46	46	45	2	0	404	411	9.2	13	54	1.2	202	4.5	3.05	90	.277	.303	-10	-14	97	95	-5.0	10	-2	-0.6
1889	Ind-N	18	22	.450	45	44	36	0	1	349	395	10.2	27	100	2.6	139	3.6	4.54	98	.301	.351	-20	-4	110	94	0.5	0	-3	-0.3
1890	Bos-N	23	17	.575	40	40	39	4	0	350	342	8.8	5	82	2.1	140	3.6	3.19	120	.271	.316	15	25	108	86	0.2	5	-2	2.8
1891	Bos-N	4	5	.444	11	9	7	0	0	89	112	11.3	4	23	2.3	29	2.9	3.84	95	.322	.364	-5	-2	109	110	-1.3	1	0	0.0
	Cle-N	0	1	.000	1	1	1	0	0	9	12	12.0	1	4	4.0	4	4.0	8.00	44	.334	.401	-5	-4	106	70	-0.4	-1	0	-0.3
	Yr	4	6	.400	12	10	8	0	0	98	124	11.4	5	27	2.5	33	3.0	4.22	86	.323	.367	-10	-6	109	70	-1.7	1	0	-0.3
1892	StL-N	5	8	.385	13	13	12	0	0	108	159	13.3	5	31	2.6	32	2.7	5.67	56	.356	.398	-29	-30	97	98	0.1	1	0	-2.4
Total	9	145	139	.511	296	292	277	11	1	2540	2670	9.5	95	602	2.1	1070	3.8	3.46	100	.284	.327	-20	-1	102	98	-2.2	6	-13	0.7
■ RUBE GEYER	Geyer, Jacob Bowman b: 3/26/1884, Allegheny, Pa. d: 10/12/62, Ford Township, Minn. BR/TR, 5'10", 170 lbs. Deb: 4/24/10																												
1910	StL-N	0	1	.000	4	0	0	0	0	4	5	11.3	0	3	6.8	5	11.3	4.50	63	.294	.400	-1	-1	93	107	-0.4	-0	-0	0.0
1911	StL-N	9	6	.600	29	11	7	1	0	149	141	8.5	7	56	3.4	46	2.8	3.26	107	.259	.335	2	4	102	108	1.6	1	-2	0.3
1912	StL-N	7	14	.333	41	18	6	0	0	181	191	9.5	4	84	4.2	61	3.0	3.28	107	.275	.356	3	4	103	112	-2.2	-0	0	0.4
1913	StL-N	1	5	.167	30	4	2	0	1	79	83	9.5	6	38	4.3	21	2.4	5.24	59	.282	.352	-18	-19	97	87	-1.5	-2	-1	-2.0
Total	4	17	26	.395	104	33	15	1	1	413	420	9.2	17	181	3.9	133	2.9	3.66	93	.271	.349	-14	-12	101	106	-2.5	-1	-2	-1.3
■ TONY GHELFI	Ghelfi, Anthony Paul b: 8/23/61, La Crosse, Wis. BR/TR, 6'3", 185 lbs. Deb: 9/01/83																												
1983	Phi-N	1	1	.500	3	3	0	0	0	14	15	9.6	2	6	3.9	14	9.0	3.21	113	.268	.339	1	1	100	140	0.0	0	1	0.1
■ BOB GIALLOMBARDO	Giallombardo, Robert Paul b: 5/20/37, Brooklyn, N.Y. BL/TL, 6', 175 lbs. Deb: 6/21/58																												
1958	LA-N	1	1	.500	6	5	0	0	0	26	29	10.0	3	15	5.2	14	4.8	3.81	110	.284	.367	0	1	106	135	0.1	-0	0	0.1
■ JOE GIARD	Giard, Joseph Oscar "Peco" b: 10/7/1898, Ware, Mass. d: 7/10/56, Worcester, Mass. BL/TL, 5'10.5", 170 lbs. Deb: 4/18/25																												
1925	StL-A	10	5	.667	30	21	9	4	0	161	179	10.0	13	87	4.9	43	2.4	5.03	94	.295	.376	-11	-5	108	104	2.3	-6	2	-0.8
1926	StL-A	3	10	.231	22	15	2	0	0	90	113	11.3	7	67	6.7	18	1.8	7.00	59	.318	.412	-30	-28	103	90	-2.8	0	-1	-2.5
1927	NY-A	0	0	—	16	0	0	0	0	27	38	12.7	1	19	6.3	10	3.3	8.00	49	.352	.425	-12	-12	94	87	0.0	0	-0	-1.1
Total	3	13	15	.464	68	36	11	4	0	278	330	10.7	21	173	5.6	71	2.3	5.96	75	.309	.393	-53	-46	105	98	-0.5	-6	1	-4.4
■ JOE GIBBON	Gibbon, Joseph Charles b: 4/10/35, Hickory, Miss. BR/TL, 6'4", 200 lbs. Deb: 4/17/60																												
1960	Pit-N	4	2	.667	27	9	0	0	0	80	87	9.8	5	31	3.5	60	6.7	4.05	90	.277	.336	-3	-4	97	102	0.4	1	0	-0.2
1961	Pit-N	13	10	.565	30	29	7	3	0	195	185	8.5	16	57	2.6	145	6.7	3.32	120	.251	.301	15	14	99	101	2.0	-2	-0	1.3
1962	Pit-N	3	4	.429	19	8	0	0	0	57	53	8.4	4	24	3.8	26	4.1	3.63	110	.250	.318	2	2	101	98	-0.8	-0	1	0.3
1963	Pit-N	5	12	.294	37	22	5	0	1	147	147	9.0	7	54	3.3	110	6.7	3.31	99	.258	.322	-0	-1	99	106	-3.1	-2	1	0.0
1964	Pit-N	10	7	.588	28	24	3	0	0	147	145	8.9	10	54	3.3	97	5.9	3.67	97	.262	.325	-2	-2	101	105	1.7	3	1	0.2
1965	Pit-N	4	9	.308	31	15	1	0	1	106	85	7.2	7	34	2.9	63	5.3	4.50	77	.221	.282	-11	-12	98	61	-2.9	-0	0	-1.1
1966	SF-N	4	6	.400	37	10	1	0	1	81	86	9.6	4	16	1.8	48	5.3	3.67	95	.275	.304	-1	-2	97	94	-1.5	0	1	0.0
1967	SF-N	6	2	.750	28	10	3	1	1	82	65	7.1	4	33	3.6	63	6.9	3.07	109	.220	.298	3	3	99	90	1.8	-1	2	0.4
1968	SF-N	1	2	.333	29	0	0	0	1	40	33	7.4	3	19	4.3	22	4.9	1.57	183	.234	.321	6	6	96	225	-0.5	-0	0	0.7
1969	SF-N	1	3	.250	16	0	0	0	2	20	15	6.7	1	13	5.8	9	4.0	3.60	100	.211	.326	-0	0	100	92	-1.0	-0	1	0.1
	Pit-N	5	1	.833	35	0	0	0	9	51	38	6.7	5	17	3.0	35	6.2	1.94	174	.208	.278	9	8	94	136	1.9	-1	1	0.9
	Yr	6	4	.600	51	0	0	0	11	71	53	6.7	6	30	3.8	44	5.6	2.41	143	.208	.289	9	8	96	136	0.9	-0	2	1.0
1970	Pit-N	0	1	.000	41	0	0	0	5	41	44	9.7	2	24	5.3	26	5.7	4.83	81	.280	.368	-4	-4	96	101	-0.4	-0	0	-0.3
1971	Cin-N	5	6	.455	50	0	0	0	11	64	54	7.6	3	32	4.5	34	4.8	2.95	113	.239	.321	4	3	96	115	-0.3	-0	1	0.4
1972	Cin-N	0	0	—	2	0	0	0	0	⅓	3	81.0	1	1	27.0	1	27.0	54.00	—	.750	.800	-2	-2	91	127	0.0	0	0	-0.1
	Hou-N	0	0	—	9	0	0	0	0	7	13	16.7	2	5	6.4	4	5.1	10.29	35	.394	.463	-5	-5	105	105	0.0	0	1	-0.4
	Yr	0	0	—	11	0	0	0	0	7	16	20.6	3	6	7.7	5	6.4	12.86	28	.432	.500	-7	-7	105	105	0.0	0	1	-0.5
Total	13	61	65	.484	419	127	20	4	32	1118	1053	8.5	74	414	3.3	743	6.0	3.53	101	.251	.315	12	4	98	104	-2.7	-2	11	2.2
■ NORWOOD GIBSON	Gibson, Norwood Ringold "Gibby" b: 3/11/1877, Peoria, Ill. d: 7/7/59, Peoria, Ill. BR/TR, 5'10", 165 lbs. Deb: 4/29/03																												
1903	Bos-A	13	9	.591	24	21	17	2	0	183	166	8.2	2	65	3.2	76	3.7	3.20	99	.263	.332	-5	-1	108	90	-1.2	4	0	0.0
1904	Bos-A	17	14	.548	33	32	29	1	0	273	216	7.1	8	81	2.7	112	3.7	2.21	119	.238	.301	12	13	101	103	-2.0	-6	-3	1.2
1905	Bos-A	4	7	.364	23	17	9	0	0	134	118	7.9	9	55	3.7	67	4.5	3.69	72	.260	.340	-16	-16	100	92	-1.6	-2	-2	-1.7
1906	Bos-A	0	2	.000	5	2	1	0	0	19	25	11.8	2	7	3.3	3	1.4	5.21	53	.345	.402	-5	-5	104	108	-0.9	0	-0	-0.5
Total	4	34	32	.515	85	72	56	3	0	609	525	7.8	21	208	3.1	258	3.8	2.93	96	.254	.323	-14	-9	103	97	-5.7	-4	-5	-1.0

YEAR	TM/L	W	L	PCT	G	GS	CG	SHO	SV	IP	H	H/G	HR	BB	BB/G	SO	SO/G	ERA	/A	OAVG	OOBP	PR	/A	PF	CPI	WAT	PB	PD	TPI
■ **PAUL GIBSON**	Gibson, Paul Marshall b: 1/4/60, Southampton, N.Y. BL/TR, 6', 165 lbs. Deb: 4/08/88																												
1988	Det-A	4	2	.667	40	1	0	0	0	92	83	8.1	6	34	3.3	50	4.9	2.93	127	.240	.305	11	8	94	111	0.8	0	0	0.8
■ **BOB GIBSON**	Gibson, Robert b: 11/9/35, Omaha, Neb. BR/TR, 6'1", 189 lbs. Deb: 4/15/59 CH																												
1959	StL-N	3	5	.375	13	9	2	1	0	76	77	9.1	4	39	4.6	48	5.7	3.32	127	.273	.351	5	7	106	131	-0.7	-1	-0	0.7
1960	StL-N	3	6	.333	27	12	2	0	0	87	97	10.0	7	48	5.0	69	7.1	5.59	73	.284	.366	-18	-15	108	89	-1.8	-0	1	-1.3
1961	StL-N	13	12	.520	35	27	10	2	1	211	186	7.9	13	119	5.1	166	7.1	3.24	140	.239	.340	19	30	113	114	0.0	2	0	3.5
1962	StL-N	15	13	.536	32	30	15	**5**	1	234	174	6.7	15	95	3.7	208	8.0	2.85	**148**	.204	.289	28	36	107	85	0.6	6	1	**4.7**
1963	StL-N	18	9	.667	36	33	14	2	0	255	224	7.9	19	96	3.4	204	7.2	3.39	102	.233	.306	-3	2	106	93	3.4	8	-2	1.0
1964	StL-N	19	12	.613	40	36	17	2	1	287	250	7.8	25	86	2.7	245	7.7	3.01	131	.232	.290	17	29	111	100	1.7	1	-1	3.3
1965	StL-N	20	12	.625	38	36	20	6	1	299	243	7.3	34	103	3.1	270	8.1	3.07	122	.222	.290	16	23	106	102	4.8	9	-2	3.5
1966	StL-N	21	12	.636	35	35	20	**5**	0	280	210	6.8	20	78	2.5	225	7.2	2.44	148	.207	.262	36	36	100	87	4.9	3	-1	4.2
1967	StL-N	13	7	.650	24	24	10	2	0	175	151	7.8	10	40	2.1	147	7.6	2.98	112	.231	.276	8	7	99	84	0.7	1	0	0.9
1968	StL-N	22	9	.710	34	34	28	**13**	0	305	198	**5.8**	11	62	1.8	**268**	7.9	**1.12**	**248**	**.184**	**.230**	**63**	**56**	93	107	5.0	4	-3	**7.5**
1969	StL-N	20	13	.606	35	35	**28**	4	0	314	251	7.2	12	95	2.7	269	7.7	2.18	163	.219	.280	50	48	99	106	3.0	8	-2	**6.3**
1970	StL-N	**23**	7	**.767**	34	34	23	3	0	294	262	8.0	13	88	2.7	274	8.4	3.12	138	.237	.292	30	39	106	90	**9.2**	12	-1	5.3
1971	StL-N	16	13	.552	31	31	20	**5**	0	246	215	7.9	14	76	2.8	185	6.8	3.04	114	.232	.290	12	12	100	89	0.0	2	0	1.6
1972	StL-N	19	11	.633	34	34	23	4	0	278	226	7.3	14	88	2.8	208	6.7	2.46	148	.224	.283	31	37	105	101	5.1	6	2	5.2
1973	StL-N	12	10	.545	25	25	13	1	0	195	159	7.3	12	57	2.6	142	6.6	2.77	119	.224	.277	20	12	90	90	1.1	3	-1	1.4
1974	StL-N	11	13	.458	33	33	9	1	0	240	236	8.9	24	104	3.9	129	4.8	3.83	98	.259	.331	-5	-2	103	105	-1.9	2	-1	-0.1
1975	StL-N	3	10	.231	22	14	1	0	2	109	120	9.9	10	62	5.1	60	5.0	5.04	75	.287	.373	-17	-16	103	102	-3.6	1	-0	-1.4
Total	17	251	174	.591	528	482	255	56	6	3885	3279	7.6	257	1336	3.1	3117	7.2	2.91	127	.228	.294	291	338	103	98	31.5	67	-10	46.3
■ **BOB GIBSON**	Gibson, Robert Louis b: 6/19/57, Philadelphia, Pa. BR/TR, 6', 195 lbs. Deb: 4/13/83																												
1983	Mil-A	3	4	.429	27	7	0	0	2	81	71	7.9	6	46	5.1	46	5.1	3.89	95	.237	.331	2	-2	91	97	-0.6	0	-1	-0.1
1984	Mil-A	2	5	.286	18	9	1	1	0	69	61	8.0	10	47	6.1	54	7.0	4.96	75	.236	.346	-7	-10	93	91	-1.0	0	0	-0.8
1985	Mil-A	6	7	.462	41	1	0	0	11	92	86	8.4	10	49	4.8	53	5.2	3.91	112	.260	.347	2	5	106	119	0.3	0	-0	0.5
1986	Mil-A	1	2	.333	11	1	0	0	0	27	23	7.7	3	23	7.7	11	3.7	4.67	92	.232	.374	-1	-1	103	101	-0.4	0	-0	0.0
1987	NY-N	0	0	—	1	0	0	0	0	1	0	0.0	0	1	9.0	2	18.0	0.00	—	.000	.250	0	0	97	0	0.0	0	0	0.1
Total	5	12	18	.400	98	18	1	1	13	270	241	8.0	29	166	5.5	166	5.5	4.23	94	.243	.344	-4	-7	98	103	-1.7	0	-1	-0.3
■ **ROBERT GIBSON**	Gibson, Robert Murray b: 8/20/1869, Duncansville, Pa. d: 12/19/49, Pittsburgh, Pa. BR/TR, 6'3", 185 lbs. Deb: 6/04/1890																												
1890	Chi-N	1	0	1.000	1	1	1	0	0	9	6	6.0	0	2	2.0	1	1.0	0.00	—	.203	.253	4	4	107	0	0.5	-0	0	0.4
	Pit-N	0	3	.000	3	3	2	0	0	12	24	18.0	0	23	17.3	3	2.3	17.25	20	.433	.599	-18	-19	95	72	-1.4	-0	0	-1.2
	Yr	1	3	.250	4	4	3	0	0	21	30	12.9	0	25	10.7	4	1.7	9.86	36	.353	.500	-15	-15	100	72	-0.9	-0	0	-0.8
■ **SAM GIBSON**	Gibson, Samuel Braxton b: 8/5/1899, King, N.C. d: 1/31/83, High Point, N.C. BL/TR, 6'2", 198 lbs. Deb: 4/19/26																												
1926	Det-A	12	9	.571	35	24	16	2	2	196	199	9.1	6	75	3.4	61	2.8	3.49	112	.269	.331	12	9	98	104	1.4	2	-0	1.1
1927	Det-A	11	12	.478	33	26	11	0	0	185	201	9.8	9	86	4.2	76	3.7	3.79	117	.285	.355	7	13	107	119	-1.3	-2	-2	1.0
1928	Det-A	5	8	.385	20	18	5	1	0	120	155	11.6	4	53	4.0	29	2.2	5.40	75	.322	.385	-18	-18	100	102	-0.8	2	-1	-1.5
1930	NY-A	0	1	.000	2	2	0	0	0	6	14	21.0	1	6	9.0	3	4.5	15.00	27	.424	.513	-7	-7	87	82	-0.4	0	0	-0.5
1932	NY-N	4	8	.333	41	5	1	1	3	82	107	11.7	7	30	3.3	39	4.3	4.83	78	.322	.377	-9	-9	98	118	-1.7	0	-1	-0.9
Total	5	32	38	.457	131	75	33	4	5	589	676	10.3	27	250	3.8	208	3.2	4.28	96	.295	.359	-15	-12	101	110	-2.8	3	-3	-0.8
■ **GEORGE GICK**	Gick, George Edward b: 10/18/15, Dunnington, Ind. BB/TR, 6', 190 lbs. Deb: 10/03/37																												
1937	Chi-A	0	0	—	1	0	0	0	1	2	0	0.0	0	0	0.0	1	4.5	0.00	—	.000	.000	1	1	102	0	0.0	0	0	0.1
1938	Chi-A	0	0	—	1	0	0	0	0	1	0	0.0	0	0	0.0	1	9.0	0.00	—	.000	.250	1	1	98	0	0.0	0	0	0.0
Total	2	0	0	—	2	0	0	0	1	3	0	0.0	0	0	0.0	2	6.0	0.00	—	.000	.100	2	2	101	0	0.0	0	0	0.1
■ **BYRON GIDEON**	Gideon, Byron Brett b: 8/8/63, Ozona, Tex. BR/TR, 6'2", 200 lbs. Deb: 7/05/87																												
1987	Pit-N	1	5	.167	29	0	0	0	3	37	34	8.3	6	10	2.4	31	7.5	4.62	92	.243	.294	-2	-1	105	81	-1.9	1	0	0.0
■ **JIM GIDEON**	Gideon, James Leslie b: 9/26/53, Taylor, Tex. BR/TR, 6'3", 190 lbs. Deb: 9/14/75																												
1975	Tex-A	0	0	—	1	1	0	0	0	6	7	10.5	1	5	7.5	2	3.0	7.50	50	.292	.414	-2	-2	100	86	0.0	0	-0	-0.1
■ **FLOYD GIEBELL**	Giebell, Floyd George b: 12/10/09, Pennsboro, W.Va. BL/TR, 6'2.5", 172 lbs. Deb: 4/21/39																												
1939	Det-A	1	1	.500	9	0	0	0	0	15	19	11.4	1	12	7.2	9	5.4	3.00	169	.317	.419	3	3	110	223	0.0	-0	-0	0.3
1940	Det-A	2	0	1.000	2	2	2	1	0	18	14	7.0	2	4	2.0	11	5.5	1.00	476	.206	.247	7	8	109	225	1.0	-1	0	0.8
1941	Det-A	0	0	—	17	2	0	0	0	34	45	11.9	3	26	6.9	10	2.6	6.09	73	.313	.413	-7	-6	107	107	0.0	0	0	-0.5
Total	3	3	1	.750	28	4	2	1	0	67	78	10.5	6	42	5.6	30	4.0	4.03	116	.287	.376	2	5	108	164	1.0	-1	-0	0.6
■ **PAUL GIEL**	Giel, Paul Robert b: 2/29/32, Winona, Minn. BR/TR, 5'11", 185 lbs. Deb: 7/10/54																												
1954	NY-N	0	0	—	6	0	0	0	0	4	8	18.0	0	2	4.5	4	9.0	9.00	46	.421	.455	-2	-2	102	95	0.0	0	0	-0.1
1955	NY-N	4	4	.500	34	2	0	0	0	82	70	7.7	8	50	5.5	47	5.2	3.40	116	.233	.338	6	5	98	115	-0.1	-2	-1	0.2
1958	SF-N	4	5	.444	29	9	0	0	0	92	89	8.7	12	55	5.4	55	5.4	4.70	84	.259	.356	-8	-8	100	101	-0.6	-2	1	-0.7
1959	Pit-N	0	0	—	4	0	0	0	0	8	17	19.1	0	6	6.8	3	3.4	13.50	30	.472	.511	-8	-8	104	80	0.0	0	0	-0.7
1960	Pit-N	2	0	1.000	16	0	0	0	0	33	35	9.5	3	15	4.1	21	5.7	5.73	63	.276	.342	-7	-8	97	79	1.0	-1	-1	-0.8
1961	Min-A	1	0	1.000	12	0	0	0	0	19	24	11.4	6	17	8.1	14	6.6	9.95	43	.289	.402	-13	-12	107	77	0.5	0	0	-1.0
	KC-A	0	0	—	1	0	0	0	0	2	6	27.0	1	3	13.5	1	4.5	31.50	13	.600	.692	-6	-6	104	70	0.0	0	0	-0.4
	Yr	1	0	1.000	13	0	0	0	0	21	30	12.9	7	20	8.6	15	6.4	12.00	36	.319	.435	-19	-18	107	70	0.5	0	0	-1.4
Total	6	11	9	.550	102	11	0	0	0	240	249	9.3	30	148	5.6	145	5.4	5.40	73	.271	.365	-38	-39	99	100	0.8	-4	0	-3.5
■ **BOB GIGGIE**	Giggie, Robert Thomas b: 8/13/33, Dorchester, Mass. BR/TR, 6'1", 200 lbs. Deb: 4/18/59																												
1959	Mil-N	1	0	1.000	13	0	0	0	1	20	24	10.8	2	10	4.5	15	6.7	4.05	91	.316	.386	-0	-1	93	143	0.5	-0	1	0.0
1960	Mil-N	0	0	—	3	0	0	0	0	4	5	11.3	0	4	9.0	5	11.3	4.50	75	.278	.409	-0	-1	89	116	0.0	0	0	0.0
	KC-A	1	0	1.000	10	0	0	0	0	19	24	11.4	1	15	7.1	8	3.8	5.68	69	.333	.424	-4	-4	101	117	0.5	-0	-0	-0.3
1962	KC-A	1	1	.500	4	2	0	0	0	14	17	10.9	5	3	1.9	4	2.6	6.43	63	.293	.328	-4	-4	101	101	0.1	-0	-0	-0.3
Total	3	3	1	.750	30	2	0	0	1	57	70	11.1	8	32	5.1	32	5.1	5.21	73	.313	.387	-8	-9	98	122	1.1	-1	1	-0.6
■ **JOE GILBERT**	Gilbert, Joe Dennis b: 4/20/52, Jasper, Tex. BR/TL, 6'1", 167 lbs. Deb: 4/30/72																												
1972	Mon-N	0	1	.000	22	0	0	0	0	33	41	11.2	3	18	4.9	25	6.8	8.45	42	.306	.383	-18	-18	104	65	-0.4	-0	-0	-1.8
1973	Mon-N	1	2	.333	21	0	0	0	1	29	30	9.3	1	19	5.9	17	5.3	4.97	77	.270	.363	-4	-4	105	88	-0.4	0	0	-0.3
Total	2	1	3	.250	43	0	0	0	1	62	71	10.3	4	37	5.4	42	6.1	6.82	54	.290	.374	-22	-22	104	76	-0.8	-0	-0	-2.1
■ **BILL GILBERT**	Gilbert, Wilmer M. b: 5/12/1870, Havre De Grace, Md 6', 180 lbs. Deb: 9/15/1892																												
1892	Bal-N	0	1	.000	2	1	1	0	0	14	14	9.0	1	17	10.9	5	3.2	5.79	58	.273	.454	-4	-4	102	104	-0.4	1	0	-0.2
■ **BILL GILBRETH**	Gilbreth, William Freeman b: 9/3/47, Abilene, Tex. BL/TL, 6', 180 lbs. Deb: 6/25/71																												
1971	Det-A	2	1	.667	9	5	2	0	0	30	28	8.4	4	21	6.3	14	4.2	4.80	69	.264	.383	-4	-5	95	112	0.4	-0	0	-0.4
1972	Det-A	0	0	—	2	0	0	0	0	5	10	18.0	1	4	7.2	2	3.6	16.20	21	.476	.519	-7	-7	112	74	0.0	-0	0	-0.6
1974	Cal-A	0	0	—	3	0	0	0	0	1	2	18.0	0	1	9.0	0	0.0	18.00	19	.400	.429	-2	-2	93	51	0.0	0	0	-0.1
Total	3	2	1	.667	14	5	2	0	0	36	40	10.0	5	26	6.5	16	4.0	6.75	49	.303	.407	-13	-14	97	105	0.4	-0	0	-1.1
■ **BOB GILKS**	Gilks, Robert James b: 7/2/1864, Cincinnati, Ohio d: 8/21/44, Brunswick, Ga. BR/TR, 5'8", 178 lbs. Deb: 8/25/1887																												
1887	Cle-a	7	5	.583	13	13	12	1	0	108	104	8.7	1	42	3.5	28	2.3	3.08	143	.266	.337	15	16	103	110	2.6	1	0	1.6
1888	Cle-a	0	2	.000	4	2	2	0	**1**	21	26	11.1	1	8	3.4	3	1.3	8.14	38	.318	.378	-12	-12	100	61	-0.9	0	0	-0.9
1890	Cle-N	2	2	.500	4	3	3	0	0	32	34	9.6	0	9	2.5	5	1.4	4.22	82	.288	.339	-2	-3	97	76	0.5	-0	0	-0.1
Total	3	9	9	.500	21	18	17	1	1	161	164	9.2	2	59	3.3	36	2.0	3.97	102	.278	.343	0	1	101	97	2.2	1	0	0.6
■ **ED GILL**	Gill, Edward James b: 8/7/1896, Somerville, Mass. BL/TR, 5'10", 165 lbs. Deb: 7/05/19																												
1919	Was-A	1	1	.500	16	2	0	0	0	37	38	9.2	0	21	5.1	7	1.7	4.86	66	.260	.361	-7	-7	99	71	0.2	-1	-1	-0.8

YEAR	TM/L	W	L	PCT	G	GS	CG	SHO	SV	IP	H	H/G	HR	BB	BB/G	SO	SO/G	ERA	/A	OAVG	OOBP	PR	/A	PF	CPI	WAT	PB	PD	TPI
■ **GEORGE GILL**	Gill, George Lloyd b: 2/13/09, Catchings, Miss. BR/TR, 6'1", 185 lbs. Deb: 5/04/37																												
1937	Det-A	11	4	.733	31	10	4	1	1	128	146	10.3	11	42	3.0	40	2.8	4.50	110	.285	.335	2	7	108	99	2.9	-3	1	0.5
1938	Det-A	12	9	.571	24	23	13	1	0	164	195	10.7	15	50	2.7	30	1.6	4.12	115	.296	.344	12	12	99	119	0.7	-4	-1	0.6
1939	Det-A	0	1	.000	3	1	0	0	0	9	14	14.0	1	3	3.0	1	1.0	8.00	63	.368	.405	-3	-3	110	92	-0.4	-0	0	-0.2
	StL-A	1	12	.077	27	11	5	0	0	95	139	13.2	10	34	3.2	24	2.3	7.11	68	.343	.389	-26	-24	105	94	-4.7	-2	1	-2.0
	Yr	1	13	.071	30	12	5	0	0	104	153	13.2	11	37	3.2	25	2.2	7.18	68	.345	.390	-30	-27	105	94	-5.1	-0	1	-2.2
Total	3	24	26	.480	85	45	22	2	1	396	494	11.2	37	129	2.9	95	2.2	5.05	96	.306	.354	-16	-8	104	106	-1.5	-9	2	-1.1
■ **HADDIE GILL**	Gill, Harold Edward b: 1/23/1899, Brockton, Mass. d: 8/1/32, Brockton, Mass. BL/TL, 5'11", 165 lbs. Deb: 8/16/23																												
1923	Cin-N	0	0	—	1	0	0	0	0	1	1	9.0	0	1	9.0	1	9.0	0.00	—	.333	.500	0	0	96	0	0.0	0	0	0.0
■ **CLARAL GILLENWATER**	Gillenwater, Claral Lewis b: 5/20/1900, Sims, Ind. d: 2/26/78, Bradenton, Fla. BR/TR, 6', 187 lbs. Deb: 8/20/23																												
1923	Chi-A	1	3	.250	5	3	1	1	0	21	28	12.0	2	6	2.6	2	0.9	5.57	71	.337	.365	-4	-4	99	104	-0.8	-1	0	-0.3
■ **JOHN GILLESPIE**	Gillespie, John Patrick "Silent John" b: 2/25/1900, Oakland, Cal. d: 2/15/54, Vallejo, Cal. BR/TR, 5'11.5", 172 lbs. Deb: 4/12/22																												
1922	Cin-N	3	3	.500	31	4	1	0	0	78	84	9.7	2	29	3.3	21	2.4	4.50	86	.294	.348	-3	-6	94	95	-0.2	-1	1	-0.4
■ **BOB GILLESPIE**	Gillespie, Robert William "Bunch" b: 10/8/18, Columbus, Ohio BR/TR, 6'4", 187 lbs. Deb: 5/11/44																												
1944	Det-A	0	1	.000	7	0	0	0	0	11	7	5.7	0	12	9.8	4	3.3	6.55	54	.194	.388	-4	-4	104	58	-0.4	-0	0	-0.3
1947	Chi-A	5	8	.385	25	17	1	0	0	118	133	10.1	4	53	4.0	36	2.7	4.73	77	.291	.354	-13	-14	99	95	-1.0	-3	3	-1.3
1948	Chi-A	0	4	.000	25	6	1	0	0	72	81	10.1	3	33	4.1	19	2.4	5.13	83	.287	.361	-7	-7	100	90	-1.9	-2	-0	-0.8
1950	Bos-A	0	0	—	1	0	0	0	0	1	2	18.0	1	4	36.0	0	0.0	27.00	19	.333	.600	-2	-2	111	85	0.0	0	0	-0.1
Total	4	5	13	.278	58	23	2	0	0	202	223	9.9	8	102	4.5	59	2.6	5.08	76	.286	.361	-26	-27	99	91	-3.3	-5	3	-2.5
■ **PAUL GILLIFORD**	Gilliford, Paul Gant "Gorilla" b: 1/12/45, Bryn Mawr, Pa. BR/TL, 5'11", 210 lbs. Deb: 9/20/67																												
1967	Bal-A	0	0	—	2	0	0	0	0	3	6	18.0	1	1	3.0	2	6.0	12.00	25	.429	.467	-3	-3	94	91	0.0	0	0	-0.2
■ **JACK GILLIGAN**	Gilligan, John Patrick b: 10/18/1884, Chicago, Ill. d: 11/19/80, Modesto, Cal. BB/TR, 6', 190 lbs. Deb: 9/16/09																												
1909	StL-A	1	2	.333	3	3	3	0	0	23	28	11.0	1	9	3.5	4	1.6	5.48	43	.315	.390	-8	-8	95	88	-0.2	-0	-1	-0.7
1910	StL-A	0	3	.000	9	5	2	0	0	39	37	8.5	0	28	6.5	10	2.3	3.69	69	.253	.377	-5	-5	101	102	-1.4	-0	0	-0.4
Total	2	1	5	.167	12	8	5	0	0	62	65	9.4	1	37	5.4	14	2.0	4.35	57	.277	.382	-13	-13	98	97	-1.6	-1	-0	-1.1
■ **GEORGE GILLPATRICK**	Gillpatrick, George F. b: 2/28/1875, Holden, Mo. d: 12/15/41, Kansas City, Mo. Deb: 5/22/1898																												
1898	StL-N	0	2	.000	7	3	1	0	0	35	42	10.8	0	19	4.9	12	3.1	6.94	57	.320	.406	-13	-12	110	67	-0.9	-2	0	-1.0
■ **FRANK GILMORE**	Gilmore, Frank T. "Shadow" b: 4/27/1864, Webster, Mass. d: 7/21/29, Hartford, Conn. BR , Deb: 9/11/1886																												
1886	Was-N	4	4	.500	9	9	9	1	0	75	57	6.8	3	22	2.6	75	9.0	2.52	131	.222	.284	7	7	100	87	1.5	-4	0	0.2
1887	Was-N	7	20	.259	28	27	27	1	0	235	247	9.5	7	92	3.5	114	4.4	3.87	103	.285	.354	5	4	99	101	-4.9	-11	0	-0.5
1888	Was-N	1	9	.100	12	11	10	0	0	96	131	12.3	5	29	2.7	23	2.2	6.66	43	.340	.386	-41	-41	101	78	-3.6	-5	0	-3.7
Total	3	12	33	.267	49	47	46	2	0	406	435	9.6	15	143	3.2	212	4.7	4.28	84	.289	.350	-29	-30	100	93	-7.0	-20	0	-4.0
■ **LEN GILMORE**	Gilmore, Leonard Preston "Meow" b: 11/3/17, Clinton, Ind. BR/TR, 6'3", 175 lbs. Deb: 10/01/44																												
1944	Pit-N	0	1	.000	1	1	1	0	0	8	13	14.6	2	0	0.0	0	0.0	7.88	48	.361	.361	-4	-4	104	90	-0.4	-0	1	-0.2
■ **JOHN GILROY**	Gilroy, John M. b: 10/26/1869, Washington, D.C. d: 8/4/1897, Norfolk, Va. Deb: 8/30/1895																												
1895	Was-N	1	4	.200	8	4	2	0	0	41	63	13.8	3	24	5.3	2	0.4	6.59	77	.374	.452	-8	-7	105	108	-0.9	-1	0	-0.5
1896	Was-N	0	0	—	1	0	0	0	0	2	0	0.0	0	1	4.5	0	0.0	0.00	—	.000	.164	1	1	96	0	0.0	-0	0	0.1
Total	2	1	4	.200	9	4	2	0	0	43	63	13.2	3	25	5.2	2	0.4	6.28	80	.363	.443	-7	-6	105	103	-0.9	-1	0	-0.4
■ **HAL GILSON**	Gilson, Harold "Lefty" b: 2/9/42, Los Angeles, Cal. BR/TL, 6'5", 195 lbs. Deb: 4/14/68																												
1968	StL-N	0	2	.000	13	0	0	0	2	22	27	11.0	1	11	4.5	19	7.8	4.50	62	.310	.376	-4	-4	93	114	-0.9	-0	-1	-0.5
	Hou-N	0	0	—	2	0	0	0	0	4	7	15.8	0	1	2.3	1	2.3	6.75	44	.412	.474	-2	-2	100	115	0.0	0	0	-0.1
	Yr	0	2	.000	15	0	0	0	2	26	34	11.8	1	12	4.2	20	6.9	4.85	58	.327	.392	-5	-6	94	115	-0.9	-0	-1	-0.6
■ **BILLY GING**	Ging, William Joseph b: 11/7/1872, Elmira, N.Y. d: 9/14/50, Elmira, N.Y. 5'10", 170 lbs. Deb: 9/25/1899																												
1899	Bos-N	1	0	1.000	1	1	1	0	0	8	5	5.6	0	5	5.6	2	2.3	1.13	352	.198	.331	2	3	103	179	0.5	-0	0	0.2
■ **JOE GINGRAS**	Gingras, Joseph Elzead John b: 1/10/1894, New York, N.Y. d: 9/6/47, Jersey City, N.J. BR/TR, 6'2", 188 lbs. Deb: 6/18/15																												
1915	KC-F	0	0	—	2	0	0	0	0	4	6	13.5	0	1	2.3	2	4.5	6.75	43	.379	.416	-2	-2	97	81	0.0	-0	0	-0.1
■ **CHARLIE GIRARD**	Girard, Charles August b: 12/16/1884, Brooklyn, N.Y. d: 8/6/36, Brooklyn, N.Y. BR/TR, 5'10", 175 lbs. Deb: 9/14/10																												
1910	Phi-N	1	2	.333	7	1	0	0	1	27	33	11.0	2	12	4.0	11	3.7	6.33	46	.308	.388	-10	-10	95	82	-0.4	-0	-1	-1.0
■ **DAVE GIUSTI**	Giusti, David John b: 11/27/39, Seneca Falls, N.Y. BR/TR, 5'11", 190 lbs. Deb: 4/13/62																												
1962	Hou-N	2	3	.400	22	5	0	0	0	74	82	10.0	7	30	3.6	43	5.2	5.59	67	.280	.343	-14	-15	95	79	0.0	2	1	-1.1
1964	Hou-N	0	0	—	8	0	0	0	0	26	24	8.3	1	8	2.8	16	5.5	3.12	112	.253	.302	1	1	98	102	0.0	1	1	0.3
1965	Hou-N	8	7	.533	38	13	4	1	3	131	132	9.1	13	46	3.2	92	6.3	4.33	74	.259	.316	-11	-16	91	89	1.8	2	1	-1.3
1966	Hou-N	15	14	.517	34	33	9	4	0	210	215	9.2	23	54	2.3	131	5.6	4.20	85	.260	.307	-14	-15	99	87	2.2	4	-1	-1.2
1967	Hou-N	11	15	.423	37	33	8	1	1	222	231	9.4	20	58	2.4	157	6.4	4.18	77	.265	.307	-20	-24	95	88	0.0	4	-2	-2.2
1968	Hou-N	11	14	.440	37	34	12	2	1	251	226	8.1	15	67	2.4	186	6.7	3.19	94	.239	.288	-6	-5	100	87	0.0	2	3	0.0
1969	StL-N	3	7	.300	22	12	2	1	0	100	96	8.6	7	37	3.3	62	5.6	3.60	99	.255	.316	-0	-0	99	99	-2.2	1	1	0.2
1970	Pit-N	9	3	.750	66	1	0	0	26	103	98	8.6	7	39	3.4	85	7.4	3.06	127	.259	.320	11	10	96	124	2.8	2	0	1.1
1971	Pit-N	5	6	.455	58	0	0	0	**30**	86	79	8.3	5	31	3.2	55	5.8	2.93	115	.241	.304	5	4	97	102	-1.3	-1	-1	0.2
1972	Pit-N	7	4	.636	54	0	0	0	22	75	59	7.1	3	20	2.4	54	6.5	1.92	180	.219	.268	13	13	100	113	0.3	-1	1	1.3
1973	Pit-N	9	2	.818	67	0	0	0	20	99	89	8.1	9	37	3.4	64	5.8	2.36	142	.241	.303	14	11	92	139	3.6	1	-2	1.1
1974	Pit-N	7	5	.583	64	2	0	0	12	106	101	8.6	2	40	3.4	53	4.5	3.31	106	.258	.317	4	2	97	97	0.6	-0	1	0.3
1975	Pit-N	5	4	.556	61	0	0	0	17	92	79	7.7	3	42	4.1	38	3.7	2.93	121	.237	.311	7	6	98	102	0.0	1	0	0.7
1976	Pit-N	5	4	.556	40	0	0	0	6	58	59	9.2	5	27	4.2	24	3.7	4.34	80	.267	.335	-5	-6	99	97	0.0	-0	0	-0.5
1977	Oak-A	3	3	.500	40	0	0	0	6	60	54	8.1	4	20	3.0	28	4.2	3.00	131	.245	.305	7	6	97	106	0.6	0	0	0.6
	Chi-N	0	2	.000	20	0	0	0	1	25	30	10.8	2	14	5.0	15	5.4	6.12	73	.297	.379	-6	-5	115	85	-0.9	-0	-0	-0.4
Total	15	100	93	.518	668	133	35	9	145	1718	1654	8.7	126	570	3.0	1103	5.8	3.60	95	.253	.309	-13	-32	97	97	7.5	17	3	-0.9
■ **DAN GLADDEN**	Gladden, Clinton Daniel b: 7/7/57, San Jose, Cal. BB/TR, 5'11", 180 lbs. Deb: 9/05/83																												
1988	Min-A	0	0	—	1	0	0	0	0	1	0	0.0	0	0	0.0	0	0.0	0.00	—	.000	.000	0	0	105	0	0.0	1	0	0.0
■ **FRED GLADDING**	Gladding, Fred Earl b: 6/28/36, Flat Rock, Mich. BL/TR, 6'1", 220 lbs. Deb: 7/01/61 C																												
1961	Det-A	1	0	1.000	8	0	0	0	0	16	18	10.1	1	11	6.2	11	6.2	3.38	112	.286	.392	1	1	94	164	0.5	-0	-0	0.0
1962	Det-A	0	0	—	6	0	0	0	0	5	3	5.4	0	2	3.6	4	7.2	0.00	—	.176	.250	2	2	110	0	0.0	0	0	0.3
1963	Det-A	1	1	.500	22	0	0	0	7	27	19	6.3	1	14	4.7	24	8.0	2.00	188	.198	.292	5	5	104	120	0.0	-0	0	0.6
1964	Det-A	7	4	.636	42	0	0	0	7	67	57	7.7	7	27	3.6	59	7.9	3.09	112	.233	.306	4	3	95	111	1.4	-1	1	0.2
1965	Det-A	6	2	.750	46	0	0	0	5	70	63	8.1	6	29	3.7	43	5.5	2.83	127	.239	.319	5	6	104	124	1.8	-1	-1	0.5
1966	Det-A	5	0	1.000	51	0	0	0	2	74	62	7.5	6	29	3.5	57	6.9	3.28	107	.230	.303	1	2	102	98	2.5	-0	-1	0.1
1967	Det-A	6	4	.600	42	1	0	0	12	77	62	7.2	6	19	2.2	64	7.5	1.99	159	.227	.281	11	10	98	144	0.5	-2	-0	0.9
1968	Hou-N	0	0	—	7	0	0	0	2	4	8	18.0	0	3	6.8	2	4.5	15.75	19	.421	.500	-6	-6	100	63	0.0	0	0	-0.5
1969	Hou-N	4	8	.333	57	0	0	0	**29**	73	83	10.2	2	27	3.3	40	4.9	4.19	87	.289	.348	-5	-4	101	99	-2.0	-1	0	-0.4
1970	Hou-N	7	4	.636	63	0	0	0	18	71	84	10.6	4	24	3.0	46	5.8	4.06	94	.293	.343	-0	-2	94	112	1.7	-1	1	-0.1
1971	Hou-N	4	5	.444	48	0	0	0	12	51	51	9.0	0	22	3.9	17	3.0	2.12	151	.268	.351	8	6	92	183	-0.3	-0	-1	0.5
1972	Hou-N	5	6	.455	42	0	0	0	14	49	38	7.0	1	12	2.2	18	3.3	2.76	132	.222	.274	4	5	105	80	-0.9	-1	-1	0.3
1973	Hou-N	2	0	1.000	16	0	0	0	1	16	18	10.1	4	4	2.3	9	5.1	4.50	77	.290	.328	-1	-2	95	121	1.0	0	0	-0.1
Total	13	48	34	.585	450	1	0	0	109	600	566	8.5	38	223	3.3	394	5.9	3.14	113	.252	.320	29	26	99	118	6.2	-6	-1	2.3
■ **FRED GLADE**	Glade, Frederick Monroe "Lucky" b: 1/25/1876, Dubuque, Iowa d: 11/21/34, Grand Island, Neb. BR/TR, 5'10", 175 lbs. Deb: 5/27/02																												
1902	Chi-N	0	1	.000	1	1	1	0	0	8	13	14.6	0	3	3.4	3	3.4	9.00	29	.391	.441	-6	-6	95	67	-0.4	1	0	-0.4

YEAR	TM/L	W	L	PCT	G	GS	CG	SHO	SV	IP	H	H/G	HR	BB	BB/G	SO	SO/G	ERA	/A	OAVG	OOBP	PR	/A	PF	CPI	WAT	PB	PD	TPI
1904	StL-A	18	15	.545	35	34	30	6	1	289	248	7.7	2	58	1.8	156	4.9	2.27	111	.254	.295	10	8	98	95	4.1	1	1	1.1
1905	StL-A	6	25	.194	32	32	28	2	0	275	257	8.4	3	58	1.9	127	4.2	2.81	88	.271	.313	-5	-10	93	95	-7.8	-6	4	-0.7
1906	StL-A	15	14	.517	35	32	28	4	1	267	215	7.2	4	59	2.0	96	3.2	2.36	110	.244	.291	10	7	97	85	0.3	-4	-3	0.5
1907	StL-A	13	9	.591	24	22	18	2	0	202	187	8.3	2	45	2.0	71	3.2	2.67	93	.269	.314	-3	-4	98	92	3.1	2	-4	-0.8
1908	NY-A	0	4	.000	5	5	2	0	0	32	30	8.4	0	14	3.9	11	3.1	4.22	57	.275	.378	-7	-6	101	96	-1.9	-1	-1	-0.6
Total	6	52	68	.433	132	126	107	14	2	1073	950	8.0	11	237	2.0	464	3.9	2.62	96	.261	.306	-0	-11	96	92	-2.6	-7	-3	-0.9

■ **JOHN GLAISER** Glaiser, John Burke "Bert" b: 7/28/1894, Yoakum, Tex. d: 3/7/59, Houston, Tex. BL/TR, 5'8", 165 lbs. Deb: 4/20/20

YEAR	TM/L	W	L	PCT	G	GS	CG	SHO	SV	IP	H	H/G	HR	BB	BB/G	SO	SO/G	ERA	/A	OAVG	OOBP	PR	/A	PF	CPI	WAT	PB	PD	TPI
1920	Det-A	0	0	—	9	1	0	0	1	17	23	12.2	1	8	4.2	3	1.6	6.35	63	.354	.432	-5	-4	106	101	0.0	-0	1	-0.2

■ **TOM GLASS** Glass, Thomas Joseph b: 4/29/1898, Greensboro, N.C. d: 12/15/81, Greensboro, N.C. BR/TR, 6'3", 170 lbs. Deb: 6/12/25

YEAR	TM/L	W	L	PCT	G	GS	CG	SHO	SV	IP	H	H/G	HR	BB	BB/G	SO	SO/G	ERA	/A	OAVG	OOBP	PR	/A	PF	CPI	WAT	PB	PD	TPI
1925	Phi-A	1	0	1.000	2	0	0	0	0	5	9	16.2	0	0	0.0	2	3.6	5.40	82	.409	.360	-1	-1	101	122	0.5	-0	-0	0.0

■ **JACK GLASSCOCK** Glasscock, John Wesley "Pebbly Jack" b: 7/22/1859, Wheeling, W.Va. d: 2/24/47, Wheeling, W.Va. BR/TR, 5'8", 160 lbs. Deb: 5/01/1879 M

YEAR	TM/L	W	L	PCT	G	GS	CG	SHO	SV	IP	H	H/G	HR	BB	BB/G	SO	SO/G	ERA	/A	OAVG	OOBP	PR	/A	PF	CPI	WAT	PB	PD	TPI
1884	Cle-N	0	0	—	2	0	0	0	0	5	8	14.4	0	2	3.6	1	1.8	5.40	59	.371	.424	-1	-1	108	113	0.0	0	0	0.0
1887	Ind-N	0	0	—	1	0	0	0	0	1	0	0.0	0	0	0.0	1	9.0	0.00	—	.000	.000	0	0	101	0	0.0	0	0	0.0
1888	Ind-N	0	0	—	1	0	0	0	0	⅓	1	27.0	0	2	54.0	1	27.0	54.00	—	1.000	1.000	-2	-2	98	58	0.0	0	0	-0.1
1889	Ind-N	0	0	—	1	0	0	0	0	1	3	27.0	0	3	27.0	0	0.0	0.00	—	.533	.695	0	0	110	0	0.0	0	0	0.0
Total	4	0	0	—	5	0	0	0	0	7	12	15.4	0	7	9.0	3	3.9	6.43	55	.389	.502	-2	-2	107	81	0.0	1	0	-0.1

■ **LUKE GLAVENICH** Glavenich, Luke Frank b: 1/17/1893, Jackson, Cal. d: 5/22/35, Stockton, Cal. 5'9.5", 189 lbs. Deb: 4/12/13

YEAR	TM/L	W	L	PCT	G	GS	CG	SHO	SV	IP	H	H/G	HR	BB	BB/G	SO	SO/G	ERA	/A	OAVG	OOBP	PR	/A	PF	CPI	WAT	PB	PD	TPI
1913	Cle-A	0	0	—	1	0	0	0	0	1	3	27.0	0	3	27.0	1	9.0	9.00	34	.500	.667	-1	-1	104	220	0.0	0	0	0.0

■ **TOM GLAVINE** Glavine, Thomas Michael b: 3/25/66, Concord, Mass. BL/TL, 6' ", 175 lbs. Deb: 8/17/87

YEAR	TM/L	W	L	PCT	G	GS	CG	SHO	SV	IP	H	H/G	HR	BB	BB/G	SO	SO/G	ERA	/A	OAVG	OOBP	PR	/A	PF	CPI	WAT	PB	PD	TPI
1987	Atl-N	2	4	.333	9	9	0	0	0	50	55	9.9	5	33	5.9	20	3.6	5.58	80	.279	.382	-8	-6	109	97	-0.6	-0	1	-0.5
1988	Atl-N	7	17	.292	34	34	1	0	0	195	201	9.3	12	63	2.9	84	3.9	4.57	81	.270	.322	-24	-19	107	86	-1.8	1	2	-1.6
Total	2	9	21	.300	43	43	1	0	0	245	256	9.4	17	96	3.5	104	3.8	4.78	81	.272	.335	-32	-25	107	88	-2.4	1	2	-2.1

■ **RALPH GLAZE** Glaze, Daniel Ralph b: 3/13/1882, Denver, Col. d: 10/31/68, Atascadero, Cal. BR/TR, 5'9", 165 lbs. Deb: 6/01/06

YEAR	TM/L	W	L	PCT	G	GS	CG	SHO	SV	IP	H	H/G	HR	BB	BB/G	SO	SO/G	ERA	/A	OAVG	OOBP	PR	/A	PF	CPI	WAT	PB	PD	TPI
1906	Bos-A	4	6	.400	19	10	7	0	0	123	110	8.0	4	32	2.3	56	4.1	3.59	78	.263	.316	-12	-11	104	75	0.6	0	0	-1.1
1907	Bos-A	9	13	.409	32	21	11	1	0	182	150	7.4	4	48	2.4	68	3.4	2.32	113	.247	.302	4	6	103	94	0.3	0	-4	0.3
1908	Bos-A	2	2	.500	10	3	2	0	0	35	43	11.1	1	5	1.3	13	3.3	3.34	69	.253	.274	-4	-4	97	72	0.1	-1	-1	-0.4
Total	3	15	21	.417	61	34	20	1	0	340	303	8.0	9	85	2.3	137	3.6	2.89	92	.254	.303	-12	-9	103	85	1.0	-1	-4	-1.2

■ **WHITEY GLAZNER** Glazner, Charles Franklin b: 9/17/1893, Sycamore, Ala. BR/TR, 5'9", 165 lbs. Deb: 9/26/20

YEAR	TM/L	W	L	PCT	G	GS	CG	SHO	SV	IP	H	H/G	HR	BB	BB/G	SO	SO/G	ERA	/A	OAVG	OOBP	PR	/A	PF	CPI	WAT	PB	PD	TPI
1920	Pit-N	0	0	—	2	0	0	0	0	9	9	9.0	0	2	2.0	1	1.0	3.00	106	.300	.333	0	0	101	116	0.0	-0	-0	0.0
1921	Pit-N	14	5	.737	36	25	15	0	1	234	214	**8.2**	5	58	2.2	88	3.4	2.77	139	**.250**	.299	26	28	102	95	3.7	-3	-3	2.1
1922	Pit-N	11	12	.478	34	26	10	1	1	193	238	11.1	9	52	2.4	77	3.6	4.38	95	.309	.345	-6	-5	101	100	-1.7	3	0	0.0
1923	Pit-N	2	1	.667	7	4	1	1	1	30	29	8.7	5	11	3.3	8	2.4	3.30	116	.250	.313	2	2	95	120	0.4	2	0	0.4
	Phi-N	7	14	.333	28	23	12	2	1	161	195	10.9	11	63	3.5	51	2.9	4.70	100	.304	.364	-12	0	118	104	0.2	-1	-0	0.0
	Yr	9	15	.375	35	27	13	3	2	191	224	10.6	16	74	3.5	59	2.8	4.48	102	.296	.356	-10	2	114	104	0.6	2	0	0.4
1924	Phi-N	7	16	.304	35	24	8	2	0	157	210	12.0	14	63	3.6	41	2.4	5.90	72	.339	.395	-36	-28	111	104	-2.1	-4	1	-2.8
Total	5	41	48	.461	142	102	46	6	4	784	895	10.3	44	249	2.9	266	3.1	4.21	99	.295	.345	-25	-3	106	101	0.5	-3	-2	-0.3

■ **JOE GLEASON** Gleason, Joseph Paul b: 7/9/1895, Phelps, N.Y. BR/TR, 5'10.5", 175 lbs. Deb: 9/11/20

YEAR	TM/L	W	L	PCT	G	GS	CG	SHO	SV	IP	H	H/G	HR	BB	BB/G	SO	SO/G	ERA	/A	OAVG	OOBP	PR	/A	PF	CPI	WAT	PB	PD	TPI
1920	Was-A	0	0	—	3	0	0	0	0	8	14	15.8	2	6	6.8	2	2.3	13.50	27	.326	.420	-9	-9	96	59	0.0	1	0	-0.6
1922	Was-A	2	2	.500	8	5	3	0	0	41	53	11.6	3	18	4.0	12	2.6	4.61	81	.319	.379	-3	-4	93	118	0.2	-0	-0	-0.3
Total	2	2	2	.500	11	5	3	0	0	49	67	12.3	5	24	4.4	14	2.6	6.06	62	.321	.387	-11	-13	93	109	0.2	0	0	-0.9

■ **BILL GLEASON** Gleason, William b: 1868, Cleveland, Ohio d: 12/2/1893, Cleveland, Ohio Deb: 4/24/1890

YEAR	TM/L	W	L	PCT	G	GS	CG	SHO	SV	IP	H	H/G	HR	BB	BB/G	SO	SO/G	ERA	/A	OAVG	OOBP	PR	/A	PF	CPI	WAT	PB	PD	TPI
1890	Cle-P	0	1	.000	1	1	0	0	0	4	14	31.5	0	6	13.5	0	0.0	27.00	15	.567	.651	-10	-10	94	69	-0.4	-0	0	-0.5

■ **KID GLEASON** Gleason, William J. b: 10/26/1866, Camden, N.J. d: 1/2/33, Philadelphia, Pa. BB/TR, 5'7", 158 lbs. Deb: 1888 MC

YEAR	TM/L	W	L	PCT	G	GS	CG	SHO	SV	IP	H	H/G	HR	BB	BB/G	SO	SO/G	ERA	/A	OAVG	OOBP	PR	/A	PF	CPI	WAT	PB	PD	TPI
1888	Phi-N	7	16	.304	24	23	23	1	0	200	199	9.0	11	53	2.4	89	4.0	2.84	113	.273	.322	-0	8	113	117	-5.4	-1	0	0.9
1889	Phi-N	9	15	.375	29	21	15	0	1	205	242	10.6	8	97	4.3	64	2.8	5.58	76	.310	.386	-35	-31	105	85	-3.3	3	0	-2.1
1890	Phi-N	38	17	.691	60	55	54	6	**2**	506	479	8.5	8	167	3.0	222	3.9	2.63	145	.265	.327	52	66	107	109	**9.8**	-7	0	5.7
1891	Phi-N	24	22	.522	53	44	40	1	1	418	431	9.3	10	165	3.6	100	2.2	3.51	91	.280	.350	-8	-15	95	94	1.7	8	-2	-0.6
1892	StL-N	20	24	.455	47	45	43	2	0	400	389	8.8	11	151	3.4	133	3.0	3.33	96	.268	.337	-2	-6	97	96	3.8	8	5	0.9
1893	StL-N	21	22	.488	48	45	37	1	1	380	436	10.3	18	187	4.4	86	2.0	4.62	101	.304	.384	3	2	100	104	3.0	4	3	0.9
1894	StL-N	2	6	.250	8	8	6	0	0	58	75	11.6	2	21	3.3	9	1.4	6.05	91	.336	.393	-5	-4	103	82	-1.6	-0	0	-0.2
	Bal-N	15	5	.750	21	20	19	0	0	172	224	11.7	3	44	2.3	35	1.8	4.45	115	.338	.379	17	13	96	104	2.1	5	0	1.5
	Yr	17	11	.607	29	28	25	0	0	230	299	11.7	5	65	2.5	44	1.7	4.85	108	.337	.383	12	9	98	104	0.5	-0	0	1.3
1895	Bal-N	2	4	.333	9	5	3	0	1	50	77	13.9	4	21	3.8	6	1.1	7.02	71	.374	.432	-12	-11	104	96	-1.4	1	0	-0.8
Total	8	138	131	.513	299	266	240	11	6	2389	2552	9.6	75	906	3.4	744	2.8	3.79	103	.289	.355	10	26	102	101	8.7	21	6	6.2

■ **JERRY GLEATON** Gleaton, Jerry Don b: 9/14/57, Brownwood, Tex. BL/TL, 6'3", 205 lbs. Deb: 7/11/79

YEAR	TM/L	W	L	PCT	G	GS	CG	SHO	SV	IP	H	H/G	HR	BB	BB/G	SO	SO/G	ERA	/A	OAVG	OOBP	PR	/A	PF	CPI	WAT	PB	PD	TPI
1979	Tex-A	0	1	.000	5	2	0	0	0	10	15	13.5	0	2	1.8	2	1.8	6.30	67	.375	.400	-2	-2	99	99	-0.4	0	0	-0.1
1980	Tex-A	0	0	—	5	0	0	0	0	7	5	6.4	0	4	5.1	2	2.6	2.57	158	.208	.300	1	1	100	99	0.0	0	0	0.1
1981	Sea-A	4	7	.364	20	13	1	0	0	85	88	9.3	10	38	4.0	31	3.3	4.76	78	.273	.347	-10	-10	101	98	-0.5	0	-1	-1.0
1982	Sea-A	0	0	—	3	0	0	0	0	5	7	12.6	3	2	3.6	1	1.8	12.60	36	.333	.417	-5	-5	110	83	0.0	0	0	-0.3
1984	Chi-A	1	2	.333	11	1	0	0	2	18	20	10.0	2	6	3.0	4	2.0	3.50	127	.286	.333	1	2	111	135	-0.3	0	-0	0.1
1985	Chi-A	1	0	1.000	31	0	0	0	1	30	37	11.1	3	13	3.9	22	6.6	5.70	73	.316	.370	-5	-5	100	101	0.5	0	-0	-0.4
1987	KC-A	4	4	.500	48	0	0	0	5	51	38	6.7	4	28	4.9	44	7.8	4.24	110	.216	.314	1	2	104	80	0.0	0	1	0.3
1988	KC-A	0	4	.000	42	0	0	0	3	38	33	7.8	2	17	4.0	29	6.9	3.55	115	.232	.323	2	2	103	94	-1.9	1	-0	0.2
Total	8	10	18	.357	165	16	1	0	11	244	243	9.0	24	110	4.1	135	5.0	4.65	88	.266	.341	-17	-15	103	97	-2.6	0	0	-1.1

■ **MARTIN GLENDON** Glendon, Martin J. b: 2/8/1877, Milwaukee, Wis. d: 11/6/50, Norwood Park, Ill. 5'8", 165 lbs. Deb: 4/18/02

YEAR	TM/L	W	L	PCT	G	GS	CG	SHO	SV	IP	H	H/G	HR	BB	BB/G	SO	SO/G	ERA	/A	OAVG	OOBP	PR	/A	PF	CPI	WAT	PB	PD	TPI
1902	Cin-N	0	1	.000	1	1	0	0	0	3	5	15.0	0	4	12.0	0	0.0	12.00	25	.397	.542	-3	-3	108	74	-0.4	-0	0	-0.2
1903	Cle-A	1	2	.333	3	3	3	0	0	28	20	6.4	0	7	2.3	9	2.9	0.96	291	.219	.275	6	6	95	159	-0.5	-1	1	0.8
Total	2	1	3	.250	4	4	3	0	0	31	25	7.3	0	11	3.2	9	2.6	2.03	139	.241	.314	3	3	96	151	-0.9	-1	1	0.6

■ **BOB GLENN** Glenn, Burdette b: 6/16/1894, W.Sunbury, Pa. d: 6/3/77, Richmond, Cal. Deb: 7/27/20

YEAR	TM/L	W	L	PCT	G	GS	CG	SHO	SV	IP	H	H/G	HR	BB	BB/G	SO	SO/G	ERA	/A	OAVG	OOBP	PR	/A	PF	CPI	WAT	PB	PD	TPI
1920	StL-N	0	0	—	2	0	0	0	0	2	2	9.0	0	0	0.0	0	0.0	0.00	—	.222	.222	1	1	98	0	0.0	0	0	0.1

■ **SAL GLIATTO** Gliatto, Salvador Michael b: 5/7/02, Chicago, Ill. BB/TR, 5'8.5", 150 lbs. Deb: 4/19/30

YEAR	TM/L	W	L	PCT	G	GS	CG	SHO	SV	IP	H	H/G	HR	BB	BB/G	SO	SO/G	ERA	/A	OAVG	OOBP	PR	/A	PF	CPI	WAT	PB	PD	TPI
1930	Cle-A	0	0	—	8	0	0	0	2	15	21	12.6	1	9	5.4	7	4.2	6.60	74	.328	.421	-3	-3	105	104	0.0	-0	-0	-0.2

■ **ED GLYNN** Glynn, Edward Paul b: 6/3/53, Flushing, N.Y. BR/TL, 6'2", 180 lbs. Deb: 9/19/75

YEAR	TM/L	W	L	PCT	G	GS	CG	SHO	SV	IP	H	H/G	HR	BB	BB/G	SO	SO/G	ERA	/A	OAVG	OOBP	PR	/A	PF	CPI	WAT	PB	PD	TPI
1975	Det-A	0	2	.000	3	1	0	0	0	15	11	6.6	1	8	4.8	8	4.8	4.20	96	.220	.322	-1	-0	106	78	-0.9	0	0	0.0
1976	Det-A	1	3	.250	5	4	1	0	0	24	22	8.3	3	20	7.5	17	6.4	6.00	61	.265	.389	-7	-6	105	94	-0.8	0	-1	-0.6
1977	Det-A	2	1	.667	8	3	0	0	0	27	36	12.0	3	12	4.0	13	4.3	5.33	80	.316	.372	-4	-3	105	106	0.6	0	-0	-0.3
1978	Det-A	0	0	—	10	0	0	0	0	15	11	6.6	3	4	2.4	9	5.4	3.00	135	.208	.250	1	2	107	103	0.0	0	1	0.3
1979	NY-N	1	4	.200	46	0	0	0	7	60	57	8.6	3	40	6.0	32	4.8	3.00	120	.259	.368	5	4	96	147	-1.1	-0	-1	0.3
1980	NY-N	3	3	.500	38	0	0	0	1	52	49	8.5	5	23	4.0	32	5.5	4.15	84	.246	.316	-3	-4	97	88	0.5	-1	1	-0.3
1981	Cle-A	0	0	—	4	0	0	0	0	8	5	5.6	0	4	4.5	4	4.5	1.13	304	.192	.300	2	2	93	191	0.0	0	-0	0.2
1982	Cle-A	5	2	.714	47	0	0	0	4	50	43	7.7	6	30	5.4	54	9.7	4.14	99	.232	.333	-0	-0	101	97	1.6	0	-0	0.0
1983	Cle-A	0	2	.000	11	0	0	0	0	12	22	16.5	2	6	4.5	13	9.8	6.00	72	.373	.424	-3	-2	106	139	-0.9	0	-0	-0.1
1985	Mon-N	0	0	—	3	0	0	0	0	2	5	22.5	0	4	18.0	2	9.0	22.50	15	.455	.563	-4	-4	94	65	0.0	0	0	-0.3
Total	10	12	17	.414	175	8	1	0	12	265	261	8.9	26	151	5.1	184	6.2	4.25	90	.261	.350	-13	-12	100	111	-1.0	-1	-1	-0.8

■ **JOT GOAR** Goar, Joshua Mercer b: 1/31/1870, New Lisbon, Ind. d: 4/4/47, New Castle, Ind. BR/TR, 5'9", 160 lbs. Deb: 4/18/1896

YEAR	TM/L	W	L	PCT	G	GS	CG	SHO	SV	IP	H	H/G	HR	BB	BB/G	SO	SO/G	ERA	/A	OAVG	OOBP	PR	/A	PF	CPI	WAT	PB	PD	TPI
1896	Pit-N	0	1	.000	3	0	0	0	0	13	36	24.9	1	8	5.5	3	2.1	17.31	23	.521	.570	-19	-19	93	77	-0.4	-0	0	-1.3

YEAR	TM/L	W	L	PCT	G	GS	CG	SHO	SV	IP	H	H/G	HR	BB	BB/G	SO	SO/G	ERA	/A	OAVG	OOBP	PR	/A	PF	CPI	WAT	PB	PD	TPI
1898	Cin-N	0	0	—	1	0	0	0	0	2	4	18.0	0	1	4.5	0	0.0	9.00	43	.439	.495	-1	-1	107	93	0.0	0	0	0.0
Total	2	0	1	.000	4	0	0	0	0	15	40	24.0	1	9	5.4	3	1.8	16.20	25	.511	.562	-20	-20	95	79	-0.4	-0	0	-1.3
■ **GEORGE GOETZ** Goetz, George Burt b: Greencastle, Ind. 6'2", 180 lbs. Deb: 6/17/1889																													
1889	Bal-a	1	0	1.000	1	1	0	0	0	9	12	12.0	0	0	0.0	2	2.0	4.00	96	.336	.336	-0	-0	99	96	0.5	-1	0	0.0
■ **JOHN GOETZ** Goetz, John Hardy b: 10/24/37, Goetzville, Mich. BR/TR, 6', 185 lbs. Deb: 4/16/60																													
1960	Chi-N	0	0	—	4	0	0	0	0	6	10	15.0	2	4	6.0	6	9.0	13.50	28	.370	.438	-6	-6	101	73	0.0	-0	0	-0.5
■ **BILL GOGOLEWSKI** Gogolewski, William Joseph b: 10/26/47, Oshkosh, Wis. BL/TR, 6'4", 190 lbs. Deb: 9/03/70																													
1970	Was-A	2	2	.500	8	5	0	0	0	34	33	8.7	2	25	6.6	19	5.0	4.76	76	.260	.381	-4	-4	97	98	0.2	-0	1	-0.3
1971	Was-A	6	5	.545	27	17	4	1	0	124	112	8.1	5	39	2.8	70	5.1	2.76	118	.241	.298	10	7	94	100	1.4	0	-0	0.8
1972	Tex-A	4	11	.267	36	21	2	1	2	151	136	8.1	9	58	3.5	95	5.7	4.23	70	.239	.313	-19	-21	97	74	-1.8	-1	-0	-2.3
1973	Tex-A	3	6	.333	49	1	0	0	6	124	139	10.1	10	48	3.5	77	5.6	4.21	91	.286	.344	-5	-5	100	105	-0.1	0	2	-0.2
1974	Cle-A	0	0	—	5	0	0	0	0	14	15	9.6	1	2	1.3	3	1.9	4.50	81	.283	.321	-1	-1	101	84	0.0	0	1	0.0
1975	Chi-A	0	0	—	19	0	0	0	2	55	61	10.0	5	28	4.6	37	6.1	5.24	75	.292	.367	-9	-8	104	97	0.0	0	1	-0.6
Total	6	15	24	.385	144	44	6	2	10	502	496	8.9	32	200	3.6	301	5.4	4.02	85	.260	.328	-29	-34	98	92	-0.3	-1	5	-2.6
■ **JIM GOLDEN** Golden, James Edward b: 3/20/36, Eldon, Mo. BL/TR, 6', 175 lbs. Deb: 9/30/60																													
1960	LA-N	1	0	1.000	1	1	0	0	0	7	6	7.7	1	4	5.1	4	5.1	6.43	67	.240	.333	-2	-2	114	69	0.5	0	0	0.0
1961	LA-N	1	1	.500	28	0	0	0	0	42	52	11.1	7	20	4.3	18	3.9	5.79	71	.306	.362	-8	-8	102	102	0.0	-0	-0	-0.7
1962	Hou-N	7	11	.389	37	18	5	2	1	153	163	9.6	13	50	2.9	88	5.2	4.06	92	.270	.322	-2	-6	95	95	-0.2	4	1	-0.1
1963	Hou-N	0	1	.000	3	1	0	0	0	6	12	18.0	0	2	3.0	5	7.5	6.00	52	.429	.467	-2	-2	95	138	-0.4	0	0	-0.1
Total	4	9	13	.409	69	20	5	2	1	208	233	10.1	21	76	3.3	115	5.0	4.54	84	.282	.336	-14	-17	97	97	-0.1	4	0	-0.9
■ **MIKE GOLDEN** Golden, Michael Henry b: 9/11/1851, Shirley, Mass. d: 1/11/29, Rockford, Ill. BR/TR, 5'7", 166 lbs. Deb: 5/05/1875																													
1875	Wes-n	1	12	.077	13																								
	Chi-n	7	7	.500	15																								
	Yr	8	19	.296	28																								
1878	Mil-N	3	13	.188	22	18	15	0	0	161	217	12.1	1	33	1.8	52	2.9	4.14	63	.333	.365	-33	-27	114	95	-2.4	-2	0	-2.3
■ **ROY GOLDEN** Golden, Roy Kramer b: 7/12/1888, Madisonville, Ill d: 10/4/61, Norwood, Ohio TR, 6'1", 195 lbs. Deb: 9/07/10																													
1910	StL-N	2	3	.400	7	6	3	0	0	43	44	9.2	3	33	6.9	31	6.5	4.40	64	.286	.418	-7	-8	93	122	0.0	1	1	-0.5
1911	StL-N	4	9	.308	30	25	6	0	0	149	127	7.7	6	129	7.8	81	4.9	5.01	70	.240	.394	-27	-25	102	87	-2.6	-1	-0	-2.5
Total	2	6	12	.333	37	31	9	0	0	192	171	8.0	9	162	7.6	112	5.3	4.88	68	.250	.399	-33	-33	100	95	-2.6	-1	1	-3.0
■ **FRED GOLDSMITH** Goldsmith, Fred Ernest b: 5/15/1852, New Haven, Conn. d: 3/28/39, Berkley, Mich. BR/TR, 6'1", 195 lbs. Deb: 10/23/1875																													
1879	Tro-N	2	4	.333	8	7	7	0	0	63	61	8.7	0	1	0.1	31	4.4	1.57	159	.260	.263	6	6	100	111	0.3	0	0	0.6
1880	Chi-N	21	3	**.875**	26	24	22	4	1	210	189	8.1	2	18	0.8	90	3.9	1.76	133	.249	.266	14	13	98	105	5.6	2	0	1.6
1881	Chi-N	24	13	.649	39	39	37	5	0	330	328	8.9	4	44	1.2	76	2.1	2.59	111	.271	.297	7	10	103	90	-0.8	1	5	1.7
1882	Chi-N	28	17	.622	45	45	45	4	0	405	377	8.4	7	38	0.8	109	2.4	2.42	113	.254	.273	21	14	95	90	-2.2	-0	-1	1.0
1883	Chi-N	25	19	.568	46	45	40	2	0	383	456	10.7	14	39	0.9	82	1.9	3.15	106	.304	.321	-0	8	107	115	-2.0	-2	2	0.9
1884	Chi-N	9	11	.450	21	21	20	1	0	188	245	11.7	11	29	1.4	34	1.6	4.26	73	.324	.349	-27	-24	105	104	-2.1	-3	0	-2.1
	Bal-a	3	1	.750	4	4	3	0	0	30	29	8.7	0	2	0.6	11	3.3	2.70	117	.262	.275	2	2	98	100	0.8	-0	0	0.1
Total	6	112	68	.622	189	185	174	16	1	1609	1685	9.4	38	171	1.0	433	2.4	2.73	106	.278	.298	23	29	101	100	-0.4	-1	5	3.8
■ **HAL GOLDSMITH** Goldsmith, Harold Eugene b: 8/18/1898, Peconic, N.Y. BR/TR, 6', 174 lbs. Deb: 6/23/26																													
1926	Bos-N	5	7	.417	19	15	5	0	0	101	135	12.0	2	28	2.5	16	1.4	4.37	77	.333	.364	-6	-11	88	115	-0.2	1	1	-0.9
1927	Bos-N	1	3	.250	22	5	1	0	1	72	83	10.4	4	26	3.3	13	1.6	3.50	107	.289	.341	3	2	95	122	-0.6	0	0	0.2
1928	Bos-N	0	0	—	4	0	0	0	0	8	14	15.8	2	1	1.1	1	1.1	3.38	120	.359	.375	1	1	101	214	0.0	-0	0	0.1
1929	StL-N	0	0	—	2	0	0	0	0	4	3	6.8	1	1	2.3	0	0.0	6.75	68	.214	.267	-1	-1	98	55	0.0	-0	-0	0.0
Total	4	6	10	.375	47	20	6	0	1	185	235	11.4	9	56	2.7	30	1.5	4.04	88	.315	.354	-3	-10	91	121	-0.8	1	1	-0.6
■ **IZZY GOLDSTEIN** Goldstein, Isidore b: 6/6/08, New York, N.Y. BB/TR, 6', 160 lbs. Deb: 4/24/32																													
1932	Det-A	3	2	.600	16	6	2	0	0	56	63	10.1	2	41	6.6	14	2.3	4.50	101	.276	.391	-0	0	102	116	0.5	1	0	0.1
■ **DAVE GOLTZ** Goltz, David Allan b: 6/23/49, Pelican Rapids, Minn. BR/TR, 6'4", 200 lbs. Deb: 7/18/72																													
1972	Min-A	3	3	.500	15	11	2	0	1	91	75	7.4	5	26	2.6	38	3.8	2.67	123	.224	.274	4	6	107	87	0.0	-1	0	0.6
1973	Min-A	6	4	.600	32	10	1	0	1	106	138	11.7	11	32	2.7	65	5.5	5.26	75	.318	.361	-17	-16	103	100	1.1	0	1	-1.4
1974	Min-A	10	10	.500	28	24	5	1	1	174	192	9.9	14	45	2.3	89	4.6	3.26	112	.282	.327	7	8	101	**123**	0.0	0	1	0.9
1975	Min-A	14	14	.500	32	32	15	1	0	243	235	8.7	18	72	2.7	128	4.7	3.67	111	.255	.308	3	11	107	92	0.7	0	1	1.2
1976	Min-A	14	14	.500	36	35	13	4	0	249	239	8.6	14	91	3.3	133	4.8	3.36	103	.254	.318	4	2	98	102	-0.7	0	0	0.2
1977	Min-A	**20**	11	.645	39	39	19	2	0	303	284	8.4	23	91	2.7	186	5.5	3.36	124	.247	.301	24	27	102	94	4.7	0	-1	2.6
1978	Min-A	15	10	.600	29	29	13	2	0	220	209	8.6	12	67	2.7	116	4.7	2.50	143	.253	.303	31	26	94	125	3.8	0	0	2.8
1979	Min-A	14	13	.519	36	35	12	1	0	251	282	10.1	22	69	2.5	132	4.7	4.16	110	.288	.332	2	12	108	104	0.4	0	-0	1.0
1980	LA-N	7	11	.389	35	27	2	2	1	171	198	10.4	12	59	3.1	91	4.8	4.32	80	.299	.348	-13	-16	96	107	-2.9	0	-0	-1.6
1981	LA-N	2	7	.222	26	8	0	0	1	77	83	9.7	4	25	2.9	48	5.6	4.09	82	.288	.339	-5	-6	96	102	-2.7	-1	1	-0.6
1982	LA-N	0	1	.000	2	1	0	0	0	4	6	13.5	0	0	0.0	3	6.8	4.50	75	.353	.353	-0	-1	94	105	-0.4	-0	0	0.0
	Cal-A	8	5	.615	28	7	1	0	3	86	82	8.6	4	32	3.3	49	5.1	4.08	99	.252	.315	0	-1	99	81	0.7	0	-1	-0.1
1983	Cal-A	0	6	.000	15	6	0	0	0	64	81	11.4	10	37	5.2	27	3.8	6.19	63	.315	.395	-15	-16	96	106	-2.9	0	-0	-1.5
Total	12	113	109	.509	353	264	83	13	8	2039	2104	9.3	149	646	2.9	1105	4.9	3.69	104	.269	.322	25	35	101	103	1.8	-1	1	4.1
■ **LUIS GOMEZ** Gomez, Jose Luis (Sanchez) b: 8/19/51, Guadalajara, Mex. BR/TR, 5'9", 150 lbs. Deb: 4/28/74																													
1981	Atl-N	0	0	—	1	0	0	0	0	1	3	27.0	0	2	18.0	0	0.0	27.00	13	.500	.625	-3	-3	100	64	0.0	0	0	-0.1
■ **RUBEN GOMEZ** Gomez, Ruben (Colon) b: 7/13/27, Arroyo, P.R. BR/TR, 6', 170 lbs. Deb: 4/17/53																													
1953	NY-N	13	11	.542	29	26	13	3	0	204	166	7.3	17	101	4.5	113	5.0	3.40	123	.218	.311	20	18	98	93	2.2	0	2	1.8
1954	NY-N	17	9	.654	37	32	10	4	0	222	202	8.2	20	109	4.4	106	4.3	2.88	144	.244	.330	29	31	102	**130**	1.0	0	2	3.3
1955	NY-N	9	10	.474	33	31	9	3	1	185	207	10.1	20	63	3.1	79	3.8	4.57	87	.285	.342	-11	-13	98	100	-0.8	4	3	-0.5
1956	NY-N	7	17	.292	40	31	4	2	0	196	191	8.8	19	77	3.5	76	3.5	4.59	82	.259	.329	-18	-18	99	86	-4.3	-0	2	-1.5
1957	NY-N	15	13	.536	38	36	16	1	0	238	233	8.8	28	71	2.7	92	3.5	3.78	106	.254	.306	3	6	103	97	2.6	1	2	1.0
1958	SF-N	10	12	.455	42	30	8	1	1	208	204	8.8	21	77	3.3	112	4.8	4.37	90	.261	.327	-10	-10	100	91	-1.5	1	2	-0.6
1959	Phi-N	3	8	.273	20	12	2	1	1	72	90	11.3	12	24	3.0	37	4.6	6.13	66	.300	.349	-17	-17	102	87	-1.9	0	2	-1.4
1960	Phi-N	0	3	.000	22	1	0	0	1	52	68	11.8	7	9	1.6	24	4.2	5.37	77	.321	.335	-9	-7	110	100	-1.4	-1	-1	-0.7
1962	Cle-A	1	2	.333	15	4	0	0	1	45	50	10.0	5	25	5.0	21	4.2	4.40	89	.292	.372	-2	-2	99	127	-0.4	0	1	-0.1
	Min-A	1	1	.500	6	2	1	0	0	19	17	8.1	3	11	5.2	8	3.8	4.74	87	.254	.341	-2	-1	104	104	0.0	-0	0	-0.1
	Yr	2	3	.400	21	6	1	0	1	64	67	9.4	8	36	5.1	29	4.1	4.50	88	.276	.356	-4	-4	100	104	-0.4	0	1	-0.2
1967	Phi-N	0	0	—	7	0	0	0	0	11	8	6.5	2	7	5.7	9	7.4	4.09	86	.211	.313	-1	-1	104	103	0.0	0	1	0.0
Total	10	76	86	.469	289	205	63	15	5	1452	1436	8.9	154	574	3.6	677	4.2	4.09	98	.259	.327	-18	-14	101	100	-4.5	5	14	1.2
■ **LEFTY GOMEZ** Gomez, Vernon Louis "Goofy" b: 11/26/08, Rodeo, Cal. BL/TL, 6'2", 173 lbs. Deb: 4/29/30 H																													
1930	NY-A	2	5	.286	15	6	2	0	1	60	66	9.9	12	28	4.2	22	3.3	5.55	73	.280	.348	-6	-10	87	103	-1.7	-1	1	-0.8
1931	NY-A	21	9	.700	40	26	17	1	3	243	206	7.6	7	85	3.1	150	5.6	2.67	154	.255	.324	46	39	94	**141**	3.9	-3	-1	3.3
1932	NY-A	24	7	.774	37	31	21	1	1	265	266	9.0	23	105	3.6	176	6.0	4.21	97	.259	.325	8	-4	91	98	4.7	-1	-3	-0.8
1933	NY-A	16	10	.615	35	30	14	4	2	235	218	8.3	16	106	4.1	**163**	**6.2**	3.18	119	.240	.315	29	16	88	111	0.3	-3	4	0.8
1934	NY-A	**26**	5	**.839**	38	33	**25**	**6**	1	**282**	223	**7.1**	12	96	3.1	**158**	5.0	**2.33**	**179**	**.215**	**.279**	**68**	**58**	93	105	**9.9**	-3	-2	5.1
1935	NY-A	12	15	.444	34	30	15	2	1	246	223	8.2	18	86	3.1	138	5.0	3.18	126	.242	.302	35	23	90	106	-3.9	-6	1	1.5
1936	NY-A	13	7	.650	31	30	10	0	0	189	184	8.8	6	122	5.8	105	5.0	4.38	103	.254	.358	14	3	90	99	-0.2	-2	-1	0.0
1937	NY-A	**21**	11	.656	34	34	25	**6**	0	278	233	**7.5**	10	93	3.0	**194**	**6.3**	**2.33**	193	**.223**	.285	**71**	**67**	97	105	-0.1	-1	-3	**6.3**
1938	NY-A	18	12	.600	32	32	20	**4**	0	239	239	9.0	7	99	3.7	129	4.9	3.35	145	.260	.328	38	40	102	110	-1.3	-3	2	3.8
1939	NY-A	12	8	.600	26	26	14	2	0	198	173	7.9	11	84	3.8	102	4.6	3.41	116	.235	.313	27	12	85	99	-1.5	-1	-1	0.8

YEAR	TM/L	W	L	PCT	G	GS	CG	SHO	SV	IP	H	H/G	HR	BB	BB/G	SO	SO/G	ERA	/A	OAVG	OOBP	PR	/A	PF	CPI	WAT	PB	PD	TPI
1940	NY-A	3	3	.500	9	5	0	0	0	27	37	12.3	2	18	6.0	14	4.7	6.67	63	.325	.418	-7	-7	96	100	-0.3	-1	-1	-0.7
1941	NY-A	15	5	**.750**	23	23	8	2	0	156	151	8.7	10	103	5.9	76	4.4	3.75	105	.250	.358	7	3	95	115	3.0	-1	-4	-0.1
1942	NY-A	6	4	.600	13	13	2	0	0	80	67	7.5	4	65	7.3	41	4.6	4.27	80	.237	.377	-5	-8	94	104	-0.4	-1	-2	-0.9
1943	Was-A	0	1	.000	1	1	0	0	0	5	4	7.2	0	5	9.0	0	0.0	5.40	62	.250	.391	-1	-1	102	90	-0.4	-0	1	0.0
Total	14	189	102	.649	368	320	173	28	9	2503	2290	8.2	138	1095	3.9	1468	5.3	3.34	125	.244	.320	322	229	93	108	12.0	-27	-15	18.3
■ JOE GONZALES	Gonzales, Joe Madrid "Smokey" b: 3/19/15, San Francisco, Cal BR/TR, 5'9", 175 lbs. Deb: 8/28/37																												
1937	Bos-A	1	2	.333	8	2	2	0	0	31	37	10.7	1	11	3.2	11	3.2	4.35	109	.291	.343	1	1	102	99	-0.5	-2	0	0.0
■ JULIO GONZALES	Gonzales, Julio Enrique b: 12/20/20, Havana, Cuba BR/TR, 5'11", 150 lbs. Deb: 8/09/49																												
1949	Was-A	0	0	—	13	0	0	0	0	34	33	8.7	3	27	7.1	5	1.3	4.76	85	.256	.379	-2	-3	96	104	0.0	1	-0	-0.1
■ VINCE GONZALES	Gonzales, Wenceslao O'Reilly b: 9/28/25, Quivican, Cuba d: 3/11/81, Ciudad Del Carmen Campeche, Mexico BL/TL, 6'1", 165 lbs. Deb: 4/13/55																												
1955	Was-A	0	0	—	1	0	0	0	0	2	6	27.0	0	3	13.5	1	4.5	27.00	14	.500	.600	-5	-5	94	58	0.0	0	0	-0.3
■ GERMAN GONZALEZ	Gonzalez, German Jose (Caraballo) b: 3/7/62, Rio Caribe, Venez. BR/TR, 6', 170 lbs. Deb: 8/05/88																												
1988	Min-A	0	0	—	16	0	0	0	1	21	20	8.6	4	8	3.4	19	8.1	3.43	122	.244	.315	1	2	105	127	0.0	0	0	0.2
■ RALPH GOOD	Good, Ralph Nelson "Holy" b: 4/25/1886, Monticello, Me. d: 11/24/65, Waterville, Maine BR/TR, 6', 165 lbs. Deb: 7/01/10																												
1910	Bos-N	0	0	—	2	0	0	0	0	9	6	6.0	0	2	2.0	4	4.0	2.00	179	.188	.278	1	2	118	66	0.0	-1	0	0.2
■ WILBUR GOOD	Good, Wilbur David "Lefty" b: 9/28/1885, Punxsutawney, Pa. d: 12/30/63, Brooksville, Fla. BL/TL, 5'6", 165 lbs. Deb: 8/18/05																												
1905	NY-A	0	2	.000	5	2	0	0	0	19	18	8.5	1	14	6.6	13	6.2	4.74	57	.274	.402	-4	-4	103	95	-0.9	1	0	-0.2
■ HERB GOODALL	Goodall, Herbert Frank b: 3/10/1870, Mansfield, Pa. d: 1/20/38, Mansfield, Pa. BR/TR, 5'9", 180 lbs. Deb: 4/29/1890																												
1890	Lou-a	8	5	.615	18	13	8	1	**4**	109	94	7.8	2	51	4.2	46	3.8	3.39	119	.247	.336	6	8	104	95	-0.4	5	0	1.2
■ JOHN GOODELL	Goodell, John Henry William "Lefty" b: 4/5/07, Muskogee, Okla. BR/TL, 5'10", 165 lbs. Deb: 4/19/28																												
1928	Chi-A	0	0	—	2	0	0	0	0	3	6	18.0	0	2	6.0	0	0.0	18.00	23	.500	.500	-5	-5	100	67	0.0	0	0	-0.3
■ DWIGHT GOODEN	Gooden, Dwight Eugene b: 11/16/64, Tampa, Fla. BR/TR, 6'2", 190 lbs. Deb: 4/07/84																												
1984	NY-N	17	9	.654	31	31	7	3	0	218	161	**6.6**	7	73	3.0	**276**	**11.4**	2.60	138	**.202**	**.268**	24	24	100	71	3.3	1	1	2.8
1985	NY-N	**24**	4	.857	35	35	**16**	8	0	**277**	198	6.4	13	69	2.2	**268**	8.7	**1.53**	**225**	.201	.253	**64**	**59**	95	115	**9.5**	6	2	**7.9**
1986	NY-N	17	6	.739	33	33	12	2	0	250	197	7.1	17	80	2.9	200	7.2	2.84	122	.215	.275	24	17	93	85	2.8	-2	3	1.8
1987	NY-N	15	7	**.682**	25	25	7	3	0	180	162	8.1	11	53	2.7	148	7.4	3.20	124	.244	.297	18	15	97	96	3.2	2	-0	1.7
1988	NY-N	18	9	.667	34	34	10	3	0	248	242	8.8	8	57	2.1	175	6.4	3.19	95	.256	.298	7	-4	88	95	1.8	3	5	0.2
Total	5	91	35	.722	158	158	52	19	0	1173	960	7.4	56	332	2.5	1067	8.2	2.62	132	.223	.277	137	111	94	94	20.6	9	10	14.4
■ ART GOODWIN	Goodwin, Arthur Ingram b: 2/27/1877, Whitley Twnshp, Pa d: 6/19/43, Franklin Township, Greene County, Pa. Deb: 10/07/05																												
1905	NY-A	0	0	—	1	0	0	0	0	⅓	2	54.0	0	2	54.0	0	0.0	81.00	—	1.000	1.000	-3	-3	103	57	0.0	0	0	-0.2
■ CLYDE GOODWIN	Goodwin, Clyde Samuel b: 11/12/1886, Shade, Ohio d: 10/12/63, Dayton, Ohio BR/TR, 5'11", 145 lbs. Deb: 9/18/06																												
1906	Was-A	0	2	.000	4	3	1	0	0	22	20	8.2	0	13	5.3	9	3.7	4.50	56	.267	.375	-4	-5	94	76	-0.9	-0	-1	-0.5
■ JIM GOODWIN	Goodwin, James Patrick b: 8/15/26, St.Louis, Mo. BL/TL, 6'1", 170 lbs. Deb: 4/24/48																												
1948	Chi-A	0	0	—	8	1	0	0	1	10	9	8.1	0	12	10.8	3	2.7	9.00	47	.237	.415	-5	-5	100	58	0.0	0	0	-0.4
■ MARV GOODWIN	Goodwin, Marvin Mardo b: 1/16/1891, Gordonsville, Va. d: 10/21/25, Houston, Tex. BR/TR, 5'11", 168 lbs. Deb: 9/07/16																												
1916	Was-A	0	0	—	3	0	0	0	0	6	5	7.5	0	3	4.5	1	1.5	3.00	94	.217	.308	-0	-0	100	71	0.0	-0	-0	0.0
1917	StL-N	6	4	.600	14	12	6	3	0	85	70	7.4	1	19	2.0	38	4.0	2.22	125	.222	.263	5	5	102	77	0.7	-0	2	0.8
1919	StL-N	11	9	.550	33	17	7	0	0	179	163	8.2	3	33	1.7	48	2.4	2.51	112	.245	.281	8	6	97	96	2.9	1	-1	0.7
1920	StL-N	3	8	.273	32	12	3	0	1	116	153	11.9	1	28	2.2	23	1.8	4.97	62	.314	.350	-24	-24	98	82	-2.4	-0	-2	-2.7
1921	StL-N	1	2	.333	14	4	1	0	1	36	47	11.8	1	9	2.3	7	1.8	3.75	93	.315	.343	0	-1	93	116	-0.5	-1	0	0.0
1922	StL-N	0	0	—	2	0	0	0	0	4	3	6.8	0	3	6.8	0	0.0	2.25	183	.250	.333	1	1	100	188	0.0	0	0	0.1
1925	Cin-N	0	2	.000	4	3	2	0	0	21	26	11.1	2	5	2.1	4	1.7	4.71	87	.317	.348	-1	-1	97	110	-0.9	0	1	0.0
Total	7	21	25	.457	102	48	19	3	2	447	467	9.4	8	100	2.0	121	2.4	3.30	91	.269	.307	-11	-15	98	91	-0.2	0	1	-1.1
■ RAY GORDINIER	Gordinier, Raymond Cornelius "Gordy" b: 4/11/1892, Rochester, N.Y. d: 11/15/60, Rochester, N.Y. BB/TR, 5'8.5", 170 lbs. Deb: 9/17/21																												
1921	Bro-N	1	0	1.000	3	3	0	0	0	12	10	7.5	0	8	6.0	4	3.0	5.25	76	.227	.340	-2	-2	105	55	0.5	0	0	0.0
1922	Bro-N	0	0	—	5	0	0	0	0	11	13	10.6	3	8	6.5	5	4.1	9.00	43	.289	.396	-6	-6	95	75	0.0	-0	0	-0.5
Total	2	1	0	1.000	8	3	0	0	0	23	23	9.0	3	16	6.3	9	3.5	7.04	56	.258	.368	-8	-8	100	64	0.5	-0	0	-0.5
■ DON GORDON	Gordon, Donald Thomas b: 10/10/59, New York, N.Y. BR/TR, 6'1", 175 lbs. Deb: 4/10/86																												
1986	Tor-A	0	1	.000	14	0	0	0	1	22	28	11.5	1	8	3.3	13	5.3	6.95	63	.311	.363	-7	-6	104	72	-0.4	0	-0	-0.6
1987	Tor-A	0	0	—	5	0	0	0	0	11	8	6.5	2	3	2.5	3	2.5	4.09	109	.200	.256	0	0	99	69	0.0	0	-0	0.0
	Cle-A	0	3	.000	21	0	0	0	1	40	49	11.0	3	12	2.7	20	4.5	4.05	115	.295	.351	2	3	105	118	-1.4	0	1	0.3
	Yr	0	3	.000	26	0	0	0	1	51	57	10.1	5	15	2.6	23	4.1	4.06	114	.277	.333	2	3	103	118	-1.4	0	1	0.3
1988	Cle-A	3	4	.429	38	0	0	0	1	59	65	9.9	5	19	2.9	20	3.1	4.42	92	.284	.333	-3	-2	102	102	-0.3	0	1	-0.1
Total	3	3	8	.273	78	0	0	0	3	132	150	10.2	11	42	2.9	56	3.8	4.70	92	.286	.338	-7	-5	103	99	-2.1	0	1	-0.4
■ TOM GORDON	Gordon, Thomas b: 11/18/67, Sebring, Fla. BR/TR, 5'9", 160 lbs. Deb: 9/08/88																												
1988	KC-A	0	2	.000	5	2	0	0	0	16	16	9.0	1	7	3.9	18	10.1	5.06	81	.267	.343	-2	-2	103	81	-0.9	0	0	-0.1
■ CHARLIE GORIN	Gorin, Charles Perry b: 2/6/28, Waco, Tex. BL/TL, 5'10", 165 lbs. Deb: 5/29/54																												
1954	Mil-N	0	1	.000	5	0	0	0	0	10	5	4.5	0	6	5.4	12	10.8	1.80	207	.152	.275	3	2	91	71	-0.4	-0	-0	0.2
1955	Mil-N	0	0	—	2	0	0	0	0	⅓	1	27.0	0	3	81.0	0	0.0	54.00	—	.500	.800	-2	-2	92	60	0.0	0	0	-0.1
Total	2	0	1	.000	7	0	0	0	0	10	6	5.4	0	9	8.1	12	10.8	3.60	103	.171	.333	1	0	91	71	-0.4	-0	-0	0.1
■ JACK GORMAN	Gorman, John F. "Stooping Jack" b: 1859, St.Louis, Mo. d: 9/9/1889, St.Louis, Mo. Deb: 1883																												
1884	Pit-a	1	2	.333	3	3	3	0	0	25	22	7.9	0	5	1.8	10	3.6	4.68	70	.244	.284	-4	-4	101	56	0.1	-0	0	-0.2
■ TOM GORMAN	Gorman, Thomas Aloysius b: 1/4/25, New York, N.Y. BR/TR, 6'1", 190 lbs. Deb: 7/16/52																												
1952	NY-A	6	2	.750	12	6	1	1	1	61	63	9.3	8	22	3.2	31	4.6	4.57	76	.272	.336	-6	-7	95	99	1.4	-1	-0	-0.8
1953	NY-A	4	5	.444	40	1	0	0	6	77	65	7.6	5	32	3.7	38	4.4	3.39	104	.226	.313	5	1	88	92	-1.4	-0	-0	0.0
1954	NY-A	0	0	—	23	0	0	0	2	37	30	7.3	1	14	3.4	31	7.5	2.19	161	.222	.292	6	5	94	111	0.0	-1	0	0.5
1955	KC-A	7	6	.538	57	0	0	0	18	109	98	8.1	11	36	3.0	46	3.8	3.55	118	.246	.306	5	8	106	100	1.5	-2	-1	0.5
1956	KC-A	9	10	.474	52	13	1	0	3	171	168	8.8	23	68	3.6	56	2.9	3.84	113	.258	.325	6	10	105	109	2.2	-4	-0	0.6
1957	KC-A	5	9	.357	38	12	3	1	3	125	125	9.0	18	33	2.4	66	4.8	3.82	101	.261	.304	-0	0	102	103	-0.5	-2	-0	-0.1
1958	KC-A	4	4	.500	50	1	0	0	8	90	86	8.6	8	20	2.0	44	4.4	3.50	115	.258	.305	3	5	107	100	0.2	-1	-1	0.4
1959	KC-A	1	0	1.000	17	0	0	0	1	20	24	10.8	3	14	6.3	9	4.0	7.20	55	.293	.386	-7	-7	103	87	0.5	0	-1	-0.7
Total	8	36	36	.500	289	33	5	2	42	690	659	8.6	77	239	3.1	321	4.2	3.77	105	.254	.316	11	15	101	102	3.9	-10	-4	0.4
■ TOM GORMAN	Gorman, Thomas David "Big Tom" b: 3/16/16, New York, N.Y. d: 8/11/86, Closter, N.J. BR/TL, 6'2", 200 lbs. Deb: 9/14/39 U																												
1939	NY-N	0	0	—	4	0	0	0	0	5	7	12.6	0	1	1.8	2	3.6	7.20	54	.350	.364	-2	-2	99	73	0.0	-0	0	-0.1
■ TOM GORMAN	Gorman, Thomas Patrick b: 12/16/57, Portland, Ore. BL/TL, 6'4", 194 lbs. Deb: 9/02/81																												
1981	Mon-N	0	0	—	9	0	0	0	0	15	12	7.2	0	6	3.6	13	7.8	4.20	81	.222	.302	-1	-1	98	59	0.0	0	1	0.0
1982	Mon-N	1	0	1.000	5	0	0	0	0	7	8	10.3	0	4	5.1	6	7.7	5.14	73	.286	.364	-1	-1	104	84	0.5	0	0	0.0
	NY-N	0	1	.000	3	1	0	0	0	9	8	8.0	0	0	0.0	7	7.0	1.00	361	.235	.222	3	3	100	142	-0.4	-0	0	0.3
	Yr	1	1	.500	8	1	0	0	0	16	16	9.0	0	4	2.3	13	7.3	2.81	131	.254	.290	1	2	102	142	0.1	0	0	0.3
1983	NY-N	1	4	.200	25	4	0	0	0	49	45	8.3	3	15	2.8	30	5.5	4.96	73	.245	.294	-7	-7	100	60	-1.2	0	0	-0.7
1984	NY-N	6	0	1.000	36	0	0	0	0	58	51	7.9	6	13	2.0	40	6.2	2.95	122	.238	.283	4	4	100	104	3.0	-0	0	0.4
1985	NY-N	4	4	.500	34	2	0	0	0	53	56	9.5	8	18	3.1	32	5.4	5.09	67	.277	.326	-9	-10	95	92	-0.6	-1	1	-0.8
1986	Phi-N	0	1	.000	8	0	0	0	0	12	21	15.8	0	5	3.8	8	6.0	7.50	52	.382	.426	-5	-5	104	93	-0.4	-0	0	-0.4
1987	SD-N	0	0	—	6	0	0	0	0	11	11	9.0	1	5	4.1	8	6.5	4.09	98	.262	.340	-0	-0	98	102	0.0	0	-0	0.0

YEAR	TM/L	W	L	PCT	G	GS	CG	SHO	SV	IP	H	H/G	HR	BB	BB/G	SO	SO/G	ERA	/A	OAVG	OOBP	PR	/A	PF	CPI	WAT	PB	PD	TPI
Total	7	12	10	.545	126	7	0	0	0	214	212	8.9	18	66	2.8	144	6.1	4.33	83	.261	.311	-17	-18	99	88	0.9	-1	2	-1.2
■ **JOE GORMLEY**	Gormley, Joseph b: 12/20/1866, Summit Hill, Pa. d: 7/2/50, Summit Hill, Pa. BL/TL, Deb: 6/16/1891																												
1891	Phi-N	0	1	.000	1	1	1	0	0	8	10	11.3	0	5	5.6	2	2.3	5.63	57	.320	.414	-2	-2	95	86	-0.4	-1	0	-0.1
■ **HANK GORNICKI**	Gornicki, Henry Frank b: 1/14/11, Niagara Falls, N.Y BR/TR, 6'1", 145 lbs. Deb: 4/17/41																												
1941	StL-N	1	0	1.000	4	1	1	1	0	11	6	4.9	0	9	7.4	6	4.9	3.27	119	.158	.327	0	1	107	71	0.5	0	-0	0.1
	Chi-N	0	0	—	1	0	0	0	0	2	3	13.5	0	0	0.0	2	9.0	4.50	76	.375	.375	-0	-0	94	120	0.0	0	0	0.0
	Yr	1	0	1.000	5	1	1	1	0	13	9	6.2	0	9	6.2	8	5.5	3.46	110	.191	.316	0	1	105	120	0.5	0	0	0.1
1942	Pit-N	5	6	.455	25	14	7	2	2	112	89	7.2	2	40	3.2	48	3.9	2.57	131	.215	.280	9	10	102	85	0.1	-1	-1	0.9
1943	Pit-N	9	13	.409	42	19	4	1	4	147	165	10.1	10	47	2.9	63	3.9	3.98	87	.286	.335	-10	-8	103	106	-2.5	-1	-1	-0.9
1946	Pit-N	0	0	—	7	0	0	0	0	13	12	8.3	0	11	7.6	4	2.8	3.46	104	.255	.371	-0	0	106	124	0.0	-0	-0	0.0
Total	4	15	19	.441	79	34	12	4	6	285	275	8.7	12	107	3.4	123	3.9	3.38	102	.254	.316	-0	2	103	98	-1.9	-2	-2	0.1
■ **JOHNNY GORSICA**	Gorsica, John Joseph Perry (born John Joseph Perry Gorczyca) b: 3/29/15, Bayonne, N.J. BR/TR, 6'2", 180 lbs. Deb: 4/22/40																												
1940	Det-A	7	7	.500	29	20	5	2	0	160	170	9.6	10	57	3.2	68	3.8	4.33	110	.272	.334	1	8	109	96	-1.0	1	5	1.4
1941	Det-A	9	11	.450	33	21	8	1	2	171	193	10.2	14	55	2.9	59	3.1	4.47	99	.281	.332	-6	-0	107	97	-0.8	4	4	0.8
1942	Det-A	3	2	.600	28	0	0	0	4	53	63	10.7	2	26	4.4	19	3.2	4.75	87	.310	.380	-6	-4	113	114	0.6	-0	4	0.0
1943	Det-A	4	5	.444	35	4	1	0	5	96	88	8.3	3	40	3.8	45	4.2	3.38	102	.247	.320	-1	1	104	97	-0.5	0	3	0.4
1944	Det-A	6	14	.300	34	19	8	1	4	162	192	10.7	5	32	1.8	47	2.6	4.11	86	.296	.328	-12	-10	104	95	-5.0	-1	3	-0.7
1946	Det-A	0	0	—	14	0	0	0	1	24	28	10.5	5	11	4.1	14	5.3	4.50	82	.301	.371	-3	-2	106	134	0.0	1	-0	0.0
1947	Det-A	2	0	1.000	31	0	0	0	1	58	44	6.8	5	26	4.0	20	3.1	3.72	102	.208	.298	-0	1	103	75	1.0	0	1	0.2
Total	7	31	39	.443	204	64	22	4	17	724	778	9.7	44	247	3.1	272	3.4	4.18	98	.276	.332	-28	-8	106	97	-5.7	5	20	2.1
■ **RICH GOSSAGE**	Gossage, Richard Michael "Goose" b: 7/5/51, Colorado Springs, Colo. BR/TR, 6'3", 180 lbs. Deb: 4/16/72																												
1972	Chi-A	7	1	.875	36	1	0	0	2	80	72	8.1	2	44	4.9	57	6.4	4.27	76	.247	.341	-11	-9	106	83	2.9	-2	-0	-1.2
1973	Chi-A	0	4	.000	20	4	1	0	0	50	57	10.3	9	37	6.7	33	5.9	7.38	53	.311	.418	-20	-19	103	96	-1.9	0	-0	-1.8
1974	Chi-A	4	6	.400	39	3	0	0	1	89	92	9.3	4	47	4.8	64	6.5	4.15	89	.272	.355	-5	-4	102	102	-1.0	0	0	-0.3
1975	Chi-A	9	8	.529	62	0	0	0	**26**	142	99	6.3	3	70	4.4	130	8.2	1.84	214	.201	.299	**31**	**33**	104	128	1.1	0	1	3.6
1976	Chi-A	9	17	.346	31	29	15	0	1	224	214	8.6	16	90	3.6	135	5.4	3.94	91	.254	.327	-10	-9	101	95	-1.9	0	-1	-0.9
1977	Pit-N	11	9	.550	72	0	0	0	26	133	78	5.3	9	49	3.3	151	10.2	1.62	245	.170	.247	**34**	35	102	95	-0.7	1	-1	3.6
1978	NY-A	10	11	.476	63	0	0	0	**27**	134	87	5.8	9	59	4.0	122	8.2	2.01	182	.187	.273	**26**	**25**	97	105	-2.5	0	-1	2.4
1979	NY-A	5	3	.625	36	0	0	0	18	58	48	7.4	5	19	2.9	41	6.4	2.64	152	.227	.286	10	9	95	109	0.6	0	-1	0.8
1980	NY-A	6	2	.750	64	0	0	0	**33**	99	74	6.7	5	37	3.4	103	9.4	2.27	174	.211	.279	19	18	98	104	1.3	0	-1	1.8
1981	NY-A	3	2	.600	32	0	0	0	20	47	22	4.2	2	14	2.7	48	9.2	0.77	473	.141	.214	15	15	99	91	0.3	0	0	1.6
1982	NY-A	4	5	.444	56	0	0	0	30	93	63	6.1	5	28	2.7	102	9.9	2.23	177	.196	.256	19	18	97	88	-0.3	0	-1	1.7
1983	NY-A	13	5	.722	57	0	0	0	22	87	82	8.5	5	25	2.6	90	9.3	2.28	175	.248	.294	17	17	98	137	3.5	0	-2	1.5
1984	SD-N	10	6	.625	62	0	0	0	25	102	75	6.6	6	36	3.2	84	7.4	2.91	121	.204	.272	8	7	98	76	1.2	0	-1	0.6
1985	SD-N	5	3	.625	50	0	0	0	26	79	64	7.3	1	17	1.9	52	5.9	1.82	200	.226	.266	16	16	101	112	1.0	-1	-1	1.5
1986	SD-N	5	7	.417	45	0	0	0	21	65	69	9.6	8	20	2.8	63	8.7	4.43	81	.273	.324	-5	-6	96	98	-0.5	-1	-1	-0.7
1987	SD-N	5	4	.556	40	0	0	0	11	52	47	8.1	4	19	3.3	44	7.6	3.12	128	.244	.304	6	5	98	108	1.2	-0	-0	0.4
1988	Chi-N	4	4	.500	46	0	0	0	13	44	50	10.2	3	15	3.1	30	6.1	4.30	84	.291	.351	-4	-3	105	109	0.2	-0	0	-0.3
Total	17	110	97	.531	811	37	16	0	302	1578	1293	7.4	96	626	3.6	1349	7.7	2.92	129	.226	.300	146	147	100	102	4.5	-3	-10	14.3
■ **JIM GOTT**	Gott, James William b: 8/3/59, Hollywood, Cal. BR/TR, 6'4", 215 lbs. Deb: 4/09/82																												
1982	Tor-A	5	10	.333	30	23	1	1	0	136	134	8.9	15	66	4.4	82	5.4	4.43	100	.255	.338	-5	0	109	95	-2.4	0	-0	0.0
1983	Tor-A	9	14	.391	34	30	6	1	0	177	195	9.9	15	68	3.5	121	6.2	4.73	93	.280	.345	-13	-7	108	95	-3.6	0	-1	-0.7
1984	Tor-A	7	6	.538	35	12	1	1	2	110	93	7.6	7	49	4.0	73	6.0	4.01	101	.233	.313	-0	0	101	82	0.0	0	-1	0.0
1985	SF-N	7	10	.412	26	26	2	0	0	148	144	8.8	10	51	3.1	78	4.7	3.89	88	.254	.312	-5	-8	95	88	0.4	4	1	-0.3
1986	SF-N	0	0	—	9	2	0	0	1	13	16	11.1	0	13	9.0	9	6.2	7.62	46	.314	.439	-6	-6	95	84	0.0	0	0	-0.5
1987	SF-N	1	0	1.000	30	3	0	0	0	56	53	8.5	4	32	5.1	63	10.1	4.50	86	.244	.344	-3	-4	95	87	0.5	1	0	-0.2
	Pit-N	0	2	.000	25	0	0	0	13	31	28	8.1	0	8	2.3	27	7.8	1.45	294	.233	.279	9	10	105	143	-0.9	-0	-0	0.9
	Yr	1	2	.333	55	3	0	0	13	87	81	8.4	4	40	4.1	90	9.3	3.41	118	.238	.317	6	6	98	143	-0.4	1	-0	0.7
1988	Pit-N	6	6	.500	67	0	0	0	34	77	68	7.9	9	22	2.6	76	8.9	3.51	96	.243	.293	-0	-1	97	102	-0.3	-0	-0	-0.1
Total	7	35	48	.422	256	96	10	3	50	748	731	8.8	60	309	3.7	529	6.4	4.18	95	.256	.327	-23	-16	102	94	-6.3	5	-1	-0.9
■ **TED GOULAIT**	Goulait, Theodore Lee b: 8/11/1889, St.Clair, Mich. d: 7/15/36, St.Clair, Mich. BR/TR, 5'9.5", 172 lbs. Deb: 9/28/12																												
1912	NY-N	0	0	—	1	1	1	0	0	7	11	14.1	0	4	5.1	6	7.7	6.43	53	.367	.441	-2	-2	99	101	0.0	0	0	-0.1
■ **AL GOULD**	Gould, Albert Frank "Pudgy" b: 1/20/1893, Muscatine, Iowa d: 8/8/82, San Jose, Cal. BR/TR, 5'6.5", 160 lbs. Deb: 7/11/16																												
1916	Cle-A	5	7	.417	30	9	6	1	1	107	101	8.5	0	40	3.4	41	3.4	2.52	111	.256	.329	4	3	99	116	-1.0	-2	-1	0.1
1917	Cle-A	4	4	.500	27	7	1	0	0	94	95	9.1	1	52	5.0	24	2.3	3.64	83	.281	.382	-10	-6	113	113	-0.4	1	2	-0.3
Total	2	9	11	.450	57	16	7	1	1	201	196	8.8	1	92	4.1	65	2.9	3.04	96	.267	.354	-7	-3	106	114	-1.4	-1	1	-0.2
■ **CHARLIE GOULD**	Gould, Charles Harvey b: 8/21/1847, Cincinnati, Ohio d: 4/10/17, Flushing, N.Y. BR/TR, 6', 172 lbs. Deb: 5/05/1871 M																												
1876	Cin-N	0	0	—	2	0	0	0	0	4	10	22.5	0	0	0.0	0	0.0	0.00	—	.474	.474	1	1	100	0	0.0	-0	0	0.1
■ **LARRY GOWELL**	Gowell, Lawrence Clyde b: 5/2/48, Lewiston, Me. BR/TR, 6'2", 182 lbs. Deb: 9/21/72																												
1972	NY-A	0	1	.000	2	1	0	0	0	7	3	3.9	0	2	2.6	7	9.0	1.29	219	.143	.208	1	1	92	46	-0.4	1	0	0.2
■ **AL GRABOWSKI**	Grabowski, Alfons Francis b: 9/6/01, Syracuse, N.Y. d: 10/29/66, Memphis, N.Y. BL/TL, 5'11.5", 175 lbs. Deb: 9/11/29																												
1929	StL-N	3	2	.600	6	6	4	2	0	50	44	7.9	0	8	1.4	22	4.0	2.52	183	.227	.255	12	12	98	62	0.5	2	0	1.3
1930	StL-N	6	4	.600	33	8	1	0	1	107	122	10.3	7	49	4.1	43	3.6	4.79	105	.295	.359	2	3	102	104	0.0	3	-0	0.5
Total	2	9	6	.600	39	14	5	2	1	157	166	9.5	7	57	3.3	65	3.7	4.07	121	.273	.328	14	15	101	91	0.5	4	-0	1.8
■ **REGGIE GRABOWSKI**	Grabowski, Reginald John b: 7/16/07, Syracuse, N.Y. d: 4/2/55, Syracuse, N.Y. BR/TR, 6'0.5", 185 lbs. Deb: 4/15/32																												
1932	Phi-N	2	2	.500	14	2	0	0	0	34	38	10.1	2	22	5.8	15	4.0	3.71	116	.273	.378	1	2	111	132	0.0	-1	-0	0.1
1933	Phi-N	1	3	.250	10	5	4	1	0	48	38	7.1	4	10	1.9	9	1.7	2.44	166	.220	.262	5	9	121	97	-0.6	-1	-1	0.8
1934	Phi-N	1	3	.250	27	5	0	0	0	65	114	15.8	13	23	3.2	13	1.8	9.28	48	.384	.427	-38	-35	111	93	-0.6	-2	-1	-3.3
Total	3	4	8	.333	51	12	4	1	0	147	190	11.6	19	55	3.4	37	2.3	5.76	75	.312	.370	-32	-23	114	103	-1.2	-4	-2	-2.4
■ **JOHN GRAFF**	Graff, John F. b: Philadelphia, Pa. Deb: 7/19/1893																												
1893	Was-N	0	1	.000	2	1	1	0	0	12	21	15.8	2	13	9.8	4	3.0	11.25	38	.400	.519	-9	-9	92	92	-0.4	-0	0	-0.6
■ **PEACHES GRAHAM**	Graham, George Frederick b: 3/23/1877, Aledo, Ill. d: 7/25/39, Long Beach, Cal. BR/TR, 5'9", 180 lbs. Deb: 9/14/02																												
1903	Chi-N	0	1	.000	1	1	0	0	0	5	9	16.2	0	3	5.4	4	7.2	5.40	57	.437	.529	-1	-1	94	153	-0.4	-0	0	0.0
■ **SKINNY GRAHAM**	Graham, Kyle b: 8/14/1899, Oak Grove, Ala. d: 12/1/73, Oak Grove, Ala. BR/TR, 6'2", 172 lbs. Deb: 9/03/24																												
1924	Bos-N	0	4	.000	5	4	1	0	0	33	33	9.0	0	11	3.0	15	4.1	3.82	100	.287	.333	0	0	99	99	-1.9	-1	-0	0.0
1925	Bos-N	7	12	.368	34	23	5	0	1	157	177	10.1	6	62	3.6	32	1.8	4.41	92	.296	.355	-3	-6	95	102	-2.0	-2	-2	-0.9
1926	Bos-N	3	3	.500	15	4	1	0	0	36	54	13.5	3	19	4.8	7	1.8	8.00	42	.370	.421	-17	-19	88	93	0.4	-1	0	-1.7
1929	Det-A	1	3	.250	13	6	2	0	1	52	70	12.1	2	33	5.7	7	1.2	5.54	75	.340	.417	-7	-8	97	119	-0.8	-1	-1	-0.8
Total	4	11	22	.333	67	37	9	0	2	278	334	10.8	11	125	4.0	61	2.0	5.02	79	.314	.375	-27	-33	95	104	-4.3	-5	-3	-3.4
■ **OSCAR GRAHAM**	Graham, Oscar M. b: 7/20/1878, Plattsmouth, Neb. d: 10/15/31, Moline, Ill. TL , 6'0.5", Deb: 4/16/07																												
1907	Was-A	4	9	.308	20	14	6	0	0	104	116	10.0	3	29	2.5	44	3.8	3.98	60	.307	.357	-17	-18	94	93	-0.3	3	0	-1.8
■ **BILL GRAHAM**	Graham, William James b: 7/22/1884, Owosso, Mich. d: 2/15/36, Holt, Mich. TL , 6', Deb: 4/18/08																												
1908	StL-A	6	7	.462	21	13	7	0	0	117	104	8.0	0	32	2.5	47	3.6	2.31	105	.240	.310	1	2	102	116	-1.0	-3	-0	0.2
1909	StL-A	8	14	.364	34	21	13	3	1	187	171	8.2	3	60	2.9	82	3.9	3.13	75	.256	.322	-14	-16	95	89	-1.2	0	1	-1.7
1910	StL-A	0	8	.000	9	6	1	0	0	43	46	9.6	2	13	2.7	12	2.5	3.56	71	.297	.366	-5	-5	101	120	-3.9	-0	-2	-0.6
Total	3	14	29	.326	64	40	21	3	1	347	321	8.3	5	105	2.7	141	3.7	2.90	82	.256	.323	-17	-20	98	102	-6.1	-3	-1	-2.1

YEAR	TM/L	W	L	PCT	G	GS	CG	SHO	SV	IP	H	H/G	HR	BB	BB/G	SO	SO/G	ERA	/A	OAVG	OOBP	PR	/A	PF	CPI	WAT	PB	PD	TPI
■ **BILL GRAHAM**	Graham, William Albert b: 1/21/37, Flemingsburg, Ky. BR/TR, 6'3", 217 lbs. Deb: 10/02/66																												
1966	Det-A	0	0	—	1	0	0	0	0	2	2	9.0	0	0	0.0	2	9.0	0.00	—	.250	.250	1	1	102	0	0.0	0	0	0.1
1967	NY-N	1	2	.333	5	3	1	0	0	27	20	6.7	3	11	3.7	14	4.7	2.67	129	.200	.279	2	2	102	96	-0.1	-0	-1	0.1
Total	2	1	2	.333	6	3	1	0	0	29	22	6.8	3	11	3.4	16	5.0	2.48	139	.204	.277	3	3	102	90	-0.1	-0	-1	0.2
■ **TOMMY GRAMLY**	Gramly, Bert Thomas b: 4/19/45, Dallas, Tex. BR/TR, 6'3", 175 lbs. Deb: 4/18/68																												
1968	Cle-A	0	1	.000	3	0	0	0	0	3	3	9.0	0	2	6.0	1	3.0	3.00	100	.250	.333	-0	-0	101	122	-0.4	0	0	0.0
■ **HANK GRAMPP**	Grampp, Henry Erchardt b: 9/28/03, New York, N.Y. d: 3/24/86, New York, N.Y. BR/TR, 6'1", 185 lbs. Deb: 6/02/27																												
1927	Chi-N	0	0	—	2	0	0	0	0	3	4	12.0	0	1	3.0	3	9.0	9.00	43	.333	.385	-2	-2	99	56	0.0	0	0	-0.1
1929	Chi-N	0	1	.000	1	1	0	0	0	2	4	18.0	0	3	13.5	0	0.0	27.00	17	.500	.615	-5	-5	98	56	-0.4	0	0	-0.3
Total	2	0	1	.000	3	1	0	0	0	5	8	14.4	0	4	7.2	3	5.4	16.20	26	.400	.500	-7	-7	98	56	-0.4	0	0	-0.4
■ **JACK GRANEY**	Graney, John Gladstone b: 6/10/1886, St.Thomas, Ont., Can. d: 4/20/78, Louisiana, Mo. BL/TL, 5'9", 180 lbs. Deb: 4/30/08																												
1908	Cle-A	0	0	—	2	0	0	0	0	3	6	18.0	0	1	3.0	0	0.0	6.00	41	.400	.438	-1	-1	103	127	0.0	0	-0	-0.1
■ **WAYNE GRANGER**	Granger, Wayne Allan b: 3/15/44, Springfield, Mass. BR/TR, 6'2", 165 lbs. Deb: 6/05/68																												
1968	StL-N	4	2	.667	34	0	0	0	4	44	40	8.2	2	12	2.5	27	5.5	2.25	124	.238	.293	4	3	93	121	0.5	0	2	0.5
1969	Cin-N	9	6	.600	**90**	0	0	0	27	145	143	8.9	10	40	2.5	68	4.2	2.79	127	.262	.311	13	12	99	129	0.9	-0	1	1.4
1970	Cin-N	6	5	.545	67	0	0	0	**35**	85	79	8.4	5	27	2.9	38	4.0	2.65	158	.252	.304	13	14	103	128	-0.7	-1	2	1.6
1971	Cin-N	7	6	.538	**70**	0	0	0	11	100	94	8.5	8	28	2.5	51	4.6	3.33	100	.251	.299	2	0	96	97	0.7	1	3	0.4
1972	Min-A	4	6	.400	63	0	0	0	19	90	83	8.3	7	28	2.8	45	4.5	3.00	110	.243	.299	1	3	107	102	-1.0	0	-0	0.3
1973	StL-N	2	4	.333	33	0	0	0	5	47	50	9.6	3	21	4.0	14	2.7	4.21	78	.284	.360	-3	-5	90	108	-0.9	0	-0	-0.4
	NY-A	0	1	.000	7	0	0	0	0	15	19	11.4	1	3	1.8	10	6.0	1.80	213	.279	.319	3	3	100	198	-0.4	0	-0	0.3
1974	Chi-A	0	0	—	5	0	0	0	0	8	16	18.0	1	3	3.4	4	4.5	7.88	47	.432	.475	-4	-4	102	118	0.0	0	0	-0.2
1975	Hou-N	2	5	.286	55	0	0	0	5	74	76	9.2	7	23	2.8	30	3.6	3.65	94	.264	.319	-0	-2	95	105	-0.9	-1	1	-0.1
1976	Mon-N	1	0	1.000	27	0	0	0	2	32	32	9.0	3	16	4.5	16	4.5	3.66	99	.264	.350	-1	-0	103	123	0.5	-0	-0	0.0
Total	9	35	35	.500	451	0	0	0	108	640	632	8.9	47	201	2.8	303	4.3	3.14	111	.260	.315	28	25	99	116	-1.3	-0	8	3.8
■ **GEORGE GRANT**	Grant, George Addison b: 1/6/03, E.Tallassee, Ala. d: 3/25/86, Montgomery, Ala. BR/TR, 5'11.5", 175 lbs. Deb: 9/17/23																												
1923	StL-A	0	0	—	4	0	0	0	0	9	15	15.0	0	3	3.0	2	2.0	5.00	83	.395	.419	-1	-1	105	138	0.0	-0	0	0.0
1924	StL-A	1	2	.333	22	2	0	0	0	51	69	12.2	4	25	4.4	11	1.9	6.35	72	.325	.382	-12	-10	108	92	-0.4	-2	-1	-1.1
1925	StL-A	0	2	.000	12	0	0	0	0	16	26	14.6	2	8	4.5	7	3.9	6.19	76	.400	.430	-3	-3	108	137	-0.9	-0	0	-0.1
1927	Cle-A	4	6	.400	25	3	2	0	1	75	85	10.2	1	40	4.8	19	2.3	4.44	92	.300	.372	-2	-3	99	108	-0.3	-2	0	-0.4
1928	Cle-A	10	8	.556	28	18	6	1	0	155	196	11.4	7	76	4.4	39	2.3	5.05	87	.319	.384	-17	-11	108	109	2.5	-2	2	-1.0
1929	Cle-A	0	2	.000	12	0	0	0	0	24	41	15.4	2	23	8.6	5	1.9	10.50	41	.414	.500	-17	-17	101	96	-0.9	-0	0	-1.4
1931	Pit-N	0	0	—	11	0	0	0	0	17	28	14.8	0	7	3.7	6	3.2	7.41	53	.364	.409	-7	-7	102	89	0.0	-0	0	-0.5
Total	7	15	20	.429	114	23	8	1	1	347	460	11.9	16	182	4.7	89	2.3	5.65	77	.331	.395	-59	-51	105	106	0.0	-8	3	-4.5
■ **JIM GRANT**	Grant, James Ronald b: 8/4/1894, Coalville, Iowa d: 11/30/85, Des Moines, Iowa BR/TL, 5'11", 180 lbs. Deb: 4/21/23																												
1923	Phi-N	0	0	—	2	0	0	0	0	4	10	22.5	0	4	9.0	0	0.0	13.50	35	.588	.652	-4	-4	118	115	0.0	-0	0	-0.3
■ **JIM GRANT**	Grant, James Timothy "Mudcat" b: 8/13/35, Lacoochee, Fla. BR/TR, 6'1", 186 lbs. Deb: 4/17/58																												
1958	Cle-A	10	11	.476	44	28	11	1	4	204	173	7.6	20	104	4.6	111	4.9	3.84	92	.228	.315	-2	-7	93	90	-0.5	-4	-2	-1.3
1959	Cle-A	10	7	.588	38	19	6	1	3	165	140	7.6	23	81	4.4	85	4.6	4.15	88	.232	.319	-5	-9	95	95	0.2	1	-0	-0.7
1960	Cle-A	9	8	.529	33	19	5	0	0	160	147	8.3	26	78	4.4	75	4.2	4.39	87	.243	.326	-9	-10	98	97	0.7	3	-1	-0.8
1961	Cle-A	15	9	.625	35	35	11	3	0	245	207	7.6	32	109	4.0	146	5.4	3.86	101	.227	.308	5	1	97	92	3.7	1	0	0.2
1962	Cle-A	7	10	.412	26	23	6	1	0	150	128	7.7	24	81	4.9	90	5.4	4.26	92	.233	.328	-5	-6	99	99	-1.4	-0	-0	-0.5
1963	Cle-A	13	14	.481	38	32	10	2	1	229	213	8.4	30	87	3.4	157	6.2	3.69	96	.243	.309	-2	-4	98	102	-0.1	3	-3	-0.3
1964	Cle-A	3	4	.429	13	9	1	0	0	62	82	11.9	11	25	3.6	43	6.2	5.95	63	.324	.380	-16	-15	103	107	-0.3	4	0	-1.0
	Min-A	11	9	.550	26	23	10	1	1	166	162	8.8	21	36	2.0	75	4.1	2.82	128	.248	.286	15	15	100	116	1.4	0	0	1.6
	Yr	14	13	.519	39	32	11	1	1	228	244	9.6	32	61	2.4	118	4.7	3.67	99	.269	.313	-1	-1	101	116	1.1	4	1	0.6
1965	Min-A	**21**	7	**.750**	41	39	14	**6**	0	270	252	8.4	34	61	2.0	142	4.7	3.30	103	.247	.286	5	3	98	102	5.2	3	1	0.7
1966	Min-A	13	13	.500	35	35	10	3	0	249	248	9.0	23	49	1.8	110	4.0	3.25	116	.260	.294	5	15	110	108	-1.3	2	2	2.1
1967	Min-A	5	6	.455	27	14	2	0	0	95	121	11.5	10	17	1.6	50	4.7	4.74	72	.315	.340	-16	-14	106	105	-1.0	0	-2	-1.6
1968	LA-N	6	4	.600	37	4	1	0	3	95	77	7.3	1	19	1.8	35	3.3	2.08	131	.226	.270	10	7	91	100	1.3	0	1	0.9
1969	Mon-N	1	6	.143	11	10	1	0	0	51	64	11.3	7	14	2.5	20	3.5	4.76	78	.299	.342	-7	-6	103	105	-1.9	-1	0	-0.5
	StL-N	7	5	.583	30	3	1	0	7	63	62	8.9	9	22	3.1	35	5.0	4.14	86	.252	.315	-4	-4	99	96	0.6	2	-1	-0.3
	Yr	8	11	.421	41	13	2	0	7	114	126	9.9	16	36	2.8	55	4.3	4.42	82	.273	.325	-10	-10	101	96	-1.3	-1	-1	-0.8
1970	Oak-A	6	2	.750	72	0	0	0	24	123	104	7.6	8	30	2.2	54	4.0	1.83	194	.235	.282	**26**	**24**	96	149	1.8	2	1	2.7
	Pit-N	2	1	.667	8	0	0	0	0	12	8	6.0	2	2	1.5	4	3.0	2.25	173	.190	.227	2	2	96	102	0.4	-0	0	0.2
1971	Pit-N	5	3	.625	42	0	0	0	7	75	79	9.5	8	28	3.4	22	2.6	3.60	93	.274	.334	-1	-2	97	120	0.3	1	1	0.0
	Oak-A	1	0	1.000	15	0	0	0	3	27	25	8.3	3	6	2.0	13	4.3	2.00	171	.243	.279	4	4	99	151	0.5	0	0	0.5
Total	14	145	119	.549	571	293	89	18	53	2441	2292	8.5	292	849	3.1	1267	4.7	3.63	99	.248	.308	5	-7	99	104	9.6	17	-3	1.9
■ **MARK GRANT**	Grant, Mark Andrew b: 10/24/63, Aurora, Ill. BR/TR, 6'2", 195 lbs. Deb: 4/27/84																												
1984	SF-N	1	4	.200	11	10	0	0	1	54	56	9.3	6	19	3.2	32	5.3	6.33	55	.272	.329	-16	-17	98	68	-1.2	-1	-0	-1.7
1986	SF-N	0	1	.000	4	1	0	0	0	10	6	5.4	0	5	4.5	5	4.5	3.60	98	.176	.282	0	-0	95	45	-0.4	-0	0	0.0
1987	SF-N	1	2	.333	16	8	0	0	1	61	66	9.7	6	21	3.1	32	4.7	3.54	109	.282	.333	4	2	95	128	-0.5	-0	-1	0.1
	SD-N	6	7	.462	17	17	2	1	0	102	104	9.2	16	52	4.6	58	5.1	4.68	85	.263	.342	-7	-8	98	103	0.7	-1	-1	-0.8
	Yr	7	9	.438	33	25	2	1	1	163	170	9.4	22	73	4.0	90	5.0	4.25	93	.269	.338	-3	-6	97	103	0.2	-0	-1	-0.7
1988	SD-N	2	8	.200	33	11	0	0	0	98	97	8.9	14	36	3.3	61	5.6	3.67	91	.268	.329	-2	-3	97	126	-3.0	-1	0	-0.4
Total	4	10	22	.313	81	47	2	1	2	325	329	9.1	42	133	3.7	188	5.2	4.40	84	.267	.333	-22	-26	97	107	-4.4	-4	-1	-2.8
■ **RICK GRAPENTHIN**	Grapenthin, Richard Ray b: 4/16/58, Linn Grove, Iowa BR/TR, 6'2", 205 lbs. Deb: 5/03/83																												
1983	Mon-N	0	1	.000	1	0	0	0	0	4	4	9.0	2	1	2.3	3	6.8	9.00	41	.267	.313	-2	-2	101	75	-0.4	-0	0	-0.1
1984	Mon-N	1	2	.333	13	1	0	0	2	23	19	7.4	3	7	2.7	9	3.5	3.52	93	.235	.283	0	-1	91	98	-0.4	0	0	0.0
1985	Mon-N	0	0	—	5	0	0	0	0	7	13	16.7	0	8	10.3	4	5.1	14.14	24	.394	.512	-8	-8	94	70	0.0	0	0	-0.7
Total	3	1	3	.250	19	1	0	0	2	34	36	9.5	5	16	4.2	16	4.2	6.35	53	.279	.351	-10	-11	93	89	-0.8	0	0	-0.8
■ **LOU GRASMICK**	Grasmick, Louis Junior b: 9/11/24, Baltimore, Md. BR/TR, 6', 195 lbs. Deb: 4/22/48																												
1948	Phi-N	0	0	—	2	0	0	0	0	5	3	5.4	1	8	14.4	2	3.6	7.20	53	.176	.440	-2	-2	97	88	0.0	0	0	0.0
■ **DON GRATE**	Grate, Donald "Buckeye" b: 8/27/23, Greenfield, Ohio BR/TR, 6'2.5", 180 lbs. Deb: 7/06/45																												
1945	Phi-N	0	1	.000	4	2	0	0	0	8	18	20.3	0	12	13.5	6	6.8	18.00	22	.439	.566	-13	-13	102	69	-0.4	-0	-0	-1.0
1946	Phi-N	1	0	1.000	3	0	0	0	0	8	4	4.5	0	2	2.3	2	2.3	1.13	297	.160	.222	2	2	98	62	0.5	-0	-0	0.2
Total	2	1	1	.500	7	2	0	0	0	16	22	12.4	0	14	7.9	8	4.5	9.56	38	.333	.450	-11	-11	100	66	0.1	-0	-1	-0.8
■ **FRANK GRAVES**	Graves, Frank M. b: 11/2/1860, Cincinnati, Ohio 6', 163 lbs. Deb: 5/10/1886																												
1886	StL-N	0	0	—	1	0	0	0	0	7	10	12.9	0	1	1.3	2	2.6	9.00	36	.349	.371	-4	-4	98	54	0.0	-0	0	-0.2
■ **CHARLIE GRAY**	Gray, Charles b: 1867, Indianapolis, Ind. Deb: 4/23/1890																												
1890	Pit-N	1	4	.200	5	4	3	0	0	31	48	13.9	0	24	7.0	10	2.9	7.55	45	.371	.470	-14	-14	95	93	0.1	-0	0	-1.1
■ **DAVE GRAY**	Gray, David Alexander b: 1/7/43, Ogden, Utah BR/TR, 6'1", 190 lbs. Deb: 6/14/64																												
1964	Bos-A	0	0	—	9	1	0	0	0	13	18	12.5	3	20	13.8	17	11.8	9.00	42	.321	.494	-8	-8	103	109	0.0	0	0	-0.6
■ **CHUMMY GRAY**	Gray, George Edward b: 7/17/1873, Rockland, Me. d: 8/14/13, Rockland, Maine TR, 5'11.5", 163 lbs. Deb: 9/14/1899																												
1899	Pit-N	3	3	.500	9	7	6	0	0	71	85	10.8	1	24	3.0	9	1.1	3.42	110	.321	.378	3	3	98	121	0.0	-3	0	0.0
■ **JEFF GRAY**	Gray, Jeffrey Edward b: 4/10/63, Richmond, Va. BR/TR, 6'1", 175 lbs. Deb: 6/21/88																												
1988	Cin-N	0	0	—	5	0	0	0	0	9	12	12.0	0	4	4.0	5	5.0	4.00	90	.333	.356	-1	-0	105	136	0.0	-0	0	0.0

YEAR	TM/L	W	L	PCT	G	GS	CG	SHO	SV	IP	H	H/G	HR	BB	BB/G	SO	SO/G	ERA	/A	OAVG	OOBP	PR	/A	PF	CPI	WAT	PB	PD	TPI
■ JOHNNY GRAY	Gray, John Leonard b: 12/11/27, W.Palm Beach, Fla. BR/TR, 6'4", 226 lbs. Deb: 7/18/54																												
1954	Phi-A	3	12	.200	18	16	5	0	0	105	111	9.5	10	91	7.8	51	4.4	6.51	60	.273	.403	-33	-31	105	85	-3.1	-4	0	-3.1
1955	KC-A	0	3	.000	8	5	0	0	0	27	28	9.3	2	24	8.0	11	3.7	6.33	66	.277	.411	-7	-6	106	90	-1.4	-1	-1	-0.6
1957	Cle-A	1	3	.250	7	3	1	1	0	20	21	9.4	1	13	5.8	3	1.3	5.85	66	.288	.378	-5	-4	102	86	-0.9	-1	0	-0.4
1958	Phi-N	0	0	—	15	0	0	0	0	17	12	6.4	3	14	7.4	10	5.3	4.24	93	.222	.356	-1	-1	100	120	0.0	-0	0	0.0
Total	4	4	18	.182	48	24	6	1	0	169	172	9.2	16	142	7.6	75	4.0	6.18	64	.271	.397	-45	-42	104	89	-5.4	-5	-1	-4.1
■ SAM GRAY	Gray, Samuel David "Sad Sam" b: 10/15/1897, Van Alstyne, Tex. d: 4/16/53, Mc Kinney, Tex. BR/TR, 5'10", 175 lbs. Deb: 4/19/24																												
1924	Phi-A	8	7	.533	34	19	8	2	2	152	169	10.0	5	89	5.3	54	3.2	3.97	108	.284	.373	4	5	101	116	1.0	-2	-1	0.2
1925	Phi-A	16	8	.667	32	28	14	4	3	204	199	8.8	11	63	2.8	80	3.5	3.26	136	.260	.311	26	27	101	102	2.9	-2	-3	2.1
1926	Phi-A	11	12	.478	38	18	5	0	0	151	164	9.8	9	50	3.0	82	4.9	3.64	128	.279	.332	6	17	116	108	-1.7	1	-2	1.7
1927	Phi-A	9	6	.600	37	13	3	1	3	133	153	10.4	4	51	3.5	49	3.3	4.60	85	.295	.354	-7	-10	95	95	0.2	-1	0	-1.0
1928	StL-A	20	12	.625	35	31	21	2	3	263	256	8.8	11	86	2.9	102	3.5	3.18	131	.260	.311	25	29	103	105	3.8	-2	3	3.1
1929	StL-A	18	15	.545	43	37	23	**4**	1	**305**	336	9.9	18	96	2.8	109	3.2	3.72	114	.285	.331	18	17	100	111	1.1	-1	-1	1.4
1930	StL-A	4	15	.211	27	24	7	0	0	168	215	11.5	17	52	2.8	51	2.7	6.27	82	.316	.358	-30	-21	110	90	-4.9	-2	-1	-2.0
1931	StL-A	11	24	.314	43	37	13	0	2	258	323	11.3	20	54	1.9	88	3.1	5.09	90	.297	.329	-20	-14	105	90	-4.8	-1	-2	-1.4
1932	StL-A	7	12	.368	52	18	7	3	4	207	250	10.9	9	53	2.3	79	3.4	4.52	102	.294	.331	-1	2	103	96	-1.0	0	-1	0.1
1933	StL-A	7	4	.636	38	6	0	0	4	112	131	10.5	7	45	3.6	36	2.9	4.10	123	.301	.361	2	12	117	126	2.5	1	-1	1.2
Total	10	111	115	.491	379	231	101	16	22	1953	2196	10.1	111	639	2.9	730	3.4	4.18	107	.286	.335	24	62	104	103	-0.9	-9	-7	5.4
■ TED GRAY	Gray, Ted Glenn b: 12/31/24, Detroit, Mich. BB/TL, 5'11", 175 lbs. Deb: 5/15/46																												
1946	Det-A	0	2	.000	3	2	0	0	1	12	17	12.8	4	5	3.8	5	3.8	8.25	45	.340	.400	-6	-6	106	97	-0.9	-0	-0	-0.5
1948	Det-A	6	2	.750	26	11	3	1	0	85	73	7.7	2	72	7.6	60	6.4	4.24	98	.236	.378	0	-1	97	103	2.0	1	-0	0.0
1949	Det-A	10	10	.500	34	27	8	3	1	195	163	7.5	11	103	4.8	96	4.4	3.51	127	.227	.321	15	20	106	92	-1.2	-3	1	1.8
1950	Det-A	10	7	.588	27	21	7	0	1	149	139	8.4	22	72	4.3	102	6.2	4.41	98	.248	.331	3	-1	95	100	-0.3	-1	-2	-0.3
1951	Det-A	7	14	.333	34	28	9	1	1	197	194	8.9	17	95	4.3	131	6.0	4.07	108	.256	.337	1	7	107	102	-3.3	-3	1	0.3
1952	Det-A	12	17	.414	35	32	13	2	0	224	212	8.5	21	101	4.1	138	5.5	4.14	91	.249	.327	-12	-9	103	92	2.3	-2	1	-0.9
1953	Det-A	10	15	.400	30	28	8	0	0	176	166	8.5	25	76	3.9	115	5.9	4.60	88	.252	.329	-12	-11	102	95	0.3	2	-1	-0.8
1954	Det-A	3	5	.375	19	10	2	0	0	72	70	8.8	8	56	7.0	29	3.6	5.38	70	.268	.386	-13	-13	101	101	-0.5	-2	-1	-1.5
1955	Chi-A	0	0	—	2	1	0	0	0	3	9	27.0	0	2	6.0	1	3.0	18.00	22	.500	.550	-5	-5	98	74	0.0	0	0	-0.3
	Cle-A	0	0	—	2	0	0	0	0	2	5	22.5	1	2	9.0	1	4.5	18.00	22	.455	.538	-3	-3	102	87	0.0	0	0	-0.2
	NY-A	0	0	—	1	1	0	0	0	3	3	9.0	0	0	0.0	1	3.0	3.00	124	.300	.273	0	0	94	108	0.0	-0	0	0.0
	Bal-A	1	2	.333	9	1	0	0	0	15	21	12.6	3	11	6.6	8	4.8	8.40	44	.344	.416	-7	-8	94	95	-0.1	-0	1	-0.6
	Yr	1	2	.333	14	3	0	0	0	23	38	14.9	4	15	5.9	11	4.3	9.78	38	.376	.438	-15	-15	95	95	-0.1	-0	1	-1.1
Total	9	59	74	.444	222	162	50	7	4	1133	1072	8.5	114	595	4.7	687	5.5	4.37	95	.251	.340	-38	-28	102	97	-1.7	-10	-3	-3.0
■ DOLLY GRAY	Gray, William Denton b: 12/4/1878, Ishpeming, Mich. d: 4/4/56, Yuba City, Cal. BL/TL, 6'2", 160 lbs. Deb: 4/13/09																												
1909	Was-A	5	19	.208	36	26	19	0	0	218	210	8.7	1	77	3.2	87	3.6	3.59	66	.258	.329	-27	-29	96	79	-3.3	-1	-1	-3.2
1910	Was-A	8	19	.296	34	29	21	3	0	229	216	8.5	3	65	2.6	84	3.3	2.63	97	.249	.309	-3	-2	102	98	-4.8	3	1	0.3
1911	Was-A	2	13	.133	28	15	6	0	0	121	160	11.9	4	40	3.0	42	3.1	5.06	65	.331	.385	-23	-23	99	99	-5.2	1	1	-2.0
Total	3	15	51	.227	98	70	46	3	0	568	586	9.3	8	182	2.9	213	3.4	3.52	75	.271	.333	-53	-55	99	91	-13.3	3	1	-4.9
■ ELI GRBA	Grba, Eli b: 8/9/34, Chicago, Ill. BR/TR, 6'2", 205 lbs. Deb: 7/10/59																												
1959	NY-A	2	5	.286	19	6	0	0	0	50	52	9.4	6	39	7.0	23	4.1	6.48	55	.269	.379	-15	-16	92	85	-1.5	1	0	-1.4
1960	NY-A	6	4	.600	24	9	1	0	1	81	65	7.2	9	46	5.1	32	3.6	3.67	97	.226	.327	2	-1	92	104	-0.2	2	-1	0.0
1961	LA-A	11	13	.458	40	30	8	0	2	212	197	8.4	26	114	4.8	105	4.5	4.25	106	.242	.338	-5	6	112	98	0.6	5	-1	1.1
1962	LA-A	8	9	.471	40	29	1	0	1	176	185	9.5	19	75	3.8	90	4.6	4.55	89	.267	.335	-11	-10	102	95	-1.0	2	1	-0.6
1963	LA-A	1	2	.333	12	1	0	0	0	17	14	7.4	2	10	5.3	5	2.6	4.76	70	.222	.325	-2	-3	92	82	-0.3	-0	0	-0.2
Total	5	28	33	.459	135	75	10	0	4	536	513	8.6	62	284	4.8	255	4.3	4.48	91	.250	.339	-31	-24	103	96	-2.4	10	-1	-1.1
■ BILL GREASON	Greason, William Henry "Booster" b: 9/3/24, Atlanta, Ga. BR/TR, 5'10", 170 lbs. Deb: 5/31/54																												
1954	StL-N	0	1	.000	3	2	0	0	0	4	8	18.0	4	4	9.0	2	4.5	13.50	30	.421	.500	-4	-4	100	130	-0.4	-0	0	-0.3
■ CHRIS GREEN	Green, Christopher De Wayne b: 9/5/60, Los Angeles, Cal. BL/TL, 6'2", 214 lbs. Deb: 4/17/84																												
1984	Pit-N	0	0	—	4	0	0	0	0	3	5	15.0	0	1	3.0	3	9.0	6.00	56	.417	.429	-1	-1	94	124	0.0	0	0	0.0
■ ED GREEN	Green, Edward M. b: 1850, Philadelphia, Pa. d: 3/22/17, Ogden, Utah Deb: 4/22/1890																												
1890	Phi-a	7	15	.318	25	22	20	1	1	191	267	12.6	4	94	4.4	56	2.6	5.80	68	.347	.419	-41	-40	101	103	-2.7	-4	0	-3.6
■ FRED GREEN	Green, Fred Allen b: 9/14/33, Titusville, N.J. BR/TL, 6'4", 190 lbs. Deb: 4/15/59																												
1959	Pit-N	1	2	.333	17	1	0	0	1	37	37	9.0	2	15	3.6	20	4.9	3.16	129	.259	.323	3	4	104	113	-0.4	-1	0	0.4
1960	Pit-N	8	4	.667	45	0	0	0	3	70	61	7.8	4	33	4.2	49	6.3	3.21	113	.243	.316	4	3	97	111	0.8	3	-1	0.6
1961	Pit-N	0	0	—	13	0	0	0	0	21	27	11.6	2	9	3.9	4	1.7	4.71	85	.321	.379	-2	-2	99	121	0.0	-0	1	0.0
1962	Was-A	0	1	.000	5	0	0	0	0	7	7	9.0	3	6	7.7	2	2.6	6.43	63	.250	.371	-2	-2	102	116	-0.4	0	0	-0.1
1964	Pit-N	0	0	—	8	0	0	0	0	7	10	12.9	1	0	0.0	2	2.6	1.29	277	.323	.313	2	2	101	388	0.0	0	-0	0.1
Total	5	9	7	.563	88	1	0	0	4	142	142	9.0	12	63	4.0	77	4.9	3.49	110	.264	.330	6	5	99	127	0.0	2	0	1.0
■ DALLAS GREEN	Green, George Dallas b: 8/4/34, Newport, Del. BL/TR, 6'5", 210 lbs. Deb: 6/18/60 M																												
1960	Phi-N	3	6	.333	23	10	5	1	0	109	100	8.3	10	44	3.6	51	4.2	4.05	102	.248	.315	-3	1	110	93	-0.5	0	-1	0.1
1961	Phi-N	2	4	.333	42	10	1	1	1	128	160	11.3	8	47	3.3	51	3.6	4.85	81	.315	.369	-12	-13	98	106	0.1	1	0	-1.1
1962	Phi-N	6	6	.500	37	10	2	0	1	129	145	10.1	10	43	3.0	58	4.0	3.84	98	.289	.346	1	-1	95	117	0.0	-1	2	0.0
1963	Phi-N	7	5	.583	40	14	4	0	2	120	134	10.1	10	38	2.9	68	5.1	3.23	104	.286	.335	1	2	102	134	0.6	-2	1	0.2
1964	Phi-N	2	1	.667	25	0	0	0	0	42	63	13.5	4	14	3.0	21	4.5	5.79	60	.362	.403	-10	-11	98	118	0.3	-0	-1	-1.1
1965	Was-A	0	0	—	6	2	0	0	0	14	14	9.0	0	3	1.9	6	3.9	3.21	110	.241	.279	0	0	102	63	0.0	-0	0	0.0
1966	NY-N	0	0	—	4	0	0	0	0	5	6	10.8	2	2	3.6	1	1.8	5.40	65	.333	.381	-1	-1	97	152	0.0	0	0	0.0
1967	Phi-N	0	0	—	8	0	0	0	0	15	25	15.0	2	6	3.6	12	7.2	9.00	39	.362	.421	-9	-9	104	83	0.0	-0	1	-0.8
Total	8	20	22	.476	185	46	12	2	4	562	647	10.4	46	197	3.2	268	4.3	4.26	88	.294	.349	-33	-32	101	112	0.5	-3	3	-2.7
■ HARVEY GREEN	Green, Harvey George "Buck" b: 2/9/15, Kenosha, Wis. d: 7/24/70, Franklin, La. BB/TR, 6'2.5", 185 lbs. Deb: 9/12/35																												
1935	Bro-N	0	0	—	2	0	0	0	0	1	2	18.0	0	3	27.0	0	0.0	9.00	42	.400	.667	-1	-1	95	200	0.0	0	0	0.0
■ JUNE GREENE	Greene, Julius Foust b: 6/25/1899, Ramseur, N.C. d: 3/19/74, Glendora, Cal. BL/TR, 6'2.5", 185 lbs. Deb: 4/20/28																												
1928	Phi-N	0	0	—	1	0	0	0	0	2	5	22.5	0	0	0.0	0	0.0	9.00	48	.556	.556	-1	-1	109	128	0.0	2	0	0.0
1929	Phi-N	0	0	—	5	0	0	0	0	14	33	21.2	2	9	5.8	4	2.6	19.29	27	.465	.529	-23	-22	112	66	0.0	0	0	-1.6
Total	2	0	0	—	6	0	0	0	0	16	38	21.4	2	9	5.1	4	2.3	18.00	29	.475	.532	-24	-23	111	74	0.0	2	1	-1.6
■ NELSON GREENE	Greene, Nelson George "Lefty" b: 9/20/1900, Philadelphia, Pa. d: 4/6/83, Lebanon, Pa. BL/TL, 6', 185 lbs. Deb: 4/28/24																												
1924	Bro-N	0	1	.000	4	1	0	0	0	9	14	14.0	1	2	2.0	3	3.0	4.00	95	.350	.381	-0	-0	98	153	-0.4	-0	0	0.0
1925	Bro-N	2	0	1.000	11	0	0	0	1	22	45	18.4	4	7	2.9	4	1.6	10.64	38	.417	.444	-16	-16	95	89	1.0	0	0	-1.3
Total	2	2	1	.667	15	1	0	0	1	31	59	17.1	5	9	2.6	7	2.0	8.71	46	.399	.428	-16	-16	96	107	0.6	0	0	-1.3
■ KENT GREENFIELD	Greenfield, Kent b: 7/1/02, Guthrie, Ky. d: 3/14/78, Guthrie, Ky. BR/TR, 6'1", 180 lbs. Deb: 9/28/24																												
1924	NY-N	0	1	.000	1	1	0	0	0	3	9	27.0	1	1	3.0	1	3.0	15.00	23	.500	.526	-4	-4	88	100	-0.4	0	-0	-0.2
1925	NY-N	12	8	.600	29	21	12	0	0	172	195	10.2	4	64	3.3	66	3.5	3.87	108	.288	.342	8	6	98	104	0.9	-6	1	0.0
1926	NY-N	13	12	.520	39	28	8	1	1	223	206	8.3	17	82	3.3	74	3.0	3.96	95	.251	.312	-3	-5	98	88	0.9	-5	-2	-1.1
1927	NY-N	2	2	.500	12	1	0	0	0	20	39	17.5	3	13	5.8	4	1.8	9.45	41	.411	.478	-12	-12	98	107	-0.2	-0	0	-1.1
	Bos-N	11	14	.440	27	26	11	1	0	190	203	9.6	3	59	2.8	59	2.8	3.84	97	.282	.327	2	-2	95	98	1.2	-2	-0	-0.3
	Yr	13	16	.448	39	27	11	1	0	210	242	10.4	6	72	3.1	63	2.7	4.37	86	.297	.343	-11	-15	96	98	1.0	-0	-0	-1.4
1928	Bos-N	3	11	.214	32	23	5	0	0	144	173	10.8	6	60	3.8	30	1.9	5.31	76	.307	.363	-21	-20	101	91	-2.5	-4	1	-2.2
1929	Bos-N	0	0	—	6	2	0	0	0	16	33	18.6	1	15	8.4	7	3.9	10.69	43	.465	.538	-11	-11	97	114	0.0	-1	1	-0.8
	Bro-N	0	0	—	6	0	0	0	0	9	13	13.0	1	3	3.0	1	1.0	8.00	57	.382	.381	-3	-3	96	94	0.0	-0	0	-0.2

YEAR	TM/L	W	L	PCT	G	GS	CG	SHO	SV	IP	H	H/G	HR	BB	BB/G	SO	SO/G	ERA	/A	OAVG	OOBP	PR	/A	PF	CPI	WAT	PB	PD	TPI
	Yr	0	0	—	12	2	0	0	0	25	46	16.6	2	18	6.5	8	2.9	9.72	47	.430	.474	-14	-14	97	94	0.0	-1	1	-1.0
Total	6	41	48	.461	152	102	36	2	1	777	871	10.1	36	297	3.4	242	2.8	4.53	87	.290	.346	-45	-52	98	96	-0.1	-18	-0	-5.9
■ **JOHN GREENING**	Greening, John A. (born John A. Greenig) b: Philadelphia, Pa. Deb: 1888																												
1888	Was-N	0	1	.000	1	1	1	0	0	9	17	17.0	2	4	4.0	2	2.0	11.00	26	.416	.468	-8	-8	101	86	-0.4	-0	0	-0.5
■ **BOB GREENWOOD**	Greenwood, Robert Chandler "Greenie" b: 3/13/28, Cananea, Mexico BR/TR, 6'4", 205 lbs. Deb: 4/21/54																												
1954	Phi-N	1	2	.333	11	4	0	0	0	37	28	6.8	2	18	4.4	9	2.2	3.16	126	.209	.297	4	3	98	78	-0.4	-1	0	0.3
1955	Phi-N	0	0	—	1	0	0	0	0	2	7	31.5	1	0	0.0	0	0.0	18.00	23	.500	.500	-3	-3	102	92	0.0	-0	0	-0.2
Total	2	1	2	.333	12	4	0	0	0	39	35	8.1	3	18	4.2	9	2.1	3.92	102	.236	.314	1	0	98	79	-0.4	-1	0	0.1
■ **DAVE GREGG**	Gregg, David Charles "Highpockets" b: 3/14/1891, Chehalis, Wash. d: 11/12/65, Clarkston, Wash. BR/TR, 6'1", 185 lbs. Deb: 6/15/13																												
1913	Cle-A	0	0	—	1	0	0	0	0	1	3	27.0	0	3	27.0	1	9.0	9.00	34	.500	.667	-1	-1	104	220	0.0	0	0	0.0
■ **HAL GREGG**	Gregg, Harold Dana "Skeets" b: 7/11/21, Anaheim, Cal. BR/TR, 6'3.5", 195 lbs. Deb: 8/18/43																												
1943	Bro-N	0	3	.000	5	4	0	0	0	19	21	9.9	2	21	9.9	7	3.3	9.47	35	.304	.447	-13	-13	99	76	-1.4	0	-0	-1.1
1944	Bro-N	9	16	.360	39	31	6	0	2	198	201	9.1	12	137	6.2	92	4.2	5.45	67	.258	.369	-41	-39	102	84	-1.6	-1	0	-3.7
1945	Bro-N	18	13	.581	42	34	13	2	2	254	221	7.8	5	120	4.3	139	4.9	3.47	104	.232	.320	9	3	95	87	0.7	4	0	0.7
1946	Bro-N	6	4	.600	26	16	4	2	2	117	103	7.9	3	44	3.4	54	4.2	3.00	114	.236	.303	5	5	100	88	0.0	-1	-2	0.3
1947	Bro-N	4	5	.444	37	16	2	1	1	104	115	10.0	6	55	4.8	59	5.1	5.88	71	.272	.358	-21	-20	103	74	-1.2	1	0	-1.6
1948	Pit-N	2	4	.333	22	8	1	0	1	74	72	8.8	3	34	4.1	25	3.0	4.62	89	.255	.339	-5	-4	104	82	-1.1	2	-0	-0.2
1949	Pit-N	1	1	.500	8	1	0	0	0	19	20	9.5	1	8	3.8	9	4.3	3.32	125	.303	.367	2	2	102	156	0.1	-0	-0	0.1
1950	Pit-N	0	1	.000	5	1	0	0	0	5	10	18.0	2	7	12.6	3	5.4	14.40	30	.400	.545	-6	-6	106	99	-0.4	-0	0	-0.4
1952	NY-N	0	1	.000	16	4	1	0	1	36	42	10.5	7	17	4.3	13	3.3	4.75	79	.286	.359	-4	-4	101	122	-0.4	-0	-1	-0.4
Total	9	40	48	.455	200	115	27	5	9	826	805	8.8	41	443	4.8	401	4.4	4.54	82	.253	.345	-73	-75	100	87	-5.3	4	-2	-6.3
■ **VEAN GREGG**	Gregg, Sylveanus Augustus b: 4/13/1885, Chehalis, Wash. d: 7/29/64, Aberdeen, Was. BR/TL, 6'1", 185 lbs. Deb: 4/12/11																												
1911	Cle-A	23	7	.767	34	26	22	5	0	245	172	**6.3**	2	86	3.2	125	4.6	**1.80**	**192**	**.205**	.286	42	45	103	96	8.5	-4	0	4.4
1912	Cle-A	20	13	.606	37	34	26	1	2	271	242	8.0	4	90	3.0	184	6.1	2.59	131	.246	.316	23	24	101	110	4.5	-3	-2	2.3
1913	Cle-A	20	13	.606	44	34	23	3	3	286	258	8.1	2	124	3.9	166	5.2	2.23	136	.246	.334	22	26	104	130	1.9	-5	-3	2.5
1914	Cle-A	9	3	.750	17	12	6	1	0	97	88	8.2	0	48	4.5	56	5.2	3.06	95	.251	.347	-3	-2	106	103	3.9	1	-0	-0.2
	Bos-A	3	4	.429	12	9	4	0	0	68	71	9.4	0	37	4.9	24	3.2	3.97	66	.283	.375	-9	-10	96	100	-0.9	0	-1	-1.1
	Yr	12	7	.632	29	21	10	1	0	165	159	8.7	0	85	4.6	80	4.4	3.44	81	.263	.354	-13	-12	102	100	3.0	1	-1	-1.3
1915	Bos-A	4	2	.667	18	9	3	1	3	75	71	8.5	2	32	3.8	43	5.2	3.36	84	.260	.348	-3	-4	96	106	0.0	2	0	-0.2
1916	Bos-A	2	5	.286	21	7	3	0	0	78	71	8.2	0	30	3.5	41	4.7	3.00	87	.259	.339	-1	-3	92	104	-1.7	-1	-0	-0.4
1918	Phi-A	9	14	.391	30	25	17	3	2	199	180	8.1	4	67	3.0	63	2.8	3.12	96	.251	.310	-8	-3	108	89	-0.4	-3	-1	-0.6
1925	Was-A	2	2	.500	26	5	1	0	2	74	87	10.6	3	38	4.6	18	2.2	4.14	101	.318	.388	2	0	95	133	-0.3	0	-1	0.0
Total	8	92	63	.594	239	161	105	14	12	1393	1240	8.0	17	552	3.6	720	4.7	2.70	117	.248	.326	63	73	102	108	15.5	-12	-8	6.7
■ **FRANK GREGORY**	Gregory, Frank Ernst b: 7/25/1888, Spring Valley Township, Wis. d: 11/5/55, Beloit, Wis. BR/TR, 5'11", 185 lbs. Deb: 9/05/12																												
1912	Cin-N	2	0	1.000	4	2	1	0	0	16	19	10.7	0	7	3.9	4	2.3	4.50	71	.288	.365	-2	-2	93	86	1.0	0	-1	-0.2
■ **LEE GREGORY**	Gregory, Grover Leroy b: 6/2/38, Bakersfield, Cal. BL/TL, 6'1", 180 lbs. Deb: 4/17/64																												
1964	Chi-N	0	0	—	11	0	0	0	0	18	23	11.5	3	5	2.5	8	4.0	3.50	107	.333	.368	0	1	106	177	0.0	0	0	0.0
■ **HOWIE GREGORY**	Gregory, Howard Watterson b: 11/18/1886, Hannibal, Mo. d: 5/30/70, Tulsa, Okla. BL/TR, 6', 175 lbs. Deb: 4/16/11																												
1911	StL-A	0	1	.000	3	1	0	0	0	7	11	14.1	0	4	5.1	1	1.3	5.14	65	.393	.469	-1	-1	100	139	-0.4	-0	0	0.0
■ **PAUL GREGORY**	Gregory, Paul Edwin "Pop" b: 6/9/08, Tomnolen, Miss. BR/TR, 6'2", 180 lbs. Deb: 4/20/32																												
1932	Chi-A	5	3	.625	33	9	3	0	0	118	125	9.5	8	51	3.9	39	3.0	4.50	90	.273	.344	-0	-6	91	100	1.8	-2	3	-0.4
1933	Chi-A	4	11	.267	23	17	5	0	0	104	124	10.7	10	47	4.1	18	1.6	4.93	89	.296	.361	-8	-6	103	109	-3.1	-2	1	-0.5
Total	2	9	14	.391	56	26	8	0	0	222	249	10.1	18	98	4.0	57	2.3	4.70	90	.284	.352	-8	-12	97	104	-1.3	-4	4	-0.9
■ **BILL GREIF**	Greif, William Briley b: 4/25/50, Ft.Stockton, Tex. BR/TR, 6'4", 196 lbs. Deb: 7/19/71																												
1971	Hou-N	1	1	.500	7	3	0	0	0	16	18	10.1	1	8	4.5	14	7.9	5.06	63	.290	.368	-3	-3	92	100	0.0	0	0	-0.2
1972	SD-N	5	16	.238	34	22	2	1	2	125	143	10.3	18	47	3.4	91	6.6	5.62	56	.287	.349	-30	-34	91	91	-4.2	-2	-2	-3.8
1973	SD-N	10	17	.370	36	31	9	3	1	199	181	8.2	20	62	2.8	120	5.4	3.21	111	.246	.301	10	8	97	107	0.0	-2	-1	0.4
1974	SD-N	9	19	.321	43	35	7	1	1	226	244	9.7	17	95	3.8	137	5.5	4.66	75	.279	.351	-26	-29	97	96	-2.1	-1	0	-3.0
1975	SD-N	4	6	.400	59	1	0	0	9	72	74	9.3	7	38	4.8	43	5.4	3.88	95	.269	.353	-2	-2	101	120	-0.4	-0	-2	-0.3
1976	SD-N	1	3	.250	5	5	0	0	0	22	27	11.0	2	11	4.5	5	2.0	8.18	38	.297	.365	-11	-12	90	63	-0.8	-1	0	-1.1
	StL-N	1	5	.167	47	0	0	0	6	55	60	9.8	5	26	4.3	32	5.2	4.09	90	.290	.361	-4	-3	105	123	-1.8	0	-0	-0.2
	Yr	2	8	.200	52	5	0	0	6	77	87	10.2	7	37	4.3	37	4.3	5.26	67	.291	.362	-15	-15	100	123	-2.6	-1	-0	-1.3
Total	6	31	67	.316	231	97	18	5	19	715	747	9.4	70	287	3.6	442	5.6	4.42	78	.272	.339	-65	-76	96	101	-9.3	-6	-4	-8.2
■ **BILL GREVELL**	Grevell, William J. b: 3/5/1898, Williamstown, N.J. d: 6/21/23, Springfield Township, Pa. BR/TR, 5'11", 170 lbs. Deb: 5/14/19																												
1919	Phi-A	0	0	—	5	2	0	0	0	12	15	11.3	0	18	13.5	3	2.3	14.25	25	.306	.500	-15	-14	112	52	0.0	-1	1	-1.2
■ **GREYSON**	Greyson Deb:8/27/1873																												
1873	Nat-n	1	7	.125	8																								
■ **LEE GRIFFETH**	Griffeth, Leon Clifford b: 5/20/25, Carmel, N.Y. BB/TL, 5'11.5", 180 lbs. Deb: 6/25/46																												
1946	Phi-A	0	0	—	10	0	0	0	0	15	13	7.8	1	6	3.6	4	2.4	3.00	125	.232	.328	1	1	107	110	0.0	0	-0	0.1
■ **HANK GRIFFIN**	Griffin, James Linton "Pepper" b: 7/11/1886, Whitehouse, Tex. d: 2/11/50, Terrell, Tex. BR/TR, 6', 165 lbs. Deb: 5/05/11																												
1911	Chi-N	0	0	—	1	1	0	0	0	1	1	9.0	1	3	27.0	1	9.0	18.00	18	.250	.571	-2	-2	94	97	0.0	0	0	-0.1
	Bos-N	0	6	.000	15	6	1	0	0	83	96	10.4	3	34	3.7	30	3.3	5.20	71	.305	.383	-17	-14	109	93	-2.9	-0	0	-1.2
	Yr	0	6	.000	16	7	1	0	0	84	97	10.4	4	37	4.0	31	3.3	5.36	69	.304	.387	-18	-15	109	93	-2.9	0	0	-1.3
1912	Bos-N	0	0	—	3	0	0	0	0	2	3	13.5	0	3	13.5	0	0.0	22.50	17	.500	.700	-4	-4	110	58	0.0	0	0	-0.3
Total	2	0	6	.000	19	7	1	0	0	86	100	10.5	4	40	4.2	31	3.2	5.76	64	.308	.395	-22	-20	109	92	-2.9	-0	0	-1.6
■ **MARTY GRIFFIN**	Griffin, Martin John b: 9/2/01, San Francisco, Cal d: 11/19/51, Los Angeles, Cal. BR/TR, 6'2", 200 lbs. Deb: 7/25/28																												
1928	Bos-A	0	3	.000	11	3	0	0	0	38	42	9.9	0	17	4.0	9	2.1	4.97	82	.300	.349	-4	-4	101	91	-1.4	1	-0	-0.2
■ **MIKE GRIFFIN**	Griffin, Michael Leroy b: 6/26/57, Colusa, Cal. BR/TR, 6'4", 195 lbs. Deb: 9/17/79																												
1979	NY-A	0	0	—	3	0	0	0	1	4	5	11.3	0	2	4.5	5	11.3	4.50	89	.313	.368	-0	-0	95	110	0.0	0	0	0.0
1980	NY-A	2	4	.333	13	9	0	0	0	54	64	10.7	6	23	3.8	25	4.2	4.83	82	.287	.352	-5	-5	98	99	-1.4	0	0	-0.4
1981	NY-A	0	0	—	2	0	0	0	0	4	5	11.3	0	0	0.0	4	9.0	2.25	161	.278	.278	1	1	99	106	0.0	0	0	0.1
	Chi-N	2	5	.286	16	9	0	0	1	52	64	11.1	4	9	1.6	20	3.5	4.50	83	.302	.320	-6	-5	106	95	-0.7	-0	0	-0.4
1982	SD-N	0	1	.000	7	0	0	0	0	10	9	8.1	0	3	2.7	4	3.6	3.60	92	.237	.293	0	-0	92	64	-0.4	-0	-0	0.0
1987	Bal-A	3	5	.375	23	6	1	0	1	74	78	9.5	9	33	4.0	42	5.1	4.38	101	.269	.344	1	1	99	107	-0.3	0	-1	0.0
Total	5	7	15	.318	64	24	1	0	3	198	225	10.2	19	70	3.2	100	4.5	4.45	91	.282	.337	-9	-9	100	99	-2.8	-1	-0	-0.7
■ **PAT GRIFFIN**	Griffin, Patrick Richard b: 5/6/1893, Niles, Ohio d: 6/7/27, Youngstown, Ohio BR/TR, 6'2", 180 lbs. Deb: 7/23/14																												
1914	Cin-N	0	0	—	1	0	0	0	0	1	3	27.0	0	2	18.0	0	0.0	9.00	33	.750	.833	-1	-1	107	235	0.0	0	0	0.0
■ **TOM GRIFFIN**	Griffin, Thomas James b: 2/22/48, Los Angeles, Cal. BR/TR, 6'3", 210 lbs. Deb: 4/10/69																												
1969	Hou-N	11	10	.524	31	31	6	3	0	188	156	7.5	19	93	4.5	200	**9.6**	3.54	103	.220	.316	1	2	101	94	0.6	2	-2	0.2
1970	Hou-N	3	13	.188	23	20	2	1	0	111	118	9.6	9	72	5.8	72	5.8	5.76	66	.275	.378	-21	-24	94	88	-5.0	-2	-1	-2.5
1971	Hou-N	0	6	.000	10	6	0	0	0	38	44	10.4	4	20	4.7	29	6.9	4.74	68	.288	.373	-5	-6	92	109	-2.9	-0	1	-0.5
1972	Hou-N	5	4	.556	39	5	1	1	3	94	92	8.8	7	38	3.6	83	7.9	3.26	112	.258	.325	2	4	105	117	0.1	3	-0	0.7
1973	Hou-N	4	6	.400	25	12	4	0	0	100	83	7.5	10	46	4.1	69	6.2	4.14	84	.229	.313	-5	-7	95	83	-1.0	1	0	-0.6
1974	Hou-N	14	10	.583	34	34	8	3	0	211	202	8.6	14	89	3.8	110	4.7	3.54	100	.250	.322	2	0	98	99	2.3	8	1	0.8
1975	Hou-N	3	8	.273	17	13	3	1	0	79	89	10.1	11	46	5.2	56	6.4	5.35	64	.288	.377	-15	-17	95	103	-1.7	-0	1	-1.5

YEAR	TM/L	W	L	PCT	G	GS	CG	SHO	SV	IP	H	H/G	HR	BB	BB/G	SO	SO/G	ERA	/A	OAVG	OOBP	PR	/A	PF	CPI	WAT	PB	PD	TPI
1976	Hou-N	5	3	.625	20	2	0	0	0	42	44	9.4	4	37	7.9	33	7.1	6.00	51	.278	.408	-12	-14	87	97	1.1	-0	0	-1.3
	SD-N	4	3	.571	11	11	2	0	0	70	56	7.2	0	42	5.4	36	4.6	2.96	106	.222	.326	4	1	90	98	0.8	-1	-0	0.0
	Yr	9	6	.600	31	13	2	0	0	112	100	8.0	4	79	6.3	69	5.5	4.10	76	.242	.356	-7	-12	88	98	1.9	-0	-0	-1.3
1977	SD-N	6	9	.400	38	20	0	0	0	151	144	8.6	17	88	5.2	79	4.7	4.47	78	.254	.353	-9	-16	89	101	-0.4	1	-2	-1.6
1978	Cal-A	3	4	.429	24	4	0	0	0	56	63	10.1	8	31	5.0	35	5.6	4.02	95	.279	.353	-1	-1	101	128	-0.6	0	1	0.0
1979	SF-N	5	6	.455	59	3	0	0	2	94	83	7.9	9	46	4.4	82	7.9	3.93	89	.237	.327	-2	-5	93	93	0.2	-1	2	-0.3
1980	SF-N	5	1	.833	42	4	0	0	0	108	80	6.7	8	49	4.1	79	6.6	2.75	126	.212	.306	10	9	96	110	2.1	0	0	1.0
1981	SF-N	8	8	.500	22	22	3	1	0	129	121	8.4	8	57	4.0	83	5.8	3.77	97	.249	.332	-4	-1	105	98	0.0	2	2	0.2
1982	Pit-N	1	3	.250	6	4	0	0	0	22	32	13.1	5	15	6.1	8	3.3	9.00	44	.330	.425	-13	-12	110	87	-0.9	0	0	-1.0
Total	14	77	94	.450	401	191	29	10	5	1493	1407	8.5	133	769	4.6	1054	6.4	4.08	87	.249	.339	-68	-87	97	99	-5.3	12	1	-6.4

■ **CLARK GRIFFITH** Griffith, Clark Calvin "The Old Fox" b: 11/20/1869, Clear Creek, Mo. d: 10/27/55, Washington, D.C. BR/TR, 5'6.5", 156 lbs. Deb: 4/11/1891 MH

YEAR	TM/L	W	L	PCT	G	GS	CG	SHO	SV	IP	H	H/G	HR	BB	BB/G	SO	SO/G	ERA	/A	OAVG	OOBP	PR	/A	PF	CPI	WAT	PB	PD	TPI
1891	StL-a	11	8	.579	27	17	12	0	0	186	195	9.4	8	58	2.8	68	3.3	3.34	124	.284	.340	8	17	112	104	-0.7	-4	0	1.3
	Bos-a	3	1	.750	7	4	3	0	0	40	47	10.6	3	15	3.4	20	4.5	5.62	62	.308	.370	-8	-9	94	80	0.4	2	0	-0.5
	Yr	14	9	.609	34	21	15	0	0	226	242	9.6	11	73	2.9	88	3.5	3.74	108	.289	.346	-1	7	108	80	-0.3	-4	0	0.8
1893	Chi-N	1	2	.333	4	2	2	0	0	20	24	10.8	1	5	2.3	9	4.0	5.40	90	.313	.356	-2	-1	104	81	-0.3	-1	0	-0.1
1894	Chi-N	21	14	.600	36	30	28	0	0	261	328	11.3	12	85	2.9	71	2.4	4.93	117	.330	.383	12	24	108	97	6.4	-1	1	2.1
1895	Chi-N	26	14	.650	42	41	39	0	0	353	434	11.1	11	91	2.3	79	2.0	3.93	126	.323	.366	34	40	103	111	5.7	6	2	4.2
1896	Chi-N	23	11	.676	36	35	35	0	0	318	370	10.5	3	70	2.0	81	2.3	3.54	134	.313	.352	29	42	108	104	5.8	2	1	4.2
1897	Chi-N	21	18	.538	41	38	**38**	1	1	344	410	10.7	2	86	2.3	102	2.7	3.72	117	.318	.361	23	24	101	103	4.3	4	4	2.9
1898	Chi-N	24	10	.706	38	38	36	4	0	326	305	8.4	1	64	1.8	97	2.7	**1.88**	**195**	.268	.307	63	65	102	**127**	6.5	-2	2	6.7
1899	Chi-N	22	14	.611	38	38	35	0	0	320	329	9.3	5	65	1.8	73	2.1	2.78	132	.289	.327	38	32	96	105	4.7	6	7	4.2
1900	Chi-N	14	13	.519	30	30	27	**4**	0	248	245	8.9	6	51	1.9	61	2.2	3.05	115	.280	.320	18	12	94	93	1.7	5	-1	1.5
1901	Chi-A	24	7	**.774**	35	30	26	**5**	1	267	275	9.3	4	50	1.7	67	2.3	2.66	132	.286	.321	30	25	96	110	7.5	13	0	3.6
1902	Chi-A	15	9	.625	28	24	20	3	0	213	247	10.4	11	47	2.0	51	2.2	4.18	80	.316	.354	-15	-20	94	96	2.3	2	-1	-1.8
1903	NY-A	14	11	.560	25	24	22	2	0	213	201	8.5	3	33	1.4	69	2.9	2.70	109	.271	.302	6	6	100	94	0.7	2	-3	0.3
1904	NY-A	7	5	.583	16	11	8	1	0	100	91	8.2	3	16	1.4	36	3.2	2.88	100	.265	.297	-3	-0	111	86	-0.2	-1	-1	0.0
1905	NY-A	9	6	.600	25	7	4	2	1	102	82	7.2	1	15	1.3	46	4.1	1.68	162	.243	.275	11	12	103	110	1.9	2	-2	1.1
1906	NY-A	2	2	.500	17	2	1	0	2	60	58	8.7	0	15	2.3	16	2.4	3.00	106	.279	.327	-2	1	118	92	-0.2	-1	1	0.2
1907	NY-A	0	0	—	4	0	0	0	0	8	15	16.9	0	6	6.8	5	5.6	9.00	31	.427	.511	-6	-6	110	94	0.0	-0	0	-0.4
1909	Cin-N	0	1	.000	1	1	1	0	0	6	11	16.5	0	2	3.0	3	4.5	6.00	41	.379	.419	-2	-2	94	110	-0.4	-0	1	-0.1
1912	Was-A	0	0	—	1	0	0	0	0	0	1	—	1	0	—	0	—	∞	—	1.000	1.000	-1	-1	97	140	0.0	-0	0	0.0
1913	Was-A	0	0	—	1	0	0	0	0	1	1	9.0	0	0	0.0	0	0.0	0.00	—	.250	.250	0	0	105	0	0.0	1	0	0.0
1914	Was-A	0	0	—	1	0	0	0	1	1	1	9.0	0	0	0.0	1	9.0	0.00	—	.250	.250	0	0	100	0	0.0	1	0	0.0
Total	20	237	146	.619	453	372	337	22	6	3387	3670	9.8	75	774	2.1	955	2.5	3.31	121	.298	.339	233	258	102	104	46.1	36	11	29.4

■ **ED GRIFFITH** Griffith, Edward Deb: 8/13/1892

YEAR	TM/L	W	L	PCT	G	GS	CG	SHO	SV	IP	H	H/G	HR	BB	BB/G	SO	SO/G	ERA	/A	OAVG	OOBP	PR	/A	PF	CPI	WAT	PB	PD	TPI
1892	Chi-N	0	1	.000	1	1	0	0	0	4	3	6.8	1	6	13.5	3	6.8	11.25	27	.220	.458	-4	-4	93	61	-0.4	-0	0	-0.2

■ **FRANK GRIFFITH** Griffith, Frank Wesley b: 11/18/1872, Gilman, Ill. d: 12/13/08, BL , Deb: N/A.

YEAR	TM/L	W	L	PCT	G	GS	CG	SHO	SV	IP	H	H/G	HR	BB	BB/G	SO	SO/G	ERA	/A	OAVG	OOBP	PR	/A	PF	CPI	WAT	PB	PD	TPI
1894	Cle-N	1	2	.333	7	6	3	0	0	42	64	13.7	5	37	7.9	15	3.2	10.07	59	.374	.485	-22	-19	111	82	-0.5	2	0	-1.1

■ **HAL GRIGGS** Griggs, Harold Lloyd b: 8/24/28, Shannon, Ga. BR/TR, 6', 170 lbs. Deb: 4/18/56

YEAR	TM/L	W	L	PCT	G	GS	CG	SHO	SV	IP	H	H/G	HR	BB	BB/G	SO	SO/G	ERA	/A	OAVG	OOBP	PR	/A	PF	CPI	WAT	PB	PD	TPI
1956	Was-A	1	6	.143	34	12	1	0	1	99	120	10.9	14	76	6.9	48	4.4	6.00	74	.307	.410	-20	-17	107	110	-2.1	-1	1	-1.5
1957	Was-A	0	1	.000	2	2	0	0	0	14	11	7.1	1	7	4.5	12	7.7	3.21	120	.229	.327	1	1	102	106	-0.4	0	0	0.1
1958	Was-A	3	11	.214	32	21	3	0	0	137	138	9.1	20	74	4.9	69	4.5	5.52	69	.262	.350	-27	-26	100	87	-3.3	-2	-0	-2.7
1959	Was-A	2	8	.200	37	10	2	1	2	98	103	9.5	8	52	4.8	43	3.9	5.23	75	.270	.352	-15	-14	102	86	-2.5	-2	-0	-1.5
Total	4	6	26	.188	105	45	6	1	3	348	372	9.6	43	209	5.4	172	4.4	5.48	73	.276	.368	-61	-57	103	94	-8.3	-5	1	-5.6

■ **GUIDO GRILLI** Grilli, Guido John b: 1/9/39, Memphis, Tenn. BL/TL, 6', 188 lbs. Deb: 4/12/66

YEAR	TM/L	W	L	PCT	G	GS	CG	SHO	SV	IP	H	H/G	HR	BB	BB/G	SO	SO/G	ERA	/A	OAVG	OOBP	PR	/A	PF	CPI	WAT	PB	PD	TPI
1966	Bos-A	0	1	.000	6	0	0	0	0	5	5	9.0	1	9	16.2	4	7.2	7.20	53	.278	.519	-2	-2	110	129	-0.4	0	0	0.0
	KC-A	0	1	.000	16	0	0	0	1	16	19	10.7	0	11	6.2	8	4.5	6.75	49	.302	.429	-6	-6	95	85	-0.4	0	-1	-0.6
	Yr	0	2	.000	22	0	0	0	1	21	24	10.3	1	20	8.6	12	5.1	6.86	50	.296	.452	-8	-8	99	85	-0.8	0	-0	-0.6

■ **STEVE GRILLI** Grilli, Stephen Joseph b: 5/2/49, Brooklyn, N.Y. BR/TR, 6'2", 170 lbs. Deb: 9/19/75

YEAR	TM/L	W	L	PCT	G	GS	CG	SHO	SV	IP	H	H/G	HR	BB	BB/G	SO	SO/G	ERA	/A	OAVG	OOBP	PR	/A	PF	CPI	WAT	PB	PD	TPI
1975	Det-A	0	0	—	3	0	0	0	0	7	3	3.9	0	6	7.7	5	6.4	1.29	314	.136	.310	2	2	106	150	0.0	0	0	0.2
1976	Det-A	3	1	.750	36	0	0	0	3	66	63	8.6	5	41	5.6	36	4.9	4.64	80	.258	.362	-8	-7	105	99	1.1	0	2	-0.4
1977	Det-A	1	2	.333	30	2	0	0	0	73	71	8.8	8	49	6.0	49	6.0	4.81	89	.265	.377	-6	-4	105	106	-0.3	0	-1	-0.4
1979	Tor-A	0	0	—	1	0	0	0	0	2	1	4.5	0	0	0.0	1	4.5	0.00	—	.143	.125	1	1	106	0	0.0	0	0	0.1
Total	4	4	3	.571	70	2	0	0	3	148	138	8.4	13	96	5.8	91	5.5	4.50	89	.255	.364	-11	-8	105	103	0.8	0	1	-0.5

■ **JOHN GRIM** Grim, John Helm b: 8/9/1867, Lebanon, Ky. d: 7/28/61, Indianapolis, Ind TR , 6'2", 175 lbs. Deb: 1888

YEAR	TM/L	W	L	PCT	G	GS	CG	SHO	SV	IP	H	H/G	HR	BB	BB/G	SO	SO/G	ERA	/A	OAVG	OOBP	PR	/A	PF	CPI	WAT	PB	PD	TPI
1890	Roc-a	0	0	—	1	0	0	0	0	3	3	9.0	0	4	12.0	3	9.0	0.00	—	.276	.470	1	1	92	0	0.0	0	0	0.1

■ **BOB GRIM** Grim, Robert Anton b: 3/8/30, New York, Ny. BR/TR, 6'1", 175 lbs. Deb: 4/18/54

YEAR	TM/L	W	L	PCT	G	GS	CG	SHO	SV	IP	H	H/G	HR	BB	BB/G	SO	SO/G	ERA	/A	OAVG	OOBP	PR	/A	PF	CPI	WAT	PB	PD	TPI
1954	NY-A	20	6	.769	37	20	8	1	0	199	175	7.9	9	85	3.8	108	4.9	3.26	108	.244	.319	10	6	94	100	4.5	-1	-1	0.3
1955	NY-A	7	5	.583	26	11	1	1	4	92	81	7.9	9	42	4.1	63	6.2	4.21	89	.238	.318	-2	-5	94	86	-0.3	-1	0	-0.5
1956	NY-A	6	1	.857	26	6	1	0	5	75	64	7.7	3	31	3.7	48	5.8	2.76	143	.235	.314	12	10	95	110	2.2	-0	-1	0.9
1957	NY-A	12	8	.600	46	0	0	0	**19**	72	60	7.5	5	36	4.5	52	6.5	2.63	130	.239	.321	9	6	90	137	-0.6	1	0	0.7
1958	NY-A	0	1	.000	11	0	0	0	0	16	12	6.8	3	10	5.6	11	6.2	5.63	66	.211	.329	-3	-3	99	76	-0.4	-0	-0	-0.3
	KC-A	7	6	.538	26	14	5	1	0	114	118	9.3	7	41	3.2	54	4.3	3.55	114	.269	.331	3	6	107	109	0.9	-1	-1	0.5
	Yr	7	7	.500	37	14	5	1	0	130	130	9.0	10	51	3.5	65	4.5	3.81	105	.262	.329	-1	3	106	109	0.5	-0	-1	0.2
1959	KC-A	6	10	.375	40	9	3	1	4	125	124	8.9	10	57	4.1	65	4.7	4.10	97	.260	.336	-3	-2	103	100	-1.0	-1	-2	-0.4
1960	Cle-A	0	1	.000	3	0	0	0	0	2	6	27.0	0	1	4.5	2	9.0	13.50	28	.500	.500	-2	-2	98	95	-0.4	0	0	-0.1
	Cin-N	2	2	.500	26	0	0	0	2	30	32	9.6	3	10	3.0	22	6.6	4.50	83	.274	.316	-2	-3	99	93	0.2	-0	-0	-0.2
	StL-N	1	0	1.000	15	0	0	0	0	21	22	9.4	1	9	3.9	15	6.4	3.00	135	.272	.337	2	2	108	133	0.5	-0	0	0.3
	Yr	3	2	.600	41	0	0	0	2	51	54	9.5	4	19	3.4	37	6.5	3.88	100	.267	.324	-1	-0	103	133	0.7	-0	-0	0.1
1962	KC-A	0	1	.000	12	0	0	0	3	13	14	9.7	0	8	5.5	3	2.1	6.23	65	.292	.379	-3	-3	101	76	-0.4	-0	1	-0.2
Total	8	61	41	.598	268	60	18	4	37	759	708	8.4	50	330	3.9	443	5.3	3.62	104	.252	.326	19	12	98	104	5.2	-4	-3	1.0

■ **BURLEIGH GRIMES** Grimes, Burleigh Arland "Ol' Stubblebeard" b: 8/9/1893, Emerald, Wis. d: 12/6/85, Clear Lake, Wis. BR/TR, 5'10", 175 lbs. Deb: 9/10/16 MCH

YEAR	TM/L	W	L	PCT	G	GS	CG	SHO	SV	IP	H	H/G	HR	BB	BB/G	SO	SO/G	ERA	/A	OAVG	OOBP	PR	/A	PF	CPI	WAT	PB	PD	TPI
1916	Pit-N	2	3	.400	6	5	4	0	0	46	40	7.8	1	10	2.0	20	3.9	2.35	120	.241	.275	1	2	107	96	0.0	-1	1	0.3
1917	Pit-N	3	16	.158	37	17	8	1	0	194	186	8.6	5	70	3.2	72	3.3	3.53	79	.260	.318	-18	-16	103	94	-5.2	2	1	-1.4
1918	Bro-N	19	9	.679	**40**	28	19	7	1	270	210	7.0	3	76	2.5	113	3.8	2.13	135	.216	.269	19	22	104	84	**6.6**	-0	4	3.0
1919	Bro-N	10	11	.476	25	21	13	1	0	181	179	8.9	2	60	3.0	82	4.1	3.48	78	.256	.311	-11	-15	94	86	-0.3	2	1	-1.3
1920	Bro-N	23	11	**.676**	40	33	25	5	2	304	271	8.0	5	67	2.0	131	3.9	2.22	153	.238	.274	31	40	108	87	3.8	10	3	6.2
1921	Bro-N	**22**	13	.629	37	35	**30**	2	0	302	313	9.3	6	76	2.3	**136**	**4.1**	2.83	140	.274	.314	32	**38**	105	112	**5.2**	2	4	**4.7**
1922	Bro-N	17	14	.548	36	34	18	1	1	259	324	11.3	17	84	2.9	99	3.4	4.76	82	.308	.355	-19	-25	95	99	2.0	4	4	-1.4
1923	Bro-N	21	18	.538	39	38	**33**	2	0	**327**	356	9.8	10	100	2.8	119	3.3	3.58	109	.280	.329	15	12	98	103	2.3	3	5	1.9
1924	Bro-N	22	13	.629	38	36	**30**	1	1	**311**	351	10.2	15	91	2.6	135	3.9	3.82	99	.287	.333	2	-1	98	104	1.7	6	5	1.0
1925	Bro-N	12	19	.387	33	31	19	0	0	247	305	11.1	15	102	3.7	73	2.7	5.03	81	.309	.367	-21	-27	95	101	-2.3	6	8	-1.2
1926	Bro-N	12	13	.480	30	29	18	1	0	225	238	9.5	4	88	3.5	64	2.6	3.72	104	.276	.332	3	3	101	101	0.4	1	3	0.6
1927	NY-N	19	8	.704	39	34	15	2	2	260	274	9.5	12	87	3.0	102	3.5	3.53	109	.276	.331	11	9	98	109	4.1	-0	5	1.3
1928	Pit-N	**25**	14	.641	**48**	37	**28**	**4**	3	**331**	311	8.5	11	77	2.1	97	2.6	2.99	139	.248	.288	37	43	105	87	4.6	10	6	6.3
1929	Pit-N	17	7	.708	33	29	18	2	2	233	245	9.5	11	70	2.7	62	2.4	3.13	**153**	.269	.318	**41**	**43**	102	116	4.2	6	3	**5.1**
1930	Bos-N	3	5	.375	11	9	1	0	0	49	72	13.2	4	22	4.0	15	2.8	7.35	67	.353	.406	-13	-13	99	94	-0.6	-0	0	-1.0
	StL-N	13	6	.684	22	19	10	1	0	152	174	10.3	5	43	2.5	58	3.4	3.02	167	.293	.336	33	34	102	139	2.3	2	1	3.7
	Yr	16	11	.593	33	28	11	1	0	201	246	11.0	9	65	2.9	73	3.3	4.07	123	.307	.352	20	21	101	**139**	1.7	-0	1	2.7
1931	StL-N	17	9	.654	29	28	17	3	0	212	240	10.2	11	59	2.5	67	2.8	3.65	109	.286	.338	5	8	103	114	0.0	-2	3	0.9

YEAR	TM/L	W	L	PCT	G	GS	CG	SHO	SV	IP	H	H/G	HR	BB	BB/G	SO	SO/G	ERA	/A	OAVG	OOBP	PR	/A	PF	CPI	WAT	PB	PD	TPI
1932	Chi-N	6	11	.353	30	18	5	1	1	141	174	11.1	8	50	3.2	36	2.3	4.79	83	.297	.350	-14	-13	103	96	-3.5	1	1	-0.9
1933	Chi-N	3	6	.333	17	7	3	1	3	70	71	9.1	2	29	3.7	12	1.5	3.47	91	.277	.341	-1	-2	95	114	-1.8	-0	0	-0.2
	StL-N	0	1	.000	4	3	0	0	1	14	15	9.6	1	8	5.1	4	2.6	5.14	65	.263	.358	-3	-3	100	86	-0.4	0	-1	-0.2
	Yr	3	7	.300	21	10	3	1	4	84	86	9.2	3	37	4.0	16	1.7	3.75	85	.274	.342	-4	-5	96	86	-2.2	-0	-0	-0.4
1934	StL-N	2	1	.667	4	0	0	0	0	8	5	5.6	1	2	2.3	1	1.1	3.38	134	.179	.233	1	1	111	57	0.2	0	0	0.1
	Pit-N	1	2	.333	8	4	0	0	0	27	36	12.0	0	10	3.3	9	3.0	7.33	58	.310	.362	-10	-9	105	64	-0.4	-0	0	-0.7
	Yr	3	3	.500	12	4	0	0	0	35	41	10.5	1	12	3.1	10	2.6	6.43	67	.285	.338	-9	-8	106	64	-0.2	0	1	-0.6
	NY-A	1	2	.333	10	0	0	0	1	18	22	11.0	0	14	7.0	5	2.5	5.50	76	.319	.435	-2	-3	93	115	-0.6	-0	1	-0.1
Total	19	270	212	.560	616	495	314	35	18	4181	4412	9.5	149	1295	2.8	1512	3.3	3.53	108	.273	.323	119	133	101	101	22.3	51	58	26.7

■ JOHN GRIMES Grimes, John Thomas b: 4/17/1869, Wooodstock, Md. d: 1/17/64, San Francisco, Cal BR/TR, 5'11", 160 lbs. Deb: 7/28/1897

YEAR	TM/L	W	L	PCT	G	GS	CG	SHO	SV	IP	H	H/G	HR	BB	BB/G	SO	SO/G	ERA	/A	OAVG	OOBP	PR	/A	PF	CPI	WAT	PB	PD	TPI
1897	StL-N	0	2	.000	3	1	1	0	0	20	24	10.8	0	8	3.6	4	1.8	6.30	67	.320	.385	-4	-5	99	67	-0.9	1	0	-0.2

■ ROSS GRIMSLEY Grimsley, Ross Albert I b: 6/4/22, Americus, Kan. BL/TL, 6', 175 lbs. Deb: 9/03/51

YEAR	TM/L	W	L	PCT	G	GS	CG	SHO	SV	IP	H	H/G	HR	BB	BB/G	SO	SO/G	ERA	/A	OAVG	OOBP	PR	/A	PF	CPI	WAT	PB	PD	TPI
1951	Chi-A	0	0	—	7	0	0	0	0	14	12	7.7	1	10	6.4	8	5.1	3.86	102	.235	.361	0	0	96	108	0.0	-0	-0	0.0

■ ROSS GRIMSLEY Grimsley, Ross Albert II b: 1/7/50, Topeka, Kan. BL/TL, 6'3", 195 lbs. Deb: 5/16/71

YEAR	TM/L	W	L	PCT	G	GS	CG	SHO	SV	IP	H	H/G	HR	BB	BB/G	SO	SO/G	ERA	/A	OAVG	OOBP	PR	/A	PF	CPI	WAT	PB	PD	TPI
1971	Cin-N	10	7	.588	26	26	6	3	0	161	151	8.4	15	43	2.4	67	3.7	3.58	93	.250	.297	-2	-4	96	91	1.8	-1	-1	-0.6
1972	Cin-N	14	8	.636	30	28	4	1	1	198	194	8.8	18	50	2.3	79	3.6	3.05	104	.260	.300	9	2	91	115	0.6	-2	-0	0.0
1973	Cin-N	13	10	.565	38	36	8	1	1	242	245	9.1	24	68	2.5	90	3.3	3.24	104	.266	.310	12	3	92	116	-0.9	-6	-1	-0.4
1974	Bal-A	18	13	.581	40	39	17	4	1	296	267	8.1	26	76	2.3	158	4.8	3.07	109	.244	.289	18	9	92	99	0.8	0	0	0.9
1975	Bal-A	10	13	.435	35	32	8	1	0	197	210	9.6	29	47	2.1	89	4.1	4.07	83	.276	.314	-6	-15	89	105	-2.9	0	0	-1.4
1976	Bal-A	8	7	.533	28	19	2	0	0	137	143	9.4	8	35	2.3	41	2.7	3.94	87	.270	.310	-6	-8	97	89	0.0	0	-1	-0.8
1977	Bal-A	14	10	.583	34	34	11	2	0	218	230	9.5	24	74	3.1	53	2.2	3.96	95	.277	.330	3	-5	92	110	-0.3	0	2	-0.2
1978	Mon-N	20	11	.645	36	36	19	3	0	263	237	8.1	17	67	2.3	84	2.9	3.05	112	.243	.287	16	11	96	95	5.9	-1	1	1.1
1979	Mon-N	10	9	.526	32	27	2	0	0	151	199	11.9	18	41	2.4	42	2.5	5.36	70	.322	.358	-27	-27	101	102	-1.1	1	-0	-2.5
1980	Mon-N	2	4	.333	11	7	0	0	0	41	61	13.4	5	12	2.6	11	2.4	6.37	56	.351	.378	-13	-13	98	102	-1.1	0	0	-1.1
	Cle-A	4	5	.444	14	11	2	0	0	75	103	12.4	11	24	2.9	18	2.2	6.72	62	.331	.374	-22	-21	103	91	-0.4	0	-1	-1.9
1982	Bal-A	1	2	.333	21	0	0	0	0	60	65	9.8	7	22	3.3	18	2.7	5.25	77	.283	.339	-8	-8	99	89	-0.5	0	0	-0.7
Total	11	124	99	.556	345	295	79	15	3	2039	2105	9.3	202	559	2.5	750	3.3	3.81	91	.270	.314	-27	-75	94	102	1.9	-8	-0	-7.6

■ DAN GRINER Griner, Donald Dexter "Rusty" b: 3/7/1888, Centerville, Tenn. d: 6/3/50, Bishopville, S.C. BL/TR, 6'1", 200 lbs. Deb: 8/17/12

YEAR	TM/L	W	L	PCT	G	GS	CG	SHO	SV	IP	H	H/G	HR	BB	BB/G	SO	SO/G	ERA	/A	OAVG	OOBP	PR	/A	PF	CPI	WAT	PB	PD	TPI
1912	StL-N	3	4	.429	12	7	2	0	0	54	59	9.8	3	15	2.5	20	3.3	3.17	110	.273	.329	1	2	103	108	0.1	-1	-1	0.0
1913	StL-N	10	22	.313	34	34	18	1	0	225	279	11.2	12	66	2.6	79	3.2	5.08	61	.312	.358	-47	-49	97	93	-1.5	5	2	-4.0
1914	StL-N	9	13	.409	37	16	11	2	2	179	163	8.2	3	57	2.9	74	3.7	2.51	115	.254	.307	5	7	104	110	-2.7	4	-1	1.1
1915	StL-N	5	11	.313	37	18	9	2	3	150	137	8.2	4	46	2.8	46	2.8	2.82	98	.259	.313	-1	-1	101	114	-2.8	4	-2	0.1
1916	StL-N	0	0	—	4	0	0	0	1	11	15	12.3	0	3	2.5	3	2.5	4.09	64	.341	.388	-2	-2	100	126	0.0	0	0	-0.1
1918	Bro-N	1	5	.167	11	6	3	1	0	54	47	7.8	0	15	2.5	22	3.7	2.17	133	.267	.337	4	4	104	154	-1.8	-1	0	0.4
Total	6	28	55	.337	135	81	43	6	6	673	700	9.4	22	202	2.7	244	3.3	3.49	85	.280	.332	-39	-38	101	109	-8.7	12	-2	-2.5

■ LEE GRISSOM Grissom, Lee Theo b: 10/23/07, Sherman, Tex. BB/TL, 6'3", 200 lbs. Deb: 9/02/34

YEAR	TM/L	W	L	PCT	G	GS	CG	SHO	SV	IP	H	H/G	HR	BB	BB/G	SO	SO/G	ERA	/A	OAVG	OOBP	PR	/A	PF	CPI	WAT	PB	PD	TPI
1934	Cin-N	0	1	.000	4	1	0	0	0	7	13	16.7	0	7	9.0	4	5.1	15.43	28	.382	.476	-9	-9	105	58	-0.4	-0	0	-0.7
1935	Cin-N	1	1	.500	3	3	1	0	0	21	31	13.3	0	4	1.7	13	5.6	3.86	99	.333	.361	0	-0	95	126	0.1	-1	0	0.0
1936	Cin-N	1	1	.500	6	4	0	0	0	24	33	12.4	1	9	3.4	13	4.9	6.38	61	.320	.372	-6	-7	97	82	0.0	-1	0	-0.6
1937	Cin-N	12	17	.414	50	30	14	**5**	6	224	193	7.8	7	93	3.7	149	6.0	3.25	112	.232	.309	16	10	93	91	1.4	-3	-2	0.4
1938	Cin-N	2	3	.400	14	7	0	0	0	51	60	10.6	4	22	3.9	16	2.8	5.29	69	.300	.365	-9	-9	96	98	-0.6	-0	-0	-0.9
1939	Cin-N	9	7	.563	33	21	3	0	0	154	145	8.5	14	56	3.3	53	3.1	4.09	96	.249	.312	-3	-3	100	87	-0.8	-2	-2	-0.6
1940	NY-A	0	0	—	5	0	0	0	0	5	4	7.2	0	2	3.6	1	1.8	0.00	—	.250	.316	2	2	96	0	0.0	0	0	0.2
	Bro-N	2	5	.286	14	10	3	1	0	74	59	7.2	3	34	4.1	56	6.8	2.80	146	.215	.299	9	11	106	98	-1.7	0	-1	1.1
1941	Bro-N	0	0	—	4	1	0	0	1	11	10	8.2	2	8	6.5	5	4.1	2.45	147	.238	.346	1	1	99	204	0.0	0	0	0.2
	Phi-N	2	13	.133	29	18	2	0	0	131	120	8.2	4	70	4.8	74	5.1	3.98	94	.242	.334	-5	-4	103	87	-4.0	-1	-1	-0.4
	Yr	2	13	.133	33	19	2	0	1	142	130	8.2	6	78	4.9	79	5.0	3.87	96	.242	.335	-4	-2	102	87	-4.0	0	-1	-0.2
Total	8	29	48	.377	162	95	23	6	7	702	668	8.6	35	305	3.9	384	4.9	3.88	98	.250	.325	-2	-7	98	92	-6.0	-8	-5	-1.3

■ MARV GRISSOM Grissom, Marvin Edward b: 3/31/18, Los Molinos, Cal. BR/TR, 6'3", 190 lbs. Deb: 9/10/46 C

YEAR	TM/L	W	L	PCT	G	GS	CG	SHO	SV	IP	H	H/G	HR	BB	BB/G	SO	SO/G	ERA	/A	OAVG	OOBP	PR	/A	PF	CPI	WAT	PB	PD	TPI
1946	NY-N	0	2	.000	4	3	0	0	0	19	17	8.1	1	13	6.2	9	4.3	4.26	83	.254	.369	-2	-2	103	103	-0.9	-0	1	0.0
1949	Det-A	2	4	.333	27	2	0	0	0	39	56	12.9	6	34	7.8	17	3.9	6.46	69	.335	.442	-10	-9	106	122	-1.2	0	0	-0.7
1952	Chi-A	12	10	.545	28	24	7	1	0	166	156	8.5	6	79	4.3	97	5.3	3.74	97	.250	.333	-1	-2	99	93	0.5	-1	-2	-0.3
1953	Bos-A	2	6	.250	13	11	1	1	0	59	61	9.3	5	30	4.6	31	4.7	4.73	91	.266	.350	-5	-3	108	93	-2.1	-3	-1	-0.5
	NY-N	4	2	.667	21	7	3	0	0	84	83	8.9	6	31	3.3	46	4.9	3.96	106	.255	.317	3	2	98	91	1.2	-1	1	0.1
1954	NY-N	10	7	.588	56	3	1	1	19	122	100	7.4	13	50	3.7	64	4.7	2.36	175	.226	.307	23	24	102	139	-0.5	-1	-0	2.3
1955	NY-N	5	4	.556	55	0	0	0	8	89	76	7.7	6	41	4.1	49	5.0	2.93	135	.237	.321	11	10	98	120	0.4	-1	0	1.0
1956	NY-N	1	1	.500	43	2	0	0	7	81	71	7.9	3	16	1.8	49	5.4	1.56	241	.241	.272	**20**	**20**	99	154	0.1	-0	-1	2.0
1957	NY-N	4	4	.500	55	0	0	0	14	83	74	8.0	6	23	2.5	51	5.5	2.60	154	.243	.293	12	13	103	118	0.4	0	1	1.5
1958	SF-N	7	5	.583	51	0	0	0	10	65	71	9.8	11	26	3.6	46	6.4	4.02	98	.287	.358	-0	-1	100	134	0.9	-1	0	0.0
1959	StL-N	0	0	—	3	0	0	0	0	2	6	27.0	2	0	0.0	0	0.0	22.50	19	.500	.500	-4	-4	106	85	0.0	0	0	-0.3
Total	10	47	45	.511	356	52	12	3	58	809	771	8.6	65	343	3.8	459	5.1	3.42	116	.254	.328	47	49	101	116	-1.2	-7	0	5.1

■ CONNIE GROB Grob, Conrad George b: 11/9/32, Cross Plains, Wis. BL/TR, 6'0.5", 180 lbs. Deb: 4/22/56

YEAR	TM/L	W	L	PCT	G	GS	CG	SHO	SV	IP	H	H/G	HR	BB	BB/G	SO	SO/G	ERA	/A	OAVG	OOBP	PR	/A	PF	CPI	WAT	PB	PD	TPI
1956	Was-A	4	5	.444	37	1	0	0	1	79	121	13.8	14	26	3.0	27	3.1	7.86	56	.353	.389	-32	-30	107	90	0.5	1	1	-2.5

■ JOHNNY GRODZICKI Grodzicki, John "Grod" b: 2/26/17, Nanticoke, Pa. BR/TR, 6'1.5", 200 lbs. Deb: 4/18/41 C

YEAR	TM/L	W	L	PCT	G	GS	CG	SHO	SV	IP	H	H/G	HR	BB	BB/G	SO	SO/G	ERA	/A	OAVG	OOBP	PR	/A	PF	CPI	WAT	PB	PD	TPI
1941	StL-N	2	1	.667	5	1	0	0	0	13	6	4.2	0	11	7.6	10	6.9	1.38	281	.130	.293	3	4	107	99	0.1	0	0	0.4
1946	StL-N	0	0	—	3	0	0	0	0	4	4	9.0	1	4	9.0	2	4.5	9.00	39	.250	.400	-2	-2	103	70	0.0	0	0	-0.1
1947	StL-N	0	1	.000	16	0	0	0	0	23	21	8.2	5	19	7.4	8	3.1	5.48	77	.253	.374	-4	-3	104	110	-0.4	-0	0	-0.2
Total	3	2	2	.500	24	1	0	0	0	40	31	7.0	6	34	7.6	20	4.5	4.50	90	.214	.351	-3	-2	105	102	-0.3	0	0	0.1

■ STEVE GROMEK Gromek, Stephen Joseph b: 1/15/20, Hamtramck, Mich. BB/TR, 6'2", 180 lbs. Deb: 8/18/41

YEAR	TM/L	W	L	PCT	G	GS	CG	SHO	SV	IP	H	H/G	HR	BB	BB/G	SO	SO/G	ERA	/A	OAVG	OOBP	PR	/A	PF	CPI	WAT	PB	PD	TPI
1941	Cle-A	1	1	.500	9	2	1	0	2	23	25	9.8	0	11	4.3	19	7.4	4.30	97	.266	.340	-0	-0	101	85	0.0	-0	-1	0.0
1942	Cle-A	2	0	1.000	14	0	0	0	0	44	46	9.4	2	23	4.7	14	2.9	3.68	92	.267	.350	-0	-1	93	114	1.0	3	-1	0.0
1943	Cle-A	0	0	—	3	0	0	0	0	4	6	13.5	0	0	0.0	4	9.0	9.00	33	.353	.353	-3	-3	90	53	0.0	1	0	-0.1
1944	Cle-A	10	9	.526	35	21	12	2	1	204	160	**7.1**	5	70	3.1	115	5.1	2.56	135	**.219**	.284	20	20	101	90	1.2	4	-2	2.4
1945	Cle-A	19	9	.679	33	30	21	3	1	251	229	8.2	6	66	2.4	101	3.6	2.55	130	.243	.291	23	21	98	103	5.6	3	-3	2.3
1946	Cle-A	5	15	.250	29	21	5	2	4	154	159	9.3	20	47	2.7	75	4.4	4.32	73	.264	.316	-14	-20	90	93	-4.6	1	-1	-1.9
1947	Cle-A	3	5	.375	29	7	0	0	4	84	77	8.3	8	36	3.9	39	4.2	3.75	93	.240	.311	-0	-2	94	94	-1.1	2	-0	0.0
1948	Cle-A	9	3	.750	38	9	4	1	2	130	109	7.5	10	51	3.5	50	3.5	2.84	142	.226	.304	21	17	94	112	2.1	-1	-1	1.4
1949	Cle-A	4	6	.400	27	12	3	0	0	92	86	8.4	8	40	3.9	22	2.2	3.33	121	.250	.328	9	7	96	114	-1.5	-0	0	0.7
1950	Cle-A	10	7	.588	31	13	4	1	0	113	94	7.5	10	36	2.9	43	3.4	3.66	119	.226	.287	11	9	95	81	0.0	-2	-0	0.6
1951	Cle-A	7	4	.636	27	8	4	0	1	107	98	8.2	6	29	2.4	40	3.4	2.78	137	.238	.291	16	12	93	103	0.5	3	1	1.6
1952	Cle-A	7	7	.500	29	13	3	1	1	123	109	8.0	14	28	2.0	65	4.8	3.66	88	.232	.275	0	-6	88	79	-1.2	-0	-2	-0.8
1953	Cle-A	1	1	.500	5	1	0	0	0	11	11	9.0	0	3	2.5	8	6.5	3.27	113	.268	.326	1	1	93	104	-0.1	-0	-0	0.0
	Det-A	6	8	.429	19	17	6	1	1	126	138	9.9	17	36	2.6	59	4.2	4.50	90	.276	.332	-7	-6	102	101	0.5	-4	-1	-1.0
	Yr	7	9	.438	24	18	6	1	1	137	149	9.8	17	39	2.6	67	4.4	4.40	91	.275	.330	-6	-6	101	101	0.4	-0	-1	-1.0
1954	Det-A	18	16	.529	36	32	17	4	1	253	236	8.4	26	57	2.0	102	3.6	2.74	138	.246	.291	28	29	101	116	3.3	1	-3	2.9
1955	Det-A	13	10	.565	28	25	8	2	0	181	183	9.1	26	37	**1.8**	73	3.6	3.98	94	.261	.301	-0	-5	95	97	1.4	4	-2	-0.2
1956	Det-A	8	6	.571	40	13	4	0	4	141	142	9.1	25	47	3.0	64	4.1	4.28	92	.263	.324	-2	-5	95	108	0.6	2	-2	-0.4
1957	Det-A	0	1	.000	15	1	0	0	1	24	32	12.0	3	13	4.9	11	4.1	6.00	68	.333	.407	-6	-5	107	111	-0.4	-0	-0	-0.5
Total	17	123	108	.532	447	225	92	17	23	2065	1940	8.5	186	630	2.7	904	3.9	3.41	108	.247	.304	96	64	96	100	7.3	15	-19	7.0

■ BOB GROOM Groom, Robert b: 9/12/1884, Belleville, Ill. d: 2/19/48, Belleville, Ill. BR/TR, 6'2", 175 lbs. Deb: 4/13/09

YEAR	TM/L	W	L	PCT	G	GS	CG	SHO	SV	IP	H	H/G	HR	BB	BB/G	SO	SO/G	ERA	/A	OAVG	OOBP	PR	/A	PF	CPI	WAT	PB	PD	TPI
1909	Was-A	7	26	.212	44	31	17	1	0	261	218	7.5	2	105	3.6	131	4.5	2.86	83	.229	.314	-11	-14	96	81	-4.5	-6	3	-1.1
1910	Was-A	12	17	.414	34	30	22	3	0	258	244	8.5	8	77	2.7	98	3.4	2.76	93	.260	.322	-7	-5	102	111	-0.8	-6	-2	-1.4
1911	Was-A	13	17	.433	37	32	20	2	2	255	280	9.9	9	67	2.4	135	4.8	3.81	87	.282	.332	-13	-14	99	91	0.6	-4	1	-1.2
1912	Was-A	24	13	.649	43	40	28	2	1	316	287	8.2	3	94	2.7	179	5.1	2.62	124	.246	.305	26	22	97	100	2.9	-6	-2	2.0
1913	Was-A	16	16	.500	37	36	17	4	0	264	258	8.8	8	81	2.8	156	5.3	3.24	95	.254	.312	-9	-5	105	86	-2.7	0	2	-0.3
1914	StL-F	13	20	.394	42	34	23	1	1	281	281	9.0	9	75	2.4	167	5.3	3.23	107	.262	.312	-1	7	108	94	-0.7	-3	1	0.7
1915	StL-F	11	11	.500	37	26	11	4	2	209	200	8.6	6	73	3.1	111	4.8	3.27	95	.261	.327	-6	-4	102	102	-1.3	-2	3	-0.2
1916	StL-A	13	9	.591	41	26	8	1	4	217	174	7.2	1	98	4.1	92	3.8	2.57	104	.226	.315	6	2	94	95	2.0	-2	2	0.2
1917	StL-A	8	19	.296	38	28	11	4	3	233	193	7.5	3	95	3.7	82	3.2	2.94	89	.233	.315	-7	-8	98	85	-3.0	-4	-2	-1.4
1918	Cle-A	2	2	.500	14	5	0	0	0	43	70	14.7	0	18	3.8	8	1.7	7.12	41	.380	.438	-21	-20	107	91	-0.2	-1	0	-2.0
Total	10	119	150	.442	367	288	157	22	13	2337	2205	8.5	49	783	3.0	1159	4.5	3.10	95	.254	.319	-43	-40	100	94	-7.7	-33	5	-4.7

■ DON GROSS Gross, Donald John b: 6/30/31, Weidman, Mich. BL/TL, 5'11", 186 lbs. Deb: 7/21/55

YEAR	TM/L	W	L	PCT	G	GS	CG	SHO	SV	IP	H	H/G	HR	BB	BB/G	SO	SO/G	ERA	/A	OAVG	OOBP	PR	/A	PF	CPI	WAT	PB	PD	TPI
1955	Cin-N	4	5	.444	17	11	2	1	0	67	79	10.6	11	16	2.1	33	4.4	4.16	101	.298	.334	-1	0	104	121	-0.3	-1	0	0.0
1956	Cin-N	3	0	1.000	19	7	2	0	0	69	69	9.0	4	20	2.6	47	6.1	1.96	204	.257	.305	14	16	106	159	1.5	-1	1	1.7
1957	Cin-N	7	9	.438	43	16	5	0	1	148	152	9.2	21	33	2.0	73	4.4	4.32	95	.264	.300	-7	-3	106	90	-1.3	-2	0	-0.5
1958	Pit-N	5	7	.417	40	3	0	0	7	75	67	8.0	5	38	4.6	59	7.1	3.96	94	.241	.327	-0	-2	94	88	-1.4	-1	1	-0.2
1959	Pit-N	1	1	.500	21	0	0	0	2	33	28	7.6	3	10	2.7	15	4.1	3.55	115	.228	.287	1	2	104	81	0.0	-0	1	0.3
1960	Pit-N	0	0	—	5	0	0	0	0	5	5	9.0	1	0	0.0	3	5.4	3.60	101	.238	.238	0	0	97	79	0.0	0	-0	0.0
Total	6	20	22	.476	145	37	9	1	10	397	400	9.1	45	117	2.7	230	5.2	3.74	108	.261	.310	7	13	103	106	-1.5	-5	3	1.3

■ GREG GROSS Gross, Gregory Eugene b: 8/1/52, York, Pa. BL/TL, 5'10", 160 lbs. Deb: 9/05/73

YEAR	TM/L	W	L	PCT	G	GS	CG	SHO	SV	IP	H	H/G	HR	BB	BB/G	SO	SO/G	ERA	/A	OAVG	OOBP	PR	/A	PF	CPI	WAT	PB	PD	TPI
1986	Phi-N	0	0	—	1	0	0	0	0	1	1	9.0	0	1	9.0	2	18.0	0.00	—	.333	.500	0	0	104	0	0.0	0	0	0.0

■ KEVIN GROSS Gross, Kevin Frank b: 6/8/61, Downey, Cal. BR/TR, 6'5", 203 lbs. Deb: 6/25/83

YEAR	TM/L	W	L	PCT	G	GS	CG	SHO	SV	IP	H	H/G	HR	BB	BB/G	SO	SO/G	ERA	/A	OAVG	OOBP	PR	/A	PF	CPI	WAT	PB	PD	TPI
1983	Phi-N	4	6	.400	17	17	1	1	0	96	100	9.4	13	35	3.3	66	6.2	3.56	102	.265	.330	1	1	100	120	-1.4	-1	0	0.0
1984	Phi-N	8	5	.615	44	14	1	0	1	129	140	9.8	8	44	3.1	84	5.9	4.12	89	.277	.334	-8	-7	101	99	1.6	-2	1	-0.7
1985	Phi-N	15	13	.536	38	31	6	2	0	206	194	8.5	11	81	3.5	151	6.6	3.41	108	.251	.323	4	6	102	102	2.2	0	1	0.8
1986	Phi-N	12	12	.500	37	36	7	2	0	242	240	8.9	28	94	3.5	154	5.7	4.02	96	.259	.329	-8	-4	104	104	-0.8	3	-1	0.0
1987	Phi-N	9	16	.360	34	33	3	1	0	201	205	9.2	26	87	3.9	110	4.9	4.34	98	.267	.344	-6	-2	105	108	-3.7	2	-2	0.0
1988	Phi-N	12	14	.462	33	33	5	1	0	232	209	8.1	18	89	3.5	162	6.3	3.69	97	.239	.312	-6	-3	103	93	1.5	1	-0	-0.2
Total	6	60	66	.476	203	164	23	7	1	1106	1088	8.9	104	430	3.5	727	5.9	3.87	98	.258	.328	-22	-9	103	103	-0.6	3	-0	-0.1

■ WAYNE GROSS Gross, Wayne Dale b: 1/14/52, Riverside, Cal. BL/TR, 6'2", 210 lbs. Deb: 8/21/76

YEAR	TM/L	W	L	PCT	G	GS	CG	SHO	SV	IP	H	H/G	HR	BB	BB/G	SO	SO/G	ERA	/A	OAVG	OOBP	PR	/A	PF	CPI	WAT	PB	PD	TPI
1983	Oak-A	0	0	—	1	0	0	0	0	2	2	9.0	0	1	4.5	0	0.0	0.00	—	.222	.364	1	1	96	0	0.0	1	0	0.1

■ HARLEY GROSSMAN Grossman, Harley Joseph b: 5/5/30, Evansville, Ind. BR/TR, 6', 170 lbs. Deb: 4/22/52

YEAR	TM/L	W	L	PCT	G	GS	CG	SHO	SV	IP	H	H/G	HR	BB	BB/G	SO	SO/G	ERA	/A	OAVG	OOBP	PR	/A	PF	CPI	WAT	PB	PD	TPI
1952	Was-A	0	0	—	1	0	0	0	0	⅓	2	54.0	1	0	0.0	0	0.0	54.00	—	.667	.667	-2	-2	100	85	0.0	0	0	-0.1

■ ERNIE GROTH Groth, Ernest John "Dango" b: 12/24/1884, Cedarsburg, Wis. d: 5/23/50, Milwaukee, Wis. BR/TR, 5'11", 175 lbs. Deb: 9/06/04

YEAR	TM/L	W	L	PCT	G	GS	CG	SHO	SV	IP	H	H/G	HR	BB	BB/G	SO	SO/G	ERA	/A	OAVG	OOBP	PR	/A	PF	CPI	WAT	PB	PD	TPI
1904	Chi-N	0	2	.000	3	2	2	0	1	16	22	12.4	1	6	3.4	9	5.1	5.63	48	.359	.425	-5	-5	99	101	-0.9	-1	-0	-0.4

■ ERNEST GROTH Groth, Ernest William b: 5/3/22, Beaver Falls, Pa. BR/TR, 5'9", 185 lbs. Deb: 9/11/47

YEAR	TM/L	W	L	PCT	G	GS	CG	SHO	SV	IP	H	H/G	HR	BB	BB/G	SO	SO/G	ERA	/A	OAVG	OOBP	PR	/A	PF	CPI	WAT	PB	PD	TPI
1947	Cle-A	0	0	—	2	0	0	0	0	1	0	0.0	0	1	9.0	1	9.0	0.00	—	.000	.250	0	0	94	0	0.0	0	0	0.0
1948	Cle-A	0	0	—	1	0	0	0	0	1	1	9.0	0	2	18.0	0	0.0	9.00	45	.250	.500	-1	-1	94	83	0.0	0	0	0.0
1949	Chi-A	0	1	.000	3	0	0	0	0	5	2	3.6	2	3	5.4	1	1.8	5.40	77	.125	.286	-1	-1	99	84	-0.4	0	-0	0.0
Total	3	0	1	.000	6	0	0	0	0	7	3	3.9	2	6	7.7	2	2.6	5.14	79	.130	.323	-1	-1	98	72	-0.4	0	-0	0.0

■ ORVAL GROVE Grove, Orval Leroy b: 8/29/19, Mineral, Kan. BR/TR, 6'3", 196 lbs. Deb: 5/28/40

YEAR	TM/L	W	L	PCT	G	GS	CG	SHO	SV	IP	H	H/G	HR	BB	BB/G	SO	SO/G	ERA	/A	OAVG	OOBP	PR	/A	PF	CPI	WAT	PB	PD	TPI
1940	Chi-A	0	0	—	3	0	0	0	0	6	4	6.0	0	4	6.0	1	1.5	3.00	150	.182	.308	1	1	103	69	0.0	-0	-0	0.1
1941	Chi-A	0	0	—	2	0	0	0	0	7	9	11.6	2	5	6.4	5	6.4	10.29	38	.321	.400	-5	-5	94	79	0.0	-0	0	-0.3
1942	Chi-A	4	6	.400	12	8	4	0	0	66	77	10.5	1	33	4.5	21	2.9	5.18	71	.283	.359	-11	-11	100	84	-0.4	1	1	-0.8
1943	Chi-A	15	9	.625	32	25	18	3	2	216	192	8.0	9	72	3.0	76	3.2	2.75	122	.239	.302	13	14	101	105	2.7	2	1	1.9
1944	Chi-A	14	15	.483	34	33	11	2	0	235	237	9.1	11	71	2.7	105	4.0	3.71	94	.263	.314	-7	-5	102	93	0.7	-4	4	-0.4
1945	Chi-A	14	12	.538	33	30	16	4	1	217	233	9.7	12	68	2.8	54	2.2	3.44	94	.273	.328	-2	-5	96	110	1.8	-4	2	-0.7
1946	Chi-A	8	13	.381	33	26	10	1	0	205	213	9.4	10	78	3.4	60	2.6	3.03	113	.272	.334	11	9	97	**126**	-2.3	-2	2	0.8
1947	Chi-A	6	8	.429	25	19	6	1	0	136	158	10.5	10	70	4.6	33	2.2	4.43	83	.296	.375	-11	-12	99	117	-0.3	-0	-1	-1.2
1948	Chi-A	2	10	.167	32	11	1	0	1	88	110	11.3	6	42	4.3	18	1.8	6.14	70	.315	.384	-18	-18	100	94	-3.0	-2	2	-1.6
1949	Chi-A	0	0	—	1	0	0	0	0	1	4	36.0	1	1	9.0	1	9.0	36.00	12	.667	.750	-4	-4	99	89	0.0	0	0	-0.2
Total	10	63	73	.463	207	152	66	11	4	1177	1237	9.5	62	444	3.4	374	2.9	3.78	93	.272	.335	-33	-36	99	106	-0.8	-9	10	-2.4

■ LEFTY GROVE Grove, Robert Moses b: 3/6/1900, Lonaconing, Md. d: 5/22/75, Norwalk, Ohio BL/TL, 6'3", 190 lbs. Deb: 4/14/25 H

YEAR	TM/L	W	L	PCT	G	GS	CG	SHO	SV	IP	H	H/G	HR	BB	BB/G	SO	SO/G	ERA	/A	OAVG	OOBP	PR	/A	PF	CPI	WAT	PB	PD	TPI
1925	Phi-A	10	12	.455	45	18	5	0	1	197	207	9.5	11	131	6.0	**116**	**5.3**	4.75	93	.278	.378	-8	-7	101	103	-2.6	-6	2	-0.9
1926	Phi-A	13	13	.500	45	33	20	1	6	258	227	**7.9**	6	101	3.5	**194**	**6.8**	**2.51**	**185**	.244	.312	**43**	**61**	116	119	-1.4	-6	-1	**5.8**
1927	Phi-A	20	13	.606	51	28	14	1	9	262	251	8.6	6	79	2.7	**174**	**6.0**	3.19	123	.252	.300	28	21	95	89	0.8	-2	-1	1.6
1928	Phi-A	**24**	8	.750	39	31	24	4	4	262	228	7.8	10	64	2.2	**183**	6.3	2.58	155	.229	.275	**43**	**41**	99	85	5.7	1	-3	**4.0**
1929	Phi-A	20	6	**.769**	42	37	19	2	4	275	278	9.1	8	81	2.7	**170**	**5.6**	**2.81**	**157**	.262	.310	**44**	**49**	104	113	3.7	0	-3	**4.6**
1930	Phi-A	**28**	5	**.848**	**50**	32	22	2	**9**	291	273	8.4	8	60	1.9	**209**	**6.5**	**2.54**	**177**	**.247**	**.284**	**68**	**63**	96	110	**10.1**	1	0	**6.0**
1931	Phi-A	**31**	4	**.886**	41	30	**27**	**4**	5	289	249	7.8	10	62	1.9	**175**	5.4	**2.06**	**215**	.229	**.269**	**75**	**76**	101	118	**11.8**	-2	-2	**7.4**
1932	Phi-A	25	10	.714	44	30	**27**	**4**	7	292	269	8.3	13	79	2.4	188	5.8	**2.84**	**175**	.241	**.289**	**53**	**69**	111	104	**5.6**	-1	-2	**6.6**
1933	Phi-A	**24**	8	**.750**	45	28	**21**	2	6	275	280	9.2	12	83	2.7	114	3.7	3.21	122	.261	.313	33	22	92	111	**8.6**	-5	0	1.5
1934	Bos-A	8	8	.500	22	12	5	0	0	109	149	12.3	5	32	2.6	43	3.6	6.52	73	.320	.360	-25	-22	105	79	0.0	-0	-1	-1.9
1935	Bos-A	20	12	.625	35	30	23	2	1	273	269	8.9	6	65	2.1	121	4.0	**2.70**	**179**	.257	**.296**	**53**	**64**	108	112	4.5	-6	2	6.3
1936	Bos-A	17	12	.586	35	30	22	**6**	2	253	237	8.4	14	65	2.3	130	4.6	**2.81**	**190**	.246	**.292**	**63**	**71**	106	115	3.5	-3	0	**6.7**
1937	Bos-A	17	9	.654	32	32	21	3	0	262	269	9.2	9	83	2.9	153	5.3	3.02	156	.261	.313	47	50	102	111	4.0	-3	-1	4.6
1938	Bos-A	14	4	.778	24	21	12	1	1	164	169	9.3	8	52	2.9	99	5.4	**3.07**	**156**	.263	.314	31	31	100	118	4.4	-1	-1	2.9
1939	Bos-A	15	4	**.789**	23	23	17	2	0	191	180	8.5	8	58	2.7	81	3.8	**2.54**	**194**	.249	.299	44	51	107	126	4.9	-2	-3	4.7
1940	Bos-A	7	6	.538	22	21	9	1	0	153	159	9.4	20	50	2.9	62	3.6	4.00	110	.269	.322	7	7	100	112	0.1	-1	0	0.5
1941	Bos-A	7	7	.500	21	21	10	0	0	134	155	10.4	8	42	2.8	54	3.6	4.37	96	.287	.333	-3	-3	101	99	-0.5	-1	-2	-0.5
Total	17	300	141	.680	616	457	298	35	55	3940	3849	8.8	162	1187	2.7	2266	5.2	3.06	148	.255	.305	595	644	103	108	63.2	-38	-15	59.9

■ CHARLIE GROVER Grover, Charles Burt "Bugs" (Born Charles Byrd Grover) b: 6/20/1890, Huntington Township, Ohio d: 5/24/71, Emmett, Mich. BL/TR, 6'1.5", 185 lbs. Deb: 9/09/13

YEAR	TM/L	W	L	PCT	G	GS	CG	SHO	SV	IP	H	H/G	HR	BB	BB/G	SO	SO/G	ERA	/A	OAVG	OOBP	PR	/A	PF	CPI	WAT	PB	PD	TPI
1913	Det-A	0	0	—	2	1	0	0	0	11	9	7.4	0	7	5.7	2	1.6	3.27	90	.265	.390	-0	-0	101	120	0.0	-0	0	0.0

■ TOM GRUBBS Grubbs, Thomas Dillard "Judge" b: 2/22/1894, Mt.Sterling, Ky. d: 1/28/86, Mt.Sterling, Ky. BR/TR, 6'2", 165 lbs. Deb: 10/03/20

YEAR	TM/L	W	L	PCT	G	GS	CG	SHO	SV	IP	H	H/G	HR	BB	BB/G	SO	SO/G	ERA	/A	OAVG	OOBP	PR	/A	PF	CPI	WAT	PB	PD	TPI
1920	NY-N	0	1	.000	1	1	0	0	0	5	9	16.2	0	0	0.0	0	0.0	7.20	42	.409	.391	-2	-2	97	86	-0.4	-0	-0	-0.2

■ HENRY GRUBER Gruber, Henry John b: 12/14/1863, Hamden, Conn. d: 9/26/32, New Haven, Conn. BR/TL, Deb: 7/28/1887

YEAR	TM/L	W	L	PCT	G	GS	CG	SHO	SV	IP	H	H/G	HR	BB	BB/G	SO	SO/G	ERA	/A	OAVG	OOBP	PR	/A	PF	CPI	WAT	PB	PD	TPI
1887	Det-N	4	3	.571	7	7	7	0	0	62	63	9.1	3	21	3.0	12	1.7	2.76	143	.278	.340	9	8	97	135	-0.3	1	0	0.8
1888	Det-N	11	14	.440	27	25	25	3	0	240	196	7.4	8	41	1.5	71	2.7	2.29	120	.236	.271	15	12	97	88	-2.2	-1	0	1.1
1889	Cle-N	7	16	.304	25	23	23	0	1	205	198	8.7	6	94	4.1	74	3.2	3.64	115	.269	.351	9	13	104	98	-4.3	-2	0	1.0
1890	Cle-P	21	23	.477	48	44	39	1	1	383	464	10.9	15	204	4.8	110	2.6	4.28	93	.312	.395	-2	-13	94	111	3.0	6	3	-0.4
1891	Cle-N	17	22	.436	44	40	35	1	0	349	407	10.5	10	119	3.1	79	2.0	4.13	86	.305	.362	-30	-23	106	94	-1.7	0	3	-1.4
Total	5	60	78	.435	151	139	129	5	2	1239	1328	9.6	42	479	3.5	346	2.5	3.67	100	.288	.355	0	-1	100	101	-5.5	3	6	1.1

■ AL GRUNWALD Grunwald, Alfred Henry "Stretch" b: 2/13/30, Los Angeles, Cal. BL/TL, 6'4", 210 lbs. Deb: 4/18/55

YEAR	TM/L	W	L	PCT	G	GS	CG	SHO	SV	IP	H	H/G	HR	BB	BB/G	SO	SO/G	ERA	/A	OAVG	OOBP	PR	/A	PF	CPI	WAT	PB	PD	TPI
1955	Pit-N	0	0	—	3	0	0	0	0	8	7	7.9	1	7	7.9	2	2.3	4.50	90	.241	.389	-0	-0	101	112	0.0	1	0	0.0
1959	KC-A	0	1	.000	6	1	0	0	1	11	18	14.7	1	11	9.0	9	7.4	8.18	48	.360	.468	-5	-5	103	105	-0.4	-1	0	-0.4
Total	2	0	1	.000	9	1	0	0	1	19	25	11.8	2	18	8.5	11	5.2	6.63	60	.316	.439	-6	-6	102	108	-0.4	0	0	-0.4

YEAR	TM/L	W	L	PCT	G	GS	CG	SHO	SV	IP	H	H/G	HR	BB	BB/G	SO	SO/G	ERA	/A	OAVG	OOBP	PR	/A	PF	CPI	WAT	PB	PD	TPI
■ JOE GRZENDA	Grzenda, Joseph Charles b: 6/8/37, Scranton, Pa. BR/TL, 6'2", 180 lbs. Deb: 4/26/61																												
1961	Det-A	1	0	1.000	4	0	0	0	0	6	9	13.5	2	2	3.0	0	0.0	7.50	50	.375	.393	-2	-2	94	118	0.5	0	0	-0.1
1964	KC-A	0	2	.000	20	0	0	0	0	25	34	12.2	2	13	4.7	17	6.1	5.40	72	.324	.397	-5	-4	108	111	-0.9	-0	1	-0.2
1966	KC-A	0	2	.000	21	0	0	0	0	22	28	11.5	1	12	4.9	14	5.7	3.27	100	.337	.404	0	0	95	188	-0.9	-0	1	0.0
1967	NY-N	0	0	—	11	0	0	0	0	17	14	7.4	0	8	4.2	9	4.8	2.12	162	.237	.329	2	2	102	149	0.0	-0	-0	0.2
1969	Min-A	4	1	.800	38	0	0	0	3	49	52	9.6	4	17	3.1	24	4.4	3.86	94	.281	.338	-1	-1	100	111	1.3	0	1	0.0
1970	Was-A	3	6	.333	49	3	0	0	6	85	86	9.1	8	34	3.6	38	4.0	4.98	72	.267	.336	-12	-13	97	84	-1.0	-1	0	-1.3
1971	Was-A	5	2	.714	46	0	0	0	5	70	54	6.9	2	17	2.2	56	7.2	1.93	169	.217	.264	12	10	94	101	1.9	-0	-0	1.1
1972	StL-N	1	0	1.000	30	0	0	0	0	35	46	11.8	1	17	4.4	15	3.9	5.66	64	.326	.400	-9	-8	105	100	0.5	-0	0	-0.7
Total	8	14	13	.519	219	3	0	0	14	309	323	9.4	20	120	3.5	173	5.0	3.99	88	.277	.341	-14	-16	99	108	1.4	-2	3	-1.0
■ CECILIO GUANTE	Guante, Cecilio (Magallane) b: 2/1/60, Villa Mella, D.R. BR/TR, 6'3", 200 lbs. Deb: 5/01/82																												
1982	Pit-N	0	0	—	10	0	0	0	0	27	28	9.3	1	5	1.7	26	8.7	3.33	119	.264	.299	1	2	110	95	0.0	-1	-0	0.1
1983	Pit-N	2	6	.250	49	0	0	0	9	100	90	8.1	5	46	4.1	82	7.4	3.33	112	.241	.320	3	5	103	98	-2.0	-1	-1	0.3
1984	Pit-N	2	3	.400	27	0	0	0	2	41	32	7.0	3	16	3.5	30	6.6	2.63	128	.224	.301	4	3	94	118	-0.2	-0	-1	0.2
1985	Pit-N	4	6	.400	63	0	0	0	5	109	84	6.9	5	40	3.3	92	7.6	2.72	138	.214	.290	11	13	104	91	0.4	-1	-0	1.1
1986	Pit-N	5	2	.714	52	0	0	0	4	78	65	7.5	11	29	3.3	63	7.3	3.35	112	.225	.298	3	3	101	103	1.9	-0	-2	0.2
1987	NY-A	3	2	.600	23	0	0	0	1	44	42	8.6	8	20	4.1	46	9.4	5.73	76	.247	.323	-6	-7	97	79	0.3	0	-1	-0.6
1988	NY-A	5	6	.455	56	0	0	0	11	75	59	7.1	10	22	2.6	61	7.3	2.88	132	.213	.280	9	8	96	105	-0.7	0	-1	0.6
	Tex-A	0	0	—	7	0	0	0	1	5	8	14.4	1	4	7.2	4	7.2	1.80	226	.400	.500	1	1	102	552	0.0	0	-0	0.1
	Yr	5	6	.455	63	0	0	0	12	80	67	7.5	11	26	2.9	65	7.3	2.81	136	.221	.281	10	9	96	552	-0.7	0	-2	0.7
Total	7	21	25	.457	287	0	0	0	33	479	408	7.7	44	182	3.4	404	7.6	3.27	116	.230	.303	27	28	101	103	-0.3	-3	-6	2.0
■ MARK GUBICZA	Gubicza, Mark Steven b: 8/14/62, Philadelphia, Pa. BR/TR, 6'6", 215 lbs. Deb: 4/06/84																												
1984	KC-A	10	14	.417	29	29	4	2	0	189	172	8.2	13	75	3.6	111	5.3	4.05	98	.243	.315	-1	-2	99	84	-2.6	0	2	0.0
1985	KC-A	14	10	.583	29	28	0	0	0	177	160	8.1	14	77	3.9	99	5.0	4.07	103	.238	.318	2	3	101	86	0.7	0	2	0.4
1986	KC-A	12	6	.667	35	24	3	2	0	181	155	7.7	8	84	4.2	118	5.9	3.63	116	.233	.319	11	11	100	89	3.6	0	2	1.4
1987	KC-A	13	18	.419	35	35	10	2	0	242	231	8.6	18	120	4.5	166	6.2	3.98	117	.259	.345	13	18	104	107	-3.2	0	4	2.1
1988	KC-A	20	8	.714	35	35	8	4	0	270	237	7.9	11	83	2.8	183	6.1	2.70	151	.234	.293	38	41	103	102	6.3	0	3	**4.8**
Total	5	69	56	.552	163	151	25	10	0	1059	955	8.1	64	439	3.7	677	5.8	3.62	117	.242	.318	63	71	102	95	4.8	0	13	8.7
■ MARV GUDAT	Gudat, Marvin John b: 8/27/05, Goliad, Tex. d: 3/1/54, Los Angeles, Cal. BL/TL, 5'11", 162 lbs. Deb: 5/21/29																												
1929	Cin-N	1	1	.500	7	2	2	0	0	27	29	9.7	0	4	1.3	0	0.0	3.33	142	.282	.297	4	4	101	96	0.1	-0	-1	0.3
1932	Chi-N	0	0	—	1	0	0	0	0	1	1	9.0	0	0	0.0	2	18.0	0.00	—	.250	.250	0	0	103	0	0.0	0	0	0.0
Total	2	1	1	.500	8	2	2	0	0	28	30	9.6	0	4	1.3	2	0.6	3.21	147	.280	.296	5	5	101	93	0.1	-0	-1	0.3
■ LEE GUETTERMAN	Guetterman, Arthur Lee b: 11/22/58, Chattanooga, Tenn. BL/TL, 6'8", 225 lbs. Deb: 9/12/84																												
1984	Sea-A	0	0	—	3	0	0	0	0	4	9	20.3	0	2	4.5	2	4.5	4.50	92	.450	.500	-0	-0	103	219	0.0	0	0	0.0
1986	Sea-A	0	4	.000	41	4	1	0	0	76	108	12.8	7	30	3.6	38	4.5	7.34	61	.347	.402	-27	-24	106	90	-1.9	0	0	-2.2
1987	Sea-A	11	4	.733	25	17	2	1	0	113	117	9.3	13	35	2.8	42	3.3	3.82	120	.267	.319	8	10	103	108	3.8	0	1	1.0
1988	NY-A	1	2	.333	20	2	0	0	0	41	49	10.8	2	14	3.1	15	3.3	4.61	82	.306	.362	-3	-4	96	105	-0.5	0	-0	-0.3
Total	4	12	10	.545	89	23	3	1	0	234	283	10.9	22	81	3.1	97	3.7	5.12	86	.304	.358	-22	-19	103	103	1.4	0	1	-1.5
■ WHITEY GUESE	Guese, Theodore b: 1/24/1872, New Bremen, Ohio d: 4/8/51, Wapakoneta, Ohio BR/TR, 6'0.5", 200 lbs. Deb: 7/13/01																												
1901	Cin-N	1	4	.200	6	5	4	0	0	44	62	12.7	5	14	2.9	11	2.3	6.14	54	.362	.420	-14	-14	100	100	-1.1	1	-2	-1.2
■ RON GUIDRY	Guidry, Ronald Ames b: 8/28/50, Lafayette, La. BL/TL, 5'11", 161 lbs. Deb: 7/27/75																												
1975	NY-A	0	1	.000	10	1	0	0	0	16	15	8.4	0	9	5.1	15	8.4	3.38	109	.259	.362	1	1	98	113	-0.4	0	-0	0.0
1976	NY-A	0	0	—	7	0	0	0	0	16	20	11.3	1	4	2.3	12	6.8	5.63	61	.294	.333	-4	-4	97	73	0.0	0	-0	-0.3
1977	NY-A	16	7	.696	31	25	9	5	1	211	174	7.4	12	65	2.8	176	7.5	2.82	140	.224	.281	29	26	97	87	2.7	0	-1	2.6
1978	NY-A	**25**	3	**.893**	35	35	16	**9**	0	274	187	**6.1**	13	72	2.4	248	8.1	**1.74**	**211**	**.193**	**.246**	**62**	**59**	97	88	**10.6**	0	2	**6.9**
1979	NY-A	18	8	.692	33	30	15	2	2	236	203	7.7	20	71	2.7	201	7.7	**2.78**	144	.236	.290	38	32	95	109	4.5	0	-0	3.2
1980	NY-A	17	10	.630	37	29	5	3	1	220	215	8.8	19	80	3.3	166	6.8	3.56	111	.260	.319	12	10	98	106	-0.1	0	2	1.1
1981	NY-A	11	5	.688	23	21	0	0	0	127	100	7.1	12	26	1.8	104	7.4	2.76	131	.214	**.256**	13	12	99	81	2.7	0	1	1.4
1982	NY-A	14	8	.636	34	33	6	1	0	222	216	8.8	22	69	2.8	162	6.6	3.81	103	.254	.306	7	3	97	94	3.5	0	-2	0.1
1983	NY-A	21	9	.700	31	31	**21**	3	0	250	232	8.4	26	60	2.2	156	5.6	3.42	117	.244	.287	18	16	98	94	5.4	0	-0	1.5
1984	NY-A	10	11	.476	29	28	5	1	0	196	223	10.2	24	44	2.0	127	5.8	4.50	83	.287	.320	-11	-17	93	98	-1.2	0	-0	-1.6
1985	NY-A	**22**	6	**.786**	34	33	11	2	0	259	243	8.4	28	42	1.5	143	5.0	3.27	119	.248	.276	25	18	94	97	**7.1**	0	-1	1.7
1986	NY-A	9	12	.429	30	30	5	0	0	192	202	9.5	28	38	**1.8**	140	6.6	3.98	108	.265	.298	4	7	103	98	-2.6	0	-1	0.5
1987	NY-A	5	8	.385	22	17	2	0	0	118	111	8.5	14	38	2.9	96	7.3	3.66	119	.248	.304	11	9	97	101	-2.0	0	-0	0.8
1988	NY-A	2	3	.400	12	10	0	0	0	56	57	9.2	7	15	2.4	32	5.1	4.18	91	.259	.310	-1	-2	96	94	-0.5	0	-1	-0.2
Total	14	170	91	.651	368	323	95	26	4	2393	2198	8.3	226	633	2.4	1778	6.7	3.29	119	.244	.290	204	169	97	96	29.7	0	-3	17.7
■ SKIP GUINN	Guinn, Drannon Eugene b: 10/25/44, St.Charles, Mo. BR/TL, 5'10", 180 lbs. Deb: 5/07/68																												
1968	Atl-N	0	0	—	3	0	0	0	0	5	3	5.4	0	3	5.4	4	7.2	3.60	78	.167	.286	-0	-0	94	41	0.0	0	-0	0.0
1969	Hou-N	1	2	.333	28	0	0	0	0	27	34	11.3	3	21	7.0	33	11.0	6.67	55	.304	.412	-9	-9	101	96	-0.4	-0	0	-0.9
1971	Hou-N	0	0	—	4	0	0	0	1	5	1	1.8	0	3	5.4	3	5.4	0.00	—	.067	.222	2	2	92	0	0.0	0	0	0.2
Total	3	1	2	.333	35	0	0	0	1	37	38	9.2	3	27	6.6	40	9.7	5.35	65	.262	.377	-8	-8	99	75	-0.4	-0	-0	-0.7
■ LEFTY GUISE	Guise, Witt Orison b: 9/18/09, Driggs, Ark. d: 8/13/68, Little Rock, Ark. BL/TL, 6'2", 172 lbs. Deb: 9/13/40																												
1940	Cin-N	0	0	—	2	0	0	0	0	8	8	9.0	0	5	5.6	1	1.1	1.13	334	.296	.412	2	2	98	485	0.0	0	0	0.3
■ DON GULLETT	Gullett, Donald Edward b: 1/6/51, Lynn, Ky. BR/TL, 6', 210 lbs. Deb: 4/10/70																												
1970	Cin-N	5	2	.714	44	2	0	0	6	78	54	6.2	4	44	5.1	76	8.8	2.42	172	.196	.303	14	15	103	108	0.8	1	-1	1.6
1971	Cin-N	16	6	**.727**	35	31	4	3	0	218	196	8.1	14	64	2.6	107	4.4	2.64	126	.242	.294	20	17	96	111	5.5	-2	-2	1.3
1972	Cin-N	9	10	.474	31	16	2	0	2	135	127	8.5	15	43	2.9	96	6.4	3.93	80	.250	.306	-7	-12	91	91	-2.3	2	-2	-1.2
1973	Cin-N	18	8	.692	45	30	7	4	2	228	198	7.8	24	69	2.7	153	6.0	3.51	96	.232	.287	4	-4	92	86	3.1	3	-0	-0.1
1974	Cin-N	17	11	.607	36	35	10	3	0	243	201	7.4	22	88	3.3	183	6.8	3.04	115	.222	.288	16	12	96	91	0.1	4	0	1.6
1975	Cin-N	15	4	**.789**	22	22	8	3	0	160	127	7.1	11	56	3.1	98	5.5	2.42	152	.218	.285	22	22	101	105	3.8	2	-1	2.7
1976	Cin-N	11	3	.786	23	20	4	0	1	126	119	8.5	8	48	3.4	64	4.6	3.00	117	.253	.316	7	7	100	115	3.1	-0	0	0.8
1977	NY-A	14	4	.778	22	22	7	1	0	158	137	7.8	14	69	3.9	116	6.6	3.59	110	.232	.310	9	6	97	90	4.0	0	-1	0.4
1978	NY-A	4	2	.667	8	8	2	0	0	45	46	9.2	3	20	4.0	28	5.6	3.60	102	.269	.345	1	0	97	113	0.4	0	0	0.0
Total	9	109	50	.686	266	186	44	14	11	1391	1205	7.8	115	501	3.2	921	6.0	3.11	113	.233	.298	85	65	96	99	18.5	10	-8	7.1
■ BILL GULLICKSON	Gullickson, William Lee b: 2/20/59, Marshall, Minn. BR/TR, 6'3", 200 lbs. Deb: 9/26/79																												
1979	Mon-N	0	0	—	1	0	0	0	0	1	2	18.0	0	0	0.0	0	0.0	0.00	—	.500	.500	0	0	101	0	0.0	0	0	0.0
1980	Mon-N	10	5	.667	24	19	5	2	0	141	127	8.1	6	50	3.2	120	7.7	3.00	118	.238	.302	10	9	98	94	2.0	0	0	1.0
1981	Mon-N	7	9	.438	22	22	3	2	0	157	142	8.1	3	34	1.9	115	6.6	2.81	122	.239	.281	12	11	98	84	-1.8	0	-1	1.1
1982	Mon-N	12	14	.462	34	34	6	0	0	237	231	8.8	25	61	2.3	155	5.9	3.57	105	.254	.299	1	5	104	97	-1.9	-3	-3	0.0
1983	Mon-N	17	12	.586	34	34	10	1	0	242	230	8.6	19	59	2.2	120	4.5	3.76	98	.251	.296	-3	-2	101	84	2.8	1	-1	-0.1
1984	Mon-N	12	9	.571	32	32	3	0	0	227	230	9.1	27	37	**1.5**	100	4.0	3.61	91	.265	.292	-0	-8	91	100	2.0	-2	-4	-1.4
1985	Mon-N	14	12	.538	29	29	4	1	0	181	187	9.3	8	47	2.3	68	3.4	3.53	96	.271	.310	1	-3	94	98	0.5	2	-1	-0.2
1986	Cin-N	15	12	.556	37	37	6	2	0	245	245	9.0	24	60	2.2	121	4.4	3.38	115	.264	.303	9	14	104	110	0.8	-4	-2	0.8
1987	Cin-N	10	11	.476	27	27	3	1	0	165	172	9.4	33	39	2.1	89	4.9	4.85	87	.267	.305	-14	-12	103	93	-0.9	2	-2	-1.0
	NY-A	4	2	.667	8	8	1	0	0	48	46	8.6	7	11	2.1	28	5.3	4.88	89	.253	.293	-2	-3	97	78	0.8	0	-0	-0.2
Total	9	101	86	.540	248	242	41	9	0	1644	1612	8.8	152	398	2.2	916	5.0	3.61	101	.257	.298	14	10	99	95	4.3	-3	-13	-0.0
■ AD GUMBERT	Gumbert, Addison Courtney b: 10/10/1868, Pittsburgh, Pa. d: 4/23/25, Pittsburgh, Pa. BR/TR, 5'10", 200 lbs. Deb: 1888																												
1888	Chi-N	3	3	.500	6	6	5	0	0	49	44	8.1	0	10	1.8	16	2.9	3.12	96	.253	.294	-2	-1	106	72	-0.3	2	0	0.2
1889	Chi-N	16	13	.552	31	28	25	2	0	246	258	9.4	16	76	2.8	91	3.3	3.62	109	.285	.341	11	9	98	106	1.6	12	-0	2.2

YEAR	TM/L	W	L	PCT	G	GS	CG	SHO	SV	IP	H	H/G	HR	BB	BB/G	SO	SO/G	ERA	/A	OAVG	OOBP	PR	/A	PF	CPI	WAT	PB	PD	TPI
1890	Bos-P	23	12	.657	39	33	27	1	0	277	338	11.0	18	86	2.8	81	2.6	3.96	111	.313	.364	8	13	104	111	1.8	5	3	2.0
1891	Chi-N	17	11	.607	32	31	24	1	0	256	282	9.9	5	90	3.2	73	2.6	3.59	98	.293	.354	-7	-2	105	98	0.0	11	0	1.0
1892	Chi-N	22	19	.537	46	45	39	0	0	383	399	9.4	11	107	2.5	118	2.8	3.41	90	.281	.332	-5	-14	93	96	3.0	6	2	-0.6
1893	Pit-N	12	7	.632	22	20	16	2	0	163	207	11.4	5	78	4.3	40	2.2	5.19	94	.326	.400	-9	-5	105	101	0.1	0	0	-0.3
1894	Pit-N	15	14	.517	37	31	26	0	0	269	372	12.4	13	84	2.8	65	2.2	6.02	84	.351	.399	-21	-29	95	90	0.6	5	2	-1.6
1895	Bro-N	11	16	.407	33	26	20	0	1	234	288	11.1	11	69	2.7	45	1.7	5.08	88	.323	.372	-7	-16	94	91	-3.9	10	0	-0.4
1896	Bro-N	0	4	.000	5	4	2	0	0	31	34	9.9	2	11	3.2	3	0.9	3.77	102	.301	.363	2	0	88	110	-1.9	0	0	0.0
	Phi-N	5	3	.625	11	10	7	1	0	77	99	11.6	0	23	2.7	14	1.6	4.56	98	.335	.383	-2	-1	102	97	1.2	1	0	0.0
	Yr	5	7	.417	16	14	9	1	0	108	133	11.1	2	34	2.8	17	1.4	4.33	99	.326	.378	0	-1	98	97	-0.7	0	0	0.0
Total	9	124	102	.549	262	234	191	7	1	1985	2321	10.5	81	634	2.9	546	2.5	4.28	95	.308	.362	-31	-44	99	98	2.2	52	6	2.5

■ HARRY GUMBERT Gumbert, Harry Edward "Gunboat" b: 11/5/09, Elizabeth, Pa. BR/TR, 6'2", 185 lbs. Deb: 9/12/35

YEAR	TM/L	W	L	PCT	G	GS	CG	SHO	SV	IP	H	H/G	HR	BB	BB/G	SO	SO/G	ERA	/A	OAVG	OOBP	PR	/A	PF	CPI	WAT	PB	PD	TPI
1935	NY-N	1	2	.333	6	3	1	0	0	24	35	13.1	1	10	3.8	11	4.1	6.00	63	.330	.385	-5	-6	95	95	-0.6	-1	-0	-0.6
1936	NY-N	11	3	.786	39	15	3	0	0	141	157	10.0	7	54	3.4	52	3.3	3.89	101	.281	.343	2	1	98	108	3.4	2	3	0.6
1937	NY-N	10	11	.476	34	24	10	1	1	200	194	8.7	11	62	2.8	65	2.9	3.69	104	.257	.307	5	3	98	94	-2.7	-1	8	1.0
1938	NY-N	15	13	.536	38	33	14	1	0	236	238	9.1	13	84	3.2	84	3.2	4.00	97	.261	.324	-6	-4	102	92	-0.4	-3	8	0.1
1939	NY-N	18	11	.621	36	34	14	2	0	244	257	9.5	21	81	3.0	81	3.0	4.32	89	.271	.324	-11	-12	99	92	3.8	0	6	-0.5
1940	NY-N	12	14	.462	35	30	14	2	2	237	230	8.7	17	81	3.1	77	2.9	3.76	102	.252	.312	2	2	100	96	-0.3	2	4	0.8
1941	NY-N	1	1	.500	5	5	1	0	0	32	34	9.6	3	18	5.1	9	2.5	4.50	84	.266	.351	-3	-3	104	102	0.0	-0	1	-0.1
	StL-N	11	5	.688	33	17	8	3	1	144	139	8.7	7	30	1.9	53	3.3	2.75	142	.251	.285	14	18	107	106	1.3	6	4	3.0
	Yr	12	6	.667	38	22	9	3	1	176	173	8.8	10	48	2.5	62	3.2	3.07	126	.254	.298	11	16	107	106	1.3	-0	5	2.9
1942	StL-N	9	5	.643	38	19	5	0	5	163	156	8.6	3	59	3.3	52	2.9	3.26	104	.250	.311	1	3	103	93	-0.4	-2	5	0.5
1943	StL-N	10	5	.667	21	19	7	3	0	133	115	7.8	4	32	2.2	40	2.7	2.84	119	.237	.280	8	8	100	87	-0.1	-2	2	0.9
1944	StL-N	4	2	.667	10	7	3	0	1	61	60	8.9	1	19	2.8	16	2.4	2.51	137	.258	.310	7	6	95	123	0.0	-0	1	0.8
	Cin-N	10	8	.556	24	19	11	2	2	155	157	9.1	7	40	2.3	40	2.3	3.31	103	.262	.305	5	2	95	100	-0.3	-2	2	0.2
	Yr	14	10	.583	34	26	14	2	3	216	217	9.0	8	59	2.5	56	2.3	3.08	111	.261	.306	13	8	95	100	-0.3	-0	3	1.0
1946	Cin-N	6	8	.429	36	10	5	0	4	119	112	8.5	8	42	3.2	44	3.3	3.25	110	.248	.308	2	4	105	98	0.0	1	1	0.7
1947	Cin-N	10	10	.500	46	0	0	0	10	90	88	8.8	3	47	4.7	43	4.3	3.90	96	.260	.342	2	-2	92	99	0.6	1	0	0.0
1948	Cin-N	10	8	.556	**61**	0	0	0	**17**	106	123	10.4	5	34	2.9	25	2.1	3.48	121	.291	.338	6	9	106	123	2.3	-2	4	1.1
1949	Cin-N	4	3	.571	29	0	0	0	2	41	58	12.7	5	8	1.8	12	2.6	5.49	72	.341	.364	-7	-7	98	110	1.0	-0	1	-0.5
	Pit-N	1	4	.200	16	0	0	0	3	28	30	9.6	5	18	5.8	5	1.6	5.79	71	.270	.361	-5	-5	102	96	-1.3	0	1	-0.3
	Yr	5	7	.417	45	0	0	0	5	69	88	11.5	10	26	3.4	17	2.2	5.61	72	.312	.360	-12	-12	100	96	-0.3	-0	2	-0.8
1950	Pit-N	0	0	—	1	0	0	0	0	2	3	13.5	0	2	9.0	0	0.0	4.50	97	.333	.455	-0	-0	106	156	0.0	0	0	0.1
Total	15	143	113	.559	508	235	96	14	48	2156	2186	9.1	121	721	3.0	709	3.0	3.68	102	.263	.318	18	19	100	99	6.3	-2	50	7.8

■ BILLY GUMBERT Gumbert, William Skeen b: 8/8/1865, Pittsburgh, Pa. d: 4/13/46, Pittsburgh, Pa. BR/TR, 6'1.5", 200 lbs. Deb: 6/19/1890

YEAR	TM/L	W	L	PCT	G	GS	CG	SHO	SV	IP	H	H/G	HR	BB	BB/G	SO	SO/G	ERA	/A	OAVG	OOBP	PR	/A	PF	CPI	WAT	PB	PD	TPI
1890	Pit-N	4	6	.400	10	10	8	0	0	79	96	10.9	0	31	3.5	18	2.1	5.24	64	.317	.380	-15	-16	95	81	1.5	2	0	-1.1
1892	Pit-N	3	2	.600	6	3	2	0	0	40	30	6.7	0	23	5.2	3	0.7	1.35	228	.220	.332	9	8	94	180	0.4	-1	0	0.7
1893	Lou-N	0	0	—	1	1	0	0	0	1	2	18.0	0	5	45.0	0	0.0	45.00	10	.432	.727	-4	-4	98	47	0.0	1	0	-0.2
Total	3	7	8	.467	17	14	10	0	0	120	128	9.6	0	59	4.4	21	1.6	4.28	77	.288	.372	-11	-13	94	114	1.9	2	0	-0.6

■ DAVE GUMPERT Gumpert, David Lawrence b: 5/5/58, South Haven, Mich. BR/TR, 6'1", 190 lbs. Deb: 7/25/82

YEAR	TM/L	W	L	PCT	G	GS	CG	SHO	SV	IP	H	H/G	HR	BB	BB/G	SO	SO/G	ERA	/A	OAVG	OOBP	PR	/A	PF	CPI	WAT	PB	PD	TPI
1982	Det-A	0	0	—	5	1	0	0	1	2	7	31.5	1	2	9.0	0	0.0	27.00	15	.700	.692	-5	-5	100	90	0.0	0	0	-0.4
1983	Det-A	0	2	.000	26	0	0	0	2	44	43	8.8	1	7	1.4	14	2.9	2.66	145	.257	.279	7	6	95	102	-0.9	0	-1	0.5
1985	Chi-N	1	0	1.000	9	0	0	0	0	10	12	10.8	0	7	6.3	4	3.6	3.60	117	.279	.365	-0	1	117	123	0.5	-0	-0	0.0
1986	Chi-N	2	0	1.000	38	0	0	0	2	60	60	9.0	4	28	4.2	45	6.8	4.35	92	.267	.344	-4	-2	108	96	1.0	-1	-1	-0.3
1987	KC-A	0	0	—	8	0	0	0	0	19	27	12.8	3	6	2.8	13	6.2	6.16	75	.333	.375	-4	-3	104	103	0.0	0	0	-0.2
Total	5	3	2	.600	86	1	0	0	5	135	149	9.9	9	50	3.3	76	5.1	4.33	94	.283	.338	-6	-4	103	101	0.6	-1	-2	-0.4

■ RANDY GUMPERT Gumpert, Randall Pennington b: 1/23/18, Monocacy, Pa. BR/TR, 6'3", 185 lbs. Deb: 6/13/36

YEAR	TM/L	W	L	PCT	G	GS	CG	SHO	SV	IP	H	H/G	HR	BB	BB/G	SO	SO/G	ERA	/A	OAVG	OOBP	PR	/A	PF	CPI	WAT	PB	PD	TPI
1936	Phi-A	1	2	.333	22	3	2	0	2	62	74	10.7	2	32	4.6	9	1.3	4.79	111	.295	.371	2	4	105	106	0.0	0	-1	0.3
1937	Phi-A	0	0	—	10	1	0	0	0	12	16	12.0	1	15	11.3	5	3.8	12.00	37	.333	.492	-10	-10	96	73	0.0	0	0	-0.8
1938	Phi-A	0	2	.000	4	2	0	0	0	12	24	18.0	1	10	7.5	1	0.8	11.25	44	.393	.472	-9	-8	105	86	-0.9	0	1	-0.5
1946	NY-A	11	3	.786	33	12	4	0	1	133	113	7.6	8	32	2.2	63	4.3	2.30	149	.229	.273	18	17	98	103	3.7	-2	-1	1.5
1947	NY-A	4	1	.800	24	6	2	0	0	56	71	11.4	4	28	4.5	25	4.0	5.46	63	.311	.384	-11	-13	92	100	1.2	-1	0	-1.3
1948	NY-A	1	0	1.000	15	0	0	0	0	25	27	9.7	0	6	2.2	12	4.3	2.88	143	.267	.312	4	3	96	109	0.5	0	0	0.3
	Chi-A	2	6	.250	16	11	6	1	0	97	103	9.6	6	13	1.2	31	2.9	3.80	112	.275	.294	5	5	100	94	-1.0	-2	-1	0.2
	Yr	3	6	.333	31	11	6	1	0	122	130	9.6	6	19	1.4	43	3.2	3.61	117	.273	.296	9	8	99	94	-0.5	0	-1	0.5
1949	Chi-A	13	16	.448	34	32	18	3	1	234	223	8.6	22	83	3.2	78	3.0	3.81	110	.253	.313	10	9	99	96	1.2	-1	0	0.8
1950	Chi-A	5	12	.294	40	17	6	1	0	155	165	9.6	15	58	3.4	48	2.8	4.76	95	.275	.338	-3	-4	99	94	-2.2	-4	-0	-0.7
1951	Chi-A	9	8	.529	33	16	7	1	2	142	156	9.9	20	34	2.2	45	2.9	4.31	91	.272	.310	-3	-6	96	97	0.1	3	-3	-0.5
1952	Bos-A	1	0	1.000	10	1	0	0	1	20	15	6.7	1	5	2.3	6	2.7	4.05	97	.205	.259	-1	-0	107	48	0.5	-1	0	0.0
	Was-A	4	9	.308	20	12	2	0	0	104	112	9.7	12	30	2.6	29	2.5	4.24	87	.273	.326	-7	-6	100	100	-2.6	0	-1	-0.6
	Yr	5	9	.357	30	13	2	0	1	124	127	9.2	13	35	2.5	35	2.5	4.21	89	.262	.314	-7	-7	101	100	-2.1	-1	-1	-0.6
Total	10	51	59	.464	261	113	47	6	7	1052	1099	9.4	92	346	3.0	352	3.0	4.17	98	.268	.323	-4	-10	99	97	0.5	-8	-5	-1.3

■ RED GUNKEL Gunkel, Woodward William b: 4/15/1894, Sheffield, Ill. d: 4/19/54, Chicago, Ill. BB/TR, 5'8", 158 lbs. Deb: 6/18/16

YEAR	TM/L	W	L	PCT	G	GS	CG	SHO	SV	IP	H	H/G	HR	BB	BB/G	SO	SO/G	ERA	/A	OAVG	OOBP	PR	/A	PF	CPI	WAT	PB	PD	TPI
1916	Cle-A	0	0	—	1	0	0	0	0	1	0	0.0	0	1	9.0	1	9.0	0.00	—	.000	.500	0	0	99	0	0.0	0	0	0.0

■ LARRY GURA Gura, Lawrence Cyril b: 11/26/47, Joliet, Ill. BB/TL, 6', 170 lbs. Deb: 4/30/70

YEAR	TM/L	W	L	PCT	G	GS	CG	SHO	SV	IP	H	H/G	HR	BB	BB/G	SO	SO/G	ERA	/A	OAVG	OOBP	PR	/A	PF	CPI	WAT	PB	PD	TPI
1970	Chi-N	1	3	.250	20	3	1	0	1	38	35	8.3	6	23	5.4	21	5.0	3.79	127	.254	.353	1	4	119	134	-0.9	-1	0	0.3
1971	Chi-N	0	0	—	6	0	0	0	1	3	6	18.0	0	1	3.0	2	6.0	6.00	64	.400	.389	-1	-1	110	124	0.0	-0	0	0.0
1972	Chi-N	0	0	—	7	0	0	0	0	12	11	8.3	3	3	2.3	13	9.8	3.75	104	.250	.286	-0	0	112	120	0.0	-0	0	0.0
1973	Chi-N	2	4	.333	21	7	0	0	0	65	79	10.9	10	11	1.5	43	6.0	4.85	82	.296	.323	-8	-6	109	96	-0.8	0	1	-0.4
1974	NY-A	5	1	.833	8	8	4	2	0	56	54	8.7	2	12	1.9	17	2.7	2.41	143	.248	.287	8	6	95	103	1.9	0	0	0.7
1975	NY-A	7	8	.467	26	20	5	0	0	151	173	10.3	13	41	2.4	65	3.9	3.52	105	.295	.339	5	3	98	126	-0.7	0	-0	0.2
1976	KC-A	4	0	1.000	20	2	1	1	1	63	47	6.7	4	20	2.9	22	3.1	2.29	152	.213	.273	9	8	99	106	2.0	0	1	1.0
1977	KC-A	8	5	.615	52	6	1	1	10	106	108	9.2	8	28	2.4	46	3.9	3.14	128	.265	.308	11	10	99	113	-0.1	0	0	1.0
1978	KC-A	16	4	.800	35	26	8	2	0	222	183	7.4	13	60	2.4	81	3.3	2.72	141	.229	.278	26	27	101	94	5.7	0	2	3.1
1979	KC-A	13	12	.520	39	33	7	1	0	234	226	8.7	29	73	2.8	85	3.3	4.46	100	.253	.309	-6	-0	105	85	0.0	0	0	0.0
1980	KC-A	18	10	.643	36	36	16	4	0	283	272	8.7	20	76	2.4	113	3.6	2.96	133	.255	.300	34	31	97	110	1.8	0	1	3.3
1981	KC-A	11	8	.579	23	23	12	2	0	172	139	7.3	11	35	1.8	61	3.2	2.72	133	.223	.262	18	17	99	86	2.0	0	0	1.9
1982	KC-A	18	12	.600	37	37	8	3	0	248	251	9.1	31	64	2.3	98	3.6	4.03	101	.261	.308	1	1	100	96	1.8	0	2	0.3
1983	KC-A	11	18	.379	34	31	5	0	0	200	220	9.9	23	76	3.4	57	2.6	4.91	85	.284	.345	-18	-17	102	99	-3.6	0	3	-1.3
1984	KC-A	12	9	.571	31	25	3	0	0	169	175	9.3	26	67	3.6	68	3.6	5.17	77	.269	.336	-22	-22	99	91	1.3	0	1	-2.0
1985	KC-A	0	0	—	3	0	0	0	1	4	7	15.8	1	4	9.0	2	4.5	13.50	31	.368	.478	-4	-4	101	76	0.0	0	0	-0.3
	Chi-N	0	3	.000	5	4	0	0	0	20	34	15.3	4	6	2.7	7	3.1	8.55	49	.370	.402	-11	-10	117	93	-1.4	-0	0	-0.8
Total	16	126	97	.565	403	261	71	16	14	2046	2020	8.9	204	600	2.6	801	3.5	3.76	106	.260	.310	41	48	101	100	9.0	-2	11	7.0

■ CHARLIE GUTH Guth, Charles J. b: 1856, Chicago, Ill. d: 7/5/1883, Boston, Mass. Deb: 9/30/1880

YEAR	TM/L	W	L	PCT	G	GS	CG	SHO	SV	IP	H	H/G	HR	BB	BB/G	SO	SO/G	ERA	/A	OAVG	OOBP	PR	/A	PF	CPI	WAT	PB	PD	TPI
1880	Chi-N	1	0	1.000	1	1	1	0	0	9	12	12.0	0	1	1.0	7	7.0	5.00	47	.329	.347	-3	-3	98	80	0.5	0	0	-0.1

■ JOSE GUZMAN Guzman, Jose Alberto (Mirabal) b: 4/9/63, Santa Isabel, P.R. BR/TR, 6'2", 160 lbs. Deb: 9/10/85

YEAR	TM/L	W	L	PCT	G	GS	CG	SHO	SV	IP	H	H/G	HR	BB	BB/G	SO	SO/G	ERA	/A	OAVG	OOBP	PR	/A	PF	CPI	WAT	PB	PD	TPI
1985	Tex-A	3	2	.600	5	5	0	0	0	33	27	7.4	3	14	3.8	24	6.5	2.73	167	.214	.293	5	7	110	102	0.9	0	0	0.7
1986	Tex-A	9	15	.375	29	29	2	0	0	172	199	10.4	23	60	3.1	87	4.6	4.55	88	.293	.350	-7	-11	95	112	-3.9	0	0	-1.0
1987	Tex-A	14	14	.500	37	30	6	0	0	208	196	8.5	30	82	3.5	143	6.2	4.67	99	.251	.319	-5	-1	104	90	1.2	0	1	0.0
1988	Tex-A	11	13	.458	30	30	6	2	0	207	180	7.8	20	82	3.6	157	6.8	3.70	110	.231	.305	6	9	102	90	0.6	0	-0	0.8
Total	4	37	44	.457	101	94	14	2	0	620	602	8.7	76	238	3.5	411	6.0	4.21	101	.254	.322	-0	4	101	97	-1.2	0	1	0.5

YEAR	TM/L	W	L	PCT	G	GS	CG	SHO	SV	IP	H	H/G	HR	BB	BB/G	SO	SO/G	ERA	/A	OAVG	OOBP	PR	/A	PF	CPI	WAT	PB	PD	TPI
■ SANTIAGO GUZMAN	Guzman, Santiago Donovan (born Santiago Donovan (Guzman)) b: 7/25/49, San Pedro De Macoris, D.R. BR/TR, 6'2", 180 lbs. Deb: 9/30/69																												
1969	StL-N	0	1	.000	1	1	0	0	0	7	9	11.6	2	3	3.9	7	9.0	5.14	69	.321	.387	-1	-1	99	139	-0.4	0	0	0.0
1970	StL-N	1	1	.500	8	3	1	0	0	14	14	9.0	1	13	8.4	9	5.8	7.07	61	.275	.422	-5	-4	106	82	0.1	-0	0	-0.3
1971	StL-N	0	0	—	2	1	0	0	0	10	6	5.4	0	2	1.8	13	11.7	0.00	—	.162	.205	4	4	100	0	0.0	-0	-0	0.4
1972	StL-N	0	0	—	1	0	0	0	0	1	1	9.0	1	0	0.0	0	0.0	9.00	40	.250	.250	-1	-1	105	105	0.0	0	0	0.0
Total	4	1	2	.333	12	5	1	0	0	32	30	8.4	4	18	5.1	29	8.2	4.50	86	.250	.348	-3	-2	103	70	-0.3	0	-0	0.1
■ BRUNO HAAS	Haas, Bruno Philip "Boon" b: 5/5/1891, Worcester, Mass. d: 6/5/52, Sarasota, Fla. BB/TL, 5'10", 180 lbs. Deb: 6/23/15																												
1915	Phi-A	0	1	.000	6	2	1	0	0	14	23	14.8	0	28	18.0	7	4.5	12.21	25	.404	.600	-14	-14	103	95	-0.4	-1	0	-1.2
■ MOOSE HAAS	Haas, Bryan Edmund b: 4/22/56, Baltimore, Md. BR/TR, 6', 180 lbs. Deb: 9/08/76																												
1976	Mil-A	0	1	.000	5	2	0	0	0	16	12	6.8	0	12	6.8	9	5.1	3.94	90	.207	.329	-1	-1	100	73	-0.4	0	1	0.0
1977	Mil-A	10	12	.455	32	32	6	0	0	198	195	8.9	21	84	3.8	113	5.1	4.32	91	.261	.333	-5	-9	97	96	0.9	0	-2	-1.0
1978	Mil-A	2	3	.400	7	6	2	0	1	31	33	9.6	6	8	2.3	32	9.3	6.10	65	.273	.313	-8	-7	104	74	-0.7	0	-0	-0.6
1979	Mil-A	11	11	.500	29	28	8	1	0	185	198	9.6	26	59	2.9	95	4.6	4.77	88	.275	.325	-11	-12	99	94	-1.8	0	-1	-1.1
1980	Mil-A	16	15	.516	33	33	14	3	0	252	246	8.8	25	56	2.0	146	5.2	3.11	121	.258	.296	26	19	93	109	-0.4	0	-0	1.9
1981	Mil-A	11	7	.611	24	22	5	0	0	137	146	9.6	10	40	2.6	64	4.2	4.47	78	.275	.321	-12	-15	95	87	1.0	0	-1	-1.5
1982	Mil-A	11	8	.579	32	27	3	0	1	193	232	10.8	15	39	1.8	104	4.8	4.48	84	.302	.332	-8	-15	92	100	0.0	0	-1	-1.5
1983	Mil-A	13	3	.813	25	25	7	3	0	179	170	8.5	12	42	2.1	75	3.8	3.27	113	.251	.292	16	9	91	96	5.0	0	-1	0.8
1984	Mil-A	9	11	.450	31	30	4	0	0	189	205	9.8	15	43	2.0	84	4.0	4.00	93	.279	.313	-0	-6	93	96	0.7	0	3	-0.3
1985	Mil-A	8	8	.500	27	26	6	1	0	162	165	9.2	21	25	**1.4**	78	4.3	3.83	114	.260	.287	6	10	106	94	0.9	0	-1	0.9
1986	Oak-A	7	2	.778	12	12	1	0	0	72	58	7.3	4	19	2.4	40	5.0	2.75	143	.218	.269	11	9	94	82	2.7	0	-0	0.9
1987	Oak-A	2	2	.500	9	9	0	0	0	41	57	12.5	7	9	2.0	13	2.9	5.71	71	.335	.365	-6	-7	91	109	0.0	0	-0	-0.6
Total	12	100	83	.546	266	252	56	8	2	1655	1717	9.3	162	436	2.4	853	4.6	4.01	97	.269	.312	8	-26	95	96	7.9	0	-5	-2.1
■ BOB HABENICHT	Habenicht, Robert Julius "Hobby" b: 2/13/26, St.Louis, Mo. d: 12/24/80, Richmond, Va. BR/TR, 6'2", 185 lbs. Deb: 4/17/51																												
1951	StL-N	0	0	—	3	0	0	0	0	5	5	9.0	0	9	16.2	1	1.8	7.20	55	.278	.519	-2	-2	101	107	0.0	0	0	0.0
1953	StL-A	0	0	—	1	0	0	0	0	2	1	4.5	0	1	4.5	1	4.5	4.50	98	.167	.375	-0	-0	111	73	0.0	0	0	0.0
Total	2	0	0	—	4	0	0	0	0	7	6	7.7	0	10	12.9	2	2.6	6.43	64	.250	.486	-2	-2	104	97	0.0	0	0	0.0
■ JOHN HABYAN	Habyan, John Gabriel b: 1/29/63, Bay Shore, N.Y. BR/TR, 6'1", 195 lbs. Deb: 9/09/85																												
1985	Bal-A	1	0	1.000	2	0	0	0	0	3	3	9.0	0	0	0.0	2	6.0	0.00	—	.250	.250	1	1	98	0	0.5	0	0	0.1
1986	Bal-A	1	3	.250	6	5	0	0	0	26	24	8.3	3	18	6.2	14	4.8	4.50	92	.250	.359	-1	-1	99	106	-0.8	0	-0	0.0
1987	Bal-A	6	7	.462	27	13	0	0	1	116	110	8.5	20	40	3.1	64	5.0	4.81	92	.248	.308	-4	-5	99	87	0.6	0	1	-0.3
1988	Bal-A	1	0	1.000	7	0	0	0	0	15	22	13.2	2	4	2.4	4	2.4	4.20	92	.355	.382	-0	-1	97	158	0.5	0	0	0.0
Total	4	9	10	.474	42	18	0	0	1	160	159	8.9	25	62	3.5	84	4.7	4.61	94	.259	.323	-4	-5	99	95	0.8	0	1	-0.2
■ WARREN HACKER	Hacker, Warren Louis b: 11/21/24, Marissa, Ill. BR/TR, 6'1", 185 lbs. Deb: 9/24/48																												
1948	Chi-N	0	1	.000	3	1	0	0	0	3	7	21.0	0	3	9.0	0	0.0	21.00	18	.438	.526	-6	-6	95	53	-0.4	0	0	-0.4
1949	Chi-N	5	8	.385	30	12	3	0	0	126	141	10.1	7	53	3.8	40	2.9	4.21	93	.283	.352	-2	-4	97	106	-0.1	-1	0	-0.3
1950	Chi-N	0	1	.000	5	3	1	0	1	15	20	12.0	3	8	4.8	5	3.0	5.40	82	.313	.384	-2	-2	107	122	-0.4	-1	1	0.0
1951	Chi-N	0	0	—	2	0	0	0	0	1	3	27.0	0	0	0.0	2	18.0	18.00	22	.500	.500	-2	-2	100	80	0.0	0	0	-0.1
1952	Chi-N	15	9	.625	33	20	12	5	1	185	144	**7.0**	17	31	1.5	84	4.1	2.58	149	**.212**	**.244**	24	26	103	84	3.4	-3	-3	2.2
1953	Chi-N	12	19	.387	39	32	9	0	2	222	225	9.1	35	54	2.2	106	4.3	4.38	104	.254	.295	-2	4	106	88	-1.5	0	-3	0.2
1954	Chi-N	6	13	.316	39	18	4	1	2	159	157	8.9	28	37	2.1	80	4.5	4.25	98	.257	.296	-3	-2	102	93	-2.4	1	-1	0.0
1955	Chi-N	11	15	.423	35	30	13	0	3	213	202	8.5	38	43	1.8	80	3.4	4.27	96	.245	.279	-5	-4	101	84	-1.4	2	-4	-0.5
1956	Chi-N	3	13	.188	34	24	4	0	0	168	190	10.2	28	44	2.4	65	3.5	4.66	81	.285	.324	-17	-16	101	100	-4.3	-2	-3	-2.0
1957	Cin-N	3	2	.600	15	6	0	0	0	43	50	10.5	5	13	2.7•	18	3.8	5.23	79	.294	.346	-6	-5	106	94	0.4	-0	-3	-0.5
	Phi-N	4	4	.500	20	10	1	0	0	74	72	8.8	10	18	2.2	33	4.0	4.50	85	.257	.299	-5	-5	99	83	0.0	1	-1	-0.4
	Yr	7	6	.538	35	16	1	0	0	117	122	9.4	15	31	2.4	51	3.9	4.77	83	.267	.311	-12	-11	102	83	0.4	-0	-1	-0.9
1958	Phi-N	0	1	.000	9	1	0	0	0	17	24	12.7	2	8	4.2	4	2.1	7.41	53	.329	.395	-7	-7	100	83	-0.4	-0	-0	-0.6
1961	Chi-A	3	3	.500	42	0	0	0	8	57	62	9.8	8	8	1.3	40	6.3	3.79	105	.272	.291	1	1	99	103	-0.1	-1	-1	0.0
Total	12	62	89	.411	306	157	47	6	17	1283	1297	9.1	181	320	2.2	557	3.9	4.22	97	.259	.301	-32	-21	102	91	-7.2	-2	-15	-2.4
■ JIM HACKETT	Hackett, James Joseph "Sunny Jim" b: 10/1/1877, Jacksonville, Ill. d: 3/28/61, Douglas, Mich. BR/TR, 6'2", 185 lbs. Deb: 9/14/02																												
1902	StL-N	0	3	.000	4	3	3	0	0	30	46	13.8	0	16	4.8	7	2.1	6.30	44	.377	.449	-12	-12	99	96	-1.4	1	-0	-0.9
1903	StL-N	1	3	.250	7	6	5	0	1	48	47	8.8	0	18	3.4	21	3.9	3.75	89	.285	.366	-3	-2	102	85	-0.3	1	0	-0.1
Total	2	1	6	.143	11	9	8	0	1	78	93	10.7	0	34	3.9	28	3.2	4.73	66	.324	.401	-14	-14	101	89	-1.7	2	-0	-1.0
■ HARVEY HADDIX	Haddix, Harvey "The Kitten" b: 9/18/25, Medway, Ohio BL/TL, 5'9.5", 170 lbs. Deb: 8/20/52 C																												
1952	StL-N	2	2	.500	7	6	3	0	0	42	31	6.6	4	10	2.1	31	6.6	2.79	130	.201	.257	4	4	97	80	-0.2	0	-1	0.4
1953	StL-N	20	9	.690	36	33	19	**6**	1	253	220	7.8	24	69	2.5	163	5.8	3.06	141	.232	.284	34	35	101	97	5.4	10	1	4.7
1954	StL-N	18	13	.581	43	35	13	3	4	260	247	8.6	26	77	2.7	184	**6.4**	3.57	114	.249	.301	15	15	100	93	3.9	3	-0	1.8
1955	StL-N	12	16	.429	37	30	9	2	1	208	216	9.3	27	62	2.7	150	6.5	4.46	93	.268	.319	-10	-8	102	93	-0.4	0	1	-0.5
1956	StL-N	1	0	1.000	4	4	1	1	0	24	28	10.5	3	10	3.8	16	6.0	5.25	71	.298	.358	-4	-4	99	98	0.5	1	-0	-0.2
	Phi-N	12	8	.600	31	26	11	2	2	207	196	8.5	23	55	2.4	154	6.7	3.48	103	.247	.295	7	3	95	94	2.9	5	-1	0.6
	Yr	13	8	.619	35	30	12	3	2	231	224	8.7	26	65	2.5	170	6.6	3.66	99	.253	.302	3	-1	96	94	3.4	1	-1	0.4
1957	Phi-N	10	13	.435	27	25	8	1	0	171	176	9.3	18	39	2.1	136	7.2	4.05	95	.264	.300	-3	-4	99	89	-1.6	7	-2	0.0
1958	Cin-N	8	7	.533	29	26	8	1	0	184	191	9.3	28	43	2.1	110	5.4	3.52	119	.268	.312	9	14	106	**117**	0.6	3	-1	1.7
1959	Pit-N	12	12	.500	31	29	14	2	0	224	189	**7.6**	26	49	2.0	149	6.0	3.13	130	.228	**.268**	20	24	104	90	-0.1	-1	-0	2.5
1960	Pit-N	11	10	.524	29	28	4	0	1	172	189	9.9	13	38	2.0	101	5.3	3.98	91	.277	.311	-4	-7	97	95	-1.7	4	3	0.1
1961	Pit-N	10	6	.625	29	22	5	2	0	156	159	9.2	15	41	2.4	99	5.7	4.10	97	.266	.313	-1	-2	99	92	2.3	0	0	-0.1
1962	Pit-N	9	6	.600	28	20	4	0	0	141	146	9.3	17	42	2.7	101	6.4	4.21	95	.264	.315	-4	-4	101	94	0.4	4	-1	0.0
1963	Pit-N	3	4	.429	49	1	0	0	1	70	67	8.6	7	20	2.6	70	9.0	3.34	97	.256	.305	-0	-1	99	111	-0.1	1	0	0.0
1964	Bal-A	5	5	.500	49	0	0	0	10	90	68	6.8	4	23	2.3	90	9.0	2.30	163	.211	.263	13	14	103	89	-0.8	-2	1	1.4
1965	Bal-A	3	2	.600	24	0	0	0	1	34	31	8.2	5	23	6.1	21	5.6	3.44	99	.248	.361	0	-0	99	146	0.1	-0	-0	0.0
Total	14	136	113	.546	453	285	99	20	21	2236	2154	8.7	240	601	2.4	1575	6.3	3.63	109	.252	.300	76	80	100	96	11.2	35	1	12.4
■ GEORGE HADDOCK	Haddock, George Silas "Gentleman George" b: 12/25/1866, Portsmouth, N.H. d: 4/18/26, Boston, Mass. BR/TR, 5'11", 155 lbs. Deb: 1888																												
1888	Was-N	0	2	.000	2	2	2	0	0	16	9	5.1	0	2	1.1	3	1.7	2.25	127	.175	.206	1	1	101	16	-0.9	0	0	0.1
1889	Was-N	11	19	.367	33	31	30	0	0	276	299	9.8	10	123	4.0	106	3.5	4.21	91	.292	.368	-5	-11	96	99	1.0	7	0	-0.3
1890	Buf-P	9	26	.257	35	34	31	0	0	291	366	11.3	15	149	4.6	123	3.8	5.78	71	.320	.398	-50	-55	97	87	-1.2	7	5	-3.1
1891	Bos-a	**34**	11	.756	51	47	37	**5**	1	380	330	7.8	8	137	3.2	169	4.0	2.49	140	.248	.318	**52**	42	94	102	**6.5**	8	6	5.1
1892	Bro-N	29	13	.690	46	44	39	3	1	381	340	8.0	11	163	3.9	153	3.6	3.14	104	.251	.332	6	5	99	94	5.2	-1	3	0.7
1893	Bro-N	8	9	.471	23	20	12	0	0	151	193	11.5	10	89	5.3	37	2.2	5.60	76	.327	.415	-16	-22	91	105	-0.6	4	0	-1.4
1894	Phi-N	4	3	.571	10	7	5	0	0	56	63	10.1	0	34	5.5	7	1.1	5.79	86	.306	.404	-3	-5	94	79	0.1	-1	0	-0.3
	Was-N	0	4	.000	4	4	4	0	0	29	50	15.5	2	17	5.3	1	0.3	8.69	61	.403	.475	-11	-11	100	93	-1.9	-1	0	-0.7
	Yr	4	7	.364	14	11	9	0	0	85	113	12.0	2	51	5.4	8	0.8	6.78	75	.342	.430	-14	-16	96	93	-1.8	-1	0	-1.0
Total	7	95	87	.522	204	189	160	8	2	1580	1650	9.4	56	714	4.1	599	3.4	4.08	93	.283	.361	-25	-54	96	95	8.2	24	14	0.1
■ BUMP HADLEY	Hadley, Irving Darius b: 7/5/04, Lynn, Mass. d: 2/15/63, Lynn, Mass. BR/TR, 5'11", 190 lbs. Deb: 4/20/26																												
1926	Was-A	0	0	—	1	0	0	0	0	3	6	18.0	0	2	6.0	0	0.0	12.00	33	.429	.471	-3	-3	97	78	0.0	0	-0	-0.1
1927	Was-A	14	6	.700	30	27	13	0	0	199	177	8.0	2	86	3.9	60	2.7	2.85	140	.244	.323	29	25	96	108	3.6	2	0	2.6
1928	Was-A	12	13	.480	33	31	16	3	0	232	236	9.2	4	100	3.9	80	3.1	3.53	116	.268	.341	13	15	101	106	-0.1	1	-0	1.6
1929	Was-A	6	16	.273	37	27	7	1	0	195	196	9.0	10	85	3.9	98	4.5	5.63	76	.263	.336	-30	-30	100	68	-4.9	-4	1	-2.9
1930	Was-A	15	11	.577	42	34	15	1	2	260	242	**8.4**	6	105	3.6	162	5.6	3.74	122	.247	.317	26	24	98	90	-0.7	1	-1	2.2
1931	Was-A	11	10	.524	**55**	11	2	1	8	180	145	**7.3**	4	92	4.6	124	**6.2**	3.05	141	**.218**	.310	27	25	98	95	-1.4	-1	2	2.4
1932	Chi-A	1	1	.500	3	2	1	0	1	19	17	8.1	2	8	3.8	13	6.2	3.79	107	.262	.333	1	1	91	122	0.3	-0	0	0.0
	StL-A	13	20	.394	40	33	12	1	1	230	244	9.5	21	163	6.4	132	5.2	5.52	83	.274	.384	-27	-24	103	101	-0.7	5	-3	-1.8

YEAR	TM/L	W	L	PCT	G	GS	CG	SHO	SV	IP	H	H/G	HR	BB	BB/G	SO	SO/G	ERA	/A	OAVG	OOBP	PR	/A	PF	CPI	WAT	PB	PD	TPI
	Yr	14	21	.400	43	35	13	1	2	249	261	9.4	23	171	6.2	145	5.2	5.39	85	.273	.381	-25	-23	102	101	-0.4	-0	-3	-1.8
1933	StL-A	15	20	.429	45	36	19	2	3	**317**	309	8.8	17	141	4.0	149	4.2	3.92	128	.256	.332	13	39	117	101	2.2	-5	-3	3.3
1934	StL-A	10	16	.385	39	32	7	2	1	213	212	9.0	14	127	5.4	79	3.3	4.35	110	.257	.356	3	10	106	102	-1.8	-1	-0	0.9
1935	Was-A	10	15	.400	35	32	13	0	0	230	268	10.5	18	102	4.0	77	3.0	4.93	84	.292	.362	-12	-21	93	102	-1.2	2	1	-1.6
1936	NY-A	14	4	.778	31	17	8	1	1	174	194	10.0	12	89	4.6	74	3.8	4.34	104	.283	.364	13	4	90	**116**	3.3	2	1	0.5
1937	NY-A	11	8	.579	29	25	6	0	0	178	199	10.1	16	83	4.2	70	3.5	5.31	85	.281	.355	-14	-16	97	91	-1.2	1	1	-1.3
1938	NY-A	9	8	.529	29	17	8	1	1	167	165	8.9	13	66	3.6	61	3.3	3.61	135	.254	.321	22	23	102	106	-1.6	-2	3	2.3
1939	NY-A	12	6	.667	26	18	7	1	2	154	132	7.7	10	85	5.0	65	3.8	2.98	132	.237	.334	28	16	85	**132**	-0.4	0	2	1.7
1940	NY-A	3	5	.375	25	2	0	0	2	80	88	9.9	4	52	5.8	39	4.4	5.74	73	.276	.369	-12	-14	96	86	-1.3	-1	0	-1.2
1941	NY-N	1	0	1.000	3	2	0	0	0	13	19	13.2	1	9	6.2	4	2.8	6.23	61	.345	.438	-4	-4	104	115	0.5	-0	-0	-0.3
	Phi-A	4	6	.400	25	9	1	0	3	102	131	11.6	13	47	4.1	31	2.7	5.03	85	.310	.378	-10	-9	103	118	-0.1	-1	-1	-0.8
Total	16	161	165	.494	528	355	135	14	25	2946	2980	9.1	167	1442	4.4	1318	4.0	4.24	105	.263	.345	65	65	100	101	-5.5	-1	1	7.5

■ **BILL HAEFFNER** Haeffner, William Bernhard b: 10/9/12, Lenzburg, Ill. d: 1/27/82, Springfield, Pa. BL/TL, 5'8", 160 lbs. Deb: 4/22/43

YEAR	TM/L	W	L	PCT	G	GS	CG	SHO	SV	IP	H	H/G	HR	BB	BB/G	SO	SO/G	ERA	/A	OAVG	OOBP	PR	/A	PF	CPI	WAT	PB	PD	TPI
1943	Was-A	11	5	.688	36	13	8	1	6	165	126	6.9	4	60	3.3	65	3.5	2.29	147	.208	.280	18	20	102	90	2.6	-0	-0	2.2
1944	Was-A	12	15	.444	31	28	18	3	1	228	221	8.7	7	71	2.8	86	3.4	3.04	102	.251	.304	10	2	91	98	0.8	-0	1	0.1
1945	Was-A	16	14	.533	37	28	19	1	3	238	226	8.5	10	69	2.6	83	3.1	3.48	89	.247	.299	-3	-10	92	84	-0.9	4	1	-0.6
1946	Was-A	14	11	.560	33	27	17	2	1	228	220	8.7	10	80	3.2	85	3.4	2.84	116	.251	.314	17	12	94	110	1.9	4	-1	1.5
1947	Was-A	10	14	.417	31	28	14	4	1	193	195	9.1	8	85	4.0	77	3.6	3.64	102	.264	.339	1	2	101	105	0.0	-1	-1	0.0
1948	Was-A	5	13	.278	28	20	4	0	0	148	151	9.2	7	61	3.7	45	2.7	4.01	114	.265	.336	4	9	107	100	-2.3	-2	2	1.0
1949	Was-A	5	5	.500	19	12	4	1	0	92	85	8.3	7	53	5.2	23	2.3	4.40	92	.249	.342	-2	-4	96	93	1.4	1	1	-0.1
	Chi-A	4	6	.400	14	12	4	1	1	80	84	9.4	9	41	4.6	17	1.9	4.39	95	.275	.363	-2	-2	99	114	0.0	2	0	0.0
	Yr	9	11	.450	33	24	8	2	1	172	169	8.8	16	94	4.9	40	2.1	4.40	93	.260	.349	-4	-6	98	114	1.4	1	1	-0.1
1950	Chi-A	1	6	.143	24	9	2	0	0	71	83	10.5	11	45	5.7	17	2.2	5.70	80	.299	.394	-9	-9	99	110	-2.2	0	-1	-0.8
	Bos-N	0	2	.000	8	2	1	0	0	24	23	8.6	3	12	4.5	10	3.8	5.63	63	.247	.330	-4	-6	85	73	-0.9	1	0	-0.4
Total	8	78	91	.462	261	179	91	13	13	1467	1414	8.7	76	577	3.5	508	3.1	3.50	102	.252	.321	31	12	97	99	0.4	8	1	2.9

■ **BUD HAFEY** Hafey, Daniel Albert b: 8/6/12, Berkeley, Cal. d: 7/27/86, Sacramento, Cal. BR/TR, 6', 185 lbs. Deb: 4/21/35

YEAR	TM/L	W	L	PCT	G	GS	CG	SHO	SV	IP	H	H/G	HR	BB	BB/G	SO	SO/G	ERA	/A	OAVG	OOBP	PR	/A	PF	CPI	WAT	PB	PD	TPI
1939	Phi-N	0	0	—	2	0	0	0	0	1	7	63.0	0	1	9.0	1	9.0	45.00	9	.700	.727	-5	-5	99	76	0.0	-0	0	-0.3

■ **LEO HAFFORD** Hafford, Leo Edgar b: 9/17/1883, Somerville, Mass. d: 10/2/11, Willimantic, Conn. TR , 6', 170 lbs. Deb: 4/15/06

YEAR	TM/L	W	L	PCT	G	GS	CG	SHO	SV	IP	H	H/G	HR	BB	BB/G	SO	SO/G	ERA	/A	OAVG	OOBP	PR	/A	PF	CPI	WAT	PB	PD	TPI
1906	Cin-N	1	1	.500	3	1	1	0	0	19	13	6.2	0	11	5.2	5	2.4	0.95	322	.220	.352	4	4	116	250	0.1	-0	-1	0.4

■ **ART HAGAN** Hagan, Arthur Charles b: 3/17/1863, Providence, R.I. d: 3/25/36, Providence, R.I. TR , Deb: 6/30/1883

YEAR	TM/L	W	L	PCT	G	GS	CG	SHO	SV	IP	H	H/G	HR	BB	BB/G	SO	SO/G	ERA	/A	OAVG	OOBP	PR	/A	PF	CPI	WAT	PB	PD	TPI
1883	Phi-N	1	14	.067	17	16	15	0	0	137	207	13.6	2	33	2.2	39	2.6	5.45	57	.356	.391	-35	-36	99	101	-4.8	-5	0	-3.2
	Buf-N	0	2	.000	2	2	1	0	0	15	17	10.2	0	6	3.6	7	4.2	3.60	86	.293	.359	-1	-1	99	108	-0.9	-1	0	-0.1
	Yr	1	16	.059	19	18	16	0	0	152	224	13.3	2	39	2.3	46	2.7	5.27	59	.350	.388	-36	-36	99	108	-5.7	-5	0	-3.3
1884	Buf-N	1	2	.333	3	3	3	0	0	26	53	18.3	1	4	1.4	4	1.4	5.88	53	.429	.447	-8	-8	105	134	-0.5	0	0	-0.5
Total	2	2	18	.100	22	21	19	0	0	178	277	14.0	3	43	2.2	50	2.5	5.36	58	.363	.397	-44	-44	100	106	-6.2	-6	0	-3.8

■ **CASEY HAGEMAN** Hageman, Kurt Moritz b: 5/12/1887, Mt.Oliver, Pa. d: 4/1/64, New Bedford, Pa. BR/TR, 5'10.5", 186 lbs. Deb: 9/18/11

YEAR	TM/L	W	L	PCT	G	GS	CG	SHO	SV	IP	H	H/G	HR	BB	BB/G	SO	SO/G	ERA	/A	OAVG	OOBP	PR	/A	PF	CPI	WAT	PB	PD	TPI
1911	Bos-A	0	2	.000	2	2	2	0	0	17	16	8.5	2	5	2.6	8	4.2	2.12	155	.262	.328	2	2	99	181	-0.9	-0	-1	0.1
1912	Bos-A	0	0	—	2	1	0	0	0	1	5	45.0	0	3	27.0	1	9.0	36.00	9	.500	.615	-4	-4	102	71	0.0	0	0	-0.2
1914	StL-N	2	4	.333	12	7	2	0	0	55	43	7.0	0	20	3.3	21	3.4	2.45	118	.215	.289	2	3	104	80	-1.0	-1	1	0.3
	Chi-N	1	1	.500	16	1	0	0	1	47	44	8.4	0	12	2.3	17	3.3	3.45	80	.254	.306	-3	-4	99	75	0.0	3	-1	-0.1
	Yr	3	5	.375	28	8	2	0	1	102	87	7.7	0	32	2.8	38	3.4	2.91	97	.230	.285	-1	-1	101	75	-1.0	-1	-0	0.2
Total	3	3	7	.300	32	11	4	0	1	120	108	8.1	2	40	3.0	47	3.5	3.08	94	.243	.309	-3	-2	101	92	-1.9	2	-1	0.1

■ **KEVIN HAGEN** Hagen, Kevin Eugene b: 3/8/60, Renton, Wash. BR/TR, 6'2", 185 lbs. Deb: 6/04/83

YEAR	TM/L	W	L	PCT	G	GS	CG	SHO	SV	IP	H	H/G	HR	BB	BB/G	SO	SO/G	ERA	/A	OAVG	OOBP	PR	/A	PF	CPI	WAT	PB	PD	TPI
1983	StL-N	2	2	.500	9	4	0	0	0	22	34	13.9	0	7	2.9	7	2.9	4.91	73	.362	.398	-3	-3	98	119	0.0	-1	0	-0.3
1984	StL-N	1	0	1.000	4	0	0	0	0	7	9	11.6	0	1	1.3	2	2.6	2.57	138	.300	.323	1	1	99	138	0.5	0	-0	0.1
Total	2	3	2	.600	13	4	0	0	0	29	43	13.3	0	8	2.5	9	2.8	4.34	82	.347	.381	-2	-3	98	124	0.5	-1	0	-0.2

■ **RIP HAGERMAN** Hagerman, Zeriah Zequiel b: 6/20/1888, Linden, Kan. d: 1/30/30, Albuquerque, N.Mex BR/TR, 6'2", 200 lbs. Deb: 09

YEAR	TM/L	W	L	PCT	G	GS	CG	SHO	SV	IP	H	H/G	HR	BB	BB/G	SO	SO/G	ERA	/A	OAVG	OOBP	PR	/A	PF	CPI	WAT	PB	PD	TPI
1909	Chi-N	4	4	.500	13	7	4	1	0	79	64	7.3	0	28	3.2	32	3.6	1.82	136	.225	.298	7	6	95	115	-1.0	-0	-0	0.6
1914	Cle-A	9	15	.375	37	26	12	3	0	198	189	8.6	3	118	5.4	112	5.1	3.09	94	.265	.374	-8	-4	106	**126**	0.9	-6	-3	-0.7
1915	Cle-A	6	14	.300	29	22	7	0	0	151	156	9.3	4	77	4.6	69	4.1	3.52	89	.277	.370	-10	-6	106	118	-2.1	-3	-3	-1.1
1916	Cle-A	0	0	—	2	0	0	0	0	4	5	11.3	1	2	4.5	1	2.3	11.25	25	.333	.474	-4	-4	99	76	0.0	-0	0	-0.3
Total	4	19	33	.365	81	55	23	4	0	432	414	8.6	8	225	4.7	214	4.5	3.08	94	.263	.360	-14	-9	104	121	-2.2	-9	-6	-1.5

■ **NOODLES HAHN** Hahn, Frank George b: 4/29/1879, Nashville, Tenn. d: 2/6/60, Candler, N.C. BL/TL, 5'9", 160 lbs. Deb: 4/18/1899

YEAR	TM/L	W	L	PCT	G	GS	CG	SHO	SV	IP	H	H/G	HR	BB	BB/G	SO	SO/G	ERA	/A	OAVG	OOBP	PR	/A	PF	CPI	WAT	PB	PD	TPI
1899	Cin-N	23	8	.742	38	34	32	4	0	309	280	8.2	3	68	2.0	**145**	4.2	2.68	151	.264	.308	40	47	105	87	7.4	-5	-4	3.8
1900	Cin-N	16	19	.457	38	36	28	**4**	0	303	296	8.8	4	88	2.6	127	3.8	3.30	104	.278	.333	14	5	93	89	0.5	1	1	0.5
1901	Cin-N	22	19	.537	42	42	**41**	2	0	**375**	370	8.9	12	69	1.7	**239**	5.7	2.71	122	.281	.320	25	25	100	108	**6.8**	-2	-1	2.5
1902	Cin-N	23	12	.657	36	36	35	6	0	321	282	7.9	2	58	1.6	142	4.0	1.77	170	.259	.301	36	44	108	115	6.6	1	-3	4.7
1903	Cin-N	22	12	.647	34	34	34	5	0	296	297	9.0	3	47	1.4	127	3.9	2.52	139	.287	.323	25	32	107	106	5.1	-2	-1	3.1
1904	Cin-N	16	18	.471	35	34	33	2	0	298	258	7.8	4	35	**1.1**	98	3.0	2.05	148	.258	.287	22	33	111	96	-3.7	0	-1	3.6
1905	Cin-N	5	3	.625	13	8	5	1	0	77	85	9.9	0	9	1.1	17	2.0	2.81	110	.310	.336	2	2	103	113	0.9	-0	-3	0.0
1906	NY-A	3	2	.600	6	6	3	1	0	42	38	8.1	0	6	1.3	17	3.6	3.86	82	.266	.295	-5	-3	118	56	0.0	1	-1	-0.3
Total	8	130	93	.583	242	230	211	25	0	2021	1906	8.5	28	380	1.7	912	4.1	2.55	133	.273	.313	158	189	104	100	23.6	-5	-11	17.9

■ **FRED HAHN** Hahn, Frederick Aloys b: 2/16/29, Nyack, N.Y. d: 8/16/84, Valhalla, N.Y. BR/TL, 6'3", 174 lbs. Deb: 4/19/52

YEAR	TM/L	W	L	PCT	G	GS	CG	SHO	SV	IP	H	H/G	HR	BB	BB/G	SO	SO/G	ERA	/A	OAVG	OOBP	PR	/A	PF	CPI	WAT	PB	PD	TPI
1952	StL-N	0	0	—	1	0	0	0	0	2	2	9.0	0	1	4.5	0	0.0	0.00	—	.250	.333	1	1	97	0	0.0	0	0	0.1

■ **HAL HAID** Haid, Harold Augustine b: 12/21/1897, Barberton, Ohio d: 8/13/52, Los Angeles, Cal. BR/TR, 5'10.5", 150 lbs. Deb: 9/05/19

YEAR	TM/L	W	L	PCT	G	GS	CG	SHO	SV	IP	H	H/G	HR	BB	BB/G	SO	SO/G	ERA	/A	OAVG	OOBP	PR	/A	PF	CPI	WAT	PB	PD	TPI
1919	StL-A	0	0	—	1	0	0	0	0	2	5	22.5	0	3	13.5	1	4.5	18.00	17	.556	.667	-3	-3	98	85	0.0	0	0	-0.2
1928	StL-N	2	2	.500	27	0	0	0	**5**	47	39	7.5	1	11	2.1	21	4.0	2.30	168	.218	.255	9	8	97	70	-0.3	1	0	0.9
1929	StL-N	9	9	.500	38	12	8	0	4	155	171	9.9	8	66	3.8	41	2.4	4.06	114	.284	.352	11	10	98	111	-0.2	-3	-1	0.5
1930	StL-N	3	2	.600	20	0	0	0	2	33	38	10.4	1	14	3.8	13	3.5	4.09	124	.297	.367	3	4	102	119	0.0	-0	1	0.4
1931	Bos-N	0	2	.000	27	0	0	0	1	56	59	9.5	3	16	2.6	20	3.2	4.50	87	.263	.317	-4	-4	102	78	-0.9	-1	2	-0.1
1933	Chi-A	0	0	—	6	0	0	0	0	15	18	10.8	2	13	7.8	7	4.2	7.80	57	.310	.434	-6	-6	103	98	0.0	0	0	-0.4
Total	6	14	15	.483	119	12	8	0	12	308	330	9.6	15	123	3.6	103	3.0	4.15	106	.275	.340	10	9	99	99	-1.4	-3	2	1.1

■ **JESSE HAINES** Haines, Jesse Joseph "Pop" b: 7/22/1893, Clayton, Ohio d: 8/5/78, Dayton, Ohio BR/TR, 6', 190 lbs. Deb: 7/20/18 CH

YEAR	TM/L	W	L	PCT	G	GS	CG	SHO	SV	IP	H	H/G	HR	BB	BB/G	SO	SO/G	ERA	/A	OAVG	OOBP	PR	/A	PF	CPI	WAT	PB	PD	TPI
1918	Cin-N	0	0	—	1	0	0	0	0	5	5	9.0	0	1	1.8	2	3.6	1.80	148	.294	.300	1	0	96	188	0.0	0	0	0.1
1920	StL-N	13	20	.394	**47**	37	19	4	2	302	303	9.0	9	80	2.4	120	3.6	2.98	103	.270	.312	5	3	98	104	-3.7	-1	-5	-0.3
1921	StL-N	18	12	.600	37	29	13	3	0	244	261	9.6	15	56	2.1	84	3.1	3.50	100	.286	.321	8	-0	93	108	1.3	-3	2	-0.1
1922	StL-N	11	9	.550	29	26	11	2	0	183	207	10.2	10	45	2.2	62	3.0	3.84	107	.284	.319	5	6	100	96	0.0	-2	1	0.4
1923	StL-N	20	13	.606	37	36	23	1	0	266	283	9.6	7	75	2.5	73	2.5	3.11	115	.275	.320	26	14	90	110	3.7	-1	0	1.1
1924	StL-N	8	19	.296	35	31	16	1	0	223	275	11.1	14	66	2.7	69	2.8	4.40	90	.309	.352	-13	-11	103	108	-4.5	-3	-1	-1.3
1925	StL-N	13	14	.481	29	25	15	0	0	207	234	10.2	11	52	2.3	63	2.7	4.57	94	.290	.325	-7	-6	101	87	-0.6	-2	-1	-0.7
1926	StL-N	13	4	.765	33	21	14	3	1	183	186	9.1	10	48	2.4	46	2.3	3.25	118	.265	.308	12	12	100	103	4.0	-0	-3	0.8
1927	StL-N	24	10	.706	38	36	**25**	**6**	1	301	273	8.2	11	77	2.3	89	2.7	2.72	152	.245	.289	40	47	106	101	**5.3**	-2	1	4.9
1928	StL-N	20	8	.714	33	28	20	1	0	240	238	8.9	14	72	2.7	77	2.9	3.19	121	.266	.314	21	18	97	110	4.1	-1	-3	1.4
1929	StL-N	13	10	.565	28	25	12	0	0	180	230	11.5	21	73	3.7	59	3.0	5.70	81	.313	.371	-20	-22	98	100	1.4	-2	-4	-2.4
1930	StL-N	13	8	.619	29	24	14	0	1	182	215	10.6	15	54	2.7	68	3.4	4.30	118	.298	.343	14	15	102	109	0.6	1	-3	1.2
1931	StL-N	12	3	.800	19	17	8	2	0	122	134	9.9	2	28	2.1	27	2.0	3.02	132	.278	.316	11	13	103	111	3.3	-3	-1	1.0
1932	StL-N	3	5	.375	20	10	4	1	0	85	116	12.3	4	16	1.7	27	2.9	4.76	82	.326	.348	-8	-8	101	104	-0.7	0	-1	-0.7
1933	StL-N	9	6	.600	32	10	5	0	1	115	113	8.8	3	37	2.9	37	2.9	2.50	134	.252	.303	11	11	100	117	1.1	-2	-2	0.8
1934	StL-N	4	4	.500	37	6	0	0	1	90	86	8.6	6	19	1.9	17	1.7	3.50	129	.262	.301	**6**	**10**	111	103	-0.7	-1	2	1.1

YEAR	TM/L	W	L	PCT	G	GS	CG	SHO	SV	IP	H	H/G	HR	BB	BB/G	SO	SO/G	ERA	/A	OAVG	OOBP	PR	/A	PF	CPI	WAT	PB	PD	TPI
1935	StL-N	6	5	.545	30	12	3	0	2	115	110	8.6	4	28	2.2	24	1.9	3.60	112	.252	.295	5	6	100	83	-0.6	1	-2	0.5
1936	StL-N	7	5	.583	25	9	4	0	1	99	110	10.0	4	21	1.9	19	1.7	3.91	97	.284	.316	1	-1	95	96	0.3	-1	0	-0.1
1937	StL-N	3	3	.500	16	6	2	0	0	66	81	11.0	5	23	3.1	18	2.5	4.50	87	.303	.355	-4	-4	100	111	-0.1	-0	-1	-0.5
Total 19		210	158	.571	555	388	208	24	10	3208	3460	9.7	165	871	2.4	981	2.8	3.64	108	.280	.322	113	102	99	104	14.2	-21	-21	7.2

■ **JIM HAISLIP**   Haislip, James Clifton "Slim"   b: 8/4/1891, Farmersville, Tex.   d: 1/22/70, Dallas, Tex.   BR/TR, 6'1", 186 lbs.   Deb: 8/27/13

YEAR	TM/L	W	L	PCT	G	GS	CG	SHO	SV	IP	H	H/G	HR	BB	BB/G	SO	SO/G	ERA	/A	OAVG	OOBP	PR	/A	PF	CPI	WAT	PB	PD	TPI
1913	Phi-N	0	0	—	1	0	0	0	0	3	4	12.0	0	3	9.0	0	0.0	6.00	59	.400	.438	-1	-1	111	137	0.0	-0	0	0.0

■ **ED HALBRITER**   Halbriter, Edward L.   b: 2/2/1860, Auburn, N.Y.   d: 8/9/36, Los Angeles, Cal.   Deb: 5/23/1882

| 1882 | Phi-a | 0 | 1 | .000 | 1 | 1 | 1 | 0 | 0 | 8 | 17 | 19.1 | 1 | 4 | 4.5 | 4 | 4.5 | 7.88 | 38 | .435 | .487 | -5 | -4 | 111 | 127 | -0.4 | -1 | 0 | -0.3 |

■ **DAD HALE**   Hale, Ray Luther   b: 2/18/1879, Allegan, Mich.   d: 2/1/46, Allegan, Mich.   BR/TR, 5'10", 180 lbs.   Deb: 4/21/02

| 1902 | Bos-N | 0 | 3 | .000 | 8 | 6 | 3 | 0 | 0 | 47 | 69 | 13.2 | 1 | 18 | 3.4 | 12 | 2.3 | 6.32 | 41 | .367 | .422 | -18 | -19 | 94 | 87 | -1.4 | -1 | -0 | -1.7 |
| | Bal-A | 1 | 0 | 1.000 | 3 | 2 | 1 | 0 | 0 | 14 | 21 | 13.5 | 0 | 6 | 3.9 | 6 | 3.9 | 4.50 | 83 | .374 | .434 | -1 | -1 | 104 | 131 | -0.4 | -1 | -1 | -0.1 |

■ **ED HALICKI**   Halicki, Edward Louis   b: 10/4/50, Newark, N.J.   BR/TR, 6'7", 220 lbs.   Deb: 7/08/74

1974	SF-N	1	8	.111	16	11	3	0	0	74	84	10.2	6	31	3.8	40	4.9	4.26	93	.275	.336	-5	-2	109	98	-3.3	1	-1	-0.1
1975	SF-N	9	13	.409	24	23	7	2	0	160	143	8.0	6	59	3.3	153	8.6	3.49	106	.240	.302	3	4	102	82	-2.1	-1	-0	0.2
1976	SF-N	12	14	.462	32	31	8	4	0	186	171	8.3	10	61	3.0	130	6.3	3.63	101	.246	.304	-3	1	104	86	0.1	1	-0	0.1
1977	SF-N	16	12	.571	37	37	7	2	0	258	241	8.4	27	70	2.4	168	5.9	3.31	124	.244	.296	17	23	105	97	3.3	2	-3	2.3
1978	SF-N	9	10	.474	29	28	9	4	1	199	166	7.5	11	45	2.0	105	4.7	2.85	114	.221	.266	16	9	91	77	-1.4	-1	-2	0.5
1979	SF-N	5	8	.385	33	19	3	1	0	126	134	9.6	12	47	3.4	61	5.8	4.57	76	.266	.327	-12	-15	93	87	-0.8	1	-1	-1.3
1980	SF-N	0	0	—	11	2	0	0	0	25	29	10.4	5	10	3.6	14	5.0	5.40	64	.293	.355	-5	-5	96	104	0.0	-0	-0	-0.5
	Cal-A	3	1	.750	10	6	2	0	0	35	39	10.0	5	11	2.8	16	4.1	4.89	80	.279	.327	-3	-4	97	91	1.2	0	-1	-0.3
Total 7		55	66	.455	192	157	36	13	1	1063	1007	8.5	82	334	2.8	707	6.0	3.62	102	.247	.302	8	9	100	88	-3.0	3	-7	0.9

■ **DREW HALL**   Hall, Andrew Clark   b: 3/27/63, Louisville, Ky.   BL/TL, 6'5", 200 lbs.   Deb: 9/14/86

1986	Chi-N	1	2	.333	5	4	1	0	1	24	24	9.0	3	10	3.8	21	7.9	4.50	89	.267	.337	-2	-1	108	99	-0.3	0	-0	-0.1
1987	Chi-N	1	1	.500	21	1	0	0	1	33	40	10.9	4	14	3.8	20	5.5	6.82	61	.308	.367	-10	-10	102	82	0.1	-0	-0	-0.9
1988	Chi-N	1	1	.500	19	0	0	0	1	22	26	10.6	4	9	3.7	22	9.0	7.77	47	.295	.350	-11	-10	105	75	0.0	-0	-0	-0.9
Total 3		3	4	.429	45	4	1	0	3	79	90	10.3	11	33	3.8	63	7.2	6.38	62	.292	.350	-23	-21	104	85	-0.2	-0	-0	-1.9

■ **SEA LION HALL**   Hall, Charles Louis (born Carlos Clolo)   b: 7/27/1885, Ventura, Cal.   d: 12/6/43, Ventura, Cal.   BL/TR, 6'1", 187 lbs.   Deb: 7/12/06

1906	Cin-N	4	8	.333	14	9	9	1	1	95	86	8.1	1	50	4.7	49	4.6	3.32	92	.275	.388	-7	-3	116	105	-1.3	-2	-0	-0.2
1907	Cin-N	4	2	.667	11	8	5	0	0	68	51	6.8	0	43	5.7	25	3.3	2.51	93	.238	.375	-0	-1	95	110	1.3	2	-1	-0.2
1909	Bos-A	4	6	.600	11	7	3	0	0	59	59	8.9	0	17	2.6	27	4.1	2.55	105	.271	.332	-1	0	108	116	0.2	-1	0	0.1
1910	Bos-A	12	9	.571	35	16	13	0	2	189	142	6.8	6	73	3.5	95	4.5	1.90	129	.207	.292	13	12	97	106	1.1	3	0	1.8
1911	Bos-A	8	7	.533	32	10	6	4	1	146	149	9.2	3	72	4.4	83	5.1	3.76	88	.279	.370	-7	-7	99	106	0.4	-1	-2	-0.9
1912	Bos-A	15	8	.652	34	20	9	2	2	191	178	8.4	3	70	3.3	83	3.9	3.02	113	.257	.329	7	9	102	106	-0.6	5	1	0.9
1913	Bos-A	4	4	.500	35	4	2	0	3	105	97	8.3	1	46	3.9	48	4.1	3.43	88	.235	.319	-6	-5	103	73	-0.1	1	-0	-0.5
1916	StL-N	0	4	.000	10	5	2	0	1	43	45	9.4	1	14	2.9	15	3.1	5.44	48	.280	.328	-13	-13	100	65	-1.9	-1	-1	-1.3
1918	Det-A	0	1	.000	6	1	0	0	0	13	14	9.7	1	6	4.2	2	1.4	6.92	39	.269	.328	-6	-6	99	56	-0.4	-0	-0	-0.6
Total 9		53	47	.530	188	80	49	3	13	910	821	8.1	16	391	3.9	427	4.2	3.09	95	.250	.336	-20	-15	102	100	-1.3	7	-3	-0.9

■ **BERT HALL**   Hall, Herbert Ernest   b: 10/15/1888, Portland, Ore.   d: 7/18/48, Seattle, Wash.   BR/TR, 5'10", 178 lbs.   Deb: 8/21/11

| 1911 | Phi-N | 0 | 1 | .000 | 7 | 1 | 0 | 0 | 0 | 18 | 19 | 9.5 | 0 | 13 | 6.5 | 9 | 4.5 | 4.00 | 92 | .297 | .423 | -1 | -1 | 108 | 130 | -0.4 | 0 | -1 | 0.0 |

■ **HERB HALL**   Hall, Herbert Silas "Iron Duke"   b: 6/5/1893, Steelville, Ill.   d: 7/1/70, Fresno, Cal.   BB/TR, 6'4", 220 lbs.   Deb: 4/28/18

| 1918 | Det-A | 0 | 0 | — | 3 | 0 | 0 | 0 | 0 | 6 | 12 | 18.0 | 0 | 7 | 10.5 | 1 | 1.5 | 15.00 | 18 | .500 | .636 | -8 | -8 | 99 | 84 | 0.0 | -0 | 0 | -0.7 |

■ **JOHN HALL**   Hall, John Sylvester   b: 1/9/24, Muskogee, Okla.   BR/TR, 6'2.5", 170 lbs.   Deb: 4/21/48

| 1948 | Bro-N | 0 | 0 | — | 3 | 0 | 0 | 0 | 0 | 4 | 4 | 9.0 | 1 | 2 | 4.5 | 2 | 4.5 | 6.75 | 60 | .267 | .316 | -1 | -1 | 103 | 85 | 0.0 | 0 | 0 | 0.0 |

■ **MARC HALL**   Hall, Marcus   b: 8/12/1887, Joplin, Mo.   d: 2/24/15, Joplin, Mo.   BR/TR,   Deb: 8/20/10

1910	StL-A	1	7	.125	8	7	5	0	0	46	50	9.8	0	31	6.1	25	4.9	4.30	59	.289	.406	-9	-9	101	109	-2.3	-2	1	-0.8
1913	Det-A	10	12	.455	30	21	8	1	0	165	154	8.4	1	79	4.3	69	3.8	3.27	90	.255	.344	-6	-6	101	97	0.5	-3	0	-0.5
1914	Det-A	4	6	.400	25	8	1	0	0	90	88	8.8	1	27	2.7	18	1.8	2.70	103	.267	.322	0	1	102	110	-1.1	-2	0	0.1
Total 3		15	25	.375	63	36	14	1	0	301	292	8.7	2	137	4.1	112	3.3	3.26	87	.264	.348	-15	-14	101	103	-2.9	-7	1	-1.2

■ **DICK HALL**   Hall, Richard Wallace   b: 9/27/30, St.Louis, Mo.   BR/TR, 6'6", 200 lbs.   Deb: 4/15/52

1955	Pit-N	6	6	.500	15	13	4	0	1	94	92	8.8	8	28	2.7	46	4.4	3.93	104	.253	.304	1	1	101	86	1.2	1	-2	0.1
1956	Pit-N	0	7	.000	19	9	1	0	1	62	64	9.3	8	21	3.0	27	3.9	4.79	81	.270	.318	-7	-6	103	87	-3.4	2	-1	-0.2
1957	Pit-N	0	0	—	8	0	0	0	0	10	17	15.3	4	5	4.5	7	6.3	10.80	34	.362	.434	-8	-8	96	91	-0.0	-0	-0	-0.7
1959	Pit-N	0	0	—	2	1	0	0	0	9	12	12.0	1	1	1.0	3	3.0	3.00	136	.333	.333	1	1	104	177	0.1	-0	1	0.1
1960	KC-A	8	13	.381	29	28	9	1	0	182	183	9.0	28	38	1.9	79	3.9	4.05	97	.261	.296	-4	-3	101	95	0.1	-2	-0	-0.5
1961	Bal-A	7	5	.583	29	13	4	2	4	122	102	7.5	10	30	2.2	92	6.8	3.10	125	.227	.270	13	10	96	84	0.0	-1	1	1.1
1962	Bal-A	6	6	.500	43	6	1	0	6	118	102	7.8	9	19	1.4	71	5.4	2.29	165	.230	.259	22	19	95	104	0.3	-1	0	2.1
1963	Bal-A	5	5	.500	47	3	0	0	12	112	91	7.3	12	16	1.3	74	5.9	2.97	114	.224	.255	8	5	93	87	-0.2	6	1	1.2
1964	Bal-A	9	1	.900	44	0	0	0	7	88	58	5.9	8	16	1.6	52	5.3	1.84	204	.188	.226	17	19	103	88	3.8	-0	0	2.0
1965	Bal-A	11	8	.579	48	0	0	0	12	94	84	8.0	8	11	1.1	79	7.6	3.06	112	.243	.258	4	4	99	88	0.0	3	1	0.5
1966	Bal-A	6	2	.750	32	0	0	0	7	66	59	8.0	9	8	1.1	44	6.0	3.95	86	.233	.261	-4	-4	99	72	1.5	0	-0	-0.3
1967	Phi-N	10	8	.556	48	1	0	0	8	86	83	8.7	5	12	1.3	49	5.1	2.20	160	.255	.280	11	13	104	132	1.4	-1	1	1.4
1968	Phi-N	4	1	.800	32	0	0	0	0	46	53	10.4	6	5	1.0	31	6.1	4.89	60	.296	.307	-10	-10	99	89	1.6	0	-0	-1.0
1969	Bal-A	5	2	.714	39	0	0	0	6	66	49	6.7	9	12	1.2	31	4.2	1.91	191	.213	.240	13	13	100	94	0.5	-1	1	1.4
1970	Bal-A	10	5	.667	32	0	0	0	3	61	51	7.5	8	6	0.9	30	4.4	3.10	113	.229	.246	4	3	94	83	0.6	-1	-1	0.1
1971	Bal-A	6	6	.500	27	0	0	0	1	43	52	10.9	4	11	2.3	26	5.4	5.02	69	.302	.330	-7	-7	100	97	-1.3	1	-1	-0.8
Total 16		93	75	.554	495	74	20	3	68	1259	1152	8.2	130	236	1.7	741	5.3	3.32	111	.244	.276	55	50	99	93	5.1	9	-5	6.6

■ **BOB HALL**   Hall, Robert Lewis   b: 12/22/23, Swissvale, Pa.   d: 3/12/83, St.Petersburg, Fla   BR/TR, 6'2", 195 lbs.   Deb: 4/23/49

1949	Bos-N	6	4	.600	31	6	2	0	0	74	77	9.4	7	41	5.0	43	5.2	4.38	89	.272	.357	-3	-4	97	110	1.2	2	-2	-0.3
1950	Bos-N	0	2	.000	21	4	0	0	0	50	58	10.4	8	33	5.9	22	4.0	7.02	50	.293	.392	-16	-19	85	89	-0.9	-0	-1	-1.8
1953	Pit-N	3	12	.200	37	17	6	1	1	152	172	10.2	17	72	4.3	68	4.0	5.39	85	.286	.358	-19	-14	106	97	-3.0	-0	-1	-1.3
Total 3		9	18	.333	89	27	8	1	1	276	307	10.0	32	146	4.8	133	4.3	5.41	77	.284	.364	-37	-37	100	97	-2.7	2	-3	-3.4

■ **TOM HALL**   Hall, Tom Edward   b: 11/23/47, Thomasville, N.C.   BL/TL, 6', 150 lbs.   Deb: 6/09/68

1968	Min-A	2	1	.667	8	4	0	0	0	30	27	8.1	1	12	3.6	18	5.4	2.40	131	.239	.315	2	3	106	126	0.5	-1	-0	0.1
1969	Min-A	8	7	.533	31	18	5	2	0	141	129	8.2	12	50	3.2	92	5.9	3.32	109	.243	.307	5	5	100	98	-0.8	1	-2	0.4
1970	Min-A	11	6	.647	52	11	1	0	4	155	94	5.5	11	66	3.8	184	10.7	2.55	141	.173	.262	20	18	97	69	1.0	-0	-2	1.6
1971	Min-A	4	7	.364	48	11	0	0	4	130	104	7.2	13	58	4.0	137	9.5	3.32	109	.216	.296	2	4	104	87	-1.1	2	1	0.7
1972	Cin-N	10	5	.909	47	7	1	1	8	124	77	5.6	13	56	4.1	134	9.7	2.61	121	.173	.265	12	7	91	79	4.3	-1	-2	0.9
1973	Cin-N	8	5	.615	54	7	0	0	8	104	74	6.4	13	48	4.2	96	8.3	3.46	97	.202	.288	2	1	92	85	0.1	-2	-2	-0.4
1974	Cin-N	3	1	.750	40	1	0	0	1	64	54	7.6	9	30	4.2	48	6.8	4.08	86	.232	.312	-3	-4	96	92	0.7	-0	-0	-0.4
1975	Cin-N	0	0	—	2	0	0	0	0	2	2	9.0	1	2	9.0	3	13.5	0.00	—	.250	.400	1	1	101	0	0.0	-0	0	-0.1
	NY-N	4	3	.571	34	4	0	0	1	61	58	8.6	10	31	4.6	48	7.1	4.72	73	.254	.338	-7	-9	95	100	0.5	-0	-0	-0.7
	Yr	4	3	.571	36	4	0	0	1	63	60	8.6	10	33	4.7	51	7.3	4.57	76	.254	.340	-7	-8	95	100	0.5	-0	-0	-0.7
1976	NY-N	1	1	.500	15	0	0	0	0	24	24	9.0	5	9	3.4	17	6.4	4.50	72	.267	.340	-1	-1	91	84	0.0	1	0	-0.1
	KC-A	1	0	1.000	16	0	0	0	0	30	28	8.4	4	18	5.4	25	7.5	5.40	77	.246	.343	-3	-3	99	98	0.0	0	0	0.1
1977	KC-A	0	0	—	6	0	0	0	0	8	4	4.5	2	6	6.8	10	11.3	3.38	119	.154	.313	1	-0	99	113	0.0	0	0	0.1
Total 10		52	33	.612	358	63	7	3	32	854	656	6.9	88	382	4.0	797	8.4	3.27	106	.211	.294	29	20	97	87	5.2	-0	-7	1.7

YEAR	TM/L	W	L	PCT	G	GS	CG	SHO	SV	IP	H	H/G	HR	BB	BB/G	SO	SO/G	ERA	/A	OAVG	OOBP	PR	/A	PF	CPI	WAT	PB	PD	TPI
■ BILL HALL	Hall, William Bernard "Beanie" b: 2/22/1894, Charleston, W.Va. d: 8/15/47, Newport, Ky. BR/TR, 6'2", 250 lbs. Deb: 7/04/13																												
1913	Bro-N	0	0	—	3	0	0	0	0	5	4	7.2	0	5	9.0	3	5.4	5.40	62	.267	.455	-1	-1	105	106	0.0	-0	0	0.0
■ JOHN HALLA	Halla, John Arthur b: 5/13/1884, St.Louis, Mo. d: 9/30/47, El Segundo, Cal. BL/TL, 5'11", 175 lbs. Deb: 8/27/05																												
1905	Cle-A	0	0	—	3	0	0	0	0	13	12	8.3	0	0	0.0	4	2.8	2.77	96	.269	.269	-0	-0	100	70	0.0	-0	0	0.0
■ BILL HALLAHAN	Hallahan, William Anthony "Wild Bill" b: 8/4/02, Binghamton, N.Y. d: 7/8/81, Binghamton, N.Y. BR/TL, 5'10.5", 170 lbs. Deb: 4/16/25																												
1925	StL-N	1	0	1.000	6	0	0	0	0	15	14	8.4	0	11	6.6	8	4.8	3.60	120	.259	.373	1	1	101	116	0.5	0	0	0.2
1926	StL-N	1	4	.200	19	3	0	0	0	57	45	7.1	1	32	5.1	28	4.4	3.63	105	.260	.368	1	1	100	114	-1.6	0	-1	0.1
1929	StL-N	4	4	.500	20	12	5	0	0	94	94	9.0	6	60	5.7	52	5.0	4.40	105	.269	.368	3	2	98	107	0.0	-1	1	0.2
1930	StL-N	15	9	.625	35	32	13	2	2	237	233	8.8	15	126	4.8	**177**	**6.7**	4.67	108	.260	.344	8	10	102	88	1.0	-6	-0	0.4
1931	StL-N	**19**	9	.679	37	30	16	3	4	249	242	8.7	10	112	4.0	**159**	5.7	3.29	121	.259	.335	16	19	103	113	1.1	-4	-2	1.3
1932	StL-N	12	7	.632	25	22	13	1	1	176	169	8.6	10	69	3.5	108	5.5	3.12	125	.253	.319	15	15	101	113	3.2	2	-1	1.7
1933	StL-N	16	13	.552	36	32	16	2	0	244	245	9.0	6	98	3.6	93	3.4	3.50	96	.260	.323	-5	-4	100	96	0.6	-0	-3	-0.7
1934	StL-N	8	12	.400	32	26	10	2	0	163	195	10.8	2	66	3.6	70	3.9	4.25	106	.294	.354	-3	5	111	102	-3.8	-2	-0	0.3
1935	StL-N	15	8	.652	40	23	8	2	1	181	196	9.7	7	57	2.8	73	3.6	3.43	118	.275	.324	12	12	100	111	1.0	-1	-1	1.0
1936	StL-N	2	2	.500	9	6	1	0	0	37	58	14.1	4	17	4.1	16	3.9	6.32	60	.360	.417	-9	-10	95	114	-0.1	3	0	-0.6
	Cin-N	5	9	.357	23	19	5	2	0	135	150	10.0	3	57	3.8	32	2.1	4.33	90	.287	.348	-5	-6	97	99	-1.8	1	1	-0.4
	Yr	7	11	.389	32	25	6	2	0	172	208	10.9	7	74	3.9	48	2.5	4.76	81	.305	.364	-14	-17	97	99	-1.9	3	1	-1.0
1937	Cin-N	3	9	.250	21	9	2	0	0	63	90	12.9	3	29	4.1	18	2.6	6.14	59	.345	.406	-16	-18	93	104	-1.9	-1	0	-1.6
1938	Phi-N	1	8	.111	21	10	1	0	0	89	107	10.8	4	45	4.6	22	2.2	5.46	73	.295	.371	-17	-14	106	90	-2.8	-0	-0	-1.3
Total	12	102	94	.520	324	224	90	14	8	1740	1838	9.5	71	779	4.0	856	4.4	4.03	102	.274	.344	2	13	101	103	-4.6	-9	-5	0.6
■ JACK HALLETT	Hallett, Jack Price b: 11/13/14, Toledo, Ohio d: 6/11/82, Toledo, Ohio BR/TR, 6'4", 215 lbs. Deb: 9/13/40																												
1940	Chi-A	1	1	.500	2	2	1	0	0	14	15	9.6	1	6	3.9	9	5.8	6.43	70	.273	.349	-3	-3	103	71	0.0	0	0	-0.1
1941	Chi-A	5	5	.500	22	6	3	0	0	75	96	11.5	7	35	4.2	25	3.0	6.00	65	.306	.373	-15	-18	94	94	0.0	0	0	-1.5
1942	Pit-N	0	1	.000	3	3	2	0	0	22	23	9.4	0	8	3.3	16	6.5	4.91	69	.274	.326	-4	-4	102	72	-0.4	2	0	-0.1
1943	Pit-N	1	2	.333	9	4	2	1	0	48	36	6.8	0	11	2.1	11	2.1	1.69	206	.212	.259	9	10	103	99	-0.4	2	-1	1.2
1946	Pit-N	5	7	.417	35	9	3	1	0	115	107	8.4	0	39	3.1	64	5.0	3.29	110	.267	.327	2	4	106	98	0.1	0	0	0.5
1948	NY-N	0	0	—	2	0	0	0	0	4	3	6.8	0	4	9.0	3	6.8	4.50	87	.214	.389	-0	-0	98	88	0.0	-0	0	0.0
Total	6	12	16	.429	73	24	11	2	0	278	280	9.1	8	103	3.3	128	4.1	4.05	92	.270	.333	-12	-11	101	93	-0.7	4	-1	0.0
■ BILL HALLMAN	Hallman, William Wilson b: 3/31/1867, Pittsburgh, Pa. d: 9/11/20, Philadelphia, Pa. BR/TR, 5'8", Deb: 1888 M																												
1896	Phi-N	0	0	—	1	0	0	0	0	2	4	18.0	0	2	9.0	0	0.0	18.00	25	.440	.541	-3	-3	102	55	0.0	0	0	-0.1
■ CHARLIE HALLSTROM	Hallstrom, Charles E. "Swedish Wonder" b: 1/22/1864, Jonkoping, Sweden d: 5/6/49, Chicago, Ill. Deb: 1885																												
1885	Pro-N	0	1	.000	1	1	1	0	0	9	18	18.0	3	6	6.0	0	0.0	11.00	24	.427	.498	-8	-8	93	106	-0.4	-1	0	-0.5
■ DOC HAMANN	Hamann, Elmer Joseph b: 12/21/1900, New Ulm, Minn. d: 1/11/73, Milwaukee, Wis. BR/TR, 6'1", 180 lbs. Deb: 9/21/22																												
1922	Cle-A	0	0	—	1	0	0	0	0	0	3	—	0	3	—	0	—	∞	—	1.000	1.000	-6	-6	103	48	0.0	0	0	-0.4
■ ROGER HAMBRIGHT	Hambright, Roger Dee b: 3/26/49, Sunnyside, Wash. BR/TR, 5'10", 180 lbs. Deb: 7/19/71																												
1971	NY-A	3	1	.750	18	0	0	0	2	27	22	7.3	5	10	3.3	14	4.7	4.33	77	.224	.291	-3	-3	97	84	1.0	0	0	-0.2
■ JOHN HAMILL	Hamill, John Alexander Charles b: 12/18/1860, New York, N.Y. d: 12/6/11, Bristol, R.I. BR/TR, 5'8", 158 lbs. Deb: 5/01/1884																												
1884	Was-a	2	17	.105	19	19	18	1	0	157	197	11.3	8	43	2.5	50	2.9	4.47	68	.316	.360	-21	-25	93	115	-5.0	-3	0	-2.4
■ DAVE HAMILTON	Hamilton, David Edward b: 12/13/47, Seattle, Wash. BL/TL, 6', 180 lbs. Deb: 5/29/72																												
1972	Oak-A	6	6	.500	25	14	1	0	0	101	94	8.4	7	31	2.8	55	4.9	2.94	99	.249	.301	1	-0	95	107	-1.0	2	0	0.1
1973	Oak-A	6	4	.600	16	11	1	0	0	70	74	9.5	8	24	3.1	34	4.4	4.37	75	.274	.334	-4	-9	86	97	0.3	0	-1	-0.9
1974	Oak-A	7	4	.636	29	18	1	1	0	117	104	8.0	10	48	3.7	69	5.3	3.15	113	.241	.320	6	5	99	111	1.1	0	-0	0.5
1975	Oak-A	1	2	.333	11	4	0	0	0	36	42	10.5	4	18	4.5	20	5.0	4.00	86	.290	.361	-1	-2	91	126	-0.6	0	0	-0.1
	Chi-A	6	5	.545	30	1	0	0	6	70	63	8.1	4	29	3.7	51	6.6	2.83	139	.246	.315	7	9	104	118	0.9	0	0	0.9
	Yr	7	7	.500	41	5	0	0	6	106	105	8.9	8	47	4.0	71	6.0	3.23	117	.261	.332	7	6	100	118	0.3	0	0	0.8
1976	Chi-A	6	6	.500	45	1	0	0	10	90	81	8.1	4	45	4.5	62	6.2	3.60	99	.243	.329	-1	-0	101	98	1.1	0	-1	0.0
1977	Chi-A	4	5	.444	55	0	0	0	9	67	71	9.5	6	33	4.4	45	6.0	3.63	111	.270	.339	3	3	99	120	-0.8	0	0	0.3
1978	StL-N	0	0	—	13	0	0	0	0	14	16	10.3	5	6	3.9	8	5.1	6.43	53	.296	.355	-4	-5	96	109	0.0	-0	0	-0.4
	Pit-N	0	2	.000	16	0	0	0	1	26	23	8.0	2	12	4.2	15	5.2	3.46	108	.221	.297	0	1	105	80	-0.9	-1	-0	0.0
	Yr	0	2	.000	29	0	0	0	1	40	39	8.8	7	18	4.0	23	5.2	4.50	81	.247	.317	-4	-4	102	80	-0.9	-0	-0	-0.4
1979	Oak-A	3	4	.429	40	7	1	0	5	83	80	8.7	5	43	4.7	52	5.6	3.69	105	.261	.343	5	2	91	112	0.5	0	0	0.2
1980	Oak-A	0	3	.000	21	1	0	0	0	30	44	13.2	6	28	8.4	23	6.9	11.40	33	.344	.457	-25	-25	94	78	-1.4	0	-0	-2.3
Total	9	39	41	.488	301	57	4	1	31	704	692	8.8	61	317	4.1	434	5.5	3.85	93	.259	.334	-11	-22	96	107	-0.8	1	-2	-1.7
■ EARL HAMILTON	Hamilton, Earl Andrew b: 7/19/1891, Gibson, Ill. d: 11/17/68, Anaheim, Cal. BL/TL, 5'8", 160 lbs. Deb: 4/14/11																												
1911	StL-A	5	12	.294	32	17	10	1	0	177	191	9.7	4	69	3.5	55	2.8	3.97	84	.284	.354	-12	-13	100	96	0.0	-1	1	-1.2
1912	StL-A	11	14	.440	41	26	17	1	2	250	228	8.2	2	86	3.1	139	5.0	3.24	106	.248	.319	3	5	103	89	2.1	-0	-2	0.3
1913	StL-A	13	12	.520	31	24	19	3	1	217	197	8.2	3	83	3.4	101	4.2	2.57	111	.241	.318	9	7	98	103	3.4	-1	-1	0.6
1914	StL-A	17	18	.486	44	35	20	5	2	302	265	7.9	5	100	3.0	111	3.3	2.50	109	.239	.307	8	8	100	99	0.9	4	-4	0.3
1915	StL-A	9	17	.346	35	27	13	1	0	204	203	9.0	4	69	3.0	63	2.8	2.87	102	.274	.346	2	1	99	**126**	-2.2	-2	-2	-0.3
1916	StL-A	0	0	—	1	0	0	0	0	4	4	9.0	0	4	9.0	0	0.0	9.00	30	.250	.400	-3	-3	94	48	0.0	0	-0	-0.2
	Det-A	1	2	.333	5	5	3	0	0	37	34	8.3	0	22	5.4	7	1.7	2.68	109	.254	.375	1	1	103	140	-0.5	-1	1	0.1
	StL-A	5	7	.417	22	12	3	0	0	91	97	9.6	2	26	2.6	25	2.5	3.07	87	.284	.339	-2	-4	94	116	-1.1	-1	-1	-0.6
	Yr	6	9	.400	28	17	6	0	0	132	135	9.2	2	52	3.5	32	2.2	3.14	87	.273	.344	-5	-6	97	116	-1.6	-1	-0	-0.7
1917	StL-A	0	9	.000	27	8	2	0	1	83	86	9.3	1	41	4.4	19	2.1	3.14	83	.274	.361	-4	-5	98	118	-4.4	3	-1	-0.2
1918	Pit-N	6	0	1.000	6	6	6	1	0	54	47	7.8	0	13	2.2	20	3.3	0.83	347	.242	.286	12	12	105	265	3.0	1	0	1.7
1919	Pit-N	8	11	.421	28	19	9	1	1	160	167	9.4	3	49	2.8	39	2.2	3.32	92	.280	.328	-7	-5	105	109	-1.8	-2	2	-0.5
1920	Pit-N	10	13	.435	39	23	12	0	3	230	223	8.7	2	69	2.7	74	2.9	3.25	98	.258	.304	-3	-2	101	80	-1.9	-3	0	-0.4
1921	Pit-N	13	15	.464	35	30	12	2	0	225	237	9.5	5	58	2.3	59	2.4	3.36	114	.272	.313	11	12	102	94	-3.3	-0	4	1.5
1922	Pit-N	11	7	.611	33	14	9	1	2	160	183	10.3	6	40	2.3	34	1.9	3.99	104	.296	.327	2	3	101	98	1.3	-2	-1	0.0
1923	Pit-N	7	9	.438	28	15	5	0	1	141	148	9.4	6	42	2.7	42	2.7	3.77	101	.271	.314	4	1	95	91	-1.9	-1	2	0.1
1924	Phi-N	0	1	.000	3	0	0	0	0	6	9	13.5	0	2	3.0	2	3.0	10.50	41	.391	.462	-4	-4	111	68	-0.4	-0	0	-0.3
Total	14	116	147	.441	410	261	140	16	13	2341	2319	8.9	43	773	3.0	790	3.0	3.16	102	.264	.324	13	15	100	104	-6.8	-9	-4	0.9
■ JACK HAMILTON	Hamilton, Jack Edwin b: 12/25/38, Burlington, Iowa BR/TR, 6', 200 lbs. Deb: 4/13/62																												
1962	Phi-N	9	12	.429	41	26	4	1	2	182	185	9.1	18	107	5.3	101	5.0	5.09	74	.268	.362	-23	-27	95	94	-1.7	-4	2	-2.6
1963	Phi-N	2	1	.667	19	1	0	0	1	30	22	6.6	3	17	5.1	23	6.9	5.40	62	.200	.302	-7	-7	102	54	0.4	-0	1	-0.6
1964	Det-A	0	1	.000	5	1	0	0	0	15	24	14.4	2	8	4.8	5	3.0	8.40	41	.364	.429	-8	-8	95	93	-0.4	-0	1	-0.7
1965	Det-A	1	1	.500	4	1	0	0	0	4	6	13.5	1	4	9.0	3	6.8	15.75	23	.316	.400	-5	-5	104	53	0.0	0	0	-0.4
1966	NY-N	6	13	.316	57	13	3	1	13	149	138	8.3	13	88	5.3	93	5.6	3.93	89	.248	.349	-5	-7	97	107	-2.3	-1	1	-0.7
1967	NY-N	2	0	1.000	17	1	0	0	1	31	24	7.0	2	16	4.6	22	6.4	3.77	91	.205	.304	-1	-1	102	71	1.0	1	-0	0.0
	Cal-A	9	6	.600	26	20	0	0	0	119	104	7.9	6	63	4.8	74	5.6	3.25	95	.239	.331	-0	-2	96	110	1.3	-0	-0	-0.2
1968	Cal-A	3	1	.750	21	2	1	0	2	38	34	8.1	0	15	3.6	18	4.3	3.32	86	.246	.312	-1	-2	96	88	1.2	-0	-0	-0.2
1969	Cle-A	0	2	.000	20	0	0	0	1	31	37	10.7	2	23	6.7	13	3.8	4.35	80	.316	.420	-3	-3	96	141	-0.9	-0	-0	-0.3
	Chi-A	0	3	.000	8	0	0	0	0	12	23	17.3	1	7	5.3	5	3.8	12.00	33	.411	.462	-11	-11	110	75	-1.4	0	0	-0.9
	Yr	0	5	.000	28	0	0	0	1	43	60	12.6	3	30	6.3	18	3.8	6.49	56	.345	.433	-14	-14	100	75	-2.3	-0	-0	-1.2
Total	8	32	40	.444	218	65	8	2	20	611	597	8.8	48	348	5.1	357	5.3	4.54	76	.259	.352	-66	-73	97	98	-2.8	-5	4	-6.6
■ STEVE HAMILTON	Hamilton, Steve Absher b: 11/30/35, Columbia, Ky. BL/TL, 6'6", 190 lbs. Deb: 4/23/61 C																												
1961	Cle-A	0	0	—	2	0	0	0	0	3	2	6.0	0	3	9.0	4	12.0	3.00	129	.200	.333	0	0	97	123	0.0	0	0	0.1
1962	Was-A	3	8	.273	41	10	1	0	2	107	103	8.7	10	39	3.3	83	7.0	3.79	107	.248	.311	2	3	102	94	-1.5	-1	1	0.3

YEAR	TM/L	W	L	PCT	G	GS	CG	SHO	SV	IP	H	H/G	HR	BB	BB/G	SO	SO/G	ERA	/A	OAVG	OOBP	PR	/A	PF	CPI	WAT	PB	PD	TPI
1963	Was-A	0	1	.000	3	0	0	0	0	2	5	22.5	0	2	9.0	1	4.5	13.50	27	.556	.538	-2	-2	101	105	-0.4	0	0	-0.1
	NY-A	5	1	.833	34	0	0	0	5	62	49	7.1	3	24	3.5	63	9.1	2.61	136	.220	.290	7	7	98	103	1.6	1	1	0.9
	Yr	5	2	.714	37	0	0	0	5	64	54	7.6	3	26	3.7	64	9.0	2.95	121	.232	.302	5	4	98	103	1.2	0	1	0.8
1964	NY-A	7	2	.778	30	3	1	0	3	60	55	8.3	6	15	2.3	49	7.4	3.30	111	.246	.285	2	2	101	96	2.0	1	0	0.3
1965	NY-A	3	1	.750	46	1	0	0	5	58	47	7.3	2	16	2.5	51	7.9	1.40	250	.214	.262	13	14	101	136	1.1	0	-2	1.3
1966	NY-A	8	3	.727	44	3	1	1	3	90	69	6.9	8	22	2.2	57	5.7	3.00	107	.218	.266	4	2	94	90	2.9	-1	-1	0.0
1967	NY-A	2	4	.333	44	0	0	0	4	62	57	8.3	7	23	3.3	55	8.0	3.48	89	.250	.310	-2	-3	96	112	-0.7	-0	0	-0.2
1968	NY-A	2	2	.500	40	0	0	0	11	51	37	6.5	0	13	2.3	42	7.4	2.12	142	.211	.262	5	5	101	86	0.0	0	0	0.6
1969	NY-A	3	4	.429	38	0	0	0	2	57	39	6.2	7	21	3.3	39	6.2	3.32	105	.194	.267	2	1	96	75	-0.4	-1	-1	0.0
1970	NY-A	4	3	.571	35	0	0	0	3	45	36	7.2	3	16	3.2	33	6.6	2.80	121	.222	.285	5	3	91	97	0.0	-1	0	0.3
	Chi-A	0	0	—	3	0	0	0	0	3	4	12.0	0	1	3.0	3	9.0	6.00	67	.333	.357	-1	-1	108	83	0.0	0	0	0.0
	Yr	4	3	.571	38	0	0	0	3	48	40	7.5	3	17	3.2	36	6.8	3.00	115	.227	.285	4	2	92	83	0.0	-1	1	0.3
1971	SF-N	2	2	.500	39	0	0	0	4	45	29	5.8	4	11	2.2	38	7.6	3.00	114	.186	.237	2	2	99	59	-0.1	-0	-0	0.2
1972	Chi-N	1	0	1.000	22	0	0	0	0	17	24	12.7	1	8	4.2	13	6.9	4.76	81	.333	.393	-2	-2	112	127	0.5	-0	0	-0.1
Total	12	40	31	.563	421	17	3	1	42	662	556	7.6	51	214	2.9	531	7.2	3.06	114	.229	.287	36	32	98	96	5.0	-2	-0	3.6
■ LUKE HAMLIN	Hamlin, Luke Daniel "Hot Potato" b: 7/3/04, Ferris Center, Mich. d: 2/18/78, Clare, Mich. BL/TR, 6'2", 168 lbs. Deb: 9/18/33																												
1933	Det-A	1	0	1.000	3	3	0	0	0	17	20	10.6	3	10	5.3	10	5.3	4.76	96	.294	.375	-1	-0	107	132	0.5	1	-1	0.0
1934	Det-A	2	3	.400	20	5	1	0	1	75	87	10.4	11	44	5.3	30	3.6	5.40	78	.289	.376	-8	-10	94	108	-0.9	0	-0	-0.8
1937	Bro-N	11	13	.458	39	25	11	1	1	186	183	8.9	4	48	2.3	93	4.5	3.58	117	.252	.294	7	13	107	79	1.3	-1	-3	0.9
1938	Bro-N	12	15	.444	44	30	10	3	6	237	243	9.2	14	65	2.5	97	3.7	3.68	99	.263	.311	3	-1	96	95	-0.6	-2	-4	-0.7
1939	Bro-N	20	13	.606	40	36	19	2	0	270	255	8.5	27	54	1.8	88	2.9	3.63	114	.248	.281	9	16	106	85	2.6	-5	-4	0.7
1940	Bro-N	9	8	.529	33	25	9	2	0	182	183	9.0	17	34	1.7	91	4.5	3.07	134	.256	.289	16	21	106	111	-0.7	-5	-3	1.4
1941	Bro-N	8	8	.500	30	20	5	1	1	136	139	9.2	14	41	2.7	58	3.8	4.24	85	.261	.313	-9	-10	99	91	-1.9	-1	-1	-1.1
1942	Pit-N	4	4	.500	23	14	6	1	0	112	128	10.3	3	19	1.5	38	3.1	3.94	86	.281	.306	-8	-7	102	86	0.4	1	-2	-0.8
1944	Phi-A	6	12	.333	29	23	9	2	0	190	204	9.7	13	38	1.8	58	2.7	3.74	94	.271	.303	-7	-5	102	93	-2.7	3	-5	-0.6
Total	9	73	76	.490	261	181	70	12	9	1405	1442	9.2	106	353	2.3	563	3.6	3.77	103	.262	.304	2	16	102	93	-2.0	-9	-24	-1.0
■ PETE HAMM	Hamm, Peter Whitfield b: 9/20/47, Buffalo, N.Y. BR/TR, 6'5", 210 lbs. Deb: 7/29/70																												
1970	Min-A	0	2	.000	10	0	0	0	0	16	17	9.6	3	7	3.9	3	1.7	5.63	64	.262	.333	-3	-4	97	82	-0.9	-0	-1	-0.3
1971	Min-A	2	4	.333	13	8	1	0	0	44	55	11.3	7	18	3.7	16	3.3	6.75	54	.309	.368	-16	-15	104	85	-0.8	1	0	-1.3
Total	2	2	6	.250	23	8	1	0	0	60	72	10.8	10	25	3.8	19	2.9	6.45	56	.296	.359	-19	-19	102	84	-1.7	1	-0	-1.6
■ ATLEE HAMMAKER	Hammaker, Charlton Atlee b: 1/24/58, Carmel, Cal. BB/TL, 6'3", 200 lbs. Deb: 8/13/81																												
1981	KC-A	1	3	.250	10	6	0	0	0	39	44	10.2	2	12	2.8	11	2.5	5.54	65	.286	.331	-8	-8	99	72	-0.9	0	-1	-0.8
1982	SF-N	12	8	.600	29	27	4	1	0	175	189	9.7	16	28	1.4	102	5.2	4.11	82	.278	.302	-10	-14	94	91	1.5	-4	1	-1.6
1983	SF-N	10	9	.526	23	23	8	3	0	172	147	7.7	9	32	**1.7**	127	6.6	**2.25**	**163**	.228	**.262**	27	27	101	96	0.8	-1	1	2.9
1984	SF-N	2	0	1.000	6	6	0	0	0	33	32	8.7	2	9	2.5	24	6.5	2.18	161	.256	.295	5	5	98	148	1.0	1	0	0.6
1985	SF-N	5	12	.294	29	29	1	1	0	171	161	8.5	17	47	2.5	100	5.3	3.74	91	.247	.292	-3	-6	95	88	-2.0	-2	1	-0.8
1987	SF-N	10	10	.500	31	27	2	0	0	168	159	8.5	22	57	3.1	107	5.7	3.59	108	.248	.310	9	5	95	107	-1.0	-1	-1	0.3
1988	SF-N	9	9	.500	43	17	3	1	5	145	136	8.4	11	41	2.5	65	4.0	3.72	87	.248	.297	-4	-8	93	89	-0.1	-0	2	-0.6
Total	7	49	51	.490	171	135	18	6	5	903	868	8.7	79	226	2.3	536	5.3	3.52	100	.252	.294	16	0	96	95	-0.7	-8	3	0.0
■ GRANNY HAMNER	Hamner, Granville Wilbur b: 4/26/27, Richmond, Va. BR/TR, 5'10", 163 lbs. Deb: 9/14/44																												
1956	Phi-N	0	1	.000	3	1	0	0	0	8	10	11.3	0	2	2.3	4	4.5	4.50	80	.294	.333	-1	-1	95	78	-0.4	1	0	0.0
1957	Phi-N	0	0	—	1	0	0	0	0	1	1	9.0	0	0	0.0	1	9.0	0.00	—	.250	.250	0	0	99	0	0.0	0	0	0.0
1962	KC-A	0	1	.000	3	0	0	0	0	4	10	22.5	0	6	13.5	0	0.0	9.00	45	.476	.593	-2	-2	101	154	-0.4	0	0	-0.1
Total	3	0	2	.000	7	1	0	0	0	13	21	14.5	0	8	5.5	5	3.5	5.54	68	.356	.433	-2	-3	97	96	-0.8	1	0	-0.1
■ RALPH HAMNER	Hamner, Ralph Conant "Bruz" b: 9/12/16, Gibsland, La. BR/TR, 6'3", 165 lbs. Deb: 4/28/46																												
1946	Chi-A	2	7	.222	25	7	1	0	1	71	80	10.1	2	39	4.9	29	3.7	4.44	77	.276	.368	-7	-8	97	98	-2.4	0	-1	-0.8
1947	Chi-N	1	2	.333	3	3	2	0	0	25	24	8.6	0	16	5.8	14	5.0	2.52	167	.267	.364	4	5	104	167	-0.3	-0	-0	0.4
1948	Chi-N	5	9	.357	27	17	5	0	0	111	110	8.9	12	69	5.6	53	4.3	4.70	80	.259	.364	-9	-12	95	103	-1.0	1	2	-0.8
1949	Chi-N	0	2	.000	6	1	0	0	0	12	22	16.5	1	8	6.0	3	2.3	9.00	44	.407	.477	-7	-7	97	105	-0.9	-0	1	-0.5
Total	4	8	20	.286	61	28	8	0	1	219	236	9.7	15	132	5.4	99	4.1	4.60	81	.275	.372	-19	-22	97	109	-4.6	0	2	-1.7
■ GARRY HANCOCK	Hancock, Ronald Garry b: 1/23/54, Tampa, Fla. BL/TL, 6', 175 lbs. Deb: 7/16/78																												
1984	Oak-A	0	0	—	1	0	0	0	0	1	0	0.0	0	0	0.0	0	0.0	0.00	—	.000	.000	0	0	92	0	0.0	0	0	0.0
■ RICH HAND	Hand, Richard Allen b: 7/10/48, Bellevue, Wash. BR/TR, 6'1", 195 lbs. Deb: 4/09/70																												
1970	Cle-A	6	13	.316	35	25	3	1	3	160	132	7.4	27	69	3.9	110	6.2	3.82	112	.228	.309	-2	8	115	101	-3.3	-2	0	0.7
1971	Cle-A	2	6	.250	15	12	0	0	0	61	74	10.9	6	38	5.6	26	3.8	5.75	65	.311	.410	-15	-14	108	105	-1.2	-0	-1	-1.4
1972	Tex-A	10	14	.417	30	28	2	1	0	171	139	7.3	12	103	5.4	109	5.7	3.32	90	.226	.329	-5	-6	97	105	1.4	1	-0	-0.6
1973	Tex-A	2	3	.400	8	7	1	0	0	42	49	10.5	2	19	4.1	14	3.0	5.36	71	.290	.359	-7	-7	100	85	0.2	0	-0	-0.7
	Cal-A	4	3	.571	16	6	0	0	0	55	58	9.5	5	21	3.4	19	3.1	3.60	102	.274	.335	1	0	96	116	0.6	0	1	0.1
	Yr	6	6	.500	24	13	1	0	0	97	107	9.9	7	40	3.7	33	3.1	4.36	86	.277	.341	-6	-7	98	116	0.8	0	0	-0.6
Total	4	24	39	.381	104	78	6	2	3	489	452	8.3	52	250	4.6	278	5.1	3.99	91	.249	.337	-28	-19	104	103	-2.3	-1	-1	-1.9
■ JIM HANDIBOE	Handiboe, James Edward "Nick" b: 7/17/1866, Columbus, Ohio d: 11/8/42, Columbus, Ohio BR/TR, 5'11", 160 lbs. Deb: 5/28/1886																												
1886	Pit-a	7	7	.500	14	14	12	1	0	114	82	6.5	1	33	2.6	83	6.6	3.32	93	.211	.272	2	-3	90	59	-1.0	-2	0	-0.3
■ VERN HANDRAHAN	Handrahan, James Vernon b: 11/27/38, Charlottetown, P.E.I., Canada BL/TR, 6'2", 185 lbs. Deb: 4/14/64																												
1964	KC-A	0	1	.000	18	1	0	0	0	36	33	8.3	9	25	6.3	18	4.5	6.00	65	.252	.373	-10	-8	108	99	-0.4	-0	0	-0.7
1966	KC-A	0	1	.000	16	1	0	0	1	25	20	7.2	5	15	5.4	18	6.5	4.32	76	.227	.340	-2	-3	95	111	-0.4	-0	0	-0.2
Total	2	0	2	.000	34	2	0	0	1	61	53	7.8	14	40	5.9	36	5.3	5.31	69	.242	.360	-12	-11	103	104	-0.8	-0	0	-0.9
■ BILL HANDS	Hands, William Alfred b: 5/6/40, Hackensack, N.J. BR/TR, 6'2", 185 lbs. Deb: 6/03/65																												
1965	SF-N	0	2	.000	4	2	0	0	0	6	13	19.5	0	6	9.0	5	7.5	16.50	23	.433	.528	-9	-8	109	65	-0.9	-0	0	-0.7
1966	Chi-N	8	13	.381	41	26	0	0	2	159	168	9.5	17	59	3.3	93	5.3	4.58	81	.272	.332	-17	-16	103	94	0.3	-3	1	-1.7
1967	Chi-N	7	8	.467	49	11	3	1	6	150	134	8.0	9	48	2.9	84	5.0	2.46	138	.239	.298	15	15	100	121	-1.0	-1	-0	1.6
1968	Chi-N	16	10	.615	38	34	11	4	0	259	221	7.7	26	36	**1.3**	148	5.1	2.88	116	.231	.260	3	13	112	90	3.0	-5	-0	1.0
1969	Chi-N	20	14	.588	41	41	18	3	0	300	268	8.0	21	73	2.2	181	5.4	2.49	152	.237	.284	37	43	105	111	1.0	-5	1	4.5
1970	Chi-N	18	15	.545	39	38	12	2	1	265	278	9.4	20	76	2.6	170	5.8	3.70	130	.269	.318	10	32	119	104	1.1	0	1	3.7
1971	Chi-N	12	18	.400	36	35	14	1	0	242	248	9.2	27	50	1.9	128	4.8	3.42	111	.260	.294	1	10	110	100	-3.7	-3	-0	0.8
1972	Chi-N	11	8	.579	32	28	6	3	0	189	168	8.0	12	47	2.2	96	4.6	3.00	129	.237	.282	10	19	112	90	0.7	-5	-2	1.4
1973	Min-A	7	10	.412	39	15	3	1	2	142	138	8.7	14	41	2.6	78	4.9	3.49	113	.252	.302	5	7	103	97	-1.5	0	-1	0.7
1974	Min-A	4	5	.444	35	10	0	0	3	115	130	10.2	9	25	2.0	74	5.8	4.46	82	.284	.323	-11	-10	101	88	-0.5	0	-1	-1.1
	Tex-A	2	0	1.000	2	2	1	1	0	14	11	7.1	0	3	1.9	4	2.6	1.93	180	.208	.250	3	2	96	62	1.0	0	0	0.3
	Yr	6	5	.545	37	12	1	1	3	129	141	9.8	9	28	2.0	78	5.4	4.19	87	.274	.308	-8	-8	100	62	0.5	0	-1	-0.8
1975	Tex-A	6	7	.462	18	18	4	1	0	110	118	9.7	12	28	2.3	67	5.5	4.01	94	.271	.318	-3	-3	100	97	-0.3	0	0	-0.2
Total	11	111	110	.502	374	260	72	17	14	1951	1895	8.7	167	492	2.3	1128	5.2	3.35	115	.253	.299	45	106	108	100	-0.8	-22	0	10.3
■ DON HANKINS	Hankins, Donald Wayne b: 2/9/02, Pendleton, Ind. d: 5/16/63, Winston-Salem, N.C BR/TR, 6'3", 183 lbs. Deb: 4/23/27																												
1927	Det-A	2	1	.667	20	1	0	0	2	43	67	14.0	1	13	2.7	10	2.1	6.28	71	.383	.404	-10	-9	107	106	0.4	-1	0	-0.8
■ FRANK HANKINSON	Hankinson, Frank Edward b: 4/29/1856, New York, N.Y. d: 4/5/11, Palisades Park, N.J BR/TR, 5'11", 168 lbs. Deb: 5/01/1878																												
1878	Chi-N	0	1	.000	1	1	1	0	0	9	11	11.0	0	0	0.0	4	4.0	6.00	41	.312	.312	-4	-4	106	45	-0.4	0	0	-0.2
1879	Chi-N	15	10	.600	26	25	25	2	0	231	248	9.7	0	27	1.1	69	2.7	2.49	105	.280	.301	0	3	104	102	0.8	-4	0	-0.2
1880	Cle-N	1	1	.500	4	2	2	0	1	25	20	7.2	0	3	1.1	8	2.9	1.08	213	.228	.253	4	3	97	126	0.0	-0	0	0.3
1885	NY-a	0	0	—	1	0	0	0	0	2	2	9.0	1	1	4.5	0	0.0	4.50	62	.272	.359	-0	-0	86	170	0.0	0	0	0.0

YEAR	TM/L	W	L	PCT	G	GS	CG	SHO	SV	IP	H	H/G	HR	BB	BB/G	SO	SO/G	ERA	/A	OAVG	OOBP	PR	/A	PF	CPI	WAT	PB	PD	TPI
Total	4	16	12	.571	32	28	28	2	1	267	281	9.5	1	31	1.0	81	2.7	2.49	103	.276	.298	-0	2	104	103	0.4	-4	0	-0.1
■ JIM HANLEY	Hanley, James Patrick b: 10/13/1885, Providence, R.I. d: 5/1/61, Elmhurst, N.J. TL, 5′11″, 165 lbs. Deb: 7/03/13																												
1913	NY-A	0	0	—	1	0	0	0	0	4	5	11.3	0	4	9.0	2	4.5	6.75	45	.313	.450	-2	-2	104	90	0.0	-0	0	-0.1
■ PRESTON HANNA	Hanna, Preston Lee b: 9/10/54, Pensacola, Fla. BR/TR, 6′1″, 195 lbs. Deb: 9/13/75																												
1975	Atl-N	0	0	—	4	0	0	0	0	6	7	10.5	0	5	7.5	2	3.0	1.50	235	.304	.467	1	1	97	431	0.0	0	-0	0.1
1976	Atl-N	0	0	—	5	0	0	0	0	8	11	12.4	0	4	4.5	3	3.4	4.50	87	.333	.405	-1	-1	112	122	0.0	-0	-0	0.0
1977	Atl-N	2	6	.250	17	9	1	0	1	60	69	10.4	6	34	5.1	37	5.6	4.95	91	.285	.372	-7	-3	115	104	-1.3	-1	1	-0.1
1978	Atl-N	7	13	.350	29	28	0	0	0	140	132	8.5	10	93	6.0	90	5.8	5.14	79	.251	.358	-24	-17	114	84	-1.9	1	-0	-1.5
1979	Atl-N	1	1	.500	6	4	0	0	0	24	27	10.1	1	15	5.6	15	5.6	3.00	138	.284	.375	2	3	110	157	0.2	-0	1	0.4
1980	Atl-N	2	0	1.000	32	2	0	0	0	79	63	7.2	3	44	5.0	35	4.0	3.19	115	.224	.326	4	4	101	101	1.0	0	-1	0.4
1981	Atl-N	2	1	.667	20	1	0	0	0	35	45	11.6	2	23	5.9	22	5.7	6.43	54	.341	.415	-11	-11	100	102	0.6	0	2	-0.9
1982	Atl-N	3	0	1.000	20	1	0	0	0	36	36	9.0	3	28	7.0	17	4.3	3.75	103	.277	.405	-1	0	107	144	1.5	1	-1	0.1
	Oak-A	0	4	.000	23	2	1	0	0	48	54	10.1	3	33	6.2	32	6.0	5.63	70	.287	.386	-8	-9	96	94	-1.9	0	-0	-0.8
Total	8	17	25	.405	156	47	2	0	1	436	444	9.2	28	279	5.8	253	5.2	4.62	86	.269	.370	-45	-31	108	107	-1.8	1	2	-2.3
■ GERRY HANNAHS	Hannahs, Gerald Ellis b: 3/6/53, Binghamton, N.Y. BL/TL, 6′3″, 210 lbs. Deb: 9/08/76																												
1976	Mon-N	2	0	1.000	3	3	0	0	0	16	20	11.3	2	12	6.8	10	5.6	6.75	53	.323	.421	-6	-6	103	101	1.0	1	-0	-0.4
1977	Mon-N	1	5	.167	8	7	0	0	0	37	43	10.5	7	17	4.1	21	5.1	4.86	80	.291	.353	-4	-4	99	115	-1.8	-0	-0	-0.3
1978	LA-N	0	0	—	1	0	0	0	0	2	3	13.5	0	0	0.0	5	22.5	9.00	39	.333	.333	-1	-1	97	46	0.0	0	0	0.0
1979	LA-N	0	2	.000	4	2	0	0	1	16	10	5.6	2	13	7.3	6	3.4	3.38	110	.175	.324	1	1	99	94	-0.9	0	0	0.1
Total	4	3	7	.300	16	12	0	0	1	71	76	9.6	11	42	5.3	42	5.3	5.07	74	.275	.362	-10	-10	100	105	-1.7	1	-0	-0.6
■ JIM HANNAN	Hannan, James John b: 1/7/40, Jersey City, N.J. BR/TR, 6′3″, 205 lbs. Deb: 4/17/62																												
1962	Was-A	2	4	.333	42	3	0	0	4	68	56	7.4	6	49	6.5	39	5.2	3.31	123	.230	.345	5	6	102	126	-0.2	-1	0	0.5
1963	Was-A	2	2	.500	13	2	0	0	0	28	23	7.4	2	17	5.5	14	4.5	4.82	76	.228	.328	-4	-4	101	75	0.5	-0	0	-0.3
1964	Was-A	4	7	.364	49	7	0	0	3	106	108	9.2	13	45	3.8	67	5.7	4.16	90	.266	.333	-6	-5	103	105	-0.2	-1	-0	-0.5
1965	Was-A	1	1	.500	4	1	1	1	0	15	18	10.8	0	6	3.6	5	3.0	4.80	73	.340	.417	-2	-2	102	115	0.1	-0	-1	-0.2
1966	Was-A	3	9	.250	30	18	2	0	0	114	125	9.9	9	59	4.7	68	5.4	4.26	78	.288	.366	-10	-12	96	119	-2.7	-1	-0	-1.3
1967	Was-A	1	1	.500	8	2	0	0	0	22	28	11.5	3	7	2.9	14	5.7	5.32	63	.315	.367	-5	-5	104	107	0.1	-0	0	-0.4
1968	Was-A	10	6	.625	25	22	4	1	0	140	147	9.4	4	50	3.2	75	4.8	3.02	92	.272	.334	-1	-4	94	123	3.2	-2	-0	-0.6
1969	Was-A	7	6	.538	35	28	1	1	0	158	138	7.9	17	91	5.2	72	4.1	3.65	96	.238	.337	-0	-3	96	109	0.1	-2	-1	-0.5
1970	Was-A	9	11	.450	42	17	1	1	0	128	119	8.4	17	54	3.8	61	4.3	4.01	90	.250	.322	-4	-6	97	101	0.4	-0	1	-0.5
1971	Det-A	1	0	1.000	7	0	0	0	0	11	7	5.7	1	7	5.7	6	4.9	3.27	101	.189	.326	0	0	95	99	0.5	-0	1	0.1
	Mil-A	1	1	.500	21	1	0	0	0	32	38	10.7	7	21	5.9	17	4.8	5.06	71	.295	.390	-6	-5	104	129	0.1	-0	-0	-0.5
	Yr	2	1	.667	28	1	0	0	0	43	45	9.4	8	28	5.9	23	4.8	4.60	77	.269	.370	-5	-5	102	129	0.6	-0	1	-0.4
Total	10	41	48	.461	276	101	9	4	7	822	807	8.8	79	406	4.4	438	4.8	3.88	89	.261	.343	-33	-39	98	112	1.9	-9	0	-4.2
■ LOY HANNING	Hanning, Loy Vernon b: 10/18/17, Bunker, Mo. d: 6/24/86, Anaconda, Mo. BR/TR, 6′2″, 175 lbs. Deb: 9/20/39																												
1939	StL-A	0	1	.000	4	1	0	0	0	10	6	5.4	1	4	3.6	8	7.2	3.60	135	.158	.233	1	1	105	36	-0.4	-0	0	0.1
1942	StL-A	1	1	.500	11	0	0	0	0	17	26	13.8	2	12	6.4	9	4.8	7.94	47	.356	.448	-8	-8	102	101	0.0	0	1	-0.6
Total	2	1	2	.333	15	1	0	0	0	27	32	10.7	3	16	5.3	17	5.7	6.33	65	.288	.377	-7	-7	103	77	-0.4	-0	1	-0.5
■ ANDY HANSEN	Hansen, Andrew Viggo "Swede" b: 11/12/24, Lake Worth, Fla. BR/TR, 6′3″, 185 lbs. Deb: 6/30/44																												
1944	NY-N	3	3	.500	23	4	0	0	1	53	63	10.7	3	32	5.4	15	2.5	6.45	59	.301	.394	-17	-16	105	86	0.4	0	1	-1.3
1945	NY-N	4	3	.571	23	13	4	0	3	93	98	9.5	7	28	2.7	37	3.6	4.65	82	.273	.322	-9	-9	100	86	0.4	-3	2	-0.9
1947	NY-N	1	5	.167	27	9	1	0	0	82	78	8.6	8	38	4.2	18	2.0	4.39	92	.248	.324	-3	-3	99	87	-2.0	-0	1	-0.2
1948	NY-N	5	3	.625	36	9	3	0	1	100	96	8.6	4	36	3.2	27	2.4	2.97	131	.255	.315	11	10	98	115	1.0	-0	-1	0.9
1949	NY-N	2	6	.250	33	2	0	0	1	66	58	7.9	7	28	3.8	26	3.5	4.64	88	.234	.307	-4	-4	101	75	-1.8	-1	0	-0.3
1950	NY-N	0	1	.000	31	1	0	0	3	57	64	10.1	8	26	4.1	19	3.0	5.53	72	.279	.353	-9	-10	97	91	-0.4	-1	-0	-0.9
1951	Phi-N	3	1	.750	24	0	0	0	0	39	34	7.8	4	7	1.6	11	2.5	2.54	151	.228	.268	6	6	97	102	1.1	1	1	0.7
1952	Phi-N	5	6	.455	43	0	0	0	4	77	76	8.9	6	27	3.2	18	2.1	3.27	113	.259	.322	4	4	99	118	-1.0	1	1	0.6
1953	Phi-N	0	2	.000	30	1	0	0	3	51	60	10.6	6	24	4.2	17	3.0	4.06	103	.296	.368	1	1	98	133	-0.9	0	1	0.1
Total	9	23	30	.434	270	39	8	0	16	618	627	9.1	53	246	3.6	188	2.7	4.22	93	.263	.330	-19	-21	99	99	-3.2	-3	5	-1.3
■ SNIPE HANSEN	Hansen, Roy Emil Frederick b: 2/21/07, Chicago, Ill. d: 9/11/78, Chicago, Ill. BB/TL, 6′3″, 195 lbs. Deb: 7/05/30																												
1930	Phi-N	0	7	.000	22	9	1	0	0	84	123	13.2	8	38	4.1	25	2.7	6.75	81	.364	.413	-17	-12	109	108	-3.4	-3	-1	-1.2
1932	Phi-N	10	10	.500	39	23	5	0	2	191	215	10.1	13	51	2.4	56	2.6	3.72	116	.278	.324	3	13	111	107	0.0	-4	-2	0.8
1933	Phi-N	6	14	.300	32	22	8	0	1	168	199	10.7	12	30	1.6	47	2.5	4.45	91	.294	.320	-21	-8	121	92	-2.6	-3	-1	-1.0
1934	Phi-N	6	12	.333	50	16	5	2	3	151	194	11.6	15	61	3.6	40	2.4	5.42	83	.307	.364	-23	-16	111	100	-1.0	0	1	-1.2
1935	Phi-N	0	1	.000	2	1	0	0	0	4	8	18.0	0	5	11.3	0	0.0	13.50	35	.421	.520	-4	-4	117	81	-0.4	-0	0	-0.3
	StL-A	0	1	.000	10	0	0	0	0	27	44	14.7	2	9	3.0	8	2.7	8.67	56	.364	.406	-13	-11	110	81	-0.4	-1	-0	-1.0
Total	5	22	45	.328	155	71	19	2	6	625	783	11.3	50	194	2.8	176	2.5	5.01	89	.306	.351	-74	-37	113	100	-7.8	-10	-3	-3.9
■ ROY HANSEN	Hansen, Roy Ingiof "Ing" b: 3/6/1898, Beloit, Wis. d: 2/9/77, Beloit, Wis. BR/TR, 6′, 165 lbs. Deb: 5/28/18																												
1918	Was-A	1	0	1.000	5	0	0	0	0	9	10	10.0	0	3	3.0	2	2.0	3.00	95	.278	.350	-0	-0	103	115	0.5	0	0	0.0
■ F. C. HANSFORD	Hansford, F. C. TL, 6′, 180 lbs. Deb: 6/09/1898																												
1898	Bro-N	0	0	—	1	0	0	0	0	7	10	12.9	0	5	6.4	0	0.0	3.86	90	.359	.457	-0	-0	96	161	0.0	-0	0	0.0
■ DON HANSKI	Hanski, Donald Thomas (born Donald Thomas Hanyzewski) b: 2/27/16, Laporte, Ind. d: 9/2/57, Worth, Ill. BL/TL, 5′11″, 180 lbs. Deb: 5/06/43																												
1943	Chi-A	0	0	—	1	0	0	0	0	1	1	9.0	0	1	9.0	0	0.0	0.00	—	.333	.500	0	0	101	0	0.0	0	0	0.0
1944	Chi-A	0	0	—	2	0	0	0	0	3	5	15.0	0	2	6.0	0	0.0	12.00	29	.357	.438	-3	-3	102	57	0.0	-0	0	-0.2
Total	2	0	0	—	3	0	0	0	0	4	6	13.5	0	3	6.8	0	0.0	9.00	39	.353	.450	-2	-2	102	43	0.0	-0	0	-0.2
■ OLLIE HANSON	Hanson, Earl Sylvester b: 1/19/1896, Holbrook, Mass. d: 8/19/51, Clifton, N.J. BR/TR, 5′11″, 178 lbs. Deb: 4/27/21																												
1921	Chi-N	0	2	.000	2	2	1	0	0	9	9	9.0	0	6	6.0	2	2.0	7.00	59	.265	.381	-3	-3	108	59	-0.9	-1	0	-0.2
■ ERIK HANSON	Hanson, Erik Brian b: 5/18/65, Kinnelon, N.J. BR/TR, 6′6″, 205 lbs. Deb: 9/05/88																												
1988	Sea-A	2	3	.400	6	6	0	0	0	42	35	7.5	4	12	2.6	36	7.7	3.21	134	.230	.286	4	5	108	96	0.0	0	-0	0.5
■ ED HANYZEWSKI	Hanyzewski, Edward Michael b: 9/18/20, Union Mills, Ind. BR/TR, 6′1″, 200 lbs. Deb: 5/12/42																												
1942	Chi-N	1	1	.500	6	1	0	0	0	19	17	8.1	2	8	3.8	6	2.8	3.79	85	.254	.325	-1	-1	98	107	0.1	-0	0	0.0
1943	Chi-N	8	7	.533	33	16	3	0	0	130	120	8.3	2	45	3.1	55	3.8	2.56	129	.243	.300	12	11	98	108	0.8	-4	2	0.9
1944	Chi-N	2	5	.286	14	7	3	0	0	58	61	9.5	6	20	3.1	19	2.9	4.50	80	.261	.318	-6	-6	100	87	-1.4	-1	3	-0.3
1945	Chi-N	0	0	—	2	1	0	0	0	5	7	12.6	1	1	1.8	0	0.0	5.40	67	.350	.364	-1	-1	95	126	0.0	0	0	0.0
1946	Chi-N	1	0	1.000	3	0	0	0	0	6	8	12.0	0	5	7.5	1	1.5	4.50	71	.348	.483	-1	-1	93	159	0.5	-0	0	0.0
Total	5	12	13	.480	58	25	6	0	0	218	213	8.8	11	79	3.3	81	3.3	3.30	103	.254	.314	3	2	98	104	0.0	-5	5	0.6
■ MEL HARDER	Harder, Melvin Leroy "Chief" b: 10/15/09, Beemer, Neb. BR/TR, 6′1″, 195 lbs. Deb: 4/24/28 MC																												
1928	Cle-A	0	2	.000	23	1	0	0	1	49	64	11.8	4	32	5.9	15	2.8	6.61	66	.335	.400	-14	-12	108	101	-0.9	-1	-1	-1.3
1929	Cle-A	1	0	1.000	11	0	0	0	0	18	24	12.0	2	5	2.5	4	2.0	5.50	78	.333	.381	-3	-2	101	114	0.5	-0	-0	-0.2
1930	Cle-A	11	10	.524	36	19	7	0	2	175	205	10.5	9	68	3.5	44	2.3	4.22	116	.295	.349	8	13	105	115	0.0	-4	-1	0.8
1931	Cle-A	13	14	.481	40	24	9	0	1	194	229	10.6	8	72	3.3	63	2.9	4.36	106	.289	.349	0	6	106	105	-0.7	1	0	0.7
1932	Cle-A	15	13	.536	39	32	17	1	0	255	277	9.8	9	68	2.4	90	3.2	3.74	128	.272	.315	21	30	107	99	-1.0	-1	3	3.2
1933	Cle-A	15	17	.469	43	31	14	2	4	253	254	9.0	10	67	2.4	81	2.9	**2.95**	**152**	.259	.302	**37**	**43**	105	115	-1.0	-1	8	**5.1**
1934	Cle-A	20	12	.625	44	29	17	**6**	4	255	246	8.7	6	81	2.9	91	3.2	2.61	172	.254	.312	53	53	100	**126**	3.2	-1	2	**5.3**
1935	Cle-A	22	11	.667	42	35	17	4	2	287	313	9.8	6	53	**1.7**	95	3.0	3.29	134	.293	.322	37	35	99	119	5.5	-1	5	3.8
1936	Cle-A	15	15	.500	36	30	13	0	1	225	294	11.8	13	71	2.8	84	3.4	5.16	102	.313	.360	-3	3	105	103	-0.6	-4	-0	0.0
1937	Cle-A	15	12	.556	38	30	13	0	2	234	269	10.3	9	86	3.3	95	3.7	4.27	105	.288	.346	9	5	97	102	0.6	-1	1	0.5

YEAR	TM/L	W	L	PCT	G	GS	CG	SHO	SV	IP	H	H/G	HR	BB	BB/G	SO	SO/G	ERA	/A	OAVG	OOBP	PR	/A	PF	CPI	WAT	PB	PD	TPI
1938	Cle-A	17	10	.630	38	29	15	2	4	240	257	9.6	16	62	2.3	102	3.8	3.83	122	.271	.316	26	23	98	100	2.3	-5	2	1.8
1939	Cle-A	15	9	.625	29	26	12	1	1	208	213	9.2	15	64	2.8	67	2.9	3.50	127	.269	.319	26	22	96	116	1.9	-2	-2	1.7
1940	Cle-A	12	11	.522	31	25	5	0	0	186	200	9.7	16	59	2.9	76	3.7	4.06	99	.278	.331	7	-1	92	109	-1.2	-0	1	0.0
1941	Cle-A	5	4	.556	15	10	1	0	1	69	76	9.9	8	37	4.8	21	2.7	5.22	80	.279	.363	-8	-8	101	100	0.6	-2	1	-0.8
1942	Cle-A	13	14	.481	29	29	13	4	0	199	179	8.1	8	82	3.7	74	3.3	3.44	99	.240	.314	5	-1	93	93	-0.1	-3	1	-0.2
1943	Cle-A	8	7	.533	19	18	6	1	0	135	126	8.4	7	61	4.1	40	2.7	3.07	96	.254	.329	3	-2	90	120	0.0	2	-0	0.0
1944	Cle-A	12	10	.545	30	27	12	2	0	196	211	9.7	5	69	3.2	64	2.9	3.72	93	.278	.336	-6	-6	101	102	1.8	0	-0	-0.5
1945	Cle-A	3	7	.300	11	11	2	0	0	76	93	11.0	3	23	2.7	16	1.9	3.67	90	.303	.346	-3	-3	98	119	-2.0	-2	1	-0.4
1946	Cle-A	5	4	.556	13	12	4	1	0	92	85	8.3	4	31	3.0	21	2.1	3.42	92	.249	.304	1	-3	90	89	1.0	-2	-2	-0.6
1947	Cle-A	6	4	.600	15	15	4	1	0	80	91	10.2	3	27	3.0	17	1.9	4.50	77	.289	.342	-7	-9	94	92	0.9	0	-1	-0.9
Total	20	223	186	.545	582	433	181	25	23	3426	3706	9.7	161	1118	2.9	1160	3.0	3.80	113	.277	.330	190	182	99	108	10.8	-27	17	18.0
■ JIM HARDIN	Hardin, James Warren b: 8/6/43, Morris Chapel, Tenn. BR/TR, 6', 175 lbs. Deb: 6/23/67																												
1967	Bal-A	8	3	.727	19	14	5	2	0	111	85	6.9	5	27	2.2	64	5.2	2.27	133	.211	.263	12	9	94	91	2.8	0	-1	0.9
1968	Bal-A	18	13	.581	35	35	16	2	0	244	188	6.9	20	70	2.6	160	5.9	2.51	120	.212	.275	13	13	101	100	0.8	-3	-0	1.1
1969	Bal-A	6	7	.462	30	20	3	1	1	138	128	8.3	18	43	2.8	64	4.2	3.59	101	.248	.307	1	1	100	104	-2.1	1	-1	0.1
1970	Bal-A	6	5	.545	36	19	3	2	1	145	150	9.3	13	26	1.6	78	4.8	3.54	99	.267	.296	3	-1	94	97	-1.0	-1	-2	-0.3
1971	Bal-A	0	0	—	6	0	0	0	0	6	12	18.0	0	3	4.5	3	4.5	4.50	77	.480	.484	-1	-1	100	216	0.0	0	0	0.0
	NY-A	0	2	.000	12	3	0	0	0	28	35	11.3	3	9	2.9	14	4.5	5.14	65	.313	.357	-5	-6	97	102	-0.9	-0	-0	-0.6
	Yr	0	2	.000	18	3	0	0	0	34	47	12.4	3	12	3.2	17	4.5	5.03	67	.343	.382	-6	-6	97	102	-0.9	0	0	-0.6
1972	Atl-N	5	2	.714	26	9	1	0	2	80	93	10.5	11	24	2.7	25	2.8	4.39	84	.287	.334	-8	-6	106	107	1.7	1	-1	-0.5
Total	6	43	32	.573	164	100	28	7	4	752	691	8.3	70	202	2.4	408	4.9	3.18	104	.244	.296	14	10	99	101	1.3	-2	-4	0.7
■ CHARLIE HARDING	Harding, Charles Harold "Slim" b: 1/3/1891, Nashville, Tenn. d: 10/30/71, Bold Srpings, Tenn BR/TR, 6'2.5", 172 lbs. Deb: 9/18/13																												
1913	Det-A	0	0	—	1	0	0	0	0	2	3	13.5	0	1	4.5	0	0.0	4.50	65	.375	.444	-0	-0	101	143	0.0	0	0	0.0
■ ALEX HARDY	Hardy, David Alexander "Dooney" b: 1877, Toronto, Ont., Canada d: 4/22/40, Toronto, Ont., Can. TL , Deb: 9/04/02																												
1902	Chi-N	2	2	.500	4	4	4	1	0	35	29	7.5	0	12	3.1	12	3.1	3.60	74	.247	.316	-3	-4	95	59	0.0	0	-1	-0.3
1903	Chi-N	1	1	.500	3	3	1	0	0	13	21	14.5	0	7	4.8	4	2.8	6.23	49	.398	.477	-4	-5	94	109	-0.1	0	0	-0.3
Total	2	3	3	.500	7	7	5	1	0	48	50	9.4	0	19	3.6	16	3.0	4.31	64	.293	.368	-7	-8	95	73	-0.1	1	-0	-0.6
■ RED HARDY	Hardy, Francis Joseph b: 1/6/23, Marmarth, N.Dak. BR/TR, 5'11", 175 lbs. Deb: 6/20/51																												
1951	NY-N	0	0	—	2	0	0	0	0	1	4	36.0	0	1	9.0	0	0.0	9.00	44	.571	.600	-1	-1	99	245	0.0	0	0	0.0
■ HARRY HARDY	Hardy, Harry b: 11/5/1875, Steubenville, Ohio d: 9/4/43, Steubenville, Ohio BL/TL, 5'6", 155 lbs. Deb: 9/26/05																												
1905	Was-A	1	1	.500	3	2	2	0	0	24	20	7.5	0	6	2.3	10	3.8	1.88	149	.249	.302	2	2	106	117	0.1	-1	-1	0.1
1906	Was-A	0	3	.000	5	3	2	0	0	20	35	15.7	0	12	5.4	4	1.8	9.00	28	.412	.484	-14	-14	94	84	-1.4	-1	1	-1.2
Total	2	1	4	.200	8	5	4	0	0	44	55	11.3	0	18	3.7	14	2.9	5.11	52	.333	.398	-12	-12	100	102	-1.3	-1	-0	-1.1
■ LARRY HARDY	Hardy, Howard Lawrence b: 1/10/48, Goose Creek, Tex. BR/TR, 5'10", 180 lbs. Deb: 4/28/74																												
1974	SD-N	9	4	.692	76	1	0	0	2	102	129	11.4	9	44	3.9	57	5.0	4.68	75	.317	.370	-12	-13	97	117	3.5	-1	1	-1.2
1975	SD-N	0	0	—	3	0	0	0	0	3	8	24.0	3	2	6.0	3	9.0	12.00	31	.500	.556	-3	-3	101	168	0.0	0	-0	-0.2
1976	Hou-N	0	0	—	15	0	0	0	3	22	34	13.9	2	10	4.1	10	4.1	6.95	44	.362	.415	-8	-10	87	100	0.0	-0	0	-0.9
Total	3	9	4	.692	94	1	0	0	5	127	171	12.1	14	56	4.0	70	5.0	5.24	65	.331	.383	-23	-26	95	115	3.5	-1	1	-2.3
■ STEVE HARGAN	Hargan, Steven Lowell b: 9/8/42, Ft.Wayne, Ind. BR/TR, 6'3", 170 lbs. Deb: 8/03/65																												
1965	Cle-A	4	3	.571	17	8	1	0	2	60	55	8.3	2	28	4.2	37	5.6	3.45	98	.246	.323	0	-1	97	97	0.3	-1	0	-0.1
1966	Cle-A	13	10	.565	38	21	7	3	0	192	173	8.1	9	45	2.1	132	6.2	2.48	140	.241	.282	20	21	102	110	1.7	-2	1	2.2
1967	Cle-A	14	13	.519	30	29	15	**6**	0	223	180	7.3	9	72	2.9	141	5.7	2.62	125	.224	.283	15	16	101	98	1.6	1	1	2.2
1968	Cle-A	8	15	.348	32	27	4	2	0	158	139	7.9	11	81	4.6	78	4.4	4.16	72	.241	.332	-21	-20	101	90	-4.3	1	-2	-2.3
1969	Cle-A	5	14	.263	32	23	1	1	0	144	145	9.1	14	81	5.1	76	4.8	5.69	61	.265	.353	-33	-35	96	80	-3.2	-0	1	-3.4
1970	Cle-A	11	3	.786	23	19	8	1	0	143	101	6.4	14	53	3.3	72	4.5	2.90	148	.201	.277	13	22	115	87	4.3	-2	1	2.4
1971	Cle-A	1	13	.071	37	16	1	0	1	113	138	11.0	18	56	4.5	52	4.1	6.21	61	.304	.380	-34	-31	108	95	-5.6	-3	-1	-3.4
1972	Cle-A	0	3	.000	12	1	0	0	0	20	23	10.3	1	15	6.7	10	4.5	5.85	57	.291	.392	-6	-6	108	90	-1.4	-0	1	-0.5
1974	Tex-A	12	9	.571	37	27	8	2	0	187	202	9.7	15	48	2.3	98	4.7	3.95	88	.275	.317	-7	-10	96	96	1.2	0	2	-0.8
1975	Tex-A	9	10	.474	33	26	8	1	0	189	203	9.7	17	62	3.0	93	4.4	3.81	99	.275	.330	-0	-1	100	108	-0.2	0	2	0.1
1976	Tex-A	8	8	.500	35	8	2	1	1	124	127	9.2	8	38	2.8	63	4.6	3.63	100	.261	.313	-1	-0	103	96	0.5	0	-0	0.0
1977	Tor-A	1	3	.250	6	5	1	0	0	29	36	11.2	2	14	4.3	11	3.4	5.28	81	.308	.373	-4	-3	105	99	-0.4	0	0	-0.2
	Tex-A	1	0	1.000	6	0	0	0	0	12	22	16.5	2	5	3.8	10	7.5	9.00	47	.393	.422	-7	-6	104	96	0.5	0	-0	-0.5
	Yr	2	3	.400	12	5	1	0	0	41	58	12.7	4	19	4.2	21	4.6	6.37	67	.335	.389	-10	-10	104	96	0.1	0	0	-0.7
	Atl-N	0	3	.000	16	5	0	0	0	37	49	11.9	3	16	3.9	18	4.4	6.81	66	.325	.378	-12	-9	115	83	-1.4	-1	1	-0.8
Total	12	87	107	.448	354	215	56	17	4	1631	1593	8.8	125	614	3.4	891	4.9	3.92	91	.257	.321	-77	-63	102	96	-6.4	-8	7	-5.1
■ ALAN HARGESHEIMER	Hargesheimer, Alan Robert b: 11/21/56, Chicago, Ill. BR/TR, 6'3", 195 lbs. Deb: 7/14/80																												
1980	SF-N	4	6	.400	15	13	0	0	0	75	82	9.8	3	32	3.8	40	4.8	4.32	80	.285	.351	-6	-7	96	98	-0.6	1	-1	-0.6
1981	SF-N	1	2	.333	6	3	0	0	0	19	20	9.5	1	9	4.3	6	2.8	4.26	86	.299	.375	-2	-1	105	118	-0.4	-0	0	0.0
1983	Chi-N	0	0	—	5	0	0	0	0	4	6	13.5	0	2	4.5	5	11.3	9.00	41	.375	.421	-2	-2	101	74	0.0	0	0	-0.2
1986	KC-A	0	1	.000	5	1	0	0	0	13	18	12.5	1	7	4.8	4	2.8	6.23	67	.340	.426	-3	-3	100	108	-0.4	0	-0	-0.2
Total	4	5	9	.357	31	17	0	0	0	111	126	10.2	5	50	4.1	55	4.5	4.70	77	.297	.367	-13	-14	98	102	-1.4	1	-0	-1.0
■ MIKE HARKEY	Harkey, Michael Anthony b: 10/25/66, San Diego, Cal. BR/TR, 6'5", 220 lbs. Deb: 9/05/88																												
1988	Chi-N	0	3	.000	5	5	0	0	0	35	33	8.5	0	15	3.9	18	4.6	2.57	141	.248	.323	3	4	105	126	-1.4	-1	-1	0.3
■ JOHN HARKINS	Harkins, John Joseph "Pa" b: 4/12/1859, New Brunswick, N.J d: 11/20/40, New Brunswick, N.J BR/TR, 6'1", 205 lbs. Deb: 5/02/1884																												
1884	Cle-N	12	32	.273	46	45	42	3	0	391	399	9.2	7	108	2.5	192	4.4	3.68	87	.273	.323	-31	-21	108	82	-4.2	-5	-0	-2.1
1885	Bro-a	14	20	.412	34	34	33	1	0	293	303	9.3	8	56	1.7	141	4.3	3.75	91	.279	.314	-16	-11	105	91	-2.9	5	4	0.0
1886	Bro-a	15	16	.484	34	33	33	0	0	292	286	8.8	6	114	3.5	118	3.6	3.61	96	.266	.337	-5	-5	100	101	-2.4	3	3	0.2
1887	Bro-a	10	14	.417	24	24	22	0	0	199	262	11.8	6	77	3.5	36	1.6	6.02	71	.332	.391	-38	-39	99	89	-0.9	0	0	-2.9
1888	Bal-a	0	1	.000	1	1	1	0	0	8	12	13.5	0	3	3.4	2	2.3	6.75	44	.361	.414	-3	-3	98	87	-0.4	-0	0	-0.2
Total	5	51	83	.381	139	137	131	4	0	1183	1262	9.6	27	358	2.7	489	3.7	4.09	86	.284	.337	-93	-78	103	90	-10.8	3	7	-5.0
■ SPEC HARKNESS	Harkness, Frederick Harvey b: 12/13/1887, Los Angeles, Cal. d: 5/16/52, Compton, Cal. BR/TR, 5'11", 180 lbs. Deb: 6/13/10																												
1910	Cle-A	10	7	.588	26	16	6	1	1	136	132	8.7	2	55	3.6	60	4.0	3.04	84	.268	.345	-8	-7	102	111	2.1	-1	-1	-1.0
1911	Cle-A	2	2	.500	12	6	3	0	0	53	62	10.5	1	21	3.6	25	4.2	4.25	81	.310	.376	-5	-5	103	104	0.0	1	-2	-0.5
Total	2	12	9	.571	38	22	9	1	1	189	194	9.2	3	76	3.6	85	4.0	3.38	83	.280	.354	-13	-12	102	109	2.1	-0	-3	-1.5
■ DICK HARLEY	Harley, Henry Risk b: 8/18/1874, Springfield, Ohio d: 5/16/61, Springfield, Ohio BR/TR, Deb: 4/15/05																												
1905	Bos-N	2	5	.286	9	4	4	1	0	66	72	9.8	5	19	2.6	19	2.6	4.64	66	.306	.361	-12	-12	102	89	-0.4	-2	2	-0.9
■ LARRY HARLOW	Harlow, Larry Duane b: 11/13/51, Colorado Springs, Colo. BL/TL, 6'2", 185 lbs. Deb: 9/20/75																												
1978	Bal-A	0	0	—	1	0	0	0	0	1	2	18.0	1	4	36.0	1	9.0	45.00	8	.500	.750	-5	-5	91	62	0.0	1	0	-0.3
■ BILL HARMAN	Harman, William Bell b: 1/2/19, Bridgewater, Va. BR/TR, 6'4", 200 lbs. Deb: 6/17/41																												
1941	Phi-N	0	0	—	5	0	0	0	0	13	15	10.4	0	8	5.5	3	2.1	4.85	77	.319	.404	-2	-2	103	114	0.0	-0	-0	-0.1
■ BOB HARMON	Harmon, Robert Green "Hickory Bob" b: 10/15/1887, Liberal, Mo. d: 11/27/61, Monroe, La. BB/TR, 6', 187 lbs. Deb: 09																												
1909	StL-N	6	11	.353	21	17	10	0	0	159	155	8.8	6	65	3.7	48	2.7	3.68	70	.265	.342	-19	-19	99	96	0.0	3	-0	-2.0
1910	StL-N	13	15	.464	43	33	15	0	2	236	227	8.7	1	133	5.1	87	3.3	4.46	63	.258	.360	-37	-43	93	79	1.5	2	2	-3.9
1911	StL-N	23	16	.590	51	41	28	2	4	348	290	7.5	10	181	4.7	144	3.7	3.13	111	.235	.336	11	14	102	100	4.3	-0	1	1.5
1912	StL-N	18	18	.500	43	34	15	3	0	268	284	9.5	4	116	3.9	73	2.5	3.93	89	.270	.344	-15	-13	103	85	3.4	0	4	-0.8
1913	StL-N	8	21	.276	42	27	16	1	2	273	291	9.6	6	99	3.3	66	2.2	3.92	79	.286	.344	-22	-25	97	100	-3.1	6	1	-1.7
1914	Pit-N	13	17	.433	37	30	19	2	3	245	226	8.3	3	55	2.0	61	2.2	2.53	102	.252	.292	7	1	93	96	-0.5	-1	-2	-0.1

YEAR	TM/L	W	L	PCT	G	GS	CG	SHO	SV	IP	H	H/G	HR	BB	BB/G	SO	SO/G	ERA	/A	OAVG	OOBP	PR	/A	PF	CPI	WAT	PB	PD	TPI
1915	Pit-N	16	17	.485	37	32	25	5	1	270	242	8.1	6	62	2.1	86	2.9	2.50	108	.247	.285	8	6	98	101	0.4	1	3	1.1
1916	Pit-N	8	11	.421	31	17	10	2	0	173	175	9.1	4	39	2.0	62	3.2	2.81	100	.267	.298	-4	-0	107	105	0.0	-3	3	0.1
1918	Pit-N	2	7	.222	16	9	5	0	0	82	76	8.3	3	12	1.3	7	0.8	2.63	110	.254	.274	1	2	105	95	-2.6	-1	0	0.2
Total	9	107	133	.446	321	240	143	15	12	2054	1966	8.6	43	762	3.3	634	2.8	3.33	90	.259	.324	-71	-77	99	95	3.4	8	12	-5.6
■ **PETE HARNISCH**	Harnisch, Peter Thomas b: 9/23/66, Commack, N.Y. BB/TR, 6'1", 195 lbs. Deb: 9/13/88																												
1988	Bal-A	0	2	.000	2	2	0	0	0	13	13	9.0	1	9	6.2	10	6.9	5.54	70	.260	.361	-2	-2	97	85	-0.9	0	0	-0.1
■ **JACK HARPER**	Harper, Charles William b: 4/2/1878, Galloway, Pa. d: 9/30/50, Jamestown, N.Y. BR/TR, 6', 178 lbs. Deb: 9/18/1899																												
1899	Cle-N	1	4	.200	5	5	5	0	0	37	44	10.7	3	12	2.9	14	3.4	3.89	95	.320	.374	-0	-1	96	117	0.2	1	0	0.0
1900	StL-N	0	1	.000	1	1	0	0	0	3	4	12.0	0	2	6.0	0	0.0	12.00	29	.345	.441	-3	-3	93	47	-0.4	-0	0	-0.1
1901	StL-N	23	13	.639	39	37	28	1	0	309	294	8.6	7	99	2.9	128	3.7	3.61	87	.275	.344	-10	-16	95	87	4.7	1	1	-1.4
1902	StL-A	15	11	.577	29	26	20	2	0	222	224	9.1	8	81	3.3	74	3.0	4.14	88	.286	.353	-14	-12	102	85	0.1	-0	1	-1.0
1903	Cin-N	8	9	.471	17	15	13	0	0	135	143	9.5	2	70	4.7	45	3.0	4.33	81	.302	.403	-16	-13	107	95	-1.0	2	1	-1.0
1904	Cin-N	23	9	.719	35	35	31	6	0	285	262	8.3	2	85	2.7	125	3.9	2.37	128	.270	.334	11	21	111	115	6.3	-3	-4	1.8
1905	Cin-N	9	13	.409	26	23	15	1	1	179	189	9.5	2	69	3.5	70	3.5	3.87	79	.302	.378	-18	-16	103	98	-2.5	1	-1	-1.6
1906	Cin-N	1	4	.200	5	5	3	0	0	37	38	9.2	1	20	4.9	10	2.4	4.14	74	.298	.401	-6	-4	116	100	-1.2	1	-1	-0.5
	Chi-N	0	0	—	1	1	0	0	0	1	0	0.0	0	0	0.0	0	0.0	0.00	—	.000	.000	0	0	99	0	0.0	0	0	0.0
	Yr	1	4	.200	6	6	3	0	0	38	38	9.0	1	20	4.7	10	2.4	4.03	76	.288	.382	-6	-4	116	0	-1.2	1	-1	-0.5
Total	8	80	64	.556	158	148	115	10	1	1208	1198	8.9	25	438	3.3	466	3.5	3.58	91	.285	.359	-55	-41	103	97	6.2	3	-3	-3.8
■ **GEORGE HARPER**	Harper, George B. b: 8/17/1866, Milwaukee, Wis. d: 12/11/31, Stockton, Cal. Deb: 7/11/1894																												
1894	Phi-N	6	6	.500	12	9	7	0	0	86	128	13.4	3	49	5.1	24	2.5	5.34	94	.368	.446	-0	-3	94	123	-0.5	-3	0	-0.4
1896	Bro-N	4	8	.333	16	11	7	0	0	86	106	11.1	4	39	4.1	22	2.3	5.55	69	.326	.398	-11	-16	88	89	-1.5	1	0	-1.2
Total	2	10	14	.417	28	20	14	0	0	172	234	12.2	7	88	4.6	46	2.4	5.44	81	.348	.423	-11	-20	91	106	-2.0	-3	0	-1.6
■ **HARRY HARPER**	Harper, Harry Clayton b: 4/24/1895, Hackensack, N.J. d: 4/23/63, New York, N.Y. BL/TL, 6'2", 165 lbs. Deb: 6/27/13																												
1913	Was-A	0	0	—	4	0	0	0	0	13	10	6.9	1	5	3.5	9	6.2	3.46	89	.204	.291	-1	-1	105	64	0.0	0	0	0.0
1914	Was-A	2	1	.667	23	3	1	0	2	57	45	7.1	1	35	5.5	50	7.9	3.47	79	.211	.336	-5	-5	100	77	0.5	0	-1	-0.5
1915	Was-A	4	4	.500	19	10	5	2	2	86	66	6.9	1	40	4.2	54	5.7	1.78	165	.222	.317	11	11	99	142	-0.3	-4	-2	0.6
1916	Was-A	14	10	.583	36	34	13	2	0	250	209	7.5	4	101	3.6	149	5.4	2.45	116	.235	.319	11	11	100	109	2.4	1	-4	0.8
1917	Was-A	11	12	.478	31	31	10	4	0	179	145	7.3	1	106	5.3	99	5.0	3.02	82	.230	.345	-7	-11	93	97	-0.1	-3	-3	-1.7
1918	Was-A	11	10	.524	35	32	14	3	1	244	182	6.7	1	104	3.8	78	2.9	2.18	131	.212	.296	16	18	103	91	-0.8	-4	-4	1.1
1919	Was-A	6	21	.222	35	31	8	0	0	208	220	9.5	3	97	4.2	87	3.8	3.72	86	.284	.370	-12	-12	99	107	-6.6	-2	-1	-1.5
1920	Bos-A	5	14	.263	27	22	11	1	0	163	163	9.0	9	66	3.6	71	3.9	3.04	121	.275	.349	14	11	97	128	-4.4	-3	-2	0.5
1921	NY-A	4	3	.571	8	7	4	0	0	53	52	8.8	3	25	4.2	22	3.7	3.74	114	.263	.336	3	3	99	105	-0.3	-1	-1	0.0
1923	Bro-N	0	1	.000	1	1	0	0	0	4	8	18.0	2	3	6.8	4	9.0	13.50	29	.421	.500	-4	-4	98	97	-0.4	-0	0	-0.3
Total	10	57	76	.429	219	171	66	12	5	1257	1100	7.9	26	582	4.2	623	4.5	2.86	105	.243	.333	27	22	99	106	-10.0	-15	-19	-1.0
■ **JACK HARPER**	Harper, John Wesley b: 8/5/1893, Hendricks, W.Va. d: 6/18/27, Halstead, Kan. BR/TR, 5'11", 180 lbs. Deb: 4/17/15																												
1915	Phi-A	0	0	—	3	0	0	0	0	9	5	5.0	0	1	1.0	3	3.0	3.00	101	.161	.188	-0	0	103	2	0.0	-0	0	0.0
■ **BILL HARPER**	Harper, William Homer "Blue Sleeve" b: 6/14/1889, Bertand, Mo. d: 6/17/51, Somerville, Tenn. BB/TR, 6'1", 180 lbs. Deb: 6/10/11																												
1911	StL-A	0	0	—	2	0	0	0	0	8	9	10.1	0	4	4.5	6	6.8	6.75	49	.300	.400	-3	-3	100	69	0.0	-0	0	-0.2
■ **SLIM HARRELL**	Harrell, Oscar Martin b: 7/31/1890, Grandview, Tex. d: 4/30/71, Hillsboro, Tex. BR/TR, 6'3", 180 lbs. Deb: 6/21/12																												
1912	Phi-A	0	0	—	1	0	0	0	0	3	4	12.0	0	0	0.0	1	3.0	0.00	—	.364	.364	1	1	97	0	0.0	-0	-0	0.1
■ **RAY HARRELL**	Harrell, Raymond James "Cowboy" b: 2/16/12, Petrolia, Tex. d: 1/28/84, Alexandria, La. BR/TR, 6'1", 185 lbs. Deb: 4/16/35																												
1935	StL-N	1	1	.500	11	1	0	0	0	30	39	11.7	4	11	3.3	13	3.9	6.60	61	.320	.368	-9	-9	100	90	-0.1	-1	-0	-0.8
1937	StL-N	3	7	.300	35	15	1	1	1	97	99	9.2	7	59	5.5	41	3.8	5.85	67	.263	.356	-21	-21	100	78	-2.1	-2	-1	-2.2
1938	StL-N	2	3	.400	32	3	1	0	2	63	78	11.1	6	29	4.1	32	4.6	4.86	87	.308	.375	-7	-5	111	117	-0.3	-2	0	-0.5
1939	Chi-N	0	2	.000	4	2	0	0	0	17	29	15.4	2	6	3.2	5	2.6	8.47	46	.387	.427	-9	-9	100	92	-0.9	-1	0	-0.7
	Phi-N	3	7	.300	22	10	4	0	0	95	101	9.6	6	56	5.3	35	3.3	5.40	72	.270	.362	-16	-16	99	85	0.0	-1	-3	-1.8
	Yr	3	9	.250	26	12	4	0	0	112	130	10.4	8	62	5.0	40	3.2	5.87	66	.290	.372	-24	-25	99	85	-0.9	-1	-3	-2.5
1940	Pit-N	0	0	—	3	0	0	0	0	3	5	15.0	0	2	6.0	3	9.0	9.00	41	.333	.412	-2	-2	95	70	0.0	0	0	-0.1
1945	NY-N	0	0	—	12	0	0	0	0	25	34	12.2	1	14	5.0	7	2.5	5.04	76	.343	.412	-3	-3	100	128	0.0	1	0	-0.1
Total	6	9	20	.310	119	31	6	1	3	330	385	10.5	26	177	4.8	136	3.7	5.70	70	.293	.371	-66	-64	102	93	-3.4	-5	-3	-6.2
■ **BILL HARRELSON**	Harrelson, William Charles b: 11/17/45, Tahlequah, Okla. BB/TR, 6'5", 215 lbs. Deb: 7/31/68																												
1968	Cal-A	1	6	.143	10	5	1	0	0	34	28	7.4	4	26	6.9	22	5.8	5.03	57	.226	.357	-8	-8	96	88	-2.2	-0	-0	-0.9
■ **ANDY HARRINGTON**	Harrington, Andrew Francis b: 11/13/1888, Wakefield, Mass. d: 11/12/38, Malden, Mass. BR/TR, 6', 193 lbs. Deb: 9/08/13																												
1913	Cin-N	0	0	—	1	0	0	0	0	4	6	13.5	0	1	2.3	1	2.3	9.00	37	.353	.350	-3	-3	104	59	0.0	0	0	-0.1
■ **BILL HARRINGTON**	Harrington, William Womble b: 10/3/27, Sanford, N.C. BR/TR, 5'11", 160 lbs. Deb: 4/16/53																												
1953	Phi-A	0	0	—	1	0	0	0	0	2	5	22.5	0	0	0.0	0	0.0	13.50	31	.500	.455	-2	-2	105	76	0.0	0	0	-0.1
1955	KC-A	3	3	.500	34	1	0	0	2	77	69	8.1	6	41	4.8	26	3.0	4.09	103	.246	.333	-1	1	106	96	0.5	-1	-1	0.0
1956	KC-A	2	2	.500	23	1	0	0	1	38	40	9.5	3	26	6.2	14	3.3	6.39	68	.274	.382	-9	-9	105	77	0.5	-1	0	-0.8
Total	3	5	5	.500	58	2	0	0	3	117	114	8.8	9	67	5.2	40	3.1	5.00	85	.261	.352	-13	-10	106	90	1.0	-1	-1	-0.9
■ **BEN HARRIS**	Harris, Ben Franklin b: 12/17/1889, Donelson, Tenn. d: 4/29/27, St.Louis, Mo. BR/TR, 6', 220 lbs. Deb: 4/19/14																												
1914	KC-F	7	7	.500	31	14	5	0	1	154	179	10.5	7	41	2.4	40	2.3	4.09	75	.303	.354	-15	-17	96	106	0.8	1	2	-1.4
1915	KC-F	0	0	—	1	0	0	0	0	2	1	4.5	0	0	0.0	0	0.0	0.00	—	.169	.169	1	1	97	0	0.0	0	0	0.1
Total	2	7	7	.500	32	14	5	0	1	156	180	10.4	7	41	2.4	40	2.3	4.04	76	.302	.353	-14	-17	96	105	0.8	1	2	-1.3
■ **LUM HARRIS**	Harris, Chalmer Luman b: 1/17/15, New Castle, Ala. BR/TR, 6'1", 180 lbs. Deb: 4/19/41 MC																												
1941	Phi-A	4	4	.500	33	10	5	0	2	132	134	9.1	16	51	3.5	49	3.3	4.77	89	.260	.327	-9	-7	103	89	0.6	2	-1	-0.6
1942	Phi-A	11	15	.423	26	20	10	1	0	166	146	7.9	14	70	3.8	60	3.3	3.74	99	.234	.308	-2	-1	101	91	1.6	-2	-1	-0.2
1943	Phi-A	7	21	.250	32	27	15	1	1	216	241	10.0	17	63	2.6	55	2.3	4.21	83	.279	.327	-22	-17	106	96	-3.4	-1	-0	-1.8
1944	Phi-A	10	9	.526	23	22	12	2	0	174	193	10.0	8	26	**1.3**	33	1.7	3.31	106	.281	.302	2	4	102	103	1.2	-1	-0	0.3
1946	Phi-A	3	14	.176	34	12	4	0	0	125	153	11.0	11	48	3.5	33	2.4	5.26	72	.308	.362	-24	-21	107	97	-3.9	1	3	-1.6
1947	Was-A	0	0	—	3	0	0	0	0	6	7	10.5	0	7	10.5	2	3.0	3.00	124	.318	.424	0	0	101	232	0.0	-0	1	0.1
Total	6	35	63	.357	151	91	46	4	3	819	874	9.6	66	265	2.9	232	2.5	4.16	89	.273	.324	-54	-42	104	97	-3.9	-1	1	-3.8
■ **BUBBA HARRIS**	Harris, Charles b: 2/15/26, Sulligent, Ala. BR/TR, 6'4", 204 lbs. Deb: 4/29/48																												
1948	Phi-A	5	2	.714	45	0	0	0	5	94	89	8.5	2	35	3.4	32	3.1	4.12	106	.249	.314	2	2	102	77	1.3	-1	-0	0.1
1949	Phi-A	1	1	.500	37	0	0	0	3	84	92	9.9	12	42	4.5	18	1.9	5.46	76	.286	.362	-12	-12	99	98	0.0	-2	2	-1.0
1951	Phi-A	0	0	—	3	0	0	0	0	4	4	9.0	0	5	11.3	2	4.5	9.00	49	.250	.455	-2	-2	106	67	0.0	0	0	-0.1
	Cle-A	0	0	—	2	0	0	0	0	4	5	11.3	0	4	9.0	1	2.3	4.50	85	.333	.450	-0	-0	93	156	0.0	0	0	0.0
	Yr	0	0	—	5	0	0	0	0	8	9	10.1	0	9	10.1	3	3.4	6.75	61	.281	.429	-2	-2	99	156	0.0	0	0	-0.1
Total	3	6	3	.667	87	0	0	0	8	186	190	9.2	14	86	4.2	53	2.6	4.84	88	.267	.343	-12	-12	100	88	1.3	-3	2	-1.0
■ **GREG HARRIS**	Harris, Greg Allen b: 11/2/55, Lynwood, Cal. BB/TR, 6', 165 lbs. Deb: 5/20/81																												
1981	NY-N	3	5	.375	16	14	0	0	1	69	65	8.5	8	28	3.7	54	7.0	4.43	81	.245	.317	-7	-7	103	85	-0.2	0	-0	-0.6
1982	Cin-N	2	6	.250	34	10	1	0	1	91	96	9.5	12	37	3.7	67	6.6	4.85	77	.274	.339	-13	-11	104	96	-1.3	-0	0	-1.0
1983	Cin-N	0	0	—	1	0	0	0	0	1	2	18.0	0	3	27.0	1	9.0	27.00	14	.500	.667	-3	-3	104	74	0.0	-0	0	-0.1
1984	Mon-N	0	1	.000	15	0	0	0	2	18	10	5.0	0	7	3.5	15	7.5	2.00	164	.172	.279	3	3	91	86	-0.4	-0	0	0.3
	SD-N	2	1	.667	19	1	0	0	1	37	28	6.8	3	18	4.4	30	7.3	2.68	131	.209	.304	4	3	98	112	0.3	1	-0	0.5
	Yr	2	2	.500	34	1	0	0	3	55	38	6.2	3	25	4.1	45	7.4	2.45	140	.196	.288	7	6	96	112	-0.1	-0	-0	0.8
1985	Tex-A	5	4	.556	58	0	0	0	11	113	74	5.9	7	43	3.4	111	8.8	2.47	185	.186	.271	21	**26**	110	85	1.3	0	1	2.8
1986	Tex-A	10	8	.556	73	0	0	0	20	111	103	8.4	12	42	3.4	95	7.7	2.84	140	.251	.316	17	14	95	137	0.4	0	1	1.5

YEAR	TM/L	W	L	PCT	G	GS	CG	SHO	SV	IP	H	H/G	HR	BB	BB/G	SO	SO/G	ERA	/A	OAVG	OOBP	PR	/A	PF	CPI	WAT	PB	PD	TPI
1987	Tex-A	5	10	.333	42	19	0	0	0	141	157	10.0	18	56	3.6	106	6.8	4.85	96	.281	.345	-6	-3	104	101	-2.1	0	0	-0.2
1988	Phi-N	4	6	.400	66	1	0	0	1	107	80	6.7	7	52	4.4	71	6.0	2.36	151	.209	.305	13	14	103	125	0.0	1	-0	1.7
Total	8	31	41	.431	324	45	1	0	37	688	615	8.0	67	286	3.7	550	7.2	3.55	114	.240	.316	29	37	103	106	-2.0	2	2	4.9
■ **GREG HARRIS**	Harris, Gregory Wade b: 12/1/63, Greensboro, N.C. BR/TR, 6'2", 190 lbs. Deb: 9/14/88																												
1988	SD-N	2	0	1.000	3	1	1	0	0	18	13	6.5	0	3	1.5	15	7.5	1.50	224	.200	.235	4	4	97	79	1.0	-1	0	0.3
■ **HERB HARRIS**	Harris, Herbert Benjamin "Hub" or "Lefty" b: 4/24/13, Chicago, Ill. BL/TL, 6'1", 175 lbs. Deb: 7/21/36																												
1936	Phi-N	0	0	—	4	0	0	0	0	7	14	18.0	0	5	6.4	0	0.0	10.29	43	.438	.513	-5	-5	111	99	0.0	-0	0	-0.3
■ **JOE HARRIS**	Harris, Joseph White b: 2/1/1882, Melrose, Mass. d: 4/12/66, Melrose, Mass. TR, 6'1", 198 lbs. Deb: 9/22/05																												
1905	Bos-A	1	2	.333	3	3	3	0	0	23	16	6.3	0	8	3.1	14	5.5	2.35	113	.217	.294	1	1	100	76	-0.4	-1	-0	0.0
1906	Bos-A	2	21	.087	30	24	20	1	2	235	211	8.1	5	67	2.6	99	3.8	3.52	79	.264	.321	-22	-19	104	77	-8.6	-2	6	-1.4
1907	Bos-A	0	7	.000	12	5	3	0	0	59	57	8.7	0	13	2.0	24	3.7	3.05	86	.278	.321	-3	-3	103	85	-3.4	-0	0	-0.2
Total	3	3	30	.091	45	32	26	1	2	317	284	8.1	5	88	2.5	137	3.9	3.35	82	.264	.319	-24	-21	103	78	-12.4	-3	6	-1.6
■ **MICKEY HARRIS**	Harris, Maurice Charles b: 1/30/17, New York, N.Y. d: 4/15/71, Farmington, Mich. BL/TL, 6', 195 lbs. Deb: 4/23/40																												
1940	Bos-A	4	2	.667	13	9	3	0	0	68	83	11.0	8	26	3.4	36	4.8	5.03	87	.292	.355	-5	-5	100	103	0.9	2	0	-0.1
1941	Bos-A	8	14	.364	35	22	11	1	1	194	189	8.8	6	86	4.0	111	5.1	3.25	129	.250	.324	19	20	101	106	-4.0	2	-1	2.2
1946	Bos-A	17	9	.654	34	30	15	0	0	223	236	9.5	18	76	3.1	131	5.3	3.63	107	.268	.323	-3	6	111	105	-0.4	3	-1	0.9
1947	Bos-A	5	4	.556	15	6	1	0	0	52	42	7.3	3	23	4.0	35	6.1	2.42	163	.225	.304	7	9	107	122	0.2	3	0	1.3
1948	Bos-A	7	10	.412	20	17	6	1	0	114	120	9.5	10	59	4.7	42	3.3	5.29	79	.273	.356	-13	-14	97	90	-3.0	-1	-2	-1.5
1949	Bos-A	2	3	.400	7	6	2	0	0	38	53	12.6	3	20	4.7	14	3.3	4.97	87	.323	.389	-3	-3	103	120	-0.8	-1	0	-0.2
	Was-A	2	12	.143	23	19	4	0	0	129	151	10.5	8	55	3.8	54	3.8	5.16	78	.292	.354	-14	-16	96	89	-4.0	2	-2	-1.5
	Yr	4	15	.211	30	25	6	0	0	167	204	11.0	11	75	4.0	68	3.7	5.12	80	.299	.361	-17	-19	98	89	-4.8	-1	-2	-1.7
1950	Was-A	5	9	.357	**53**	0	0	0	**15**	98	93	8.5	10	46	4.2	41	3.8	4.78	97	.247	.326	-2	-2	101	82	-1.3	1	-1	-0.1
1951	Was-A	6	8	.429	41	0	0	0	4	87	87	9.0	6	43	4.4	47	4.9	3.83	104	.260	.340	3	2	97	108	0.3	0	-1	0.1
1952	Was-A	0	0	—	1	0	0	0	0	1	1	9.0	1	0	0.0	0	0.0	9.00	41	.250	.250	-1	-1	100	105	0.0	0	0	0.0
	Cle-A	3	0	1.000	29	0	0	0	1	47	42	8.0	6	21	4.0	23	4.4	4.60	70	.249	.325	-5	-7	88	91	1.5	0	0	-0.6
	Yr	3	0	1.000	30	0	0	0	1	48	43	8.1	7	21	3.9	23	4.3	4.69	69	.249	.323	-5	-8	88	91	1.5	0	0	-0.6
Total	9	59	71	.454	271	109	42	2	21	1051	1097	9.4	79	455	3.9	534	4.6	4.18	98	.267	.336	-16	-9	101	100	-10.6	11	-7	0.5
■ **BOB HARRIS**	Harris, Robert Arthur b: 5/1/16, Gillette, Wyo. BR/TR, 6', 185 lbs. Deb: 9/19/38																												
1938	Det-A	1	0	1.000	3	1	1	0	0	10	14	12.6	0	4	3.6	7	6.3	7.20	66	.318	.375	-3	-3	99	70	0.5	0	0	-0.1
1939	Det-A	1	1	.500	5	1	0	0	0	18	18	9.0	4	8	4.0	9	4.5	4.00	127	.269	.342	1	2	110	139	0.0	0	0	0.2
	StL-A	3	12	.200	28	16	6	0	0	126	162	11.6	5	71	5.1	48	3.4	5.71	85	.321	.394	-15	-12	105	104	-2.2	-0	3	-0.8
	Yr	4	13	.235	33	17	6	0	0	144	180	11.3	9	79	4.9	57	3.6	5.50	89	.315	.388	-14	-10	105	104	-2.2	0	3	-0.6
1940	StL-A	11	15	.423	35	28	8	1	1	194	225	10.4	24	85	3.9	49	2.3	4.92	96	.290	.357	-12	-4	108	108	-0.3	3	-0	0.0
1941	StL-A	12	14	.462	34	29	9	2	1	187	237	11.4	18	85	4.1	57	2.7	5.20	81	.312	.380	-22	-21	101	110	0.2	-2	-2	-2.2
1942	StL-A	1	5	.167	6	6	0	0	0	34	37	9.8	2	17	4.5	9	2.4	5.56	67	.268	.344	-7	-7	102	76	-2.0	-1	-1	-0.7
	Phi-A	1	5	.167	16	8	2	1	0	78	77	8.9	5	24	2.8	26	3.0	2.88	128	.253	.302	7	7	101	116	-1.5	1	2	1.1
	Yr	2	10	.167	22	14	2	1	0	112	114	9.2	7	41	3.3	35	2.8	3.70	100	.258	.316	-0	0	101	116	-3.5	-1	2	0.4
Total	5	30	52	.366	127	89	26	4	2	647	770	10.7	58	294	4.1	205	2.9	4.95	89	.297	.364	-51	-38	104	108	-5.3	1	3	-2.5
■ **BUDDY HARRIS**	Harris, Walter Francis b: 12/5/48, Philadelphia, Pa. BR/TR, 6'7", 245 lbs. Deb: 9/10/70																												
1970	Hou-N	0	0	—	2	0	0	0	0	6	6	9.0	3	0	0.0	2	3.0	6.00	63	.240	.240	-1	-1	94	87	0.0	-0	0	-0.1
1971	Hou-N	1	1	.500	20	0	0	0	0	31	33	9.6	3	16	4.6	21	6.1	6.39	50	.275	.355	-10	-11	92	72	0.0	-0	-1	-1.1
Total	2	1	1	.500	22	0	0	0	0	37	39	9.5	6	16	3.9	23	5.6	6.32	52	.269	.337	-11	-12	93	74	0.0	-0	-1	-1.2
■ **BILL HARRIS**	Harris, William Milton b: 6/23/1900, Wylie, Tex. d: 8/21/65, Indian Trail, N.C. BR/TR, 6'1", 180 lbs. Deb: 4/22/23																												
1923	Cin-N	3	2	.600	22	3	1	0	0	70	79	10.2	3	18	2.3	18	2.3	5.14	75	.292	.332	-9	-10	96	78	0.1	1	0	-0.7
1924	Cin-N	0	0	—	3	0	0	0	0	7	10	12.9	0	2	2.6	5	6.4	9.00	43	.323	.364	-4	-4	99	51	0.0	0	0	-0.2
1931	Pit-N	2	2	.500	4	4	3	1	0	31	21	6.1	0	9	2.6	10	2.9	0.87	451	.194	.248	10	11	102	162	0.1	-1	0	1.1
1932	Pit-N	10	9	.526	37	17	4	0	2	168	178	9.5	6	38	2.0	63	3.4	3.64	106	.271	.310	4	4	100	95	-0.5	-1	-2	0.1
1933	Pit-N	4	4	.500	31	0	0	0	5	59	68	10.4	1	14	2.1	19	2.9	3.20	98	.289	.323	1	-0	94	114	-0.4	-1	-1	-0.1
1934	Pit-N	0	0	—	11	2	0	0	0	19	28	13.3	2	7	3.3	8	3.8	6.63	64	.350	.396	-5	-5	105	103	0.0	0	0	-0.3
1938	Bos-A	5	5	.500	13	11	5	1	1	80	83	9.3	5	21	2.4	26	2.9	4.05	118	.268	.310	7	7	100	93	-0.7	-0	-0	0.6
Total	7	24	22	.522	121	37	13	2	8	434	467	9.7	17	109	2.3	149	3.1	3.92	101	.276	.316	4	1	99	99	-1.4	-1	-2	0.5
■ **BILL HARRIS**	Harris, William Thomas b: 12/3/31, Duguayville, N.B., Canada BL/TR, 5'8", 187 lbs. Deb: 9/27/57																												
1957	Bro-N	0	1	.000	1	1	0	0	0	7	9	11.6	1	1	1.3	3	3.9	3.86	115	.321	.333	0	0	114	136	-0.4	0	0	0.1
1959	LA-N	0	0	—	1	0	0	0	0	2	0	0.0	0	3	13.5	0	0.0	0.00	—	.000	.375	1	1	101	0	0.0	0	0	0.1
Total	2	0	1	.000	2	1	0	0	0	9	9	9.0	1	4	4.0	3	3.0	3.00	145	.273	.342	1	1	111	106	-0.4	0	0	0.2
■ **BOB HARRISON**	Harrison, Robert Lee b: 9/22/30, St.Louis, Mo. BL/TR, 5'11", 178 lbs. Deb: 9/23/55																												
1955	Bal-A	0	0	—	1	0	0	0	0	2	3	13.5	0	4	18.0	0	0.0	9.00	41	.500	.636	-1	-1	94	147	0.0	0	0	0.0
1956	Bal-A	0	0	—	1	1	0	0	0	2	3	13.5	0	5	22.5	0	0.0	13.50	30	.375	.615	-2	-2	97	91	0.0	0	0	-0.1
Total	2	0	0	—	2	1	0	0	0	4	6	13.5	0	9	20.3	0	0.0	11.25	34	.429	.625	-3	-3	95	119	0.0	0	0	-0.1
■ **RORIC HARRISON**	Harrison, Roric Edward b: 9/20/46, Los Angeles, Cal. BR/TR, 6'3", 195 lbs. Deb: 4/18/72																												
1972	Bal-A	3	4	.429	39	2	0	0	4	94	68	6.5	2	34	3.3	62	5.9	2.30	128	.209	.285	8	7	96	95	-0.5	1	-0	0.8
1973	Atl-N	11	8	.579	38	22	3	0	5	177	161	8.2	15	98	5.0	130	6.6	4.17	99	.242	.337	-10	-1	113	92	2.1	-2	-1	-0.3
1974	Atl-N	6	11	.353	20	20	3	0	0	126	148	10.6	12	49	3.5	46	3.3	4.71	80	.294	.356	-15	-13	104	102	-3.1	3	-2	-1.2
1975	Atl-N	3	4	.429	15	7	2	0	1	55	58	9.5	7	19	3.1	22	3.6	4.75	74	.266	.321	-7	-7	97	86	0.1	1	0	-0.6
	Cle-A	7	7	.500	19	19	4	0	0	126	137	9.8	9	46	3.3	52	3.7	4.79	79	.274	.335	-14	-14	100	84	0.0	0	-1	-1.4
1978	Min-A	0	1	.000	9	0	0	0	0	12	18	13.5	0	11	8.3	7	5.3	7.50	48	.346	.453	-5	-5	94	94	-0.4	0	-0	-0.5
Total	5	30	35	.462	140	70	12	0	10	590	590	9.0	45	257	3.9	319	4.9	4.24	88	.261	.334	-43	-34	103	92	-1.8	2	-5	-3.2
■ **TOM HARRISON**	Harrison, Thomas James b: 1/18/45, Trail, B.C., Canada BR/TR, 6'3", 200 lbs. Deb: 5/07/65																												
1965	KC-A	0	0	—	1	0	0	0	0	1	2	18.0	0	1	9.0	0	0.0	9.00	38	.667	.750	-1	-1	100	154	0.0	0	0	0.0
■ **SLIM HARRISS**	Harriss, William Jennings Bryan b: 12/11/1896, Brownwood, Tex. d: 9/19/63, Temple, Tex. BR/TR, 6'6", 180 lbs. Deb: 4/19/20																												
1920	Phi-A	9	14	.391	31	25	11	1	0	192	226	10.6	5	57	2.7	60	2.8	4.08	92	.305	.359	-6	-7	99	103	1.5	-6	3	-1.0
1921	Phi-A	11	16	.407	39	28	14	0	2	228	258	10.2	16	73	2.9	92	3.6	4.26	108	.290	.343	0	8	107	102	1.5	-7	-1	0.0
1922	Phi-A	9	20	.310	47	32	13	0	3	230	262	10.3	19	94	3.7	102	4.0	5.01	86	.290	.351	-25	-18	106	91	-4.4	-4	0	-1.9
1923	Phi-A	10	16	.385	46	28	9	0	6	209	221	9.5	9	95	4.1	89	3.8	4.00	102	.280	.348	-1	1	102	103	-2.2	-8	5	0.0
1924	Phi-A	6	10	.375	36	12	4	1	2	123	138	10.1	5	62	4.5	45	3.3	4.68	91	.291	.362	-6	-6	101	99	-1.6	-3	4	-0.3
1925	Phi-A	19	12	.613	46	33	15	2	1	253	263	9.4	8	95	3.4	95	3.4	3.49	127	.268	.330	25	27	101	101	1.5	-2	4	2.7
1926	Phi-A	3	5	.375	12	10	2	0	0	57	66	10.4	0	22	3.5	13	2.1	4.11	113	.289	.337	-1	3	116	93	-1.2	-2	0	0.2
	Bos-A	6	10	.375	21	18	6	1	0	113	135	10.8	0	33	2.6	34	2.7	4.46	95	.311	.344	-6	-3	106	96	0.9	-0	1	-0.1
	Yr	9	15	.375	33	28	8	1	0	170	201	10.6	0	55	2.9	47	2.5	4.34	101	.304	.342	-6	1	109	96	-0.3	-2	1	0.1
1927	Bos-A	14	21	.400	44	27	11	1	1	218	253	10.4	8	66	2.7	77	3.2	4.17	98	.298	.341	-1	-2	99	104	2.3	-5	1	-0.5
1928	Bos-A	8	11	.421	27	15	4	1	1	128	141	9.9	5	33	2.3	37	2.6	4.64	88	.287	.321	-8	-8	101	84	0.8	-3	-2	-1.1
Total	9	95	135	.413	349	228	89	7	16	1751	1963	10.1	75	630	3.2	644	3.3	4.25	100	.290	.344	-27	-3	103	99	-0.9	-40	14	-2.0
■ **EARL HARRIST**	Harrist, Earl "Irish" b: 8/20/19, Dubach, La. BR/TR, 6', 175 lbs. Deb: 8/18/45																												
1945	Cin-N	2	4	.333	14	5	1	0	0	62	60	8.7	2	27	3.9	15	2.2	3.63	102	.249	.321	1	0	97	93	-0.4	-2	-1	-0.2
1947	Chi-A	3	8	.273	33	4	0	0	5	94	85	8.1	3	49	4.7	55	5.3	3.54	103	.248	.337	2	1	99	103	-2.2	-0	1	0.2
1948	Chi-A	1	3	.250	11	1	0	0	0	23	23	9.0	4	13	5.1	14	5.5	5.87	73	.267	.368	-4	-4	100	98	-0.4	-1	0	-0.4
	Was-A	3	3	.500	23	4	0	0	0	60	70	10.5	1	37	5.6	21	3.2	4.65	99	.293	.390	-2	-0	107	110	0.7	-1	-1	-0.1
	Yr	4	6	.400	34	5	0	0	0	83	93	10.1	5	50	5.4	35	3.8	4.99	90	.284	.376	-7	-5	105	110	0.3	-1	-1	-0.5

YEAR	TM/L	W	L	PCT	G	GS	CG	SHO	SV	IP	H	H/G	HR	BB	BB/G	SO	SO/G	ERA	/A	OAVG	OOBP	PR	/A	PF	CPI	WAT	PB	PD	TPI
1952	StL-A	2	8	.200	36	9	1	0	5	117	119	9.2	7	47	3.6	49	3.8	4.00	91	.269	.348	-4	-4	100	104	-2.6	-2	1	-0.5
1953	Chi-A	1	0	1.000	7	0	0	0	0	8	9	10.1	1	5	5.6	1	1.1	7.88	53	.290	.389	-3	-3	104	72	0.5	-0	0	-0.3
	Det-A	0	2	.000	8	1	0	0	0	19	25	11.8	2	15	7.1	7	3.3	8.53	48	.333	.421	-10	-9	102	84	-0.9	-0	1	-0.7
	Yr	1	2	.333	15	1	0	0	0	27	34	11.3	3	20	6.7	8	2.7	8.33	49	.321	.412	-13	-13	102	84	-0.4	-0	1	-1.0
Total	5	12	28	.300	132	24	2	0	10	383	391	9.2	20	193	4.5	162	3.8	4.35	89	.268	.354	-21	-20	100	101	-5.3	-7	0	-2.0

■ JACK HARSHMAN Harshman, John Elvin b: 7/12/27, San Diego, Cal. BL/TL, 6'2", 178 lbs. Deb: 9/16/48

YEAR	TM/L	W	L	PCT	G	GS	CG	SHO	SV	IP	H	H/G	HR	BB	BB/G	SO	SO/G	ERA	/A	OAVG	OOBP	PR	/A	PF	CPI	WAT	PB	PD	TPI
1952	NY-N	0	2	.000	2	2	0	0	0	6	12	18.0	2	6	9.0	6	9.0	15.00	25	.429	.500	-8	-7	101	86	-0.9	-0	0	-0.5
1954	Chi-A	14	8	.636	35	21	9	4	1	177	157	8.0	7	96	4.9	134	6.8	2.95	126	.238	.334	15	15	100	114	0.8	3	-1	1.9
1955	Chi-A	11	7	.611	32	23	9	0	0	179	144	7.2	16	97	4.9	116	5.8	3.37	115	.224	.322	12	10	98	104	0.5	4	-0	1.3
1956	Chi-A	15	11	.577	34	30	15	4	0	227	183	7.3	14	102	4.0	143	5.7	3.09	137	.221	.303	27	29	102	92	0.9	6	-2	3.3
1957	Chi-A	8	8	.500	30	26	6	0	1	151	142	8.5	16	82	4.9	83	4.9	4.11	89	.250	.343	-5	-8	97	102	-1.2	5	-3	-0.4
1958	Bal-A	12	15	.444	34	29	17	3	4	236	204	7.8	20	75	2.9	161	6.1	2.90	124	.231	.289	23	18	95	101	-1.2	7	1	3.1
1959	Bal-A	0	6	.000	14	8	0	0	0	47	58	11.1	6	28	5.4	24	4.6	6.89	55	.319	.398	-16	-16	98	95	-2.9	1	1	-1.2
	Bos-A	2	3	.400	8	2	0	0	0	25	29	10.4	2	10	3.6	14	5.0	6.48	63	.284	.342	-7	-7	105	69	-0.4	0	-0	-0.6
	Cle-A	5	1	.833	13	6	5	1	1	66	46	6.3	6	13	1.8	35	4.8	2.59	141	.179	.213	9	8	95	42	1.8	2	0	1.0
	Yr	7	10	.412	35	16	5	1	1	138	133	8.7	14	51	3.3	73	4.8	4.76	79	.244	.301	-14	-15	98	42	-1.5	2	1	-0.8
1960	Cle-A	2	4	.333	15	8	0	0	0	54	50	8.3	7	30	5.0	25	4.2	4.00	95	.243	.333	-1	-1	98	103	-0.9	-0	-1	-0.1
Total	8	69	65	.515	217	155	61	12	7	1168	1025	7.9	96	539	4.2	741	5.7	3.51	109	.235	.316	49	40	98	97	-3.5	29	-5	7.8

■ OSCAR HARSTAD Harstad, Oscar Theander b: 5/24/1892, Parkland, Wash. d: 11/14/85, Corvallis, Ore. 6', 174 lbs. Deb: 4/23/15

YEAR	TM/L	W	L	PCT	G	GS	CG	SHO	SV	IP	H	H/G	HR	BB	BB/G	SO	SO/G	ERA	/A	OAVG	OOBP	PR	/A	PF	CPI	WAT	PB	PD	TPI
1915	Cle-A	3	5	.375	32	7	4	0	1	82	81	8.9	1	35	3.8	35	3.8	3.40	92	.270	.348	-4	-2	106	104	0.0	-1	2	-0.1

■ BILLY HART Hart, Joseph L. 5'8", Deb: 7/13/1890

YEAR	TM/L	W	L	PCT	G	GS	CG	SHO	SV	IP	H	H/G	HR	BB	BB/G	SO	SO/G	ERA	/A	OAVG	OOBP	PR	/A	PF	CPI	WAT	PB	PD	TPI
1890	StL-a	12	8	.600	26	24	20	0	0	201	188	8.4	6	66	3.0	95	4.3	3.67	121	.263	.325	4	17	115	90	0.7	-1	0	1.7

■ BILL HART Hart, William Franklin b: 7/19/1865, Louisville, Ky. d: 9/19/36, Cincinnati, Ohio TR, 5'10", 163 lbs. Deb: 7/26/1886

YEAR	TM/L	W	L	PCT	G	GS	CG	SHO	SV	IP	H	H/G	HR	BB	BB/G	SO	SO/G	ERA	/A	OAVG	OOBP	PR	/A	PF	CPI	WAT	PB	PD	TPI
1886	Phi-a	9	13	.409	22	22	22	2	0	186	183	8.9	7	66	3.2	78	3.8	3.19	111	.267	.332	5	7	103	115	-1.5	-5	0	0.2
1887	Phi-a	1	2	.333	3	3	3	0	0	26	28	9.7	1	17	5.9	4	1.4	4.50	95	.289	.395	-1	-1	100	110	-0.4	-2	0	-0.1
1892	Bro-N	9	12	.429	28	23	16	2	1	195	188	8.7	3	96	4.4	65	3.0	3.28	100	.266	.354	0	-0	99	103	-3.4	2	0	0.2
1895	Pit-N	14	17	.452	36	29	24	0	1	262	293	10.1	4	135	4.6	85	2.9	4.77	97	.303	.388	0	-5	96	92	-3.0	-2	6	0.0
1896	StL-N	12	29	.293	42	41	37	0	0	336	411	11.0	11	141	3.8	65	1.7	5.12	84	.324	.392	-28	-31	98	92	-1.3	-5	6	-2.4
1897	StL-N	9	27	.250	39	38	31	0	0	295	395	12.1	10	148	4.5	67	2.0	6.28	68	.344	.419	-65	-67	99	87	0.9	-0	4	-5.0
1898	Pit-N	5	9	.357	16	15	13	1	1	125	141	10.2	4	44	3.2	19	1.4	4.82	73	.307	.367	-17	-18	98	83	-1.9	0	0	-1.5
1901	Cle-A	7	11	.389	20	19	16	0	0	158	180	10.3	3	57	3.2	48	2.7	3.76	95	.307	.368	-2	-3	97	106	-0.2	-1	2	0.0
Total	8	66	120	.355	206	190	162	5	3	1583	1819	10.3	43	704	4.0	431	2.5	4.66	86	.307	.381	-106	-116	99	96	-10.8	-13	18	-8.6

■ CHUCK HARTENSTEIN Hartenstein, Charles Oscar "Twiggy" b: 5/26/42, Seguin, Tex. BR/TR, 5'11", 165 lbs. Deb: 9/11/65 C

YEAR	TM/L	W	L	PCT	G	GS	CG	SHO	SV	IP	H	H/G	HR	BB	BB/G	SO	SO/G	ERA	/A	OAVG	OOBP	PR	/A	PF	CPI	WAT	PB	PD	TPI
1966	Chi-N	0	0	—	5	0	0	0	0	9	8	8.0	0	3	3.0	4	4.0	2.00	185	.222	.300	2	2	103	107	0.0	0	0	0.2
1967	Chi-N	9	5	.643	45	0	0	0	10	73	74	9.1	4	17	2.1	20	2.5	3.08	110	.278	.315	2	2	100	122	1.7	-1	0	0.1
1968	Chi-N	2	4	.333	28	0	0	0	1	36	41	10.3	3	11	2.8	17	4.3	4.50	75	.291	.340	-6	-5	112	98	-1.0	-0	-0	-0.5
1969	Pit-N	5	4	.556	56	0	0	0	10	96	84	7.9	9	27	2.5	44	4.1	3.94	86	.241	.296	-4	-6	94	84	0.1	-1	1	-0.5
1970	Pit-N	1	1	.500	17	0	0	0	1	24	25	9.4	3	8	3.0	14	5.3	4.50	86	.278	.320	-1	-2	96	102	0.0	-0	1	0.0
	StL-N	0	0	—	6	0	0	0	0	13	24	16.6	1	5	3.5	9	6.2	9.00	48	.375	.408	-7	-7	106	83	0.0	0	0	-0.5
	Yr	1	1	.500	23	0	0	0	1	37	49	11.9	4	13	3.2	23	5.6	6.08	66	.316	.356	-8	-8	100	83	0.0	-0	1	-0.5
	Bos-A	0	3	.000	17	0	0	0	1	19	21	9.9	6	12	5.7	12	5.7	8.05	51	.288	.386	-9	-8	110	89	-1.4	0	-0	-0.8
1977	Tor-A	0	2	.000	13	0	0	0	0	27	40	13.3	8	6	2.0	15	5.0	6.67	64	.348	.382	-8	-7	105	114	-0.9	0	0	-0.6
Total	6	17	19	.472	187	0	0	0	23	297	317	9.6	34	89	2.7	135	4.1	4.52	80	.280	.329	-31	-30	101	100	-1.5	-2	2	-2.6

■ FRANK HARTER Harter, Franklin Pierce "Chief" b: 9/19/1886, Keyesport, Ill. d: 4/14/59, Breese, Ill. BR/TR, 5'11", 165 lbs. Deb: 8/31/12

YEAR	TM/L	W	L	PCT	G	GS	CG	SHO	SV	IP	H	H/G	HR	BB	BB/G	SO	SO/G	ERA	/A	OAVG	OOBP	PR	/A	PF	CPI	WAT	PB	PD	TPI
1912	Cin-N	1	2	.333	6	3	1	0	0	29	25	7.8	1	11	3.4	12	3.7	3.10	103	.225	.295	1	0	93	67	-0.4	-1	-1	-0.1
1913	Cin-N	1	1	.500	17	2	0	0	0	47	47	9.0	3	19	3.6	10	1.9	3.83	87	.272	.333	-3	-3	104	102	0.1	-1	-1	-0.3
1914	Ind-F	1	2	.333	6	1	1	0	0	25	33	11.9	0	7	2.5	8	2.9	3.96	87	.350	.395	-2	-1	108	116	-0.5	-1	0	-0.2
Total	3	3	5	.375	29	6	2	0	0	101	105	9.4	4	37	3.3	30	2.7	3.65	91	.278	.337	-4	-4	102	95	-0.8	-3	-2	-0.6

■ CHARLIE HARTMAN Hartman, Charles Otto b: 8/10/1888, Los Angeles, Cal. d: 10/22/60, Los Angeles, Cal. Deb: 6/24/08

YEAR	TM/L	W	L	PCT	G	GS	CG	SHO	SV	IP	H	H/G	HR	BB	BB/G	SO	SO/G	ERA	/A	OAVG	OOBP	PR	/A	PF	CPI	WAT	PB	PD	TPI
1908	Bos-A	0	0	—	1	0	0	0	0	2	1	4.5	0	2	9.0	1	4.5	4.50	52	.143	.333	-0	-0	97	48	0.0	0	0	0.0

■ BOB HARTMAN Hartman, Robert Louis b: 8/28/37, Kenosha, Wis. BR/TL, 5'11", 185 lbs. Deb: 4/26/59

YEAR	TM/L	W	L	PCT	G	GS	CG	SHO	SV	IP	H	H/G	HR	BB	BB/G	SO	SO/G	ERA	/A	OAVG	OOBP	PR	/A	PF	CPI	WAT	PB	PD	TPI
1959	Mil-N	0	0	—	3	0	0	0	0	2	6	27.0	0	2	9.0	1	4.5	22.50	16	.545	.615	-4	-4	93	69	0.0	0	0	-0.3
1962	Cle-A	0	1	.000	8	2	0	0	0	17	14	7.4	1	8	4.2	11	5.8	3.18	123	.209	.289	1	1	99	75	-0.4	-1	-0	0.0
Total	2	0	1	.000	11	2	0	0	0	19	20	9.5	1	10	4.7	12	5.7	5.21	75	.256	.337	-3	-3	98	74	-0.4	-1	-0	-0.3

■ RAY HARTRANFT Hartranft, Raymond Joseph b: 9/19/1890, Quakertown, Pa. d: 2/10/55, Spring City, Pa. BL/TL, 6'1", 195 lbs. Deb: 6/16/13

YEAR	TM/L	W	L	PCT	G	GS	CG	SHO	SV	IP	H	H/G	HR	BB	BB/G	SO	SO/G	ERA	/A	OAVG	OOBP	PR	/A	PF	CPI	WAT	PB	PD	TPI
1913	Phi-N	0	0	—	1	0	0	0	0	1	3	27.0	0	1	9.0	1	9.0	9.00	39	.500	.571	-1	-1	111	160	0.0	0	0	0.0

■ CLINT HARTUNG Hartung, Clinton Clarence "Floppy" or "The Hondo Hurricane" b: 8/10/22, Hondo, Tex. BR/TR, 6'5", 210 lbs. Deb: 4/15/47

YEAR	TM/L	W	L	PCT	G	GS	CG	SHO	SV	IP	H	H/G	HR	BB	BB/G	SO	SO/G	ERA	/A	OAVG	OOBP	PR	/A	PF	CPI	WAT	PB	PD	TPI
1947	NY-N	9	7	.563	23	20	8	1	0	138	140	9.1	15	69	4.5	54	3.5	4.57	89	.263	.347	-8	-8	99	98	0.7	9	-1	0.4
1948	NY-N	8	8	.500	36	19	6	2	1	153	146	8.6	15	72	4.2	42	2.5	4.76	82	.258	.340	-14	-15	98	91	0.0	2	-0	-1.2
1949	NY-N	9	11	.450	33	25	8	0	0	155	156	9.1	16	86	5.0	48	2.8	4.99	82	.260	.355	-16	-16	101	92	-0.5	4	1	-0.9
1950	NY-N	3	3	.500	20	8	1	0	0	65	87	12.0	10	44	6.1	23	3.2	6.65	60	.326	.422	-18	-19	97	108	-0.2	4	2	-0.9
Total	4	29	29	.500	112	72	23	3	1	511	529	9.3	56	271	4.8	167	2.9	5.02	80	.269	.358	-56	-58	99	95	-0.0	19	3	-2.6

■ PAUL HARTZELL Hartzell, Paul Franklin b: 11/2/53, Bloomsburg, Pa. BR/TR, 6'5", 200 lbs. Deb: 4/10/76

YEAR	TM/L	W	L	PCT	G	GS	CG	SHO	SV	IP	H	H/G	HR	BB	BB/G	SO	SO/G	ERA	/A	OAVG	OOBP	PR	/A	PF	CPI	WAT	PB	PD	TPI
1976	Cal-A	7	4	.636	37	15	7	2	2	166	166	9.0	6	43	2.3	51	2.8	2.77	118	.266	.316	14	9	93	**124**	1.8	0	1	1.1
1977	Cal-A	8	12	.400	41	23	6	0	4	189	200	9.5	14	38	1.8	79	3.8	3.57	108	.274	.305	11	6	95	101	-1.3	0	1	0.6
1978	Cal-A	6	10	.375	54	12	5	0	6	157	168	9.6	8	41	2.4	55	3.2	3.44	111	.278	.325	6	7	101	107	-2.5	0	1	0.8
1979	Min-A	6	10	.375	28	26	4	0	0	163	193	10.7	18	44	2.4	44	2.4	5.36	85	.301	.342	-20	-14	108	91	-2.1	0	1	-1.2
1980	Bal-A	0	2	.000	6	0	0	0	0	18	22	11.0	3	9	4.5	5	2.5	6.50	62	.310	.387	-5	-5	99	94	-0.9	0	-0	-0.4
1984	Mil-A	0	1	.000	4	1	0	0	0	10	17	15.3	0	6	5.4	3	2.7	8.10	46	.370	.426	-5	-5	93	87	-0.4	0	0	-0.4
Total	6	27	39	.409	170	77	22	2	12	703	766	9.8	49	181	2.3	237	3.0	3.90	99	.282	.325	1	-2	99	105	-5.4	0	3	0.5

■ BRYAN HARVEY Harvey, Bryan Stanley b: 6/2/63, Chattanooga, Tenn. BR/TR, 6'3", 205 lbs. Deb: 5/16/87

YEAR	TM/L	W	L	PCT	G	GS	CG	SHO	SV	IP	H	H/G	HR	BB	BB/G	SO	SO/G	ERA	/A	OAVG	OOBP	PR	/A	PF	CPI	WAT	PB	PD	TPI
1987	Cal-A	0	0	—	3	0	0	0	0	5	6	10.8	0	2	3.6	3	5.4	0.00	—	.300	.364	2	2	100	0	0.0	0	-0	0.2
1988	Cal-A	7	5	.583	50	0	0	0	17	76	59	7.0	4	20	2.4	67	7.9	2.13	177	.214	.264	16	14	95	105	1.4	0	-1	1.3
Total	2	7	5	.583	53	0	0	0	17	81	65	7.2	4	22	2.4	70	7.8	2.00	190	.220	.271	18	16	95	98	1.4	0	-2	1.5

■ ERWIN HARVEY Harvey, Ervin King "Zaza" b: 1/5/1879, Saratoga, Cal. d: 6/3/54, Santa Monica, Cal. BL , Deb: 5/03/00

YEAR	TM/L	W	L	PCT	G	GS	CG	SHO	SV	IP	H	H/G	HR	BB	BB/G	SO	SO/G	ERA	/A	OAVG	OOBP	PR	/A	PF	CPI	WAT	PB	PD	TPI
1900	Chi-N	0	0	—	1	0	0	0	0	4	3	6.8	0	1	2.3	0	0.0	0.00	—	.228	.283	2	2	94	0	0.0	-0	0	0.2
1901	Chi-A	3	6	.333	16	9	5	0	1	92	91	8.9	2	34	3.3	27	2.6	3.62	97	.278	.346	0	-1	96	91	-1.9	2	2	-2.9
Total	2	3	6	.333	17	9	5	0	1	96	94	8.8	2	35	3.3	27	2.5	3.47	101	.276	.343	2	0	96	87	-1.9	1	2	-2.7

■ HERB HASH Hash, Herbert Howard b: 2/13/11, Woolwine, Va. BR/TR, 6'1", 180 lbs. Deb: 4/19/40

YEAR	TM/L	W	L	PCT	G	GS	CG	SHO	SV	IP	H	H/G	HR	BB	BB/G	SO	SO/G	ERA	/A	OAVG	OOBP	PR	/A	PF	CPI	WAT	PB	PD	TPI
1940	Bos-A	7	7	.500	34	12	3	1	3	120	123	9.2	11	84	6.3	36	2.7	4.95	89	.266	.380	-8	-8	100	106	-0.4	-0	1	-0.5
1941	Bos-A	1	0	1.000	4	0	0	0	1	8	7	7.9	1	7	7.9	3	3.4	5.63	75	.226	.359	-1	-1	101	82	0.5	-0	0	0.0
Total	2	8	7	.533	38	12	3	1	4	128	130	9.1	12	91	6.4	39	2.7	4.99	88	.264	.379	-9	-9	100	104	0.1	-0	1	-0.5

■ ANDY HASSLER Hassler, Andrew Earl b: 10/18/51, Texas City, Tex. BL/TL, 6'5", 220 lbs. Deb: 5/30/71

YEAR	TM/L	W	L	PCT	G	GS	CG	SHO	SV	IP	H	H/G	HR	BB	BB/G	SO	SO/G	ERA	/A	OAVG	OOBP	PR	/A	PF	CPI	WAT	PB	PD	TPI
1971	Cal-A	0	3	.000	6	4	0	0	0	19	25	11.8	0	15	7.1	13	6.2	3.79	91	.333	.446	-1	-1	99	167	-1.4	-1	0	0.0
1973	Cal-A	0	4	.000	7	4	1	0	0	32	33	9.3	0	19	5.3	19	5.3	3.66	101	.262	.367	1	0	96	107	-1.9	0	-0	0.0
1974	Cal-A	7	11	.389	23	22	10	2	1	162	132	7.3	10	79	4.4	76	4.2	2.61	129	.225	.322	18	14	93	121	-0.6	0	0	1.5
1975	Cal-A	3	12	.200	30	18	6	1	0	133	158	10.7	12	53	3.6	82	5.5	5.95	61	.303	.363	-32	-34	96	86	-4.2	0	1	-3.2

YEAR	TM/L	W	L	PCT	G	GS	CG	SHO	SV	IP	H	H/G	HR	BB	BB/G	SO	SO/G	ERA	/A	OAVG	OOBP	PR	/A	PF	CPI	WAT	PB	PD	TPI
1976	Cal-A	0	6	.000	14	4	0	0	0	47	50	9.6	3	17	3.3	16	3.1	5.17	63	.284	.335	-9	-10	93	82	-2.9	0	0	-0.9
	KC-A	5	6	.455	19	14	4	1	0	100	89	8.0	2	39	3.5	45	4.1	2.88	120	.242	.309	7	7	99	100	-1.0	0	1	0.8
	Yr	5	12	.294	33	18	4	1	0	147	139	8.5	5	56	3.4	61	3.7	3.61	94	.254	.318	-1	-3	97	100	-3.9	0	1	-0.1
1977	KC-A	9	6	.600	29	27	3	1	0	156	166	9.6	7	75	4.3	83	4.8	4.21	96	.270	.351	-2	-3	99	97	-0.3	0	0	-0.2
1978	KC-A	1	4	.200	11	9	1	0	0	58	76	11.8	1	24	3.7	26	4.0	4.34	88	.317	.378	-4	-3	101	114	-1.5	0	-0	-0.3
	Bos-A	2	1	.667	13	2	0	0	1	30	38	11.4	0	13	3.9	23	6.9	3.00	134	.302	.367	3	3	106	144	0.2	0	-0	0.3
	Yr	3	5	.375	24	11	1	0	1	88	114	11.7	1	37	3.8	49	5.0	3.89	100	.308	.369	-1	-0	103	144	-1.3	0	-1	0.0
1979	Bos-A	1	2	.333	8	0	0	0	0	15	23	13.8	0	7	4.2	7	4.2	9.00	50	.365	.431	-8	-8	106	74	-0.5	0	-0	-0.6
	NY-N	4	5	.444	29	8	1	0	4	80	74	8.3	5	42	4.7	53	6.0	3.71	97	.252	.338	0	-1	96	103	0.4	-2	1	-0.2
1980	Pit-N	0	0	—	6	0	0	0	0	12	9	6.8	2	4	3.0	4	3.0	3.75	99	.243	.289	-0	-0	103	112	0.0	-0	1	0.0
	Cal-A	5	1	.833	41	0	0	0	10	83	67	7.3	8	37	4.0	75	8.1	2.49	157	.214	.297	14	13	97	113	2.2	0	-1	1.3
1981	Cal-A	4	3	.571	42	0	0	0	5	76	72	8.5	8	33	3.9	44	5.2	3.20	119	.262	.333	4	5	104	133	0.7	0	1	0.6
1982	Cal-A	2	1	.667	54	0	0	0	4	71	58	7.4	5	40	5.1	38	4.8	2.79	144	.232	.338	10	10	99	137	0.3	0	2	1.2
1983	Cal-A	0	5	.000	42	0	0	0	4	36	42	10.5	2	17	4.3	20	5.0	5.50	71	.302	.369	-6	-6	96	92	-2.4	0	1	-0.5
1984	StL-N	1	0	1.000	3	0	0	0	0	2	4	18.0	2	2	9.0	1	4.5	13.50	26	.364	.462	-2	-2	99	119	0.5	0	0	-0.1
1985	StL-N	0	1	.000	10	0	0	0	0	10	9	8.1	0	4	3.6	5	4.5	1.80	187	.225	.289	2	2	93	119	-0.4	0	-0	0.2
Total	14	44	71	.383	387	112	26	5	29	1122	1125	9.0	67	520	4.2	630	5.1	3.83	97	.264	.343	-4	-16	98	109	-12.8	-3	5	-0.1

■ **CHARLIE HASTINGS** Hastings, Charles Morton b: 11/11/1870, Ironton, Ohio d: 8/3/34, Parkersburg, W.Va. 5'11", 179 lbs. Deb: 5/03/1893

YEAR	TM/L	W	L	PCT	G	GS	CG	SHO	SV	IP	H	H/G	HR	BB	BB/G	SO	SO/G	ERA	/A	OAVG	OOBP	PR	/A	PF	CPI	WAT	PB	PD	TPI
1893	Cle-N	4	5	.444	15	9	6	0	1	92	128	12.5	5	33	3.2	14	1.4	4.70	102	.346	.400	-0	1	103	121	-1.0	0	0	0.1
1896	Pit-N	5	10	.333	17	13	9	0	1	104	126	10.9	1	44	3.8	19	1.6	5.88	69	.322	.391	-18	-21	93	76	-2.7	0	0	-1.6
1897	Pit-N	5	4	.556	16	10	9	0	0	118	138	10.5	3	47	3.6	42	3.2	4.58	94	.314	.381	-3	-3	100	93	0.9	3	0	0.0
1898	Pit-N	4	10	.286	19	13	12	0	0	137	142	9.3	2	52	3.4	40	2.6	3.42	104	.289	.357	3	2	98	102	-3.0	2	0	0.4
Total	4	18	29	.383	67	45	36	0	2	451	534	10.7	11	176	3.5	115	2.3	4.55	90	.316	.380	-18	-22	98	98	-5.8	5	0	-1.1

■ **BOB HASTY** Hasty, Robert Keller b: 5/3/1896, Canton, Ga. d: 5/28/72, Dallas, Ga. BR/TR, 6'3", 210 lbs. Deb: 9/11/19

YEAR	TM/L	W	L	PCT	G	GS	CG	SHO	SV	IP	H	H/G	HR	BB	BB/G	SO	SO/G	ERA	/A	OAVG	OOBP	PR	/A	PF	CPI	WAT	PB	PD	TPI
1919	Phi-A	0	2	.000	2	2	1	0	0	12	15	11.3	1	4	3.0	5	3.8	5.25	69	.306	.358	-3	-2	112	87	-0.9	0	-1	-0.2
1920	Phi-A	1	3	.250	19	4	1	0	0	72	91	11.4	5	28	3.5	12	1.5	5.00	75	.323	.384	-10	-10	99	104	-0.3	0	1	-0.7
1921	Phi-A	5	16	.238	35	22	9	0	0	179	238	12.0	8	40	**2.0**	46	2.3	4.88	94	.331	.349	-12	-6	107	103	-3.5	2	1	-0.2
1922	Phi-A	9	14	.391	28	26	14	1	0	192	225	10.5	20	41	1.9	33	1.5	4.27	101	.298	.323	-5	1	106	103	-0.9	-2	-2	-0.2
1923	Phi-A	13	15	.464	44	36	10	1	1	243	274	10.1	11	72	2.7	56	2.1	4.44	91	.291	.333	-12	-10	102	91	0.3	-2	-1	-1.2
1924	Phi-A	1	3	.250	18	4	0	0	0	53	57	9.7	4	30	5.1	15	2.5	5.60	76	.282	.358	-8	-8	101	86	-0.8	-1	2	-0.6
Total	6	29	53	.354	146	94	35	2	1	751	900	10.8	49	215	2.6	167	2.0	4.65	91	.305	.341	-49	-35	104	98	-6.1	-3	-1	-3.1

■ **GIL HATFIELD** Hatfield, Gilbert "Colonel" b: 1/27/1855, Hoboken, N.J. d: 5/27/21, Hoboken, N.J. TR, 5'9.5", 168 lbs. Deb: 1885

YEAR	TM/L	W	L	PCT	G	GS	CG	SHO	SV	IP	H	H/G	HR	BB	BB/G	SO	SO/G	ERA	/A	OAVG	OOBP	PR	/A	PF	CPI	WAT	PB	PD	TPI
1889	NY-N	2	4	.333	6	5	5	0	0	52	53	9.2	2	25	4.3	28	4.8	3.98	102	.279	.363	0	1	101	99	-1.4	-0	0	0.0
1890	NY-P	1	1	.500	3	0	0	0	1	8	8	9.0	1	4	4.5	3	3.4	3.38	135	.272	.359	1	1	107	126	0.0	0	0	0.1
1891	Was-a	0	0	—	4	0	0	0	0	18	29	14.5	1	14	7.0	3	1.5	11.00	34	.379	.475	-15	-15	101	69	0.0	1	0	-1.0
Total	3	3	5	.375	13	5	5	0	1	78	90	10.4	4	43	5.0	34	3.9	5.54	73	.304	.393	-14	-13	102	95	-1.4	1	0	-0.9

■ **JOHN HATFIELD** Hatfield, John Van Buskirk b: 7/20/1847, New Jersey d: 2/20/09, Long Island City, N.Y. 5'10", 165 lbs. Deb: 5/18/1871 M

YEAR	TM/L	W	L	PCT	G	GS	CG	SHO	SV	IP	H	H/G	HR	BB	BB/G	SO	SO/G	ERA	/A	OAVG	OOBP	PR	/A	PF	CPI	WAT	PB	PD	TPI
1874	Mut-n	0	0	—	1																								

■ **RAY HATHAWAY** Hathaway, Ray Wilson b: 10/13/16, Greenville, Ohio BR/TR, 6', 165 lbs. Deb: 4/20/45

YEAR	TM/L	W	L	PCT	G	GS	CG	SHO	SV	IP	H	H/G	HR	BB	BB/G	SO	SO/G	ERA	/A	OAVG	OOBP	PR	/A	PF	CPI	WAT	PB	PD	TPI
1945	Bro-N	0	1	.000	4	1	0	0	0	9	11	11.0	1	6	6.0	3	3.0	4.00	90	.297	.395	-0	-0	95	147	-0.4	-0	0	0.0

■ **JOE HATTEN** Hatten, Joseph Hilarian b: 11/17/16, Bancroft, Iowa BR/TL, 6', 176 lbs. Deb: 4/21/46

YEAR	TM/L	W	L	PCT	G	GS	CG	SHO	SV	IP	H	H/G	HR	BB	BB/G	SO	SO/G	ERA	/A	OAVG	OOBP	PR	/A	PF	CPI	WAT	PB	PD	TPI
1946	Bro-N	14	11	.560	42	30	13	1	2	222	207	8.4	10	110	4.5	85	3.4	2.84	120	.253	.341	14	14	100	**129**	-1.2	-6	-2	0.7
1947	Bro-N	17	8	.680	42	32	11	3	0	225	211	8.4	9	105	4.2	76	3.0	3.64	115	.252	.332	11	13	103	99	2.6	0	3	1.6
1948	Bro-N	13	10	.565	42	30	11	1	0	209	228	9.8	9	94	4.0	73	3.1	3.57	114	.283	.355	9	11	103	125	0.6	1	4	1.7
1949	Bro-N	12	8	.600	37	29	11	2	2	187	194	9.3	15	69	3.3	58	2.8	4.19	94	.271	.335	-3	-5	98	100	-0.4	-1	0	-0.5
1950	Bro-N	2	2	.500	23	8	2	1	0	69	82	10.7	10	31	4.0	29	3.8	4.57	95	.294	.363	-3	-2	104	119	-0.2	-1	-0	-0.2
1951	Bro-N	1	0	1.000	11	6	0	0	0	49	55	10.1	3	21	3.9	22	4.0	4.59	82	.281	.349	-3	-5	95	94	0.5	-1	1	-0.4
	Chi-N	2	6	.250	23	6	1	0	0	75	82	9.8	8	37	4.4	23	2.8	5.16	77	.281	.359	-10	-10	100	95	-1.5	0	-0	-0.9
	Yr	3	6	.333	34	12	1	0	0	124	137	9.9	11	58	4.2	45	3.3	4.94	78	.281	.355	-13	-15	98	95	-1.0	-1	1	-1.3
1952	Chi-N	4	4	.500	13	8	2	0	0	50	65	11.7	6	25	4.5	15	2.7	6.12	63	.314	.387	-13	-13	103	98	0.0	-1	1	-1.1
Total	7	65	49	.570	233	149	51	8	4	1086	1124	9.3	70	492	4.1	381	3.2	3.88	101	.271	.346	1	5	101	111	0.4	-8	6	0.9

■ **CLYDE HATTER** Hatter, Clyde Melno b: 8/7/08, Poplar Hill, Ky. d: 10/16/37, Yosemite, Ky. BR/TL, 5'11", 170 lbs. Deb: 4/23/35

YEAR	TM/L	W	L	PCT	G	GS	CG	SHO	SV	IP	H	H/G	HR	BB	BB/G	SO	SO/G	ERA	/A	OAVG	OOBP	PR	/A	PF	CPI	WAT	PB	PD	TPI
1935	Det-A	0	0	—	8	2	0	0	0	33	44	12.0	2	30	8.2	15	4.1	7.64	54	.319	.436	-12	-13	93	92	0.0	0	-1	-1.1
1937	Det-A	1	0	1.000	3	0	0	0	0	9	17	17.0	0	11	11.0	4	4.0	12.00	41	.415	.537	-7	-7	108	91	0.5	-0	-0	-0.5
Total	2	1	0	1.000	11	2	0	0	0	42	61	13.1	2	41	8.8	19	4.1	8.57	50	.341	.460	-19	-20	96	91	0.5	0	-1	-1.6

■ **CHRIS HAUGHEY** Haughey, Christopher Francis "Bud" b: 10/3/25, Astoria, N.Y. BR/TR, 6'1", 180 lbs. Deb: 10/03/43

YEAR	TM/L	W	L	PCT	G	GS	CG	SHO	SV	IP	H	H/G	HR	BB	BB/G	SO	SO/G	ERA	/A	OAVG	OOBP	PR	/A	PF	CPI	WAT	PB	PD	TPI
1943	Bro-N	0	1	.000	1	0	0	0	0	7	5	6.4	0	10	12.9	0	0.0	3.86	87	.238	.455	-0	-0	99	153	-0.4	-0	0	0.0

■ **PHIL HAUGSTAD** Haugstad, Philip Donald b: 2/23/24, Black River Falls Wis. BR/TR, 6'2", 165 lbs. Deb: 9/01/47

YEAR	TM/L	W	L	PCT	G	GS	CG	SHO	SV	IP	H	H/G	HR	BB	BB/G	SO	SO/G	ERA	/A	OAVG	OOBP	PR	/A	PF	CPI	WAT	PB	PD	TPI
1947	Bro-N	1	0	1.000	6	1	0	0	0	13	14	9.7	1	4	2.8	4	2.8	2.77	151	.298	.346	2	2	103	169	0.5	-0	-0	0.2
1948	Bro-N	0	0	—	1	0	0	0	0	1	1	9.0	0	0	0.0	0	0.0	0.00	—	.333	.250	0	0	103	0	0.0	0	0	0.1
1951	Bro-N	0	1	.000	21	1	0	0	0	31	28	8.1	4	24	7.0	22	6.4	6.39	59	.233	.372	-8	-9	95	75	-0.4	0	0	-0.7
1952	Cin-N	0	0	—	9	0	0	0	0	12	8	6.0	1	13	9.8	2	1.5	6.75	55	.190	.373	-4	-4	100	66	0.0	-0	0	-0.3
Total	4	1	1	.500	37	2	0	0	0	57	51	8.1	6	41	6.5	28	4.4	5.53	70	.241	.365	-10	-11	98	93	0.1	-0	1	-0.7

■ **TOM HAUSMAN** Hausman, Thomas Matthew b: 3/31/53, Mobridge, S.D. BR/TR, 6'4", 190 lbs. Deb: 4/26/75

YEAR	TM/L	W	L	PCT	G	GS	CG	SHO	SV	IP	H	H/G	HR	BB	BB/G	SO	SO/G	ERA	/A	OAVG	OOBP	PR	/A	PF	CPI	WAT	PB	PD	TPI
1975	Mil-A	3	6	.333	29	9	1	0	0	112	110	8.8	7	47	3.8	46	3.7	4.10	94	.258	.331	-4	-3	101	92	-0.9	0	1	-0.2
1976	Mil-A	0	0	—	3	0	0	0	0	3	3	9.0	0	3	9.0	1	3.0	6.00	59	.250	.400	-1	-1	100	75	0.0	0	0	0.0
1978	NY-N	3	3	.500	10	10	0	0	0	52	58	10.0	6	9	1.6	16	2.8	4.67	76	.287	.315	-6	-6	99	91	0.5	0	0	-0.5
1979	NY-N	2	6	.250	19	10	1	0	2	79	65	7.4	6	19	2.2	33	3.8	2.73	132	.226	.279	9	8	96	96	-1.4	-1	0	0.7
1980	NY-N	6	5	.545	55	4	0	0	1	122	125	9.2	12	26	1.9	53	3.9	3.98	88	.266	.300	-5	-7	97	91	1.3	-1	1	-0.6
1981	NY-N	0	1	.000	20	0	0	0	0	33	28	7.6	2	7	1.9	13	3.5	2.18	164	.235	.269	5	5	103	119	-0.4	0	0	0.6
1982	NY-N	1	2	.333	21	0	0	0	0	37	44	10.7	4	6	1.5	16	3.9	4.38	82	.295	.321	-3	-3	100	101	-0.2	-0	-1	-0.3
	Atl-N	0	0	—	3	0	0	0	0	4	6	13.5	0	4	9.0	2	4.5	4.50	85	.500	.526	-0	-0	107	230	0.0	0	0	0.0
	Yr	1	2	.333	24	0	0	0	0	41	50	11.0	4	10	2.2	18	4.0	4.39	83	.299	.331	-4	-3	101	230	-0.2	-0	-0	-0.3
Total	7	15	23	.395	160	33	2	0	3	442	439	8.9	37	121	2.5	180	3.7	3.79	96	.262	.309	-6	-8	99	96	-1.1	-2	2	-0.3

■ **CLEM HAUSMANN** Hausmann, Clemens Raymond b: 8/17/19, Houston, Tex. d: 8/29/72, Baytown, Tex. BR/TR, 5'9", 165 lbs. Deb: 4/28/44

YEAR	TM/L	W	L	PCT	G	GS	CG	SHO	SV	IP	H	H/G	HR	BB	BB/G	SO	SO/G	ERA	/A	OAVG	OOBP	PR	/A	PF	CPI	WAT	PB	PD	TPI
1944	Bos-A	4	7	.364	32	12	3	0	2	137	139	9.1	6	69	4.5	43	2.8	3.42	97	.266	.350	0	-2	97	118	-1.5	-2	-0	-0.3
1945	Bos-A	5	7	.417	31	13	4	2	2	125	131	9.4	5	60	4.3	30	2.2	5.04	64	.270	.345	-23	-25	96	80	-0.5	-2	2	-2.6
1949	Phi-A	0	0	—	1	0	0	0	0	1	0	0.0	0	2	18.0	0	0.0	9.00	46	.000	.500	-1	-1	99	54	0.0	0	0	0.0
Total	3	9	14	.391	64	25	7	2	4	263	270	9.2	11	131	4.5	73	2.5	4.21	78	.267	.348	-24	-27	96	100	-2.0	-5	2	-2.9

■ **BRAD HAVENS** Havens, Bradley David b: 11/17/59, Highland Park, Mich BL/TL, 6'1", 180 lbs. Deb: 6/05/81

YEAR	TM/L	W	L	PCT	G	GS	CG	SHO	SV	IP	H	H/G	HR	BB	BB/G	SO	SO/G	ERA	/A	OAVG	OOBP	PR	/A	PF	CPI	WAT	PB	PD	TPI
1981	Min-A	3	6	.333	14	12	1	1	0	78	76	8.8	6	24	2.8	43	5.0	3.58	109	.257	.313	1	3	107	98	-0.5	0	-0	0.2
1982	Min-A	10	14	.417	33	32	4	1	0	209	201	8.7	32	80	3.4	129	5.6	4.31	96	.250	.315	-5	-4	102	95	1.0	0	-3	-0.6
1983	Min-A	5	8	.385	16	14	1	0	0	80	110	12.4	11	38	4.3	40	4.5	8.21	53	.333	.392	-37	-34	106	80	-0.7	0	-2	-3.2
1985	Bal-A	0	1	.000	8	1	0	0	0	14	20	12.9	4	10	6.4	19	12.2	9.00	45	.333	.429	-8	-8	98	94	-0.4	0	0	-0.6
1986	Bal-A	3	3	.500	46	0	0	0	1	71	64	8.1	7	29	3.7	57	7.2	4.56	91	.248	.316	-3	-3	99	84	0.3	0	1	-0.2
1987	LA-N	0	0	—	31	1	0	0	1	35	30	7.7	2	23	5.9	23	5.9	4.37	86	.227	.344	-1	-2	92	82	0.0	-0	-1	-0.2
1988	LA-N	0	0	—	9	0	0	0	0	10	15	13.5	1	4	3.6	8	7.2	4.50	81	.357	.404	-1	-1	105	152	0.0	-0	1	0.0
	Cle-A	2	3	.400	28	0	0	0	1	57	62	9.8	7	17	2.7	30	4.7	3.16	129	.273	.319	5	6	102	135	-0.3	0	-0	0.5

YEAR	TM/L	W	L	PCT	G	GS	CG	SHO	SV	IP	H	H/G	HR	BB	BB/G	SO	SO/G	ERA	/A	OAVG	OOBP	PR	/A	PF	CPI	WAT	PB	PD	TPI
Total	7	23	35	.397	185	60	6	2	3	554	578	9.4	70	225	3.7	349	5.7	4.81	85	.269	.334	-49	-43	102	96	-0.6	-0	-5	-4.1
■ **ED HAWK**	Hawk, Edward b: 5/11/1890, Neosho, Mo. d: 3/26/36, Neosho, Mo. BL/TR, 5'11", 175 lbs. Deb: 9/07/11																												
1911	StL-A	0	4	.000	5	4	4	0	0	38	38	9.0	1	8	1.9	14	3.3	3.32	100	.253	.309	0	0	100	80	-1.9	-1	0	0.0
■ **BILL HAWKE**	Hawke, William Victor "Dick" b: 4/28/1870, Elsmere, Del. d: 12/11/02, Wilmington, Del. BR/TR, 5'8.5", 169 lbs. Deb: 7/28/1892																												
1892	StL-N	5	5	.500	14	11	10	1	0	97	108	10.0	2	45	4.2	55	5.1	3.71	86	.295	.372	-5	-6	97	110	1.1	-4	0	-0.8
1893	StL-N	0	1	.000	1	1	0	0	0	5	9	16.2	0	3	5.4	1	1.8	5.40	87	.407	.477	-0	-0	100	148	-0.4	0	0	0.0
	Bal-N	11	16	.407	29	29	22	1	0	225	248	9.9	8	108	4.3	69	2.8	4.76	106	.295	.376	-2	7	108	93	-1.8	-5	0	0.2
	Yr	11	17	.393	30	30	22	1	0	230	257	10.1	8	111	4.3	70	2.7	4.77	105	.298	.378	-2	6	107	93	-2.2	0	0	0.2
1894	Bal-N	16	9	.640	32	25	17	0	3	205	264	11.6	9	78	3.4	68	3.0	5.84	88	.335	.395	-12	-16	96	87	-1.1	3	0	-0.9
Total	3	32	31	.508	76	66	49	2	3	532	629	10.6	19	234	4.0	193	3.3	4.99	95	.312	.384	-19	-15	101	94	-2.2	-6	0	-1.5
■ **ANDY HAWKINS**	Hawkins, Melton Andrew b: 1/21/60, Waco, Tex. BR/TR, 6'4", 200 lbs. Deb: 7/17/82																												
1982	SD-N	2	5	.286	15	10	1	0	0	64	66	9.3	4	27	3.8	25	3.5	4.08	81	.274	.338	-3	-6	92	103	-1.4	-2	-1	-0.7
1983	SD-N	5	7	.417	21	19	4	1	0	120	106	8.0	8	48	3.6	59	4.4	2.93	123	.244	.317	9	9	99	118	-1.0	-1	1	0.9
1984	SD-N	8	9	.471	36	22	2	1	0	146	143	8.8	13	72	4.4	77	4.7	4.68	75	.254	.334	-18	-19	98	86	-1.5	1	-1	-1.9
1985	SD-N	18	8	.692	33	33	5	2	0	229	229	9.0	18	65	2.6	69	2.7	3.14	116	.267	.313	12	13	101	119	5.3	-4	-1	0.8
1986	SD-N	10	8	.556	37	35	3	1	0	209	218	9.4	24	75	3.2	117	5.0	4.31	83	.268	.329	-14	-17	96	99	1.8	-0	-2	-1.9
1987	SD-N	3	10	.231	24	20	0	0	0	118	131	10.0	16	49	3.7	51	3.9	5.03	79	.287	.353	-12	-14	98	102	-2.8	-0	0	-1.3
1988	SD-N	14	11	.560	33	33	4	2	0	218	196	8.1	16	76	3.1	91	3.8	3.34	100	.244	.307	3	0	97	102	1.3	-2	-3	-0.3
Total	7	60	58	.508	199	172	19	7	0	1104	1089	8.9	99	412	3.4	489	4.0	3.84	93	.261	.324	-23	-33	98	105	1.7	-8	-7	-4.4
■ **WYNN HAWKINS**	Hawkins, Wynn Firth "Hawk" b: 2/20/36, E.Palestine, Ohio BR/TR, 6'3", 195 lbs. Deb: 4/22/60																												
1960	Cle-A	4	4	.500	15	9	1	0	0	66	68	9.3	10	39	5.3	39	5.3	4.23	90	.269	.364	-3	-3	98	121	0.1	-1	1	-0.2
1961	Cle-A	7	9	.438	30	21	3	1	1	133	139	9.4	16	59	4.0	51	3.5	4.06	96	.270	.341	-1	-3	97	113	-0.8	-1	-1	-0.4
1962	Cle-A	1	0	1.000	3	0	0	0	0	4	9	20.3	1	1	2.3	0	0.0	6.75	58	.429	.455	-1	-1	99	156	0.5	0	-0	0.0
Total	3	12	13	.480	48	30	4	1	1	203	216	9.6	27	99	4.4	90	4.0	4.17	93	.274	.351	-4	-7	97	116	-0.2	-2	-0	-0.6
■ **PINK HAWLEY**	Hawley, Emerson P. b: 12/5/1872, Beaver Dam, Wis. d: 9/19/38, Beaver Dam, Wis. BL/TR, 5'10", 185 lbs. Deb: 8/13/1892																												
1892	StL-N	6	14	.300	20	20	18	0	0	166	160	8.7	4	63	3.4	63	3.4	3.20	100	.266	.335	2	-0	97	98	-2.1	-2	0	-0.1
1893	StL-N	5	17	.227	31	24	21	0	1	227	249	9.9	6	103	4.1	73	2.9	4.60	102	.294	.371	2	2	100	93	-5.6	7	0	0.7
1894	StL-N	19	27	.413	53	41	36	0	0	393	481	11.0	14	149	3.4	120	2.7	4.90	112	.324	.386	19	25	103	96	-0.8	1	3	2.4
1895	Pit-N	31	22	.585	**56**	50	44	**4**	1	**444**	449	9.1	7	122	2.5	142	2.9	3.18	145	.282	.333	**79**	**70**	96	101	4.2	12	3	**7.3**
1896	Pit-N	22	21	.512	49	43	37	2	0	378	382	9.1	3	157	3.7	137	3.3	3.57	113	.284	.359	33	20	93	96	0.0	3	4	2.2
1897	Pit-N	18	18	.500	40	39	33	0	0	311	362	10.5	6	94	2.7	88	2.5	4.80	90	.313	.365	-17	-17	100	82	1.9	-3	1	-1.4
1898	Cin-N	27	11	.711	43	37	32	3	0	331	357	9.7	5	91	2.5	69	1.9	3.37	114	.297	.347	9	18	107	101	6.2	-4	-4	1.0
1899	Cin-N	14	17	.452	34	29	25	0	1	250	289	10.4	7	65	2.3	46	1.7	4.25	95	.314	.359	-11	-5	105	90	-3.3	-2	-2	-0.6
1900	NY-N	18	18	.500	41	38	**34**	2	0	329	377	10.3	7	89	2.4	80	2.2	3.53	104	.311	.358	6	5	99	107	2.7	-2	4	0.7
1901	Mil-A	7	14	.333	26	23	17	0	0	182	228	11.3	3	41	2.0	50	2.5	4.60	78	.328	.365	-19	-20	98	91	-0.5	3	0	-1.7
Total	10	167	179	.483	393	344	297	11	3	3011	3334	10.0	62	974	2.9	868	2.6	3.96	107	.302	.358	103	99	100	96	2.7	12	9	10.5
■ **SCOTT HAWLEY**	Hawley, Scott Deb: 9/22/1894																												
1894	Bos-N	0	1	.000	1	1	1	0	0	7	10	12.9	0	7	9.0	1	1.3	7.71	77	.359	.488	-2	-1	111	93	-0.4	-1	0	0.0
■ **HAL HAYDEL**	Haydel, John Harold b: 7/9/44, Houma, La. BR/TR, 6', 190 lbs. Deb: 9/07/70																												
1970	Min-A	2	0	1.000	4	0	0	0	0	9	7	7.0	2	4	4.0	4	4.0	3.00	120	.226	.297	1	1	97	144	1.0	2	0	0.3
1971	Min-A	4	2	.667	31	0	0	0	1	40	33	7.4	3	20	4.5	29	6.5	4.27	85	.243	.333	-4	-3	104	90	1.2	0	0	-0.2
Total	2	6	2	.750	35	0	0	0	1	49	40	7.3	5	24	4.4	33	6.1	4.04	89	.240	.327	-3	-2	103	100	2.2	2	0	0.1
■ **LEFTY HAYDEN**	Hayden, Eugene Franklin b: 4/14/35, San Francisco, Cal BL/TL, 6'2", 175 lbs. Deb: 6/26/58																												
1958	Cin-N	0	0	—	3	0	0	0	0	4	5	11.3	0	1	2.3	3	6.8	4.50	93	.313	.353	-0	-0	106	92	0.0	0	0	0.0
■ **BEN HAYES**	Hayes, Ben Joseph b: 8/4/57, Niagara Falls, N.Y. BR/TR, 6'1", 180 lbs. Deb: 6/25/82																												
1982	Cin-N	2	0	1.000	26	0	0	0	2	46	37	7.2	3	22	4.3	38	7.4	1.96	191	.219	.299	8	9	104	148	1.0	-0	-1	0.9
1983	Cin-N	4	6	.400	60	0	0	0	7	69	82	10.7	8	37	4.8	44	5.7	6.52	58	.301	.377	-22	-21	104	86	-0.6	-1	0	-2.1
Total	2	6	6	.500	86	0	0	0	9	115	119	9.3	11	59	4.6	82	6.4	4.70	80	.270	.348	-14	-12	104	111	0.4	-1	-0	-1.2
■ **JIM HAYES**	Hayes, James Millard "Whitey" b: 2/25/12, Montevallo, Ala. BL/TR, 6'1", 168 lbs. Deb: 7/13/35																												
1935	Was-A	2	4	.333	7	4	1	0	0	28	38	12.2	0	23	7.4	9	2.9	8.36	49	.322	.427	-12	-13	93	75	-0.6	-0	-1	-1.1
■ **JOE HAYNES**	Haynes, Joseph Walton b: 9/21/17, Lincolnton, Ga. d: 1/6/67, Hopkins, Minn. BR/TR, 6'2.5", 190 lbs. Deb: 4/24/39 C																												
1939	Was-A	8	12	.400	27	20	10	1	0	173	186	9.7	10	78	4.1	64	3.3	5.36	79	.276	.345	-14	-22	91	84	-0.6	0	-1	-2.0
1940	Was-A	3	6	.333	22	7	1	0	0	63	85	12.1	4	34	4.9	23	3.3	6.57	63	.327	.403	-15	-17	95	95	-0.8	-1	-1	-1.6
1941	Chi-A	0	0	—	8	0	0	0	0	28	30	9.6	0	11	3.5	18	5.8	3.86	101	.280	.342	1	0	94	102	0.0	0	-0	0.0
1942	Chi-A	8	5	.615	**40**	1	1	0	6	103	88	7.7	6	47	4.1	35	3.1	2.62	140	.234	.319	12	12	100	130	2.1	0	0	1.3
1943	Chi-A	7	2	.778	35	2	1	0	3	109	114	9.4	2	32	2.6	37	3.1	2.97	112	.263	.314	4	4	101	106	2.4	2	-1	0.6
1944	Chi-A	5	6	.455	33	12	8	0	2	154	148	8.6	5	43	2.5	44	2.6	2.57	136	.254	.298	15	16	102	116	0.0	1	0	2.0
1945	Chi-A	5	5	.500	14	13	8	1	1	104	92	8.0	5	29	2.5	34	2.9	3.55	91	.237	.286	-2	-4	96	75	0.2	-2	1	-0.5
1946	Chi-A	7	9	.438	32	23	9	0	2	177	203	10.3	14	60	3.1	60	3.1	3.76	91	.289	.345	-5	-7	97	118	-0.7	3	1	-0.3
1947	Chi-A	14	6	.700	29	22	7	2	0	182	174	8.6	5	61	3.0	50	2.5	**2.42**	**151**	.250	.309	26	25	99	**124**	4.8	2	0	3.0
1948	Chi-A	9	10	.474	27	22	6	0	0	150	167	10.0	13	52	3.1	40	2.4	3.96	108	.284	.338	5	5	100	115	2.2	-1	-2	0.2
1949	Was-A	2	9	.182	37	10	0	0	2	96	106	9.9	6	55	5.2	19	1.8	6.28	64	.283	.370	-22	-24	96	78	-2.4	1	1	-2.0
1950	Was-A	7	5	.583	27	10	1	1	0	102	124	10.9	14	46	4.1	15	1.3	5.82	79	.305	.376	-14	-14	101	101	1.7	1	0	-1.0
1951	Was-A	1	4	.200	26	3	1	0	2	73	85	10.5	9	37	4.6	18	2.2	4.56	88	.290	.368	-4	-5	97	118	-1.2	2	-1	-0.2
1952	Was-A	0	3	.000	22	2	0	0	3	66	70	9.5	2	35	4.8	18	2.5	4.50	82	.275	.358	-6	-6	100	94	-1.4	-1	-1	-0.6
Total	14	76	82	.481	379	147	53	5	21	1580	1672	9.5	95	620	3.5	475	2.7	4.01	95	.272	.336	-20	-33	98	106	6.3	7	-2	-1.1
■ **RAY HAYWARD**	Hayward, Raymond Alton b: 4/27/61, Enid, Okla. BL/TL, 6'1", 190 lbs. Deb: 9/20/86																												
1986	SD-N	0	2	.000	3	3	0	0	0	10	16	14.4	1	4	3.6	6	5.4	9.00	40	.340	.392	-6	-6	96	71	-0.9	-0	-0	-0.5
1987	SD-N	0	0	—	4	0	0	0	0	6	12	18.0	3	3	4.5	2	3.0	16.50	24	.444	.484	-8	-8	98	80	0.0	-0	1	-0.6
1988	Tex-A	4	6	.400	12	12	1	1	0	63	63	9.0	6	35	5.0	37	5.3	5.43	75	.276	.362	-10	-10	102	92	-0.3	0	1	-0.7
Total	3	4	8	.333	19	15	1	1	0	79	91	10.4	10	42	4.8	45	5.1	6.72	59	.301	.377	-24	-24	101	88	-1.2	-1	1	-1.8
■ **BILL HAYWOOD**	Haywood, William Kiernan b: 4/21/37, Colon, Panama BR/TR, 6'3", 205 lbs. Deb: 7/28/68																												
1968	Was-A	0	0	—	14	0	0	0	0	23	27	10.6	1	12	4.7	10	3.9	4.70	60	.314	.383	-4	-5	94	118	0.0	0	0	-0.5
■ **ED HEAD**	Head, Edward Marvin b: 1/25/18, Selma, La. d: 1/31/80, Bastrop, La. BR/TR, 6'1", 175 lbs. Deb: 7/27/40																												
1940	Bro-N	1	2	.333	13	5	2	0	0	39	40	9.2	0	18	4.2	13	3.0	4.15	99	.260	.330	-1	-0	106	85	-0.5	-0	-1	-0.1
1942	Bro-N	10	6	.625	36	15	5	1	4	137	118	7.8	11	47	3.1	78	5.1	3.55	91	.231	.294	-4	-5	97	86	-0.6	4	0	0.0
1943	Bro-N	9	10	.474	47	18	7	3	6	170	166	8.8	8	66	3.5	83	4.4	3.65	91	.250	.313	-5	-6	99	89	-1.0	-2	1	-0.6
1944	Bro-N	4	3	.571	9	8	5	1	0	63	54	7.7	2	19	2.7	17	2.4	2.71	135	.232	.286	6	7	102	94	1.0	1	-1	0.7
1946	Bro-N	3	2	.600	13	7	3	1	1	56	56	9.0	3	24	3.9	17	2.7	3.21	106	.267	.333	1	1	100	118	0.0	1	-1	0.2
Total	5	27	23	.540	118	53	22	6	11	465	434	8.4	24	174	3.4	208	4.0	3.48	98	.245	.308	-3	-4	99	92	-1.1	5	-1	0.2
■ **RALPH HEAD**	Head, Ralph b: 8/30/1893, Tallapoosa, Ga. d: 10/8/62, Muscadine, Ala. BR/TR, 5'10", 175 lbs. Deb: 4/18/23																												
1923	Phi-N	2	9	.182	35	13	5	0	0	132	185	12.6	13	57	3.9	24	1.6	6.68	71	.341	.389	-39	-29	118	94	-2.4	-6	-1	-3.0
■ **TOM HEALEY**	Healey, Thomas b: 1853, Cranston, R.I. d: 2/6/1891, Lewiston, Maine Deb: 6/13/1878																												
1878	Pro-N	0	3	.000	3	3	3	0	0	24	27	10.1	1	7	2.6	2	0.8	3.00	74	.294	.344	-2	-2	97	112	-1.4	0	0	-0.1
	Ind-N	6	4	.600	11	10	9	0	1	89	98	9.9	1	13	1.3	18	1.8	2.22	91	.290	.316	1	-2	88	118	1.9	-1	0	-0.2
	Yr	6	7	.462	14	13	12	0	**1**	113	125	10.0	2	20	1.6	20	1.6	2.39	87	.291	.322	-1	-4	90	118	0.5	0	0	-0.3

YEAR	TM/L	W	L	PCT	G	GS	CG	SHO	SV	IP	H	H/G	HR	BB	BB/G	SO	SO/G	ERA	/A	OAVG	OOBP	PR	/A	PF	CPI	WAT	PB	PD	TPI
■ EGYPTIAN HEALY	Healy, John J. "Long John" b: 10/27/1866, Cairo, Ill. d: 3/16/1899, St.Louis, Mo. BR/TR, 6'2", 158 lbs. Deb: 9/11/1885																												
1885	StL-N	1	7	.125	8	8	8	0	0	66	54	7.4	0	20	2.7	32	4.4	3.00	91	.233	.294	-1	-2	97	73	-2.5	-3	0	-0.4
1886	StL-N	17	23	.425	42	41	39	3	0	354	315	8.0	5	118	3.0	213	5.4	2.87	112	.251	.315	17	14	98	96	3.2	-11	-2	0.0
1887	Ind-N	12	29	.293	41	41	40	3	0	341	415	11.0	24	108	2.9	75	2.0	5.17	79	.316	.368	-42	-40	101	94	0.0	-4	-5	-3.8
1888	Ind-N	12	24	.333	37	37	36	1	0	321	347	9.7	12	87	2.4	124	3.5	3.90	71	.290	.338	-38	-40	98	93	-2.3	4	0	-3.3
1889	Was-N	1	11	.083	13	12	10	0	0	101	139	12.4	2	38	3.4	49	4.4	6.24	62	.344	.400	-25	-27	96	85	-4.5	1	0	-2.0
	Chi-N	1	4	.200	5	5	5	0	0	46	48	9.4	4	18	3.5	22	4.3	4.50	88	.284	.353	-2	-3	98	93	-1.4	-2	0	-0.3
	Yr	2	15	.118	18	17	15	0	0	147	187	11.4	6	56	3.4	71	4.3	5.69	68	.326	.386	-27	-30	96	93	-5.9	1	0	-2.3
1890	Tol-a	22	21	.512	46	46	44	2	0	389	326	7.5	5	127	2.9	225	5.2	2.89	137	.242	.307	42	46	102	92	-0.1	5	-1	4.9
1891	Bal-a	9	10	.474	23	22	19	0	0	170	179	9.5	6	57	3.0	54	2.9	3.76	99	.285	.345	-1	-0	100	93	-1.0	-2	0	-0.1
1892	Bal-N	3	6	.333	9	8	5	0	0	68	82	10.9	4	21	2.8	24	3.2	4.76	71	.312	.363	-11	-11	102	92	0.1	1	0	-0.8
	Lou-N	1	1	.500	2	2	2	0	0	18	15	7.5	0	5	2.5	4	2.0	2.00	153	.238	.295	3	2	93	101	0.1	1	0	0.3
	Yr	4	7	.364	11	10	7	0	0	86	97	10.2	4	26	2.7	28	2.9	4.19	79	.298	.350	-9	-8	100	101	0.2	1	0	-0.5
Total	8	79	136	.367	226	222	208	9	0	1874	1920	9.2	62	599	2.9	822	3.9	3.84	92	.279	.337	-59	-63	100	92	-8.4	-11	-7	-5.5
■ CHARLIE HEARD	Heard, Charles b: 1/30/1872, Philadelphia, Pa. d: 2/20/45, Philadelphia, Pa. BR/TR, 6'2", 190 lbs. Deb: 7/14/1890																												
1890	Pit-N	0	6	.000	6	6	5	0	0	44	75	15.3	5	32	6.5	13	2.7	8.39	40	.394	.481	-24	-25	95	101	-2.9	-1	0	-1.8
■ JAY HEARD	Heard, Jehosie b: 1/17/20, Atlanta, Ga. BL/TL, 5'7", 155 lbs. Deb: 4/24/54																												
1954	Bal-A	0	0	—	2	0	0	0	0	3	6	18.0	1	3	9.0	2	6.0	15.00	25	.375	.474	-4	-4	99	74	0.0	0	0	-0.2
■ BUNNY HEARN	Hearn, Bunn b: 5/21/1891, Chapel Hill, N.C. d: 10/19/59, Wilson, N.C. BL/TL, 5'11", 190 lbs. Deb: 9/17/10																												
1910	StL-N	1	3	.250	5	5	4	0	0	39	49	11.3	2	16	3.7	14	3.2	5.08	55	.322	.391	-9	-10	93	101	-0.7	0	-1	-0.9
1911	StL-N	0	0	—	2	0	0	0	0	3	7	21.0	1	0	0.0	1	3.0	12.00	29	.538	.538	-3	-3	102	109	0.0	-0	-0	-0.2
1913	NY-N	1	1	.500	2	2	1	0	0	13	13	9.0	0	7	4.8	8	5.5	2.77	115	.277	.357	1	1	100	142	-0.2	1	0	0.1
1915	Pit-F	6	11	.353	29	17	8	1	0	176	187	9.6	6	37	1.9	49	2.5	3.38	92	.285	.326	-7	-5	102	107	-3.3	0	2	-0.2
1918	Bos-N	5	6	.455	17	12	9	1	0	126	119	8.5	2	29	2.1	30	2.1	2.50	105	.256	.291	4	2	95	105	0.3	-1	1	0.2
1920	Bos-N	0	3	.000	11	4	2	0	0	43	54	11.3	3	11	2.3	9	1.9	5.65	55	.329	.349	-12	-12	99	87	-1.4	-1	0	-1.2
Total	6	13	24	.351	66	40	24	2	0	400	429	9.7	14	100	2.3	111	2.5	3.56	82	.287	.327	-26	-28	99	105	-5.3	-1	2	-2.2
■ BUNNY HEARN	Hearn, Elmer Lafayette b: 1/13/04, Brooklyn, N.Y. d: 3/31/74, Venice, Fla. BL/TL, 5'8", 160 lbs. Deb: 4/13/26																												
1926	Bos-N	4	9	.308	34	12	3	0	2	117	121	9.3	2	56	4.3	40	3.1	4.23	79	.276	.346	-5	-11	88	93	-1.9	-2	2	-1.1
1927	Bos-N	0	2	.000	8	0	0	0	0	13	16	11.1	0	9	6.2	5	3.5	4.15	90	.327	.424	-0	-1	95	141	-0.9	1	0	0.0
1928	Bos-N	1	0	1.000	7	0	0	0	0	10	6	5.4	0	8	7.2	8	7.2	6.30	64	.167	.333	-3	-3	101	33	0.5	-0	-0	-0.2
1929	Bos-N	2	0	1.000	10	1	0	0	0	18	18	9.0	2	9	4.5	12	6.0	4.50	102	.277	.351	0	0	97	111	1.0	0	1	0.1
Total	4	7	11	.389	59	13	3	0	2	158	161	9.2	4	82	4.7	65	3.7	4.39	81	.273	.353	-8	-15	90	95	-1.3	-2	2	-1.2
■ JIM HEARN	Hearn, James Tolbert b: 4/11/21, Atlanta, Ga. BR/TR, 6'3", 205 lbs. Deb: 4/17/47																												
1947	StL-N	12	7	.632	37	21	4	1	1	162	151	8.4	9	63	3.5	57	3.2	3.22	131	.248	.316	15	18	104	104	1.4	-1	-1	1.5
1948	StL-N	8	6	.571	34	13	3	0	1	90	92	9.2	9	35	3.5	27	2.7	4.20	93	.271	.336	-2	-3	99	105	0.3	-0	-2	-0.4
1949	StL-N	1	3	.250	17	4	0	0	0	42	48	10.3	3	23	4.9	18	3.9	5.14	85	.294	.372	-5	-4	108	104	-1.1	-1	0	-0.3
1950	StL-N	0	1	.000	6	0	0	0	0	9	12	12.0	1	6	6.0	4	4.0	10.00	43	.333	.400	-6	-6	103	69	-0.4	0	0	-0.4
	NY-N	11	3	.786	16	16	11	5	0	125	72	5.2	8	38	2.7	54	3.9	1.94	206	.169	.236	31	29	97	72	3.8	-0	0	3.1
	Yr	11	4	.733	22	16	11	**5**	0	134	84	5.6	9	44	3.0	58	3.9	2.49	162	.182	.250	25	23	97	72	3.4	0	0	2.7
1951	NY-N	17	9	.654	34	34	11	0	0	211	204	8.7	21	82	3.5	66	2.8	3.63	108	.251	.319	8	7	99	103	1.2	-0	5	1.2
1952	NY-N	14	7	.667	37	34	11	1	1	224	208	8.4	16	97	3.9	89	3.6	3.78	100	.245	.322	-1	-0	101	96	2.0	4	4	0.7
1953	NY-N	9	12	.429	36	32	6	0	0	197	206	9.4	22	84	3.8	77	3.5	4.52	93	.266	.336	-5	-7	98	97	-0.6	1	1	-0.4
1954	NY-N	8	8	.500	29	18	3	2	1	130	137	9.5	10	66	4.6	45	3.1	4.15	100	.272	.353	-1	-0	102	105	-1.7	-1	1	0.0
1955	NY-N	14	16	.467	39	33	11	1	0	227	225	8.9	27	66	2.6	86	3.4	3.73	106	.260	.309	8	6	98	102	-1.7	1	2	0.9
1956	NY-N	5	11	.313	30	19	2	0	1	129	124	8.7	17	44	3.1	66	4.6	3.98	94	.254	.309	-3	-3	99	96	-2.3	-3	0	-0.5
1957	Phi-N	5	1	.833	36	4	1	0	3	74	79	9.6	6	18	2.2	46	5.6	3.65	105	.274	.316	2	2	99	104	2.0	-2	1	0.0
1958	Phi-N	5	3	.625	39	1	0	0	0	73	88	10.8	6	27	3.3	33	4.1	4.19	94	.292	.343	-2	-2	100	107	1.3	-1	-0	-0.3
1959	Phi-N	0	2	.000	6	0	0	0	0	11	15	12.3	2	6	4.9	1	0.8	5.73	70	.333	.396	-2	-2	102	123	-0.9	0	0	-0.1
Total	13	109	89	.551	396	229	63	10	8	1704	1661	8.8	157	655	3.5	669	3.5	3.81	105	.255	.321	35	33	100	99	3.3	-3	11	5.0
■ SPENCER HEATH	Heath, Spencer Paul b: 11/5/1894, Chicago, Ill. d: 1/25/30, Chicago, Ill. BB/TR, 6', 170 lbs. Deb: 5/04/20																												
1920	Chi-A	0	0	—	4	0	0	0	0	7	19	24.4	1	2	2.6	0	0.0	15.43	23	.475	.500	-9	-9	94	77	0.0	-0	0	-0.8
■ JEFF HEATHCOCK	Heathcock, Ronald Jeffrey b: 11/18/59, Covina, Cal. BR/TR, 6'4", 205 lbs. Deb: 9/03/83																												
1983	Hou-N	2	1	.667	6	3	0	0	1	28	19	6.1	1	4	1.3	12	3.9	3.21	102	.181	.216	1	0	90	22	0.5	-1	0	0.0
1985	Hou-N	3	1	.750	14	7	1	0	1	56	50	8.0	9	13	2.1	25	4.0	3.38	102	.239	.283	1	0	96	104	1.0	0	0	0.1
1987	Hou-N	4	2	.667	19	2	0	0	1	43	44	9.2	4	9	1.9	15	3.1	3.14	121	.277	.310	5	3	93	128	1.1	-1	-0	0.2
1988	Hou-N	0	5	.000	17	1	0	0	0	31	33	9.6	2	16	4.6	12	3.5	5.81	56	.275	.350	-8	-9	93	79	-2.4	-0	0	-0.8
Total	4	9	9	.500	56	13	1	0	3	158	146	8.3	16	42	2.4	64	3.6	3.76	92	.246	.294	-1	-5	94	91	0.2	-2	0	-0.5
■ NEAL HEATON	Heaton, Neal b: 3/3/60, Holtsville, N.Y. BL/TL, 6'1", 205 lbs. Deb: 9/03/82																												
1982	Cle-A	0	2	.000	8	4	0	0	0	31	32	9.3	1	16	4.6	14	4.1	5.23	79	.260	.338	-4	-4	101	71	-0.9	0	-0	-0.3
1983	Cle-A	11	7	.611	39	16	4	3	7	149	157	9.5	11	44	2.7	75	4.5	4.17	104	.269	.317	-2	3	106	91	3.1	0	-2	0.1
1984	Cle-A	12	15	.444	38	34	4	1	0	199	231	10.4	21	75	3.4	75	3.4	5.20	81	.293	.348	-27	-21	106	93	-0.5	0	-3	-2.2
1985	Cle-A	9	17	.346	36	33	5	1	0	208	244	10.6	19	80	3.5	82	3.5	4.89	81	.298	.359	-17	-22	95	105	-0.9	0	-3	-2.2
1986	Cle-A	3	6	.333	12	12	2	0	0	74	73	8.9	8	34	4.1	24	2.9	4.26	96	.254	.333	-1	-1	98	96	-1.6	0	-0	-0.1
	Min-A	4	9	.308	21	17	3	0	1	124	128	9.3	18	47	3.4	66	4.8	3.99	115	.273	.335	3	8	109	118	-2.0	0	-1	0.7
	Yr	7	15	.318	33	29	5	0	1	198	201	9.1	26	81	3.7	90	4.1	4.09	107	.266	.333	2	7	105	118	-3.6	0	-1	0.6
1987	Mon-N	13	10	.565	32	32	3	1	0	193	207	9.7	25	37	1.7	105	4.9	4.52	96	.273	.306	-9	-4	106	90	0.1	2	-1	-0.3
1988	Mon-N	3	10	.231	32	11	0	0	2	97	98	9.1	14	43	4.0	43	4.0	5.01	72	.271	.347	-17	-15	105	99	-3.5	-0	-0	-1.5
Total	7	55	76	.420	218	159	21	6	10	1075	1170	9.8	117	376	3.1	484	4.1	4.65	90	.279	.336	-73	-56	103	97	-6.2	1	-9	-5.8
■ DAVE HEAVERLO	Heaverlo, David Wallace b: 8/25/50, Ellensburg, Wash. BR/TR, 6'2", 200 lbs. Deb: 4/14/75																												
1975	SF-N	3	1	.750	42	0	0	0	1	64	62	8.7	2	31	4.4	35	4.9	2.39	155	.262	.342	9	9	102	156	1.0	1	0	1.1
1976	SF-N	4	4	.500	61	0	0	0	1	75	85	10.2	2	15	1.8	40	4.8	4.44	82	.289	.317	-8	-7	104	83	0.3	0	1	-0.5
1977	SF-N	5	1	.833	56	0	0	0	1	99	92	8.4	10	21	1.9	58	5.3	2.55	161	.251	.291	15	17	105	131	2.1	-0	2	1.9
1978	Oak-A	3	6	.333	69	0	0	0	10	130	141	9.8	11	41	2.8	71	4.9	3.25	119	.281	.327	8	9	103	128	-0.9	0	3	1.2
1979	Oak-A	4	11	.267	62	0	0	0	9	86	97	10.2	7	42	4.4	40	4.2	4.19	92	.294	.365	0	-3	91	123	-1.5	0	0	-0.2
1980	Sea-A	6	3	.667	60	0	0	0	4	79	75	8.5	9	35	4.0	42	4.8	3.87	110	.253	.337	1	3	105	108	2.2	0	-1	0.2
1981	Oak-A	1	0	1.000	6	0	0	0	0	6	7	10.5	0	3	4.5	2	3.0	1.50	232	.292	.370	1	1	95	287	0.5	0	-0	0.1
Total	7	26	26	.500	356	0	0	0	26	539	559	9.3	41	188	3.1	288	4.8	3.41	115	.273	.330	27	31	102	124	3.7	1	4	3.8
■ WALLY HEBERT	Hebert, Wallace Andrew "Preacher" b: 8/21/07, Lake Charles, La. BL/TL, 6'1", 195 lbs. Deb: 5/01/31																												
1931	StL-A	6	7	.462	23	13	5	0	0	103	128	11.2	11	43	3.8	26	2.3	5.07	91	.306	.374	-8	-5	105	113	0.6	-1	-2	-0.7
1932	StL-A	1	12	.077	35	15	2	0	1	108	145	12.1	6	45	3.8	29	2.4	6.50	71	.322	.381	-24	-23	103	89	-5.3	3	0	-1.7
1933	StL-A	4	6	.400	33	10	3	0	0	88	114	11.7	4	35	3.6	19	1.9	5.32	95	.308	.367	-10	-3	117	97	0.3	3	-1	0.0
1943	Pit-N	10	11	.476	34	23	12	1	0	184	197	9.6	3	45	2.2	41	2.0	2.98	116	.272	.311	8	10	103	108	-0.9	1	1	1.4
Total	4	21	36	.368	125	61	22	1	1	483	584	10.9	24	168	3.1	115	2.1	4.64	91	.298	.351	-34	-22	106	103	-5.3	6	-1	-1.0
■ GUY HECKER	Hecker, Guy Jackson b: 4/3/1856, Youngville, Pa. d: 12/3/38, Wooster, Ohio BR/TR, 6', 190 lbs. Deb: 5/02/1882 M																												
1882	Lou-a	6	6	.500	13	11	10	0	0	104	75	**6.5**	0	5	**0.4**	33	2.9	1.30	186	**.207**	**.218**	16	13	90	71	-0.2	4	0	1.2
1883	Lou-a	26	23	.531	51	50	49	3	0	451	509	10.2	4	72	1.4	153	3.1	3.33	93	.290	.318	-2	-12	94	109	-0.4	10	3	0.3
1884	Lou-a	**52**	20	.722	**75**	73	**72**	6	0	**671**	526	7.1	4	56	0.8	**385**	5.2	**1.80**	157	.224	**.242**	**108**	**76**	87	104	**18.0**	30	7	**10.7**
1885	Lou-a	30	23	.566	53	53	51	2	0	480	454	8.5	6	54	1.0	209	3.9	2.18	**154**	.261	.283	57	63	103	**120**	7.7	8	5	**7.8**
1886	Lou-a	26	23	.531	49	48	45	2	0	421	390	8.3	5	118	2.5	133	2.8	2.86	130	.256	.309	27	40	108	104	3.2	18	1	7.3

YEAR	TM/L	W	L	PCT	G	GS	CG	SHO	SV	IP	H	H/G	HR	BB	BB/G	SO	SO/G	ERA	/A	OAVG	OOBP	PR	/A	PF	CPI	WAT	PB	PD	TPI
1887	Lou-a	18	12	.600	34	32	32	2	1	285	325	10.3	9	50	**1.6**	58	1.8	4.17	109	.301	.331	4	12	106	93	1.8	10	0	1.0
1888	Lou-a	8	17	.320	26	25	25	0	0	223	251	10.1	5	43	1.7	63	2.5	3.39	84	.297	.331	-8	-13	93	**109**	-1.4	3	0	-1.1
1889	Lou-a	5	13	.278	19	16	15	0	0	151	215	12.8	7	47	2.8	33	2.0	5.60	70	.351	.397	-29	-28	102	99	1.0	3	0	-2.1
1890	Pit-N	2	9	.182	14	12	11	0	0	120	160	12.0	9	44	3.3	32	2.4	5.18	65	.337	.393	-21	-24	95	103	0.1	1	0	-1.9
Total	9	173	146	.542	334	320	310	15	1	2906	2905	9.0	49	489	1.5	1099	3.4	2.93	113	.270	.302	152	121	97	105	29.8	87	16	23.2
■ HARRY HEDGPETH	Hedgpeth, Harry Malcolm b: 9/4/1888, Fayetteville, N.C. d: 7/30/66, Richmond, Va. BL/TL, 6'1.5", 194 lbs. Deb: 10/03/13																												
1913	Was-A	0	0	—	1	0	0	0	1	1	1	9.0	0	0	0.0	0	0.0	0.00	—	.250	.250	0	0	105	0	0.0	0	0	0.1
■ MIKE HEDLUND	Hedlund, Michael David "Red" b: 8/11/46, Dallas, Tex. BB/TR, 6'1", 182 lbs. Deb: 5/08/65																												
1965	Cle-A	0	0	—	6	0	0	0	0	5	6	10.8	0	5	9.0	4	7.2	5.40	62	.286	.407	-1	-1	97	102	0.0	-0	-0	0.0
1968	Cle-A	0	0	—	3	0	0	0	0	2	6	27.0	0	2	9.0	0	0.0	9.00	33	.545	.643	-1	-1	101	186	0.0	0	0	0.0
1969	KC-A	3	6	.333	34	16	1	0	2	125	123	8.9	8	40	2.9	74	5.3	3.24	116	.259	.308	5	7	104	106	-0.9	-1	1	0.9
1970	KC-A	2	3	.400	9	0	0	0	0	15	18	10.8	6	7	4.2	5	3.0	7.20	51	.300	.362	-6	-6	100	104	0.0	-0	-0	-0.6
1971	KC-A	15	8	.652	32	30	7	1	0	206	168	7.3	15	72	3.1	76	3.3	2.71	126	.227	.289	17	16	98	104	3.4	-3	3	1.7
1972	KC-A	5	7	.417	29	16	1	0	0	113	119	9.5	10	41	3.3	52	4.1	4.78	64	.275	.336	-21	-22	100	87	-0.9	-0	1	-2.2
Total	6	25	24	.510	113	62	9	1	2	466	440	8.5	39	167	3.2	211	4.1	3.55	96	.253	.313	-7	-7	100	101	1.6	-5	5	-0.2
■ DANNY HEEP	Heep, Daniel William b: 7/3/57, San Antonio, Tex. BL/TL, 5'11", 185 lbs. Deb: 8/31/79																												
1988	LA-N	0	0	—	1	0	0	0	0	2	2	9.0	1	0	0.0	0	0.0	9.00	40	.222	.222	-1	-1	105	51	0.0	0	0	0.0
■ BOB HEFFNER	Heffner, Robert Frederic b: 9/13/38, Allentown, Pa. BR/TR, 6'4", 200 lbs. Deb: 6/19/63																												
1963	Bos-A	4	9	.308	20	19	3	1	0	125	131	9.4	15	36	2.6	77	5.5	4.25	91	.267	.315	-9	-5	107	95	-2.3	-1	0	-0.6
1964	Bos-A	7	9	.438	55	10	1	1	6	159	152	8.6	20	44	2.5	112	6.3	4.08	92	.251	.301	-8	-6	103	89	0.0	0	-1	-0.6
1965	Bos-A	0	2	.000	27	1	0	0	0	49	59	10.8	9	18	3.3	42	7.7	7.16	53	.304	.355	-20	-18	109	81	-0.9	-1	-1	-1.9
1966	Cle-A	0	1	.000	5	1	0	0	0	13	12	8.3	1	3	2.1	7	4.8	3.46	101	.240	.278	-0	0	102	83	-0.4	0	-0	0.0
1968	Cal-A	0	0	—	7	0	0	0	0	8	6	6.8	0	6	6.8	3	3.4	2.25	127	.240	.364	1	1	96	174	0.0	0	0	0.1
Total	5	11	21	.344	114	31	4	2	6	354	360	9.2	45	107	2.7	241	6.1	4.50	84	.264	.314	-36	-29	105	92	-3.6	-1	-2	-3.0
■ RANDY HEFLIN	Heflin, Randolph Rutherford b: 9/11/18, Fredericksburg, Va. BL/TR, 6', 185 lbs. Deb: 6/09/45																												
1945	Bos-A	4	10	.286	20	14	6	2	0	102	102	9.0	3	61	5.4	39	3.4	4.06	80	.272	.370	-8	-9	96	110	-2.7	-3	1	-1.1
1946	Bos-A	0	1	.000	5	1	0	0	0	15	16	9.6	0	12	7.2	6	3.6	2.40	162	.296	.408	2	2	111	228	-0.4	1	1	0.4
Total	2	4	11	.267	25	15	6	2	0	117	118	9.1	3	73	5.6	45	3.5	3.85	86	.275	.375	-6	-7	98	125	-3.1	-2	2	-0.7
■ JAKE HEHL	Hehl, Herman Jacob b: 12/8/1899, Brooklyn, N.Y. d: 7/4/61, Brooklyn, N.Y. BR/TR, 5'11", 180 lbs. Deb: 6/20/18																												
1918	Bro-N	0	0	—	1	0	0	0	0	1	0	0.0	0	0	0.0	0	0.0	0.00	—	.000	.250	0	0	104	0	0.0	0	0	0.1
■ EMMETT HEIDRICK	Heidrick, R. Emmet "Snags" b: 7/9/1876, Queenstown, Pa. d: 1/20/16, Clarion, Pa. BL/TR, 6', 185 lbs. Deb: 9/14/1898																												
1902	StL-A	0	0	—	1	0	0	0	0	1	0	0.0	0	0	0.0	0	0.0	0.00	—	.000	.000	0	0	102	0	0.0	0	0	0.0
■ FRANK HEIFER	Heifer, Franklin "Heck" b: 1/18/1854, Reading, Pa. d: 8/29/1893, Reading, Pa. 5'10.5", 175 lbs. Deb: 6/04/1875																												
1875	Bos-n	0	0	—	1																								
■ FRED HEIMACH	Heimach, Frederick Amos "Lefty" b: 1/27/01, Camden, N.J. d: 6/1/73, Ft.Myers, Fla. BL/TL, 6', 175 lbs. Deb: 10/01/20																												
1920	Phi-A	0	1	.000	1	1	0	0	0	5	13	23.4	0	1	1.8	0	0.0	14.40	26	.542	.560	-6	-6	99	83	-0.4	-0	1	-0.3
1921	Phi-A	1	0	1.000	1	1	1	1	0	9	7	7.0	0	1	1.0	1	1.0	0.00	—	.226	.250	4	5	107	0	0.5	-0	1	0.7
1922	Phi-A	7	11	.389	37	19	7	0	1	172	220	11.5	18	63	3.3	47	2.5	5.02	86	.316	.365	-19	-14	106	107	-0.7	2	1	-0.9
1923	Phi-A	6	12	.333	40	19	10	0	0	208	238	10.3	14	69	3.0	63	2.7	4.33	94	.292	.339	-8	-6	102	100	-2.5	2	0	-0.1
1924	Phi-A	14	12	.538	40	26	10	0	0	198	243	11.0	2	60	2.7	60	2.7	4.73	90	.306	.346	-11	-10	101	89	2.0	6	2	-0.1
1925	Phi-A	0	1	.000	10	0	0	0	0	20	24	10.8	2	9	4.0	6	2.7	4.05	110	.312	.382	1	1	101	139	-0.4	-0	0	0.1
1926	Phi-A	1	0	1.000	13	1	0	0	0	32	28	7.9	1	5	1.4	8	2.3	2.81	165	.239	.264	4	7	116	76	0.5	-1	2	0.7
	Bos-A	2	9	.182	20	13	6	0	0	102	119	10.5	5	42	3.7	17	1.5	5.65	75	.303	.358	-18	-16	106	83	-2.2	2	3	-0.9
	Yr	3	9	.250	33	14	6	0	0	134	147	9.9	6	47	3.2	25	1.7	4.97	87	.288	.337	-14	-9	108	83	-1.7	-1	5	-0.2
1928	NY-A	2	3	.400	13	9	5	0	0	68	66	8.7	3	16	2.1	25	3.3	3.31	108	.250	.286	6	2	89	84	-0.9	-1	0	0.1
1929	NY-A	11	6	.647	35	10	3	3	4	135	141	9.4	4	29	1.9	26	1.7	4.00	103	.272	.306	4	2	97	82	1.7	0	1	0.3
1930	Bro-N	0	2	.000	9	0	0	0	1	7	14	18.0	0	3	3.9	1	1.3	5.14	95	.424	.436	-0	-0	99	170	-0.9	-0	0	0.0
1931	Bro-N	9	7	.563	31	10	7	1	1	135	145	9.7	6	23	1.5	43	2.9	3.47	113	.274	.299	6	7	101	96	0.8	1	4	1.1
1932	Bro-N	9	4	.692	36	15	7	0	0	168	203	10.9	7	28	1.5	30	1.6	3.96	94	.299	.326	-2	-5	96	104	2.4	1	1	-0.2
1933	Bro-N	0	1	.000	10	3	0	0	0	30	49	14.7	2	11	3.3	7	2.1	9.90	33	.374	.419	-22	-22	98	72	-0.4	-0	-0	-2.0
Total	13	62	69	.473	296	127	56	5	7	1289	1510	10.5	64	360	2.5	334	2.3	4.46	91	.296	.336	-61	-56	101	94	-0.5	12	16	-1.5
■ GORMAN HEIMUELLER	Heimueller, Gorman John b: 9/24/55, Los Angeles, Cal. BL/TL, 6'4", 195 lbs. Deb: 7/12/83																												
1983	Oak-A	3	5	.375	16	14	2	1	0	84	93	10.0	8	29	3.1	31	3.3	4.39	89	.286	.340	-3	-4	96	105	-0.6	0	2	-0.1
1984	Oak-A	0	1	.000	6	0	0	0	0	15	21	12.6	2	7	4.2	3	1.8	6.00	61	.344	.389	-3	-4	92	113	-0.4	0	0	-0.3
Total	2	3	6	.333	22	14	2	1	0	99	114	10.4	10	36	3.3	34	3.1	4.64	84	.295	.348	-6	-8	96	106	-1.0	0	3	-0.4
■ DON HEINKEL	Heinkel, Donald Elliott b: 10/20/59, Racine, Wis. BL/TR, 6', 185 lbs. Deb: 4/07/88																												
1988	Det-A	0	0	—	21	0	0	0	1	36	30	7.5	4	12	3.0	30	7.5	4.00	93	.219	.285	-0	-1	94	73	0.0	0	0	0.0
■ KEN HEINTZELMAN	Heintzelman, Kenneth Alphonse b: 10/14/15, Peruque, Mo. BR/TL, 5'11.5", 185 lbs. Deb: 10/03/37																												
1937	Pit-N	1	0	1.000	1	1	1	0	0	9	6	6.0	0	3	3.0	4	4.0	2.00	198	.207	.294	2	2	101	123	0.5	-1	-0	0.1
1938	Pit-N	0	0	—	1	0	0	0	0	2	1	4.5	0	3	13.5	1	4.5	9.00	42	.167	.444	-1	-1	99	52	0.0	0	0	0.0
1939	Pit-N	1	1	.500	17	2	1	1	0	36	35	8.8	2	18	4.5	18	4.5	5.00	79	.250	.329	-4	-4	101	72	0.1	0	-0	-0.3
1940	Pit-N	8	8	.500	39	16	5	2	3	165	193	10.5	7	65	3.5	71	3.9	4.47	82	.292	.353	-11	-15	95	104	0.0	-1	2	-1.3
1941	Pit-N	11	11	.500	35	24	13	2	0	196	206	9.5	8	83	3.8	81	3.7	3.44	107	.272	.340	4	5	102	117	-0.5	-2	1	0.4
1942	Pit-N	8	11	.421	27	18	5	3	0	130	143	9.9	9	63	4.4	39	2.7	4.57	74	.281	.355	-18	-17	102	101	-0.6	-2	-2	-2.0
1946	Pit-N	8	12	.400	32	24	6	2	1	158	165	9.4	7	86	4.9	57	3.2	3.76	96	.271	.355	-6	-3	106	110	-0.2	-1	2	-0.1
1947	Pit-N	0	0	—	2	1	0	0	0	4	9	20.3	2	6	13.5	2	4.5	20.25	21	.409	.536	-7	-7	102	76	0.0	0	-0	-0.5
	Phi-N	7	10	.412	24	19	8	0	1	136	144	9.5	12	46	3.0	55	3.6	4.04	103	.277	.336	0	2	102	105	0.1	-2	-3	-0.3
	Yr	7	10	.412	26	20	8	0	1	140	153	9.8	14	52	3.3	57	3.7	4.50	92	.282	.346	-7	-6	102	105	0.1	0	-3	-0.8
1948	Phi-N	6	11	.353	27	16	5	2	2	130	117	8.1	10	45	3.1	57	3.9	4.29	89	.241	.304	-5	-7	97	77	-1.6	-1	-1	-0.8
1949	Phi-N	17	10	.630	33	32	15	**5**	0	250	239	8.6	19	93	3.3	65	2.3	3.02	134	.255	.320	28	29	101	123	3.4	-1	-2	2.6
1950	Phi-N	3	9	.250	23	17	4	1	0	125	122	8.8	10	54	3.9	39	2.8	4.10	97	.250	.322	1	-2	96	89	-3.5	-3	-2	-0.6
1951	Phi-N	6	12	.333	35	12	3	0	2	118	119	9.1	13	53	4.0	55	4.2	4.19	92	.267	.341	-3	-5	97	108	-2.8	-1	-1	-0.6
1952	Phi-N	1	3	.250	23	1	0	0	1	43	41	8.6	1	12	2.5	20	4.2	3.14	118	.266	.312	3	3	99	108	-1.0	-0	-1	0.2
Total	13	77	98	.440	319	183	66	18	10	1502	1540	9.2	100	630	3.8	564	3.4	3.93	97	.267	.336	-18	-20	100	105	-6.1	-16	-7	-3.2
■ CLARENCE HEISE	Heise, Clarence Edward "Lefty" b: 8/7/07, Topeka, Kan. BL/TL, 5'10", 172 lbs. Deb: 4/22/34																												
1934	StL-N	0	0	—	1	0	0	0	0	2	3	13.5	1	0	0.0	1	4.5	4.50	100	.300	.300	-0	0	111	154	0.0	0	0	0.0
■ JIM HEISE	Heise, James Edward b: 10/2/32, Scottdale, Pa. BR/TR, 6'1", 185 lbs. Deb: 6/29/57																												
1957	Was-A	0	3	.000	8	2	0	0	0	19	25	11.8	2	16	7.6	8	3.8	8.05	48	.329	.427	-9	-9	102	88	-1.4	-0	0	-0.8
■ ROY HEISER	Heiser, Le Roy Barton b: 6/22/42, Baltimore, Md. BR/TR, 6'4", 190 lbs. Deb: 9/02/61																												
1961	Was-A	0	0	—	3	0	0	0	0	6	6	9.0	1	9	13.5	1	1.5	6.00	65	.261	.485	-1	-1	97	134	0.0	-0	-0	-0.1
■ CRESE HEISMANN	Heismann, Christian Ernest b: 4/16/1880, Cincinnati, Ohio d: 11/19/51, Cincinnati, Ohio BR/TL, 6'2", 175 lbs. Deb: 9/25/01																												
1901	Cin-N	0	1	.000	3	2	1	0	0	14	16	10.3	1	6	3.9	6	3.9	5.79	57	.329	.433	-4	-4	100	90	-0.4	0	-0	-0.3
1902	Cin-N	2	1	.667	5	3	2	0	0	33	33	9.0	1	10	2.7	15	4.1	2.45	123	.283	.340	1	2	108	126	0.5	0	0	0.2
	Bal-A	0	3	.000	3	3	2	0	0	16	20	11.3	1	12	6.8	2	1.1	8.44	44	.332	.443	-9	-8	104	71	-1.4	-1	-0	-0.6
Total	2	2	5	.286	11	8	5	0	0	63	69	9.9	3	28	4.0	23	3.3	4.71	69	.306	.390	-11	-10	105	104	-1.3	0	-1	-0.7

YEAR	TM/L	W	L	PCT	G	GS	CG	SHO	SV	IP	H	H/G	HR	BB	BB/G	SO	SO/G	ERA	/A	OAVG	OOBP	PR	/A	PF	CPI	WAT	PB	PD	TPI
■ HARRY HEITMANN	Heitmann, Henry Anton b: 10/6/1896, Albany, N.Y. d: 12/15/58, Brooklyn, N.Y. BR/TR, 6', 175 lbs. Deb: 7/27/18																												
1918	Bro-N	0	1	.000	1	1	0	0	0	⅓	4	108.0	0	0	0.0	0	0.0	108.00	—	1.000	1.000	-4	-4	104	55	-0.4	0	0	-0.3
■ MEL HELD	Held, Melvin Nicholas "Country" b: 4/12/29, Edon, Ohio BR/TR, 6'1", 178 lbs. Deb: 4/27/56																												
1956	Bal-A	0	0	—	4	0	0	0	0	7	7	9.0	1	3	3.9	4	5.1	5.14	78	.318	.345	-1	-1	97	118	0.0	0	0	0.0
■ HORACE HELMBOLD	Helmbold, Horace b: Philadelphia, Pa. Deb: 10/11/1890																												
1890	Phi-a	0	1	.000	1	1	1	0	0	7	17	21.9	0	6	7.7	3	3.9	14.14	28	.480	.556	-8	-8	101	84	-0.4	-0	0	-0.5
■ RUSS HEMAN	Heman, Russell Fredrick b: 2/10/33, Olive, Cal. BR/TR, 6'4", 200 lbs. Deb: 4/20/61																												
1961	Cle-A	0	0	—	6	0	0	0	1	10	8	7.2	0	8	7.2	4	3.6	3.60	108	.216	.370	0	0	97	97	0.0	-0	0	0.0
	LA-A	0	0	—	6	0	0	0	0	10	4	3.6	1	2	1.8	2	1.8	1.80	251	.125	.184	2	3	112	49	0.0	-0	0	0.3
	Yr	0	0	—	12	0	0	0	1	20	12	5.4	1	10	4.5	6	2.7	2.70	155	.171	.274	3	3	104	49	0.0	-0	0	0.3
■ GEORGE HEMMING	Hemming, George Earl "Old Wax Figger" b: 12/15/1868, Carrollton, Ohio d: 6/3/30, Springfield, Mass. BR/TR, 5'11", 170 lbs. Deb: 4/21/1890																												
1890	Cle-P	0	1	.000	3	1	1	0	0	21	25	10.7	1	19	8.1	3	1.3	6.86	58	.308	.439	-6	-7	94	84	-0.4	-1	0	-0.4
	Bro-P	8	4	.667	19	11	11	0	3	123	117	8.6	3	59	4.3	32	2.3	3.80	117	.262	.348	6	9	105	84	1.4	-4	0	0.4
	Yr	8	5	.615	22	12	12	0	**3**	144	142	8.9	4	78	4.9	35	2.2	4.25	103	.269	.363	-0	2	104	84	1.0	-1	0	0.0
1891	Bro-N	8	15	.348	27	22	19	1	1	200	231	10.4	11	84	3.8	83	3.7	5.00	66	.303	.373	-37	-38	98	85	-2.8	-1	0	-3.2
1892	Cin-N	0	1	.000	1	0	0	0	0	6	10	15.0	1	2	3.0	0	0.0	7.50	45	.385	.429	-3	-3	103	101	-0.4	0	0	-0.1
	Lou-N	2	2	.500	4	4	4	0	0	35	36	9.3	1	17	4.4	12	3.1	4.63	66	.279	.363	-5	-6	93	82	0.3	-1	0	-0.5
	Yr	2	3	.400	5	4	4	0	0	41	46	10.1	2	19	4.2	12	2.6	5.05	62	.297	.373	-8	-9	95	82	-0.1	0	0	-0.6
1893	Lou-N	18	17	.514	41	33	33	1	1	332	373	10.1	7	176	4.8	79	2.1	5.18	89	.299	.386	-18	-22	98	88	4.3	-3	3	-1.7
1894	Lou-N	13	19	.406	35	32	32	1	1	294	358	11.0	7	133	4.1	66	2.0	4.38	110	.323	.395	31	15	91	109	3.6	3	-0	1.2
	Bal-N	4	0	1.000	6	6	4	0	0	45	48	9.6	0	26	5.2	4	0.8	3.60	143	.295	.392	9	8	96	116	2.0	1	0	0.7
	Yr	17	19	.472	41	38	36	1	1	339	406	10.8	7	159	4.2	70	1.9	4.27	114	.319	.395	40	22	91	116	5.6	3	-0	1.9
1895	Bal-N	20	13	.606	34	31	26	1	0	262	288	9.9	10	96	3.3	43	1.5	4.05	123	.299	.363	21	27	104	100	-1.9	3	-2	2.3
1896	Bal-N	15	6	.714	25	21	20	3	0	202	233	10.4	9	54	2.4	33	1.5	4.19	103	.312	.358	4	3	99	96	0.7	3	0	0.6
1897	Lou-N	3	4	.429	9	8	7	0	0	67	80	10.7	5	25	3.4	7	0.9	5.10	82	.319	.381	-6	-7	97	92	0.2	-1	0	-0.6
Total	8	91	82	.526	204	169	157	7	6	1587	1799	10.2	55	691	3.9	362	2.1	4.56	98	.304	.377	-4	-20	98	95	7.0	1	0	-1.3
■ BERNIE HENDERSON	Henderson, Bernard "Barnyard" b: 4/12/1899, Douglassville, Tex d: 6/6/66, Linden, Tex. BR/TR, 5'9", 175 lbs. Deb: 9/05/21																												
1921	Cle-A	0	1	.000	2	1	0	0	0	3	5	15.0	0	0	0.0	1	3.0	9.00	46	.333	.333	-2	-2	96	45	-0.4	0	-0	-0.1
■ ED HENDERSON	Henderson, Edward J. (born Eugene J. Ball) b: 12/25/1884, Newark, N.J. d: 1/15/64, New York, N.Y. BL/TL, 5'9", 168 lbs. Deb: 5/15/14																												
1914	Pit-F	0	1	.000	6	1	1	0	0	16	14	7.9	2	8	4.5	4	2.3	3.94	78	.263	.359	-1	-2	96	100	-0.4	-0	0	-0.1
	Ind-F	1	0	1.000	2	1	1	0	0	10	8	7.2	0	4	3.6	1	0.9	4.50	77	.246	.328	-1	-1	108	52	0.5	-1	0	-0.1
	Yr	1	1	.500	8	2	2	0	0	26	22	7.6	2	12	4.2	5	1.7	4.15	78	.256	.348	-3	-3	101	52	0.1	-0	0	-0.2
■ HARDIE HENDERSON	Henderson, James Harding b: 10/31/1862, Philadelphia, Pa. d: 2/6/03, Philadelphia, Pa. BR/TR, Deb: 5/02/1883																												
1883	Phi-N	0	1	.000	1	1	1	0	0	9	26	26.0	0	2	2.0	2	2.0	19.00	16	.514	.532	-16	-16	99	65	-0.4	0	0	-0.8
	Bal-a	10	32	.238	45	42	38	0	0	358	383	9.6	5	87	2.2	145	3.6	4.02	93	.279	.322	-29	-11	113	90	-5.9	-9	-2	-1.6
1884	Bal-a	27	23	.540	52	52	50	4	0	439	382	7.8	10	116	2.4	346	**7.1**	2.62	121	.242	.294	30	26	98	112	-3.9	5	1	3.0
1885	Bal-a	25	35	.417	61	61	59	0	0	539	539	9.0	7	117	2.0	263	4.4	3.19	111	.272	.313	4	22	109	100	4.0	0	-1	2.2
1886	Bal-a	3	15	.167	19	19	19	0	0	171	188	9.9	0	66	3.5	88	4.6	4.63	70	.290	.355	-22	-26	94	88	-5.1	3	0	-1.9
	Bro-a	10	4	.714	14	14	14	0	0	124	112	8.1	2	51	3.7	49	3.6	2.90	119	.251	.328	8	8	100	113	2.7	-1	0	0.6
	Yr	13	19	.406	33	33	33	0	0	295	300	9.2	2	117	3.6	137	4.2	3.91	85	.274	.344	-15	-19	97	113	-2.4	3	0	-1.3
1887	Bro-a	5	8	.385	13	12	12	0	0	112	127	10.2	3	63	5.1	28	2.3	3.94	108	.299	.390	4	4	99	124	-0.9	-3	0	0.1
1888	Pit-N	1	3	.250	5	5	4	0	0	35	43	11.1	0	20	5.1	9	2.3	5.40	50	.317	.404	-10	-11	95	91	-0.9	1	0	-0.8
Total	6	81	121	.401	210	206	197	4	0	1787	1800	9.1	27	522	2.6	930	4.7	3.51	99	.271	.324	-31	-4	104	102	-10.4	-3	-3	0.8
■ JOE HENDERSON	Henderson, Joseph Lee b: 7/4/46, Lake Cormorant, Miss. BL/TR, 6'2", 195 lbs. Deb: 6/07/74																												
1974	Chi-A	1	0	1.000	5	3	0	0	0	15	21	12.6	2	11	6.6	12	7.2	8.40	44	.328	.421	-8	-8	102	83	0.5	0	0	-0.7
1976	Cin-N	2	0	1.000	4	0	0	0	0	11	9	7.4	0	8	6.5	7	5.7	0.00	—	.225	.354	4	4	100	0	1.0	0	0	0.5
1977	Cin-N	0	2	.000	7	0	0	0	0	9	17	17.0	2	6	6.0	8	8.0	12.00	32	.386	.460	-8	-8	99	80	-0.9	-0	-0	-0.7
Total	3	3	2	.600	16	3	0	0	0	35	47	12.1	4	25	6.4	27	6.9	6.69	55	.318	.414	-12	-12	101	56	0.6	0	-0	-0.9
■ BILL HENDERSON	Henderson, William Maxwell b: 11/4/01, Pensacola, Fla. d: 10/6/66, Pensacola, Fla. BR/TR, 6', 190 lbs. Deb: 6/20/30																												
1930	NY-A	0	0	—	3	0	0	0	0	8	7	7.9	1	4	4.5	2	2.3	4.50	90	.250	.314	0	-0	87	102	0.0	0	0	0.0
■ BOB HENDLEY	Hendley, Charles Robert b: 4/30/39, Macon, Ga. BR/TL, 6'2", 190 lbs. Deb: 6/23/61																												
1961	Mil-N	5	7	.417	19	13	3	0	0	97	96	8.9	8	39	3.6	44	4.1	3.90	94	.262	.328	1	-2	91	100	-1.3	-3	1	-0.3
1962	Mil-N	11	13	.458	35	29	7	2	1	200	188	8.5	17	59	2.7	112	5.0	3.60	107	.247	.296	8	6	98	89	-1.8	1	0	0.7
1963	Mil-N	9	9	.500	41	24	7	3	3	169	153	8.1	16	64	3.4	105	5.6	3.94	83	.244	.308	-12	-12	100	88	-0.3	-1	1	-1.2
1964	SF-N	10	11	.476	30	29	4	1	0	163	161	8.9	18	59	3.3	104	5.7	3.64	96	.258	.319	-2	-3	99	110	-1.6	-1	-2	-0.5
1965	SF-N	0	0	—	8	2	0	0	0	15	27	16.2	6	13	7.8	8	4.8	12.60	31	.397	.471	-15	-15	109	95	0.0	-0	0	-1.3
	Chi-N	4	4	.500	18	10	2	0	0	62	59	8.6	9	25	3.6	38	5.5	4.35	84	.244	.311	-6	-5	103	91	0.4	-1	1	-0.5
	Yr	4	4	.500	26	12	2	0	0	77	86	10.1	15	38	4.4	46	5.4	5.96	62	.277	.347	-21	-19	104	91	0.4	-0	1	-1.8
1966	Chi-N	4	5	.444	43	6	0	0	7	90	98	9.8	10	39	3.9	65	6.5	3.90	95	.285	.348	-3	-2	103	123	0.6	1	1	0.0
1967	Chi-N	2	0	1.000	7	0	0	0	1	12	17	12.8	4	3	2.3	10	7.5	6.75	50	.315	.351	-4	-4	100	102	1.0	-1	-0	-0.5
	NY-N	3	3	.500	15	13	2	0	0	71	65	8.2	11	28	3.5	36	4.6	3.42	100	.241	.309	-0	0	102	115	0.6	-0	-2	-0.1
	Yr	5	3	.625	22	13	2	0	1	83	82	8.9	15	31	3.4	46	5.0	3.90	88	.253	.316	-5	-4	102	115	1.6	-1	-2	-0.6
Total	7	48	52	.480	216	126	25	6	12	879	864	8.8	99	329	3.4	522	5.3	3.97	91	.257	.318	-34	-37	99	100	-2.4	-6	0	-3.7
■ ED HENDRICKS	Hendricks, Edward "Big Ed" b: 6/20/1886, Zeeland, Mich. d: 11/28/30, Jackson, Mich. 6'3", 200 lbs. Deb: 9/15/10																												
1910	NY-N	0	1	.000	4	1	1	0	1	12	12	9.0	0	4	3.0	2	1.5	3.75	75	.261	.320	-1	-1	92	74	-0.4	-1	-0	-0.1
■ ELLIE HENDRICKS	Hendricks, Elrod Jerome b: 12/22/40, Charlotte Amalie, V.I. BL/TR, 6'1", 175 lbs. Deb: 4/13/68 C																												
1978	Bal-A	0	0	—	1	0	0	0	0	2	1	4.5	0	1	4.5	0	0.0	0.00	—	.125	.222	1	1	91	0	0.0	1	0	0.1
■ DON HENDRICKSON	Hendrickson, Donald Williamson b: 7/14/13, Rochester, Ind. d: 1/19/77, Norfolk, Va. BR/TR, 6'2", 195 lbs. Deb: 7/04/45																												
1945	Bos-N	4	8	.333	37	2	1	0	5	73	74	9.1	8	39	4.8	14	1.7	4.93	87	.261	.343	-9	-5	113	93	-1.5	-1	-1	-0.5
1946	Bos-N	0	1	.000	2	0	0	0	0	2	4	18.0	0	2	9.0	2	9.0	4.50	71	.364	.462	-0	-0	94	183	-0.4	-0	0	0.0
Total	2	4	9	.308	39	2	1	0	5	75	78	9.4	8	41	4.9	16	1.9	4.92	86	.265	.348	-9	-6	112	95	-1.9	-1	-1	-0.5
■ CLAUDE HENDRIX	Hendrix, Claude Raymond b: 4/13/1889, Olathe, Kan. d: 3/22/44, Allentown, Pa. BR/TR, 6', 195 lbs. Deb: 6/07/11																												
1911	Pit-N	4	6	.400	22	12	6	1	1	119	85	6.4	1	53	4.0	57	4.3	2.72	122	.204	.295	9	8	97	73	-1.3	-2	4	0.9
1912	Pit-N	24	9	**.727**	39	32	25	4	1	289	256	8.0	6	105	3.3	176	5.5	2.58	126	.239	.313	26	21	95	97	5.7	15	5	4.2
1913	Pit-N	14	15	.483	42	25	17	2	3	241	216	8.1	3	89	3.3	138	5.2	2.84	106	.248	.313	10	5	94	101	-1.3	9	2	1.6
1914	Chi-F	**29**	10	.744	**49**	37	**34**	6	5	362	262	**6.5**	6	77	1.9	189	4.7	**1.69**	169	**.203**	**.251**	**61**	47	89	80	**9.4**	6	9	**6.7**
1915	Chi-F	16	15	.516	40	31	26	5	4	285	256	8.1	7	84	2.7	107	3.4	3.00	96	.241	.298	1	-4	95	86	-1.6	11	-0	0.7
1916	Chi-N	8	16	.333	36	24	15	3	2	218	193	8.0	4	67	2.8	117	4.8	2.68	115	.242	.297	-2	10	117	97	-3.2	2	2	1.7
1917	Chi-N	10	12	.455	40	21	13	1	1	215	202	8.5	3	72	3.0	81	3.4	2.60	110	.257	.312	3	6	105	117	-0.6	5	-2	1.0
1918	Chi-N	20	7	**.741**	32	27	21	3	0	233	229	8.8	2	54	2.1	86	3.3	2.78	98	.259	.298	-0	-2	98	96	4.1	9	2	0.9
1919	Chi-N	10	14	.417	33	25	15	2	0	206	208	9.1	3	42	1.8	69	3.0	2.62	110	.266	.302	7	6	99	113	-3.0	-0	1	0.8
1920	Chi-N	9	12	.429	27	23	12	0	0	204	216	9.5	6	54	2.4	72	3.2	3.57	87	.273	.313	-10	-11	99	86	-1.3	-2	-0	-1.2
Total	10	144	116	.554	360	257	184	27	17	2372	2123	8.1	41	697	2.6	1092	4.1	2.65	113	.243	.297	105	90	98	94	6.9	53	21	17.3
■ LAFAYETTE HENION	Henion, Lafayette Marion b: 6/7/1899, Eureka, Cal. d: 7/22/55, San Luis Obispo, Cal. BR/TR, 5'11", 154 lbs. Deb: 9/10/19																												
1919	Bro-N	0	0	—	1	0	0	0	0	3	2	6.0	0	2	6.0	2	6.0	6.00	45	.200	.333	-1	-1	94	43	0.0	-0	0	0.0

YEAR	TM/L	W	L	PCT	G	GS	CG	SHO	SV	IP	H	H/G	HR	BB	BB/G	SO	SO/G	ERA	/A	OAVG	OOBP	PR	/A	PF	CPI	WAT	PB	PD	TPI
■ TOM HENKE	Henke, Thomas Anthony b: 12/21/57, Kansas City, Mo. BR/TR, 6'5", 215 lbs. Deb: 9/10/82																												
1982	Tex-A	1	0	1.000	8	0	0	0	0	16	14	7.9	0	8	4.5	9	5.1	1.13	342	.246	.343	5	5	94	306	0.5	0	0	0.5
1983	Tex-A	1	0	1.000	8	0	0	0	1	16	16	9.0	1	4	2.3	17	9.6	3.38	122	.262	.308	1	1	101	101	0.5	0	0	0.1
1984	Tex-A	1	1	.500	25	0	0	0	2	28	36	11.6	0	20	6.4	25	8.0	6.43	63	.313	.404	-8	-7	101	88	0.1	0	-0	-0.7
1985	Tor-A	3	3	.500	28	0	0	0	13	40	29	6.5	4	8	1.8	42	9.4	2.02	203	.206	.242	9	9	99	112	-0.5	0	-0	0.9
1986	Tor-A	9	5	.643	63	0	0	0	27	91	63	6.2	6	32	3.2	118	11.7	3.36	130	.191	.259	8	10	104	58	1.8	0	-1	0.8
1987	Tor-A	0	6	.000	72	0	0	0	**34**	94	62	5.9	10	25	2.4	128	12.3	2.49	178	.188	.240	**21**	20	99	82	-2.9	0	1	2.1
1988	Tor-A	4	4	.500	52	0	0	0	25	68	60	7.9	6	24	3.2	66	8.7	2.91	135	.237	.302	8	8	99	115	-0.2	0	0	0.8
Total	7	19	19	.500	256	0	0	0	102	353	280	7.1	27	121	3.1	405	10.3	3.03	139	.218	.281	45	46	100	97	-0.7	0	-0	4.5
■ WELDON HENLEY	Henley, Weldon b: 10/25/1880, Jasper, Ga. d: 11/16/60, Palatka, Fla. BR/TR, 6', 175 lbs. Deb: 4/23/03																												
1903	Phi-A	12	9	.571	29	21	13	1	0	186	186	9.0	3	67	3.2	86	4.2	3.92	77	.282	.349	-20	-19	102	87	0.4	-3	-1	-1.8
1904	Phi-A	15	17	.469	36	34	31	5	0	296	245	7.4	3	76	2.3	130	4.0	2.52	104	.247	.300	2	3	101	87	-2.4	2	3	0.7
1905	Phi-A	4	11	.267	25	19	13	1	0	184	155	7.6	4	67	3.3	82	4.0	2.59	109	.251	.325	1	5	106	105	-4.4	-1	4	0.9
1907	Bro-N	1	5	.167	7	7	5	0	0	56	54	8.7	2	21	3.4	11	1.8	3.05	78	.283	.357	-4	-4	96	107	-1.8	1	2	-0.2
Total	4	32	42	.432	97	81	62	7	0	722	640	8.0	12	231	2.9	309	3.9	2.94	93	.260	.324	-20	-16	102	93	-8.2	-2	8	-0.4
■ MIKE HENNEMAN	Henneman, Michael Alan b: 12/11/61, St.Charles, Mo. BR/TR, 6'4", 205 lbs. Deb: 5/11/87																												
1987	Det-A	11	3	.786	55	0	0	0	7	97	86	8.0	8	30	2.8	75	7.0	2.97	144	.238	.298	16	14	96	107	3.4	0	0	1.3
1988	Det-A	9	6	.600	65	0	0	0	22	91	72	7.1	7	24	2.4	58	5.7	1.88	199	.218	.269	**21**	**19**	94	135	1.0	0	-1	1.8
Total	2	20	9	.690	120	0	0	0	29	188	158	7.6	15	54	2.6	133	6.4	2.44	164	.228	.284	37	33	95	121	4.4	0	-1	3.1
■ GEORGE HENNESSEY	Hennessey, George "Three Star" b: 10/28/07, Slatington, Pa. d: 1/15/88, Princeton, N.J. BR/TR, 5'10", 168 lbs. Deb: 9/02/37																												
1937	StL-A	0	1	.000	5	0	0	0	0	7	15	19.3	2	6	7.7	4	5.1	10.29	46	.500	.553	-4	-4	103	140	-0.4	0	0	-0.3
1942	Phi-N	1	1	.500	5	1	0	0	0	17	11	5.8	1	10	5.3	2	1.1	2.65	126	.180	.296	1	1	101	87	0.3	-1	-0	0.0
1945	Chi-N	0	0	—	2	0	0	0	0	4	7	15.8	0	1	2.3	2	4.5	6.75	54	.438	.471	-1	-1	95	117	0.0	0	0	0.0
Total	3	1	2	.333	12	1	0	0	0	28	33	10.6	3	17	5.5	8	2.6	5.14	73	.308	.397	-4	-4	101	105	-0.1	-1	-0	-0.3
■ PHIL HENNIGAN	Hennigan, Phillip Winston b: 4/10/46, Jasper, Tex. BR/TR, 5'11.5", 185 lbs. Deb: 9/02/69																												
1969	Cle-A	2	1	.667	9	0	0	0	0	16	14	7.9	0	4	2.3	10	5.6	3.38	103	.241	.288	0	0	96	74	0.7	-0	-1	0.0
1970	Cle-A	6	3	.667	42	1	0	0	3	72	69	8.6	7	44	5.5	43	5.4	4.00	107	.263	.370	-2	2	115	120	1.7	1	1	0.4
1971	Cle-A	4	3	.571	57	0	0	0	14	82	80	8.8	13	51	5.6	69	7.6	4.94	76	.261	.360	-13	-11	108	103	1.2	-0	-1	-1.1
1972	Cle-A	5	3	.625	38	1	0	0	5	67	54	7.3	8	18	2.4	44	5.9	2.69	123	.226	.277	3	5	108	111	1.3	-0	-1	0.4
1973	NY-N	0	4	.000	30	0	0	0	3	43	50	10.5	6	16	3.3	22	4.6	6.28	59	.289	.344	-12	-12	100	79	-1.9	0	-0	-1.2
Total	5	17	14	.548	176	2	0	0	25	280	267	8.6	34	133	4.3	188	6.0	4.28	88	.257	.338	-25	-16	108	104	3.0	1	-2	-1.5
■ PETE HENNING	Henning, Ernest Herman b: 12/28/1887, Crown Point, Ind. d: 11/4/39, Dyer, Ind. BR/TR, 5'11", 185 lbs. Deb: 4/17/14																												
1914	KC-F	5	10	.333	28	14	7	0	2	138	153	10.0	5	58	3.8	45	2.9	4.83	64	.291	.369	-25	-27	96	91	-1.9	1	1	-2.4
1915	KC-F	9	15	.375	40	20	15	1	2	207	181	7.9	5	76	3.3	73	3.2	3.17	92	.235	.307	-3	-6	97	84	-3.8	-0	6	0.0
Total	2	14	25	.359	68	34	22	1	4	345	334	8.7	10	134	3.5	118	3.1	3.83	78	.258	.332	-28	-32	96	87	-5.7	0	7	-2.4
■ RICK HENNINGER	Henninger, Richard Lee b: 1/11/48, Hastings, Neb. BR/TR, 6'6", 225 lbs. Deb: 9/03/73																												
1973	Tex-A	1	0	1.000	6	2	0	0	0	23	23	9.0	1	11	4.3	6	2.3	2.74	139	.261	.333	3	3	100	135	0.5	0	-1	0.2
■ DWAYNE HENRY	Henry, Dwayne Allen b: 2/16/62, Elkton, Md. BR/TR, 6'3", 205 lbs. Deb: 9/07/84																												
1984	Tex-A	0	1	.000	3	0	0	0	0	4	5	11.3	0	7	15.8	2	4.5	9.00	45	.294	.480	-2	-2	101	87	-0.4	0	0	-0.1
1985	Tex-A	2	2	.500	16	0	0	0	3	21	16	6.9	0	7	3.0	20	8.6	2.57	177	.211	.267	4	5	110	74	0.4	0	0	0.5
1986	Tex-A	1	0	1.000	19	0	0	0	0	19	14	6.6	1	22	10.4	17	8.1	4.74	84	.209	.398	-1	-2	95	100	0.5	0	0	0.0
1987	Tex-A	0	0	—	5	0	0	0	0	10	12	10.8	2	9	8.1	7	6.3	9.00	52	.293	.420	-5	-5	104	78	0.0	0	0	-0.3
1988	Tex-A	0	1	.000	11	0	0	0	1	10	15	13.5	1	9	8.1	10	9.0	9.00	45	.326	.458	-6	-5	102	91	-0.4	0	-0	-0.5
Total	5	3	4	.429	54	0	0	0	4	64	62	8.7	4	54	7.6	56	7.9	5.63	76	.251	.383	-10	-9	103	86	0.1	0	0	-0.4
■ EARL HENRY	Henry, Earl Clifford "Hook" b: 6/10/17, Roseville, Ohio BL/TL, 5'11", 172 lbs. Deb: 9/23/44																												
1944	Cle-A	1	1	.500	2	2	1	0	0	18	18	9.0	0	3	1.5	5	2.5	4.50	77	.269	.296	-2	-2	101	63	0.1	-0	0	-0.1
1945	Cle-A	0	3	.000	15	1	0	0	0	22	20	8.2	0	20	8.2	10	4.1	5.32	62	.253	.406	-5	-5	98	87	-1.4	1	1	-0.3
Total	2	1	4	.200	17	3	1	0	0	40	38	8.5	0	23	5.2	15	3.4	4.95	68	.260	.360	-7	-7	99	76	-1.3	0	1	-0.4
■ DUTCH HENRY	Henry, Frank John b: 5/12/02, Cleveland, Ohio d: 8/23/68, Cleveland, Ohio BL/TL, 6'1", 175 lbs. Deb: 9/16/21																												
1921	StL-A	0	0	—	1	0	0	0	0	2	2	9.0	0	0	0.0	1	4.5	4.50	96	.250	.222	-0	-0	101	34	0.0	0	0	0.0
1922	StL-A	0	0	—	4	0	0	0	0	5	7	12.6	0	5	9.0	3	5.4	5.40	76	.280	.387	-1	-1	102	89	0.0	0	0	0.0
1923	Bro-N	4	6	.400	17	9	5	2	0	94	105	10.1	9	28	2.7	28	2.7	3.93	99	.281	.327	1	-0	98	105	-0.9	1	-0	0.0
1924	Bro-N	1	2	.333	16	4	0	0	0	46	69	13.5	0	15	2.9	11	2.2	5.67	67	.352	.389	-9	-10	98	99	-0.6	0	0	-0.8
1927	NY-N	11	6	.647	45	15	7	1	4	164	184	10.1	6	31	1.7	40	2.2	4.23	91	.278	.302	-6	-7	98	78	1.2	1	-2	-0.6
1928	NY-N	3	6	.333	17	8	4	0	1	64	82	11.5	4	25	3.5	23	3.2	3.80	104	.325	.375	1	1	99	142	-2.0	-1	1	0.2
1929	NY-N	5	6	.455	27	9	4	0	1	101	129	11.5	10	31	2.8	27	2.4	3.83	119	.316	.359	10	8	97	141	-1.0	2	-1	0.8
	Chi-A	1	0	1.000	2	1	1	0	0	15	20	12.0	1	7	4.2	2	1.2	6.00	69	.308	.370	-3	-3	98	86	0.5	0	-1	-0.2
1930	Chi-A	2	17	.105	35	16	4	0	0	155	211	12.3	12	48	2.8	34	2.0	4.88	100	.331	.373	-4	0	105	**122**	-7.2	1	2	0.3
Total	8	27	43	.386	164	62	25	3	6	646	809	11.3	42	190	2.6	169	2.4	4.39	96	.308	.348	-10	-12	100	110	-10.0	5	1	-0.3
■ JIM HENRY	Henry, James Francis b: 6/26/10, Danville, Pa. d: 8/15/76, Memphis, Tenn. BR/TR, 6'2", 175 lbs. Deb: 4/23/36																												
1936	Bos-A	5	1	.833	21	8	2	0	0	76	75	8.9	10	40	4.7	36	4.3	4.62	115	.255	.344	4	6	106	104	2.1	-1	0	0.5
1937	Bos-A	1	0	1.000	3	2	1	0	0	15	15	9.0	2	11	6.6	8	4.8	5.40	88	.263	.371	-1	-1	102	100	0.5	-1	0	-0.1
1939	Phi-N	0	1	.000	9	1	0	0	1	23	24	9.4	3	8	3.1	7	2.7	5.09	77	.276	.333	-3	-3	99	92	-0.4	-1	-1	-0.3
Total	3	6	2	.750	33	11	3	0	1	114	114	9.0	15	59	4.7	51	4.0	4.82	103	.260	.346	-1	2	104	101	2.2	-2	-1	0.1
■ JOHN HENRY	Henry, John Michael b: 9/2/1863, Springfield, Mass. d: 6/11/39, Hartford, Conn. Deb: 8/13/1884																												
1884	Cle-N	1	4	.200	5	5	5	1	0	42	46	9.9	2	26	5.6	23	4.9	3.64	88	.288	.387	-3	-2	108	126	-0.8	-1	0	-0.2
1885	Bal-a	2	7	.222	9	9	9	0	0	71	71	9.0	0	13	1.6	31	3.9	4.31	82	.272	.306	-8	-6	109	69	-1.8	1	0	-0.3
1886	Was-N	1	3	.250	4	4	4	0	0	28	35	11.3	1	15	4.8	19	6.1	4.18	79	.320	.402	-3	-3	100	127	0.0	1	0	-0.1
Total	3	4	14	.222	18	18	18	1	0	141	152	9.7	3	54	3.4	73	4.7	4.09	83	.287	.352	-14	-11	107	98	-2.6	1	0	-0.6
■ BILL HENRY	Henry, William Francis b: 2/15/42, Long Beach, Cal. BL/TL, 6'3", 195 lbs. Deb: 9/13/66																												
1966	NY-A	0	0	—	2	0	0	0	0	3	0	0.0	0	2	6.0	3	9.0	0.00	—	.000	.182	1	1	94	0	0.0	0	0	0.2
■ BILL HENRY	Henry, William Rodman b: 10/15/27, Alice, Tex. BL/TL, 6'2", 180 lbs. Deb: 4/17/52																												
1952	Bos-A	5	4	.556	13	10	5	0	0	77	75	8.8	7	36	4.2	23	2.7	3.86	102	.254	.335	-2	1	107	104	0.6	2	-1	0.2
1953	Bos-A	5	5	.500	21	12	4	1	1	86	86	9.0	4	33	3.5	56	5.9	3.24	133	.260	.331	7	10	108	113	-0.4	-0	-0	1.0
1954	Bos-A	3	7	.300	24	13	3	1	0	96	104	9.8	9	49	4.6	38	3.6	4.50	83	.270	.348	-8	-8	101	97	-1.6	-1	-1	-0.9
1955	Bos-A	2	4	.333	17	7	0	0	0	60	56	8.4	7	21	3.2	23	3.5	3.30	147	.247	.303	4	10	122	108	-1.1	-2	0	1.0
1958	Chi-N	5	4	.556	44	0	0	0	6	81	63	7.0	8	17	1.9	58	6.4	2.89	138	.214	.258	10	10	101	77	0.8	1	1	1.0
1959	Chi-N	9	8	.529	**65**	0	0	0	12	134	111	7.5	19	26	1.7	115	7.7	2.69	145	.227	.262	19	**18**	99	108	0.9	0	-1	1.8
1960	Cin-N	1	5	.167	51	0	0	0	17	68	62	8.2	8	20	2.6	58	7.7	3.18	118	.247	.309	4	4	99	117	-1.8	-1	1	0.4
1961	Cin-N	2	1	.667	47	0	0	0	16	53	50	8.5	8	15	2.5	53	9.0	2.21	188	.244	.290	11	11	103	160	0.2	-1	0	1.1
1962	Cin-N	4	2	.667	40	0	0	0	11	37	40	9.7	5	20	4.9	35	8.5	4.62	86	.280	.363	-3	-3	100	113	0.5	0	-1	-0.2
1963	Cin-N	1	3	.250	47	0	0	0	14	52	55	9.5	4	11	1.9	45	7.8	4.15	82	.279	.310	-5	-4	103	92	-1.0	-0	-0	-0.4
1964	Cin-N	2	2	.500	37	0	0	0	6	52	31	5.4	2	12	2.1	28	4.8	0.87	415	.170	.228	15	16	102	132	-0.1	1	-0	1.8
1965	Cin-N	2	0	1.000	3	0	0	0	0	5	3	5.4	0	1	1.8	5	9.0	0.00	—	.176	.222	2	2	102	0	1.0	0	-0	0.2
	SF-N	2	2	.500	35	0	0	0	4	42	40	8.6	2	8	1.7	35	7.5	3.64	106	.248	.283	-0	1	109	77	-0.2	0	-0	0.1
	Yr	4	2	.667	38	0	0	0	4	47	43	8.2	2	9	1.7	40	7.7	3.26	118	.242	.277	1	3	108	77	0.8	0	-0	0.3
1966	SF-N	1	1	.500	35	0	0	0	1	22	15	6.1	3	10	4.1	15	6.1	2.45	142	.190	.280	3	3	97	114	0.0	-0	0	0.2
1967	SF-N	2	0	1.000	28	1	0	0	2	22	16	6.5	1	9	3.7	23	9.4	2.05	164	.198	.287	3	3	99	111	1.0	-0	-0	0.3

YEAR	TM/L	W	L	PCT	G	GS	CG	SHO	SV	IP	H	H/G	HR	BB	BB/G	SO	SO/G	ERA	/A	OAVG	OOBP	PR	/A	PF	CPI	WAT	PB	PD	TPI
1968	SF-N	0	2	.000	7	1	0	0	0	5	4	7.2	0	3	5.4	0	0.0	5.40	53	.250	.381	-1	-1	96	78	-0.9	0	0	0.0
	Pit-N	0	0	—	10	0	0	0	0	17	29	15.4	2	3	1.6	9	4.8	7.94	38	.382	.420	-9	-9	100	93	0.0	-0	-1	-1.0
	Yr	0	2	.000	17	1	0	0	0	22	33	13.5	2	6	2.5	9	3.7	7.36	40	.355	.402	-11	-11	99	93	-0.9	0	-0	-1.0
1969	Hou-N	0	0	—	3	0	0	0	0	5	2	3.6	0	2	3.6	2	3.6	0.00	—	.111	.200	2	2	101	0	0.0	0	-0	0.2
Total	16	46	50	.479	527	44	12	2	90	914	842	8.3	89	296	2.9	621	6.1	3.26	120	.244	.303	52	65	103	106	-2.1	-1	-5	6.8
■ **ROY HENSHAW**	Henshaw, Roy Knikelbine b: 7/29/11, Chicago, Ill. BR/TL, 5'8", 155 lbs. Deb: 4/15/33																												
1933	Chi-N	2	1	.667	21	0	0	0	0	39	32	7.4	0	20	4.6	16	3.7	4.15	76	.230	.331	-4	-4	95	71	0.4	-0	-1	-0.4
1935	Chi-N	13	5	.722	31	18	7	3	1	143	135	8.5	6	68	4.3	53	3.3	3.27	117	.249	.334	12	9	95	112	2.1	2	-3	0.7
1936	Chi-N	6	5	.545	39	14	6	1	1	129	152	10.6	8	56	3.9	69	4.8	3.98	103	.296	.364	1	2	102	124	-0.1	-2	-2	-0.2
1937	Bro-N	5	12	.294	42	16	5	0	2	156	176	10.2	14	69	4.0	98	5.7	5.08	83	.278	.348	-20	-15	107	91	-2.4	-2	-0	-1.6
1938	StL-N	5	11	.313	27	15	4	0	0	130	132	9.1	7	48	3.3	34	2.4	4.02	105	.266	.328	-3	3	111	95	-2.8	-0	-1	0.2
1942	Det-A	2	4	.333	23	2	0	0	1	62	63	9.1	3	27	3.9	24	3.5	4.06	101	.269	.341	-3	0	113	101	-0.8	-1	-1	0.0
1943	Det-A	0	2	.000	26	3	0	0	2	71	75	9.5	2	33	4.2	33	4.2	3.80	90	.276	.348	-4	-3	104	110	-0.9	-1	0	-0.3
1944	Det-A	0	0	—	7	1	0	0	0	12	17	12.8	0	6	4.5	10	7.5	9.00	39	.315	.383	-7	-7	104	55	0.0	-1	0	-0.7
Total	8	33	40	.452	216	69	22	4	7	742	782	9.5	40	327	4.0	337	4.1	4.16	95	.271	.344	-29	-16	104	102	-4.5	-6	-8	-2.3
■ **PHIL HENSIEK**	Hensiek, Philip Frank "Sid" b: 10/13/01, St.Louis, Mo. d: 2/21/72, St.Louis, Mo. BR/TR, 6', 160 lbs. Deb: 8/15/35																												
1935	Was-A	0	3	.000	6	1	0	0	1	13	21	14.5	2	9	6.2	6	4.2	9.69	43	.356	.429	-8	-8	93	85	-1.4	1	0	-0.5
■ **CHUCK HENSLEY**	Hensley, Charles Floyd b: 3/11/59, Tulare, Cal. BL/TL, 6'3", 190 lbs. Deb: 5/10/86																												
1986	SF-N	0	0	—	11	0	0	0	1	7	5	6.4	2	2	2.6	6	7.7	2.57	137	.179	.233	1	1	95	104	0.0	0	0	0.1
■ **BILL HEPLER**	Hepler, William Lewis b: 9/25/45, Covington, Va. BL/TL, 6', 160 lbs. Deb: 4/23/66																												
1966	NY-N	3	3	.500	37	3	0	0	0	69	71	9.3	3	51	6.7	25	3.3	3.52	99	.274	.393	1	-0	97	141	0.5	0	-1	0.0
■ **RON HERBEL**	Herbel, Ronald Samuel b: 1/16/38, Denver, Colo. BR/TR, 6'1", 195 lbs. Deb: 9/10/63																												
1963	SF-N	0	0	—	2	0	0	0	0	1	1	9.0	0	1	9.0	1	9.0	9.00	34	.200	.333	-1	-1	94	26	0.0	0	0	0.0
1964	SF-N	9	9	.500	40	22	7	2	1	161	162	9.1	7	61	3.4	98	5.5	3.07	114	.259	.324	8	8	99	115	-0.9	-4	2	0.6
1965	SF-N	12	9	.571	47	21	1	0	1	171	172	9.1	16	47	2.5	106	5.6	3.84	101	.261	.309	-6	0	109	96	-0.2	-5	2	-0.1
1966	SF-N	4	5	.444	32	18	0	0	1	130	149	10.3	15	39	2.7	55	3.8	4.15	84	.291	.338	-8	-10	97	112	-1.0	-3	-1	-1.3
1967	SF-N	4	5	.444	42	11	1	1	1	126	125	8.9	10	35	2.5	52	3.7	3.07	109	.268	.314	4	4	99	124	-0.9	0	4	0.8
1968	SF-N	0	0	—	28	2	0	0	0	43	55	11.5	5	15	3.1	18	3.8	3.35	86	.309	.362	-2	-2	96	158	0.0	-0	1	-0.1
1969	SF-N	4	1	.800	39	4	2	0	1	87	92	9.5	7	23	2.4	34	3.5	4.03	89	.275	.314	-4	-4	100	96	1.4	-2	0	-0.5
1970	SD-N	7	5	.583	64	1	0	0	9	111	114	9.2	14	39	3.2	53	4.3	4.95	79	.266	.326	-11	-13	97	89	2.0	-1	-0	-1.3
	NY-N	2	2	.500	12	0	0	0	1	13	14	9.7	1	2	1.4	8	5.5	1.38	302	.275	.296	4	4	103	258	0.0	0	-0	0.4
	Yr	9	7	.563	**76**	1	0	0	10	124	128	9.3	15	41	3.0	61	4.4	4.57	86	.262	.316	-7	-9	97	258	2.0	-1	-1	-0.9
1971	Atl-N	0	1	.000	25	0	0	0	1	52	61	10.6	6	23	4.0	22	3.8	5.19	74	.300	.373	-10	-8	111	105	-0.4	-1	0	-0.8
Total	9	42	37	.532	331	79	11	3	16	895	945	9.5	81	285	2.9	447	4.5	3.82	94	.273	.326	-25	-21	101	111	-0.0	-16	8	-2.3
■ **ERNIE HERBERT**	Herbert, Ernie Albert "Tex" b: 1/30/1887, Hale, Mo. d: 1/13/68, Dallas, Tex. BR/TR, 5'10", 165 lbs. Deb: 7/27/13																												
1913	Cin-N	0	0	—	6	0	0	0	0	17	12	6.4	0	5	2.6	5	2.6	2.12	157	.179	.247	2	2	104	28	0.0	0	-1	0.2
1914	StL-F	1	1	.500	18	2	0	0	1	50	56	10.1	2	27	4.9	24	4.3	3.78	92	.293	.392	-3	-2	108	130	0.2	3	0	0.1
1915	StL-F	1	0	1.000	11	1	1	0	0	48	48	9.0	1	18	3.4	23	4.3	3.38	92	.253	.327	-2	-1	102	94	0.5	1	0	0.0
Total	3	2	1	.667	35	3	1	0	1	115	116	9.1	3	50	3.9	52	4.1	3.37	98	.259	.344	-3	-1	105	100	0.7	4	-1	0.3
■ **FRED HERBERT**	Herbert, Frederick (born Herbert Frederick Kemman) b: 3/4/1887, Lagrange, Ill. d: 5/29/63, Tice, Fla. BR/TR, 6', 185 lbs. Deb: 9/25/15																												
1915	NY-N	1	1	.500	2	2	1	0	0	17	12	6.4	0	4	2.1	6	3.2	1.06	240	.197	.246	3	3	92	101	0.1	-0	0	0.3
■ **RAY HERBERT**	Herbert, Raymond Ernest b: 12/15/29, Detroit, Mich. BR/TR, 5'11", 185 lbs. Deb: 8/27/50																												
1950	Det-A	1	2	.333	8	3	1	0	1	22	20	8.2	1	12	4.9	5	2.0	3.68	118	.244	.333	2	2	95	99	-0.6	0	1	0.2
1951	Det-A	4	0	1.000	5	0	0	0	0	13	8	5.5	0	9	6.2	9	6.2	1.38	317	.190	.333	4	4	107	200	2.0	-0	-0	0.4
1953	Det-A	4	6	.400	43	3	0	0	6	88	109	11.1	5	46	4.7	37	3.8	5.22	78	.308	.382	-12	-11	102	102	0.1	-0	3	-0.7
1954	Det-A	3	6	.333	42	4	0	0	0	84	114	12.2	6	50	5.4	44	4.7	5.89	64	.334	.413	-20	-20	101	108	-1.1	2	2	-1.5
1955	KC-A	1	8	.111	23	11	2	0	0	88	99	10.1	10	40	4.1	30	3.1	6.24	67	.292	.354	-22	-20	106	82	-3.2	0	2	-1.6
1958	KC-A	8	8	.500	42	16	5	0	3	175	161	8.3	20	55	2.8	108	5.6	3.50	115	.248	.306	5	10	107	104	0.4	1	2	1.5
1959	KC-A	11	11	.500	37	26	10	2	1	184	196	9.6	24	62	3.0	99	4.8	4.84	82	.275	.326	-20	-18	103	93	1.6	2	-1	-1.6
1960	KC-A	14	15	.483	37	33	14	0	1	253	256	9.1	17	72	2.6	122	4.3	3.27	120	.267	.315	17	18	101	111	2.9	1	2	2.3
1961	KC-A	3	6	.333	13	12	1	0	0	84	103	11.0	10	30	3.2	34	3.6	5.36	78	.303	.354	-12	-11	104	98	-0.5	-1	0	-1.0
	Chi-A	9	6	.600	21	20	4	0	0	138	142	9.3	15	36	2.3	50	3.3	4.04	98	.265	.304	-0	-1	99	94	1.2	4	1	0.3
	Yr	12	12	.500	34	32	5	0	0	222	245	9.9	25	66	2.7	84	3.4	4.54	89	.278	.322	-13	-12	101	94	0.7	-1	1	-0.7
1962	Chi-A	20	9	**.690**	35	35	12	2	0	237	228	8.7	13	74	2.8	115	4.4	3.27	115	.255	.308	19	13	94	102	5.7	5	3	2.1
1963	Chi-A	13	10	.565	33	33	14	**7**	0	225	230	9.2	12	35	1.4	105	4.2	3.24	115	.265	.292	10	12	102	97	-0.2	5	2	2.2
1964	Chi-A	6	7	.462	20	19	1	1	0	112	117	9.4	14	17	1.4	40	3.2	3.46	98	.275	.299	2	-1	93	114	-1.5	-1	-1	-0.2
1965	Phi-N	5	8	.385	25	19	4	1	1	131	162	11.1	13	19	1.3	51	3.5	3.85	87	.309	.331	-4	-7	95	121	-1.8	3	1	-0.3
1966	Phi-N	2	5	.286	23	2	0	0	2	50	55	9.9	7	14	2.5	15	2.7	4.32	84	.293	.333	-4	-4	100	113	-1.6	-1	-0	-0.4
Total	14	104	107	.493	407	236	68	13	15	1884	2000	9.6	167	571	2.7	864	4.1	4.01	96	.276	.324	-37	-34	100	103	3.4	20	18	1.7
■ **UBALDO HEREDIA**	Heredia, Ubaldo Jose (Martinez) b: 5/4/56, Ciudad Bolivar, Ven. BR/TR, 6'2", 180 lbs. Deb: 5/12/87																												
1987	Mon-N	0	1	.000	2	2	0	0	0	10	10	9.0	2	3	2.7	6	5.4	5.40	80	.263	.333	-1	-1	106	90	-0.4	-0	0	0.0
■ **ART HERMAN**	Herman, Arthur b: 5/11/1871, Ohio d: 9/20/55, Los Angeles, Cal. Deb: 6/29/1896																												
1896	Lou-N	4	6	.400	14	12	9	0	0	94	122	11.7	4	36	3.4	13	1.2	5.65	79	.337	.397	-13	-13	102	89	0.8	-4	0	-1.2
1897	Lou-N	0	1	.000	3	2	1	0	0	18	23	11.5	1	5	2.5	4	2.0	4.00	105	.334	.379	1	0	97	118	-0.4	1	0	0.2
Total	2	4	7	.364	17	14	10	0	0	112	145	11.7	5	41	3.3	17	1.4	5.38	82	.337	.394	-13	-12	101	94	0.4	-2	0	-1.0
■ **JESUS HERNAIZ**	Hernaiz, Jesus Rafael (Rodriguez) b: 1/8/48, Santurce, P.R. BR/TR, 6'2", 175 lbs. Deb: 6/14/74																												
1974	Phi-N	2	3	.400	27	0	0	0	1	41	53	11.6	6	25	5.5	16	3.5	5.93	63	.323	.406	-10	-10	104	111	-0.4	-0	-0	-1.0
■ **EVELIO HERNANDEZ**	Hernandez, Gregorio Evelio (Lopez) b: 12/24/30, Guanabacoa, Havana, Cuba BR/TR, 6'1", 195 lbs. Deb: 9/12/56																												
1956	Was-A	1	1	.500	4	4	1	0	0	23	24	9.4	2	8	3.1	9	3.5	4.70	94	.276	.330	-1	-1	107	88	0.2	-1	-0	0.0
1957	Was-A	0	0	—	14	2	0	0	0	36	38	9.5	2	20	5.0	15	3.8	4.25	91	.268	.354	-2	-2	102	98	0.0	-1	-1	-0.2
Total	2	1	1	.500	18	6	1	0	0	59	62	9.5	4	28	4.3	24	3.7	4.42	92	.271	.345	-3	-2	104	95	0.2	-1	-1	-0.2
■ **WILLIE HERNANDEZ**	Hernandez, Guillermo (Villanueva) b: 11/14/54, Aguada, P.R. BL/TL, 6'3", 180 lbs. Deb: 4/09/77																												
1977	Chi-N	8	7	.533	67	1	0	0	4	110	94	7.7	11	28	2.3	78	6.4	3.03	148	.234	.281	11	18	115	97	0.5	-2	3	2.0
1978	Chi-N	8	2	.800	54	0	0	0	3	60	57	8.6	6	35	5.3	38	5.7	3.75	106	.263	.352	-1	2	111	125	3.1	-0	1	0.2
1979	Chi-N	4	4	.500	51	2	0	0	0	79	85	9.7	8	39	4.4	53	6.0	5.01	84	.281	.357	-11	-7	112	97	0.1	0	0	-0.6
1980	Chi-N	1	9	.100	53	7	0	0	0	108	115	9.6	8	45	3.8	75	6.3	4.42	88	.276	.342	-10	-6	108	97	-3.7	0	2	-0.4
1981	Chi-N	0	0	—	12	0	0	0	2	14	14	9.0	0	8	5.1	13	8.4	3.86	96	.280	.355	-1	-0	106	111	0.0	0	0	0.0
1982	Chi-N	4	6	.400	75	0	0	0	10	75	74	8.9	3	24	2.9	54	6.5	3.00	125	.268	.317	5	6	104	119	-0.5	-0	2	0.9
1983	Chi-N	1	0	1.000	11	1	0	0	1	20	16	7.2	0	6	2.7	18	8.1	3.15	117	.222	.275	1	1	101	63	0.5	0	0	0.2
	Phi-N	8	4	.667	63	0	0	0	7	96	93	8.7	9	26	2.4	75	7.0	3.28	111	.254	.302	4	4	100	103	1.6	1	-0	0.5
	Yr	9	4	.692	74	1	0	0	8	116	109	8.5	9	32	2.5	93	7.2	3.26	112	.249	.297	5	5	100	103	2.1	0	0	0.7
1984	Det-A	9	3	.750	**80**	0	0	0	32	140	96	6.2	6	36	2.3	112	7.2	1.93	195	.194	.248	**32**	**29**	94	86	1.9	0	-1	2.8
1985	Det-A	8	10	.444	74	0	0	0	31	107	82	6.9	13	14	1.2	76	6.4	2.69	163	.210	.234	17	20	106	84	-1.4	0	-1	1.9
1986	Det-A	8	7	.533	64	0	0	0	24	89	87	8.8	13	21	2.1	77	7.8	3.54	112	.251	.301	6	4	95	107	0.0	0	1	0.5
1987	Det-A	3	4	.429	45	0	0	0	8	49	53	9.7	8	20	3.7	30	5.5	3.67	116	.276	.336	4	3	96	136	-1.0	0	-1	0.2
1988	Det-A	6	5	.545	63	0	0	0	10	68	50	6.6	8	31	4.1	59	7.8	3.04	123	.208	.299	7	5	94	110	0.0	0	1	0.7
Total	12	68	61	.527	712	11	0	0	132	1015	916	8.1	93	333	3.0	758	6.7	3.30	121	.243	.301	66	79	103	101	1.1	1	7	8.9

YEAR TM/L	W	L	PCT	G	GS	CG	SHO	SV	IP	H	H/G	HR	BB	BB/G	SO	SO/G	ERA	/A	OAVG	OOBP	PR	/A	PF	CPI	WAT	PB	PD	TPI
■ MANNY HERNANDEZ	Hernandez, Manuel Antonio (Montas) b: 5/7/61, La Romana, D.R. BR/TR, 6', 150 lbs. Deb: 6/05/86																											
1986 Hou-N	2	3	.400	9	4	0	0	0	28	33	10.6	2	12	3.9	9	2.9	3.86	98	.306	.360	-0	-0	102	132	-0.7	-1	0	0.0
1987 Hou-N	0	4	.000	6	3	0	0	0	22	25	10.2	1	5	2.0	12	4.9	5.32	71	.301	.326	-3	-4	93	83	-1.9	-0	0	-0.3
Total 2	2	7	.222	15	7	0	0	0	50	58	10.4	3	17	3.1	21	3.8	4.50	84	.304	.345	-3	-4	98	111	-2.6	-1	0	-0.3
■ RAMON HERNANDEZ	Hernandez, Ramon (Gonzalez) b: 8/31/40, Carolina, P.R. BB/TL, 5'11", 165 lbs. Deb: 4/11/67																											
1967 Atl-N	0	2	.000	46	0	0	0	5	52	60	10.4	5	14	2.4	28	4.8	4.15	85	.296	.339	-4	-4	105	112	-0.9	-0	1	-0.3
1968 Chi-N	0	0	—	8	0	0	0	0	9	14	14.0	1	0	0.0	3	3.0	9.00	37	.350	.357	-6	-6	112	65	0.0	0	0	-0.5
1971 Pit-N	0	1	.000	10	0	0	0	4	12	5	3.8	0	2	1.5	7	5.3	0.75	447	.122	.159	4	3	97	92	-0.4	0	0	0.4
1972 Pit-N	5	0	1.000	53	0	0	0	14	70	50	6.4	3	22	2.8	47	6.0	1.67	207	.194	.263	14	14	100	102	2.5	0	0	1.6
1973 Pit-N	4	5	.444	59	0	0	0	11	90	71	7.1	5	25	2.5	64	6.4	2.40	140	.218	.277	13	10	92	99	-0.4	0	1	1.1
1974 Pit-N	5	2	.714	58	0	0	0	2	69	68	8.9	3	18	2.3	33	4.3	2.74	128	.258	.306	7	6	97	113	1.3	1	-1	0.6
1975 Pit-N	7	2	.778	46	0	0	0	5	64	62	8.7	0	28	3.9	43	6.0	2.95	120	.252	.321	5	4	98	101	2.2	-0	1	0.5
1976 Pit-N	2	2	.500	37	0	0	0	3	43	42	8.8	3	16	3.3	17	3.6	3.56	98	.262	.321	-0	-0	99	107	-0.1	-0	-0	0.0
Chi-N	0	0	—	2	0	0	0	0	2	2	9.0	0	0	0.0	1	4.5	0.00	—	.333	.286	1	1	111	0	0.0	0	0	0.1
Yr	2	2	.500	39	0	0	0	3	45	44	8.8	3	16	3.2	18	3.6	3.40	103	.257	.314	1	0	100	0	-0.1	-0	-0	0.1
1977 Chi-N	0	0	—	6	0	0	0	1	8	11	12.4	1	3	3.4	4	4.5	7.88	57	.306	.359	-4	-3	115	66	0.0	-0	0	-0.2
Bos-A	0	1	.000	12	0	0	0	1	13	14	9.7	2	7	4.8	8	5.5	5.54	85	.280	.379	-2	-1	116	99	-0.4	0	0	0.0
Total 9	23	15	.605	337	0	0	0	46	432	399	8.3	23	135	2.8	255	5.3	3.02	117	.245	.302	26	24	99	102	3.8	1	2	3.3
■ RUDY HERNANDEZ	Hernandez, Rudolph Albert (Fuentes) b: 12/10/31, Santiago, D.R. BR/TR, 6'3", 185 lbs. Deb: 7/03/60																											
1960 Was-A	4	1	.800	21	0	0	0	0	35	34	8.7	2	21	5.4	22	5.7	4.37	91	.262	.354	-2	-2	102	99	1.6	-0	-0	-0.1
1961 Was-A	0	1	.000	7	0	0	0	0	9	8	8.0	0	3	3.0	4	4.0	3.00	131	.250	.297	1	1	97	97	-0.4	0	0	0.1
Total 2	4	2	.667	28	0	0	0	0	44	42	8.6	2	24	4.9	26	5.3	4.09	97	.259	.344	-1	-1	101	98	1.2	-0	0	0.0
■ WALT HERRELL	Herrell, Walter William "Reds" b: 2/19/1889, Rockville, Md. d: 1/23/49, Front Royal, Va. Deb: 6/10/11																											
1911 Was-A	0	0	—	1	0	0	0	0	2	5	22.5	0	2	9.0	0	0.0	18.00	18	.556	.636	-3	-3	99	78	0.0	-0	0	-0.2
■ BOBBY HERRERA	Herrera, Procopio Rodriguez "Tito" b: 7/26/26, Nuevo Laredo, Mex BR/TR, 6', 184 lbs. Deb: 4/19/51																											
1951 StL-A	0	0	—	3	0	0	0	0	2	6	27.0	2	4	18.0	1	4.5	31.50	14	.462	.611	-6	-6	109	80	0.0	0	0	-0.4
■ TROY HERRIAGE	Herriage, William Troy "Dutch" b: 12/20/30, Tipton, Okla. BR/TR, 6'1", 170 lbs. Deb: 4/25/56																											
1956 KC-A	1	13	.071	31	16	1	0	0	103	135	11.8	16	64	5.6	59	5.2	6.64	66	.321	.409	-28	-26	105	103	-5.5	-1	-2	-2.6
■ TOM HERRIN	Herrin, Thomas Edward b: 9/12/29, Shreveport, La. BR/TR, 6'3", 190 lbs. Deb: 4/13/54																											
1954 Bos-A	1	2	.333	14	1	0	0	0	28	34	10.9	3	22	7.1	8	2.6	7.39	51	.315	.415	-11	-11	101	88	-0.3	-0	1	-0.9
■ ART HERRING	Herring, Arthur L "Red" or "Sandy" b: 3/10/07, Altus, Okla. BR/TR, 5'7", 168 lbs. Deb: 9/12/29																											
1929 Det-A	2	1	.667	4	4	2	0	0	32	38	10.7	0	19	5.3	15	4.2	4.78	86	.302	.395	-2	-2	97	104	0.6	1	0	0.0
1930 Det-A	3	3	.500	23	6	1	0	0	78	97	11.2	2	36	4.2	16	1.8	5.31	93	.315	.379	-6	-3	106	104	0.1	-2	-0	-0.4
1931 Det-A	7	13	.350	35	16	9	0	1	165	186	10.1	8	67	3.7	64	3.5	4.31	108	.281	.351	1	7	107	107	-1.2	-1	2	0.8
1932 Det-A	1	2	.333	12	0	0	0	2	22	25	10.2	2	15	6.1	12	4.9	5.32	86	.284	.390	-2	-2	102	108	-0.4	-0	0	-0.1
1933 Det-A	1	2	.333	24	3	1	0	0	61	61	9.0	6	20	3.0	20	3.0	3.84	119	.264	.318	3	5	107	110	-0.4	-1	-0	0.4
1934 Bro-N	2	4	.333	14	4	2	0	0	49	63	11.6	2	29	5.3	15	2.8	6.24	62	.307	.387	-12	-13	95	88	-0.8	1	-0	-1.1
1939 Chi-A	0	0	—	7	0	0	0	0	14	13	8.4	2	5	3.2	8	5.1	5.79	85	.250	.317	-2	-1	106	76	0.0	-0	0	0.0
1944 Bro-N	3	4	.429	12	6	3	1	1	55	59	9.7	3	17	2.8	19	3.1	3.44	107	.277	.324	1	1	102	115	0.1	0	0	0.2
1945 Bro-N	7	4	.636	22	15	7	2	2	124	103	7.5	11	43	3.1	34	2.5	3.48	103	.222	.287	4	2	95	83	1.0	-2	1	0.0
1946 Bro-N	7	2	.778	35	2	0	1	5	86	91	9.5	2	29	3.0	34	3.6	3.35	102	.277	.324	1	1	100	108	2.0	0	2	0.3
1947 Pit-N	1	3	.250	11	0	0	0	2	11	18	14.7	3	4	3.3	6	4.9	8.18	51	.360	.400	-5	-5	102	100	-0.7	-0	-0	-0.4
Total 11	34	38	.472	199	56	25	4	13	697	754	9.7	41	284	3.7	243	3.1	4.33	96	.276	.342	-18	-12	102	101	0.3	-5	4	-0.3
■ HERB HERRING	Herring, Herbert Lee b: 7/22/1891, Danville, Ark. d: 4/22/64, Tucson, Ariz. BR/TR, 5'11", 178 lbs. Deb: 9/04/12																											
1912 Was-A	0	0	—	1	0	0	0	0	1	1	9.0	0	1	9.0	0	0.0	0.00	—	.250	.400	0	0	97	0	0.0	0	0	0.0
■ LEFTY HERRING	Herring, Silas Clarke b: 3/4/1880, Philadelphia, Pa. d: 2/11/65, Massapequa, N.Y. BL/TL, 5'11", 160 lbs. Deb: 5/16/1899																											
1899 Was-N	0	0	—	2	0	0	0	0	2	0	0.0	0	2	9.0	0	0.0	0.00	—	.000	.283	1	1	98	0	0.0	1	0	0.2
■ BILL HERRING	Herring, William Francis "Smoke" b: 10/31/1893, New York, N.Y. d: 9/10/62, Honesdale, Pa. 6'3", 185 lbs. Deb: 6/26/15																											
1915 Bro-F	0	0	—	3	0	0	0	0	3	5	15.0	1	2	6.0	3	9.0	15.00	20	.404	.487	-4	-4	98	67	0.0	0	0	-0.3
■ LEROY HERRMANN	Herrmann, Leroy George b: 2/27/06, Steward, Ill. d: 7/3/72, Livermore, Cal. BR/TR, 5'10", 185 lbs. Deb: 7/30/32																											
1932 Chi-N	2	1	.667	7	0	0	0	0	13	18	12.5	0	9	6.2	5	3.5	6.23	64	.346	.435	-3	-3	103	106	0.3	0	0	-0.2
1933 Chi-N	0	1	.000	9	1	0	0	1	21	26	11.1	3	8	3.4	4	1.7	5.57	57	.299	.369	-5	-6	95	104	-0.4	-0	-1	-0.6
1935 Cin-N	3	5	.375	29	8	2	0	0	108	124	10.3	9	31	2.6	30	2.5	3.58	107	.297	.348	5	3	95	137	-0.6	1	-0	0.4
Total 3	5	7	.417	45	9	2	0	1	142	168	10.6	12	48	3.0	39	2.5	4.12	91	.302	.360	-3	-6	96	129	-0.7	2	-1	-0.4
■ MARTY HERRMANN	Herrmann, Martin John "Lefty" b: 1/10/1893, Oldenburg, Ind. d: 9/11/56, Cincinnati, Ohio BL/TL, 5'10", 150 lbs. Deb: 7/10/18																											
1918 Bro-N	0	0	—	1	0	0	0	0	1	0	0.0	0	0	0.0	0	0.0	0.00	—	.000	.250	0	0	104	0	0.0	0	0	0.1
■ FRANK HERSHEY	Hershey, Frank b: 12/13/1877, Gorham, N.Y. d: 12/15/49, Canadaigua, N.Y. TR , Deb: 4/20/05																											
1905 Bos-N	0	1	.000	1	1	0	0	0	4	5	11.3	0	2	4.5	1	2.3	6.75	45	.335	.413	-2	-2	102	72	-0.4	-0	-0	-0.1
■ OREL HERSHISER	Hershiser, Orel Leonard b: 9/16/58, Buffalo, N.Y. BR/TR, 6'3", 190 lbs. Deb: 9/01/83																											
1983 LA-N	0	0	—	8	0	0	0	1	8	7	7.9	1	6	6.8	5	5.6	3.38	107	.233	.351	0	0	100	130	0.0	0	0	0.0
1984 LA-N	11	8	.579	45	20	8	**4**	2	190	160	7.6	9	50	2.4	150	7.1	2.65	141	.225	.278	20	23	104	89	1.9	1	1	2.7
1985 LA-N	19	3	**.864**	36	34	9	5	0	240	179	6.7	8	68	2.6	157	5.9	2.03	163	.206	.265	42	34	92	93	7.7	3	2	4.4
1986 LA-N	14	14	.500	35	35	8	1	0	231	213	8.3	13	86	3.4	153	6.0	3.86	91	.243	.308	-3	-9	95	83	1.5	4	1	-0.4
1987 LA-N	16	16	.500	37	35	10	1	1	**265**	247	8.4	17	74	2.5	190	6.5	3.06	123	.247	.302	30	21	92	104	1.8	5	1	2.6
1988 LA-N	**23**	8	.742	35	34	**15**	**8**	1	**267**	208	7.0	18	73	2.5	178	6.0	2.26	161	.213	.267	**35**	**41**	105	104	6.7	-1	6	**5.4**
Total 6	83	49	.629	196	158	50	19	5	1201	1014	7.6	66	357	2.7	833	6.2	2.77	130	.227	.285	124	111	97	95	19.6	12	11	14.7
■ JOE HESKETH	Hesketh, Joseph Thomas b: 2/15/59, Lackawanna, N.Y. BR/TL, 6'2", 170 lbs. Deb: 8/07/84																											
1984 Mon-N	2	2	.500	11	5	1	1	1	45	38	7.6	2	15	3.0	32	6.4	1.80	182	.233	.291	9	7	91	153	0.1	0	0	0.8
1985 Mon-N	10	5	.667	25	25	2	1	0	155	125	7.3	10	45	2.6	113	6.6	2.50	135	.222	.275	19	15	94	99	2.4	-1	-1	1.4
1986 Mon-N	6	5	.545	15	15	0	0	0	83	92	10.0	11	31	3.4	67	7.3	4.99	73	.283	.345	-12	-12	98	97	0.7	-2	-1	-1.4
1987 Mon-N	0	0	—	18	0	0	0	1	29	23	7.1	2	15	4.7	31	9.6	3.10	139	.211	.313	3	4	106	96	0.0	-0	-1	0.3
1988 Mon-N	4	3	.571	60	0	0	0	9	73	63	7.8	1	35	4.3	64	7.9	2.84	128	.242	.322	5	6	105	115	0.5	0	1	0.9
Total 5	22	15	.595	129	45	3	2	11	385	341	8.0	26	141	3.3	307	7.2	3.06	116	.240	.305	24	21	97	108	3.7	-2	-1	2.0
■ OTTO HESS	Hess, Otto C. b: 10/10/1878, Berne, Switzerland d: 2/25/26, Tucson, Ariz. BL/TL, 6'1", 170 lbs. Deb: 8/03/02																											
1902 Cle-A	2	4	.333	7	4	4	0	0	44	67	13.7	0	23	4.7	13	2.7	5.93	58	.377	.449	-12	-12	96	106	-1.0	-1	1	-0.9
1904 Cle-A	8	7	.533	21	16	15	4	0	151	134	8.0	2	31	1.8	64	3.8	1.67	152	.260	.302	16	15	98	142	-0.4	-3	-1	1.6
1905 Cle-A	10	15	.400	26	25	22	4	0	214	179	7.5	1	72	3.0	109	4.6	3.15	84	.250	.319	-12	-12	100	79	-2.6	5	0	-1.2
1906 Cle-A	20	17	.541	43	36	33	7	**3**	334	274	7.4	4	85	2.3	167	4.5	1.83	146	.247	.301	32	31	99	118	-1.6	1	-1	3.4
1907 Cle-A	6	6	.500	17	14	7	0	1	93	84	8.1	1	37	3.6	36	3.5	2.90	81	.264	.341	-4	-6	93	98	-0.6	-0	-1	-0.6
1908 Cle-A	0	0	—	4	0	0	0	0	7	11	14.1	0	1	1.3	2	2.6	5.14	48	.407	.429	-2	-2	103	123	0.0	-1	0	-0.1
1912 Bos-N	12	17	.414	33	31	21	1	0	254	270	9.6	3	90	3.2	80	2.8	3.76	100	.274	.344	-10	-0	110	90	2.0	2	-3	0.0
1913 Bos-N	7	17	.292	29	27	19	2	0	218	231	9.5	12	70	2.9	80	3.3	3.84	80	.279	.329	-15	-19	96	101	-4.7	9	1	-0.9
1914 Bos-N	5	6	.455	14	11	7	1	1	89	89	9.0	2	33	3.3	24	2.4	3.03	94	.271	.339	-2	-2	102	115	-1.4	1	2	-0.1
1915 Bos-N	0	1	.000	4	1	1	0	0	14	16	10.3	0	6	3.9	5	3.2	3.86	69	.286	.369	-2	-2	97	110	-0.4	1	0	0.0
Total 10	70	90	.438	198	165	129	19	5	1418	1355	8.6	25	448	2.8	580	3.7	2.98	98	.268	.328	-11	-10	100	105	-10.7	14	-3	1.2

YEAR	TM/L	W	L	PCT	G	GS	CG	SHO	SV	IP	H	H/G	HR	BB	BB/G	SO	SO/G	ERA	/A	OAVG	OOBP	PR	/A	PF	CPI	WAT	PB	PD	TPI
■ **GEORGE HESSELBACHER** Hesselbacher, George Edward b: 1/18/1895, Philadelphia, Pa. d: 2/18/80, Rydal, Pa. BR/TR, 6'2", 175 lbs. Deb: 6/29/16																													
1916	Phi-A	0	4	.000	6	4	2	0	0	26	37	12.8	3	22	7.6	6	2.1	7.27	41	.349	.461	-13	-12	105	105	-1.9	-1	1	-1.1
■ **LARRY HESTERFER** Hesterfer, Lawrence b: 6/9/1878, Newark, N.J. d: 9/22/43, Cedar Grove, N.J. BR/TL, 5'8", 145 lbs. Deb: 9/05/01																													
1901	NY-N	0	1	.000	1	1	1	0	0	6	15	22.5	0	3	4.5	2	3.0	7.50	42	.495	.541	-3	-3	95	146	-0.4	0	0	-0.2
■ **JOHNNY HETKI** Hetki, John Edward b: 5/12/22, Leavenworth, Kan. BR/TR, 6'1", 202 lbs. Deb: 9/14/45																													
1945	Cin-N	1	2	.333	5	2	2	0	0	33	28	7.6	1	11	3.0	9	2.5	3.55	104	.235	.289	1	1	97	79	-0.1	-1	1	0.0
1946	Cin-N	6	6	.500	32	11	4	0	1	126	121	8.6	3	31	2.2	41	2.9	3.00	119	.253	.293	6	8	105	90	0.7	3	-0	1.1
1947	Cin-N	3	4	.429	37	5	2	0	0	96	110	10.3	7	48	4.5	33	3.1	5.81	64	.287	.363	-19	-22	92	83	-0.2	1	0	-1.9
1948	Cin-N	0	1	.000	3	0	0	0	0	7	8	10.3	0	3	3.9	3	3.9	9.00	47	.286	.333	-4	-4	106	45	-0.4	0	-0	-0.3
1950	Cin-N	1	2	.333	22	1	0	0	0	53	53	9.0	9	27	4.6	21	3.6	5.09	86	.265	.356	-6	-4	106	102	-0.2	0	-0	-0.3
1952	StL-A	0	1	.000	3	1	0	0	0	9	15	15.0	2	2	2.0	4	4.0	4.00	91	.357	.378	-0	-0	100	183	-0.4	0	0	0.0
1953	Pit-N	3	6	.333	54	2	0	0	3	118	120	9.2	9	33	2.5	37	2.8	3.97	115	.266	.309	4	8	106	94	0.1	1	0	0.9
1954	Pit-N	4	4	.500	58	1	0	0	9	83	102	11.1	11	30	3.3	27	2.9	4.99	83	.297	.344	-8	-8	102	99	1.0	0	-1	-0.8
Total	8	18	26	.409	214	23	8	0	13	525	557	9.5	42	185	3.2	175	3.0	4.39	92	.272	.327	-26	-22	102	93	0.5	5	-1	-1.3
■ **ED HEUSSER** Heusser, Edward Burlton "The Wild Elk Of The Wasatch" b: 5/7/09, Mill Creek, Utah d: 3/1/56, Aurora, Cal. BB/TR, 6'0.5", 187 lbs. Deb: 4/25/35																													
1935	StL-N	5	5	.500	33	11	2	0	2	123	125	9.1	5	27	2.0	39	2.9	2.93	138	.263	.301	15	15	100	111	-0.9	-1	-1	1.3
1936	StL-N	7	3	.700	42	3	0	0	3	104	130	11.3	6	38	3.3	26	2.3	5.45	70	.310	.364	-17	-19	95	94	1.6	3	-0	-1.5
1938	Phi-N	0	0	—	1	0	0	0	0	1	2	18.0	1	1	9.0	0	0.0	27.00	15	.400	.500	-3	-3	106	64	0.0	0	0	-0.1
1940	Phi-A	6	13	.316	41	6	2	0	5	110	144	11.8	11	42	3.4	39	3.2	4.99	87	.308	.363	-7	-8	99	110	-1.0	1	1	-0.5
1943	Cin-N	4	3	.571	26	10	2	1	0	91	97	9.6	4	23	2.3	28	2.8	3.46	96	.275	.316	-1	-2	98	102	0.1	-1	-1	-0.2
1944	Cin-N	13	11	.542	30	23	17	4	2	193	165	7.7	9	42	2.0	42	2.0	**2.38**	**144**	.231	**.270**	26	22	95	102	-0.8	1	-1	2.3
1945	Cin-N	11	16	.407	31	30	18	4	1	223	248	10.0	10	60	2.4	56	2.3	3.71	99	.280	.322	2	-1	97	103	0.3	4	-0	0.3
1946	Cin-N	7	14	.333	29	21	9	1	2	168	167	8.9	11	39	2.1	47	2.5	3.21	111	.260	.299	4	7	105	98	-2.6	1	-2	0.7
1948	Phi-N	3	2	.600	33	0	0	0	3	74	89	10.8	9	28	3.4	22	2.7	4.99	77	.299	.355	-8	-10	97	105	0.8	-1	0	-0.9
Total	9	56	67	.455	266	104	50	10	18	1087	1167	9.7	66	300	2.5	299	2.5	3.69	101	.274	.319	11	3	98	103	-2.5	8	-4	1.4
■ **JOE HEVING** Heving, Joseph William b: 9/2/1900, Covington, Ky. d: 4/11/70, Covington, Ky. BR/TR, 6'1", 185 lbs. Deb: 4/29/30																													
1930	NY-N	7	5	.583	41	2	0	0	6	90	109	10.9	7	27	2.7	37	3.7	5.20	92	.309	.344	-2	-4	96	96	0.3	-0	4	0.0
1931	NY-N	1	6	.143	22	0	0	0	3	42	48	10.3	4	11	2.4	26	5.6	4.93	73	.277	.321	-5	-6	93	84	-2.6	-0	1	-0.5
1933	Chi-A	7	5	.583	40	6	3	1	6	118	113	8.6	6	27	2.1	47	3.6	2.67	165	.249	.289	21	**23**	103	118	1.6	0	0	2.3
1934	Chi-A	1	7	.125	33	2	0	0	4	88	133	13.6	12	48	4.9	40	4.1	7.26	64	.343	.411	-27	-26	103	102	-2.5	1	1	-2.0
1937	Cle-A	8	4	.667	40	0	0	0	5	73	92	11.3	6	30	3.7	35	4.3	4.81	93	.311	.368	-2	-3	97	115	1.8	1	1	0.0
1938	Cle-A	1	1	.500	3	0	0	0	0	6	10	15.0	0	5	7.5	0	0.0	9.00	52	.370	.469	-3	-3	98	89	0.0	-0	-0	-0.2
	Bos-A	8	1	.889	16	11	7	1	2	82	94	10.3	5	22	2.4	34	3.7	3.73	128	.283	.329	10	10	100	111	3.3	-1	2	1.0
	Yr	9	2	.818	19	11	7	1	2	88	104	10.6	5	27	2.8	34	3.5	4.09	117	.290	.340	7	7	100	111	3.3	-0	2	0.8
1939	Bos-A	11	3	.786	46	5	1	0	7	107	124	10.4	8	34	2.9	43	3.6	3.70	133	.295	.340	**11**	**15**	107	130	3.5	-1	0	1.3
1940	Bos-A	12	7	.632	39	7	4	0	3	119	129	9.8	7	42	3.2	55	4.2	4.01	109	.272	.331	5	5	100	102	2.2	0	0	0.5
1941	Cle-A	5	2	.714	27	3	2	1	5	71	63	8.0	2	31	3.9	18	2.3	2.28	183	.240	.319	15	15	101	143	1.6	-1	2	1.6
1942	Cle-A	5	3	.625	27	2	0	0	3	46	55	10.8	4	25	4.9	13	2.5	4.89	69	.294	.380	-6	-8	93	111	1.1	-1	0	-0.7
1943	Cle-A	1	1	.500	30	1	0	0	9	72	58	7.3	1	34	4.3	34	4.3	2.75	107	.230	.318	4	2	90	108	0.0	-0	2	0.3
1944	Cle-A	8	3	.727	**63**	1	0	0	10	120	106	8.0	2	41	3.1	46	3.5	1.95	177	.239	.299	**20**	**20**	101	139	2.8	-1	1	2.2
1945	Bos-N	1	0	1.000	3	0	0	0	0	5	5	9.0	0	3	5.4	1	1.8	3.60	119	.294	.409	0	0	113	151	0.5	-0	1	0.1
Total	13	76	48	.613	430	40	17	3	63	1039	1139	9.9	64	380	3.3	429	3.7	3.90	109	.279	.337	41	39	100	115	13.6	-4	14	5.9
■ **JAKE HEWITT** Hewitt, Charles Jacob b: 6/6/1870, Maidsville, W.Va. d: 5/18/59, Morgantown, W.Va. BL/TL, 5'7", 150 lbs. Deb: 8/06/1895																													
1895	Pit-N	1	0	1.000	4	2	1	0	2	13	13	9.0	0	2	1.4	4	2.8	4.15	111	.280	.309	1	1	96	65	0.5	-1	0	0.0
■ **GREG HEYDEMAN** Heydeman, Gregory George b: 1/2/52, Carmel, Cal. BR/TR, 6', 180 lbs. Deb: 9/02/73																													
1973	LA-N	0	0	—	1	0	0	0	0	2	2	9.0	0	1	4.5	1	4.5	4.50	81	.222	.364	-0	-0	99	73	0.0	0	0	0.0
■ **JOHN HEYNER** Heyner, John b: Hyde Park, Ill. Deb: 8/19/1890																													
1890	Pit-N	0	0	—	1	0	0	0	0	4	7	15.8	2	5	11.3	1	2.3	13.50	25	.400	.533	-4	-5	95	97	0.0	-0	0	-0.3
■ **JOHN HIBBARD** Hibbard, John Denison b: 12/2/1864, Chicago, Ill. d: 11/17/37, Hollywood, Cal. TL , Deb: 7/31/1884																													
1884	Chi-N	1	1	.500	2	2	2	1	0	17	18	9.5	1	9	4.8	4	2.1	2.65	118	.281	.369	1	1	105	160	0.0	-1	0	0.0
■ **JIM HICKEY** Hickey, James Robert "Sid" b: 10/22/20, N.Abington, Mass. BR/TR, 6'1", 204 lbs. Deb: 4/25/42																													
1942	Bos-N	0	1	.000	1	1	0	0	0	1	4	36.0	1	2	18.0	0	0.0	27.00	12	.500	.545	-3	-3	98	102	-0.4	-0	0	-0.2
1944	Bos-N	0	0	—	8	0	0	0	0	9	15	15.0	0	5	5.0	3	3.0	5.00	69	.366	.447	-1	-2	96	144	0.0	-0	0	0.0
Total	2	0	1	.000	9	1	0	0	0	10	19	17.1	1	7	6.3	3	2.7	7.20	48	.388	.466	-4	-4	96	140	-0.4	-0	0	-0.2
■ **JOHN HICKEY** Hickey, John William b: 11/3/1881, Minneapolis, Minn. d: 12/28/41, Seattle, Wash. Deb: 4/16/04																													
1904	Cle-A	0	1	.000	2	2	1	0	0	12	14	10.5	0	11	8.3	5	3.8	7.50	34	.316	.452	-7	-7	98	75	-0.4	-1	0	-0.5
■ **KEVIN HICKEY** Hickey, Kevin John b: 2/25/57, Chicago, Ill. BR/TL, 6'1", 170 lbs. Deb: 4/14/81																													
1981	Chi-A	0	2	.000	41	0	0	0	3	44	38	7.8	3	18	3.7	17	3.5	3.68	98	.232	.303	-0	-0	99	84	-0.9	0	1	0.0
1982	Chi-A	4	4	.500	60	0	0	0	6	78	73	8.4	4	30	3.5	38	4.4	3.00	132	.256	.321	9	8	97	121	-0.2	0	2	1.0
1983	Chi-A	1	2	.333	23	0	0	0	5	21	23	9.9	5	11	4.7	8	3.4	5.14	81	.264	.347	-2	-2	102	105	-0.6	0	0	-0.1
Total	3	5	8	.385	124	0	0	0	14	143	134	8.4	12	59	3.7	63	4.0	3.52	110	.250	.320	7	6	98	108	-1.7	0	3	0.9
■ **CHARLIE HICKMAN** Hickman, Charles Taylor "Cheerful Charlie" or "Piano Legs" b: 5/4/1876, Taylortown, Pa. d: 4/19/34, Morgantown, W.Va. BR/TR, 5'11.5", 215 lbs. Deb: 9/08/1897																													
1897	Bos-N	0	0	—	2	0	0	0	1	8	10	11.3	0	5	5.6	0	0.0	6.75	66	.329	.424	-2	-2	103	76	0.0	2	0	0.0
1898	Bos-N	1	2	.333	6	3	3	1	2	33	22	6.0	0	13	3.5	9	2.5	2.18	167	.207	.294	5	5	101	74	-0.7	0	0	0.5
1899	Bos-N	6	0	1.000	11	9	5	2	1	66	52	7.1	3	40	5.5	14	1.9	4.50	88	.237	.355	-5	-4	103	69	3.0	6	0	0.7
1901	NY-N	3	5	.375	9	9	6	0	0	65	76	10.5	1	26	3.6	11	1.5	4.57	69	.318	.392	-9	-10	95	96	0.0	2	1	-0.8
1902	Cle-A	0	1	.000	1	1	1	0	0	8	11	12.4	0	5	5.6	1	1.1	7.88	44	.353	.443	-4	-4	96	74	-0.3	1	0	-0.4
1907	Was-A	0	0	—	1	0	0	0	0	5	4	7.2	0	5	9.0	2	3.6	3.60	66	.241	.417	-1	-1	94	110	0.0	0	1	0.0
Total	6	10	8	.556	30	22	15	3	4	185	175	8.5	4	94	4.6	37	1.8	4.33	82	.273	.368	-15	-16	99	81	2.0	11	1	0.0
■ **ERNIE HICKMAN** Hickman, Ernest P. b: 1856, E.St.Louis, Ill. d: 11/19/1891, E.St.Louis, Ill Deb: 6/07/1884																													
1884	KC-U	4	13	.235	17	17	15	0	0	137	172	11.3	5	36	2.4	68	4.5	4.53	61	.312	.354	-23	-27	92	103	0.4	-3	0	-2.5
■ **JIM HICKMAN** Hickman, James Lucius b: 5/10/37, Henning, Tenn. BR/TR, 6'3", 192 lbs. Deb: 4/14/62																													
1967	LA-N	0	0	—	1	0	0	0	0	2	2	9.0	1	0	0.0	0	0.0	4.50	67	.286	.286	-0	-0	89	149	0.0	0	0	0.0
■ **JESSE HICKMAN** Hickman, Jesse Owens b: 2/18/39, Lecompte, La. BR/TR, 6'2", 186 lbs. Deb: 6/05/65																													
1965	KC-A	0	1	.000	12	0	0	0	0	15	9	5.4	3	8	4.8	16	9.6	6.00	57	.184	.288	-4	-4	100	59	-0.4	0	0	-0.4
1966	KC-A	0	0	—	1	0	0	0	0	1	0	0.0	0	1	9.0	0	0.0	0.00	—	.000	.333	0	0	95	0	0.0	0	0	0.0
Total	2	0	1	.000	13	0	0	0	0	16	9	5.1	3	9	5.1	16	9.0	5.63	61	.176	.290	-4	-4	99	56	-0.4	0	0	-0.4
■ **KIRBY HIGBE** Higbe, Walter Kirby b: 4/8/15, Columbia, S.C. d: 5/6/85, Columbia, S.C. BR/TR, 5'11", 190 lbs. Deb: 10/03/37																													
1937	Chi-N	1	0	1.000	1	0	0	0	0	5	4	7.2	1	1	1.8	2	3.6	5.40	73	.182	.217	-1	-1	100	28	0.5	-0	-0	0.0
1938	Chi-N	0	0	—	2	2	0	0	0	10	10	9.0	1	6	5.4	4	3.6	5.40	72	.263	.356	-2	-2	103	87	0.0	-0	1	0.0
1939	Chi-N	2	1	.667	9	2	0	0	0	23	12	4.7	0	22	8.6	16	6.3	3.13	125	.158	.337	2	2	100	81	0.4	1	-0	0.2
	Phi-N	10	14	.417	34	26	14	1	2	187	208	10.0	10	101	4.9	79	3.8	4.86	80	.283	.369	-20	-20	99	99	2.3	-2	-4	-2.5
	Yr	12	15	.444	43	28	14	1	2	210	220	9.4	10	123	5.3	95	4.1	4.67	83	.272	.366	-18	-18	99	99	2.7	1	-4	-2.3
1940	Phi-N	14	19	.424	41	36	20	1	1	283	242	7.7	12	121	3.8	**137**	4.4	3.72	105	.232	.307	4	6	102	84	2.9	-2	-1	0.4
1941	Bro-N	**22**	9	.710	**48**	39	19	2	3	298	244	7.4	17	132	4.0	121	3.7	3.14	115	.220	.302	16	15	99	92	3.2	1	-4	1.2
1942	Bro-N	16	11	.593	38	32	13	2	0	222	180	7.3	17	106	4.3	115	4.7	3.24	99	.223	.310	2	-1	97	99	-1.9	-4	-1	-0.6

YEAR	TM/L	W	L	PCT	G	GS	CG	SHO	SV	IP	H	H/G	HR	BB	BB/G	SO	SO/G	ERA	/A	OAVG	OOBP	PR	/A	PF	CPI	WAT	PB	PD	TPI
1943	Bro-N	13	10	.565	35	27	8	1	0	185	189	9.2	4	95	4.6	108	5.3	3.70	90	.264	.351	-7	-7	99	104	1.0	-2	-1	-1.0
1946	Bro-N	17	8	.680	42	29	11	3	1	211	178	7.6	6	107	4.6	134	**5.7**	3.03	113	.229	.316	9	9	100	94	2.4	-4	1	0.6
1947	Bro-N	2	0	1.000	4	3	0	0	0	16	18	10.1	0	12	6.8	10	5.6	5.06	83	.295	.408	-2	-2	103	106	1.0	0	0	0.0
	Pit-N	11	17	.393	46	30	10	1	5	225	204	8.2	22	110	4.4	99	4.0	3.72	112	.240	.325	9	11	102	100	-0.3	-1	-4	0.5
	Yr	13	17	.433	50	33	10	1	5	241	222	8.3	22	122	4.6	109	4.1	3.81	109	.243	.330	7	9	102	100	0.7	0	-4	0.5
1948	Pit-N	8	7	.533	56	8	3	0	10	158	140	8.0	11	83	4.7	86	4.9	3.36	123	.240	.332	10	13	104	112	0.0	1	-2	1.3
1949	Pit-N	0	2	.000	7	1	0	0	0	15	25	15.0	2	12	7.2	5	3.0	13.80	30	.379	.457	-16	-16	102	65	-0.9	-0	0	-1.4
	NY-N	2	0	1.000	37	2	0	0	2	81	72	8.0	12	41	4.6	38	4.2	3.44	118	.242	.331	5	6	101	126	1.0	-0	-1	0.4
	Yr	2	2	.500	44	3	0	0	2	96	97	9.1	14	53	5.0	43	4.0	5.06	81	.266	.355	-11	-10	101	126	0.1	-0	-1	-1.0
1950	NY-N	0	3	.000	18	1	0	0	0	35	37	9.5	2	30	7.7	17	4.4	4.89	82	.285	.404	-3	-3	97	117	-1.4	0	1	-0.1
Total	12	118	101	.539	418	238	98	11	24	1954	1763	8.1	117	979	4.5	971	4.5	3.68	101	.241	.328	8	10	100	98	10.2	-14	-16	-1.0
■ **IRV HIGGINBOTHAM**	Higginbotham, Irving Clinton b: 4/26/1882, Homer, Neb. d: 6/12/59, Seattle, Wash. TR , 6'1", 196 lbs. Deb: 8/11/06																												
1906	StL-N	1	4	.200	7	6	4	0	0	47	50	9.6	1	11	2.1	14	2.7	3.26	84	.303	.350	-3	-3	104	103	-1.0	0	0	-0.1
1908	StL-N	3	8	.273	19	11	7	1	0	107	113	9.5	0	33	2.8	38	3.2	3.20	73	.303	.364	-10	-10	100	105	-0.7	-2	-1	-1.2
1909	StL-N	1	0	1.000	3	1	1	0	0	11	5	4.1	0	2	1.6	2	1.6	1.64	158	.143	.189	1	1	99	4	0.5	-0	-0	0.1
	Chi-N	5	2	.714	19	6	4	0	1	78	64	7.4	0	20	2.3	32	3.7	2.19	113	.213	.269	4	2	95	66	0.4	1	-1	0.1
	Yr	6	2	.750	22	7	5	0	1	89	69	7.0	0	22	2.2	34	3.4	2.12	117	.205	.260	5	4	96	66	0.9	-0	-2	0.2
Total	3	10	14	.417	48	24	16	1	1	243	232	8.6	1	66	2.4	86	3.2	2.81	88	.265	.322	-9	-9	99	87	-0.8	-1	-2	-1.1
■ **DENNIS HIGGINS**	Higgins, Dennis Dean b: 8/4/39, Jefferson City, Mo. BR/TR, 6'3", 180 lbs. Deb: 4/12/66																												
1966	Chi-A	1	0	1.000	42	1	0	0	5	93	66	6.4	9	33	3.2	86	8.3	2.52	127	.202	.280	9	7	93	109	0.5	0	1	0.8
1967	Chi-A	1	2	.333	9	0	0	0	0	12	13	9.8	0	10	7.5	8	6.0	6.00	50	.271	.419	-4	-4	93	91	-0.5	-0	0	-0.3
1968	Was-A	4	4	.500	59	0	0	0	13	100	81	7.3	8	46	4.1	66	5.9	3.24	86	.226	.307	-3	-5	94	102	0.7	0	-1	-0.6
1969	Was-A	10	9	.526	55	0	0	0	16	85	79	8.4	7	56	5.9	71	7.5	3.49	100	.252	.360	1	-0	96	128	0.0	-1	-1	-0.1
1970	Cle-A	4	6	.400	58	0	0	0	11	90	82	8.2	8	54	5.4	82	8.2	4.00	107	.248	.349	-3	3	115	105	-0.7	1	1	0.5
1971	StL-N	1	0	1.000	3	0	0	0	0	7	6	7.7	0	2	2.6	6	7.7	3.86	90	.240	.276	-0	-0	100	62	0.5	-0	0	0.0
1972	StL-N	1	2	.333	15	1	0	0	1	23	19	7.4	0	22	8.6	20	7.8	3.91	93	.226	.383	-1	-1	105	100	-0.4	-0	-0	0.0
Total	7	22	23	.489	241	2	0	0	46	410	346	7.6	32	223	4.9	339	7.4	3.42	99	.233	.330	-0	-1	100	109	0.1	0	-1	0.3
■ **EDDIE HIGGINS**	Higgins, Thomas Edward "Doc" or "Irish" b: 3/18/1888, Nevada, Ill. d: 2/14/59, Elgin, Ill. BR/TR, 6'0.5", 174 lbs. Deb: 09																												
1909	StL-N	3	3	.500	16	5	5	0	0	66	68	9.3	4	17	2.3	15	2.0	4.50	57	.273	.322	-14	-14	99	77	0.7	-0	0	-1.3
1910	StL-N	0	1	.000	2	0	0	0	0	10	15	13.5	0	7	6.3	1	0.9	4.50	63	.349	.440	-2	-2	93	141	-0.4	1	1	0.0
Total	2	3	4	.429	18	5	5	0	0	76	83	9.8	4	24	2.8	16	1.9	4.50	58	.284	.341	-16	-16	99	85	0.3	0	1	-1.3
■ **ED HIGH**	High, Edward T. "Lefty" b: 12/26/1876, Baltimore, Md. d: 2/10/26, Baltimore, Md. TL , Deb: 7/04/01																												
1901	Det-A	1	0	1.000	4	1	1	0	0	18	21	10.5	0	6	3.0	4	2.0	3.50	114	.312	.368	0	1	109	112	0.5	-1	-0	0.1
■ **TEDDY HIGUERA**	Higuera, Teodoro Valenzuela (Valenzuela) b: 11/9/58, Los Mochis, Mexico BB/TL, 5'10", 178 lbs. Deb: 4/23/85																												
1985	Mil-A	15	8	.652	32	30	7	2	0	212	186	7.9	22	63	2.7	127	5.4	3.91	112	.235	.288	6	11	106	82	4.8	0	-3	0.9
1986	Mil-A	20	11	.645	34	34	15	4	0	248	226	8.2	26	74	2.7	207	7.5	2.79	154	.241	.294	38	42	103	119	5.7	0	-1	4.2
1987	Mil-A	18	10	.643	35	35	14	3	0	262	236	8.1	24	87	3.0	240	8.2	3.85	119	.241	.300	18	21	102	87	3.0	0	-2	1.8
1988	Mil-A	16	9	.640	31	31	8	1	0	227	168	6.7	15	59	2.3	192	7.6	2.46	166	.207	**.260**	**38**	41	103	90	3.2	0	1	4.6
Total	4	69	38	.645	132	130	44	10	0	949	816	7.7	87	283	2.7	766	7.3	3.25	134	.232	.287	100	115	103	95	16.7	0	-5	11.5
■ **WHITEY HILCHER**	Hilcher, Walter Frank b: 2/28/09, Chicago, Ill. d: 11/21/62, Minneapolis, Minn. BR/TR, 6', 174 lbs. Deb: 9/17/31																												
1931	Cin-N	0	1	.000	2	1	0	0	0	12	16	12.0	0	4	3.0	5	3.8	3.00	126	.320	.382	1	1	98	167	-0.4	-1	-0	0.0
1932	Cin-N	0	3	.000	11	2	0	0	0	19	24	11.4	3	10	4.7	4	1.9	7.58	51	.316	.391	-8	-8	99	85	-1.4	1	0	-0.6
1935	Cin-N	2	0	1.000	4	2	1	1	0	19	19	9.0	0	5	2.4	9	4.3	2.84	135	.264	.300	2	2	95	109	1.0	-0	1	0.3
1936	Cin-N	1	2	.333	14	1	0	0	0	35	44	11.3	3	14	3.6	10	2.6	6.17	63	.299	.362	-8	-9	97	82	-0.4	-1	-1	-0.9
Total	4	3	6	.333	31	6	1	1	0	85	103	10.9	6	33	3.5	28	3.0	5.29	73	.299	.358	-13	-14	97	100	-1.2	-1	0	-1.2
■ **ORAL HILDEBRAND**	Hildebrand, Oral Clyde b: 4/7/07, Indianapolis, Ind. d: 9/8/77, Southport, Ind. BR/TR, 6'3", 175 lbs. Deb: 9/08/31																												
1931	Cle-A	2	1	.667	5	2	2	0	0	27	25	8.3	0	13	4.3	6	2.0	4.33	107	.243	.339	0	1	106	82	0.5	-1	-0	0.0
1932	Cle-A	8	6	.571	27	15	7	0	0	129	124	8.7	7	62	4.3	49	3.4	3.70	129	.249	.327	11	16	107	104	0.0	-3	-2	1.0
1933	Cle-A	16	11	.593	36	31	15	**6**	0	220	205	8.4	8	88	3.6	90	3.7	3.76	119	.245	.314	13	18	105	90	3.0	-2	-0	1.6
1934	Cle-A	11	9	.550	33	28	10	1	1	198	225	10.2	14	99	4.5	72	3.3	4.50	100	.282	.358	-0	-0	100	108	0.0	-1	1	0.0
1935	Cle-A	9	8	.529	34	20	8	0	5	171	171	9.0	12	63	3.3	49	2.6	3.95	111	.263	.322	10	9	99	101	0.0	-2	0	0.6
1936	Cle-A	10	11	.476	36	21	9	0	4	175	197	10.1	10	83	4.3	65	3.3	4.89	108	.283	.357	3	8	105	99	-0.9	-0	-1	0.6
1937	StL-A	8	17	.320	30	27	12	1	1	201	228	10.2	18	87	3.9	75	3.4	5.15	93	.284	.352	-12	-8	103	93	0.5	-1	-1	-0.8
1938	StL-A	8	10	.444	23	23	10	0	0	163	194	10.7	18	73	4.0	66	3.6	5.69	87	.297	.367	-16	-14	103	96	1.3	1	-4	-1.3
1939	NY-A	10	4	.714	21	15	7	1	2	127	102	7.2	11	41	2.9	50	3.5	3.05	129	.219	.280	22	13	85	95	0.3	-0	-1	1.0
1940	NY-A	1	1	.500	13	0	0	0	0	19	19	9.0	1	14	6.6	5	2.4	1.89	222	.268	.386	5	5	96	273	0.0	-0	-0	0.4
Total	10	83	78	.516	258	182	80	9	13	1430	1490	9.4	99	623	3.9	527	3.3	4.36	107	.267	.338	36	46	101	100	4.7	-9	-8	3.1
■ **TOM HILGENDORF**	Hilgendorf, Thomas Eugene b: 3/10/42, Clinton, Iowa BB/TL, 6'1.5", 187 lbs. Deb: 8/15/69																												
1969	StL-N	0	0	—	6	0	0	0	2	6	3	4.5	0	2	3.0	2	3.0	1.50	237	.150	.200	1	1	99	40	0.0	1	0	0.2
1970	StL-N	0	4	.000	23	0	0	0	3	21	22	9.4	0	13	5.6	13	5.6	3.86	112	.272	.361	0	1	106	109	-1.9	-0	0	0.1
1972	Cle-A	3	1	.750	19	5	1	0	0	47	51	9.8	4	21	4.0	25	4.8	2.68	124	.283	.357	2	3	108	173	1.1	-1	0	0.3
1973	Cle-A	5	3	.625	48	1	1	0	6	95	87	8.2	9	36	3.4	58	5.5	3.13	121	.242	.313	7	7	99	109	1.4	0	1	0.8
1974	Cle-A	4	3	.571	35	0	0	0	3	48	58	10.9	6	17	3.2	23	4.3	4.88	75	.302	.349	-7	-6	101	105	0.7	0	0	-0.6
1975	Phi-N	7	3	.700	53	0	0	0	0	97	81	7.5	6	38	3.5	52	4.8	2.13	172	.230	.298	16	17	101	136	1.9	1	1	1.9
Total	6	19	14	.576	184	6	2	0	14	314	302	8.7	25	127	3.6	173	5.0	3.04	122	.255	.322	21	23	102	125	3.2	1	3	2.7
■ **CARMEN HILL**	Hill, Carmen Proctor "Specs" or "Bunker" b: 10/1/1895, Royalton, Minn. BR/TR, 6'1", 180 lbs. Deb: 8/24/15																												
1915	Pit-N	2	1	.667	8	3	2	1	0	47	42	8.0	0	13	2.5	24	4.6	1.15	234	.255	.306	8	8	98	242	0.6	0	1	1.1
1916	Pit-N	0	0	—	2	0	0	0	0	6	11	16.5	0	5	7.5	5	7.5	9.00	31	.611	.708	-4	-4	107	135	0.0	0	-0	-0.3
1918	Pit-N	2	3	.400	6	4	3	0	0	44	24	4.9	0	17	3.5	15	3.1	1.23	236	.160	.241	8	8	105	59	-0.5	0	0	1.1
1919	Pit-N	0	0	—	4	0	0	0	0	5	12	21.6	0	1	1.8	1	1.8	9.00	34	.480	.481	-3	-3	105	111	0.0	0	0	-0.2
1922	NY-N	2	1	.667	8	4	0	0	0	28	33	10.6	0	5	1.6	6	1.9	4.82	85	.295	.314	-2	-2	100	69	0.2	-0	1	-0.1
1926	Pit-N	3	3	.500	6	6	4	1	0	40	42	9.4	2	9	2.0	8	1.8	3.37	126	.288	.323	2	4	111	118	-0.2	-1	1	0.4
1927	Pit-N	22	11	.667	43	31	22	2	3	278	260	8.4	12	80	2.6	95	3.1	3.24	120	.249	.295	21	20	99	92	2.9	2	0	2.3
1928	Pit-N	16	10	.615	36	31	16	1	2	237	229	8.7	16	81	3.1	73	2.8	3.53	118	.259	.312	12	17	105	98	1.9	2	-3	1.6
1929	Pit-N	2	3	.400	27	3	0	0	3	79	94	10.7	4	35	4.0	28	3.2	3.99	120	.297	.358	6	7	102	120	-0.7	-3	0	0.3
	StL-N	0	0	—	3	1	0	0	0	9	10	10.0	2	8	8.0	1	1.0	8.00	58	.303	.442	-3	-3	98	99	0.0	-0	0	-0.2
	Yr	2	3	.400	30	4	0	0	3	88	104	10.6	6	43	4.4	29	3.0	4.40	108	.297	.367	**3**	**4**	101	99	-0.7	-3	0	0.1
1930	StL-N	0	1	.000	4	2	0	0	0	15	12	7.2	2	13	7.8	8	4.8	7.20	70	.240	.373	-4	-4	102	75	-0.4	0	0	-0.2
Total	10	49	33	.598	147	85	47	5	8	788	769	8.8	38	267	3.0	264	3.0	3.44	116	.261	.315	40	47	102	104	3.8	0	1	5.8
■ **RED HILL**	Hill, Clifford Joseph b: 1/20/1893, Marshall, Tex. d: 8/11/38, El Paso, Tex. BB/TL, Deb: 4/21/17																												
1917	Phi-A	0	0	—	1	0	0	0	0	3	5	15.0	0	1	3.0	0	0.0	6.00	43	.385	.429	-1	-1	97	106	0.0	0	0	0.0
■ **DAVE HILL**	Hill, David Burnham b: 11/11/37, New Orleans, La. BR/TL, 6'2", 170 lbs. Deb: 8/22/57																												
1957	KC-A	0	0	—	2	0	0	0	0	2	6	27.0	3	3	13.5	1	4.5	31.50	12	.462	.563	-6	-6	102	83	0.0	0	0	-0.4
■ **GARRY HILL**	Hill, Garry Alton b: 11/3/46, Rutherfordton, N.C. BR/TR, 6'2", 195 lbs. Deb: 6/12/69																												
1969	Atl-N	0	1	.000	1	1	0	0	0	2	6	27.0	1	1	4.5	2	9.0	18.00	21	.462	.500	-3	-3	103	87	-0.4	0	0	-0.2
■ **HERBERT HILL**	Hill, Herbert Lee b: 8/19/1891, Hutchins, Tex. d: 9/2/70, Farmers Branch, Tex. 5'11.5", 175 lbs. Deb: 7/17/15																												
1915	Cle-A	0	0	—	1	0	0	0	0	2	1	4.5	0	2	9.0	0	0.0	0.00	—	.250	.500	1	1	106	0	0.0	0	0	0.1

YEAR	TM/L	W	L	PCT	G	GS	CG	SHO	SV	IP	H	H/G	HR	BB	BB/G	SO	SO/G	ERA	/A	OAVG	OOBP	PR	/A	PF	CPI	WAT	PB	PD	TPI
■ KEN HILL	Hill, Kenneth Wade b: 12/14/65, Lynn, Mass. BR/TR, 6'2", 175 lbs. Deb: 9/03/88																												
1988	StL-N	0	1	.000	4	1	0	0	0	14	16	10.3	0	6	3.9	6	3.9	5.14	70	.286	.355	-3	-2	105	79	-0.4	-0	0	-0.2
■ BILL HILL	Hill, William Cicero "Still Bill" b: 8/2/1874, Chattanooga, Tenn. d: 1/28/38, Cincinnati, Ohio BL/TL, 6'1", 201 lbs. Deb: 4/18/1896																												
1896	Lou-N	9	28	.243	43	39	32	0	2	320	353	9.9	14	155	4.4	104	2.9	4.33	102	.302	.384	1	4	102	101	-3.8	-5	4	0.2
1897	Lou-N	7	17	.292	27	26	20	1	0	199	209	9.5	6	69	3.1	55	2.5	3.62	116	.292	.354	15	13	97	99	-3.7	-8	0	0.4
1898	Cin-N	13	14	.481	33	32	26	2	0	262	261	9.0	3	119	4.1	75	2.6	3.98	97	.281	.362	-11	-4	107	87	-3.1	-8	2	-0.6
1899	Cle-N	3	6	.333	11	10	7	0	0	72	96	12.0	0	39	4.9	26	3.3	7.00	53	.345	.426	-25	-26	96	75	1.1	-2	0	-2.2
	Bal-N	3	4	.429	8	7	6	0	0	61	64	9.4	1	18	2.7	17	2.5	3.25	126	.293	.347	4	6	106	102	-0.9	1	0	0.6
	Bro-N	1	0	1.000	2	1	1	0	1	11	11	9.0	0	6	4.9	3	2.5	0.82	482	.283	.379	4	4	102	444	0.5	2	0	0.6
	Yr	7	10	.412	21	18	14	0	1	144	171	10.7	1	63	3.9	46	2.9	4.94	79	.319	.391	-17	-17	101	444	0.7	-2	0	-1.0
Total	4	36	69	.343	124	115	92	3	3	925	994	9.7	24	406	4.0	280	2.7	4.17	99	.297	.373	-12	-3	102	99	-9.9	-20	5	-1.0
■ HOMER HILLEBRAND	Hillebrand, Homer Hiller Henry "Doc" b: 10/10/1879, Freeport, Ill. d: 1/20/74, Elsinore, Cal. 5'8", 165 lbs. Deb: 4/24/05																												
1905	Pit-N	5	2	.714	10	6	4	0	1	61	43	6.3	0	19	2.8	37	5.5	2.80	108	.223	.300	1	2	102	62	0.8	1	-1	0.2
1906	Pit-N	3	2	.600	7	5	4	1	0	53	42	7.1	1	21	3.6	32	5.4	2.21	120	.244	.330	2	3	101	111	0.0	1	1	0.6
1908	Pit-N	0	0	—	1	0	0	0	0	1	1	9.0	0	0	0.0	1	9.0	0.00	—	.289	.289	0	0	92	0	0.0	0	0	0.0
Total	3	8	4	.667	18	11	8	1	1	115	86	6.7	1	40	3.1	70	5.5	2.50	114	.234	.314	4	4	101	84	0.8	2	1	0.8
■ SHAWN HILLEGAS	Hillegas, Shawn Patrick b: 8/21/64, Dos Palos, Cal. BR/TR, 6'3", 205 lbs. Deb: 8/09/87																												
1987	LA-N	4	3	.571	12	10	0	0	0	58	52	8.1	5	31	4.8	51	7.9	3.57	105	.241	.329	3	1	92	107	0.8	-1	-1	0.0
1988	LA-N	3	4	.429	11	10	0	0	0	57	54	8.5	5	17	2.7	30	4.7	4.11	88	.250	.310	-4	-3	105	87	-0.9	-0	-1	-0.3
	Chi-A	3	2	.600	6	6	0	0	0	40	30	6.7	4	18	4.0	26	5.8	3.15	124	.207	.295	4	3	99	94	0.7	0	-0	0.3
Total	2	10	9	.526	29	26	0	0	0	155	136	7.9	14	66	3.8	107	6.2	3.66	103	.236	.314	3	2	98	96	0.6	-1	-2	0.0
■ FRANK HILLER	Hiller, Frank Walter "Dutch" b: 7/13/20, Newark, N.J. d: 1/8/87, West Chester, Pa. BR/TR, 6', 200 lbs. Deb: 5/25/46																												
1946	NY-A	0	2	.000	3	1	0	0	0	11	13	10.6	2	6	4.9	4	3.3	4.91	70	.295	.380	-2	-2	98	120	-0.9	0	0	-0.1
1948	NY-A	5	2	.714	22	5	1	0	0	62	59	8.6	8	30	4.4	25	3.6	4.06	101	.244	.326	1	0	96	102	1.0	2	0	0.2
1949	NY-A	0	2	.000	4	0	0	0	1	8	9	10.1	0	7	7.9	3	3.4	5.63	72	.290	.421	-1	-1	97	95	-0.9	0	0	0.0
1950	Chi-N	12	5	.706	38	17	9	2	1	153	153	9.0	16	32	1.9	55	3.2	3.53	126	.258	.297	10	15	107	100	4.5	-3	0	1.3
1951	Chi-N	6	12	.333	24	21	6	2	1	141	147	9.4	17	31	2.0	50	3.2	4.85	81	.268	.315	-14	-14	100	83	-1.6	-2	1	-1.3
1952	Cin-N	5	8	.385	28	15	6	1	1	124	129	9.4	7	37	2.7	50	3.6	4.65	81	.271	.328	-13	-12	100	83	-0.9	1	0	-1.1
1953	NY-N	2	1	.667	19	1	0	0	0	34	43	11.4	6	15	4.0	10	2.6	6.09	69	.303	.380	-7	-7	98	102	0.6	1	1	-0.4
Total	7	30	32	.484	138	60	22	5	4	533	553	9.3	56	158	2.7	197	3.3	4.42	92	.266	.322	-24	-21	101	92	1.8	-1	3	-1.4
■ JOHN HILLER	Hiller, John Frederick b: 4/8/43, Toronto, Ont., Canada BR/TL, 6'1", 185 lbs. Deb: 9/06/65																												
1965	Det-A	0	0	—	5	0	0	0	1	6	5	7.5	0	1	1.5	4	6.0	0.00	—	.227	.261	2	2	104	0	0.0	0	-0	0.2
1966	Det-A	0	0	—	1	0	0	0	0	2	2	9.0	0	2	9.0	1	4.5	9.00	39	.286	.400	-1	-1	102	63	0.0	0	0	0.0
1967	Det-A	4	3	.571	23	6	2	2	3	65	57	7.9	4	9	1.2	49	6.8	2.63	120	.233	.258	4	4	98	88	0.1	-0	-0	0.4
1968	Det-A	9	6	.600	39	12	4	1	2	128	92	6.5	9	51	3.6	78	5.5	2.39	129	.200	.276	8	10	103	97	-0.4	-2	-0	0.8
1969	Det-A	4	4	.500	40	8	1	1	4	99	97	8.8	13	44	4.0	74	6.7	4.00	93	.257	.329	-4	-3	102	106	-0.3	2	-1	-0.2
1970	Det-A	6	6	.500	47	5	1	1	3	104	82	7.1	12	46	4.0	89	7.7	3.03	128	.219	.301	8	10	104	107	0.2	-2	-1	0.7
1972	Det-A	1	2	.333	24	3	1	0	3	44	39	8.0	4	13	2.7	26	5.3	2.05	169	.232	.296	5	7	112	145	-0.5	-0	1	0.8
1973	Det-A	10	5	.667	**65**	0	0	0	**38**	125	89	6.4	7	39	2.8	124	8.9	1.44	269	.198	.257	**33**	**34**	101	127	2.4	0	0	3.6
1974	Det-A	17	14	.548	59	0	0	0	13	150	127	7.6	10	62	3.7	134	8.0	2.64	148	.231	.303	16	21	108	115	3.4	0	-2	2.0
1975	Det-A	2	3	.400	36	0	0	0	14	71	52	6.6	6	36	4.6	87	11.0	2.15	187	.205	.298	13	15	106	129	0.2	0	0	1.5
1976	Det-A	12	8	.600	56	1	1	1	13	121	93	6.9	7	67	5.0	117	8.7	2.38	155	.219	.318	15	**18**	105	135	2.9	0	-1	1.8
1977	Det-A	8	14	.364	45	8	3	0	7	124	120	8.7	15	61	4.4	115	8.3	3.56	120	.258	.338	7	10	105	123	-2.4	0	-1	0.8
1978	Det-A	9	4	.692	51	0	0	0	15	92	64	6.3	6	35	3.4	74	7.2	2.35	172	.202	.273	15	17	107	98	2.4	0	-1	1.7
1979	Det-A	4	7	.364	43	0	0	0	9	79	83	9.5	14	55	6.3	46	5.2	5.24	78	.274	.371	-9	-10	96	110	-1.7	0	-0	-0.9
1980	Det-A	1	0	1.000	11	0	0	0	0	31	38	11.0	3	14	4.1	18	5.2	4.35	97	.309	.371	-1	-0	105	124	0.5	0	-0	0.0
Total	15	87	76	.534	545	43	13	6	125	1241	1040	7.5	110	535	3.9	1036	7.5	2.84	134	.229	.305	112	132	104	114	6.8	-3	-7	13.2
■ DAVE HILLMAN	Hillman, Darius Dutton b: 9/14/27, Dungannon, Va. BR/TR, 5'11", 168 lbs. Deb: 4/30/55																												
1955	Chi-N	0	0	—	25	3	0	0	0	58	63	9.8	10	25	3.9	23	3.6	5.28	78	.283	.344	-8	-8	101	99	0.0	0	0	-0.6
1956	Chi-N	0	2	.000	2	2	0	0	0	12	11	8.3	0	5	3.8	6	4.5	2.25	169	.216	.286	2	2	101	69	-0.9	-1	0	0.2
1957	Chi-N	6	11	.353	32	14	1	0	1	103	115	10.0	13	37	3.2	53	4.6	4.37	87	.280	.337	-6	-7	98	104	-1.1	-2	-0	-0.8
1958	Chi-N	4	8	.333	31	16	3	0	1	126	132	9.4	12	31	2.2	65	4.6	3.14	127	.265	.302	11	12	101	110	-1.7	-1	-0	1.1
1959	Chi-N	8	11	.421	39	24	4	1	0	191	178	8.4	17	43	2.0	88	4.1	3.53	110	.248	.285	9	8	99	88	-1.2	1	1	1.0
1960	Bos-A	0	3	.000	16	3	0	0	0	37	41	10.0	6	12	2.9	14	3.4	5.59	73	.281	.329	-7	-6	105	84	-1.4	-1	0	-0.5
1961	Bos-A	3	2	.600	28	1	0	0	0	78	70	8.1	8	23	2.7	39	4.5	2.77	149	.242	.290	11	12	103	119	0.6	-2	0	1.0
1962	Cin-N	0	0	—	2	0	0	0	0	4	8	18.0	0	1	2.3	0	0.0	9.00	44	.421	.450	-2	-2	100	87	0.0	0	-0	-0.1
	NY-N	0	0	—	13	1	0	0	1	16	21	11.8	5	8	4.5	8	4.5	6.19	69	.333	.395	-4	-3	108	131	0.0	-0	0	-0.2
	Yr	0	0	—	15	1	0	0	1	20	29	13.0	5	9	4.0	8	3.6	6.75	62	.354	.406	-6	-6	107	131	0.0	0	0	-0.3
Total	8	21	37	.362	188	64	8	1	3	625	639	9.2	71	185	2.7	296	4.3	3.86	103	.264	.310	6	7	100	101	-5.7	-5	1	1.1
■ CHARLIE HILSEY	Hilsey, Charles T. b: 3/23/1864, Philadelphia, Pa. d: 10/31/18, Philadelphia, Pa. 5'7", 180 lbs. Deb: 9/27/1883																												
1883	Phi-N	0	3	.000	3	3	3	0	0	26	36	12.5	1	4	1.4	8	2.8	5.54	56	.336	.360	-7	-7	99	86	-1.4	-1	0	-0.5
1884	Phi-a	2	1	.667	3	3	3	0	0	27	29	9.7	0	5	1.7	10	3.3	4.67	78	.283	.316	-4	-3	113	77	0.3	-0	0	-0.2
Total	2	2	4	.333	6	6	6	0	0	53	65	11.0	1	9	1.5	18	3.1	5.09	67	.310	.339	-11	-10	106	81	-1.1	-1	0	-0.7
■ SAM HINDS	Hinds, Samuel Russell b: 7/11/53, Frederick, Md. BR/TR, 6'6", 215 lbs. Deb: 5/21/77																												
1977	Mil-A	0	3	.000	29	1	0	0	2	72	72	9.0	5	40	5.0	46	5.8	4.75	83	.266	.352	-5	-7	97	93	-1.4	0	-0	-0.6
■ PAUL HINES	Hines, Paul A. b: 3/1/1852, Washington, D.C. d: 7/10/35, Hyattsville, Md. BR/TR, 5'9.5", 173 lbs. Deb: 4/20/1872																												
1884	Pro-N	0	0	—	1	0	0	0	0	1	3	27.0	0	0	0.0	0	0.0	0.00	—	.525	.525	0	0	96	0	0.0	0	0	0.0
■ PAUL HINRICHS	Hinrichs, Paul Edwin "Herky" b: 8/31/25, Marengo, Iowa BR/TR, 6', 180 lbs. Deb: 5/16/51																												
1951	Bos-A	0	0	—	4	0	0	0	0	3	7	21.0	1	4	12.0	1	3.0	24.00	18	.412	.524	-7	-7	106	58	0.0	0	0	-0.5
■ DUTCH HINRICHS	Hinrichs, William Louis b: 4/27/1889, Orange, Cal. d: 8/18/72, Kingsburg, Cal. BR/TR, 6'3", 195 lbs. Deb: 6/25/10																												
1910	Was-A	0	1	.000	3	0	0	0	1	7	10	12.9	0	3	3.9	5	6.4	2.57	100	.357	.419	-0	-0	102	221	-0.4	-1	-0	0.0
■ JERRY HINSLEY	Hinsley, Jerry Dean b: 4/9/44, Hugo, Okla. BR/TR, 5'11", 165 lbs. Deb: 4/18/64																												
1964	NY-N	0	2	.000	9	2	0	0	0	15	21	12.6	0	7	4.2	11	6.6	8.40	41	.313	.368	-8	-8	98	58	-0.9	-0	-0	-0.8
1967	NY-N	0	0	—	2	0	0	0	0	5	6	10.8	0	4	7.2	3	5.4	3.60	95	.316	.435	-0	-0	102	162	0.0	0	0	0.0
Total	2	0	2	.000	11	2	0	0	0	20	27	12.1	0	11	4.9	14	6.3	7.20	48	.314	.384	-8	-8	99	84	-0.9	-0	-0	-0.8
■ RICH HINTON	Hinton, Richard Michael b: 5/22/47, Tucson, Ariz. BL/TL, 6'2", 185 lbs. Deb: 7/17/71																												
1971	Chi-A	3	4	.429	18	2	0	0	0	24	27	10.1	1	6	2.3	15	5.6	4.50	75	.310	.337	-3	-3	97	100	-0.3	-0	1	-0.1
1972	NY-A	1	0	1.000	7	3	0	0	0	17	20	10.6	2	8	4.2	13	6.9	4.76	59	.299	.354	-3	-4	92	110	0.5	-0	-0	-0.4
	Tex-A	0	1	.000	5	0	0	0	0	11	7	5.7	1	10	8.2	4	3.3	2.45	121	.171	.327	1	1	97	121	-0.4	1	0	0.2
	Yr	1	1	.500	12	3	0	0	0	28	27	8.7	3	18	5.8	17	5.5	3.86	75	.245	.344	-2	-3	94	121	0.1	-0	-0	-0.2
1975	Chi-A	1	0	1.000	15	0	0	0	0	37	41	10.0	3	15	3.6	30	7.3	4.86	81	.270	.329	-4	-4	104	81	0.5	0	1	-0.2
1976	Cin-N	1	2	.333	12	1	0	0	0	18	30	15.0	4	11	5.5	8	4.0	7.50	47	.380	.446	-8	-8	100	120	-0.6	-0	-0	-0.8
1978	Chi-A	2	6	.250	29	4	2	0	1	81	78	8.7	5	28	3.1	48	5.3	4.00	96	.261	.321	-2	-1	102	90	-1.7	0	-1	-0.2
1979	Chi-A	1	2	.333	16	2	0	0	2	42	57	12.2	4	8	1.7	27	5.8	6.00	72	.331	.356	-8	-8	103	92	-0.3	0	1	-0.6
	Sea-A	0	2	.000	14	1	0	0	0	20	23	10.3	4	5	2.3	7	3.1	5.40	79	.284	.333	-3	-2	101	96	-0.9	0	-0	-0.2
	Yr	1	4	.200	30	3	0	0	2	62	80	11.6	8	13	1.9	34	4.9	5.81	74	.310	.342	-11	-10	102	96	-1.2	0	0	-0.8
Total	6	9	17	.346	116	13	2	0	3	250	283	10.2	24	91	3.3	152	5.5	4.86	78	.289	.344	-30	-30	101	95	-3.2	0	1	-2.3

YEAR TM/L	W	L	PCT	G	GS	CG	SHO	SV	IP	H	H/G	HR	BB	BB/G	SO	SO/G	ERA	/A	OAVG	OOBP	PR	/A	PF	CPI	WAT	PB	PD	TPI
■ **HERB HIPPAUF**	Hippauf, Herbert August b: 5/9/40, New York, N.Y. BR/TL, 6', 180 lbs. Deb: 4/27/66																											
1966 Atl-N	0	1	.000	3	0	0	0	0	3	6	18.0	0	1	3.0	1	3.0	12.00	29	.462	.467	-3	-3	97	75	-0.4	0	-0	-0.2
■ **HARLEY HISNER**	Hisner, Harley Parnell b: 11/6/26, Naples, Ind. BR/TR, 6'1", 185 lbs. Deb: 9/30/51																											
1951 Bos-A	0	1	.000	1	1	0	0	0	6	7	10.5	0	4	6.0	3	4.5	4.50	97	.292	.393	-0	-0	106	109	-0.4	0	0	0.0
■ **BRUCE HITT**	Hitt, Bruce Smith b: 3/14/1897, Comanche, Tex. d: 11/10/73, Portland, Ore. BR/TR, 6'1", 190 lbs. Deb: 9/23/17																											
1917 StL-N	0	0	—	2	0	0	0	0	4	7	15.8	1	1	2.3	1	2.3	9.00	31	.368	.400	-3	-3	102	89	0.0	-0	0	-0.2
■ **ROY HITT**	Hitt, Roy Wesley "Rhino" b: 6/22/1887, Carleton, Neb. d: 2/8/56, Pomona, Cal. TL, 5'10", 200 lbs. Deb: 4/27/07																											
1907 Cin-N	6	10	.375	21	18	14	2	0	153	143	8.4	2	56	3.3	63	3.7	3.41	69	.282	.366	-16	-18	95	90	-1.1	1	-1	-2.0
■ **LLOYD HITTLE**	Hittle, Lloyd Eldon "Red" b: 2/21/24, Lodi, Cal. BR/TL, 5'10.5", 164 lbs. Deb: 6/12/49																											
1949 Was-A	5	7	.417	36	9	3	2	0	109	123	10.2	2	57	4.7	32	2.6	4.21	96	.285	.359	-0	-2	96	103	0.9	-2	-1	-0.4
1950 Was-A	2	4	.333	11	4	1	0	0	43	60	12.6	1	17	3.6	9	1.9	5.02	92	.326	.377	-2	-2	101	106	-0.6	-1	1	-0.1
Total 2	7	11	.389	47	13	4	2	0	152	183	10.8	3	74	4.4	41	2.4	4.44	95	.298	.365	-2	-4	98	104	0.3	-3	0	-0.5
■ **MYRIL HOAG**	Hoag, Myril Oliver b: 3/9/08, Davis, Cal. d: 7/28/71, High Springs, Fla BR/TR, 5'11", 180 lbs. Deb: 4/15/31																											
1939 StL-A	0	0	—	1	0	0	0	0	1	0	0.0	0	0	0.0	0	0.0	0.00	—	.000	.000	1	1	105	0	0.0	0	0	0.1
1945 Cle-A	0	0	—	2	0	0	0	0	3	3	9.0	0	1	3.0	0	0.0	0.00	—	.300	.364	1	1	98	0	0.0	0	0	0.1
Total 2	0	0	—	3	0	0	0	0	4	3	6.8	0	1	2.3	0	0.0	0.00	—	.214	.267	2	2	100	0	0.0	1	0	0.2
■ **ED HOBAUGH**	Hobaugh, Edward Russell b: 6/27/34, Kittanning, Pa. BR/TR, 6', 176 lbs. Deb: 4/19/61																											
1961 Was-A	7	9	.438	26	18	3	0	0	126	142	10.1	12	64	4.6	67	4.8	4.43	88	.281	.359	-6	-7	97	108	0.8	-2	0	-0.8
1962 Was-A	2	1	.667	26	2	0	0	1	69	66	8.6	9	25	3.3	37	4.8	3.78	107	.258	.313	1	2	102	109	0.7	0	-1	0.2
1963 Was-A	0	0	—	9	1	0	0	0	16	20	11.3	3	6	3.4	11	6.2	6.19	59	.308	.364	-5	-4	101	101	0.0	2	0	-0.2
Total 3	9	10	.474	61	21	3	0	1	211	228	9.7	24	95	4.1	115	4.9	4.35	91	.276	.345	-9	-9	99	108	1.5	-0	-1	-0.8
■ **GLEN HOBBIE**	Hobbie, Glen Frederick b: 4/24/36, Witt, Ill. BR/TR, 6'2", 195 lbs. Deb: 9/20/57																											
1957 Chi-N	0	0	—	2	0	0	0	0	4	6	13.5	0	5	11.3	3	6.8	11.25	34	.333	.458	-3	-3	98	68	0.0	-0	0	-0.2
1958 Chi-N	10	6	.625	55	16	2	1	2	168	163	8.7	13	93	5.0	91	4.9	3.75	106	.252	.348	4	4	101	107	2.6	-2	4	0.6
1959 Chi-N	16	13	.552	46	33	10	3	0	234	204	7.8	15	106	4.1	138	5.3	3.69	106	.236	.319	7	5	99	90	2.4	-3	1	0.3
1960 Chi-N	16	20	.444	46	36	16	4	1	259	253	8.8	27	101	3.5	134	4.7	3.96	96	.256	.325	-6	-5	101	101	2.1	1	4	0.0
1961 Chi-N	7	13	.350	36	29	7	2	2	199	207	9.4	26	54	2.4	103	4.7	4.25	97	.268	.315	-5	-3	102	97	-1.7	2	3	0.2
1962 Chi-N	5	14	.263	42	23	5	0	0	162	198	11.0	19	62	3.4	87	4.8	5.22	82	.304	.359	-23	-17	109	101	-2.8	-2	0	-1.6
1963 Chi-N	7	10	.412	36	24	4	1	0	165	172	9.4	17	49	2.7	94	5.1	3.93	88	.270	.324	-12	-9	105	103	-1.6	-2	-1	-1.2
1964 Chi-N	0	3	.000	8	4	0	0	0	27	39	13.0	4	10	3.3	14	4.7	8.00	47	.325	.382	-13	-13	106	78	-1.4	0	0	-1.1
StL-N	1	2	.333	13	5	1	0	1	44	41	8.4	4	15	3.1	18	3.7	4.30	92	.241	.302	-4	-2	111	78	-0.5	1	1	0.0
Yr	1	5	.167	21	9	1	0	1	71	80	10.1	8	25	3.2	32	4.1	5.70	68	.275	.331	-17	-14	109	78	-1.9	0	1	-1.1
Total 8	62	81	.434	284	170	45	11	6	1262	1283	9.1	125	495	3.5	682	4.9	4.21	93	.264	.331	-55	-41	103	98	-0.9	-5	12	-3.0
■ **JOHN HOBBS**	Hobbs, John Douglas b: 11/11/56, Philadelphia, Pa. BR/TL, 6'3", 190 lbs. Deb: 8/31/81																											
1981 Min-A	0	0	—	4	0	0	0	0	6	5	7.5	0	6	9.0	1	1.5	3.00	130	.238	.448	0	1	107	180	0.0	0	-0	0.0
■ **HARRY HOCH**	Hoch, Harry Keller b: 1/9/1887, Woodside, Del. d: 10/26/81, Lewes, Del. BR/TR, 5'10.5", 165 lbs. Deb: 4/16/08																											
1908 Phi-N	2	1	.667	3	3	2	0	0	26	20	6.9	0	13	4.5	4	1.4	2.77	83	.244	.361	-1	-1	98	94	0.4	1	0	0.0
1914 StL-A	0	2	.000	15	2	1	0	0	54	55	9.2	1	27	4.5	13	2.2	3.00	91	.284	.377	-2	-2	100	138	-0.9	-2	2	0.0
1915 StL-A	0	4	.000	12	3	1	0	0	40	52	11.7	2	26	5.8	9	2.0	7.20	40	.311	.413	-19	-19	99	80	-1.9	0	-0	-1.8
Total 3	2	7	.222	30	8	4	0	0	120	127	9.5	3	66	5.0	26	2.0	4.35	62	.287	.388	-22	-22	99	109	-2.4	-1	2	-1.8
■ **CHUCK HOCKENBERY**	Hockenbery, Charles Marion b: 12/15/50, Lacrosse, Wis. BB/TR, 6'1", 195 lbs. Deb: 7/04/75																											
1975 Cal-A	0	5	.000	16	4	0	0	1	41	48	10.5	3	19	4.2	15	3.3	5.27	69	.296	.378	-7	-7	96	96	-2.4	0	-0	-0.7
■ **GEORGE HOCKETTE**	Hockette, George Edward "Lefty" b: 4/7/08, Perth, Miss. d: 1/20/74, Plantation, Fla. BL/TL, 6', 174 lbs. Deb: 9/17/34																											
1934 Bos-A	2	1	.667	3	3	3	2	0	27	22	7.3	3	6	2.0	14	4.7	1.67	284	.218	.259	8	9	105	158	0.5	0	-0	1.0
1935 Bos-A	2	3	.400	23	4	0	0	0	61	83	12.2	6	12	1.8	11	1.6	5.16	94	.329	.353	-5	-2	108	108	-0.5	-1	3	0.0
Total 2	4	4	.500	26	7	3	2	0	88	105	10.7	9	18	1.8	25	2.6	4.09	117	.297	.326	4	7	107	124	0.0	-0	3	1.0
■ **SHOVEL HODGE**	Hodge, Clarence Clemet b: 7/6/1893, Mount Andrew, Ala. d: 12/31/67, Ft.Walton Beach, Fla. BL/TR, 6'4", 190 lbs. Deb: 9/06/20																											
1920 Chi-A	1	1	.500	4	2	1	0	0	20	15	6.7	0	12	5.4	5	2.3	2.25	158	.224	.342	3	3	94	126	-0.1	-1	-0	0.1
1921 Chi-A	6	8	.429	36	10	5	0	2	143	191	12.0	7	54	3.4	25	1.6	6.55	67	.335	.382	-36	-35	102	86	0.3	3	3	-2.5
1922 Chi-A	7	6	.538	35	8	2	0	1	139	154	10.0	3	65	4.2	37	2.4	4.14	99	.300	.365	-2	-1	101	111	0.5	-1	2	0.0
Total 3	14	15	.483	75	20	8	0	3	302	360	10.7	10	131	3.9	67	2.0	5.16	81	.313	.372	-34	-33	101	100	0.7	1	4	-2.4
■ **ED HODGE**	Hodge, Ed Oliver b: 4/19/58, Bellflower, Cal. BL/TL, 6'2", 192 lbs. Deb: 5/01/84																											
1984 Min-A	4	3	.571	25	15	0	0	0	100	116	10.4	13	29	2.6	59	5.3	4.77	89	.291	.338	-9	-6	106	100	0.5	0	-2	-0.7
■ **ELI HODKEY**	Hodkey, Aloysius Joseph b: 11/3/17, Lorain, Ohio BL/TL, 6'4", 185 lbs. Deb: 9/12/46																											
1946 Phi-N	0	1	.000	2	1	0	0	0	4	9	20.3	0	5	11.3	0	0.0	13.50	25	.391	.500	-4	-5	98	75	-0.4	-0	-0	-0.4
■ **CHARLIE HODNETT**	Hodnett, Charles b: 1861, Iowa Deb: 5/03/1883																											
1883 StL-a	2	2	.500	4	4	3	0	0	32	28	7.9	1	7	2.0	6	1.7	1.41	246	.241	.284	7	7	105	192	-0.4	-0	0	0.7
1884 StL-U	12	2	.857	14	14	12	1	0	121	121	9.0	0	16	1.2	41	3.0	2.01	147	.265	.290	13	13	98	**139**	1.2	1	0	1.2
Total 2	14	4	.778	18	18	15	1	0	153	149	8.8	1	23	1.4	47	2.8	1.88	162	.260	.289	20	20	100	150	0.8	1	0	1.9
■ **GEORGE HODSON**	Hodson, George S. b: 1876, Hartford, Conn. Deb: 8/09/1894																											
1894 Bos-N	4	4	.500	12	11	8	0	0	74	103	12.5	4	35	4.3	12	1.5	5.84	102	.353	.422	-4	1	111	102	-0.8	-5	0	-0.1
1895 Phi-N	1	2	.333	4	2	1	0	0	17	27	14.3	4	9	4.8	6	3.2	9.53	49	.381	.451	-9	-9	98	89	-0.6	-1	0	-0.6
Total 2	5	6	.455	16	13	9	0	0	91	130	12.9	8	44	4.4	18	1.8	6.53	87	.358	.428	-13	-8	109	99	-1.4	-5	0	-0.7
■ **BILLY HOEFT**	Hoeft, William Frederick b: 5/17/32, Oshkosh, Wis. BL/TL, 6'3", 180 lbs. Deb: 4/18/52																											
1952 Det-A	2	7	.222	34	10	1	0	4	125	123	8.9	14	63	4.5	67	4.8	4.32	87	.260	.345	-9	-8	103	104	-1.4	-1	1	-0.7
1953 Det-A	9	14	.391	29	27	9	0	2	198	223	10.1	24	58	2.6	90	4.1	4.82	84	.283	.330	-18	-17	102	94	0.0	0	-1	-1.6
1954 Det-A	7	15	.318	34	25	10	4	1	175	180	9.3	22	59	3.0	114	5.9	4.58	82	.266	.323	-17	-16	101	90	-3.3	4	-2	-1.3
1955 Det-A	16	7	.696	32	29	17	**7**	0	220	187	7.7	17	75	3.1	133	5.4	2.99	126	.229	.295	24	19	95	96	**4.8**	4	-3	1.9
1956 Det-A	20	14	.588	38	34	18	4	0	248	276	10.0	22	104	3.8	172	6.2	4.06	97	.287	.352	3	-3	95	116	2.5	6	-3	0.0
1957 Det-A	9	11	.450	34	28	10	1	1	207	188	8.2	15	69	3.0	111	4.8	3.48	117	.244	.301	7	13	107	92	-1.2	1	-2	1.5
1958 Det-A	10	9	.526	36	21	6	0	3	143	148	9.3	15	49	3.1	94	5.9	4.15	93	.268	.322	-6	-4	103	98	0.6	4	-2	-0.1
1959 Det-A	1	1	.500	2	2	0	0	0	9	6	6.0	0	4	4.0	2	2.0	5.00	86	.188	.297	-1	-1	111	39	0.0	0	0	0.0
Bos-A	0	3	.000	5	3	0	0	0	18	22	11.0	1	8	4.0	8	4.0	5.50	74	.319	.373	-3	-3	105	102	-1.4	-0	0	-0.2
Bal-A	1	1	.500	16	3	0	0	0	41	50	11.0	6	19	4.2	30	6.6	5.71	66	.307	.371	-8	-9	98	102	0.0	1	0	-0.7
Yr	2	5	.286	23	8	0	0	0	68	78	10.3	7	31	4.1	40	5.3	5.56	71	.290	.356	-13	-12	102	102	-1.4	-0	0	-0.9
1960 Bal-A	2	1	.667	19	0	0	0	0	19	18	8.5	2	14	6.6	14	6.6	4.26	91	.240	.360	-1	-1	101	100	0.3	-0	0	0.0
1961 Bal-A	7	4	.636	35	12	3	1	3	138	106	6.9	7	55	3.6	100	6.5	2.02	191	.216	.289	**31**	28	96	130	0.7	1	1	3.1
1962 Bal-A	4	8	.333	57	4	0	0	7	114	103	8.1	7	43	3.4	73	5.8	4.58	82	.243	.307	-8	-10	95	72	-1.8	2	0	-0.7
1963 SF-N	2	0	1.000	23	0	0	0	4	24	26	9.8	5	10	3.8	8	3.0	4.50	69	.271	.333	-3	-4	94	113	1.0	1	-0	-0.3
1964 Mil-N	4	0	1.000	42	0	0	0	4	73	76	9.4	9	18	2.2	47	5.8	3.82	89	.271	.314	-2	-3	96	108	2.0	1	0	-0.1
1965 Chi-N	2	2	.500	29	2	1	0	1	51	41	7.2	3	20	3.5	44	7.8	2.82	129	.215	.281	4	5	103	89	0.2	1	-1	0.5
1966 Chi-N	1	2	.333	36	0	0	0	3	41	43	9.4	4	14	3.1	30	6.6	4.61	80	.264	.322	-5	-4	103	84	0.0	0	1	-0.3
SF-N	0	2	.000	4	0	0	0	0	4	4	9.0	0	3	6.8	3	6.8	6.75	52	.250	.368	-1	-1	97	56	-0.9	0	0	-0.1
Yr	1	4	.200	40	0	0	0	3	45	47	9.4	4	17	3.4	33	6.6	4.80	77	.261	.322	-6	-6	102	56	-0.9	0	1	-0.4
Total 15	97	101	.490	505	200	75	17	33	1848	1820	8.9	173	685	3.3	1140	5.6	3.94	98	.259	.321	-14	-18	100	99	2.1	24	-10	0.9

YEAR	TM/L	W	L	PCT	G	GS	CG	SHO	SV	IP	H	H/G	HR	BB	BB/G	SO	SO/G	ERA	/A	OAVG	OOBP	PR	/A	PF	CPI	WAT	PB	PD	TPI
■ ART HOELSKOETTER Hoelskoetter, Arthur "Holley" or "Hoss" (a.k.a. Arthur H. Hostetter) b: 9/30/1882, St.Louis, Mo. d: 8/3/54, St.Louis, Mo. BR/TR, 6'2", Deb: 9/10/05																													
1905	StL-N	0	1	.000	1	1	1	0	0	6	6	9.0	1	5	7.5	4	6.0	1.50	190	.287	.424	1	1	95	390	-0.4	0	0	0.1
1906	StL-N	1	4	.200	12	3	2	0	0	58	53	8.2	1	34	5.3	20	3.1	4.66	59	.271	.382	-13	-12	104	76	-1.0	1	-1	-1.2
1907	StL-N	0	0	—	2	0	0	0	0	11	9	7.4	0	10	8.2	8	6.5	5.73	43	.264	.456	-4	-4	100	74	0.0	0	-1	-0.3
Total	3	1	5	.167	15	4	3	0	0	75	68	8.2	2	49	5.9	32	3.8	4.56	59	.272	.397	-16	-15	103	101	-1.4	1	-1	-1.4
■ JOE HOERNER Hoerner, Joseph Walter b: 11/12/36, Dubuque, Iowa BR/TL, 6'1", 200 lbs. Deb: 9/27/63																													
1963	Hou-N	0	0	—	1	0	0	0	0	3	2	6.0	0	0	0.0	2	6.0	0.00	—	.182	.182	1	1	95	0	0.0	-0	0	0.1
1964	Hou-N	0	0	—	7	0	0	0	0	11	13	10.6	3	6	4.9	4	3.3	4.91	71	.310	.380	-2	-2	98	145	0.0	-0	0	-0.1
1966	StL-N	5	1	.833	57	0	0	0	13	76	57	6.8	5	21	2.5	63	7.5	1.54	234	.212	.271	17	17	100	154	2.0	1	-0	1.9
1967	StL-N	4	4	.500	57	0	0	0	15	66	52	7.1	5	20	2.7	50	6.8	2.59	129	.225	.272	6	6	99	109	-0.7	0	-0	0.6
1968	StL-N	8	2	.800	47	0	0	0	17	49	34	6.2	2	12	2.2	42	7.7	1.47	189	.192	.237	8	7	93	96	2.6	-1	-0	0.7
1969	StL-N	2	3	.400	45	0	0	0	15	53	44	7.5	5	9	1.5	35	5.9	2.89	123	.230	.261	4	4	99	92	-0.6	-1	0	0.4
1970	Phi-N	9	5	.643	44	0	0	0	9	58	53	8.2	5	20	3.1	39	6.1	2.64	150	.247	.302	9	9	98	134	2.6	1	-2	0.8
1971	Phi-N	4	5	.444	49	0	0	0	9	73	57	7.0	6	21	2.6	57	7.0	1.97	184	.215	.267	12	13	105	123	0.2	-1	-0	1.4
1972	Phi-N	0	2	.000	15	0	0	0	3	22	21	8.6	2	5	2.0	12	4.9	2.05	167	.259	.293	3	3	99	174	-0.9	-0	-0	0.3
	Atl-N	1	3	.250	25	0	0	0	2	23	34	13.3	4	8	3.1	19	7.4	6.65	55	.351	.387	-8	-8	106	106	-0.8	-0	-0	-0.8
	Yr	1	5	.167	40	0	0	0	5	45	55	11.0	6	13	2.6	31	6.2	4.40	81	.301	.340	-5	-4	102	106	-1.7	-0	-1	-0.5
1973	Atl-N	2	2	.500	20	0	0	0	2	13	17	11.8	1	4	2.8	10	6.9	6.23	66	.333	.375	-4	-3	113	88	0.1	0	-0	-0.3
	KC-A	2	0	1.000	22	0	0	0	4	19	28	13.3	0	13	6.2	15	7.1	5.21	80	.329	.410	-3	-2	109	112	1.0	0	-0	-0.2
1974	KC-A	2	3	.400	30	0	0	0	2	35	32	8.2	3	12	3.1	24	6.2	3.86	100	.244	.314	-1	-0	106	92	-0.3	0	-1	0.0
1975	Phi-N	0	0	—	25	0	0	0	0	21	25	10.7	3	8	3.4	20	8.6	2.57	143	.298	.354	2	3	101	206	0.0	-0	-1	0.2
1976	Tex-A	0	4	.000	41	0	0	0	8	35	41	10.5	3	19	4.9	15	3.9	5.14	70	.315	.373	-6	-6	103	112	-1.9	0	-1	-0.6
1977	Cin-N	0	0	—	8	0	0	0	0	6	9	13.5	3	3	4.5	5	7.5	12.00	32	.375	.469	-5	-5	99	100	0.0	0	-0	-0.4
Total	14	39	34	.534	493	0	0	0	99	563	519	8.3	50	181	2.9	412	6.6	2.99	120	.249	.302	35	37	101	122	3.3	-1	-6	4.0
■ LEFTY HOERST Hoerst, Frank Joseph b: 8/11/17, Philadelphia, Pa. BL/TL, 6'3", 192 lbs. Deb: 4/26/40																													
1940	Phi-N	1	0	1.000	6	0	0	0	0	12	12	9.0	1	8	6.0	3	2.3	5.25	75	.250	.351	-2	-2	102	84	0.5	-0	1	0.0
1941	Phi-N	3	10	.231	37	11	1	0	0	106	111	9.4	7	50	4.2	33	2.8	5.18	72	.275	.348	-18	-17	103	86	-1.1	0	2	-1.4
1942	Phi-N	4	16	.200	33	22	5	0	1	151	162	9.7	11	78	4.6	52	3.1	5.19	65	.271	.352	-31	-31	101	86	-3.0	-0	2	-2.9
1946	Phi-N	1	6	.143	18	7	2	0	0	68	77	10.2	4	36	4.8	17	2.3	4.63	72	.288	.369	-9	-10	98	102	-2.3	-1	-1	-1.1
1947	Phi-N	1	1	.500	4	1	0	0	0	11	19	15.5	1	3	2.5	0	0.0	8.18	51	.358	.393	-5	-5	102	80	0.2	1	0	-0.3
Total	5	10	33	.233	98	41	8	0	1	348	381	9.9	24	175	4.5	105	2.7	5.17	68	.279	.356	-66	-64	101	89	-5.7	-1	3	-5.7
■ RED HOFF Hoff, Chester Cornelius b: 5/8/1891, Ossining, N.Y. BL/TL, 5'9", 162 lbs. Deb: 9/06/11																													
1911	NY-A	0	1	.000	5	1	0	0	0	21	21	9.0	0	7	3.0	10	4.3	2.14	173	.262	.322	3	4	111	131	-0.4	0	1	0.5
1912	NY-A	0	1	.000	5	1	0	0	0	16	20	11.3	0	6	3.4	14	7.9	6.75	52	.303	.361	-6	-6	105	63	-0.4	-0	0	-0.5
1913	NY-A	0	0	—	2	0	0	0	0	3	0	0.0	0	1	3.0	2	6.0	0.00	—	.000	.111	1	1	104	0	0.0	-0	-0	0.1
1915	StL-A	2	2	.500	11	3	2	0	0	44	26	5.3	0	24	4.9	23	4.7	1.23	238	.169	.285	8	8	99	109	0.3	-1	1	0.9
Total	4	2	4	.333	23	5	2	0	0	84	67	7.2	0	38	4.1	49	5.3	2.46	131	.218	.305	6	7	103	102	-0.5	-1	2	1.0
■ BILL HOFFER Hoffer, William Leopold "Chick" or "Wizard" b: 11/8/1870, Cedar Rapids, Iowa d: 7/21/59, Cedar Rapids, Ia. BR/TR, 5'9", 155 lbs. Deb: 4/26/1895																													
1895	Bal-N	31	6	**.838**	41	38	32	**4**	0	314	296	8.5	9	124	3.6	80	2.3	3.21	155	.268	.342	55	61	104	103	**11.0**	-5	-2	4.8
1896	Bal-N	25	7	**.781**	35	35	32	3	0	309	317	9.2	1	95	2.8	93	2.7	3.38	127	.287	.343	34	32	99	94	5.4	10	2	4.0
1897	Bal-N	22	11	.667	38	33	29	1	0	303	350	10.4	5	104	3.1	62	1.8	4.31	92	.312	.370	0	-11	92	93	-0.7	2	1	-0.6
1898	Bal-N	0	4	.000	4	4	4	0	0	34	62	16.4	0	16	4.2	5	1.3	7.41	48	.417	.473	-14	-14	100	101	-1.9	0	0	-1.1
	Pit-N	3	0	1.000	4	3	3	0	0	31	26	7.5	0	15	4.4	11	3.2	1.74	203	.247	.341	6	6	98	155	1.5	-1	0	0.6
	Yr	3	4	.429	8	7	7	0	0	65	88	12.2	0	31	4.3	16	2.2	4.71	76	.347	.418	-8	-8	99	155	-0.4	0	0	-0.5
1899	Pit-N	8	10	.444	23	19	15	2	0	164	169	9.3	5	64	3.5	44	2.4	3.62	104	.289	.360	4	3	98	99	-1.2	-2	0	0.1
1901	Cle-A	3	8	.273	16	10	10	0	**3**	99	113	10.3	2	35	3.2	19	1.7	4.55	78	.307	.368	-10	-11	97	88	-1.8	-1	0	-0.8
Total	6	92	46	.667	161	142	125	10	3	1254	1333	9.6	22	453	3.3	314	2.3	3.75	112	.294	.358	76	65	98	98	12.3	3	2	7.0
■ DANNY HOFFMAN Hoffman, Daniel John b: 3/2/1880, Canaan, Conn. d: 3/14/22, Manchester, Conn. BL/TL, 5'9", 175 lbs. Deb: 4/20/03																													
1903	Phi-A	0	0	—	1	0	0	0	0	3	2	6.0	0	2	6.0	0	0.0	3.00	100	.208	.344	-0	0	102	82	0.0	0	-0	0.0
■ FRANK HOFFMAN Hoffman, Frank J. "The Texas Wonder" b: Houston, Tex. Deb: 1888																													
1888	KC-a	3	9	.250	12	12	12	0	0	104	102	8.8	5	42	3.6	38	3.3	2.77	124	.269	.342	3	8	112	135	-1.4	-2	0	0.7
■ GUY HOFFMAN Hoffman, Guy Alan b: 7/9/56, Ottawa, Ill. BL/TL, 5'9", 175 lbs. Deb: 7/04/79																													
1979	Chi-A	0	5	.000	24	0	0	0	2	30	30	9.0	0	23	6.9	18	5.4	5.40	80	.261	.380	-4	-4	103	80	-2.4	0	0	-0.2
1980	Chi-A	1	0	1.000	23	1	0	0	1	38	38	9.0	1	17	4.0	24	5.7	2.61	152	.268	.342	6	6	98	144	0.5	0	-1	0.5
1983	Chi-A	1	0	1.000	11	0	0	0	0	6	14	21.0	1	2	3.0	2	3.0	7.50	55	.483	.500	-2	-2	102	157	0.5	0	0	-0.1
1986	Chi-N	6	2	.750	32	8	1	0	0	84	92	9.9	6	29	3.1	47	5.0	3.86	104	.288	.345	-1	2	108	116	2.3	-1	-1	0.0
1987	Cin-N	9	10	.474	36	22	0	0	0	159	160	9.1	20	49	2.8	87	4.9	4.36	97	.265	.318	-5	-3	103	96	-0.8	-2	-1	-0.5
1988	Tex-A	0	0	—	11	0	0	0	0	22	22	9.0	5	8	3.3	9	3.7	5.32	76	.247	.313	-3	-3	102	86	0.0	0	0	-0.2
Total	6	17	17	.500	137	31	1	0	3	339	356	9.5	33	128	3.4	187	5.0	4.25	97	.274	.337	-9	-4	104	105	0.1	-2	-3	-0.5
■ BILL HOFFMAN Hoffman, William Joseph b: 3/3/18, Philadelphia, Pa. BL/TL, 5'9", 170 lbs. Deb: 8/13/39																													
1939	Phi-N	0	0	—	3	0	0	0	0	6	8	12.0	2	7	10.5	1	1.5	13.50	29	.333	.529	-6	-6	99	84	0.0	-0	0	-0.5
■ JOHN HOFFNER Hoffner, John Alexander b: 8/18/1871, Danville, Pa. d: 11/22/46, Danville, Pa. Deb: 1888																													
1888	KC-a	0	2	.000	2	2	2	0	0	18	24	12.0	0	16	8.0	5	2.5	7.00	49	.334	.455	-8	-7	112	93	-0.9	-1	0	-0.5
■ JOHN HOFFORD Hofford, John William b: 5/25/1863, Philadelphia, Pa. d: 12/16/15, Philadelphia, Pa. Deb: 1885																													
1885	Pit-a	0	3	.000	3	3	3	0	0	25	28	10.1	1	9	3.2	21	7.6	3.60	96	.295	.356	-1	-0	107	122	-1.4	-1	0	0.0
1886	Pit-a	3	6	.333	9	9	9	0	0	81	88	9.8	1	40	4.4	25	2.8	4.33	71	.287	.370	-8	-11	90	101	-1.9	3	0	-0.6
Total	2	3	9	.250	12	12	12	0	0	106	116	9.8	2	49	4.2	46	3.9	4.16	77	.289	.366	-9	-11	94	106	-3.3	3	0	-0.6
■ GEORGE HOGAN Hogan, George A. b: 9/25/1885, Marion, Ohio d: 2/22/22, Bartlesville, Okla BR/TR, 6', 160 lbs. Deb: 4/18/14																													
1914	KC-F	0	1	.000	4	1	0	0	0	13	12	8.3	1	7	4.8	7	4.8	4.15	74	.273	.373	-1	-2	96	94	-0.4	-1	0	-0.1
■ EDDIE HOGAN Hogan, Robert Edward b: 4/1860, St.Louis, Mo. BR , 5'7", 153 lbs. Deb: 7/05/1882																													
1882	StL-a	0	1	.000	1	1	1	0	0	8	10	11.3	0	0	0.0	4	4.5	1.13	248	.311	.311	1	1	104	301	-0.4	0	0	0.2
■ BRAD HOGG Hogg, Carter Bradley b: 3/26/1888, Buena Vista, Ga. d: 4/2/35, Buena Vista, Ga. BR/TR, 6', 185 lbs. Deb: 9/01/11																													
1911	Bos-N	0	3	.000	8	3	2	0	1	26	33	11.4	0	14	4.8	8	2.8	6.58	56	.337	.425	-9	-8	109	87	-1.4	1	0	-0.5
1912	Bos-N	1	1	.500	10	1	0	0	1	31	37	10.7	2	16	4.6	12	3.5	6.97	54	.289	.377	-12	-11	110	66	0.2	-1	-0	-1.0
1915	Chi-N	1	0	1.000	2	2	1	1	0	13	12	8.3	1	6	4.2	0	0.0	2.08	137	.245	.333	1	1	103	176	0.5	-0	0	0.1
1918	Phi-N	13	13	.500	29	25	17	3	1	228	201	7.9	3	61	2.4	81	3.2	2.53	122	.245	.290	6	14	111	100	1.5	3	2	2.3
1919	Phi-N	5	12	.294	22	19	13	0	0	150	163	9.8	7	55	3.3	48	2.9	4.44	71	.292	.346	-25	-21	109	97	-1.3	3	-2	-2.0
Total	5	20	29	.408	71	50	33	4	3	448	446	9.0	13	152	3.1	149	3.0	3.70	86	.270	.325	-40	-26	110	98	-0.5	6	0	-1.1
■ BILL HOGG Hogg, William "Buffalo Bill" b: 1880, Port Huron, Mich. d: 12/8/09, New Orleans, La. BR/TR, 6', Deb: 4/25/05																													
1905	NY-A	9	13	.409	39	22	9	3	1	205	178	7.8	1	101	4.4	125	5.5	3.20	85	.257	.352	-13	-11	103	96	-1.7	-5	-5	-1.6
1906	NY-A	14	13	.519	28	25	15	3	0	206	171	7.5	5	72	3.1	107	4.7	2.93	109	.249	.320	-5	6	118	88	-2.0	-5	-5	0.1
1907	NY-A	10	8	.556	25	21	13	0	0	167	173	9.3	3	83	4.5	64	3.4	3.07	91	.292	.379	-10	-5	110	125	1.6	-0	-1	-0.6
1908	NY-A	4	16	.200	24	21	6	0	0	152	155	9.2	4	63	3.7	72	4.3	3.02	80	.262	.337	-11	-10	101	119	-4.2	-3	-2	-1.2
Total	4	37	50	.425	116	89	43	6	1	730	677	8.3	13	319	3.9	368	4.5	3.06	91	.264	.347	-39	-21	108	105	-6.3	-14	-13	-3.3
■ CHIEF HOGSETT Hogsett, Elon Chester b: 11/2/03, Brownell, Kan. BL/TL, 6', 190 lbs. Deb: 9/18/29																													
1929	Det-A	1	2	.333	4	4	2	1	0	29	34	10.6	0	9	2.8	9	2.8	2.79	148	.312	.364	5	4	97	163	-0.3	-0	0	0.4
1930	Det-A	9	8	.529	33	17	4	0	1	146	174	10.7	9	63	3.9	54	3.3	5.42	91	.300	.367	-13	-8	106	98	0.8	2	2	-0.3

YEAR	TM/L	W	L	PCT	G	GS	CG	SHO	SV	IP	H	H/G	HR	BB	BB/G	SO	SO/G	ERA	/A	OAVG	OOBP	PR	/A	PF	CPI	WAT	PB	PD	TPI
1931	Det-A	3	9	.250	22	12	5	0	2	112	150	12.1	8	33	2.7	47	3.8	5.95	79	.324	.372	-19	-16	107	96	-2.2	-0	0	-1.3
1932	Det-A	11	9	.550	47	15	7	0	7	178	201	10.2	8	66	3.3	56	2.8	3.54	129	.286	.344	19	20	102	**129**	1.1	3	2	2.4
1933	Det-A	6	10	.375	45	2	0	0	9	116	137	10.6	7	56	4.3	39	3.0	4.50	102	.296	.370	-3	1	107	117	-1.9	-1	1	0.2
1934	Det-A	3	2	.600	26	0	0	0	3	50	61	11.0	4	19	3.4	23	4.1	4.32	98	.303	.357	1	-1	94	121	-0.1	0	1	0.0
1935	Det-A	6	6	.500	40	0	0	0	5	97	109	10.1	1	49	4.5	39	3.6	3.53	117	.288	.368	10	6	93	133	-1.1	2	3	1.0
1936	Det-A	0	1	.000	3	0	0	0	0	4	8	18.0	1	1	2.3	1	2.3	9.00	53	.400	.409	-2	-2	95	107	-0.4	0	0	0.0
	StL-A	13	15	.464	39	29	10	0	1	215	278	11.6	15	90	3.8	67	2.8	5.53	98	.310	.380	-12	-3	107	104	2.4	-3	1	-0.3
	Yr	13	16	.448	42	29	10	0	1	219	286	11.8	16	91	3.7	68	2.8	5.59	96	.312	.380	-13	-5	107	104	2.0	0	1	-0.3
1937	StL-A	6	19	.240	37	26	8	1	2	177	245	12.5	19	75	3.8	68	3.5	6.31	76	.328	.386	-33	-30	103	100	-2.7	0	-1	-2.6
1938	Was-A	5	6	.455	31	9	1	0	3	91	107	10.6	12	36	3.6	33	3.3	6.03	76	.292	.361	-13	-15	96	92	-0.4	3	0	-0.9
1944	Det-A	0	0	—	3	0	0	0	0	6	7	10.5	1	4	6.0	5	7.5	0.00	—	.250	.382	2	2	104	0	0.0	-0	0	0.2
Total	11	63	87	.420	330	114	37	2	33	1221	1511	11.1	85	501	3.7	441	3.3	5.03	94	.305	.369	-57	-41	103	110	-4.8	7	9	-1.2

■ CAL HOGUE Hogue, Calvin Grey b: 10/24/27, Dayton, Ohio BR/TR, 6', 185 lbs. Deb: 7/15/52

YEAR	TM/L	W	L	PCT	G	GS	CG	SHO	SV	IP	H	H/G	HR	BB	BB/G	SO	SO/G	ERA	/A	OAVG	OOBP	PR	/A	PF	CPI	WAT	PB	PD	TPI
1952	Pit-N	1	8	.111	19	12	3	0	0	84	79	8.5	7	68	7.3	34	3.6	4.82	81	.258	.392	-10	-8	105	109	-2.6	1	-2	-0.8
1953	Pit-N	1	1	.500	3	2	2	0	0	19	19	9.0	4	16	7.6	10	4.7	5.21	87	.250	.387	-2	-1	106	113	0.3	-1	0	-0.1
1954	Pit-N	0	1	.000	3	2	0	0	0	11	11	9.0	1	12	9.8	7	5.7	4.91	84	.282	.442	-1	-1	102	131	-0.4	-0	0	0.0
Total	3	2	10	.167	25	16	5	0	0	114	109	8.6	12	96	7.6	51	4.0	4.89	83	.259	.396	-13	-11	105	111	-2.7	0	-2	-0.9

■ BOBBY HOGUE Hogue, Robert Clinton b: 4/5/21, Miami, Fla. d: 12/22/87, Miami, Fla. BR/TR, 5'10", 195 lbs. Deb: 4/24/48

YEAR	TM/L	W	L	PCT	G	GS	CG	SHO	SV	IP	H	H/G	HR	BB	BB/G	SO	SO/G	ERA	/A	OAVG	OOBP	PR	/A	PF	CPI	WAT	PB	PD	TPI
1948	Bos-N	8	2	.800	40	1	0	0	2	86	88	9.2	4	19	2.0	43	4.5	3.24	120	.265	.304	7	6	99	103	2.6	-1	-1	0.4
1949	Bos-N	2	2	.500	33	0	0	0	3	72	78	9.8	4	25	3.1	23	2.9	3.13	125	.280	.334	7	6	97	134	0.1	1	2	0.9
1950	Bos-N	3	5	.375	36	1	0	0	7	63	69	9.9	8	31	4.4	15	2.1	5.00	71	.280	.366	-6	-10	85	104	-1.2	1	0	-0.8
1951	Bos-N	0	0	—	3	0	0	0	0	5	4	7.2	1	3	5.4	0	0.0	5.40	71	.235	.350	-1	-1	97	91	0.0	0	-0	0.0
	StL-A	1	1	.500	18	0	0	0	1	30	31	9.3	1	23	6.9	11	3.3	5.10	88	.279	.394	-3	-2	109	101	0.2	1	1	0.0
	NY-A	1	0	1.000	7	0	0	0	0	7	4	5.1	0	3	3.9	2	2.6	0.00	—	.174	.269	3	3	88	0	0.5	0	0	0.3
	Yr	2	1	.667	25	0	0	0	1	37	35	8.5	1	26	6.3	13	3.2	4.14	105	.261	.374	-0	1	105	0	0.7	1	1	0.3
1952	NY-A	3	5	.375	27	0	0	0	4	47	52	10.0	6	25	4.8	12	2.3	5.36	65	.294	.375	-9	-10	95	104	-1.5	0	-1	-1.0
	StL-A	0	1	.000	8	1	0	0	0	16	10	5.6	1	13	7.3	2	1.1	2.81	130	.179	.329	2	2	100	104	-0.4	-0	0	0.1
	Yr	3	6	.333	35	1	0	0	4	63	62	8.9	7	38	5.4	14	2.0	4.71	75	.265	.360	-7	-8	96	104	-1.9	0	-1	-0.9
Total	5	18	16	.529	172	3	0	0	17	326	336	9.3	25	142	3.9	108	3.0	3.98	96	.271	.343	-0	-6	96	108	0.3	3	1	-0.1

■ WALLY HOLBOROW Holborow, Walter Albert b: 11/30/13, New York, N.Y. d: 7/14/86, Ft.Lauderdale, Fla. BR/TR, 5'11", 187 lbs. Deb: 9/27/44

YEAR	TM/L	W	L	PCT	G	GS	CG	SHO	SV	IP	H	H/G	HR	BB	BB/G	SO	SO/G	ERA	/A	OAVG	OOBP	PR	/A	PF	CPI	WAT	PB	PD	TPI
1944	Was-A	0	0	—	1	0	0	0	0	3	0	0.0	0	2	6.0	1	3.0	0.00	—	.000	.182	1	1	91	0	0.0	0	0	0.1
1945	Was-A	1	1	.500	15	1	1	1	0	31	20	5.8	0	16	4.6	14	4.1	2.32	133	.189	.290	4	3	92	83	0.0	-0	-1	0.2
1948	Phi-A	1	2	.333	5	1	1	0	0	17	32	16.9	1	7	3.7	3	1.6	5.82	75	.421	.443	-3	-3	102	152	-0.5	1	1	0.0
Total	3	2	3	.400	21	2	2	1	0	51	52	9.2	1	25	4.4	18	3.2	3.35	104	.272	.345	2	1	95	101	-0.5	1	0	0.3

■ KEN HOLCOMBE Holcombe, Kenneth Edward b: 8/23/18, Burnsville, N.C. BR/TR, 5'11.5", 169 lbs. Deb: 4/27/45

YEAR	TM/L	W	L	PCT	G	GS	CG	SHO	SV	IP	H	H/G	HR	BB	BB/G	SO	SO/G	ERA	/A	OAVG	OOBP	PR	/A	PF	CPI	WAT	PB	PD	TPI
1945	NY-A	3	3	.500	23	2	0	0	0	55	43	7.0	2	27	4.4	20	3.3	1.80	198	.226	.308	10	11	106	168	-0.1	-1	-0	1.0
1948	Cin-N	0	0	—	2	0	0	0	0	2	3	13.5	0	0	0.0	2	9.0	9.00	47	.300	.300	-1	-1	106	35	0.0	0	0	0.0
1950	Chi-A	3	10	.231	24	15	5	0	1	96	122	11.4	10	45	4.2	37	3.5	4.59	99	.307	.372	-0	-1	99	121	-2.7	-2	-0	-0.1
1951	Chi-A	11	12	.478	28	23	12	2	0	159	142	8.0	9	68	3.8	39	2.2	3.79	104	.241	.315	6	3	96	90	-1.1	1	3	0.6
1952	Chi-A	0	5	.000	7	7	1	0	0	35	38	9.8	3	18	4.6	12	3.1	6.17	59	.286	.374	-10	-10	99	82	-2.4	-1	0	-0.9
	StL-A	0	2	.000	12	1	0	0	0	21	20	8.6	1	9	3.9	7	3.0	3.86	95	.263	.326	-0	-0	100	99	-0.9	0	0	0.0
	Yr	0	7	.000	19	8	1	0	0	56	58	9.3	4	27	4.3	19	3.1	5.30	69	.275	.348	-10	-10	99	99	-3.3	-1	1	-0.9
1953	Bos-A	1	0	1.000	3	0	0	0	1	6	9	13.5	0	3	4.5	1	1.5	6.00	72	.333	.400	-1	-1	108	93	0.5	-0	0	0.0
Total	6	18	32	.360	99	48	18	2	2	374	377	9.1	25	170	4.1	118	2.8	3.99	100	.265	.337	3	0	99	109	-6.7	-3	3	0.6

■ FRED HOLDSWORTH Holdsworth, Fredrick William b: 5/29/52, Detroit, Mich. BR/TR, 6'1", 190 lbs. Deb: 7/27/72

YEAR	TM/L	W	L	PCT	G	GS	CG	SHO	SV	IP	H	H/G	HR	BB	BB/G	SO	SO/G	ERA	/A	OAVG	OOBP	PR	/A	PF	CPI	WAT	PB	PD	TPI
1972	Det-A	0	1	.000	2	2	0	0	0	7	13	16.7	0	2	2.6	5	6.4	12.86	27	.419	.441	-8	-7	112	58	-0.4	0	0	-0.6
1973	Det-A	0	1	.000	5	2	0	0	0	15	13	7.8	3	6	3.6	9	5.4	6.60	59	.236	.306	-5	-5	101	62	-0.4	0	-0	-0.4
1974	Det-A	0	3	.000	8	5	0	0	0	36	40	10.0	4	14	3.5	16	4.0	4.25	92	.286	.348	-3	-1	108	110	-1.4	0	-1	-0.2
1976	Bal-A	4	1	.800	16	0	0	0	2	40	24	5.4	0	13	2.9	24	5.4	2.02	169	.179	.248	7	6	97	61	1.4	0	-0	0.6
1977	Bal-A	0	1	.000	12	0	0	0	0	14	17	10.9	0	16	10.3	4	2.6	6.43	59	.333	.466	-4	-4	92	117	-0.4	0	-0	-0.3
	Mon-N	3	3	.500	14	6	0	0	0	42	35	7.5	6	18	3.9	21	4.5	3.21	121	.230	.306	3	3	99	113	0.2	-1	0	0.2
1978	Mon-N	0	0	—	6	0	0	0	0	9	16	16.0	3	8	8.0	3	3.0	7.00	49	.381	.480	-3	-4	96	155	0.0	0	0	-0.3
1980	Mil-A	0	0	—	9	0	0	0	0	20	24	10.8	2	9	4.0	12	5.4	4.50	84	.286	.355	-1	-2	93	103	0.0	0	0	0.0
Total	7	7	10	.412	72	15	0	0	2	183	182	9.0	18	86	4.2	94	4.6	4.38	85	.264	.341	-13	-13	100	96	-1.0	-1	-1	-1.0

■ WALTER HOLKE Holke, Walter Henry "Union Man" b: 12/25/1892, St.Louis, Mo. d: 10/12/54, St.Louis, Mo. BB/TL, 6'1.5", 185 lbs. Deb: 10/06/14 C

YEAR	TM/L	W	L	PCT	G	GS	CG	SHO	SV	IP	H	H/G	HR	BB	BB/G	SO	SO/G	ERA	/A	OAVG	OOBP	PR	/A	PF	CPI	WAT	PB	PD	TPI
1923	Phi-N	0	0	—	1	0	0	0	0	⅓	1	27.0	0	0	0.0	0	0.0	0.00	—	.500	.500	0	0	118	0	0.0	0	0	0.0

■ AL HOLLAND Holland, Alfred Willis b: 8/16/52, Roanoke, Va. BR/TL, 5'11", 207 lbs. Deb: 9/05/77

YEAR	TM/L	W	L	PCT	G	GS	CG	SHO	SV	IP	H	H/G	HR	BB	BB/G	SO	SO/G	ERA	/A	OAVG	OOBP	PR	/A	PF	CPI	WAT	PB	PD	TPI
1977	Pit-N	0	0	—	2	0	0	0	0	2	4	18.0	0	0	0.0	1	4.5	9.00	44	.400	.400	-1	-1	102	74	0.0	0	0	0.0
1979	SF-N	0	0	—	3	0	0	0	0	7	3	3.9	0	5	6.4	7	9.0	0.00	—	.125	.276	3	3	93	0	0.0	0	-0	0.3
1980	SF-N	5	3	.625	54	0	0	0	7	82	71	7.8	2	34	3.7	65	7.1	1.76	198	.233	.304	17	16	96	157	1.2	1	0	1.9
1981	SF-N	7	5	.583	47	3	0	0	7	101	87	7.8	4	44	3.9	78	7.0	2.41	152	.233	.309	12	14	105	125	1.0	-1	-1	1.4
1982	SF-N	7	3	.700	58	7	0	0	5	130	115	8.0	12	40	2.8	97	6.7	3.32	102	.231	.286	4	1	94	86	1.8	-2	0	-0.1
1983	Phi-N	8	4	.667	68	0	0	0	25	92	63	6.2	8	30	2.9	100	9.8	2.25	162	.188	.251	14	14	100	80	1.6	-1	-2	1.2
1984	Phi-N	5	10	.333	68	0	0	0	29	98	82	7.5	14	30	2.8	61	5.6	3.40	107	.225	.280	2	3	101	94	-2.6	-1	-2	0.0
1985	Phi-N	0	1	.000	3	0	0	0	1	4	5	11.3	0	4	9.0	1	2.3	4.50	82	.333	.429	-0	-0	102	153	-0.4	0	0	0.0
	Pit-N	1	3	.250	38	0	0	0	4	59	48	7.3	5	17	2.6	47	7.2	3.36	112	.227	.277	2	3	104	84	-0.5	2	-1	0.4
	Yr	1	4	.200	41	0	0	0	5	63	53	7.6	5	21	3.0	48	6.9	3.43	109	.233	.289	1	2	104	84	-0.9	0	-0	0.4
	Cal-A	0	1	.000	15	0	0	0	0	24	17	6.4	4	10	3.8	14	5.3	1.50	278	.193	.273	7	7	101	194	-0.4	0	-0	0.7
1986	NY-A	1	0	1.000	25	1	0	0	0	41	44	9.7	5	9	2.0	37	8.1	5.05	85	.268	.299	-4	-3	103	76	0.5	0	-1	-0.3
1987	NY-A	0	0	—	3	0	0	0	0	6	9	13.5	1	9	13.5	5	7.5	15.00	29	.321	.486	-7	-7	97	62	0.0	0	0	-0.5
Total	10	34	30	.531	384	11	0	0	78	646	548	7.6	55	232	3.2	513	7.1	2.98	122	.227	.290	49	48	100	104	2.2	-2	-5	5.0

■ MUL HOLLAND Holland, Howard Arthur b: 1/6/03, Franklin, Va. d: 2/16/69, Winchester, Va. BR/TR, 6'4", 185 lbs. Deb: 5/25/26

YEAR	TM/L	W	L	PCT	G	GS	CG	SHO	SV	IP	H	H/G	HR	BB	BB/G	SO	SO/G	ERA	/A	OAVG	OOBP	PR	/A	PF	CPI	WAT	PB	PD	TPI
1926	Cin-N	0	0	—	3	0	0	0	0	7	3	3.9	0	5	6.4	0	0.0	1.29	277	.136	.286	2	2	93	114	0.0	0	1	0.3
1927	NY-N	1	0	1.000	2	0	0	0	0	2	0	0.0	0	3	13.5	0	0.0	0.00	—	.000	.333	1	1	98	0	0.5	0	0	0.1
1929	StL-N	0	1	.000	8	0	0	0	0	14	13	8.4	3	7	4.5	5	3.2	9.64	48	.232	.323	-8	-8	98	46	-0.4	0	-0	-0.6
Total	3	1	1	.500	13	0	0	0	0	23	16	6.3	3	15	5.9	5	2.0	6.26	67	.190	.314	-5	-5	97	62	0.1	1	1	-0.2

■ BILL HOLLAND Holland, William David "Dutch" b: 6/4/15, Varina, N.C. BL/TL, 6'1", 190 lbs. Deb: 9/17/39

YEAR	TM/L	W	L	PCT	G	GS	CG	SHO	SV	IP	H	H/G	HR	BB	BB/G	SO	SO/G	ERA	/A	OAVG	OOBP	PR	/A	PF	CPI	WAT	PB	PD	TPI
1939	Was-A	0	1	.000	3	0	0	0	0	4	6	13.5	1	5	11.3	2	4.5	11.25	38	.400	.524	-3	-3	91	104	-0.4	0	0	-0.2

■ ED HOLLEY Holley, Edward Edgar b: 7/23/1899, Benton, Ky. d: 10/26/86, Paducah, Ky. BR/TR, 6'1.5", 195 lbs. Deb: 5/24/28

YEAR	TM/L	W	L	PCT	G	GS	CG	SHO	SV	IP	H	H/G	HR	BB	BB/G	SO	SO/G	ERA	/A	OAVG	OOBP	PR	/A	PF	CPI	WAT	PB	PD	TPI
1928	Chi-N	0	0	—	13	1	0	0	0	31	31	9.0	1	16	4.6	10	2.9	3.77	98	.265	.358	1	-0	93	105	0.0	-0	-1	0.0
1932	Phi-N	11	14	.440	34	30	16	2	0	228	247	9.8	15	55	2.2	87	3.4	3.95	109	.273	.316	-2	9	111	95	-1.8	-6	-2	0.3
1933	Phi-N	13	15	.464	30	28	12	3	0	207	219	9.5	18	62	2.7	56	2.4	3.52	115	.273	.328	-4	12	121	116	1.9	-3	-3	0.9
1934	Phi-N	1	8	.111	15	13	2	0	0	73	85	10.5	10	31	3.8	14	1.7	7.15	63	.294	.366	-25	-22	111	77	-3.1	-1	-1	-2.0
	Pit-N	0	3	.000	5	4	0	0	0	9	20	20.0	1	6	6.0	2	2.0	16.00	27	.426	.509	-12	-12	105	70	-1.4	2	0	-0.8
	Yr	1	11	.083	20	17	2	0	0	82	105	11.5	11	37	4.1	16	1.8	8.12	55	.309	.376	-37	-33	110	70	-4.5	-1	-1	-2.8
Total	4	25	40	.385	97	76	30	5	0	548	602	9.9	45	170	2.8	169	2.8	4.40	96	.279	.334	-42	-11	114	100	-4.4	-9	-6	-1.6

■ BUG HOLLIDAY Holliday, James Wear b: 2/8/1867, St.Louis, Mo. d: 2/15/10, Cincinnati, Ohio BR/TR, 5'11", 151 lbs. Deb: 4/17/1889

YEAR	TM/L	W	L	PCT	G	GS	CG	SHO	SV	IP	H	H/G	HR	BB	BB/G	SO	SO/G	ERA	/A	OAVG	OOBP	PR	/A	PF	CPI	WAT	PB	PD	TPI
1892	Cin-N	0	0	—	1	0	0	0	0	4	13	29.3	0	1	2.3	0	0.0	11.25	30	.550	.568	-4	-3	103	124	0.0	0	0	-0.2
1896	Cin-N	0	0	—	1	0	0	0	0	1	4	36.0	0	2	18.0	0	0.0	0.00	—	.611	.702	0	1	103	0	0.0	0	0	0.0

YEAR	TM/L	W	L	PCT	G	GS	CG	SHO	SV	IP	H	H/G	HR	BB	BB/G	SO	SO/G	ERA	/A	OAVG	OOBP	PR	/A	PF	CPI	WAT	PB	PD	TPI
Total	2	0	0	—	2	0	0	0	0	5	17	30.6	0	3	5.4	0	0.0	9.00	40	.563	.603	-3	-3	103	99	0.0	1	0	-0.2
■ **CARL HOLLING**	Holling, Carl b: 7/9/1896, Dana, Cal. d: 7/18/62, Sonoma, Cal. BR/TR, 6'1", 172 lbs. Deb: 4/19/21																												
1921	Det-A	3	7	.300	35	11	4	0	4	136	162	10.7	8	58	3.8	38	2.5	4.30	95	.305	.363	-0	-3	96	115	-1.7	2	2	0.0
1922	Det-A	1	1	.500	5	1	0	0	0	9	21	21.0	1	5	5.0	2	2.0	16.00	25	.525	.560	-12	-12	97	84	0.0	-0	0	-1.0
Total	2	4	8	.333	40	12	4	0	4	145	183	11.4	9	63	3.9	40	2.5	5.03	81	.320	.378	-12	-15	96	113	-1.7	1	2	-1.0
■ **AL HOLLINGSWORTH**	Hollingsworth, Albert Wayne "Boots" b: 2/25/08, St.Louis, Mo. BL/TL, 6', 174 lbs. Deb: 4/16/35 C																												
1935	Cin-N	6	13	.316	38	22	8	0	0	173	165	8.6	5	76	4.0	89	4.6	3.90	98	.243	.316	2	-1	95	81	-2.9	-2	1	-0.2
1936	Cin-N	9	10	.474	29	25	9	0	0	184	204	10.0	4	66	3.2	76	3.7	4.16	94	.281	.340	-3	-5	97	96	-0.1	7	-2	0.0
1937	Cin-N	9	15	.375	43	24	11	1	5	202	224	10.0	8	73	3.3	74	3.3	3.92	93	.278	.334	-0	-6	93	101	0.3	3	1	-0.2
1938	Cin-N	2	2	.500	9	4	1	0	0	34	43	11.4	2	12	3.2	13	3.4	7.15	51	.307	.350	-13	-13	96	69	-0.1	1	0	-1.1
	Phi-N	5	16	.238	24	21	11	1	0	174	177	9.2	4	77	4.0	80	4.1	3.83	105	.264	.336	-1	3	106	97	-2.3	-0	-3	0.1
	Yr	7	18	.280	33	25	12	1	0	208	220	9.5	6	89	3.9	93	4.0	4.37	90	.272	.339	-13	-10	104	97	-2.4	1	-2	-1.0
1939	Phi-N	1	9	.100	15	10	3	0	0	60	78	11.7	2	27	4.1	24	3.6	5.85	67	.317	.371	-13	-13	99	89	-3.3	-1	-0	-1.3
	Bro-N	1	2	.333	8	5	1	0	0	27	33	11.0	1	11	3.7	11	3.7	5.33	78	.311	.369	-4	-4	106	95	-0.5	-1	1	-0.2
	Yr	2	11	.154	23	15	4	0	0	87	111	11.5	3	38	3.9	35	3.6	5.69	70	.315	.370	-17	-17	101	95	-3.8	-1	1	-1.5
1940	Was-A	1	0	1.000	3	2	0	0	0	18	18	9.0	0	11	5.5	7	3.5	5.50	76	.261	.358	-2	-3	95	73	0.5	0	1	-0.1
1942	StL-A	10	6	.625	33	18	7	1	4	161	173	9.7	4	52	2.9	60	3.4	2.96	126	.272	.323	12	14	102	124	1.6	-0	0	1.5
1943	StL-A	6	13	.316	35	20	9	1	3	154	169	9.9	7	51	3.0	63	3.7	4.21	79	.281	.332	-16	-15	101	95	-3.4	-1	-1	-1.7
1944	StL-A	5	7	.417	26	10	3	2	1	93	108	10.5	3	37	3.6	22	2.1	4.45	77	.291	.348	-11	-11	100	96	-1.7	-1	-1	-1.2
1945	StL-A	12	9	.571	26	22	15	1	1	173	164	8.5	4	68	3.5	64	3.3	2.71	142	.251	.315	13	22	114	116	0.9	0	2	2.8
1946	StL-A	0	0	—	5	0	0	0	0	11	23	18.8	1	4	3.3	3	2.5	6.55	53	.411	.450	-4	-4	100	134	0.0	-0	-0	-0.3
	Chi-A	3	2	.600	21	2	0	0	1	55	63	10.3	2	22	3.6	22	3.6	4.58	74	.288	.344	-7	-7	97	91	0.6	-1	-0	-0.8
	Yr	3	2	.600	26	2	0	0	1	66	86	11.7	3	26	3.5	25	3.4	4.91	70	.313	.365	-10	-11	98	91	0.6	-0	-1	-1.1
Total	11	70	104	.402	315	185	78	7	15	1519	1642	9.7	47	587	3.5	608	3.6	3.99	94	.275	.335	-45	-41	101	99	-10.4	2	-2	-2.7
■ **BONNIE HOLLINGSWORTH**	Hollingsworth, John Burnette b: 12/26/1895, Jacksboro, Tenn. BR/TR, 5'10", 170 lbs. Deb: 5/30/22																												
1922	Pit-N	0	0	—	9	0	0	0	0	14	17	10.9	0	8	5.1	7	4.5	7.71	54	.315	.394	-6	-6	101	68	0.0	0	-0	-0.4
1923	Was-A	3	7	.300	17	8	1	0	0	73	72	8.9	3	50	6.2	26	3.2	4.07	93	.272	.375	-1	-2	95	115	-1.9	-1	-1	-0.3
1924	Bro-N	1	0	1.000	3	1	1	0	0	9	8	8.0	0	10	10.0	7	7.0	6.00	63	.267	.429	-2	-2	98	92	0.5	-0	0	-0.1
1928	Bos-N	0	2	.000	7	2	0	0	0	22	30	12.3	2	13	5.3	10	4.1	5.32	76	.341	.406	-3	-3	101	124	-0.9	-0	0	-0.2
Total	4	4	9	.308	36	11	2	0	0	118	127	9.7	5	81	6.2	50	3.8	4.88	79	.291	.388	-12	-13	97	109	-2.3	-2	-1	-1.0
■ **JOHN HOLLISON**	Hollison, John Henry "Swede" b: 5/3/1870, Chicago, Ill. d: 8/19/69, Chicago, Ill. BR/TL, 5'8", 162 lbs. Deb: 8/13/1892																												
1892	Chi-N	0	0	—	1	0	0	0	0	4	1	2.3	1	0	0.0	2	4.5	2.25	136	.086	.086	0	0	93	11	0.0	-0	0	0.0
■ **BOBO HOLLOMAN**	Holloman, Alva Lee b: 3/7/25, Thomaston, Ga. d: 5/1/87, Athens, Ga. BR/TR, 6'2", 207 lbs. Deb: 4/18/53																												
1953	StL-A	3	7	.300	22	10	1	1	0	65	69	9.6	2	50	6.9	25	3.5	5.26	84	.275	.393	-9	-6	111	94	-0.7	-2	0	-0.7
■ **JIM HOLLOWAY**	Holloway, James Madison b: 9/22/08, Plaquemine, La. BR/TR, 6'1", 165 lbs. Deb: 5/17/29																												
1929	Phi-N	0	0	—	3	0	0	0	0	5	10	18.0	2	5	9.0	1	1.8	12.60	42	.455	.556	-4	-4	112	112	0.0	0	-0	-0.2
■ **KEN HOLLOWAY**	Holloway, Kenneth Eugene (born Kenneth Eugene Hollaway) b: 8/8/1897, Thomas County, Ga. d: 9/25/68, Thomasville, Ga. BR/TR, 6', 185 lbs. Deb: 8/27/22																												
1922	Det-A	0	0	—	1	0	0	0	0	1	1	9.0	0	0	0.0	1	9.0	0.00	—	.250	.200	0	0	97	0	0.0	0	0	0.0
1923	Det-A	11	10	.524	42	24	7	1	1	194	232	10.8	12	75	3.5	55	2.6	4.45	85	.302	.361	-10	-14	95	108	-0.2	-5	1	-1.6
1924	Det-A	14	6	.700	49	14	5	0	3	181	209	10.4	6	61	3.0	46	2.3	4.08	102	.299	.348	3	2	99	108	3.5	-1	2	0.2
1925	Det-A	13	4	.765	38	14	6	0	2	158	170	9.7	8	67	3.8	29	1.7	4.61	93	.282	.343	-4	-5	98	91	4.5	-0	-2	-0.7
1926	Det-A	4	6	.400	36	12	3	0	2	139	192	12.4	2	42	2.7	43	2.8	5.12	77	.343	.381	-17	-18	98	107	-1.1	1	0	-1.6
1927	Det-A	11	12	.478	36	23	11	1	6	183	210	10.3	10	61	3.0	36	1.8	4.08	109	.299	.342	1	7	107	111	-1.3	-6	2	0.3
1928	Det-A	4	8	.333	30	11	5	0	2	120	137	10.3	2	32	2.4	32	2.4	4.35	93	.291	.328	-4	-4	100	91	-1.5	-2	1	-0.4
1929	Cle-A	6	5	.545	25	11	6	2	0	119	118	8.9	2	37	2.8	32	2.4	3.03	141	.264	.317	16	16	101	108	0.2	-1	-2	1.3
1930	Cle-A	1	1	.500	12	2	0	0	2	30	49	14.7	5	14	4.2	8	2.4	8.40	58	.374	.420	-12	-12	105	100	0.0	-2	1	-1.0
	NY-A	0	0	—	16	0	0	0	0	34	52	13.8	3	8	2.1	11	2.9	5.29	77	.374	.385	-2	-5	87	134	0.0	-0	0	-0.4
	Yr	1	1	.500	28	2	0	0	2	64	101	14.2	8	22	3.1	19	2.7	6.75	66	.374	.402	-15	-16	96	134	0.0	-2	1	-1.4
Total	9	64	52	.552	285	111	43	4	18	1159	1370	10.6	50	397	3.1	293	2.3	4.40	94	.303	.351	-29	-32	99	105	4.1	-18	4	-3.9
■ **JEFF HOLLY**	Holly, Jeffrey Owen b: 3/1/53, San Pedro, Cal. BL/TL, 6'5", 210 lbs. Deb: 5/01/77																												
1977	Min-A	2	3	.400	18	5	0	0	0	48	57	10.7	8	12	2.3	32	6.0	6.94	60	.300	.338	-15	-15	102	75	-0.5	0	-1	-1.4
1978	Min-A	1	1	.500	15	1	0	0	0	35	28	7.2	1	18	4.6	12	3.1	3.60	99	.222	.307	1	-0	94	77	0.1	0	0	0.0
1979	Min-A	0	0	—	6	0	0	0	0	6	10	15.0	0	3	4.5	5	7.5	7.50	61	.385	.419	-2	-2	108	96	0.0	0	0	-0.1
Total	3	3	4	.429	39	6	0	0	0	89	95	9.6	9	33	3.3	49	5.0	5.66	70	.278	.332	-17	-17	99	77	-0.4	0	-0	-1.5
■ **BRIAN HOLMAN**	Holman, Brian Scott b: 1/25/65, Denver, Colo. BR/TR, 6'4", 185 lbs. Deb: 6/25/88																												
1988	Mon-N	4	8	.333	18	16	1	1	0	100	101	9.1	3	34	3.1	58	5.2	3.24	112	.264	.320	2	4	105	107	-2.0	-1	-1	0.2
■ **SCOTT HOLMAN**	Holman, Randy Scott b: 9/18/58, Santa Paula, Cal. BR/TR, 6'1", 190 lbs. Deb: 9/20/80																												
1980	NY-N	0	0	—	4	0	0	0	0	7	6	7.7	0	1	1.3	3	3.9	1.29	272	.250	.269	2	2	97	185	0.0	0	-0	0.1
1982	NY-N	2	1	.667	4	4	1	0	0	27	23	7.7	2	7	2.3	11	3.7	2.33	155	.232	.280	4	4	100	116	0.7	0	1	0.5
1983	NY-N	1	7	.125	35	10	0	0	0	101	90	8.0	7	52	4.6	44	3.9	3.74	97	.242	.326	-1	-1	100	97	-2.8	0	2	0.1
Total	3	3	8	.273	43	14	1	0	0	135	119	7.9	9	60	4.0	58	3.9	3.33	109	.240	.315	4	4	100	105	-2.1	1	2	0.7
■ **CHICK HOLMES**	Holmes, Elwood Marter b: 3/22/1896, Beverly, N.J. d: 4/15/54, Camden, N, J. TR , Deb: 6/27/18																												
1918	Phi-A	0	0	—	2	0	0	0	0	2	4	18.0	0	1	4.5	0	0.0	13.50	22	.400	.500	-2	-2	108	68	0.0	0	0	-0.2
■ **JIM HOLMES**	Holmes, James Scott b: 8/2/1882, Lawrenceburg, Ky. d: 3/10/60, Jacksonville, Fla. Deb: 9/08/06																												
1906	Phi-A	0	1	.000	3	1	0	0	0	9	10	10.0	0	8	8.0	1	1.0	4.00	62	.308	.444	-1	-2	93	132	-0.4	1	0	-0.1
1908	Bro-N	1	4	.200	13	1	1	0	0	40	37	8.3	0	20	4.5	10	2.3	3.37	68	.280	.386	-5	-5	99	100	-1.0	-1	-2	-0.6
Total	2	1	5	.167	16	2	1	0	0	49	47	8.6	0	28	5.1	11	2.0	3.49	67	.285	.398	-6	-6	97	106	-1.4	0	-2	-0.7
■ **DUCKY HOLMES**	Holmes, James William b: 1/28/1869, Des Moines, Iowa d: 8/6/32, Truro, Iowa BL/TR, 5'6", 170 lbs. Deb: 8/08/1895																												
1895	Lou-N	1	0	1.000	2	1	1	0	0	14	16	10.3	1	4	2.6	0	0.0	5.79	82	.307	.357	-2	-2	99	75	0.5	1	0	0.0
1896	Lou-N	0	1	.000	2	1	0	0	0	12	26	19.5	0	8	6.0	3	2.3	7.50	59	.459	.526	-4	-4	102	131	-0.4	0	0	-0.2
Total	2	1	1	.500	4	2	1	0	0	26	42	14.5	1	12	4.2	3	1.0	6.58	70	.387	.448	-6	-6	100	101	0.1	1	0	-0.2
■ **HERM HOLSHOUSER**	Holshouser, Herman Alexander b: 1/20/07, Rockwell, N.C. BR/TR, 6', 170 lbs. Deb: 4/15/30																												
1930	StL-A	0	1	.000	25	1	0	0	1	62	103	15.0	8	28	4.1	37	5.4	7.84	65	.376	.427	-22	-19	110	106	-0.4	-1	-0	-1.6
■ **VERN HOLTGRAVE**	Holtgrave, Lavern George "Woody" b: 10/18/42, Aviston, Ill. BR/TR, 6'1", 183 lbs. Deb: 9/26/65																												
1965	Det-A	0	0	—	1	0	0	0	0	3	4	12.0	0	2	6.0	2	6.0	6.00	60	.308	.400	-1	-1	104	87	0.0	0	0	0.0
■ **BRIAN HOLTON**	Holton, Brian John b: 11/29/59, Mc Keesport, Pa. BR/TR, 6'2", 190 lbs. Deb: 9/09/85																												
1985	LA-N	1	1	.500	3	0	0	0	0	4	9	20.3	0	1	2.3	1	2.3	9.00	37	.450	.476	-2	-3	92	102	0.0	0	0	-0.2
1986	LA-N	2	3	.400	12	3	0	0	0	24	28	10.5	1	6	2.3	24	9.0	4.50	78	.292	.330	-2	-3	95	91	-0.2	-0	0	-0.2
1987	LA-N	3	2	.600	53	1	0	0	2	83	87	9.4	11	32	3.5	58	6.3	3.90	96	.269	.331	2	-1	92	114	0.7	0	1	0.0
1988	LA-N	7	3	.700	45	0	0	0	1	85	69	7.3	1	26	2.8	49	5.2	1.69	214	.228	.283	17	18	105	145	1.5	-1	-0	1.9
Total	4	13	9	.591	113	4	0	0	3	196	193	8.9	13	65	3.0	132	6.1	3.12	118	.260	.315	14	12	98	125	2.0	-1	1	1.5
■ **KEN HOLTZMAN**	Holtzman, Kenneth Dale b: 11/3/45, St.Louis, Mo. BR/TL, 6'2", 175 lbs. Deb: 9/04/65																												
1965	Chi-N	0	0	—	3	0	0	0	0	4	2	4.5	1	3	6.8	3	6.8	2.25	162	.143	.278	1	1	103	150	0.0	0	0	0.1
1966	Chi-N	11	16	.407	34	33	9	0	0	221	194	7.9	27	68	2.8	171	7.0	3.79	98	.235	.292	-4	-2	103	86	1.1	-3	-2	-0.6
1967	Chi-N	9	0	1.000	12	12	3	0	0	93	76	7.4	11	44	4.3	62	6.0	2.52	134	.222	.311	9	9	100	137	4.5	1	0	1.1
1968	Chi-N	11	14	.440	34	32	6	3	1	215	201	8.4	17	76	3.2	151	6.3	3.35	100	.248	.312	-9	0	112	102	-2.1	-3	1	0.0

YEAR	TM/L	W	L	PCT	G	GS	CG	SHO	SV	IP	H	H/G	HR	BB	BB/G	SO	SO/G	ERA	/A	OAVG	OOBP	PR	/A	PF	CPI	WAT	PB	PD	TPI
1969	Chi-N	17	13	.567	39	39	12	6	0	261	248	8.6	18	93	3.2	176	6.1	3.59	106	.247	.311	0	6	105	92	0.0	-0	-1	0.5
1970	Chi-N	17	11	.607	39	38	15	1	0	288	271	8.5	30	94	2.9	202	6.3	3.38	142	.248	.305	22	46	119	107	3.0	1	0	5.2
1971	Chi-N	9	15	.375	30	29	9	3	0	195	213	9.8	18	64	3.0	143	6.6	4.48	85	.276	.329	-22	-14	110	91	-3.5	-1	-0	-1.5
1972	Oak-A	19	11	.633	39	37	16	4	0	265	232	7.9	23	52	1.8	134	4.6	2.51	115	.236	.272	16	11	95	107	1.5	1	0	1.4
1973	Oak-A	21	13	.618	40	40	16	4	0	297	275	8.3	22	66	2.0	157	4.8	2.97	110	.243	.285	28	10	86	94	1.9	0	-1	0.9
1974	Oak-A	19	17	.528	39	38	9	3	0	255	273	9.6	14	51	1.8	117	4.1	3.07	116	.272	.305	16	14	99	107	-1.0	0	0	1.5
1975	Oak-A	18	14	.563	39	38	13	2	0	266	217	7.3	16	108	3.7	122	4.1	3.15	110	.222	.299	19	9	91	87	-1.3	0	3	1.2
1976	Bal-A	5	4	.556	13	13	6	1	0	98	100	9.2	4	35	3.2	25	2.3	2.85	121	.271	.329	7	6	97	131	0.1	0	1	0.8
	NY-A	9	7	.563	21	21	10	2	0	149	165	10.0	14	35	2.1	41	2.5	4.17	82	.283	.319	-11	-12	97	97	-0.6	0	-0	-1.2
	Yr	14	11	.560	34	34	16	3	0	247	265	9.7	18	70	2.6	66	2.4	3.64	94	.277	.322	-3	-6	97	97	-0.5	0	1	-0.4
1977	NY-A	2	3	.400	18	11	0	0	0	72	105	13.1	7	24	3.0	14	1.8	5.75	68	.362	.402	-13	-14	97	116	-0.8	0	2	-1.1
1978	NY-A	1	0	1.000	5	3	0	0	0	18	21	10.5	2	9	4.5	3	1.5	4.00	92	.313	.385	-0	-1	97	144	0.5	0	1	0.0
	Chi-N	0	3	.000	23	6	0	0	2	53	61	10.4	10	35	5.9	36	6.1	6.11	65	.286	.388	-15	-13	111	100	-1.4	1	-0	-1.2
1979	Chi-N	6	9	.400	23	20	3	2	0	118	133	10.1	15	53	4.0	44	3.4	4.58	92	.287	.363	-11	-5	112	112	-1.4	2	-1	-0.3
Total	15	174	150	.537	451	410	127	31	3	2868	2787	8.7	249	910	2.9	1601	5.0	3.49	105	.255	.310	33	51	102	101	0.5	-1	1	6.8
■ RICK HONEYCUTT	Honeycutt, Frederick Wayne b: 6/29/52, Chattanooga, Tenn. BL/TL, 6'1", 185 lbs. Deb: 8/24/77																												
1977	Sea-A	0	1	.000	10	3	0	0	0	29	26	8.1	7	11	3.4	17	5.3	4.34	92	.239	.320	-1	-1	98	108	-0.4	0	-1	-0.1
1978	Sea-A	5	11	.313	26	24	4	1	0	134	150	10.1	12	49	3.3	50	3.4	4.90	80	.285	.340	-17	-14	104	91	-0.8	0	1	-1.2
1979	Sea-A	11	12	.478	33	28	8	1	0	194	201	9.3	22	67	3.1	83	3.9	4.04	106	.268	.327	4	5	101	105	1.5	0	-1	0.3
1980	Sea-A	10	17	.370	30	30	9	1	0	203	221	9.8	22	60	2.7	79	3.5	3.95	108	.280	.326	2	7	105	108	0.2	0	-0	0.6
1981	Tex-A	11	6	.647	20	20	8	2	0	128	120	8.4	12	17	**1.2**	40	2.8	3.30	100	.246	.269	5	-0	90	85	2.2	0	1	0.1
1982	Tex-A	5	17	.227	30	26	4	1	0	164	201	11.0	20	54	3.0	64	3.5	5.27	73	.305	.354	-22	-26	94	100	-5.0	0	1	-2.3
1983	Tex-A	14	8	.636	25	25	5	2	0	175	168	8.6	9	37	1.9	56	2.9	**2.42**	**170**	.262	.304	**32**	33	101	**140**	3.7	0	3	3.9
	LA-N	2	3	.400	9	7	1	0	0	39	46	10.6	6	13	3.0	18	4.2	5.77	63	.297	.355	-9	-9	100	92	-0.6	-1	2	-0.7
1984	LA-N	10	9	.526	29	28	6	2	0	184	180	8.8	11	51	2.5	75	3.7	2.84	132	.258	.306	15	18	104	117	0.8	-1	2	2.2
1985	LA-N	8	12	.400	31	25	1	0	1	142	141	8.9	9	49	3.1	67	4.2	3.42	96	.261	.318	3	-2	92	105	-3.4	0	3	0.1
1986	LA-N	11	9	.550	32	28	0	0	0	171	164	8.6	9	45	2.4	100	5.3	3.32	106	.249	.297	8	4	95	90	2.0	0	2	0.6
1987	LA-N	2	12	.143	27	20	1	1	0	116	133	10.3	10	45	3.5	92	7.1	4.58	82	.278	.343	-6	-10	92	95	-4.8	2	-0	-0.8
	Oak-A	1	4	.200	7	4	0	0	0	24	25	9.4	3	9	3.4	10	3.8	5.25	77	.275	.340	-2	-3	91	92	-1.4	0	-0	-0.2
1988	Oak-A	3	2	.600	55	0	0	0	7	80	74	8.3	6	25	2.8	47	5.3	3.49	106	.253	.309	4	2	93	104	-0.1	0	1	0.3
Total	12	93	123	.431	364	268	47	11	8	1783	1850	9.3	158	532	2.7	798	4.0	3.82	100	.269	.320	17	2	98	104	-6.1	1	13	2.8
■ DON HOOD	Hood, Donald Harris b: 10/16/49, Florence, S.C. BL/TL, 6'2", 180 lbs. Deb: 7/16/73																												
1973	Bal-A	3	2	.600	8	4	1	1	1	32	31	8.7	1	6	1.7	18	5.1	3.94	102	.256	.288	-0	0	105	70	0.0	0	-0	0.0
1974	Bal-A	1	1	.500	20	2	0	0	1	57	47	7.4	1	20	3.2	26	4.1	3.47	96	.223	.286	1	-1	92	63	0.0	0	-0	0.0
1975	Cle-A	6	10	.375	29	19	2	0	0	135	136	9.1	16	57	3.8	51	3.4	4.40	86	.268	.337	-9	-9	100	99	-2.0	0	-2	-1.0
1976	Cle-A	3	5	.375	33	6	0	0	1	78	89	10.3	5	41	4.7	32	3.7	4.85	72	.296	.383	-11	-12	100	106	-1.0	0	0	-1.1
1977	Cle-A	2	1	.667	41	5	1	0	0	105	87	7.5	3	49	4.2	62	5.3	3.00	133	.224	.313	13	12	98	92	0.6	0	-1	1.0
1978	Cle-A	5	6	.455	36	19	1	0	0	155	166	9.6	13	77	4.5	73	4.2	4.47	79	.278	.354	-12	-16	94	101	0.2	0	0	-1.5
1979	Cle-A	1	0	1.000	13	0	0	0	1	22	13	5.3	1	14	5.7	7	2.9	3.68	122	.169	.304	1	2	106	58	0.5	0	0	0.2
	NY-A	3	1	.750	27	6	0	0	1	67	62	8.3	3	30	4.0	22	3.0	3.09	130	.252	.326	8	7	95	117	0.9	0	1	0.7
	Yr	4	1	.800	40	6	0	0	2	89	75	7.6	4	44	4.4	29	2.9	3.24	128	.231	.318	10	9	98	117	1.4	0	1	0.9
1980	StL-N	4	6	.400	33	8	1	0	0	82	90	9.9	2	34	3.7	35	3.8	3.40	109	.288	.351	2	3	102	125	-0.6	-0	1	0.3
1982	KC-A	4	0	1.000	30	3	0	0	1	67	71	9.5	7	22	3.0	31	4.2	3.49	116	.276	.330	4	4	100	125	2.0	0	0	0.5
1983	KC-A	2	3	.400	27	0	0	0	0	48	48	9.0	5	14	2.6	17	3.2	2.25	185	.273	.322	10	10	102	191	-0.4	0	1	1.2
Total	10	34	35	.493	297	72	6	1	6	848	840	8.9	57	364	3.9	374	4.0	3.79	100	.263	.335	6	0	98	106	0.2	-0	0	0.3
■ WALLY HOOD	Hood, Wallace James Jr. b: 9/24/25, Los Angeles, Cal. BR/TR, 6'1", 190 lbs. Deb: 9/23/49																												
1949	NY-A	0	0	—	2	0	0	0	0	2	0	0.0	0	1	4.5	2	9.0	0.00	—	.000	.143	1	1	97	0	0.0	0	0	0.1
■ JAY HOOK	Hook, James Wesley b: 11/18/36, Waukegan, Ill. BL/TR, 6'2", 182 lbs. Deb: 9/03/57																												
1957	Cin-N	0	1	.000	3	2	0	0	0	10	6	5.4	0	8	7.2	6	5.4	4.50	91	.176	.311	-1	-0	106	54	-0.4	-0	0	0.0
1958	Cin-N	0	1	.000	1	1	0	0	0	3	3	9.0	2	2	6.0	5	15.0	12.00	35	.250	.357	-3	-3	106	71	-0.4	-0	0	-0.1
1959	Cin-N	5	5	.500	17	15	4	0	0	79	79	9.0	11	39	4.4	37	4.2	5.13	79	.266	.355	-10	-9	103	94	0.2	-1	-1	-1.0
1960	Cin-N	11	18	.379	36	33	10	2	0	222	222	9.0	31	73	3.0	103	4.2	4.50	83	.263	.319	-18	-19	99	95	-2.1	-3	-1	-2.2
1961	Cin-N	1	3	.250	22	5	0	0	0	63	83	11.9	14	22	3.1	36	5.1	7.71	54	.322	.378	-26	-25	103	87	-1.1	-1	-1	-2.4
1962	NY-N	8	19	.296	37	34	13	0	0	214	230	9.7	31	71	3.0	113	4.8	4.84	88	.273	.329	-21	-13	108	94	1.0	2	-1	-1.0
1963	NY-N	4	14	.222	41	20	3	0	1	153	168	9.9	21	53	3.1	89	5.2	5.47	62	.281	.342	-37	-35	104	88	-2.8	2	-1	-3.4
1964	NY-N	0	1	.000	3	2	0	0	0	10	17	15.3	2	7	6.3	5	4.5	9.00	39	.395	.471	-6	-6	98	107	-0.4	-0	0	-0.5
Total	8	29	62	.319	160	112	30	2	1	754	808	9.6	112	275	3.3	394	4.7	5.22	75	.276	.338	-122	-111	104	92	-6.0	-1	-4	-10.6
■ BUCK HOOKER	Hooker, William Edward b: 8/28/1880, Richmond, Va. d: 7/2/29, Richmond, Va. TR , 5'6", Deb: 9/05/02																												
1902	Cin-N	0	1	.000	1	1	1	0	0	8	11	12.4	1	0	0.0	0	0.0	4.50	67	.352	.352	-2	-1	108	106	-0.4	-0	-0	-0.1
1903	Cin-N	0	0	—	1	0	0	0	0	2	2	9.0	0	2	9.0	0	0.0	0.00	—	.284	.443	1	1	107	0	0.0	-0	0	0.1
Total	2	0	1	.000	2	1	1	0	0	10	13	11.7	1	2	1.8	0	0.0	3.60	86	.339	.372	-1	-1	108	85	-0.4	-1	-0	0.0
■ HARRY HOOPER	Hooper, Harry Bartholomew b: 8/24/1887, Bell Station, Cal. d: 12/18/74, Santa Cruz, Cal. BL/TR, 5'10", 168 lbs. Deb: 4/16/09 H																												
1913	Bos-A	0	0	—	1	0	0	0	0	2	2	9.0	0	1	4.5	0	0.0	0.00	—	.333	.429	1	1	103	0	0.0	0	0	0.1
■ BOB HOOPER	Hooper, Robert Nelson b: 5/30/22, Leamington, Ont., Canada d: 3/17/80, New Brunswick, N.J BR/TR, 5'11", 195 lbs. Deb: 4/19/50																												
1950	Phi-A	15	10	.600	45	20	3	0	5	170	181	9.6	15	91	4.8	58	3.1	5.03	85	.272	.358	-9	-14	93	93	**5.5**	-2	3	-1.2
1951	Phi-A	12	10	.545	38	23	9	0	5	189	192	9.1	13	61	2.9	64	3.0	4.38	100	.267	.324	-5	-0	106	88	2.1	-1	1	0.0
1952	Phi-A	8	15	.348	43	14	4	0	6	144	158	9.9	13	68	4.3	40	2.5	5.19	79	.279	.354	-24	-17	112	90	-4.0	1	3	-1.2
1953	Cle-A	5	4	.556	43	0	0	0	7	69	50	6.5	4	38	5.0	16	2.1	4.04	92	.206	.313	-0	-3	93	73	-0.2	-1	1	-0.2
1954	Cle-A	0	0	—	17	0	0	0	2	35	39	10.0	3	16	4.1	12	3.1	4.89	77	.289	.361	-5	-4	101	98	0.0	-1	0	-0.4
1955	Cin-N	0	2	.000	8	0	0	0	0	13	20	13.8	2	6	4.2	6	4.2	7.62	55	.357	.400	-5	-5	104	96	-0.9	-0	0	-0.4
Total	6	40	41	.494	194	57	16	0	25	620	640	9.3	50	280	4.1	196	2.8	4.80	87	.268	.344	-48	-42	102	89	2.5	-3	8	-3.4
■ LEON HOOTEN	Hooten, Michael Leon b: 4/4/48, Downey, Cal. BR/TR, 5'11", 180 lbs. Deb: 4/13/74																												
1974	Oak-A	0	0	—	6	0	0	0	0	8	6	6.8	1	4	4.5	1	1.1	3.38	106	.207	.314	0	0	99	101	0.0	0	0	0.0
■ BURT HOOTON	Hooton, Burt Carlton b: 2/17/50, Greenville, Tex. BR/TR, 6'1", 210 lbs. Deb: 6/17/71																												
1971	Chi-N	2	0	1.000	3	3	2	1	0	21	8	3.4	2	10	4.3	22	9.4	2.14	178	.111	.220	3	4	110	29	1.0	-1	-0	0.3
1972	Chi-N	11	14	.440	33	31	9	3	0	218	201	8.3	13	81	3.3	132	5.4	2.81	138	.246	.309	16	26	112	115	-2.7	-1	1	3.0
1973	Chi-N	14	17	.452	42	34	9	2	0	240	248	9.3	12	73	2.7	134	5.0	3.68	109	.270	.321	-0	8	109	98	-1.0	-1	-1	0.8
1974	Chi-N	7	11	.389	48	21	3	1	1	176	214	10.9	16	51	2.6	94	4.8	4.81	77	.299	.339	-23	-22	102	96	-0.4	-3	3	-2.2
1975	Chi-N	0	2	.000	3	3	0	0	0	11	18	14.7	2	4	3.3	5	4.1	8.18	47	.383	.407	-6	-5	105	98	-0.9	-0	1	-0.4
	LA-N	18	7	.720	31	30	12	4	0	224	172	6.9	16	64	2.6	148	5.9	2.81	120	.210	.264	20	14	93	74	5.3	1	-2	1.3
	Yr	18	9	.667	34	33	12	4	0	235	190	7.3	18	68	2.6	153	5.9	3.06	111	.219	.272	15	9	94	74	4.4	-0	-1	0.9
1976	LA-N	11	15	.423	33	33	8	4	0	227	203	8.0	16	60	2.4	116	4.6	3.25	106	.241	.285	6	5	99	89	-3.7	-2	-1	0.2
1977	LA-N	12	7	.632	32	31	6	2	1	223	184	7.4	14	60	2.4	153	6.2	2.62	146	.225	.275	32	30	98	94	0.7	-0	0	3.1
1978	LA-N	19	10	.655	32	32	10	3	0	236	196	7.5	17	61	2.3	104	4.0	2.71	128	.226	.273	23	20	97	93	2.8	1	-1	2.2
1979	LA-N	11	10	.524	29	29	12	1	0	212	191	8.1	11	63	2.7	129	5.5	2.97	125	.244	.293	18	18	99	97	0.8	-1	-0	1.7
1980	LA-N	14	8	.636	34	33	4	2	1	207	194	8.4	22	64	2.8	118	5.1	3.65	95	.249	.301	-1	-4	96	95	2.0	-3	-0	-0.8
1981	LA-N	11	6	.647	23	23	5	4	0	142	124	7.9	3	33	2.1	74	4.7	2.28	147	.237	.278	19	17	96	105	1.7	2	-1	2.0
1982	LA-N	4	7	.364	21	21	2	2	0	121	130	9.7	5	33	2.5	51	3.8	4.02	84	.275	.321	-5	-9	94	90	-1.8	-1	0	-0.8
1983	LA-N	9	8	.529	33	27	2	0	0	160	156	8.8	21	59	3.3	87	4.9	4.22	86	.254	.317	-10	-11	100	93	-0.4	1	-0	-1.0
1984	LA-N	3	6	.333	54	6	0	0	4	110	109	8.9	5	43	3.5	62	5.1	3.44	109	.263	.328	2	4	104	106	-1.4	-1	-0	0.2

YEAR	TM/L	W	L	PCT	G	GS	CG	SHO	SV	IP	H	H/G	HR	BB	BB/G	SO	SO/G	ERA	/A	OAVG	OOBP	PR	/A	PF	CPI	WAT	PB	PD	TPI
1985	Tex-A	5	8	.385	29	20	2	0	0	124	149	10.8	18	40	2.9	62	4.5	5.23	87	.297	.346	-15	-9	110	100	0.0	0	-1	-0.9
Total	15	151	136	.526	480	377	86	29	7	2652	2497	8.5	193	799	2.7	1491	5.1	3.38	109	.250	.301	79	86	101	95	2.0	-9	-3	8.7
■ **DICK HOOVER**	Hoover, Richard Lloyd b: 12/11/25, Columbus, Ohio d: 4/12/81, Lake Placid, Fla. BL/TL, 6', 170 lbs. Deb: 4/16/52																												
1952	Bos-N	0	0	—	2	0	0	0	0	5	8	14.4	1	3	5.4	0	0.0	7.20	50	.348	.423	-2	-2	97	111	0.0	0	-0	-0.1
■ **SAM HOPE**	Hope, Samuel b: 12/4/1878, Brooklyn, N.Y. d: 6/30/46, Greenport, N.Y. TR , 5'10", Deb: 8/05/07																												
1907	Phi-A	0	0	—	1	0	0	0	0	⅓	3	81.0	0	0	0.0	0	0.0	0.00	—	1.000	1.000	0	0	104	0	0.0	0	0	0.0
■ **PAUL HOPKINS**	Hopkins, Paul Henry b: 9/25/04, Chester, Conn. BR/TR, 6', 175 lbs. Deb: 9/29/27																												
1927	Was-A	1	0	1.000	2	1	0	0	0	9	13	13.0	1	4	4.0	5	5.0	5.00	80	.361	.405	-1	-1	96	141	0.5	1	0	0.0
1929	Was-A	0	1	.000	7	0	0	0	0	16	15	8.4	1	9	5.1	5	2.8	2.25	189	.250	.343	4	4	100	172	-0.4	-1	-0	0.3
	StL-A	0	0	—	2	0	0	0	0	2	0	0.0	0	2	9.0	1	4.5	0.00	—	.000	.286	1	1	100	0	0.0	0	0	0.1
	Yr	0	1	.000	9	0	0	0	0	18	15	7.5	1	11	5.5	6	3.0	2.00	213	.231	.338	4	5	100	0	-0.4	-1	-0	0.4
Total	2	1	1	.500	11	1	0	0	0	27	28	9.3	2	15	5.0	11	3.7	3.00	139	.277	.361	4	3	99	149	0.1	1	0	0.4
■ **LEFTY HOPPER**	Hopper, C. F. b: Ridgewood, N.J. TL , Deb: 10/10/1898																												
1898	Bro-N	0	2	.000	2	2	2	0	0	11	14	11.5	0	5	4.1	5	4.1	4.91	71	.333	.404	-2	-2	96	96	-0.9	-1	0	-0.1
■ **JIM HOPPER**	Hopper, James Mc Daniel b: 9/1/19, Charlotte, N.C. d: 1/23/82, Charlotte, N.C. BR/TR, 6'1", 175 lbs. Deb: 4/21/46																												
1946	Pit-N	0	1	.000	2	1	0	0	0	4	6	13.5	1	3	6.8	1	2.3	11.25	32	.316	.409	-3	-3	106	67	-0.4	0	0	-0.2
■ **BILL HOPPER**	Hopper, William Booth "Bird Dog" b: 10/26/1890, Jackson, Tenn. d: 1/14/65, Allen Park, Mich. BR/TR, 6', 175 lbs. Deb: 9/11/13																												
1913	StL-N	0	3	.000	3	3	2	0	0	24	20	7.5	2	8	3.0	3	1.1	3.75	83	.230	.304	-1	-2	97	83	-1.4	1	-0	0.0
1914	StL-N	0	0	—	3	0	0	0	0	5	6	10.8	0	5	9.0	1	1.8	3.60	80	.286	.423	-0	-0	104	146	0.0	0	0	0.0
1915	Was-A	0	1	.000	13	0	0	0	1	31	39	11.3	0	16	4.6	8	2.3	4.65	63	.348	.434	-6	-6	99	124	-0.4	0	1	-0.4
Total	3	0	4	.000	19	3	2	0	1	60	65	9.8	2	29	4.3	12	1.8	4.20	71	.295	.381	-8	-8	99	110	-1.8	2	1	-0.4
■ **JOHN HORAN**	Horan, John J. b: 1863, Ireland d: 12/21/05, Chicago, Ill. Deb: 5/17/1884																												
1884	CP-U	3	6	.333	13	10	9	0	0	98	94	8.6	0	24	2.2	55	5.1	3.49	86	.257	.303	-5	-5	100	83	-1.2	-5	0	-1.0
■ **JOE HORLEN**	Horlen, Joel Edward b: 8/14/37, San Antonio, Tex. BR/TR, 6', 170 lbs. Deb: 9/04/61																												
1961	Chi-A	1	3	.250	5	4	0	0	0	18	25	12.5	2	13	6.5	11	5.5	6.50	61	.338	.432	-5	-5	99	110	-1.0	-1	0	-0.4
1962	Chi-A	7	6	.538	20	19	5	1	0	109	108	8.9	10	43	3.6	63	5.2	4.87	77	.262	.330	-11	-14	94	83	0.2	-3	2	-1.3
1963	Chi-A	11	7	.611	33	21	3	0	0	124	122	8.9	10	55	4.0	61	4.4	3.27	114	.261	.336	5	6	102	125	0.7	1	2	0.9
1964	Chi-A	13	9	.591	32	28	9	2	0	211	142	**6.1**	11	55	2.3	138	5.9	1.88	180	**.190**	**.247**	41	35	93	86	-0.2	-1	3	4.2
1965	Chi-A	13	13	.500	34	34	7	4	0	219	203	8.3	16	39	1.6	125	5.1	2.88	109	.245	.275	14	6	91	97	-2.1	1	0	0.6
1966	Chi-A	10	13	.435	37	29	4	2	1	211	185	7.9	14	53	2.3	124	5.3	2.43	132	.233	.282	24	18	93	114	-1.9	-3	6	2.3
1967	Chi-A	19	7	**.731**	35	35	13	**6**	0	258	188	6.6	13	58	2.0	103	3.6	**2.06**	**146**	.203	**.251**	**34**	**27**	93	91	5.8	1	3	**3.5**
1968	Chi-A	12	14	.462	35	35	4	1	0	224	197	7.9	16	70	2.8	102	4.1	2.37	128	.238	.303	15	17	102	**133**	1.2	-1	2	2.1
1969	Chi-A	13	16	.448	36	35	7	2	0	236	237	9.0	20	77	2.9	121	4.6	3.78	105	.261	.319	-4	5	110	98	0.9	-1	-1	0.4
1970	Chi-A	6	16	.273	28	26	4	0	0	172	198	10.4	18	41	2.1	77	4.0	4.87	82	.287	.327	-22	-16	108	88	-2.5	-2	4	-1.3
1971	Chi-A	8	9	.471	34	18	3	0	2	137	150	9.9	12	30	2.0	82	5.4	4.27	79	.284	.322	-12	-14	97	94	-0.2	-2	1	-1.5
1972	Oak-A	3	4	.429	32	6	0	0	1	84	74	7.9	3	20	2.1	58	6.2	3.00	97	.236	.289	1	-1	95	83	-0.9	-0	1	0.0
Total	12	116	117	.498	361	290	59	18	4	2003	1829	8.2	145	554	2.5	1065	4.8	3.10	109	.243	.296	79	64	98	101	0.0	-12	23	9.5
■ **TRADER HORNE**	Horne, Berlyn Dale "Sonny" b: 4/12/1899, Bachman, Ohio d: 2/3/83, Franklin, Ohio BB/TR, 5'9", 155 lbs. Deb: 4/24/29																												
1929	Chi-N	1	1	.500	11	1	0	0	0	23	24	9.4	3	21	8.2	6	2.3	5.09	91	.273	.405	-1	-1	98	119	-0.1	0	0	0.0
■ **JACK HORNER**	Horner, William Frank b: 9/21/1863, Baltimore, Md. d: 7/14/10, New Orleans, La. Deb: 5/07/1894																												
1894	Bal-N	0	1	.000	2	1	1	0	1	11	15	12.3	0	7	5.7	2	1.6	9.00	57	.348	.439	-4	-5	96	65	-0.4	-0	0	-0.2
■ **MIKE HORNUNG**	Hornung, Michael Joseph "Ubbo Ubbo" b: 6/12/1857, Carthage, N.Y. d: 10/30/31, Howard Beach, N.Y. BR/TR, 5'8.5", 164 lbs. Deb: 5/01/1879																												
1880	Buf-N	0	0	—	1	0	0	0	0	3	2	6.0	0	1	3.0	0	0.0	6.00	38	.197	.269	-1	-1	96	21	0.0	0	0	0.0
■ **HANSON HORSEY**	Horsey, Hanson b: 11/26/1889, Galena, Md. d: 12/1/49, Millington, Md. BR/TR, 5'11", 165 lbs. Deb: 4/27/12																												
1912	Cin-N	0	0	—	1	0	0	0	0	4	14	31.5	0	3	6.8	0	0.0	22.50	14	.583	.630	-8	-9	93	76	0.0	-0	-0	-0.5
■ **OSCAR HORSTMANN**	Horstmann, Oscar Theodore b: 6/2/1891, Alma, Mo. d: 5/11/77, Salina, Kan. BR/TR, 5'11", 165 lbs. Deb: 4/18/17																												
1917	StL-N	9	4	.692	35	11	4	1	1	139	111	7.2	5	54	3.5	50	3.2	3.43	81	.225	.299	-11	-10	102	76	2.3	0	0	-1.0
1918	StL-N	0	2	.000	9	2	0	0	0	23	29	11.3	0	14	5.5	6	2.3	5.48	48	.349	.422	-7	-7	95	108	-0.9	-0	1	-0.6
1919	StL-N	0	1	.000	6	2	0	0	0	15	14	8.4	0	12	7.2	5	3.0	3.00	94	.264	.388	-0	-0	97	147	-0.4	0	0	0.0
Total	3	9	7	.563	50	15	4	1	1	177	154	7.8	5	80	4.1	61	3.1	3.66	75	.245	.324	-18	-18	101	86	1.0	0	1	-1.6
■ **ELMER HORTON**	Horton, Elmer E. "Herky Jerky" b: 9/4/1869, Hamilton, Ohio d: 8/12/20, Vienna, N.Y. Deb: 9/24/1896																												
1896	Pit-N	0	2	.000	2	2	2	0	0	15	22	13.2	0	9	5.4	3	1.8	9.60	42	.365	.448	-9	-9	93	64	-0.9	-1	0	-0.7
1898	Bro-N	0	1	.000	1	1	1	0	0	9	16	16.0	0	6	6.0	0	0.0	10.00	35	.411	.489	-6	-7	96	78	-0.4	-0	0	-0.4
Total	2	0	3	.000	3	3	3	0	0	24	38	14.3	0	15	5.6	3	1.1	9.75	39	.383	.464	-15	-16	94	69	-1.3	-1	0	-1.1
■ **RICKY HORTON**	Horton, Ricky Neal b: 7/30/59, Poughkeepsie, N.Y. BL/TL, 6'2", 195 lbs. Deb: 4/07/84																												
1984	StL-N	9	4	.692	37	18	1	1	1	126	140	10.0	14	39	2.8	76	5.4	3.43	103	.285	.335	2	2	99	132	2.5	-2	3	0.3
1985	StL-N	3	2	.600	49	3	0	0	1	90	84	8.4	5	34	3.4	59	5.9	2.90	116	.251	.317	7	5	93	120	0.0	-0	2	0.6
1986	StL-N	4	3	.571	42	9	1	0	3	100	77	6.9	7	26	2.3	49	4.4	2.25	171	.218	.269	16	18	103	108	0.6	0	2	2.1
1987	StL-N	8	3	.727	67	6	0	0	7	125	127	9.1	15	42	3.0	55	4.0	3.82	104	.263	.317	4	2	97	107	2.0	1	3	0.5
1988	Chi-A	6	10	.375	52	9	1	0	2	109	120	9.9	6	36	3.0	28	2.3	4.87	80	.291	.342	-11	-12	99	93	-1.2	0	1	-1.0
	LA-N	1	1	.500	12	0	0	0	0	9	11	11.0	2	2	2.0	8	8.0	5.00	73	.306	.317	-2	-1	105	115	0.0	0	1	0.0
Total	5	31	23	.574	259	45	3	1	14	559	559	9.0	49	179	2.9	275	4.4	3.53	106	.265	.318	17	13	98	112	3.9	-1	10	2.5
■ **DAVE HOSKINS**	Hoskins, David Taylor b: 8/3/25, Greenwood, Miss. d: 4/2/70, Flint, Mich. BL/TR, 6'1", 180 lbs. Deb: 4/18/53																												
1953	Cle-A	9	3	.750	26	7	3	0	1	113	102	8.1	9	38	3.0	55	4.4	3.98	93	.243	.308	0	-4	93	84	2.4	4	0	0.0
1954	Cle-A	0	1	.000	14	1	0	0	0	27	29	9.7	3	10	3.3	9	3.0	3.00	126	.284	.339	2	2	101	152	-0.4	-1	0	0.1
Total	2	9	4	.692	40	8	3	0	1	140	131	8.4	12	48	3.1	64	4.1	3.79	98	.251	.314	2	-1	94	97	2.0	3	0	0.1
■ **GENE HOST**	Host, Eugene Earl "Twinkles" or "Slick" b: 1/1/33, Leeper, Pa. BB/TL, 5'11", 190 lbs. Deb: 9/16/56																												
1956	Det-A	0	0	—	1	1	0	0	0	5	9	16.2	2	2	3.6	5	9.0	7.20	55	.409	.458	-2	-2	95	149	0.0	-0	-0	-0.1
1957	KC-A	0	2	.000	11	2	0	0	0	24	29	10.9	5	14	5.3	9	3.4	7.13	54	.315	.394	-9	-9	102	95	-0.9	-1	0	-0.8
Total	2	0	2	.000	12	3	0	0	0	29	38	11.8	7	16	5.0	14	4.3	7.14	54	.333	.406	-11	-11	100	105	-0.9	-1	0	-0.9
■ **BYRON HOUCK**	Houck, Byron Simon "Duke" b: 8/28/1891, Prosper, Minn. d: 6/17/69, Santa Cruz, Cal. BR/TR, 6', 175 lbs. Deb: 5/15/12																												
1912	Phi-A	8	8	.500	30	17	10	0	1	181	148	7.4	1	74	3.7	75	3.7	2.93	111	.234	.326	8	6	97	97	-1.3	-7	-1	0.6
1913	Phi-A	14	6	.700	41	19	4	1	0	176	147	7.5	3	122	6.2	71	3.6	4.14	65	.214	.337	-24	-28	93	65	2.2	-3	-2	-2.9
1914	Phi-A	0	0	—	3	3	0	0	0	11	14	11.5	0	6	4.9	4	3.3	3.27	78	.318	.400	-1	-1	93	152	0.0	0	0	0.0
	Bro-F	2	6	.250	17	9	3	0	0	92	95	9.3	4	43	4.2	45	4.4	3.13	103	.272	.355	1	1	101	128	-2.0	2	0	0.4
1918	StL-A	2	4	.333	27	2	0	0	2	72	58	7.3	0	29	3.6	29	3.6	2.38	116	.225	.299	**3**	**3**	100	87	-0.8	-1	-1	0.2
Total	4	26	24	.520	118	50	17	1	3	532	462	7.8	8	274	4.6	224	3.8	3.30	91	.234	.333	-12	-18	97	91	-1.9	-8	-3	-1.7
■ **CHARLIE HOUGH**	Hough, Charles Oliver b: 1/5/48, Honolulu, Hawaii BR/TR, 6'2", 190 lbs. Deb: 8/12/70																												
1970	LA-N	0	0	—	8	0	0	0	2	17	18	9.5	7	11	5.8	8	4.2	5.29	68	.265	.367	-2	-3	89	136	0.0	0	0	-0.2
1971	LA-N	0	0	—	4	0	0	0	0	4	3	6.8	1	3	6.8	4	9.0	4.50	75	.200	.316	-0	-0	98	100	0.0	0	0	0.0
1972	LA-N	0	0	—	2	0	0	0	0	3	2	6.0	0	2	6.0	4	12.0	3.00	107	.200	.385	0	0	93	120	0.0	0	0	0.0
1973	LA-N	4	2	.667	37	0	0	0	5	72	52	6.5	3	45	5.6	70	8.8	2.75	132	.207	.333	7	7	99	114	0.6	0	0	0.8
1974	LA-N	9	4	.692	49	0	0	0	1	96	65	6.1	12	40	3.8	63	5.9	3.75	87	.196	.280	-1	-5	90	76	1.2	-1	-0	-0.6
1975	LA-N	3	7	.300	38	0	0	0	4	61	43	6.3	3	34	5.0	34	5.0	2.95	115	.195	.320	5	3	93	91	-2.2	1	-1	0.3
1976	LA-N	12	8	.600	77	0	0	0	18	143	102	6.4	6	77	4.8	81	5.1	2.20	157	.200	.312	**21**	**20**	99	120	0.8	2	-0	2.3

YEAR	TM/L	W	L	PCT	G	GS	CG	SHO	SV	IP	H	H/G	HR	BB	BB/G	SO	SO/G	ERA	/A	OAVG	OOBP	PR	/A	PF	CPI	WAT	PB	PD	TPI
1977	LA-N	6	12	.333	70	1	0	0	22	127	98	6.9	10	70	5.0	105	7.4	3.33	115	.213	.318	8	7	98	96	-4.2	1	-0	0.7
1978	LA-N	5	5	.500	55	0	0	0	7	93	69	6.7	6	48	4.6	66	6.4	3.29	106	.205	.313	3	2	97	85	-0.7	1	-0	0.3
1979	LA-N	7	5	.583	42	14	0	0	0	151	152	9.1	16	66	3.9	76	4.5	4.77	78	.264	.341	-17	-18	99	91	1.2	-0	0	-1.7
1980	LA-N	1	3	.250	19	1	0	0	1	32	37	10.4	4	21	5.9	25	7.0	5.63	61	.291	.385	-7	-8	96	104	-1.0	0	-0	-0.7
	Tex-A	2	2	.500	16	2	2	1	0	61	54	8.0	2	37	5.5	47	6.9	3.98	102	.240	.348	0	0	100	92	0.1	0	-0	0.0
1981	Tex-A	4	1	.800	21	5	2	0	1	82	61	6.7	4	31	3.4	69	7.6	2.96	111	.207	.288	6	3	90	80	1.4	0	-1	0.2
1982	Tex-A	16	13	.552	34	34	12	2	0	228	217	8.6	21	72	2.8	128	5.1	3.95	98	.251	.310	3	-2	94	90	4.3	0	1	-0.1
1983	Tex-A	15	13	.536	34	33	11	3	0	252	219	7.8	22	95	3.4	152	5.4	3.18	129	.238	.308	25	26	101	107	1.9	0	4	3.1
1984	Tex-A	16	14	.533	36	36	**17**	1	0	266	260	8.8	26	94	3.2	164	5.5	3.76	107	.255	.320	7	8	101	101	3.2	0	3	1.1
1985	Tex-A	14	16	.467	34	34	14	1	0	250	198	7.1	23	83	3.0	141	5.1	3.31	138	.215	.283	23	35	110	84	2.4	0	1	3.7
1986	Tex-A	17	10	.630	33	33	7	2	0	230	188	7.4	32	89	3.5	146	5.7	3.80	105	.221	.299	10	5	95	90	3.1	0	1	0.5
1987	Tex-A	18	13	.581	40	40	13	0	0	**285**	238	7.5	36	124	3.9	223	7.0	3.79	122	.223	.310	22	27	104	94	4.0	0	3	2.9
1988	Tex-A	15	16	.484	34	34	10	0	0	252	202	7.2	20	126	4.5	174	6.2	3.32	122	.221	.319	18	21	102	102	1.6	0	4	2.6
Total	19	164	144	.532	683	267	88	10	61	2705	2278	7.6	254	1168	3.9	1780	5.9	3.55	112	.228	.312	131	125	100	96	17.7	4	14	15.2

■ PAT HOUSE House, Patrick Lory b: 9/1/40, Boise, Idaho BL/TL, 6'3", 185 lbs. Deb: 9/06/67

YEAR	TM/L	W	L	PCT	G	GS	CG	SHO	SV	IP	H	H/G	HR	BB	BB/G	SO	SO/G	ERA	/A	OAVG	OOBP	PR	/A	PF	CPI	WAT	PB	PD	TPI
1967	Hou-N	1	0	1.000	6	0	0	0	1	4	3	6.8	0	0	0.0	2	4.5	4.50	71	.214	.267	-0	-1	95	40	0.5	0	0	0.0
1968	Hou-N	1	1	.500	18	0	0	0	0	16	21	11.8	0	6	3.4	6	3.4	7.88	38	.323	.387	-9	-9	100	65	0.1	0	-0	-0.9
Total	2	2	1	.667	24	0	0	0	1	20	24	10.8	0	6	2.7	8	3.6	7.20	42	.304	.367	-9	-9	99	60	0.6	0	0	-0.9

■ TOM HOUSE House, Thomas Ross b: 4/29/47, Seattle, Wash. BL/TL, 5'11", 190 lbs. Deb: 6/23/71 C

YEAR	TM/L	W	L	PCT	G	GS	CG	SHO	SV	IP	H	H/G	HR	BB	BB/G	SO	SO/G	ERA	/A	OAVG	OOBP	PR	/A	PF	CPI	WAT	PB	PD	TPI
1971	Atl-N	1	0	1.000	11	1	0	0	0	21	20	8.6	2	3	1.3	11	4.7	3.00	128	.263	.293	1	2	111	115	0.5	1	0	0.3
1972	Atl-N	0	0	—	8	0	0	0	2	9	7	7.0	1	6	6.0	7	7.0	3.00	122	.226	.368	0	1	106	146	0.0	-0	0	0.1
1973	Atl-N	4	2	.667	52	0	0	0	4	67	58	7.8	13	31	4.2	42	5.6	4.70	88	.243	.323	-8	-4	113	97	1.1	0	-0	-0.3
1974	Atl-N	6	2	.750	56	0	0	0	11	103	74	6.5	5	27	2.4	64	5.6	1.92	195	.203	.257	20	21	104	98	1.9	1	1	2.5
1975	Atl-N	7	7	.500	58	0	0	0	11	79	79	9.0	2	36	4.1	36	4.1	3.19	110	.262	.333	4	3	97	112	1.1	-0	1	0.3
1976	Bos-A	1	3	.250	36	0	0	0	4	44	39	8.0	4	19	3.9	27	5.5	4.30	90	.241	.323	-4	-2	110	85	-0.9	0	1	0.0
1977	Bos-A	1	0	1.000	8	0	0	0	0	8	15	16.9	0	6	6.8	6	6.8	12.38	38	.405	.488	-7	-7	116	70	0.5	0	-0	-0.6
	Sea-A	4	5	.444	26	11	1	0	1	89	94	9.5	12	19	1.9	39	3.9	3.94	102	.268	.310	1	1	98	101	0.4	0	-1	0.0
	Yr	5	5	.500	34	11	1	0	1	97	109	10.1	12	25	2.3	45	4.2	4.64	88	.281	.329	-6	-6	100	101	0.9	0	-1	-0.6
1978	Sea-A	5	4	.556	34	9	3	0	0	116	130	10.1	10	35	2.7	29	2.3	4.66	85	.289	.336	-11	-9	104	95	1.5	0	-0	-0.9
Total	8	29	23	.558	289	21	4	0	33	536	516	8.7	49	182	3.1	261	4.4	3.79	102	.256	.316	-4	5	104	100	6.1	2	1	1.4

■ FRED HOUSE House, Willard Edwin b: 10/3/1890, Cabool, Mo. d: 11/16/23, Kansas City, Mo. BR/TR, 6'3", 190 lbs. Deb: 4/22/13

YEAR	TM/L	W	L	PCT	G	GS	CG	SHO	SV	IP	H	H/G	HR	BB	BB/G	SO	SO/G	ERA	/A	OAVG	OOBP	PR	/A	PF	CPI	WAT	PB	PD	TPI
1913	Det-A	1	2	.333	19	2	0	0	0	54	64	10.7	1	17	2.8	16	2.7	5.17	57	.325	.384	-13	-13	101	91	-0.2	-1	1	-1.2

■ CHARLIE HOUSEHOLDER Householder, Charles F. b: 1856, Harrisburg, Pa. 5'7", 150 lbs. Deb: 4/20/1884

YEAR	TM/L	W	L	PCT	G	GS	CG	SHO	SV	IP	H	H/G	HR	BB	BB/G	SO	SO/G	ERA	/A	OAVG	OOBP	PR	/A	PF	CPI	WAT	PB	PD	TPI
1884	CP-U	0	0	—	2	0	0	0	0	3	4	12.0	0	0	0.0	3	9.0	3.00	100	.325	.325	0	0	100	135	0.0	0	0	0.0

■ FRANK HOUSEMAN Houseman, Frank b: Holland Deb: 9/02/1886

YEAR	TM/L	W	L	PCT	G	GS	CG	SHO	SV	IP	H	H/G	HR	BB	BB/G	SO	SO/G	ERA	/A	OAVG	OOBP	PR	/A	PF	CPI	WAT	PB	PD	TPI
1886	Bal-a	0	1	.000	1	1	1	0	0	8	6	6.8	0	1	1.1	5	5.6	3.38	96	.218	.245	0	-0	94	47	-0.4	-0	0	0.0

■ JOE HOUSER Houser, Joseph William b: 7/3/1891, Steubenville, Ohio d: 1/3/53, Orlando, Fla. BL/TL, 5'9.5", 160 lbs. Deb: 4/24/14

YEAR	TM/L	W	L	PCT	G	GS	CG	SHO	SV	IP	H	H/G	HR	BB	BB/G	SO	SO/G	ERA	/A	OAVG	OOBP	PR	/A	PF	CPI	WAT	PB	PD	TPI
1914	Buf-F	0	1	.000	7	2	0	0	0	23	21	8.2	1	20	7.8	6	2.3	5.48	61	.271	.421	-6	-5	104	83	-0.4	-0	0	-0.5

■ ART HOUTTEMAN Houtteman, Arthur Joseph b: 8/7/27, Detroit, Mich. BR/TR, 6'2", 188 lbs. Deb: 4/29/45

YEAR	TM/L	W	L	PCT	G	GS	CG	SHO	SV	IP	H	H/G	HR	BB	BB/G	SO	SO/G	ERA	/A	OAVG	OOBP	PR	/A	PF	CPI	WAT	PB	PD	TPI
1945	Det-A	0	2	.000	13	0	0	0	0	25	27	9.7	1	11	4.0	9	3.2	5.40	65	.270	.336	-6	-5	105	73	-0.9	-1	1	-0.4
1946	Det-A	0	1	.000	1	1	0	0	0	8	15	16.9	1	0	0.0	2	2.3	9.00	41	.385	.375	-5	-5	106	77	-0.4	0	-0	-0.3
1947	Det-A	7	2	.778	23	9	7	2	0	111	106	8.6	6	36	2.9	58	4.7	3.41	112	.247	.305	4	5	103	90	2.3	2	-0	0.7
1948	Det-A	2	16	.111	43	20	4	0	10	164	186	10.2	11	52	2.9	74	4.1	4.66	89	.287	.335	-7	-9	97	95	-7.1	-2	4	-0.6
1949	Det-A	15	10	.600	34	25	13	2	0	204	227	10.0	19	59	2.6	85	3.8	3.71	120	.282	.332	11	17	106	115	1.2	0	5	2.3
1950	Det-A	19	12	.613	41	34	21	**4**	4	275	257	8.4	29	99	3.2	88	2.9	3.53	123	.251	.317	32	24	95	110	0.0	-2	2	2.3
1952	Det-A	8	20	.286	35	28	10	2	1	221	218	8.9	19	65	2.6	109	4.4	4.36	87	.253	.305	-17	-14	103	78	-1.9	-5	1	-1.7
1953	Det-A	2	6	.250	16	9	3	1	1	69	87	11.3	11	29	3.8	28	3.7	5.87	69	.309	.380	-14	-14	102	102	-1.4	0	-0	-1.2
	Cle-A	7	7	.500	22	13	6	1	3	109	113	9.3	4	25	2.1	40	3.3	3.80	98	.269	.313	2	-1	93	90	-1.1	-1	0	-0.1
	Yr	9	13	.409	38	22	9	2	4	178	200	10.1	15	54	2.7	68	3.4	4.60	83	.283	.335	-12	-15	96	90	-2.5	0	-0	-1.3
1954	Cle-A	15	7	.682	32	25	11	1	0	188	198	9.5	14	59	2.8	68	3.3	3.35	112	.273	.323	8	9	101	114	-0.6	4	2	1.6
1955	Cle-A	10	6	.625	35	12	3	1	0	124	126	9.1	15	44	3.2	53	3.8	3.99	101	.265	.325	-0	1	102	104	0.5	-1	2	0.2
1956	Cle-A	2	2	.500	22	4	0	0	1	47	60	11.5	5	31	5.9	19	3.6	6.51	63	.317	.406	-12	-13	99	100	-0.2	-1	0	-1.1
1957	Cle-A	0	0	—	3	0	0	0	0	4	6	13.5	1	3	6.8	3	6.8	6.75	57	.353	.450	-1	-1	102	129	0.0	0	0	0.0
	Bal-A	0	0	—	5	1	0	0	0	7	20	25.7	0	3	3.9	3	3.9	16.71	21	.513	.548	-10	-10	93	75	0.0	0	0	-0.8
	Yr	0	0	—	8	1	0	0	0	11	26	21.3	1	6	4.9	6	4.9	13.09	28	.464	.516	-11	-12	96	75	0.0	0	0	-0.8
Total	12	87	91	.489	325	181	78	14	20	1556	1646	9.5	136	516	3.0	639	3.7	4.14	98	.272	.328	-16	-16	100	100	-9.6	-4	17	0.9

■ ED HOVLIK Hovlik, Edward Charles b: 8/20/1891, Cleveland, Ohio d: 3/19/55, Painesville, Ohio BR/TR, 6', 180 lbs. Deb: 7/14/18

YEAR	TM/L	W	L	PCT	G	GS	CG	SHO	SV	IP	H	H/G	HR	BB	BB/G	SO	SO/G	ERA	/A	OAVG	OOBP	PR	/A	PF	CPI	WAT	PB	PD	TPI
1918	Was-A	2	1	.667	8	2	1	0	0	28	25	8.0	0	10	3.2	10	3.2	1.29	222	.272	.330	5	5	103	246	0.4	-1	-0	0.4
1919	Was-A	0	0	—	3	0	0	0	0	6	12	18.0	0	9	13.5	3	4.5	12.00	27	.480	.618	-6	-6	99	104	0.0	-0	0	-0.5
Total	2	2	1	.667	11	2	1	0	0	34	37	9.8	0	19	5.0	13	3.4	3.18	92	.316	.400	-1	-1	102	221	0.4	-1	0	-0.1

■ JOE HOVLIK Hovlik, Joseph b: 8/16/1884, Czechoslovakia d: 11/3/51, Oxford Junction, Ia BR/TR, 5'10.5", 194 lbs. Deb: 7/10/09

YEAR	TM/L	W	L	PCT	G	GS	CG	SHO	SV	IP	H	H/G	HR	BB	BB/G	SO	SO/G	ERA	/A	OAVG	OOBP	PR	/A	PF	CPI	WAT	PB	PD	TPI
1909	Was-A	0	0	—	3	0	0	0	0	6	13	19.5	0	3	4.5	1	1.5	4.50	53	.419	.486	-1	-1	96	199	0.0	0	0	0.0
1910	Was-A	0	0	—	1	0	0	0	0	2	6	27.0	0	0	0.0	0	0.0	13.50	19	.500	.538	-2	-2	102	95	0.0	0	0	-0.1
1911	Chi-A	2	0	1.000	12	3	1	1	0	47	47	9.0	1	20	3.8	24	4.6	3.06	104	.257	.330	1	1	95	99	1.0	-0	1	0.2
Total	3	2	0	1.000	16	3	1	1	0	55	66	10.8	1	23	3.8	25	4.1	3.60	85	.292	.363	-2	-3	95	110	1.0	-0	1	0.1

■ BRUCE HOWARD Howard, Bruce Ernest b: 3/23/43, Salisbury, Md. BB/TR, 6'2", 180 lbs. Deb: 9/04/63

YEAR	TM/L	W	L	PCT	G	GS	CG	SHO	SV	IP	H	H/G	HR	BB	BB/G	SO	SO/G	ERA	/A	OAVG	OOBP	PR	/A	PF	CPI	WAT	PB	PD	TPI
1963	Chi-A	2	1	.667	7	0	0	0	1	17	12	6.4	0	14	7.4	9	4.8	2.65	140	.207	.351	2	2	102	125	0.3	0	-0	0.2
1964	Chi-A	2	1	.667	3	3	1	1	0	22	10	4.1	0	8	3.3	17	7.0	0.82	413	.139	.232	7	6	93	74	0.2	-1	0	0.6
1965	Chi-A	9	8	.529	30	22	1	1	0	148	123	7.5	13	72	4.4	120	7.3	3.47	90	.224	.313	-0	-6	91	94	-0.8	2	-1	-0.4
1966	Chi-A	9	5	.643	27	21	4	2	0	149	110	6.6	14	44	2.7	85	5.1	2.30	139	.202	.261	19	15	93	101	2.0	-1	0	1.5
1967	Chi-A	3	10	.231	30	17	1	0	0	113	102	8.1	9	52	4.1	76	6.1	3.42	88	.240	.322	-2	-5	93	106	-3.8	1	1	-0.3
1968	Bal-A	0	2	.000	10	5	0	0	0	31	30	8.7	2	26	7.5	19	5.5	3.77	79	.268	.400	-3	-3	101	142	-0.9	2	0	0.0
	Was-A	1	4	.200	13	7	0	0	0	49	62	11.4	7	23	4.2	23	4.2	5.33	52	.330	.386	-13	-14	94	119	-1.2	-2	1	-1.5
	Yr	1	6	.143	23	12	0	0	0	80	92	10.3	9	49	5.5	42	4.7	4.72	61	.302	.386	-16	-16	96	119	-2.1	2	1	-1.5
Total	6	26	31	.456	120	75	7	4	1	529	449	7.6	45	239	4.1	349	5.9	3.18	98	.231	.312	9	-4	93	104	-4.2	2	2	0.1

■ EARL HOWARD Howard, Earl Nycum b: 6/25/1893, Everett, Pa. d: 4/4/37, Everett, Pa. TR, 6'1", 160 lbs. Deb: 4/18/18

YEAR	TM/L	W	L	PCT	G	GS	CG	SHO	SV	IP	H	H/G	HR	BB	BB/G	SO	SO/G	ERA	/A	OAVG	OOBP	PR	/A	PF	CPI	WAT	PB	PD	TPI
1918	StL-N	0	0	—	1	0	0	0	0	2	0	0.0	0	2	9.0	0	0.0	0.00	—	.000	.286	1	1	95	0	0.0	0	1	0.1

■ FRED HOWARD Howard, Fred Irving b: 9/2/56, Portland, Maine BR/TR, 6'3", 190 lbs. Deb: 5/26/79

YEAR	TM/L	W	L	PCT	G	GS	CG	SHO	SV	IP	H	H/G	HR	BB	BB/G	SO	SO/G	ERA	/A	OAVG	OOBP	PR	/A	PF	CPI	WAT	PB	PD	TPI
1979	Chi-A	1	5	.167	28	6	0	0	0	68	73	9.7	5	32	4.2	36	4.8	3.57	121	.283	.351	5	6	103	130	-1.8	0	-1	0.5

■ DEL HOWARD Howard, George Elmer b: 12/24/1877, Kenney, Ill. d: 12/24/56, Seattle, Wash. BL/TR, 6', 180 lbs. Deb: 4/15/05

YEAR	TM/L	W	L	PCT	G	GS	CG	SHO	SV	IP	H	H/G	HR	BB	BB/G	SO	SO/G	ERA	/A	OAVG	OOBP	PR	/A	PF	CPI	WAT	PB	PD	TPI
1905	Pit-N	0	0	—	1	0	0	0	0	6	4	6.0	0	1	1.5	0	0.0	0.00	—	.223	.301	2	2	102	0	0.0	0	0	0.2

■ LEE HOWARD Howard, Lee Vincent b: 11/11/23, Staten Island, N.Y BL/TL, 6'2", 175 lbs. Deb: 9/22/46

YEAR	TM/L	W	L	PCT	G	GS	CG	SHO	SV	IP	H	H/G	HR	BB	BB/G	SO	SO/G	ERA	/A	OAVG	OOBP	PR	/A	PF	CPI	WAT	PB	PD	TPI
1946	Pit-N	0	1	.000	3	2	1	0	0	13	14	9.7	0	9	6.2	6	4.2	2.08	174	.286	.377	2	2	106	223	-0.4	-1	-0	0.1
1947	Pit-N	0	0	—	2	0	0	0	0	3	4	12.0	1	0	0.0	2	6.0	3.00	138	.333	.333	0	0	102	225	0.0	0	0	0.1
Total	2	0	1	.000	5	2	1	0	0	16	18	10.1	1	9	5.1	8	4.5	2.25	165	.295	.370	2	3	105	223	-0.4	-1	-0	0.2

■ CAL HOWE Howe, Calvin Earl b: 11/27/24, Rock Falls, Ill. BL/TL, 6'3", 205 lbs. Deb: 9/26/52

YEAR	TM/L	W	L	PCT	G	GS	CG	SHO	SV	IP	H	H/G	HR	BB	BB/G	SO	SO/G	ERA	/A	OAVG	OOBP	PR	/A	PF	CPI	WAT	PB	PD	TPI
1952	Chi-N	0	0	—	1	0	0	0	0	2	0	0.0	0	1	4.5	2	9.0	0.00	—	.000	.143	1	1	103	0	0.0	0	0	0.1

YEAR	TM/L	W	L	PCT	G	GS	CG	SHO	SV	IP	H	H/G	HR	BB	BB/G	SO	SO/G	ERA	/A	OAVG	OOBP	PR	/A	PF	CPI	WAT	PB	PD	TPI
■ **LES HOWE**	Howe, Lester Curtis "Lucky" b: 8/24/1895, Brooklyn, N.Y. d: 7/16/76, Woodmere, N.Y. BR/TR, 5'11.5", 170 lbs. Deb: 8/18/23																												
1923	Bos-A	1	0	1.000	12	2	0	0	0	30	23	6.9	0	7	2.1	7	2.1	2.40	175	.211	.254	5	6	106	60	0.5	-1	0	0.5
1924	Bos-A	1	0	1.000	4	0	0	0	0	7	11	14.1	1	2	2.6	3	3.9	7.71	58	.423	.452	-3	-3	105	115	0.5	0	0	-0.1
Total	2	2	0	1.000	16	2	0	0	0	37	34	8.3	1	9	2.2	10	2.4	3.41	125	.252	.294	3	3	105	70	1.0	-1	0	0.4
■ **STEVE HOWE**	Howe, Steven Roy b: 3/10/58, Pontiac, Mich. BL/TL, 6'1", 180 lbs. Deb: 4/11/80																												
1980	LA-N	7	9	.438	59	0	0	0	17	85	83	8.8	1	22	2.3	39	4.1	2.65	131	.256	.298	9	8	96	107	-1.8	-1	1	0.8
1981	LA-N	5	3	.625	41	0	0	0	8	54	51	8.5	2	18	3.0	32	5.3	2.50	134	.254	.304	6	5	96	127	0.5	0	-1	0.5
1982	LA-N	7	5	.583	66	0	0	0	13	99	87	7.9	3	17	1.5	49	4.5	2.09	161	.240	.265	17	14	94	111	0.6	-1	-0	1.4
1983	LA-N	4	7	.364	46	0	0	0	18	69	55	7.2	2	12	1.6	52	6.8	1.43	252	.217	.248	17	17	100	120	-1.9	0	1	1.9
1985	LA-N	1	1	.500	19	0	0	0	3	22	30	12.3	2	5	2.0	11	4.5	4.91	67	.319	.346	-3	-4	92	106	0.0	0	0	-0.3
	Min-A	2	3	.400	13	0	0	0	0	19	28	13.3	1	7	3.3	10	4.7	6.16	70	.333	.372	-4	-4	104	93	-0.3	0	-0	-0.3
1987	Tex-A	3	3	.500	24	0	0	0	1	31	33	9.6	2	8	2.3	19	5.5	4.35	107	.280	.336	0	1	104	97	0.2	0	0	0.1
Total	6	29	31	.483	268	0	0	0	60	379	367	8.7	13	89	2.1	212	5.0	2.71	132	.255	.293	42	36	97	112	-2.7	-1	1	4.1
■ **HARRY HOWELL**	Howell, Henry Harry b: 11/14/1876, New Jersey d: 5/22/56, Spokane, Wash. BR/TR, 5'9", Deb: 10/10/1898																												
1898	Bro-N	2	0	1.000	2	2	2	0	0	18	15	7.5	0	11	5.5	2	1.0	5.00	70	.246	.362	-3	-3	96	60	1.0	0	0	-0.1
1899	Bal-N	13	8	.619	28	25	21	0	1	209	248	10.7	1	69	3.0	58	2.5	3.92	105	.319	.375	-2	4	106	102	1.1	-4	0	0.1
1900	Bro-N	6	5	.545	21	10	7	2	0	110	131	10.7	4	36	2.9	26	2.1	3.76	104	.319	.374	-1	2	106	114	-0.5	4	0	0.5
1901	Bal-A	14	21	.400	37	34	32	1	0	295	333	10.2	5	79	2.4	93	2.8	3.66	107	.305	.352	0	8	107	100	-4.7	1	-2	0.9
1902	Bal-A	9	15	.375	26	23	19	1	0	199	243	11.0	5	48	2.2	33	1.5	4.12	90	.327	.368	-12	-9	104	101	0.3	6	4	-0.7
1903	NY-A	9	6	.600	25	15	13	0	0	156	140	8.1	4	44	2.5	62	3.6	3.52	84	.261	.317	-10	-10	100	78	1.1	2	3	-0.2
1904	StL-A	13	21	.382	34	33	32	2	0	300	254	7.6	1	60	1.8	122	3.7	2.19	116	.251	.293	14	11	98	95	-2.1	4	9	2.9
1905	StL-A	15	22	.405	38	37	**35**	4	0	323	252	7.0	2	101	2.8	198	5.5	1.98	125	.237	.303	24	18	93	109	1.9	3	18	4.4
1906	StL-A	15	14	.517	35	33	30	6	1	277	233	7.6	1	61	2.0	140	4.5	2.11	123	.252	.298	18	15	97	99	0.3	-3	7	2.1
1907	StL-A	16	15	.516	42	35	26	2	3	316	258	7.3	3	88	2.5	118	3.4	1.94	129	.245	.303	21	19	98	108	2.2	6	8	3.9
1908	StL-A	18	18	.500	41	32	27	2	1	324	279	7.8	1	70	1.9	117	3.3	1.89	129	.240	.293	18	20	102	127	-1.8	1	0	2.5
1909	StL-A	1	1	.500	10	3	0	0	0	37	42	10.2	0	8	1.9	16	3.9	3.16	74	.294	.344	-3	-3	95	109	0.2	0	-0	-0.3
1910	StL-A	0	0	—	1	0	0	0	0	3	7	21.0	0	2	6.0	1	3.0	12.00	21	.467	.529	-3	-3	101	88	0.0	-0	0	-0.2
Total	13	131	146	.473	340	282	244	20	6	2567	2435	8.5	27	677	2.4	986	3.5	2.74	108	.271	.323	61	64	100	104	-1.0	20	47	15.8
■ **JAY HOWELL**	Howell, Jay Canfield b: 11/26/55, Miami, Fla. BR/TR, 6'3", 200 lbs. Deb: 8/10/80																												
1980	Cin-N	0	0	—	5	0	0	0	0	3	8	24.0	0	0	0.0	1	3.0	15.00	24	.471	.474	-4	-4	101	72	0.0	0	0	-0.3
1981	Chi-N	2	0	1.000	10	2	0	0	0	22	23	9.4	3	10	4.1	10	4.1	4.91	76	.277	.361	-3	-3	106	105	1.0	0	1	-0.1
1982	NY-A	2	3	.400	6	6	0	0	0	28	42	13.5	1	13	4.2	21	6.8	7.71	51	.341	.399	-11	-12	97	78	-0.4	0	-0	-1.0
1983	NY-A	1	5	.167	19	12	2	0	0	82	89	9.8	7	35	3.8	61	6.7	5.38	74	.275	.345	-12	-13	98	83	-2.0	0	0	-1.1
1984	NY-A	9	4	.692	61	1	0	0	7	104	86	7.4	5	34	2.9	109	9.4	2.68	139	.223	.282	15	12	93	91	2.3	0	2	1.4
1985	Oak-A	9	8	.529	63	0	0	0	29	98	98	9.0	5	31	2.8	68	6.2	2.85	136	.261	.314	14	11	93	124	1.0	0	0	1.1
1986	Oak-A	3	6	.333	38	0	0	0	16	53	53	9.0	3	23	3.9	42	7.1	3.40	116	.262	.335	5	3	94	115	-1.3	0	-0	0.3
1987	Oak-A	3	4	.429	36	0	0	0	16	44	48	9.8	6	21	4.3	35	7.2	5.93	69	.277	.350	-7	-9	91	85	-0.4	0	-0	-0.8
1988	LA-N	5	3	.625	50	0	0	0	21	65	44	6.1	1	21	2.9	70	9.7	2.08	175	.188	.252	10	11	105	72	0.4	-0	0	1.2
Total	9	34	33	.507	288	21	2	0	89	499	491	8.9	31	188	3.4	417	7.5	3.90	99	.256	.320	6	-2	96	95	0.6	-0	2	0.7
■ **KEN HOWELL**	Howell, Kenneth b: 11/28/60, Detroit, Mich. BR/TR, 6'3", 200 lbs. Deb: 6/25/84																												
1984	LA-N	5	5	.500	32	1	0	0	6	51	51	9.0	1	9	1.6	54	9.5	3.35	111	.267	.295	1	2	104	90	0.1	-1	0	0.2
1985	LA-N	4	7	.364	56	0	0	0	12	86	66	6.9	8	35	3.7	85	8.9	3.77	88	.208	.284	-2	-4	92	70	-2.1	-0	0	-0.4
1986	LA-N	6	12	.333	62	0	0	0	12	98	86	7.9	7	63	5.8	104	9.6	3.86	91	.239	.348	-1	-4	95	105	-2.5	-0	-1	-0.5
1987	LA-N	3	4	.429	40	2	0	0	1	55	54	8.8	7	29	4.7	60	9.8	4.91	77	.265	.347	-5	-7	92	97	-0.1	0	0	-0.6
1988	LA-N	0	1	.000	4	1	0	0	0	13	16	11.1	0	4	2.8	12	8.3	6.23	58	.320	.364	-4	-4	105	75	-0.4	-0	-0	-0.3
Total	5	18	29	.383	194	4	0	0	31	303	273	8.1	23	140	4.2	315	9.4	4.04	88	.243	.322	-11	-17	95	90	-5.0	-1	-1	-1.6
■ **DIXIE HOWELL**	Howell, Millard b: 1/7/20, Bowman, Ky. d: 3/18/60, Hollywood, Fla. BL/TR, 6'2", 210 lbs. Deb: 9/14/40																												
1940	Cle-A	0	0	—	3	0	0	0	0	5	2	3.6	0	4	7.2	2	3.6	1.80	224	.143	.316	1	1	92	145	0.0	0	0	0.1
1949	Cin-N	0	1	.000	5	1	0	0	0	13	21	14.5	3	8	5.5	7	4.8	8.31	48	.362	.439	-6	-6	98	105	-0.4	-0	0	-0.5
1955	Chi-A	8	3	.727	35	0	0	0	9	74	70	8.5	1	25	3.0	25	3.0	2.92	133	.250	.303	9	8	98	97	1.9	2	1	1.1
1956	Chi-A	5	6	.455	34	1	0	0	4	64	79	11.1	3	36	5.1	28	3.9	4.64	91	.309	.393	-3	-3	102	116	-0.9	2	0	0.0
1957	Chi-A	6	5	.545	37	0	0	0	6	68	64	8.5	6	30	4.0	37	4.9	3.31	110	.255	.330	4	3	97	117	-0.3	4	1	0.7
1958	Chi-A	0	0	—	1	0	0	0	0	2	0	0.0	0	0	0.0	0	0.0	0.00	—	.000	.000	1	1	98	0	0.0	0	0	0.1
Total	6	19	15	.559	115	2	0	0	19	226	236	9.4	13	103	4.1	99	3.9	3.78	103	.273	.346	5	3	98	109	0.3	8	2	1.5
■ **ROLAND HOWELL**	Howell, Roland Boatner "Billiken" b: 1/3/1892, Napoleonville, La. d: 3/31/73, Baton Rouge, La. 6'4", 210 lbs. Deb: 6/14/12																												
1912	StL-N	0	0	—	3	0	0	0	0	2	5	22.5	0	5	22.5	0	0.0	22.50	16	.556	.714	-4	-4	103	81	0.0	0	0	-0.3
■ **TEX HOYLE**	Hoyle, Roland Edison b: 7/17/21, Carbondale, Pa. BR/TR, 6'4", 170 lbs. Deb: 4/18/52																												
1952	Phi-A	0	0	—	3	0	0	0	0	2	9	40.5	2	1	4.5	1	4.5	31.50	13	.563	.588	-6	-6	112	85	0.0	0	0	-0.5
■ **LaMARR HOYT**	Hoyt, Dewey LaMarr b: 1/1/55, Columbia, S.C. BR/TR, 6'3", 195 lbs. Deb: 9/14/79																												
1979	Chi-A	0	0	—	2	0	0	0	0	3	2	6.0	0	0	0.0	0	0.0	0.00	—	.200	.200	1	1	103	0	0.0	0	0	0.1
1980	Chi-A	9	3	.750	24	13	3	1	0	112	123	9.9	8	41	3.3	55	4.4	4.58	87	.281	.335	-7	-8	98	92	3.4	0	-2	-0.8
1981	Chi-A	9	3	.750	43	1	0	0	10	91	80	7.9	10	28	2.8	60	5.9	3.56	102	.240	.299	1	1	99	97	3.1	0	-1	0.0
1982	Chi-A	**19**	15	.559	39	32	14	2	0	240	248	9.3	17	48	1.8	124	4.7	3.53	112	.266	.299	15	11	97	96	1.0	0	-1	1.0
1983	Chi-A	**24**	10	.706	36	36	11	1	0	261	236	8.1	27	31	**1.1**	148	5.1	3.66	113	.238	**.259**	12	14	102	74	4.9	0	5	1.9
1984	Chi-A	13	18	.419	34	34	11	1	0	236	244	9.3	31	43	**1.6**	126	4.8	4.46	100	.266	.299	-12	-1	111	86	-1.4	0	1	0.0
1985	SD-N	16	8	.667	31	31	8	3	0	210	210	9.0	20	20	**0.9**	83	3.6	3.47	105	.261	.277	3	4	101	90	4.2	-4	1	0.1
1986	SD-N	8	11	.421	35	25	1	0	0	159	170	9.6	27	68	3.8	85	4.8	5.15	69	.276	.345	-25	-28	96	99	-0.7	-1	-2	-2.9
Total	8	98	68	.590	244	172	48	8	10	1312	1313	9.0	140	279	1.9	681	4.7	3.99	99	.260	.297	-12	-5	101	89	14.5	-5	1	-0.6
■ **WAITE HOYT**	Hoyt, Waite Charles "Schoolboy" b: 9/9/1899, Brooklyn, N.Y. d: 8/25/84, Cincinnati, Ohio BR/TR, 6', 180 lbs. Deb: 7/24/18 H																												
1918	NY-N	0	0	—	1	0	0	0	0	1	0	0.0	0	0	0.0	2	18.0	0.00	—	.000	.000	0	0	96	0	0.0	-0	0	0.0
1919	Bos-A	4	6	.400	13	11	6	1	0	105	99	8.5	1	22	1.9	28	2.4	3.26	90	.262	.303	-0	-4	91	78	-0.8	-2	1	-0.5
1920	Bos-A	6	6	.500	22	11	6	2	1	121	123	9.1	2	47	3.5	45	3.3	4.39	84	.270	.339	-8	-10	97	76	0.4	-3	1	-1.0
1921	NY-A	19	13	.594	43	32	21	1	3	282	301	9.6	3	81	2.6	102	3.3	3.10	137	.276	.322	37	36	99	107	-1.3	-2	-1	3.2
1922	NY-A	19	12	.613	37	31	17	3	0	265	271	9.2	13	76	2.6	95	3.2	3.43	117	.269	.319	18	17	99	101	0.1	1	-2	1.6
1923	NY-A	17	9	.654	37	28	19	1	1	239	227	8.5	9	66	2.5	60	2.3	3.01	133	.253	.299	26	27	101	95	0.4	-2	-1	2.4
1924	NY-A	18	13	.581	46	32	14	2	4	247	295	10.7	8	76	2.8	71	2.6	3.79	108	.300	.344	12	9	97	112	-0.1	-5	-0	0.3
1925	NY-A	11	14	.440	46	30	17	1	6	243	283	10.5	14	78	2.9	86	3.2	4.00	107	.292	.337	11	7	97	105	-0.2	5	2	1.3
1926	NY-A	16	12	.571	40	28	12	1	4	218	224	9.2	4	62	2.6	79	3.3	3.84	102	.264	.306	4	1	97	78	-0.5	-0	-3	-0.1
1927	NY-A	**22**	7	**.759**	36	32	23	3	1	256	242	8.5	10	54	1.9	86	3.0	2.64	147	.251	.287	43	35	94	103	2.7	0	-0	3.4
1928	NY-A	23	7	.767	42	31	19	3	**8**	273	279	9.2	16	60	2.0	67	2.2	3.36	107	.272	.304	21	7	89	105	5.6	2	-1	0.6
1929	NY-A	10	9	.526	30	25	12	0	1	202	219	9.8	9	69	3.1	57	2.5	4.23	97	.279	.329	0	-3	97	92	-0.7	1	-2	-0.3
1930	NY-A	2	2	.500	8	7	2	0	0	48	64	12.0	7	9	1.7	10	1.9	4.50	90	.317	.343	1	-2	87	124	-0.1	-2	-0	-0.3
	Det-A	9	8	.529	26	20	8	1	4	136	176	11.6	7	47	3.1	25	1.7	4.76	103	.313	.358	-2	2	106	110	0.8	-3	-3	-0.2
	Yr	11	10	.524	34	27	10	1	4	184	240	11.7	14	56	2.7	35	1.7	4.70	100	.314	.354	-1	0	101	110	0.7	-2	-3	-0.5
1931	Det-A	3	8	.273	16	12	5	0	0	92	124	12.1	2	32	3.1	10	1.0	5.87	80	.319	.368	-15	-12	107	90	-1.7	-3	-0	-1.2
	Phi-A	10	5	.667	16	14	9	2	0	111	130	10.5	9	37	3.0	30	2.4	4.22	105	.298	.349	2	3	101	119	-0.3	3	1	0.6
	Yr	13	13	.500	32	26	14	2	0	203	254	11.3	11	69	3.1	40	1.8	4.97	91	.307	.356	-13	-10	104	119	-2.0	-3	0	-0.6
1932	Bro-N	1	3	.250	8	4	0	0	1	27	38	12.7	3	12	4.0	7	2.3	7.67	48	.342	.391	-11	-12	96	86	-1.0	-1	1	-0.9
	NY-N	5	7	.417	18	12	3	0	0	97	103	9.6	6	25	2.3	29	2.7	3.43	110	.275	.317	5	4	98	114	-0.6	-2	1	0.2
	Yr	6	10	.375	26	16	3	0	1	124	141	10.2	9	37	2.7	36	2.6	4.35	87	.290	.334	-7	-8	97	114	-1.6	-1	2	-0.7

YEAR	TM/L	W	L	PCT	G	GS	CG	SHO	SV	IP	H	H/G	HR	BB	BB/G	SO	SO/G	ERA	/A	OAVG	OOBP	PR	/A	PF	CPI	WAT	PB	PD	TPI
1933	Pit-N	5	7	.417	36	8	4	1	4	117	118	9.1	3	19	1.5	44	3.4	2.92	107	.262	.289	5	3	94	94	-1.6	-1	1	0.3
1934	Pit-N	15	6	.714	48	15	8	3	5	191	184	8.7	6	43	2.0	105	4.9	2.92	146	.252	.292	24	28	105	100	5.0	-1	-1	2.7
1935	Pit-N	7	11	.389	39	11	5	0	6	164	187	10.3	8	27	1.5	63	3.5	3.40	124	.285	.310	11	15	105	110	-2.9	2	-0	1.7
1936	Pit-N	7	5	.583	22	9	6	0	1	117	115	8.8	5	20	1.5	37	2.8	2.69	144	.255	.286	17	15	96	108	0.5	-1	1	1.5
1937	Pit-N	1	2	.333	11	0	0	0	2	28	31	10.0	3	6	1.9	21	6.8	4.50	88	.270	.306	-2	-2	101	84	-0.5	-1	-1	-0.2
	Bro-N	7	7	.500	27	19	10	1	0	167	180	9.7	5	30	1.6	44	2.4	3.23	130	.270	.297	13	18	107	97	1.2	-3	-1	1.5
	Yr	8	9	.471	38	19	10	1	2	195	211	9.7	8	36	1.7	65	3.0	3.42	122	.270	.298	11	16	106	97	0.7	-1	-2	1.3
1938	Bro-N	0	3	.000	6	1	0	0	0	16	24	13.5	1	5	2.8	3	1.7	5.06	72	.333	.372	-2	-3	96	112	-1.4	-0	-0	-0.2
Total	21	237	182	.566	674	423	226	26	52	3763	4037	9.7	154	1003	2.4	1206	2.9	3.59	112	.276	.318	210	179	98	100	3.0	-17	-7	16.4

■ **AL HRABOSKY** Hrabosky, Alan Thomas b: 7/21/49, Oakland, Cal. BR/TL, 5'11", 185 lbs. Deb: 6/16/70

YEAR	TM/L	W	L	PCT	G	GS	CG	SHO	SV	IP	H	H/G	HR	BB	BB/G	SO	SO/G	ERA	/A	OAVG	OOBP	PR	/A	PF	CPI	WAT	PB	PD	TPI
1970	StL-N	2	1	.667	16	1	0	0	0	19	22	10.4	2	7	3.3	12	5.7	4.74	91	.286	.341	-1	-1	106	99	0.6	-0	-1	-0.1
1971	StL-N	0	0	—	1	0	0	0	0	2	2	9.0	0	0	0.0	2	9.0	0.00	—	.250	.250	1	1	100	0	0.0	0	0	0.1
1972	StL-N	1	0	1.000	5	0	0	0	0	7	2	2.6	0	3	3.9	9	11.6	0.00	—	.087	.185	3	3	105	0	0.5	-0	-0	0.3
1973	StL-N	2	4	.333	44	0	0	0	5	56	45	7.2	2	21	3.4	57	9.2	2.09	158	.220	.291	10	8	90	117	-0.9	-0	-1	0.7
1974	StL-N	8	1	.889	65	0	0	0	9	88	71	7.3	3	38	3.9	82	8.4	2.97	126	.221	.299	6	8	103	87	3.5	1	-1	0.8
1975	StL-N	13	3	.813	65	0	0	0	**22**	97	72	6.7	3	33	3.1	82	7.6	1.67	225	.205	.270	**21**	**22**	103	113	5.2	1	-2	2.3
1976	StL-N	8	6	.571	68	0	0	0	13	95	89	8.4	5	39	3.7	73	6.9	3.32	110	.252	.324	2	4	105	108	1.7	0	-0	0.4
1977	StL-N	6	5	.545	65	0	0	0	10	86	82	8.6	12	41	4.3	68	7.1	4.40	85	.256	.337	-5	-6	95	102	0.4	-1	-1	-0.7
1978	KC-A	8	7	.533	58	0	0	0	20	75	52	6.2	6	35	4.2	60	7.2	2.88	133	.200	.286	7	8	101	91	-0.4	0	-0	0.8
1979	KC-A	9	4	.692	58	0	0	0	11	65	67	9.3	3	41	5.7	39	5.4	3.74	119	.272	.371	4	5	105	123	2.4	0	-1	0.3
1980	Atl-N	4	2	.667	45	0	0	0	3	60	50	7.5	8	31	4.7	31	4.7	3.60	102	.223	.310	0	0	101	99	1.0	-0	-1	0.0
1981	Atl-N	1	1	.500	24	0	0	0	1	34	24	6.4	1	9	2.4	13	3.4	1.06	329	.207	.252	9	9	100	180	0.1	-0	-1	0.9
1982	Atl-N	2	1	.667	31	0	0	0	3	37	41	10.0	5	17	4.1	20	4.9	5.59	69	.285	.349	-8	-7	107	90	0.4	0	-1	-0.7
Total	13	64	35	.646	545	1	0	0	97	721	619	7.7	50	315	3.9	548	6.8	3.11	121	.234	.310	49	53	101	106	14.5	0	-10	5.1

■ **CARL HUBBELL** Hubbell, Carl Owen "King Carl" or "The Mealticket" b: 6/22/03, Carthage, Mo. d: 11/21/88, Scottsdale, Ariz. BR/TL, 6', 170 lbs. Deb: 7/26/28 H

YEAR	TM/L	W	L	PCT	G	GS	CG	SHO	SV	IP	H	H/G	HR	BB	BB/G	SO	SO/G	ERA	/A	OAVG	OOBP	PR	/A	PF	CPI	WAT	PB	PD	TPI
1928	NY-N	10	6	.625	20	14	8	1	1	124	117	8.5	7	21	1.5	37	2.7	2.83	140	.248	.276	16	16	99	91	0.5	-3	2	1.5
1929	NY-N	18	11	.621	39	35	19	1	1	268	273	9.2	17	67	2.3	106	3.6	3.69	124	.265	.306	30	26	97	95	2.5	-6	5	2.3
1930	NY-N	17	12	.586	37	32	17	3	2	242	263	9.8	11	58	2.2	117	4.4	3.87	123	.278	.320	30	24	96	97	0.9	-5	-1	1.5
1931	NY-N	14	12	.538	36	30	21	4	3	248	211	**7.7**	14	67	2.4	155	5.6	2.65	136	**.227**	**.279**	34	26	93	94	-0.8	4	-2	2.9
1932	NY-N	18	11	.621	40	32	22	0	2	284	260	8.2	20	40	1.3	137	4.3	2.50	151	.238	**.264**	43	41	98	100	4.8	4	6	**5.4**
1933	NY-N	**23**	12	.657	45	33	22	**10**	5	**309**	256	7.5	6	47	1.4	156	4.5	**1.66**	**193**	.227	**.254**	**58**	**53**	96	113	3.2	1	8	**7.1**
1934	NY-N	21	12	.636	49	34	**25**	5	**8**	313	286	8.2	17	37	**1.1**	118	3.4	**2.30**	167	.239	**.259**	**61**	54	95	104	1.5	-1	4	5.9
1935	NY-N	23	12	.657	42	35	24	1	0	303	314	9.3	27	49	1.5	150	4.5	3.27	117	.263	.289	25	18	95	105	3.3	4	4	2.6
1936	NY-N	**26**	6	**.813**	42	34	25	3	3	304	265	**7.8**	7	57	1.7	123	3.6	**2.31**	**171**	.236	**.272**	**58**	**55**	98	101	**9.5**	0	1	**5.9**
1937	NY-N	**22**	8	**.733**	39	32	18	4	4	262	261	9.0	18	55	1.9	**159**	5.5	3.19	120	.257	.293	21	18	98	102	5.0	1	-1	1.8
1938	NY-N	13	10	.565	24	22	13	1	1	179	171	8.6	16	33	1.7	104	**5.2**	3.07	126	.249	**.281**	14	16	102	101	0.4	-2	-1	1.3
1939	NY-N	11	9	.550	29	18	10	0	2	154	150	8.8	11	24	1.4	62	3.6	2.75	141	.249	**.275**	20	19	99	101	0.9	-1	1	2.0
1940	NY-N	11	12	.478	31	27	11	2	0	214	220	9.3	22	59	2.5	86	3.6	3.66	105	.259	.307	5	5	100	104	0.1	-0	1	0.6
1941	NY-N	11	9	.550	26	22	11	1	1	164	169	9.3	10	53	2.9	75	4.1	3.57	106	.266	.318	1	4	104	105	1.5	-2	-3	0.0
1942	NY-N	11	8	.579	24	20	11	0	0	157	158	9.1	17	34	1.9	61	3.5	3.96	85	.259	.292	-11	-10	101	90	0.5	-0	-1	-1.1
1943	NY-N	4	4	.500	12	11	3	0	0	66	87	11.9	7	24	3.3	31	4.2	4.91	68	.322	.371	-11	-12	99	115	0.9	-0	-1	-1.1
Total	16	253	154	.622	535	431	260	36	33	3591	3461	8.7	227	725	1.8	1677	4.2	2.98	130	.251	.286	394	354	98	101	34.7	-5	22	38.6

■ **BILL HUBBELL** Hubbell, Wilbert William b: 6/17/1897, San Francisco, Cal. d: 8/3/80, Lakewood, Colo. BR/TR, 6'1.5", 195 lbs. Deb: 9/24/19

YEAR	TM/L	W	L	PCT	G	GS	CG	SHO	SV	IP	H	H/G	HR	BB	BB/G	SO	SO/G	ERA	/A	OAVG	OOBP	PR	/A	PF	CPI	WAT	PB	PD	TPI
1919	NY-N	1	1	.500	2	2	2	0	0	18	19	9.5	0	2	1.0	3	1.5	2.00	140	.260	.295	2	2	96	128	-0.1	-1	-0	0.1
1920	NY-N	0	1	.000	14	0	0	0	2	30	26	7.8	2	15	4.5	8	2.4	2.10	144	.239	.323	3	3	97	154	-0.4	-0	1	0.4
	Phi-N	9	9	.500	24	20	9	1	2	150	176	10.6	3	42	2.5	26	1.6	3.84	91	.301	.336	-12	-6	112	100	1.6	-4	-2	-1.0
	Yr	9	10	.474	38	20	9	1	4	180	202	10.1	5	57	2.8	34	1.7	3.55	97	.291	.333	-8	-2	109	100	1.2	-0	-1	-0.6
1921	Phi-N	9	16	.360	36	30	15	1	2	220	269	11.0	18	38	1.6	43	1.8	4.34	93	.306	.325	-14	-7	107	98	0.6	-1	-1	-0.7
1922	Phi-N	7	15	.318	35	24	11	1	1	189	257	12.2	14	41	2.0	33	1.6	5.00	96	.317	.346	-19	-5	117	94	-1.7	-2	0	-0.4
1923	Phi-N	1	6	.143	22	5	1	0	0	55	102	16.7	13	17	2.8	8	1.3	8.35	56	.394	.428	-27	-22	118	107	-1.9	0	0	-1.9
1924	Phi-N	10	9	.526	36	22	9	2	2	179	233	11.7	9	45	2.3	30	1.5	4.83	89	.324	.358	-19	-11	111	102	2.7	-0	0	-0.9
1925	Phi-N	0	0	—	2	0	0	0	0	3	5	15.0	0	1	3.0	0	0.0	0.00	—	.385	.429	1	2	118	0	0.0	-0	1	0.2
	Bro-N	3	6	.333	33	5	3	0	1	87	120	12.4	8	24	2.5	16	1.7	5.28	77	.337	.372	-10	-12	95	109	-1.1	0	1	-0.9
	Yr	3	6	.333	35	5	3	0	1	90	125	12.5	8	25	2.5	16	1.6	5.10	80	.339	.373	-8	-10	96	109	-1.1	-0	1	-0.7
Total	7	40	63	.388	204	108	50	5	10	931	1207	11.7	67	225	2.2	167	1.6	4.68	88	.317	.348	-93	-56	109	102	-0.3	-8	0	-5.1

■ **EARL HUCKLEBERRY** Huckleberry, Earl Eugene b: 5/23/10, Konawa, Okla. BR/TR, 5'11", 165 lbs. Deb: 9/13/35

YEAR	TM/L	W	L	PCT	G	GS	CG	SHO	SV	IP	H	H/G	HR	BB	BB/G	SO	SO/G	ERA	/A	OAVG	OOBP	PR	/A	PF	CPI	WAT	PB	PD	TPI
1935	Phi-A	1	0	1.000	1	1	0	0	0	7	8	10.3	1	4	5.1	2	2.6	9.00	51	.296	.375	-4	-3	102	66	0.5	-0	0	-0.2

■ **WILLIS HUDLIN** Hudlin, George Willis "Ace" b: 5/23/06, Wagoner, Okla. BR/TR, 6', 190 lbs. Deb: 8/15/26 C

YEAR	TM/L	W	L	PCT	G	GS	CG	SHO	SV	IP	H	H/G	HR	BB	BB/G	SO	SO/G	ERA	/A	OAVG	OOBP	PR	/A	PF	CPI	WAT	PB	PD	TPI
1926	Cle-A	1	3	.250	8	2	1	0	0	32	25	7.0	1	13	3.7	6	1.7	2.81	139	.227	.303	4	4	97	102	-1.0	0	2	0.6
1927	Cle-A	18	12	.600	43	30	18	1	0	265	291	9.9	3	83	2.8	65	2.2	4.01	102	.283	.333	4	2	99	93	5.2	3	3	0.7
1928	Cle-A	14	14	.500	42	26	10	1	7	220	231	9.4	7	90	3.7	62	2.5	4.05	108	.279	.343	-0	8	108	102	2.7	-1	2	1.0
1929	Cle-A	17	15	.531	40	33	22	2	1	280	299	9.6	7	73	2.3	60	1.9	3.34	128	.272	.311	28	29	101	99	0.0	-3	7	3.2
1930	Cle-A	13	16	.448	37	33	13	1	1	217	255	10.6	12	76	3.2	60	2.5	4.56	107	.293	.344	2	8	105	102	-2.5	-1	4	1.1
1931	Cle-A	15	14	.517	44	34	15	1	4	254	313	11.1	14	88	3.1	83	2.9	4.61	100	.301	.353	-6	1	106	107	0.4	1	3	0.5
1932	Cle-A	12	8	.600	33	21	12	0	2	182	204	10.1	10	59	2.9	65	3.2	4.70	102	.278	.330	-4	2	107	89	0.7	1	1	0.4
1933	Cle-A	5	13	.278	34	17	6	0	1	147	161	9.9	7	61	3.7	44	2.7	3.98	113	.275	.341	5	8	105	108	-4.1	-1	3	1.1
1934	Cle-A	15	10	.600	36	26	15	1	4	195	210	9.7	8	65	3.0	58	2.7	4.75	94	.277	.334	-6	-6	100	86	1.6	3	5	0.2
1935	Cle-A	15	11	.577	36	29	14	3	5	232	252	9.8	8	61	2.4	45	1.7	3.69	119	.277	.319	20	18	99	102	1.4	6	0	2.3
1936	Cle-A	1	5	.167	27	7	1	0	0	64	112	15.8	1	31	4.4	20	2.8	9.00	59	.397	.446	-28	-26	105	92	-2.0	-1	1	-2.1
1937	Cle-A	12	11	.522	35	23	10	2	2	176	213	10.9	8	43	2.2	31	1.6	4.09	109	.295	.331	10	7	97	104	-0.3	-1	3	0.9
1938	Cle-A	8	8	.500	29	15	8	0	1	127	158	11.2	13	45	3.2	27	1.9	4.89	96	.303	.356	-1	-3	98	108	-0.9	-2	1	-0.3
1939	Cle-A	9	10	.474	27	20	7	0	3	143	175	11.0	6	42	2.6	28	1.8	4.91	91	.303	.339	-5	-7	96	95	-1.6	1	5	-0.1
1940	Cle-A	2	1	.667	4	4	2	0	0	24	31	11.6	3	2	0.8	8	3.0	4.88	83	.316	.330	-1	-2	92	104	0.3	-0	0	-0.1
	Was-A	1	2	.333	8	6	1	0	0	37	50	12.2	9	5	1.2	9	2.2	6.57	64	.314	.337	-9	-10	95	94	-0.2	-1	0	-0.8
	StL-A	0	1	.000	6	1	0	0	0	11	19	15.5	0	8	6.5	4	3.3	11.45	41	.358	.443	-9	-8	108	64	-0.4	0	0	-0.6
	Yr	3	4	.429	18	11	3	0	0	72	100	12.5	12	15	1.9	21	2.6	6.75	62	.321	.348	-19	-20	96	64	-0.3	-1	0	-1.5
	NY-N	0	1	.000	1	1	0	0	0	5	9	16.2	1	1	1.8	1	1.8	10.80	36	.409	.435	-4	-4	100	82	-0.4	-0	0	-0.2
1944	StL-A	0	1	.000	1	0	0	0	0	2	3	13.5	0	0	0.0	1	4.5	4.50	76	.300	.300	-0	-0	100	69	-0.4	0	0	0.0
Total	16	158	156	.503	491	328	155	11	31	2613	3011	10.4	118	846	2.9	677	2.3	4.41	102	.289	.339	-0	21	102	99	-1.5	4	40	7.8

■ **CHARLIE HUDSON** Hudson, Charles b: 8/18/49, Ada, Okla. BL/TL, 6'3", 185 lbs. Deb: 5/21/72

YEAR	TM/L	W	L	PCT	G	GS	CG	SHO	SV	IP	H	H/G	HR	BB	BB/G	SO	SO/G	ERA	/A	OAVG	OOBP	PR	/A	PF	CPI	WAT	PB	PD	TPI
1972	StL-N	1	0	1.000	12	0	0	0	0	12	10	7.5	0	7	5.3	4	3.0	5.25	69	.233	.333	-2	-2	105	63	0.5	0	0	-0.1
1973	Tex-A	4	2	.667	25	4	1	1	1	62	59	8.6	3	31	4.5	34	4.9	4.65	82	.254	.331	-6	-6	100	79	1.5	0	0	-0.5
1975	Cal-A	0	1	.000	3	1	0	0	0	6	7	10.5	0	4	6.0	0	0.0	9.00	40	.304	.379	-3	-4	96	57	-0.4	0	0	-0.2
Total	3	5	3	.625	40	5	1	1	1	80	76	8.5	3	42	4.7	38	4.3	5.06	75	.255	.335	-12	-11	100	75	1.6	0	0	-0.8

■ **CHARLES HUDSON** Hudson, Charles Lynn b: 3/16/58, Ennis, Tex. BB/TR, 6'3", 185 lbs. Deb: 5/31/83

YEAR	TM/L	W	L	PCT	G	GS	CG	SHO	SV	IP	H	H/G	HR	BB	BB/G	SO	SO/G	ERA	/A	OAVG	OOBP	PR	/A	PF	CPI	WAT	PB	PD	TPI
1983	Phi-N	8	8	.500	26	26	3	0	0	169	158	8.4	13	53	2.8	101	5.4	3.36	109	.248	.301	5	5	100	95	-0.8	-2	-1	0.3
1984	Phi-N	9	11	.450	30	30	1	1	0	174	181	9.4	12	52	2.7	94	4.9	4.03	90	.265	.314	-9	-8	101	90	-1.0	-2	-2	-1.1
1985	Phi-N	8	13	.381	38	26	3	0	0	193	188	8.8	23	74	3.5	122	5.7	3.78	97	.252	.316	-4	-2	102	102	-2.0	-1	-2	-0.4
1986	Phi-N	7	10	.412	33	23	0	0	0	144	165	10.3	20	58	3.6	82	5.1	4.94	78	.291	.350	-19	-17	104	104	-2.0	-3	-0	-2.0
1987	NY-A	11	7	.611	35	16	6	2	0	155	137	8.0	19	57	3.3	100	5.8	3.60	121	.239	.307	15	13	97	103	1.4	0	-1	1.1
1988	NY-A	6	6	.500	28	12	1	0	2	106	93	7.9	9	36	3.1	58	4.9	4.50	84	.235	.298	-6	-8	96	73	-0.2	0	-0	-0.8

YEAR	TM/L	W	L	PCT	G	GS	CG	SHO	SV	IP	H	H/G	HR	BB	BB/G	SO	SO/G	ERA	/A	OAVG	OOBP	PR	/A	PF	CPI	WAT	PB	PD	TPI
Total	6	49	55	.471	190	133	14	3	2	941	922	8.8	96	330	3.2	557	5.3	3.98	96	.256	.315	-18	-16	100	96	-4.6	-9	-6	-2.9
■ HAL HUDSON	Hudson, Hal Campbell "Bud" or "Lefty" b: 5/4/27, Grosse Pointe, Mich. BL/TL, 5'10", 175 lbs. Deb: 4/20/52																												
1952	StL-A	0	0	—	3	0	0	0	0	6	9	13.5	0	6	9.0	0	0.0	12.00	30	.360	.469	-6	-6	100	64	0.0	-0	-0	-0.5
	Chi-A	0	0	—	2	0	0	0	0	4	7	15.8	0	1	2.3	4	9.0	2.25	162	.389	.421	1	1	99	297	0.0	0	0	0.1
	Yr	0	0	—	5	0	0	0	0	10	16	14.4	0	7	6.3	4	3.6	8.10	45	.372	.451	-5	-5	99	297	0.0	-0	-0	-0.4
1953	Chi-A	0	0	—	1	0	0	0	0	1	0	0.0	0	0	0.0	0	0.0	0.00	—	.000	.000	0	0	104	0	0.0	0	0	0.0
Total	2	0	0	—	6	0	0	0	0	11	16	13.1	0	7	5.7	4	3.3	7.36	50	.364	.442	-4	-4	100	143	0.0	-0	-0	-0.4
■ JESSE HUDSON	Hudson, Jesse James b: 7/22/48, Mansfield, La. BL/TL, 6'2", 165 lbs. Deb: 9/19/69																												
1969	NY-N	0	0	—	1	0	0	0	0	2	2	9.0	0	2	9.0	3	13.5	4.50	79	.250	.400	-0	-0	99	100	0.0	0	0	0.0
■ NAT HUDSON	Hudson, Nathaniel P. b: 1/12/1859, Chicago, Ill. d: 3/14/28, Chicago, Ill. TR, Deb: 4/18/1886																												
1886	StL-a	16	10	.615	29	27	25	0	**1**	234	224	8.6	3	62	2.4	100	3.8	3.04	120	.262	.312	11	16	106	102	-1.2	-0	0	1.6
1887	StL-a	4	4	.500	9	9	7	0	0	67	91	12.2	2	20	2.7	15	2.0	4.97	90	.339	.384	-5	-4	105	106	-1.1	0	0	-0.1
1888	StL-a	25	10	**.714**	39	37	36	5	0	333	283	7.6	8	59	1.6	130	3.5	2.54	128	.242	.279	19	26	106	90	2.3	6	-0	3.5
1889	StL-a	3	2	.600	9	5	4	0	0	60	71	10.7	2	15	2.3	13	2.0	4.20	99	.310	.352	-2	-0	109	96	-0.2	1	0	0.1
Total	4	48	26	.649	86	78	72	5	1	694	669	8.7	15	156	2.0	258	3.3	3.09	116	.265	.308	23	39	106	96	-0.2	6	-0	5.1
■ REX HUDSON	Hudson, Rex Haughton b: 8/11/53, Tulsa, Okla. BB/TR, 5'11", 165 lbs. Deb: 7/27/74																												
1974	LA-N	0	0	—	1	0	0	0	0	2	6	27.0	2	0	0.0	0	0.0	22.50	14	.500	.500	-4	-4	90	85	0.0	0	0	-0.3
■ SID HUDSON	Hudson, Sidney Charles b: 1/3/17, Coalfield, Tenn. BR/TR, 6'4", 180 lbs. Deb: 4/18/40 C																												
1940	Was-A	17	16	.515	38	31	19	3	1	252	272	9.7	20	81	2.9	96	3.4	4.57	91	.274	.327	-5	-11	95	91	3.4	2	1	-0.8
1941	Was-A	13	14	.481	33	33	17	3	0	250	242	8.7	12	97	3.5	108	3.9	3.46	119	.253	.317	19	18	99	101	0.8	-0	2	2.0
1942	Was-A	10	17	.370	35	31	19	1	2	239	266	10.0	9	70	2.6	72	2.7	4.37	83	.276	.325	-19	-20	99	86	-1.5	1	3	-1.5
1946	Was-A	8	11	.421	31	15	6	1	1	142	160	10.1	9	37	2.3	35	2.2	3.61	91	.280	.326	-2	-5	94	106	-1.5	3	2	0.0
1947	Was-A	6	9	.400	20	17	5	1	0	106	113	9.6	8	58	4.9	37	3.1	5.60	66	.272	.360	-22	-22	101	81	-0.2	2	1	-1.8
1948	Was-A	4	16	.200	39	29	4	0	1	182	217	10.7	11	107	5.3	53	2.6	5.88	78	.299	.386	-32	-26	107	94	-4.8	2	3	-1.9
1949	Was-A	8	17	.320	40	27	11	2	1	209	234	10.1	11	91	3.9	54	2.3	4.22	96	.283	.353	-1	-4	96	103	-0.1	2	3	0.1
1950	Was-A	14	14	.500	30	30	17	0	0	238	261	9.9	17	98	3.7	75	2.8	4.08	113	.284	.348	13	14	101	113	1.9	-1	3	1.5
1951	Was-A	5	12	.294	23	19	8	0	0	139	168	10.9	8	52	3.4	43	2.8	5.12	78	.302	.361	-15	-17	97	96	-2.4	2	2	-1.2
1952	Was-A	3	4	.429	7	7	6	0	0	63	59	8.4	4	29	4.1	24	3.4	2.71	136	.257	.332	7	7	100	142	-0.5	-0	2	1.0
	Bos-A	7	9	.438	21	18	7	0	0	134	145	9.7	9	36	2.4	50	3.4	3.63	108	.276	.325	1	5	107	108	-0.9	-1	4	0.8
	Yr	10	13	.435	28	25	13	0	0	197	204	9.3	13	65	3.0	74	3.4	3.34	116	.270	.327	7	11	105	108	-1.4	-0	6	1.8
1953	Bos-A	6	9	.400	30	17	4	0	2	156	164	9.5	13	49	2.8	60	3.5	3.52	123	.269	.326	8	14	108	112	-2.1	-2	1	1.2
1954	Bos-A	3	4	.429	33	5	0	0	5	71	83	10.5	5	30	3.8	27	3.4	4.44	85	.296	.359	-6	-5	101	108	-0.1	-1	0	-0.5
Total	12	104	152	.406	380	279	123	11	13	2181	2384	9.8	136	835	3.4	734	3.0	4.28	95	.278	.341	-54	-54	100	101	-8.0	9	26	-1.1
■ AL HUENKE	Huenke, Albert A. b: 6/26/1891, New Bremen, Ohio d: 9/20/74, St. Mary's, Ohio BR/TR, 6', 175 lbs. Deb: 10/06/14																												
1914	NY-N	0	0	—	1	0	0	0	0	2	2	9.0	0	0	0.0	2	9.0	4.50	58	.250	.250	-0	-0	94	33	0.0	-0	0	0.0
■ PHIL HUFFMAN	Huffman, Phillip Lee b: 6/20/58, Freeport, Tex. BR/TR, 6'2", 180 lbs. Deb: 4/10/79																												
1979	Tor-A	6	18	.250	31	31	2	1	0	173	220	11.4	25	68	3.5	56	2.9	5.77	77	.304	.359	-30	-25	106	94	-3.1	0	0	-2.3
1985	Bal-A	0	0	—	2	1	0	0	0	5	7	12.6	1	5	9.0	2	3.6	14.40	28	.350	.462	-6	-6	98	63	0.0	0	0	-0.4
Total	2	6	18	.250	33	32	2	1	0	178	227	11.5	26	73	3.7	58	2.9	6.02	74	.305	.362	-35	-31	105	94	-3.1	0	0	-2.7
■ ED HUGHES	Hughes, Edward J. b: 10/5/1880, Chicago, Ill. d: 10/11/27, Mc Henry, Ill. 6'1", 180 lbs. Deb: 8/29/02																												
1905	Bos-A	3	2	.600	6	4	2	0	0	33	38	10.4	0	9	2.5	8	2.2	4.64	57	.315	.362	-7	-7	100	83	0.5	-0	-2	-0.8
1906	Bos-A	0	0	—	2	0	0	0	0	10	15	13.5	0	3	2.7	3	2.7	5.40	52	.375	.419	-3	-3	104	102	0.0	-0	-0	-0.2
Total	2	3	2	.600	8	4	2	0	0	43	53	11.1	0	12	2.5	11	2.3	4.81	56	.330	.376	-10	-10	101	87	0.5	-1	-2	-1.0
■ JIM HUGHES	Hughes, James Jay "Jay" b: 1/22/1874, Sacramento, Cal. d: 6/2/24, Sacramento, Cal. BR/TR, Deb: 4/18/1898																												
1898	Bal-N	23	12	.657	38	35	31	5	0	301	268	8.0	4	100	3.0	81	2.4	3.20	112	.259	.324	14	13	100	82	0.8	4	3	2.1
1899	Bro-N	**28**	6	**.824**	35	35	30	3	0	292	250	7.7	6	119	3.7	99	3.1	2.68	147	.253	.333	38	41	102	101	**8.7**	5	2	4.7
1901	Bro-N	17	12	.586	31	29	24	0	0	251	265	9.5	3	102	3.7	96	3.4	3.26	105	.297	.377	2	4	103	117	0.2	-1	1	0.5
1902	Bro-N	15	11	.577	31	30	28	0	0	254	228	8.1	3	55	1.9	94	3.3	2.87	91	.264	.315	-3	-8	94	80	1.2	5	2	-0.5
Total	4	83	41	.669	135	129	113	8	0	1098	1011	8.3	16	376	3.1	370	3.0	3.00	114	.268	.337	51	49	100	95	10.9	13	8	6.8
■ JIM HUGHES	Hughes, James Michael b: 7/2/51, Los Angeles, Cal. BR/TR, 6'3", 190 lbs. Deb: 9/14/74																												
1974	Min-A	0	2	.000	2	2	1	0	0	10	8	7.2	2	4	3.6	8	7.2	5.40	68	.216	.286	-2	-2	101	66	-0.9	0	0	-0.1
1975	Min-A	16	14	.533	37	34	12	2	0	250	241	8.7	17	127	4.6	130	4.7	3.82	106	.255	.346	-1	7	107	105	1.9	0	1	0.7
1976	Min-A	9	14	.391	37	26	3	0	0	177	190	9.7	17	73	3.7	87	4.4	4.98	69	.281	.352	-29	-30	98	94	-3.2	0	-1	-3.1
1977	Min-A	0	0	—	2	0	0	0	0	4	4	9.0	0	1	2.3	1	2.3	2.25	185	.250	.278	1	1	102	105	0.0	-0	-0	0.1
Total	4	25	30	.455	78	62	16	2	0	441	443	9.0	36	205	4.2	226	4.6	4.31	88	.265	.347	-31	-25	103	99	-2.2	0	-1	-2.4
■ JIM HUGHES	Hughes, James Robert b: 3/21/23, Chicago, Ill. BR/TR, 6'1", 200 lbs. Deb: 9/13/52																												
1952	Bro-N	2	1	.667	6	0	0	0	0	19	16	7.6	0	11	5.2	8	3.8	1.42	258	.235	.342	5	5	98	229	0.2	-0	-1	0.4
1953	Bro-N	4	3	.571	48	0	0	0	9	86	80	8.4	6	41	4.3	49	5.1	3.45	123	.245	.328	8	8	100	107	-0.5	1	-1	0.7
1954	Bro-N	8	4	.667	**60**	0	0	0	**24**	87	76	7.9	7	44	4.6	58	6.0	3.21	128	.239	.322	8	9	101	110	1.1	-0	-1	0.7
1955	Bro-N	0	2	.000	24	0	0	0	6	43	41	8.6	10	19	4.0	20	4.2	4.19	97	.256	.330	-1	-1	101	120	-0.9	-2	0	-0.1
1956	Bro-N	0	0	—	5	0	0	0	0	12	10	7.5	3	4	3.0	8	6.0	5.25	72	.233	.292	-2	-2	100	80	0.0	-0	-0	-0.2
	Chi-N	1	3	.250	25	1	0	0	0	45	43	8.6	4	30	6.0	20	4.0	5.20	73	.259	.374	-7	-7	101	92	-0.6	1	-0	-0.6
	Yr	1	3	.250	30	1	0	0	0	57	53	8.4	7	34	5.4	28	4.4	5.21	73	.254	.358	-9	-9	101	92	-0.6	-0	-1	-0.8
1957	Chi-A	0	0	—	4	0	0	0	0	5	12	21.6	0	3	5.4	2	3.6	10.80	34	.462	.517	-4	-4	97	99	0.0	0	0	-0.3
Total	6	15	13	.536	172	1	0	0	39	297	278	8.4	30	152	4.6	165	5.0	3.82	106	.251	.337	7	8	100	114	-0.7	-1	-3	0.6
■ MICKEY HUGHES	Hughes, Michael J. b: 10/25/1866, New York, N.Y. d: 4/10/31, Jersey City, N.J. TR, 5'6", 165 lbs. Deb: 1888																												
1888	Bro-a	25	13	.658	40	40	40	2	0	363	281	7.0	5	98	2.4	159	3.9	2.13	146	.225	.282	37	40	102	98	2.0	-7	0	3.2
1889	Bro-a	9	8	.529	20	17	13	0	0	153	172	10.1	7	86	5.1	54	3.2	4.35	81	.299	.390	-9	-14	92	108	-2.0	-2	0	-1.3
1890	Bro-N	4	4	.500	9	8	6	0	0	66	77	10.5	1	30	4.1	22	3.0	5.18	66	.308	.382	-12	-13	96	83	-0.9	-4	0	-1.3
	Phi-a	1	3	.250	6	5	4	0	0	41	64	14.0	0	21	4.6	15	3.3	5.49	71	.373	.441	-7	-7	101	121	-0.7	-1	0	-0.6
Total	3	39	28	.582	75	70	63	2	0	623	594	8.6	13	235	3.4	250	3.6	3.22	103	.265	.335	10	7	99	100	-1.6	-14	0	0.0
■ DICK HUGHES	Hughes, Richard Henry b: 2/13/38, Stephens, Ark. BR/TR, 6'3", 195 lbs. Deb: 9/11/66																												
1966	StL-N	2	1	.667	6	2	1	1	1	21	12	5.1	0	7	3.0	20	8.6	1.71	210	.162	.247	4	4	100	53	0.5	1	0	0.6
1967	StL-N	16	6	**.727**	37	27	12	3	3	222	164	**6.6**	22	48	1.9	161	6.5	2.68	125	**.203**	**.249**	17	16	99	80	3.3	-2	-2	1.4
1968	StL-N	2	2	.500	25	5	0	0	4	64	45	6.3	7	21	3.0	49	6.9	3.52	79	.202	.265	-4	-5	93	71	-0.2	-1	1	-0.5
Total	3	20	9	.690	68	34	13	4	8	307	221	6.5	29	76	2.2	230	6.7	2.79	116	.200	.252	18	15	98	76	3.6	-2	-1	1.5
■ TOM HUGHES	Hughes, Thomas Edward b: 9/13/34, Ancon, C.Z., Pan. BL/TR, 6'2", 180 lbs. Deb: 9/13/59																												
1959	StL-N	0	2	.000	2	2	0	0	0	4	9	20.3	2	2	4.5	2	4.5	15.75	27	.409	.458	-5	-5	106	79	-0.9	-0	-0	-0.4
■ TOM HUGHES	Hughes, Thomas James "Long Tom" b: 11/29/1878, Chicago, Ill. d: 2/8/56, Chicago, Ill. BR/TR, 6'1", Deb: 9/07/00																												
1900	Chi-N	1	1	.500	3	3	3	0	0	21	31	13.3	0	7	3.0	12	5.1	5.14	68	.368	.416	-3	-4	94	105	0.1	-0	0	-0.3
1901	Chi-N	10	23	.303	37	35	32	1	0	308	309	9.0	4	115	3.4	225	**6.6**	3.24	105	.286	.361	3	5	103	107	-4.1	-8	-2	0.3
1902	Bal-A	7	5	.583	13	13	12	1	0	108	120	10.0	2	32	2.7	45	3.8	3.92	95	.306	.359	-4	-2	104	95	2.2	-3	1	0.0
	Bos-A	3	3	.500	9	8	4	0	0	49	51	9.4	0	24	4.4	15	2.8	3.31	106	.293	.378	1	1	98	114	-0.2	2	-0	0.1
	Yr	10	8	.556	22	21	16	1	0	157	171	9.8	2	56	3.2	60	3.4	3.73	98	.302	.365	-3	-1	102	114	2.0	-3	1	0.1
1903	Bos-A	20	7	.741	33	31	25	5	0	245	232	8.5	4	60	2.2	112	4.1	2.57	123	.271	.319	10	16	108	110	3.8	6	-4	2.0
1904	NY-A	7	11	.389	19	18	12	1	0	136	141	9.3	3	48	3.2	75	5.0	3.71	78	.291	.355	-17	-13	111	97	-3.4	1	-2	-1.5
	Was-A	2	13	.133	16	14	14	0	1	124	133	9.7	4	34	2.5	48	3.5	3.48	74	.298	.348	-12	-13	99	104	-3.6	3	-1	-1.3

YEAR	TM/L	W	L	PCT	G	GS	CG	SHO	SV	IP	H	H/G	HR	BB	BB/G	SO	SO/G	ERA	/A	OAVG	OOBP	PR	/A	PF	CPI	WAT	PB	PD	TPI
	Yr	9	24	.273	35	32	26	1	1	260	274	9.5	7	82	2.8	123	4.3	3.60	76	.294	.351	-29	-25	105	104	-7.0	1	-3	-2.8
1905	Was-A	17	20	.459	39	35	26	6	0	291	239	7.4	3	79	2.4	149	4.6	2.35	119	.247	.303	10	14	106	97	1.5	4	-4	1.1
1906	Was-A	7	17	.292	30	24	18	1	0	204	230	10.1	5	81	3.6	90	4.0	3.62	70	.311	.379	-21	-25	94	115	-2.7	3	-4	-2.9
1907	Was-A	7	14	.333	34	23	18	2	**4**	211	206	8.8	1	47	2.0	102	4.4	3.11	77	.280	.323	-13	-17	94	86	0.2	4	-1	-1.8
1908	Was-A	18	15	.545	43	31	24	3	4	276	224	7.3	3	77	2.5	165	5.4	2.22	104	.227	.287	5	3	97	101	3.8	2	1	0.4
1909	Was-A	4	7	.364	22	13	7	2	1	120	113	8.5	1	33	2.5	77	5.8	2.70	88	.246	.303	-3	-4	96	85	0.7	-2	-0	-0.4
1911	Was-A	11	17	.393	34	27	17	2	0	223	251	10.1	7	77	3.1	86	3.5	3.47	95	.288	.348	-3	-4	99	109	-0.8	-1	-2	-0.7
1912	Was-A	13	10	.565	31	26	11	1	0	196	201	9.2	8	78	3.6	108	5.0	2.94	111	.270	.344	9	7	97	**129**	-0.7	1	0	0.7
1913	Was-A	4	12	.250	36	12	4	0	6	130	129	8.9	6	61	4.2	59	4.1	4.29	72	.253	.350	-20	-18	105	83	-4.7	-1	1	-1.6
Total	13	131	175	.428	399	313	227	25	16	2642	2610	8.9	51	853	2.9	1368	4.7	3.10	94	.274	.336	-59	-53	101	103	-7.9	11	-20	-5.9
■ TOM HUGHES	Hughes, Thomas L. "Salida Tom" b: 1/28/1884, Coal Creek, Colo. d: 11/1/61, Los Angeles, Cal. BR/TR, 6'2", 175 lbs. Deb: 9/18/06																												
1906	NY-A	1	0	1.000	3	1	1	0	0	15	11	6.6	2	1	0.6	5	3.0	4.20	76	.227	.242	-3	-2	118	51	0.5	0	-1	-0.2
1907	NY-A	2	0	1.000	4	3	2	0	0	27	16	5.3	0	11	3.7	10	3.3	2.67	105	.191	.285	-0	0	110	48	1.0	-0	-1	0.0
1909	NY-A	7	8	.467	24	16	9	2	1	119	109	8.2	3	37	2.8	69	5.2	2.65	93	.249	.313	-2	-2	99	99	-0.3	1	-1	-0.3
1910	NY-A	7	9	.438	23	15	11	0	1	152	153	9.1	2	37	2.2	64	3.8	3.49	76	.271	.320	-16	-14	106	86	-2.1	-1	1	-1.3
1914	Bos-N	2	0	1.000	2	2	1	0	0	17	14	7.4	0	4	2.1	11	5.8	2.65	107	.226	.269	0	0	102	62	1.0	-1	1	0.0
1915	Bos-N	16	14	.533	**50**	25	17	4	**9**	280	208	6.7	4	58	1.9	171	5.5	2.12	126	.213	.259	20	17	97	80	-0.3	-3	-2	1.2
1916	Bos-N	16	3	**.842**	40	14	7	1	5	161	121	6.8	2	51	2.9	97	5.4	2.35	101	.215	.284	5	1	91	86	6.2	2	-1	0.1
1917	Bos-N	5	3	.625	11	8	6	2	0	74	54	6.6	1	30	3.6	40	4.9	1.95	134	.216	.291	6	6	97	122	1.2	-3	-0	0.3
1918	Bos-N	0	2	.000	3	3	1	0	0	18	17	8.5	0	6	3.0	9	4.5	3.50	75	.250	.299	-1	-2	95	74	-0.9	1	0	0.0
Total	9	56	39	.589	160	87	55	9	16	863	703	7.3	14	235	2.5	476	5.0	2.56	102	.230	.287	8	5	99	86	6.3	-4	-4	-0.2
■ TOMMY HUGHES	Hughes, Thomas Owen b: 10/7/19, Wilkes-Barre, Pa. BR/TR, 6'1", 190 lbs. Deb: 4/19/41																												
1941	Phi-N	9	14	.391	34	24	5	2	0	170	187	9.9	12	82	4.3	59	3.1	4.45	84	.280	.357	-15	-14	103	105	2.0	0	0	-1.2
1942	Phi-N	12	18	.400	40	31	19	0	1	253	224	8.0	8	99	3.5	77	2.7	3.06	109	.238	.302	7	8	101	96	3.0	-5	2	0.6
1946	Phi-N	6	9	.400	29	13	3	2	1	111	123	10.0	5	44	3.6	34	2.8	4.38	76	.281	.342	-12	-13	98	92	-0.8	-1	-1	-1.5
1947	Phi-N	4	11	.267	29	15	4	1	1	127	121	8.6	5	59	4.2	44	3.1	3.47	119	.265	.347	8	9	102	115	-2.6	-4	0	0.6
1948	Cin-N	0	4	.000	12	4	0	0	0	27	43	14.3	3	24	8.0	7	2.3	9.00	47	.364	.456	-15	-14	106	96	-1.9	-0	-0	-1.3
Total	5	31	56	.356	144	87	31	5	3	688	698	9.1	33	308	4.0	221	2.9	3.92	92	.266	.338	-27	-23	101	101	-0.3	-10	2	-2.8
■ VERN HUGHES	Hughes, Vernon Alexander "Lefty" b: 4/15/1893, Etna, Pa. d: 9/26/61, Sewickley, Pa. BL/TL, 5'10", 155 lbs. Deb: 7/06/14																												
1914	Bal-F	0	0	—	3	0	0	0	0	6	5	7.5	0	3	4.5	0	0.0	3.00	106	.253	.352	0	0	99	93	0.0	-0	0	0.0
■ BILL HUGHES	Hughes, William Nesbert b: 11/18/1896, Philadelphia, Pa. d: 2/25/63, Birmingham, Ala. BR/TR, 5'10.5", 155 lbs. Deb: 9/15/21																												
1921	Pit-N	0	0	—	1	0	0	0	0	2	3	13.5	0	1	4.5	2	9.0	4.50	85	.375	.455	-0	-0	102	177	0.0	0	0	0.0
■ BILL HUGHES	Hughes, William R. b: 11/25/1866, Bladensville, Ill. d: 8/25/43, Santa Ana, Cal. BL/TL, Deb: 9/28/1884																												
1885	Phi-a	0	2	.000	2	2	2	0	0	17	18	9.5	0	10	5.3	4	2.1	5.29	63	.283	.381	-4	-4	102	83	-0.9	0	0	-0.2
■ JIM HUGHEY	Hughey, James Ulysses "Coldwater Jim" b: 3/8/1869, Wakashma, Mich. d: 3/29/45, Coldwater, Mich. TR, 6', Deb: 9/29/1891																												
1891	CM-a	1	0	1.000	2	1	1	0	0	15	18	10.8	0	3	1.8	9	5.4	3.00	140	.313	.347	1	2	113	119	0.5	-1	0	0.1
1893	Chi-N	0	1	.000	2	2	1	0	0	9	14	14.0	0	3	3.0	4	4.0	11.00	44	.372	.418	-6	-6	104	55	-0.4	-0	0	-0.3
1896	Pit-N	6	8	.429	25	14	11	0	0	155	171	9.9	3	67	3.9	48	2.8	4.99	81	.302	.376	-11	-16	93	81	-1.1	-1	0	-1.4
1897	Pit-N	6	10	.375	25	17	13	0	1	149	193	11.7	3	45	2.7	38	2.3	5.07	85	.337	.385	-13	-13	100	91	-1.5	-5	0	-1.4
1898	StL-N	7	24	.226	35	33	31	0	0	284	325	10.3	2	71	2.3	74	2.3	3.93	101	.310	.353	-10	1	110	91	-2.4	-6	-1	-0.3
1899	Cle-N	4	30	.118	36	34	32	0	0	283	403	12.8	9	88	2.8	54	1.7	5.41	68	.360	.407	-49	-54	96	98	-1.9	-5	0	-4.9
1900	StL-N	5	7	.417	20	12	11	0	0	113	147	11.7	3	40	3.2	23	1.8	5.26	66	.339	.395	-20	-23	93	92	-0.6	1	0	-1.9
Total	7	29	80	.266	145	113	100	0	1	1008	1271	11.3	20	317	2.8	250	2.2	4.88	80	.331	.382	-107	-107	100	92	-7.4	-17	-1	-10.1
■ TEX HUGHSON	Hughson, Cecil Carlton b: 2/9/16, Kyle, Tex. BR/TR, 6'3", 198 lbs. Deb: 4/16/41																												
1941	Bos-A	5	3	.625	12	8	4	0	0	61	70	10.3	3	13	1.9	22	3.2	4.13	101	.289	.323	0	0	101	98	0.7	-1	0	0.0
1942	Bos-A	**22**	6	.786	38	30	**22**	4	4	**281**	258	8.3	10	75	2.4	**113**	3.6	2.59	142	.245	.290	33	34	100	111	**7.0**	1	1	3.9
1943	Bos-A	12	15	.444	35	32	**20**	4	2	266	242	8.2	23	73	2.5	114	3.9	2.64	130	.247	.294	19	24	104	**124**	0.0	-4	1	2.4
1944	Bos-A	18	5	**.783**	28	23	19	2	5	203	172	7.6	4	41	1.8	112	5.0	2.26	147	.225	**.264**	26	24	97	85	7.0	-0	-0	2.5
1946	Bos-A	20	11	.645	39	35	21	6	3	278	252	8.2	15	51	**1.7**	172	5.6	2.75	141	.238	.270	23	35	111	86	-0.8	-3	-2	3.4
1947	Bos-A	12	11	.522	29	26	13	3	0	189	173	8.2	17	71	3.4	119	5.7	3.33	119	.244	.308	8	13	107	104	-0.3	-6	-0	0.8
1948	Bos-A	3	1	.750	15	0	0	0	0	19	21	9.9	0	7	3.3	6	2.8	5.21	80	.276	.333	-2	-2	97	71	0.7	-0	-1	-0.2
1949	Bos-A	4	2	.667	29	2	0	0	3	78	82	9.5	5	41	4.7	35	4.0	5.31	82	.268	.355	-10	-8	103	80	0.4	-3	-2	-1.1
Total	8	96	54	.640	225	156	99	19	17	1375	1270	8.3	77	372	2.4	693	4.5	2.95	126	.245	.292	98	119	104	101	14.7	-17	-2	11.7
■ MARK HUISMANN	Huismann, Mark Lawrence b: 5/11/58, Littleton, Colo. BR/TR, 6'3", 195 lbs. Deb: 8/16/83																												
1983	KC-A	2	1	.667	13	0	0	0	0	31	29	8.4	1	17	4.9	20	5.8	5.52	75	.250	.341	-5	-5	102	67	0.5	0	-0	-0.4
1984	KC-A	3	3	.500	38	0	0	0	3	75	84	10.1	7	21	2.5	54	6.5	4.20	95	.286	.327	-2	-2	99	103	0.0	0	0	-0.1
1985	KC-A	1	0	1.000	9	0	0	0	0	19	14	6.6	1	3	1.4	9	4.3	1.89	222	.219	.243	5	5	101	119	0.5	0	0	0.5
1986	KC-A	0	1	.000	10	0	0	0	1	17	18	9.5	1	6	3.2	13	6.9	4.24	99	.269	.324	-0	-0	100	89	-0.4	0	0	0.0
	Sea-A	3	3	.500	36	1	0	0	4	80	80	9.0	18	19	2.1	59	6.6	3.71	120	.256	.299	4	7	106	119	0.5	0	0	0.6
	Yr	3	4	.429	46	1	0	0	5	97	98	9.1	19	25	2.3	72	6.7	3.80	116	.258	.304	4	6	105	119	0.1	0	0	0.6
1987	Sea-A	0	0	—	6	0	0	0	0	15	10	6.0	1	4	2.4	15	9.0	4.80	96	.196	.262	-1	-0	103	51	0.0	0	0	0.0
	Cle-A	2	3	.400	20	0	0	0	2	35	38	9.8	6	8	2.1	23	5.9	5.14	91	.271	.305	-3	-2	105	85	0.1	0	-0	-0.1
	Yr	2	3	.400	26	0	0	0	2	50	48	8.6	7	12	2.2	38	6.8	5.04	92	.247	.283	-3	-2	104	85	0.1	0	0	-0.1
1988	Det-A	1	0	1.000	5	0	0	0	0	5	6	10.8	0	2	3.6	6	10.8	5.40	69	.286	.348	-1	-1	94	72	0.5	0	0	0.0
Total	6	12	11	.522	137	1	0	0	10	277	279	9.1	35	80	2.6	199	6.5	4.22	101	.262	.310	-2	2	103	98	1.7	0	1	0.5
■ HARRY HULIHAN	Hulihan, Harry Joseph b: 4/18/1899, Rutland, Vt. d: 9/11/80, Rutland, Vt. BR/TL, 5'11", 170 lbs. Deb: 8/16/22																												
1922	Bos-N	2	3	.400	7	6	2	0	0	40	40	9.0	0	26	5.8	16	3.6	3.15	127	.274	.395	4	4	98	142	0.2	-0	-1	0.2
■ HANK HULVEY	Hulvey, James Hensel b: 7/18/1897, Mt.Sidney, Va. d: 4/9/82, Mount Sydney, Va. BB/TR, 6', 180 lbs. Deb: 9/05/23																												
1923	Phi-A	0	1	.000	1	1	0	0	0	7	10	12.9	1	2	2.6	2	2.6	7.71	53	.357	.387	-3	-3	102	86	-0.4	0	0	-0.1
■ TOM HUME	Hume, Thomas Hubert b: 3/29/53, Cincinnati, Ohio BR/TR, 6'1", 185 lbs. Deb: 5/25/77																												
1977	Cin-N	3	3	.500	14	5	0	0	0	43	54	11.3	5	17	3.6	22	4.6	7.12	54	.305	.360	-15	-15	99	74	-0.1	1	-0	-1.3
1978	Cin-N	8	11	.421	42	23	3	0	1	174	198	10.2	12	50	2.6	90	4.7	4.14	89	.289	.336	-11	-9	102	103	-2.6	-3	0	-1.1
1979	Cin-N	10	9	.526	57	12	2	0	17	163	162	8.9	12	33	1.8	80	4.4	2.76	130	.262	.291	18	15	96	**117**	-0.5	0	0	1.6
1980	Cin-N	9	10	.474	78	0	0	0	25	137	121	7.9	6	38	2.5	68	4.5	2.56	143	.240	.292	16	17	101	107	-1.4	0	3	2.1
1981	Cin-N	9	4	.692	51	0	0	0	13	68	63	8.3	7	31	4.1	27	3.6	3.44	102	.259	.338	0	1	101	124	1.5	-0	0	0.0
1982	Cin-N	2	6	.250	46	0	0	0	17	64	57	8.0	2	21	3.0	22	3.1	3.09	121	.245	.300	4	5	104	95	-1.3	-1	-1	0.4
1983	Cin-N	3	5	.375	48	0	0	0	9	66	66	9.0	8	41	5.6	34	4.6	4.77	79	.264	.365	-8	-7	104	104	-0.6	-1	1	-0.6
1984	Cin-N	4	13	.235	54	8	0	0	3	113	142	11.3	14	41	3.3	59	4.7	5.65	68	.309	.355	-26	-23	107	96	-4.0	-1	1	-2.2
1985	Cin-N	3	5	.375	56	0	0	0	3	80	65	7.3	7	35	3.9	50	5.6	3.26	116	.224	.311	3	5	105	99	-1.2	-1	0	0.4
1986	Phi-N	4	1	.800	48	1	0	0	4	94	89	8.5	5	34	3.3	51	4.9	2.78	139	.252	.313	10	11	104	123	1.4	-1	1	1.2
1987	Phi-N	1	4	.200	38	6	0	0	0	71	75	9.5	10	41	5.2	29	3.7	5.58	77	.277	.369	-12	-10	105	98	-1.4	0	0	-0.8
	Cin-N	1	0	1.000	11	0	0	0	0	13	14	9.7	0	2	1.4	4	2.8	4.15	101	.292	.315	-0	0	103	89	0.5	0	0	0.0
	Yr	2	4	.333	49	6	0	0	0	84	89	9.5	10	43	4.6	33	3.5	5.36	80	.274	.351	-12	-10	104	89	-0.9	0	0	-0.8
Total	11	57	71	.445	543	55	5	0	92	1086	1106	9.2	88	384	3.2	536	4.4	3.85	97	.268	.326	-22	-12	102	106	-9.7	-5	5	-0.3
■ BILL HUMPHREYS	Humphreys, Bryon William b: 6/17/11, Vienna, Mo. BR/TR, 6', 180 lbs. Deb: 4/24/38																												
1938	Bos-A	0	0	—	2	0	0	0	0	2	5	22.5	0	1	4.5	0	0.0	9.00	53	.500	.500	-1	-1	100	135	0.0	0	0	0.0
■ BOB HUMPHREYS	Humphreys, Robert William b: 8/18/35, Covington, Va. BR/TR, 5'11", 165 lbs. Deb: 9/08/62																												
1962	Det-A	0	1	.000	4	0	0	0	1	5	8	14.4	3	2	3.6	3	5.4	7.20	61	.381	.417	-2	-2	110	158	-0.4	0	0	0.0

YEAR	TM/L	W	L	PCT	G	GS	CG	SHO	SV	IP	H	H/G	HR	BB	BB/G	SO	SO/G	ERA	/A	OAVG	OOBP	PR	/A	PF	CPI	WAT	PB	PD	TPI
1963	StL-N	0	1	.000	9	0	0	0	0	11	11	9.0	4	7	5.7	8	6.5	4.91	71	.282	.396	-2	-2	106	154	-0.4	0	0	-0.1
1964	StL-N	2	0	1.000	28	0	0	0	2	43	32	6.7	3	15	3.1	36	7.5	2.51	157	.213	.282	5	7	111	107	1.0	1	-0	0.8
1965	Chi-N	2	0	1.000	41	0	0	0	0	66	59	8.0	6	27	3.7	38	5.2	3.14	116	.244	.320	3	4	103	118	1.0	-0	-1	0.3
1966	Was-A	7	3	.700	58	1	0	0	3	112	91	7.3	6	28	2.3	88	7.1	2.81	118	.229	.280	8	6	96	96	2.4	1	-0	0.7
1967	Was-A	6	2	.750	48	2	0	0	4	106	93	7.9	13	41	3.5	54	4.6	4.16	81	.238	.311	-11	-10	104	90	2.2	0	-1	-1.0
1968	Was-A	5	7	.417	56	0	0	0	2	93	78	7.5	13	30	2.9	56	5.4	3.68	76	.233	.286	-7	-9	94	94	0.1	1	1	-0.8
1969	Was-A	3	3	.500	47	0	0	0	5	80	69	7.8	3	38	4.3	43	4.8	3.04	115	.233	.317	5	4	96	100	-0.1	-1	0	0.4
1970	Was-A	0	0	—	5	0	0	0	0	7	4	5.1	1	9	11.6	6	7.7	1.29	281	.200	.433	2	2	97	461	0.0	0	0	0.2
	Mil-A	2	4	.333	23	1	0	0	3	46	37	7.2	3	22	4.3	32	6.3	3.13	119	.222	.310	3	3	100	98	-0.4	-1	0	0.2
	Yr	2	4	.333	28	1	0	0	3	53	41	7.0	4	31	5.3	38	6.5	2.89	128	.219	.326	5	5	100	98	-0.4	0	0	0.4
Total	9	27	21	.563	319	4	0	0	20	569	482	7.6	55	219	3.5	364	5.8	3.34	102	.234	.305	4	3	100	105	5.4	1	-1	0.7

■ BERT HUMPHRIES Humphries, Albert b: 9/26/1880, California, Pa. d: 9/21/45, Orlando, Fla. 5'11.5", 182 lbs. Deb: 4/16/10

YEAR	TM/L	W	L	PCT	G	GS	CG	SHO	SV	IP	H	H/G	HR	BB	BB/G	SO	SO/G	ERA	/A	OAVG	OOBP	PR	/A	PF	CPI	WAT	PB	PD	TPI
1910	Phi-N	0	0	—	5	0	0	0	2	10	13	11.7	0	3	2.7	3	2.7	4.50	64	.317	.378	-2	-2	95	101	0.0	0	0	-0.1
1911	Phi-N	3	1	.750	11	5	2	0	1	41	56	12.3	1	10	2.2	13	2.9	4.17	88	.339	.398	-3	-2	108	132	1.0	3	-0	0.0
	Cin-N	4	3	.571	14	7	3	0	0	65	62	8.6	3	18	2.5	16	2.2	2.35	133	.266	.335	8	6	92	153	0.8	-1	0	0.5
	Yr	7	4	.636	25	12	5	0	1	106	118	10.0	4	28	2.4	29	2.5	3.06	109	.292	.347	4	3	98	153	1.8	3	-0	0.5
1912	Cin-N	9	11	.450	30	15	9	2	2	159	162	9.2	6	36	2.0	58	3.3	3.23	99	.259	.308	3	-1	93	85	-0.8	-1	-2	-0.3
1913	Chi-N	16	4	**.800**	28	20	13	2	1	181	169	8.4	10	24	1.2	61	3.0	2.69	116	.250	.273	10	8	97	93	5.6	1	-2	0.7
1914	Chi-N	10	11	.476	34	22	8	2	0	171	162	8.5	5	37	1.9	62	3.3	2.68	103	.250	.284	2	1	99	90	-0.6	2	2	0.5
1915	Chi-N	8	13	.381	31	22	10	4	3	172	183	9.6	6	23	1.2	45	2.4	2.30	123	.280	.301	9	10	103	**140**	-2.3	-0	-2	0.9
Total	6	50	43	.538	153	91	45	10	9	799	807	9.1	31	151	1.7	258	2.9	2.78	109	.265	.302	27	21	98	108	3.7	4	-3	2.2

■ JOHNNY HUMPHRIES Humphries, John William b: 6/23/15, Clifton Forge, Va d: 6/24/65, New Orleans, La. BR/TR, 6'1", 185 lbs. Deb: 5/08/38

YEAR	TM/L	W	L	PCT	G	GS	CG	SHO	SV	IP	H	H/G	HR	BB	BB/G	SO	SO/G	ERA	/A	OAVG	OOBP	PR	/A	PF	CPI	WAT	PB	PD	TPI
1938	Cle-A	9	8	.529	**45**	6	1	0	6	103	105	9.2	6	63	5.5	56	4.9	5.24	89	.264	.360	-5	-6	98	88	-0.5	-1	-1	-0.7
1939	Cle-A	2	4	.333	15	1	0	0	2	28	30	9.6	0	32	10.3	12	3.9	8.36	53	.294	.438	-12	-12	96	80	-1.2	-1	-0	-1.1
1940	Cle-A	0	2	.000	19	1	1	0	1	34	35	9.3	5	29	7.7	17	4.5	8.21	49	.269	.398	-14	-16	92	76	-0.9	-1	-1	-1.4
1941	Chi-A	4	2	.667	14	6	4	4	1	73	63	7.8	2	22	2.7	25	3.1	1.85	210	.230	.287	19	17	94	137	1.0	-1	-1	1.4
1942	Chi-A	12	12	.500	28	28	17	2	0	228	227	9.0	9	59	2.3	71	2.8	2.68	137	.257	.303	25	25	100	121	1.4	4	-2	3.0
1943	Chi-A	11	11	.500	28	27	8	2	0	188	198	9.5	7	54	2.6	51	2.4	3.30	101	.268	.318	-0	1	101	105	-0.7	5	-1	0.6
1944	Chi-A	8	10	.444	30	20	8	0	1	169	170	9.1	9	57	3.0	42	2.2	3.67	95	.267	.325	-5	-3	102	101	-0.3	0	-3	-0.6
1945	Chi-A	6	14	.300	22	21	10	1	1	153	172	10.1	11	48	2.8	33	1.9	4.24	76	.282	.333	-15	-17	96	97	-3.9	-2	-4	-2.3
1946	Phi-N	0	0	—	10	1	0	0	0	25	24	8.6	1	9	3.2	10	3.6	3.96	84	.258	.330	-2	-2	98	86	0.0	0	-1	-0.2
Total	9	52	63	.452	211	111	49	9	12	1001	1024	9.2	50	373	3.4	317	2.9	3.79	97	.265	.328	-9	-13	99	105	-5.1	4	-13	-1.3

■ BEN HUNT Hunt, Benjamin Franklin "High Pockets" b: 1888, Eufaula, Okla. BL/TL, 6'1", 190 lbs. Deb: 8/24/10

YEAR	TM/L	W	L	PCT	G	GS	CG	SHO	SV	IP	H	H/G	HR	BB	BB/G	SO	SO/G	ERA	/A	OAVG	OOBP	PR	/A	PF	CPI	WAT	PB	PD	TPI
1910	Bos-A	2	3	.400	7	7	3	0	0	47	45	8.6	4	20	3.8	19	3.6	4.02	61	.266	.344	-8	-8	97	97	-0.5	-2	-1	-0.8
1913	StL-N	0	1	.000	2	1	0	0	0	8	6	6.8	0	9	10.1	6	6.8	3.38	92	.240	.410	-0	-0	97	154	-0.4	-0	1	0.0
Total	2	2	4	.333	9	8	3	0	0	55	51	8.3	4	29	4.7	25	4.1	3.93	65	.263	.355	-8	-8	97	105	-0.9	-2	0	-0.8

■ KEN HUNT Hunt, Kenneth Raymond b: 12/14/38, Ogden, Utah BR/TR, 6'4", 200 lbs. Deb: 4/16/61

YEAR	TM/L	W	L	PCT	G	GS	CG	SHO	SV	IP	H	H/G	HR	BB	BB/G	SO	SO/G	ERA	/A	OAVG	OOBP	PR	/A	PF	CPI	WAT	PB	PD	TPI
1961	Cin-N	9	10	.474	29	22	4	0	0	136	130	8.6	13	66	4.4	75	5.0	3.97	104	.257	.345	1	3	103	107	-2.2	0	-1	0.2

■ GEORGE HUNTER Hunter, George Henry b: 7/8/1887, Buffalo, N.Y. d: 1/11/68, Harrisburg, Pa. BB , 5'8.5", 165 lbs. Deb: 09

YEAR	TM/L	W	L	PCT	G	GS	CG	SHO	SV	IP	H	H/G	HR	BB	BB/G	SO	SO/G	ERA	/A	OAVG	OOBP	PR	/A	PF	CPI	WAT	PB	PD	TPI
1909	Bro-N	4	10	.286	16	13	10	0	0	113	104	8.3	2	38	3.0	43	3.4	2.47	108	.254	.322	2	3	103	118	-1.4	2	0	0.3

■ JIM HUNTER Hunter, James Augustus "Catfish" b: 4/8/46, Hertford, N.C. BR/TR, 6', 190 lbs. Deb: 5/13/65 H

YEAR	TM/L	W	L	PCT	G	GS	CG	SHO	SV	IP	H	H/G	HR	BB	BB/G	SO	SO/G	ERA	/A	OAVG	OOBP	PR	/A	PF	CPI	WAT	PB	PD	TPI
1965	KC-A	8	8	.500	32	20	3	2	0	133	124	8.4	21	46	3.1	82	5.5	4.26	81	.246	.303	-12	-12	100	92	1.9	-0	-2	-1.4
1966	KC-A	9	11	.450	30	25	4	0	0	177	158	8.0	17	64	3.3	103	5.2	4.02	82	.239	.303	-11	-15	95	85	-0.2	1	-3	-1.7
1967	KC-A	13	17	.433	35	35	13	5	0	260	209	7.2	16	84	2.9	196	6.8	2.80	117	.219	.280	12	14	102	92	1.4	3	-5	1.5
1968	Oak-A	13	13	.500	36	34	11	2	1	234	210	8.1	29	69	2.7	172	6.6	3.35	87	.238	.292	-10	-11	98	101	-0.1	5	-3	-1.0
1969	Oak-A	12	15	.444	38	35	10	3	0	247	210	7.7	34	85	3.1	150	5.5	3.35	99	.234	.299	8	-1	91	105	-2.7	4	-0	0.2
1970	Oak-A	18	14	.563	40	40	9	1	0	262	253	8.7	32	74	2.5	178	6.1	3.81	93	.250	.301	-3	-8	96	93	0.6	4	-2	-0.6
1971	Oak-A	21	11	.656	37	37	16	4	0	274	225	7.4	27	80	2.6	181	5.9	2.96	116	.223	.279	16	14	99	91	1.5	12	-3	2.6
1972	Oak-A	21	7	**.750**	38	37	16	5	0	295	200	6.1	21	70	2.1	191	5.8	2.04	142	.189	.238	34	28	95	76	5.9	2	-2	3.3
1973	Oak-A	21	5	**.808**	36	36	11	3	0	256	222	7.8	39	69	2.4	124	4.4	3.34	98	.232	.281	14	-2	86	97	**7.6**	0	-4	-0.4
1974	Oak-A	**25**	12	.676	41	41	23	6	0	318	268	7.6	25	46	1.3	143	4.0	**2.49**	144	.229	**.256**	**40**	38	99	92	6.0	0	-4	3.8
1975	NY-A	**23**	14	.622	39	39	**30**	7	0	**328**	248	**6.8**	25	83	2.3	177	4.9	2.58	143	**.208**	**.260**	44	41	98	81	4.8	0	-4	3.9
1976	NY-A	17	15	.531	36	36	21	2	0	299	268	8.1	28	68	2.0	173	5.2	3.52	97	.241	.280	0	-3	97	85	-2.4	0	-2	-0.5
1977	NY-A	9	9	.500	22	22	8	1	0	143	137	8.6	29	47	3.0	52	3.3	4.72	83	.250	.308	-10	-12	97	91	-1.8	0	-3	-1.4
1978	NY-A	12	6	.667	21	20	5	1	0	118	98	7.5	16	35	2.7	56	4.3	3.58	102	.226	.281	3	1	97	86	1.4	0	-1	0.0
1979	NY-A	2	9	.182	19	19	1	0	0	105	128	11.0	15	34	2.9	34	2.9	5.31	76	.312	.354	-13	-15	95	105	-3.7	0	-1	-1.4
Total	15	224	166	.574	500	476	181	42	1	3449	2958	7.7	374	954	2.5	2012	5.3	3.26	105	.231	.282	111	59	96	91	20.2	31	-38	6.9

■ LEM HUNTER Hunter, Robert Lemuel b: 1/16/1863, Warren, Ohio d: 11/9/56, W.Lafayette, Ohio Deb: 9/01/1883

YEAR	TM/L	W	L	PCT	G	GS	CG	SHO	SV	IP	H	H/G	HR	BB	BB/G	SO	SO/G	ERA	/A	OAVG	OOBP	PR	/A	PF	CPI	WAT	PB	PD	TPI
1883	Cle-N	0	0	—	1	0	0	0	0	6	10	15.0	0	2	3.0	4	6.0	1.50	217	.379	.423	1	1	104	429	0.0	-0	0	0.1

■ WILLARD HUNTER Hunter, Willard Mitchell b: 3/8/34, Newark, N.J. BR/TL, 6'2", 180 lbs. Deb: 4/16/62

YEAR	TM/L	W	L	PCT	G	GS	CG	SHO	SV	IP	H	H/G	HR	BB	BB/G	SO	SO/G	ERA	/A	OAVG	OOBP	PR	/A	PF	CPI	WAT	PB	PD	TPI
1962	LA-N	0	0	—	1	0	0	0	0	2	6	27.0	1	4	18.0	1	4.5	40.50	9	.545	.588	-8	-8	91	54	0.0	0	0	-0.5
	NY-N	1	6	.143	27	6	1	0	0	63	67	9.6	9	34	4.9	40	5.7	5.57	77	.270	.355	-11	-9	108	89	-1.4	0	-1	-0.9
	Yr	1	6	.143	28	6	1	0	0	65	73	10.1	10	38	5.3	41	5.7	6.65	64	.281	.368	-20	-17	108	89	-1.4	0	-1	-1.4
1964	NY-N	3	3	.500	41	0	0	0	5	49	54	9.9	4	9	1.7	22	4.0	4.41	79	.284	.319	-5	-5	98	92	0.8	0	-0	-0.4
Total	2	4	9	.308	69	6	1	0	5	114	127	10.0	14	47	3.7	63	5.0	5.68	69	.283	.348	-24	-22	104	89	-0.6	1	-1	-1.8

■ WALT HUNTZINGER Huntzinger, Walter Henry "Shakes" b: 2/6/1899, Pottsville, Pa. d: 8/11/81, Upper Darby, Pa. BR/TR, 6', 150 lbs. Deb: 9/29/23

YEAR	TM/L	W	L	PCT	G	GS	CG	SHO	SV	IP	H	H/G	HR	BB	BB/G	SO	SO/G	ERA	/A	OAVG	OOBP	PR	/A	PF	CPI	WAT	PB	PD	TPI
1923	NY-N	0	1	.000	2	1	0	0	0	8	9	10.1	0	1	1.1	2	2.3	7.88	50	.290	.303	-3	-3	99	40	-0.4	-0	-0	-0.3
1924	NY-N	1	1	.500	12	2	0	0	1	32	41	11.5	3	9	2.5	6	1.7	4.50	75	.318	.350	-2	-4	88	114	-0.1	1	-0	-0.2
1925	NY-N	5	1	.833	26	1	0	0	0	64	68	9.6	3	17	2.4	19	2.7	3.52	119	.281	.315	**5**	**5**	98	106	1.9	-1	-1	0.3
1926	StL-N	0	4	.000	9	4	2	0	0	34	35	9.3	4	14	3.7	9	2.4	4.24	90	.267	.331	-2	-2	100	100	-1.9	-1	1	-0.1
	Chi-N	1	1	.500	11	0	0	0	2	29	26	8.1	0	8	2.5	4	1.2	0.93	430	.260	.314	9	10	105	350	0.0	-1	0	1.0
	Yr	1	5	.167	20	4	2	0	2	63	61	8.7	4	22	3.1	13	1.9	2.71	144	.264	.323	8	8	102	350	-1.9	-1	1	0.9
Total	4	7	8	.467	60	8	2	0	3	167	179	9.6	10	49	2.6	40	2.2	3.61	108	.283	.324	7	6	98	145	-0.5	-1	-0	0.7

■ TOM HURD Hurd, Thomas Carr "Whitey" b: 5/27/24, Danville, Va. d: 9/5/82, Waterloo, Iowa BR/TR, 5'9", 155 lbs. Deb: 7/30/54

YEAR	TM/L	W	L	PCT	G	GS	CG	SHO	SV	IP	H	H/G	HR	BB	BB/G	SO	SO/G	ERA	/A	OAVG	OOBP	PR	/A	PF	CPI	WAT	PB	PD	TPI
1954	Bos-A	2	0	1.000	16	0	0	0	1	30	21	6.3	2	12	3.6	14	4.2	3.00	125	.198	.277	2	2	101	73	1.0	1	0	0.3
1955	Bos-A	8	6	.571	43	0	0	0	5	81	72	8.0	7	38	4.2	48	5.3	3.00	162	.242	.323	9	17	122	122	0.4	-1	0	1.6
1956	Bos-A	3	4	.429	40	0	0	0	5	76	84	9.9	5	47	5.6	34	4.0	5.33	80	.289	.381	-10	-9	102	97	-0.7	2	-1	-0.7
Total	3	13	10	.565	99	0	0	0	11	187	177	8.5	14	97	4.7	96	4.6	3.95	112	.255	.341	1	10	111	104	0.7	1	-1	1.2

■ BRUCE HURST Hurst, Bruce Vee b: 3/24/58, St.George, Utah BL/TL, 6'4", 200 lbs. Deb: 4/12/80

YEAR	TM/L	W	L	PCT	G	GS	CG	SHO	SV	IP	H	H/G	HR	BB	BB/G	SO	SO/G	ERA	/A	OAVG	OOBP	PR	/A	PF	CPI	WAT	PB	PD	TPI
1980	Bos-A	2	2	.500	12	7	0	0	0	31	39	11.3	4	16	4.6	16	4.6	9.00	46	.307	.388	-17	-17	102	66	0.0	0	-0	-1.5
1981	Bos-A	2	0	1.000	5	5	0	0	0	23	23	9.0	1	12	4.7	11	4.3	4.30	90	.258	.346	-2	-1	106	91	1.0	0	-0	-0.1
1982	Bos-A	3	7	.300	28	19	0	0	0	117	161	12.4	16	40	3.1	53	4.1	5.77	78	.333	.381	-22	-17	110	108	-2.2	0	1	-1.4
1983	Bos-A	12	12	.500	33	32	6	2	0	211	241	10.3	22	62	2.6	115	4.9	4.09	101	.290	.339	-0	1	102	113	0.5	0	1	0.2
1984	Bos-A	12	12	.500	33	33	9	2	0	218	232	9.6	25	88	3.6	136	5.6	3.92	112	.271	.340	2	11	110	113	-0.7	0	0	1.2
1985	Bos-A	11	13	.458	35	31	6	1	0	229	243	9.6	31	70	2.8	189	7.4	4.52	93	.273	.325	-9	-8	102	99	-1.1	0	0	-0.7
1986	Bos-A	13	8	.619	25	25	11	4	0	174	169	8.7	18	50	2.6	167	8.6	3.00	138	.256	.308	23	22	99	**123**	0.8	0	-1	2.1
1987	Bos-A	15	13	.536	33	33	15	3	0	239	239	9.0	35	76	2.9	190	7.2	4.41	100	.262	.316	2	0	99	97	1.7	0	0	0.0
1988	Bos-A	18	6	.750	33	32	7	1	0	217	222	9.2	21	65	2.7	166	6.9	3.65	117	.264	.313	8	15	108	106	5.8	0	0	1.6
Total	9	88	73	.547	237	217	54	13	0	1459	1569	9.7	173	479	3.0	1043	6.4	4.23	101	.276	.331	-16	9	104	107	5.8	0	1	1.4

YEAR	TM/L	W	L	PCT	G	GS	CG	SHO	SV	IP	H	H/G	HR	BB	BB/G	SO	SO/G	ERA	/A	OAVG	OOBP	PR	/A	PF	CPI	WAT	PB	PD	TPI
■ BILL HUSTED	Husted, William J. b: 10/9/1867, Gloucester, N.J. Deb: 4/29/1890																												
1890	Phi-P	5	10	.333	18	17	12	0	0	129	148	10.3	2	67	4.7	33	2.3	4.88	88	.300	.384	-9	-9	101	86	-2.8	-6	0	-1.0
■ BERT HUSTING	Husting, Berthold Juneau "Pete" b: 3/6/1878, Fond Du Lac, Wis. d: 9/3/48, Milwaukee, Wis. BR/TR, Deb: 8/16/00																												
1900	Pit-N	0	0	—	2	0	0	0	0	8	10	11.3	2	5	5.6	7	7.9	5.63	66	.330	.425	-2	-2	101	125	0.0	-1	0	-0.1
1901	Mil-A	10	15	.400	34	26	19	0	1	217	234	9.7	5	95	3.9	67	2.8	4.27	84	.295	.371	-15	-16	98	92	1.1	-1	5	-0.9
1902	Bos-A	0	1	.000	1	1	1	0	0	8	15	16.9	0	8	9.0	4	4.5	9.00	39	.427	.533	-5	-5	98	104	-0.4	0	0	-0.3
	Phi-A	14	5	.737	32	27	17	1	0	204	240	10.6	7	91	4.0	44	1.9	3.79	100	.319	.392	-5	-0	106	121	3.4	-3	2	0.2
	Yr	14	6	.700	33	28	18	1	0	212	255	10.8	7	99	4.2	48	2.0	3.99	95	.324	.399	-10	-5	106	121	3.0	0	2	-0.1
Total	3	24	21	.533	69	54	37	1	1	437	499	10.3	14	199	4.1	122	2.5	4.16	89	.310	.386	-26	-23	102	106	4.1	-5	7	-1.1
■ JIM HUTCHENSON	Hutchenson, James F. b: 1863, New York, N.Y. d: 12/24/41, New York, N.Y. Deb: 6/10/1884																												
1884	KC-U	1	1	.500	2	2	2	0	0	17	14	7.4	0	1	0.5	5	2.6	2.65	104	.229	.242	1	0	92	65	0.4	-0	0	0.0
■ JOHNNY HUTCHINGS	Hutchings, John Richard Joseph b: 4/14/16, Chicago, Ill. d: 4/27/63, Indianapolis, Ind. BB/TR, 6'2", 250 lbs. Deb: 4/26/40																												
1940	Cin-N	2	1	.667	19	4	0	0	0	54	53	8.8	3	18	3.0	18	3.0	3.50	107	.260	.316	2	2	98	106	0.1	0	-1	0.0
1941	Cin-N	0	0	—	8	0	0	0	0	11	12	9.8	0	4	3.3	5	4.1	4.09	87	.279	.333	-1	-1	98	91	0.0	0	0	0.0
	Bos-N	1	6	.143	36	7	1	1	2	96	110	10.3	6	22	2.1	36	3.4	4.13	84	.287	.325	-5	-7	96	100	-2.2	0	0	-0.6
	Yr	1	6	.143	44	7	1	1	2	107	122	10.3	6	26	2.2	41	3.4	4.12	84	.286	.326	-6	-8	96	100	-2.2	0	0	-0.6
1942	Bos-N	1	0	1.000	20	3	0	0	0	66	66	9.0	2	34	4.6	27	3.7	4.36	74	.260	.351	-8	-8	98	89	0.5	-2	-1	-1.0
1944	Bos-N	1	4	.200	14	7	1	0	1	57	55	8.7	3	26	4.1	26	4.1	3.95	88	.252	.333	-2	-3	96	93	-1.2	-1	-1	-0.3
1945	Bos-N	7	6	.538	57	12	3	2	3	185	173	8.4	21	75	3.6	99	4.8	3.75	114	.244	.315	1	11	113	102	1.2	1	0	1.3
1946	Bos-N	0	1	.000	1	1	0	0	0	3	5	15.0	1	1	3.0	1	3.0	9.00	36	.357	.400	-2	-2	94	93	-0.4	-0	0	-0.1
Total	6	12	18	.400	155	34	5	3	6	472	474	9.0	36	180	3.4	212	4.0	3.95	96	.260	.326	-14	-9	103	99	-2.0	-1	-2	-0.7
■ FRED HUTCHINSON	Hutchinson, Frederick Charles b: 8/12/19, Seattle, Wash. d: 11/12/64, Bradenton, Fla. BL/TR, 6'2", 190 lbs. Deb: 5/02/39 M																												
1939	Det-A	3	6	.333	13	12	3	0	0	85	95	10.1	9	51	5.4	22	2.3	5.19	98	.287	.373	-5	-1	110	107	-1.6	3	0	0.2
1940	Det-A	3	7	.300	17	10	1	0	0	76	85	10.1	6	26	3.1	32	3.8	5.68	84	.281	.337	-11	-8	109	79	-2.4	0	0	-0.5
1946	Det-A	14	11	.560	28	26	16	3	2	207	184	8.0	14	66	2.9	138	6.0	3.09	120	.236	.293	10	14	106	90	-0.8	8	3	2.8
1947	Det-A	18	10	.643	33	25	18	3	2	220	211	8.6	14	61	2.5	113	4.6	3.03	126	.251	.301	17	19	103	105	3.3	11	2	3.6
1948	Det-A	13	11	.542	33	28	15	0	0	221	223	9.1	32	48	**2.0**	92	3.7	4.32	96	.258	**.294**	-1	-4	97	89	1.0	5	3	-0.3
1949	Det-A	15	7	.682	33	21	9	4	1	189	167	8.0	18	52	**2.5**	54	2.6	2.95	151	.237	**.289**	26	31	106	102	3.3	4	2	3.9
1950	Det-A	17	8	.680	39	26	10	1	0	232	269	10.4	18	48	**1.9**	71	2.8	3.96	109	.290	.326	16	10	95	107	2.4	11	2	2.2
1951	Det-A	10	10	.500	31	20	9	2	2	188	204	9.8	11	27	**1.3**	53	2.5	3.69	119	.275	.298	9	15	107	93	0.6	-2	2	1.5
1952	Det-A	2	1	.667	12	1	0	0	0	37	40	9.7	4	9	2.2	12	2.9	3.41	111	.276	.318	1	2	103	120	0.8	-1	2	0.2
1953	Det-A	0	0	—	3	0	0	0	0	10	9	8.1	0	0	0.0	4	3.6	2.70	150	.243	.243	1	2	102	64	0.0	0	-0	0.2
Total	10	95	71	.572	242	169	81	13	7	1465	1487	9.1	126	388	2.4	591	3.6	3.72	113	.262	.308	63	80	103	98	6.6	40	15	13.8
■ IRA HUTCHINSON	Hutchinson, Ira Kendall b: 8/31/10, Chicago, Ill. d: 8/21/73, Chicago, Ill. BR/TR, 5'10.5", 180 lbs. Deb: 9/24/33																												
1933	Chi-A	0	0	—	1	1	0	0	0	4	7	15.8	1	3	6.8	2	4.5	13.50	33	.368	.455	-4	-4	103	72	0.0	0	-0	-0.2
1937	Bos-N	4	6	.400	31	8	1	0	0	92	99	9.7	4	35	3.4	29	2.8	3.72	95	.286	.343	2	-2	90	118	-1.1	-1	1	-0.2
1938	Bos-N	9	8	.529	36	12	4	1	4	151	150	8.9	3	61	3.6	38	2.3	2.74	123	.258	.328	18	10	89	126	0.4	-1	1	1.0
1939	Bro-N	5	2	.714	41	1	0	0	1	106	103	8.7	9	51	4.3	46	3.9	4.33	96	.265	.338	-5	-2	106	100	1.3	-3	1	-0.3
1940	StL-N	4	2	.667	20	2	1	0	1	63	68	9.7	3	19	2.7	19	2.7	3.14	124	.271	.318	5	5	101	119	0.8	0	0	0.6
1941	StL-N	1	5	.167	29	0	0	0	5	47	32	6.1	3	19	3.6	19	3.6	3.83	102	.196	.286	-1	0	107	65	-2.1	0	0	0.1
1944	Bos-N	9	7	.563	40	8	1	1	1	120	136	10.2	8	53	4.0	22	1.7	4.20	83	.296	.363	-8	-10	96	118	2.1	-1	1	-0.9
1945	Bos-N	2	3	.400	11	0	0	0	1	29	33	10.2	2	8	2.5	4	1.2	4.97	86	.277	.326	-4	-2	113	80	-0.1	-1	1	-0.2
Total	8	34	33	.507	209	32	7	2	13	612	628	9.2	33	249	3.7	179	2.6	3.75	98	.270	.336	3	-4	97	111	1.3	-7	5	-0.1
■ BILL HUTCHINSON	Hutchinson, William Forrest "Wild Bill" b: 12/17/1859, New Haven, Conn. d: 3/19/26, Kansas City, Mo. TR , Deb: N/A.																												
1889	Chi-N	16	17	.485	37	36	33	3	0	318	306	8.7	11	117	3.3	136	3.8	3.54	112	.268	.336	17	15	98	94	-0.9	-4	5	1.4
1890	Chi-N	**42**	25	.627	**71**	66	**65**	5	**2**	**603**	505	7.5	20	199	3.0	289	4.3	2.70	141	.242	.308	58	74	107	91	2.2	-5	4	7.1
1891	Chi-N	**44**	19	.698	**66**	58	**56**	4	1	**561**	508	8.1	26	178	2.9	261	4.2	2.81	125	.254	.315	34	43	105	94	**11.4**	-2	-1	3.9
1892	Chi-N	**37**	36	.507	**75**	71	**67**	5	0	**627**	572	8.2	11	187	2.7	**316**	4.5	2.74	112	.255	.313	38	23	93	95	3.6	6	5	3.0
1893	Chi-N	16	24	.400	44	40	38	2	0	348	420	10.9	9	156	4.0	80	2.1	4.76	103	.315	.386	-3	5	104	101	-2.5	0	-2	0.3
1894	Chi-N	14	16	.467	36	34	28	0	0	278	373	12.1	9	140	4.5	59	1.9	6.09	95	.344	.420	-23	-10	108	92	1.2	5	-1	-0.1
1895	Chi-N	13	21	.382	38	35	30	2	0	291	371	11.5	13	129	4.0	85	2.6	4.73	104	.331	.400	2	7	103	110	-6.3	-6	0	0.1
1897	StL-N	1	4	.200	6	5	2	0	0	40	55	12.4	5	22	4.9	5	1.1	6.07	70	.350	.430	-8	-8	99	107	-0.1	1	0	-0.5
Total	8	183	162	.530	373	345	319	21	3	3066	3110	9.1	104	1128	3.3	1231	3.6	3.59	112	.279	.345	114	142	102	96	8.6	-5	12	15.2
■ HERB HUTSON	Hutson, George Herbert b: 7/17/49, Savannah, Ga. BR/TR, 6'2", 205 lbs. Deb: 4/10/74																												
1974	Chi-N	0	2	.000	20	2	0	0	0	29	24	7.4	3	15	4.7	22	6.8	3.41	108	.233	.317	1	1	102	111	-0.9	-0	-0	0.0
■ TOM HUTTON	Hutton, Thomas George b: 4/20/46, Los Angeles, Cal. BL/TL, 5'11", 180 lbs. Deb: 9/16/66																												
1980	Mon-N	0	0	—	1	0	0	0	0	1	3	27.0	1	1	9.0	1	9.0	27.00	13	.500	.571	-3	-3	98	81	0.0	0	0	-0.1
■ DICK HYDE	Hyde, Richard Elde b: 8/3/28, Hindsboro, Ill. BR/TR, 5'11", 170 lbs. Deb: 4/23/55																												
1955	Was-A	0	0	—	3	0	0	0	0	2	2	9.0	0	1	4.5	1	4.5	4.50	83	.286	.333	-0	-0	94	94	0.0	0	0	0.0
1957	Was-A	4	3	.571	52	2	0	0	1	109	104	8.6	4	56	4.6	46	3.8	4.13	93	.261	.346	-4	-3	102	98	1.2	-0	1	-0.2
1958	Was-A	10	3	.769	53	0	0	0	18	103	82	7.2	1	35	3.1	49	4.3	1.75	217	.220	.286	**23**	**23**	100	127	4.2	-2	2	2.5
1959	Was-A	2	5	.286	37	0	0	0	4	54	56	9.3	5	27	4.5	29	4.8	5.00	78	.269	.344	-7	-6	102	92	-1.0	-1	2	-0.4
1960	Was-A	0	1	.000	9	0	0	0	0	9	11	11.0	2	5	5.0	4	4.0	4.00	99	.355	.436	-0	-0	102	204	-0.4	0	-0	0.0
1961	Bal-A	1	2	.333	15	0	0	0	0	21	18	7.7	1	13	5.6	15	6.4	5.57	69	.228	.333	-4	-4	96	63	-0.6	0	1	-0.1
Total	6	17	14	.548	169	2	0	0	23	298	273	8.2	13	137	4.1	144	4.3	3.56	108	.249	.328	8	9	101	107	3.4	-2	6	1.8
■ JIM HYNDMAN	Hyndman, James William b: 1864, Kingston, Pa. Deb: 7/23/1886																												
1886	Phi-a	0	1	.000	1	1	0	0	0	2	5	22.5	1	5	22.5	1	4.5	27.00	13	.481	.650	-5	-5	103	77	-0.4	-1	0	-0.3
■ PAT HYNES	Hynes, Patrick J. b: 3/12/1884, St.Louis, Mo. d: 3/12/07, St.Louis, Mo. TL , Deb: 03																												
1903	StL-N	0	1	.000	1	1	1	0	0	9	10	10.0	0	6	6.0	1	1.0	4.00	83	.306	.414	-1	-1	102	112	-0.4	-0	-1	0.0
1904	StL-A	1	0	1.000	5	2	1	0	0	26	35	12.1	1	7	2.4	6	2.1	6.23	41	.348	.390	-11	-11	98	81	0.5	0	-1	-0.9
Total	2	1	1	.500	6	3	2	0	0	35	45	11.6	1	13	3.3	7	1.8	5.66	48	.337	.396	-11	-11	99	88	0.1	0	-2	-0.9
■ HAM IBURG	Iburg, Herman Edward b: 10/29/1877, San Francisco, Cal d: 2/11/45, San Francisco, Cal BR/TR, 5'11", 165 lbs. Deb: 4/17/02																												
1902	Phi-N	11	18	.379	30	30	20	1	0	236	286	10.9	1	62	2.4	106	4.0	3.89	78	.327	.378	-29	-23	109	100	-1.2	-5	-0	-2.2
■ GARY IGNASIAK	Ignasiak, Gary Raymond b: 9/1/49, Mt.Clemens, Mich. BR/TL, 5'11", 185 lbs. Deb: 9/20/73																												
1973	Det-A	0	0	—	3	0	0	0	0	5	5	9.0	0	3	5.4	4	7.2	3.60	108	.278	.364	0	0	101	118	0.0	0	0	0.0
■ DOC IMLAY	Imlay, Harry Miller b: 1/12/1889, Allentown, N.J. d: 10/7/48, Bordentown, N.J. BR/TR, 5'11", 168 lbs. Deb: 7/07/13																												
1913	Phi-N	0	0	—	9	0	0	0	0	14	19	12.2	1	7	4.5	7	4.5	7.07	50	.358	.413	-6	-5	111	93	0.0	-0	0	-0.5
■ BOB INGERSOLL	Ingersoll, Robert Randolph b: 1/8/1883, Rapid City, S.D. d: 1/13/27, Minneapolis, Minn. BR/TR, 5'11.5", 175 lbs. Deb: 4/23/14																												
1914	Cin-N	0	0	—	4	0	0	0	0	6	5	7.5	0	5	7.5	2	3.0	3.00	100	.250	.423	-0	-0	107	150	0.0	0	0	0.0
■ BERT INKS	Inks, Albert Preston (born Albert Preston Inkstein) b: 1/27/1871, Ligonier, Ind. d: 10/3/41, Ligonier, Ind. BL/TL, 6'3", 175 lbs. Deb: 9/02/1891																												
1891	Bro-N	3	10	.231	13	13	11	1	0	96	99	9.3	2	43	4.0	47	4.4	4.03	81	.280	.358	-7	-8	98	85	-3.2	2	0	-0.5
1892	Bro-N	4	2	.667	9	8	4	1	0	58	48	7.4	0	33	5.1	25	3.9	3.88	84	.237	.344	-4	-4	99	72	0.4	3	0	0.0
	Was-N	1	2	.333	3	3	3	0	0	21	29	12.4	0	10	4.3	11	4.7	5.14	68	.342	.411	-4	-4	106	103	-0.1	1	0	-0.2
	Yr	5	4	.556	12	11	7	1	0	79	77	8.8	0	43	4.9	36	4.1	4.22	79	.268	.363	-8	-8	101	103	0.3	3	0	-0.2
1894	Bal-N	9	4	.692	22	14	10	0	1	133	181	12.2	4	54	3.7	30	2.0	5.55	93	.348	.409	-3	-6	96	98	0.0	2	0	-0.2
	Lou-N	2	6	.250	8	8	8	0	0	60	87	13.1	2	34	5.1	8	1.2	6.60	73	.362	.441	-8	-12	91	96	-0.3	3	0	-0.6

YEAR	TM/L	W	L	PCT	G	GS	CG	SHO	SV	IP	H	H/G	HR	BB	BB/G	SO	SO/G	ERA	/A	OAVG	OOBP	PR	/A	PF	CPI	WAT	PB	PD	TPI
	Yr	11	10	.524	30	22	18	0	1	193	268	12.5	6	88	4.1	38	1.8	5.88	86	.352	.419	-12	-18	94	96	-0.3	2	0	-0.8
1895	Lou-N	7	20	.259	28	27	21	0	0	205	294	12.9	3	78	3.4	42	1.8	6.41	74	.358	.413	-37	-38	99	87	-0.4	-0	0	-2.9
1896	Phi-N	0	1	.000	3	1	0	0	0	10	21	18.9	1	5	4.5	2	1.8	8.10	55	.452	.505	-4	-4	102	121	-0.4	-0	0	-0.2
	Cin-N	1	1	.500	3	3	2	0	0	20	21	9.4	0	9	4.0	2	0.9	4.50	100	.292	.370	-0	0	103	82	-0.1	-1	0	0.0
	Yr	1	2	.333	6	4	2	0	0	30	42	12.6	1	14	4.2	4	1.2	5.70	79	.355	.423	-4	-4	103	82	-0.5	-0	0	-0.2
Total	5	27	46	.370	89	77	59	2	1	603	780	11.6	12	266	4.0	167	2.5	5.54	80	.333	.401	-68	-75	98	90	-4.1	9	0	-4.6
JEFF INNIS	Innis, Jeffrey David b: 7/5/62, Decatur, Ill. BR/TR, 6'1", 170 lbs. Deb: 5/16/87																												
1987	NY-N	0	1	.000	17	1	0	0	0	26	29	10.0	5	4	1.4	28	9.7	3.12	127	.279	.312	3	2	97	148	-0.4	-0	0	0.2
1988	NY-N	1	1	.500	12	0	0	0	0	19	19	9.0	0	2	0.9	14	6.6	1.89	160	.250	.262	3	2	88	113	-0.1	0	-1	0.2
Total	2	1	2	.333	29	1	0	0	0	45	48	9.6	5	6	1.2	42	8.4	2.60	137	.267	.291	6	5	93	133	-0.5	-0	-1	0.4
DANE IORG	Iorg, Dane Charles b: 5/11/50, Eureka, Cal. BL/TR, 6', 180 lbs. Deb: 4/09/77																												
1986	SD-N	0	0	—	2	0	0	0	0	3	5	15.0	2	1	3.0	2	6.0	12.00	30	.357	.400	-3	-3	96	92	0.0	0	0	-0.2
HOOKS IOTT	Iott, Clarence Eugene b: 12/3/19, Mountain Grove, Mo. d: 8/17/80, St.Petersburg, Fla BB/TL, 6'2", 200 lbs. Deb: 9/06/41																												
1941	StL-A	0	0	—	2	0	0	0	0	2	2	9.0	0	1	4.5	1	4.5	9.00	47	.250	.333	-1	-1	101	36	0.0	0	0	0.0
1947	StL-A	0	1	.000	4	0	0	0	0	8	15	16.9	4	14	15.8	6	6.8	16.88	23	.375	.537	-12	-12	106	86	-0.4	-0	0	-0.9
	NY-N	3	8	.273	20	9	2	1	0	71	67	8.5	3	52	6.6	46	5.8	5.96	68	.251	.366	-15	-15	99	72	-2.7	1	-0	-1.3
Total	2	3	9	.250	26	9	2	1	0	81	84	9.3	7	67	7.4	53	5.9	7.11	57	.267	.389	-28	-28	100	73	-3.1	1	0	-2.2
ARTHUR IRWIN	Irwin, Arthur Albert "Doc" or "Sandy" b: 2/14/1858, Toronto, Ont., Can. d: 7/16/21, Atlantic Ocean BL/TR, 5'8.5", 158 lbs. Deb: 5/01/1880 M																												
1884	Pro-N	0	0	—	1	0	0	0	0	3	5	15.0	0	1	3.0	0	0.0	3.00	95	.381	.424	-0	-0	96	209	0.0	0	0	0.0
1889	Was-N	0	0	—	1	0	0	0	0	1	1	9.0	0	0	0.0	0	0.0	0.00	—	.276	.276	0	0	96	0	0.0	0	0	0.0
Total	2	0	0	—	2	0	0	0	0	4	6	13.5	0	1	2.3	0	0.0	2.25	138	.358	.394	0	0	96	157	0.0	0	0	0.0
BILL IRWIN	Irwin, William Franklin "Phil" b: 9/16/1859, Neville, Ohio d: 8/7/33, Ft.Thomas, Ky. BR/TR, 6', 195 lbs. Deb: 8/30/1886																												
1886	Cin-a	0	2	.000	2	2	2	0	0	17	18	9.5	2	8	4.2	6	3.2	5.82	57	.282	.362	-4	-5	96	86	-0.9	-1	0	-0.3
FRANK ISBELL	Isbell, William Frank "Bald Eagle" b: 8/21/1875, Delevan, N.Y. d: 7/15/41, Wichita, Kan. BL/TR, 5'11", 190 lbs. Deb: 5/01/1898																												
1898	Chi-N	4	7	.364	13	9	7	0	0	81	86	9.6	0	42	4.7	16	1.8	3.56	103	.294	.383	0	1	102	109	-2.0	-0	0	0.1
1901	Chi-A	0	0	—	1	0	0	0	0	1	2	18.0	0	0	0.0	0	0.0	9.00	39	.438	.438	-1	-1	96	80	0.0	0	0	0.0
1902	Chi-A	0	0	—	1	1	0	0	0	1	3	27.0	0	1	9.0	1	9.0	9.00	37	.544	.614	-1	-1	94	166	0.0	0	1	0.0
1906	Chi-A	0	0	—	1	0	0	0	0	2	1	4.5	0	0	0.0	2	9.0	0.00	—	.167	.167	1	1	89	0	0.0	0	0	0.1
1907	Chi-A	0	0	—	1	0	0	0	1	⅓	0	0.0	0	0	0.0	0	0.0	0.00	—	—	—	0	0	101	0	0.0	0	0	0.0
Total	5	4	7	.364	17	10	7	0	1	85	92	9.7	0	43	4.6	19	2.0	3.60	101	.298	.384	-0	0	101	107	-2.0	0	1	0.2
AL JACKSON	Jackson, Alvin Neil b: 12/25/35, Waco, Tex. BL/TL, 5'10", 169 lbs. Deb: 6/01/59 C																												
1959	Pit-N	0	0	—	8	3	0	0	0	18	30	15.0	1	8	4.0	13	6.5	6.50	63	.405	.452	-5	-5	104	123	0.0	-0	0	-0.4
1961	Pit-N	1	0	1.000	3	2	1	0	0	24	20	7.5	2	4	1.5	15	5.6	3.38	118	.233	.264	2	2	99	76	0.5	-1	1	0.2
1962	NY-N	8	20	.286	36	33	12	4	0	231	244	9.5	16	78	3.0	118	4.6	4.40	97	.273	.328	-12	-3	108	90	0.8	-5	4	-0.2
1963	NY-N	13	17	.433	37	34	11	0	1	227	237	9.4	25	84	3.3	142	5.6	3.96	86	.267	.333	-17	-14	104	108	3.1	2	2	-1.0
1964	NY-N	11	16	.407	40	31	11	3	1	213	229	9.7	18	60	2.5	112	4.7	4.27	81	.272	.320	-17	-19	98	92	1.9	2	0	-1.6
1965	NY-N	8	20	.286	37	31	7	3	1	205	217	9.5	17	61	2.7	120	5.3	4.35	85	.271	.324	-18	-15	104	92	-1.1	-2	2	-1.4
1966	StL-N	13	15	.464	36	30	11	3	0	233	222	8.6	18	45	1.7	90	3.5	2.51	144	.250	.284	28	28	100	**117**	-1.5	2	4	4.0
1967	StL-N	9	4	.692	38	11	1	1	1	107	117	9.8	7	29	2.4	43	3.6	3.95	85	.279	.320	-7	-7	99	98	1.2	2	2	-0.2
1968	NY-N	3	7	.300	25	9	0	0	3	93	88	8.5	5	17	1.6	59	5.7	3.68	83	.249	.285	-7	-6	103	74	-1.6	1	1	-0.4
1969	NY-N	0	0	—	9	0	0	0	0	11	18	14.7	1	4	3.3	10	8.2	10.64	34	.353	.397	-9	-9	99	64	0.0	-0	0	-0.7
	Cin-N	1	0	1.000	33	0	0	0	3	27	27	9.0	5	17	5.7	16	5.3	5.33	66	.260	.373	-5	-5	99	104	0.5	0	-0	-0.5
	Yr	1	0	1.000	42	0	0	0	3	38	45	10.7	6	21	5.0	26	6.2	6.87	52	.285	.375	-14	-14	99	104	0.5	-0	-0	-1.2
Total	10	67	99	.404	302	184	54	14	10	1389	1449	9.4	115	407	2.6	738	4.8	3.98	91	.268	.319	-67	-54	102	98	3.8	3	16	-2.2
CHARLIE JACKSON	Jackson, Charles Bernard b: 8/4/1876, Versailles, Ohio d: 11/23/57, Scottsbluff, Neb. Deb: 8/11/05																												
1905	Det-A	0	2	.000	2	2	1	0	0	11	14	11.5	1	7	5.7	3	2.5	5.73	46	.337	.432	-4	-4	100	107	-0.9	0	-0	-0.3
DANNY JACKSON	Jackson, Danny Lynn b: 1/5/62, San Antonio, Tex. BR/TL, 6', 190 lbs. Deb: 9/11/83																												
1983	KC-A	1	1	.500	4	3	0	0	0	19	26	12.3	1	6	2.8	9	4.3	5.21	80	.325	.368	-2	-2	102	101	0.0	0	0	-0.1
1984	KC-A	2	6	.250	15	11	1	0	0	76	84	9.9	4	35	4.1	40	4.7	4.26	93	.285	.367	-2	-2	99	109	-2.0	0	-0	-0.2
1985	KC-A	14	12	.538	32	32	4	3	0	208	209	9.0	7	76	3.3	114	4.9	3.42	123	.261	.326	17	18	101	104	-0.5	0	-1	1.7
1986	KC-A	11	12	.478	32	27	4	1	1	186	177	8.6	13	79	3.8	115	5.6	3.19	131	.256	.330	21	21	100	121	0.2	0	-1	2.0
1987	KC-A	9	18	.333	36	34	11	2	0	224	219	8.8	11	109	4.4	152	6.1	4.02	116	.258	.341	11	16	104	98	-5.2	0	-2	1.3
1988	Cin-N	**23**	8	.742	35	35	**15**	6	0	261	206	7.1	13	71	2.4	161	5.6	2.72	133	.218	.270	21	26	105	87	7.6	-0	2	3.1
Total	6	60	57	.513	154	142	35	12	1	974	921	8.5	49	376	3.5	591	5.5	3.43	120	.252	.320	65	76	102	102	0.1	-0	-2	7.8
DARRELL JACKSON	Jackson, Darrell Preston b: 4/3/56, Los Angeles, Cal. BB/TL, 5'10", 150 lbs. Deb: 6/16/78																												
1978	Min-A	4	6	.400	19	15	1	1	0	92	89	8.7	9	48	4.7	54	5.3	4.50	79	.256	.344	-7	-10	94	93	-0.5	0	-1	-0.9
1979	Min-A	4	4	.500	24	8	1	0	0	69	89	11.6	5	26	3.4	43	5.6	4.30	106	.319	.373	-1	2	108	125	0.0	0	1	0.3
1980	Min-A	9	9	.500	32	25	1	0	1	172	161	8.4	15	69	3.6	90	4.7	3.87	114	.250	.320	3	10	109	94	0.4	0	-0	1.0
1981	Min-A	3	3	.500	14	5	0	0	0	33	35	9.5	1	19	5.2	26	7.1	4.36	89	.282	.379	-3	-2	107	106	0.6	0	-1	-0.2
1982	Min-A	0	5	.000	13	7	0	0	0	45	51	10.2	6	24	4.8	16	3.2	6.20	67	.297	.376	-11	-10	102	92	-2.4	0	-0	-0.9
Total	5	20	27	.426	102	60	3	1	1	411	425	9.3	36	186	4.1	229	5.0	4.38	95	.272	.346	-18	-9	105	100	-1.9	0	-1	-0.7
GRANT JACKSON	Jackson, Grant Dwight "Buck" b: 9/28/42, Fostoria, Ohio BL/TL, 6', 180 lbs. Deb: 9/03/65 C																												
1965	Phi-N	1	1	.500	6	2	0	0	0	14	17	10.9	4	5	3.2	15	9.6	7.07	47	.304	.361	-5	-6	95	92	0.0	-0	0	-0.5
1966	Phi-N	0	0	—	2	0	0	0	0	2	2	9.0	0	3	13.5	0	0.0	4.50	80	.333	.556	-0	-0	100	181	0.0	0	0	0.0
1967	Phi-N	2	3	.400	43	4	0	0	1	84	86	9.2	3	43	4.6	83	8.9	3.86	91	.267	.348	-4	-3	104	105	-0.4	-0	-2	-0.5
1968	Phi-N	1	6	.143	33	6	1	0	1	61	59	8.7	4	20	3.0	49	7.2	2.95	100	.248	.299	-0	-0	99	106	-2.4	1	0	0.1
1969	Phi-N	14	18	.438	38	35	13	4	1	253	237	8.4	16	92	3.3	180	6.4	3.34	107	.249	.312	7	7	100	101	1.6	-1	-2	0.4
1970	Phi-N	5	15	.250	32	23	1	0	0	150	170	10.2	17	61	3.7	104	6.2	5.28	75	.288	.347	-20	-22	98	94	-4.7	-2	0	-2.2
1971	Bal-A	4	3	.571	29	9	0	0	0	78	72	8.3	7	20	2.3	51	5.9	3.12	111	.249	.296	3	3	100	104	-0.3	0	-0	0.3
1972	Bal-A	1	1	.500	32	0	0	0	8	41	33	7.2	1	9	2.0	34	7.5	2.63	112	.217	.261	2	1	96	65	0.0	-0	0	0.1
1973	Bal-A	8	0	1.000	45	0	0	0	9	80	54	6.1	5	24	2.7	47	5.3	1.91	210	.198	.256	17	19	105	104	4.0	0	0	1.9
1974	Bal-A	6	4	.600	49	0	0	0	12	67	48	6.4	7	22	3.0	56	7.5	2.55	131	.198	.261	8	6	92	89	0.5	0	-1	0.5
1975	Bal-A	4	3	.571	41	0	0	0	7	48	42	7.9	3	21	3.9	39	7.3	3.38	100	.241	.317	2	0	89	100	0.0	0	0	0.0
1976	Bal-A	1	1	.500	13	0	0	0	3	19	19	9.0	1	9	4.3	14	6.6	5.21	66	.268	.361	-4	-4	97	83	0.0	0	0	-0.3
	NY-A	6	0	1.000	21	2	1	1	1	59	38	5.8	1	16	2.4	25	3.8	1.68	204	.186	.242	12	11	97	80	3.0	0	-1	1.1
	Yr	7	1	.875	34	2	1	1	4	78	57	6.6	2	25	2.9	39	4.5	2.54	135	.205	.268	9	8	97	80	3.0	0	-1	0.8
1977	Pit-N	5	3	.625	49	2	0	0	4	91	81	8.0	11	39	3.9	41	4.1	3.86	103	.240	.314	1	1	102	97	0.3	2	-1	0.2
1978	Pit-N	7	5	.583	60	0	0	0	5	77	89	10.4	5	32	3.7	45	5.3	3.27	115	.298	.353	3	4	105	147	0.5	1	0	0.5
1979	Pit-N	8	5	.615	72	0	0	0	14	82	67	7.4	9	35	3.8	39	4.3	2.96	131	.230	.307	7	8	104	117	0.2	-1	-1	0.7
1980	Pit-N	8	4	.667	61	0	0	0	9	71	71	9.0	4	20	2.5	31	3.9	2.92	128	.275	.315	5	6	103	129	2.0	-1	-0	0.5
1981	Pit-N	1	2	.333	35	0	0	0	4	32	30	8.4	1	10	2.8	17	4.8	2.53	133	.248	.296	3	3	96	114	-0.3	-0	-1	0.2
	Mon-N	1	0	1.000	10	0	0	0	0	11	14	11.5	2	9	7.4	4	3.3	7.36	46	.333	.426	-5	-5	98	105	0.5	0	0	-0.4
	Yr	2	2	.500	45	0	0	0	4	43	44	9.2	3	19	4.0	21	4.4	3.77	90	.267	.333	-1	-2	97	105	0.2	-0	-1	-0.2
1982	KC-A	3	1	.750	20	0	0	0	0	38	42	9.9	7	21	5.0	15	3.6	5.21	78	.271	.361	-5	-5	100	104	0.9	0	-0	-0.4
	Pit-N	0	0	—	1	0	0	0	0	1	1	9.0	1	0	0.0	0	0.0	9.00	44	.333	.333	-1	-1	110	130	0.0	0	0	0.0
Total	18	86	75	.534	692	83	16	5	79	1359	1272	8.4	109	511	3.4	889	5.9	3.46	105	.251	.314	27	25	100	103	5.4	-2	-8	2.2
JOHN JACKSON	Jackson, John Lewis b: 7/15/09, Wynnefield, Pa. d: 10/24/56, Somers Point, N.J. BR/TR, 6'2", 180 lbs. Deb: 6/20/33																												
1933	Phi-N	2	2	.500	10	7	1	0	0	54	74	12.3	3	35	5.8	11	1.8	6.00	67	.329	.427	-16	-12	121	108	0.4	-1	-2	-1.3

YEAR	TM/L	W	L	PCT	G	GS	CG	SHO	SV	IP	H	H/G	HR	BB	BB/G	SO	SO/G	ERA	/A	OAVG	OOBP	PR	/A	PF	CPI	WAT	PB	PD	TPI
■ **LARRY JACKSON**	Jackson, Lawrence Curtis b: 6/2/31, Nampa, Idaho BR/TR, 6'1.5", 175 lbs. Deb: 4/17/55																												
1955	StL-N	9	14	.391	37	25	4	1	2	177	189	9.6	25	72	3.7	88	4.5	4.32	96	.277	.348	-6	-4	102	113	-1.4	-6	0	-0.8
1956	StL-N	2	2	.500	51	1	0	0	9	85	75	7.9	5	45	4.8	50	5.3	4.13	91	.240	.331	-3	-4	99	83	0.0	-0	2	-0.1
1957	StL-N	15	9	.625	41	22	6	2	1	210	196	8.4	21	57	2.4	96	4.1	3.47	111	.248	.298	9	9	99	96	1.9	0	4	1.4
1958	StL-N	13	13	.500	49	23	11	1	8	198	211	9.6	21	51	2.3	124	5.6	3.68	116	.272	.322	6	13	108	108	0.9	-2	-2	0.9
1959	StL-N	14	13	.519	40	37	12	3	0	256	271	9.5	13	64	2.3	145	5.1	3.30	127	.270	.314	18	25	106	104	1.7	-3	-0	2.3
1960	StL-N	18	13	.581	43	38	14	3	0	**282**	277	8.8	22	70	2.2	171	5.5	3.48	117	.257	.298	9	18	108	97	1.0	2	-2	2.0
1961	StL-N	14	11	.560	33	28	12	3	0	211	203	8.7	20	56	2.4	113	4.8	3.75	121	.252	.299	7	18	113	89	1.2	-0	1	2.1
1962	StL-N	16	11	.593	36	35	11	2	0	252	267	9.5	25	64	2.3	112	4.0	3.75	112	.269	.314	5	13	107	102	2.4	2	1	1.7
1963	Chi-N	14	18	.438	37	37	13	4	0	275	256	8.4	11	54	1.8	153	5.0	2.55	136	.245	.281	22	28	105	102	-2.5	3	2	3.8
1964	Chi-N	**24**	11	.686	40	38	19	3	0	298	265	8.0	17	58	1.8	148	4.5	3.14	120	.235	.270	13	21	106	79	**8.2**	0	7	3.1
1965	Chi-N	14	21	.400	39	39	12	4	0	257	268	9.4	28	57	2.0	131	4.6	3.85	95	.267	.306	-9	-6	103	99	-2.1	1	3	-0.1
1966	Chi-N	0	2	.000	3	2	0	0	0	8	14	15.8	3	4	4.5	5	5.6	13.50	27	.368	.419	-9	-9	103	71	-0.9	-0	0	-0.7
	Phi-N	15	13	.536	35	33	12	5	0	247	243	8.9	22	58	2.1	107	3.9	2.99	121	.259	.302	17	17	100	115	0.0	-0	1	2.0
	Yr	15	15	.500	38	35	12	5	0	255	257	9.1	25	62	2.2	112	4.0	3.32	109	.264	.307	8	9	100	115	-0.9	-0	2	1.3
1967	Phi-N	13	15	.464	40	37	11	4	0	262	242	8.3	17	54	1.9	139	4.8	3.09	113	.241	.280	8	12	104	89	-1.3	-0	4	1.9
1968	Phi-N	13	17	.433	34	34	12	2	0	244	229	8.4	9	60	2.2	127	4.7	2.77	107	.248	.294	6	5	99	100	-1.3	-0	1	0.6
Total	14	194	183	.515	558	429	149	37	20	3262	3206	8.8	259	824	2.3	1709	4.7	3.40	113	.256	.301	95	156	105	98	7.8	-5	24	20.1
■ **MICHAEL JACKSON**	Jackson, Michael Ray b: 12/22/64, Houston, Tex. BR/TR, 6'1", 185 lbs. Deb: 8/11/86																												
1986	Phi-N	0	0	—	9	0	0	0	0	13	12	8.3	2	4	2.8	3	2.1	3.46	112	.250	.333	0	1	104	126	0.0	0	-0	0.0
1987	Phi-N	3	10	.231	55	7	0	0	1	109	88	7.3	16	56	4.6	93	7.7	4.21	101	.219	.314	-2	1	105	88	-3.5	-0	-1	0.0
1988	Sea-A	6	5	.545	62	0	0	0	4	99	74	6.7	10	43	3.9	76	6.9	2.64	163	.209	.289	15	18	108	115	1.2	0	-0	1.8
Total	3	9	15	.375	126	7	0	0	5	221	174	7.1	28	103	4.2	172	7.0	3.46	123	.216	.304	14	20	106	102	-2.3	-0	-1	1.8
■ **MIKE JACKSON**	Jackson, Michael Warren b: 3/27/46, Paterson, N.J. BL/TL, 6'3", 190 lbs. Deb: 5/10/70																												
1970	Phi-N	1	1	.500	5	0	0	0	0	6	6	9.0	0	4	6.0	4	6.0	1.50	264	.286	.400	2	2	98	324	0.1	0	0	0.2
1971	StL-N	0	0	—	1	0	0	0	0	1	1	9.0	0	1	9.0	0	0.0	0.00	—	.333	.500	0	0	100	0	0.0	-0	0	0.0
1972	KC-A	1	2	.333	7	3	0	0	0	20	24	10.8	0	14	6.3	15	6.7	6.30	49	.320	.413	-7	-7	100	87	-0.4	-1	1	-0.6
1973	KC-A	0	0	—	9	0	0	0	0	22	25	10.2	3	20	8.2	13	5.3	6.95	60	.301	.434	-8	-7	109	99	0.0	0	0	-0.6
	Cle-A	0	0	—	1	0	0	0	0	1	1	9.0	0	0	0.0	1	9.0	0.00	—	.333	.333	0	0	99	0	0.0	0	0	0.0
	Yr	0	0	—	10	0	0	0	0	23	26	10.2	3	20	7.8	14	5.5	6.65	62	.295	.422	-7	-6	109	0	0.0	0	0	-0.6
Total	4	2	3	.400	23	3	0	0	0	50	57	10.3	3	39	7.0	33	5.9	5.76	64	.308	.422	-12	-12	104	117	-0.3	-0	1	-1.0
■ **ROY LEE JACKSON**	Jackson, Roy Lee b: 5/1/54, Opelika, Ala. BR/TR, 6'2", 190 lbs. Deb: 9/13/77																												
1977	NY-N	0	2	.000	4	4	0	0	0	24	25	9.4	2	15	5.6	13	4.9	6.00	63	.263	.371	-6	-6	97	80	-0.9	-1	-1	-0.6
1978	NY-N	0	0	—	4	2	0	0	0	13	21	14.5	2	6	4.2	6	4.2	9.00	40	.429	.475	-8	-8	99	106	0.0	1	0	-0.5
1979	NY-N	1	0	1.000	8	0	0	0	0	16	11	6.2	1	5	2.8	10	5.6	2.25	160	.200	.279	3	2	96	99	0.5	0	0	0.3
1980	NY-N	1	7	.125	24	8	1	0	1	71	78	9.9	4	20	2.5	58	7.4	4.18	84	.287	.328	-5	-5	97	96	-2.7	1	-1	-0.6
1981	Tor-A	1	2	.333	39	0	0	0	7	62	65	9.4	5	25	3.6	27	3.9	2.61	158	.275	.342	7	11	113	165	0.0	0	0	1.1
1982	Tor-A	8	8	.500	48	2	0	0	6	97	77	7.1	7	31	2.9	71	6.6	3.06	145	.218	.279	11	15	109	84	0.3	0	0	1.5
1983	Tor-A	8	3	.727	49	0	0	0	7	92	92	9.0	6	41	4.0	48	4.7	4.50	98	.267	.338	-4	-1	108	94	2.3	0	0	0.0
1984	Tor-A	7	8	.467	54	0	0	0	10	86	73	7.6	12	31	3.2	58	6.1	3.56	113	.230	.296	4	5	101	98	-1.1	0	0	0.5
1985	SD-N	2	3	.400	22	2	0	0	2	40	32	7.2	4	13	2.9	28	6.3	2.70	135	.224	.282	4	4	101	111	-0.5	-1	0	0.4
1986	Min-A	0	1	.000	28	0	0	0	1	58	57	8.8	7	16	2.5	32	5.0	3.88	118	.256	.305	2	4	109	99	-0.4	0	-0	0.4
Total	10	28	34	.452	280	18	1	0	34	559	531	8.5	50	203	3.3	351	5.7	3.77	109	.254	.317	9	21	105	103	-2.5	1	-1	2.5
■ **TONY JACOBS**	Jacobs, Anthony Robert b: 8/5/25, Dixmoor, Ill. d: 12/21/80, Nashville, Tenn. BB/TR, 5'9", 150 lbs. Deb: 9/19/48																												
1948	Chi-N	0	0	—	1	0	0	0	0	2	3	13.5	1	0	0.0	2	9.0	4.50	83	.333	.333	-0	-0	95	180	0.0	0	0	0.0
1955	StL-N	0	0	—	1	0	0	0	0	2	6	27.0	1	1	4.5	1	4.5	18.00	23	.500	.538	-3	-3	102	93	0.0	-0	0	-0.2
Total	2	0	0	—	2	0	0	0	0	4	9	20.3	2	1	2.3	3	6.8	11.25	35	.429	.455	-3	-3	99	137	0.0	-0	0	-0.2
■ **ART JACOBS**	Jacobs, Arthur Edward b: 8/28/02, Luckey, Ohio d: 6/8/67, Inglewood, Cal. BL/TL, 5'10", 170 lbs. Deb: 6/18/39																												
1939	Cin-N	0	0	—	1	0	0	0	1	1	2	18.0	0	1	9.0	0	0.0	9.00	43	.400	.500	-1	-1	100	105	0.0	0	0	0.0
■ **BUCKY JACOBS**	Jacobs, Newton Smith b: 3/21/13, Altavista, Va. BR/TR, 5'11", 155 lbs. Deb: 6/27/37																												
1937	Was-A	1	1	.500	11	1	0	0	0	22	26	10.6	0	11	4.5	8	3.3	4.91	90	.295	.366	-1	-1	96	94	0.0	-1	0	-0.1
1939	Was-A	0	0	—	2	0	0	0	0	3	1	3.0	0	0	0.0	1	3.0	0.00	—	.100	.100	2	1	91	0	0.0	0	0	0.1
1940	Was-A	0	1	.000	9	0	0	0	0	15	16	9.6	1	9	5.4	6	3.6	6.00	70	.271	.375	-3	-3	95	85	-0.4	-0	1	-0.1
Total	3	1	2	.333	22	1	0	0	0	40	43	9.7	1	20	4.5	15	3.4	4.95	87	.274	.355	-2	-3	95	84	-0.4	-1	2	-0.1
■ **ELMER JACOBS**	Jacobs, William Elmer b: 8/10/1892, Salem, Mo. d: 2/10/58, Salem, Mo. BR/TR, 6', 165 lbs. Deb: 4/23/14																												
1914	Phi-N	1	3	.250	14	7	1	0	0	51	65	11.5	2	20	3.5	17	3.0	4.76	59	.342	.391	-11	-11	101	116	-0.9	-2	0	-1.2
1916	Pit-N	6	10	.375	34	17	8	0	0	153	151	8.9	2	38	2.2	46	2.7	2.94	95	.258	.298	-5	-2	107	93	-0.9	-2	-1	-0.5
1917	Pit-N	6	19	.240	38	25	10	1	2	227	214	8.5	3	76	3.0	58	2.3	2.81	99	.262	.313	-3	-1	103	113	-3.8	-1	2	0.0
1918	Pit-N	0	1	.000	8	4	0	0	0	23	31	12.1	0	14	5.5	2	0.8	5.87	49	.344	.405	-8	-8	105	100	-0.4	0	1	-0.6
	Phi-N	9	5	.643	18	14	12	4	1	123	96	7.0	3	42	3.1	33	2.4	2.41	127	.221	.287	5	9	111	94	2.7	-1	-2	0.8
	Yr	9	6	.600	26	18	12	4	1	146	127	7.8	3	56	3.5	35	2.2	2.96	103	.242	.309	-3	1	110	94	2.3	0	-1	0.2
1919	Phi-N	6	10	.375	17	15	13	0	0	129	150	10.5	5	44	3.1	37	2.6	3.84	82	.304	.359	-13	-10	109	119	0.4	-1	1	-0.9
	StL-N	3	6	.333	17	8	4	1	1	85	81	8.6	2	25	2.6	31	3.3	2.54	111	.264	.321	4	3	97	130	-0.6	3	-0	0.6
	Yr	9	16	.360	34	23	17	1	1	214	231	9.7	7	69	2.9	68	2.9	3.32	91	.287	.338	-10	-7	104	130	-0.2	-1	1	-0.3
1920	StL-N	4	8	.333	23	9	1	0	1	78	91	10.5	2	33	3.8	21	2.4	5.19	59	.296	.359	-18	-18	98	82	-1.9	-0	1	-1.7
1924	Chi-N	11	12	.478	38	22	13	1	1	190	181	8.6	9	72	3.4	50	2.4	3.74	104	.258	.322	3	3	101	93	-1.2	-4	1	0.0
1925	Chi-N	2	3	.400	18	4	1	1	1	56	63	10.1	9	22	3.5	19	3.1	5.14	82	.274	.337	-5	-6	98	90	-0.1	-0	0	-0.4
1927	Chi-A	2	4	.333	25	8	2	1	0	74	105	12.8	3	37	4.5	22	2.7	4.62	92	.354	.414	-4	-3	103	143	-0.7	-1	2	-0.2
Total	9	50	81	.382	250	133	65	9	7	1189	1228	9.3	40	423	3.2	336	2.5	3.55	91	.276	.333	-57	-42	103	106	-7.4	-9	5	-4.1
■ **BEANY JACOBSON**	Jacobson, Albert L. (born Albin L. Jacobson) b: 6/5/1881, Port Washington, Wis. d: 1/31/33, Decatur, Ill. BL/TL, 6', 170 lbs. Deb: 4/30/04																												
1904	Was-A	6	23	.207	33	30	23	1	0	254	276	9.8	6	57	2.0	75	2.7	3.54	73	.301	.342	-27	-27	99	99	-3.0	-5	1	-2.7
1905	Was-A	7	8	.467	22	17	12	0	0	144	139	8.7	1	35	2.2	50	3.1	3.31	84	.278	.325	-11	-8	106	87	0.6	1	-2	-1.0
1906	StL-A	9	9	.500	24	15	12	0	0	155	146	8.5	3	27	1.6	53	3.1	2.50	104	.274	.309	3	2	97	104	-0.1	-4	0	0.2
1907	StL-A	1	6	.143	7	7	6	0	0	57	55	8.7	1	26	4.1	16	2.5	3.00	83	.277	.361	-3	-3	98	112	-2.3	-0	-0	-0.3
	Bos-A	0	0	—	2	1	0	0	0	2	2	9.0	0	3	13.5	1	4.5	9.00	29	.285	.499	-1	-1	103	70	0.0	0	0	0.0
	Yr	1	6	.143	9	8	6	0	0	59	57	8.7	1	29	4.4	17	2.6	3.20	78	.278	.367	-4	-5	98	70	-2.3	-0	-0	-0.3
Total	4	23	46	.333	88	70	53	1	0	612	618	9.1	11	148	2.2	195	2.9	3.19	82	.286	.332	-38	-39	100	98	-4.8	-9	-1	-3.8
■ **LARRY JACOBUS**	Jacobus, Stuart Louis b: 12/18/1893, Cincinnati, Ohio d: 8/19/65, N.College Hill, O. BB/TR, 6'2", 186 lbs. Deb: 7/15/18																												
1918	Cin-N	0	1	.000	5	0	0	0	0	17	25	13.2	0	1	0.5	8	4.2	5.82	46	.368	.351	-6	-6	96	86	-0.4	-1	-0	-0.6
■ **PAT JACQUEZ**	Jacquez, Patrick Thomas b: 4/23/47, Stockton, Cal. BR/TR, 6', 200 lbs. Deb: 4/18/71																												
1971	Chi-A	0	0	—	2	0	0	0	0	2	4	18.0	0	2	9.0	1	4.5	4.50	75	.444	.500	-0	-0	97	231	0.0	-0	0	0.0
■ **JAKE JAECKEL**	Jaeckel, Paul Henry b: 4/1/42, E.Los Angeles, Cal. BR/TR, 5'10", 170 lbs. Deb: 9/19/64																												
1964	Chi-N	1	0	1.000	4	0	0	0	1	8	4	4.5	0	3	3.4	2	2.3	0.00	—	.160	.250	3	3	106	0	0.5	-0	0	0.4
■ **CHARLIE JAEGER**	Jaeger, Charles Thomas b: 4/17/1875, Ottawa, Ill. d: 9/27/42, Ottawa, Ill. BR/TR, Deb: 9/09/04																												
1904	Det-A	3	3	.500	8	6	5	0	0	49	49	9.0	0	15	2.8	13	2.4	2.57	99	.284	.341	0	-0	98	121	0.5	-1	-1	0.0
■ **JOE JAEGER**	Jaeger, Joseph Peter "Zip" b: 3/3/1895, St.Cloud, Minn. d: 12/13/63, Hampton, Iowa BR/TR, 6'1", 190 lbs. Deb: 7/28/20																												
1920	Chi-N	0	0	—	2	0	0	0	0	3	6	18.0	0	4	12.0	0	0.0	12.00	26	.500	.556	-3	-3	99	102	0.0	-0	0	-0.2

YEAR	TM/L	W	L	PCT	G	GS	CG	SHO	SV	IP	H	H/G	HR	BB	BB/G	SO	SO/G	ERA	/A	OAVG	OOBP	PR	/A	PF	CPI	WAT	PB	PD	TPI
■ SIG JAKUCKI	Jakucki, Sigmund "Jack" b: 8/20/09, Camden, N.J. d: 5/28/79, Galveston, Tex. BR/TR, 6'2.5", 198 lbs. Deb: 8/30/36																												
1936	StL-A	0	3	.000	7	2	0	0	0	21	32	13.7	2	12	5.1	9	3.9	8.57	63	.348	.417	-8	-7	107	87	-1.4	-1	0	-0.6
1944	StL-A	13	9	.591	35	24	12	4	3	198	211	9.6	17	54	2.5	67	3.0	3.55	97	.268	.314	-3	-3	100	105	0.4	-1	1	-0.2
1945	StL-A	12	10	.545	30	24	15	1	2	192	188	8.8	9	65	3.0	55	2.6	3.52	109	.257	.311	-3	7	114	94	0.3	-0	0	0.9
Total	3	25	22	.532	72	50	27	5	5	411	431	9.4	28	131	2.9	131	2.9	3.79	98	.268	.319	-14	-3	107	99	-0.7	-3	2	0.1
■ LEFTY JAMERSON	Jamerson, Charles Dewey "Charlie" b: 1/26/1900, Enfield, Ill. d: 8/4/80, Mockville, N.C. BL/TL, 6'1", 195 lbs. Deb: 8/16/24																												
1924	Bos-A	0	0	—	1	0	0	0	0	1	1	9.0	0	3	27.0	0	0.0	18.00	25	.250	.571	-2	-2	105	55	0.0	0	0	0.0
■ JEFF JAMES	James, Jeffrey Lynn "Jesse" b: 9/29/41, Indianapolis, Ind. BR/TR, 6'3", 195 lbs. Deb: 4/13/68																												
1968	Phi-N	4	4	.500	29	13	1	1	0	116	112	8.7	8	46	3.6	83	6.4	4.27	69	.256	.327	-17	-17	99	86	0.2	-1	0	-1.9
1969	Phi-N	2	2	.500	6	5	1	0	0	32	36	10.1	5	14	3.9	21	5.9	5.34	67	.288	.352	-6	-6	100	98	0.4	-0	-0	-0.6
Total	2	6	6	.500	35	18	2	1	0	148	148	9.0	13	60	3.6	104	6.3	4.50	69	.263	.333	-23	-23	99	89	0.6	-1	-0	-2.5
■ JOHNNY JAMES	James, John Phillip b: 7/23/33, Bonner's Ferry, Idaho BL/TR, 5'10", 160 lbs. Deb: 9/06/58																												
1958	NY-A	0	0	—	1	0	0	0	0	3	2	6.0	0	4	12.0	1	3.0	0.00	—	.250	.500	1	1	99	0	0.0	-0	0	0.1
1960	NY-A	5	1	.833	28	0	0	0	2	43	38	8.0	3	26	5.4	29	6.1	4.40	81	.248	.354	-3	-4	92	97	1.7	-0	1	-0.3
1961	NY-A	0	0	—	1	0	0	0	0	1	1	9.0	0	0	0.0	2	18.0	0.00	—	.250	.250	0	0	93	0	0.0	0	0	0.0
	LA-A	0	2	.000	36	3	0	0	0	71	66	8.4	12	54	6.8	41	5.2	5.32	85	.246	.370	-10	-6	112	99	-0.9	-2	-0	-0.7
	Yr	0	2	.000	37	3	0	0	0	72	67	8.4	12	54	6.8	43	5.4	5.25	86	.246	.368	-10	-6	112	99	-0.9	0	-0	-0.7
Total	3	5	3	.625	66	3	0	0	2	118	107	8.2	15	84	6.4	73	5.6	4.81	86	.247	.366	-11	-9	104	95	0.8	-2	0	-0.9
■ RICK JAMES	James, Richard Lee b: 10/11/47, Sheffield, Ala. BR/TR, 6'2.5", 205 lbs. Deb: 9/20/67																												
1967	Chi-N	0	1	.000	3	1	0	0	0	5	9	16.2	1	2	3.6	2	3.6	12.60	27	.529	.524	-5	-5	100	90	-0.4	-0	-0	-0.4
■ BOB JAMES	James, Robert Harvey b: 8/15/58, Glendale, Cal. BR/TR, 6'4", 215 lbs. Deb: 9/07/78																												
1978	Mon-N	0	1	.000	4	1	0	0	0	4	4	9.0	1	4	9.0	3	6.8	9.00	38	.267	.421	-2	-2	96	78	-0.4	0	0	-0.1
1979	Mon-N	0	0	—	2	0	0	0	0	2	2	9.0	0	3	13.5	1	4.5	13.50	28	.250	.455	-2	-2	101	43	0.0	0	0	-0.1
1982	Mon-N	0	0	—	7	0	0	0	0	9	10	10.0	0	8	8.0	11	11.0	6.00	63	.294	.409	-2	-2	104	91	0.0	0	0	-0.1
	Det-A	0	2	.000	12	1	0	0	0	20	22	9.9	4	8	3.6	20	9.0	4.95	82	.278	.345	-2	-2	100	106	-0.9	0	0	-0.1
1983	Det-A	0	0	—	4	0	0	0	0	4	5	11.3	2	3	6.8	4	9.0	11.25	34	.313	.421	-3	-3	95	85	0.0	0	0	-0.2
	Mon-N	1	0	1.000	27	0	0	0	7	50	37	6.7	3	23	4.1	56	10.1	2.88	128	.210	.303	4	4	101	98	0.5	0	1	0.6
1984	Mon-N	6	6	.500	62	0	0	0	10	96	92	8.6	6	45	4.2	91	8.5	3.66	90	.251	.328	-1	-4	91	103	0.2	-0	-1	-0.5
1985	Chi-A	8	7	.533	69	0	0	0	32	110	90	7.4	5	23	1.9	88	7.2	2.13	195	.226	.264	25	25	100	111	0.1	0	-1	2.4
1986	Chi-A	5	4	.556	49	0	0	0	14	58	61	9.5	8	23	3.6	32	5.0	5.28	80	.268	.335	-7	-7	101	88	0.9	0	-0	-0.6
1987	Chi-A	4	6	.400	43	0	0	0	10	54	54	9.0	10	17	2.8	34	5.7	4.67	104	.256	.315	-1	1	109	97	-0.7	0	0	0.1
Total	8	24	26	.480	279	2	0	0	73	407	377	8.3	39	157	3.5	340	7.5	3.80	104	.246	.314	8	7	99	101	-0.3	0	-1	1.4
■ LEFTY JAMES	James, William A. b: 7/1/1889, Glenroy, Ohio d: 5/3/33, Portsmouth, Ohio BL/TL, 5'11.5", 175 lbs. Deb: 4/13/12																												
1912	Cle-A	0	1	.000	3	1	0	0	1	6	8	12.0	0	4	6.0	2	3.0	7.50	45	.348	.483	-3	-3	101	96	-0.4	-0	0	-0.2
1913	Cle-A	2	2	.500	11	4	3	0	0	39	42	9.7	0	9	2.1	18	4.2	3.00	101	.273	.325	-0	0	104	100	-0.1	-0	-1	0.0
1914	Cle-A	0	3	.000	17	6	1	0	0	51	44	7.8	0	32	5.6	16	2.8	3.18	91	.251	.373	-2	-2	106	113	-1.4	-1	1	0.0
Total	3	2	6	.250	31	11	4	0	1	96	94	8.8	0	45	4.2	36	3.4	3.38	89	.267	.361	-6	-4	105	107	-1.9	-1	0	-0.2
■ BILL JAMES	James, William Henry "Big Bill" b: 1/20/1887, Detroit, Mich. d: 5/24/42, Venice, Cal. BB/TR, 6'4", 195 lbs. Deb: 6/12/11																												
1911	Cle-A	2	4	.333	8	6	4	0	0	52	58	10.0	1	32	5.5	21	3.6	4.85	71	.284	.387	-9	-8	103	91	-1.0	-2	-1	-0.7
1912	Cle-A	0	0	—	3	0	0	0	0	14	15	9.6	0	9	5.8	5	3.2	4.50	75	.288	.393	-2	-2	101	102	0.0	-0	-1	-0.1
1914	StL-A	15	14	.517	44	35	20	3	1	284	269	8.5	4	109	3.5	109	3.5	2.85	96	.257	.330	-4	-4	100	106	1.7	-3	5	0.1
1915	StL-A	7	10	.412	34	23	8	0	1	170	155	8.2	2	92	4.9	58	3.1	3.60	81	.255	.359	-12	-13	99	99	0.0	0	2	-1.1
	Det-A	7	3	.700	11	9	3	1	0	67	57	7.7	1	33	4.4	24	3.2	2.42	128	.243	.336	4	5	105	127	0.8	2	1	0.9
	Yr	14	13	.519	45	32	11	1	1	237	212	8.1	3	125	4.7	82	3.1	3.27	91	.249	.345	-8	-8	101	127	0.8	0	3	-0.2
1916	Det-A	8	12	.400	30	20	8	0	1	152	141	8.3	1	79	4.7	61	3.6	3.67	79	.255	.360	-14	-13	103	96	-3.1	-3	-0	-1.7
1917	Det-A	13	10	.565	34	23	10	2	1	198	163	7.4	2	96	4.4	62	2.8	2.09	123	.229	.330	13	10	96	127	1.5	3	-0	1.4
1918	Det-A	6	11	.353	19	18	8	1	0	122	127	9.4	3	68	5.0	42	3.1	3.76	73	.279	.366	-13	-14	99	110	-1.7	-3	2	-1.5
1919	Det-A	1	0	1.000	2	1	0	0	0	9	12	12.0	0	7	7.0	3	3.0	6.00	50	.324	.432	-3	-3	92	96	0.5	0	0	-0.2
	Bos-A	3	5	.375	13	7	4	0	0	73	74	9.1	2	39	4.8	12	1.5	4.07	72	.280	.379	-7	-9	91	103	-0.8	-1	0	-0.9
	Chi-A	3	2	.600	5	5	3	2	0	39	39	9.0	0	14	3.2	11	2.5	2.54	129	.281	.355	3	3	102	139	0.0	-1	-1	0.2
	Yr	7	7	.500	20	13	7	2	0	121	125	9.3	2	60	4.5	26	1.9	3.72	82	.282	.370	-7	-9	95	139	-0.3	-0	-0	-0.9
Total	8	65	71	.478	203	147	68	9	4	1180	1110	8.5	16	578	4.4	408	3.1	3.20	89	.258	.351	-44	-47	99	109	-2.1	-8	8	-3.6
■ BILL JAMES	James, William Lawrence "Seattle Bill" b: 3/12/1892, Iowa Hill, Cal. d: 3/10/71, Oroville, Cal. BR/TR, 6'3", 196 lbs. Deb: 4/17/13																												
1913	Bos-N	6	10	.375	24	14	10	1	0	136	134	8.9	4	57	3.8	73	4.8	2.78	110	.264	.336	6	4	96	130	-1.5	2	0	0.6
1914	Bos-N	26	7	**.788**	46	37	30	4	2	332	261	7.1	7	118	3.2	156	4.2	1.90	150	.225	.298	**33**	**35**	102	121	**8.4**	4	-1	**4.3**
1915	Bos-N	5	4	.556	13	10	4	0	0	68	68	9.0	3	22	2.9	23	3.0	3.04	88	.269	.321	-2	-3	97	116	0.1	-2	1	-0.3
1919	Bos-N	0	0	—	1	0	0	0	0	5	6	10.8	0	2	3.6	1	1.8	3.60	81	.273	.333	-0	-0	100	93	0.0	-0	0	0.0
Total	4	37	21	.638	84	61	44	5	2	541	469	7.8	14	199	3.3	253	4.2	2.28	126	.242	.311	37	36	100	122	7.0	4	1	4.6
■ CHARLIE JAMIESON	Jamieson, Charles Devine "Cuckoo" b: 2/7/1893, Paterson, N.J. d: 10/27/69, Paterson, N.J. BL/TL, 5'8.5", 165 lbs. Deb: 9/20/15																												
1916	Was-A	0	0	—	1	0	0	0	0	4	2	4.5	0	3	6.8	2	4.5	4.50	63	.143	.294	-1	-1	100	26	0.0	0	0	0.0
1917	Was-A	0	0	—	1	0	0	0	0	2	10	45.0	0	2	9.0	1	4.5	45.00	5	.625	.667	-9	-9	93	53	0.0	0	0	-0.6
1918	Phi-A	2	1	.667	5	2	1	0	0	23	24	9.4	0	13	5.1	2	0.8	4.30	69	.261	.358	-4	-3	108	83	0.7	0	-0	-0.3
1919	Cle-A	0	0	—	4	1	0	0	0	13	12	8.3	0	8	5.5	0	0.0	5.54	61	.250	.357	-3	-3	104	59	0.0	0	-0	-0.2
1922	Cle-A	0	0	—	2	0	0	0	0	6	7	10.5	0	4	6.0	2	3.0	3.00	138	.318	.423	1	1	103	182	0.0	1	-0	0.1
Total	5	2	1	.667	13	3	1	0	0	48	55	10.3	0	30	5.6	7	1.3	6.19	52	.286	.385	-17	-16	105	83	0.7	2	-1	-1.0
■ JERRY JANESKI	Janeski, Gerard Joseph b: 4/18/46, Pasadena, Cal. BR/TR, 6'4", 205 lbs. Deb: 4/10/70																												
1970	Chi-A	10	17	.370	35	35	4	1	0	206	247	10.8	22	63	2.8	79	3.5	4.76	84	.300	.347	-24	-17	108	102	0.6	-5	1	-1.9
1971	Was-A	1	5	.167	23	10	0	0	1	62	72	10.5	5	34	4.9	19	2.8	4.94	66	.304	.388	-10	-12	94	111	-1.7	1	1	-1.0
1972	Tex-A	0	1	.000	4	1	0	0	0	13	11	7.6	0	7	4.8	7	4.8	2.77	107	.229	.310	0	0	97	99	-0.4	-0	0	0.0
Total	3	11	23	.324	62	46	4	1	1	281	330	10.6	27	104	3.3	105	3.4	4.71	80	.298	.355	-34	-29	104	103	-1.5	-4	2	-2.9
■ LARRY JANSEN	Jansen, Lawrence Joseph b: 7/16/20, Verboort, Ore. BR/TR, 6'2", 190 lbs. Deb: 4/17/47 C																												
1947	NY-N	21	5	**.808**	42	30	20	1	1	248	241	8.7	23	57	2.1	104	3.8	3.16	128	.262	.304	25	24	99	114	**8.3**	0	-0	2.4
1948	NY-N	18	12	.600	42	36	15	4	2	277	283	9.2	25	54	1.8	126	4.1	3.61	108	.265	.299	11	9	98	100	3.4	-2	2	0.9
1949	NY-N	15	16	.484	37	35	17	3	0	260	271	9.4	36	62	2.1	113	3.9	3.84	106	.263	.304	6	7	101	103	0.4	-1	2	0.9
1950	NY-N	19	13	.594	40	35	21	**5**	3	275	238	7.8	31	55	1.8	161	5.3	3.01	133	.232	**.269**	35	30	97	94	1.6	-0	2	3.2
1951	NY-N	**23**	11	.676	39	34	18	3	0	279	254	8.2	26	56	1.8	145	4.7	3.03	129	.239	.276	29	28	99	94	2.9	-5	3	2.7
1952	NY-N	11	11	.500	34	27	8	1	2	167	183	9.9	16	47	2.5	74	4.0	4.10	92	.281	.330	-7	-6	101	106	-1.9	3	1	-0.1
1953	NY-N	11	16	.407	36	26	6	0	1	185	185	9.0	24	55	2.7	88	4.3	4.14	101	.256	.308	3	1	98	94	-1.6	-1	-1	0.0
1954	NY-N	2	2	.500	13	7	0	0	0	41	57	12.5	5	15	3.3	15	3.3	5.93	70	.337	.386	-8	-8	102	105	-0.3	1	1	-0.5
1956	Cin-N	2	3	.400	8	7	2	0	1	35	39	10.0	5	9	2.3	16	4.1	5.14	78	.281	.325	-5	-4	106	85	-0.7	-1	-0	-0.5
Total	9	122	89	.578	291	237	107	17	10	1767	1751	8.9	191	410	2.1	842	4.3	3.58	111	.258	.299	87	81	99	100	12.1	-6	10	9.0
■ RAY JARVIS	Jarvis, Raymond Arnold b: 5/10/46, Providence, R.I. BR/TR, 6'2", 198 lbs. Deb: 4/15/69																												
1969	Bos-A	5	6	.455	29	12	2	0	1	100	105	9.5	8	43	3.9	36	3.2	4.77	80	.274	.345	-13	-11	105	91	-0.8	-2	1	-1.1
1970	Bos-A	0	1	.000	15	0	0	0	0	16	17	9.6	1	14	7.9	8	4.5	3.94	104	.274	.402	-0	0	110	144	-0.4	0	0	0.0
Total	2	5	7	.417	44	12	2	0	1	116	122	9.5	9	57	4.4	44	3.4	4.66	82	.274	.354	-13	-11	105	98	-1.2	-2	1	-1.1
■ PAT JARVIS	Jarvis, Robert Patrick b: 3/18/41, Carlyle, Ill. BR/TR, 5'10.5", 180 lbs. Deb: 8/04/66																												
1966	Atl-N	6	2	.750	10	9	3	1	0	62	46	6.7	1	12	1.7	41	6.0	2.32	151	.206	.248	9	8	97	63	1.9	-2	-1	0.5
1967	Atl-N	15	10	.600	32	30	7	1	0	194	195	9.0	15	62	2.9	118	5.5	3.66	96	.260	.315	-6	-3	105	99	3.4	-3	-2	-0.7

YEAR	TM/L	W	L	PCT	G	GS	CG	SHO	SV	IP	H	H/G	HR	BB	BB/G	SO	SO/G	ERA	/A	OAVG	OOBP	PR	/A	PF	CPI	WAT	PB	PD	TPI
1968	Atl-N	16	12	.571	34	34	14	1	0	256	202	7.1	15	50	1.8	157	5.5	2.60	107	.214	.250	11	5	94	75	2.3	1	-2	0.4
1969	Atl-N	13	11	.542	37	33	4	1	0	217	204	8.5	25	73	3.0	123	5.1	4.44	83	.246	.303	-20	-18	103	80	-0.7	-3	-0	-2.0
1970	Atl-N	16	16	.500	36	34	11	1	0	254	240	8.5	21	72	2.6	173	6.1	3.61	117	.247	.294	12	18	105	89	1.1	-0	2	2.0
1971	Atl-N	6	14	.300	35	23	3	3	1	162	162	9.0	16	51	2.8	68	3.8	4.11	93	.261	.315	-12	-5	111	91	-4.3	-2	1	-0.6
1972	Atl-N	11	7	.611	37	6	0	0	2	99	94	8.5	7	44	4.0	56	5.1	4.09	90	.260	.326	-7	-5	106	96	2.8	-0	1	-0.3
1973	Mon-N	2	1	.667	28	0	0	0	0	39	37	8.5	6	16	3.7	19	4.4	3.23	119	.250	.321	2	3	105	129	0.5	-0	-0	0.2
Total	8	85	73	.538	249	169	42	8	3	1283	1180	8.3	106	380	2.7	755	5.3	3.58	100	.243	.294	-11	2	103	87	7.0	-11	-2	-0.5
■ **HI JASPER**	Jasper, Henry W. b: 11/15/1880, St.Louis, Mo. d: 5/22/37, St.Louis, Mo. BR/TR, 5'11", 180 lbs. Deb: 4/19/14																												
1914	Chi-A	1	0	1.000	16	0	0	0	0	32	22	6.2	0	20	5.6	19	5.3	3.38	85	.210	.341	-2	-2	105	78	0.5	-1	1	0.0
1915	Chi-A	0	1	.000	3	2	1	0	0	16	8	4.5	2	9	5.1	15	8.4	4.50	61	.157	.283	-3	-3	94	51	-0.4	0	1	-0.1
1916	StL-N	5	6	.455	21	11	2	0	1	107	97	8.2	0	42	3.5	37	3.1	3.28	80	.254	.328	-8	-8	100	94	0.6	1	1	-0.5
1919	Cle-A	4	5	.444	12	10	5	0	0	83	83	9.0	1	28	3.0	25	2.7	3.58	94	.269	.330	-3	-2	104	86	-1.2	-2	1	-0.3
Total	4	10	12	.455	52	23	8	0	1	238	210	7.9	3	99	3.7	96	3.6	3.48	84	.248	.328	-16	-15	102	86	-0.5	-2	4	-0.9
■ **LARRY JASTER**	Jaster, Larry Edward b: 1/13/44, Midland, Mich. BL/TL, 6'3", 190 lbs. Deb: 9/17/65																												
1965	StL-N	3	0	1.000	4	3	3	0	0	28	21	6.8	1	7	2.3	10	3.2	1.61	233	.206	.255	6	7	106	111	1.5	0	-1	0.8
1966	StL-N	11	5	.688	26	21	6	**5**	0	152	124	7.3	17	45	2.7	92	5.4	3.26	111	.227	.286	6	6	100	94	3.1	1	-1	0.6
1967	StL-N	9	7	.563	34	23	2	1	3	152	141	8.3	12	44	2.6	87	5.2	3.02	111	.244	.294	6	5	99	104	-0.8	-1	-2	0.2
1968	StL-N	9	13	.409	31	21	3	1	0	154	153	8.9	13	38	2.2	70	4.1	3.51	79	.262	.306	-9	-12	93	101	-3.7	1	-2	-1.4
1969	Mon-N	1	6	.143	24	11	1	0	0	77	95	11.1	17	28	3.3	39	4.6	5.49	68	.302	.354	-16	-15	103	109	-1.9	3	-2	-1.3
1970	Atl-N	1	1	.500	14	0	0	0	0	22	33	13.5	5	8	3.3	9	3.7	6.95	61	.359	.390	-7	-7	105	112	0.1	-0	1	-0.5
1972	Atl-N	1	1	.500	5	1	0	0	0	12	12	9.0	4	8	6.0	6	4.5	5.25	70	.267	.377	-2	-2	106	128	0.1	-0	0	-0.1
Total	7	35	33	.515	138	80	15	7	3	597	579	8.7	69	178	2.7	313	4.7	3.65	92	.256	.308	-17	-19	99	102	-1.6	4	-6	-1.7
■ **AL JAVERY**	Javery, Alva William "Beartracks" b: 6/5/18, Worcester, Mass. d: 9/13/77, Woodstock, Conn. BR/TR, 6'3", 183 lbs. Deb: 4/23/40																												
1940	Bos-N	2	4	.333	29	4	1	0	1	83	99	10.7	2	36	3.9	42	4.6	5.53	70	.293	.361	-16	-15	101	84	-0.6	-1	-2	-1.6
1941	Bos-N	10	11	.476	34	23	9	1	1	161	181	10.1	5	65	3.6	54	3.0	4.30	81	.283	.350	-12	-15	96	99	1.5	-3	1	-1.7
1942	Bos-N	12	16	.429	42	37	19	5	0	261	251	8.7	8	78	2.7	85	2.9	3.03	107	.251	.300	8	6	98	99	0.8	-4	2	0.4
1943	Bos-N	17	16	.515	41	35	19	5	0	**303**	288	8.6	13	99	2.9	134	4.0	3.21	114	.248	.304	6	15	109	95	2.6	-3	2	1.7
1944	Bos-N	10	19	.345	40	33	11	3	3	254	248	8.8	12	118	4.2	137	4.9	3.54	98	.262	.338	2	-2	96	111	-3.0	-2	-2	-0.6
1945	Bos-N	2	7	.222	17	14	2	1	0	77	92	10.8	4	51	6.0	18	2.1	6.31	68	.295	.384	-21	-17	113	85	-2.2	-1	1	-1.5
1946	Bos-N	0	1	.000	2	1	0	0	0	3	5	15.0	0	5	15.0	0	0.0	15.00	21	.417	.556	-4	-4	94	74	-0.4	-0	-0	-0.3
Total	7	53	74	.417	205	147	61	15	5	1142	1164	9.2	44	452	3.6	470	3.7	3.81	93	.264	.328	-37	-32	101	98	-1.3	-16	2	-3.6
■ **JOEY JAY**	Jay, Joseph Richard b: 8/15/35, Middletown, Conn. BB/TR, 6'4", 228 lbs. Deb: 7/21/53																												
1953	Mil-N	1	0	1.000	3	1	1	1	0	10	6	5.4	0	5	4.5	4	3.6	0.00	—	.188	.297	5	4	92	0	0.5	-0	-0	0.4
1954	Mil-N	1	0	1.000	15	1	0	0	0	18	21	10.5	2	16	8.0	13	6.5	6.50	57	.304	.432	-5	-6	91	103	0.5	0	0	-0.4
1955	Mil-N	0	0	—	12	1	0	0	0	19	23	10.9	2	13	6.2	3	1.4	4.74	78	.324	.419	-1	-2	92	139	0.0	1	-0	-0.1
1957	Mil-N	0	0	—	1	0	0	0	1	1	0	0.0	0	0	0.0	0	0.0	0.00	—	.000	.000	0	0	88	0	0.0	0	0	0.1
1958	Mil-N	7	5	.583	18	12	6	3	0	97	60	5.6	8	43	4.0	74	6.9	2.13	161	.177	.269	20	14	87	90	-0.1	-1	0	1.4
1959	Mil-N	6	11	.353	34	19	4	1	0	136	130	8.6	11	64	4.2	88	5.8	4.10	89	.248	.331	-2	-7	93	92	-3.2	-1	2	-0.5
1960	Mil-N	9	8	.529	32	11	3	0	1	133	128	8.7	10	59	4.0	90	6.1	3.25	103	.254	.332	8	2	89	121	-0.6	0	-0	0.1
1961	Cin-N	**21**	10	.677	34	34	14	**4**	0	247	217	7.9	25	92	3.4	157	5.7	3.53	117	.236	.304	14	17	103	95	3.4	-6	-1	1.0
1962	Cin-N	21	14	.600	39	37	16	4	0	273	269	8.9	26	100	3.3	155	5.1	3.76	105	.260	.320	6	6	100	103	-0.1	3	-2	0.8
1963	Cin-N	7	18	.280	30	22	4	1	1	170	172	9.1	19	73	3.9	116	6.1	4.29	79	.266	.338	-19	-17	103	102	-6.3	0	-0	-1.7
1964	Cin-N	11	11	.500	34	23	10	0	2	183	167	8.2	17	36	1.8	134	6.6	3.39	106	.245	.280	3	4	102	91	-1.4	-3	-2	0.0
1965	Cin-N	9	8	.529	37	24	4	1	1	156	150	8.7	21	63	3.6	102	5.9	4.21	86	.252	.322	-12	-10	102	99	-0.2	-3	-0	-1.3
1966	Cin-N	6	2	.750	12	10	1	1	0	74	78	9.5	8	23	2.8	44	5.4	3.89	106	.275	.332	-2	2	114	109	2.1	-1	-1	0.0
	Atl-N	0	4	.000	9	8	0	0	1	30	39	11.7	4	20	6.0	19	5.7	7.80	45	.315	.405	-14	-14	97	83	-1.9	-0	-0	-1.3
	Yr	6	6	.500	21	18	1	1	1	104	117	10.1	12	43	3.7	63	5.5	5.02	78	.285	.349	-16	-12	109	83	0.2	-1	-1	-1.3
Total	13	99	91	.521	310	203	63	16	7	1547	1460	8.5	153	607	3.5	999	5.8	3.77	99	.251	.319	-1	-6	99	99	-7.3	-10	-5	-1.5
■ **TEX JEANES**	Jeanes, Ernest Lee b: 12/19/1900, Maypearl, Tex. d: 4/5/73, Longview, Tex. BR/TR, 6', 176 lbs. Deb: 4/20/21																												
1922	Cle-A	0	0	—	1	0	0	0	0	0	0	—	0	1	—	0	—	—	—	—	1.000	0	0	103	0	0.0	0	0	0.0
1927	NY-N	0	0	—	1	0	0	0	0	1	2	18.0	0	2	18.0	0	0.0	9.00	43	.400	.571	-1	-1	98	136	0.0	0	0	0.0
Total	2	0	0	—	2	0	0	0	0	1	2	18.0	0	3	27.0	0	0.0	9.00	43	.400	.625	-1	-1	98	136	0.0	0	0	0.0
■ **GEORGE JEFFCOAT**	Jeffcoat, George Edward b: 12/24/13, New Brookland, S.C d: 10/13/78, Leesville, S.C. BR/TR, 5'11.5", 175 lbs. Deb: 4/20/36																												
1936	Bro-N	5	6	.455	40	5	3	0	3	96	84	7.9	7	63	5.9	46	4.3	4.50	95	.239	.359	-5	-2	107	96	0.2	-1	-1	-0.3
1937	Bro-N	1	3	.250	21	3	1	1	0	54	58	9.7	4	27	4.5	29	4.8	5.17	81	.274	.354	-8	-6	107	88	-0.7	-2	-0	-0.7
1939	Bro-N	0	0	—	1	0	0	0	0	2	2	9.0	0	0	0.0	1	4.5	0.00	—	.286	.250	1	1	106	0	0.0	0	0	0.1
1943	Bos-N	1	2	.333	8	1	0	0	0	18	15	7.5	1	10	5.0	10	5.0	3.00	122	.217	.316	1	1	109	97	-0.3	1	0	0.2
Total	4	7	11	.389	70	9	4	1	3	170	159	8.4	12	100	5.3	86	4.6	4.50	93	.248	.352	-11	-6	107	92	-0.8	-3	-1	-0.7
■ **HAL JEFFCOAT**	Jeffcoat, Harold Bentley b: 9/6/24, W.Columbia, S.C. BR/TR, 5'10.5", 185 lbs. Deb: 4/20/48																												
1954	Chi-N	5	6	.455	43	3	1	0	7	104	110	9.5	12	58	5.0	35	3.0	5.19	80	.276	.362	-13	-12	102	95	0.4	2	1	-0.7
1955	Chi-N	8	6	.571	50	1	0	0	6	101	107	9.5	5	53	4.7	32	2.9	2.94	139	.276	.362	12	13	101	152	1.4	1	1	1.4
1956	Cin-N	8	2	.800	38	16	2	0	2	171	189	9.9	12	55	2.9	55	2.9	3.84	104	.281	.335	-1	3	106	105	2.6	-1	3	0.5
1957	Cin-N	12	13	.480	37	31	10	1	0	207	236	10.3	29	46	2.0	63	2.7	4.52	91	.294	.331	-15	-9	106	106	-1.0	6	-1	-0.3
1958	Cin-N	6	8	.429	49	0	0	0	9	75	76	9.1	8	26	3.1	35	4.2	3.72	113	.268	.321	2	4	106	110	-0.9	2	2	0.8
1959	Cin-N	0	1	.000	17	0	0	0	1	22	21	8.6	3	10	4.1	12	4.9	3.27	124	.253	.333	2	2	103	129	-0.4	1	0	0.3
	StL-N	0	1	.000	11	0	0	0	0	18	33	16.5	4	9	4.5	7	3.5	9.00	47	.402	.462	-10	-10	106	106	-0.4	-0	0	-0.9
	Yr	0	2	.000	28	0	0	0	1	40	54	12.1	7	19	4.3	19	4.3	5.85	70	.327	.397	-8	-8	104	106	-0.8	1	0	-0.6
Total	6	39	37	.513	245	51	13	1	25	698	772	10.0	73	257	3.3	239	3.1	4.22	97	.285	.344	-23	-9	105	112	1.7	11	6	1.1
■ **MIKE JEFFCOAT**	Jeffcoat, James Michael b: 8/3/59, Pine Bluff, Ark. BL/TL, 6'2", 187 lbs. Deb: 8/21/83																												
1983	Cle-A	1	3	.250	11	2	0	0	0	33	32	8.7	1	13	3.5	9	2.5	3.27	132	.256	.329	3	4	106	106	-0.8	0	-0	0.4
1984	Cle-A	5	2	.714	63	1	0	0	1	75	82	9.8	7	24	2.9	41	4.9	3.00	141	.281	.327	8	10	106	144	1.7	0	1	1.1
1985	Cle-A	0	0	—	9	0	0	0	0	10	8	7.2	1	6	5.4	4	3.6	2.70	146	.235	.318	2	1	95	157	0.0	0	1	0.2
	SF-N	0	2	.000	19	1	0	0	0	22	27	11.0	1	6	2.5	10	4.1	5.32	64	.307	.354	-4	-5	95	109	-0.9	0	1	-0.3
1987	Tex-A	0	1	.000	2	2	0	0	0	7	11	14.1	4	4	5.1	1	1.3	12.86	36	.355	.429	-7	-6	104	85	-0.4	0	-0	-0.5
1988	Tex-A	0	2	.000	5	2	0	0	0	10	19	17.1	1	5	4.5	5	4.5	11.70	35	.432	.500	-9	-8	102	87	-0.9	0	0	-0.7
Total	5	6	10	.375	109	8	0	0	1	157	179	10.3	18	58	3.3	70	4.0	4.36	95	.292	.349	-6	-4	103	125	-1.3	0	2	0.2
■ **JESSE JEFFERSON**	Jefferson, Jesse Harrison b: 3/3/49, Midlothian, Va. BR/TR, 6'3", 188 lbs. Deb: 6/23/73																												
1973	Bal-A	6	5	.545	18	15	3	0	0	101	104	9.3	15	46	4.1	52	4.6	4.10	98	.267	.342	-3	-1	105	113	-0.4	0	1	0.0
1974	Bal-A	1	0	1.000	20	2	0	0	0	57	55	8.7	2	38	6.0	31	4.9	4.42	76	.261	.368	-5	-7	92	95	0.5	0	0	-0.6
1975	Bal-A	0	2	.000	4	0	0	0	0	8	5	5.6	0	8	9.0	4	4.5	2.25	150	.227	.394	1	1	89	207	-0.9	0	0	0.1
	Chi-A	5	9	.357	22	21	1	0	0	108	100	8.3	10	94	7.8	67	5.6	5.08	77	.249	.388	-16	-14	104	98	-1.6	0	0	-1.3
	Yr	5	11	.313	26	21	1	0	0	116	105	8.1	10	102	7.9	71	5.5	4.89	80	.248	.388	-14	-13	103	98	-2.5	0	1	-1.2
1976	Chi-A	2	5	.286	19	9	0	0	0	62	86	12.5	3	42	6.1	30	4.4	8.56	42	.339	.423	-35	-34	101	77	-0.9	0	2	-3.1
1977	Tor-A	9	17	.346	33	33	8	0	0	217	224	9.3	23	83	3.4	114	4.7	4.31	99	.269	.328	-6	-1	105	97	0.2	0	0	0.0
1978	Tor-A	7	16	.304	31	30	9	2	0	212	214	9.1	28	86	3.7	97	4.1	4.37	88	.267	.334	-14	-12	102	100	-2.1	0	0	-1.2
1979	Tor-A	2	10	.167	34	10	2	0	1	116	150	11.6	19	45	3.5	43	3.3	5.51	81	.328	.384	-16	-13	106	116	-3.0	0	1	-1.1
1980	Tor-A	4	13	.235	29	18	2	2	0	122	130	9.6	12	52	3.8	53	3.9	5.46	75	.281	.344	-19	-19	101	85	-3.8	0	1	-1.6
	Pit-N	1	0	1.000	1	1	0	0	0	7	3	3.9	0	2	2.6	4	5.1	1.29	289	.143	.217	2	2	103	52	0.5	-0	0	0.2
1981	Cal-A	2	4	.333	26	5	0	0	0	77	80	9.4	4	24	2.8	27	3.2	3.62	105	.269	.318	0	1	104	101	-0.8	0	-1	0.1
Total	9	39	81	.325	237	144	25	4	1	1087	1151	9.5	116	520	4.3	522	4.3	4.80	83	.277	.352	-110	-97	103	99	-12.3	-0	3	-8.5

YEAR	TM/L	W	L	PCT	G	GS	CG	SHO	SV	IP	H	H/G	HR	BB	BB/G	SO	SO/G	ERA	/A	OAVG	OOBP	PR	/A	PF	CPI	WAT	PB	PD	TPI
■ FERGUSON JENKINS	Jenkins, Ferguson Arthur b: 12/13/43, Chatham, Ont., Can. BR/TR, 6'5", 205 lbs. Deb: 9/10/65																												
1965	Phi-N	2	1	.667	7	0	0	0	1	12	7	5.3	2	2	1.5	10	7.5	2.25	149	.159	.196	2	1	95	59	0.4	-0	-0	0.1
1966	Phi-N	0	0	—	1	0	0	0	0	2	3	13.5	0	1	4.5	2	9.0	4.50	80	.273	.333	-0	-0	100	72	0.0	0	0	0.0
	Chi-N	6	8	.429	60	12	2	1	5	182	147	7.3	24	51	2.5	148	7.3	3.31	112	.219	.272	6	8	103	87	0.8	0	-2	0.7
	Yr	6	8	.429	61	12	2	1	5	184	150	7.3	24	52	2.5	150	7.3	3.33	111	.220	.273	6	8	103	87	0.8	0	-2	0.7
1967	Chi-N	20	13	.606	38	38	**20**	3	0	289	230	7.2	30	83	2.6	236	7.3	2.80	121	.217	.274	18	19	100	96	2.9	2	2	2.5
1968	Chi-N	20	15	.571	40	40	20	3	0	308	255	7.5	26	65	1.9	260	7.6	2.63	128	.222	.262	12	25	112	90	2.4	2	-1	3.2
1969	Chi-N	21	15	.583	43	42	23	7	1	311	284	8.2	27	71	2.1	**273**	7.9	3.21	118	.242	.285	13	20	105	94	0.8	0	0	2.2
1970	Chi-N	22	16	.579	40	39	**24**	3	0	313	265	7.6	30	60	**1.7**	274	7.9	3.39	142	.224	**.262**	23	**49**	119	75	3.0	-4	-1	4.9
1971	Chi-N	**24**	13	.649	39	39	**30**	3	0	**325**	304	8.4	29	37	**1.0**	263	7.3	2.77	138	.246	.266	25	38	110	98	**6.2**	12	1	6.2
1972	Chi-N	20	12	.625	36	36	23	5	0	289	253	7.9	32	62	1.9	184	5.7	3.21	121	.234	.274	8	22	112	91	3.3	1	3	3.1
1973	Chi-N	14	16	.467	38	38	7	2	0	271	267	8.9	35	57	1.9	170	5.6	3.89	103	.259	.293	-6	3	109	94	-0.3	-2	3	0.6
1974	Tex-A	**25**	12	.676	41	41	**29**	6	0	328	286	7.8	27	45	**1.2**	225	6.2	2.83	123	.232	.260	29	24	96	84	**7.0**	1	-0	2.6
1975	Tex-A	17	18	.486	37	37	22	4	0	270	261	8.7	37	56	**1.9**	157	5.2	3.93	96	.251	.291	-4	-5	100	88	0.0	0	1	-0.3
1976	Bos-A	12	11	.522	30	29	12	2	0	209	201	8.7	20	43	1.9	142	6.1	3.27	118	.253	.291	6	14	110	100	0.3	0	-1	1.4
1977	Bos-A	10	10	.500	28	28	11	1	0	193	190	8.9	30	36	1.7	105	4.9	3.68	128	.257	.286	8	22	116	100	-1.8	0	1	2.4
1978	Tex-A	18	8	.692	34	30	16	4	0	249	228	8.2	21	41	**1.5**	157	5.7	3.04	119	.245	.275	21	16	96	92	4.9	0	2	1.9
1979	Tex-A	16	14	.533	37	37	10	3	0	259	252	8.8	40	81	2.8	164	5.7	4.07	103	.256	.309	5	4	99	100	0.8	0	4	0.7
1980	Tex-A	12	12	.500	29	29	12	0	0	198	190	8.6	22	52	2.4	129	5.9	3.77	107	.250	.297	6	6	100	90	0.7	0	1	0.7
1981	Tex-A	5	8	.385	19	16	1	0	0	106	122	10.4	14	40	3.4	63	5.3	4.50	73	.290	.347	-10	-14	90	110	-2.0	0	2	-1.2
1982	Chi-N	14	15	.483	34	34	4	1	0	217	221	9.2	19	68	2.8	134	5.6	3.15	119	.264	.315	11	14	104	120	1.0	-1	-0	1.3
1983	Chi-N	6	9	.400	33	29	1	1	0	167	176	9.5	19	46	2.5	96	5.2	4.31	85	.275	.323	-13	-12	101	97	-0.6	3	-1	-0.9
Total	19	284	226	.557	664	594	267	49	7	4498	4142	8.3	484	997	2.0	3192	6.4	3.34	115	.243	.284	160	255	105	93	29.8	15	14	32.1
■ JACK JENKINS	Jenkins, Warren Washington b: 12/22/42, Covington, Va. BR/TR, 6'2", 195 lbs. Deb: 9/13/62																												
1962	Was-A	0	1	.000	3	1	1	0	0	13	12	8.3	4	7	4.8	10	6.9	4.15	98	.245	.339	-0	-0	102	135	-0.4	-1	-0	0.0
1963	Was-A	0	2	.000	4	2	0	0	0	12	16	12.0	2	12	9.0	5	3.8	6.00	61	.340	.459	-3	-3	101	140	-0.9	0	0	-0.2
1969	LA-N	0	0	—	1	0	0	0	0	1	0	0.0	0	0	0.0	1	9.0	0.00	—	.000	.000	0	0	97	0	0.0	0	0	0.0
Total	3	0	3	.000	8	3	1	0	0	26	28	9.7	6	19	6.6	16	5.5	4.85	80	.283	.392	-3	-3	102	132	-1.3	-0	0	-0.2
■ WILLIE JENSEN	Jensen, William Christian b: 11/17/1889, Philadelphia, Pa. d: 3/27/17, Philadelphia, Pa. BL/TR, 5'11.5", 170 lbs. Deb: 9/10/12																												
1912	Det-A	1	2	.333	5	4	1	0	0	33	43	11.7	1	18	4.9	8	2.2	4.91	65	.339	.429	-6	-6	96	124	-0.3	-2	-0	-0.5
1914	Phi-A	0	1	.000	1	1	1	0	0	9	7	7.0	1	2	2.0	1	1.0	2.00	127	.226	.273	1	1	93	129	-0.4	0	0	0.1
Total	2	1	3	.250	6	5	2	0	0	42	50	10.7	2	20	4.3	9	1.9	4.29	71	.316	.400	-5	-6	95	125	-0.7	-2	-0	-0.4
■ VIRGIL JESTER	Jester, Virgil Milton b: 7/23/27, Denver, Colo. BR/TR, 5'11", 188 lbs. Deb: 6/18/52																												
1952	Bos-N	3	5	.375	19	8	4	1	0	73	80	9.9	5	23	2.8	25	3.1	3.33	108	.283	.333	3	2	97	127	-0.3	1	-1	0.2
1953	Mil-N	0	0	—	2	0	0	0	0	2	4	18.0	1	4	18.0	0	0.0	22.50	17	.400	.571	-4	-4	92	72	0.0	0	0	-0.3
Total	2	3	5	.375	21	8	4	1	0	75	84	10.1	6	27	3.2	25	3.0	3.84	94	.287	.344	-1	-2	96	126	-0.3	1	-1	-0.1
■ GERMAN JIMENEZ	Jimenez, German (Camarena) b: 12/5/62, Santiago, Mex. BL/TL, Deb: 6/28/88																												
1988	Atl-N	1	6	.143	15	9	0	0	0	56	65	10.4	4	12	1.9	26	4.2	4.98	74	.294	.324	-10	-8	107	86	-2.0	-1	-1	-1.0
■ JUAN JIMENEZ	Jimenez, Juan Antonio (Martes) b: 3/8/49, La Torre, La Vega, D.R. BR/TR, 6'1", 165 lbs. Deb: 9/09/74																												
1974	Pit-N	0	0	—	4	0	0	0	0	4	6	13.5	0	2	4.5	2	4.5	6.75	52	.353	.421	-1	-1	97	90	0.0	0	0	-0.1
■ TOMMY JOHN	John, Thomas Edward b: 5/22/43, Terre Haute, Ind. BR/TL, 6'3", 180 lbs. Deb: 9/06/63																												
1963	Cle-A	0	2	.000	6	3	0	0	0	20	23	10.3	1	6	2.7	9	4.0	2.25	158	.284	.319	3	3	98	176	-0.9	-1	0	0.2
1964	Cle-A	2	9	.182	25	14	2	1	0	94	97	9.3	10	35	3.4	65	6.2	3.93	95	.262	.320	-3	-2	103	100	-3.4	0	1	-0.1
1965	Chi-A	14	7	.667	39	27	6	1	3	184	162	7.9	12	58	2.8	126	6.2	3.08	102	.237	.295	8	1	91	95	2.3	2	3	0.6
1966	Chi-A	14	11	.560	34	33	10	**5**	0	223	195	7.9	13	57	2.3	138	5.6	2.62	122	.235	.287	20	14	93	108	1.4	2	1	1.9
1967	Chi-A	10	13	.435	31	29	9	**6**	0	178	143	7.2	12	47	2.4	110	5.6	2.48	121	.219	.273	15	10	93	101	-2.6	-0	6	1.8
1968	Chi-A	10	5	.667	25	25	5	1	0	177	135	6.9	10	49	2.5	117	5.9	1.98	153	.212	.278	20	21	102	119	3.4	2	6	3.6
1969	Chi-A	9	11	.450	33	33	6	2	0	232	230	8.9	16	90	3.5	128	5.0	3.26	122	.261	.326	10	19	110	114	0.6	-2	7	2.6
1970	Chi-A	12	17	.414	37	37	10	3	0	269	253	8.5	19	101	3.4	138	4.6	3.28	122	.251	.320	13	22	108	107	1.8	1	4	3.0
1971	Chi-A	13	16	.448	38	35	10	3	0	229	244	9.6	17	58	2.3	131	5.1	3.62	93	.274	.315	-4	-6	97	102	-1.3	-1	-1	-0.8
1972	LA-N	11	5	.688	29	29	4	1	0	187	172	8.3	14	40	1.9	117	5.6	2.89	111	.244	.281	12	7	93	99	2.7	-1	4	1.0
1973	LA-N	16	7	**.696**	36	31	4	2	0	218	202	8.3	16	50	2.1	116	4.8	3.10	117	.246	.288	14	13	99	95	3.3	2	7	2.3
1974	LA-N	13	3	.813	22	22	5	3	0	153	133	7.8	4	42	2.5	78	4.6	2.59	126	.235	.286	18	11	90	92	4.2	-1	2	1.2
1976	LA-N	10	10	.500	31	31	6	2	0	207	207	9.0	7	61	2.7	91	4.0	3.09	112	.261	.309	10	9	99	104	-1.2	-2	-1	0.6
1977	LA-N	20	7	.741	31	31	11	3	0	220	225	9.2	12	50	2.0	123	5.0	2.78	138	.267	.307	28	26	98	120	5.2	1	2	3.1
1978	LA-N	17	10	.630	33	30	7	0	1	213	230	9.7	11	53	2.2	124	5.2	3.30	105	.271	.316	7	4	97	106	1.7	-1	2	0.5
1979	NY-A	21	9	.700	37	36	17	3	0	276	268	8.7	9	65	2.1	111	3.6	2.97	135	.260	.302	**39**	32	95	104	5.6	0	2	3.4
1980	NY-A	22	9	.710	36	36	16	**6**	0	265	270	9.2	13	56	1.9	78	2.6	3.43	115	.268	.305	18	15	98	96	3.7	0	1	1.6
1981	NY-A	9	8	.529	20	20	7	0	0	140	135	8.7	10	39	2.5	50	3.2	2.64	137	.256	.305	16	15	99	128	-0.3	0	1	1.8
1982	NY-A	10	10	.500	30	26	9	2	0	187	190	9.1	11	34	1.6	54	2.6	3.66	108	.266	.296	9	6	97	90	0.3	0	2	0.7
	Cal-A	4	2	.667	7	7	1	0	0	35	49	12.6	4	5	1.3	14	3.6	3.86	104	.336	.355	1	1	99	143	0.7	0	1	0.1
	Yr	14	12	.538	37	33	10	2	0	222	239	9.7	15	39	**1.6**	68	2.8	3.69	107	.274	.303	10	7	97	143	1.0	0	2	0.8
1983	Cal-A	11	13	.458	34	34	9	0	0	235	287	11.0	20	49	1.9	65	2.5	4.33	91	.304	.335	-7	-11	96	107	0.6	0	1	-0.9
1984	Cal-A	7	13	.350	32	29	4	1	0	181	223	11.1	15	56	2.8	47	2.3	4.52	90	.306	.355	-11	-9	101	109	-3.2	0	0	-0.8
1985	Cal-A	2	4	.333	12	6	0	0	0	38	51	12.1	3	15	3.6	17	4.0	4.74	88	.329	.381	-2	-2	101	125	-1.1	0	1	0.0
	Oak-A	2	6	.250	11	11	0	0	0	48	66	12.4	6	13	2.4	8	1.5	6.19	62	.332	.362	-11	-12	93	97	-1.8	0	1	-1.0
	Yr	4	10	.286	23	17	0	0	0	86	117	12.2	9	28	2.9	25	2.6	5.55	72	.328	.368	-13	-15	96	97	-2.9	0	2	-1.0
1986	NY-A	5	3	.625	13	10	1	0	0	71	73	9.3	8	15	1.9	28	3.5	2.92	147	.275	.310	10	11	103	142	0.7	0	1	1.2
1987	NY-A	13	6	.684	33	33	3	1	0	188	212	10.1	12	47	2.3	63	3.0	4.02	108	.288	.330	9	7	97	105	3.1	0	-1	0.5
1988	NY-A	9	8	.529	35	32	0	0	0	176	221	11.3	11	46	2.4	81	4.1	4.50	84	.308	.352	-10	-14	96	107	0.0	0	2	-1.1
Total	25	286	224	.561	750	690	162	46	4	4644	4696	9.1	296	1237	2.4	2227	4.3	3.31	111	.264	.311	230	189	98	106	25.5	1	54	27.0
■ AUGIE JOHNS	Johns, Augustus Francis "Lefty" b: 9/10/1899, St.Louis, Mo. d: 9/12/75, San Antonio, Tex. BL/TL, 5'8.5", 170 lbs. Deb: 4/16/26																												
1926	Det-A	6	4	.600	35	14	3	1	1	113	117	9.3	6	69	5.5	40	3.2	5.34	73	.271	.364	-17	-18	98	84	0.9	-1	-2	-1.9
1927	Det-A	0	0	—	1	0	0	0	0	1	1	9.0	0	1	9.0	1	9.0	9.00	49	.333	.400	-1	-1	107	77	0.0	0	0	0.0
Total	2	6	4	.600	36	14	3	1	1	114	118	9.3	6	70	5.5	41	3.2	5.37	73	.271	.364	-17	-18	98	84	0.9	-1	-2	-1.9
■ OLLIE JOHNS	Johns, Oliver Tracy b: 8/21/1879, Trenton, Ohio d: 6/17/61, Hamilton, Ohio BL/TL, Deb: 9/24/05																												
1905	Cin-N	1	0	1.000	4	1	1	0	1	18	31	15.5	1	4	2.0	8	4.0	3.50	88	.409	.439	-1	-1	103	196	0.5	-0	-0	0.0
■ ABE JOHNSON	Johnson, Abraham b: London, Ont., Can. Deb: 7/16/1893																												
1893	Chi-N	0	0	—	1	0	0	0	1	1	2	18.0	0	2	18.0	0	0.0	36.00	14	.432	.604	-3	-3	104	36	0.0	0	0	-0.2
■ RANKIN JOHNSON	Johnson, Adam Rankin Jr. b: 3/1/17, Hayden, Ariz. BR/TR, 6'3", 177 lbs. Deb: 4/17/41																												
1941	Phi-A	1	0	1.000	7	0	0	0	0	10	14	12.6	0	3	2.7	0	0.0	3.60	119	.326	.362	1	1	103	138	0.5	-0	0	0.1
■ RANKIN JOHNSON	Johnson, Adam Rankin Sr. "Tex" b: 2/4/1888, Burnet, Tex. d: 7/2/72, Williamsport, Pa. BR/TR, 6'1.5", 185 lbs. Deb: 4/20/14																												
1914	Bos-A	4	9	.308	16	13	4	2	0	99	92	8.4	2	34	3.1	24	2.2	3.09	85	.265	.336	-4	-5	96	105	-3.2	-1	-2	-0.6
	Chi-F	9	5	.643	16	14	12	2	0	120	88	6.6	4	29	2.2	60	4.5	1.58	181	.209	.267	22	17	89	114	1.4	-2	0	1.6
1915	Chi-F	2	4	.333	11	6	3	0	1	57	58	9.2	2	23	3.6	19	3.0	4.42	65	.293	.366	-9	-10	95	85	-1.2	-2	0	-1.1
	Bal-F	7	11	.389	23	19	12	2	1	151	143	8.5	3	58	3.5	62	3.7	3.34	101	.278	.351	-5	1	111	97	1.2	-2	0	0.0
	Yr	9	15	.375	34	25	15	2	2	208	201	8.7	5	81	3.5	81	3.5	3.63	89	.282	.355	-14	-9	107	97	0.0	-2	0	-1.1
1918	StL-N	1	1	.500	6	1	0	0	0	23	20	7.8	0	7	2.7	4	1.6	2.74	96	.263	.300	0	-0	95	108	0.2	0	1	0.1
Total	3	23	30	.434	72	53	31	6	2	450	401	8.0	11	151	3.0	169	3.4	2.92	102	.258	.325	4	3	99	102	-1.6	-7	-1	-0.0

YEAR	TM/L	W	L	PCT	G	GS	CG	SHO	SV	IP	H	H/G	HR	BB	BB/G	SO	SO/G	ERA	/A	OAVG	OOBP	PR	/A	PF	CPI	WAT	PB	PD	TPI
■ **ART JOHNSON**	Johnson, Arthur Gilbert b: 2/15/1897, Warren, Pa. d: 6/7/82, Sarasota, Fla. BB/TL, 6'1", 167 lbs. Deb: 9/18/27																												
1927	NY-N	0	0	—	1	0	0	0	0	3	1	3.0	0	1	3.0	0	0.0	0.00	—	.125	.182	1	1	98	0	0.0	0	0	0.1
■ **ART JOHNSON**	Johnson, Arthur Henry "Lefty" b: 7/16/16, Winchester, Mass. BL/TL, 6'2", 185 lbs. Deb: 9/22/40																												
1940	Bos-N	0	1	.000	2	1	0	0	0	6	10	15.0	0	3	4.5	1	1.5	10.50	37	.345	.424	-4	-4	101	64	-0.4	-0	0	-0.3
1941	Bos-N	7	15	.318	43	18	6	0	1	183	189	9.3	7	71	3.5	70	3.4	3.54	98	.270	.334	2	-1	96	111	-2.5	-2	0	-0.2
1942	Bos-N	0	0	—	4	0	0	0	0	6	4	6.0	0	5	7.5	0	0.0	1.50	217	.190	.370	1	1	98	222	0.0	-0	0	0.1
Total	3	7	16	.304	49	19	6	0	1	195	203	9.4	7	79	3.6	71	3.3	3.69	94	.271	.339	-1	-5	96	113	-2.9	-2	1	-0.4
■ **BEN JOHNSON**	Johnson, Benjamin Franklin b: 5/16/31, Greenwood, S.C. BR/TR, 6'2", 190 lbs. Deb: 9/06/59																												
1959	Chi-N	0	0	—	4	2	0	0	0	17	17	9.0	1	4	2.1	6	3.2	2.12	184	.262	.304	3	3	99	152	0.0	-0	-0	0.3
1960	Chi-N	2	1	.667	17	0	0	0	1	29	39	12.1	3	11	3.4	9	2.8	4.97	76	.355	.392	-4	-4	101	135	0.7	-0	1	-0.3
Total	2	2	1	.667	21	2	0	0	1	46	56	11.0	4	15	2.9	15	2.9	3.91	98	.320	.362	-0	-0	100	141	0.7	-1	0	0.0
■ **CHET JOHNSON**	Johnson, Chester Lillis "Chesty Chet" b: 8/1/17, Redmond, Wash. d: 4/10/83, Seattle, Wash. BL/TL, 6', 175 lbs. Deb: 9/12/46																												
1946	StL-A	0	0	—	5	3	0	0	0	18	20	10.0	0	13	6.5	8	4.0	5.00	70	.286	.393	-3	-3	100	95	0.0	-1	-1	-0.3
■ **BART JOHNSON**	Johnson, Clair Barth b: 1/3/50, Torrance, Cal. BR/TR, 6'5", 190 lbs. Deb: 9/08/69																												
1969	Chi-A	1	3	.250	4	3	0	0	0	22	22	9.0	2	6	2.5	18	7.4	3.27	122	.259	.308	1	2	110	106	-0.7	0	-0	0.3
1970	Chi-A	4	7	.364	18	15	2	1	0	90	92	9.2	11	46	4.6	71	7.1	4.80	84	.268	.356	-11	-8	108	98	0.2	2	-0	-0.5
1971	Chi-A	12	10	.545	53	16	4	0	14	178	148	7.5	9	111	5.6	153	7.7	2.93	115	.227	.338	11	9	97	117	1.4	1	-1	0.9
1972	Chi-A	0	3	.000	9	0	0	0	1	14	18	11.6	2	13	8.4	9	5.8	9.00	36	.327	.451	-9	-9	106	85	-1.4	-0	0	-0.9
1973	Chi-A	3	3	.500	22	9	0	0	0	81	76	8.4	6	40	4.4	56	6.2	4.11	96	.252	.335	-3	-2	103	94	0.1	0	-0	-0.1
1974	Chi-A	10	4	.714	18	18	8	2	0	122	105	7.7	6	32	2.4	76	5.6	2.73	136	.229	.280	12	13	102	86	3.2	0	-2	1.2
1976	Chi-A	9	16	.360	32	32	8	3	0	211	231	9.9	20	62	2.6	91	3.9	4.73	75	.282	.326	-28	-27	101	89	-1.3	0	0	-2.6
1977	Chi-A	4	5	.444	29	4	0	0	2	92	114	11.2	5	38	3.7	46	4.5	4.01	100	.302	.362	1	0	99	120	-0.8	0	-0	0.0
Total	8	43	51	.457	185	97	22	6	17	810	806	9.0	61	348	3.9	520	5.8	3.93	94	.261	.333	-27	-22	101	100	0.7	3	-4	-1.7
■ **CONNIE JOHNSON**	Johnson, Clifford b: 12/27/22, Stone Mountain, Ga BR/TR, 6'4", 200 lbs. Deb: 4/17/53																												
1953	Chi-A	4	4	.500	14	10	2	1	0	61	55	8.1	4	38	5.6	44	6.5	3.54	117	.238	.349	3	4	104	109	-0.5	-2	-1	0.2
1955	Chi-A	7	4	.636	17	16	5	2	0	99	95	8.6	5	52	4.7	72	6.5	3.45	112	.251	.339	6	5	98	106	0.7	-1	-1	0.2
1956	Chi-A	0	1	.000	5	2	0	0	0	12	11	8.3	1	7	5.3	6	4.5	3.75	113	.234	.321	1	1	102	94	-0.4	-0	0	0.0
	Bal-A	9	10	.474	26	25	9	2	0	184	165	8.1	12	62	3.0	130	6.4	3.42	117	.239	.298	15	12	97	87	0.5	3	-3	1.2
	Yr	9	11	.450	31	27	9	2	0	196	176	8.1	13	69	3.2	136	6.2	3.44	117	.239	.299	16	13	97	87	0.1	-0	-3	1.2
1957	Bal-A	14	11	.560	35	30	14	3	0	242	212	7.9	17	66	2.5	177	6.6	3.20	110	.235	.285	16	8	93	86	1.8	-4	-3	0.1
1958	Bal-A	6	9	.400	26	17	4	0	1	118	116	8.8	13	32	2.4	68	5.2	3.89	92	.260	.304	-2	-4	95	95	-1.3	1	-2	-0.4
Total	5	40	39	.506	123	100	34	8	1	716	654	8.2	52	257	3.2	497	6.2	3.44	109	.243	.306	38	26	96	92	0.8	-3	-10	1.3
■ **DAVE JOHNSON**	Johnson, David Charles b: 10/4/48, Abilene, Tex. BR/TR, 6'1", 183 lbs. Deb: 7/02/74																												
1974	Bal-A	2	2	.500	11	0	0	0	2	15	17	10.2	1	5	3.0	6	3.6	3.00	111	.274	.328	1	1	92	124	-0.1	0	-0	0.0
1975	Bal-A	0	1	.000	6	0	0	0	0	9	8	8.0	0	7	7.0	4	4.0	4.00	84	.250	.366	-0	-1	89	101	-0.4	0	0	0.0
1977	Min-A	2	5	.286	30	6	0	0	0	73	86	10.6	7	23	2.8	33	4.1	4.56	91	.299	.356	-4	-3	102	108	-1.5	0	0	-0.2
1978	Min-A	0	2	.000	6	1	0	0	0	12	15	11.3	1	9	6.8	7	5.3	7.50	48	.313	.414	-5	-5	94	82	-0.9	0	0	-0.4
Total	4	4	10	.286	53	7	0	0	2	109	126	10.4	9	44	3.6	50	4.1	4.62	84	.293	.360	-8	-9	99	107	-2.9	0	0	-0.6
■ **DAVE JOHNSON**	Johnson, David Wayne b: 10/24/59, Baltimore, Md. BR/TR, 5'10", 180 lbs. Deb: 5/29/87																												
1987	Pit-N	0	0	—	5	0	0	0	0	6	13	19.5	1	2	3.0	4	6.0	10.50	41	.448	.484	-4	-4	105	100	0.0	0	0	-0.3
■ **DON JOHNSON**	Johnson, Donald Roy b: 11/12/26, Portland, Ore. BR/TR, 6'3", 200 lbs. Deb: 4/20/47																												
1947	NY-A	4	3	.571	15	8	2	0	0	54	57	9.5	2	23	3.8	16	2.7	3.67	93	.270	.340	0	-2	92	106	-0.2	-1	-0	-0.3
1950	NY-A	1	0	1.000	8	0	0	0	0	18	35	17.5	2	12	6.0	9	4.5	10.00	44	.398	.470	-11	-11	96	93	0.5	-0	-0	-0.9
	StL-A	5	6	.455	25	12	4	1	1	96	126	11.8	14	55	5.2	31	2.9	6.09	83	.325	.400	-16	-11	111	111	0.7	-3	-1	-1.2
	Yr	6	6	.500	33	12	4	1	1	114	161	12.7	16	67	5.3	40	3.2	6.71	74	.338	.413	-27	-22	108	111	1.2	-0	-1	-2.1
1951	StL-A	0	1	.000	6	3	0	0	0	15	27	16.2	4	18	10.8	8	4.8	12.60	36	.391	.505	-14	-13	109	94	-0.4	0	0	-1.1
	Was-A	7	11	.389	21	20	8	1	0	144	138	8.6	9	58	3.6	52	3.3	3.94	101	.255	.326	3	1	97	94	-0.2	-5	-0	-0.3
	Yr	7	12	.368	27	23	8	1	0	159	165	9.3	13	76	4.3	60	3.4	4.75	85	.270	.348	-11	-13	98	94	-0.6	0	-0	-1.4
1952	Was-A	0	5	.000	29	6	0	0	2	69	80	10.4	4	33	4.3	37	4.8	4.43	83	.287	.367	-6	-6	100	106	-2.4	-1	-0	-0.6
1954	Chi-A	8	7	.533	46	16	3	3	7	144	129	8.1	14	43	2.7	68	4.3	3.13	119	.243	.296	10	9	100	103	-0.9	-3	0	0.6
1955	Bal-A	2	4	.333	31	5	0	0	1	68	89	11.8	4	35	4.6	27	3.6	5.82	64	.333	.394	-14	-16	94	102	-0.2	-1	0	-1.6
1958	SF-N	0	1	.000	17	0	0	0	1	23	31	12.1	2	8	3.1	14	5.5	6.26	63	.323	.380	-6	-6	100	90	-0.4	-0	-0	-0.5
Total	7	27	38	.415	198	70	17	5	12	631	712	10.2	55	285	4.1	262	3.7	4.78	84	.288	.358	-54	-55	100	102	-3.5	-16	-2	-5.9
■ **EARL JOHNSON**	Johnson, Earl Douglas "Lefty" b: 4/2/19, Redmond, Was. BL/TL, 6'3", 190 lbs. Deb: 7/20/40																												
1940	Bos-A	6	2	.750	17	10	2	0	0	70	69	8.9	0	39	5.0	26	3.3	4.11	107	.260	.356	2	2	100	97	1.9	-3	1	0.0
1941	Bos-A	4	5	.444	17	12	4	0	0	94	90	8.6	4	51	4.9	46	4.4	4.50	93	.247	.343	-4	-3	101	84	-0.8	2	2	0.1
1946	Bos-A	5	4	.556	29	5	0	0	3	80	78	8.8	5	39	4.4	40	4.5	3.71	104	.250	.334	-2	1	111	98	-0.7	2	-0	0.3
1947	Bos-A	12	11	.522	45	17	6	3	8	142	129	8.2	7	62	3.9	65	4.1	2.98	133	.246	.324	11	15	107	115	-0.3	1	2	2.0
1948	Bos-A	10	4	.714	35	3	1	0	5	91	98	9.7	7	42	4.2	45	4.5	4.55	91	.276	.348	-3	-4	97	100	1.9	-3	2	-0.3
1949	Bos-A	3	6	.333	19	3	0	0	0	49	65	11.9	1	29	5.3	20	3.7	7.53	58	.327	.414	-18	-17	103	79	-2.1	-1	-1	-1.7
1950	Bos-A	0	0	—	11	0	0	0	0	14	18	11.6	0	8	5.1	6	3.9	7.07	72	.333	.415	-4	-3	111	86	0.0	-0	1	-0.2
1951	Det-A	0	0	—	6	0	0	0	1	6	9	13.5	0	2	3.0	2	3.0	6.00	73	.375	.423	-1	-1	107	107	0.0	0	0	0.0
Total	8	40	32	.556	179	50	13	3	17	546	556	9.2	24	272	4.5	250	4.1	4.30	97	.265	.349	-18	-9	104	98	-0.1	-2	7	0.2
■ **WALT JOHNSON**	Johnson, Ellis Walter b: 12/8/1892, Minneapolis, Minn. d: 1/4/65, Minneapolis, Minn. BR/TR, 6'0.5", 180 lbs. Deb: 7/06/12																												
1912	Chi-A	0	0	—	3	0	0	0	0	12	11	8.3	0	7	5.3	7	5.3	3.75	88	.262	.380	-1	-1	99	107	0.0	-0	-0	0.0
1915	Chi-A	0	0	—	1	0	0	0	0	2	3	13.5	0	0	0.0	3	13.5	9.00	31	.333	.333	-1	-1	94	45	0.0	0	0	0.0
1917	Phi-A	0	2	.000	4	2	0	0	0	14	15	9.6	0	5	3.2	8	5.1	7.07	37	.294	.357	-7	-7	97	52	-0.9	0	0	-0.5
Total	3	0	2	.000	8	2	0	0	0	28	29	9.3	0	12	3.9	18	5.8	5.79	50	.284	.365	-9	-9	98	75	-0.9	0	0	-0.5
■ **ERNIE JOHNSON**	Johnson, Ernest Thorwald b: 6/16/24, Brattleboro, Vt. BR/TR, 6'3.5", 190 lbs. Deb: 4/28/50																												
1950	Bos-N	2	0	1.000	16	1	0	0	0	21	37	15.9	1	13	5.6	15	6.4	6.86	51	.394	.455	-6	-8	85	121	1.0	0	1	-0.5
1952	Bos-N	6	3	.667	29	10	2	1	1	92	100	9.8	7	31	3.0	45	4.4	4.11	88	.270	.328	-4	-5	97	96	2.0	-0	1	-0.3
1953	Mil-N	4	3	.571	36	1	0	0	0	81	79	8.8	4	22	2.4	36	4.0	2.67	147	.263	.314	15	11	92	134	-0.1	-1	0	1.0
1954	Mil-N	5	2	.714	40	4	1	0	2	99	77	7.0	11	34	3.1	68	6.2	2.82	132	.219	.286	14	10	91	102	1.2	0	1	1.1
1955	Mil-N	5	7	.417	40	2	0	0	4	92	81	7.9	5	55	5.4	43	4.2	3.42	108	.240	.342	6	3	92	108	-1.5	-1	-0	0.1
1956	Mil-N	4	3	.571	36	0	0	0	6	51	54	9.5	9	21	3.7	26	4.6	3.71	98	.270	.339	0	-0	96	128	-0.1	0	0	0.0
1957	Mil-N	7	3	.700	30	0	0	0	4	65	67	9.3	9	26	3.6	44	6.1	3.88	88	.265	.331	0	-3	88	113	1.1	3	1	0.0
1958	Mil-N	3	1	.750	15	0	0	0	1	23	35	13.7	4	10	3.9	13	5.1	8.22	42	.357	.404	-11	-12	87	91	0.8	0	0	-1.1
1959	Bal-A	4	1	.800	31	1	0	0	1	50	57	10.3	6	19	3.4	29	5.2	4.14	92	.286	.343	-2	-2	98	120	1.6	0	0	0.0
Total	9	40	23	.635	273	19	3	1	19	574	587	9.2	56	231	3.6	319	5.0	3.78	97	.266	.334	12	-7	92	112	6.0	2	5	0.3
■ **FRED JOHNSON**	Johnson, Frederick Edward "Deacon" or "Cactus" b: 3/10/1894, Tolar, Tex. d: 6/14/73, Kerrville, Tex. BR/TR, 6', 185 lbs. Deb: 9/27/22																												
1922	NY-N	0	2	.000	2	2	1	0	0	18	20	10.0	3	1	0.5	8	4.0	4.00	103	.294	.292	0	0	100	108	-0.9	-1	0	0.0
1923	NY-N	2	0	1.000	3	2	1	0	0	17	11	5.8	2	7	3.7	5	2.6	4.24	93	.177	.261	-0	-1	99	44	1.0	-1	1	0.0
1938	StL-A	3	7	.300	17	6	3	0	3	69	91	11.9	7	27	3.5	24	3.1	5.61	88	.316	.373	-6	-5	103	103	-0.8	-0	-2	-0.5
1939	StL-A	0	1	.000	5	2	1	0	0	14	23	14.8	0	9	5.8	2	1.3	6.43	75	.383	.457	-3	-2	105	122	-0.4	-1	1	-0.1
Total	4	5	10	.333	27	12	6	0	3	118	145	11.1	12	44	3.4	39	3.0	5.26	88	.303	.358	-9	-8	102	97	-1.1	-2	0	-0.6
■ **CHIEF JOHNSON**	Johnson, George Howard "Murphy" or "Big Murph" b: 3/30/1886, Winnebago, Neb. d: 6/11/22, Des Moines, Iowa BR/TR, 5'11.5", 190 lbs. Deb: 4/16/13																												
1913	Cin-N	14	16	.467	44	31	13	3	0	269	251	8.4	8	86	2.9	107	3.6	3.01	110	.256	.311	6	9	104	102	1.5	-3	0	0.7
1914	Cin-N	0	0	—	1	1	0	0	0	4	6	13.5	0	2	4.5	1	2.3	6.75	44	.333	.400	-2	-2	107	79	0.0	0	-0	-0.1

YEAR	TM/L	W	L	PCT	G	GS	CG	SHO	SV	IP	H	H/G	HR	BB	BB/G	SO	SO/G	ERA	/A	OAVG	OOBP	PR	/A	PF	CPI	WAT	PB	PD	TPI
	KC-F	9	10	.474	20	19	12	2	0	134	157	10.5	2	33	2.2	78	5.2	3.16	97	.298	.345	1	-1	96	124	0.6	-1	-2	-0.4
1915	KC-F	17	17	.500	46	34	19	4	2	281	253	8.1	5	71	2.3	118	3.8	2.75	106	.242	.295	9	6	97	91	-1.1	-2	5	0.9
Total	3	40	43	.482	111	85	44	9	2	688	667	8.7	15	192	2.5	304	4.0	2.96	105	.259	.312	13	12	99	102	1.0	-6	3	1.1
■ **HANK JOHNSON**	Johnson, Henry Ward b: 5/21/06, Bradenton, Fla. d: 8/20/82, Bradenton, Fla. BR/TR, 5'11.5", 175 lbs. Deb: 4/17/25																												
1925	NY-A	1	3	.250	24	4	2	1	0	67	88	11.8	3	37	5.0	25	3.4	6.85	62	.319	.403	-18	-19	97	85	-0.8	-1	1	-1.7
1926	NY-A	0	0	—	1	0	0	0	1	1	2	18.0	0	2	18.0	0	0.0	18.00	22	.400	.571	-2	-2	97	68	0.0	0	0	0.0
1928	NY-A	14	9	.609	31	22	10	1	0	199	188	8.5	16	104	4.7	110	5.0	4.30	83	.250	.344	-6	-16	89	95	-0.9	2	0	-1.3
1929	NY-A	3	3	.500	12	8	2	0	0	43	37	7.7	5	39	8.2	24	5.0	5.02	82	.237	.376	-4	-4	97	99	-0.3	-1	-1	-0.5
1930	NY-A	14	11	.560	44	15	7	1	2	175	177	9.1	12	104	5.3	115	5.9	4.68	87	.265	.358	-1	-12	87	101	0.1	5	2	-0.5
1931	NY-A	13	8	.619	40	23	8	0	4	196	176	8.1	13	102	4.7	106	4.9	4.73	87	.234	.323	-8	-14	94	76	0.1	1	-3	-1.4
1932	NY-A	2	2	.500	5	4	2	0	0	31	34	9.9	7	15	4.4	27	7.8	4.94	83	.266	.340	-2	-3	91	111	-0.5	0	0	-0.2
1933	Bos-A	8	6	.571	25	21	7	0	1	155	156	9.1	13	74	4.3	65	3.8	4.06	108	.263	.340	4	5	102	110	1.9	3	-2	0.7
1934	Bos-A	6	8	.429	31	14	7	1	1	124	162	11.8	12	53	3.8	66	4.8	5.37	88	.316	.378	-12	-9	105	110	-1.0	1	-1	-0.7
1935	Bos-A	2	1	.667	13	2	0	0	1	31	41	11.9	3	14	4.1	14	4.1	5.52	88	.331	.387	-4	-2	108	114	0.5	-1	-1	-0.3
1936	Phi-A	0	2	.000	3	3	0	0	0	12	16	12.0	4	10	7.5	6	4.5	7.50	71	.296	.415	-3	-3	105	111	-0.9	-0	-0	-0.2
1939	Cin-N	0	3	.000	20	0	0	0	1	31	30	8.7	1	13	3.8	10	2.9	2.03	193	.268	.323	6	6	100	189	-1.4	1	-1	0.6
Total	12	63	56	.529	249	116	45	4	11	1065	1107	9.4	89	567	4.8	568	4.8	4.76	87	.268	.353	-48	-72	95	100	-3.2	9	-6	-5.5
■ **JIM JOHNSON**	Johnson, James Brian b: 11/3/45, Muskegon, Mich. BL/TL, 5'11", 175 lbs. Deb: 4/13/70																												
1970	SF-N	1	0	1.000	3	0	0	0	0	7	8	10.3	0	5	6.4	2	2.6	7.71	50	.320	.394	-3	-3	96	76	0.5	0	0	-0.2
■ **JERRY JOHNSON**	Johnson, Jerry Michael b: 12/3/43, Miami, Fla. BR/TR, 6'3", 200 lbs. Deb: 7/17/68																												
1968	Phi-N	4	4	.500	16	11	2	0	0	81	82	9.1	5	29	3.2	40	4.4	3.22	91	.264	.328	-2	-2	99	114	0.2	-0	1	-0.1
1969	Phi-N	6	13	.316	33	21	4	2	1	147	151	9.2	18	57	3.5	82	5.0	4.29	84	.268	.332	-11	-12	100	102	-1.9	1	-1	-1.0
1970	StL-N	2	0	1.000	7	0	0	0	1	11	6	4.9	1	3	2.5	5	4.1	3.27	131	.146	.205	1	1	106	18	1.0	0	-0	0.1
	SF-N	3	4	.429	33	1	0	0	3	65	67	9.3	5	38	5.3	44	6.1	4.29	90	.266	.358	-2	-3	96	107	-0.6	-1	-0	-0.4
	Yr	5	4	.556	40	1	0	0	4	76	73	8.6	6	41	4.9	49	5.8	4.14	95	.249	.338	-1	-2	97	107	0.4	0	-1	-0.3
1971	SF-N	12	9	.571	67	0	0	0	18	109	93	7.7	9	48	4.0	85	7.0	2.97	115	.230	.303	6	6	99	107	0.4	-0	0	0.6
1972	SF-N	8	6	.571	48	0	0	0	8	73	73	9.0	4	40	4.9	57	7.0	4.44	78	.261	.340	-8	-8	100	91	1.7	-1	0	-0.8
1973	Cle-A	5	6	.455	39	1	0	0	5	60	70	10.5	7	39	5.8	45	6.8	6.15	62	.299	.388	-16	-16	99	94	0.2	0	0	-1.4
1974	Hou-N	2	1	.667	34	0	0	0	0	45	47	9.4	2	24	4.8	32	6.4	4.80	74	.276	.353	-6	-6	98	90	0.5	-0	0	-0.6
1975	SD-N	3	1	.750	21	4	0	0	0	54	60	10.0	3	31	5.2	18	3.0	5.17	71	.282	.364	-9	-9	101	89	1.1	-1	-1	-0.9
1976	SD-N	1	3	.250	24	1	0	0	0	39	39	9.0	0	26	6.0	27	6.2	5.31	59	.260	.363	-8	-9	90	74	-0.8	-0	-0	-1.0
1977	Tor-A	2	4	.333	43	0	0	0	5	86	91	9.5	9	54	5.7	54	5.7	4.60	93	.279	.370	-5	-3	105	112	0.0	0	-0	-0.3
Total	10	48	51	.485	365	39	6	2	41	770	779	9.1	63	389	4.5	489	5.7	4.31	83	.265	.343	-60	-62	99	100	1.8	-2	-1	-5.8
■ **JOHNNY JOHNSON**	Johnson, John Clifford "Swede" b: 9/29/14, Belmore, Ohio BL/TL, 6', 182 lbs. Deb: 4/19/44																												
1944	NY-A	0	2	.000	22	1	0	0	3	27	25	8.3	0	24	8.0	11	3.7	4.00	90	.243	.373	-2	-1	105	105	-0.9	1	-1	0.0
1945	Chi-A	3	0	1.000	29	0	0	0	4	70	85	10.9	2	35	4.5	38	4.9	4.24	76	.306	.375	-7	-8	96	117	1.5	2	-1	-0.6
Total	2	3	2	.600	51	1	0	0	7	97	110	10.2	2	59	5.5	49	4.5	4.18	80	.289	.374	-9	-9	99	114	0.6	3	-1	-0.6
■ **JOHN HENRY JOHNSON**	Johnson, John Henry b: 8/21/56, Houston, Tex. BL/TL, 6'2", 190 lbs. Deb: 4/10/78																												
1978	Oak-A	11	10	.524	33	30	7	2	0	186	164	7.9	18	82	4.0	91	4.4	3.39	114	.238	.312	8	10	103	102	2.0	0	-3	0.7
1979	Oak-A	2	8	.200	14	13	1	0	0	85	89	9.4	13	36	3.8	50	5.3	4.34	89	.269	.339	-1	-5	91	108	-2.0	0	-1	-0.4
	Tex-A	2	6	.250	17	12	1	0	0	82	79	8.7	12	36	4.0	46	5.0	4.94	85	.255	.325	-6	-7	99	88	-2.0	0	-0	-0.6
	Yr	4	14	.222	31	25	2	0	0	167	168	9.1	25	72	3.9	96	5.2	4.63	87	.261	.331	-7	-11	95	88	-4.0	0	-1	-1.0
1980	Tex-A	2	2	.500	33	0	0	0	4	39	27	6.2	2	15	3.5	44	10.2	2.31	176	.199	.279	8	8	100	95	0.1	0	0	0.8
1981	Tex-A	3	1	.750	24	0	0	0	2	24	19	7.1	2	6	2.3	8	3.0	2.63	125	.232	.277	3	2	90	115	0.9	0	1	0.3
1983	Bos-A	3	2	.600	34	1	0	0	1	53	58	9.8	3	20	3.4	51	8.7	3.74	111	.283	.338	2	2	102	116	0.6	0	-0	0.2
1984	Bos-A	1	2	.333	30	3	0	0	1	64	64	9.0	7	27	3.8	57	8.0	3.52	125	.260	.331	3	6	110	117	-0.5	0	-0	0.6
1986	Mil-A	2	1	.667	19	0	0	0	1	44	43	8.8	2	10	2.0	42	8.6	2.66	162	.251	.288	7	8	103	107	0.5	0	-1	0.7
1987	Mil-A	0	1	.000	10	2	0	0	0	26	42	14.5	1	18	6.2	18	6.2	9.69	47	.365	.448	-15	-15	102	78	-0.4	0	0	-1.2
Total	8	26	33	.441	214	61	9	2	9	603	585	8.7	60	250	3.7	407	6.1	3.90	104	.256	.324	9	10	101	103	-0.8	0	-5	1.1
■ **JOHN JOHNSON**	Johnson, John Louis "Youngy" (born John Louis Mercer) b: 11/18/1869, Pekin, Ill. d: 1/28/41, Kansas City, Mo. TL, 165 lbs. Deb: 9/11/1894																												
1894	Phi-N	1	1	.500	4	3	2	0	0	33	44	12.0	3	15	4.1	10	2.7	6.27	80	.343	.412	-3	-5	94	94	0.0	-1	0	-0.3
■ **JOE JOHNSON**	Johnson, Joseph Richard b: 10/30/61, Brookline, Mass. BR/TR, 6'2", 195 lbs. Deb: 7/25/85																												
1985	Atl-N	4	4	.500	15	14	1	0	0	86	95	9.9	9	24	2.5	34	3.6	4.08	95	.285	.332	-5	-2	108	109	0.7	-1	-2	-0.3
1986	Atl-N	6	7	.462	17	15	2	0	0	87	101	10.4	8	35	3.6	49	5.1	4.97	77	.289	.354	-12	-11	103	96	0.2	-1	2	-0.9
	Tor-A	7	2	.778	16	15	0	0	0	88	94	9.6	3	22	2.3	39	4.0	3.89	112	.281	.323	3	5	104	97	2.4	0	-1	0.4
1987	Tor-A	3	5	.375	14	14	0	0	0	67	77	10.3	10	18	2.4	27	3.6	5.10	87	.289	.336	-5	-5	99	97	-1.4	0	-0	-0.4
Total	3	20	18	.526	62	58	3	0	0	328	367	10.1	30	99	2.7	149	4.1	4.47	92	.286	.337	-18	-13	104	100	1.9	-2	-1	-1.2
■ **KEN JOHNSON**	Johnson, Kenneth Travis b: 6/16/33, W.Palm Beach, Fla. BR/TR, 6'4", 210 lbs. Deb: 9/13/58																												
1958	KC-A	0	0	—	2	0	0	0	0	2	6	27.0	1	3	13.5	1	4.5	31.50	13	.429	.529	-6	-6	107	55	0.0	0	0	-0.4
1959	KC-A	1	1	.500	2	2	0	0	0	11	11	9.0	2	5	4.1	8	6.5	4.09	97	.268	.340	-0	-0	103	124	0.1	-0	0	0.0
1960	KC-A	5	10	.333	42	6	2	0	3	120	120	9.0	16	45	3.4	83	6.2	4.28	92	.263	.328	-5	-5	101	102	-0.8	-1	2	-0.3
1961	KC-A	0	4	.000	6	1	0	0	0	9	11	11.0	2	7	7.0	4	4.0	11.00	38	.297	.400	-7	-7	104	63	-1.9	-0	1	-0.5
	Cin-N	6	2	.750	15	11	3	1	1	83	71	7.7	11	22	2.4	42	4.6	3.25	127	.229	.279	7	8	103	95	1.5	1	1	1.0
1962	Hou-N	7	16	.304	33	31	5	1	0	197	195	8.9	18	46	2.1	178	8.1	3.84	97	.257	.300	2	-2	95	89	-3.0	-3	1	-0.3
1963	Hou-N	11	17	.393	37	32	6	1	1	224	204	8.2	12	50	2.0	148	5.9	2.65	118	.242	.285	16	12	95	104	-0.5	-4	2	1.1
1964	Hou-N	11	16	.407	35	35	7	1	0	218	209	8.6	15	44	1.8	117	4.8	3.63	96	.250	.286	-2	-4	98	84	0.0	-2	1	-0.4
1965	Hou-N	3	2	.600	8	8	1	0	0	52	52	9.0	4	11	1.9	28	4.8	4.15	78	.267	.312	-4	-5	91	90	0.8	-0	1	-0.4
	Mil-N	13	8	.619	29	26	8	1	2	180	165	8.3	15	37	1.9	123	6.2	3.20	114	.240	.279	7	9	103	89	2.2	-2	-3	0.4
	Yr	16	10	.615	37	34	9	1	2	232	217	8.4	19	48	1.9	151	5.9	3.41	104	.244	.282	3	4	100	89	3.0	-0	-2	0.0
1966	Atl-N	14	8	.636	32	31	11	2	0	216	213	8.9	24	46	1.9	105	4.4	3.29	107	.262	.297	8	5	97	109	2.9	0	0	0.6
1967	Atl-N	13	9	.591	29	29	6	0	0	210	191	8.2	19	38	1.6	85	3.6	2.74	129	.244	.280	15	18	105	110	2.7	-1	-2	1.9
1968	Atl-N	5	8	.385	31	16	1	0	0	135	145	9.7	10	25	1.7	57	3.8	3.47	81	.279	.316	-7	-10	94	111	-1.5	0	-1	-1.2
1969	Atl-N	0	1	.000	9	2	0	0	1	29	32	9.9	4	9	2.8	20	6.2	4.97	74	.283	.325	-4	-4	103	93	-0.4	-0	0	-0.4
	NY-A	1	2	.333	12	0	0	0	0	26	19	6.6	1	11	3.8	21	7.3	3.46	100	.202	.278	0	0	96	61	-0.4	-0	1	0.1
	Chi-N	1	2	.333	9	1	0	0	1	19	17	8.1	2	13	6.2	18	8.5	2.84	133	.230	.345	2	2	105	139	-0.5	-0	-0	0.1
1970	Mon-N	0	0	—	3	0	0	0	0	6	9	13.5	1	1	1.5	4	6.0	7.50	55	.321	.387	-2	-2	102	87	0.0	0	0	-0.1
Total	13	91	106	.462	334	231	50	7	9	1737	1670	8.7	157	413	2.1	1042	5.4	3.46	101	.253	.297	18	8	99	98	1.2	-12	5	1.2
■ **KEN JOHNSON**	Johnson, Kenneth Wandersee "Hook" b: 1/14/23, Topeka, Kan. BL/TL, 6'1", 185 lbs. Deb: 9/18/47																												
1947	StL-N	1	0	1.000	2	1	1	0	0	10	2	1.8	0	5	4.5	8	7.2	0.00	—	.063	.211	5	5	104	0	0.5	1	0	0.6
1948	StL-N	2	4	.333	13	4	0	0	0	45	43	8.6	1	30	6.0	20	4.0	4.80	81	.262	.374	-4	-4	99	92	-1.1	2	-0	-0.2
1949	StL-N	0	1	.000	14	2	0	0	0	34	29	7.7	1	35	9.3	18	4.8	6.35	68	.250	.419	-9	-8	108	86	-0.4	0	1	-0.5
1950	StL-N	0	0	—	2	0	0	0	0	2	1	4.5	0	3	13.5	1	4.5	0.00	—	.167	.400	1	1	103	0	0.0	0	0	0.1
	Phi-N	4	1	.800	14	8	3	1	0	61	61	9.0	3	43	6.3	32	4.7	3.98	99	.260	.372	1	-0	96	113	1.3	-0	0	0.0
	Yr	4	1	.800	16	8	3	1	0	63	62	8.9	3	46	6.6	33	4.7	3.86	103	.257	.373	2	1	96	113	1.3	0	0	0.1
1951	Phi-N	5	8	.385	20	18	4	3	0	106	103	8.7	8	68	5.8	58	4.9	4.58	84	.259	.367	-7	-9	97	100	-1.2	-1	-0	-0.9
1952	Det-A	0	0	—	9	1	0	0	0	11	12	9.8	1	11	9.0	10	8.2	6.55	58	.273	.418	-4	-3	103	90	0.0	0	0	-0.2
Total	6	12	14	.462	74	34	8	4	0	269	251	8.4	14	195	6.5	147	4.9	4.58	86	.252	.374	-17	-19	99	95	-0.9	2	1	-1.1
■ **LLOYD JOHNSON**	Johnson, Lloyd William "Eppa" b: 12/24/10, Santa Rosa, Cal. d: 10/8/80, Stockton, Cal. BL/TL, 6'4", 204 lbs. Deb: 4/21/34																												
1934	Pit-N	0	0	—	1	0	0	0	0	1	1	9.0	0	0	0.0	0	0.0	0.00	—	.333	.333	0	0	105	0	0.0	0	0	0.0

YEAR	TM/L	W	L	PCT	G	GS	CG	SHO	SV	IP	H	H/G	HR	BB	BB/G	SO	SO/G	ERA	/A	OAVG	OOBP	PR	/A	PF	CPI	WAT	PB	PD	TPI
■ **MIKE JOHNSON**	Johnson, Michael Norton b: 3/2/51, Slayton, Minn. BR/TR, 6'1", 185 lbs. Deb: 7/25/74																											
1974	SD-N	0	2	.000	18	0	0	0	0	21	29	12.4	1	15	6.4	15	6.4	4.71	75	.326	.413	-3	-3	97	134	-0.9	0	-0	-0.2
■ **RANDY JOHNSON**	Johnson, Randall David b: 9/10/63, Walnut Creek, Cal. BL/TR, 6'10", 225 lbs. Deb: 9/15/88																											
1988	Mon-N	3	0	1.000	4	4	1	0	0	26	23	8.0	3	7	2.4	25	8.7	2.42	150	.225	.275	3	3	105	117	1.5	-0	-1	0.2
■ **BOB JOHNSON**	Johnson, Robert Dale b: 4/25/43, Aurora, Ill. BL/TR, 6'4", 220 lbs. Deb: 9/19/69																											
1969	NY-N	0	0	—	2	0	0	0	1	2	1	4.5	0	1	4.5	1	4.5	0.00	—	.167	.286	1	1	99	0	0.0	0	0	0.1
1970	KC-A	8	13	.381	40	26	10	1	4	214	178	7.5	18	82	3.4	206	8.7	3.07	120	.228	.303	15	15	100	102	-0.5	-1	-1	1.4
1971	Pit-N	9	10	.474	31	27	7	1	0	175	170	8.7	19	55	2.8	101	5.2	3.45	97	.259	.317	0	-2	97	112	-2.1	-1	-1	-0.4
1972	Pit-N	4	4	.500	31	11	1	0	3	116	98	7.6	14	46	3.6	79	6.1	2.95	117	.231	.306	7	7	100	118	-0.7	-0	-2	0.5
1973	Pit-N	4	2	.667	50	2	0	0	4	92	98	9.6	12	34	3.3	68	6.7	3.62	93	.276	.341	1	-3	92	128	1.1	-1	-2	-0.5
1974	Cle-A	3	4	.429	14	10	0	0	0	72	75	9.4	12	37	4.6	36	4.5	4.38	84	.273	.355	-6	-6	101	118	-0.3	0	0	-0.5
1977	Atl-N	0	1	.000	15	0	0	0	0	22	24	9.8	7	14	5.7	16	6.5	7.36	61	.270	.377	-8	-7	115	91	-0.4	0	-0	-0.6
Total	7	28	34	.452	183	76	18	2	12	693	644	8.4	82	269	3.5	507	6.6	3.48	102	.249	.321	9	5	99	112	-2.9	-3	-6	0.0
■ **ROY JOHNSON**	Johnson, Roy J "Hardrock" b: 10/1/1895, Madill, Okla. d: 1/10/86, Scottsdale, Ariz. BR/TR, 6', 185 lbs. Deb: 8/07/18 MC																											
1918	Phi-A	1	5	.167	10	8	3	0	0	50	47	8.5	0	34	6.1	12	2.2	3.42	87	.254	.358	-4	-2	108	107	-1.7	-2	-0	-0.4
■ **JING JOHNSON**	Johnson, Russell Conwell b: 10/9/1894, Parker Ford, Pa. d: 12/6/50, Pottstown, Pa. BR/TR, 5'9", 172 lbs. Deb: 6/27/16																											
1916	Phi-A	2	8	.200	12	12	8	0	0	84	90	9.6	3	39	4.2	25	2.7	3.75	79	.288	.368	-9	-7	105	113	-0.7	-1	2	-0.5
1917	Phi-A	9	12	.429	34	23	13	0	0	191	184	8.7	3	56	2.6	55	2.6	2.78	93	.260	.319	-2	-4	97	103	1.3	3	2	0.0
1919	Phi-A	9	15	.375	34	25	12	0	0	202	222	9.9	8	62	2.8	67	3.0	3.61	100	.291	.346	-9	0	112	106	2.2	-0	4	0.5
1927	Phi-A	4	2	.667	17	3	2	0	0	52	42	7.3	2	16	2.8	16	2.8	3.46	113	.235	.302	4	3	95	84	0.6	-0	1	0.3
1928	Phi-A	0	0	—	3	0	0	0	0	11	13	10.6	1	5	4.1	3	2.5	4.91	81	.310	.375	-1	-1	99	111	0.0	1	0	0.0
Total	5	24	37	.393	100	63	35	0	0	540	551	9.2	17	178	3.0	166	2.8	3.35	95	.275	.337	-17	-10	104	104	3.4	2	10	0.3
■ **SI JOHNSON**	Johnson, Silas Kenneth b: 10/5/06, Marseilles, Ill. BR/TR, 5'11.5", 185 lbs. Deb: 5/02/28																											
1928	Cin-N	0	0	—	3	0	0	0	0	10	9	8.1	0	5	4.5	1	0.9	4.50	86	.250	.333	-1	-1	97	71	0.0	0	0	0.0
1929	Cin-N	0	0	—	1	0	0	0	0	2	2	9.0	0	1	4.5	0	0.0	4.50	105	.250	.333	0	0	101	69	0.0	0	0	0.0
1930	Cin-N	3	1	.750	35	3	0	0	0	78	86	9.9	5	31	3.6	47	5.4	4.96	93	.286	.351	0	-3	93	93	1.2	0	-0	-0.2
1931	Cin-N	11	19	.367	42	33	14	0	0	262	273	9.4	5	74	2.5	95	3.3	3.78	100	.269	.317	3	0	98	90	-0.4	-3	-5	-0.7
1932	Cin-N	13	15	.464	42	27	14	2	2	245	246	9.0	8	57	2.1	94	3.5	3.27	117	.259	.298	17	15	99	93	2.0	-4	0	1.1
1933	Cin-N	7	18	.280	34	28	14	4	1	211	212	9.0	7	54	2.3	51	2.2	3.50	97	.263	.303	-4	-2	102	90	-3.7	-7	-1	-1.1
1934	Cin-N	7	22	.241	46	31	9	0	3	216	264	11.0	15	84	3.5	89	3.7	5.21	82	.297	.358	-27	-23	105	94	-4.9	-4	-3	-2.6
1935	Cin-N	5	11	.313	30	20	4	1	0	130	155	10.7	14	59	4.1	40	2.8	6.23	62	.293	.360	-32	-35	95	84	-2.5	-4	-1	-3.5
1936	Cin-N	0	0	—	2	0	0	0	0	4	7	15.8	1	0	0.0	2	4.5	13.50	29	.368	.368	-4	-4	97	55	0.0	0	-0	-0.3
	StL-N	5	3	.625	12	9	3	1	0	62	82	11.9	4	11	1.6	21	3.0	4.35	87	.314	.342	-2	-4	95	108	0.6	-0	-1	-0.4
	Yr	5	3	.625	14	9	3	1	0	66	89	12.1	5	11	1.5	23	3.1	4.91	77	.318	.344	-7	-8	95	108	0.6	0	-1	-0.7
1937	StL-N	12	12	.500	38	21	12	1	1	192	222	10.4	14	43	2.0	64	3.0	3.33	117	.292	.324	12	12	100	**128**	-0.6	-3	-2	0.8
1938	StL-N	0	3	.000	6	3	0	0	0	16	27	15.2	0	6	3.4	4	2.3	7.31	58	.380	.418	-6	-6	111	94	-1.4	-0	0	-0.4
1940	Phi-N	5	14	.263	37	14	5	0	1	138	145	9.5	13	42	2.7	58	3.8	4.89	80	.268	.318	-16	-15	102	84	-2.0	-2	-2	-1.8
1941	Phi-N	5	12	.294	39	21	6	1	2	163	207	11.4	8	54	3.0	80	4.4	4.53	82	.309	.355	-16	-14	103	107	0.2	-2	-1	-1.6
1942	Phi-N	8	19	.296	39	26	10	1	0	195	198	9.1	6	72	3.3	78	3.6	3.69	91	.266	.325	-8	-7	101	98	0.4	-4	-3	-1.4
1943	Phi-N	8	3	.727	21	14	9	1	2	113	110	8.8	4	25	2.0	46	3.7	3.27	99	.252	.285	1	-1	96	84	3.0	0	-0	0.0
1946	Phi-N	0	0	—	1	0	0	0	0	3	7	21.0	1	0	0.0	2	6.0	3.00	111	.538	.438	0	0	98	433	0.0	0	0	0.1
	Bos-N	6	5	.545	28	12	5	1	1	127	134	9.5	8	35	2.5	41	2.9	2.76	116	.272	.318	9	6	94	131	0.2	-1	-1	0.4
	Yr	6	5	.545	29	12	5	1	1	130	141	9.8	9	35	2.4	43	3.0	2.77	116	.279	.321	9	6	94	131	0.2	0	-1	0.5
1947	Bos-N	6	8	.429	36	10	3	0	2	113	124	9.9	7	34	2.7	27	2.2	4.22	92	.275	.323	-2	-4	95	90	-1.7	-3	3	-0.4
Total	17	101	165	.380	492	272	108	13	15	2280	2510	9.9	120	687	2.7	840	3.3	4.09	92	.279	.326	-76	-84	99	98	-9.6	-36	-17	-12.0
■ **SYL JOHNSON**	Johnson, Sylvester W b: 12/31/1900, Portland, Ore. d: 2/20/85, Portland, Ore. BR/TR, 5'11", 180 lbs. Deb: 4/24/22 C																											
1922	Det-A	7	3	.700	29	8	3	0	1	97	99	9.2	7	30	2.8	29	2.7	3.71	106	.273	.327	4	2	97	104	2.0	-0	-2	0.0
1923	Det-A	12	7	.632	37	18	7	0	0	176	181	9.3	12	47	2.4	93	**4.8**	3.99	95	.274	.315	-0	-4	95	92	2.1	-0	-5	-0.9
1924	Det-A	5	4	.556	29	9	2	0	3	104	117	10.1	8	42	3.6	55	4.8	4.93	85	.287	.351	-8	-9	99	92	0.0	-0	-1	-0.9
1925	Det-A	0	2	.000	6	0	0	0	0	13	11	7.6	1	10	6.9	5	3.5	3.46	124	.250	.368	1	1	98	136	-0.9	-1	0	0.1
1926	StL-N	0	3	.000	19	6	1	0	1	49	54	9.9	3	15	2.8	10	1.8	4.22	90	.297	.341	-2	-2	100	107	-1.4	-2	-1	-0.4
1927	StL-N	0	0	—	2	0	0	0	0	3	3	9.0	1	0	0.0	2	6.0	6.00	69	.250	.250	-1	-1	106	70	0.0	0	0	0.0
1928	StL-N	8	4	.667	34	6	2	0	3	120	117	8.8	6	33	2.5	66	5.0	3.90	99	.259	.306	1	-0	97	81	0.8	-0	-1	-0.1
1929	StL-N	13	7	.650	42	19	12	3	3	182	186	9.2	11	56	2.8	80	4.0	3.61	128	.265	.319	22	20	98	102	3.1	-2	-4	1.3
1930	StL-N	12	10	.545	32	24	9	2	2	188	215	10.3	13	38	1.8	92	4.4	4.64	109	.293	.324	7	9	102	91	-1.0	-0	-3	0.4
1931	StL-N	11	9	.550	32	24	12	2	2	186	186	9.0	9	29	**1.4**	82	4.0	3.00	133	.255	.283	18	20	103	93	-1.7	2	-3	2.0
1932	StL-N	5	14	.263	32	22	7	1	2	165	199	10.9	14	35	1.9	70	3.8	4.91	80	.299	.331	-19	-18	101	93	-4.4	-1	-1	-1.8
1933	StL-N	3	3	.500	35	1	0	0	3	84	89	9.5	7	16	1.7	28	3.0	4.29	78	.271	.305	-9	-9	100	84	-0.1	0	-2	-0.9
1934	Cin-N	0	0	—	2	0	0	0	0	7	9	11.6	2	0	0.0	0	0.0	2.57	165	.310	.310	1	1	105	225	0.0	1	-0	0.2
	Phi-N	5	9	.357	42	10	4	3	3	134	122	8.2	14	24	1.6	54	3.6	3.49	129	.242	.274	8	15	111	88	-0.3	-0	-4	1.1
	Yr	5	9	.357	44	10	4	3	3	141	131	8.4	16	24	1.5	54	3.4	3.45	130	.245	.276	10	16	110	88	-0.3	1	-4	1.3
1935	Phi-N	10	8	.556	37	18	8	1	6	175	182	9.4	15	31	1.6	89	4.6	3.55	133	.265	.293	9	23	117	99	2.3	1	-3	2.2
1936	Phi-N	5	7	.417	39	8	1	0	7	111	129	10.5	10	29	2.4	48	3.9	4.30	104	.288	.332	-3	2	111	102	0.7	0	-2	0.0
1937	Phi-N	4	10	.286	32	15	4	0	3	138	155	10.1	20	22	1.4	46	3.0	5.02	86	.288	.312	-17	-11	111	90	-2.0	-3	-1	-1.2
1938	Phi-N	2	7	.222	22	6	2	0	0	83	87	9.4	4	11	1.2	21	2.3	4.23	95	.267	.287	-4	-2	106	73	-1.1	-3	-2	-0.6
1939	Phi-N	8	8	.500	22	14	6	0	2	111	112	9.1	10	15	1.2	37	3.0	3.81	102	.264	.283	1	1	99	87	2.5	-1	-1	0.0
1940	Phi-N	2	2	.500	17	2	2	0	2	41	37	8.1	6	5	1.1	13	2.9	4.17	94	.236	.255	-1	-1	102	74	0.5	-1	-0	-0.1
Total	19	112	117	.489	542	210	82	12	43	2167	2290	9.5	173	488	2.0	920	3.8	4.06	104	.273	.310	9	39	103	93	1.1	-10	-36	0.4
■ **TOM JOHNSON**	Johnson, Thomas G. b: Scranton, Pa. Deb: 4/29/1897																											
1897	Phi-N	1	2	.333	5	2	1	0	0	29	39	12.1	0	12	3.7	7	2.2	4.66	89	.345	.408	-1	-2	96	107	-0.2	-2	0	-0.2
1899	NY-N	0	0	—	1	0	0	0	0	2	0	0.0	0	2	9.0	1	4.5	0.00	—	.000	.283	1	1	99	0	0.0	-0	0	0.1
Total	2	1	2	.333	6	2	1	0	0	31	39	11.3	0	14	4.1	8	2.3	4.35	95	.330	.401	-0	-1	96	100	-0.2	-2	0	-0.1
■ **TOM JOHNSON**	Johnson, Thomas Raymond b: 4/2/51, St.Paul, Minn. BR/TR, 6'1", 185 lbs. Deb: 9/10/74																											
1974	Min-A	2	0	1.000	4	0	0	0	1	7	4	5.1	0	0	0.0	4	5.1	0.00	—	.167	.167	3	3	101	0	1.0	0	0	0.3
1975	Min-A	1	2	.333	18	0	0	0	3	39	40	9.2	4	21	4.8	17	3.9	4.15	98	.263	.352	-2	-0	107	109	-0.4	0	0	0.0
1976	Min-A	3	1	.750	18	1	0	0	0	48	44	8.3	2	8	1.5	37	6.9	2.63	131	.243	.272	5	4	98	92	1.0	0	0	0.5
1977	Min-A	16	7	.696	71	0	0	0	15	147	152	9.3	11	47	2.9	87	5.3	3.12	133	.272	.324	16	17	102	127	4.6	0	1	1.7
1978	Min-A	1	4	.200	18	0	0	0	3	33	42	11.5	2	17	4.6	21	5.7	5.45	65	.318	.394	-6	-7	94	104	-1.3	0	0	-0.6
Total	5	23	14	.622	129	1	0	0	22	274	282	9.3	19	93	3.1	166	5.5	3.38	116	.269	.326	15	17	101	112	4.9	0	1	1.9
■ **VIC JOHNSON**	Johnson, Victor Oscar b: 8/3/20, Eau Claire, Wis. BR/TL, 6', 160 lbs. Deb: 5/03/44																											
1944	Bos-A	0	3	.000	7	5	0	0	0	27	42	14.0	0	15	5.0	7	2.3	6.33	52	.362	.422	-9	-9	97	104	-1.4	-1	1	-0.8
1945	Bos-A	6	4	.600	26	9	4	1	2	85	90	9.5	4	46	4.9	21	2.2	4.02	80	.276	.359	-6	-7	96	111	1.4	-1	1	-0.7
1946	Cle-A	0	1	.000	9	1	0	0	0	14	20	12.9	1	8	5.1	3	1.9	9.00	35	.357	.438	-9	-9	90	77	-0.4	-0	1	-0.8
Total	3	6	8	.429	42	15	4	1	2	126	152	10.9	5	69	4.9	31	2.2	5.07	64	.305	.383	-23	-26	96	105	-0.4	-3	2	-2.3
■ **WALTER JOHNSON**	Johnson, Walter Perry "Barney" or "The Big Train" b: 11/6/1887, Humboldt, Kan. d: 12/10/46, Washington, D.C. BR/TR, 6'1", 200 lbs. Deb: 8/02/07 MH																											
1907	Was-A	5	9	.357	14	12	11	2	0	111	98	7.9	1	17	1.4	68	5.5	1.86	128	.260	.292	8	6	94	110	0.4	-1	-2	0.3
1908	Was-A	14	14	.500	36	29	23	6	1	257	194	6.8	0	53	1.9	160	5.6	1.65	140	.211	.262	21	19	97	99	1.8	2	-4	1.9
1909	Was-A	13	25	.342	40	36	27	4	1	297	247	7.5	1	84	2.5	164	5.0	2.21	107	.221	.284	9	5	96	76	2.2	-2	-3	0.0
1910	Was-A	25	17	.595	**45**	42	**38**	8	1	**374**	269	6.5	1	76	1.8	**313**	**7.5**	1.35	**190**	.210	.262	49	**51**	102	107	7.4	0	-2	5.9

YEAR	TM/L	W	L	PCT	G	GS	CG	SHO	SV	IP	H	H/G	HR	BB	BB/G	SO	SO/G	ERA	/A	OAVG	OOBP	PR	/A	PF	CPI	WAT	PB	PD	TPI
1911	Was-A	25	13	.658	40	37	**36**	**6**	1	323	292	8.1	8	70	2.0	207	5.8	1.89	175	.238	.283	**52**	**51**	99	109	**9.2**	3	3	**6.1**
1912	Was-A	33	12	.733	50	37	34	7	2	368	259	**6.3**	2	76	1.9	**303**	**7.4**	**1.39**	**233**	**.196**	**.248**	**80**	**76**	97	84	9.4	9	1	**9.5**
1913	Was-A	**36**	7	**.837**	48	36	**29**	**11**	2	**346**	232	**6.0**	9	38	**1.0**	**243**	**6.3**	**1.14**	**268**	**.187**	**.217**	**69**	**74**	105	54	**14.7**	10	0	**8.8**
1914	Was-A	**28**	18	.609	**51**	40	**33**	**9**	1	**372**	287	6.9	3	74	1.8	**225**	5.4	1.72	159	.217	.265	42	**42**	100	90	5.3	8	2	**6.3**
1915	Was-A	**27**	13	.675	47	39	**35**	**7**	4	**337**	258	6.9	1	56	**1.5**	**203**	5.4	1.55	189	.214	**.260**	**52**	**52**	99	95	**6.6**	6	2	**6.9**
1916	Was-A	**25**	20	.556	48	38	**36**	3	1	**371**	290	7.0	0	82	2.0	**228**	5.5	1.89	150	.220	.270	39	**39**	100	86	3.6	8	-5	4.8
1917	Was-A	23	16	.590	47	34	30	8	3	328	259	7.1	3	67	1.8	**188**	**5.2**	2.30	107	.220	.270	13	6	93	70	5.0	10	-0	1.7
1918	Was-A	**23**	13	.639	39	29	29	**8**	3	325	241	6.7	2	70	1.9	**162**	4.5	**1.27**	**224**	.210	**.253**	**54**	**57**	103	103	4.1	6	-2	**8.3**
1919	Was-A	20	14	.588	39	29	27	**7**	2	290	235	**7.3**	0	51	1.6	**147**	4.6	**1.49**	**214**	**.219**	**.259**	**56**	**55**	99	85	6.4	2	0	**6.6**
1920	Was-A	8	10	.444	21	15	12	4	3	144	135	8.4	5	27	1.7	78	4.9	3.13	117	.245	.286	11	9	96	73	0.0	4	-1	1.1
1921	Was-A	17	14	.548	35	32	25	1	1	264	265	9.0	7	92	3.1	**143**	**4.9**	3.51	121	.263	.321	23	22	99	92	1.0	3	-3	2.1
1922	Was-A	15	16	.484	41	31	23	4	4	280	283	9.1	8	99	3.2	105	3.4	2.99	125	.267	.326	33	23	93	114	1.2	-0	0	2.2
1923	Was-A	17	12	.586	42	34	18	3	4	261	265	9.1	9	73	2.5	**130**	4.5	3.48	109	.271	.326	15	9	95	102	3.2	1	-2	0.7
1924	Was-A	**23**	7	**.767**	38	38	20	**6**	0	278	233	**7.5**	10	77	2.5	**158**	**5.1**	**2.72**	**149**	**.224**	**.279**	**47**	**42**	96	79	**7.1**	6	-1	**4.6**
1925	Was-A	20	7	.741	30	29	16	3	0	229	211	**8.3**	7	78	3.1	108	4.2	3.07	136	**.243**	.306	34	28	95	91	4.5	16	-4	**3.9**
1926	Was-A	15	16	.484	33	33	22	2	0	262	259	8.9	13	73	2.5	125	4.3	3.61	108	.263	.306	12	9	97	91	-1.9	1	-5	0.4
1927	Was-A	5	6	.455	18	15	7	1	0	108	113	9.4	7	26	2.2	48	4.0	5.08	78	.278	.317	-11	-13	96	76	-0.9	6	0	-0.6
Total	21	417	279	.599	802	665	531	110	34	5925	4925	7.5	97	1359	2.1	3506	5.3	2.17	147	.228	.277	705	665	98	90	90.3	98	-23	81.5
■ **BILL JOHNSON**	Johnson, William C. b: 10/6/60, Wilmington, Del. BR/TR, 6'5", 205 lbs. Deb: 9/06/83																												
1983	Chi-N	1	0	1.000	10	0	0	0	0	12	17	12.8	0	3	2.3	4	3.0	4.50	82	.347	.364	-1	-1	101	115	0.5	0	0	0.0
1984	Chi-N	0	0	—	4	0	0	0	0	5	4	7.2	0	1	1.8	3	5.4	1.80	217	.235	.263	1	1	109	124	0.0	0	0	0.2
Total	2	1	0	1.000	14	0	0	0	0	17	21	11.1	0	4	2.1	7	3.7	3.71	101	.318	.338	-0	0	103	118	0.5	0	1	0.2
■ **ROY JOINER**	Joiner, Roy Merrill "Pop" b: 10/30/06, Red Bluff, Cal. BL/TL, 6', 170 lbs. Deb: 4/30/34																												
1934	Chi-N	0	1	.000	20	2	0	0	0	34	61	16.1	3	8	2.1	9	2.4	8.21	48	.391	.408	-16	-16	97	93	-0.4	-0	-0	-1.5
1935	Chi-N	0	0	—	2	0	0	0	0	3	6	18.0	0	2	6.0	0	0.0	6.00	64	.429	.444	-1	-1	95	158	0.0	-0	0	0.0
1940	NY-N	3	2	.600	30	2	0	0	1	53	66	11.2	8	17	2.9	25	4.2	3.40	113	.308	.364	3	3	100	175	0.6	1	0	0.4
Total	3	3	3	.500	52	4	0	0	1	90	133	13.3	11	27	2.7	34	3.4	5.30	73	.346	.385	-14	-14	99	143	0.2	0	0	-1.1
■ **DAVE JOLLY**	Jolly, David "Gabby" b: 10/14/24, Stony Point, N.C. d: 5/27/63, Durham, N.C. BR/TR, 6', 160 lbs. Deb: 5/09/53																												
1953	Mil-N	0	1	.000	24	0	0	0	0	38	34	8.1	4	27	6.4	23	5.4	3.55	111	.239	.360	3	2	92	127	-0.4	1	0	0.2
1954	Mil-N	11	6	.647	47	1	0	0	10	111	87	7.1	6	64	5.2	62	5.0	2.43	153	.215	.319	20	16	91	121	1.5	3	1	1.9
1955	Mil-N	2	3	.400	36	0	0	0	1	58	58	9.0	6	51	7.9	23	3.6	5.74	64	.258	.389	-11	-13	92	91	-0.6	0	1	-1.1
1956	Mil-N	2	3	.400	29	0	0	0	7	46	39	7.6	7	35	6.8	20	3.9	3.72	97	.228	.354	0	-0	96	119	-0.7	-0	-1	-0.1
1957	Mil-N	1	1	.500	23	0	0	0	1	38	37	8.8	4	21	5.0	27	6.4	4.97	68	.264	.359	-5	-7	88	97	-0.1	1	0	-0.4
Total	5	16	14	.533	159	1	0	0	19	291	255	7.9	27	198	6.1	155	4.8	3.77	98	.236	.350	8	-3	92	112	-0.3	5	1	0.5
■ **COWBOY JONES**	Jones, Albert Edward "Bronco" b: 8/23/1874, Golden, Colo. d: 2/9/58, Inglewood, Cal. BL/TL, 5'11", 160 lbs. Deb: 6/24/1898																												
1898	Cle-N	4	4	.500	9	9	7	0	0	72	76	9.5	0	29	3.6	26	3.3	3.00	114	.293	.364	5	3	95	118	-0.2	-2	0	0.1
1899	StL-N	6	5	.545	12	12	9	0	0	85	111	11.8	1	22	2.3	28	3.0	3.60	114	.340	.382	2	5	107	123	0.0	0	0	0.5
1900	StL-N	13	19	.406	39	36	29	3	0	293	334	10.3	7	82	2.5	68	2.1	3.56	97	.310	.359	4	-4	93	107	-2.4	-2	6	0.0
1901	StL-N	2	6	.250	10	9	7	0	0	76	97	11.5	4	22	2.6	25	3.0	4.50	70	.337	.390	-10	-11	95	108	-2.1	0	2	-0.8
Total	4	25	34	.424	70	66	52	3	0	526	618	10.6	12	155	2.7	147	2.5	3.63	97	.317	.368	2	-7	96	111	-4.7	-4	7	-0.2
■ **ALEX JONES**	Jones, Alexander b: 12/25/1869, Pittsburgh, Pa. d: 4/4/41, Woodville, Pa. BL/TL, 5'6", 135 lbs. Deb: 9/25/1889																												
1889	Pit-N	1	0	1.000	1	1	1	0	0	9	7	7.0	0	1	1.0	10	10.0	3.00	121	.228	.253	1	1	90	48	0.5	0	0	0.1
1892	Lou-N	5	11	.313	18	16	13	1	0	147	130	8.0	3	56	3.4	44	2.7	3.31	93	.249	.322	-0	-4	93	82	-2.0	-1	0	-0.4
	Was-N	0	3	.000	4	4	3	0	0	27	33	11.0	0	14	4.7	7	2.3	4.00	87	.315	.395	-2	-2	106	115	-1.4	0	0	0.0
	Yr	5	14	.263	22	20	16	1	0	174	163	8.4	3	70	3.6	51	2.6	3.41	92	.260	.335	-2	-5	95	115	-3.4	-1	0	-0.4
1894	Phi-N	1	0	1.000	1	1	1	0	0	9	10	10.0	0	0	0.0	2	2.0	2.00	250	.303	.303	3	3	94	140	0.5	-0	0	0.2
1903	Det-A	0	1	.000	2	2	0	0	0	9	19	19.0	0	6	6.0	2	2.0	12.00	24	.454	.522	-9	-9	96	81	-0.4	-1	0	-0.7
Total	4	7	15	.318	26	24	18	1	0	201	199	8.9	3	77	3.4	65	2.9	3.72	87	.272	.341	-7	-11	95	88	-2.8	-1	0	-0.8
■ **AL JONES**	Jones, Alfornia b: 2/10/59, Charleston, Miss. BR/TR, 6'4", 210 lbs. Deb: 8/06/83																												
1983	Chi-A	0	0	—	2	0	0	0	0	2	3	13.5	0	2	9.0	2	9.0	4.50	92	.375	.500	-0	-0	102	183	0.0	0	0	0.0
1984	Chi-A	1	1	.500	20	0	0	0	5	20	23	10.3	3	11	4.9	15	6.7	4.50	99	.299	.376	-1	-0	111	133	0.1	0	0	0.0
1985	Chi-A	1	0	1.000	5	0	0	0	0	6	3	4.5	0	3	4.5	2	3.0	1.50	276	.167	.286	2	2	100	130	0.5	0	0	0.2
Total	3	2	1	.667	27	0	0	0	5	28	29	9.3	3	16	5.1	19	6.1	3.86	113	.282	.371	1	2	108	136	0.6	0	0	0.2
■ **ART JONES**	Jones, Arthur Lennox b: 2/7/06, Kershaw, S.C. d: 11/25/80, Columbia, S.C. BR/TR, 6', 165 lbs. Deb: 4/23/32																												
1932	Bro-N	0	0	—	1	0	0	0	0	1	2	18.0	0	1	9.0	0	0.0	18.00	21	.667	.600	-2	-2	96	80	0.0	0	0	0.0
■ **BARRY JONES**	Jones, Barry Louis b: 2/15/63, Centerville, Ind. BR/TR, 6'2", 215 lbs. Deb: 7/18/86																												
1986	Pit-N	3	4	.429	26	0	0	0	3	37	29	7.1	3	21	5.1	29	7.1	2.92	128	.215	.314	3	3	101	109	0.2	0	1	0.4
1987	Pit-N	2	4	.333	32	0	0	0	1	43	55	11.5	6	23	4.8	28	5.9	5.65	76	.314	.384	-7	-7	105	110	-0.9	-0	0	-0.5
1988	Pit-N	1	1	.500	42	0	0	0	2	56	57	9.2	3	21	3.4	31	5.0	3.05	110	.271	.328	2	2	97	132	0.0	-0	0	0.1
	Chi-A	2	2	.500	17	0	0	0	1	26	15	5.2	3	17	5.9	17	5.9	2.42	162	.170	.302	4	4	99	120	0.2	0	0	0.5
Total	3	8	11	.421	117	0	0	0	7	162	156	8.7	15	82	4.6	105	5.8	3.61	104	.257	.337	3	3	100	119	-0.5	-0	1	0.5
■ **DEACON JONES**	Jones, Carroll Elmer b: 12/20/1892, Arcadia, Kan. d: 12/28/52, Pittsburg, Kan. BR/TR, 6'1", 174 lbs. Deb: 9/23/16																												
1916	Det-A	0	0	—	1	0	0	0	0	7	7	9.0	0	5	6.4	2	2.6	2.57	113	.269	.387	0	0	103	161	0.0	-0	0	0.0
1917	Det-A	4	4	.500	24	6	2	0	0	77	69	8.1	0	26	3.0	28	3.3	2.92	88	.256	.334	-2	-3	96	100	0.0	-1	1	-0.2
1918	Det-A	3	1	.750	21	4	1	0	0	67	60	8.1	0	38	5.1	15	2.0	3.09	88	.244	.341	-2	-3	99	97	1.1	-1	1	-0.1
Total	3	7	5	.583	46	10	3	0	0	151	136	8.1	0	69	4.1	45	2.7	2.98	89	.251	.340	-4	-5	98	102	1.1	-2	2	-0.3
■ **BUMPUS JONES**	Jones, Charles Leander b: 1/1/1870, Cedarville, Ohio d: 6/25/38, Xenia, Ohio BR/TR, Deb: 10/15/1892																												
1892	Cin-N	1	0	1.000	1	1	1	0	0	9	0	0.0	0	4	4.0	3	3.0	0.00	—	.000	.143	3	3	103	0	0.5	-0	0	0.4
1893	Cin-N	1	3	.250	6	5	2	0	0	29	37	11.5	1	23	7.1	6	1.9	10.24	47	.327	.440	-18	-18	102	60	-0.9	1	0	-1.2
	NY-N	0	1	.000	1	1	0	0	0	4	5	11.3	0	10	22.5	1	2.3	11.25	43	.322	.588	-3	-3	103	94	-0.4	0	0	-0.1
	Yr	1	4	.200	7	6	2	0	0	33	42	11.5	1	33	9.0	7	1.9	10.36	46	.326	.464	-21	-21	102	94	-1.3	1	0	-1.3
Total	2	2	4	.333	8	7	3	0	0	42	42	9.0	1	37	7.9	10	2.1	8.14	55	.275	.417	-18	-17	102	50	-0.8	1	0	-0.9
■ **CHARLEY JONES**	Jones, Charles Wesley "Baby" (born Benjamin Wesley Rippay) b: 4/30/1850, Alamance Co., N.C. BR/TR, Deb: N/A.																												
1887	NY-a	0	0	—	2	0	0	0	0	3	2	6.0	0	4	12.0	0	0.0	3.00	132	.201	.430	0	0	92	149	0.0	0	0	0.0
■ **DALE JONES**	Jones, Dale Eldon "Nubs" b: 12/17/18, Marquette, Neb. d: 11/8/80, Orlando, Fla. BR/TR, 6'1", 172 lbs. Deb: 9/07/41																												
1941	Phi-N	0	1	.000	2	1	0	0	0	8	13	14.6	0	6	6.8	2	2.3	7.88	47	.342	.422	-4	-4	103	85	-0.4	1	-0	-0.2
■ **JACK JONES**	Jones, Daniel Albion "Jumping Jack" b: 10/23/1860, Litchfield, Conn. d: 10/19/36, Wallingford, Conn. TR, Deb: 7/09/1883																												
1883	Det-N	6	5	.545	12	12	9	0	0	93	103	10.0	0	19	1.8	33	3.2	3.48	84	.288	.324	-4	-6	94	92	1.4	-1	0	-0.5
	Phi-a	5	2	.714	7	7	7	0	0	65	58	8.0	1	6	0.8	28	3.9	2.63	124	.244	.263	5	5	99	88	0.5	0	0	0.4
■ **DICK JONES**	Jones, Decatur Poindexter b: 5/22/02, Meadville, Miss. BL/TR, 6', 184 lbs. Deb: 9/11/26																												
1926	Was-A	2	1	.667	4	3	1	0	0	21	20	8.6	0	11	4.7	3	1.3	4.29	91	.263	.341	-1	-1	97	84	0.4	-0	0	0.0
1927	Was-A	0	0	—	2	0	0	0	0	3	8	24.0	0	5	15.0	1	3.0	24.00	17	.444	.542	-7	-7	96	58	0.0	0	0	-0.5
Total	2	2	1	.667	6	3	1	0	0	24	28	10.5	0	16	6.0	4	1.5	6.75	58	.298	.383	-7	-8	97	81	0.4	-0	0	-0.5
■ **DOUG JONES**	Jones, Douglas Reid b: 6/24/57, Lebanon, Ind. BR/TR, 6'3", 195 lbs. Deb: 4/09/82																												
1982	Mil-A	0	0	—	4	0	0	0	0	3	5	15.0	1	1	3.0	1	3.0	9.00	42	.385	.429	-2	-2	92	103	0.0	0	0	-0.1
1986	Cle-A	1	0	1.000	11	0	0	0	1	18	18	9.0	0	6	3.0	12	6.0	2.50	164	.257	.316	3	3	98	124	0.5	0	0	0.4
1987	Cle-A	6	5	.545	49	0	0	0	8	91	101	10.0	4	24	2.4	87	8.6	3.16	148	.281	.327	13	15	105	125	1.6	0	1	1.5

YEAR	TM/L	W	L	PCT	G	GS	CG	SHO	SV	IP	H	H/G	HR	BB	BB/G	SO	SO/G	ERA	/A	OAVG	OOBP	PR	/A	PF	CPI	WAT	PB	PD	TPI
1988	Cle-A	3	4	.429	51	0	0	0	37	83	69	7.5	1	16	1.7	72	7.8	2.28	178	.218	.257	16	16	102	75	-0.3	0	0	1.7
Total	4	10	9	.526	115	0	0	0	46	195	193	8.9	6	47	2.2	172	7.9	2.82	154	.254	.300	31	33	103	103	1.8	0	1	3.5
■ **EARL JONES**	Jones, Earl Leslie "Lefty" b: 6/11/19, Fresno, Cal. BL/TL, 5'10.5", 190 lbs. Deb: 7/06/45																												
1945	StL-A	0	0	—	10	0	0	0	1	28	18	5.8	0	18	5.8	13	4.2	2.57	150	.184	.300	2	4	114	81	0.0	1	-0	0.5
■ **ELIJAH JONES**	Jones, Elijah Albert "Bumpus" b: 1/27/1882, Oxford, Mich. d: 4/29/43, Pontiac, Mich. BR/TR, Deb: 4/13/07																												
1907	Det-A	0	1	.000	4	1	1	0	1	16	23	12.9	0	4	2.3	9	5.1	5.06	49	.364	.402	-4	-5	98	98	-0.4	-1	-0	-0.4
1909	Det-A	1	1	.500	2	2	0	0	0	10	10	9.0	0	0	0.0	2	1.8	2.70	98	.278	.278	-0	-0	106	82	-0.1	0	-0	0.0
Total	2	1	2	.333	6	3	1	0	1	26	33	11.4	0	4	1.4	11	3.8	4.15	61	.333	.358	-5	-5	101	92	-0.5	-0	-1	-0.4
■ **GARY JONES**	Jones, Gareth Howell b: 6/12/45, Huntington Park, Cal. BL/TL, 6', 191 lbs. Deb: 9/25/70																												
1970	NY-A	0	0	—	2	0	0	0	0	2	3	13.5	0	1	4.5	2	9.0	0.00	—	.375	.444	1	1	91	0	0.0	0	0	0.1
1971	NY-A	0	0	—	12	0	0	0	0	14	19	12.2	1	7	4.5	10	6.4	9.00	37	.317	.377	-9	-9	97	61	0.0	-0	-0	-0.8
Total	2	0	0	—	14	0	0	0	0	16	22	12.4	1	8	4.5	12	6.8	7.88	43	.324	.385	-8	-8	96	53	0.0	-0	-0	-0.7
■ **GORDON JONES**	Jones, Gordon Bassett b: 4/2/30, Portland, Ore. BR/TR, 6', 185 lbs. Deb: 8/06/54 C																												
1954	StL-N	4	4	.500	11	10	4	2	0	81	78	8.7	3	19	2.1	48	5.3	2.00	204	.248	.290	19	19	100	128	0.3	-1	-0	1.9
1955	StL-N	1	4	.200	15	9	0	0	0	57	66	10.4	10	28	4.4	46	7.3	5.84	71	.286	.363	-11	-11	102	93	-1.3	-1	-1	-1.1
1956	StL-N	0	2	.000	5	1	0	0	0	11	14	11.5	2	5	4.1	6	4.9	5.73	65	.311	.358	-2	-2	99	105	-0.9	-0	0	-0.2
1957	NY-N	0	1	.000	10	0	0	0	0	12	16	12.0	1	3	2.3	5	3.8	6.00	67	.320	.351	-3	-3	103	88	-0.4	0	-0	-0.2
1958	SF-N	3	1	.750	11	1	0	0	1	30	33	9.9	2	5	1.5	8	2.4	2.40	164	.284	.312	5	5	100	156	1.0	-1	1	0.5
1959	SF-N	3	2	.600	31	0	0	0	2	44	45	9.2	6	19	3.9	29	5.9	4.30	86	.280	.339	-2	-3	94	116	0.3	-0	-0	-0.3
1960	Bal-A	1	1	.500	29	0	0	0	2	55	59	9.7	9	13	2.1	30	4.9	4.42	88	.281	.320	-3	-3	101	104	0.0	1	0	-0.2
1961	Bal-A	0	0	—	3	0	0	0	1	5	5	9.0	3	0	0.0	4	7.2	5.40	71	.250	.250	-1	-1	96	118	0.0	0	0	0.0
1962	KC-A	3	2	.600	21	0	0	0	6	33	31	8.5	10	14	3.8	28	7.6	6.27	64	.252	.317	-8	-8	101	87	0.7	-1	-0	-0.8
1964	Hou-N	0	1	.000	34	0	0	0	0	50	58	10.4	3	14	2.5	28	5.0	4.14	84	.290	.327	-3	-4	98	101	-0.4	0	-0	-0.3
1965	Hou-N	0	0	—	1	0	0	0	0	1	0	0.0	0	0	0.0	0	0.0	0.00	—	.000	.000	0	0	91	0	0.0	0	0	0.0
Total	11	15	18	.455	171	21	4	2	12	379	405	9.6	49	120	2.8	232	5.5	4.16	94	.275	.324	-10	-11	100	110	-0.7	-3	-2	-0.7
■ **HENRY JONES**	Jones, Henry M. "Baldy" b: Cadillac, Mich. Deb: 8/20/1884																												
1890	Pit-N	2	1	.667	5	4	2	0	0	31	35	10.2	1	14	4.1	13	3.8	3.48	97	.301	.376	0	-0	95	122	0.9	-0	0	0.0
■ **JIMMY JONES**	Jones, James Condia b: 4/20/64, Dallas, Tex. BR/TR, 6'2", 175 lbs. Deb: 9/21/86																												
1986	SD-N	2	0	1.000	3	3	1	1	0	18	10	5.0	1	3	1.5	15	7.5	2.50	143	.164	.200	2	2	96	33	1.0	-0	0	0.2
1987	SD-N	9	7	.563	30	22	2	1	0	146	154	9.5	14	54	3.3	51	3.1	4.13	97	.270	.333	-1	-2	98	103	2.3	1	1	0.0
1988	SD-N	9	14	.391	29	29	3	0	0	179	192	9.7	14	44	2.2	82	4.1	4.12	81	.277	.314	-13	-15	97	96	-3.0	2	1	-1.2
Total	3	20	21	.488	62	54	6	2	0	343	356	9.3	29	101	2.7	148	3.9	4.04	90	.269	.318	-12	-15	97	96	0.3	3	3	-1.0
■ **JIM JONES**	Jones, James Tilford "Sheriff" b: 12/25/1876, London, Ky. d: 5/6/53, London, Ky. TR, 5'10", 162 lbs. Deb: 6/29/1897																												
1897	Lou-N	0	0	—	1	0	0	0	0	7	19	24.4	1	5	6.4	0	0.0	20.57	20	.516	.573	-13	-13	97	67	0.0	1	0	-0.7
1901	NY-N	0	1	.000	1	1	1	0	0	5	6	10.8	0	2	3.6	3	5.4	10.80	29	.320	.386	-4	-4	95	40	-0.4	0	0	-0.2
Total	2	0	1	.000	2	1	1	0	0	12	25	18.8	1	7	5.3	3	2.3	16.50	23	.450	.511	-17	-17	96	55	-0.4	1	0	-0.9
■ **JEFF JONES**	Jones, Jeffrey Allen b: 7/29/56, Detroit, Mich. BR/TR, 6'3", 210 lbs. Deb: 4/10/80																												
1980	Oak-A	1	3	.250	35	0	0	0	5	44	32	6.5	2	26	5.3	34	7.0	2.86	133	.204	.307	6	5	94	96	-0.9	0	1	0.6
1981	Oak-A	4	1	.800	33	0	0	0	3	61	51	7.5	7	40	5.9	43	6.3	3.39	103	.233	.344	2	1	95	128	1.3	0	-1	0.0
1982	Oak-A	3	1	.750	18	2	0	0	0	37	44	10.7	6	26	6.3	18	4.4	5.11	77	.306	.401	-4	-5	96	130	1.2	0	-0	-0.4
1983	Oak-A	1	1	.500	13	1	0	0	0	30	43	12.9	7	8	2.4	14	4.2	5.70	69	.339	.384	-5	-6	96	125	0.1	0	0	-0.5
1984	Oak-A	0	3	.000	13	0	0	0	0	33	31	8.5	4	12	3.3	19	5.2	3.55	104	.258	.319	2	0	92	116	-1.4	0	0	0.0
Total	5	9	9	.500	112	3	0	0	8	205	201	8.8	26	112	4.9	128	5.6	3.95	94	.262	.350	-0	-5	95	119	0.3	0	0	-0.3
■ **BROADWAY JONES**	Jones, Jesse Frank b: 11/15/1898, Millsboro, Del. d: 9/7/77, Lewes, Del. BR/TR, 5'9", 154 lbs. Deb: 7/04/23																												
1923	Phi-N	0	0	—	3	0	0	0	0	8	5	5.6	0	7	7.9	1	1.1	9.00	52	.185	.343	-4	-4	118	31	0.0	0	-0	-0.2
■ **JOHNNY JONES**	Jones, John Paul "Admiral" b: 8/25/1892, Arcadia, La. d: 6/5/80, Ruston, La. BR/TR, 6'1", 151 lbs. Deb: 4/24/19																												
1919	NY-N	0	0	—	2	0	0	0	1	7	9	11.6	0	3	3.9	3	3.9	5.14	55	.310	.371	-2	-2	96	97	0.0	-0	0	-0.1
1920	Bos-N	1	0	1.000	3	1	0	0	0	10	16	14.4	1	5	4.5	6	5.4	6.30	49	.372	.438	-4	-4	99	114	0.5	1	0	-0.2
Total	2	1	0	1.000	5	1	0	0	1	17	25	13.2	1	8	4.2	9	4.8	5.82	51	.347	.410	-5	-5	98	107	0.5	0	0	-0.3
■ **KEN JONES**	Jones, Kenneth Frederick "Broadway" b: 4/13/04, Dover, N.J. BR/TR, 6'3", 193 lbs. Deb: 5/19/24																												
1924	Det-A	0	0	—	1	0	0	0	0	2	1	4.5	0	1	4.5	0	0.0	0.00	—	.143	.250	1	1	99	0	0.0	0	0	0.1
1930	Bos-N	0	1	.000	8	1	0	0	0	20	28	12.6	1	4	1.8	4	1.8	5.85	84	.359	.352	-2	-2	99	103	-0.4	-0	0	-0.1
Total	2	0	1	.000	9	1	0	0	0	22	29	11.9	1	5	2.0	4	1.6	5.32	91	.341	.343	-1	-1	99	94	-0.4	-0	0	0.0
■ **MIKE JONES**	Jones, Michael b: Hamilton, Ont., Canada d: 3/24/1894, Hamilton, Ont., Can BL, Deb: 8/12/1890																												
1890	Lou-a	2	0	1.000	3	3	2	0	0	22	21	8.6	2	9	3.7	6	2.5	3.27	123	.267	.342	1	2	104	124	1.0	2	0	0.3
■ **MIKE JONES**	Jones, Michael Carl b: 7/30/59, Penfield, N.Y. BL/TL, 6'6", 215 lbs. Deb: 9/06/80																												
1980	KC-A	0	1	.000	3	1	0	0	0	5	6	10.8	0	5	9.0	2	3.6	10.80	36	.333	.458	-4	-4	97	64	-0.4	0	-0	-0.3
1981	KC-A	6	3	.667	12	11	0	0	0	76	74	8.8	7	28	3.3	29	3.4	3.20	113	.256	.322	4	4	99	119	1.7	0	0	0.4
1984	KC-A	2	3	.400	23	12	0	0	0	81	86	9.6	10	36	4.0	43	4.8	4.89	81	.270	.343	-8	-8	99	93	-0.5	0	-1	-0.8
1985	KC-A	3	3	.500	33	1	0	0	0	64	62	8.7	6	39	5.5	32	4.5	4.78	88	.257	.348	-4	-4	101	96	-0.2	0	0	-0.3
Total	4	11	10	.524	71	25	0	0	0	226	228	9.1	23	108	4.3	106	4.2	4.42	89	.263	.340	-12	-13	100	102	0.6	0	-1	-1.0
■ **ODELL JONES**	Jones, Odell b: 1/13/53, Tulare, Cal. BR/TR, 6'3", 175 lbs. Deb: 9/11/75																												
1975	Pit-N	0	0	—	2	0	0	0	0	3	1	3.0	0	0	0.0	2	6.0	0.00	—	.100	.100	1	1	98	0	0.0	0	0	0.1
1977	Pit-N	3	7	.300	34	15	1	0	0	108	118	9.8	14	31	2.6	66	5.5	5.08	78	.278	.326	-14	-13	102	86	-2.4	-1	-2	-1.5
1978	Pit-N	2	0	1.000	3	1	0	0	0	9	7	7.0	0	4	4.0	10	10.0	2.00	187	.206	.289	2	2	105	93	1.0	-0	0	0.2
1979	Sea-A	3	11	.214	25	19	3	0	0	119	151	11.4	16	58	4.4	72	5.4	6.05	71	.317	.383	-24	-23	101	102	-3.4	0	-2	-2.3
1981	Pit-N	4	5	.444	13	8	0	0	0	54	51	8.5	3	23	3.8	30	5.0	3.33	101	.250	.319	1	0	96	103	0.0	0	0	0.0
1983	Tex-A	3	6	.333	42	0	0	0	10	67	56	7.5	4	22	3.0	50	6.7	3.09	133	.223	.285	7	8	101	85	-1.3	0	-1	0.7
1984	Tex-A	2	4	.333	33	0	0	0	2	59	62	9.5	7	23	3.5	28	4.3	3.66	110	.281	.343	2	2	101	131	-0.6	0	1	0.3
1986	Bal-A	2	2	.500	21	0	0	0	0	49	58	10.7	4	23	4.2	32	5.9	3.86	108	.305	.370	2	2	99	138	0.2	0	-0	0.1
1988	Mil-A	5	0	1.000	28	2	0	0	1	81	75	8.3	8	29	3.2	48	5.3	4.33	94	.251	.310	-3	-2	103	87	2.5	0	-1	-0.2
Total	9	24	35	.407	201	45	4	0	13	549	579	9.5	56	213	3.5	338	5.5	4.43	91	.275	.336	-26	-24	101	100	-4.0	-1	-5	-2.6
■ **OSCAR JONES**	Jones, Oscar Winfield "Flip Flap" b: 1/21/1879, London Grove, Pa. d: 10/8/46, Perkasie, Pa. BR/TR, 5'7", 163 lbs. Deb: 4/20/03																												
1903	Bro-N	19	14	.576	38	36	31	4	0	324	320	8.9	4	77	2.1	95	2.6	2.94	113	.286	.343	12	14	102	99	2.6	2	-4	1.0
1904	Bro-N	17	25	.405	46	41	38	0	0	377	387	9.2	7	92	2.2	96	2.3	2.75	97	.293	.347	-1	-3	98	117	1.7	-1	-7	-1.0
1905	Bro-N	8	15	.348	29	20	14	0	1	174	197	10.2	6	56	2.9	66	3.4	4.66	65	.317	.382	-32	-31	102	90	0.6	-0	-4	-3.3
Total	3	44	54	.449	113	97	83	4	1	875	904	9.3	17	225	2.3	257	2.6	3.20	93	.296	.353	-21	-21	100	105	4.9	1	-15	-3.3
■ **PERCY JONES**	Jones, Percy Lee b: 10/28/1899, Harwood, Tex. d: 3/18/79, Dallas, Tex. BR/TL, 5'11.5", 175 lbs. Deb: 8/06/20																												
1920	Chi-N	0	0	—	4	0	0	0	0	7	15	19.3	1	3	3.9	0	0.0	11.57	27	.455	.514	-7	-7	99	92	0.0	-0	0	-0.6
1921	Chi-N	3	5	.375	32	5	1	0	0	99	116	10.5	2	39	3.5	46	4.2	4.55	90	.295	.357	-8	-5	108	92	-0.3	-0	-2	-0.6
1922	Chi-N	8	9	.471	44	26	7	2	1	162	197	10.9	10	68	3.8	45	2.5	4.78	82	.310	.369	-12	-16	96	106	-0.8	-4	0	-1.7
1925	Chi-N	6	6	.500	28	13	6	1	0	124	123	8.9	12	71	5.2	60	4.4	4.65	90	.263	.357	-5	-6	98	98	0.7	-2	2	-0.5
1926	Chi-N	12	7	.632	30	20	10	2	2	160	151	8.5	3	90	5.1	80	4.5	3.09	129	.256	.350	13	16	105	**122**	2.2	3	-1	1.8
1927	Chi-N	7	8	.467	30	11	5	1	0	113	123	9.8	3	72	5.7	37	2.9	4.06	95	.285	.380	-2	-3	99	120	-1.2	3	2	0.2
1928	Chi-N	10	6	.625	39	18	9	1	3	154	167	9.8	4	56	3.3	41	2.4	4.03	92	.288	.345	-1	-6	93	101	0.7	-0	-0	-0.6
1929	Bos-N	7	15	.318	35	22	11	1	0	188	219	10.5	15	84	4.0	69	3.3	4.64	99	.298	.361	1	-1	97	111	-1.5	-3	1	-0.2

YEAR	TM/L	W	L	PCT	G	GS	CG	SHO	SV	IP	H	H/G	HR	BB	BB/G	SO	SO/G	ERA	/A	OAVG	OOBP	PR	/A	PF	CPI	WAT	PB	PD	TPI
1930	Pit-N	0	1	.000	9	2	0	0	0	19	26	12.3	3	11	5.2	3	1.4	6.63	73	.329	.417	-4	-4	98	111	-0.4	-0	-0	-0.3
Total	9	53	57	.482	251	117	49	8	6	1026	1137	10.0	53	494	4.3	381	3.3	4.34	94	.288	.362	-24	-30	99	108	-0.6	-5	1	-2.5

■ RANDY JONES Jones, Randall Leo b: 1/12/50, Fullerton, Cal. BR/TL, 6', 178 lbs. Deb: 6/16/73

YEAR	TM/L	W	L	PCT	G	GS	CG	SHO	SV	IP	H	H/G	HR	BB	BB/G	SO	SO/G	ERA	/A	OAVG	OOBP	PR	/A	PF	CPI	WAT	PB	PD	TPI
1973	SD-N	7	6	.538	20	19	6	1	0	140	129	8.3	13	37	2.4	77	5.0	3.15	113	.241	.286	8	6	97	94	1.8	-0	0	0.6
1974	SD-N	8	22	.267	40	34	4	1	2	208	217	9.4	16	78	3.4	124	5.4	4.46	79	.270	.330	-19	-22	97	90	-4.7	-1	2	-2.0
1975	SD-N	20	12	.625	37	36	18	6	0	285	242	7.6	17	56	1.8	103	3.3	**2.24**	**164**	.232	.265	44	**45**	101	104	6.1	-1	5	**5.5**
1976	SD-N	**22**	14	.611	40	40	**25**	5	0	**315**	274	7.8	15	50	1.4	93	2.7	2.74	115	.234	**.262**	27	14	90	82	**6.2**	-5	8	1.7
1977	SD-N	6	12	.333	27	25	1	0	0	147	173	10.6	12	36	2.2	44	2.7	4.59	76	.291	.326	-11	-18	89	91	-2.0	-1	4	-1.5
1978	SD-N	13	14	.481	37	36	7	2	0	253	263	9.4	6	64	2.3	71	2.5	2.88	115	.272	.309	20	12	93	114	-1.0	1	1	1.5
1979	SD-N	11	12	.478	39	39	6	0	0	263	257	8.8	17	64	2.2	112	3.8	3.63	100	.259	.298	3	0	97	89	1.3	-0	4	0.4
1980	SD-N	5	13	.278	24	24	4	3	0	154	165	9.6	14	29	1.7	53	3.1	3.92	86	.276	.304	-5	-9	94	95	-3.6	-3	3	-0.9
1981	NY-N	1	8	.111	13	12	0	0	0	59	65	9.9	8	38	5.8	14	2.1	4.88	73	.274	.366	-9	-9	103	109	-3.2	-1	2	-0.7
1982	NY-N	7	10	.412	28	20	2	1	0	108	130	10.8	11	51	4.3	44	3.7	4.58	79	.304	.375	-12	-12	100	120	0.2	0	3	-0.8
Total	10	100	123	.448	305	285	73	19	2	1932	1915	8.9	129	503	2.3	735	3.4	3.42	101	.260	.302	46	9	95	97	1.1	-11	31	3.8

■ SAM JONES Jones, Samuel "Toothpick Sam" b: 12/14/25, Stewartsville, Ohio d: 11/5/71, Morgantown, W.Va. BR/TR, 6'4", 192 lbs. Deb: 9/22/51

YEAR	TM/L	W	L	PCT	G	GS	CG	SHO	SV	IP	H	H/G	HR	BB	BB/G	SO	SO/G	ERA	/A	OAVG	OOBP	PR	/A	PF	CPI	WAT	PB	PD	TPI
1951	Cle-A	0	1	.000	2	1	0	0	0	9	4	4.0	0	5	5.0	4	4.0	2.00	191	.143	.265	2	2	93	71	-0.4	-0	0	0.1
1952	Cle-A	2	3	.400	14	4	0	0	1	36	38	9.5	6	37	9.3	28	7.0	7.25	45	.270	.429	-14	-16	88	94	-0.8	-1	-0	-1.6
1955	Chi-N	14	20	.412	36	34	12	4	0	242	175	**6.5**	22	185	6.9	**198**	**7.4**	4.09	100	**.206**	.350	-1	0	101	93	-2.5	-2	-0	-0.1
1956	Chi-N	9	14	.391	33	28	8	2	0	189	155	7.4	21	115	5.5	**176**	**8.4**	3.90	97	.221	.334	-3	-2	101	93	0.0	-0	-1	-0.3
1957	StL-N	12	9	.571	28	27	10	2	0	183	164	8.1	17	71	3.5	154	**7.6**	3.59	107	.239	.314	6	5	99	95	0.2	-1	0	0.5
1958	StL-N	14	13	.519	35	35	14	2	0	250	204	**7.3**	23	107	3.9	**225**	**8.1**	2.88	148	.223	.305	30	**39**	108	106	1.5	-6	-0	**3.5**
1959	SF-N	**21**	15	.583	50	35	16	**4**	4	271	232	7.7	18	109	3.6	209	6.9	**2.82**	131	**.228**	.304	**34**	26	94	104	2.2	-1	-2	2.3
1960	SF-N	18	14	.563	39	35	13	3	0	234	200	7.7	18	91	3.5	190	7.3	3.19	105	.230	.302	15	4	89	97	2.0	2	-2	0.3
1961	SF-N	8	8	.500	37	17	2	0	1	128	134	9.4	12	57	4.0	105	7.4	4.50	86	.264	.344	-7	-9	96	95	-0.7	-1	-2	-1.0
1962	Det-A	2	4	.333	30	6	1	0	1	81	77	8.6	13	35	3.9	73	8.1	3.67	119	.254	.325	3	6	110	123	-1.0	-1	-0	0.6
1963	StL-N	2	0	1.000	11	0	0	0	2	11	15	12.3	0	5	4.1	8	6.5	9.00	39	.319	.385	-7	-7	106	55	1.0	0	0	-0.6
1964	Bal-A	0	0	—	7	0	0	0	0	10	5	4.5	1	5	4.5	6	5.4	2.70	139	.152	.263	1	1	103	70	0.0	0	0	0.1
Total	12	102	101	.502	322	222	76	17	9	1644	1403	7.7	151	822	4.5	1376	7.5	3.59	107	.230	.323	58	49	99	99	1.5	-11	-7	3.8

■ SAM JONES Jones, Samuel Pond "Sad Sam" b: 7/26/1892, Woodsfield, Ohio d: 7/6/66, Barnesville, Ohio BR/TR, 6', 170 lbs. Deb: 6/13/14

YEAR	TM/L	W	L	PCT	G	GS	CG	SHO	SV	IP	H	H/G	HR	BB	BB/G	SO	SO/G	ERA	/A	OAVG	OOBP	PR	/A	PF	CPI	WAT	PB	PD	TPI
1914	Cle-A	0	0	—	1	0	0	0	0	3	2	6.0	0	2	6.0	0	0.0	3.00	97	.200	.333	-0	-0	106	80	0.0	0	0	0.0
1915	Cle-A	4	9	.308	48	9	2	0	4	146	131	8.1	0	63	3.9	42	2.6	3.64	86	.252	.334	-11	-8	106	83	-1.2	-0	0	-0.8
1916	Bos-A	0	1	.000	12	0	0	0	1	27	25	8.3	0	10	3.3	7	2.3	3.67	71	.272	.343	-3	-3	92	90	-0.4	0	-0	-0.2
1917	Bos-A	0	1	.000	9	1	0	0	1	16	15	8.4	1	6	3.4	5	2.8	4.50	63	.259	.328	-3	-3	106	74	-0.4	-1	1	-0.2
1918	Bos-A	16	5	**.762**	24	21	16	5	0	184	151	7.4	1	70	3.4	44	2.2	2.25	114	.230	.305	11	6	93	102	**4.8**	2	-1	0.8
1919	Bos-A	12	20	.375	35	31	21	5	1	245	258	9.5	4	95	3.5	67	2.5	3.75	78	.278	.350	-14	-22	91	95	-4.2	-0	3	-2.0
1920	Bos-A	13	16	.448	37	33	21	3	0	274	302	9.9	9	79	2.6	86	2.8	3.94	93	.297	.350	-4	-8	97	102	-0.7	1	-1	-0.8
1921	Bos-A	23	16	.590	40	38	25	**5**	1	299	318	9.6	1	78	2.3	98	2.9	3.22	133	.279	.320	35	36	100	103	4.9	4	-3	3.5
1922	NY-A	13	13	.500	45	28	20	0	**8**	260	270	9.3	16	76	2.6	81	2.8	3.67	109	.275	.321	11	10	99	101	-2.6	8	-1	1.6
1923	NY-A	21	8	.724	39	27	18	3	4	243	239	8.9	11	69	2.6	68	2.5	3.63	111	.257	.306	10	10	101	83	3.8	2	1	1.3
1924	NY-A	9	6	.600	36	21	8	3	3	179	187	9.4	6	76	3.8	53	2.7	3.62	113	.276	.342	12	10	97	108	0.3	-0	-1	0.8
1925	NY-A	15	21	.417	43	31	14	1	2	247	267	9.7	14	104	3.8	92	3.4	4.63	92	.281	.345	-6	-10	97	91	-1.5	-3	0	-1.1
1926	NY-A	9	8	.529	39	23	6	1	5	161	186	10.4	6	80	4.5	69	3.9	4.98	78	.298	.367	-17	-19	97	96	-0.9	1	-2	-1.8
1927	StL-A	8	14	.364	30	26	11	0	0	190	211	10.0	13	102	4.8	72	3.4	4.31	105	.282	.360	-4	4	109	108	-0.6	-3	-2	0.0
1928	Was-A	17	7	.708	30	27	19	4	0	225	209	8.4	5	78	3.1	63	2.5	2.84	144	.252	.313	30	31	101	110	5.7	6	0	3.9
1929	Was-A	9	9	.500	24	24	8	1	0	154	156	9.1	5	49	2.9	36	2.1	3.92	109	.264	.316	6	6	100	86	0.6	0	-2	0.5
1930	Was-A	15	7	.682	25	25	14	1	0	183	195	9.6	4	61	3.0	60	3.0	4.08	112	.277	.329	12	10	98	97	2.3	-1	-1	0.6
1931	Was-A	9	10	.474	25	24	8	1	1	148	185	11.3	10	47	2.9	58	3.5	4.32	100	.304	.353	1	-0	98	118	-2.1	4	-0	0.3
1932	Chi-A	10	15	.400	30	28	10	0	0	200	217	9.8	9	75	3.4	64	2.9	4.23	96	.270	.330	6	-4	91	96	1.6	2	2	0.0
1933	Chi-A	10	12	.455	27	25	11	2	0	177	181	9.2	13	65	3.3	60	3.1	3.36	132	.265	.329	18	21	103	124	0.2	-1	-1	1.9
1934	Chi-A	8	12	.400	27	26	11	1	0	183	217	10.7	16	60	3.0	60	3.0	5.11	91	.289	.340	-13	-10	103	91	0.9	2	-2	-0.8
1935	Chi-A	8	7	.533	21	19	7	0	0	140	162	10.4	8	51	3.3	38	2.4	4.05	120	.284	.339	6	13	109	107	0.7	-0	0	1.3
Total	22	229	217	.513	647	487	250	36	31	3884	4084	9.5	152	1396	3.2	1223	2.8	3.84	104	.275	.334	81	67	99	100	11.2	25	-9	8.8

■ SHELDON JONES Jones, Sheldon Leslie "Available" b: 2/2/22, Tecumseh, Neb. BR/TR, 6', 180 lbs. Deb: 9/09/46

YEAR	TM/L	W	L	PCT	G	GS	CG	SHO	SV	IP	H	H/G	HR	BB	BB/G	SO	SO/G	ERA	/A	OAVG	OOBP	PR	/A	PF	CPI	WAT	PB	PD	TPI
1946	NY-N	1	2	.333	6	4	1	0	0	28	21	6.8	4	17	5.5	24	7.7	3.21	110	.208	.320	1	1	103	112	-0.1	0	0	0.1
1947	NY-N	2	2	.500	15	6	0	0	0	56	51	8.2	2	29	4.7	24	3.9	3.86	105	.250	.346	1	1	99	99	0.0	-1	-1	0.0
1948	NY-N	16	8	.667	55	21	8	2	5	201	204	9.1	16	90	4.0	82	3.7	3.36	116	.263	.341	13	12	98	126	4.4	2	0	1.3
1949	NY-N	15	12	.556	42	27	11	1	0	207	198	8.6	19	88	3.8	79	3.4	3.35	122	.248	.328	16	17	101	116	2.5	-3	-0	1.3
1950	NY-N	13	16	.448	40	28	11	2	2	199	188	8.5	26	90	4.1	97	4.4	4.61	87	.249	.332	-10	-14	97	92	-3.3	-2	-2	-1.6
1951	NY-N	6	11	.353	41	12	2	0	4	120	119	8.9	12	52	3.9	58	4.3	4.28	92	.260	.335	-4	-5	99	98	-3.8	-1	0	-0.4
1952	Bos-N	1	4	.200	39	1	0	0	1	70	81	10.4	8	31	4.0	40	5.1	4.76	76	.286	.352	-8	-9	97	105	-1.2	-0	0	-0.8
1953	Chi-N	0	2	.000	22	2	0	0	0	38	47	11.1	3	16	3.8	9	2.1	5.45	84	.299	.380	-5	-4	106	98	-0.9	-1	0	-0.3
Total	8	54	57	.486	260	101	33	5	12	919	909	8.9	90	413	4.0	413	4.0	3.97	100	.258	.338	4	-0	99	108	-2.4	-7	-3	-0.4

■ SHERMAN JONES Jones, Sherman Jarvis "Roadblock" b: 2/10/35, Winton, N.C. BL/TR, 6'4", 205 lbs. Deb: 8/02/60

YEAR	TM/L	W	L	PCT	G	GS	CG	SHO	SV	IP	H	H/G	HR	BB	BB/G	SO	SO/G	ERA	/A	OAVG	OOBP	PR	/A	PF	CPI	WAT	PB	PD	TPI
1960	SF-N	1	1	.500	16	0	0	0	1	32	37	10.4	3	11	3.1	10	2.8	3.09	108	.291	.343	2	1	89	153	0.0	0	-1	0.0
1961	Cin-N	1	1	.500	24	2	0	0	2	55	51	8.3	6	27	4.4	32	5.2	4.42	94	.256	.335	-2	-2	103	99	-0.1	0	-0	-0.1
1962	NY-N	0	4	.000	8	3	0	0	0	23	31	12.1	3	8	3.1	11	4.3	7.83	55	.326	.373	-10	-9	108	78	-1.9	1	0	-0.6
Total	3	2	6	.250	48	5	0	0	3	110	119	9.7	12	46	3.8	53	4.3	4.75	83	.283	.346	-10	-10	100	110	-2.0	1	-1	-0.7

■ STEVE JONES Jones, Steven Howell b: 4/22/41, Huntington Park, Cal. BL/TL, 5'10", 175 lbs. Deb: 8/15/67

YEAR	TM/L	W	L	PCT	G	GS	CG	SHO	SV	IP	H	H/G	HR	BB	BB/G	SO	SO/G	ERA	/A	OAVG	OOBP	PR	/A	PF	CPI	WAT	PB	PD	TPI
1967	Chi-A	2	2	.500	11	3	0	0	0	26	21	7.3	1	12	4.2	17	5.9	4.15	72	.223	.306	-3	-3	93	69	-0.1	0	-0	-0.2
1968	Was-A	1	2	.333	7	0	0	0	0	11	8	6.5	3	7	5.7	11	9.0	5.73	49	.205	.326	-3	-4	94	82	-0.2	-0	-0	-0.4
1969	KC-A	2	3	.400	20	4	0	0	0	45	45	9.0	3	24	4.8	31	6.2	4.20	90	.260	.355	-3	-2	104	101	-0.1	0	0	-0.1
Total	3	5	7	.417	38	7	0	0	0	82	74	8.1	7	43	4.7	59	6.5	4.39	77	.242	.336	-9	-9	99	88	-0.4	1	-0	-0.7

■ RICK JONES Jones, Thomas Fredrick b: 4/16/55, Jacksonville, Fla. BL/TL, 6'5", 190 lbs. Deb: 4/18/76

YEAR	TM/L	W	L	PCT	G	GS	CG	SHO	SV	IP	H	H/G	HR	BB	BB/G	SO	SO/G	ERA	/A	OAVG	OOBP	PR	/A	PF	CPI	WAT	PB	PD	TPI
1976	Bos-A	5	3	.625	24	14	1	0	0	104	133	11.5	6	26	2.3	45	3.9	3.38	115	.311	.345	2	6	110	137	1.0	0	-0	0.6
1977	Sea-A	1	4	.200	10	10	0	0	0	42	47	10.1	10	37	7.9	16	3.4	5.14	78	.283	.414	-5	-5	98	135	-1.2	0	-0	-0.4
1978	Sea-A	0	2	.000	3	2	0	0	0	12	17	12.8	1	7	5.3	11	8.3	6.00	66	.315	.393	-3	-3	104	96	-0.9	0	0	-0.2
Total	3	6	9	.400	37	26	1	0	0	158	197	11.2	17	70	4.0	72	4.1	4.04	97	.304	.368	-6	-2	106	133	-1.1	0	-0	0.0

■ TIM JONES Jones, Timmothy Byron b: 1/24/54, Sacramento, Cal. BB/TR, 6'5", 220 lbs. Deb: 9/04/77

YEAR	TM/L	W	L	PCT	G	GS	CG	SHO	SV	IP	H	H/G	HR	BB	BB/G	SO	SO/G	ERA	/A	OAVG	OOBP	PR	/A	PF	CPI	WAT	PB	PD	TPI
1977	Pit-N	1	0	1.000	3	1	0	0	0	10	4	3.6	0	3	2.7	5	4.5	0.00	—	.118	.189	4	4	102	0	0.5	-0	-0	0.4

■ CLAUDE JONNARD Jonnard, Claude Alfred b: 11/23/1897, Nashville, Tenn. d: 8/27/59, Nashville, Tenn. BR/TR, 6'1", 165 lbs. Deb: 10/01/21

YEAR	TM/L	W	L	PCT	G	GS	CG	SHO	SV	IP	H	H/G	HR	BB	BB/G	SO	SO/G	ERA	/A	OAVG	OOBP	PR	/A	PF	CPI	WAT	PB	PD	TPI
1921	NY-N	0	0	—	1	0	0	0	1	4	4	9.0	0	0	0.0	7	15.8	0.00	—	.267	.267	2	2	94	0	0.0	-0	0	0.1
1922	NY-N	6	1	.857	33	0	0	0	**5**	96	96	9.0	7	28	2.6	44	4.1	3.84	107	.272	.316	3	3	100	98	2.3	-3	-1	0.0
1923	NY-N	4	3	.571	**45**	1	1	0	**5**	96	105	9.8	6	35	3.3	45	4.2	3.28	120	.279	.333	8	7	99	120	-0.2	-3	-1	0.3
1924	NY-N	4	5	.444	34	3	1	0	5	90	80	8.0	2	24	2.4	40	4.0	2.40	141	.229	.277	**15**	**10**	88	85	-1.2	-2	-0	0.7
1926	StL-A	0	2	.000	12	3	0	0	1	36	46	11.5	1	24	6.0	13	3.3	6.00	69	.313	.393	-8	-7	103	92	-0.9	-1	1	-0.5
1929	Chi-N	0	1	.000	12	2	0	0	0	28	41	13.2	4	11	3.5	11	3.5	7.39	62	.320	.373	-8	-9	98	82	-0.4	1	0	-0.6
Total	6	14	12	.538	137	9	2	0	17	350	372	9.6	20	122	3.1	160	4.1	3.78	104	.272	.324	11	5	97	98	-0.4	-8	-1	0.0

■ CHARLIE JORDAN Jordan, Charles T. "Kid" b: 10/4/1871, Baltimore, Md. d: 6/1/28, Hazleton, Pa. Deb: 7/31/1896

YEAR	TM/L	W	L	PCT	G	GS	CG	SHO	SV	IP	H	H/G	HR	BB	BB/G	SO	SO/G	ERA	/A	OAVG	OOBP	PR	/A	PF	CPI	WAT	PB	PD	TPI
1896	Phi-N	0	0	—	2	0	0	0	0	5	9	16.2	0	2	3.6	3	5.4	9.00	50	.414	.463	-3	-3	102	81	0.0	0	0	-0.1

YEAR	TM/L	W	L	PCT	G	GS	CG	SHO	SV	IP	H	H/G	HR	BB	BB/G	SO	SO/G	ERA	/A	OAVG	OOBP	PR	/A	PF	CPI	WAT	PB	PD	TPI
■ **HARRY JORDAN**	Jordan, Harry J. b: 2/14/1873, Pittsburgh, Pa. d: 3/1/20, Pittsburgh, Pa. Deb: 9/25/1894																												
1894	Pit-N	1	0	1.000	1	1	1	0	0	9	10	10.0	0	2	2.0	1	1.0	4.00	126	.303	.343	1	1	95	85	0.5	-0	0	0.1
1895	Pit-N	0	2	.000	2	2	2	0	0	17	24	12.7	0	6	3.2	4	2.1	4.24	109	.354	.407	1	1	96	125	-0.9	-0	0	0.0
Total	2	1	2	.333	3	3	3	0	0	26	34	11.8	0	8	2.8	5	1.7	4.15	115	.337	.386	2	2	96	111	-0.4	-0	0	0.1
■ **MILT JORDAN**	Jordan, Milton Mignot b: 5/24/27, Mineral Springs, Pa. BR/TR, 6'2.5", 207 lbs. Deb: 4/16/53																												
1953	Det-A	0	1	.000	8	1	0	0	0	17	26	13.8	3	5	2.6	4	2.1	5.82	70	.366	.397	-3	-3	102	126	-0.4	0	0	-0.2
■ **NILES JORDAN**	Jordan, Niles Chapman b: 12/1/25, Lyman, Wash. BL/TL, 5'11", 180 lbs. Deb: 8/26/51																												
1951	Phi-N	2	3	.400	5	5	2	1	0	37	35	8.5	4	8	1.9	11	2.7	3.16	121	.250	.289	3	3	97	104	-0.3	-1	-0	0.2
1952	Cin-N	0	1	.000	3	1	0	0	0	6	14	21.0	1	3	4.5	2	3.0	10.50	36	.452	.500	-5	-5	100	109	-0.4	-0	0	-0.3
Total	2	2	4	.333	8	6	2	1	0	43	49	10.3	5	11	2.3	13	2.7	4.19	91	.287	.328	-1	-2	97	105	-0.7	-1	-0	-0.1
■ **RIP JORDAN**	Jordan, Raymond Willis "Lanky" b: 9/28/1889, Portland, Me. d: 6/5/60, Meriden, Conn. BL/TR, 6', 172 lbs. Deb: 6/25/12																												
1912	Chi-A	0	0	—	4	0	0	0	0	12	13	9.8	2	3	2.3	1	0.8	5.25	63	.289	.347	-3	-3	99	95	0.0	-1	-0	-0.2
1919	Was-A	0	0	—	1	1	0	0	0	4	6	13.5	1	2	4.5	2	4.5	11.25	28	.353	.421	-4	-4	99	69	0.0	-0	-0	-0.2
Total	2	0	0	—	5	1	0	0	0	16	19	10.7	3	5	2.8	3	1.7	6.75	49	.306	.368	-6	-6	99	89	0.0	-1	-0	-0.4
■ **ORVILLE JORGENS**	Jorgens, Orville Edward b: 6/4/08, Rockford, Ill. BR/TR, 6'1", 180 lbs. Deb: 4/19/35																												
1935	Phi-N	10	15	.400	**53**	24	6	0	2	188	216	10.3	12	96	4.6	57	2.7	4.84	97	.283	.364	-17	-3	117	100	-0.5	-6	3	-0.3
1936	Phi-N	8	8	.500	39	21	4	0	0	167	196	10.6	16	69	3.7	58	3.1	4.80	93	.290	.356	-14	-6	111	103	2.0	-1	1	-0.5
1937	Phi-N	3	4	.429	52	11	1	0	3	141	159	10.1	12	68	4.3	34	2.2	4.40	98	.298	.374	-8	-1	111	122	0.2	-1	1	0.0
Total	3	21	27	.438	144	56	11	0	5	496	571	10.4	40	233	4.2	149	2.7	4.70	96	.290	.364	-39	-10	113	107	1.7	-8	5	-0.8
■ **ADDIE JOSS**	Joss, Adrian b: 4/12/1880, Juneau, Wis. d: 4/14/11, Toledo, Ohio BR/TR, 6'3", 185 lbs. Deb: 4/26/02 H																												
1902	Cle-A	17	13	.567	32	29	28	**5**	0	269	225	7.5	2	75	2.5	106	3.5	2.78	123	.250	.307	24	19	96	80	2.2	-5	6	2.5
1903	Cle-A	18	13	.581	32	31	31	3	0	284	232	7.4	3	37	1.2	120	3.8	2.19	128	.243	**.272**	24	20	95	82	1.3	0	4	2.6
1904	Cle-A	14	10	.583	25	24	20	5	0	192	160	7.5	0	30	1.4	83	3.9	**1.59**	159	.248	.281	21	20	98	117	0.5	-3	-0	2.4
1905	Cle-A	20	12	.625	33	32	31	3	0	286	246	7.7	4	46	1.4	132	4.2	2.01	132	.255	.289	20	20	100	109	4.9	-0	5	2.9
1906	Cle-A	21	9	.700	34	31	28	9	1	282	220	7.0	3	43	1.4	106	3.4	1.72	155	.238	.272	30	30	99	97	4.9	2	2	3.8
1907	Cle-A	**27**	11	.711	42	38	34	6	2	339	279	7.4	3	54	1.4	127	3.4	1.83	129	.247	**.281**	27	20	93	98	7.8	-4	8	3.3
1908	Cle-A	24	11	.686	42	35	29	9	2	325	232	**6.4**	2	30	**0.8**	130	3.6	**1.16**	**212**	**.197**	**.218**	44	**47**	103	78	5.2	2	2	6.2
1909	Cle-A	14	13	.519	33	28	24	4	0	243	198	7.3	0	31	**1.1**	67	2.5	1.70	150	.226	.255	21	23	103	78	1.6	-3	-0	2.7
1910	Cle-A	5	5	.500	13	12	9	1	0	107	96	8.1	2	18	1.5	49	4.1	2.27	113	.245	.282	3	4	102	95	0.3	-1	2	0.5
Total	9	160	97	.623	286	260	234	45	5	2327	1888	7.3	19	364	1.4	920	3.6	1.89	142	.237	.271	214	204	99	92	28.7	-13	29	26.9
■ **MIKE JOYCE**	Joyce, Michael Lewis b: 2/12/41, Detroit, Mich. BR/TR, 6'2", 193 lbs. Deb: 7/02/62																												
1962	Chi-A	2	1	.667	25	1	0	0	2	43	40	8.4	2	14	2.9	9	1.9	3.35	112	.247	.297	3	2	94	92	0.5	1	0	0.3
1963	Chi-A	0	0	—	6	0	0	0	0	11	13	10.6	1	8	6.5	7	5.7	8.18	45	.289	.396	-6	-5	102	68	0.0	0	-0	-0.5
Total	2	2	1	.667	31	1	0	0	2	54	53	8.8	3	22	3.7	16	2.7	4.33	86	.256	.319	-3	-4	96	87	0.5	1	0	-0.2
■ **DICK JOYCE**	Joyce, Richard Edward b: 11/18/43, Portland, Me. BL/TL, 6'5", 225 lbs. Deb: 9/03/65																												
1965	KC-A	0	1	.000	5	3	0	0	0	13	12	8.3	0	4	2.8	7	4.8	2.77	124	.240	.291	1	1	100	87	-0.4	-0	0	0.0
■ **BOB JOYCE**	Joyce, Robert Emmett b: 1/14/15, Stockton, Cal. d: 12/10/81, San Francisco, Cal BR/TR, 6'1", 180 lbs. Deb: 5/04/39																												
1939	Phi-A	3	5	.375	30	6	1	0	0	108	156	13.0	13	37	3.1	25	2.1	6.67	71	.337	.375	-25	-23	102	97	0.1	-3	1	-2.2
1946	NY-N	3	4	.429	14	7	2	0	0	61	79	11.7	3	20	3.0	24	3.5	5.31	66	.315	.360	-13	-12	103	90	0.2	0	1	-1.0
Total	2	6	9	.400	44	13	3	0	0	169	235	12.5	16	57	3.0	49	2.6	6.18	69	.329	.370	-37	-35	102	94	0.3	-3	2	-3.2
■ **RALPH JUDD**	Judd, Ralph Wesley b: 12/7/01, Perrysburg, Ohio d: 5/6/57, Lapeer, Mich. BL/TR, 5'10", 170 lbs. Deb: 10/02/27																												
1927	Was-A	0	0	—	1	0	0	0	1	4	8	18.0	0	2	4.5	2	4.5	6.75	59	.400	.455	-1	-1	96	119	0.0	-0	-0	0.0
1929	NY-N	3	0	1.000	18	0	0	0	0	51	49	8.6	4	11	1.9	21	3.7	2.65	172	.261	.293	12	11	97	131	1.5	-2	0	0.8
1930	NY-N	0	0	—	2	0	0	0	0	8	13	14.6	0	3	3.4	0	0.0	5.63	85	.406	.444	-1	-1	96	115	0.0	-1	0	0.0
Total	3	3	0	1.000	21	0	0	0	1	63	70	10.0	4	16	2.3	23	3.3	3.29	139	.292	.327	10	9	97	128	1.5	-3	0	0.8
■ **OSCAR JUDD**	Judd, Thomas William Oscar "Ossie" b: 2/14/08, London, Ont., Can. BL/TL, 6'0.5", 180 lbs. Deb: 4/16/41																												
1941	Bos-A	0	0	—	7	0	0	0	1	12	15	11.3	1	10	7.5	5	3.8	9.00	47	.300	.417	-6	-6	101	70	0.0	2	0	-0.3
1942	Bos-A	8	10	.444	31	19	11	0	2	150	135	8.1	3	90	5.4	70	4.2	3.90	94	.239	.342	-4	-4	100	91	-2.6	6	-0	0.2
1943	Bos-A	11	6	.647	23	20	8	1	0	155	131	7.6	2	69	4.0	53	3.1	2.90	119	.230	.311	7	9	104	96	3.3	3	2	1.7
1944	Bos-A	1	1	.500	9	6	1	0	0	30	30	9.0	1	15	4.5	9	2.7	3.60	92	.261	.341	-1	-1	97	104	0.0	1	-0	0.0
1945	Bos-A	0	1	.000	2	1	0	0	0	6	10	15.0	1	3	4.5	5	7.5	9.00	36	.333	.382	-4	-4	96	77	-0.4	0	0	-0.2
	Phi-N	5	4	.556	23	9	3	1	2	83	80	8.7	3	40	4.3	36	3.9	3.80	102	.254	.332	0	1	102	97	1.7	3	1	0.5
1946	Phi-N	11	12	.478	30	24	12	1	2	173	169	8.8	6	90	4.7	65	3.4	3.54	94	.260	.342	-2	-4	98	105	0.7	8	4	0.8
1947	Phi-N	4	15	.211	32	19	8	1	0	147	155	9.5	6	69	4.2	54	3.3	4.59	90	.279	.355	-9	-7	102	95	-4.7	2	1	-0.3
1948	Phi-N	0	2	.000	4	1	0	0	0	14	19	12.2	1	11	7.1	7	4.5	7.07	54	.317	.411	-5	-5	97	92	-0.9	0	-0	-0.3
Total	8	40	51	.440	161	99	43	4	7	770	744	8.7	24	397	4.6	304	3.6	3.90	94	.256	.341	-24	-21	101	97	-2.9	26	8	2.1
■ **HOWIE JUDSON**	Judson, Howard Kolls b: 2/16/26, Hebron, Ill. BR/TR, 6'1", 195 lbs. Deb: 4/22/48																												
1948	Chi-A	4	5	.444	40	5	1	0	8	107	102	8.6	7	56	4.7	38	3.2	4.79	89	.255	.346	-6	-6	100	88	0.8	-2	0	-0.7
1949	Chi-A	1	14	.067	26	12	3	0	1	108	114	9.5	13	70	5.8	36	3.0	4.58	91	.274	.373	-5	-5	99	114	-6.3	-3	0	-0.6
1950	Chi-A	2	3	.400	46	3	1	0	0	112	105	8.4	10	63	5.1	34	2.7	3.94	115	.252	.349	**8**	**7**	99	110	0.0	-1	-2	0.5
1951	Chi-A	5	6	.455	27	14	3	0	1	122	124	9.1	9	55	4.1	43	3.2	3.76	105	.264	.339	5	2	96	110	-0.7	-2	0	0.0
1952	Chi-A	0	1	.000	21	0	0	0	1	34	30	7.9	4	22	5.8	15	4.0	4.24	86	.244	.340	-2	-2	99	106	-0.4	-0	-0	-0.2
1953	Cin-N	0	1	.000	10	6	0	0	0	39	58	13.4	8	11	2.5	11	2.5	5.54	78	.341	.377	-5	-5	100	124	-0.4	1	0	-0.3
1954	Cin-N	5	7	.417	37	8	0	0	3	93	86	8.3	9	42	4.1	27	2.6	3.97	107	.251	.330	1	3	104	98	-0.8	-2	-2	0.0
Total	7	17	37	.315	207	48	8	0	14	615	619	9.1	60	319	4.7	204	3.0	4.29	98	.265	.350	-4	-6	99	106	-7.8	-9	-3	-1.3
■ **KEN JUNGELS**	Jungels, Kenneth Peter "Curly" b: 6/23/16, Aurora, Ill. d: 9/9/75, West Bend, Wis. BR/TR, 6'1", 180 lbs. Deb: 9/15/37																												
1937	Cle-A	0	0	—	2	0	0	0	0	3	3	9.0	0	1	3.0	0	0.0	0.00	—	.273	.333	2	1	97	0	0.0	0	0	0.1
1938	Cle-A	1	0	1.000	9	0	0	0	0	15	21	12.6	1	18	10.8	7	4.2	9.00	52	.339	.488	-7	-7	98	98	0.5	-1	0	-0.6
1940	Cle-A	0	0	—	2	0	0	0	0	3	3	9.0	0	1	3.0	1	3.0	3.00	134	.273	.308	0	0	92	123	0.0	-0	0	0.0
1941	Cle-A	0	0	—	6	0	0	0	0	14	17	10.9	4	8	5.1	6	3.9	7.07	59	.293	.388	-5	-5	101	100	0.0	-0	-0	-0.4
1942	Pit-N	0	0	—	6	0	0	0	0	14	12	7.7	0	4	2.6	7	4.5	6.43	52	.235	.281	-5	-5	102	37	0.0	0	0	-0.3
Total	5	1	0	1.000	25	0	0	0	0	49	56	10.3	5	32	5.9	21	3.9	6.80	61	.290	.391	-14	-15	99	77	0.5	-1	-0	-1.2
■ **MIKE JUREWICZ**	Jurewicz, Michael Allen b: 9/20/45, Buffalo, N.Y. BB/TL, 6'3", 205 lbs. Deb: 9/07/65																												
1965	NY-A	0	0	—	2	0	0	0	0	2	5	22.5	0	1	4.5	2	9.0	9.00	39	.417	.462	-1	-1	101	104	0.0	0	0	0.0
■ **AL JURISICH**	Jurisich, Alvin Joseph b: 8/25/21, New Orleans, La. d: 11/3/81, New Orleans, La. BR/TR, 6'2", 193 lbs. Deb: 4/26/44																												
1944	StL-N	7	9	.438	30	14	5	2	1	130	102	7.1	7	65	4.5	53	3.7	3.39	101	.221	.319	3	1	95	94	-3.0	-0	-1	0.0
1945	StL-N	3	3	.500	27	6	1	0	0	72	61	7.6	7	41	5.1	42	5.3	5.13	72	.232	.329	-11	-12	97	76	-0.5	-2	-1	-1.3
1946	Phi-N	4	3	.571	13	10	2	1	1	68	71	9.4	9	31	4.1	34	4.5	3.71	90	.263	.338	-2	-3	98	117	0.8	-0	-1	-0.4
1947	Phi-N	1	7	.125	34	12	5	0	3	118	110	8.4	15	52	4.0	48	3.7	4.96	84	.258	.334	-12	-11	102	89	-2.7	-3	-2	-1.4
Total	4	15	22	.405	104	42	13	3	5	388	344	8.0	38	189	4.4	177	4.1	4.24	87	.242	.329	-21	-24	98	93	-5.4	-6	-5	-3.1
■ **WALT JUSTIS**	Justis, Walter Newton "Smoke" b: 8/17/1883, Moores Hill, Ind. d: 10/4/41, Lawrenceburg, Ind. 5'11.5", 195 lbs. Deb: 8/01/05																												
1905	Det-A	0	0	—	2	0	0	0	0	3	4	12.0	0	6	18.0	0	0.0	9.00	29	.347	.571	-2	-2	100	106	0.0	0	-0	-0.1
■ **HEROLD JUUL**	Juul, Earl Herold b: 5/21/1893, Chicago, Ill. d: 1/4/42, Chicago, Ill. BR/TR, 5'9.5", 150 lbs. Deb: 4/24/14																												
1914	Bro-F	0	3	.000	9	3	0	0	0	29	26	8.1	0	31	9.6	16	5.0	6.21	52	.268	.445	-10	-10	101	75	-1.4	-0	0	-0.8
■ **HERB JUUL**	Juul, Herbert Victor b: 2/2/1886, Chicago, Ill. d: 11/14/28, Chicago, Ill. BL/TL, 5'11", 150 lbs. Deb: 7/11/11																												
1911	Cin-N	0	0	—	1	0	0	0	0	4	3	6.8	0	4	9.0	2	4.5	4.50	70	.231	.412	-0	-1	92	95	0.0	-0	-0	0.0

YEAR	TM/L	W	L	PCT	G	GS	CG	SHO	SV	IP	H	H/G	HR	BB	BB/G	SO	SO/G	ERA	/A	OAVG	OOBP	PR	/A	PF	CPI	WAT	PB	PD	TPI
■ JIM KAAT	Kaat, James Lee b: 11/7/38, Zeeland, Mich. BL/TL, 6'4.5", 205 lbs. Deb: 8/02/59 C																												
1959	Was-A	0	2	.000	3	2	0	0	0	5	7	12.6	1	4	7.2	2	3.6	12.60	31	.350	.448	-5	-5	102	76	-0.9	-0	0	-0.4
1960	Was-A	1	5	.167	13	9	0	0	0	50	48	8.6	8	31	5.6	25	4.5	5.58	71	.255	.368	-9	-9	102	93	-1.9	-1	0	-0.8
1961	Min-A	9	17	.346	36	29	8	1	0	201	188	8.4	12	82	3.7	122	5.5	3.90	111	.248	.325	3	9	107	92	-3.0	4	3	1.7
1962	Min-A	18	14	.563	39	35	16	**5**	1	269	243	8.1	23	75	2.5	173	5.8	3.14	131	.243	.302	25	29	104	106	0.0	3	6	4.1
1963	Min-A	10	10	.500	31	27	7	1	1	178	195	9.9	24	38	1.9	105	5.3	4.20	85	.274	.317	-11	-13	98	101	-1.2	-0	4	-0.8
1964	Min-A	17	11	.607	36	34	13	0	1	243	231	8.6	23	60	2.2	171	6.3	3.22	112	.251	.297	11	11	100	105	3.8	5	3	2.0
1965	Min-A	18	11	.621	45	42	7	2	2	264	267	9.1	25	63	2.1	154	5.3	2.83	120	.258	.300	18	17	98	**123**	-0.1	7	3	3.0
1966	Min-A	**25**	13	.658	41	41	**19**	3	0	**305**	271	8.0	29	55	**1.6**	205	6.0	2.74	138	.235	.268	23	**35**	110	102	5.6	4	0	**4.6**
1967	Min-A	16	13	.552	42	38	13	2	0	263	269	9.2	21	42	1.4	211	7.2	3.05	112	.260	.291	5	11	106	108	-0.2	3	1	1.7
1968	Min-A	14	12	.538	30	29	9	2	0	208	192	8.3	16	40	1.7	130	5.6	2.94	107	.243	.275	1	5	106	96	1.5	0	-0	0.6
1969	Min-A	14	13	.519	40	32	10	0	1	242	252	9.4	23	75	2.8	139	5.2	3.50	104	.265	.321	4	3	100	110	-2.0	6	-3	0.8
1970	Min-A	14	10	.583	45	34	4	1	0	230	244	9.5	26	58	2.3	120	4.7	3.56	101	.273	.314	4	1	97	111	-0.4	4	2	0.6
1971	Min-A	13	14	.481	39	38	15	4	0	260	275	9.5	16	47	1.6	137	4.7	3.32	109	.268	.299	4	8	104	97	0.6	-1	-0	0.9
1972	Min-A	10	2	.833	15	15	5	0	0	113	94	7.5	6	20	1.6	64	5.1	2.07	159	.227	.257	13	15	107	102	4.1	5	0	2.6
1973	Min-A	11	12	.478	29	28	7	2	0	182	206	10.2	26	39	1.9	93	4.6	4.40	90	.282	.320	-12	-9	103	98	-0.5	0	-1	-1.0
	Chi-A	4	1	.800	7	7	3	1	0	43	44	9.2	4	4	0.8	16	3.3	4.19	94	.260	.277	-2	-1	103	70	1.6	0	-1	-0.1
	Yr	15	13	.536	36	35	10	3	0	225	250	10.0	30	43	**1.7**	109	4.4	4.36	90	.276	.308	-13	-10	103	70	1.1	0	-2	-1.1
1974	Chi-A	21	13	.618	42	39	15	3	0	277	263	8.5	18	63	2.0	142	4.6	2.92	127	.250	.292	22	24	102	100	4.8	0	-2	2.4
1975	Chi-A	20	14	.588	43	41	12	1	0	304	321	9.5	20	77	2.3	142	4.2	3.11	127	.274	.318	23	28	104	**119**	4.7	0	-2	2.7
1976	Phi-N	12	14	.462	38	35	7	1	0	228	241	9.5	21	32	1.3	83	3.3	3.47	106	.274	.295	1	5	105	103	-3.7	2	-3	0.4
1977	Phi-N	6	11	.353	35	27	2	0	0	160	211	11.9	20	40	2.3	55	3.1	5.40	71	.320	.357	-26	-28	98	100	-3.8	1	-2	-2.7
1978	Phi-N	8	5	.615	26	24	2	1	0	140	150	9.6	9	32	2.1	48	3.1	4.11	90	.280	.319	-8	-6	104	94	0.9	-1	-2	-0.8
1979	Phi-N	1	0	1.000	3	1	0	0	0	8	9	10.1	1	5	5.6	2	2.3	4.50	81	.281	.378	-1	-1	97	117	0.5	0	0	0.0
	NY-A	2	3	.400	40	1	0	0	2	58	64	9.9	4	14	2.2	23	3.6	3.88	104	.287	.321	2	1	95	107	-0.6	0	-1	0.0
1980	NY-A	0	1	.000	4	0	0	0	0	5	8	14.4	0	4	7.2	1	1.8	7.20	55	.381	.444	-2	-2	98	108	-0.4	0	1	0.0
	StL-N	8	7	.533	49	14	6	1	4	130	140	9.7	6	33	2.3	36	2.5	3.81	97	.281	.317	-3	-2	102	97	1.1	1	-2	-0.2
1981	StL-N	6	6	.500	41	1	0	0	4	53	60	10.2	2	17	2.9	8	1.4	3.40	104	.299	.336	1	1	101	127	-0.8	1	1	0.3
1982	StL-N	5	3	.625	62	2	0	0	2	75	79	9.5	6	23	2.8	35	4.2	4.08	91	.276	.324	-4	-3	102	100	0.6	-1	1	-0.3
1983	StL-N	0	0	—	24	0	0	0	0	35	48	12.3	5	10	2.6	19	4.9	3.86	93	.327	.358	-1	-1	98	150	0.0	-0	0	-0.1
Total	25	283	237	.544	898	625	180	31	18	4529	4620	9.2	395	1083	2.2	2461	4.9	3.45	107	.264	.306	75	125	103	104	10.3	42	6	21.2
■ GEORGE KAHLER	Kahler, George Runnells "Krum" b: 9/6/1889, Athens, Ohio d: 2/7/24, Battle Creek, Va. BR/TR, 6', 183 lbs. Deb: 8/13/10																												
1910	Cle-A	6	4	.600	12	12	8	2	0	95	80	7.6	0	46	4.4	38	3.6	1.61	159	.237	.335	10	10	102	173	1.3	-2	-1	0.9
1911	Cle-A	9	8	.529	30	17	10	0	1	154	153	8.9	1	66	3.9	97	5.7	3.27	105	.270	.360	1	3	103	110	0.1	-3	-1	0.0
1912	Cle-A	12	19	.387	41	32	17	3	1	246	263	9.6	1	121	4.4	104	3.8	3.70	92	.291	.382	-10	-8	101	120	-3.8	-5	-4	-1.2
1913	Cle-A	5	11	.313	24	15	5	0	0	118	118	9.0	1	32	2.4	43	3.3	3.13	97	.266	.322	-3	-1	104	94	-3.7	-3	-4	-0.4
1914	Cle-A	0	1	.000	2	1	1	0	0	14	17	10.9	0	7	4.5	3	1.9	3.86	75	.309	.387	-2	-1	106	118	-0.4	-0	-0	-0.1
Total	5	32	43	.427	109	77	41	5	2	627	631	9.1	3	272	3.9	285	4.1	3.17	101	.274	.358	-3	2	102	121	-6.5	-14	-9	-0.8
■ DON KAINER	Kainer, Donald Wayne b: 9/3/55, Houston, Tex. BR/TR, 6'3", 205 lbs. Deb: 9/06/80																												
1980	Tex-A	0	0	—	4	3	0	0	0	20	22	9.9	0	9	4.0	10	4.5	1.80	225	.289	.374	5	5	100	252	0.0	0	1	0.7
■ DON KAISER	Kaiser, Clyde Donald "Tiger" b: 2/3/35, Byng, Okla. BR/TR, 6'5", 195 lbs. Deb: 7/20/55																												
1955	Chi-N	0	0	—	11	0	0	0	0	18	20	10.0	2	5	2.5	11	5.5	5.50	74	.274	.329	-3	-3	101	75	0.0	-0	-0	-0.2
1956	Chi-N	4	9	.308	27	22	5	1	0	150	144	8.6	15	52	3.1	74	4.4	3.60	105	.247	.308	3	3	101	92	-1.4	-5	-0	-0.1
1957	Chi-N	2	6	.250	20	13	1	0	0	72	91	11.4	4	28	3.5	23	2.9	5.00	76	.316	.371	-9	-10	98	102	-1.5	-1	2	-0.8
Total	3	6	15	.286	58	35	6	1	0	240	255	9.6	21	85	3.2	108	4.1	4.16	92	.270	.329	-9	-9	100	94	-2.9	-6	1	-1.1
■ JEFF KAISER	Kaiser, Jeffrey Patrick b: 7/24/60, Wyandotte, Mich. BR/TL, 6'3", 195 lbs. Deb: 4/11/85																												
1985	Oak-A	0	0	—	15	0	0	0	0	17	25	13.2	6	20	10.6	10	5.3	14.29	27	.342	.474	-19	-20	93	75	0.0	0	1	-1.7
1987	Cle-A	0	0	—	2	0	0	0	0	3	4	12.0	1	3	9.0	2	6.0	18.00	26	.286	.444	-5	-4	105	49	0.0	0	0	-0.3
1988	Cle-A	0	0	—	3	0	0	0	0	3	2	6.0	0	1	3.0	0	0.0	0.00	—	.286	.273	1	1	102	0	0.0	0	0	0.2
Total	3	0	0	—	20	0	0	0	0	23	31	12.1	7	24	9.4	12	4.7	12.91	31	.330	.452	-22	-23	96	62	0.0	0	1	-1.8
■ BOB KAISER	Kaiser, Robert Thomas b: 4/29/50, Cincinnati, Ohio BB/TL, 5'10", 175 lbs. Deb: 9/03/71																												
1971	Cle-A	0	0	—	5	0	0	0	0	6	8	12.0	2	3	4.5	4	6.0	4.50	84	.333	.448	-1	-0	108	198	0.0	0	0	0.0
■ GEORGE KAISERLING	Kaiserling, George b: 5/12/1893, Steubenville, Ohio d: 3/2/18, Steubenville, Ohio BR/TR, 6', 175 lbs. Deb: 4/20/14																												
1914	Ind-F	17	10	.630	37	33	20	1	0	275	288	9.4	8	72	2.4	75	2.5	3.11	111	.274	.330	3	11	108	112	2.0	-6	-2	0.5
1915	New-F	15	15	.500	41	29	16	5	2	261	246	8.5	1	73	2.5	75	2.6	2.24	127	.257	.316	23	17	94	130	-0.8	-2	2	1.9
Total	2	32	25	.561	78	62	36	6	2	536	534	9.0	9	145	2.4	150	2.5	2.69	117	.266	.323	26	28	101	120	1.2	-7	1	2.4
■ BILL KALFASS	Kalfass, William Philip "Lefty" b: 3/3/16, New York, N.Y. d: 9/8/68, Brooklyn, N.Y. BR/TL, 6'3.5", 190 lbs. Deb: 9/15/37																												
1937	Phi-A	1	0	1.000	3	1	1	0	0	12	10	7.5	0	10	7.5	9	6.8	3.00	148	.233	.370	2	2	96	132	0.5	-1	-0	0.1
■ RUDY KALLIO	Kallio, Rudolph b: 12/14/1892, Portland, Ore. d: 4/6/79, Newport, Ore. BR/TR, 5'10", 160 lbs. Deb: 4/25/18																												
1918	Det-A	8	14	.364	30	22	10	2	0	181	178	8.9	0	76	3.8	70	3.5	3.63	75	.261	.325	-17	-18	99	82	-2.0	-1	-0	-2.0
1919	Det-A	0	0	—	12	1	0	0	1	22	28	11.5	0	8	3.3	3	1.2	5.73	52	.326	.389	-6	-7	92	83	0.0	-1	-0	-0.7
1925	Bos-A	1	4	.200	7	4	0	0	0	19	28	13.3	0	9	4.3	2	0.9	7.58	58	.364	.422	-7	-7	99	86	-0.8	0	-0	-0.5
Total	3	9	18	.333	49	27	10	2	1	222	234	9.5	0	93	3.8	75	3.0	4.18	69	.277	.340	-30	-32	98	83	-2.8	-1	-1	-3.2
■ BOB KAMMEYER	Kammeyer, Robert Lynn b: 12/2/50, Kansas City, Kan. BR/TR, 6'4", 210 lbs. Deb: 7/03/78																												
1978	NY-A	0	0	—	7	0	0	0	0	22	24	9.8	1	6	2.5	11	4.5	5.73	64	.276	.327	-5	-5	97	66	0.0	0	1	-0.3
1979	NY-A	0	0	—	1	0	0	0	0	0	7	—	2	0	—	0	—	∞	—	1.000	1.000	-8	-8	95	73	0.0	0	0	-0.5
Total	2	0	0	—	8	0	0	0	0	22	31	12.7	3	6	2.5	11	4.5	9.00	41	.330	.377	-13	-13	97	66	0.0	0	1	-0.8
■ IKE KAMP	Kamp, Alphonse Francis b: 9/5/1900, Roxbury, Mass. d: 2/25/55, Boston, Mass. BB/TL, 6', 170 lbs. Deb: 9/16/24																												
1924	Bos-N	0	1	.000	1	1	0	0	0	7	9	11.6	0	5	6.4	4	5.1	5.14	74	.360	.438	-1	-1	99	132	-0.4	-0	0	0.0
1925	Bos-N	2	4	.333	24	4	1	0	0	58	68	10.6	0	35	5.4	20	3.1	5.12	79	.301	.381	-5	-7	95	95	-0.7	-0	0	-0.5
Total	2	2	5	.286	25	5	1	0	0	65	77	10.7	0	40	5.5	24	3.3	5.12	79	.307	.387	-6	-8	96	99	-1.1	-0	1	-0.5
■ HARRY KANE	Kane, Harry "Klondike" (born Harry Cohen) b: 7/27/1883, Hamburg, Ark. d: 9/15/32, Portland, Ore. BL/TL, Deb: 8/08/02																												
1902	StL-A	0	1	.000	4	1	1	0	0	23	34	13.3	2	16	6.3	7	2.7	5.48	66	.370	.464	-5	-5	102	131	-0.4	-1	0	-0.3
1903	Det-A	0	2	.000	3	3	2	0	0	18	26	13.0	0	8	4.0	10	5.0	8.50	33	.362	.426	-11	-11	96	68	-0.9	-0	-1	-0.9
1905	Phi-N	1	1	.500	2	2	2	1	0	17	12	6.4	0	8	4.2	12	6.4	1.59	192	.221	.321	3	3	102	133	0.0	-0	-0	0.3
1906	Phi-N	1	3	.250	6	3	2	0	0	28	28	9.0	0	18	5.8	14	4.5	3.86	63	.297	.425	-4	-4	93	110	-0.8	-1	0	-0.3
Total	4	2	7	.222	15	9	7	1	0	86	100	10.5	2	50	5.2	43	4.5	4.81	61	.320	.419	-17	-18	98	111	-2.1	-2	-1	-1.2
■ ERV KANTLEHNER	Kantlehner, Erving Leslie "Peanuts" b: 7/31/1892, San Jose, Cal. BL/TL, 6', 190 lbs. Deb: 4/17/14																												
1914	Pit-N	3	2	.600	21	5	3	2	0	67	51	6.9	0	39	5.2	26	3.5	3.09	84	.218	.324	-2	-4	93	84	0.7	-0	-0	-0.4
1915	Pit-N	5	12	.294	29	18	10	1	3	163	135	7.5	1	58	3.2	64	3.5	2.26	119	.230	.294	9	8	98	105	-3.4	3	1	1.2
1916	Pit-N	5	15	.250	34	21	7	2	2	165	151	8.2	1	57	3.1	49	2.7	3.16	89	.249	.305	-10	-7	107	87	-4.3	-0	1	-0.5
	Phi-N	0	0	—	3	0	0	0	0	4	7	15.8	0	3	6.8	2	4.5	9.00	27	.500	.526	-3	-3	94	110	0.0	0	0	-0.2
	Yr	5	15	.250	37	21	7	2	2	169	158	8.4	1	60	3.2	51	2.7	3.30	85	.253	.305	-13	-9	107	110	-4.3	-0	1	-0.7
Total	3	13	29	.310	87	44	20	5	5	399	344	7.8	2	157	3.5	141	3.2	2.84	96	.239	.307	-6	-5	101	94	-7.0	2	2	0.1
■ PAUL KARDOW	Kardow, Paul Otto "Tex" b: 9/19/15, Humble, Tex. d: 4/27/68, San Antonio, Tex. BR/TR, 6'6", 210 lbs. Deb: 7/01/36																												
1936	Cle-A	0	0	—	2	0	0	0	0	2	1	4.5	0	2	9.0	0	0.0	4.50	117	.167	.333	0	0	105	80	0.0	0	0	0.0

YEAR	TM/L	W	L	PCT	G	GS	CG	SHO	SV	IP	H	H/G	HR	BB	BB/G	SO	SO/G	ERA	/A	OAVG	OOBP	PR	/A	PF	CPI	WAT	PB	PD	TPI
■ ED KARGER	Karger, Edwin "Loose" b: 5/6/1883, San Angelo, Tex. d: 9/9/57, Delta, Colo. BR/TL, 5'11", 185 lbs. Deb: 4/15/06																												
1906	Pit-N	2	3	.400	6	2	0	0	0	28	21	6.8	0	9	2.9	8	2.6	1.93	137	.238	.322	2	2	101	105	-0.8	-1	1	0.4
	StL-N	5	16	.238	25	20	17	0	1	192	193	9.0	0	43	2.0	73	3.4	2.72	101	.292	.342	-2	0	104	107	-3.5	3	3	0.4
	Yr	7	19	.269	31	22	17	0	1	220	214	8.8	0	52	2.1	81	3.3	2.62	104	.285	.337	0	3	103	107	-4.3	-1	4	0.8
1907	StL-N	15	19	.441	38	31	28	6	1	310	251	7.3	2	64	1.9	132	3.8	2.03	122	.250	.301	15	15	100	91	3.2	1	4	2.2
1908	StL-N	4	9	.308	22	15	9	1	0	141	148	9.4	1	50	3.2	34	2.2	3.06	76	.301	.367	-11	-11	100	113	-0.1	2	-1	-1.3
1909	Cin-N	1	3	.250	9	5	1	0	0	34	26	6.9	0	30	7.9	8	2.1	4.50	54	.217	.382	-7	-8	94	78	-0.9	1	0	-0.7
	Bos-A	5	2	.714	12	6	3	0	0	68	71	9.4	0	22	2.9	17	2.3	3.18	84	.273	.337	-5	-4	108	98	1.1	-0	-0	-0.4
1910	Bos-A	11	7	.611	27	25	16	1	1	183	162	8.0	5	53	2.6	81	4.0	3.20	77	.230	.289	-14	-15	97	68	1.7	7	-2	-1.1
1911	Bos-A	5	8	.385	25	18	6	1	0	131	134	9.2	4	42	2.9	57	3.9	3.37	98	.272	.334	-0	-1	99	100	-1.6	3	-0	0.2
Total	6	48	67	.417	164	122	80	9	3	1087	1006	8.3	12	313	2.6	410	3.4	2.79	94	.263	.325	-23	-21	100	94	-0.9	17	4	-0.3
■ ANDY KARL	Karl, Anton Andrew b: 4/8/14, Mt.Vernon, N.Y. BR/TR, 6'1.5", 175 lbs. Deb: 4/24/43																												
1943	Bos-A	1	1	.500	11	0	0	0	1	26	31	10.7	0	13	4.5	6	2.1	3.46	99	.310	.376	-0	-0	104	140	0.1	0	1	0.2
	Phi-N	1	2	.333	9	2	0	0	0	27	44	14.7	0	11	3.7	4	1.3	7.00	46	.383	.417	-11	-11	96	97	-0.2	1	0	-0.9
1944	Phi-N	3	2	.600	38	0	0	0	2	89	76	7.7	1	21	2.1	26	2.6	2.33	159	.237	.279	**13**	**14**	103	105	0.9	1	1	1.6
1945	Phi-N	8	8	.500	**67**	2	1	0	**15**	181	175	8.7	7	50	2.5	51	2.5	2.98	130	.253	.300	**16**	**18**	102	104	2.5	-2	1	1.7
1946	Phi-N	3	7	.300	39	0	0	0	5	65	84	11.6	6	22	3.0	15	2.1	4.98	67	.321	.366	-11	-12	98	107	-1.6	-0	1	-1.1
1947	Bos-N	2	3	.400	27	0	0	0	3	35	41	10.5	2	13	3.3	5	1.3	3.86	101	.318	.367	1	0	95	136	-0.6	-0	2	0.2
Total	5	18	23	.439	191	4	1	0	26	423	451	9.6	16	130	2.8	107	2.3	3.51	105	.279	.326	7	9	101	109	1.1	-1	5	1.7
■ BILL KARNS	Karns, William Arthur b: Chicago, Ill. TL , Deb: 8/14/01																												
1901	Bal-A	1	0	1.000	3	1	1	0	0	17	30	15.9	0	9	4.8	5	2.6	6.35	61	.407	.472	-5	-5	107	117	0.5	-1	-0	-0.3
■ HERB KARPEL	Karpel, Herbert "Lefty" b: 12/27/17, Brooklyn, N.Y. BL/TL, 5'9.5", 180 lbs. Deb: 4/19/46																												
1946	NY-A	0	0	—	2	0	0	0	0	2	4	18.0	0	0	0.0	0	0.0	9.00	38	.500	.500	-1	-1	98	99	0.0	0	0	0.0
■ BENN KARR	Karr, Benjamin Joyce "Baldy" b: 11/28/1893, Mt.Pleasant, Miss. d: 12/8/68, Memphis, Tenn. BL/TR, 6', 175 lbs. Deb: 4/20/20																												
1920	Bos-A	3	8	.273	26	2	0	0	1	92	109	10.7	3	24	2.3	21	2.1	4.79	77	.304	.349	-10	-11	97	85	-2.3	5	-1	-1.0
1921	Bos-A	8	7	.533	26	7	5	0	0	118	123	9.4	8	38	2.9	37	2.8	3.66	117	.283	.325	8	8	100	112	0.7	1	-0	0.8
1922	Bos-A	5	12	.294	41	13	7	0	1	183	212	10.4	10	45	2.2	41	2.0	4.48	90	.302	.334	-9	-10	99	96	-2.3	-1	-1	-0.9
1925	Cle-A	11	12	.478	32	24	12	1	0	198	248	11.3	8	80	3.6	41	1.9	4.77	98	.317	.372	-8	-2	107	107	0.6	3	2	0.4
1926	Cle-A	5	6	.455	30	7	4	0	1	113	137	10.9	9	41	3.3	23	1.8	5.02	78	.291	.344	-13	-14	97	90	-1.1	2	1	-1.0
1927	Cle-A	3	3	.500	22	5	1	0	2	77	92	10.8	5	32	3.7	17	2.0	5.03	81	.315	.367	-8	-8	99	105	0.4	1	2	-0.4
Total	6	35	48	.422	177	58	29	1	5	781	921	10.6	43	260	3.0	180	2.1	4.60	91	.303	.349	-39	-37	101	100	-4.0	11	2	-2.1
■ JACK KATOLL	Katoll, John "Big Jack" b: 6/24/1872, Germany d: 6/18/55, Hartland, Ill. BR/TR, 5'11", 195 lbs. Deb: 9/09/1898																												
1898	Chi-N	0	1	.000	2	1	1	0	0	11	8	6.5	0	1	0.8	3	2.5	0.82	448	.222	.243	3	3	102	129	-0.4	-1	0	0.3
1899	Chi-N	1	1	.500	2	2	2	0	0	18	17	8.5	0	4	2.0	1	0.5	6.00	61	.272	.316	-4	-5	96	41	0.0	-1	0	-0.3
1901	Chi-A	11	10	.524	27	25	19	0	0	208	231	10.0	3	53	2.3	59	2.6	2.81	125	.302	.347	20	16	96	**125**	-1.6	-4	2	1.7
1902	Chi-A	0	0	—	1	0	0	0	0	1	1	9.0	0	0	0.0	2	18.0	0.00	—	.284	.284	0	0	94	0	0.0	-0	0	0.0
	Bal-A	5	10	.333	15	13	13	0	0	123	175	12.8	5	32	2.3	25	1.8	4.02	92	.361	.401	-6	-4	104	133	-0.6	-0	4	0.0
	Yr	5	10	.333	16	13	13	0	0	124	176	12.8	5	32	2.3	27	2.0	3.99	93	.361	.400	-6	-4	104	133	-0.6	-0	4	0.0
Total	4	17	22	.436	47	41	35	0	0	361	432	10.8	8	90	2.2	90	2.2	3.32	109	.319	.362	13	11	99	123	-2.6	-6	6	1.7
■ BOB KATZ	Katz, Robert Clyde b: 1/30/11, Lancaster, Pa. d: 12/14/62, St.Joseph, Mich. BR/TR, 5'11.5", 190 lbs. Deb: 5/12/44																												
1944	Cin-N	0	1	.000	6	2	0	0	0	18	17	8.5	0	7	3.5	4	2.0	4.00	85	.254	.320	-1	-1	95	78	-0.4	-1	1	0.0
■ CURT KAUFMAN	Kaufman, Curt Gerrard b: 7/19/57, Omaha, Neb. BR/TR, 6'2", 175 lbs. Deb: 9/10/82																												
1982	NY-A	1	0	1.000	7	0	0	0	0	9	9	9.0	2	6	6.0	1	1.0	5.00	79	.265	.375	-1	-1	97	117	0.5	0	-0	0.0
1983	NY-A	0	0	—	4	0	0	0	0	9	10	10.0	0	4	4.0	8	8.0	3.00	133	.303	.359	1	1	98	155	0.0	0	0	0.1
1984	Cal-A	2	3	.400	29	1	0	0	1	69	68	8.9	13	20	2.6	41	5.3	4.57	89	.254	.301	-4	-4	101	91	-0.4	0	0	-0.3
Total	3	3	3	.500	40	1	0	0	1	87	87	9.0	15	30	3.1	50	5.2	4.45	91	.260	.315	-4	-4	101	100	0.1	0	0	-0.2
■ TONY KAUFMANN	Kaufmann, Anthony Charles b: 12/16/1900, Chicago, Ill. d: 6/4/82, Elgin, Ill. BR/TR, 5'11", 165 lbs. Deb: 9/23/21 C																												
1921	Chi-N	1	0	1.000	2	1	1	0	1	13	12	8.3	0	3	2.1	6	4.2	4.15	99	.240	.278	-1	-0	108	46	0.5	1	-0	0.0
1922	Chi-N	7	13	.350	37	9	4	1	3	153	161	9.5	15	57	3.4	45	2.6	4.06	96	.273	.334	1	-2	96	102	-3.5	2	-1	-0.1
1923	Chi-N	14	10	.583	33	24	18	2	3	206	209	9.1	14	67	2.9	72	3.1	3.10	133	.264	.326	21	24	103	**117**	1.3	3	-1	2.5
1924	Chi-N	16	11	.593	34	26	16	3	0	208	218	9.4	21	66	2.9	79	3.4	4.02	97	.272	.324	-4	-3	101	100	2.1	6	-1	0.2
1925	Chi-N	13	13	.500	31	23	14	2	2	196	221	10.1	9	77	3.5	49	2.3	4.50	93	.292	.356	-5	-7	98	99	1.6	2	-0	-0.4
1926	Chi-N	9	7	.563	26	21	14	1	2	170	169	8.9	6	44	2.3	52	2.8	3.02	133	.262	.308	15	19	105	106	0.6	1	-2	1.9
1927	Chi-N	3	3	.500	9	6	3	0	0	53	75	12.7	8	19	3.2	21	3.6	6.45	60	.338	.386	-15	-15	99	103	-0.2	3	2	-0.9
	Phi-N	0	3	.000	5	5	1	0	0	19	37	17.5	2	8	3.8	4	1.9	10.42	38	.425	.450	-14	-14	100	88	-1.4	0	-0	-1.1
	StL-N	0	0	—	1	0	0	0	0	⅓	4	108.0	0	1	27.0	0	0.0	81.00	—	1.000	1.000	-3	-3	106	84	0.0	0	0	-0.2
	Yr	3	6	.333	15	11	4	0	0	72	116	14.5	10	28	3.5	25	3.1	7.88	49	.366	.401	-32	-32	99	84	-1.6	3	1	-2.2
1928	StL-N	0	0	—	4	1	0	0	0	5	8	14.4	1	4	7.2	2	3.6	9.00	43	.444	.500	-3	-3	97	126	0.0	0	0	-0.2
1930	StL-N	0	1	.000	2	1	0	0	0	10	15	13.5	2	4	3.6	2	1.8	8.10	62	.357	.396	-3	-3	102	95	-0.4	0	-0	-0.2
1931	StL-N	1	1	.500	15	1	0	0	1	49	65	11.9	3	17	3.1	13	2.4	6.06	66	.319	.366	-12	-11	103	87	-0.1	-1	0	-1.1
1935	StL-N	0	0	—	3	0	0	0	0	4	4	9.0	0	1	2.3	0	0.0	2.25	179	.286	.313	1	1	100	166	0.0	0	0	0.1
Total	11	64	62	.508	202	118	71	9	12	1086	1198	9.9	81	368	3.0	345	2.9	4.19	96	.284	.339	-22	-18	101	103	0.5	17	-4	0.5
■ STEVE KEALEY	Kealey, Steven William b: 5/13/47, Torrance, Cal. BR/TR, 6', 185 lbs. Deb: 9/09/68																												
1968	Cal-A	0	1	.000	6	0	0	0	0	10	10	9.0	0	5	4.5	4	3.6	2.70	106	.256	.341	0	0	96	125	-0.4	0	-0	0.0
1969	Cal-A	2	0	1.000	15	3	1	1	0	37	48	11.7	4	13	3.2	17	4.1	3.89	94	.322	.376	-1	-1	101	145	1.0	-1	-1	-0.2
1970	Cal-A	1	0	1.000	17	0	0	0	1	22	19	7.8	2	6	2.5	14	5.7	4.09	83	.260	.301	-1	-2	92	91	0.5	0	-1	-0.1
1971	Chi-A	2	2	.500	54	1	0	0	6	77	69	8.1	10	26	3.0	50	5.8	3.86	87	.239	.290	-3	-4	97	88	0.0	1	-0	-0.3
1972	Chi-A	3	2	.600	40	0	0	0	4	57	50	7.9	4	12	1.9	37	5.8	3.32	98	.234	.267	-2	-0	106	74	0.2	-0	-1	-0.1
1973	Chi-A	0	0	—	7	0	0	0	0	11	23	18.8	2	7	5.7	4	3.3	15.55	25	.418	.462	-14	-14	103	66	0.0	0	-0	-1.2
Total	6	8	5	.615	139	4	1	1	11	214	219	9.2	22	69	2.9	126	5.3	4.29	79	.267	.315	-21	-21	100	95	1.3	-0	-3	-1.9
■ ED KEAS	Keas, Edward James b: 2/2/1863, Dubuque, Iowa d: 1/12/40, Dubuque, Iowa Deb: 1888																												
1888	Cle-a	3	3	.500	6	6	6	0	0	51	53	9.4	1	12	2.1	18	3.2	2.29	134	.281	.324	4	4	100	146	0.6	-2	0	0.2
■ RAY KEATING	Keating, Raymond Herbert b: 7/21/1891, Bridgeport, Conn. d: 12/28/63, Sacramento, Cal. BR/TR, 5'11", 185 lbs. Deb: 9/12/12																												
1912	NY-A	0	3	.000	6	5	3	0	0	36	36	9.0	0	18	4.5	21	5.3	5.75	61	.265	.355	-10	-9	105	63	-1.4	2	0	-0.7
1913	NY-A	6	12	.333	28	21	9	2	0	151	147	8.8	3	51	3.0	83	4.9	3.22	94	.253	.316	-5	-3	104	86	-1.1	-3	-2	-0.4
1914	NY-A	7	11	.389	34	25	14	0	1	210	198	8.5	1	67	2.9	109	4.7	2.96	93	.253	.316	-5	-5	100	90	-1.3	-0	2	-0.2
1915	NY-A	3	6	.333	11	10	8	1	0	79	66	7.5	3	45	5.1	37	4.2	3.65	80	.228	.337	-6	-7	99	85	-1.1	-1	1	-0.6
1916	NY-A	5	6	.455	14	12	6	0	0	91	91	9.0	4	37	3.7	35	3.5	3.07	93	.272	.349	-2	-2	101	123	-0.6	1	2	0.1
1918	NY-A	2	2	.500	15	6	1	0	0	48	39	7.3	0	30	5.6	16	3.0	3.94	66	.238	.353	-6	-7	94	81	0.0	-0	0	-0.7
1919	Bos-N	7	11	.389	22	13	9	1	0	136	129	8.5	2	45	3.0	48	3.2	2.98	98	.261	.315	-1	-1	100	106	-0.4	-1	2	0.0
Total	7	30	51	.370	130	92	50	4	1	751	706	8.5	13	293	3.5	349	4.2	3.30	88	.254	.326	-35	-34	101	94	-5.9	-2	5	-2.5
■ BOB KEATING	Keating, Robert M. b: 9/22/1862, Springfield, Mass d: 1/19/22, Springfield, Mass. BL/TL, 6'4", Deb: 8/27/1887																												
1887	Bal-a	0	1	.000	1	1	1	0	0	9	16	16.0	0	6	6.0	0	0.0	11.00	37	.401	.479	-7	-7	94	75	-0.4	-0	0	-0.4
■ CACTUS KECK	Keck, Frank Joseph b: 1/13/1899, St.Louis, Mo. d: 2/6/81, Kirkwood, Mo. BR/TR, 5'11", 170 lbs. Deb: 5/26/22																												
1922	Cin-N	7	6	.538	27	15	5	1	1	131	138	9.5	4	29	2.0	27	1.9	3.37	115	.276	.313	11	7	94	98	-0.2	-1	-3	0.2
1923	Cin-N	3	6	.333	35	6	1	0	2	87	84	8.7	5	32	3.3	16	1.7	3.72	104	.254	.317	3	1	96	90	-1.9	-1	1	0.1
Total	2	10	12	.455	62	21	6	1	3	218	222	9.2	9	61	2.5	43	1.8	3.51	110	.267	.315	13	9	95	95	-2.1	-2	-3	0.3

YEAR	TM/L	W	L	PCT	G	GS	CG	SHO	SV	IP	H	H/G	HR	BB	BB/G	SO	SO/G	ERA	/A	OAVG	OOBP	PR	/A	PF	CPI	WAT	PB	PD	TPI
■ **DAVE KEEFE**	Keefe, David Edwin b: 1/9/1897, Williston, Vt. d: 2/4/78, Kansas City, Mo. BL/TR, 5'9", 165 lbs. Deb: 4/21/17 C																												
1917	Phi-A	1	0	1.000	3	0	0	0	0	5	5	9.0	0	4	7.2	1	1.8	1.80	144	.278	.409	0	0	97	252	0.5	-0	0	0.0
1919	Phi-A	0	1	.000	1	1	1	0	0	9	8	8.0	0	3	3.0	5	5.0	4.00	90	.242	.306	-1	-0	112	57	-0.4	-1	0	0.0
1920	Phi-A	6	7	.462	31	13	7	1	0	130	129	8.9	2	30	2.1	41	2.8	2.98	126	.262	.313	12	11	99	94	1.5	0	1	1.2
1921	Phi-A	2	9	.182	44	12	4	0	1	173	214	11.1	19	64	3.3	68	3.5	4.68	98	.311	.361	-8	-2	107	114	-2.6	-3	-2	-0.5
1922	Cle-A	0	0	—	18	1	0	0	0	36	47	11.8	2	12	3.0	11	2.8	6.25	66	.333	.371	-9	-8	103	86	0.0	1	0	-0.7
Total	5	9	17	.346	97	27	12	1	1	353	403	10.3	23	113	2.9	126	3.2	4.16	100	.294	.345	-5	1	104	104	-1.0	-3	-1	0.0
■ **GEORGE KEEFE**	Keefe, George W. b: 1/7/1867, Washington, D.C. d: 8/24/35, Washington, D.C. BL/TL, 5'9", 168 lbs. Deb: 7/30/1886																												
1886	Was-N	0	3	.000	4	4	4	0	0	31	28	8.1	0	15	4.4	5	1.5	5.23	63	.253	.343	-7	-7	100	60	-1.4	-2	0	-0.6
1887	Was-N	0	1	.000	1	1	1	0	0	8	16	18.0	1	4	4.5	0	0.0	9.00	44	.432	.487	-4	-4	99	108	-0.4	-1	0	-0.3
1888	Was-N	6	7	.462	13	13	13	1	0	114	87	6.9	2	43	3.4	52	4.1	2.84	101	.224	.301	-0	0	101	77	1.1	1	0	0.2
1889	Was-N	8	18	.308	30	27	24	0	0	230	266	10.4	6	143	5.6	90	3.5	5.13	75	.306	.404	-28	-33	96	96	-1.0	-1	0	-2.8
1890	Buf-P	6	16	.273	25	22	22	0	0	196	280	12.9	11	138	6.3	55	2.5	6.52	63	.348	.444	-50	-53	97	99	0.0	1	0	-3.8
1891	Was-a	0	3	.000	5	4	4	0	1	37	44	10.7	0	17	4.1	11	2.7	2.68	140	.311	.384	4	4	101	158	-1.4	-0	0	0.4
Total	6	20	48	.294	78	71	68	1	1	616	721	10.5	20	360	5.3	213	3.1	5.06	74	.306	.398	-85	-91	97	96	-3.1	-2	0	-6.9
■ **JOHN KEEFE**	Keefe, John Thomas b: 5/5/1867, Fitchburg, Mass. d: 8/9/37, Fitchburg, Mass. TL , Deb: 4/28/1890																												
1890	Syr-a	17	24	.415	43	41	36	2	0	352	355	9.1	9	148	3.8	120	3.1	4.32	82	.277	.352	-18	-30	92	90	-1.2	-4	1	-2.8
■ **BOBBY KEEFE**	Keefe, Robert Francis b: 6/16/1882, Folsom, Cal. d: 12/7/64, Sacramento, Cal. BR/TR, 5'11", 155 lbs. Deb: 4/15/07																												
1907	NY-A	3	5	.375	19	3	0	0	3	58	60	9.3	1	20	3.1	20	3.1	2.48	112	.292	.354	0	2	110	137	-0.8	-2	0	0.2
1911	Cin-N	12	13	.480	39	26	15	0	3	234	196	7.5	7	76	2.9	105	4.0	2.69	116	.229	.294	18	11	92	88	0.6	-2	-5	0.3
1912	Cin-N	1	3	.250	17	6	0	0	2	69	78	10.2	0	33	4.3	29	3.8	5.22	61	.283	.367	-14	-16	93	74	-0.9	-0	0	-1.4
Total	3	16	21	.432	75	35	15	0	8	361	334	8.3	8	129	3.2	154	3.8	3.14	99	.249	.319	5	-1	95	93	-1.1	-4	-5	-0.9
■ **TIM KEEFE**	Keefe, Timothy John "Smiling Tim" or "Sir Timothy" b: 1/1/1857, Cambridge, Mass. d: 4/23/33, Cambridge, Mass. BR/TR, 5'10.5", 185 lbs. Deb: 8/06/1880 H																												
1880	Tro-N	6	6	.500	12	12	12	0	0	105	71	**6.1**	0	17	1.5	43	3.7	**0.86**	**309**	**.199**	.236	18	21	112	100	0.1	-0	0	2.3
1881	Tro-N	18	27	.400	45	45	45	4	0	402	442	9.9	4	81	1.8	103	2.3	3.25	86	.291	.327	-21	-20	101	94	-5.7	5	-0	-1.3
1882	Tro-N	17	26	.395	43	42	41	1	0	375	368	8.8	4	81	1.9	116	2.8	2.50	113	.264	.305	16	13	98	109	-2.5	5	5	2.2
1883	NY-a	41	27	.603	**68**	68	**68**	5	0	**619**	486	**7.1**	6	98	1.4	**361**	**5.2**	2.41	144	**.221**	**.255**	61	73	105	80	8.8	3	4	**7.6**
1884	NY-a	37	17	.685	58	58	57	4	0	492	388	7.1	5	75	1.4	323	5.9	2.29	136	.225	.257	52	45	96	93	-1.1	11	-1	5.3
1885	NY-N	32	13	.711	46	46	45	7	0	398	297	**6.7**	6	103	2.3	230	5.2	**1.58**	**182**	**.217**	.272	55	57	102	115	-2.2	-2	0	5.6
1886	NY-N	**42**	20	.677	**64**	64	**62**	2	0	**540**	478	8.0	9	100	1.7	291	4.8	2.53	111	.250	.287	46	17	85	93	7.3	4	-0	1.5
1887	NY-N	35	19	.648	56	56	54	2	0	479	447	8.4	11	108	2.0	186	3.5	3.10	138	.262	.306	51	63	106	90	**8.8**	4	2	6.2
1888	NY-N	**35**	12	**.745**	51	51	51	**8**	0	434	316	**6.6**	5	91	1.9	**333**	**6.9**	**1.74**	144	**.215**	**.261**	**53**	37	89	87	9.1	-4	1	3.2
1889	NY-N	28	13	.683	47	45	38	3	1	364	310	**7.7**	9	151	3.7	209	**5.2**	3.31	123	**.245**	**.325**	29	31	101	86	2.1	-4	2	2.6
1890	NY-P	17	11	.607	30	30	23	1	0	229	228	9.0	6	85	3.3	88	3.5	3.38	134	.271	.338	22	30	107	92	1.7	-6	0	2.1
1891	NY-N	2	5	.286	8	7	4	0	0	55	71	11.6	1	27	4.4	29	4.7	5.24	59	.327	.402	-12	-13	93	92	-1.6	-1	0	-1.1
	Phi-N	3	6	.333	11	10	9	0	1	78	84	9.7	2	28	3.2	35	4.0	3.92	81	.289	.351	-5	-6	95	88	-1.4	1	0	-0.4
	Yr	5	11	.313	19	17	13	0	1	133	155	10.5	3	55	3.7	64	4.3	4.47	71	.305	.373	-17	-19	94	88	-3.0	-1	0	-1.5
1892	Phi-N	19	16	.543	39	38	31	2	0	313	264	7.6	4	100	2.9	127	3.7	2.36	143	.241	.304	32	35	103	97	-0.9	-7	-1	2.7
1893	Phi-N	10	7	.588	22	22	17	0	0	178	202	10.2	3	79	4.0	53	2.7	4.40	104	.302	.375	6	4	98	99	0.7	1	0	0.3
Total	14	342	225	.603	600	594	557	39	2	5061	4452	7.9	75	1224	2.2	2527	4.5	2.62	126	.247	.295	402	382	99	93	23.2	8	12	38.8
■ **ED KEEGAN**	Keegan, Edward Charles b: 7/8/39, Camden, N.J. BR/TR, 6'3", 165 lbs. Deb: 8/24/59																												
1959	Phi-N	0	3	.000	3	3	0	0	0	9	19	19.0	2	13	13.0	3	3.0	18.00	22	.432	.559	-14	-14	102	76	-1.4	-0	-0	-1.1
1961	KC-A	0	0	—	6	0	0	0	1	6	6	9.0	0	5	7.5	3	4.5	4.50	93	.261	.393	-0	-0	104	99	0.0	0	0	0.0
1962	Phi-N	0	0	—	4	0	0	0	0	8	6	6.8	1	5	5.6	5	5.6	2.25	167	.214	.353	2	1	95	183	0.0	0	-0	0.1
Total	3	0	3	.000	13	3	0	0	1	23	31	12.1	3	23	9.0	11	4.3	9.00	44	.326	.463	-13	-13	100	119	-1.4	-0	-0	-1.0
■ **BOB KEEGAN**	Keegan, Robert Charles "Smiley" b: 8/4/20, Rochester, N.Y. BR/TR, 6'2.5", 207 lbs. Deb: 5/24/53																												
1953	Chi-A	7	5	.583	22	11	4	2	1	99	80	7.3	4	33	3.0	32	2.9	2.73	152	.223	.289	14	15	104	94	0.1	2	1	1.9
1954	Chi-A	16	9	.640	31	27	14	2	2	210	211	9.0	16	82	3.5	61	2.6	3.09	120	.266	.329	15	15	100	**126**	1.1	-2	-1	1.2
1955	Chi-A	2	5	.286	18	11	1	0	0	59	83	12.7	4	28	4.3	29	4.4	5.80	67	.336	.396	-12	-13	98	104	-1.7	2	0	-1.0
1956	Chi-A	5	7	.417	20	16	4	0	0	105	119	10.2	15	35	3.0	32	2.7	3.94	107	.286	.337	3	3	102	122	-1.5	-1	-0	0.2
1957	Chi-A	10	8	.556	30	20	6	2	2	143	131	8.2	22	37	2.3	36	2.3	3.52	104	.243	.291	4	2	97	100	-0.4	-1	-1	0.0
1958	Chi-A	0	2	.000	14	2	0	0	0	30	44	13.2	9	18	5.4	8	2.4	6.00	61	.358	.428	-7	-8	98	147	-0.9	-1	1	-0.7
Total	6	40	36	.526	135	87	29	6	5	646	668	9.3	70	233	3.2	198	2.8	3.65	106	.270	.328	16	15	100	114	-3.3	-2	-1	1.6
■ **BURT KEELEY**	Keeley, Burton Elwood "Speed" b: 11/2/1879, Wilmington, Ill. d: 5/3/52, Ely, Minn. BR/TR, 5'9", 170 lbs. Deb: 4/18/08																												
1908	Was-A	6	11	.353	28	16	12	1	1	170	173	9.2	3	48	2.5	68	3.6	2.96	78	.259	.313	-11	-12	97	103	-1.8	-3	1	-1.1
1909	Was-A	0	0	—	2	0	0	0	0	7	12	15.4	0	1	1.3	0	0.0	11.57	21	.364	.400	-7	-7	96	49	0.0	0	1	-0.5
Total	2	6	11	.353	30	16	12	1	1	177	185	9.4	3	49	2.5	68	3.5	3.31	70	.264	.317	-18	-20	97	101	-1.8	-2	2	-1.6
■ **VIC KEEN**	Keen, Howard Victor b: 3/16/1899, Belair, Md. d: 12/10/76, Salisbury, Md. BR/TR, 5'9", 165 lbs. Deb: 8/13/18																												
1918	Phi-A	0	1	.000	1	1	0	0	0	8	9	10.1	1	1	1.1	1	1.1	3.38	88	.300	.323	-1	-0	108	123	-0.4	-0	-0	0.0
1921	Chi-N	0	3	.000	5	4	1	0	0	25	29	10.4	0	9	3.2	9	3.2	4.68	88	.319	.371	-2	-2	108	99	-1.4	-1	0	-0.1
1922	Chi-N	1	2	.333	7	3	2	0	1	35	36	9.3	4	10	2.6	11	2.8	3.86	102	.275	.320	1	0	96	106	-0.4	1	-0	0.1
1923	Chi-N	12	8	.600	35	17	10	0	1	177	169	8.6	8	57	2.9	46	2.3	3.00	138	.255	.313	20	22	103	107	1.5	-3	-2	1.8
1924	Chi-N	15	14	.517	40	28	15	0	3	235	242	9.3	17	80	3.1	75	2.9	3.79	103	.272	.328	2	3	101	103	-0.3	-4	-3	-0.4
1925	Chi-N	2	6	.250	30	8	1	0	1	83	125	13.6	8	41	4.4	19	2.1	6.29	67	.359	.420	-19	-19	98	112	-1.7	0	1	-1.6
1926	StL-N	10	9	.526	26	21	12	1	0	152	179	10.6	15	42	2.5	29	1.7	4.56	84	.295	.337	-12	-13	100	99	-0.9	-6	-2	-1.9
1927	StL-N	2	1	.667	21	0	0	0	0	34	39	10.3	3	8	2.1	12	3.2	4.76	87	.293	.322	-3	-2	106	94	0.3	-0	0	-0.1
Total	8	42	44	.488	165	82	41	1	6	749	828	9.9	56	248	3.0	202	2.4	4.11	97	.287	.338	-15	-10	101	104	-3.3	-13	-6	-2.2
■ **KID KEENAN**	Keenan, Harry Leon b: 1875, Louisville, Ky. d: 6/11/03, Covington, Ky. TR , 095 lbs. Deb: 8/11/1891																												
1891	CM-a	0	1	.000	1	1	1	0	0	8	6	6.8	0	4	4.5	5	5.6	0.00	—	.221	.321	3	4	113	0	-0.4	1	0	0.5
■ **JIM KEENAN**	Keenan, James W. b: 2/10/1858, New Haven, Conn. d: 9/21/26, Cincinnati, Ohio BR/TR, 5'10", 186 lbs. Deb: 5/17/1875																												
1884	Ind-a	0	0	—	1	0	0	0	0	3	2	6.0	0	0	0.0	0	0.0	3.00	108	.197	.197	0	0	100	33	0.0	0	0	0.0
1885	Cin-a	0	0	—	1	0	0	0	0	8	7	7.9	0	1	1.1	0	0.0	1.13	296	.246	.272	2	2	103	196	0.0	0	0	0.2
1886	Cin-a	0	1	.000	2	0	0	0	0	8	8	9.0	0	3	3.4	2	2.3	3.38	98	.271	.338	0	-0	96	105	-0.4	1	0	0.0
Total	3	0	1	.000	4	0	0	0	0	19	17	8.1	0	4	1.9	2	0.9	2.37	140	.249	.291	2	2	99	132	-0.4	1	0	0.2
■ **JIMMIE KEENAN**	Keenan, James William "Sparkplug" b: 5/25/1898, Avon, N.Y. d: 6/5/80, Seminole, Fla. BL/TL, 5'6", 155 lbs. Deb: 9/09/20																												
1920	Phi-N	0	0	—	1	0	0	0	0	3	3	9.0	0	1	3.0	2	6.0	3.00	117	.333	.333	0	0	112	151	0.0	0	0	0.0
1921	Phi-N	1	2	.333	15	2	0	0	0	32	48	13.5	3	15	4.2	7	2.0	6.75	60	.364	.416	-11	-10	107	103	0.0	-1	-1	-1.0
Total	2	1	2	.333	16	2	0	0	0	35	51	13.1	3	16	4.1	9	2.3	6.43	62	.362	.410	-11	-9	107	107	0.0	-2	-1	-1.0
■ **JEFF KEENER**	Keener, Jeffrey Bruce b: 1/14/59, Pana, Ill. BL/TR, 6', 170 lbs. Deb: 6/08/82																												
1982	StL-N	1	1	.500	19	0	0	0	0	22	19	7.8	1	19	7.8	25	10.2	1.64	226	.235	.365	5	5	102	258	0.0	0	0	0.6
1983	StL-N	0	0	—	4	0	0	0	0	4	6	13.5	0	1	2.3	4	9.0	9.00	40	.333	.381	-2	-2	98	61	0.0	0	0	-0.1
Total	2	1	1	.500	23	0	0	0	0	26	25	8.7	1	20	6.9	29	10.0	2.77	133	.253	.368	2	3	102	228	0.0	0	0	0.5
■ **JOE KEENER**	Keener, Joseph Donald b: 4/21/53, San Pedro, Cal. BR/TR, 6'4", 200 lbs. Deb: 9/18/76																												
1976	Mon-N	0	1	.000	2	2	0	0	0	4	7	15.8	0	8	18.0	1	2.3	11.25	32	.389	.593	-3	-3	103	109	-0.4	-0	0	-0.2
■ **HARRY KEENER**	Keener, Joshua Harry "Beans" b: 1869, Easton, Pa. d: 3/5/12, Easton, Pa. Deb: 6/27/1896																												
1896	Phi-N	3	11	.214	16	13	11	0	0	113	144	11.5	5	39	3.1	28	2.2	5.89	76	.333	.389	-19	-18	102	82	-4.0	2	0	-1.2

YEAR	TM/L	W	L	PCT	G	GS	CG	SHO	SV	IP	H	H/G	HR	BB	BB/G	SO	SO/G	ERA	/A	OAVG	OOBP	PR	/A	PF	CPI	WAT	PB	PD	TPI
■ **RICKEY KEETON**	Keeton, Rickey b: 3/18/57, Cincinnati, Ohio BR/TR, 6'2", 190 lbs. Deb: 5/27/80																												
1980	Mil-A	2	2	.500	5	5	0	0	0	28	35	11.3	4	9	2.9	8	2.6	4.82	78	.307	.346	-2	-3	93	110	0.0	0	0	-0.2
1981	Mil-A	1	0	1.000	17	0	0	0	0	35	47	12.1	4	11	2.8	9	2.3	5.14	68	.329	.367	-6	-6	95	112	0.5	0	0	-0.5
Total	2	3	2	.600	22	5	0	0	0	63	82	11.7	8	20	2.9	17	2.4	5.00	72	.319	.358	-8	-10	94	111	0.5	0	0	-0.7
■ **FRANK KEFFER**	Keffer, C. Frank b: Philadelphia, Pa. d: 3/25/12, Easton, Pa. Deb: 4/19/1890																												
1890	Syr-a	1	1	.500	2	1	1	0	0	16	15	8.4	0	9	5.1	4	2.3	5.63	63	.263	.364	-3	-4	92	66	0.1	-0	0	-0.2
■ **CHET KEHN**	Kehn, Chester Lawrence b: 10/30/21, San Diego, Cal. d: 4/5/84, San Diego, Cal. BR/TR, 5'11", 168 lbs. Deb: 4/30/42																												
1942	Bro-N	0	0	—	3	1	0	0	0	8	8	9.0	2	4	4.5	3	3.4	6.75	48	.267	.353	-3	-3	97	84	0.0	1	0	-0.1
■ **KATIE KEIFER**	Keifer, Sherman C. b: 1892, BB/TL, Deb: 10/08/14																												
1914	Ind-F	1	0	1.000	1	1	1	0	0	9	6	6.0	0	2	2.0	2	2.0	2.00	173	.214	.266	1	1	108	58	0.5	0	0	0.2
■ **MIKE KEKICH**	Kekich, Michael Dennis b: 4/2/45, San Diego, Cal. BR/TL, 6'1", 196 lbs. Deb: 6/09/65																												
1965	LA-N	0	1	.000	5	1	0	0	0	10	10	9.0	2	13	11.7	9	8.1	9.90	32	.263	.451	-7	-7	90	75	-0.4	-0	-0	-0.7
1968	LA-N	2	10	.167	25	20	1	1	0	115	116	9.1	9	46	3.6	84	6.6	3.91	70	.267	.331	-12	-15	91	102	-3.9	-1	-1	-1.8
1969	NY-A	4	6	.400	28	13	1	0	1	105	91	7.8	11	49	4.2	66	5.7	4.54	76	.236	.318	-11	-13	96	80	-0.9	-1	-1	-1.4
1970	NY-A	6	3	.667	26	14	1	0	0	99	103	9.4	12	55	5.0	63	5.7	4.82	71	.267	.357	-12	-16	91	98	1.0	-1	-1	-1.7
1971	NY-A	10	9	.526	37	24	3	0	0	170	167	8.8	13	82	4.3	93	4.9	4.08	82	.257	.338	-11	-14	97	96	0.4	-0	1	-1.3
1972	NY-A	10	13	.435	29	28	2	0	0	175	172	8.8	13	76	3.9	78	4.0	3.70	76	.263	.337	-12	-17	92	107	-1.8	-1	-1	-2.0
1973	NY-A	1	1	.500	5	4	0	0	0	15	20	12.0	1	14	8.4	4	2.4	9.00	43	.351	.486	-9	-9	100	89	0.0	0	0	-0.7
	Cle-A	1	4	.200	16	6	0	0	0	50	73	13.1	6	35	6.3	26	4.7	7.02	54	.349	.437	-18	-18	99	105	-1.3	0	-1	-1.8
	Yr	2	5	.286	21	10	0	0	0	65	93	12.9	7	49	6.8	30	4.2	7.48	51	.346	.442	-26	-27	99	105	-1.3	0	-1	-2.5
1975	Tex-A	0	0	—	23	0	0	0	2	31	33	9.6	2	21	6.1	19	5.5	3.77	100	.282	.380	0	0	100	133	0.0	0	1	0.1
1977	Sea-A	5	4	.556	41	2	0	0	3	90	90	9.0	11	51	5.1	55	5.5	5.60	72	.265	.359	-15	-16	98	86	1.2	0	-0	-1.5
Total	9	39	51	.433	235	112	8	1	6	860	875	9.2	80	442	4.6	497	5.2	4.59	72	.268	.351	-107	-125	95	98	-5.7	-5	-4	-12.8
■ **GEORGE KELB**	Kelb, George Francis "Pugger" or "Lefty" b: 7/17/1870, Toledo, Ohio d: 10/20/36, Toledo, Ohio TL , Deb: 4/17/1898																												
1898	Cle-N	0	1	.000	3	1	1	0	0	16	23	12.9	0	1	0.6	8	4.5	4.50	76	.360	.370	-2	-2	95	99	-0.4	-0	0	-0.1
■ **HAL KELLEHER**	Kelleher, Harold Joseph b: 6/24/13, Philadelphia, Pa. BR/TR, 6', 165 lbs. Deb: 9/17/35																												
1935	Phi-N	2	0	1.000	3	3	2	1	0	25	26	9.4	0	12	4.3	12	4.3	1.80	262	.260	.342	6	8	117	200	1.0	1	0	1.1
1936	Phi-N	0	5	.000	14	4	1	0	0	44	60	12.3	2	29	5.9	13	2.7	5.32	84	.331	.424	-6	-4	111	124	-2.4	-0	0	-0.3
1937	Phi-N	2	4	.333	27	2	1	0	0	58	72	11.2	3	31	4.8	20	3.1	6.67	65	.308	.397	-18	-15	111	86	-0.4	-0	-0	-1.4
1938	Phi-N	0	0	—	6	0	0	0	0	7	16	20.6	0	9	11.6	4	5.1	19.29	21	.432	.543	-12	-12	106	61	0.0	0	0	-0.9
Total	4	4	9	.308	50	9	4	1	0	134	174	11.7	5	81	5.4	49	3.3	5.98	74	.315	.407	-30	-23	112	118	-1.8	1	0	-1.5
■ **RON KELLER**	Keller, Ronald Lee b: 6/3/43, Indianapolis, Ind. BR/TR, 6'2", 200 lbs. Deb: 7/09/66																												
1966	Min-A	0	0	—	2	0	0	0	0	5	7	12.6	1	1	1.8	1	1.8	5.40	70	.318	.333	-1	-1	110	109	0.0	-0	0	0.0
1968	Min-A	0	1	.000	7	1	0	0	0	16	18	10.1	2	4	2.3	11	6.2	2.81	112	.305	.348	0	1	106	182	-0.4	-0	0	0.1
Total	2	0	1	.000	9	1	0	0	0	21	25	10.7	3	5	2.1	12	5.1	3.43	96	.309	.344	-1	-0	107	165	-0.4	-0	0	0.1
■ **AL KELLETT**	Kellett, Alfred Henry b: 10/30/01, Red Bank, N.J. d: 7/14/60, New York, N.Y. 6'3", 200 lbs. Deb: 7/01/23																												
1923	Phi-A	0	1	.000	5	0	0	0	0	10	11	9.9	0	8	7.2	1	0.9	6.30	65	.282	.388	-3	-2	102	75	-0.4	0	1	-0.1
1924	Bos-A	0	0	—	1	0	0	0	0	0	0	—	0	2	—	0	—	∞	—	—	1.000	-2	-2	105	31	0.0	0	0	-0.1
Total	2	0	1	.000	6	0	0	0	0	10	11	9.9	0	10	9.0	1	0.9	8.10	50	.282	.412	-5	-4	102	75	-0.4	0	1	-0.2
■ **HARRY KELLEY**	Kelley, Harry Leroy b: 2/13/06, Parkin, Ark. d: 3/23/58, Parkin, Ark. BR/TR, 5'9.5", 170 lbs. Deb: 4/16/25																												
1925	Was-A	1	1	.500	6	1	0	0	0	16	30	16.9	0	12	6.8	7	3.9	9.00	46	.405	.472	-8	-9	95	96	-0.1	-1	1	-0.7
1926	Was-A	0	0	—	7	1	0	0	0	10	17	15.3	0	8	7.2	6	5.4	8.10	48	.405	.510	-5	-5	97	109	0.0	-0	0	-0.4
1936	Phi-A	15	12	.556	35	27	20	1	3	235	250	9.6	21	75	2.9	82	3.1	3.87	137	.275	.326	31	37	105	115	4.9	-2	-2	3.2
1937	Phi-A	13	21	.382	41	29	14	0	0	205	267	11.7	16	79	3.5	68	3.0	5.36	83	.306	.362	-17	-21	96	97	0.8	2	-1	-1.7
1938	Phi-A	0	2	.000	4	3	0	0	0	8	17	19.1	0	10	11.3	3	3.4	16.88	30	.436	.551	-11	-11	105	69	-0.9	-0	-0	-0.8
	Was-A	9	8	.529	38	14	7	2	1	148	162	9.9	12	46	2.8	44	2.7	4.50	102	.276	.326	5	1	96	93	0.6	1	0	0.2
	Yr	9	10	.474	42	17	7	2	1	156	179	10.3	12	56	3.2	47	2.7	5.13	90	.286	.342	-6	-9	96	93	-0.3	-0	0	-0.6
1939	Was-A	4	3	.571	15	3	2	0	1	54	69	11.5	2	14	2.3	20	3.3	4.67	90	.314	.357	-0	-3	91	107	0.9	1	-0	-0.1
Total	6	42	47	.472	146	78	43	3	5	676	812	10.8	51	244	3.2	230	3.1	4.86	98	.296	.351	-5	-9	99	103	6.2	0	-2	-0.3
■ **DICK KELLEY**	Kelley, Richard Anthony b: 1/8/40, Boston, Mass BR/TL, 5'11.5", 174 lbs. Deb: 4/15/64																												
1964	Mil-N	0	0	—	2	0	0	0	0	2	2	9.0	0	3	13.5	2	9.0	18.00	19	.250	.455	-3	-3	96	33	0.0	0	0	-0.2
1965	Mil-N	1	1	.500	21	4	0	0	0	45	37	7.4	5	20	4.0	31	6.2	3.00	122	.226	.306	3	3	103	114	0.0	-1	-0	0.2
1966	Atl-N	7	5	.583	20	13	2	2	0	81	75	8.3	6	21	2.3	50	5.6	3.22	109	.247	.297	3	3	97	97	0.8	-3	-2	-0.1
1967	Atl-N	2	9	.182	39	9	1	1	2	98	88	8.1	8	42	3.9	75	6.9	3.77	94	.247	.316	-4	-3	105	98	-3.4	1	1	0.0
1968	Atl-N	2	4	.333	31	11	1	1	1	98	86	7.9	4	45	4.1	73	6.7	2.76	101	.238	.315	3	0	94	114	-0.9	-1	1	0.1
1969	SD-N	4	8	.333	27	23	1	1	0	136	113	7.5	11	61	4.0	96	6.4	3.57	101	.230	.313	0	0	100	94	0.1	-2	1	0.0
1971	SD-N	2	3	.400	48	1	0	0	2	60	52	7.8	5	23	3.5	42	6.3	3.45	98	.232	.309	0	-0	98	93	0.1	0	0	0.0
Total	7	18	30	.375	188	61	5	5	5	520	453	7.8	39	215	3.7	369	6.4	3.39	100	.237	.311	2	0	99	100	-3.3	-5	2	0.0
■ **TOM KELLEY**	Kelley, Thomas Henry b: 1/5/44, Manchester, Conn. BR/TR, 6', 185 lbs. Deb: 5/05/64																												
1964	Cle-A	0	0	—	6	0	0	0	0	10	9	8.1	1	9	8.1	7	6.3	5.40	69	.237	.396	-2	-2	103	93	0.0	0	0	-0.1
1965	Cle-A	2	1	.667	4	4	1	0	0	30	19	5.7	3	13	3.9	31	9.3	2.40	140	.186	.278	4	3	97	102	0.4	1	-0	0.4
1966	Cle-A	4	8	.333	31	7	1	0	0	95	97	9.2	14	42	4.0	64	6.1	4.36	80	.264	.333	-10	-9	102	107	-2.0	-1	-1	-1.1
1967	Cle-A	0	0	—	1	0	0	0	0	1	0	0.0	0	2	18.0	0	0.0	0.00	—	.000	.500	0	0	101	0	0.0	0	-0	0.1
1971	Atl-N	9	5	.643	28	20	5	0	0	143	140	8.8	8	69	4.3	68	4.3	2.96	130	.262	.343	8	14	111	132	2.1	-4	-0	1.0
1972	Atl-N	5	7	.417	27	14	2	1	0	116	122	9.5	12	65	5.0	59	4.6	4.58	80	.272	.361	-14	-12	106	103	-0.4	-2	-3	-1.5
1973	Atl-N	0	1	.000	7	0	0	0	0	13	13	9.0	0	7	4.8	5	3.5	2.77	149	.289	.364	1	2	113	158	-0.4	-2	-0	0.1
Total	7	20	22	.476	104	45	9	1	0	408	400	8.8	38	207	4.6	234	5.2	3.75	98	.260	.344	-13	-3	106	115	-0.3	-7	-4	-1.1
■ **ALEX KELLNER**	Kellner, Alexander Raymond b: 8/26/24, Tucson, Ariz. BR/TL, 6', 200 lbs. Deb: 4/29/48																												
1948	Phi-A	0	0	—	13	1	0	0	0	23	21	8.2	0	16	6.3	14	5.5	7.83	56	.239	.364	-9	-9	102	49	0.0	-1	-0	-0.8
1949	Phi-A	20	12	.625	38	27	19	0	1	245	243	8.9	18	129	4.7	94	3.5	3.75	111	.261	.350	12	11	99	112	4.0	1	-0	1.1
1950	Phi-A	8	20	.286	36	29	15	0	2	225	253	10.1	28	112	4.5	85	3.4	5.48	78	.282	.359	-23	-30	93	93	-2.4	-0	-3	-2.9
1951	Phi-A	11	14	.440	33	29	11	1	2	210	218	9.3	20	93	4.0	94	4.0	4.46	98	.272	.347	-8	-2	106	102	-0.4	-1	-1	-0.2
1952	Phi-A	12	14	.462	34	33	14	2	0	231	223	8.7	21	86	3.4	105	4.1	4.36	94	.252	.316	-18	-6	112	84	-1.4	0	-2	-0.6
1953	Phi-A	11	12	.478	25	25	14	2	0	202	210	9.4	8	51	2.3	81	3.6	3.92	107	.269	.312	2	6	105	87	2.0	1	-2	0.6
1954	Phi-A	6	17	.261	27	27	8	1	0	174	204	10.6	16	88	4.6	69	3.6	5.38	72	.301	.376	-32	-29	105	100	-2.7	-0	0	-2.7
1955	KC-A	11	8	.579	30	24	6	3	0	163	164	9.1	18	60	3.3	75	4.1	4.20	100	.265	.325	-4	0	106	99	3.0	2	0	0.2
1956	KC-A	7	4	.636	20	17	5	0	0	92	103	10.1	15	33	3.2	44	4.3	4.30	101	.289	.346	-1	0	105	120	2.6	-0	0	0.1
1957	KC-A	6	5	.545	28	21	3	0	0	133	141	9.5	18	41	2.8	72	4.9	4.26	90	.278	.329	-7	-6	102	105	1.5	4	0	-0.1
1958	KC-A	0	2	.000	7	6	0	0	0	34	40	10.6	5	8	2.1	22	5.8	5.82	69	.315	.353	-8	-7	107	92	-0.9	-0	0	-0.6
	Cin-N	7	3	.700	18	7	4	0	0	82	74	8.1	8	20	2.2	42	4.6	2.30	182	.243	.293	15	17	106	134	2.1	3	-2	2.0
1959	StL-N	2	1	.667	12	4	0	0	0	37	31	7.5	9	10	2.4	19	4.6	3.16	133	.220	.273	3	4	106	116	0.6	0	-0	0.4
Total	12	101	112	.474	321	250	99	9	5	1851	1925	9.4	184	747	3.6	816	4.0	4.41	95	.270	.338	-78	-47	104	100	8.0	8	-8	-3.5
■ **WALT KELLNER**	Kellner, Walter Joseph b: 4/26/29, Tucson, Ariz. BR/TR, 6', 200 lbs. Deb: 9/06/52																												
1952	Phi-A	0	0	—	1	0	0	0	1	4	4	9.0	0	3	6.8	2	4.5	6.75	61	.250	.368	-1	-1	112	57	0.0	-0	-0	0.0
1953	Phi-A	0	0	—	2	0	0	0	0	3	1	3.0	0	4	12.0	4	12.0	6.00	70	.111	.429	-1	-1	105	65	0.0	0	0	0.0
Total	2	0	0	—	3	0	0	0	1	7	5	6.4	0	7	9.0	6	7.7	6.43	65	.200	.394	-2	-2	109	60	0.0	-0	0	0.0

YEAR	TM/L	W	L	PCT	G	GS	CG	SHO	SV	IP	H	H/G	HR	BB	BB/G	SO	SO/G	ERA	/A	OAVG	OOBP	PR	/A	PF	CPI	WAT	PB	PD	TPI
■ **AL KELLOGG**	Kellogg, Albert C. Deb: 9/25/08																												
1908	Phi-A	0	2	.000	3	3	2	0	0	17	20	10.6	1	9	4.8	8	4.2	5.82	45	.294	.385	-6	-6	110	88	-0.9	-1	0	-0.5
■ **WIN KELLUM**	Kellum, Winford Ansley b: 4/11/1876, Waterford, Ont., Canada d: 8/10/51, Big Rapids, Mich. BB/TL, 5'10", 190 lbs. Deb: 4/26/01																												
1901	Bos-A	2	3	.400	6	6	5	0	0	48	61	11.4	3	7	1.3	8	1.5	6.38	54	.331	.355	-14	-16	94	69	-0.7	-1	1	-1.1
1904	Cin-N	15	10	.600	31	24	22	1	2	225	206	8.2	1	46	1.8	70	2.8	2.60	117	.270	.320	3	11	111	94	0.9	1	0	1.2
1905	StL-N	3	3	.500	11	7	5	1	0	74	70	8.5	1	10	1.2	19	2.3	2.92	97	.277	.307	1	-1	95	86	0.6	1	1	0.0
Total	3	20	16	.556	48	37	32	2	2	347	337	8.7	5	63	1.6	97	2.5	3.19	96	.281	.323	-11	-4	106	89	0.8	1	2	0.1
■ **BRYAN KELLY**	Kelly, Bryan Keith b: 2/24/59, Silver Spring, Md. BR/TR, 6'2", 195 lbs. Deb: 9/02/86																												
1986	Det-A	1	2	.333	6	4	0	0	0	20	21	9.4	4	10	4.5	18	8.1	4.50	88	.269	.352	-1	-1	95	118	-0.5	0	0	0.0
1987	Det-A	0	1	.000	5	0	0	0	0	11	12	9.8	2	7	5.7	10	8.2	4.91	87	.286	.380	-1	-1	96	124	-0.4	0	-0	0.0
Total	2	1	3	.250	11	4	0	0	0	31	33	9.6	6	17	4.9	28	8.1	4.65	88	.275	.362	-1	-2	95	120	-0.9	0	0	0.0
■ **ED KELLY**	Kelly, Edward Leo b: 12/10/1888, Pawtucket, R.I. d: 11/4/28, Red Lodge, Mont. BR/TR, 5'11.5", 173 lbs. Deb: 4/14/14																												
1914	Bos-A	0	0	—	3	0	0	0	0	2	1	4.5	0	1	4.5	4	18.0	0.00	—	.100	.182	1	1	96	0	0.0	-0	0	0.1
■ **GEORGE KELLY**	Kelly, George Lange "Highpockets" b: 9/10/1895, San Francisco, Cal. d: 10/13/84, Burlingame, Cal. BR/TR, 6'4", 190 lbs. Deb: 8/18/15 CH																												
1917	NY-N	1	0	1.000	1	0	0	0	0	5	4	7.2	0	1	1.8	2	3.6	0.00	—	.211	.250	2	1	93	0	0.5	-0	-0	0.0
■ **HERB KELLY**	Kelly, Herbert Barrett "Moke" b: 6/4/1892, Mobile, Ala. d: 5/18/73, Torrance, Cal. BL/TL, 5'9", 160 lbs. Deb: 9/25/14																												
1914	Pit-N	0	2	.000	5	2	2	0	0	26	24	8.3	1	7	2.4	6	2.1	2.42	107	.253	.295	1	0	93	112	-0.9	0	0	0.0
1915	Pit-N	1	1	.500	5	1	0	0	0	11	10	8.2	0	4	3.3	6	4.9	4.09	66	.250	.313	-2	-2	98	74	0.0	1	1	0.0
Total	2	1	3	.250	10	3	2	0	0	37	34	8.3	1	11	2.7	12	2.9	2.92	90	.252	.301	-1	-1	94	100	-0.9	1	1	0.0
■ **MIKE KELLY**	Kelly, Michael J. b: 11/9/02, St.Louis, Mo. BR/TR, 6'1", 178 lbs. Deb: 9/03/26																												
1926	Phi-N	0	0	—	4	0	0	0	0	7	9	11.6	0	4	5.1	2	2.6	9.00	46	.346	.424	-4	-4	107	71	0.0	-1	-0	-0.3
■ **KING KELLY**	Kelly, Michael Joseph b: 12/31/1857, Troy, N.Y. d: 11/8/1894, Boston, Mass. BR/TR, 5'10", 170 lbs. Deb: 5/01/1878 MH																												
1880	Chi-N	0	0	—	1	0	0	0	0	3	3	9.0	0	1	3.0	1	3.0	0.00	—	.269	.329	1	1	98	0	0.0	0	0	0.1
1883	Chi-N	0	0	—	1	0	0	0	0	1	1	9.0	0	0	0.0	0	0.0	0.00	—	.268	.268	0	0	107	0	0.0	0	0	0.0
1884	Chi-N	0	1	.000	2	0	0	0	0	5	12	21.6	2	2	3.6	1	1.8	9.00	35	.469	.508	-3	-3	105	146	-0.4	1	0	-0.2
1887	Bos-N	1	0	1.000	3	0	0	0	0	13	17	11.8	1	14	9.7	0	0.0	3.46	114	.332	.475	1	1	97	216	0.5	1	0	0.1
1890	Bos-P	1	0	1.000	1	0	0	0	0	2	1	4.5	0	2	9.0	2	9.0	4.50	98	.157	.359	-0	-0	104	48	0.5	0	0	0.0
1891	CM-a	0	1	.000	3	0	0	0	0	15	21	12.6	2	7	4.2	0	0.0	5.40	78	.347	.414	-3	-2	113	117	-0.3	1	0	-0.6
1892	Bos-N	0	0	—	1	0	0	0	0	6	8	12.0	0	4	6.0	0	0.0	1.50	243	.334	.429	1	1	111	372	0.0	-0	0	0.1
Total	7	2	2	.500	12	0	0	0	0	45	63	12.6	5	30	6.0	4	0.8	4.20	90	.345	.437	-3	-2	105	169	0.3	4	0	-0.5
■ **REN KELLY**	Kelly, Reynolds Joseph b: 11/18/1899, San Francisco, Cal d: 8/24/63, Millbrae, Cal. BR/TR, 6', 183 lbs. Deb: 9/18/23																												
1923	Phi-A	0	0	—	1	0	0	0	0	7	7	9.0	0	4	5.1	1	1.3	2.57	158	.259	.333	1	1	102	135	0.0	-1	-0	0.0
■ **BOB KELLY**	Kelly, Robert Edward b: 10/4/27, Cleveland, Ohio BR/TR, 6', 180 lbs. Deb: 5/04/51																												
1951	Chi-N	7	4	.636	35	11	4	0	0	124	130	9.4	8	55	4.0	48	3.5	4.65	85	.275	.348	-9	-10	100	92	2.2	-1	0	-0.9
1952	Chi-N	4	9	.308	31	15	3	2	0	125	114	8.2	7	46	3.3	50	3.6	3.60	107	.236	.300	2	4	103	83	-2.5	0	1	0.5
1953	Chi-N	0	1	.000	14	0	0	0	0	17	27	14.3	2	9	4.8	6	3.2	9.53	48	.375	.446	-10	-9	106	85	-0.4	-0	0	-0.8
	Cin-N	1	2	.333	28	5	0	0	2	66	71	9.7	7	26	3.5	29	4.0	4.36	99	.276	.340	-1	-0	100	104	-0.3	-1	0	0.0
	Yr	1	3	.250	42	5	0	0	2	83	98	10.6	9	35	3.8	35	3.8	5.42	80	.297	.361	-10	-10	102	104	-0.7	-0	1	-0.8
1958	Cin-N	0	0	—	2	1	0	0	0	2	3	13.5	0	3	13.5	1	4.5	4.50	93	.500	.545	-0	-0	106	264	0.0	0	0	0.0
	Cle-A	0	2	.000	13	3	0	0	0	28	29	9.3	4	13	4.2	12	3.9	5.14	68	.282	.361	-4	-5	93	101	-0.9	0	0	-0.4
Total	4	12	18	.400	123	35	7	2	2	362	374	9.3	28	152	3.8	146	3.6	4.50	88	.268	.338	-23	-21	101	93	-1.9	-1	1	-1.6
■ **BILL KELSO**	Kelso, William Eugene b: 2/19/40, Kansas City, Mo. BR/TR, 6'4", 215 lbs. Deb: 7/31/64																												
1964	LA-A	2	0	1.000	10	1	1	1	0	24	19	7.1	3	9	3.4	21	7.9	2.25	143	.218	.299	4	3	89	142	1.0	-0	0	0.3
1966	Cal-A	1	1	.500	5	0	0	0	0	11	11	9.0	1	6	4.9	11	9.0	2.45	139	.244	.346	1	1	100	168	0.0	-0	0	0.1
1967	Cal-A	5	3	.625	69	1	0	0	11	112	85	6.8	6	63	5.1	91	7.3	2.97	104	.219	.323	3	2	96	112	0.9	-1	1	0.1
1968	Cin-N	4	1	.800	35	0	0	0	1	54	56	9.3	6	15	2.5	39	6.5	4.00	83	.277	.318	-6	-4	111	108	1.5	-1	-1	-0.5
Total	4	12	5	.706	119	2	1	1	12	201	171	7.7	16	93	4.2	162	7.3	3.13	102	.237	.320	2	1	99	118	3.4	-2	0	0.0
■ **RUSS KEMMERER**	Kemmerer, Russell Paul "Rusty" or "Dutch" b: 11/1/31, Pittsburgh, Pa. BR/TR, 6'2", 198 lbs. Deb: 6/27/54																												
1954	Bos-A	5	3	.625	19	9	2	1	0	75	71	8.5	4	41	4.9	37	4.4	3.84	98	.257	.348	-1	-1	101	104	1.3	-0	0	0.0
1955	Bos-A	1	1	.500	7	2	0	0	0	17	18	9.5	3	15	7.9	13	6.9	7.41	65	.269	.402	-7	-5	122	82	0.0	-0	-0	-0.4
1957	Bos-A	0	0	—	1	0	0	0	0	4	5	11.3	0	2	4.5	1	2.3	4.50	92	.333	.368	-0	-0	109	121	0.0	-0	-0	0.0
	Was-A	7	11	.389	39	26	6	0	0	172	214	11.2	20	71	3.7	81	4.2	4.97	77	.309	.370	-23	-21	102	110	0.5	-1	-3	-2.4
	Yr	7	11	.389	40	26	6	0	0	176	219	11.2	20	73	3.7	82	4.2	4.96	78	.309	.370	-23	-22	102	110	0.5	-0	-3	-2.4
1958	Was-A	6	15	.286	40	30	6	0	0	224	234	9.4	25	74	3.0	111	4.5	4.62	82	.270	.322	-21	-21	100	90	-3.1	-2	0	-2.2
1959	Was-A	8	17	.320	37	28	8	0	0	206	221	9.7	20	71	3.1	89	3.9	4.50	87	.276	.331	-15	-13	102	96	-3.0	-1	0	-1.3
1960	Was-A	0	2	.000	3	3	0	0	0	17	18	9.5	2	10	5.3	10	5.3	7.94	50	.269	.367	-8	-8	102	62	-0.9	0	1	-0.5
	Chi-A	6	3	.667	36	7	2	1	2	121	111	8.3	5	45	3.3	76	5.7	2.98	129	.248	.310	12	11	99	105	1.1	-3	0	0.9
	Yr	6	5	.545	39	10	2	1	2	138	129	8.4	7	55	3.6	86	5.6	3.59	107	.250	.316	4	4	99	105	0.2	0	1	0.4
1961	Chi-A	3	3	.500	47	2	0	0	2	97	102	9.5	10	26	2.4	35	3.2	4.36	91	.278	.317	-4	-4	99	96	-0.1	1	1	-0.1
1962	Chi-A	2	1	.667	20	0	0	0	0	28	30	9.6	3	11	3.5	17	5.5	3.86	97	.270	.328	0	-0	94	111	0.5	1	1	0.1
	Hou-N	5	3	.625	36	2	0	0	3	68	72	9.5	10	15	2.0	23	3.0	4.10	91	.272	.318	-1	-3	95	103	1.5	1	0	-0.1
1963	Hou-N	0	0	—	17	0	0	0	1	37	48	11.7	1	8	1.9	12	2.9	5.59	56	.320	.341	-9	-10	95	81	0.0	0	1	-0.9
Total	9	43	59	.422	302	109	24	2	8	1066	1144	9.7	103	389	3.3	505	4.3	4.47	86	.277	.335	-76	-75	100	98	-2.2	-5	1	-6.9
■ **DUTCH KEMNER**	Kemner, Herman John b: 3/4/1899, Quincy, Ill. BR/TR, 5'10.5", 175 lbs. Deb: 4/19/29																												
1929	Cin-N	0	0	—	9	0	0	0	1	15	19	11.4	0	8	4.8	10	6.0	7.80	61	.328	.380	-5	-5	101	72	0.0	0	0	-0.3
■ **ED KENNA**	Kenna, Edward Benninghaus "The Pitching Poet" b: 10/17/1877, Charleston, W.Va. d: 3/22/12, Grant, Fla. TR , 6', 180 lbs. Deb: 5/05/02																												
1902	Phi-A	1	1	.500	2	1	1	0	0	17	19	10.1	1	11	5.8	5	2.6	5.29	72	.308	.412	-3	-3	106	95	-0.1	-0	0	-0.1
■ **VERN KENNEDY**	Kennedy, Lloyd Vernon b: 3/20/07, Kansas City, Mo. BL/TR, 6', 175 lbs. Deb: 9/18/34																												
1934	Chi-A	0	2	.000	3	3	1	0	0	19	21	9.9	1	9	4.3	7	3.3	3.79	122	.300	.375	1	2	103	138	-0.9	0	1	0.2
1935	Chi-A	11	11	.500	31	25	16	2	1	212	211	9.0	17	95	4.0	65	2.8	3.91	125	.262	.340	13	23	109	109	0.3	0	2	2.5
1936	Chi-A	21	9	.700	35	34	20	1	0	274	282	9.3	13	147	4.8	99	3.3	4.63	107	.268	.356	12	10	99	99	**6.1**	6	1	1.4
1937	Chi-A	14	13	.519	32	30	15	1	0	221	238	9.7	16	124	5.0	114	4.6	5.09	92	.273	.362	-12	-9	102	93	-1.1	2	0	-0.6
1938	Det-A	12	9	.571	33	26	11	0	2	190	215	10.2	13	113	5.4	53	2.5	5.07	94	.287	.375	-6	-7	99	104	0.7	4	2	0.0
1939	Det-A	0	3	.000	4	4	1	0	0	21	25	10.7	4	9	3.9	9	3.9	6.43	79	.301	.368	-4	-3	110	97	-1.4	0	1	-0.1
	StL-A	9	17	.346	33	27	12	1	0	192	229	10.7	18	115	5.4	55	2.6	5.72	85	.297	.381	-23	-19	105	100	1.4	-3	-1	-1.8
	Yr	9	20	.310	37	31	13	1	0	213	254	10.7	22	124	5.2	64	2.7	5.79	84	.297	.379	-28	-22	105	100	0.0	0	-0	-1.9
1940	StL-A	12	17	.414	34	32	18	0	0	222	263	10.7	18	122	4.9	70	2.8	5.59	85	.298	.380	-30	-21	108	99	-0.8	6	2	-1.0
1941	StL-A	2	4	.333	6	6	2	0	0	45	44	8.8	5	27	5.4	6	1.2	4.40	95	.259	.359	-1	-1	101	108	-0.7	3	0	0.2
	Was-A	1	7	.125	17	7	2	0	0	66	77	10.5	5	39	5.3	22	3.0	5.73	72	.297	.384	-12	-12	99	98	-2.8	-1	0	-1.1
	Yr	3	11	.214	23	13	4	0	0	111	121	9.8	10	66	5.4	28	2.3	5.19	80	.282	.374	-13	-13	100	98	-3.5	3	0	-0.9
1942	Cle-A	4	8	.333	28	12	4	0	1	108	99	8.3	1	50	4.2	37	3.1	4.08	83	.244	.325	-5	-8	93	78	-1.9	1	0	-0.6
1943	Cle-A	10	7	.588	28	17	8	1	0	147	130	8.0	4	59	3.6	63	3.9	2.45	120	.242	.317	14	8	90	125	1.1	1	1	1.1
1944	Cle-A	2	5	.286	12	10	2	0	0	59	66	10.1	0	37	5.6	17	2.6	5.03	69	.289	.377	-11	-10	101	92	-1.3	-2	1	-1.1
	Phi-N	1	5	.167	12	7	3	0	0	55	60	9.8	3	20	3.3	23	3.8	4.25	87	.269	.328	-4	-3	103	89	-1.7	1	0	-0.2
1945	Phi-N	0	3	.000	12	3	0	0	0	36	43	10.8	2	14	3.5	13	3.3	5.50	71	.297	.352	-7	-6	102	85	-1.4	-0	1	-0.4
	Cin-N	5	12	.294	24	20	11	0	1	158	170	9.7	10	69	3.9	38	2.2	3.99	93	.280	.349	-3	-5	97	112	-2.3	2	1	-0.1
	Yr	5	15	.250	36	23	11	1	1	194	213	9.9	12	83	3.9	51	2.4	4.27	87	.283	.350	-10	-12	98	112	-3.7	-0	2	-0.5

YEAR	TM/L	W	L	PCT	G	GS	CG	SHO	SV	IP	H	H/G	HR	BB	BB/G	SO	SO/G	ERA	/A	OAVG	OOBP	PR	/A	PF	CPI	WAT	PB	PD	TPI
Total	12	104	132	.441	344	263	126	7	5	2025	2173	9.7	130	1049	4.7	691	3.1	4.68	94	.277	.358	-77	-66	101	101	-6.7	20	11	-1.6
■ **MONTE KENNEDY**	Kennedy, Montia Calvin b: 5/11/22, Amelia, Va. BR/TL, 6'2", 185 lbs. Deb: 4/18/46																												
1946	NY-N	9	10	.474	38	27	10	1	1	187	153	**7.4**	14	116	5.6	71	3.4	3.42	103	.224	.335	-0	2	103	102	1.4	2	-0	0.4
1947	NY-N	9	12	.429	34	24	9	0	0	148	158	9.6	8	88	5.4	60	3.6	4.86	83	.272	.368	-13	-13	99	94	-2.1	-0	-0	-1.3
1948	NY-N	3	9	.250	25	16	7	1	0	114	118	9.3	10	57	4.5	63	5.0	4.03	97	.264	.349	-1	-2	98	109	-3.1	-1	-1	-0.2
1949	NY-N	12	14	.462	38	32	14	4	1	223	208	8.4	13	100	4.0	95	3.8	3.43	119	.242	.321	15	16	101	99	-0.3	-1	-3	1.2
1950	NY-N	5	4	.556	36	17	5	0	2	114	120	9.5	14	53	4.2	41	3.2	4.74	84	.269	.343	-8	-9	97	99	0.0	-3	-0	-1.1
1951	NY-N	1	2	.333	29	5	1	0	0	68	68	9.0	0	31	4.1	22	2.9	2.25	175	.270	.346	13	13	99	165	-0.6	0	-0	1.3
1952	NY-N	3	4	.429	31	6	2	1	0	83	73	7.9	6	31	3.4	48	5.2	3.04	124	.230	.299	6	7	101	100	-0.9	-1	1	0.6
1953	NY-N	0	0	—	18	0	0	0	0	23	30	11.7	2	19	7.4	11	4.3	7.04	59	.337	.442	-7	-7	98	106	0.0	-0	0	-0.6
Total	8	42	55	.433	249	127	48	7	4	960	928	8.7	67	495	4.6	411	3.9	3.84	101	.253	.340	6	6	100	105	-5.6	-5	-4	0.3
■ **TED KENNEDY**	Kennedy, Theodore A. b: 2/1865, Henry, Ill. d: 10/31/07, St.Louis, Mo. BL , Deb: 6/12/1885																												
1885	Chi-N	7	2	.778	9	9	8	0	0	79	91	10.4	5	28	3.2	36	4.1	3.42	87	.300	.359	-5	-4	106	131	0.0	-4	0	-0.6
1886	Phi-a	5	15	.250	20	19	19	0	0	173	196	10.2	4	65	3.4	68	3.5	4.53	78	.296	.359	-21	-19	103	97	-4.9	-10	0	-2.2
	Lou-a	0	4	.000	4	4	4	0	0	32	53	14.9	1	16	4.5	14	3.9	5.34	70	.381	.444	-7	-6	108	139	-1.9	-1	0	-0.5
	Yr	5	19	.208	24	23	23	0	0	205	249	10.9	5	81	3.6	82	3.6	4.65	77	.311	.374	-27	-25	104	139	-6.8	-10	0	-2.7
Total	2	12	21	.364	33	32	31	0	0	284	340	10.8	10	109	3.5	118	3.7	4.31	79	.308	.370	-33	-28	104	111	-6.8	-15	0	-3.3
■ **BILL KENNEDY**	Kennedy, William Aulton "Lefty" b: 3/14/21, Carnesville, Ga. d: 4/9/83, Seattle, Wash. BL/TL, 6'2.5", 200 lbs. Deb: 4/26/48																												
1948	Cle-A	1	0	1.000	6	3	0	0	0	11	16	13.1	0	13	10.6	12	9.8	11.45	35	.333	.468	-9	-9	94	67	0.5	1	0	-0.6
	StL-A	7	8	.467	26	20	3	0	0	132	132	9.0	10	104	7.1	77	5.3	4.70	99	.259	.386	-6	-1	109	108	1.1	1	-1	0.0
	Yr	8	8	.500	32	23	3	0	0	143	148	9.3	10	117	7.4	89	5.6	5.22	88	.265	.394	-15	-10	108	108	1.6	1	-1	-0.6
1949	StL-A	4	11	.267	48	16	2	0	1	154	172	10.1	12	73	4.3	69	4.0	4.68	93	.285	.356	-8	-5	104	101	-1.7	-2	-2	-0.7
1950	StL-A	0	0	—	1	0	0	0	0	2	1	4.5	0	2	9.0	1	4.5	0.00	—	.143	.333	1	1	111	0	0.0	0	-0	0.1
1951	StL-A	1	5	.167	19	5	1	0	0	56	76	12.2	4	37	5.9	29	4.7	5.79	78	.332	.419	-10	-8	109	115	-1.4	-2	1	-0.7
1952	Chi-A	2	2	.500	**47**	1	0	0	5	71	54	6.8	4	38	4.8	46	5.8	2.79	130	.213	.316	7	7	99	107	0.0	0	-1	0.6
1953	Bos-A	0	0	—	16	0	0	0	2	24	24	9.0	2	17	6.4	14	5.3	3.75	115	.255	.362	1	2	108	125	0.0	0	-0	0.2
1956	Cin-N	0	0	—	1	0	0	0	0	2	6	27.0	1	0	0.0	0	0.0	18.00	22	.667	.545	-3	-3	106	105	0.0	0	0	-0.2
1957	Cin-N	0	2	.000	8	0	0	0	3	13	16	11.1	1	5	3.5	8	5.5	6.23	66	.314	.367	-3	-3	106	87	-0.9	0	0	-0.2
Total	8	15	28	.349	172	45	6	0	11	465	497	9.6	34	289	5.6	256	5.0	4.72	92	.275	.372	-31	-20	105	105	-2.4	-1	-2	-1.5
■ **BILL KENNEDY**	Kennedy, William Gorman b: 12/22/18, Alexandria, Va. BL/TL, 6'1", 175 lbs. Deb: 5/01/42																												
1942	Was-A	0	1	.000	8	2	1	0	2	18	21	10.5	1	10	5.0	4	2.0	8.00	45	.296	.373	-9	-9	99	65	-0.4	-1	1	-0.7
1946	Was-A	1	2	.333	21	2	0	0	3	39	40	9.2	1	29	6.7	18	4.2	6.00	55	.270	.379	-11	-12	94	76	-0.4	-0	0	-1.1
1947	Was-A	0	0	—	2	0	0	0	0	7	10	12.9	1	5	6.4	1	1.3	7.71	48	.370	.441	-3	-3	101	107	0.0	-0	0	-0.2
Total	3	1	3	.250	31	4	1	0	5	64	71	10.0	3	44	6.2	23	3.2	6.75	51	.289	.385	-23	-24	96	76	-0.8	-1	1	-2.0
■ **BRICKYARD KENNEDY**	Kennedy, William P. b: 10/7/1867, Bellaire, Ohio d: 9/23/15, Bellaire, Ohio BR/TR, 5'11", 160 lbs. Deb: 4/26/1892																												
1892	Bro-N	13	8	.619	26	21	18	0	1	191	189	8.9	3	95	4.5	108	**5.1**	3.86	85	.271	.358	-12	-13	99	91	0.1	-1	0	-1.1
1893	Bro-N	25	20	.556	46	44	40	2	1	383	376	8.8	15	168	3.9	107	2.5	3.74	114	.272	.351	40	22	91	100	3.2	3	6	2.4
1894	Bro-N	24	20	.545	48	41	34	0	2	361	445	11.1	15	149	3.7	107	2.7	4.94	102	.326	.392	16	3	94	99	0.8	4	4	0.7
1895	Bro-N	19	12	.613	39	33	26	2	1	280	335	10.8	13	93	3.0	39	1.3	5.14	87	.317	.372	-11	-21	94	88	3.0	4	0	-1.4
1896	Bro-N	17	20	.459	42	38	28	1	1	306	334	9.8	12	130	3.8	76	2.2	4.44	87	.300	.373	-3	-20	88	93	0.8	-5	3	-2.0
1897	Bro-N	18	20	.474	44	40	36	2	1	343	370	9.7	6	149	3.9	81	2.1	3.91	113	.297	.372	15	19	102	99	0.6	2	4	2.2
1898	Bro-N	16	22	.421	40	39	38	0	0	339	360	9.6	11	123	3.3	73	1.9	3.37	103	.294	.358	9	4	96	110	1.9	4	6	1.2
1899	Bro-N	22	9	.710	40	33	27	2	2	277	297	9.6	10	86	2.8	55	1.8	2.79	141	.298	.353	33	35	102	**129**	1.6	4	0	3.8
1900	Bro-N	20	13	.606	42	35	26	2	0	292	316	9.7	5	111	3.4	75	2.3	3.91	100	.299	.366	-7	0	106	96	0.2	7	2	1.0
1901	Bro-N	3	5	.375	14	8	6	0	0	85	80	8.5	1	24	2.5	28	3.0	3.07	112	.270	.327	2	3	103	91	-1.4	-1	-0	0.3
1902	NY-N	1	4	.200	6	6	4	1	0	39	44	10.2	0	16	3.7	9	2.1	3.92	74	.308	.378	-5	-4	104	96	-1.0	1	-1	-0.4
1903	Pit-N	9	6	.600	18	15	10	0	0	125	130	9.4	0	57	4.1	39	2.8	3.46	96	.294	.377	-3	-2	101	103	-0.5	8	-1	0.4
Total	12	187	159	.540	405	353	293	12	9	3021	3276	9.8	91	1201	3.6	797	2.4	3.97	103	.297	.366	75	35	97	101	9.3	29	22	7.1
■ **ART KENNEY**	Kenney, Arthur Joseph b: 4/29/16, Milford, Mass. BL/TL, 6', 175 lbs. Deb: 7/01/38																												
1938	Bos-N	0	0	—	2	0	0	0	0	2	3	13.5	0	8	36.0	2	9.0	18.00	19	.300	.611	-3	-3	89	79	0.0	0	0	-0.2
■ **ED KENT**	Kent, Edward C. b: 1859, New York TL , 5'6.5", 152 lbs. Deb: 8/14/1884																												
1884	Tol-a	0	1	.000	1	1	1	0	0	9	14	14.0	0	3	3.0	4	4.0	6.00	57	.364	.410	-3	-3	105	107	-0.4	-1	0	-0.2
■ **MAURY KENT**	Kent, Maurice Allen b: 9/17/1885, Marshalltown, Ia. d: 4/19/66, Iowa City, Iowa BR/TR, 6', 168 lbs. Deb: 4/15/12																												
1912	Bro-N	5	5	.500	20	9	2	1	0	93	107	10.4	3	46	4.5	24	2.3	4.84	68	.284	.363	-15	-16	97	83	1.0	1	1	-1.3
1913	Bro-N	0	0	—	3	0	0	0	0	7	5	6.4	0	3	3.9	1	1.3	2.57	130	.192	.276	0	1	105	53	0.0	-0	-0	0.0
Total	2	5	5	.500	23	9	2	1	0	100	112	10.1	3	49	4.4	25	2.3	4.68	71	.278	.358	-14	-15	98	81	1.0	1	1	-1.3
■ **MATT KEOUGH**	Keough, Matthew Lon b: 7/3/55, Pomona, Cal. BR/TR, 6'3", 190 lbs. Deb: 9/03/77																												
1977	Oak-A	1	3	.250	7	6	0	0	0	43	39	8.2	4	22	4.6	23	4.8	4.81	82	.247	.339	-4	-4	97	83	-0.6	0	-1	-0.4
1978	Oak-A	8	15	.348	32	32	6	0	0	197	178	8.1	9	85	3.9	108	4.9	3.24	119	.241	.319	12	14	103	97	-2.3	0	1	1.6
1979	Oak-A	2	17	.105	30	28	7	1	0	177	220	11.2	18	78	4.0	95	4.8	5.03	77	.315	.381	-16	-23	91	114	-6.7	0	2	-1.9
1980	Oak-A	16	13	.552	34	32	20	2	0	250	218	7.8	24	94	3.4	121	4.4	2.92	130	.236	.305	31	25	94	113	1.4	0	-1	2.4
1981	Oak-A	10	6	.625	19	19	10	2	0	140	125	8.0	11	45	2.9	60	3.9	3.41	102	.239	.294	4	1	95	90	0.8	0	-2	0.0
1982	Oak-A	11	18	.379	34	34	10	2	0	209	233	10.0	38	101	4.3	75	3.2	5.73	69	.284	.358	-38	-42	96	97	-1.6	0	-3	-4.1
1983	Oak-A	2	3	.400	14	4	0	0	0	44	50	10.2	7	31	6.3	28	5.7	5.52	71	.284	.386	-7	-8	96	108	-0.2	0	-1	-0.7
	NY-A	3	4	.429	12	12	0	0	0	56	59	9.5	12	20	3.2	26	4.2	5.14	78	.266	.329	-7	-7	98	97	-0.8	0	-0	-0.6
	Yr	5	7	.417	26	16	0	0	0	100	109	9.8	19	51	4.6	54	4.9	5.31	75	.273	.355	-14	-15	97	97	-1.0	0	-1	-1.3
1985	StL-N	0	1	.000	4	1	0	0	0	10	10	9.0	0	4	3.6	10	9.0	4.50	75	.278	.349	-1	-1	93	90	-0.4	-0	0	0.0
1986	Chi-N	2	2	.500	19	2	0	0	0	29	36	11.2	4	12	3.7	19	5.9	4.97	81	.316	.380	-4	-3	108	120	0.2	1	0	-0.1
	Hou-N	3	2	.600	10	5	0	0	0	35	22	5.7	5	18	4.6	25	6.4	3.09	123	.180	.287	2	3	102	92	0.0	1	-1	0.4
	Yr	5	4	.556	29	7	0	0	0	64	58	8.2	9	30	4.2	44	6.2	3.94	99	.245	.327	-2	-0	104	92	0.2	1	-1	0.3
Total	9	58	84	.408	215	175	53	7	0	1190	1190	9.0	132	510	3.9	590	4.5	4.17	92	.262	.335	-27	-45	96	102	-10.2	2	-4	-3.4
■ **KURT KEPSHIRE**	Kepshire, Kurt David b: 7/3/59, Bridgeport, Conn. BL/TR, 6'1", 180 lbs. Deb: 7/04/84																												
1984	StL-N	6	5	.545	17	16	2	2	0	109	100	8.3	7	44	3.6	71	5.9	3.30	107	.249	.318	4	3	99	105	0.3	-2	-2	0.0
1985	StL-N	10	9	.526	32	29	0	0	0	153	155	9.1	16	71	4.2	67	3.9	4.76	70	.264	.337	-20	-24	93	90	-1.5	-0	-2	-2.6
1986	StL-N	0	1	.000	2	1	0	0	0	8	8	9.0	2	4	4.5	6	6.8	4.50	85	.258	.343	-1	-1	103	119	-0.4	-0	0	0.0
Total	3	16	15	.516	51	46	2	2	0	270	263	8.8	25	119	4.0	144	4.8	4.17	83	.258	.330	-17	-22	96	97	-1.6	-3	-3	-2.6
■ **CHARLIE KERFELD**	Kerfeld, Charles Patrick b: 9/28/63, Knob Knoster, Mo. BR/TR, 6'6", 225 lbs. Deb: 7/27/85																												
1985	Hou-N	4	2	.667	11	6	0	0	0	44	44	9.0	2	25	5.1	30	6.1	4.09	84	.268	.358	-2	-3	96	105	1.0	-1	-1	-0.4
1986	Hou-N	11	2	.846	61	0	0	0	7	94	71	6.8	5	42	4.0	77	7.4	2.68	141	.213	.295	11	12	102	102	4.2	-0	-1	1.1
1987	Hou-N	0	2	.000	21	0	0	0	0	30	34	10.2	3	21	6.3	17	5.1	6.60	58	.309	.409	-8	-9	93	96	-0.9	-0	0	-0.9
Total	3	15	6	.714	93	6	0	0	7	168	149	8.0	10	88	4.7	124	6.6	3.75	99	.245	.333	0	-1	99	102	4.3	-2	-1	-0.2
■ **GUS KERIAZAKOS**	Keriazakos, Constantine Nicholas b: 7/28/31, W.Orange, N.J. BR/TR, 6'3", 187 lbs. Deb: 10/01/50																												
1950	Chi-A	0	1	.000	1	1	0	0	0	2	7	31.5	0	5	22.5	1	4.5	22.50	20	.500	.632	-4	-4	99	88	-0.4	0	0	-0.2
1954	Was-A	2	3	.400	22	3	2	0	0	60	59	8.9	4	30	4.5	33	5.0	3.75	98	.262	.338	-0	-0	99	107	-0.1	-1	0	-0.1
1955	KC-A	0	1	.000	5	1	0	0	0	12	15	11.3	4	7	5.3	8	6.0	12.00	35	.333	.407	-11	-10	106	69	-0.4	-0	-0	-0.9
Total	3	2	5	.286	28	5	2	0	0	74	81	9.9	8	42	5.1	42	5.1	5.59	68	.285	.366	-15	-15	100	100	-0.9	-1	-0	-1.2
■ **BILL KERKSIECK**	Kerksieck, Wayman William b: 12/6/13, Ulm, Ark. d: 3/11/70, Stuttgart, Ark. BR/TR, 6'1", 183 lbs. Deb: 6/21/39																												
1939	Phi-N	0	2	.000	23	2	1	0	0	63	81	11.6	13	32	4.6	13	1.9	7.14	55	.328	.390	-23	-23	99	98	-0.9	-0	-1	-2.2

YEAR	TM/L	W	L	PCT	G	GS	CG	SHO	SV	IP	H	H/G	HR	BB	BB/G	SO	SO/G	ERA	/A	OAVG	OOBP	PR	/A	PF	CPI	WAT	PB	PD	TPI
■ **JIM KERN**	Kern, James Lester b: 3/15/49, Gladwin, Mich. BR/TR, 6'5", 185 lbs. Deb: 9/06/74																												
1974	Cle-A	0	1	.000	4	3	1	0	0	15	16	9.6	1	14	8.4	11	6.6	4.80	76	.262	.395	-2	-2	101	106	-0.4	0	-0	-0.1
1975	Cle-A	1	2	.333	13	7	0	0	0	72	60	7.5	5	45	5.6	55	6.9	3.75	101	.233	.354	0	0	100	104	-0.4	0	0	0.0
1976	Cle-A	10	7	.588	50	2	0	0	15	118	91	6.9	2	50	3.8	111	8.5	2.36	148	.222	.304	15	15	100	114	1.5	0	0	1.6
1977	Cle-A	8	10	.444	60	0	0	0	18	92	85	8.3	3	47	4.6	91	8.9	3.42	117	.260	.351	7	6	98	118	0.1	0	0	0.6
1978	Cle-A	10	10	.500	58	0	0	0	13	99	77	7.0	4	58	5.3	95	8.6	3.09	114	.224	.326	8	5	94	107	1.3	0	1	0.6
1979	Tex-A	13	5	.722	71	0	0	0	29	143	99	6.2	5	62	3.9	136	8.6	1.57	267	.199	.282	**42**	**42**	99	141	4.1	0	-1	4.1
1980	Tex-A	3	11	.214	38	1	0	0	2	63	65	9.3	4	45	6.4	40	5.7	4.86	83	.279	.380	-6	-6	100	107	-3.9	0	0	-0.4
1981	Tex-A	1	2	.333	23	0	0	0	6	30	21	6.3	0	22	6.6	20	6.0	2.70	122	.204	.336	3	2	90	111	-0.5	0	-0	0.2
1982	Cin-N	3	5	.375	50	0	0	0	2	76	61	7.2	3	48	5.7	43	5.1	2.84	132	.222	.331	6	8	104	116	0.0	-1	1	0.8
	Chi-A	2	1	.667	13	1	0	0	3	28	20	6.4	3	12	3.9	23	7.4	5.14	77	.204	.286	-3	-4	97	56	0.4	0	0	-0.3
1983	Chi-A	0	0	—	1	0	0	0	0	1	1	9.0	0	0	0.0	0	0.0	0.00	—	.333	.333	0	0	102	0	0.0	0	0	0.0
1984	Phi-N	0	1	.000	8	0	0	0	0	13	20	13.8	3	10	6.9	8	5.5	10.38	35	.339	.429	-10	-10	101	80	-0.4	-0	0	-0.9
	Mil-A	1	0	1.000	6	0	0	0	0	5	6	10.8	0	3	5.4	4	7.2	0.00	—	.300	.391	2	2	93	0	0.5	0	0	0.2
1985	Mil-A	0	1	.000	5	0	0	0	0	11	14	11.5	1	5	4.1	3	2.5	6.55	67	.318	.380	-3	-3	106	88	-0.4	0	1	-0.1
1986	Cle-A	1	1	.500	16	0	0	0	0	27	34	11.3	1	23	7.7	11	3.7	8.00	51	.298	.423	-11	-12	98	76	0.0	0	0	-1.0
Total	13	53	57	.482	416	14	1	0	88	793	670	7.6	35	444	5.0	651	7.4	3.33	115	.235	.334	49	45	99	112	1.9	-0	2	5.3
■ **DICKIE KERR**	Kerr, Richard Henry b: 7/3/1893, St.Louis, Mo. d: 5/4/63, Houston, Tex. BL/TL, 5'7", 155 lbs. Deb: 4/25/19																												
1919	Chi-A	13	7	.650	39	17	10	1	0	212	208	8.8	2	64	2.7	79	3.4	2.89	114	.259	.316	8	9	102	94	0.7	4	1	1.6
1920	Chi-A	21	9	.700	45	28	19	3	**5**	254	266	9.4	7	72	2.6	72	2.6	3.37	106	.278	.331	12	5	94	101	3.6	-3	3	0.4
1921	Chi-A	19	17	.528	44	37	25	3	1	309	357	10.4	12	96	2.8	80	2.3	4.72	93	.295	.341	-15	-12	102	89	4.6	5	-1	-0.7
1925	Chi-A	0	1	.000	12	2	0	0	0	37	45	10.9	3	18	4.4	4	1.0	5.11	82	.304	.376	-3	-4	95	103	-0.4	1	0	-0.2
Total	4	53	34	.609	140	84	54	7	6	812	876	9.7	24	250	2.8	235	2.6	3.83	100	.281	.333	2	-1	99	94	8.5	7	4	1.1
■ **JOE KERRIGAN**	Kerrigan, Joseph Thomas b: 11/30/54, Philadelphia, Pa. BR/TR, 6'5", 205 lbs. Deb: 7/09/76 C																												
1976	Mon-N	2	6	.250	38	0	0	0	1	57	63	9.9	3	23	3.6	22	3.5	3.79	95	.289	.361	-2	-1	103	118	-1.0	-0	0	0.0
1977	Mon-N	3	5	.375	66	0	0	0	11	89	80	8.1	4	33	3.3	43	4.3	3.24	120	.241	.306	7	6	99	94	-0.7	-1	1	0.6
1978	Bal-A	3	1	.750	26	2	0	0	3	72	75	9.4	10	36	4.5	41	5.1	4.75	72	.273	.354	-8	-11	91	103	0.9	0	2	-0.8
1980	Bal-A	0	0	—	1	0	0	0	0	2	3	13.5	0	0	0.0	1	4.5	4.50	89	.273	.273	-0	-0	99	37	0.0	0	0	0.0
Total	4	8	12	.400	131	2	0	0	15	220	221	9.0	17	92	3.8	107	4.4	3.89	94	.264	.336	-3	-5	97	103	-0.8	-1	3	-0.2
■ **RICK KESTER**	Kester, Richard Lee b: 7/7/46, Iola, Kan. BR/TR, 6', 190 lbs. Deb: 8/18/68																												
1968	Atl-N	0	0	—	5	0	0	0	0	6	8	12.0	0	3	4.5	9	13.5	6.00	47	.308	.379	-2	-2	94	79	0.0	0	0	-0.2
1969	Atl-N	0	0	—	1	0	0	0	0	2	5	22.5	1	0	0.0	2	9.0	13.50	27	.455	.455	-2	-2	103	95	0.0	0	0	-0.1
1970	Atl-N	0	0	—	15	0	0	0	0	32	36	10.1	3	19	5.3	20	5.6	5.63	75	.283	.369	-6	-5	105	92	0.0	-1	-1	-0.6
Total	3	0	0	—	21	0	0	0	0	40	49	11.0	4	22	4.9	31	7.0	6.07	66	.299	.376	-10	-9	103	90	0.0	-1	-1	-0.9
■ **GUS KETCHUM**	Ketchum, Augustus Franklin b: 3/21/1897, Royce City, Tex. d: 9/6/80, Oklahoma City, Okla. BR/TR, 5'9.5", 170 lbs. Deb: 8/07/22																												
1922	Phi-A	0	1	.000	6	0	0	0	0	16	19	10.7	2	8	4.5	4	2.3	5.63	76	.302	.378	-3	-2	106	100	-0.4	-1	-1	-0.2
■ **HENRY KEUPPER**	Keupper, Henry J. b: 6/24/1887, Staunton, Ill. d: 8/14/60, Marion, Ill. BL/TL, 6'1", 185 lbs. Deb: 4/19/14																												
1914	StL-F	8	20	.286	42	25	12	1	0	213	256	10.8	3	49	2.1	70	3.0	4.27	81	.291	.332	-25	-19	108	84	-4.8	2	5	-1.1
■ **JIMMY KEY**	Key, James Edward b: 4/22/61, Huntsville, Ala. BR/TL, 6'1", 185 lbs. Deb: 4/06/84																												
1984	Tor-A	4	5	.444	63	0	0	0	10	62	70	10.2	8	32	4.6	44	6.4	4.65	87	.286	.361	-4	-4	101	113	-0.8	0	1	-0.2
1985	Tor-A	14	6	.700	35	32	3	0	0	213	188	7.9	22	50	2.1	85	3.6	3.00	137	.237	.280	27	26	99	103	2.4	0	4	3.2
1986	Tor-A	14	11	.560	36	35	4	2	0	232	222	8.6	24	74	2.9	141	5.5	3.57	122	.256	.312	16	21	104	107	0.9	0	3	2.4
1987	Tor-A	17	8	.680	36	36	8	1	0	261	210	**7.2**	24	66	2.3	161	5.6	**2.76**	**161**	**.221**	**.269**	**50**	**49**	99	96	3.1	0	2	**5.1**
1988	Tor-A	12	5	.706	21	21	2	2	0	131	127	8.7	13	30	2.1	65	4.5	3.30	119	.250	.294	10	9	99	102	3.3	0	0	0.9
Total	5	61	35	.635	191	124	17	5	10	899	817	8.2	91	252	2.5	496	5.0	3.23	131	.243	.294	98	101	101	102	8.9	0	10	11.4
■ **JOE KIEFER**	Kiefer, Joseph William "Harlem Joe" or "Smoke" b: 7/19/1899, W.Leyden, N.Y. d: 7/5/75, Utica, N.Y. BR/TR, 5'11", 190 lbs. Deb: 10/01/20																												
1920	Chi-A	0	1	.000	2	1	0	0	0	5	7	12.6	0	5	9.0	1	1.8	14.40	25	.333	.481	-6	-6	94	50	-0.4	-0	-0	-0.5
1925	Bos-A	0	2	.000	2	2	0	0	0	15	20	12.0	1	9	5.4	4	2.4	6.00	73	.351	.400	-3	-3	99	108	-0.9	-1	1	-0.1
1926	Bos-A	0	2	.000	11	1	0	0	0	30	29	8.7	2	16	4.8	4	1.2	4.80	89	.266	.351	-3	-2	106	92	-0.9	-0	0	-0.1
Total	3	0	5	.000	15	4	0	0	0	50	56	10.1	2	30	5.4	9	1.6	6.12	69	.299	.381	-11	-11	103	92	-2.2	-1	1	-0.7
■ **LEO KIELY**	Kiely, Leo Patrick "Kiki" b: 11/30/29, Hoboken, N.J. d: 1/18/84, Montclair, N.J. BL/TL, 6'2", 180 lbs. Deb: 6/27/51																												
1951	Bos-A	7	7	.500	17	16	4	0	0	113	106	8.4	9	39	3.1	46	3.7	3.35	131	.251	.310	10	13	106	108	-0.8	-1	1	1.4
1954	Bos-A	5	8	.385	28	19	4	1	0	131	153	10.5	12	58	4.0	59	4.1	3.50	107	.295	.360	3	4	101	140	-0.9	1	-1	0.3
1955	Bos-A	3	3	.500	33	4	0	0	6	90	91	9.1	5	37	3.7	36	3.6	2.80	173	.269	.333	12	**20**	122	139	-0.2	-1	1	2.3
1956	Bos-A	2	2	.500	23	0	0	0	3	31	47	13.6	1	14	4.1	9	2.6	5.23	81	.362	.406	-4	-3	102	128	-0.1	-0	0	-0.3
1958	Bos-A	5	2	.714	47	0	0	0	12	81	77	8.6	3	18	2.0	26	2.9	3.00	132	.254	.292	7	9	105	98	1.5	-2	1	0.8
1959	Bos-A	3	3	.500	41	0	0	0	7	56	67	10.8	8	18	2.9	30	4.8	4.18	97	.299	.345	-2	-1	105	125	0.1	-1	1	0.0
1960	KC-A	1	2	.333	20	0	0	0	1	21	21	9.0	1	5	2.1	6	2.6	1.71	229	.266	.314	5	5	101	197	-0.1	0	1	0.7
Total	7	26	27	.491	209	39	8	1	29	523	562	9.7	39	189	3.3	212	3.6	3.37	124	.279	.335	31	46	107	126	-0.5	-4	5	5.2
■ **JOHN KILEY**	Kiley, John Frederick b: 7/1/1859, S.Dedham, Mass. d: 12/18/40, Norwood, Mass. BL/TL, Deb: 5/01/1884																												
1891	Bos-N	0	1	.000	1	1	1	0	0	8	13	14.6	3	5	5.6	1	1.1	6.75	54	.380	.459	-3	-3	109	142	-0.4	-0	0	-0.1
■ **PAUL KILGUS**	Kilgus, Paul Nelson b: 2/2/62, Bowling Green, Ky. BL/TL, 6'1", 175 lbs. Deb: 6/07/87																												
1987	Tex-A	2	7	.222	25	12	0	0	0	89	95	9.6	14	31	3.1	42	4.2	4.15	112	.271	.332	3	5	104	113	-2.3	0	-1	0.4
1988	Tex-A	12	15	.444	32	32	5	3	0	203	190	8.4	18	71	3.1	88	3.9	4.17	98	.243	.311	-4	-2	102	84	0.3	0	1	-0.1
Total	2	14	22	.389	57	44	5	3	0	292	285	8.8	32	102	3.1	130	4.0	4.16	102	.252	.318	-1	3	103	93	-2.0	0	0	0.3
■ **MIKE KILKENNY**	Kilkenny, Michael David b: 4/11/45, Bradford, Ont., Can. BR/TL, 6'3.5", 175 lbs. Deb: 4/11/69																												
1969	Det-A	8	6	.571	39	15	6	4	2	128	99	7.0	13	63	4.4	97	6.8	3.38	110	.211	.305	4	5	102	91	0.3	-3	0	0.2
1970	Det-A	7	6	.538	36	21	3	0	0	129	141	9.8	10	70	4.9	105	7.3	5.16	75	.279	.362	-21	-19	104	91	0.7	-3	0	-2.0
1971	Det-A	4	5	.444	30	11	2	0	1	86	83	8.7	8	44	4.6	47	4.9	5.02	66	.247	.333	-15	-17	95	76	-0.9	-1	-0	-1.8
1972	Det-A	0	0	—	1	0	0	0	0	1	1	9.0	1	0	0.0	0	0.0	9.00	38	.250	.250	-1	-1	112	105	0.0	0	0	0.0
	Oak-A	0	0	—	1	0	0	0	0	1	0	0.0	0	0	0.0	0	0.0	0.00	—	.000	.000	0	0	95	0	0.0	0	0	0.0
	Yr	0	0	—	2	0	0	0	0	2	1	4.5	1	0	0.0	0	0.0	4.50	71	.143	.143	-0	-0	103	0	0.0	0	0	0.0
	SD-N	0	0	—	5	0	0	0	0	4	7	15.8	1	3	6.8	5	11.3	9.00	35	.350	.435	-2	-3	91	98	0.0	0	0	-0.2
	Cle-A	4	1	.800	22	7	1	0	1	58	51	7.9	5	39	6.1	44	6.8	3.41	97	.237	.353	-2	-1	108	117	1.6	-1	1	0.0
1973	Cle-A	0	0	—	5	0	0	0	0	2	5	22.5	1	5	22.5	3	13.5	22.50	17	.455	.647	-4	-4	99	94	0.0	0	0	-0.3
Total	5	23	18	.561	139	54	12	4	4	409	387	8.5	39	224	4.9	301	6.6	4.44	81	.248	.340	-41	-38	102	91	1.7	-8	1	-4.1
■ **EVANS KILLEEN**	Killeen, Evans Henry b: 2/27/36, Brooklyn, N.Y. BR/TR, 6', 190 lbs. Deb: 9/07/59																												
1959	KC-A	0	0	—	4	0	0	0	0	6	4	6.0	0	4	6.0	1	1.5	4.50	88	.211	.348	-0	-0	103	70	0.0	0	-0	0.0
■ **HENRY KILLEEN**	Killeen, Henry b: 1871, Troy, N.Y. Deb: 9/11/1891																												
1891	Cle-N	0	1	.000	1	1	1	0	0	9	11	11.0	1	8	8.0	3	3.0	7.00	51	.315	.443	-4	-3	106	90	-0.4	-0	0	-0.2
■ **FRANK KILLEN**	Killen, Frank Bissell "Lefty" b: 11/30/1870, Pittsburgh, Pa. d: 12/3/39, Pittsburgh, Pa. BL/TL, 6'1", 200 lbs. Deb: 8/27/1891																												
1891	CM-a	7	4	.636	11	11	11	2	0	97	73	6.8	1	51	4.7	38	3.5	1.67	251	.222	.326	22	27	113	139	1.8	2	0	3.0
1892	Was-N	29	26	.527	60	52	46	2	0	460	448	8.8	15	182	3.6	147	2.9	3.31	106	.268	.340	-1	9	106	100	8.9	7	3	2.1
1893	Pit-N	**34**	14	.708	55	48	38	2	0	415	401	8.7	12	140	3.0	99	2.1	3.64	134	.269	.332	48	58	105	91	7.3	12	3	6.4
1894	Pit-N	14	11	.560	28	28	20	1	0	204	261	11.5	3	86	3.8	62	2.7	4.50	112	.334	.400	19	12	95	110	1.8	1	0	1.0
1895	Pit-N	5	5	.500	13	11	6	0	0	95	113	10.7	2	57	5.4	25	2.4	5.49	84	.316	.410	-7	-9	96	92	-0.3	3	0	-0.4
1896	Pit-N	**30**	18	.625	**52**	50	**44**	**5**	0	**432**	476	9.9	7	119	2.5	134	2.8	3.42	118	.302	.351	46	30	93	105	7.8	9	2	3.5

YEAR	TM/L	W	L	PCT	G	GS	CG	SHO	SV	IP	H	H/G	HR	BB	BB/G	SO	SO/G	ERA	/A	OAVG	OOBP	PR	/A	PF	CPI	WAT	PB	PD	TPI
1897	Pit-N	17	23	.425	42	41	**38**	1	0	337	417	11.1	4	76	2.0	99	2.6	4.46	97	.327	.364	-5	-6	100	90	-1.9	4	1	0.0
1898	Pit-N	10	11	.476	23	23	17	0	0	178	201	10.2	3	41	2.1	48	2.4	3.74	95	.307	.348	-3	-4	98	95	-0.2	2	0	-0.1
	Was-N	6	9	.400	17	16	15	0	0	128	149	10.5	4	29	2.0	43	3.0	3.59	105	.313	.353	0	3	105	106	0.8	3	0	0.7
	Yr	16	20	.444	40	39	32	0	0	306	350	10.3	7	70	2.1	91	2.7	3.68	99	.310	.350	-2	-1	101	106	0.6	2	0	0.6
1899	Was-N	0	2	.000	2	2	1	0	0	12	18	13.5	0	4	3.0	3	2.3	6.00	63	.372	.420	-3	-3	98	91	-0.9	-0	0	-0.2
	Bos-N	7	5	.583	12	12	11	0	0	99	108	9.8	3	26	2.4	23	2.1	4.27	93	.301	.349	-5	-3	103	82	-0.3	-2	0	-0.4
	Yr	7	7	.500	14	14	12	0	0	111	126	10.2	3	30	2.4	26	2.1	4.46	88	.310	.357	-7	-6	102	82	-1.2	-0	0	-0.6
1900	Chi-N	3	3	.500	6	6	6	0	0	54	65	10.8	1	11	1.8	4	0.7	4.67	75	.322	.357	-6	-7	94	83	0.2	-1	0	-0.6
Total	10	162	131	.553	321	300	253	13	0	2511	2730	9.8	55	822	2.9	725	2.6	3.78	111	.296	.354	105	112	101	99	25.0	40	8	15.0

■ **ED KILLIAN** Killian, Edwin Henry "Twilight Ed" b: 11/12/1876, Racine, Wis. d: 7/18/28, Detroit, Mich. BL/TL, 5'11", 170 lbs. Deb: 8/25/03

YEAR	TM/L	W	L	PCT	G	GS	CG	SHO	SV	IP	H	H/G	HR	BB	BB/G	SO	SO/G	ERA	/A	OAVG	OOBP	PR	/A	PF	CPI	WAT	PB	PD	TPI
1903	Cle-A	3	4	.429	9	8	7	3	0	62	61	8.9	1	13	1.9	18	2.6	2.47	114	.279	.320	3	2	95	118	-0.7	-0	-0	0.2
1904	Det-A	14	20	.412	40	34	32	4	1	332	293	7.9	0	93	2.5	124	3.4	2.44	104	.259	.315	6	4	98	100	0.1	-3	-5	-0.1
1905	Det-A	23	14	.622	39	37	33	**8**	0	313	263	7.6	0	102	2.9	110	3.2	2.27	117	.251	.317	13	13	100	108	5.0	7	-4	1.0
1906	Det-A	10	6	.625	21	16	14	0	2	150	165	9.9	0	54	3.2	47	2.8	3.42	87	.305	.369	-12	-8	110	109	2.5	-1	-2	-1.0
1907	Det-A	25	13	.658	41	34	29	3	1	314	286	8.2	1	91	2.6	96	2.8	1.78	140	.266	.323	27	25	98	**143**	2.8	10	-2	4.0
1908	Det-A	12	9	.571	27	23	15	0	1	181	170	8.5	3	53	2.6	47	2.3	2.98	79	.252	.314	-12	-13	99	100	-0.2	-3	3	-1.0
1909	Det-A	11	9	.550	25	19	14	3	1	173	150	7.8	1	49	2.5	54	2.8	1.72	153	.236	.297	15	18	106	121	-1.6	-2	-1	2.0
1910	Det-A	4	3	.571	11	9	5	1	0	74	75	9.1	2	27	3.3	20	2.4	3.04	83	.268	.345	-4	-4	100	115	0.1	-1	-1	-0.6
Total	8	102	78	.567	213	180	149	22	6	1599	1463	8.2	8	482	2.7	516	2.9	2.38	109	.261	.322	35	38	101	114	8.0	7	-13	4.5

■ **JACK KILLILAY** Killilay, John William b: 5/24/1887, Leavenworth, Kan. d: 10/21/68, Tulsa, Okla. BR/TR, 5'11", 165 lbs. Deb: 5/13/11

YEAR	TM/L	W	L	PCT	G	GS	CG	SHO	SV	IP	H	H/G	HR	BB	BB/G	SO	SO/G	ERA	/A	OAVG	OOBP	PR	/A	PF	CPI	WAT	PB	PD	TPI
1911	Bos-A	4	2	.667	14	7	1	0	0	61	65	9.6	0	36	5.3	28	4.1	3.54	93	.302	.425	-1	-2	99	144	1.0	-2	0	-0.1

■ **MATT KILROY** Kilroy, Matthew Aloysius "Matches" b: 6/21/1866, Philadelphia, Pa. d: 3/2/40, Philadelphia, Pa. TL , 5'9", 175 lbs. Deb: 4/17/1886

YEAR	TM/L	W	L	PCT	G	GS	CG	SHO	SV	IP	H	H/G	HR	BB	BB/G	SO	SO/G	ERA	/A	OAVG	OOBP	PR	/A	PF	CPI	WAT	PB	PD	TPI
1886	Bal-a	29	34	.460	**68**	68	**66**	5	0	583	476	7.3	10	182	2.8	**513**	**7.9**	3.37	96	.232	.295	5	-8	94	76	7.9	-4	6	-0.6
1887	Bal-a	**46**	19	.708	**69**	69	**66**	**6**	0	**589**	585	8.9	9	157	2.4	217	3.3	3.07	132	.272	.322	**80**	64	94	106	**15.4**	9	10	**6.9**
1888	Bal-a	17	21	.447	40	40	35	2	0	321	347	9.7	5	79	2.2	135	3.8	4.04	74	.289	.333	-35	-37	98	88	1.4	-0	-1	-3.3
1889	Bal-a	29	25	.537	59	56	**55**	5	0	481	476	8.9	8	142	2.7	217	4.1	2.86	134	.273	.328	53	51	99	108	1.7	11	9	**6.5**
1890	Bos-P	9	15	.375	30	27	18	0	0	218	268	11.1	14	87	3.6	48	2.0	4.29	102	.315	.378	-1	3	104	109	-5.3	-0	0	0.2
1891	CM-a	1	4	.200	7	6	4	0	0	45	51	10.2	1	19	3.8	6	1.2	3.00	140	.300	.371	4	6	113	134	-1.4	-1	0	0.5
1892	Was-N	1	1	.500	4	3	2	0	0	26	20	6.9	0	15	5.2	1	0.3	2.42	144	.224	.336	2	3	106	104	0.2	-0	0	0.3
1893	Lou-N	3	2	.600	5	5	5	1	0	35	57	14.7	2	23	5.9	4	1.0	9.00	51	.383	.465	-17	-17	98	86	0.9	3	0	-1.0
1894	Lou-N	0	5	.000	8	7	3	0	0	37	46	11.2	2	20	4.9	11	2.7	3.89	124	.327	.411	6	4	91	138	-2.4	-2	0	0.2
1898	Chi-N	6	7	.462	13	11	10	0	0	100	119	10.7	2	30	2.7	18	1.6	4.32	85	.318	.369	-8	-7	102	94	-1.2	2	0	-0.6
Total	10	141	133	.515	303	292	264	19	0	2435	2445	9.0	53	754	2.8	1170	4.3	3.48	107	.274	.331	89	62	97	97	17.2	18	24	9.1

■ **MIKE KILROY** Kilroy, Michael Joseph b: 11/4/1872, Philadelphia, Pa. d: 10/2/60, Philadelphia, Pa. TR , Deb: 1888

YEAR	TM/L	W	L	PCT	G	GS	CG	SHO	SV	IP	H	H/G	HR	BB	BB/G	SO	SO/G	ERA	/A	OAVG	OOBP	PR	/A	PF	CPI	WAT	PB	PD	TPI
1888	Bal-a	0	1	.000	1	1	1	0	0	9	12	12.0	1	5	5.0	1	1.0	8.00	37	.334	.415	-5	-5	98	80	-0.4	-1	0	-0.3
1891	Phi-N	0	2	.000	3	1	0	0	0	10	15	13.5	1	4	3.6	3	2.7	9.90	32	.361	.417	-7	-7	95	63	-0.9	1	0	-0.4
Total	2	0	3	.000	4	2	1	0	0	19	27	12.8	2	9	4.3	4	1.9	9.00	34	.349	.416	-12	-12	97	71	-1.3	0	0	-0.7

■ **NEWT KIMBALL** Kimball, Newell W. b: 3/27/15, Logan, Utah BR/TR, 6'2.5", 190 lbs. Deb: 5/07/37

YEAR	TM/L	W	L	PCT	G	GS	CG	SHO	SV	IP	H	H/G	HR	BB	BB/G	SO	SO/G	ERA	/A	OAVG	OOBP	PR	/A	PF	CPI	WAT	PB	PD	TPI
1937	Chi-N	0	0	—	2	0	0	0	0	5	12	21.6	1	1	1.8	0	0.0	10.80	36	.444	.464	-4	-4	100	100	0.0	-0	0	-0.2
1938	Chi-N	0	0	—	1	0	0	0	0	1	3	27.0	0	0	0.0	1	9.0	9.00	43	.500	.500	-1	-1	103	130	0.0	0	0	0.0
1940	Bro-N	3	1	.750	21	0	0	0	1	34	29	7.7	2	15	4.0	21	5.6	3.18	129	.238	.310	3	3	106	110	0.8	-1	-0	0.3
	StL-N	1	0	1.000	2	1	1	0	0	14	11	7.1	1	6	3.9	6	3.9	2.57	151	.208	.288	2	2	101	102	0.5	1	-0	0.3
	Yr	4	1	.800	23	1	1	0	1	48	40	7.5	3	21	3.9	27	5.1	3.00	135	.229	.303	5	6	105	102	1.3	-1	-0	0.6
1941	Bro-N	3	1	.750	15	5	1	0	1	52	43	7.4	0	29	5.0	17	2.9	3.63	99	.225	.320	-0	-0	99	79	0.6	0	0	0.0
1942	Bro-N	2	0	1.000	14	1	0	0	0	29	27	8.4	0	19	5.9	8	2.5	3.72	86	.265	.379	-1	-2	97	115	1.0	-0	-1	-0.2
1943	Bro-N	1	1	.500	5	0	0	0	1	11	9	7.4	0	5	4.1	2	1.6	1.64	204	.214	.298	2	2	99	130	0.0	-0	-0	0.2
	Phi-N	1	6	.143	34	6	2	0	2	90	85	8.5	4	42	4.2	33	3.3	4.10	79	.253	.326	-7	-9	96	88	-2.2	1	-2	-0.9
	Yr	2	7	.222	39	6	2	0	3	101	94	8.4	4	47	4.2	35	3.1	3.83	84	.249	.323	-5	-7	96	88	-2.2	-0	-2	-0.7
Total	6	11	9	.550	94	13	4	0	5	236	219	8.4	8	117	4.5	88	3.4	3.78	92	.249	.330	-6	-8	99	96	0.7	1	-4	-0.5

■ **SAM KIMBER** Kimber, Samuel Jackson b: 10/29/1852, Philadelphia, Pa. d: 11/7/25, Philadelphia, Pa. BR/TR, 5'10.5", 165 lbs. Deb: 5/01/1884

YEAR	TM/L	W	L	PCT	G	GS	CG	SHO	SV	IP	H	H/G	HR	BB	BB/G	SO	SO/G	ERA	/A	OAVG	OOBP	PR	/A	PF	CPI	WAT	PB	PD	TPI
1884	Bro-a	17	20	.459	40	40	40	3	0	352	363	9.3	6	69	1.8	119	3.0	3.91	83	.275	.311	-26	-27	100	90	3.3	-5	-2	-2.8
1885	Pro-N	0	1	.000	1	1	1	0	0	8	15	16.9	1	5	5.6	4	4.5	11.25	23	.411	.482	-7	-8	93	83	-0.4	-0	0	-0.5
Total	2	17	21	.447	41	41	41	3	0	360	378	9.4	7	74	1.9	123	3.1	4.07	79	.278	.316	-34	-34	99	90	2.9	-5	-2	-3.3

■ **HARRY KIMBERLIN** Kimberlin, Harry Lydle "Murphy" or "Mule Trader" b: 3/13/09, Sullivan, Mo. BR/TR, 6'3", 175 lbs. Deb: 7/11/36

YEAR	TM/L	W	L	PCT	G	GS	CG	SHO	SV	IP	H	H/G	HR	BB	BB/G	SO	SO/G	ERA	/A	OAVG	OOBP	PR	/A	PF	CPI	WAT	PB	PD	TPI
1936	StL-A	0	0	—	13	0	0	0	0	20	24	10.8	3	16	7.2	4	1.8	5.40	100	.296	.408	-1	-0	107	126	0.0	-0	-0	0.0
1937	StL-A	0	2	.000	3	2	1	0	0	15	16	9.6	2	9	5.4	5	3.0	2.40	199	.254	.347	4	4	103	187	-0.9	0	0	0.4
1938	StL-A	0	0	—	1	1	1	0	0	8	8	9.0	1	3	3.4	1	1.1	3.38	146	.286	.344	1	1	103	154	0.0	-0	-0	0.1
1939	StL-A	1	2	.333	17	3	0	0	0	41	59	13.0	6	19	4.2	11	2.4	5.49	88	.326	.390	-4	-3	105	123	0.1	0	0	-0.1
Total	4	1	4	.200	34	6	2	0	0	84	107	11.5	12	47	5.0	21	2.3	4.71	105	.303	.383	0	2	105	138	-0.8	0	-1	0.4

■ **HAL KIME** Kime, Harold Lee "Lefty" b: 3/15/1899, W.Salem, Ohio d: 5/16/39, Columbus, Ohio BL/TL, 5'9", 160 lbs. Deb: 6/19/20

YEAR	TM/L	W	L	PCT	G	GS	CG	SHO	SV	IP	H	H/G	HR	BB	BB/G	SO	SO/G	ERA	/A	OAVG	OOBP	PR	/A	PF	CPI	WAT	PB	PD	TPI
1920	StL-N	0	0	—	4	0	0	0	0	7	9	11.6	0	2	2.6	1	1.3	2.57	119	.333	.400	0	0	98	192	0.0	-0	0	0.0

■ **CHAD KIMSEY** Kimsey, Clyde Elias b: 8/6/06, Copperhill, Tenn. d: 12/3/42, Pryor, Okla. BL/TR, 6'2", 200 lbs. Deb: 4/21/29

YEAR	TM/L	W	L	PCT	G	GS	CG	SHO	SV	IP	H	H/G	HR	BB	BB/G	SO	SO/G	ERA	/A	OAVG	OOBP	PR	/A	PF	CPI	WAT	PB	PD	TPI
1929	StL-A	3	6	.333	24	3	1	0	1	64	88	12.4	2	19	2.7	13	1.8	5.06	83	.370	.399	-6	-6	100	124	-1.6	3	3	0.0
1930	StL-A	6	10	.375	42	4	1	0	1	113	139	11.1	8	45	3.6	32	2.5	6.37	80	.312	.368	-22	-16	110	87	-0.8	7	1	-0.5
1931	StL-A	4	6	.400	42	1	0	0	7	94	121	11.6	1	27	2.6	27	2.6	4.40	104	.312	.353	-0	**2**	105	109	0.0	5	2	0.9
1932	StL-A	4	2	.667	33	0	0	0	3	78	85	9.8	3	33	3.8	13	1.5	4.04	114	.281	.343	4	5	103	111	1.3	2	1	0.7
	Chi-A	1	1	.500	7	0	0	0	2	11	8	6.5	0	5	4.1	6	4.9	2.45	166	.211	.311	2	2	91	115	0.3	-0	1	0.3
	Yr	5	3	.625	40	0	0	0	5	89	93	9.4	3	38	3.8	19	1.9	3.84	118	.274	.339	6	**7**	101	115	1.6	2	2	1.0
1933	Chi-A	4	1	.800	28	2	0	0	0	96	124	11.6	7	36	3.4	19	1.8	5.53	80	.318	.373	-13	-12	103	104	1.6	-2	1	-1.1
1936	Det-A	2	3	.400	22	0	0	0	3	52	58	10.0	2	29	5.0	11	1.9	4.85	98	.284	.370	1	-0	95	103	-0.6	2	2	0.3
Total	6	24	29	.453	198	10	2	0	17	508	623	11.0	23	194	3.4	121	2.1	5.08	91	.311	.365	-34	-25	103	105	0.2	16	11	0.6

■ **ELLIS KINDER** Kinder, Ellis Raymond "Old Folks" b: 7/26/14, Atkins, Ark. d: 10/16/68, Jackson, Tenn. BR/TR, 6', 195 lbs. Deb: 4/30/46

YEAR	TM/L	W	L	PCT	G	GS	CG	SHO	SV	IP	H	H/G	HR	BB	BB/G	SO	SO/G	ERA	/A	OAVG	OOBP	PR	/A	PF	CPI	WAT	PB	PD	TPI
1946	StL-A	3	3	.500	33	7	1	0	1	87	78	8.1	8	36	3.7	59	6.1	3.31	106	.241	.311	2	2	100	104	0.4	-1	-1	0.0
1947	StL-A	8	15	.348	34	26	10	2	1	194	201	9.3	11	82	3.8	110	5.1	4.50	87	.264	.334	-17	-13	106	85	-1.1	-4	-3	-1.8
1948	Bos-A	10	7	.588	28	22	10	1	0	178	183	9.3	10	63	3.2	53	2.7	3.74	111	.266	.325	11	8	97	103	-0.4	-3	-3	0.2
1949	Bos-A	23	6	**.793**	43	30	19	**6**	4	252	251	9.0	21	99	3.5	138	4.9	3.36	129	.260	.324	24	27	103	114	7.3	-4	-4	1.9
1950	Bos-A	14	12	.538	48	23	11	1	9	207	212	9.2	23	78	3.4	95	4.1	4.26	119	.263	.322	7	19	111	97	-1.7	-2	-2	1.6
1771	Bos-A	11	2	.846	**63**	2	1	0	**14**	127	108	7.7	9	46	3.3	84	6.0	2.55	172	.230	.293	**22**	**26**	106	117	4.3	-3	-1	2.2
1952	Bos-A	5	6	.455	23	10	4	0	4	98	85	7.8	11	28	2.6	50	4.6	2.57	153	.234	.285	12	15	107	121	-0.4	-5	0	1.1
1953	Bos-A	10	6	.625	**69**	0	0	0	**27**	107	84	7.1	8	38	3.2	39	3.3	1.85	234	.215	.281	**25**	**29**	108	142	1.5	3	0	3.4
1954	Bos-A	8	8	.500	48	2	0	0	15	107	106	8.9	7	36	3.0	67	5.6	3.62	104	.260	.311	1	2	101	96	0.8	1	-2	0.1
1955	Bos-A	5	5	.500	43	0	0	0	18	67	57	7.7	5	15	2.0	31	4.2	2.82	172	.229	.269	9	15	122	88	-0.3	0	-1	1.5
1956	StL-N	2	0	1.000	22	0	0	0	6	26	23	8.0	3	9	3.1	4	1.4	3.46	108	.245	.296	1	1	99	101	1.0	-0	-1	0.0
	Chi-A	3	1	.750	29	0	0	0	3	30	33	9.9	2	8	2.4	19	5.7	2.70	157	.277	.315	5	5	102	138	0.9	-0	-0	0.4
1957	Chi-A	0	0	—	1	0	0	0	0	1	0	0.0	0	1	9.0	0	0.0	0.00	—	.000	.200	0	0	97	0	0.0	0	0	0.0
Total	12	102	71	.590	484	122	56	10	102	1481	1421	8.6	118	539	3.3	749	4.6	3.43	124	.252	.312	102	136	105	106	12.3	-19	-16	10.6

■ **SILVER KING** King, Charles Frederick (born Charles Frederick Koenig) b: 1/11/1868, St.Louis, Mo. d: 5/21/38, St.Louis, Mo. BR/TR, 6', 170 lbs. Deb: 9/02/1886

YEAR	TM/L	W	L	PCT	G	GS	CG	SHO	SV	IP	H	H/G	HR	BB	BB/G	SO	SO/G	ERA	/A	OAVG	OOBP	PR	/A	PF	CPI	WAT	PB	PD	TPI
1886	KC-N	1	3	.250	5	5	5	0	0	39	43	9.9	1	9	2.1	23	5.3	4.85	78	.293	.334	-7	-5	114	75	0.0	-2	0	-0.5
1887	StL-a	32	12	.727	46	44	43	2	1	390	401	9.3	4	109	2.5	128	3.0	3.78	119	.279	.330	22	31	105	91	2.5	-4	-2	2.1

YEAR	TM/L	W	L	PCT	G	GS	CG	SHO	SV	IP	H	H/G	HR	BB	BB/G	SO	SO/G	ERA	/A	OAVG	OOBP	PR	/A	PF	CPI	WAT	PB	PD	TPI
1888	StL-a	**45**	21	.682	**66**	65	**64**	**6**	0	**586**	437	6.7	6	76	**1.2**	258	4.0	**1.64**	**198**	.219	**.248**	**92**	**105**	106	93	0.1	10	0	**11.9**
1889	StL-a	35	16	.686	56	53	47	3	1	458	462	9.1	15	125	2.5	188	3.7	3.14	133	.277	.327	36	52	109	103	2.3	2	0	5.1
1890	Chi-P	30	22	.577	56	56	48	**4**	0	461	420	**8.2**	5	163	3.2	185	3.6	**2.69**	**161**	**.254**	.321	**79**	**84**	103	94	2.6	-6	8	**7.4**
1891	Pit-N	14	29	.326	48	44	40	3	1	384	382	9.0	7	144	3.4	160	3.8	3.12	110	.273	.341	10	13	102	97	-5.7	-2	-1	1.0
1892	NY-N	23	24	.489	52	47	46	1	0	419	397	8.5	15	174	3.7	177	3.8	3.24	100	.263	.339	2	-1	98	100	1.2	6	-1	0.4
1893	NY-N	3	4	.429	7	7	4	0	0	49	69	12.7	4	26	4.8	13	2.4	8.63	56	.349	.425	-22	-21	103	75	-0.5	1	0	-1.4
	Cin-N	5	6	.455	17	15	8	1	1	105	119	10.2	2	56	4.8	30	2.6	4.89	98	.301	.388	-2	-1	102	95	-0.5	-0	0	0.0
	Yr	8	10	.444	24	22	12	1	1	154	188	11.0	6	82	4.8	43	2.5	6.08	79	.317	.400	-24	-22	102	95	-1.0	1	0	-1.4
1896	Was-N	10	7	.588	22	16	12	0	1	145	179	11.1	3	43	2.7	35	2.2	4.10	102	.326	.375	4	2	96	106	2.5	4	0	0.5
1897	Was-N	6	9	.400	23	19	12	0	1	154	196	11.5	7	45	2.6	32	1.9	4.79	91	.333	.380	-8	-7	102	97	-1.0	0	0	-0.4
Total	10	204	153	.571	398	371	329	20	6	3190	3105	8.8	69	970	2.7	1229	3.5	3.18	123	.269	.326	207	253	104	96	3.5	10	5	26.1
■ **CLYDE KING**	King, Clyde Edward b: 5/23/25, Goldsboro, N.C. BB/TR, 6'1", 175 lbs. Deb: 6/21/44 MC																												
1944	Bro-N	2	1	.667	14	3	1	0	0	44	42	8.6	1	12	2.5	14	2.9	3.07	120	.256	.307	3	3	102	101	0.7	-0	-1	0.2
1945	Bro-N	5	5	.500	42	2	0	0	3	112	131	10.5	8	48	3.9	29	2.3	4.10	88	.295	.356	-4	-6	95	119	-0.5	-2	1	-0.6
1947	Bro-N	6	5	.545	29	9	2	0	0	88	85	8.7	11	29	3.0	31	3.2	2.76	151	.252	.309	13	14	103	137	-0.5	-1	-1	1.2
1948	Bro-N	0	1	.000	9	0	0	0	0	12	14	10.5	3	6	4.5	5	3.8	8.25	49	.286	.375	-6	-6	103	77	-0.4	-0	0	-0.4
1951	Bro-N	14	7	.667	48	3	1	0	6	121	118	8.8	15	50	3.7	33	2.5	4.17	90	.263	.335	-3	-6	95	106	1.5	0	0	-0.4
1952	Bro-N	2	0	1.000	23	0	0	0	0	43	56	11.7	5	12	2.5	17	3.6	5.02	73	.318	.361	-6	-6	98	110	1.0	-1	1	-0.5
1953	Cin-N	3	6	.333	35	4	0	0	2	76	78	9.2	15	32	3.8	21	2.5	5.21	83	.271	.344	-8	-8	100	101	-1.1	-1	-0	-0.7
Total	7	32	25	.561	200	21	4	0	11	496	524	9.5	58	189	3.4	150	2.7	4.14	93	.275	.338	-11	-15	98	113	0.7	-4	0	-1.2
■ **ERIC KING**	King, Eric Steven b: 4/10/64, Oxnard, Cal. BR/TR, 6'2", 180 lbs. Deb: 5/15/86																												
1986	Det-A	11	4	.733	33	16	3	1	3	138	108	7.0	11	63	4.1	79	5.2	3.52	112	.216	.309	10	7	95	88	3.4	0	0	0.7
1987	Det-A	6	9	.400	55	4	0	0	9	116	111	8.6	15	60	4.7	89	6.9	4.89	87	.251	.341	-5	-8	96	91	-2.6	0	2	-0.4
1988	Det-A	4	1	.800	23	5	0	0	3	69	60	7.8	5	34	4.4	45	5.9	3.39	110	.233	.327	4	3	94	108	1.4	0	-0	0.2
Total	3	21	14	.600	111	25	3	1	15	323	279	7.8	31	157	4.4	213	5.9	3.98	101	.232	.325	9	1	95	93	2.2	0	2	0.5
■ **NELLIE KING**	King, Nelson Joseph b: 3/15/28, Shenandoah, Pa. BR/TR, 6'6", 185 lbs. Deb: 4/15/54																												
1954	Pit-N	0	0	—	4	0	0	0	0	7	10	12.9	0	1	1.3	3	3.9	5.14	81	.400	.355	-1	-1	102	121	0.0	0	0	0.0
1955	Pit-N	1	3	.250	17	4	0	0	0	54	60	10.0	2	14	2.3	21	3.5	3.00	136	.286	.328	6	6	101	129	-0.6	-2	-0	0.4
1956	Pit-N	4	1	.800	38	0	0	0	5	60	54	8.1	8	19	2.9	25	3.8	3.15	124	.241	.301	4	5	103	109	1.6	-1	-1	0.3
1957	Pit-N	2	1	.667	36	0	0	0	1	52	69	11.9	7	16	2.8	23	4.0	4.50	83	.337	.380	-4	-5	96	138	0.7	-1	-0	-0.5
Total	4	7	5	.583	95	4	0	0	6	173	193	10.0	17	50	2.6	72	3.7	3.59	109	.291	.336	6	6	100	124	1.7	-3	-1	0.2
■ **BRIAN KINGMAN**	Kingman, Brian Paul b: 7/27/54, Los Angeles, Cal. BR/TR, 6'2", 200 lbs. Deb: 6/28/79																												
1979	Oak-A	8	7	.533	18	17	5	1	0	113	113	9.0	10	33	2.6	58	4.6	4.30	90	.258	.310	-1	-6	91	83	2.4	0	-2	-0.6
1980	Oak-A	8	20	.286	32	30	10	1	0	211	209	8.9	21	82	3.5	116	4.9	3.84	99	.256	.323	5	-1	94	99	-6.8	0	-2	-0.2
1981	Oak-A	3	6	.333	18	15	3	1	0	100	112	10.1	10	32	2.9	52	4.7	3.96	88	.286	.340	-3	-5	95	115	-1.9	0	-2	-0.6
1982	Oak-A	4	12	.250	23	20	3	0	1	123	131	9.6	11	57	4.2	46	3.4	4.46	88	.279	.356	-5	-7	96	107	-3.3	0	-2	-0.9
1983	SF-N	0	0	—	3	0	0	0	0	5	10	18.0	0	1	1.8	1	1.8	7.20	51	.417	.440	-2	-2	101	105	0.0	0	-0	-0.1
Total	5	23	45	.338	94	82	21	3	1	552	575	9.4	52	205	3.3	273	4.5	4.13	92	.269	.332	-7	-21	94	100	-9.6	0	-8	-2.4
■ **DAVE KINGMAN**	Kingman, David Arthur b: 12/21/48, Pendleton, Ore. BR/TR, 6'6", 210 lbs. Deb: 7/30/71																												
1973	SF-N	0	0	—	2	0	0	0	0	4	3	6.8	0	6	13.5	4	9.0	9.00	43	.200	.429	-2	-2	104	51	0.0	1	0	-0.1
■ **DENNIS KINNEY**	Kinney, Dennis Paul b: 2/26/52, Toledo, Ohio BL/TL, 6'1", 175 lbs. Deb: 4/09/78																												
1978	Cle-A	0	2	.000	18	0	0	0	5	39	37	8.5	3	14	3.2	19	4.4	4.38	81	.259	.317	-3	-4	94	85	-0.9	0	-0	-0.3
	SD-N	0	1	.000	7	0	0	0	0	7	6	7.7	3	4	5.1	2	2.6	6.43	52	.222	.323	-2	-2	93	92	-0.4	-0	-0	-0.2
1979	SD-N	0	0	—	13	0	0	0	0	18	17	8.5	2	8	4.0	11	5.5	3.50	104	.250	.333	0	0	97	115	0.0	-0	-0	0.0
1980	SD-N	4	6	.400	50	0	0	0	1	83	79	8.6	3	37	4.0	40	4.3	4.23	80	.252	.326	-6	-8	94	81	-0.5	-0	-0	-0.8
1981	Det-A	0	0	—	6	0	0	0	0	4	5	11.3	0	4	9.0	3	6.8	9.00	43	.313	.450	-2	-2	105	70	0.0	0	0	-0.1
1982	Oak-A	0	0	—	3	0	0	0	0	4	9	20.3	1	4	9.0	0	0.0	9.00	44	.474	.542	-2	-2	96	153	0.0	0	0	-0.1
Total	5	4	9	.308	97	0	0	0	6	155	153	8.9	12	71	4.1	75	4.4	4.53	77	.261	.336	-15	-18	94	88	-1.8	-1	-1	-1.5
■ **WALT KINNEY**	Kinney, Walter William b: 9/9/1893, Denison, Tex. d: 7/1/71, Escondido, Cal. BL/TL, 6'2", 186 lbs. Deb: 7/26/18																												
1918	Bos-A	0	0	—	5	0	0	0	0	15	5	3.0	0	8	4.8	4	2.4	1.80	143	.106	.263	2	1	93	25	0.0	-1	0	0.0
1919	Phi-A	9	15	.375	43	21	13	0	2	203	199	8.8	7	91	4.0	97	4.3	3.64	99	.262	.347	-9	-1	112	96	2.2	5	3	1.0
1920	Phi-A	2	4	.333	10	8	5	1	0	61	59	8.7	3	28	4.1	19	2.8	3.10	121	.261	.345	5	4	99	116	0.1	2	0	0.7
1923	Phi-A	0	1	.000	5	1	0	0	0	12	11	8.3	0	9	6.8	9	6.8	7.50	54	.229	.339	-5	-5	102	40	-0.4	1	-0	-0.3
Total	4	11	20	.355	63	30	18	1	2	291	274	8.5	10	136	4.2	129	4.0	3.59	101	.254	.343	-8	1	108	94	1.9	7	2	1.4
■ **MIKE KINNUNEN**	Kinnunen, Michael John b: 4/1/58, Seattle, Wash. BL/TL, 6'1", 185 lbs. Deb: 6/12/80																												
1980	Min-A	0	0	—	21	0	0	0	0	25	29	10.4	1	9	3.2	8	2.9	5.04	88	.290	.348	-3	-2	109	84	0.0	0	0	0.0
1986	Bal-A	0	0	—	9	0	0	0	0	7	8	10.3	1	5	6.4	1	1.3	6.43	65	.308	.419	-2	-2	99	102	0.0	0	0	-0.1
1987	Bal-A	0	0	—	18	0	0	0	0	20	27	12.1	3	16	7.2	14	6.3	4.95	90	.338	.443	-1	-1	99	157	0.0	0	-0	0.0
Total	3	0	0	—	48	0	0	0	0	52	64	11.1	5	30	5.2	23	4.0	5.19	85	.311	.396	-6	-5	104	115	0.0	0	0	-0.1
■ **ED KINSELLA**	Kinsella, Edward William "Rube" b: 1/15/1882, Lexington, Ill. d: 1/17/76, Bloomington, Ill. BR/TR, 6'1.5", 175 lbs. Deb: 9/16/05																												
1905	Pit-N	0	1	.000	3	2	2	0	0	17	19	10.1	0	3	1.6	11	5.8	2.65	115	.315	.358	1	1	102	132	-0.4	-0	-1	0.0
1910	StL-A	1	3	.250	10	5	2	0	0	50	62	11.2	0	16	2.9	10	1.8	3.78	67	.321	.379	-7	-7	101	118	-0.3	2	1	-0.4
Total	2	1	4	.200	13	7	4	0	0	67	81	10.9	0	19	2.6	21	2.8	3.49	76	.320	.374	-6	-6	101	122	-0.7	2	0	-0.4
■ **HARRY KINZY**	Kinzy, Henry Hershel "Slim" b: 7/19/10, Hallsville, Tex. BR/TR, 6'4", 185 lbs. Deb: 6/08/34																												
1934	Chi-A	0	1	.000	13	2	1	0	0	34	38	10.1	1	31	8.2	12	3.2	5.03	92	.290	.432	-2	-1	103	124	-0.4	1	-0	0.0
■ **FRED KIPP**	Kipp, Fred Leo b: 10/1/31, Piqua, Kan. BL/TL, 6'4", 200 lbs. Deb: 9/10/57																												
1957	Bro-N	0	0	—	1	0	0	0	0	4	6	13.5	2	0	0.0	3	6.8	9.00	49	.333	.333	-2	-2	114	89	0.0	-0	0	-0.1
1958	LA-N	6	6	.500	40	9	0	0	0	102	107	9.4	16	45	4.0	58	5.1	5.03	84	.273	.345	-12	-9	106	96	0.5	1	0	-0.7
1959	LA-N	0	0	—	2	0	0	0	0	3	2	6.0	0	3	9.0	1	3.0	0.00	—	.222	.385	1	1	101	0	0.0	0	0	0.2
1960	NY-A	0	1	.000	4	0	0	0	0	4	4	9.0	0	0	0.0	2	4.5	6.75	53	.250	.235	-1	-1	92	24	-0.4	0	0	0.0
Total	4	6	7	.462	47	9	0	0	0	113	119	9.5	18	48	3.8	64	5.1	5.10	82	.274	.342	-14	-12	106	90	0.1	1	1	-0.6
■ **BOB KIPPER**	Kipper, Robert Wayne b: 7/8/64, Aurora, Ill. BR/TL, 6'2", 200 lbs. Deb: 4/12/85																												
1985	Cal-A	0	1	.000	2	1	0	0	0	3	7	21.0	1	3	9.0	0	0.0	24.00	17	.467	.500	-7	-7	101	61	-0.4	0	0	-0.5
	Pit-N	1	2	.333	5	4	0	0	0	25	21	7.6	4	7	2.5	13	4.7	5.04	75	.221	.269	-4	-4	104	60	0.0	0	0	-0.2
1986	Pit-N	6	8	.429	20	19	0	0	0	114	123	9.7	17	34	2.7	81	6.4	4.03	93	.271	.321	-4	-4	101	109	0.4	-3	-1	-0.6
1987	Pit-N	5	9	.357	24	20	1	1	0	111	117	9.5	25	52	4.2	83	6.7	5.92	72	.271	.347	-23	-20	105	93	-2.0	2	-0	-1.7
1988	Pit-N	2	6	.250	50	0	0	0	0	65	54	7.5	7	26	3.6	39	5.4	3.74	90	.234	.307	-2	-3	97	98	-2.1	-0	1	-0.1
Total	4	14	26	.350	101	44	1	1	0	318	322	9.1	54	122	3.5	216	6.1	4.90	79	.262	.326	-39	-37	102	97	-4.1	-1	0	-3.1
■ **THORNTON KIPPER**	Kipper, Thornton John b: 9/27/28, Bagley, Wis. BR/TR, 6'3", 190 lbs. Deb: 6/07/53																												
1953	Phi-N	3	3	.500	20	3	0	0	0	46	59	11.5	8	12	2.3	15	2.9	4.70	89	.319	.351	-2	-3	98	125	-0.1	-1	-0	-0.3
1954	Phi-N	0	0	—	11	0	0	0	1	14	22	14.1	0	12	7.7	5	3.2	7.71	52	.379	.486	-6	-6	98	105	0.0	-0	0	-0.5
1955	Phi-N	0	1	.000	24	0	0	0	0	40	47	10.6	4	22	4.9	15	3.4	4.95	83	.301	.385	-4	-4	102	112	-0.4	0	-0	-0.3
Total	3	3	4	.429	55	3	0	0	1	100	128	11.5	12	46	4.1	35	3.2	5.22	79	.321	.386	-12	-12	99	117	-0.5	-1	-0	-1.1
■ **CLAY KIRBY**	Kirby, Clayton Laws b: 6/25/48, Washington, D.C. BR/TR, 6'3", 175 lbs. Deb: 4/11/69																												
1969	SD-N	7	20	.259	35	35	2	0	0	216	204	8.5	18	100	4.2	113	4.7	3.79	95	.252	.333	-5	-4	100	103	-2.9	-2	-2	-0.8
1970	SD-N	10	16	.385	36	34	6	1	0	215	198	8.3	29	120	5.0	154	6.4	4.52	87	.248	.345	-11	-15	97	102	-0.1	-0	-2	-1.6
1971	SD-N	15	13	.536	38	36	13	2	0	267	213	7.2	20	103	3.5	231	7.8	2.83	120	.216	.288	19	17	98	92	4.1	-3	-0	1.4

YEAR	TM/L	W	L	PCT	G	GS	CG	SHO	SV	IP	H	H/G	HR	BB	BB/G	SO	SO/G	ERA	/A	OAVG	OOBP	PR	/A	PF	CPI	WAT	PB	PD	TPI
1972	SD-N	12	14	.462	34	34	9	2	0	239	197	7.4	21	116	4.4	175	6.6	3.13	100	.226	.314	9	0	91	105	2.0	-3	-1	-0.4
1973	SD-N	8	18	.308	34	31	4	2	0	192	214	10.0	30	66	3.1	129	6.0	4.78	74	.282	.334	-24	-26	97	100	-2.4	-3	-2	-3.0
1974	Cin-N	12	9	.571	36	35	7	1	0	231	210	8.2	15	91	3.5	160	6.2	3.27	107	.242	.309	9	6	96	98	-0.6	-3	-2	0.0
1975	Cin-N	10	6	.625	26	19	1	0	0	111	113	9.2	13	54	4.4	48	3.9	4.70	78	.263	.345	-13	-13	101	95	-0.5	1	-2	-1.3
1976	Mon-N	1	8	.111	22	15	0	0	0	79	81	9.2	10	63	7.2	51	5.8	5.70	63	.273	.395	-19	-18	103	100	-3.0	-1	-1	-1.9
Total	8	75	104	.419	261	239	42	8	0	1550	1430	8.3	156	713	4.1	1061	6.2	3.83	92	.246	.325	-35	-53	97	99	-3.4	-15	-12	-7.6
■ **JOHN KIRBY**	Kirby, John F. b: 1/13/1865, St.Louis, Mo. d: 10/6/31, St.Louis, Mo. TR, 5'8", 172 lbs. Deb: 8/01/1884																												
1884	KC-U	0	1	.000	2	2	1	0	0	11	13	10.6	0	2	1.6	1	0.8	4.09	67	.299	.330	-1	-2	92	93	-0.4	-1	0	-0.1
1885	StL-N	5	8	.385	14	14	14	0	0	129	118	8.2	0	44	3.1	46	3.2	3.56	77	.254	.318	-11	-12	97	78	0.6	-5	0	-1.5
1886	StL-N	11	25	.306	41	41	38	1	0	325	329	9.1	9	134	3.7	129	3.6	3.30	98	.276	.349	0	-2	98	112	-3.1	-9	-2	-1.2
1887	Ind-N	1	6	.143	8	8	5	0	0	62	70	10.2	3	43	6.2	7	1.0	6.10	67	.300	.409	-14	-14	101	87	-1.7	-2	0	-1.2
	Cle-a	0	5	.000	5	5	5	0	0	41	62	13.6	1	28	6.1	6	1.3	9.00	49	.363	.453	-21	-21	103	79	-2.4	-1	0	-1.4
1888	KC-a	1	4	.200	5	5	5	0	0	43	48	10.0	0	7	1.5	11	2.3	4.19	82	.296	.325	-5	-4	112	81	-0.9	-2	0	-0.4
Total	5	18	49	.269	75	75	68	1	0	611	640	9.4	13	258	3.8	200	2.9	4.09	80	.282	.355	-53	-54	99	98	-7.9	-21	-2	-5.8
■ **LA RUE KIRBY**	Kirby, La Rue b: 12/30/1889, Eureka, Mich. d: 6/10/61, Lansing, Mich. BB/TR, 6', 185 lbs. Deb: 8/07/12																												
1912	NY-N	1	0	1.000	3	1	1	0	0	11	13	10.6	1	6	4.9	2	1.6	5.73	59	.289	.385	-3	-3	99	87	0.5	0	0	-0.1
1915	StL-F	0	0	—	1	0	0	0	0	7	7	9.0	1	2	2.6	7	9.0	5.14	60	.289	.343	-2	-2	102	81	0.0	0	0	-0.1
Total	2	1	0	1.000	4	1	1	0	0	18	20	10.0	2	8	4.0	9	4.5	5.50	60	.289	.371	-4	-4	100	84	0.5	0	0	-0.2
■ **MIKE KIRCHER**	Kircher, Michael Andrew (born Wolfgang Andrew Kerscher) b: 9/30/1897, Rochester, N.Y. d: 6/26/72, Rochester.N.Y. BB/TR, 6', 180 lbs. Deb: 8/08/19																												
1919	Phi-A	0	0	—	2	0	0	0	0	8	15	16.9	0	3	3.4	2	2.3	7.88	46	.429	.474	-4	-4	112	101	0.0	-1	-0	-0.3
1920	StL-N	2	1	.667	9	3	1	0	0	37	50	12.2	0	5	1.2	5	1.2	5.35	57	.333	.354	-9	-9	98	80	0.5	0	-1	-1.0
1921	StL-N	0	1	.000	3	0	0	0	0	3	4	12.0	0	1	3.0	2	6.0	9.00	39	.364	.400	-2	-2	93	73	-0.4	0	0	-0.1
Total	3	2	2	.500	14	3	1	0	0	48	69	12.9	0	9	1.7	9	1.7	6.00	53	.352	.379	-15	-15	100	83	0.1	-0	-1	-1.4
■ **BILL KIRK**	Kirk, William Partlemore b: 7/19/35, Coatesville, Pa. BL/TL, 6', 165 lbs. Deb: 9/23/61																												
1961	KC-A	0	0	—	1	1	0	0	0	3	6	18.0	2	1	3.0	3	9.0	12.00	35	.375	.412	-3	-3	104	99	0.0	0	0	-0.1
■ **DON KIRKWOOD**	Kirkwood, Donald Paul b: 9/24/49, Pontiac, Mich. BR/TR, 6'3", 175 lbs. Deb: 9/13/74																												
1974	Cal-A	0	0	—	3	0	0	0	0	7	12	15.4	0	6	7.7	4	5.1	9.00	37	.375	.474	-4	-4	93	87	0.0	0	-0	-0.3
1975	Cal-A	6	5	.545	44	2	0	0	7	84	85	9.1	6	28	3.0	49	5.3	3.11	117	.270	.317	6	5	96	122	1.0	0	-0	0.4
1976	Cal-A	6	12	.333	28	26	4	0	0	158	167	9.5	12	57	3.2	78	4.4	4.61	71	.278	.333	-19	-23	93	90	-2.7	0	1	-2.2
1977	Cal-A	1	0	1.000	13	0	0	0	1	18	20	10.0	3	9	4.5	10	5.0	5.00	77	.290	.372	-2	-2	95	111	0.5	0	1	0.0
	Chi-A	1	1	.500	16	0	0	0	0	40	49	11.0	3	10	2.3	24	5.4	5.17	78	.310	.343	-5	-5	99	92	0.0	0	0	-0.4
	Yr	2	1	.667	29	0	0	0	1	58	69	10.7	6	19	2.9	34	5.3	5.12	78	.304	.352	-7	-7	97	92	0.5	0	1	-0.4
1978	Tor-A	4	5	.444	16	9	3	0	0	68	76	10.1	6	25	3.3	29	3.8	4.24	91	.289	.345	-3	-3	102	106	0.6	0	0	-0.2
Total	5	18	23	.439	120	37	7	0	8	375	409	9.8	30	135	3.2	194	4.7	4.37	82	.284	.338	-27	-33	96	101	-0.6	0	2	-2.7
■ **HARRY KIRSCH**	Kirsch, Harry Louis "Casey" b: 10/17/1887, Pittsburgh, Pa. d: 12/25/25, Overbrook, Pa. TR, 5'11", 170 lbs. Deb: 4/16/10																												
1910	Cle-A	0	0	—	2	0	0	0	0	3	5	15.0	0	1	3.0	5	15.0	6.00	43	.385	.429	-1	-1	102	107	0.0	0	0	0.0
■ **RUBE KISINGER**	Kisinger, Charles Samuel b: 12/13/1876, Adrian, Mich. d: 7/14/41, Huron, Ohio BR/TR, 6', 190 lbs. Deb: 9/10/02																												
1902	Det-A	2	3	.400	5	5	5	0	0	43	48	10.0	0	14	2.9	7	1.5	3.14	114	.307	.364	2	2	101	117	0.1	-1	-0	0.2
1903	Det-A	7	9	.438	16	14	13	2	0	119	118	8.9	0	27	2.0	33	2.5	2.95	96	.281	.324	0	-2	96	97	-0.7	-2	1	0.0
Total	2	9	12	.429	21	19	18	2	0	162	166	9.2	0	41	2.3	40	2.2	3.00	101	.288	.335	2	1	97	103	-0.6	-3	0	0.2
■ **BRUCE KISON**	Kison, Bruce Eugene b: 2/18/50, Pasco, Wash. BR/TR, 6'4", 178 lbs. Deb: 7/04/71																												
1971	Pit-N	6	5	.545	18	13	2	1	0	95	93	8.8	6	36	3.4	60	5.7	3.41	98	.259	.333	1	-1	97	110	-0.4	-1	1	0.0
1972	Pit-N	9	7	.563	32	18	6	1	3	152	123	7.3	11	69	4.1	102	6.0	3.26	106	.220	.314	3	4	100	94	-0.7	2	-1	0.5
1973	Pit-N	3	0	1.000	7	7	0	0	0	44	36	7.4	4	24	4.9	26	5.3	3.07	110	.232	.337	3	1	92	122	1.5	0	0	0.2
1974	Pit-N	9	8	.529	40	16	1	0	2	129	123	8.6	8	57	4.0	71	5.0	3.49	100	.247	.333	2	0	97	103	-0.1	-0	1	0.1
1975	Pit-N	12	11	.522	33	29	6	0	0	192	160	7.5	10	92	4.3	89	4.2	3.23	110	.227	.313	9	7	98	93	-1.0	-2	2	0.7
1976	Pit-N	14	9	.609	31	29	6	1	1	193	180	8.4	10	52	2.4	98	4.6	3.08	113	.247	.294	9	9	99	95	1.2	4	1	1.4
1977	Pit-N	9	10	.474	33	32	3	1	0	193	209	9.7	25	55	2.6	122	5.7	4.90	81	.278	.325	-21	-20	102	90	-2.0	5	1	-1.4
1978	Pit-N	6	6	.500	28	11	0	0	0	96	81	7.6	3	39	3.7	62	5.8	3.19	118	.229	.307	4	6	105	89	-0.4	1	1	0.8
1979	Pit-N	13	7	.650	33	25	3	1	0	172	157	8.2	13	45	2.4	105	5.5	3.19	122	.246	.293	10	13	104	97	1.3	0	1	1.6
1980	Cal-A	3	6	.333	13	13	2	1	0	73	73	9.0	5	32	3.9	28	3.5	4.93	79	.264	.336	-7	-8	97	81	-0.7	0	-1	-0.8
1981	Cal-A	1	1	.500	11	4	0	0	0	44	40	8.2	8	14	2.9	19	3.9	3.48	109	.241	.300	1	2	104	112	0.1	0	1	0.2
1982	Cal-A	10	5	.667	33	16	3	1	1	142	120	7.6	15	44	2.8	86	5.5	3.17	127	.226	.290	14	14	99	95	1.8	0	2	1.6
1983	Cal-A	11	5	.688	26	17	4	1	2	127	128	9.1	13	43	3.0	83	5.9	4.04	97	.264	.324	1	-2	96	102	3.8	0	1	0.0
1984	Cal-A	4	5	.444	20	7	0	0	2	65	72	10.0	10	28	3.9	66	9.1	5.40	75	.280	.361	-10	-10	101	97	-0.4	0	-1	-0.9
1985	Bos-A	5	3	.625	22	9	0	0	1	92	98	9.6	9	32	3.1	56	5.5	4.11	102	.274	.329	0	1	102	105	1.0	0	2	0.3
Total	15	115	88	.567	380	246	36	8	12	1809	1693	8.4	150	662	3.3	1073	5.3	3.66	102	.248	.316	19	16	100	97	5.0	8	12	4.3
■ **BILL KISSINGER**	Kissinger, William Francis "Shang" b: 8/15/1871, Dayton, Ky. d: 4/20/29, Cincinnati, Ohio BR/TR, 185 lbs. Deb: 5/30/1895																												
1895	Bal-N	1	0	1.000	2	2	1	0	0	11	18	14.7	0	2	1.6	3	2.5	4.09	121	.389	.414	1	1	104	145	0.5	-0	0	0.1
	StL-N	4	12	.250	24	14	9	0	0	141	222	14.2	8	51	3.3	31	2.0	6.77	72	.379	.429	-31	-29	102	97	-1.3	-2	0	-2.3
	Yr	5	12	.294	26	16	10	0	0	152	240	14.2	8	53	3.1	34	2.0	6.57	75	.380	.428	-30	-28	102	97	-0.8	-0	0	-2.2
1896	StL-N	2	9	.182	20	12	11	0	1	136	209	13.8	5	55	3.6	22	1.5	6.49	66	.376	.432	-32	-33	98	96	-2.3	2	0	-2.4
1897	StL-N	0	4	.000	7	4	2	0	0	31	51	14.8	2	15	4.4	5	1.5	11.61	37	.392	.455	-25	-25	99	62	-1.9	2	0	-1.8
Total	3	7	25	.219	53	32	23	0	1	319	500	14.1	15	123	3.5	61	1.7	7.03	65	.380	.433	-87	-87	100	95	-5.0	2	0	-6.4
■ **FRANK KITSON**	Kitson, Frank L. b: 4/11/1872, Hopkins, Mich. d: 4/14/30, Allegan, Mich. BL/TR, 5'11", 165 lbs. Deb: 5/19/1898																												
1898	Bal-N	8	5	.615	17	13	13	1	0	119	123	9.3	0	35	2.6	32	2.4	3.25	110	.288	.342	5	4	100	96	-0.2	3	0	1.1
1899	Bal-N	22	16	.579	40	37	35	3	0	330	329	9.0	6	66	1.8	75	2.0	2.75	149	.283	.321	40	49	106	101	0.0	-2	-2	4.5
1900	Bro-N	15	13	.536	40	30	21	2	**4**	253	283	10.1	12	56	2.0	55	2.0	4.20	93	.306	.346	-14	-8	106	89	-1.8	5	-4	-0.4
1901	Bro-N	19	11	.633	38	32	26	5	2	281	312	10.0	9	67	2.1	127	4.1	2.98	115	.306	.355	11	14	103	**125**	2.3	5	-3	1.1
1902	Bro-N	19	12	.613	31	30	28	3	0	260	251	8.7	4	48	1.7	107	3.7	2.84	92	.278	.320	-2	-7	94	90	2.9	8	0	-0.6
1903	Det-A	15	16	.484	31	28	28	2	0	258	277	9.7	8	38	1.3	102	3.6	2.58	110	.297	.325	11	7	96	**128**	0.2	-1	-2	0.5
1904	Det-A	8	13	.381	26	24	19	0	1	200	211	9.5	7	38	1.7	69	3.1	3.06	83	.295	.330	-10	-11	98	109	-0.7	0	-1	-1.2
1905	Det-A	12	14	.462	33	27	21	3	1	226	230	9.2	3	57	2.3	78	3.1	3.46	76	.289	.336	-21	-20	100	93	-1.5	-1	-3	-2.3
1906	Was-A	6	14	.300	30	21	15	1	0	197	196	9.0	2	57	2.6	59	2.7	3.65	69	.285	.339	-21	-25	94	85	-1.9	8	-1	-2.5
1907	Was-A	0	3	.000	5	3	2	0	0	32	41	11.5	1	9	2.5	11	3.1	3.94	61	.338	.383	-5	-6	94	115	-1.4	-0	-1	-0.5
	NY-A	4	0	1.000	12	4	3	0	0	61	75	11.1	0	17	2.5	14	2.1	3.10	90	.329	.375	-4	-2	110	130	2.0	1	-2	-0.3
	Yr	4	3	.571	17	7	5	0	0	93	116	11.2	1	26	2.5	25	2.4	3.39	78	.332	.378	-9	-8	104	130	0.6	-0	-2	-0.8
Total	10	128	117	.522	303	249	211	20	8	2217	2328	9.5	52	488	2.0	729	3.0	3.17	99	.294	.336	-10	-8	100	104	-0.1	27	-16	-0.6
■ **MALACHI KITTRIDGE**	Kittridge, Malachi Jedediah "Jedediah" b: 10/12/1869, Clinton, Mass. d: 6/23/28, Gary, Ind. BR/TR, 5'7", 170 lbs. Deb: 4/19/1890 M																												
1896	Chi-N	0	0	—	1	0	0	0	0	2	2	9.0	0	1	4.5	0	0.0	9.00	53	.282	.370	-1	-1	108	40	0.0	-0	0	0.0
■ **HUGO KLAERNER**	Klaerner, Hugo Emil "Dutch" b: 10/15/08, Fredericksburg, Tex. d: 2/3/82, Fredericksburg, Tex. BR/TR, 5'11", 190 lbs. Deb: 9/10/34																												
1934	Chi-A	0	2	.000	3	3	1	0	0	17	24	12.7	4	16	8.5	9	4.8	11.12	42	.329	.435	-13	-12	103	78	-0.9	1	1	-0.7
■ **FRED KLAGES**	Klages, Frederick Albert Antony b: 10/31/43, Ambridge, Pa. BR/TR, 6'2", 185 lbs. Deb: 9/11/66																												
1966	Chi-A	1	0	1.000	3	3	0	0	0	16	9	5.1	0	7	3.9	6	3.4	1.69	190	.167	.258	3	3	93	78	0.5	1	0	0.4
1967	Chi-A	4	4	.500	11	9	0	0	0	45	43	8.6	6	16	3.2	17	3.4	3.80	79	.256	.321	-3	-4	93	110	-0.3	-1	-1	-0.6
Total	2	5	4	.556	14	12	0	0	0	61	52	7.7	6	23	3.4	23	3.4	3.25	94	.234	.305	0	-1	93	101	0.2	-0	-1	-0.2

YEAR	TM/L	W	L	PCT	G	GS	CG	SHO	SV	IP	H	H/G	HR	BB	BB/G	SO	SO/G	ERA	/A	OAVG	OOBP	PR	/A	PF	CPI	WAT	PB	PD	TPI
■ **AL KLAWITTER**	Klawitter, Albert "Dutch" b: 4/12/1888, Wilkes-Barre, Pa. d: 5/2/50, Milwaukee, Wis. BR/TR, 5'11.5", 187 lbs. Deb: 09																												
1909	NY-N	1	1	.500	6	3	2	0	1	27	24	8.0	1	13	4.3	6	2.0	2.00	134	.247	.336	2	2	103	162	-0.1	1	1	0.3
1910	NY-N	0	0	—	1	0	0	0	0	1	2	18.0	0	2	18.0	0	0.0	9.00	31	.400	.571	-1	-1	92	134	0.0	0	-0	0.0
1913	Det-A	1	2	.333	8	3	1	0	0	32	39	11.0	0	15	4.2	10	2.8	5.91	50	.305	.378	-11	-11	101	74	-0.2	-2	0	-0.9
Total	3	2	3	.400	15	6	3	0	1	60	65	9.8	1	30	4.5	16	2.4	4.20	67	.283	.365	-9	-9	102	114	-0.3	-0	1	-0.6
■ **TOM KLAWITTER**	Klawitter, Thomas Carl b: 6/24/58, La Crosse, Wis. BR/TL, 6'2", 190 lbs. Deb: 4/14/85																												
1985	Min-A	0	0	—	7	2	0	0	0	9	7	7.0	2	13	13.0	5	5.0	7.00	62	.226	.444	-3	-3	104	104	0.0	0	0	-0.2
■ **HAL KLEINE**	Kleine, Harold John b: 6/8/23, St.Louis, Mo. d: 12/10/57, St.Louis, Mo. BL/TL, 6'2", 193 lbs. Deb: 4/26/44																												
1944	Cle-A	1	2	.333	11	6	1	0	0	41	38	8.3	0	36	7.9	13	2.9	5.71	61	.248	.392	-10	-10	101	75	-0.3	-1	-1	-1.0
1945	Cle-A	0	0	—	3	0	0	0	0	7	8	10.3	0	7	9.0	5	6.4	3.86	86	.286	.429	-0	-0	98	144	0.0	0	0	0.0
Total	2	1	2	.333	14	6	1	0	0	48	46	8.6	0	43	8.1	18	3.4	5.44	63	.254	.397	-11	-11	100	85	-0.3	-0	-1	-1.0
■ **TED KLEINHANS**	Kleinhans, Theodore Otto b: 4/8/1899, Deer Park, Wis. d: 7/24/85, Redington Beach, Fla. BR/TL, 6', 170 lbs. Deb: 4/20/34																												
1934	Phi-N	0	0	—	5	0	0	0	0	6	11	16.5	1	3	4.5	2	3.0	9.00	50	.379	.424	-3	-3	111	96	0.0	-0	0	-0.2
	Cin-N	2	6	.250	24	9	0	0	0	80	107	12.0	2	38	4.3	23	2.6	5.74	74	.321	.382	-15	-13	105	96	-1.0	-1	1	-1.1
	Yr	2	6	.250	29	9	0	0	0	86	118	12.3	3	41	4.3	25	2.6	5.97	72	.326	.386	-18	-16	105	96	-1.0	-0	2	-1.3
1936	NY-A	1	1	.500	19	0	0	0	1	29	36	11.2	0	23	7.1	10	3.1	5.90	77	.300	.407	-3	-4	90	97	-0.2	-0	0	-0.3
1937	Cin-N	1	2	.333	7	3	1	0	0	27	29	9.7	1	12	4.0	13	4.3	2.33	156	.271	.347	5	4	93	175	0.0	0	-1	0.3
1938	Cin-N	0	0	—	1	0	0	0	0	1	2	18.0	0	0	0.0	0	0.0	9.00	40	.400	.400	-1	-1	96	75	0.0	0	0	0.0
Total	4	4	9	.308	56	12	1	0	1	143	185	11.6	4	76	4.8	48	3.0	5.29	80	.311	.383	-17	-17	100	111	-1.2	-2	1	-1.3
■ **NUB KLEINKE**	Kleinke, Norbert Georbe b: 5/19/11, Fond Du Lac, Wis. d: 3/16/50, Off Marin Coast, Cal. BR/TR, 6'1", 170 lbs. Deb: 4/25/35																												
1935	StL-N	0	0	—	4	2	0	0	0	13	19	13.2	1	3	2.1	5	3.5	4.85	83	.358	.386	-1	-1	100	130	0.0	-0	0	0.0
1937	StL-N	1	1	.500	5	2	1	0	0	21	25	10.7	0	7	3.0	9	3.9	4.71	83	.321	.368	-2	-2	100	102	0.0	-1	0	-0.2
Total	2	1	1	.500	9	4	1	0	0	34	44	11.6	1	10	2.6	14	3.7	4.76	83	.336	.375	-3	-3	100	113	0.0	-1	0	-0.2
■ **ED KLEPFER**	Klepfer, Edward Lloyd "Big Ed" b: 3/17/1888, Summerville, Pa. d: 8/9/50, Tulsa, Okla. BR/TR, 6', 185 lbs. Deb: 7/04/11																												
1911	NY-A	0	0	—	2	0	0	0	0	4	5	11.3	0	2	4.5	4	9.0	6.75	55	.250	.318	-2	-1	111	35	0.0	-0	0	0.0
1913	NY-A	0	1	.000	8	1	0	0	0	25	38	13.7	2	12	4.3	10	3.6	7.56	40	.373	.448	-13	-13	104	95	-0.4	0	0	-1.1
1915	Chi-A	1	0	1.000	3	2	1	0	0	13	11	7.6	0	5	3.5	3	2.1	2.77	100	.234	.308	0	-0	94	86	0.5	-0	-0	0.0
	Cle-A	1	6	.143	8	7	2	0	0	43	47	9.8	0	11	2.3	13	2.7	2.09	150	.283	.328	4	5	106	156	-2.1	-0	1	0.6
	Yr	2	6	.250	11	9	3	0	0	56	58	9.3	0	16	2.6	16	2.6	2.25	135	.272	.323	4	5	103	156	-1.6	-0	0	0.6
1916	Cle-A	6	6	.500	31	13	4	1	2	143	136	8.6	0	46	2.9	62	3.9	2.52	111	.262	.327	5	5	99	118	0.0	-4	-0	0.0
1917	Cle-A	14	4	.778	41	27	9	0	1	213	208	8.8	0	55	2.3	66	2.8	2.37	128	.264	.312	7	15	113	112	4.6	-7	-1	0.9
1919	Cle-A	0	0	—	5	0	0	0	0	7	12	15.4	1	6	7.7	7	9.0	7.71	44	.375	.474	-3	-3	104	114	0.0	-0	0	-0.2
Total	6	22	17	.564	98	50	16	1	3	448	457	9.2	3	137	2.8	165	3.3	2.81	106	.273	.330	-2	8	107	116	2.6	-11	-1	0.2
■ **ED KLIEMAN**	Klieman, Edward Frederick "Specs" or "Babe" b: 3/21/18, Norwood, Ohio d: 11/15/79, Homosassa, Fla. BR/TR, 6'1", 190 lbs. Deb: 9/24/43																												
1943	Cle-A	0	1	.000	1	1	1	0	0	9	8	8.0	0	5	5.0	2	2.0	1.00	295	.286	.382	2	2	90	445	-0.4	-0	0	0.2
1944	Cle-A	11	13	.458	47	19	5	1	5	178	185	9.4	4	70	3.5	44	2.2	3.39	102	.274	.343	1	1	101	114	-0.2	-3	1	0.0
1945	Cle-A	5	8	.385	38	12	4	1	4	126	123	8.8	3	49	3.5	33	2.4	3.86	86	.261	.327	-7	-8	98	91	-1.5	1	3	-0.3
1946	Cle-A	0	0	—	9	0	0	0	0	15	18	10.8	0	10	6.0	2	1.2	6.60	48	.290	.389	-5	-6	90	71	0.0	-0	-1	-0.6
1947	Cle-A	5	4	.556	**58**	0	0	0	**17**	92	78	7.6	5	39	3.8	21	2.1	3.03	115	.231	.310	7	5	94	102	0.4	-1	2	0.6
1948	Cle-A	3	2	.600	44	0	0	0	4	80	62	7.0	3	46	5.2	18	2.0	2.59	155	.229	.333	**15**	**13**	94	142	0.0	-0	1	1.3
1949	Was-A	0	0	—	2	0	0	0	0	3	8	24.0	0	3	9.0	1	3.0	18.00	22	.500	.550	-5	-5	96	75	0.0	0	0	-0.3
	Chi-A	2	0	1.000	18	0	0	0	3	33	33	9.0	2	15	4.1	9	2.5	3.00	139	.273	.336	4	4	99	142	1.0	0	1	0.5
	Yr	2	0	1.000	20	0	0	0	3	36	41	10.3	2	18	4.5	10	2.5	4.25	98	.299	.362	-0	-0	99	142	1.0	0	1	0.2
1950	Phi-A	0	0	—	5	0	0	0	0	6	10	15.0	0	2	3.0	0	0.0	9.00	47	.357	.438	-3	-3	93	77	0.0	-0	-0	-0.2
Total	8	26	28	.481	222	32	10	2	33	542	525	8.7	17	239	4.0	130	2.2	3.49	102	.261	.337	10	4	97	116	-0.7	-3	6	1.2
■ **RON KLIMKOWSKI**	Klimkowski, Ronald Bernard b: 3/1/44, Jersey City, N.J. BR/TR, 6'2", 190 lbs. Deb: 9/15/69																												
1969	NY-A	0	0	—	3	1	0	0	0	14	6	3.9	0	5	3.2	3	1.9	0.64	540	.130	.212	5	4	96	37	0.0	-0	-0	0.4
1970	NY-A	6	7	.462	45	3	1	1	1	98	80	7.3	7	33	3.0	40	3.7	2.66	128	.223	.291	11	8	91	102	-1.3	-1	0	0.7
1971	Oak-A	2	2	.500	26	0	0	0	2	45	37	7.4	3	23	4.6	25	5.0	3.40	101	.220	.313	0	0	99	88	-0.3	1	1	0.2
1972	NY-A	0	3	.000	16	2	0	0	1	31	32	9.3	3	15	4.4	11	3.2	4.06	69	.271	.350	-3	-4	92	110	-1.4	-1	0	-0.5
Total	4	8	12	.400	90	6	1	1	4	188	155	7.4	13	76	3.6	79	3.8	2.92	114	.224	.301	13	8	94	95	-3.0	-1	1	0.8
■ **BOBBY KLINE**	Kline, John Robert b: 1/27/29, St.Petersburg, Fla BR/TR, 6', 179 lbs. Deb: 4/11/55																												
1955	Was-A	0	0	—	1	0	0	0	0	1	4	36.0	1	1	9.0	0	0.0	27.00	14	.667	.625	-3	-3	94	108	0.0	0	0	-0.1
■ **BOB KLINE**	Kline, Robert George "Junior" b: 12/9/09, Enterprise, Ohio d: 3/16/87, Westerville, Ohio BR/TR, 6'3", 200 lbs. Deb: 9/17/30																												
1930	Bos-A	0	0	—	1	0	0	0	0	1	1	9.0	0	0	0.0	0	0.0	0.00	—	.333	.250	1	0	96	0	0.0	0	0	0.0
1931	Bos-A	5	5	.500	28	10	3	0	0	98	110	10.1	3	35	3.2	25	2.3	4.41	96	.298	.357	-0	-2	97	110	0.8	2	2	0.2
1932	Bos-A	11	13	.458	47	19	4	1	2	172	203	10.6	10	76	4.0	31	1.6	5.28	87	.294	.357	-15	-13	102	95	3.4	-3	3	-1.2
1933	Bos-A	7	8	.467	46	8	1	0	4	127	127	9.0	5	67	4.7	16	1.1	4.54	96	.265	.354	-4	-2	102	98	0.6	-1	3	0.0
1934	Phi-A	6	2	.750	20	0	0	0	1	40	50	11.2	6	13	2.9	14	3.1	6.30	70	.314	.354	-8	-8	98	94	2.2	1	1	-0.5
	Was-A	1	0	1.000	6	0	0	0	0	4	10	22.5	0	4	9.0	1	2.3	15.75	29	.500	.556	-5	-5	102	90	0.5	0	0	-0.3
	Yr	7	2	.778	26	0	0	0	1	44	60	12.3	6	17	3.5	15	3.1	7.16	62	.335	.380	-13	-13	99	90	2.7	1	2	-0.8
Total	5	30	28	.517	148	37	8	1	7	442	501	10.2	24	195	4.0	87	1.8	5.05	88	.291	.359	-32	-30	101	99	7.5	-1	9	-1.8
■ **RON KLINE**	Kline, Ronald Lee b: 3/9/32, Callery, Pa. BR/TR, 6'3", 205 lbs. Deb: 4/21/52																												
1952	Pit-N	0	7	.000	27	11	0	0	0	79	74	8.4	3	66	7.5	27	3.1	5.47	72	.253	.397	-15	-14	105	89	-3.4	-2	-1	-1.6
1955	Pit-N	6	13	.316	36	19	2	1	2	137	161	10.6	13	53	3.5	48	3.2	4.14	98	.298	.358	-2	-1	101	120	-1.9	-2	2	0.0
1956	Pit-N	14	18	.438	44	39	9	2	2	264	263	9.0	26	81	2.8	125	4.3	3.38	115	.263	.317	12	15	103	110	0.3	-3	1	1.3
1957	Pit-N	9	16	.360	40	31	11	2	0	205	214	9.4	28	61	2.7	88	3.9	4.04	92	.268	.317	-4	-7	96	103	-1.4	-5	-1	-1.3
1958	Pit-N	13	16	.448	32	32	11	2	0	237	220	8.4	25	92	3.5	109	4.1	3.53	105	.252	.316	11	5	94	106	-3.0	-6	1	0.0
1959	Pit-N	11	13	.458	33	29	7	0	0	186	186	9.0	23	70	3.4	91	4.4	4.26	96	.263	.324	-6	-3	104	99	-1.2	-2	-1	-0.5
1960	StL-N	4	9	.308	34	17	1	0	1	118	133	10.1	21	43	3.3	54	4.1	6.03	67	.284	.337	-30	-26	108	85	-3.0	-2	0	-2.5
1961	LA-A	3	6	.333	26	12	0	0	1	105	119	10.2	16	44	3.8	70	6.0	4.89	92	.288	.353	-10	-4	112	107	-1.0	-2	1	-0.4
	Det-A	5	3	.625	10	8	3	1	0	56	53	8.5	3	17	2.7	27	4.3	2.73	138	.245	.295	8	6	94	108	0.0	0	-1	0.6
	Yr	8	9	.471	36	20	3	1	1	161	172	9.6	19	61	3.4	97	5.4	4.14	103	.272	.332	-2	2	106	108	-1.0	-2	0	0.2
1962	Det-A	3	6	.333	36	4	0	0	2	77	88	10.3	9	28	3.3	47	5.5	4.32	101	.284	.344	-3	0	110	109	-1.6	-1	1	0.0
1963	Was-A	3	8	.273	62	1	0	0	17	94	85	8.1	3	30	2.9	49	4.7	2.78	132	.249	.308	9	9	101	114	-1.1	-0	-0	0.9
1964	Was-A	10	7	.588	61	0	0	0	14	81	81	9.0	4	21	2.3	40	4.4	2.33	160	.262	.302	12	13	103	141	3.0	0	-0	1.3
1965	Was-A	7	6	.538	74	0	0	0	**29**	99	106	9.6	7	32	2.9	52	4.7	2.64	134	.275	.323	9	10	102	151	1.3	-1	-1	0.9
1966	Was-A	6	4	.600	63	0	0	0	23	90	79	7.9	12	17	1.7	46	4.6	2.40	138	.237	.270	10	9	96	133	1.5	0	-2	0.8
1967	Min-A	7	1	.875	54	0	0	0	5	72	71	8.9	10	15	1.9	36	4.5	3.75	91	.261	.296	-4	-3	106	104	2.9	-1	-0	-0.3
1968	Pit-N	12	5	.706	56	0	0	0	7	113	94	7.5	3	31	2.5	48	3.8	1.67	179	.234	.283	**16**	**16**	100	150	3.8	-1	-1	1.6
1969	Pit-N	1	3	.250	20	0	0	0	3	31	37	10.7	3	5	1.5	15	4.4	5.81	58	.296	.321	-8	-8	94	74	-1.0	-1	-0	-0.8
	SF-N	0	2	.000	7	0	0	0	0	11	16	13.1	1	6	4.9	7	5.7	4.09	88	.364	.423	-1	-1	100	176	-0.9	0	0	0.0
	Yr	1	5	.167	27	0	0	0	3	42	53	11.4	4	11	2.4	22	4.7	5.36	64	.310	.344	-8	-9	96	176	-1.9	-1	-0	-0.8
	Bos-A	0	1	.000	16	0	0	0	1	17	24	12.7	4	17	9.0	7	3.7	4.76	80	.329	.446	-2	-2	105	180	-0.4	0	0	-0.1
1970	Atl-N	0	0	—	5	0	0	0	1	6	9	13.5	4	2	3.0	3	4.5	7.50	57	.321	.367	-2	-2	105	132	0.0	0	-0	-0.1
Total	17	114	144	.442	736	203	44	8	108	2078	2113	9.2	218	731	3.2	989	4.3	3.75	101	.266	.324	1	13	101	113	-7.1	-28	-4	-0.2
■ **STEVE KLINE**	Kline, Steven Jack b: 10/6/47, Wenatchee, Wash. BR/TR, 6'3", 200 lbs. Deb: 7/10/70																												
1970	NY-A	6	6	.500	16	15	5	0	0	100	99	8.9	8	24	2.2	49	4.4	3.42	99	.254	.293	3	-0	91	92	-0.7	2	1	0.2
1971	NY-A	12	13	.480	31	30	15	1	0	222	206	8.4	21	37	1.5	81	3.3	2.96	113	.244	.274	13	10	97	94	-0.7	-0	3	1.3

YEAR TM/L	W	L	PCT	G	GS	CG	SHO	SV	IP	H	H/G	HR	BB	BB/G	SO	SO/G	ERA	/A	OAVG	OOBP	PR	/A	PF	CPI	WAT	PB	PD	TPI
1972 NY-A	16	9	.640	32	32	11	4	0	236	210	8.0	11	44	1.7	58	2.2	2.40	117	.237	.276	18	11	92	100	3.8	-2	2	1.1
1973 NY-A	4	7	.364	14	13	2	1	0	74	76	9.2	5	31	3.8	19	2.3	4.01	95	.270	.338	-2	-2	100	100	-1.4	0	-0	-0.1
1974 NY-A	2	2	.500	4	4	0	0	0	26	26	9.0	3	5	1.7	6	2.1	3.46	100	.263	.302	0	-0	95	104	-0.1	0	-0	0.0
Cle-A	3	8	.273	16	11	1	0	0	71	70	8.9	9	31	3.9	17	2.2	5.07	72	.266	.347	-11	-11	101	90	-2.3	0	1	-0.9
Yr	5	10	.333	20	15	1	0	0	97	96	8.9	12	36	3.3	23	2.1	4.64	78	.264	.333	-11	-11	100	90	-2.4	0	1	-0.9
1977 Atl-N	0	0	—	16	0	0	0	1	20	21	9.4	4	12	5.4	10	4.5	6.75	67	.259	.355	-6	-5	115	76	0.0	0	-0	-0.4
Total 6	43	45	.489	129	105	34	6	1	749	708	8.5	61	184	2.2	240	2.9	3.27	101	.249	.294	15	2	96	96	-1.4	-1	5	1.2

■ BILL KLING Kling, William b: 1/14/1867, Kansas City, Mo. d: 8/26/34, Kansas City, Mo. BL/TR, 6', 190 lbs. Deb: 8/13/1891

YEAR TM/L	W	L	PCT	G	GS	CG	SHO	SV	IP	H	H/G	HR	BB	BB/G	SO	SO/G	ERA	/A	OAVG	OOBP	PR	/A	PF	CPI	WAT	PB	PD	TPI
1891 Phi-N	4	2	.667	12	7	4	0	0	75	90	10.8	2	32	3.8	26	3.1	4.32	74	.311	.380	-8	-9	95	99	1.0	1	0	-0.6
1892 Bal-N	0	2	.000	2	2	0	0	0	11	17	13.9	1	7	5.7	7	5.7	11.45	29	.367	.451	-10	-10	102	63	-0.9	1	0	-0.6
1895 Lou-N	0	0	—	1	0	0	0	0	1	0	0.0	0	1	9.0	0	0.0	0.00	—	.000	.280	1	1	99	0	0.0	-0	0	0.0
Total 3	4	4	.500	15	9	4	0	0	87	107	11.1	3	40	4.1	33	3.4	5.17	62	.317	.389	-18	-19	96	93	0.1	2	0	-1.2

■ BOB KLINGER Klinger, Robert Harold b: 6/4/08, Allenton, Mo. d: 8/19/77, Villa Ridge, Mo. BR/TR, 6', 180 lbs. Deb: 4/19/38

YEAR TM/L	W	L	PCT	G	GS	CG	SHO	SV	IP	H	H/G	HR	BB	BB/G	SO	SO/G	ERA	/A	OAVG	OOBP	PR	/A	PF	CPI	WAT	PB	PD	TPI
1938 Pit-N	12	5	.706	28	21	10	1	1	159	152	8.6	7	42	2.4	58	3.3	3.00	125	.253	.303	14	13	99	106	2.9	-1	0	1.2
1939 Pit-N	14	17	.452	37	33	10	2	0	225	251	10.0	11	81	3.2	64	2.6	4.36	90	.284	.339	-11	-10	101	96	0.2	0	3	-0.6
1940 Pit-N	8	13	.381	39	22	3	0	3	142	196	12.4	5	53	3.4	48	3.0	5.39	68	.329	.384	-24	-27	95	105	-2.8	-1	1	-2.6
1941 Pit-N	9	4	.692	35	9	3	0	4	117	127	9.8	5	30	2.3	36	2.8	3.92	94	.276	.317	-4	-3	102	94	2.4	2	0	0.0
1942 Pit-N	8	11	.421	37	19	8	1	1	153	151	8.9	6	45	2.6	58	3.4	3.24	104	.252	.303	1	2	102	95	-0.6	1	1	0.5
1943 Pit-N	11	8	.579	33	25	14	3	0	195	185	8.5	6	58	2.7	65	3.0	2.72	127	.252	.300	14	16	103	109	1.3	3	0	2.1
1946 Bos-A	3	2	.600	28	1	0	0	**9**	57	49	7.7	1	25	3.9	16	2.5	2.37	164	.238	.318	7	10	111	124	-0.2	1	-0	1.1
1947 Bos-A	1	1	.500	28	0	0	0	5	42	42	9.0	5	24	5.1	12	2.6	3.86	103	.253	.345	-1	0	107	115	0.0	-1	-0	0.0
Total 8	66	61	.520	265	130	48	7	23	1090	1153	9.5	46	358	3.0	357	2.9	3.67	100	.271	.325	-3	1	101	103	3.2	3	4	1.7

■ JOE KLINK Klink, Joseph Charles b: 2/3/62, Johnstown, Pa. BL/TL, 5'11", 170 lbs. Deb: 4/09/87

YEAR TM/L	W	L	PCT	G	GS	CG	SHO	SV	IP	H	H/G	HR	BB	BB/G	SO	SO/G	ERA	/A	OAVG	OOBP	PR	/A	PF	CPI	WAT	PB	PD	TPI
1987 Min-A	0	1	.000	12	0	0	0	0	23	37	14.5	4	11	4.3	17	6.7	6.65	65	.359	.414	-6	-6	96	117	-0.4	0	-0	-0.5

■ JOHNNY KLIPPSTEIN Klippstein, John Calvin b: 10/17/27, Washington, D.C. BR/TR, 6'1", 173 lbs. Deb: 5/03/50

YEAR TM/L	W	L	PCT	G	GS	CG	SHO	SV	IP	H	H/G	HR	BB	BB/G	SO	SO/G	ERA	/A	OAVG	OOBP	PR	/A	PF	CPI	WAT	PB	PD	TPI
1950 Chi-N	2	9	.182	33	11	3	0	1	105	112	9.6	9	64	5.5	51	4.4	5.23	85	.279	.375	-13	-9	107	98	-3.1	4	-1	-0.5
1951 Chi-N	6	6	.500	35	11	1	1	2	124	125	9.1	10	53	3.8	56	4.1	4.28	92	.263	.337	-4	-5	100	96	1.0	-1	0	-0.5
1952 Chi-N	9	14	.391	41	25	7	2	3	203	208	9.2	17	89	3.9	110	4.9	4.43	87	.265	.342	-16	-13	103	96	-2.7	1	1	-0.9
1953 Chi-N	10	11	.476	48	20	5	0	6	168	169	9.1	15	107	5.7	113	6.1	4.82	95	.258	.366	-10	-5	106	97	1.1	-1	-2	-0.6
1954 Chi-N	4	11	.267	36	21	4	0	1	148	155	9.4	13	96	5.8	69	4.2	5.29	78	.272	.368	-20	-19	102	92	-2.8	-2	1	-1.8
1955 Cin-N	9	10	.474	39	14	3	2	0	138	120	7.8	13	60	3.9	68	4.4	3.39	124	.233	.313	10	13	104	99	-0.2	-2	-0	1.1
1956 Cin-N	12	11	.522	37	29	11	0	1	211	219	9.3	26	82	3.5	86	3.7	4.09	98	.275	.340	-8	-2	106	112	-1.5	-4	1	-0.4
1957 Cin-N	8	11	.421	46	18	3	1	3	146	146	9.0	17	68	4.2	99	6.1	5.05	81	.261	.337	-19	-15	106	86	-1.9	-3	-1	-1.8
1958 Cin-N	3	2	.600	12	4	0	0	1	33	37	10.1	5	14	3.8	22	6.0	4.91	85	.285	.354	-4	-3	106	103	0.5	-0	-1	-0.3
LA-N	3	5	.375	45	0	0	0	9	90	81	8.1	12	44	4.4	73	7.3	3.80	111	.248	.333	2	4	106	111	-0.7	-2	-0	0.2
Yr	6	7	.462	57	4	0	0	10	123	118	8.6	17	58	4.2	95	7.0	4.10	102	.258	.337	-2	1	106	111	-0.2	-0	-1	-0.1
1959 LA-N	4	0	1.000	28	0	0	0	2	46	48	9.4	8	33	6.5	30	5.9	5.87	68	.276	.388	-10	-10	101	102	2.0	-0	-0	-0.9
1960 Cle-A	5	5	.500	49	0	0	0	**14**	74	53	6.4	8	35	4.3	46	5.6	2.92	130	.205	.294	8	7	98	103	0.1	-0	0	0.7
1961 Was-A	2	2	.500	42	1	0	0	0	72	83	10.4	13	43	5.4	41	5.1	6.75	58	.297	.387	-22	-23	97	94	0.4	-0	1	-2.1
1962 Cin-N	7	6	.538	40	7	0	0	4	109	113	9.3	13	64	5.3	67	5.5	4.46	89	.278	.369	-6	-6	100	118	-0.7	1	0	-0.4
1963 Phi-N	5	6	.455	49	1	0	0	8	112	80	6.4	3	46	3.7	86	6.9	1.93	173	.204	.287	17	18	102	115	-0.8	-2	-1	1.6
1964 Phi-N	2	1	.667	11	0	0	0	1	22	22	9.0	6	8	3.3	13	5.3	4.09	85	.250	.327	-1	-2	98	126	0.3	-0	1	-0.1
Min-A	0	4	.000	33	0	0	0	2	46	44	8.6	4	20	3.9	39	7.6	1.96	185	.260	.330	9	9	100	208	-1.9	0	1	1.0
1965 Min-A	9	3	.750	56	0	0	0	5	76	59	7.0	8	31	3.7	59	7.0	2.25	151	.217	.296	10	10	98	140	2.1	-1	-1	0.9
1966 Min-A	1	1	.500	26	0	0	0	3	40	35	7.9	2	20	4.5	26	5.8	3.37	112	.238	.331	0	2	110	106	0.0	-0	-0	0.1
1967 Det-A	0	0	—	5	0	0	0	0	7	6	7.7	1	1	1.3	4	5.1	5.14	62	.250	.269	-1	-2	98	69	0.0	0	0	-0.1
Total 18	101	118	.461	711	162	37	6	66	1970	1915	8.7	203	978	4.5	1158	5.3	4.24	94	.258	.342	-79	-51	103	105	-8.8	-15	0	-4.8

■ FRED KLOBEDANZ Klobedanz, Frederick Augustus "Duke" b: 6/13/1871, Waterbury, Conn. d: 4/12/40, Waterbury, Conn. BL/TL, 5'11", 190 lbs. Deb: 8/20/1896

YEAR TM/L	W	L	PCT	G	GS	CG	SHO	SV	IP	H	H/G	HR	BB	BB/G	SO	SO/G	ERA	/A	OAVG	OOBP	PR	/A	PF	CPI	WAT	PB	PD	TPI
1896 Bos-N	6	4	.600	10	9	9	0	0	81	69	7.7	5	31	3.4	26	2.9	3.00	155	.250	.326	12	15	107	99	0.4	2	0	1.6
1897 Bos-N	26	7	**.788**	38	37	30	2	0	309	344	10.0	12	125	3.6	92	2.7	4.60	97	.304	.373	-10	-5	103	90	5.7	8	-3	0.4
1898 Bos-N	19	10	.655	35	33	25	0	0	271	281	9.3	13	99	3.3	51	1.7	3.89	94	.289	.355	-8	-7	101	95	-0.7	-0	0	-0.5
1899 Bos-N	1	4	.200	5	5	4	0	0	33	39	10.6	2	9	2.5	8	2.2	4.91	81	.318	.365	-4	-3	103	86	-1.6	1	0	-0.1
1902 Bos-N	1	0	1.000	1	1	1	0	0	8	9	10.1	0	2	2.3	4	4.5	1.13	232	.308	.352	1	1	94	293	0.5	1	-0	0.1
Total 5	53	25	.679	89	85	69	2	0	702	742	9.5	32	266	3.4	181	2.3	4.12	100	.293	.360	-8	0	103	95	4.3	13	-3	1.5

■ STAN KLOPP Klopp, Stanley Harold "Betz" b: 12/22/10, Womelsdorf, Pa. d: 3/11/80, Robesonia, Pa. BR/TR, 6'1.5", 180 lbs. Deb: 4/30/44

YEAR TM/L	W	L	PCT	G	GS	CG	SHO	SV	IP	H	H/G	HR	BB	BB/G	SO	SO/G	ERA	/A	OAVG	OOBP	PR	/A	PF	CPI	WAT	PB	PD	TPI
1944 Bos-N	1	2	.333	24	0	0	0	0	46	47	9.2	1	33	6.5	17	3.3	4.30	81	.272	.377	-4	-4	96	108	-0.2	0	-1	-0.4

■ CHRIS KNAPP Knapp, Robert Christian b: 9/16/53, Cherry Point, N.C. BR/TR, 6'5", 195 lbs. Deb: 9/04/75

YEAR TM/L	W	L	PCT	G	GS	CG	SHO	SV	IP	H	H/G	HR	BB	BB/G	SO	SO/G	ERA	/A	OAVG	OOBP	PR	/A	PF	CPI	WAT	PB	PD	TPI
1975 Chi-A	0	0	—	2	0	0	0	0	2	2	9.0	0	4	18.0	3	13.5	4.50	87	.250	.500	-0	-0	104	161	0.0	0	0	0.0
1976 Chi-A	3	1	.750	11	6	1	0	0	52	54	9.3	5	32	5.5	41	7.1	4.85	74	.273	.373	-8	-7	101	102	1.2	0	-0	-0.7
1977 Chi-A	12	7	.632	27	26	4	0	0	146	166	10.2	16	61	3.8	103	6.3	4.81	84	.283	.352	-12	-13	99	99	1.8	0	-0	-1.2
1978 Cal-A	14	8	.636	30	29	6	0	0	188	178	8.5	25	67	3.2	126	6.0	4.21	91	.250	.310	-9	-8	101	90	2.6	0	-2	-1.0
1979 Cal-A	5	5	.500	20	18	3	0	0	98	109	10.0	8	35	3.2	36	3.3	5.51	70	.275	.332	-14	-18	92	74	-0.3	0	-0	-1.6
1980 Cal-A	2	11	.154	32	20	1	0	1	117	133	10.2	18	51	3.9	46	3.5	6.15	64	.289	.359	-27	-29	97	88	-4.1	0	-1	-2.8
Total 6	36	32	.529	122	99	15	0	1	603	642	9.6	72	250	3.7	355	5.3	5.00	78	.272	.340	-70	-75	98	91	1.2	0	-4	-7.3

■ FRANK KNAUSS Knauss, Frank H. b: 1868, Cleveland, Ohio BL/TL, 170 lbs. Deb: 6/25/1890

YEAR TM/L	W	L	PCT	G	GS	CG	SHO	SV	IP	H	H/G	HR	BB	BB/G	SO	SO/G	ERA	/A	OAVG	OOBP	PR	/A	PF	CPI	WAT	PB	PD	TPI
1890 Col-a	17	12	.586	37	34	28	3	2	276	206	**6.7**	3	106	3.5	148	4.8	2.80	132	**.221**	.301	33	28	96	84	0.0	4	0	2.9
1891 Cle-N	0	3	.000	3	3	1	0	0	15	23	13.8	2	8	4.8	6	3.6	7.20	49	.366	.438	-6	-6	106	98	-1.4	-0	0	-0.4
1892 Cin-N	0	0	—	1	0	0	0	0	8	13	14.6	0	5	5.6	2	2.3	3.38	100	.379	.458	-0	0	103	205	0.0	0	0	0.0
1894 Cle-N	0	1	.000	2	2	1	0	0	11	7	5.7	0	14	11.5	2	1.6	5.73	103	.200	.428	-0	0	111	69	-0.4	-1	0	0.0
1895 NY-N	0	0	—	1	1	0	0	0	4	9	20.3	0	2	4.5	1	2.3	20.25	22	.466	.516	-7	-7	94	49	0.0	-0	0	-0.4
Total 5	17	16	.515	44	40	30	3	2	314	258	7.4	5	135	3.9	159	4.6	3.35	113	.238	.323	19	15	97	87	-1.8	4	0	2.1

■ RUDY KNEISCH Kneisch, Rudolph Frank b: 4/10/1899, Baltimore, Md. d: 4/6/65, Baltimore, Md. BR/TL, 5'10.5", 175 lbs. Deb: 9/21/26

YEAR TM/L	W	L	PCT	G	GS	CG	SHO	SV	IP	H	H/G	HR	BB	BB/G	SO	SO/G	ERA	/A	OAVG	OOBP	PR	/A	PF	CPI	WAT	PB	PD	TPI
1926 Det-A	0	1	.000	2	2	1	0	0	17	18	9.5	2	6	3.2	4	2.1	2.65	148	.273	.347	3	2	98	170	-0.4	-1	0	0.2

■ PHIL KNELL Knell, Philip Louis b: 3/12/1865, San Francisco, Cal d: 6/5/44, Santa Monica, Cal. BR/TL, 5'7.5", 154 lbs. Deb: 1888

YEAR TM/L	W	L	PCT	G	GS	CG	SHO	SV	IP	H	H/G	HR	BB	BB/G	SO	SO/G	ERA	/A	OAVG	OOBP	PR	/A	PF	CPI	WAT	PB	PD	TPI
1888 Pit-N	1	2	.333	3	3	3	0	0	26	20	6.9	1	18	6.2	15	5.2	3.81	71	.225	.355	-3	-3	95	86	-0.4	-1	0	-0.3
1890 Phi-P	22	11	.667	35	31	30	2	0	287	287	9.0	10	166	5.2	99	3.1	3.83	112	.272	.371	13	14	101	99	**6.1**	-1	0	1.1
1891 Col-a	28	27	.509	58	52	47	**5**	0	462	363	**7.1**	4	226	4.4	228	4.4	2.92	114	**.229**	.326	41	22	90	82	4.9	-7	5	1.4
1892 Was-N	9	13	.409	22	21	17	1	0	170	156	8.3	4	76	4.0	74	3.9	3.65	96	.256	.339	-7	-3	106	85	0.5	-5	0	-0.6
Phi-N	5	5	.500	11	9	7	0	0	80	87	9.8	0	35	3.9	43	4.8	4.05	83	.290	.364	-7	-6	103	92	-0.5	-3	0	-0.7
Yr	14	18	.438	33	30	24	1	0	250	243	8.7	4	111	4.0	117	4.2	3.78	91	.268	.347	-14	-9	105	92	0.0	-5	0	-1.3
1894 Pit-N	0	0	—	1	0	0	0	0	7	11	14.1	0	6	7.7	0	0.0	11.57	44	.381	.488	-5	-5	95	65	0.0	-1	0	-0.3
Lou-N	7	21	.250	32	28	25	0	0	247	330	12.0	9	104	3.8	67	2.4	5.32	91	.344	.408	0	-14	91	101	-1.6	2	-2	-1.1
Yr	7	21	.250	33	28	25	0	0	254	341	12.1	9	110	3.9	67	2.4	5.49	88	.345	.410	-4	-19	91	101	-1.6	1	-2	-1.4
1895 Lou-N	0	6	.000	10	6	3	0	0	57	75	11.8	3	21	3.3	19	3.0	6.63	71	.338	.395	-12	-12	99	79	-2.9	0	0	-0.8
Cle-N	7	5	.583	20	13	9	0	0	117	149	11.5	7	53	4.1	30	2.3	5.46	83	.331	.401	-9	-12	95	98	-0.5	-2	0	-1.0
Yr	7	11	.389	30	19	12	0	0	174	224	11.6	10	74	3.8	49	2.5	5.84	79	.333	.399	-20	-24	96	98	-3.4	0	0	-1.8
Total 6	79	90	.467	192	163	141	8	0	1453	1478	9.2	38	705	4.4	575	3.6	4.06	97	.279	.364	13	-17	96	90	5.6	-18	3	-2.3

■ CHARLIE KNEPPER Knepper, Charles b: 2/18/1871, Anderson, Ind. d: 2/6/46, Muncie, Ind. BR/TR, 6'4", 190 lbs. Deb: 5/26/1899

YEAR TM/L	W	L	PCT	G	GS	CG	SHO	SV	IP	H	H/G	HR	BB	BB/G	SO	SO/G	ERA	/A	OAVG	OOBP	PR	/A	PF	CPI	WAT	PB	PD	TPI
1899 Cle-N	4	22	.154	27	26	26	0	0	220	307	12.6	11	77	3.1	43	1.8	5.81	64	.355	.408	-48	-52	96	93	0.4	-5	0	-4.6

YEAR	TM/L	W	L	PCT	G	GS	CG	SHO	SV	IP	H	H/G	HR	BB	BB/G	SO	SO/G	ERA	/A	OAVG	OOBP	PR	/A	PF	CPI	WAT	PB	PD	TPI
■ BOB KNEPPER Knepper, Robert Wesley b: 5/25/54, Akron, Ohio BL/TL, 6'3", 195 lbs. Deb: 9/10/76																													
1976	SF-N	1	2	.333	4	4	0	0	0	25	26	9.4	0	7	2.5	11	4.0	3.24	113	.277	.317	1	1	104	102	-0.3	-0	0	0.1
1977	SF-N	11	9	.550	27	27	6	2	0	166	151	8.2	14	72	3.9	100	5.4	3.36	122	.242	.318	10	14	105	104	1.8	1	-1	1.4
1978	SF-N	17	11	.607	36	35	16	**6**	0	260	218	7.5	10	85	2.9	147	5.1	2.63	124	.229	.289	**27**	18	91	98	2.1	-3	-2	1.3
1979	SF-N	9	12	.429	34	34	6	2	0	207	241	10.5	30	77	3.3	123	5.3	4.65	75	.289	.347	-21	-27	93	107	-0.2	3	-1	-2.5
1980	SF-N	9	16	.360	35	33	8	1	0	215	242	10.1	15	61	2.6	103	4.3	4.10	85	.281	.330	-12	-15	96	99	-3.1	-0	2	-1.3
1981	Hou-N	9	5	.643	22	22	6	5	0	157	128	7.3	5	38	2.2	75	4.3	2.18	139	.226	.276	23	15	87	105	1.5	1	-0	1.7
1982	Hou-N	5	15	.250	33	29	4	0	1	180	193	9.6	14	60	3.0	108	5.4	4.45	81	.278	.332	-17	-17	100	93	-5.0	-3	1	-1.8
1983	Hou-N	6	13	.316	35	29	4	3	0	203	202	9.0	12	71	3.1	125	5.5	3.19	103	.261	.319	10	2	90	111	-4.0	3	1	0.6
1984	Hou-N	15	10	.600	35	34	11	3	0	234	223	8.6	26	55	2.1	140	5.4	3.19	103	.251	.292	10	3	92	107	3.0	4	-1	0.5
1985	Hou-N	15	13	.536	37	37	4	0	0	241	253	9.4	21	54	2.0	131	4.9	3.55	97	.271	.305	1	-3	96	104	0.8	0	-3	-0.5
1986	Hou-N	17	12	.586	40	38	8	**5**	0	258	232	8.1	19	62	2.2	143	5.0	3.14	121	.242	.283	17	18	102	94	-0.1	-3	2	1.8
1987	Hou-N	8	17	.320	33	31	1	0	0	178	226	11.4	26	54	2.7	76	3.8	5.26	72	.313	.359	-23	-29	93	107	-4.3	-1	1	-2.7
1988	Hou-N	14	5	.737	27	27	3	2	0	175	156	8.0	13	67	3.4	103	5.3	3.14	103	.243	.310	6	2	93	111	4.7	-0	2	0.3
Total	13	136	140	.493	398	380	77	29	1	2499	2491	9.0	205	763	2.7	1385	5.0	3.54	98	.261	.313	33	-18	95	103	-3.1	2	0	-1.1
■ LOU KNERR Knerr, Wallace Luther b: 8/21/21, Strasburg, Pa. d: 3/23/80, Denver, Pa. BR/TR, 6'1", 210 lbs. Deb: 4/17/45																													
1945	Phi-A	5	11	.313	27	17	5	0	0	130	142	9.8	6	74	5.1	41	2.8	4.22	77	.283	.365	-12	-14	96	110	-0.8	-1	0	-1.5
1946	Phi-A	3	16	.158	30	22	6	0	0	148	171	10.4	13	67	4.1	58	3.5	5.41	70	.288	.355	-31	-27	107	87	-5.0	-0	-0	-2.6
1947	Was-A	0	0	—	6	0	0	0	0	9	17	17.0	1	8	8.0	5	5.0	11.00	34	.405	.472	-7	-7	101	91	0.0	0	-0	-0.5
Total	3	8	27	.229	63	39	11	0	0	287	330	10.3	20	149	4.7	104	3.3	5.05	70	.290	.364	-51	-49	102	98	-5.8	-1	-0	-4.6
■ ELMER KNETZER Knetzer, Elmer Ellsworth "Baron" b: 7/22/1885, Carrick, Pa. d: 10/3/75, Pittsburgh, Pa. BR/TR, 5'10", 180 lbs. Deb: 09																													
1909	Bro-N	1	3	.250	5	4	3	0	0	36	33	8.3	2	22	5.5	7	1.8	3.00	89	.252	.359	-2	-1	103	128	-0.5	-2	1	0.0
1910	Bro-N	7	5	.583	20	15	10	3	0	133	122	8.3	1	60	4.1	56	3.8	3.18	93	.255	.339	-2	-3	98	98	1.8	-2	-1	-0.6
1911	Bro-N	11	12	.478	35	20	11	3	0	204	202	8.9	1	93	4.1	66	2.9	3.49	97	.277	.359	-2	-2	99	110	1.2	-4	-1	-0.7
1912	Bro-N	7	9	.438	33	16	4	1	0	140	135	8.7	6	70	4.5	61	3.9	4.56	73	.250	.340	-18	-19	97	71	0.8	-1	-0	-1.9
1914	Pit-F	20	12	.625	37	30	20	3	1	272	257	8.5	9	88	2.9	146	4.8	2.88	107	.254	.315	10	6	96	104	6.4	-7	3	0.2
1915	Pit-F	18	14	.563	41	33	22	3	3	279	256	8.3	5	89	2.9	120	3.9	2.58	120	.251	.311	14	16	102	112	0.0	-5	3	1.5
1916	Bos-N	0	2	.000	2	0	0	0	0	5	11	19.8	0	2	3.6	2	3.6	7.20	33	.524	.542	-3	-3	91	148	-0.9	0	1	-0.1
	Cin-N	5	12	.294	36	16	12	0	1	171	161	8.5	6	48	2.5	70	3.7	2.89	91	.252	.298	-5	-5	101	98	-2.2	-1	3	-0.3
	Yr	5	14	.263	38	16	12	0	1	176	172	8.8	6	50	2.6	72	3.7	3.02	87	.261	.306	-8	-8	100	98	-3.1	0	3	-0.4
1917	Cin-N	0	0	—	11	0	0	0	1	27	29	9.7	0	12	4.0	7	2.3	3.00	84	.282	.336	-1	-1	93	133	0.0	-0	0	-0.1
Total	8	69	69	.500	220	134	82	13	6	1267	1206	8.6	30	484	3.4	535	3.8	3.15	97	.258	.327	-8	-13	99	103	6.6	-22	7	-2.0
■ LON KNIGHT Knight, Alonzo P. b: 6/16/1853, Philadelphia, Pa. d: 4/23/32, Philadelphia, Pa. BR/TR, 5'11.5", 165 lbs. Deb: 9/04/1875 M																													
1875	Ath-n	6	5	.545	13																								
1876	Phi-N	10	22	.313	34	32	27	0	0	282	383	12.2	0	34	1.1	12	0.4	2.62	93	.328	.347	-10	-6	105	**133**	3.1	-1	0	-0.4
1884	Phi-a	0	1	.000	2	1	1	0	0	14	24	15.4	0	4	2.6	2	1.3	9.00	41	.386	.424	-9	-8	113	79	-0.4	0	0	-0.5
1885	Phi-a	0	0	—	1	0	0	0	0	5	4	7.2	0	2	3.6	1	1.8	1.80	184	.230	.310	1	1	102	144	0.0	0	0	0.1
	Pro-N	0	0	—	1	0	0	0	0	4	4	9.0	1	4	9.0	1	2.3	6.75	39	.271	.427	-2	-2	93	103	0.0	-0	0	-0.1
Total	3	10	23	.303	38	33	28	0	0	305	415	12.2	1	44	1.3	16	0.5	2.95	85	.329	.352	-20	-15	105	130	2.7	-1	0	-0.9
■ JACK KNIGHT Knight, Elma Russell b: 1/12/1895, Pittsboro, Miss. d: 7/30/76, San Antonio, Tex. BL/TR, 6', 175 lbs. Deb: 9/20/22																													
1922	StL-N	0	0	—	1	1	0	0	0	4	9	20.3	0	3	6.8	1	2.3	9.00	46	.474	.522	-2	-2	100	123	0.0	0	0	-0.1
1925	Phi-N	7	6	.538	33	11	4	0	3	105	161	13.8	14	36	3.1	19	1.6	6.86	73	.354	.391	-30	-21	118	99	1.2	-1	-1	-2.0
1926	Phi-N	3	12	.200	35	15	5	0	2	143	206	13.0	14	48	3.0	29	1.8	6.61	62	.347	.380	-44	-40	107	94	-3.7	1	5	-3.1
1927	Bos-N	0	0	—	3	0	0	0	0	3	6	18.0	0	2	6.0	0	0.0	15.00	25	.429	.500	-4	-4	95	62	0.0	0	1	-0.2
Total	4	10	18	.357	72	27	9	0	5	255	382	13.5	28	89	3.1	49	1.7	6.85	65	.353	.389	-80	-68	111	96	-2.5	-0	4	-5.4
■ GEORGE KNIGHT Knight, George Henry b: 11/24/1855, Lakeville, Conn. d: 10/4/12, Lakeville, Conn. Deb: 9/28/1875																													
1875	NH-n	1	0	1.000	0																								
■ JOE KNIGHT Knight, Jonas William "Quiet Joe" b: 9/28/1859, Point Stanley, Ont., Canada d: 10/18/38, St.Thomas, Ont., Can. BL/TL, 5'11", 185 lbs. Deb: 5/16/1884																													
1884	Phi-N	2	4	.333	6	6	6	0	0	51	66	11.6	2	21	3.7	8	1.4	5.47	53	.323	.386	-14	-15	97	90	0.0	1	0	-1.0
■ HUB KNOLLS Knolls, Oscar Edward b: 12/18/1883, Valparaiso, Ind. d: 7/1/46, Chicago, Ill. TR , Deb: 5/01/06																													
1906	Bro-N	0	0	—	2	0	0	0	0	7	13	16.7	0	2	2.6	3	3.9	3.86	61	.429	.464	-1	-1	90	185	0.0	1	-0	-0.1
■ JACK KNOTT Knott, John Henry b: 3/2/07, Dallas, Tex. d: 10/13/81, Brownwood, Tex. BR/TR, 6'2.5", 200 lbs. Deb: 4/13/33																													
1933	StL-A	1	8	.111	20	9	0	0	0	83	88	9.5	11	33	3.6	19	2.1	4.99	101	.269	.333	-7	0	117	96	-3.1	0	-1	0.0
1934	StL-A	10	3	.769	45	10	2	0	4	138	149	9.7	17	67	4.4	56	3.7	4.96	96	.278	.353	-7	-3	106	103	4.0	-1	1	-0.2
1935	StL-A	11	8	.579	48	19	7	2	**7**	188	219	10.5	8	78	3.7	45	2.2	4.60	106	.287	.349	-3	6	110	97	2.8	-6	1	0.2
1936	StL-A	9	17	.346	47	23	9	0	6	193	272	12.7	15	93	4.3	60	2.8	7.27	74	.330	.397	-48	-40	107	89	-1.1	-6	-1	-3.9
1937	StL-A	8	18	.308	38	22	8	0	2	191	220	10.4	25	91	4.3	74	3.5	4.90	98	.291	.365	-6	-3	103	112	0.2	-4	-3	-0.7
1938	StL-A	1	2	.333	7	4	0	0	0	30	35	10.5	3	15	4.5	8	2.4	4.80	103	.285	.362	-0	0	103	105	0.0	-1	-0	0.0
	Chi-A	5	10	.333	20	18	9	0	0	131	135	9.3	8	54	3.7	35	2.4	4.05	116	.271	.333	11	10	98	105	-1.9	-2	1	0.7
	Yr	6	12	.333	27	22	9	0	0	161	170	9.5	11	69	3.9	43	2.4	4.19	113	.273	.339	11	10	99	105	-1.9	-1	1	0.7
1939	Chi-A	11	6	.647	25	23	8	0	0	150	157	9.4	13	41	2.5	56	3.4	4.14	119	.269	.310	8	13	106	96	2.0	-3	-1	0.8
1940	Chi-A	11	9	.550	25	23	4	2	0	158	166	9.5	12	52	3.0	44	2.5	4.56	99	.265	.321	-3	-1	103	86	0.4	-4	-1	-0.4
1941	Phi-A	13	11	.542	27	26	11	0	0	194	212	9.8	20	81	3.8	54	2.5	4.41	97	.279	.344	-6	-3	103	107	2.9	-3	-3	-0.7
1942	Phi-A	2	10	.167	20	14	4	0	0	95	127	12.0	7	36	3.4	31	2.9	5.59	66	.310	.360	-20	-20	101	94	-3.2	-1	1	-1.8
1946	Phi-A	0	1	.000	3	1	0	0	0	6	7	10.5	1	1	1.5	2	3.0	6.00	63	.280	.321	-2	-1	107	78	-0.4	0	-0	-0.1
Total	11	82	103	.443	325	192	62	4	19	1557	1787	10.3	140	642	3.7	484	2.8	4.97	95	.287	.350	-82	-42	105	99	2.6	-30	-5	-6.1
■ ED KNOUFF Knouff, Edward "Fred" b: 1867, Philadelphia, Pa. d: 9/14/1900, Philadelphia, Pa. BR/TR, 210 lbs. Deb: 1885																													
1885	Phi-a	7	6	.538	14	13	12	0	0	106	103	8.7	0	44	3.7	43	3.7	3.65	91	.266	.341	-5	-4	102	96	0.7	-1	0	-0.4
1886	Bal-a	0	1	.000	1	1	1	0	0	9	2	2.0	0	5	5.0	8	8.0	2.00	162	.076	.224	1	1	94	7	-0.4	-1	0	0.1
1887	Bal-a	2	6	.250	9	9	6	0	0	63	79	11.3	0	41	5.9	27	3.9	7.57	54	.321	.418	-23	-25	94	73	-2.2	1	0	-1.7
	StL-a	4	2	.667	6	6	6	1	0	50	40	7.2	1	36	6.5	18	3.2	4.50	100	.232	.364	-1	-0	105	80	-0.1	-1	0	0.0
	Yr	6	8	.429	15	15	12	1	0	113	119	9.5	1	77	6.1	45	3.6	6.21	68	.284	.395	-24	-25	99	80	-2.3	1	0	-1.7
1888	StL-a	5	4	.556	9	9	9	0	0	81	66	7.3	0	37	4.1	25	2.8	2.67	122	.235	.324	4	5	106	101	-0.8	-2	0	0.3
	Cle-a	0	1	.000	2	2	1	0	0	9	8	8.0	0	3	3.0	2	2.0	1.00	307	.251	.315	2	2	100	272	-0.4	0	0	0.2
	Yr	5	5	.500	11	11	10	0	0	90	74	7.4	0	40	4.0	27	2.7	2.50	129	.236	.323	6	7	106	272	-1.2	-2	0	0.5
1889	Phi-a	2	0	1.000	3	3	2	0	0	25	37	13.3	2	9	3.2	5	1.8	3.96	93	.360	.411	-0	-1	96	156	1.0	0	0	0.0
Total	5	20	20	.500	44	43	37	1	0	343	335	8.8	3	175	4.6	128	3.4	4.17	87	.268	.358	-22	-20	101	97	-2.2	-4	0	-1.5
■ DAROLD KNOWLES Knowles, Darold Duane b: 12/9/41, Brunswick, Mo. BL/TL, 6', 180 lbs. Deb: 4/18/65 C																													
1965	Bal-A	0	1	.000	5	1	0	0	0	15	14	8.4	2	10	6.0	12	7.2	9.00	38	.250	.391	-9	-9	99	59	-0.4	-0	0	-0.8
1966	Phi-N	6	5	.545	69	0	0	0	13	100	98	8.8	4	46	4.1	88	7.9	3.06	118	.260	.343	6	6	100	126	0.1	0	2	0.9
1967	Was-A	6	8	.429	61	1	0	0	14	113	91	7.2	5	52	4.1	85	6.8	2.71	124	.228	.316	7	8	104	117	-0.6	-1	2	1.0
1968	Was-A	1	1	.500	32	0	0	0	4	41	38	8.3	0	12	2.6	37	8.1	2.20	127	.241	.291	4	3	94	112	0.2	1	0	0.4
1969	Was-A	9	2	.818	53	0	0	0	13	84	73	7.8	8	31	3.3	59	6.3	2.25	155	.236	.307	13	12	96	150	3.5	0	1	1.2
1970	Was-A	2	14	.125	71	0	0	0	27	119	100	7.6	4	58	4.4	71	5.4	2.04	177	.231	.318	22	21	97	151	-5.8	-1	2	2.2
1971	Was-A	2	2	.500	12	0	0	0	2	15	17	10.2	2	6	3.6	16	9.6	3.60	91	.266	.329	-0	-1	94	115	0.4	-0	0	0.0
	Oak-A	5	2	.714	43	0	0	0	7	53	40	6.8	3	16	2.7	40	6.8	3.57	96	.221	.285	-1	-1	99	74	0.8	-0	1	0.0
	Yr	7	4	.636	55	0	0	0	9	68	57	7.5	5	22	2.9	56	7.4	3.57	95	.233	.296	-1	-1	98	74	1.2	-0	1	0.0
1972	Oak-A	5	1	.833	54	0	0	0	11	66	49	6.7	1	37	5.0	36	4.9	1.36	213	.212	.316	13	**11**	95	191	1.8	1	3	1.7
1973	Oak-A	6	8	.429	52	5	1	1	9	99	87	7.9	7	49	4.5	46	4.2	3.09	106	.246	.329	8	2	86	123	-1.9	0	2	0.3

YEAR	TM/L	W	L	PCT	G	GS	CG	SHO	SV	IP	H	H/G	HR	BB	BB/G	SO	SO/G	ERA	/A	OAVG	OOBP	PR	/A	PF	CPI	WAT	PB	PD	TPI
1974	Oak-A	3	3	.500	45	1	0	0	3	53	61	10.4	6	35	5.9	18	3.1	4.25	84	.296	.392	-4	-4	99	136	-0.2	0	1	-0.2
1975	Chi-N	6	9	.400	58	0	0	0	15	88	107	10.9	3	36	3.7	63	6.4	5.83	66	.298	.356	-21	-20	105	77	-1.0	-1	3	-1.7
1976	Chi-N	5	7	.417	58	0	0	0	9	72	61	7.6	6	22	2.8	39	4.9	2.88	135	.242	.299	5	8	111	116	-0.5	1	2	1.2
1977	Tex-A	5	2	.714	42	0	0	0	4	50	50	9.0	3	23	4.1	14	2.5	3.24	130	.272	.347	5	5	104	133	1.2	0	1	0.6
1978	Mon-N	3	3	.500	60	0	0	0	6	72	63	7.9	5	30	3.8	34	4.3	2.38	144	.250	.316	10	8	96	154	0.2	-0	2	1.0
1979	StL-N	2	5	.286	48	0	0	0	6	49	54	9.9	5	17	3.1	22	4.0	4.04	96	.277	.332	-2	-1	104	104	-1.6	-0	-1	-0.1
1980	StL-N	0	1	.000	2	0	0	0	0	2	3	13.5	1	0	0.0	1	4.5	9.00	41	.375	.375	-1	-1	102	102	-0.4	0	0	0.0
Total	16	66	74	.471	765	8	1	1	143	1091	1006	8.3	65	480	4.0	681	5.6	3.12	113	.250	.327	53	48	99	126	-4.2	-2	20	7.7
■ TOM KNOWLSON	Knowlson, Thomas Herbert "Doc" b: 4/23/1895, Pittsburgh, Pa. d: 4/11/43, Miami Shores, Fla. BR/TR, 5'11", 178 lbs. Deb: 7/03/15																												
1915	Phi-A	4	6	.400	18	9	8	0	0	101	99	8.8	1	60	5.3	24	2.1	3.48	87	.273	.386	-6	-5	103	122	0.9	-3	-0	-0.8
■ BILL KNOWLTON	Knowlton, William Young b: 8/18/1892, Philadelphia, Pa. d: 2/25/44, Philadelphia, Pa. BR/TR, Deb: 9/03/20																												
1920	Phi-A	0	1	.000	1	1	0	0	0	6	9	13.5	0	3	4.5	5	7.5	4.50	83	.346	.469	-0	-1	99	158	-0.4	-0	0	0.0
■ MARK KNUDSON	Knudson, Mark Richard b: 10/28/60, Denver, Colo. BR/TR, 6'5", 215 lbs. Deb: 7/08/85																												
1985	Hou-N	0	2	.000	2	2	0	0	0	11	21	17.2	0	3	2.5	4	3.3	9.00	38	.429	.453	-7	-7	96	89	-0.9	0	0	-0.5
1986	Hou-N	1	5	.167	9	7	0	0	0	43	48	10.0	5	15	3.1	20	4.2	4.19	90	.279	.335	-2	-2	102	108	-2.1	-1	-1	-0.3
	Mil-A	0	1	.000	4	1	0	0	0	18	22	11.0	7	5	2.5	9	4.5	7.50	57	.286	.329	-7	-6	103	86	-0.4	0	0	-0.5
1987	Mil-A	4	4	.500	15	8	1	0	0	62	88	12.8	7	14	2.0	26	3.8	5.37	85	.331	.354	-6	-6	102	106	-0.4	0	-1	-0.5
1988	Mil-A	0	0	—	5	0	0	0	0	16	17	9.6	1	2	1.1	7	3.9	1.13	363	.279	.302	5	5	103	314	0.0	0	0	0.6
Total	4	5	12	.294	35	18	1	0	0	150	196	11.8	20	39	2.3	66	4.0	5.10	82	.314	.349	-17	-15	102	125	-3.8	-1	-2	-1.2
■ KEVIN KOBEL	Kobel, Kevin Richard b: 10/2/53, Buffalo, N.Y. BR/TL, 6', 180 lbs. Deb: 9/08/73																												
1973	Mil-A	0	1	.000	2	1	0	0	0	8	9	10.1	2	8	9.0	4	4.5	9.00	41	.273	.415	-5	-5	96	77	-0.4	0	0	-0.3
1974	Mil-A	6	14	.300	34	24	3	2	0	169	166	8.8	16	54	2.9	74	3.9	3.99	93	.258	.312	-7	-5	103	90	-3.8	0	1	-0.4
1976	Mil-A	0	1	.000	3	0	0	0	0	4	6	13.5	3	3	6.8	1	2.3	11.25	31	.375	.455	-3	-3	100	123	-0.4	0	0	-0.2
1978	NY-N	5	6	.455	32	11	1	0	0	108	95	7.9	9	30	2.5	51	4.3	2.92	122	.239	.287	8	8	99	104	0.5	0	-1	0.8
1979	NY-N	6	8	.429	30	27	1	1	0	162	169	9.4	14	46	2.6	67	3.7	3.50	103	.274	.319	4	2	96	113	0.5	1	1	0.3
1980	NY-N	1	4	.200	14	1	0	0	0	24	36	13.5	5	11	4.1	8	3.0	7.13	49	.353	.412	-9	-10	97	107	-1.2	-0	-0	-0.9
Total	6	18	34	.346	115	64	5	3	0	475	481	9.1	49	152	2.9	205	3.9	3.88	93	.266	.318	-12	-13	99	102	-4.8	0	1	-0.7
■ ALAN KOCH	Koch, Alan Goodman b: 3/25/38, Decatur, Ala. BR/TR, 6'4", 195 lbs. Deb: 7/26/63																												
1963	Det-A	1	1	.500	7	1	0	0	0	10	21	18.9	3	9	8.1	5	4.5	10.80	35	.467	.544	-8	-8	104	126	0.0	1	0	-0.6
1964	Det-A	0	0	—	3	0	0	0	0	4	6	13.5	1	3	6.8	1	2.3	6.75	51	.375	.474	-1	-1	95	138	0.0	0	-0	-0.1
	Was-A	3	10	.231	32	14	1	0	0	114	110	8.7	18	43	3.4	67	5.3	4.89	77	.253	.318	-16	-15	103	87	-2.6	2	-2	-1.4
	Yr	3	10	.231	35	14	1	0	0	118	116	8.8	19	46	3.5	68	5.2	4.96	75	.258	.324	-17	-16	103	87	-2.6	0	-2	-1.5
Total	2	4	11	.267	42	15	1	0	0	128	137	9.6	22	55	3.9	73	5.1	5.41	69	.277	.346	-25	-24	103	91	-2.6	3	-2	-2.1
■ DICK KOECHER	Koecher, Richard Finlay "Highpockets" b: 3/30/26, Philadelphia, Pa. BL/TL, 6'5", 196 lbs. Deb: 9/29/46																												
1946	Phi-N	0	1	.000	1	1	0	0	0	3	7	21.0	0	1	3.0	2	6.0	9.00	37	.467	.500	-2	-2	98	110	-0.4	-0	0	-0.1
1947	Phi-N	0	2	.000	3	2	1	0	0	17	20	10.6	1	10	5.3	4	2.1	4.76	87	.299	.392	-1	-1	102	114	-0.9	-1	0	0.0
1948	Phi-N	0	1	.000	3	0	0	0	0	6	4	6.0	0	3	4.5	2	3.0	3.00	127	.235	.333	1	1	97	118	-0.4	0	0	0.0
Total	3	0	4	.000	7	3	1	0	0	26	31	10.7	1	14	4.8	8	2.8	4.85	82	.313	.397	-3	-3	100	114	-1.7	-1	0	-0.1
■ MARK KOENIG	Koenig, Mark Anthony b: 7/19/02, San Francisco, Cal BB/TR, 6', 180 lbs. Deb: 9/08/25																												
1930	Det-A	0	1	.000	2	1	0	0	0	9	11	11.0	0	8	8.0	6	6.0	10.00	49	.314	.455	-5	-5	106	67	-0.3	0	0	-0.3
1931	Det-A	0	0	—	3	0	0	0	0	7	7	9.0	0	11	14.1	3	3.9	6.43	73	.280	.500	-2	-1	107	116	0.0	0	0	0.0
Total	2	0	1	.000	5	1	0	0	0	16	18	10.1	0	19	10.7	9	5.1	8.44	57	.300	.475	-7	-6	106	88	-0.3	0	0	-0.3
■ WILL KOENIGSMARK	Koenigsmark, William Thomas b: 2/27/1896, Waterloo, Ill. d: 7/1/72, Waterloo, Ill. BR/TR, 6'4", 180 lbs. Deb: 9/10/19																												
1919	StL-N	0	0	—	1	0	0	0	0	0	2	—	0	1	—	0	—	∞	—	1.000	1.000	-2	-2	97	70	0.0	0	0	-0.1
■ ELMER KOESTNER	Koestner, Elmer Joseph "Bob" b: 11/30/1885, Piper City, Ill. d: 10/27/59, Fairbury, Ill. BR/TR, 6'1.5", 175 lbs. Deb: 4/23/10																												
1910	Cle-A	5	10	.333	27	13	8	1	2	145	145	9.0	0	63	3.9	44	2.7	3.04	84	.282	.367	-8	-8	102	124	-2.2	3	-1	-0.6
1914	Chi-N	0	0	—	4	0	0	0	0	6	6	9.0	0	4	6.0	6	9.0	3.00	92	.261	.333	-0	-0	99	123	0.0	-0	0	0.0
	Cin-N	0	0	—	5	1	0	0	0	18	18	9.0	0	9	4.5	6	3.0	4.50	66	.265	.329	-3	-3	107	74	0.0	1	0	-0.1
	Yr	0	0	—	9	1	0	0	0	24	24	9.0	0	13	4.9	12	4.5	4.13	71	.264	.330	-4	-3	105	74	0.0	-0	0	-0.1
Total	2	5	10	.333	36	14	8	1	2	169	169	9.0	0	76	4.0	56	3.0	3.20	82	.279	.361	-12	-11	102	118	-2.2	3	-1	-0.7
■ JOE KOHLMAN	Kohlman, Joseph James "Blackie" b: 1/28/13, Philadelphia, Pa. d: 3/16/74, Philadelphia, Pa. BR/TR, 6', 160 lbs. Deb: 9/26/37																												
1937	Was-A	1	0	1.000	2	2	1	0	0	13	15	10.4	0	3	2.1	3	2.1	4.15	106	.283	.321	1	0	96	83	0.5	-0	-0	0.0
1938	Was-A	0	0	—	7	0	0	0	0	14	12	7.7	1	11	7.1	5	3.2	6.43	71	.240	.365	-3	-3	96	73	0.0	-0	0	-0.2
Total	2	1	0	1.000	9	2	1	0	0	27	27	9.0	1	14	4.7	8	2.7	5.33	84	.262	.345	-2	-2	96	78	0.5	-1	0	-0.2
■ EDDIE KOLB	Kolb, Edward William b: 7/20/1880, Cincinnati, Ohio BR/TR, Deb: 10/15/1899																												
1899	Cle-N	0	1	.000	1	1	1	0	0	8	18	20.3	0	5	5.6	1	1.1	10.13	37	.471	.532	-6	-6	96	99	-0.4	-0	0	-0.3
■ RAY KOLP	Kolp, Raymond Carl "Jockey" b: 10/1/1894, New Berlin, Ohio d: 7/29/67, New Orleans, La. BR/TR, 5'10.5", 187 lbs. Deb: 4/16/21																												
1921	StL-A	8	7	.533	37	18	5	1	0	167	208	11.2	12	51	2.7	43	2.3	4.96	87	.314	.349	-13	-12	101	98	0.1	-5	1	-1.4
1922	StL-A	14	4	.778	32	18	9	1	0	170	199	10.5	10	36	1.9	54	2.9	3.92	105	.292	.325	2	4	102	100	4.2	5	-4	0.4
1923	StL-A	5	12	.294	34	17	11	1	1	171	178	9.4	11	54	2.8	44	2.3	3.89	107	.273	.323	2	5	105	97	-3.5	-4	-2	0.0
1924	StL-A	5	7	.417	25	12	5	1	0	97	131	12.2	4	25	2.3	29	2.7	5.66	81	.329	.366	-15	-12	108	90	-0.8	-0	-1	-1.1
1927	Cin-N	3	3	.500	24	5	2	1	3	82	86	9.4	5	29	3.2	28	3.1	3.07	127	.278	.330	8	8	100	132	0.1	-0	0	0.8
1928	Cin-N	13	10	.565	44	24	12	1	3	209	219	9.4	9	55	2.4	61	2.6	3.19	121	.280	.318	19	16	97	114	1.4	3	1	1.9
1929	Cin-N	8	10	.444	30	16	4	1	0	145	151	9.4	8	39	2.4	27	1.7	4.03	117	.278	.313	11	11	101	97	0.3	-2	1	1.0
1930	Cin-N	7	12	.368	37	19	5	2	3	168	180	9.6	10	34	1.8	40	2.1	4.23	109	**.240**	**.265**	14	7	93	47	-0.3	2	-1	0.6
1931	Cin-N	4	9	.308	30	10	2	0	1	107	144	12.1	8	39	3.3	24	2.0	4.96	76	.332	.382	-13	-14	98	118	-1.2	-1	-1	-1.5
1932	Cin-N	6	10	.375	32	19	7	2	1	160	176	9.9	13	27	1.5	42	2.4	3.88	99	.280	.309	-0	-1	99	99	-0.2	-1	-2	-0.3
1933	Cin-N	6	9	.400	30	14	4	0	3	150	168	10.1	7	23	1.4	28	1.7	3.54	96	.290	.313	-3	-2	102	104	0.2	-1	1	-0.2
1934	Cin-N	0	2	.000	28	2	0	0	3	62	78	11.3	1	12	1.7	19	2.8	4.50	94	.312	.341	-3	-2	105	98	-0.9	-1	2	0.0
Total	12	79	95	.454	383	174	66	11	18	1688	1918	10.2	98	424	2.3	439	2.3	4.08	101	.288	.323	8	9	100	98	-0.6	-7	-6	0.2
■ HAL KOLSTAD	Kolstad, Harold Everette b: 6/1/35, Rice Lake, Wis. BR/TR, 5'9", 190 lbs. Deb: 4/22/62																												
1962	Bos-A	0	2	.000	27	2	0	0	2	61	65	9.6	11	35	5.2	36	5.3	5.46	75	.269	.362	-10	-9	103	99	-0.9	-2	0	-1.0
1963	Bos-A	0	2	.000	7	0	0	0	0	11	16	13.1	4	6	4.9	6	4.9	13.09	30	.340	.436	-12	-11	107	71	-0.9	-0	0	-1.0
Total	2	0	4	.000	34	2	0	0	2	72	81	10.1	15	41	5.1	42	5.3	6.63	61	.280	.374	-22	-21	103	94	-1.8	-2	0	-2.0
■ ED KONETCHY	Konetchy, Edward Joseph "Big Ed" b: 9/3/1885, Lacrosse, Wis. d: 5/27/47, Ft.Worth, Tex. BR/TR, 6'2.5", 195 lbs. Deb: 6/29/07																												
1910	StL-N	0	0	—	1	0	0	0	0	4	4	9.0	0	1	2.3	0	0.0	4.50	63	.267	.313	-1	-1	93	61	0.0	0	-0	0.0
1913	StL-N	1	0	1.000	1	0	0	0	0	5	1	1.8	0	4	7.2	3	5.4	0.00	—	.071	.278	2	2	97	0	0.5	0	-0	0.2
1918	Bos-N	0	1	.000	1	1	1	0	0	8	14	15.8	1	2	2.3	3	3.4	6.75	39	.378	.400	-4	-4	95	107	-0.4	0	-0	-0.2
Total	3	1	1	.500	3	1	1	0	0	17	19	10.1	1	7	3.7	6	3.2	4.24	66	.288	.351	-2	-3	95	64	0.1	1	-1	0.0
■ DOUG KONIECZNY	Konieczny, Douglas James b: 9/27/51, Detroit, Mich. BR/TR, 6'4", 220 lbs. Deb: 9/11/73																												
1973	Hou-N	0	1	.000	2	2	0	0	0	13	12	8.3	0	4	2.8	6	4.2	5.54	63	.279	.327	-3	-3	95	64	-0.4	-0	-0	-0.2
1974	Hou-N	0	3	.000	6	3	0	0	0	16	18	10.1	0	12	6.8	8	4.5	7.88	45	.290	.416	-8	-8	98	67	-1.4	-1	0	-0.7
1975	Hou-N	6	13	.316	32	29	4	1	0	171	184	9.7	15	87	4.6	89	4.7	4.47	77	.280	.357	-16	-20	95	104	-2.1	1	-1	-2.0
1977	Hou-N	1	1	.500	4	4	0	0	0	21	26	11.1	1	8	3.4	7	3.0	6.00	60	.302	.361	-5	-6	92	79	0.0	-0	0	-0.4
Total	4	7	18	.280	44	38	4	1	0	221	240	9.8	16	111	4.5	110	4.5	4.93	70	.283	.360	-31	-36	95	96	-3.9	-0	-1	-3.3

YEAR	TM/L	W	L	PCT	G	GS	CG	SHO	SV	IP	H	H/G	HR	BB	BB/G	SO	SO/G	ERA	/A	OAVG	OOBP	PR	/A	PF	CPI	WAT	PB	PD	TPI
■ ALEX KONIKOWSKI	Konikowski, Alexander James "Whitey" b: 6/8/28, Throop, Pa. BR/TR, 6'1", 187 lbs. Deb: 6/16/48																												
1948	NY-N	2	3	.400	22	1	0	0	1	33	46	12.5	7	17	4.6	9	2.5	7.64	51	.346	.409	-13	-14	98	101	-0.4	0	1	-1.1
1951	NY-N	0	0	—	3	0	0	0	0	4	2	4.5	0	0	0.0	5	11.3	0.00	—	.154	.154	2	2	99	0	0.0	0	0	0.2
1954	NY-N	0	0	—	10	0	0	0	0	12	10	7.5	1	12	9.0	6	4.5	7.50	55	.244	.393	-5	-4	102	69	0.0	-0	-0	-0.4
Total	3	2	3	.400	35	1	0	0	1	49	58	10.7	8	29	5.3	20	3.7	6.98	57	.310	.390	-16	-16	99	85	-0.4	0	0	-1.3
■ JIM KONSTANTY	Konstanty, Casimir James b: 3/2/17, Strykersville, N.Y. d: 6/11/76, Oneonta, N.Y. BR/TR, 6'1.5", 202 lbs. Deb: 6/18/44																												
1944	Cin-N	6	4	.600	20	12	5	1	0	113	113	9.0	11	33	2.6	19	1.5	2.79	123	.266	.314	10	8	95	141	0.3	2	1	1.1
1946	Bos-N	0	1	.000	10	1	0	0	0	15	17	10.2	2	7	4.2	9	5.4	5.40	59	.283	.358	-3	-4	94	91	-0.4	0	1	-0.2
1948	Phi-N	1	0	1.000	6	0	0	0	2	10	7	6.3	0	2	1.8	7	6.3	0.90	425	.233	.273	3	3	97	283	0.5	-0	-0	0.3
1949	Phi-N	9	5	.643	53	0	0	0	7	97	98	9.1	9	29	2.7	43	4.0	3.25	125	.280	.332	9	**9**	101	135	1.9	-0	1	1.0
1950	Phi-N	16	7	.696	**74**	0	0	0	**22**	152	108	6.4	11	50	3.0	56	3.3	2.66	149	.205	.266	**25**	**22**	96	90	3.3	-2	-1	1.8
1951	Phi-N	4	11	.267	58	1	0	0	9	116	127	9.9	9	31	2.4	27	2.1	4.03	95	.282	.320	-1	-3	97	100	-3.4	-0	1	0.0
1952	Phi-N	5	3	.625	42	2	2	1	6	80	87	9.8	9	21	2.4	16	1.8	3.94	94	.274	.316	-2	-2	99	104	0.6	-0	-0	-0.2
1953	Phi-N	14	10	.583	48	19	7	0	5	171	198	10.4	18	42	2.2	45	2.4	4.42	95	.290	.331	-3	-4	98	102	1.3	-0	-0	-0.3
1954	Phi-N	2	3	.400	33	1	0	0	3	50	62	11.2	7	12	2.2	11	2.0	3.78	105	.316	.344	2	1	98	140	-0.4	-2	0	0.0
	NY-A	1	1	.500	9	0	0	0	2	18	11	5.5	0	6	3.0	3	1.5	1.00	351	.183	.243	5	5	94	130	-0.2	-0	0	0.5
1955	NY-A	7	2	.778	45	0	0	0	11	74	68	8.3	5	24	2.9	19	2.3	2.31	162	.247	.299	14	12	94	137	1.9	-0	0	1.1
1956	NY-A	0	0	—	8	0	0	0	2	11	15	12.3	3	6	4.9	6	4.9	4.91	80	.319	.396	-1	-1	95	148	0.0	-0	-0	-0.1
	StL-N	1	1	.500	27	0	0	0	5	39	46	10.6	4	6	1.4	7	1.6	4.62	81	.301	.311	-4	-4	99	93	0.0	0	-1	-0.3
Total	11	66	48	.579	433	36	14	2	74	946	957	9.1	88	269	2.6	268	2.5	3.46	112	.268	.313	55	42	97	115	5.4	-4	3	4.7
■ ERNIE KOOB	Koob, Ernest Gerald b: 9/11/1893, Keeler, Mich. d: 11/12/41, Lemay, Mo. BL/TL, 5'10", 160 lbs. Deb: 6/23/15																												
1915	StL-A	4	5	.444	28	13	6	0	1	134	119	8.0	2	50	3.4	37	2.5	2.35	124	.254	.339	9	8	99	138	0.3	-1	-2	0.6
1916	StL-A	11	8	.579	33	20	10	2	2	167	153	8.2	1	56	3.0	26	1.4	2.53	105	.252	.321	5	2	94	110	1.4	-1	-3	-0.1
1917	StL-A	6	14	.300	39	18	3	1	1	134	139	9.3	1	57	3.8	47	3.2	3.90	67	.280	.361	-18	-19	98	96	-2.0	-1	0	-2.0
1919	StL-A	2	3	.400	25	4	0	0	0	66	77	10.5	3	23	3.1	11	1.5	4.64	68	.296	.358	-10	-11	98	90	-0.3	-2	0	-1.2
Total	4	23	30	.434	125	55	19	3	4	501	488	8.8	7	186	3.3	121	2.2	3.13	89	.266	.342	-14	-19	97	111	-0.6	-5	-4	-2.7
■ CAL KOONCE	Koonce, Calvin Lee b: 11/18/40, Fayetteville, N.C. BR/TR, 6'1", 185 lbs. Deb: 4/14/62																												
1962	Chi-N	10	10	.500	35	30	3	1	0	191	200	9.4	17	86	4.1	84	4.0	3.96	108	.271	.347	-0	7	109	112	2.4	-4	-1	0.3
1963	Chi-N	2	6	.250	21	13	0	0	0	73	75	9.2	9	32	3.9	44	5.4	4.56	76	.273	.343	-10	-9	105	103	-2.0	-0	1	-0.8
1964	Chi-N	3	0	1.000	6	2	0	0	0	31	30	8.7	1	7	2.0	17	4.9	2.03	185	.254	.289	5	6	106	141	1.5	-1	2	0.8
1965	Chi-N	7	9	.438	38	23	3	1	0	173	181	9.4	17	52	2.7	88	4.6	3.69	99	.271	.324	-3	-1	103	112	0.0	-0	0	0.0
1966	Chi-N	5	5	.500	45	5	0	0	2	109	113	9.3	13	35	2.9	65	5.4	3.80	97	.268	.316	-2	-1	103	108	1.1	0	1	0.1
1967	Chi-N	2	2	.500	34	0	0	0	2	51	52	9.2	2	21	3.7	28	4.9	4.59	74	.268	.338	-7	-7	100	84	-0.1	-1	1	-0.6
	NY-N	3	3	.500	11	6	2	1	0	45	45	9.0	2	7	1.4	24	4.8	2.80	123	.259	.284	3	3	102	101	0.6	-0	1	0.5
	Yr	5	5	.500	45	6	2	1	2	96	97	9.1	4	28	2.6	52	4.9	3.75	91	.262	.311	-4	-4	101	101	0.5	-1	2	-0.1
1968	NY-N	6	4	.600	55	2	0	0	11	97	80	7.4	4	32	3.0	50	4.6	2.41	127	.235	.294	6	7	103	116	1.4	-1	-0	0.7
1969	NY-N	6	3	.667	40	0	0	0	7	83	85	9.2	8	42	4.6	48	5.2	4.99	72	.269	.354	-13	-13	99	92	0.6	0	1	-1.1
1970	NY-N	0	2	.000	13	0	0	0	0	22	25	10.2	2	14	5.7	10	4.1	3.27	128	.301	.404	2	2	103	182	-0.9	-0	0	0.2
	Bos-A	3	4	.429	23	8	1	0	2	76	64	7.6	7	29	3.4	37	4.4	3.55	115	.231	.307	1	5	110	91	-0.6	-0	2	0.7
1971	Bos-A	0	1	.000	13	1	0	0	0	21	22	9.4	3	11	4.7	9	3.9	5.57	65	.278	.363	-5	-4	105	91	-0.4	0	1	-0.3
Total	10	47	49	.490	334	90	9	3	24	972	972	9.0	85	368	3.4	504	4.7	3.78	98	.264	.328	-23	-6	104	108	3.6	-7	9	0.5
■ JERRY KOOSMAN	Koosman, Jerome Martin b: 12/23/42, Appleton, Minn. BR/TL, 6'2", 205 lbs. Deb: 4/14/67																												
1967	NY-N	0	2	.000	9	3	0	0	0	22	22	9.0	3	19	7.8	11	4.5	6.14	56	.259	.390	-7	-7	102	90	-0.9	0	0	-0.6
1968	NY-N	19	12	.613	35	34	17	7	0	264	221	7.5	16	69	2.4	178	6.1	2.08	147	.228	.282	27	29	103	123	5.3	-3	-1	3.0
1969	NY-N	17	9	.654	32	32	16	6	0	241	187	7.0	14	68	2.5	180	6.7	2.28	157	.216	.271	35	35	99	103	1.5	-6	-1	3.0
1970	NY-N	12	7	.632	30	29	5	1	0	212	189	8.0	22	71	3.0	118	5.0	3.14	133	.237	.296	21	24	103	106	2.5	-2	-3	2.0
1971	NY-N	6	11	.353	26	24	4	0	0	166	160	8.7	12	51	2.8	96	5.2	3.04	110	.256	.305	8	5	96	111	-2.8	0	-1	0.5
1972	NY-N	11	12	.478	34	24	4	1	1	163	155	8.6	14	52	2.9	147	8.1	4.14	80	.250	.308	-12	-15	96	83	-1.2	-3	0	-1.8
1973	NY-N	14	15	.483	35	35	12	3	0	263	234	8.0	18	76	2.6	156	5.3	2.84	129	.242	.293	24	24	100	106	-0.8	-3	-1	2.2
1974	NY-N	15	11	.577	35	35	13	0	0	265	258	8.8	16	85	2.9	188	6.4	3.36	108	.257	.313	8	8	100	101	3.6	2	0	1.0
1975	NY-N	14	13	.519	36	34	11	4	2	240	234	8.8	19	98	3.7	173	6.5	3.41	101	.261	.330	6	1	95	114	0.4	1	-0	0.1
1976	NY-N	21	10	.677	34	32	17	3	0	247	205	7.5	19	66	2.4	200	7.3	2.70	118	.226	.274	22	13	91	96	5.6	3	0	1.7
1977	NY-N	8	20	.286	32	32	6	1	0	227	195	7.7	17	81	3.2	192	**7.6**	3.49	109	.232	.298	11	8	97	85	-4.3	-3	-2	0.2
1978	NY-N	3	15	.167	38	32	3	0	2	235	221	8.5	17	84	3.2	160	6.1	3.75	95	.255	.317	-4	-5	99	97	-5.5	-3	2	-0.6
1979	Min-A	20	13	.606	37	36	10	2	0	264	268	9.1	19	83	2.8	157	5.4	3.38	136	.268	.322	25	35	108	113	4.0	0	2	3.8
1980	Min-A	16	13	.552	38	34	8	0	2	243	252	9.3	24	69	2.6	149	5.5	4.04	109	.272	.319	0	10	109	99	2.4	0	1	1.1
1981	Min-A	3	9	.250	19	13	2	1	5	94	98	9.4	8	34	3.3	55	5.3	4.21	93	.272	.327	-6	-3	107	97	-2.1	0	0	-0.3
	Chi-A	1	4	.200	8	3	1	0	0	27	27	9.0	2	7	2.3	21	7.0	3.33	109	.260	.301	1	1	99	101	-1.4	0	-0	0.1
	Yr	4	13	.235	27	16	3	1	5	121	125	9.3	10	41	3.0	76	5.7	4.02	96	.267	.321	-5	-2	105	101	-3.5	0	-0	-0.2
1982	Chi-A	11	7	.611	42	19	3	1	3	173	194	10.1	9	38	2.0	88	4.6	3.85	103	.287	.322	4	2	97	102	1.6	0	0	0.2
1983	Chi-A	11	7	.611	37	24	2	1	2	170	176	9.3	19	53	2.8	90	4.8	4.76	87	.266	.322	-13	-12	102	87	0.0	0	0	-1.1
1984	Phi-N	14	15	.483	36	34	3	1	0	224	232	9.3	8	60	2.4	137	5.5	3.25	112	.267	.311	8	10	101	103	-0.5	-3	-1	0.6
1985	Phi-N	6	4	.600	19	18	3	1	0	99	107	9.7	14	34	3.1	60	5.5	4.64	79	.276	.333	-11	-11	102	100	1.3	-2	-0	-1.2
Total	19	222	209	.515	612	527	140	33	17	3839	3635	8.5	290	1198	2.8	2556	6.0	3.36	111	.252	.307	148	151	100	102	8.7	-22	-4	13.9
■ HOWIE KOPLITZ	Koplitz, Howard Dean b: 5/4/38, Oshkosh, Wis. BR/TR, 5'10.5", 190 lbs. Deb: 9/08/61																												
1961	Det-A	2	0	1.000	4	1	1	0	0	12	16	12.0	0	8	6.0	9	6.8	2.25	168	.327	.407	2	2	94	259	1.0	-0	-0	0.1
1962	Det-A	3	0	1.000	10	6	1	0	0	38	54	12.8	5	10	2.4	10	2.4	5.21	84	.342	.372	-5	-4	110	119	1.5	1	0	-0.2
1964	Was-A	0	0	—	6	1	0	0	0	17	20	10.6	3	13	6.9	9	4.8	4.76	79	.290	.402	-2	-2	103	133	0.0	-0	0	-0.1
1965	Was-A	4	7	.364	33	11	0	0	1	107	97	8.2	11	48	4.0	59	5.0	4.04	87	.249	.327	-7	-6	102	99	-0.8	-1	1	-0.5
1966	Was-A	0	0	—	1	0	0	0	0	2	0	0.0	0	1	4.5	0	0.0	0.00	—	.000	.200	1	1	96	0	0.0	0	0	0.1
Total	5	9	7	.563	54	19	2	0	1	176	187	9.6	19	80	4.1	87	4.4	4.19	89	.280	.350	-11	-9	103	116	1.7	-1	1	-0.6
■ GEORGE KORINCE	Korince, George Eugene "Moose" b: 1/10/46, Ottawa, Ont., Canada BR/TR, 6'3", 210 lbs. Deb: 9/10/66																												
1966	Det-A	0	0	—	2	0	0	0	0	3	1	3.0	0	3	9.0	2	6.0	0.00	—	.091	.333	1	1	102	0	0.0	-0	0	0.1
1967	Det-A	1	0	1.000	9	0	0	0	0	14	10	6.4	1	11	7.1	11	7.1	5.14	62	.204	.328	-3	-3	98	71	0.5	-0	0	-0.2
Total	2	1	0	1.000	11	0	0	0	0	17	11	5.8	1	14	7.4	13	6.9	4.24	76	.183	.329	-2	-2	99	58	0.5	-0	0	-0.1
■ JIM KORWAN	Korwan, James "Long Jim" b: 3/4/1874, Brooklyn, N.Y. d: 8/1899, Brooklyn, N.Y. BR/TR, 6'1", 181 lbs. Deb: 4/24/1894																												
1894	Bro-N	0	0	—	1	0	0	0	0	5	9	16.2	1	5	9.0	2	3.6	14.40	35	.414	.523	-5	-5	94	74	0.0	-0	0	-0.3
1897	Chi-N	1	2	.333	5	4	3	0	0	34	47	12.4	1	28	7.4	12	3.2	5.82	75	.351	.464	-6	-6	101	112	-0.3	-2	0	-0.5
Total	2	1	2	.333	6	4	3	0	0	39	56	12.9	2	33	7.6	14	3.2	6.92	64	.360	.472	-11	-11	100	107	-0.3	-2	0	-0.8
■ BILL KOSKI	Koski, William John "T-Bone" b: 2/6/32, Madera, Cal. BR/TR, 6'4", 185 lbs. Deb: 4/28/51																												
1951	Pit-N	0	1	.000	13	1	0	0	0	27	26	8.7	2	28	9.3	6	2.0	6.67	65	.257	.412	-8	-7	110	83	-0.4	-1	-1	-0.7
■ DAVE KOSLO	Koslo, George Bernard (born George Bernard Koslowski) b: 3/31/20, Menasha, Wis. d: 12/1/75, Menasha, Wis. BL/TL, 5'11", 180 lbs. Deb: 9/12/41																												
1941	NY-N	1	2	.333	4	3	2	0	0	24	17	6.4	0	10	3.8	12	4.5	1.88	201	.202	.287	5	5	104	108	-0.4	-1	-1	0.4
1942	NY-N	3	6	.333	19	11	3	1	0	78	79	9.1	7	32	3.7	42	4.8	5.08	66	.261	.326	-15	-15	101	79	-1.8	-0	-1	-1.5
1946	NY-N	14	19	.424	40	35	17	3	1	265	251	8.5	15	101	3.4	121	4.1	3.63	97	.249	.314	-6	-3	103	89	1.0	-4	1	-0.5
1947	NY-N	15	10	.600	39	31	10	3	0	217	223	9.2	23	82	3.4	86	3.6	4.40	92	.259	.322	-8	-8	99	90	2.3	-1	-1	-0.9
1948	NY-N	8	10	.444	35	18	5	3	3	149	168	10.1	7	62	3.7	58	3.5	3.87	101	.290	.353	2	0	98	118	-1.1	-1	-1	-0.1
1949	NY-N	11	14	.440	38	23	15	0	4	212	193	8.2	13	43	**1.8**	64	2.7	**2.50**	**163**	.239	**.276**	**36**	37	101	106	-1.0	1	0	4.0
1950	NY-N	13	15	.464	40	22	7	2	3	187	190	9.1	18	68	3.3	56	2.7	3.90	103	.268	.331	5	2	97	109	-2.7	-0	-0	0.1
1951	NY-N	10	9	.526	39	16	5	2	3	150	153	9.2	18	45	2.7	54	3.2	3.30	119	.258	.311	11	10	99	115	-1.6	-1	2	1.1

YEAR	TM/L	W	L	PCT	G	GS	CG	SHO	SV	IP	H	H/G	HR	BB	BB/G	SO	SO/G	ERA	/A	OAVG	OOBP	PR	/A	PF	CPI	WAT	PB	PD	TPI
1952	NY-N	10	7	.588	41	17	8	2	5	166	154	8.3	10	47	2.5	67	3.6	3.20	118	.242	.294	10	10	101	93	0.0	-4	1	0.8
1953	NY-N	6	12	.333	37	12	2	0	2	112	135	10.8	8	36	2.9	36	2.9	4.74	88	.296	.347	-6	-7	98	97	-2.5	-3	1	-0.8
1954	Bal-A	0	1	.000	3	1	0	0	0	14	20	12.9	1	3	1.9	3	1.9	3.21	115	.333	.365	1	1	99	162	-0.4	-0	-0	0.0
	Mil-N	1	1	.500	12	0	0	0	1	17	13	6.9	0	9	4.8	7	3.7	3.18	117	.228	.310	2	1	91	92	0.0	-0	-1	0.0
1955	Mil-N	0	1	.000	1	0	0	0	0	0	1	—	1	0	—	0	—	∞	—	1.000	1.000	-1	-1	92	140	-0.4	0	0	0.0
Total	12	92	107	.462	348	189	74	16	22	1591	1597	9.0	121	538	3.0	606	3.4	3.68	105	.260	.317	34	33	100	100	-8.6	-15	1	2.6
■ JOE KOSTAL	Kostal, Joseph William "Cudgey" b: 3/17/1876, Chicago, Ill. d: 10/17/33, Guelph, Ont., Can. BR/TR, 5'6", 130 lbs. Deb: 7/14/1896																												
1896	Lou-N	0	0	—	2	0	0	0	0	2	4	18.0	0	0	0.0	0	0.0	0.00	—	.440	.440	1	1	102	0	0.0	0	0	0.1
■ SANDY KOUFAX	Koufax, Sanford b: 12/30/35, Brooklyn, N.Y. BR/TL, 6'2", 210 lbs. Deb: 6/24/55 H																												
1955	Bro-N	2	2	.500	12	5	2	2	0	42	33	7.1	2	28	6.0	30	6.4	3.00	136	.216	.339	5	5	101	108	-0.3	-2	-0	0.3
1956	Bro-N	2	4	.333	16	10	0	0	0	59	66	10.1	10	29	4.4	30	4.6	4.88	78	.286	.364	-7	-7	100	109	-1.3	-0	-1	-0.8
1957	Bro-N	5	4	.556	34	13	2	0	0	104	83	7.2	14	51	4.4	122	10.6	3.89	114	.216	.306	-0	6	114	86	0.1	-4	-2	0.1
1958	LA-N	11	11	.500	40	26	5	0	1	159	132	7.5	19	105	5.9	131	7.4	4.47	94	**.220**	.333	-9	-5	106	82	0.9	-2	-0	-0.6
1959	LA-N	8	6	.571	35	23	6	1	2	153	136	8.0	23	92	5.4	173	10.2	4.06	98	.235	.336	-2	-1	101	104	0.1	-1	-1	-0.2
1960	LA-N	8	13	.381	37	26	7	2	1	175	133	**6.8**	20	100	5.1	197	**10.1**	3.91	110	**.207**	.311	-3	7	114	84	-3.2	-3	-1	0.4
1961	LA-N	18	13	.581	42	35	15	2	1	256	212	**7.5**	27	96	3.4	**269**	**9.5**	3.52	116	**.222**	.291	15	16	102	85	0.1	-5	-3	0.9
1962	LA-N	14	7	.667	28	26	11	2	1	184	134	**6.6**	13	57	2.8	216	**10.6**	**2.54**	141	**.197**	**.259**	29	21	91	74	1.5	-2	-2	1.6
1963	LA-N	**25**	5	.833	40	40	20	**11**	0	311	214	**6.2**	18	58	1.7	**306**	8.9	**1.88**	163	**.189**	**.227**	**49**	41	94	69	**9.3**	-3	-4	3.8
1964	LA-N	19	5	**.792**	29	28	15	**7**	1	223	154	**6.2**	13	53	2.1	223	**9.0**	**1.74**	**186**	**.191**	**.238**	45	37	91	90	7.5	-1	-3	3.6
1965	LA-N	**26**	8	**.765**	43	41	**27**	8	2	**336**	216	**5.8**	26	71	1.9	**382**	**10.2**	**2.04**	156	**.179**	**.225**	**56**	43	90	69	**8.0**	5	-2	5.0
1966	LA-N	**27**	9	.750	41	41	**27**	**5**	0	**323**	241	6.7	19	77	2.1	**317**	**8.8**	**1.73**	**199**	.205	.250	**67**	**61**	95	104	8.2	-5	-4	**5.9**
Total	12	165	87	.655	397	314	137	40	9	2325	1754	6.8	204	817	3.2	2396	9.3	2.76	131	.205	.273	244	223	98	85	30.9	-24	-23	20.0
■ JOE KOUKALIK	Koukalik, Joseph b: 3/3/1880, Chicago, Ill. d: 12/27/45, Chicago, Ill. 5'8", 160 lbs. Deb: 9/01/04																												
1904	Bro-N	0	1	.000	1	1	1	0	0	8	10	11.3	0	4	4.5	1	1.1	1.13	237	.332	.410	1	1	98	423	-0.4	-0	-0	0.1
■ LOU KOUPAL	Koupal, Louis Laddie b: 12/19/1898, Tabor, S.D. d: 12/8/61, San Gabriel, Cal. BR/TR, 5'11", 175 lbs. Deb: 4/17/25																												
1925	Pit-N	0	0	—	6	0	0	0	0	9	14	14.0	1	7	7.0	0	0.0	9.00	47	.378	.467	-5	-5	99	95	0.0	-0	0	-0.3
1926	Pit-N	0	2	.000	6	2	1	0	0	20	22	9.9	0	8	3.6	7	3.1	3.15	135	.289	.356	1	2	111	131	-0.9	0	-0	0.3
1928	Bro-N	1	0	1.000	17	1	1	0	1	37	43	10.5	0	15	3.6	10	2.4	2.43	161	.303	.358	6	6	99	179	0.5	-1	1	0.7
1929	Bro-N	0	1	.000	18	3	0	0	4	40	49	11.0	3	25	5.6	17	3.8	5.40	84	.308	.385	-3	-4	96	108	-0.4	-1	-0	-0.4
	Phi-N	5	5	.500	15	12	3	0	2	87	106	11.0	5	29	3.0	18	1.9	4.76	111	.305	.350	-0	5	112	102	0.4	-2	-1	0.2
	Yr	5	6	.455	33	15	3	0	6	127	155	11.0	8	54	3.8	35	2.5	4.96	101	.306	.362	-3	1	107	102	0.0	-1	-1	-0.2
1930	Phi-N	0	4	.000	13	4	1	0	0	37	52	12.6	4	17	4.1	11	2.7	8.51	64	.344	.400	-15	-13	109	80	-1.9	-2	-1	-1.2
1937	StL-A	4	9	.308	26	13	6	0	0	106	150	12.7	10	55	4.7	24	2.0	6.54	73	.339	.406	-23	-21	103	103	0.1	-3	-0	-2.0
Total	6	10	21	.323	101	35	12	0	7	336	436	11.7	23	156	4.2	87	2.3	5.57	86	.322	.383	-37	-29	105	111	-2.2	-9	-1	-2.7
■ FABIAN KOWALIK	Kowalik, Fabian Lorenz b: 4/22/08, Falls City, Tex. d: 8/14/54, Karnes City, Tex. BB/TR, 5'11", 185 lbs. Deb: 9/04/32																												
1932	Chi-A	0	1	.000	2	1	1	0	0	10	16	14.4	2	4	3.6	2	1.8	7.20	56	.340	.404	-3	-3	91	107	-0.4	1	0	-0.2
1935	Chi-N	2	2	.500	20	2	1	0	1	55	60	9.8	2	19	3.1	20	3.3	4.42	86	.280	.331	-2	-4	95	91	-0.4	-0	1	-0.2
1936	Chi-N	0	2	.000	6	0	0	0	1	16	24	13.5	1	7	3.9	1	0.6	6.75	61	.358	.413	-5	-5	102	99	-0.9	-1	0	-0.4
	Phi-N	1	5	.167	22	8	2	0	0	77	100	11.7	5	31	3.6	19	2.2	5.38	83	.308	.364	-12	-8	111	96	-1.5	-0	-2	-0.8
	Bos-N	0	1	.000	1	1	1	0	0	9	18	18.0	0	2	2.0	0	0.0	8.00	48	.419	.426	-4	-4	96	99	-0.4	1	0	-0.2
	Yr	1	8	.111	29	9	3	0	1	102	142	12.5	6	40	3.5	20	1.8	5.82	75	.325	.374	-20	-17	108	99	-2.8	-1	-1	-1.4
Total	3	3	11	.214	51	12	4	0	2	167	218	11.7	10	63	3.4	42	2.3	5.44	76	.313	.365	-26	-24	103	95	-3.6	0	-1	-1.8
■ JOE KRAKAUSKAS	Krakauskas, Joseph Victor Lawrence b: 3/28/15, Montreal, Que., Can d: 7/8/60, Hamilton, Ont., Can BL/TL, 6'1", 203 lbs. Deb: 9/09/37																												
1937	Was-A	4	1	.800	5	4	3	0	0	40	33	7.4	0	22	4.9	18	4.0	2.70	163	.226	.327	9	8	96	109	1.6	-0	-1	0.6
1938	Was-A	7	5	.583	29	10	5	1	0	121	99	7.4	4	88	6.5	104	7.7	3.12	147	.220	.345	22	20	96	116	1.1	1	-1	1.8
1939	Was-A	11	17	.393	39	29	12	0	1	217	230	9.5	13	114	4.7	110	4.6	4.60	92	.276	.357	0	-9	91	102	-1.3	3	-2	-0.8
1940	Was-A	1	6	.143	32	10	2	0	2	109	137	11.3	7	73	6.0	68	5.6	6.44	65	.309	.398	-25	-27	95	93	-2.2	1	1	-2.2
1941	Cle-A	1	2	.333	12	5	0	0	0	42	39	8.4	3	29	6.2	25	5.4	4.07	102	.245	.360	0	0	101	106	-0.4	-1	1	0.0
1942	Cle-A	0	0	—	3	0	0	0	0	7	7	9.0	1	4	5.1	2	2.6	3.86	88	.259	.344	-0	-0	93	127	0.0	-0	1	0.0
1946	Cle-A	2	5	.286	29	5	0	0	1	47	60	11.5	2	25	4.8	20	3.8	5.55	57	.314	.385	-11	-12	90	96	-1.2	-1	1	-1.2
Total	7	26	36	.419	149	63	22	1	4	583	605	9.3	30	355	5.5	347	5.4	4.54	93	.269	.363	-4	-22	94	104	-2.4	2	-1	-1.8
■ JACK KRALICK	Kralick, John Francis b: 6/1/35, Youngstown, Ohio BL/TL, 6'2", 180 lbs. Deb: 4/15/59																												
1959	Was-A	0	0	—	6	0	0	0	0	12	13	9.8	5	6	4.5	7	5.3	6.75	58	.289	.358	-4	-4	102	112	0.0	-0	1	-0.2
1960	Was-A	8	6	.571	35	18	7	2	1	151	139	8.3	12	45	2.7	71	4.2	3.04	130	.245	.300	14	15	102	104	1.4	-1	-1	1.5
1961	Min-A	13	11	.542	33	33	11	2	0	242	257	9.6	21	64	2.4	137	5.1	3.61	120	.274	.317	11	19	107	109	2.5	-2	1	1.9
1962	Min-A	12	11	.522	39	37	7	1	0	243	239	8.9	30	61	2.3	139	5.1	3.85	107	.258	.300	3	7	104	97	-0.8	3	1	1.2
1963	Min-A	1	4	.200	5	5	1	1	0	26	28	9.7	2	8	2.8	13	4.5	3.81	93	.280	.333	-1	-1	98	111	-1.5	1	0	0.1
	Cle-A	13	9	.591	28	27	10	3	0	197	187	8.5	19	41	1.9	116	5.3	2.92	121	.249	.284	15	14	98	108	2.5	1	-1	1.5
	Yr	14	13	.519	33	32	11	4	0	223	215	8.7	21	49	2.0	129	5.2	3.03	117	.252	.289	15	13	98	108	1.0	1	-1	1.6
1964	Cle-A	12	7	.632	30	29	8	3	0	191	196	9.2	17	51	2.4	119	5.6	3.20	116	.267	.317	9	11	103	119	2.9	-1	0	1.1
1965	Cle-A	5	11	.313	30	16	1	0	0	86	106	11.1	9	21	2.2	34	3.6	4.92	68	.298	.333	-14	-15	97	94	-3.4	-0	-1	-1.6
1966	Cle-A	3	4	.429	27	4	0	0	0	68	69	9.1	9	20	2.6	31	4.1	3.84	91	.268	.313	-3	-3	102	112	-0.4	-1	1	-0.2
1967	Cle-A	0	2	.000	2	0	0	0	0	2	4	18.0	0	1	4.5	1	4.5	9.00	36	.444	.500	-1	-1	101	102	-0.9	0	1	0.0
Total	9	67	65	.508	235	169	45	12	1	1218	1238	9.1	124	318	2.3	668	4.9	3.56	109	.264	.308	30	42	102	107	2.3	-0	3	5.3
■ STEVE KRALY	Kraly, Steve Charles "Lefty" b: 4/18/29, Whiting, Ind. BL/TL, 5'10", 152 lbs. Deb: 8/09/53																												
1953	NY-A	0	2	.000	5	3	0	0	1	25	19	6.8	2	16	5.8	8	2.9	3.24	109	.209	.333	2	1	88	107	-0.9	-1	0	0.0
■ JACK KRAMER	Kramer, John Henry b: 1/5/18, New Orleans, La. BR/TR, 6'2", 190 lbs. Deb: 4/25/39																												
1939	StL-A	9	16	.360	40	31	10	2	0	212	269	11.4	18	127	5.4	68	2.9	5.82	83	.318	.400	-28	-23	105	109	1.6	-1	-1	-2.1
1940	StL-A	3	7	.300	16	9	1	0	0	65	86	11.9	4	26	3.6	12	1.7	6.23	76	.327	.382	-13	-11	108	93	-1.5	-1	0	-0.9
1941	StL-A	4	3	.571	29	3	0	0	2	59	69	10.5	5	40	6.1	20	3.1	5.19	81	.289	.384	-7	-7	101	107	0.8	1	0	-0.4
1943	StL-A	0	0	—	3	0	0	0	0	9	11	11.0	0	8	8.0	4	4.0	8.00	41	.297	.435	-5	-5	101	74	0.0	1	0	-0.3
1944	StL-A	17	13	.567	33	31	18	1	0	257	233	8.2	3	75	2.6	124	4.3	2.49	138	.241	.292	27	27	100	102	-0.3	2	3	3.6
1945	StL-A	10	15	.400	29	25	15	3	2	193	190	8.9	13	73	3.4	99	4.6	3.36	115	.254	.315	0	10	114	103	-3.5	-1	1	1.3
1946	StL-A	13	11	.542	31	28	13	3	0	195	190	8.8	6	68	3.1	69	3.2	3.18	110	.257	.315	7	7	100	99	2.7	-1	-0	0.5
1947	StL-A	11	16	.407	33	28	9	1	1	199	206	9.3	16	89	4.0	77	3.5	4.97	79	.270	.343	-28	-24	106	86	0.6	-2	1	-2.3
1948	Bos-A	18	5	**.783**	29	29	14	2	0	205	233	10.2	12	64	2.8	72	3.2	4.35	96	.284	.333	-1	-4	97	97	5.4	-0	-3	-0.6
1949	Bos-A	6	8	.429	21	18	7	2	1	112	126	10.1	8	49	3.9	24	1.9	5.14	84	.286	.355	-12	-10	103	89	-2.2	3	-1	-0.6
1950	NY-N	3	6	.333	35	9	1	0	1	87	91	9.4	6	39	4.0	27	2.8	3.52	114	.268	.338	6	5	97	119	-1.8	1	0	0.6
1951	NY-N	0	0	—	4	1	0	0	0	5	11	19.8	0	3	5.4	2	3.6	14.40	27	.524	.538	-6	-6	99	81	0.0	0	0	-0.4
	NY-A	1	3	.250	19	3	0	0	0	41	46	10.1	1	21	4.6	15	3.3	4.61	79	.280	.353	-2	-4	88	94	-1.1	-0	-1	-0.5
Total	12	95	103	.480	322	215	88	14	7	1639	1761	9.7	92	682	3.7	613	3.4	4.24	94	.276	.341	-62	-43	103	99	0.7	1	0	-2.1
■ RANDY KRAMER	Kramer, Randall John b: 9/20/60, Palo Alto, Cal. BB/TR, 6'2", 170 lbs. Deb: 9/11/88																												
1988	Pit-N	1	2	.333	5	1	0	0	0	10	12	10.8	1	1	0.9	7	6.3	5.40	62	.316	.333	-2	-2	97	93	-0.5	-0	-0	-0.2
■ GENE KRAPP	Krapp, Eugene Hamley "Rubber Arm" b: 5/12/1887, Rochester, N.Y. d: 4/13/23, Detroit, Mich. BR/TR, 5'5", 165 lbs. Deb: 4/14/11																												
1911	Cle-A	13	9	.591	35	26	14	1	1	222	188	7.6	1	138	5.6	132	5.4	3.41	101	.232	.353	-2	1	103	90	1.8	3	4	0.9
1912	Cle-A	2	5	.286	9	7	4	0	0	59	57	8.7	0	42	6.4	22	3.4	4.58	74	.273	.404	-8	-8	101	101	-1.4	1	2	-0.4
1914	Buf-F	16	14	.533	36	29	18	1	0	253	198	7.0	4	115	4.1	106	3.8	2.49	134	.210	.304	20	24	104	88	0.1	-1	7	3.3
1915	Buf-F	9	19	.321	38	30	14	1	0	231	188	7.3	6	123	4.8	93	3.6	3.51	87	.230	.333	-12	-11	101	88	-5.3	-2	8	-0.4
Total	4	40	47	.460	118	92	50	3	1	765	631	7.4	11	418	4.9	353	4.2	3.22	102	.227	.335	-2	6	103	89	-4.8	2	22	3.4

YEAR	TM/L	W	L	PCT	G	GS	CG	SHO	SV	IP	H	H/G	HR	BB	BB/G	SO	SO/G	ERA	/A	OAVG	OOBP	PR	/A	PF	CPI	WAT	PB	PD	TPI
■ JACK KRAUS	Kraus, John William "Tex" or "Texas Jack" b: 4/26/18, San Antonio, Tex. d: 1/2/76, San Antonio, Tex. BR/TL, 6'4", 190 lbs. Deb: 4/25/43																												
1943	Phi-N	9	15	.375	34	25	10	1	2	200	197	8.9	7	78	3.5	48	2.2	3.15	102	.259	.319	5	2	96	109	-1.3	-4	1	-0.1
1945	Phi-N	4	9	.308	19	13	0	0	0	82	96	10.5	3	40	4.4	28	3.1	5.38	72	.293	.371	-14	-14	102	90	0.1	-1	0	-1.3
1946	NY-N	2	1	.667	17	1	0	0	0	25	25	9.0	4	15	5.4	7	2.5	6.12	58	.260	.360	-8	-7	103	82	0.7	-0	1	-0.6
Total	3	15	25	.375	70	39	10	1	2	307	318	9.3	14	133	3.9	83	2.4	3.99	86	.268	.337	-17	-19	98	101	-0.5	-6	2	-2.0
■ HARRY KRAUSE	Krause, Harry William "Hal" b: 7/12/1887, San Francisco, Cal. d: 10/23/40, San Francisco, Cal BB/TL, 5'10", 165 lbs. Deb: 4/20/08																												
1908	Phi-A	1	1	.500	4	2	2	0	0	21	20	8.6	0	4	1.7	10	4.3	2.57	102	.247	.307	-0	0	110	105	0.1	-1	-1	0.0
1909	Phi-A	18	8	.692	32	21	16	7	0	213	151	6.4	2	49	2.1	139	5.9	**1.39**	**173**	.204	.266	26	24	97	98	2.8	-1	-2	2.6
1910	Phi-A	6	6	.500	16	11	9	2	0	112	99	8.0	4	42	3.4	60	4.8	2.89	84	.254	.339	-5	-6	97	114	-1.6	1	-2	-0.7
1911	Phi-A	11	8	.579	27	19	12	1	2	169	155	8.3	2	47	2.5	85	4.5	3.04	97	.251	.313	6	-2	88	87	-1.3	3	-3	-0.4
1912	Phi-A	0	2	.000	4	2	0	0	0	5	10	18.0	0	2	3.6	3	5.4	14.40	23	.435	.500	-6	-6	97	64	-0.9	-0	0	-0.5
	Cle-A	0	1	.000	2	2	0	0	0	5	11	19.8	0	2	3.6	1	1.8	10.80	31	.500	.542	-4	-4	101	98	-0.4	0	-0	-0.3
	Yr	0	3	.000	6	4	0	0	0	10	21	18.9	0	4	3.6	4	3.6	12.60	26	.457	.500	-10	-10	99	98	-1.3	-0	-0	-0.8
Total	5	36	26	.581	85	57	39	10	2	525	446	7.6	8	146	2.5	298	5.1	2.50	105	.238	.305	16	8	95	98	-1.3	1	-9	0.7
■ LEW KRAUSSE	Krausse, Lewis Bernard Jr. b: 4/25/43, Media, Pa. BR/TR, 6', 175 lbs. Deb: 6/16/61																												
1961	KC-A	2	5	.286	12	8	2	1	0	56	49	7.9	3	46	7.4	32	5.1	4.82	87	.243	.376	-5	-4	104	94	-0.8	-1	-1	-0.5
1964	KC-A	0	2	.000	5	4	0	0	0	15	22	13.2	1	9	5.4	9	5.4	7.20	54	.349	.423	-6	-5	108	99	-0.9	0	-0	-0.5
1965	KC-A	2	4	.333	7	5	0	0	0	25	29	10.4	1	8	2.9	22	7.9	5.04	68	.284	.336	-4	-4	100	78	-0.2	-1	-1	-0.5
1966	KC-A	14	9	.609	36	22	4	1	3	178	144	7.3	8	63	3.2	87	4.4	2.98	110	.222	.291	9	6	95	90	3.5	1	-3	0.3
1967	KC-A	7	17	.292	48	19	0	0	6	160	140	7.9	17	67	3.8	96	5.4	4.27	77	.236	.310	-19	-18	102	85	-3.2	1	-0	-1.7
1968	Oak-A	10	11	.476	36	25	2	0	4	185	147	7.2	16	62	3.0	105	5.1	3.11	93	.217	.280	-3	-4	98	87	-0.6	3	-2	-0.3
1969	Oak-A	7	7	.500	43	16	4	2	7	140	134	8.6	23	48	3.1	85	5.5	4.44	75	.256	.317	-13	-17	91	97	-0.5	4	-1	-1.4
1970	Mil-A	13	18	.419	37	35	8	1	0	216	235	9.8	33	67	2.8	130	5.4	4.75	78	.275	.324	-25	-25	100	95	0.6	1	-0	-2.4
1971	Mil-A	8	12	.400	43	22	1	0	0	180	164	8.2	23	62	3.1	92	4.6	2.95	122	.239	.304	10	13	104	118	-0.7	-3	-1	1.0
1972	Bos-A	1	3	.250	24	7	0	0	1	61	74	10.9	9	28	4.1	35	5.2	6.34	51	.308	.375	-22	-21	105	92	-1.0	-0	1	-2.2
1973	StL-N	0	0	—	1	0	0	0	0	2	2	9.0	0	1	4.5	1	4.5	0.00	—	.250	.333	1	1	90	0	0.0	0	0	0.1
1974	Atl-N	4	3	.571	29	4	0	0	0	67	65	8.7	3	32	4.3	27	3.6	4.16	90	.258	.328	-4	-3	104	90	0.2	2	-0	-0.1
Total	12	68	91	.428	321	167	21	5	21	1285	1205	8.4	137	493	3.5	721	5.0	4.00	86	.248	.316	-80	-82	100	94	-3.6	6	-9	-8.2
■ LEW KRAUSSE	Krausse, Lewis Bernard Sr. b: 6/8/12, Media, Pa. d: 9/6/88, Sarasota, Fla. BR/TR, 6'0.5", 167 lbs. Deb: 6/11/31																												
1931	Phi-A	1	0	1.000	3	1	1	0	0	11	6	4.9	2	6	4.9	1	0.8	4.09	108	.150	.261	0	0	101	58	0.5	0	0	0.1
1932	Phi-A	4	1	.800	20	3	2	1	0	57	64	10.1	3	24	3.8	16	2.5	4.58	108	.281	.344	-1	2	111	98	1.2	-0	1	0.3
Total	2	5	1	.833	23	4	3	1	0	68	70	9.3	5	30	4.0	17	2.3	4.50	108	.261	.331	-0	3	109	92	1.7	-0	1	0.4
■ KEN KRAVEC	Kravec, Kenneth Peter b: 7/29/51, Cleveland, Ohio BL/TL, 6'2", 185 lbs. Deb: 9/04/75																												
1975	Chi-A	0	1	.000	2	1	0	0	0	4	1	2.3	0	8	18.0	1	2.3	6.75	58	.071	.409	-1	-1	104	44	-0.4	0	1	0.0
1976	Chi-A	1	5	.167	9	8	1	0	0	50	49	8.8	3	32	5.8	38	6.8	4.86	73	.257	.363	-7	-7	101	88	-1.7	0	-0	-0.7
1977	Chi-A	11	8	.579	26	25	6	1	0	167	161	8.7	12	57	3.1	125	6.7	4.10	98	.250	.312	-0	-1	99	82	0.6	0	0	0.0
1978	Chi-A	11	16	.407	30	30	7	2	0	203	188	8.3	22	95	4.2	154	6.8	4.08	94	.245	.329	-7	-5	102	96	-1.1	0	-1	-0.6
1979	Chi-A	15	13	.536	36	35	10	3	1	250	208	7.5	20	111	4.0	132	4.8	3.74	116	.233	.320	14	16	103	94	2.4	0	-1	1.5
1980	Chi-A	3	6	.333	20	15	0	0	0	82	100	11.0	13	44	4.8	37	4.1	6.91	57	.298	.378	-26	-27	98	85	-1.0	0	0	-2.4
1981	Chi-N	1	6	.143	24	12	0	0	0	78	80	9.2	5	39	4.5	50	5.8	5.08	73	.268	.346	-14	-12	106	86	-2.1	-1	1	-1.2
1982	Chi-N	1	1	.500	13	2	0	0	0	25	27	9.7	3	18	6.5	20	7.2	6.12	61	.267	.366	-7	-7	104	84	0.1	-0	1	-0.6
Total	8	43	56	.434	160	128	24	6	1	859	814	8.5	78	404	4.2	557	5.8	4.46	90	.251	.334	-49	-44	102	90	-3.2	-1	-1	-4.0
■ RAY KRAWCZYK	Krawczyk, Raymond Allen b: 10/9/59, Pittsburgh, Pa. BR/TR, 6'1", 184 lbs. Deb: 6/29/84																												
1984	Pit-N	0	0	—	4	0	0	0	0	5	7	12.6	0	4	7.2	3	5.4	3.60	94	.350	.440	-0	-0	94	190	0.0	0	-0	0.0
1985	Pit-N	0	2	.000	8	0	0	0	0	8	20	22.5	1	6	6.8	9	10.1	14.63	26	.455	.529	-10	-10	104	86	-0.9	0	0	-0.8
1986	Pit-N	0	1	.000	12	0	0	0	0	12	17	12.8	3	10	7.5	7	5.3	7.50	50	.321	.415	-5	-5	101	107	-0.4	0	-0	-0.4
1988	Cal-A	0	1	.000	14	1	0	0	1	24	29	10.9	2	8	3.0	17	6.4	4.88	77	.299	.361	-2	-3	95	103	-0.4	0	1	-0.1
Total	4	0	4	.000	38	1	0	0	1	49	73	13.4	6	28	5.1	36	6.6	6.98	53	.341	.418	-17	-18	98	110	-1.7	0	0	-1.3
■ RAY KREMER	Kremer, Remy Peter "Wiz" b: 3/23/1893, Oakland, Cal. d: 2/8/65, Pinole, Cal. BR/TR, 6'1", 190 lbs. Deb: 4/18/24																												
1924	Pit-N	18	10	.643	**41**	30	17	4	1	259	262	9.1	7	51	1.8	64	2.2	3.20	126	.265	.297	19	24	104	93	2.2	-4	-2	1.8
1925	Pit-N	17	8	.680	40	27	14	0	2	215	232	9.7	19	47	2.0	62	2.6	3.68	114	.278	.315	14	13	99	105	2.3	1	-3	1.0
1926	Pit-N	**20**	6	**.769**	37	26	18	3	5	231	221	8.6	9	51	2.0	74	2.9	**2.61**	**162**	.252	.289	**31**	**42**	111	106	**7.0**	2	-3	**4.4**
1927	Pit-N	19	8	.704	35	28	18	3	2	226	205	8.2	9	53	2.1	63	2.5	**2.47**	157	.244	.278	36	35	99	106	3.7	-1	-3	3.3
1928	Pit-N	15	13	.536	34	31	17	1	0	219	253	10.4	15	68	2.8	61	2.5	4.64	90	.297	.337	-16	-12	105	95	-0.6	-0	-4	-1.4
1929	Pit-N	18	10	.643	34	27	14	0	0	222	226	9.2	21	60	2.4	66	2.7	4.26	112	.271	.309	11	13	102	94	2.6	-2	-3	0.7
1930	Pit-N	**20**	12	.625	39	38	18	1	0	**276**	366	11.9	29	63	2.1	58	1.9	5.02	97	.322	.349	-2	-5	98	107	4.2	-4	-4	-1.1
1931	Pit-N	11	15	.423	30	30	15	1	0	230	246	9.6	6	65	2.5	58	2.3	3.33	118	.271	.318	14	15	102	103	-1.9	4	-5	1.4
1932	Pit-N	4	3	.571	11	10	3	1	0	57	61	9.6	5	16	2.5	6	0.9	4.26	91	.270	.318	-2	-3	100	91	0.1	-1	-1	-0.4
1933	Pit-N	1	0	1.000	7	0	0	0	0	20	36	16.2	2	9	4.0	4	1.8	10.35	30	.387	.433	-16	-16	94	77	0.5	-1	1	-1.4
Total	10	143	85	.627	308	247	134	14	10	1955	2108	9.7	122	483	2.2	516	2.4	3.76	113	.278	.315	90	108	102	101	20.1	-7	-28	8.3
■ JIM KREMMEL	Kremmel, James Louis b: 2/28/48, Belleville, Ill. BL/TL, 6', 175 lbs. Deb: 7/04/73																												
1973	Tex-A	0	2	.000	4	2	0	0	0	9	15	15.0	1	6	6.0	6	6.0	9.00	42	.366	.460	-5	-5	100	94	-0.9	0	0	-0.4
1974	Chi-N	0	2	.000	23	2	0	0	0	31	37	10.7	3	18	5.2	22	6.4	5.23	71	.303	.381	-5	-5	102	108	-0.9	-0	0	-0.5
Total	2	0	4	.000	27	4	0	0	0	40	52	11.7	4	24	5.4	28	6.3	6.07	61	.319	.401	-11	-10	101	105	-1.8	-0	0	-0.9
■ RED KRESS	Kress, Ralph b: 1/2/07, Columbia, Cal. d: 11/29/62, Los Angeles, Cal. BR/TR, 5'11.5", 165 lbs. Deb: 9/24/27 C																												
1935	Was-A	0	0	—	3	0	0	0	0	6	8	12.0	0	5	7.5	5	7.5	12.00	34	.333	.419	-5	-5	93	56	0.0	1	0	-0.4
1946	NY-N	0	0	—	1	0	0	0	0	4	5	11.3	1	1	2.3	1	2.3	11.25	31	.333	.412	-3	-3	103	65	0.0	0	1	-0.1
Total	2	0	0	—	4	0	0	0	0	10	13	11.7	1	6	5.4	6	5.4	11.70	33	.333	.417	-9	-9	97	59	0.0	1	1	-0.5
■ LOU KRETLOW	Kretlow, Louis Henry "Lena" b: 6/27/23, Apache, Okla. BR/TR, 6'2", 185 lbs. Deb: 9/26/46																												
1946	Det-A	1	0	1.000	1	1	1	0	0	9	7	7.0	2	2	2.0	4	4.0	3.00	123	.206	.250	1	1	106	96	0.5	1	-0	0.2
1948	Det-A	2	1	.667	5	2	1	0	0	23	21	8.2	1	11	4.3	9	3.5	4.70	88	.233	.317	-1	-1	97	66	0.5	1	0	0.0
1949	Det-A	3	2	.600	25	10	1	0	0	76	85	10.1	5	69	8.2	40	4.7	6.16	72	.290	.421	-17	-14	106	97	0.2	-4	2	-1.4
1950	StL-A	0	2	.000	9	2	0	0	0	14	25	16.1	2	18	11.6	10	6.4	12.21	42	.403	.536	-12	-11	111	95	-0.9	-1	0	-0.9
	Chi-A	0	0	—	11	1	0	0	0	22	17	7.0	1	27	11.0	14	5.7	3.68	123	.221	.419	2	2	99	139	0.0	-1	-1	0.1
	Yr	0	2	.000	20	3	0	0	0	36	42	10.5	3	45	11.3	24	6.0	7.00	68	.298	.460	-10	-9	104	139	-0.9	-1	-1	-0.8
1951	Chi-A	6	9	.400	26	18	7	1	0	137	129	8.5	7	74	4.9	89	5.8	4.20	94	.250	.342	-1	-4	96	92	-1.8	-5	-0	-0.8
1952	Chi-A	4	4	.500	19	11	4	2	1	79	52	5.9	5	56	6.4	63	7.2	2.96	123	.186	.317	6	6	99	95	-0.1	-1	-1	0.5
1953	Chi-A	0	0	—	9	3	0	0	0	21	12	5.1	2	30	12.9	15	6.4	3.43	121	.171	.422	1	2	104	148	0.0	-0	1	0.2
	StL-A	1	5	.167	22	11	0	0	0	81	93	10.3	5	52	5.8	37	4.1	5.11	86	.286	.382	-10	-6	111	99	-1.5	-1	-2	-0.7
	Yr	1	5	.167	31	14	0	0	0	102	105	9.3	7	82	7.2	52	4.6	4.76	92	.265	.388	-9	-5	109	99	-1.5	-0	-1	-0.5
1954	Bal-A	6	11	.353	32	20	5	0	0	167	169	9.1	12	82	4.4	82	4.4	4.37	84	.269	.345	-12	-13	99	96	0.0	-0	0	-1.2
1955	Bal-A	0	4	.000	15	5	0	0	0	38	50	11.8	3	27	6.4	26	6.2	8.29	45	.316	.406	-18	-19	94	75	-1.9	-1	1	-1.7
1956	KC-A	4	9	.308	25	20	3	0	0	119	121	9.2	17	74	5.6	61	4.6	5.29	82	.262	.360	-15	-12	105	93	-0.5	-3	-1	-1.4
Total	10	27	47	.365	199	104	22	3	1	786	781	8.9	62	522	6.0	450	5.2	4.87	83	.261	.366	-76	-72	101	96	-5.5	-13	-0	-7.1
■ RICK KREUGER	Kreuger, Richard Allen b: 11/3/48, Grand Rapids, Mich. BR/TL, 6'2", 185 lbs. Deb: 9/06/75																												
1975	Bos-A	0	0	—	2	0	0	0	0	4	3	6.8	0	1	2.3	1	2.3	4.50	91	.200	.250	-0	-0	108	25	0.0	0	0	0.0
1976	Bos-A	2	1	.667	8	4	1	0	0	31	31	9.0	3	16	4.6	12	3.5	4.06	95	.272	.351	-2	-1	110	114	0.5	0	1	0.0
1977	Bos-A	0	1	.000	1	0	0	0	0	0	2	—	0	0	—	0	—	∞	—	1.000	1.000	-2	-2	116	55	-0.4	0	0	-0.1
1978	Cle-A	0	0	—	6	0	0	0	0	9	6	6.0	1	3	3.0	7	7.0	4.00	88	.194	.237	-0	-0	94	58	0.0	0	0	0.0

YEAR	TM/L	W	L	PCT	G	GS	CG	SHO	SV	IP	H	H/G	HR	BB	BB/G	SO	SO/G	ERA	/A	OAVG	OOBP	PR	/A	PF	CPI	WAT	PB	PD	TPI
Total	4	2	2	.500	17	4	1	0	0	44	42	8.6	4	20	4.1	20	4.1	4.50	85	.259	.326	-4	-3	106	94	0.1	0	1	-0.1

■ **FRANK KREUTZER** Kreutzer, Franklin James b: 2/7/39, Buffalo, N.Y. BR/TL, 6'1", 175 lbs. Deb: 9/20/62

YEAR	TM/L	W	L	PCT	G	GS	CG	SHO	SV	IP	H	H/G	HR	BB	BB/G	SO	SO/G	ERA	/A	OAVG	OOBP	PR	/A	PF	CPI	WAT	PB	PD	TPI
1962	Chi-A	0	0	—	1	0	0	0	0	1	0	0.0	0	1	9.0	1	9.0	0.00	—	.000	.200	0	0	94	0	0.0	0	0	0.0
1963	Chi-A	1	0	1.000	1	1	0	0	0	5	3	5.4	1	1	1.8	0	0.0	1.80	206	.188	.235	1	1	102	157	0.5	-0	0	0.1
1964	Chi-A	3	1	.750	17	2	0	0	1	40	37	8.3	1	18	4.0	32	7.2	3.37	100	.239	.313	1	0	93	86	0.7	0	1	0.1
	Was-A	2	6	.250	13	9	0	0	0	45	48	9.6	6	23	4.6	27	5.4	4.80	78	.267	.350	-6	-5	103	98	-1.3	-1	0	-0.6
	Yr	5	7	.417	30	11	0	0	1	85	85	9.0	7	41	4.3	59	6.2	4.13	87	.253	.332	-5	-5	99	98	-0.6	0	1	-0.5
1965	Was-A	2	6	.250	33	14	2	1	0	85	73	7.7	7	54	5.7	65	6.9	4.34	81	.232	.340	-8	-8	102	89	-1.6	-1	-2	-1.0
1966	Was-A	0	5	.000	9	6	0	0	0	31	30	8.7	9	10	2.9	24	7.0	6.10	54	.236	.297	-9	-10	96	76	-2.4	0	0	-0.8
1969	Was-A	0	0	—	4	0	0	0	0	2	3	13.5	0	2	9.0	2	9.0	4.50	78	.333	.455	-0	-0	96	153	0.0	0	0	0.0
Total	6	8	18	.308	78	32	2	1	1	209	194	8.4	24	109	4.7	151	6.5	4.44	79	.241	.329	-21	-21	100	90	-4.1	-2	-1	-2.2

■ **KRIEGER** Krieger Deb:7/28/1884

YEAR	TM/L	W	L	PCT	G	GS	CG	SHO	SV	IP	H	H/G	HR	BB	BB/G	SO	SO/G	ERA	/A	OAVG	OOBP	PR	/A	PF	CPI	WAT	PB	PD	TPI
1884	KC-U	0	1	.000	1	1	0	0	0	7	9	11.6	0	5	6.4	3	3.9	0.00	—	.317	.420	2	2	92	0	-0.4	-0	0	0.2

■ **KURT KRIEGER** Krieger, Kurt Ferdinand "Dutch" b: 9/16/26, Traisen, Austria d: 8/16/70, St.Louis, Mo. BR/TR, 6'3", 212 lbs. Deb: 4/21/49

YEAR	TM/L	W	L	PCT	G	GS	CG	SHO	SV	IP	H	H/G	HR	BB	BB/G	SO	SO/G	ERA	/A	OAVG	OOBP	PR	/A	PF	CPI	WAT	PB	PD	TPI
1949	StL-N	0	0	—	1	0	0	0	0	1	0	0.0	0	1	9.0	0	0.0	0.00	—	.000	.250	0	0	108	0	0.0	0	0	0.0
1951	StL-N	0	0	—	2	0	0	0	0	4	6	13.5	1	5	11.3	3	6.8	15.75	25	.353	.478	-5	-5	101	65	0.0	0	0	-0.4
Total	2	0	0	—	3	0	0	0	0	5	6	10.8	1	6	10.8	3	5.4	12.60	32	.300	.444	-5	-5	102	52	0.0	0	0	-0.4

■ **HOWIE KRIST** Krist, Howard Wilbur "Spud" b: 2/28/16, W.Henrietta, N.Y. BL/TR, 6'1", 175 lbs. Deb: 9/12/37

YEAR	TM/L	W	L	PCT	G	GS	CG	SHO	SV	IP	H	H/G	HR	BB	BB/G	SO	SO/G	ERA	/A	OAVG	OOBP	PR	/A	PF	CPI	WAT	PB	PD	TPI
1937	StL-N	3	1	.750	6	4	1	0	0	28	34	10.9	0	10	3.2	6	1.9	4.18	93	.304	.358	-1	-1	100	105	1.0	-1	-1	-0.2
1938	StL-N	0	0	—	2	0	0	0	0	1	1	9.0	0	0	0.0	1	9.0	0.00	—	.250	.250	0	0	111	0	0.0	0	0	0.0
1941	StL-N	10	0	1.000	37	8	2	0	2	114	107	8.4	10	35	2.8	36	2.8	4.03	97	.246	.300	-5	-2	107	84	5.0	1	-1	-0.1
1942	StL-N	13	3	.813	34	8	3	0	1	118	103	7.9	2	43	3.3	47	3.6	2.52	135	.233	.300	10	12	103	106	3.4	-1	-2	0.9
1943	StL-N	11	5	.688	34	17	9	2	3	164	141	7.7	5	62	3.4	57	3.1	2.91	116	.233	.303	8	9	100	97	0.2	-2	-5	0.2
1946	StL-N	0	2	.000	15	0	0	0	0	19	22	10.4	3	8	3.8	3	1.4	6.63	53	.306	.369	-7	-7	103	87	-0.9	0	0	-0.6
Total	6	37	11	.771	128	37	15	2	6	444	408	8.3	20	158	3.2	150	3.0	3.32	107	.244	.308	7	11	103	96	8.7	-3	-9	0.2

■ **GUS KROCK** Krock, August H. b: 5/9/1866, Milwaukee, Wis. d: 3/22/05, Pasadena, Cal. TL, 6', 196 lbs. Deb: 1888

YEAR	TM/L	W	L	PCT	G	GS	CG	SHO	SV	IP	H	H/G	HR	BB	BB/G	SO	SO/G	ERA	/A	OAVG	OOBP	PR	/A	PF	CPI	WAT	PB	PD	TPI
1888	Chi-N	25	14	.641	39	39	39	4	0	340	295	7.8	20	45	1.2	161	4.3	2.44	123	.247	.274	15	21	106	96	4.2	-3	-4	1.6
1889	Chi-N	3	3	.500	7	7	5	0	0	61	86	12.7	10	14	2.1	16	2.4	5.02	79	.349	.384	-7	-7	98	122	0.0	-1	0	-0.6
	Ind-N	2	2	.500	4	4	3	0	0	32	48	13.5	2	14	3.9	10	2.8	7.31	61	.363	.424	-12	-10	110	87	0.2	1	0	-0.6
	Was-N	2	4	.333	6	6	6	0	0	48	65	12.2	1	22	4.1	17	3.2	5.25	73	.340	.408	-7	-7	96	103	0.0	-2	0	-0.7
	Yr	7	9	.438	17	17	14	0	0	141	199	12.7	13	50	3.2	43	2.7	5.62	72	.349	.402	-25	-25	100	103	0.2	0	0	-1.9
1890	Buf-P	0	3	.000	4	3	3	0	0	25	43	15.5	1	15	5.4	5	1.8	6.12	67	.391	.464	-5	-6	97	123	-1.4	-1	0	-0.4
Total	3	32	26	.552	60	59	56	4	0	506	537	9.6	34	110	2.0	209	3.7	3.50	96	.286	.326	-15	-8	104	101	3.0	-7	-4	-0.7

■ **RUBE KROH** Kroh, Floyd Myron b: 8/25/1886, Friendship, N.Y. d: 3/17/44, New Orleans, La. BL/TL, 6'2", 186 lbs. Deb: 9/30/06

YEAR	TM/L	W	L	PCT	G	GS	CG	SHO	SV	IP	H	H/G	HR	BB	BB/G	SO	SO/G	ERA	/A	OAVG	OOBP	PR	/A	PF	CPI	WAT	PB	PD	TPI
1906	Bos-A	1	0	1.000	1	1	1	0	0	9	2	2.0	0	4	4.0	5	5.0	0.00	—	.082	.210	3	3	104	0	0.5	-0	0	0.4
1907	Bos-A	1	4	.200	7	5	1	0	0	34	33	8.7	0	8	2.1	8	2.1	2.65	99	.279	.324	-0	-0	103	100	-1.2	0	0	0.0
1908	Chi-N	0	0	—	2	1	0	0	0	12	9	6.8	0	4	3.0	11	8.3	1.50	160	.234	.306	1	1	102	122	0.0	-0	0	0.2
1909	Chi-N	9	4	.692	17	13	10	1	0	120	97	7.3	2	30	2.3	51	3.8	1.65	150	.224	.276	13	11	95	114	0.3	-0	1	1.4
1910	Chi-N	3	1	.750	6	4	1	0	0	34	33	8.7	1	15	4.0	16	4.2	4.50	65	.254	.340	-6	-6	96	73	0.5	0	1	-0.4
1912	Bos-N	0	0	—	3	1	0	0	0	6	8	12.0	0	6	9.0	1	1.5	6.00	63	.364	.500	-2	-1	110	123	0.0	0	1	0.0
Total	6	14	9	.609	36	25	13	2	0	215	182	7.6	3	67	2.8	92	3.9	2.30	113	.237	.301	9	7	98	101	0.1	0	3	1.6

■ **GARY KROLL** Kroll, Gary Melvin b: 7/8/41, Culver City, Cal. BR/TR, 6'6", 220 lbs. Deb: 7/26/64

YEAR	TM/L	W	L	PCT	G	GS	CG	SHO	SV	IP	H	H/G	HR	BB	BB/G	SO	SO/G	ERA	/A	OAVG	OOBP	PR	/A	PF	CPI	WAT	PB	PD	TPI
1964	Phi-N	0	0	—	2	0	0	0	0	3	3	9.0	0	2	6.0	2	6.0	3.00	115	.250	.357	0	0	98	122	0.0	0	0	0.0
	NY-N	0	1	.000	8	2	0	0	0	22	19	7.8	1	15	6.1	24	9.8	4.09	85	.241	.361	-1	-2	98	101	-0.4	0	1	0.0
	Yr	0	1	.000	10	2	0	0	0	25	22	7.9	1	17	6.1	26	9.4	3.96	88	.242	.360	-1	-1	98	101	-0.4	0	1	0.0
1965	NY-N	6	6	.500	32	11	1	0	1	87	83	8.6	12	41	4.2	62	6.4	4.45	83	.249	.332	-9	-7	104	99	1.8	-1	0	-0.8
1966	Hou-N	0	0	—	10	0	0	0	0	24	26	9.8	2	11	4.1	22	8.3	3.75	95	.280	.343	-0	-1	99	120	0.0	-0	0	0.0
1969	Cle-A	0	0	—	19	0	0	0	0	24	16	6.0	3	22	8.3	28	10.5	4.13	85	.188	.349	-1	-2	96	94	0.0	0	0	-0.1
Total	4	6	7	.462	71	13	1	0	1	160	147	8.3	18	91	5.1	138	7.8	4.22	85	.244	.341	-12	-11	101	102	1.4	-1	1	-0.9

■ **BILL KRUEGER** Krueger, William Culp b: 4/24/58, Waukegan, Ill. BL/TL, 6'5", 205 lbs. Deb: 4/10/83

YEAR	TM/L	W	L	PCT	G	GS	CG	SHO	SV	IP	H	H/G	HR	BB	BB/G	SO	SO/G	ERA	/A	OAVG	OOBP	PR	/A	PF	CPI	WAT	PB	PD	TPI
1983	Oak-A	7	6	.538	17	16	2	0	0	110	104	8.5	7	53	4.3	58	4.7	3.60	109	.252	.336	6	4	96	107	1.0	0	-2	0.2
1984	Oak-A	10	10	.500	26	24	1	0	0	142	156	9.9	9	85	5.4	61	3.9	4.75	77	.285	.376	-12	-17	92	105	0.5	0	-2	-1.7
1985	Oak-A	9	10	.474	32	23	2	0	0	151	165	9.8	13	69	4.1	56	3.3	4.53	85	.276	.350	-6	-11	93	101	0.0	0	-1	-1.1
1986	Oak-A	1	2	.333	11	3	0	0	1	34	40	10.6	4	13	3.4	10	2.6	6.09	64	.301	.356	-7	-8	94	86	-0.3	0	1	-0.6
1987	Oak-A	0	3	.000	9	0	0	0	0	6	9	13.5	0	8	12.0	2	3.0	9.00	45	.360	.515	-3	-3	91	98	-1.4	0	-0	-0.2
	LA-N	0	0	—	2	0	0	0	0	2	3	13.5	0	1	4.5	2	9.0	0.00	—	.250	.308	1	1	92	0	0.0	0	0	0.1
1988	LA-N	0	0	—	1	1	0	0	0	2	4	18.0	0	2	9.0	1	4.5	13.50	27	.364	.500	-2	-2	105	73	0.0	0	0	-0.1
Total	6	27	31	.466	98	67	5	0	1	447	481	9.7	33	231	4.7	190	3.8	4.57	84	.277	.359	-24	-37	94	102	-0.2	0	-4	-3.4

■ **ABE KRUGER** Kruger, Abraham b: 2/14/1885, Morris Run, Pa. d: 7/4/62, Elmira, N.Y. BR/TR, 6'2", 190 lbs. Deb: 10/06/08

YEAR	TM/L	W	L	PCT	G	GS	CG	SHO	SV	IP	H	H/G	HR	BB	BB/G	SO	SO/G	ERA	/A	OAVG	OOBP	PR	/A	PF	CPI	WAT	PB	PD	TPI
1908	Bro-N	0	1	.000	2	1	0	0	0	6	5	7.5	0	3	4.5	2	3.0	4.50	51	.299	.484	-1	-1	99	91	-0.4	-0	1	0.0

■ **MIKE KRUKOW** Krukow, Michael Edward b: 1/21/52, Long Beach, Cal. BR/TR, 6'5", 205 lbs. Deb: 9/06/76

YEAR	TM/L	W	L	PCT	G	GS	CG	SHO	SV	IP	H	H/G	HR	BB	BB/G	SO	SO/G	ERA	/A	OAVG	OOBP	PR	/A	PF	CPI	WAT	PB	PD	TPI
1976	Chi-N	0	0	—	2	0	0	0	0	4	6	13.5	0	2	4.5	1	2.3	9.00	43	.333	.400	-2	-2	111	62	0.0	-0	-0	-0.2
1977	Chi-N	8	14	.364	34	33	1	1	0	172	195	10.2	16	61	3.2	106	5.5	4.40	102	.281	.338	-9	2	115	98	-3.2	-1	1	0.3
1978	Chi-N	9	3	.750	27	20	3	1	0	138	125	8.2	11	53	3.5	81	5.3	3.91	102	.243	.314	-5	1	111	88	3.2	3	-0	0.4
1979	Chi-N	9	9	.500	28	28	0	0	0	165	172	9.4	13	81	4.4	119	6.5	4.20	100	.275	.355	-8	0	112	107	0.1	5	-1	0.4
1980	Chi-N	10	15	.400	34	34	3	0	0	205	200	8.8	13	80	3.5	130	5.7	4.39	88	.258	.326	-18	-12	108	85	0.1	3	-3	-1.1
1981	Chi-N	9	9	.500	25	25	2	1	0	144	146	9.1	11	55	3.4	101	6.3	3.69	101	.264	.326	-3	0	106	106	2.2	-0	0	0.1
1982	Phi-N	13	11	.542	33	33	7	2	0	208	211	9.1	8	82	3.5	138	6.0	3.12	108	.268	.331	11	6	94	120	-0.1	0	2	0.7
1983	SF-N	11	11	.500	31	31	2	1	0	184	189	9.2	17	76	3.7	136	6.7	3.96	93	.261	.328	-7	-6	101	99	0.3	5	-2	-0.3
1984	SF-N	11	12	.478	35	33	3	1	1	199	234	10.6	22	78	3.5	141	6.4	4.57	77	.290	.351	-22	-23	98	107	1.6	-1	-1	-2.6
1985	SF-N	8	11	.421	28	28	6	1	0	195	176	8.1	19	49	2.3	150	6.9	3.37	101	.238	.284	5	1	95	89	0.7	4	-0	0.4
1986	SF-N	20	9	.690	34	34	10	2	0	245	204	7.5	24	55	2.0	178	6.5	2.94	120	.223	.266	21	16	95	88	6.0	0	-1	1.6
1987	SF-N	5	6	.455	30	28	3	0	0	163	182	10.0	24	46	2.5	104	5.7	4.80	81	.288	.329	-13	-17	95	101	-1.0	1	1	-1.3
1988	SF-N	7	4	.636	20	20	1	0	0	125	111	8.0	13	31	2.2	75	5.4	3.53	91	.236	.284	-1	-4	93	90	1.5	-0	-0	-0.4
Total	13	120	114	.513	361	347	41	10	1	2147	2151	9.0	191	749	3.1	1460	6.1	3.89	96	.261	.320	-51	-39	101	98	11.4	19	-4	-2.0

■ **AL KRUMM** Krumm, Albert b: Columbus, Ohio TR, Deb: 5/17/1889

YEAR	TM/L	W	L	PCT	G	GS	CG	SHO	SV	IP	H	H/G	HR	BB	BB/G	SO	SO/G	ERA	/A	OAVG	OOBP	PR	/A	PF	CPI	WAT	PB	PD	TPI
1889	Pit-N	0	1	.000	1	1	1	0	0	9	8	8.0	0	10	10.0	4	4.0	10.00	36	.253	.432	-6	-6	90	48	-0.4	-1	0	-0.4

■ **JOHNNY KUCAB** Kucab, John Albert b: 12/17/19, Olyphant, Pa. d: 5/26/77, Youngstown, Ohio BR/TR, 6'2", 185 lbs. Deb: 9/14/50

YEAR	TM/L	W	L	PCT	G	GS	CG	SHO	SV	IP	H	H/G	HR	BB	BB/G	SO	SO/G	ERA	/A	OAVG	OOBP	PR	/A	PF	CPI	WAT	PB	PD	TPI
1950	Phi-A	1	1	.500	4	2	2	0	0	26	29	10.0	4	8	2.8	8	2.8	3.46	123	.282	.330	3	2	93	138	0.2	-0	-0	0.1
1951	Phi-A	4	3	.571	30	1	0	0	4	75	76	9.1	9	23	2.8	23	2.8	4.20	104	.265	.317	-1	1	106	99	0.8	-2	-2	-0.1
1952	Phi-A	0	1	.000	25	0	0	0	2	51	64	11.3	5	20	3.5	17	3.0	5.29	78	.312	.368	-9	-7	112	102	-0.4	-0	-0	-0.6
Total	3	5	5	.500	59	3	2	0	6	152	169	10.0	18	51	3.0	48	2.8	4.44	97	.284	.337	-7	-3	106	107	0.6	-2	-2	-0.6

■ **JACK KUCEK** Kucek, John Andrew Charles b: 6/8/53, Warren, Ohio BR/TR, 6'2", 200 lbs. Deb: 8/08/74

YEAR	TM/L	W	L	PCT	G	GS	CG	SHO	SV	IP	H	H/G	HR	BB	BB/G	SO	SO/G	ERA	/A	OAVG	OOBP	PR	/A	PF	CPI	WAT	PB	PD	TPI
1974	Chi-A	1	4	.200	9	7	0	0	0	38	48	11.4	3	21	5.0	25	5.9	5.21	71	.320	.400	-7	-6	102	112	-1.4	0	1	-0.5
1975	Chi-A	0	0	—	2	0	0	0	0	4	9	20.3	0	4	9.0	2	4.5	4.50	87	.500	.591	-0	-0	104	273	0.0	0	0	0.0
1976	Chi-A	0	0	—	2	0	0	0	0	5	9	16.2	2	4	7.2	2	3.6	9.00	40	.429	.500	-3	-3	101	136	0.0	0	-0	-0.2
1977	Chi-A	0	1	.000	8	3	0	0	0	35	35	9.0	4	10	2.6	25	6.4	3.60	112	.267	.318	2	2	99	115	-0.4	0	0	0.3
1978	Chi-A	2	3	.400	10	5	3	0	1	52	42	7.3	5	27	4.7	30	5.2	3.29	117	.220	.309	3	3	102	97	-0.1	0	-0	0.3

YEAR	TM/L	W	L	PCT	G	GS	CG	SHO	SV	IP	H	H/G	HR	BB	BB/G	SO	SO/G	ERA	/A	OAVG	OOBP	PR	/A	PF	CPI	WAT	PB	PD	TPI
1979	Chi-A	0	0	—	1	0	0	0	0	1	0	0.0	0	3	27.0	0	0.0	0.00	—	.000	.500	0	0	103	0	0.0	0	0	0.0
	Phi-N	1	0	1.000	4	0	0	0	0	4	6	13.5	2	1	2.3	2	4.5	9.00	40	.333	.350	-2	-2	97	96	0.5	0	0	-0.2
1980	Tor-A	3	8	.273	23	12	0	0	1	68	83	11.0	9	41	5.4	35	4.6	6.75	61	.300	.385	-20	-20	101	86	-1.9	0	-1	-1.9
Total	7	7	16	.304	59	27	3	0	2	207	232	10.1	25	111	4.8	121	5.3	5.09	77	.287	.367	-28	-27	101	103	-3.3	0	1	-2.2
■ **JOHNNY KUCKS**	Kucks, John Charles b: 7/27/33, Hoboken, N.J. BR/TR, 6'3", 170 lbs. Deb: 4/17/55																												
1955	NY-A	8	7	.533	29	13	3	1	0	127	122	8.6	8	44	3.1	49	3.5	3.40	110	.252	.313	8	5	94	97	-1.1	-4	-0	0.0
1956	NY-A	18	9	.667	34	31	12	3	0	224	223	9.0	19	72	2.9	67	2.7	3.86	102	.261	.322	8	2	95	97	1.6	-2	0	0.0
1957	NY-A	8	10	.444	37	23	4	1	2	179	169	8.5	13	59	3.0	78	3.9	3.57	96	.251	.311	4	-3	90	97	-2.9	-2	3	-0.1
1958	NY-A	8	8	.500	34	15	4	1	4	126	132	9.4	14	39	2.8	46	3.3	3.93	95	.269	.325	-2	-3	99	106	-1.3	-1	1	-0.2
1959	NY-A	0	1	.000	9	1	0	0	0	17	21	11.1	5	9	4.8	9	4.8	8.47	42	.323	.395	-9	-9	92	90	-0.4	-0	0	-0.8
	KC-A	8	11	.421	33	23	6	1	1	151	163	9.7	10	42	2.5	51	3.0	3.87	102	.278	.334	-0	2	103	106	-0.1	-3	1	0.0
	Yr	8	12	.400	42	24	6	1	1	168	184	9.9	15	51	2.7	60	3.2	4.34	90	.282	.341	-9	-8	102	106	-0.5	-0	1	-0.8
1960	KC-A	4	10	.286	31	17	1	0	0	114	140	11.1	22	43	3.4	38	3.0	6.00	65	.306	.355	-27	-26	101	97	-1.7	-1	-0	-2.6
Total	6	54	56	.491	207	123	30	7	7	938	970	9.3	91	308	3.0	338	3.2	4.10	92	.269	.327	-18	-33	96	100	-5.9	-12	5	-3.7
■ **BERT KUCZYNSKI**	Kuczynski, Bernard Carl b: 1/8/20, Philadelphia, Pa. BR/TR, 6', 195 lbs. Deb: 6/02/43																												
1943	Phi-A	0	1	.000	6	1	0	0	0	25	36	13.0	2	9	3.2	8	2.9	3.96	88	.336	.395	-2	-1	106	155	-0.4	-0	-0	-0.1
■ **FRED KUHAULUA**	Kuhaulua, Fred Mahele b: 2/23/53, Honolulu, Hawaii BL/TL, 5'11", 175 lbs. Deb: 8/02/77																												
1977	Cal-A	0	0	—	3	1	0	0	0	6	15	22.5	1	7	10.5	3	4.5	16.50	23	.455	.550	-8	-8	95	82	0.0	0	0	-0.6
1981	SD-N	1	0	1.000	5	4	0	0	0	29	28	8.7	1	9	2.8	16	5.0	2.48	133	.257	.311	3	3	95	127	0.5	-0	-1	0.1
Total	2	1	0	1.000	8	5	0	0	0	35	43	11.1	2	16	4.1	19	4.9	4.89	70	.303	.371	-5	-6	95	119	0.5	-0	-1	-0.5
■ **BUB KUHN**	Kuhn, Bernard Daniel b: 10/12/1899, Vicksburg, Mich. d: 11/20/56, Detroit, Mich. BL/TR, 6'1.5", 182 lbs. Deb: 9/01/24																												
1924	Cle-A	0	1	.000	1	0	0	0	0	1	4	36.0	1	0	0.0	0	0.0	27.00	15	.667	.571	-3	-3	97	99	-0.4	0	0	-0.1
■ **JOHN KULL**	Kull, John A. b: 6/24/1882, Shenandoah, Pa. d: 3/30/36, Schuylkill, Pa. BL/TL, 6'2", 190 lbs. Deb: 10/02/09																												
1909	Phi-A	1	0	1.000	1	0	0	0	0	3	3	9.0	0	5	15.0	4	12.0	3.00	80	.250	.500	-0	-0	97	233	0.5	0	0	0.0
■ **MIKE KUME**	Kume, John Michael b: 5/19/26, Premier, W.Va. BR/TR, 6'1", 195 lbs. Deb: 8/26/55																												
1955	KC-A	0	2	.000	6	4	0	0	0	24	35	13.1	1	15	5.6	7	2.6	7.88	53	.354	.438	-10	-10	106	90	-0.9	-1	0	-0.9
■ **JEFF KUNKEL**	Kunkel, Jeffrey William b: 3/25/62, W.Palm Beach, Fla. BR/TR, 6'2", 180 lbs. Deb: 7/23/84																												
1988	Tex-A	0	0	—	1	0	0	0	0	1	0	0.0	0	0	0.0	1	9.0	0.00	—	.000	.000	0	0	102	0	0.0	1	0	0.0
■ **BILL KUNKEL**	Kunkel, William Gustave James b: 7/7/36, Hoboken, N.J. d: 5/4/85, Red Bank, N.J. BR/TR, 6'1", 187 lbs. Deb: 4/15/61 U																												
1961	KC-A	3	4	.429	58	2	0	0	4	89	103	10.4	11	32	3.2	46	4.7	5.16	81	.289	.341	-11	-9	104	94	0.3	-0	0	-0.8
1962	KC-A	0	0	—	9	0	0	0	0	8	8	9.0	3	4	4.5	6	6.8	3.38	119	.258	.333	1	1	101	188	0.0	0	0	0.0
1963	NY-A	3	2	.600	22	0	0	0	0	46	42	8.2	3	13	2.5	31	6.1	2.74	130	.239	.288	5	4	98	104	-0.1	1	-1	0.5
Total	3	6	6	.500	89	2	0	0	4	143	153	9.6	17	49	3.1	83	5.2	4.28	93	.272	.324	-6	-5	102	102	0.2	1	-1	-0.3
■ **EARL KUNZ**	Kunz, Earl Dewey "Pinches" b: 12/25/1899, Sacramento, Cal. d: 4/14/63, Sacramento, Cal. BR/TR, 5'10", 170 lbs. Deb: 4/19/23																												
1923	Pit-N	1	2	.333	21	2	1	0	1	46	48	9.4	2	24	4.7	12	2.3	5.48	70	.293	.358	-8	-9	95	87	-0.5	-1	-1	-0.9
■ **RYAN KUROSAKI**	Kurosaki, Ryan Yoshitomo b: 7/3/52, Honolulu, Hawaii BR/TR, 5'10", 160 lbs. Deb: 5/20/75																												
1975	StL-N	0	0	—	7	0	0	0	0	13	15	10.4	3	7	4.8	6	4.2	7.62	49	.283	.361	-6	-6	103	77	0.0	-0	-0	-0.5
■ **HAL KURTZ**	Kurtz, Harold James "Bud" b: 8/20/43, Washington, D.C. BR/TR, 6'3", 205 lbs. Deb: 4/18/68																												
1968	Cle-A	1	0	1.000	28	0	0	0	1	38	37	8.8	2	15	3.6	16	3.8	5.21	58	.255	.337	-9	-9	101	74	0.5	-0	-0	-1.0
■ **ED KUSEL**	Kusel, Edward D. b: 2/15/1886, Cleveland, Ohio d: 10/20/48, Cleveland, Ohio Deb: 9/18/09																												
1909	StL-A	0	3	.000	3	3	3	0	0	24	43	16.1	1	1	0.4	2	0.8	7.13	33	.384	.389	-12	-13	95	84	-1.4	1	-1	-1.1
■ **EMIL KUSH**	Kush, Emil Benedict b: 11/4/16, Chicago, Ill. d: 11/26/69, River Grove, Ill. BR/TR, 5'11", 185 lbs. Deb: 9/21/41																												
1941	Chi-N	0	0	—	2	0	0	0	0	4	2	4.5	0	0	0.0	2	4.5	2.25	151	.143	.143	1	1	94	28	0.0	-0	-0	0.0
1942	Chi-N	0	0	—	1	0	0	0	0	2	1	4.5	0	1	4.5	1	4.5	0.00	—	.167	.250	1	1	98	0	0.0	-0	0	0.1
1946	Chi-N	9	2	.818	40	6	1	1	2	130	120	8.3	4	43	3.0	50	3.5	3.05	104	.253	.310	5	2	93	101	3.4	0	2	0.5
1947	Chi-N	8	3	.727	47	1	1	0	5	91	80	7.9	8	53	5.2	44	4.4	3.36	125	.247	.351	7	**9**	104	128	2.9	1	1	1.1
1948	Chi-N	1	4	.200	34	1	0	0	3	72	70	8.8	5	37	4.6	31	3.9	4.38	86	.253	.334	-3	-5	95	92	-1.2	0	1	-0.3
1949	Chi-N	3	3	.500	26	0	0	0	2	48	51	9.6	7	24	4.5	22	4.1	3.75	105	.283	.368	2	1	97	146	0.5	1	1	0.3
Total	6	21	12	.636	150	8	2	1	12	347	324	8.4	24	158	4.1	150	3.9	3.48	106	.254	.332	12	8	97	111	5.6	2	5	1.7
■ **CRAIG KUSICK**	Kusick, Craig Robert b: 9/30/48, Milwaukee, Wis. BR/TR, 6'3", 210 lbs. Deb: 9/08/73																												
1979	Tor-A	0	0	—	1	0	0	0	0	4	3	6.8	1	0	0.0	0	0.0	4.50	99	.214	.214	-0	-0	106	67	0.0	1	0	-0.1
■ **MARTY KUTYNA**	Kutyna, Marion John b: 11/14/32, Philadelphia, Pa. BR/TR, 6', 190 lbs. Deb: 9/19/59																												
1959	KC-A	0	0	—	4	0	0	0	1	7	7	9.0	0	1	1.3	1	1.3	0.00	—	.250	.267	3	3	103	0	0.0	0	0	0.4
1960	KC-A	3	2	.600	51	0	0	0	4	62	64	9.3	7	32	4.6	20	2.9	3.92	100	.274	.348	-0	0	101	121	0.9	-0	0	0.0
1961	Was-A	6	8	.429	50	6	0	0	3	143	147	9.3	12	48	3.0	64	4.0	3.97	99	.271	.321	1	-1	97	102	0.6	0	3	0.2
1962	Was-A	5	6	.455	54	0	0	0	0	78	83	9.6	9	27	3.1	25	2.9	4.04	101	.275	.320	-1	0	102	108	0.8	-0	1	0.1
Total	4	14	16	.467	159	6	0	0	8	290	301	9.3	28	108	3.4	110	3.4	3.88	102	.272	.325	3	3	100	105	2.3	-0	4	0.7
■ **BOB KUZAVA**	Kuzava, Robert Leroy "Sarge" b: 5/28/23, Wyandotte, Mich. BB/TL, 6'2", 202 lbs. Deb: 9/21/46																												
1946	Cle-A	1	0	1.000	2	2	0	0	0	12	9	6.8	0	11	8.3	4	3.0	3.00	106	.191	.350	1	0	90	95	0.5	0	0	0.0
1947	Cle-A	1	1	.500	4	4	1	1	0	22	22	9.0	1	9	3.7	9	3.7	4.09	85	.265	.340	-1	-1	94	95	0.0	-1	1	0.0
1949	Chi-A	10	6	.625	29	18	9	1	0	157	139	8.0	6	91	5.2	83	4.8	4.01	104	.240	.337	3	3	99	88	3.1	-6	-2	-0.5
1950	Chi-A	1	3	.250	10	7	1	0	0	44	43	8.8	5	27	5.5	21	4.3	5.73	79	.257	.357	-6	-6	99	82	-0.6	-0	0	-0.5
	Was-A	8	7	.533	22	22	8	1	0	155	156	9.1	8	75	4.4	84	4.9	3.95	117	.263	.342	11	12	101	102	1.4	-2	-1	0.8
	Yr	9	10	.474	32	29	9	1	0	199	199	9.0	13	102	4.6	105	4.7	4.34	106	.261	.345	5	6	101	102	0.8	-0	-1	0.3
1951	Was-A	3	3	.500	8	8	3	0	0	52	57	9.9	5	28	4.8	22	3.8	5.54	72	.284	.369	-8	-9	97	94	0.5	-0	0	-0.7
	NY-A	8	4	.667	23	8	4	1	5	82	76	8.3	5	27	3.0	50	5.5	2.41	151	.241	.301	16	11	88	127	0.5	0	-1	1.0
	Yr	11	7	.611	31	16	7	1	5	134	133	8.9	10	55	3.7	72	4.8	3.63	104	.257	.325	7	2	92	127	1.0	-0	-1	0.3
1952	NY-A	8	8	.500	28	12	6	1	3	133	115	7.8	7	63	4.3	67	4.5	3.45	101	.240	.323	3	0	95	99	-1.6	-2	-2	-0.2
1953	NY-A	6	5	.545	33	6	2	2	4	92	92	9.0	9	34	3.3	48	4.7	3.33	106	.264	.326	7	2	88	122	-0.9	-1	-2	0.0
1954	NY-A	1	3	.250	20	3	0	0	1	40	46	10.3	3	18	4.0	22	4.9	5.40	65	.297	.364	-7	-8	94	90	-1.2	-0	-1	-0.9
	Bal-A	1	3	.250	4	4	0	0	0	24	30	11.3	0	11	4.1	15	5.6	4.13	89	.323	.383	-1	-1	99	121	-0.5	-1	-0	-0.2
	Yr	2	6	.250	24	7	0	0	1	64	76	10.7	3	29	4.1	37	5.2	4.92	73	.306	.371	-9	-10	96	121	-1.7	-0	-1	-1.1
1955	Bal-A	0	1	.000	6	1	0	0	0	12	10	7.5	0	4	3.0	5	3.8	3.75	99	.222	.275	0	-0	94	53	-0.4	-0	-0	0.0
	Phi-N	1	0	1.000	17	4	0	0	0	32	47	13.2	5	12	3.4	13	3.7	7.31	56	.333	.383	-12	-11	102	87	0.5	-0	0	-1.0
1957	Pit-N	0	0	—	4	0	0	0	0	2	3	13.5	0	3	13.5	1	4.5	9.00	41	.333	.500	-1	-1	96	92	0.0	0	0	0.0
	StL-N	0	0	—	3	0	0	0	0	2	4	18.0	0	2	9.0	2	9.0	4.50	86	.364	.462	-0	-0	99	182	0.0	0	0	0.0
	Yr	0	0	—	7	0	0	0	0	4	7	15.8	0	5	11.3	3	6.8	6.75	56	.350	.480	-1	-1	98	182	0.0	0	0	0.0
Total	10	49	44	.527	213	99	34	7	13	861	849	8.9	54	415	4.3	446	4.7	4.06	97	.260	.339	5	-11	96	100	1.3	-13	-7	-2.2
■ **CLEM LABINE**	Labine, Clement Walter b: 8/6/26, Lincoln, R.I. BR/TR, 6', 180 lbs. Deb: 4/18/50																												
1950	Bro-N	0	0	—	1	0	0	0	0	2	2	9.0	0	1	4.5	0	0.0	4.50	96	.286	.375	-0	-0	104	97	0.0	0	0	0.0
1951	Bro-N	5	1	.833	14	6	5	2	0	65	52	7.2	4	20	2.8	39	5.4	2.22	169	.223	.279	13	11	95	117	1.7	-0	-1	1.0
1952	Bro-N	8	4	.667	25	9	0	0	0	77	76	8.9	3	47	5.5	43	5.0	5.14	71	.259	.362	-12	-13	98	82	0.7	-2	1	-1.2
1953	Bro-N	11	6	.647	37	7	0	0	7	110	92	7.5	9	30	2.5	44	3.6	2.78	153	.225	.275	18	18	100	96	-0.4	-1	0	1.7
1954	Bro-N	7	6	.538	47	2	0	0	5	108	101	8.4	7	56	4.7	43	3.6	4.17	98	.247	.329	-1	-1	101	86	-0.6	-2	1	-0.1
1955	Bro-N	13	5	.722	**60**	8	1	0	11	144	121	7.6	12	55	3.4	67	4.2	3.25	125	.229	.297	13	13	101	92	2.3	1	3	1.7
1956	Bro-N	10	6	.625	62	3	1	0	**19**	116	111	8.6	11	39	3.0	75	5.8	3.34	113	.253	.311	6	6	100	105	0.5	-1	0	0.5

YEAR	TM/L	W	L	PCT	G	GS	CG	SHO	SV	IP	H	H/G	HR	BB	BB/G	SO	SO/G	ERA	/A	OAVG	OOBP	PR	/A	PF	CPI	WAT	PB	PD	TPI
1957	Bro-N	5	7	.417	58	0	0	0	**17**	105	104	8.9	8	27	2.3	67	5.7	3.43	129	.259	.297	5	12	114	97	-1.4	-2	2	1.3
1958	LA-N	6	6	.500	52	2	0	0	14	104	112	9.7	8	33	2.9	43	3.7	4.15	101	.283	.332	-2	1	106	100	0.5	-1	0	0.0
1959	LA-N	5	10	.333	56	0	0	0	9	85	91	9.6	11	25	2.6	37	3.9	3.92	102	.282	.327	0	1	101	116	-3.2	-2	1	0.0
1960	LA-N	0	1	.000	13	0	0	0	1	17	26	13.8	1	8	4.2	15	7.9	5.82	74	.356	.420	-4	-3	114	115	-0.4	1	0	-0.1
	Det-A	0	3	.000	14	0	0	0	2	19	19	9.0	2	12	5.7	6	2.8	5.21	76	.257	.344	-3	-3	102	86	-1.4	-0	0	-0.2
	Pit-N	3	0	1.000	15	0	0	0	3	30	29	8.7	0	11	3.3	21	6.3	1.50	242	.254	.318	8	7	97	207	1.5	-0	0	0.7
1961	Pit-N	4	1	.800	56	1	0	0	8	93	102	9.9	4	31	3.0	49	4.7	3.68	109	.284	.338	4	3	99	110	1.5	-0	-0	0.2
1962	NY-N	0	0	—	3	0	0	0	0	4	5	11.3	1	1	2.3	2	4.5	11.25	38	.278	.316	-3	-3	108	44	0.0	0	0	-0.2
Total	13	77	56	.579	513	38	7	2	96	1079	1043	8.7	81	396	3.3	551	4.6	3.63	111	.256	.317	40	49	102	102	1.3	-11	8	5.3
■ **BOB LACEY**	Lacey, Robert Joseph b: 8/25/53, Fredericksburg, Va. BR/TL, 6'5", 210 lbs. Deb: 5/13/77																												
1977	Oak-A	6	8	.429	64	0	0	0	7	122	100	7.4	13	43	3.2	69	5.1	3.02	130	.234	.291	14	12	97	110	0.5	0	3	1.5
1978	Oak-A	8	9	.471	**74**	0	0	0	5	120	126	9.4	10	35	2.6	60	4.5	3.00	129	.270	.315	10	12	103	125	0.7	0	2	1.4
1979	Oak-A	1	5	.167	42	0	0	0	4	48	66	12.4	7	24	4.5	33	6.2	5.81	66	.327	.396	-8	-10	91	112	-1.4	0	0	-0.9
1980	Oak-A	3	2	.600	47	1	1	1	6	80	68	7.6	7	21	2.4	45	5.1	2.93	130	.234	.280	10	8	94	98	0.5	0	0	0.8
1981	Cle-A	0	0	—	14	0	0	0	0	21	36	15.4	5	3	1.3	11	4.7	7.71	44	.371	.379	-9	-10	93	99	0.0	0	0	-0.9
	Tex-A	0	0	—	1	0	0	0	0	1	1	9.0	1	0	0.0	0	0.0	9.00	37	.250	.250	-1	-1	90	105	0.0	0	0	0.0
	Yr	0	0	—	15	0	0	0	0	22	37	15.1	6	3	1.2	11	4.5	7.77	44	.356	.374	-10	-11	93	105	0.0	0	0	-0.9
1983	Cal-A	1	2	.333	8	0	0	0	0	9	12	12.0	1	0	0.0	7	7.0	5.00	78	.343	.343	-1	-1	96	107	-0.2	0	0	0.0
1984	SF-N	1	3	.250	34	1	0	0	0	51	55	9.7	5	13	2.3	26	4.6	3.88	90	.276	.315	-2	-2	98	103	-0.7	1	0	-0.1
Total	7	20	29	.408	284	2	1	1	22	452	464	9.2	49	139	2.8	251	5.0	3.66	104	.269	.316	13	8	97	111	-0.6	1	5	1.8
■ **MARCEL LACHEMANN**	Lachemann, Marcel Ernest b: 6/13/41, Los Angeles, Cal. BR/TR, 6', 185 lbs. Deb: 6/04/69 C																												
1969	Oak-A	4	1	.800	28	0	0	0	2	43	43	9.0	1	19	4.0	16	3.3	3.98	83	.261	.340	-2	-3	91	90	1.4	-0	1	-0.2
1970	Oak-A	3	3	.500	41	0	0	0	3	58	58	9.0	6	18	2.8	39	6.1	2.79	127	.266	.321	6	5	96	143	-0.2	-1	1	0.6
1971	Oak-A	0	0	—	1	0	0	0	0	⅓	2	54.0	0	1	27.0	0	0.0	54.00	—	1.000	.750	-2	-2	99	69	0.0	0	0	-0.1
Total	3	7	4	.636	70	0	0	0	5	101	103	9.2	7	38	3.4	55	4.9	3.48	99	.268	.333	2	-0	94	120	1.2	-1	2	0.3
■ **AL LACHOWICZ**	Lachowicz, Allen Richard b: 9/6/60, Pittsburgh, Pa. BR/TR, 6'3", 198 lbs. Deb: 9/13/83																												
1983	Tex-A	0	1	.000	2	1	0	0	0	8	9	10.1	0	2	2.3	8	9.0	2.25	183	.281	.324	2	2	101	151	-0.4	0	0	0.2
■ **GEORGE LaCLAIRE**	LaClaire, George Lewis "Frenchy" b: 10/18/1886, Milton, Vt. d: 10/10/18, Farnham, Que., Can. TR, 5'9", 170 lbs. Deb: 6/05/14																												
1914	Pit-F	5	2	.714	22	7	5	1	0	103	99	8.7	1	25	2.2	49	4.3	4.02	77	.262	.309	-9	-11	96	71	1.8	-1	1	-1.1
1915	Pit-F	1	2	.333	14	3	1	0	1	46	43	8.4	1	13	2.5	10	2.0	3.33	93	.275	.331	-2	-1	102	87	-0.5	-1	0	-0.1
	Buf-F	0	0	—	1	0	0	0	0	3	4	12.0	0	1	3.0	2	6.0	6.00	51	.351	.404	-1	-1	101	81	0.0	0	0	0.0
	Bal-F	1	8	.111	18	9	6	1	1	84	76	8.1	2	22	2.4	30	3.2	2.46	137	.269	.322	5	9	111	110	-2.8	-2	0	0.7
	Yr	2	10	.167	33	12	7	1	2	133	123	8.3	3	36	2.4	42	2.8	2.84	115	.273	.327	3	6	108	110	-3.3	-1	0	0.6
Total	2	7	12	.368	55	19	12	2	2	236	222	8.5	4	61	2.3	91	3.5	3.36	95	.268	.319	-7	-4	103	88	-1.5	-4	1	-0.5
■ **FRANK LaCORTE**	LaCorte, Frank Joseph b: 10/13/51, San Jose, Cal. BR/TR, 6'1", 180 lbs. Deb: 9/08/75																												
1975	Atl-N	0	3	.000	3	2	0	0	0	14	13	8.4	1	6	3.9	10	6.4	5.14	69	.245	.322	-2	-3	97	65	-1.4	-1	0	-0.2
1976	Atl-N	3	12	.200	19	17	1	0	0	105	97	8.3	6	53	4.5	79	6.8	4.71	83	.249	.335	-14	-9	112	82	-4.1	-2	-0	-1.1
1977	Atl-N	1	8	.111	14	7	0	0	0	37	67	16.3	10	29	7.1	28	6.8	11.68	39	.394	.478	-32	-29	115	91	-3.1	-0	0	-2.6
1978	Atl-N	0	1	.000	2	2	0	0	0	15	9	5.4	0	4	2.4	7	4.2	3.60	113	.180	.232	-0	1	114	30	-0.4	-1	-0	0.0
1979	Atl-N	0	0	—	6	0	0	0	0	8	9	10.1	2	5	5.6	6	6.8	7.88	52	.273	.368	-4	-3	110	75	0.0	-0	-0	-0.3
	Hou-N	1	2	.333	12	3	0	0	0	27	21	7.0	3	10	3.3	24	8.0	5.00	68	.208	.272	-4	-5	90	51	-0.5	-0	-1	-0.5
	Yr	1	2	.333	18	3	0	0	0	35	30	7.7	5	15	3.9	30	7.7	5.66	63	.224	.296	-7	-8	95	51	-0.5	-0	-1	-0.8
1980	Hou-N	8	5	.615	55	0	0	0	11	83	61	6.6	4	43	4.7	66	7.2	2.82	124	.210	.304	7	6	97	97	0.7	0	-2	0.5
1981	Hou-N	4	2	.667	37	0	0	0	5	42	41	8.8	1	21	4.5	40	8.6	3.64	83	.258	.337	-1	-3	87	99	0.8	0	-0	-0.2
1982	Hou-N	1	5	.167	55	0	0	0	7	76	71	8.4	5	46	5.4	51	6.0	4.50	80	.247	.339	-8	-8	100	87	-1.9	-1	-2	-1.0
1983	Hou-N	4	4	.500	37	0	0	0	3	53	35	5.9	8	28	4.8	48	8.2	5.09	64	.190	.295	-9	-11	90	62	-0.1	0	-0	-1.0
1984	Cal-A	1	2	.333	13	1	0	0	0	29	33	10.2	9	13	4.0	13	4.0	7.14	57	.282	.351	-10	-10	101	88	-0.4	0	-0	-0.9
Total	10	23	44	.343	253	32	1	0	26	489	457	8.4	49	258	4.7	372	6.8	5.02	73	.249	.336	-75	-73	101	82	-10.4	-4	-6	-7.3
■ **MIKE LaCOSS**	LaCoss, Michael James b: 5/30/56, Glendale, Cal. BR/TR, 6'5", 185 lbs. Deb: 7/18/78																												
1978	Cin-N	4	8	.333	16	15	2	1	0	96	104	9.8	5	46	4.3	31	2.9	4.50	81	.288	.360	-10	-9	102	103	-2.5	-2	-0	-1.0
1979	Cin-N	14	8	.636	35	32	6	1	0	206	202	8.8	13	79	3.5	73	3.2	3.50	103	.263	.326	6	2	96	106	2.2	-1	1	0.2
1980	Cin-N	10	12	.455	34	29	4	2	0	169	207	11.0	9	68	3.6	59	3.1	4.63	79	.303	.362	-19	-18	101	103	-2.0	-3	1	-2.0
1981	Cin-N	4	7	.364	20	13	1	1	1	78	102	11.8	7	30	3.5	22	2.5	6.12	57	.325	.376	-23	-23	101	93	-2.3	-2	0	-2.4
1982	Hou-N	6	6	.500	41	8	0	0	0	115	107	8.4	3	54	4.2	51	4.0	2.90	124	.252	.338	9	9	100	121	0.3	1	-1	1.0
1983	Hou-N	5	7	.417	38	17	2	0	1	138	142	9.3	10	56	3.7	53	3.5	4.43	74	.273	.339	-12	-18	90	93	-1.2	-1	1	-1.8
1984	Hou-N	7	5	.583	39	18	2	1	3	132	132	9.0	3	55	3.8	86	5.9	4.02	82	.261	.331	-6	-11	92	86	1.1	-0	0	-1.1
1985	KC-A	1	1	.500	21	0	0	0	1	41	49	10.8	2	29	6.4	26	5.7	5.05	83	.304	.404	-4	-4	101	114	0.0	0	0	-0.2
1986	SF-N	10	13	.435	37	31	4	1	0	204	179	7.9	14	70	3.1	86	3.8	3.57	99	.240	.303	3	-1	95	90	-1.9	5	1	0.5
1987	SF-N	13	10	.565	39	26	2	1	0	171	184	9.7	16	63	3.3	79	4.2	3.68	105	.283	.342	8	4	95	**124**	0.3	-2	4	0.4
1988	SF-N	7	7	.500	19	19	1	1	0	114	99	7.8	5	47	3.7	70	5.5	3.63	89	.234	.308	-2	-5	93	84	-0.1	2	3	0.0
Total	11	81	84	.491	339	208	24	9	6	1464	1507	9.3	87	597	3.7	636	3.9	4.01	89	.271	.338	-51	-73	96	101	-6.1	-3	10	-6.4
■ **PETER LADD**	Ladd, Peter Linwood b: 7/17/56, Portland, Maine BR/TR, 6'3", 228 lbs. Deb: 8/17/79																												
1979	Hou-N	1	1	.500	10	0	0	0	0	12	8	6.0	1	8	6.0	6	4.5	3.00	113	.178	.321	1	1	90	93	0.0	-0	0	0.1
1982	Mil-A	1	3	.250	16	0	0	0	3	18	16	8.0	5	6	3.0	12	6.0	4.00	94	.239	.293	0	-0	92	116	-1.1	0	-0	0.0
1983	Mil-A	3	4	.429	44	0	0	0	25	49	30	5.5	3	16	2.9	41	7.5	2.57	144	.172	.242	8	6	91	56	-0.6	0	-0	0.6
1984	Mil-A	4	9	.308	54	1	0	0	3	91	94	9.3	16	38	3.8	75	7.4	5.24	71	.266	.335	-13	-16	93	92	-1.7	0	-1	-1.6
1985	Mil-A	0	0	—	29	0	0	0	2	46	58	11.3	5	10	2.0	22	4.3	4.50	97	.315	.347	-2	-1	106	118	0.0	0	-0	0.0
1986	Sea-A	8	6	.571	52	0	0	0	6	71	69	8.7	10	18	2.3	53	6.7	3.80	117	.258	.306	3	5	106	106	2.0	0	-1	0.4
Total	6	17	23	.425	205	1	0	0	39	287	275	8.6	40	96	3.0	209	6.6	4.14	96	.252	.312	-2	-5	98	95	-1.4	-0	-3	-0.5
■ **DOYLE LADE**	Lade, Doyle Marion "Porky" b: 2/17/21, Fairbury, Neb. BR/TR, 5'10", 183 lbs. Deb: 9/18/46																												
1946	Chi-N	0	2	.000	3	2	0	0	0	15	15	9.0	0	3	1.8	8	4.8	4.20	76	.238	.284	-1	-2	93	46	-0.9	-0	0	-0.1
1947	Chi-N	11	10	.524	34	25	7	1	0	187	202	9.7	15	79	3.8	62	3.0	3.95	107	.276	.341	3	6	104	110	1.6	2	2	1.0
1948	Chi-N	5	6	.455	19	12	6	0	0	87	99	10.2	4	31	3.2	29	3.0	4.03	93	.283	.339	-1	-3	95	103	0.4	-1	1	-0.1
1949	Chi-N	4	5	.444	36	13	5	1	1	130	141	9.8	14	58	4.0	43	3.0	4.98	79	.274	.346	-14	-15	97	93	0.4	2	0	-1.2
1950	Chi-N	5	6	.455	34	12	2	0	2	118	126	9.6	14	50	3.8	36	2.7	4.73	94	.275	.345	-8	-4	107	99	0.4	3	3	0.2
Total	5	25	29	.463	126	64	20	2	3	537	583	9.8	47	221	3.7	178	3.0	4.39	93	.275	.341	-21	-18	101	100	1.9	5	7	-0.2
■ **STEVE LADEW**	Ladew, Stephen b: St.Louis, Mo. Deb: 9/27/1889																												
1889	KC-a	0	0	—	1	0	0	0	0	2	1	4.5	0	3	13.5	0	0.0	4.50	93	.160	.432	-0	-0	109	86	0.0	-0	0	0.0
■ **FLIP LAFFERTY**	Lafferty, Frank Bernard b: 5/4/1854, Scranton, Pa. d: 2/8/10, Wilmington, Del. TR, Deb: 9/15/1876																												
1876	Phi-N	0	1	.000	1	1	1	0	0	9	5	5.0	0	0	0.0	0	0.0	0.00	—	.167	.167	2	2	105	0	-0.4	-1	0	0.2
■ **ED LAFITTE**	Lafitte, Edward Francis "Doc" b: 4/7/1886, New Orleans, La. d: 4/12/71, Jenkintown, Pa. BR/TR, 6'2", 188 lbs. Deb: 4/16/09																												
1909	Det-A	0	1	.000	3	1	1	0	1	14	22	14.1	2	2	1.3	11	7.1	3.86	68	.344	.373	-2	-2	106	153	-0.4	0	0	-0.1
1911	Det-A	11	8	.579	29	20	15	0	1	172	205	10.7	2	52	2.7	63	3.3	3.92	91	.302	.356	-11	-7	107	101	0.0	-3	-2	-0.9
1912	Det-A	0	0	—	1	0	0	0	0	2	2	9.0	0	2	9.0	0	0.0	13.50	24	.333	.500	-2	-2	96	49	0.0	0	0	-0.1
1914	Bro-F	18	15	.545	42	33	23	0	2	291	260	8.0	7	127	3.9	137	4.2	2.63	123	.248	.338	19	20	101	125	1.9	4	5	3.2
1915	Bro-F	6	9	.400	17	16	7	0	0	118	126	9.6	7	57	4.3	34	2.6	3.97	75	.303	.387	-12	-13	98	111	-1.0	3	0	-1.0
	Buf-F	2	2	.500	14	5	1	0	1	50	53	9.5	0	22	4.0	17	3.1	3.42	90	.301	.379	-2	-2	101	111	0.1	-1	0	-0.2
	Yr	8	11	.421	31	21	8	0	1	168	179	9.6	7	79	4.2	51	2.7	3.80	79	.302	.384	-14	-15	99	111	-0.9	3	0	-1.2
Total	5	37	35	.514	106	75	47	0	5	647	668	9.3	18	262	3.6	262	3.6	3.34	97	.280	.356	-11	-6	102	115	0.6	3	4	0.9

YEAR	TM/L	W	L	PCT	G	GS	CG	SHO	SV	IP	H	H/G	HR	BB	BB/G	SO	SO/G	ERA	/A	OAVG	OOBP	PR	/A	PF	CPI	WAT	PB	PD	TPI
■ ED LAGGER	Lagger, Edwin Joseph b: 7/14/12, Joliet, Ill. d: 11/10/81, Joliet, Ill. BR/TR, 6'3", 200 lbs. Deb: 6/15/34																												
1934	Phi-A	0	0	—	8	0	0	0	0	18	27	13.5	1	14	7.0	2	1.0	11.00	40	.342	.442	-13	-13	98	68	0.0	-1	1	-1.0
■ LERRIN LaGROW	LaGrow, Lerrin Harris b: 7/8/48, Phoenix, Ariz. BR/TR, 6'5", 220 lbs. Deb: 7/28/70																												
1970	Det-A	0	1	.000	10	0	0	0	0	12	16	12.0	2	6	4.5	7	5.3	7.50	52	.308	.373	-5	-5	104	80	-0.4	-0	0	-0.4
1972	Det-A	0	1	.000	16	0	0	0	2	27	22	7.3	0	6	2.0	9	3.0	1.33	259	.222	.264	5	6	112	127	-0.4	0	0	0.7
1973	Det-A	1	5	.167	21	3	0	0	3	54	54	9.0	8	23	3.8	33	5.5	4.33	89	.263	.333	-3	-3	101	104	-2.0	0	1	-0.1
1974	Det-A	8	19	.296	37	34	11	0	0	216	245	10.2	21	80	3.3	85	3.5	4.67	84	.287	.346	-25	-18	108	97	-5.0	0	3	-1.5
1975	Det-A	7	14	.333	32	26	7	2	0	164	183	10.0	15	66	3.6	75	4.1	4.39	92	.280	.341	-11	-7	106	100	-0.7	0	-2	-0.8
1976	StL-N	0	1	.000	8	2	1	0	0	24	21	7.9	0	7	2.6	10	3.8	1.50	244	.241	.293	5	6	105	173	-0.4	-1	0	0.6
1977	Chi-A	7	3	.700	66	0	0	0	25	99	81	7.4	10	35	3.2	63	5.7	2.45	164	.230	.292	18	17	99	130	1.7	0	1	1.8
1978	Chi-A	6	5	.545	52	0	0	0	16	88	85	8.7	9	38	3.9	41	4.2	4.40	88	.260	.337	-6	-5	102	94	1.1	0	1	-0.3
1979	Chi-A	0	3	.000	11	2	0	0	1	18	27	13.5	2	16	8.0	9	4.5	9.00	48	.346	.463	-10	-9	103	89	-1.4	0	-0	-0.8
	LA-N	5	1	.833	31	0	0	0	4	37	38	9.2	2	18	4.4	22	5.4	3.41	109	.270	.348	1	1	99	119	2.0	0	-0	0.1
1980	Phi-N	0	2	.000	25	0	0	0	3	39	42	9.7	5	17	3.9	21	4.8	4.15	92	.276	.341	-2	-1	106	113	-0.9	0	0	-0.1
Total	10	34	55	.382	309	67	19	2	54	778	814	9.4	74	312	3.6	375	4.3	4.12	95	.271	.336	-32	-17	105	107	-6.4	-0	3	-0.8
■ JEFF LAHTI	Lahti, Jeffrey Allen b: 10/8/56, Oregon City, Ore. BR/TR, 6', 180 lbs. Deb: 6/27/82																												
1982	StL-N	5	4	.556	33	1	0	0	0	57	53	8.4	3	21	3.3	22	3.5	3.79	98	.245	.310	-1	-1	102	85	0.0	-1	2	0.0
1983	StL-N	3	3	.500	53	0	0	0	0	74	64	7.8	2	29	3.5	26	3.2	3.16	113	.240	.308	4	3	98	93	0.1	-1	1	0.3
1984	StL-N	4	2	.667	63	0	0	0	1	85	69	7.3	6	34	3.6	45	4.8	3.71	96	.225	.297	-1	-2	99	81	0.9	-0	0	0.0
1985	StL-N	5	2	.714	52	0	0	0	19	68	63	8.3	3	26	3.4	41	5.4	1.85	181	.251	.319	13	11	93	179	0.9	-1	-0	1.1
1986	StL-N	0	0	—	4	0	0	0	0	2	3	13.5	0	1	4.5	3	13.5	0.00	—	.333	.400	1	1	103	0	0.0	0	0	0.1
Total	5	17	11	.607	205	1	0	0	20	286	252	7.9	14	111	3.5	137	4.3	3.12	114	.240	.309	16	13	98	107	1.9	-3	3	1.5
■ EDDIE LAKE	Lake, Edward Erving "Sparky" b: 3/18/16, Antioch, Cal. BR/TR, 5'7", 159 lbs. Deb: 9/26/39																												
1944	Bos-A	0	0	—	6	0	0	0	0	19	20	9.5	2	11	5.2	7	3.3	4.26	78	.278	.391	-2	-2	97	128	0.0	1	0	-0.1
■ JOE LAKE	Lake, Joseph Henry b: 1/6/1881, Brooklyn, N.Y. d: 6/30/50, Brooklyn, N.Y. BR/TR, 6', 185 lbs. Deb: 4/21/08																												
1908	NY-A	9	22	.290	38	27	19	2	0	269	252	8.4	6	77	2.6	118	3.9	3.18	76	.242	.298	-24	-23	101	84	-2.2	1	-5	-2.9
1909	NY-A	14	11	.560	31	26	17	3	1	215	180	7.5	2	59	2.5	117	4.9	1.88	131	.225	.283	14	14	99	94	2.0	1	5	2.2
1910	StL-A	11	17	.393	35	29	24	1	2	261	243	8.4	3	77	2.7	141	4.9	2.21	115	.248	.304	9	9	101	112	2.1	2	0	1.1
1911	StL-A	10	15	.400	30	25	14	2	0	215	245	10.3	3	40	1.7	69	2.9	3.31	101	.282	.316	1	1	100	91	2.1	2	5	0.8
1912	StL-A	1	7	.125	11	6	4	0	0	57	70	11.1	0	16	2.5	28	4.4	4.42	78	.314	.363	-7	-6	103	98	-2.5	-1	2	-0.4
	Det-A	9	11	.450	26	14	11	0	1	163	190	10.5	3	39	2.2	86	4.7	3.09	104	.296	.340	5	2	96	125	0.0	-3	0	0.2
	Yr	10	18	.357	37	20	15	0	1	220	260	10.6	3	55	2.3	114	4.7	3.44	95	.301	.345	-2	-4	98	125	-2.5	-1	2	-0.2
1913	Det-A	8	7	.533	28	12	6	0	1	137	149	9.8	3	24	1.6	35	2.3	3.28	90	.278	.309	-5	-5	101	90	1.5	4	3	-0.1
Total	6	62	90	.408	199	139	95	8	5	1317	1329	9.1	20	332	2.3	594	4.1	2.85	98	.261	.309	-7	-8	100	99	3.0	5	10	0.9
■ AL LAKEMAN	Lakeman, Albert Wesley "Moose" b: 12/31/18, Cincinnati, Ohio d: 5/25/76, Spartanburg, S.C. BR/TR, 6'2", 195 lbs. Deb: 4/19/42 C																												
1948	Phi-N	0	0	—	1	0	0	0	0	1	1	9.0	1	0	0.0	0	0.0	9.00	42	.333	.333	-1	-1	97	131	0.0	0	0	0.0
■ JACK LAMABE	Lamabe, John Alexander b: 10/3/36, Farmingdale, N.Y. BR/TR, 6'1", 198 lbs. Deb: 4/17/62																												
1962	Pit-N	3	1	.750	46	0	0	0	2	78	70	8.1	4	40	4.6	56	6.5	2.88	138	.238	.323	9	10	101	115	0.8	-1	1	0.9
1963	Bos-A	7	4	.636	65	2	0	0	6	151	139	8.3	8	46	2.7	93	5.5	3.16	122	.247	.300	8	12	107	100	1.8	-1	1	1.2
1964	Bos-A	9	13	.409	39	25	3	0	1	177	235	11.9	25	57	2.9	109	5.5	5.90	64	.318	.363	-45	-42	103	96	-0.9	-1	-0	-4.2
1965	Bos-A	0	3	.000	14	0	0	0	0	25	34	12.2	5	14	5.0	17	6.1	8.28	46	.340	.418	-13	-13	109	93	-1.4	-0	0	-1.2
	Hou-N	0	2	.000	3	2	0	0	0	13	17	11.8	3	3	2.1	6	4.2	4.15	78	.315	.351	-1	-1	91	146	-0.9	0	-0	0.0
1966	Chi-A	7	9	.438	34	17	3	2	0	121	116	8.6	9	35	2.6	67	5.0	3.94	81	.251	.301	-7	-10	93	85	-1.2	-2	-0	-1.2
1967	Chi-A	1	0	1.000	3	0	0	0	0	5	7	12.6	0	1	1.8	3	5.4	1.80	167	.318	.348	1	1	93	241	0.5	0	0	0.1
	NY-N	0	3	.000	16	2	0	0	1	32	24	6.8	4	8	2.3	23	6.5	3.94	87	.200	.248	-2	-2	102	56	-1.4	-0	0	-0.1
	StL-N	3	4	.429	23	1	1	1	4	48	43	8.1	2	10	1.9	30	5.6	2.81	119	.244	.279	3	3	99	94	-1.0	0	-0	0.3
	Yr	3	7	.300	39	3	1	1	5	80	67	7.5	6	18	2.0	53	6.0	3.26	104	.226	.266	1	1	100	94	-2.4	-0	-0	0.2
1968	Chi-N	3	2	.600	42	0	0	0	1	61	68	10.0	7	24	3.5	30	4.4	4.28	78	.289	.342	-9	-6	112	113	0.4	0	-0	-0.6
Total	7	33	41	.446	285	49	7	3	15	711	753	9.5	67	238	3.0	434	5.5	4.24	85	.272	.325	-56	-49	102	98	-3.3	-6	0	-4.8
■ AL LaMACCHIA	LaMacchia, Alfred Anthony b: 7/22/21, St.Louis, Mo. BR/TR, 5'10.5", 190 lbs. Deb: 9/27/43																												
1943	StL-A	0	1	.000	1	1	0	0	0	4	9	20.3	0	2	4.5	2	4.5	11.25	29	.450	.478	-4	-4	101	88	-0.4	-0	-0	-0.2
1945	StL-A	2	0	1.000	5	0	0	0	0	9	6	6.0	0	3	3.0	2	2.0	2.00	192	.207	.265	1	2	114	100	1.0	-0	0	0.2
1946	StL-A	0	0	—	8	0	0	0	0	15	17	10.2	2	7	4.2	3	1.8	6.00	58	.279	.343	-4	-4	100	80	0.0	-0	-0	-0.4
	Was-A	0	1	.000	2	0	0	0	0	3	6	18.0	1	2	6.0	0	0.0	15.00	22	.462	.533	-4	-4	94	84	-0.4	0	0	-0.3
	Yr	0	1	.000	10	0	0	0	0	18	23	11.5	3	9	4.5	3	1.5	7.50	46	.311	.376	-8	-8	99	84	-0.4	-0	-0	-0.7
Total	3	2	2	.500	16	1	0	0	0	31	38	11.0	3	14	4.1	7	2.0	6.39	56	.309	.366	-10	-10	104	87	0.2	-1	-0	-0.7
■ HANK LaMANNA	LaManna, Frank b: 8/22/19, Watertown, Pa. d: 9/1/80, Syracuse, N.Y. BR/TR, 6'2.5", 195 lbs. Deb: 4/16/40																												
1940	Bos-N	1	0	1.000	5	1	1	0	0	13	13	9.0	1	8	5.5	3	2.1	4.85	80	.271	.368	-1	-1	101	102	0.5	0	0	0.0
1941	Bos-N	5	4	.556	35	4	0	0	1	73	77	9.5	5	56	6.9	23	2.8	5.30	65	.285	.392	-14	-15	96	106	1.2	1	1	-1.1
1942	Bos-N	0	1	.000	5	0	0	0	0	7	5	6.4	1	3	3.9	2	2.6	5.14	63	.208	.296	-1	-1	98	65	-0.4	-0	0	-0.1
Total	3	6	5	.545	45	5	1	0	1	93	95	9.2	7	67	6.5	28	2.7	5.23	67	.278	.383	-16	-18	96	102	1.3	1	1	-1.2
■ FRANK LAMANSKE	Lamanske, Frank James "Lefty" b: 9/30/06, Oglesby, Ill. d: 8/4/71, Olney, Ill. BL/TL, 5'11", 170 lbs. Deb: 4/27/35																												
1935	Bro-N	0	0	—	2	0	0	0	0	4	5	11.3	0	1	2.3	1	2.3	6.75	56	.313	.353	-1	-1	95	65	0.0	-0	0	0.0
■ WAYNE LaMASTER	LaMaster, Wayne Lee b: 2/13/07, Speed, Ind. BL/TL, 5'8", 170 lbs. Deb: 4/19/37																												
1937	Phi-N	15	19	.441	50	30	10	1	4	220	255	10.4	24	82	3.4	135	5.5	5.32	81	.290	.348	-34	-24	111	92	1.5	-2	-4	-2.8
1938	Phi-N	4	7	.364	18	12	1	1	0	64	80	11.3	8	31	4.4	35	4.9	7.73	52	.301	.377	-28	-27	106	74	0.5	4	1	-2.0
	Bro-N	0	1	.000	3	0	0	0	0	11	17	13.9	0	3	2.5	3	2.5	4.91	74	.340	.377	-1	-2	96	108	-0.4	-0	0	-0.1
	Yr	4	8	.333	21	12	1	1	0	75	97	11.6	8	34	4.1	38	4.6	7.32	54	.304	.369	-29	-28	104	108	0.1	4	1	-2.1
Total	2	19	27	.413	71	42	11	2	4	295	352	10.7	32	116	3.5	173	5.3	5.83	73	.295	.356	-64	-52	109	89	1.6	1	-4	-4.9
■ JOHN LAMB	Lamb, John Andrew b: 7/20/46, Sharon, Conn. BR/TR, 6'3", 180 lbs. Deb: 8/12/70																												
1970	Pit-N	0	1	.000	23	0	0	0	3	32	23	6.5	2	13	3.7	24	6.8	2.81	138	.209	.299	4	4	96	102	-0.4	-0	-1	0.3
1971	Pit-N	0	0	—	2	0	0	0	0	4	3	6.8	0	1	2.3	1	2.3	0.00	—	.188	.222	2	1	97	0	0.0	-0	0	0.2
1973	Pit-N	0	1	.000	22	0	0	0	2	30	37	11.1	3	10	3.0	11	3.3	6.00	56	.308	.351	-8	-9	92	84	-0.4	-0	0	-0.8
Total	3	0	2	.000	47	0	0	0	5	66	63	8.6	5	24	3.3	36	4.9	4.09	88	.256	.319	-2	-3	94	88	-0.8	-1	-1	-0.3
■ RAY LAMB	Lamb, Raymond Richard b: 12/23/44, Glendale, Cal. BR/TR, 6'1", 170 lbs. Deb: 8/01/69																												
1969	LA-N	0	1	.000	10	0	0	0	1	15	12	7.2	2	7	4.2	11	6.6	1.80	195	.235	.317	3	3	97	221	-0.4	-0	0	0.3
1970	LA-N	6	1	.857	35	0	0	0	0	57	59	9.3	4	27	4.3	32	5.1	3.79	95	.277	.360	2	-1	89	125	2.4	-0	-1	-0.2
1971	Cle-A	6	12	.333	43	21	3	1	1	158	147	8.4	11	69	3.9	91	5.2	3.36	112	.247	.320	2	7	108	103	-0.9	-2	-2	0.3
1972	Cle-A	5	6	.455	34	9	0	0	0	108	101	8.4	5	29	2.4	64	5.3	3.08	107	.248	.293	-0	3	108	91	0.0	-1	-1	0.1
1973	Cle-A	3	3	.500	32	1	0	0	2	86	98	10.3	7	42	4.4	60	6.3	4.60	82	.291	.368	-7	-8	99	106	0.3	0	-0	-0.7
Total	5	20	23	.465	154	31	3	1	4	424	417	8.9	29	174	3.7	258	5.5	3.54	103	.260	.329	-1	5	103	108	1.4	-4	-4	-0.2
■ CLAYTON LAMBERT	Lambert, Clayton Patrick b: 3/26/17, Summitt, Ill. d: 4/3/81, Ogden, Utah BR/TR, 6'2", 185 lbs. Deb: 4/22/46																												
1946	Cin-N	2	2	.500	23	4	2	0	1	53	48	8.2	3	20	3.4	20	3.4	4.25	84	.251	.322	-5	-4	105	80	0.2	-1	-1	-0.5
1947	Cin-N	0	0	—	3	0	0	0	0	6	12	18.0	3	6	9.0	1	1.5	15.00	25	.444	.545	-7	-8	92	97	0.0	-0	0	-0.6
Total	2	2	2	.500	26	4	2	0	1	59	60	9.2	6	26	4.0	21	3.2	5.34	68	.275	.352	-12	-11	104	81	0.2	-1	-1	-1.1
■ GENE LAMBERT	Lambert, Eugene Marion b: 4/26/21, Crenshaw, Miss. BR/TR, 5'11", 175 lbs. Deb: 9/14/41																												
1941	Phi-N	0	1	.000	2	1	0	0	0	9	11	11.0	0	2	2.0	3	3.0	2.00	187	.297	.325	2	2	103	190	-0.4	-0	-0	0.1

YEAR	TM/L	W	L	PCT	G	GS	CG	SHO	SV	IP	H	H/G	HR	BB	BB/G	SO	SO/G	ERA	/A	OAVG	OOBP	PR	/A	PF	CPI	WAT	PB	PD	TPI
1942	Phi-N	0	0	—	1	0	0	0	0	1	3	27.0	0	0	0.0	1	9.0	9.00	37	.500	.500	-1	-1	101	129	0.0	0	0	0.0
Total	2	0	1	.000	3	1	0	0	0	10	14	12.6	0	2	1.8	4	3.6	2.70	137	.326	.348	1	1	103	184	-0.4	-0	0	0.1
■ OTIS LAMBETH	Lambeth, Otis Samuel b: 5/13/1890, Berlin, Kan. d: 6/5/76, Moran, Kan. BR/TR, 6', 175 lbs. Deb: 7/16/16																												
1916	Cle-A	4	3	.571	15	9	3	0	1	74	69	8.4	1	38	4.6	28	3.4	2.92	96	.256	.354	-1	-1	99	119	0.5	-1	-2	-0.3
1917	Cle-A	7	6	.538	26	10	2	0	2	97	97	9.0	2	30	2.8	27	2.5	3.15	96	.274	.349	-5	-1	113	112	-0.3	-0	-1	-0.2
1918	Cle-A	0	0	—	2	0	0	0	0	7	10	12.9	0	6	7.7	3	3.9	6.43	46	.370	.485	-3	-3	107	111	0.0	0	0	-0.1
Total	3	11	9	.550	43	19	5	0	3	178	176	8.9	3	74	3.7	58	2.9	3.19	92	.270	.357	-9	-5	107	115	0.2	-1	-3	-0.6
■ FRED LAMLINE	Lamline, Frederick Arthur "Dutch" (born Frederick Arthur Lamlein) b: 8/14/1887, Port Huron, Mich. d: 9/20/70, Port Huron, Mich. BR/TR, 5'11", 171 lbs. Deb: 9/18/12																												
1912	Chi-A	0	0	—	1	0	0	0	0	2	7	31.5	0	2	9.0	1	4.5	31.50	11	.583	.643	-6	-6	99	57	0.0	0	0	-0.4
1915	StL-N	0	0	—	4	0	0	0	0	19	21	9.9	0	3	1.4	11	5.2	1.42	195	.300	.333	3	3	101	264	0.0	-0	0	0.3
Total	2	0	0	—	5	0	0	0	0	21	28	12.0	0	5	2.1	12	5.1	4.29	66	.341	.380	-3	-3	100	245	0.0	-0	0	-0.1
■ DENNIS LAMP	Lamp, Dennis Patrick b: 9/23/52, Los Angeles, Cal. BR/TR, 6'4", 200 lbs. Deb: 8/21/77																												
1977	Chi-N	0	2	.000	11	3	0	0	0	30	43	12.9	3	8	2.4	12	3.6	6.30	71	.344	.387	-8	-6	115	98	-0.9	1	0	-0.4
1978	Chi-N	7	15	.318	37	36	6	3	0	224	221	8.9	16	56	2.3	73	2.9	3.29	121	.258	.303	7	17	111	101	-4.1	0	3	2.3
1979	Chi-N	11	10	.524	38	32	6	1	0	200	223	10.0	14	46	2.1	86	3.9	3.51	120	.287	.325	5	15	112	114	0.7	-1	3	1.9
1980	Chi-N	10	14	.417	41	37	2	1	0	203	259	11.5	16	82	3.6	83	3.7	5.19	75	.317	.371	-36	-29	108	104	0.5	-3	3	-2.9
1981	Chi-A	7	6	.538	27	10	3	0	0	127	103	7.3	4	43	3.0	71	5.0	2.41	150	.222	.286	18	17	99	98	0.4	0	1	1.9
1982	Chi-A	11	8	.579	44	27	3	2	5	190	206	9.8	9	59	2.8	78	3.7	3.98	99	.279	.332	2	-1	97	99	1.0	0	2	0.1
1983	Chi-A	7	7	.500	49	5	1	0	15	116	123	9.5	6	29	2.3	44	3.4	3.72	111	.275	.323	5	5	102	101	-1.3	0	0	0.5
1984	Tor-A	8	8	.500	56	4	0	0	9	85	97	10.3	9	38	4.0	45	4.8	4.55	89	.285	.351	-5	-5	101	106	-0.7	0	1	-0.3
1985	Tor-A	11	0	1.000	53	1	0	0	2	106	96	8.2	7	27	2.3	68	5.8	3.31	124	.247	.289	10	9	99	95	5.5	0	2	1.2
1986	Tor-A	2	6	.250	40	2	0	0	2	73	93	11.5	5	23	2.8	30	3.7	5.05	86	.309	.353	-7	-6	104	96	-2.1	0	0	-0.4
1987	Oak-A	1	3	.250	36	5	0	0	0	57	76	12.0	5	22	3.5	36	5.7	5.05	80	.326	.378	-4	-6	91	116	-0.9	0	0	-0.5
1988	Bos-A	7	6	.538	46	0	0	0	0	83	92	10.0	3	19	2.1	49	5.3	3.47	124	.284	.323	5	8	108	110	0.0	0	1	0.9
Total	12	82	85	.491	478	162	21	7	33	1494	1632	9.8	97	452	2.7	675	4.1	3.92	103	.281	.330	-8	21	105	103	-1.9	-3	16	4.3
■ HENRY LAMPE	Lampe, Henry Joseph b: 9/19/1872, Boston, Mass. d: 9/16/36, Dorchester, Mass. BR/TL, 5'11.5", 175 lbs. Deb: 5/14/1894																												
1894	Bos-N	0	1	.000	2	1	0	0	0	5	17	30.6	5	7	12.6	1	1.8	12.60	47	.571	.653	-4	-4	111	205	-0.4	-1	0	-0.2
1895	Phi-N	0	2	.000	7	3	2	0	0	44	68	13.9	3	33	6.8	18	3.7	7.57	62	.375	.471	-14	-14	98	100	-0.9	-1	0	-1.0
Total	2	0	3	.000	9	4	2	0	0	49	85	15.6	8	40	7.3	19	3.5	8.08	60	.403	.498	-18	-18	100	111	-1.3	-1	0	-1.2
■ DICK LANAHAN	Lanahan, Richard Anthony b: 9/27/11, Washington, D.C. d: 3/12/75, Rochester, Minn. BL/TL, 6', 186 lbs. Deb: 9/15/35																												
1935	Was-A	0	3	.000	3	3	0	0	0	21	27	11.6	2	17	7.3	10	4.3	5.57	74	.314	.434	-3	-3	93	126	-1.4	-0	0	-0.2
1937	Was-A	0	1	.000	6	2	0	0	0	11	16	13.1	2	13	10.6	2	1.6	13.09	34	.320	.462	-10	-11	96	67	-0.4	0	0	-0.7
1940	Pit-N	6	8	.429	40	8	4	0	2	108	121	10.1	8	42	3.5	45	3.8	4.25	86	.279	.341	-5	-7	95	105	-1.1	-2	0	-0.8
1941	Pit-N	0	1	.000	7	0	0	0	0	12	13	9.8	1	3	2.3	5	3.8	5.25	70	.283	.346	-2	-2	102	88	-0.4	-0	0	-0.1
Total	4	6	13	.316	56	13	4	0	2	152	177	10.5	13	75	4.4	62	3.7	5.15	73	.288	.366	-20	-23	95	104	-3.3	-2	1	-1.8
■ LESTER LANCASTER	Lancaster, Lester Wayne b: 4/21/62, Dallas, Tex. BR/TR, 6'2", 205 lbs. Deb: 4/07/87																												
1987	Chi-N	8	3	.727	27	18	0	0	0	132	138	9.4	14	51	3.5	78	5.3	4.91	85	.268	.329	-12	-11	102	86	2.8	-2	-1	-1.3
1988	Chi-N	4	6	.400	44	3	1	0	5	86	89	9.3	4	34	3.6	36	3.8	3.77	96	.273	.334	-3	-1	105	107	-0.7	-1	1	-0.2
Total	2	12	9	.571	71	21	1	0	5	218	227	9.4	18	85	3.5	114	4.7	4.46	89	.270	.331	-15	-12	103	95	2.1	-4	-0	-1.5
■ GARY LANCE	Lance, Gary Dean b: 9/21/48, Greenville, S.C. BB/TR, 6'3", 195 lbs. Deb: 9/28/77																												
1977	KC-A	0	1	.000	1	0	0	0	0	2	2	9.0	0	2	9.0	0	0.0	4.50	89	.286	.400	-0	-0	99	126	-0.4	0	0	0.0
■ DOC LANDIS	Landis, Samuel H. b: 8/16/1854, Philadelphia, Pa. 5'11", 172 lbs. Deb: 5/02/1882																												
1882	Phi-a	1	1	.500	2	2	2	0	0	17	16	8.5	1	1	0.5	13	6.9	3.18	94	.254	.266	-1	-0	111	78	0.0	-1	-0	0.0
	Bal-a	11	27	.289	42	39	35	0	0	341	409	10.8	7	46	1.2	62	1.6	3.33	83	.303	.326	-24	-22	102	110	1.5	-7	-3	-2.8
	Yr	12	28	.300	44	41	37	0	0	358	425	10.7	8	47	1.2	75	1.9	3.32	83	.300	.323	-25	-22	103	110	1.5	-1	-4	-2.8
■ BILL LANDIS	Landis, William Henry b: 10/8/42, Hanford, Cal. BL/TL, 6'2", 178 lbs. Deb: 9/28/63																												
1963	KC-A	0	0	—	1	0	0	0	0	2	0	0.0	0	1	4.5	3	13.5	0.00	—	.000	.167	1	1	109	0	0.0	0	0	0.1
1967	Bos-A	1	0	1.000	18	1	0	0	0	26	24	8.3	6	11	3.8	23	8.0	5.19	70	.253	.318	-6	-4	113	96	0.5	-0	-1	-0.5
1968	Bos-A	3	3	.500	38	1	0	0	3	60	48	7.2	4	30	4.5	59	8.9	3.15	95	.223	.316	-1	-1	101	103	-0.1	-1	-1	-0.2
1969	Bos-A	5	5	.500	45	5	0	0	1	82	82	9.0	7	49	5.4	50	5.5	5.27	72	.269	.363	-15	-13	105	90	-0.3	-0	0	-1.3
Total	4	9	8	.529	102	7	0	0	4	170	154	8.2	17	91	4.8	135	7.1	4.45	78	.248	.339	-21	-18	105	95	0.1	-1	-1	-1.9
■ LARRY LANDRETH	Landreth, Larry Robert b: 3/11/55, Stratford, Ont., Can BR/TR, 6'1", 175 lbs. Deb: 9/16/76																												
1976	Mon-N	1	2	.333	3	3	0	0	0	11	13	10.6	1	10	8.2	7	5.7	4.09	88	.310	.434	-1	-1	103	163	0.0	-0	-0	0.0
1977	Mon-N	0	2	.000	4	1	0	0	0	9	16	16.0	0	8	8.0	5	5.0	10.00	39	.381	.471	-6	-6	99	83	-0.9	-0	-0	-0.5
Total	2	1	4	.200	7	4	0	0	0	20	29	13.0	1	18	8.1	12	5.4	6.75	55	.345	.452	-7	-7	101	127	-0.9	-1	-0	-0.5
■ JOE LANDRUM	Landrum, Joseph Butler b: 12/13/28, Columbia, S.C. BR/TR, 5'11", 180 lbs. Deb: 7/13/50																												
1950	Bro-N	0	0	—	7	0	0	0	1	7	12	15.4	2	1	1.3	5	6.4	7.71	56	.414	.412	-3	-3	104	126	0.0	0	0	-0.1
1952	Bro-N	1	3	.250	9	5	2	0	0	38	46	10.9	3	10	2.4	17	4.0	5.21	70	.301	.343	-6	-7	98	90	-1.1	-0	-0	-0.6
Total	2	1	3	.250	16	5	2	0	1	45	58	11.6	5	11	2.2	22	4.4	5.60	67	.319	.355	-9	-9	99	95	-1.1	-0	0	-0.7
■ BILL LANDRUM	Landrum, Thomas William b: 8/17/57, Columbia, S.C. BR/TR, 6'2", 185 lbs. Deb: 8/31/86																												
1986	Cin-N	0	0	—	10	0	0	0	0	13	23	15.9	0	4	2.8	14	9.7	6.92	56	.390	.415	-5	-4	104	100	0.0	-0	-0	-0.4
1987	Cin-N	3	2	.600	44	2	0	0	2	65	68	9.4	3	34	4.7	42	5.8	4.71	89	.292	.370	-4	-4	103	104	0.4	0	1	-0.2
1988	Chi-N	1	0	1.000	7	0	0	0	0	12	19	14.3	1	3	2.3	6	4.5	6.00	60	.365	.400	-3	-3	105	110	0.5	-0	-0	-0.3
Total	3	4	2	.667	61	2	0	0	2	90	110	11.0	4	41	4.1	62	6.2	5.20	79	.320	.381	-13	-11	103	104	0.9	-0	0	-0.9
■ JERRY LANE	Lane, Jerald Hal b: 2/7/26, Ashland, N.Y. d: 7/24/88, Chattanooga, Tenn. BR/TR, 6'0.5", 205 lbs. Deb: 7/07/53																												
1953	Was-A	1	4	.200	20	2	0	0	0	57	64	10.1	3	16	2.5	26	4.1	4.89	76	.288	.328	-6	-7	93	84	-1.4	0	-0	-0.7
1954	Cin-N	1	0	1.000	3	0	0	0	0	11	9	7.4	0	3	2.5	2	1.6	1.64	260	.237	.293	3	3	104	143	0.5	-0	-0	0.3
1955	Cin-N	0	2	.000	8	0	0	0	1	11	11	9.0	2	6	4.9	5	4.1	4.91	86	.289	.362	-1	-1	104	120	-0.9	0	0	0.0
Total	3	2	6	.250	31	2	0	0	1	79	84	9.6	5	25	2.8	33	3.8	4.44	87	.282	.328	-4	-5	96	97	-1.8	0	-1	-0.4
■ SAM LANFORD	Lanford, Lewis Grover b: 1/8/1886, Woodruff, S.C. d: 9/14/70, Woodruff, S.C. BR/TR, 5'9", 155 lbs. Deb: 8/19/07																												
1907	Was-A	0	1	.000	2	1	0	0	0	7	10	12.9	0	5	6.4	2	2.6	5.14	46	.362	.460	-2	-2	94	121	-0.4	0	-0	-0.1
■ WALT LANFRANCONI	Lanfranconi, Walter Oswald b: 11/9/16, Barre, Vt. d: 8/18/86, Barre, Vt. BR/TR, 5'7.5", 155 lbs. Deb: 9/12/41																												
1941	Chi-N	0	1	.000	2	1	0	0	0	6	7	10.5	0	2	3.0	1	1.5	3.00	113	.280	.333	0	0	94	120	-0.4	-0	0	0.0
1947	Bos-N	4	4	.500	36	4	1	0	1	64	65	9.1	2	27	3.8	18	2.5	2.95	131	.272	.339	8	7	95	132	-0.3	-1	1	0.6
Total	2	4	5	.444	38	5	1	0	1	70	72	9.3	2	29	3.7	19	2.4	2.96	130	.273	.339	8	7	95	131	-0.7	-1	1	0.6
■ MARTY LANG	Lang, Martin John b: 9/27/05, Hooper, Neb. d: 1/13/68, Lakewood, Colo. BR/TL, 5'11", 160 lbs. Deb: 7/04/30																												
1930	Pit-N	0	0	—	2	0	0	0	0	2	9	40.5	2	3	13.5	2	9.0	45.00	11	.692	.750	-9	-9	98	75	0.0	0	0	-0.6
■ CHIP LANG	Lang, Robert David b: 8/21/52, Pittsburgh, Pa. BR/TR, 6'4", 205 lbs. Deb: 9/08/75																												
1975	Mon-N	0	0	—	1	1	0	0	0	2	2	9.0	0	3	13.5	2	9.0	9.00	44	.333	.556	-1	-1	109	90	0.0	0	0	0.0
1976	Mon-N	1	3	.250	29	2	0	0	0	62	56	8.1	3	34	4.9	30	4.4	4.21	86	.242	.338	-5	-4	103	87	-0.4	-0	0	-0.3
Total	2	1	3	.250	30	3	0	0	0	64	58	8.2	3	37	5.2	32	4.5	4.36	83	.245	.345	-6	-5	103	87	-0.4	-0	0	-0.3
■ FRANK LANGE	Lange, Frank Herman "Seagan" b: 10/28/1883, Columbia, Wis. d: 12/26/45, Madison, Wis. BR/TR, 5'11", 180 lbs. Deb: 5/16/10																												
1910	Chi-A	9	4	.692	23	15	6	1	0	131	93	6.4	2	54	3.7	98	6.7	1.65	145	.204	.301	13	11	95	123	3.0	3	-2	1.3
1911	Chi-A	8	8	.500	29	22	8	1	0	162	151	8.4	3	77	4.3	104	5.8	3.22	99	.251	.339	2	-1	95	97	-0.1	8	-0	0.6
1912	Chi-A	10	10	.500	31	20	11	2	3	165	165	9.0	4	68	3.7	96	5.2	3.27	101	.270	.347	1	1	99	114	0.0	2	-1	0.0

YEAR	TM/L	W	L	PCT	G	GS	CG	SHO	SV	IP	H	H/G	HR	BB	BB/G	SO	SO/G	ERA	/A	OAVG	OOBP	PR	/A	PF	CPI	WAT	PB	PD	TPI
1913	Chi-A	1	3	.250	12	3	0	0	0	41	46	10.1	0	20	4.4	20	4.4	4.83	58	.295	.379	-9	-9	95	87	-0.9	1	1	-0.7
Total	4	28	25	.528	95	60	25	4	3	499	455	8.2	9	219	3.9	318	5.7	2.96	101	.249	.335	8	1	96	108	2.0	13	-2	1.2
■ **ERV LANGE**	Lange, Erwin Henry b: 8/12/1887, Forest Park, Ill. d: 4/24/71, Maywood, Ill. BR/TR, 5'10", 170 lbs. Deb: 4/19/14																												
1914	Chi-F	12	11	.522	36	22	10	2	2	190	162	7.7	3	55	2.6	87	4.1	2.23	128	.224	.282	21	13	89	88	-0.9	3	-1	1.5
■ **DICK LANGE**	Lange, Richard Otto b: 9/1/48, Harbor Beach, Mich. BR/TR, 5'10", 185 lbs. Deb: 9/09/72																												
1972	Cal-A	0	0	—	2	1	0	0	0	8	7	7.9	0	2	2.3	8	9.0	4.50	61	.233	.281	-1	-2	90	45	0.0	-0	0	-0.1
1973	Cal-A	2	1	.667	17	4	1	0	0	53	61	10.4	9	21	3.6	27	4.6	4.42	83	.292	.349	-3	-4	96	121	0.5	0	0	-0.3
1974	Cal-A	3	8	.273	21	18	1	0	0	114	111	8.8	10	47	3.7	57	4.5	3.79	89	.248	.321	-2	-5	93	93	-1.9	0	-1	-0.6
1975	Cal-A	4	6	.400	30	8	1	0	1	102	119	10.5	12	53	4.7	45	4.0	5.21	70	.292	.370	-16	-18	96	101	-0.5	0	-0	-1.7
Total	4	9	15	.375	70	31	3	0	1	277	298	9.7	31	123	4.0	137	4.5	4.45	79	.272	.344	-23	-29	94	100	-1.9	-0	-1	-2.7
■ **RICK LANGFORD**	Langford, James Rick b: 3/20/52, Farmville, Va. BR/TR, 6', 180 lbs. Deb: 6/13/76																												
1976	Pit-N	0	1	.000	12	1	0	0	0	23	27	10.6	2	14	5.5	17	6.7	6.26	56	.307	.390	-7	-7	99	91	-0.4	0	0	-0.6
1977	Oak-A	8	19	.296	37	31	6	1	0	208	223	9.6	18	73	3.2	141	6.1	4.02	98	.273	.331	1	-2	97	100	-3.7	0	1	0.0
1978	Oak-A	7	13	.350	37	34	4	2	0	176	169	8.6	15	56	2.9	92	4.7	3.43	113	.253	.308	7	9	103	100	-1.9	0	1	1.0
1979	Oak-A	12	16	.429	34	29	14	1	0	219	233	9.6	22	57	2.3	101	4.2	4.27	90	.273	.315	-1	-10	91	93	2.3	0	2	-0.7
1980	Oak-A	19	12	.613	35	33	**28**	2	0	**290**	276	8.6	29	64	2.0	102	3.2	3.26	117	.255	.292	25	17	94	102	3.8	0	1	1.9
1981	Oak-A	12	10	.545	24	24	**18**	2	0	195	190	8.8	14	58	2.7	84	3.9	3.00	116	.255	.305	14	10	95	112	-0.9	0	-1	0.9
1982	Oak-A	11	16	.407	32	31	15	2	0	237	265	10.1	33	49	1.9	79	3.0	4.22	93	.281	.314	-4	-7	96	102	-0.4	0	1	-0.6
1983	Oak-A	0	4	.000	7	7	0	0	0	20	43	19.3	4	10	4.5	2	0.9	12.15	32	.448	.491	-18	-18	96	95	-1.9	0	-0	-1.5
1984	Oak-A	0	0	—	3	2	0	0	0	9	15	15.0	2	2	2.0	2	2.0	8.00	46	.366	.395	-4	-4	92	95	0.0	0	-0	-0.3
1985	Oak-A	3	5	.375	23	3	0	0	0	59	60	9.2	8	15	2.3	21	3.2	3.51	110	.261	.304	4	2	93	112	-0.8	0	0	0.2
1986	Oak-A	1	10	.091	16	11	0	0	0	55	69	11.3	13	18	2.9	30	4.9	7.36	53	.300	.351	-19	-21	94	81	-4.4	0	-1	-1.9
Total	11	73	106	.408	260	206	85	10	0	1491	1570	9.5	160	416	2.5	671	4.1	4.01	95	.271	.317	-1	-31	96	101	-8.3	0	3	-1.6
■ **MARK LANGSTON**	Langston, Mark Edward b: 8/20/60, San Diego, Cal. BR/TL, 6'2", 177 lbs. Deb: 4/07/84																												
1984	Sea-A	17	10	.630	35	33	5	2	0	225	188	7.5	16	118	4.7	**204**	**8.2**	3.40	121	.230	.325	15	18	103	103	4.8	0	1	2.0
1985	Sea-A	7	14	.333	24	24	2	0	0	127	122	8.6	22	91	6.4	72	5.1	5.46	73	.255	.373	-18	-21	95	100	-3.0	0	2	-1.7
1986	Sea-A	12	14	.462	37	36	9	0	0	239	234	8.8	30	123	4.6	**245**	**9.2**	4.86	92	.255	.342	-18	-11	106	91	1.2	0	-1	-1.1
1987	Sea-A	19	13	.594	35	35	14	3	0	272	242	8.0	30	114	3.8	**262**	**8.7**	3.84	120	.238	.313	19	23	103	96	4.1	0	1	2.3
1988	Sea-A	15	11	.577	35	35	9	3	0	261	222	7.7	32	110	3.8	235	8.1	3.34	129	.233	.311	18	28	108	110	3.9	0	3	3.2
Total	5	70	62	.530	166	163	39	8	0	1124	1008	8.1	130	556	4.5	1018	8.2	4.04	107	.241	.328	16	37	104	100	11.0	0	6	4.7
■ **MAX LANIER**	Lanier, Hubert Max b: 8/18/15, Denton, N.C. BR/TL, 5'11", 180 lbs. Deb: 4/20/38																												
1938	StL-N	0	3	.000	18	3	1	0	0	45	57	11.4	1	28	5.6	14	2.8	4.20	100	.317	.405	-2	0	111	138	-1.4	-1	0	0.0
1939	StL-N	2	1	.667	7	6	2	0	0	38	29	6.9	0	13	3.1	14	3.3	2.37	170	.220	.289	7	7	103	96	0.3	1	-0	0.8
1940	StL-N	9	6	.600	35	11	4	2	3	105	113	9.7	1	38	3.3	49	4.2	3.34	117	.276	.332	6	6	101	115	0.9	-0	1	0.8
1941	StL-N	10	8	.556	35	18	8	2	3	153	126	7.4	4	59	3.5	93	5.5	2.82	138	.225	.296	14	18	107	93	-1.1	-1	2	2.1
1942	StL-N	13	8	.619	34	20	8	2	2	161	137	7.7	4	60	3.4	93	5.2	2.96	115	.234	.303	6	8	103	95	-1.1	3	1	1.2
1943	StL-N	15	7	.682	32	25	14	2	3	213	195	8.2	3	75	3.2	123	5.2	**1.90**	**178**	.246	.308	**35**	**35**	100	**151**	0.0	-3	1	3.8
1944	StL-N	17	12	.586	33	30	16	5	0	224	192	7.7	5	71	2.9	141	**5.7**	2.65	130	.234	.293	24	20	95	99	-2.3	-0	0	2.0
1945	StL-N	2	2	.500	4	3	3	0	0	26	22	7.6	0	8	2.8	16	5.5	1.73	213	.222	.278	6	6	97	117	-0.3	-0	-0	0.6
1946	StL-N	6	0	1.000	6	6	6	2	0	56	45	7.2	1	19	3.1	36	5.8	1.93	183	.228	.294	9	10	103	126	3.0	-0	0	1.2
1949	StL-N	5	4	.556	15	15	4	1	0	92	92	9.0	5	35	3.4	37	3.6	3.82	114	.261	.321	2	5	108	97	-0.4	-2	-1	0.3
1950	StL-N	11	9	.550	27	27	10	2	0	181	173	8.6	13	68	3.4	89	4.4	3.13	136	.249	.314	20	22	103	110	0.9	-1	0	2.2
1951	StL-N	11	9	.550	31	23	9	2	1	160	149	8.4	14	50	2.8	59	3.3	3.26	122	.248	.303	12	13	101	103	0.6	-2	0	1.1
1952	NY-N	7	12	.368	37	16	6	1	5	137	124	8.1	11	65	4.3	47	3.1	3.94	95	.244	.329	-3	-3	101	96	-3.8	3	3	0.3
1953	NY-N	0	0	—	3	0	0	0	0	5	8	14.4	1	3	5.4	2	3.6	7.20	58	.381	.423	-2	-2	98	124	0.0	-0	0	-0.1
	StL-A	0	1	.000	10	1	0	0	0	22	28	11.5	2	19	7.8	8	3.3	7.36	60	.322	.431	-8	-7	111	94	-0.4	-0	0	-0.6
Total	14	108	82	.568	327	204	91	21	17	1618	1490	8.3	65	611	3.4	821	4.6	3.01	126	.247	.313	126	139	102	109	-5.1	-3	6	15.7
■ **JOHNNY LANNING**	Lanning, John Young "Tobacco Chewin' Johnny" b: 9/6/10, Asheville, N.C. BR/TR, 6'1", 185 lbs. Deb: 4/17/36																												
1936	Bos-N	7	11	.389	28	20	3	1	0	153	154	9.1	9	55	3.2	33	1.9	3.65	106	.263	.322	6	4	96	102	-1.5	-2	-1	0.0
1937	Bos-N	5	7	.417	32	11	4	1	2	117	107	8.2	10	40	3.1	37	2.8	3.92	90	.236	.297	-0	-5	90	80	-1.2	-1	-0	-0.6
1938	Bos-N	8	7	.533	32	18	4	1	0	138	146	9.5	5	52	3.4	39	2.5	3.72	91	.267	.328	1	-5	89	99	0.4	-1	-1	-0.7
1939	Bos-N	5	6	.455	37	6	3	0	4	129	120	8.4	6	53	3.7	45	3.1	3.42	107	.252	.319	7	3	93	102	0.4	-1	0	0.2
1940	Pit-N	8	4	.667	38	7	2	0	2	116	119	9.2	8	39	3.0	42	3.3	4.03	90	.268	.323	-2	-5	95	99	2.1	1	-0	-0.3
1941	Pit-N	11	11	.500	34	23	9	0	1	176	175	8.9	6	47	2.4	41	2.1	3.12	118	.256	.299	10	11	102	98	-0.5	-2	1	1.1
1942	Pit-N	6	8	.429	34	8	2	1	1	119	125	9.5	7	26	2.0	31	2.3	3.33	101	.274	.306	-0	1	102	108	-0.3	-0	-0	0.0
1943	Pit-N	4	1	.800	12	2	0	0	2	27	23	7.7	0	9	3.0	11	3.7	2.33	149	.223	.281	3	3	103	87	1.5	-0	-1	0.3
1945	Pit-N	0	0	—	1	0	0	0	0	2	8	36.0	1	0	0.0	0	0.0	36.00	11	.571	.571	-7	-7	102	56	0.0	0	0	-0.4
1946	Pit-N	4	5	.444	27	9	3	0	1	91	97	9.6	3	31	3.1	16	1.6	3.07	118	.269	.322	4	5	106	112	0.3	-1	1	0.6
1947	Bos-N	0	0	—	3	0	0	0	0	4	4	9.0	0	6	13.5	0	0.0	9.00	43	.400	.556	-2	-2	95	106	0.0	0	0	-0.1
Total	11	58	60	.492	278	104	30	4	13	1072	1078	9.1	55	358	3.0	295	2.5	3.58	101	.261	.315	19	4	97	99	1.2	-6	-1	0.1
■ **RED LANNING**	Lanning, Lester Alfred b: 5/13/1895, Harvard, Ill. d: 6/13/62, Bristol, Conn. BL/TL, 5'9", 165 lbs. Deb: 6/20/16																												
1916	Phi-A	0	3	.000	6	3	1	0	0	24	38	14.3	1	17	6.4	9	3.4	8.25	36	.362	.460	-14	-14	105	90	-1.4	1	0	-1.3
■ **TOM LANNING**	Lanning, Thomas Newton b: 4/22/07, Asheville, N.C. d: 11/4/67, Marietta, Ga. BL/TL, 6'1", 165 lbs. Deb: 9/14/38																												
1938	Phi-N	0	1	.000	3	1	0	0	0	7	9	11.6	0	2	2.6	2	2.6	6.43	62	.300	.333	-2	-2	106	63	-0.4	0	-0	-0.1
■ **GENE LANSING**	Lansing, Eugene Hewitt "Jigger" b: 1/11/1898, Albany, N.Y. d: 1/18/45, Rensselaer, N.Y. BR/TR, 6'1", 185 lbs. Deb: 4/27/22																												
1922	Bos-N	0	1	.000	15	1	0	0	0	41	46	10.1	1	22	4.8	14	3.1	5.93	68	.301	.372	-8	-9	98	80	-0.4	-1	-0	-0.8
■ **PAUL LaPALME**	LaPalme, Paul Edmore "Lefty" b: 12/14/23, Springfield, Mass. BL/TL, 5'10", 175 lbs. Deb: 5/28/51																												
1951	Pit-N	1	5	.167	22	8	1	1	0	54	79	13.2	6	31	5.2	24	4.0	6.33	68	.333	.408	-14	-12	110	106	-1.7	-0	-1	-1.1
1952	Pit-N	1	2	.333	31	2	0	0	0	60	56	8.4	6	37	5.6	25	3.8	3.90	101	.253	.355	-1	0	105	118	0.1	-0	1	0.0
1953	Pit-N	8	16	.333	35	24	7	1	2	176	191	9.8	20	64	3.3	86	4.4	4.60	99	.272	.328	-6	-1	106	94	0.2	-5	-2	-0.7
1954	Pit-N	4	10	.286	33	15	2	0	0	121	147	10.9	15	54	4.0	57	4.2	5.50	75	.302	.364	-19	-18	102	97	-1.2	-0	-0	-1.7
1955	StL-N	4	3	.571	56	0	0	0	3	92	76	7.4	10	34	3.3	39	3.8	2.74	151	.228	.294	13	14	102	116	0.8	0	1	1.5
1956	StL-N	0	0	—	1	0	0	0	0	1	4	36.0	0	2	18.0	0	0.0	54.00	7	.667	.750	-6	-6	99	45	0.0	0	0	-0.3
	Cin-N	2	4	.333	11	2	0	0	0	27	26	8.7	7	4	1.3	4	1.3	4.67	86	.257	.273	-3	-2	106	93	-1.2	1	0	0.0
	Yr	2	4	.333	12	2	0	0	0	28	30	9.6	7	6	1.9	4	1.3	6.43	62	.280	.305	-8	-8	106	93	-1.2	0	0	-0.3
	Chi-A	3	1	.750	29	0	0	0	2	46	31	6.1	2	27	5.3	23	4.5	2.35	180	.195	.301	9	10	102	109	0.9	-1	1	0.9
1957	Chi-A	1	4	.200	35	0	0	0	7	40	35	7.9	5	19	4.3	19	4.3	3.37	108	.235	.325	2	1	97	112	-1.6	1	1	0.4
Total	7	24	45	.348	253	51	10	2	14	617	645	9.4	71	272	4.0	277	4.0	4.42	95	.269	.338	-25	-14	104	104	-3.7	-5	-0	-1.0
■ **ANDY LAPIHUSKA**	Lapihuska, Andrew "Apples" b: 11/1/22, Delmont, N.J. BL/TR, 5'10.5", 175 lbs. Deb: 9/12/42																												
1942	Phi-N	0	2	.000	3	2	0	0	0	21	17	7.3	0	13	5.6	8	3.4	5.14	65	.221	.340	-4	-4	101	62	-0.9	0	0	-0.3
1943	Phi-N	0	0	—	1	0	0	0	0	2	5	22.5	1	3	13.5	0	0.0	27.00	12	.417	.533	-5	-5	96	59	0.0	-0	0	-0.4
Total	2	0	2	.000	4	2	0	0	0	23	22	8.6	1	16	6.3	8	3.1	7.04	47	.247	.367	-10	-9	101	62	-0.9	0	0	-0.7
■ **DAVE LaPOINT**	LaPoint, David Jeffrey b: 7/29/59, Glens Falls, N.Y. BL/TL, 6'3", 205 lbs. Deb: 9/10/80																												
1980	Mil-A	1	0	1.000	5	3	0	0	1	15	17	10.2	2	13	7.8	5	3.0	6.00	63	.293	.400	-3	-4	93	107	0.5	0	-1	-0.3
1981	StL-N	1	0	1.000	3	2	0	0	0	11	12	9.8	1	2	1.6	4	3.3	4.09	86	.293	.333	-1	-1	101	109	0.5	-1	0	0.0
1982	StL-N	9	3	.750	42	21	0	0	0	153	170	10.0	8	52	3.1	81	4.8	3.41	108	.290	.343	3	5	102	126	2.6	-3	-3	0.0
1983	StL-N	12	9	.571	37	29	1	0	0	191	191	9.0	12	84	4.0	113	5.3	3.96	90	.267	.335	-7	-8	98	102	1.9	1	-1	-0.8
1984	StL-N	12	10	.545	33	33	2	1	0	193	205	9.6	9	77	3.6	130	6.1	3.96	89	.278	.342	-8	-9	99	103	0.7	-3	-2	-1.4

YEAR	TM/L	W	L	PCT	G	GS	CG	SHO	SV	IP	H	H/G	HR	BB	BB/G	SO	SO/G	ERA	/A	OAVG	OOBP	PR	/A	PF	CPI	WAT	PB	PD	TPI
1985	SF-N	7	17	.292	31	31	2	1	0	207	215	9.3	18	74	3.2	122	5.3	3.57	96	.269	.326	1	-4	95	112	-3.1	2	-2	-0.4
1986	Det-A	3	6	.333	16	8	0	0	0	68	85	11.3	11	32	4.2	36	4.8	5.69	70	.307	.373	-11	-13	95	105	-1.7	0	-0	-1.2
	SD-N	1	4	.200	24	4	0	0	0	61	67	9.9	8	24	3.5	41	6.0	4.28	83	.276	.336	-4	-5	96	108	-1.3	-1	-0	-0.5
1987	StL-N	1	1	.500	6	2	0	0	0	16	26	14.6	4	5	2.8	8	4.5	6.75	59	.351	.392	-5	-5	97	113	0.0	-0	0	-0.4
	Chi-A	6	3	.667	14	12	2	1	0	83	69	7.5	7	31	3.4	43	4.7	2.93	166	.224	.296	14	18	109	102	1.7	0	2	2.0
1988	Chi-A	10	11	.476	25	25	1	1	0	161	151	8.4	10	47	2.6	79	4.4	3.41	115	.245	.295	10	9	99	90	0.8	0	-2	0.7
	Pit-N	4	2	.667	8	8	1	0	0	52	54	9.3	4	10	1.7	19	3.3	2.77	121	.271	.298	4	3	97	131	0.9	-1	0	0.3
Total	9	67	66	.504	244	178	9	4	1	1211	1262	9.4	94	451	3.4	681	5.1	3.81	97	.271	.331	-6	-13	99	107	3.5	-6	-9	-2.0

■ **TERRY LARKIN** Larkin, Frank S. d: 9/6/1894, Brooklyn, N.Y. BR/TR, Deb: 5/20/1876

YEAR	TM/L	W	L	PCT	G	GS	CG	SHO	SV	IP	H	H/G	HR	BB	BB/G	SO	SO/G	ERA	/A	OAVG	OOBP	PR	/A	PF	CPI	WAT	PB	PD	TPI
1876	NY-N	0	1	.000	1	1	1	0	0	9	9	9.0	0	0	0.0	0	0.0	3.00	71	.265	.265	-1	-1	93	48	-0.4	-1	0	0.0
1877	Har-N	29	25	.537	56	56	55	4	0	501	510	9.2	2	53	1.0	96	1.7	2.14	114	.272	.292	38	17	87	102	2.0	5	-1	1.5
1878	Chi-N	29	26	.527	56	56	56	1	0	506	511	9.1	4	31	0.6	163	2.9	2.24	109	.272	.284	4	11	106	85	**11.2**	14	-4	2.2
1879	Chi-N	31	23	.574	58	58	57	3	0	513	514	9.0	5	30	0.5	142	2.5	2.44	107	.266	.277	3	10	104	86	-1.1	1	-6	0.5
1880	Tro-N	0	5	.000	5	5	3	0	0	38	83	19.7	1	10	2.4	5	1.2	8.76	30	.446	.474	-27	-26	112	101	-2.4	-1	0	-1.9
Total	5	89	80	.527	176	176	172	8	0	1567	1627	9.3	12	124	0.7	406	2.3	2.44	103	.276	.290	17	13	99	91	9.3	19	-11	2.3

■ **PAT LARKIN** Larkin, Patrick Clibborn b: 6/14/60, Arcadia, Cal. BL/TL, 6', 180 lbs. Deb: 7/16/83

YEAR	TM/L	W	L	PCT	G	GS	CG	SHO	SV	IP	H	H/G	HR	BB	BB/G	SO	SO/G	ERA	/A	OAVG	OOBP	PR	/A	PF	CPI	WAT	PB	PD	TPI
1983	SF-N	0	0	—	5	0	0	0	0	10	13	11.7	1	3	2.7	6	5.4	4.50	82	.317	.375	-1	-1	101	128	0.0	-0	0	0.0

■ **STEVE LARKIN** Larkin, Stephen Patrick b: 12/9/10, Cincinnati, Ohio d: 5/2/69, Norristown, Pa. BR/TR, 6'1", 195 lbs. Deb: 5/06/34

YEAR	TM/L	W	L	PCT	G	GS	CG	SHO	SV	IP	H	H/G	HR	BB	BB/G	SO	SO/G	ERA	/A	OAVG	OOBP	PR	/A	PF	CPI	WAT	PB	PD	TPI
1934	Det-A	0	0	—	2	1	0	0	0	6	8	12.0	0	5	7.5	8	12.0	1.50	281	.296	.406	2	2	94	365	0.0	1	0	0.3

■ **DAVE LaROCHE** LaRoche, David Eugene b: 5/14/48, Colorado Springs, Colo. BL/TL, 6'2", 200 lbs. Deb: 5/11/70

YEAR	TM/L	W	L	PCT	G	GS	CG	SHO	SV	IP	H	H/G	HR	BB	BB/G	SO	SO/G	ERA	/A	OAVG	OOBP	PR	/A	PF	CPI	WAT	PB	PD	TPI
1970	Cal-A	4	1	.800	38	0	0	0	4	50	41	7.4	6	21	3.8	44	7.9	3.42	99	.224	.313	2	-0	92	102	1.5	1	0	0.1
1971	Cal-A	5	1	.833	56	0	0	0	9	72	55	6.9	3	27	3.4	63	7.9	2.50	138	.212	.281	8	8	99	91	2.1	-0	-1	0.7
1972	Min-A	5	7	.417	62	0	0	0	10	95	72	6.8	9	39	3.7	79	7.5	2.84	116	.209	.295	2	5	107	99	-1.0	0	0	0.6
1973	Chi-N	4	1	.800	45	0	0	0	4	54	55	9.2	7	29	4.8	34	5.7	5.83	68	.274	.351	-13	-11	109	85	1.6	1	1	-0.8
1974	Chi-N	5	6	.455	49	4	0	0	5	92	103	10.1	9	47	4.6	49	4.8	4.79	77	.286	.363	-12	-11	102	104	0.5	3	-0	-0.8
1975	Cle-A	5	3	.625	61	0	0	0	17	82	61	6.7	5	57	6.3	94	10.3	2.20	172	.210	.334	15	14	100	153	1.1	0	1	1.6
1976	Cle-A	1	4	.200	61	0	0	0	21	96	57	5.3	2	49	4.6	104	9.8	2.25	156	.175	.275	14	13	100	81	-1.4	0	-1	1.3
1977	Cle-A	2	2	.500	13	0	0	0	4	19	15	7.1	3	7	3.3	18	8.5	5.21	77	.234	.293	-2	-3	98	75	0.2	0	-0	-0.2
	Cal-A	6	5	.545	46	0	0	0	13	81	64	7.1	8	37	4.1	61	6.8	3.11	124	.218	.302	9	7	95	101	1.0	0	-0	0.6
	Yr	8	7	.533	59	0	0	0	17	100	79	7.1	11	44	4.0	79	7.1	3.51	111	.220	.300	6	4	95	101	1.2	0	-0	0.4
1978	Cal-A	10	9	.526	59	0	0	0	25	96	73	6.8	7	48	4.5	70	6.6	2.81	136	.215	.305	10	11	101	107	-0.1	0	0	1.1
1979	Cal-A	7	11	.389	53	1	0	0	10	86	107	11.2	13	32	3.3	59	6.2	5.55	70	.314	.364	-13	-16	92	105	-2.7	0	1	-1.4
1980	Cal-A	3	5	.375	52	9	1	0	4	128	122	8.6	14	39	2.7	89	6.3	4.08	96	.256	.309	-0	-2	97	92	-0.2	0	-1	-0.2
1981	NY-A	4	1	.800	26	1	0	0	0	47	38	7.3	3	16	3.1	24	4.6	2.49	146	.229	.286	6	6	99	117	1.4	0	-0	0.6
1982	NY-A	4	2	.667	25	0	0	0	0	50	54	9.7	4	11	2.0	31	5.6	3.42	115	.273	.311	4	3	97	108	1.1	0	-1	0.2
1983	NY-A	0	0	—	1	0	0	0	0	1	2	18.0	1	0	0.0	0	0.0	18.00	22	.400	.400	-2	-2	98	80	0.0	0	0	0.0
Total	14	65	58	.528	647	15	1	0	126	1049	919	7.9	94	459	3.9	819	7.0	3.53	106	.239	.316	27	23	99	102	5.1	5	0	3.4

■ **JOHN LaROSE** LaRose, Henry John b: 10/25/51, Pawtucket, R.I. BL/TL, 6'1", 185 lbs. Deb: 9/20/78

YEAR	TM/L	W	L	PCT	G	GS	CG	SHO	SV	IP	H	H/G	HR	BB	BB/G	SO	SO/G	ERA	/A	OAVG	OOBP	PR	/A	PF	CPI	WAT	PB	PD	TPI
1978	Bos-A	0	0	—	1	0	0	0	0	2	3	13.5	1	3	13.5	0	0.0	22.50	18	.375	.545	-4	-4	106	59	0.0	0	0	-0.2

■ **DON LARSEN** Larsen, Don James b: 8/7/29, Michigan City, Ind. BR/TR, 6'4", 215 lbs. Deb: 4/18/53

YEAR	TM/L	W	L	PCT	G	GS	CG	SHO	SV	IP	H	H/G	HR	BB	BB/G	SO	SO/G	ERA	/A	OAVG	OOBP	PR	/A	PF	CPI	WAT	PB	PD	TPI
1953	StL-A	7	12	.368	38	22	7	2	2	193	201	9.4	11	64	3.0	96	4.5	4.15	106	.267	.325	-3	6	111	90	0.3	5	-1	1.3
1954	Bal-A	3	21	.125	29	28	12	1	0	202	213	9.5	18	89	4.0	80	3.6	4.37	84	.274	.340	-14	-15	99	99	-8.1	8	0	-0.7
1955	NY-A	9	2	.818	19	13	5	1	2	97	81	7.5	8	51	4.7	44	4.1	3.06	122	.229	.325	10	7	94	113	2.9	2	-0	0.8
1956	NY-A	11	5	.688	38	20	6	1	1	180	133	6.7	19	96	4.8	107	5.3	3.25	121	.204	.311	18	14	95	95	1.4	6	-1	1.8
1957	NY-A	10	4	.714	27	20	4	1	0	140	113	7.3	12	87	5.6	81	5.2	3.73	92	.220	.331	1	-5	90	93	1.6	5	-0	-0.1
1958	NY-A	9	6	.600	19	19	5	3	0	114	100	7.9	4	52	4.1	55	4.3	3.08	121	.233	.318	9	8	99	98	0.1	8	-1	1.5
1959	NY-A	6	7	.462	25	18	3	1	3	125	122	8.8	14	76	5.5	69	5.0	4.32	82	.260	.357	-6	-11	92	110	-0.6	4	-0	-0.6
1960	KC-A	1	10	.091	22	15	0	0	0	84	97	10.4	11	42	4.5	43	4.6	5.36	73	.293	.365	-14	-13	101	99	-4.1	0	-1	-1.3
1961	KC-A	1	0	1.000	8	1	0	0	0	15	21	12.6	2	11	6.6	13	7.8	4.20	100	.344	.440	-0	-0	104	185	0.5	1	0	0.0
	Chi-A	7	2	.778	25	3	0	0	2	74	64	7.8	5	29	3.5	53	6.4	4.14	96	.231	.298	-1	-1	99	73	2.4	3	0	0.1
	Yr	8	2	.800	33	4	0	0	2	89	85	8.6	7	40	4.0	66	6.7	4.15	97	.251	.323	-1	-1	100	73	2.9	1	1	0.1
1962	SF-N	5	4	.556	49	0	0	0	11	86	83	8.7	9	47	4.9	58	6.1	4.40	88	.256	.347	-4	-5	99	100	-0.4	1	0	-0.3
1963	SF-N	7	7	.500	46	0	0	0	3	62	46	6.7	8	30	4.4	44	6.4	3.05	102	.203	.291	2	0	94	98	-0.5	0	0	0.1
1964	SF-N	0	1	.000	6	0	0	0	0	10	10	9.0	0	6	5.4	6	5.4	4.50	78	.256	.348	-1	-1	99	82	-0.4	-0	-0	0.0
	Hou-N	4	8	.333	30	10	2	1	1	103	92	8.0	4	20	1.7	58	5.1	2.27	153	.233	.267	14	14	98	100	-1.1	0	0	1.5
	Yr	4	9	.308	36	10	2	1	1	113	102	8.1	4	26	2.1	64	5.1	2.47	141	.235	.274	13	13	98	100	-1.5	-0	0	1.5
1965	Hou-N	0	0	—	1	1	0	0	0	5	8	14.4	0	3	5.4	1	1.8	5.40	60	.348	.407	-1	-1	91	119	0.0	-0	1	0.0
	Bal-A	1	2	.333	27	1	0	0	1	54	53	8.8	4	20	3.3	40	6.7	2.67	128	.255	.316	5	5	99	135	-0.5	1	1	0.7
1967	Chi-N	0	0	—	3	0	0	0	0	4	5	11.3	1	2	4.5	1	2.3	9.00	38	.333	.389	-2	-2	100	82	0.0	0	0	-0.1
Total	14	81	91	.471	412	171	44	11	26	1548	1442	8.4	130	725	4.2	849	4.9	3.78	100	.247	.327	10	-2	98	99	-6.5	43	-1	4.7

■ **DAN LARSON** Larson, Daniel James b: 7/4/54, Los Angeles, Cal. BR/TR, 6', 175 lbs. Deb: 7/18/76

YEAR	TM/L	W	L	PCT	G	GS	CG	SHO	SV	IP	H	H/G	HR	BB	BB/G	SO	SO/G	ERA	/A	OAVG	OOBP	PR	/A	PF	CPI	WAT	PB	PD	TPI
1976	Hou-N	5	8	.385	13	13	5	0	0	92	81	7.9	3	28	2.7	42	4.1	3.03	100	.236	.290	5	0	87	86	-1.4	3	0	0.3
1977	Hou-N	1	7	.125	32	10	1	0	1	98	108	9.9	13	45	4.1	44	4.0	5.79	62	.280	.350	-20	-24	92	85	-2.9	1	0	-2.2
1978	Phi-N	0	0	—	1	0	0	0	0	1	1	9.0	1	1	9.0	2	18.0	9.00	41	.250	.400	-1	-1	104	135	0.0	0	0	0.0
1979	Phi-N	1	1	.500	3	3	0	0	0	19	17	8.1	1	9	4.3	9	4.3	4.26	85	.250	.333	-1	-1	97	88	0.0	-1	0	-0.1
1980	Phi-N	0	5	.000	12	7	0	0	0	46	46	9.0	4	24	4.7	17	3.3	3.13	123	.271	.348	2	4	106	144	-2.4	0	-1	0.3
1981	Phi-N	3	0	1.000	5	4	1	0	0	28	27	8.7	4	15	4.8	15	4.8	4.18	94	.260	.344	-2	-1	112	113	1.5	0	0	0.0
1982	Chi-N	0	4	.000	12	6	0	0	0	40	51	11.5	4	18	4.0	22	4.9	5.62	67	.327	.388	-9	-8	104	108	-1.9	0	1	-0.6
Total	7	10	25	.286	78	43	7	0	1	324	331	9.2	30	140	3.9	151	4.2	4.39	80	.269	.337	-26	-31	96	99	-7.1	4	1	-2.3

■ **AL LARY** Lary, Alfred Allen b: 9/26/29, Northport, Ala. BR/TR, 6'3", 185 lbs. Deb: 9/06/54

YEAR	TM/L	W	L	PCT	G	GS	CG	SHO	SV	IP	H	H/G	HR	BB	BB/G	SO	SO/G	ERA	/A	OAVG	OOBP	PR	/A	PF	CPI	WAT	PB	PD	TPI
1954	Chi-N	0	0	—	1	1	0	0	0	6	3	4.5	0	7	10.5	4	6.0	3.00	138	.150	.370	1	1	102	92	0.0	0	0	0.1
1962	Chi-N	0	1	.000	15	3	0	0	0	34	42	11.1	5	15	4.0	18	4.8	7.15	60	.311	.368	-12	-11	109	82	-0.4	0	-0	-0.9
Total	2	0	1	.000	16	4	0	0	0	40	45	10.1	5	22	4.9	22	4.9	6.52	65	.290	.368	-11	-10	107	83	-0.4	1	-0	-0.8

■ **FRANK LARY** Lary, Frank Strong "Mule" or "The Yankee Killer" b: 4/10/30, Northport, Ala. BR/TR, 5'11", 175 lbs. Deb: 9/14/54

YEAR	TM/L	W	L	PCT	G	GS	CG	SHO	SV	IP	H	H/G	HR	BB	BB/G	SO	SO/G	ERA	/A	OAVG	OOBP	PR	/A	PF	CPI	WAT	PB	PD	TPI
1954	Det-A	0	0	—	3	0	0	0	0	4	4	9.0	0	3	6.8	5	11.3	2.25	168	.286	.412	1	1	101	217	0.0	0	0	0.1
1955	Det-A	14	15	.483	36	31	16	2	1	235	232	8.9	10	89	3.4	98	3.8	3.10	121	.262	.328	22	17	95	115	-0.9	1	1	1.9
1956	Det-A	**21**	13	.618	41	38	20	3	1	**294**	289	8.8	20	116	3.6	165	5.1	3.15	125	.257	.329	33	26	95	**117**	3.8	1	-0	2.6
1957	Det-A	11	16	.407	40	35	12	2	3	238	250	9.5	23	72	2.7	107	4.0	3.97	102	.276	.330	-5	2	107	106	-3.0	-4	1	0.0
1958	Det-A	16	15	.516	39	34	**19**	3	1	**260**	249	8.6	20	68	2.4	131	4.5	2.91	133	.251	.303	25	28	103	113	0.6	-0	-0	2.9
1959	Det-A	17	10	.630	32	32	11	3	0	223	225	9.1	23	46	1.9	137	5.5	3.55	121	.261	.303	8	18	111	103	4.2	-3	-0	1.7
1960	Det-A	15	15	.500	38	36	**15**	2	1	**274**	262	8.6	25	62	2.0	149	4.9	3.51	112	.249	.299	11	13	102	92	1.3	4	-2	1.6
1961	Det-A	23	9	.719	36	36	**22**	4	0	275	252	8.2	24	66	2.2	146	4.8	3.24	116	.243	.287	24	16	94	95	4.7	5	4	2.5
1962	Det-A	2	6	.250	17	14	2	1	0	80	98	11.0	17	21	2.4	41	4.6	5.74	76	.297	.339	-16	-12	110	98	-2.1	0	-1	-1.1
1963	Det-A	4	9	.308	16	14	6	0	0	107	90	7.6	15	26	2.2	46	3.9	3.28	115	.226	.279	4	6	104	96	-2.4	1	1	0.9
1964	Det-A	0	2	.000	6	4	0	0	0	18	24	12.0	3	10	5.0	6	3.0	7.00	49	.316	.411	-7	-7	95	98	-0.9	-0	-1	-0.7
	NY-N	2	3	.400	13	8	3	1	1	57	62	9.8	7	14	2.2	27	4.3	4.58	76	.279	.329	-7	-7	98	98	0.3	1	-0	-0.6
	Mil-N	1	0	1.000	5	2	0	0	0	12	15	11.3	4	0	0.0	4	3.0	4.50	75	.306	.294	-1	-1	96	132	0.5	-0	1	0.0
	Yr	3	3	.500	18	10	3	1	1	69	77	10.0	11	14	1.8	31	4.0	4.57	76	.279	.310	-8	-8	98	132	0.8	1	1	-0.6
1965	NY-N	1	3	.250	14	7	0	0	1	57	48	7.6	2	16	2.5	23	3.6	3.00	123	.233	.283	3	4	104	88	-0.3	0	0	0.5
	Chi-A	1	0	1.000	14	1	0	0	2	27	23	7.7	4	7	2.3	14	4.7	4.00	78	.230	.288	-2	-3	91	86	0.5	0	0	-0.1

YEAR	TM/L	W	L	PCT	G	GS	CG	SHO	SV	IP	H	H/G	HR	BB	BB/G	SO	SO/G	ERA	/A	OAVG	OOBP	PR	/A	PF	CPI	WAT	PB	PD	TPI
Total	12	128	116	.525	350	292	126	21	11	2161	2123	8.8	197	616	2.6	1099	4.6	3.49	112	.257	.311	94	103	101	104	6.3	6	3	12.2

■ **FRED LASHER** Lasher, Frederick Walter b: 8/19/41, Poughkeepsie, N.Y. BR/TR, 6'3", 190 lbs. Deb: 4/12/63

YEAR	TM/L	W	L	PCT	G	GS	CG	SHO	SV	IP	H	H/G	HR	BB	BB/G	SO	SO/G	ERA	/A	OAVG	OOBP	PR	/A	PF	CPI	WAT	PB	PD	TPI
1963	Min-A	0	0	—	11	0	0	0	0	11	12	9.8	1	11	9.0	10	8.2	4.91	72	.286	.397	-2	-2	98	129	0.0	-0	0	0.0
1967	Det-A	2	1	.667	17	0	0	0	9	30	25	7.5	1	11	3.3	28	8.4	3.90	81	.221	.294	-2	-2	98	65	0.4	-0	0	-0.2
1968	Det-A	5	1	.833	34	0	0	0	5	49	37	6.8	5	22	4.0	32	5.9	3.31	93	.215	.295	-2	-1	103	95	1.7	-0	1	0.0
1969	Det-A	2	1	.667	32	0	0	0	0	44	34	7.0	5	22	4.5	26	5.3	3.07	121	.224	.320	3	3	102	121	0.4	-0	0	0.3
1970	Det-A	1	3	.250	12	0	0	0	3	9	10	10.0	0	12	12.0	8	8.0	5.00	77	.278	.460	-1	-1	104	130	-0.9	-0	0	0.0
	Cle-A	1	7	.125	43	1	0	0	5	58	57	8.8	6	30	4.7	44	6.8	4.03	106	.264	.349	-2	2	115	113	-2.9	-1	-1	0.0
	Yr	2	10	.167	55	1	0	0	8	67	67	9.0	6	42	5.6	52	7.0	4.16	101	.264	.364	-3	0	114	113	-3.8	-0	-1	0.0
1971	Cal-A	0	0	—	2	0	0	0	0	1	4	36.0	0	2	18.0	0	0.0	36.00	10	.667	.667	-4	-4	99	66	0.0	0	0	-0.3
Total	6	11	13	.458	151	1	0	0	22	202	179	8.0	18	110	4.9	148	6.6	3.88	93	.243	.336	-10	-6	105	105	-1.3	-2	0	-0.2

■ **BILL LASKEY** Laskey, William Alan b: 12/20/57, Toledo, Ohio BR/TR, 6'5", 190 lbs. Deb: 4/23/82

YEAR	TM/L	W	L	PCT	G	GS	CG	SHO	SV	IP	H	H/G	HR	BB	BB/G	SO	SO/G	ERA	/A	OAVG	OOBP	PR	/A	PF	CPI	WAT	PB	PD	TPI
1982	SF-N	13	12	.520	32	31	7	1	0	189	186	8.9	14	43	2.0	88	4.2	3.14	108	.261	.296	10	5	94	106	-0.4	-1	0	0.3
1983	SF-N	13	10	.565	25	25	1	0	0	148	151	9.2	18	45	2.7	81	4.9	4.20	87	.266	.317	-9	-9	101	96	2.0	0	-1	-1.0
1984	SF-N	9	14	.391	35	34	2	0	0	208	222	9.6	20	50	2.2	71	3.1	4.33	81	.273	.315	-17	-19	98	91	-0.4	-3	-2	-2.4
1985	SF-N	5	11	.313	19	19	0	0	0	114	110	8.7	10	39	3.1	42	3.3	3.55	96	.255	.307	1	-2	95	101	-1.5	1	0	-0.1
	Mon-N	0	5	.000	11	7	0	0	0	34	55	14.6	9	14	3.7	18	4.8	9.53	35	.362	.415	-22	-23	94	89	-2.4	-0	1	-2.1
	Yr	5	16	.238	30	26	0	0	0	148	165	10.0	19	53	3.2	60	3.6	4.93	69	.281	.335	-22	-25	95	89	-3.9	1	1	-2.2
1986	SF-N	1	1	.500	20	0	0	0	1	27	28	9.3	5	13	4.3	8	2.7	4.33	81	.275	.350	-2	-2	95	122	0.0	-0	0	-0.1
1988	Cle-A	1	0	1.000	17	0	0	0	1	24	32	12.0	0	6	2.3	17	6.4	5.25	77	.320	.345	-3	-3	102	86	0.5	0	0	-0.2
Total	6	42	53	.442	159	116	10	1	2	744	784	9.5	76	210	2.5	325	3.9	4.15	84	.272	.317	-43	-53	97	98	-2.2	-4	-2	-5.6

■ **BILL LASLEY** Lasley, Willard Almond b: 7/13/02, Marietta, Ohio BB/TR, 6', 175 lbs. Deb: 9/19/24

YEAR	TM/L	W	L	PCT	G	GS	CG	SHO	SV	IP	H	H/G	HR	BB	BB/G	SO	SO/G	ERA	/A	OAVG	OOBP	PR	/A	PF	CPI	WAT	PB	PD	TPI
1924	StL-A	0	0	—	2	0	0	0	0	4	7	15.8	0	2	4.5	0	0.0	6.75	68	.412	.429	-1	-1	108	118	0.0	-0	-0	0.0

■ **TOM LASORDA** Lasorda, Thomas Charles b: 9/22/27, Norristown, Pa. BL/TL, 5'10", 175 lbs. Deb: 8/05/54 MC

YEAR	TM/L	W	L	PCT	G	GS	CG	SHO	SV	IP	H	H/G	HR	BB	BB/G	SO	SO/G	ERA	/A	OAVG	OOBP	PR	/A	PF	CPI	WAT	PB	PD	TPI
1954	Bro-N	0	0	—	4	0	0	0	0	9	8	8.0	2	5	5.0	5	5.0	5.00	82	.242	.333	-1	-1	101	97	0.0	-0	-0	0.0
1955	Bro-N	0	0	—	4	1	0	0	0	4	5	11.3	1	6	13.5	4	9.0	13.50	30	.313	.500	-4	-4	101	76	0.0	0	0	-0.3
1956	KC-A	0	4	.000	18	5	0	0	1	45	40	8.0	6	45	9.0	28	5.6	6.20	70	.240	.400	-10	-9	105	90	-1.9	-1	0	-0.9
Total	3	0	4	.000	26	6	0	0	1	58	53	8.2	9	56	8.7	37	5.7	6.52	66	.245	.399	-15	-14	104	90	-1.9	-2	0	-1.2

■ **BILL LATHAM** Latham, William Carol b: 8/29/60, Birmingham, Ala. BL/TL, 6'2", 190 lbs. Deb: 4/15/85

YEAR	TM/L	W	L	PCT	G	GS	CG	SHO	SV	IP	H	H/G	HR	BB	BB/G	SO	SO/G	ERA	/A	OAVG	OOBP	PR	/A	PF	CPI	WAT	PB	PD	TPI
1985	NY-N	1	3	.250	7	3	0	0	0	23	21	8.2	1	7	2.7	10	3.9	3.91	88	.250	.301	-1	-1	95	79	-1.1	1	1	0.0
1986	Min-A	0	1	.000	7	2	0	0	0	16	24	13.5	1	6	3.4	8	4.5	7.31	63	.358	.403	-6	-5	109	91	-0.4	0	-0	-0.4
Total	2	1	4	.200	14	5	0	0	0	39	45	10.4	2	13	3.0	18	4.2	5.31	73	.298	.347	-6	-6	101	84	-1.5	1	0	-0.4

■ **BILL LATHROP** Lathrop, William George b: 8/12/1891, Hanover, Wis. d: 11/20/58, Janesville, Wis. BR/TR, 6'2.5", 184 lbs. Deb: 7/29/13

YEAR	TM/L	W	L	PCT	G	GS	CG	SHO	SV	IP	H	H/G	HR	BB	BB/G	SO	SO/G	ERA	/A	OAVG	OOBP	PR	/A	PF	CPI	WAT	PB	PD	TPI
1913	Chi-A	0	1	.000	6	0	0	0	0	17	16	8.5	0	12	6.4	9	4.8	4.24	66	.262	.392	-2	-3	95	96	-0.4	-1	0	-0.2
1914	Chi-A	1	2	.333	19	1	0	0	0	48	41	7.7	0	19	3.6	7	1.3	2.63	109	.241	.325	1	1	105	101	-0.3	-1	1	0.2
Total	2	1	3	.250	25	1	0	0	0	65	57	7.9	0	31	4.3	16	2.2	3.05	94	.247	.343	-2	-1	102	100	-0.7	-2	1	0.0

■ **BARRY LATMAN** Latman, Arnold Barry b: 5/21/36, Los Angeles, Cal. BR/TR, 6'3", 210 lbs. Deb: 9/10/57

YEAR	TM/L	W	L	PCT	G	GS	CG	SHO	SV	IP	H	H/G	HR	BB	BB/G	SO	SO/G	ERA	/A	OAVG	OOBP	PR	/A	PF	CPI	WAT	PB	PD	TPI
1957	Chi-A	1	2	.333	7	2	0	0	1	12	12	9.0	2	13	9.8	9	6.8	8.25	44	.267	.433	-6	-6	97	82	-0.6	-0	0	-0.5
1958	Chi-A	3	0	1.000	13	3	1	1	0	48	27	5.1	1	17	3.2	28	5.3	0.75	491	.162	.239	16	16	98	130	1.5	-0	-1	1.6
1959	Chi-A	8	5	.615	37	21	5	2	0	156	138	8.0	15	72	4.2	97	5.6	3.75	98	.235	.317	2	-1	95	96	0.1	-1	-3	-0.4
1960	Cle-A	7	7	.500	31	20	4	0	0	147	146	8.9	19	72	4.4	94	5.8	4.04	94	.258	.341	-3	-4	98	110	0.1	-1	-1	-0.3
1961	Cle-A	13	5	.722	45	18	4	2	5	177	163	8.3	23	54	2.7	108	5.5	4.02	97	.244	.302	0	-3	97	91	4.4	-3	-3	-0.8
1962	Cle-A	8	13	.381	45	21	7	1	5	179	179	9.0	23	72	3.6	117	5.9	4.17	94	.261	.331	-4	-5	99	104	-2.6	2	-1	-0.3
1963	Cle-A	7	12	.368	38	21	4	2	2	149	146	8.8	23	52	3.1	133	8.0	4.95	72	.257	.319	-22	-23	98	87	-2.4	2	3	-1.8
1964	LA-A	6	10	.375	40	18	2	1	2	138	128	8.3	15	52	3.4	81	5.3	3.85	84	.244	.316	-3	-10	89	96	-2.1	-1	-1	-1.1
1965	Cal-A	1	1	.500	18	0	0	0	0	32	30	8.4	3	16	4.5	18	5.1	2.81	121	.254	.336	2	2	98	146	0.1	-0	-1	0.1
1966	Hou-N	2	7	.222	31	9	1	1	1	103	88	7.7	5	35	3.1	74	6.5	2.71	131	.233	.304	10	10	99	108	-2.2	-0	0	1.0
1967	Hou-N	3	6	.333	39	1	0	0	0	78	73	8.4	13	34	3.9	70	8.1	4.50	71	.252	.334	-10	-11	95	103	-0.9	-1	0	-1.1
Total	11	59	68	.465	344	134	28	10	16	1219	1130	8.3	142	489	3.6	829	6.1	3.91	93	.246	.319	-17	-36	96	101	-4.6	-0	-7	-3.6

■ **BILL LATTIMORE** Lattimore, William Hershel "Slothful Bill" b: 5/25/1884, Roxton, Tex. d: 10/30/19, Colorado Springs, Colo. BL/TL, 5'9", 165 lbs. Deb: 4/17/08

YEAR	TM/L	W	L	PCT	G	GS	CG	SHO	SV	IP	H	H/G	HR	BB	BB/G	SO	SO/G	ERA	/A	OAVG	OOBP	PR	/A	PF	CPI	WAT	PB	PD	TPI
1908	Cle-A	1	2	.333	4	4	1	1	0	24	24	9.0	0	7	2.6	5	1.9	4.50	55	.247	.298	-6	-5	103	57	-0.6	1	-1	-0.5

■ **CHUCK LAUER** Lauer, John Charles b: 1865, Pittsburgh, Pa. TR , Deb: 7/17/1884

YEAR	TM/L	W	L	PCT	G	GS	CG	SHO	SV	IP	H	H/G	HR	BB	BB/G	SO	SO/G	ERA	/A	OAVG	OOBP	PR	/A	PF	CPI	WAT	PB	PD	TPI
1884	Pit-a	0	2	.000	3	3	2	0	0	19	23	10.9	0	9	4.3	8	3.8	7.58	43	.308	.382	-9	-9	101	67	-0.9	-1	0	-0.6

■ **GEORGE LAUZERIQUE** Lauzerique, George Albert b: 7/22/47, Havana, Cuba BR/TR, 6'1", 180 lbs. Deb: 9/17/67

YEAR	TM/L	W	L	PCT	G	GS	CG	SHO	SV	IP	H	H/G	HR	BB	BB/G	SO	SO/G	ERA	/A	OAVG	OOBP	PR	/A	PF	CPI	WAT	PB	PD	TPI
1967	KC-A	0	2	.000	3	2	0	0	0	16	11	6.2	2	6	3.4	10	5.6	2.25	146	.193	.273	2	2	102	123	-0.9	-0	0	0.2
1968	Oak-A	0	0	—	1	0	0	0	0	1	0	0.0	0	1	9.0	0	0.0	0.00	—	.000	.250	0	0	98	0	0.0	0	0	0.1
1969	Oak-A	3	4	.429	19	8	1	0	0	61	58	8.6	14	27	4.0	39	5.8	4.72	70	.250	.331	-7	-10	91	103	-0.7	-1	1	-0.9
1970	Mil-A	1	2	.333	11	4	1	0	0	35	41	10.5	7	14	3.6	24	6.2	6.94	53	.295	.354	-13	-13	100	82	-0.2	1	-0	-1.1
Total	4	4	8	.333	34	14	2	0	0	113	110	8.8	23	48	3.8	73	5.8	5.02	68	.256	.330	-18	-20	96	99	-1.8	0	1	-1.7

■ **GARY LAVELLE** Lavelle, Gary Robert b: 1/3/49, Scranton, Pa. BB/TL, 6'2", 190 lbs. Deb: 9/10/74

YEAR	TM/L	W	L	PCT	G	GS	CG	SHO	SV	IP	H	H/G	HR	BB	BB/G	SO	SO/G	ERA	/A	OAVG	OOBP	PR	/A	PF	CPI	WAT	PB	PD	TPI
1974	SF-N	0	3	.000	10	0	0	0	0	17	14	7.4	1	10	5.3	12	6.4	2.12	187	.222	.320	3	3	109	149	-1.4	-0	-0	0.3
1975	SF-N	6	3	.667	65	0	0	0	8	82	80	8.8	3	48	5.3	51	5.6	2.96	125	.260	.354	6	7	102	136	1.6	-0	0	0.7
1976	SF-N	10	6	.625	65	0	0	0	12	110	102	8.3	6	52	4.3	71	5.8	2.70	135	.246	.326	10	12	104	130	2.7	-1	-1	1.0
1977	SF-N	7	7	.500	73	0	0	0	20	118	106	8.1	4	37	2.8	93	7.1	2.06	199	.239	.295	24	27	105	129	0.5	-2	1	2.7
1978	SF-N	13	10	.565	67	0	0	0	14	98	96	8.8	3	44	4.0	63	5.8	3.31	99	.263	.335	3	-0	91	113	0.5	-1	0	0.0
1979	SF-N	7	9	.438	70	0	0	0	20	97	86	8.0	5	42	3.9	80	7.4	2.51	139	.247	.319	13	11	93	138	0.0	0	0	1.1
1980	SF-N	6	8	.429	62	0	0	0	9	100	106	9.5	4	36	3.2	66	5.9	3.42	102	.275	.327	2	1	96	110	-0.5	-1	0	0.0
1981	SF-N	2	6	.250	34	3	0	0	4	66	58	7.9	3	23	3.1	45	6.1	3.82	96	.244	.309	-2	-1	105	83	-2.0	1	1	0.1
1982	SF-N	10	7	.588	68	0	0	0	8	105	97	8.3	6	29	2.5	76	6.5	2.66	127	.247	.294	11	8	94	112	1.0	0	2	1.1
1983	SF-N	7	4	.636	56	0	0	0	20	87	73	7.6	4	19	2.0	68	7.0	2.59	142	.229	.264	10	10	101	87	1.7	-2	2	1.1
1984	SF-N	5	4	.556	77	0	0	0	12	101	92	8.2	5	42	3.7	71	6.3	2.76	127	.246	.317	9	8	98	121	1.2	-0	-1	0.8
1985	Tor-A	5	7	.417	69	0	0	0	8	73	54	6.7	5	36	4.4	50	6.2	3.08	134	.214	.302	9	8	99	101	-1.9	0	-0	0.8
1987	Tor-A	2	3	.400	23	0	0	0	1	28	36	11.6	2	19	6.1	17	5.5	5.46	81	.313	.399	-3	-3	99	111	-0.7	0	0	-0.2
	Oak-A	0	0	—	6	0	0	0	0	4	4	9.0	0	3	6.8	6	13.5	9.00	45	.267	.368	-2	-2	91	50	0.0	0	0	-0.1
	Yr	2	3	.400	29	0	0	0	1	32	40	11.3	2	22	6.2	23	6.5	5.91	74	.305	.395	-5	-5	98	50	-0.7	0	0	-0.3
Total	13	80	77	.510	745	3	0	0	136	1086	1004	8.3	51	440	3.6	769	6.4	2.93	125	.249	.316	93	88	99	116	2.7	-6	4	9.4

■ **JIMMY LAVENDER** Lavender, James Sanford b: 3/25/1884, Barnesville, Ga. d: 1/12/60, Cartersville, Ga. BR/TR, 5'11", 165 lbs. Deb: 4/23/12

YEAR	TM/L	W	L	PCT	G	GS	CG	SHO	SV	IP	H	H/G	HR	BB	BB/G	SO	SO/G	ERA	/A	OAVG	OOBP	PR	/A	PF	CPI	WAT	PB	PD	TPI
1912	Chi-N	16	13	.552	42	31	15	3	3	252	240	8.6	9	89	3.2	109	3.9	3.04	115	.251	.321	10	12	102	94	-1.5	-3	0	1.0
1913	Chi-N	10	14	.417	40	20	10	0	2	204	206	9.1	6	98	4.3	91	4.0	3.66	85	.267	.352	-10	-13	97	106	-3.6	-4	-2	-1.8
1914	Chi-N	11	11	.500	37	28	11	2	0	214	191	8.0	11	87	3.7	87	3.7	3.07	90	.247	.318	-7	-8	99	104	-0.1	2	3	-0.2
1915	Chi-N	10	16	.385	41	24	13	1	4	220	178	7.3	5	67	2.7	117	4.8	2.58	110	.228	.288	4	6	103	92	-2.8	-2	3	0.8
1916	Chi-N	10	14	.417	36	25	9	4	2	188	163	7.8	3	62	3.0	91	4.4	2.82	109	.240	.304	-4	5	117	93	-0.6	-2	-1	0.4
1917	Phi-N	6	8	.429	28	14	7	0	1	129	119	8.3	5	44	3.1	52	3.6	3.56	81	.250	.310	-12	-10	106	86	-1.8	-1	2	-1.3
Total	6	63	76	.453	224	142	65	10	12	1207	1097	8.2	39	447	3.3	547	4.1	3.09	99	.247	.316	-19	-5	104	97	-10.4	-10	2	-1.1

■ **RON LAW** Law, Ronald David b: 3/14/46, Hamilton, Ont., Can. BR/TR, 6'2", 165 lbs. Deb: 6/29/69

YEAR	TM/L	W	L	PCT	G	GS	CG	SHO	SV	IP	H	H/G	HR	BB	BB/G	SO	SO/G	ERA	/A	OAVG	OOBP	PR	/A	PF	CPI	WAT	PB	PD	TPI
1969	Cle-A	3	4	.429	35	1	0	0	1	52	68	11.8	2	34	5.9	29	5.0	5.02	70	.325	.409	-8	-9	96	121	0.3	-0	0	-0.8

YEAR TM/L	W	L	PCT	G	GS	CG	SHO	SV	IP	H	H/G	HR	BB	BB/G	SO	SO/G	ERA	/A	OAVG	OOBP	PR	/A	PF	CPI	WAT	PB	PD	TPI
■ VANCE LAW	Law, Vance Aaron b: 10/1/56, Boise, Idaho BR/TR, 6'2", 185 lbs. Deb: 6/01/80																											
1986 Mon-N	0	0	—	3	0	0	0	0	4	3	6.8	0	2	4.5	0	0.0	2.25	163	.214	.313	1	1	98	110	0.0	1	0	0.1
1987 Mon-N	0	0	—	3	0	0	0	0	3	5	15.0	0	0	0.0	2	6.0	6.00	72	.333	.333	-1	-1	106	71	0.0	1	0	0.0
Total 2	0	0	—	6	0	0	0	0	7	8	10.3	0	2	2.6	2	2.6	3.86	102	.276	.323	0	0	102	93	0.0	2	0	0.1
■ VERN LAW	Law, Vernon Sanders "Deacon" b: 3/12/30, Meridian, Idaho BR/TR, 6'2", 195 lbs. Deb: 6/11/50 C																											
1950 Pit-N	7	9	.438	27	17	5	1	0	128	137	9.6	11	49	3.4	57	4.0	4.92	89	.272	.338	-11	-8	106	86	0.9	-2	-2	-1.0
1951 Pit-N	6	9	.400	28	14	2	1	2	114	109	8.6	9	51	4.0	41	3.2	4.50	96	.253	.333	-7	-2	110	88	-0.2	5	-1	0.3
1954 Pit-N	9	13	.409	39	18	7	0	3	162	201	11.2	20	56	3.1	57	3.2	5.50	75	.311	.357	-26	-24	102	97	1.2	4	-1	-1.9
1955 Pit-N	10	10	.500	43	24	8	1	1	201	221	9.9	19	61	2.7	82	3.7	3.81	107	.280	.327	5	6	101	110	2.0	3	0	1.0
1956 Pit-N	8	16	.333	39	32	6	0	2	196	218	10.0	24	49	2.3	60	2.8	4.32	90	.281	.321	-12	-9	103	98	-2.9	1	-1	-0.8
1957 Pit-N	10	8	.556	31	25	9	3	1	173	172	8.9	18	32	1.7	55	2.9	2.86	130	.256	.288	20	16	96	113	2.5	1	-1	1.6
1958 Pit-N	14	12	.538	35	29	6	1	3	202	235	10.5	16	39	1.7	56	2.5	3.97	94	.297	.322	-0	-6	94	105	-0.1	6	-0	0.0
1959 Pit-N	18	9	.667	34	33	20	2	1	266	245	8.3	25	53	1.8	110	3.7	2.98	**137**	.243	.278	29	**33**	104	98	5.0	1	1	**3.7**
1960 Pit-N	20	9	.690	35	35	**18**	3	0	272	266	8.8	25	40	1.3	120	4.0	3.08	118	.257	.284	21	17	97	104	3.2	3	2	2.3
1961 Pit-N	3	4	.429	11	10	1	0	0	59	72	11.0	10	18	2.7	20	3.1	4.73	84	.305	.353	-5	-5	99	116	-0.3	1	1	-0.2
1962 Pit-N	10	7	.588	23	20	7	2	0	139	156	10.1	21	27	1.7	78	5.1	3.95	101	.276	.309	-0	1	101	105	0.2	5	1	0.6
1963 Pit-N	4	5	.444	18	12	1	1	0	77	91	10.6	11	13	1.5	31	3.6	4.91	66	.296	.320	-14	-14	99	94	0.0	1	1	-1.2
1964 Pit-N	12	13	.480	35	29	7	5	0	192	203	9.5	18	32	1.5	93	4.4	3.61	99	.270	.297	-2	-1	101	99	-0.3	8	1	0.8
1965 Pit-N	17	9	.654	29	28	13	4	0	217	182	7.5	17	35	1.5	101	4.2	2.16	161	.229	.260	33	32	98	**115**	3.3	4	1	4.2
1966 Pit-N	12	8	.600	31	28	8	4	0	178	203	10.3	19	24	1.2	88	4.4	4.04	88	.292	.313	-9	-9	99	103	0.8	5	2	-0.3
1967 Pit-N	2	6	.250	25	10	1	0	0	97	122	11.3	5	18	1.7	43	4.0	4.18	81	.308	.330	-9	-9	100	104	-2.0	-0	-0	-0.9
Total 16	162	147	.524	483	364	119	28	13	2673	2833	9.5	268	597	2.0	1092	3.7	3.76	101	.272	.309	14	16	100	103	13.3	45	1	8.2
■ BROOKS LAWRENCE	Lawrence, Brooks Ulysses "Bull" b: 1/30/25, Springfield, Ohio BR/TR, 6', 205 lbs. Deb: 6/24/54																											
1954 StL-N	15	6	.714	35	18	8	0	1	159	141	8.0	17	72	4.1	72	4.1	3.74	109	.243	.328	6	6	100	103	5.3	0	0	0.7
1955 StL-N	3	8	.273	46	10	2	1	1	96	102	9.6	11	58	5.4	52	4.9	6.56	63	.278	.378	-27	-26	102	81	-2.1	-2	1	-2.5
1956 Cin-N	19	10	.655	49	30	11	1	0	219	210	8.6	26	71	2.9	96	3.9	3.99	100	.256	.310	-5	0	106	94	2.7	-1	3	0.4
1957 Cin-N	16	13	.552	49	32	12	1	4	250	234	8.4	26	76	2.7	121	4.4	3.53	117	.247	.304	10	16	106	98	1.2	-0	-0	1.7
1958 Cin-N	8	13	.381	46	23	6	2	5	181	194	9.6	12	55	2.7	74	3.7	4.13	101	.275	.327	-4	1	106	92	-2.6	-2	0	0.0
1959 Cin-N	7	12	.368	43	14	3	0	10	128	144	10.1	17	45	3.2	64	4.5	4.78	85	.281	.342	-12	-10	103	98	-2.3	-1	-0	-1.0
1960 Cin-N	1	0	1.000	7	0	0	0	1	8	9	10.1	1	8	9.0	2	2.3	10.13	37	.310	.447	-6	-6	99	72	0.5	0	0	-0.4
Total 7	69	62	.527	275	127	42	5	22	1041	1034	8.9	110	385	3.3	481	4.2	4.24	96	.261	.326	-38	-18	104	95	2.7	-5	4	-1.1
■ BOB LAWRENCE	Lawrence, Robert Andrew "Larry" b: 12/14/1899, Brooklyn, N.Y. d: 11/6/83, Jamaica, N.Y. BR/TR, 5'11", 180 lbs. Deb: 7/19/24																											
1924 Chi-A	0	0	—	1	0	0	0	0	1	1	9.0	0	1	9.0	1	9.0	9.00	46	.250	.400	-1	-1	98	48	0.0	0	0	0.0
■ AL LAWSON	Lawson, Alfred William b: 3/24/1869, London, England d: 11/29/54, San Antonio, Tex. BR/TR, 5'11", 161 lbs. Deb: 5/13/1890																											
1890 Bos-N	0	1	.000	1	1	1	0	0	9	10	10.0	0	4	4.0	1	1.0	4.00	96	.297	.372	-0	-0	108	97	-0.4	-0	0	0.0
Pit-N	0	2	.000	2	2	1	0	0	10	15	13.5	0	10	9.0	2	1.8	9.00	37	.364	.488	-6	-6	95	82	-0.9	-1	0	-0.4
Yr	0	3	.000	3	3	2	0	0	19	25	11.8	0	14	6.6	3	1.4	6.63	54	.334	.439	-6	-6	101	82	-1.3	-0	0	-0.4
■ ROXIE LAWSON	Lawson, Alfred Voyle b: 4/13/06, Donnellson, Iowa d: 4/9/77, Stockport, Iowa BR/TR, 6', 170 lbs. Deb: 8/03/30																											
1930 Cle-A	1	2	.333	7	4	2	0	0	34	46	12.2	1	23	6.1	10	2.6	6.09	80	.324	.406	-5	-4	105	103	-0.5	-1	-0	-0.4
1931 Cle-A	0	2	.000	17	3	0	0	0	56	72	11.6	5	36	5.8	20	3.2	7.55	61	.304	.391	-20	-18	106	80	-0.9	-0	-1	-1.6
1933 Det-A	0	1	.000	4	2	0	0	0	16	17	9.6	2	17	9.6	6	3.4	7.31	62	.270	.425	-5	-5	107	89	-0.4	-1	0	-0.4
1935 Det-A	3	1	.750	7	4	4	2	2	40	34	7.6	3	24	5.4	16	3.6	1.57	262	.233	.337	13	11	93	245	0.7	1	-1	1.1
1936 Det-A	8	6	.571	41	8	3	0	3	128	139	9.8	13	71	5.0	34	2.4	5.48	87	.281	.370	-6	-10	95	99	0.5	1	1	-0.7
1937 Det-A	18	7	.720	37	29	15	0	1	217	236	9.8	17	115	4.8	68	2.8	5.27	94	.271	.354	-16	-7	108	86	4.7	2	-1	-0.4
1938 Det-A	8	9	.471	27	16	5	0	1	127	154	10.9	13	82	5.8	39	2.8	5.46	87	.299	.387	-9	-10	99	109	-1.2	-5	0	-1.2
1939 Det-A	1	1	.500	2	1	0	0	0	11	7	5.7	1	7	5.7	4	3.3	4.91	103	.167	.280	-0	0	110	43	0.0	-1	0	0.0
StL-A	3	7	.300	36	14	5	0	0	151	181	10.8	10	83	4.9	43	2.6	5.30	91	.307	.384	-11	-8	105	108	0.2	-1	-1	-0.7
Yr	4	8	.333	38	15	5	0	0	162	188	10.4	11	90	5.0	47	2.6	5.28	92	.297	.377	-12	-7	105	108	0.2	-1	-0	-0.7
1940 StL-A	5	3	.625	30	2	0	0	4	72	77	9.6	5	54	6.8	18	2.3	5.13	92	.278	.389	-6	-3	108	106	1.4	-3	-0	-0.5
Total 9	47	39	.547	208	83	34	2	11	852	963	10.2	70	512	5.4	258	2.7	5.37	89	.285	.374	-67	-54	103	104	4.5	-7	-2	-4.8
■ BOB LAWSON	Lawson, Robert Baker b: 8/23/1876, Brookneal, Va. d: 10/28/52, Chapel Hill, N.C. BR/TR, 5'10", 170 lbs. Deb: 5/07/01																											
1901 Bos-N	2	2	.500	6	4	4	0	0	46	45	8.8	0	28	5.5	12	2.3	3.33	112	.281	.394	-0	2	112	117	0.0	-0	1	0.3
1902 Bal-A	0	2	.000	3	2	1	0	0	13	21	14.5	0	3	2.1	5	3.5	4.85	77	.391	.423	-2	-2	104	122	-0.9	-0	1	0.0
Total 2	2	4	.333	9	6	5	0	0	59	66	10.1	0	31	4.7	17	2.6	3.66	102	.308	.401	-2	0	110	118	-0.9	-1	1	0.3
■ STEVE LAWSON	Lawson, Steven George b: 12/28/50, Oakland, Cal. BR/TL, 6'1", 175 lbs. Deb: 8/03/72																											
1972 Tex-A	0	0	—	13	0	0	0	1	16	13	7.3	1	10	5.6	13	7.3	2.81	106	.213	.324	0	0	97	106	0.0	0	0	0.1
■ BILL LAXTON	Laxton, William Harry b: 1/5/48, Camden, N.J. BL/TL, 6'1", 190 lbs. Deb: 9/15/70																											
1970 Phi-N	0	0	—	2	0	0	0	0	2	2	9.0	2	2	9.0	2	9.0	13.50	29	.250	.455	-2	-2	98	101	0.0	0	0	-0.1
1971 SD-N	0	2	.000	18	0	0	0	0	28	32	10.3	4	26	8.4	23	7.4	6.75	50	.305	.437	-10	-10	98	104	-0.9	0	0	-1.0
1974 SD-N	0	1	.000	30	1	0	0	0	45	37	7.4	5	38	7.6	40	8.0	4.00	88	.226	.371	-2	-2	97	115	-0.4	0	-0	-0.2
1976 Det-A	0	5	.000	26	3	0	0	2	95	77	7.3	13	51	4.8	74	7.0	4.07	91	.221	.327	-6	-4	105	95	-2.4	0	-2	-0.5
1977 Sea-A	3	2	.600	43	0	0	0	3	73	62	7.6	10	39	4.8	49	6.0	4.93	81	.233	.332	-7	-7	98	83	0.9	0	-1	-0.8
Cle-A	0	0	—	2	0	0	0	0	2	2	9.0	0	2	9.0	1	4.5	4.50	89	.286	.444	-0	-0	98	126	0.0	0	0	0.0
Yr	3	2	.600	45	0	0	0	3	75	64	7.7	10	41	4.9	50	6.0	4.92	81	.228	.323	-7	-8	98	126	0.9	0	-1	-0.8
Total 5	3	10	.231	121	4	0	0	5	245	212	7.8	34	158	5.8	189	6.9	4.70	79	.236	.353	-27	-27	100	96	-2.8	0	-3	-2.6
■ DANNY LAZAR	Lazar, John Dan b: 11/14/43, East Chicago, Ind. BL/TL, 6'1", 190 lbs. Deb: 6/21/68																											
1968 Chi-A	0	1	.000	8	1	0	0	0	13	14	9.7	1	4	2.8	11	7.6	4.15	73	.269	.316	-2	-2	102	91	-0.4	0	0	-0.1
1969 Chi-A	0	0	—	9	3	0	0	0	21	21	9.0	5	11	4.7	9	3.9	6.43	62	.280	.363	-7	-6	110	95	0.0	-0	-0	-0.5
Total 2	0	1	.000	17	4	0	0	0	34	35	9.3	6	15	4.0	20	5.3	5.56	65	.276	.345	-8	-7	107	93	-0.4	0	0	-0.6
■ JACK LAZORKO	Lazorko, Jack Thomas b: 3/30/56, Hoboken, N.J. BR/TR, 5'11", 200 lbs. Deb: 6/04/84																											
1984 Mil-A	0	1	.000	15	1	0	0	1	40	37	8.3	7	22	4.9	24	5.4	4.27	87	.245	.343	-1	-3	93	109	-0.4	0	0	-0.2
1985 Sea-A	0	0	—	15	0	0	0	1	20	23	10.3	1	8	3.6	7	3.1	3.60	110	.291	.370	1	1	95	138	0.0	0	1	0.1
1986 Det-A	0	0	—	3	0	0	0	0	7	8	10.3	0	4	5.1	3	3.9	3.86	103	.296	.387	0	0	95	123	0.0	0	0	0.0
1987 Cal-A	5	6	.455	26	11	2	0	0	118	108	8.2	20	44	3.4	55	4.2	4.58	97	.248	.316	-1	-2	100	94	0.0	0	2	0.0
1988 Cal-A	0	1	.000	10	3	0	0	0	38	37	8.8	5	16	3.8	19	4.5	3.32	113	.255	.327	3	2	95	130	-0.4	0	0	0.2
Total 5	5	8	.385	69	15	2	0	2	223	213	8.6	33	94	3.8	108	4.4	4.20	98	.254	.331	2	-2	97	108	-0.8	0	2	0.1
■ CHARLIE LEA	Lea, Charles William b: 12/25/56, Orleans, France BR/TR, 6'4", 194 lbs. Deb: 6/12/80																											
1980 Mon-N	7	5	.583	21	19	0	0	0	104	103	8.9	5	55	4.8	56	4.8	3.72	95	.262	.349	-1	-2	98	109	0.4	-2	-1	-0.4
1981 Mon-N	5	4	.556	16	11	2	2	0	64	63	8.9	4	26	3.7	31	4.4	4.64	74	.268	.337	-8	-9	98	86	0.0	-0	-0	-0.8
1982 Mon-N	12	10	.545	27	27	4	2	0	178	145	7.3	16	56	2.8	115	5.8	3.24	116	.222	.278	7	10	104	83	0.4	-1	-1	0.9
1983 Mon-N	16	11	.593	33	33	8	4	0	222	195	7.9	15	84	3.4	137	5.6	3.12	118	.238	.305	13	14	101	99	2.7	-2	-1	1.1
1984 Mon-N	15	10	.600	30	30	8	0	0	224	198	8.0	19	68	2.7	123	4.9	2.89	113	.239	.293	17	10	91	109	3.2	-2	0	0.7
1987 Mon-N	0	1	.000	1	1	0	0	0	1	4	36.0	1	2	18.0	1	9.0	36.00	12	.571	.667	-4	-4	106	83	-0.4	0	0	-0.2
1988 Min-A	7	7	.500	24	23	0	0	0	130	156	10.8	19	50	3.5	72	5.0	4.85	86	.301	.361	-13	-9	105	115	-0.7	0	-1	-0.9
Total 7	62	48	.564	152	144	22	8	0	923	864	8.4	79	341	3.3	535	5.2	3.54	103	.250	.314	12	10	99	101	5.6	-7	-4	0.4
■ RICK LEACH	Leach, Richard Max b: 5/4/57, Ann Arbor, Mich. BL/TL, 6'1", 180 lbs. Deb: 4/30/81																											
1984 Tor-A	0	0	—	1	0	0	0	0	1	2	18.0	1	2	18.0	0	0.0	27.00	15	.400	.571	-3	-3	101	74	0.0	0	0	-0.1

YEAR	TM/L	W	L	PCT	G	GS	CG	SHO	SV	IP	H	H/G	HR	BB	BB/G	SO	SO/G	ERA	/A	OAVG	OOBP	PR	/A	PF	CPI	WAT	PB	PD	TPI
■ **TERRY LEACH**	Leach, Terry Hester b: 3/13/54, Selma, Ala. BR/TR, 6', 215 lbs. Deb: 8/12/81																												
1981	NY-N	1	1	.500	21	1	0	0	0	35	26	6.7	2	12	3.1	16	4.1	2.57	139	.205	.273	4	4	103	82	0.2	0	0	0.5
1982	NY-N	2	1	.667	21	1	1	1	3	45	46	9.2	2	18	3.6	30	6.0	4.20	86	.271	.330	-3	-3	100	91	0.7	-0	0	-0.3
1985	NY-N	3	4	.429	22	4	1	1	1	56	48	7.7	3	14	2.3	30	4.8	2.89	119	.235	.279	4	3	95	92	-1.0	1	1	0.5
1986	NY-N	0	0	—	6	0	0	0	0	7	6	7.7	0	3	3.9	4	5.1	2.57	135	.222	.300	1	1	93	87	0.0	0	0	0.1
1987	NY-N	11	1	.917	44	12	1	1	0	131	132	9.1	14	29	2.0	61	4.2	3.23	123	.262	.299	12	11	97	113	4.9	-2	1	1.0
1988	NY-N	7	2	.778	52	0	0	0	3	92	95	9.3	5	24	2.3	51	5.0	2.54	119	.268	.311	9	5	88	143	1.9	0	2	0.8
Total	6	24	9	.727	166	18	3	3	7	366	353	8.7	26	100	2.5	192	4.7	3.05	117	.255	.301	28	21	95	111	6.7	-1	5	2.6
■ **LUIS LEAL**	Leal, Luis Enrique (born Luis Enrique Albarado (Leal)) b: 3/21/57, Barquisimeto, Venz. BR/TR, 6'3", 205 lbs. Deb: 5/25/80																												
1980	Tor-A	3	4	.429	13	10	1	0	0	60	72	10.8	6	31	4.7	26	3.9	4.50	91	.314	.385	-3	-3	101	129	0.1	0	-1	-0.2
1981	Tor-A	7	13	.350	29	19	3	0	1	130	127	8.8	8	44	3.0	71	4.9	3.67	113	.254	.313	-0	7	113	94	0.0	0	-1	0.6
1982	Tor-A	12	15	.444	38	38	10	0	0	250	250	9.0	24	79	2.8	111	4.0	3.92	113	.262	.315	4	15	109	98	-1.1	0	-1	1.4
1983	Tor-A	13	12	.520	35	35	7	1	0	217	216	9.0	23	65	2.7	116	4.8	4.31	102	.257	.313	-6	2	108	88	-0.7	0	-1	0.1
1984	Tor-A	13	8	.619	35	35	6	2	0	222	221	9.0	27	77	3.1	134	5.4	3.89	104	.258	.318	3	4	101	103	1.8	0	0	0.4
1985	Tor-A	3	6	.333	15	14	0	0	0	67	82	11.0	13	24	3.2	33	4.4	5.78	71	.303	.360	-12	-12	99	103	-2.0	0	0	-1.1
Total	6	51	58	.468	165	151	27	3	1	946	968	9.2	101	320	3.0	491	4.7	4.14	103	.265	.323	-14	12	106	99	-1.9	0	-2	1.2
■ **KING LEAR**	Lear, Charles Bernard b: 1/23/1891, Greencastle, Pa. d: 10/31/76, Greencastle, Pa. BR/TR, 6', 175 lbs. Deb: 5/02/14																												
1914	Cin-N	1	2	.333	17	4	3	1	1	56	55	8.8	3	19	3.1	20	3.2	3.05	98	.271	.325	-2	-0	107	118	-0.1	0	-0	0.0
1915	Cin-N	6	10	.375	40	15	9	0	0	168	169	9.1	7	45	2.4	46	2.5	3.00	95	.270	.315	-5	-3	104	113	-1.5	-1	-4	-0.7
Total	2	7	12	.368	57	19	12	1	1	224	224	9.0	10	64	2.6	66	2.7	3.01	96	.270	.318	-6	-3	105	114	-1.6	-0	-4	-0.7
■ **FRANK LEARY**	Leary, Francis Patrick b: 2/26/1881, Wayland, Mass. d: 10/4/07, Natick, Mass. Deb: 4/30/07																												
1907	Cin-N	0	1	.000	2	1	0	0	0	8	7	7.9	0	6	6.8	4	4.5	1.13	208	.262	.398	1	1	95	315	-0.4	-0	0	0.2
■ **JACK LEARY**	Leary, John J. b: 1858, New Haven, Conn. TL, 5'11", 186 lbs. Deb: 8/21/1880																												
1880	Bos-N	0	1	.000	1	1	0	0	0	3	8	24.0	0	0	0.0	1	3.0	15.00	15	.495	.495	-4	-4	93	69	-0.4	-0	0	-0.3
1881	Det-N	0	2	.000	2	2	1	0	0	13	13	9.0	0	2	1.4	2	1.4	4.15	71	.272	.302	-2	-2	106	56	-0.9	1	0	0.0
1882	Pit-a	1	0	1.000	3	2	1	0	0	19	28	13.3	0	3	1.4	5	2.4	6.16	42	.348	.371	-7	-8	97	80	0.5	1	0	-0.5
	Bal-a	2	1	.667	3	3	3	0	0	26	29	10.0	1	8	2.8	2	0.7	1.38	199	.288	.340	4	4	102	280	0.8	0	0	0.4
	Yr	3	1	.750	6	5	4	0	0	45	57	11.4	1	11	2.2	7	1.4	3.40	79	.314	.353	-4	-4	100	280	1.3	1	0	-0.1
1884	Alt-U	0	3	.000	3	3	2	0	0	24	31	11.6	0	2	0.8	7	2.6	5.25	62	.318	.332	-6	-5	109	78	-1.4	-2	0	-0.3
	CP-U	0	2	.000	2	1	1	0	0	10	14	12.6	0	5	4.5	6	5.4	5.40	56	.336	.407	-3	-3	100	107	-0.9	-0	0	-0.1
	Yr	0	5	.000	5	4	3	0	0	34	45	11.9	0	7	1.9	13	3.4	5.29	60	.324	.356	-9	-8	106	107	-2.3	-2	0	-0.4
Total	4	3	9	.250	14	12	8	0	0	95	123	11.7	1	20	1.9	23	2.2	4.55	63	.320	.354	-18	-18	103	133	-2.3	-1	0	-0.8
■ **TIM LEARY**	Leary, Timothy James b: 12/23/58, Santa Monica, Cal. BR/TR, 6'3", 205 lbs. Deb: 4/12/81																												
1981	NY-N	0	0	—	1	1	0	0	0	2	0	0.0	0	1	4.5	3	13.5	0.00	—	.000	.143	1	1	103	0	0.0	-0	0	0.1
1983	NY-N	1	1	.500	2	2	1	0	0	11	15	12.3	0	4	3.3	9	7.4	3.27	111	.319	.358	0	0	100	143	0.1	0	0	0.1
1984	NY-N	3	3	.500	20	7	0	0	0	54	61	10.2	2	18	3.0	29	4.8	4.00	90	.285	.342	-2	-2	100	102	-0.2	2	-1	-0.1
1985	Mil-A	1	4	.200	5	5	0	0	0	33	40	10.9	5	8	2.2	29	7.9	4.09	107	.296	.336	0	1	106	124	-1.3	0	1	0.2
1986	Mil-A	12	12	.500	33	30	3	2	0	188	216	10.3	20	53	2.5	110	5.3	4.21	102	.289	.338	-1	2	103	110	0.6	0	1	0.3
1987	LA-N	3	11	.214	39	12	0	0	1	108	121	10.1	15	36	3.0	61	5.1	4.75	79	.285	.339	-8	-12	92	102	-3.7	2	1	-0.8
1988	LA-N	17	11	.607	35	34	9	6	0	229	201	7.9	13	56	2.2	180	7.1	2.91	125	.234	.282	14	18	105	93	0.9	5	2	2.7
Total	7	37	42	.468	135	91	13	8	1	625	654	9.4	55	176	2.5	421	6.1	3.77	103	.269	.319	4	9	102	103	-3.6	9	3	2.5
■ **RAZOR LEDBETTER**	Ledbetter, Ralph Overton b: 12/8/1894, Rutherford College N.C. d: 2/1/69, W.Palm Beach, Fla. BR/TR, 6'3", 190 lbs. Deb: 4/16/15																												
1915	Det-A	0	0	—	1	0	0	0	0	1	1	9.0	0	0	0.0	0	0.0	0.00	—	.333	.333	0	0	105	0	0.0	0	0	0.1
■ **DON LEE**	Lee, Donald Edward b: 2/26/34, Globe, Ariz. BR/TR, 6'4", 205 lbs. Deb: 4/23/57																												
1957	Det-A	1	3	.250	11	6	0	0	0	39	48	11.1	6	18	4.2	19	4.4	4.62	88	.308	.374	-4	-2	107	128	-0.9	-1	-0	-0.2
1958	Det-A	0	0	—	1	0	0	0	0	2	1	4.5	1	1	4.5	0	0.0	9.00	43	.143	.333	-1	-1	103	66	0.0	0	0	0.0
1960	Was-A	8	7	.533	44	20	1	0	3	165	160	8.7	16	64	3.5	88	4.8	3.44	115	.258	.325	8	10	102	113	0.9	-0	1	1.1
1961	Min-A	3	6	.333	37	10	4	0	3	115	93	7.3	12	35	2.7	65	5.1	3.52	122	.221	.283	6	10	107	83	-1.0	-3	2	1.0
1962	Min-A	3	3	.500	9	9	1	0	0	52	51	8.8	8	24	4.2	28	4.8	4.50	91	.256	.353	-3	-2	104	108	-0.2	0	0	-0.1
	LA-A	8	8	.500	27	22	4	2	2	153	153	9.0	12	39	2.3	74	4.4	3.12	130	.256	.301	14	16	102	108	-0.4	-0	-2	1.4
	Yr	11	11	.500	36	31	5	2	2	205	204	9.0	20	63	2.8	102	4.5	3.47	117	.254	.307	11	14	102	108	-0.6	0	-1	1.3
1963	LA-A	8	11	.421	40	22	3	2	1	154	148	8.6	12	51	3.0	89	5.2	3.68	91	.251	.315	-1	-6	92	97	-0.2	-1	-1	-0.6
1964	LA-A	5	4	.556	33	8	0	0	2	89	99	10.0	6	25	2.5	73	7.4	2.73	118	.279	.322	9	5	89	142	0.5	2	-1	0.6
1965	Cal-A	0	1	.000	10	0	0	0	0	14	21	13.5	4	5	3.2	12	7.7	6.43	53	.350	.397	-5	-5	98	125	-0.4	1	0	-0.3
	Hou-N	0	0	—	7	0	0	0	0	8	8	9.0	0	3	3.4	3	3.4	3.38	95	.267	.353	0	-0	91	111	0.0	-0	0	0.0
1966	Hou-N	2	0	1.000	9	0	0	0	0	18	17	8.5	1	4	2.0	9	4.5	2.50	142	.250	.284	2	2	99	114	1.0	0	1	0.4
	Chi-N	2	1	.667	16	0	0	0	0	19	28	13.3	3	12	5.7	7	3.3	7.11	52	.346	.417	-7	-7	103	105	0.7	0	0	-0.6
	Yr	4	1	.800	25	0	0	0	0	37	45	10.9	4	16	3.9	16	3.9	4.86	75	.302	.359	-5	-5	101	105	1.7	0	1	-0.2
Total	9	40	44	.476	244	97	13	4	11	828	827	9.0	81	281	3.1	467	5.1	3.61	106	.260	.321	19	18	100	108	-0.0	-1	1	2.7
■ **MARK LEE**	Lee, Mark Linden b: 6/14/53, Inglewood, Cal. BR/TR, 6'4", 225 lbs. Deb: 4/23/78																												
1978	SD-N	5	1	.833	56	0	0	0	2	85	74	7.8	2	36	3.8	31	3.3	3.28	101	.240	.314	3	0	93	94	2.0	-1	1	0.1
1979	SD-N	2	4	.333	46	1	0	0	5	65	88	12.2	3	25	3.5	25	3.5	4.29	85	.332	.381	-4	-5	97	129	-0.6	1	1	-0.3
1980	Pit-N	0	1	.000	4	0	0	0	0	6	5	7.5	0	3	4.5	2	3.0	4.50	83	.227	.308	-1	-1	103	59	-0.4	0	0	0.0
1981	Pit-N	0	2	.000	12	0	0	0	2	20	17	7.6	1	5	2.3	5	2.3	2.70	124	.233	.265	2	1	96	94	-0.9	0	1	0.3
Total	4	7	8	.467	118	1	0	0	9	176	184	9.4	6	69	3.5	63	3.2	3.63	95	.275	.335	0	-4	95	106	0.1	1	4	0.1
■ **MARK LEE**	Lee, Mark Owen b: 7/20/64, Williston, N.Dak. BL/TL, 6'3", 198 lbs. Deb: 9/08/88																												
1988	KC-A	0	0	—	4	0	0	0	0	5	6	10.8	0	1	1.8	0	0.0	3.60	113	.300	.333	0	0	103	106	0.0	0	0	0.0
■ **MIKE LEE**	Lee, Michael Randall b: 5/19/41, Bell, Cal. BL/TL, 6'5", 220 lbs. Deb: 5/06/60																												
1960	Cle-A	0	0	—	7	0	0	0	0	9	6	6.0	1	11	11.0	6	6.0	2.00	190	.207	.429	2	2	98	283	0.0	0	-0	0.2
1963	LA-A	1	1	.500	6	4	0	0	0	26	30	10.4	3	14	4.8	11	3.8	3.81	88	.300	.388	-1	-1	92	150	0.1	-1	1	0.0
Total	2	1	1	.500	13	4	0	0	0	35	36	9.3	4	25	6.4	17	4.4	3.34	104	.279	.399	1	0	94	184	0.1	-1	1	0.2
■ **BOB LEE**	Lee, Robert Dean "Moose" or "Horse" b: 11/26/37, Ottumwa, Iowa BR/TR, 6'3", 225 lbs. Deb: 4/15/64																												
1964	LA-A	6	5	.545	64	5	0	0	19	137	87	5.7	6	58	3.8	111	7.3	1.51	213	.182	.268	**32**	**26**	89	119	0.5	-2	-2	2.3
1965	Cal-A	9	7	.563	69	0	0	0	23	131	95	6.5	11	42	2.9	89	6.1	1.92	177	.205	.262	22	**21**	98	123	1.6	1	-1	2.3
1966	Cal-A	5	4	.556	61	0	0	0	16	102	90	7.9	8	31	2.7	46	4.1	2.74	125	.237	.290	8	8	100	114	0.6	-0	-1	0.7
1967	LA-N	0	0	—	4	0	0	0	0	7	6	7.7	2	3	3.9	2	2.6	5.14	58	.222	.313	-1	-2	89	95	0.0	0	0	-0.1
	Cin-N	3	3	.500	27	1	0	0	2	51	51	9.0	0	25	4.4	33	5.8	4.41	83	.262	.335	-6	-4	109	80	-0.1	1	-1	-0.3
	Yr	3	3	.500	31	1	0	0	2	58	57	8.8	2	28	4.3	35	5.4	4.50	80	.254	.328	-7	-6	106	80	-0.1	0	-1	-0.4
1968	Cin-N	2	4	.333	44	1	0	0	3	65	73	10.1	4	37	5.1	34	4.7	5.12	65	.302	.379	-15	-13	111	102	-1.0	0	-1	-1.5
Total	5	25	23	.521	269	7	0	0	63	493	402	7.3	31	196	3.6	315	5.8	2.70	125	.225	.295	40	37	99	112	1.6	-1	-5	3.4
■ **ROY LEE**	Lee, Roy Edwin b: 9/28/17, Elmira, N.Y. d: 11/11/85, St.Louis, Mo. BL/TL, 5'11.5", 175 lbs. Deb: 9/23/45																												
1945	NY-N	0	2	.000	3	1	0	0	0	7	8	10.3	3	3	3.9	0	0.0	11.57	33	.267	.333	-6	-6	100	58	-0.9	-0	-0	-0.5
■ **TOM LEE**	Lee, Thomas F. b: 3/23/1864, Philadelphia, Pa. d: 3/4/1886, Milwaukee, Wis. Deb: 6/14/1884																												
1884	Chi-N	1	4	.200	5	5	5	0	0	45	55	11.0	12	15	3.0	14	2.8	3.80	82	.311	.364	-4	-3	105	160	-1.5	-2	0	-0.4
	Bal-U	5	8	.385	15	14	12	0	0	122	121	8.9	1	29	2.1	81	6.0	3.39	97	.264	.308	-5	-1	110	91	-2.1	1	0	0.1
■ **THORNTON LEE**	Lee, Thornton Starr "Lefty" b: 9/13/06, Sonoma, Cal. BL/TL, 6'3", 205 lbs. Deb: 9/19/33																												
1933	Cle-A	1	1	.500	3	2	2	0	0	17	13	6.9	1	11	5.8	7	3.7	4.24	106	.203	.320	0	0	105	72	0.0	1	-0	0.2

YEAR	TM/L	W	L	PCT	G	GS	CG	SHO	SV	IP	H	H/G	HR	BB	BB/G	SO	SO/G	ERA	/A	OAVG	OOBP	PR	/A	PF	CPI	WAT	PB	PD	TPI
1934	Cle-A	1	1	.500	24	6	0	0	0	86	105	11.0	8	44	4.6	41	4.3	5.02	89	.308	.380	-5	-5	100	117	0.0	-1	0	-0.5
1935	Cle-A	7	10	.412	32	20	8	1	1	181	179	8.9	6	71	3.5	81	4.0	4.03	109	.259	.324	9	7	99	90	-2.1	-1	2	0.8
1936	Cle-A	3	5	.375	43	8	2	0	3	127	138	9.8	2	67	4.7	49	3.5	4.89	108	.271	.354	**2**	**5**	105	87	-1.1	-3	2	0.5
1937	Chi-A	12	10	.545	30	25	13	2	0	205	209	9.2	17	60	2.6	80	3.5	3.51	134	.260	.308	25	27	102	103	-0.2	0	-1	2.6
1938	Chi-A	13	12	.520	33	30	18	1	1	245	252	9.3	12	94	3.5	77	2.8	3.49	135	.263	.325	35	33	98	110	2.1	6	-2	3.6
1939	Chi-A	15	11	.577	33	29	15	2	3	235	260	10.0	14	70	2.7	81	3.1	4.21	117	.285	.330	11	18	106	103	0.9	-3	0	1.5
1940	Chi-A	12	13	.480	28	27	24	1	0	228	223	8.8	13	56	2.2	87	3.4	3.47	129	.254	.296	23	26	103	94	-1.3	4	-3	2.7
1941	Chi-A	22	11	.667	35	34	**30**	3	1	300	258	7.7	18	92	2.8	130	3.9	**2.37**	**164**	.232	**.289**	**59**	**51**	94	**122**	6.4	6	-1	**5.7**
1942	Chi-A	2	6	.250	11	8	6	1	0	76	82	9.7	4	31	3.7	25	3.0	3.32	111	.278	.344	3	3	100	130	-1.7	0	-2	0.1
1943	Chi-A	5	9	.357	19	19	7	1	0	127	129	9.1	8	50	3.5	35	2.5	4.18	80	.266	.333	-12	-12	101	94	-2.4	-4	-3	-1.8
1944	Chi-A	3	9	.250	15	14	6	0	0	113	105	8.4	3	25	2.0	39	3.1	3.03	116	.246	.284	5	6	102	85	-2.8	-4	2	0.5
1945	Chi-A	15	12	.556	29	28	19	1	0	228	208	8.2	6	76	3.0	108	4.3	2.45	132	.245	.309	23	20	96	121	2.4	-1	-1	1.9
1946	Chi-A	2	4	.333	7	7	2	0	0	43	39	8.2	1	23	4.8	23	4.8	3.56	96	.244	.337	-0	-1	97	95	-0.8	1	-0	0.0
1947	Chi-A	3	7	.300	21	11	2	1	1	87	86	8.9	5	56	5.8	57	5.9	4.45	82	.261	.365	-7	-8	99	100	-1.7	0	0	-0.6
1948	NY-N	1	3	.250	11	4	1	0	0	33	41	11.2	3	12	3.3	17	4.6	4.36	89	.304	.360	-1	-2	98	118	-0.9	-1	0	-0.1
Total	16	117	124	.485	374	272	155	14	10	2331	2327	9.0	121	838	3.2	937	3.6	3.56	118	.260	.321	169	168	100	105	-3.2	2	-7	17.1
■ BILL LEE	Lee, William Crutcher "Big Bill" b: 10/21/09, Plaquemine, La. d: 6/15/77, Plaquemine, La. BR/TR, 6'3", 195 lbs. Deb: 4/29/34																												
1934	Chi-N	13	14	.481	35	29	16	4	1	214	218	9.2	9	74	3.1	104	4.4	3.41	115	.263	.323	16	12	97	106	-2.4	-2	1	1.1
1935	Chi-N	20	6	**.769**	39	32	18	3	1	252	241	8.6	11	84	3.0	100	3.6	2.96	129	.251	.312	30	24	95	111	5.0	3	-0	2.6
1936	Chi-N	18	11	.621	43	33	20	4	1	259	238	8.3	14	93	3.2	102	3.5	3.30	124	.246	.309	21	23	102	99	2.2	-3	1	2.1
1937	Chi-N	14	15	.483	42	33	17	2	3	272	289	9.6	14	73	2.4	108	3.6	3.54	111	.273	.316	11	12	100	104	-3.3	-1	3	1.4
1938	Chi-N	**22**	9	**.710**	44	37	19	**9**	2	291	281	8.7	18	74	2.3	121	3.7	**2.66**	**146**	.252	.299	**37**	**40**	103	**119**	**5.4**	1	1	**4.4**
1939	Chi-N	19	15	.559	37	36	20	1	0	282	295	9.4	18	85	2.7	105	3.4	3.45	114	.272	.317	15	15	100	109	0.6	-4	5	1.5
1940	Chi-N	9	17	.346	37	30	9	1	0	211	246	10.5	12	70	3.0	70	3.0	5.03	75	.294	.343	-28	-29	99	91	-4.2	-2	-1	-3.0
1941	Chi-N	8	14	.364	28	22	12	0	1	167	179	9.6	6	43	2.3	62	3.3	3.77	90	.270	.310	-3	-7	94	91	-2.4	1	1	-0.4
1942	Chi-N	13	13	.500	32	30	18	1	0	220	221	9.0	4	67	2.7	75	3.1	3.85	84	.258	.308	-13	-15	98	80	1.6	1	1	-1.3
1943	Chi-N	3	7	.300	13	12	4	0	0	78	83	9.6	4	27	3.1	18	2.1	3.58	93	.273	.327	-2	-2	98	106	-1.9	1	-1	-0.1
	Phi-N	1	5	.167	13	7	2	0	3	61	70	10.3	4	21	3.1	17	2.5	4.57	71	.298	.352	-8	-9	96	101	-1.7	-2	-1	-1.1
	Yr	4	12	.250	26	19	6	0	3	139	153	9.9	8	48	3.1	35	2.3	4.01	82	.284	.338	-10	-11	97	101	-3.6	1	-2	-1.2
1944	Phi-N	10	11	.476	31	28	11	3	1	208	199	8.6	9	57	2.5	50	2.2	3.16	117	.248	.297	10	13	103	94	1.5	-0	2	1.5
1945	Phi-N	3	6	.333	13	13	2	0	0	77	107	12.5	0	30	3.5	13	1.5	4.68	83	.318	.367	-7	-7	102	104	0.2	-1	0	-0.6
	Bos-N	6	3	.667	16	13	6	1	0	106	112	9.5	6	36	3.1	12	1.0	2.80	153	.279	.331	12	17	113	146	1.9	-1	1	1.9
	Yr	9	9	.500	29	26	8	1	0	183	219	10.8	6	66	3.2	25	1.2	3.59	115	.297	.348	4	11	108	146	2.1	-1	1	1.3
1946	Bos-N	10	9	.526	25	21	8	0	0	140	148	9.5	7	45	2.9	32	2.1	4.18	77	.273	.322	-12	-15	94	87	0.0	-1	1	-1.5
1947	Chi-N	0	2	.000	14	2	0	0	0	24	26	9.8	2	14	5.3	9	3.4	4.50	94	.268	.353	-1	-1	104	103	-0.9	0	0	0.0
Total	14	169	157	.518	462	378	182	29	13	2862	2953	9.3	138	893	2.8	998	3.1	3.54	106	.266	.318	77	70	99	103	1.6	-10	14	8.5
■ BILL LEE	Lee, William Francis b: 12/28/46, Burbank, Cal. BL/TL, 6'3", 205 lbs. Deb: 6/25/69																												
1969	Bos-A	1	3	.250	20	1	0	0	0	52	56	9.7	9	28	4.8	45	7.8	4.50	84	.281	.371	-5	-4	105	124	-1.0	-1	-0	-0.5
1970	Bos-A	2	2	.500	11	5	0	0	1	37	48	11.7	3	14	3.4	19	4.6	4.62	88	.320	.371	-4	-2	110	116	0.0	-1	1	-0.2
1971	Bos-A	9	2	.818	47	3	0	0	2	102	102	9.0	7	46	4.1	74	6.5	2.74	133	.256	.330	8	10	105	135	3.5	0	0	1.2
1972	Bos-A	7	4	.636	47	0	0	0	5	84	75	8.0	5	32	3.4	43	4.6	3.21	100	.248	.312	-1	0	105	103	1.1	1	2	0.5
1973	Bos-A	17	11	.607	38	33	18	1	1	285	275	8.7	20	76	2.4	120	3.8	2.75	146	.257	.303	34	40	105	**120**	2.1	0	1	4.5
1974	Bos-A	17	15	.531	38	37	16	1	0	282	320	10.2	25	67	2.1	95	3.0	3.51	110	.290	.329	4	11	106	119	0.5	0	4	1.5
1975	Bos-A	17	9	.654	41	34	17	4	0	260	274	9.5	20	69	2.4	78	2.7	3.95	103	.273	.317	-5	4	108	95	2.2	0	1	0.5
1976	Bos-A	5	7	.417	24	14	1	0	3	96	124	11.6	13	28	2.6	29	2.7	5.63	69	.307	.352	-22	-19	110	94	-1.1	0	1	-1.7
1977	Bos-A	9	5	.643	27	16	4	0	1	128	155	10.9	14	29	2.0	31	2.2	4.43	107	.306	.339	-5	4	116	108	0.8	0	2	0.6
1978	Bos-A	10	10	.500	28	24	8	1	0	177	198	10.1	20	59	3.0	44	2.2	3.46	116	.285	.337	6	11	106	**131**	-1.9	0	0	1.1
1979	Mon-N	16	10	.615	33	33	6	3	0	222	230	9.3	20	46	1.9	59	2.4	3.04	124	.265	.299	17	18	101	113	0.8	2	1	2.2
1980	Mon-N	4	6	.400	24	18	2	0	0	118	156	11.9	13	22	1.7	34	2.6	4.96	72	.319	.347	-18	-18	98	103	-1.4	1	0	-1.7
1981	Mon-N	5	6	.455	31	7	0	0	6	89	90	9.1	6	14	1.4	34	3.4	2.93	117	.265	.290	6	5	98	110	-1.0	3	3	1.2
1982	Mon-N	0	0	—	7	0	0	0	0	12	19	14.3	1	1	0.8	8	6.0	4.50	84	.352	.357	-1	-1	104	125	0.0	0	0	0.0
Total	14	119	90	.569	416	225	72	10	19	1944	2122	9.8	176	531	2.5	713	3.3	3.63	107	.280	.324	14	57	105	113	4.6	5	16	9.2
■ WATTY LEE	Lee, Wyatt Arnold b: 8/12/1879, Lynch's Station, Va. d: 3/6/36, Washington, D.C. TL, 5'10.5", 171 lbs. Deb: 4/30/01																												
1901	Was-A	16	16	.500	36	33	25	2	0	262	328	11.3	14	45	1.5	63	2.2	4.40	84	.327	.356	-21	-21	100	98	1.7	4	1	-1.2
1902	Was-A	5	7	.417	13	10	10	0	0	98	118	10.8	5	20	1.8	24	2.2	5.05	71	.324	.359	-16	-16	100	83	-0.4	3	1	-1.3
1903	Was-A	8	12	.400	22	20	15	2	0	167	169	9.1	5	40	2.2	70	3.8	3.07	107	.285	.330	-2	4	111	105	1.4	1	2	0.4
1904	Pit-N	1	2	.333	5	3	1	0	0	23	34	13.3	0	9	3.5	5	2.0	8.61	31	.382	.456	-15	-15	98	69	-0.5	1	0	-1.2
Total	4	30	37	.448	76	66	51	4	0	550	649	10.6	24	114	1.9	162	2.7	4.29	82	.317	.354	-55	-48	104	96	2.2	10	4	-3.3
■ SAM LEEVER	Leever, Samuel "Deacon" or "The Goshen Schoolmaster" b: 12/23/1871, Goshen, Ohio d: 5/19/53, Goshen, Ohio BR/TR, 5'10.5", 175 lbs. Deb: 5/26/1898																												
1898	Pit-N	1	0	1.000	5	3	2	0	0	33	26	7.1	0	5	1.4	15	4.1	2.45	144	.236	.269	4	4	98	62	0.5	0	0	0.4
1899	Pit-N	21	23	.477	**51**	39	35	4	**3**	**379**	353	8.4	7	122	2.9	121	2.9	3.18	119	.269	.331	28	25	98	88	-1.9	3	2	2.8
1900	Pit-N	15	13	.536	30	29	25	3	0	233	236	9.1	2	48	1.9	84	3.2	2.70	138	.285	.325	26	27	101	106	-0.9	-0	0	2.5
1901	Pit-N	14	5	.737	21	20	18	2	0	176	182	9.3	2	39	2.0	82	4.2	2.86	111	.291	.339	9	6	96	110	2.7	-0	1	0.8
1902	Pit-N	16	7	.696	28	26	23	4	2	222	203	8.2	2	31	1.3	86	3.5	2.39	114	.267	.301	10	8	98	89	-0.7	-0	-4	0.5
1903	Pit-N	25	7	**.781**	36	34	30	**7**	1	284	255	8.1	2	60	1.9	90	2.9	**2.06**	**161**	.264	.311	38	40	101	109	**7.0**	-4	-1	3.9
1904	Pit-N	18	11	.621	34	32	26	0	0	253	224	8.0	2	54	1.9	63	2.2	2.17	123	.262	.309	16	14	98	105	2.1	7	-1	1.3
1905	Pit-N	20	5	**.800**	33	29	20	3	1	230	199	7.8	3	54	2.1	81	3.2	2.70	113	.262	.321	7	9	102	92	6.3	-4	0	0.9
1906	Pit-N	22	7	.759	36	31	25	6	0	260	232	8.0	3	48	1.7	76	2.6	2.32	114	.267	.311	9	10	101	99	**6.3**	2	-6	0.4
1907	Pit-N	14	9	.609	31	24	17	5	0	217	182	7.5	3	46	1.9	65	2.7	1.66	152	.257	.310	19	21	102	125	0.6	-1	-5	1.8
1908	Pit-N	15	7	.682	38	20	14	4	2	193	179	8.3	1	41	1.9	28	1.3	2.10	103	.277	.326	5	1	92	119	1.6	0	-3	-0.1
1909	Pit-N	8	1	.889	19	4	2	0	2	70	74	9.5	0	14	1.8	23	3.0	2.83	91	.276	.322	-2	-2	99	107	2.8	0	0	-0.1
1910	Pit-N	6	5	.545	26	8	4	0	2	111	104	8.4	2	25	2.0	33	2.7	2.76	121	.259	.313	3	7	110	102	-0.1	-3	1	0.6
Total	13	195	100	.661	388	299	241	38	13	2661	2449	8.3	29	587	2.0	847	2.9	2.47	123	.269	.318	174	169	99	102	26.3	1	-15	15.7
■ BILL LeFEBVRE	LeFebvre, Wilfrid Henry "Lefty" b: 11/11/15, Natick, R.I. BL/TL, 5'11.5", 180 lbs. Deb: 6/10/38																												
1938	Bos-A	0	0	—	1	0	0	0	0	4	8	18.0	2	0	0.0	0	0.0	13.50	36	.400	.429	-4	-4	100	84	0.0	1	-0	-0.1
1939	Bos-A	1	1	.500	5	3	0	0	0	26	35	12.1	2	14	4.8	8	2.8	5.88	84	.333	.402	-4	-3	107	111	-0.1	1	-0	-0.1
1943	Was-A	2	0	1.000	6	3	1	0	0	32	33	9.3	3	16	4.5	10	2.8	4.50	75	.268	.350	-4	-4	102	99	1.0	2	0	-0.2
1944	Was-A	2	4	.333	24	4	2	0	3	70	86	11.1	3	21	2.7	18	2.3	4.50	69	.305	.348	-8	-11	91	100	-0.5	3	-0	-1.0
Total	4	5	5	.500	36	10	3	0	3	132	162	11.0	10	51	3.5	36	2.5	5.05	71	.306	.363	-20	-22	97	101	0.4	7	-1	-1.4
■ CRAIG LEFFERTS	Lefferts, Craig Lindsey b: 9/29/57, Munich, W.Germany BL/TL, 6'1", 180 lbs. Deb: 4/07/83																												
1983	Chi-N	3	4	.429	56	5	0	0	1	89	80	8.1	13	29	2.9	60	6.1	3.13	117	.243	.302	5	5	101	119	0.0	-1	0	0.5
1984	SD-N	3	4	.429	62	0	0	0	10	106	88	7.5	4	24	2.0	56	4.8	2.12	166	.229	.269	17	16	98	109	-0.8	1	-1	1.7
1985	SD-N	7	6	.538	60	0	0	0	2	83	75	8.1	7	30	3.3	48	5.2	3.36	109	.244	.304	2	3	101	101	0.4	0	-0	0.2
1986	SD-N	9	8	.529	**83**	0	0	0	4	108	98	8.2	7	44	3.7	72	6.0	3.08	116	.253	.321	8	6	96	120	1.3	1	2	0.8
1987	SD-N	2	2	.500	33	0	0	0	2	51	56	9.9	9	15	2.6	39	6.9	4.41	90	.272	.324	-2	-2	98	106	0.3	0	-1	-0.2
	SF-N	3	3	.500	44	0	0	0	4	47	36	6.9	4	18	3.4	18	3.4	3.26	119	.216	.283	4	3	95	87	-0.2	0	-0	0.3
	Yr	5	5	.500	77	0	0	0	6	98	92	8.4	13	33	3.0	57	5.2	3.86	102	.245	.300	2	1	96	87	0.1	0	-1	0.1
1988	SF-N	3	8	.273	64	0	0	0	11	92	74	7.2	7	23	2.3	58	5.7	2.93	110	.225	.271	5	3	93	92	-2.6	-1	-1	0.1
Total	6	30	35	.462	402	5	0	0	34	576	507	7.9	51	183	2.9	351	5.5	3.06	117	.240	.296	40	34	97	106	-1.6	2	-2	3.4
■ REGIS LEHENY	Leheny, Regis Francis b: 1/5/08, Pittsburgh, Pa. d: 11/2/76, Pittsburgh, Pa. BL/TL, 6'0.5", 180 lbs. Deb: 5/21/32																												
1932	Bos-A	0	0	—	2	0	0	0	0	3	5	15.0	0	3	9.0	1	3.0	15.00	31	.417	.500	-4	-3	102	66	0.0	-0	0	-0.2

YEAR	TM/L	W	L	PCT	G	GS	CG	SHO	SV	IP	H	H/G	HR	BB	BB/G	SO	SO/G	ERA	/A	OAVG	OOBP	PR	/A	PF	CPI	WAT	PB	PD	TPI
■ **JIM LEHEW**	Lehew, James Anthony b: 8/19/37, Baltimore, Md. BR/TR, 6', 185 lbs. Deb: 9/13/61																												
1961	Bal-A	0	0	—	2	0	0	0	0	2	1	4.5	0	0	0.0	0	0.0	0.00	—	.167	.143	1	1	96	0	0.0	0	0	0.1
1962	Bal-A	0	0	—	6	0	0	0	0	10	10	9.0	0	3	2.7	2	1.8	1.80	209	.303	.333	2	2	95	236	0.0	-0	0	0.2
Total	2	0	0	—	8	0	0	0	0	12	11	8.3	0	3	2.3	2	1.5	1.50	252	.282	.304	3	3	95	197	0.0	-0	0	0.3
■ **KEN LEHMAN**	Lehman, Kenneth Karl b: 6/10/28, Seattle, Wash. BL/TL, 6', 170 lbs. Deb: 9/05/52																												
1952	Bro-N	1	2	.333	4	3	0	0	0	15	19	11.4	1	6	3.6	7	4.2	5.40	68	.297	.357	-3	-3	98	88	-0.6	0	0	-0.2
1956	Bro-N	2	3	.400	25	4	0	0	0	49	65	11.9	11	23	4.2	29	5.3	5.69	66	.325	.381	-10	-10	100	120	-0.8	1	1	-0.8
1957	Bro-N	0	0	—	3	0	0	0	0	7	7	9.0	0	1	1.3	3	3.9	0.00	—	.259	.286	3	3	114	0	0.0	0	0	0.4
	Bal-A	8	3	.727	30	3	1	0	6	68	57	7.5	1	22	2.9	32	4.2	2.78	126	.232	.287	8	6	93	87	2.6	1	-0	0.7
1958	Bal-A	2	1	.667	31	1	1	0	0	62	64	9.3	5	18	2.6	36	5.2	3.48	103	.276	.319	2	1	95	117	0.5	-1	0	0.0
1961	Phi-N	1	1	.500	41	2	0	0	1	63	61	8.7	6	25	3.6	27	3.9	4.29	92	.260	.323	-2	-2	98	93	0.3	-1	1	-0.1
Total	5	14	10	.583	134	13	2	0	7	264	273	9.3	24	95	3.2	134	4.6	3.92	95	.272	.327	-2	-6	97	99	2.0	1	2	-0.0
■ **NORM LEHR**	Lehr, Norman Carl Michael "King" b: 5/28/01, Rochester, N.Y. d: 7/17/68, Livonia, N.Y. BR/TR, 6', 168 lbs. Deb: 5/20/26																												
1926	Cle-A	0	0	—	4	0	0	0	0	15	11	6.6	0	4	2.4	4	2.4	3.00	130	.216	.259	2	2	97	60	0.0	-1	1	0.1
■ **HANK LEIBER**	Leiber, Henry Edward b: 1/17/11, Phoenix, Ariz. BR/TR, 6'1.5", 205 lbs. Deb: 4/16/33																												
1942	NY-N	0	1	.000	1	1	1	0	0	9	9	9.0	0	5	5.0	5	5.0	6.00	56	.290	.357	-3	-3	101	81	-0.4	0	0	-0.1
■ **CHARLIE LEIBRANDT**	Leibrandt, Charles Louis b: 10/4/56, Chicago, Ill. BR/TL, 6'3", 195 lbs. Deb: 9/17/79																												
1979	Cin-N	0	0	—	3	0	0	0	0	4	2	4.5	0	2	4.5	1	2.3	0.00	—	.154	.250	2	2	96	0	0.0	0	0	0.2
1980	Cin-N	10	9	.526	36	27	5	2	0	174	200	10.3	15	54	2.8	62	3.2	4.24	86	.292	.340	-12	-11	101	106	-0.3	1	1	-0.8
1981	Cin-N	1	1	.500	7	4	1	1	0	30	28	8.4	0	15	4.5	9	2.7	3.60	97	.262	.336	-0	-0	101	101	-0.1	-0	0	0.0
1982	Cin-N	5	7	.417	36	11	0	0	2	108	130	10.8	4	48	4.0	34	2.8	5.08	74	.308	.372	-18	-16	104	97	0.4	-1	-0	-1.7
1984	KC-A	11	7	.611	23	23	0	0	0	144	158	9.9	11	38	2.4	53	3.3	3.63	110	.277	.320	6	6	99	108	1.9	0	-1	0.4
1985	KC-A	17	9	.654	33	33	8	3	0	238	223	8.4	17	68	2.6	108	4.1	2.68	157	.248	.298	39	40	101	**121**	3.1	0	4	4.7
1986	KC-A	14	11	.560	35	34	8	1	0	231	238	9.3	18	63	2.5	108	4.2	4.09	103	.268	.313	2	3	100	92	2.5	0	2	0.4
1987	KC-A	16	11	.593	35	35	8	3	0	240	235	8.8	23	74	2.8	151	5.7	3.41	136	.253	.305	28	33	104	104	2.6	0	4	3.7
1988	KC-A	13	12	.520	35	35	7	2	0	243	244	9.0	20	62	2.3	125	4.6	3.19	128	.264	.309	21	24	103	116	0.0	0	2	2.7
Total	9	87	67	.565	243	202	37	12	2	1412	1458	9.3	108	424	2.7	651	4.1	3.61	114	.268	.318	68	79	102	107	10.1	-0	12	9.6
■ **LEFTY LEIFIELD**	Leifield, Albert Peter b: 9/5/1883, Trenton, Ill. d: 10/10/70, Alexandria, Va. BL/TL, 6'1", 165 lbs. Deb: 9/03/05 C																												
1905	Pit-N	5	2	.714	8	7	6	1	0	56	52	8.4	0	14	2.3	10	1.6	2.89	105	.278	.341	1	1	102	96	0.8	3	1	0.2
1906	Pit-N	18	13	.581	37	31	24	8	1	256	214	7.5	3	68	2.4	111	3.9	1.86	142	.257	.323	22	22	101	125	-0.8	-3	1	2.7
1907	Pit-N	20	16	.556	40	33	24	6	1	286	270	8.5	1	100	3.1	112	3.5	2.33	108	.281	.356	4	6	102	125	-1.3	-0	3	1.0
1908	Pit-N	15	14	.517	34	26	18	5	2	219	168	6.9	1	86	3.5	87	3.6	2.10	103	.242	.336	6	2	92	109	-3.1	4	-0	0.1
1909	Pit-N	19	8	.704	32	27	13	3	0	202	172	7.7	4	54	2.4	43	1.9	2.36	109	.229	.286	5	5	99	89	-0.4	2	-2	0.3
1910	Pit-N	15	13	.536	40	30	13	3	2	218	197	8.1	6	67	2.8	64	2.6	2.64	126	.253	.320	9	17	110	111	-0.7	0	3	2.2
1911	Pit-N	16	16	.500	42	37	26	2	1	318	301	8.5	7	82	2.3	111	3.1	2.63	126	.260	.318	27	24	97	117	-1.8	7	-1	3.0
1912	Pit-N	1	2	.333	6	1	1	1	0	24	29	10.9	0	10	3.8	8	3.0	4.13	79	.290	.366	-2	-2	95	95	-0.6	0	1	0.0
	Chi-N	7	2	.778	13	9	4	1	0	71	68	8.6	0	21	2.7	23	2.9	2.41	144	.250	.311	8	8	102	100	2.0	-1	1	0.9
	Yr	8	4	.667	19	10	5	2	0	95	97	9.2	0	31	2.9	31	2.9	2.84	120	.259	.321	6	6	100	100	1.4	0	2	0.9
1913	Chi-N	0	1	.000	6	1	0	0	0	21	28	12.0	0	5	2.1	4	1.7	5.57	56	.329	.355	-6	-6	97	82	-0.4	-1	1	-0.5
1918	StL-A	2	6	.250	15	6	3	1	0	67	61	8.2	1	19	2.6	22	3.0	2.55	108	.252	.308	2	2	100	102	-1.9	-2	1	0.1
1919	StL-A	6	4	.600	19	9	6	2	0	92	96	9.4	4	25	2.4	18	1.8	2.93	107	.270	.325	3	2	98	110	1.2	-2	1	0.0
1920	StL-A	0	0	—	4	0	0	0	0	9	17	17.0	0	3	3.0	3	3.0	7.00	60	.405	.444	-3	-3	111	105	0.0	-0	-0	-0.2
Total	12	124	97	.561	296	217	138	33	7	1839	1673	8.2	27	554	2.7	616	3.0	2.47	115	.259	.325	77	77	100	112	-7.0	7	9	9.8
■ **DAVE LEIPER**	Leiper, David Paul b: 6/18/62, Whittier, Cal. BL/TL, 6'1", 160 lbs. Deb: 9/02/84																												
1984	Oak-A	1	0	1.000	8	0	0	0	0	7	12	15.4	2	5	6.4	3	3.9	9.00	41	.353	.436	-4	-4	92	101	0.5	0	0	-0.3
1986	Oak-A	2	2	.500	33	0	0	0	1	32	28	7.9	3	18	5.1	15	4.2	4.78	82	.252	.353	-2	-3	94	96	0.1	0	0	-0.2
1987	Oak-A	2	1	.667	45	0	0	0	1	52	49	8.5	6	18	3.1	33	5.7	3.81	107	.246	.304	4	1	91	97	0.5	0	1	0.2
	SD-N	1	0	1.000	12	0	0	0	1	16	16	9.0	2	5	2.8	10	5.6	4.50	89	.267	.313	-1	-1	98	93	0.5	0	-0	0.2
1988	SD-N	3	0	1.000	35	0	0	0	1	54	45	7.5	1	14	2.3	33	5.5	2.17	155	.231	.272	8	7	97	110	1.5	0	0	0.8
Total	4	9	3	.750	133	0	0	0	4	161	150	8.4	14	60	3.4	94	5.3	3.75	101	.250	.312	5	1	94	101	3.1	0	2	0.5
■ **JACK LEIPER**	Leiper, John Henry Thomas b: 12/23/1867, Chester, Pa. d: 8/23/60, West Goshen, Pa. BL/TL, 5'11", Deb: 9/04/1891																												
1891	Col-a	2	2	.500	6	5	4	0	0	45	41	8.2	3	39	7.8	19	3.8	5.40	62	.257	.402	-8	-10	90	83	0.2	-1	0	-0.9
■ **JOHN LEISTER**	Leister, John William b: 1/3/61, San Antonio, Tex. BR/TR, 6'2", 200 lbs. Deb: 5/28/87																												
1987	Bos-A	0	2	.000	8	6	0	0	0	30	49	14.7	9	12	3.6	16	4.8	9.30	48	.368	.418	-16	-16	99	95	-0.9	0	-0	-1.4
■ **AL LEITER**	Leiter, Alois Terry b: 10/23/65, Toms River, N.J. BL/TL, 6'2", 200 lbs. Deb: 9/15/87																												
1987	NY-A	2	2	.500	4	4	0	0	0	23	24	9.4	2	15	5.9	28	11.0	6.26	69	.273	.375	-5	-5	97	80	-0.1	0	-0	-0.4
1988	NY-A	4	4	.500	14	14	0	0	0	57	49	7.7	7	33	5.2	60	9.5	3.95	96	.231	.347	0	-1	96	108	-0.1	0	1	0.0
Total	2	6	6	.500	18	18	0	0	0	80	73	8.2	9	48	5.4	88	9.9	4.61	86	.243	.355	-4	-6	96	100	-0.2	0	1	-0.4
■ **SHADY BILL LEITH**	Leith, William b: 5/31/1873, Matteawan, N.Y. d: 7/16/40, Beacon, N.Y. Deb: 9/25/1899																												
1899	Was-N	0	0	—	1	0	0	0	0	2	4	18.0	0	2	9.0	1	4.5	18.00	21	.442	.542	-3	-3	98	54	0.0	-0	0	-0.2
■ **DOC LEITNER**	Leitner, George Aloysius b: 9/14/1865, Piermont, N.Y. d: 5/18/37, New York, N.Y. BR/TR, 5'11.5", 185 lbs. Deb: 8/10/1887																												
1887	Ind-N	2	6	.250	8	8	8	0	0	65	69	9.6	6	41	5.7	27	3.7	5.68	72	.287	.391	-12	-11	101	90	-0.5	-3	0	-1.0
■ **DUMMY LEITNER**	Leitner, George Michael b: 6/19/1871, Parkton, Md. d: 2/20/60, Baltimore, Md. 5'7", 120 lbs. Deb: 6/29/01																												
1901	Phi-A	0	0	—	1	0	0	0	0	2	1	4.5	0	1	4.5	1	4.5	0.00	—	.163	.280	1	1	100	0	0.0	-0	0	0.1
	NY-N	0	2	.000	2	2	2	0	0	18	27	13.5	0	4	2.0	3	1.5	4.50	70	.376	.416	-2	-3	95	120	-0.9	-0	-0	-0.2
1902	Cle-A	0	0	—	1	1	0	0	0	8	11	12.4	0	1	1.1	0	0.0	4.50	76	.353	.374	-1	-1	96	98	0.0	0	0	0.0
	Chi-A	0	0	—	1	0	0	0	0	4	9	20.3	0	2	4.5	0	0.0	13.50	25	.472	.522	-4	-5	94	73	0.0	-0	0	-0.2
	Yr	0	0	—	2	1	0	0	0	12	20	15.0	0	3	2.3	0	0.0	7.50	45	.399	.432	-5	-5	95	73	0.0	0	1	-0.2
Total	2	0	2	.000	5	3	2	0	0	32	48	13.5	0	8	2.3	4	1.1	5.34	61	.374	.415	-7	-7	96	101	-0.9	-1	0	-0.3
■ **BILL LELIVELT**	Lelivelt, William John b: 10/21/1884, Chicago, Ill. d: 2/14/68, Chicago, Ill. BR/TR, 6', 195 lbs. Deb: 7/19/09																												
1909	Det-A	0	1	.000	4	2	1	0	1	20	27	12.1	0	2	0.9	4	1.8	4.50	59	.325	.341	-4	-4	106	84	-0.4	1	0	-0.3
1910	Det-A	0	1	.000	1	1	1	0	0	9	6	6.0	0	3	3.0	2	2.0	1.00	251	.207	.281	2	2	100	171	-0.4	1	0	0.2
Total	2	0	2	.000	5	3	2	0	1	29	33	10.2	0	5	1.6	6	1.9	3.41	76	.295	.325	-3	-3	104	111	-0.8	2	0	-0.1
■ **DAVE LEMANCZYK**	Lemanczyk, David Lawrence b: 8/17/50, Syracuse, N.Y. BR/TR, 6'4", 235 lbs. Deb: 4/15/73																												
1973	Det-A	0	0	—	1	0	0	0	0	2	4	18.0	0	0	0.0	0	0.0	13.50	29	.364	.364	-2	-2	101	39	0.0	0	0	-0.1
1974	Det-A	2	1	.667	22	3	0	0	0	79	79	9.0	12	44	5.0	52	5.9	3.99	98	.261	.355	-3	-1	108	121	0.6	0	1	0.0
1975	Det-A	2	7	.222	26	6	4	0	0	109	120	9.9	8	46	3.8	67	5.5	4.46	90	.281	.347	-8	-5	106	98	-1.7	0	0	-0.4
1976	Det-A	4	6	.400	20	10	1	0	0	81	86	9.6	7	34	3.8	51	5.7	5.11	72	.271	.338	-14	-13	105	82	-0.6	0	1	-1.1
1977	Tor-A	13	16	.448	34	34	11	0	0	252	278	9.9	20	87	3.1	105	3.8	4.25	100	.282	.338	-5	0	105	100	2.9	0	0	0.0
1978	Tor-A	4	14	.222	29	20	3	0	0	137	170	11.2	16	65	4.3	62	4.1	6.24	62	.313	.384	-37	-36	102	92	-3.7	0	-0	-3.5
1979	Tor-A	8	10	.444	22	20	11	3	0	143	137	8.6	12	45	2.8	63	4.0	3.71	120	.258	.315	8	12	106	101	1.7	0	0	1.2
1980	Tor-A	2	5	.286	10	8	0	0	0	43	57	11.9	4	15	3.1	10	2.1	5.44	75	.322	.369	-7	-6	101	100	-1.0	0	1	-0.5
	Cal-A	2	4	.333	21	2	0	0	0	67	81	10.9	8	27	3.6	19	2.6	4.30	91	.301	.363	-2	-3	97	123	-0.5	0	-1	-0.3
	Yr	4	9	.308	31	10	0	0	0	110	138	11.3	12	42	3.4	29	2.4	4.75	84	.308	.365	-9	-9	99	123	-1.5	0	-1	-0.8
Total	8	37	63	.370	185	103	30	3	0	913	1012	10.0	87	363	3.6	429	4.2	4.62	89	.284	.348	-71	-54	104	100	-2.3	0	0	-4.7
■ **DENNY LEMASTER**	Lemaster, Denver Clayton b: 2/25/39, Corona, Cal. BR/TL, 6'1", 182 lbs. Deb: 7/15/62																												
1962	Mil-N	3	4	.429	17	12	4	1	0	87	75	7.8	11	32	3.3	69	7.1	3.00	129	.233	.304	9	8	98	117	-0.6	-1	-2	0.5

YEAR	TM/L	W	L	PCT	G	GS	CG	SHO	SV	IP	H	H/G	HR	BB	BB/G	SO	SO/G	ERA	/A	OAVG	OOBP	PR	/A	PF	CPI	WAT	PB	PD	TPI
1963	Mil-N	11	14	.440	46	31	10	1	1	237	199	7.6	30	85	3.2	190	7.2	3.04	108	.227	.292	7	6	100	107	-2.1	3	-3	0.7
1964	Mil-N	17	11	.607	39	35	9	3	1	221	216	8.8	27	75	3.1	185	7.5	4.15	82	.252	.311	-15	-19	96	93	2.3	1	0	-1.8
1965	Mil-N	7	13	.350	32	23	4	1	0	146	140	8.6	12	58	3.6	111	6.8	4.44	82	.251	.322	-15	-13	103	84	-3.6	-2	-0	-1.4
1966	Atl-N	11	8	.579	27	27	10	3	0	171	170	8.9	25	41	2.2	139	7.3	3.74	94	.258	.299	-2	-4	97	102	1.2	-1	-2	-0.6
1967	Atl-N	9	9	.500	31	31	8	2	0	215	184	7.7	20	72	3.0	148	6.2	3.35	105	.229	.291	1	4	105	90	0.5	-2	-0	0.2
1968	Hou-N	10	15	.400	33	32	7	2	0	224	231	9.3	11	72	2.9	146	5.9	2.81	107	.262	.318	4	5	100	122	-1.4	-4	-3	-0.1
1969	Hou-N	13	17	.433	38	37	11	1	1	245	232	8.5	20	72	2.6	173	6.4	3.16	115	.246	.296	12	13	101	99	-2.3	3	-1	1.6
1970	Hou-N	7	12	.368	39	21	3	0	3	162	169	9.4	22	65	3.6	103	5.7	4.56	83	.268	.333	-9	-14	94	100	-2.4	2	-1	-1.2
1971	Hou-N	0	2	.000	42	0	0	0	2	60	59	8.9	4	22	3.3	28	4.2	3.45	93	.262	.324	0	-2	92	107	-0.9	-0	0	-0.1
1972	Mon-N	2	0	1.000	13	0	0	0	0	20	28	12.6	2	6	2.7	13	5.8	7.65	47	.329	.376	-9	-9	104	75	1.0	1	-0	-0.8
Total	11	90	105	.462	357	249	66	14	8	1788	1703	8.6	184	600	3.0	1305	6.6	3.58	97	.249	.308	-18	-22	99	101	-8.3	-0	-12	-3.0

■ **DICK LeMAY** LeMay, Richard Paul b: 8/28/38, Cincinnati, Ohio BL/TL, 6'3", 190 lbs. Deb: 6/13/61

YEAR	TM/L	W	L	PCT	G	GS	CG	SHO	SV	IP	H	H/G	HR	BB	BB/G	SO	SO/G	ERA	/A	OAVG	OOBP	PR	/A	PF	CPI	WAT	PB	PD	TPI
1961	SF-N	3	6	.333	27	5	1	0	3	83	65	7.0	11	36	3.9	54	5.9	3.58	108	.217	.302	4	3	96	95	-1.7	-1	-0	0.1
1962	SF-N	0	1	.000	9	0	0	0	1	9	9	9.0	2	9	9.0	5	5.0	8.00	49	.265	.400	-4	-4	99	84	-0.4	0	0	-0.3
1963	Chi-N	0	1	.000	9	1	0	0	0	15	26	15.6	1	4	2.4	10	6.0	5.40	64	.394	.405	-4	-3	105	135	-0.4	-0	0	-0.3
Total	3	3	8	.273	45	6	1	0	4	107	100	8.4	14	49	4.1	69	5.8	4.21	91	.250	.328	-3	-4	98	99	-2.5	-1	-0	-0.5

■ **BOB LEMON** Lemon, Robert Granville b: 9/22/20, San Bernardino, Cal. BL/TR, 6', 180 lbs. Deb: 9/09/41 MCH

YEAR	TM/L	W	L	PCT	G	GS	CG	SHO	SV	IP	H	H/G	HR	BB	BB/G	SO	SO/G	ERA	/A	OAVG	OOBP	PR	/A	PF	CPI	WAT	PB	PD	TPI
1946	Cle-A	4	5	.444	32	5	1	0	1	94	77	7.4	1	68	6.5	39	3.7	2.49	127	.229	.352	11	7	90	138	0.0	2	4	1.3
1947	Cle-A	11	5	.688	37	15	6	1	3	167	150	8.1	7	97	5.2	65	3.5	3.45	101	.242	.346	5	1	94	107	3.0	8	4	1.6
1948	Cle-A	20	14	.588	43	37	**20**	**10**	2	**294**	231	7.1	12	129	3.9	147	4.5	2.82	143	.216	.299	**48**	39	94	97	-1.2	13	9	**6.3**
1949	Cle-A	22	10	.688	37	33	22	2	1	280	211	6.8	19	137	4.4	138	4.4	2.99	135	.211	.305	38	32	96	96	4.9	15	6	5.6
1950	Cle-A	**23**	11	.676	44	37	**22**	3	3	**288**	281	8.8	28	146	4.6	**170**	5.3	3.84	114	.257	.342	23	17	95	111	4.1	16	5	3.6
1951	Cle-A	17	14	.548	42	34	17	1	2	263	244	8.3	19	124	4.2	132	4.5	3.52	108	.244	.325	17	9	93	103	-1.6	4	4	1.6
1952	Cle-A	22	11	.667	42	36	**28**	5	4	**310**	236	**6.9**	15	105	3.0	131	3.8	2.50	129	**.208**	.277	41	25	88	88	3.2	7	7	4.0
1953	Cle-A	21	15	.583	41	36	23	5	1	**287**	283	8.9	16	110	3.4	98	3.1	3.36	110	.262	.332	20	11	93	113	-0.4	8	8	2.8
1954	Cle-A	**23**	7	.767	36	33	**21**	2	0	258	228	8.0	12	92	3.2	110	3.8	2.72	138	.237	.301	29	30	101	104	2.9	5	4	**4.3**
1955	Cle-A	**18**	10	.643	35	31	5	0	2	211	218	9.3	17	74	3.2	100	4.3	3.88	104	.266	.327	2	4	102	99	1.6	6	2	1.2
1956	Cle-A	20	14	.588	39	35	**21**	2	3	255	230	8.1	23	89	3.1	94	3.3	3.04	136	.239	.303	32	31	99	106	0.8	5	4	4.1
1957	Cle-A	6	11	.353	21	17	2	0	0	117	129	9.9	9	64	4.9	45	3.5	4.62	84	.287	.370	-11	-10	102	110	-2.6	-3	3	-0.9
1958	Cle-A	0	1	.000	11	1	0	0	0	25	41	14.8	3	16	5.8	8	2.9	5.40	65	.376	.453	-5	-5	93	154	-0.4	0	1	-0.3
Total	13	207	128	.618	460	350	188	31	22	2849	2559	8.1	181	1251	4.0	1277	4.0	3.23	119	.241	.320	250	190	95	104	14.3	86	59	35.2

■ **DAVE LEMONDS** Lemonds, David Lee b: 7/5/48, Charlotte, N.C. BL/TL, 6'1.5", 180 lbs. Deb: 6/30/69

YEAR	TM/L	W	L	PCT	G	GS	CG	SHO	SV	IP	H	H/G	HR	BB	BB/G	SO	SO/G	ERA	/A	OAVG	OOBP	PR	/A	PF	CPI	WAT	PB	PD	TPI
1969	Chi-N	0	1	.000	2	1	0	0	0	5	5	9.0	0	5	9.0	0	0.0	3.60	105	.313	.476	-0	0	105	175	-0.4	-0	0	0.0
1972	Chi-A	4	7	.364	31	18	0	0	0	95	87	8.2	6	38	3.6	69	6.5	2.94	111	.247	.315	1	3	106	113	-2.0	-1	-0	0.3
Total	2	4	8	.333	33	19	0	0	0	100	92	8.3	6	43	3.9	69	6.2	2.97	110	.250	.323	1	3	106	116	-2.4	-1	-0	0.3

■ **MARK LEMONGELLO** Lemongello, Mark b: 7/21/55, Jersey City, N.J. BR/TR, 6'1", 180 lbs. Deb: 9/14/76

YEAR	TM/L	W	L	PCT	G	GS	CG	SHO	SV	IP	H	H/G	HR	BB	BB/G	SO	SO/G	ERA	/A	OAVG	OOBP	PR	/A	PF	CPI	WAT	PB	PD	TPI
1976	Hou-N	3	1	.750	4	4	1	0	0	29	26	8.1	2	7	2.2	9	2.8	2.79	109	.236	.270	2	1	87	95	1.0	-0	1	0.1
1977	Hou-N	9	14	.391	34	30	5	0	0	215	237	9.9	20	52	2.2	83	3.5	3.47	104	.281	.321	11	3	92	116	-2.7	-3	-0	0.0
1978	Hou-N	9	14	.391	33	30	9	1	1	210	204	8.7	20	66	2.8	77	3.3	3.94	86	.259	.312	-8	-13	95	96	-1.8	1	-0	-1.2
1979	Tor-A	1	9	.100	18	10	2	0	0	83	97	10.5	14	34	3.7	40	4.3	6.29	71	.299	.363	-19	-17	106	91	-3.4	0	1	-1.4
Total	4	22	38	.367	89	74	17	1	1	537	564	9.5	56	159	2.7	209	3.5	4.06	89	.273	.322	-15	-26	95	103	-6.9	-3	1	-2.5

■ **ED LENNON** Lennon, Edward Francis b: 8/17/1897, Philadelphia, Pa. d: 9/13/47, Philadelphia, Pa. BR/TR, 5'11", 170 lbs. Deb: 6/30/28

YEAR	TM/L	W	L	PCT	G	GS	CG	SHO	SV	IP	H	H/G	HR	BB	BB/G	SO	SO/G	ERA	/A	OAVG	OOBP	PR	/A	PF	CPI	WAT	PB	PD	TPI
1928	Phi-N	0	0	—	5	0	0	0	0	12	19	14.3	0	10	7.5	6	4.5	9.00	48	.373	.446	-7	-6	109	84	0.0	-1	-0	-0.6

■ **IZZY LEON** Leon, Isidoro (Becerra) b: 1/4/11, Cruces, Las Villas, Cuba BR/TR, 5'10", 160 lbs. Deb: 6/21/45

YEAR	TM/L	W	L	PCT	G	GS	CG	SHO	SV	IP	H	H/G	HR	BB	BB/G	SO	SO/G	ERA	/A	OAVG	OOBP	PR	/A	PF	CPI	WAT	PB	PD	TPI
1945	Phi-N	0	4	.000	14	4	0	0	0	39	49	11.3	3	19	4.4	11	2.5	5.31	73	.312	.380	-7	-6	102	105	-1.9	-0	0	-0.5

■ **MAX LEON** Leon, Maximino (Molino) b: 2/4/50, Pozo Hondo, Aculo, Mexico BR/TR, 5'10", 145 lbs. Deb: 7/18/73

YEAR	TM/L	W	L	PCT	G	GS	CG	SHO	SV	IP	H	H/G	HR	BB	BB/G	SO	SO/G	ERA	/A	OAVG	OOBP	PR	/A	PF	CPI	WAT	PB	PD	TPI
1973	Atl-N	2	2	.500	12	1	1	0	0	27	30	10.0	6	9	3.0	18	6.0	5.33	78	.278	.341	-5	-4	113	101	0.1	0	-0	-0.3
1974	Atl-N	4	7	.364	34	2	1	1	3	75	68	8.2	5	14	1.7	38	4.6	2.64	142	.242	.279	8	9	104	100	-1.8	-1	1	1.0
1975	Atl-N	2	1	.667	50	1	0	0	6	85	90	9.5	5	33	3.5	53	5.6	4.13	85	.274	.341	-5	-6	97	100	0.7	1	1	-0.3
1976	Atl-N	2	4	.333	30	0	0	0	3	36	32	8.0	2	15	3.8	16	4.0	2.75	143	.234	.314	3	5	112	113	-0.6	-0	-1	0.4
1977	Atl-N	4	4	.500	31	9	0	0	1	82	89	9.8	9	25	2.7	44	4.8	3.95	114	.280	.343	-0	5	115	116	0.8	1	0	0.7
1978	Atl-N	0	0	—	5	0	0	0	0	6	6	9.0	1	4	6.0	1	1.5	6.00	68	.273	.379	-2	-1	114	101	0.0	0	0	0.0
Total	6	14	18	.438	162	13	2	1	13	311	315	9.1	28	100	2.9	170	4.9	3.70	107	.264	.325	-0	8	107	106	-0.8	1	1	1.5

■ **DENNIS LEONARD** Leonard, Dennis Patrick b: 5/18/51, Brooklyn, N.Y. BR/TR, 6'1", 190 lbs. Deb: 9/04/74

YEAR	TM/L	W	L	PCT	G	GS	CG	SHO	SV	IP	H	H/G	HR	BB	BB/G	SO	SO/G	ERA	/A	OAVG	OOBP	PR	/A	PF	CPI	WAT	PB	PD	TPI
1974	KC-A	0	4	.000	5	4	0	0	0	22	28	11.5	0	12	4.9	8	3.3	5.32	72	.329	.410	-4	-4	106	109	-1.9	0	1	-0.2
1975	KC-A	15	7	.682	32	30	8	0	0	212	212	9.0	18	90	3.8	146	6.2	3.78	101	.263	.340	0	1	101	108	3.3	0	0	0.1
1976	KC-A	17	10	.630	35	34	16	2	0	259	247	8.6	16	70	2.4	150	5.2	3.51	99	.255	.306	0	-1	99	95	2.6	0	-4	-0.4
1977	KC-A	**20**	12	.625	38	37	21	5	1	293	246	7.6	18	79	2.4	244	7.5	3.04	132	.227	.281	34	32	99	83	0.0	0	-2	3.1
1978	KC-A	21	17	.553	40	40	20	4	0	295	283	8.6	27	78	2.4	183	5.6	3.33	115	.254	.304	15	16	101	102	-0.6	0	0	1.7
1979	KC-A	14	12	.538	32	32	12	**5**	0	236	226	8.6	33	56	2.1	126	4.8	4.08	109	.253	.294	4	9	105	90	0.4	0	0	0.9
1980	KC-A	20	11	.645	38	38	9	3	0	280	271	8.7	30	80	2.6	155	5.0	3.79	104	.253	.300	8	4	97	92	2.2	0	-0	0.4
1981	KC-A	13	11	.542	26	26	9	2	0	**202**	202	9.0	15	41	1.8	107	4.8	2.99	121	.258	.294	15	14	99	107	1.7	0	0	1.6
1982	KC-A	10	6	.625	21	21	2	0	0	131	145	10.0	20	46	3.2	58	4.0	5.08	80	.279	.333	-15	-15	100	94	1.4	0	0	-1.3
1983	KC-A	6	3	.667	10	10	1	0	0	63	69	9.9	3	19	2.7	31	4.4	3.71	112	.277	.326	3	3	102	102	1.6	0	0	0.3
1985	KC-A	0	0	—	2	0	0	0	0	2	1	4.5	0	0	0.0	1	4.5	0.00	—	.143	.143	1	1	101	0	0.0	0	0	0.1
1986	KC-A	8	13	.381	33	30	5	2	0	193	207	9.7	22	51	2.4	114	5.3	4.43	95	.275	.319	-5	-5	100	95	-2.1	0	0	-0.4
Total	12	144	106	.576	312	302	103	23	1	2188	2137	8.8	202	622	2.6	1323	5.4	3.69	106	.257	.307	56	57	100	96	8.6	0	-3	5.9

■ **ELMER LEONARD** Leonard, Elmer Ellsworth "Tiny" b: 11/12/1888, Napa, Cal. d: 5/27/81, Napa, Cal. BR/TR, 6'3.5", 210 lbs. Deb: 6/22/11

YEAR	TM/L	W	L	PCT	G	GS	CG	SHO	SV	IP	H	H/G	HR	BB	BB/G	SO	SO/G	ERA	/A	OAVG	OOBP	PR	/A	PF	CPI	WAT	PB	PD	TPI
1911	Phi-A	2	2	.500	5	1	1	0	0	19	26	12.3	0	10	4.7	10	4.7	2.84	104	.329	.418	1	0	88	194	-0.4	1	-0	0.0

■ **DUTCH LEONARD** Leonard, Emil John b: 3/25/09, Auburn, Ill. d: 4/17/83, Springfield, Ill. BR/TR, 6', 175 lbs. Deb: 8/31/33 C

YEAR	TM/L	W	L	PCT	G	GS	CG	SHO	SV	IP	H	H/G	HR	BB	BB/G	SO	SO/G	ERA	/A	OAVG	OOBP	PR	/A	PF	CPI	WAT	PB	PD	TPI
1933	Bro-N	2	3	.400	10	3	2	0	0	40	42	9.4	0	10	2.3	6	1.3	2.93	112	.261	.301	2	2	98	92	-0.1	-1	0	0.0
1934	Bro-N	14	11	.560	44	20	11	2	5	184	210	10.3	12	33	1.6	58	2.8	3.28	118	.286	.318	16	12	95	121	2.5	-1	1	1.2
1935	Bro-N	2	9	.182	43	11	4	0	**8**	138	152	9.9	11	29	1.9	41	2.7	3.91	97	.280	.314	2	-2	95	102	-3.3	-4	-1	-0.6
1936	Bro-N	0	0	—	16	0	0	0	1	32	34	9.6	2	5	1.4	8	2.3	3.66	117	.262	.281	1	2	107	83	0.0	0	1	0.4
1938	Was-A	12	15	.444	33	31	15	3	0	223	221	8.9	11	53	**2.1**	68	2.7	3.43	134	.256	**.299**	34	29	96	96	-1.6	3	0	2.9
1939	Was-A	20	8	.714	34	34	21	2	0	269	273	9.1	16	59	2.0	88	2.9	3.55	119	.262	.297	32	20	91	98	**7.7**	1	2	2.0
1940	Was-A	14	19	.424	35	35	23	2	0	289	328	10.2	19	78	2.4	124	3.9	3.49	120	.286	.328	29	22	95	122	0.3	-4	4	2.1
1941	Was-A	18	13	.581	34	33	19	4	0	256	271	9.5	6	54	1.9	91	3.2	3.45	119	.270	.306	20	19	99	96	4.2	-5	-1	1.2
1942	Was-A	2	2	.500	6	5	1	1	0	35	28	7.2	1	5	1.3	15	3.9	4.11	88	.214	.239	-2	-2	99	40	0.3	-0	0	-0.1
1943	Was-A	11	13	.458	31	30	15	2	1	220	218	8.9	9	46	**1.9**	51	2.1	3.27	103	.257	.294	1	2	102	91	-2.2	-5	2	0.0
1944	Was-A	14	14	.500	32	31	17	3	0	229	222	8.7	8	37	1.5	62	2.4	3.07	101	.252	.280	9	1	91	85	2.4	2	1	0.4
1945	Was-A	17	7	.708	31	29	12	4	1	216	208	8.7	5	35	1.5	96	4.0	2.13	146	.248	.277	30	23	92	112	4.4	1	0	2.6
1946	Was-A	10	10	.500	26	23	7	2	0	162	182	10.1	9	36	2.0	62	3.4	3.56	93	.281	.319	-1	-5	94	103	0.1	-0	3	-0.2
1947	Phi-N	17	12	.586	32	29	19	3	0	235	224	8.6	14	57	2.2	103	3.9	2.68	155	.258	.300	36	38	102	123	5.1	-1	2	4.2
1948	Phi-N	12	17	.414	34	31	16	1	0	226	226	9.0	9	54	2.2	92	3.7	2.51	152	.265	.309	36	33	97	**135**	-0.5	-2	3	3.6
1949	Chi-N	7	16	.304	33	28	10	1	0	180	198	9.9	4	43	2.2	83	4.2	4.15	95	.272	.315	-2	-4	97	81	-2.9	0	1	-0.2
1950	Chi-N	5	1	.833	35	1	0	0	6	74	70	8.5	7	27	3.3	28	3.4	3.77	118	.248	.311	3	5	107	97	2.2	-2	0	0.4
1951	Chi-N	10	6	.625	41	1	0	0	3	82	69	7.6	3	28	3.1	30	3.3	2.63	150	.234	.294	12	12	100	108	3.2	-3	2	1.1
1952	Chi-N	2	2	.500	45	0	0	0	11	67	56	7.5	3	24	3.2	37	5.0	2.15	179	.235	.294	12	13	103	146	0.0	-0	2	1.6

YEAR	TM/L	W	L	PCT	G	GS	CG	SHO	SV	IP	H	H/G	HR	BB	BB/G	SO	SO/G	ERA	/A	OAVG	OOBP	PR	/A	PF	CPI	WAT	PB	PD	TPI
1953	Chi-N	2	3	.400	45	0	0	0	8	63	72	10.3	9	24	3.4	27	3.9	4.57	100	.289	.351	-2	-0	106	113	0.0	1	0	0.1
Total	20	191	181	.513	640	375	192	30	44	3220	3304	9.2	158	737	2.1	1170	3.3	3.25	119	.265	.304	267	221	97	105	21.8	-20	23	22.7
■ DUTCH LEONARD		Leonard, Hubert Benjamin b: 4/16/1892, Birmingham, Ohio d: 7/11/52, Fresno, Cal. BL/TL, 5'10.5", 185 lbs. Deb: 4/12/13																											
1913	Bos-A	14	16	.467	42	28	14	3	1	259	245	8.5	0	94	3.3	144	5.0	2.40	125	.253	.321	15	18	103	113	-2.0	1	-2	1.7
1914	Bos-A	19	5	.792	36	25	17	7	3	225	139	**5.6**	3	60	2.4	176	**7.0**	**0.96**	**274**	**.180**	**.246**	**44**	42	96	98	**6.3**	-1	-3	4.6
1915	Bos-A	15	7	.682	32	21	10	2	0	183	130	**6.4**	3	67	3.3	116	**5.7**	2.36	120	**.208**	.299	12	9	96	91	0.5	5	-4	1.0
1916	Bos-A	18	12	.600	48	34	17	6	6	274	244	8.0	6	66	2.2	144	4.7	2.36	110	.247	.300	14	7	92	108	0.4	2	-6	0.3
1917	Bos-A	16	17	.485	37	36	26	4	1	294	257	7.9	5	72	2.2	144	4.4	2.17	130	.236	.286	16	21	106	95	-3.5	-7	-5	1.1
1918	Bos-A	8	6	.571	16	16	12	3	0	126	119	8.5	0	53	3.8	47	3.4	2.71	95	.254	.321	1	-2	93	105	-0.2	1	-2	-0.3
1919	Det-A	14	13	.519	29	28	18	4	0	217	212	8.8	7	65	2.7	102	4.2	2.78	107	.254	.313	11	5	92	99	-1.4	-3	-3	-0.2
1920	Det-A	10	17	.370	28	27	10	3	0	191	192	9.0	8	63	3.0	76	3.6	4.34	93	.271	.338	-11	-7	106	82	-0.9	1	-1	-0.6
1921	Det-A	11	13	.458	36	32	16	1	1	245	273	10.0	15	63	2.3	120	4.4	3.75	109	.286	.327	15	10	96	105	-0.1	-4	-2	0.3
1924	Det-A	3	2	.600	9	7	3	0	1	51	68	12.0	1	18	3.2	26	4.6	4.59	91	.327	.375	-2	-2	99	111	0.2	-0	-0	-0.2
1925	Det-A	11	4	.733	18	18	9	0	0	126	143	10.2	7	43	3.1	65	4.6	4.50	96	.289	.337	-2	-3	98	92	3.5	-1	-2	-0.5
Total	11	139	112	.554	331	272	152	33	13	2191	2022	8.3	55	664	2.7	1160	4.8	2.76	115	.249	.309	113	98	98	100	2.8	-5	-31	7.2
■ DAVE LEONHARD		Leonhard, David Paul b: 1/22/42, Arlington, Va. BR/TR, 5'11", 165 lbs. Deb: 9/21/67																											
1967	Bal-A	0	0	—	3	2	0	0	1	14	11	7.1	1	6	3.9	9	5.8	3.21	94	.200	.290	0	-0	94	76	0.0	0	0	0.0
1968	Bal-A	7	7	.500	28	18	5	2	1	126	95	6.8	10	57	4.1	61	4.4	3.14	95	.216	.304	-2	-2	101	97	-0.7	-1	1	-0.1
1969	Bal-A	7	4	.636	37	3	1	1	1	94	78	7.5	8	38	3.6	37	3.5	2.49	146	.228	.302	12	12	100	124	-0.2	-0	-0	1.2
1970	Bal-A	0	0	—	23	0	0	0	1	28	32	10.3	5	18	5.8	14	4.5	5.14	68	.294	.379	-4	-5	94	119	0.0	0	1	-0.3
1971	Bal-A	2	3	.400	12	6	1	1	1	54	51	8.5	5	19	3.2	18	3.0	2.83	123	.252	.314	4	4	100	126	-0.9	1	1	0.6
1972	Bal-A	0	0	—	14	0	0	0	0	20	20	9.0	3	12	5.4	7	3.1	4.50	66	.260	.348	-3	-3	96	107	0.0	1	0	-0.2
Total	6	16	14	.533	117	29	7	4	5	336	287	7.7	32	150	4.0	146	3.9	3.16	104	.234	.314	6	5	99	111	-1.8	1	3	1.2
■ RUDY LEOPOLD		Leopold, Rudolph Matas b: 7/27/05, Grand Cane, La. d: 9/3/65, Baton Rouge, La. BL/TL, 6', 160 lbs. Deb: 7/04/28																											
1928	Chi-A	0	0	—	2	0	0	0	0	2	3	13.5	0	0	0.0	0	0.0	4.50	90	.273	.250	-0	-0	100	39	0.0	-0	-0	0.0
■ RANDY LERCH		Lerch, Randy Louis b: 10/9/54, Sacramento, Cal. BL/TL, 6'5", 190 lbs. Deb: 9/14/75																											
1975	Phi-N	0	0	—	3	0	0	0	0	7	6	7.7	1	1	1.3	8	10.3	6.43	57	.231	.259	-2	-2	101	43	0.0	0	-0	-0.1
1976	Phi-N	0	0	—	1	0	0	0	1	3	3	9.0	0	0	0.0	0	0.0	3.00	122	.250	.250	0	0	105	57	0.0	1	0	0.1
1977	Phi-N	10	6	.625	32	28	3	0	0	169	207	11.0	20	75	4.0	81	4.3	5.06	76	.312	.372	-22	-23	98	112	0.0	0	2	-1.9
1978	Phi-N	11	8	.579	33	28	5	0	0	184	183	9.0	15	70	3.4	96	4.7	3.96	94	.263	.324	-8	-5	104	98	0.6	7	1	0.3
1979	Phi-N	10	13	.435	37	35	6	1	0	214	228	9.6	20	60	2.5	92	3.9	3.74	97	.281	.324	-0	-2	97	111	-2.0	2	2	0.0
1980	Phi-N	4	14	.222	30	22	2	0	0	150	178	10.7	15	55	3.3	57	3.4	5.16	74	.302	.351	-26	-22	106	97	-5.6	4	1	-1.7
1981	Mil-A	7	9	.438	23	18	1	0	0	111	134	10.9	8	43	3.5	53	4.3	4.30	81	.303	.358	-8	-10	95	114	-2.0	0	0	-0.9
1982	Mil-A	8	7	.533	21	20	1	1	0	109	123	10.2	12	51	4.2	33	2.7	4.95	76	.286	.359	-11	-14	92	102	-0.6	0	-1	-1.4
	Mon-N	2	0	1.000	6	4	0	0	0	24	26	9.8	0	8	3.0	4	1.5	3.38	111	.289	.333	1	1	104	113	1.0	0	0	0.1
1983	Mon-N	1	3	.250	19	5	0	0	0	39	45	10.4	6	18	4.2	24	5.5	6.69	55	.292	.364	-13	-13	101	81	-0.9	1	-0	-1.2
	SF-N	1	0	1.000	7	0	0	0	0	11	9	7.4	1	8	6.5	6	4.9	3.27	112	.231	.354	0	0	101	126	0.5	0	0	0.1
	Yr	2	3	.400	26	5	0	0	0	50	54	9.7	7	26	4.7	30	5.4	5.94	62	.277	.357	-13	-13	101	126	-0.4	1	-0	-1.1
1984	SF-N	5	3	.625	37	4	0	0	2	72	80	10.0	3	36	4.5	48	6.0	4.25	83	.287	.359	-5	-6	98	108	1.5	1	1	-0.4
1986	Phi-N	1	1	.500	4	0	0	0	0	8	10	11.3	0	7	7.9	5	5.6	7.88	49	.286	.405	-4	-4	104	65	0.0	1	0	-0.2
Total	11	60	64	.484	253	164	18	2	3	1101	1232	10.1	101	432	3.5	507	4.1	4.52	82	.289	.347	-97	-99	100	105	-7.5	15	4	-7.2
■ LOUIS LeROY		LeRoy, Louis Paul "Chief" b: 2/18/1879, Omro Village, Wis. d: 10/10/44, Shawano, Wis. BR/TR, 5'10", 180 lbs. Deb: 9/22/05																											
1905	NY-A	1	1	.500	3	3	2	0	0	24	26	9.8	2	1	0.4	8	3.0	3.75	72	.302	.310	-3	-3	103	93	0.0	-0	-0	-0.2
1906	NY-A	2	0	1.000	11	2	1	0	1	45	33	6.6	0	12	2.4	28	5.6	2.20	144	.227	.286	2	5	118	76	1.0	-1	1	0.7
1910	Bos-A	0	0	—	1	0	0	0	0	4	7	15.8	1	2	4.5	3	6.8	11.25	22	.389	.450	-4	-4	97	80	0.0	-0	0	-0.3
Total	3	3	1	.750	15	5	3	0	1	73	66	8.1	3	15	1.8	39	4.8	3.21	93	.264	.306	-4	-2	112	82	1.0	-1	1	0.2
■ BARRY LERSCH		Lersch, Barry Lee b: 9/7/44, Denver, Colo. BL/TR, 6', 175 lbs. Deb: 4/08/69																											
1969	Phi-N	0	3	.000	10	0	0	0	2	18	20	10.0	6	10	5.0	13	6.5	7.00	51	.286	.373	-7	-7	100	101	-1.4	-0	1	-0.6
1970	Phi-N	6	3	.667	42	11	3	0	3	138	119	7.8	17	47	3.1	92	6.0	3.26	121	.232	.291	12	11	98	103	1.8	-2	-0	0.8
1971	Phi-N	5	14	.263	38	30	3	0	0	214	203	8.5	28	50	2.1	113	4.8	3.79	96	.252	.293	-7	-4	105	93	-3.6	1	-0	-0.2
1972	Phi-N	4	6	.400	36	8	3	1	0	101	86	7.7	8	33	2.9	48	4.3	3.03	113	.231	.293	5	4	99	98	0.2	-2	0	0.2
1973	Phi-N	3	6	.333	42	4	0	0	1	98	105	9.6	10	27	2.5	51	4.7	4.41	91	.279	.321	-8	-5	109	94	-1.0	-0	-0	-0.4
1974	StL-N	0	0	—	1	0	0	0	0	1	3	27.0	1	5	45.0	0	0.0	54.00	7	.429	.667	-6	-6	103	57	0.0	0	0	-0.4
Total	6	18	32	.360	169	53	9	1	6	570	536	8.5	70	172	2.7	317	5.0	3.82	98	.250	.302	-11	-5	102	97	-4.0	-3	-0	-0.6
■ DON LESHNOCK		Leshnock, Donald Lee b: 11/25/46, Youngstown, Ohio BR/TL, 6'3", 195 lbs. Deb: 6/07/72																											
1972	Det-A	0	0	—	1	0	0	0	0	1	2	18.0	0	0	0.0	2	18.0	0.00	—	.400	.400	0	0	112	0	0.0	0	0	0.0
■ BRAD LESLEY		Lesley, Bradley Jay b: 9/11/58, Turlock, Cal. BR/TR, 6'6", 230 lbs. Deb: 7/31/82																											
1982	Cin-N	0	2	.000	28	0	0	0	4	38	27	6.4	1	13	3.1	29	6.9	2.61	144	.197	.265	4	5	104	65	-0.9	-0	0	0.5
1983	Cin-N	0	0	—	5	0	0	0	0	8	9	10.1	1	0	0.0	5	5.6	2.25	168	.290	.281	1	1	104	170	0.0	-0	0	0.1
1984	Cin-N	0	1	.000	16	0	0	0	2	19	17	8.1	3	14	6.6	7	3.3	5.21	74	.246	.356	-3	-3	107	98	-0.4	0	0	-0.2
1985	Mil-A	1	0	1.000	5	0	0	0	0	6	8	12.0	2	2	3.0	5	7.5	10.50	42	.296	.345	-4	-4	106	62	0.5	0	0	-0.3
Total	4	1	3	.250	54	0	0	0	6	71	61	7.7	7	29	3.7	46	5.8	3.93	98	.231	.301	-2	-1	105	85	-0.8	0	0	0.1
■ WALT LEVERENZ		Leverenz, Walter Fred "Tiny" b: 7/21/1887, Chicago, Ill. d: 3/19/73, Atascadero, Cal. BL/TL, 5'10", 175 lbs. Deb: 4/18/13																											
1913	StL-A	6	17	.261	30	27	13	2	1	203	159	7.0	3	89	3.9	87	3.9	2.57	111	.222	.318	8	6	98	95	-3.8	-1	-1	0.5
1914	StL-A	1	12	.077	27	16	5	0	0	111	107	8.7	5	63	5.1	41	3.3	3.81	72	.264	.368	-13	-13	100	105	-5.4	-0	-1	-1.5
1915	StL-A	0	2	.000	5	1	0	0	1	9	11	11.0	0	8	8.0	3	3.0	8.00	36	.333	.476	-5	-5	99	83	-0.9	-0	0	-0.4
Total	3	7	31	.184	62	44	18	2	2	323	277	7.7	8	160	4.5	131	3.7	3.15	89	.240	.341	-10	-12	98	98	-10.1	-1	-3	-1.4
■ DIXIE LEVERETT		Leverett, Gorham Vance b: 3/29/1894, Georgetown, Tex. d: 2/20/57, Beaverton, Ore. BR/TR, 5'11", 190 lbs. Deb: 5/06/22																											
1922	Chi-A	13	10	.565	33	27	16	4	2	224	224	9.0	11	79	3.2	60	2.4	3.33	122	.264	.318	18	19	101	104	1.7	3	-1	2.1
1923	Chi-A	10	13	.435	38	24	9	0	3	193	212	9.9	6	64	3.0	64	3.0	4.06	97	.280	.329	-2	-2	99	91	-0.3	4	-0	0.1
1924	Chi-A	2	3	.400	21	11	4	0	0	99	123	11.2	2	41	3.7	29	2.6	5.82	71	.314	.365	-17	-18	98	84	-0.1	-1	0	-1.6
1926	Chi-A	1	1	.500	6	3	1	0	0	24	31	11.6	1	7	2.6	12	4.5	6.00	61	.316	.349	-5	-6	90	78	0.0	-0	0	-0.5
1929	Bos-N	3	7	.300	24	12	3	0	1	98	135	12.4	5	30	2.8	28	2.6	6.34	72	.339	.375	-18	-19	97	92	-0.8	-0	-0	-1.6
Total	5	29	34	.460	122	77	33	4	6	638	725	10.2	25	221	3.1	193	2.7	4.50	91	.291	.339	-24	-27	99	94	0.5	6	-1	-1.5
■ HOD LEVERETTE		Leverette, Horace Wilbur "Levy" b: 2/4/1889, Shreveport, La. d: 4/10/58, St.Petersburg, Fla BR/TR, 6', 180 lbs. Deb: 4/22/20																											
1920	StL-A	0	2	.000	3	2	0	0	0	10	9	8.1	1	12	10.8	0	0.0	5.40	78	.250	.438	-2	-1	111	107	-0.9	-1	1	0.0
■ DUTCH LEVSEN		Levsen, Emil Henry b: 4/29/1898, Wyoming, Iowa d: 3/12/72, St.Louis Park, Minn. BR/TR, 6', 180 lbs. Deb: 9/28/23																											
1923	Cle-A	0	0	—	3	0	0	0	0	4	4	9.0	0	0	0.0	1	2.3	0.00	—	.267	.250	2	2	99	0	0.0	-0	1	0.3
1924	Cle-A	1	1	.500	4	1	1	0	0	16	22	12.4	0	4	2.3	3	1.7	4.50	92	.333	.361	-0	-1	97	106	0.1	-1	0	0.0
1925	Cle-A	1	2	.333	4	3	2	0	0	24	30	11.3	1	16	6.0	9	3.4	5.63	83	.313	.412	-3	-2	107	102	-0.3	0	-1	-0.2
1926	Cle-A	16	13	.552	33	31	18	2	0	237	235	8.9	11	85	3.2	53	2.0	3.42	114	.261	.322	16	13	97	101	-0.5	0	-1	1.2
1927	Cle-A	3	7	.300	25	13	2	1	0	80	96	10.8	1	37	4.2	15	1.7	5.51	74	.303	.370	-12	-13	99	85	-1.5	-1	1	-1.1
1928	Cle-A	0	3	.000	11	3	0	0	0	41	39	8.6	4	31	6.8	7	1.5	5.49	80	.258	.367	-7	-5	108	93	-1.4	-2	0	-0.6
Total	6	21	26	.447	80	51	23	3	0	402	426	9.5	17	173	3.9	88	2.0	4.19	97	.276	.343	-5	-6	99	96	-3.6	-4	1	-0.4
■ DENNIS LEWALLYN		Lewallyn, Dennis Dale b: 8/11/53, Pensacola, Fla. BR/TR, 6'4", 200 lbs. Deb: 9/21/75																											
1975	LA-N	0	0	—	2	0	0	0	0	3	1	3.0	0	0	0.0	0	0.0	0.00	—	.100	.100	1	1	93	0	0.0	0	0	0.1
1976	LA-N	1	1	.500	4	2	0	0	0	17	12	6.4	1	6	3.2	4	2.1	2.12	163	.207	.269	3	3	99	112	0.0	-1	0	0.3
1977	LA-N	3	1	.750	5	1	0	0	1	17	22	11.6	1	4	2.1	8	4.2	4.24	90	.306	.342	-1	-1	98	103	0.7	-1	-0	-0.1

YEAR	TM/L	W	L	PCT	G	GS	CG	SHO	SV	IP	H	H/G	HR	BB	BB/G	SO	SO/G	ERA	/A	OAVG	OOBP	PR	/A	PF	CPI	WAT	PB	PD	TPI
1978	LA-N	0	0	—	1	0	0	0	0	2	2	9.0	0	0	0.0	0	0.0	0.00	—	.250	.250	1	1	97	0	0.0	0	0	0.1
1979	LA-N	0	1	.000	7	0	0	0	0	12	19	14.3	0	5	3.8	1	0.8	5.25	71	.358	.410	-2	-2	99	120	-0.4	0	0	0.0
1980	Tex-A	0	0	—	4	0	0	0	0	6	7	10.5	0	4	6.0	1	1.5	7.50	54	.304	.407	-2	-2	100	68	0.0	0	0	-0.1
1981	Cle-A	0	0	—	7	0	0	0	0	13	16	11.1	1	2	1.4	11	7.6	5.54	62	.296	.316	-3	-3	93	73	0.0	0	-0	-0.2
1982	Cle-A	0	1	.000	4	0	0	0	0	10	13	11.7	3	1	0.9	3	2.7	7.20	57	.310	.311	-3	-3	101	84	-0.4	0	-0	-0.2
Total	8	4	4	.500	34	3	0	0	1	80	92	10.3	6	22	2.5	28	3.1	4.50	82	.287	.328	-6	-7	98	91	-0.1	-1	1	-0.1
■ DAN LEWANDOWSKI	Lewandowski, Daniel William b: 1/6/28, Buffalo, N.Y. BR/TR, 6', 180 lbs. Deb: 9/22/51																												
1951	StL-N	0	1	.000	2	0	0	0	0	1	3	27.0	0	1	9.0	1	9.0	9.00	44	.500	.500	-1	-1	101	160	-0.4	0	0	0.0
■ LEWIS	Lewis b:Brooklyn, N.Y. Deb: 7/12/1890																												
1890	Buf-P	0	1	.000	1	1	0	0	0	3	13	39.0	3	7	21.0	1	3.0	60.00	7	.618	.714	-19	-19	97	55	-0.4	-0	0	-0.9
■ TED LEWIS	Lewis, Edward Morgan "Parson" b: 12/25/1872, Machynlleth, Wales d: 5/24/36, Durham, N.H. 5'10.5", 158 lbs. Deb: 7/06/1896																												
1896	Bos-N	1	4	.200	6	5	4	0	0	42	37	7.9	2	27	5.8	12	2.6	3.21	145	.257	.374	5	7	107	116	-1.5	-2	0	0.4
1897	Bos-N	21	12	.636	38	34	30	2	1	290	316	9.8	11	125	3.9	65	2.0	3.85	116	.299	.373	15	20	103	106	-2.0	-2	-3	1.4
1898	Bos-N	26	8	**.765**	41	33	29	1	2	313	267	7.7	9	109	3.1	72	2.1	2.90	125	.251	.320	24	26	101	90	5.2	5	-0	3.0
1899	Bos-N	17	11	.607	29	25	23	2	0	235	245	9.4	10	73	2.8	60	2.3	3.49	114	.292	.348	10	12	103	101	-0.4	1	0	1.3
1900	Bos-N	13	12	.520	30	22	19	1	0	209	215	9.3	11	86	3.7	66	2.8	4.13	107	.289	.362	-10	7	120	93	1.2	-5	0	0.4
1901	Bos-A	16	17	.485	39	34	31	1	1	316	299	8.5	14	91	2.6	103	2.9	3.53	98	.269	.324	5	-3	94	85	-3.3	-2	-2	-0.3
Total	6	94	64	.595	183	153	136	7	4	1405	1379	8.8	57	511	3.3	378	2.4	3.53	112	.278	.345	49	69	103	95	-0.8	-4	-5	6.2
■ DUFFY LEWIS	Lewis, George Edward b: 4/18/1888, San Francisco, Cal d: 6/17/79, Salem, N.H. BL/TL, 5'10.5", 165 lbs. Deb: 4/16/10 C																												
1913	Bos-A	0	0	—	1	0	0	0	0	1	3	27.0	0	0	0.0	1	9.0	18.00	17	.500	.500	-2	-2	103	64	0.0	0	0	-0.1
■ JIM LEWIS	Lewis, James Martin b: 10/12/55, Miami, Fla. BR/TR, 6'3", 190 lbs. Deb: 9/12/79																												
1979	Sea-A	0	0	—	2	0	0	0	0	2	10	45.0	1	1	4.5	0	0.0	18.00	24	.625	.647	-3	-3	101	148	0.0	0	-0	-0.2
1982	NY-A	0	0	—	1	0	0	0	0	1	3	27.0	0	3	27.0	0	0.0	36.00	11	.500	.667	-4	-4	97	55	0.0	0	0	-0.2
1983	Min-A	0	0	—	6	0	0	0	0	18	24	12.0	5	7	3.5	8	4.0	6.50	67	.324	.390	-5	-4	106	113	0.0	0	0	-0.3
1985	Sea-A	0	1	.000	2	1	0	0	0	5	8	14.4	1	1	1.8	1	1.8	7.20	55	.421	.478	-2	-2	95	138	-0.4	0	-0	-0.1
Total	4	0	1	.000	11	1	0	0	0	26	45	15.6	7	12	4.2	9	3.1	8.65	49	.391	.458	-13	-13	103	118	-0.4	0	-0	-0.8
■ BERT LEWIS	Lewis, William Burton b: 10/3/1895, Tonawanda, N.Y. d: 3/24/50, Tonawanda, N.Y. BR/TR, 6'2", 176 lbs. Deb: 4/19/24																												
1924	Phi-N	0	0	—	12	0	0	0	0	18	23	11.5	1	7	3.5	3	1.5	6.00	71	.315	.373	-4	-3	111	87	0.0	-1	0	-0.3
■ TERRY LEY	Ley, Terrence Richard b: 2/21/47, Portland, Ore. BL/TL, 6', 190 lbs. Deb: 8/20/71																												
1971	NY-A	0	0	—	6	0	0	0	0	9	9	9.0	1	9	9.0	7	7.0	5.00	67	.257	.408	-2	-2	97	123	0.0	0	0	0.0
■ AL LIBKE	Libke, Albert Walter b: 9/12/18, Tacoma, Wash. BL/TR, 6'4", 215 lbs. Deb: 4/19/45																												
1945	Cin-N	0	0	—	4	0	0	0	0	4	3	6.8	0	3	6.8	2	4.5	0.00	—	.200	.333	2	2	97	0	0.0	1	0	0.2
1946	Cin-N	0	0	—	1	1	0	0	0	5	4	7.2	0	3	5.4	2	3.6	3.60	100	.235	.350	-0	-0	105	89	0.0	0	-0	0.0
Total	2	0	0	—	5	1	0	0	0	9	7	7.0	0	6	6.0	4	4.0	2.00	182	.219	.342	2	2	101	50	0.0	2	0	0.2
■ DON LIDDLE	Liddle, Donald Eugene b: 5/25/25, Mt.Carmel, Ill. BL/TL, 5'10", 165 lbs. Deb: 4/17/53																												
1953	Mil-N	7	6	.538	31	15	4	0	2	129	119	8.3	6	55	3.8	63	4.4	3.07	128	.248	.324	17	12	92	114	-0.6	-2	-1	0.9
1954	NY-N	9	4	.692	28	19	4	3	0	127	100	7.1	5	55	3.9	44	3.1	3.05	136	.223	.303	14	15	102	89	1.2	2	-1	1.7
1955	NY-N	10	4	.714	33	13	4	0	1	106	97	8.2	18	61	5.2	56	4.8	4.25	93	.246	.347	-2	-3	98	111	3.0	1	-1	-0.2
1956	NY-N	1	2	.333	11	5	1	0	1	41	45	9.9	5	14	3.1	21	4.6	3.95	95	.278	.326	-1	-1	99	111	-0.3	0	0	0.0
	StL-N	1	2	.333	14	2	0	0	0	25	36	13.0	8	18	6.5	14	5.0	8.28	45	.353	.443	-13	-13	99	110	-0.4	-0	-0	-1.2
	Yr	2	4	.333	25	7	1	0	1	66	81	11.0	13	32	4.4	35	4.8	5.59	67	.302	.369	-13	-14	99	110	-0.7	0	-0	-1.2
Total	4	28	18	.609	117	54	13	3	4	428	397	8.3	42	203	4.3	198	4.2	3.74	106	.250	.332	16	11	97	105	2.9	1	-2	1.2
■ DUTCH LIEBER	Lieber, Charles Edwin b: 2/1/10, Alameda, Cal. d: 12/31/61, Sawtelle, Cal. BR/TR, 6'0.5", 180 lbs. Deb: 4/18/35																												
1935	Phi-A	1	1	.500	18	1	0	0	2	47	45	8.6	1	19	3.6	14	2.7	3.06	149	.263	.333	7	8	102	124	0.2	-1	0	0.7
1936	Phi-A	0	1	.000	3	0	0	0	0	12	17	12.8	0	6	4.5	1	0.8	7.50	71	.362	.426	-3	-3	105	91	-0.4	-0	1	-0.1
Total	2	1	2	.333	21	1	0	0	2	59	62	9.5	1	25	3.8	15	2.3	3.97	119	.284	.353	4	5	103	117	-0.2	-2	1	0.6
■ GLENN LIEBHARDT	Liebhardt, Glenn Ignatius "Sandy" b: 7/31/10, Cleveland, Ohio BR/TR, 5'10.5", 170 lbs. Deb: 4/22/30																												
1930	Phi-A	0	1	.000	5	0	0	0	0	9	14	14.0	2	8	8.0	2	2.0	11.00	41	.359	.458	-6	-7	96	86	-0.4	-0	-0	-0.5
1936	StL-A	0	0	—	24	0	0	0	0	55	98	16.0	4	27	4.4	20	3.3	8.84	61	.375	.436	-23	-21	107	91	0.0	-2	-1	-2.0
1938	StL-A	0	0	—	2	0	0	0	0	3	4	12.0	1	0	0.0	1	3.0	6.00	82	.308	.308	-0	-0	103	102	0.0	0	0	0.0
Total	3	0	1	.000	31	0	0	0	0	67	116	15.6	7	35	4.7	23	3.1	9.00	58	.371	.435	-30	-28	105	91	-0.4	-2	-2	-2.5
■ GLENN LIEBHARDT	Liebhardt, Glenn John b: 3/10/1883, Milton, Ind. d: 7/13/56, Cleveland, Ohio 5'10", 175 lbs. Deb: 10/02/06																												
1906	Cle-A	2	0	1.000	2	2	2	0	0	18	13	6.5	0	1	0.5	9	4.5	1.50	178	.224	.237	2	2	99	69	1.0	-1	0	0.3
1907	Cle-A	18	14	.563	38	34	27	4	1	280	254	8.2	1	85	2.7	110	3.5	2.06	115	.265	.325	15	9	93	124	0.2	-0	1	1.1
1908	Cle-A	15	16	.484	38	26	19	3	0	262	222	7.6	2	81	2.8	146	5.0	2.20	112	.235	.297	6	8	103	112	-3.1	-0	1	1.0
1909	Cle-A	1	5	.167	12	4	1	0	1	52	54	9.3	0	16	2.8	15	2.6	2.94	87	.314	.376	-3	-2	103	135	-1.8	-2	-2	-0.4
Total	4	36	35	.507	90	66	49	7	2	612	543	8.0	3	183	2.7	280	4.1	2.18	112	.254	.315	20	18	98	118	-3.7	-3	-0	2.0
■ GENE LILLARD	Lillard, Robert Eugene b: 11/12/13, Santa Barbara, Cal BR/TR, 5'10.5", 178 lbs. Deb: 5/08/36																												
1939	Chi-N	3	5	.375	20	7	2	0	0	55	68	11.1	2	36	5.9	31	5.1	6.55	60	.309	.405	-16	-16	100	87	-1.2	1	0	-1.3
1940	StL-N	0	1	.000	2	1	0	0	0	5	8	14.4	1	4	7.2	2	3.6	12.60	31	.364	.481	-5	-5	101	77	-0.4	0	0	-0.3
Total	2	3	6	.333	22	8	2	0	0	60	76	11.4	3	40	6.0	33	5.0	7.05	56	.314	.412	-21	-21	100	87	-1.6	1	0	-1.6
■ JIM LILLIE	Lillie, James J. "Grasshopper" b: 1862, New Haven, Conn. d: 11/9/1890, Kansas City, Mo. Deb: 5/17/1883																												
1883	Buf-N	0	1	.000	3	0	0	0	0	12	16	12.0	0	2	1.5	4	3.0	3.00	104	.328	.354	0	0	99	142	-0.4	0	0	0.0
1884	Buf-N	0	1	.000	2	1	0	0	0	13	22	15.2	0	5	3.5	4	2.8	6.23	50	.384	.434	-5	-4	105	105	-0.4	-0	0	-0.3
1886	KC-N	0	0	—	1	0	0	0	0	6	8	12.0	0	1	1.5	0	0.0	4.50	84	.334	.361	-1	-0	114	98	0.0	-0	0	0.0
Total	3	0	2	.000	6	1	0	0	0	31	46	13.4	0	8	2.3	8	2.3	4.65	70	.354	.391	-5	-5	105	118	-0.8	-0	0	-0.3
■ EZRA LINCOLN	Lincoln, Ezra Perry b: 11/17/1868, Raynham, Mass. d: 5/7/51, Taunton, Mass. TL , 5'11", 160 lbs. Deb: 5/02/1890																												
1890	Cle-N	3	11	.214	15	15	13	0	0	118	157	12.0	1	53	4.0	22	1.7	4.42	78	.336	.404	-11	-13	97	114	-2.6	-3	0	-1.2
	Syr-a	0	3	.000	3	3	2	0	0	20	33	14.8	1	4	1.8	6	2.7	10.35	34	.386	.413	-14	-15	92	64	-1.4	-1	0	-1.1
■ VIVE LINDAMAN	Lindaman, Vivan Alexander b: 10/28/1877, Charles City, Iowa d: 2/13/27, Charles City, Iowa BR/TR, 6'1", 200 lbs. Deb: 4/14/06																												
1906	Bos-N	12	23	.343	39	37	32	2	0	307	303	8.9	4	90	2.6	115	3.4	2.43	114	.288	.351	7	12	106	128	0.6	-2	-2	1.1
1907	Bos-N	11	15	.423	34	28	24	2	1	260	252	8.7	10	108	3.7	90	3.1	3.63	67	.287	.375	-34	-35	99	97	0.8	-2	-3	-3.9
1908	Bos-N	12	16	.429	43	30	21	2	1	271	246	8.2	7	70	2.3	68	2.3	2.36	105	.273	.332	-0	4	106	115	0.6	0	-3	0.1
1909	Bos-N	1	6	.143	15	6	6	1	0	66	75	10.2	1	28	3.8	13	1.8	4.64	57	.299	.371	-15	-15	102	92	-1.7	1	-1	-1.5
Total	4	36	60	.375	131	101	83	7	2	904	876	8.7	22	296	2.9	286	2.8	2.92	88	.284	.354	-42	-34	103	112	0.3	-3	-9	-4.2
■ PAUL LINDBLAD	Lindblad, Paul Aaron b: 8/9/41, Chanute, Kan. BL/TL, 6'1", 185 lbs. Deb: 9/15/65																												
1965	KC-A	0	1	.000	4	0	0	0	0	7	12	15.4	3	0	0.0	12	15.4	11.57	30	.353	.371	-6	-6	100	75	-0.4	-0	0	-0.5
1966	KC-A	5	10	.333	38	14	0	0	1	121	138	10.3	14	37	2.8	69	5.1	4.17	79	.292	.342	-10	-12	95	117	-2.1	0	0	-1.1
1967	KC-A	5	8	.385	46	10	1	1	6	116	106	8.2	15	35	2.7	83	6.4	3.57	92	.241	.302	-4	-4	102	102	0.0	2	-0	-0.2
1968	Oak-A	4	3	.571	47	1	0	0	2	56	51	8.2	6	14	2.3	42	6.8	2.41	121	.237	.277	4	3	98	125	0.5	1	0	0.5
1969	Oak-A	9	6	.600	60	0	0	0	9	78	72	8.3	8	33	3.8	64	7.4	4.15	80	.240	.316	-5	-7	91	85	1.0	1	-0	-0.5
1970	Oak-A	8	2	.800	62	0	0	0	3	63	52	7.4	7	28	4.0	42	6.0	2.71	131	.222	.301	7	6	96	117	2.9	-1	0	0.5
1971	Oak-A	1	0	1.000	8	0	0	0	0	16	18	10.1	1	2	1.1	4	2.3	3.94	87	.295	.323	-1	-1	99	100	0.5	0	0	0.0
	Was-A	6	4	.600	43	0	0	0	8	84	58	6.2	6	29	3.1	50	5.4	2.57	127	.196	.269	8	6	94	82	1.8	0	1	0.8
	Yr	7	4	.636	51	0	0	0	8	100	76	6.8	7	31	2.8	54	4.9	2.79	118	.212	.275	8	6	95	82	2.3	0	1	0.8
1972	Tex-A	5	8	.385	**66**	0	0	0	9	100	95	8.6	7	29	2.6	51	4.6	2.61	114	.257	.302	5	4	97	126	0.4	0	-1	0.4

YEAR	TM/L	W	L	PCT	G	GS	CG	SHO	SV	IP	H	H/G	HR	BB	BB/G	SO	SO/G	ERA	/A	OAVG	OOBP	PR	/A	PF	CPI	WAT	PB	PD	TPI
1973	Oak-A	1	5	.167	36	3	0	0	2	78	89	10.3	8	28	3.2	33	3.8	3.69	89	.292	.352	1	-4	86	129	-2.1	0	-1	-0.3
1974	Oak-A	4	4	.500	45	2	0	0	6	101	85	7.6	4	30	2.7	46	4.1	2.05	174	.231	.284	18	17	99	122	-0.3	0	0	1.9
1975	Oak-A	9	1	.900	68	0	0	0	7	122	105	7.7	6	43	3.2	58	4.3	2.73	126	.237	.297	14	10	91	105	3.8	0	1	1.1
1976	Oak-A	6	5	.545	65	0	0	0	5	115	111	8.7	5	24	1.9	37	2.9	3.05	114	.253	.287	6	5	98	94	0.1	0	1	0.6
1977	Tex-A	4	5	.444	42	1	0	0	4	99	103	9.4	16	29	2.6	46	4.2	4.18	101	.270	.319	-1	0	104	106	-1.0	0	0	0.0
1978	Tex-A	1	1	.500	18	0	0	0	2	40	41	9.2	2	15	3.4	25	5.6	3.60	100	.279	.341	1	0	96	115	0.0	0	-0	0.0
	NY-A	0	0	—	7	1	0	0	0	18	21	10.5	4	8	4.0	9	4.5	4.50	82	.284	.345	-1	-2	97	123	0.0	0	0	0.0
	Yr	1	1	.500	25	1	0	0	2	58	62	9.6	6	23	3.6	34	5.3	3.88	94	.276	.335	-1	-2	96	123	0.0	0	0	0.0
Total	14	68	63	.519	655	32	1	1	64	1214	1157	8.6	112	384	2.8	671	5.0	3.28	104	.253	.308	36	17	96	109	5.1	5	3	3.2
■ LYMAN LINDE	Linde, Lyman Gilbert b: 9/20/20, Beaver Dam, Wis. BR/TR, 5'11", 185 lbs. Deb: 9/11/47																												
1947	Cle-A	0	0	—	1	0	0	0	0	1	3	27.0	0	1	9.0	0	0.0	18.00	19	.600	.667	-2	-2	94	93	0.0	0	0	-0.1
1948	Cle-A	0	0	—	3	0	0	0	0	10	9	8.1	1	4	3.6	0	0.0	5.40	74	.243	.317	-1	-2	94	69	0.0	-0	-0	-0.1
Total	2	0	0	—	4	0	0	0	0	11	12	9.8	1	5	4.1	0	0.0	6.55	61	.286	.362	-3	-3	94	71	0.0	-0	-0	-0.2
■ JOHNNY LINDELL	Lindell, John Harlan b: 8/30/16, Greeley, Colo. d: 8/27/85, Newport Beach, Cal. BR/TR, 6'4.5", 217 lbs. Deb: 4/18/41																												
1942	NY-A	2	1	.667	23	2	0	0	1	53	52	8.8	3	22	3.7	28	4.8	3.74	92	.254	.325	-0	-2	94	98	0.0	1	-0	0.0
1953	Pit-N	5	16	.238	27	23	13	1	0	176	173	8.8	17	116	5.9	102	5.2	4.70	97	.262	.370	-8	-3	106	105	-3.0	7	2	-0.2
	Phi-N	1	1	.500	5	3	2	0	0	23	22	8.6	0	23	9.0	16	6.3	4.30	97	.259	.402	-0	-0	98	116	0.0	2	-0	0.0
	Yr	6	17	.261	32	26	15	1	0	199	195	8.8	17	139	6.3	118	5.3	4.66	97	.259	.367	-8	-3	105	116	-3.0	7	2	-0.2
Total	2	8	18	.308	55	28	15	1	1	252	247	8.8	20	161	5.8	146	5.2	4.46	96	.260	.364	-9	-5	103	105	-3.0	9	2	-0.2
■ ERNIE LINDEMANN	Lindemann, Ernest b: 6/10/1883, New York, N.Y. d: 12/27/51, Brooklyn, N.Y. BR/TR, Deb: 6/28/07																												
1907	Bos-N	0	0	—	1	1	0	0	0	6	6	9.0	0	4	6.0	3	4.5	6.00	41	.289	.404	-2	-2	99	65	0.0	0	0	-0.1
■ CARL LINDQUIST	Lindquist, Carl Emil b: 5/9/19, Morris Run, Pa. BR/TR, 6'2", 185 lbs. Deb: 9/27/43																												
1943	Bos-N	0	2	.000	2	2	0	0	0	13	17	11.8	3	4	2.8	1	0.7	6.23	59	.315	.362	-4	-4	109	100	-0.9	-1	0	-0.3
1944	Bos-N	0	0	—	5	0	0	0	0	9	8	8.0	1	2	2.0	4	4.0	3.00	116	.222	.256	1	0	96	83	0.0	-0	-0	0.0
Total	2	0	2	.000	7	2	0	0	0	22	25	10.2	4	6	2.5	5	2.0	4.91	73	.278	.320	-4	-3	104	93	-0.9	-1	0	-0.3
■ JIM LINDSEY	Lindsey, James Kendrick b: 1/24/1898, Greensburg, La. d: 10/25/63, Jackson, La. BR/TR, 6'1", 175 lbs. Deb: 5/01/22																												
1922	Cle-A	4	5	.444	29	5	0	0	1	84	105	11.3	4	24	2.6	29	3.1	6.00	69	.324	.355	-18	-17	103	84	-0.5	-1	-1	-1.7
1924	Cle-A	0	0	—	3	0	0	0	0	3	8	24.0	0	3	9.0	0	0.0	21.00	20	.500	.524	-6	-6	97	64	0.0	-1	0	-0.4
1929	StL-N	1	1	.500	2	2	1	0	0	16	20	11.3	1	2	1.1	8	4.5	5.63	82	.290	.319	-2	-2	98	68	0.0	-0	0	-0.1
1930	StL-N	7	5	.583	39	6	3	0	5	106	131	11.1	6	46	3.9	50	4.2	4.42	115	.312	.370	7	8	102	122	-0.1	0	-3	0.5
1931	StL-N	6	4	.600	35	2	1	1	7	75	77	9.2	2	45	5.4	32	3.8	2.76	144	.270	.362	**9**	**10**	103	156	-0.4	-0	-0	1.0
1932	StL-N	3	3	.500	33	5	0	0	3	89	96	9.7	6	38	3.8	31	3.1	4.96	79	.279	.347	-11	-10	101	90	0.2	-1	-1	-1.1
1933	StL-N	0	0	—	1	0	0	0	0	2	2	9.0	0	1	4.5	1	4.5	4.50	74	.286	.375	-0	-0	100	93	0.0	0	0	0.0
1934	Cin-N	0	0	—	4	0	0	0	0	4	4	9.0	0	2	4.5	2	4.5	4.50	94	.286	.350	-0	-0	105	114	0.0	0	0	0.0
	StL-N	0	1	.000	11	0	0	0	1	14	21	13.5	2	3	1.9	7	4.5	6.43	70	.328	.353	-4	-3	111	91	-0.4	-0	-0	-0.2
	Yr	0	1	.000	15	0	0	0	1	18	25	12.5	2	5	2.5	9	4.5	6.00	74	.316	.341	-4	-3	110	91	-0.4	0	-0	-0.2
1937	Bro-N	0	1	.000	20	0	0	0	2	38	43	10.2	4	12	2.8	15	3.6	3.55	118	.295	.341	2	3	107	138	-0.4	-0	-0	0.2
Total	9	21	20	.512	177	20	5	1	19	431	507	10.6	25	176	3.7	175	3.7	4.70	92	.300	.358	-23	-18	103	112	-1.6	-3	-5	-1.8
■ AXEL LINDSTROM	Lindstrom, Axel Olaf b: 8/26/1895, Gustavsberg, Sweden d: 6/24/40, Asheville, N.C. BR/TR, 5'10", 180 lbs. Deb: 10/03/16																												
1916	Phi-A	0	0	—	1	0	0	0	1	4	2	4.5	0	0	0.0	1	2.3	4.50	66	.182	.250	-1	-1	105	30	0.0	0	0	0.0
■ DICK LINES	Lines, Richard George b: 8/17/38, Montreal, Que., Can. BR/TL, 6'1", 175 lbs. Deb: 4/16/66																												
1966	Was-A	5	2	.714	53	0	0	0	2	83	63	6.8	4	24	2.6	49	5.3	2.28	145	.213	.270	11	10	96	101	1.7	-1	2	1.1
1967	Was-A	2	5	.286	54	0	0	0	4	86	83	8.7	6	24	2.5	54	5.7	3.35	100	.245	.289	-1	0	104	91	-1.3	1	0	0.1
Total	2	7	7	.500	107	0	0	0	6	169	146	7.8	10	48	2.6	103	5.5	2.82	118	.230	.280	10	10	100	95	0.4	-1	2	1.2
■ FRED LINK	Link, Edward Theodore "Laddie" b: 3/11/1886, Columbus, Ohio d: 5/22/39, Houston, Tex. BL/TL, 6' 1", 700 lbs. Deb: 4/15/1910																												
1910	Cle-A	5	6	.455	22	13	6	1	1	128	121	8.5	0	50	3.5	55	3.9	3.16	81	.259	.340	-9	-8	102	98	-0.1	-1	-1	-1.0
	StL-A	0	1	.000	3	3	0	0	0	17	24	12.7	0	13	6.9	5	2.6	4.24	60	.375	.487	-3	-3	101	169	-0.4	-0	-0	-0.3
	Yr	5	7	.417	25	16	6	1	1	145	145	9.0	0	63	3.9	60	3.7	3.29	78	.270	.347	-12	-12	102	169	-0.5	-1	-1	-1.3
■ ED LINKE	Linke, Edward Karl "Babe" b: 11/9/11, Chicago, Ill. d: 6/21/88, Chicago, Ill. BR/TR, 5'11", 180 lbs. Deb: 4/27/33																												
1933	Was-A	1	0	1.000	3	2	0	0	0	16	15	8.4	0	11	6.2	6	3.4	5.06	79	.250	.361	-1	-2	93	80	0.5	0	0	-0.1
1934	Was-A	2	2	.500	7	4	2	0	0	35	38	9.8	1	9	2.3	9	2.3	4.11	112	.277	.315	1	2	102	90	0.2	0	0	0.2
1935	Was-A	11	7	.611	40	22	10	1	3	178	211	10.7	6	80	4.0	51	2.6	5.01	82	.296	.361	-11	-17	93	95	3.0	6	-1	-1.1
1936	Was-A	1	5	.167	13	6	1	0	0	52	73	12.6	4	14	2.4	11	1.9	7.10	68	.330	.363	-12	-13	96	82	-2.0	4	1	-0.5
1937	Was-A	6	1	.857	36	7	0	0	3	129	158	11.0	11	59	4.1	61	4.3	5.58	79	.304	.374	-14	-17	96	98	2.6	1	-0	-1.4
1938	StL-A	1	7	.125	21	2	0	0	0	40	60	13.5	6	33	7.4	18	4.0	7.87	63	.357	.451	-14	-13	103	110	-2.6	0	1	-1.0
Total	6	22	22	.500	120	43	13	1	6	450	555	11.1	28	206	4.1	156	3.1	5.60	78	.305	.371	-50	-60	96	95	1.7	12	0	-3.9
■ ROYCE LINT	Lint, Royce James b: 1/1/21, Birmingham, Ala. BL/TL, 6'1", 165 lbs. Deb: 4/13/54																												
1954	StL-N	2	3	.400	30	4	1	1	0	70	75	9.6	9	30	3.9	36	4.6	4.89	84	.273	.335	-6	-6	100	91	-0.3	1	1	-0.3
■ FRANK LINZY	Linzy, Frank Alfred b: 9/15/40, Ft.Gibson, Okla. BR/TR, 6'1", 190 lbs. Deb: 8/14/63																												
1963	SF-N	0	0	—	8	1	0	0	0	17	22	11.6	0	10	5.3	14	7.4	4.76	65	.324	.412	-3	-3	94	118	0.0	-0	0	-0.2
1965	SF-N	9	3	.750	57	0	0	0	21	82	76	8.3	2	23	2.5	35	3.8	1.43	271	.250	.305	**19**	**22**	109	210	2.5	1	5	3.1
1966	SF-N	7	11	.389	51	0	0	0	16	100	107	9.6	4	34	3.1	57	5.1	2.97	117	.273	.326	7	6	97	124	-3.1	0	1	0.7
1967	SF-N	7	7	.500	57	0	0	0	17	96	67	6.3	4	34	3.2	38	3.6	1.50	223	.203	.269	20	20	99	144	-0.7	-2	3	2.4
1968	SF-N	9	8	.529	57	0	0	0	12	95	76	7.2	1	27	2.6	36	3.4	2.08	138	.218	.269	10	8	96	93	-0.1	-1	4	1.3
1969	SF-N	14	9	.609	58	0	0	0	11	116	129	10.0	5	38	2.9	62	4.8	3.65	99	.283	.330	-1	-1	100	110	1.6	3	3	0.6
1970	SF-N	2	1	.667	20	0	0	0	1	26	33	11.4	2	11	3.8	16	5.5	6.92	56	.327	.385	-8	-9	96	86	0.4	-0	0	-0.8
	StL-N	3	5	.375	47	0	0	0	2	61	66	9.7	3	23	3.4	19	2.8	3.69	117	.282	.338	2	4	106	115	-0.7	-1	1	0.4
	Yr	5	6	.455	67	0	0	0	3	87	99	10.2	5	34	3.5	35	3.6	4.66	90	.293	.350	-6	-5	103	115	-0.3	-0	1	-0.4
1971	StL-N	4	3	.571	50	0	0	0	6	59	49	7.5	2	27	4.1	24	3.7	2.14	163	.226	.304	9	9	100	128	0.1	1	1	1.1
1972	Mil-A	2	2	.500	47	0	0	0	12	77	70	8.2	4	27	3.2	24	2.8	3.04	98	.248	.306	0	-1	97	105	0.3	-0	1	0.0
1973	Mil-A	2	6	.250	42	1	0	0	13	63	68	9.7	7	21	3.0	21	3.0	3.57	103	.282	.337	2	1	96	124	-1.8	0	0	0.1
1974	Phi-N	3	2	.600	22	0	0	0	0	25	27	9.7	1	7	2.5	12	4.3	3.24	116	.284	.330	1	1	104	116	0.5	0	1	0.2
Total	11	62	57	.521	516	2	0	0	111	817	790	8.7	35	282	3.1	358	3.9	2.85	122	.257	.314	58	58	100	126	-1.0	0	20	8.9
■ ANGELO LiPETRI	LiPetri, Michael Angelo b: 7/6/30, Brooklyn, N.Y. BR/TR, 6'1.5", 180 lbs. Deb: 4/25/56																												
1956	Phi-N	0	0	—	6	0	0	0	0	11	7	5.7	2	3	2.5	8	6.5	3.27	110	.175	.244	1	0	95	67	0.0	-0	0	0.0
1958	Phi-N	0	0	—	4	0	0	0	0	4	6	13.5	1	0	0.0	1	2.3	11.25	35	.353	.389	-3	-3	100	65	0.0	0	0	-0.2
Total	2	0	0	—	10	0	0	0	0	15	13	7.8	3	3	1.8	9	5.4	5.40	68	.228	.286	-3	-3	97	66	0.0	0	0	-0.2
■ TOM LIPP	Lipp, Thomas C. (born Thomas C. Lieb) b: 6/4/1870, Baltimore, Md. d: 5/30/32, Baltimore, Md. 5'11.5", 170 lbs. Deb: 9/18/1897																												
1897	Phi-N	0	1	.000	1	1	0	0	0	3	8	24.0	0	2	6.0	1	3.0	15.00	28	.511	.566	-4	-4	96	82	-0.4	0	0	-0.1
■ NIG LIPSCOMB	Lipscomb, Gerard b: 2/24/11, Rutherfordton, N.C d: 2/27/78, Huntersville, N.C. BR/TR, 6', 175 lbs. Deb: 4/23/37																												
1937	StL-A	0	0	—	3	0	0	0	0	10	13	11.7	3	5	4.5	1	0.9	6.30	76	.333	.400	-2	-2	103	128	0.0	1	-0	-0.1
■ HOD LISENBEE	Lisenbee, Horace Milton b: 9/23/1898, Clarksville, Tenn d: 11/14/87, Clarksville, Tenn. BR/TR, 5'11", 170 lbs. Deb: 4/23/27																												
1927	Was-A	18	9	.667	39	34	17	**4**	0	242	221	8.2	6	78	2.9	105	3.9	3.57	111	.245	.297	15	11	96	77	4.0	-4	-2	0.3
1928	Was-A	2	6	.250	16	9	3	0	0	77	102	11.9	4	32	3.7	13	1.5	6.08	67	.326	.381	-17	-17	101	94	-1.9	-0	-1	-1.6
1929	Bos-A	0	0	—	5	0	0	0	0	9	10	10.0	1	4	4.0	2	2.0	5.00	89	.294	.350	-1	-1	105	103	0.0	-0	0	0.0
1930	Bos-A	10	17	.370	37	31	15	0	0	237	254	9.6	20	86	3.3	47	1.8	4.41	101	.280	.336	7	2	96	105	0.8	1	-4	0.0
1931	Bos-A	5	12	.294	41	17	6	0	0	165	190	10.4	13	49	2.7	42	2.3	5.18	82	.281	.328	-15	-17	97	85	-2.5	0	-1	-1.6

YEAR	TM/L	W	L	PCT	G	GS	CG	SHO	SV	IP	H	H/G	HR	BB	BB/G	SO	SO/G	ERA	/A	OAVG	OOBP	PR	/A	PF	CPI	WAT	PB	PD	TPI
1932	Bos-A	0	4	.000	19	6	3	0	0	73	87	10.7	9	25	3.1	13	1.6	5.67	81	.296	.347	-10	-9	102	94	-1.9	-2	-1	-1.0
1936	Phi-A	1	7	.125	19	7	4	0	0	86	115	12.0	9	24	2.5	17	1.8	6.17	86	.322	.359	-11	-8	105	94	-2.5	-1	-1	-0.8
1945	Cin-N	1	3	.250	31	3	0	0	1	80	97	10.9	12	16	1.8	14	1.6	5.51	67	.294	.329	-15	-16	97	88	-0.7	-3	-1	-1.8
Total	8	37	58	.389	207	107	48	4	1	969	1076	10.0	74	314	2.9	253	2.3	4.81	89	.282	.331	-47	-56	98	90	-4.7	-9	-11	-6.5
■ AD LISKA	Liska, Adolph James b: 7/10/06, Dwight, Neb. BR/TR, 5'11.5", 160 lbs. Deb: 4/17/29																												
1929	Was-A	3	9	.250	24	10	4	0	0	94	87	8.3	1	42	4.0	33	3.2	4.79	89	.249	.326	-6	-6	100	68	-2.8	-1	3	-0.2
1930	Was-A	9	7	.563	32	16	7	1	1	151	140	8.3	6	71	4.2	40	2.4	3.28	139	.250	.333	23	22	98	117	-0.6	-4	6	2.2
1931	Was-A	0	1	.000	2	1	0	0	0	4	9	20.3	0	1	2.3	2	4.5	6.75	64	.450	.476	-1	-1	98	143	-0.4	-0	0	0.0
1932	Phi-N	2	0	1.000	8	0	0	0	1	27	22	7.3	0	10	3.3	6	2.0	1.67	259	.239	.306	7	8	111	178	1.0	-1	1	0.9
1933	Phi-N	3	1	.750	45	1	0	0	1	76	96	11.4	5	26	3.1	23	2.7	4.50	90	.310	.355	-10	-4	121	108	1.2	-2	4	-0.1
Total	5	17	18	.486	111	28	11	1	3	352	354	9.1	12	150	3.8	104	2.7	3.86	114	.266	.336	13	21	105	107	-1.6	-7	14	2.8
■ MARK LITTELL	Littell, Mark Alan b: 1/17/53, Cape Girardeau, Mo. BL/TR, 6'3", 210 lbs. Deb: 6/14/73																												
1973	KC-A	1	3	.250	8	7	1	0	0	38	44	10.4	5	23	5.4	16	3.8	5.68	73	.288	.374	-8	-6	109	95	-1.0	0	-0	-0.6
1975	KC-A	1	2	.333	7	3	1	0	0	24	19	7.1	1	15	5.6	19	7.1	3.75	102	.229	.333	0	0	101	93	-0.5	0	1	0.1
1976	KC-A	8	4	.667	60	1	0	0	16	104	68	5.9	1	60	5.2	92	8.0	2.08	167	.188	.299	**17**	16	99	102	1.6	0	-1	1.6
1977	KC-A	8	4	.667	48	5	0	0	12	105	73	6.3	6	55	4.7	106	9.1	3.60	112	.198	.297	6	5	99	71	0.6	0	-1	0.4
1978	StL-N	4	8	.333	72	2	0	0	11	106	80	6.8	8	59	5.0	130	11.0	2.80	122	.213	.320	9	7	96	115	-1.3	-0	-0	0.7
1979	StL-N	9	4	.692	63	0	0	0	13	82	60	6.6	2	39	4.3	67	7.4	2.20	178	.203	.289	14	16	104	98	2.4	-1	-0	1.4
1980	StL-N	0	2	.000	14	0	0	0	2	11	14	11.5	2	7	5.7	7	5.7	9.00	41	.318	.404	-7	-6	102	76	-0.9	-0	-0	-0.6
1981	StL-N	1	3	.250	28	1	0	0	2	41	36	7.9	2	31	6.8	22	4.8	4.39	80	.237	.360	-4	-4	101	91	-1.1	0	-0	-0.3
1982	StL-N	0	1	.000	16	0	0	0	0	21	22	9.4	1	15	6.4	7	3.0	5.14	72	.272	.378	-4	-3	102	92	-0.4	-0	-1	-0.3
Total	9	32	31	.508	316	19	2	0	56	532	416	7.0	28	304	5.1	466	7.9	3.32	112	.217	.320	23	24	100	95	-0.6	-2	-3	2.4
■ JEFF LITTLE	Little, Donald Jeffrey b: 12/25/54, Fremont, Ohio BR/TL, 6'6", 220 lbs. Deb: 9/06/80																												
1980	StL-N	1	1	.500	7	2	0	0	0	19	18	8.5	0	9	4.3	17	8.1	3.79	98	.250	.333	-0	-0	102	83	0.1	-0	-0	0.0
1982	Min-A	2	0	1.000	33	0	0	0	0	36	33	8.3	6	27	6.8	26	6.5	4.25	98	.244	.364	-1	-0	102	120	1.0	0	-0	0.0
Total	2	3	1	.750	40	2	0	0	0	55	51	8.3	6	36	5.9	43	7.0	4.09	98	.246	.354	-1	-1	102	107	1.1	-0	-1	0.0
■ JOHN LITTLEFIELD	Littlefield, John Andrew b: 1/5/54, Covina, Cal. BR/TR, 6'2", 200 lbs. Deb: 6/08/80																												
1980	StL-N	5	5	.500	52	0	0	0	9	66	71	9.7	2	20	2.7	22	3.0	3.14	118	.282	.329	3	4	102	121	0.4	-1	0	0.3
1981	SD-N	2	3	.400	42	0	0	0	2	64	53	7.5	5	28	3.9	21	3.0	3.66	90	.235	.317	-1	-2	95	93	0.1	-0	-0	-0.2
Total	2	7	8	.467	94	0	0	0	11	130	124	8.6	7	48	3.3	43	3.0	3.39	103	.259	.323	2	2	99	107	0.5	-1	0	0.1
■ DICK LITTLEFIELD	Littlefield, Richard Bernard b: 3/18/26, Detroit, Mich. BL/TL, 6', 180 lbs. Deb: 7/07/50																												
1950	Bos-A	2	2	.500	15	2	0	0	1	23	27	10.6	6	24	9.4	13	5.1	9.39	54	.297	.444	-12	-11	111	88	-0.3	-1	1	-0.9
1951	Chi-A	1	1	.500	4	2	0	0	0	10	9	8.1	1	17	15.3	7	6.3	8.10	49	.243	.481	-4	-5	96	90	0.0	0	0	-0.3
1952	Det-A	0	3	.000	28	1	0	0	1	48	46	8.6	4	25	4.7	32	6.0	4.31	87	.257	.335	-3	-3	103	96	-1.4	-0	-1	-0.3
	StL-A	2	3	.400	7	5	3	0	0	46	35	6.8	4	17	3.3	34	6.7	2.74	133	.205	.274	5	5	100	86	0.0	-2	-1	0.2
	Yr	2	6	.250	35	6	3	0	1	94	81	7.8	8	42	4.0	66	6.3	3.54	105	.231	.306	1	2	101	86	-1.4	-0	-2	-0.1
1953	StL-A	7	12	.368	36	22	2	0	0	152	153	9.1	17	84	5.0	104	6.2	5.09	87	.264	.354	-19	-11	111	93	0.3	-1	-0	-1.1
1954	Bal-A	0	0	—	3	0	0	0	0	6	8	12.0	0	6	9.0	5	7.5	10.50	35	.333	.484	-5	-5	99	69	0.0	-0	-0	-0.4
	Pit-N	10	11	.476	23	21	7	1	0	155	140	8.1	10	85	4.9	92	5.3	3.60	115	.239	.331	8	9	102	96	2.4	0	-3	0.7
1955	Pit-N	5	12	.294	35	17	4	1	0	130	148	10.2	15	68	4.7	70	4.8	5.12	79	.290	.365	-16	-15	101	102	-2.2	0	-2	-1.6
1956	Pit-N	0	0	—	6	2	0	0	0	13	14	9.7	2	6	4.2	10	6.9	4.15	94	.286	.364	-1	-0	103	124	0.0	-0	-0	0.0
	StL-N	0	2	.000	3	2	0	0	0	10	9	8.1	2	4	3.6	5	4.5	7.20	52	.237	.302	-4	-4	99	55	-0.9	-0	-0	-0.3
	NY-N	4	4	.500	31	7	0	0	2	97	78	7.2	16	39	3.6	65	6.0	4.08	92	.231	.295	-3	-4	99	92	0.5	-2	0	-0.4
	Yr	4	6	.400	40	11	0	0	2	120	101	7.6	20	49	3.7	80	6.0	4.35	87	.238	.304	-8	-8	100	92	-0.4	-1	-1	-0.7
1957	Chi-N	2	3	.400	48	2	0	0	4	66	76	10.4	12	37	5.0	51	7.0	5.32	71	.295	.373	-11	-11	98	113	0.0	0	-1	-1.1
1958	Mil-N	0	1	.000	4	0	0	0	1	6	7	10.5	2	1	1.5	7	10.5	4.50	76	.280	.333	-0	-1	87	131	-0.4	0	-0	0.0
Total	9	33	54	.379	243	83	16	2	9	762	750	8.9	91	413	4.9	495	5.8	4.71	86	.260	.346	-65	-56	103	96	-2.0	-5	-9	-5.5
■ CARLISLE LITTLEJOHN	Littlejohn, Charles Carlisle b: 10/6/01, Irene, Tex. d: 10/27/77, Kansas City, Mo. BR/TR, 5'10", 175 lbs. Deb: 5/11/27																												
1927	StL-N	3	1	.750	14	2	1	0	0	42	47	10.1	4	14	3.0	16	3.4	4.50	92	.292	.343	-3	-2	106	102	0.8	2	-1	0.0
1928	StL-N	2	1	.667	12	2	1	0	0	32	36	10.1	2	14	3.9	6	1.7	3.66	106	.286	.347	1	1	97	118	0.2	-2	-0	0.0
Total	2	5	2	.714	26	4	2	0	0	74	83	10.1	6	28	3.4	22	2.7	4.14	97	.289	.345	-2	-1	102	109	1.0	-0	-1	0.0
■ BUDDY LIVELY	Lively, Everett Adrian "Red" b: 2/14/25, Birmingham, Ala. BR/TR, 6'0.5", 200 lbs. Deb: 4/17/47																												
1947	Cin-N	4	7	.364	38	17	3	1	0	123	126	9.2	16	63	4.6	52	3.8	4.68	80	.265	.342	-8	-13	92	99	-1.3	2	-0	-1.0
1948	Cin-N	0	0	—	10	0	0	0	0	23	13	5.1	0	11	4.3	12	4.7	2.35	179	.165	.272	4	5	106	61	0.0	-0	-0	0.4
1949	Cin-N	4	6	.400	31	10	3	1	1	103	91	8.0	11	53	4.6	30	2.6	3.93	101	.245	.335	1	0	98	105	0.0	0	-1	0.0
Total	3	8	13	.381	79	27	6	2	1	249	230	8.3	27	127	4.6	94	3.4	4.16	93	.248	.333	-3	-8	96	98	-1.3	2	-2	-0.6
■ JACK LIVELY	Lively, Henry Everett b: 5/29/1885, Joppa, Ala. d: 12/5/67, Arab, Ala. BR , 5'9", 185 lbs. Deb: 4/16/11																												
1911	Det-A	7	5	.583	18	14	10	0	0	114	143	11.3	1	34	2.7	45	3.6	4.58	78	.313	.369	-16	-13	107	95	0.1	2	-1	-0.9
■ WES LIVENGOOD	Livengood, Wesley Amos b: 7/18/10, Salisbury, N.C. BR/TR, 6'2", 172 lbs. Deb: 5/30/39																												
1939	Cin-N	0	0	—	5	0	0	0	0	6	9	13.5	3	3	4.5	4	6.0	9.00	43	.360	.429	-3	-3	100	114	0.0	0	0	-0.2
■ JAKE LIVINGSTON	Livingston, Jacob M. (born Jacob M. Livingstone) b: 1/1/1880, Russia d: 3/22/49, Wassaic, N.Y. Deb: 9/06/01																												
1901	NY-N	0	0	—	2	0	0	0	0	12	26	19.5	0	7	5.3	6	4.5	9.00	35	.485	.566	-8	-8	95	114	0.0	0	-0	-0.6
■ CLEM LLEWELLYN	Llewellyn, Clement Manley "Lew" b: 8/1/1895, Dobson, N.C. d: 11/26/69, Concord, N.C. BL/TR, 6'2", 195 lbs. Deb: 6/18/22																												
1922	NY-A	0	0	—	1	0	0	0	0	1	1	9.0	0	0	0.0	0	0.0	0.00	—	.250	.250	0	0	99	0	0.0	0	0	0.0
■ HARRY LOCHHEAD	Lochhead, Robert Henry b: 3/29/1876, Stockton, Cal. d: 8/22/09, Stockton, Cal. TR , Deb: 4/16/1899																												
1899	Cle-N	0	0	—	1	0	0	0	0	4	4	9.0	0	2	4.5	0	0.0	0.00	—	.283	.372	2	2	96	0	0.0	0	0	0.2
■ CHUCK LOCKE	Locke, Charles Edward b: 5/5/32, Malden, Mo. BR/TR, 5'11", 185 lbs. Deb: 9/16/55																												
1955	Bal-A	0	0	—	2	0	0	0	0	3	0	0.0	0	1	3.0	1	3.0	0.00	—	.000	.091	1	1	94	0	0.0	0	0	0.1
■ BOBBY LOCKE	Locke, Lawrence Donald b: 3/3/34, Rowes Run, Pa. BR/TR, 5'11", 185 lbs. Deb: 6/18/59																												
1959	Cle-A	3	2	.600	24	7	0	0	2	78	66	7.6	6	41	4.7	40	4.6	3.12	117	.233	.325	6	5	95	119	0.1	3	0	0.8
1960	Cle-A	3	5	.375	32	11	2	2	2	123	121	8.9	10	37	2.7	53	3.9	3.37	113	.255	.307	7	6	98	100	-0.9	3	2	1.1
1961	Cle-A	4	4	.500	37	4	0	0	2	95	112	10.6	12	40	3.8	37	3.5	4.55	85	.300	.362	-6	-7	97	119	0.1	0	1	-0.5
1962	StL-N	0	0	—	1	0	0	0	0	2	1	4.5	0	2	9.0	1	4.5	0.00	—	.143	.333	1	1	107	0	0.0	0	0	0.1
	Phi-N	1	0	1.000	5	0	0	0	0	16	16	9.0	4	10	5.6	9	5.1	5.63	67	.262	.361	-3	-3	95	103	0.5	0	1	-0.1
	Yr	1	0	1.000	6	0	0	0	0	18	17	8.5	4	12	6.0	10	5.0	5.00	76	.250	.358	-2	-2	97	103	0.5	0	1	0.0
1963	Phi-N	0	0	—	9	0	0	0	0	11	10	8.2	0	5	4.1	7	5.7	5.73	58	.244	.326	-3	-3	102	51	0.0	-0	-0	-0.2
1964	Phi-N	0	0	—	8	0	0	0	0	19	21	9.9	2	6	2.8	11	5.2	2.84	122	.276	.325	1	1	98	149	0.0	-0	0	0.1
1965	Cin-N	0	1	.000	11	0	0	0	0	17	20	10.6	2	8	4.2	8	4.2	5.82	62	.299	.364	-4	-4	102	93	-0.4	0	1	-0.3
1967	Cal-A	3	0	1.000	9	1	0	0	2	19	14	6.6	1	3	1.4	7	3.3	2.37	131	.203	.243	2	2	96	75	1.5	1	0	0.3
1968	Cal-A	2	3	.400	29	0	0	0	2	36	51	12.8	3	13	3.3	21	5.3	6.50	44	.331	.378	-14	-15	96	90	0.0	-0	-0	-1.6
Total	9	16	15	.516	165	23	2	2	10	416	432	9.3	40	165	3.6	194	4.2	4.02	91	.269	.334	-12	-17	97	106	0.9	7	4	-0.3
■ RON LOCKE	Locke, Ronald Thomas b: 4/4/42, Wakefield, R.I. BR/TL, 5'11", 168 lbs. Deb: 4/23/64																												
1964	NY-N	1	2	.333	25	3	0	0	0	41	46	10.1	3	22	4.8	17	3.7	3.51	99	.289	.367	0	-0	98	144	0.0	-0	-0	0.0
■ BOB LOCKER	Locker, Robert Awtry b: 3/15/38, George, Iowa BB/TR, 6'3", 200 lbs. Deb: 4/14/65																												
1965	Chi-A	5	2	.714	51	0	0	0	2	91	71	7.0	6	30	3.0	69	6.8	3.16	99	.216	.278	3	-0	91	80	1.1	-1	4	0.2
1966	Chi-A	9	8	.529	56	0	0	0	12	95	73	6.9	2	23	2.2	70	6.6	2.46	130	.206	.263	10	8	93	72	0.3	1	3	1.3

YEAR	TM/L	W	L	PCT	G	GS	CG	SHO	SV	IP	H	H/G	HR	BB	BB/G	SO	SO/G	ERA	/A	OAVG	OOBP	PR	/A	PF	CPI	WAT	PB	PD	TPI
1967	Chi-A	7	5	.583	**77**	0	0	0	20	125	102	7.3	5	23	1.7	80	5.8	2.09	144	.222	.268	16	13	93	109	0.5	-1	5	1.9
1968	Chi-A	5	4	.556	70	0	0	0	10	90	78	7.8	4	27	2.7	62	6.2	2.30	132	.234	.285	7	7	102	116	1.1	-1	2	1.1
1969	Chi-A	2	3	.400	17	0	0	0	4	22	26	10.6	6	6	2.5	15	6.1	6.55	61	.292	.333	-7	-6	110	88	0.0	-0	0	-0.5
	Sea-A	3	3	.500	51	0	0	0	6	78	69	8.0	3	26	3.0	46	5.3	2.19	166	.234	.298	12	13	100	123	0.5	-0	2	1.5
	Yr	5	6	.455	68	0	0	0	10	100	95	8.6	9	32	2.9	61	5.5	3.15	118	.247	.306	5	6	102	123	0.5	-0	2	1.0
1970	Mil-A	0	1	.000	28	0	0	0	3	32	37	10.4	1	10	2.8	19	5.3	3.38	110	.306	.377	1	1	100	143	-0.4	-0	-0	0.1
	Oak-A	3	3	.500	38	0	0	0	4	56	49	7.9	1	19	3.1	33	5.3	2.89	123	.232	.292	5	4	96	84	-0.2	-0	1	0.5
	Yr	3	4	.429	66	0	0	0	7	88	86	8.8	2	29	3.0	52	5.3	3.07	118	.254	.310	6	5	97	84	-0.6	-0	0	0.6
1971	Oak-A	7	2	.778	47	0	0	0	6	72	68	8.5	3	19	2.4	46	5.8	2.88	119	.249	.293	5	4	99	98	1.9	-0	1	0.6
1972	Oak-A	6	1	.857	56	0	0	0	10	78	69	8.0	1	16	1.8	47	5.4	2.65	109	.235	.274	4	2	95	80	2.3	0	-1	0.2
1973	Chi-N	10	6	.625	63	0	0	0	18	106	96	8.2	6	42	3.6	76	6.5	2.55	157	.244	.316	13	17	109	130	2.4	-1	2	1.9
1975	Chi-N	0	1	.000	22	0	0	0	0	33	38	10.4	3	16	4.4	14	3.8	4.91	78	.306	.378	-5	-4	105	112	-0.4	0	1	-0.3
Total	10	57	39	.594	576	0	0	0	95	878	776	8.0	41	257	2.6	577	5.9	2.76	122	.237	.293	64	58	98	102	9.1	-4	19	8.5

■ SKIP LOCKWOOD Lockwood, Claude Edward b: 8/17/46, Boston, Mass. BR/TR, 6'1", 175 lbs. Deb: 4/23/65

YEAR	TM/L	W	L	PCT	G	GS	CG	SHO	SV	IP	H	H/G	HR	BB	BB/G	SO	SO/G	ERA	/A	OAVG	OOBP	PR	/A	PF	CPI	WAT	PB	PD	TPI
1969	Sea-A	0	1	.000	6	3	0	0	0	23	24	9.4	3	6	2.3	10	3.9	3.52	103	.279	.316	0	0	100	123	-0.4	-1	0	0.0
1970	Mil-A	5	12	.294	27	26	3	1	0	174	173	8.9	22	79	4.1	93	4.8	4.29	87	.266	.343	-11	-11	100	106	-2.4	2	-1	-0.9
1971	Mil-A	10	15	.400	33	32	5	1	0	208	191	8.3	13	91	3.9	115	5.0	3.33	108	.246	.324	3	6	104	103	-0.9	-2	-3	0.2
1972	Mil-A	8	15	.348	29	27	5	3	0	170	148	7.8	11	71	3.8	106	5.6	3.60	82	.232	.309	-10	-12	97	84	-2.1	-0	-2	-1.6
1973	Mil-A	5	12	.294	37	15	3	0	0	155	164	9.5	10	59	3.4	87	5.1	3.89	94	.280	.345	-1	-4	96	109	-3.1	0	0	-0.3
1974	Cal-A	2	5	.286	37	2	0	0	1	81	81	9.0	8	32	3.6	39	4.3	4.33	78	.264	.332	-6	-9	93	96	-1.1	0	-0	-0.8
1975	NY-N	1	3	.250	24	0	0	0	2	48	28	5.3	3	25	4.7	61	11.4	1.50	230	.174	.281	11	10	95	141	-0.9	-0	-1	1.0
1976	NY-N	10	7	.588	56	0	0	0	19	94	62	5.9	6	34	3.3	108	10.3	2.68	118	.186	.261	9	5	91	70	1.1	3	-0	0.7
1977	NY-N	4	8	.333	63	0	0	0	20	104	87	7.5	5	31	2.7	84	7.3	3.38	112	.227	.286	6	5	97	74	-0.9	-0	-2	0.3
1978	NY-N	7	13	.350	57	0	0	0	15	91	78	7.7	10	31	3.1	73	7.2	3.56	100	.236	.294	0	-0	99	94	-1.5	1	-2	0.0
1979	NY-N	2	5	.286	27	0	0	0	9	42	33	7.1	3	14	3.0	42	9.0	1.50	240	.224	.287	10	10	96	183	-0.9	-0	-0	1.0
1980	Bos-A	3	1	.750	24	1	0	0	2	46	61	11.9	4	17	3.3	11	2.2	5.28	78	.321	.370	-6	-6	102	103	1.0	0	-1	-0.6
Total	12	57	97	.370	420	106	16	5	68	1236	1130	8.2	98	490	3.6	829	6.0	3.55	99	.246	.317	5	-5	98	100	-12.1	3	-12	-1.0

■ MILO LOCKWOOD Lockwood, Milo Hathaway b: 4/7/1858, Solon, Ohio d: 10/9/1897, Economy, Pa. 5'10", 160 lbs. Deb: 4/17/1884

YEAR	TM/L	W	L	PCT	G	GS	CG	SHO	SV	IP	H	H/G	HR	BB	BB/G	SO	SO/G	ERA	/A	OAVG	OOBP	PR	/A	PF	CPI	WAT	PB	PD	TPI
1884	Was-U	1	9	.100	11	10	6	0	0	68	99	13.1	4	15	2.0	48	6.4	7.41	40	.345	.377	-33	-34	98	77	-3.8	0	0	-2.5

■ BILLY LOES Loes, William b: 12/13/29, Long Island City, N.Y. BR/TR, 6'1", 165 lbs. Deb: 5/18/50

YEAR	TM/L	W	L	PCT	G	GS	CG	SHO	SV	IP	H	H/G	HR	BB	BB/G	SO	SO/G	ERA	/A	OAVG	OOBP	PR	/A	PF	CPI	WAT	PB	PD	TPI
1950	Bro-N	0	0	—	10	0	0	0	0	13	16	11.1	5	5	3.5	2	1.4	7.62	57	.314	.375	-5	-5	104	101	0.0	0	-0	-0.4
1952	Bro-N	13	8	.619	39	21	8	4	1	187	154	7.4	12	71	3.4	115	5.5	2.70	136	.224	.296	22	20	98	106	-0.1	-3	-0	1.8
1953	Bro-N	14	8	.636	32	25	9	1	0	163	165	9.1	21	53	2.9	75	4.1	4.53	94	.261	.320	-4	-5	100	92	-0.7	-2	3	-0.3
1954	Bro-N	13	5	.722	28	21	6	0	0	148	154	9.4	14	60	3.6	97	5.9	4.14	99	.269	.333	-1	-1	101	98	3.0	-2	-0	-0.3
1955	Bro-N	10	4	.714	22	19	6	0	0	128	116	8.2	16	46	3.2	85	6.0	3.59	114	.240	.304	6	7	101	98	1.5	-3	0	0.4
1956	Bro-N	0	1	.000	1	1	0	0	0	1	5	45.0	1	1	9.0	2	18.0	54.00	7	.556	.600	-6	-6	100	54	-0.4	0	0	-0.3
	Bal-A	2	7	.222	21	6	1	0	3	57	65	10.3	4	23	3.6	22	3.5	4.74	85	.291	.352	-4	-5	97	99	-2.2	-1	1	-0.3
1957	Bal-A	12	7	.632	31	18	8	3	4	155	142	8.2	8	37	2.1	86	5.0	3.25	108	.245	.291	9	5	93	86	2.8	-3	2	0.3
1958	Bal-A	3	9	.250	32	10	1	0	5	114	106	8.4	10	44	3.5	44	3.5	3.63	99	.252	.324	2	-1	95	106	-2.9	-2	0	-0.2
1959	Bal-A	4	7	.364	37	0	0	0	14	64	58	8.2	5	25	3.5	34	4.8	4.08	93	.239	.313	-2	-2	98	83	-1.3	-0	1	0.0
1960	SF-N	3	2	.600	37	0	0	0	5	46	40	7.8	9	17	3.3	28	5.5	4.89	68	.247	.321	-6	-8	89	96	0.5	0	1	-0.6
1961	SF-N	6	5	.545	26	18	3	1	0	115	114	8.9	13	39	3.1	55	4.3	4.23	92	.258	.320	-2	-4	96	93	0.0	-0	0	-0.4
Total	11	80	63	.559	316	139	42	9	32	1191	1135	8.6	118	421	3.2	645	4.9	3.88	99	.252	.315	9	-4	97	96	0.2	-17	6	-0.3

■ FRANK LOFTUS Loftus, Francis Patrick b: 3/10/1898, Scranton, Pa. d: 10/27/80, Belchertown, Mass. BR/TR, 5'9", 190 lbs. Deb: 9/26/26

YEAR	TM/L	W	L	PCT	G	GS	CG	SHO	SV	IP	H	H/G	HR	BB	BB/G	SO	SO/G	ERA	/A	OAVG	OOBP	PR	/A	PF	CPI	WAT	PB	PD	TPI
1926	Was-A	0	0	—	1	0	0	0	0	1	3	27.0	0	2	18.0	0	0.0	9.00	43	.600	.714	-1	-1	97	219	0.0	0	0	0.0

■ BOB LOGAN Logan, Robert Dean "Lefty" b: 2/10/10, Thompson, Neb. d: 5/20/78, Indianapolis, Ind. BR/TL, 5'10", 170 lbs. Deb: 4/18/35

YEAR	TM/L	W	L	PCT	G	GS	CG	SHO	SV	IP	H	H/G	HR	BB	BB/G	SO	SO/G	ERA	/A	OAVG	OOBP	PR	/A	PF	CPI	WAT	PB	PD	TPI
1935	Bro-N	0	1	.000	2	0	0	0	0	3	2	6.0	0	1	3.0	1	3.0	3.00	127	.182	.250	0	0	95	38	-0.4	0	0	0.1
1937	Det-A	0	0	—	1	0	0	0	0	1	1	9.0	0	1	9.0	1	9.0	0.00	—	.333	.500	1	1	108	0	0.0	0	0	0.0
	Chi-N	0	0	—	4	0	0	0	1	6	6	9.0	0	4	6.0	2	3.0	1.50	261	.261	.357	2	2	100	272	0.0	-0	-0	0.1
1938	Chi-N	0	2	.000	14	0	0	0	2	23	18	7.0	0	17	6.7	10	3.9	2.74	142	.222	.360	3	3	103	129	-0.9	-0	-0	0.2
1941	Cin-N	0	1	.000	2	0	0	0	0	3	5	15.0	0	5	15.0	0	0.0	9.00	39	.333	.500	-2	-2	98	100	-0.4	0	0	0.0
1945	Bos-N	7	11	.389	34	25	5	1	1	187	213	10.3	9	53	2.6	53	2.6	3.18	135	.283	.328	13	23	113	**124**	-1.1	0	0	2.5
Total	5	7	15	.318	57	25	5	1	4	223	245	9.9	9	81	3.3	67	2.7	3.15	134	.277	.335	16	27	111	127	-2.8	-0	1	2.9

■ BILL LOHRMAN Lohrman, William Le Roy b: 5/22/13, Brooklyn, N.Y. BR/TR, 6'1", 185 lbs. Deb: 6/19/34

YEAR	TM/L	W	L	PCT	G	GS	CG	SHO	SV	IP	H	H/G	HR	BB	BB/G	SO	SO/G	ERA	/A	OAVG	OOBP	PR	/A	PF	CPI	WAT	PB	PD	TPI
1934	Phi-N	0	1	.000	4	0	0	0	1	6	5	7.5	0	1	1.5	2	3.0	4.50	100	.217	.250	-0	-0	111	33	-0.4	0	0	0.0
1937	NY-N	1	0	1.000	2	1	1	0	1	10	5	4.5	0	2	1.8	3	2.7	0.90	424	.152	.200	3	3	98	42	0.5	-0	0	0.4
1938	NY-N	9	6	.600	31	14	3	0	0	152	152	9.0	9	33	2.0	52	3.1	3.32	117	.253	.293	8	9	102	92	0.9	-4	2	0.7
1939	NY-N	12	13	.480	38	24	9	1	1	186	200	9.7	15	45	2.2	70	3.4	4.06	95	.282	.322	-3	-4	99	100	-0.8	4	-0	0.0
1940	NY-N	10	15	.400	31	28	11	**5**	1	195	200	9.2	19	43	2.0	73	3.4	3.78	102	.264	.304	1	1	100	100	-2.2	-2	2	0.1
1941	NY-N	9	10	.474	33	20	6	2	3	159	184	10.4	7	40	2.3	61	3.5	4.02	94	.286	.324	-7	-4	104	97	-0.1	3	0	0.0
1942	StL-N	1	1	.500	5	0	0	0	0	13	11	7.6	0	2	1.4	6	4.2	1.38	245	.244	.260	3	3	103	167	-0.2	1	0	0.4
	NY-N	13	4	.765	26	19	12	2	0	158	143	8.1	11	33	1.9	41	2.3	2.56	131	.240	.277	13	14	101	108	4.2	-3	-1	1.1
	Yr	14	5	.737	31	19	12	2	0	171	154	8.1	11	35	1.8	47	2.5	2.47	136	.240	.276	16	17	101	108	4.0	1	-1	1.5
1943	NY-N	5	6	.455	17	12	3	0	1	80	110	12.4	7	25	2.8	16	1.8	5.17	65	.324	.370	-16	-16	99	106	0.9	-3	-1	-1.9
	Bro-N	0	2	.000	6	2	2	0	0	28	29	9.3	2	10	3.2	5	1.6	3.54	94	.274	.331	-1	-1	99	116	-0.9	0	0	0.0
	Yr	5	8	.385	23	14	5	0	1	108	139	11.6	9	35	2.9	21	1.8	4.75	70	.311	.356	-17	-17	99	116	0.0	-3	-1	-1.9
1944	Bro-N	0	0	—	3	0	0	0	0	3	4	12.0	0	4	12.0	1	3.0	0.00	—	.500	.667	1	1	102	0	0.0	0	0	0.1
	Cin-N	0	1	.000	2	1	0	0	0	2	5	22.5	0	2	9.0	0	0.0	22.50	15	.500	.583	-4	-4	95	58	-0.4	0	0	-0.3
	Yr	0	1	.000	5	1	0	0	0	5	9	16.2	0	6	10.8	1	1.8	9.00	40	.500	.625	-3	-3	99	58	-0.4	0	0	-0.2
Total	9	60	59	.504	198	121	47	10	8	992	1048	9.5	70	240	2.2	330	3.0	3.68	101	.271	.312	-1	2	101	100	1.5	-3	3	0.6

■ MICKEY LOLICH Lolich, Michael Stephen b: 9/12/40, Portland, Ore. BB/TL, 6'1", 170 lbs. Deb: 5/12/63

YEAR	TM/L	W	L	PCT	G	GS	CG	SHO	SV	IP	H	H/G	HR	BB	BB/G	SO	SO/G	ERA	/A	OAVG	OOBP	PR	/A	PF	CPI	WAT	PB	PD	TPI
1963	Det-A	5	9	.357	33	18	4	0	0	144	145	9.1	13	56	3.5	103	6.4	3.56	106	.265	.332	1	3	104	116	-1.9	-1	-1	0.2
1964	Det-A	18	9	.667	44	33	12	6	2	232	196	7.6	26	64	2.5	192	7.4	3.26	106	.225	.279	9	5	95	88	4.6	1	-2	0.4
1965	Det-A	15	9	.625	43	37	7	3	3	244	216	8.0	23	72	2.7	226	8.3	3.43	105	.236	.296	1	5	104	93	2.3	-6	-2	-0.3
1966	Det-A	14	14	.500	40	33	5	1	3	204	204	9.0	24	83	3.7	173	7.6	4.76	73	.257	.328	-30	-29	102	88	-1.2	1	-3	-3.0
1967	Det-A	14	13	.519	31	30	11	**6**	0	204	165	7.3	14	56	2.5	174	7.7	3.04	104	.221	.278	4	3	98	86	-1.1	3	-2	0.4
1968	Det-A	17	9	.654	39	32	8	4	1	220	178	7.3	23	65	2.7	197	8.1	3.19	96	.219	.281	-5	-3	103	90	0.8	0	-2	-0.5
1969	Det-A	19	11	.633	37	36	15	1	1	281	214	6.9	22	122	3.9	271	8.7	3.14	118	.210	.299	15	18	102	90	3.1	-3	-0	1.6
1970	Det-A	14	19	.424	40	39	13	3	0	273	272	9.0	27	109	3.6	230	7.6	3.79	102	.260	.327	-2	2	104	105	-2.5	0	1	0.5
1971	Det-A	**25**	14	.641	45	45	**29**	4	0	**376**	336	8.0	36	92	2.2	**308**	7.4	2.92	113	.237	.283	23	15	95	99	4.4	2	-4	1.4
1972	Det-A	22	14	.611	41	41	23	4	0	327	282	7.8	29	74	2.0	250	6.9	2.50	138	.234	.278	21	34	112	111	3.0	-1	-4	3.6
1973	Det-A	16	15	.516	42	42	17	3	0	309	315	9.2	35	79	2.3	214	6.2	3.82	101	.266	.310	0	2	101	100	-0.2	0	-0	0.1
1974	Det-A	16	21	.432	41	41	27	3	0	308	310	9.1	38	78	2.3	202	5.9	4.15	94	.268	.310	-18	-8	108	95	-0.5	0	-4	-1.2
1975	Det-A	12	18	.400	32	32	19	1	0	241	260	9.7	19	64	2.4	139	5.2	3.77	107	.279	.319	0	7	106	103	1.2	0	-2	0.5
1976	NY-N	8	13	.381	31	30	5	2	0	193	184	8.6	14	52	2.4	120	5.6	3.22	99	.252	.296	6	-1	91	99	-3.2	0	-1	-0.1
1978	SD-N	2	1	.667	20	2	0	0	1	35	30	7.7	0	11	2.8	13	3.3	1.54	215	.240	.300	8	7	93	170	0.5	-0	0	0.7
1979	SD-N	0	2	.000	27	5	0	0	0	49	59	10.8	4	22	4.0	20	3.7	4.78	76	.304	.363	-6	-6	97	107	-0.9	-0	0	-0.6
Total	16	217	191	.532	586	496	195	41	11	3640	3366	8.3	347	1099	2.7	2832	7.0	3.44	104	.246	.301	28	55	102	98	8.4	-3	-25	3.7

■ TIM LOLLAR Lollar, William Timothy b: 3/17/56, Poplar Bluff, Mo. BL/TL, 6'3", 200 lbs. Deb: 6/28/80

YEAR	TM/L	W	L	PCT	G	GS	CG	SHO	SV	IP	H	H/G	HR	BB	BB/G	SO	SO/G	ERA	/A	OAVG	OOBP	PR	/A	PF	CPI	WAT	PB	PD	TPI
1980	NY-A	1	0	1.000	14	1	0	0	2	32	33	9.3	3	20	5.6	13	3.7	3.38	117	.280	.368	2	2	98	151	0.5	0	0	0.2

YEAR	TM/L	W	L	PCT	G	GS	CG	SHO	SV	IP	H	H/G	HR	BB	BB/G	SO	SO/G	ERA	/A	OAVG	OOBP	PR	/A	PF	CPI	WAT	PB	PD	TPI
1981	SD-N	2	8	.200	24	11	0	0	1	77	87	10.2	4	51	6.0	38	4.4	6.08	54	.293	.391	-22	-24	95	88	-2.3	1	2	-2.0
1982	SD-N	16	9	.640	34	34	4	2	0	233	192	7.4	20	87	3.4	150	5.8	3.13	106	.224	.294	12	4	92	94	3.9	9	0	1.3
1983	SD-N	7	12	.368	30	30	1	0	0	176	170	8.7	22	85	4.3	135	6.9	4.60	78	.258	.342	-19	-20	99	96	-2.6	5	-2	-1.5
1984	SD-N	11	13	.458	31	31	3	2	0	196	168	7.7	18	105	4.8	131	6.0	3.90	90	.234	.328	-7	-8	98	95	-2.5	7	-2	-0.3
1985	Chi-A	3	5	.375	18	13	0	0	0	83	83	9.0	10	58	6.3	61	6.6	4.66	89	.266	.376	-5	-5	100	114	-1.1	0	-0	-0.4
	Bos-A	5	5	.500	16	10	1	0	1	67	57	7.7	9	40	5.4	44	5.9	4.57	92	.230	.337	-3	-3	102	91	0.0	0	-1	-0.3
	Yr	8	10	.444	34	23	1	0	1	150	140	8.4	19	98	5.9	105	6.3	4.62	90	.248	.357	-8	-7	101	91	-1.1	0	-1	-0.7
1986	Bos-A	2	0	1.000	32	1	0	0	0	43	51	10.7	7	34	7.1	28	5.9	6.91	60	.304	.417	-13	-13	99	101	1.0	0	1	-1.1
Total	7	47	52	.475	199	131	9	4	4	907	841	8.3	93	480	4.8	600	6.0	4.27	85	.249	.340	-54	-66	97	98	-3.1	23	-2	-4.1
■ **VIC LOMBARDI**	Lombardi, Victor Alvin b: 9/20/22, Reedley, Cal. BL/TL, 5'7", 158 lbs. Deb: 4/18/45																												
1945	Bro-N	10	11	.476	38	24	9	0	4	204	195	8.6	11	86	3.8	64	2.8	3.31	109	.252	.325	11	7	95	110	-1.8	-0	-0	0.5
1946	Bro-N	13	10	.565	41	25	13	2	3	193	170	7.9	10	84	3.9	60	2.8	2.89	118	.235	.309	11	11	100	103	-1.0	1	0	1.4
1947	Bro-N	12	11	.522	33	20	7	3	3	175	156	8.0	12	65	3.3	72	3.7	2.98	140	.241	.307	21	23	103	110	-1.8	2	1	2.6
1948	Pit-N	10	9	.526	38	17	9	0	4	163	156	8.6	9	67	3.7	54	3.0	3.70	112	.255	.327	5	8	104	100	-0.2	1	1	1.0
1949	Pit-N	5	5	.500	34	12	4	0	1	134	149	10.0	14	68	4.6	64	4.3	4.57	90	.286	.367	-8	-7	102	113	0.4	5	1	0.0
1950	Pit-N	0	5	.000	39	2	0	0	1	76	93	11.0	14	48	5.7	26	3.1	6.63	66	.310	.402	-21	-19	106	102	-2.4	1	0	-1.6
Total	6	50	51	.495	223	100	42	5	16	945	919	8.8	70	418	4.0	340	3.2	3.68	106	.257	.332	19	23	101	107	-6.8	10	2	3.9
■ **LOU LOMBARDO**	Lombardo, Louis b: 11/18/28, Carlstadt, N.J. BL/TL, 6'2", 210 lbs. Deb: 9/22/48																												
1948	NY-N	0	0	—	2	0	0	0	0	5	5	9.0	1	5	9.0	0	0.0	7.20	54	.250	.407	-2	-2	98	93	0.0	-0	0	-0.1
■ **JIM LONBORG**	Lonborg, James Reynold b: 4/16/42, Santa Maria, Cal. BR/TR, 6'5", 200 lbs. Deb: 4/23/65																												
1965	Bos-A	9	17	.346	32	31	7	1	0	185	193	9.4	20	65	3.2	113	5.5	4.48	84	.262	.321	-21	-14	109	88	-1.4	0	-2	-1.5
1966	Bos-A	10	10	.500	45	23	3	1	2	182	173	8.6	18	55	2.7	131	6.5	3.86	98	.249	.306	-9	-1	110	93	1.1	-2	-1	-0.2
1967	Bos-A	**22**	9	.710	39	39	15	2	0	273	228	7.5	23	83	2.7	**246**	8.1	3.16	115	.225	.292	2	15	113	95	**5.8**	-2	-2	1.3
1968	Bos-A	6	10	.375	23	17	4	1	0	113	89	7.1	11	59	4.7	73	5.8	4.30	70	.216	.324	-17	-16	101	82	-2.4	4	-2	-1.5
1969	Bos-A	7	11	.389	29	23	4	0	0	144	148	9.3	15	65	4.1	100	6.3	4.50	84	.270	.350	-14	-11	105	100	-2.6	-1	-0	-1.1
1970	Bos-A	4	1	.800	9	4	0	0	0	34	33	8.7	3	9	2.4	21	5.6	3.18	129	.260	.304	2	3	110	110	1.4	2	0	0.7
1971	Bos-A	10	7	.588	27	26	5	1	0	168	167	8.9	15	67	3.6	100	5.4	4.13	88	.259	.337	-12	-9	105	97	1.3	0	1	-0.7
1972	Mil-A	14	12	.538	33	30	11	2	1	223	197	8.0	17	76	3.1	143	5.8	2.83	105	.238	.306	6	4	97	112	3.1	-0	-2	0.1
1973	Phi-N	13	16	.448	38	30	6	0	0	199	218	9.9	25	80	3.6	106	4.8	4.88	82	.279	.347	-27	-20	109	97	0.3	-0	-1	-2.0
1974	Phi-N	17	13	.567	39	39	16	3	0	283	280	8.9	22	70	2.2	121	3.8	3.21	117	.261	.305	13	17	104	106	2.6	-4	-4	1.0
1975	Phi-N	8	6	.571	27	26	6	2	0	159	161	9.1	12	45	2.5	72	4.1	4.13	89	.257	.309	-9	-8	101	80	0.7	-3	0	-1.0
1976	Phi-N	18	10	.643	33	32	8	1	1	222	210	8.5	18	50	2.0	118	4.8	3.08	119	.249	.289	10	14	105	100	0.9	1	-3	1.4
1977	Phi-N	11	4	.733	25	25	4	1	0	158	157	8.9	15	50	2.8	76	4.3	4.10	94	.261	.318	-3	-4	98	92	2.3	-2	-1	-0.7
1978	Phi-N	8	10	.444	22	22	1	0	0	114	132	10.4	16	45	3.6	48	3.8	5.21	71	.293	.354	-21	-19	104	99	-1.9	1	-0	-1.8
1979	Phi-N	0	1	.000	4	1	0	0	0	7	14	18.0	3	4	5.1	7	9.0	11.57	31	.389	.463	-6	-6	97	100	-0.4	-0	0	-0.5
Total	15	157	137	.534	425	368	90	15	4	2464	2400	8.8	233	823	3.0	1475	5.4	3.86	95	.255	.317	-104	-56	105	97	10.8	-6	-17	-6.5
■ **LEP LONG**	Long, Lester b: 7/12/1888, Summit, N.J. d: 10/21/58, Birmingham, Ala. BR/TR, 5'10", 153 lbs. Deb: 6/29/11																												
1911	Phi-A	0	0	—	4	0	0	0	0	8	15	16.9	0	5	5.6	4	4.5	4.50	66	.405	.476	-1	-1	88	180	0.0	-0	0	0.0
■ **RED LONG**	Long, Nelson b: 9/28/1876, Burlington, Ont., Canada d: 8/11/29, Hamilton, Ont., Can BR/TR, 6'1", 190 lbs. Deb: 9/11/02																												
1902	Bos-N	0	0	—	1	1	1	0	0	8	4	4.5	0	3	3.4	5	5.6	1.13	232	.165	.257	1	1	94	58	0.0	-0	-0	0.1
■ **BOB LONG**	Long, Robert Earl b: 11/11/54, Jasper, Tenn. BR/TR, 6'3", 178 lbs. Deb: 9/02/81																												
1981	Pit-N	1	2	.333	5	3	0	0	0	20	23	10.3	2	10	4.5	8	3.6	5.85	57	.299	.367	-5	-6	96	91	-0.3	-0	-0	-0.5
1985	Sea-A	0	0	—	28	0	0	0	0	38	30	7.1	7	17	4.0	29	6.9	3.79	104	.210	.302	2	1	95	96	0.0	-0	-0	0.0
Total	2	1	2	.333	33	3	0	0	0	58	53	8.2	9	27	4.2	37	5.7	4.50	83	.241	.325	-4	-5	96	94	-0.3	-0	-1	-0.5
■ **TOM LONG**	Long, Thomas Francis "Little Hawk" b: 4/22/1898, Memphis, Tenn. d: 9/16/73, Louisville, Ky. BL/TL, 5'9", 154 lbs. Deb: 4/26/24																												
1924	Bro-N	0	0	—	1	0	0	0	0	2	2	9.0	0	2	9.0	0	0.0	9.00	42	.333	.444	-1	-1	98	76	0.0	0	0	0.0
■ **BILL LONG**	Long, William Douglas b: 2/29/60, Cincinnati, Ohio BR/TR, 6', 185 lbs. Deb: 7/21/85																												
1985	Chi-A	0	1	.000	4	3	0	0	0	14	25	16.1	4	5	3.2	13	8.4	10.29	40	.391	.423	-10	-10	100	91	-0.4	0	0	-0.7
1987	Chi-A	8	8	.500	29	23	5	2	1	169	179	9.5	20	28	**1.5**	72	3.8	4.37	111	.272	.300	2	9	109	89	0.4	0	0	0.8
1988	Chi-A	8	11	.421	47	18	3	0	2	174	187	9.7	21	43	2.2	77	4.0	4.03	97	.280	.320	-1	-2	99	109	-0.4	0	-0	-0.2
Total	3	16	20	.444	80	44	8	2	3	357	391	9.9	45	76	1.9	162	4.1	4.44	98	.281	.316	-9	-3	103	99	-0.4	0	0	-0.1
■ **PETE LOOS**	Loos, Ivan b: 3/23/1878, Philadelphia, Pa. d: 2/23/56, Darby, Pa. TR , Deb: 5/02/01																												
1901	Phi-A	0	1	.000	1	1	0	0	0	1	2	18.0	0	4	36.0	0	0.0	27.00	14	.438	.700	-3	-3	100	68	-0.4	0	0	-0.1
■ **EDDIE LOPAT**	Lopat, Edmund Walter (born Edmund Walter Lopatynski) b: 6/21/18, New York, N.Y. BL/TL, 5'10", 185 lbs. Deb: 4/30/44 MC																												
1944	Chi-A	11	10	.524	27	25	13	1	0	210	217	9.3	12	59	2.5	75	3.2	3.26	108	.265	.310	4	6	102	106	1.4	6	1	1.5
1945	Chi-A	10	13	.435	26	24	17	1	1	199	226	10.2	8	56	2.5	74	3.3	4.12	78	.285	.330	-17	-20	96	95	-1.1	6	-1	-1.5
1946	Chi-A	13	13	.500	29	29	20	2	0	231	216	8.4	18	48	1.9	89	3.5	2.73	125	.248	.284	20	18	97	107	0.6	6	1	2.7
1947	Chi-A	16	13	.552	31	31	22	3	0	253	241	8.6	17	73	2.6	109	3.9	2.81	130	.253	.302	25	24	99	117	3.1	0	-1	2.5
1948	NY-A	17	11	.607	33	31	13	3	0	227	246	9.8	16	66	2.6	83	3.3	3.65	113	.284	.328	16	12	96	118	0.0	-1	1	1.2
1949	NY-A	15	10	.600	31	30	14	4	1	215	222	9.3	19	69	2.9	70	2.9	3.27	125	.269	.326	22	19	97	122	-0.6	7	0	2.6
1950	NY-A	18	8	.692	35	32	15	3	1	236	244	9.3	19	65	2.5	72	2.7	3.47	126	.266	.313	29	24	96	108	2.3	7	1	3.1
1951	NY-A	21	9	.700	31	31	20	4	0	235	209	8.0	12	71	2.7	93	3.6	2.91	125	.239	**.293**	32	19	88	101	3.1	2	1	2.1
1952	NY-A	10	5	.667	20	19	10	2	0	149	127	7.7	11	53	3.2	56	3.4	2.54	137	.234	.303	19	16	95	123	1.1	0	0	1.7
1953	NY-A	16	4	**.800**	25	24	9	3	0	178	169	8.5	13	32	**1.6**	50	2.5	**2.43**	145	.250	.285	31	22	88	123	4.5	2	1	2.5
1954	NY-A	12	4	.750	26	23	7	0	0	170	189	10.0	14	33	**1.7**	54	2.9	3.55	99	.288	.319	3	-1	94	114	2.1	-5	-1	-0.6
1955	NY-A	4	8	.333	16	12	3	1	0	87	101	10.4	12	16	1.7	24	2.5	3.72	100	.294	.324	2	0	94	123	-2.8	-1	-1	-0.2
	Bal-A	3	4	.429	10	7	1	0	0	49	57	10.5	8	9	1.7	10	1.8	4.22	88	.294	.329	-1	-3	94	116	0.3	0	1	-0.1
	Yr	7	12	.368	26	19	4	1	0	136	158	10.5	20	25	1.7	34	2.3	3.90	95	.293	.324	1	-3	94	116	-2.5	-1	-0	-0.3
Total	12	166	112	.597	340	318	164	27	3	2439	2464	9.1	179	650	2.4	859	3.2	3.21	116	.264	.310	185	138	95	112	14.0	28	4	17.5
■ **ART LOPATKA**	Lopatka, Arthur Joseph b: 5/28/19, Chicago, Ill. BB/TL, 5'10", 170 lbs. Deb: 9/12/45																												
1945	StL-N	1	0	1.000	4	1	1	0	0	12	7	5.3	0	3	2.3	5	3.8	1.50	246	.159	.229	3	3	97	35	0.5	0	-0	0.3
1946	Phi-N	0	1	.000	4	1	0	0	0	5	13	23.4	1	4	7.2	4	7.2	18.00	19	.448	.515	-8	-8	98	71	-0.4	0	0	-0.7
Total	2	1	1	.500	8	2	1	0	0	17	20	10.6	1	7	3.7	9	4.8	6.35	56	.274	.346	-5	-5	97	46	0.1	0	-0	-0.4
■ **AURELIO LOPEZ**	Lopez, Aurelio Alejandro (Rios) b: 9/21/48, Tecamachalco Puebla, Mexico BR/TR, 6', 185 lbs. Deb: 9/01/74																												
1974	KC-A	0	0	—	8	1	0	0	0	16	21	11.8	0	10	5.6	5	2.8	5.63	68	.344	.408	-4	-3	106	107	0.0	0	0	-0.2
1978	StL-N	4	2	.667	25	4	0	0	0	65	52	7.2	4	32	4.4	46	6.4	4.29	80	.218	.305	-5	-6	96	68	1.3	0	-1	-0.7
1979	Det-A	10	5	.667	61	0	0	0	21	127	95	6.7	12	51	3.6	106	7.5	2.41	169	.210	.287	26	23	96	117	2.4	0	0	2.3
1980	Det-A	13	6	.684	67	1	0	0	21	124	125	9.1	15	45	3.3	97	7.0	3.77	112	.263	.324	4	6	105	109	3.5	0	1	-0.5
1981	Det-A	5	2	.714	29	3	0	0	3	82	70	7.7	8	31	3.4	53	5.8	3.62	106	.233	.305	0	2	105	92	1.3	0	-0	0.2
1982	Det-A	3	1	.750	19	0	0	0	3	41	41	9.0	8	19	4.2	26	5.7	5.27	77	.268	.341	-5	-5	100	98	1.0	0	0	-0.4
1983	Det-A	9	8	.529	57	0	0	0	18	115	87	6.8	12	49	3.8	90	7.0	2.82	137	.210	.290	16	13	95	105	-0.5	0	-1	1.2
1984	Det-A	10	1	.909	71	0	0	0	14	138	109	7.1	16	52	3.4	94	6.1	2.93	128	.221	.292	16	13	94	109	4.2	0	-2	1.1
1985	Det-A	3	7	.300	51	0	0	0	5	86	82	8.6	15	41	4.3	53	5.5	4.81	91	.250	.327	-6	-4	106	96	-2.1	0	-0	-0.3
1986	Hou-N	3	3	.500	45	0	0	0	7	78	64	7.4	6	25	2.9	44	5.1	3.46	109	.221	.277	2	3	102	75	-0.4	-1	-2	0.0
1987	Hou-N	2	1	.667	26	0	0	0	1	38	39	9.2	6	12	2.8	21	5.0	4.50	84	.273	.323	-2	-3	93	106	0.6	-0	0	-0.2
Total	11	62	36	.633	459	9	0	0	93	910	785	7.8	102	367	3.6	635	6.3	3.56	111	.234	.306	42	39	99	100	11.3	-1	-7	3.5
■ **RAMON LOPEZ**	Lopez, Jose Ramon (Hevia) b: 5/26/33, Las Villas, Cuba d: 9/4/82, Miami, Fla. BR/TR, 6', 175 lbs. Deb: 8/21/66																												
1966	Cal-A	0	1	.000	4	1	0	0	0	7	4	5.1	1	4	5.1	2	2.6	5.14	67	.154	.267	-1	-1	100	41	-0.4	0	-0	-0.1

YEAR	TM/L	W	L	PCT	G	GS	CG	SHO	SV	IP	H	H/G	HR	BB	BB/G	SO	SO/G	ERA	/A	OAVG	OOBP	PR	/A	PF	CPI	WAT	PB	PD	TPI
■ MARCELINO LOPEZ	Lopez, Marcelino Pons b: 9/23/43, Havana, Cuba BR/TL, 6'3", 195 lbs. Deb: 4/14/63																												
1963	Phi-N	1	0	1.000	4	2	0	0	0	6	8	12.0	0	7	10.5	2	3.0	6.00	56	.333	.469	-2	-2	102	122	0.5	-0	0	-0.1
1965	Cal-A	14	13	.519	35	32	8	1	1	215	185	7.7	12	82	3.4	122	5.1	2.93	116	.230	.301	13	11	98	99	1.6	3	4	2.0
1966	Cal-A	7	14	.333	37	32	6	2	1	199	188	8.5	20	68	3.1	132	6.0	3.93	87	.251	.315	-11	-11	100	97	-3.6	1	2	-0.8
1967	Cal-A	0	2	.000	4	3	0	0	0	9	11	11.0	1	9	9.0	6	6.0	9.00	34	.324	.435	-6	-6	96	83	-0.9	0	-0	-0.5
	Bal-A	1	0	1.000	4	4	0	0	0	18	15	7.5	1	10	5.0	15	7.5	2.50	121	.227	.329	1	1	94	134	0.5	-0	0	0.0
	Yr	1	2	.333	8	7	0	0	0	27	26	8.7	2	19	6.3	21	7.0	4.67	65	.257	.369	-4	-5	94	134	-0.4	0	-1	-0.5
1969	Bal-A	5	3	.625	27	4	0	0	0	69	65	8.5	3	34	4.4	57	7.4	4.43	82	.252	.338	-6	-6	100	82	-0.2	1	-1	-0.6
1970	Bal-A	1	1	.500	25	3	0	0	0	61	47	6.9	2	37	5.5	49	7.2	2.07	169	.217	.322	11	10	94	145	-0.2	0	-1	0.9
1971	Mil-A	2	7	.222	31	11	0	0	0	68	64	8.5	5	60	7.9	42	5.6	4.63	78	.251	.380	-9	-8	104	104	-2.1	-1	1	-0.8
1972	Cle-A	0	0	—	4	2	0	0	0	8	8	9.0	0	10	11.3	1	1.1	5.63	59	.276	.450	-2	-2	108	105	0.0	-0	0	-0.2
Total	8	31	40	.437	171	93	14	3	2	653	591	8.1	44	317	4.4	426	5.9	3.62	95	.243	.327	-11	-13	99	102	-4.4	4	4	-0.1
■ BRIS LORD	Lord, Bristol Robotham "The Human Eyeball" b: 9/21/1883, Upland, Pa. d: 11/13/64, Annapolis, Md. BR/TR, 5'9", 185 lbs. Deb: 4/21/05																												
1907	Phi-A	0	0	—	1	0	0	0	0	1	3	27.0	0	0	0.0	0	0.0	9.00	29	.544	.544	-1	-1	104	131	0.0	0	0	0.0
■ LEFTY LORENZEN	Lorenzen, Adolph Andreas b: 1/12/1893, Davenport, Iowa d: 3/5/63, Davenport, Iowa BL/TL, 5'10", 164 lbs. Deb: 9/12/13																												
1913	Det-A	0	0	—	1	0	0	0	0	2	4	18.0	0	3	13.5	0	0.0	18.00	16	.667	.778	-3	-3	101	83	0.0	0	1	-0.2
■ JOE LOTZ	Lotz, Joseph Peter "Smokey" b: 1/2/1891, Remsen, Iowa d: 1/1/71, Castro Valley, Cal. BR/TR, 5'8.5", 175 lbs. Deb: 7/15/16																												
1916	StL-N	0	3	.000	12	3	1	0	0	40	31	7.0	1	17	3.8	18	4.0	4.27	61	.225	.304	-7	-7	100	61	-1.4	1	-0	-0.6
■ ART LOUDELL	Loudell, Arthur (born Arthur Laudel) b: 4/10/1882, Latham, Mo. d: 2/19/61, Kansas City, Mo. BR/TR, 5'11", 173 lbs. Deb: 8/13/10																												
1910	Det-A	1	1	.500	5	2	1	0	0	21	23	9.9	0	14	6.0	12	5.1	3.43	73	.284	.389	-2	-2	100	127	0.0	-0	-1	-0.2
■ LARRY LOUGHLIN	Loughlin, Larry John b: 8/16/41, Tacoma, Wash. BL/TL, 6'1", 190 lbs. Deb: 5/27/67																												
1967	Phi-N	0	0	—	3	0	0	0	0	5	9	16.2	1	4	7.2	5	9.0	16.20	22	.375	.464	-7	-7	104	58	0.0	1	-0	-0.5
■ DON LOUN	Loun, Donald Nelson b: 11/9/40, Frederick, Md. BR/TL, 6'2", 185 lbs. Deb: 9/23/64																												
1964	Was-A	1	1	.500	2	2	1	1	0	13	13	9.0	0	3	2.1	3	2.1	2.08	180	.250	.291	2	2	103	113	0.2	-0	0	0.3
■ SLIM LOVE	Love, Edward Haughton b: 8/1/1890, Love, Miss. d: 11/30/42, Memphis, Tenn. BL/TL, 6'7", 195 lbs. Deb: 9/08/13																												
1913	Was-A	1	0	1.000	5	1	0	0	1	17	14	7.4	0	6	3.2	5	2.6	1.59	193	.226	.294	3	3	105	124	0.5	0	-1	0.2
1916	NY-A	2	0	1.000	20	1	0	0	0	48	46	8.6	2	23	4.3	21	3.9	4.88	59	.274	.361	-11	-11	101	81	1.0	-2	-0	-1.2
1917	NY-A	6	5	.545	33	9	2	0	1	130	115	8.0	0	57	3.9	82	5.7	2.35	122	.251	.335	4	7	107	123	0.9	-1	-2	0.5
1918	NY-A	13	12	.520	38	29	13	1	1	229	207	8.1	3	116	4.6	95	3.7	3.07	85	.253	.346	-8	-12	94	108	1.0	3	-4	-1.4
1919	Det-A	6	4	.600	22	8	4	0	1	90	92	9.2	3	40	4.0	46	4.6	3.00	99	.275	.363	2	-0	92	130	0.4	0	-2	-0.1
1920	Det-A	0	0	—	1	0	0	0	0	4	6	13.5	0	4	9.0	2	4.5	9.00	45	.375	.500	-2	-2	106	88	0.0	0	0	-0.1
Total	6	28	21	.571	119	48	19	1	4	518	480	8.3	8	246	4.3	251	4.4	3.04	92	.259	.348	-12	-15	98	113	3.8	0	-8	-2.1
■ VANCE LOVELACE	Lovelace, Vance Odell b: 8/9/63, Tampa, Fla. BL/TL, 6'5", 205 lbs. Deb: 9/10/88																												
1988	Cal-A	0	0	—	3	0	0	0	0	1	2	18.0	1	3	27.0	0	0.0	18.00	21	.400	.625	-2	-2	95	127	0.0	0	0	-0.1
■ LYNN LOVENGUTH	Lovenguth, Lynn Richard b: 11/29/22, Camden, N.Y. BL/TR, 5'10.5", 170 lbs. Deb: 4/18/55																												
1955	Phi-N	0	1	.000	14	0	0	0	0	18	17	8.5	1	10	5.0	14	7.0	4.50	91	.258	.354	-1	-1	102	97	-0.4	-0	-0	0.0
1957	StL-N	0	1	.000	2	1	0	0	0	9	6	6.0	0	6	6.0	6	6.0	2.00	193	.182	.308	2	2	99	95	-0.4	-0	-0	0.1
Total	2	0	2	.000	16	1	0	0	0	27	23	7.7	1	16	5.3	20	6.7	3.67	110	.232	.339	1	1	101	96	-0.8	-1	-0	0.1
■ JOHN LOVETT	Lovett, John b: 5/6/1877, Monday, Ohio d: 12/5/37, Murray City, Ohio Deb: 03																												
1903	StL-N	0	0	—	3	1	0	0	0	5	6	10.8	0	5	9.0	3	5.4	5.40	62	.341	.509	-1	-1	102	118	0.0	0	0	0.0
■ LEN LOVETT	Lovett, Leonard Walker b: 7/17/1852, Lancaster Co., Pa d: 11/18/22, Newark, Del. BR/TR, Deb: 8/04/1873																												
1873	Res-n	0	1	.000	1																								
■ TOM LOVETT	Lovett, Thomas Joseph b: 12/7/1863, Providence, R.I. d: 3/20/28, Providence, R.I. BR , 5'8", 162 lbs. Deb: 1885																												
1885	Phi-a	7	8	.467	16	16	15	1	0	139	130	8.4	3	38	2.5	56	3.6	3.69	90	.259	.311	-7	-6	102	84	-0.3	0	0	-0.4
1889	Bro-a	17	10	.630	29	28	23	1	0	229	234	9.2	3	65	2.6	92	3.6	4.32	82	.280	.331	-12	-20	92	74	-1.1	0	0	-1.6
1890	Bro-N	30	11	**.732**	44	41	39	4	0	372	327	7.9	14	141	3.4	124	3.0	2.78	123	.251	.324	32	27	96	102	5.4	-1	0	2.3
1891	Bro-N	23	19	.548	44	43	39	3	0	366	361	8.9	14	129	3.2	129	3.2	3.69	89	.271	.335	-14	-17	98	84	5.2	-4	-1	-1.9
1893	Bro-N	3	5	.375	14	8	6	0	1	96	134	12.6	2	35	3.3	15	1.4	6.56	65	.347	.401	-20	-25	91	83	-1.0	-1	0	-2.0
1894	Bos-N	8	6	.571	15	13	10	0	0	104	155	13.4	12	36	3.1	23	2.0	5.97	99	.369	.418	-7	-0	111	110	-0.6	-6	0	-0.3
Total	6	88	59	.599	162	149	132	9	1	1306	1341	9.2	48	444	3.1	439	3.0	3.93	93	.280	.342	-28	-42	97	89	7.6	-12	-1	-3.9
■ PETE LOVRICH	Lovrich, Peter b: 10/16/42, Blue Island, Ill. BR/TR, 6'4", 200 lbs. Deb: 4/26/63																												
1963	KC-A	1	1	.500	20	1	0	0	0	21	25	10.7	5	10	4.3	16	6.9	7.71	51	.291	.364	-10	-9	109	81	0.1	0	-0	-0.9
■ GROVER LOWDERMILK	Lowdermilk, Grover Cleveland "Slim" b: 1/15/1885, Sandborn, Ind. d: 3/31/68, Odin, Ill. BR/TR, 6'4", 190 lbs. Deb: 09																												
1909	StL-N	0	2	.000	7	3	1	0	0	29	28	8.7	1	30	9.3	14	4.3	6.21	42	.292	.473	-12	-12	99	99	-0.9	-1	0	-1.1
1911	StL-N	0	1	.000	11	2	1	1	0	33	37	10.1	1	33	9.0	15	4.1	7.36	47	.301	.456	-15	-14	102	86	-0.4	-1	0	-1.3
1912	Chi-N	0	1	.000	2	1	1	0	0	13	17	11.8	1	14	9.7	8	5.5	9.69	36	.293	.431	-9	-9	102	63	-0.4	-1	0	-0.7
1915	StL-A	9	17	.346	38	29	14	1	0	222	183	7.4	1	133	5.4	130	5.3	3.12	93	.234	.357	-4	-5	99	105	-2.2	-3	-0	-0.7
	Det-A	4	1	.800	7	5	0	0	0	28	17	5.5	0	24	7.7	18	5.8	4.18	74	.185	.359	-4	-3	105	67	1.1	-0	0	-0.3
	Yr	13	18	.419	45	34	14	1	0	250	200	7.2	1	157	5.7	148	5.3	3.24	91	.225	.342	-8	-8	100	67	-1.1	-3	0	-1.0
1916	Det-A	0	0	—	1	0	0	0	0	⅓	0	0.0	0	3	81.0	0	0.0	0.00	—	.000	.750	0	0	103	0	0.0	0	0	0.0
	Cle-A	1	5	.167	10	9	2	0	0	51	52	9.2	0	45	7.9	28	4.9	3.18	88	.277	.424	-2	-2	99	156	-1.9	-0	0	-0.1
	Yr	1	5	.167	11	9	2	0	0	51	52	9.2	0	48	8.5	28	4.9	3.18	88	.275	.429	-2	-2	99	156	-1.9	0	0	-0.1
1917	StL-A	2	1	.667	3	2	2	1	0	19	16	7.6	0	4	1.9	9	4.3	1.42	184	.225	.267	3	3	98	106	0.7	-1	0	0.2
1918	StL-A	2	6	.250	13	11	4	0	0	80	74	8.3	1	38	4.3	25	2.8	3.15	88	.255	.337	-3	-3	100	102	-1.9	1	2	0.0
1919	StL-A	0	0	—	7	0	0	0	0	12	6	4.5	0	4	3.0	6	4.5	0.75	419	.176	.349	3	3	98	335	0.0	-0	0	0.3
	Chi-A	5	5	.500	20	11	5	0	0	97	95	8.8	0	43	4.0	43	4.0	2.78	118	.268	.353	5	5	102	121	-1.0	-3	1	0.3
	Yr	5	5	.500	27	11	5	0	0	109	101	8.3	0	47	3.9	49	4.0	2.56	128	.256	.342	8	9	101	121	-1.0	-0	1	0.6
1920	Chi-A	0	0	—	3	0	0	0	0	5	9	16.2	0	5	9.0	0	0.0	7.20	49	.409	.519	-2	-2	94	128	0.0	0	1	0.0
Total	9	23	39	.371	122	73	30	3	0	589	534	8.2	5	376	5.7	296	4.5	3.59	83	.253	.374	-40	-40	100	112	-6.9	-8	5	-3.4
■ LOU LOWDERMILK	Lowdermilk, Louis Bailey b: 2/23/1887, Sandborn, Ind. d: 12/27/75, Centralia, Ill. BR/TL, 6'1", 180 lbs. Deb: 4/20/11																												
1911	StL-N	3	4	.429	16	3	3	0	0	65	72	10.0	0	29	4.0	20	2.8	3.46	101	.304	.391	-0	0	102	135	-0.4	-1	-2	-0.1
1912	StL-N	1	1	.500	4	1	1	0	1	15	14	8.4	0	9	5.4	2	1.2	3.00	117	.233	.333	1	1	103	85	0.2	-0	0	0.1
Total	2	4	5	.444	20	4	4	0	1	80	86	9.7	0	38	4.3	22	2.5	3.37	103	.290	.379	0	1	102	125	-0.2	-1	-2	0.0
■ GEORGE LOWE	Lowe, George Wesley "Doc" b: 4/25/1895, Ridgefield Park, N.J. d: 9/2/81, Somers Point, N.J. 6'2", 180 lbs. Deb: 7/28/20																												
1920	Cin-N	0	0	—	1	0	0	0	0	2	1	4.5	0	1	4.5	0	0.0	0.00	—	.167	.286	1	1	88	0	0.0	0	0	0.1
■ BOBBY LOWE	Lowe, Robert Lincoln "Link" b: 7/10/1868, Pittsburgh, Pa. d: 12/8/51, Detroit, Mich. BR/TR, 5'10", 150 lbs. Deb: 4/19/1890 M																												
1891	Bos-N	0	0	—	1	0	0	0	0	1	3	27.0	0	1	9.0	0	0.0	9.00	41	.531	.601	-1	-1	109	163	0.0	0	0	0.0
■ TURK LOWN	Lown, Omar Joseph b: 5/30/24, Brooklyn, N.Y. BR/TR, 6', 180 lbs. Deb: 4/24/51																												
1951	Chi-N	4	9	.308	31	18	3	1	0	127	125	8.9	14	90	6.4	39	2.8	5.46	72	.260	.370	-21	-21	100	92	-1.5	1	0	-1.8
1952	Chi-N	4	11	.267	33	19	5	0	0	157	154	8.8	13	93	5.3	73	4.2	4.36	88	.257	.355	-11	-9	103	102	-3.6	-0	1	-0.7
1953	Chi-N	8	7	.533	49	12	2	0	3	148	166	10.1	20	84	5.1	76	4.6	5.17	88	.282	.370	-15	-10	106	104	1.6	-2	2	-0.8
1954	Chi-N	0	2	.000	15	0	0	0	0	22	23	9.4	1	15	6.1	16	6.5	6.14	67	.261	.358	-5	-5	102	68	-0.9	0	1	-0.3
1956	Chi-N	9	8	.529	61	0	0	0	13	111	95	7.7	10	78	6.3	74	6.0	3.57	106	.240	.356	3	3	101	119	2.1	2	-1	0.5
1957	Chi-N	5	7	.417	**67**	0	0	0	12	93	74	7.2	10	51	4.9	51	4.9	3.77	101	.221	.318	1	0	98	92	0.2	0	2	0.2
1958	Chi-N	0	0	—	4	0	0	0	0	4	2	4.5	0	3	6.8	4	9.0	4.50	89	.154	.313	-0	-0	101	41	0.0	0	0	0.0

YEAR	TM/L	W	L	PCT	G	GS	CG	SHO	SV	IP	H	H/G	HR	BB	BB/G	SO	SO/G	ERA	/A	OAVG	OOBP	PR	/A	PF	CPI	WAT	PB	PD	TPI
	Cin-N	0	2	.000	11	0	0	0	0	12	12	9.0	2	12	9.0	9	6.8	5.25	80	.273	.421	-2	-1	106	123	-0.9	-0	-0	-0.1
	Yr	0	2	.000	15	0	0	0	0	16	14	7.9	2	15	8.4	13	7.3	5.06	82	.246	.397	-2	-2	105	123	-0.9	0	-0	-0.1
	Chi-A	3	3	.500	27	0	0	0	8	41	49	10.8	1	28	6.1	40	8.8	3.95	93	.308	.395	-1	-1	98	139	-0.1	1	0	0.0
1959	Chi-A	9	2	.818	60	0	0	0	**15**	93	73	7.1	12	42	4.1	63	6.1	2.90	127	.215	.299	10	8	95	115	3.0	1	1	0.9
1960	Chi-A	2	3	.400	45	0	0	0	5	67	60	8.1	6	34	4.6	39	5.2	3.90	98	.239	.322	-0	-0	99	92	-0.6	1	0	0.0
1961	Chi-A	7	5	.583	59	0	0	0	11	101	87	7.8	13	35	3.1	50	4.5	2.76	144	.238	.293	14	14	99	130	0.7	-2	-1	1.1
1962	Chi-A	4	2	.667	42	0	0	0	6	56	58	9.3	3	25	4.0	40	6.4	3.05	123	.269	.337	6	4	94	133	0.9	-0	1	0.5
Total	11	55	61	.474	504	49	10	1	73	1032	978	8.5	105	590	5.1	574	5.0	4.12	96	.252	.345	-21	-20	100	108	0.9	1	7	-0.5
■ SAM LOWRY	Lowry, Samuel Joseph b: 3/25/20, Philadelphia, Pa. BR/TR, 5'11", 170 lbs. Deb: 9/19/42																												
1942	Phi-A	0	0	—	1	0	0	0	0	3	3	9.0	0	1	3.0	0	0.0	6.00	62	.250	.308	-1	-1	101	47	0.0	-0	-0	0.0
1943	Phi-A	0	0	—	5	0	0	0	0	18	18	9.0	1	9	4.5	3	1.5	5.00	70	.269	.342	-3	-3	106	84	0.0	-0	0	-0.2
Total	2	0	0	—	6	0	0	0	0	21	21	9.0	1	10	4.3	3	1.3	5.14	68	.266	.337	-4	-4	105	79	0.0	-0	0	-0.2
■ MIKE LOYND	Loynd, Michael Wallace b: 3/26/64, St.Louis, Mo. BR/TR, 6'4", 210 lbs. Deb: 7/24/86																												
1986	Tex-A	2	2	.500	9	8	0	0	1	42	49	10.5	4	19	4.1	33	7.1	5.36	74	.290	.363	-5	-6	95	94	0.0	0	0	-0.5
1987	Tex-A	1	5	.167	26	8	0	0	1	69	82	10.7	14	38	5.0	48	6.3	6.13	76	.287	.369	-13	-11	104	97	-1.8	0	-1	-1.1
Total	2	3	7	.300	35	16	0	0	2	111	131	10.6	18	57	4.6	81	6.6	5.84	75	.288	.367	-18	-18	101	96	-1.8	0	-1	-1.6
■ PAT LUBY	Luby, John Perkins b: 1868, Charleston, S.C. d: 4/24/1899, Charleston, S.C. TR , 6', 185 lbs. Deb: 6/16/1890																												
1890	Chi-N	20	9	.690	34	31	26	0	1	268	226	7.6	6	95	3.2	85	2.9	3.19	119	.243	.313	11	18	107	78	3.5	7	0	2.5
1891	Chi-N	8	11	.421	30	24	18	0	1	206	221	9.7	11	94	4.1	52	2.3	4.76	74	.288	.366	-32	-29	105	82	-3.1	6	0	-1.7
1892	Chi-N	10	16	.385	31	26	24	1	1	247	247	9.0	10	106	3.9	64	2.3	3.13	98	.273	.349	4	-2	93	114	-2.9	2	0	0.0
1895	Lou-N	1	5	.167	11	6	5	0	0	71	115	14.6	5	19	2.4	12	1.5	6.85	69	.386	.423	-16	-17	99	97	-1.1	2	0	-0.9
Total	4	39	41	.488	106	87	73	1	3	792	809	9.2	32	314	3.6	213	2.4	3.91	91	.279	.350	-33	-29	101	92	-3.6	17	0	-0.1
■ RED LUCAS	Lucas, Charles Frederick "The Nashville Narcissus" b: 4/28/02, Columbia, Tenn. d: 7/9/86, Nashville, Tenn. BL/TR, 5'9.5", 170 lbs. Deb: 4/19/23																												
1923	NY-N	0	0	—	3	0	0	0	1	5	9	16.2	0	4	7.2	3	5.4	0.00	—	.346	.433	2	2	99	0	0.0	-0	1	0.2
1924	Bos-N	1	4	.200	27	4	1	0	0	84	112	12.0	5	18	1.9	30	3.2	5.14	74	.332	.365	-12	-12	99	103	-1.0	2	1	-0.8
1926	Cin-N	8	5	.615	39	11	7	1	2	154	161	9.4	6	30	1.8	34	2.0	3.68	97	.277	.302	2	-2	93	92	0.8	6	-1	0.6
1927	Cin-N	18	11	.621	37	23	19	4	2	240	231	8.7	6	39	1.5	51	1.9	3.38	116	.256	**.277**	14	14	100	78	4.3	6	-1	1.4
1928	Cin-N	13	9	.591	27	19	13	**4**	1	167	164	8.8	9	42	2.3	35	1.9	3.40	114	.258	.297	11	9	97	89	2.0	6	-0	1.4
1929	Cin-N	19	12	.613	32	32	**28**	2	0	270	267	**8.9**	14	58	1.9	72	2.4	3.60	132	**.257**	**.290**	33	34	101	85	**5.8**	10	0	3.3
1930	Cin-N	14	16	.467	33	28	18	1	1	211	270	11.5	15	44	1.9	53	2.3	5.37	86	.315	.340	-9	-17	93	90	2.4	15	-3	-1.4
1931	Cin-N	14	13	.519	29	29	**24**	3	0	238	261	9.9	10	39	1.5	56	2.1	3.59	105	.280	.305	7	5	98	96	3.6	10	0	0.5
1932	Cin-N	13	17	.433	31	31	**28**	0	0	269	261	8.7	10	35	1.2	63	2.1	2.94	130	.249	.269	28	27	99	85	1.3	13	0	2.8
1933	Cin-N	10	16	.385	29	29	21	3	0	220	248	10.1	13	18	**0.7**	40	1.6	3.40	100	.289	.297	-1	-0	102	104	0.1	12	0	0.0
1934	Pit-N	10	9	.526	29	21	12	1	0	173	198	10.3	14	40	2.1	44	2.3	4.37	98	.283	.321	-6	-2	105	94	0.7	2	-3	-0.1
1935	Pit-N	8	6	.571	20	19	8	2	0	126	136	9.7	10	23	1.6	29	2.1	3.43	123	.272	.302	8	11	105	107	0.2	7	-1	1.1
1936	Pit-N	15	4	.789	27	22	12	0	0	176	178	9.1	7	26	**1.3**	53	2.7	3.17	122	.257	.284	17	14	96	88	5.4	5	-1	1.4
1937	Pit-N	8	10	.444	20	20	9	1	0	126	150	10.7	12	23	1.6	20	1.4	4.29	93	.290	.317	-5	-4	101	99	-1.9	5	-2	-0.3
1938	Pit-N	6	3	.667	13	13	4	0	0	84	90	9.6	5	16	1.7	19	2.0	3.54	106	.283	.313	2	2	99	109	1.0	-2	-1	0.2
Total	15	157	135	.538	396	301	204	22	7	2543	2736	9.7	136	455	1.6	602	2.1	3.72	108	.275	.302	92	80	99	92	24.7	97	-9	10.3
■ GARY LUCAS	Lucas, Gary Paul b: 11/8/54, Riverside, Cal. BL/TL, 6'5", 200 lbs. Deb: 4/16/80																												
1980	SD-N	5	8	.385	46	18	0	0	3	150	138	8.3	8	43	2.6	85	5.1	3.24	104	.250	.296	6	2	94	96	-0.9	-0	1	0.3
1981	SD-N	7	7	.500	**57**	0	0	0	13	90	78	7.8	1	36	3.6	53	5.3	2.00	165	.247	.317	**15**	13	95	158	1.6	-1	0	1.4
1982	SD-N	1	10	.091	65	0	0	0	16	97	89	8.3	5	29	2.7	64	5.9	3.25	102	.245	.292	4	1	92	91	-4.5	-1	1	0.0
1983	SD-N	5	8	.385	62	0	0	0	17	91	85	8.4	9	34	3.4	60	5.9	2.87	126	.245	.304	8	7	99	120	-1.5	-1	-1	0.5
1984	Mon-N	0	3	.000	55	0	0	0	8	53	54	9.2	4	20	3.4	42	7.1	2.72	121	.267	.329	5	3	91	145	-1.4	-0	2	0.5
1985	Mon-N	6	2	.750	49	0	0	0	1	68	63	8.3	6	24	3.2	31	4.1	3.18	106	.251	.306	3	1	94	112	2.0	-0	0	0.1
1986	Cal-A	4	1	.800	27	0	0	0	2	46	45	8.8	1	6	1.2	31	6.1	3.13	127	.253	.276	5	4	95	78	1.4	0	1	0.5
1987	Cal-A	1	5	.167	48	0	0	0	3	74	66	8.0	7	35	4.3	44	5.4	3.65	122	.241	.322	7	7	100	105	-1.8	0	1	0.7
Total	8	29	44	.397	409	18	0	0	63	669	618	8.3	41	227	3.1	410	5.5	3.01	117	.249	.305	53	39	95	112	-5.1	-4	4	4.0
■ RAY LUCAS	Lucas, Ray Wesley "Luke" b: 10/2/08, Springfield, Ohio d: 10/9/69, Harrison, Mich. BR/TR, 6'2", 175 lbs. Deb: 9/28/29																												
1929	NY-N	0	0	—	3	0	0	0	1	8	3	3.4	0	3	3.4	1	1.1	0.00	—	.111	.200	4	4	97	0	0.0	0	0	0.5
1930	NY-N	0	0	—	6	0	0	0	0	10	9	8.1	2	10	9.0	1	0.9	7.20	66	.265	.408	-2	-3	96	99	0.0	-0	1	-0.1
1931	NY-N	0	0	—	1	0	0	0	0	2	1	4.5	1	1	4.5	0	0.0	4.50	80	.143	.250	-0	-0	93	98	0.0	0	0	0.0
1933	Bro-N	0	0	—	2	0	0	0	0	5	6	10.8	0	4	7.2	0	0.0	7.20	45	.316	.440	-2	-2	98	88	0.0	0	0	-0.1
1934	Bro-N	1	1	.500	10	2	0	0	0	31	39	11.3	2	14	4.1	3	0.9	6.68	58	.328	.392	-9	-10	95	92	0.1	1	1	-0.6
Total	5	1	1	.500	22	2	0	0	1	56	58	9.3	5	32	5.1	5	0.8	5.79	70	.282	.373	-10	-11	96	80	0.1	1	2	-0.3
■ JOE LUCEY	Lucey, Joseph Earl "Scootch" b: 3/27/1897, Holyoke, Mass. d: 7/30/80, Holyoke, Mass. BR/TR, 6', 168 lbs. Deb: 7/06/20																												
1925	Bos-A	0	1	.000	7	2	0	0	0	11	18	14.7	0	14	11.5	2	1.6	9.00	49	.360	.485	-6	-6	99	95	-0.4	-1	1	-0.5
■ CON LUCID	Lucid, Cornelius Cecil b: 2/24/1874, Dublin, Ireland d: 6/25/31, Houston, Tex. Deb: 5/01/1893																												
1893	Lou-N	0	1	.000	2	1	0	0	0	6	10	15.0	0	10	15.0	0	0.0	15.00	31	.388	.559	-7	-7	98	69	-0.4	0	0	-0.4
1894	Bro-N	5	3	.625	10	9	7	0	0	71	87	11.0	6	44	5.6	15	1.9	6.59	76	.324	.420	-10	-12	94	87	0.8	-2	0	-1.0
1895	Bro-N	10	7	.588	21	19	12	2	0	137	164	10.8	4	72	4.7	24	1.6	5.52	81	.317	.401	-11	-16	94	89	1.0	2	0	-1.0
	Phi-N	6	3	.667	10	10	7	1	0	70	80	10.3	3	35	4.5	19	2.4	5.91	80	.307	.390	-9	-9	98	79	0.8	3	0	-0.4
	Yr	16	10	.615	31	29	19	3	0	207	244	10.6	7	107	4.7	43	1.9	5.65	81	.314	.397	-20	-25	95	79	1.8	2	0	-1.4
1896	Phi-N	1	4	.200	5	5	5	0	0	42	75	16.1	2	17	3.6	3	0.6	8.36	53	.412	.462	-19	-18	102	91	-1.4	-2	0	-1.4
1897	StL-N	1	5	.167	6	6	5	0	0	49	66	12.1	0	26	4.8	4	0.7	3.67	116	.346	.424	3	3	99	145	-0.7	-0	0	0.3
Total	5	23	23	.500	54	50	36	3	0	375	482	11.6	15	204	4.9	65	1.6	6.02	76	.334	.416	-52	-59	96	94	0.1	2	0	-3.9
■ LOU LUCIER	Lucier, Louis Joseph b: 3/23/18, Northbridge, Mass. BR/TR, 5'8", 160 lbs. Deb: 4/23/43																												
1943	Bos-A	3	4	.429	16	9	3	0	0	74	94	11.4	1	33	4.0	23	2.8	3.89	88	.322	.389	-5	-4	104	134	-0.1	-0	3	0.0
1944	Bos-A	0	0	—	3	0	0	0	0	5	7	12.6	0	7	12.6	2	3.6	5.40	61	.292	.452	-1	-1	97	125	0.0	-0	-0	-0.1
	Phi-N	0	0	—	1	0	0	0	0	2	3	13.5	0	2	9.0	1	4.5	13.50	27	.333	.455	-2	-2	103	52	0.0	0	0	-0.1
1945	Phi-N	0	1	.000	13	0	0	0	1	20	14	6.3	1	5	2.3	5	2.3	2.25	173	.194	.237	3	4	102	74	-0.4	0	1	0.5
Total	3	3	5	.375	33	9	3	0	1	101	118	10.5	2	47	4.2	31	2.8	3.83	92	.297	.368	-5	-3	104	120	-0.5	-0	4	0.3
■ HOWARD LUCKEY	Luckey, Howard J. b: Philadelphia, Pa. Deb: 10/02/1890																												
1890	Phi-a	0	0	—	1	0	0	0	0	2	1	4.5	0	3	13.5	1	4.5	9.00	44	.160	.432	-1	-1	101	46	0.0	-0	0	0.0
■ WILLIE LUDOLPH	Ludolph, William Francis "Wee Willie" b: 1/21/1900, San Francisco, Cal d: 4/8/52, Oakland, Cal. BR/TR, 6'1.5", 170 lbs. Deb: 5/28/24																												
1924	Det-A	0	0	—	3	0	0	0	0	6	5	7.5	0	2	3.0	1	1.5	4.50	93	.250	.348	-0	-0	99	76	0.0	-0	0	0.0
■ STEVE LUEBBER	Luebber, Stephen Lee b: 7/9/49, Clinton, Mo. BR/TR, 6'3", 185 lbs. Deb: 6/27/71																												
1971	Min-A	2	5	.286	18	12	0	0	1	68	73	9.7	7	37	4.9	35	4.6	5.03	72	.278	.370	-12	-11	104	98	-1.3	-2	0	-1.2
1972	Min-A	0	0	—	2	0	0	0	0	2	3	13.5	0	2	9.0	1	4.5	0.00	—	.333	.417	1	1	107	0	0.0	0	0	0.1
1976	Min-A	4	5	.444	38	12	2	1	2	119	109	8.2	9	62	4.7	45	3.4	4.01	86	.248	.339	-6	-7	98	96	-0.6	0	-1	-0.8
1979	Tor-A	0	0	—	1	0	0	0	0	0	2	—	0	1	—	0	—	∞	—	1.000	1.000	-1	-1	106	140	0.0	0	0	0.0
1981	Bal-A	0	0	—	7	0	0	0	0	17	26	13.8	3	4	2.1	12	6.4	7.41	49	.366	.403	-7	-7	99	98	0.0	0	0	-0.6
Total	5	6	10	.375	66	24	2	1	3	206	213	9.3	19	106	4.6	93	4.1	4.63	76	.271	.358	-26	-26	100	96	-1.9	-2	-1	-2.5
■ DICK LUEBKE	Luebke, Richard Raymond b: 4/8/35, Chicago, Ill. d: 12/4/74, San Diego, Cal. BR/TL, 6'4", 200 lbs. Deb: 8/11/62																												
1962	Bal-A	0	1	.000	10	0	0	0	0	13	12	8.3	0	6	4.2	7	4.8	2.77	136	.250	.321	2	1	95	116	-0.4	0	-0	0.1

YEAR	TM/L	W	L	PCT	G	GS	CG	SHO	SV	IP	H	H/G	HR	BB	BB/G	SO	SO/G	ERA	/A	OAVG	OOBP	PR	/A	PF	CPI	WAT	PB	PD	TPI
■ **HENRY LUFF**	Luff, Henry T. b: 9/14/1856, Philadelphia, Pa. d: 10/11/16, Philadelphia, Pa. Deb: 4/21/1875																												
1875	NH-n	1	7	.125	8																								
■ **RAFAEL LUGO**	Lugo, Rafael Urbano (Colina) b: 8/12/62, Punto Fijo, Venez. BR/TR, 6', 185 lbs. Deb: 4/28/85																												
1985	Cal-A	3	4	.429	20	10	1	0	0	83	86	9.3	10	29	3.1	42	4.6	3.69	113	.274	.339	4	4	101	126	-0.7	0	0	0.5
1986	Cal-A	1	1	.500	6	3	0	0	0	21	21	9.0	4	6	2.6	9	3.9	3.86	103	.266	.314	1	0	95	119	0.0	0	-0	0.0
1987	Cal-A	0	2	.000	7	5	0	0	0	28	42	13.5	8	18	5.8	24	7.7	9.32	48	.339	.420	-15	-15	100	90	-0.9	0	-0	-1.2
1988	Cal-A	0	0	—	1	0	0	0	0	2	2	9.0	1	1	4.5	1	4.5	9.00	42	.250	.333	-1	-1	95	78	0.0	0	0	0.0
Total	4	4	7	.364	34	18	1	0	0	134	151	10.1	23	54	3.6	76	5.1	4.97	84	.288	.355	-11	-12	99	117	-1.6	0	-0	-0.7
■ **WILD BILL LUHRSEN**	Luhrsen, William Ferdinand b: 4/14/1884, Buckley, Ill. d: 8/15/73, Little Rock, Ark. BR/TR, 5'9", 165 lbs. Deb: 8/23/13																												
1913	Pit-N	3	1	.750	5	3	2	0	0	29	25	7.8	3	16	5.0	11	3.4	2.48	122	.248	.358	2	2	94	171	1.0	-1	1	0.1
■ **AL LUKENS**	Lukens, Albert P. b: 11/1868, Pennsylvania Deb: 6/23/1894																												
1894	Phi-N	0	1	.000	3	2	1	0	0	15	26	15.6	0	10	6.0	0	0.0	10.20	49	.404	.485	-8	-9	94	77	-0.4	-2	0	-0.6
■ **RALPH LUMENTI**	Lumenti, Raphael Anthony b: 12/21/36, Milford, Mass. BL/TL, 6'3", 185 lbs. Deb: 9/07/57																												
1957	Was-A	0	1	.000	3	2	0	0	0	9	9	9.0	1	5	5.0	8	8.0	7.00	55	.250	.357	-3	-3	102	63	-0.4	-0	0	-0.2
1958	Was-A	1	2	.333	8	4	0	0	0	21	21	9.0	2	36	15.4	20	8.6	8.57	44	.266	.496	-11	-11	100	92	-0.1	0	0	-0.9
1959	Was-A	0	0	—	2	0	0	0	0	3	2	6.0	0	1	3.0	2	6.0	0.00	—	.200	.273	1	1	102	0	0.0	0	0	0.1
Total	3	1	3	.250	13	6	0	0	0	33	32	8.7	3	42	11.5	30	8.2	7.36	52	.256	.447	-13	-13	101	76	-0.5	-0	0	-1.0
■ **MEMO LUNA**	Luna, Guillermo Romero b: 6/25/30, Tacubaya, Mexico BL/TL, 6', 168 lbs. Deb: 4/20/54																												
1954	StL-N	0	1	.000	1	1	0	0	0	1	2	18.0	0	2	18.0	0	0.0	18.00	23	.667	.667	-2	-2	100	95	-0.4	0	0	0.0
■ **JACK LUNDBOM**	Lundbom, John Frederick b: 3/10/1877, Manistee, Mich. d: 10/31/49, Manistee, Mich. BR/TR, 6'2", 187 lbs. Deb: 5/09/02																												
1902	Cle-A	1	1	.500	8	3	1	0	0	34	48	12.7	1	16	4.2	7	1.9	6.62	52	.360	.428	-12	-12	96	87	0.0	1	-0	-1.0
■ **CARL LUNDGREN**	Lundgren, Carl Leonard b: 2/16/1880, Marengo, Ill. d: 8/21/34, Marengo, Ill. BR/TR, 5'11", 175 lbs. Deb: 6/19/02																												
1902	Chi-N	9	9	.500	18	18	17	1	0	160	158	8.9	2	45	2.5	68	3.8	1.97	135	.284	.345	14	12	95	**150**	0.1	-4	-3	1.0
1903	Chi-N	11	9	.550	27	20	16	0	**3**	193	191	8.9	1	60	2.8	67	3.1	2.94	104	.285	.349	7	3	94	102	-0.8	-1	-3	0.0
1904	Chi-N	17	9	.654	31	27	25	2	1	242	203	7.5	2	77	2.9	106	3.9	2.60	103	.251	.319	3	2	99	90	1.8	4	-1	0.1
1905	Chi-N	13	5	.722	23	19	16	3	0	169	132	7.0	3	53	2.8	69	3.7	2.24	134	.243	.321	14	14	100	104	3.0	1	1	1.6
1906	Chi-N	17	6	.739	27	24	21	5	2	208	160	6.9	3	89	3.9	103	4.5	2.21	118	.240	.337	10	9	99	111	-0.3	2	-1	0.9
1907	Chi-N	18	7	.720	28	25	21	7	0	207	130	**5.7**	0	92	4.0	84	3.7	1.17	214	**.204**	.306	**30**	**31**	102	129	0.8	-3	-1	3.7
1908	Chi-N	6	9	.400	23	15	9	1	0	139	149	9.6	5	56	3.6	38	2.5	4.21	57	.304	.375	-29	-28	102	92	-2.9	-2	-1	-3.0
1909	Chi-N	0	1	.000	2	1	0	0	0	4	6	13.5	0	4	9.0	0	0.0	4.50	55	.353	.476	-1	-1	95	163	-0.4	0	-0	0.0
Total	8	91	55	.623	179	149	125	19	6	1322	1129	7.7	16	476	3.2	535	3.6	2.42	112	.257	.335	49	43	99	111	1.3	-1	-8	4.3
■ **DEL LUNDGREN**	Lundgren, Ebin Delmar b: 9/21/1899, Lindsborg, Kan. d: 10/19/84, Lindsborg, Kan. BR/TR, 5'8", 160 lbs. Deb: 4/27/24																												
1924	Pit-N	0	1	.000	8	1	0	0	0	17	25	13.2	0	3	1.6	4	2.1	6.35	63	.403	.392	-5	-4	104	104	-0.4	-1	0	-0.3
1926	Bos-A	0	2	.000	18	1	0	0	0	31	35	10.2	2	28	8.1	11	3.2	7.55	56	.307	.426	-12	-11	106	88	-0.9	-0	0	-1.0
1927	Bos-A	5	12	.294	30	17	5	2	0	136	160	10.6	7	87	5.8	39	2.6	6.29	65	.302	.392	-32	-33	99	87	-1.0	-2	-2	-3.3
Total	3	5	15	.250	56	19	5	2	0	184	220	10.8	9	118	5.8	54	2.6	6.51	63	.312	.398	-49	-49	100	89	-2.3	-3	-2	-4.6
■ **DOLF LUQUE**	Luque, Adolfo "The Pride Of Havana" b: 8/4/1890, Havana, Cuba d: 7/3/57, Havana, Cuba BR/TR, 5'7", 160 lbs. Deb: 5/20/14 C																												
1914	Bos-N	0	1	.000	2	1	1	0	0	9	5	5.0	0	4	4.0	1	1.0	4.00	71	.167	.257	-1	-1	102	24	-0.4	-0	-0	-0.1
1915	Bos-N	0	0	—	2	1	0	0	0	5	6	10.8	0	4	7.2	3	5.4	3.60	74	.286	.400	-0	-1	97	135	0.0	-0	0	0.0
1918	Cin-N	6	3	.667	12	10	9	1	0	83	84	9.1	1	32	3.5	26	2.8	3.80	70	.277	.335	-10	-10	96	95	1.4	4	-0	-0.6
1919	Cin-N	10	3	.769	30	9	6	2	3	106	89	7.6	2	36	3.1	40	3.4	2.63	112	.237	.296	3	4	101	101	1.9	-0	1	0.5
1920	Cin-N	13	9	.591	37	23	10	1	1	208	168	**7.3**	5	60	2.6	72	3.1	2.51	110	**.225**	.281	14	6	88	77	1.5	5	-2	0.9
1921	Cin-N	17	19	.472	41	36	25	3	3	304	318	9.4	13	64	1.9	102	3.0	3.38	114	.273	.304	14	16	101	93	0.6	5	0	2.1
1922	Cin-N	13	23	.361	39	32	18	0	0	261	266	9.2	7	72	2.5	79	2.7	3.31	117	.268	.310	23	16	94	94	-7.4	2	0	1.7
1923	Cin-N	**27**	8	**.771**	41	37	28	**6**	2	322	279	**7.8**	2	88	2.5	151	4.2	**1.93**	**200**	**.235**	.286	**74**	**69**	96	115	**8.8**	2	1	**7.4**
1924	Cin-N	10	15	.400	31	28	13	2	0	219	229	9.4	5	53	2.2	86	3.5	3.16	121	.271	.307	17	16	99	101	-3.6	-1	1	1.7
1925	Cin-N	16	18	.471	36	36	22	**4**	0	291	263	**8.1**	7	78	2.4	140	4.3	**2.63**	**157**	**.239**	**.287**	**53**	**48**	97	91	-2.0	5	4	**5.8**
1926	Cin-N	13	16	.448	34	30	16	1	0	234	231	8.9	7	77	3.0	83	3.2	3.42	104	.260	.312	10	4	93	94	-3.4	8	2	1.3
1927	Cin-N	13	12	.520	29	27	17	2	0	231	225	8.8	10	56	2.2	76	3.0	3.19	123	.260	.296	19	19	100	97	0.9	2	4	2.4
1928	Cin-N	11	10	.524	33	29	11	1	1	234	254	9.8	12	84	3.2	72	2.8	3.58	108	.284	.337	11	7	97	113	0.3	-1	-2	0.4
1929	Cin-N	5	16	.238	32	22	8	1	0	176	213	10.9	7	56	2.9	43	2.2	4.50	105	.310	.351	4	5	101	107	-4.9	3	0	0.8
1930	Bro-N	14	8	.636	31	24	16	2	2	199	221	10.0	18	58	2.6	62	2.8	4.30	114	.287	.329	15	13	99	103	2.2	1	1	1.4
1931	Bro-N	7	6	.538	19	15	5	0	0	103	122	10.7	6	27	2.4	25	2.2	4.54	86	.297	.339	-8	-7	101	96	0.3	0	-1	-0.7
1932	NY-N	6	7	.462	38	5	1	0	5	110	128	10.5	4	32	2.6	32	2.6	4.01	95	.290	.331	-2	-3	98	101	0.0	-2	1	-0.2
1933	NY-N	8	2	.800	35	0	0	0	4	80	75	8.4	4	19	2.1	23	2.6	2.70	119	.251	.287	6	5	96	107	2.6	1	0	0.6
1934	NY-N	4	3	.571	26	0	0	0	7	42	54	11.6	3	17	3.6	12	2.6	3.86	100	.316	.369	1	-0	95	143	-0.1	1	1	0.2
1935	NY-N	1	0	1.000	2	0	0	0	0	4	1	2.3	0	1	2.3	2	4.5	0.00	—	.077	.143	2	2	95	0	0.5	0	-0	0.2
Total	20	194	179	.520	550	365	206	26	28	3221	3231	9.0	113	918	2.6	1130	3.2	3.24	118	.265	.310	245	205	97	99	-0.8	35	12	25.8
■ **JOHNNY LUSH**	Lush, John Charles b: 10/8/1885, Williamsport, Pa. d: 11/18/46, Beverly Hills, Cal BL/TL, 5'9.5", 165 lbs. Deb: 4/22/04																												
1904	Phi-N	0	6	.000	7	6	3	0	0	43	52	10.9	0	27	5.7	27	5.7	3.56	74	.339	.459	-4	-4	97	151	-2.9	2	1	-0.3
1905	Phi-N	2	0	1.000	2	2	1	0	0	17	12	6.4	0	8	4.2	8	4.2	1.59	192	.225	.337	3	3	102	143	1.0	0	0	0.3
1906	Phi-N	18	15	.545	37	35	24	4	0	281	254	8.1	2	119	3.8	151	4.8	2.37	103	.272	.364	8	2	93	130	3.1	7	2	0.2
1907	Phi-N	3	5	.375	8	8	5	2	0	57	48	7.6	0	21	3.3	20	3.2	3.00	85	.259	.344	-3	-3	103	82	-1.3	0	1	-0.2
	StL-N	7	10	.412	20	19	15	4	0	144	132	8.3	2	42	2.6	71	4.4	2.50	99	.276	.344	-1	-0	100	109	1.0	6	-1	0.8
	Yr	10	15	.400	28	27	20	6	0	201	180	8.1	2	63	2.8	91	4.1	2.64	94	.270	.340	-4	-3	101	109	-0.3	0	0	0.6
1908	StL-N	11	18	.379	38	32	23	3	1	251	221	7.9	6	57	2.0	93	3.3	2.12	111	.267	.323	6	6	100	118	1.6	1	0	0.8
1909	StL-N	11	18	.379	34	28	21	2	0	221	215	8.8	1	69	2.8	66	2.7	3.14	82	.260	.324	-13	-14	99	93	0.7	4	-1	-0.9
1910	StL-N	14	13	.519	36	24	13	2	1	225	235	9.4	6	70	2.8	54	2.2	3.20	88	.276	.336	-4	-10	93	107	2.9	5	-2	-0.7
Total	7	66	85	.437	182	154	105	17	2	1239	1169	8.5	17	413	3.0	490	3.6	2.68	95	.271	.344	-8	-19	97	113	6.1	26	-0	0.0
■ **SPARKY LYLE**	Lyle, Albert Walter b: 7/22/44, Du Bois, Pa. BL/TL, 6'1", 182 lbs. Deb: 7/04/67																												
1967	Bos-A	1	2	.333	27	0	0	0	5	43	33	6.9	3	14	2.9	42	8.8	2.30	158	.213	.283	4	6	113	114	-0.5	1	-0	0.8
1968	Bos-A	6	1	.857	49	0	0	0	11	66	67	9.1	6	14	1.9	52	7.1	2.73	110	.261	.296	2	2	101	125	2.5	-0	-1	0.1
1969	Bos-A	8	3	.727	71	0	0	0	17	103	91	8.0	8	48	4.2	93	8.1	2.53	150	.240	.319	13	14	105	138	2.4	-1	1	1.6
1970	Bos-A	1	7	.125	63	0	0	0	20	67	62	8.3	5	34	4.6	51	6.9	3.90	105	.244	.327	-1	1	110	94	-3.0	-1	-1	0.0
1971	Bos-A	6	4	.600	50	0	0	0	16	52	41	7.1	5	23	4.0	37	6.4	2.77	132	.228	.306	4	5	105	120	0.8	1	0	0.7
1972	NY-A	9	5	.643	59	0	0	0	**35**	108	84	7.0	3	29	2.4	75	6.3	1.92	147	.216	.265	**14**	11	92	101	2.0	1	-1	1.2
1973	NY-A	5	9	.357	51	0	0	0	27	82	66	7.2	4	18	2.0	63	6.9	2.52	152	.216	.255	12	12	100	73	-2.0	0	0	1.2
1974	NY-A	9	3	.750	66	0	0	0	15	114	93	7.3	6	43	3.4	89	7.0	1.66	208	.226	.292	**25**	23	95	162	2.8	0	-1	2.3
1975	NY-A	5	7	.417	49	0	0	0	6	89	94	9.5	1	36	3.6	65	6.6	3.13	118	.275	.341	6	6	98	118	-1.2	0	0	0.6
1976	NY-A	7	8	.467	64	0	0	0	**23**	104	82	7.1	5	42	3.6	61	5.3	2.25	153	.225	.295	15	14	97	125	-1.8	0	-1	1.3
1977	NY-A	13	5	.722	**72**	0	0	0	26	137	131	8.6	7	33	2.2	68	4.5	2.17	182	.257	.300	**29**	27	97	145	2.7	0	-1	2.6
1978	NY-A	9	3	.750	59	0	0	0	9	112	116	9.3	6	33	2.7	33	2.7	3.46	106	.278	.326	4	3	97	112	2.2	0	0	0.3
1979	Tex-A	5	8	.385	67	0	0	0	13	95	78	7.4	9	28	2.7	48	4.5	3.13	134	.226	.276	12	11	99	90	-1.6	0	-1	1.0
1980	Tex-A	3	2	.600	49	0	0	0	8	81	97	10.8	9	28	3.1	43	4.8	4.67	87	.306	.354	-6	-6	100	110	0.6	0	-0	-0.5
	Phi-N	0	0	—	10	0	0	0	2	14	11	7.1	0	6	3.9	6	3.9	1.93	199	.220	.288	3	3	106	121	0.0	0	-0	0.3
1981	Phi-N	9	6	.600	48	0	0	0	2	75	85	10.2	4	33	4.0	29	3.5	4.44	88	.301	.358	-8	-4	112	110	0.9	1	1	-0.1
1982	Phi-N	3	3	.500	34	0	0	0	2	37	50	12.2	3	12	2.9	12	2.9	5.11	66	.327	.371	-6	-7	94	107	-0.2	1	1	-0.5
	Chi-A	0	0	—	11	0	0	0	1	12	11	8.3	0	7	5.3	6	4.5	3.00	132	.262	.360	1	1	97	132	0.0	0	0	0.1
Total	16	99	76	.566	899	0	0	0	238	1391	1292	8.4	84	481	3.1	873	5.6	2.88	127	.251	.308	122	122	100	118	6.6	2	-4	13.0

YEAR	TM/L	W	L	PCT	G	GS	CG	SHO	SV	IP	H	H/G	HR	BB	BB/G	SO	SO/G	ERA	/A	OAVG	OOBP	PR	/A	PF	CPI	WAT	PB	PD	TPI
■ **JIM LYLE**	Lyle, James Charles b: 7/24/1900, Lake, Miss. d: 10/10/77, Williamsport, Pa. BR/TR, 6'1", 180 lbs. Deb: 10/02/25																												
1925	Was-A	0	0	—	1	0	0	0	0	3	5	15.0	0	1	3.0	3	9.0	6.00	70	.333	.375	-1	-1	95	82	0.0	0	0	0.0
■ **ADRIAN LYNCH**	Lynch, Adrian Ryan b: 2/9/1897, Laurens, Iowa d: 3/16/34, Davenport, Iowa BR/TR, Deb: 8/04/20																												
1920	StL-A	2	0	1.000	5	3	1	0	0	22	23	9.4	1	17	7.0	8	3.3	5.32	79	.277	.406	-4	-3	111	93	1.0	-0	-0	-0.2
■ **ED LYNCH**	Lynch, Edward Francis b: 2/25/56, Brooklyn, N.Y. BR/TR, 6'6", 230 lbs. Deb: 8/31/80																												
1980	NY-N	1	1	.500	5	4	0	0	0	19	24	11.4	0	5	2.4	9	4.3	5.21	67	.304	.349	-3	-4	97	79	0.1	0	0	-0.2
1981	NY-N	4	5	.444	17	13	0	0	0	80	79	8.9	6	21	2.4	27	3.0	2.93	122	.254	.301	5	6	103	111	0.4	1	-1	0.6
1982	NY-N	4	8	.333	43	12	0	0	2	139	145	9.4	6	40	2.6	51	3.3	3.56	101	.273	.318	1	1	100	101	-1.0	-3	-1	-0.3
1983	NY-N	10	10	.500	30	27	1	0	0	175	208	10.7	17	41	2.1	44	2.3	4.27	85	.302	.336	-12	-12	100	108	1.5	-1	-1	-1.4
1984	NY-N	9	8	.529	40	13	0	0	2	124	169	12.3	14	24	1.7	62	4.5	4.50	80	.324	.354	-12	-12	100	120	-0.3	1	-1	-1.2
1985	NY-N	10	8	.556	31	29	6	1	0	191	188	8.9	19	27	1.3	65	3.1	3.44	100	.256	.278	3	-0	95	91	-0.7	-2	-3	-0.5
1986	NY-N	0	0	—	1	0	0	0	0	2	2	9.0	0	0	0.0	1	4.5	0.00	—	.286	.286	1	1	93	0	0.0	0	0	0.1
	Chi-N	7	5	.583	23	13	1	1	0	100	105	9.5	10	23	2.1	57	5.1	3.78	106	.279	.315	-1	3	108	108	1.6	-2	-0	0.0
	Yr	7	5	.583	24	13	1	1	0	102	107	9.4	10	23	2.0	58	5.1	3.71	108	.279	.315	0	3	108	108	1.6	0	-0	0.1
1987	Chi-N	2	9	.182	58	8	0	0	4	110	130	10.6	17	48	3.9	80	6.5	5.40	77	.295	.361	-16	-15	102	102	-3.4	0	1	-1.3
Total	8	47	54	.465	248	119	8	2	8	940	1050	10.1	89	229	2.2	396	3.8	4.00	92	.284	.323	-35	-34	100	104	-1.8	-6	-8	-4.2
■ **JACK LYNCH**	Lynch, John H. b: 2/5/1857, New York, N.Y d: 4/20/23, BR/TR, 5'8", 185 lbs. Deb: 5/02/1881																												
1881	Buf-N	10	9	.526	20	19	17	0	0	166	203	11.0	1	29	1.6	32	1.7	3.58	79	.314	.343	-15	-14	101	99	-0.3	-3	0	-1.4
1883	NY-a	13	15	.464	29	29	29	1	0	255	263	9.3	6	25	0.9	119	4.2	4.09	85	.272	.290	-22	-17	105	75	-3.1	-4	-1	-1.7
1884	NY-a	37	15	.712	54	53	53	5	0	487	410	7.6	10	42	0.8	286	5.3	2.64	118	.236	.254	33	26	96	86	1.7	-6	-4	1.4
1885	NY-a	23	21	.523	44	43	43	1	0	379	410	9.7	17	42	**1.0**	177	4.2	3.61	77	.288	.308	-15	-34	86	98	6.4	4	-6	-3.4
1886	NY-a	20	30	.400	51	50	50	1	0	433	485	10.1	11	116	2.4	193	4.0	3.95	93	.294	.340	-24	-14	106	102	0.5	-8	-3	-1.9
1887	NY-a	7	14	.333	21	21	21	0	0	187	245	11.8	9	36	1.7	45	2.2	5.10	77	.331	.362	-17	-24	92	96	0.0	-3	0	-2.1
1890	BB-a	0	1	.000	1	1	1	0	0	9	22	22.0	1	5	5.0	1	1.0	12.00	33	.482	.533	-8	-8	103	100	-0.4	2	0	-0.3
Total	7	110	105	.512	220	216	214	8	0	1916	2038	9.6	55	295	1.4	853	4.0	3.69	89	.283	.311	-69	-86	98	93	4.8	-17	-14	-9.4
■ **MIKE LYNCH**	Lynch, Michael Joseph b: 6/28/1880, Holyoke, Mass. d: 4/2/27, Garrison, N.Y. BR/TR, 5'10", 155 lbs. Deb: 6/21/04																												
1904	Pit-N	15	11	.577	27	24	24	1	0	223	200	8.1	1	91	3.7	95	3.8	2.70	99	.268	.359	1	-1	98	111	0.3	4	-3	-0.3
1905	Pit-N	17	8	.680	33	22	13	0	2	206	191	8.3	3	107	4.7	106	4.6	3.80	80	.274	.374	-19	-17	102	93	2.1	-2	0	-1.6
1906	Pit-N	6	5	.545	18	12	7	0	0	119	101	7.6	2	31	2.3	48	3.6	2.42	109	.261	.328	3	3	101	102	-0.5	0	-1	0.2
1907	Pit-N	2	2	.500	7	4	2	0	0	36	37	9.3	0	22	5.5	9	2.3	2.25	112	.297	.406	1	1	102	177	-0.2	1	1	0.3
	NY-N	3	6	.333	12	10	7	0	1	72	68	8.5	3	30	3.8	34	4.3	3.38	76	.277	.356	-7	-7	104	97	-1.7	2	0	-0.6
	Yr	5	8	.385	19	14	9	0	1	108	105	8.8	3	52	4.3	43	3.6	3.00	85	.283	.371	-6	-5	103	97	-1.9	1	2	-0.3
Total	4	43	32	.573	97	72	53	1	3	656	597	8.2	9	281	3.9	292	4.0	3.05	91	.271	.361	-22	-21	100	105	-0.0	6	-2	-2.0
■ **DUMMY LYNCH**	Lynch, Thomas b: 1863, Peru, Ill. d: 5/13/03, Peru, Ill. 5'11", 175 lbs. Deb: 8/05/1884																												
1884	Chi-N	0	0	—	1	1	0	0	0	7	7	9.0	1	3	3.9	2	2.6	2.57	121	.269	.345	0	0	105	168	0.0	-1	0	0.0
■ **RED LYNN**	Lynn, Japhet Monroe b: 12/27/13, Kenney, Tex. d: 10/27/77, Bellville, Tex. BR/TR, 6', 162 lbs. Deb: 4/25/39																												
1939	Det-A	0	1	.000	4	0	0	0	0	8	11	12.4	2	3	3.4	3	3.4	9.00	56	.324	.375	-4	-3	110	82	-0.4	-0	0	-0.2
	NY-N	1	0	1.000	26	0	0	0	1	50	44	7.9	3	21	3.8	22	4.0	3.06	126	.240	.313	5	4	99	111	0.5	-1	-1	0.2
1940	NY-N	4	3	.571	33	0	0	0	3	42	40	8.6	3	24	5.1	25	5.4	3.86	100	.247	.344	-0	-0	100	107	0.7	-1	-1	-0.1
1944	Chi-N	5	4	.556	22	7	4	1	1	84	80	8.6	4	37	4.0	35	3.8	4.07	89	.251	.329	-4	-4	100	87	0.6	0	1	-0.2
Total	3	10	8	.556	85	7	4	1	5	184	175	8.6	12	85	4.2	85	4.2	3.96	96	.251	.330	-3	-3	100	98	1.4	-1	-1	-0.3
■ **AL LYONS**	Lyons, Albert Harold b: 7/18/18, St.Joseph, Mo. d: 12/20/65, Inglewood, Cal. BR/TR, 6'2", 195 lbs. Deb: 4/19/44																												
1944	NY-A	0	0	—	11	0	0	0	0	40	43	9.7	2	24	5.4	15	3.4	4.50	80	.291	.385	-5	-4	105	114	0.0	2	-1	-0.1
1946	NY-A	0	1	.000	2	1	0	0	0	8	11	12.4	0	6	6.8	4	4.5	5.63	61	.314	.429	-2	-2	98	106	-0.4	-1	0	-0.1
1947	NY-A	1	0	1.000	6	0	0	0	0	11	18	14.7	2	9	7.4	7	5.7	9.00	38	.367	.458	-6	-7	92	100	0.5	1	0	-0.3
	Pit-N	1	2	.333	13	0	0	0	0	28	36	11.6	4	12	3.9	16	5.1	7.39	56	.300	.368	-10	-10	102	75	-0.2	1	1	-0.6
1948	Bos-N	1	0	1.000	7	0	0	0	0	13	17	11.8	1	8	5.5	5	3.5	7.62	51	.309	.391	-5	-5	99	77	0.5	0	1	-0.4
Total	4	3	3	.500	39	1	0	0	0	100	125	11.3	9	59	5.3	47	4.2	6.30	60	.307	.394	-29	-28	101	96	0.4	5	2	-1.5
■ **GEORGE LYONS**	Lyons, George Tony "Smooth" b: 1/25/1891, Bible Grove, Ill. d: 8/12/81, Nevada, Mo. BR/TR, 5'11", 180 lbs. Deb: 9/06/20																												
1920	StL-N	2	1	.667	7	2	1	0	0	23	21	8.2	2	9	3.5	5	2.0	3.13	98	.262	.333	0	-0	98	121	0.5	-0	1	0.0
1924	StL-A	3	2	.600	26	6	2	0	0	78	97	11.2	2	45	5.2	25	2.9	5.19	88	.323	.409	-8	-5	108	111	0.6	-0	1	-0.3
Total	2	5	3	.625	33	8	3	0	0	101	118	10.5	4	54	4.8	30	2.7	4.72	89	.311	.394	-8	-6	105	114	1.1	-0	2	-0.3
■ **HARRY LYONS**	Lyons, Harry P. b: 3/25/1866, Chester, Pa. d: 6/30/12, Mauricetown, N.J. BR/TR, 5'10.5", 157 lbs. Deb: 8/29/1887																												
1890	Roc-a	0	0	—	1	0	0	0	0	4	8	18.0	0	1	2.3	2	4.5	13.50	26	.432	.461	-4	-4	92	60	0.0	0	0	-0.2
■ **HERSH LYONS**	Lyons, Herschel Englebert b: 7/23/15, Fresno, Cal. BR/TR, 5'11", 195 lbs. Deb: 4/17/41																												
1941	StL-N	0	0	—	1	0	0	0	0	1	1	9.0	0	3	27.0	1	9.0	0.00	—	.200	.500	0	0	107	0	0.0	0	0	0.1
■ **TED LYONS**	Lyons, Theodore Amar b: 12/28/1900, Lake Charles, La. d: 7/25/86, Sulphur, La. BB/TR, 5'11", 200 lbs. Deb: 7/02/23 MCH																												
1923	Chi-A	2	1	.667	9	1	0	0	0	23	30	11.7	2	15	5.9	6	2.3	6.26	63	.323	.407	-6	-6	99	101	0.6	0	1	-0.4
1924	Chi-A	12	11	.522	41	22	12	0	3	216	279	11.6	10	72	3.0	52	2.2	4.88	85	.322	.360	-15	-17	98	103	2.1	0	-3	-1.8
1925	Chi-A	**21**	11	.656	43	32	19	**5**	3	263	274	9.4	7	83	2.8	45	1.5	3.25	128	.278	.323	33	27	95	111	5.5	-3	2	2.4
1926	Chi-A	18	16	.529	39	31	24	3	2	284	268	8.5	6	106	3.4	51	1.6	3.01	121	.252	.310	32	20	90	99	0.0	0	3	2.2
1927	Chi-A	**22**	14	.611	39	34	**30**	2	2	**308**	291	8.5	7	67	2.0	71	2.1	2.83	150	.251	.284	**45**	**49**	103	90	**6.1**	5	0	**5.5**
1928	Chi-A	15	14	.517	39	27	21	0	6	240	276	10.4	11	68	2.6	60	2.3	3.98	102	.295	.332	2	2	100	106	1.6	1	2	0.4
1929	Chi-A	14	20	.412	37	31	21	1	2	259	276	9.6	11	76	2.6	57	2.0	4.10	101	.278	.321	4	1	98	91	0.8	2	2	0.5
1930	Chi-A	22	15	.595	42	36	**29**	1	1	**298**	331	10.0	12	57	1.7	69	2.1	3.78	129	.285	.310	29	37	105	103	7.1	7	3	4.5
1931	Chi-A	4	6	.400	22	12	7	0	0	101	117	10.4	6	33	2.9	16	1.4	4.01	105	.296	.345	4	2	96	119	0.3	-1	-1	0.0
1932	Chi-A	10	15	.400	33	26	19	1	2	231	243	9.5	10	71	2.8	58	2.3	3.27	124	.272	.324	31	20	91	121	1.6	5	-1	2.2
1933	Chi-A	10	21	.323	36	27	14	2	1	228	260	10.3	10	74	2.9	74	2.9	4.38	101	.280	.329	-3	1	103	93	-5.0	6	0	0.6
1934	Chi-A	11	13	.458	30	24	21	0	1	205	249	10.9	15	66	2.9	53	2.3	4.87	95	.293	.342	-9	-5	103	95	2.3	1	2	0.0
1935	Chi-A	15	8	.652	23	22	19	3	0	191	194	9.1	15	56	2.6	54	2.5	3.02	161	.262	.312	31	39	109	**125**	4.1	-1	-1	3.9
1936	Chi-A	10	13	.435	26	24	15	1	0	182	227	11.2	21	45	**2.2**	48	2.4	5.14	97	.305	.342	-2	-4	99	103	-2.4	-2	1	-0.3
1937	Chi-A	12	7	.632	22	22	11	0	0	169	182	9.7	21	45	2.4	45	2.4	4.15	113	.278	.323	9	10	102	107	1.8	1	0	1.1
1938	Chi-A	9	11	.450	23	23	17	1	0	195	238	11.0	13	52	2.4	54	2.5	3.69	128	.299	.336	24	22	98	**125**	0.2	-1	2	2.1
1939	Chi-A	14	6	.700	21	21	16	0	0	173	162	8.4	7	26	**1.4**	65	3.4	2.76	178	.247	**.269**	36	41	106	98	3.6	4	-1	4.5
1940	Chi-A	12	8	.600	22	22	17	**4**	0	186	188	9.1	17	37	**1.8**	72	3.5	3.24	139	.252	.285	24	26	103	99	1.6	2	-2	2.6
1941	Chi-A	12	10	.545	22	22	19	2	0	187	199	9.6	9	37	**1.8**	63	3.0	3.71	105	.269	.302	9	4	94	93	1.1	4	1	0.8
1942	Chi-A	14	6	.700	20	20	20	1	0	180	167	8.4	11	26	1.3	50	2.5	**2.10**	**174**	.245	.271	31	31	100	131	4.9	4	1	**4.1**
1946	Chi-A	1	4	.200	5	5	5	0	0	43	38	8.0	2	9	1.9	10	2.1	2.30	148	.235	.270	6	5	97	100	-1.4	-1	0	0.5
Total	21	260	230	.531	594	484	356	27	23	4162	4489	9.7	223	1121	2.4	1073	2.3	3.67	118	.276	.317	314	304	99	105	36.5	31	10	35.4
■ **TOBY LYONS**	Lyons, Thomas A. b: 3/27/1869, Cambridge, Mass. d: 8/29/20, Boston, Mass. Deb: 4/18/1890																												
1890	Syr-a	0	2	.000	3	3	2	0	0	22	40	16.4	1	21	8.6	6	2.5	10.64	33	.409	.514	-17	-17	92	90	-0.9	1	0	-1.1
■ **RICK LYSANDER**	Lysander, Richard Eugene b: 2/21/53, Huntington Park, Cal. BR/TR, 6'2", 190 lbs. Deb: 4/12/80																												
1980	Oak-A	0	0	—	5	0	0	0	0	14	24	15.4	3	4	2.6	5	3.2	7.71	49	.381	.418	-6	-6	94	105	0.0	0	0	-0.4
1983	Min-A	5	12	.294	61	4	1	1	3	125	132	9.5	8	43	3.1	58	4.2	3.38	128	.275	.326	10	13	106	120	-2.8	0	0	1.4
1984	Min-A	4	3	.571	36	0	0	0	5	57	62	9.8	2	27	4.3	22	3.5	3.47	122	.283	.353	3	5	106	125	0.5	0	0	0.5
1985	Min-A	0	2	.000	35	1	0	0	3	61	72	10.6	3	22	3.2	26	3.8	6.05	71	.305	.359	-13	-12	104	80	-0.9	0	-0	-1.1
Total	4	9	17	.346	137	5	1	1	11	257	290	10.2	16	96	3.4	111	3.9	4.27	100	.291	.345	-6	0	105	111	-3.2	0	0	0.4

YEAR	TM/L	W	L	PCT	G	GS	CG	SHO	SV	IP	H	H/G	HR	BB	BB/G	SO	SO/G	ERA	/A	OAVG	OOBP	PR	/A	PF	CPI	WAT	PB	PD	TPI
■ **BILL LYSTON**	Lyston, William Edward b: 1863, Near Baltimore, Md. d: 8/44, Baltimore, Md. TR , Deb: 8/29/1891																												
1891	Col-a	0	1	.000	1	1	1	0	0	6	10	15.0	0	6	9.0	1	1.5	10.50	32	.387	.503	-5	-5	90	77	-0.4	0	0	-0.3
1894	Cle-N	0	0	—	1	1	0	0	0	4	5	11.3	1	4	9.0	0	0.0	11.25	52	.329	.468	-3	-2	111	73	0.0	-0	0	-0.1
Total	2	0	1	.000	2	2	1	0	0	10	15	13.5	1	10	9.0	1	0.9	10.80	40	.365	.490	-7	-7	98	75	-0.4	-0	0	-0.4
■ **DUKE MAAS**	Maas, Duane Fredrick b: 1/31/29, Utica, Mich. d: 12/7/76, Mt.Clemens, Mich. BR/TR, 5'10", 170 lbs. Deb: 4/21/55																												
1955	Det-A	5	6	.455	18	16	5	2	0	87	91	9.4	7	50	5.2	42	4.3	4.86	77	.271	.364	-9	-11	95	95	-0.6	0	0	-0.9
1956	Det-A	0	7	.000	26	7	0	0	0	63	81	11.6	9	32	4.6	34	4.9	6.57	60	.313	.386	-17	-18	95	95	-3.4	0	-0	-1.7
1957	Det-A	10	14	.417	45	26	8	2	6	219	210	8.6	23	65	2.7	116	4.8	3.29	124	.252	.302	12	19	107	107	-2.3	-4	1	1.7
1958	KC-A	4	5	.444	10	7	3	1	1	55	49	8.0	3	13	2.1	19	3.1	3.93	103	.241	.286	-1	1	107	71	-0.2	0	0	0.1
	NY-A	7	3	.700	22	13	2	1	0	101	93	8.3	9	36	3.2	50	4.5	3.83	98	.242	.306	-1	-1	99	87	1.3	-2	-1	-0.3
	Yr	11	8	.579	32	20	5	2	1	156	142	8.2	12	49	2.8	69	4.0	3.87	99	.241	.298	-2	-0	102	87	1.1	0	-1	-0.2
1959	NY-A	14	8	.636	38	21	3	1	4	138	149	9.7	14	53	3.5	67	4.4	4.43	80	.278	.340	-9	-14	92	102	3.1	-1	1	-1.3
1960	NY-A	5	1	.833	35	1	0	0	4	70	70	9.0	6	35	4.5	28	3.6	4.11	87	.265	.339	-2	-4	92	104	1.7	-1	1	-0.3
1961	NY-A	0	0	—	1	0	0	0	0	⅓	2	54.0	0	0	0.0	0	0.0	54.00	—	1.000	.667	-2	-2	93	54	0.0	0	0	-0.1
Total	7	45	44	.506	195	91	21	7	15	733	745	9.1	71	284	3.5	356	4.4	4.20	91	.264	.328	-28	-30	99	98	-0.4	-7	0	-2.8
■ **BOB MABE**	Mabe, Robert Lee b: 10/8/29, Danville, Va. BR/TR, 5'11", 165 lbs. Deb: 4/18/58																												
1958	StL-N	3	9	.250	31	13	4	0	0	112	113	9.1	11	41	3.3	74	5.9	4.50	95	.260	.324	-7	-3	108	85	-2.8	-2	0	-0.4
1959	Cin-N	4	2	.667	18	1	0	0	3	30	29	8.7	6	19	5.7	8	2.4	5.40	75	.254	.358	-5	-4	103	97	1.1	-1	-0	-0.5
1960	Bal-A	0	0	—	2	0	0	0	0	1	4	36.0	0	1	9.0	0	0.0	18.00	22	.571	.625	-2	-2	101	106	0.0	0	0	-0.1
Total	3	7	11	.389	51	14	4	0	3	143	146	9.2	17	61	3.8	82	5.2	4.78	88	.263	.335	-13	-9	107	88	-1.7	-3	0	-1.0
■ **MAC MacARTHUR**	MacArthur, Malcolm b: 1/19/1862, Glasgow, Scotland d: 10/18/32, Detroit, Mich. TR , Deb: 5/02/1884																												
1884	Ind-a	1	5	.167	6	6	6	0	0	52	57	9.9	1	21	3.6	19	3.3	5.02	65	.287	.355	-10	-10	100	88	-1.1	-2	0	-0.9
■ **FRANK MacCORMACK**	MacCormack, Frank Louis b: 9/21/54, Jersey City, N.J. BR/TR, 6'4", 210 lbs. Deb: 6/14/76																												
1976	Det-A	0	5	.000	9	8	0	0	0	33	35	9.5	1	34	9.3	14	3.8	5.73	64	.294	.449	-8	-7	105	108	-2.4	0	-0	-0.7
1977	Sea-A	0	0	—	3	3	0	0	0	7	4	5.1	0	12	15.4	4	5.1	3.86	104	.174	.500	0	0	98	161	0.0	0	0	0.0
Total	2	0	5	.000	12	11	0	0	0	40	39	8.8	1	46	10.3	18	4.0	5.40	69	.275	.459	-8	-7	104	118	-2.4	0	-0	-0.7
■ **BILL MACDONALD**	Macdonald, William Paul b: 3/28/29, Alameda, Cal. BR/TR, 5'10", 170 lbs. Deb: 5/06/50																												
1950	Pit-N	8	10	.444	32	20	6	2	1	153	138	8.1	17	88	5.2	60	3.5	4.29	102	.243	.342	-3	1	106	98	1.2	-2	-3	-0.2
1953	Pit-N	0	1	.000	4	1	0	0	0	7	12	15.4	0	8	10.3	4	5.1	12.86	35	.400	.538	-7	-6	106	78	-0.4	0	0	-0.5
Total	2	8	11	.421	36	21	6	2	1	160	150	8.4	17	96	5.4	64	3.6	4.67	94	.251	.353	-9	-5	106	97	0.8	-2	-3	-0.7
■ **JIMMY MACE**	Mace, Harry L. b: Washington, D.C. 5'11", 185 lbs. Deb: 5/05/1891																												
1891	Was-a	0	1	.000	3	1	1	0	0	16	18	10.1	1	8	4.5	3	1.7	7.31	51	.299	.381	-6	-6	101	62	-0.4	-1	0	-0.5
■ **DANNY MacFAYDEN**	MacFayden, Daniel Knowles "Deacon Danny" b: 6/10/05, N.Truro, Mass. d: 8/26/72, Brunswick, Me. BR/TR, 5'11", 170 lbs. Deb: 8/25/26																												
1926	Bos-A	0	1	.000	3	1	1	0	0	13	10	6.9	0	7	4.8	1	0.7	4.85	88	.217	.315	-1	-1	106	51	-0.4	0	1	0.0
1927	Bos-A	5	8	.385	34	16	6	1	2	160	176	9.9	9	59	3.3	42	2.4	4.27	96	.294	.348	-2	-3	99	107	0.6	4	-2	0.0
1928	Bos-A	9	15	.375	33	28	9	0	0	195	215	9.9	12	78	3.6	61	2.8	4.75	86	.289	.348	-15	-14	101	96	0.1	-1	-1	-1.5
1929	Bos-A	10	18	.357	32	26	14	**4**	0	221	225	9.2	8	81	3.3	61	2.5	3.62	123	.271	.332	15	20	105	105	-0.8	-3	2	1.9
1930	Bos-A	11	14	.440	36	33	18	1	2	269	293	9.8	9	93	3.1	76	2.5	4.22	106	.281	.335	13	7	96	100	2.2	-4	1	0.4
1931	Bos-A	16	12	.571	35	32	17	2	0	231	263	10.2	4	79	3.1	74	2.9	4.01	105	.281	.337	9	6	97	102	4.5	-5	2	0.3
1932	Bos-A	1	10	.091	12	11	6	0	0	78	91	10.5	3	33	3.8	29	3.3	5.08	90	.289	.351	-5	-4	102	92	-3.7	-2	0	-0.4
	NY-A	7	5	.583	17	15	9	0	1	121	137	10.2	11	37	2.8	33	2.5	3.94	104	.281	.331	7	2	91	114	-0.9	-2	-2	-0.2
	Yr	8	15	.348	29	26	15	0	1	199	228	10.3	14	70	3.2	62	2.8	4.39	98	.284	.338	2	-2	96	114	-4.6	-2	-1	-0.6
1933	NY-A	3	2	.600	25	6	2	0	0	90	120	12.0	8	37	3.7	28	2.8	5.90	64	.319	.377	-16	-21	88	100	0.0	-4	0	-2.2
1934	NY-A	4	3	.571	22	11	4	0	0	96	110	10.3	5	31	2.9	41	3.8	4.50	93	.288	.339	-0	-4	93	98	-0.1	-2	-1	-0.5
1935	Cin-N	1	2	.333	7	4	1	0	0	36	39	9.8	1	13	3.3	13	3.3	4.75	81	.281	.338	-3	-4	95	85	-0.3	-1	1	-0.2
	Bos-N	5	13	.278	28	20	7	1	0	152	200	11.8	8	34	2.0	46	2.7	5.09	79	.314	.348	-18	-18	100	95	0.4	-1	2	-1.6
	Yr	6	15	.286	35	24	8	1	0	188	239	11.4	9	47	2.3	59	2.8	5.03	79	.308	.346	-21	-22	99	95	0.1	-1	3	-1.8
1936	Bos-N	17	13	.567	37	31	21	2	0	267	268	9.0	5	66	2.2	86	2.9	2.87	135	.259	.304	34	30	96	106	3.5	-5	3	2.8
1937	Bos-N	14	14	.500	32	32	16	2	0	246	250	9.1	5	60	2.2	70	2.6	2.93	120	.268	.307	27	16	90	112	-0.5	-1	1	1.5
1938	Bos-N	14	9	.609	29	29	19	5	0	220	208	8.5	6	64	2.6	58	2.4	2.95	114	.247	.300	21	10	89	98	2.7	-4	-1	0.5
1939	Bos-N	8	14	.364	33	28	8	0	2	192	221	10.4	11	59	2.8	46	2.2	3.89	94	.291	.336	1	-5	93	111	-1.5	-1	1	-0.4
1940	Pit-N	5	4	.556	35	8	0	0	2	91	112	11.1	5	27	2.7	24	2.4	3.56	102	.302	.350	3	1	95	135	0.5	-0	0	0.1
1941	Was-A	0	1	.000	5	0	0	0	0	7	12	15.4	1	5	6.4	3	3.9	10.29	40	.375	.459	-5	-5	99	86	-0.4	0	0	-0.3
1943	Bos-N	2	1	.667	10	1	0	0	0	21	31	13.3	1	9	3.9	5	2.1	6.00	61	.344	.410	-6	-5	109	103	0.6	0	0	-0.5
Total	17	132	159	.454	465	332	158	18	9	2706	2981	9.9	112	872	2.9	797	2.7	3.96	101	.281	.333	58	7	96	104	6.5	-31	10	-0.3
■ **CHUCK MACHEMEHL**	Machemehl, Charles Walter b: 4/20/47, Brenham, Tex. BR/TR, 6'4", 200 lbs. Deb: 4/06/71																												
1971	Cle-A	0	2	.000	14	0	0	0	3	18	16	8.0	2	15	7.5	9	4.5	6.50	58	.246	.369	-6	-5	108	76	-0.9	0	0	-0.4
■ **DENNY MACK**	Mack, Dennis Joseph (born Dennis Joseph Mc Gee) b: 1851, Easton, Pa. d: 4/10/1888, Wilkes-Barre, Pa. BR/TR, 5'7", 164 lbs. Deb: 5/06/1871 M																												
1871	Rok-n	0	1	.000	1																								
■ **FRANK MACK**	Mack, Frank George "Stubby" b: 2/2/1900, Okahoma City, Okla. d: 7/2/71, Clearwater, Fla. BR/TR, 6'1.5", 180 lbs. Deb: 8/16/22																												
1922	Chi-A	2	2	.500	8	4	1	1	0	34	36	9.5	2	16	4.2	11	2.9	3.71	110	.281	.349	1	1	101	116	0.0	1	-1	0.1
1923	Chi-A	0	1	.000	11	0	0	0	0	23	23	9.0	0	11	4.3	6	2.3	4.30	92	.284	.343	-1	-1	99	94	-0.4	-1	0	-0.1
1925	Chi-A	0	0	—	8	0	0	0	0	13	24	16.6	1	13	9.0	6	4.2	9.69	43	.444	.529	-8	-8	95	113	0.0	0	-0	-0.6
Total	3	2	3	.400	27	4	1	1	0	70	83	10.7	3	40	5.1	23	3.0	5.01	81	.316	.387	-7	-7	99	108	-0.4	0	-1	-0.6
■ **TONY MACK**	Mack, Tony Lynn b: 4/30/61, Lexington, Ky. BR/TR, 5'10", 177 lbs. Deb: 7/27/85																												
1985	Cal-A	0	1	.000	1	1	0	0	0	2	8	36.0	0	0	0.0	0	0.0	18.00	23	.571	.571	-3	-3	101	92	-0.4	0	0	-0.2
■ **BILL MACK**	Mack, William Francis b: 2/12/1885, Elmira, N.Y. d: 9/30/71, Elmira, N.Y. 6'1", 155 lbs. Deb: 7/14/08																												
1908	Chi-N	0	0	—	2	0	0	0	0	6	5	7.5	1	1	1.5	2	3.0	3.00	80	.267	.338	-0	-0	102	118	0.0	1	0	0.0
■ **KEN MacKENZIE**	MacKenzie, Kenneth Purvis b: 3/10/34, Gore Bay, Ont., Can. BR/TL, 6', 185 lbs. Deb: 5/02/60																												
1960	Mil-N	0	1	.000	9	0	0	0	0	8	9	10.1	2	3	3.4	9	10.1	6.75	50	.281	.324	-3	-3	89	83	-0.4	-0	-0	-0.2
1961	Mil-N	0	1	.000	5	0	0	0	0	7	8	10.3	1	2	2.6	5	6.4	5.14	71	.296	.355	-1	-1	91	104	-0.4	-0	0	0.0
1962	NY-N	5	4	.556	42	1	0	0	1	80	87	9.8	10	34	3.8	51	5.7	4.95	86	.280	.349	-9	-6	108	98	1.9	-1	0	-0.5
1963	NY-N	3	1	.750	34	0	0	0	3	58	63	9.8	11	12	1.9	41	6.4	4.97	69	.267	.306	-11	-10	104	87	1.3	-1	-1	-1.2
	StL-N	0	0	—	8	0	0	0	0	9	9	9.0	1	3	3.0	7	7.0	4.00	87	.250	.308	-1	-1	106	88	0.0	0	-0	0.0
	Yr	3	1	.750	42	0	0	0	3	67	72	9.7	12	15	2.0	48	6.4	4.84	71	.262	.299	-12	-11	104	88	1.3	-1	-1	-1.2
1964	SF-N	0	0	—	10	0	0	0	1	9	9	9.0	1	3	3.0	3	3.0	5.00	70	.265	.293	-1	-1	99	81	0.0	0	0	0.0
1965	Hou-N	0	3	.000	21	0	0	0	0	37	46	11.2	7	6	1.5	26	6.3	3.89	83	.299	.323	-1	-3	91	130	-1.4	1	-0	-0.1
Total	6	8	10	.444	129	1	0	0	5	208	231	10.0	33	63	2.7	142	6.1	4.80	77	.278	.328	-27	-25	102	99	1.0	-2	-0	-2.0
■ **JOHN MACKINSON**	Mackinson, John Joseph b: 10/29/23, Orange, N.J. BR/TR, 5'10.5", 160 lbs. Deb: 4/16/53																												
1953	Phi-A	0	0	—	1	0	0	0	0	1	1	9.0	0	2	18.0	0	0.0	0.00	—	.200	.429	0	0	105	0	0.0	0	0	0.0
1955	StL-N	0	1	.000	8	1	0	0	0	21	24	10.3	3	10	4.3	8	3.4	7.71	54	.296	.357	-9	-8	102	73	-0.4	-0	0	-0.7
Total	2	0	1	.000	9	1	0	0	0	22	25	10.2	3	12	4.9	8	3.3	7.36	56	.291	.362	-8	-8	102	69	-0.4	-0	0	-0.7
■ **BILLY MacLEOD**	MacLeod, William Daniel b: 5/13/42, Gloucester, Mass. BL/TL, 6'2", 190 lbs. Deb: 9/13/62																												
1962	Bos-A	0	1	.000	2	0	0	0	0	2	4	18.0	0	1	4.5	2	9.0	4.50	91	.444	.500	-0	-0	103	205	-0.4	0	0	0.0
■ **MAX MACON**	Macon, Max Cullen b: 10/14/15, Pensacola, Fla. BL/TL, 6'3", 175 lbs. Deb: 4/21/38																												
1938	StL-N	4	11	.267	38	12	5	1	2	129	133	9.3	9	61	4.3	39	2.7	4.12	102	.268	.344	-5	1	111	105	-3.3	2	1	0.4

YEAR	TM/L	W	L	PCT	G	GS	CG	SHO	SV	IP	H	H/G	HR	BB	BB/G	SO	SO/G	ERA	/A	OAVG	OOBP	PR	/A	PF	CPI	WAT	PB	PD	TPI
1940	Bro-N	1	0	1.000	2	0	0	0	0	2	5	22.5	2	0	0.0	1	4.5	22.50	18	.455	.455	-4	-4	106	76	0.5	0	0	-0.2
1942	Bro-N	5	3	.625	14	8	4	1	1	84	67	7.2	3	33	3.5	27	2.9	1.93	167	.220	.293	13	12	97	136	-0.2	4	-0	1.8
1943	Bro-N	7	5	.583	25	9	0	0	0	77	89	10.4	4	32	3.7	21	2.5	5.96	56	.284	.354	-22	-22	99	74	0.7	-1	1	-2.3
1944	Bos-N	0	0	—	1	0	0	0	0	3	10	30.0	2	1	3.0	1	3.0	21.00	17	.556	.550	-6	-6	96	96	0.0	0	0	-0.4
1947	Bos-N	0	0	—	1	0	0	0	0	2	1	4.5	0	1	4.5	1	4.5	0.00	—	.167	.286	1	1	95	0	0.0	-0	0	0.1
Total	6	17	19	.472	81	29	9	2	3	297	305	9.2	20	128	3.9	90	2.7	4.24	87	.265	.337	-23	-19	104	105	-2.3	5	1	-0.6
■ **HARRY MacPHERSON**	MacPherson, Harry William b: 7/10/26, N.Andover, Mass. BR/TR, 5'10", 150 lbs. Deb: 8/14/44																												
1944	Bos-N	0	0	—	1	0	0	0	0	1	0	0.0	0	1	9.0	1	9.0	0.00	—	.000	.250	0	0	96	0	0.0	0	0	0.0
■ **JIMMY MACULLAR**	Macullar, James F. "Little Mac" b: 1/6/1855, Boston, Mass. d: 4/8/24, Baltimore, Md. BR/TL, Deb: 5/05/1879 M																												
1886	Bal-a	0	0	—	1	0	0	0	0	2	4	18.0	0	0	0.0	1	4.5	9.00	36	.426	.426	-1	-1	94	83	0.0	0	0	0.0
■ **KEITH MacWHORTER**	MacWhorter, Keith b: 12/30/55, Worcester, Mass. BR/TR, 6'4", 190 lbs. Deb: 5/10/80																												
1980	Bos-A	0	3	.000	14	2	0	0	0	42	46	9.9	3	18	3.9	21	4.5	5.57	74	.280	.349	-7	-7	102	80	-1.4	0	0	-0.5
■ **LEN MADDEN**	Madden, Leonard Joseph "Lefty" b: 7/2/1890, Toledo, Ohio d: 9/9/49, Toledo, Ohio BL/TL, 6'2", 165 lbs. Deb: 8/31/12																												
1912	Chi-N	0	1	.000	6	2	0	0	0	12	16	12.0	1	9	6.8	5	3.8	3.00	116	.291	.400	1	1	102	181	-0.4	-0	-0	0.0
■ **MIKE MADDEN**	Madden, Michael Anthony b: 1/13/58, Denver, Colo. BL/TL, 6'1", 190 lbs. Deb: 4/05/83																												
1983	Hou-N	9	5	.643	28	13	0	0	0	95	76	7.2	4	45	4.3	44	4.2	3.13	105	.231	.315	5	2	90	100	1.9	-1	0	0.0
1984	Hou-N	2	3	.400	17	7	0	0	0	41	46	10.1	1	35	7.7	29	6.4	5.49	60	.297	.420	-9	-10	92	103	-0.4	1	-1	-0.9
1985	Hou-N	0	0	—	13	0	0	0	0	19	29	13.7	1	11	5.2	16	7.6	4.26	81	.363	.435	-1	-2	96	165	0.0	0	-0	-0.1
1986	Hou-N	1	2	.333	13	6	0	0	0	40	47	10.6	3	22	4.9	30	6.7	4.05	93	.297	.373	-1	-1	102	129	-0.6	-1	-0	-0.1
Total	4	12	10	.545	71	26	0	0	0	195	198	9.1	9	113	5.2	119	5.5	3.92	87	.274	.364	-6	-11	93	113	0.9	-1	-1	-1.1
■ **KID MADDEN**	Madden, Michael Joseph b: 10/2/1866, Portland, Me. d: 3/16/1896, Portland, Maine TL, 5'7.5", 130 lbs. Deb: 5/06/1887																												
1887	Bos-N	21	14	.600	37	37	36	3	0	321	317	8.9	20	122	3.4	81	2.3	3.79	104	.273	.342	10	5	97	100	4.4	4	-2	0.6
1888	Bos-N	7	11	.389	20	18	17	1	0	165	142	7.7	6	24	1.3	53	2.9	2.95	101	.245	.275	-2	1	105	74	-2.5	-2	0	0.0
1889	Bos-N	10	10	.500	22	19	18	1	1	178	194	9.8	7	71	3.6	64	3.2	4.40	90	.293	.362	-7	-9	98	93	-2.5	3	0	-0.4
1890	Bos-P	3	2	.600	10	7	5	1	1	62	85	12.3	2	25	3.6	24	3.5	4.79	92	.339	.399	-4	-3	104	108	0.0	-1	0	-0.2
1891	Bos-a	0	1	.000	1	1	1	0	0	8	10	11.3	2	6	6.8	6	6.8	6.75	52	.321	.431	-3	-3	94	107	-0.4	1	0	0.0
	Bal-a	13	12	.520	32	27	20	1	1	224	239	9.6	4	88	3.5	56	2.3	4.10	91	.288	.356	-9	-9	100	87	-0.1	5	0	-0.2
	Yr	13	13	.500	33	28	21	1	1	232	249	9.7	6	94	3.6	62	2.4	4.19	89	.289	.359	-12	-12	100	87	-0.5	1	0	-0.2
Total	5	54	50	.519	122	109	97	7	2	958	987	9.3	41	336	3.2	284	2.7	3.92	96	.281	.343	-16	-16	100	92	-1.1	9	-2	-0.2
■ **MORRIS MADDEN**	Madden, Morris De Wayne b: 8/31/60, Laurens, S.C. BL/TL, 6' ", 155 lbs. Deb: 6/11/87																												
1987	Det-A	0	0	—	2	0	0	0	0	2	4	18.0	0	3	13.5	0	0.0	13.50	32	.444	.583	-2	-2	96	90	0.0	0	-0	-0.1
1988	Pit-N	0	0	—	5	0	0	0	0	6	5	7.5	0	7	10.5	3	4.5	0.00	—	.294	.480	2	2	97	0	0.0	0	0	0.3
Total	2	0	0	—	7	0	0	0	0	8	9	10.1	0	10	11.3	3	3.4	3.38	106	.346	.514	0	0	97	23	0.0	0	0	0.2
■ **NICK MADDOX**	Maddox, Nicholas b: 11/9/1886, Gavanstown, Md. d: 11/27/54, Pittsburgh, Pa. TR, 6', 175 lbs. Deb: 9/13/07																												
1907	Pit-N	5	1	.833	6	6	6	1	0	54	32	5.3	0	13	2.2	38	6.3	0.83	302	.199	.275	10	10	102	115	1.8	2	-0	1.3
1908	Pit-N	23	8	.742	36	32	22	4	1	261	209	7.2	5	90	3.1	70	2.4	2.28	95	.249	.330	2	-3	92	105	5.3	9	-0	-0.3
1909	Pit-N	13	8	.619	31	27	17	4	0	203	173	7.7	2	39	1.7	56	2.5	2.22	116	.232	.283	9	8	99	91	-1.6	4	-1	0.8
1910	Pit-N	2	3	.400	20	7	2	0	0	87	73	7.6	0	28	2.9	29	3.0	3.41	98	.246	.321	-4	-1	110	78	-0.6	1	-0	0.0
Total	4	43	20	.683	93	72	47	9	1	605	487	7.2	7	170	2.5	193	2.9	2.29	109	.238	.308	17	14	98	97	4.9	15	-1	1.8
■ **GREG MADDUX**	Maddux, Gregory Alan b: 4/14/66, San Angelo, Tex. BR/TR, 6', 150 lbs. Deb: 9/03/86																												
1986	Chi-N	2	4	.333	6	5	1	0	0	31	44	12.8	3	11	3.2	20	5.8	5.52	73	.336	.389	-6	-5	108	110	-0.6	1	0	-0.3
1987	Chi-N	6	14	.300	30	27	1	1	0	156	181	10.4	17	74	4.3	101	5.8	5.60	74	.294	.369	-26	-25	102	95	-3.9	-2	6	-1.9
1988	Chi-N	18	8	.692	34	34	9	3	0	249	230	8.3	13	81	2.9	140	5.1	3.18	114	.244	.306	8	12	105	100	5.9	2	2	1.9
Total	3	26	26	.500	70	66	11	4	0	436	455	9.4	33	166	3.4	261	5.4	4.21	91	.269	.336	-25	-18	104	99	1.4	1	8	-0.3
■ **MIKE MADDUX**	Maddux, Michael Ausley b: 8/27/61, Dayton, Ohio BL/TR, 6'2", 180 lbs. Deb: 6/03/86																												
1986	Phi-N	3	7	.300	16	16	0	0	0	78	88	10.2	6	34	3.9	44	5.1	5.42	71	.286	.356	-15	-13	104	87	-2.2	-2	-1	-1.4
1987	Phi-N	2	0	1.000	7	2	0	0	0	17	17	9.0	0	5	2.6	15	7.9	2.65	161	.254	.306	3	3	105	103	1.0	-0	-0	0.2
1988	Phi-N	4	3	.571	25	11	0	0	0	89	91	9.2	6	34	3.4	59	6.0	3.74	95	.275	.342	-3	-2	103	116	1.0	-0	1	0.0
Total	3	9	10	.474	48	29	0	0	0	184	196	9.6	12	73	3.6	118	5.8	4.35	86	.278	.345	-15	-12	104	102	-0.2	-2	-0	-1.2
■ **TONY MADIGAN**	Madigan, William "Tice" b: 1868, Washington, D.C. d: 12/4/54, Washington, D.C. TR, 5'5.5", 126 lbs. Deb: 7/10/1886																												
1886	Was-N	1	13	.071	14	14	13	0	0	116	159	12.3	3	44	3.4	29	2.3	5.12	65	.340	.397	-23	-23	100	105	-4.9	-4	0	-2.2
■ **DAVE MADISON**	Madison, David Pledger b: 2/1/21, Boroksville, Miss. d: 12/8/85, Macon, Miss. BR/TR, 6'3", 190 lbs. Deb: 9/26/50																												
1950	NY-A	0	0	—	1	0	0	0	0	3	3	9.0	1	1	3.0	1	3.0	6.00	73	.273	.333	-0	-1	96	102	0.0	0	0	0.0
1952	StL-A	4	2	.667	31	4	0	0	0	78	78	9.0	7	48	5.5	35	4.0	4.38	83	.264	.364	-6	-6	100	108	1.3	-1	0	-0.6
	Det-A	1	1	.500	10	1	0	0	0	15	16	9.6	1	10	6.0	7	4.2	7.80	48	.291	.409	-7	-7	103	71	0.3	0	-0	-0.6
	Yr	5	3	.625	41	5	0	0	0	93	94	9.1	8	58	5.6	42	4.1	4.94	74	.265	.362	-13	-13	100	71	1.6	-1	0	-1.2
1953	Det-A	3	4	.429	32	1	0	0	0	62	76	11.0	7	44	6.4	27	3.9	6.82	59	.303	.401	-19	-19	102	92	0.2	-1	0	-1.8
Total	3	8	7	.533	74	6	0	0	0	158	173	9.9	16	103	5.9	70	4.0	5.70	67	.282	.383	-33	-33	101	98	1.8	-2	0	-3.0
■ **ALEX MADRID**	Madrid, Alexander b: 4/18/63, Springerville, Ariz BR/TR, 6'3", 200 lbs. Deb: 7/20/87																												
1987	Mil-A	0	0	—	3	0	0	0	0	5	11	19.8	1	1	1.8	1	1.8	16.20	28	.440	.429	-7	-6	102	64	0.0	0	-0	-0.5
1988	Phi-N	1	1	.500	5	2	1	0	0	16	15	8.4	0	6	3.4	2	1.1	2.81	126	.246	.300	1	1	103	102	0.2	-0	-0	0.1
Total	2	1	1	.500	8	2	1	0	0	21	26	11.1	1	7	3.0	3	1.3	6.00	63	.302	.337	-5	-5	103	92	0.2	-0	-0	-0.4
■ **HECTOR MAESTRI**	Maestri, Hector Anibal b: 4/19/35, Havana, Cuba BR/TR, 5'10", 158 lbs. Deb: 9/24/60																												
1960	Was-A	0	0	—	1	0	0	0	0	2	1	4.5	0	1	4.5	1	4.5	0.00	—	.167	.286	1	1	102	0	0.0	0	0	0.1
1961	Was-A	0	1	.000	1	1	0	0	0	6	6	9.0	1	2	3.0	2	3.0	1.50	261	.250	.308	2	2	97	263	-0.4	-0	0	0.2
Total	2	0	1	.000	2	1	0	0	0	7	7	7.9	1	3	3.4	3	3.4	1.13	349	.233	.303	3	2	99	197	-0.4	-0	0	0.3
■ **BILL MAGEE**	Magee, William J. (born William Fitzgerald) b: 1/13/1864, Cambridge, Mass. d: 8/12/22, Tuftonboro, N.H. 5'10", 154 lbs. Deb: 5/18/1897																												
1897	Lou-N	4	12	.250	22	16	13	1	0	155	186	10.8	6	99	5.7	44	2.6	5.40	78	.320	.419	-19	-21	97	96	-3.2	-2	0	-1.8
1898	Lou-N	16	15	.516	38	33	29	3	0	295	294	9.0	8	129	3.9	55	1.7	4.06	87	.281	.360	-15	-18	98	87	1.9	-9	-1	-2.4
1899	Lou-N	3	7	.300	12	10	6	1	0	71	91	11.5	1	28	3.5	13	1.6	5.20	76	.336	.398	-11	-10	103	90	-1.9	-2	0	-0.9
	Phi-N	3	5	.375	9	9	7	0	0	70	82	10.5	0	32	4.1	4	0.5	5.66	65	.316	.392	-14	-15	95	75	-1.5	-2	0	-1.3
	Was-N	1	4	.200	8	7	4	0	0	42	54	11.6	3	28	6.0	11	2.4	8.57	44	.337	.436	-22	-22	98	69	-1.0	1	0	-1.6
	Yr	7	16	.304	29	26	17	1	0	183	227	11.2	4	88	4.3	28	1.4	6.15	62	.329	.405	-47	-48	99	69	-4.4	-3	0	-3.8
1901	StL-N	0	0	—	1	1	0	0	0	8	8	9.0	0	4	4.5	3	3.4	4.50	70	.282	.370	-1	-1	95	79	0.0	1	-0	0.0
	NY-N	0	4	.000	6	5	4	0	0	42	56	12.0	4	11	2.4	14	3.0	6.00	53	.348	.396	-13	-13	95	90	-1.9	-0	0	-1.1
	Yr	0	4	.000	7	6	4	0	0	50	64	11.5	4	15	2.7	17	3.1	5.76	55	.338	.392	-14	-14	95	90	-1.9	1	-0	-1.1
1902	NY-N	0	0	—	2	1	0	0	0	5	5	9.0	0	1	1.8	2	3.6	3.60	80	.283	.322	-0	-0	104	71	0.0	-0	0	0.0
	Phi-N	2	4	.333	8	6	6	0	0	54	61	10.2	1	18	3.0	15	2.5	3.67	83	.309	.366	-5	-4	109	101	-0.5	-1	-0	-0.3
	Yr	2	4	.333	10	7	6	0	0	59	66	10.1	1	19	2.9	17	2.6	3.66	82	.306	.363	-6	-4	109	101	-0.5	-1	-0	-0.3
Total	5	29	51	.363	106	88	69	5	0	742	837	10.2	23	350	4.2	161	2.0	4.94	74	.307	.387	-99	-104	99	88	-8.1	-12	-2	-9.4
■ **SAL MAGLIE**	Maglie, Salvatore Anthony "The Barber" b: 4/26/17, Niagara Falls, N.Y BR/TR, 6'2", 180 lbs. Deb: 8/09/45 C																												
1945	NY-N	5	4	.556	13	10	7	3	0	84	72	7.7	2	22	2.4	32	3.4	2.36	162	.231	.282	13	14	100	103	0.4	-1	0	1.4
1950	NY-N	18	4	**.818**	47	16	12	**5**	1	206	169	7.4	14	86	3.8	96	4.2	**2.71**	148	.226	.310	33	30	97	116	**6.9**	-1	3	3.2
1951	NY-N	**23**	6	.793	42	37	22	3	4	298	254	**7.7**	27	86	2.6	146	4.4	2.93	**134**	**.230**	.286	**34**	**33**	99	99	7.3	-3	1	**3.3**
1952	NY-N	18	8	.692	35	31	12	5	1	216	199	8.3	16	75	3.1	112	4.7	2.92	129	.244	.310	20	20	101	116	3.5	-4	1	1.9
1953	NY-N	8	9	.471	27	24	9	3	0	145	158	9.8	19	47	2.9	80	5.0	4.16	101	.278	.332	2	0	98	110	0.3	2	-2	0.1

YEAR	TM/L	W	L	PCT	G	GS	CG	SHO	SV	IP	H	H/G	HR	BB	BB/G	SO	SO/G	ERA	/A	OAVG	OOBP	PR	/A	PF	CPI	WAT	PB	PD	TPI
1954	NY-N	14	6	.700	34	32	9	1	2	218	222	9.2	21	70	2.9	117	4.8	3.26	127	.262	.317	20	21	102	112	2.1	-2	0	2.0
1955	NY-N	9	5	.643	23	21	6	0	0	130	142	9.8	18	48	3.3	71	4.9	3.74	106	.278	.337	4	3	98	125	1.9	-2	-2	0.0
	Cle-A	0	2	.000	10	2	0	0	2	26	26	9.0	1	7	2.4	11	3.8	3.81	106	.252	.304	0	1	102	68	-0.9	-0	-1	0.0
1956	Cle-A	0	0	—	2	0	0	0	0	5	6	10.8	1	2	3.6	2	3.6	3.60	114	.300	.364	0	0	99	161	0.0	0	-0	0.0
	Bro-N	13	5	.722	28	26	9	3	0	191	154	**7.3**	21	52	2.5	108	5.1	2.87	132	.222	.278	19	19	100	95	2.9	-3	-2	1.5
1957	Bro-N	6	6	.500	19	17	4	1	1	101	94	8.4	12	26	2.3	50	4.5	2.94	151	.245	.295	11	17	114	115	-0.4	-4	-1	1.4
	NY-A	2	0	1.000	6	3	1	1	3	26	22	7.6	1	7	2.4	9	3.1	1.73	197	.227	.283	6	5	90	136	1.0	0	0	0.5
1958	NY-A	1	1	.500	7	3	0	0	0	23	27	10.6	3	9	3.5	7	2.7	4.70	80	.300	.356	-2	-2	99	112	-0.1	1	0	-0.1
	StL-N	2	6	.250	10	10	2	0	0	53	46	7.8	14	25	4.2	21	3.6	4.75	90	.232	.317	-5	-3	108	99	-1.8	-1	-1	-0.3
Total	10	119	62	.657	303	232	93	25	14	1722	1591	8.3	169	562	2.9	862	4.5	3.15	126	.245	.306	155	158	100	109	23.1	-17	-2	14.9
■ JIM MAGNUSON	Magnuson, James Robert b: 8/18/46, Marinette, Wis. BR/TL, 6'2", 190 lbs. Deb: 6/28/70																												
1970	Chi-A	1	5	.167	13	6	0	0	0	45	45	9.0	7	16	3.2	20	4.0	4.80	84	.263	.326	-5	-4	108	91	-1.5	-1	-0	-0.5
1971	Chi-A	1	1	.500	15	4	0	0	0	30	30	9.0	0	16	4.8	11	3.3	4.50	75	.265	.366	-3	-4	97	85	0.0	-0	-0	-0.4
1973	NY-A	0	1	.000	8	0	0	0	0	27	38	12.7	2	9	3.0	9	3.0	4.33	88	.342	.379	-2	-2	100	134	-0.4	0	0	0.0
Total	3	2	7	.222	36	10	0	0	0	102	113	10.0	9	41	3.6	40	3.5	4.59	82	.286	.353	-10	-9	103	101	-1.9	-2	0	-0.9
■ JOE MAGRANE	Magrane, Joseph David b: 7/2/64, Des Moines, Iowa BR/TL, 6'6", 225 lbs. Deb: 4/25/87																												
1987	StL-N	9	7	.563	27	26	4	2	0	170	157	8.3	9	60	3.2	101	5.3	3.55	112	.245	.314	10	8	97	94	-0.3	2	0	0.9
1988	StL-N	5	9	.357	24	24	4	3	0	165	133	7.3	6	51	2.8	100	5.5	**2.18**	**166**	.217	.275	23	26	105	105	-1.7	1	2	3.5
Total	2	14	16	.467	51	50	8	5	0	335	290	7.8	15	111	3.0	201	5.4	2.87	133	.232	.295	34	35	101	99	-2.0	3	2	4.4
■ PETE MAGRINI	Magrini, Peter Alexander b: 6/8/42, San Francisco, Cal. BR/TR, 6', 195 lbs. Deb: 4/13/66																												
1966	Bos-A	0	1	.000	3	1	0	0	0	7	8	10.3	0	8	10.3	3	3.9	10.29	37	.308	.459	-5	-5	110	69	-0.4	-0	-0	-0.4
■ ART MAHAFFEY	Mahaffey, Arthur b: 6/4/38, Cincinnati, Ohio BR/TR, 6'1", 185 lbs. Deb: 7/30/60																												
1960	Phi-N	7	3	.700	14	12	5	1	0	93	78	7.5	9	34	3.3	56	5.4	2.32	179	.229	.296	15	19	110	137	2.7	-2	-1	1.8
1961	Phi-N	11	19	.367	36	32	12	3	0	219	205	8.4	27	70	2.9	158	6.5	4.11	96	.249	.308	-2	-4	98	91	1.6	-2	-2	-0.7
1962	Phi-N	19	14	.576	41	39	20	2	0	274	253	8.3	36	81	2.7	177	5.8	3.94	95	.246	.304	-0	-6	95	94	2.9	1	-4	-0.8
1963	Phi-N	7	10	.412	26	22	6	1	0	149	143	8.6	18	48	2.9	97	5.9	3.99	84	.255	.311	-12	-11	102	97	-2.1	2	-1	-0.9
1964	Phi-N	12	9	.571	34	29	2	2	0	157	161	9.2	17	82	4.7	80	4.6	4.53	76	.269	.357	-17	-19	98	106	0.1	0	-2	-2.0
1965	Phi-N	2	5	.286	22	9	1	0	0	71	82	10.4	11	32	4.1	52	6.6	6.21	54	.294	.368	-21	-23	95	93	-1.5	-1	-1	-2.4
1966	StL-N	1	4	.200	12	5	0	0	1	35	37	9.5	7	21	5.4	19	4.9	6.43	56	.276	.371	-11	-11	100	90	-1.4	-1	-0	-1.1
Total	7	59	64	.480	185	148	46	9	1	998	959	8.6	125	368	3.3	639	5.8	4.18	88	.255	.321	-48	-53	99	99	2.3	-2	-11	-6.1
■ ROY MAHAFFEY	Mahaffey, Lee Roy "Popeye" b: 2/9/03, Belton, S.C. d: 7/23/69, Anderson, S.C. BR/TR, 6', 180 lbs. Deb: 8/31/26																												
1926	Pit-N	0	0	—	4	0	0	0	0	5	5	9.0	0	1	1.8	3	5.4	0.00	—	.294	.350	2	2	111	0	0.0	-0	-0	0.2
1927	Pit-N	1	0	1.000	2	1	0	0	0	9	9	9.0	0	9	9.0	4	4.0	8.00	49	.300	.467	-4	-4	99	87	0.5	0	-0	-0.2
1930	Phi-A	9	5	.643	33	16	6	0	0	153	186	10.9	16	53	3.1	38	2.2	5.00	90	.298	.349	-6	-9	96	104	-0.1	-5	-1	-1.3
1931	Phi-A	15	4	.789	30	20	8	0	2	162	161	8.9	9	82	4.6	59	3.3	4.22	105	.281	.370	3	4	101	118	3.0	1	-3	0.2
1932	Phi-A	13	13	.500	37	28	13	0	0	223	245	9.9	27	96	3.9	106	4.3	5.09	97	.274	.345	-15	-3	111	97	-2.6	-3	-2	-0.5
1933	Phi-A	13	10	.565	33	23	9	0	0	179	198	10.0	5	74	3.7	66	3.3	5.18	76	.275	.339	-18	-25	92	80	1.2	1	-2	-2.4
1934	Phi-A	6	7	.462	37	14	3	0	2	129	142	9.9	10	55	3.8	37	2.6	5.37	82	.276	.343	-13	-14	98	83	0.1	2	-2	-1.1
1935	Phi-A	8	4	.667	27	17	5	0	0	136	153	10.1	11	42	2.8	39	2.6	3.90	117	.283	.336	8	10	102	114	2.9	-2	-1	0.6
1936	StL-A	2	6	.250	21	9	1	0	1	60	82	12.3	6	40	6.0	13	2.0	8.10	67	.315	.405	-20	-18	107	82	-1.3	-1	-2	-1.7
Total	9	67	49	.578	224	128	45	0	5	1056	1181	10.1	84	452	3.9	365	3.1	5.01	90	.283	.352	-62	-57	101	98	3.7	-7	-13	-6.2
■ LOU MAHAFFEY	Mahaffey, Louis Wood b: 1/3/1874, Kentucky d: 10/26/49, Torrance, Cal. 5'9", 170 lbs. Deb: 4/26/1898																												
1898	Lou-N	0	1	.000	1	1	1	0	0	9	10	10.0	0	5	5.0	1	1.0	3.00	117	.303	.395	1	1	98	141	-0.4	-0	0	0.0
■ ART MAHAN	Mahan, Arthur Leo b: 6/8/13, Somerville, Mass. BL/TL, 5'11", 178 lbs. Deb: 4/30/40																												
1940	Phi-N	0	0	—	1	0	0	0	0	1	1	9.0	0	0	0.0	0	0.0	0.00	—	.333	.333	0	0	102	0	0.0	0	0	0.0
■ MICKEY MAHLER	Mahler, Michael James b: 7/30/52, Montgomery, Ala. BB/TL, 6'3", 189 lbs. Deb: 9/13/77																												
1977	Atl-N	1	2	.333	5	5	0	0	0	23	31	12.1	4	9	3.5	14	5.5	6.26	72	.326	.376	-6	-4	115	103	-0.1	2	-0	-0.2
1978	Atl-N	4	11	.267	34	21	1	0	0	135	130	8.7	16	66	4.4	92	6.1	4.67	87	.255	.340	-16	-9	114	94	-2.9	-3	-1	-1.2
1979	Atl-N	5	11	.313	26	18	1	0	0	100	123	11.1	11	47	4.2	71	6.4	5.85	71	.304	.368	-23	-19	110	93	-2.0	-1	-0	-1.9
1980	Pit-N	0	0	—	2	0	0	0	0	1	4	36.0	1	3	27.0	1	9.0	63.00	6	.571	.700	-7	-7	103	52	0.0	0	0	-0.5
1981	Cal-A	0	0	—	6	0	0	0	0	6	1	1.5	0	2	3.0	5	7.5	0.00	—	.056	.150	2	3	104	0	0.0	0	0	0.3
1982	Cal-A	2	0	1.000	6	0	0	0	0	8	9	10.1	0	6	6.8	5	5.6	1.13	358	.300	.405	3	3	99	475	1.0	0	0	0.3
1985	Mon-N	1	4	.200	9	7	1	1	1	48	40	7.5	3	24	4.5	32	6.0	3.56	95	.229	.320	0	-1	94	92	-1.5	1	-1	0.0
	Det-A	1	2	.333	3	2	0	0	0	21	19	8.1	2	4	1.7	14	6.0	1.71	256	.241	.274	6	6	106	172	-0.4	0	-0	0.7
1986	Tex-A	0	2	.000	29	5	0	0	3	63	71	10.1	3	29	4.1	28	4.0	4.14	96	.295	.371	0	-1	95	118	-0.9	0	-0	0.0
	Tor-A	0	0	—	2	0	0	0	0	1	1	9.0	0	0	0.0	0	0.0	0.00	—	.200	.333	0	0	104	0	0.0	0	0	0.1
	Yr	0	2	.000	31	5	0	0	3	64	72	10.1	3	29	4.1	28	3.9	4.08	98	.285	.359	1	-1	95	0	-0.9	0	0	0.1
Total	8	14	32	.304	122	58	3	1	4	406	429	9.5	40	190	4.2	262	5.8	4.68	86	.274	.350	-41	-29	107	108	-6.8	-1	-2	-2.4
■ RICKY MAHLER	Mahler, Richard Keith b: 8/5/53, Austin, Tex. BR/TR, 6'1", 195 lbs. Deb: 4/20/79																												
1979	Atl-N	0	0	—	15	0	0	0	0	22	28	11.5	4	11	4.5	12	4.9	6.14	67	.311	.386	-6	-5	110	101	0.0	0	-0	-0.4
1980	Atl-N	0	0	—	2	0	0	0	0	4	2	4.5	0	0	0.0	1	2.3	2.25	163	.154	.154	1	1	101	8	0.0	0	0	0.1
1981	Atl-N	8	6	.571	34	14	1	0	2	112	109	8.8	5	43	3.5	54	4.3	2.81	124	.258	.320	8	8	100	124	1.5	-0	1	0.9
1982	Atl-N	9	10	.474	39	33	5	2	0	205	213	9.4	18	62	2.7	105	4.6	4.21	91	.272	.322	-14	-8	107	94	-1.4	2	2	-0.4
1983	Atl-N	0	0	—	10	0	0	0	0	14	16	10.3	0	9	5.8	7	4.5	5.14	74	.296	.379	-2	-2	104	94	0.0	-0	-0	-0.2
1984	Atl-N	13	10	.565	38	29	9	1	0	222	209	8.5	13	62	2.5	106	4.3	3.12	126	.251	.298	12	20	110	101	1.8	5	2	**3.1**
1985	Atl-N	17	15	.531	39	39	6	1	0	267	272	9.2	24	79	2.7	107	3.6	3.47	112	.268	.318	4	13	108	111	4.0	-1	1	1.4
1986	Atl-N	14	18	.438	39	39	7	1	0	238	283	10.7	25	95	3.6	137	5.2	4.88	79	.301	.361	-31	-27	103	106	-0.3	2	1	-2.3
1987	Atl-N	8	13	.381	39	28	3	1	0	197	212	9.7	24	85	3.9	95	4.3	4.98	90	.283	.352	-20	-11	109	99	-1.2	1	2	-0.7
1988	Atl-N	9	16	.360	39	34	5	0	0	249	279	10.1	17	42	1.5	131	4.7	3.69	100	.282	.310	-6	0	107	104	0.5	-2	1	0.0
Total	10	78	88	.470	294	216	36	6	2	1530	1623	9.5	130	488	2.9	755	4.4	3.97	98	.276	.327	-54	-12	107	104	4.9	7	10	1.5
■ AL MAHON	Mahon, Alfred Gwinn "Lefty" b: 9/23/09, Albion, Neb. d: 12/26/77, New Haven, Conn. BL/TL, 5'11", 160 lbs. Deb: 4/22/30																												
1930	Phi-A	0	0	—	3	0	0	0	0	4	11	24.8	0	7	15.8	0	0.0	24.75	18	.579	.621	-9	-9	96	74	0.0	0	0	-0.6
■ CHRIS MAHONEY	Mahoney, Christopher John b: 6/11/1885, Milton, Mass. d: 7/15/54, Visalia, Cal. BR/TR, 5'9", 160 lbs. Deb: 7/12/10																												
1910	Bos-A	0	1	.000	2	1	0	0	1	11	16	13.1	1	5	4.1	6	4.9	3.27	75	.327	.389	-1	-1	97	176	-0.4	-0	1	0.0
■ MIKE MAHONEY	Mahoney, George W. "Big Mike" b: 12/5/1873, Boston, Mass. d: 1/3/40, Boston, Mass. BR , 6'4", 220 lbs. Deb: 5/18/1897																												
1897	Bos-N	0	0	—	1	0	0	0	0	1	3	27.0	0	1	9.0	1	9.0	18.00	25	.540	.611	-2	-2	103	82	0.0	0	0	0.0
■ BOB MAHONEY	Mahoney, Robert Paul b: 6/20/28, Le Roy, Minn. BR/TR, 6'1", 185 lbs. Deb: 5/03/51																												
1951	Chi-A	0	0	—	3	0	0	0	0	7	5	6.4	1	5	6.4	3	3.9	5.14	77	.208	.345	-1	-1	96	81	0.0	0	-0	0.0
	StL-A	2	5	.286	30	4	0	0	0	81	86	9.6	7	41	4.6	30	3.3	4.44	101	.274	.353	-3	1	109	104	-0.5	-0	-1	0.0
	Yr	2	5	.286	33	4	0	0	0	88	91	9.3	8	46	4.7	33	3.4	4.50	99	.269	.352	-4	-0	108	104	-0.5	0	-1	0.0
1952	StL-A	0	0	—	3	0	0	0	0	3	8	24.0	0	4	12.0	1	3.0	18.00	20	.500	.571	-5	-5	100	80	0.0	0	0	-0.4
Total	2	2	5	.286	36	4	0	0	0	91	99	9.8	8	50	4.9	34	3.4	4.95	90	.280	.363	-8	-5	108	102	-0.5	-0	-1	-0.4
■ WALTER MAILS	Mails, John Walter "Duster" or "The Great" b: 10/1/1895, San Quentin, Cal. d: 7/5/74, San Francisco, Cal BL/TL, 6', 195 lbs. Deb: 9/28/15																												
1915	Bro-N	0	1	.000	2	0	0	0	0	5	6	10.8	2	5	9.0	3	5.4	3.60	78	.333	.458	-0	-0	102	269	-0.4	-0	0	0.0
1916	Bro-N	0	1	.000	11	0	0	0	0	17	15	7.9	1	9	4.8	13	6.9	3.71	71	.242	.329	-2	-2	100	92	-0.4	0	-0	-0.2
1920	Cle-A	7	0	1.000	9	8	6	2	0	63	54	7.7	1	18	2.6	25	3.6	1.86	204	.230	.285	14	14	100	104	3.5	0	-1	1.3
1921	Cle-A	14	8	.636	34	24	10	2	2	194	210	9.7	4	89	4.1	87	4.0	3.94	104	.283	.350	7	4	96	103	0.8	-4	-3	-0.3

YEAR	TM/L	W	L	PCT	G	GS	CG	SHO	SV	IP	H	H/G	HR	BB	BB/G	SO	SO/G	ERA	/A	OAVG	OOBP	PR	/A	PF	CPI	WAT	PB	PD	TPI
1922	Cle-A	4	7	.364	26	13	4	1	0	104	122	10.6	8	40	3.5	54	4.7	5.28	78	.291	.348	-14	-13	103	86	-1.5	-0	0	-1.1
1925	StL-N	7	7	.500	21	14	9	0	0	131	145	10.0	11	58	4.0	49	3.4	4.60	94	.279	.355	-5	-4	101	98	0.0	-2	-1	-0.7
1926	StL-N	0	1	.000	1	0	0	0	0	1	2	18.0	0	1	9.0	1	9.0	0.00	—	.400	.375	0	0	100	0	-0.4	0	0	0.0
Total	7	32	25	.561	104	59	29	5	2	515	554	9.7	27	220	3.8	232	4.1	4.11	99	.277	.344	-0	-2	99	100	1.6	-6	-5	-1.0
■ WOODY MAIN	Main, Forrest Harry b: 2/12/22, Delano, Cal. BR/TR, 6'3.5", 195 lbs. Deb: 4/21/48																												
1948	Pit-N	1	1	.500	17	0	0	0	0	27	35	11.7	4	19	6.3	12	4.0	8.33	50	.324	.415	-13	-13	104	85	0.0	-0	0	-1.1
1950	Pit-N	1	0	1.000	12	0	0	0	1	20	21	9.4	2	11	4.9	12	5.4	4.95	88	.256	.347	-2	-1	106	87	0.5	1	0	0.0
1952	Pit-N	2	12	.143	48	11	2	0	2	153	149	8.8	14	52	3.1	79	4.6	4.47	88	.253	.308	-13	-9	105	81	-3.4	-3	-3	-1.5
1953	Pit-N	0	0	—	2	0	0	0	0	4	5	11.3	1	2	4.5	4	9.0	11.25	40	.294	.368	-3	-3	106	56	0.0	0	0	-0.2
Total	4	4	13	.235	79	11	2	0	3	204	210	9.3	21	84	3.7	107	4.7	5.16	78	.264	.329	-31	-26	105	82	-2.9	-3	-3	-2.8
■ ALEX MAIN	Main, Miles Grant b: 5/13/1884, Montrose, Mich. d: 12/29/65, Royal Oak, Mich. BL/TR, 6'5", 195 lbs. Deb: 4/18/14																												
1914	Det-A	6	6	.500	32	12	5	1	3	138	131	8.5	2	59	3.8	55	3.6	2.67	104	.259	.340	1	2	102	120	-0.2	-2	4	0.7
1915	KC-F	13	14	.481	35	28	18	2	3	230	181	7.1	4	75	2.9	91	3.6	2.54	115	.222	.291	12	10	97	88	-1.4	1	7	1.9
1918	Phi-N	2	2	.500	8	4	1	1	0	35	30	7.7	1	16	4.1	14	3.6	4.63	66	.240	.336	-7	-6	111	73	0.2	-1	0	-0.6
Total	3	21	22	.488	75	44	24	4	6	403	342	7.6	7	150	3.3	160	3.6	2.77	105	.236	.312	6	6	100	98	-1.4	-2	11	2.0
■ JIM MAINS	Mains, James Royal b: 6/12/22, Bridgton, Maine d: 3/17/69, Bridgton, Maine BR/TR, 6'2", 190 lbs. Deb: 8/22/43																												
1943	Phi-A	0	1	.000	1	1	1	0	0	8	9	10.1	0	3	3.4	4	4.5	5.63	62	.281	.333	-2	-2	106	66	-0.4	0	-0	-0.1
■ WILLARD MAINS	Mains, Willard Eben "Grasshopper" b: 7/7/1868, N.Windham, Maine d: 5/23/23, Bridgton, Maine TR, 6'2", 190 lbs. Deb: 1888																												
1888	Chi-N	1	1	.500	2	2	1	0	0	11	8	6.5	0	6	4.9	5	4.1	4.91	61	.215	.324	-3	-2	106	48	0.0	-0	0	-0.1
1891	CM-a	12	14	.462	32	25	20	0	0	214	210	8.8	4	117	4.9	78	3.3	3.07	136	.271	.367	15	27	113	117	-0.2	2	0	2.7
1896	Bos-N	3	2	.600	8	5	3	0	1	43	43	9.0	1	31	6.5	13	2.7	5.65	83	.282	.403	-6	-5	107	77	0.2	-0	0	-0.3
Total	3	16	17	.485	42	32	24	0	1	268	261	8.8	5	154	5.2	96	3.2	3.56	118	.271	.371	7	20	111	108	0.0	2	0	2.3
■ FRANK MAKOSKY	Makosky, Frank b: 1/20/10, Boonton, N.J. d: 1/10/87, Stroudsburg, Pa. BR/TR, 6'1", 185 lbs. Deb: 4/30/37																												
1937	NY-A	5	2	.714	26	1	1	0	3	58	64	9.9	6	24	3.7	27	4.2	4.97	90	.277	.332	-2	-3	97	93	0.6	1	2	0.0
■ TOM MAKOWSKI	Makowski, Thomas Anthony b: 12/22/50, Buffalo, N.Y. BR/TL, 5'11", 185 lbs. Deb: 5/01/75																												
1975	Det-A	0	0	—	3	0	0	0	0	9	10	10.0	2	9	9.0	3	3.0	5.00	81	.278	.396	-1	-1	106	139	0.0	0	0	0.0
■ JOHN MALARKEY	Malarkey, John S. "Liz" b: 5/4/1872, Springfield, Ohio d: 10/29/49, Cincinnati, Ohio TR, 5'11", 155 lbs. Deb: 9/21/1894																												
1894	Was-N	2	1	.667	3	3	3	0	0	26	42	14.5	1	5	1.7	3	1.0	4.15	128	.388	.415	3	3	100	149	0.8	-2	0	0.1
1895	Was-N	0	8	.000	22	8	5	0	2	101	135	12.0	3	60	5.3	32	2.9	6.06	83	.342	.429	-14	-11	105	96	-3.9	-4	0	-1.1
1896	Was-N	0	1	.000	1	1	0	0	0	7	9	11.6	1	3	3.9	0	0.0	1.29	326	.335	.402	2	2	96	457	-0.4	1	0	0.3
1899	Chi-N	0	1	.000	1	1	1	0	0	9	19	19.0	0	5	5.0	7	7.0	13.00	28	.455	.513	-9	-9	96	70	-0.4	0	0	-0.5
1902	Bos-N	9	11	.450	21	19	17	1	1	170	158	8.4	0	58	3.1	39	2.1	2.59	101	.269	.334	3	0	94	101	-1.7	3	2	0.3
1903	Bos-N	11	16	.407	32	27	25	2	0	253	266	9.5	5	96	3.4	98	3.5	3.09	104	.298	.373	5	3	98	118	-0.4	0	1	0.5
Total	6	22	38	.367	80	59	51	3	3	566	629	10.0	10	227	3.6	179	2.8	3.66	94	.306	.378	-9	-13	98	114	-6.0	-3	4	-0.4
■ BILL MALARKEY	Malarkey, William John b: 11/26/1878, Port Byron, Ill. d: 12/12/56, Phoenix, Ariz. BR/TR, 5'10", 185 lbs. Deb: 4/16/08																												
1908	NY-N	0	2	.000	15	0	0	0	2	35	31	8.0	1	10	2.6	12	3.1	2.57	91	.267	.331	-1	-1	100	104	-0.9	-1	-0	0.0
■ CY MALIS	Malis, Cyrus Sol b: 2/26/07, Philadelphia, Pa. d: 1/12/71, N.Hollywood, Cal. BR/TR, 5'11", 175 lbs. Deb: 8/17/34																												
1934	Phi-N	0	0	—	1	0	0	0	0	4	4	9.0	0	2	4.5	1	2.3	4.50	100	.267	.353	-0	-0	111	85	0.0	0	0	0.0
■ MAL MALLETTE	Mallette, Malcolm Francis b: 1/30/22, Syracuse, N.Y. BL/TL, 6'2", 200 lbs. Deb: 9/25/50																												
1950	Bro-N	0	0	—	2	0	0	0	0	1	2	18.0	0	1	9.0	2	18.0	0.00	—	.333	.429	0	0	104	0	0.0	0	0	0.0
■ ROB MALLICOAT	Mallicoat, Robbin Dale b: 11/16/64, St.Helens, Ore. BL/TL, 6'3", 180 lbs. Deb: 9/11/87																												
1987	Hou-N	0	0	—	4	1	0	0	0	7	8	10.3	0	6	7.7	4	5.1	6.43	59	.320	.452	-2	-2	93	97	0.0	0	0	-0.1
■ ALEX MALLOY	Malloy, Archibald Alexander "Lick" b: 10/31/1886, Laurinburg, N.C. d: 3/1/61, Ferris, Tex. BR/TR, 6'2", 180 lbs. Deb: 9/10/10																												
1910	StL-A	0	6	.000	7	6	4	0	0	53	47	8.0	0	17	2.9	27	4.6	2.55	99	.261	.332	-0	-0	101	116	-2.9	-1	0	0.0
■ HERM MALLOY	Malloy, Herman "Tug" b: 6/1/1885, Massillon, Ohio d: 5/9/42, Nimishillen, Ohio BR/TR, 6', Deb: 10/06/07																												
1907	Det-A	0	1	.000	1	1	1	0	0	8	13	14.6	1	5	5.6	6	6.8	5.63	44	.393	.472	-3	-3	98	140	-0.4	0	0	-0.2
1908	Det-A	0	2	.000	3	2	2	0	0	17	20	10.6	1	4	2.1	8	4.2	3.71	64	.278	.333	-2	-3	99	108	-0.9	1	1	-0.1
Total	2	0	3	.000	4	3	3	0	0	25	33	11.9	2	9	3.2	14	5.0	4.32	56	.314	.379	-5	-5	99	118	-1.3	1	1	-0.3
■ BOB MALLOY	Malloy, Robert Paul b: 5/28/18, Canonsburg, Pa. BR/TR, 5'11", 185 lbs. Deb: 5/04/43																												
1943	Cin-N	0	0	—	6	0	0	0	0	10	14	12.6	1	8	7.2	4	3.6	6.30	52	.778	.759	-3	-3	98	196	0.0	1	-0	-0.2
1944	Cin-N	1	1	.500	9	0	0	0	0	23	22	8.6	0	11	4.3	4	1.6	3.13	109	.265	.347	1	1	95	118	0.0	-1	0	0.0
1946	Cin-N	2	5	.286	27	3	1	0	2	72	71	8.9	2	26	3.3	24	3.0	2.75	130	.265	.324	5	7	105	125	-1.1	1	-1	0.7
1947	Cin-N	0	0	—	1	0	0	0	0	1	3	27.0	1	0	0.0	1	9.0	18.00	21	.600	.600	-2	-2	92	121	0.0	0	0	0.0
1949	StL-A	1	1	.500	5	0	0	0	0	10	6	5.4	0	7	6.3	2	1.8	2.70	162	.200	.333	2	2	104	117	0.2	-0	0	0.1
Total	5	4	7	.364	48	3	1	0	2	116	116	9.0	4	52	4.0	35	2.7	3.26	110	.287	.359	3	4	102	129	-0.9	1	-1	0.6
■ BOB MALLOY	Malloy, Robert William b: 11/24/64, Garland, Tex. BR/TR, 6'5", 200 lbs. Deb: 5/26/87																												
1987	Tex-A	0	0	—	2	2	0	0	0	11	13	10.6	6	3	2.5	8	6.5	6.55	71	.271	.314	-3	-2	104	109	0.0	0	-0	-0.1
■ MALONE	Malone Deb:6/20/1872																												
1872	Eck-n	0	3	.000	3																								
■ PAT MALONE	Malone, Perce Leigh b: 9/25/02, Altoona, Pa. d: 5/13/43, Altoona, Pa. BL/TR, 6', 200 lbs. Deb: 4/12/28																												
1928	Chi-N	18	13	.581	42	25	16	2	2	251	218	7.8	15	99	3.5	155	5.6	2.83	130	.236	.308	32	24	93	105	-0.2	1	0	2.4
1929	Chi-N	**22**	10	.688	40	30	19	**5**	2	267	283	9.5	12	102	3.4	**166**	**5.6**	3.57	129	.276	.339	34	31	98	115	2.4	2	-3	2.7
1930	Chi-N	**20**	9	.690	45	35	**22**	2	4	272	290	9.6	14	96	3.2	142	4.7	3.94	130	.271	.327	31	36	103	97	4.3	4	-2	3.5
1931	Chi-N	16	9	.640	36	30	12	2	0	228	229	9.0	9	88	3.5	112	4.4	3.91	93	.258	.325	-1	-7	94	89	3.0	2	-0	-0.5
1932	Chi-N	15	17	.469	37	33	17	2	0	237	222	8.4	13	78	3.0	120	4.6	3.38	118	.244	.306	13	16	103	92	-3.7	-0	-3	1.3
1933	Chi-N	10	14	.417	31	26	13	2	0	186	186	9.0	10	59	2.9	72	3.5	3.92	81	.258	.314	-12	-16	95	85	-3.3	-2	-1	-1.8
1934	Chi-N	14	7	.667	34	21	8	1	0	191	200	9.4	14	55	2.6	111	5.2	3.53	111	.270	.317	11	8	97	110	2.7	-2	-1	0.5
1935	NY-A	3	5	.375	29	2	0	0	3	56	53	8.5	7	33	5.3	25	4.0	5.46	73	.252	.343	-6	-9	90	87	-1.4	-2	-0	-1.0
1936	NY-A	12	4	.750	35	9	5	0	**9**	135	144	9.6	4	60	4.0	72	4.8	3.80	119	.273	.344	19	11	90	114	2.2	-0	-2	0.7
1937	NY-A	4	4	.500	28	9	3	0	6	92	109	10.7	5	35	3.4	49	4.8	5.48	82	.291	.352	-9	-10	97	85	-0.9	-4	-2	-1.4
Total	10	134	92	.593	357	220	115	16	26	1915	1934	9.1	103	705	3.3	1024	4.8	3.74	110	.262	.324	112	83	97	99	5.1	-2	-13	6.4
■ CHARLIE MALONEY	Maloney, Charles Michael b: 5/22/1886, Cambridge, Mass. d: 1/17/67, Arlington, Mass. BR/TR, 5'8", 155 lbs. Deb: 8/10/08																												
1908	Bos-N	0	0	—	1	0	0	0	0	2	3	13.5	0	1	4.5	0	0.0	4.50	55	.379	.449	-0	-0	106	133	0.0	0	0	0.0
■ JIM MALONEY	Maloney, James William b: 6/2/40, Fresno, Cal. BL/TR, 6'2", 190 lbs. Deb: 7/27/60																												
1960	Cin-N	2	6	.250	11	10	2	1	0	64	61	8.6	5	37	5.2	48	6.8	4.64	80	.255	.356	-6	-6	99	93	-1.7	-0	-0	-0.6
1961	Cin-N	6	7	.462	27	11	1	0	2	95	86	8.1	16	59	5.6	57	5.4	4.36	95	.242	.344	-3	-2	103	107	-1.5	4	-1	0.1
1962	Cin-N	9	7	.563	22	17	3	0	1	115	90	7.0	11	66	5.2	105	8.2	3.52	112	.214	.319	5	6	100	94	-0.5	0	-1	0.4
1963	Cin-N	23	7	.767	33	33	13	6	0	250	183	6.6	17	88	3.2	265	**9.5**	2.77	122	.202	.274	14	17	103	80	8.3	1	-2	1.8
1964	Cin-N	15	10	.600	31	31	11	2	0	216	175	7.3	16	83	3.5	214	8.9	2.71	133	.222	.293	20	21	102	107	1.1	1	-2	2.3
1965	Cin-N	20	9	.690	33	33	14	**5**	0	255	189	6.7	13	110	3.9	244	8.6	2.54	142	.206	.290	28	30	102	99	5.1	7	-1	4.2
1966	Cin-N	16	8	.667	32	32	10	5	0	225	174	7.0	18	90	3.6	216	8.6	2.80	147	.214	.295	20	33	114	101	4.8	3	-0	4.1
1967	Cin-N	15	11	.577	30	29	6	3	0	196	181	8.3	8	72	3.3	153	7.0	3.26	112	.247	.311	3	9	109	97	1.3	0	-1	1.0
1968	Cin-N	16	10	.615	33	32	8	5	0	207	183	8.0	17	80	3.5	181	7.9	3.61	92	.239	.307	-14	-7	111	91	3.1	6	-1	-0.1
1969	Cin-N	12	5	.706	30	27	6	3	0	179	135	6.8	11	86	4.3	102	5.1	2.77	128	.208	.297	17	15	99	96	3.2	7	-1	2.3
1970	Cin-N	0	1	.000	7	3	0	0	1	17	26	13.8	3	15	7.9	7	3.7	11.12	38	.366	.467	-13	-13	103	84	-0.4	-0	0	-1.1

YEAR	TM/L	W	L	PCT	G	GS	CG	SHO	SV	IP	H	H/G	HR	BB	BB/G	SO	SO/G	ERA	/A	OAVG	OOBP	PR	/A	PF	CPI	WAT	PB	PD	TPI
1971	Cal-A	0	3	.000	13	4	0	0	0	30	35	10.5	3	24	7.2	13	3.9	5.10	68	.294	.408	-5	-6	99	118	-1.4	0	0	-0.5
Total	12	134	84	.615	302	262	74	30	4	1849	1518	7.4	138	810	3.9	1605	7.8	3.19	115	.224	.305	64	98	105	96	21.4	28	-9	13.9
■ PAUL MALOY	Maloy, Paul Augustus "Biff" b: 6/4/1892, Bascom, Ohio d: 3/18/76, Sandusky, Ohio BR/TR, 5'11", 185 lbs. Deb: 7/11/13																												
1913	Bos-A	0	0	—	2	0	0	0	0	2	2	9.0	0	1	4.5	0	0.0	9.00	33	.286	.500	-1	-1	103	75	0.0	0	-0	-0.1
■ GORDON MALTZBERGER	Maltzberger, Gordon Ralph "Maltzy" b: 9/4/12, Utopia, Tex. d: 12/11/74, Rialto, Cal. BR/TR, 6', 170 lbs. Deb: 4/27/43 C																												
1943	Chi-A	7	4	.636	37	0	0	0	**14**	99	86	7.8	8	24	2.2	48	4.4	2.45	136	.236	.283	9	10	101	118	1.3	0	0	1.1
1944	Chi-A	10	5	.667	46	0	0	0	**12**	91	81	8.0	2	19	1.9	49	4.8	2.97	118	.235	.272	5	5	102	75	3.0	-1	-0	0.5
1946	Chi-A	2	0	1.000	19	0	0	0	2	40	30	6.7	3	6	1.3	17	3.8	1.57	217	.205	.240	9	8	97	109	1.0	-0	-1	0.8
1947	Chi-A	1	4	.200	33	0	0	0	5	64	61	8.6	4	25	3.5	22	3.1	3.38	108	.257	.321	2	2	99	110	-1.3	1	1	0.4
Total	4	20	13	.606	135	0	0	0	33	294	258	7.9	17	74	2.3	136	4.2	2.69	129	.236	.282	25	25	101	102	4.0	-0	0	2.8
■ AL MAMAUX	Mamaux, Albert Leon b: 5/30/1894, Pittsburgh, Pa. d: 1/2/63, Santa Monica, Cal. BR/TR, 6'0.5", 168 lbs. Deb: 9/23/13																												
1913	Pit-N	0	0	—	1	0	0	0	0	3	2	6.0	0	2	6.0	2	6.0	3.00	101	.167	.286	0	0	94	35	0.0	-0	0	0.0
1914	Pit-N	5	2	.714	13	6	4	2	0	63	41	5.9	1	24	3.4	30	4.3	1.71	151	.186	.270	8	6	93	79	1.7	1	1	0.9
1915	Pit-N	21	8	.724	38	31	17	8	0	252	182	6.5	3	96	3.4	152	5.4	2.04	132	.208	.286	20	18	98	99	7.7	-1	-3	1.2
1916	Pit-N	21	15	.583	45	38	26	1	2	310	264	7.7	3	136	3.9	163	4.7	2.53	111	.239	.317	3	10	107	112	6.0	1	0	1.3
1917	Pit-N	2	11	.154	16	13	5	0	0	86	92	9.6	1	50	5.2	22	2.3	5.23	53	.278	.368	-24	-23	103	82	-3.5	0	-1	-2.4
1918	Bro-N	0	1	.000	2	1	0	0	0	8	14	15.8	0	2	2.3	2	2.3	6.75	43	.438	.444	-4	-3	104	111	-0.4	-0	1	-0.2
1919	Bro-N	10	12	.455	30	22	16	2	0	199	174	7.9	2	66	3.0	80	3.6	2.67	102	.245	.302	5	1	94	102	-0.9	1	-0	0.1
1920	Bro-N	12	8	.600	41	18	9	2	4	191	172	8.1	2	63	3.0	101	**4.8**	2.69	126	.255	.313	10	15	108	103	0.0	-1	-1	1.5
1921	Bro-N	3	3	.500	12	1	0	0	1	43	36	7.5	1	13	2.7	21	4.4	3.14	126	.240	.289	3	4	105	82	0.0	-0	1	0.4
1922	Bro-N	1	4	.200	37	7	1	0	3	88	97	9.9	7	33	3.4	35	3.6	3.68	106	.290	.345	4	2	95	122	-1.4	3	0	0.5
1923	Bro-N	0	2	.000	5	1	0	0	0	13	20	13.8	0	6	4.2	5	3.5	8.31	47	.385	.426	-6	-6	98	83	-0.9	0	0	-0.4
1924	NY-A	1	1	.500	14	2	0	0	0	38	44	10.4	2	20	4.7	12	2.8	5.68	72	.308	.378	-6	-7	97	93	0.0	-1	-1	-0.7
Total	12	76	67	.531	254	140	78	15	10	1294	1138	7.9	22	511	3.6	625	4.3	2.89	104	.245	.315	13	18	101	102	8.3	2	-2	2.2
■ HAL MANDERS	Manders, Harold Carl b: 6/14/17, Waukee, Iowa BR/TR, 6', 187 lbs. Deb: 8/12/41																												
1941	Det-A	1	0	1.000	8	0	0	0	0	15	13	7.8	0	8	4.8	7	4.2	2.40	185	.236	.338	3	3	107	140	0.5	-1	-0	0.3
1942	Det-A	2	0	1.000	18	0	0	0	0	33	39	10.6	4	15	4.1	14	3.8	4.09	101	.307	.377	-2	0	113	142	1.0	0	0	0.0
1946	Det-A	0	0	—	2	0	0	0	0	6	8	12.0	1	2	3.0	3	4.5	10.50	35	.364	.423	-5	-5	106	71	0.0	0	-0	-0.3
	Chi-N	0	1	.000	2	1	0	0	0	6	11	16.5	1	3	4.5	4	6.0	9.00	35	.423	.500	-4	-4	93	111	-0.4	-0	-0	-0.3
Total	3	3	1	.750	30	1	0	0	0	60	71	10.7	6	28	4.2	28	4.2	4.80	85	.309	.386	-7	-5	109	131	1.1	-0	-0	-0.3
■ LEO MANGUM	Mangum, Leo Allan "Blackie" b: 5/24/1896, Durham, N.C. d: 7/9/74, Lima, Ohio BR/TR, 6'1", 187 lbs. Deb: 7/11/24																												
1924	Chi-A	1	4	.200	13	7	1	0	0	47	69	13.2	3	25	4.8	12	2.3	7.09	59	.359	.422	-15	-15	98	98	-1.3	-1	0	-1.3
1925	Chi-A	1	0	1.000	7	0	0	0	0	15	25	15.0	0	6	3.6	6	3.6	7.80	53	.373	.419	-6	-6	95	84	0.5	1	-0	-0.4
1928	NY-N	0	0	—	1	1	0	0	0	3	6	18.0	0	5	15.0	1	3.0	15.00	26	.500	.550	-4	-4	99	91	0.0	0	1	-0.1
1932	Bos-N	0	0	—	7	0	0	0	0	10	17	15.3	1	0	0.0	3	2.7	5.40	67	.333	.315	-2	-2	93	95	0.0	-0	1	0.0
1933	Bos-N	4	3	.571	25	5	2	1	0	84	93	10.0	2	11	1.2	28	3.0	3.32	96	.280	.295	0	-1	96	94	0.3	-2	2	0.0
1934	Bos-N	5	3	.625	29	3	1	0	1	94	127	12.2	9	23	2.2	28	2.7	5.74	61	.315	.346	-18	-23	86	90	0.9	2	1	-1.8
1935	Bos-N	0	0	—	3	0	0	0	0	5	6	10.8	0	2	3.6	0	0.0	3.60	112	.300	.364	0	0	100	123	0.0	0	0	0.0
Total	7	11	10	.524	85	16	4	1	1	258	343	12.0	15	72	2.5	78	2.7	5.37	67	.318	.353	-43	-51	93	93	0.4	1	4	-3.6
■ ERNIE MANNING	Manning, Ernest Devon "Ed" b: 10/9/1890, Florala, Ala. d: 4/28/73, Pensacola, Fla. BL/TR, 6', 175 lbs. Deb: 5/03/14																												
1914	StL-A	0	0	—	4	0	0	0	0	10	11	9.9	0	3	2.7	3	2.7	3.60	76	.297	.350	-1	-1	100	102	0.0	-0	0	0.0
■ JIM MANNING	Manning, James Benjamin b: 7/21/43, L'Anse, Mich. BR/TR, 6'1", 185 lbs. Deb: 4/15/62																												
1962	Min-A	0	0	—	5	1	0	0	0	7	14	18.0	0	1	1.3	3	3.9	5.14	80	.389	.410	-1	-1	104	138	0.0	-0	0	0.0
■ JACK MANNING	Manning, John E. b: 12/20/1853, Braintree, Mass. d: 8/15/29, Boston, Mass. BR/TR, 5'8.5", 158 lbs. Deb: 4/23/1873																												
1874	Bal-n	4	14	.222	19																								
1875	Bos-n	13	3	.813	17																								
1876	Bos-N	18	5	.783	34	20	13	0	**5**	197	213	9.7	1	32	1.5	24	1.1	2.15	101	.280	.309	4	1	94	108	7.0	4	1	0.0
1877	Cin-N	0	4	.000	10	4	2	0	1	44	83	17.0	1	7	1.4	6	1.2	6.95	36	.409	.429	-20	-22	90	96	-1.9	4	0	-1.7
1878	Bos-N	1	0	1.000	3	1	1	0	0	11	24	19.6	1	5	4.1	2	1.6	14.73	16	.447	.494	-15	-15	105	63	0.5	0	0	-1.1
Total	2 n	17	17	.500	36																								
Total	3	19	9	.679	47	25	16	0	6	252	320	11.4	3	44	1.6	32	1.1	3.54	64	.315	.343	-32	-36	94	104	5.6	8	1	-2.8
■ RUBE MANNING	Manning, Walter S. b: 4/29/1883, Chambersburg, Pa. d: 4/23/30, Williamsport, Pa. BR/TR, 6', 180 lbs. Deb: 9/25/07																												
1907	NY-A	0	1	.000	1	1	1	0	0	9	8	8.0	0	3	3.0	3	3.0	3.00	93	.261	.327	-0	-0	110	84	-0.4	-0	-0	0.0
1908	NY-A	13	16	.448	41	26	19	2	1	245	228	8.4	4	86	3.2	113	4.2	2.94	82	.256	.334	-15	-14	101	114	3.0	1	-2	-1.7
1909	NY-A	7	11	.389	26	21	11	2	1	173	167	8.7	2	48	2.5	71	3.7	3.17	78	.265	.326	-13	-14	99	91	-2.0	0	-1	-1.5
1910	NY-A	2	4	.333	16	9	4	0	0	75	80	9.6	4	25	3.0	25	3.0	3.72	72	.283	.349	-10	-9	106	106	-1.2	0	-1	-0.9
Total	4	22	32	.407	84	57	35	4	2	502	483	8.7	10	162	2.9	212	3.8	3.14	79	.263	.334	-39	-37	101	104	-0.6	0	-3	-4.1
■ TOM MANSELL	Mansell, Thomas E. "Brick" b: 1/1/1855, Auburn, N.Y. d: 10/6/34, Auburn, N.Y. BL/TL, 5'8", 160 lbs. Deb: 5/01/1879																												
1883	Det-N	0	0	—	1	0	0	0	0	7	21	27.0	2	5	6.4	3	3.9	18.00	16	.523	.576	-12	-12	94	92	0.0	0	0	-0.6
■ LOU MANSKE	Manske, Louis Hugo b: 7/4/1884, Milwaukee, Wis. d: 4/27/63, Milwaukee, Wis. BL/TL, 6', Deb: 8/31/06																												
1906	Pit-N	0	0	—	2	1	0	0	0	8	12	13.5	0	5	5.6	6	6.8	5.63	47	.378	.462	-3	-3	101	113	0.0	-1	-0	-0.2
■ MOXIE MANUEL	Manuel, Mark Garfield b: 10/16/1881, Metropolis, Ill. d: 4/26/24, Memphis, Tenn. BR/TB, 5'11", 170 lbs. Deb: 9/25/05																												
1905	Was-A	0	0	—	3	1	1	0	0	10	9	8.1	0	3	2.7	3	2.7	5.40	52	.264	.324	-3	-3	106	49	0.0	0	0	-0.2
1908	Chi-A	3	4	.429	18	6	3	0	1	60	52	7.8	0	25	3.8	25	3.8	3.30	67	.251	.338	-6	-7	93	96	-0.8	-1	0	-0.7
Total	2	3	4	.429	21	7	4	0	1	70	61	7.8	0	28	3.6	28	3.6	3.60	64	.253	.336	-9	-10	94	90	-0.8	-1	0	-0.9
■ DICK MANVILLE	Manville, Richard Wesley b: 12/25/26, Des Moines, Iowa BR/TR, 6'4", 192 lbs. Deb: 4/30/50																												
1950	Bos-N	0	0	—	1	0	0	0	0	2	0	0.0	0	3	13.5	2	9.0	0.00	—	.000	.300	1	1	85	0	0.0	0	0	0.1
1952	Chi-N	0	0	—	11	0	0	0	0	17	25	13.2	2	12	6.4	6	3.2	7.94	49	.362	.446	-8	-8	103	100	0.0	0	0	-0.6
Total	2	0	0	—	12	0	0	0	0	19	25	11.8	2	15	7.1	8	3.8	7.11	54	.329	.430	-7	-7	101	89	0.0	0	0	-0.5
■ RAVELO MANZANILLO	Manzanillo, Ravelo (Adams) b: 10/17/63, San Pedro De Macoris, D.R. BL/TL, 5'10", 190 lbs. Deb: 9/25/88																												
1988	Chi-A	0	1	.000	2	2	0	0	0	9	7	7.0	1	12	12.0	10	10.0	6.00	65	.212	.435	-2	-2	99	98	-0.4	0	0	-0.1
■ ROLLA MAPEL	Mapel, Rolla Hamilton "Lefty" b: 3/9/1890, Lee'S Summitt, Mo. d: 4/6/66, San Diego, Cal. BL/TL, 5'11.5", 165 lbs. Deb: 8/31/19																												
1919	StL-A	0	3	.000	4	3	2	0	0	20	17	7.6	0	17	7.6	2	0.9	4.50	70	.262	.435	-3	-3	98	107	-1.4	-0	1	-0.1
■ GEORGES MARANDA	Maranda, Georges Henri b: 1/15/32, Levis, Que., Can. BR/TR, 6'2", 195 lbs. Deb: 4/26/60																												
1960	SF-N	1	4	.200	17	4	0	0	0	51	50	8.8	6	30	5.3	28	4.9	4.59	73	.254	.348	-5	-7	89	98	-1.4	-0	2	-0.5
1962	Min-A	1	3	.250	32	4	0	0	0	73	69	8.5	11	35	4.3	36	4.4	4.44	93	.252	.340	-4	-3	104	103	-1.0	1	1	0.0
Total	2	2	7	.222	49	8	0	0	0	124	119	8.6	17	65	4.7	64	4.6	4.50	84	.253	.343	-8	-10	97	101	-2.4	1	2	-0.5
■ FIRPO MARBERRY	Marberry, Fredrick b: 11/30/1898, Streetman, Tex. d: 8/76, Mexia, Tex. BR/TR, 6'1", 190 lbs. Deb: 8/11/23 U																												
1923	Was-A	4	0	1.000	11	4	2	0	0	45	42	8.4	1	17	3.4	18	3.6	2.80	135	.258	.326	6	5	95	121	2.0	-1	-0	0.4
1924	Was-A	11	12	.478	**50**	15	6	0	**15**	195	190	8.8	3	70	3.2	68	3.1	3.09	131	.262	.322	25	21	96	108	-2.5	-4	-1	1.5
1925	Was-A	9	5	.643	**55**	0	0	0	**15**	93	84	8.1	4	45	4.4	53	5.1	3.48	120	.246	.333	**9**	**7**	95	100	0.2	1	1	0.9
1926	Was-A	12	7	.632	**64**	5	3	0	**22**	138	120	7.8	4	66	4.3	43	2.8	3.00	130	.243	.321	16	14	97	108	2.1	-1	-1	1.2
1927	Was-A	10	7	.588	56	10	2	0	9	155	177	10.3	4	68	3.9	74	4.3	4.65	86	.296	.357	-9	-12	96	98	0.8	-3	-1	-1.5
1928	Was-A	13	13	.500	**48**	11	7	1	3	161	160	8.9	4	42	2.3	76	4.2	3.86	106	.268	.307	3	4	101	86	0.4	-4	-1	0.0
1929	Was-A	19	12	.613	**49**	26	16	0	**11**	250	233	8.4	6	69	2.5	121	4.4	3.06	139	.252	**.300**	33	33	100	96	5.0	2	-3	3.1
1930	Was-A	15	5	.750	33	22	9	2	1	185	190	9.2	15	53	2.6	56	2.7	4.09	112	.270	.314	12	10	98	99	3.9	5	-1	1.2

YEAR	TM/L	W	L	PCT	G	GS	CG	SHO	SV	IP	H	H/G	HR	BB	BB/G	SO	SO/G	ERA	/A	OAVG	OOBP	PR	/A	PF	CPI	WAT	PB	PD	TPI
1931	Was-A	16	4	.800	45	25	11	1	7	219	211	8.7	13	63	2.6	88	3.6	3.45	125	.252	.303	23	21	98	101	5.4	1	-2	1.9
1932	Was-A	8	4	.667	**54**	15	8	1	**13**	198	202	9.2	13	72	3.3	66	3.0	4.00	109	.268	.326	11	8	98	104	1.0	-2	1	0.7
1933	Det-A	16	11	.593	37	32	15	1	2	238	232	8.8	13	61	2.3	84	3.2	3.29	139	.254	**.297**	26	34	107	102	3.2	-6	-3	2.5
1934	Det-A	15	5	.750	38	19	6	1	3	156	174	10.0	12	48	2.8	64	3.7	4.56	92	.276	.325	-1	-6	94	90	3.0	3	-2	-0.4
1935	Det-A	0	1	.000	5	2	1	0	0	19	22	10.4	2	9	4.3	7	3.3	4.26	97	.289	.348	0	-0	93	121	-0.4	0	-0	0.0
1936	NY-N	0	0	—	1	0	0	0	0	⅓	1	27.0	0	0	0.0	0	0.0	0.00	—	.500	.333	0	0	98	0	0.0	-0	0	0.0
	Was-A	0	2	.000	5	1	0	0	0	14	11	7.1	2	3	1.9	4	2.6	3.86	126	.208	.259	2	2	96	73	-0.9	-0	0	0.1
Total	14	148	88	.627	551	187	86	7	101	2066	2049	8.9	96	686	3.0	822	3.6	3.63	117	.262	.317	155	141	99	100	23.2	-8	-12	11.6

■ **WALT MARBET** Marbet, Walter William b: 9/13/1890, Plymouth Co., Ia. d: 9/24/56, Hohenwald, Tenn. 6'1", 175 lbs. Deb: 6/17/13

YEAR	TM/L	W	L	PCT	G	GS	CG	SHO	SV	IP	H	H/G	HR	BB	BB/G	SO	SO/G	ERA	/A	OAVG	OOBP	PR	/A	PF	CPI	WAT	PB	PD	TPI
1913	StL-N	0	1	.000	3	1	0	0	0	3	9	27.0	0	4	12.0	1	3.0	18.00	17	.500	.591	-5	-5	97	85	-0.4	0	-0	-0.4

■ **PHIL MARCHILDON** Marchildon, Philip Joseph "Babe" b: 10/25/13, Penetanguishene, Ont., Canada BR/TR, 5'10.5", 170 lbs. Deb: 9/22/40

YEAR	TM/L	W	L	PCT	G	GS	CG	SHO	SV	IP	H	H/G	HR	BB	BB/G	SO	SO/G	ERA	/A	OAVG	OOBP	PR	/A	PF	CPI	WAT	PB	PD	TPI
1940	Phi-A	0	2	.000	2	2	1	0	0	10	12	10.8	1	8	7.2	4	3.6	7.20	60	.286	.392	-3	-3	99	82	-0.9	-0	0	-0.2
1941	Phi-A	10	15	.400	30	27	14	1	0	204	188	8.3	15	118	5.2	74	3.3	3.57	120	.245	.344	13	16	103	114	-0.5	0	-3	1.3
1942	Phi-A	17	14	.548	38	31	18	1	1	244	215	7.9	14	140	5.2	110	4.1	4.20	88	.235	.332	-15	-14	101	87	5.4	3	-3	-1.3
1945	Phi-A	0	1	.000	3	2	0	0	0	9	5	5.0	0	11	11.0	2	2.0	4.00	81	.179	.390	-1	-1	96	98	-0.4	1	0	0.0
1946	Phi-A	13	16	.448	36	29	16	1	1	227	197	7.8	14	114	4.5	95	3.8	3.49	108	.237	.327	0	7	107	98	3.3	-6	-2	0.0
1947	Phi-A	19	9	.679	35	35	21	2	0	277	228	7.4	15	141	4.6	128	4.2	3.22	115	.224	.321	15	15	100	98	**5.5**	-1	-3	1.1
1948	Phi-A	9	15	.375	33	30	12	1	0	226	214	8.5	19	131	5.2	66	2.6	4.54	96	.251	.347	-6	-5	102	96	-4.1	-6	-1	-1.0
1949	Phi-A	0	3	.000	7	6	0	0	0	16	24	13.5	3	19	10.7	2	1.1	11.81	35	.358	.494	-14	-14	99	83	-1.4	-0	-0	-1.1
1950	Bos-A	0	0	—	1	0	0	0	0	1	1	9.0	0	2	18.0	0	0.0	9.00	57	.200	.429	-0	-0	111	53	0.0	0	0	0.0
Total	9	68	75	.476	185	162	82	6	2	1214	1084	8.0	81	684	5.1	481	3.6	3.93	100	.240	.337	-11	1	102	98	6.9	-10	-11	-1.2

■ **JOHNNY MARCUM** Marcum, John Alfred "Footsie" b: 9/9/09, Campbellsburg, Ky. d: 9/10/84, Louisville, Ky. BL/TR, 5'11", 197 lbs. Deb: 9/07/33

YEAR	TM/L	W	L	PCT	G	GS	CG	SHO	SV	IP	H	H/G	HR	BB	BB/G	SO	SO/G	ERA	/A	OAVG	OOBP	PR	/A	PF	CPI	WAT	PB	PD	TPI
1933	Phi-A	3	2	.600	5	5	4	2	0	37	28	6.8	0	20	4.9	14	3.4	1.95	201	.200	.298	10	8	92	113	0.4	0	0	0.9
1934	Phi-A	14	11	.560	37	31	17	2	0	232	257	10.0	13	88	3.4	92	3.6	4.50	98	.280	.339	-0	-2	98	97	2.8	5	-0	0.2
1935	Phi-A	17	12	.586	39	27	19	2	3	243	256	9.5	9	83	3.1	99	3.7	4.07	112	.268	.321	10	13	102	91	5.4	9	-3	1.8
1936	Bos-A	8	13	.381	31	23	9	1	1	174	194	10.0	14	52	2.7	57	2.9	4.81	111	.281	.328	4	10	106	92	-2.3	1	-0	1.0
1937	Bos-A	13	11	.542	37	23	9	1	3	184	230	11.3	17	47	2.3	59	2.9	4.84	98	.306	.345	-5	-2	102	102	0.5	5	1	0.4
1938	Bos-A	5	6	.455	15	11	7	0	0	92	113	11.1	11	25	2.4	25	2.4	4.11	117	.298	.338	7	7	100	121	-1.2	-1	-1	0.5
1939	StL-A	2	5	.286	12	6	2	0	0	48	66	12.4	12	10	1.9	14	2.6	7.69	63	.332	.360	-16	-15	105	90	0.0	3	-0	-1.0
	Chi-A	3	3	.500	19	6	2	0	0	90	125	12.5	15	19	1.9	32	3.2	6.00	82	.326	.347	-14	-11	106	101	-0.2	2	-1	-0.9
	Yr	5	8	.385	31	12	4	0	0	138	191	12.5	27	29	1.9	46	3.0	6.59	74	.327	.350	-30	-26	106	101	-0.2	3	-1	-1.9
Total	7	65	63	.508	195	132	69	8	7	1100	1269	10.4	91	344	2.8	392	3.2	4.66	101	.287	.335	-4	7	102	98	5.4	25	-4	2.9

■ **LEO MARENTETTE** Marentette, Leo John b: 2/18/41, Detroit, Mich. BR/TR, 6'2", 200 lbs. Deb: 9/26/65

YEAR	TM/L	W	L	PCT	G	GS	CG	SHO	SV	IP	H	H/G	HR	BB	BB/G	SO	SO/G	ERA	/A	OAVG	OOBP	PR	/A	PF	CPI	WAT	PB	PD	TPI
1965	Det-A	0	0	—	2	0	0	0	0	3	1	3.0	0	1	3.0	3	9.0	0.00	—	.111	.200	1	1	104	0	0.0	0	0	0.1
1969	Mon-N	0	0	—	3	0	0	0	0	5	9	16.2	1	1	1.8	4	7.2	7.20	52	.391	.400	-2	-2	103	113	0.0	-0	0	-0.1
Total	2	0	0	—	5	0	0	0	0	8	10	11.3	1	2	2.3	7	7.9	4.50	82	.313	.343	-1	-1	104	71	0.0	-0	0	0.0

■ **JOE MARGONERI** Margoneri, Joseph Emanuel b: 1/13/30, Somerset, Pa. BL/TL, 6', 185 lbs. Deb: 4/25/56

YEAR	TM/L	W	L	PCT	G	GS	CG	SHO	SV	IP	H	H/G	HR	BB	BB/G	SO	SO/G	ERA	/A	OAVG	OOBP	PR	/A	PF	CPI	WAT	PB	PD	TPI
1956	NY-N	6	6	.500	23	13	2	0	0	92	88	8.6	12	49	4.8	49	4.8	3.91	96	.254	.338	-1	-2	99	110	0.7	-1	-0	-0.2
1957	NY-N	1	1	.500	13	2	1	0	0	34	44	11.6	1	21	5.6	18	4.8	5.29	76	.314	.400	-5	-5	103	105	0.1	-1	0	-0.5
Total	2	7	7	.500	36	15	3	0	0	126	132	9.4	13	70	5.0	67	4.8	4.29	89	.271	.356	-7	-7	100	108	0.8	-2	-0	-0.7

■ **JUAN MARICHAL** Marichal, Juan Antonio (Sanchez) "Manito" b: 10/20/37, Laguna Verde, D.R. BR/TR, 6', 185 lbs. Deb: 7/19/60 H

YEAR	TM/L	W	L	PCT	G	GS	CG	SHO	SV	IP	H	H/G	HR	BB	BB/G	SO	SO/G	ERA	/A	OAVG	OOBP	PR	/A	PF	CPI	WAT	PB	PD	TPI
1960	SF-N	6	2	.750	11	11	6	1	0	81	59	6.6	5	28	3.1	58	6.4	2.67	125	.200	.265	10	6	89	77	2.0	0	0	0.6
1961	SF-N	13	10	.565	29	27	9	3	0	185	183	8.9	24	48	2.3	124	6.0	3.89	100	.257	.303	3	-0	96	96	0.4	-2	-1	-0.3
1962	SF-N	18	11	.621	37	36	18	3	1	263	233	8.0	34	90	3.1	153	5.2	3.35	116	.234	.296	17	15	99	101	0.0	4	-1	1.8
1963	SF-N	**25**	8	.758	41	40	18	5	0	**321**	259	7.3	27	61	1.7	248	7.0	2.41	128	.216	.254	31	24	94	89	8.7	3	-3	2.6
1964	SF-N	21	8	.724	33	33	**22**	4	0	269	241	8.1	18	52	1.7	206	6.9	2.48	142	.236	.270	32	31	99	104	6.2	-0	1	3.4
1965	SF-N	22	13	.629	39	37	24	**10**	1	295	224	6.8	27	46	**1.4**	240	7.3	2.14	**181**	.205	.238	46	**57**	109	90	2.2	-0	0	**6.7**
1966	SF-N	25	6	**.806**	37	36	25	4	0	307	228	**6.7**	32	36	**1.1**	222	6.5	2.23	157	**.202**	**.228**	47	43	97	80	**9.2**	7	0	5.7
1967	SF-N	14	10	.583	26	26	18	2	0	202	195	8.7	20	42	1.9	166	7.4	2.76	121	.249	.284	14	13	99	114	0.7	2	-1	1.6
1968	SF-N	**26**	9	.743	38	38	**30**	5	0	**326**	295	8.1	21	46	1.3	218	6.0	2.43	118	.238	.265	20	16	96	100	**8.7**	2	3	2.5
1969	SF-N	21	11	.656	37	36	27	**8**	0	300	244	7.3	15	54	**1.6**	205	6.2	**2.10**	**172**	.222	**.259**	**50**	**50**	100	101	4.3	-1	4	6.1
1970	SF-N	12	10	.545	34	33	14	1	0	243	269	10.0	28	48	1.8	123	4.6	4.11	94	.277	.307	-2	-6	96	98	0.4	-6	2	-1.0
1971	SF-N	18	11	.621	37	37	18	4	0	279	244	7.9	27	56	1.8	159	5.1	2.94	117	.233	.270	17	15	99	91	2.5	0	3	2.0
1972	SF-N	6	16	.273	25	24	6	0	0	165	176	9.6	15	46	2.5	72	3.9	3.71	93	.277	.322	-5	-5	100	109	-4.6	1	0	-0.3
1973	SF-N	11	15	.423	34	32	9	2	0	207	231	10.0	22	37	**1.6**	87	3.8	3.83	100	.277	.303	-4	0	104	98	-3.2	1	4	0.5
1974	Bos-A	5	1	.833	11	9	0	0	0	57	61	9.6	3	14	2.2	21	3.3	4.89	79	.270	.316	-8	-7	106	69	2.0	0	-0	-0.6
1975	LA-N	0	1	.000	2	2	0	0	0	6	11	16.5	2	5	7.5	1	1.5	13.50	25	.407	.471	-7	-7	93	84	-0.4	-0	0	-0.5
Total	16	243	142	.631	471	457	244	52	2	3506	3153	8.1	320	709	1.8	2303	5.9	2.89	122	.237	.274	262	246	99	96	39.1	11	11	30.8

■ **DAN MARION** Marion, Donald G. "Rube" b: 7/31/1890, Cleveland, Ohio d: 1/18/33, Milwaukee, Wis. BR/TR, 6'1", 187 lbs. Deb: 4/23/14

YEAR	TM/L	W	L	PCT	G	GS	CG	SHO	SV	IP	H	H/G	HR	BB	BB/G	SO	SO/G	ERA	/A	OAVG	OOBP	PR	/A	PF	CPI	WAT	PB	PD	TPI
1914	Bro-F	3	2	.600	17	9	4	0	0	89	97	9.8	1	38	3.8	41	4.1	3.94	82	.281	.362	-7	-7	101	101	0.5	-1	0	-0.7
1915	Bro-F	12	9	.571	35	25	15	2	0	208	193	8.4	1	64	2.8	46	2.0	3.20	93	.248	.308	-4	-5	98	84	2.4	-0	3	-0.2
Total	2	15	11	.577	52	34	19	2	0	297	290	8.8	2	102	3.1	87	2.6	3.42	89	.258	.325	-11	-12	99	89	2.9	-1	3	-0.9

■ **DUKE MARKELL** Markell, Harry Duquesne (born Harry Duquesne Makowsky) b: 8/17/23, Paris, France d: 6/14/84, Ft.Lauderdale, Fla. BR/TR, 6'1.5", 209 lbs. Deb: 9/06/51

YEAR	TM/L	W	L	PCT	G	GS	CG	SHO	SV	IP	H	H/G	HR	BB	BB/G	SO	SO/G	ERA	/A	OAVG	OOBP	PR	/A	PF	CPI	WAT	PB	PD	TPI
1951	StL-A	1	1	.500	5	2	1	0	0	21	25	10.7	3	20	8.6	10	4.3	6.43	70	.298	.433	-5	-4	109	108	0.2	-0	-0	-0.4

■ **CLIFF MARKLE** Markle, Clifford Monroe b: 5/3/1894, Dravosburg, Pa. d: 5/24/74, Temple City, Cal. BR/TR, 5'9", 163 lbs. Deb: 9/18/15

YEAR	TM/L	W	L	PCT	G	GS	CG	SHO	SV	IP	H	H/G	HR	BB	BB/G	SO	SO/G	ERA	/A	OAVG	OOBP	PR	/A	PF	CPI	WAT	PB	PD	TPI
1915	NY-A	2	0	1.000	3	2	2	0	0	23	15	5.9	1	6	2.3	12	4.7	0.39	742	.185	.241	7	6	99	307	1.0	0	-1	0.7
1916	NY-A	4	3	.571	11	7	3	1	0	46	41	8.0	0	31	6.1	14	2.7	4.50	64	.256	.390	-9	-8	101	89	0.4	-1	-0	-1.0
1921	Cin-N	2	6	.250	10	6	5	0	0	67	75	10.1	0	20	2.7	23	3.1	3.76	102	.291	.331	0	1	101	94	-1.8	-2	-1	-0.1
1922	Cin-N	4	5	.444	25	3	2	1	0	76	75	8.9	3	33	3.9	34	4.0	3.79	102	.268	.329	3	1	94	98	-0.9	-0	-0	0.0
1924	NY-A	0	3	.000	7	3	0	0	0	23	29	11.3	5	20	7.8	7	2.7	9.00	46	.333	.438	-12	-13	97	91	-1.4	-1	-1	-1.1
Total	5	12	17	.414	56	21	12	2	0	235	235	9.0	9	110	4.2	90	3.4	4.10	88	.271	.346	-11	-13	98	115	-2.7	-5	-2	-1.5

■ **DICK MARLOWE** Marlowe, Richard Burton b: 6/27/29, Hickory, N.C. d: 12/30/68, Toledo, Ohio BR/TR, 6'2", 165 lbs. Deb: 9/19/51

YEAR	TM/L	W	L	PCT	G	GS	CG	SHO	SV	IP	H	H/G	HR	BB	BB/G	SO	SO/G	ERA	/A	OAVG	OOBP	PR	/A	PF	CPI	WAT	PB	PD	TPI
1951	Det-A	0	1	.000	2	1	0	0	0	2	5	22.5	0	2	9.0	1	4.5	27.00	16	.500	.583	-5	-5	107	49	-0.4	0	0	-0.3
1952	Det-A	0	2	.000	4	1	0	0	0	11	21	17.2	1	3	2.5	3	2.5	7.36	51	.420	.453	-5	-4	103	115	-0.9	-0	-0	-0.4
1953	Det-A	6	7	.462	42	11	2	0	0	120	152	11.4	13	42	3.2	52	3.9	5.25	77	.319	.366	-17	-16	102	107	0.8	-0	-1	-1.6
1954	Det-A	5	4	.556	38	2	0	0	2	84	76	8.1	11	40	4.3	39	4.2	4.18	90	.244	.320	-4	-4	101	94	1.0	0	-1	-0.4
1955	Det-A	1	0	1.000	4	1	1	0	1	15	12	7.2	1	4	2.4	9	5.4	1.80	208	.218	.271	4	3	95	125	0.5	-0	-0	0.3
1956	Det-A	1	1	.500	7	1	0	0	0	11	12	9.8	1	9	7.4	4	3.3	5.73	69	.279	.396	-2	-2	95	97	0.0	-0	0	-0.1
	Chi-A	0	0	—	1	0	0	0	0	1	2	18.0	1	1	9.0	0	0.0	9.00	47	.500	.600	-1	-1	102	217	0.0	0	0	0.0
	Yr	1	1	.500	8	1	0	0	0	12	14	10.5	2	10	7.5	4	3.0	6.00	66	.298	.414	-2	-3	96	217	0.0	-0	0	-0.1
Total	6	13	15	.464	98	17	3	0	3	244	280	10.3	28	101	3.7	108	4.0	4.98	79	.295	.354	-29	-29	101	104	1.0	-1	-2	-2.5

■ **LOU MARONE** Marone, Louis Stephen b: 12/3/45, San Diego, Cal. BR/TL, 5'11", 185 lbs. Deb: 5/30/69

YEAR	TM/L	W	L	PCT	G	GS	CG	SHO	SV	IP	H	H/G	HR	BB	BB/G	SO	SO/G	ERA	/A	OAVG	OOBP	PR	/A	PF	CPI	WAT	PB	PD	TPI
1969	Pit-N	1	1	.500	29	0	0	0	0	35	24	6.2	2	13	3.3	25	6.4	2.57	131	.195	.279	4	3	94	86	0.0	0	-0	0.3
1970	Pit-N	0	0	—	1	0	0	0	0	2	2	9.0	1	0	0.0	0	0.0	4.50	86	.222	.222	-0	-0	96	99	0.0	0	0	0.0
Total	2	1	1	.500	30	0	0	0	0	37	26	6.3	3	13	3.2	25	6.1	2.68	127	.197	.275	4	3	94	87	0.0	0	-0	0.3

■ **RUBE MARQUARD** Marquard, Richard William b: 10/9/1889, Cleveland, Ohio d: 6/1/80, Baltimore, Md. BB/TL, 6'3", 180 lbs. Deb: 9/25/08 H

YEAR	TM/L	W	L	PCT	G	GS	CG	SHO	SV	IP	H	H/G	HR	BB	BB/G	SO	SO/G	ERA	/A	OAVG	OOBP	PR	/A	PF	CPI	WAT	PB	PD	TPI
1908	NY-N	0	1	.000	1	1	0	0	0	5	4	7.2	0	2	3.6	2	3.6	3.60	65	.262	.383	-1	-1	100	78	-0.4	-0	0	0.0
1909	NY-N	5	13	.278	29	21	8	0	1	173	155	8.1	2	73	3.8	109	5.7	2.60	103	.248	.335	-0	2	103	117	-5.0	-2	-0	0.1

YEAR	TM/L	W	L	PCT	G	GS	CG	SHO	SV	IP	H	H/G	HR	BB	BB/G	SO	SO/G	ERA	/A	OAVG	OOBP	PR	/A	PF	CPI	WAT	PB	PD	TPI
1910	NY-N	4	4	.500	13	8	2	0	0	71	65	8.2	2	40	5.1	52	6.6	4.44	63	.254	.363	-11	-13	92	83	-0.5	-1	-0	-1.4
1911	NY-N	24	7	**.774**	45	33	22	5	3	278	221	7.2	9	106	3.4	**237**	**7.7**	2.49	134	.219	.296	28	27	99	93	6.4	-1	-4	2.2
1912	NY-N	**26**	11	.703	43	38	22	1	1	295	286	8.7	9	80	2.4	175	5.3	2.56	132	.249	.300	28	27	99	95	1.6	2	-3	2.5
1913	NY-N	23	10	.697	42	33	20	4	3	288	248	7.8	10	49	1.5	151	4.7	2.50	128	.237	.267	23	22	100	87	2.0	1	-5	1.9
1914	NY-N	12	22	.353	39	33	15	4	2	268	261	8.8	9	47	1.6	92	3.1	3.06	85	.262	.285	-8	-13	94	87	-6.9	-1	0	-1.4
1915	NY-N	9	8	.529	27	20	10	2	2	169	178	9.5	8	33	1.8	79	4.2	3.73	68	.272	.302	-18	-22	92	86	1.3	-2	-0	-2.6
	Bro-N	2	2	.500	6	3	0	0	1	25	29	10.4	0	5	1.8	13	4.7	6.12	46	.276	.304	-9	-9	102	48	0.0	-0	-0	-0.9
	Yr	11	10	.524	33	23	10	2	3	194	207	9.6	8	38	1.8	92	4.3	4.04	64	.272	.301	-28	-32	94	48	1.3	-2	-0	-3.5
1916	Bro-N	13	6	.684	36	20	15	2	5	205	169	7.4	2	38	1.7	107	4.7	1.58	**166**	.229	.261	24	24	100	114	2.0	-1	-4	2.3
1917	Bro-N	19	12	.613	37	29	14	2	0	233	200	7.7	5	60	2.3	117	4.5	2.55	111	.232	.276	4	8	105	85	5.1	0	-4	0.5
1918	Bro-N	9	18	.333	34	29	19	4	0	239	231	8.7	7	59	2.2	89	3.4	2.64	109	.260	.297	3	6	104	109	-4.1	-2	-2	0.3
1919	Bro-N	3	3	.500	8	7	3	0	0	59	54	8.2	1	10	1.5	29	4.4	2.29	119	.244	.269	4	3	94	96	0.0	1	-1	0.3
1920	Bro-N	10	7	.588	28	26	10	1	0	190	181	8.6	5	35	1.7	89	4.2	3.22	105	.251	.279	-2	4	108	69	-0.1	-2	-4	-0.1
1921	Cin-N	17	14	.548	39	35	18	2	0	266	291	9.8	8	50	1.7	88	3.0	3.38	113	.285	.312	12	13	101	99	3.1	-2	-3	0.8
1922	Bos-N	11	15	.423	39	24	7	0	1	198	255	11.6	12	66	3.0	57	2.6	5.09	79	.322	.363	-22	-24	98	99	1.8	-1	1	-2.1
1923	Bos-N	11	14	.440	38	29	11	3	0	239	265	10.0	10	65	2.4	78	2.9	3.73	110	.288	.327	7	10	102	104	2.0	-6	0	0.3
1924	Bos-N	1	2	.333	6	6	1	0	0	36	33	8.3	3	13	3.3	10	2.5	3.00	127	.254	.313	3	3	99	122	0.0	0	0	0.4
1925	Bos-N	2	8	.200	26	8	0	1	0	72	105	13.1	5	27	3.4	19	2.4	5.75	71	.341	.380	-12	-13	95	103	-2.8	-1	-2	-1.5
Total	18	201	177	.532	536	403	197	31	19	3309	3231	8.8	107	858	2.3	1593	4.3	3.07	105	.259	.303	53	52	100	95	5.5	-18	-31	1.6

■ **JIM MARQUIS** Marquis, James Milburn b: 11/18/1900, Yoakum, Tex. BR/TR, 5'11", 174 lbs. Deb: 8/08/25

YEAR	TM/L	W	L	PCT	G	GS	CG	SHO	SV	IP	H	H/G	HR	BB	BB/G	SO	SO/G	ERA	/A	OAVG	OOBP	PR	/A	PF	CPI	WAT	PB	PD	TPI
1925	NY-A	0	0	—	2	0	0	0	0	7	12	15.4	1	6	7.7	0	0.0	10.29	41	.414	.474	-5	-5	97	98	0.0	-0	0	-0.3

■ **CONNIE MARRERO** Marrero, Conrado Eugenio (Ramos) b: 4/25/11, Las Villas, Cuba BR/TR, 5'7", 158 lbs. Deb: 4/21/50

YEAR	TM/L	W	L	PCT	G	GS	CG	SHO	SV	IP	H	H/G	HR	BB	BB/G	SO	SO/G	ERA	/A	OAVG	OOBP	PR	/A	PF	CPI	WAT	PB	PD	TPI
1950	Was-A	6	10	.375	27	19	8	1	1	152	159	9.4	17	55	3.3	63	3.7	4.50	103	.269	.329	1	2	101	96	-1.1	-2	-3	-0.1
1951	Was-A	11	9	.550	25	25	16	2	0	187	198	9.5	8	71	3.4	66	3.2	3.90	102	.268	.332	5	2	97	97	2.7	-2	-2	-0.1
1952	Was-A	11	8	.579	22	22	16	2	0	184	175	8.6	9	53	2.6	77	3.8	2.89	128	.249	.301	16	16	100	105	1.6	-5	-3	0.9
1953	Was-A	8	7	.533	22	20	10	2	2	146	130	8.0	14	48	3.0	65	4.0	3.02	123	.241	.303	16	11	93	114	0.6	-1	-1	0.8
1954	Was-A	3	6	.333	22	8	1	0	0	66	74	10.1	12	22	3.0	26	3.5	4.77	77	.287	.334	-8	-8	99	106	-0.9	-1	-1	-0.9
Total	5	39	40	.494	118	94	51	7	3	735	736	9.0	60	249	3.0	297	3.6	3.67	108	.260	.319	30	24	98	103	2.9	-11	-10	0.6

■ **BUCK MARROW** Marrow, Charles Kennon b: 8/29/09, Tarboro, N.C. d: 11/21/82, Newport News, Va. BR/TR, 6'4", 200 lbs. Deb: 7/03/32

YEAR	TM/L	W	L	PCT	G	GS	CG	SHO	SV	IP	H	H/G	HR	BB	BB/G	SO	SO/G	ERA	/A	OAVG	OOBP	PR	/A	PF	CPI	WAT	PB	PD	TPI
1932	Det-A	2	5	.286	18	7	2	0	1	64	70	9.8	6	29	4.1	31	4.4	4.78	95	.278	.365	-2	-2	102	107	-1.5	-0	1	0.0
1937	Bro-N	1	2	.333	6	3	1	0	0	16	19	10.7	2	9	5.1	2	1.1	6.75	62	.284	.368	-5	-5	107	78	-0.2	-1	0	-0.4
1938	Bro-N	0	1	.000	15	0	0	0	0	20	23	10.3	1	11	4.9	6	2.7	4.50	81	.291	.385	-2	-2	96	119	-0.4	-0	0	-0.1
Total	3	3	8	.273	39	10	3	0	1	100	112	10.1	9	49	4.4	39	3.5	5.04	85	.281	.370	-9	-8	101	105	-2.1	-1	1	-0.5

■ **ED MARS** Mars, Edward M. b: 12/4/1866, Chicago, Ill. d: 12/9/41, Chicago, Ill. 5'9", 166 lbs. Deb: 8/12/1890

YEAR	TM/L	W	L	PCT	G	GS	CG	SHO	SV	IP	H	H/G	HR	BB	BB/G	SO	SO/G	ERA	/A	OAVG	OOBP	PR	/A	PF	CPI	WAT	PB	PD	TPI
1890	Syr-a	9	5	.643	16	14	14	0	0	121	132	9.8	2	49	3.6	59	4.4	4.69	76	.293	.363	-11	-15	92	89	2.8	4	0	-0.9

■ **CUDDLES MARSHALL** Marshall, Clarence Westly b: 4/28/25, Bellingham, Wash. BR/TR, 6'3", 200 lbs. Deb: 4/24/46

YEAR	TM/L	W	L	PCT	G	GS	CG	SHO	SV	IP	H	H/G	HR	BB	BB/G	SO	SO/G	ERA	/A	OAVG	OOBP	PR	/A	PF	CPI	WAT	PB	PD	TPI
1946	NY-A	3	4	.429	23	11	1	0	0	81	96	10.7	4	56	6.2	32	3.6	5.33	64	.308	.406	-16	-17	98	106	-0.8	-1	1	-1.6
1948	NY-A	0	0	—	1	0	0	0	0	1	0	0.0	0	3	27.0	0	0.0	0.00	—	.000	.500	0	0	96	0	0.0	0	0	0.0
1949	NY-A	3	0	1.000	21	2	0	0	3	49	48	8.8	3	48	8.8	13	2.4	5.14	79	.259	.412	-5	-6	97	105	1.5	-0	1	-0.4
1950	StL-A	1	3	.250	28	2	0	0	1	54	72	12.0	1	51	8.5	24	4.0	7.83	65	.321	.443	-20	-17	111	86	-0.6	0	-1	-1.5
Total	4	7	7	.500	73	15	1	0	4	185	216	10.5	8	158	7.7	69	3.4	5.98	68	.298	.420	-41	-40	101	99	0.1	-0	0	-3.5

■ **MIKE MARSHALL** Marshall, Michael Grant b: 1/15/43, Adrian, Mich. BR/TR, 5'10", 180 lbs. Deb: 5/31/67

YEAR	TM/L	W	L	PCT	G	GS	CG	SHO	SV	IP	H	H/G	HR	BB	BB/G	SO	SO/G	ERA	/A	OAVG	OOBP	PR	/A	PF	CPI	WAT	PB	PD	TPI
1967	Det-A	1	3	.250	37	0	0	0	10	59	51	7.8	6	20	3.1	41	6.3	1.98	160	.233	.299	8	8	98	167	-1.0	0	1	0.9
1969	Sea-A	3	10	.231	20	14	3	1	0	88	99	10.1	8	35	3.6	47	4.8	5.11	71	.281	.344	-15	-14	100	87	-2.7	3	3	-0.8
1970	Hou-N	0	1	.000	4	0	0	0	0	5	8	14.4	0	4	7.2	5	9.0	9.00	42	.400	.481	-3	-3	94	100	-0.4	0	1	-0.1
	Mon-N	3	7	.300	24	5	0	0	3	65	56	7.8	4	29	4.0	38	5.3	3.46	119	.225	.302	4	5	102	84	-1.6	0	2	0.6
	Yr	3	8	.273	28	5	0	0	3	70	64	8.2	4	33	4.2	43	5.5	3.86	106	.237	.315	2	2	101	84	-2.0	0	2	0.5
1971	Mon-N	5	8	.385	66	0	0	0	23	111	100	8.1	9	50	4.1	85	6.9	4.30	81	.247	.326	-10	-10	100	87	-0.8	1	3	-0.6
1972	Mon-N	14	8	.636	**65**	0	0	0	18	116	82	6.4	3	47	3.6	95	7.4	1.78	201	.202	.282	**22**	**23**	104	120	4.1	0	0	2.6
1973	Mon-N	14	11	.560	**92**	0	0	0	**31**	179	163	8.2	10	75	3.8	124	6.2	2.66	144	.252	.324	20	**23**	105	**134**	2.0	1	3	2.9
1974	LA-N	15	12	.556	**106**	0	0	0	**21**	208	191	8.3	9	56	2.4	143	6.2	2.42	135	.247	.289	**28**	19	90	116	-1.8	1	1	2.1
1975	LA-N	9	14	.391	57	0	0	0	13	109	98	8.1	8	39	3.2	64	5.3	3.30	103	.242	.301	4	1	93	98	-3.5	-1	2	0.1
1976	LA-N	4	3	.571	30	0	0	0	8	63	64	9.1	2	25	3.6	39	5.6	4.43	78	.270	.330	-6	-7	99	85	0.0	0	2	-0.4
	Atl-N	2	1	.667	24	0	0	0	6	37	35	8.5	4	14	3.4	17	4.1	3.16	124	.259	.318	1	3	112	129	0.6	0	0	0.4
	Yr	6	4	.600	54	0	0	0	14	100	99	8.9	6	39	3.5	56	5.0	3.96	92	.264	.323	-5	-4	104	129	0.6	0	2	0.0
1977	Atl-N	1	0	1.000	4	0	0	0	0	6	12	18.0	1	2	3.0	6	9.0	9.00	50	.400	.438	-3	-3	115	98	0.5	0	-0	-0.2
	Tex-A	2	2	.500	12	4	0	0	1	36	42	10.5	0	13	3.3	18	4.5	4.00	105	.304	.363	0	1	104	112	-0.2	0	0	0.1
1978	Min-A	10	12	.455	54	0	0	0	21	99	80	7.3	3	37	3.4	56	5.1	2.45	145	.225	.292	15	12	94	103	0.1	0	1	1.4
1979	Min-A	10	15	.400	**90**	1	0	0	**32**	143	132	8.3	8	48	3.0	81	5.1	2.64	173	.254	.314	25	31	108	131	-2.9	0	3	3.3
1980	Min-A	1	3	.250	18	0	0	0	1	32	42	11.8	2	12	3.4	13	3.7	6.19	71	.323	.373	-8	-6	109	89	-0.9	0	1	-0.5
1981	NY-N	3	2	.600	20	0	0	0	0	31	26	7.5	2	8	2.3	8	2.3	2.61	137	.224	.268	3	3	103	91	0.9	0	0	0.4
Total	14	97	112	.464	723	24	3	1	188	1387	1281	8.3	79	514	3.3	880	5.7	3.14	118	.249	.313	85	85	100	112	-7.6	7	20	12.2

■ **RUBE MARSHALL** Marshall, Roy De Verne "Cy" b: 1/19/1890, Salineville, Ohio d: 6/11/80, Dover, Ohio BR/TR, 5'11", 170 lbs. Deb: 9/28/12

YEAR	TM/L	W	L	PCT	G	GS	CG	SHO	SV	IP	H	H/G	HR	BB	BB/G	SO	SO/G	ERA	/A	OAVG	OOBP	PR	/A	PF	CPI	WAT	PB	PD	TPI
1912	Phi-N	0	1	.000	2	1	0	0	0	3	12	36.0	0	1	3.0	2	6.0	21.00	16	.545	.565	-6	-6	101	79	-0.4	0	0	-0.4
1913	Phi-N	0	1	.000	14	3	0	0	1	45	54	10.8	2	22	4.4	18	3.6	4.60	77	.297	.370	-7	-5	111	102	-0.4	-1	0	-0.5
1914	Phi-N	6	7	.462	27	19	7	0	1	134	144	9.7	2	50	3.4	49	3.3	3.76	75	.279	.337	-15	-14	101	95	-0.2	-2	1	-1.5
1915	Buf-F	2	1	.667	21	4	2	0	0	59	62	9.5	1	33	5.0	21	3.2	3.97	77	.281	.379	-6	-6	101	111	0.5	1	0	-0.4
Total	4	8	10	.444	64	27	9	0	2	241	272	10.2	5	106	4.0	90	3.4	4.18	72	.289	.358	-33	-31	103	100	-0.5	-1	1	-2.8

■ **PHONNEY MARTIN** Martin, Alphonse Case b: 8/4/1845, New York, N.Y. d: 5/24/33, Hollis, N.Y. 5'7", 148 lbs. Deb: 4/26/1872

YEAR	TM/L	W	L	PCT	G	GS	CG	SHO	SV	IP	H	H/G	HR	BB	BB/G	SO	SO/G	ERA	/A	OAVG	OOBP	PR	/A	PF	CPI	WAT	PB	PD	TPI
1872	Tro-n	1	2	.333	3																								
	Eck-n	2	8	.200	10																								
	Yr	3	10	.231	13																								
1873	Mut-n	0	2	.000	2																								
Total	2 n	3	12	.200	15																								

■ **BARNEY MARTIN** Martin, Barnes Robertson b: 3/3/23, Columbia, S.C. BR/TR, 5'11", 170 lbs. Deb: 4/22/53

YEAR	TM/L	W	L	PCT	G	GS	CG	SHO	SV	IP	H	H/G	HR	BB	BB/G	SO	SO/G	ERA	/A	OAVG	OOBP	PR	/A	PF	CPI	WAT	PB	PD	TPI
1953	Cin-N	0	0	—	1	0	0	0	0	2	3	13.5	0	1	4.5	1	4.5	9.00	48	.333	.400	-1	-1	100	63	0.0	0	0	0.0

■ **RENIE MARTIN** Martin, Donald Renie b: 8/30/55, Dover, Del. BR/TR, 6'4", 190 lbs. Deb: 5/09/79

YEAR	TM/L	W	L	PCT	G	GS	CG	SHO	SV	IP	H	H/G	HR	BB	BB/G	SO	SO/G	ERA	/A	OAVG	OOBP	PR	/A	PF	CPI	WAT	PB	PD	TPI
1979	KC-A	0	3	.000	25	0	0	0	5	35	32	8.2	1	14	3.6	25	6.4	5.14	86	.248	.315	-4	-3	105	63	-1.4	0	1	-0.1
1980	KC-A	10	10	.500	32	20	2	0	2	137	133	8.7	18	70	4.6	68	4.5	4.40	89	.255	.341	-5	-7	97	99	-1.7	0	-0	-0.6
1981	KC-A	4	5	.444	29	0	0	0	4	62	55	8.0	2	29	4.2	25	3.6	2.76	131	.244	.318	6	6	99	120	-0.3	0	1	0.7
1982	SF-N	7	10	.412	29	25	1	0	0	141	148	9.4	14	64	4.1	63	4.0	4.66	73	.274	.342	-16	-20	94	96	-2.1	3	1	-1.6
1983	SF-N	2	4	.333	37	6	0	0	1	94	95	9.1	11	51	4.9	43	4.1	4.21	87	.268	.360	-6	-6	101	114	-0.9	4	1	0.0
1984	SF-N	1	1	.500	12	0	0	0	0	23	29	11.3	2	16	6.3	8	3.1	3.91	90	.305	.402	-1	-1	98	151	0.2	1	1	0.1
	Phi-N	0	2	.000	9	0	0	0	0	16	17	9.6	2	12	6.8	5	2.8	4.50	81	.274	.377	-2	-2	101	123	-0.9	-0	1	0.0
	Yr	1	3	.250	21	0	0	0	0	39	46	10.6	4	28	6.5	13	3.0	4.15	86	.293	.392	-2	-3	99	123	-0.7	1	2	0.1
Total	6	24	35	.407	173	51	3	0	12	508	509	9.0	50	256	4.5	237	4.2	4.27	87	.264	.345	-28	-32	98	104	-7.1	8	5	-1.5

■ **SPEED MARTIN** Martin, Elwood Good b: 9/15/1893, Wawawai, Wash. d: 6/14/83, Lemon Grove, Cal. BR/TR, 6', 165 lbs. Deb: 7/05/17

YEAR	TM/L	W	L	PCT	G	GS	CG	SHO	SV	IP	H	H/G	HR	BB	BB/G	SO	SO/G	ERA	/A	OAVG	OOBP	PR	/A	PF	CPI	WAT	PB	PD	TPI
1917	StL-A	0	2	.000	9	2	0	0	0	16	20	11.3	0	5	2.8	5	2.8	5.63	47	.339	.391	-5	-5	98	84	-0.9	-0	1	-0.4
1918	Chi-N	5	2	.714	9	5	4	1	1	54	47	7.8	0	14	2.3	16	2.7	1.83	148	.246	.283	6	5	98	132	0.7	-0	1	0.7

YEAR TM/L	W	L	PCT	G	GS	CG	SHO	SV	IP	H	H/G	HR	BB	BB/G	SO	SO/G	ERA	/A	OAVG	OOBP	PR	/A	PF	CPI	WAT	PB	PD	TPI
1919 Chi-N	8	8	.500	35	14	7	2	2	164	158	8.7	2	52	2.9	54	3.0	2.47	117	.259	.315	8	8	99	123	-0.5	-1	2	0.9
1920 Chi-N	4	15	.211	35	13	6	0	2	136	165	10.9	2	50	3.3	44	2.9	4.83	64	.305	.350	-26	-26	99	85	-5.6	-0	1	-2.5
1921 Chi-N	11	15	.423	37	28	13	1	1	217	245	10.2	12	68	2.8	86	3.6	4.35	94	.298	.341	-14	-6	108	97	0.1	1	2	-0.1
1922 Chi-N	1	0	1.000	1	1	0	0	0	6	10	15.0	0	2	3.0	2	3.0	7.50	52	.385	.429	-2	-2	96	88	0.5	0	-0	-0.1
Total 6	29	42	.408	126	63	30	4	6	593	645	9.8	16	191	2.9	207	3.1	3.78	89	.287	.333	-33	-28	102	104	-5.7	-1	7	-1.5

■ **FRED MARTIN** Martin, Fred Turner b: 6/27/15, Williams, Okla. d: 6/11/79, Chicago, Ill. BR/TR, 6'1", 185 lbs. Deb: 4/21/46 C

YEAR TM/L	W	L	PCT	G	GS	CG	SHO	SV	IP	H	H/G	HR	BB	BB/G	SO	SO/G	ERA	/A	OAVG	OOBP	PR	/A	PF	CPI	WAT	PB	PD	TPI
1946 StL-N	2	1	.667	6	3	2	0	0	29	29	9.0	0	8	2.5	19	5.9	4.03	87	.254	.301	-2	-2	103	63	0.2	0	0	0.0
1949 StL-N	6	0	1.000	21	5	3	0	0	70	65	8.4	3	20	2.6	30	3.9	2.44	178	.243	.291	12	15	108	115	3.0	1	0	1.6
1950 StL-N	4	2	.667	30	2	0	0	0	63	87	12.4	4	30	4.3	19	2.7	5.14	83	.331	.396	-7	-6	103	117	1.0	1	1	-0.4
Total 3	12	3	.800	57	10	5	0	0	162	181	10.1	7	58	3.2	68	3.8	3.78	110	.281	.337	3	7	105	106	4.2	2	1	1.2

■ **DOC MARTIN** Martin, Harold Winthrop b: 9/23/1887, Roxbury, Mass. d: 4/14/35, Milton, Mass. BR/TR, 5'11", 165 lbs. Deb: 10/07/08

YEAR TM/L	W	L	PCT	G	GS	CG	SHO	SV	IP	H	H/G	HR	BB	BB/G	SO	SO/G	ERA	/A	OAVG	OOBP	PR	/A	PF	CPI	WAT	PB	PD	TPI
1908 Phi-A	0	1	.000	1	1	0	0	0	2	2	9.0	0	3	13.5	2	9.0	13.50	19	.286	.545	-2	-2	110	62	-0.4	-0	0	-0.1
1911 Phi-A	1	1	.500	11	3	1	0	0	38	40	9.5	1	17	4.0	21	5.0	4.50	66	.272	.367	-5	-7	88	87	-0.2	0	0	-0.5
1912 Phi-A	0	0	—	2	0	0	0	0	4	5	11.3	0	5	11.3	4	9.0	11.25	29	.333	.524	-4	-4	97	73	0.0	-0	0	-0.2
Total 3	1	2	.333	14	4	1	0	0	44	47	9.6	1	25	5.1	27	5.5	5.52	54	.278	.393	-11	-12	90	85	-0.6	-0	1	-0.8

■ **PEPPER MARTIN** Martin, John Leonard Roosevelt "The Wild Horse Of The Osage" b: 2/29/04, Temple, Okla. d: 3/5/65, Mc Alester, Okla. BR/TR, 5'8", 170 lbs. Deb: 4/16/28 C

YEAR TM/L	W	L	PCT	G	GS	CG	SHO	SV	IP	H	H/G	HR	BB	BB/G	SO	SO/G	ERA	/A	OAVG	OOBP	PR	/A	PF	CPI	WAT	PB	PD	TPI
1934 StL-N	0	0	—	1	0	0	0	0	2	1	4.5	0	0	0.0	0	0.0	4.50	100	.167	.167	-0	0	111	12	0.0	0	0	0.0
1936 StL-N	0	0	—	1	0	0	0	0	2	1	4.5	0	2	9.0	0	0.0	0.00	—	.200	.429	1	1	95	0	0.0	1	0	0.1
Total 2	0	0	—	2	0	0	0	0	4	2	4.5	0	2	4.5	0	0.0	2.25	185	.182	.308	1	1	103	6	0.0	1	0	0.1

■ **JOHN MARTIN** Martin, John Robert b: 4/11/56, Wyandotte, Mich. BB/TL, 6', 190 lbs. Deb: 8/27/80

YEAR TM/L	W	L	PCT	G	GS	CG	SHO	SV	IP	H	H/G	HR	BB	BB/G	SO	SO/G	ERA	/A	OAVG	OOBP	PR	/A	PF	CPI	WAT	PB	PD	TPI
1980 StL-N	2	3	.400	9	5	1	0	0	42	39	8.4	1	9	1.9	23	4.9	4.29	86	.247	.284	-3	-3	102	59	-0.2	1	-0	-0.2
1981 StL-N	8	5	.615	17	15	4	0	0	103	85	7.4	10	26	2.3	36	3.1	3.41	103	.228	.278	1	1	101	84	0.6	2	0	0.4
1982 StL-N	4	5	.444	24	7	0	0	0	66	56	7.6	6	30	4.1	21	2.9	4.23	87	.230	.312	-5	-4	102	78	-0.9	-0	-1	-0.5
1983 StL-N	3	1	.750	26	5	0	0	0	66	60	8.2	6	26	3.5	29	4.0	3.55	101	.242	.310	1	0	98	98	1.0	1	1	0.1
Det-A	0	0	—	15	0	0	0	1	13	15	10.4	2	4	2.8	11	7.6	7.62	51	.294	.339	-5	-5	95	67	0.0	0	0	-0.4
Total 4	17	14	.548	91	32	5	0	1	290	255	7.9	25	95	2.9	120	3.7	3.94	92	.238	.297	-11	-10	101	81	0.5	3	-1	-0.6

■ **MORRIE MARTIN** Martin, Morris Webster "Lefty" b: 9/3/22, Dixon, Mo. BL/TL, 6', 173 lbs. Deb: 4/25/49

YEAR TM/L	W	L	PCT	G	GS	CG	SHO	SV	IP	H	H/G	HR	BB	BB/G	SO	SO/G	ERA	/A	OAVG	OOBP	PR	/A	PF	CPI	WAT	PB	PD	TPI
1949 Bro-N	1	3	.250	10	4	0	0	0	31	39	11.3	5	15	4.4	15	4.4	6.97	57	.320	.392	-10	-10	98	95	-1.1	-0	0	-0.9
1951 Phi-A	11	4	.733	35	13	3	1	0	138	139	9.1	13	63	4.1	35	2.3	3.78	116	.259	.340	5	9	106	112	4.0	-1	2	1.0
1952 Phi-A	0	2	.000	5	5	0	0	0	25	32	11.5	1	15	5.4	13	4.7	6.48	64	.302	.398	-8	-7	112	83	-0.9	-1	-0	-0.6
1953 Phi-A	10	12	.455	58	11	2	0	7	156	158	9.1	12	59	3.4	64	3.7	4.44	95	.262	.331	-8	-4	105	89	1.5	-4	-0	-0.7
1954 Phi-A	2	4	.333	13	6	2	0	0	53	57	9.7	9	19	3.2	24	4.1	5.43	72	.278	.336	-10	-9	105	90	0.0	0	-0	-0.8
Chi-A	5	4	.556	35	2	1	0	5	70	52	6.7	5	24	3.1	31	4.0	2.06	180	.210	.275	13	13	100	116	-0.3	-0	-0	1.3
Yr	7	8	.467	48	8	3	0	5	123	109	8.0	14	43	3.1	55	4.0	3.51	108	.240	.299	3	4	102	116	-0.3	0	-1	0.5
1955 Chi-A	2	3	.400	37	0	0	0	2	52	50	8.7	4	20	3.5	22	3.8	3.63	107	.259	.323	2	1	98	106	-0.7	1	1	0.3
1956 Chi-A	1	0	1.000	10	0	0	0	0	18	21	10.5	1	7	3.5	9	4.5	5.00	85	.292	.350	-2	-2	102	88	0.5	0	0	0.0
Bal-A	1	1	.500	9	0	0	0	0	5	10	18.0	1	2	3.6	3	5.4	10.80	37	.400	.448	-4	-4	97	90	0.1	0	0	-0.3
Yr	2	1	.667	19	0	0	0	0	23	31	12.1	2	9	3.5	12	4.7	6.26	67	.316	.376	-5	-5	101	90	0.6	0	0	-0.3
1957 StL-N	0	0	—	4	1	0	0	0	11	5	4.1	0	4	3.3	7	5.7	2.45	157	.143	.244	2	2	99	37	0.0	-0	0	0.2
1958 StL-N	3	1	.750	17	0	0	0	0	25	19	6.8	3	12	4.3	16	5.8	4.68	91	.211	.317	-2	-1	108	70	1.1	-1	-0	-0.1
Cle-A	2	0	1.000	14	0	0	0	1	19	20	9.5	0	8	3.8	5	2.4	2.37	148	.294	.350	3	2	93	179	1.0	0	-0	0.2
1959 Chi-N	0	0	—	3	0	0	0	0	2	5	22.5	2	1	4.5	1	4.5	22.50	17	.455	.500	-4	-4	99	87	0.0	0	0	-0.3
Total 10	38	34	.528	250	42	8	1	15	605	607	9.0	56	249	3.7	245	3.6	4.28	95	.262	.335	-22	-14	103	100	5.2	-6	2	-0.7

■ **PAT MARTIN** Martin, Patrick Francis b: 4/13/1892, Brooklyn, N.Y. d: 2/4/49, Brooklyn, N.Y. BL/TL, 5'11.5", 170 lbs. Deb: 9/20/19

YEAR TM/L	W	L	PCT	G	GS	CG	SHO	SV	IP	H	H/G	HR	BB	BB/G	SO	SO/G	ERA	/A	OAVG	OOBP	PR	/A	PF	CPI	WAT	PB	PD	TPI
1919 Phi-A	0	2	.000	2	2	1	0	0	11	11	9.0	0	8	6.5	6	4.9	4.09	88	.256	.373	-1	-1	112	89	-0.9	-1	-0	0.0
1920 Phi-A	1	4	.200	8	5	2	0	0	32	48	13.5	2	25	7.0	14	3.9	6.19	61	.364	.478	-8	-9	99	127	-0.8	1	-1	-0.7
Total 2	1	6	.143	10	7	3	0	0	43	59	12.3	2	33	6.9	20	4.2	5.65	66	.337	.453	-10	-9	102	117	-1.7	1	-1	-0.7

■ **PAUL MARTIN** Martin, Paul Charles b: 3/10/32, Brownstone, Pa. BR/TR, 6'6", 235 lbs. Deb: 7/02/55

YEAR TM/L	W	L	PCT	G	GS	CG	SHO	SV	IP	H	H/G	HR	BB	BB/G	SO	SO/G	ERA	/A	OAVG	OOBP	PR	/A	PF	CPI	WAT	PB	PD	TPI
1955 Pit-N	0	1	.000	7	1	0	0	0	7	13	16.7	0	17	21.9	3	3.9	14.14	29	.464	.633	-8	-8	101	107	-0.4	0	0	-0.6

■ **RAY MARTIN** Martin, Raymond Joseph b: 3/13/25, Norwood, Mass. BR/TR, 6'2", 177 lbs. Deb: 8/15/43

YEAR TM/L	W	L	PCT	G	GS	CG	SHO	SV	IP	H	H/G	HR	BB	BB/G	SO	SO/G	ERA	/A	OAVG	OOBP	PR	/A	PF	CPI	WAT	PB	PD	TPI
1943 Bos-N	0	0	—	2	0	0	0	0	3	3	9.0	0	1	3.0	1	3.0	9.00	41	.231	.286	-2	-2	109	22	0.0	-0	0	-0.1
1947 Bos-N	1	0	1.000	1	1	1	0	0	9	7	7.0	0	4	4.0	2	2.0	1.00	388	.212	.297	3	3	95	215	0.5	-0	0	0.4
1948 Bos-N	0	0	—	2	0	0	0	0	2	0	0.0	0	1	4.5	0	0.0	0.00	—	.000	.125	1	1	99	0	0.0	0	0	0.1
Total 3	1	0	1.000	5	1	1	0	0	14	10	6.4	0	6	3.9	3	1.9	2.57	150	.189	.271	2	2	99	143	0.5	-0	1	0.4

■ **JOE MARTINA** Martina, Joseph John "Oyster Joe" b: 7/8/1889, New Orleans, La. d: 3/22/62, New Orleans, La. BR/TR, 6', 183 lbs. Deb: 4/19/24

YEAR TM/L	W	L	PCT	G	GS	CG	SHO	SV	IP	H	H/G	HR	BB	BB/G	SO	SO/G	ERA	/A	OAVG	OOBP	PR	/A	PF	CPI	WAT	PB	PD	TPI
1924 Was-A	6	8	.429	24	13	8	0	0	125	129	9.3	7	56	4.0	57	4.1	4.68	87	.271	.340	-6	-9	96	88	-2.0	3	-2	-0.6

■ **ALFREDO MARTINEZ** Martinez, Alfredo b: 3/15/57, Los Angeles, Cal. BR/TR, 6'3", 185 lbs. Deb: 4/20/80

YEAR TM/L	W	L	PCT	G	GS	CG	SHO	SV	IP	H	H/G	HR	BB	BB/G	SO	SO/G	ERA	/A	OAVG	OOBP	PR	/A	PF	CPI	WAT	PB	PD	TPI
1980 Cal-A	7	9	.438	30	23	4	1	0	149	150	9.1	14	59	3.6	57	3.4	4.53	86	.259	.324	-8	-10	97	84	0.5	0	-2	-1.1
1981 Cal-A	0	0	—	2	0	0	0	0	6	5	7.5	1	3	4.5	4	6.0	3.00	127	.227	.320	0	1	104	133	0.0	0	0	0.1
Total 2	7	9	.438	32	23	4	1	0	155	155	9.0	15	62	3.6	61	3.5	4.47	87	.257	.323	-8	-10	97	86	0.5	0	-2	-1.0

■ **TIPPY MARTINEZ** Martinez, Felix Anthony b: 5/31/50, La Junta, Colo. BL/TL, 5'10", 180 lbs. Deb: 8/09/74

YEAR TM/L	W	L	PCT	G	GS	CG	SHO	SV	IP	H	H/G	HR	BB	BB/G	SO	SO/G	ERA	/A	OAVG	OOBP	PR	/A	PF	CPI	WAT	PB	PD	TPI
1974 NY-A	0	0	—	10	0	0	0	0	13	14	9.7	0	9	6.2	10	6.9	4.15	83	.286	.400	-1	-1	95	117	0.0	0	0	0.0
1975 NY-A	1	2	.333	23	2	0	0	8	37	27	6.6	2	32	7.8	20	4.9	2.68	138	.208	.359	5	4	98	140	-0.4	0	-1	0.3
1976 NY-A	2	0	1.000	11	0	0	0	2	28	18	5.8	1	14	4.5	14	4.5	1.93	178	.191	.296	5	5	97	119	1.0	0	1	0.6
Bal-A	3	1	.750	28	0	0	0	8	42	32	6.9	0	28	6.0	31	6.6	2.57	133	.222	.341	4	4	97	125	0.9	0	1	0.5
Yr	5	1	.833	39	0	0	0	10	70	50	6.4	1	42	5.4	45	5.8	2.31	148	.210	.324	9	9	97	125	1.9	0	2	1.1
1977 Bal-A	5	1	.833	41	0	0	0	9	50	47	8.5	2	27	4.9	29	5.2	2.70	139	.266	.352	8	6	92	154	1.8	0	1	0.7
1978 Bal-A	3	3	.500	42	0	0	0	5	69	77	10.0	4	40	5.2	57	7.4	4.83	71	.281	.371	-8	-11	91	96	-0.2	0	1	-0.9
1979 Bal-A	10	3	.769	39	0	0	0	3	78	59	6.8	0	31	3.6	61	7.0	2.88	140	.210	.286	12	10	96	70	2.4	0	1	1.0
1980 Bal-A	4	4	.500	53	0	0	0	10	81	69	7.7	5	34	3.8	68	7.6	3.00	134	.240	.316	9	9	99	111	-0.7	0	2	1.1
1981 Bal-A	3	3	.500	37	0	0	0	11	59	48	7.3	4	32	4.9	50	7.6	2.90	125	.231	.323	5	5	99	121	-0.2	0	1	0.6
1982 Bal-A	8	8	.500	76	0	0	0	16	95	81	7.7	6	37	3.5	78	7.4	3.41	118	.240	.306	7	7	99	98	-1.1	0	-0	0.6
1983 Bal-A	9	3	.750	65	0	0	0	21	103	76	6.6	10	37	3.2	81	7.1	2.36	171	.211	.278	20	19	99	118	2.3	0	2	2.1
1984 Bal-A	4	9	.308	55	0	0	0	17	90	88	8.8	9	51	5.1	72	7.2	3.90	96	.260	.346	1	-1	94	115	-2.7	0	0	0.0
1985 Bal-A	3	3	.500	49	0	0	0	4	70	70	9.0	8	37	4.8	47	6.0	5.40	75	.261	.343	-10	-10	98	85	0.0	0	1	-0.9
1986 Bal-A	0	2	.000	14	0	0	0	1	16	18	10.1	1	12	6.8	11	6.2	5.63	74	.295	.405	-3	-3	99	101	-0.9	0	0	-0.2
1988 Min-A	0	0	—	3	0	0	0	0	4	8	18.0	1	4	9.0	3	6.8	18.00	23	.471	.542	-6	-6	105	77	0.0	0	0	-0.5
Total 14	55	42	.567	546	2	0	0	115	835	732	7.9	53	425	4.6	632	6.8	3.45	111	.242	.329	48	36	97	109	2.2	0	9	5.0

■ **BUCK MARTINEZ** Martinez, John Albert b: 11/7/48, Redding, Cal. BR/TR, 5'10", 190 lbs. Deb: 6/18/69

YEAR TM/L	W	L	PCT	G	GS	CG	SHO	SV	IP	H	H/G	HR	BB	BB/G	SO	SO/G	ERA	/A	OAVG	OOBP	PR	/A	PF	CPI	WAT	PB	PD	TPI
1979 Mil-A	0	0	—	1	0	0	0	0	1	1	9.0	0	1	9.0	0	0.0	9.00	47	.250	.400	-1	-1	99	50	0.0	1	0	0.0

■ **DENNIS MARTINEZ** Martinez, Jose Dennis (Emilia) b: 5/14/55, Granada, Nicaragua BR/TR, 6'1", 160 lbs. Deb: 9/14/76

YEAR TM/L	W	L	PCT	G	GS	CG	SHO	SV	IP	H	H/G	HR	BB	BB/G	SO	SO/G	ERA	/A	OAVG	OOBP	PR	/A	PF	CPI	WAT	PB	PD	TPI
1976 Bal-A	1	2	.333	4	2	1	0	0	28	23	7.4	1	8	2.6	18	5.8	2.57	133	.237	.292	3	3	97	106	-0.5	0	0	0.3
1977 Bal-A	14	7	.667	42	13	5	0	4	167	157	8.5	10	64	3.4	107	5.8	4.10	92	.253	.323	-0	-6	92	87	1.9	0	0	-0.5
1978 Bal-A	16	11	.593	40	38	15	2	0	276	257	8.4	20	93	3.0	142	4.6	3.52	97	.250	.310	8	-3	91	94	1.2	0	4	0.0
1979 Bal-A	15	16	.484	40	39	**18**	3	0	**292**	279	8.6	28	78	2.4	132	4.1	3.67	110	.253	.297	18	12	96	93	-4.4	0	3	1.5
1980 Bal-A	6	4	.600	25	12	2	0	1	100	103	9.3	12	44	4.0	42	3.8	3.96	101	.272	.348	1	1	99	116	0.0	0	0	0.1
1981 Bal-A	**14**	5	.737	25	24	9	2	0	179	173	8.7	10	62	3.1	88	4.4	3.32	109	.254	.315	7	6	99	101	4.3	0	4	1.1
1982 Bal-A	16	12	.571	40	39	10	2	0	252	262	9.4	30	87	3.1	111	4.0	4.21	96	.267	.326	-4	-5	99	101	-0.2	0	0	-0.4

YEAR	TM/L	W	L	PCT	G	GS	CG	SHO	SV	IP	H	H/G	HR	BB	BB/G	SO	SO/G	ERA	/A	OAVG	OOBP	PR	/A	PF	CPI	WAT	PB	PD	TPI
1983	Bal-A	7	16	.304	32	25	4	0	0	153	209	12.3	21	45	2.6	71	4.2	5.53	73	.330	.372	-25	-26	99	109	-6.1	0	5	-1.9
1984	Bal-A	6	9	.400	34	20	2	0	0	142	145	9.2	26	37	2.3	77	4.9	5.01	75	.263	.312	-16	-20	94	87	-1.8	0	1	-1.7
1985	Bal-A	13	11	.542	33	31	3	1	0	180	203	10.1	29	63	3.2	68	3.4	5.15	79	.288	.349	-20	-22	98	103	0.8	0	0	-1.9
1986	Bal-A	0	0	—	4	0	0	0	0	7	11	14.1	0	2	2.6	2	2.6	6.43	65	.367	.394	-2	-2	99	94	0.0	0	0	0.0
	Mon-N	3	6	.333	19	15	1	1	0	98	103	9.5	11	28	2.6	63	5.8	4.59	80	.274	.322	-9	-10	98	92	-1.4	-0	1	-0.9
1987	Mon-N	11	4	.733	22	22	2	1	0	145	133	8.3	9	40	2.5	84	5.2	3.29	131	.244	.299	13	17	106	93	3.1	-2	0	1.5
1988	Mon-N	15	13	.536	34	34	9	2	0	235	215	8.2	21	55	2.1	120	4.6	2.72	133	.239	.285	19	24	105	112	1.2	2	0	2.9
Total	13	137	116	.542	394	314	81	14	5	2254	2273	9.1	228	706	2.8	1125	4.5	3.97	97	.263	.318	-7	-30	98	99	-1.9	-1	20	0.1
■ MARTY MARTINEZ	Martinez, Orlando (Oliva) b: 8/23/41, Havana, Cuba BB/TR, 6', 170 lbs. Deb: 5/02/62 MC																												
1969	Hou-N	0	0	—	1	0	0	0	0	1	1	9.0	1	0	0.0	0	0.0	9.00	41	.333	.333	-1	-1	101	130	0.0	0	0	0.0
■ RAMON MARTINEZ	Martinez, Ramon Jaime b: 3/22/68, Santo Domingo, D.R. BR/TR, 6'416", 508 lbs. Deb: /13/1988																												
1988	LA-N	1	3	.250	9	6	0	0	0	36	27	6.8	0	22	5.5	23	5.8	3.75	97	.216	.325	-1	-0	105	78	-1.1	-1	-0	-0.1
■ ROGELIO MARTINEZ	Martinez, Rogelio (Ulloa) "Limonar" b: 11/5/18, Matanzas, Cuba BR/TR, 6', 180 lbs. Deb: 7/13/50																												
1950	Was-A	0	1	.000	2	1	0	0	0	1	4	36.0	0	2	18.0	0	0.0	36.00	13	.500	.600	-3	-3	101	54	-0.4	0	0	-0.2
■ SILVIO MARTINEZ	Martinez, Silvio Ramon (Cabrera) b: 8/19/55, Santiago, D.R. BR/TR, 5'10", 170 lbs. Deb: 4/09/77																												
1977	Chi-A	0	1	.000	10	0	0	0	1	21	28	12.0	4	12	5.1	10	4.3	5.57	72	.337	.404	-3	-4	99	131	-0.4	0	0	-0.2
1978	StL-N	9	8	.529	22	22	5	2	0	138	114	7.4	11	71	4.6	45	2.9	3.65	94	.228	.319	-1	-3	96	93	1.7	0	-1	-0.4
1979	StL-N	15	8	.652	32	29	7	2	0	207	204	8.9	14	67	2.9	102	4.4	3.26	120	.259	.313	11	15	104	105	3.3	-2	-3	1.0
1980	StL-N	5	10	.333	25	20	2	0	0	120	127	9.5	8	48	3.6	39	2.9	4.80	77	.273	.337	-16	-15	102	85	-2.1	-2	-2	-1.8
1981	StL-N	2	5	.286	18	16	0	0	0	97	95	8.8	4	39	3.6	34	3.2	3.99	88	.260	.327	-5	-5	101	89	-1.7	1	-1	-0.4
Total	5	31	32	.492	107	87	14	4	1	583	568	8.8	41	237	3.7	230	3.6	3.87	95	.258	.325	-15	-12	101	96	0.8	-3	-6	-1.8
■ WEDO MARTINI	Martini, Guido Joe "Southern" b: 7/1/13, Birmingham, Ala. d: 10/28/70, Philadelphia, Pa. BR/TR, 5'10", 165 lbs. Deb: 7/28/35																												
1935	Phi-A	0	2	.000	3	2	0	0	0	6	8	12.0	0	11	16.5	1	1.5	18.00	25	.333	.528	-9	-9	102	53	-0.9	-0	1	-0.6
■ JOE MARTY	Marty, Joseph Anton b: 9/1/13, Sacramento, Cal. d: 10/4/84, Sacramento, Cal. BR/TR, 6', 182 lbs. Deb: 4/22/37																												
1939	Phi-N	0	0	—	1	0	0	0	0	4	2	4.5	0	3	6.8	1	2.3	4.50	87	.154	.294	-0	-0	99	43	0.0	0	0	-0.1
■ RANDY MARTZ	Martz, Randy Carl b: 5/28/56, Harrisburg, Pa. BL/TR, 6'4", 210 lbs. Deb: 9/06/80																												
1980	Chi-N	1	2	.333	6	6	0	0	0	30	28	8.4	1	11	3.3	5	1.5	2.10	185	.241	.300	5	6	108	134	-0.1	-1	1	0.7
1981	Chi-N	5	7	.417	33	14	1	0	6	108	103	8.6	6	49	4.1	32	2.7	3.67	101	.256	.330	-2	1	106	102	0.5	1	0	0.2
1982	Chi-N	11	10	.524	28	24	1	0	1	148	157	9.5	17	36	2.2	40	2.4	4.20	89	.272	.312	-10	-7	104	95	1.6	1	1	-0.5
1983	Chi-A	0	0	—	1	1	0	0	0	5	4	7.2	0	4	7.2	1	1.8	3.60	115	.211	.348	0	0	102	84	0.0	0	0	0.0
Total	4	17	19	.472	68	45	2	0	7	291	292	9.0	24	100	3.1	78	2.4	3.77	100	.262	.318	-6	-1	105	101	2.0	1	1	0.4
■ DEL MASON	Mason, Adelbert William b: 10/29/1883, Newfane, N.Y. d: 12/31/62, Winter Park, Fla. BR/TR, 6', 160 lbs. Deb: 4/23/04																												
1904	Was-A	0	3	.000	5	3	2	0	0	33	45	12.3	1	13	3.5	16	4.4	6.00	43	.350	.410	-12	-13	99	90	-1.4	-2	-1	-1.2
1906	Cin-N	0	1	.000	2	1	1	0	0	12	10	7.5	1	6	4.5	4	3.0	4.50	68	.259	.372	-2	-2	116	80	-0.4	-1	-0	-0.1
1907	Cin-N	5	12	.294	25	17	13	1	0	146	144	8.9	2	55	3.4	45	2.8	3.14	75	.289	.367	-11	-13	95	104	-2.8	0	1	-1.3
Total	3	5	16	.238	32	21	16	1	0	191	199	9.4	4	74	3.5	65	3.1	3.72	65	.299	.376	-26	-28	97	100	-4.6	-3	-0	-2.6
■ ERNIE MASON	Mason, Ernest b: New Orleans, La. d: 7/30/04, Covington, La. Deb: 7/17/1894																												
1894	StL-N	0	3	.000	4	2	2	0	0	23	34	13.3	1	10	3.9	3	1.2	7.43	74	.367	.428	-5	-5	103	83	-1.4	-0	0	-0.3
■ HANK MASON	Mason, Henry b: 6/19/31, Marshall, Mo. BR/TR, 6', 185 lbs. Deb: 9/12/58																												
1958	Phi-N	0	0	—	1	0	0	0	0	5	7	12.6	0	2	3.6	3	5.4	10.80	37	.368	.417	-4	-4	100	62	0.0	-0	-0	-0.3
1960	Phi-N	0	0	—	3	0	0	0	0	6	9	13.5	1	5	7.5	3	4.5	9.00	46	.375	.452	-3	-3	110	100	0.0	-0	0	-0.2
Total	2	0	0	—	4	0	0	0	0	11	16	13.1	1	7	5.7	6	4.9	9.82	41	.372	.436	-7	-7	106	83	0.0	-0	-0	-0.5
■ MIKE MASON	Mason, Michael Paul b: 11/21/58, Faribault, Minn. BL/TL, 6'2", 205 lbs. Deb: 9/13/82																												
1982	Tex-A	1	2	.333	4	4	0	0	0	23	21	8.2	3	9	3.5	8	3.1	5.09	76	.244	.313	-3	-3	94	75	-0.1	0	0	-0.2
1983	Tex-A	0	2	.000	5	0	0	0	0	11	10	8.2	0	6	4.9	9	7.4	5.73	72	.244	.340	-2	-2	101	62	-0.9	0	0	-0.1
1984	Tex-A	9	13	.409	36	24	4	0	0	184	159	7.8	18	51	2.5	113	5.5	3.62	111	.233	.283	8	8	101	83	-0.5	0	-1	0.7
1985	Tex-A	8	15	.348	38	30	1	1	0	179	212	10.7	22	73	3.7	92	4.6	4.83	95	.299	.360	-13	-5	110	111	-1.2	0	-0	-0.4
1986	Tex-A	7	3	.700	27	22	2	1	0	135	135	9.0	11	56	3.7	85	5.7	4.33	92	.257	.325	-2	-5	95	88	1.8	0	0	-0.4
1987	Tex-A	0	2	.000	8	6	0	0	0	29	37	11.5	6	22	6.8	21	6.5	5.59	83	.322	.444	-4	-3	104	143	-0.9	0	0	-0.2
	Chi-N	4	1	.800	17	4	0	0	0	38	43	10.2	4	23	5.4	28	6.6	5.68	73	.303	.387	-7	-6	102	104	1.6	1	0	-0.5
1988	Min-A	0	1	.000	5	0	0	0	0	7	8	10.3	1	9	11.6	7	9.0	10.29	41	.286	.459	-5	-5	105	73	-0.4	0	-0	-0.4
Total	7	29	39	.426	140	90	7	2	0	606	625	9.3	65	249	3.7	363	5.4	4.53	93	.268	.336	-28	-22	102	96	-0.6	1	-1	-1.5
■ ROGER MASON	Mason, Roger Le Roy b: 9/18/58, Bellaire, Mich. BR/TR, 6'6", 215 lbs. Deb: 9/04/84																												
1984	Det-A	1	1	.500	5	2	0	0	1	22	23	9.4	1	10	4.1	15	6.1	4.50	84	.271	.340	-1	-2	94	89	-0.1	0	0	-0.1
1985	SF-N	1	3	.250	5	5	1	1	0	30	28	8.4	1	11	3.3	26	7.8	2.10	162	.243	.305	5	4	95	139	-0.6	-0	-0	0.4
1986	SF-N	3	4	.429	11	11	1	0	0	60	56	8.4	5	30	4.5	43	6.5	4.80	73	.250	.340	-7	-8	95	84	-0.5	-2	-1	-1.0
1987	SF-N	1	1	.500	5	5	0	0	0	26	30	10.4	4	10	3.5	18	6.2	4.50	86	.303	.364	-1	-2	95	125	0.0	0	0	-0.1
Total	4	6	9	.400	26	23	2	1	1	138	137	8.9	11	61	4.0	102	6.7	4.11	88	.262	.337	-5	-8	95	104	-1.2	-2	-1	-0.8
■ WALT MASTERS	Masters, Walter Thomas b: 3/28/07, Pen Argyl, Pa. BR/TR, 5'10.5", 180 lbs. Deb: 7/09/31																												
1931	Was-A	0	0	—	3	0	0	0	1	9	7	7.0	0	4	4.0	1	1.0	2.00	215	.226	.306	2	2	98	148	0.0	-0	1	0.2
1937	Phi-N	0	0	—	1	0	0	0	0	1	5	45.0	0	1	9.0	0	0.0	36.00	12	.714	.750	-4	-4	111	74	0.0	0	0	-0.2
1939	Phi-A	0	0	—	4	0	0	0	0	11	15	12.3	0	8	6.5	2	1.6	6.55	72	.306	.397	-2	-2	102	85	0.0	-0	0	-0.1
Total	3	0	0	—	8	0	0	0	1	21	27	11.6	0	13	5.6	3	1.3	6.00	75	.310	.392	-4	-3	101	111	0.0	-1	1	-0.1
■ PAUL MASTERSON	Masterson, Paul Nickalis "Lefty" b: 10/16/15, Chicago, Ill. BL/TL, 5'11", 165 lbs. Deb: 9/15/40																												
1940	Phi-N	0	0	—	2	0	0	0	0	5	5	9.0	0	2	3.6	3	5.4	7.20	54	.263	.333	-2	-2	102	49	0.0	-0	0	-0.1
1941	Phi-N	1	0	1.000	2	1	1	0	0	11	11	9.0	0	6	4.9	8	6.5	4.91	76	.250	.340	-2	-1	103	68	0.5	-1	0	-0.1
1942	Phi-N	0	0	—	4	0	0	0	0	8	10	11.3	1	5	5.6	3	3.4	6.75	50	.303	.385	-3	-3	101	89	0.0	0	0	-0.2
Total	3	1	0	1.000	8	1	1	0	0	24	26	9.8	1	13	4.9	14	5.3	6.00	61	.271	.355	-6	-6	102	71	0.5	-1	0	-0.4
■ WALT MASTERSON	Masterson, Walter Edward b: 6/22/20, Philadelphia, Pa. BR/TR, 6'2", 189 lbs. Deb: 5/08/39																												
1939	Was-A	2	2	.500	24	5	1	0	0	58	66	10.2	2	48	7.4	12	1.9	5.59	76	.293	.404	-6	-9	91	106	0.3	-0	-1	-0.8
1940	Was-A	3	13	.188	31	19	3	0	2	130	128	8.9	6	88	6.1	68	4.7	4.92	85	.257	.364	-8	-11	95	92	-4.5	0	-1	-1.0
1941	Was-A	4	3	.571	34	6	1	0	3	78	101	11.7	3	53	6.1	40	4.6	6.00	68	.321	.412	-16	-16	99	103	0.8	-1	1	-1.5
1942	Was-A	5	9	.357	25	15	8	4	2	143	138	8.7	6	54	3.4	63	4.0	3.34	108	.251	.314	5	4	99	102	-0.9	-0	-2	0.2
1945	Was-A	1	2	.333	4	2	1	1	0	25	21	7.6	1	10	3.6	14	5.0	1.08	286	.228	.298	6	6	92	252	-0.5	-1	0	0.6
1946	Was-A	5	6	.455	29	9	2	0	1	91	105	10.4	8	67	6.6	61	6.0	6.03	55	.295	.402	-26	-28	94	96	-0.4	-1	0	-2.8
1947	Was-A	12	16	.429	35	31	14	4	1	253	215	7.6	11	97	3.5	135	4.8	3.13	119	.234	.303	16	17	101	94	0.4	-3	2	1.7
1948	Was-A	8	15	.348	33	27	9	2	2	188	171	8.2	12	122	5.8	72	3.4	3.83	120	.247	.358	9	16	107	113	-0.6	-1	-2	1.3
1949	Was-A	3	2	.600	10	7	3	0	0	53	42	7.1	4	21	3.6	17	2.9	3.23	125	.216	.301	6	5	96	88	1.0	-1	1	0.4
	Bos-A	3	4	.429	18	5	1	0	4	55	58	9.5	2	35	5.7	19	3.1	4.25	102	.283	.381	-0	1	103	113	-1.0	-0	-1	0.0
	Yr	6	6	.500	28	12	4	0	4	108	100	8.3	6	56	4.7	36	3.0	3.75	112	.249	.337	5	5	100	113	0.0	-1	0	0.4
1950	Bos-A	8	6	.571	33	15	6	0	1	129	145	10.1	15	82	5.7	60	4.2	5.65	90	.287	.383	-15	-8	111	99	-0.4	-3	1	-0.7
1951	Bos-A	3	0	1.000	30	1	0	0	2	59	53	8.1	1	32	4.9	39	5.9	3.36	131	.228	.320	5	7	106	86	1.5	-1	0	0.6
1952	Bos-A	1	1	.500	5	1	0	0	0	9	18	18.0	1	11	11.0	3	3.0	12.00	33	.400	.509	-8	-8	107	91	0.0	0	0	-0.7
	Was-A	9	8	.529	24	21	11	0	2	161	153	8.6	11	72	4.0	89	5.0	3.69	100	.253	.332	-0	-0	100	102	0.4	-2	1	0.0
	Yr	10	9	.526	29	22	11	0	2	170	171	9.1	12	83	4.4	92	4.9	4.13	90	.263	.346	-9	-8	101	102	0.4	0	1	-0.7
1953	Was-A	10	12	.455	29	20	10	4	0	166	145	7.9	16	62	3.4	95	5.2	3.63	102	.232	.301	7	2	93	89	-1.1	-1	0	0.1
1956	Det-A	1	1	.500	35	0	0	0	0	50	54	9.7	2	32	5.8	28	5.0	4.14	96	.289	.377	0	-1	95	122	0.0	0	-0	0.0

YEAR	TM/L	W	L	PCT	G	GS	CG	SHO	SV	IP	H	H/G	HR	BB	BB/G	SO	SO/G	ERA	/A	OAVG	OOBP	PR	/A	PF	CPI	WAT	PB	PD	TPI
Total	14	78	100	.438	399	184	70	15	20	1648	1613	8.8	101	886	4.8	815	4.5	4.15	97	.258	.347	-25	-26	100	102	-5.0	-14	-0	-2.6
■ LEN MATARAZZO	Matarazzo, Leonard b: 9/12/28, New Castle, Pa. BR/TR, 6'4", 195 lbs. Deb: 9/06/52																												
1952	Phi-A	0	0	—	1	0	0	0	0	1	1	9.0	0	1	9.0	0	0.0	0.00	—	.250	.400	0	0	112	0	0.0	0	0	0.0
■ GREG MATHEWS	Mathews, Gregory Inman b: 5/17/62, Harbor City, Cal. BR/TL, 6'2", 180 lbs. Deb: 6/03/86																												
1986	StL-N	11	8	.579	23	22	1	0	0	145	139	8.6	15	44	2.7	67	4.2	3.66	105	.259	.313	1	3	103	104	1.8	-3	-2	-0.1
1987	StL-N	11	11	.500	32	32	2	1	0	198	184	8.4	17	71	3.2	108	4.9	3.73	107	.249	.310	8	5	97	95	-1.7	2	-1	0.6
1988	StL-N	4	6	.400	13	13	1	0	0	68	61	8.1	4	33	4.4	31	4.1	4.24	85	.247	.336	-6	-5	105	90	-0.7	0	0	-0.4
Total	3	26	25	.510	68	67	4	1	0	411	384	8.4	36	148	3.2	206	4.5	3.79	102	.252	.315	3	4	101	97	-0.6	-1	-3	0.1
■ BOBBY MATHEWS	Mathews, Robert T. b: 11/21/1851, Baltimore, Md. d: 4/17/1898, Baltimore, Md. BR/TR, 5'5.5", 140 lbs. Deb: 5/04/1871																												
1871	Kek-n	7	12	.368	19																								
1872	Bal-n	25	16	.610	45																								
1873	Mut-n	29	22	.569	51																								
1874	Mut-n	42	23	.646	65																								
1875	Mut-n	29	38	.433	70																								
1876	NY-N	21	34	.382	56	56	55	2	0	516	693	12.1	8	24	0.4	37	0.6	2.86	75	.326	.333	-32	-41	93	116	10.5	-9	-1	-4.4
1877	Cin-N	3	12	.200	15	15	13	0	0	129	208	14.5	0	17	1.2	9	0.6	4.05	63	.372	.390	-18	-22	90	**126**	-2.2	-3	0	-2.0
1879	Pro-N	12	6	.667	27	25	15	0	**1**	189	194	9.2	4	26	1.2	90	4.3	2.29	103	.271	.296	4	1	94	111	-0.5	-0	0	0.0
1881	Pro-N	4	8	.333	14	14	10	1	0	102	121	10.7	2	21	1.9	28	2.5	3.18	81	.307	.342	-5	-7	92	112	-2.6	-2	0	-0.6
	Bos-N	1	0	1.000	5	1	1	0	2	23	22	8.6	0	11	4.3	5	2.0	2.35	110	.264	.349	1	1	93	129	0.5	-1	0	0.1
	Yr	5	8	.385	19	15	11	1	**2**	125	143	10.3	2	32	2.3	33	2.4	3.02	85	.300	.344	-3	-6	92	129	-2.1	-2	0	-0.5
1882	Bos-N	19	15	.559	34	32	31	0	0	285	278	8.8	5	22	**0.7**	153	**4.8**	2.87	102	.263	.278	0	2	102	82	1.4	-2	-4	-0.3
1883	Phi-a	30	13	.698	44	44	41	1	0	381	396	9.4	11	31	**0.7**	203	4.8	2.46	133	.273	.289	36	34	99	**127**	2.7	-6	-1	2.5
1884	Phi-a	30	18	.625	49	49	48	3	0	431	401	8.4	10	49	1.0	286	6.0	3.32	110	.255	.277	-4	16	113	85	5.0	-7	-2	0.9
1885	Phi-a	30	17	.638	48	48	46	2	0	422	394	8.4	4	57	1.2	286	**6.1**	2.43	137	.259	.285	38	42	102	107	9.7	-6	-1	3.3
1886	Phi-a	13	9	.591	24	24	22	0	0	198	226	10.3	3	53	2.4	93	4.2	3.95	90	.297	.343	-11	-9	103	103	2.9	-1	0	-0.7
1887	Phi-a	3	4	.429	7	7	7	0	0	58	75	11.6	4	25	3.9	9	1.4	6.67	64	.328	.394	-15	-15	100	84	-0.3	-0	0	-1.1
Total	5 n	132	111	.543	250																								
Total	10	166	136	.550	323	315	289	9	3	2734	3008	9.9	51	336	1.1	1199	3.9	3.00	100	.287	.309	-4	-4	100	106	27.1	-36	-8	-2.3
■ CHRISTY MATHEWSON	Mathewson, Christopher "Matty" or "Big Six" b: 8/12/1880, Factoryville, Pa. d: 10/7/25, Saranac Lake, N.Y. BR/TR, 6'1.5", 195 lbs. Deb: 7/17/00 MH																												
1900	NY-N	0	2	.000	5	1	1	0	0	30	35	10.5	1	14	4.2	15	4.5	5.40	68	.315	.392	-6	-6	99	84	-0.9	0	0	-0.4
1901	NY-N	20	17	.541	40	38	36	5	0	336	288	7.7	3	97	2.6	221	5.9	2.41	131	.254	.318	34	28	95	101	6.0	-0	7	3.6
1902	NY-N	13	18	.419	34	32	29	**8**	0	277	241	7.8	3	73	2.4	159	5.2	2.11	137	.258	.318	21	24	104	109	2.0	-0	3	3.1
1903	NY-N	30	13	.698	45	42	37	3	2	366	321	7.9	4	100	2.5	**267**	**6.6**	2.26	149	.260	.321	**41**	45	103	105	6.6	3	2	**5.1**
1904	NY-N	33	12	.733	48	46	33	4	1	368	306	7.5	7	78	1.9	**212**	5.2	2.03	134	.249	.296	29	28	100	102	4.0	6	5	3.7
1905	NY-N	**31**	8	.795	43	37	32	**8**	2	339	252	6.7	4	64	1.7	**206**	5.5	**1.27**	**225**	.230	**.274**	**65**	**60**	96	126	**8.1**	9	6	**7.6**
1906	NY-N	22	12	.647	38	35	22	5	1	267	262	8.8	3	77	2.6	128	4.3	2.97	86	.285	.342	-10	-12	97	101	0.9	8	3	-0.9
1907	NY-N	**24**	12	.667	41	36	31	**8**	2	315	250	7.1	6	53	1.5	**178**	5.1	2.00	128	.244	**.283**	16	20	104	85	6.1	1	1	2.4
1908	NY-N	**37**	11	.771	**56**	44	**34**	**11**	**5**	**391**	285	6.6	6	42	**1.0**	**259**	6.0	**1.43**	**164**	.229	**.256**	**40**	**40**	100	87	**11.0**	1	10	**6.1**
1909	NY-N	25	6	**.806**	37	33	26	8	2	275	192	**6.3**	2	36	**1.2**	149	4.9	**1.15**	**234**	.200	**.228**	44	**47**	103	79	**8.8**	7	6	**6.5**
1910	NY-N	**27**	9	.750	38	35	**27**	2	0	318	292	8.3	5	60	1.7	184	5.2	1.90	148	.248	.286	**40**	32	92	117	**8.2**	8	7	**5.2**
1911	NY-N	26	13	.667	45	37	29	5	3	307	303	8.9	5	38	**1.1**	141	4.1	**1.99**	**168**	.259	.283	**48**	**46**	99	122	1.4	0	7	**5.7**
1912	NY-N	23	12	.657	43	34	27	0	4	**310**	311	9.0	6	34	**1.0**	134	3.9	2.12	160	.253	**.275**	**44**	**44**	99	93	-0.7	5	0	**5.0**
1913	NY-N	25	11	.694	40	35	25	4	2	306	291	8.6	8	21	**0.6**	93	2.7	**2.06**	**155**	.252	.261	**39**	**38**	100	104	2.0	-0	4	**4.6**
1914	NY-N	24	13	.649	41	35	29	5	2	312	314	9.1	16	23	**0.7**	80	2.3	3.00	87	.263	.271	-7	-14	94	83	5.2	6	2	-0.7
1915	NY-N	8	14	.364	27	24	11	1	0	186	199	9.6	9	20	**1.0**	57	2.8	3.58	71	.277	.286	-17	-22	92	87	-2.4	2	1	-2.0
1916	NY-N	3	4	.429	12	6	4	1	2	66	59	8.0	3	7	1.0	16	2.2	2.32	106	.243	.258	2	1	94	93	-0.8	-1	2	0.2
	Cin-N	1	0	1.000	1	1	1	0	0	9	15	15.0	1	1	1.0	3	3.0	8.00	33	.366	.372	-5	-5	101	79	0.5	1	0	-0.2
	Yr	4	4	.500	13	7	5	1	2	75	74	8.9	4	8	1.0	19	2.3	3.00	82	.261	.274	-3	-4	94	79	-0.3	-1	2	0.0
Total	17	372	187	.665	634	551	434	78	28	4778	4216	7.9	92	838	1.6	2502	4.7	2.13	135	.251	.287	418	396	99	100	66.0	56	65	54.6
■ HENRY MATHEWSON	Mathewson, Henry b: 12/24/1886, Factoryville, Pa. d: 7/1/17, Factoryville, Pa. 6'3", 175 lbs. Deb: 9/28/06																												
1906	NY-N	0	1	.000	2	1	1	0	1	10	7	6.3	0	14	12.6	2	1.8	5.40	47	.228	.481	-3	-3	97	90	-0.4	-0	0	-0.2
1907	NY-N	0	0	—	1	0	0	0	1	1	1	9.0	0	0	0.0	0	0.0	0.00	—	.289	.289	0	0	104	0	0.0	0	0	0.0
Total	2	0	1	.000	3	1	1	0	2	11	8	6.5	0	14	11.5	2	1.6	4.91	52	.234	.468	-3	-3	98	82	-0.4	-0	0	-0.2
■ CARL MATHIAS	Mathias, Carl Lynwood "Stubby" b: 6/13/36, Bechtelsville, Pa BB/TL, 5'11", 195 lbs. Deb: 7/31/60																												
1960	Cle-A	0	1	.000	7	0	0	0	0	15	14	8.4	2	8	4.8	13	7.8	3.60	106	.233	.324	0	0	98	102	-0.4	-0	0	0.0
1961	Was-A	0	1	.000	4	3	0	0	0	14	22	14.1	3	4	2.6	7	4.5	10.93	36	.361	.397	-11	-11	97	70	-0.4	-0	0	-0.9
Total	2	0	2	.000	11	3	0	0	0	29	36	11.2	5	12	3.7	20	6.2	7.14	54	.298	.360	-10	-11	98	87	-0.8	-0	0	-0.9
■ RON MATHIS	Mathis, Ronald Vance b: 9/25/58, Kansas City, Mo. BR/TR, 6', 175 lbs. Deb: 4/13/85																												
1985	Hou-N	3	5	.375	23	8	0	0	1	70	83	10.7	7	27	3.5	34	4.4	6.04	57	.293	.348	-19	-20	96	80	-1.0	-1	-0	-2.0
1987	Hou-N	0	1	.000	8	0	0	0	0	12	10	7.5	2	11	8.3	8	6.0	5.25	72	.233	.382	-2	-2	93	102	-0.4	-0	0	-0.1
Total	2	3	6	.333	31	8	0	0	1	82	93	10.2	9	38	4.2	42	4.6	5.93	59	.285	.353	-21	-22	95	84	-1.4	-1	-0	-2.1
■ JON MATLACK	Matlack, Jonathan Trumpbour b: 1/19/50, West Chester, Pa. BL/TL, 6'3", 205 lbs. Deb: 7/11/71																												
1971	NY-N	0	3	.000	7	6	0	0	0	37	31	7.5	2	15	3.6	24	5.8	4.14	80	.228	.301	-3	-3	96	68	-1.4	1	-1	-0.2
1972	NY-N	15	10	.600	34	32	8	4	0	244	215	7.9	14	71	2.6	169	6.2	2.32	143	.234	.287	31	27	96	115	2.1	1	-1	3.0
1973	NY-N	14	16	.467	34	34	14	3	0	242	210	7.8	16	99	3.7	205	7.6	3.20	115	.236	.308	13	13	100	97	-1.4	2	1	1.6
1974	NY-N	13	15	.464	34	34	14	**7**	0	265	221	7.5	8	76	2.6	195	6.6	2.41	151	.226	.281	36	36	100	93	0.8	-4	-0	3.5
1975	NY-N	16	12	.571	33	32	8	3	0	229	224	8.8	15	58	2.3	154	6.1	3.38	102	.254	.297	6	2	95	90	2.2	0	-2	0.0
1976	NY-N	17	10	.630	35	35	16	**6**	0	262	236	8.1	18	57	2.0	153	5.3	2.95	108	.242	.281	16	6	91	95	3.3	4	-1	0.9
1977	NY-N	7	15	.318	26	26	5	3	0	169	175	9.3	19	43	2.3	123	6.6	4.21	90	.273	.313	-6	-8	97	96	-2.3	-2	0	-0.9
1978	Tex-A	15	13	.536	35	33	18	2	1	270	252	8.4	14	51	1.7	157	5.2	2.27	159	.245	.280	45	40	96	114	0.0	0	0	4.5
1979	Tex-A	5	4	.556	13	13	2	0	0	85	98	10.4	9	15	1.6	35	3.7	4.13	102	.293	.321	1	1	99	104	0.4	0	0	0.1
1980	Tex-A	10	10	.500	35	34	8	1	1	235	265	10.1	17	48	**1.8**	142	5.4	3.68	110	.287	.318	10	10	100	106	0.6	0	-3	0.7
1981	Tex-A	4	7	.364	17	16	1	1	0	104	101	8.7	8	41	3.5	43	3.7	4.15	79	.258	.320	-6	-10	90	91	-1.9	0	0	-0.9
1982	Tex-A	7	7	.500	33	14	1	0	1	148	158	9.6	14	37	2.3	78	4.7	3.53	109	.275	.317	9	5	94	113	1.3	0	0	0.5
1983	Tex-A	2	4	.333	25	9	2	0	0	73	90	11.1	7	27	3.3	38	4.7	4.68	88	.307	.364	-5	-5	101	114	-0.8	0	1	-0.3
Total	13	125	126	.498	361	318	97	30	3	2363	2276	8.7	161	638	2.4	1516	5.8	3.18	114	.254	.300	148	114	97	101	2.9	2	-5	12.5
■ AL MATTERN	Mattern, Alonzo Albert b: 6/16/1883, W.Rush, N.Y. d: 11/6/58, West Rush, N.Y. BL/TR, 5'10", 165 lbs. Deb: 9/16/08																												
1908	Bos-N	1	2	.333	5	3	1	1	0	30	30	9.0	0	6	1.8	8	2.4	2.10	118	.289	.328	1	1	106	128	-0.2	-0	-0	0.1
1909	Bos-N	15	21	.417	47	32	24	2	3	316	322	9.2	4	108	3.1	98	2.8	2.85	93	.268	.330	-9	-7	102	111	3.9	-0	2	-0.5
1910	Bos-N	16	19	.457	**51**	37	17	6	1	305	288	8.5	5	121	3.6	94	2.8	2.98	120	.257	.332	2	21	118	103	3.7	-6	1	1.8
1911	Bos-N	4	15	.211	33	21	11	0	0	186	228	11.0	13	63	3.0	51	2.5	4.98	74	.320	.376	-33	-26	109	103	-2.8	-2	1	-2.4
1912	Bos-N	0	1	.000	2	1	0	0	0	6	10	15.0	0	1	1.5	3	4.5	7.50	50	.294	.314	-3	-2	110	38	-0.4	-0	0	-0.1
Total	5	36	58	.383	138	94	53	9	4	843	878	9.4	22	299	3.2	254	2.7	3.37	95	.277	.341	-42	-15	110	107	4.2	-8	4	-1.1
■ C. V. MATTERSON	Matterson, C. V. b: Ohio Deb: 6/13/1884																												
1884	StL-U	1	0	1.000	1	1	1	0	0	6	9	13.5	1	3	4.5	3	4.5	9.00	33	.352	.420	-4	-4	98	84	0.5	-1	0	-0.3
■ EDDIE MATTESON	Matteson, Henry Edson "Matty" b: 9/7/1884, Guys Mills, Pa. d: 9/1/43, Westfield, N.Y. BR/TR, 5'10.5", 160 lbs. Deb: 5/30/14																												
1914	Phi-N	3	2	.600	15	3	2	0	0	58	58	9.0	1	23	3.6	28	4.3	3.10	91	.278	.337	-2	-2	101	116	0.6	-0	-2	-0.3
1918	Was-A	5	3	.625	14	6	2	0	0	68	57	7.5	2	15	2.0	17	2.3	1.72	166	.238	.284	8	9	103	128	0.6	-2	-1	0.7
Total	2	8	5	.615	29	9	4	0	0	126	115	8.2	3	38	2.7	45	3.2	2.36	120	.257	.310	6	7	102	122	1.2	-2	-2	0.4

YEAR	TM/L	W	L	PCT	G	GS	CG	SHO	SV	IP	H	H/G	HR	BB	BB/G	SO	SO/G	ERA	/A	OAVG	OOBP	PR	/A	PF	CPI	WAT	PB	PD	TPI
■ **JOE MATTHEWS**	Matthews, John Joseph "Lefty" b: 9/29/1898, Baltimore, Md. d: 2/8/68, Hagerstown, Md. BB/TL, 6', 170 lbs. Deb: 9/18/22																												
1922	Bos-N	0	1	.000	3	1	0	0	0	10	5	4.5	1	6	5.4	0	0.0	3.60	111	.143	.273	1	0	98	48	-0.4	-0	-0	0.0
■ **WILLIAM MATTHEWS**	Matthews, William Calvin b: 1/12/1878, Mahanoy City, Pa. d: 1/23/46, Mahanoy City, Pa. TR , Deb: 8/28/09																												
1909	Bos-A	0	0	—	5	1	0	0	0	17	16	8.5	1	10	5.3	6	3.2	3.18	84	.271	.377	-1	-1	108	131	0.0	-1	-0	-0.1
■ **DALE MATTHEWSON**	Matthewson, Dale Wesley b: 5/15/23, Catasaqua, Pa. d: 2/20/84, Blairsville, Ga. BR/TR, 5'11.5", 145 lbs. Deb: 7/03/43																												
1943	Phi-N	0	3	.000	11	1	0	0	0	26	26	9.0	1	8	2.8	8	2.8	4.85	67	.271	.315	-4	-5	96	74	-1.4	-0	-0	-0.4
1944	Phi-N	0	0	—	17	1	0	0	0	32	27	7.6	1	16	4.5	8	2.3	3.94	94	.237	.321	-1	-1	103	84	0.0	0	-0	0.0
Total	2	0	3	.000	28	2	0	0	0	58	53	8.2	2	24	3.7	16	2.5	4.34	80	.252	.318	-5	-6	99	79	-1.4	-0	-0	-0.4
■ **MIKE MATTIMORE**	Mattimore, Michael Joseph b: 1859, Renovo, Pa. d: 4/28/31, Butte, Mont. BL/TR, 5'8.5", 160 lbs. Deb: 5/03/1887																												
1887	NY-N	3	3	.500	7	7	6	1	0	57	47	7.4	2	28	4.4	12	1.9	2.37	180	.238	.333	11	12	106	129	-0.2	-1	0	1.1
1888	Phi-a	15	10	.600	26	24	24	4	0	221	221	9.0	6	65	2.6	80	3.3	3.38	88	.273	.327	-8	-10	97	100	-0.1	7	0	0.0
1889	Phi-a	2	1	.667	5	1	1	0	1	31	43	12.5	0	13	3.8	6	1.7	5.81	64	.345	.407	-7	-7	96	91	0.4	1	0	-0.5
	KC-a	0	0	—	1	0	0	0	0	3	3	9.0	1	2	6.0	1	3.0	3.00	139	.275	.388	0	0	109	219	0.0	-0	0	0.0
	Yr	2	1	.667	6	1	1	0	1	34	46	12.2	1	15	4.0	7	1.9	5.56	67	.339	.405	-6	-7	97	219	0.4	1	0	-0.5
1890	BB-a	6	13	.316	19	19	19	0	0	178	201	10.2	3	76	3.8	33	1.7	4.55	87	.301	.372	-14	-12	103	97	0.1	-3	0	-1.2
Total	4	26	27	.491	58	51	50	5	1	490	515	9.5	12	184	3.4	132	2.4	3.84	92	.285	.351	-17	-17	100	102	0.2	4	0	-0.6
■ **EARL MATTINGLY**	Mattingly, Laurence Earl b: 11/4/04, Newport, Md. BR/TR, 5'10.5", 164 lbs. Deb: 4/15/31																												
1931	Bro-N	0	1	.000	8	0	0	0	0	14	15	9.6	0	10	6.4	6	3.9	2.57	152	.268	.397	2	2	101	182	-0.4	-0	1	0.2
■ **RICK MATULA**	Matula, Richard Carlton b: 11/22/53, Wharton, Tex. BR/TR, 6', 190 lbs. Deb: 4/08/79																												
1979	Atl-N	8	10	.444	28	28	1	0	0	171	193	10.2	14	64	3.4	67	3.5	4.16	99	.286	.345	-8	-1	110	107	0.5	-3	0	-0.2
1980	Atl-N	11	13	.458	33	30	3	1	0	177	195	9.9	17	60	3.1	62	3.2	4.58	80	.286	.335	-19	-18	101	97	-1.1	-3	1	-1.9
1981	Atl-N	0	0	—	5	0	0	0	0	7	8	10.3	1	2	2.6	0	0.0	6.43	54	.286	.333	-2	-2	100	72	0.0	-0	0	-0.2
Total	3	19	23	.452	66	58	4	1	0	355	396	10.0	32	126	3.2	129	3.3	4.41	88	.286	.340	-29	-21	106	101	-0.6	-6	1	-2.3
■ **HARRY MATUZAK**	Matuzak, Harry George "Matty" b: 1/27/10, Omer, Mich. d: 11/16/78, Fair Hope, Ala. BR/TR, 5'11.5", 185 lbs. Deb: 4/19/34																												
1934	Phi-A	0	3	.000	11	0	0	0	0	24	28	10.5	2	10	3.8	9	3.4	4.88	91	.292	.351	-1	-1	98	104	-1.4	0	0	0.0
1936	Phi-A	0	1	.000	6	1	0	0	0	15	21	12.6	0	4	2.4	8	4.8	7.20	74	.318	.352	-4	-3	105	66	-0.4	-0	0	-0.2
Total	2	0	4	.000	17	1	0	0	0	39	49	11.3	2	14	3.2	17	3.9	5.77	82	.302	.352	-5	-4	101	89	-1.8	-0	0	-0.2
■ **HAL MAUCK**	Mauck, Alfred Maris b: 3/6/1869, Princeton, Ind. d: 4/27/21, Princeton, Ind. BR/TR, 5'11", 185 lbs. Deb: 4/29/1893																												
1893	Chi-N	8	10	.444	23	18	12	1	0	143	168	10.6	2	60	3.8	23	1.4	4.41	111	.309	.378	4	8	104	102	0.1	-6	0	0.2
■ **AL MAUL**	Maul, Albert Joseph "Smiling Al" b: 10/9/1865, Philadelphia, Pa. d: 5/3/58, Philadelphia, Pa. BR/TR, 6', 175 lbs. Deb: 6/20/1884																												
1884	Phi-U	0	1	.000	1	1	1	0	0	8	10	11.3	0	1	1.1	7	7.9	4.50	64	.311	.332	-1	-1	95	89	-0.4	-1	0	-0.1
1887	Phi-N	4	2	.667	7	5	4	0	0	50	72	13.0	2	15	2.7	18	3.2	5.58	68	.354	.398	-8	-10	94	102	0.5	4	0	-0.7
1888	Pit-N	0	2	.000	3	1	1	0	0	17	26	13.8	0	5	2.6	12	6.4	6.35	42	.366	.408	-7	-7	95	88	-0.9	0	0	-0.5
1889	Pit-N	1	4	.200	6	4	4	0	0	42	64	13.7	3	28	6.0	11	2.4	9.86	37	.367	.455	-27	-29	90	73	-1.3	2	0	-2.0
1890	Pit-P	16	12	.571	30	28	26	2	0	247	258	9.4	14	104	3.8	81	3.0	3.79	103	.281	.354	12	3	92	99	3.3	6	0	0.8
1891	Pit-N	1	2	.333	8	3	3	0	1	39	44	10.2	0	16	3.7	13	3.0	2.31	148	.298	.367	5	5	102	158	-0.2	0	0	0.4
1893	Was-N	12	21	.364	37	33	29	1	0	297	355	10.8	17	144	4.4	72	2.2	5.30	81	.313	.390	-21	-33	92	96	1.7	11	1	-1.6
1894	Was-N	11	15	.423	28	26	21	0	0	202	272	12.1	12	73	3.3	34	1.5	6.01	88	.345	.401	-15	-16	100	91	2.0	1	2	-0.7
1895	Was-N	10	5	.667	16	16	14	0	0	136	136	9.0	5	37	2.4	34	2.3	**2.45**	**206**	.280	.331	35	39	105	**135**	4.0	1	0	3.7
1896	Was-N	5	2	.714	8	8	7	0	0	62	75	10.9	0	20	2.9	18	2.6	3.63	116	.322	.375	5	4	96	113	1.8	2	0	0.5
1897	Was-N	0	1	.000	1	1	0	0	0	2	4	18.0	0	1	4.5	0	0.0	9.00	49	.439	.495	-1	-1	102	94	-0.4	-0	0	0.0
	Bal-N	0	0	—	2	2	0	0	0	8	9	10.1	0	8	9.0	2	2.3	7.88	50	.306	.454	-3	-3	92	70	0.0	0	0	-0.2
	Yr	0	1	.000	3	3	0	0	0	10	13	11.7	0	9	8.1	2	1.8	8.10	50	.338	.463	-4	-4	94	70	-0.4	-0	0	-0.2
1898	Bal-N	20	7	.741	28	28	26	1	0	240	207	7.8	3	49	1.8	31	1.2	2.10	171	.253	.295	40	40	100	101	4.2	3	-4	4.0
1899	Bro-N	2	0	1.000	4	4	2	0	0	26	35	12.1	1	6	2.1	2	0.7	4.50	88	.347	.384	-2	-2	102	105	1.0	0	0	0.0
1900	Phi-N	2	3	.400	5	4	3	0	0	38	53	12.6	2	3	0.7	6	1.4	6.16	59	.355	.367	-10	-11	98	77	-0.6	0	0	-0.8
1901	NY-N	0	3	.000	3	3	2	0	0	19	39	18.5	1	8	3.8	5	2.4	11.37	28	.451	.503	-17	-17	95	80	-1.4	1	0	-1.2
Total	15	84	80	.512	187	167	143	4	1	1433	1659	10.4	60	518	3.3	346	2.2	4.44	94	.308	.369	-16	-40	96	101	13.3	32	-1	1.6
■ **ERNIE MAUN**	Maun, Ernest Gerald b: 2/3/01, Clearwater, Kan. d: 1/1/87, Corpus Christi, Tex. BL/TR, 6', 165 lbs. Deb: 5/16/24																												
1924	NY-N	1	1	.500	22	0	0	0	1	35	46	11.8	2	10	2.6	5	1.3	5.91	57	.326	.363	-8	-10	88	88	-0.1	1	-1	-0.8
1926	Phi-N	1	4	.200	14	5	0	0	0	38	57	13.5	4	18	4.3	9	2.1	6.39	64	.339	.400	-11	-10	107	102	-1.1	-0	-0	-0.8
Total	2	2	5	.286	36	5	0	0	1	73	103	12.7	6	28	3.5	14	1.7	6.16	61	.333	.383	-19	-20	98	95	-1.2	1	-1	-1.6
■ **DICK MAUNEY**	Mauney, Richard b: 1/26/20, Concord, N.C. d: 2/6/70, Albermarle, N.C. BR/TR, 5'11.5", 164 lbs. Deb: 6/13/45																												
1945	Phi-N	6	10	.375	20	16	6	2	1	123	127	9.3	7	27	2.0	35	2.6	3.07	126	.268	.306	10	11	102	113	1.0	-0	1	1.2
1946	Phi-N	6	4	.600	24	7	3	2	2	90	98	9.8	4	18	1.8	31	3.1	2.70	124	.279	.315	7	6	98	129	1.4	-0	0	0.6
1947	Phi-N	0	0	—	9	1	0	0	1	16	15	8.4	1	7	3.9	6	3.4	3.94	105	.288	.371	0	0	102	126	0.0	-0	1	0.1
Total	3	12	14	.462	53	24	9	4	4	229	240	9.4	12	52	2.0	72	2.8	2.99	123	.274	.314	17	18	100	120	2.4	-1	2	1.9
■ **HARRY MAUPIN**	Maupin, Henry Carr b: 7/11/1872, Wellesville, Mo. d: 8/23/52, Deb: 10/05/1898																												
1898	StL-N	0	2	.000	2	2	2	0	0	18	22	11.0	0	3	1.5	3	1.5	5.50	72	.324	.353	-4	-3	110	67	-0.9	1	0	-0.1
1899	Cle-N	0	3	.000	5	3	2	0	0	25	55	19.8	0	7	2.5	3	1.1	12.60	29	.465	.495	-24	-25	96	70	-1.4	-2	0	-1.9
Total	2	0	5	.000	7	5	4	0	0	43	77	16.1	0	10	2.1	6	1.3	9.63	40	.414	.443	-28	-28	102	68	-2.3	-1	0	-2.0
■ **RALPH MAURIELLO**	Mauriello, Ralph "Tami" b: 8/25/34, Brooklyn, N.Y. BR/TR, 6'3", 195 lbs. Deb: 9/13/58																												
1958	LA-N	1	1	.500	3	2	0	0	0	12	10	7.5	1	8	6.0	11	8.3	4.50	93	.238	.353	-1	-0	106	91	0.1	-1	-0	0.0
■ **LARRY MAXIE**	Maxie, Larry Hans b: 10/10/40, Upland, Cal. BR/TR, 6'4", 220 lbs. Deb: 8/30/69																												
1969	Atl-N	0	0	—	2	0	0	0	0	3	1	3.0	0	1	3.0	1	3.0	3.00	123	.111	.250	0	0	103	36	0.0	0	0	0.1
■ **BERT MAXWELL**	Maxwell, James Albert b: 10/17/1886, Texarkana, Ark. d: 12/10/61, Brady, Tex. BB/TR, 6', 180 lbs. Deb: 9/12/06																												
1906	Pit-N	0	1	.000	1	1	0	0	0	8	8	9.0	0	2	2.3	1	1.1	5.63	47	.288	.336	-3	-3	101	51	-0.4	-0	0	-0.1
1908	Phi-A	0	0	—	4	0	0	0	0	13	23	15.9	0	9	6.2	7	4.8	11.08	24	.348	.442	-13	-12	110	67	0.0	-1	0	-1.1
1911	NY-N	1	2	.333	4	3	3	0	0	31	37	10.7	0	7	2.0	8	2.3	2.90	115	.311	.359	2	2	99	145	-0.6	-0	1	0.2
1914	Bro-F	3	4	.429	12	8	6	1	1	71	76	9.6	0	24	3.0	19	2.4	3.30	98	.276	.337	-1	-0	101	103	-0.4	-2	0	-0.1
Total	4	4	7	.364	21	12	9	1	1	123	144	10.5	0	42	3.1	35	2.6	4.17	76	.295	.357	-14	-14	101	106	-1.4	-3	1	-1.1
■ **JAKIE MAY**	May, Frank Spruiell b: 11/25/1895, Youngville, N.C. d: 6/3/70, Wendell, N.C. BR/TL, 5'8", 178 lbs. Deb: 6/26/17																												
1917	StL-N	0	0	—	15	1	0	0	0	29	29	9.0	0	11	3.4	18	5.6	3.41	81	.302	.371	-2	-2	102	129	0.0	-1	2	0.0
1918	StL-N	5	6	.455	29	16	6	0	0	153	149	8.8	2	69	4.1	61	3.6	3.82	69	.264	.345	-18	-20	95	96	0.6	-1	-2	-2.4
1919	StL-N	3	12	.200	28	19	8	1	0	126	99	7.1	1	87	6.2	58	4.1	3.21	87	.230	.362	-4	-6	97	114	-3.8	-1	-1	-0.8
1920	StL-N	1	4	.200	16	5	3	0	0	71	65	8.2	0	37	4.7	33	4.2	3.04	101	.251	.344	1	0	98	108	-1.4	1	-2	0.0
1921	StL-N	1	3	.250	5	5	1	0	0	21	29	12.4	0	12	5.1	5	2.1	4.71	74	.333	.414	-2	-3	93	117	-1.0	1	-1	-0.2
1924	Cin-N	3	3	.500	38	4	2	0	**6**	99	104	9.5	2	29	2.6	59	5.4	3.00	128	.276	.330	10	9	99	120	-0.1	-2	-0	0.7
1925	Cin-N	8	9	.471	36	12	7	1	2	137	146	9.6	3	45	3.0	74	4.9	3.88	106	.272	.332	6	4	97	91	-0.8	0	0	0.4
1926	Cin-N	13	9	.591	45	15	9	1	3	168	175	9.4	4	44	2.4	103	5.5	3.21	111	.276	.321	11	6	93	109	0.8	-1	-1	0.4
1927	Cin-N	15	12	.556	44	28	17	2	1	236	242	9.2	4	70	2.7	121	4.6	3.51	112	.274	.325	11	11	100	102	2.0	0	1	1.1
1928	Cin-N	3	5	.375	21	11	1	0	1	79	99	11.3	1	35	4.0	39	4.4	4.44	87	.315	.373	-4	-5	97	109	-1.0	1	-1	-0.4
1929	Cin-N	10	14	.417	41	24	10	0	3	199	219	9.9	7	75	3.4	92	4.2	4.61	103	.285	.342	2	3	101	92	-0.3	-1	-1	0.1
1930	Cin-N	3	11	.214	26	18	5	1	0	112	147	11.8	6	41	3.3	44	3.5	5.79	80	.320	.374	-10	-14	93	93	-3.2	-1	0	-1.2
1931	Chi-N	5	5	.500	31	4	1	0	2	79	81	9.2	2	43	4.9	38	4.3	3.87	94	.275	.363	-0	-2	94	114	-0.3	1	0	0.0
1932	Chi-N	2	2	.500	35	0	0	0	1	54	61	10.2	3	19	3.2	20	3.3	4.33	92	.281	.333	-3	-2	103	97	-0.2	-0	-0	-0.2
Total	14	72	95	.431	410	162	70	7	19	1563	1645	9.5	35	617	3.6	765	4.4	3.88	97	.278	.344	-3	-22	97	103	-8.7	-4	-5	-2.5

YEAR	TM/L	W	L	PCT	G	GS	CG	SHO	SV	IP	H	H/G	HR	BB	BB/G	SO	SO/G	ERA	/A	OAVG	OOBP	PR	/A	PF	CPI	WAT	PB	PD	TPI
■ **RUDY MAY**	May, Rudolph b: 7/18/44, Coffeyville, Kan. BL/TL, 6'2", 205 lbs. Deb: 4/18/65																												
1965	Cal-A	4	9	.308	30	19	2	1	0	124	111	8.1	7	78	5.7	76	5.5	3.92	87	.245	.354	-6	-7	98	103	-2.2	3	-2	-0.5
1969	Cal-A	10	13	.435	43	25	4	0	2	180	142	7.1	20	66	3.3	133	6.7	3.45	106	.220	.292	4	4	101	89	0.0	-2	-1	0.2
1970	Cal-A	7	13	.350	38	34	2	2	0	209	190	8.2	20	81	3.5	164	7.1	4.00	85	.245	.314	-7	-14	92	89	-3.6	-2	0	-1.6
1971	Cal-A	11	12	.478	32	31	7	2	0	208	160	6.9	12	87	3.8	156	6.8	3.03	114	.213	.292	10	10	99	84	0.2	-0	-1	0.9
1972	Cal-A	12	11	.522	35	30	10	3	1	205	162	7.1	15	82	3.6	169	7.4	2.94	93	.215	.287	3	-4	90	88	1.0	-1	-2	-0.8
1973	Cal-A	7	17	.292	34	28	10	4	0	185	177	8.6	20	80	3.9	134	6.5	4.38	84	.254	.326	-11	-14	96	90	-5.2	0	2	-1.2
1974	Cal-A	0	1	.000	18	3	0	0	2	27	29	9.7	2	10	3.3	12	4.0	7.00	48	.274	.328	-10	-11	93	58	-0.4	0	1	-0.9
	NY-A	8	4	.667	17	15	8	2	0	114	75	5.9	5	48	3.8	90	7.1	2.29	151	.188	.277	17	15	95	86	1.7	0	-1	1.4
	Yr	8	5	.615	35	18	8	2	2	141	104	6.6	7	58	3.7	102	6.5	3.19	108	.204	.286	7	4	95	86	1.3	0	-0	0.5
1975	NY-A	14	12	.538	32	31	13	1	0	212	179	7.6	9	99	4.2	145	6.2	3.06	121	.231	.313	17	15	98	98	0.6	0	-1	1.4
1976	NY-A	4	3	.571	11	11	2	1	0	68	49	6.5	5	28	3.7	38	5.0	3.57	96	.206	.289	-0	-1	97	73	-0.1	0	0	0.0
	Bal-A	11	7	.611	24	21	5	1	0	152	156	9.2	11	42	2.5	71	4.2	3.79	91	.267	.311	-5	-6	97	95	1.5	0	-1	-0.6
	Yr	15	10	.600	35	32	7	2	0	220	205	8.4	16	70	2.9	109	4.5	3.72	92	.249	.303	-5	-7	97	95	1.4	0	-1	-0.6
1977	Bal-A	18	14	.563	37	37	11	4	0	252	243	8.7	25	78	2.8	105	3.8	3.61	104	.255	.311	13	4	92	100	-1.2	0	-3	0.1
1978	Mon-N	8	10	.444	27	23	4	1	0	144	141	8.8	15	42	2.6	87	5.4	3.88	88	.255	.308	-5	-7	96	95	-0.4	1	-2	-0.8
1979	Mon-N	10	3	.769	33	7	2	1	0	94	88	8.4	4	31	3.0	67	6.4	2.30	164	.255	.313	15	15	101	145	2.9	-0	1	1.6
1980	NY-A	15	5	.750	41	17	3	1	3	175	144	7.4	14	39	2.0	133	6.8	**2.47**	**160**	.224	**.265**	31	29	98	97	3.4	0	0	3.0
1981	NY-A	6	11	.353	27	22	4	0	1	148	137	8.3	10	41	2.5	79	4.8	4.14	88	.246	.295	-8	-8	99	74	-3.3	0	1	-0.7
1982	NY-A	6	6	.500	41	6	0	0	3	106	109	9.3	4	14	1.2	85	7.2	2.89	136	.267	.283	14	12	97	103	0.2	0	1	1.3
1983	NY-A	1	5	.167	15	0	0	0	0	18	22	11.0	1	12	6.0	16	8.0	7.00	57	.293	.389	-6	-6	98	78	-2.0	0	0	-0.5
Total	16	152	156	.494	535	360	87	24	12	2621	2314	7.9	199	958	3.3	1760	6.0	3.46	102	.238	.304	66	25	96	93	-6.9	-2	-7	2.3
■ **SCOTT MAY**	May, Scott Francis b: 11/11/61, West Bend, Wis. BR/TR, 6', 185 lbs. Deb: 9/2/88																												
1988	Tex-A	0	0	—	3	1	0	0	0	7	8	10.3	3	4	5.1	4	5.1	9.00	45	.296	.364	-4	-4	102	90	0.0	0	0	-0.3
■ **BUCKSHOT MAY**	May, William Herbert b: 12/13/1899, Bakersfield, Cal. d: 3/15/84, Bakersfield, Cal. BR/TR, 6'2", 169 lbs. Deb: 5/09/24																												
1924	Pit-N	0	0	—	1	0	0	0	0	1	2	18.0	0	0	0.0	1	9.0	0.00	—	.500	.500	0	0	104	0	0.0	0	0	0.0
■ **ED MAYER**	Mayer, Edwin David b: 11/30/31, San Francisco, Cal BL/TL, 6'2", 185 lbs. Deb: 9/15/57																												
1957	Chi-N	0	0	—	3	1	0	0	0	8	8	9.0	2	2	2.3	3	3.4	5.63	67	.258	.324	-2	-2	98	88	0.0	0	0	0.0
1958	Chi-N	2	2	.500	19	0	0	0	1	24	15	5.6	0	16	6.0	14	5.3	3.75	106	.190	.340	1	1	101	74	0.1	-0	-0	0.0
Total	2	2	2	.500	22	1	0	0	1	32	23	6.5	2	18	5.1	17	4.8	4.22	93	.209	.336	-1	-1	100	77	0.1	0	0	0.0
■ **ERSKINE MAYER**	Mayer, Erskine John (born James Erskine) b: 1/16/1889, Atlanta, Ga. d: 3/10/57, Los Angeles, Cal. BR/TR, 6', 168 lbs. Deb: 9/04/12																												
1912	Phi-N	0	1	.000	7	1	0	0	0	21	27	11.6	1	7	3.0	5	2.1	6.43	53	.310	.368	-7	-7	101	71	-0.4	-0	0	-0.6
1913	Phi-N	9	9	.500	39	20	7	2	1	171	172	9.1	6	46	2.4	51	2.7	3.11	114	.272	.322	2	8	111	111	-1.3	-3	0	0.7
1914	Phi-N	21	19	.525	48	39	24	4	2	321	308	8.6	8	91	2.6	116	3.3	2.58	109	.256	.307	7	8	101	109	2.2	3	4	1.7
1915	Phi-N	21	15	.583	43	33	20	2	2	275	240	7.9	9	59	1.9	114	3.7	2.36	122	.243	.287	12	16	104	109	-0.2	5	1	2.4
1916	Phi-N	7	7	.500	28	16	7	2	0	140	148	9.5	7	33	2.1	62	4.0	3.15	78	.281	.319	-8	-11	94	114	-1.1	-0	3	-0.8
1917	Phi-N	11	6	.647	28	18	11	1	0	160	160	9.0	6	33	1.9	64	3.6	2.76	104	.268	.304	-1	2	106	114	1.6	-0	-0	0.2
1918	Phi-N	7	4	.636	13	13	7	0	0	104	108	9.3	2	26	2.3	16	1.4	3.12	99	.276	.319	-4	-0	111	106	2.0	1	0	0.1
	Pit-N	9	3	.750	15	14	11	1	0	123	122	8.9	1	27	2.0	25	1.8	2.27	127	.268	.301	7	9	105	128	3.0	2	-2	1.0
	Yr	16	7	.696	28	27	18	1	0	227	230	9.1	3	53	2.1	41	1.6	2.66	112	.270	.305	3	8	108	128	5.0	1	-2	1.1
1919	Pit-N	5	3	.625	18	10	6	0	1	88	100	10.2	2	12	1.2	20	2.0	4.50	68	.267	.289	-16	-14	105	61	1.0	0	-1	-1.5
	Chi-A	1	3	.250	6	2	0	0	0	24	30	11.3	1	11	4.1	9	3.4	8.25	40	.316	.387	-13	-13	102	59	-1.1	-1	-0	-1.2
Total	8	91	70	.565	245	166	93	12	6	1427	1415	8.9	43	345	2.2	482	3.0	2.96	99	.264	.307	-21	-3	104	107	5.7	5	5	2.0
■ **SAM MAYER**	Mayer, Samuel Frankel (born Samuel Frankel Erskine) b: 2/28/1893, Atlanta, Ga. d: 7/1/62, Atlanta, Ga. BR/TL, 5'10", 164 lbs. Deb: 9/14/15																												
1915	Was-A	0	0	—	1	0	0	0	0	0	0	—	0	2	—	0	—	—	—	—	1.000	0	0	99	0	0.0	0	0	0.0
■ **AL MAYS**	Mays, Albert C. b: 5/17/1865, Canal Dover, Ohio d: 5/7/05, Parkersburg, W.Va. BR , Deb: 1885																												
1885	Lou-a	6	11	.353	17	17	17	0	0	150	129	7.7	3	43	2.6	61	3.7	2.76	122	.243	.300	8	10	103	99	-2.3	-0	0	0.9
1886	NY-a	11	28	.282	41	41	39	1	0	350	330	8.5	7	140	3.6	163	4.2	3.39	108	.259	.332	2	10	106	102	-6.8	-11	-1	0.0
1887	NY-a	17	34	.333	52	52	50	0	0	441	551	11.2	11	136	2.8	124	2.5	4.73	83	.320	.370	-21	-38	92	100	0.2	2	9	-2.3
1888	Bro-a	9	9	.500	18	18	17	1	0	161	150	8.4	1	32	1.8	67	3.7	2.80	111	.259	.298	5	6	102	93	-2.0	-5	0	0.2
1889	Col-a	10	7	.588	21	19	13	1	0	140	167	10.7	4	56	3.6	52	3.3	4.82	74	.312	.377	-15	-20	92	93	2.5	-1	0	-1.6
1890	Col-a	0	1	.000	1	1	1	0	0	9	14	14.0	0	8	8.0	2	2.0	8.00	46	.372	.482	-4	-4	96	96	-0.4	-0	0	-0.2
Total	6	53	90	.371	150	148	137	3	0	1251	1341	9.6	26	415	3.0	469	3.4	3.91	94	.287	.345	-26	-33	99	99	-8.8	-15	9	-3.0
■ **CARL MAYS**	Mays, Carl William "Sub" b: 11/12/1891, Liberty, Ky. d: 4/4/71, El Cajon, Cal. BL/TR, 5'11.5", 195 lbs. Deb: 4/15/15																												
1915	Bos-A	6	5	.545	38	6	2	0	**7**	132	119	8.1	0	21	1.4	65	4.4	2.59	109	.244	.282	5	3	96	81	-1.0	2	2	0.7
1916	Bos-A	18	13	.581	44	24	14	2	3	245	208	7.6	3	74	2.7	76	2.8	2.39	109	.234	.299	12	6	92	97	-0.2	8	9	2.5
1917	Bos-A	22	9	.710	35	33	27	2	0	289	230	7.2	1	74	2.3	91	2.8	1.74	162	.221	.282	30	34	106	100	**5.2**	5	8	**6.0**
1918	Bos-A	21	13	.618	35	33	**30**	**8**	0	293	230	7.1	2	81	2.5	114	3.5	2.21	116	.221	.277	18	12	93	80	1.3	10	9	3.5
1919	Bos-A	5	11	.313	21	16	14	2	2	146	131	8.1	3	40	2.5	53	3.3	2.47	119	.247	.306	12	8	91	101	-2.9	-1	3	0.9
	NY-A	9	3	.750	13	13	12	1	0	120	96	7.2	2	37	2.8	54	4.1	1.65	203	.216	.283	21	23	104	104	2.6	3	2	3.2
	Yr	14	14	.500	34	29	26	3	2	266	227	7.7	5	77	2.6	107	3.6	2.10	149	.231	.291	33	30	97	104	-0.3	-1	4	4.1
1920	NY-A	26	11	.703	45	37	26	**6**	2	312	310	8.9	13	84	2.4	92	2.7	3.06	123	.263	.316	26	24	99	100	5.1	2	6	3.2
1921	NY-A	**27**	9	**.750**	**49**	38	30	1	**7**	**337**	332	8.9	11	76	2.0	70	1.9	3.04	139	.257	.298	46	45	99	92	6.6	12	2	5.8
1922	NY-A	12	14	.462	34	29	21	1	2	240	257	9.6	12	50	1.9	41	1.5	3.60	111	.285	.318	12	11	99	103	-3.5	1	6	1.7
1923	NY-A	5	2	.714	23	7	2	0	0	81	119	13.2	8	32	3.6	16	1.8	6.22	65	.357	.405	-20	-20	101	108	0.7	1	3	-1.5
1924	Cin-N	20	9	.690	37	27	15	2	0	226	238	9.5	3	36	1.4	63	2.5	3.15	122	.270	.296	18	17	99	91	5.4	7	8	3.3
1925	Cin-N	3	5	.375	12	5	3	0	2	52	60	10.4	0	13	2.3	10	1.7	3.29	125	.294	.333	6	5	97	114	-1.1	1	1	0.6
1926	Cin-N	19	12	.613	39	33	**24**	3	1	281	286	9.2	3	53	1.7	58	1.9	3.14	113	.269	.296	21	13	93	93	2.1	3	10	2.6
1927	Cin-N	3	7	.300	14	9	6	0	0	82	89	9.8	1	10	1.1	17	1.9	3.51	112	.276	.292	4	4	100	84	-1.9	5	4	1.3
1928	Cin-N	4	1	.800	14	7	4	1	1	63	67	9.6	3	22	3.1	10	1.4	3.86	100	.275	.331	1	-0	97	95	1.5	1	0	0.1
1929	NY-N	7	2	.778	37	8	1	0	4	123	140	10.2	8	31	2.3	32	2.3	4.32	106	.287	.322	5	3	97	96	2.3	4	2	0.9
Total	15	207	126	.622	490	325	231	29	31	3022	2912	8.7	73	734	2.2	862	2.6	2.92	119	.257	.302	217	187	98	95	22.2	62	73	34.8
■ **JACK McADAMS**	McAdams, George D. b: 12/17/1886, Benton, Ark. d: 5/21/37, San Francisco, Cal BR/TR, 6'1.5", 170 lbs. Deb: 7/22/11																												
1911	StL-N	0	0	—	6	0	0	0	0	10	7	6.3	0	5	4.5	4	3.6	3.60	97	.226	.368	-0	-0	102	95	0.0	-0	0	0.0
■ **BILL McAFEE**	McAfee, William Fort b: 9/7/07, Smithville, Ga. d: 7/8/58, Culpepper, Va. BR/TR, 6'2", 186 lbs. Deb: 5/12/30																												
1930	Chi-N	0	0	—	2	0	0	0	0	1	3	27.0	0	2	18.0	0	0.0	0.00	—	.375	.500	1	1	103	0	0.0	0	0	0.0
1931	Bos-N	0	1	.000	18	1	0	0	0	30	39	11.7	2	10	3.0	9	2.7	6.30	62	.333	.380	-8	-8	102	90	-0.4	-0	0	-0.7
1932	Was-A	6	1	.857	8	5	2	0	0	41	47	10.3	3	22	4.8	10	2.2	3.95	111	.287	.365	2	2	98	131	2.3	-1	1	0.1
1933	Was-A	3	2	.600	27	1	0	0	5	53	64	10.9	3	21	3.6	14	2.4	6.62	60	.296	.351	-14	-15	93	75	-0.1	2	0	-1.1
1934	StL-A	1	0	1.000	28	0	0	0	0	62	84	12.2	4	26	3.8	11	1.6	5.81	82	.332	.392	-9	-7	106	106	0.5	0	-1	-0.6
Total	5	10	4	.714	83	7	2	0	5	187	237	11.4	12	81	3.9	44	2.1	5.68	76	.313	.374	-28	-28	100	99	2.3	0	1	-2.3
■ **JIMMY McALEER**	McAleer, James Robert "Loafer" b: 7/10/1864, Youngstown, Ohio d: 4/29/31, Youngstown, Ohio BR/TR, 6', 175 lbs. Deb: 4/24/1889 M																												
1901	Cle-A	0	0	—	1	0	0	0	0	⅓	2	54.0	0	3	81.0	0	0.0	0.00	—	1.000	1.000	0	0	97	0	0.0	-0	0	0.0
■ **JACK McALEESE**	McAleese, John James b: 1877, Sharon, Pa. d: 11/15/50, New York, N.Y. TR , 5'8", Deb: 8/10/01																												
1901	Chi-A	0	0	—	1	0	0	0	0	3	7	21.0	0	1	3.0	1	3.0	9.00	39	.476	.509	-2	-2	96	108	0.0	-0	0	-0.1
■ **SPORT McALLISTER**	McAllister, Lewis William b: 7/23/1874, Austin, Miss. d: 7/17/62, Wyandotte, Mich. BB/TR, 5'11", 180 lbs. Deb: 8/07/1896																												
1896	Cle-N	0	0	—	1	0	0	0	0	4	9	20.3	0	2	4.5	0	0.0	6.75	70	.469	.519	-1	-1	108	145	0.0	-0	0	0.0
1897	Cle-N	1	2	.333	4	3	3	0	0	28	29	9.3	3	9	2.9	10	3.2	4.50	105	.289	.347	-1	1	110	89	-0.5	-0	0	0.1

YEAR	TM/L	W	L	PCT	G	GS	CG	SHO	SV	IP	H	H/G	HR	BB	BB/G	SO	SO/G	ERA	/A	OAVG	OOBP	PR	/A	PF	CPI	WAT	PB	PD	TPI
1898	Cle-N	3	4	.429	9	7	6	0	0	65	73	10.1	2	23	3.2	9	1.2	4.57	75	.306	.367	-7	-8	95	87	-0.7	1	0	-0.5
1899	Cle-N	0	1	.000	3	1	1	0	0	16	29	16.3	0	10	5.6	2	1.1	9.56	39	.417	.491	-10	-10	96	82	-0.4	0	0	-0.7
Total	4	4	7	.364	17	11	10	0	0	113	140	11.2	5	44	3.5	21	1.7	5.34	71	.327	.390	-19	-19	99	89	-1.6	1	0	-1.1
■ **ERNIE McANALLY**	McAnally, Ernest Lee b: 8/15/46, Pittsburg, Tex. BR/TR, 6'1", 190 lbs. Deb: 4/11/71																												
1971	Mon-N	11	12	.478	31	25	8	2	0	178	150	7.6	9	87	4.4	98	5.0	3.89	89	.228	.322	-8	-8	100	80	0.9	-2	0	-1.0
1972	Mon-N	6	15	.286	29	27	4	2	0	170	165	8.7	13	71	3.8	102	5.4	3.81	94	.259	.330	-7	-4	104	102	-4.1	-2	3	-0.2
1973	Mon-N	7	9	.438	27	24	4	0	0	147	158	9.7	13	54	3.3	72	4.4	4.04	95	.274	.333	-6	-3	105	102	-0.8	-1	-0	-0.4
1974	Mon-N	6	13	.316	25	21	5	2	0	129	126	8.8	10	56	3.9	79	5.5	4.47	85	.256	.332	-12	-10	104	85	-3.6	-2	1	-1.0
Total	4	30	49	.380	112	97	21	6	0	624	599	8.6	45	268	3.9	351	5.1	4.02	91	.253	.329	-33	-26	103	92	-7.6	-6	3	-2.6
■ **JIM McANDREW**	McAndrew, James Clement b: 1/11/44, Lost Nation, Iowa BR/TR, 6'2", 185 lbs. Deb: 7/21/68																												
1968	NY-N	4	7	.364	12	12	2	1	0	79	66	7.5	5	17	1.9	46	5.2	2.28	134	.230	.277	6	7	103	113	-1.0	-1	-0	0.6
1969	NY-N	6	7	.462	27	21	4	2	0	135	112	7.5	12	44	2.9	90	6.0	3.47	103	.225	.286	2	2	99	83	-1.6	0	-1	0.0
1970	NY-N	10	14	.417	32	27	9	3	2	184	166	8.1	18	38	1.9	111	5.4	3.57	117	.239	.277	10	12	103	84	-2.4	1	-2	1.2
1971	NY-N	2	5	.286	24	10	0	0	0	90	78	7.8	10	32	3.2	42	4.2	4.40	76	.227	.291	-9	-11	96	68	-1.5	-1	1	-1.1
1972	NY-N	11	8	.579	28	23	4	0	1	161	133	7.4	12	38	2.1	81	4.5	2.80	119	.225	.274	12	9	96	90	1.1	-2	-1	0.6
1973	NY-N	3	8	.273	23	12	0	0	1	80	109	12.3	9	31	3.5	38	4.3	5.40	68	.330	.384	-15	-15	100	111	-2.6	2	-1	-1.4
1974	SD-N	1	4	.200	15	5	1	0	0	42	48	10.3	7	13	2.8	16	3.4	5.57	63	.284	.324	-9	-10	97	86	-1.1	0	-1	-0.9
Total	7	37	53	.411	161	110	20	6	4	771	712	8.3	73	213	2.5	424	4.9	3.65	98	.245	.295	-4	-6	99	89	-9.1	-3	-5	-1.0
■ **DIXIE McARTHUR**	McArthur, Oland Alexander b: 2/1/1892, Vernon, Ala. d: 5/31/86, West Point, Miss. BR/TR, 6'1", 185 lbs. Deb: 7/10/14																												
1914	Pit-N	0	0	—	1	0	0	0	0	1	1	9.0	0	0	0.0	1	9.0	0.00	—	.250	.250	0	0	93	0	0.0	0	0	0.0
■ **WICKEY McAVOY**	McAvoy, James Eugene b: 10/22/1894, Rochester, N.Y. d: 7/5/73, Rochester, N.Y. BR/TR, 5'11", 172 lbs. Deb: 9/29/13																												
1918	Phi-A	0	0	—	1	0	0	0	0	1	1	9.0	1	0	0.0	0	0.0	9.00	33	.500	.500	-1	-1	108	148	0.0	0	0	0.0
■ **TOM McAVOY**	McAvoy, Thomas John b: 8/12/36, Brooklyn, N.Y. BL/TL, 6'3", 200 lbs. Deb: 9/27/59																												
1959	Was-A	0	0	—	1	0	0	0	0	3	1	3.0	0	2	6.0	0	0.0	0.00	—	.125	.300	1	1	102	0	0.0	-0	0	0.1
■ **AL McBEAN**	McBean, Alvin O'Neal b: 5/15/38, Charlotte Amalie, V.I. BR/TR, 5'11.5", 165 lbs. Deb: 7/02/61																												
1961	Pit-N	3	2	.600	27	2	0	0	0	74	72	8.8	4	42	5.1	49	6.0	3.77	106	.263	.358	2	2	99	116	0.6	1	2	0.5
1962	Pit-N	15	10	.600	33	29	6	2	0	190	212	10.0	11	65	3.1	119	5.6	3.69	108	.285	.345	5	6	101	114	0.8	2	0	0.8
1963	Pit-N	13	3	.813	55	7	2	1	11	122	100	7.4	5	39	2.9	74	5.5	2.58	126	.222	.283	10	9	99	93	5.4	2	2	1.3
1964	Pit-N	8	3	.727	58	0	0	0	22	90	76	7.6	4	17	1.7	41	4.1	1.90	187	.234	.273	**16**	**17**	101	134	2.6	-1	4	2.1
1965	Pit-N	6	6	.500	62	1	0	0	18	114	111	8.8	5	42	3.3	54	4.3	2.29	152	.260	.323	16	15	98	158	-0.5	1	1	1.9
1966	Pit-N	4	3	.571	47	0	0	0	3	87	95	9.8	9	24	2.5	54	5.6	3.21	111	.280	.328	4	3	99	131	0.0	-1	1	0.4
1967	Pit-N	7	4	.636	51	8	5	0	4	131	118	8.1	6	43	3.0	54	3.7	2.54	133	.248	.306	12	12	100	124	1.6	2	0	1.6
1968	Pit-N	9	12	.429	36	28	9	2	0	198	204	9.3	10	63	2.9	100	4.5	3.59	83	.269	.324	-13	-13	100	102	-1.5	2	4	-0.7
1969	SD-N	0	1	.000	1	1	0	0	0	7	10	12.9	1	2	2.6	1	1.3	5.14	70	.345	.387	-1	-1	100	124	-0.4	0	0	0.0
	LA-N	2	6	.250	31	0	0	0	4	48	46	8.6	6	21	3.9	26	4.9	3.94	89	.258	.332	-2	-2	97	111	-2.0	-0	-1	-0.3
	Yr	2	7	.222	32	1	0	0	4	55	56	9.2	7	23	3.8	27	4.4	4.09	86	.271	.339	-3	-4	98	111	-2.4	0	-1	-0.3
1970	LA-N	0	0	—	1	0	0	0	0	1	1	9.0	0	0	0.0	0	0.0	0.00	—	.333	.333	0	0	89	0	0.0	0	0	0.0
	Pit-N	0	0	—	7	0	0	0	1	10	13	11.7	2	7	6.3	3	2.7	8.10	48	.317	.417	-4	-5	96	89	0.0	-0	0	-0.4
	Yr	0	0	—	8	0	0	0	1	11	14	11.5	2	7	5.7	3	2.5	7.36	53	.318	.412	-4	-4	95	89	0.0	0	0	-0.4
Total	10	67	50	.573	409	76	22	5	63	1072	1058	8.9	63	365	3.1	575	4.8	3.13	112	.262	.322	45	43	100	118	6.6	9	13	7.2
■ **PRYOR McBEE**	McBee, Pryor Edward "Lefty" b: 6/20/01, Blanco, Okla. d: 4/19/63, Roseville, Cal. BR/TL, 6'1", 190 lbs. Deb: 5/22/26																												
1926	Chi-A	0	0	—	1	0	0	0	0	1	1	9.0	0	3	27.0	1	9.0	9.00	40	.250	.500	-1	-1	90	110	0.0	0	0	0.0
■ **DICK McBRIDE**	McBride, James Dickson b: 1845, Philadelphia, Pa. d: 10/10/16, Philadelphia, Pa. TR, 5'9", 150 lbs. Deb: 5/20/1871 M																												
1871	Ath-n	20	5	.800	25																								
1872	Ath-n	30	14	.682	46																								
1873	Ath-n	25	21	.543	46																								
1874	Ath-n	33	22	.600	55																								
1875	Ath-n	44	14	.759	60																								
1876	Bos-N	0	4	.000	4	4	3	0	0	33	53	14.5	1	5	1.4	2	0.5	2.73	80	.366	.387	-2	-2	94	183	-1.9	-1	0	-0.2
Total	5 n	152	76	.667	232																								
■ **KEN McBRIDE**	McBride, Kenneth Faye b: 8/12/35, Huntsville, Ala. BR/TR, 6'1", 190 lbs. Deb: 8/04/59 C																												
1959	Chi-A	0	1	.000	11	2	0	0	1	23	20	7.8	1	17	6.7	12	4.7	3.13	117	.230	.352	2	1	95	119	-0.4	-0	1	0.2
1960	Chi-A	0	1	.000	5	0	0	0	0	5	6	10.8	0	3	5.4	4	7.2	3.60	106	.333	.417	0	0	99	175	-0.4	0	0	0.0
1961	LA-A	12	15	.444	38	36	11	1	1	242	229	8.5	28	102	3.8	180	6.7	3.64	124	.252	.326	10	23	112	112	0.3	-6	4	2.4
1962	LA-A	11	5	.688	24	23	6	4	0	149	136	8.2	9	70	4.2	83	5.0	3.50	115	.249	.336	8	9	102	110	2.9	-0	5	1.4
1963	LA-A	13	12	.520	36	36	11	2	0	251	198	7.1	22	82	2.9	147	5.3	3.26	103	.218	.288	10	3	92	88	2.2	2	3	0.7
1964	LA-A	4	13	.235	29	21	0	0	1	116	104	8.1	14	75	5.8	66	5.1	5.28	61	.239	.366	-21	-27	89	88	-4.7	3	3	-2.0
1965	Cal-A	0	3	.000	8	4	0	0	0	22	24	9.8	1	14	5.7	11	4.5	6.14	55	.270	.377	-7	-7	98	76	-1.4	-0	-0	-0.6
Total	7	40	50	.444	151	122	28	7	3	808	717	8.0	75	363	4.0	503	5.6	3.79	101	.240	.326	2	2	100	100	-1.5	-1	15	2.1
■ **PETE McBRIDE**	McBride, Peter William b: 7/9/1875, Adams, Mass. d: 7/3/44, N.Adams, Mass. 5'10", 170 lbs. Deb: 9/20/1898																												
1898	Cle-N	0	1	.000	1	1	1	0	0	7	9	11.6	0	4	5.1	6	7.7	6.43	53	.335	.421	-2	-2	95	80	-0.4	1	0	0.0
1899	StL-N	2	4	.333	11	6	4	0	0	64	65	9.1	4	40	5.6	26	3.7	4.08	101	.286	.393	-2	0	107	108	-1.1	0	0	0.1
Total	2	2	5	.286	12	7	5	0	0	71	74	9.4	4	44	5.6	32	4.1	4.31	94	.292	.396	-4	-2	106	105	-1.5	1	0	0.1
■ **RALPH McCABE**	McCabe, Ralph Herbert "Mack" b: 10/21/18, Napanee, Ont., Can. d: 5/3/74, Windsor, Ont., Can. BR/TR, 6'4", 195 lbs. Deb: 9/18/46																												
1946	Cle-A	0	1	.000	1	1	0	0	0	4	5	11.3	3	2	4.5	3	6.8	11.25	28	.313	.421	-3	-4	90	100	-0.4	-0	0	-0.2
■ **DICK McCABE**	McCabe, Richard James b: 2/21/1896, Mamaroneck, N.Y. d: 4/11/50, Buffalo, N.Y. BR/TR, 5'10.5", 159 lbs. Deb: 5/30/18																												
1918	Bos-A	0	1	.000	3	1	0	0	0	10	13	11.7	0	2	1.8	3	2.7	2.70	95	.351	.375	0	-0	93	174	-0.4	-0	0	0.0
1922	Chi-A	1	0	1.000	3	0	0	0	0	3	4	12.0	0	0	0.0	1	3.0	6.00	68	.308	.308	-1	-1	101	53	0.5	0	-0	0.0
Total	2	1	1	.500	6	1	0	0	0	13	17	11.8	0	2	1.4	4	2.8	3.46	84	.340	.358	-1	-1	95	146	0.1	-0	0	0.0
■ **TIM McCABE**	McCabe, Timothy J. b: 10/19/1894, Ironton, Mo. d: 4/12/77, Ironton, Mo. BR/TR, 6', 190 lbs. Deb: 8/16/15																												
1915	StL-A	3	1	.750	7	4	4	1	0	42	25	5.4	1	9	1.9	17	3.6	1.29	227	.177	.232	8	8	99	72	1.2	-1	-1	0.7
1916	StL-A	2	0	1.000	13	0	0	0	0	26	29	10.0	0	7	2.4	7	2.4	3.12	86	.282	.339	-1	-1	94	110	1.0	-0	1	0.0
1917	StL-A	0	0	—	1	0	0	0	0	2	4	18.0	1	4	18.0	2	9.0	27.00	10	.400	.571	-5	-5	98	59	0.0	0	0	-0.3
1918	StL-A	0	0	—	1	0	0	0	0	1	2	18.0	0	1	9.0	0	0.0	18.00	15	.333	.375	-2	-2	100	39	0.0	0	0	-0.1
Total	4	5	1	.833	22	4	4	1	0	71	60	7.6	2	21	2.7	26	3.3	2.92	96	.231	.295	-0	-1	97	85	2.2	-1	1	0.3
■ **HARRY McCAFFERY**	McCaffery, Harry Charles b: 11/25/1858, St.Louis, Mo. d: 4/19/28, St.Louis, Mo. BR/TR, 5'10.5", 185 lbs. Deb: 6/15/1882																												
1885	Cin-a	1	0	1.000	1	1	1	0	0	9	13	13.0	1	2	2.0	2	2.0	6.00	56	.350	.384	-3	-3	103	103	0.5	-1	0	-0.2
■ **BILL McCAHAN**	McCahan, William Glenn b: 6/7/21, Philadelphia, Pa. d: 7/3/86, Fort Worth, Tex. BR/TR, 5'11", 200 lbs. Deb: 9/15/46																												
1946	Phi-A	1	1	.500	4	2	2	1	0	18	16	8.0	0	9	4.5	6	3.0	1.00	376	.246	.325	5	6	107	314	0.3	1	0	0.7
1947	Phi-A	10	5	.667	29	19	10	1	0	165	160	8.7	7	62	3.4	47	2.6	3.33	111	.252	.316	7	7	100	97	2.6	-1	1	0.8
1948	Phi-A	4	7	.364	17	15	5	0	0	87	98	10.1	8	65	6.7	20	2.1	5.69	76	.284	.391	-14	-13	102	100	-1.8	1	-1	-1.1
1949	Phi-A	1	1	.500	7	4	0	0	0	21	23	9.9	0	9	3.9	3	1.3	2.57	161	.291	.352	4	4	99	163	0.0	-0	-0	0.3
Total	4	16	14	.533	57	40	17	2	0	291	297	9.2	15	145	4.5	76	2.4	3.84	102	.264	.343	2	3	101	116	1.1	1	-0	0.7
■ **WINDY McCALL**	McCall, John William b: 7/18/25, San Francisco, Cal BL/TL, 6', 180 lbs. Deb: 4/25/48																												
1948	Bos-A	0	1	.000	1	1	0	0	0	1	6	54.0	1	1	9.0	0	0.0	27.00	15	.600	.636	-3	-3	97	128	-0.4	0	0	-0.1
1949	Bos-A	0	0	—	5	0	0	0	0	9	13	13.0	2	10	10.0	8	8.0	12.00	36	.333	.469	-8	-8	103	75	0.0	1	-0	-0.6

YEAR	TM/L	W	L	PCT	G	GS	CG	SHO	SV	IP	H	H/G	HR	BB	BB/G	SO	SO/G	ERA	/A	OAVG	OOBP	PR	/A	PF	CPI	WAT	PB	PD	TPI
1950	Pit-N	0	0	—	2	0	0	0	0	7	12	15.4	2	4	5.1	5	6.4	9.00	49	.387	.457	-4	-4	106	109	0.0	0	0	-0.2
1954	NY-N	2	5	.286	33	4	0	0	2	61	50	7.4	5	29	4.3	38	5.6	3.25	128	.219	.311	6	6	102	92	-1.9	-1	-1	0.4
1955	NY-N	6	5	.545	42	6	4	0	3	95	86	8.1	8	37	3.5	50	4.7	3.69	107	.244	.322	4	3	98	96	0.3	-1	1	0.3
1956	NY-N	3	4	.429	46	4	0	0	7	77	74	8.6	7	20	2.3	41	4.8	3.62	103	.252	.296	1	1	99	88	0.0	-0	-1	0.0
1957	NY-N	0	0	—	5	0	0	0	0	3	8	24.0	1	2	6.0	2	6.0	15.00	27	.533	.579	-4	-4	103	112	0.0	0	0	-0.3
Total 7		11	15	.423	134	15	4	0	12	253	249	8.9	26	103	3.7	144	5.1	4.23	94	.257	.330	-7	-8	100	93	-2.0	-1	-2	-0.5
■ **LARRY McCALL**	McCall, Larry Stephen b: 9/8/52, Asheville, N.C. BL/TR, 6'2", 195 lbs. Deb: 9/10/77																												
1977	NY-A	0	1	.000	2	0	0	0	0	6	12	18.0	1	1	1.5	0	0.0	7.50	53	.375	.394	-2	-2	97	100	-0.4	0	-0	-0.1
1978	NY-A	1	1	.500	5	1	0	0	0	16	20	11.3	2	6	3.4	7	3.9	5.63	65	.323	.380	-3	-3	97	105	-0.1	0	0	-0.2
1979	Tex-A	1	0	1.000	2	1	0	0	0	8	7	7.9	0	3	3.4	3	3.4	2.25	187	.226	.286	2	2	99	94	0.5	0	0	0.2
Total 3		2	2	.500	9	2	0	0	0	30	39	11.7	3	10	3.0	10	3.0	5.10	76	.312	.360	-4	-4	98	101	0.0	0	0	-0.1
■ **DUTCH McCALL**	McCall, Robert Leonard b: 12/27/20, Columbia, Tenn. BL/TL, 6'1", 184 lbs. Deb: 4/27/48																												
1948	Chi-N	4	13	.235	30	20	5	0	0	151	158	9.4	14	85	5.1	89	5.3	4.83	78	.268	.357	-15	-18	95	97	-3.8	1	1	-1.5
■ **GENE McCANN**	McCann, Henry Eugene "Mike" b: 6/13/1876, Baltimore, Md. d: 4/26/43, New York, N.Y. TR, 5'10", Deb: 4/19/01																												
1901	Bro-N	2	3	.400	6	5	3	0	0	34	34	9.0	1	16	4.2	9	2.4	3.44	99	.291	.395	-0	-0	103	118	-0.7	-1	0	0.0
1902	Bro-N	1	2	.333	3	3	3	0	0	30	32	9.6	0	12	3.6	9	2.7	2.40	108	.296	.367	1	1	94	143	-0.5	-1	1	0.1
Total 2		3	5	.375	9	8	6	0	0	64	66	9.3	1	28	3.9	18	2.5	2.95	102	.294	.382	1	1	99	130	-1.2	-2	1	0.1
■ **ARCH McCARTHY**	McCarthy, Archibald J. b: Ypsilanti, Mich. Deb: 8/14/02																												
1902	Det-A	2	7	.222	10	8	8	0	0	72	90	11.3	2	31	3.9	10	1.3	6.13	59	.332	.401	-20	-20	101	79	-1.9	-3	-2	-1.8
■ **JOHNNY McCARTHY**	McCarthy, John Joseph b: 1/7/10, Chicago, Ill. d: 9/13/73, Mundelein, Ill. BL/TL, 6'1.5", 185 lbs. Deb: 9/02/34																												
1939	NY-N	0	0	—	1	0	0	0	0	5	8	14.4	1	2	3.6	0	0.0	7.20	54	.364	.417	-2	-2	99	109	0.0	0	0	-0.1
■ **TOMMY McCARTHY**	McCarthy, Thomas Francis Michael b: 7/24/1863, Boston, Mass. d: 8/5/22, Boston, Mass. BR/TR, 5'7", 170 lbs. Deb: 7/10/1884 MH																												
1884	Bos-U	0	7	.000	7	6	5	0	0	56	73	11.7	2	14	2.3	18	2.9	4.82	61	.320	.360	-11	-12	98	101	-3.4	-0	0	-0.9
1886	Phi-N	0	0	—	1	0	0	0	0	1	0	0.0	0	1	9.0	1	9.0	0.00	—	.000	.273	0	0	96	0	0.0	0	0	0.0
1888	StL-a	0	0	—	2	0	0	0	0	4	3	6.8	1	2	4.5	1	2.3	4.50	72	.220	.320	-1	-1	106	98	0.0	0	0	0.0
1889	StL-a	0	0	—	1	0	0	0	0	5	4	7.2	0	6	10.8	1	1.8	7.20	58	.233	.432	-2	-2	109	63	0.0	0	0	0.0
1891	StL-a	0	0	—	1	0	0	0	0	1	2	18.0	0	0	0.0	0	0.0	9.00	46	.431	.431	-1	-1	112	78	0.0	0	0	0.0
1894	Bos-N	0	0	—	1	0	0	0	0	2	1	4.5	0	3	13.5	0	0.0	4.50	132	.164	.439	0	0	111	86	0.0	0	0	0.0
Total 6		0	7	.000	13	6	5	0	0	69	83	10.8	3	26	3.4	21	2.7	4.96	63	.305	.366	-14	-14	99	96	-3.4	1	0	-0.9
■ **TOM McCARTHY**	McCarthy, Thomas Michael b: 6/18/61, Lundstahl, W.Ger. BR/TR, 6', 180 lbs. Deb: 7/05/85 H																												
1985	Bos-A	0	0	—	3	0	0	0	0	5	7	12.6	1	4	7.2	2	3.6	10.80	39	.350	.440	-4	-4	102	79	0.0	0	0	-0.2
1988	Chi-A	2	0	1.000	6	0	0	0	1	13	9	6.2	0	2	1.4	5	3.5	1.38	283	.191	.255	4	4	99	97	1.0	0	0	0.4
Total 2		2	0	1.000	9	0	0	0	1	18	16	8.0	1	6	3.0	7	3.5	4.00	100	.239	.316	0	-0	99	92	1.0	0	0	0.2
■ **TOM McCARTHY**	McCarthy, Thomas Patrick b: 5/22/1884, Ft.Wayne, Ind. d: 3/28/33, Mishawaka, Ind. TR, 5'7", 170 lbs. Deb: 5/10/08																												
1908	Cin-N	0	1	.000	1	1	0	0	0	4	6	13.5	0	3	6.8	3	6.8	9.00	27	.379	.478	-3	-3	104	74	-0.4	-0	0	-0.2
	Pit-N	0	0	—	2	1	0	0	0	6	3	4.5	0	6	9.0	1	1.5	0.00	—	.169	.379	2	1	92	0	0.0	-0	1	0.3
	Bos-N	7	3	.700	14	11	7	2	0	94	77	7.4	0	28	2.7	27	2.6	1.63	152	.251	.316	7	9	106	129	2.5	-0	0	1.1
	Yr	7	4	.636	17	13	7	2	0	104	86	7.4	0	37	3.2	31	2.7	1.82	135	.253	.328	6	7	105	129	2.1	-1	1	1.2
1909	Bos-N	0	5	.000	8	7	3	0	0	46	47	9.2	3	28	5.5	11	2.2	3.52	75	.272	.379	-5	-4	102	128	-2.4	-0	0	-0.4
Total 2		7	9	.438	25	20	10	2	0	150	133	8.0	3	65	3.9	42	2.5	2.34	108	.259	.346	1	3	104	122	-0.3	-1	1	0.8
■ **BILL McCARTHY**	McCarthy, William Thomas b: 4/11/1882, Ashland, Mass. d: 5/29/39, Boston, Mass. BR/TR, 5'11", 180 lbs. Deb: 4/21/06																												
1906	Bos-N	0	0	—	1	0	0	0	0	2	2	9.0	0	3	13.5	0	0.0	9.00	31	.288	.503	-1	-1	106	70	0.0	-0	0	-0.1
■ **JOHN McCARTY**	McCarty, John A. b: St.Louis, Mo. TR, Deb: 4/18/1889																												
1889	KC-a	8	6	.571	15	14	13	0	0	120	147	11.0	3	61	4.6	36	2.7	3.90	107	.317	.397	-1	4	109	126	2.1	-2	0	0.2
■ **KIRK McCASKILL**	McCaskill, Kirk Edward b: 4/9/61, Kapuskasing, Ont.Can BR/TR, 6'1", 195 lbs. Deb: 5/01/85																												
1985	Cal-A	12	12	.500	30	29	6	1	0	190	189	9.0	23	64	3.0	102	4.8	4.69	89	.258	.318	-11	-11	101	87	-1.3	0	-0	-1.0
1986	Cal-A	17	10	.630	34	33	10	2	0	246	207	7.6	19	92	3.4	202	7.4	3.37	119	.229	.300	22	17	95	91	2.2	0	0	1.7
1987	Cal-A	4	6	.400	14	13	1	1	0	75	84	10.1	14	34	4.1	56	6.7	5.64	79	.286	.359	-10	-10	100	100	-0.6	0	1	-0.8
1988	Cal-A	8	6	.571	23	23	4	2	0	146	155	9.6	9	61	3.8	98	6.0	4.32	87	.274	.342	-6	-9	95	98	1.5	0	0	-0.8
Total 4		41	34	.547	101	98	21	6	0	657	635	8.7	65	251	3.4	458	6.3	4.22	96	.254	.322	-4	-13	97	92	1.8	0	1	-0.9
■ **STEVE McCATTY**	McCatty, Steven Earl b: 3/20/54, Detroit, Mich. BR/TR, 6'3", 195 lbs. Deb: 9/17/77																												
1977	Oak-A	0	0	—	4	2	0	0	0	14	16	10.3	1	7	4.5	9	5.8	5.14	76	.276	.364	-2	-2	97	88	0.0	0	-0	-0.1
1978	Oak-A	0	0	—	9	0	0	0	0	20	26	11.7	1	9	4.0	10	4.5	4.50	86	.310	.361	-2	-1	103	111	0.0	0	-0	-0.1
1979	Oak-A	11	12	.478	31	23	8	0	0	186	207	10.0	17	80	3.9	87	4.2	4.21	92	.284	.353	0	-7	91	114	2.8	0	-2	-0.8
1980	Oak-A	14	14	.500	33	31	11	1	0	222	202	8.2	27	99	4.0	114	4.6	3.85	99	.240	.322	5	-1	94	98	-0.3	0	-1	-0.2
1981	Oak-A	**14**	7	.667	22	22	16	**4**	0	186	140	**6.8**	12	61	3.0	91	4.4	**2.32**	150	**.211**	.274	**28**	**24**	95	103	2.4	0	-1	**2.6**
1982	Oak-A	6	3	.667	21	20	2	0	0	129	124	8.7	16	70	4.9	66	4.6	3.98	99	.255	.347	2	-1	96	115	2.0	0	-1	0.0
1983	Oak-A	6	9	.400	38	24	3	2	5	167	156	8.4	16	82	4.4	65	3.5	3.99	98	.247	.330	2	-1	96	99	-0.9	0	-2	-0.3
1984	Oak-A	8	14	.364	33	30	4	0	0	180	206	10.3	24	71	3.6	63	3.2	4.75	77	.289	.351	-15	-21	92	106	-2.8	0	-2	-2.2
1985	Oak-A	4	4	.500	30	9	1	0	0	86	95	9.9	10	41	4.3	36	3.8	5.55	70	.286	.366	-13	-16	93	95	0.2	0	0	-1.4
Total 9		63	63	.500	221	161	45	7	5	1190	1172	8.9	124	520	3.9	541	4.1	3.99	95	.258	.333	4	-27	94	104	3.4	0	-8	-2.5
■ **AL McCAULEY**	McCauley, Allen A. b: 3/4/1863, Indianapolis, Ind. d: 8/24/17, Wayne Twnshp., Ind BL/TL, 6', 180 lbs. Deb: 6/21/1884																												
1884	Ind-a	2	7	.222	10	9	9	0	0	76	87	10.3	2	25	3.0	34	4.0	5.09	64	.296	.351	-16	-16	100	89	-0.8	1	0	-1.0
■ **JOE McCLAIN**	McClain, Joseph Fred b: 5/5/33, Johnson City, Tenn. BR/TR, 6', 183 lbs. Deb: 4/14/61																												
1961	Was-A	8	18	.308	33	29	7	2	1	212	221	9.4	22	48	2.0	76	3.2	3.86	101	.270	.306	4	1	97	100	-2.7	2	-3	0.0
1962	Was-A	0	4	.000	10	4	0	0	0	24	33	12.4	8	11	4.1	6	2.3	9.38	43	.327	.393	-14	-14	102	86	-1.9	-0	0	-1.2
Total 2		8	22	.267	43	33	7	2	1	236	254	9.7	30	59	2.3	82	3.1	4.42	89	.276	.316	-11	-13	98	98	-4.6	1	-3	-1.2
■ **JIM McCLOSKEY**	McCloskey, James Ellwood "Irish" b: 5/26/10, Danville, Pa. d: 8/18/71, Jersey City, N.J. BL/TL, 5'9.5", 180 lbs. Deb: 4/21/36																												
1936	Bos-N	0	0	—	4	1	0	0	0	8	14	15.8	1	3	3.4	2	2.3	11.25	34	.378	.429	-6	-7	96	72	0.0	-0	0	-0.5
■ **JOHN McCLOSKEY**	McCloskey, James John b: 8/20/1882, Wyoming, Pa. d: 3/1/19, Lewisburg, Pa. Deb: 5/03/06																												
1906	Phi-N	3	2	.600	9	4	3	0	0	41	46	10.1	2	9	2.0	6	1.3	2.85	86	.314	.358	-1	-2	93	133	0.7	0	-1	-0.2
1907	Phi-N	0	0	—	3	0	0	0	0	9	15	15.0	0	6	6.0	3	3.0	7.00	36	.415	.510	-5	-4	103	107	0.0	-0	0	-0.4
Total 2		3	2	.600	12	4	3	0	0	50	61	11.0	2	15	2.7	9	1.6	3.60	68	.334	.391	-6	-6	95	128	0.7	0	-1	-0.6
■ **BOB McCLURE**	McClure, Robert Craig b: 4/29/52, Oakland, Cal. BR/TL, 5'11", 170 lbs. Deb: 8/13/75																												
1975	KC-A	1	0	1.000	12	0	0	0	1	15	4	2.4	0	14	8.4	15	9.0	0.00	—	.077	.273	6	6	101	0	0.5	0	-0	0.6
1976	KC-A	0	0	—	8	0	0	0	0	4	3	6.8	0	8	18.0	3	6.8	9.00	39	.214	.500	-2	-2	99	74	0.0	0	0	-0.2
1977	Mil-A	2	1	.667	68	0	0	0	6	71	64	8.1	2	34	4.3	57	7.2	2.54	155	.249	.328	12	11	97	136	0.7	0	2	1.3
1978	Mil-A	2	6	.250	44	0	0	0	9	65	53	7.3	8	30	4.2	47	6.5	3.74	105	.223	.314	0	1	104	96	-2.2	0	-0	0.1
1979	Mil-A	5	2	.714	36	0	0	0	5	51	53	9.4	6	24	4.2	37	6.5	3.88	108	.269	.349	2	2	99	121	1.1	0	-0	0.1
1980	Mil-A	5	8	.385	52	5	2	1	10	91	83	8.2	6	37	3.7	47	4.6	3.07	123	.241	.313	10	7	93	105	-1.8	0	-1	0.6
1981	Mil-A	0	0	—	4	0	0	0	0	8	7	7.9	1	4	4.5	6	6.8	3.38	103	.233	.324	0	0	95	112	0.0	0	-0	0.0
1982	Mil-A	12	7	.632	34	26	5	0	0	173	160	8.3	21	74	3.8	99	5.2	4.21	89	.248	.324	-3	-9	92	95	1.2	0	-1	-0.8
1983	Mil-A	9	9	.500	24	23	4	0	0	142	152	9.6	11	68	4.3	68	4.3	4.50	82	.277	.360	-7	-12	91	104	-0.6	0	-1	-1.2
1984	Mil-A	4	8	.333	39	18	1	0	1	140	154	9.9	9	52	3.3	68	4.4	4.37	85	.282	.338	-6	-10	93	97	-1.2	0	-0	-1.0
1985	Mil-A	4	1	.800	38	1	0	0	3	86	91	9.5	10	30	3.1	57	6.0	4.29	102	.274	.335	-1	1	106	106	1.6	0	0	0.1
1986	Mil-A	2	1	.667	13	0	0	0	0	16	18	10.1	2	10	5.6	11	6.2	3.94	110	.286	.373	0	1	103	140	0.5	0	-0	0.0

YEAR	TM/L	W	L	PCT	G	GS	CG	SHO	SV	IP	H	H/G	HR	BB	BB/G	SO	SO/G	ERA	/A	OAVG	OOBP	PR	/A	PF	CPI	WAT	PB	PD	TPI
	Mon-N	2	5	.286	52	0	0	0	6	63	53	7.6	2	23	3.3	42	6.0	3.00	122	.232	.300	5	5	98	93	-1.4	0	0	0.5
1987	Mon-N	6	1	.857	52	0	0	0	5	52	47	8.1	8	20	3.5	33	5.7	3.46	125	.241	.302	4	5	106	113	2.4	-0	0	0.5
1988	Mon-N	1	3	.250	19	0	0	0	2	19	23	10.9	3	6	2.8	12	5.7	6.16	59	.307	.345	-6	-5	105	92	-0.9	-0	0	-0.5
	NY-N	1	0	1.000	14	0	0	0	1	11	12	9.8	1	2	1.6	7	5.7	4.09	74	.279	.326	-1	-1	88	101	0.5	0	-0	-0.1
	Yr	2	3	.400	33	0	0	0	3	30	35	10.5	4	8	2.4	19	5.7	5.40	63	.289	.331	-6	-7	99	101	-0.4	-0	0	-0.6
Total	14	56	52	.519	509	73	12	1	49	1007	977	8.7	90	436	3.9	609	5.4	3.88	100	.256	.331	15	-1	96	103	0.4	-0	-2	0.0

■ **HARRY McCLUSKEY** McCluskey, Harry Robert b: 3/29/1892, Clay Center, Ohio d: 6/7/62, Toledo, Ohio BL/TL, 5'11.5", 173 lbs. Deb: 7/29/15

YEAR	TM/L	W	L	PCT	G	GS	CG	SHO	SV	IP	H	H/G	HR	BB	BB/G	SO	SO/G	ERA	/A	OAVG	OOBP	PR	/A	PF	CPI	WAT	PB	PD	TPI
1915	Cin-N	0	0	—	3	0	0	0	0	5	4	7.2	0	0	0.0	2	3.6	5.40	53	.182	.174	-1	-1	104	11	0.0	-0	-0	-0.1

■ **ALEX McCOLL** McColl, Alexander Boyd "Red" b: 3/29/1894, Eagleville, Ohio BB/TR, 6'1", 178 lbs. Deb: 8/27/33

YEAR	TM/L	W	L	PCT	G	GS	CG	SHO	SV	IP	H	H/G	HR	BB	BB/G	SO	SO/G	ERA	/A	OAVG	OOBP	PR	/A	PF	CPI	WAT	PB	PD	TPI
1933	Was-A	1	0	1.000	4	1	1	0	0	17	13	6.9	0	7	3.7	5	2.6	2.65	151	.210	.290	3	3	93	85	0.5	1	0	0.3
1934	Was-A	3	4	.429	42	2	1	0	1	112	129	10.4	6	36	2.9	29	2.3	3.86	119	.291	.337	8	9	102	116	0.0	-2	2	0.9
Total	2	4	4	.500	46	3	2	0	1	129	142	9.9	6	43	3.0	34	2.4	3.70	122	.281	.332	11	12	101	112	0.5	-1	2	1.2

■ **RALPH McCONNAUGHEY** McConnaughey, Ralph James b: 8/5/1889, Pennsylvania d: 6/4/66, Detroit, Mich. BR/TR, 5'8.5", 166 lbs. Deb: 7/08/14

YEAR	TM/L	W	L	PCT	G	GS	CG	SHO	SV	IP	H	H/G	HR	BB	BB/G	SO	SO/G	ERA	/A	OAVG	OOBP	PR	/A	PF	CPI	WAT	PB	PD	TPI
1914	Ind-F	0	2	.000	7	2	1	0	0	26	23	8.0	3	16	5.5	7	2.4	4.85	71	.265	.379	-5	-4	108	87	-0.9	-0	0	-0.3

■ **GEORGE McCONNELL** McConnell, George Neely "Slats" b: 9/16/1877, Shelbyville, Tenn d: 5/10/64, Chattanooga, Tenn. BR/TR, 6'3", 190 lbs. Deb: 4/13/09

YEAR	TM/L	W	L	PCT	G	GS	CG	SHO	SV	IP	H	H/G	HR	BB	BB/G	SO	SO/G	ERA	/A	OAVG	OOBP	PR	/A	PF	CPI	WAT	PB	PD	TPI
1909	NY-A	0	1	.000	2	1	0	0	0	4	3	6.8	0	3	6.8	4	9.0	2.25	109	.231	.375	0	0	99	146	-0.4	0	1	0.0
1912	NY-A	8	12	.400	23	20	19	0	0	177	172	8.7	3	52	2.6	91	4.6	2.75	128	.269	.328	12	15	105	121	1.2	3	5	2.8
1913	NY-A	4	15	.211	35	20	8	0	3	180	162	8.1	2	60	3.0	72	3.6	3.20	95	.245	.314	-5	-3	104	81	-4.4	-1	4	0.1
1914	Chi-N	0	1	.000	1	1	0	0	0	7	3	3.9	0	3	3.9	3	3.9	1.29	214	.125	.222	1	1	99	12	-0.4	-0	0	0.1
1915	Chi-F	**25**	10	**.714**	44	35	23	4	1	303	262	7.8	8	89	2.6	151	4.5	2.20	131	.232	.292	28	23	95	110	**7.1**	6	7	4.0
1916	Chi-N	4	12	.250	28	20	8	1	0	171	137	7.2	8	35	1.8	82	4.3	2.58	119	.223	.260	1	9	117	80	-3.6	-2	2	1.1
Total	6	41	51	.446	133	97	58	5	4	842	739	7.9	21	242	2.6	403	4.3	2.60	119	.240	.298	37	47	104	99	-0.5	5	18	8.1

■ **BILLY McCOOL** McCool, William John b: 7/14/44, Batesville, Ind. BR/TL, 6'2", 195 lbs. Deb: 4/24/64

YEAR	TM/L	W	L	PCT	G	GS	CG	SHO	SV	IP	H	H/G	HR	BB	BB/G	SO	SO/G	ERA	/A	OAVG	OOBP	PR	/A	PF	CPI	WAT	PB	PD	TPI
1964	Cin-N	6	5	.545	40	3	0	0	7	89	66	6.7	3	29	2.9	87	8.8	2.43	148	.206	.268	11	12	102	85	-0.1	-2	-1	0.9
1965	Cin-N	9	10	.474	62	2	0	0	21	105	93	8.0	9	47	4.0	120	10.3	4.29	84	.237	.321	-9	-8	102	83	-1.4	-2	0	-0.9
1966	Cin-N	8	8	.500	57	0	0	0	18	105	76	6.5	5	41	3.5	104	8.9	2.49	166	.205	.283	13	19	114	94	0.4	-0	2	2.3
1967	Cin-N	3	7	.300	31	11	0	0	2	97	92	8.5	8	56	5.2	83	7.7	3.43	107	.246	.346	-1	2	109	120	-2.2	-1	-1	0.1
1968	Cin-N	3	4	.429	30	4	0	0	2	51	59	10.4	4	41	7.2	30	5.3	4.94	67	.294	.403	-11	-9	111	117	-0.5	-0	-1	-1.0
1969	SD-N	3	5	.375	54	0	0	0	7	59	59	9.0	2	42	6.4	35	5.3	4.27	84	.266	.388	-4	-4	100	112	0.3	-0	-0	-0.4
1970	StL-N	0	3	.000	18	0	0	0	1	22	20	8.2	0	16	6.5	12	4.9	6.14	70	.250	.364	-5	-4	106	66	-1.4	-0	0	-0.4
Total	7	32	42	.432	292	20	0	0	58	528	465	7.9	31	272	4.6	471	8.0	3.60	103	.237	.329	-6	7	106	98	-4.9	-6	-1	0.6

■ **JIM McCORMICK** McCormick, James b: 1856, Glasgow, Scotland d: 3/10/18, Paterson, N.J. BR/TR, 5'10.5", 195 lbs. Deb: 5/20/1878 M

YEAR	TM/L	W	L	PCT	G	GS	CG	SHO	SV	IP	H	H/G	HR	BB	BB/G	SO	SO/G	ERA	/A	OAVG	OOBP	PR	/A	PF	CPI	WAT	PB	PD	TPI
1878	Ind-N	5	8	.385	14	14	12	1	0	117	128	9.8	1	15	1.2	36	2.8	1.69	120	.288	.312	8	4	88	**148**	-0.2	-2	0	0.1
1879	Cle-N	20	40	.333	62	60	59	3	0	546	582	9.6	4	74	1.2	197	3.2	2.42	107	.278	.303	4	10	103	108	0.7	-2	4	1.1
1880	Cle-N	**45**	28	.616	**74**	74	**72**	7	0	**658**	585	8.0	2	75	1.0	260	3.6	1.85	125	.247	.270	39	**34**	97	98	**19.4**	2	3	**3.7**
1881	Cle-N	26	30	.464	59	58	**57**	2	0	526	484	**8.3**	5	84	1.4	178	3.0	2.45	109	**.256**	.288	19	13	96	83	4.7	5	-3	1.4
1882	Cle-N	**36**	30	.545	**68**	67	**65**	4	0	**596**	550	8.3	14	103	1.6	200	3.0	2.37	109	.252	.286	34	15	90	101	**9.0**	-2	-1	0.7
1883	Cle-N	28	12	**.700**	43	41	36	1	1	342	316	8.3	1	65	1.7	145	3.8	**1.84**	**177**	.253	.290	49	54	104	**121**	8.6	-2	7	5.6
1884	Cle-N	19	22	.463	42	41	39	3	0	359	357	8.9	17	75	1.9	182	4.6	2.86	112	.268	.307	5	14	108	103	6.3	2	0	1.7
	Cin-U	21	3	**.875**	24	24	24	**7**	0	210	151	6.5	3	14	0.6	161	6.9	**1.54**	**205**	.206	**.221**	34	38	105	86	8.3	-1	0	3.5
1885	Pro-N	1	3	.250	4	4	4	0	0	37	34	8.3	1	20	4.9	8	1.9	2.43	108	.255	.352	2	1	93	146	-0.9	0	0	0.1
	Chi-N	20	4	.833	24	24	24	3	0	215	187	7.8	8	40	1.7	88	3.7	2.43	122	.244	.282	9	13	106	99	3.6	1	0	1.4
	Yr	21	7	.750	28	28	28	3	0	252	221	7.9	9	60	2.1	96	3.4	2.43	120	.246	.293	11	14	104	99	2.7	0	0	1.5
1886	Chi-N	31	11	.738	42	42	38	2	0	348	341	8.8	18	100	2.6	172	4.4	2.82	129	.269	.323	19	31	110	120	1.4	2	1	3.5
1887	Pit-N	13	23	.361	36	36	36	0	0	322	377	10.5	12	84	2.3	77	2.2	4.30	90	.308	.352	-9	-15	96	98	-4.3	-0	5	-0.9
Total	10	265	214	.553	492	485	466	33	1	4276	4092	8.6	86	749	1.6	1704	3.6	2.43	118	.261	.295	213	208	100	103	56.6	2	17	21.9

■ **JERRY McCORMICK** McCormick, John b: Philadelphia, Pa. d: 9/19/05, Philadelphia, Pa. Deb: 5/01/1883

YEAR	TM/L	W	L	PCT	G	GS	CG	SHO	SV	IP	H	H/G	HR	BB	BB/G	SO	SO/G	ERA	/A	OAVG	OOBP	PR	/A	PF	CPI	WAT	PB	PD	TPI
1884	Phi-U	0	0	—	1	0	0	0	0	2	5	22.5	1	0	0.0	3	13.5	9.00	32	.475	.475	-1	-1	95	151	0.0	0	0	-0.1

■ **MIKE McCORMICK** McCormick, Michael Francis b: 9/29/38, Pasadena, Cal. BL/TL, 6'2", 195 lbs. Deb: 9/03/56

YEAR	TM/L	W	L	PCT	G	GS	CG	SHO	SV	IP	H	H/G	HR	BB	BB/G	SO	SO/G	ERA	/A	OAVG	OOBP	PR	/A	PF	CPI	WAT	PB	PD	TPI
1956	NY-N	0	1	.000	3	2	0	0	0	7	7	9.0	1	10	12.9	4	5.1	9.00	42	.269	.472	-4	-4	99	82	-0.4	-0	0	-0.3
1957	NY-N	3	1	.750	24	5	1	0	0	75	79	9.5	7	32	3.8	50	6.0	4.08	98	.280	.355	-2	-1	103	114	1.1	1	-1	0.0
1958	SF-N	11	8	.579	42	28	8	2	1	178	192	9.7	19	60	3.0	82	4.1	4.60	85	.276	.330	-13	-13	100	92	1.3	1	2	-0.9
1959	SF-N	12	16	.429	47	31	7	3	4	226	213	8.5	24	86	3.4	151	6.0	3.98	93	.248	.309	-1	-7	94	91	-3.3	-1	1	-0.8
1960	SF-N	15	12	.556	40	34	15	4	3	253	228	8.1	15	65	2.3	154	5.5	**2.70**	123	.241	.285	**30**	18	89	105	1.4	2	3	2.2
1961	SF-N	13	16	.448	40	35	13	3	0	250	235	8.5	33	75	2.7	163	5.9	3.20	121	.249	.302	23	19	96	115	-3.1	1	-2	1.8
1962	SF-N	5	5	.500	28	15	1	0	0	99	112	10.2	18	45	4.1	42	3.8	5.36	72	.286	.353	-16	-16	99	101	-0.9	0	-1	-1.5
1963	Bal-A	6	8	.429	25	21	2	0	0	136	132	8.7	18	66	4.4	75	5.0	4.30	79	.256	.335	-10	-14	93	102	-1.3	1	-0	-1.3
1964	Bal-A	0	2	.000	4	2	0	0	0	17	21	11.1	1	8	4.2	13	6.9	5.29	71	.288	.358	-3	-3	103	85	-0.9	-0	0	-0.2
1965	Was-A	8	8	.500	44	21	3	1	1	158	158	9.0	17	36	2.1	88	5.0	3.36	105	.260	.297	2	3	102	106	1.0	-1	-1	0.1
1966	Was-A	11	14	.440	41	32	8	3	0	216	193	8.0	23	51	2.1	101	4.2	3.46	96	.236	.278	-1	-4	96	88	-0.1	4	-1	-0.1
1967	SF-N	**22**	10	.688	40	35	14	5	0	262	220	7.6	25	81	2.8	150	5.2	2.85	117	.226	.285	15	14	99	102	**5.3**	-0	-2	1.4
1968	SF-N	12	14	.462	38	28	9	2	1	198	196	8.9	17	49	2.2	121	5.5	3.59	80	.254	.295	-13	-16	96	91	-2.2	2	-2	-1.8
1969	SF-N	11	9	.550	32	28	9	0	0	197	175	8.0	20	77	3.5	76	3.5	3.34	108	.237	.307	6	6	100	102	0.0	0	-1	0.5
1970	SF-N	3	4	.429	23	11	1	0	2	78	80	9.2	15	36	4.2	37	4.3	6.23	62	.262	.339	-19	-20	96	81	-0.6	0	1	-1.8
	NY-A	2	0	1.000	9	4	0	0	0	21	26	11.1	2	13	5.6	12	5.1	6.00	57	.295	.386	-5	-6	91	90	1.0	0	-0	-0.5
1971	KC-A	0	0	—	4	1	0	0	0	10	14	12.6	0	5	4.5	2	1.8	9.00	38	.350	.413	-6	-6	98	65	0.0	-0	1	-0.4
Total	16	134	128	.511	484	333	91	23	12	2381	2281	8.6	255	795	3.0	1321	5.0	3.73	95	.251	.308	-17	-50	97	99	-1.7	9	-4	-3.6

■ **HARRY McCORMICK** McCormick, Patrick Henry b: 10/25/1855, Syracuse, N.Y. d: 8/8/1889, Syracuse, N.Y. TR, 5'9", 155 lbs. Deb: 5/01/1879

YEAR	TM/L	W	L	PCT	G	GS	CG	SHO	SV	IP	H	H/G	HR	BB	BB/G	SO	SO/G	ERA	/A	OAVG	OOBP	PR	/A	PF	CPI	WAT	PB	PD	TPI
1879	Syr-N	18	33	.353	54	54	49	5	0	457	517	10.2	3	31	0.6	96	1.9	2.99	79	.291	.303	-25	-32	95	92	4.6	-0	-6	-3.5
1881	Wor-N	1	8	.111	9	9	9	1	0	78	89	10.3	1	15	1.7	7	0.8	3.58	83	.299	.333	-7	-5	107	91	-3.2	-2	0	-0.6
1882	Cin-a	14	11	.560	25	25	24	3	0	220	177	7.2	3	42	1.7	33	1.4	1.51	177	.225	.265	29	29	100	121	-3.0	-5	0	2.2
1883	Cin-a	8	6	.571	15	15	14	1	0	129	139	9.7	1	27	1.9	21	1.5	2.86	113	.281	.318	6	5	98	123	-0.6	4	0	0.8
Total	4	41	58	.414	103	103	96	10	0	884	922	9.4	8	115	1.2	157	1.6	2.66	99	.275	.299	3	-3	98	103	-2.2	-4	-6	-1.1

■ **BILL McCORRY** McCorry, William Charles b: 7/9/1887, Saranac Lake, N.Y. d: 3/22/73, Augusta, Ga. BL/TR, 5'9", 157 lbs. Deb: 9/17/09

YEAR	TM/L	W	L	PCT	G	GS	CG	SHO	SV	IP	H	H/G	HR	BB	BB/G	SO	SO/G	ERA	/A	OAVG	OOBP	PR	/A	PF	CPI	WAT	PB	PD	TPI
1909	StL-A	0	2	.000	2	2	2	0	0	15	29	17.4	1	6	3.6	10	6.0	9.00	26	.397	.443	-11	-11	95	86	-0.9	-0	-1	-0.9

■ **LES McCRABB** McCrabb, Lester William "Buster" b: 11/4/14, Wakefield, Pa. BR/TR, 5'11", 175 lbs. Deb: 9/07/39 C

YEAR	TM/L	W	L	PCT	G	GS	CG	SHO	SV	IP	H	H/G	HR	BB	BB/G	SO	SO/G	ERA	/A	OAVG	OOBP	PR	/A	PF	CPI	WAT	PB	PD	TPI
1939	Phi-A	1	2	.333	5	4	2	0	0	36	42	10.5	4	10	2.5	11	2.8	4.00	118	.290	.331	2	3	102	120	0.0	-2	0	0.1
1940	Phi-A	0	0	—	4	0	0	0	0	12	19	14.3	2	2	1.5	4	3.0	6.75	64	.365	.379	-3	-3	99	110	0.0	0	0	-0.2
1941	Phi-A	9	13	.409	26	23	11	1	2	157	188	10.8	16	49	2.8	40	2.3	5.50	78	.293	.339	-24	-21	103	88	-0.1	-2	-2	-2.2
1942	Phi-A	0	0	—	1	0	0	0	0	4	14	31.5	2	2	4.5	0	0.0	31.50	12	.560	.586	-12	-12	101	66	0.0	-0	0	-0.7
1950	Phi-A	0	0	—	2	0	0	0	0	1	7	63.0	0	0	0.0	2	18.0	36.00	12	.636	.636	-3	-4	93	80	0.0	0	0	-0.2
Total	5	10	15	.400	38	27	13	1	2	210	270	11.6	24	63	2.7	57	2.4	5.96	73	.309	.351	-40	-38	103	94	-0.1	-4	-1	-3.2

■ **ED McCREERY** McCreery, Esley Porterfield "Big Ed" b: 12/24/1889, Cripple Creek, Colo. d: 10/19/60, Sacramento, Cal. BR/TR, 6', 190 lbs. Deb: 8/16/14

YEAR	TM/L	W	L	PCT	G	GS	CG	SHO	SV	IP	H	H/G	HR	BB	BB/G	SO	SO/G	ERA	/A	OAVG	OOBP	PR	/A	PF	CPI	WAT	PB	PD	TPI
1914	Det-A	1	0	1.000	3	1	0	0	0	4	6	13.5	0	3	6.8	4	9.0	11.25	25	.316	.409	-4	-4	102	50	0.5	-0	0	-0.3

■ **TOM McCREERY** McCreery, Thomas Livingston b: 10/19/1874, Beaver, Pa. d: 7/3/41, Beaver, Pa. BB, 5'11", 180 lbs. Deb: 6/08/1895

YEAR	TM/L	W	L	PCT	G	GS	CG	SHO	SV	IP	H	H/G	HR	BB	BB/G	SO	SO/G	ERA	/A	OAVG	OOBP	PR	/A	PF	CPI	WAT	PB	PD	TPI
1895	Lou-N	3	1	.750	8	4	3	1	1	49	51	9.4	0	38	7.0	14	2.6	5.51	86	.288	.414	-4	-4	99	84	1.3	1	0	-0.2
1896	Lou-N	0	1	.000	1	1	0	0	0	1	4	36.0	1	5	45.0	0	0.0	36.00	12	.611	.779	-4	-4	102	107	-0.4	0	0	-0.2
1900	Pit-N	0	0	—	1	0	0	0	0	3	3	9.0	2	1	3.0	0	0.0	12.00	31	.283	.345	-3	-3	101	68	0.0	0	0	-0.1

YEAR	TM/L	W	L	PCT	G	GS	CG	SHO	SV	IP	H	H/G	HR	BB	BB/G	SO	SO/G	ERA	/A	OAVG	OOBP	PR	/A	PF	CPI	WAT	PB	PD	TPI
Total	3	3	2	.600	10	5	3	1	1	53	58	9.8	3	44	7.5	14	2.4	6.45	72	.298	.428	-10	-11	99	83	0.9	2	0	-0.5
■ LANCE McCULLERS	McCullers, Lance Graye b: 3/8/64, Tampa, Fla. BR/TR, 6'1", 185 lbs. Deb: 8/12/85																												
1985	SD-N	0	2	.000	21	0	0	0	5	35	23	5.9	3	16	4.1	27	6.9	2.31	158	.195	.282	5	5	101	117	-0.9	-0	0	0.5
1986	SD-N	10	10	.500	70	7	0	0	5	136	103	6.8	12	58	3.8	92	6.1	2.78	128	.216	.300	14	12	96	111	0.9	1	-1	1.2
1987	SD-N	8	10	.444	78	0	0	0	16	123	115	8.4	11	59	4.3	126	9.2	3.73	107	.244	.326	5	4	98	101	0.7	-1	0	0.3
1988	SD-N	3	6	.333	60	0	0	0	10	98	70	6.4	8	55	5.1	81	7.4	2.48	135	.205	.307	11	10	97	126	-1.6	1	0	1.1
Total	4	21	28	.429	229	7	0	0	36	392	311	7.1	34	188	4.3	326	7.5	2.96	123	.221	.309	35	30	97	112	-0.9	0	-1	3.1
■ CHARLIE McCULLOUGH	McCullough, Charles F. b: 1867, Dublin, Ireland Deb: 4/23/1890																												
1890	BB-a	4	21	.160	26	25	24	0	0	216	247	10.3	5	102	4.3	61	2.5	4.58	86	.303	.381	-17	-15	103	102	-6.6	-12	0	-2.2
	Syr-a	1	2	.333	3	3	3	0	0	26	29	10.0	1	14	4.8	8	2.8	7.27	49	.298	.386	-10	-11	92	66	-0.3	0	0	-0.7
	Yr	5	23	.179	29	28	27	0	0	242	276	10.3	6	116	4.3	69	2.6	4.87	80	.303	.382	-27	-26	101	66	-6.9	-12	0	-2.9
■ PAUL McCULLOUGH	McCullough, Paul Willard b: 7/28/1898, New Castle, Pa. d: 11/7/70, New Castle, Pa. BR/TR, 5'9.5", 190 lbs. Deb: 7/02/29																												
1929	Was-A	0	0	—	3	0	0	0	0	7	7	9.0	1	2	2.6	3	3.9	9.00	47	.250	.300	-4	-4	100	39	0.0	-0	-0	-0.3
■ PHIL McCULLOUGH	McCullough, Pinson Lamar b: 7/22/17, Stockbridge, Ga. BR/TR, 6'4", 204 lbs. Deb: 4/22/42																												
1942	Was-A	0	0	—	1	0	0	0	0	3	5	15.0	0	2	6.0	2	6.0	6.00	60	.333	.412	-1	-1	99	105	0.0	-0	0	0.0
■ LINDY McDANIEL	McDaniel, Lyndall Dale b: 12/13/35, Hollis, Okla. BR/TR, 6'3", 195 lbs. Deb: 9/02/55																												
1955	StL-N	0	0	—	4	2	0	0	0	19	22	10.4	4	7	3.3	7	3.3	4.74	87	.293	.345	-1	-1	102	118	0.0	-0	0	0.0
1956	StL-N	7	6	.538	39	7	1	0	0	116	121	9.4	7	42	3.3	59	4.6	3.41	110	.273	.327	5	4	99	111	0.6	2	1	0.7
1957	StL-N	15	9	.625	30	26	10	1	0	191	196	9.2	13	53	2.5	75	3.5	3.49	110	.266	.313	8	8	99	101	1.9	5	0	1.3
1958	StL-N	5	7	.417	26	17	2	1	0	109	139	11.5	17	31	2.6	47	3.9	5.78	74	.305	.350	-22	-18	108	90	-0.6	-3	1	-1.8
1959	StL-N	14	12	.538	62	7	1	0	**15**	132	144	9.8	11	41	2.8	86	5.9	3.82	110	.283	.331	2	6	106	111	2.2	-2	2	0.6
1960	StL-N	12	4	.750	65	2	1	0	**26**	116	85	6.6	8	24	1.9	105	8.1	2.09	194	.207	.246	**22**	**25**	108	97	3.7	1	1	2.9
1961	StL-N	10	6	.625	55	0	0	0	9	94	117	11.2	11	31	3.0	65	6.2	4.88	93	.305	.354	-9	-4	113	106	1.9	-0	1	-0.1
1962	StL-N	3	10	.231	55	2	0	0	14	107	96	8.1	12	29	2.4	79	6.6	4.12	102	.239	.284	-2	1	107	77	-3.6	-1	2	0.2
1963	Chi-N	13	7	.650	57	0	0	0	**22**	88	82	8.4	9	27	2.8	75	7.7	2.86	121	.251	.299	4	6	105	123	3.2	-0	0	0.6
1964	Chi-N	1	7	.125	63	0	0	0	15	95	104	9.9	4	23	2.2	71	6.7	3.88	97	.276	.313	-4	-1	106	92	-2.9	-1	0	-0.1
1965	Chi-N	5	6	.455	71	0	0	0	2	129	115	8.0	12	47	3.3	92	6.4	2.58	141	.241	.301	14	15	103	132	0.1	-1	2	1.8
1966	SF-N	10	5	.667	64	0	0	0	6	122	103	7.6	5	35	2.6	93	6.9	2.66	131	.228	.279	13	11	97	90	1.7	-1	1	1.2
1967	SF-N	2	6	.250	41	3	0	0	3	73	69	8.5	5	24	3.0	48	5.9	3.70	91	.248	.307	-3	-3	99	90	-2.2	-1	2	-0.1
1968	SF-N	0	0	—	12	0	0	0	0	19	30	14.2	2	5	2.4	9	4.3	7.58	38	.357	.389	-10	-10	96	84	0.0	-0	0	-1.0
	NY-A	4	1	.800	24	0	0	0	10	51	30	5.3	5	12	2.1	43	7.6	1.76	170	.166	.221	7	7	101	76	1.5	-1	2	0.9
1969	NY-A	5	6	.455	51	0	0	0	5	84	84	9.0	4	23	2.5	60	6.4	3.54	98	.261	.301	1	-1	96	90	-0.4	-1	1	0.0
1970	NY-A	9	5	.643	62	0	0	0	29	112	88	7.1	7	23	1.8	81	6.5	2.01	169	.217	.255	21	17	91	102	1.2	0	1	1.9
1971	NY-A	5	10	.333	44	0	0	0	4	70	82	10.5	12	24	3.1	39	5.0	5.01	67	.296	.342	-12	-13	97	104	-2.6	-0	0	-1.3
1972	NY-A	3	1	.750	37	0	0	0	0	68	54	7.1	4	25	3.3	47	6.2	2.25	125	.217	.283	6	4	92	108	1.0	1	1	0.8
1973	NY-A	12	6	.667	47	3	1	0	10	160	148	8.3	11	49	2.8	93	5.2	2.87	134	.250	.301	17	17	100	112	3.3	0	3	2.1
1974	KC-A	1	4	.200	38	5	2	0	1	107	109	9.2	6	24	2.0	47	4.0	3.45	112	.265	.300	2	5	106	92	-1.4	0	1	0.6
1975	KC-A	5	1	.833	40	0	0	0	1	78	81	9.3	3	24	2.8	40	4.6	4.15	92	.273	.315	-3	-3	101	85	1.9	0	-0	-0.2
Total	21	141	119	.542	987	74	18	2	172	2140	2099	8.8	172	623	2.6	1361	5.7	3.45	109	.258	.305	56	72	102	101	10.5	-3	22	11.0
■ VON McDANIEL	McDaniel, Max Von b: 4/18/39, Hollis, Okla. BR/TR, 6'2.5", 180 lbs. Deb: 6/13/57																												
1957	StL-N	7	5	.583	17	13	4	2	0	87	71	7.3	7	31	3.2	45	4.7	3.21	120	.225	.289	6	6	99	89	0.3	-3	-1	0.2
1958	StL-N	0	0	—	2	1	0	0	0	2	5	22.5	0	5	22.5	0	0.0	13.50	32	.500	.625	-2	-2	108	127	0.0	0	0	-0.1
Total	2	7	5	.583	19	14	4	2	0	89	76	7.7	7	36	3.6	45	4.6	3.44	112	.233	.304	4	4	99	90	0.3	-3	-1	0.1
■ JOE McDERMOTT	McDermott, Joseph Deb: 5/04/1871																												
1872	Eck-n	0	7	.000	7																								
■ MICKEY McDERMOTT	McDermott, Maurice Joseph b: 8/29/28, Poughkeepsie, N.Y. BL/TL, 6'2", 170 lbs. Deb: 4/24/48																												
1948	Bos-A	0	0	—	7	0	0	0	0	23	16	6.3	2	35	13.7	17	6.7	6.26	66	.208	.456	-5	-5	97	100	0.0	1	1	-0.2
1949	Bos-A	5	4	.556	12	12	6	2	0	80	63	7.1	5	52	5.8	50	5.6	4.05	107	.220	.338	1	3	103	87	-0.4	1	-0	0.4
1950	Bos-A	7	3	.700	38	15	4	0	5	130	119	8.2	8	124	8.6	96	6.6	5.19	98	.249	.402	-9	-1	111	99	1.2	7	1	0.6
1951	Bos-A	8	8	.500	34	19	9	1	3	172	141	7.4	10	92	4.8	127	**6.6**	3.35	131	.226	.326	15	20	106	102	-0.9	3	1	2.4
1952	Bos-A	10	9	.526	30	21	7	2	0	162	139	7.7	14	92	5.1	117	**6.5**	3.72	106	.234	.338	-1	4	107	102	0.7	3	-0	0.7
1953	Bos-A	18	10	.643	32	30	8	4	0	206	169	7.4	9	109	4.8	92	4.0	3.01	143	.224	.320	22	30	108	102	3.4	7	1	**4.1**
1954	Was-A	7	15	.318	30	26	11	1	1	196	172	7.9	8	110	5.1	95	4.4	3.44	107	.239	.335	6	5	99	99	-3.1	2	0	0.8
1955	Was-A	10	10	.500	31	20	8	1	1	156	140	8.1	9	100	5.8	78	4.5	3.75	100	.243	.356	4	-0	94	108	2.6	7	0	0.0
1956	NY-A	2	6	.250	23	9	1	0	0	87	85	8.8	10	47	4.9	38	3.9	4.24	93	.261	.344	-1	-3	95	106	-2.4	3	-0	-0.2
1957	KC-A	1	4	.200	29	4	0	0	0	69	68	8.9	9	50	6.5	29	3.8	5.48	70	.266	.373	-13	-13	102	96	-1.1	4	1	-1.2
1958	Det-A	0	0	—	2	0	0	0	0	2	6	27.0	0	2	9.0	0	0.0	9.00	43	.500	.571	-1	-1	103	158	0.0	0	0	0.0
1961	StL-N	1	0	1.000	19	0	0	0	4	27	29	9.7	3	15	5.0	15	5.0	3.67	124	.271	.352	1	3	113	129	0.5	-1	-0	0.1
	KC-A	0	0	—	4	0	0	0	0	6	14	21.0	0	10	15.0	3	4.5	13.50	31	.452	.585	-6	-6	104	99	0.0	1	-0	-0.4
Total	12	69	69	.500	291	156	54	11	14	1316	1161	7.9	87	838	5.7	757	5.2	3.91	106	.240	.349	13	34	103	102	0.5	36	5	7.1
■ MIKE McDERMOTT	McDermott, Michael Joseph b: 9/7/1862, St.Louis, Mo. d: 6/30/43, St.Louis, Mo. TR , 5'8", 145 lbs. Deb: 9/02/1889																												
1889	Lou-a	1	8	.111	9	9	9	0	0	84	108	11.6	4	34	3.6	22	2.4	4.18	94	.328	.391	-3	-2	102	122	-1.9	-1	0	-0.2
1895	Lou-N	4	19	.174	33	26	18	0	0	207	258	11.2	8	103	4.5	42	1.8	6.00	79	.326	.404	-28	-29	99	86	-4.4	-2	0	-2.4
1896	Lou-N	2	7	.222	12	10	4	1	0	65	87	12.0	4	44	6.1	12	1.7	7.34	60	.344	.442	-21	-21	102	85	-1.0	1	0	-1.5
1897	Cle-N	4	5	.444	9	7	4	0	0	62	75	10.9	2	25	3.6	12	1.7	4.50	105	.322	.387	-1	2	110	101	-0.6	1	0	0.2
	StL-N	1	2	.333	4	4	1	0	0	21	23	9.9	1	19	8.1	3	1.3	9.43	45	.300	.439	-12	-12	99	58	0.2	-0	0	-0.8
	Yr	5	7	.417	13	11	5	0	0	83	98	10.6	3	44	4.8	15	1.6	5.75	80	.316	.401	-13	-10	107	58	-0.4	1	0	-0.6
Total	4	12	41	.226	67	56	36	1	0	439	551	11.3	19	225	4.6	91	1.9	5.80	78	.327	.407	-66	-63	101	94	-7.7	-1	0	-4.7
■ DANNY McDEVITT	McDevitt, Daniel Eugene b: 11/18/32, New York, N.YI BL/TL, 5'10", 175 lbs. Deb: 6/17/57																												
1957	Bro-N	7	4	.636	22	17	5	2	0	119	105	7.9	5	72	5.4	90	6.8	3.25	136	.238	.348	8	16	114	113	1.2	-1	2	1.8
1958	LA-N	2	6	.250	13	10	2	0	0	48	71	13.3	6	31	5.8	26	4.9	7.50	56	.355	.429	-19	-18	106	100	-1.8	-1	-0	-1.6
1959	LA-N	10	8	.556	39	22	6	2	4	145	149	9.2	16	51	3.2	106	6.6	3.97	100	.263	.332	-0	0	101	106	-0.1	-2	0	0.0
1960	LA-N	0	4	.000	24	7	0	0	0	53	51	8.7	7	42	7.1	30	5.1	4.25	101	.260	.399	-3	0	114	135	-1.9	0	-0	0.0
1961	NY-A	1	2	.333	8	2	0	0	1	13	18	12.5	2	8	5.5	8	5.5	7.62	49	.353	.443	-5	-6	93	103	-0.7	0	0	-0.4
	Min-A	1	0	1.000	16	1	0	0	0	27	20	6.7	1	19	6.3	15	5.0	2.33	185	.213	.352	5	6	107	160	0.5	-0	0	0.6
	Yr	2	2	.500	24	3	0	0	1	40	38	8.5	3	27	6.1	23	5.2	4.05	102	.259	.377	-0	0	103	160	-0.2	0	0	0.2
1962	KC-A	0	3	.000	33	1	0	0	2	51	47	8.3	5	41	7.2	28	4.9	5.82	69	.250	.379	-11	-10	101	85	-1.4	0	1	-0.8
Total	6	21	27	.438	155	60	13	4	7	456	461	9.1	42	264	5.2	303	6.0	4.40	95	.265	.365	-25	-11	107	111	-4.2	-3	3	-0.4
■ HANK McDONALD	McDonald, Henry Monroe b: 1/16/11, Santa Monica, Cal. d: 10/17/82, Hemet, Cal. BR/TR, 6'3", 200 lbs. Deb: 4/16/31																												
1931	Phi-A	2	4	.333	19	10	1	1	0	70	62	8.0	3	41	5.3	23	3.0	3.73	119	.239	.341	5	5	101	104	-1.5	-1	-1	0.3
1933	Phi-A	1	1	.500	4	1	0	0	0	12	14	10.5	0	4	3.0	1	0.8	5.25	75	.264	.310	-1	-2	92	60	0.0	-0	0	-0.1
	StL-A	0	4	.000	25	5	0	0	0	58	83	12.9	6	34	5.3	22	3.4	8.69	58	.332	.408	-28	-24	117	81	-1.9	-1	-0	-2.1
	Yr	1	5	.167	29	6	0	0	0	70	97	12.5	6	38	4.9	23	3.0	8.10	60	.320	.392	-30	-25	113	81	-1.9	-0	-0	-2.2
Total	2	3	9	.250	48	16	1	1	0	140	159	10.2	9	79	5.1	46	3.0	5.91	78	.283	.368	-25	-20	107	91	-3.4	-2	-1	-1.9
■ JIM McDONALD	McDonald, Jimmie Le Roy "Hot Rod" b: 5/17/27, Grants Pass, Ore. BR/TR, 5'10.5", 185 lbs. Deb: 7/27/50																												
1950	Bos-A	1	0	1.000	9	0	0	0	0	19	23	10.9	1	10	4.7	5	2.4	3.79	134	.329	.400	2	3	111	163	0.5	1	1	0.4
1951	StL-A	4	7	.364	16	11	5	0	1	84	84	9.0	5	46	4.9	28	3.0	4.07	111	.260	.352	0	4	109	104	0.2	-0	1	0.5
1952	NY-A	3	4	.429	26	5	1	0	0	69	71	9.3	1	40	5.2	20	2.6	3.52	99	.268	.362	1	-0	95	117	-1.0	3	3	0.5

YEAR	TM/L	W	L	PCT	G	GS	CG	SHO	SV	IP	H	H/G	HR	BB	BB/G	SO	SO/G	ERA	/A	OAVG	OOBP	PR	/A	PF	CPI	WAT	PB	PD	TPI
1953	NY-A	9	7	.563	27	18	6	2	0	130	128	8.9	4	39	2.7	43	3.0	3.81	93	.260	.312	3	-4	88	85	-1.2	-2	2	-0.4
1954	NY-A	4	1	.800	16	10	3	1	0	71	54	6.8	3	45	5.7	20	2.5	3.17	111	.213	.331	4	3	94	96	1.0	2	1	0.5
1955	Bal-A	3	5	.375	21	8	0	0	0	52	76	13.2	5	30	5.2	20	3.5	7.10	52	.345	.419	-18	-20	94	96	0.0	1	1	-1.6
1956	Chi-A	0	2	.000	8	3	0	0	0	19	29	13.7	2	7	3.3	10	4.7	8.53	50	.377	.420	-9	-9	102	87	-0.9	-0	0	-0.8
1957	Chi-A	0	1	.000	10	0	0	0	0	22	18	7.4	2	10	4.1	12	4.9	2.05	179	.234	.304	4	4	97	171	-0.4	0	0	0.4
1958	Chi-A	0	0	—	3	0	0	0	0	2	6	27.0	1	4	18.0	0	0.0	22.50	16	.429	.556	-4	-4	98	83	0.0	0	0	-0.3
Total	9	24	27	.471	136	55	15	3	1	468	489	9.4	24	231	4.4	158	3.0	4.27	89	.273	.353	-17	-24	96	103	-1.8	4	8	-0.8
■ **JOHN McDONALD**	McDonald, John Joseph (born John Joseph Mc Donnell) b: 1/27/1883, Throop, Pa. d: 4/9/50, Roselle, N.J. BR/TR, 6'1", 170 lbs. Deb: 9/13/07																												
1907	Was-A	0	0	—	1	0	0	0	0	6	12	18.0	0	2	3.0	3	4.5	9.00	27	.443	.481	-4	-4	94	88	0.0	0	0	-0.3
■ **MC DOOLAN**	McDoolan Deb: 4/14/1873																												
1873	Mar-n	0	1	.000	1																								
■ **SANDY McDOUGAL**	McDougal, John Auchanbolt b: 5/21/1874, Buffalo, N.Y. d: 10/2/10, Buffalo, N.Y. BR/TR, 5'10", 155 lbs. Deb: 6/12/1895																												
1895	Bro-N	0	0	—	1	0	0	0	1	3	3	9.0	0	5	15.0	2	6.0	12.00	37	.280	.509	-2	-3	94	58	0.0	-0	0	-0.1
1905	StL-N	1	4	.200	5	5	5	0	0	45	50	10.0	0	12	2.4	10	2.0	3.40	84	.309	.357	-2	-3	95	104	-1.1	-1	3	0.0
Total	2	1	4	.200	6	5	5	0	1	48	53	9.9	0	17	3.2	12	2.3	3.94	75	.307	.369	-4	-5	95	101	-1.1	-1	3	-0.1
■ **DEWEY McDOUGAL**	McDougal, John H. b: 9/19/1871, Aledo, Ill. d: 4/28/36, Galesburg, Ill. 170 lbs. Deb: 4/24/1895																												
1895	StL-N	3	10	.231	18	14	10	0	0	115	187	14.6	11	46	3.6	23	1.8	8.37	59	.387	.440	-46	-44	102	86	-1.5	-2	0	-3.3
1896	StL-N	0	1	.000	3	1	0	0	0	10	13	11.7	2	4	3.6	0	0.0	8.10	53	.338	.400	-4	-4	98	78	-0.4	-1	0	-0.3
Total	2	3	11	.214	21	15	10	0	0	125	200	14.4	13	50	3.6	23	1.7	8.35	58	.383	.437	-50	-49	102	86	-1.9	-3	0	-3.6
■ **JACK McDOWELL**	McDowell, Jack Burns b: 1/16/66, Van Nuys, Cal. BR/TR, 6'5", 180 lbs. Deb: 9/15/87																												
1987	Chi-A	3	0	1.000	4	4	0	0	0	28	16	5.1	1	6	1.9	15	4.8	1.93	252	.168	.233	8	9	109	61	1.5	0	0	1.0
1988	Chi-A	5	10	.333	26	26	1	0	0	159	147	8.3	12	68	3.8	84	4.8	3.96	99	.245	.323	0	-1	99	94	-1.9	0	-1	-0.1
Total	2	8	10	.444	30	30	1	0	0	187	163	7.8	13	74	3.6	99	4.8	3.66	111	.235	.311	8	8	100	89	-0.4	0	-1	0.9
■ **ROGER McDOWELL**	McDowell, Roger Alan b: 12/21/60, Cincinnati, Ohio BR/TR, 6'1", 175 lbs. Deb: 4/11/85																												
1985	NY-N	6	5	.545	62	2	0	0	17	127	108	7.7	9	37	2.6	70	5.0	2.83	121	.230	.283	11	8	95	96	-0.5	0	2	1.2
1986	NY-N	14	9	.609	75	0	0	0	22	128	107	7.5	4	42	3.0	65	4.6	3.02	115	.228	.290	10	6	93	84	-1.0	1	3	1.1
1987	NY-N	7	5	.583	56	0	0	0	25	89	95	9.6	7	28	2.8	32	3.2	4.15	96	.276	.326	-1	-2	97	99	0.2	1	1	0.0
1988	NY-N	5	5	.500	62	0	0	0	16	89	80	8.1	1	31	3.1	46	4.7	2.63	115	.238	.302	8	4	88	105	-1.0	2	2	0.8
Total	4	32	24	.571	255	2	0	0	80	433	390	8.1	21	138	2.9	213	4.4	3.12	111	.241	.298	28	17	93	95	-2.3	5	7	3.1
■ **SAM McDOWELL**	McDowell, Samuel Edward Thomas "Sudden Sam" b: 9/21/42, Pittsburgh, Pa. BL/TL, 6'5", 190 lbs. Deb: 9/15/61																												
1961	Cle-A	0	0	—	1	1	0	0	0	6	3	4.5	0	5	7.5	5	7.5	0.00	—	.136	.296	3	3	97	0	0.0	-0	0	0.3
1962	Cle-A	3	7	.300	25	13	0	0	1	88	81	8.3	9	70	7.2	70	7.2	6.03	65	.243	.378	-20	-21	99	80	-1.9	-1	-0	-2.0
1963	Cle-A	3	5	.375	14	12	3	1	0	65	63	8.7	6	44	6.1	63	8.7	4.85	73	.256	.366	-9	-9	98	96	-0.9	0	-0	-0.8
1964	Cle-A	11	6	.647	31	24	6	2	1	173	148	7.7	8	100	5.2	177	**9.2**	2.71	138	.229	.330	18	20	103	**122**	2.9	-0	-1	2.1
1965	Cle-A	17	11	.607	42	35	14	3	4	273	178	**5.9**	9	132	4.4	**325**	**10.7**	**2.18**	**155**	**.185**	.283	**39**	**36**	97	91	2.5	-2	1	**3.9**
1966	Cle-A	9	8	.529	35	28	8	**5**	3	194	130	**6.0**	12	102	4.7	**225**	**10.4**	2.88	121	**.188**	.295	12	13	102	87	0.6	1	1	1.7
1967	Cle-A	13	15	.464	37	37	10	1	0	236	201	7.7	21	123	4.7	236	9.0	3.85	85	.233	.326	-16	-15	101	97	0.0	1	-1	-1.5
1968	Cle-A	15	14	.517	38	37	11	3	0	269	181	6.1	13	110	3.7	**283**	**9.5**	1.81	166	.189	.274	35	36	101	113	-0.5	-0	-1	4.3
1969	Cle-A	18	14	.563	39	38	18	4	1	285	222	7.0	13	102	3.2	**279**	**8.8**	2.94	119	.213	.284	22	18	96	79	5.4	0	-0	1.7
1970	Cle-A	20	12	.625	39	39	19	1	0	**305**	236	7.0	25	131	3.9	**304**	**9.0**	2.92	**146**	.213	.298	27	**46**	115	96	**5.5**	-5	-2	**4.5**
1971	Cle-A	13	17	.433	35	31	8	2	1	215	160	6.7	22	153	6.4	192	8.0	3.39	111	.207	.335	2	9	108	105	1.8	-1	-2	0.7
1972	SF-N	10	8	.556	28	25	4	0	0	164	155	8.5	12	86	4.7	122	6.7	4.34	79	.253	.344	-16	-16	100	93	2.0	-1	-0	-1.8
1973	SF-N	1	2	.333	18	3	0	0	3	40	45	10.1	4	29	6.5	35	7.9	4.50	85	.285	.389	-4	-3	104	121	-0.5	-0	0	-0.2
	NY-A	5	8	.385	16	15	2	1	0	96	73	6.8	4	64	6.0	75	7.0	3.94	97	.212	.329	-1	-1	100	77	-1.4	0	0	0.0
1974	NY-A	1	6	.143	13	7	0	0	0	48	42	7.9	6	41	7.7	33	6.2	4.69	74	.236	.371	-6	-7	95	101	-2.5	0	-1	-0.7
1975	Pit-N	2	1	.667	14	1	0	0	0	35	30	7.7	0	20	5.1	29	7.5	2.83	125	.242	.336	3	3	98	115	0.3	-1	0	0.2
Total	15	141	134	.513	425	346	103	23	14	2492	1948	7.0	164	1312	4.7	2453	8.9	3.17	112	.215	.313	88	109	102	96	13.3	-9	-4	12.4
■ **JIM McELROY**	McElroy, James D. b: 1863, San Francisco, Cal. d: 7/24/1889, Needles, Cal. Deb: 5/26/1884																												
1884	Phi-N	1	12	.077	13	13	13	0	0	111	115	9.3	1	54	4.4	45	3.6	4.86	60	.276	.359	-23	-24	97	75	-5.1	-3	0	-2.2
	WiL-U	0	1	.000	1	1	0	0	0	5	10	18.0	0	0	0.0	3	5.4	10.80	30	.420	.420	-4	-4	109	68	-0.4	-0	0	-0.2
■ **WILL McENANEY**	McEnaney, William Henry b: 2/14/52, Springfield, Ohio BL/TL, 6', 180 lbs. Deb: 7/03/74																												
1974	Cin-N	2	1	.667	24	0	0	0	2	27	24	8.0	4	9	3.0	13	4.3	4.33	81	.250	.303	-2	-3	96	91	0.2	0	-1	-0.2
1975	Cin-N	5	2	.714	70	0	0	0	15	91	92	9.1	6	23	2.3	48	4.7	2.47	149	.264	.308	12	12	101	137	0.5	-2	-1	1.0
1976	Cin-N	2	6	.250	55	0	0	0	7	72	97	12.1	3	23	2.9	28	3.5	4.88	72	.323	.363	-11	-11	100	104	-2.4	1	0	-1.0
1977	Mon-N	3	5	.375	69	0	0	0	3	87	92	9.5	6	22	2.3	38	3.9	3.93	99	.271	.312	-0	-0	99	92	-0.7	-1	-0	-0.1
1978	Pit-N	0	0	—	6	0	0	0	0	9	15	15.0	3	2	2.0	6	6.0	10.00	37	.395	.429	-6	-6	105	95	0.0	0	0	-0.5
1979	StL-N	0	3	.000	45	0	0	0	2	64	60	8.4	3	16	2.3	15	2.1	2.95	132	.251	.292	6	7	104	100	-1.4	-0	2	0.8
Total	6	12	17	.414	269	0	0	0	29	350	380	9.8	25	95	2.4	148	3.8	3.75	99	.279	.321	-2	-1	101	108	-3.8	-2	-0	0.0
■ **LOU McEVOY**	McEvoy, Louis Anthony b: 5/30/02, Williamsburg, Kan. d: 12/17/53, Webster Groves, Mo BR/TR, 6'2.5", 203 lbs. Deb: 4/28/30																												
1930	NY-A	1	3	.250	28	1	0	0	3	52	64	11.1	4	29	5.0	14	2.4	6.75	60	.288	.358	-12	-16	87	78	-1.0	-1	-1	-1.4
1931	NY-A	0	0	—	6	0	0	0	1	12	19	14.3	1	12	9.0	3	2.3	12.75	32	.358	.478	-11	-12	94	71	0.0	-1	0	-0.9
Total	2	1	3	.250	34	1	0	0	4	64	83	11.7	5	41	5.8	17	2.4	7.88	52	.302	.383	-23	-27	88	76	-1.0	-1	-1	-2.3
■ **BARNEY McFADDEN**	McFadden, Bernard Joseph b: 2/22/1874, Eckley, Pa. d: 4/28/24, Mauch Chunk, Pa. BR/TR, 6'1", 195 lbs. Deb: 4/24/01																												
1901	Cin-N	3	4	.429	8	5	4	0	0	46	54	10.6	2	40	7.8	11	2.2	6.07	55	.327	.473	-14	-14	100	101	0.3	-1	1	-1.1
1902	Phi-N	0	1	.000	1	1	1	0	0	9	14	14.0	0	7	7.0	3	3.0	8.00	38	.381	.480	-5	-5	109	85	-0.4	-0	0	-0.3
Total	2	3	5	.375	9	6	5	0	0	55	68	11.1	2	47	7.7	14	2.3	6.38	51	.336	.474	-19	-19	101	99	-0.1	-2	1	-1.4
■ **DAN McFARLAN**	McFarlan, Anderson Daniel b: 11/1/1873, Gainesville, Tex. d: 9/23/24, Louisville, Ky. Deb: 9/02/1895																												
1895	Lou-N	0	7	.000	7	7	6	0	0	46	80	15.7	4	15	2.9	10	2.0	6.65	71	.403	.445	-10	-10	99	113	-3.4	-1	0	-0.7
1899	Bro-N	0	0	—	1	0	0	0	0	6	6	9.0	1	3	4.5	0	0.0	1.50	263	.283	.372	2	2	102	319	0.0	-0	0	0.1
	Was-N	8	18	.308	32	28	22	1	0	212	268	11.4	5	64	2.7	41	1.7	4.75	80	.333	.382	-21	-23	98	93	-1.9	-0	0	-1.9
	Yr	8	18	.308	33	28	22	1	0	218	274	11.3	6	67	2.8	41	1.7	4.67	81	.332	.382	-20	-21	98	93	-1.9	-0	0	-1.8
Total	2	8	25	.242	40	35	28	1	0	264	354	12.1	10	82	2.8	51	1.7	5.01	79	.346	.394	-29	-31	98	102	-5.3	-1	0	-2.5
■ **CHAPPIE McFARLAND**	McFarland, Charles A. b: 3/13/1875, White Hill, Ill. d: 12/14/24, Houston, Tex. TR, 6'1", Deb: 9/15/02																												
1902	StL-N	0	1	.000	2	1	1	0	0	11	11	9.0	1	3	2.5	3	2.5	5.73	48	.283	.335	-4	-4	99	61	-0.4	-1	0	-0.2
1903	StL-N	9	19	.321	28	26	25	1	0	229	253	9.9	2	48	1.9	76	3.0	3.07	109	.307	.350	5	7	102	108	0.2	-4	2	0.8
1904	StL-N	14	18	.438	32	31	28	1	0	269	266	8.9	7	56	1.9	111	3.7	3.21	84	.283	.326	-14	-15	99	90	-1.9	-3	6	-0.9
1905	StL-N	8	18	.308	31	28	22	3	1	250	281	10.1	3	65	2.3	85	3.1	3.82	75	.313	.364	-23	-27	95	98	-2.7	1	1	-2.5
1906	StL-N	2	1	.667	6	4	2	0	1	37	33	8.0	1	8	1.9	16	3.9	1.95	140	.265	.309	3	3	104	125	0.7	-1	1	0.4
	Pit-N	1	3	.250	6	5	2	1	0	35	39	10.0	0	7	1.8	11	2.8	2.57	103	.316	.362	0	0	101	133	-1.1	1	0	0.0
	Bro-N	0	1	.000	1	1	1	0	0	9	10	10.0	1	5	5.0	5	5.0	8.00	29	.310	.403	-5	-6	90	64	-0.4	-0	-0	-0.4
	Yr	3	5	.375	13	10	5	1	1	81	82	9.1	2	20	2.2	32	3.6	2.89	92	.290	.337	-3	-2	101	64	-0.8	1	1	0.0
Total	5	34	61	.358	106	96	81	6	2	840	893	9.6	15	192	2.1	307	3.3	3.35	87	.300	.346	-38	-42	99	100	-5.6	-6	10	-2.8
■ **CHRIS McFARLAND**	McFarland, Christopher b: 8/17/1861, Fall River, Mass. d: 5/24/18, New Bedford, Mass. 5'9", 170 lbs. Deb: 4/19/1884																												
1884	Bal-U	0	1	.000	1	1	0	0	0	3	9	27.0	1	1	3.0	3	9.0	15.00	22	.520	.546	-4	-4	110	105	-0.4	-0	0	-0.2
■ **MONTE McFARLAND**	McFarland, La Mont A. b: 1873, Illinois d: 11/15/13, Peoria, Ill. Deb: 9/14/1895																												
1895	Chi-N	2	0	1.000	2	2	2	0	0	14	21	13.5	0	5	3.2	5	3.2	5.14	96	.368	.419	-1	-0	103	112	1.0	-1	0	0.0
1896	Chi-N	0	4	.000	4	3	2	0	0	25	32	11.5	0	21	7.6	3	1.1	7.20	66	.334	.454	-8	-7	108	82	-1.9	-2	0	-0.6

YEAR	TM/L	W	L	PCT	G	GS	CG	SHO	SV	IP	H	H/G	HR	BB	BB/G	SO	SO/G	ERA	/A	OAVG	OOBP	PR	/A	PF	CPI	WAT	PB	PD	TPI
Total	2	2	4	.333	6	5	4	0	0	39	53	12.2	0	26	6.0	8	1.8	6.46	74	.347	.442	-8	-7	106	93	-0.9	-3	0	-0.6
■ JACK McFETRIDGE	McFetridge, John Reed b: 8/25/1869, Philadelphia, Pa. d: 1/10/17, Philadelphia, Pa. 6', 175 lbs. Deb: 6/07/1890																												
1890	Phi-N	1	0	1.000	1	1	1	0	0	9	5	5.0	0	2	2.0	4	4.0	1.00	381	.175	.229	3	3	107	50	0.5	1	0	0.4
1903	Phi-N	1	11	.083	14	13	11	0	0	103	120	10.5	2	49	4.3	31	2.7	4.89	63	.319	.401	-19	-21	94	90	-4.6	1	-1	-1.9
Total	2	2	11	.154	15	14	12	0	0	112	125	10.0	2	51	4.1	35	2.8	4.58	69	.309	.390	-16	-18	95	87	-4.1	2	-1	-1.5
■ ANDY McGAFFIGAN	McGaffigan, Andrew Joseph b: 10/25/56, W.Palm Beach, Fla. BR/TR, 6'3", 185 lbs. Deb: 9/22/81																												
1981	NY-A	0	0	—	2	0	0	0	0	7	5	6.4	1	3	3.9	2	2.6	2.57	141	.200	.258	1	1	99	115	0.0	0	-0	0.1
1982	SF-N	1	0	1.000	4	0	0	0	0	8	5	5.6	0	1	1.1	4	4.5	0.00	—	.179	.233	3	3	94	0	0.5	-0	-0	0.3
1983	SF-N	3	9	.250	43	16	0	0	2	134	131	8.8	17	39	2.6	93	6.2	4.30	85	.255	.305	-10	-9	101	86	-2.9	-1	-3	-1.4
1984	Mon-N	3	4	.429	21	3	0	0	1	46	37	7.2	2	15	2.9	39	7.6	2.54	129	.220	.283	5	4	91	94	-0.3	-1	0	0.3
	Cin-N	0	2	.000	9	3	0	0	0	23	23	9.0	2	8	3.1	18	7.0	5.48	70	.261	.316	-5	-4	107	69	-0.9	-0	-1	-0.4
	Yr	3	6	.333	30	6	0	0	1	69	60	7.8	4	23	3.0	57	7.4	3.52	99	.233	.294	1	-0	97	69	-1.2	-1	-1	-0.1
1985	Cin-N	3	3	.500	15	15	2	0	0	94	88	8.4	4	30	2.9	83	7.9	3.73	101	.247	.306	-1	0	105	81	-0.2	-2	0	0.0
1986	Mon-N	10	5	.667	48	14	1	1	2	143	114	7.2	9	55	3.5	104	6.5	2.64	138	.223	.293	17	16	98	108	2.8	-2	-1	1.3
1987	Mon-N	5	2	.714	69	0	0	0	12	120	105	7.9	5	42	3.2	100	7.5	2.40	180	.235	.300	22	26	106	119	1.3	-1	-0	2.4
1988	Mon-N	6	0	1.000	63	0	0	0	4	91	81	8.0	4	37	3.7	71	7.0	2.77	131	.233	.306	7	9	105	109	3.0	-0	-1	0.8
Total	8	31	25	.554	274	51	3	1	21	666	589	8.0	44	230	3.1	514	6.9	3.16	119	.237	.300	40	45	102	98	3.3	-8	-6	3.4
■ JACK McGEACHEY	McGeachey, John Charles b: 5/23/1864, Clinton, Mass. d: 4/5/30, Cambridge, Mass. BR, 5'8", 165 lbs. Deb: 6/17/1886																												
1887	Ind-N	0	1	.000	1	0	0	0	0	6	13	19.5	2	4	6.0	3	4.5	12.00	34	.451	.518	-5	-5	101	105	-0.4	0	0	-0.3
1888	Ind-N	0	0	—	1	0	0	0	0	5	5	9.0	2	3	5.4	0	0.0	7.20	38	.274	.376	-2	-2	98	96	0.0	0	0	-0.1
1889	Ind-N	0	0	—	3	0	0	0	0	5	7	12.6	2	6	10.8	3	5.4	12.60	35	.348	.497	-5	-5	110	84	0.0	0	0	-0.3
Total	3	0	1	.000	5	0	0	0	0	16	25	14.1	6	13	7.3	6	3.4	10.69	35	.372	.474	-12	-12	103	96	-0.4	0	0	-0.7
■ BILL McGEE	McGee, William Henry "Fiddler Bill" b: 11/16/09, Batchtown, Ill. d: 2/11/87, St.Louis, Mo. BR/TR, 6'1", 215 lbs. Deb: 9/29/35																												
1935	StL-N	1	0	1.000	1	1	1	0	0	9	3	3.0	0	1	1.0	2	2.0	1.00	404	.103	.133	3	3	100	87	0.5	0	-0	0.3
1936	StL-N	1	1	.500	7	2	0	0	0	16	23	12.9	3	4	2.3	8	4.5	7.88	48	.359	.386	-7	-7	95	91	0.0	0	0	-0.5
1937	StL-N	1	0	1.000	4	1	1	0	0	14	13	8.4	1	4	2.6	9	5.8	2.57	151	.255	.316	2	2	100	143	0.5	-0	0	0.2
1938	StL-N	7	12	.368	47	25	10	1	5	216	216	9.0	4	78	3.3	104	4.3	3.21	131	.257	.317	14	24	111	101	-2.2	0	-0	2.5
1939	StL-N	12	5	.706	43	17	5	4	0	156	155	8.9	14	59	3.4	56	3.2	3.81	106	.261	.324	2	4	103	103	2.4	-2	0	0.2
1940	StL-N	16	10	.615	38	31	11	3	0	218	222	9.2	13	96	4.0	78	3.2	3.80	103	.263	.335	1	2	101	107	2.2	-1	-3	0.0
1941	StL-N	0	1	.000	4	3	0	0	0	14	17	10.9	1	13	8.4	2	1.3	5.14	76	.298	.437	-2	-2	107	127	-0.4	-1	0	-0.2
	NY-N	2	9	.182	22	14	1	0	0	106	117	9.9	9	54	4.6	41	3.5	4.92	77	.285	.360	-15	-14	104	100	-3.4	-1	-2	-1.5
	Yr	2	10	.167	26	17	1	0	0	120	134	10.1	10	67	5.0	43	3.2	4.95	77	.286	.368	-18	-15	104	100	-3.8	-1	-2	-1.7
1942	NY-N	6	3	.667	31	8	2	1	1	104	95	8.2	8	46	4.0	40	3.5	2.94	114	.244	.318	4	5	101	123	1.1	-2	-1	0.2
Total	8	46	41	.529	197	102	31	9	6	853	861	9.1	53	355	3.7	340	3.6	3.74	105	.263	.331	2	17	104	106	0.7	-6	-5	1.2
■ CONNY McGEEHAN	McGeehan, Cornelius Bernard b: 8/25/1882, Drifton, Pa. d: 7/4/07, Hazleton, Pa. Deb: 03																												
1903	Phi-A	1	0	1.000	3	0	0	0	0	10	9	8.1	0	1	0.9	4	3.6	4.50	67	.262	.282	-2	-2	102	46	0.5	-1	0	-0.1
■ PAT McGEHEE	McGehee, Patrick Henry b: 7/2/1888, Meadville, Miss. d: 12/30/46, Paducah, Ky. BL/TR, 6'2.5", 180 lbs. Deb: 8/23/12																												
1912	Det-A	0	0	—	1	1	0	0	0	0	1	—	0	1	—	0	—	—	—	1.000	1.000	0	0	96	0	0.0	0	0	0.0
■ RANDY McGILBERRY	McGilberry, Randall Kent b: 10/29/53, Mobile, Ala. BB/TR, 6'1", 195 lbs. Deb: 9/06/77																												
1977	KC-A	0	1	.000	3	0	0	0	0	7	7	9.0	1	1	1.3	1	1.3	5.14	78	.280	.308	-1	-1	99	82	-0.4	0	0	0.0
1978	KC-A	0	1	.000	18	0	0	0	0	26	27	9.3	2	18	6.2	12	4.2	4.15	92	.276	.375	-1	-1	101	120	-0.4	0	0	0.0
Total	2	0	2	.000	21	0	0	0	0	33	34	9.3	3	19	5.2	13	3.5	4.36	89	.276	.363	-2	-2	101	112	-0.8	0	0	0.0
■ BILL McGILL	McGill, William John "Parson" b: 6/29/1880, Galva, Kan. d: 8/7/59, Alva, Okla. BR/TR, 6'2", Deb: 9/16/07																												
1907	StL-A	1	0	1.000	2	2	1	0	0	18	22	11.0	0	2	1.0	8	4.0	3.50	71	.327	.347	-2	-2	98	101	0.5	-1	0	-0.1
■ WILLIE McGILL	McGill, William Vaness "Kid" b: 11/10/1873, Atlanta, Ga. d: 8/29/44, Indianapolis, Ind. TL, 5'6.5", 170 lbs. Deb: 5/08/1890																												
1890	Cle-P	11	9	.550	24	20	19	0	0	184	222	10.9	5	96	4.7	82	4.0	4.16	96	.311	.392	2	-4	94	111	2.5	2	0	-0.1
1891	CM-a	2	5	.286	8	8	6	0	0	65	69	9.6	1	37	5.1	19	2.6	4.98	84	.287	.382	-9	-6	113	81	-1.3	0	0	-0.3
	StL-a	19	10	.655	35	31	22	1	1	249	225	8.1	10	131	4.7	154	5.6	2.93	142	.255	.351	22	34	112	113	1.5	1	0	3.4
	Yr	21	15	.583	43	39	28	1	1	314	294	8.4	11	168	4.8	173	5.0	3.35	124	.262	.358	13	28	112	113	0.2	0	0	3.1
1892	Cin-N	1	1	.500	3	3	1	0	0	17	18	9.5	0	5	2.6	7	3.7	5.29	64	.285	.337	-4	-4	103	60	0.0	0	0	-0.2
1893	Chi-N	17	18	.486	39	34	26	1	0	303	311	9.2	6	181	5.4	91	2.7	4.63	105	.281	.382	1	8	104	92	1.9	1	-4	0.5
1894	Chi-N	7	19	.269	27	23	22	0	0	208	272	11.8	2	117	5.1	58	2.5	5.84	99	.339	.423	-12	-2	108	93	-5.5	-0	0	0.0
1895	Phi-N	10	8	.556	20	20	13	0	0	146	177	10.9	2	81	5.0	70	4.3	5.55	85	.320	.407	-12	-14	98	90	-0.6	-0	0	-1.0
1896	Phi-N	5	4	.556	12	11	7	0	0	80	87	9.8	0	53	6.0	29	3.3	5.40	83	.299	.407	-9	-8	102	82	0.7	-0	0	-0.6
Total	7	72	74	.493	168	150	116	2	1	1252	1381	9.9	26	701	5.0	510	3.7	4.61	101	.297	.389	-21	6	104	97	-0.8	4	-4	1.7
■ JOHN McGILLEN	McGillen, John Joseph b: 8/6/17, Eddystone, Pa. BL/TL, 6'1", 175 lbs. Deb: 4/20/44																												
1944	Phi-A	0	0	—	2	0	0	0	0	1	1	9.0	0	2	18.0	0	0.0	18.00	19	.333	.600	-2	-2	102	53	0.0	0	0	-0.1
■ JIM McGINLEY	McGinley, James William b: 10/2/1878, Groveland, Mass. d: 9/20/61, Haverhill, Mass. 5'9.5", 165 lbs. Deb: 9/22/04																												
1904	StL-N	2	1	.667	3	3	3	0	0	27	28	9.3	0	6	2.0	6	2.0	2.00	135	.301	.363	2	2	99	162	0.5	-1	-1	0.1
1905	StL-N	0	1	.000	1	1	0	0	0	3	5	15.0	1	2	6.0	0	0.0	15.00	19	.401	.484	-4	-4	95	66	-0.4	0	-0	-0.3
Total	2	2	2	.500	4	4	3	0	0	30	33	9.9	1	8	2.4	6	1.8	3.30	82	.313	.378	-2	-2	98	153	0.1	-0	-1	-0.2
■ DAN McGINN	McGinn, Daniel Michael b: 11/29/43, Omaha, Neb. BL/TL, 6', 185 lbs. Deb: 9/03/68																												
1968	Cin-N	0	1	.000	14	0	0	0	0	12	13	9.8	1	11	8.3	16	12.0	5.25	63	.271	.417	-3	-3	111	109	-0.4	-0	0	-0.2
1969	Mon-N	7	10	.412	74	1	0	0	6	132	123	8.4	8	65	4.4	112	7.6	3.95	94	.245	.334	-5	-4	103	91	1.3	1	1	-0.1
1970	Mon-N	7	10	.412	52	19	3	2	0	131	154	10.6	13	78	5.4	83	5.7	5.43	76	.296	.389	-20	-19	102	106	-0.7	-2	2	-1.8
1971	Mon-N	1	4	.200	28	6	1	0	0	71	74	9.4	7	42	5.3	40	5.1	5.96	58	.274	.368	-20	-20	100	82	-1.3	0	1	-1.8
1972	Chi-N	0	5	.000	42	2	0	0	4	63	78	11.1	5	29	4.1	42	6.0	5.86	66	.301	.374	-17	-14	112	89	-2.4	1	-1	-1.3
Total	5	15	30	.333	210	28	4	2	10	409	442	9.7	34	225	5.0	293	6.4	5.11	75	.276	.367	-65	-58	104	94	-3.5	-0	3	-5.2
■ GUS McGINNIS	McGinnis, August b: 1870, Painesville, Ohio 5'11", 168 lbs. Deb: 4/27/1893																												
1893	Chi-N	2	5	.286	13	5	3	0	0	67	85	11.4	2	31	4.2	13	1.7	5.37	91	.326	.397	-5	-4	104	96	-1.2	2	0	-0.1
	Phi-N	1	3	.250	5	4	4	1	0	37	39	9.5	0	17	4.1	12	2.9	4.38	105	.286	.365	1	1	98	88	-1.0	-1	0	0.0
	Yr	3	8	.273	18	9	7	1	0	104	124	10.7	2	48	4.2	25	2.2	5.02	95	.312	.386	-4	-3	102	88	-2.2	2	0	-0.1
■ JUMBO McGINNIS	McGinnis, George Washington b: 2/22/1864, Alton, Mo. d: 5/18/34, St.Louis, Mo. 5'10", 197 lbs. Deb: 5/02/1882																												
1882	StL-a	25	17	.595	44	44	42	3	0	379	376	8.9	2	52	1.2	134	3.2	2.47	113	.264	.290	9	14	104	103	8.6	1	-6	0.9
1883	StL-a	28	16	.636	45	45	41	**6**	0	383	325	7.6	4	69	1.6	128	3.0	2.33	149	.235	.271	41	48	105	99	-1.5	-6	-0	4.0
1884	StL-a	24	16	.600	40	40	39	5	0	354	331	8.4	4	35	0.9	141	3.6	2.85	124	.256	.275	16	26	109	95	-1.2	1	-1	2.7
1885	StL-a	6	6	.500	13	13	12	3	0	112	98	7.9	1	19	1.5	41	3.3	3.38	85	.246	.281	-2	-6	89	71	-1.8	0	0	-0.5
1886	StL-a	5	5	.500	10	10	10	1	0	88	107	10.9	2	27	2.8	30	3.1	3.78	97	.311	.361	-3	-1	106	122	-1.2	-1	0	-0.1
	Bal-a	11	13	.458	26	25	24	0	0	209	235	10.1	5	48	2.1	70	3.0	3.49	93	.294	.334	-1	-6	94	113	2.1	-0	0	-0.5
	Yr	16	18	.471	36	35	34	1	0	297	342	10.4	7	75	2.3	100	3.0	3.58	94	.299	.342	-4	-7	97	113	0.9	-1	0	-0.6
1887	Cin-a	3	5	.375	8	8	8	0	0	69	85	11.1	3	43	5.6	18	2.3	5.48	83	.317	.411	-9	-7	106	103	-1.5	-1	0	-0.5
Total	6	102	78	.567	186	185	176	18	0	1594	1557	8.8	21	293	1.7	562	3.2	2.92	113	.263	.298	51	69	103	100	3.5	-6	-7	6.0
■ JOE McGINNITY	McGinnity, Joseph Jerome "Iron Man" b: 3/19/1871, Rock Island, Ill. d: 11/14/29, Brooklyn, N.Y. BR/TR, 5'11", 206 lbs. Deb: 4/18/1899 CH																												
1899	Bal-N	**28**	16	.636	48	41	38	4	2	366	358	8.8	2	93	2.3	74	1.8	2.68	153	.279	.328	48	58	106	103	3.9	-6	2	5.2
1900	Bro-N	**28**	8	**.778**	44	37	32	1	0	**343**	350	9.2	5	113	3.0	93	2.4	2.94	133	.287	.347	29	37	106	112	**9.3**	-5	-1	3.0
1901	Bal-A	26	20	.565	**48**	43	**39**	1	1	**382**	412	9.7	7	96	2.3	75	1.8	3.56	110	.296	.341	4	15	107	95	3.7	-5	-2	1.1
1902	Bal-A	13	10	.565	25	23	19	0	0	199	219	9.9	3	46	2.1	39	1.8	3.44	108	.304	.346	3	6	104	101	4.1	5	-2	0.4

YEAR	TM/L	W	L	PCT	G	GS	CG	SHO	SV	IP	H	H/G	HR	BB	BB/G	SO	SO/G	ERA	/A	OAVG	OOBP	PR	/A	PF	CPI	WAT	PB	PD	TPI
	NY-N	8	8	.500	19	16	16	1	0	153	122	7.2	1	32	1.9	67	3.9	2.06	141	.243	.299	12	14	104	88	2.0	-4	1	1.7
1903	NY-N	**31**	20	.608	**55**	48	**44**	3	2	**434**	391	8.1	4	109	2.3	171	3.5	2.43	139	.267	.326	41	**46**	103	101	0.4	-3	-4	4.1
1904	NY-N	**35**	8	**.814**	**51**	44	38	**9**	**5**	**408**	307	6.8	8	86	1.9	144	3.2	**1.61**	**169**	.232	**.286**	**51**	**50**	100	109	**10.2**	-1	2	**5.9**
1905	NY-N	21	15	.583	**46**	38	26	2	3	320	289	8.1	6	71	2.0	125	3.5	2.87	100	.270	.324	4	-0	96	93	-3.3	7	1	0.1
1906	NY-N	**27**	12	.692	**45**	37	32	3	2	340	316	8.4	1	71	1.9	105	2.8	2.25	114	.275	.321	14	12	97	110	4.1	-4	0	1.4
1907	NY-N	18	18	.500	**47**	34	23	3	**4**	310	320	9.3	6	58	1.7	120	3.5	3.16	81	.299	.344	-24	-21	104	96	-1.4	-1	2	-2.0
1908	NY-N	11	7	.611	37	20	7	5	**5**	186	192	9.3	8	37	1.8	55	2.7	2.27	103	.299	.344	1	1	100	**144**	-0.3	-0	-1	0.1
Total	10	246	142	.634	465	381	314	32	24	3441	3276	8.6	51	812	2.1	1068	2.8	2.66	121	.277	.328	184	214	102	104	32.7	-17	-3	21.0
■ **LYNN McGLOTHEN**	McGlothen, Lynn Everatt b: 3/27/50, Monroe, La. d: 8/14/84, Dubach, La. BL/TR, 6'2", 185 lbs. Deb: 6/25/72																												
1972	Bos-A	8	7	.533	22	22	4	1	0	145	135	8.4	9	59	3.7	112	7.0	3.41	94	.247	.324	-6	-3	105	100	-0.1	1	3	0.1
1973	Bos-A	1	2	.333	6	3	0	0	0	23	39	15.3	6	8	3.1	16	6.3	8.22	49	.386	.421	-11	-11	105	107	-0.5	0	0	-0.9
1974	StL-N	16	12	.571	31	31	8	3	0	237	212	8.1	12	89	3.4	142	5.4	2.70	139	.241	.307	25	28	103	112	1.3	-1	1	3.0
1975	StL-N	15	13	.536	35	34	9	2	0	239	231	8.7	21	97	3.7	146	5.5	3.92	96	.254	.323	-8	-4	103	95	1.0	-5	-2	-1.1
1976	StL-N	13	15	.464	33	32	10	4	0	205	209	9.2	10	68	3.0	106	4.7	3.91	94	.268	.324	-9	-6	105	94	0.6	2	-1	-0.4
1977	SF-N	2	9	.182	21	15	2	0	0	80	94	10.6	9	52	5.8	42	4.7	5.62	73	.299	.394	-15	-14	105	104	-3.3	-1	-2	-1.5
1978	SF-N	0	0	—	5	1	0	0	0	13	15	10.4	0	4	2.8	9	6.2	4.85	67	.313	.339	-2	-2	91	90	0.0	-0	0	-0.2
	Chi-N	5	3	.625	49	1	0	0	0	80	77	8.7	7	39	4.4	60	6.7	3.04	131	.257	.338	5	8	111	133	1.1	1	-2	0.8
	Yr	5	3	.625	54	2	0	0	0	93	92	8.9	7	43	4.2	69	6.7	3.29	118	.264	.338	3	6	108	133	1.1	-0	-2	0.6
1979	Chi-N	13	14	.481	42	29	6	1	2	212	236	10.0	27	55	2.3	147	6.2	4.12	102	.283	.325	-9	2	112	107	-0.3	2	-2	0.2
1980	Chi-N	12	14	.462	39	27	2	2	0	182	211	10.4	24	64	3.2	119	5.9	4.80	81	.293	.343	-24	-19	108	104	1.7	2	-2	-1.8
1981	Chi-N	1	4	.200	20	6	0	0	0	55	71	11.6	1	28	4.6	26	4.3	4.75	78	.317	.385	-8	-6	106	111	-1.1	-1	1	-0.6
	Chi-A	0	0	—	11	0	0	0	0	22	14	5.7	0	7	2.9	12	4.9	4.09	88	.189	.265	-1	-1	99	39	0.0	0	-0	-0.1
1982	NY-A	0	0	—	4	0	0	0	0	5	9	16.2	1	2	3.6	2	3.6	10.80	36	.375	.423	-4	-4	97	77	0.0	0	0	-0.3
Total	11	86	93	.480	318	201	41	13	2	1498	1553	9.3	127	572	3.4	939	5.6	3.98	95	.270	.332	-66	-32	106	103	0.4	-1	-6	-2.8
■ **PAT McGLOTHIN**	McGlothin, Ezra Mac b: 10/20/20, Coalfield, Tenn. BL/TR, 6'3.5", 180 lbs. Deb: 4/25/49																												
1949	Bro-N	1	1	.500	7	0	0	0	0	16	13	7.3	2	5	2.8	11	6.2	4.50	88	.224	.286	-1	-1	98	70	-0.1	-0	1	0.0
1950	Bro-N	0	0	—	1	0	0	0	0	2	5	22.5	0	1	4.5	2	9.0	13.50	32	.455	.500	-2	-2	104	78	0.0	0	0	-0.1
Total	2	1	1	.500	8	0	0	0	0	18	18	9.0	2	6	3.0	13	6.5	5.50	72	.261	.320	-3	-3	98	71	-0.1	-0	1	-0.1
■ **JIM McGLOTHLIN**	McGlothlin, James Milton "Red" b: 10/6/43, Los Angeles, Cal. d: 12/23/75, Union, Ky. BR/TR, 6'1", 185 lbs. Deb: 9/20/65																												
1965	Cal-A	0	3	.000	3	3	1	0	0	18	18	9.0	1	7	3.5	9	4.5	3.50	97	.261	.329	-0	-0	98	104	-1.4	-1	-0	0.0
1966	Cal-A	3	1	.750	19	11	0	0	0	68	79	10.5	9	19	2.5	41	5.4	4.50	76	.292	.337	-8	-8	100	108	1.0	-0	-0	-0.8
1967	Cal-A	12	8	.600	32	29	9	**6**	0	197	163	7.4	13	56	2.6	137	6.3	2.97	104	.226	.281	6	3	96	92	1.8	0	1	0.4
1968	Cal-A	10	15	.400	40	32	8	0	3	208	187	8.1	19	60	2.6	135	5.8	3.55	81	.244	.300	-13	-16	96	94	-0.4	-1	2	-1.6
1969	Cal-A	8	16	.333	37	35	4	1	0	201	188	8.4	19	58	2.6	96	4.3	3.18	115	.249	.304	10	11	101	107	-3.1	-1	2	1.2
1970	Cin-N	14	10	.583	35	34	5	3	0	211	192	8.2	19	86	3.7	97	4.1	3.58	117	.245	.315	11	14	103	103	-0.9	1	5	2.1
1971	Cin-N	8	12	.400	30	26	6	0	0	171	151	7.9	15	47	2.5	93	4.9	3.21	104	.243	.296	5	2	96	99	-1.9	1	1	0.4
1972	Cin-N	9	8	.529	31	21	3	1	0	145	165	10.2	15	49	3.0	69	4.3	3.91	81	.287	.337	-7	-12	91	115	-1.2	3	0	-1.0
1973	Cin-N	3	3	.500	24	9	0	0	0	63	91	13.0	13	23	3.3	18	2.6	6.71	50	.340	.386	-21	-23	92	102	-0.5	0	1	-2.1
	Chi-A	0	1	.000	5	1	0	0	0	18	13	6.5	2	13	6.5	14	7.0	4.00	98	.203	.333	-0	-0	103	89	-0.4	0	0	0.0
Total	9	67	77	.465	256	201	36	11	3	1300	1247	8.6	125	418	2.9	709	4.9	3.61	94	.255	.312	-19	-31	98	101	-7.0	1	11	-1.4
■ **STONEY McGLYNN**	McGlynn, Ulysses Simpson Grant b: 5/26/1872, Lancaster, Pa. d: 8/26/41, Manitowoc, Wis. BR/TR, 5'11", 185 lbs. Deb: 9/20/06																												
1906	StL-N	2	2	.500	6	6	6	0	0	48	43	8.1	0	15	2.8	25	4.7	2.44	112	.268	.334	1	2	104	106	0.5	-1	2	0.4
1907	StL-N	14	25	.359	45	39	**33**	3	1	**352**	329	8.4	6	112	2.9	109	2.8	2.91	85	.276	.340	-18	-17	100	96	0.7	3	-2	-2.0
1908	StL-N	1	6	.143	16	6	4	0	1	76	76	9.0	0	17	2.0	23	2.7	3.43	68	.292	.340	-9	-9	100	82	-1.9	-1	1	-0.8
Total	3	17	33	.340	67	51	43	3	2	476	448	8.5	6	144	2.7	157	3.0	2.95	84	.278	.340	-26	-25	100	95	-0.7	1	1	-2.4
■ **MICKEY McGOWAN**	McGowan, Tullis Earl b: 11/26/21, Dothan, Ala. BL/TL, 6'2", 200 lbs. Deb: 4/22/48																												
1948	NY-N	0	0	—	3	0	0	0	0	4	3	6.8	1	4	9.0	2	4.5	6.75	58	.231	.389	-1	-1	98	96	0.0	-0	0	0.0
■ **HOWARD McGRANER**	McGraner, Howard "Muck" b: 9/11/1889, Hanley Run, Ohio d: 10/22/52, Zaleski, Ohio BL/TL, 5'7", 155 lbs. Deb: 9/12/12																												
1912	Cin-N	1	0	1.000	4	0	0	0	0	19	22	10.4	2	7	3.3	5	2.4	7.11	45	.286	.353	-8	-8	93	62	0.5	1	1	-0.6
1914	Bro-F	0	0	—	1	0	0	0	0	2	0	0.0	0	0	0.0	2	9.0	0.00	—	.000	.000	1	1	101	0	0.0	0	0	0.1
Total	2	1	0	1.000	5	0	0	0	0	21	22	9.4	2	7	3.0	7	3.0	6.43	50	.269	.334	-7	-8	94	56	0.5	1	1	-0.5
■ **TUG McGRAW**	McGraw, Frank Edwin b: 8/30/44, Martinez, Cal. BR/TL, 6', 170 lbs. Deb: 4/18/65																												
1965	NY-N	2	7	.222	37	9	2	0	1	98	88	8.1	8	48	4.4	57	5.2	3.31	111	.249	.334	3	4	104	122	-1.2	-1	-1	0.3
1966	NY-N	2	9	.182	15	12	1	0	0	62	72	10.5	11	25	3.6	34	4.9	5.37	65	.294	.351	-12	-13	97	101	-3.1	1	-0	-1.2
1967	NY-N	0	3	.000	4	4	0	0	0	17	13	6.9	3	13	6.9	18	9.5	7.94	43	.206	.333	-9	-9	102	53	-1.4	0	0	-0.6
1969	NY-N	9	3	.750	42	4	1	0	12	100	89	8.0	6	47	4.2	92	8.3	2.25	159	.243	.321	**15**	**15**	99	155	2.2	0	1	1.7
1970	NY-N	4	6	.400	57	0	0	0	10	91	77	7.6	6	49	4.8	81	8.0	3.26	128	.231	.319	8	9	103	108	-1.1	1	1	1.2
1971	NY-N	11	4	.733	51	1	0	0	8	111	73	5.9	4	41	3.3	109	8.8	1.70	195	.189	.265	**22**	20	96	104	3.6	2	-1	2.3
1972	NY-N	8	6	.571	54	0	0	0	27	106	71	6.0	3	40	3.4	92	7.8	1.70	195	.197	.272	21	19	96	120	0.6	-0	0	2.0
1973	NY-N	5	6	.455	60	2	0	0	25	119	106	8.0	11	55	4.2	81	6.1	3.86	95	.243	.326	-2	-2	100	96	-0.5	0	1	-0.1
1974	NY-N	6	11	.353	41	4	1	1	3	89	96	9.7	12	32	3.2	54	5.5	4.15	88	.279	.328	-5	-5	100	110	-1.7	-0	-1	-0.5
1975	Phi-N	9	6	.600	56	0	0	0	14	103	84	7.3	6	36	3.1	55	4.8	2.97	123	.226	.294	8	8	101	91	1.2	-0	-0	0.8
1976	Phi-N	7	6	.538	58	0	0	0	11	97	81	7.5	4	42	3.9	76	7.1	2.51	146	.226	.301	11	13	105	109	-0.9	0	-1	1.3
1977	Phi-N	7	3	.700	45	0	0	0	9	79	62	7.1	6	24	2.7	58	6.6	2.62	147	.221	.280	11	11	98	100	1.1	2	0	1.3
1978	Phi-N	8	7	.533	55	1	0	0	9	90	82	8.2	6	23	2.3	63	6.3	3.20	116	.245	.289	4	5	104	92	-0.2	-0	0	0.5
1979	Phi-N	4	3	.571	65	1	0	0	16	84	83	8.9	9	29	3.1	57	6.1	5.14	71	.259	.319	-13	-14	97	75	0.4	-0	-1	-1.5
1980	Phi-N	5	4	.556	57	0	0	0	20	92	62	6.1	3	23	2.3	75	7.3	1.47	261	.194	.245	**22**	**24**	106	108	0.0	0	0	2.7
1981	Phi-N	2	4	.333	34	0	0	0	10	44	35	7.2	2	14	2.9	26	5.3	2.66	147	.219	.275	4	6	112	87	-1.1	-0	-0	0.6
1982	Phi-N	3	3	.500	34	0	0	0	5	40	50	11.2	3	12	2.7	25	5.6	4.27	79	.305	.348	-3	-4	94	111	-0.2	-0	0	-0.3
1983	Phi-N	2	1	.667	34	1	0	0	0	56	58	9.3	4	19	3.1	30	4.8	3.54	103	.271	.326	1	1	100	109	0.4	0	0	0.1
1984	Phi-N	2	0	1.000	25	0	0	0	0	38	36	8.5	1	10	2.4	26	6.2	3.79	96	.245	.287	-1	-1	101	69	1.0	0	0	0.0
Total	19	96	92	.511	824	39	5	1	180	1516	1318	7.8	108	582	3.5	1109	6.6	3.13	116	.237	.304	83	87	101	105	-0.9	5	-1	10.6
■ **JOHN McGRAW**	McGraw, John b: 1890, d: 11/14/18, Cleveland, Ohio 190 lbs. Deb: 7/29/14																												
1914	Bro-F	0	0	—	1	0	0	0	0	2	0	0.0	0	0	0.0	2	9.0	0.00	—	.000	.000	1	1	101	0	0.0	0	0	0.1
■ **BOB McGRAW**	McGraw, Robert Emmett b: 4/10/1895, La Veta, Colo. d: 6/2/78, Boise, Idaho BR/TR, 6'2", 160 lbs. Deb: 9/25/17																												
1917	NY-A	0	1	.000	2	2	1	0	0	11	9	7.4	0	3	2.5	3	2.5	0.82	350	.257	.316	2	2	107	323	-0.4	-0	-0	0.2
1918	NY-A	0	1	.000	1	1	0	0	0	0	0	—	0	4	—	0	—	∞	—	—	1.000	-4	-4	94	31	-0.4	0	0	-0.3
1919	NY-A	1	0	1.000	6	0	0	0	0	16	11	6.2	1	10	5.6	3	1.7	3.38	99	.216	.355	-0	-0	104	100	0.5	-0	-0	0.0
	Bos-A	0	2	.000	10	1	0	0	0	27	33	11.0	0	17	5.7	6	2.0	6.67	44	.347	.461	-10	-11	91	93	-0.9	-1	-1	-1.1
	Yr	1	2	.333	16	1	0	0	0	43	44	9.2	1	27	5.7	9	1.9	5.44	57	.299	.418	-11	-11	96	93	-0.4	-0	-1	-1.1
1920	NY-A	0	0	—	15	0	0	0	0	27	24	8.0	1	20	6.7	11	3.7	4.67	80	.240	.372	-3	-3	99	81	0.0	-1	-1	-0.3
1925	Bro-N	0	2	.000	2	2	2	0	0	20	14	6.3	0	13	5.8	3	1.3	3.15	129	.222	.338	2	2	95	105	-0.9	0	-1	0.1
1926	Bro-N	9	13	.409	33	21	10	0	1	174	197	10.2	12	67	3.5	49	2.5	4.60	84	.292	.343	-15	-15	101	99	-1.4	-2	-1	-1.6
1927	Bro-N	0	1	.000	1	1	0	0	0	4	5	11.3	1	2	4.5	2	4.5	9.00	45	.313	.368	-2	-2	104	76	-0.4	-0	0	-0.1
	StL-N	4	5	.444	18	12	4	1	0	94	121	11.6	3	30	2.9	37	3.5	5.07	82	.323	.358	-12	-10	106	97	-1.1	1	1	-0.7
	Yr	4	6	.400	19	13	4	1	0	98	126	11.6	4	32	2.9	39	3.6	5.23	79	.322	.358	-14	-12	106	97	-1.5	-0	1	-0.8
1928	Phi-N	7	8	.467	39	3	0	0	1	132	150	10.2	7	56	3.8	28	1.9	4.64	94	.326	.378	-10	-4	109	117	2.1	-3	-1	-0.6
1929	Phi-N	5	5	.500	41	4	0	0	4	86	113	11.8	6	43	4.5	22	2.3	5.76	91	.324	.383	-10	-5	112	104	0.4	-0	1	-0.2
Total	9	26	38	.406	168	47	17	1	6	591	677	10.3	31	265	4.0	164	2.5	4.89	85	.305	.366	-61	-50	104	107	-2.5	-6	-2	-4.6

YEAR	TM/L	W	L	PCT	G	GS	CG	SHO	SV	IP	H	H/G	HR	BB	BB/G	SO	SO/G	ERA	/A	OAVG	OOBP	PR	/A	PF	CPI	WAT	PB	PD	TPI
■ SCOTT McGREGOR	McGregor, Scott Houston b: 1/18/54, Inglewood, Cal. BB/TL, 6'1", 190 lbs. Deb: 9/19/76																												
1976	Bal-A	0	1	.000	3	2	0	0	0	15	17	10.2	0	5	3.0	6	3.6	3.60	95	.293	.349	-0	-0	97	108	-0.4	0	0	0.0
1977	Bal-A	3	5	.375	29	5	1	0	4	114	119	9.4	8	30	2.4	55	4.3	4.42	85	.275	.325	-4	-8	92	89	-1.5	0	-1	-0.8
1978	Bal-A	15	13	.536	35	32	13	4	1	233	217	8.4	19	47	1.8	94	3.6	3.32	103	.248	.283	12	3	91	88	-0.6	0	0	0.3
1979	Bal-A	13	6	.684	27	23	7	2	0	175	165	8.5	19	23	**1.2**	81	4.2	3.34	121	.248	**.269**	17	14	96	90	1.3	0	-1	1.2
1980	Bal-A	20	8	.714	36	36	12	4	0	252	254	9.1	16	58	2.1	119	4.3	3.32	121	.265	.303	20	19	99	101	4.1	0	-3	1.7
1981	Bal-A	13	5	.722	24	22	8	3	0	160	167	9.4	13	40	2.3	82	4.6	3.26	111	.273	.312	7	7	99	116	3.7	0	1	0.8
1982	Bal-A	14	12	.538	37	37	7	1	0	226	238	9.5	31	52	2.1	84	3.3	4.62	87	.267	.304	-13	-15	99	86	-1.0	0	-1	-1.4
1983	Bal-A	18	7	.720	36	36	12	2	0	260	271	9.4	24	45	1.6	86	3.0	3.18	126	.269	.296	26	24	99	113	4.1	0	-1	2.4
1984	Bal-A	15	12	.556	30	30	10	3	0	196	216	9.9	18	54	2.5	67	3.1	3.95	95	.280	.327	1	-4	94	105	1.0	0	1	-0.2
1985	Bal-A	14	14	.500	35	34	8	1	0	204	226	10.0	34	65	2.9	86	3.8	4.81	85	.283	.330	-15	-17	98	104	-0.4	0	-1	-1.6
1986	Bal-A	11	15	.423	34	33	4	2	0	203	216	9.6	35	57	2.5	95	4.2	4.52	92	.270	.318	-8	-8	99	100	-0.8	0	-1	-0.8
1987	Bal-A	2	7	.222	26	15	1	1	0	85	112	11.9	15	35	3.7	39	4.1	6.67	67	.326	.382	-21	-21	99	99	-2.0	0	3	-1.6
1988	Bal-A	0	3	.000	4	4	0	0	0	17	27	14.3	3	7	3.7	10	5.3	9.00	43	.370	.415	-9	-10	97	88	-1.4	0	1	-0.7
Total	13	138	108	.561	356	309	83	23	5	2140	2245	9.4	235	518	2.2	904	3.8	3.99	98	.271	.311	12	-17	97	99	6.1	0	-2	-0.7
■ SLIM McGREW	McGrew, Walter Howard b: 8/5/1899, Yoakum, Tex. d: 8/21/67, Houston, Tex. BR/TR, 6'7.5", 235 lbs. Deb: 4/18/22																												
1922	Was-A	0	0	—	1	0	0	0	0	2	4	18.0	0	2	9.0	1	4.5	9.00	42	.500	.500	-1	-1	93	131	0.0	-0	0	0.0
1923	Was-A	0	0	—	3	0	0	0	0	5	11	19.8	0	3	5.4	1	1.8	12.60	30	.440	.500	-5	-5	95	77	0.0	-0	0	-0.3
1924	Was-A	0	1	.000	6	2	0	0	0	23	25	9.8	1	12	4.7	8	3.1	5.09	80	.281	.352	-2	-3	96	85	-0.4	-1	-1	-0.3
Total	3	0	1	.000	10	2	0	0	0	30	40	12.0	1	17	5.1	10	3.0	6.60	61	.328	.393	-8	-9	96	87	-0.4	-2	0	-0.6
■ DEACON McGUIRE	McGuire, James Thomas b: 11/2/1865, Youngstown, Ohio d: 10/31/36, Albion, Mich. BR/TL, 6'1", 185 lbs. Deb: 6/21/1884 M																												
1890	Roc-a	0	0	—	1	0	0	0	0	4	10	22.5	0	1	2.3	1	2.3	6.75	53	.488	.512	-1	-1	92	157	0.0	0	0	0.0
■ MURRAY McGUIRE	McGuire, Murray Mason b: 1/19/1872, Richmond, Va. d: 9/10/45, Richmond, Va. TL , Deb: 6/16/1894																												
1894	Cin-N	0	0	—	1	0	0	0	0	6	15	22.5	0	5	7.5	1	1.5	10.50	52	.495	.566	-3	-3	102	116	0.0	-0	0	-0.1
■ TOM McGUIRE	McGuire, Thomas Patrick "Elmer" b: 2/1/1892, Chicago, Ill. d: 12/7/59, Phoenix, Ariz. BR/TR, 6', 175 lbs. Deb: 4/18/14																												
1914	Chi-F	5	6	.455	24	12	7	0	0	131	143	9.8	7	57	3.9	37	2.5	3.71	77	.288	.366	-7	-12	89	120	-1.0	4	1	-0.4
1919	Chi-A	0	0	—	1	0	0	0	0	3	5	15.0	0	3	9.0	0	0.0	9.00	36	.500	.615	-2	-2	102	117	0.0	-0	0	-0.1
Total	2	5	6	.455	25	12	7	0	0	134	148	9.9	7	60	4.0	37	2.5	3.83	75	.292	.371	-9	-14	89	119	-1.0	4	2	-0.5
■ BILL McGUNNIGLE	McGunnigle, William Henry "Gunner" b: 1/1/1855, Boston, Mass. d: 3/9/1899, Brockton, Mass. BR/TR, 5'9", 155 lbs. Deb: 5/02/1879 M																												
1879	Buf-N	9	5	.643	14	13	13	2	0	120	113	**8.5**	0	16	1.2	62	**4.7**	2.63	108	**.254**	.280	-2	3	114	74	1.1	-3	0	0.3
1880	Buf-N	2	3	.400	5	5	4	1	0	37	43	10.5	0	8	1.9	3	0.7	3.41	67	.300	.337	-4	-5	96	101	0.4	-1	0	-1.2
Total	2	11	8	.579	19	18	17	3	0	157	156	8.9	0	24	1.4	65	3.7	2.81	96	.265	.294	-6	-2	109	80	1.5	-4	0	-0.9
■ MARTY McHALE	McHale, Martin Joseph b: 10/30/1888, Stoneham, Mass. d: 5/7/79, Hempstead, N.Y. BR/TR, 5'11.5", 174 lbs. Deb: 9/28/10																												
1910	Bos-A	0	2	.000	2	2	1	0	0	14	15	9.6	0	6	3.9	14	9.0	4.50	55	.259	.338	-3	-3	97	70	-0.9	-1	0	-0.2
1911	Bos-A	0	0	—	4	1	0	0	0	9	19	19.0	1	3	3.0	3	3.0	10.00	33	.475	.523	-7	-7	99	106	0.0	-0	0	-0.5
1913	NY-A	2	4	.333	7	6	4	1	0	49	49	9.0	1	10	1.8	11	2.0	2.94	103	.266	.308	-0	1	104	95	-0.3	-2	-1	0.0
1914	NY-A	7	16	.304	31	23	12	0	1	191	195	9.2	3	33	**1.6**	75	3.5	2.97	92	.268	.303	-5	-5	100	92	-4.1	2	-3	-0.8
1915	NY-A	3	7	.300	13	11	6	0	0	78	86	9.9	1	19	2.2	25	2.9	4.27	68	.277	.318	-11	-12	99	73	-1.7	1	0	-1.1
1916	Bos-A	0	1	.000	2	1	0	0	0	6	7	10.5	0	4	6.0	1	1.5	3.00	87	.280	.400	-0	-0	92	157	-0.4	0	0	0.0
	Cle-A	0	0	—	5	0	0	0	0	11	10	8.2	1	6	4.9	2	1.6	5.73	49	.270	.372	-4	-4	99	78	0.0	-0	-0	-0.3
	Yr	0	1	.000	7	1	0	0	0	17	17	9.0	1	10	5.3	3	1.6	4.76	57	.270	.370	-4	-4	97	78	-0.4	0	0	-0.3
Total	6	12	30	.286	64	44	23	1	1	358	381	9.6	7	81	2.0	131	3.3	3.57	79	.275	.319	-30	-30	100	88	-7.4	-0	-4	-2.9
■ VANCE McILREE	McIlree, Vance Elmer b: 10/14/1897, Riverside, Iowa d: 5/6/59, Kansas City, Mo. BR/TR, 6', 160 lbs. Deb: 9/13/21																												
1921	Was-A	0	0	—	1	0	0	0	0	1	1	9.0	0	0	0.0	0	0.0	9.00	47	.200	.200	-1	-1	99	12	0.0	0	0	0.0
■ IRISH McILVEEN	McIlveen, Henry Cooke b: 7/27/1880, Belfast, Ireland d: 10/18/60, Lorain, Ohio TL , 5'11.5", 180 lbs. Deb: 7/10/06																												
1906	Pit-N	0	1	.000	2	1	0	0	0	7	10	12.9	1	2	2.6	3	3.9	7.71	34	.366	.409	-4	-4	101	80	-0.4	1	0	-0.3
■ STOVER McILWAIN	McIlwain, Stover William "Smokey" b: 9/22/39, Savannah, Ga. d: 1/15/66, Buffalo, N.Y. BR/TR, 6'2", 195 lbs. Deb: 9/25/57																												
1957	Chi-A	0	0	—	1	0	0	0	0	1	2	18.0	0	1	9.0	0	0.0	0.00	—	.500	.600	0	0	97	0	0.0	0	0	0.0
1958	Chi-A	0	0	—	1	1	0	0	0	4	4	9.0	1	0	0.0	4	9.0	2.25	164	.250	.250	1	1	98	162	0.0	-0	0	0.1
Total	2	0	0	—	2	1	0	0	0	5	6	10.8	1	1	1.8	4	7.2	1.80	204	.300	.333	1	1	97	129	0.0	-0	0	0.1
■ HARRY McINTIRE	McIntire, John Reid b: 1/11/1879, Dayton, Ohio d: 1/9/49, Daytona Beach, Fla. BR/TR, 5'11", 180 lbs. Deb: 4/14/05																												
1905	Bro-N	8	25	.242	40	35	29	1	1	309	340	9.9	6	101	2.9	135	3.9	3.70	82	.312	.381	-24	-23	102	108	-4.5	5	-3	-2.5
1906	Bro-N	13	21	.382	39	31	25	4	3	276	254	8.3	2	89	2.9	121	3.9	2.97	79	.275	.348	-10	-19	90	96	-2.4	1	-1	-2.0
1907	Bro-N	7	15	.318	28	22	19	3	0	200	178	8.0	6	79	3.6	49	2.2	2.39	99	.268	.352	2	-0	96	124	-3.3	4	-1	-0.1
1908	Bro-N	11	20	.355	40	35	26	4	2	288	259	8.1	5	90	2.8	108	3.4	2.69	86	.274	.349	-11	-12	99	106	0.3	2	-2	-1.5
1909	Bro-N	7	17	.292	32	26	20	2	1	228	200	7.9	5	91	3.6	84	3.3	3.63	74	.246	.337	-26	-24	103	86	-2.5	1	-0	-2.5
1910	Chi-N	13	9	.591	28	19	10	3	0	176	152	7.8	5	50	2.6	65	3.3	3.07	95	.240	.305	-1	-3	96	83	-1.5	-3	-1	-0.3
1911	Chi-N	11	7	.611	25	17	9	1	0	149	147	8.9	5	33	2.0	56	3.4	4.11	78	.257	.302	-12	-15	94	68	0.3	5	-0	-1.0
1912	Chi-N	1	2	.333	4	3	2	0	0	24	22	8.3	0	6	2.3	8	3.0	3.75	93	.247	.295	-1	-1	102	57	-0.6	1	0	0.0
1913	Cin-N	0	1	.000	1	0	0	0	0	1	3	27.0	0	0	0.0	0	0.0	27.00	12	.600	.600	-3	-3	104	51	-0.4	0	0	-0.1
Total	9	71	117	.378	237	188	140	18	7	1651	1555	8.5	34	539	2.9	626	3.4	3.22	83	.271	.344	-86	-99	97	98	-14.6	17	-9	-10.0
■ JOE McINTOSH	McIntosh, Joseph Anthony b: 8/4/51, Billings, Mont. BB/TR, 6'2", 185 lbs. Deb: 4/05/74																												
1974	SD-N	0	4	.000	10	5	0	0	0	37	36	8.8	3	17	4.1	22	5.4	3.65	96	.250	.329	-0	-1	97	101	-1.9	-1	-0	-0.1
1975	SD-N	8	15	.348	37	28	4	1	0	183	195	9.6	14	60	3.0	71	3.5	3.69	100	.273	.326	-1	-0	101	105	-2.6	2	-0	0.1
Total	2	8	19	.296	47	33	4	1	0	220	231	9.4	17	77	3.1	93	3.8	3.68	99	.270	.326	-1	-1	100	105	-4.5	0	-1	0.0
■ FRANK McINTYRE	McIntyre, Frank W. b: Detroit d: 7/8/1887, Detroit, Mich. Deb: 5/16/1883																												
1883	Det-N	1	0	1.000	1	1	1	0	0	11	11	9.0	0	1	0.8	0	0.0	0.82	359	.268	.285	3	3	94	284	0.5	-0	0	0.2
	Col-a	1	1	.500	2	2	2	0	0	19	20	9.5	0	7	3.3	6	2.8	5.21	58	.276	.340	-4	-5	91	72	0.3	-0	0	-0.3
■ DOC McJAMES	McJames, James McCutchen (born James Mc Cutchen James) b: 8/27/1873, Williamsburg, S.C. d: 9/23/01, Charleston, S.C. TR , Deb: 9/24/1895																												
1895	Was-N	1	1	.500	2	2	2	0	0	17	17	9.0	0	16	8.5	9	4.8	1.59	318	.280	.430	6	7	105	308	0.2	-1	0	0.5
1896	Was-N	12	20	.375	37	33	29	0	1	280	310	10.0	2	135	4.3	103	3.3	4.28	98	.303	.384	3	-2	96	96	-3.0	-8	-0	-0.8
1897	Was-N	15	23	.395	44	39	33	**3**	2	324	361	10.0	7	137	3.8	**156**	4.3	3.61	121	.304	.376	25	28	102	112	-3.6	-7	1	1.9
1898	Bal-N	27	15	.643	45	42	40	2	0	374	327	7.9	5	113	2.7	178	4.3	2.36	152	.255	.316	52	51	100	105	0.0	-4	-3	4.4
1899	Bro-N	19	15	.559	37	34	27	1	1	275	295	9.7	4	122	4.0	105	3.4	3.50	113	.298	.375	11	13	102	109	-3.7	-5	3	1.1
1901	Bro-N	5	6	.455	13	12	6	0	0	91	104	10.3	1	40	4.0	42	4.2	4.75	72	.316	.402	-14	-13	103	93	-1.2	-4	-2	-1.3
Total	6	79	80	.497	178	162	137	6	4	1361	1414	9.4	19	563	3.7	593	3.9	3.43	116	.290	.365	82	83	100	107	-11.3	-29	-0	5.8
■ ARCHIE McKAIN	McKain, Archie Richard "Happy" b: 5/12/11, Delphos, Kan. d: 5/21/85, Salina, Kan. BB/TL, 5'10", 175 lbs. Deb: 4/25/37																												
1937	Bos-A	8	8	.500	36	18	3	0	2	137	152	10.0	7	64	4.2	66	4.3	4.66	101	.276	.346	-1	1	102	92	-0.3	3	0	0.4
1938	Bos-A	5	4	.556	37	5	1	0	6	100	119	10.7	6	44	4.0	27	2.4	4.50	107	.297	.364	3	3	100	112	-0.2	-2	2	0.2
1939	Det-A	5	6	.455	32	11	4	0	4	130	120	8.3	6	54	3.7	49	3.4	3.67	138	.247	.314	14	20	110	96	-0.7	4	-2	2.2
1940	Det-A	5	0	1.000	27	0	0	0	3	51	48	8.5	2	25	4.4	24	4.2	2.82	169	.247	.326	9	11	109	128	2.5	0	1	1.2
1941	Det-A	2	1	.667	15	0	0	0	0	43	58	12.1	3	11	2.3	14	2.9	5.02	89	.330	.358	-4	-3	107	109	0.5	-1	2	-0.1
	StL-A	0	1	.000	8	0	0	0	1	10	16	14.4	2	4	3.6	2	1.8	8.10	52	.364	.429	-4	-4	101	102	-0.4	-0	1	-0.3
	Yr	2	2	.500	23	0	0	0	1	53	74	12.6	5	15	2.5	16	2.7	5.60	79	.336	.372	-9	-7	106	102	0.1	-1	3	-0.4
1943	StL-A	1	1	.500	10	0	0	0	0	16	16	9.0	0	6	3.4	6	3.4	3.94	84	.242	.306	-1	-1	101	65	0.1	-0	0	0.0
Total	6	26	21	.553	165	34	8	0	16	487	529	9.8	26	208	3.8	188	3.5	4.25	112	.276	.341	15	27	105	102	1.5	3	4	3.6

YEAR	TM/L	W	L	PCT	G	GS	CG	SHO	SV	IP	H	H/G	HR	BB	BB/G	SO	SO/G	ERA	/A	OAVG	OOBP	PR	/A	PF	CPI	WAT	PB	PD	TPI
■ **HAL McKAIN**	McKain, Harold Le Roy b: 7/10/06, Logan, Iowa d: 1/24/70, Sacramento, Cal. BL/TR, 5'11", 185 lbs. Deb: 9/22/27																												
1927	Cle-A	0	1	.000	2	1	0	0	0	11	18	14.7	0	4	3.3	5	4.1	4.09	100	.391	.431	0	-0	99	171	-0.4	-1	0	0.0
1929	Chi-A	6	9	.400	34	10	4	1	1	158	158	9.0	10	85	4.8	33	1.9	3.65	114	.275	.361	11	9	98	**130**	0.2	3	4	1.4
1930	Chi-A	6	4	.600	32	5	0	0	5	89	108	10.9	0	42	4.2	52	5.3	5.56	88	.299	.368	-9	-7	105	87	1.7	7	1	0.1
1931	Chi-A	6	9	.400	27	8	3	0	0	112	134	10.8	10	57	4.6	39	3.1	5.71	74	.295	.372	-16	-19	96	97	0.4	-1	1	-1.5
1932	Chi-A	0	0	—	8	0	0	0	0	11	17	13.9	1	5	4.1	7	5.7	11.45	36	.340	.386	-9	-9	91	59	0.0	-0	0	-0.7
Total	5	18	23	.439	103	24	7	1	6	381	435	10.3	21	193	4.6	136	3.2	4.94	88	.293	.369	-23	-26	99	109	1.9	8	7	-0.7
■ **REEVE McKAY**	McKay, Reeve Stewart "Rip" b: 11/16/1881, Morgan, Tex. d: 1/18/46, Dallas, Tex. TR, 6'1.5", 168 lbs. Deb: 10/02/15																												
1915	StL-A	0	0	—	1	0	0	0	0	1	1	9.0	0	0	0.0	0	0.0	9.00	32	.500	.500	-1	-1	99	65	0.0	0	0	0.0
■ **JIM McKEE**	McKee, James Marion b: 2/1/47, Columbus, Ohio BR/TR, 6'7", 215 lbs. Deb: 9/15/72																												
1972	Pit-N	1	0	1.000	2	0	0	0	0	5	2	3.6	0	1	1.8	4	7.2	0.00	—	.125	.167	2	2	100	0	0.5	0	-0	0.2
1973	Pit-N	0	1	.000	15	1	0	0	0	27	31	10.3	2	17	5.7	13	4.3	5.67	59	.287	.377	-6	-7	92	91	-0.4	-0	-0	-0.7
Total	2	1	1	.500	17	1	0	0	0	32	33	9.3	2	18	5.1	17	4.8	4.78	71	.266	.351	-4	-5	93	77	0.1	-0	-0	-0.5
■ **ROGERS McKEE**	McKee, Rogers Hornsby b: 9/16/26, Shelby, N.C. BL/TL, 6'1", 160 lbs. Deb: 8/18/43																												
1943	Phi-N	1	0	1.000	4	1	1	0	0	13	12	8.3	0	5	3.5	1	0.7	6.23	52	.226	.288	-4	-4	96	34	0.5	0	0	-0.3
1944	Phi-N	0	0	—	1	0	0	0	0	2	2	9.0	1	1	4.5	0	0.0	4.50	82	.250	.333	-0	-0	103	156	0.0	0	0	0.0
Total	2	1	0	1.000	5	1	1	0	0	15	14	8.4	1	6	3.6	1	0.6	6.00	55	.230	.294	-4	-5	97	50	0.5	0	0	-0.3
■ **TIM McKEITHAN**	McKeithan, Emmett James b: 11/2/06, Lawndale, N.C. d: 8/20/69, Forest City, N.C. BR/TR, 6'2", 182 lbs. Deb: 7/21/32																												
1932	Phi-A	0	1	.000	4	2	0	0	0	13	18	12.5	0	5	3.5	0	0.0	6.92	71	.340	.390	-4	-3	111	84	-0.4	0	0	-0.1
1933	Phi-A	1	0	1.000	3	1	0	0	0	9	10	10.0	0	4	4.0	3	3.0	4.00	98	.278	.341	0	-0	92	102	0.5	0	0	0.0
1934	Phi-A	0	0	—	3	0	0	0	0	4	7	15.8	2	5	11.3	0	0.0	15.75	28	.389	.522	-5	-5	98	86	0.0	-0	-0	-0.4
Total	3	1	1	.500	10	3	0	0	0	26	35	12.1	2	14	4.8	3	1.0	7.27	62	.327	.398	-8	-8	102	90	0.1	0	0	-0.5
■ **RUSS McKELVY**	McKelvy, Russell Errett b: 9/8/1856, Meadville, Pa. d: 10/19/15, Omaha, Neb. TR, Deb: 5/01/1878																												
1878	Ind-N	0	2	.000	4	1	1	0	0	25	38	13.7	1	3	1.1	3	1.1	2.16	94	.360	.378	0	-0	88	222	-0.9	0	0	0.0
■ **KIT McKENNA**	McKenna, James William b: 2/10/1873, Lynchburg, Va. d: 3/31/41, Lynchburg, Va. Deb: 7/07/1898																												
1898	Bro-N	2	6	.250	14	9	7	0	0	101	118	10.5	4	57	5.1	27	2.4	5.70	61	.314	.404	-24	-25	96	85	-1.3	1	0	-2.0
1899	Bal-N	2	3	.400	8	4	4	0	1	45	66	13.2	1	19	3.8	7	1.4	4.60	89	.367	.427	-4	-3	106	125	-0.7	-1	0	-0.2
Total	2	4	9	.308	22	13	11	0	1	146	184	11.3	5	76	4.7	34	2.1	5.36	68	.331	.412	-27	-28	99	97	-2.0	-0	0	-2.2
■ **LIMB McKENRY**	McKenry, Frank Gordon "Big Pete" b: 8/13/1888, Piney Flats, Tenn. d: 11/1/56, Fresno, Cal. BR/TR, 6'4", 205 lbs. Deb: 8/27/15																												
1915	Cin-N	5	5	.500	21	11	5	0	0	110	94	7.7	2	39	3.2	37	3.0	2.95	97	.238	.300	-2	-1	104	90	0.4	0	1	0.1
1916	Cin-N	1	1	.500	6	1	0	0	0	15	14	8.4	0	8	4.8	2	1.2	4.20	63	.259	.364	-3	-3	101	91	0.2	2	0	0.0
Total	2	6	6	.500	27	12	5	0	0	125	108	7.8	2	47	3.4	39	2.8	3.10	92	.241	.308	-5	-4	104	90	0.6	2	1	0.1
■ **JOEL McKEON**	McKeon, Joel Jacob b: 2/25/63, Covington, Ky. BL/TL, 6', 185 lbs. Deb: 5/06/86																												
1986	Chi-A	3	1	.750	30	0	0	0	1	33	18	4.9	2	17	4.6	18	4.9	2.45	173	.165	.271	6	7	101	82	1.1	0	-0	0.6
1987	Chi-A	1	2	.333	13	0	0	0	0	21	27	11.6	8	15	6.4	14	6.0	9.43	51	.318	.412	-12	-11	109	92	-0.4	0	-0	-0.9
Total	2	4	3	.571	43	0	0	0	1	54	45	7.5	10	32	5.3	32	5.3	5.17	87	.232	.333	-5	-4	104	86	0.7	0	-1	-0.3
■ **LARRY McKEON**	McKeon, Lawrence G. b: 3/25/1866, New York d: 7/18/15, Indianapolis, Ind 5'10", 168 lbs. Deb: 5/01/1884																												
1884	Ind-a	18	41	.305	61	60	59	2	0	512	488	8.6	20	94	1.7	308	5.4	3.50	93	.259	.295	-14	-14	100	93	2.9	-3	7	-0.9
1885	Cin-a	20	13	.606	33	33	32	2	0	290	273	8.5	5	50	1.6	117	3.6	2.86	117	.260	.294	13	15	103	98	2.2	-5	-1	0.9
1886	Cin-a	8	8	.500	19	19	16	0	0	156	174	10.0	6	54	3.1	46	2.7	5.08	65	.293	.352	-28	-31	96	85	0.5	2	0	-2.3
	KC-N	0	2	.000	3	3	3	0	0	21	44	18.9	0	8	3.4	3	1.3	10.71	35	.441	.482	-17	-16	114	82	-0.9	-2	0	-1.2
Total	3	46	64	.418	116	115	110	4	0	979	979	9.0	31	206	1.9	474	4.4	3.71	89	.270	.309	-47	-46	100	93	4.7	-8	6	-3.5
■ **DENNY McLAIN**	McLain, Dennis Dale b: 3/29/44, Chicago, Ill. BR/TR, 6'1", 185 lbs. Deb: 9/21/63																												
1963	Det-A	2	1	.667	3	3	2	0	0	21	20	8.6	2	16	6.9	22	9.4	4.29	88	.253	.375	-2	-1	104	113	0.5	1	1	0.0
1964	Det-A	4	5	.444	19	16	3	0	0	100	84	7.6	16	37	3.3	70	6.3	4.05	85	.225	.293	-5	-7	95	86	-0.6	-1	-2	-0.9
1965	Det-A	16	6	.727	33	29	13	4	1	220	174	7.1	25	62	2.5	192	7.9	2.62	138	.216	.270	21	24	104	103	4.7	-4	-0	2.2
1966	Det-A	20	14	.588	38	38	14	4	0	264	205	7.0	42	104	3.5	192	6.5	3.92	89	.214	.289	-14	-12	102	88	2.1	1	-1	-1.1
1967	Det-A	17	16	.515	37	37	10	3	0	235	209	8.0	35	73	2.8	161	6.2	3.79	83	.237	.292	-15	-16	98	96	-1.6	-2	-2	-2.2
1968	Det-A	**31**	6	**.838**	41	41	**28**	6	0	**336**	241	6.5	31	63	1.7	280	7.5	1.96	157	.200	.241	38	**42**	103	100	**11.4**	-0	1	**5.3**
1969	Det-A	**24**	9	.727	42	41	23	**9**	0	**325**	288	8.0	25	67	1.9	181	5.0	2.80	132	.237	.275	30	33	102	96	**7.3**	-1	-5	2.9
1970	Det-A	3	5	.375	14	14	1	0	0	91	100	9.9	19	28	2.8	52	5.1	4.65	83	.273	.326	-9	-8	104	105	-0.9	-2	0	-0.9
1971	Was-A	10	22	.313	33	32	9	3	0	217	233	9.7	31	72	3.0	103	4.3	4.27	76	.281	.331	-19	-24	94	109	-3.9	-0	-1	-2.6
1972	Oak-A	1	2	.333	5	5	0	0	0	22	32	13.1	4	8	3.3	8	3.3	6.14	47	.323	.370	-7	-8	95	101	-0.6	-0	0	-0.7
	Atl-N	3	5	.375	15	8	2	0	1	54	60	10.0	12	18	3.0	21	3.5	6.50	56	.279	.333	-18	-17	106	80	-0.6	-0	-1	-1.7
Total	10	131	91	.590	280	264	105	29	2	1885	1646	7.9	242	548	2.6	1282	6.1	3.39	101	.234	.288	-1	5	101	97	17.8	-9	-10	0.3
■ **BARNEY McLAUGHLIN**	McLaughlin, Bernard b: 1857, Ireland d: 2/13/21, Lowell, Mass. BR/TR, Deb: N/A.																												
1884	KC-U	1	3	.250	7	4	4	0	0	49	62	11.4	2	15	2.8	14	2.6	5.51	50	.314	.362	-14	-15	92	89	0.1	1	0	-1.1
■ **BYRON McLAUGHLIN**	McLaughlin, Byron Scott b: 9/29/55, Van Nuys, Cal. BR/TR, 6'1", 175 lbs. Deb: 9/18/77																												
1977	Sea-A	0	0	—	1	0	0	0	0	1	5	45.0	1	0	0.0	1	9.0	36.00	11	.625	.625	-4	-4	98	81	0.0	0	0	-0.2
1978	Sea-A	4	8	.333	20	17	4	0	0	107	97	8.2	15	39	3.3	87	7.3	4.37	90	.238	.311	-7	-5	104	84	-0.2	0	-2	-0.6
1979	Sea-A	7	7	.500	47	7	1	0	14	124	114	8.3	13	60	4.4	74	5.4	4.21	102	.251	.333	0	1	101	98	1.1	0	-2	0.0
1980	Sea-A	3	6	.333	45	4	0	0	2	91	124	12.3	15	50	4.9	41	4.1	6.82	62	.331	.401	-28	-26	105	101	-0.3	0	-2	-2.6
1983	Cal-A	2	4	.333	16	7	0	0	0	56	63	10.1	3	22	3.5	45	7.2	5.14	76	.286	.348	-7	-8	96	87	-0.6	0	0	-0.7
Total	5	16	25	.390	129	35	5	0	16	379	403	9.6	47	171	4.1	248	5.9	5.11	81	.275	.348	-45	-41	102	93	0.0	0	-5	-4.1
■ **FRANK McLAUGHLIN**	McLaughlin, Francis Edward b: 6/19/1856, Lowell, Mass. d: 4/5/17, Lowell, Mass. BR/TR, 5'9", 160 lbs. Deb: 8/09/1882																												
1883	Pit-a	0	0	—	2	0	0	0	0	9	14	14.0	0	3	3.0	1	1.0	13.00	25	.360	.406	-10	-10	98	47	0.0	0	0	-0.6
1884	KC-U	0	0	—	2	1	0	0	0	10	15	13.5	0	2	1.8	3	2.7	5.40	51	.352	.381	-3	-3	92	100	0.0	0	0	-0.4
Total	2	0	0	—	4	1	0	0	0	19	29	13.7	0	5	2.4	4	1.9	9.00	33	.356	.393	-12	-13	94	75	0.0	0	0	-1.0
■ **JIM McLAUGHLIN**	McLaughlin, James C. b: 1860, Cleveland, Ohio d: 11/16/1895, Cleveland, Ohio TL, Deb: 5/03/1884																												
1884	Bal-a	1	2	.333	3	2	2	0	0	22	27	11.0	2	11	4.5	8	3.3	3.68	86	.311	.388	-1	-1	98	161	-0.6	0	0	0.0
■ **JOEY McLAUGHLIN**	McLaughlin, Joey Richard b: 7/11/56, Tulsa, Okla. BR/TR, 6'2", 205 lbs. Deb: 6/11/77																												
1977	Atl-N	0	0	—	3	2	0	0	0	6	10	15.0	3	3	4.5	0	0.0	15.00	30	.385	.419	-7	-7	115	73	0.0	-0	0	-0.5
1979	Atl-N	5	3	.625	37	0	0	0	5	69	54	7.0	3	34	4.4	40	5.2	2.48	167	.224	.312	10	13	110	121	1.5	0	-1	1.3
1980	Tor-A	6	9	.400	55	10	0	0	4	136	159	10.5	16	53	3.5	70	4.6	4.50	91	.302	.360	-7	-6	101	117	-0.2	0	-0	-0.6
1981	Tor-A	1	5	.167	40	0	0	0	10	60	55	8.3	2	21	3.2	38	5.7	2.85	145	.249	.305	5	9	113	108	-1.5	0	-0	0.9
1982	Tor-A	8	6	.571	44	0	0	0	8	70	54	6.9	7	30	3.9	49	6.3	3.21	138	.212	.293	7	10	109	91	1.3	0	1	1.0
1983	Tor-A	7	4	.636	50	0	0	0	9	65	63	8.7	11	37	5.1	47	6.5	4.43	99	.259	.351	-3	-0	108	114	1.1	0	0	0.0
1984	Tor-A	0	0	—	6	0	0	0	0	11	12	9.8	0	7	5.7	3	2.5	2.45	165	.286	.380	2	2	101	187	0.0	0	0	0.2
	Tex-A	2	1	.667	15	0	0	0	0	33	33	9.0	4	13	3.5	21	5.7	4.36	92	.260	.324	-1	-1	101	94	0.6	0	-0	-0.1
	Yr	2	1	.667	21	0	0	0	0	44	45	9.2	4	20	4.1	24	4.9	3.89	104	.265	.339	1	1	101	94	0.6	0	0	0.1
Total	7	29	28	.509	250	12	0	0	36	450	440	8.8	46	198	4.0	268	5.4	3.84	110	.262	.333	6	18	106	112	2.8	-0	0	2.2
■ **JUD McLAUGHLIN**	McLaughlin, Justin Theodore b: 3/24/12, Brighton, Mass. d: 9/27/64, Cambridge, Mass. BL/TL, 5'11", 155 lbs. Deb: 6/23/31																												
1931	Bos-A	0	0	—	9	1	0	0	0	12	23	17.3	1	8	6.0	3	2.3	12.00	35	.397	.463	-10	-10	97	78	0.0	0	0	-0.8
1932	Bos-A	0	0	—	1	0	0	0	0	3	5	15.0	0	4	12.0	0	0.0	15.00	31	.385	.529	-4	-3	102	66	0.0	-0	0	-0.2
1933	Bos-A	0	0	—	6	0	0	0	0	9	14	14.0	1	5	5.0	1	1.0	6.00	73	.359	.432	-2	-2	102	129	0.0	0	-0	-0.1
Total	3	0	0	—	16	1	0	0	0	24	42	15.8	2	17	6.4	4	1.5	10.13	43	.382	.461	-15	-15	99	95	0.0	-0	0	-1.1

■ BO McLAUGHLIN McLaughlin, Michael Duane b: 10/23/53, Oakland, Cal. BR/TR, 6'5", 210 lbs. Deb: 7/20/76

YEAR	TM/L	W	L	PCT	G	GS	CG	SHO	SV	IP	H	H/G	HR	BB	BB/G	SO	SO/G	ERA	/A	OAVG	OOBP	PR	/A	PF	CPI	WAT	PB	PD	TPI
1976	Hou-N	4	5	.444	17	11	4	2	1	79	71	8.1	6	17	1.9	32	3.6	2.85	107	.244	.286	6	2	87	104	-0.4	-1	0	0.0
1977	Hou-N	4	7	.364	46	6	0	0	5	85	81	8.6	6	34	3.6	59	6.2	4.24	85	.260	.337	-3	-6	92	94	-1.5	-1	1	-0.5
1978	Hou-N	0	1	.000	12	1	0	0	2	23	30	11.7	2	16	6.3	10	3.9	5.09	67	.313	.414	-4	-4	95	125	-0.4	-0	-0	-0.4
1979	Hou-N	1	2	.333	12	0	0	0	0	16	22	12.4	2	4	2.3	12	6.8	5.63	60	.314	.342	-3	-4	90	92	-0.5	-0	0	-0.3
	Atl-N	1	1	.500	37	1	0	0	0	50	63	11.3	2	16	2.9	45	8.1	4.86	85	.303	.352	-6	-4	110	92	0.2	-1	-1	-0.5
	Yr	2	3	.400	49	1	0	0	0	66	85	11.6	4	20	2.7	57	7.8	5.05	78	.305	.350	-10	-8	105	92	-0.3	-0	-1	-0.8
1981	Oak-A	0	0	—	11	0	0	0	1	12	17	12.8	1	9	6.8	3	2.3	11.25	31	.333	.443	-10	-10	95	63	0.0	0	0	-0.9
1982	Oak-A	0	4	.000	21	2	1	0	0	48	51	9.6	3	27	5.1	27	5.1	4.88	81	.267	.354	-4	-5	96	89	-1.9	0	0	-0.4
Total	6	10	20	.333	156	21	5	2	9	313	335	9.6	22	123	3.5	188	5.4	4.49	79	.275	.342	-25	-32	95	96	-4.5	-3	0	-3.0

■ PAT McLAUGHLIN McLaughlin, Patrick Elmer b: 8/17/10, Taylor, Tex. BR/TR, 6'2", 175 lbs. Deb: 4/25/37

YEAR	TM/L	W	L	PCT	G	GS	CG	SHO	SV	IP	H	H/G	HR	BB	BB/G	SO	SO/G	ERA	/A	OAVG	OOBP	PR	/A	PF	CPI	WAT	PB	PD	TPI
1937	Det-A	0	2	.000	10	3	0	0	0	33	39	10.6	3	16	4.4	8	2.2	6.27	79	.291	.367	-6	-5	108	81	-0.9	-1	-1	-0.5
1940	Phi-A	0	0	—	1	0	0	0	0	2	4	18.0	1	1	4.5	0	0.0	13.50	32	.444	.500	-2	-2	99	99	0.0	0	0	-0.1
1945	Det-A	0	0	—	1	0	0	0	0	1	2	18.0	0	0	0.0	0	0.0	9.00	39	.400	.400	-1	-1	105	74	0.0	0	-0	0.0
Total	3	0	2	.000	12	3	0	0	0	36	45	11.3	4	17	4.3	8	2.0	6.75	73	.304	.376	-9	-7	107	82	-0.9	-1	-1	-0.6

■ WARREN McLAUGHLIN McLaughlin, Warren A. b: 1/22/1876, N.Plainfield, N.J. d: 10/22/23, Plainfield, N.J. TL , Deb: 7/07/00

YEAR	TM/L	W	L	PCT	G	GS	CG	SHO	SV	IP	H	H/G	HR	BB	BB/G	SO	SO/G	ERA	/A	OAVG	OOBP	PR	/A	PF	CPI	WAT	PB	PD	TPI
1900	Phi-N	0	0	—	1	0	0	0	0	6	4	6.0	0	6	9.0	1	1.5	4.50	80	.208	.396	-1	-1	98	73	0.0	1	0	0.0
1902	Pit-N	3	0	1.000	3	3	3	0	0	26	27	9.3	0	9	3.1	13	4.5	2.77	98	.291	.354	0	-0	98	114	1.5	1	-1	0.0
1903	Phi-N	0	3	.000	3	2	2	0	0	23	38	14.9	0	11	4.3	3	1.2	7.04	44	.400	.468	-10	-10	94	96	-1.4	0	-1	-0.8
Total	3	3	3	.500	7	5	5	0	0	55	69	11.3	0	26	4.3	17	2.8	4.75	63	.333	.410	-10	-11	97	102	0.1	2	-2	-0.8

■ AL McLEAN McLean, Albert Eldon "Elrod" b: 9/20/12, Chicago, Ill. BR/TR, 6', 175 lbs. Deb: 7/16/35

YEAR	TM/L	W	L	PCT	G	GS	CG	SHO	SV	IP	H	H/G	HR	BB	BB/G	SO	SO/G	ERA	/A	OAVG	OOBP	PR	/A	PF	CPI	WAT	PB	PD	TPI
1935	Was-A	0	0	—	4	0	0	0	0	9	12	12.0	0	5	5.0	3	3.0	7.00	59	.324	.405	-3	-3	93	81	0.0	-0	-0	-0.2

■ WAYNE McLELAND McLeland, Wayne Gaffney "Nubbin" b: 8/29/24, Milton, Iowa BR/TR, 6', 180 lbs. Deb: 4/20/51

YEAR	TM/L	W	L	PCT	G	GS	CG	SHO	SV	IP	H	H/G	HR	BB	BB/G	SO	SO/G	ERA	/A	OAVG	OOBP	PR	/A	PF	CPI	WAT	PB	PD	TPI
1951	Det-A	0	1	.000	6	1	0	0	0	11	20	16.4	1	4	3.3	0	0.0	8.18	54	.400	.455	-5	-5	107	103	-0.4	-0	0	-0.3
1952	Det-A	0	0	—	4	0	0	0	0	3	4	12.0	0	6	18.0	0	0.0	9.00	42	.444	.556	-2	-2	103	133	0.0	0	0	-0.1
Total	2	0	1	.000	10	1	0	0	0	14	24	15.4	1	10	6.4	0	0.0	8.36	51	.407	.479	-7	-6	106	110	-0.4	-0	0	-0.4

■ CAL McLISH McLish, Calvin Coolidge Julius Caesar Tuskahoma "Buster" b: 12/1/25, Anadarko, Okla. BB/TR, 6', 179 lbs. Deb: 5/13/44 C

YEAR	TM/L	W	L	PCT	G	GS	CG	SHO	SV	IP	H	H/G	HR	BB	BB/G	SO	SO/G	ERA	/A	OAVG	OOBP	PR	/A	PF	CPI	WAT	PB	PD	TPI
1944	Bro-N	3	10	.231	23	13	3	0	0	84	110	11.8	10	48	5.1	24	2.6	7.82	47	.321	.396	-39	-39	102	82	-2.9	0	-2	-3.7
1946	Bro-N	0	0	—	1	0	0	0	0	0	1	—	0	0	—	0	—	∞	—	1.000	.500	-2	-2	100	27	0.0	0	0	-0.1
1947	Pit-N	0	0	—	1	0	0	0	0	1	2	18.0	0	0	0.0	0	0.0	18.00	23	.400	.500	-2	-2	102	53	0.0	0	0	0.0
1948	Pit-N	0	0	—	2	1	0	0	0	5	8	14.4	0	2	3.6	1	1.8	9.00	46	.400	.455	-3	-3	104	81	0.0	-0	0	-0.1
1949	Chi-N	1	1	.500	8	2	0	0	0	23	31	12.1	5	12	4.7	6	2.3	5.87	67	.341	.402	-5	-5	97	129	0.2	2	1	-0.2
1951	Chi-N	4	10	.286	30	17	5	1	0	146	159	9.8	16	52	3.2	46	2.8	4.44	89	.283	.341	-8	-8	100	105	-2.1	-1	0	-0.8
1956	Cle-A	2	4	.333	37	2	0	0	1	62	67	9.7	5	32	4.6	27	3.9	4.94	83	.282	.359	-5	-6	99	95	-1.2	1	1	-0.2
1957	Cle-A	9	7	.563	42	7	2	0	1	144	118	7.4	11	67	4.2	88	5.5	2.75	141	.220	.304	17	18	102	107	1.1	3	1	2.3
1958	Cle-A	16	8	.667	39	30	13	0	1	226	214	8.5	25	70	2.8	97	3.9	2.99	118	.251	.303	20	13	93	**121**	4.4	-0	0	1.3
1959	Cle-A	19	8	.704	35	32	13	0	1	235	253	9.7	26	72	2.8	113	4.3	3.64	101	.270	.323	6	1	95	114	4.6	1	3	0.5
1960	Cin-N	4	14	.222	37	21	2	1	0	151	170	10.1	16	48	2.9	56	3.3	4.17	89	.287	.339	-7	-7	99	112	-4.6	-3	1	-0.9
1961	Chi-A	10	13	.435	31	27	4	0	1	162	178	9.9	21	47	2.6	80	4.4	4.39	90	.280	.322	-7	-8	99	102	-2.3	-1	2	-0.6
1962	Phi-N	11	5	.688	32	24	5	1	1	155	184	10.7	15	45	2.6	71	4.1	4.24	89	.293	.339	-5	-8	95	107	3.2	-1	-1	-0.9
1963	Phi-N	13	11	.542	32	32	10	2	0	210	184	7.9	14	56	2.4	98	4.2	3.26	103	.239	.288	1	2	102	89	0.1	3	2	0.8
1964	Phi-N	0	1	.000	2	1	0	0	0	5	6	10.8	0	1	1.8	6	10.8	3.60	96	.261	.292	-0	-0	98	68	-0.4	-0	0	0.0
Total	15	92	92	.500	352	209	57	5	6	1609	1685	9.4	164	552	3.1	713	4.0	4.01	93	.270	.326	-39	-52	98	106	0.1	4	8	-2.6

■ SAM McMACKIN McMackin, Samuel b: 1872, Cleveland, Ohio d: 2/11/03, Columbus, Ohio TL , Deb: 9/04/02

YEAR	TM/L	W	L	PCT	G	GS	CG	SHO	SV	IP	H	H/G	HR	BB	BB/G	SO	SO/G	ERA	/A	OAVG	OOBP	PR	/A	PF	CPI	WAT	PB	PD	TPI
1902	Chi-A	0	0	—	1	0	0	0	0	3	1	3.0	0	0	0.0	2	6.0	0.00	—	.117	.117	1	1	94	0	0.0	-0	0	0.1
	Det-A	0	1	.000	1	1	1	0	0	8	9	10.1	0	4	4.5	2	2.3	3.38	106	.309	.393	0	0	101	125	-0.4	1	0	0.0
	Yr	0	1	.000	2	1	1	0	0	11	10	8.2	0	4	3.3	4	3.3	2.45	144	.265	.336	1	1	99	125	-0.4	-0	1	0.1

■ JACK McMAHAN McMahan, Jack Wally b: 7/25/32, Hot Springs, Ark. BR/TL, 6', 175 lbs. Deb: 4/18/56

YEAR	TM/L	W	L	PCT	G	GS	CG	SHO	SV	IP	H	H/G	HR	BB	BB/G	SO	SO/G	ERA	/A	OAVG	OOBP	PR	/A	PF	CPI	WAT	PB	PD	TPI
1956	Pit-N	0	0	—	11	0	0	0	0	13	18	12.5	1	9	6.2	9	6.2	6.23	63	.340	.422	-4	-3	103	108	0.0	-0	0	-0.2
	KC-A	0	5	.000	23	9	0	0	0	62	69	10.0	7	31	4.5	13	1.9	4.79	91	.290	.366	-4	-3	105	109	-2.4	-2	-0	-0.4

■ DON McMAHON McMahon, Donald John b: 1/4/30, Brooklyn, N.Y. d: 7/22/87, Los Angeles, Cal. BR/TR, 6'2", 215 lbs. Deb: 6/30/57 C

YEAR	TM/L	W	L	PCT	G	GS	CG	SHO	SV	IP	H	H/G	HR	BB	BB/G	SO	SO/G	ERA	/A	OAVG	OOBP	PR	/A	PF	CPI	WAT	PB	PD	TPI
1957	Mil-N	2	3	.400	32	0	0	0	9	47	33	6.3	0	29	5.6	46	8.8	1.53	222	.196	.310	12	10	88	146	-0.8	1	-0	1.1
1958	Mil-N	7	2	.778	38	0	0	0	8	59	50	7.6	4	29	4.4	37	5.6	3.66	94	.235	.324	2	-2	87	93	2.1	0	-0	-0.1
1959	Mil-N	5	3	.625	60	0	0	0	**15**	81	81	9.0	5	37	4.1	55	6.1	2.56	144	.259	.331	13	10	93	149	0.7	1	-1	1.0
1960	Mil-N	3	6	.333	48	0	0	0	10	64	66	9.3	9	32	4.5	50	7.0	5.91	57	.263	.347	-15	-18	89	80	-1.8	-1	0	-1.8
1961	Mil-N	6	4	.600	53	0	0	0	8	92	84	8.2	4	51	5.0	55	5.4	2.84	129	.249	.341	12	8	91	134	0.7	0	1	1.0
1962	Mil-N	0	1	.000	2	0	0	0	0	3	3	9.0	1	0	0.0	3	9.0	6.00	64	.250	.250	-1	-1	98	71	-0.4	0	0	0.0
	Hou-N	5	5	.500	51	0	0	0	8	77	53	6.2	4	33	3.9	69	8.1	1.52	245	.201	.284	21	19	95	159	0.9	-1	0	1.8
	Yr	5	6	.455	53	0	0	0	8	80	56	6.3	5	33	3.7	72	8.1	1.69	221	.203	.283	20	18	95	159	0.5	0	0	1.8
1963	Hou-N	1	5	.167	49	2	0	0	5	80	83	9.3	10	26	2.9	51	5.7	4.05	77	.270	.317	-7	-8	95	104	-1.7	0	-0	-0.8
1964	Cle-A	6	4	.600	70	0	0	0	16	101	67	6.0	7	52	4.6	92	8.2	2.41	155	.189	.289	14	15	103	102	1.2	-1	-1	1.4
1965	Cle-A	3	3	.500	58	0	0	0	11	85	79	8.4	8	37	3.9	60	6.4	3.28	103	.248	.324	2	1	97	116	-0.1	0	1	0.2
1966	Cle-A	1	1	.500	12	0	0	0	1	12	8	6.0	1	6	4.5	5	3.8	3.00	116	.190	.280	1	1	102	87	0.0	-0	0	0.0
	Bos-A	8	7	.533	49	0	0	0	9	78	65	7.5	7	38	4.4	57	6.6	2.65	143	.232	.317	7	10	110	140	1.3	-0	-0	1.0
	Yr	9	8	.529	61	0	0	0	10	90	73	7.3	8	44	4.4	62	6.2	2.70	139	.226	.313	7	11	109	140	1.3	-0	-0	1.0
1967	Bos-A	1	2	.333	11	0	0	0	2	18	14	7.0	4	13	6.5	10	5.0	3.50	104	.215	.342	-1	0	113	138	-0.5	-0	0	0.0
	Chi-A	5	0	1.000	52	0	0	0	3	92	54	5.3	5	27	2.6	74	7.2	1.66	181	.173	.246	16	14	93	99	2.5	0	-0	1.5
	Yr	6	2	.750	63	0	0	0	5	110	68	5.6	9	40	3.3	84	6.9	1.96	158	.180	.264	15	14	96	99	2.0	-0	0	1.5
1968	Chi-A	2	1	.667	25	0	0	0	0	46	31	6.1	2	20	3.9	32	6.3	1.96	155	.190	.284	5	6	102	112	0.7	0	-1	0.6
	Det-A	3	1	.750	20	0	0	0	1	36	22	5.5	2	10	2.5	33	8.3	2.00	154	.180	.237	4	4	103	77	0.6	-0	-0	0.4
	Yr	5	2	.714	45	0	0	0	1	82	53	5.8	4	30	3.3	65	7.1	1.98	155	.183	.255	9	10	103	77	1.3	0	-1	1.0
1969	Det-A	3	5	.375	34	0	0	0	11	37	25	6.1	2	18	4.4	38	9.2	3.89	95	.192	.288	-1	-1	102	60	-1.2	-1	0	0.0
	SF-N	3	1	.750	13	0	0	0	2	24	13	4.9	1	9	3.4	21	7.9	3.00	120	.157	.239	2	2	100	35	0.9	0	0	0.2
1970	SF-N	9	5	.643	61	0	0	0	19	94	70	6.7	9	45	4.3	74	7.1	2.97	131	.202	.293	11	9	96	94	1.8	0	-0	0.9
1971	SF-N	10	6	.625	61	0	0	0	4	82	73	8.0	9	37	4.1	71	7.8	4.06	84	.242	.329	-5	-6	99	97	1.4	-1	1	-0.5
1972	SF-N	3	3	.500	44	0	0	0	5	63	46	6.6	8	21	3.0	45	6.4	3.71	93	.206	.269	-2	-2	100	75	0.3	0	-0	-0.1
1973	SF-N	4	0	1.000	22	0	0	0	6	30	21	6.3	1	7	2.1	20	6.0	1.50	255	.189	.235	7	8	104	74	2.0	0	0	0.9
1974	SF-N	0	0	—	9	0	0	0	0	12	13	9.8	2	2	1.5	5	3.8	3.00	132	.283	.300	1	1	109	146	0.0	0	-0	0.1
Total	18	90	68	.570	874	2	0	0	153	1313	1054	7.2	105	579	4.0	1003	6.9	2.95	119	.221	.303	97	82	97	109	10.6	-1	1	8.8

■ DOC McMAHON McMahon, Henry John b: 12/19/1886, Woburn, Mass. d: 12/11/29, Woburn, Mass. Deb: 10/06/08

YEAR	TM/L	W	L	PCT	G	GS	CG	SHO	SV	IP	H	H/G	HR	BB	BB/G	SO	SO/G	ERA	/A	OAVG	OOBP	PR	/A	PF	CPI	WAT	PB	PD	TPI
1908	Bos-A	1	0	1.000	1	1	1	0	0	9	14	14.0	0	0	0.0	3	3.0	3.00	77	.350	.350	-1	-1	97	158	0.5	1	-0	0.0

■ SADIE McMAHON McMahon, John Joseph b: 9/19/1867, Wilmington, Del. d: 2/20/54, Delaware City, Del BR/TR, 5'9.5", 165 lbs. Deb: 7/05/1889

YEAR	TM/L	W	L	PCT	G	GS	CG	SHO	SV	IP	H	H/G	HR	BB	BB/G	SO	SO/G	ERA	/A	OAVG	OOBP	PR	/A	PF	CPI	WAT	PB	PD	TPI
1889	Phi-a	14	12	.538	28	27	27	2	0	242	230	8.6	5	102	3.8	117	4.4	3.53	105	.265	.342	8	5	96	92	-0.6	-5	0	0.0
1890	Phi-a	29	18	.617	48	46	44	0	1	410	414	9.1	5	133	2.9	225	4.9	3.34	118	.278	.337	24	27	101	105	10.7	2	10	3.6
	BB-a	7	3	.700	12	11	11	1	0	99	84	7.6	1	33	3.0	66	6.0	3.00	132	.244	.310	10	11	103	91	2.9	-4	0	0.6
	Yr	**36**	21	.632	**60**	57	**55**	1	1	**509**	498	8.8	6	166	2.9	**291**	5.1	3.27	120	.271	.332	34	37	102	91	**13.6**	2	10	4.2
1891	Bal-a	**34**	24	.586	61	58	**53**	**5**	1	**503**	493	8.8	13	149	2.7	219	3.9	2.81	133	.271	.326	51	52	100	105	5.9	-3	5	4.8
1892	Bal-N	20	25	.444	48	46	44	2	0	397	430	9.7	9	145	3.3	118	2.7	3.24	104	.289	.352	2	6	102	113	5.7	-9	0	-0.1
1893	Bal-N	23	18	.561	43	40	35	0	1	346	378	9.8	6	156	4.1	79	2.1	4.37	115	.294	.370	12	25	108	96	5.1	-5	-0	1.9

YEAR	TM/L	W	L	PCT	G	GS	CG	SHO	SV	IP	H	H/G	HR	BB	BB/G	SO	SO/G	ERA	/A	OAVG	OOBP	PR	/A	PF	CPI	WAT	PB	PD	TPI
1894	Bal-N	25	8	.758	35	33	26	0	0	276	317	10.3	7	111	3.6	60	2.0	4.21	122	.310	.378	35	28	96	102	4.2	2	3	2.6
1895	Bal-N	10	4	.714	15	15	15	**4**	0	122	110	8.1	1	32	2.4	37	2.7	2.95	168	.259	.311	25	27	104	87	1.1	1	0	2.5
1896	Bal-N	11	9	.550	22	22	19	0	0	176	195	10.0	4	55	2.8	33	1.7	3.48	124	.303	.358	17	16	99	108	-2.3	-7	0	0.8
1897	Bro-N	0	6	.000	9	7	5	0	0	63	75	10.7	1	29	4.1	13	1.9	5.86	75	.318	.393	-11	-10	102	76	-2.9	-1	0	-0.8
Total	9	173	127	.577	321	305	279	14	3	2634	2726	9.3	52	945	3.2	967	3.3	3.51	118	.283	.347	173	187	101	102	29.8	-29	18	15.9
■ **JOHN McMAKIN** McMakin, John Weaver "Spartanburg John" b: 3/6/1878, Spartanburg, S.C. d: 9/25/56, Lyman, S.C. BR/TL, 5'11", 165 lbs. Deb: 4/19/02																													
1902	Bro-N	2	2	.500	4	4	4	0	0	32	34	9.6	0	11	3.1	6	1.7	3.09	84	.296	.357	-1	-2	94	105	-0.1	0	0	-0.1
■ **JOE McMANUS** McManus, Joab Logan b: 9/7/1887, Palmyra, Ill. d: 12/23/55, Beckley, W.Va. BR/TR, 5'11", 180 lbs. Deb: 4/12/13																													
1913	Cin-N	0	0	—	1	0	0	0	0	2	3	13.5	0	4	18.0	1	4.5	18.00	18	.375	.583	-3	-3	104	60	0.0	0	0	-0.2
■ **PAT McMANUS** McManus, Patrick b: Ireland d: 10/6/17, Brooklyn, N.Y. Deb: 5/22/1879																													
1879	Tro-N	0	2	.000	2	2	2	0	0	21	24	10.3	1	1	0.4	6	2.6	3.00	83	.293	.301	-1	-1	100	102	-0.9	-1	0	-0.1
■ **GEORGE McMULLEN** McMullen, George b: California Deb: 7/02/1887																													
1887	NY-a	2	1	.667	3	3	2	0	0	21	25	10.7	2	19	8.1	2	0.9	7.71	51	.310	.441	-8	-9	92	86	0.8	-2	0	-0.7
■ **JOHN McMULLIN** McMullin, John F. "Lefty" b: 1848, Philadelphia, Pa. d: 4/11/1881, Philadelphia, Pa. BL/TL, 5'9", 160 lbs. Deb: 5/09/1871																													
1871	Tro-n	13	15	.464	29																								
1872	Mut-n	1	0	1.000	2																								
1873	Ath-n	1	0	1.000	1																								
1875	Phi-n	0	1	.000	1																								
Total	4 n	15	16	.484	33																								
■ **CRAIG McMURTRY** McMurtry, Joe Craig b: 11/5/59, Troy, Tex. BR/TR, 6'5", 195 lbs. Deb: 4/10/83																													
1983	Atl-N	15	9	.625	36	35	6	3	0	225	204	8.2	13	88	3.5	105	4.2	3.08	123	.243	.311	14	18	104	103	2.4	-4	3	1.9
1984	Atl-N	9	17	.346	37	30	0	0	0	183	184	9.0	16	102	5.0	99	4.9	4.33	91	.268	.354	-15	-8	110	106	-4.3	-2	4	-0.4
1985	Atl-N	0	3	.000	17	6	0	0	1	45	56	11.2	6	27	5.4	28	5.6	6.60	59	.306	.382	-15	-14	108	92	-1.4	-1	1	-1.3
1986	Atl-N	1	6	.143	37	5	0	0	0	80	82	9.2	7	43	4.8	50	5.6	4.72	81	.265	.357	-9	-8	103	95	-2.3	-0	0	-0.7
1988	Tex-A	3	3	.500	32	0	0	0	3	60	37	5.6	5	24	3.6	35	5.3	2.25	181	.180	.263	11	12	102	98	0.4	0	1	1.3
Total	5	28	38	.424	159	76	6	3	4	593	563	8.5	47	284	4.3	317	4.8	3.87	100	.253	.332	-13	1	106	101	-5.2	-6	9	0.8
■ **EDGAR McNABB** McNabb, Edgar J. "Texas" b: 10/24/1865, Mt.Vernon, Ohio d: 2/28/1894, Pittsburgh, Pa. TL, 5'11.5", 170 lbs. Deb: 5/12/1893																													
1893	Bal-N	8	7	.533	21	14	12	0	0	142	167	10.6	5	53	3.4	18	1.1	4.12	122	.309	.371	9	14	108	110	1.1	-3	0	1.0
■ **DAVE McNALLY** McNally, David Arthur b: 10/31/42, Billings, Mont. BR/TL, 5'11", 185 lbs. Deb: 9/26/62																													
1962	Bal-A	1	0	1.000	1	1	1	1	0	9	2	2.0	0	3	3.0	4	4.0	0.00	—	.071	.161	4	4	95	0	0.5	-0	0	0.4
1963	Bal-A	7	8	.467	29	20	2	0	1	126	133	9.5	9	55	3.9	78	5.6	4.57	74	.276	.349	-13	-17	93	97	-0.9	-2	-1	-1.9
1964	Bal-A	9	11	.450	30	23	5	3	0	159	157	8.9	15	51	2.9	88	5.0	3.68	102	.260	.324	-1	1	103	105	-2.6	-0	0	0.1
1965	Bal-A	11	6	.647	35	29	6	2	0	199	163	7.4	15	73	3.3	116	5.2	2.85	120	.222	.294	13	13	99	100	1.5	-2	0	1.1
1966	Bal-A	13	6	.684	34	33	5	1	0	213	212	9.0	22	64	2.7	158	6.7	3.17	107	.256	.309	6	5	99	**118**	2.1	2	0	0.8
1967	Bal-A	7	7	.500	24	22	3	1	0	119	134	10.1	13	39	2.9	70	5.3	4.54	67	.295	.346	-17	-20	94	108	0.4	0	-2	-2.2
1968	Bal-A	22	10	.688	35	35	18	5	0	273	175	5.8	24	55	1.8	202	6.7	1.95	154	.182	**.231**	31	32	101	83	5.3	3	-3	4.0
1969	Bal-A	20	7	.741	41	40	11	4	0	269	232	7.8	21	84	2.8	166	5.6	3.21	113	.234	.294	12	13	100	92	3.2	-2	-3	0.8
1970	Bal-A	**24**	9	.727	40	40	16	1	0	296	277	8.4	29	78	2.4	185	5.6	3.22	109	.250	.297	16	9	94	104	3.6	4	-2	1.1
1971	Bal-A	21	5	**.808**	30	30	11	1	0	224	188	7.6	24	58	2.3	91	3.7	2.89	120	.229	.279	14	14	100	99	**6.7**	2	-0	1.8
1972	Bal-A	13	17	.433	36	36	12	6	0	241	220	8.2	15	68	2.5	120	4.5	2.95	100	.247	.296	3	0	96	101	-2.9	2	1	0.2
1973	Bal-A	17	17	.500	38	38	17	4	0	266	247	8.4	16	81	2.7	87	2.9	3.21	125	.251	.307	18	24	105	100	-3.3	0	1	2.6
1974	Bal-A	16	10	.615	39	37	13	4	1	259	260	9.0	19	81	2.8	111	3.9	3.58	93	.270	.325	1	-7	92	107	1.9	0	2	-0.4
1975	Mon-N	3	6	.333	12	12	0	0	0	77	88	10.3	8	36	4.2	36	4.2	5.26	75	.280	.358	-14	-11	109	90	-1.2	2	-0	-0.8
Total	14	184	119	.607	424	396	120	33	2	2730	2488	8.2	230	826	2.7	1512	5.0	3.24	106	.245	.302	75	60	99	100	14.3	9	-7	7.6
■ **TIM McNAMARA** McNamara, Timothy Aloysius b: 11/20/1898, Millville, Mass. BR/TR, 5'11", 170 lbs. Deb: 4/27/22																													
1922	Bos-N	3	4	.429	24	5	4	2	0	71	55	7.0	2	26	3.3	16	2.0	2.41	166	.225	.293	**13**	**13**	98	104	0.5	-1	-0	1.1
1923	Bos-N	3	13	.188	32	16	3	0	0	139	185	12.0	8	29	1.9	32	2.1	4.92	83	.320	.350	-14	-13	102	96	-3.8	0	-2	-1.2
1924	Bos-N	8	12	.400	35	21	6	2	0	179	242	12.2	9	31	1.6	35	1.8	5.18	74	.334	.348	-26	-27	99	97	0.9	-1	1	-2.5
1925	Bos-N	0	0	—	1	0	0	0	0	1	6	54.0	0	2	18.0	1	9.0	54.00	8	.857	.889	-6	-6	95	69	0.0	0	0	-0.3
1926	NY-N	0	0	—	6	0	0	0	0	6	7	10.5	0	4	6.0	4	6.0	9.00	42	.304	.379	-3	-4	98	57	0.0	0	0	-0.2
Total	5	14	29	.326	98	42	13	4	0	396	495	11.3	19	92	2.1	88	2.0	4.77	83	.314	.343	-36	-36	100	97	-2.4	-1	-2	-3.1
■ **GORDON McNAUGHTON** McNaughton, Gordon Joseph b: 7/31/10, Chicago, Ill. d: 8/6/42, Chicago, Ill. BR/TR, 6'1", 190 lbs. Deb: 8/13/32																													
1932	Bos-A	0	1	.000	6	2	0	0	0	21	21	9.0	1	22	9.4	6	2.6	6.43	71	.259	.434	-5	-4	102	94	-0.4	0	1	-0.2
■ **HARRY McNEAL** McNeal, John Harley b: 8/11/1877, Iberia, Ohio d: 1/11/45, Cleveland, Ohio BR/TR, 6'3", 175 lbs. Deb: 8/05/01																													
1901	Cle-A	5	5	.500	12	10	9	0	0	85	120	12.7	4	30	3.2	15	1.6	4.45	80	.354	.407	-7	-8	97	125	0.9	-2	-2	-0.8
■ **ED McNICHOL** McNichol, Edwin Briggs b: 1/10/1879, Martins Ferry, O. d: 11/1/52, Salineville, O. BR/TR, 5'5", 170 lbs. Deb: 7/09/04																													
1904	Bos-N	2	12	.143	17	15	12	1	0	122	120	8.9	3	74	5.5	39	2.9	4.28	65	.284	.397	-21	-20	102	95	-4.3	-4	-2	-2.1
■ **FRANK McPARTLIN** McPartlin, Frank b: 2/16/1872, Hoosick Falls, N.Y d: 11/13/43, New York, N.Y. TR, 6', 180 lbs. Deb: 8/22/1899																													
1899	NY-N	0	0	—	1	0	0	0	0	4	4	9.0	0	3	6.8	2	4.5	4.50	85	.283	.409	-0	-0	99	93	0.0	-0	0	0.0
■ **JOHN McPHERSON** McPherson, John Jacob b: 3/9/1869, Easton, Pa. d: 9/30/41, Easton, Pa. Deb: 7/12/01																													
1901	Phi-A	0	1	.000	1	1	0	0	0	4	7	15.8	0	4	9.0	0	0.0	11.25	32	.405	.517	-3	-3	100	77	-0.4	-0	0	-0.1
1904	Phi-N	1	12	.077	15	12	11	1	0	128	130	9.1	1	46	3.2	32	2.3	3.66	72	.291	.365	-13	-14	97	93	-5.0	-4	0	-1.3
Total	2	1	13	.071	16	13	11	1	0	132	137	9.3	1	50	3.4	32	2.2	3.89	69	.295	.371	-17	-18	97	93	-5.4	-4	0	-1.4
■ **HERB McQUAID** McQuaid, Herbert George b: 3/29/1899, San Francisco, Cal d: 4/4/66, Richmond, Cal. BR/TR, 6'2", 185 lbs. Deb: 6/22/23																													
1923	Cin-N	1	0	1.000	12	1	0	0	0	34	31	8.2	0	10	2.6	9	2.4	2.38	162	.238	.306	6	6	96	102	0.5	-1	1	0.5
1926	NY-A	1	0	1.000	17	1	0	0	0	38	48	11.4	5	13	3.1	6	1.4	6.16	63	.329	.360	-9	-10	97	98	0.5	-1	0	-0.9
Total	2	2	0	1.000	29	2	0	0	0	72	79	9.9	5	23	2.9	15	1.9	4.38	89	.286	.335	-3	-4	97	100	1.0	-2	1	-0.4
■ **MIKE McQUEEN** McQueen, Michael Robert b: 8/30/50, Oklahoma City, Okla BL/TL, 6', 188 lbs. Deb: 10/02/69																													
1969	Atl-N	0	0	—	1	1	0	0	0	3	2	6.0	0	3	9.0	3	9.0	3.00	123	.182	.357	0	0	103	97	0.0	0	0	0.0
1970	Atl-N	1	5	.167	22	8	1	0	1	66	67	9.1	10	31	4.2	54	7.4	5.59	76	.266	.340	-11	-10	105	87	-1.9	2	-1	-0.7
1971	Atl-N	4	1	.800	17	3	0	0	1	56	47	7.6	7	23	3.7	38	6.1	3.54	109	.228	.306	-0	2	111	98	1.5	0	-1	0.1
1972	Atl-N	0	5	.000	23	7	1	0	1	78	79	9.1	11	44	5.1	40	4.6	4.62	79	.260	.347	-10	-8	106	102	-2.4	-2	-1	-1.0
1974	Cin-N	0	0	—	10	0	0	0	0	15	17	10.2	4	11	6.6	5	3.0	5.40	65	.288	.394	-3	-3	96	127	0.0	-0	-0	-0.2
Total	5	5	11	.313	73	19	2	0	3	218	212	8.8	32	112	4.6	140	5.8	4.67	83	.255	.339	-24	-19	106	98	-2.8	1	-3	-1.8
■ **GEORGE McQUILLAN** McQuillan, George Watt b: 5/1/1885, Brooklyn, N.Y. d: 3/30/40, Columbus, Ohio BR/TR, 5'11.5", 175 lbs. Deb: 5/08/07																													
1907	Phi-N	4	0	1.000	6	5	5	3	0	41	21	4.6	0	11	2.4	28	6.1	0.66	386	.174	.248	8	9	103	76	2.0	3	-2	0.9
1908	Phi-N	23	17	.575	48	42	32	7	2	360	263	6.6	1	91	2.3	114	2.8	1.52	151	.230	.291	33	31	98	104	2.1	-1	-3	3.5
1909	Phi-N	13	16	.448	41	28	16	4	2	248	202	7.3	5	54	2.0	96	3.5	2.14	129	.226	.271	13	17	106	87	-1.2	-4	-2	1.7
1910	Phi-N	9	6	.600	24	17	13	3	1	152	109	6.5	2	50	3.0	71	4.2	1.60	181	.204	.276	24	22	95	100	1.5	-0	-0	2.3
1911	Cin-N	2	6	.250	19	5	2	0	0	77	92	10.8	2	31	3.6	28	3.3	4.68	67	.308	.380	-11	-13	92	102	-1.8	-1	-1	-1.4
1913	Pit-N	8	6	.571	25	16	7	0	1	142	144	9.1	1	35	2.2	59	3.7	3.42	88	.273	.310	-3	-6	94	90	0.8	-1	-1	-0.8
1914	Pit-N	13	17	.433	45	28	15	0	4	259	248	8.6	8	60	2.1	96	3.3	2.99	87	.261	.301	-6	-11	93	95	-0.5	-4	0	-1.6
1915	Pit-N	8	10	.444	30	20	9	0	1	149	160	9.7	1	39	2.4	56	3.4	2.84	95	.284	.322	-1	-2	98	120	-0.5	-3	0	-0.5
	Phi-N	4	3	.571	9	8	5	0	0	64	60	8.4	1	11	1.5	13	1.8	2.11	136	.247	.274	5	5	104	107	0.0	-2	-1	0.3
	Yr	12	13	.480	39	28	14	0	1	213	220	9.3	2	50	2.1	69	2.9	2.62	105	.272	.305	3	3	100	107	-0.5	-3	-1	-0.2
1916	Phi-N	1	7	.125	21	3	1	0	2	62	58	8.4	2	15	2.2	22	3.2	2.76	89	.251	.292	-1	-2	94	100	-3.1	-0	-0	-0.2

YEAR	TM/L	W	L	PCT	G	GS	CG	SHO	SV	IP	H	H/G	HR	BB	BB/G	SO	SO/G	ERA	/A	OAVG	OOBP	PR	/A	PF	CPI	WAT	PB	PD	TPI
1918	Cle-A	0	1	.000	5	1	0	0	1	23	25	9.8	0	4	1.6	7	2.7	2.35	126	.284	.305	1	2	107	123	-0.4	-0	0	0.2
Total	10	85	89	.489	273	173	105	17	14	1577	1382	7.9	23	401	2.3	590	3.4	2.38	112	.247	.297	61	51	98	99	-1.1	-14	-9	4.4
■ **HUGH McQUILLAN**	McQuillan, Hugh A. "Handsome Hugh" b: 9/15/1897, New York, N.Y. d: 8/26/47, New York, N.Y. BR/TR, 6', 170 lbs. Deb: 7/26/18																												
1918	Bos-N	1	0	1.000	1	1	1	0	0	9	7	7.0	0	5	5.0	1	1.0	3.00	88	.219	.308	-0	-0	95	84	0.5	0	0	0.0
1919	Bos-N	2	3	.400	16	7	2	0	1	60	66	9.9	3	14	2.1	13	2.0	3.45	84	.288	.318	-4	-4	100	111	0.0	0	-1	-0.3
1920	Bos-N	11	15	.423	38	27	17	1	5	226	230	9.2	3	70	2.8	53	2.1	3.54	88	.273	.318	-10	-11	99	87	0.4	6	2	-0.3
1921	Bos-N	13	17	.433	45	31	13	2	5	250	284	10.2	9	90	3.2	94	3.4	4.00	87	.291	.343	-6	-14	92	100	-2.8	2	0	-1.1
1922	Bos-N	5	10	.333	28	17	7	0	0	136	154	10.2	3	56	3.7	33	2.2	4.24	95	.299	.353	-2	-3	98	103	-0.2	-1	1	-0.3
	NY-N	6	5	.545	15	13	5	0	1	94	111	10.6	7	34	3.3	24	2.3	3.83	108	.301	.351	3	3	100	120	-0.5	-1	-1	0.0
	Yr	11	15	.423	43	30	12	0	1	230	265	10.4	10	90	3.5	57	2.2	4.07	100	.299	.351	1	-0	99	120	-0.7	-1	-0	-0.3
1923	NY-N	15	14	.517	38	32	15	5	0	230	224	8.8	12	66	2.6	75	2.9	3.40	116	.259	.307	15	14	99	95	-2.8	-2	-1	1.0
1924	NY-N	14	8	.636	27	23	14	1	3	184	179	8.8	8	43	2.1	49	2.4	2.69	126	.259	.297	24	14	88	113	0.9	-0	-2	1.1
1925	NY-N	2	3	.400	14	11	2	0	1	70	95	12.2	9	23	3.0	23	3.0	6.04	69	.343	.385	-14	-14	98	105	-0.7	-1	1	-1.2
1926	NY-N	11	10	.524	33	22	12	1	0	167	171	9.2	7	42	2.3	47	2.5	3.72	101	.271	.310	2	0	98	91	0.8	-3	2	0.0
1927	NY-N	5	4	.556	11	9	5	0	0	58	73	11.3	4	22	3.4	17	2.6	4.50	85	.309	.364	-4	-4	98	112	-0.2	1	0	-0.2
	Bos-N	3	5	.375	13	11	2	0	0	78	109	12.6	2	24	2.8	17	2.0	5.54	67	.332	.363	-14	-16	95	94	-0.1	0	0	-1.3
	Yr	8	9	.471	24	20	7	0	0	136	182	12.0	6	46	3.0	34	2.3	5.10	74	.322	.362	-18	-20	96	94	-0.3	1	0	-1.5
Total	10	88	94	.484	279	204	95	10	16	1562	1703	9.8	67	489	2.8	446	2.6	3.83	95	.284	.330	-10	-35	96	100	-4.7	1	1	-2.6
■ **NORM McRAE**	McRae, Norman b: 9/26/47, Elizabeth, N.J. BR/TR, 6'1", 195 lbs. Deb: 9/13/69																												
1969	Det-A	0	0	—	3	0	0	0	0	3	2	6.0	0	1	3.0	3	9.0	6.00	62	.200	.250	-1	-1	102	29	0.0	0	0	0.0
1970	Det-A	0	0	—	19	0	0	0	0	31	26	7.5	1	25	7.3	16	4.6	2.90	133	.226	.364	3	3	104	130	0.0	-0	1	0.4
Total	2	0	0	—	22	0	0	0	0	34	28	7.4	1	26	6.9	19	5.0	3.18	121	.224	.355	2	3	104	121	0.0	-0	1	0.4
■ **TRICK McSORLEY**	McSorley, John Bernard b: 12/6/1858, St.Louis, Mo. d: 2/9/36, St.Louis, Mo. TR, 5'4", 142 lbs. Deb: 5/06/1875																												
1884	Tol-a	0	0	—	1	0	0	0	0	2	5	22.5	0	0	0.0	1	4.5	4.50	76	.479	.479	-0	-0	105	228	0.0	0	0	0.0
■ **BILL McTIGUE**	McTigue, William Patrick "Rebel" b: 1/3/1891, Nashville, Tenn. d: 5/8/20, Nashville, Tenn. BL/TL, 6'1.5", 175 lbs. Deb: 5/02/11																												
1911	Bos-N	0	5	.000	14	8	0	0	0	37	37	9.0	3	49	11.9	23	5.6	7.05	53	.280	.481	-15	-14	109	100	-2.4	-1	-1	-1.4
1912	Bos-N	2	0	1.000	10	1	1	0	0	35	39	10.0	0	18	4.6	17	4.4	5.40	70	.285	.368	-8	-6	110	71	1.0	-1	1	-0.6
1916	Det-A	0	0	—	3	0	0	0	0	5	5	9.0	0	5	9.0	1	1.8	5.40	54	.278	.435	-1	-1	103	96	0.0	-0	0	0.0
Total	3	2	5	.286	27	9	1	0	0	77	81	9.5	3	72	8.4	41	4.8	6.19	59	.282	.429	-24	-22	109	87	-1.4	-2	0	-2.0
■ **CAL McVEY**	McVey, Calvin Alexander b: 8/30/1850, Montrose, Iowa d: 8/20/26, San Francisco, Cal BR/TR, 5'9", 170 lbs. Deb: 5/05/1871 M																												
1875	Bos-n	1	0	1.000	2																								
1876	Chi-N	5	2	.714	11	6	5	0	2	59	57	8.7	0	2	0.3	9	1.4	1.53	171	.258	.265	5	7	113	90	-0.3	2	0	0.6
1877	Chi-N	4	8	.333	17	10	6	0	**2**	92	129	12.6	2	11	1.1	20	2.0	4.50	62	.340	.358	-17	-18	99	94	-1.6	8	0	-1.4
1879	Cin-N	0	2	.000	3	1	1	0	0	14	34	21.9	1	2	1.3	7	4.5	8.36	28	.468	.482	-9	-9	94	118	-0.9	1	0	-0.7
Total	3	9	12	.429	31	17	12	0	4	165	220	12.0	3	15	0.8	36	2.0	3.76	72	.327	.341	-21	-20	103	95	-2.8	11	0	-1.5
■ **DOUG McWEENY**	McWeeny, Douglas Lawrence "Buzz" b: 8/17/1896, Chicago, Ill. d: 1/1/53, Melrose Park, Ill. BR/TR, 6'2", 190 lbs. Deb: 4/24/21																												
1921	Chi-A	3	6	.333	27	8	3	0	2	98	127	11.7	7	45	4.1	46	4.2	6.06	72	.325	.387	-19	-18	102	93	-0.7	-4	-1	-2.0
1922	Chi-A	0	1	.000	4	1	0	0	0	11	13	10.6	0	7	5.7	5	4.1	5.73	71	.325	.385	-2	-2	101	97	-0.4	0	-0	-0.1
1924	Chi-A	1	3	.250	13	5	2	0	0	43	47	9.8	2	17	3.6	18	3.8	4.60	90	.294	.361	-2	-2	98	99	-0.8	-0	3	0.0
1926	Bro-N	11	13	.458	42	24	10	1	1	216	213	8.9	6	84	3.5	96	4.0	3.04	127	.258	.324	19	19	101	111	-0.1	-5	-1	1.4
1927	Bro-N	4	8	.333	34	22	6	0	1	164	167	9.2	13	70	3.8	73	4.0	3.57	114	.266	.338	6	9	104	116	-1.3	-4	1	0.6
1928	Bro-N	14	14	.500	42	32	12	**4**	1	244	218	8.0	11	114	4.2	79	2.9	3.17	124	.235	.314	22	20	99	93	0.0	-1	3	2.2
1929	Bro-N	4	10	.286	36	24	4	0	1	146	167	10.3	17	93	5.7	59	3.6	6.10	74	.288	.380	-23	-25	96	92	-2.7	-2	-2	-2.5
1930	Cin-N	0	2	.000	8	2	0	0	0	26	28	9.7	0	20	6.9	10	3.5	7.27	64	.283	.393	-7	-8	93	68	-0.9	-0	0	-0.6
Total	8	37	57	.394	206	118	37	5	6	948	980	9.3	56	450	4.3	386	3.7	4.17	99	.269	.344	-5	-6	100	101	-6.9	-16	2	-1.0
■ **LARRY McWILLIAMS**	McWilliams, Larry Dean b: 2/10/54, Wichita, Kan. BL/TL, 6'5", 180 lbs. Deb: 7/17/78																												
1978	Atl-N	9	3	.750	15	15	3	1	0	99	84	7.6	11	35	3.2	42	3.8	2.82	145	.224	.290	8	14	114	107	3.5	-2	1	1.5
1979	Atl-N	3	2	.600	13	13	1	0	0	66	69	9.4	4	22	3.0	32	4.4	5.59	74	.272	.331	-14	-11	110	70	0.8	1	1	-0.7
1980	Atl-N	9	14	.391	30	30	4	1	0	164	188	10.3	27	39	2.1	77	4.2	4.94	74	.285	.327	-24	-23	101	97	-2.8	0	-0	-2.3
1981	Atl-N	2	1	.667	6	5	2	1	0	38	31	7.3	2	8	1.9	23	5.4	3.08	113	.230	.265	2	2	100	78	0.6	-0	1	0.3
1982	Atl-N	2	3	.400	27	2	0	0	0	38	52	12.3	3	20	4.7	24	5.7	6.16	62	.327	.400	-11	-10	107	100	-0.6	0	2	-0.7
	Pit-N	6	5	.545	19	18	2	2	1	122	106	7.8	9	24	1.8	94	6.9	3.10	128	.232	.272	7	12	110	83	0.3	-0	2	1.5
	Yr	8	8	.500	46	20	2	2	1	160	158	8.9	12	44	2.5	118	6.6	3.82	103	.255	.304	-4	2	109	83	-0.3	0	4	0.8
1983	Pit-N	15	8	.652	35	35	8	4	0	238	205	7.8	19	87	3.3	199	7.5	3.25	115	.230	.294	10	13	103	90	3.6	-3	1	1.1
1984	Pit-N	12	11	.522	34	32	7	2	1	227	226	9.0	18	78	3.1	149	5.9	2.93	115	.263	.320	17	11	94	**129**	1.4	-2	0	0.8
1985	Pit-N	7	9	.438	30	19	2	0	0	126	139	9.9	9	62	4.4	52	3.7	4.71	80	.283	.366	-16	-13	104	101	1.1	-1	-0	-1.4
1986	Pit-N	3	11	.214	49	15	0	0	0	122	129	9.5	16	49	3.6	80	5.9	5.16	72	.268	.339	-20	-19	101	89	-3.3	0	-0	-1.9
1987	Atl-N	0	1	.000	9	2	0	0	0	20	25	11.2	2	7	3.1	13	5.8	5.85	76	.301	.358	-4	-3	109	90	-0.4	0	0	-0.2
1988	StL-N	6	9	.400	42	17	2	1	1	136	130	8.6	10	45	3.0	70	4.6	3.90	93	.253	.308	-7	-4	105	92	-1.1	1	-0	-0.3
Total	11	74	77	.490	309	203	31	12	3	1396	1384	8.9	130	476	3.1	855	5.5	3.94	95	.258	.318	-51	-33	103	98	3.1	-7	8	-2.3
■ **JOHNNY MEADOR**	Meador, John Davis b: 12/4/1892, Madison, N.C. d: 4/11/70, Winston-Salem, N.C BR/TR, 5'10.5", 165 lbs. Deb: 4/24/20																												
1920	Pit-N	0	2	.000	12	2	0	0	0	36	48	12.0	1	7	1.8	5	1.3	4.25	75	.340	.359	-4	-4	101	111	-0.9	-0	1	-0.3
■ **LEE MEADOWS**	Meadows, Henry Lee "Specs" b: 7/12/1894, Oxford, N.C. d: 1/29/63, Daytona Beach, Fla BL/TR, 5'9", 190 lbs. Deb: 4/19/15																												
1915	StL-N	13	11	.542	39	26	14	1	0	244	232	8.6	5	88	3.2	104	3.8	2.99	93	.259	.320	-6	-6	101	107	1.9	-4	-3	-1.3
1916	StL-N	12	23	.343	**51**	36	11	1	2	289	261	8.1	3	119	3.7	120	3.7	2.58	101	.247	.324	1	1	100	116	-2.6	-1	1	0.1
1917	StL-N	15	9	.625	43	37	18	4	2	266	253	8.6	5	90	3.0	100	3.4	3.08	90	.262	.320	-11	-9	102	104	2.6	-6	-3	-1.9
1918	StL-N	8	14	.364	30	21	12	0	1	165	176	9.6	1	56	3.1	49	2.7	3.60	73	.280	.339	-15	-18	95	100	-0.9	-2	-1	-2.2
1919	StL-N	4	10	.286	22	12	3	1	0	92	100	9.8	3	30	2.9	28	2.7	3.03	93	.292	.339	-1	-2	97	134	-2.0	-2	3	-0.1
	Phi-N	8	10	.444	18	17	15	3	0	158	128	7.3	2	49	2.8	88	5.0	2.34	135	.229	.291	10	14	109	103	1.6	-4	-1	1.2
	Yr	12	20	.375	40	29	18	4	0	250	228	8.2	5	79	2.8	116	4.2	2.59	117	.252	.308	9	12	104	103	-0.4	-2	2	1.1
1920	Phi-N	16	14	.533	35	33	19	3	0	247	249	9.1	5	90	3.3	95	3.5	2.84	123	.270	.333	8	18	112	**116**	3.8	-4	0	1.7
1921	Phi-N	11	16	.407	28	27	15	2	0	194	226	10.5	10	62	2.9	52	2.4	4.31	94	.288	.334	-11	-6	107	90	1.8	2	4	0.1
1922	Phi-N	12	18	.400	33	33	19	2	0	237	264	10.0	8	71	2.7	62	2.4	4.03	119	.288	.337	2	20	117	97	0.8	4	3	2.8
1923	Phi-N	1	3	.250	8	5	0	0	1	20	40	18.0	0	15	6.7	10	4.5	13.05	36	.430	.505	-20	-19	118	73	-0.4	2	0	-1.4
	Pit-N	16	10	.615	31	25	17	1	0	227	250	9.9	3	44	1.7	66	2.6	3.01	127	.284	.313	25	20	95	109	1.8	4	2	2.5
	Yr	17	13	.567	39	30	17	1	1	247	290	10.6	3	59	2.1	76	2.8	3.83	102	.298	.332	5	2	97	109	1.4	2	2	1.1
1924	Pit-N	13	12	.520	36	30	15	3	0	229	240	9.4	7	51	2.0	61	2.4	3.26	123	.278	.314	15	19	104	106	-1.6	-2	-1	1.7
1925	Pit-N	19	10	.655	35	31	20	1	1	255	272	9.6	11	67	2.4	87	3.1	3.67	115	.273	.318	17	15	99	95	1.6	-0	1	1.5
1926	Pit-N	**20**	9	.690	36	31	15	1	0	227	254	10.1	10	52	2.1	54	2.1	3.96	107	.287	.321	-4	7	111	96	5.2	-2	3	0.9
1927	Pit-N	19	10	.655	40	38	**25**	2	0	299	315	9.5	11	66	2.0	84	2.5	3.40	114	.273	.308	17	16	99	99	2.0	-4	-1	1.0
1928	Pit-N	1	1	.500	4	2	1	0	0	10	18	16.2	0	5	4.5	3	2.7	8.10	51	.383	.426	-5	-4	105	88	0.0	1	0	-0.3
1929	Pit-N	0	0	—	1	0	0	0	0	1	2	18.0	0	1	9.0	0	0.0	9.00	53	.500	.600	-0	-0	102	136	0.0	-0	0	0.0
Total	15	188	180	.511	490	404	219	25	7	3160	3280	9.3	84	956	2.7	1063	3.0	3.38	105	.274	.324	22	65	104	104	15.6	-18	5	6.3
■ **RUFUS MEADOWS**	Meadows, Rufus Rivers b: 8/25/07, Chase City, Va. d: 5/10/70, Wichita, Kan. BL/TL, 5'11", 175 lbs. Deb: 4/23/26																												
1926	Cin-N	0	0	—	1	0	0	0	0	⅓	0	0.0	0	0	0.0	0	0.0	0.00	—	.000	.000	0	0	93	0	0.0	-0	0	0.0
■ **DAVE MEADS**	Meads, David Donald b: 1/7/64, Montclair, N.J. BL/TL, 6' ", 175 lbs. Deb: 4/13/87																												
1987	Hou-N	5	3	.625	45	0	0	0	0	49	60	11.0	8	16	2.9	32	5.9	5.51	69	.321	.368	-8	-9	93	110	1.2	1	-1	-0.8
1988	Hou-N	3	1	.750	22	2	0	0	0	40	37	8.3	4	14	3.1	27	6.1	3.15	102	.240	.298	1	0	93	107	1.0	1	0	0.1
Total	2	8	4	.667	67	2	0	0	0	89	97	9.8	12	30	3.0	59	6.0	4.45	80	.284	.337	-6	-9	93	109	2.2	1	-1	-0.7

■ GEORGE MEAKIM Meakim, George Clinton b: 7/11/1865, Brooklyn, N.Y. d: 2/17/23, Queens, N.Y. 5'7.5", 154 lbs. Deb: 5/02/1890

YEAR	TM/L	W	L	PCT	G	GS	CG	SHO	SV	IP	H	H/G	HR	BB	BB/G	SO	SO/G	ERA	/A	OAVG	OOBP	PR	/A	PF	CPI	WAT	PB	PD	TPI
1890	Lou-a	12	7	.632	28	21	16	3	1	192	173	8.1	4	63	3.0	123	5.8	2.91	138	.255	.319	20	24	104	105	-0.5	-3	0	2.0
1891	Phi-a	1	4	.200	6	6	4	0	0	35	51	13.1	1	22	5.7	13	3.3	6.94	55	.356	.441	-13	-12	103	90	-1.5	0	0	-0.9
1892	Chi-N	0	1	.000	1	1	1	0	0	9	18	18.0	0	2	2.0	0	0.0	11.00	28	.429	.455	-8	-8	93	70	-0.4	1	0	-0.4
	Cin-N	1	1	.500	3	3	1	0	0	14	19	12.2	1	9	5.8	4	2.6	9.00	38	.338	.429	-9	-9	103	69	0.0	-1	0	-0.7
	Yr	1	2	.333	4	4	2	0	0	23	37	14.5	1	11	4.3	4	1.6	9.78	33	.377	.440	-17	-17	99	69	-0.4	1	0	-1.1
1895	Lou-N	1	0	1.000	1	1	1	0	0	7	7	9.0	0	4	5.1	2	2.6	2.57	184	.280	.379	2	2	99	150	0.5	0	0	0.1
Total	4	15	13	.536	39	32	23	3	1	257	268	9.4	6	100	3.5	142	5.0	4.06	97	.284	.353	-7	-3	103	101	-1.9	-3	0	0.1

■ DOC MEDICH Medich, George Francis b: 12/9/48, Aliquippa, Pa. BR/TR, 6'5", 225 lbs. Deb: 9/05/72

YEAR	TM/L	W	L	PCT	G	GS	CG	SHO	SV	IP	H	H/G	HR	BB	BB/G	SO	SO/G	ERA	/A	OAVG	OOBP	PR	/A	PF	CPI	WAT	PB	PD	TPI
1972	NY-A	0	0	—	1	1	0	0	0	0	2	—	0	2	—	0	—	∞	—	1.000	1.000	-2	-2	92	85	0.0	0	0	-0.1
1973	NY-A	14	9	.609	34	32	11	3	0	235	217	8.3	20	74	2.8	145	5.6	2.95	130	.241	.297	23	23	100	103	2.9	0	-2	2.2
1974	NY-A	19	15	.559	38	38	17	4	0	280	275	8.8	24	91	2.9	154	5.0	3.60	96	.259	.319	1	-5	95	101	0.4	0	-1	-0.5
1975	NY-A	16	16	.500	38	37	15	2	0	272	271	9.0	25	72	2.4	132	4.4	3.51	105	.264	.307	9	6	98	103	-0.6	0	-3	0.3
1976	Pit-N	8	11	.421	29	26	3	0	0	179	193	9.7	10	48	2.4	86	4.3	3.52	99	.281	.320	-0	-1	99	109	-2.6	-2	1	0.0
1977	Oak-A	10	6	.625	26	25	1	0	0	148	155	9.4	19	49	3.0	74	4.5	4.68	84	.265	.320	-10	-12	97	88	3.3	0	-1	-1.2
	Sea-A	2	0	1.000	3	3	1	0	0	22	26	10.6	1	4	1.6	3	1.2	3.68	109	.286	.327	1	1	98	103	1.0	0	-1	0.0
	Yr	12	6	.667	29	28	2	0	0	170	181	9.6	20	53	2.8	77	4.1	4.55	87	.265	.317	-9	-12	97	103	4.3	0	-2	-1.2
	NY-N	0	1	.000	1	1	0	0	0	7	6	7.7	0	1	1.3	3	3.9	3.86	98	.261	.280	0	-0	97	71	-0.4	-0	-0	0.0
1978	Tex-A	9	8	.529	28	22	6	2	2	171	166	8.7	10	52	2.7	71	3.7	3.74	97	.255	.308	1	-2	96	87	0.0	0	1	-0.1
1979	Tex-A	10	7	.588	29	19	4	1	0	149	156	9.4	9	49	3.0	58	3.5	4.17	101	.269	.323	1	1	99	90	1.5	0	1	0.2
1980	Tex-A	14	11	.560	34	32	6	0	0	204	230	10.1	13	56	2.5	91	4.0	3.93	103	.285	.330	3	3	100	102	2.4	0	-1	0.2
1981	Tex-A	10	6	.625	20	20	4	**4**	0	143	136	8.6	8	33	2.1	65	4.1	3.08	107	.252	.292	9	3	90	97	1.6	0	1	0.5
1982	Tex-A	7	11	.389	21	21	2	0	0	123	146	10.7	8	61	4.5	37	2.7	5.05	76	.307	.377	-13	-16	94	107	-0.1	0	0	-1.5
	Mil-A	5	4	.556	10	10	1	0	0	63	57	8.1	4	32	4.6	36	5.1	5.00	75	.242	.332	-6	-9	92	72	-0.1	0	-1	-0.8
	Yr	12	15	.444	31	31	3	0	0	186	203	9.8	12	93	4.5	73	3.5	5.03	76	.281	.359	-20	-25	94	72	-0.2	0	-0	-2.3
Total	11	124	105	.541	312	287	71	16	2	1996	2036	9.2	151	624	2.8	955	4.3	3.78	99	.266	.318	15	-11	97	98	9.3	-2	-5	-0.8

■ IRV MEDLINGER Medlinger, Irving John b: 6/18/27, Chicago, Ill. d: 9/3/75, Wheeling, Ill. BL/TL, 5'11", 185 lbs. Deb: 4/20/49

YEAR	TM/L	W	L	PCT	G	GS	CG	SHO	SV	IP	H	H/G	HR	BB	BB/G	SO	SO/G	ERA	/A	OAVG	OOBP	PR	/A	PF	CPI	WAT	PB	PD	TPI
1949	StL-A	0	0	—	3	0	0	0	0	4	11	24.8	1	3	6.8	4	9.0	27.00	16	.478	.538	-10	-10	104	53	0.0	0	0	-0.8
1951	StL-A	0	0	—	6	0	0	0	0	10	10	9.0	1	12	10.8	5	4.5	8.10	56	.270	.440	-4	-4	109	82	0.0	0	-0	-0.3
Total	2	0	0	—	9	0	0	0	0	14	21	13.5	2	15	9.6	9	5.8	13.50	33	.350	.474	-15	-14	108	74	0.0	0	-0	-1.1

■ SCOTT MEDVIN Medvin, Scott Howard b: 9/16/61, North Olmstead, O. BR/TR, 6', 190 lbs. Deb: 5/11/88

YEAR	TM/L	W	L	PCT	G	GS	CG	SHO	SV	IP	H	H/G	HR	BB	BB/G	SO	SO/G	ERA	/A	OAVG	OOBP	PR	/A	PF	CPI	WAT	PB	PD	TPI
1988	Pit-N	3	0	1.000	17	0	0	0	0	28	23	7.4	1	9	2.9	16	5.1	4.82	70	.230	.295	-4	-5	97	58	1.5	-0	0	-0.4

■ PETE MEEGAN Meegan, Peter J. "Steady Pete" b: 11/13/1863, San Francisco, Cal d: 3/15/05, San Francisco, Cal Deb: 8/12/1884

YEAR	TM/L	W	L	PCT	G	GS	CG	SHO	SV	IP	H	H/G	HR	BB	BB/G	SO	SO/G	ERA	/A	OAVG	OOBP	PR	/A	PF	CPI	WAT	PB	PD	TPI
1884	Ric-a	5	9	.357	17	17	17	1	0	140	140	9.0	7	27	1.7	71	4.6	4.37	76	.269	.305	-18	-16	102	82	1.0	-3	0	-1.6
1885	Pit-a	7	8	.467	18	16	14	1	0	146	146	9.0	1	38	2.3	58	3.6	3.39	102	.272	.320	-2	1	107	96	-0.5	-2	0	0.0
Total	2	12	17	.414	35	33	31	2	0	286	286	9.0	8	65	2.0	129	4.1	3.87	88	.270	.313	-20	-15	104	89	0.5	-5	0	-1.6

■ BILL MEEHAN Meehan, William Thomas b: 9/4/1889, Osceola Mills, Pa. d: 10/8/82, Douglas, Wyo. BR/TR, 5'9", 155 lbs. Deb: 9/17/15

YEAR	TM/L	W	L	PCT	G	GS	CG	SHO	SV	IP	H	H/G	HR	BB	BB/G	SO	SO/G	ERA	/A	OAVG	OOBP	PR	/A	PF	CPI	WAT	PB	PD	TPI
1915	Phi-A	0	1	.000	1	1	0	0	0	4	7	15.8	0	3	6.8	4	9.0	11.25	27	.389	.476	-4	-4	103	71	-0.4	0	0	-0.2

■ ROY MEEKER Meeker, Charles Roy b: 9/15/1900, Lead Mines, Mo. d: 3/25/29, Orlando, Fla. BL/TL, 5'9", 175 lbs. Deb: 9/22/23

YEAR	TM/L	W	L	PCT	G	GS	CG	SHO	SV	IP	H	H/G	HR	BB	BB/G	SO	SO/G	ERA	/A	OAVG	OOBP	PR	/A	PF	CPI	WAT	PB	PD	TPI
1923	Phi-A	3	0	1.000	5	2	2	0	0	25	24	8.6	0	13	4.7	12	4.3	3.60	113	.253	.333	1	1	102	88	1.5	-1	-0	0.0
1924	Phi-A	5	12	.294	30	14	5	1	0	146	166	10.2	7	81	5.0	37	2.3	4.68	91	.288	.373	-7	-7	101	101	-3.3	-0	-1	-0.7
1926	Cin-N	0	2	.000	7	1	1	0	0	21	24	10.3	1	9	3.9	5	2.1	6.43	55	.324	.375	-6	-7	93	84	-0.9	-1	0	-0.6
Total	3	8	14	.364	42	17	8	1	0	192	214	10.0	8	103	4.8	54	2.5	4.73	88	.287	.368	-12	-12	100	98	-2.7	-2	-1	-1.3

■ JOUETT MEEKIN Meekin, Jouett b: 2/21/1867, New Albany, Ind. d: 12/14/44, New Albany, Ind. 6'1", 180 lbs. Deb: 6/13/1891

YEAR	TM/L	W	L	PCT	G	GS	CG	SHO	SV	IP	H	H/G	HR	BB	BB/G	SO	SO/G	ERA	/A	OAVG	OOBP	PR	/A	PF	CPI	WAT	PB	PD	TPI
1891	Lou-a	10	16	.385	29	26	25	2	0	228	227	9.0	2	113	4.5	144	**5.7**	4.30	80	.274	.361	-15	-22	92	80	-0.3	5	0	-1.4
1892	Lou-N	7	10	.412	19	18	17	0	0	156	168	9.7	3	78	4.5	67	3.9	4.04	76	.288	.372	-13	-17	93	99	0.0	-4	0	-1.8
	Was-N	3	10	.231	14	14	13	1	0	112	112	9.0	2	48	3.9	58	4.7	3.46	101	.273	.349	-2	0	106	98	-2.6	-1	0	0.0
	Yr	10	20	.333	33	32	30	1	0	268	280	9.4	5	126	4.2	125	4.2	3.79	85	.282	.363	-15	-16	99	98	-2.6	-4	0	-1.8
1893	Was-N	10	15	.400	31	28	24	1	0	245	289	10.6	6	140	5.1	91	3.3	4.96	87	.310	.400	-8	-18	92	101	2.0	4	0	-1.0
1894	NY-N	33	9	**.786**	52	48	40	1	2	409	404	8.9	13	171	3.8	133	2.9	3.70	142	.279	**.355**	74	70	98	97	**9.4**	7	-1	6.0
1895	NY-N	16	11	.593	29	29	24	1	0	226	296	11.8	10	73	2.9	76	3.0	5.30	85	.337	.388	-13	-19	94	95	2.9	4	0	-1.1
1896	NY-N	26	14	.650	42	41	34	0	0	334	378	10.2	8	127	3.4	110	3.0	3.83	112	.307	.372	20	18	99	106	**8.0**	11	-3	2.2
1897	NY-N	20	11	.645	37	34	30	2	0	304	328	9.7	9	99	2.9	83	2.5	3.76	111	.297	.355	19	14	96	97	0.6	5	-2	1.5
1898	NY-N	16	18	.471	38	37	34	1	0	320	329	9.3	9	108	3.0	82	2.3	3.77	90	.287	.349	-6	-13	94	91	-1.7	1	-5	-1.5
1899	NY-N	5	11	.313	18	18	16	0	0	148	169	10.3	4	70	4.3	30	1.8	4.38	87	.311	.390	-9	-9	99	99	-1.8	1	0	-0.7
	Bos-N	7	6	.538	13	13	12	0	0	108	111	9.3	0	23	1.9	23	1.9	2.83	140	.289	.329	12	13	103	100	-0.9	-1	0	1.2
	Yr	12	17	.414	31	31	28	0	0	256	280	9.8	4	93	3.3	53	1.9	3.73	104	.302	.365	4	4	100	100	-2.7	1	0	0.5
1900	Pit-N	0	2	.000	2	2	1	0	0	13	20	13.8	1	8	5.5	3	2.1	6.92	54	.377	.459	-5	-5	101	103	-0.9	-1	0	-0.3
Total	10	153	133	.535	324	308	270	9	2	2603	2831	9.8	67	1058	3.7	900	3.1	4.07	101	.297	.367	56	12	96	97	14.7	32	-9	3.1

■ PHIL MEELER Meeler, Charles Phillip b: 7/3/48, South Boston, Va. BR/TR, 6'5", 215 lbs. Deb: 5/10/72

YEAR	TM/L	W	L	PCT	G	GS	CG	SHO	SV	IP	H	H/G	HR	BB	BB/G	SO	SO/G	ERA	/A	OAVG	OOBP	PR	/A	PF	CPI	WAT	PB	PD	TPI
1972	Det-A	0	1	.000	7	0	0	0	0	8	10	11.3	0	7	7.9	5	5.6	4.50	77	.303	.405	-1	-1	112	124	-0.4	-0	0	0.0

■ RUSS MEERS Meers, Russell Harlan "Babe" b: 11/28/18, Tilton, Ill. BL/TL, 5'10", 170 lbs. Deb: 9/28/41

YEAR	TM/L	W	L	PCT	G	GS	CG	SHO	SV	IP	H	H/G	HR	BB	BB/G	SO	SO/G	ERA	/A	OAVG	OOBP	PR	/A	PF	CPI	WAT	PB	PD	TPI
1941	Chi-N	0	1	.000	1	1	0	0	0	8	5	5.6	0	0	0.0	5	5.6	1.13	302	.172	.200	2	2	94	30	-0.4	-0	-0	0.2
1946	Chi-N	1	2	.333	7	2	0	0	0	11	10	8.2	0	10	8.2	2	1.6	3.27	97	.238	.377	0	-0	93	120	-0.5	0	0	0.0
1947	Chi-N	2	0	1.000	35	1	0	0	0	64	61	8.6	5	38	5.3	28	3.9	4.50	94	.263	.363	-3	-2	104	103	1.0	-1	-0	-0.2
Total	3	3	3	.500	43	4	0	0	0	83	76	8.2	5	48	5.2	35	3.8	4.01	100	.251	.352	-1	-0	101	98	0.1	-0	-0	0.0

■ HEINIE MEINE Meine, Henry William "The Count Of Luxemburg" b: 5/1/1896, St.Louis, Mo. d: 3/18/68, St.Louis, Mo. BR/TR, 5'11", 180 lbs. Deb: 8/16/22

YEAR	TM/L	W	L	PCT	G	GS	CG	SHO	SV	IP	H	H/G	HR	BB	BB/G	SO	SO/G	ERA	/A	OAVG	OOBP	PR	/A	PF	CPI	WAT	PB	PD	TPI
1922	StL-A	0	0	—	1	0	0	0	0	4	5	11.3	1	2	4.5	0	0.0	4.50	92	.313	.389	-0	-0	102	149	0.0	-0	0	0.0
1929	Pit-N	7	6	.538	22	13	7	1	1	108	120	10.0	4	34	2.8	19	1.6	4.50	106	.291	.344	3	3	102	98	-0.4	-2	-2	0.0
1930	Pit-N	6	8	.429	20	16	4	0	1	117	168	12.9	6	44	3.4	18	1.4	6.15	79	.346	.394	-15	-17	98	101	-1.2	-3	2	-1.4
1931	Pit-N	**19**	13	.594	36	35	22	3	0	**284**	278	8.8	8	87	2.8	58	1.8	2.98	132	.254	.309	28	30	102	104	4.0	-3	-0	2.8
1932	Pit-N	12	9	.571	28	25	13	1	1	172	193	10.1	6	45	2.4	32	1.7	3.87	100	.278	.320	0	-0	100	94	0.4	-2	-1	-0.2
1933	Pit-N	15	8	.652	32	29	12	2	0	207	227	9.9	10	50	2.2	50	2.2	3.65	86	.278	.314	-7	-12	94	98	2.6	-1	-3	-1.6
1934	Pit-N	7	6	.538	26	14	2	0	0	106	134	11.4	12	25	2.1	22	1.9	4.33	98	.306	.339	-3	-1	105	116	0.6	-1	-1	-0.2
Total	7	66	50	.569	165	132	60	7	3	998	1125	10.1	47	287	2.6	199	1.8	3.96	101	.284	.330	5	2	99	102	6.0	-12	-4	-0.6

■ FRANK MEINKE Meinke, Frank Louis b: 10/18/1863, Chicago, Ill. d: 11/8/31, Chicago, Ill. 5'10.5", 172 lbs. Deb: 5/01/1884

YEAR	TM/L	W	L	PCT	G	GS	CG	SHO	SV	IP	H	H/G	HR	BB	BB/G	SO	SO/G	ERA	/A	OAVG	OOBP	PR	/A	PF	CPI	WAT	PB	PD	TPI
1884	Det-N	8	23	.258	35	31	31	1	0	289	341	10.6	10	63	2.0	124	3.9	3.18	93	.303	.340	-6	-7	99	**119**	0.2	-3	-2	-0.5
1885	Det-N	0	1	.000	1	1	0	0	0	5	13	23.4	0	4	7.2	0	0.0	3.60	77	.492	.558	-0	-0	99	346	-0.4	-0	0	0.0
Total	2	8	24	.250	36	32	31	1	0	294	354	10.8	10	67	2.1	124	3.8	3.18	93	.307	.346	-7	-8	99	123	-0.2	-4	-2	-0.5

■ SAM MEJIAS Mejias, Samuel Elias b: 5/9/52, Santiago, D.R. BR/TR, 6', 170 lbs. Deb: 9/06/76

YEAR	TM/L	W	L	PCT	G	GS	CG	SHO	SV	IP	H	H/G	HR	BB	BB/G	SO	SO/G	ERA	/A	OAVG	OOBP	PR	/A	PF	CPI	WAT	PB	PD	TPI
1978	Mon-N	0	0	—	1	0	0	0	0	1	0	0.0	0	0	0.0	0	0.0	0.00	—	.000	.250	0	0	96	0	0.0	0	0	0.0

■ STEVE MELTER Melter, Stephen Blazius b: 1/2/1886, Cherokee, Iowa d: 1/28/62, Mishawaka, Ind. BR/TR, 6'2", 180 lbs. Deb: 09

YEAR	TM/L	W	L	PCT	G	GS	CG	SHO	SV	IP	H	H/G	HR	BB	BB/G	SO	SO/G	ERA	/A	OAVG	OOBP	PR	/A	PF	CPI	WAT	PB	PD	TPI
1909	StL-N	0	1	.000	23	1	0	0	3	64	79	11.1	1	20	2.8	24	3.4	3.52	74	.322	.378	-7	-7	99	131	-0.4	-0	1	-0.5

■ CLIFF MELTON Melton, Clifford George "Mickey Mouse" or "Mountain Music" b: 1/3/12, Brevard, N.C. d: 7/28/86, Baltimore, Md. BL/TL, 6'5.5", 203 lbs. Deb: 4/25/37

YEAR	TM/L	W	L	PCT	G	GS	CG	SHO	SV	IP	H	H/G	HR	BB	BB/G	SO	SO/G	ERA	/A	OAVG	OOBP	PR	/A	PF	CPI	WAT	PB	PD	TPI
1937	NY-N	20	9	.690	46	27	14	2	**7**	248	216	7.8	9	55	2.0	142	5.2	2.61	146	.233	.276	36	**33**	98	94	3.0	-5	4	3.3
1938	NY-N	14	14	.500	36	31	10	1	0	243	266	9.9	19	61	2.3	101	3.7	3.89	99	.276	.315	-3	-1	102	100	-1.5	-1	2	0.0
1939	NY-N	12	15	.444	41	23	9	2	5	207	214	9.3	7	65	2.8	95	4.1	3.57	108	.269	.319	8	7	99	99	-2.0	-1	1	0.6

YEAR	TM/L	W	L	PCT	G	GS	CG	SHO	SV	IP	H	H/G	HR	BB	BB/G	SO	SO/G	ERA	/A	OAVG	OOBP	PR	/A	PF	CPI	WAT	PB	PD	TPI
1940	NY-N	10	11	.476	37	21	4	1	2	167	185	10.0	9	68	3.7	91	**4.9**	4.90	79	.285	.347	-20	-20	100	93	0.1	2	2	-1.5
1941	NY-N	8	11	.421	42	22	9	3	1	194	181	8.4	14	61	2.8	100	4.6	3.02	125	.246	.298	13	16	104	109	-1.3	-4	3	1.7
1942	NY-N	11	5	.688	23	17	12	2	1	144	122	7.6	9	33	2.1	61	3.8	2.63	128	.229	.273	11	12	101	97	2.5	2	3	1.8
1943	NY-N	9	13	.409	34	28	6	2	0	186	184	8.9	7	69	3.3	55	2.7	3.19	105	.257	.318	4	3	99	106	1.0	1	3	0.8
1944	NY-N	2	2	.500	13	10	1	0	0	64	78	11.0	5	19	2.7	15	2.1	4.08	93	.294	.337	-3	-2	105	111	0.2	-2	1	-0.2
Total	8	86	80	.518	272	179	65	13	16	1453	1446	9.0	79	431	2.7	660	4.1	3.42	109	.259	.308	46	49	100	100	2.0	-9	19	6.5
■ RUBE MELTON	Melton, Reuben Franklin b: 2/27/17, Cramerton, N.C. d: 9/11/71, Greer, S.C. BR/TR, 6'5", 205 lbs. Deb: 4/17/41																												
1941	Phi-N	1	5	.167	25	5	2	0	0	84	81	8.7	7	47	5.0	57	6.1	4.71	79	.258	.347	-10	-9	103	93	-1.1	-1	-1	-1.1
1942	Phi-N	9	20	.310	42	29	10	1	4	209	180	7.8	7	114	4.9	107	4.6	3.70	90	.234	.329	-9	-8	101	90	0.8	-1	-2	-1.1
1943	Bro-N	5	8	.385	30	17	4	2	0	119	102	7.7	3	79	6.0	63	4.8	3.93	85	.233	.352	-7	-8	99	92	-1.8	-2	-1	-1.1
1944	Bro-N	9	13	.409	37	23	6	1	0	187	178	8.6	1	96	4.6	91	4.4	3.47	106	.254	.336	3	4	102	102	0.0	-3	0	0.2
1946	Bro-N	6	3	.667	24	12	3	2	1	100	72	6.5	3	52	4.7	44	4.0	1.98	172	.206	.308	16	16	100	128	0.6	-2	-0	1.5
1947	Bro-N	0	1	.000	4	1	0	0	0	5	7	12.6	1	7	12.6	1	1.8	12.60	33	.350	.519	-5	-5	103	80	-0.4	0	-0	-0.3
Total	6	30	50	.375	162	87	25	6	5	704	620	7.9	22	395	5.0	363	4.6	3.62	97	.239	.336	-12	-10	101	99	-1.9	-9	-5	-1.9
■ MARIO MENDOZA	Mendoza, Mario (Aizpuru) b: 12/26/50, Chihuahua, Mex. BR/TR, 5'11", 170 lbs. Deb: 4/26/74 C																												
1977	Pit-N	0	0	—	1	0	0	0	0	2	3	13.5	1	2	9.0	0	0.0	13.50	30	.375	.500	-2	-2	102	89	0.0	0	0	-0.1
■ MIKE MENDOZA	Mendoza, Michael Joseph b: 11/26/55, Inglewood, Cal. BR/TR, 6'5", 215 lbs. Deb: 9/07/79																												
1979	Hou-N	0	0	—	1	0	0	0	0	1	0	0.0	0	0	0.0	0	0.0	0.00	—	.000	.000	0	0	90	0	0.0	0	0	0.0
■ JOCK MENEFEE	Menefee, John b: 1/15/1868, West Virginia d: 3/11/53, Belle Vernon, Pa. BR/TR, 6', Deb: 8/17/1892																												
1892	Pit-N	0	0	—	1	0	0	0	0	4	10	22.5	0	2	4.5	0	0.0	11.25	27	.484	.530	-4	-4	94	97	0.0	-0	0	-0.2
1893	Lou-N	8	7	.533	15	15	14	1	0	129	150	10.5	3	40	2.8	30	2.1	4.26	108	.307	.359	6	5	98	98	1.8	3	0	0.8
1894	Lou-N	8	17	.320	28	24	20	1	0	212	258	11.0	3	50	2.1	43	1.8	4.29	113	.323	.363	25	13	91	96	0.9	-5	0	0.5
	Pit-N	5	8	.385	13	13	13	0	0	112	159	12.8	4	39	3.1	33	2.7	5.46	92	.357	.409	-2	-5	95	103	-1.5	1	0	-0.3
	Yr	13	25	.342	41	37	33	1	0	324	417	11.6	7	89	2.5	76	2.1	4.69	104	.335	.380	23	7	92	103	-0.6	-5	0	0.2
1895	Pit-N	0	1	.000	2	1	0	0	0	2	2	9.0	0	7	31.5	0	0.0	22.50	20	.280	.636	-4	-4	96	53	-0.4	0	0	-0.2
1898	NY-N	0	1	.000	1	1	1	0	0	9	11	11.0	0	2	2.0	3	3.0	5.00	68	.324	.362	-1	-2	94	77	-0.4	-1	0	-0.1
1900	Chi-N	9	4	.692	16	13	11	0	0	117	140	10.8	1	35	2.7	30	2.3	3.85	91	.320	.371	-2	-5	94	104	2.9	-4	0	-0.7
1901	Chi-N	8	12	.400	21	20	19	0	0	182	201	9.9	4	34	1.7	55	2.7	3.81	89	.305	.345	-10	-8	103	91	0.4	3	-1	-0.7
1902	Chi-N	12	10	.545	22	21	20	4	0	197	202	9.2	2	26	1.2	60	2.7	2.42	109	.291	.322	8	5	95	110	1.3	2	-1	0.5
1903	Chi-N	8	10	.444	20	17	13	1	0	147	157	9.6	3	38	2.3	39	2.4	3.00	102	.301	.356	4	1	94	113	-2.4	1	3	0.4
Total	9	58	70	.453	139	125	111	7	0	1111	1290	10.5	20	273	2.2	293	2.4	3.84	100	.314	.359	21	-2	95	101	2.6	0	2	0.0
■ MIKE MEOLA	Meola, Emile Michael b: 10/19/05, New York, N.Y. d: 9/1/76, Fair Lawn, N.J. BR/TR, 5'11", 175 lbs. Deb: 4/24/33																												
1933	Bos-A	0	0	—	3	0	0	0	0	2	5	22.5	0	2	9.0	1	4.5	27.00	16	.417	.500	-5	-5	102	41	0.0	0	0	-0.3
1936	StL-A	0	1	.000	9	0	0	0	0	19	29	13.7	0	13	6.2	6	2.8	9.47	57	.358	.453	-9	-9	107	78	-0.4	1	0	-0.6
	Bos-A	0	2	.000	6	3	1	0	1	21	29	12.4	0	10	4.3	8	3.4	5.57	96	.326	.381	-1	-1	106	104	-0.9	-1	1	0.0
	Yr	0	3	.000	15	3	1	0	1	40	58	13.0	0	23	5.2	14	3.1	7.42	72	.339	.410	-11	-9	106	104	-1.3	1	1	-0.6
Total	2	0	3	.000	18	3	1	0	1	42	63	13.5	0	25	5.4	15	3.2	8.36	64	.346	.421	-16	-14	106	89	-1.3	0	1	-0.9
■ WIN MERCER	Mercer, George Barclay b: 6/20/1874, Chester, W.Va. d: 1/12/03, San Francisco, Cal TR, 5'7", 140 lbs. Deb: 4/21/1894																												
1894	Was-N	17	23	.425	49	38	30	0	3	333	431	11.6	9	125	3.4	69	1.9	3.76	142	.336	.395	58	58	100	**133**	3.5	2	2	5.0
1895	Was-N	13	23	.361	43	38	32	0	2	311	430	12.4	17	96	2.8	84	2.4	4.46	113	.349	.396	12	20	105	122	0.9	-1	-1	1.7
1896	Was-N	25	18	.581	46	45	38	2	0	366	456	11.2	10	117	2.9	94	2.3	4.13	102	.328	.380	10	3	96	109	7.1	0	1	0.4
1897	Was-N	20	20	.500	45	42	34	**3**	2	332	395	10.7	5	102	2.8	88	2.4	3.25	135	.318	.370	39	42	102	**124**	2.0	8	0	4.5
1898	Was-N	12	18	.400	33	30	24	0	0	234	309	11.9	3	71	2.7	52	2.0	4.81	78	.341	.389	-31	-27	105	97	1.8	8	0	-2.3
1899	Was-N	7	14	.333	23	21	21	0	0	186	234	11.3	1	53	2.6	28	1.4	4.60	82	.332	.379	-15	-17	98	92	-0.6	5	0	-1.4
1900	NY-N	13	17	.433	32	29	26	1	0	242	303	11.3	5	58	2.2	39	1.5	3.87	95	.330	.370	-4	-5	99	109	0.0	6	2	-0.4
1901	Was-A	9	13	.409	24	22	19	1	1	180	217	10.9	8	50	2.5	31	1.5	4.55	81	.319	.366	-18	-17	100	94	-1.2	6	0	-1.4
1902	Det-A	15	18	.455	35	33	28	4	1	282	282	9.0	5	80	2.6	40	1.3	3.03	118	.284	.338	17	17	101	103	2.4	-2	3	1.8
Total	9	131	164	.444	330	298	252	11	9	2466	3057	11.2	63	752	2.7	525	1.9	3.98	107	.327	.377	67	73	101	112	15.9	33	7	7.9
■ JACK MERCER	Mercer, John Deb: 8/02/10																												
1910	Pit-N	0	0	—	1	0	0	0	0	1	0	0.0	0	2	18.0	1	9.0	0.00	—	.000	.500	0	0	110	0	0.0	0	0	0.0
■ MARK MERCER	Mercer, Mark Kenneth b: 5/22/54, Fort Bragg, N.C. BL/TL, 6'5", 220 lbs. Deb: 9/01/81																												
1981	Tex-A	0	1	.000	7	0	0	0	2	8	7	7.9	1	7	7.9	8	9.0	4.50	73	.241	.389	-1	-1	90	113	-0.4	0	0	0.0
■ SPIKE MERENA	Merena, John Joseph b: 11/18/09, Paterson, N.J. d: 3/9/77, Bridgeport, Conn. BL/TL, 6', 185 lbs. Deb: 9/16/34																												
1934	Bos-A	1	2	.333	4	3	2	1	0	25	20	7.2	2	16	5.8	7	2.5	2.88	164	.222	.343	4	5	105	136	-0.4	-0	-1	0.4
■ RON MERIDITH	Meridith, Ronald Knox b: 11/26/56, San Pedro, Cal. BL/TL, 6', 175 lbs. Deb: 9/16/84																												
1984	Chi-N	0	0	—	3	0	0	0	0	5	6	10.8	1	2	3.6	4	7.2	3.60	109	.273	.320	-0	0	109	137	0.0	0	0	0.0
1985	Chi-N	3	2	.600	32	0	0	0	1	46	53	10.4	3	24	4.7	23	4.5	4.50	93	.301	.373	-5	-2	117	116	0.6	0	0	0.0
1986	Tex-A	1	0	1.000	5	0	0	0	0	3	2	6.0	0	1	3.0	2	6.0	3.00	133	.286	.300	0	0	95	143	0.5	0	0	0.1
1987	Tex-A	1	0	1.000	11	0	0	0	0	21	25	10.7	7	12	5.1	17	7.3	6.00	77	.298	.385	-4	-3	104	122	0.5	0	0	-0.2
Total	4	5	2	.714	51	0	0	0	1	75	86	10.3	11	39	4.7	46	5.5	4.80	90	.298	.371	-8	-4	112	120	1.6	0	1	-0.1
■ GEORGE MERRITT	Merritt, George Washington b: 4/14/1880, Paterson, N.J. d: 2/21/38, Memphis, Tenn. TR, 6', 160 lbs. Deb: 9/06/01																												
1901	Pit-N	3	0	1.000	3	3	3	0	0	24	28	10.5	0	5	1.9	5	1.9	4.88	65	.321	.372	-4	-5	96	78	1.5	1	-0	-0.3
1903	Pit-N	0	0	—	1	0	0	0	0	4	4	9.0	0	1	2.3	2	4.5	2.25	147	.284	.332	0	0	101	122	0.0	-0	0	0.0
Total	2	3	0	1.000	4	3	3	0	0	28	32	10.3	0	6	1.9	7	2.3	4.50	71	.316	.366	-4	-4	97	84	1.5	1	-0	-0.3
■ JIM MERRITT	Merritt, James Joseph b: 12/9/43, Altadena, Cal. BL/TL, 6'3", 175 lbs. Deb: 8/02/65																												
1965	Min-A	5	4	.556	16	9	1	0	2	77	68	7.9	11	20	2.3	61	7.1	3.16	108	.239	.283	3	2	98	108	-0.5	0	0	0.3
1966	Min-A	7	14	.333	31	18	5	1	3	144	112	7.0	17	33	2.1	124	7.8	3.38	112	.212	.254	1	7	110	75	-4.4	-1	-0	0.6
1967	Min-A	13	7	.650	37	28	11	4	0	228	196	7.7	21	30	**1.2**	161	6.4	2.53	135	.230	.256	18	22	106	102	2.2	1	-2	2.5
1968	Min-A	12	16	.429	38	34	11	1	1	238	207	7.8	21	52	2.0	181	6.8	3.25	97	.232	.275	-7	-3	106	85	-1.9	0	0	-0.2
1969	Cin-N	17	9	.654	42	36	8	1	0	251	269	9.6	33	61	2.2	144	5.2	4.37	81	.273	.313	-22	-23	99	95	3.4	1	-3	-2.4
1970	Cin-N	20	12	.625	35	35	12	1	0	234	248	9.5	21	53	2.0	136	5.2	4.08	103	.270	.307	-1	3	103	93	0.0	2	-2	0.3
1971	Cin-N	1	11	.083	28	11	0	0	0	107	115	9.7	14	31	2.6	38	3.2	4.37	76	.279	.327	-11	-12	96	101	-4.9	0	-2	-1.3
1972	Cin-N	1	0	1.000	4	1	0	0	0	8	13	14.6	1	2	2.3	4	4.5	4.50	70	.361	.395	-1	-1	91	149	0.5	-0	0	-0.1
1973	Tex-A	5	13	.278	35	19	8	1	1	160	191	10.7	18	34	1.9	65	3.7	4.05	94	.296	.326	-4	-4	100	109	-2.0	0	-1	-0.5
1974	Tex-A	0	0	—	26	1	0	0	0	33	46	12.5	3	6	1.6	18	4.9	4.09	85	.329	.349	-2	-2	96	124	0.0	0	-0	-0.2
1975	Tex-A	0	0	—	5	0	0	0	0	4	3	6.8	0	0	0.0	0	0.0	0.00	—	.214	.267	2	2	100	0	0.0	0	-0	0.2
Total	11	81	86	.485	297	192	56	9	7	1484	1468	8.9	160	322	2.0	932	5.7	3.65	98	.257	.294	-24	-10	102	95	-7.6	3	-9	-0.8
■ LLOYD MERRITT	Merritt, Lloyd Wesley b: 4/8/33, St.Louis, Mo. BR/TR, 6', 189 lbs. Deb: 4/22/57																												
1957	StL-N	1	2	.333	44	0	0	0	7	65	60	8.3	7	28	3.9	35	4.8	3.32	116	.251	.329	4	4	99	123	-0.5	-0	0	0.4
■ SAM MERTES	Mertes, Samuel Blair "Sandow" b: 8/6/1872, San Francisco, Cal. d: 3/11/45, San Francisco, Cal BR/TR, 5'10", 185 lbs. Deb: 6/30/1896																												
1902	Chi-A	1	0	1.000	1	0	0	0	0	8	6	6.8	0	0	0.0	0	0.0	1.13	298	.230	.230	2	2	94	84	0.5	0	-0	0.2
■ JIM MERTZ	Mertz, James Verlin b: 8/10/16, Lima, Ohio BR/TR, 5'10.5", 170 lbs. Deb: 5/01/43																												
1943	Was-A	5	7	.417	33	10	2	0	3	117	109	8.4	7	58	4.5	53	4.1	4.62	73	.251	.335	-17	-16	102	82	-1.4	0	0	-1.6
■ JOSE MESA	Mesa, Jose Ramon b: 5/22/66, Pueblo Viejo, D.R. BR/TR, 6'3", 170 lbs. Deb: 9/10/87																												
1987	Bal-A	1	3	.250	6	5	0	0	0	31	38	11.0	7	15	4.4	17	4.9	6.10	73	.297	.371	-6	-6	99	102	-0.7	0	-1	-0.5

YEAR	TM/L	W	L	PCT	G	GS	CG	SHO	SV	IP	H	H/G	HR	BB	BB/G	SO	SO/G	ERA	/A	OAVG	OOBP	PR	/A	PF	CPI	WAT	PB	PD	TPI
BUD MESSENGER	Messenger, Andrew Warren b: 2/1/1898, Grand Blanc, Mich. d: 11/4/71, Lansing, Mich. BR/TR, 6', 175 lbs. Deb: 7/31/24																												
1924	Cle-A	2	0	1.000	5	2	1	0	0	25	28	10.1	4	14	5.0	4	1.4	4.32	95	.283	.368	-0	-1	97	124	1.0	-0	-0	0.0
ANDY MESSERSMITH	Messersmith, John Alexander b: 8/6/45, Toms River, N.J. BR/TR, 6'1", 200 lbs. Deb: 7/04/68																												
1968	Cal-A	4	2	.667	28	5	2	1	4	81	44	4.9	3	35	3.9	74	8.2	2.22	129	.157	.249	7	6	96	57	1.3	-1	0	0.6
1969	Cal-A	16	11	.593	40	33	10	2	2	250	169	**6.1**	17	100	3.6	211	7.6	2.52	145	**.190**	.272	31	32	101	83	4.2	1	-1	3.5
1970	Cal-A	11	10	.524	37	26	6	1	5	195	144	**6.6**	21	78	3.6	162	7.5	3.00	113	**.205**	.287	16	9	92	92	-0.1	1	-1	0.9
1971	Cal-A	20	13	.606	38	38	14	4	0	277	224	7.3	16	121	3.9	179	5.8	2.99	115	.218	.301	15	14	99	90	5.0	3	1	2.0
1972	Cal-A	8	11	.421	25	21	10	3	2	170	125	6.6	5	68	3.6	142	7.5	2.81	98	.207	.283	5	-1	90	77	-1.3	2	0	0.1
1973	LA-N	14	10	.583	33	33	10	3	0	250	196	7.1	24	77	2.8	177	6.4	2.70	134	.214	.275	27	26	99	94	-0.1	1	0	2.9
1974	LA-N	**20**	6	**.769**	39	39	13	3	0	292	227	7.0	24	94	2.9	221	6.8	2.59	126	.212	**.275**	34	22	90	92	**5.4**	9	0	3.3
1975	LA-N	19	14	.576	42	40	**19**	**7**	1	**322**	244	**6.8**	22	96	2.7	213	6.0	2.29	148	**.213**	.270	**48**	39	93	100	1.4	2	-2	4.2
1976	Atl-N	11	11	.500	29	28	12	3	1	207	166	7.2	14	74	3.2	135	5.9	3.04	129	.219	.286	11	20	112	86	1.5	0	1	2.5
1977	Atl-N	5	4	.556	16	16	1	0	0	102	101	8.9	12	39	3.4	69	6.1	4.41	102	.256	.318	-6	1	115	89	1.3	-0	0	0.2
1978	NY-A	0	3	.000	6	5	0	0	0	22	24	9.8	7	15	6.1	16	6.5	5.73	64	.267	.377	-5	-5	97	114	-1.4	0	0	-0.4
1979	LA-N	2	4	.333	11	11	1	0	0	62	55	8.0	9	34	4.9	26	3.8	4.94	75	.244	.335	-8	-8	99	88	-0.9	-1	0	-0.8
Total	12	130	99	.568	344	295	98	27	15	2230	1719	6.9	174	831	3.4	1625	6.6	2.86	122	.212	.284	174	153	98	89	16.3	18	-0	19.0
TOM METCALF	Metcalf, Thomas John b: 7/16/40, Amherst, Wis. BR/TR, 6'2.5", 174 lbs. Deb: 8/04/63																												
1963	NY-A	1	0	1.000	8	0	0	0	0	13	12	8.3	1	3	2.1	3	2.1	2.77	129	.250	.294	1	1	98	114	0.5	0	-0	0.1
DEWEY METIVIER	Metivier, George Dewey b: 5/6/1898, Cambridge, Mass. d: 3/2/47, Cambridge, Mass. BL/TR, 5'11", 175 lbs. Deb: 9/15/22																												
1922	Cle-A	2	0	1.000	2	2	2	0	0	18	18	9.0	1	3	1.5	1	0.5	4.50	92	.265	.306	-1	-1	103	69	1.0	-0	-1	0.0
1923	Cle-A	4	2	.667	26	5	1	0	1	73	111	13.7	1	38	4.7	9	1.1	6.53	60	.368	.419	-21	-21	99	105	0.9	-0	0	-1.9
1924	Cle-A	1	5	.167	26	6	1	0	3	76	110	13.0	3	34	4.0	14	1.7	5.33	77	.358	.401	-9	-10	97	120	-1.8	-2	-1	-1.1
Total	3	7	7	.500	54	13	4	0	4	167	239	12.9	5	75	4.0	24	1.3	5.77	70	.353	.401	-31	-32	99	108	0.1	-2	-1	-3.0
BUTCH METZGER	Metzger, Clarence Edward b: 5/23/52, Lafayette, Ind. BR/TR, 6'1", 185 lbs. Deb: 9/08/74																												
1974	SF-N	1	0	1.000	10	0	0	0	0	13	11	7.6	0	12	8.3	5	3.5	3.46	114	.239	.383	0	1	109	121	0.5	0	-0	0.1
1975	SD-N	1	0	1.000	4	0	0	0	0	5	6	10.8	1	4	7.2	6	10.8	7.20	51	.316	.417	-2	-2	101	101	0.5	0	0	-0.1
1976	SD-N	11	4	.733	77	0	0	0	16	123	119	8.7	5	52	3.8	89	6.5	2.93	107	.258	.330	8	3	90	123	4.0	-0	-0	0.2
1977	SD-N	0	0	—	17	1	0	0	0	23	27	10.6	5	12	4.7	6	2.3	5.48	64	.307	.381	-4	-5	89	121	0.0	-0	-0	-0.5
	StL-N	4	2	.667	58	0	0	0	7	93	78	7.5	8	38	3.7	48	4.6	3.10	120	.228	.301	8	6	95	100	1.0	-0	-1	0.5
	Yr	4	2	.667	75	1	0	0	7	116	105	8.1	13	50	3.9	54	4.2	3.57	103	.242	.316	4	1	94	100	1.0	-0	-1	0.0
1978	NY-N	1	3	.250	25	0	0	0	0	37	48	11.7	4	22	5.4	21	5.1	6.57	54	.324	.394	-12	-12	99	98	-0.7	0	-0	-1.2
Total	5	18	9	.667	191	1	0	0	23	294	289	8.8	23	140	4.3	175	5.4	3.73	92	.262	.338	-2	-9	94	112	5.3	-1	-2	-1.0
BRIAN MEYER	Meyer, Brian Scott b: 1/29/63, Camden, N.J. BR/TR, 6'1", 190 lbs. Deb: 9/03/88																												
1988	Hou-N	0	0	—	8	0	0	0	0	12	9	6.8	2	4	3.0	10	7.5	1.50	215	.225	.283	3	2	93	249	0.0	0	1	0.3
JACK MEYER	Meyer, John Robert b: 3/23/32, Philadelphia, Pa. d: 3/6/67, Philadelphia, Pa. BR/TR, 6'1", 175 lbs. Deb: 4/16/55																												
1955	Phi-N	6	11	.353	50	5	0	0	**16**	110	75	6.1	14	66	5.4	97	7.9	3.44	120	.190	.306	7	8	102	88	-2.6	0	-0	0.8
1956	Phi-N	7	11	.389	41	7	2	0	2	96	86	8.1	8	51	4.8	66	6.2	4.41	82	.242	.337	-7	-9	95	85	-1.5	1	0	-0.6
1957	Phi-N	0	2	.000	19	2	0	0	0	38	44	10.4	7	28	6.6	34	8.1	5.68	67	.297	.406	-8	-8	99	116	-0.9	0	0	-0.6
1958	Phi-N	3	6	.333	37	5	1	0	2	90	77	7.7	8	33	3.3	87	8.7	3.60	110	.232	.297	4	4	100	84	-1.1	1	-1	0.3
1959	Phi-N	5	3	.625	47	1	1	0	1	94	76	7.3	9	53	5.1	71	6.8	3.35	120	.222	.321	6	7	102	104	1.5	-1	0	0.6
1960	Phi-N	3	1	.750	7	4	0	0	0	25	25	9.0	2	11	4.0	18	6.5	4.32	96	.272	.330	-2	-0	110	101	1.2	-0	0	0.0
1961	Phi-N	0	0	—	1	0	0	0	0	2	2	9.0	1	2	9.0	2	9.0	9.00	44	.286	.444	-1	-1	98	106	0.0	0	0	0.0
Total	7	24	34	.414	202	24	4	0	21	455	385	7.6	49	244	4.8	375	7.4	3.92	100	.230	.325	0	1	100	93	-3.4	1	-1	0.5
BOB MEYER	Meyer, Robert Bernard b: 8/4/39, Toledo, Ohio BR/TL, 6'2", 185 lbs. Deb: 4/20/64																												
1964	NY-A	0	3	.000	7	1	0	0	0	18	16	8.0	1	12	6.0	12	6.0	5.00	73	.235	.341	-3	-3	101	74	-1.4	-0	1	-0.2
	LA-A	1	1	.500	6	5	0	0	0	18	25	12.5	2	13	6.5	13	6.5	5.00	64	.333	.438	-3	-4	89	143	0.0	-1	0	-0.3
	KC-A	1	4	.200	9	7	2	0	0	42	37	7.9	2	33	7.1	30	6.4	3.86	101	.248	.372	-1	0	108	115	-1.0	-1	-1	-0.1
	Yr	2	8	.200	22	13	2	0	0	78	78	9.0	5	58	6.7	55	6.3	4.38	84	.266	.379	-7	-6	102	115	-2.4	-1	-0	-0.6
1969	Sea-A	0	3	.000	6	5	1	0	0	33	30	8.2	4	10	2.7	17	4.6	3.27	111	.252	.311	1	1	100	119	-1.4	-1	-1	0.0
1970	Mil-A	0	1	.000	10	0	0	0	0	18	24	12.0	3	12	6.0	20	10.0	6.50	57	.329	.409	-6	-6	100	109	-0.4	0	0	-0.4
Total	3	2	12	.143	38	18	3	0	0	129	132	9.2	12	80	5.6	92	6.4	4.40	84	.273	.369	-11	-10	101	113	-4.2	-3	-1	-1.0
RUSS MEYER	Meyer, Russell Charles "Rowdy" or "The Mad Monk" b: 10/25/23, Peru, Ill. BB/TR, 6'1", 175 lbs. Deb: 9/13/46																												
1946	Chi-N	0	0	—	4	1	0	0	1	17	21	11.1	2	10	5.3	10	5.3	3.18	100	.309	.397	0	0	93	184	0.0	0	0	0.0
1947	Chi-N	3	2	.600	23	2	1	0	0	45	43	8.6	4	14	2.8	22	4.4	3.40	124	.257	.314	3	4	104	109	0.7	0	-0	0.4
1948	Chi-N	10	10	.500	29	26	8	3	0	165	157	8.6	8	77	4.2	89	4.9	3.65	103	.254	.335	6	2	95	103	1.6	-3	-0	-0.1
1949	Phi-N	17	8	.680	37	28	14	2	1	213	199	8.4	14	70	3.0	78	3.3	3.08	132	.250	.308	23	23	101	110	4.6	-1	-2	2.1
1950	Phi-N	9	11	.450	32	25	3	0	1	160	193	10.9	21	67	3.8	74	4.2	5.29	75	.304	.369	-20	-24	96	106	-2.5	-1	1	-2.2
1951	Phi-N	8	9	.471	28	24	7	2	0	168	172	9.2	13	55	2.9	65	3.5	3.48	110	.263	.318	9	7	97	106	0.0	-2	-2	0.2
1952	Phi-N	13	14	.481	37	32	14	1	1	232	235	9.1	10	65	2.5	92	3.6	3.14	117	.260	.308	15	14	99	105	-2.2	-2	-2	1.0
1953	Bro-N	15	5	.750	34	32	10	2	0	191	201	9.5	25	63	3.0	106	5.0	4.57	93	.269	.324	-6	-6	100	95	2.4	-2	-0	-0.8
1954	Bro-N	11	6	.647	36	28	6	2	0	180	193	9.6	17	49	2.5	70	3.5	4.00	102	.275	.318	1	2	101	97	1.2	-3	-2	-0.2
1955	Bro-N	6	2	.750	18	11	2	1	0	73	86	10.6	8	31	3.8	26	3.2	5.42	75	.300	.358	-11	-11	101	95	1.3	-3	1	-1.1
1956	Chi-N	1	6	.143	20	9	0	0	0	57	71	11.2	11	26	4.1	28	4.4	6.32	60	.313	.375	-16	-16	101	99	-2.2	-1	2	-1.4
	Cin-N	0	0	—	1	0	0	0	0	1	1	9.0	0	0	0.0	1	9.0	0.00	—	.250	.250	0	0	106	0	0.0	0	0	0.1
	Yr	1	6	.143	21	9	0	0	0	58	72	11.2	11	26	4.0	29	4.5	6.21	61	.305	.366	-16	-16	101	0	-2.2	-1	2	-1.3
1957	Bos-A	0	0	—	2	1	0	0	0	5	10	18.0	0	3	5.4	1	1.8	5.40	76	.417	.464	-1	-1	109	161	0.0	0	1	0.0
1959	KC-A	1	0	1.000	18	0	0	0	1	24	24	9.0	3	11	4.1	10	3.8	4.50	88	.261	.336	-2	-1	103	101	0.5	-0	-0	-0.1
Total	13	94	73	.563	319	219	65	13	5	1531	1606	9.4	136	541	3.2	672	4.0	3.99	99	.271	.329	2	-7	99	104	5.4	-18	-4	-2.1
LEVI MEYERLE	Meyerle, Levi Samuel "Long Levi" b: 7/1845, Philadelphia, Pa. d: 11/4/21, Philadelphia, Pa. BR/TR, 6'1", 177 lbs. Deb: 5/20/1871																												
1876	Phi-N	0	2	.000	2	2	2	0	0	18	28	14.0	0	1	0.5	0	0.0	5.00	49	.359	.367	-5	-5	105	85	-0.9	1	0	-0.3
GENE MICHAEL	Michael, Eugene Richard "Stick" b: 6/2/38, Kent, Ohio BB/TR, 6'2", 183 lbs. Deb: 7/15/66 MC																												
1968	NY-A	0	0	—	1	0	0	0	0	3	5	15.0	0	0	0.0	3	9.0	0.00	—	.357	.375	1	1	101	0	0.0	0	0	0.1
JOHN MICHAELS	Michaels, John Joseph b: 7/10/07, Bridgeport, Conn. BL/TL, 5'10.5", 154 lbs. Deb: 4/16/32																												
1932	Bos-A	1	6	.143	28	8	2	0	0	81	101	11.2	4	27	3.0	16	1.8	5.11	90	.304	.354	-6	-5	102	98	-1.7	-1	1	-0.3
JOHN MICHAELSON	Michaelson, John August "Mike" b: 8/12/1893, Tivalkoski, Finland d: 4/16/68, Woodruff, Wis. BR/TR, 5'9", 165 lbs. Deb: 8/28/21																												
1921	Chi-A	0	0	—	2	0	0	0	0	3	4	12.0	0	1	3.0	1	3.0	9.00	49	.400	.455	-2	-2	102	75	0.0	0	-0	-0.1
GLENN MICKENS	Mickens, Glenn Roger b: 7/26/30, Wilmar, Cal. BR/TR, 6', 175 lbs. Deb: 7/19/53																												
1953	Bro-N	0	1	.000	4	2	0	0	0	6	11	16.5	2	4	6.0	5	7.5	12.00	36	.393	.455	-5	-5	100	89	-0.4	-0	0	-0.4
JIM MIDDLETON	Middleton, James Blaine "Rifle Jim" b: 5/28/1889, Argos, Ind. d: 1/12/74, Argos, Ind. BR/TR, 5'11.5", 165 lbs. Deb: 4/18/17																												
1917	NY-N	1	1	.500	13	0	0	0	1	36	35	8.8	1	8	2.0	9	2.3	2.75	92	.255	.286	-0	-1	93	101	-0.1	-1	1	-0.1
1921	Det-A	6	11	.353	38	10	2	0	**7**	122	149	11.0	5	44	3.2	31	2.3	5.02	82	.302	.351	-10	-12	96	89	-2.1	-2	1	-1.1
Total	2	7	12	.368	51	10	2	0	8	158	184	10.5	6	52	3.0	40	2.3	4.50	83	.292	.337	-10	-13	95	91	-2.2	-3	2	-1.2
JOHN MIDDLETON	Middleton, John Wayne "Lefty" b: 4/11/1900, Mt.Calm, Tex. d: 11/3/86, Amarillo, Tex. BL/TL, 6'1", 185 lbs. Deb: 9/06/22																												
1922	Cle-A	0	1	.000	2	1	0	0	0	7	8	10.3	1	6	7.7	2	2.6	7.71	54	.286	.400	-3	-3	103	79	-0.4	0	0	-0.1
DICK MIDKIFF	Midkiff, Richard b: 9/28/14, Gonzales, Tex. d: 10/30/56, Temple, Tex. BR/TR, 6'2", 185 lbs. Deb: 4/24/38																												
1938	Bos-A	1	1	.500	13	2	0	0	0	35	43	11.1	5	21	5.4	10	2.6	5.14	93	.305	.379	-1	-1	100	123	-0.1	0	0	0.0

YEAR TM/L	W	L	PCT	G	GS	CG	SHO	SV	IP	H	H/G	HR	BB	BB/G	SO	SO/G	ERA	/A	OAVG	OOBP	PR	/A	PF	CPI	WAT	PB	PD	TPI
■ **GARY MIELKE** Mielke, Gary Roger b: 1/28/63, St.James, Minn. BR/TR, 6'3", 185 lbs. Deb: 8/19/87																												
1987 Tex-A	0	0	—	3	0	0	0	0	3	3	9.0	2	1	3.0	3	9.0	6.00	77	.250	.286	-1	-0	104	130	0.0	0	0	0.0
■ **PETE MIKKELSEN** Mikkelsen, Peter James b: 10/25/39, Staten Island, N.Y. BR/TR, 6'2", 210 lbs. Deb: 4/17/64																												
1964 NY-A	7	4	.636	50	0	0	0	12	86	79	8.3	3	41	4.3	63	6.6	3.56	103	.247	.333	1	1	101	98	0.4	-1	1	0.1
1965 NY-A	4	9	.308	41	3	0	0	1	82	78	8.6	10	36	4.0	69	7.6	3.29	106	.249	.328	2	2	101	124	-2.3	-1	1	0.3
1966 Pit-N	9	8	.529	71	0	0	0	14	126	106	7.6	8	51	3.6	76	5.4	3.07	116	.234	.315	7	7	99	104	-0.5	-0	-0	0.7
1967 Pit-N	1	2	.333	32	0	0	0	2	56	50	8.0	7	19	3.1	30	4.8	4.34	78	.237	.303	-6	-6	100	82	-0.4	-0	-1	-0.7
Chi-N	0	0	—	7	0	0	0	0	7	9	11.6	1	5	6.4	0	0.0	6.43	53	.333	.417	-2	-2	100	118	0.0	0	0	-0.2
Yr	1	2	.333	39	0	0	0	2	63	59	8.4	8	24	3.4	30	4.3	4.57	74	.244	.307	-8	-8	100	118	-0.4	-0	-1	-0.9
1968 Chi-N	0	0	—	3	0	0	0	0	5	7	12.6	3	1	1.8	5	9.0	7.20	47	.350	.364	-2	-2	112	135	0.0	0	0	-0.1
StL-N	0	0	—	5	0	0	0	0	16	10	5.6	0	7	3.9	8	4.5	1.13	247	.179	.262	3	3	93	124	0.0	-0	-0	0.3
Yr	0	0	—	8	0	0	0	0	21	17	7.3	3	8	3.4	13	5.6	2.57	114	.224	.287	1	1	98	124	0.0	0	-0	0.2
1969 LA-N	7	5	.583	48	0	0	0	4	81	57	6.3	9	30	3.3	51	5.7	2.78	126	.193	.271	7	7	97	88	0.8	-0	1	0.8
1970 LA-N	4	2	.667	33	0	0	0	6	62	48	7.0	5	20	2.9	47	6.8	2.76	131	.211	.282	9	6	89	96	0.8	1	0	0.7
1971 LA-N	8	5	.615	41	0	0	0	5	74	67	8.1	10	17	2.1	46	5.6	3.65	93	.242	.282	-1	-2	98	90	1.0	0	1	0.0
1972 LA-N	5	5	.500	33	0	0	0	5	58	65	10.1	3	23	3.6	41	6.4	4.03	80	.283	.351	-4	-5	93	109	-0.4	-0	0	-0.5
Total 9	45	40	.529	364	3	0	0	49	653	576	7.9	59	250	3.4	436	6.0	3.38	103	.237	.310	13	7	98	101	-0.6	-2	3	1.4
■ **HANK MIKLOS** Miklos, John Joseph b: 11/27/10, Chicago, Ill. BL/TL, 5'11", 175 lbs. Deb: 4/23/44																												
1944 Chi-N	0	0	—	2	0	0	0	0	7	9	11.6	1	3	3.9	0	0.0	7.71	47	.333	.387	-3	-3	100	84	0.0	-0	1	-0.2
■ **BOB MILACKI** Milacki, Robert b: 7/28/64, Trenton, N.J. BR/TR, 6'4", 220 lbs. Deb: 9/18/88																												
1988 Bal-A	2	0	1.000	3	3	1	1	0	25	9	3.2	1	9	3.2	18	6.5	0.72	538	.110	.198	9	9	97	24	1.0	0	0	1.1
■ **CARL MILES** Miles, Carl Thomas b: 3/22/18, Trenton, Mo. BB/TL, 5'11", 178 lbs. Deb: 6/08/40																												
1940 Phi-A	0	0	—	2	0	0	0	0	8	9	10.1	2	8	9.0	6	6.8	13.50	32	.281	.415	-8	-8	99	56	0.0	2	0	-0.4
■ **JIM MILES** Miles, James Charlie b: 8/8/43, Grenada, Miss. BR/TR, 6'2", 210 lbs. Deb: 9/07/68																												
1968 Was-A	0	0	—	3	0	0	0	0	4	8	18.0	0	2	4.5	5	11.3	13.50	21	.421	.435	-5	-5	94	63	0.0	0	0	-0.4
1969 Was-A	0	1	.000	10	1	0	0	0	20	19	8.5	2	15	6.7	15	6.7	6.30	55	.257	.392	-6	-6	96	86	-0.4	0	1	-0.4
Total 2	0	1	.000	13	1	0	0	0	24	27	10.1	2	17	6.4	20	7.5	7.50	45	.290	.400	-11	-11	96	82	-0.4	0	1	-0.8
■ **JOHNNY MILJUS** Miljus, John Kenneth "Jovo" or "Big Serb" b: 6/30/1895, Pittsburgh, Pa. d: 2/11/76, Poulson, Montana BR/TR, 6'1", 178 lbs. Deb: 10/02/15																												
1915 Pit-F	0	0	—	1	0	0	0	0	1	1	9.0	0	0	0.0	0	0.0	0.00	—	.289	.289	0	0	102	0	0.0	0	0	0.0
1917 Bro-N	0	1	.000	4	1	1	0	0	15	14	8.4	0	8	4.8	9	5.4	0.60	474	.250	.357	4	4	105	631	-0.4	-1	-0	0.3
1920 Bro-N	1	0	1.000	9	0	0	0	0	23	24	9.4	2	4	1.6	9	3.5	3.13	109	.267	.283	0	1	108	97	0.5	1	1	0.3
1921 Bro-N	6	3	.667	28	9	3	0	1	94	115	11.0	1	27	2.6	37	3.5	4.21	94	.312	.353	-4	-3	105	100	1.5	-2	2	-0.2
1927 Pit-N	8	3	.727	19	6	3	2	0	76	62	7.3	0	17	2.0	24	2.8	1.89	205	.228	.266	17	17	99	103	1.7	-1	2	1.8
1928 Pit-N	5	7	.417	21	10	3	0	1	70	90	11.6	2	33	4.2	26	3.3	5.27	79	.313	.377	-10	-9	105	96	-1.5	1	-0	-0.6
Cle-A	1	4	.200	11	4	1	0	1	51	46	8.1	1	20	3.5	19	3.4	2.65	166	.243	.306	8	10	108	110	-1.2	-0	-0	0.9
1929 Cle-A	8	8	.500	34	15	4	0	2	128	174	12.2	10	64	4.5	42	3.0	5.20	82	.331	.391	-14	-13	101	118	-0.4	2	0	-1.0
Total 7	29	26	.527	127	45	15	2	5	458	526	10.3	16	173	3.4	166	3.3	3.91	104	.293	.347	1	7	103	123	0.2	1	4	1.5
■ **BURT MILLER** Miller, Burt b: Kalamazoo, Mich. Deb: 7/15/1897																												
1897 Lou-N	0	1	.000	4	1	1	0	0	17	32	16.9	0	3	1.6	3	1.6	7.94	53	.425	.447	-7	-7	97	88	-0.4	-0	0	-0.5
■ **DYAR MILLER** Miller, Dyar K b: 5/29/46, Batesville, Ind. BR/TR, 6'1", 195 lbs. Deb: 6/09/75 C																												
1975 Bal-A	6	3	.667	30	0	0	0	8	46	32	6.3	3	16	3.1	33	6.5	2.74	123	.199	.261	5	3	89	77	1.1	0	0	0.3
1976 Bal-A	2	4	.333	49	0	0	0	7	89	79	8.0	5	36	3.6	37	3.7	2.93	117	.246	.314	6	5	97	115	-1.1	0	-1	0.4
1977 Bal-A	2	2	.500	12	0	0	0	1	22	25	10.2	6	10	4.1	9	3.7	5.73	66	.278	.350	-4	-5	92	101	-0.2	0	-0	-0.4
Cal-A	4	4	.500	41	0	0	0	4	92	81	7.9	10	30	2.9	49	4.8	3.03	127	.242	.296	11	8	95	112	0.3	0	-1	0.7
Yr	6	6	.500	53	0	0	0	5	114	106	8.4	16	40	3.2	58	4.6	3.55	108	.249	.307	7	4	94	112	0.1	0	-1	0.3
1978 Cal-A	6	2	.750	41	0	0	0	1	85	85	9.0	3	41	4.3	34	3.6	2.65	145	.264	.350	11	11	101	148	1.9	0	-2	1.0
1979 Cal-A	1	0	1.000	14	1	0	0	0	35	44	11.3	2	13	3.3	16	4.1	3.34	116	.319	.376	3	2	92	161	0.5	0	-1	0.1
Tor-A	0	0	—	10	0	0	0	0	15	27	16.2	3	5	3.0	7	4.2	10.80	41	.391	.427	-11	-11	106	79	0.0	0	-0	-0.9
Yr	1	0	1.000	24	1	0	0	0	50	71	12.8	5	18	3.2	23	4.1	5.58	73	.333	.384	-7	-8	96	79	0.5	0	-1	-0.8
1980 NY-N	1	2	.333	31	0	0	0	1	42	37	7.9	1	11	2.4	28	6.0	1.93	182	.242	.282	8	7	97	134	-0.2	-0	-1	0.7
1981 NY-N	1	0	1.000	23	0	0	0	0	38	49	11.6	2	15	3.6	22	5.2	3.32	108	.327	.374	1	1	103	166	0.5	0	-1	0.1
Total 7	23	17	.575	251	1	0	0	22	464	459	8.9	35	177	3.4	235	4.6	3.24	114	.264	.326	30	23	97	124	2.8	0	-6	2.0
■ **ELMER MILLER** Miller, Elmer Joseph "Lefty" b: 4/17/03, Detroit, Mich. BL/TL, 5'11", 189 lbs. Deb: 6/21/29																												
1929 Phi-N	0	1	.000	8	2	0	0	0	11	12	9.8	1	21	17.2	5	4.1	11.45	46	.279	.529	-8	-8	112	82	-0.4	0	0	-0.6
■ **FRANK MILLER** Miller, Frank Lee "Bullet" b: 5/13/1886, Allegan, Mich. d: 2/19/74, Allegan, Mich. BR/TR, 6', 188 lbs. Deb: 7/12/13																												
1913 Chi-A	0	1	.000	1	1	0	0	0	2	4	18.0	0	3	13.5	2	9.0	22.50	12	.571	.700	-4	-4	95	62	-0.4	0	0	-0.3
1916 Pit-N	7	10	.412	30	20	10	2	1	173	135	7.0	4	49	2.5	88	4.6	2.29	123	.226	.282	6	10	107	98	-0.1	-1	-1	1.0
1917 Pit-N	10	19	.345	38	28	14	5	1	224	216	8.7	1	60	2.4	92	3.7	3.13	89	.251	.292	-11	-9	103	83	0.4	-4	1	-1.3
1918 Pit-N	11	8	.579	23	23	14	2	0	170	152	8.0	1	37	2.0	47	2.5	2.38	121	.250	.290	7	10	105	105	1.3	-4	0	0.7
1919 Pit-N	13	12	.520	32	26	16	3	0	202	170	7.6	6	34	1.5	59	2.6	3.03	101	.234	.263	-3	1	105	71	0.3	-5	1	-0.2
1922 Bos-N	11	13	.458	31	23	14	2	1	200	213	9.6	7	60	2.7	65	2.9	3.51	114	.279	.323	13	11	98	102	2.4	-5	1	0.6
1923 Bos-N	0	3	.000	8	6	0	0	1	39	54	12.5	2	11	2.5	6	1.4	4.62	89	.335	.378	-3	-2	102	119	-1.4	-0	-1	-0.2
Total 7	52	66	.441	163	127	68	14	4	1010	944	8.4	21	254	2.3	359	3.2	3.01	105	.253	.296	7	17	103	92	2.5	-19	1	0.3
■ **FRED MILLER** Miller, Frederick Holman "Speedy" b: 6/28/1886, Fairfield, Ind. d: 5/2/53, Brookville, Ind. BL/TL, 6'2", 190 lbs. Deb: 7/08/10																												
1910 Bro-N	1	1	.500	6	2	0	0	0	21	25	10.7	1	13	5.6	2	0.9	4.71	63	.309	.423	-4	-4	98	120	0.1	0	0	-0.2
■ **OX MILLER** Miller, John Anthony b: 5/4/15, Gause, Tex. BR/TR, 6'1", 190 lbs. Deb: 8/07/43																												
1943 Was-A	0	0	—	3	0	0	0	0	6	10	15.0	1	5	7.5	1	1.5	10.50	32	.370	.455	-5	-5	102	86	0.0	-0	1	-0.3
StL-A	0	0	—	2	0	0	0	0	6	7	10.5	2	3	4.5	3	4.5	12.00	28	.304	.414	-6	-6	101	68	0.0	-0	1	-0.4
Yr	0	0	—	5	0	0	0	0	12	17	12.8	3	8	6.0	4	3.0	11.25	30	.340	.435	-11	-11	101	68	0.0	-0	1	-0.7
1945 StL-A	2	1	.667	4	3	3	0	0	28	23	7.4	2	5	1.6	4	1.3	1.61	239	.219	.252	5	7	114	129	0.4	-1	-1	0.6
1946 StL-A	1	3	.250	11	3	0	0	1	35	52	13.4	5	15	3.9	12	3.1	6.94	50	.338	.392	-13	-13	100	94	-0.7	1	1	-1.1
1947 Chi-N	1	2	.333	4	4	1	0	0	16	31	17.4	2	5	2.8	7	3.9	10.13	42	.397	.434	-11	-10	104	82	-0.3	2	-0	-0.7
Total 4	4	6	.400	24	10	4	0	1	91	123	12.2	12	33	3.3	27	2.7	6.43	58	.318	.370	-29	-27	105	100	-0.6	2	0	-1.9
■ **JOHN MILLER** Miller, John Ernest b: 5/30/41, Baltimore, Md. BR/TR, 6'2", 210 lbs. Deb: 9/22/62																												
1962 Bal-A	1	1	.500	2	1	0	0	0	10	2	1.8	0	5	4.5	4	3.6	0.90	419	.065	.194	3	3	95	60	0.0	-0	0	0.3
1963 Bal-A	1	1	.500	3	2	0	0	0	17	12	6.4	0	14	7.4	16	8.5	3.18	107	.194	.338	1	0	93	87	0.0	-1	-0	0.2
1965 Bal-A	6	4	.600	16	16	1	0	0	93	75	7.3	4	58	5.6	71	6.9	3.19	107	.223	.332	3	2	99	104	0.3	-1	0	0.2
1966 Bal-A	4	8	.333	23	16	0	0	0	101	92	8.2	15	58	5.2	81	7.2	4.72	72	.241	.338	-14	-15	99	94	-2.7	-1	1	-1.5
1967 Bal-A	0	0	—	2	0	0	0	0	6	7	10.5	1	3	4.5	6	9.0	7.50	40	.304	.429	-3	-3	94	93	0.0	0	0	-0.2
Total 5	12	14	.462	46	35	1	0	0	227	188	7.5	20	138	5.5	178	7.1	3.89	88	.225	.333	-10	-12	98	96	-2.4	-3	1	-1.2
■ **CYCLONE MILLER** Miller, Joseph H. b: 9/24/1859, Springfield, Mass d: 10/13/16, New London, Conn. TL, 5'9.5", 165 lbs. Deb: 7/11/1884																												
1884 CP-U	1	0	1.000	1	1	1	0	0	9	4	4.0	0	0	0.0	13	13.0	1.00	301	.138	.138	2	2	100	31	0.5	-0	0	0.2
Pro-N	2	2	.500	6	5	2	0	0	35	36	9.3	0	11	2.8	12	3.1	2.06	138	.275	.331	4	3	96	148	-0.6	-3	0	0.0
Phi-N	0	1	.000	1	1	1	0	0	9	17	17.0	5	6	6.0	1	1.0	10.00	29	.410	.485	-7	-7	97	125	-0.4	-1	0	-0.4
Yr	2	3	.400	7	6	3	0	0	44	53	10.8	5	17	3.5	13	2.7	3.68	78	.307	.370	-3	-4	96	125	-1.0	-3	0	-0.4
1886 Phi-a	10	8	.556	19	19	19	1	0	170	158	8.4	6	59	3.1	99	5.2	2.96	120	.256	.321	9	11	103	114	1.7	-1	0	0.9
Total 2	13	11	.542	27	26	23	1	0	223	215	8.7	11	76	3.1	125	5.0	3.03	112	.263	.326	8	9	101	116	1.2	-5	0	0.7

YEAR	TM/L	W	L	PCT	G	GS	CG	SHO	SV	IP	H	H/G	HR	BB	BB/G	SO	SO/G	ERA	/A	OAVG	OOBP	PR	/A	PF	CPI	WAT	PB	PD	TPI
■ **WHITEY MILLER**	Miller, Kenneth Albert b: 5/2/15, St.Louis, Mo. BR/TR, 6'1", 195 lbs. Deb: 9/15/44																												
1944	NY-N	0	1	.000	4	0	0	0	0	5	1	1.8	0	4	7.2	2	3.6	0.00	—	.059	.238	2	2	105	0	-0.4	-0	0	0.2
■ **LARRY MILLER**	Miller, Larry Don b: 6/19/37, Topeka, Kan. BL/TL, 6', 195 lbs. Deb: 6/21/64																												
1964	LA-N	4	8	.333	16	14	1	0	0	80	87	9.8	1	28	3.1	50	5.6	4.16	78	.275	.329	-6	-8	91	88	-2.0	2	-1	-0.7
1965	NY-N	1	4	.200	28	5	0	0	0	57	66	10.4	6	25	3.9	36	5.7	5.05	73	.289	.354	-10	-9	104	99	-0.8	-0	-0	-0.8
1966	NY-N	0	2	.000	4	1	0	0	0	8	9	10.1	3	4	4.5	7	7.9	7.88	44	.273	.351	-4	-4	97	84	-0.9	0	-0	-0.3
Total	3	5	14	.263	48	20	1	0	0	145	162	10.1	10	57	3.5	93	5.8	4.72	73	.281	.340	-19	-21	97	92	-3.7	2	-1	-1.8
■ **RED MILLER**	Miller, Leo Alphonso b: 2/11/1897, Philadelphia, Pa. d: 10/20/73, Orlando, Fla. BR/TR, 5'11", 195 lbs. Deb: 4/13/23																												
1923	Phi-N	0	0	—	1	0	0	0	0	2	6	27.0	0	1	4.5	0	0.0	27.00	17	.545	.583	-5	-5	118	52	0.0	-0	0	-0.3
■ **RALPH MILLER**	Miller, Ralph Darwin b: 3/15/1873, Cincinnati, Ohio d: 5/8/73, Cincinnati, Ohio BR/TR, 5'11", 170 lbs. Deb: 5/04/1898																												
1898	Bro-N	4	14	.222	23	21	16	0	0	152	161	9.5	4	86	5.1	43	2.5	5.39	65	.293	.389	-30	-32	96	78	-3.8	-1	0	-2.8
1899	Bal-N	1	3	.250	5	4	3	0	0	34	42	11.1	0	13	3.4	3	0.8	4.76	86	.328	.390	-3	-3	106	91	-1.1	1	0	0.0
Total	2	5	17	.227	28	25	19	0	0	186	203	9.8	4	99	4.8	46	2.2	5.27	68	.300	.389	-34	-35	98	80	-4.9	0	0	-2.8
■ **RALPH MILLER**	Miller, Ralph Henry "Moose" or "Lefty" b: 1/14/1899, Vinton, Iowa d: 2/18/67, White Bear Lake, Minn. BR/TL, 6'1.5", 190 lbs. Deb: 9/16/21																												
1921	Was-A	0	0	—	1	0	0	0	0	1	1	9.0	0	0	0.0	0	0.0	9.00	47	.200	.200	-1	-1	99	12	0.0	0	0	0.0
■ **RANDY MILLER**	Miller, Randall Scott b: 3/18/53, Oxnard, Cal. BR/TR, 6'1", 180 lbs. Deb: 9/07/77																												
1977	Bal-A	0	0	—	1	0	0	0	0	1	4	36.0	0	0	0.0	0	0.0	27.00	14	.800	.667	-3	-3	92	79	0.0	0	0	-0.1
1978	Mon-N	0	1	.000	5	0	0	0	0	7	11	14.1	1	3	3.9	6	7.7	10.29	33	.393	.389	-5	-5	96	79	-0.4	-0	0	-0.4
Total	2	0	1	.000	6	0	0	0	0	8	15	16.9	1	3	3.4	6	6.8	12.38	28	.455	.429	-8	-8	95	79	-0.4	-0	0	-0.5
■ **BOB MILLER**	Miller, Robert Gerald b: 7/15/35, Berwyn, Ill. BR/TL, 6'1", 185 lbs. Deb: 6/25/53																												
1953	Det-A	1	2	.333	13	1	0	0	0	36	43	10.8	2	21	5.3	9	2.3	6.00	68	.289	.380	-8	-8	102	83	-0.1	-1	0	-0.7
1954	Det-A	1	1	.500	32	1	0	0	1	70	62	8.0	1	26	3.3	27	3.5	2.44	154	.244	.307	10	10	101	115	0.1	-0	-1	1.0
1955	Det-A	2	1	.667	7	3	1	0	0	25	26	9.4	4	12	4.3	11	4.0	2.52	149	.263	.339	4	3	95	183	0.5	0	-0	0.3
1956	Det-A	0	2	.000	11	3	0	0	0	32	37	10.4	5	22	6.2	16	4.5	5.63	70	.308	.404	-5	-6	95	116	-0.9	0	-0	-0.5
1962	Cin-N	0	0	—	6	0	0	0	0	5	14	25.2	1	3	5.4	4	7.2	23.40	17	.538	.576	-11	-11	100	69	0.0	-0	0	-0.9
	NY-N	2	2	.500	17	0	0	0	1	20	24	10.8	2	8	3.6	8	3.6	7.20	59	.312	.375	-7	-7	108	77	0.7	-0	0	-0.5
	Yr	2	2	.500	23	0	0	0	1	25	38	13.7	3	11	4.0	12	4.3	10.44	40	.355	.413	-18	-17	107	77	0.7	-0	0	-1.4
Total	5	6	8	.429	86	8	1	0	2	188	206	9.9	15	92	4.4	75	3.6	4.74	83	.284	.361	-17	-17	100	113	0.3	-1	-1	-1.3
■ **BOB MILLER**	Miller, Robert John b: 6/16/26, Detroit, Mich. BR/TR, 6'3", 190 lbs. Deb: 9/16/49																												
1949	Phi-N	0	0	—	3	0	0	0	0	3	2	6.0	0	2	6.0	0	0.0	0.00	—	.200	.333	1	1	101	0	0.0	0	0	0.1
1950	Phi-N	11	6	.647	35	22	7	2	1	174	190	9.8	9	57	2.9	44	2.3	3.57	111	.277	.334	11	8	96	111	1.3	-0	2	0.8
1951	Phi-N	2	1	.667	17	3	0	0	0	34	47	12.4	2	18	4.8	10	2.6	6.88	56	.331	.402	-11	-11	97	89	0.6	1	-1	-1.0
1952	Phi-N	0	1	.000	3	1	0	0	0	9	13	13.0	2	1	1.0	2	2.0	6.00	61	.351	.368	-2	-2	99	113	-0.4	-0	0	-0.1
1953	Phi-N	8	9	.471	35	20	8	3	2	157	169	9.7	14	42	2.4	63	3.6	4.01	105	.271	.315	5	3	98	97	-1.1	-1	-1	0.1
1954	Phi-N	7	9	.438	30	16	5	0	0	150	176	10.6	14	39	2.3	42	2.5	4.56	87	.300	.336	-8	-10	98	101	-0.8	1	1	-0.7
1955	Phi-N	8	4	.667	40	0	0	0	1	90	80	8.0	6	28	2.8	28	2.8	2.40	171	.242	.294	16	17	102	127	2.1	1	0	1.8
1956	Phi-N	3	6	.333	49	6	3	1	5	122	115	8.5	14	34	2.5	53	3.9	3.25	111	.248	.296	7	5	95	103	-1.2	-1	-0	0.3
1957	Phi-N	2	5	.286	32	1	0	0	6	60	61	9.2	4	17	2.6	12	1.8	2.70	142	.265	.311	8	8	99	131	-1.4	2	-1	0.9
1958	Phi-N	1	1	.500	17	0	0	0	0	22	36	14.7	7	9	3.7	9	3.7	11.86	33	.360	.398	-19	-19	100	72	0.1	-0	-0	-1.8
Total	10	42	42	.500	261	69	23	6	15	821	889	9.7	72	247	2.7	263	2.9	3.97	100	.277	.325	8	-1	98	106	-0.8	1	1	0.4
■ **BOB MILLER**	Miller, Robert Lane b: 2/18/39, St.Louis, Mo. BR/TR, 6'1", 180 lbs. Deb: 6/26/57 C																												
1957	StL-N	0	0	—	5	0	0	0	0	9	13	13.0	2	5	5.0	7	7.0	7.00	55	.325	.391	-3	-3	99	102	0.0	0	0	-0.2
1959	StL-N	4	3	.571	11	10	3	0	0	71	66	8.4	2	21	2.7	43	5.5	3.30	127	.248	.299	5	7	106	87	0.7	0	1	0.9
1960	StL-N	4	3	.571	15	7	0	0	0	53	53	9.0	2	17	2.9	33	5.6	3.40	119	.262	.316	2	4	108	101	0.1	-1	0	0.4
1961	StL-N	1	3	.250	34	5	0	0	3	74	82	10.0	6	46	5.6	39	4.7	4.26	107	.290	.384	-2	2	113	124	-1.0	2	1	0.5
1962	NY-N	1	12	.077	33	21	1	0	0	144	146	9.1	20	62	3.9	91	5.7	4.88	88	.259	.331	-15	-10	108	90	-4.5	-1	2	-0.7
1963	LA-N	10	8	.556	42	23	2	0	1	187	171	8.2	7	65	3.1	125	6.0	2.89	106	.244	.306	8	4	94	104	-0.8	-2	5	0.7
1964	LA-N	7	7	.500	**74**	2	0	0	9	138	115	7.5	1	63	4.1	94	6.1	2.61	124	.226	.309	14	10	91	102	0.1	1	2	1.3
1965	LA-N	6	7	.462	61	1	0	0	9	103	82	7.2	9	26	2.3	77	6.7	2.97	107	.225	.268	7	2	90	95	-1.5	-1	2	0.3
1966	LA-N	4	2	.667	46	0	0	0	5	84	70	7.5	5	29	3.1	58	6.2	2.79	123	.230	.291	8	6	95	100	0.6	-1	-1	0.4
1967	LA-N	2	9	.182	52	4	0	0	0	86	88	9.2	9	27	2.8	32	3.3	4.29	70	.273	.325	-9	-12	89	99	-3.3	-0	1	-1.1
1968	Min-A	0	3	.000	45	0	0	0	2	72	65	8.1	1	24	3.0	41	5.1	2.75	115	.239	.310	2	3	106	102	-1.4	-0	1	0.4
1969	Min-A	5	5	.500	48	11	1	0	3	119	118	8.9	9	32	2.4	57	4.3	3.03	120	.264	.309	8	8	100	116	-0.8	-3	1	0.6
1970	Cle-A	2	2	.500	15	2	0	0	1	28	35	11.3	1	15	4.8	15	4.8	4.18	102	.310	.376	-1	0	115	123	0.1	0	-1	0.0
	Chi-A	4	6	.400	15	12	0	0	0	70	88	11.3	11	33	4.2	36	4.6	5.01	80	.315	.385	-10	-8	108	124	0.4	0	2	-0.4
	Yr	6	8	.429	30	14	0	0	1	98	123	11.3	12	48	4.4	51	4.7	4.78	86	.313	.382	-12	-8	110	124	0.5	0	1	-0.4
	Chi-N	0	0	—	7	1	0	0	2	9	6	6.0	3	6	6.0	4	4.0	5.00	96	.194	.308	-1	-0	119	102	0.0	0	0	0.0
1971	Chi-N	0	0	—	2	0	0	0	0	7	10	12.9	0	1	1.3	2	2.6	5.14	74	.357	.367	-1	-1	110	99	0.0	0	0	0.0
	SD-N	7	3	.700	38	0	0	0	7	64	53	7.5	0	26	3.7	36	5.1	1.41	242	.227	.303	15	14	98	173	2.7	-1	1	1.5
	Pit-N	1	2	.333	16	0	0	0	3	28	20	6.4	1	13	4.2	13	4.2	1.29	261	.200	.287	7	6	97	169	-0.6	0	0	0.7
	Yr	8	5	.615	56	0	0	0	10	99	83	7.5	1	40	3.6	51	4.6	1.64	209	.229	.301	20	20	98	169	2.1	-1	2	2.2
1972	Pit-N	5	2	.714	36	0	0	0	3	54	54	9.0	3	24	4.0	18	3.0	2.67	130	.263	.333	5	5	100	145	0.9	-0	-0	0.4
1973	SD-N	0	0	—	18	0	0	0	0	31	29	8.4	4	12	3.5	15	4.4	4.06	87	.244	.308	-1	-2	97	90	0.0	-0	-1	-0.2
	NY-N	0	0	—	1	0	0	0	0	1	0	0.0	0	0	0.0	1	9.0	0.00	—	.000	.000	0	0	100	0	0.0	0	0	0.0
	Yr	0	0	—	19	0	0	0	0	32	29	8.2	4	12	3.4	16	4.5	3.94	90	.236	.301	-1	-1	97	0	0.0	-0	-1	-0.2
	Det-A	4	2	.667	22	0	0	0	1	42	34	7.3	3	22	4.7	23	4.9	3.43	113	.230	.322	2	2	101	99	0.9	0	0	0.2
1974	NY-N	2	2	.500	58	0	0	0	2	78	89	10.3	2	39	4.5	35	4.0	3.58	102	.296	.365	0	1	100	129	0.2	-0	0	0.0
Total	17	69	81	.460	694	99	7	0	51	1552	1487	8.6	101	608	3.5	895	5.2	3.37	106	.255	.321	39	37	100	110	-7.2	-8	18	5.7
■ **BOB MILLER**	Miller, Robert W. b: 1862, Deb: 8/30/1890																												
1890	Roc-a	3	7	.300	13	12	11	0	1	92	89	8.7	2	26	2.5	20	2.0	4.30	83	.269	.322	-4	-8	92	76	-2.0	-1	0	-0.7
1891	Was-a	2	5	.286	7	7	3	0	0	42	53	11.4	3	24	5.1	13	2.8	4.29	87	.323	.410	-3	-3	101	127	-0.4	-2	0	-0.3
Total	2	5	12	.294	20	19	14	0	1	134	142	9.5	5	50	3.4	33	2.2	4.30	84	.287	.353	-7	-10	95	92	-2.4	-3	0	-1.0
■ **ROGER MILLER**	Miller, Roger Wesley b: 8/1/54, Connellsville, Pa. BR/TR, 6'3", 200 lbs. Deb: 9/08/74																												
1974	Mil-A	0	0	—	2	0	0	0	0	2	3	13.5	1	0	0.0	2	9.0	13.50	28	.300	.364	-2	-2	103	61	0.0	0	0	-0.1
■ **RONNIE MILLER**	Miller, Roland Arthur b: 8/28/18, Mason City, Iowa BB/TR, 5'11", 167 lbs. Deb: 9/10/41																												
1941	Was-A	0	0	—	1	0	0	0	0	2	2	9.0	0	1	4.5	0	0.0	4.50	91	.333	.429	-0	-0	99	127	0.0	0	0	0.0
■ **ROSCOE MILLER**	Miller, Roscoe Clyde "Roxy" or "Rubberlegs" b: 12/2/1876, Greenville, Ind. d: 4/18/13, Corydon, Ind. 6'2", 190 lbs. Deb: 4/25/01																												
1901	Det-A	23	13	.639	38	36	35	3	1	332	339	9.2	1	98	2.7	79	2.1	2.95	136	.284	.339	26	39	109	105	4.6	-0	4	4.1
1902	Det-A	6	12	.333	20	18	15	1	1	149	158	9.5	3	57	3.4	39	2.4	3.68	97	.297	.365	-2	-2	101	101	-1.3	-2	1	0.0
	NY-N	1	8	.111	10	9	7	0	0	73	77	9.5	1	11	1.4	15	1.8	4.56	63	.294	.323	-14	-14	104	61	-3.0	-3	-1	-1.3
1903	NY-N	2	5	.286	15	8	6	0	**3**	85	101	10.7	1	24	2.5	30	3.2	4.13	82	.322	.372	-8	-7	103	94	-1.8	-1	-1	-0.6
1904	Pit-N	7	7	.500	19	17	11	2	0	134	133	8.9	4	39	2.6	35	2.4	3.36	79	.285	.345	-9	-10	98	96	-0.8	-4	-2	-1.1
Total	4	39	45	.464	102	88	74	6	5	773	808	9.4	10	229	2.7	198	2.3	3.45	102	.292	.347	-8	5	104	97	-2.3	-9	1	1.1
■ **RUSS MILLER**	Miller, Russell Lewis b: 3/25/1900, Etna, Ohio d: 4/30/62, Bucyrus, Ohio BR/TR, 5'11", 165 lbs. Deb: 9/24/27																												
1927	Phi-N	1	1	.500	2	2	1	0	0	15	21	12.6	2	3	1.8	4	2.4	5.40	73	.339	.357	-2	-2	100	112	0.3	0	0	-0.1
1928	Phi-N	0	12	.000	33	12	1	0	1	108	137	11.4	14	34	2.8	19	1.6	5.42	80	.315	.353	-17	-13	109	99	-5.9	-1	0	-1.2
Total	2	1	13	.071	35	14	2	0	1	123	158	11.6	16	37	2.7	23	1.7	5.41	79	.318	.353	-20	-15	108	100	-5.6	-1	0	-1.3

YEAR	TM/L	W	L	PCT	G	GS	CG	SHO	SV	IP	H	H/G	HR	BB	BB/G	SO	SO/G	ERA	/A	OAVG	OOBP	PR	/A	PF	CPI	WAT	PB	PD	TPI
■ **STU MILLER**	Miller, Stuart Leonard b: 12/26/27, Northampton, Mass. BR/TR, 5'11.5", 165 lbs. Deb: 8/12/52																												
1952	StL-N	6	3	.667	12	11	6	2	0	88	63	6.4	3	26	2.7	64	6.5	2.05	177	.197	.259	16	15	97	87	1.0	-1	3	1.9
1953	StL-N	7	8	.467	40	18	8	2	4	138	161	10.5	19	47	3.1	79	5.2	5.54	78	.293	.345	-19	-19	101	92	-1.0	0	5	-1.2
1954	StL-N	2	3	.400	19	4	0	0	2	47	55	10.5	5	29	5.6	22	4.2	5.74	71	.307	.397	-9	-9	100	105	-0.3	1	2	-0.4
1956	StL-N	0	1	.000	3	0	0	0	1	7	12	15.4	3	5	6.4	5	6.4	5.14	73	.387	.459	-1	-1	99	215	-0.4	-0	0	0.0
	Phi-N	5	8	.385	24	15	2	0	0	107	109	9.2	16	51	4.3	55	4.6	4.46	81	.263	.343	-8	-10	95	103	-1.1	2	0	-0.7
	Yr	5	9	.357	27	15	2	0	1	114	121	9.6	19	56	4.4	60	4.7	4.50	80	.271	.351	-9	-11	96	103	-1.5	-0	0	-0.7
1957	NY-N	7	9	.438	38	13	0	0	1	124	110	8.0	15	45	3.3	60	4.4	3.63	110	.242	.307	3	5	103	101	-0.1	-3	2	0.4
1958	SF-N	6	9	.400	41	20	4	1	0	182	160	7.9	16	49	2.4	119	5.9	**2.47**	**159**	.233	**.284**	30	30	100	111	-1.8	-0	1	3.2
1959	SF-N	8	7	.533	59	9	2	0	8	168	164	8.8	15	57	3.1	95	5.1	2.84	130	.260	.316	**21**	16	94	**135**	0.0	-3	3	1.6
1960	SF-N	7	6	.538	47	3	2	0	2	102	100	8.8	9	31	2.7	65	5.7	3.88	86	.256	.307	-1	-6	89	93	0.4	1	1	-0.3
1961	SF-N	14	5	.737	63	0	0	0	**17**	122	95	7.0	4	37	2.7	89	6.6	2.66	146	.215	.273	**19**	**17**	96	79	4.2	1	2	2.0
1962	SF-N	5	8	.385	59	0	0	0	19	107	107	9.0	8	42	3.5	78	6.6	4.12	94	.268	.328	-2	-3	99	98	-2.5	-0	0	-0.2
1963	Bal-A	5	8	.385	**71**	0	0	0	**27**	112	93	7.5	5	53	4.3	114	9.2	2.25	151	.232	.316	17	14	93	144	-1.8	2	2	1.9
1964	Bal-A	7	7	.500	66	0	0	0	23	97	77	7.1	7	34	3.2	87	8.1	3.06	122	.222	.290	6	7	103	92	-1.1	-0	1	0.8
1965	Bal-A	14	7	.667	67	0	0	0	24	119	87	6.6	5	32	2.4	104	7.9	1.89	181	.207	.260	21	20	99	105	2.4	-0	1	2.2
1966	Bal-A	9	4	.692	51	0	0	0	18	92	65	6.4	5	22	2.2	67	6.6	2.25	150	.201	.253	12	12	99	89	1.5	-1	-1	1.1
1967	Bal-A	3	10	.231	42	0	0	0	8	81	63	7.0	5	36	4.0	60	6.7	2.56	118	.220	.296	6	4	94	117	-3.4	-1	-0	0.3
1968	Atl-N	0	0	—	2	0	0	0	0	1	1	9.0	0	4	36.0	1	9.0	36.00	8	.500	.714	-4	-4	94	47	0.0	0	0	-0.3
Total	16	105	103	.505	704	93	24	5	154	1694	1522	8.1	140	600	3.2	1164	6.2	3.24	114	.242	.305	107	88	97	105	-4.0	-2	22	12.3
■ **JAKE MILLER**	Miller, Walter Jacob b: 2/28/1897, Wagram, Ohio d: 8/20/75, Venice, Fla. BL/TL, 6'1", 185 lbs. Deb: 9/11/24																												
1924	Cle-A	0	1	.000	2	2	1	0	0	12	13	9.8	0	5	3.8	4	3.0	3.00	137	.265	.327	2	1	97	105	-0.4	-1	0	0.1
1925	Cle-A	10	13	.435	32	22	13	0	2	190	207	9.8	4	62	2.9	51	2.4	3.32	141	.279	.331	23	29	107	110	-0.5	-4	0	2.5
1926	Cle-A	7	4	.636	18	11	5	3	1	83	99	10.7	1	18	2.0	24	2.6	3.25	120	.307	.336	7	6	97	126	0.9	-2	-1	0.3
1927	Cle-A	10	8	.556	34	23	11	0	0	185	189	9.2	4	48	2.3	53	2.6	3.21	127	.271	.313	19	18	99	104	2.2	-4	0	1.4
1928	Cle-A	8	9	.471	25	24	8	0	0	158	203	11.6	6	43	2.4	37	2.1	4.44	99	.332	.369	-7	-1	108	**119**	1.1	-5	1	-0.4
1929	Cle-A	14	12	.538	29	29	14	2	0	206	227	9.9	7	60	2.6	58	2.5	3.58	119	.279	.328	15	16	101	104	0.2	-3	1	1.4
1930	Cle-A	4	4	.500	24	9	1	0	0	88	147	15.0	6	38	3.9	31	3.2	7.16	68	.373	.419	-24	-22	105	107	-0.1	1	2	-1.6
1931	Cle-A	2	1	.667	10	5	1	1	0	41	45	9.9	2	19	4.2	17	3.7	4.39	105	.273	.344	-0	1	106	99	0.5	-2	1	0.0
1933	Chi-A	5	6	.455	26	14	4	2	0	106	130	11.0	3	47	4.0	30	2.5	5.60	79	.297	.367	-16	-14	103	89	0.1	-1	1	-1.2
Total	9	60	58	.508	200	139	58	8	3	1069	1260	10.6	33	340	2.9	305	2.6	4.09	107	.298	.346	19	34	103	107	4.0	-20	6	2.5
■ **WALT MILLER**	Miller, Walter W. b: 10/19/1884, Gas City, Ind. d: 3/1/56, Marion, Ind. BR/TR, 5'11.5", 180 lbs. Deb: 9/20/11																												
1911	Bro-N	0	1	.000	3	2	0	0	0	11	16	13.1	0	6	4.9	0	0.0	6.55	52	.356	.442	-4	-4	99	99	-0.4	-1	-0	-0.3
■ **BILL MILLER**	Miller, William Francis "Wild Bill" b: 4/12/10, Hannibal, Mo. d: 2/26/82, Hannibal, Mo. BR/TR, 6', 180 lbs. Deb: 10/02/37																												
1937	StL-A	0	1	.000	1	1	0	0	0	4	7	15.8	1	4	9.0	1	2.3	13.50	35	.389	.500	-4	-4	103	86	-0.4	-0	0	-0.2
■ **BILL MILLER**	Miller, William Paul "Lefty" or "Hooks" b: 7/26/27, Minersville, Pa. BL/TL, 6', 175 lbs. Deb: 4/20/52																												
1952	NY-A	4	6	.400	21	13	5	2	0	88	78	8.0	4	49	5.0	45	4.6	3.48	100	.241	.339	2	-0	95	105	-1.7	1	-0	0.0
1953	NY-A	2	1	.667	13	3	0	0	1	34	46	12.2	3	19	5.0	17	4.5	4.76	74	.324	.405	-3	-5	88	130	0.0	0	1	-0.3
1954	NY-A	0	1	.000	2	1	0	0	0	6	9	13.5	0	1	1.5	6	9.0	6.00	59	.375	.385	-2	-2	94	95	-0.4	-0	-0	-0.1
1955	Bal-A	0	1	.000	5	1	0	0	0	4	3	6.8	0	10	22.5	4	9.0	13.50	27	.200	.520	-4	-4	94	55	-0.4	0	0	-0.3
Total	4	6	9	.400	41	18	5	2	1	132	136	9.3	7	79	5.4	72	4.9	4.23	83	.270	.367	-7	-11	93	109	-2.5	1	1	-0.7
■ **JOHN MILLIGAN**	Milligan, John Alexander b: 1/22/04, Schuylersville, N.Y. d: 5/15/72, Fort Pierce, Fla. BR/TL, 5'10", 172 lbs. Deb: 8/11/28																												
1928	Phi-N	2	5	.286	13	7	3	0	0	68	69	9.1	2	32	4.2	22	2.9	4.37	100	.274	.348	-3	-0	109	91	0.0	-3	1	-0.1
1929	Phi-N	0	1	.000	8	3	0	0	0	10	29	26.1	0	10	9.0	2	1.8	16.20	32	.527	.603	-13	-12	112	97	-0.4	0	0	-0.9
1930	Phi-N	1	2	.333	9	2	1	0	0	28	26	8.4	0	21	6.8	7	2.3	3.21	169	.255	.380	5	7	109	137	0.0	-1	1	0.7
1931	Phi-N	0	0	—	3	0	0	0	0	8	11	12.4	0	4	4.5	5	5.6	3.38	125	.324	.410	0	1	109	169	0.0	-0	-0	0.0
1934	Was-A	0	0	—	2	0	0	0	0	3	6	18.0	0	0	0.0	1	3.0	9.00	51	.500	.500	-2	-1	102	105	0.0	0	0	0.0
Total	5	3	8	.273	35	12	4	0	0	117	141	10.8	2	67	5.2	37	2.8	5.15	91	.310	.396	-11	-6	109	108	-0.4	-4	2	-0.3
■ **BILLY MILLIGAN**	Milligan, William Joseph b: 8/19/1878, Buffalo, N.Y. d: 10/14/28, Buffalo, N.Y. TL, 5'7", Deb: 4/30/01																												
1901	Phi-A	0	3	.000	6	3	2	0	0	33	43	11.7	1	14	3.8	5	1.4	4.36	84	.336	.402	-3	-3	100	116	-1.4	2	-0	-0.2
1904	NY-N	0	1	.000	5	1	1	0	2	25	36	13.0	2	4	1.4	6	2.2	5.40	50	.367	.398	-7	-7	100	101	-0.4	0	-0	-0.6
Total	2	0	4	.000	11	4	3	0	2	58	79	12.3	3	18	2.8	11	1.7	4.81	67	.350	.400	-10	-10	100	110	-1.8	2	-0	-0.8
■ **BOB MILLIKEN**	Milliken, Robert Fogle "Bobo" b: 8/25/26, Majorsville, W.Va. BR/TR, 6', 195 lbs. Deb: 4/22/53 C																												
1953	Bro-N	8	4	.667	37	10	3	0	2	118	94	7.2	13	42	3.2	65	5.0	3.36	127	.214	.280	12	12	100	84	0.0	-1	-2	0.8
1954	Bro-N	5	2	.714	24	3	0	0	2	63	58	8.3	12	18	2.6	25	3.6	4.00	102	.246	.299	1	1	101	99	1.1	-0	-1	0.0
Total	2	13	6	.684	61	13	3	0	4	181	152	7.6	25	60	3.0	90	4.5	3.58	117	.225	.287	13	13	100	89	1.1	-2	-3	0.8
■ **ART MILLS**	Mills, Arthur Grant b: 3/2/03, Utica, N.Y. d: 7/23/75, Utica, N.Y. BR/TR, 5'10", 155 lbs. Deb: 4/16/27 C																												
1927	Bos-N	0	1	.000	15	1	0	0	0	38	41	9.7	1	18	4.3	7	1.7	3.79	99	.287	.358	1	-0	95	120	-0.4	-1	1	0.0
1928	Bos-N	0	0	—	4	0	0	0	0	8	17	19.1	3	8	9.0	0	0.0	12.38	33	.472	.563	-7	-7	101	121	0.0	-0	-0	-0.6
Total	2	0	1	.000	19	1	0	0	0	46	58	11.3	4	26	5.1	7	1.4	5.28	72	.324	.403	-7	-8	96	120	-0.4	-1	1	-0.6
■ **LEFTY MILLS**	Mills, Howard Robinson b: 5/12/10, Dedham, Mass. d: 9/23/82, Riverside, Cal. BL/TL, 6'1", 187 lbs. Deb: 6/10/34																												
1934	StL-A	0	0	—	4	0	0	0	0	9	10	10.0	0	11	11.0	2	2.0	4.00	119	.303	.477	0	1	106	175	0.0	0	-0	0.1
1937	StL-A	1	1	.500	2	2	1	0	0	13	16	11.1	1	10	6.9	10	6.9	6.23	77	.286	.394	-2	-2	103	89	0.3	-1	0	-0.1
1938	StL-A	10	12	.455	30	27	15	1	0	210	216	9.3	16	116	5.0	134	5.7	5.31	93	.262	.353	-12	-9	103	85	1.8	-3	-2	-1.1
1939	StL-A	4	11	.267	34	14	4	0	2	144	147	9.2	16	113	7.1	103	6.4	6.56	74	.264	.386	-31	-27	105	85	-0.3	1	-1	-2.1
1940	StL-A	0	6	.000	26	5	1	0	0	59	64	9.8	7	52	7.9	18	2.7	7.78	61	.275	.409	-22	-20	108	79	-2.9	-1	0	-1.7
Total	5	15	30	.333	96	48	21	1	2	435	453	9.4	40	302	6.2	267	5.5	6.06	80	.266	.376	-67	-57	104	86	-1.1	-3	-3	-4.9
■ **DICK MILLS**	Mills, Richard Alan b: 1/29/45, Boston, Mass. BR/TR, 6'3", 195 lbs. Deb: 9/07/70																												
1970	Bos-A	0	0	—	2	0	0	0	0	4	6	13.5	0	3	6.8	3	6.8	2.25	182	.353	.455	1	1	110	331	0.0	0	0	0.1
■ **WILLIE MILLS**	Mills, William Grant "Wee Willie" b: 8/15/1877, Schenevus, N.Y. d: 7/5/14, Norwood, N.Y. 5'7", 150 lbs. Deb: 7/13/01																												
1901	NY-N	0	2	.000	2	2	2	0	0	16	21	11.8	2	4	2.3	3	1.7	8.44	37	.345	.395	-9	-9	95	66	-0.9	0	-0	-0.7
■ **AL MILNAR**	Milnar, Albert Joseph "Happy" b: 12/26/13, Cleveland, Ohio BL/TL, 6'2", 195 lbs. Deb: 4/30/36																												
1936	Cle-A	1	2	.333	4	3	1	0	0	22	26	10.6	0	18	7.4	9	3.7	7.36	72	.286	.396	-6	-5	105	72	-0.4	0	0	-0.3
1938	Cle-A	3	1	.750	23	5	2	0	1	68	90	11.9	5	26	3.4	29	3.8	5.03	93	.320	.372	-2	-3	98	112	0.9	-0	0	-0.2
1939	Cle-A	14	12	.538	37	26	12	2	3	209	212	9.1	11	99	4.3	76	3.3	3.79	117	.264	.338	19	15	96	110	-0.6	3	0	1.8
1940	Cle-A	18	10	.643	37	33	15	**4**	3	242	242	9.0	14	99	3.7	99	3.7	3.27	123	.257	.326	30	20	92	115	2.5	-1	-5	1.3
1941	Cle-A	12	19	.387	35	30	9	1	0	229	236	9.3	9	116	4.6	82	3.2	4.36	96	.266	.347	-5	-5	101	95	-3.7	1	-3	-0.5
1942	Cle-A	6	8	.429	28	19	8	2	0	157	146	8.4	3	85	4.9	35	2.0	4.13	82	.251	.343	-8	-13	93	97	-0.8	2	1	-1.0
1943	Cle-A	1	3	.250	16	6	0	0	0	39	51	11.8	0	35	8.1	12	2.8	8.08	37	.329	.448	-21	-22	90	81	-1.0	0	0	-2.1
	StL-A	1	2	.333	3	2	1	0	0	15	23	13.8	0	9	5.4	7	4.2	5.40	61	.354	.421	-4	-3	101	120	-0.4	1	0	-0.1
	Yr	2	5	.286	19	8	1	0	0	54	74	12.3	0	44	7.3	19	3.2	7.33	42	.335	.437	-24	-26	93	120	-1.4	0	0	-2.2
1946	StL-A	1	1	.500	4	2	1	1	0	15	15	9.0	1	6	3.6	1	0.6	2.40	146	.278	.344	2	2	100	175	0.1	1	0	0.3
	Phi-N	0	0	—	1	1	0	0	0	⅓	2	54.0	0	2	54.0	0	0.0	108.00	—	1.000	1.000	-2	-4	98	43	0.0	0	0	-0.2
Total	8	57	58	.496	188	127	49	10	7	996	1043	9.4	43	495	4.5	350	3.2	4.22	96	.270	.349	2	-18	96	104	-3.4	9	-6	-1.0
■ **GEORGE MILSTEAD**	Milstead, George Earl "Cowboy" b: 6/26/03, Cleburne, Tex. d: 8/9/77, Cleburne, Tex. BL/TL, 5'10", 144 lbs. Deb: 6/27/24																												
1924	Chi-N	1	1	.500	13	2	1	0	0	30	41	12.3	3	13	3.9	6	1.8	6.00	65	.328	.387	-7	-7	101	100	0.0	0	0	-0.5
1925	Chi-N	1	1	.500	5	3	1	0	0	21	26	11.1	0	8	3.4	7	3.0	3.00	140	.310	.370	3	3	98	149	0.1	-1	0	0.2
1926	Chi-N	1	5	.167	18	4	0	0	2	55	63	10.3	0	24	3.9	14	2.3	3.60	111	.309	.365	1	2	105	130	-2.0	-3	2	0.2

YEAR	TM/L	W	L	PCT	G	GS	CG	SHO	SV	IP	H	H/G	HR	BB	BB/G	SO	SO/G	ERA	/A	OAVG	OOBP	PR	/A	PF	CPI	WAT	PB	PD	TPI
Total	3	3	7	.300	36	9	2	0	2	106	130	11.0	3	45	3.8	27	2.3	4.16	97	.315	.373	-3	-2	102	125	-1.9	-3	3	-0.1
■ LARRY MILTON	Milton, Samuel Lawrence "Tug" b: 5/4/1879, Owensboro, Ky. d: 5/16/42, Hannibal, Mo. TR , Deb: 03																												
1903	StL-N	0	0	—	1	0	0	0	0	4	3	6.8	0	1	2.3	0	0.0	2.25	148	.229	.284	0	0	102	67	0.0	0	0	0.1
■ COTTON MINAHAN	Minahan, Edmund Joseph b: 12/10/1882, Springfield, Ohio d: 5/20/58, E.Orange, N.J. BR/TR, 6', 190 lbs. Deb: 4/21/07																												
1907	Cin-N	0	2	.000	2	2	1	0	0	14	12	7.7	0	13	8.4	4	2.6	1.29	182	.264	.437	2	2	95	323	-0.9	-1	-1	0.1
■ RUDY MINARCIN	Minarcin, Rudy Anthony "Buster" b: 3/25/30, N.Vandergrift, Pa. BR/TR, 6', 195 lbs. Deb: 4/11/55																												
1955	Cin-N	5	9	.357	41	12	3	1	1	116	116	9.0	17	51	4.0	45	3.5	4.89	86	.261	.336	-11	-9	104	92	-1.9	-1	2	-0.6
1956	Bos-A	1	0	1.000	3	1	0	0	0	10	9	8.1	2	8	7.2	5	4.5	2.70	157	.250	.400	2	2	102	221	0.5	1	0	0.3
1957	Bos-A	0	0	—	26	0	0	0	2	45	44	8.8	5	30	6.0	20	4.0	4.40	94	.267	.366	-3	-1	109	115	0.0	0	0	0.0
Total	3	6	9	.400	70	13	3	1	3	171	169	8.9	24	89	4.7	70	3.7	4.63	91	.262	.348	-12	-8	105	106	-1.4	0	2	-0.3
■ RAY MINER	Miner, Raymond Theadore "Lefty" b: 4/4/1897, Glens Falls, N.Y. d: 9/15/63, Glenridge, N.Y. BR/TL, 5'11", 160 lbs. Deb: 9/15/21																												
1921	Phi-A	0	0	—	1	0	0	0	0	1	2	18.0	0	3	27.0	0	0.0	36.00	13	.400	.625	-4	-3	107	41	0.0	0	0	-0.2
■ CRAIG MINETTO	Minetto, Craig Stephen b: 4/25/54, Stockton, Cal. BL/TL, 6', 185 lbs. Deb: 7/04/78																												
1978	Oak-A	0	0	—	4	1	0	0	0	12	13	9.8	1	7	5.3	3	2.3	3.75	103	.283	.393	0	0	103	143	0.0	0	0	0.0
1979	Oak-A	1	5	.167	36	13	0	0	0	118	131	10.0	16	58	4.4	64	4.9	5.57	69	.282	.356	-18	-22	91	92	-1.4	0	-2	-2.2
1980	Oak-A	0	2	.000	7	1	0	0	1	8	11	12.4	2	3	3.4	5	5.6	7.88	48	.324	.368	-3	-4	94	86	-0.9	0	-0	-0.3
1981	Oak-A	0	0	—	8	0	0	0	0	7	7	9.0	0	4	5.1	4	5.1	2.57	135	.280	.387	1	1	95	182	0.0	0	-0	0.0
Total	4	1	7	.125	55	15	0	0	1	145	162	10.1	19	72	4.5	76	4.7	5.40	71	.284	.361	-20	-25	92	100	-2.3	0	-2	-2.5
■ STEVE MINGORI	Mingori, Stephen Bernard b: 2/29/44, Kansas City, Mo. BL/TL, 5'10", 165 lbs. Deb: 8/05/70																												
1970	Cle-A	1	0	1.000	21	0	0	0	1	20	17	7.6	2	12	5.4	16	7.2	2.70	158	.227	.333	2	4	115	139	0.5	-0	0	0.4
1971	Cle-A	1	2	.333	54	0	0	0	4	57	31	4.9	2	24	3.8	45	7.1	1.42	265	.166	.253	13	15	108	107	-0.1	0	1	1.7
1972	Cle-A	0	6	.000	41	0	0	0	10	57	67	10.6	4	36	5.7	47	7.4	3.95	84	.293	.387	-6	-4	108	133	-2.9	-0	1	-0.3
1973	Cle-A	0	0	—	5	0	0	0	0	12	10	7.5	3	10	7.5	4	3.0	6.00	63	.233	.377	-3	-3	99	95	0.0	0	1	-0.1
	KC-A	3	3	.500	19	1	0	0	1	56	59	9.5	6	23	3.7	46	7.4	3.05	137	.267	.343	5	7	109	140	-0.1	0	-0	0.7
	Yr	3	3	.500	24	1	0	0	1	68	69	9.1	9	33	4.4	50	6.6	3.57	115	.261	.349	2	4	107	140	-0.1	0	1	0.6
1974	KC-A	2	3	.400	36	0	0	0	2	67	53	7.1	4	23	3.1	43	5.8	2.82	136	.212	.278	6	8	106	80	-0.3	0	2	1.0
1975	KC-A	0	3	.000	36	0	0	0	2	50	42	7.6	2	20	3.6	25	4.5	2.52	152	.226	.297	7	7	101	104	-1.4	0	0	0.8
1976	KC-A	5	5	.500	55	0	0	0	10	85	73	7.7	3	25	2.6	38	4.0	2.33	149	.238	.296	11	11	99	119	-0.4	0	3	1.4
1977	KC-A	2	4	.333	43	0	0	0	4	64	59	8.3	4	19	2.7	19	2.7	3.09	130	.254	.302	7	7	99	108	-1.3	0	1	0.7
1978	KC-A	1	4	.200	45	0	0	0	7	69	64	8.3	5	16	2.1	28	3.7	2.74	139	.242	.287	8	8	101	103	-1.5	0	0	0.9
1979	KC-A	3	3	.500	30	1	0	0	1	47	69	13.2	10	17	3.3	18	3.4	5.74	77	.348	.390	-8	-7	105	128	0.0	0	-1	-0.6
Total	10	18	33	.353	385	2	0	0	42	584	544	8.4	45	225	3.5	329	5.1	3.04	127	.248	.316	43	52	104	113	-7.5	-0	7	6.6
■ PAUL MINNER	Minner, Paul Edison "Lefty" b: 7/30/23, New Wilmington, Pa. BL/TL, 6'5", 200 lbs. Deb: 9/12/46																												
1946	Bro-N	0	1	.000	3	0	0	0	0	4	6	13.5	1	3	6.8	3	6.8	6.75	51	.333	.409	-1	-1	100	120	-0.4	0	-0	-0.1
1948	Bro-N	4	3	.571	28	2	0	0	1	63	61	8.7	5	26	3.7	23	3.3	2.43	167	.257	.323	11	11	103	161	0.2	1	0	1.3
1949	Bro-N	3	1	.750	27	1	0	0	2	47	49	9.4	7	18	3.4	17	3.3	3.83	103	.272	.335	1	1	98	125	0.7	-0	0	0.1
1950	Chi-N	8	13	.381	39	24	9	1	4	190	217	10.3	18	72	3.4	99	4.7	4.12	108	.287	.346	0	7	107	113	-1.0	2	3	1.2
1951	Chi-N	6	17	.261	33	28	14	3	1	202	219	9.8	20	64	2.9	68	3.0	3.79	104	.277	.329	4	4	100	111	-4.4	5	3	1.3
1952	Chi-N	14	9	.609	28	27	12	2	0	181	180	9.0	13	54	2.7	61	3.0	3.73	103	.258	.308	0	3	103	94	2.8	6	2	1.1
1953	Chi-N	12	15	.444	31	27	9	2	1	201	227	10.2	15	40	1.8	64	2.9	4.21	108	.283	.314	2	8	106	94	0.6	2	4	1.4
1954	Chi-N	11	11	.500	32	29	12	0	1	218	236	9.7	19	50	2.1	79	3.3	3.96	104	.280	.314	3	4	102	97	1.8	3	1	0.9
1955	Chi-N	9	9	.500	22	22	7	1	0	158	173	9.9	15	47	2.7	53	3.0	3.47	118	.283	.327	10	11	101	**123**	0.6	2	2	1.5
1956	Chi-N	2	5	.286	10	9	1	0	0	47	60	11.5	9	19	3.6	14	2.7	6.89	55	.324	.380	-16	-16	101	94	-0.9	2	0	-1.3
Total	10	69	84	.451	253	169	64	9	10	1311	1428	9.8	122	393	2.7	481	3.3	3.94	105	.279	.326	13	30	103	108	-0.0	23	15	7.4
■ DON MINNICK	Minnick, Donald Athey b: 4/14/31, Lynchburg, Va. BR/TR, 6'3", 195 lbs. Deb: 9/23/57																												
1957	Was-A	0	1	.000	2	1	0	0	0	9	14	14.0	1	2	2.0	7	7.0	5.00	77	.341	.364	-1	-1	102	117	-0.4	-0	0	-0.1
■ JIM MINSHALL	Minshall, James Edward b: 7/4/47, Covington, Ky. BR/TR, 6'6", 215 lbs. Deb: 9/14/74																												
1974	Pit-N	0	1	.000	5	0	0	0	0	4	1	2.3	0	2	4.5	3	6.8	0.00	—	.083	.200	2	2	97	0	-0.4	0	0	0.2
1975	Pit-N	0	0	—	1	0	0	0	0	1	0	0.0	0	2	18.0	2	18.0	0.00	—	.000	.400	0	0	98	0	0.0	0	0	0.0
Total	2	0	1	.000	6	0	0	0	0	5	1	1.8	0	4	7.2	5	9.0	0.00	—	.067	.250	2	2	97	0	-0.4	0	0	0.2
■ GREG MINTON	Minton, Gregory Brian b: 7/29/51, Lubbock, Tex. BB/TR, 6'2", 180 lbs. Deb: 9/07/75																												
1975	SF-N	1	1	.500	4	2	0	0	0	17	19	10.1	1	11	5.8	6	3.2	6.88	54	.288	.392	-6	-6	102	75	0.0	-1	0	-0.5
1976	SF-N	0	3	.000	10	2	0	0	0	26	32	11.1	0	12	4.2	7	2.4	4.85	75	.317	.385	-4	-3	104	103	-1.4	-0	0	-0.3
1977	SF-N	1	1	.500	2	2	0	0	0	14	14	9.0	0	4	2.6	5	3.2	4.50	91	.264	.316	-1	-1	105	66	0.1	1	1	0.0
1978	SF-N	0	1	.000	11	0	0	0	0	16	22	12.4	3	8	4.5	6	3.4	7.88	41	.338	.408	-8	-8	91	92	-0.4	-0	0	-0.7
1979	SF-N	4	3	.571	46	0	0	0	4	80	59	6.6	0	27	3.0	33	3.7	1.80	194	.215	.280	17	15	93	115	0.9	-0	2	1.8
1980	SF-N	4	6	.400	68	0	0	0	19	91	81	8.0	0	34	3.4	42	4.2	2.47	141	.243	.305	11	10	96	110	-0.6	-0	2	1.2
1981	SF-N	4	5	.444	55	0	0	0	21	84	84	9.0	0	36	3.9	29	3.1	2.89	127	.267	.334	6	7	105	121	-0.5	-1	3	0.9
1982	SF-N	10	4	.714	78	0	0	0	30	123	108	7.9	5	42	3.1	58	4.2	1.83	185	.244	.306	**24**	21	94	168	2.8	0	1	2.3
1983	SF-N	7	11	.389	73	0	0	0	22	107	117	9.8	6	47	4.0	38	3.2	3.53	104	.283	.345	1	2	101	122	-1.9	4	-0	0.6
1984	SF-N	4	9	.308	74	1	0	0	19	124	130	9.4	6	57	4.1	48	3.5	3.77	93	.267	.336	-2	-4	98	104	-1.6	-1	2	-0.2
1985	SF-N	5	4	.556	68	0	0	0	4	97	98	9.1	6	54	5.0	37	3.4	3.53	97	.272	.358	1	-1	95	127	1.3	-0	2	0.0
1986	SF-N	4	4	.500	48	0	0	0	5	69	63	8.2	4	34	4.4	34	4.4	3.91	90	.251	.331	-1	-3	95	97	0.0	2	2	0.0
1987	SF-N	1	0	1.000	15	0	0	0	1	23	30	11.7	2	10	3.9	9	3.5	3.52	110	.323	.390	1	1	95	167	0.5	-0	0	0.1
	Cal-A	5	4	.556	41	0	0	0	10	76	71	8.4	4	29	3.4	35	4.1	3.08	145	.257	.323	12	12	100	121	0.8	0	2	1.3
1988	Cal-A	4	5	.444	44	0	0	0	7	79	67	7.6	1	34	3.9	46	5.2	2.85	132	.233	.314	10	8	95	103	-0.1	0	2	1.0
Total	14	54	61	.470	637	7	0	0	142	1026	995	8.7	38	439	3.9	433	3.8	3.18	114	.261	.331	61	50	97	119	-0.1	2	18	7.5
■ PAUL MIRABELLA	Mirabella, Paul Thomas b: 3/20/54, Belleville, N.J. BL/TL, 6'1", 190 lbs. Deb: 7/28/78																												
1978	Tex-A	3	2	.600	10	4	0	0	1	28	30	9.6	2	17	5.5	23	7.4	5.79	62	.286	.376	-6	-7	96	86	0.3	0	-0	-0.6
1979	NY-A	0	4	.000	10	1	0	0	0	14	16	10.3	3	10	6.4	4	2.6	9.00	45	.276	.380	-7	-8	95	69	-1.9	0	-0	-0.6
1980	Tor-A	5	12	.294	33	22	3	1	0	131	151	10.4	11	66	4.5	53	3.6	4.33	95	.294	.369	-4	-3	101	118	-2.6	0	0	-0.2
1981	Tor-A	0	0	—	8	1	0	0	0	15	20	12.0	2	7	4.2	9	5.4	7.20	57	.313	.384	-6	-5	113	84	0.0	0	-0	-0.5
1982	Tex-A	1	1	.500	40	0	0	0	3	51	46	8.1	4	22	3.9	29	5.1	4.76	81	.241	.323	-4	-5	94	74	0.2	0	-0	-0.4
1983	Bal-A	0	0	—	3	2	0	0	0	10	9	8.1	1	7	6.3	4	3.6	5.40	75	.243	.356	-1	-2	99	83	0.0	0	-0	-0.1
1984	Sea-A	2	5	.286	52	1	0	0	3	68	74	9.8	6	32	4.2	41	5.4	4.37	94	.282	.353	-3	-2	103	109	-1.2	0	1	0.0
1985	Sea-A	0	0	—	10	0	0	0	0	14	9	5.8	0	4	2.6	8	5.1	1.29	308	.188	.263	4	4	95	137	0.0	0	-0	0.4
1986	Sea-A	0	0	—	8	0	0	0	0	6	13	19.5	1	3	4.5	6	9.0	9.00	49	.419	.471	-3	-3	106	113	0.0	0	0	-0.2
1987	Mil-A	2	1	.667	29	0	0	0	2	29	30	9.3	0	16	5.0	14	4.3	4.97	92	.268	.346	-2	-1	102	79	0.4	0	1	0.0
1988	Mil-A	2	2	.500	38	0	0	0	4	60	44	6.6	3	21	3.2	33	5.0	1.65	247	.204	.270	15	16	103	132	0.0	0	1	1.7
Total	11	15	27	.357	241	31	3	1	13	426	442	9.3	33	205	4.3	224	4.7	4.39	93	.270	.347	-17	-16	101	105	-4.8	0	1	-0.5
■ ROY MITCHELL	Mitchell, Albert Roy b: 4/19/1885, Belton, Tex. d: 9/8/59, Temple, Tex. BR/TR, 5'9.5", 170 lbs. Deb: 9/10/10																												
1910	StL-A	4	2	.667	6	6	6	0	0	52	43	7.4	0	12	2.1	23	4.0	2.60	98	.244	.300	-0	-0	101	89	1.6	0	1	0.0
1911	StL-A	4	8	.333	28	12	8	1	0	133	134	9.1	4	45	3.0	40	2.7	3.86	86	.273	.341	-8	-8	100	91	0.3	2	-0	-0.5
1912	StL-A	3	4	.429	13	7	5	0	0	62	81	11.8	2	17	2.5	22	3.2	4.65	74	.323	.375	-9	-8	103	107	0.5	3	-1	-0.8
1913	StL-A	13	16	.448	33	27	21	4	1	245	265	9.7	6	47	1.7	59	2.2	3.01	95	.280	.318	-2	-4	98	105	2.1	-1	-1	-0.5
1914	StL-A	4	5	.444	28	9	4	0	**4**	103	134	11.7	1	38	3.3	38	3.3	4.37	62	.320	.384	-19	-19	100	109	-0.1	1	0	-1.9
1918	Chi-A	0	1	.000	2	2	0	0	0	12	18	13.5	1	4	3.0	3	2.3	7.50	37	.346	.373	-6	-6	100	77	-0.4	-0	0	-0.5
	Cin-N	4	0	1.000	5	3	3	2	0	36	27	6.8	0	5	1.3	9	2.3	0.75	355	.208	.234	8	8	96	140	2.0	0	-0	0.9

YEAR	TM/L	W	L	PCT	G	GS	CG	SHO	SV	IP	H	H/G	HR	BB	BB/G	SO	SO/G	ERA	/A	OAVG	OOBP	PR	/A	PF	CPI	WAT	PB	PD	TPI
1919	Cin-N	0	1	.000	7	1	0	0	0	31	32	9.3	0	9	2.6	10	2.9	2.32	127	.276	.315	2	2	101	139	-0.4	-1	1	0.2
Total	7	32	37	.464	122	67	47	7	5	674	734	9.8	14	177	2.4	204	2.7	3.43	86	.284	.335	-34	-36	99	105	5.6	3	-1	-3.1

■ **CHARLIE MITCHELL** Mitchell, Charles Ross b: 6/24/62, Dickson, Tenn. BR/TR, 6'3", 170 lbs. Deb: 8/09/84

YEAR	TM/L	W	L	PCT	G	GS	CG	SHO	SV	IP	H	H/G	HR	BB	BB/G	SO	SO/G	ERA	/A	OAVG	OOBP	PR	/A	PF	CPI	WAT	PB	PD	TPI
1984	Bos-A	0	0	—	10	0	0	0	0	16	14	7.9	1	6	3.4	7	3.9	2.81	156	.226	.310	2	3	110	106	0.0	0	0	0.3
1985	Bos-A	0	0	—	2	0	0	0	0	2	5	22.5	1	0	0.0	2	9.0	13.50	31	.500	.500	-2	-2	102	106	0.0	0	0	-0.1
Total	2	0	0	—	12	0	0	0	0	18	19	9.5	2	6	3.0	9	4.5	4.00	109	.264	.333	0	1	109	106	0.0	0	0	0.2

■ **CLARENCE MITCHELL** Mitchell, Clarence Elmer b: 2/22/1891, Franklin, Neb. d: 11/6/63, Grand Island, Neb. BL/TL, 5'11.5", 190 lbs. Deb: 6/02/11

YEAR	TM/L	W	L	PCT	G	GS	CG	SHO	SV	IP	H	H/G	HR	BB	BB/G	SO	SO/G	ERA	/A	OAVG	OOBP	PR	/A	PF	CPI	WAT	PB	PD	TPI
1911	Det-A	1	0	1.000	5	1	0	0	0	14	20	12.9	1	7	4.5	4	2.6	8.36	43	.351	.422	-8	-7	107	76	0.5	1	-0	-0.5
1916	Cin-N	11	10	.524	29	24	17	1	0	195	211	9.7	4	45	2.1	52	2.4	3.14	84	.285	.325	-11	-11	101	113	2.5	2	1	-0.6
1917	Cin-N	9	15	.375	32	20	10	2	1	159	166	9.4	4	34	1.9	37	2.1	3.23	78	.268	.301	-9	-13	93	93	-3.4	4	0	-0.7
1918	Bro-N	0	1	.000	1	1	0	0	0	⅓	4	108.0	0	0	0.0	0	0.0	108.00	—	1.000	1.000	-4	-4	104	55	-0.4	0	0	-0.3
1919	Bro-N	7	5	.583	23	11	9	0	0	109	123	10.2	0	23	1.9	43	3.6	3.06	89	.297	.324	-2	-4	94	117	1.2	7	1	0.4
1920	Bro-N	5	2	.714	19	7	3	1	1	79	85	9.7	1	23	2.6	18	2.1	3.08	110	.288	.328	1	3	108	111	1.0	1	1	0.3
1921	Bro-N	11	9	.550	37	18	13	3	2	190	206	9.8	7	46	2.2	39	1.8	2.89	137	.280	.318	19	23	105	118	1.0	4	3	3.1
1922	Bro-N	0	3	.000	5	3	0	0	0	13	28	19.4	0	7	4.8	1	0.7	13.85	28	.467	.493	-14	-14	95	74	-1.4	2	1	-1.1
1923	Phi-N	9	10	.474	29	19	8	1	0	139	170	11.0	8	46	3.0	41	2.7	4.73	100	.299	.350	-11	-0	118	94	2.3	3	-3	0.1
1924	Phi-N	6	13	.316	30	26	9	1	1	165	223	12.2	10	58	3.2	36	2.0	5.62	76	.321	.370	-32	-25	111	94	-1.3	-0	3	-2.2
1925	Phi-N	10	17	.370	32	26	12	1	1	199	245	11.1	23	51	2.3	46	2.1	5.29	95	.302	.341	-23	-6	118	91	-2.5	-2	4	-0.1
1926	Phi-N	9	14	.391	28	25	12	0	1	179	232	11.7	7	55	2.8	52	2.6	4.58	90	.318	.361	-15	-10	107	106	0.2	1	4	-0.2
1927	Phi-N	6	3	.667	13	12	8	1	0	95	99	9.4	7	28	2.7	17	1.6	4.07	96	.271	.322	-2	-2	100	93	2.3	2	0	0.1
1928	Phi-N	0	0	—	3	0	0	0	0	6	13	19.5	0	2	3.0	0	0.0	9.00	48	.542	.536	-3	-3	109	124	0.0	-0	0	-0.2
	StL-N	8	9	.471	19	18	9	1	0	150	149	8.9	8	38	2.3	31	1.9	3.30	117	.265	.305	11	9	97	100	-2.1	-3	3	0.8
	Yr	8	9	.471	22	18	9	1	0	156	162	9.3	8	40	2.3	31	1.8	3.52	110	.276	.315	8	6	97	100	-2.1	-0	3	0.6
1929	StL-N	8	11	.421	25	22	16	0	0	173	221	11.5	13	60	3.1	39	2.0	4.27	108	.320	.370	9	7	98	129	-1.8	4	-1	0.9
1930	StL-N	1	0	1.000	1	1	0	0	0	3	5	15.0	0	2	6.0	1	3.0	6.00	84	.357	.438	-0	-0	102	115	0.5	0	0	0.0
	NY-N	10	3	.769	24	16	5	0	0	129	151	10.5	10	36	2.5	40	2.8	3.98	120	.298	.338	14	11	96	116	3.2	0	2	1.2
	Yr	11	3	.786	25	17	5	0	0	132	156	10.6	10	38	2.6	41	2.8	4.02	118	.300	.340	14	11	96	116	3.7	0	2	1.2
1931	NY-N	13	11	.542	27	25	13	0	0	190	221	10.5	12	52	2.5	39	1.8	4.07	89	.285	.329	-4	-10	93	100	-0.7	2	-2	-0.9
1932	NY-N	1	3	.250	8	3	1	0	2	30	41	12.3	1	11	3.3	7	2.1	4.20	90	.325	.376	-1	-1	98	129	-0.8	0	-1	-0.1
Total	18	125	139	.473	390	278	145	12	9	2217	2613	10.6	116	624	2.5	543	2.2	4.12	94	.297	.340	-86	-60	103	105	0.3	28	16	-0.0

■ **CRAIG MITCHELL** Mitchell, Craig Seton b: 4/14/54, Santa Rosa, Cal. BR/TR, 6'3", 180 lbs. Deb: 9/25/75

YEAR	TM/L	W	L	PCT	G	GS	CG	SHO	SV	IP	H	H/G	HR	BB	BB/G	SO	SO/G	ERA	/A	OAVG	OOBP	PR	/A	PF	CPI	WAT	PB	PD	TPI
1975	Oak-A	0	1	.000	1	1	0	0	0	4	6	13.5	0	2	4.5	2	4.5	11.25	31	.375	.444	-3	-3	91	59	-0.4	0	0	-0.2
1976	Oak-A	0	0	—	1	0	0	0	0	3	3	9.0	0	0	0.0	0	0.0	3.00	116	.231	.231	0	0	98	32	0.0	0	0	0.0
1977	Oak-A	0	1	.000	3	1	0	0	0	6	9	13.5	1	2	3.0	1	1.5	7.50	52	.346	.379	-2	-2	97	90	-0.4	0	0	-0.1
Total	3	0	2	.000	5	2	0	0	0	13	18	12.5	1	4	2.8	3	2.1	7.62	48	.327	.367	-5	-6	95	67	-0.8	0	0	-0.3

■ **FRED MITCHELL** Mitchell, Frederick Francis (born Frederick Francis Yapp) b: 6/5/1878, Cambridge, Mass. d: 10/13/70, Newton, Mass. BR/TR, 5'9.5", 185 lbs. Deb: 4/27/01 M

YEAR	TM/L	W	L	PCT	G	GS	CG	SHO	SV	IP	H	H/G	HR	BB	BB/G	SO	SO/G	ERA	/A	OAVG	OOBP	PR	/A	PF	CPI	WAT	PB	PD	TPI
1901	Bos-A	6	6	.500	17	13	10	0	0	109	115	9.5	2	51	4.2	34	2.8	3.80	91	.291	.372	-2	-4	94	102	-0.8	-1	0	-0.4
1902	Bos-A	0	1	.000	1	0	0	0	0	4	8	18.0	1	5	11.3	2	4.5	11.25	31	.443	.564	-3	-3	98	112	-0.4	-0	0	-0.2
	Phi-A	5	7	.417	18	14	9	0	1	108	120	10.0	4	59	4.9	22	1.8	3.58	106	.306	.397	-0	2	106	127	-1.9	-1	2	0.4
	Yr	5	8	.385	19	14	9	0	1	112	128	10.3	5	64	5.1	24	1.9	3.86	98	.312	.405	-4	-1	106	127	-2.3	-0	3	0.2
1903	Phi-N	11	16	.407	28	28	24	1	0	227	250	9.9	4	102	4.0	69	2.7	4.48	69	.311	.402	-30	-35	94	93	1.2	-0	-3	-3.4
1904	Phi-N	4	7	.364	13	13	11	0	0	109	133	11.0	3	25	2.1	29	2.4	3.39	78	.332	.381	-8	-9	97	125	0.2	1	3	-0.3
	Bro-N	2	5	.286	8	8	8	1	0	66	73	10.0	0	23	3.1	16	2.2	3.82	70	.309	.377	-8	-8	98	98	-0.7	2	1	-0.4
	Yr	6	12	.333	21	21	19	1	0	175	206	10.6	3	48	2.5	45	2.3	3.55	75	.320	.370	-16	-17	97	98	-0.5	1	4	-0.7
1905	Bro-N	3	7	.300	12	10	9	0	0	96	107	10.0	2	38	3.6	44	4.1	4.78	64	.314	.391	-19	-19	102	88	-0.2	-0	1	-1.7
Total	5	31	49	.387	97	86	71	2	1	719	806	10.1	16	303	3.8	216	2.7	4.09	77	.312	.391	-71	-76	98	104	-2.6	1	4	-6.0

■ **JOHN MITCHELL** Mitchell, John Kyle b: 8/11/65, Dickson, Tenn. BR/TR, 6'2", 165 lbs. Deb: 9/08/86

YEAR	TM/L	W	L	PCT	G	GS	CG	SHO	SV	IP	H	H/G	HR	BB	BB/G	SO	SO/G	ERA	/A	OAVG	OOBP	PR	/A	PF	CPI	WAT	PB	PD	TPI
1986	NY-N	0	1	.000	4	1	0	0	0	10	10	9.0	1	4	3.6	2	1.8	3.60	96	.278	.350	0	-0	93	126	-0.4	-0	0	0.0
1987	NY-N	3	6	.333	20	19	1	0	0	112	124	10.0	6	36	2.9	57	4.6	4.10	97	.279	.329	-0	-2	97	97	-1.8	-1	1	-0.1
1988	NY-N	0	0	—	1	0	0	0	0	1	2	18.0	0	1	9.0	1	9.0	0.00	—	.500	.600	0	0	88	0	0.0	-0	0	0.0
Total	3	3	7	.300	25	20	1	0	0	123	136	10.0	7	41	3.0	60	4.4	4.02	97	.281	.333	0	-2	97	99	-2.2	-1	1	-0.1

■ **MONROE MITCHELL** Mitchell, Monroe Barr b: 9/11/01, Starkville, Miss. d: 9/4/76, Valdosta, Ga. BR/TL, 6'1.5", 170 lbs. Deb: 7/11/23

YEAR	TM/L	W	L	PCT	G	GS	CG	SHO	SV	IP	H	H/G	HR	BB	BB/G	SO	SO/G	ERA	/A	OAVG	OOBP	PR	/A	PF	CPI	WAT	PB	PD	TPI
1923	Was-A	2	4	.333	10	6	3	1	2	42	57	12.2	0	22	4.7	8	1.7	6.43	59	.350	.406	-11	-12	95	94	-0.9	1	-1	-1.0

■ **PAUL MITCHELL** Mitchell, Paul Michael b: 8/19/49, Worcester, Mass. BR/TR, 6'1", 195 lbs. Deb: 7/01/75

YEAR	TM/L	W	L	PCT	G	GS	CG	SHO	SV	IP	H	H/G	HR	BB	BB/G	SO	SO/G	ERA	/A	OAVG	OOBP	PR	/A	PF	CPI	WAT	PB	PD	TPI
1975	Bal-A	3	0	1.000	11	4	1	0	0	57	41	6.5	8	19	3.0	31	4.9	3.63	93	.204	.268	1	-2	89	76	1.5	0	-1	-0.2
1976	Oak-A	9	7	.563	26	26	4	1	0	142	169	10.7	15	30	1.9	67	4.2	4.25	82	.294	.325	-11	-12	98	103	0.4	0	-1	-1.3
1977	Oak-A	0	3	.000	5	3	0	0	0	14	21	13.5	3	7	4.5	5	3.2	10.29	38	.339	.394	-10	-10	97	71	-1.4	0	0	-0.8
	Sea-A	3	3	.500	9	9	0	0	0	40	50	11.2	7	16	3.6	20	4.5	4.95	81	.311	.366	-4	-4	98	121	0.5	0	0	-0.3
	Yr	3	6	.333	14	12	0	0	0	54	71	11.8	10	23	3.8	25	4.2	6.33	63	.318	.374	-14	-14	98	121	-0.9	0	1	-1.1
1978	Sea-A	8	14	.364	29	29	4	2	0	168	173	9.3	21	79	4.2	75	4.0	4.18	94	.270	.346	-7	-4	104	110	0.3	0	-1	-0.5
1979	Sea-A	1	4	.200	10	6	1	0	0	37	46	11.2	4	15	3.6	18	4.4	4.38	98	.309	.367	-1	-0	101	123	-1.2	0	-0	0.0
	Mil-A	3	3	.500	18	8	0	0	0	75	81	9.7	11	10	1.2	32	3.8	5.76	73	.276	.301	-13	-13	99	72	-0.4	0	-1	-1.2
	Yr	4	7	.364	28	14	1	0	0	112	127	10.2	15	25	2.0	50	4.0	5.30	80	.287	.324	-13	-13	100	72	-1.6	0	-1	-1.2
1980	Mil-A	5	5	.500	17	11	1	1	1	89	92	9.3	7	15	1.5	29	2.9	3.54	106	.267	.293	5	2	93	94	-0.2	0	0	0.3
Total	6	32	39	.451	125	96	11	4	1	622	673	9.7	76	191	2.8	277	4.0	4.44	86	.278	.326	-40	-44	99	99	-0.5	0	-3	-4.0

■ **BOBBY MITCHELL** Mitchell, Robert Mc Kasha b: 2/6/1856, Cincinnati, Ohio d: 5/1/33, Springfield, Ohio BL/TL, 5'5", 135 lbs. Deb: 9/06/1877

YEAR	TM/L	W	L	PCT	G	GS	CG	SHO	SV	IP	H	H/G	HR	BB	BB/G	SO	SO/G	ERA	/A	OAVG	OOBP	PR	/A	PF	CPI	WAT	PB	PD	TPI
1877	Cin-N	6	5	.545	12	12	11	1	0	100	123	11.1	0	11	1.0	41	**3.7**	3.51	72	.311	.329	-8	-11	90	91	2.4	-0	0	-0.9
1878	Cin-N	7	2	.778	9	9	9	1	0	80	69	**7.8**	0	18	2.0	51	**5.7**	2.14	100	**.242**	.287	1	-0	93	75	2.1	1	0	0.0
1879	Cle-N	7	15	.318	23	22	20	0	0	195	236	10.9	0	42	1.9	90	4.2	3.28	79	.305	.340	-17	-15	103	107	-0.4	-5	0	-1.7
1882	StL-a	0	1	.000	1	1	0	0	0	7	12	15.4	0	2	2.6	2	2.6	7.71	36	.383	.420	-4	-4	104	84	-0.4	-1	0	-0.2
Total	4	20	23	.465	45	44	40	2	0	382	440	10.4	0	73	1.7	184	4.3	3.18	78	.296	.329	-27	-30	98	95	3.7	-5	0	-2.8

■ **WILLIE MITCHELL** Mitchell, William b: 12/1/1889, Pleasant Grove, Miss. d: 11/23/73, Sardis, Miss. BR/TL, 6', 176 lbs. Deb: 9/22/09

YEAR	TM/L	W	L	PCT	G	GS	CG	SHO	SV	IP	H	H/G	HR	BB	BB/G	SO	SO/G	ERA	/A	OAVG	OOBP	PR	/A	PF	CPI	WAT	PB	PD	TPI
1909	Cle-A	1	2	.333	3	3	3	0	0	23	18	7.0	0	10	3.9	8	3.1	1.57	163	.225	.340	2	3	103	170	-0.3	1	0	0.3
1910	Cle-A	12	8	.600	35	18	11	1	0	184	155	7.6	2	55	2.7	102	5.0	2.59	99	.236	.310	-2	-1	102	95	2.8	-3	-2	-0.5
1911	Cle-A	7	14	.333	30	22	9	0	0	177	190	9.7	1	60	3.1	78	4.0	3.76	92	.284	.354	-8	-6	103	98	-4.1	-5	-1	-1.1
1912	Cle-A	5	8	.385	29	15	8	0	1	164	149	8.2	0	56	3.1	94	5.2	2.80	121	.240	.309	10	11	101	90	-1.4	-4	-3	0.8
1913	Cle-A	14	8	.636	35	22	14	4	0	217	153	6.3	1	88	3.6	141	5.8	1.91	159	.199	.288	25	27	104	86	2.0	-2	-3	2.8
1914	Cle-A	12	17	.414	39	32	16	3	1	257	228	8.0	3	124	4.3	179	6.3	3.19	91	.238	.330	-13	-8	106	88	2.1	-4	-5	-1.3
1915	Cle-A	11	14	.440	36	30	12	1	1	236	210	8.0	1	84	3.2	149	5.7	2.82	111	.241	.309	3	8	106	89	1.5	-5	-4	0.0
1916	Cle-A	2	5	.286	12	6	1	0	1	44	55	11.3	2	19	3.9	24	4.9	5.11	55	.309	.376	-11	-11	99	93	-1.4	-1	-1	-1.3
	Det-A	7	5	.583	23	17	7	2	0	128	119	8.4	0	48	3.4	60	4.2	3.30	88	.253	.329	-7	-6	103	88	0.3	2	-3	-0.6
	Yr	9	10	.474	35	23	8	2	1	172	174	9.1	2	67	3.5	84	4.4	3.77	77	.269	.342	-18	-17	102	88	-1.1	-1	-4	-1.9
1917	Det-A	12	8	.600	30	22	12	5	0	185	172	8.4	2	46	2.2	80	3.9	2.19	117	.250	.309	10	8	96	116	2.1	-3	-2	0.2
1918	Det-A	0	1	.000	1	1	0	0	0	4	3	6.8	0	5	11.3	2	4.5	9.00	30	.200	.400	-3	-3	99	41	-0.4	-0	0	-0.2
1919	Det-A	1	2	.333	3	2	0	0	0	14	12	7.7	2	10	6.4	4	2.6	5.14	58	.255	.397	-3	-3	92	99	-0.5	0	0	-0.2
Total	11	84	92	.477	276	190	93	16	4	1633	1464	8.1	14	605	3.3	921	5.1	2.88	104	.243	.320	4	18	103	94	2.7	-24	-23	-1.1

■ **VINEGAR BEND MIZELL** Mizell, Wilmer David b: 8/13/30, Leakesville, Miss. BR/TL, 6'3.5", 205 lbs. Deb: 4/22/52

YEAR	TM/L	W	L	PCT	G	GS	CG	SHO	SV	IP	H	H/G	HR	BB	BB/G	SO	SO/G	ERA	/A	OAVG	OOBP	PR	/A	PF	CPI	WAT	PB	PD	TPI
1952	StL-N	10	8	.556	30	30	7	2	0	190	171	8.1	12	103	4.9	146	**6.9**	3.65	99	.237	.330	2	-1	97	98	-0.2	-5	-2	-0.7
1953	StL-N	13	11	.542	33	33	10	1	0	224	193	7.8	12	114	4.6	173	**7.0**	3.50	123	.227	.317	20	20	101	90	0.1	-4	-0	1.6

YEAR	TM/L	W	L	PCT	G	GS	CG	SHO	SV	IP	H	H/G	HR	BB	BB/G	SO	SO/G	ERA	/A	OAVG	OOBP	PR	/A	PF	CPI	WAT	PB	PD	TPI
1956	StL-N	14	14	.500	33	33	11	3	0	209	172	7.4	20	92	4.0	153	6.6	3.62	104	.222	.308	4	3	99	84	0.2	-3	0	0.0
1957	StL-N	8	10	.444	33	21	7	2	0	149	136	8.2	18	51	3.1	87	5.3	3.74	103	.241	.300	2	2	99	92	-2.0	-2	1	0.1
1958	StL-N	10	14	.417	30	29	8	2	0	190	178	8.4	17	91	4.3	80	3.8	3.41	125	.252	.330	11	18	108	114	-1.4	-4	-1	1.5
1959	StL-N	13	10	.565	31	30	8	1	0	201	196	8.8	21	89	4.0	108	4.8	4.21	100	.252	.329	-6	-0	106	94	2.5	1	-3	-0.1
1960	StL-N	1	3	.250	9	9	0	0	0	55	64	10.5	7	28	4.6	42	6.9	4.58	89	.291	.365	-5	-3	108	117	-1.0	-1	0	-0.2
	Pit-N	13	5	.722	23	23	8	3	0	156	141	8.1	7	46	2.7	71	4.1	3.12	117	.247	.301	11	9	97	99	2.7	-1	-2	0.6
	Yr	14	8	.636	32	32	8	3	0	211	205	8.7	14	74	3.2	113	4.8	3.50	107	.259	.319	6	6	100	99	1.7	-1	-2	0.4
1961	Pit-N	7	10	.412	25	17	2	1	0	100	120	10.8	16	31	2.8	37	3.3	5.04	79	.299	.346	-11	-12	99	104	-1.3	-1	-3	-1.3
1962	Pit-N	1	1	.500	4	3	0	0	0	16	15	8.4	3	10	5.6	6	3.4	5.06	79	.254	.361	-2	-2	101	106	0.0	-0	0	-0.1
	NY-N	0	2	.000	17	2	0	0	0	38	48	11.4	10	25	5.9	15	3.6	7.34	58	.324	.407	-14	-13	108	106	-0.9	0	-1	-1.2
	Yr	1	3	.250	21	5	0	0	0	54	63	10.5	13	35	5.8	21	3.5	6.67	63	.301	.390	-16	-15	106	106	-0.9	-0	-0	-1.3
Total	9	90	88	.506	268	230	61	15	0	1528	1434	8.4	143	680	4.0	918	5.4	3.85	103	.247	.324	11	21	101	97	-1.3	-18	-9	0.2

■ MIKE MODAK Modak, Michael Joseph Aloysius b: 5/18/22, Campbell, Ohio BR/TR, 5'10.5", 195 lbs. Deb: 7/04/45

YEAR	TM/L	W	L	PCT	G	GS	CG	SHO	SV	IP	H	H/G	HR	BB	BB/G	SO	SO/G	ERA	/A	OAVG	OOBP	PR	/A	PF	CPI	WAT	PB	PD	TPI
1945	Cin-N	1	2	.333	20	3	1	1	1	42	52	11.1	0	23	4.9	7	1.5	5.79	64	.308	.385	-9	-10	97	86	-0.1	-1	-1	-1.0

■ JOE MOELLER Moeller, Joseph Douglas b: 2/15/43, Blue Island, Ill. BR/TR, 6'5", 192 lbs. Deb: 4/12/62

YEAR	TM/L	W	L	PCT	G	GS	CG	SHO	SV	IP	H	H/G	HR	BB	BB/G	SO	SO/G	ERA	/A	OAVG	OOBP	PR	/A	PF	CPI	WAT	PB	PD	TPI
1962	LA-N	6	5	.545	19	15	1	0	1	86	87	9.1	10	58	6.1	46	4.8	5.23	68	.266	.373	-12	-16	91	96	-0.6	1	1	-1.3
1964	LA-N	7	13	.350	27	24	1	0	0	145	153	9.5	14	31	1.9	97	6.0	4.22	77	.265	.301	-11	-16	91	87	-3.1	-2	-0	-1.8
1966	LA-N	2	4	.333	29	8	0	0	0	79	73	8.3	4	14	1.6	31	3.5	2.51	137	.244	.276	10	8	95	105	-1.2	0	1	1.1
1967	LA-N	0	0	—	6	0	0	0	0	5	9	16.2	1	3	5.4	2	3.6	9.00	33	.409	.444	-3	-3	89	108	0.0	0	0	-0.2
1968	LA-N	1	1	.500	3	3	0	0	0	16	17	9.6	1	2	1.1	11	6.2	5.06	54	.270	.299	-4	-4	91	65	0.1	-1	0	-0.4
1969	LA-N	1	0	1.000	23	4	0	0	1	51	54	9.5	4	13	2.3	25	4.4	3.35	105	.278	.315	1	1	97	116	0.5	0	1	0.2
1970	LA-N	7	9	.438	31	19	2	1	4	135	131	8.7	16	43	2.9	63	4.2	3.93	92	.248	.303	2	-5	89	92	-1.6	0	-2	-0.6
1971	LA-N	2	4	.333	28	1	0	0	1	66	72	9.8	5	12	1.6	32	4.4	3.82	89	.279	.300	-3	-3	98	95	-1.1	-0	1	-0.2
Total	8	26	36	.419	166	74	4	1	7	583	596	9.2	55	176	2.7	307	4.7	4.01	85	.263	.312	-20	-38	92	95	-7.0	-1	2	-3.2

■ RON MOELLER Moeller, Ronald Ralph "The Kid" b: 10/13/38, Cincinnati, Ohio BL/TL, 6', 180 lbs. Deb: 9/08/56

YEAR	TM/L	W	L	PCT	G	GS	CG	SHO	SV	IP	H	H/G	HR	BB	BB/G	SO	SO/G	ERA	/A	OAVG	OOBP	PR	/A	PF	CPI	WAT	PB	PD	TPI
1956	Bal-A	0	1	.000	4	1	0	0	0	9	10	10.0	0	3	3.0	2	2.0	4.00	100	.286	.333	0	0	97	92	-0.4	-0	-0	0.0
1958	Bal-A	0	0	—	4	0	0	0	0	4	6	13.5	0	3	6.8	3	6.8	4.50	80	.333	.429	-0	-0	95	139	0.0	0	0	0.0
1961	LA-A	4	8	.333	33	18	1	1	0	113	122	9.7	15	83	6.6	87	6.9	5.81	78	.275	.388	-22	-16	112	97	-1.4	2	1	-1.2
1963	LA-A	0	0	—	3	0	0	0	0	3	5	15.0	1	1	3.0	2	6.0	6.00	56	.385	.429	-1	-1	92	155	0.0	0	0	0.0
	Was-A	2	0	1.000	8	3	0	0	0	24	31	11.6	4	10	3.8	10	3.8	6.38	58	.316	.382	-7	-7	101	98	1.0	0	-1	-0.7
	Yr	2	0	1.000	11	3	0	0	0	27	36	12.0	5	11	3.7	12	4.0	6.33	57	.324	.387	-8	-8	100	98	1.0	0	-0	-0.7
Total	4	6	9	.400	52	22	1	1	0	153	174	10.2	20	100	5.9	104	6.1	5.76	75	.287	.386	-31	-25	109	99	-0.8	2	0	-1.9

■ SAM MOFFETT Moffett, Samuel R. b: 3/14/1857, Wheeling, W.Va. d: 5/5/07, Butte, Mont. TR , Deb: 5/15/1884

YEAR	TM/L	W	L	PCT	G	GS	CG	SHO	SV	IP	H	H/G	HR	BB	BB/G	SO	SO/G	ERA	/A	OAVG	OOBP	PR	/A	PF	CPI	WAT	PB	PD	TPI
1884	Cle-N	3	19	.136	24	22	21	0	0	198	236	10.7	9	58	2.6	84	3.8	3.86	83	.305	.354	-20	-15	108	107	-6.7	-3	0	-1.2
1887	Ind-N	1	5	.167	6	6	6	0	0	50	47	8.5	1	23	4.1	3	0.5	3.78	109	.263	.347	2	2	101	91	-1.2	-2	0	-0.1
1888	Ind-N	2	5	.286	7	7	6	1	0	56	62	10.0	3	17	2.7	7	1.1	4.66	59	.295	.347	-11	-12	98	85	-0.7	-0	0	-1.0
Total	3	6	29	.171	37	35	33	1	0	304	345	10.2	13	98	2.9	94	2.8	4.00	82	.297	.352	-29	-24	105	101	-8.6	-6	0	-2.3

■ RANDY MOFFITT Moffitt, Randall James b: 10/13/48, Long Beach, Cal. BR/TR, 6'3", 190 lbs. Deb: 6/11/72

YEAR	TM/L	W	L	PCT	G	GS	CG	SHO	SV	IP	H	H/G	HR	BB	BB/G	SO	SO/G	ERA	/A	OAVG	OOBP	PR	/A	PF	CPI	WAT	PB	PD	TPI
1972	SF-N	1	5	.167	40	0	0	0	4	71	72	9.1	5	30	3.8	37	4.7	3.68	94	.266	.339	-2	-2	100	109	-1.8	-1	0	-0.2
1973	SF-N	4	4	.500	60	0	0	0	14	100	86	7.7	9	31	2.8	65	5.9	2.43	158	.225	.282	14	16	104	109	-0.2	-1	-1	1.4
1974	SF-N	5	7	.417	61	1	0	0	15	102	99	8.7	9	29	2.6	49	4.3	4.50	88	.256	.302	-10	-6	109	76	-0.3	2	1	-0.3
1975	SF-N	4	5	.444	55	0	0	0	11	74	73	8.9	6	32	3.9	39	4.7	3.89	95	.257	.330	-2	-2	102	99	-0.4	1	-0	0.0
1976	SF-N	6	6	.500	58	0	0	0	14	103	92	8.0	6	35	3.1	50	4.4	2.27	161	.238	.293	14	16	104	130	0.5	-0	-0	1.6
1977	SF-N	4	9	.308	64	0	0	0	11	88	91	9.3	4	39	4.0	68	7.0	3.58	115	.273	.343	3	5	105	115	-2.2	-0	1	0.6
1978	SF-N	8	4	.667	70	0	0	0	12	82	79	8.7	5	33	3.6	52	5.7	3.29	99	.258	.324	3	-0	91	114	1.7	0	-1	-0.1
1979	SF-N	2	5	.286	28	0	0	0	2	35	53	13.6	5	14	3.6	16	4.1	7.71	45	.356	.406	-15	-16	93	93	-1.2	-0	-0	-1.6
1980	SF-N	1	1	.500	13	0	0	0	0	17	18	9.5	2	4	2.1	10	5.3	4.76	73	.281	.333	-2	-2	96	92	0.1	-0	0	-0.2
1981	SF-N	0	0	—	10	0	0	0	0	11	15	12.3	2	2	1.6	11	9.0	8.18	45	.313	.333	-6	-6	105	66	0.0	0	-0	-0.5
1982	Hou-N	2	4	.333	30	0	0	0	3	42	36	7.7	3	13	2.8	20	4.3	3.00	120	.228	.302	3	3	100	99	-0.8	-0	-1	0.2
1983	Tor-A	6	2	.750	45	0	0	0	10	57	52	8.2	5	24	3.8	38	6.0	3.79	116	.243	.312	2	4	108	95	1.8	0	0	0.4
Total	12	43	52	.453	534	1	0	0	96	782	766	8.8	61	286	3.3	455	5.2	3.65	103	.257	.318	1	8	102	105	-2.8	-1	-2	1.3

■ HERB MOFORD Moford, Herbert b: 8/6/28, Brooksville, Ky. BR/TR, 6'1", 175 lbs. Deb: 4/12/55

YEAR	TM/L	W	L	PCT	G	GS	CG	SHO	SV	IP	H	H/G	HR	BB	BB/G	SO	SO/G	ERA	/A	OAVG	OOBP	PR	/A	PF	CPI	WAT	PB	PD	TPI
1955	StL-N	1	1	.500	14	1	0	0	2	24	29	10.9	5	15	5.6	8	3.0	7.88	52	.299	.388	-10	-10	102	83	0.1	-0	1	-0.8
1958	Det-A	4	9	.308	25	11	6	0	1	110	83	6.8	10	42	3.4	58	4.7	3.60	108	.214	.299	2	3	103	84	-2.5	-4	1	0.1
1959	Bos-A	0	2	.000	4	2	0	0	0	9	10	10.0	3	6	6.0	7	7.0	11.00	37	.286	.390	-7	-7	105	66	-0.9	-0	0	-0.5
1962	NY-N	0	1	.000	7	0	0	0	0	15	21	12.6	3	1	0.6	5	3.0	7.20	59	.318	.319	-5	-5	108	75	-0.4	0	-0	-0.4
Total	4	5	13	.278	50	14	6	0	3	158	143	8.1	21	64	3.6	78	4.4	5.01	79	.244	.322	-21	-18	103	82	-3.7	-5	2	-1.6

■ GEORGE MOGRIDGE Mogridge, George Anthony b: 2/18/1889, Rochester, N.Y. d: 3/4/62, Rochester, N.Y. BL/TL, 6'2", 165 lbs. Deb: 8/17/11

YEAR	TM/L	W	L	PCT	G	GS	CG	SHO	SV	IP	H	H/G	HR	BB	BB/G	SO	SO/G	ERA	/A	OAVG	OOBP	PR	/A	PF	CPI	WAT	PB	PD	TPI
1911	Chi-A	0	2	.000	4	1	0	0	0	13	12	8.3	1	1	0.7	5	3.5	4.85	66	.255	.271	-2	-2	95	53	-0.9	0	0	-0.1
1912	Chi-A	3	4	.429	17	8	2	0	3	65	69	9.6	2	15	2.1	31	4.3	4.02	83	.264	.307	-5	-5	99	74	-0.5	-0	-1	-0.5
1915	NY-A	2	3	.400	6	5	3	1	0	41	33	7.2	0	11	2.4	11	2.4	1.76	165	.219	.285	5	5	99	105	-0.2	-1	-0	0.5
1916	NY-A	6	12	.333	30	21	10	2	0	195	174	8.0	3	45	2.1	66	3.0	2.31	124	.252	.305	11	12	101	114	-3.4	1	1	1.6
1917	NY-A	9	11	.450	29	25	15	1	0	196	185	8.5	5	39	1.8	46	2.1	2.98	96	.255	.301	-7	-3	107	87	-0.2	-2	1	-0.2
1918	NY-A	16	13	.552	**45**	19	13	1	**7**	239	232	8.7	6	43	1.6	62	2.3	2.18	119	.263	.298	15	11	94	122	2.3	1	3	1.6
1919	NY-A	10	7	.588	35	18	13	3	0	169	159	8.5	6	46	2.4	58	3.1	2.77	121	.250	.307	9	11	104	96	0.3	-1	1	1.2
1920	NY-A	5	9	.357	26	15	7	0	1	125	146	10.5	4	36	2.6	35	2.5	4.32	87	.287	.338	-7	-8	99	84	-3.0	-1	1	-0.7
1921	Was-A	18	14	.563	38	36	21	4	0	288	301	9.4	12	66	2.1	101	3.2	3.00	142	.269	.307	41	40	99	106	1.6	-5	2	3.4
1922	Was-A	18	13	.581	34	32	18	3	0	252	300	10.7	12	72	2.6	61	2.2	3.57	105	.304	.347	13	5	93	**125**	4.4	5	-1	0.7
1923	Was-A	13	13	.500	33	30	17	3	1	211	228	9.7	10	56	2.4	62	2.6	3.11	122	.285	.324	20	16	95	122	0.3	1	1	1.8
1924	Was-A	16	11	.593	30	30	13	2	0	213	217	9.2	2	61	2.6	48	2.0	3.76	108	.270	.315	11	7	96	86	0.0	-2	0	0.4
1925	Was-A	3	4	.429	10	8	3	0	0	53	58	9.8	2	18	3.1	12	2.0	4.08	103	.291	.349	2	1	95	107	-1.1	-2	-0	0.0
	StL-A	1	1	.500	2	2	1	0	0	15	17	10.2	2	5	3.0	8	4.8	6.00	79	.279	.338	-3	-2	108	75	0.0	-0	0	-0.1
	Yr	4	5	.444	12	10	4	0	0	68	75	9.9	4	23	3.0	20	2.6	4.50	96	.284	.333	-1	-1	98	75	-1.1	-2	0	-0.1
1926	Bos-N	6	10	.375	39	10	2	0	3	142	173	11.0	6	36	2.3	46	2.9	4.50	74	.311	.342	-11	-18	88	101	-1.1	-1	2	-1.6
1927	Bos-N	6	4	.600	20	1	0	0	5	49	48	8.8	4	15	2.8	26	4.8	3.67	102	.257	.308	1	0	95	97	1.8	-0	1	0.1
Total	15	132	131	.502	398	261	138	20	20	2266	2352	9.3	77	565	2.2	678	2.7	3.23	109	.273	.317	95	73	98	104	0.3	-7	11	8.1

■ GEORGE MOHART Mohart, George Benjamin b: 3/6/1892, Buffalo, N.Y. d: 10/2/70, Silver Creek, N.Y. BR/TR, 5'9", 165 lbs. Deb: 4/15/20

YEAR	TM/L	W	L	PCT	G	GS	CG	SHO	SV	IP	H	H/G	HR	BB	BB/G	SO	SO/G	ERA	/A	OAVG	OOBP	PR	/A	PF	CPI	WAT	PB	PD	TPI
1920	Bro-N	0	1	.000	13	1	0	0	0	36	33	8.3	0	7	1.8	13	3.3	1.75	194	.250	.297	6	7	108	131	-0.4	-0	1	0.8
1921	Bro-N	0	0	—	2	0	0	0	0	7	8	10.3	0	1	1.3	1	1.3	3.86	103	.296	.323	-0	0	105	95	0.0	0	-0	0.0
Total	2	0	1	.000	15	1	0	0	0	43	41	8.6	0	8	1.7	14	2.9	2.09	167	.258	.301	5	7	108	125	-0.4	0	1	0.8

■ DALE MOHORCIC Mohorcic, Dale Robert b: 1/25/56, Cleveland, Ohio BL/TL, 6'3", 220 lbs. Deb: 5/31/86

YEAR	TM/L	W	L	PCT	G	GS	CG	SHO	SV	IP	H	H/G	HR	BB	BB/G	SO	SO/G	ERA	/A	OAVG	OOBP	PR	/A	PF	CPI	WAT	PB	PD	TPI
1986	Tex-A	2	4	.333	58	0	0	0	7	79	86	9.8	5	15	1.7	29	3.3	2.51	159	.279	.314	15	13	95	148	-1.1	0	0	1.3
1987	Tex-A	7	6	.538	74	0	0	0	16	99	88	8.0	11	19	1.7	48	4.4	3.00	155	.244	.279	16	18	104	110	1.0	0	2	1.9
1988	Tex-A	2	6	.250	43	0	0	0	5	52	62	10.7	6	20	3.5	25	4.3	4.85	84	.295	.363	-5	-5	102	110	-1.7	0	0	-0.3
	NY-A	2	2	.500	13	0	0	0	1	23	21	8.2	1	9	3.5	19	7.4	2.74	139	.239	.324	3	3	96	123	0.0	0	-0	0.2
	Yr	4	8	.333	56	0	0	0	6	75	83	10.0	7	29	3.5	44	5.3	4.20	95	.269	.336	-2	-2	100	123	-1.7	0	0	-0.1
Total	3	13	18	.419	188	0	0	0	29	253	257	9.1	23	63	2.2	121	4.3	3.20	132	.266	.313	29	29	100	123	-1.8	0	2	3.1

■ BILL MOISAN Moisan, William Joseph b: 7/30/25, Bradford, Mass. BL/TR, 6'1", 170 lbs. Deb: 9/17/53

YEAR	TM/L	W	L	PCT	G	GS	CG	SHO	SV	IP	H	H/G	HR	BB	BB/G	SO	SO/G	ERA	/A	OAVG	OOBP	PR	/A	PF	CPI	WAT	PB	PD	TPI
1953	Chi-N	0	0	—	3	0	0	0	0	5	5	9.0	0	2	3.6	1	1.8	5.40	84	.278	.364	-1	-0	106	82	0.0	0	0	0.0

YEAR TM/L	W	L	PCT	G	GS	CG	SHO	SV	IP	H	H/G	HR	BB	BB/G	SO	SO/G	ERA	/A	OAVG	OOBP	PR	/A	PF	CPI	WAT	PB	PD	TPI
■ CARLTON MOLESWORTH Molesworth, Carlton b: 2/15/1876, Frederick, Md. d: 7/25/61, Frederick, Md. TL, 5'6", 200 lbs. Deb: 9/14/1895																												
1895 Was-N	0	2	.000	4	3	1	0	0	16	33	18.6	1	15	8.4	7	3.9	14.63	35	.445	.538	-17	-17	105	73	-0.9	-1	0	-1.2
■ RICHIE MOLONEY Moloney, Richard Henry b: 6/7/50, Brookline, Mass. BR/TR, 6'3", 185 lbs. Deb: 9/20/70																												
1970 Chi-A	0	0	—	1	0	0	0	0	1	2	18.0	0	0	0.0	1	9.0	0.00	—	.400	.400	0	0	108	0	0.0	0	0	0.0
■ VINCE MOLYNEAUX Molyneaux, Vincent Leo b: 8/17/1888, Lewiston, N.Y. d: 5/4/50, Stamford, Conn. BR/TR, 6', 180 lbs. Deb: 7/05/17																												
1917 StL-A	0	0	—	7	0	0	0	0	22	18	7.4	0	20	8.2	4	1.6	4.91	53	.237	.396	-5	-6	98	79	0.0	-1	0	-0.5
1918 Bos-A	1	0	1.000	6	0	0	0	0	11	3	2.5	0	8	6.5	1	0.8	3.27	78	.086	.256	-1	-1	93	3	0.5	-0	0	0.0
Total 2	1	0	1.000	13	0	0	0	0	33	21	5.7	0	28	7.6	5	1.4	4.36	60	.189	.353	-6	-6	97	53	0.5	-1	0	-0.5
■ RINTY MONAHAN Monahan, Edward Francis b: 4/28/28, Brooklyn, N.Y. BR/TR, 6'1.5", 195 lbs. Deb: 8/09/53																												
1953 Phi-A	0	0	—	4	0	0	0	0	11	11	9.0	0	7	5.7	2	1.6	4.09	103	.275	.383	-0	0	105	107	0.0	-0	-0	0.0
■ BILL MONBOUQUETTE Monbouquette, William Charles b: 8/11/36, Medford, Mass. BR/TR, 5'11", 190 lbs. Deb: 7/18/58 C																												
1958 Bos-A	3	4	.429	10	8	3	0	0	54	52	8.7	4	20	3.3	30	5.0	3.33	118	.251	.312	3	4	105	103	-0.5	-1	-1	0.3
1959 Bos-A	7	7	.500	34	17	4	0	0	152	165	9.8	15	33	2.0	87	5.2	4.14	98	.285	.319	-5	-1	105	103	0.2	-4	-0	-0.4
1960 Bos-A	14	11	.560	35	30	12	3	0	215	217	9.1	18	68	2.8	134	5.6	3.64	112	.263	.316	5	10	105	100	3.4	-3	-0	0.8
1961 Bos-A	14	14	.500	32	32	12	1	0	236	233	8.9	24	100	3.8	161	6.1	3.39	122	.254	.323	17	19	103	114	1.0	-0	-1	1.8
1962 Bos-A	15	13	.536	35	35	11	4	0	235	227	8.7	22	65	2.5	153	5.9	3.33	123	.251	.300	17	20	103	102	1.9	-3	-4	1.3
1963 Bos-A	20	10	.667	37	36	13	1	0	267	258	8.7	31	42	1.4	174	5.9	3.81	101	.250	.275	-5	2	107	84	6.3	-4	1	0.0
1964 Bos-A	13	14	.481	36	35	7	5	1	234	258	9.9	34	40	**1.5**	120	4.6	4.04	93	.277	.303	-11	-8	103	102	1.1	-2	0	-0.9
1965 Bos-A	10	18	.357	35	35	10	2	0	229	239	9.4	32	40	1.6	110	4.3	3.69	102	.269	.295	-6	2	109	106	-1.0	-3	0	0.0
1966 Det-A	7	8	.467	30	14	2	1	0	103	120	10.5	14	22	1.9	61	5.3	4.72	74	.293	.327	-15	-14	102	101	-1.0	-0	-1	-1.4
1967 Det-A	0	0	—	2	0	0	0	0	2	1	4.5	0	0	0.0	2	9.0	0.00	—	.143	.143	1	1	98	0	0.0	0	0	0.1
NY-A	6	5	.545	33	10	2	1	1	133	122	8.3	6	17	1.2	53	3.6	2.37	131	.246	.272	13	11	96	110	1.1	-0	-1	1.1
Yr	6	5	.545	35	10	2	1	1	135	123	8.2	6	17	1.1	55	3.7	2.33	133	.245	.270	13	11	96	110	1.1	0	-1	1.2
1968 NY-A	5	7	.417	17	11	2	0	0	89	92	9.3	7	13	1.3	32	3.2	4.45	68	.264	.292	-15	-14	101	74	-1.1	-0	1	-1.4
SF-N	0	1	.000	7	0	0	0	1	12	11	8.3	4	2	1.5	5	3.8	3.75	77	.239	.260	-1	-1	96	121	-0.4	0	0	0.0
Total 11	114	112	.504	343	263	78	18	3	1961	1995	9.2	211	462	2.1	1122	5.1	3.69	104	.263	.302	-2	30	104	100	11.0	-21	-6	1.3
■ SID MONGE Monge, Isidro Pedroza b: 4/11/51, Agua Preita, Mexico BB/TL, 6'2", 185 lbs. Deb: 9/12/75																												
1975 Cal-A	0	2	.000	4	2	2	0	0	24	22	8.3	3	10	3.8	17	6.4	4.13	88	.242	.320	-1	-1	96	92	-0.9	-0	-0	-0.1
1976 Cal-A	6	7	.462	32	13	2	0	0	118	108	8.2	10	49	3.7	53	4.0	3.36	98	.248	.322	2	-1	93	109	0.0	-0	-1	-0.1
1977 Cal-A	0	1	.000	4	0	0	0	1	12	14	10.5	2	6	4.5	4	3.0	3.00	129	.304	.357	1	1	95	199	-0.4	0	0	0.1
Cle-A	1	2	.333	33	0	0	0	3	39	47	10.8	6	27	6.2	25	5.8	6.23	64	.309	.398	-9	-10	98	105	-0.3	0	-1	-0.9
Yr	1	3	.250	37	0	0	0	4	51	61	10.8	8	33	5.8	29	5.1	5.47	73	.307	.388	-8	-9	97	105	-0.7	0	-0	-0.8
1978 Cle-A	4	3	.571	48	2	0	0	6	85	71	7.5	4	51	5.4	54	5.7	2.75	128	.225	.326	10	7	94	114	0.9	0	-0	0.7
1979 Cle-A	12	10	.545	76	0	0	0	19	131	96	6.6	9	64	4.4	108	7.4	2.40	187	.209	.297	27	30	106	118	1.1	0	-0	3.0
1980 Cle-A	3	5	.375	67	0	0	0	14	94	80	7.7	12	40	3.8	61	5.8	3.54	118	.227	.307	5	6	103	96	-0.9	0	-1	0.5
1981 Cle-A	3	5	.375	31	0	0	0	4	58	58	9.0	9	21	3.3	41	6.4	4.34	79	.266	.324	-4	-6	93	103	-1.0	0	-1	-0.6
1982 Phi-N	7	1	.875	47	0	0	0	2	72	70	8.8	8	22	2.8	43	5.4	3.75	90	.256	.308	-1	-3	94	101	2.9	-0	1	-0.2
1983 Phi-N	3	0	1.000	14	0	0	0	0	12	20	15.0	4	6	4.5	7	5.3	6.75	54	.377	.426	-4	-4	100	140	1.5	-0	-0	-0.4
SD-N	7	3	.700	47	0	0	0	7	69	65	8.5	4	31	4.0	32	4.2	3.13	115	.257	.331	4	4	99	120	2.1	-0	-0	0.3
Yr	10	3	.769	61	0	0	0	7	81	85	9.4	8	37	4.1	39	4.3	3.67	98	.277	.347	-0	-1	99	120	3.6	-0	-0	-0.1
1984 SD-N	2	1	.667	13	0	0	0	0	15	17	10.2	3	17	10.2	7	4.2	4.80	73	.293	.436	-2	-2	98	160	0.3	-0	-0	-0.2
Det-A	1	0	1.000	19	0	0	0	0	36	40	10.0	5	12	3.0	19	4.8	4.25	89	.282	.340	-1	-2	94	113	0.5	0	-1	-0.2
Total 10	49	40	.551	435	17	4	0	56	765	708	8.3	79	356	4.2	471	5.5	3.53	106	.248	.327	26	19	98	112	5.8	-1	-5	1.9
■ ED MONROE Monroe, Edward Oliver "Peck" b: 2/22/1895, Louisville, Ky. d: 4/29/69, Louisville, Ky. BR/TR, 6'5", 187 lbs. Deb: 5/29/17																												
1917 NY-A	1	0	1.000	9	1	1	0	1	29	35	10.9	1	6	1.9	12	3.7	3.41	84	.310	.355	-2	-2	107	122	0.5	-0	0	-0.1
1918 NY-A	0	0	—	1	0	0	0	0	2	1	4.5	0	2	9.0	1	4.5	4.50	58	.143	.333	-0	-0	94	39	0.0	0	0	0.0
Total 2	1	0	1.000	10	1	1	0	1	31	36	10.5	1	8	2.3	13	3.8	3.48	82	.300	.354	-3	-2	107	117	0.5	-0	0	-0.1
■ LARRY MONROE Monroe, Lawrence James b: 6/20/56, Detroit, Mich. BR/TR, 6'4", 200 lbs. Deb: 8/23/76																												
1976 Chi-A	0	1	.000	8	2	0	0	0	22	23	9.4	0	13	5.3	9	3.7	4.09	87	.284	.375	-1	-1	101	107	-0.4	0	0	0.0
■ ZACH MONROE Monroe, Zachary Charles b: 7/8/31, Peoria, Ill. BR/TR, 6', 198 lbs. Deb: 6/27/58																												
1958 NY-A	4	2	.667	21	6	1	0	1	58	57	8.8	8	27	4.2	18	2.8	3.26	115	.263	.336	3	3	99	140	0.5	-1	0	0.3
1959 NY-A	0	0	—	3	0	0	0	0	3	3	9.0	2	2	6.0	1	3.0	6.00	59	.231	.333	-1	-1	92	133	0.0	0	0	0.0
Total 2	4	2	.667	24	6	1	0	1	61	60	8.9	10	29	4.3	19	2.8	3.39	110	.261	.336	3	2	99	139	0.5	-1	0	0.3
■ JOHN MONTAGUE Montague, John Evans b: 9/12/47, Newport News, Va. BR/TR, 6'2", 213 lbs. Deb: 9/09/73																												
1973 Mon-N	0	0	—	4	0	0	0	0	8	8	9.0	0	2	2.3	7	7.9	3.38	114	.286	.344	0	0	105	114	0.0	-0	-0	0.0
1974 Mon-N	3	4	.429	46	1	0	0	3	83	73	7.9	5	38	4.1	43	4.7	3.14	121	.241	.327	4	6	104	110	-0.4	-0	-2	0.4
1975 Mon-N	0	1	.000	12	0	0	0	2	18	23	11.5	4	6	3.0	9	4.5	5.50	72	.324	.383	-4	-3	109	122	-0.4	-0	-0	-0.2
Phi-N	0	0	—	3	0	0	0	0	5	8	14.4	1	4	7.2	1	1.8	9.00	41	.400	.480	-3	-3	101	108	0.0	0	-0	-0.2
Yr	0	1	.000	15	0	0	0	2	23	31	12.1	5	10	3.9	10	3.9	6.26	62	.326	.387	-7	-6	107	108	-0.4	-0	0	-0.4
1977 Sea-A	8	12	.400	47	15	2	0	4	182	193	9.5	20	75	3.7	98	4.8	4.30	93	.272	.342	-5	-6	98	102	0.1	0	1	-0.4
1978 Sea-A	1	3	.250	19	0	0	0	2	44	52	10.6	2	24	4.9	14	2.9	6.14	64	.308	.384	-12	-11	104	85	-0.5	0	-1	-1.0
1979 Sea-A	6	4	.600	41	1	0	0	1	116	125	9.7	14	47	3.6	60	4.7	5.59	77	.284	.343	-17	-17	101	87	1.7	0	0	-1.5
Cal-A	2	0	1.000	14	0	0	0	6	18	16	8.0	3	9	4.5	6	3.0	5.00	78	.242	.333	-2	-2	92	87	1.0	0	-1	-0.2
Yr	8	4	.667	55	1	0	0	7	134	141	9.5	17	56	3.8	66	4.4	5.51	77	.273	.338	-19	-19	100	87	2.7	0	-0	-1.7
1980 Cal-A	4	2	.667	37	0	0	0	3	74	97	11.8	8	21	2.6	22	2.7	5.11	77	.324	.361	-9	-10	97	108	1.3	0	0	-0.8
Total 7	24	26	.480	223	17	2	0	21	548	595	9.8	57	226	3.7	260	4.3	4.75	84	.283	.348	-46	-45	100	100	2.8	-0	-1	-3.9
■ RAFAEL MONTALVO Montalvo, Rafael Edgardo (Torres) b: 3/31/64, Rio Piedras, P.R. BR/TR, 6', 185 lbs. Deb: 4/13/86																												
1986 Hou-N	0	0	—	1	0	0	0	0	1	1	9.0	0	2	18.0	0	0.0	9.00	42	.250	.500	-1	-1	102	81	0.0	0	0	0.0
■ AURELIO MONTEAGUDO Monteagudo, Aurelio Faustino (Cintra) b: 11/19/43, Caibarien, Cuba BR/TR, 5'11", 180 lbs. Deb: 9/01/63																												
1963 KC-A	0	0	—	4	0	0	0	0	7	4	5.1	0	3	3.9	3	3.9	2.57	154	.182	.250	1	1	109	72	0.0	0	0	0.1
1964 KC-A	0	4	.000	11	6	0	0	0	31	40	11.6	11	10	2.9	14	4.1	9.00	43	.317	.370	-19	-18	108	82	-1.9	1	-0	-1.5
1965 KC-A	0	0	—	4	0	0	0	0	7	5	6.4	1	4	5.1	5	6.4	3.86	89	.185	.290	-0	-0	100	71	0.0	0	-0	0.0
1966 KC-A	0	0	—	6	0	0	0	0	13	12	8.3	0	7	4.8	3	2.1	2.77	118	.261	.352	1	1	95	137	0.0	0	0	0.1
Hou-N	0	0	—	10	0	0	0	1	15	14	8.4	1	11	6.6	7	4.2	4.80	74	.241	.352	-2	-2	99	85	0.0	-0	0	-0.1
1967 Chi-A	0	1	.000	1	1	0	0	0	1	4	36.0	1	2	18.0	0	0.0	27.00	11	.500	.600	-3	-3	93	102	-0.4	0	0	-0.2
1970 KC-A	1	1	.500	21	0	0	0	0	27	20	6.7	2	9	3.0	18	6.0	3.00	123	.200	.270	2	2	100	70	0.2	-0	-0	0.1
1973 Cal-A	2	1	.667	15	0	0	0	3	30	23	6.9	2	16	4.8	8	2.4	4.20	88	.215	.333	-1	-2	96	80	0.5	0	0	-0.1
Total 7	3	7	.300	72	7	0	0	4	131	122	8.4	18	62	4.3	58	4.0	5.08	72	.247	.332	-21	-20	101	84	-1.6	1	-0	-1.6
■ RENE MONTEAGUDO Monteagudo, Rene (Miranda) b: 3/12/16, Havana, Cuba d: 9/14/73, Hialeah, Fla. BL/TL, 5'7", 165 lbs. Deb: 9/06/38																												
1938 Was-A	1	1	.500	5	3	2	0	0	22	26	10.6	3	15	6.1	13	5.3	5.73	80	.286	.387	-2	-3	96	102	0.0	1	-1	-0.1
1940 Was-A	2	6	.250	27	8	3	0	2	101	128	11.4	7	52	4.6	64	5.7	6.06	69	.316	.391	-19	-21	95	98	-1.5	0	-1	-1.9
1945 Phi-N	0	0	—	14	0	0	0	0	46	67	13.1	1	28	5.5	16	3.1	7.43	52	.347	.418	-19	-18	102	89	0.0	2	-1	-1.6
Total 3	3	7	.300	46	11	5	0	2	169	221	11.8	11	95	5.1	93	5.0	6.39	65	.321	.398	-40	-42	97	96	-1.5	4	-2	-3.6
■ JOHN MONTEFUSCO Montefusco, John Joseph "Count" b: 5/25/50, Long Branch, N.J. BR/TR, 6'1", 180 lbs. Deb: 9/03/74																												
1974 SF-N	3	2	.600	7	5	1	1	0	39	41	9.5	3	19	4.4	34	7.8	4.85	82	.256	.335	-5	-4	109	77	0.7	3	-0	-0.1
1975 SF-N	15	9	.625	35	34	10	4	0	244	210	7.7	11	86	3.2	215	**7.9**	2.88	128	.233	.299	20	22	102	96	3.4	-2	-1	2.0
1976 SF-N	16	14	.533	37	36	11	**6**	0	253	224	8.0	11	74	2.6	172	6.1	2.85	128	.238	.289	19	23	104	95	2.5	-2	-3	1.9
1977 SF-N	7	12	.368	26	25	4	0	0	157	170	9.7	10	46	2.6	110	6.3	3.50	117	.273	.318	7	11	105	106	-2.0	-1	-2	0.8

YEAR	TM/L	W	L	PCT	G	GS	CG	SHO	SV	IP	H	H/G	HR	BB	BB/G	SO	SO/G	ERA	/A	OAVG	OOBP	PR	/A	PF	CPI	WAT	PB	PD	TPI
1978	SF-N	11	9	.550	36	36	3	0	0	239	233	8.8	25	68	2.6	177	6.7	3.80	86	.255	.304	-6	-14	91	95	0.0	-3	-2	-1.9
1979	SF-N	3	8	.273	22	22	0	0	0	137	145	9.5	15	51	3.4	76	5.0	3.94	89	.279	.338	-3	-7	93	114	-2.1	2	0	-0.5
1980	SF-N	4	8	.333	22	17	1	0	0	113	120	9.6	15	39	3.1	85	6.8	4.38	79	.265	.323	-10	-11	96	96	-1.7	-2	-1	-1.4
1981	Atl-N	2	3	.400	26	9	0	0	1	77	75	8.8	9	27	3.2	34	4.0	3.51	99	.260	.316	-0	-0	100	114	-0.3	-1	0	0.0
1982	SD-N	10	11	.476	32	32	1	0	0	184	177	8.7	17	41	2.0	83	4.1	4.01	82	.251	.287	-8	-14	92	80	-0.5	-2	-1	-1.7
1983	SD-N	9	4	.692	31	10	1	0	4	95	94	8.9	6	32	3.0	52	4.9	3.32	109	.265	.319	3	3	99	110	2.6	-1	-1	0.1
	NY-A	5	0	1.000	6	6	0	0	0	38	39	9.2	3	10	2.4	15	3.6	3.32	120	.271	.318	3	3	98	117	2.5	0	-1	0.2
1984	NY-A	5	3	.625	11	11	0	0	0	55	55	9.0	5	13	2.1	23	3.8	3.60	103	.253	.295	2	1	93	91	0.8	0	-0	0.0
1985	NY-A	0	0	—	3	1	0	0	0	7	12	15.4	3	2	2.6	2	2.6	10.29	38	.387	.412	-5	-5	94	98	0.0	0	0	-0.3
1986	NY-A	0	0	—	4	0	0	0	0	12	9	6.8	2	5	3.8	3	2.3	2.25	191	.200	.280	3	3	103	131	0.0	0	0	0.3
Total	13	90	83	.520	298	244	32	11	5	1650	1604	8.7	135	513	2.8	1081	5.9	3.55	101	.255	.307	21	9	98	98	5.9	-9	-11	-0.6
■ **MANNY MONTEJO**	Montejo, Manuel (Bofill) b: 10/16/35, Caibarien, Cuba BR/TR, 5'11", 150 lbs. Deb: 7/25/61																												
1961	Det-A	0	0	—	12	0	0	0	0	16	13	7.3	2	6	3.4	15	8.4	3.94	96	.217	.309	0	-0	94	84	0.0	0	-0	0.0
■ **RICH MONTELEONE**	Monteleone, Richard b: 3/22/63, Tampa, Fla. BR/TR, 6'2", 205 lbs. Deb: 4/15/87																												
1987	Sea-A	0	0	—	3	0	0	0	0	7	10	12.9	2	4	5.1	2	2.6	6.43	72	.345	.441	-2	-1	103	137	0.0	0	0	0.0
1988	Cal-A	0	0	—	3	0	0	0	0	4	4	9.0	0	1	2.3	3	6.8	0.00	—	.222	.300	2	2	95	0	0.0	0	0	0.2
Total	2	0	0	—	6	0	0	0	0	11	14	11.5	2	5	4.1	5	4.1	4.09	105	.298	.389	0	0	100	87	0.0	0	0	0.2
■ **JEFF MONTGOMERY**	Montgomery, Jeffrey Thomas b: 1/7/62, Wellston, Ohio BR/TR, 5'11", 170 lbs. Deb: 8/01/87																												
1987	Cin-N	2	2	.500	14	1	0	0	0	19	25	11.8	2	9	4.3	13	6.2	6.63	64	.313	.382	-5	-5	103	86	0.0	-0	0	-0.4
1988	KC-A	7	2	.778	45	0	0	0	1	63	54	7.7	6	30	4.3	47	6.7	3.43	119	.231	.317	4	5	103	105	2.5	0	0	0.5
Total	2	9	4	.692	59	1	0	0	1	82	79	8.7	8	39	4.3	60	6.6	4.17	99	.252	.333	-2	-1	103	100	2.5	-0	0	0.1
■ **MONTY MONTGOMERY**	Montgomery, Monty Bryson b: 9/1/46, Albermarle, N.C. BR/TR, 6'3", 200 lbs. Deb: 9/14/71																												
1971	KC-A	3	0	1.000	3	2	0	0	0	21	16	6.9	0	3	1.3	12	5.1	2.14	159	.205	.232	3	3	98	47	1.5	-0	0	0.3
1972	KC-A	3	3	.500	9	8	1	1	0	56	55	8.8	2	17	2.7	24	3.9	3.05	100	.263	.313	0	0	100	105	0.0	0	-0	0.0
Total	2	6	3	.667	12	10	1	1	0	77	71	8.3	2	20	2.3	36	4.2	2.81	113	.247	.292	3	3	99	89	1.5	0	-0	0.3
■ **RAMON MONZANT**	Monzant, Ramon Segundo (Espina) b: 1/4/33, Maracaibo, Venez. BR/TR, 6', 160 lbs. Deb: 7/02/54																												
1954	NY-N	0	0	—	6	1	0	0	0	8	8	9.0	0	11	12.4	5	5.6	4.50	92	.276	.463	-0	-0	102	141	0.0	-0	-0	0.0
1955	NY-N	4	8	.333	28	12	3	0	0	95	98	9.3	11	43	4.1	54	5.1	3.98	99	.278	.351	1	-0	98	121	-2.2	-1	-1	-0.1
1956	NY-N	1	0	1.000	4	1	1	0	0	13	8	5.5	4	7	4.8	11	7.6	4.15	90	.170	.278	-1	-1	99	85	0.5	-1	0	0.0
1957	NY-N	3	2	.600	24	2	0	0	0	50	55	9.9	6	16	2.9	37	6.7	3.96	101	.286	.336	-0	0	103	119	0.7	0	-1	0.0
1958	SF-N	8	11	.421	43	16	4	1	1	151	160	9.5	21	57	3.4	93	5.5	4.71	84	.273	.336	-13	-13	100	97	-1.9	-1	1	-1.2
1960	SF-N	0	0	—	1	0	0	0	0	1	1	9.0	1	0	0.0	1	9.0	9.00	37	.250	.250	-1	-1	89	105	0.0	0	0	0.0
Total	6	16	21	.432	106	32	8	1	1	318	330	9.3	43	134	3.8	201	5.7	4.36	91	.273	.342	-14	-14	100	108	-2.9	-3	-1	-1.3
■ **LEO MOON**	Moon, Leo "Lefty" b: 6/22/1899, Belmont, N.C. d: 8/25/70, New Orleans, La. BR/TL, 5'11", 165 lbs. Deb: 7/09/32																												
1932	Cle-A	0	0	—	1	0	0	0	0	6	11	16.5	0	7	10.5	1	1.5	10.50	46	.379	.500	-4	-4	107	90	0.0	0	0	-0.2
■ **JIM MOONEY**	Mooney, Jim Irving b: 9/4/06, Mooresburg, Tenn. d: 4/27/79, Johnson City, Tenn BR/TL, 5'11", 168 lbs. Deb: 8/14/31																												
1931	NY-N	7	1	.875	10	8	6	2	0	72	71	8.9	1	16	2.0	38	4.8	2.00	181	.262	.301	15	13	93	149	2.9	-1	-1	1.2
1932	NY-N	6	10	.375	29	18	4	1	0	125	154	11.1	18	42	3.0	37	2.7	5.04	75	.299	.347	-16	-17	98	104	-1.6	-2	-1	-1.9
1933	StL-N	2	5	.286	21	8	2	0	1	77	87	10.2	1	26	3.0	14	1.6	3.74	90	.296	.343	-3	-3	100	109	-1.6	-2	1	-0.4
1934	StL-N	2	4	.333	32	7	1	0	1	82	114	12.5	3	49	5.4	27	3.0	5.49	82	.326	.411	-13	-9	111	112	-1.3	-2	-1	-1.1
Total	4	17	20	.459	92	41	13	3	2	356	426	10.8	23	133	3.4	116	2.9	4.25	90	.298	.354	-18	-17	101	116	-1.6	-7	-3	-2.2
■ **BILL MOONEYHAM**	Mooneyham, William Craig b: 8/16/60, Livermore, Cal. BR/TR, 6', 175 lbs. Deb: 4/19/86																												
1986	Oak-A	4	5	.444	45	6	0	0	2	100	103	9.3	4	67	6.0	75	6.8	4.50	87	.270	.379	-3	-6	94	104	-0.1	0	1	-0.5
■ **BALOR MOORE**	Moore, Balor Lilbon b: 1/25/51, Smithville, Tex. BL/TL, 6'2", 178 lbs. Deb: 5/21/70																												
1970	Mon-N	0	2	.000	6	2	0	0	0	10	14	12.6	0	8	7.2	6	5.4	7.20	57	.368	.458	-3	-3	102	103	-0.9	0	0	-0.2
1972	Mon-N	9	9	.500	22	22	6	3	0	148	122	7.4	15	59	3.6	161	9.8	3.47	103	.226	.304	-0	2	104	93	0.9	-0	0	0.2
1973	Mon-N	7	16	.304	35	32	3	1	0	176	151	7.7	18	109	5.6	151	7.7	4.50	85	.233	.339	-16	-13	105	87	-4.6	-3	-1	-1.6
1974	Mon-N	0	2	.000	8	2	0	0	0	14	13	8.4	1	15	9.6	16	10.3	3.86	98	.245	.412	-0	-0	104	134	-0.9	-0	-0	0.0
1977	Cal-A	0	2	.000	7	3	0	0	0	23	28	11.0	7	10	3.9	14	5.5	3.91	99	.298	.366	0	-0	95	178	-0.9	0	-0	0.0
1978	Tor-A	6	9	.400	37	18	2	0	0	144	165	10.3	16	54	3.4	75	4.7	4.94	78	.294	.356	-19	-17	102	100	0.4	0	1	-1.6
1979	Tor-A	5	7	.417	34	16	5	0	0	139	135	8.7	17	79	5.1	51	3.3	4.86	92	.262	.362	-10	-6	106	101	0.9	0	-1	-0.6
1980	Tor-A	1	1	.500	31	3	0	0	1	65	76	10.5	6	31	4.3	22	3.0	5.26	78	.309	.383	-9	-8	101	107	0.1	0	-0	-0.8
Total	8	28	48	.368	180	98	16	4	1	719	704	8.8	80	365	4.6	496	6.2	4.52	87	.261	.348	-57	-46	103	99	-5.0	-4	-1	-4.6
■ **BRAD MOORE**	Moore, Bradley Alan b: 6/21/64, Loveland, Colo. BR/TR, 6', 185 lbs. Deb: 6/14/88																												
1988	Phi-N	0	0	—	5	0	0	0	0	6	4	6.0	0	4	6.0	2	3.0	0.00	—	.267	.381	2	2	103	0	0.0	0	0	0.3
■ **CARLOS MOORE**	Moore, Carlos Whitman b: 8/13/06, Clinton, Tenn. d: 7/2/58, New Orleans, La. BR/TR, 6'1.5", 180 lbs. Deb: 5/04/30																												
1930	Was-A	0	0	—	4	0	0	0	0	12	9	6.8	0	4	3.0	2	1.5	2.25	203	.225	.277	3	3	98	118	0.0	-1	-0	0.2
■ **DEE MOORE**	Moore, D C b: 4/6/14, Hedley, Tex. BR/TR, 5'11", 190 lbs. Deb: 9/12/36																												
1936	Cin-N	0	0	—	2	1	0	0	0	7	3	3.9	0	2	2.6	3	3.9	0.00	—	.120	.185	3	3	97	0	0.0	1	0	0.3
■ **DONNIE MOORE**	Moore, Donnie Ray b: 2/13/54, Lubbock, Tex. BL/TR, 6', 185 lbs. Deb: 9/14/75																												
1975	Chi-N	0	0	—	4	1	0	0	0	9	12	12.0	1	4	4.0	8	8.0	4.00	96	.316	.381	-0	-0	105	140	0.0	-0	0	0.0
1977	Chi-N	4	2	.667	27	1	0	0	0	49	51	9.4	1	18	3.3	34	6.2	4.04	111	.285	.333	-1	2	115	99	1.0	1	1	0.5
1978	Chi-N	9	7	.563	71	1	0	0	4	103	117	10.2	7	31	2.7	50	4.4	4.11	97	.287	.333	-6	-1	111	102	1.3	1	0	0.0
1979	Chi-N	1	4	.200	39	1	0	0	1	73	95	11.7	8	25	3.1	43	5.3	5.18	81	.321	.370	-12	-8	112	108	-1.4	0	1	-0.6
1980	StL-N	1	1	.500	11	0	0	0	0	22	25	10.2	1	5	2.0	10	4.1	6.14	60	.298	.333	-6	-6	102	69	0.1	2	-1	-0.4
1981	Mil-A	0	0	—	3	0	0	0	0	4	4	9.0	0	4	9.0	2	4.5	6.75	52	.286	.421	-1	-1	95	84	0.0	0	0	0.0
1982	Atl-N	3	1	.750	16	0	0	0	1	28	32	10.3	1	7	2.3	17	5.5	4.18	92	.294	.339	-2	-1	107	99	0.9	-0	0	0.0
1983	Atl-N	2	3	.400	43	0	0	0	6	69	72	9.4	6	10	1.3	41	5.3	3.65	104	.279	.297	-0	1	104	100	-0.6	1	-1	0.2
1984	Atl-N	4	5	.444	47	0	0	0	16	64	63	8.9	3	18	2.5	47	6.6	2.95	133	.258	.303	5	7	110	110	-0.4	-0	0	0.7
1985	Cal-A	8	8	.500	65	0	0	0	31	103	91	8.0	9	21	1.8	72	6.3	1.92	217	.237	.269	**25**	26	101	148	-0.8	0	-1	2.5
1986	Cal-A	4	5	.444	49	0	0	0	21	73	60	7.4	10	22	2.7	53	6.5	2.96	135	.228	.278	10	8	95	112	-0.9	0	-1	0.7
1987	Cal-A	2	2	.500	14	0	0	0	5	27	28	9.3	2	13	4.3	17	5.7	2.67	167	.259	.336	5	5	100	149	0.1	0	-0	0.5
1988	Cal-A	5	2	.714	27	0	0	0	4	33	48	13.1	4	8	2.2	22	6.0	4.91	77	.343	.373	-3	-4	95	125	1.7	0	0	-0.3
Total	13	43	40	.518	416	4	0	0	89	657	698	9.6	53	186	2.5	416	5.7	3.66	111	.276	.319	14	29	105	114	1.0	5	-1	3.8
■ **EARL MOORE**	Moore, Earl Alonzo "Big Ebbie" or "Crossfire" b: 7/29/1879, Pickerington, O. d: 11/28/61, Columbus, Ohio BR/TR, 6', 195 lbs. Deb: 4/25/01																												
1901	Cle-A	16	14	.533	31	30	28	4	0	251	234	8.4	4	107	3.8	99	3.5	2.90	123	.266	.346	21	18	97	107	4.0	-5	-5	1.2
1902	Cle-A	17	17	.500	36	34	29	4	1	293	304	9.3	8	101	3.1	84	2.6	2.95	116	.292	.355	20	16	96	121	-0.2	-0	-1	1.4
1903	Cle-A	19	9	.679	29	27	27	3	1	248	196	**7.1**	0	62	2.3	148	5.4	**1.74**	**161**	**.237**	.290	**33**	29	95	110	4.7	-5	-3	2.9
1904	Cle-A	12	11	.522	26	24	22	1	0	228	186	7.3	2	61	2.4	139	5.5	2.25	113	.244	.300	9	7	98	96	-1.0	-2	-7	0.0
1905	Cle-A	15	15	.500	31	30	28	3	0	269	232	7.8	6	92	3.1	131	4.4	2.64	100	.256	.324	0	0	100	105	0.2	-4	-2	-0.1
1906	Cle-A	1	1	.500	5	4	2	0	0	30	27	8.1	1	18	5.4	8	2.4	3.90	68	.265	.375	-4	-4	99	94	0.0	-1	-1	-0.4
1907	Cle-A	1	1	.500	3	2	1	0	0	19	18	8.5	0	8	3.8	7	3.3	4.74	50	.274	.353	-5	-5	93	64	0.0	-1	0	-0.4
	NY-A	2	6	.250	12	9	3	0	1	64	72	10.1	1	30	4.2	28	3.9	3.94	71	.309	.388	-10	-8	110	106	-1.8	1	-0	-0.8
	Yr	3	7	.300	15	11	4	0	1	83	90	9.8	1	38	4.1	35	3.8	4.12	65	.301	.380	-15	-13	106	106	-1.8	-1	-0	-1.2
1908	Phi-N	2	1	.667	3	3	3	1	0	26	20	6.9	0	8	2.8	16	5.5	0.00	—	.244	.327	7	7	98	0	0.4	0	-1	0.8
1909	Phi-N	18	12	.600	38	34	24	4	0	300	238	7.1	6	108	3.2	173	5.2	2.10	132	.210	.283	17	22	106	87	4.0	-5	-5	1.9
1910	Phi-N	22	15	.595	46	35	18	7	0	283	228	7.3	5	121	3.8	**185**	5.9	2.58	112	.228	.318	14	10	95	99	4.0	3	-3	0.9

YEAR	TM/L	W	L	PCT	G	GS	CG	SHO	SV	IP	H	H/G	HR	BB	BB/G	SO	SO/G	ERA	/A	OAVG	OOBP	PR	/A	PF	CPI	WAT	PB	PD	TPI
1911	Phi-N	15	19	.441	42	36	21	5	1	308	265	7.7	11	164	4.8	174	5.1	2.63	139	.240	.345	26	35	108	**130**	-3.1	-7	-3	2.7
1912	Phi-N	9	14	.391	31	24	10	1	0	182	186	9.2	3	77	3.8	79	3.9	3.31	104	.268	.347	2	2	101	103	-2.3	-4	-2	-0.3
1913	Phi-N	1	3	.250	12	4	0	0	1	52	50	8.7	3	40	6.9	24	4.2	5.02	71	.254	.370	-10	-8	111	88	-1.1	-2	1	-0.9
	Chi-N	1	1	.500	7	2	0	0	0	28	34	10.9	3	12	3.9	12	3.9	4.50	69	.321	.362	-4	-4	97	125	0.0	-0	1	-0.3
	Yr	2	4	.333	19	6	0	0	1	80	84	9.4	6	52	5.8	36	4.0	4.84	70	.276	.365	-15	-13	106	125	-1.1	-2	2	-1.2
1914	Buf-F	11	15	.423	36	27	14	2	2	195	184	8.5	3	99	4.6	96	4.4	4.29	78	.263	.362	-24	-21	104	88	-2.9	-1	-1	-2.2
Total	14	162	154	.513	388	325	230	35	7	2776	2474	8.0	56	1108	3.6	1403	4.5	2.78	111	.252	.330	93	97	100	104	4.9	-32	-32	6.4
■ **EUEL MOORE**	Moore, Euel Walton "Chief" b: 5/27/08, Reagan, Okla. BR/TR, 6'2", 185 lbs. Deb: 7/08/34																												
1934	Phi-N	5	7	.417	20	16	3	0	1	122	145	10.7	9	41	3.0	38	2.8	4.06	111	.288	.335	0	6	111	109	0.4	-4	-2	0.1
1935	Phi-N	1	6	.143	15	8	1	0	1	40	63	14.2	5	20	4.5	15	3.4	7.87	60	.354	.417	-17	-14	117	95	-2.2	1	0	-1.1
	NY-N	1	0	1.000	6	0	0	0	0	8	9	10.1	0	4	4.5	3	3.4	5.63	68	.281	.351	-1	-2	95	74	0.5	-0	0	-0.1
	Yr	2	6	.250	21	8	1	0	1	48	72	13.5	5	24	4.5	18	3.4	7.50	61	.340	.398	-19	-16	113	74	-1.7	1	0	-1.2
1936	Phi-N	2	3	.400	20	5	1	0	1	54	76	12.7	4	12	2.0	19	3.2	7.00	64	.311	.344	-18	-15	111	68	0.2	-0	-1	-1.5
Total	3	9	16	.360	61	29	5	0	3	224	293	11.8	18	77	3.1	75	3.0	5.50	82	.306	.353	-36	-25	111	96	-1.1	-3	-3	-2.6
■ **GENE MOORE**	Moore, Eugene Sr. "Blue Goose" b: 11/9/1885, Lancaster, Tex. d: 8/31/38, Dallas, Tex. BL/TL, 6'2", 185 lbs. Deb: 09																												
1909	Pit-N	0	0	—	1	0	0	0	0	2	4	18.0	0	3	13.5	2	9.0	18.00	14	.364	.500	-3	-3	99	54	0.0	-0	0	-0.2
1910	Pit-N	2	1	.667	4	1	0	0	0	17	19	10.1	1	7	3.7	9	4.8	3.18	105	.268	.333	-0	0	110	112	0.4	-1	0	0.0
1912	Cin-N	0	1	.000	5	2	0	0	1	15	17	10.2	0	11	6.6	6	3.6	4.80	66	.298	.429	-2	-3	93	109	-0.4	-1	-0	-0.2
Total	3	2	2	.500	10	3	0	0	1	34	40	10.6	1	21	5.6	17	4.5	4.76	68	.288	.389	-6	-6	102	107	0.0	-2	0	-0.4
■ **GEORGE MOORE**	Moore, George Raymond b: 11/25/1872, Cambridge, Mass. d: 11/17/48, Hyannis, Mass. BB/TR, 5'10", 165 lbs. Deb: 6/14/05																												
1905	Pit-N	0	0	—	1	0	0	0	0	3	2	6.0	0	0	0.0	1	3.0	0.00	—	.211	.211	1	1	102	0	0.0	-0	-0	0.1
■ **JIM MOORE**	Moore, James Stanford b: 12/14/03, Prescott, Ark. d: 5/19/73, Seattle, Wash. BR/TR, 6', 165 lbs. Deb: 9/21/28																												
1928	Cle-A	0	1	.000	1	1	1	0	0	9	5	5.0	0	5	5.0	1	1.0	2.00	219	.161	.278	2	2	108	63	-0.4	-1	-0	0.2
1929	Cle-A	0	0	—	2	0	0	0	0	6	6	9.0	1	4	6.0	0	0.0	9.00	47	.273	.357	-3	-3	101	62	0.0	-0	0	-0.2
1930	Chi-A	2	1	.667	9	5	2	0	1	40	42	9.4	0	12	2.7	11	2.5	3.60	136	.268	.305	5	6	105	93	0.7	-0	0	0.5
1931	Chi-A	0	2	.000	33	4	0	0	0	84	93	10.0	3	27	2.9	15	1.6	4.93	85	.282	.330	-5	-7	96	85	-0.9	-1	1	-0.6
1932	Chi-A	0	0	—	1	0	0	0	0	1	1	9.0	0	1	9.0	2	18.0	0.00	—	.250	.400	0	0	91	0	0.0	-0	0	0.0
Total	5	2	4	.333	46	10	3	0	1	140	147	9.4	4	49	3.2	29	1.9	4.50	98	.270	.321	-1	-1	99	84	-0.6	-2	1	-0.1
■ **WHITEY MOORE**	Moore, Lloyd Albert b: 6/10/12, Tuscarawas, Ohio d: 12/10/87, Ulrichsville, O. BR/TR, 6'1", 195 lbs. Deb: 9/27/36																												
1936	Cin-N	1	0	1.000	1	0	0	0	0	5	3	5.4	0	3	5.4	4	7.2	5.40	72	.167	.286	-1	-1	97	28	0.5	-0	-0	0.0
1937	Cin-N	0	3	.000	13	6	0	0	0	39	32	7.4	1	39	9.0	27	6.2	4.85	75	.239	.414	-4	-5	93	106	-1.4	-1	-0	-0.5
1938	Cin-N	6	4	.600	19	11	3	1	0	90	66	6.6	4	42	4.2	38	3.8	3.50	104	.205	.298	3	1	96	74	0.6	-2	-1	-0.1
1939	Cin-N	13	12	.520	42	24	9	2	3	188	177	8.5	10	95	4.5	81	3.9	3.45	114	.254	.339	10	10	100	113	-2.4	-4	-1	0.5
1940	Cin-N	8	8	.500	25	15	5	1	1	117	100	7.7	8	56	4.3	60	4.6	3.62	104	.231	.325	3	2	98	100	-1.9	-1	-3	-0.2
1941	Cin-N	2	1	.667	23	4	1	0	0	62	62	9.0	2	45	6.5	17	2.5	4.35	82	.256	.379	-5	-6	98	102	0.3	-1	-1	-0.6
1942	Cin-N	0	0	—	1	0	0	0	0	1	0	0.0	0	1	9.0	0	0.0	0.00	—	.000	.250	0	0	102	0	0.0	0	0	0.0
	StL-N	0	1	.000	9	0	0	0	0	12	10	7.5	0	11	8.3	1	0.8	4.50	75	.217	.379	-2	-1	103	84	-0.4	-0	-0	-0.1
	Yr	0	1	.000	10	0	0	0	0	13	10	6.9	0	12	8.3	1	0.7	4.15	82	.204	.371	-1	-1	102	84	-0.4	0	-0	-0.1
Total	7	30	29	.508	133	60	18	4	4	514	450	7.9	25	292	5.1	228	4.0	3.75	100	.237	.341	5	0	98	100	-4.7	-10	-6	-1.0
■ **MIKE MOORE**	Moore, Michael Wayne b: 11/26/59, Eakly, Okla. BR/TR, 6'4", 205 lbs. Deb: 4/11/82																												
1982	Sea-A	7	14	.333	28	27	1	1	0	144	159	9.9	21	79	4.9	73	4.6	5.38	83	.285	.369	-21	-14	110	102	-3.2	0	1	-1.2
1983	Sea-A	6	8	.429	22	21	3	2	0	128	130	9.1	10	60	4.2	108	7.6	4.71	88	.267	.347	-9	-8	101	92	0.7	0	2	-0.6
1984	Sea-A	7	17	.292	34	33	6	0	0	212	236	10.0	16	85	3.6	158	6.7	4.97	83	.282	.348	-23	-20	103	90	-4.7	0	3	-1.6
1985	Sea-A	17	10	.630	35	34	14	2	0	247	230	8.4	18	70	2.6	155	5.6	3.46	114	.247	.299	19	14	95	94	4.8	0	2	1.6
1986	Sea-A	11	13	.458	38	37	11	1	1	266	279	9.4	28	94	3.2	146	4.9	4.30	104	.273	.336	-3	5	106	103	1.1	0	-1	0.3
1987	Sea-A	9	19	.321	33	33	12	0	0	231	268	10.4	29	84	3.3	115	4.5	4.71	98	.292	.345	-6	-3	103	106	-5.2	0	1	-0.1
1988	Sea-A	9	15	.375	37	32	9	3	1	229	196	7.7	24	63	2.5	182	7.2	3.77	114	.232	.285	5	14	108	82	-1.5	0	1	1.4
Total	7	66	96	.407	227	217	56	9	2	1457	1498	9.3	146	535	3.3	937	5.8	4.38	98	.267	.330	-38	-13	104	96	-8.0	0	9	-0.2
■ **RAY MOORE**	Moore, Raymond Leroy "Farmer" b: 6/1/26, Meadows, Md. BR/TR, 6', 195 lbs. Deb: 8/01/52																												
1952	Bro-N	1	2	.333	14	2	0	0	0	28	29	9.3	3	26	8.4	11	3.5	4.82	76	.274	.416	-3	-4	98	128	-0.6	-0	-0	-0.3
1953	Bro-N	0	1	.000	1	1	1	0	0	8	6	6.8	1	4	4.5	4	4.5	3.38	126	.214	.294	1	1	100	104	-0.4	-0	-0	0.0
1955	Bal-A	10	10	.500	46	14	3	1	6	152	128	7.6	14	80	4.7	80	4.7	3.91	95	.229	.322	1	-3	94	90	2.3	-2	-2	-0.6
1956	Bal-A	12	7	.632	32	27	9	1	0	185	161	7.8	12	99	4.8	105	5.1	4.18	96	.238	.330	-1	-4	97	85	3.4	5	-2	0.0
1957	Bal-A	11	13	.458	34	32	7	1	0	227	196	7.8	17	112	4.4	117	4.6	3.73	94	.236	.322	2	-5	93	93	-1.1	4	-2	-0.4
1958	Chi-A	9	7	.563	32	20	4	2	2	137	107	7.0	10	70	4.6	73	4.8	3.81	97	.220	.311	-1	-2	98	83	0.6	2	-1	0.0
1959	Chi-A	3	6	.333	29	8	0	0	0	90	86	8.6	10	46	4.6	49	4.9	4.10	90	.261	.342	-2	-4	95	111	-2.0	-1	-1	-0.5
1960	Chi-A	1	1	.500	14	0	0	0	0	21	19	8.1	5	11	4.7	3	1.3	5.57	69	.253	.337	-4	-4	99	95	0.0	-0	0	-0.3
	Was-A	3	2	.600	37	0	0	0	13	66	49	6.7	5	27	3.7	29	4.0	2.86	138	.213	.291	7	8	102	97	0.6	-1	-1	0.5
	Yr	4	3	.571	51	0	0	0	13	87	68	7.0	10	38	3.9	32	3.3	3.52	112	.222	.302	3	4	101	97	0.6	-0	-1	0.2
1961	Min-A	4	4	.500	46	0	0	0	14	56	49	7.9	8	38	6.1	45	7.2	3.70	117	.233	.345	2	4	107	121	0.5	0	-0	0.4
1962	Min-A	8	3	.727	49	0	0	0	9	65	55	7.6	8	30	4.2	58	8.0	4.71	87	.231	.313	-5	-4	104	80	2.2	-1	-1	-0.5
1963	Min-A	1	3	.250	31	1	0	0	2	39	50	11.5	8	17	3.9	38	8.8	6.92	51	.309	.374	-14	-15	98	91	-1.0	0	0	-1.4
Total	11	63	59	.516	365	105	24	5	46	1074	935	7.8	101	560	4.7	612	5.1	4.06	93	.238	.327	-18	-33	97	93	4.5	5	-9	-3.1
■ **BARRY MOORE**	Moore, Robert Barry b: 4/3/43, Statesville, N.C. BL/TL, 6'1", 190 lbs. Deb: 5/29/65																												
1965	Was-A	0	0	—	1	0	0	0	0	1	1	9.0	0	1	9.0	0	0.0	0.00	—	.333	.400	0	0	102	0	0.0	0	0	0.0
1966	Was-A	3	3	.500	12	11	1	0	0	62	55	8.0	3	39	5.7	28	4.1	3.77	88	.240	.351	-2	-3	96	103	0.3	-1	0	-0.3
1967	Was-A	7	11	.389	27	26	3	1	0	144	127	7.9	15	71	4.4	74	4.6	3.75	89	.240	.326	-8	-6	104	105	-1.6	-0	1	-0.5
1968	Was-A	4	6	.400	32	18	0	0	3	118	116	8.8	8	42	3.2	56	4.3	3.36	83	.261	.318	-5	-7	94	110	0.0	-1	1	-0.8
1969	Was-A	9	8	.529	31	25	4	0	0	134	123	8.3	12	67	4.5	51	3.4	4.30	81	.246	.330	-10	-12	96	90	0.0	1	-2	-1.2
1970	Cle-A	3	5	.375	13	12	0	0	0	70	70	9.0	8	46	5.9	35	4.5	4.24	101	.262	.368	-4	0	115	114	-0.7	-2	1	0.0
	Chi-A	0	4	.000	24	7	0	0	0	71	85	10.8	12	34	4.3	34	4.3	6.34	63	.302	.383	-21	-18	108	97	-1.9	1	1	-1.6
	Yr	3	9	.250	37	19	0	0	0	141	155	9.9	20	80	5.1	69	4.4	5.30	78	.281	.374	-25	-18	111	97	-2.6	-2	1	-1.6
Total	6	26	37	.413	140	99	8	1	3	600	577	8.7	58	300	4.5	278	4.2	4.16	83	.256	.340	-50	-47	101	102	-3.9	-2	2	-4.4
■ **BOBBY MOORE**	Moore, Robert Devell b: 11/8/58, Sweetwater, La. BR/TR, 6'4", 200 lbs. Deb: 9/11/85																												
1985	SF-N	0	0	—	11	0	0	0	0	17	18	9.5	1	10	5.3	10	5.3	3.18	107	.269	.359	1	0	95	138	0.0	-0	-0	0.0
■ **ROY MOORE**	Moore, Roy Daniel b: 10/26/1898, Austin, Tex. d: 4/5/51, Seattle, Wash. BB/TL, 6', 185 lbs. Deb: 4/15/20																												
1920	Phi-A	1	13	.071	24	14	5	0	0	133	161	10.9	6	64	4.3	45	3.0	4.67	80	.314	.393	-13	-14	99	109	-5.4	-1	-1	-1.2
1921	Phi-A	10	10	.500	29	26	12	0	0	192	206	9.7	4	122	5.7	64	3.0	4.50	102	.280	.372	-5	2	107	100	2.6	3	2	0.8
1922	Phi-A	0	3	.000	15	6	0	0	0	51	65	11.5	1	32	5.6	29	5.1	7.59	57	.319	.408	-20	-19	106	74	-1.4	1	-0	-1.5
	Det-A	0	0	—	9	0	0	0	2	20	29	13.0	0	10	4.5	9	4.0	5.85	67	.367	.454	-4	-4	97	122	0.0	1	0	-0.2
	Yr	0	3	.000	24	6	0	0	2	71	94	11.9	1	42	5.3	38	4.8	7.10	59	.329	.412	-24	-23	104	122	-1.4	1	-0	-1.7
1923	Det-A	0	0	—	3	0	0	0	1	12	15	11.3	0	11	8.3	7	5.3	3.00	126	.288	.413	1	1	95	171	0.0	-0	1	0.1
Total	4	11	26	.297	80	46	17	0	3	408	476	10.5	11	239	5.3	154	3.4	4.96	85	.300	.389	-40	-34	103	103	-4.2	4	4	-2.0
■ **TERRY MOORE**	Moore, Terry Bluford b: 5/27/12, Vernon, Ala. BR/TR, 5'11", 195 lbs. Deb: 4/16/35 MC																												
1939	StL-N	0	0	—	1	0	0	0	0	1	0	0.0	0	0	0.0	1	9.0	0.00	—	.000	.000	0	0	103	0	0.0	0	0	0.0
■ **TOMMY MOORE**	Moore, Tommy Joe b: 7/7/48, Lynwood, Cal. BR/TR, 5'11", 175 lbs. Deb: 9/15/72																												
1972	NY-N	0	0	—	3	1	0	0	0	12	12	9.0	1	1	0.8	5	3.8	3.00	111	.273	.277	1	0	96	111	0.0	0	0	0.1
1973	NY-N	0	1	.000	3	1	0	0	0	3	6	18.0	1	3	9.0	1	3.0	12.00	31	.400	.500	-3	-3	100	99	-0.4	0	0	-0.2

YEAR	TM/L	W	L	PCT	G	GS	CG	SHO	SV	IP	H	H/G	HR	BB	BB/G	SO	SO/G	ERA	/A	OAVG	OOBP	PR	/A	PF	CPI	WAT	PB	PD	TPI
1975	StL-N	0	0	—	10	0	0	0	0	19	15	7.1	2	12	5.7	6	2.8	3.79	99	.203	.314	-0	-0	103	78	0.0	0	0	0.1
	Tex-A	0	2	.000	12	0	0	0	0	21	31	13.3	1	12	5.1	15	6.4	8.14	46	.352	.427	-10	-10	100	83	-0.9	0	0	-0.9
1977	Sea-A	2	1	.667	14	1	0	0	0	33	36	9.8	1	21	5.7	13	3.5	4.91	82	.281	.387	-3	-3	98	100	0.7	0	-1	-0.3
Total	4	2	4	.333	42	3	0	0	0	88	100	10.2	6	49	5.0	40	4.1	5.42	70	.287	.374	-16	-16	100	92	-0.6	1	0	-1.2
■ CY MOORE	Moore, William Austin b: 2/7/05, Elberton, Ga. d: 3/28/72, Augusta, Ga. BR/TR, 6'1", 178 lbs. Deb: 6/07/29																												
1929	Bro-N	3	3	.500	32	4	0	0	2	68	87	11.5	3	31	4.1	17	2.3	5.56	82	.320	.372	-6	-8	96	99	0.2	-0	-1	-0.7
1930	Bro-N	0	0	—	1	0	0	0	0	0	2	—	0	0	—	0	—	—	—	1.000	1.000	0	0	99	0	0.0	0	0	0.0
1931	Bro-N	1	2	.333	23	1	1	0	0	62	62	9.0	5	13	1.9	35	5.1	3.77	104	.262	.307	1	1	101	94	-0.4	-1	0	0.0
1932	Bro-N	0	3	.000	20	2	0	0	0	49	56	10.3	3	17	3.1	21	3.9	4.78	78	.293	.344	-5	-6	96	96	-1.4	0	0	-0.4
1933	Phi-N	8	9	.471	36	18	9	3	1	161	177	9.9	7	42	2.3	53	3.0	3.75	108	.279	.322	-7	5	121	98	1.2	-5	-0	0.1
1934	Phi-N	4	9	.308	35	15	3	0	0	127	163	11.6	11	65	4.6	55	3.9	6.45	70	.309	.383	-34	-28	111	88	-1.2	-3	-1	-2.8
Total	6	16	26	.381	147	40	13	3	3	467	547	10.5	29	168	3.2	181	3.5	4.86	87	.293	.348	-52	-33	109	95	-1.6	-9	-2	-3.8
■ BILL MOORE	Moore, William Christopher b: 9/3/02, Corning, N.Y. d: 1/24/84, Corning, N.Y. BR/TR, 6'3", 195 lbs. Deb: 4/15/25																												
1925	Det-A	0	0	—	1	0	0	0	0	0	0	—	0	3	—	0	—	∞	—	—	1.000	-2	-2	98	46	0.0	0	0	-0.1
■ WILCY MOORE	Moore, William Wilcy "Cy" b: 5/20/1897, Bonita, Tex. d: 3/29/63, Hollis, Okla. BR/TR, 6', 195 lbs. Deb: 4/14/27																												
1927	NY-A	19	7	.731	50	12	6	1	**13**	213	185	**7.8**	2	59	2.5	75	3.2	**2.28**	**170**	**.234**	.282	44	38	94	97	0.9	-6	8	3.9
1928	NY-A	4	4	.500	35	2	0	0	2	60	71	10.7	4	31	4.7	18	2.7	4.20	85	.286	.349	-1	-4	89	111	-0.9	-0	1	-0.2
1929	NY-A	6	4	.600	41	0	0	0	8	61	64	9.4	4	19	2.8	21	3.1	4.13	99	.268	.318	1	-0	97	87	0.4	-2	2	0.0
1931	Bos-A	11	13	.458	53	15	8	1	**10**	185	195	9.5	7	55	2.7	37	1.8	3.89	109	.269	.315	10	7	97	97	1.2	-3	6	0.9
1932	Bos-A	4	10	.286	37	2	0	0	4	84	98	10.5	5	42	4.5	28	3.0	5.25	87	.284	.353	-7	-6	102	93	0.1	-3	3	-0.5
	NY-A	2	0	1.000	10	1	0	0	4	25	27	9.7	1	6	2.2	8	2.9	2.52	162	.273	.308	5	4	91	146	1.0	-1	0	0.3
	Yr	6	10	.375	47	3	0	0	8	109	125	10.3	6	48	4.0	36	3.0	4.62	97	.281	.342	-2	-2	100	146	1.1	-3	3	-0.2
1933	NY-A	5	6	.455	35	0	0	0	8	62	92	13.4	1	20	2.9	17	2.5	5.52	69	.333	.376	-9	-12	88	100	-1.4	-1	0	-1.1
Total	6	51	44	.537	261	32	14	2	49	690	732	9.5	24	232	3.0	204	2.7	3.70	109	.269	.320	44	26	95	99	1.3	-16	20	3.3
■ BOB MOORHEAD	Moorhead, Charles Robert b: 1/23/38, Chambersburg, Pa. d: 12/3/86, Lemoyne, Pa. BR/TR, 6'1", 208 lbs. Deb: 4/11/62																												
1962	NY-N	0	2	.000	38	7	0	0	0	105	118	10.1	13	42	3.6	63	5.4	4.54	94	.289	.355	-7	-3	108	111	-0.9	-1	2	0.0
1965	NY-N	0	1	.000	9	0	0	0	0	14	16	10.3	0	5	3.2	5	3.2	4.50	82	.271	.328	-1	-1	104	74	-0.4	0	0	0.0
Total	2	0	3	.000	47	7	0	0	0	119	134	10.1	13	47	3.6	68	5.1	4.54	93	.287	.352	-9	-4	108	106	-1.3	-1	3	0.0
■ BOB MOOSE	Moose, Robert Ralph b: 10/9/47, Export, Pa. d: 10/9/76, Martins Ferry, Ohio BR/TR, 6', 200 lbs. Deb: 9/19/67																												
1967	Pit-N	1	0	1.000	2	2	1	0	0	15	14	8.4	1	4	2.4	7	4.2	3.60	94	.259	.322	-0	-0	100	100	0.5	1	0	0.1
1968	Pit-N	8	12	.400	38	22	3	3	3	171	136	7.2	5	41	2.2	126	6.6	2.74	109	.218	.263	5	5	100	72	-2.0	-2	2	0.5
1969	Pit-N	14	3	.824	44	19	6	1	4	170	149	7.9	9	62	3.3	165	8.7	2.91	116	.231	.302	13	9	94	97	5.4	-1	1	0.9
1970	Pit-N	11	10	.524	28	27	9	2	0	190	186	8.8	14	64	3.0	119	5.6	3.98	98	.262	.323	2	-2	96	96	-0.5	3	-1	0.0
1971	Pit-N	11	7	.611	30	18	3	1	1	140	169	10.9	12	35	2.3	68	4.4	4.11	82	.301	.334	-10	-12	97	110	0.3	-1	0	-1.2
1972	Pit-N	13	10	.565	31	30	6	3	1	226	213	8.5	11	47	1.9	144	5.7	2.91	119	.248	.285	14	14	100	95	-1.1	2	1	1.9
1973	Pit-N	12	13	.480	33	29	6	3	0	201	219	9.8	11	70	3.1	111	5.0	3.54	95	.280	.337	3	-4	92	113	-0.3	0	2	-0.2
1974	Pit-N	1	5	.167	7	6	0	0	0	36	59	14.8	4	7	1.8	15	3.8	7.50	47	.386	.402	-15	-16	97	96	-2.0	0	2	-1.2
1975	Pit-N	2	2	.500	23	5	1	0	0	68	63	8.3	4	25	3.3	34	4.5	3.71	96	.246	.314	-1	-1	98	87	-0.2	0	1	0.0
1976	Pit-N	3	9	.250	53	2	0	0	10	88	100	10.2	4	32	3.3	38	3.9	3.68	95	.294	.351	-2	-2	99	122	-3.4	2	-0	0.0
Total	10	76	71	.517	289	160	35	13	19	1305	1308	9.0	75	387	2.7	827	5.7	3.50	98	.262	.314	8	-9	97	98	-3.3	4	8	0.8
■ JAKE MOOTY	Mooty, J T b: 4/13/13, Bennett, Tex. d: 4/20/70, Fort Worth, Tex. BR/TR, 5'10.5", 170 lbs. Deb: 9/09/36																												
1936	Cin-N	0	0	—	8	0	0	0	1	14	10	6.4	0	4	2.6	11	7.1	3.86	101	.204	.264	0	0	97	44	0.0	-0	-0	0.0
1937	Cin-N	0	3	.000	14	2	0	0	1	39	54	12.5	2	22	5.1	11	2.5	8.31	44	.327	.398	-19	-20	93	73	-1.4	-1	-0	-1.9
1940	Chi-N	6	6	.500	20	12	6	0	1	114	101	8.0	11	49	3.9	42	3.3	2.92	130	.243	.320	12	11	99	133	0.2	1	-2	1.1
1941	Chi-N	8	9	.471	33	14	7	1	4	153	143	8.4	9	56	3.3	45	2.6	3.35	101	.251	.313	5	1	94	104	0.3	1	1	0.2
1942	Chi-N	2	5	.286	19	10	1	0	1	84	89	9.5	11	44	4.7	28	3.0	4.71	69	.265	.346	-13	-14	98	100	-1.2	0	0	-1.3
1943	Chi-N	0	0	—	2	0	0	0	0	1	2	18.0	0	1	9.0	1	9.0	0.00	—	.400	.500	0	0	98	0	0.0	0	0	0.0
1944	Det-A	0	0	—	15	0	0	0	0	28	35	11.3	0	18	5.8	7	2.3	4.50	79	.310	.394	-3	-3	104	118	0.0	-0	-0	-0.3
Total	7	16	23	.410	111	38	14	1	8	433	434	9.0	33	194	4.0	145	3.0	4.03	87	.263	.335	-18	-25	96	107	-2.1	1	-1	-2.2
■ HIKER MORAN	Moran, Albert Thomas b: 1/1/12, Rochester, N.Y. BR/TR, 6'4.5", 185 lbs. Deb: 9/29/38																												
1938	Bos-N	0	0	—	1	0	0	0	0	3	1	3.0	0	1	3.0	0	0.0	0.00	—	.111	.200	1	1	89	0	0.0	-0	-0	0.1
1939	Bos-N	1	1	.500	6	2	1	0	0	20	21	9.4	3	11	4.9	4	1.8	4.50	81	.276	.356	-1	-2	93	117	0.1	1	-0	-0.1
Total	2	1	1	.500	7	2	1	0	0	23	22	8.6	3	12	4.7	4	1.6	3.91	92	.259	.340	-0	-1	93	102	0.1	0	-0	0.0
■ BILL MORAN	Moran, Carl William "Bugs" b: 9/26/50, Portsmouth, Va. BR/TR, 6'4", 210 lbs. Deb: 4/12/74																												
1974	Chi-A	1	3	.250	15	5	0	0	0	46	57	11.2	5	23	4.5	17	3.3	4.70	79	.302	.389	-5	-5	102	121	-0.9	0	-1	-0.5
■ CHARLIE MORAN	Moran, Charles Barthell "Uncle Charlie" b: 2/22/1878, Nashville, Tenn. d: 6/14/49, Horse Cave, Ky. BR/TR, 5'8", 180 lbs. Deb: 03																												
1903	StL-N	0	1	.000	3	2	2	0	0	24	30	11.3	0	19	7.1	7	2.6	5.25	63	.335	.457	-5	-5	102	107	-0.4	1	-1	-0.3
■ HARRY MORAN	Moran, Harry Edwin b: 4/2/1889, Slater, W.Va. d: 11/28/62, Beckley, W.Va. BL/TL, 6'1", 165 lbs. Deb: 6/23/12																												
1912	Det-A	0	1	.000	5	2	1	0	0	15	19	11.4	1	12	7.2	3	1.8	4.80	67	.339	.471	-2	-3	96	152	-0.4	-0	0	-0.2
1914	Buf-F	10	7	.588	34	16	7	2	2	154	159	9.3	7	53	3.1	73	4.3	4.27	78	.276	.348	-18	-16	104	92	1.2	1	-0	-1.5
1915	New-F	13	9	.591	34	23	13	2	0	206	193	8.4	2	66	2.9	87	3.8	2.53	112	.262	.337	11	7	94	**132**	1.7	1	3	1.1
Total	3	23	17	.575	73	41	21	4	2	375	371	8.9	10	131	3.1	163	3.9	3.34	92	.271	.348	-9	-12	98	117	2.5	1	3	-0.6
■ SAM MORAN	Moran, Samuel b: 9/16/1870, Rochester, N.Y. d: 8/29/1897, Rochester, N.Y. TL, 160 lbs. Deb: 8/28/1895																												
1895	Pit-N	2	4	.333	10	6	6	0	0	63	78	11.1	2	51	7.3	19	2.7	7.57	61	.325	.443	-19	-21	96	79	-1.1	-1	0	-1.5
■ FORREST MORE	More, Forrest b: 9/30/1883, Hayden, Ind. d: 8/17/68, Columbus, Ind. 6', 180 lbs. Deb: 09																												
1909	StL-N	1	5	.167	15	3	1	0	0	50	48	8.6	0	20	3.6	17	3.1	5.04	51	.258	.340	-14	-14	99	62	-1.5	0	1	-1.3
	Bos-N	1	5	.167	10	4	3	0	0	49	47	8.6	0	20	3.7	10	1.8	4.41	60	.270	.359	-10	-10	102	80	-1.2	-1	0	-0.9
	Yr	2	10	.167	25	7	4	0	0	99	95	8.6	0	40	3.6	27	2.5	4.73	55	.262	.342	-23	-23	100	80	-2.7	0	1	-2.2
■ DAVE MOREHEAD	Morehead, David Michael "Moe" b: 9/5/42, San Diego, Cal. BR/TR, 6'1", 185 lbs. Deb: 4/13/63																												
1963	Bos-A	10	13	.435	29	29	6	1	0	175	137	7.0	20	99	5.1	136	7.0	3.81	102	.211	.314	-3	1	107	88	-0.9	-3	1	0.0
1964	Bos-A	8	15	.348	32	30	3	1	0	167	156	8.4	14	112	6.0	139	7.5	4.96	76	.248	.356	-25	-22	103	88	-2.7	-2	-1	-2.5
1965	Bos-A	10	18	.357	34	33	5	2	0	193	157	7.3	18	113	5.3	163	7.6	4.06	93	.217	.323	-13	-6	109	84	-1.0	0	-2	-0.7
1966	Bos-A	1	2	.333	12	5	0	0	0	28	31	10.0	7	7	2.3	20	6.4	5.46	69	.274	.311	-6	-5	110	94	-0.3	1	-0	-0.4
1967	Bos-A	5	4	.556	10	9	1	1	0	48	48	9.0	0	22	4.1	40	7.5	4.31	85	.264	.346	-6	-4	113	85	0.0	-1	-1	-0.4
1968	Bos-A	1	4	.200	11	9	3	1	0	55	52	8.5	3	20	3.3	28	4.6	2.45	122	.249	.318	3	3	101	137	-1.5	-0	-1	0.2
1969	KC-A	2	3	.400	21	2	0	0	0	33	28	7.6	3	28	7.6	32	8.7	5.73	66	.239	.378	-8	-7	104	99	-0.1	0	-0	-0.7
1970	KC-A	3	5	.375	28	17	1	0	1	122	121	8.9	9	62	4.6	69	5.1	3.61	102	.261	.343	1	1	100	113	-0.2	0	-2	0.0
Total	8	40	64	.385	177	134	19	6	1	821	730	8.0	78	463	5.1	627	6.9	4.14	90	.237	.334	-56	-39	105	94	-6.7	-5	-6	-4.5
■ SETH MOREHEAD	Morehead, Seth Marvin "Moe" b: 8/15/34, Houston, Tex. BL/TL, 6'0.5", 195 lbs. Deb: 4/27/57																												
1957	Phi-N	1	1	.500	34	1	1	0	1	59	57	8.7	1	20	3.1	36	5.5	3.66	105	.254	.312	1	1	99	84	0.0	-1	-1	0.0
1958	Phi-N	1	6	.143	27	11	0	0	0	92	121	11.8	8	26	2.5	54	5.3	5.87	67	.319	.356	-20	-20	100	87	-2.3	0	-2	-1.9
1959	Phi-N	0	2	.000	3	3	0	0	0	10	15	13.5	3	3	2.7	8	7.2	9.90	41	.333	.388	-7	-7	102	76	-0.9	-0	0	-0.5
	Chi-N	0	1	.000	11	2	0	0	0	19	25	11.8	1	8	3.8	9	4.3	4.74	82	.313	.375	-2	-2	99	107	-0.4	1	-1	-0.1
	Yr	0	3	.000	14	5	0	0	0	29	40	12.4	4	11	3.4	17	5.3	6.52	60	.317	.372	-8	-8	100	107	-1.3	-0	-1	-0.6
1960	Chi-N	2	9	.182	45	7	2	0	4	123	123	9.0	17	46	3.4	64	4.7	3.95	96	.258	.322	-3	-2	101	106	-2.9	-1	-0	-0.2
1961	Mil-N	1	0	1.000	12	0	0	0	0	15	16	9.6	4	7	4.2	13	7.8	6.60	56	.271	.343	-4	-5	91	89	0.5	0	-0	-0.4
Total	5	5	19	.208	132	24	3	0	5	318	357	10.1	34	110	3.1	184	5.2	4.81	80	.282	.337	-33	-34	100	95	-6.0	-1	-3	-3.1

YEAR	TM/L	W	L	PCT	G	GS	CG	SHO	SV	IP	H	H/G	HR	BB	BB/G	SO	SO/G	ERA	/A	OAVG	OOBP	PR	/A	PF	CPI	WAT	PB	PD	TPI
■ LEW MOREN	Moren, Lewis Howard "Hicks" b: 8/4/1883, Pittsburgh, Pa. d: 11/2/66, Pittsburgh, Pa. TR, 5'11", 150 lbs. Deb: 03																												
1903	Pit-N	0	1	.000	1	1	1	0	0	6	9	13.5	0	2	3.0	2	3.0	9.00	37	.389	.460	-4	-4	101	66	-0.4	-0	0	-0.2
1904	Pit-N	0	0	—	1	0	0	0	0	4	7	15.8	1	4	9.0	0	0.0	9.00	30	.435	.569	-3	-3	98	125	0.0	-0	0	-0.1
1907	Phi-N	11	18	.379	37	31	21	3	1	255	202	7.1	3	101	3.6	98	3.5	2.54	100	.246	.335	-2	-0	103	92	-5.4	-3	-1	0.0
1908	Phi-N	8	9	.471	28	16	9	4	0	154	146	8.5	1	49	2.9	72	4.2	2.92	79	.280	.344	-10	-11	98	97	-1.1	2	0	-1.1
1909	Phi-N	16	15	.516	40	31	19	2	1	258	226	7.9	6	93	3.2	110	3.8	2.65	104	.239	.309	-1	3	106	98	1.2	-3	-5	-0.1
1910	Phi-N	13	14	.481	34	26	12	2	1	205	207	9.1	6	82	3.6	74	3.2	3.56	81	.269	.347	-12	-15	95	100	-0.8	-1	-0	-1.6
Total	6	48	57	.457	141	105	62	11	3	882	797	8.1	17	331	3.4	356	3.6	2.95	90	.257	.334	-32	-29	101	97	-6.5	-5	-5	-3.1
■ ANGEL MORENO	Moreno, Angel (Veneroso) b: 6/6/55, La Mendosa Soledad Mex. BL/TL, 5'9", 165 lbs. Deb: 8/15/81																												
1981	Cal-A	1	3	.250	8	4	1	0	0	31	27	7.8	2	14	4.1	12	3.5	2.90	131	.233	.313	3	3	104	109	-0.8	0	-0	0.3
1982	Cal-A	3	7	.300	13	8	2	0	1	49	55	10.1	7	23	4.2	22	4.0	4.78	84	.288	.362	-4	-4	99	112	-2.4	0	0	-0.3
Total	2	4	10	.286	21	12	3	0	1	80	82	9.2	9	37	4.2	34	3.8	4.05	97	.267	.344	-1	-1	101	111	-3.2	0	-0	0.0
■ JULIO MORENO	Moreno, Julio (Gonzalez) b: 1/28/21, Guines, Cuba d: 1/2/87, Miami, Fla. BR/TR, 5'8", 165 lbs. Deb: 9/08/50																												
1950	Was-A	1	1	.500	4	3	1	0	0	21	22	9.4	1	12	5.1	7	3.0	4.71	98	.268	.368	-0	-0	101	95	0.1	-1	0	0.0
1951	Was-A	5	11	.313	31	18	5	0	2	133	132	8.9	18	80	5.4	37	2.5	4.87	82	.256	.356	-11	-13	97	99	-1.8	-1	0	-1.3
1952	Was-A	9	9	.500	26	22	7	0	0	147	154	9.4	10	52	3.2	62	3.8	3.98	93	.270	.333	-5	-5	100	100	0.0	-2	-1	-0.7
1953	Was-A	3	1	.750	12	2	1	0	0	35	41	10.5	2	13	3.3	13	3.3	2.83	131	.291	.346	5	3	93	156	1.0	-1	-0	0.2
Total	4	18	22	.450	73	45	14	0	2	336	349	9.3	31	157	4.2	119	3.2	4.26	91	.267	.346	-12	-14	98	105	-0.7	-5	-1	-1.8
■ ROGELIO MORET	Moret, Rogelio (Torres) b: 9/16/49, Guayama, P.R. BB/TL, 6'4", 170 lbs. Deb: 9/13/70																												
1970	Bos-A	1	0	1.000	3	1	0	0	0	8	7	7.9	0	4	4.5	2	2.3	3.38	121	.226	.314	0	1	110	73	0.5	-0	0	0.0
1971	Bos-A	4	3	.571	13	7	4	1	0	71	50	6.3	5	40	5.1	47	6.0	2.92	125	.205	.316	4	6	105	103	0.4	-1	-0	0.5
1972	Bos-A	0	0	—	3	0	0	0	0	5	5	9.0	0	6	10.8	4	7.2	3.60	90	.263	.440	-0	-0	105	151	0.0	-0	-0	0.0
1973	Bos-A	13	2	.867	30	15	5	2	3	156	138	8.0	19	67	3.9	90	5.2	3.17	126	.238	.316	11	14	105	116	5.4	0	-0	1.5
1974	Bos-A	9	10	.474	31	21	10	1	2	173	158	8.2	15	79	4.1	111	5.8	3.75	103	.243	.321	-2	2	106	95	-0.8	0	-2	0.0
1975	Bos-A	14	3	.824	36	16	4	1	1	145	132	8.2	8	76	4.7	80	5.0	3.60	113	.248	.337	3	8	108	102	5.0	0	-1	0.6
1976	Atl-N	3	5	.375	27	12	1	0	1	77	84	9.8	7	27	3.2	30	3.5	5.03	78	.280	.334	-13	-9	112	86	-0.5	-1	-0	-1.0
1977	Tex-A	3	3	.500	18	8	0	0	4	72	59	7.4	6	38	4.8	39	4.9	3.75	112	.220	.308	3	4	104	83	-0.3	0	-1	0.2
1978	Tex-A	0	1	.000	7	2	0	0	1	15	23	13.8	1	2	1.2	5	3.0	4.80	75	.390	.400	-2	-2	96	140	-0.4	0	-0	-0.1
Total	9	47	27	.635	168	82	24	5	12	722	656	8.2	61	339	4.2	408	5.1	3.66	108	.245	.325	4	23	106	101	9.3	-3	-5	1.7
■ DAVE MOREY	Morey, David Beale b: 2/25/1889, Malden, Mass. d: 1/4/86, Oak Bluff, Mass. BL/TR, 6', 185 lbs. Deb: 7/04/13																												
1913	Phi-A	0	0	—	2	0	0	0	0	4	2	4.5	0	2	4.5	1	2.3	4.50	60	.182	.357	-1	-1	93	60	0.0	-0	0	0.0
■ CY MORGAN	Morgan, Cyril Arlon b: 12/11/1896, Lakeville, Mass. d: 9/11/46, Lakeville, Mass. BR/TR, 6', 170 lbs. Deb: 6/08/21																												
1921	Bos-N	1	1	.500	17	0	0	0	1	30	37	11.1	0	17	5.1	8	2.4	6.60	53	.314	.393	-9	-10	92	76	0.0	-1	1	-0.9
1922	Bos-N	0	0	—	2	0	0	0	0	1	8	72.0	0	2	18.0	0	0.0	36.00	11	.667	.714	-4	-4	98	109	0.0	0	0	-0.2
Total	2	1	1	.500	19	0	0	0	1	31	45	13.1	0	19	5.5	8	2.3	7.55	47	.346	.422	-13	-14	93	77	0.0	-1	1	-1.1
■ DAN MORGAN	Morgan, Daniel b: 5/1855, Missouri Deb: 5/04/1875																												
1875	RS-n	1	3	.250	5																								
■ CY MORGAN	Morgan, Harry Richard b: 11/10/1878, Pomeroy, Ohio d: 6/28/62, Wheeling, W.Va. BR/TR, 6', 175 lbs. Deb: 03																												
1903	StL-A	0	2	.000	2	1	1	0	0	13	12	8.3	0	6	4.2	6	4.2	4.15	68	.266	.353	-2	-2	96	76	-0.9	0	-0	-0.1
1904	StL-A	0	2	.000	8	3	2	0	0	51	51	9.0	3	10	1.8	24	4.2	3.71	68	.284	.321	-6	-7	98	88	-0.9	-2	1	-0.5
1905	StL-A	2	5	.286	13	8	5	1	0	77	82	9.6	1	37	4.3	44	5.1	3.62	68	.298	.381	-8	-10	93	113	-0.6	2	2	-0.8
1907	StL-A	2	5	.286	10	6	4	0	0	55	77	12.6	3	17	2.8	14	2.3	6.05	41	.358	.405	-21	-22	98	88	-1.2	-1	1	-1.9
	Bos-A	6	6	.500	16	13	9	2	0	114	77	6.1	1	34	2.7	50	3.9	1.97	133	.212	.279	7	8	103	74	1.1	-4	-1	0.8
	Yr	8	11	.421	26	19	13	2	0	169	154	8.2	4	51	2.7	64	3.4	3.30	78	.266	.326	-14	-14	101	74	-0.1	-1	1	-1.1
1908	Bos-A	14	13	.519	30	26	17	2	1	205	166	7.3	7	90	4.0	99	4.3	2.46	94	.226	.319	-2	-3	97	119	1.0	-3	1	-0.2
1909	Bos-A	2	6	.250	12	10	5	0	1	65	52	7.2	0	31	4.3	30	4.2	2.35	114	.240	.350	1	2	108	125	-2.2	-2	2	0.5
	Phi-A	16	11	.593	28	26	21	5	0	229	152	6.0	3	71	2.8	81	3.2	1.65	146	.191	.271	21	19	97	80	-0.6	-3	-1	2.1
	Yr	18	17	.514	40	36	26	5	1	294	204	**6.2**	3	102	3.1	111	3.4	1.81	137	**.200**	.283	22	22	100	80	-2.8	-2	1	2.6
1910	Phi-A	18	12	.600	36	34	23	3	0	291	214	6.6	0	117	3.6	134	4.1	1.55	158	.216	.310	31	29	97	**142**	-2.0	-4	1	3.0
1911	Phi-A	15	7	.682	38	30	15	2	1	250	217	7.8	0	113	4.1	136	4.9	2.70	109	.243	.341	18	7	88	109	0.5	-4	3	0.5
1912	Phi-A	3	8	.273	16	14	5	0	0	94	75	7.2	0	51	4.9	47	4.5	3.73	87	.226	.338	-4	-5	97	78	-3.0	-3	2	-0.2
1913	Cin-N	0	1	.000	1	1	0	0	0	2	5	22.5	0	1	4.5	2	9.0	18.00	18	.500	.583	-3	-3	104	72	-0.4	-0	0	-0.2
Total	10	78	78	.500	210	172	107	15	3	1446	1180	7.3	18	578	3.6	667	4.2	2.51	104	.234	.322	32	16	96	107	-9.2	-24	12	3.0
■ BILL MORGAN	Morgan, Henry William b: 10/1857, Washington, D.C. Deb: N/A.																												
1884	Ric-a	2	3	.400	5	5	5	0	0	39	37	8.5	0	2	0.5	35	8.1	4.15	80	.258	.269	-4	-4	102	62	0.4	-0	0	-1.3
■ MIKE MORGAN	Morgan, Michael Thomas b: 10/8/59, Tulare, Cal. BR/TR, 6'3", 195 lbs. Deb: 6/11/78																												
1978	Oak-A	0	3	.000	3	3	1	0	0	12	19	14.3	1	8	6.0	0	0.0	7.50	52	.373	.450	-5	-5	103	104	-1.4	0	1	-0.3
1979	Oak-A	2	10	.167	13	13	2	0	0	77	102	11.9	7	50	5.8	17	2.0	5.96	65	.332	.421	-15	-18	91	113	-3.0	0	1	-1.5
1982	NY-A	7	11	.389	30	23	2	0	0	150	167	10.0	15	67	4.0	71	4.3	4.38	90	.285	.357	-5	-7	97	111	-1.9	0	1	-0.6
1983	Tor-A	0	3	.000	16	4	0	0	0	45	48	9.6	6	21	4.2	22	4.4	5.20	84	.273	.348	-6	-4	108	92	-1.4	0	1	-0.3
1985	Sea-A	1	1	.500	2	2	0	0	0	6	11	16.5	2	5	7.5	2	3.0	12.00	33	.393	.485	-5	-5	95	93	0.1	0	0	-0.4
1986	Sea-A	11	17	.393	37	33	9	1	1	216	243	10.1	24	86	3.6	116	4.8	4.54	98	.286	.350	-9	-2	106	106	-0.7	0	-0	-0.2
1987	Sea-A	12	17	.414	34	31	8	2	0	207	245	10.7	25	53	2.3	85	3.7	4.65	99	.296	.337	-4	-1	103	105	-2.3	0	1	0.0
1988	Bal-A	1	6	.143	22	10	2	0	1	71	70	8.9	6	23	2.9	29	3.7	5.45	71	.255	.314	-12	-12	97	67	-1.9	0	0	-1.1
Total	8	34	68	.333	157	119	24	3	2	784	905	10.4	86	313	3.6	342	3.9	4.90	87	.292	.356	-60	-55	101	103	-12.5	0	4	-4.4
■ TOM MORGAN	Morgan, Tom Stephen "Plowboy" b: 5/20/30, El Monte, Cal. d: 1/13/87, Anaheim, Cal. BR/TR, 6'1", 180 lbs. Deb: 4/20/51 C																												
1951	NY-A	9	3	.750	27	16	4	2	2	125	119	8.6	11	36	2.6	57	4.1	3.67	99	.253	.306	6	-0	88	97	2.0	2	1	0.3
1952	NY-A	5	4	.556	16	12	2	1	2	94	86	8.2	8	33	3.2	35	3.4	3.06	113	.252	.322	6	4	95	122	-0.4	1	3	0.8
1954	NY-A	11	5	.688	32	17	7	4	1	143	149	9.4	8	40	2.5	34	2.1	3.34	105	.274	.322	6	3	94	111	0.5	-0	3	0.5
1955	NY-A	7	3	.700	40	1	0	0	10	72	72	9.0	3	24	3.0	17	2.1	3.25	115	.267	.329	6	4	94	114	1.1	0	2	0.7
1956	NY-A	6	7	.462	41	0	0	0	11	71	74	9.4	2	27	3.4	20	2.5	4.18	94	.284	.342	-0	-2	95	100	-1.8	-0	1	0.0
1957	KC-A	9	7	.563	46	13	5	0	7	144	160	10.0	19	61	3.8	32	2.0	4.63	83	.299	.362	-13	-12	102	116	2.5	-2	4	-1.0
1958	Det-A	2	5	.286	39	1	0	0	1	63	70	10.0	7	4	0.6	32	4.6	3.14	123	.286	.293	4	5	103	122	-1.4	-0	-0	0.5
1959	Det-A	1	4	.200	46	1	0	0	9	93	94	9.1	11	18	1.7	39	3.8	3.97	108	.265	.306	-1	3	111	99	-1.4	4	-0	0.7
1960	Det-A	3	2	.600	22	0	0	0	1	29	33	10.2	6	10	3.1	12	3.7	4.66	85	.295	.339	-3	-2	102	119	0.7	0	0	-0.1
	Was-A	1	3	.250	14	0	0	0	0	24	36	13.5	6	5	1.9	11	4.1	3.75	106	.343	.372	0	1	102	187	-0.9	-1	0	0.0
	Yr	4	5	.444	36	0	0	0	1	53	69	11.7	12	15	2.5	23	3.9	4.25	93	.315	.354	-2	-2	102	187	-0.2	0	0	-0.1
1961	LA-A	8	2	.800	59	0	0	0	10	92	74	7.2	7	17	1.7	39	3.8	2.35	192	.224	.264	17	**22**	112	107	3.3	-1	1	2.2
1962	LA-A	5	2	.714	48	0	0	0	9	59	53	8.1	6	19	2.9	29	4.4	2.90	140	.247	.302	7	8	102	124	1.4	-1	-1	0.6
1963	LA-A	0	0	—	13	0	0	0	1	16	20	11.3	1	6	3.4	7	3.9	5.63	60	.313	.382	-4	-4	92	100	0.0	-0	-0	-0.4
Total	12	67	47	.588	443	61	18	7	64	1025	1040	9.1	95	300	2.6	364	3.2	3.60	107	.270	.321	33	29	99	112	5.6	2	13	4.8
■ GENE MORIARITY	Moriarity, Eugene John b: Holyoke, Mass. BL/TL, 5'8", 190 lbs. Deb: 6/18/1884																												
1884	Ind-a	0	2	.000	2	2	2	0	0	14	16	10.3	0	7	4.5	4	2.6	5.79	56	.296	.376	-4	-4	100	83	-0.9	0	0	-0.2
1885	Det-N	0	0	—	1	0	0	0	0	2	3	13.5	0	1	4.5	1	4.5	9.00	31	.358	.427	-1	-1	99	68	0.0	-0	0	0.0
Total	2	0	2	.000	3	2	2	0	0	16	19	10.7	0	8	4.5	5	2.8	6.19	52	.304	.383	-5	-5	100	81	-0.9	-0	0	-0.2
■ JOHN MORLAN	Morlan, John Glen b: 11/22/47, Columbus, Ohio BR/TR, 6', 178 lbs. Deb: 7/20/73																												
1973	Pit-N	2	2	.500	10	7	1	0	0	41	42	9.2	4	23	5.0	23	5.0	3.95	85	.276	.359	-1	-3	92	122	0.0	1	-1	-0.2
1974	Pit-N	0	3	.000	39	0	0	0	0	65	54	7.5	2	48	6.6	38	5.3	4.29	82	.227	.354	-5	-6	97	85	-1.4	-1	-1	-0.6

YEAR	TM/L	W	L	PCT	G	GS	CG	SHO	SV	IP	H	H/G	HR	BB	BB/G	SO	SO/G	ERA	/A	OAVG	OOBP	PR	/A	PF	CPI	WAT	PB	PD	TPI
Total	2	2	5	.286	49	7	1	0	0	106	96	8.2	6	71	6.0	61	5.2	4.16	83	.246	.356	-6	-8	95	99	-1.4	0	-1	-0.8
■ DAN MOROGIELLO	Morogiello, Daniel Joseph b: 3/26/55, Brooklyn, N.Y. BL/TL, 6'1", 200 lbs. Deb: 5/20/83																												
1983	Bal-A	0	1	.000	22	0	0	0	1	38	39	9.2	1	10	2.4	15	3.6	2.37	170	.265	.313	7	7	99	139	-0.4	0	-1	0.6
■ JIM MORONEY	Moroney, James Francis b: 12/4/1885, Boston, Mass. d: 2/26/29, Philadelphia, Pa. BL/TL, Deb: 4/24/06																												
1906	Bos-N	0	3	.000	3	3	3	0	0	27	28	9.3	1	12	4.0	11	3.7	5.33	52	.315	.431	-8	-8	106	84	-1.4	-1	0	-0.6
1910	Phi-N	1	2	.333	12	2	1	0	1	42	43	9.2	1	11	2.4	13	2.8	2.14	135	.295	.360	4	3	95	186	-0.4	-1	-0	0.2
1912	Chi-N	1	1	.500	10	3	1	0	1	24	25	9.4	0	17	6.4	5	1.9	4.50	77	.294	.434	-3	-3	102	116	-0.1	1	-0	-0.1
Total	3	2	6	.250	25	8	5	0	2	93	96	9.3	2	40	3.9	29	2.8	3.68	82	.300	.401	-7	-7	100	138	-1.9	-1	-0	-0.5
■ BILL MORRELL	Morrell, Willard Blackmer b: 4/9/1900, Boston, Mass. d: 8/5/75, Brimingham, Ala. BR/TR, 6', 172 lbs. Deb: 4/20/26																												
1926	Was-A	3	3	.500	26	2	1	0	1	70	83	10.7	5	29	3.7	16	2.1	5.27	74	.311	.370	-10	-11	97	99	-0.1	1	-1	-0.9
1930	NY-N	0	0	—	2	0	0	0	0	8	6	6.8	0	1	1.1	3	3.4	1.13	423	.214	.241	3	3	96	130	0.0	-0	0	0.3
1931	NY-N	5	3	.625	20	7	2	0	1	66	83	11.3	4	27	3.7	16	2.2	4.36	83	.306	.365	-4	-6	93	115	0.5	-0	-0	-0.5
Total	3	8	6	.571	48	9	3	0	2	144	172	10.8	9	57	3.6	35	2.2	4.63	83	.304	.362	-10	-13	95	108	0.4	0	-1	-1.1
■ JOHN MORRILL	Morrill, John Francis "Honest John" b: 2/19/1855, Boston, Mass. d: 4/2/32, Boston, Mass. BR/TR, 5'10.5", 155 lbs. Deb: 4/24/1876 M																												
1880	Bos-N	0	0	—	3	0	0	0	0	11	9	7.4	0	1	0.8	0	0.0	0.82	269	.232	.251	2	2	93	167	0.0	0	0	0.2
1881	Bos-N	0	1	.000	3	0	0	0	1	6	9	13.5	0	1	1.5	0	0.0	7.50	34	.359	.384	-3	-3	93	65	-0.4	1	0	-0.2
1882	Bos-N	0	0	—	1	0	0	0	0	2	3	13.5	0	0	0.0	2	9.0	0.00	—	.354	.354	1	1	102	0	0.0	0	0	0.1
1883	Bos-N	1	0	1.000	2	1	1	0	0	13	15	10.4	0	4	2.8	5	3.5	2.77	115	.297	.349	1	1	102	134	0.5	1	0	0.1
1884	Bos-N	0	1	.000	7	1	1	0	**2**	23	34	13.3	0	6	2.3	13	5.1	7.43	37	.353	.391	-11	-12	93	69	-0.4	2	0	-0.9
1886	Bos-N	0	0	—	1	0	0	0	0	4	5	11.3	0	0	0.0	2	4.5	0.00	—	.320	.320	1	1	97	0	0.0	0	0	0.1
1889	Was-N	0	0	—	1	0	0	0	0	⅓	0	0.0	0	0	0.0	0	0.0	0.00	—	—	—	0	0	96	0	0.0	0	0	0.0
Total	7	1	2	.333	18	2	2	0	3	59	75	11.4	0	12	1.8	22	3.4	4.42	63	.319	.352	-10	-11	96	94	-0.3	4	0	-0.6
■ DANNY MORRIS	Morris, Danny Walker b: 6/11/46, Greenville, Ky. BR/TR, 6'1", 200 lbs. Deb: 9/10/68																												
1968	Min-A	0	1	.000	3	2	0	0	0	11	11	9.0	0	4	3.3	6	4.9	1.64	193	.262	.326	2	2	106	194	-0.4	-0	0	0.2
1969	Min-A	0	1	.000	3	1	0	0	0	5	5	9.0	1	4	7.2	1	1.8	5.40	67	.238	.346	-1	-1	100	93	-0.4	0	0	0.0
Total	2	0	2	.000	6	3	0	0	0	16	16	9.0	1	8	4.5	7	3.9	2.81	118	.254	.333	1	1	104	162	-0.8	-0	0	0.2
■ E. MORRIS	Morris, E. b: Trenton, N.J. Deb: 9/11/1884																												
1884	Bal-U	0	0	—	1	0	0	0	0	1	2	18.0	0	2	18.0	0	0.0	9.00	37	.420	.591	-1	-1	110	143	0.0	-1	0	0.0
■ ED MORRIS	Morris, Edward "Cannonball" b: 9/29/1862, Brooklyn, N.Y. d: 4/12/37, Pittsburgh, Pa. BR/TL, 165 lbs. Deb: 5/01/1884																												
1884	Col-a	34	13	**.723**	52	52	47	3	0	430	335	**7.0**	3	51	1.1	302	6.3	2.18	142	**.223**	.248	51	44	96	90	8.2	1	2	4.4
1885	Pit-a	39	24	.619	**63**	63	**63**	**6**	0	**581**	459	**7.1**	5	101	1.6	**298**	4.6	2.35	147	**.228**	**.265**	58	**71**	107	84	**12.9**	-8	-1	6.1
1886	Pit-a	**41**	20	.672	64	63	63	**12**	**1**	555	455	7.4	5	118	1.9	326	5.3	2.45	127	.233	**.277**	62	40	90	92	10.0	-4	0	2.9
1887	Pit-N	14	22	.389	38	38	37	1	0	318	375	10.6	13	71	2.0	91	2.6	4.33	89	.309	.348	-10	-16	96	96	-2.9	-4	-2	-1.8
1888	Pit-N	29	23	.558	**55**	55	**54**	5	0	480	470	8.8	7	74	1.4	135	2.5	2.31	117	.270	.299	28	21	95	114	5.0	-11	-0	0.9
1889	Pit-N	6	13	.316	21	21	18	0	0	170	196	10.4	4	48	2.5	40	2.1	4.13	88	.305	.353	-2	-10	90	96	-3.2	-4	0	-1.2
1890	Pit-P	8	7	.533	18	15	15	1	0	144	178	11.1	5	35	2.2	25	1.6	4.88	80	.316	.356	-10	-16	92	83	1.0	-3	0	-1.4
Total	7	171	122	.584	311	307	297	28	1	2678	2468	8.3	42	498	1.7	1217	4.1	2.82	116	.256	.293	177	137	96	94	31.0	-34	-2	9.9
■ JACK MORRIS	Morris, John Scott b: 5/16/55, St.Paul, Minn. BR/TR, 6'3", 195 lbs. Deb: 7/26/77																												
1977	Det-A	1	1	.500	7	6	1	0	0	46	38	7.4	4	23	4.5	28	5.5	3.72	115	.235	.323	2	3	105	97	0.1	0	0	0.3
1978	Det-A	3	5	.375	28	7	0	0	0	106	107	9.1	8	49	4.2	48	4.1	4.33	93	.268	.339	-6	-3	107	97	-1.1	0	-0	-0.3
1979	Det-A	17	7	.708	27	27	9	1	0	198	179	8.1	19	59	2.7	113	5.1	3.27	124	.244	.300	21	17	96	102	5.1	0	-1	1.6
1980	Det-A	16	15	.516	36	36	11	2	0	250	252	9.1	20	87	3.1	112	4.0	4.18	101	.262	.319	-4	2	105	89	0.0	0	3	0.4
1981	Det-A	**14**	7	.667	25	25	15	1	0	198	153	7.0	14	78	3.5	97	4.4	3.05	126	.218	.292	14	17	105	93	3.2	0	-0	1.9
1982	Det-A	17	16	.515	37	37	17	3	0	266	247	8.4	37	96	3.2	135	4.6	4.06	100	.247	.310	1	1	100	95	0.1	0	-0	0.0
1983	Det-A	20	13	.606	37	37	20	1	0	**294**	257	7.9	30	83	2.5	**232**	7.1	3.34	115	.233	.285	24	17	95	92	1.8	0	-1	1.6
1984	Det-A	19	11	.633	35	35	9	1	0	240	221	8.3	20	87	3.3	148	5.6	3.60	105	.241	.305	11	4	94	90	-0.1	0	2	0.6
1985	Det-A	16	11	.593	35	35	13	4	0	257	212	7.4	21	110	3.9	191	6.7	3.33	132	.225	.304	23	30	106	96	2.3	0	-1	3.1
1986	Det-A	21	8	.724	35	35	15	**6**	0	267	229	7.7	40	82	2.8	223	7.5	3.27	121	.229	.285	27	20	95	102	6.6	0	0	2.1
1987	Det-A	18	11	.621	34	34	13	0	0	266	227	7.7	39	93	3.1	208	7.0	3.38	126	.228	.292	32	26	96	102	0.7	0	-2	2.4
1988	Det-A	15	13	.536	34	34	10	2	0	235	225	8.6	20	83	3.2	168	6.4	3.94	95	.251	.313	1	-6	94	92	-0.1	0	0	-0.5
Total	12	177	118	.600	370	348	133	21	0	2623	2347	8.1	272	930	3.2	1703	5.8	3.59	113	.239	.302	145	131	99	95	18.6	0	-0	13.2
■ JOHN MORRIS	Morris, John Wallace b: 8/23/41, Lewes, Del. BR/TL, 6'2", 195 lbs. Deb: 7/19/66																												
1966	Phi-N	1	1	.500	13	0	0	0	0	14	15	9.6	2	3	1.9	8	5.1	5.14	70	.278	.328	-2	-2	100	86	0.0	0	0	-0.1
1968	Bal-A	2	0	1.000	19	0	0	0	0	32	19	5.3	4	17	4.8	22	6.2	2.53	119	.173	.301	2	2	101	116	1.0	-1	0	0.1
1969	Sea-A	0	0	—	6	0	0	0	0	13	16	11.1	2	8	5.5	8	5.5	6.23	58	.308	.387	-4	-4	100	100	0.0	1	1	-0.1
1970	Mil-A	4	3	.571	20	9	2	0	0	73	70	8.6	4	22	2.7	40	4.9	3.95	94	.253	.310	-2	-2	100	81	1.0	0	1	0.0
1971	Mil-A	2	2	.500	43	1	0	0	1	68	69	9.1	4	27	3.6	42	5.6	3.71	97	.270	.329	-2	-1	104	105	0.3	-0	1	0.0
1972	SF-N	0	0	—	7	0	0	0	0	6	9	13.5	2	2	3.0	5	7.5	4.50	77	.310	.355	-1	-1	100	154	0.0	0	0	0.0
1973	SF-N	1	0	1.000	7	0	0	0	0	6	12	18.0	0	3	4.5	3	4.5	9.00	43	.429	.469	-4	-3	104	96	0.5	-0	0	-0.3
1974	SF-N	1	1	.500	17	0	0	0	1	21	17	7.3	1	4	1.7	9	3.9	3.00	132	.215	.253	1	2	109	58	0.1	0	-1	0.2
Total	8	11	7	.611	132	10	2	0	2	233	227	8.8	19	86	3.3	137	5.3	3.94	91	.256	.322	-11	-9	102	94	2.9	1	2	-0.2
■ BUGS MORRIS	Morris, Joseph Harley (a.k.a. Joseph Harley Bennett 1918) b: 4/19/1892, Kansas City, Mo. d: 11/21/57, Noel, Mo. BR/TR, 5'9.5", 163 lbs. Deb: 7/20/18																												
1918	StL-A	0	2	.000	4	2	0	0	0	10	12	10.8	1	7	6.3	0	0.0	3.60	77	.308	.396	-1	-1	100	160	-0.9	0	0	0.0
1921	Chi-A	0	3	.000	3	2	1	0	0	18	19	9.5	1	16	8.0	2	1.0	6.00	73	.297	.412	-3	-3	102	100	-1.4	0	1	-0.1
	StL-A	0	0	—	3	1	0	0	0	6	11	16.5	1	6	9.0	3	4.5	13.50	32	.407	.543	-6	-6	101	86	0.0	0	-0	-0.4
	Yr	0	3	.000	6	3	1	0	0	24	30	11.3	2	22	8.3	5	1.9	7.88	55	.330	.450	-10	-9	102	86	-1.4	0	0	-0.5
Total	2	0	5	.000	10	5	1	0	0	34	42	11.1	3	29	7.7	5	1.3	6.62	59	.323	.435	-11	-10	101	115	-2.3	1	1	-0.5
■ ED MORRIS	Morris, Walter Edward "Big Ed" b: 12/7/1899, Foshee, Ala. d: 3/3/32, Century, Fla. BR/TR, 6'2", 185 lbs. Deb: 8/05/22																												
1922	Chi-N	0	0	—	5	0	0	0	0	12	22	16.5	1	6	4.5	5	3.8	8.25	47	.386	.431	-6	-6	96	95	0.0	0	-0	-0.4
1928	Bos-A	19	15	.559	47	29	20	0	5	258	255	8.9	7	80	2.8	104	3.6	3.52	116	.264	.313	15	16	101	95	6.0	-4	-2	1.0
1929	Bos-A	14	14	.500	33	26	17	2	1	208	227	9.8	7	95	4.1	73	3.2	4.46	100	.282	.348	-5	0	105	95	3.2	2	-2	0.0
1930	Bos-A	4	9	.308	18	9	3	0	0	65	67	9.3	1	38	5.3	28	3.9	4.15	107	.260	.342	4	2	96	96	-0.5	2	-0	0.3
1931	Bos-A	5	7	.417	37	14	3	0	0	131	131	9.0	4	74	5.1	46	3.2	4.74	89	.260	.354	-5	-7	97	91	0.1	-1	0	-0.7
Total	5	42	45	.483	140	78	43	2	6	674	702	9.4	20	293	3.9	256	3.4	4.19	102	.271	.338	3	6	101	94	8.8	-2	-4	0.2
■ BILL MORRISETTE	Morrisette, William Lee b: 1/17/1893, Baltimore, Md. d: 3/25/66, Virginia Beach, Va BR/TR, 6', 176 lbs. Deb: 9/19/15																												
1915	Phi-A	2	0	1.000	4	1	1	0	0	20	15	6.7	0	5	2.3	11	4.9	1.35	225	.195	.244	4	4	103	62	1.0	0	0	0.4
1916	Phi-A	0	0	—	1	0	0	0	0	4	6	13.5	0	5	11.3	2	4.5	6.75	44	.429	.579	-2	-2	105	142	0.0	0	1	0.0
1920	Det-A	1	1	.500	8	3	1	0	0	27	25	8.3	0	19	6.3	15	5.0	4.33	93	.245	.379	-2	-1	106	85	0.2	-1	-0	-0.2
Total	3	3	1	.750	13	4	2	0	0	51	46	8.1	0	29	5.1	28	4.9	3.35	106	.238	.347	0	1	105	81	1.2	-1	0	0.2
■ JIM MORRISON	Morrison, James Forrest b: 9/23/52, Pensacola, Fla. BR/TR, 5'11", 175 lbs. Deb: 9/18/77																												
1988	Atl-N	0	0	—	3	0	0	0	0	4	3	6.8	0	2	4.5	1	2.3	0.00	—	.214	.313	2	2	107	0	0.0	0	-0	0.2
■ JOHNNY MORRISON	Morrison, John Dewey "Jughandle Johnny" b: 10/22/1895, Pellville, Ky. d: 3/20/66, Louisville, Ky. BR/TR, 5'11", 188 lbs. Deb: 9/28/20																												
1920	Pit-N	1	0	1.000	2	1	1	1	0	7	4	5.1	0	1	1.3	3	3.9	0.00	—	.167	.200	2	2	101	0	0.5	-0	0	0.2
1921	Pit-N	9	7	.563	21	17	11	3	0	144	131	8.2	3	33	2.1	52	3.3	2.88	134	.258	.294	15	15	102	96	-0.3	-1	0	1.4
1922	Pit-N	17	11	.607	45	33	20	5	1	286	315	9.9	10	87	2.7	104	3.3	3.43	121	.286	.331	21	23	101	110	2.1	-3	0	1.9
1923	Pit-N	25	13	.658	42	37	27	2	2	302	287	8.6	6	110	3.3	114	3.4	3.49	109	.253	.317	17	11	95	86	5.0	-3	-0	0.7
1924	Pit-N	11	16	.407	**41**	25	10	0	2	238	213	8.1	7	73	2.8	85	3.2	3.74	107	.245	.296	3	7	104	75	-4.6	-3	-2	0.3

YEAR	TM/L	W	L	PCT	G	GS	CG	SHO	SV	IP	H	H/G	HR	BB	BB/G	SO	SO/G	ERA	/A	OAVG	OOBP	PR	/A	PF	CPI	WAT	PB	PD	TPI
1925	Pit-N	17	14	.548	**44**	26	10	0	**4**	211	245	10.5	12	60	2.6	60	2.6	3.88	109	.291	.335	9	8	99	107	-2.1	-2	-2	0.3
1926	Pit-N	6	8	.429	26	13	6	2	2	122	119	8.8	2	44	3.2	39	2.9	3.39	125	.267	.322	6	11	111	102	-1.6	-4	-2	0.6
1927	Pit-N	3	2	.600	21	2	1	0	3	54	63	10.5	2	21	3.5	21	3.5	4.17	93	.304	.356	-1	-2	99	112	0.0	-0	-1	-0.2
1929	Bro-N	13	7	.650	39	10	4	0	**8**	137	150	9.9	11	61	4.0	57	3.7	4.47	102	.279	.347	4	1	96	102	3.9	-1	-3	-0.3
1930	Bro-N	1	2	.333	16	0	0	0	1	35	47	12.1	4	16	4.1	11	2.8	5.40	91	.346	.396	-2	-2	99	126	-0.5	-1	-0	-0.2
Total	10	103	80	.563	297	164	90	13	23	1536	1574	9.2	57	506	3.0	546	3.2	3.64	112	.271	.323	74	77	100	97	2.4	-18	-11	4.7
■ **MIKE MORRISON**	Morrison, Michael b: 2/6/1867, Erie, Pa. d: 6/16/55, Erie, Pa. BR/TR, 5'8.5", 156 lbs. Deb: 4/19/1887																												
1887	Cle-a	12	25	.324	40	40	35	0	0	317	385	10.9	12	205	5.8	158	4.5	4.94	89	.314	.412	-23	-19	103	113	1.0	-5	10	-0.9
1888	Cle-a	1	3	.250	4	4	4	0	0	35	40	10.3	3	19	4.9	14	3.6	5.40	57	.301	.388	-9	-9	100	97	-0.6	-0	0	-0.7
1890	Syr-a	6	9	.400	17	14	13	1	0	127	131	9.3	4	81	5.7	69	4.9	5.88	60	.282	.389	-28	-33	92	79	-0.5	3	0	-2.6
	BB-a	1	2	.333	4	4	3	0	0	26	15	5.2	0	20	6.9	13	4.5	3.81	104	.180	.339	0	0	103	66	0.1	-1	0	0.0
	Yr	7	11	.389	21	18	16	1	0	153	146	8.6	4	101	5.9	82	4.8	5.53	66	.267	.381	-28	-32	94	66	-0.4	3	0	-2.6
Total	3	20	39	.339	65	62	55	1	0	505	571	10.2	19	325	5.8	254	4.5	5.15	79	.299	.401	-60	-60	100	101	-0.0	-3	10	-4.2
■ **PHIL MORRISON**	Morrison, Philip Melvin b: 10/18/1894, Rockport, Ind. d: 1/18/55, Lexington, Ky. BB/TR, 6'2", 190 lbs. Deb: 9/30/21																												
1921	Pit-N	0	0	—	1	0	0	0	0	1	1	9.0	0	0	0.0	1	9.0	0.00	—	.333	.333	0	0	102	0	0.0	0	0	0.0
■ **HANK MORRISON**	Morrison, Stephen Henry b: 5/22/1866, Olneyville, R.I. d: 9/30/27, Attleboro, Mass. BR/TR, 5'10", 180 lbs. Deb: 5/28/1887																												
1887	Ind-N	3	4	.429	7	7	5	0	0	57	79	12.5	2	27	4.3	13	2.1	7.58	54	.345	.414	-22	-22	101	77	0.7	-2	0	-1.7
■ **GUY MORRISON**	Morrison, Walter Guy b: 8/29/1895, Hinton, W.Va. d: 8/14/34, Grand Rapids, Mich BR/TR, 5'11", 185 lbs. Deb: 8/31/27																												
1927	Bos-N	1	2	.333	11	3	1	0	0	34	40	10.6	1	15	4.0	6	1.6	4.50	83	.296	.348	-2	-3	95	100	-0.1	1	1	0.0
1928	Bos-N	0	0	—	1	0	0	0	0	3	4	12.0	1	3	9.0	0	0.0	12.00	34	.308	.438	-3	-3	101	71	0.0	0	0	-0.1
Total	2	1	2	.333	12	3	1	0	0	37	44	10.7	2	18	4.4	6	1.5	5.11	74	.297	.356	-5	-6	96	97	-0.1	1	1	-0.1
■ **FRANK MORRISSEY**	Morrissey, Michael Joseph "Deacon" b: 5/5/1876, Baltimore, Md. d: 2/22/39, Baltimore, Md. TR , 5'4", 140 lbs. Deb: 7/13/01																												
1901	Bos-A	0	0	—	1	0	0	0	0	4	5	11.3	0	2	4.5	1	2.3	2.25	153	.327	.405	1	1	94	213	0.0	-0	0	0.1
1902	Chi-N	1	3	.250	5	5	5	0	0	40	40	9.0	0	8	1.8	13	2.9	2.25	118	.283	.322	2	2	95	114	-0.9	-1	0	0.2
Total	2	1	3	.250	6	5	5	0	0	44	45	9.2	0	10	2.0	14	2.9	2.25	121	.287	.330	3	2	95	123	-0.9	-1	1	0.3
■ **CARL MORTON**	Morton, Carl Wendle b: 1/18/44, Kansas City, Mo. d: 4/12/83, Tulsa, Okla. BR/TR, 6', 200 lbs. Deb: 4/11/69																												
1969	Mon-N	0	3	.000	8	5	0	0	0	29	29	9.0	2	18	5.6	16	5.0	4.66	80	.264	.360	-3	-3	103	100	-1.4	-0	1	-0.2
1970	Mon-N	18	11	.621	43	37	10	4	0	285	281	8.9	27	125	3.9	154	4.9	3.60	114	.262	.337	14	16	102	118	5.1	2	1	1.9
1971	Mon-N	10	18	.357	36	35	9	0	1	214	252	10.6	22	83	3.5	84	3.5	4.79	72	.295	.354	-31	-31	100	102	-3.0	2	2	-2.7
1972	Mon-N	7	13	.350	27	27	3	1	0	172	170	8.9	16	53	2.8	51	2.7	3.92	91	.258	.313	-9	-6	104	92	-2.3	1	1	-0.4
1973	Atl-N	15	10	.600	38	37	10	4	0	256	254	8.9	18	70	2.5	112	3.9	3.41	121	.259	.305	7	21	113	98	3.4	3	0	2.7
1974	Atl-N	16	12	.571	38	38	7	1	0	275	293	9.6	10	89	2.9	113	3.7	3.14	120	.277	.327	15	19	104	**117**	1.0	-4	-1	1.6
1975	Atl-N	17	16	.515	39	39	11	2	0	278	302	9.8	19	82	2.7	78	2.5	3.50	101	.278	.323	4	1	97	110	3.4	0	0	0.0
1976	Atl-N	4	9	.308	26	24	1	1	0	140	172	11.1	6	45	2.9	42	2.7	4.18	94	.306	.352	-10	-4	112	111	-1.9	-0	2	-0.1
Total	8	87	92	.486	255	242	51	13	1	1649	1753	9.6	120	565	3.1	650	3.5	3.73	102	.275	.330	-13	12	104	108	4.3	4	5	2.8
■ **CHARLIE MORTON**	Morton, Charles Hazen b: 10/12/1854, Kingsville, Ohio d: 12/9/21, Massillon, Ohio TR , Deb: 5/02/1882 M																												
1884	Tol-a	0	1	.000	3	1	1	0	0	23	18	7.0	0	5	2.0	7	2.7	3.13	109	.223	.269	0	1	105	70	-0.4	-0	0	0.1
■ **GUY MORTON**	Morton, Guy Sr. "The Alabama Blossom" b: 6/1/1893, Vernon, Ala. d: 10/18/34, Sheffield, Ala. BR/TR, 6'1", 175 lbs. Deb: 6/20/14																												
1914	Cle-A	1	13	.071	25	13	5	0	1	128	116	8.2	1	55	3.9	80	5.6	3.02	96	.257	.341	-4	-2	106	104	-5.5	-4	-1	-0.3
1915	Cle-A	16	15	.516	34	27	15	6	1	240	189	7.1	5	60	2.3	134	5.0	2.14	147	.216	.268	22	27	106	80	4.2	-4	-0	2.3
1916	Cle-A	12	8	.600	27	18	9	0	0	150	139	8.3	1	42	2.5	88	5.3	2.88	97	.246	.302	-1	-1	99	84	2.2	-0	-1	-0.2
1917	Cle-A	10	10	.500	35	18	6	1	2	161	158	8.8	3	59	3.3	62	3.5	2.74	110	.266	.335	-1	5	113	117	-1.3	-5	-2	0.0
1918	Cle-A	14	8	.636	30	28	13	1	0	215	189	7.9	1	77	3.2	123	**5.1**	2.64	112	.240	.302	3	7	107	90	1.9	-1	-1	0.7
1919	Cle-A	9	9	.500	26	20	9	3	0	147	128	7.8	3	47	2.9	64	3.9	2.82	119	.233	.293	7	9	104	75	-1.6	-2	-1	0.6
1920	Cle-A	8	6	.571	29	17	6	1	1	137	140	9.2	2	57	3.7	72	4.7	4.47	85	.270	.344	-10	-10	100	77	-0.7	-1	-2	-1.2
1921	Cle-A	8	3	.727	30	7	3	2	0	108	98	8.2	1	32	2.7	45	3.8	2.75	149	.244	.295	18	16	96	91	1.7	-2	-2	1.2
1922	Cle-A	14	9	.609	38	23	13	3	0	203	218	9.7	7	85	3.8	102	**4.5**	3.99	104	.277	.341	1	3	103	97	2.7	-2	3	0.5
1923	Cle-A	6	6	.500	33	14	3	2	1	129	133	9.3	3	56	3.9	54	3.8	4.26	92	.276	.338	-4	-5	99	90	-0.3	-2	-1	-0.6
1924	Cle-A	0	1	.000	10	0	0	0	0	12	12	9.0	0	13	9.8	6	4.5	6.75	61	.250	.403	-3	-4	97	68	-0.4	-0	-0	-0.3
Total	11	98	88	.527	317	185	82	19	6	1630	1520	8.4	27	583	3.2	830	4.6	3.13	109	.251	.315	27	50	104	90	2.9	-25	-7	2.7
■ **SPARROW MORTON**	Morton, William P. TL , Deb: 7/15/1884																												
1884	Phi-N	0	2	.000	2	2	2	0	0	17	16	8.5	0	11	5.8	5	2.6	5.29	55	.258	.369	-4	-5	97	67	-0.9	1	0	-0.2
■ **EARL MOSELEY**	Moseley, Earl Victor "Vic" b: 9/7/1884, Middleburg, Ohio d: 7/1/63, Alliance, Ohio BR/TR, 5'9.5", 168 lbs. Deb: 6/17/13																												
1913	Bos-A	9	5	.643	24	15	7	3	0	121	105	7.8	1	49	3.6	62	4.6	3.12	96	.245	.322	-3	-2	103	87	1.8	-2	1	0.0
1914	Ind-F	19	18	.514	43	38	29	4	1	317	303	8.6	5	123	3.5	205	5.8	3.46	100	.258	.330	-9	0	108	92	-2.4	-7	2	-0.3
1915	New-F	15	15	.500	38	32	22	5	1	268	222	7.5	2	99	3.3	142	4.8	**1.91**	149	.229	.302	33	28	94	126	-0.8	-2	0	2.8
1916	Cin-N	7	10	.412	31	15	7	0	1	150	145	8.7	5	69	4.1	60	3.6	3.90	68	.257	.328	-21	-21	101	87	0.3	-2	-2	-2.6
Total	4	50	48	.510	136	100	65	12	3	856	775	8.1	13	340	3.6	469	4.9	3.01	102	.247	.320	0	5	102	101	-1.1	-14	1	-0.1
■ **WALTER MOSER**	Moser, Walter Fredrick b: 2/27/1881, Concord, N.C. d: 12/10/46, Philadelphia, Pa. BR/TR, 5'9", 170 lbs. Deb: 9/03/06																												
1906	Phi-N	0	4	.000	6	4	4	0	0	43	49	10.3	0	15	3.1	17	3.6	3.56	69	.317	.382	-4	-5	93	109	-1.9	-2	-1	-0.5
1911	Bos-A	0	1	.000	6	3	1	0	0	25	37	13.3	0	11	4.0	11	4.0	3.96	83	.366	.434	-2	-2	99	156	-0.4	-1	0	-0.1
	StL-A	0	2	.000	2	2	0	0	0	3	11	33.0	0	4	12.0	2	6.0	24.00	14	.478	.556	-7	-7	100	67	-0.9	0	0	-0.5
	Yr	0	3	.000	8	5	1	0	0	28	48	15.4	0	15	4.8	13	4.2	6.11	54	.384	.450	-9	-9	99	67	-1.3	-1	0	-0.6
Total	2	0	7	.000	14	9	5	0	0	71	97	12.3	0	30	3.8	30	3.8	4.56	61	.348	.416	-13	-14	95	123	-3.2	-2	-1	-1.1
■ **PAUL MOSKAU**	Moskau, Paul Richard b: 12/20/53, St.Joseph, Mo. BR/TR, 6'2", 200 lbs. Deb: 6/21/77																												
1977	Cin-N	6	6	.500	20	19	2	2	0	108	116	9.7	10	40	3.3	71	5.9	4.00	97	.278	.336	-1	-2	99	107	-0.4	2	1	0.1
1978	Cin-N	6	4	.600	26	25	2	1	1	145	139	8.6	17	57	3.5	88	5.5	3.97	92	.255	.325	-6	-5	102	101	0.4	3	-2	-0.3
1979	Cin-N	5	4	.556	21	15	1	0	1	106	107	9.1	9	51	4.3	58	4.9	3.91	92	.263	.336	-2	-4	96	105	0.0	-2	1	-0.4
1980	Cin-N	9	7	.563	33	19	2	1	2	153	147	8.6	13	41	2.4	94	5.5	4.00	91	.257	.300	-7	-6	101	86	0.3	-1	0	-0.6
1981	Cin-N	2	1	.667	27	1	0	0	2	55	54	8.8	4	32	5.2	32	5.2	4.91	71	.258	.354	-9	-9	101	87	0.2	-0	1	-0.8
1982	Pit-N	1	3	.250	13	5	0	0	0	35	43	11.1	7	8	2.1	15	3.9	4.37	91	.303	.336	-3	-2	110	123	-0.9	-1	-0	-0.2
1983	Chi-N	3	2	.600	8	8	0	0	0	32	44	12.4	7	14	3.9	16	4.5	6.75	54	.331	.389	-11	-11	101	102	0.7	0	0	-0.9
Total	7	32	27	.542	148	92	7	4	5	634	650	9.2	67	243	3.4	374	5.3	4.22	88	.268	.330	-39	-37	101	99	0.3	2	0	-3.1
■ **JIM MOSOLF**	Mosolf, James Frederick b: 8/21/05, Puyallup, Wash. d: 12/28/79, Dallasyore. BL/TR, 5'10", 186 lbs. Deb: 9/09/29																												
1930	Pit-N	0	0	—	1	0	0	0	0	1/3	1	27.0	0	0	0.0	1	27.0	27.00	—	.500	.500	-1	-1	98	25	0.0	0	0	0.0
■ **MAL MOSS**	Moss, Charles Malcolm b: 4/18/05, Sullivan, Ind. d: 2/5/83, Savannah, Ga. BR/TL, 6', 175 lbs. Deb: 4/29/30																												
1930	Chi-N	0	0	—	12	1	0	0	1	19	18	8.5	0	14	6.6	4	1.9	6.16	83	.254	.368	-3	-2	103	66	0.0	-0	0	-0.1
■ **RAY MOSS**	Moss, Raymond Earl b: 12/5/01, Chattanooga, Tenn. BR/TR, 6'1", 185 lbs. Deb: 4/17/26																												
1926	Bro-N	0	0	—	1	0	0	0	0	1	3	27.0	0	0	0.0	0	0.0	9.00	43	.600	.500	-1	-1	101	156	0.0	-0	0	0.0
1927	Bro-N	1	0	1.000	1	1	1	0	0	8	11	12.4	0	1	1.1	1	1.1	3.38	121	.333	.343	0	1	104	133	0.5	1	-0	0.1
1928	Bro-N	0	3	.000	22	5	1	1	1	60	62	9.3	5	35	5.3	5	0.8	4.95	79	.279	.362	-6	-7	99	97	-1.4	2	0	-0.4
1929	Bro-N	11	6	.647	39	20	7	2	0	182	214	10.6	9	81	4.0	59	2.9	5.04	90	.296	.364	-7	-10	96	97	3.2	-5	-2	-1.5
1930	Bro-N	9	6	.600	36	11	5	0	1	118	127	9.7	13	55	4.2	30	2.3	5.11	96	.270	.346	-2	-3	99	89	0.8	-2	-2	-0.5
1931	Bro-N	0	0	—	1	0	0	0	0	1	1	9.0	0	1	9.0	0	0.0	0.00	—	.333	.400	0	0	101	0	0.0	0	0	0.1
	Bos-N	1	3	.250	12	5	0	0	0	45	56	11.2	2	16	3.2	14	2.8	4.60	85	.306	.351	-4	-3	102	103	-0.7	-1	-0	-0.3
	Yr	1	3	.250	13	5	0	0	0	46	57	11.2	2	17	3.3	14	2.7	4.50	87	.306	.352	-3	-3	102	103	-0.7	0	0	-0.2
Total	6	22	18	.550	112	42	13	3	2	415	474	10.3	29	189	4.1	109	2.4	4.97	90	.289	.357	-18	-22	98	96	2.4	-5	-4	-2.5

YEAR	TM/L	W	L	PCT	G	GS	CG	SHO	SV	IP	H	H/G	HR	BB	BB/G	SO	SO/G	ERA	/A	OAVG	OOBP	PR	/A	PF	CPI	WAT	PB	PD	TPI
■ **DON MOSSI**	Mossi, Donald Louis "The Sphinx" b: 1/11/29, St.Helena, Cal. BL/TL, 6'1", 195 lbs. Deb: 4/17/54																												
1954	Cle-A	6	1	.857	40	5	2	0	7	93	56	5.4	5	39	3.8	55	5.3	1.94	195	.176	.261	**18**	**19**	101	89	1.8	0	-1	2.0
1955	Cle-A	4	3	.571	57	1	0	0	9	82	81	8.9	4	18	2.0	69	7.6	2.41	168	.253	.288	14	15	102	117	-0.1	-0	2	1.7
1956	Cle-A	6	5	.545	48	3	0	0	11	88	79	8.1	6	33	3.4	59	6.0	3.58	115	.240	.304	6	5	99	88	-0.2	0	0	0.5
1957	Cle-A	11	10	.524	36	22	6	1	2	159	165	9.3	16	57	3.2	97	5.5	4.13	94	.265	.323	-6	-5	102	96	0.6	2	-1	-0.3
1958	Cle-A	7	8	.467	43	5	0	0	3	102	106	9.4	6	30	2.6	55	4.9	3.88	90	.269	.317	-1	-4	93	95	-0.5	-1	0	-0.5
1959	Det-A	17	9	.654	34	30	15	3	0	228	210	8.3	20	49	1.9	125	4.9	3.36	128	.243	.283	13	24	111	90	4.7	-0	0	2.6
1960	Det-A	9	8	.529	23	22	9	2	0	158	158	9.0	17	32	1.8	69	3.9	3.47	113	.258	.289	7	8	102	97	1.2	-0	-0	0.8
1961	Det-A	15	7	.682	35	34	12	1	1	240	237	8.9	29	47	**1.8**	137	5.1	2.96	127	.258	.290	28	22	94	119	1.9	2	0	2.3
1962	Det-A	11	13	.458	35	27	8	1	1	180	195	9.8	24	36	1.8	121	6.1	4.20	104	.270	.300	-5	4	110	93	-1.7	1	-2	0.3
1963	Det-A	7	7	.500	24	16	3	0	2	123	110	8.0	20	17	1.2	68	5.0	3.73	101	.236	.264	-1	0	104	87	0.2	2	0	0.3
1964	Chi-A	3	1	.750	34	0	0	0	7	40	37	8.3	9	7	1.6	36	8.1	2.93	116	.240	.276	3	2	93	130	0.7	-0	0	0.2
1965	KC-A	5	8	.385	51	0	0	0	7	55	59	9.7	0	20	3.3	41	6.7	3.76	91	.278	.326	-2	-2	100	96	0.2	-1	-0	-0.2
Total	12	101	80	.558	460	165	55	8	50	1548	1493	8.7	156	385	2.2	932	5.4	3.43	115	.252	.293	74	88	102	99	8.8	4	-1	9.7
■ **EARL MOSSOR**	Mossor, Earl Dalton b: 7/21/25, Forbes, Tenn. BL/TR, 6'1", 175 lbs. Deb: 4/30/51																												
1951	Bro-N	0	0	—	3	0	0	0	0	2	2	9.0	1	7	31.5	1	4.5	27.00	14	.333	.692	-5	-5	95	66	0.0	0	0	-0.3
■ **GLEN MOULDER**	Moulder, Glen Hubert b: 9/28/17, Cleveland, Okla. BR/TR, 6', 180 lbs. Deb: 4/28/46																												
1946	Bro-N	0	0	—	1	0	0	0	0	2	2	9.0	1	1	4.5	1	4.5	4.50	76	.286	.375	-0	-0	100	177	0.0	0	0	0.0
1947	StL-A	4	2	.667	32	2	0	0	2	73	78	9.6	4	43	5.3	23	2.8	3.82	102	.283	.368	-1	1	106	126	1.4	-0	1	0.2
1948	Chi-A	3	6	.333	33	9	0	0	2	86	108	11.3	8	54	5.7	26	2.7	6.38	67	.316	.400	-20	-20	100	99	0.0	1	-0	-1.7
Total	3	7	8	.467	66	11	0	0	4	161	188	10.5	13	98	5.5	50	2.8	5.20	79	.301	.385	-21	-20	102	112	1.4	1	1	-1.5
■ **FRANK MOUNTAIN**	Mountain, Frank Henry b: 5/17/1860, Ft.Edward, N.Y. d: 11/19/39, Schenectady, N.Y. TR, 5'11", 185 lbs. Deb: 7/19/1880																												
1880	Tro-N	1	1	.500	2	2	2	0	0	17	23	12.2	0	6	3.2	2	1.1	5.29	50	.333	.386	-6	-5	112	90	0.0	-0	0	-0.4
1881	Det-N	3	4	.429	7	7	7	0	0	60	80	12.0	2	18	2.7	13	2.0	5.25	56	.333	.379	-16	-15	106	89	-0.4	-0	0	-1.2
1882	Wor-N	0	5	.000	5	5	3	0	0	42	54	11.6	4	10	2.1	8	1.7	3.00	103	.320	.358	-1	0	107	165	-2.4	-3	0	-0.1
	Phi-a	2	6	.250	8	8	8	0	0	69	72	9.4	1	11	1.4	15	2.0	3.91	76	.274	.303	-9	-7	111	75	-2.2	3	0	-0.2
	Wor-N	2	11	.154	13	13	13	0	0	102	131	11.6	0	25	2.2	21	1.9	3.97	78	.320	.359	-12	-10	107	107	-2.0	2	0	-0.4
1883	Col-a	26	33	.441	59	59	57	4	0	503	546	9.8	8	123	2.2	159	2.8	3.60	84	.282	.325	-17	-33	91	103	9.9	7	1	-2.2
1884	Col-a	23	17	.575	42	41	40	5	**1**	361	289	7.2	7	78	1.9	156	3.9	2.44	127	.227	.272	32	26	96	99	-2.9	7	3	3.8
1885	Pit-a	1	4	.200	5	5	5	0	0	46	56	11.0	1	24	4.7	7	1.4	4.30	80	.313	.394	-5	-4	107	121	-1.4	-1	0	-0.4
1886	Pit-a	0	2	.000	2	2	2	0	0	16	22	12.4	0	14	7.9	2	1.1	7.88	39	.338	.455	-8	-8	90	86	-0.9	0	0	-0.5
Total	7	58	83	.411	143	142	137	9	1	1216	1273	9.4	23	309	2.3	383	2.8	3.47	88	.277	.322	-42	-54	97	102	-2.3	15	4	-1.6
■ **BILL MOUNTJOY**	Mountjoy, William R. "Medicine Bill" b: 1857, Port Huron, Mich. d: 5/19/34, London, Ont., Can. Deb: 1883																												
1883	Cin-a	0	1	.000	1	1	1	0	0	8	9	10.1	0	2	2.3	3	3.4	2.25	144	.289	.332	1	1	98	169	-0.4	-0	0	0.0
1884	Cin-a	19	12	.613	33	33	32	3	0	289	274	8.5	4	43	1.3	96	3.0	2.93	114	.258	.287	10	13	103	100	-0.3	-4	1	1.1
1885	Cin-a	10	7	.588	17	17	17	1	0	154	149	8.7	5	52	3.0	50	2.9	3.16	106	.265	.328	2	3	103	111	0.6	-1	0	0.3
	Bal-a	2	4	.333	6	6	6	1	0	53	72	12.2	1	13	2.2	15	2.5	5.43	65	.337	.375	-13	-11	109	94	-0.3	-0	0	-0.8
	Yr	12	11	.522	23	23	23	2	0	207	221	9.6	6	65	2.8	65	2.8	3.74	91	.285	.340	-11	-8	104	94	0.3	-1	0	-0.5
Total	3	31	24	.564	57	57	56	5	0	504	504	9.0	10	110	2.0	164	2.9	3.25	103	.270	.311	-0	6	103	104	-0.4	-6	1	0.6
■ **ED MOYER**	Moyer, Charles Edward b: 8/15/1885, Andover, Ohio d: 11/18/62, Jacksonville, Fla. Deb: 7/20/10																												
1910	Was-A	0	3	.000	6	3	2	0	0	25	22	7.9	1	13	4.7	3	1.1	3.24	79	.253	.369	-2	-2	102	118	-1.4	-1	1	0.0
■ **JAMIE MOYER**	Moyer, Jamie b: 11/18/62, Sellersville, Pa. BL/TL, 6', 170 lbs. Deb: 6/16/86																												
1986	Chi-N	7	4	.636	16	16	1	1	0	87	107	11.1	10	42	4.3	45	4.7	5.07	79	.311	.385	-13	-10	108	115	2.0	-0	1	-0.8
1987	Chi-N	12	15	.444	35	33	1	0	0	201	210	9.4	28	97	4.3	147	6.6	5.10	81	.271	.347	-23	-21	102	96	-0.8	4	2	-1.4
1988	Chi-N	9	15	.375	34	30	3	1	0	202	212	9.4	20	55	2.5	121	5.4	3.48	104	.272	.317	-0	3	105	118	-2.8	-2	3	0.4
Total	3	28	34	.452	85	79	5	2	0	490	529	9.7	58	194	3.6	313	5.7	4.43	88	.279	.342	-36	-28	104	108	-1.6	1	6	-1.8
■ **RON MROZINSKI**	Mrozinski, Ronald Frank b: 9/16/30, White Haven, Pa. BR/TL, 5'11", 160 lbs. Deb: 6/20/54																												
1954	Phi-N	1	1	.500	15	4	1	0	0	48	49	9.2	10	25	4.7	26	4.9	4.50	88	.261	.346	-2	-3	98	111	0.0	-1	-1	-0.4
1955	Phi-N	0	2	.000	22	1	0	0	1	34	38	10.1	2	19	5.0	18	4.8	6.62	62	.299	.391	-10	-9	102	83	-0.9	-1	-0	-0.9
Total	2	1	3	.250	37	5	1	0	1	82	87	9.5	12	44	4.8	44	4.8	5.38	75	.276	.365	-12	-12	99	99	-0.9	-2	-1	-1.3
■ **PHIL MUDROCK**	Mudrock, Philip Ray b: 6/12/37, Louisville, Colo. BR/TR, 6'1", 190 lbs. Deb: 4/19/63																												
1963	Chi-N	0	0	—	1	0	0	0	0	1	2	18.0	0	0	0.0	0	0.0	9.00	38	.400	.400	-1	-1	105	74	0.0	0	0	0.0
■ **GORDIE MUELLER**	Mueller, Joseph Gordon b: 12/10/22, Baltimore, Md. BR/TR, 6'4", 200 lbs. Deb: 4/19/50																												
1950	Bos-A	0	0	—	8	0	0	0	0	7	11	14.1	1	13	16.7	1	1.3	10.29	49	.344	.533	-4	-4	111	106	0.0	-0	0	-0.3
■ **LESLIE MUELLER**	Mueller, Leslie Clyde b: 3/4/19, Belleville, Ill. BR/TR, 6'3", 190 lbs. Deb: 8/15/41																												
1941	Det-A	0	0	—	4	0	0	0	0	13	9	6.2	1	10	6.9	8	5.5	4.85	92	.205	.333	-1	-1	107	78	0.0	-0	0	0.0
1945	Det-A	6	8	.429	26	18	6	2	1	135	117	7.8	8	58	3.9	42	2.8	3.67	96	.234	.311	-5	-2	105	85	-1.8	1	-2	-0.3
Total	2	6	8	.429	30	18	6	2	1	148	126	7.7	9	68	4.1	50	3.0	3.77	95	.231	.313	-6	-3	105	84	-1.8	0	-2	-0.3
■ **WILLIE MUELLER**	Mueller, Willard Lawrence b: 8/30/56, West Bend, Wis. BR/TR, 6'4", 220 lbs. Deb: 8/12/78																												
1978	Mil-A	1	0	1.000	5	0	0	0	0	13	16	11.1	1	6	4.2	6	4.2	6.23	63	.291	.361	-4	-3	104	75	0.5	0	0	-0.2
1981	Mil-A	0	0	—	1	0	0	0	0	2	4	18.0	0	0	0.0	1	4.5	4.50	78	.400	.400	-0	-0	95	147	0.0	0	0	0.0
Total	2	1	0	1.000	6	0	0	0	0	15	20	12.0	1	6	3.6	7	4.2	6.00	65	.308	.366	-4	-4	103	84	0.5	0	0	-0.2
■ **BILLY MUFFETT**	Muffett, Billy Arnold "Muff" b: 9/21/30, Hammond, Ind. BR/TR, 6'1", 198 lbs. Deb: 8/03/57 C																												
1957	StL-N	3	2	.600	23	0	0	0	8	44	35	7.2	1	13	2.7	21	4.3	2.25	171	.222	.276	8	8	99	96	0.2	-1	-1	0.6
1958	StL-N	4	6	.400	35	6	1	0	5	84	107	11.5	11	42	4.5	41	4.4	4.93	87	.316	.389	-9	-6	108	124	-0.7	0	-1	-0.5
1959	SF-N	0	0	—	5	0	0	0	0	7	11	14.1	2	3	3.9	3	3.9	5.14	72	.407	.452	-1	-1	94	187	0.0	0	0	0.0
1960	Bos-A	6	4	.600	23	14	4	1	0	125	116	8.4	6	36	2.6	75	5.4	3.24	126	.242	.296	9	12	105	86	1.6	2	0	1.5
1961	Bos-A	3	11	.214	38	11	2	0	2	113	130	10.4	18	36	2.9	47	3.7	5.65	73	.291	.335	-20	-19	103	90	-3.9	2	-0	-1.6
1962	Bos-A	0	0	—	1	1	0	0	0	4	8	18.0	0	2	4.5	1	2.3	9.00	45	.471	.500	-2	-2	103	109	0.0	-0	-0	-0.1
Total	6	16	23	.410	125	32	7	1	15	377	407	9.7	38	132	3.2	188	4.5	4.32	95	.277	.333	-16	-9	104	99	-2.8	3	-2	-0.1
■ **JOE MUICH**	Muich, Ignatius Andrew b: 11/23/03, St.Louis, Mo. BR/TR, 6'2", 175 lbs. Deb: 9/04/24																												
1924	Bos-N	0	0	—	3	0	0	0	0	9	19	19.0	1	5	5.0	1	1.0	11.00	35	.432	.480	-7	-7	99	92	0.0	-1	0	-0.6
■ **JOE MUIR**	Muir, Joseph Allen b: 11/26/22, Oriole, Md. d: 6/25/80, Baltimore, Md. BL/TL, 6'1", 172 lbs. Deb: 4/21/51																												
1951	Pit-N	0	2	.000	9	1	0	0	0	16	11	6.2	2	7	3.9	5	2.8	2.81	154	.180	.257	2	3	110	74	-0.9	-0	1	0.3
1952	Pit-N	2	3	.400	12	5	1	0	0	36	42	10.5	3	18	4.5	17	4.3	6.25	63	.288	.366	-10	-9	105	79	0.4	-0	0	-0.8
Total	2	2	5	.286	21	6	1	0	0	52	53	9.2	5	25	4.3	22	3.8	5.19	78	.256	.333	-8	-7	106	77	-0.5	-0	1	-0.5
■ **HUGH MULCAHY**	Mulcahy, Hugh Noyes "Losing Pitcher" b: 9/9/13, Brighton, Mass. BR/TR, 6'2", 190 lbs. Deb: 7/24/35 C																												
1935	Phi-N	1	5	.167	18	5	0	0	1	53	62	10.5	2	25	4.2	11	1.9	4.75	99	.295	.374	-4	-0	117	106	-1.7	-3	1	-0.1
1936	Phi-N	1	1	.500	3	2	2	0	0	23	20	7.8	0	12	4.7	2	0.8	3.13	142	.238	.340	2	3	111	108	0.2	0	0	0.4
1937	Phi-N	8	18	.308	**56**	25	9	1	3	216	256	10.7	17	97	4.0	54	2.3	5.13	84	.296	.368	-29	-19	111	100	-3.3	-3	3	-1.7
1938	Phi-N	10	20	.333	46	34	15	0	1	267	294	9.9	14	120	4.0	90	3.0	4.62	87	.278	.350	-25	-18	106	94	0.9	-3	0	-1.9
1939	Phi-N	9	16	.360	38	31	14	1	4	226	246	9.8	19	93	3.7	59	2.3	4.98	78	.282	.348	-27	-27	99	93	1.3	-2	-0	-2.8
1940	Phi-N	13	22	.371	36	36	21	3	0	280	283	9.1	12	91	2.9	82	2.6	3.60	109	.261	.317	8	10	102	99	1.5	0	3	1.4
1945	Phi-N	1	3	.250	5	4	1	0	0	28	33	10.6	1	9	2.9	2	0.6	3.86	101	.295	.336	-0	0	102	111	-0.2	-1	1	0.0
1946	Phi-N	2	4	.333	16	5	1	0	0	63	69	9.9	3	33	4.7	12	1.7	4.43	75	.295	.377	-7	-8	98	113	-0.7	1	1	-0.5
1947	Pit-N	0	0	—	2	1	0	0	0	7	8	10.3	1	7	9.0	2	2.6	3.86	108	.333	.484	0	0	102	209	0.0	0	1	0.1
Total	9	45	89	.336	220	143	63	5	9	1163	1271	9.8	69	487	3.8	314	2.4	4.48	90	.280	.348	-82	-59	105	99	-2.0	-9	10	-5.1

YEAR TM/L	W	L	PCT	G	GS	CG	SHO	SV	IP	H	H/G	HR	BB	BB/G	SO	SO/G	ERA	/A	OAVG	OOBP	PR	/A	PF	CPI	WAT	PB	PD	TPI
■ **TERRY MULHOLLAND**	Mulholland, Terence John b: 3/9/63, Uniontown, Pa. BR/TL, 6'3", 200 lbs. Deb: 6/08/86																											
1986 SF-N	1	7	.125	15	10	0	0	0	55	51	8.3	3	35	5.7	27	4.4	4.91	72	.251	.355	-7	-8	95	85	-3.0	-1	-1	-0.9
1988 SF-N	2	1	.667	9	6	2	1	0	46	50	9.8	3	7	1.4	18	3.5	3.72	87	.281	.304	-1	-3	93	100	0.5	-1	0	-0.2
Total 2	3	8	.273	24	16	2	1	0	101	101	9.0	6	42	3.7	45	4.0	4.37	78	.265	.333	-9	-11	94	92	-2.5	-2	-0	-1.1
■ **TONY MULLANE**	Mullane, Anthony John "Count" or "The Apollo Of The Box" b: 1/20/1859, Cork, Ireland d: 4/25/44, Chicago, Ill. BB/TB, 5'10.5", 165 lbs. Deb: 8/27/1881																											
1881 Det-N	1	4	.200	5	5	5	0	0	44	55	11.3	2	17	3.5	7	1.4	4.91	60	.319	.380	-10	-10	106	93	-1.4	-0	0	-0.7
1882 Lou-a	30	24	.556	**55**	55	51	5	0	460	418	8.2	3	78	1.5	**170**	3.3	1.88	128	.247	.281	41	27	90	119	4.7	11	10	4.6
1883 StL-a	35	15	**.700**	53	49	49	3	**1**	461	372	7.3	3	74	1.4	191	3.7	2.19	**158**	.226	.259	57	65	105	92	5.0	1	1	6.6
1884 Tol-a	37	26	.587	68	66	65	**8**	0	576	485	7.6	5	90	1.4	329	5.1	2.48	137	.236	.268	49	59	105	96	14.8	17	8	9.2
1886 Cin-a	33	27	.550	63	56	55	1	0	530	501	8.5	11	166	2.8	250	4.2	3.70	89	.260	.318	-15	-24	96	88	7.1	4	3	-1.3
1887 Cin-a	31	17	.646	48	48	47	**6**	0	416	414	9.0	11	121	2.6	97	2.1	3.25	141	.273	.326	49	61	106	105	4.0	-1	-2	5.3
1888 Cin-a	26	16	.619	44	42	41	4	**1**	380	341	8.1	9	75	1.8	186	4.4	2.84	107	.252	.292	9	8	99	90	1.6	6	1	1.6
1889 Cin-a	11	9	.550	33	24	17	0	**5**	220	218	8.9	4	89	3.6	112	4.6	2.99	133	.273	.346	21	24	103	**114**	0.1	9	0	3.8
1890 Cin-N	12	10	.545	25	21	21	0	1	209	175	7.5	7	96	4.1	91	3.9	2.24	169	.242	.331	31	36	106	**126**	-0.7	5	0	3.4
1891 Cin-N	23	26	.469	51	47	42	1	0	426	390	8.2	15	187	4.0	124	2.6	3.23	97	.257	.338	5	-5	93	91	3.7	-4	3	-0.6
1892 Cin-N	21	13	.618	37	34	30	3	1	295	222	**6.8**	11	127	3.9	109	3.3	2.59	131	**.220**	.308	23	26	103	90	3.3	-2	0	2.4
1893 Cin-N	6	6	.500	15	13	11	0	1	122	130	9.6	4	65	4.8	24	1.8	4.43	108	.288	.378	3	5	102	99	0.0	2	0	0.6
Bal-N	12	16	.429	34	26	23	0	1	245	277	10.2	4	124	4.6	71	2.6	4.44	113	.301	.384	6	16	108	102	-1.1	-4	3	1.4
Yr	18	22	.450	49	39	34	0	**2**	367	407	10.0	8	189	4.6	95	2.3	4.44	111	.297	.382	10	21	106	102	-1.1	2	3	2.0
1894 Bal-N	6	9	.400	21	15	9	0	4	123	155	11.3	4	90	6.6	43	3.1	6.37	81	.330	.438	-14	-17	96	92	-3.3	6	0	-0.7
Cle-N	1	2	.333	4	4	3	0	0	33	46	12.5	3	10	2.7	3	0.8	7.64	77	.353	.399	-8	-6	111	75	-0.5	-1	0	-0.4
Yr	7	11	.389	25	19	12	0	**4**	156	201	11.6	7	100	5.8	46	2.7	6.63	80	.335	.430	-23	-23	99	75	-3.8	6	0	-1.1
Total 13	285	220	.564	556	505	469	31	15	4540	4199	8.3	96	1409	2.8	1807	3.6	3.05	117	.256	.315	247	258	101	99	37.3	50	27	35.2
■ **JOE MULLIGAN**	Mulligan, Joseph Ignatius b: 7/31/13, E.Weymouth, Mass. d: 6/5/86, W.Roxbury, Mass. BR/TR, 6'4", 210 lbs. Deb: 6/28/34																											
1934 Bos-A	1	0	1.000	14	2	1	0	0	45	46	9.2	1	27	5.4	13	2.6	3.60	131	.279	.379	4	6	105	136	0.5	-2	0	0.4
■ **DICK MULLIGAN**	Mulligan, Richard Charles b: 3/18/18, Wilkes-Barre, Pa. BL/TL, 6', 167 lbs. Deb: 9/24/41																											
1941 Was-A	0	1	.000	1	1	1	0	0	9	11	11.0	0	2	2.0	2	2.0	5.00	82	.306	.333	-1	-1	99	83	-0.4	-0	0	0.0
1946 Phi-N	2	2	.500	19	5	1	0	1	55	61	10.0	0	27	4.4	16	2.6	4.75	70	.289	.371	-8	-9	98	92	0.2	-1	0	-0.9
Bos-N	1	0	1.000	4	0	0	0	0	15	6	3.6	1	9	5.4	4	2.4	2.40	133	.122	.259	2	1	94	48	0.5	0	-0	0.1
Yr	3	2	.600	23	5	1	0	1	70	67	8.6	1	36	4.6	20	2.6	4.24	78	.254	.337	-6	-7	97	48	0.7	-1	-0	-0.8
1947 Bos-N	0	0	—	1	0	0	0	0	2	1	4.5	0	1	4.5	1	4.5	0.00	—	.167	.286	1	1	95	0	0.0	0	0	0.1
Total 3	3	3	.500	25	6	2	0	1	81	79	8.8	1	39	4.3	23	2.6	4.22	81	.262	.347	-6	-7	97	80	0.3	-1	-0	-0.7
■ **GEORGE MULLIN**	Mullin, George Joseph "Wabash George" b: 7/4/1880, Toledo, Ohio d: 1/7/44, Wabash, Ind. BR/TR, 5'11", 188 lbs. Deb: 5/04/02																											
1902 Det-A	13	16	.448	35	30	25	0	0	260	282	9.8	4	95	3.3	78	2.7	3.67	98	.301	.366	-3	-2	101	102	1.8	10	2	1.0
1903 Det-A	19	15	.559	41	36	31	6	**2**	321	284	8.0	4	106	3.0	170	4.8	2.24	126	.258	.323	25	21	96	121	3.3	8	5	3.8
1904 Det-A	17	23	.425	45	44	42	7	0	382	345	8.1	1	131	3.1	161	3.8	2.40	106	.263	.330	8	6	98	114	0.8	11	8	3.1
1905 Det-A	21	21	.500	44	41	**35**	1	0	**348**	303	7.8	4	138	3.6	168	4.3	2.51	106	.258	.336	5	5	100	115	-0.8	7	6	2.2
1906 Det-A	21	18	.538	40	40	35	2	0	330	315	8.6	3	108	2.9	123	3.4	2.78	107	.276	.339	-3	7	110	108	3.0	3	3	1.6
1907 Det-A	20	20	.500	46	42	35	5	3	357	346	8.7	1	106	2.7	146	3.7	2.60	96	.278	.335	-2	-4	98	109	-4.6	4	4	0.6
1908 Det-A	17	13	.567	39	30	26	1	0	291	301	9.3	1	71	2.2	121	3.7	3.09	76	.271	.319	-23	-24	99	103	-0.6	8	3	-1.4
1909 Det-A	**29**	8	**.784**	40	35	29	3	1	304	258	7.6	1	78	2.3	124	3.7	2.22	119	.234	.289	9	14	106	87	**8.5**	4	1	2.5
1910 Det-A	21	12	.636	38	32	27	5	0	289	260	8.1	7	102	3.2	98	3.1	2.87	88	.254	.330	-11	-11	100	107	3.5	6	0	-0.2
1911 Det-A	18	10	.643	30	29	25	2	0	234	245	9.4	7	61	2.3	87	3.3	3.08	116	.276	.331	7	13	107	109	2.5	7	-2	2.0
1912 Det-A	12	17	.414	30	29	22	2	0	226	214	8.5	3	92	3.7	88	3.5	3.54	90	.255	.335	-5	-8	96	92	-1.3	9	0	0.0
1913 Det-A	1	6	.143	7	7	4	0	0	52	53	9.2	1	18	3.1	16	2.8	2.77	106	.268	.335	1	1	101	118	-2.3	3	1	0.5
Was-A	3	5	.375	11	9	3	0	0	57	69	10.9	1	25	3.9	14	2.2	5.05	61	.283	.361	-13	-13	105	79	-1.4	0	1	-1.0
Yr	4	11	.267	18	16	7	0	0	109	122	10.1	2	43	3.6	30	2.5	3.96	76	.275	.346	-13	-12	103	79	-3.7	3	1	-0.5
1914 Ind-F	14	10	.583	36	20	11	1	2	203	202	9.0	4	91	4.0	74	3.3	2.70	128	.261	.346	11	17	108	131	0.3	9	-2	2.7
1915 New-F	2	2	.500	5	4	3	0	0	32	41	11.5	0	16	4.5	14	3.9	5.91	48	.342	.420	-10	-11	94	86	0.0	-0	0	-1.0
Total 14	228	196	.538	487	428	353	35	8	3686	3518	8.6	42	1238	3.0	1482	3.6	2.82	101	.266	.332	-5	11	101	108	12.7	90	28	16.4
■ **DOMINIC MULRENAN**	Mulrenan, Dominic Joseph b: 12/18/1893, Woburn, Mass. d: 7/27/64, Melrose, Mass. TR , 5'11", 170 lbs. Deb: 4/24/21																											
1921 Chi-A	2	8	.200	12	10	3	0	0	56	84	13.5	2	36	5.8	10	1.6	7.23	60	.359	.437	-18	-18	102	97	-2.5	-1	0	-1.5
■ **FRANK MULRONEY**	Mulroney, Francis Joseph b: 4/8/03, Mallard, Iowa d: 11/11/85, Aberdeen, Wash. BR/TR, 6', 170 lbs. Deb: 4/15/30																											
1930 Bos-A	0	1	.000	2	0	0	0	0	3	3	9.0	0	0	0.0	2	6.0	3.00	149	.273	.250	1	0	96	93	-0.4	0	0	0.1
■ **BOB MUNCRIEF**	Muncrief, Robert Cleveland b: 1/28/16, Madill, Okla. BR/TR, 6'2", 190 lbs. Deb: 9/30/37																											
1937 StL-A	0	0	—	1	1	0	0	0	2	3	13.5	1	2	9.0	0	0.0	4.50	106	.300	.417	0	0	103	214	0.0	0	0	0.0
1939 StL-A	0	0	—	2	0	0	0	0	3	7	21.0	1	3	9.0	1	3.0	15.00	32	.500	.556	-3	-3	105	104	0.0	0	0	-0.2
1941 StL-A	13	9	.591	36	24	12	2	1	214	221	9.3	18	53	2.2	67	2.8	3.66	114	.266	.311	12	13	101	104	3.1	2	-1	1.4
1942 StL-A	6	8	.429	24	18	7	1	0	134	149	10.0	11	31	2.1	39	2.6	3.90	96	.280	.315	-4	-2	102	103	-1.5	-1	-0	-0.3
1943 StL-A	13	12	.520	35	27	12	3	1	205	211	9.3	13	48	2.1	80	3.5	2.81	118	.264	.305	11	12	101	120	1.3	-2	-3	0.8
1944 StL-A	13	8	.619	33	27	12	3	1	219	216	8.9	11	50	2.1	88	3.6	3.08	111	.258	.297	8	8	100	100	1.2	2	-1	1.0
1945 StL-A	13	4	.765	27	15	10	0	1	146	132	8.1	8	44	2.7	54	3.3	2.71	142	.239	.293	11	18	114	104	4.4	-4	-1	1.5
1946 StL-A	3	12	.200	29	14	4	1	0	115	149	11.7	6	31	2.4	49	3.8	5.01	70	.314	.350	-19	-19	100	93	-4.1	-3	-1	-2.3
1947 StL-A	8	14	.364	31	23	7	0	0	176	210	10.7	14	51	2.6	74	3.8	4.91	80	.299	.342	-24	-20	106	94	-0.5	-4	0	-2.2
1948 Cle-A	5	4	.556	21	9	1	1	0	72	76	9.5	8	31	3.9	24	3.0	4.00	101	.279	.346	2	0	94	122	-0.4	-1	-0	0.0
1949 Pit-N	1	5	.167	13	4	1	0	3	36	44	11.0	8	13	3.3	11	2.8	6.25	66	.310	.358	-9	-8	102	100	-1.8	-0	1	-0.7
Chi-N	5	6	.455	34	3	1	0	2	75	80	9.6	9	31	3.7	36	4.3	4.56	86	.276	.339	-4	-5	97	103	0.6	2	-0	-0.3
Yr	6	11	.353	47	7	2	0	5	111	124	10.1	17	44	3.6	47	3.8	5.11	78	.287	.346	-13	-14	99	103	-1.2	-0	1	-1.0
1951 NY-A	0	0	—	2	0	0	0	0	3	5	15.0	0	4	12.0	2	6.0	9.00	40	.417	.529	-2	-2	88	116	0.0	0	0	0.0
Total 12	80	82	.494	288	165	67	11	9	1400	1503	9.7	108	392	2.5	525	3.4	3.81	99	.275	.320	-21	-8	102	104	2.3	-10	-6	-1.3
■ **RED MUNGER**	Munger, George David b: 10/4/18, Houston, Tex. BR/TR, 6'2", 200 lbs. Deb: 5/01/43																											
1943 StL-N	9	5	.643	32	9	5	0	2	93	101	9.8	2	42	4.1	45	4.4	3.97	85	.281	.347	-6	-6	100	103	-0.3	1	1	-0.3
1944 StL-N	11	3	.786	21	12	7	2	2	121	92	6.8	2	41	3.0	55	4.1	1.34	257	.212	.282	31	28	95	161	2.4	-2	3	3.2
1946 StL-N	2	2	.500	10	7	2	0	1	49	47	8.6	0	12	2.2	28	5.1	3.31	106	.255	.296	1	1	103	78	-0.3	1	2	0.4
1947 StL-N	16	5	.762	40	31	13	6	3	224	218	8.8	12	76	3.1	123	4.9	3.38	125	.255	.316	17	21	104	100	5.0	1	2	2.4
1948 StL-N	10	11	.476	39	25	7	2	0	166	179	9.7	13	74	4.0	72	3.9	4.50	87	.272	.344	-10	-11	99	97	-1.5	1	2	-0.8
1949 StL-N	15	8	.652	35	28	12	2	2	188	179	8.6	13	87	4.2	82	3.9	3.88	112	.255	.334	3	10	108	102	1.0	4	1	1.5
1950 StL-N	7	8	.467	32	20	5	1	0	155	158	9.2	15	70	4.1	61	3.5	3.89	109	.262	.339	4	6	103	109	-0.6	-2	0	0.5
1951 StL-N	4	6	.400	23	11	3	0	0	95	106	10.0	13	46	4.4	44	4.2	5.31	75	.286	.358	-14	-14	101	98	-1.2	-0	2	-1.1
1952 StL-N	0	1	.000	1	1	0	0	0	4	7	15.8	2	1	2.3	1	2.3	13.50	27	.389	.429	-4	-4	97	84	-0.4	-0	0	-0.3
Pit-N	0	3	.000	5	4	0	0	0	26	30	10.4	6	10	3.5	8	2.8	7.27	54	.283	.339	-10	-10	105	77	-1.4	-1	1	-0.8
Yr	0	4	.000	6	5	0	0	0	30	37	11.1	8	11	3.3	9	2.7	8.10	48	.296	.345	-15	-14	104	77	-1.8	-0	1	-1.1
1956 Pit-N	3	4	.429	35	13	0	0	2	107	126	10.6	8	41	3.4	45	3.8	4.04	96	.299	.352	-3	-2	103	115	0.0	-1	-1	-0.2
Total 10	77	56	.579	273	161	54	13	12	1228	1243	9.1	86	500	3.7	564	4.1	3.83	104	.264	.332	8	19	102	107	2.7	0	13	4.5
■ **VAN MUNGO**	Mungo, Van Lingle b: 6/8/11, Pageland, S.C. d: 2/12/85, Pageland, S.C. BR/TR, 6'2", 185 lbs. Deb: 9/07/31																											
1931 Bro-N	3	1	.750	5	4	2	1	0	31	27	7.8	0	13	3.8	12	3.5	2.32	168	.241	.325	5	5	101	129	1.0	1	-0	0.6
1932 Bro-N	13	11	.542	39	33	11	1	2	223	224	9.0	9	115	4.6	107	4.3	4.44	84	.260	.350	-14	-18	96	90	0.5	1	2	-1.5
1933 Bro-N	16	15	.516	41	28	18	3	0	248	223	8.1	7	84	3.0	110	4.0	2.72	120	.236	.293	17	15	98	94	3.0	-0	1	1.7
1934 Bro-N	18	16	.529	45	38	22	3	3	**315**	300	8.6	15	104	3.0	184	5.3	3.37	115	.249	.306	24	18	95	96	2.5	4	1	2.3
1935 Bro-N	16	10	.615	37	26	18	**4**	2	214	205	8.6	13	90	3.8	143	**6.0**	3.66	104	.252	.323	9	4	95	101	4.3	5	1	0.9

YEAR	TM/L	W	L	PCT	G	GS	CG	SHO	SV	IP	H	H/G	HR	BB	BB/G	SO	SO/G	ERA	/A	OAVG	OOBP	PR	/A	PF	CPI	WAT	PB	PD	TPI
1936	Bro-N	18	19	.486	45	37	22	2	3	312	275	7.9	8	118	3.4	**238**	**6.9**	3.35	128	**.234**	.302	23	32	107	82	2.2	-4	2	3.0
1937	Bro-N	9	11	.450	25	21	14	0	3	161	136	**7.6**	3	56	3.1	122	**6.8**	2.91	144	**.229**	.293	18	23	107	89	0.9	2	3	3.0
1938	Bro-N	4	11	.267	24	18	6	2	0	133	133	9.0	11	72	4.9	72	4.9	3.92	92	.259	.350	-2	-4	96	110	-3.3	2	1	-0.1
1939	Bro-N	4	5	.444	14	10	1	0	0	77	70	8.2	7	33	3.9	34	4.0	3.27	127	.239	.316	6	8	106	108	-0.8	2	-1	0.8
1940	Bro-N	1	0	1.000	7	0	0	0	1	22	24	9.8	1	10	4.1	9	3.7	2.45	167	.282	.354	3	4	106	184	0.5	-1	-0	0.3
1941	Bro-N	0	0	—	2	0	0	0	0	2	1	4.5	0	2	9.0	0	0.0	4.50	80	.143	.333	-0	-0	99	48	0.0	0	0	0.0
1942	NY-N	1	2	.333	9	5	0	0	0	36	38	9.5	4	21	5.3	27	6.8	6.00	56	.273	.364	-11	-11	101	83	-0.5	-0	0	-0.9
1943	NY-N	3	7	.300	45	13	2	2	2	154	140	8.2	7	79	4.6	83	4.9	3.92	85	.243	.331	-9	-10	99	91	-0.8	-1	1	-0.9
1945	NY-N	14	7	.667	26	26	7	2	0	183	161	7.9	4	71	3.5	101	5.0	3.20	119	.238	.306	12	12	100	93	3.7	4	-0	1.7
Total	14	120	115	.511	364	259	123	20	16	2111	1957	8.3	89	868	3.7	1242	5.3	3.47	110	.245	.317	82	78	100	95	13.2	13	10	10.9
■ **MANNY MUNIZ**	Muniz, Manuel (Rodriguez) b: 12/31/47, Caguas, P.R. BR/TR, 5'11", 190 lbs. Deb: 9/03/71																												
1971	Phi-N	0	1	.000	5	0	0	0	0	10	9	8.1	2	8	7.2	6	5.4	7.20	50	.225	.354	-4	-4	105	66	-0.4	-0	-0	-0.3
■ **SCOTT MUNNINGHOFF**	Munninghoff, Scott Andrew b: 12/5/58, Cincinnati, Ohio BR/TR, 6', 175 lbs. Deb: 4/13/80																												
1980	Phi-N	0	0	—	4	0	0	0	0	6	8	12.0	0	5	7.5	2	3.0	4.50	85	.320	.419	-1	-0	106	134	0.0	1	0	0.1
■ **LES MUNNS**	Munns, Leslie Ernest "Big Ed" or "Nemo" b: 12/1/08, Fort Bragg, Cal. BR/TR, 6'5", 212 lbs. Deb: 4/22/34																												
1934	Bro-N	3	7	.300	33	9	4	0	0	99	106	9.6	7	60	5.5	41	3.7	4.73	82	.280	.374	-7	-9	95	106	-1.8	2	2	-0.5
1935	Bro-N	1	3	.250	21	5	0	0	1	58	74	11.5	5	33	5.1	13	2.0	5.59	68	.319	.407	-10	-11	95	113	-0.8	-0	-2	-1.2
1936	StL-N	0	3	.000	7	1	0	0	1	24	23	8.6	2	12	4.5	4	1.5	3.00	127	.240	.321	3	2	95	118	-1.4	-1	1	0.2
Total	3	4	13	.235	61	15	4	0	2	181	203	10.1	14	105	5.2	58	2.9	4.77	81	.287	.378	-15	-19	95	110	-4.0	1	1	-1.5
■ **STEVE MURA**	Mura, Stephen Andrew b: 2/12/55, New Orleans, La. BR/TR, 6'2", 188 lbs. Deb: 9/05/78																												
1978	SD-N	0	2	.000	5	2	0	0	0	8	15	16.9	1	5	5.6	5	5.6	11.25	29	.441	.500	-7	-7	93	90	-0.9	-0	-0	-0.6
1979	SD-N	4	4	.500	38	5	0	0	2	73	57	7.0	6	37	4.6	59	7.3	3.08	118	.217	.307	5	5	97	100	0.6	-1	-0	0.3
1980	SD-N	8	7	.533	37	23	3	1	2	169	149	7.9	9	86	4.6	109	5.8	3.67	92	.246	.331	-1	-5	94	100	1.2	-0	0	-0.5
1981	SD-N	5	14	.263	23	22	2	0	0	139	156	10.1	10	50	3.2	70	4.5	4.27	77	.285	.336	-12	-15	95	101	-3.1	-0	1	-1.4
1982	StL-N	12	11	.522	35	30	7	1	0	184	196	9.6	16	80	3.9	84	4.1	4.06	91	.278	.347	-9	-7	102	110	-1.0	-4	-1	-1.2
1983	Chi-A	0	0	—	6	0	0	0	0	12	13	9.8	1	6	4.5	4	3.0	4.50	92	.260	.333	-1	-0	102	89	0.0	0	-0	0.0
1985	Oak-A	1	1	.500	23	1	0	0	1	48	41	7.7	3	25	4.7	29	5.4	4.13	94	.225	.316	0	-1	93	77	0.0	0	-0	-0.1
Total	7	30	39	.435	167	83	12	2	5	633	627	8.9	46	289	4.1	360	5.1	4.00	89	.263	.336	-24	-32	97	101	-3.2	-5	-0	-3.5
■ **MASANORI MURAKAMI**	Murakami, Masanori b: 5/6/44, Otsuki, Japan BL/TL, 6', 180 lbs. Deb: 9/01/64																												
1964	SF-N	1	0	1.000	9	0	0	0	1	15	8	4.8	1	1	0.6	15	9.0	1.80	195	.163	.170	3	3	99	45	0.5	-0	-0	0.2
1965	SF-N	4	1	.800	45	1	0	0	8	74	57	6.9	9	22	2.7	85	10.3	3.77	103	.205	.270	-2	1	109	68	1.3	-0	-1	0.0
Total	2	5	1	.833	54	1	0	0	9	89	65	6.6	10	23	2.3	100	10.1	3.44	111	.199	.255	1	4	107	64	1.8	-1	-2	0.2
■ **TIM MURCHISON**	Murchison, Thomas Malcolm b: 10/8/1896, Liberty, N.C. d: 10/20/62, Liberty, N.C. BR/TL, 6', 185 lbs. Deb: 6/21/17																												
1917	StL-N	0	0	—	1	0	0	0	0	1	0	0.0	0	2	18.0	2	18.0	0.00	—	.000	.400	0	0	102	0	0.0	0	0	0.0
1920	Cle-A	0	0	—	2	0	0	0	0	5	3	5.4	0	4	7.2	0	0.0	0.00	—	.200	.368	2	2	100	0	0.0	-0	1	0.3
Total	2	0	0	—	3	0	0	0	0	6	3	4.5	0	6	9.0	2	3.0	0.00	—	.167	.375	2	2	100	0	0.0	-0	1	0.3
■ **RED MURFF**	Murff, John Robert b: 4/1/21, Burlington, Tex. BR/TR, 6'3", 195 lbs. Deb: 4/21/56																												
1956	Mil-N	0	0	—	14	1	0	0	1	24	25	9.4	3	7	2.6	18	6.8	4.50	81	.272	.311	-2	-2	96	90	0.0	-0	0	-0.1
1957	Mil-N	2	2	.500	12	1	0	0	2	26	31	10.7	3	11	3.8	13	4.5	4.85	70	.301	.365	-3	-4	88	108	-0.3	-1	1	-0.3
Total	2	2	2	.500	26	2	0	0	3	50	56	10.1	6	18	3.2	31	5.6	4.68	75	.287	.339	-5	-6	92	99	-0.3	-1	1	-0.4
■ **CON MURPHY**	Murphy, Cornelius B. "Monk" or "Razzle Dazzle" b: 10/15/1863, Worcester, Mass. d: 8/1/14, Worcester, Mass. 5'9", 130 lbs. Deb: 9/11/1884																												
1884	Phi-N	0	3	.000	3	3	3	0	0	26	37	12.8	1	6	2.1	10	3.5	6.58	44	.344	.379	-10	-11	97	77	-1.4	-1	0	-0.8
1890	Bro-P	4	10	.286	20	14	11	0	2	139	168	10.9	2	82	5.3	29	1.9	4.79	93	.311	.402	-9	-5	105	99	-3.6	-1	0	-0.3
	BB-a	3	9	.250	12	12	10	0	0	96	121	11.3	6	46	4.3	26	2.4	5.72	69	.324	.398	-20	-19	103	97	-1.1	-0	0	-1.4
Total	2	7	22	.241	35	29	24	0	2	261	326	11.2	9	134	4.6	65	2.2	5.31	77	.319	.398	-39	-35	104	96	-6.1	-3	0	-2.5
■ **DANNY MURPHY**	Murphy, Daniel Francis b: 8/23/42, Beverly, Mass. BL/TR, 5'11", 185 lbs. Deb: 6/18/60																												
1969	Chi-A	2	1	.667	17	0	0	0	4	31	28	8.1	2	10	2.9	16	4.6	2.03	196	.252	.317	5	7	110	173	0.6	0	-0	0.7
1970	Chi-A	2	3	.400	51	0	0	0	5	81	82	9.1	11	49	5.4	42	4.7	5.67	71	.273	.368	-18	-15	108	94	0.2	2	-1	-1.3
Total	2	4	4	.500	68	0	0	0	9	112	110	8.8	13	59	4.7	58	4.7	4.66	86	.268	.355	-12	-8	108	116	0.8	2	-1	-0.6
■ **ED MURPHY**	Murphy, Edward J. b: 1/22/1877, Auburn, N.Y. d: 1/29/35, Weedsport, N.Y. TR, 6'1", 186 lbs. Deb: 4/23/1898																												
1898	Phi-N	1	2	.333	7	3	2	0	0	30	41	12.3	3	10	3.0	8	2.4	5.10	67	.349	.400	-5	-6	94	110	-0.5	1	0	-0.3
1901	StL-N	10	9	.526	23	21	16	0	0	165	201	11.0	5	32	1.7	42	2.3	4.20	75	.324	.358	-16	-19	95	96	-0.2	4	2	-1.6
1902	StL-N	10	6	.625	23	17	12	1	1	164	187	10.3	7	31	1.7	37	2.0	3.02	91	.312	.349	-4	-5	99	119	3.1	1	2	-0.3
1903	StL-N	4	8	.333	15	12	9	0	0	106	108	9.2	2	38	3.2	16	1.4	3.31	100	.293	.368	-0	0	102	104	0.2	-1	0	0.0
Total	4	25	25	.500	68	53	39	1	1	465	537	10.4	17	111	2.1	103	2.0	3.64	84	.315	.360	-26	-30	98	107	2.6	5	3	-2.2
■ **JOHN MURPHY**	Murphy, John H. b: 3/8/1867, Philadelphia, Pa. Deb: 4/17/1884																												
1884	WiL-U	0	6	.000	7	6	5	0	0	48	52	9.8	3	2	0.4	27	5.1	3.00	110	.281	.289	0	2	109	114	-2.9	-3	0	-0.1
	Alt-U	5	6	.455	14	10	10	0	0	112	141	11.3	3	9	0.7	46	3.7	3.86	85	.313	.326	-11	-7	109	107	2.3	-5	0	-1.0
	Yr	5	12	.294	21	16	15	0	0	160	193	10.9	6	11	0.6	73	4.1	3.60	91	.304	.315	-10	-6	109	107	-0.6	-3	0	-1.1
■ **JOHNNY MURPHY**	Murphy, John Joseph "Grandma" "Fireman" Or "Fordham Johnny" b: 7/14/08, New York, N.Y. d: 1/14/70, New York, N.Y. BR/TR, 6'2", 190 lbs. Deb: 5/19/32																												
1932	NY-A	0	0	—	2	0	0	0	0	3	7	21.0	0	3	9.0	2	6.0	18.00	23	.438	.526	-5	-5	91	64	0.0	0	0	-0.2
1934	NY-A	14	10	.583	40	20	10	0	4	208	193	8.4	11	76	3.3	70	3.0	3.12	134	.250	.313	32	24	93	113	-0.5	-3	1	2.1
1935	NY-A	10	5	.667	40	8	4	0	5	117	110	8.5	7	55	4.2	28	2.2	4.08	98	.243	.324	5	-1	90	86	1.4	2	-1	0.0
1936	NY-A	9	3	.750	27	5	2	0	5	88	90	9.2	5	36	3.7	34	3.5	3.38	134	.262	.332	16	11	90	120	1.6	4	1	1.4
1937	NY-A	13	4	.765	39	4	0	0	10	110	121	9.9	7	50	4.1	36	2.9	4.17	108	.277	.346	5	4	97	106	2.8	1	4	0.8
1938	NY-A	8	2	.800	32	2	1	0	**11**	91	90	8.9	5	41	4.1	43	4.3	4.25	114	.256	.332	**5**	**6**	102	91	2.2	-3	1	0.4
1939	NY-A	3	6	.333	38	0	0	0	**19**	61	57	8.4	2	28	4.1	30	4.4	4.43	89	.252	.327	1	-3	85	84	-2.3	1	0	-0.1
1940	NY-A	8	4	.667	35	1	0	0	9	63	58	8.3	5	15	2.1	23	3.3	3.71	113	.247	.286	5	3	96	87	1.4	-0	1	0.4
1941	NY-A	8	3	.727	35	0	0	0	**15**	77	68	7.9	1	40	4.7	29	3.4	1.99	198	.237	.324	**18**	**17**	95	162	1.2	-1	-1	1.4
1942	NY-A	4	10	.286	31	0	0	0	**11**	58	66	10.2	2	23	3.6	24	3.7	3.41	100	.293	.350	2	0	94	135	-4.1	0	0	0.0
1943	NY-A	12	4	.750	37	0	0	0	8	68	44	5.8	2	30	4.0	31	4.1	2.51	123	.183	.269	6	4	94	69	2.7	-2	-0	0.2
1946	NY-A	4	2	.667	27	0	0	0	7	45	40	8.0	4	19	3.8	19	3.8	3.40	101	.240	.307	1	0	98	99	0.7	-0	1	0.1
1947	Bos-A	0	0	—	32	0	0	0	3	55	41	6.7	1	28	4.6	9	1.5	2.78	142	.206	.299	6	7	107	84	0.0	1	0	0.9
Total	13	93	53	.637	415	40	17	0	107	1044	985	8.5	52	444	3.8	378	3.3	3.50	117	.249	.321	98	69	94	104	7.1	-0	8	7.4
■ **JOE MURPHY**	Murphy, Joseph Akin b: 9/7/1866, St.Louis, Mo. d: 3/28/51, Coral Gables, Fla. 5'11", 160 lbs. Deb: 4/28/1886																												
1886	Cin-a	2	3	.400	5	5	5	0	0	46	50	9.8	0	21	4.1	11	2.2	4.89	68	.287	.364	-7	-8	96	86	-0.3	-3	0	-0.8
	StL-N	0	4	.000	4	4	3	0	0	33	45	12.3	3	16	4.4	11	3.0	7.09	46	.339	.410	-14	-14	98	87	-1.9	0	0	-1.0
	StL-a	1	0	1.000	1	1	1	0	0	7	5	6.4	0	3	3.9	3	3.9	9.00	41	.209	.298	-4	-4	106	25	0.5	-1	0	-0.2
1887	StL-a	1	0	1.000	1	1	1	0	0	9	13	13.0	0	4	4.0	5	5.0	5.00	90	.352	.416	-1	-1	105	118	0.5	-1	0	0.0
Total	2	4	7	.364	11	11	10	0	0	95	113	10.7	3	44	4.2	30	2.8	5.97	57	.307	.381	-26	-27	98	85	-1.2	-4	0	-2.0
■ **ROB MURPHY**	Murphy, Robert Albert b: 5/26/60, Miami, Fla. BL/TL, 6'2", 200 lbs. Deb: 9/13/85																												
1985	Cin-N	0	0	—	2	0	0	0	0	3	2	6.0	1	2	6.0	1	3.0	6.00	63	.200	.333	-1	-1	105	88	0.0	0	0	0.0
1986	Cin-N	6	0	1.000	34	0	0	0	1	50	26	4.7	0	21	3.8	36	6.5	0.72	538	.155	.241	17	18	104	128	3.0	-0	0	1.9
1987	Cin-N	8	5	.615	87	0	0	0	3	101	91	8.1	7	32	2.9	99	8.8	3.03	139	.239	.296	12	13	103	100	1.4	0	0	1.4
1988	Cin-N	0	6	.000	**76**	0	0	0	3	85	69	7.3	3	38	4.0	74	7.8	3.07	118	.229	.309	4	5	105	100	-2.9	0	1	0.6
Total	4	14	11	.560	199	0	0	0	7	239	188	7.1	11	93	3.5	210	7.9	2.60	151	.219	.290	31	35	104	105	1.5	-0	1	3.9

■ BOB MURPHY   Murphy, Robert J.   b: 12/26/1866, Dutchess Co., N.Y.   Deb: 4/24/1890

■ TOM MURPHY   Murphy, Thomas Andrew   b: 12/30/45, Cleveland, Ohio   BR/TR, 6'3", 185 lbs.   Deb: 6/13/68

■ WALTER MURPHY   Murphy, Walter Joseph   b: 9/27/07, New York, N.Y.   BR/TR, 6'1.5", 180 lbs.   Deb: 4/19/31

■ DALE MURRAY   Murray, Dale Albert   b: 2/2/50, Cuero, Tex.   BR/TR, 6'4", 205 lbs.   Deb: 7/07/74

■ GEORGE MURRAY   Murray, George King "Smiler"   b: 9/23/1898, Charlotte, N.C.   d: 10/18/55, Memphis, Tenn.   BR/TR, 6'2", 200 lbs.   Deb: 5/08/22

■ JIM MURRAY   Murray, James Francis "Big Jim"   b: 12/31/1900, Scranton, Pa.   d: 7/15/73, New York, N.Y.   BB/TL, 6'2", 210 lbs.   Deb: 7/03/22

■ AMBY MURRAY   Murray, Joseph Ambrose   b: 6/4/13, Fall River, Mass.   BL/TL, 5'7", 150 lbs.   Deb: 7/05/36

■ JOE MURRAY   Murray, Joseph Ambrose   b: 11/11/20, Wilkes-Barre, Pa.   BL/TL, 6', 165 lbs.   Deb: 8/17/50

■ PAT MURRAY   Murray, Patrick Joseph   b: 7/18/1897, Scottsville, N.Y.   d: 11/5/83, Rochester, N.Y.   BR/TL, 6', 175 lbs.   Deb: 7/01/19

■ DENNIS MUSGRAVES   Musgraves, Dennis Eugene   b: 12/25/43, Indianapolis, Ind.   BR/TR, 6'4", 188 lbs.   Deb: 7/09/65

■ STAN MUSIAL   Musial, Stanley Frank "Stan The Man"   b: 11/21/20, Donora, Pa.   BL/TL, 6', 175 lbs.   Deb: 9/17/41   H

■ JEFF MUSSELMAN   Musselman, Jeffrey Joseph   b: 6/21/63, Doylestown, Pa.   BL/TL, 6', 180 lbs.   Deb: 9/02/86

■ RON MUSSELMAN   Musselman, Ralph Ronald   b: 11/11/54, Wilmington, N.C.   BR/TR, 6'2", 185 lbs.   Deb: 8/18/82

■ PAUL MUSSER   Musser, Paul   b: 6/24/1889, Millheim, Pa.   d: 7/7/73, State College, Pa.   BR/TR, 6', 175 lbs.   Deb: 6/06/12

■ BARNEY MUSSILL   Mussill, Bernard James   b: 10/1/19, Woodville, Pa.   BR/TL, 6'1", 200 lbs.   Deb: 4/20/44

■ ALEX MUSTAIKIS   Mustaikis, Alexander Dominick   b: 3/26/09, Chelsea, Mass.   d: 1/17/70, Scranton, Pa.   BR/TR, 6'3", 180 lbs.   Deb: 7/07/40

■ ELMER MYERS   Myers, Elmer Glenn   b: 3/2/1894, York Springs, Pa.   d: 7/29/76, Collingwood, N.J.   BR/TR, 6'2", 185 lbs.   Deb: 10/06/15

YEAR	TM/L	W	L	PCT	G	GS	CG	SHO	SV	IP	H	H/G	HR	BB	BB/G	SO	SO/G	ERA	/A	OAVG	OOBP	PR	/A	PF	CPI	WAT	PB	PD	TPI
BOB MURPHY																													
1890	NY-N	1	0	1.000	2	1	1	0	0	18	23	11.5	0	10	5.0	8	4.0	5.50	61	.327	.411	-4	-4	94	92	0.5	-1	0	-0.3
TOM MURPHY																													
1968	Cal-A	5	6	.455	15	15	3	0	0	99	67	6.1	5	28	2.5	56	5.1	2.18	131	.191	.256	9	7	96	83	0.4	-2	-1	0.4
1969	Cal-A	10	16	.385	36	35	4	0	0	216	213	8.9	12	69	2.9	100	4.2	4.21	87	.260	.330	-14	-13	101	87	-1.8	-1	1	-1.2
1970	Cal-A	16	13	.552	39	38	5	2	0	227	223	8.8	32	81	3.2	99	3.9	4.24	80	.261	.326	-13	-21	92	100	0.8	3	-1	-1.9
1971	Cal-A	6	17	.261	37	36	7	0	0	243	228	8.4	24	82	3.0	89	3.3	3.78	91	.256	.318	-8	-9	99	99	-5.4	1	1	-0.7
1972	Cal-A	0	0	—	6	0	0	0	0	10	13	11.7	0	8	7.2	2	1.8	5.40	51	.342	.438	-3	-3	90	118	0.0	-0	1	-0.2
	KC-A	4	4	.500	18	9	1	1	1	70	77	9.9	3	16	2.1	34	4.4	3.09	99	.287	.339	-0	-0	100	127	0.1	-1	1	0.0
	Yr	4	4	.500	24	9	1	1	1	80	90	10.1	3	24	2.7	36	4.0	3.37	90	.293	.353	-3	-3	98	127	0.1	-0	1	-0.2
1973	StL-N	3	7	.300	19	13	2	0	0	89	89	9.0	8	22	2.2	42	4.2	3.74	88	.269	.311	-1	-4	90	94	-2.0	1	1	-0.3
1974	Mil-A	10	10	.500	70	0	0	0	20	123	97	7.1	6	51	3.7	47	3.4	1.90	195	.224	.302	24	25	103	147	0.7	1	2	2.9
1975	Mil-A	1	9	.100	52	0	0	0	20	72	85	10.6	3	27	3.4	32	4.0	4.63	83	.295	.358	-7	-6	101	102	-3.8	0	0	-0.5
1976	Mil-A	0	1	.000	15	0	0	0	1	18	25	12.5	2	9	4.5	7	3.5	7.50	47	.313	.383	-8	-8	100	81	-0.4	0	0	-0.7
	Bos-A	4	5	.444	37	0	0	0	8	81	91	10.1	5	25	2.8	32	3.6	3.44	112	.290	.336	1	4	110	124	-0.5	-0	0	0.4
	Yr	4	6	.400	52	0	0	0	9	99	116	10.5	7	34	3.1	39	3.5	4.18	91	.293	.342	-7	-4	108	124	-0.9	0	0	-0.5
1977	Bos-A	0	1	.000	16	0	0	0	0	31	44	12.8	6	12	3.5	13	3.8	6.68	71	.338	.392	-9	-7	116	103	-0.4	-0	0	-0.5
	Tor-A	2	1	.667	19	1	0	0	2	52	63	10.9	6	18	3.1	26	4.5	3.63	117	.304	.355	3	4	105	142	0.8	-0	0	0.3
	Yr	2	2	.500	35	1	0	0	2	83	107	11.6	12	30	3.3	39	4.2	4.77	93	.317	.369	-6	-3	109	142	0.4	0	0	-0.2
1978	Tor-A	6	9	.400	50	0	0	0	7	94	87	8.3	11	37	3.5	36	3.4	3.93	98	.256	.313	-2	-1	102	102	0.4	0	2	0.1
1979	Tor-A	1	2	.333	10	0	0	0	0	18	23	11.5	1	8	4.0	6	3.0	5.50	81	.311	.378	-3	-2	106	93	0.0	0	1	0.0
Total 12		68	101	.402	439	147	22	3	59	1443	1425	8.9	123	493	3.1	621	3.9	3.78	94	.263	.325	-31	-35	99	105	-11.1	0	7	-1.9
WALTER MURPHY																													
1931	Bos-A	0	0	—	2	0	0	0	0	2	4	18.0	0	1	4.5	0	0.0	9.00	47	.444	.500	-1	-1	97	108	0.0	0	0	0.0
DALE MURRAY																													
1974	Mon-N	1	1	.500	32	0	0	0	10	70	46	5.9	1	23	3.0	31	4.0	1.03	368	.187	.255	20	21	104	130	0.0	-1	0	2.2
1975	Mon-N	15	8	.652	63	0	0	0	9	111	134	10.9	3	39	3.2	43	3.5	3.97	100	.305	.353	-4	-0	109	107	4.5	1	3	0.3
1976	Mon-N	4	9	.308	81	0	0	0	13	113	117	9.3	1	37	2.9	35	2.8	3.27	111	.277	.322	3	4	103	109	-0.6	-1	4	0.8
1977	Cin-N	7	2	.778	61	1	0	0	4	102	125	11.0	13	46	4.1	42	3.7	4.94	78	.314	.379	-12	-12	99	118	2.4	-0	0	-1.1
1978	Cin-N	1	1	.500	15	0	0	0	2	33	34	9.3	1	17	4.6	25	6.8	4.09	90	.272	.354	-2	-2	102	102	-0.1	-0	1	-0.1
	NY-N	8	5	.615	53	0	0	0	5	86	85	8.9	4	36	3.8	37	3.9	3.66	97	.266	.330	-1	-1	99	106	2.4	-0	2	0.0
	Yr	9	6	.600	68	0	0	0	7	119	119	9.0	5	53	4.0	62	4.7	3.78	95	.266	.335	-3	-3	100	106	2.4	-0	2	-0.1
1979	NY-N	4	8	.333	58	0	0	0	4	97	105	9.7	6	52	4.8	37	3.4	4.82	75	.287	.367	-12	-13	96	98	-0.8	-0	1	-1.2
	Mon-N	1	2	.333	9	0	0	0	1	13	14	9.7	1	3	2.1	4	2.8	2.77	136	.292	.321	1	1	101	150	-0.6	-0	0	0.1
	Yr	5	10	.333	67	0	0	0	5	110	119	9.7	7	55	4.5	41	3.4	4.58	79	.285	.362	-10	-12	97	150	-1.4	-0	1	-1.1
1980	Mon-N	0	1	.000	16	0	0	0	0	29	39	12.1	3	12	3.7	16	5.0	6.21	57	.315	.372	-8	-9	98	89	-0.4	-0	-1	-0.9
1981	Tor-A	1	0	1.000	11	0	0	0	0	15	12	7.2	0	5	3.0	12	7.2	1.20	345	.211	.274	4	5	113	140	0.5	0	1	0.6
1982	Tor-A	8	7	.533	56	0	0	0	11	111	115	9.3	3	32	2.6	60	4.9	3.16	141	.268	.319	11	16	109	108	0.8	0	3	1.9
1983	NY-A	2	4	.333	40	0	0	0	1	94	113	10.8	5	22	2.1	45	4.3	4.50	89	.297	.328	-4	-5	98	94	-1.1	0	0	-0.4
1984	NY-A	1	2	.333	19	0	0	0	0	24	30	11.3	2	5	1.9	13	4.9	4.88	76	.306	.349	-2	-3	93	99	-0.5	-0	0	-0.2
1985	NY-A	0	0	—	3	0	0	0	0	2	4	18.0	0	2	9.0	0	0.0	13.50	29	.400	.400	-2	-2	94	50	0.0	0	0	-0.1
	Tex-A	0	0	—	1	0	0	0	0	1	3	27.0	0	0	0.0	0	0.0	18.00	25	.750	.600	-2	-1	110	92	0.0	0	0	0.0
	Yr	0	0	—	4	0	0	0	0	3	7	21.0	0	2	6.0	0	0.0	15.00	27	.500	.467	-4	-4	99	92	0.0	0	0	-0.1
Total 12		53	50	.515	518	1	0	0	60	901	976	9.7	40	329	3.3	400	4.0	3.86	100	.282	.337	-9	-0	102	108	6.6	-3	13	1.9
GEORGE MURRAY																													
1922	NY-A	4	2	.667	22	2	0	0	0	57	53	8.4	9	26	4.1	14	2.2	3.95	101	.255	.332	1	0	99	81	0.4	2	0	0.2
1923	Bos-A	7	11	.389	39	18	5	0	0	178	190	9.6	9	87	4.4	40	2.0	4.90	86	.291	.363	-18	-14	106	96	-0.2	-3	-2	-1.6
1924	Bos-A	2	9	.182	28	7	0	0	0	80	97	10.9	6	32	3.6	27	3.0	6.75	60	.307	.365	-22	-21	105	77	-3.2	-1	0	-1.8
1926	Was-A	6	3	.667	12	12	5	0	0	81	89	9.9	1	37	4.1	28	3.1	5.67	69	.287	.357	-15	-16	97	76	1.3	-2	-1	-1.6
1927	Was-A	1	1	.500	7	3	0	0	0	18	18	9.0	1	15	7.5	5	2.5	7.00	57	.265	.393	-6	-6	96	74	0.0	-0	-1	-0.5
1933	Chi-A	0	0	—	2	0	0	0	0	2	3	13.5	0	2	9.0	0	0.0	9.00	49	.375	.455	-1	-1	103	95	0.0	0	0	0.0
Total 6		20	26	.435	110	42	10	0	0	416	450	9.7	17	199	4.3	114	2.5	5.39	77	.288	.360	-62	-57	102	85	-1.7	-4	-3	-5.3
JIM MURRAY																													
1922	Bro-N	0	0	—	4	0	0	0	1	6	8	12.0	0	3	4.5	3	4.5	4.50	87	.320	.393	-0	-0	95	110	0.0	0	-0	0.0
AMBY MURRAY																													
1936	Bos-N	0	0	—	4	1	0	0	0	11	15	12.3	1	3	2.5	2	1.6	4.09	95	.319	.353	-0	-0	96	129	0.0	0	0	0.0
JOE MURRAY																													
1950	Phi-A	0	3	.000	8	2	0	0	0	30	34	10.2	1	21	6.3	18	5.4	5.70	75	.283	.385	-4	-5	93	87	-1.4	-2	0	-0.4
PAT MURRAY																													
1919	Phi-N	0	2	.000	8	2	1	0	0	34	50	13.2	0	12	3.2	11	2.9	6.35	50	.347	.402	-13	-12	109	91	-0.9	-2	-0	-1.3
DENNIS MUSGRAVES																													
1965	NY-N	0	0	—	5	1	0	0	0	16	11	6.2	0	7	3.9	11	6.2	0.56	654	.200	.308	5	6	104	425	0.0	-0	0	0.6
STAN MUSIAL																													
1952	StL-N	0	0	—	1	0	0	0	0	0	0	—	0	0	—	0	—	—	—	.000	.000				97	0.0	1	0	0.0
JEFF MUSSELMAN																													
1986	Tor-A	0	0	—	6	0	0	0	0	5	8	14.4	1	5	9.0	4	7.2	10.80	40	.333	.448	-4	-4	104	79	0.0	0	0	-0.2
1987	Tor-A	12	5	.706	68	1	0	0	3	89	75	7.6	7	54	5.5	54	5.5	4.15	107	.237	.346	3	3	99	100	2.6	0	1	0.4
1988	Tor-A	8	5	.615	15	15	0	0	0	85	80	8.5	4	30	3.2	39	4.1	3.18	124	.252	.319	8	7	99	108	1.2	0	-1	0.6
Total 3		20	10	.667	89	16	0	0	3	179	163	8.2	12	89	4.5	97	4.9	3.87	108	.248	.338	7	6	99	103	3.8	0	0	0.8
RON MUSSELMAN																													
1982	Sea-A	1	0	1.000	12	0	0	0	0	16	18	10.1	2	6	3.4	9	5.1	3.38	133	.300	.362	1	2	110	161	0.5	0	0	0.2
1984	Tor-A	0	2	.000	11	0	0	0	0	21	18	7.7	2	10	4.3	9	3.9	2.14	188	.225	.301	4	4	101	149	-0.9	0	0	0.4
1985	Tor-A	3	0	1.000	25	4	0	0	1	52	59	10.2	2	24	4.2	29	5.0	4.50	91	.284	.352	-2	-2	99	97	1.5	0	-1	-0.2
Total 3		4	2	.667	48	4	0	0	1	89	95	9.6	6	40	4.0	47	4.8	3.74	111	.273	.342	4	4	102	121	1.1	0	-1	0.4
PAUL MUSSER																													
1912	Was-A	0	0	—	7	2	0	0	2	21	16	6.9	0	16	6.9	10	4.3	2.57	126	.225	.382	2	2	97	144	0.0	-1	0	0.2
1919	Bos-A	0	2	.000	5	4	1	0	2	20	26	11.7	0	8	3.6	14	6.3	4.05	73	.342	.405	-2	-2	91	127	-0.9	-1	-0	-0.3
Total 2		0	2	.000	12	6	1	0	2	41	42	9.2	0	24	5.3	24	5.3	3.29	94	.286	.393	-0	-1	94	136	-0.9	-2	-0	-0.1
BARNEY MUSSILL																													
1944	Phi-N	0	1	.000	16	0	0	0	0	19	20	9.5	1	13	6.2	5	2.4	6.16	60	.267	.359	-5	-5	103	75	-0.4	-0	0	-0.4
ALEX MUSTAIKIS																													
1940	Bos-A	0	1	.000	6	1	0	0	0	15	15	9.0	1	15	9.0	6	3.6	9.00	49	.254	.395	-8	-8	100	60	-0.4	1	1	-0.4
ELMER MYERS																													
1915	Phi-A	1	0	1.000	1	1	1	1	0	9	5	5.0	0	12	12.0	12	12.0	0.00	—	.074	.219	3	3	103	0	0.5	-0	-0	0.2
1916	Phi-A	14	23	.378	44	35	31	2	1	315	280	8.0	1	168	4.8	182	5.2	3.66	81	.248	.353	-29	-24	105	94	4.3	2	5	-1.7
1917	Phi-A	9	16	.360	38	23	13	2	3	202	221	9.8	1	79	3.5	88	3.9	4.41	59	.283	.353	-39	-41	97	82	0.0	2	1	-3.9

YEAR	TM/L	W	L	PCT	G	GS	CG	SHO	SV	IP	H	H/G	HR	BB	BB/G	SO	SO/G	ERA	/A	OAVG	OOBP	PR	/A	PF	CPI	WAT	PB	PD	TPI
1918	Phi-A	4	8	.333	18	15	5	1	1	95	101	9.6	4	42	4.0	17	1.6	4.64	64	.283	.353	-20	-18	108	87	-1.1	-3	2	-1.8
1919	Cle-A	8	7	.533	23	15	6	1	1	135	134	8.9	3	43	2.9	38	2.5	3.73	90	.264	.334	-8	-6	104	85	-0.9	2	1	-0.1
1920	Cle-A	2	4	.333	16	7	2	0	1	72	93	11.6	1	23	2.9	16	2.0	4.75	80	.316	.374	-8	-8	100	96	-1.4	0	0	-0.6
	Bos-A	9	1	.900	12	10	9	1	0	97	90	8.4	1	24	2.2	34	3.2	2.13	172	.249	.299	18	17	97	111	4.1	3	-1	1.9
	Yr	11	5	.688	28	17	11	1	1	169	183	9.7	2	47	2.5	50	2.7	3.25	115	.277	.327	10	9	98	111	2.7	0	-1	1.3
1921	Bos-A	8	12	.400	30	20	11	0	0	172	217	11.4	11	53	2.8	40	2.1	4.87	88	.315	.359	-11	-11	100	103	-1.9	-2	0	-1.1
1922	Bos-A	0	1	.000	3	1	0	0	0	6	10	15.0	1	3	4.5	1	1.5	16.50	24	.370	.469	-8	-8	99	54	-0.4	-0	0	-0.6
Total	8	55	72	.433	185	127	78	8	7	1103	1148	9.4	29	440	3.6	428	3.5	4.06	81	.275	.349	-102	-94	102	92	3.2	4	7	-7.7
■ **HENRY MYERS**	Myers, Henry C. b: 5/1858, Philadelphia, Pa. d: 4/18/1895, Philadelphia, Pa. BR/TR, 5'9", 159 lbs. Deb: 8/20/1881 M																												
1882	Bal-a	0	2	.000	6	2	1	0	0	26	30	10.4	2	4	1.4	7	2.4	6.58	42	.295	.321	-11	-11	102	60	-0.9	-1	0	-0.8
■ **JOSEPH MYERS**	Myers, Joseph William b: 3/18/1882, Wilmington, Del. d: 2/11/56, Delaware City, Del BR/TR, Deb: 10/07/05																												
1905	Phi-A	0	0	—	1	1	1	0	0	5	3	5.4	0	3	5.4	5	9.0	3.60	78	.193	.324	-1	-0	106	56	0.0	-0	0	0.0
■ **RANDY MYERS**	Myers, Randall Kirk b: 9/19/62, Vancouver, Wash. BL/TL, 6'1", 190 lbs. Deb: 10/06/85																												
1985	NY-N	0	0	—	1	0	0	0	0	2	0	0.0	0	1	4.5	2	9.0	0.00	—	.000	.143	1	1	95	0	0.0	0	0	0.1
1986	NY-N	0	0	—	10	0	0	0	0	11	11	9.0	1	9	7.4	13	10.6	4.09	85	.256	.396	-0	-1	93	127	0.0	0	0	0.0
1987	NY-N	3	6	.333	54	0	0	0	6	75	61	7.3	6	30	3.6	92	11.0	3.96	100	.225	.290	1	0	97	77	-1.8	0	0	0.1
1988	NY-N	7	3	.700	55	0	0	0	26	68	45	6.0	5	17	2.3	69	9.1	1.72	176	.190	.245	13	10	88	111	1.1	1	-1	1.0
Total	4	10	9	.526	120	0	0	0	32	156	117	6.7	12	57	3.3	176	10.2	2.94	119	.210	.279	14	10	93	94	-0.7	1	-1	1.2
■ **BOB MYRICK**	Myrick, Robert Howard b: 10/1/52, Hattiesburg, Miss. BR/TL, 6'1", 195 lbs. Deb: 5/28/76																												
1976	NY-N	1	1	.500	21	1	0	0	0	28	34	10.9	2	13	4.2	11	3.5	3.21	99	.306	.373	1	-0	91	161	0.0	-0	0	0.0
1977	NY-N	2	2	.500	44	4	0	0	2	87	86	8.9	5	33	3.4	49	5.1	3.62	105	.265	.327	3	2	97	104	0.4	-0	0	0.2
1978	NY-N	0	3	.000	17	0	0	0	0	25	18	6.5	3	13	4.7	13	4.7	3.24	110	.207	.304	1	1	99	101	-1.4	-0	0	0.1
Total	3	3	6	.333	82	5	0	0	2	140	138	8.9	10	59	3.8	73	4.7	3.47	104	.264	.333	5	2	96	114	-1.0	-1	1	0.3
■ **JACK NABORS**	Nabors, Herman John b: 11/19/1887, Montevallo, Ala. d: 11/20/23, Wilton, Ala. BR/TR, 6'3", 185 lbs. Deb: 8/09/15																												
1915	Phi-A	0	5	.000	10	7	2	0	0	54	58	9.7	1	35	5.8	18	3.0	5.50	55	.304	.424	-15	-15	103	96	-2.4	-1	-0	-1.5
1916	Phi-A	1	20	.048	40	30	11	0	1	213	206	8.7	2	95	4.0	74	3.1	3.46	86	.266	.349	-15	-12	105	100	-8.5	-5	-3	-1.9
1917	Phi-A	0	0	—	2	0	0	0	0	3	2	6.0	0	1	3.0	2	6.0	3.00	86	.200	.273	-0	-0	97	48	0.0	0	0	0.0
Total	3	1	25	.038	52	37	13	0	1	270	266	8.9	3	131	4.4	94	3.1	3.87	77	.273	.364	-30	-26	105	98	-10.9	-6	-2	-3.4
■ **BILL NAGEL**	Nagel, William Taylor b: 8/19/15, Memphis, Tenn. d: 10/8/81, Freehold, N.J. BR/TR, 6'1", 190 lbs. Deb: 4/20/39																												
1939	Phi-A	0	0	—	1	0	0	0	0	3	7	21.0	1	1	3.0	0	0.0	12.00	39	.438	.444	-2	-2	102	101	0.0	0	0	-0.1
■ **JUDGE NAGLE**	Nagle, Walter Harold "Lucky" b: 3/10/1880, Santa Rosa, Cal. d: 5/27/71, Santa Rosa, Cal. 6', 176 lbs. Deb: 4/26/11																												
1911	Pit-N	4	2	.667	8	3	1	0	1	27	33	11.0	3	6	2.0	11	3.7	3.67	90	.324	.367	-1	-1	97	145	0.8	-0	0	0.0
	Bos-A	1	1	.500	5	1	0	0	0	27	27	9.0	2	6	2.0	12	4.0	3.33	99	.262	.303	0	-0	99	91	0.0	-1	-1	0.0
■ **STEVE NAGY**	Nagy, Stephen b: 5/28/19, Franklin, N.J. BL/TL, 5'9", 174 lbs. Deb: 4/20/47																												
1947	Pit-N	1	3	.250	6	1	0	0	0	14	18	11.6	1	9	5.8	4	2.6	5.79	72	.310	.397	-3	-3	102	101	-0.7	0	0	-0.1
1950	Was-A	2	5	.286	9	9	2	0	0	53	69	11.7	5	29	4.9	17	2.9	6.62	70	.307	.380	-12	-12	101	85	-1.1	2	-0	-0.8
Total	2	3	8	.273	15	10	2	0	0	67	87	11.7	6	38	5.1	21	2.8	6.45	70	.307	.383	-15	-14	101	89	-1.8	2	-0	-0.9
■ **MIKE NAGY**	Nagy, Michael Timothy b: 3/25/48, Bronx, N.Y. BR/TR, 6'3", 195 lbs. Deb: 4/21/69																												
1969	Bos-A	12	2	.857	33	28	7	1	0	197	183	8.4	10	106	4.8	84	3.8	3.11	122	.245	.345	11	15	105	119	5.0	-2	0	1.4
1970	Bos-A	6	5	.545	23	20	4	0	0	129	138	9.6	16	64	4.5	56	3.9	4.47	92	.275	.355	-11	-5	110	108	0.1	2	-1	-0.3
1971	Bos-A	1	3	.250	12	7	0	0	0	38	46	10.9	4	20	4.7	9	2.1	6.63	55	.315	.388	-13	-13	105	87	-1.0	-1	-0	-1.2
1972	Bos-A	0	0	—	1	0	0	0	0	2	3	13.5	0	0	0.0	2	9.0	9.00	36	.375	.400	-1	-1	105	72	0.0	0	0	0.0
1973	StL-N	0	2	.000	9	7	0	0	0	41	44	9.7	4	15	3.3	14	3.1	4.17	79	.282	.341	-2	-4	90	107	-0.9	-1	-0	-0.4
1974	Hou-N	1	1	.500	9	0	0	0	0	13	17	11.8	3	5	3.5	5	3.5	8.31	43	.309	.371	-7	-7	98	77	0.0	-0	0	-0.6
Total	6	20	13	.606	87	62	11	1	0	420	431	9.2	37	210	4.5	170	3.6	4.14	92	.267	.353	-23	-15	105	110	3.2	-2	-1	-1.1
■ **SAM NAHEM**	Nahem, Samuel Ralph "Subway Sam" b: 10/19/15, New York, N.Y. BR/TR, 6'1.5", 190 lbs. Deb: 10/02/38																												
1938	Bro-N	1	0	1.000	1	1	1	0	0	9	6	6.0	0	4	4.0	2	2.0	3.00	121	.194	.286	1	1	96	64	0.5	1	-0	0.1
1941	StL-N	5	2	.714	26	8	2	0	1	82	76	8.3	2	38	4.2	31	3.4	2.96	131	.243	.323	6	8	107	110	0.8	-1	1	0.9
1942	Phi-N	1	3	.250	35	2	0	0	0	75	72	8.6	2	40	4.8	38	4.6	4.92	68	.254	.342	-13	-13	101	76	-0.1	-1	1	-1.3
1948	Phi-N	3	3	.500	28	1	0	0	0	59	68	10.4	4	45	6.9	30	4.6	7.02	54	.288	.401	-20	-21	97	82	0.4	-0	-1	-2.0
Total	4	10	8	.556	90	12	3	0	1	225	222	8.9	8	127	5.1	101	4.0	4.68	79	.257	.350	-27	-25	102	90	1.6	-2	1	-2.3
■ **PETE NAKTENIS**	Naktenis, Peter Ernest b: 6/12/14, Aberdeen, Wash. BL/TL, 6'1", 185 lbs. Deb: 6/13/36																												
1936	Phi-A	0	1	.000	7	1	0	0	0	19	24	11.4	2	27	12.8	18	8.5	12.32	43	.324	.510	-15	-15	105	76	-0.4	-0	-0	-1.2
1939	Cin-N	0	0	—	3	0	0	0	0	4	2	4.5	0	0	0.0	1	2.3	2.25	174	.154	.267	1	1	100	55	0.0	0	0	0.1
Total	2	0	1	.000	10	1	0	0	0	23	26	10.2	2	27	10.6	19	7.4	10.57	48	.299	.479	-15	-14	104	72	-0.4	-0	-0	-1.1
■ **BUDDY NAPIER**	Napier, Skelton Le Roy b: 12/18/1889, Byronville, Ga. d: 3/29/68, Hutchins, Tex. BR/TR, 5'11", 165 lbs. Deb: 8/14/12																												
1912	StL-A	1	2	.333	7	2	0	0	0	25	33	11.9	0	5	1.8	10	3.6	5.04	68	.317	.366	-5	-4	103	89	0.0	-1	0	-0.3
1918	Chi-N	0	0	—	1	0	0	0	0	7	10	12.9	0	4	5.1	2	2.6	5.14	53	.357	.438	-2	-2	98	120	0.0	0	0	-0.1
1920	Cin-N	4	2	.667	9	5	5	1	0	49	47	8.6	0	7	1.3	17	3.1	1.29	215	.254	.281	10	8	88	158	0.9	1	0	1.0
1921	Cin-N	0	2	.000	22	6	1	0	1	57	72	11.4	2	13	2.1	14	2.2	5.53	69	.329	.348	-11	-11	101	85	-0.9	1	1	-0.7
Total	4	5	6	.455	39	13	6	1	1	138	162	10.6	2	29	1.9	43	2.8	3.91	85	.302	.334	-8	-9	97	113	0.0	1	1	-0.1
■ **GONZALO NARANJO**	Naranjo, Lazaro Ramon Gonzalo b: 11/25/34, Havana, Cuba BL/TR, 5'11.5", 165 lbs. Deb: 7/08/56																												
1956	Pit-N	1	2	.333	17	3	0	0	0	34	37	9.8	7	17	4.5	26	6.9	4.50	87	.282	.355	-3	-2	103	125	-0.2	-0	1	0.0
■ **RAY NARLESKI**	Narleski, Raymond Edmond b: 11/25/28, Camden, N.J. BR/TR, 6'1", 175 lbs. Deb: 4/17/54																												
1954	Cle-A	3	3	.500	42	2	1	0	13	89	59	6.0	8	44	4.4	52	5.3	2.22	169	.189	.290	15	15	101	111	-0.8	-2	-1	1.3
1955	Cle-A	9	1	.900	**60**	1	1	0	**19**	112	91	7.3	11	52	4.2	94	7.6	3.70	109	.220	.304	3	4	102	84	3.8	1	-2	0.4
1956	Cle-A	3	2	.600	32	0	0	0	4	59	36	5.5	5	19	2.9	42	6.4	1.53	270	.170	.239	**17**	**17**	99	91	0.2	0	-1	1.7
1957	Cle-A	11	5	.688	46	15	7	1	16	154	136	7.9	14	70	4.1	93	5.4	3.10	125	.235	.317	12	13	102	111	3.2	-2	-4	0.8
1958	Cle-A	13	10	.565	44	24	7	0	1	183	179	8.8	21	91	4.5	102	5.0	4.08	86	.255	.339	-6	-12	93	104	1.7	1	-3	-1.3
1959	Det-A	4	12	.250	42	10	1	0	5	104	105	9.1	21	59	5.1	71	6.1	5.80	74	.254	.339	-22	-17	111	87	-4.1	-1	-2	-1.9
Total	6	43	33	.566	266	52	17	1	58	701	606	7.8	80	335	4.3	454	5.8	3.61	107	.230	.315	18	21	101	100	4.0	-3	-12	1.0
■ **BUSTER NARUM**	Narum, Leslie Ferdinand b: 11/16/40, Philadelphia, Pa. BR/TR, 6'1", 194 lbs. Deb: 4/14/63																												
1963	Bal-A	0	0	—	7	0	0	0	0	9	8	8.0	0	5	5.0	5	5.0	3.00	113	.242	.342	1	0	93	109	0.0	1	0	0.2
1964	Was-A	9	15	.375	38	32	7	2	0	199	195	8.8	31	73	3.3	121	5.5	4.30	87	.259	.323	-15	-12	103	101	-0.2	-5	-3	-1.9
1965	Was-A	4	12	.250	46	24	2	0	0	174	176	9.1	16	91	4.7	86	4.4	4.45	79	.267	.350	-19	-18	102	103	-3.5	-2	2	-1.8
1966	Was-A	0	0	—	3	0	0	0	0	3	11	33.0	2	4	12.0	0	0.0	24.00	14	.579	.600	-7	-7	96	102	0.0	0	0	-0.6
1967	Was-A	1	0	1.000	2	2	0	0	0	12	8	6.0	1	4	3.0	8	6.0	3.00	112	.195	.267	0	0	104	77	0.5	-1	-0	0.0
Total	5	14	27	.341	96	58	9	2	0	397	398	9.0	50	177	4.0	220	5.0	4.44	82	.264	.338	-40	-36	102	101	-3.2	-6	-1	-4.1
■ **JIM NASH**	Nash, James Edwin b: 2/9/45, Hawthorne, Nev. BR/TR, 6'5", 215 lbs. Deb: 7/03/66																												
1966	KC-A	12	1	.923	18	17	5	0	1	127	95	6.7	6	47	3.3	98	6.9	2.06	159	.204	.275	19	17	95	107	**5.6**	-1	-3	1.4
1967	KC-A	12	17	.414	37	34	8	2	0	222	200	8.1	21	87	3.5	186	7.5	3.77	87	.242	.312	-13	-12	102	96	0.8	-2	-2	-1.7
1968	Oak-A	13	13	.500	34	33	12	6	0	229	185	7.3	18	55	2.2	169	6.6	2.28	128	.219	.267	18	16	98	106	-0.1	-2	-3	1.3
1969	Oak-A	8	8	.500	26	19	3	1	0	115	112	8.8	17	30	2.3	75	5.9	3.68	90	.247	.296	-1	-5	91	96	-0.6	-0	-1	-0.5
1970	Atl-N	13	9	.591	34	33	6	2	0	212	211	9.0	22	90	3.8	153	6.5	4.08	104	.257	.327	-1	4	105	101	2.8	-3	0	0.1
1971	Atl-N	9	7	.563	32	19	2	0	2	133	166	11.2	17	50	3.4	65	4.4	4.94	78	.314	.363	-22	-16	111	112	1.0	-2	-1	-1.8
1972	Atl-N	1	1	.500	11	4	0	0	1	31	35	10.2	2	25	7.3	10	2.9	5.52	66	.307	.420	-7	-6	106	110	0.1	0	-0	-0.6

YEAR	TM/L	W	L	PCT	G	GS	CG	SHO	SV	IP	H	H/G	HR	BB	BB/G	SO	SO/G	ERA	/A	OAVG	OOBP	PR	/A	PF	CPI	WAT	PB	PD	TPI
	Phi-N	0	8	.000	9	8	0	0	0	37	46	11.2	5	17	4.1	15	3.6	6.32	54	.311	.371	-12	-12	99	95	-3.9	-0	0	-1.1
	Yr	1	9	.100	20	12	0	0	1	68	81	10.7	7	42	5.6	25	3.3	5.96	59	.305	.393	-19	-18	102	95	-3.8	0	-0	-1.7
Total	7	68	64	.515	201	167	36	11	4	1106	1050	8.5	108	401	3.3	771	6.3	3.59	97	.250	.313	-18	-15	101	103	5.7	-11	-10	-2.9
■ BILLY NASH	Nash, William Mitchell b: 6/24/1865, Richmond, Va. d: 11/15/29, E.Orange, N.J. BR/TR, 5'8.5", 167 lbs. Deb: 8/05/1884 M																												
1889	Bos-N	0	0	—	1	0	0	0	0	1	0	0.0	0	1	9.0	0	0.0	0.00	—	.000	.276	0	0	98	0	0.0	0	0	0.0
1890	Bos-P	0	0	—	1	0	0	0	0	⅓	1	27.0	0	0	0.0	0	0.0	0.00	—	1.000	1.000	0	0	104	0	0.0	0	0	0.0
Total	2	0	0	—	2	0	0	0	0	1	1	9.0	0	1	9.0	0	0.0	0.00	—	.276	.432	0	0	98	0	0.0	1	0	0.0
■ PHILIP NASTU	Nastu, Philip b: 3/8/55, Bridgeport, Conn. BL/TL, 6'2", 180 lbs. Deb: 9/15/78																												
1978	SF-N	0	1	.000	3	1	0	0	0	8	8	9.0	1	2	2.3	5	5.6	5.63	58	.258	.303	-2	-2	91	65	-0.4	-0	-0	-0.1
1979	SF-N	3	4	.429	25	14	1	0	0	100	105	9.5	14	41	3.7	47	4.2	4.32	81	.272	.340	-6	-9	93	107	0.0	-1	0	-0.9
1980	SF-N	0	0	—	6	0	0	0	0	6	10	15.0	1	5	7.5	1	1.5	6.00	58	.357	.455	-2	-2	96	143	0.0	0	0	-0.1
Total	3	3	5	.375	34	15	1	0	0	114	123	9.7	16	48	3.8	53	4.2	4.50	77	.276	.345	-10	-13	93	106	-0.4	-1	0	-1.1
■ JULIO NAVARRO	Navarro, Julio (Ventura) "Whiplash" b: 1/9/36, Vieques, P.R. BR/TR, 6', 175 lbs. Deb: 9/03/62																												
1962	LA-A	1	1	.500	9	0	0	0	0	15	20	12.0	2	4	2.4	11	6.6	4.80	84	.317	.348	-1	-1	102	114	0.0	0	-0	0.0
1963	LA-A	4	5	.444	57	0	0	0	12	90	75	7.5	7	32	3.2	53	5.3	2.90	116	.228	.291	7	5	92	104	0.1	1	1	0.7
1964	LA-A	0	0	—	5	0	0	0	1	9	5	5.0	0	5	5.0	8	8.0	2.00	161	.167	.324	2	1	89	111	0.0	-0	0	0.1
	Det-A	2	1	.667	26	0	0	0	2	41	40	8.8	9	16	3.5	36	7.9	3.95	87	.250	.319	-1	-2	95	118	0.5	-1	-0	-0.2
	Yr	2	1	.667	31	0	0	0	3	50	45	8.1	9	21	3.8	44	7.9	3.60	95	.234	.311	0	-1	94	118	0.5	-0	0	-0.1
1965	Det-A	0	2	.000	15	1	0	0	1	30	25	7.5	5	12	3.6	22	6.6	4.20	86	.238	.301	-2	-2	104	97	-0.9	-0	0	-0.1
1966	Det-A	0	0	—	1	0	0	0	0	⅓	2	54.0	2	0	0.0	0	0.0	81.00	—	1.000	1.000	-3	-3	102	104	0.0	0	0	-0.2
1970	Atl-N	0	0	—	17	0	0	0	1	26	24	8.3	7	1	0.3	21	7.3	4.15	102	.233	.248	-0	0	105	87	0.0	-0	0	0.0
Total	6	7	9	.438	130	1	0	0	17	211	191	8.1	32	70	3.0	151	6.4	3.67	97	.241	.301	0	-3	97	105	-0.3	-0	2	0.3
■ EARL NAYLOR	Naylor, Earl Eugene b: 5/19/19, Kansas City, Mo. BR/TR, 6', 190 lbs. Deb: 4/15/42																												
1942	Phi-N	0	5	.000	20	4	1	0	0	60	68	10.2	5	29	4.3	19	2.9	6.15	54	.286	.357	-19	-19	101	78	-2.4	1	-0	-1.8
■ ROLLIE NAYLOR	Naylor, Roleine Cecil b: 2/4/1892, Crum, Tex. d: 6/18/66, Fort Worth, Tex. BR/TR, 6'1.5", 180 lbs. Deb: 9/14/17																												
1917	Phi-A	2	2	.500	5	5	3	0	0	33	30	8.2	1	11	3.0	11	3.0	1.64	158	.265	.336	4	3	97	200	0.4	-1	1	0.4
1919	Phi-A	5	18	.217	31	23	17	0	0	205	210	9.2	2	64	2.8	68	3.0	3.34	108	.280	.339	-3	6	112	100	-2.0	-3	-1	0.4
1920	Phi-A	10	23	.303	42	36	20	0	0	251	306	11.0	7	86	3.1	90	3.2	3.48	108	.312	.371	9	8	99	**130**	-0.5	-5	2	0.3
1921	Phi-A	3	13	.188	32	19	6	0	0	169	214	11.4	10	53	2.8	39	2.1	4.85	95	.315	.355	-11	-5	107	101	-3.8	-4	-2	-0.8
1922	Phi-A	10	15	.400	35	26	11	0	0	171	212	11.2	7	51	2.7	37	1.9	4.74	91	.309	.344	-13	-8	106	95	-0.7	1	1	-0.5
1923	Phi-A	12	7	.632	26	20	9	2	0	143	149	9.4	5	59	3.7	27	1.7	3.46	117	.273	.334	8	10	102	108	3.4	1	-2	0.9
1924	Phi-A	0	5	.000	10	7	1	0	0	38	53	12.6	2	20	4.7	10	2.4	6.39	67	.333	.392	-9	-9	101	93	-2.4	1	0	-0.6
Total	7	42	83	.336	181	136	67	2	0	1010	1174	10.5	34	344	3.1	282	2.5	3.94	101	.300	.352	-15	5	105	111	-5.6	-11	0	0.1
■ MIKE NAYMICK	Naymick, Michael John b: 9/6/17, Berlin, Pa. BR/TR, 6'8", 225 lbs. Deb: 9/24/39																												
1939	Cle-A	0	1	.000	2	1	1	0	0	5	3	5.4	0	5	9.0	3	5.4	1.80	247	.188	.364	2	1	96	208	-0.4	-0	-0	0.1
1940	Cle-A	1	2	.333	13	4	0	0	0	30	36	10.8	1	17	5.1	15	4.5	5.10	79	.290	.386	-2	-4	92	102	-0.5	0	1	-0.2
1943	Cle-A	4	4	.500	29	4	0	0	2	63	32	4.6	3	47	6.7	41	5.9	2.29	129	.160	.312	7	5	90	116	-0.2	-0	1	0.5
1944	Cle-A	0	0	—	7	0	0	0	0	13	16	11.1	1	10	6.9	4	2.8	9.69	36	.314	.394	-9	-9	101	65	0.0	-0	0	-0.8
	StL-N	0	0	—	1	0	0	0	0	2	2	9.0	0	1	4.5	1	4.5	4.50	76	.333	.375	-0	-0	95	121	0.0	0	0	0.0
Total	4	5	7	.417	52	9	1	0	2	113	89	7.1	5	80	6.4	64	5.1	3.90	86	.224	.347	-3	-7	92	111	-1.1	-1	1	-0.4
■ JACK NEAGLE	Neagle, John Henry b: 1/2/1858, Syracuse, N.Y. d: 9/20/04, Syracuse, N.Y. BR/TR, 5'6", 155 lbs. Deb: 7/08/1879																												
1879	Cin-N	0	1	.000	2	2	1	0	0	13	13	9.0	0	5	3.5	4	2.8	3.46	68	.266	.334	-1	-2	94	85	-0.4	-0	0	-0.1
1883	Phi-N	1	7	.125	8	7	6	0	0	61	88	13.0	0	21	3.1	13	1.9	6.93	45	.346	.395	-26	-26	99	77	-1.1	-2	0	-1.9
	Bal-a	1	4	.200	6	5	4	0	0	46	48	9.4	1	20	3.9	9	1.8	4.89	76	.274	.349	-8	-6	113	83	-0.7	1	0	-0.2
	Pit-a	3	12	.200	16	16	12	0	0	114	156	12.3	9	25	2.0	41	3.2	5.84	55	.331	.365	-32	-33	98	95	-3.0	-1	0	-2.8
	Yr	4	16	.200	22	21	16	0	0	160	204	11.5	10	45	2.5	50	2.8	5.57	61	.316	.360	-40	-39	102	95	-3.7	1	0	-3.0
1884	Pit-a	11	26	.297	38	38	37	2	0	326	354	9.8	6	70	1.9	85	2.3	3.73	88	.285	.323	-17	-16	101	104	0.8	-5	-3	-2.2
Total	3	16	50	.242	70	68	60	2	0	560	659	10.6	16	141	2.3	152	2.4	4.60	71	.301	.343	-85	-83	101	97	-4.4	-8	-3	-7.2
■ JOE NEALE	Neale, Joseph Hunt b: 5/7/1866, Wadsworth, Ohio d: 12/30/13, Akron, Ohio BR/TR, 5'8", 153 lbs. Deb: 6/21/1886																												
1886	Lou-a	0	1	.000	1	1	0	0	0	7	11	14.1	0	7	9.0	0	0.0	7.71	48	.368	.488	-3	-3	108	106	-0.4	-0	0	-0.1
1887	Lou-a	1	4	.200	5	4	4	0	0	41	60	13.2	4	15	3.3	11	2.4	7.02	65	.355	.408	-12	-11	106	93	-1.5	-2	0	-0.9
1890	StL-a	5	3	.625	10	9	8	0	0	69	53	6.9	4	15	2.0	23	3.0	3.39	131	.226	.273	4	8	115	70	0.5	-3	0	0.5
1891	StL-a	6	4	.600	15	11	9	1	1	110	109	8.9	4	36	2.9	24	2.0	4.25	98	.273	.333	-7	-1	112	74	-0.1	-4	0	-0.2
Total	4	12	12	.500	31	25	21	1	1	227	233	9.2	12	73	2.9	58	2.3	4.60	93	.280	.338	-19	-8	111	77	-1.5	-9	0	-0.7
■ RON NECCIAI	Necciai, Ronald Andrew b: 6/18/32, Manown, Pa. BR/TR, 6'5", 185 lbs. Deb: 8/10/52																												
1952	Pit-N	1	6	.143	12	9	0	0	0	55	63	10.3	5	32	5.2	31	5.1	7.04	56	.296	.387	-20	-19	105	79	-1.6	-1	-0	-1.8
■ RON NEGRAY	Negray, Ronald Alvin b: 2/26/30, Akron, Ohio BR/TR, 6'1", 185 lbs. Deb: 9/14/52																												
1952	Bro-N	0	0	—	4	1	0	0	0	13	15	10.4	0	5	3.5	5	3.5	3.46	106	.294	.357	0	0	98	121	0.0	-0	-0	0.0
1955	Phi-N	4	3	.571	19	10	2	0	0	72	71	8.9	13	21	2.6	30	3.8	3.50	118	.257	.306	4	5	102	119	0.5	-3	-0	0.1
1956	Phi-N	2	3	.400	39	4	0	0	3	67	72	9.7	6	24	3.2	44	5.9	4.16	86	.280	.334	-3	-4	95	102	-0.2	1	0	-0.2
1958	LA-N	0	0	—	4	0	0	0	0	11	12	9.8	4	7	5.7	2	1.6	7.36	57	.279	.373	-4	-4	106	96	0.0	-0	0	-0.3
Total	4	6	6	.500	66	15	2	0	3	163	170	9.4	23	57	3.1	81	4.5	4.03	96	.271	.327	-2	-3	99	110	0.3	-3	-0	-0.4
■ JIM NEHER	Neher, James Gilmore b: 2/5/1889, Rochester, N.Y. d: 11/11/51, Buffalo, N.Y. BR/TR, 5'11", 185 lbs. Deb: 9/10/12																												
1912	Cle-A	0	0	—	1	0	0	0	0	1	0	0.0	0	0	0.0	0	0.0	0.00	—	.000	.000	0	0	101	0	0.0	0	0	0.0
■ ART NEHF	Nehf, Arthur Neukom b: 7/31/1892, Terre Haute, Ind. d: 12/18/60, Phoenix, Ariz. BL/TL, 5'9.5", 176 lbs. Deb: 8/13/15																												
1915	Bos-N	5	4	.556	12	10	6	4	0	78	60	6.9	0	21	2.4	39	4.5	2.54	106	.214	.270	2	1	97	68	0.1	-1	0	0.0
1916	Bos-N	7	5	.583	22	12	6	1	0	121	110	8.2	1	20	1.5	36	2.7	2.01	119	.244	.275	8	5	91	106	0.0	-0	-1	0.4
1917	Bos-N	17	8	.680	38	23	17	5	0	233	197	7.6	4	39	1.5	101	3.9	2.16	121	.231	.263	14	12	97	89	5.5	5	0	1.8
1918	Bos-N	15	15	.500	32	31	**28**	2	0	284	274	8.7	2	76	2.4	96	3.0	2.69	97	.259	.305	2	-2	95	103	2.4	2	3	0.3
1919	Bos-N	8	9	.471	22	19	13	1	0	169	151	8.0	6	40	2.1	53	2.8	3.09	94	.242	.286	-3	-3	100	84	1.0	2	1	0.0
	NY-N	9	2	.818	13	12	9	2	0	102	70	6.2	2	19	1.7	24	2.1	1.50	187	.196	.236	16	15	96	81	3.0	3	-1	2.1
	Yr	17	11	.607	35	31	22	3	0	271	221	7.3	8	59	2.0	77	2.6	2.49	115	.224	.262	13	12	99	81	4.0	2	0	2.1
1920	NY-N	21	12	.636	40	33	22	5	0	281	273	8.7	8	45	1.4	79	2.5	3.07	98	.260	.283	2	-1	97	79	3.5	5	3	0.6
1921	NY-N	20	10	.667	41	34	18	2	1	261	266	9.2	18	55	1.9	67	2.3	3.62	98	.271	.303	5	-2	94	92	2.4	1	3	0.0
1922	NY-N	19	13	.594	37	35	20	3	1	268	286	9.6	15	64	2.1	60	2.0	3.29	125	.276	.315	24	25	100	106	-0.2	3	1	2.7
1923	NY-N	13	10	.565	34	27	7	1	2	196	219	10.1	14	49	2.3	50	2.3	4.50	88	.281	.321	-11	-12	99	84	-1.1	1	1	-0.9
1924	NY-N	14	4	.778	30	20	11	0	2	172	167	8.7	14	42	2.2	72	3.8	3.61	94	.254	.297	5	-4	88	88	4.2	6	2	0.3
1925	NY-N	11	9	.550	29	20	8	1	1	155	193	11.2	7	50	2.9	63	3.7	3.77	111	.308	.357	9	7	98	**122**	-0.2	1	2	0.9
1926	NY-N	0	0	—	2	0	0	0	0	2	2	9.0	0	1	4.5	0	0.0	9.00	42	.286	.375	-1	-1	98	47	0.0	-0	0	0.0
	Cin-N	0	1	.000	7	0	0	0	0	17	25	13.2	0	5	2.6	4	2.1	3.71	96	.379	.408	0	-0	93	172	-0.4	-0	1	0.0
	Yr	0	1	.000	9	0	0	0	0	19	27	12.8	0	6	2.8	4	1.9	4.26	84	.370	.405	-1	-1	94	172	-0.4	-0	1	0.0
1927	Cin-N	3	5	.375	21	5	1	0	4	45	59	11.8	2	14	2.8	21	4.2	5.60	70	.319	.360	-8	-8	100	87	-0.9	-1	1	-0.7
	Chi-N	1	1	.500	8	2	2	1	1	26	25	8.7	0	9	3.1	12	4.2	1.38	279	.260	.309	7	7	99	223	0.0	1	0	0.9
	Yr	4	6	.400	29	7	3	1	5	71	84	10.6	2	23	2.9	33	4.2	4.06	96	.299	.342	-1	-1	99	223	-0.9	-1	1	0.2
1928	Chi-N	13	7	.650	31	21	10	2	0	177	190	9.7	3	52	2.6	40	2.0	2.64	140	.281	.322	26	21	93	**133**	1.6	3	1	2.4
1929	Chi-N	8	5	.615	32	15	4	0	1	121	148	11.0	11	39	2.9	27	2.0	5.58	83	.310	.357	-12	-13	98	94	-0.2	4	0	-0.7
Total	15	184	120	.605	451	319	182	30	13	2708	2715	9.0	107	640	2.1	844	2.8	3.20	105	.265	.304	85	44	96	97	20.7	33	17	10.1

YEAR	TM/L	W	L	PCT	G	GS	CG	SHO	SV	IP	H	H/G	HR	BB	BB/G	SO	SO/G	ERA	/A	OAVG	OOBP	PR	/A	PF	CPI	WAT	PB	PD	TPI
■ GARY NEIBAUER	Neibauer, Gary Wayne b: 10/29/44, Billings, Mont. BR/TR, 6'3", 200 lbs. Deb: 4/12/69																												
1969	Atl-N	1	2	.333	29	0	0	0	0	58	42	6.5	9	31	4.8	42	6.5	3.88	95	.204	.302	-2	-1	103	91	-0.5	-1	-0	-0.1
1970	Atl-N	0	3	.000	7	0	0	0	0	13	11	7.6	0	8	5.5	9	6.2	4.85	88	.239	.339	-1	-1	105	72	-1.4	-0	-0	0.0
1971	Atl-N	1	0	1.000	6	1	0	0	1	21	14	6.0	3	9	3.9	6	2.6	2.14	179	.187	.279	3	4	111	126	0.5	-1	0	0.4
1972	Atl-N	0	0	—	8	0	0	0	0	17	27	14.3	6	6	3.2	8	4.2	7.41	49	.360	.410	-7	-7	106	119	0.0	-0	-0	-0.7
	Phi-N	0	2	.000	9	2	0	0	0	19	17	8.1	1	14	6.6	7	3.3	5.21	65	.239	.368	-4	-4	99	80	-0.9	0	-0	-0.3
	Yr	0	2	.000	17	2	0	0	0	36	44	11.0	7	20	5.0	15	3.8	6.25	57	.297	.382	-11	-11	102	80	-0.9	-0	-0	-1.0
1973	Atl-N	2	1	.667	16	1	0	0	0	21	24	10.3	3	19	8.1	9	3.9	7.29	57	.282	.421	-8	-7	113	89	0.6	1	-1	-0.6
Total	5	4	8	.333	75	4	0	0	1	149	135	8.2	22	87	5.3	81	4.9	4.77	79	.242	.343	-19	-16	105	96	-1.7	-1	-1	-1.3
■ AL NEIGER	Neiger, Alvin Edward b: 3/26/39, Wilmington, Del. BL/TL, 6', 195 lbs. Deb: 7/30/60																												
1960	Phi-N	0	0	—	6	0	0	0	0	13	16	11.1	2	4	2.8	3	2.1	5.54	75	.340	.373	-3	-2	110	123	0.0	0	0	-0.1
■ ERNIE NEITZKE	Neitzke, Ernest Fredrich b: 11/13/1894, Toledo, Ohio d: 4/27/77, Sylvania, Ohio BR/TR, 5'10", 180 lbs. Deb: 6/02/21																												
1921	Bos-A	0	0	—	2	0	0	0	0	7	8	10.3	0	4	5.1	1	1.3	6.43	67	.333	.375	-2	-2	100	89	0.0	0	0	0.0
■ BOTS NEKOLA	Nekola, Francis Joseph b: 12/10/06, New York, N.Y. d: 3/11/87, Rockville Ctr., Md BL/TL, 5'11.5", 175 lbs. Deb: 7/19/29																												
1929	NY-A	0	0	—	9	1	0	0	0	19	21	9.9	0	15	7.1	2	0.9	4.26	96	.296	.409	-0	-0	97	125	0.0	1	1	0.1
1933	Det-A	0	0	—	2	0	0	0	0	1	4	36.0	1	1	9.0	0	0.0	36.00	13	.500	.556	-4	-3	107	69	0.0	0	0	-0.2
Total	2	0	0	—	11	1	0	0	0	20	25	11.2	1	16	7.2	2	0.9	5.85	71	.316	.423	-4	-4	97	122	0.0	1	1	-0.1
■ RED NELSON	Nelson, Albert Francis (born Albert W. Horazdovsky) b: 5/19/1886, Cleveland, Ohio d: 10/26/56, St.Petersburg, Fla BR/TR, 5'11", 190 lbs. Deb: 9/09/10																												
1910	StL-A	5	1	.833	7	6	6	1	0	60	57	8.6	0	14	2.1	30	4.5	2.55	99	.261	.318	-0	-0	101	108	2.3	2	4	0.4
1911	StL-A	3	9	.250	16	13	6	0	0	81	103	11.4	1	44	4.9	24	2.7	5.22	64	.324	.417	-17	-17	100	104	-0.9	-2	-1	-1.6
1912	StL-A	0	2	.000	8	3	0	0	1	18	21	10.5	0	13	6.5	9	4.5	7.00	49	.318	.430	-7	-7	103	80	-0.9	1	-1	-0.6
	Phi-N	2	0	1.000	4	2	1	0	0	19	25	11.8	2	6	2.8	2	0.9	3.79	91	.301	.363	-1	-1	101	127	1.0	-1	0	-0.1
1913	Phi-N	0	0	—	2	0	0	0	0	8	9	10.1	0	4	4.5	3	3.4	2.25	158	.290	.371	1	1	111	185	0.0	0	0	0.2
	Cin-N	0	0	—	2	0	0	0	0	2	6	27.0	1	4	18.0	0	0.0	31.50	11	.667	.688	-6	-6	104	81	0.0	0	0	-0.5
	Yr	0	0	—	4	0	0	0	0	10	15	13.5	1	8	7.2	3	2.7	8.10	43	.375	.471	-5	-5	109	81	0.0	0	0	-0.3
Total	4	10	12	.455	39	24	13	1	1	188	221	10.6	4	85	4.1	68	3.3	4.55	68	.305	.387	-31	-30	101	108	1.5	0	2	-2.2
■ ANDY NELSON	Nelson, Andrew "Peaches" TL , Deb: 5/26/08																												
1908	Chi-A	0	0	—	2	1	0	0	0	9	11	11.0	0	4	4.0	1	1.0	2.00	110	.282	.364	0	0	93	213	0.0	0	-1	0.0
■ EMMETT NELSON	Nelson, George Emmett "Ramrod" b: 2/26/05, Viborg, S.Dak. d: 8/25/67, Sioux Falls, S.D. BR/TR, 6'3", 180 lbs. Deb: 6/24/35																												
1935	Cin-N	4	4	.500	19	7	3	1	1	60	70	10.5	2	23	3.5	14	2.1	4.35	88	.295	.354	-2	-3	95	106	0.4	-1	1	-0.3
1936	Cin-N	1	0	1.000	6	1	0	0	0	17	24	12.7	1	4	2.1	3	1.6	3.18	123	.333	.372	2	1	97	174	0.5	-0	0	0.1
Total	2	5	4	.556	25	8	3	1	1	77	94	11.0	3	27	3.2	17	2.0	4.09	94	.304	.358	-1	-2	96	121	0.9	-1	1	-0.2
■ JIM NELSON	Nelson, James Lorin b: 7/4/47, Birmingham, Ala. BR/TR, 6', 180 lbs. Deb: 5/30/70																												
1970	Pit-N	4	2	.667	15	10	1	1	0	68	64	8.5	5	38	5.0	42	5.6	3.44	113	.255	.352	5	3	96	127	0.8	0	-1	0.3
1971	Pit-N	2	2	.500	17	2	0	0	0	35	27	6.9	0	26	6.7	11	2.8	2.31	145	.225	.379	4	4	97	164	-0.2	2	-0	0.6
Total	2	6	4	.600	32	12	1	1	0	103	91	8.0	5	64	5.6	53	4.6	3.06	121	.245	.361	9	7	96	139	0.6	2	-1	0.9
■ LUKE NELSON	Nelson, Luther Martin b: 12/4/1893, Cable, Ill. BR/TR, 6', 180 lbs. Deb: 5/25/19																												
1919	NY-A	3	0	1.000	9	1	0	0	0	24	22	8.3	1	11	4.1	11	4.1	3.00	112	.244	.333	1	1	104	103	1.5	-0	-0	0.1
■ LYNN NELSON	Nelson, Lynn Bernard "Line Drive" b: 2/24/05, Sheldon, N.Dak. d: 2/15/55, Kansas City, Mo. BL/TR, 5'10.5", 170 lbs. Deb: 4/18/30																												
1930	Chi-N	3	2	.600	37	3	0	0	0	81	97	10.8	10	28	3.1	29	3.2	5.11	100	.300	.359	-1	0	103	105	0.1	0	1	0.2
1933	Chi-N	5	5	.500	24	3	3	0	1	76	65	7.7	2	30	3.6	20	2.4	3.20	99	.232	.294	1	-0	95	84	-0.5	2	0	0.2
1934	Chi-N	0	1	.000	2	1	0	0	0	1	4	36.0	1	1	9.0	0	0.0	36.00	11	.667	.714	-4	-4	97	82	-0.4	0	0	-0.2
1937	Phi-A	4	9	.308	30	4	1	0	2	116	140	10.9	12	51	4.0	49	3.8	5.90	75	.300	.363	-16	-19	96	92	-0.9	7	-2	-1.6
1938	Phi-A	10	11	.476	32	23	13	0	2	191	215	10.1	29	79	3.7	75	3.5	5.65	89	.277	.344	-18	-14	105	89	2.3	4	-1	-1.1
1939	Phi-A	10	13	.435	35	24	12	2	1	198	233	10.6	27	64	2.9	75	3.4	4.77	99	.292	.342	-3	-1	102	109	1.5	-2	-1	-0.3
1940	Det-A	1	1	.500	6	2	0	0	0	14	23	14.8	5	9	5.8	7	4.5	10.93	44	.371	.438	-10	-10	109	93	0.0	2	0	-0.7
Total	7	33	42	.440	166	60	29	2	6	677	777	10.3	86	262	3.5	255	3.4	5.25	88	.287	.346	-52	-48	101	97	2.1	13	-1	-3.5
■ MEL NELSON	Nelson, Melvin Frederick b: 5/30/36, San Diego, Cal. BR/TL, 6', 185 lbs. Deb: 9/27/60																												
1960	StL-N	0	1	.000	2	1	0	0	0	8	7	7.9	1	2	2.3	7	7.9	3.38	120	.226	.273	0	1	108	83	-0.4	0	0	0.1
1963	LA-A	2	3	.400	36	3	0	0	1	53	55	9.3	7	32	5.4	41	7.0	5.26	64	.263	.356	-10	-11	92	95	-0.1	-1	1	-1.0
1965	Min-A	0	4	.000	28	3	0	0	3	55	57	9.3	7	23	3.8	31	5.1	4.09	83	.261	.332	-4	-4	98	106	-1.9	-0	-0	-0.4
1967	Min-A	0	0	—	1	0	0	0	0	⅓	3	81.0	1	0	0.0	0	0.0	54.00	—	.750	.750	-2	-2	106	113	0.0	0	0	-0.1
1968	StL-N	2	1	.667	18	4	1	0	1	53	49	8.3	3	9	1.5	16	2.7	2.89	96	.254	.274	1	-1	93	99	0.3	0	-0	0.0
1969	StL-N	0	1	.000	8	0	0	0	0	5	13	23.4	0	3	5.4	3	5.4	12.60	28	.520	.533	-5	-5	99	99	-0.4	0	-0	-0.4
Total	6	4	10	.286	93	11	1	0	5	174	184	9.5	19	69	3.6	98	5.1	4.40	73	.271	.331	-20	-23	95	99	-2.5	-0	1	-1.8
■ ROGER NELSON	Nelson, Roger Eugene "Spider" b: 6/7/44, Altadena, Cal. BR/TR, 6'3", 200 lbs. Deb: 9/09/67																												
1967	Chi-A	0	1	.000	5	0	0	0	0	7	4	5.1	1	0	0.0	4	5.1	1.29	234	.182	.250	2	1	93	198	-0.4	0	0	0.2
1968	Bal-A	4	3	.571	19	6	0	0	1	71	49	6.2	3	26	3.3	70	8.9	2.41	125	.192	.269	5	5	101	77	0.1	-0	-0	0.5
1969	KC-A	7	13	.350	29	29	8	1	0	193	170	7.9	12	65	3.0	82	3.8	3.31	114	.243	.305	7	10	104	96	-1.9	-1	-1	0.9
1970	KC-A	0	2	.000	4	2	0	0	0	9	18	18.0	3	0	0.0	3	3.0	10.00	37	.419	.422	-6	-6	100	99	-0.9	0	0	-0.5
1971	KC-A	0	1	.000	13	1	0	0	0	34	35	9.3	1	5	1.3	29	7.7	5.29	64	.269	.288	-7	-7	98	54	-0.4	1	1	-0.5
1972	KC-A	11	6	.647	34	19	10	6	3	173	120	6.2	13	31	1.6	120	6.2	2.08	147	.196	**.233**	19	19	100	77	2.8	-2	1	2.1
1973	Cin-N	3	2	.600	14	8	1	0	0	55	49	8.0	4	24	3.9	17	2.8	3.44	98	.246	.325	1	-0	92	107	0.0	-1	1	0.0
1974	Cin-N	4	4	.500	14	12	1	0	0	85	67	7.1	7	35	3.7	42	4.4	3.39	103	.213	.292	2	1	96	78	-0.6	0	0	0.0
1976	KC-A	0	0	—	3	0	0	0	0	9	4	4.0	0	4	4.0	4	4.0	2.00	174	.138	.278	2	1	99	69	0.0	0	-1	0.2
Total	9	29	32	.475	135	77	20	7	5	636	516	7.3	44	190	2.7	371	5.3	3.06	111	.224	.283	24	23	100	86	-1.3	-3	2	2.9
■ GENE NELSON	Nelson, Wayland Eugene b: 12/3/60, Tampa, Fla. BR/TR, 6', 172 lbs. Deb: 5/04/81																												
1981	NY-A	3	1	.750	8	7	0	0	0	39	40	9.2	5	23	5.3	16	3.7	4.85	75	.261	.358	-5	-5	99	99	0.9	0	0	-0.5
1982	Sea-A	6	9	.400	22	19	2	1	0	123	133	9.7	16	60	4.4	71	5.2	4.61	97	.279	.358	-7	-2	110	109	-1.1	0	1	0.0
1983	Sea-A	0	3	.000	10	5	1	0	0	32	38	10.7	6	21	5.9	11	3.1	7.88	52	.295	.392	-14	-13	101	82	-1.4	0	0	-1.1
1984	Chi-A	3	5	.375	20	9	2	0	1	75	72	8.6	9	17	2.0	36	4.3	4.44	100	.254	.296	-4	0	111	80	-0.6	0	0	0.0
1985	Chi-A	10	10	.500	46	18	1	0	2	146	144	8.9	23	67	4.1	101	6.2	4.25	97	.258	.339	-2	-2	100	112	-0.4	0	0	-0.1
1986	Chi-A	6	6	.500	54	1	0	0	6	115	118	9.2	7	41	3.2	70	5.5	3.83	111	.271	.332	4	5	101	104	0.6	0	1	0.6
1987	Oak-A	6	5	.545	54	6	0	0	3	124	120	8.7	12	35	2.5	94	6.8	3.92	104	.249	.302	8	2	91	88	0.5	0	-1	0.1
1988	Oak-A	9	6	.600	54	1	0	0	3	112	93	7.5	9	38	3.1	67	5.4	3.05	121	.228	.294	11	8	93	100	-0.4	0	-1	0.7
Total	8	43	45	.489	268	66	6	1	15	766	758	8.9	87	302	3.5	466	5.5	4.22	98	.259	.328	-8	-6	100	100	-1.9	0	1	-0.3
■ BILL NELSON	Nelson, William F. b: 9/28/1863, Terre Haute, Ind. d: 6/23/41, Terre Haute, Ind. TR , Deb: 9/03/1884																												
1884	Pit-a	1	2	.333	3	3	3	0	0	26	26	9.0	1	8	2.8	6	2.1	4.50	73	.269	.325	-4	-4	101	85	0.1	-1	0	-0.3
■ HAL NEUBAUER	Neubauer, Harold Charles b: 5/13/02, Hoboken, N.J. d: 9/9/49, Barrington, R.I. BR/TR, 6'0.5", 185 lbs. Deb: 6/12/25																												
1925	Bos-A	1	0	1.000	7	0	0	0	0	10	17	15.3	2	11	9.9	4	3.6	12.60	35	.378	.467	-9	-9	99	81	0.5	0	0	-0.7
■ TEX NEUER	Neuer, John S. b: 6/8/1877, Fremont, Ohio d: 1/14/66, Northumberland, Pa TL , Deb: 8/28/07																												
1907	NY-A	4	2	.667	7	6	6	3	0	54	40	6.7	1	19	3.2	22	3.7	2.17	129	.228	.303	2	4	110	92	1.1	-2	-1	0.3
■ DAN NEUMEIER	Neumeier, Daniel George b: 3/9/48, Shawano, Wis. BR/TR, 6'5", 205 lbs. Deb: 9/08/72																												
1972	Chi-A	0	0	—	3	0	0	0	0	3	2	6.0	0	3	9.0	0	0.0	9.00	36	.200	.385	-2	-2	106	39	0.0	-0	0	-0.1
■ ERNIE NEVEL	Nevel, Ernie Wyre b: 8/17/19, Charleston, Mo. BR/TR, 5'11", 190 lbs. Deb: 9/26/50																												
1950	NY-A	0	1	.000	3	1	0	0	0	6	10	15.0	0	6	9.0	3	4.5	10.50	42	.345	.457	-4	-4	96	71	-0.4	-0	0	-0.3

YEAR	TM/L	W	L	PCT	G	GS	CG	SHO	SV	IP	H	H/G	HR	BB	BB/G	SO	SO/G	ERA	/A	OAVG	OOBP	PR	/A	PF	CPI	WAT	PB	PD	TPI
1951	NY-A	0	0	—	1	0	0	0	1	4	1	2.3	0	1	2.3	1	2.3	0.00	—	.083	.154	2	2	88	0	0.0	-0	-0	0.1
1953	Cin-N	0	0	—	10	0	0	0	0	10	16	14.4	0	1	0.9	5	4.5	6.30	68	.390	.386	-2	-2	100	100	0.0	0	0	-0.1
Total	3	0	1	.000	14	1	0	0	1	20	27	12.1	0	8	3.6	9	4.0	6.30	67	.329	.380	-4	-5	97	71	-0.4	-0	0	-0.3
■ **ERNIE NEVERS**	Nevers, Ernest Alonzo b: 6/11/03, Willow River, Minn. d: 5/3/76, San Rafael, Cal. BR/TR, 6', 205 lbs. Deb: 4/26/26																												
1926	StL-A	2	4	.333	11	7	4	0	0	75	82	9.8	4	24	2.9	16	1.9	4.44	94	.290	.328	-3	-2	103	94	-0.4	-1	2	0.0
1927	StL-A	3	8	.273	27	5	2	0	2	95	105	9.9	8	35	3.3	22	2.1	4.93	92	.311	.358	-8	-4	109	106	-1.6	-1	1	-0.3
1928	StL-A	1	0	1.000	6	0	0	0	0	9	9	9.0	1	2	2.0	1	1.0	3.00	139	.281	.306	1	1	103	141	0.5	-0	0	0.1
Total	3	6	12	.333	44	12	6	0	2	179	196	9.9	13	61	3.1	39	2.0	4.63	94	.300	.343	-11	-6	106	103	-1.5	-2	3	-0.2
■ **DON NEWCOMBE**	Newcombe, Donald "Newk" b: 6/14/26, Madison, N.J. BL/TR, 6'4", 220 lbs. Deb: 5/20/49																												
1949	Bro-N	17	8	.680	38	31	19	**5**	1	244	223	8.2	17	73	2.7	149	**5.5**	3.17	124	.243	.298	24	21	98	99	2.0	4	1	2.5
1950	Bro-N	19	11	.633	40	35	20	4	3	267	258	8.7	22	75	2.5	130	4.4	3.71	117	.254	.304	13	18	104	92	2.4	7	-0	2.5
1951	Bro-N	20	9	.690	40	36	18	3	0	272	235	7.8	19	91	3.0	**164**	5.4	3.28	114	.230	.295	21	14	95	88	3.2	6	1	2.1
1954	Bro-N	9	8	.529	29	25	6	0	0	144	158	9.9	24	49	3.1	82	5.1	4.56	90	.274	.331	-8	-8	101	101	-1.0	4	-1	-0.3
1955	Bro-N	20	5	**.800**	34	31	17	1	0	234	222	8.5	35	38	**1.5**	143	5.5	3.19	128	.249	.277	22	23	101	105	**6.1**	20	-2	**4.4**
1956	Bro-N	**27**	7	**.794**	38	36	18	5	0	268	219	7.4	33	46	1.5	139	4.7	3.06	124	**.221**	**.255**	21	22	100	79	**9.2**	9	0	**3.4**
1957	Bro-N	11	12	.478	28	28	12	4	0	199	199	9.0	28	33	**1.5**	90	4.1	3.48	127	.258	.286	9	21	114	102	-1.5	4	1	3.0
1958	LA-N	0	6	.000	11	8	1	0	0	34	53	14.0	11	8	2.1	16	4.2	7.94	53	.346	.374	-15	-14	106	96	-2.9	2	0	-1.0
	Cin-N	7	7	.500	20	18	7	0	1	133	159	10.8	20	28	1.9	53	3.6	3.86	109	.298	.329	1	5	106	124	0.1	8	-2	1.2
	Yr	7	13	.350	31	26	8	0	1	167	212	11.4	31	36	1.9	69	3.7	4.69	89	.309	.339	-14	-9	106	124	-2.8	2	-2	0.2
1959	Cin-N	13	8	.619	30	29	17	2	1	222	216	8.8	25	27	**1.1**	100	4.1	3.16	128	.253	.276	19	22	103	99	3.1	15	-1	2.3
1960	Cin-N	4	6	.400	16	15	1	0	0	83	99	10.7	12	14	1.5	36	3.9	4.55	82	.304	.328	-7	-8	99	110	-0.3	-0	-1	-0.8
	Cle-A	2	3	.400	20	2	0	0	1	54	61	10.2	6	8	1.3	27	4.5	4.33	88	.289	.309	-3	-3	98	94	-0.4	2	-1	-0.2
Total	10	149	90	.623	344	294	136	24	7	2154	2102	8.8	252	490	2.0	1129	4.7	3.56	113	.254	.295	97	114	102	97	20.0	81	-5	19.1
■ **TOM NEWELL**	Newell, Thomas Dean b: 5/17/63, Monrovia, Cal. BR/TR, 6'1", 185 lbs. Deb: 9/09/87																												
1987	Phi-N	0	0	—	2	0	0	0	0	1	4	36.0	1	3	27.0	1	9.0	36.00	12	.571	.700	-4	-4	105	91	0.0	0	0	-0.2
■ **DON NEWHAUSER**	Newhauser, Donald Louis b: 11/7/47, Miami, Fla. BR/TR, 6'4", 200 lbs. Deb: 6/15/72																												
1972	Bos-A	4	2	.667	31	0	0	0	4	37	30	7.3	2	25	6.1	27	6.6	2.43	133	.226	.348	3	3	105	150	0.8	-0	0	0.3
1973	Bos-A	0	0	—	9	0	0	0	1	12	9	6.8	0	13	9.8	8	6.0	0.00	—	.205	.390	5	5	105	0	0.0	0	-0	0.5
1974	Bos-A	0	1	.000	2	0	0	0	0	4	5	11.3	0	4	9.0	2	4.5	9.00	43	.357	.450	-2	-2	106	81	-0.4	0	0	-0.1
Total	3	4	3	.571	42	0	0	0	5	53	44	7.5	2	42	7.1	37	6.3	2.38	145	.230	.366	5	6	105	111	0.4	-0	-0	0.7
■ **HAL NEWHOUSER**	Newhouser, Harold b: 5/20/21, Detroit, Mich. BL/TL, 6'2", 180 lbs. Deb: 9/29/39																												
1939	Det-A	0	1	.000	1	1	1	0	0	5	3	5.4	0	4	7.2	4	7.2	5.40	94	.188	.318	-0	-0	110	59	-0.4	-0	0	0.0
1940	Det-A	9	9	.500	28	20	7	0	0	133	149	10.1	12	76	5.1	89	6.0	4.87	98	.282	.370	-7	-2	109	107	-1.3	-1	2	0.0
1941	Det-A	9	11	.450	33	27	5	1	0	173	166	8.6	6	137	7.1	106	5.5	4.79	93	.249	.375	-12	-6	107	92	-0.8	-2	2	-0.5
1942	Det-A	8	14	.364	38	23	11	1	5	184	137	**6.7**	4	114	5.6	103	**5.0**	2.45	169	**.207**	.321	25	**34**	113	117	-2.8	-1	2	3.9
1943	Det-A	8	17	.320	37	25	10	1	1	196	163	7.5	3	111	5.1	144	6.6	3.03	113	.224	.322	6	9	104	96	-5.0	-0	3	1.2
1944	Det-A	**29**	9	.763	47	34	25	6	2	312	264	7.6	6	102	2.9	**187**	**5.4**	2.22	160	.230	.289	42	46	104	108	**9.8**	4	1	5.9
1945	Det-A	**25**	9	**.735**	40	36	**29**	**8**	2	**313**	239	**6.9**	5	110	3.2	**212**	**6.1**	**1.81**	**194**	**.211**	.277	**54**	**59**	105	111	**7.4**	5	3	**8.1**
1946	Det-A	**26**	9	.743	37	34	29	6	1	293	215	**6.6**	10	98	3.0	275	**8.4**	**1.94**	**191**	**.201**	**.267**	51	**57**	106	91	7.4	-1	2	**6.8**
1947	Det-A	17	17	.500	40	36	**24**	3	2	285	268	8.5	9	110	3.5	176	5.6	2.87	133	.249	.313	26	**30**	103	110	-1.9	2	3	**3.8**
1948	Det-A	**21**	12	.636	39	35	19	2	1	272	249	8.2	10	99	3.3	143	4.7	3.01	138	.242	.305	38	34	97	102	5.2	1	1	3.8
1949	Det-A	18	11	.621	38	35	22	3	1	292	277	8.5	19	111	3.4	144	4.4	3.36	132	.251	.316	27	35	106	101	2.2	1	3	4.0
1950	Det-A	15	13	.536	35	30	15	1	3	214	232	9.8	23	81	3.4	87	3.7	4.33	100	.279	.341	6	-0	95	107	-2.1	-1	-0	-0.1
1951	Det-A	6	6	.500	15	14	7	1	0	96	98	9.2	10	19	1.8	37	3.5	3.94	112	.268	.305	2	5	107	98	0.3	2	1	0.8
1952	Det-A	9	9	.500	25	19	8	0	0	154	148	8.6	13	47	2.7	57	3.3	3.74	101	.254	.303	-1	1	103	92	2.6	3	1	0.5
1953	Det-A	0	1	.000	7	4	0	0	1	22	31	12.7	4	8	3.3	6	2.5	6.95	58	.348	.402	-7	-7	102	105	-0.4	2	0	-0.4
1954	Cle-A	7	2	.778	26	1	0	0	7	47	34	6.5	3	18	3.4	25	4.8	2.49	151	.209	.278	6	7	101	98	1.0	-1	0	0.6
1955	Cle-A	0	0	—	2	0	0	0	0	2	1	4.5	0	4	18.0	1	4.5	0.00	—	.125	.417	1	1	102	0	0.0	0	0	0.1
Total	17	207	150	.580	488	374	212	33	26	2993	2674	8.0	137	1249	3.8	1796	5.4	3.06	130	.239	.312	256	305	104	103	21.2	12	22	38.5
■ **FLOYD NEWKIRK**	Newkirk, Floyd Elmo "Three-Finger" b: 7/16/08, Norris City, Ill. d: 4/15/76, Clayton, Mo. BR/TR, 5'11", 178 lbs. Deb: 8/21/34																												
1934	NY-A	0	0	—	1	0	0	0	0	1	1	9.0	0	1	9.0	0	0.0	0.00	—	.333	.400	0	0	93	0	0.0	0	0	0.1
■ **JOEL NEWKIRK**	Newkirk, Joel Inez "Sailor" b: 5/1/1896, Kyana, Ind. d: 1/22/66, Eldorado, Ill. BR/TR, 6', 180 lbs. Deb: 8/20/19																												
1919	Chi-N	0	0	—	1	0	0	0	0	2	2	9.0	0	3	13.5	1	4.5	13.50	21	.286	.545	-2	-2	99	61	0.0	-0	0	-0.1
1920	Chi-N	0	1	.000	2	1	0	0	0	7	8	10.3	1	6	7.7	2	2.6	5.14	60	.333	.452	-2	-2	99	139	-0.4	-0	-0	-0.2
Total	2	0	1	.000	3	1	0	0	0	9	10	10.0	1	9	9.0	3	3.0	7.00	44	.323	.476	-4	-4	99	122	-0.4	-1	-0	-0.3
■ **MAURY NEWLIN**	Newlin, Maurice Milton b: 6/22/14, Bloomingdale, Ind d: 8/14/78, Houston, Tex. BR/TR, 6', 176 lbs. Deb: 9/20/40																												
1940	StL-A	1	0	1.000	1	1	0	0	0	6	4	6.0	1	2	3.0	3	4.5	6.00	79	.190	.261	-1	-1	108	47	0.5	0	-0	0.0
1941	StL-A	0	2	.000	14	0	0	0	1	28	43	13.8	4	12	3.9	10	3.2	6.43	65	.361	.407	-7	-7	101	117	-0.9	-1	1	-0.6
Total	2	1	2	.333	15	1	0	0	1	34	47	12.4	5	14	3.7	13	3.4	6.35	67	.336	.386	-8	-8	102	105	-0.4	-1	0	-0.6
■ **FRED NEWMAN**	Newman, Frederick William b: 2/21/42, Boston, Mass. d: 6/24/87, Framingham, Mass. BR/TR, 6'3", 180 lbs. Deb: 9/16/62																												
1962	LA-A	0	1	.000	4	1	0	0	0	6	11	16.5	0	3	4.5	4	6.0	10.50	39	.393	.452	-4	-4	102	73	-0.4	-0	-0	-0.3
1963	LA-A	1	5	.167	12	8	0	0	0	44	56	11.5	6	15	3.1	16	3.3	5.32	63	.316	.372	-8	-10	92	109	-1.8	1	-0	-0.9
1964	LA-A	13	10	.565	32	28	7	2	0	190	177	8.4	9	39	1.8	83	3.9	2.75	117	.246	.286	19	10	89	100	1.6	2	4	1.7
1965	Cal-A	14	16	.467	36	36	10	2	0	261	225	7.8	15	64	2.2	109	3.8	2.93	116	.234	.278	15	14	98	89	0.1	-0	8	2.3
1966	Cal-A	4	7	.364	21	19	1	0	0	103	112	9.8	7	31	2.7	42	3.7	4.72	73	.289	.344	-15	-15	100	96	-1.4	1	1	-1.3
1967	Cal-A	1	0	1.000	3	1	0	0	0	6	8	12.0	1	2	3.0	0	0.0	1.50	207	.320	.379	1	1	96	433	0.5	-0	-0	0.1
Total	6	33	39	.458	108	93	18	4	0	610	589	8.7	38	154	2.3	254	3.7	3.41	98	.256	.303	8	-4	95	98	-1.4	3	12	1.6
■ **JEFF NEWMAN**	Newman, Jeffrey Lynn b: 9/11/48, Fort Worth, Tex. BR/TR, 6'2", 215 lbs. Deb: 6/30/76 MC																												
1977	Oak-A	0	0	—	1	0	0	0	0	1	1	9.0	0	0	0.0	0	0.0	0.00	—	.250	.400	0	0	97	0	0.0	0	0	0.0
■ **RAY NEWMAN**	Newman, Raymond Francis b: 6/20/45, Evansville, Ind. BL/TL, 6'5", 205 lbs. Deb: 5/16/71																												
1971	Chi-N	1	2	.333	30	0	0	0	2	38	30	7.1	4	17	4.0	35	8.3	3.55	107	.219	.301	-0	1	110	88	-0.4	-1	0	0.1
1972	Mil-A	0	0	—	4	0	0	0	1	7	4	5.1	0	2	2.6	1	1.3	0.00	—	.182	.240	2	2	97	0	0.0	0	0	0.3
1973	Mil-A	2	1	.667	11	0	0	0	1	18	19	9.5	2	5	2.5	10	5.0	3.00	122	.260	.300	2	1	96	118	0.6	0	1	0.2
Total	3	3	3	.500	45	0	0	0	4	63	53	7.6	6	24	3.4	46	6.6	3.00	123	.228	.295	4	5	104	87	0.2	-0	1	0.6
■ **BOBO NEWSOM**	Newsom, Louis Norman "Buck" b: 8/11/07, Hartsville, S.C. d: 12/7/62, Orlando, Fla. BR/TR, 6'3", 200 lbs. Deb: 9/11/29																												
1929	Bro-N	0	3	.000	3	2	0	0	0	9	15	15.0	0	5	5.0	6	6.0	11.00	41	.375	.426	-6	-6	96	66	-1.4	-0	0	-0.5
1930	Bro-N	0	0	—	2	0	0	0	0	3	2	6.0	0	2	6.0	1	3.0	0.00	—	.167	.286	2	2	99	0	0.0	0	0	0.1
1932	Chi-N	0	0	—	1	0	0	0	0	1	1	9.0	0	0	0.0	0	0.0	0.00	—	.333	.333	0	0	103	0	0.0	0	0	0.0
1934	StL-A	16	20	.444	47	32	15	2	5	262	259	8.9	15	149	5.1	135	4.6	4.02	119	.261	.353	14	22	106	109	0.2	-3	0	1.9
1935	StL-A	0	6	.000	7	6	1	0	1	43	54	11.3	2	13	2.7	22	4.6	4.81	102	.303	.347	-2	0	110	96	-2.9	-1	0	0.0
	Was-A	11	12	.478	28	23	17	2	2	198	222	10.1	9	84	3.8	65	3.0	4.45	93	.288	.356	0	-7	93	104	1.0	5	-2	-0.4
	Yr	11	18	.379	35	29	18	2	3	241	276	10.3	11	97	3.6	87	3.2	4.52	94	.291	.354	-2	-7	96	104	-1.9	-1	-2	-0.4
1936	Was-A	17	15	.531	43	38	24	4	2	286	294	9.3	13	146	4.6	156	4.9	4.31	112	.268	.352	23	17	96	103	-0.1	-0	1	1.5
1937	Was-A	3	4	.429	11	10	3	0	0	68	76	10.1	4	48	6.4	39	5.2	5.82	76	.287	.396	-9	-11	96	95	-0.3	-1	0	-0.9
	Bos-A	13	10	.565	30	27	14	1	0	208	193	8.4	14	119	5.1	127	5.5	4.46	106	.243	.340	4	6	102	88	1.1	2	-2	0.7
	Yr	16	14	.533	41	37	17	1	0	276	269	8.8	18	167	5.4	166	5.4	4.79	97	.253	.352	-5	-4	101	88	0.8	-1	-1	-0.2
1938	StL-A	20	16	.556	44	40	**31**	0	1	**330**	334	9.1	30	192	5.2	226	6.2	5.07	97	.265	.360	-10	-5	103	95	**6.5**	2	-4	-0.5
1939	StL-A	3	1	.750	6	6	3	0	0	46	50	9.8	5	22	4.3	28	5.5	4.70	103	.266	.346	-0	1	105	98	1.3	-0	0	0.1

YEAR	TM/L	W	L	PCT	G	GS	CG	SHO	SV	IP	H	H/G	HR	BB	BB/G	SO	SO/G	ERA	/A	OAVG	OOBP	PR	/A	PF	CPI	WAT	PB	PD	TPI
	Det-A	17	10	.630	35	31	21	2	2	246	222	8.1	14	104	3.8	164	6.0	3.37	150	.238	.312	34	46	110	100	3.4	-4	-1	4.1
	Yr	20	11	.645	41	37	**24**	2	2	292	272	8.4	19	126	3.9	192	5.9	3.58	141	.243	.317	34	47	109	100	4.7	-0	-1	4.2
1940	Det-A	21	5	.808	36	34	20	3	0	264	235	8.0	19	100	3.4	164	5.6	2.83	**168**	.238	.307	46	**57**	109	119	**7.6**	-1	-3	**5.5**
1941	Det-A	12	20	.375	43	36	12	2	2	250	265	9.5	15	118	4.2	175	6.3	4.61	97	.264	.342	-13	-4	107	89	-4.3	-6	-2	-1.0
1942	Was-A	11	17	.393	30	29	15	2	0	214	236	9.9	5	92	3.9	**113**	4.8	4.92	73	.280	.346	-30	-31	99	85	-0.6	-2	-3	-3.3
	Bro-N	2	2	.500	6	5	2	1	0	32	28	7.9	1	14	3.9	21	5.9	3.38	95	.235	.319	-0	-1	97	91	-0.4	-1	-1	-0.2
1943	Bro-N	9	4	.692	22	12	6	1	1	125	113	8.1	4	57	4.1	75	5.4	3.02	110	.244	.326	5	4	99	108	2.4	1	0	0.6
	StL-A	1	6	.143	10	9	0	0	0	52	69	11.9	7	35	6.1	37	6.4	7.44	45	.318	.409	-24	-24	101	90	-2.4	1	-1	-2.2
	Was-A	3	3	.500	6	6	2	0	0	40	38	8.5	1	21	4.7	11	2.5	3.82	88	.247	.341	-2	-2	102	93	-0.2	-1	-1	-0.3
	Yr	4	9	.308	16	15	2	0	0	92	107	10.5	8	56	5.5	48	4.7	5.87	57	.288	.378	-26	-26	101	93	-2.6	1	-2	-2.5
1944	Phi-A	13	15	.464	37	33	18	2	1	265	243	8.3	11	82	2.8	142	4.8	2.82	124	.244	.300	18	20	102	103	0.0	-6	-1	1.4
1945	Phi-A	8	20	.286	36	34	16	3	0	257	255	8.9	12	103	3.6	127	4.4	3.29	99	.260	.323	2	-1	96	109	-2.8	-3	-4	-0.9
1946	Phi-A	3	5	.375	10	9	3	1	0	59	61	9.3	2	30	4.6	32	4.9	3.36	112	.266	.360	1	3	107	122	0.4	-1	-1	0.1
	Was-A	11	8	.579	24	22	14	2	1	178	163	8.2	5	60	3.0	82	4.1	2.78	119	.242	.302	14	10	94	99	1.8	-2	-3	0.5
	Yr	14	13	.519	34	31	17	3	1	237	224	8.5	7	90	3.4	114	4.3	2.92	117	.247	.313	15	13	97	99	2.2	-1	-4	0.6
1947	Was-A	4	6	.400	14	13	1	0	0	84	99	10.6	2	37	4.0	40	4.3	4.07	91	.296	.360	-3	-3	101	111	-0.1	1	-2	-0.3
	NY-A	7	5	.583	17	15	6	2	0	116	109	8.5	8	30	2.3	42	3.3	2.79	122	.250	.297	12	8	92	113	-0.4	-3	-2	0.3
	Yr	11	11	.500	31	28	7	2	0	200	208	9.4	10	67	3.0	82	3.7	3.33	106	.270	.324	8	5	96	113	-0.5	1	-3	0.0
1948	NY-N	0	4	.000	11	4	0	0	0	26	35	12.1	1	13	4.5	9	3.1	4.15	94	.330	.390	-1	-1	98	141	-1.9	1	-0	0.0
1952	Was-A	1	1	.500	10	0	0	0	2	13	16	11.1	2	9	6.2	5	3.5	4.85	76	.302	.397	-2	-2	100	131	0.0	-0	0	-0.1
	Phi-A	3	3	.500	14	5	1	0	1	48	38	7.1	2	23	4.3	22	4.1	3.56	116	.220	.313	1	3	112	82	0.0	-1	0	0.3
	Yr	4	4	.500	24	5	1	0	3	61	54	8.0	4	32	4.7	27	4.0	3.84	105	.239	.333	-1	1	110	82	0.0	-0	1	0.2
1953	Phi-A	2	1	.667	17	2	1	0	0	39	44	10.2	3	24	5.5	16	3.7	4.85	87	.282	.390	-4	-3	105	110	0.7	-0	0	-0.2
Total	20	211	222	.487	600	483	246	30	21	3762	3769	9.0	206	1732	4.1	2082	5.0	3.98	106	.261	.338	69	95	102	101	8.6	-26	-29	6.4

■ DICK NEWSOME Newsome, Heber Hampton b: 12/13/09, Ahoskie, N.C. d: 12/15/65, Ahoskie, N.C. BR/TR, 6', 185 lbs. Deb: 4/25/41

YEAR	TM/L	W	L	PCT	G	GS	CG	SHO	SV	IP	H	H/G	HR	BB	BB/G	SO	SO/G	ERA	/A	OAVG	OOBP	PR	/A	PF	CPI	WAT	PB	PD	TPI
1941	Bos-A	19	10	.655	36	29	17	2	0	214	235	9.9	13	79	3.3	58	2.4	4.12	102	.277	.340	1	2	101	104	4.1	2	3	0.7
1942	Bos-A	8	10	.444	24	23	11	0	0	158	174	9.9	11	67	3.8	40	2.3	5.01	73	.278	.344	-24	-24	100	88	-2.6	2	1	-2.0
1943	Bos-A	8	13	.381	25	22	8	2	0	154	166	9.7	8	68	4.0	40	2.3	4.50	76	.274	.347	-21	-18	104	93	-1.7	-1	-2	-2.0
Total	3	35	33	.515	85	74	36	4	0	526	575	9.8	32	214	3.7	138	2.4	4.50	85	.276	.343	-44	-40	102	96	-0.2	3	2	-3.3

■ DOC NEWTON Newton, Eustace James b: 10/26/1877, Indianapolis, Ind. d: 5/14/31, Memphis, Tenn. BL/TL, 6', 185 lbs. Deb: 4/27/00

YEAR	TM/L	W	L	PCT	G	GS	CG	SHO	SV	IP	H	H/G	HR	BB	BB/G	SO	SO/G	ERA	/A	OAVG	OOBP	PR	/A	PF	CPI	WAT	PB	PD	TPI
1900	Cin-N	9	15	.375	35	27	22	1	0	235	255	9.8	4	100	3.8	88	3.4	4.14	83	.300	.373	-11	-18	93	94	-2.1	-0	0	-1.6
1901	Cin-N	4	13	.235	20	18	17	0	0	168	190	10.2	6	59	3.2	65	3.5	4.13	80	.314	.387	-15	-15	100	104	-3.3	-4	1	-1.3
	Bro-N	6	5	.545	13	12	9	0	0	105	110	9.4	1	30	2.6	45	3.9	2.83	121	.297	.361	6	7	103	123	-0.3	1	-0	0.7
	Yr	10	18	.357	33	30	26	0	0	273	300	9.9	7	89	2.9	110	3.6	3.63	93	.303	.365	-9	-8	101	123	-3.6	-4	1	-0.6
1902	Bro-N	15	14	.517	31	28	26	4	2	264	208	**7.1**	2	87	3.0	107	3.6	2.42	107	**.240**	.314	10	5	94	85	-0.8	-0	-2	0.4
1905	NY-A	2	2	.500	11	7	2	0	0	60	61	9.2	1	24	3.6	15	2.3	2.10	129	.288	.361	4	4	103	174	0.1	-1	-1	0.3
1906	NY-A	7	5	.583	21	15	6	2	0	125	118	8.5	3	33	2.4	52	3.7	3.17	100	.274	.326	-7	0	118	91	0.0	-1	2	0.2
1907	NY-A	7	10	.412	19	15	11	0	0	133	132	8.9	0	31	2.1	70	4.7	3.18	88	.283	.328	-9	-6	110	86	-1.1	-1	1	-0.5
1908	NY-A	4	5	.444	23	13	6	1	1	88	78	8.0	0	41	4.2	49	5.0	2.97	81	.242	.341	-6	-5	101	108	0.8	-0	-0	-0.5
1909	NY-A	0	3	.000	4	4	1	0	0	22	27	11.0	0	11	4.5	11	4.5	2.86	86	.300	.394	-1	-1	99	160	-1.4	0	1	0.0
Total	8	54	72	.429	177	139	100	8	3	1200	1179	8.8	17	416	3.1	502	3.8	3.23	94	.280	.350	-29	-27	101	101	-8.1	-7	0	-2.3

■ KID NICHOLS Nichols, Charles Augustus b: 9/14/1869, Madison, Wis. d: 4/11/53, Kansas City, Mo. BB/TR, 5'10.5", 175 lbs. Deb: 4/23/1890 MH

YEAR	TM/L	W	L	PCT	G	GS	CG	SHO	SV	IP	H	H/G	HR	BB	BB/G	SO	SO/G	ERA	/A	OAVG	OOBP	PR	/A	PF	CPI	WAT	PB	PD	TPI
1890	Bos-N	27	19	.587	48	47	47	**7**	0	427	374	7.9	8	112	2.4	222	4.7	2.21	174	.250	.303	64	77	108	106	1.2	0	0	**7.7**
1891	Bos-N	30	17	.638	52	48	45	5	**3**	426	413	8.7	15	103	**2.2**	240	5.1	2.39	**153**	.268	**.313**	**45**	**60**	109	112	0.7	-3	7	**6.2**
1892	Bos-N	35	16	.686	53	51	50	5	0	454	404	8.0	15	121	2.4	187	3.7	2.83	129	.251	.303	23	41	111	89	0.8	-0	4	4.6
1893	Bos-N	**34**	14	.708	52	45	44	1	1	425	426	9.0	15	118	2.5	94	2.0	3.52	134	.276	**.328**	55	56	101	96	4.4	-1	-0	4.8
1894	Bos-N	32	13	.711	50	46	40	**3**	0	407	488	10.8	23	121	2.7	113	2.5	4.75	125	.320	.370	26	53	111	95	6.8	2	1	4.8
1895	Bos-N	26	16	.619	48	42	42	1	**3**	380	417	9.9	15	86	2.0	140	3.3	3.41	143	.299	.340	58	62	102	108	4.8	-2	1	5.2
1896	Bos-N	**30**	14	.682	49	43	37	3	1	372	387	9.4	14	101	2.4	102	2.5	2.83	165	.290	.340	**64**	**76**	107	**121**	7.8	-4	2	6.8
1897	Bos-N	**31**	11	.738	**46**	40	37	2	**3**	**368**	362	8.9	9	68	1.7	127	3.1	2.64	**169**	.278	**.314**	**68**	**74**	103	104	3.3	3	-1	**7.3**
1898	Bos-N	**31**	12	.721	**50**	42	40	5	**3**	388	316	**7.3**	7	85	2.0	138	3.2	2.13	171	**.242**	**.288**	**63**	**65**	101	93	3.3	3	-1	**6.7**
1899	Bos-N	21	19	.525	42	37	37	4	1	343	326	8.6	11	82	2.2	108	2.8	2.99	132	.273	.320	33	37	103	93	-4.0	-4	0	3.2
1900	Bos-N	13	16	.448	29	27	25	**4**	0	231	215	8.4	11	72	2.8	53	2.1	3.08	144	.268	.329	16	35	120	99	-1.0	-3	0	3.3
1901	Bos-N	20	15	.571	38	34	33	4	0	321	306	8.6	8	90	2.5	143	4.0	3.22	116	.274	.333	3	18	112	93	3.2	10	-1	3.5
1904	StL-N	21	13	.618	36	35	35	3	1	317	268	7.6	3	50	1.4	134	3.8	2.02	134	.252	.289	25	24	99	96	5.2	-1	-1	2.5
1905	StL-N	1	5	.167	7	7	5	0	0	52	64	11.1	1	18	3.1	16	2.8	5.37	53	.331	.388	-14	-15	95	84	-1.6	0	-1	-1.4
	Phi-N	10	6	.625	17	16	15	1	0	139	129	8.4	1	28	1.8	50	3.2	2.27	135	.274	.320	11	12	102	114	1.5	-0	-4	0.9
	Yr	11	11	.500	24	23	20	1	0	191	193	9.1	2	46	2.2	66	3.1	3.11	96	.291	.340	-3	-2	100	114	-0.1	0	-5	-0.5
1906	Phi-N	0	1	.000	4	2	1	0	0	11	17	13.9	0	13	10.6	1	0.8	9.82	25	.403	.559	-9	-9	93	88	-0.4	-0	-1	-0.8
Total	15	362	207	.636	621	562	533	48	16	5061	4912	8.7	156	1268	2.3	1868	3.3	2.95	140	.274	.322	533	667	106	101	36.0	-0	5	65.3

■ CHET NICHOLS Nichols, Chester Raymond Jr. b: 2/22/31, Pawtucket, R.I. BB/TL, 6'1.5", 165 lbs. Deb: 4/19/51

YEAR	TM/L	W	L	PCT	G	GS	CG	SHO	SV	IP	H	H/G	HR	BB	BB/G	SO	SO/G	ERA	/A	OAVG	OOBP	PR	/A	PF	CPI	WAT	PB	PD	TPI
1951	Bos-N	11	8	.579	33	19	12	3	2	156	142	8.2	4	69	4.0	71	4.1	**2.88**	133	.246	.320	19	16	97	112	1.8	-2	2	1.6
1954	Mil-N	9	11	.450	35	20	5	1	1	122	132	9.7	5	65	4.8	55	4.1	4.43	84	.286	.369	-5	-10	91	105	-2.4	-2	1	-1.0
1955	Mil-N	9	8	.529	34	21	6	0	1	144	139	8.7	20	67	4.2	44	2.8	4.00	92	.253	.331	1	-5	92	106	-0.3	-2	2	-0.5
1956	Mil-N	0	1	.000	2	0	0	0	0	4	9	20.3	1	3	6.8	2	4.5	6.75	54	.563	.600	-1	-1	96	218	-0.4	-0	0	0.0
1960	Bos-A	0	2	.000	6	1	0	0	0	13	12	8.3	0	4	2.8	11	7.6	4.15	98	.240	.291	-0	-0	105	56	-0.9	-0	0	0.0
1961	Bos-A	3	2	.600	26	2	0	0	3	52	40	6.9	3	26	4.5	20	3.5	2.08	199	.221	.307	11	12	103	151	0.6	-0	3	1.5
1962	Bos-A	1	1	.500	29	1	0	0	3	57	61	9.6	3	22	3.5	33	5.2	3.00	136	.276	.332	6	7	103	135	0.0	-1	1	0.8
1963	Bos-A	1	3	.250	21	7	0	0	0	53	61	10.4	8	24	4.1	27	4.6	4.75	81	.298	.360	-7	-5	107	117	-0.9	0	-0	-0.5
1964	Cin-N	0	0	—	3	0	0	0	0	3	4	12.0	1	0	0.0	3	9.0	6.00	60	.308	.308	-1	-1	102	100	0.0	0	0	0.0
Total	9	34	36	.486	189	71	23	4	10	604	600	8.9	45	280	4.2	266	4.0	3.64	106	.264	.338	23	14	97	114	-2.5	-8	9	1.9

■ CHET NICHOLS Nichols, Chester Raymond Sr. "Nick" b: 7/3/1897, Woonsocket, R.I. d: 7/11/82, Pawtucket, R.I. BR/TR, 5'11", 160 lbs. Deb: 7/30/26

YEAR	TM/L	W	L	PCT	G	GS	CG	SHO	SV	IP	H	H/G	HR	BB	BB/G	SO	SO/G	ERA	/A	OAVG	OOBP	PR	/A	PF	CPI	WAT	PB	PD	TPI
1926	Pit-N	0	0	—	3	0	0	0	0	8	13	14.6	0	5	5.6	2	2.3	7.88	54	.342	.419	-4	-3	111	79	0.0	0	0	-0.2
1927	Pit-N	0	3	.000	8	0	0	0	0	28	34	10.9	1	17	5.5	9	2.9	5.79	67	.309	.394	-6	-6	99	95	-1.4	-0	0	-0.5
1928	NY-N	0	0	—	3	0	0	0	0	3	11	33.0	0	3	9.0	1	3.0	21.00	19	.611	.625	-6	-6	99	96	0.0	0	0	-0.4
1930	Phi-N	1	2	.333	16	5	1	0	0	60	76	11.4	8	16	2.4	15	2.3	6.75	81	.306	.344	-12	-9	109	78	0.0	0	1	-0.5
1931	Phi-N	0	1	.000	3	0	0	0	0	6	10	15.0	0	1	1.5	1	1.5	9.00	47	.435	.423	-3	-3	109	84	-0.4	-0	0	-0.2
1932	Phi-N	0	2	.000	11	0	0	0	1	19	23	10.9	2	14	6.6	5	2.4	7.11	61	.299	.398	-7	-6	111	86	-0.9	-1	0	-0.5
Total	6	1	8	.111	44	5	1	0	1	124	167	12.1	11	56	4.1	33	2.4	7.11	67	.325	.384	-37	-33	107	84	-2.7	-1	1	-2.3

■ DOLAN NICHOLS Nichols, Dolan Levon "Nick" b: 2/28/30, Tishomingo, Miss. BR/TR, 6', 195 lbs. Deb: 4/15/58

YEAR	TM/L	W	L	PCT	G	GS	CG	SHO	SV	IP	H	H/G	HR	BB	BB/G	SO	SO/G	ERA	/A	OAVG	OOBP	PR	/A	PF	CPI	WAT	PB	PD	TPI
1958	Chi-N	0	4	.000	24	0	0	0	1	41	46	10.1	1	16	3.5	9	2.0	5.05	79	.295	.352	-5	-5	101	86	-1.9	-1	1	-0.4

■ TRICKY NICHOLS Nichols, Frederick C. b: 7/26/1850, Bridgeport, Conn. d: 8/22/1897, Bridgeport, Conn. BR/TR, 5'7.5", 150 lbs. Deb: 4/21/1875

YEAR	TM/L	W	L	PCT	G	GS	CG	SHO	SV	IP	H	H/G	HR	BB	BB/G	SO	SO/G	ERA	/A	OAVG	OOBP	PR	/A	PF	CPI	WAT	PB	PD	TPI
1875	NH-n	4	28	.125	32																								
1876	Bos-N	1	0	1.000	1	1	1	0	0	9	7	7.0	0	0	0.0	0	0.0	1.00	217	.219	.219	1	1	94	39	0.5	-1	0	0.0
1877	StL-N	18	23	.439	42	39	35	1	0	350	376	9.7	2	53	1.4	80	2.1	2.60	112	.283	.310	8	12	103	100	-3.3	-8	0	0.3
1878	Pro-N	4	7	.364	11	10	10	0	0	98	157	14.4	0	8	0.7	21	1.9	4.22	53	.372	.384	-21	-22	97	113	-2.0	-0	0	-1.8
1880	Wor-N	0	2	.000	2	2	2	0	0	18	29	14.5	0	4	2.0	4	2.0	4.00	66	.372	.403	-3	-3	111	143	-0.9	-1	0	-0.2
1882	Bal-a	1	12	.077	16	13	12	0	0	118	155	11.8	2	17	1.3	21	1.6	5.03	55	.322	.345	-31	-30	102	84	-4.7	-2	0	-2.6
Total	5	24	44	.353	72	65	60	1	0	593	724	11.0	4	82	1.2	126	1.9	3.37	81	.309	.332	-45	-41	102	99	-10.4	-13	0	-4.3

■ ROD NICHOLS Nichols, Rodney Lea b: 12/29/64, Burlington, Iowa BR/TR, 6'2", 190 lbs. Deb: 7/30/88

YEAR	TM/L	W	L	PCT	G	GS	CG	SHO	SV	IP	H	H/G	HR	BB	BB/G	SO	SO/G	ERA	/A	OAVG	OOBP	PR	/A	PF	CPI	WAT	PB	PD	TPI
1988	Cle-A	1	7	.125	11	10	3	0	0	69	73	9.5	5	23	3.0	31	4.0	5.09	80	.272	.330	-9	-8	102	80	-2.9	0	-0	-0.7

■ FRANK NICHOLSON Nicholson, Frank Collins b: 8/29/1889, Berlin, Pa. d: 11/10/72, Jersey Shore, Pa. BR/TR, 6'2", 175 lbs. Deb: 9/06/12

YEAR	TM/L	W	L	PCT	G	GS	CG	SHO	SV	IP	H	H/G	HR	BB	BB/G	SO	SO/G	ERA	/A	OAVG	OOBP	PR	/A	PF	CPI	WAT	PB	PD	TPI
1912	Phi-N	0	0	—	2	0	0	0	0	4	8	18.0	1	2	4.5	1	2.3	6.75	51	.471	.526	-1	-1	101	170	0.0	0	0	0.0

■ GEORGE NICOL Nicol, George Edward b: 10/17/1870, Barry, Ill. d: 8/10/24, Milwaukee, Wis. TL, 5'7", 155 lbs. Deb: 9/23/1890

YEAR	TM/L	W	L	PCT	G	GS	CG	SHO	SV	IP	H	H/G	HR	BB	BB/G	SO	SO/G	ERA	/A	OAVG	OOBP	PR	/A	PF	CPI	WAT	PB	PD	TPI
1890	StL-a	2	1	.667	3	3	2	0	0	17	11	5.8	1	19	10.1	16	8.5	4.76	93	.198	.402	-2	-1	115	90	0.3	1	0	0.1
1891	Chi-N	0	1	.000	3	2	0	0	0	11	14	11.5	0	10	8.2	12	9.8	4.91	71	.324	.451	-2	-2	105	117	-0.4	1	0	0.0
1894	Pit-N	3	4	.429	8	5	3	0	0	44	57	11.7	2	33	6.8	11	2.3	6.55	77	.337	.445	-6	-7	95	94	-0.4	2	0	-0.3
	Lou-N	0	1	.000	1	1	1	0	0	9	19	19.0	2	5	5.0	3	3.0	15.00	32	.453	.511	-10	-10	91	74	-0.4	0	0	-0.5
	Yr	3	5	.375	9	6	4	0	0	53	76	12.9	4	38	6.5	14	2.4	7.98	63	.360	.457	-16	-18	94	74	-0.8	2	0	-0.8
Total	3	5	7	.417	15	11	6	0	0	81	101	11.2	5	67	7.4	42	4.7	6.89	69	.326	.445	-19	-19	100	94	-0.9	5	0	-0.7

■ TOM NIEDENFUER Niedenfuer, Thomas Edward b: 8/13/59, St.Louis Park, Minn BR/TR, 6'5", 225 lbs. Deb: 8/15/81

YEAR	TM/L	W	L	PCT	G	GS	CG	SHO	SV	IP	H	H/G	HR	BB	BB/G	SO	SO/G	ERA	/A	OAVG	OOBP	PR	/A	PF	CPI	WAT	PB	PD	TPI
1981	LA-N	3	1	.750	17	0	0	0	2	26	25	8.7	1	6	2.1	12	4.2	3.81	88	.258	.299	-1	-1	96	82	0.8	0	-0	-0.1
1982	LA-N	3	4	.429	55	0	0	0	9	70	71	9.1	3	25	3.2	60	7.7	2.70	125	.269	.328	7	5	94	139	-0.7	-0	-1	0.5
1983	LA-N	8	3	.727	66	0	0	0	11	95	55	5.2	6	29	2.7	66	6.3	1.89	191	.170	.232	18	18	100	72	2.2	-0	-1	1.8
1984	LA-N	2	5	.286	33	0	0	0	11	47	39	7.5	3	23	4.4	45	8.6	2.49	150	.227	.315	6	7	104	132	-1.4	-0	-0	0.6
1985	LA-N	7	9	.438	64	0	0	0	19	106	86	7.3	6	24	2.0	102	8.7	2.72	121	.223	.267	10	7	92	84	-2.1	-0	-1	0.6
1986	LA-N	6	6	.500	60	0	0	0	11	80	86	9.7	11	29	3.3	55	6.2	3.71	95	.280	.336	0	-2	95	128	0.6	1	0	0.0
1987	LA-N	1	0	1.000	15	0	0	0	1	16	13	7.3	1	9	5.1	10	5.6	2.81	134	.220	.329	2	2	92	119	0.5	0	0	0.2
	Bal-A	3	5	.375	45	0	0	0	13	52	55	9.5	11	22	3.8	37	6.4	5.02	88	.266	.335	-3	-3	99	102	-0.3	0	-1	-0.3
1988	Bal-A	3	4	.429	52	0	0	0	18	59	59	9.0	8	19	2.9	40	6.1	3.51	110	.259	.317	3	2	97	119	0.5	0	-1	0.2
Total	8	36	37	.493	407	0	0	0	95	551	489	8.0	50	186	3.0	427	7.0	3.05	118	.239	.300	43	34	96	106	0.1	-0	-4	3.5

■ DICK NIEHAUS Niehaus, Richard J. b: 10/24/1892, Covington, Ky. d: 3/12/57, Atlanta, Ga. BL/TL, 5'11", 165 lbs. Deb: 9/09/13

YEAR	TM/L	W	L	PCT	G	GS	CG	SHO	SV	IP	H	H/G	HR	BB	BB/G	SO	SO/G	ERA	/A	OAVG	OOBP	PR	/A	PF	CPI	WAT	PB	PD	TPI
1913	StL-N	0	2	.000	3	3	2	0	0	24	20	7.5	1	13	4.9	4	1.5	4.13	75	.241	.317	-2	-3	97	83	-0.9	1	0	-0.1
1914	StL-N	1	0	1.000	8	1	1	0	0	17	18	9.5	1	8	4.2	6	3.2	3.18	91	.269	.342	-1	-1	104	119	0.5	1	-0	0.0
1915	StL-N	2	1	.667	15	2	0	0	0	45	48	9.6	2	22	4.4	21	4.2	4.00	69	.281	.351	-6	-6	101	107	0.6	-1	0	-0.6
1920	Cle-A	1	2	.333	19	3	0	0	2	40	42	9.4	0	16	3.6	12	2.7	3.60	105	.269	.341	1	1	100	90	-0.6	2	-1	0.1
Total	4	4	5	.444	45	9	3	0	2	126	128	9.1	4	59	4.2	43	3.1	3.79	84	.268	.341	-9	-9	100	98	-0.4	2	-1	-0.6

■ JOE NIEKRO Niekro, Joseph Franklin b: 11/7/44, Martins Ferry, Ohio BR/TR, 6'1", 185 lbs. Deb: 4/16/67

YEAR	TM/L	W	L	PCT	G	GS	CG	SHO	SV	IP	H	H/G	HR	BB	BB/G	SO	SO/G	ERA	/A	OAVG	OOBP	PR	/A	PF	CPI	WAT	PB	PD	TPI
1967	Chi-N	10	7	.588	36	22	7	2	0	170	171	9.1	15	32	1.7	77	4.1	3.34	101	.257	.290	1	1	100	97	1.0	1	-1	0.2
1968	Chi-N	14	10	.583	34	29	2	1	2	177	204	10.4	18	59	3.0	65	3.3	4.32	78	.294	.346	-26	-19	112	109	1.9	-2	0	-2.1
1969	Chi-N	0	1	.000	4	3	0	0	0	19	24	11.4	3	6	2.8	7	3.3	3.79	100	.304	.349	-0	-0	105	141	-0.4	0	1	0.1
	SD-N	8	17	.320	37	31	8	3	0	202	213	9.5	15	45	2.0	55	2.5	3.70	97	.273	.306	-2	-2	100	98	0.0	0	-2	-0.3
	Yr	8	18	.308	41	34	8	3	0	221	237	9.7	18	51	2.1	62	2.5	3.71	98	.275	.310	-3	-2	101	98	-0.4	0	-1	-0.2
1970	Det-A	12	13	.480	38	34	6	2	0	213	221	9.3	28	72	3.0	101	4.3	4.06	95	.266	.324	-8	-5	104	103	-0.1	3	1	0.0
1971	Det-A	6	7	.462	31	15	0	0	1	122	136	10.0	13	49	3.6	43	3.2	4.50	73	.283	.346	-14	-16	95	102	-1.1	0	1	-1.5
1972	Det-A	3	2	.600	18	7	1	0	1	47	62	11.9	3	8	1.5	24	4.6	3.83	90	.330	.357	-4	-2	112	128	0.3	1	-0	-0.1
1973	Atl-N	2	4	.333	20	0	0	0	3	24	23	8.6	2	11	4.1	12	4.5	4.13	100	.277	.343	-1	0	113	110	-0.8	0	1	0.1
1974	Atl-N	3	2	.600	27	2	0	0	0	43	36	7.5	5	18	3.8	31	6.5	3.56	106	.237	.315	0	1	104	105	0.3	-1	1	0.1
1975	Hou-N	6	4	.600	40	4	1	1	4	88	79	8.1	3	39	4.0	54	5.5	3.07	112	.240	.317	6	4	95	100	1.8	1	0	0.5
1976	Hou-N	4	8	.333	36	13	0	0	0	118	107	8.2	8	56	4.3	77	5.9	3.36	90	.238	.318	2	-4	87	100	-2.0	2	-1	-0.2
1977	Hou-N	13	8	.619	44	14	9	2	5	181	155	7.7	14	64	3.2	101	5.0	3.03	119	.237	.299	18	12	92	104	2.8	-1	2	1.2
1978	Hou-N	14	14	.500	35	29	10	1	0	203	190	8.4	13	73	3.2	97	4.3	3.86	88	.248	.316	-6	-10	95	88	1.3	-1	-1	-1.3
1979	Hou-N	**21**	11	.656	38	38	11	**5**	0	264	221	7.5	17	107	3.6	119	4.1	3.00	113	.228	.306	22	11	90	98	4.5	-1	0	0.9
1980	Hou-N	20	12	.625	37	36	11	2	0	256	268	9.4	12	79	2.8	127	4.5	3.55	99	.270	.320	2	-1	97	101	2.4	7	-0	0.4
1981	Hou-N	9	9	.500	24	24	5	2	0	166	150	8.1	8	47	2.5	77	4.2	2.82	107	.243	.291	12	4	87	101	-0.9	1	-1	0.4
1982	Hou-N	17	12	.586	35	35	16	5	0	270	224	7.5	12	64	2.1	130	4.3	2.47	146	.229	.275	34	34	100	97	3.6	-4	0	3.2
1983	Hou-N	15	14	.517	38	38	9	1	0	264	238	8.1	15	101	3.4	152	5.2	3.48	94	.241	.307	5	-6	90	89	-0.2	-3	-2	-1.1
1984	Hou-N	16	12	.571	38	38	6	1	0	248	223	8.1	16	89	3.2	127	4.6	3.05	108	.241	.308	15	7	92	104	2.5	-1	1	0.6
1985	Hou-N	9	12	.429	32	32	4	1	0	213	197	8.3	21	99	4.2	117	4.9	3.72	93	.247	.325	-3	-6	96	104	-1.8	3	0	-0.2
	NY-A	2	1	.667	3	3	0	0	0	12	14	10.5	3	8	6.0	4	3.0	6.00	65	.280	.379	-2	-3	94	107	0.2	0	0	-0.1
1986	NY-A	9	10	.474	25	25	0	0	0	126	139	9.9	15	63	4.5	59	4.2	4.86	88	.275	.356	-9	-8	103	99	-1.5	0	-1	-0.8
1987	NY-A	3	4	.429	8	8	1	0	0	51	40	7.1	4	19	3.4	30	5.3	3.53	123	.215	.299	5	5	97	83	-0.7	0	-0	0.4
	Min-A	4	9	.308	19	18	0	0	0	96	115	10.8	11	45	4.2	54	5.1	6.28	68	.296	.374	-19	-21	96	88	-2.7	0	-1	-1.9
	Yr	7	13	.350	27	26	1	0	0	147	155	9.5	15	64	3.9	84	5.1	5.33	81	.268	.344	-14	-17	96	88	-3.4	0	-1	-1.5
1988	Min-A	1	1	.500	5	2	0	0	0	12	16	12.0	2	9	6.8	7	5.3	9.75	43	.320	.424	-8	-7	105	74	0.0	0	1	-0.6
Total	22	221	204	.520	702	500	107	29	16	3585	3466	8.7	276	1262	3.2	1747	4.4	3.59	98	.255	.316	17	-32	97	99	10.4	6	-2	-2.1

■ PHIL NIEKRO Niekro, Philip Henry b: 4/1/39, Blaine, Ohio BR/TR, 6'1", 180 lbs. Deb: 4/15/64

YEAR	TM/L	W	L	PCT	G	GS	CG	SHO	SV	IP	H	H/G	HR	BB	BB/G	SO	SO/G	ERA	/A	OAVG	OOBP	PR	/A	PF	CPI	WAT	PB	PD	TPI
1964	Mil-N	0	0	—	10	0	0	0	0	15	15	9.0	1	7	4.2	8	4.8	4.80	71	.273	.348	-2	-2	96	94	0.0	0	-0	-0.2
1965	Mil-N	2	3	.400	41	1	0	0	6	75	73	8.8	5	26	3.1	49	5.9	2.88	127	.258	.315	5	6	103	128	-0.5	-0	1	0.7
1966	Atl-N	4	3	.571	28	0	0	0	2	50	48	8.6	4	23	4.1	17	3.1	4.14	85	.249	.326	-3	-4	97	90	0.4	-1	2	-0.2
1967	Atl-N	11	9	.550	46	20	10	1	9	207	164	7.1	9	55	2.4	129	5.6	**1.87**	**189**	.218	.273	35	38	105	121	1.6	-1	1	4.4
1968	Atl-N	14	12	.538	37	34	15	5	2	257	228	8.0	16	45	1.6	140	4.9	2.59	108	.239	.273	11	6	94	99	1.2	-1	3	0.9
1969	Atl-N	23	13	.639	40	35	21	4	1	284	235	7.4	21	57	1.8	193	6.1	2.57	144	.221	.260	33	36	103	88	3.4	3	2	4.6
1970	Atl-N	12	18	.400	34	32	10	3	0	230	222	8.7	40	68	2.7	168	6.6	4.27	100	.248	.302	-5	-1	105	95	-2.5	-1	2	0.0
1971	Atl-N	15	14	.517	42	36	18	4	2	269	248	8.3	27	70	2.3	173	5.8	2.98	129	.245	.292	15	26	111	107	0.4	-3	2	2.8
1972	Atl-N	16	12	.571	38	36	17	1	0	282	254	8.1	22	53	1.7	164	5.2	3.06	120	.236	.271	12	19	106	85	3.5	2	1	2.4
1973	Atl-N	13	10	.565	42	30	9	1	4	245	214	7.9	21	89	3.3	131	4.8	3.31	125	.234	.301	10	23	113	94	2.3	-2	2	2.6
1974	Atl-N	**20**	13	.606	41	39	**18**	6	1	**302**	249	7.4	19	88	2.6	195	5.8	2.38	158	.225	.281	**42**	**46**	104	106	2.8	0	1	**5.2**
1975	Atl-N	15	15	.500	39	37	13	1	0	276	285	9.3	29	72	2.3	144	4.7	3.20	110	.269	.317	13	10	97	122	2.6	0	1	1.1
1976	Atl-N	17	11	.607	38	37	10	2	0	271	249	8.3	18	101	3.4	173	5.7	3.29	120	.242	.309	7	19	112	98	4.9	1	1	2.4
1977	Atl-N	16	20	.444	44	43	**20**	2	0	**330**	315	8.6	26	164	4.5	**262**	7.1	4.04	112	.255	.341	-4	18	115	99	2.4	-4	2	1.8
1978	Atl-N	19	18	.514	44	42	**22**	4	1	**334**	295	7.9	16	102	2.7	248	6.7	2.88	141	.235	.295	26	**44**	114	96	3.5	3	4	**6.0**
1979	Atl-N	**21**	20	.512	44	44	**23**	1	0	**342**	311	8.2	41	113	3.0	208	5.5	3.39	122	.241	.303	13	**28**	110	102	4.4	1	3	**3.6**
1980	Atl-N	15	18	.455	40	38	11	3	1	275	256	8.4	30	85	2.8	176	5.8	3.63	101	.249	.303	-1	1	101	97	-1.9	-2	1	0.0
1981	Atl-N	7	7	.500	22	22	3	3	0	139	120	7.8	6	56	3.6	62	4.0	3.11	112	.233	.306	6	6	100	94	0.4	-4	0	0.3
1982	Atl-N	17	4	**.810**	35	35	4	2	0	234	225	8.7	23	73	2.8	144	5.5	3.62	106	.255	.311	-0	6	107	100	**6.4**	2	1	1.0
1983	Atl-N	11	10	.524	34	33	2	0	0	202	212	9.4	18	105	4.7	128	5.7	3.97	96	.275	.359	-7	-4	104	117	-0.3	1	0	-0.2
1984	NY-A	16	8	.667	32	31	5	1	0	216	219	9.1	15	76	3.2	136	5.7	3.08	121	.267	.325	22	15	93	**125**	3.8	0	2	1.8
1985	NY-A	16	12	.571	33	33	7	1	0	220	203	8.3	29	120	4.9	149	6.1	4.09	95	.245	.340	1	-5	94	107	-0.8	0	-2	-0.5
1986	Cle-A	11	11	.500	34	32	5	0	0	210	241	10.3	24	95	4.1	81	3.5	4.33	95	.287	.360	-3	-5	98	117	-0.4	0	-1	-0.5
1987	Tor-A	0	2	.000	3	3	0	0	0	12	15	11.3	4	7	5.3	7	5.3	8.25	54	.306	.393	-5	-5	99	92	-0.9	0	-0	-0.4
	Cle-A	7	11	.389	22	22	2	0	0	124	142	10.3	18	53	3.8	57	4.1	5.88	80	.286	.355	-19	-17	105	89	0.2	0	0	-1.4
	Yr	7	13	.350	25	25	2	0	0	136	157	10.4	22	60	4.0	64	4.2	6.09	76	.288	.358	-24	-22	104	89	-0.7	0	-0	-1.8
	Atl-N	0	0	—	1	1	0	0	0	3	6	18.0	0	6	18.0	0	0.0	15.00	30	.429	.600	-4	-4	109	87	0.0	-0	0	-0.2
Total	24	318	274	.537	864	716	245	45	29	5404	5044	8.4	482	1809	3.0	3342	5.6	3.35	115	.247	.308	196	302	105	103	36.9	-6	27	38.0

■ SCOTT NIELSEN Nielsen, Jeffrey Scott b: 12/18/58, Salt Lake City, Ut. BR/TR, 6'1", 190 lbs. Deb: 7/07/86

YEAR	TM/L	W	L	PCT	G	GS	CG	SHO	SV	IP	H	H/G	HR	BB	BB/G	SO	SO/G	ERA	/A	OAVG	OOBP	PR	/A	PF	CPI	WAT	PB	PD	TPI
1986	NY-A	4	4	.500	10	9	2	2	0	56	66	10.6	12	12	1.9	20	3.2	4.02	107	.299	.340	1	2	103	138	-0.3	0	-1	0.1
1987	Chi-A	3	5	.375	19	7	1	1	2	66	83	11.3	9	25	3.4	23	3.1	6.27	77	.307	.365	-13	-10	109	90	-0.8	0	-1	-0.9
1988	NY-A	1	2	.333	7	2	0	0	0	20	27	12.1	5	13	5.8	4	1.8	6.75	56	.333	.426	-6	-7	96	118	-0.5	0	0	-0.5
Total	3	8	11	.421	36	18	3	3	2	142	176	11.2	26	50	3.2	47	3.0	5.45	82	.308	.365	-18	-15	104	113	-1.6	0	-1	-1.3

YEAR	TM/L	W	L	PCT	G	GS	CG	SHO	SV	IP	H	H/G	HR	BB	BB/G	SO	SO/G	ERA	/A	OAVG	OOBP	PR	/A	PF	CPI	WAT	PB	PD	TPI
■ RANDY NIEMANN	Niemann, Randal Harold b: 11/15/55, Scotia, Cal. BL/TL, 6'4", 200 lbs. Deb: 5/20/79																												
1979	Hou-N	3	2	.600	26	7	3	2	1	67	68	9.1	1	22	3.0	24	3.2	3.76	90	.272	.317	-0	-3	90	92	0.3	-0	-1	-0.3
1980	Hou-N	0	1	.000	22	1	0	0	1	33	40	10.9	2	12	3.3	18	4.9	5.45	64	.299	.354	-7	-7	97	84	-0.4	0	1	-0.5
1982	Pit-N	1	1	.500	20	0	0	0	1	35	34	8.7	1	17	4.4	26	6.7	5.14	77	.254	.338	-6	-5	110	71	0.0	1	1	-0.2
1983	Pit-N	0	1	.000	8	1	0	0	0	14	20	12.9	2	7	4.5	8	5.1	9.00	42	.357	.424	-8	-8	103	83	-0.4	-0	0	-0.7
1984	Chi-A	0	0	—	5	0	0	0	0	5	5	9.0	0	5	9.0	5	9.0	1.80	247	.263	.417	1	1	111	277	0.0	0	0	0.2
1985	NY-N	0	0	—	4	0	0	0	0	5	5	9.0	0	0	0.0	2	3.6	0.00	—	.278	.278	2	2	95	0	0.0	0	0	0.2
1986	NY-N	2	3	.400	31	1	0	0	0	36	44	11.0	2	12	3.0	18	4.5	3.75	92	.308	.354	-0	-1	93	127	-0.9	1	1	0.0
1987	Min-A	1	0	1.000	6	0	0	0	0	5	3	5.4	0	7	12.6	1	1.8	9.00	48	.158	.429	-3	-3	96	48	0.5	0	0	-0.1
Total	8	7	8	.467	122	10	3	2	3	200	219	9.9	8	82	3.7	102	4.6	4.64	78	.283	.347	-21	-23	97	94	-0.9	2	2	-1.4
■ JACK NIEMES	Niemes, Jacob Leland b: 10/19/19, Cincinnati, Ohio d: 3/4/66, Hamilton, Ohio BR/TL, 6'1", 180 lbs. Deb: 5/30/43																												
1943	Cin-N	0	0	—	3	0	0	0	0	3	5	15.0	0	2	6.0	1	3.0	6.00	55	.385	.467	-1	-1	98	127	0.0	0	0	0.0
■ CHUCK NIESON	Nieson, Charles Bassett b: 9/24/42, Hanford, Cal. BR/TR, 6'2", 185 lbs. Deb: 9/18/64																												
1964	Min-A	0	0	—	2	0	0	0	0	2	1	4.5	1	1	4.5	5	22.5	4.50	80	.143	.250	-0	-0	100	101	0.0	0	0	0.0
■ JUAN NIEVES	Nieves, Juan Manuel (Cruz) b: 1/5/65, Las Lomas, P.R. BL/TL, 6'3", 175 lbs. Deb: 4/10/86																												
1986	Mil-A	11	12	.478	35	33	4	3	0	185	224	10.9	17	77	3.7	116	5.6	4.91	88	.299	.362	-15	-12	103	103	0.0	0	-2	-1.3
1987	Mil-A	14	8	.636	34	33	3	1	0	196	199	9.1	24	100	4.6	163	7.5	4.87	94	.264	.347	-9	-7	102	96	2.1	0	-1	-0.7
1988	Mil-A	7	5	.583	25	15	1	1	1	110	84	6.9	13	50	4.1	73	6.0	4.09	100	.208	.295	-1	-0	103	75	0.6	0	0	0.0
Total	3	32	25	.561	94	81	8	5	1	491	507	9.3	54	227	4.2	352	6.5	4.71	93	.266	.342	-25	-19	103	94	2.7	0	-4	-2.0
■ JOHNNY NIGGELING	Niggeling, John Arnold b: 7/10/03, Remsen, Iowa d: 9/16/63, Le Mars, Iowa BR/TR, 6', 170 lbs. Deb: 4/30/38																												
1938	Bos-N	1	0	1.000	2	0	0	0	0	2	4	18.0	0	1	4.5	1	4.5	9.00	37	.400	.455	-1	-1	89	91	0.5	0	0	0.0
1939	Cin-N	2	1	.667	10	5	2	1	0	40	51	11.5	2	13	2.9	20	4.5	5.85	67	.309	.357	-9	-9	100	83	0.2	-0	-0	-0.8
1940	StL-A	7	11	.389	28	20	10	0	0	154	148	8.6	9	69	4.0	82	4.8	4.44	106	.250	.331	-1	5	108	85	-1.0	-2	-0	0.3
1941	StL-A	7	9	.438	24	20	13	1	0	168	168	9.0	17	63	3.4	68	3.6	3.80	110	.255	.317	6	7	101	102	-0.2	-1	-1	0.5
1942	StL-A	15	11	.577	28	27	16	3	0	206	173	7.6	10	93	4.1	107	4.7	2.67	140	.226	.313	23	25	102	118	1.1	-2	-1	2.3
1943	StL-A	6	8	.429	20	20	7	0	0	150	122	7.3	7	57	3.4	73	4.4	3.18	104	.220	.295	2	2	101	83	-0.6	-4	-0	-0.2
	Was-A	4	2	.667	6	6	5	3	0	51	27	4.8	0	17	3.0	24	4.2	0.88	382	.153	.226	14	14	102	59	0.8	1	0	2.0
	Yr	10	10	.500	26	26	12	3	0	201	149	6.7	7	74	3.3	97	4.3	2.60	128	.202	.271	16	16	101	59	0.2	-4	0	1.8
1944	Was-A	10	8	.556	24	24	14	2	0	206	164	7.2	5	88	3.8	121	5.3	2.32	134	.221	.302	26	18	91	112	2.4	-2	-1	1.6
1945	Was-A	7	12	.368	26	25	8	2	0	177	161	8.2	7	73	3.7	90	4.6	3.15	98	.240	.314	4	-1	92	97	-3.5	-3	-2	-0.6
1946	Was-A	3	2	.600	8	6	3	0	0	38	39	9.2	1	21	5.0	10	2.4	4.03	82	.265	.353	-2	-3	94	99	0.5	0	-0	-0.2
	Bos-N	2	5	.286	8	8	3	0	0	58	54	8.4	2	21	3.3	24	3.7	3.26	98	.243	.308	1	-0	94	87	-1.6	-1	0	0.0
Total	9	64	69	.481	184	161	81	12	0	1250	1111	8.0	60	516	3.7	620	4.5	3.22	112	.236	.312	62	55	98	98	-1.4	-14	-6	4.9
■ AL NIPPER	Nipper, Albert Samuel b: 4/2/59, San Diego, Cal. BR/TR, 6', 188 lbs. Deb: 9/06/83																												
1983	Bos-A	1	1	.500	3	2	1	0	0	16	17	9.6	0	7	3.9	5	2.8	2.25	184	.293	.373	3	3	102	202	0.0	0	0	0.3
1984	Bos-A	11	6	.647	29	24	6	0	0	183	183	9.0	18	52	2.6	84	4.1	3.89	113	.257	.311	2	10	110	93	2.3	0	3	1.3
1985	Bos-A	9	12	.429	25	25	5	0	0	162	157	8.7	14	82	4.6	85	4.7	4.06	104	.256	.348	2	3	102	107	-1.6	0	2	0.5
1986	Bos-A	10	12	.455	26	26	3	0	0	159	186	10.5	24	47	2.7	79	4.5	5.38	77	.290	.338	-21	-22	99	92	-2.7	0	3	-1.7
1987	Bos-A	11	12	.478	30	30	6	0	0	174	196	10.1	30	62	3.2	89	4.6	5.43	81	.284	.341	-19	-19	99	96	0.0	0	1	-1.6
1988	Chi-N	2	4	.333	22	12	0	0	1	80	72	8.1	9	34	3.8	27	3.0	3.04	119	.238	.320	4	5	105	124	-0.8	-1	-1	0.3
Total	6	44	47	.484	135	119	21	0	1	774	811	9.4	95	284	3.3	369	4.3	4.45	95	.269	.333	-29	-19	103	102	-2.8	-1	7	-0.9
■ MERLIN NIPPERT	Nippert, Merlin Lee b: 9/1/38, Mangum, Okla. BR/TR, 6'1", 175 lbs. Deb: 9/12/62																												
1962	Bos-A	0	0	—	4	0	0	0	0	6	4	6.0	1	4	6.0	3	4.5	4.50	91	.200	.296	-0	-0	103	90	0.0	0	0	0.0
■ RON NISCHWITZ	Nischwitz, Ronald Lee b: 7/1/37, Dayton, Ohio BB/TL, 6'3", 205 lbs. Deb: 9/04/61																												
1961	Det-A	0	1	.000	6	1	0	0	0	11	13	10.6	2	8	6.5	8	6.5	5.73	66	.295	.375	-2	-2	94	113	-0.4	-0	-0	-0.2
1962	Det-A	4	5	.444	48	0	0	0	4	65	73	10.1	5	26	3.6	28	3.9	3.88	113	.285	.345	1	4	110	117	-0.6	2	0	0.6
1963	Cle-A	0	2	.000	14	0	0	0	1	17	17	9.0	3	8	4.2	10	5.3	6.35	56	.262	.333	-5	-5	98	76	-0.9	-0	0	-0.4
1965	Det-A	1	0	1.000	20	0	0	0	1	23	21	8.2	2	6	2.3	12	4.7	2.74	132	.259	.300	2	2	104	131	0.5	-0	-0	0.2
Total	4	5	8	.385	88	1	0	0	6	116	124	9.6	12	48	3.7	58	4.5	4.19	96	.278	.339	-5	-2	106	114	-1.4	1	0	0.2
■ OTHO NITCHOLAS	Nitcholas, Otho James b: 9/13/08, Mc Kinney, Tex. BR/TR, 6', 190 lbs. Deb: 4/18/45																												
1945	Bro-N	1	0	1.000	7	0	0	0	0	19	19	9.0	4	1	0.5	4	1.9	5.21	69	.257	.256	-3	-3	95	74	0.5	0	-0	-0.2
■ WILLARD NIXON	Nixon, Willard Lee b: 6/17/28, Taylorsville, Ga. BL/TR, 6'2", 195 lbs. Deb: 7/07/50																												
1950	Bos-A	8	6	.571	22	15	2	0	2	101	126	11.2	8	58	5.2	57	5.1	6.06	84	.310	.391	-17	-11	111	96	-0.4	-2	0	-1.0
1951	Bos-A	7	4	.636	33	14	2	1	1	125	136	9.8	12	56	4.0	70	5.0	4.90	90	.285	.361	-11	-7	106	103	1.0	3	0	-0.3
1952	Bos-A	5	4	.556	23	13	5	0	0	104	115	10.0	12	61	5.3	50	4.3	4.85	81	.290	.385	-14	-11	107	115	0.6	1	1	-0.8
1953	Bos-A	4	8	.333	23	15	5	1	0	117	114	8.8	6	59	4.5	57	4.4	3.92	110	.254	.337	1	5	108	97	-2.4	0	-0	0.6
1954	Bos-A	11	12	.478	31	30	8	2	0	200	182	8.2	16	87	3.9	102	4.6	4.05	93	.248	.327	-7	-7	101	91	0.7	6	1	0.1
1955	Bos-A	12	10	.545	31	31	7	3	0	208	207	9.0	10	85	3.7	95	4.1	4.07	119	.259	.327	-2	18	122	87	0.0	4	2	2.8
1956	Bos-A	9	8	.529	23	22	9	1	0	145	142	8.8	9	57	3.5	74	4.6	4.22	101	.255	.328	-1	0	102	86	-0.2	-0	2	0.2
1957	Bos-A	12	13	.480	29	29	11	1	0	191	207	9.8	10	56	2.6	96	4.5	3.68	112	.280	.334	2	10	109	107	-1.3	5	-1	1.5
1958	Bos-A	1	7	.125	10	8	2	0	0	43	48	10.0	7	11	2.3	15	3.1	6.07	65	.281	.316	-11	-10	105	75	-3.0	1	0	-0.8
Total	9	69	72	.489	225	177	51	9	3	1234	1277	9.3	90	530	3.9	616	4.5	4.39	98	.270	.343	-59	-13	109	96	-5.0	18	5	2.3
■ THE ONLY NOLAN	Nolan, Edward Sylvester b: 11/7/1857, Paterson, N.J. d: 5/18/13, Paterson, N.J. BL/TR, 5'8", 171 lbs. Deb: 5/01/1878																												
1878	Ind-N	13	22	.371	38	38	37	1	0	347	357	9.3	1	56	1.5	125	3.2	2.57	79	.276	.306	-10	-21	88	87	-2.6	5	3	-1.3
1881	Cle-N	8	14	.364	22	21	20	0	0	180	183	9.1	3	38	1.9	54	2.7	3.05	88	.276	.315	-5	-7	96	89	-2.0	1	0	-0.5
1883	Pit-a	0	7	.000	7	7	6	0	0	55	81	13.3	0	10	1.6	23	3.8	4.25	76	.348	.375	-6	-6	98	126	-3.4	1	0	-0.3
1884	WiL-U	1	4	.200	5	5	5	0	0	40	44	9.9	1	7	1.6	52	11.7	2.93	112	.284	.315	0	2	109	123	0.3	1	0	0.3
1885	Phi-N	1	5	.167	7	7	6	0	0	54	55	9.2	1	24	4.0	20	3.3	4.17	70	.275	.352	-8	-7	104	89	-2.0	-2	0	-0.7
Total	5	23	52	.307	79	78	74	1	0	676	720	9.6	6	135	1.8	274	3.6	2.98	81	.283	.319	-29	-42	94	93	-9.7	6	3	-2.5
■ GARY NOLAN	Nolan, Gary Lynn b: 5/27/48, Herlong, Cal. BR/TR, 6'2.5", 197 lbs. Deb: 4/15/67																												
1967	Cin-N	14	8	.636	33	32	8	5	0	227	193	7.7	18	62	2.5	206	**8.2**	2.58	142	.228	.279	20	27	109	106	2.6	-1	-1	2.9
1968	Cin-N	9	4	.692	23	22	4	2	0	150	105	6.3	10	49	2.9	111	6.7	2.40	138	.196	.264	10	15	111	85	2.5	2	-2	1.9
1969	Cin-N	8	8	.500	16	15	2	1	0	109	102	8.4	11	40	3.3	83	6.9	3.55	100	.247	.309	1	-0	99	100	-0.7	4	-1	0.2
1970	Cin-N	18	7	.720	37	37	4	2	0	251	226	8.1	25	96	3.4	181	6.5	3.26	128	.240	.307	22	26	103	108	3.5	0	-1	2.5
1971	Cin-N	12	15	.444	35	35	9	0	0	245	208	7.6	12	59	2.2	146	5.4	3.16	106	.227	.271	8	5	96	71	-1.3	-1	1	0.5
1972	Cin-N	15	5	**.750**	25	25	6	2	0	176	147	7.5	13	30	1.5	90	4.6	1.99	158	.227	.258	29	23	91	115	3.8	-0	-1	2.3
1973	Cin-N	0	1	.000	2	2	0	0	0	10	6	5.4	1	7	6.3	3	2.7	3.60	93	.167	.295	0	-0	92	68	-0.4	0	-0	0.0
1975	Cin-N	15	9	.625	32	32	5	1	0	211	202	8.6	18	29	**1.2**	74	3.2	3.16	117	.251	.272	11	12	101	89	-0.8	2	-2	1.3
1976	Cin-N	15	9	.625	34	34	7	1	0	239	232	8.7	28	27	**1.0**	113	4.3	3.46	101	.254	.273	1	1	100	91	0.0	-3	-3	-0.5
1977	Cin-N	4	1	.800	8	8	0	0	0	39	53	12.2	5	12	2.8	28	6.5	4.85	80	.321	.363	-4	-4	99	115	1.4	-1	0	-0.4
	Cal-A	0	3	.000	5	5	0	0	0	18	31	15.5	5	2	1.0	4	2.0	9.00	43	.365	.371	-10	-10	95	85	-1.4	0	-0	-0.9
Total	10	110	70	.611	250	247	45	14	0	1675	1505	8.1	146	413	2.2	1039	5.6	3.08	117	.239	.283	88	95	101	95	9.2	1	-11	9.8
■ DICK NOLD	Nold, Richard Louis b: 5/4/43, San Francisco, Cal. BR/TR, 6'2", 190 lbs. Deb: 8/19/67																												
1967	Was-A	0	2	.000	7	3	0	0	0	20	19	8.5	1	13	5.8	10	4.5	4.95	68	.241	.348	-4	-4	104	77	-0.9	-0	-0	-0.3
■ DICKIE NOLES	Noles, Dickie Ray b: 11/19/56, Charlotte, N.C. BR/TR, 6'2", 160 lbs. Deb: 7/05/79																												
1979	Phi-N	3	4	.429	14	14	0	0	0	90	80	8.0	6	38	3.8	42	4.2	3.80	96	.246	.318	-1	-2	97	92	-0.5	-1	1	-0.1
1980	Phi-N	1	4	.200	48	3	0	0	6	81	80	8.9	5	42	4.7	57	6.3	3.89	99	.254	.335	-3	-0	106	98	-1.5	1	-0	0.0
1981	Phi-N	2	2	.500	13	8	0	0	0	58	57	8.8	2	23	3.6	34	5.3	4.19	93	.260	.333	-4	-2	112	87	-0.1	-1	-1	-0.3

YEAR	TM/L	W	L	PCT	G	GS	CG	SHO	SV	IP	H	H/G	HR	BB	BB/G	SO	SO/G	ERA	/A	OAVG	OOBP	PR	/A	PF	CPI	WAT	PB	PD	TPI
1982	Chi-N	10	13	.435	31	30	2	2	0	171	180	9.5	11	61	3.2	85	4.5	4.42	85	.274	.331	-15	-13	104	91	-0.4	-2	0	-1.4
1983	Chi-N	5	10	.333	24	18	1	1	0	116	133	10.3	9	37	2.9	59	4.6	4.73	78	.287	.338	-14	-14	101	90	-1.8	2	-0	-1.2
1984	Chi-N	2	2	.500	21	1	0	0	0	51	60	10.6	4	16	2.8	14	2.5	5.12	76	.305	.356	-9	-7	109	95	-0.2	-1	-1	-0.8
	Tex-A	2	3	.400	18	6	0	0	0	58	60	9.3	6	30	4.7	39	6.1	5.12	79	.262	.360	-7	-7	101	89	-0.1	0	-1	-0.7
1985	Tex-A	4	8	.333	28	13	0	0	1	110	129	10.6	11	33	2.7	59	4.8	5.07	90	.289	.344	-11	-6	110	92	-0.8	0	1	-0.5
1986	Cle-A	3	2	.600	32	0	0	0	0	55	56	9.2	9	30	4.9	32	5.2	5.07	81	.269	.363	-5	-6	98	107	0.4	0	0	-0.5
1987	Chi-N	4	2	.667	41	1	0	0	2	64	59	8.3	1	27	3.8	33	4.6	3.52	118	.239	.319	4	5	102	86	1.1	-1	1	0.4
	Det-A	0	0	—	4	0	0	0	2	2	2	9.0	0	1	4.5	0	0.0	4.50	95	.250	.333	-0	-0	96	71	0.0	0	0	0.0
1988	Bal-A	0	2	.000	2	2	0	0	0	3	11	33.0	2	0	0.0	1	3.0	27.00	14	.500	.522	-8	-8	97	72	-0.9	0	0	-0.6
Total	10	36	52	.409	276	96	3	3	11	859	907	9.5	66	338	3.5	455	4.8	4.56	86	.272	.339	-73	-60	104	92	-4.8	-3	-2	-5.7
■ ERIC NOLTE	Nolte, Eric Carl b: 4/28/64, Canoga Park, Cal. BL/TL, 6'3", 205 lbs. Deb: 8/01/87																												
1987	SD-N	2	6	.250	12	12	1	0	0	67	57	7.7	6	36	4.8	44	5.9	3.22	124	.226	.324	6	6	98	109	-1.5	-1	-0	0.4
1988	SD-N	0	0	—	2	0	0	0	0	3	3	9.0	1	2	6.0	1	3.0	6.00	56	.273	.357	-1	-1	97	117	0.0	0	0	0.0
Total	2	2	6	.250	14	12	1	0	0	70	60	7.7	7	38	4.9	45	5.8	3.34	119	.228	.326	6	5	98	109	-1.5	-1	-0	0.4
■ JERRY NOPS	Nops, Jeremiah H. b: 6/23/1875, Toledo, Ohio d: 3/26/37, Camden, N.J. TL , Deb: 9/07/1896																												
1896	Phi-N	1	0	1.000	1	1	1	0	0	7	11	14.1	0	1	1.3	1	1.3	5.14	87	.381	.402	-1	-1	102	105	0.5	-1	0	0.0
	Bal-N	2	1	.667	3	3	3	0	0	22	29	11.9	0	2	0.8	8	3.3	6.14	70	.341	.356	-4	-4	99	65	0.0	-1	0	-0.3
	Yr	3	1	.750	4	4	4	0	0	29	40	12.4	0	3	0.9	9	2.8	5.90	74	.351	.368	-5	-5	99	65	0.5	-1	0	-0.3
1897	Bal-N	20	6	.769	30	25	23	1	0	221	235	9.6	5	52	2.1	69	2.8	2.81	141	.294	.337	37	29	92	117	3.8	-2	0	2.3
1898	Bal-N	16	9	.640	33	29	23	2	0	235	241	9.2	5	78	3.0	91	3.5	3.56	101	.287	.347	1	1	100	94	0.0	2	0	0.2
1899	Bal-N	17	11	.607	33	33	26	2	0	259	296	10.3	1	71	2.5	60	2.1	4.03	102	.311	.359	-5	2	106	89	1.1	1	-2	0.2
1900	Bro-N	4	4	.500	9	8	6	1	0	68	79	10.5	1	18	2.4	22	2.9	3.84	102	.314	.360	-1	1	106	99	-0.6	-1	0	0.0
1901	Bal-A	12	10	.545	27	23	17	1	1	177	192	9.8	5	59	3.0	43	2.2	4.07	96	.297	.355	-8	-3	107	91	0.9	-0	-5	-0.6
Total	6	72	41	.637	136	122	99	7	1	989	1083	9.9	17	281	2.6	294	2.7	3.69	106	.301	.351	19	25	101	97	5.7	-2	-7	1.8
■ WAYNE NORDHAGEN	Nordhagen, Wayne Oren b: 7/4/48, Thief River Falls, Minn. BR/TR, 6'2", 205 lbs. Deb: 7/16/76																												
1979	Chi-A	0	0	—	2	0	0	0	0	2	2	9.0	0	1	4.5	2	9.0	9.00	48	.286	.375	-1	-1	103	48	0.0	2	0	0.0
■ JOHN NORIEGA	Noriega, John Alan b: 12/20/43, Ogden, Utah BR/TR, 6'4", 185 lbs. Deb: 5/01/69																												
1969	Cin-N	0	0	—	5	0	0	0	0	8	12	13.5	1	3	3.4	4	4.5	5.63	63	.400	.417	-2	-2	99	140	0.0	0	-0	-0.1
1970	Cin-N	0	0	—	8	0	0	0	0	18	25	12.5	0	10	5.0	6	3.0	8.00	52	.333	.411	-8	-8	103	76	0.0	0	1	-0.5
Total	2	0	0	—	13	0	0	0	0	26	37	12.8	1	13	4.5	10	3.5	7.27	55	.352	.413	-10	-10	102	96	0.0	0	1	-0.6
■ FRED NORMAN	Norman, Fredie Hubert b: 8/20/42, San Antonio, Tex. BB/TL, 5'8", 155 lbs. Deb: 9/21/62																												
1962	KC-A	0	0	—	2	0	0	0	0	4	4	9.0	0	1	2.3	2	4.5	2.25	179	.250	.294	1	1	101	109	0.0	0	-0	0.1
1963	KC-A	0	1	.000	2	2	0	0	0	6	9	13.5	1	7	10.5	6	9.0	12.00	33	.346	.457	-6	-5	109	76	-0.4	-0	0	-0.4
1964	Chi-N	0	4	.000	8	5	0	0	0	32	34	9.6	9	21	5.9	20	5.6	6.47	58	.279	.389	-10	-10	106	104	-1.9	-1	-0	-0.9
1966	Chi-N	0	0	—	2	0	0	0	0	4	5	11.3	0	2	4.5	6	13.5	4.50	82	.313	.389	-0	-0	103	108	0.0	0	0	0.0
1967	Chi-N	0	0	—	1	0	0	0	0	1	0	0.0	0	0	0.0	3	27.0	0.00	—	.000	.000	0	0	100	0	0.0	0	0	0.0
1970	LA-N	2	0	1.000	30	0	0	0	1	62	65	9.4	8	33	4.8	47	6.8	5.23	69	.273	.355	-8	-11	89	98	1.0	1	-1	-1.0
	StL-N	0	0	—	1	0	0	0	0	1	1	9.0	0	0	0.0	0	0.0	0.00	—	.333	.250	0	0	106	0	0.0	0	0	0.1
	Yr	2	0	1.000	31	0	0	0	1	63	66	9.4	8	33	4.7	47	6.7	5.14	70	.269	.346	-8	-11	89	0	1.0	1	-1	-0.9
1971	StL-N	0	0	—	4	0	0	0	0	4	7	15.8	1	7	15.8	4	9.0	11.25	31	.438	.583	-3	-3	100	123	0.0	0	0	-0.3
	SD-N	3	12	.200	20	18	5	0	0	127	114	8.1	7	56	4.0	77	5.5	3.33	102	.240	.317	2	1	98	97	-3.6	2	-1	0.2
	Yr	3	12	.200	24	18	5	0	0	131	121	8.3	8	63	4.3	81	5.6	3.57	95	.246	.328	-1	-3	98	97	-3.6	0	-1	-0.1
1972	SD-N	9	11	.450	42	28	10	6	2	212	195	8.3	18	88	3.7	167	7.1	3.44	91	.244	.315	0	-7	91	102	1.3	1	-1	-0.7
1973	SD-N	1	7	.125	12	11	1	0	0	74	72	8.8	9	29	3.5	49	6.0	4.26	83	.262	.326	-5	-6	97	98	-2.6	-0	1	-0.5
	Cin-N	12	6	.667	24	24	7	3	0	166	136	7.4	18	72	3.9	112	6.1	3.31	102	.224	.301	7	1	92	97	1.4	-3	-1	-0.3
	Yr	13	13	.500	36	35	8	3	0	240	208	7.8	27	101	3.8	161	6.0	3.60	95	.235	.308	2	-5	93	97	-1.2	-0	-0	-0.8
1974	Cin-N	13	12	.520	35	26	8	2	0	186	170	8.2	15	68	3.3	141	6.8	3.15	111	.241	.303	10	7	96	101	-1.9	-2	-3	0.2
1975	Cin-N	12	4	.750	34	26	2	0	0	188	163	7.8	23	84	4.0	119	5.7	3.73	99	.235	.311	-2	-1	101	96	2.2	-2	-2	-0.4
1976	Cin-N	12	7	.632	33	24	8	3	0	180	153	7.7	10	70	3.5	126	6.3	3.10	113	.231	.303	8	8	100	95	0.1	-1	-3	0.4
1977	Cin-N	14	13	.519	35	34	8	1	0	221	200	8.1	28	98	4.0	160	6.5	3.38	115	.241	.319	13	12	99	113	-0.6	-2	-1	0.9
1978	Cin-N	11	9	.550	36	31	0	0	1	177	173	8.8	19	82	4.2	111	5.6	3.71	99	.255	.332	-3	-1	102	110	-0.3	-1	-1	-0.2
1979	Cin-N	11	13	.458	34	31	5	0	0	195	193	8.9	14	57	2.6	95	4.4	3.65	99	.258	.306	2	-1	96	91	-2.4	1	-1	-0.1
1980	Mon-N	4	4	.500	48	8	2	0	4	98	96	8.8	8	40	3.7	58	5.3	4.13	86	.259	.326	-6	-6	98	95	-0.3	-2	-1	-0.9
Total	16	104	103	.502	403	268	56	15	8	1938	1790	8.3	188	815	3.8	1303	6.1	3.64	97	.246	.317	1	-21	97	100	-8.0	-10	-13	-3.8
■ MIKE NORRIS	Norris, Michael Kelvin b: 3/19/55, San Francisco, Cal. BR/TR, 6'2", 175 lbs. Deb: 4/10/75																												
1975	Oak-A	1	0	1.000	4	3	1	1	0	17	6	3.2	0	8	4.2	5	2.6	0.00	—	.107	.215	7	7	91	0	0.5	0	0	0.8
1976	Oak-A	4	5	.444	24	19	1	1	0	96	91	8.5	10	56	5.3	44	4.1	4.78	73	.250	.347	-13	-14	98	90	-0.7	0	3	-1.0
1977	Oak-A	2	7	.222	16	12	1	1	0	77	77	9.0	14	31	3.6	35	4.1	4.79	82	.260	.334	-6	-7	97	98	-1.9	0	1	-0.5
1978	Oak-A	0	5	.000	14	5	1	0	0	49	46	8.4	2	35	6.4	36	6.6	5.51	70	.249	.367	-9	-9	103	76	-2.4	0	-0	-0.8
1979	Oak-A	5	8	.385	29	18	3	0	0	146	146	9.0	11	94	5.8	96	5.9	4.81	80	.265	.372	-9	-15	91	100	0.5	0	-1	-1.5
1980	Oak-A	22	9	.710	33	33	24	1	0	284	215	**6.8**	18	83	2.6	180	5.7	2.54	150	**.209**	.268	**48**	**40**	94	85	7.1	0	3	**4.6**
1981	Oak-A	12	9	.571	23	23	12	2	0	173	145	7.5	17	63	3.3	78	4.1	3.75	93	.228	.302	-2	-5	95	87	-0.2	0	-0	-0.5
1982	Oak-A	7	11	.389	28	28	7	1	0	166	154	8.3	25	84	4.6	83	4.5	4.77	82	.242	.332	-13	-15	96	90	-0.6	0	1	-1.4
1983	Oak-A	4	5	.444	16	16	2	0	0	89	68	6.9	11	36	3.6	63	6.4	3.74	105	.213	.293	3	2	96	86	0.0	0	-2	0.0
Total	9	57	59	.491	187	157	52	7	0	1097	948	7.8	108	490	4.0	620	5.1	3.91	96	.233	.316	5	-18	95	88	2.3	0	5	-0.3
■ LOU NORTH	North, Louis Alexander b: 6/15/1891, Elgin, Ill. d: 5/16/74, Shelton, Conn. BR/TR, 5'11", 175 lbs. Deb: 8/22/13																												
1913	Det-A	0	1	.000	1	1	0	0	0	6	10	15.0	1	9	13.5	3	4.5	15.00	20	.357	.514	-8	-8	101	68	-0.4	-0	-0	-0.5
1917	StL-N	0	0	—	5	0	0	0	0	11	14	11.5	1	4	3.3	4	3.3	4.09	68	.350	.391	-2	-2	102	147	0.0	-0	0	-0.1
1920	StL-N	3	2	.600	24	6	3	0	1	88	90	9.2	3	32	3.3	37	3.8	3.27	94	.278	.336	-1	-2	98	109	0.6	0	-1	-0.2
1921	StL-N	4	4	.500	40	0	0	0	**7**	86	81	8.5	5	32	3.3	28	2.9	3.56	98	.256	.318	**2**	-1	93	93	-0.4	-1	-2	-0.3
1922	StL-N	10	3	.769	**53**	11	4	0	4	150	164	9.8	4	64	3.8	84	5.0	4.44	93	.283	.353	-6	-5	100	91	3.3	1	4	0.0
1923	StL-N	3	4	.429	34	3	0	0	1	72	90	11.3	8	31	3.9	24	3.0	5.13	70	.308	.375	-9	-12	90	107	-0.5	-0	1	-1.1
1924	StL-N	0	0	—	6	0	0	0	0	15	15	9.0	1	9	5.4	8	4.8	6.60	60	.273	.375	-5	-4	103	70	0.0	-0	-0	-0.4
	Bos-N	1	2	.333	9	4	1	0	0	35	45	11.6	1	19	4.9	11	2.8	5.40	71	.321	.393	-6	-6	99	101	0.0	-1	-0	-0.6
	Yr	1	2	.333	15	4	1	0	0	50	60	10.8	2	28	5.0	19	3.4	5.76	67	.308	.388	-11	-11	100	101	0.0	-0	-1	-1.0
Total	7	21	16	.568	172	25	8	0	13	463	509	9.9	24	200	3.9	199	3.9	4.43	82	.287	.355	-34	-40	97	99	2.6	-1	1	-3.2
■ JAKE NORTHROP	Northrop, George Howard "Jerky" b: 3/5/1888, Monroeton, Pa. d: 11/16/45, Monroeton, Pa. BL/TR, 5'11", 170 lbs. Deb: 7/29/18																												
1918	Bos-N	5	1	.833	7	4	4	1	0	40	26	5.8	0	3	0.7	4	0.9	1.35	195	.183	.193	6	6	95	22	2.2	-1	0	0.6
1919	Bos-N	1	5	.167	11	3	2	0	0	37	43	10.5	2	10	2.4	9	2.2	4.62	63	.301	.338	-7	-7	100	94	-1.7	3	1	-0.2
Total	2	6	6	.500	18	7	6	1	0	77	69	8.1	2	13	1.5	13	1.5	2.92	95	.242	.268	-1	-1	97	56	0.5	2	1	0.4
■ EFFIE NORTON	Norton, Elisha Strong "Leiter" b: 8/17/1873, Conneaut, Ohio d: 3/5/50, Aspinwall, Pa. BR/TR, Deb: 8/08/1896																												
1896	Was-N	3	1	.750	8	5	2	0	0	44	49	10.0	2	14	2.9	13	2.7	3.07	137	.304	.360	6	6	96	129	1.1	-0	0	0.4
1897	Was-N	2	1	.667	4	2	1	0	0	17	31	16.4	0	11	5.8	3	1.6	6.88	64	.417	.492	-5	-5	102	117	0.6	1	0	-0.2
Total	2	5	2	.714	12	7	3	0	0	61	80	11.8	2	25	3.7	16	2.4	4.13	103	.340	.403	2	1	98	126	1.7	0	0	0.2
■ TOM NORTON	Norton, Thomas John b: 4/26/50, Elyria, Ohio BR/TR, 6'1", 200 lbs. Deb: 4/18/72																												
1972	Min-A	0	1	.000	21	0	0	0	0	32	31	8.7	1	14	3.9	22	6.2	2.81	117	.252	.331	1	2	107	118	-0.4	0	1	0.3
■ DON NOTTEBART	Nottebart, Donald Edward b: 1/23/36, West Newton, Mass. BR/TR, 6'1", 190 lbs. Deb: 7/01/60																												
1960	Mil-N	1	0	1.000	5	1	0	0	1	15	14	8.4	0	15	9.0	8	4.8	4.20	80	.233	.377	-1	-1	89	97	0.5	-1	1	0.0
1961	Mil-N	6	7	.462	38	11	2	0	3	126	117	8.4	11	48	3.4	66	4.7	4.07	90	.251	.314	-1	-6	91	90	-0.9	1	2	-0.3

YEAR	TM/L	W	L	PCT	G	GS	CG	SHO	SV	IP	H	H/G	HR	BB	BB/G	SO	SO/G	ERA	/A	OAVG	OOBP	PR	/A	PF	CPI	WAT	PB	PD	TPI
1962	Mil-N	2	2	.500	39	0	0	0	2	64	64	9.0	4	20	2.8	36	5.1	3.23	120	.258	.317	5	4	98	109	0.0	1	2	0.7
1963	Hou-N	11	8	.579	31	27	9	2	0	193	170	7.9	10	39	1.8	118	5.5	3.17	98	.234	.268	3	-1	95	76	3.0	0	-0	-0.1
1964	Hou-N	6	11	.353	28	24	2	0	0	157	165	9.5	12	37	2.1	90	5.2	3.90	89	.275	.309	-6	-7	98	98	-1.2	-2	4	-0.6
1965	Hou-N	4	15	.211	29	25	3	0	0	158	166	9.5	14	55	3.1	77	4.4	4.67	69	.273	.330	-20	-25	91	90	-4.7	-1	2	-2.4
1966	Cin-N	5	4	.556	59	1	0	0	11	111	97	7.9	11	43	3.5	69	5.6	3.08	134	.235	.304	6	13	114	108	0.7	-1	1	1.4
1967	Cin-N	0	3	.000	47	0	0	0	4	79	75	8.5	4	19	2.2	48	5.5	1.94	189	.253	.297	13	15	109	160	-1.4	-0	1	1.7
1969	NY-A	0	0	—	4	0	0	0	0	6	6	9.0	1	0	0.0	5	7.5	4.50	77	.261	.292	-1	-1	96	85	0.0	0	0	0.0
	Chi-N	1	1	.500	16	0	0	0	0	18	28	14.0	2	7	3.5	8	4.0	7.00	54	.350	.393	-7	-6	105	95	0.0	0	0	-0.5
Total	9	36	51	.414	296	89	16	2	21	927	902	8.8	69	283	2.7	525	5.1	3.66	96	.256	.307	-8	-15	98	98	-4.0	-2	11	-0.1
■ **CHET NOURSE** Nourse, Chester Linwood b: 8/7/1887, Ipswich, Mass. d: 4/20/58, Clearwater, Fla. 6'3", 185 lbs. Deb: 7/27/09																													
1909	Bos-A	0	0	—	3	0	0	0	0	5	5	9.0	0	5	9.0	3	5.4	7.20	37	.263	.417	-3	-3	108	64	0.0	-0	0	-0.2
■ **WIN NOYES** Noyes, Winfield Charles b: 6/16/1889, Pleasanton, Neb. d: 4/8/69, Cashmere, Wash. BR/TR, 6', 180 lbs. Deb: 5/19/13																													
1913	Bos-N	0	0	—	11	0	0	0	0	21	22	9.4	1	6	2.6	5	2.1	4.71	65	.289	.368	-4	-4	96	95	0.0	0	0	-0.3
1917	Phi-A	10	10	.500	27	22	11	1	1	171	156	8.2	5	77	4.1	64	3.4	2.95	88	.258	.345	-5	-7	97	114	2.4	-2	-1	-1.0
1919	Phi-A	1	5	.167	10	6	3	0	0	49	66	12.1	1	15	2.8	20	3.7	5.69	63	.332	.381	-13	-11	112	85	-1.0	-1	0	-1.1
	Chi-A	0	0	—	1	1	0	0	0	6	10	15.0	0	0	0.0	4	6.0	7.50	44	.385	.385	-3	-3	102	73	0.0	0	0	-0.1
	Yr	1	5	.167	11	7	3	0	0	55	76	12.4	1	15	2.5	24	3.9	5.89	61	.336	.378	-16	-14	111	73	-1.0	-1	0	-1.2
Total	3	11	15	.423	49	29	14	1	1	247	254	9.3	7	98	3.6	93	3.4	3.75	76	.280	.356	-25	-25	100	106	1.4	-3	-1	-2.5
■ **ED NUNEZ** Nunez, Edwin (Martinez) b: 5/27/63, Humacao, P.R. BR/TR, 6'5", 235 lbs. Deb: 4/07/82																													
1982	Sea-A	1	2	.333	8	5	0	0	0	35	36	9.3	7	16	4.1	27	6.9	4.63	97	.269	.340	-2	-1	110	112	-0.3	0	0	0.0
1983	Sea-A	0	4	.000	14	5	0	0	0	37	40	9.7	3	22	5.4	35	8.5	4.38	94	.278	.382	-1	-1	101	117	-1.9	0	0	0.0
1984	Sea-A	2	2	.500	37	0	0	0	7	68	55	7.3	8	21	2.8	57	7.5	3.18	130	.218	.282	6	7	103	92	0.2	0	-0	0.7
1985	Sea-A	7	3	.700	70	0	0	0	16	90	79	7.9	13	34	3.4	58	5.8	3.10	128	.234	.299	10	9	95	119	2.3	0	0	0.9
1986	Sea-A	1	2	.333	14	1	0	0	0	22	25	10.2	5	5	2.0	17	7.0	5.73	78	.284	.323	-4	-3	106	90	-0.2	0	-0	-0.2
1987	Sea-A	3	4	.429	48	0	0	0	12	47	45	8.6	7	18	3.4	34	6.5	3.83	120	.262	.323	3	4	103	120	-0.3	0	-0	0.3
1988	Sea-A	1	4	.200	14	3	0	0	0	29	45	14.0	4	14	4.3	19	5.9	8.07	53	.366	.421	-13	-12	108	97	-1.2	0	1	-1.0
	NY-N	1	0	1.000	10	0	0	0	0	14	21	13.5	1	3	1.9	8	5.1	4.50	67	.339	.369	-2	-2	88	124	0.5	0	0	-0.2
Total	7	16	21	.432	215	14	0	0	35	342	346	9.1	48	133	3.5	255	6.7	4.16	100	.264	.329	-2	1	102	109	-0.9	0	0	0.5
■ **JOSE NUNEZ** Nunez, Jose (Jimenez) b: 1/13/64, Jarabacoa, D.R. BR/TR, 6'3", 175 lbs. Deb: 4/09/87																													
1987	Tor-A	5	2	.714	37	9	0	0	0	97	91	8.4	12	58	5.4	99	9.2	5.01	89	.256	.349	-6	-6	99	95	1.1	0	-1	-0.6
1988	Tor-A	0	1	.000	13	2	0	0	0	29	28	8.7	3	17	5.3	18	5.6	3.10	127	.259	.362	3	3	99	153	-0.4	0	0	0.3
Total	2	5	3	.625	50	11	0	0	0	126	119	8.5	15	75	5.4	117	8.4	4.57	95	.256	.352	-3	-3	99	108	0.7	0	-1	-0.3
■ **HOWIE NUNN** Nunn, Howard Ralph b: 10/18/35, Westfield, N.C. BR/TR, 6', 173 lbs. Deb: 4/11/59																													
1959	StL-N	2	2	.500	16	0	0	0	0	21	23	9.9	3	15	6.4	20	8.6	7.71	54	.291	.392	-9	-8	106	78	0.1	-0	1	-0.7
1961	Cin-N	2	1	.667	24	0	0	0	0	38	35	8.3	0	24	5.7	26	6.2	3.55	117	.252	.353	2	2	103	106	0.2	0	0	0.2
1962	Cin-N	0	0	—	6	0	0	0	0	10	15	13.5	0	3	2.7	4	3.6	5.40	73	.375	.400	-2	-2	100	114	0.0	-0	0	-0.1
Total	3	4	3	.571	46	0	0	0	0	69	73	9.5	3	42	5.5	50	6.5	5.09	81	.283	.372	-8	-7	104	99	0.3	-0	1	-0.6
■ **JOE NUXHALL** Nuxhall, Joseph Henry b: 7/30/28, Hamilton, Ohio BL/TL, 6'3", 195 lbs. Deb: 6/10/44																													
1944	Cin-N	0	0	—	1	0	0	0	0	1	2	18.0	0	5	45.0	0	0.0	45.00	8	.500	.778	-5	-5	95	51	0.0	0	0	-0.3
1952	Cin-N	1	4	.200	37	5	2	0	1	92	83	8.1	4	42	4.1	52	5.1	3.23	116	.246	.330	5	5	100	110	-1.3	-1	2	0.6
1953	Cin-N	9	11	.450	30	17	5	1	2	142	136	8.6	13	69	4.4	52	3.3	4.31	100	.252	.339	-0	-0	100	97	0.2	8	-2	0.5
1954	Cin-N	12	5	.706	35	14	5	1	0	167	188	10.1	11	59	3.2	85	4.6	3.88	109	.292	.348	4	7	104	115	3.9	4	0	1.1
1955	Cin-N	17	12	.586	50	33	14	**5**	3	257	240	8.4	25	78	2.7	98	3.4	3.47	121	.249	.304	16	21	104	99	3.3	4	-2	2.4
1956	Cin-N	13	11	.542	44	32	10	2	3	201	196	8.8	18	87	3.9	120	5.4	3.72	108	.257	.334	1	6	106	104	-1.1	3	-1	0.9
1957	Cin-N	10	10	.500	39	28	6	2	1	174	192	9.9	24	53	2.7	99	5.1	4.76	86	.275	.328	-17	-12	106	93	-0.3	3	-2	-1.0
1958	Cin-N	12	11	.522	36	26	5	0	0	176	169	8.6	15	63	3.2	111	5.7	3.78	111	.257	.317	3	8	106	96	0.7	-0	0	0.7
1959	Cin-N	9	9	.500	28	21	6	1	1	132	155	10.6	10	35	2.4	75	5.1	4.23	96	.292	.333	-4	-2	103	101	0.4	3	-1	0.0
1960	Cin-N	1	8	.111	38	6	0	0	0	112	130	10.4	8	27	2.2	72	5.8	4.42	84	.297	.334	-8	-9	99	101	-3.3	-1	2	-0.7
1961	KC-A	5	8	.385	37	13	1	0	1	128	135	9.5	12	65	4.6	81	5.7	5.34	79	.268	.350	-19	-16	104	84	0.1	8	-1	-0.8
1962	LA-A	0	0	—	5	0	0	0	0	5	7	12.6	0	5	9.0	2	3.6	10.80	37	.304	.448	-4	-4	102	61	0.0	0	0	-0.2
	Cin-N	5	0	1.000	12	9	1	0	1	66	59	8.0	4	25	3.4	57	7.8	2.45	161	.240	.308	11	11	100	128	2.5	3	-0	1.4
1963	Cin-N	15	8	.652	35	29	14	2	2	217	194	8.0	14	39	1.6	169	7.0	2.61	130	.237	.272	16	19	103	98	3.3	-0	-1	2.0
1964	Cin-N	9	8	.529	32	22	7	4	2	155	146	8.5	19	51	3.0	111	6.4	4.06	88	.250	.313	-9	-8	102	96	-0.5	-1	-2	-0.9
1965	Cin-N	11	4	.733	32	16	5	1	2	149	142	8.6	18	31	1.9	117	7.1	3.44	105	.252	.293	2	3	102	102	3.2	1	-2	0.1
1966	Cin-N	6	8	.429	35	16	2	1	0	130	136	9.4	14	42	2.9	71	4.9	4.50	91	.270	.332	-13	-6	114	94	-0.6	-3	-1	-0.8
Total	16	135	117	.536	526	287	83	20	19	2304	2310	9.0	209	776	3.0	1372	5.4	3.90	102	.262	.322	-21	18	104	100	10.5	29	-11	5.0
■ **RICH NYE** Nye, Richard Raymond b: 8/4/44, Oakland, Cal. BL/TL, 6'4", 185 lbs. Deb: 9/16/66																													
1966	Chi-N	0	2	.000	3	2	0	0	0	17	16	8.5	1	7	3.7	9	4.8	2.12	175	.254	.324	3	3	103	167	-0.9	0	-0	0.3
1967	Chi-N	13	10	.565	35	30	7	0	0	205	179	7.9	15	52	2.3	119	5.2	3.20	106	.234	.279	4	4	100	86	0.7	3	0	0.8
1968	Chi-N	7	12	.368	27	20	6	1	1	133	145	9.8	16	34	2.3	74	5.0	3.79	88	.276	.316	-12	-6	112	109	-2.9	-0	-0	-0.6
1969	Chi-N	3	5	.375	34	5	1	0	3	69	72	9.4	13	21	2.7	39	5.1	5.09	74	.271	.320	-11	-10	105	93	-1.3	-1	-1	-1.1
1970	StL-N	0	0	—	6	0	0	0	0	8	13	14.6	2	6	6.8	5	5.6	4.50	96	.371	.442	-0	-0	106	211	0.0	1	0	0.0
	Mon-N	3	2	.600	8	6	2	0	0	46	47	9.2	3	20	3.9	21	4.1	4.11	100	.260	.330	-0	0	102	93	0.7	0	0	0.0
	Yr	3	2	.600	14	6	2	0	0	54	60	10.0	5	26	4.3	26	4.3	4.17	99	.276	.350	-1	-0	102	93	0.7	1	0	0.0
Total	5	26	31	.456	113	63	16	1	4	478	472	8.9	50	140	2.6	267	5.0	3.71	95	.257	.306	-17	-9	105	99	-3.7	2	-1	-0.6
■ **JERRY NYMAN** Nyman, Gerald Smith b: 11/23/42, Logan, Utah BL/TL, 5'10", 165 lbs. Deb: 8/24/68																													
1968	Chi-A	2	1	.667	8	7	1	1	0	40	38	8.5	1	16	3.6	27	6.1	2.02	150	.247	.309	4	5	102	151	0.7	-0	0	0.5
1969	Chi-A	4	4	.500	20	10	2	1	0	65	58	8.0	7	39	5.4	40	5.5	5.26	76	.244	.344	-12	-9	110	80	0.6	-1	-0	-1.0
1970	SD-N	0	2	.000	2	2	0	0	0	5	8	14.4	1	2	3.6	2	3.6	16.20	24	.364	.385	-7	-7	97	49	-0.9	0	-0	-0.5
Total	3	6	7	.462	30	19	3	2	0	110	104	8.5	9	57	4.7	69	5.6	4.58	79	.251	.333	-14	-12	106	104	0.4	-1	-1	-1.0
■ **PRINCE OANA** Oana, Henry Kauhane b: 1/22/08, Waipahu, Hawaii d: 6/19/76, Austin, Tex. BR/TR, 6'2", 193 lbs. Deb: 4/22/34																													
1943	Det-A	3	2	.600	10	0	0	0	0	34	34	9.0	4	19	5.0	15	4.0	4.50	76	.262	.355	-5	-4	104	106	0.5	5	-0	-0.3
1945	Det-A	0	0	—	3	1	0	0	1	11	3	2.5	0	7	5.7	3	2.5	1.64	215	.086	.238	2	2	105	9	0.0	-0	-0	0.2
Total	2	3	2	.600	13	1	0	0	1	45	37	7.4	4	26	5.2	18	3.6	3.80	91	.224	.330	-2	-2	104	82	0.5	5	-0	-0.1
■ **HENRY OBERBECK** Oberbeck, Henry A. b: 5/17/1858, Missouri d: 8/26/21, St.Louis, Mo. Deb: 5/07/1883																													
1884	Bal-U	0	0	—	2	1	0	0	0	6	9	13.5	0	2	3.0	1	1.5	3.00	110	.352	.399	0	0	110	193	0.0	-0	0	0.0
	KC-U	0	5	.000	6	4	3	0	0	30	47	14.1	0	3	0.9	6	1.8	6.00	46	.362	.376	-10	-11	92	91	-2.4	-0	0	-0.8
	Yr	0	5	.000	8	5	3	0	0	36	56	14.0	0	5	1.3	7	1.8	5.50	52	.360	.380	-10	-11	95	91	-2.4	-0	0	-0.8
■ **DOC OBERLANDER** Oberlander, Hartman Louis b: 5/12/1864, Waukegan, Ill. d: 11/14/22, Pryor, Montana Deb: 1888																													
1888	Cle-a	1	2	.333	3	3	3	0	0	26	27	9.3	2	18	6.2	23	8.0	5.54	55	.281	.394	-7	-7	100	91	-0.1	0	0	-0.5
■ **FRANK OBERLIN** Oberlin, Frank Rufus "Flossie" b: 3/29/1876, Elsie, Mich. d: 1/6/52, Ashley, Ind. BR/TR, 6'1", 165 lbs. Deb: 9/20/06																													
1906	Bos-A	1	3	.250	4	4	4	0	0	34	38	10.1	0	13	3.4	13	3.4	3.18	88	.309	.375	-2	-1	104	122	-0.3	-0	1	0.0
1907	Bos-A	1	5	.167	12	4	2	0	0	46	48	9.4	2	24	4.7	18	3.5	4.30	61	.293	.384	-9	-9	103	96	-1.7	-0	-1	-0.9
	Was-A	2	6	.250	11	8	3	0	0	49	57	10.5	0	12	2.2	18	3.3	4.59	52	.316	.359	-11	-12	94	79	-0.9	-2	-1	-1.2
	Yr	3	11	.214	23	12	5	0	0	95	105	9.9	2	36	3.4	36	3.4	4.45	56	.305	.371	-20	-21	98	79	-2.6	-0	-2	-2.1
1909	Was-A	1	4	.200	9	4	1	0	0	41	41	9.0	1	16	3.5	13	2.9	3.73	64	.266	.358	-6	-6	96	96	-0.6	-1	-1	-0.7
1910	Was-A	0	6	.000	8	6	6	0	0	57	52	8.2	0	23	3.6	18	2.8	3.00	85	.259	.341	-3	-3	102	103	-2.9	-2	-1	-0.3
Total	4	5	24	.172	44	26	16	0	0	227	236	9.4	3	88	3.5	80	3.2	3.77	67	.287	.362	-31	-31	100	98	-6.4	-4	-2	-3.1

YEAR	TM/L	W	L	PCT	G	GS	CG	SHO	SV	IP	H	H/G	HR	BB	BB/G	SO	SO/G	ERA	/A	OAVG	OOBP	PR	/A	PF	CPI	WAT	PB	PD	TPI
■ DAN O'BRIEN	O'Brien, Daniel Jogues b: 4/22/54, St.Petersburg, Fla. BR/TR, 6'4", 215 lbs. Deb: 9/04/78																												
1978	StL-N	0	2	.000	7	2	0	0	0	18	22	11.0	1	8	4.0	12	6.0	4.50	76	.301	.372	-2	-2	96	115	-0.9	-0	-0	-0.2
1979	StL-N	1	1	.500	6	0	0	0	0	11	21	17.2	0	3	2.5	5	4.1	8.18	48	.420	.436	-5	-5	104	95	0.0	-0	-0	-0.5
Total	2	1	3	.250	13	2	0	0	0	29	43	13.3	1	11	3.4	17	5.3	5.90	61	.350	.397	-7	-7	99	107	-0.9	-1	-0	-0.7
■ EDDIE O'BRIEN	O'Brien, Edward Joseph b: 12/11/30, S.Amboy, N.J. BR/TR, 5'9", 165 lbs. Deb: 4/25/53 C																												
1956	Pit-N	0	0	—	1	0	0	0	0	2	1	4.5	0	0	0.0	0	0.0	0.00	—	.167	.286	1	1	103	0	0.0	0	0	0.1
1957	Pit-N	1	0	1.000	3	1	1	0	0	12	11	8.3	2	3	2.3	10	7.5	2.25	165	.229	.275	2	2	96	135	0.5	-0	0	0.2
1958	Pit-N	0	0	—	1	0	0	0	0	2	4	18.0	1	1	4.5	1	4.5	13.50	27	.444	.500	-2	-2	94	96	0.0	0	0	-0.1
Total	3	1	0	1.000	5	1	1	0	0	16	16	9.0	3	4	2.3	11	6.2	3.38	111	.254	.309	1	1	97	113	0.5	-0	0	0.2
■ DARBY O'BRIEN	O'Brien, John F. b: 4/15/1867, Troy, N.Y. d: 3/11/1892, W.Troy, N.Y. BR/TR, 5'10", 165 lbs. Deb: 1888																												
1888	Cle-a	11	19	.367	30	30	30	1	0	259	245	8.5	5	99	3.4	135	4.7	3.30	93	.262	.333	-7	-7	100	100	-0.5	-3	0	-0.8
1889	Cle-N	22	17	.564	41	41	39	1	0	347	345	8.9	9	167	4.3	122	3.2	4.15	101	.274	.360	-5	2	104	90	5.0	3	2	0.7
1890	Cle-P	8	16	.333	25	25	22	0	0	206	229	10.0	9	93	4.1	54	2.4	3.41	117	.293	.369	19	13	94	119	-2.9	-5	0	0.5
1891	Bos-a	18	13	.581	40	30	22	0	1	269	300	10.0	13	127	4.2	87	2.9	3.65	96	.297	.375	2	-5	94	117	-2.9	1	0	-0.3
Total	4	59	65	.476	136	126	113	2	1	1081	1119	9.3	36	486	4.0	398	3.3	3.68	101	.281	.359	9	4	99	105	-1.3	-5	2	0.1
■ JOHNNY O'BRIEN	O'Brien, John Thomas b: 12/11/30, S.Amboy, N.J. BR/TR, 5'9", 170 lbs. Deb: 4/19/53																												
1956	Pit-N	1	0	1.000	8	0	0	0	0	19	8	3.8	2	9	4.3	9	4.3	2.84	137	.133	.260	2	2	103	62	0.5	-0	-1	0.2
1957	Pit-N	0	3	.000	16	1	0	0	0	40	46	10.3	7	24	5.4	19	4.3	6.07	61	.293	.378	-10	-10	96	99	-1.4	2	-1	-0.9
1958	StL-N	0	0	—	1	0	0	0	0	2	7	31.5	0	2	9.0	2	9.0	22.50	19	.538	.600	-4	-4	108	74	0.0	0	0	-0.2
Total	3	1	3	.250	25	1	0	0	0	61	61	9.0	9	35	5.2	30	4.4	5.61	68	.265	.359	-12	-12	99	87	-0.9	2	-2	-0.9
■ BOB O'BRIEN	O'Brien, Robert Allen b: 4/23/49, Pittsburgh, Pa. BL/TL, 5'10", 170 lbs. Deb: 4/11/71																												
1971	LA-N	2	2	.500	14	4	1	1	0	42	42	9.0	4	13	2.8	15	3.2	3.00	113	.262	.316	2	2	98	125	-0.1	-0	-1	0.0
■ TOM O'BRIEN	O'Brien, Thomas H. b: 6/22/1860, Salem, Mass. d: 4/21/21, Worcester, Mass. Deb: 6/14/1882																												
1887	NY-a	0	0	—	1	0	0	0	0	4	4	9.0	0	5	11.3	0	0.0	9.00	44	.274	.459	-2	-2	92	66	0.0	-0	0	-0.1
■ BUCK O'BRIEN	O'Brien, Thomas Joseph b: 5/9/1882, Brockton, Mass. d: 7/25/59, Boston, Mass. BR/TR, 5'10", 188 lbs. Deb: 9/09/11																												
1911	Bos-A	5	1	.833	6	5	5	2	0	48	30	5.6	0	21	3.9	31	5.8	0.38	878	.180	.275	16	16	99	317	2.0	-1	1	1.9
1912	Bos-A	20	13	.606	37	34	25	2	0	276	237	7.7	3	90	2.9	115	3.8	2.58	133	.237	.306	24	26	102	100	-2.4	-5	0	2.7
1913	Bos-A	4	9	.308	15	12	6	0	0	90	103	10.3	0	35	3.5	54	5.4	3.70	81	.305	.370	-8	-7	103	112	-2.7	0	1	-0.5
	Chi-A	0	2	.000	6	3	0	0	0	18	21	10.5	0	13	6.5	4	2.0	4.00	70	.318	.430	-2	-2	95	135	-0.9	-0	-0	-0.2
	Yr	4	11	.267	21	15	6	0	0	108	124	10.3	0	48	4.0	58	4.8	3.75	79	.307	.381	-10	-9	101	135	-3.6	0	1	-0.7
Total	3	29	25	.537	64	54	36	4	0	432	391	8.1	3	159	3.3	204	4.3	2.63	125	.249	.322	30	32	102	128	-4.0	-6	1	3.9
■ DARBY O'BRIEN	O'Brien, William D. b: 9/1/1863, Peoria, Ill. d: 6/15/1893, Peoria, Ill. BR/TR, 6'1", 186 lbs. Deb: 4/16/1887																												
1887	NY-a	0	0	—	1	0	0	0	0	1	1	9.0	0	1	9.0	0	0.0	0.00	—	.274	.430	0	0	92	0	0.0	0	0	0.0
■ BILLY O'BRIEN	O'Brien, William Smith b: 3/14/1860, Albany, N.Y. d: 5/26/11, Kansas City, Mo. BR , 6', 185 lbs. Deb: 9/27/1884																												
1884	StP-U	1	0	1.000	2	0	0	0	0	10	8	7.2	0	3	2.7	7	6.3	1.80	167	.224	.284	1	1	100	126	0.5	0	0	-0.1
■ WALTER OCKEY	Ockey, Walter Andrew "Footie" (born Walter Andrew Okpych) b: 1/4/20, New York, N.Y. d: 12/4/71, Staten Island, N.Y. BR/TR, 6', 175 lbs. Deb: 5/03/44																												
1944	NY-N	0	0	—	2	0	0	0	0	3	2	6.0	1	2	6.0	1	3.0	3.00	127	.200	.333	0	0	105	178	0.0	0	0	0.1
■ PAT O'CONNELL	O'Connell, Patrick H. b: 6/10/1861, Bangor, Me. d: 1/24/43, Lewiston, Maine BR/TR, 5'10", 175 lbs. Deb: 7/22/1886																												
1886	Bal-a	0	0	—	1	0	0	0	0	3	4	12.0	0	2	6.0	1	3.0	6.00	54	.331	.426	-1	-1	94	100	0.0	-0	0	0.0
■ ANDY O'CONNOR	O'Connor, Andrew James b: 9/14/1884, Roxbury, Mass. d: 9/26/80, Norwood, Mass. 6', 160 lbs. Deb: 10/06/08																												
1908	NY-A	0	1	.000	1	1	1	0	0	8	15	16.9	0	7	7.9	5	5.6	10.13	24	.429	.556	-7	-7	101	104	-0.4	-0	-0	-0.5
■ FRANK O'CONNOR	O'Connor, Frank Henry b: 9/15/1870, Keeseville, N.Y. d: 12/26/13, Brattleboro, Vt. BL/TL, 6', 185 lbs. Deb: 8/03/1893																												
1893	Phi-N	0	0	—	3	1	0	0	1	4	2	4.5	0	9	20.3	0	0.0	11.25	41	.160	.511	-3	-3	98	54	0.0	2	0	0.0
■ JACK O'CONNOR	O'Connor, Jack William b: 6/2/58, Twenty-Nine Palms, Cal. BL/TL, 6'3", 215 lbs. Deb: 4/09/81																												
1981	Min-A	3	2	.600	28	0	0	0	0	35	46	11.8	3	30	7.7	16	4.1	5.91	66	.336	.451	-9	-8	107	125	0.9	0	1	-0.7
1982	Min-A	8	9	.471	23	19	6	1	0	126	122	8.7	13	57	4.1	56	4.0	4.29	97	.255	.333	-3	-2	102	96	1.5	0	-3	-0.4
1983	Min-A	2	3	.400	27	8	0	0	0	83	107	11.6	13	36	3.9	56	6.1	5.86	74	.315	.373	-16	-14	106	104	-0.1	0	-1	-1.4
1984	Min-A	0	0	—	2	0	0	0	0	5	1	1.8	1	4	7.2	0	0.0	1.80	235	.067	.263	1	1	106	114	0.0	0	-0	0.1
1985	Mon-N	0	2	.000	20	1	0	0	0	24	21	7.9	1	13	4.9	16	6.0	4.88	69	.239	.321	-3	-4	94	70	-0.9	0	-1	-0.4
1987	Bal-A	1	1	.500	29	0	0	0	2	46	46	9.0	5	23	4.5	33	6.5	4.30	103	.263	.342	1	1	99	105	0.1	0	-1	0.0
Total	6	14	17	.452	129	28	6	1	2	319	343	9.7	36	163	4.6	177	5.0	4.88	85	.278	.358	-29	-26	103	101	1.5	0	-5	-2.8
■ HANK O'DAY	O'Day, Henry Francis b: 7/8/1862, Chicago, Ill. d: 7/2/35, Chicago, Ill. TR , Deb: 5/02/1884 MU																												
1884	Tol-a	7	28	.200	39	38	33	0	1	309	326	9.5	6	65	1.9	154	4.5	3.99	85	.279	.317	-26	-20	105	93	-11.2	-1	4	-1.3
1885	Pit-a	5	7	.417	12	12	10	0	0	103	110	9.6	4	16	1.4	36	3.1	3.67	94	.285	.314	-5	-2	107	97	-1.0	1	0	0.0
1886	Was-N	1	2	.333	6	6	6	0	0	49	41	7.5	1	17	3.1	47	8.6	1.65	200	.239	.308	9	9	100	156	0.2	-2	0	0.6
1887	Was-N	8	20	.286	30	30	29	0	0	255	255	9.0	15	109	3.8	86	3.0	4.16	96	.275	.352	-3	-5	99	95	-4.0	-3	0	-0.6
1888	Was-N	16	29	.356	46	46	46	3	0	403	359	8.0	20	117	2.6	186	4.2	3.10	92	.252	.308	-12	-11	101	91	-0.1	-7	-4	-2.0
1889	Was-N	2	10	.167	13	13	11	0	0	108	117	9.8	7	57	4.8	23	1.9	4.33	89	.292	.380	-4	-6	96	106	-3.0	0	0	-0.5
	NY-N	9	1	.900	10	10	8	0	0	78	83	9.6	2	35	4.0	28	3.2	4.27	95	.288	.365	-2	-2	101	93	3.6	-2	0	-0.2
	Yr	11	11	.500	23	23	19	0	0	186	200	9.7	9	92	4.5	51	2.5	4.31	92	.290	.374	-6	-8	98	93	0.6	-0	0	-0.7
1890	NY-P	22	13	.629	43	35	32	1	3	329	356	9.7	11	163	4.5	94	2.6	4.21	108	.288	.371	1	12	107	94	3.3	-2	-1	0.8
Total	7	70	110	.389	199	190	175	4	4	1634	1647	9.1	66	579	3.2	654	3.6	3.79	96	.274	.338	-42	-25	103	96	-12.2	-17	-2	-3.2
■ PAUL O'DEA	O'Dea, Paul "Lefty" b: 7/3/20, Cleveland, Ohio d: 12/11/78, Cleveland, Ohio BL/TL, 6', 200 lbs. Deb: 4/19/44																												
1944	Cle-A	0	0	—	3	0	0	0	0	4	5	11.3	0	6	13.5	0	0.0	2.25	154	.333	.500	1	1	101	367	0.0	1	-0	0.1
1945	Cle-A	0	0	—	1	0	0	0	0	2	4	18.0	0	2	9.0	0	0.0	13.50	25	.400	.462	-2	-2	98	70	0.0	0	0	-0.1
Total	2	0	0	—	4	0	0	0	0	6	9	13.5	0	8	12.0	0	0.0	6.00	57	.360	.486	-2	-2	100	268	0.0	1	-0	0.0
■ BILLY O'DELL	O'Dell, William Oliver b: 2/10/33, Whitmire, S.C. BB/TL, 5'11", 170 lbs. Deb: 6/20/54																												
1954	Bal-A	1	1	.500	7	2	1	0	0	16	15	8.4	0	5	2.8	6	3.4	2.81	131	.242	.299	2	2	99	83	0.2	-0	0	0.2
1956	Bal-A	0	0	—	4	1	0	0	1	8	6	6.8	0	6	6.8	6	6.8	1.13	357	.222	.353	3	3	97	307	0.0	-0	-0	0.2
1957	Bal-A	4	10	.286	35	15	2	1	4	140	107	6.9	12	39	2.5	97	6.2	2.70	130	.212	.270	17	13	93	91	-3.1	-1	-2	1.0
1958	Bal-A	14	11	.560	41	25	12	3	8	221	201	8.2	13	51	2.1	137	5.6	2.97	121	.241	.280	20	15	95	92	2.1	-1	-0	1.4
1959	Bal-A	10	12	.455	38	24	6	2	1	199	163	7.4	18	67	3.0	88	4.0	2.94	129	.220	.280	20	19	98	94	-0.6	-3	1	1.8
1960	SF-N	8	13	.381	43	24	6	1	2	203	198	8.8	16	72	3.2	145	6.4	3.19	105	.252	.312	13	3	89	110	-2.9	1	-1	0.2
1961	SF-N	7	5	.583	46	14	4	1	2	130	132	9.1	10	33	2.3	110	7.6	3.60	108	.260	.300	6	4	96	93	0.5	-2	-1	0.1
1962	SF-N	19	14	.576	43	39	20	2	0	281	282	9.0	18	66	2.1	195	6.2	3.52	110	.258	.301	13	11	99	91	-1.5	-1	-2	0.7
1963	SF-N	14	10	.583	36	33	10	3	1	222	218	8.8	14	70	2.8	116	4.7	3.16	98	.253	.310	3	-2	94	105	1.2	4	-4	-0.2
1964	SF-N	8	7	.533	36	8	1	0	2	85	82	8.7	10	35	3.7	54	5.7	5.40	65	.252	.326	-18	-18	99	76	-0.2	-2	-1	-2.0
1965	Mil-N	10	6	.625	62	1	0	0	18	111	87	7.1	10	30	2.4	78	6.3	2.19	167	.215	.266	17	18	103	116	1.7	0	-0	1.9
1966	Atl-N	2	3	.400	24	0	0	0	6	41	44	9.7	3	18	4.0	20	4.4	2.41	145	.272	.350	5	5	97	176	-0.5	0	-0	0.5
	Pit-N	3	2	.600	37	2	0	0	4	71	74	9.4	3	23	2.9	47	6.0	2.79	128	.275	.332	6	6	99	138	0.2	-1	-1	0.4
	Yr	5	5	.500	61	2	0	0	10	112	118	9.5	6	41	3.3	67	5.4	2.65	134	.273	.335	12	11	98	138	-0.3	0	-1	0.9
1967	Pit-N	5	6	.455	27	11	1	0	0	87	88	9.1	10	41	4.2	34	3.5	5.79	58	.265	.346	-23	-23	100	78	-0.4	-0	-1	-2.4
Total	13	105	100	.512	479	199	63	13	48	1815	1697	8.4	137	556	2.8	1133	5.6	3.30	108	.246	.300	84	56	96	100	-3.3	-6	-11	3.8
■ TED ODENWALD	Odenwald, Theodore Joseph "Lefty" b: 1/4/02, Hudson, Wis. d: 10/23/65, Shakopee, Minn. BR/TL, 5'10", 147 lbs. Deb: 4/13/21																												
1921	Cle-A	1	0	1.000	10	0	0	0	0	17	16	8.5	0	6	3.2	4	2.1	1.59	259	.262	.324	5	5	96	208	0.5	-1	0	0.4
1922	Cle-A	0	0	—	1	0	0	0	0	1	6	54.0	0	2	18.0	2	18.0	54.00	8	.600	.667	-6	-6	103	55	0.0	0	0	-0.3

YEAR	TM/L	W	L	PCT	G	GS	CG	SHO	SV	IP	H	H/G	HR	BB	BB/G	SO	SO/G	ERA	/A	OAVG	OOBP	PR	/A	PF	CPI	WAT	PB	PD	TPI
Total	2	1	0	1.000	11	0	0	0	0	18	22	11.0	0	8	4.0	6	3.0	4.50	91	.310	.373	-0	-1	96	199	0.5	-1	0	0.1

■ **DAVE ODOM** Odom, David Everett "Blimp" or "Porky" b: 6/5/18, Dinuba, Cal. BR/TR, 5'10", 185 lbs. Deb: 5/31/43

YEAR	TM/L	W	L	PCT	G	GS	CG	SHO	SV	IP	H	H/G	HR	BB	BB/G	SO	SO/G	ERA	/A	OAVG	OOBP	PR	/A	PF	CPI	WAT	PB	PD	TPI
1943	Bos-N	0	3	.000	22	3	1	0	2	55	54	8.8	3	30	4.9	17	2.8	5.24	70	.269	.370	-11	-10	109	86	-1.4	-2	-1	-1.2

■ **BLUE MOON ODOM** Odom, Johnny Lee b: 5/29/45, Macon, Ga. BR/TR, 6', 178 lbs. Deb: 9/05/64

YEAR	TM/L	W	L	PCT	G	GS	CG	SHO	SV	IP	H	H/G	HR	BB	BB/G	SO	SO/G	ERA	/A	OAVG	OOBP	PR	/A	PF	CPI	WAT	PB	PD	TPI
1964	KC-A	1	2	.333	5	5	1	1	0	17	29	15.4	5	11	5.8	10	5.3	10.06	39	.363	.440	-12	-12	108	92	0.0	-0	0	-1.0
1965	KC-A	0	0	—	1	0	0	0	0	1	2	18.0	0	2	18.0	0	0.0	9.00	38	.400	.571	-1	-1	100	136	0.0	0	0	0.0
1966	KC-A	5	5	.500	14	14	4	2	0	90	70	7.0	1	53	5.3	47	4.7	2.50	131	.215	.323	9	8	95	115	0.4	-1	2	1.0
1967	KC-A	3	8	.273	29	17	0	0	0	104	94	8.1	9	68	5.9	67	5.8	5.02	65	.243	.353	-21	-20	102	86	-1.6	2	0	-1.8
1968	Oak-A	16	10	.615	32	31	9	4	0	231	179	7.0	9	98	3.8	143	5.6	2.45	119	.216	.299	13	12	98	107	3.3	6	1	2.2
1969	Oak-A	15	6	.714	32	32	10	3	0	231	179	7.0	15	112	4.4	150	5.8	2.92	113	.215	.308	18	10	91	99	4.3	11	1	2.3
1970	Oak-A	9	8	.529	29	29	4	1	0	156	128	7.4	14	100	5.8	88	5.1	3.81	93	.227	.343	-2	-4	96	102	-0.2	6	2	0.4
1971	Oak-A	10	12	.455	25	25	3	1	0	141	147	9.4	13	71	4.5	69	4.4	4.28	80	.271	.346	-13	-13	99	103	-3.3	1	-1	-1.2
1972	Oak-A	15	6	.714	31	30	4	2	0	194	164	7.6	10	87	4.0	86	4.0	2.51	116	.234	.316	12	9	95	123	3.3	0	0	1.0
1973	Oak-A	5	12	.294	30	24	3	0	0	150	153	9.2	14	67	4.0	83	5.0	4.50	73	.263	.337	-11	-21	86	90	-4.3	0	-1	-2.1
1974	Oak-A	1	5	.167	34	5	1	0	1	87	85	8.8	4	52	5.4	52	5.4	3.83	93	.267	.365	-2	-2	99	114	-2.0	0	1	-0.1
1975	Oak-A	0	2	.000	7	2	0	0	0	11	19	15.5	1	11	9.0	4	3.3	12.27	28	.422	.525	-10	-11	91	85	-0.9	0	0	-0.9
	Cle-A	1	0	1.000	3	1	1	1	0	10	4	3.6	1	8	7.2	10	9.0	2.70	140	.118	.286	1	1	100	64	0.5	0	-0	0.1
	Yr	1	2	.333	10	3	1	1	0	21	23	9.9	2	19	8.1	14	6.0	7.71	47	.284	.416	-9	-10	95	64	-0.4	0	-0	-0.8
	Atl-N	1	7	.125	15	10	0	0	0	56	78	12.5	5	28	4.5	30	4.8	7.07	50	.342	.403	-21	-22	97	90	-2.7	-1	0	-2.1
1976	Chi-A	2	2	.500	8	4	0	0	0	28	31	10.0	2	20	6.4	18	5.8	5.79	62	.282	.391	-7	-7	101	91	0.3	0	-1	-0.7
Total	13	84	85	.497	295	229	40	15	1	1507	1362	8.1	103	788	4.7	857	5.1	3.70	88	.244	.335	-45	-72	95	103	-2.9	25	6	-2.9

■ **GEORGE O'DONNELL** O'Donnell, George Dana b: 5/27/29, Winchester, Ill. BR/TR, 6'3", 175 lbs. Deb: 4/18/54

YEAR	TM/L	W	L	PCT	G	GS	CG	SHO	SV	IP	H	H/G	HR	BB	BB/G	SO	SO/G	ERA	/A	OAVG	OOBP	PR	/A	PF	CPI	WAT	PB	PD	TPI
1954	Pit-N	3	9	.250	21	10	3	0	1	87	105	10.9	4	21	2.2	8	0.8	4.55	91	.315	.343	-5	-4	102	102	-1.6	-1	1	-0.3

■ **JOHN O'DONOGHUE** O'Donoghue, John Eugene b: 10/7/39, Kansas City, Mo. BR/TL, 6'4", 203 lbs. Deb: 9/29/63

YEAR	TM/L	W	L	PCT	G	GS	CG	SHO	SV	IP	H	H/G	HR	BB	BB/G	SO	SO/G	ERA	/A	OAVG	OOBP	PR	/A	PF	CPI	WAT	PB	PD	TPI
1963	KC-A	0	1	.000	1	1	0	0	0	6	6	9.0	0	2	3.0	1	1.5	1.50	263	.286	.348	1	2	109	255	-0.4	-0	-0	0.1
1964	KC-A	10	14	.417	39	32	2	1	0	174	202	10.4	24	65	3.4	79	4.1	4.91	79	.286	.343	-25	-20	108	99	1.4	2	-1	-1.8
1965	KC-A	9	18	.333	34	30	4	1	0	178	183	9.3	15	66	3.3	82	4.1	3.94	87	.267	.327	-10	-10	100	101	-1.2	3	0	-0.7
1966	Cle-A	6	8	.429	32	13	2	0	0	108	109	9.1	13	23	1.9	49	4.1	3.83	91	.264	.299	-5	-4	102	101	-1.0	-1	1	-0.3
1967	Cle-A	8	9	.471	33	17	5	2	2	131	120	8.2	10	33	2.3	81	5.6	3.23	101	.247	.292	0	1	101	99	0.1	-0	3	0.4
1968	Bal-A	0	0	—	16	0	0	0	2	22	34	13.9	2	7	2.9	11	4.5	6.14	49	.374	.406	-8	-8	101	112	0.0	-0	0	-0.8
1969	Sea-A	2	2	.500	55	0	0	0	6	70	58	7.5	5	37	4.8	48	6.2	2.96	123	.230	.328	5	5	100	119	0.4	-1	-0	0.5
1970	Mil-A	2	0	1.000	25	0	0	0	0	23	29	11.3	4	9	3.5	13	5.1	5.09	73	.299	.349	-3	-4	100	107	1.0	-0	1	-0.2
	Mon-N	2	3	.400	9	3	0	0	0	22	20	8.2	2	11	4.5	6	2.5	5.32	77	.263	.351	-3	-3	102	90	-0.2	-0	0	-0.2
1971	Mon-N	0	0	—	13	0	0	0	0	17	19	10.1	3	7	3.7	7	3.7	4.76	73	.271	.333	-2	-2	100	100	0.0	0	0	-0.2
Total	9	39	55	.415	257	96	13	4	10	751	780	9.3	78	260	3.1	377	4.5	4.07	87	.269	.326	-49	-43	102	103	0.1	2	4	-3.2

■ **LEFTY O'DOUL** O'Doul, Francis Joseph b: 3/4/1897, San Francisco, Cal. d: 12/7/69, San Francisco, Cal. BL/TL, 6', 180 lbs. Deb: 4/29/19

YEAR	TM/L	W	L	PCT	G	GS	CG	SHO	SV	IP	H	H/G	HR	BB	BB/G	SO	SO/G	ERA	/A	OAVG	OOBP	PR	/A	PF	CPI	WAT	PB	PD	TPI
1919	NY-A	0	0	—	3	0	0	0	0	5	7	12.6	0	4	7.2	2	3.6	3.60	93	.304	.407	-0	-0	104	144	0.0	0	-0	0.0
1920	NY-A	0	0	—	2	0	0	0	0	4	4	9.0	0	2	4.5	2	4.5	4.50	83	.286	.412	-0	-0	99	105	0.0	-0	-0	0.0
1922	NY-A	0	0	—	6	0	0	0	0	16	24	13.5	0	12	6.8	5	2.8	3.38	119	.353	.450	1	1	99	200	0.0	1	0	0.2
1923	Bos-A	1	1	.500	23	1	0	0	0	53	69	11.7	2	31	5.3	10	1.7	5.43	77	.337	.419	-9	-7	106	115	0.2	-1	1	-0.7
Total	4	1	1	.500	34	1	0	0	0	78	104	12.0	2	49	5.7	19	2.2	4.85	84	.335	.425	-8	-7	104	134	0.2	-1	1	-0.5

■ **BRYAN OELKERS** Oelkers, Bryan Alois b: 3/1/61, Zaragoza, Spain BL/TL, 6'3", 192 lbs. Deb: 4/09/83

YEAR	TM/L	W	L	PCT	G	GS	CG	SHO	SV	IP	H	H/G	HR	BB	BB/G	SO	SO/G	ERA	/A	OAVG	OOBP	PR	/A	PF	CPI	WAT	PB	PD	TPI
1983	Min-A	0	5	.000	10	8	0	0	0	34	56	14.8	7	17	4.5	13	3.4	8.74	50	.376	.437	-18	-17	106	98	-2.4	0	-1	-1.5
1986	Cle-A	3	3	.500	35	4	0	0	1	69	70	9.1	13	40	5.2	33	4.3	4.70	87	.262	.365	-4	-5	98	117	0.0	0	-1	-0.5
Total	2	3	8	.273	45	12	0	0	1	103	126	11.0	20	57	5.0	46	4.0	6.03	69	.303	.390	-22	-21	101	111	-2.4	0	-2	-2.0

■ **JOE OESCHGER** Oeschger, Joseph Carl b: 5/24/1892, Chicago, Ill. d: 7/28/86, Rohnert Park, Cal BR/TR, 6' ", 190 lbs. Deb: 4/21/14

YEAR	TM/L	W	L	PCT	G	GS	CG	SHO	SV	IP	H	H/G	HR	BB	BB/G	SO	SO/G	ERA	/A	OAVG	OOBP	PR	/A	PF	CPI	WAT	PB	PD	TPI
1914	Phi-N	4	8	.333	32	10	5	0	1	124	129	9.4	5	54	3.9	47	3.4	3.77	75	.279	.353	-14	-13	101	108	-1.8	-4	-1	-1.8
1915	Phi-N	1	0	1.000	6	1	1	0	0	24	21	7.9	1	9	3.4	8	3.0	3.38	85	.247	.303	-2	-1	104	91	0.5	-1	0	-0.2
1916	Phi-N	1	0	1.000	14	0	0	0	0	30	18	5.4	2	14	4.2	17	5.1	2.40	102	.184	.277	1	0	94	91	0.5	-1	1	0.0
1917	Phi-N	15	14	.517	42	30	18	5	1	262	241	8.3	7	72	2.5	123	4.2	2.75	104	.249	.300	-1	3	106	100	-1.6	-4	-3	-0.3
1918	Phi-N	6	18	.250	30	23	13	2	3	184	159	7.8	3	83	4.1	60	2.9	3.03	101	.238	.320	-5	1	111	96	-5.8	-5	-2	-0.4
1919	Phi-N	0	1	.000	5	4	2	0	0	38	52	12.3	1	16	3.8	5	1.2	5.92	53	.340	.395	-13	-12	109	96	-0.4	-2	-0	-1.2
	NY-N	0	1	.000	5	1	0	0	0	8	12	13.5	0	2	2.3	3	3.4	4.50	62	.400	.424	-1	-2	96	142	-0.4	-0	0	-0.1
	Bos-N	4	2	.667	7	7	4	1	0	57	63	9.9	0	21	3.3	16	2.5	2.53	115	.300	.357	2	2	100	164	1.3	-1	-1	0.0
	Yr	4	4	.500	17	12	6	1	0	103	127	11.1	1	39	3.4	24	2.1	3.93	76	.322	.373	-12	-11	103	164	0.5	-2	-1	-1.3
1920	Bos-N	15	13	.536	38	30	20	5	0	299	294	8.8	10	99	3.0	80	2.4	3.46	90	.265	.321	-11	-12	99	91	3.5	-3	-3	-1.7
1921	Bos-N	20	14	.588	46	36	19	3	0	299	303	9.1	11	97	2.9	68	2.0	3.52	99	.274	.333	9	-1	92	103	3.1	3	2	0.3
1922	Bos-N	6	21	.222	46	23	10	1	1	196	234	10.7	8	81	3.7	51	2.3	5.05	79	.303	.363	-21	-23	98	93	-5.4	-0	1	-2.0
1923	Bos-N	5	15	.250	44	19	6	1	2	166	227	12.3	4	54	2.9	33	1.8	5.69	72	.330	.377	-31	-29	102	90	-3.1	-0	0	-2.7
1924	NY-N	2	0	1.000	10	2	0	0	0	29	35	10.9	1	14	4.3	10	3.1	3.10	109	.287	.358	2	1	88	138	1.0	1	-1	0.1
	Phi-N	2	7	.222	19	8	0	0	0	65	88	12.2	6	16	2.2	8	1.1	4.43	97	.333	.366	-4	-1	111	127	-1.7	-0	-0	-0.1
	Yr	4	7	.364	29	10	0	0	0	94	123	11.8	7	30	2.9	18	1.7	4.02	100	.319	.364	-2	-0	103	127	-0.7	1	-1	0.0
1925	Bro-N	1	2	.333	21	3	1	0	0	37	60	14.6	2	19	4.6	6	1.5	6.08	67	.382	.435	-7	-8	95	125	-0.3	-0	-0	-0.7
Total	12	82	116	.414	365	197	99	18	8	1818	1936	9.6	61	651	3.2	535	2.6	3.81	88	.281	.340	-96	-90	101	101	-10.6	-18	-7	-10.8

■ **JACK OGDEN** Ogden, John Mahlon b: 11/5/1897, Ogden, Pa. d: 11/9/77, Philadelphia, Pa. BR/TR, 6', 190 lbs. Deb: 6/22/18

YEAR	TM/L	W	L	PCT	G	GS	CG	SHO	SV	IP	H	H/G	HR	BB	BB/G	SO	SO/G	ERA	/A	OAVG	OOBP	PR	/A	PF	CPI	WAT	PB	PD	TPI
1918	NY-N	0	0	—	5	0	0	0	0	9	8	8.0	0	3	3.0	1	1.0	3.00	88	.296	.371	-0	-0	96	147	0.0	-0	-0	0.0
1928	StL-A	15	16	.484	38	31	18	1	2	243	257	9.5	23	80	3.0	67	2.5	4.15	100	.274	.322	-3	0	103	99	-1.6	-1	-4	-0.3
1929	StL-A	4	8	.333	34	14	7	0	0	131	154	10.6	8	44	3.0	32	2.2	4.95	85	.301	.346	-10	-11	100	94	-2.2	1	0	-0.8
1931	Cin-N	4	8	.333	22	9	3	1	1	89	79	8.0	3	32	3.2	24	2.4	2.93	129	.242	.296	9	8	98	102	-0.6	-1	-1	0.6
1932	Cin-N	2	2	.500	24	3	1	0	0	57	72	11.4	5	22	3.5	20	3.2	5.21	74	.310	.363	-8	-9	99	102	0.4	0	1	-0.7
Total	5	25	34	.424	123	57	29	2	3	529	570	9.7	39	181	3.1	144	2.4	4.24	96	.280	.329	-12	-11	101	99	-4.0	-1	-4	-1.2

■ **CURLY OGDEN** Ogden, Warren Harvey b: 1/24/01, Ogden, Pa. d: 8/6/64, Chester, Pa. BR/TR, 6'1.5", 180 lbs. Deb: 7/18/22

YEAR	TM/L	W	L	PCT	G	GS	CG	SHO	SV	IP	H	H/G	HR	BB	BB/G	SO	SO/G	ERA	/A	OAVG	OOBP	PR	/A	PF	CPI	WAT	PB	PD	TPI
1922	Phi-A	1	4	.200	15	6	4	0	0	72	59	7.4	4	33	4.1	20	2.5	3.13	138	.237	.327	7	9	106	109	-1.2	-0	-0	0.9
1923	Phi-A	1	2	.333	18	2	0	0	0	46	63	12.3	2	32	6.3	14	2.7	5.67	72	.330	.417	-9	-8	102	112	-0.3	1	0	-0.6
1924	Phi-A	0	3	.000	5	1	0	0	0	13	14	9.7	1	7	4.8	4	2.8	4.85	88	.275	.361	-1	-1	101	96	-1.4	-1	-0	-0.1
	Was-A	9	5	.643	16	16	9	3	0	108	83	6.9	3	51	4.3	23	1.9	2.58	157	.221	.304	20	18	96	105	0.9	2	-0	1.9
	Yr	9	8	.529	21	17	9	3	0	121	97	7.2	4	58	4.3	27	2.0	2.83	145	.227	.309	19	17	97	105	-0.5	-1	1	1.8
1925	Was-A	3	1	.750	17	4	2	1	0	42	45	9.6	1	18	3.9	6	1.3	4.50	93	.288	.359	-1	-1	95	97	0.6	-0	-0	-0.1
1926	Was-A	4	4	.500	22	9	4	0	0	96	114	10.7	2	45	4.2	21	2.0	4.31	91	.305	.368	-3	-4	97	112	-0.2	-1	-1	-0.5
Total	5	18	19	.486	93	38	19	4	0	377	378	9.0	13	186	4.4	88	2.1	3.80	108	.271	.349	14	12	99	107	-1.6	1	-2	1.5

■ **JOE OGRODOWSKI** Ogrodowski, Joseph Anthony b: 11/20/06, Hoytville, Pa. d: 6/24/59, Elmira, N.Y. BR/TR, 5'11", 165 lbs. Deb: 4/27/25

YEAR	TM/L	W	L	PCT	G	GS	CG	SHO	SV	IP	H	H/G	HR	BB	BB/G	SO	SO/G	ERA	/A	OAVG	OOBP	PR	/A	PF	CPI	WAT	PB	PD	TPI
1925	Bos-N	0	0	—	1	0	0	0	0	1	6	54.0	0	3	27.0	0	0.0	54.00	8	.600	.692	-6	-6	95	60	0.0	0	0	-0.3

■ **BILL O'HARA** O'Hara, William Alexander b: 8/14/1883, Toronto, Ont., Can. d: 6/15/31, Jersey City, N.J. BL/TR, 5'10", Deb: 09

YEAR	TM/L	W	L	PCT	G	GS	CG	SHO	SV	IP	H	H/G	HR	BB	BB/G	SO	SO/G	ERA	/A	OAVG	OOBP	PR	/A	PF	CPI	WAT	PB	PD	TPI
1910	StL-N	0	0	—	1	0	0	0	0	1	0	0.0	0	0	0.0	0	0.0	0.00	—	.000	.000	0	0	93	0	0.0	-0	0	0.0

■ **JOE OHL** Ohl, Joseph Earl b: 1/10/1888, Jobstown, N.J. d: 12/18/51, Camden, N.J. BL/TL, Deb: 7/29/09

YEAR	TM/L	W	L	PCT	G	GS	CG	SHO	SV	IP	H	H/G	HR	BB	BB/G	SO	SO/G	ERA	/A	OAVG	OOBP	PR	/A	PF	CPI	WAT	PB	PD	TPI
1909	Was-A	0	0	—	4	0	0	0	0	9	7	7.0	0	1	1.0	2	2.0	2.00	119	.194	.237	0	0	96	26	0.0	-0	0	0.0

■ **BOBBY OJEDA** Ojeda, Robert Michael b: 12/17/57, Los Angeles, Cal. BL/TL, 6'1", 185 lbs. Deb: 7/13/80

YEAR	TM/L	W	L	PCT	G	GS	CG	SHO	SV	IP	H	H/G	HR	BB	BB/G	SO	SO/G	ERA	/A	OAVG	OOBP	PR	/A	PF	CPI	WAT	PB	PD	TPI
1980	Bos-A	1	1	.500	7	7	0	0	0	26	39	13.5	2	14	4.8	12	4.2	6.92	60	.361	.434	-8	-8	102	102	0.0	0	-0	-0.7

YEAR	TM/L	W	L	PCT	G	GS	CG	SHO	SV	IP	H	H/G	HR	BB	BB/G	SO	SO/G	ERA	/A	OAVG	OOBP	PR	/A	PF	CPI	WAT	PB	PD	TPI
1981	Bos-A	6	2	.750	10	10	2	0	0	66	50	6.8	6	25	3.4	28	3.8	3.14	123	.212	.288	4	5	106	89	1.9	0	-0	0.5
1982	Bos-A	4	6	.400	22	14	0	0	0	78	95	11.0	13	29	3.3	52	6.0	5.65	79	.296	.355	-14	-10	110	96	-1.3	0	-1	-1.0
1983	Bos-A	12	7	.632	29	28	5	0	0	174	173	8.9	15	73	3.8	94	4.9	4.03	103	.265	.334	1	2	102	104	3.0	0	0	0.2
1984	Bos-A	12	12	.500	33	32	8	**5**	0	217	211	8.8	17	96	4.0	137	5.7	3.98	110	.259	.333	0	10	110	99	-0.7	0	1	1.0
1985	Bos-A	9	11	.450	39	22	5	0	1	158	166	9.5	11	48	2.7	102	5.8	3.99	106	.273	.322	3	4	102	100	-1.0	0	0	0.4
1986	NY-N	18	5	**.783**	32	30	7	2	0	217	185	7.7	15	52	2.2	148	6.1	2.57	135	.230	.274	28	22	93	101	4.4	-2	1	2.1
1987	NY-N	3	5	.375	10	7	0	0	0	46	45	8.8	5	10	2.0	21	4.1	3.91	101	.253	.286	1	0	97	86	-1.3	-0	0	0.0
1988	NY-N	10	13	.435	29	29	5	5	0	190	158	7.5	6	33	1.6	133	6.3	2.89	105	.225	.259	12	3	88	72	-3.8	1	2	0.6
Total	9	75	62	.547	211	179	32	12	1	1172	1122	8.6	90	380	2.9	727	5.6	3.68	105	.253	.310	27	26	100	95	1.2	-1	2	3.1
■ **FRANK OKRIE**	Okrie, Frank Anthony "Lefty" b: 10/28/1896, Detroit, Mich. d: 10/16/59, Detroit, Mich. BL/TL, 5'11", 175 lbs. Deb: 4/20/20																												
1920	Det-A	1	2	.333	21	1	1	0	0	41	44	9.7	2	18	4.0	9	2.0	5.27	76	.295	.390	-7	-6	106	91	-0.1	-0	6	0.0
■ **RED OLDHAM**	Oldham, John Cyrus b: 7/15/1893, Zion, Md. d: 1/28/61, Costa Mesa, Cal. BB/TL, 6' ", 176 lbs. Deb: 8/19/14																												
1914	Det-A	2	4	.333	9	7	3	0	0	45	42	8.4	1	8	1.6	23	4.6	3.40	82	.243	.288	-3	-3	102	65	-1.0	1	-1	-0.3
1915	Det-A	3	0	1.000	17	2	1	0	4	58	52	8.1	1	17	2.6	17	2.6	2.79	111	.243	.311	1	2	105	95	1.5	-0	-0	0.1
1920	Det-A	8	13	.381	39	22	10	1	1	215	248	10.4	5	91	3.8	62	2.6	3.85	105	.302	.376	-1	4	106	116	-0.4	-2	4	0.6
1921	Det-A	11	14	.440	40	28	12	1	1	229	258	10.1	11	81	3.2	67	2.6	4.24	97	.288	.341	1	-4	96	97	-0.7	3	1	0.0
1922	Det-A	10	13	.435	43	27	9	0	3	212	256	10.9	14	59	2.5	72	3.1	4.67	84	.305	.348	-15	-17	97	99	-1.9	4	1	-1.1
1925	Pit-N	3	2	.600	11	4	3	0	1	53	66	11.2	2	18	3.1	10	1.7	3.91	108	.313	.369	2	2	99	124	0.0	2	0	0.4
1926	Pit-N	2	2	.500	17	2	0	0	2	42	56	12.0	1	18	3.9	16	3.4	5.57	76	.359	.405	-8	-6	111	112	-0.1	0	0	-0.5
Total	7	39	48	.448	176	92	38	2	12	854	978	10.3	35	292	3.1	267	2.8	4.15	95	.295	.352	-23	-21	101	103	-2.6	8	4	-0.8
■ **DIOMEDES OLIVO**	Olivo, Diomedes Antonio (Maldonado) b: 1/22/19, Guayubin, D.R. d: 2/15/77, Santo Domingo, D.R. BL/TL, 6'1", 195 lbs. Deb: 9/05/60																												
1960	Pit-N	0	0	—	4	0	0	0	0	10	8	7.2	1	5	4.5	10	9.0	2.70	135	.216	.310	1	1	97	117	0.0	-0	0	0.1
1962	Pit-N	5	1	.833	62	1	0	0	7	84	88	9.4	5	25	2.7	66	7.1	2.79	143	.277	.317	11	11	101	138	1.8	0	-1	1.1
1963	StL-N	0	5	.000	19	0	0	0	0	13	16	11.1	1	9	6.2	9	6.2	5.54	63	.296	.394	-3	-3	106	104	-2.4	0	0	-0.2
Total	3	5	6	.455	85	1	0	0	7	107	112	9.4	7	39	3.3	85	7.1	3.11	125	.274	.328	9	9	101	132	-0.6	0	-0	1.0
■ **CHI-CHI OLIVO**	Olivo, Federico Emilio (Moldonado) b: 3/18/28, Guayubin, D.R. d: 2/3/77, Guaybin, D.R. BR/TR, 6'2", 215 lbs. Deb: 6/05/61																												
1961	Mil-N	0	0	—	3	0	0	0	0	2	3	13.5	1	5	22.5	1	4.5	18.00	20	.500	.667	-3	-3	91	103	0.0	0	0	-0.2
1964	Mil-N	2	1	.667	38	0	0	0	5	60	55	8.3	7	21	3.2	45	6.8	3.75	91	.247	.303	-1	-2	96	99	0.4	0	1	-0.1
1965	Mil-N	0	1	.000	8	0	0	0	0	13	12	8.3	1	5	3.5	11	7.6	1.38	263	.267	.315	3	3	103	297	-0.4	0	-0	0.3
1966	Atl-N	5	4	.556	47	0	0	0	7	66	59	8.0	4	19	2.6	41	5.6	4.23	83	.240	.287	-5	-5	97	68	0.3	-0	-1	-0.6
Total	4	7	6	.538	96	0	0	0	12	141	129	8.2	13	50	3.2	98	6.3	3.96	88	.248	.304	-6	-8	97	103	0.3	-0	-0	-0.6
■ **JIM OLLOM**	Ollom, James Donald b: 7/8/45, Snohomish, Wash. BR/TL, 6'4", 210 lbs. Deb: 9/03/66																												
1966	Min-A	0	0	—	3	1	0	0	0	10	6	5.4	1	1	0.9	11	9.9	3.60	105	.167	.211	-0	0	110	34	0.0	-0	0	0.0
1967	Min-A	0	1	.000	21	2	0	0	0	35	33	8.5	4	11	2.8	17	4.4	5.40	63	.258	.322	-8	-8	106	78	-0.4	0	-0	-0.8
Total	2	0	1	.000	24	3	0	0	0	45	39	7.8	5	12	2.4	28	5.6	5.00	70	.238	.299	-9	-8	107	68	-0.4	-0	-0	-0.8
■ **FRED OLMSTEAD**	Olmstead, Frederic William b: 7/3/1881, Grand Rapids, Mich d: 10/22/36, Muskogee, Okla. BR/TR, 5'11", 170 lbs. Deb: 7/02/08																												
1908	Chi-A	0	0	—	1	0	0	0	0	2	6	27.0	0	1	4.5	1	4.5	13.50	16	.600	.636	-2	-3	93	110	0.0	1	0	-0.2
1909	Chi-A	3	2	.600	8	6	5	0	0	55	52	8.5	1	12	2.0	21	3.4	1.80	133	.277	.323	4	4	97	166	0.5	-1	0	0.4
1910	Chi-A	10	12	.455	32	20	14	4	0	184	174	8.5	1	50	2.4	68	3.3	1.96	123	.260	.316	11	9	95	141	0.2	-2	1	0.8
1911	Chi-A	6	6	.500	25	11	7	1	2	118	146	11.1	3	30	2.3	45	3.4	4.19	76	.309	.358	-11	-13	95	100	0.0	-0	-1	-1.3
Total	4	19	20	.487	66	37	26	5	2	359	378	9.5	5	93	2.3	135	3.4	2.73	97	.283	.334	2	-3	95	131	0.7	-3	0	-0.3
■ **AL OLMSTED**	Olmsted, Alan Ray b: 3/18/57, St.Louis, Mo. BR/TL, 6'2", 195 lbs. Deb: 9/12/80																												
1980	StL-N	1	1	.500	5	5	0	0	0	35	32	8.2	2	14	3.6	14	3.6	2.83	131	.244	.320	3	3	102	117	0.1	-0	1	0.4
■ **HANK OLMSTED**	Olmsted, Henry Theodore b: 1/12/1879, Saginaw Bay, Mich. d: 1/6/69, Bradenton, Fla. 5'8.5", 147 lbs. Deb: 7/15/05																												
1905	Bos-A	1	2	.333	3	3	3	0	0	25	18	6.5	0	12	4.3	6	2.2	3.24	82	.223	.324	-2	-2	100	70	-0.4	-0	-0	-0.1
■ **OLE OLSEN**	Olsen, Arthur b: 9/12/1894, S.Norwalk, Conn. BR/TR, 5'10", 163 lbs. Deb: 4/12/22																												
1922	Det-A	7	6	.538	37	15	5	0	3	137	147	9.7	8	40	2.6	52	3.4	4.53	87	.281	.337	-7	-9	97	90	0.4	-1	1	-0.9
1923	Det-A	1	1	.500	17	2	1	0	0	41	42	9.2	1	17	3.7	12	2.6	6.37	60	.290	.356	-11	-12	95	71	0.0	-1	-1	-1.2
Total	2	8	7	.533	54	17	6	0	3	178	189	9.6	9	57	2.9	64	3.2	4.96	79	.283	.341	-18	-21	97	86	0.4	-1	-0	-2.1
■ **VERN OLSEN**	Olsen, Vern Jarl b: 3/16/18, Hillsboro, Ore. BR/TL, 6'0.5", 175 lbs. Deb: 9/08/39																												
1939	Chi-N	1	0	1.000	4	0	0	0	0	8	2	2.3	0	7	7.9	3	3.4	0.00	—	.087	.300	3	3	100	0	0.5	0	-0	0.4
1940	Chi-N	13	9	.591	34	20	9	4	0	173	172	8.9	5	62	3.2	71	3.7	2.97	128	.260	.322	17	16	99	119	2.5	3	4	2.4
1941	Chi-N	10	8	.556	37	23	10	2	1	186	202	9.8	7	59	2.9	73	3.5	3.15	108	.276	.325	10	5	94	**120**	1.8	3	2	1.1
1942	Chi-N	6	9	.400	32	17	4	1	1	140	161	10.4	6	55	3.5	46	3.0	4.50	72	.283	.343	-18	-20	98	93	-0.7	1	1	-1.7
1946	Chi-N	0	0	—	5	0	0	0	0	10	10	9.0	0	9	8.1	8	7.2	2.70	118	.294	.432	1	1	93	203	0.0	0	0	0.1
Total	5	30	26	.536	112	60	23	7	2	517	547	9.5	18	192	3.3	201	3.5	3.39	103	.271	.331	13	6	96	112	4.1	8	7	2.3
■ **GREG OLSON**	Olson, Greggory William b: 10/11/66, Scribner, Neb. BR/TR, 6'4", 210 lbs. Deb: 9/02/88																												
1988	Bal-A	1	1	.500	10	0	0	0	0	11	10	8.2	1	10	8.2	9	7.4	3.27	118	.244	.392	1	1	97	154	0.2	0	0	0.1
■ **TED OLSON**	Olson, Theodore Otto b: 8/27/12, Quincy, Mass. d: 12/9/80, Weymouth, Mass. BR/TR, 6'0.5", 185 lbs. Deb: 6/21/36																												
1936	Bos-A	1	1	.500	5	3	1	0	0	18	24	12.0	3	8	4.0	5	2.5	7.50	71	.324	.376	-5	-4	106	90	0.0	-0	0	-0.3
1937	Bos-A	0	0	—	11	0	0	0	0	32	42	11.8	4	15	4.2	11	3.1	7.31	65	.318	.375	-10	-9	102	84	0.0	1	1	-0.6
1938	Bos-A	0	0	—	2	0	0	0	0	7	9	11.6	0	2	2.6	2	2.6	6.43	75	.310	.355	-1	-1	100	70	0.0	-0	0	0.0
Total	3	1	1	.500	18	3	1	0	0	57	75	11.8	7	25	3.9	18	2.8	7.26	68	.319	.373	-16	-15	103	84	0.0	1	1	-0.9
■ **ED OLWINE**	Olwine, Edward R. b: 5/28/58, Greenville, Ohio BR/TL, 6'2", 165 lbs. Deb: 6/02/86																												
1986	Atl-N	0	0	—	37	0	0	0	1	48	35	6.6	5	17	3.2	37	6.9	3.38	114	.207	.280	2	3	103	81	0.0	1	-0	0.3
1987	Atl-N	0	1	.000	27	0	0	0	1	23	25	9.8	4	8	3.1	12	4.7	5.09	88	.269	.327	-3	-2	109	93	-0.4	0	-0	-0.1
1988	Atl-N	0	0	—	16	0	0	0	1	19	22	10.4	4	4	1.9	5	2.4	6.63	56	.286	.329	-7	-6	107	78	0.0	0	-0	-0.6
Total	3	0	1	.000	80	0	0	0	3	90	82	8.2	13	29	2.9	54	5.4	4.50	88	.242	.304	-7	-5	106	83	-0.4	1	-1	-0.4
■ **SKINNY O'NEAL**	O'Neal, Oran Herbert b: 5/2/1899, Gatewood, Mo. d: 6/2/81, Springfield, Mo. BR/TR, 5'11", 160 lbs. Deb: 4/18/25																												
1925	Phi-N	0	0	—	11	1	0	0	0	20	35	15.7	2	12	5.4	6	2.7	9.45	53	.407	.461	-12	-10	118	95	0.0	-0	-0	-0.8
1927	Phi-N	0	0	—	2	0	0	0	0	5	9	16.2	0	2	3.6	2	3.6	9.00	44	.409	.440	-3	-3	100	86	0.0	-0	1	-0.1
Total	2	0	0	—	13	1	0	0	0	25	44	15.8	2	14	5.0	8	2.9	9.36	51	.407	.457	-14	-13	114	93	0.0	-0	0	-0.9
■ **RANDY O'NEAL**	O'Neal, Randall Jeffrey b: 8/30/60, Ashland, Ky. BR/TR, 6'2", 195 lbs. Deb: 9/12/84																												
1984	Det-A	2	1	.667	4	3	0	0	0	19	16	7.6	0	6	2.8	12	5.7	3.32	114	.222	.282	1	1	94	59	0.1	0	-0	0.1
1985	Det-A	5	5	.500	28	12	1	0	1	94	82	7.9	8	36	3.4	52	5.0	3.26	135	.240	.309	9	12	106	108	-0.1	0	1	1.3
1986	Det-A	3	7	.300	37	11	1	0	2	123	121	8.9	13	44	3.2	68	5.0	4.32	92	.260	.322	-2	-5	95	93	-2.2	0	1	-0.3
1987	Atl-N	4	2	.667	16	10	0	0	0	61	79	11.7	12	24	3.5	33	4.9	5.61	80	.316	.376	-10	-8	109	114	1.3	-1	1	-0.6
	StL-N	0	0	—	1	1	0	0	0	5	2	3.6	0	2	3.6	4	7.2	1.80	221	.111	.190	1	1	97	32	0.0	0	0	0.2
	Yr	4	2	.667	17	11	0	0	0	66	81	11.0	12	26	3.5	37	5.0	5.32	83	.298	.357	-9	-7	108	32	1.3	-1	1	-0.4
1988	StL-N	2	3	.400	10	8	0	0	0	53	57	9.7	7	10	1.7	20	3.4	4.58	79	.274	.311	-7	-6	105	91	-0.3	-2	1	-0.6
Total	5	16	18	.471	96	45	2	0	3	355	357	9.1	40	122	3.1	189	4.8	4.21	98	.263	.323	-7	-4	102	98	-1.2	-2	4	0.1
■ **ED O'NEIL**	O'Neil, Edward J. b: 3/11/1859, Fall River, Mass. d: 9/30/1892, Fall River, Mass. TR , 5'11", 180 lbs. Deb: 6/20/1890																												
1890	Tol-a	0	1	.000	2	2	2	0	0	16	27	15.2	0	13	7.3	2	1.1	7.88	50	.391	.488	-7	-7	102	103	-0.4	-2	0	-0.5
	Phi-a	0	6	.000	6	6	6	0	0	52	84	14.5	0	32	5.5	17	2.9	9.69	40	.381	.459	-34	-33	101	75	-2.9	-1	0	-2.4
	Yr	0	7	.000	8	8	8	0	0	68	111	14.7	0	45	6.0	19	2.5	9.26	42	.383	.466	-41	-40	102	75	-3.3	-2	0	-2.9

YEAR	TM/L	W	L	PCT	G	GS	CG	SHO	SV	IP	H	H/G	HR	BB	BB/G	SO	SO/G	ERA	/A	OAVG	OOBP	PR	/A	PF	CPI	WAT	PB	PD	TPI
■ **O'NEILL**	O'Neill b:Bedford, Pa. Deb: 10/09/1875																												
1875	Atl-n	0	4	.000	4																								
■ **TIP O'NEILL**	O'Neill, James Edward b: 5/25/1858, Woodstock, Ont., Canada d: 12/31/15, Woodstock, Ont., Canada. BR/TR, 6'1.5", 167 lbs. Deb: 5/05/1883																												
1883	NY-N	5	12	.294	19	19	15	0	0	148	182	11.1	5	64	3.9	55	3.3	4.07	78	.310	.378	-15	-15	101	116	-3.6	-2	0	-1.3
1884	StL-a	11	4	.733	17	14	14	0	0	141	125	8.0	3	51	3.3	36	2.3	2.68	131	.246	.314	9	13	109	**122**	2.4	4	0	1.2
Total	2	16	16	.500	36	33	29	0	0	289	307	9.6	8	115	3.6	91	2.8	3.39	98	.280	.349	-7	-2	105	119	-1.2	2	0	-0.1
■ **HARRY O'NEILL**	O'Neill, Joseph Henry b: 2/20/1897, Ridgetown, Ont., Canada d: 9/5/69, Ridgetown, Ont., Can. BR/TR, 6', 180 lbs. Deb: 9/15/22																												
1922	Phi-A	0	0	—	1	0	0	0	0	3	2	6.0	0	1	3.0	0	0.0	3.00	143	.200	.333	0	0	106	85	0.0	-0	0	0.0
1923	Phi-A	0	0	—	3	0	0	0	0	2	1	4.5	0	3	13.5	2	9.0	0.00	—	.167	.444	1	1	102	0	0.0	0	0	0.1
Total	2	0	0	—	4	0	0	0	0	5	3	5.4	0	4	7.2	2	3.6	1.80	234	.188	.381	1	1	105	51	0.0	-0	0	0.1
■ **MIKE O'NEILL**	O'Neill, Michael Joyce (played under name of Michael Joyce In 1901) b: 9/7/1877, Galway, Ireland d: 8/12/59, Scranton, Pa. BR/TR, 5'11", 185 lbs. Deb: 9/20/01																												
1901	StL-N	2	2	.500	5	4	4	1	0	41	29	6.4	2	10	2.2	16	3.5	1.32	239	.224	.300	9	8	95	157	-0.1	3	-1	0.8
1902	StL-N	16	15	.516	36	32	29	2	2	288	297	9.3	3	66	2.1	105	3.3	2.91	95	.293	.342	-4	-5	99	103	3.2	9	0	0.8
1903	StL-N	4	13	.235	19	17	12	0	0	115	184	14.4	2	43	3.4	39	3.1	4.77	70	.393	.451	-19	-18	102	133	-2.2	2	1	-1.5
1904	StL-N	10	14	.417	25	24	23	1	0	220	229	9.4	1	50	2.0	68	2.8	2.09	129	.294	.338	16	15	99	146	-1.9	4	1	1.7
Total	4	32	44	.421	85	77	68	4	2	664	739	10.0	8	169	2.3	228	3.1	2.86	100	.309	.360	2	-0	99	126	-1.0	18	1	1.8
■ **PAUL O'NEILL**	O'Neill, Paul Andrew b: 2/25/63, Columbus, Ohio BL/TL, 6'4", 200 lbs. Deb: 9/03/85																												
1987	Cin-N	0	0	—	1	0	0	0	0	2	2	9.0	1	4	18.0	2	9.0	13.50	31	.286	.545	-2	-2	103	92	0.0	0	0	-0.1
■ **EMMETT O'NEILL**	O'Neill, Robert Emmett "Pinky" b: 1/13/18, San Mateo, Cal. BR/TR, 6'3", 185 lbs. Deb: 8/03/43																												
1943	Bos-A	1	4	.200	11	5	1	0	0	58	56	8.7	3	46	7.1	20	3.1	4.50	76	.256	.379	-8	-7	104	104	-1.3	0	0	-0.5
1944	Bos-A	6	11	.353	28	22	8	1	0	152	154	9.1	6	89	5.3	68	4.0	4.62	72	.265	.360	-20	-22	97	91	-2.6	-0	-2	-2.4
1945	Bos-A	8	11	.421	24	22	10	1	0	142	134	8.5	5	117	7.4	55	3.5	5.13	63	.258	.392	-28	-30	96	93	-0.8	2	0	-2.7
1946	Chi-N	0	0	—	1	0	0	0	0	1	0	0.0	0	3	27.0	1	9.0	0.00	—	.000	.500	0	0	93	0	0.0	0	0	0.0
	Chi-A	0	0	—	2	0	0	0	0	4	4	9.0	0	5	11.3	0	0.0	0.00	—	.333	.500	2	2	97	0	0.0	-0	0	0.2
Total	4	15	26	.366	66	49	19	2	0	357	348	8.8	14	260	6.6	144	3.6	4.74	70	.261	.378	-54	-57	98	92	-4.7	2	-2	-5.4
■ **STEVE ONTIVEROS**	Ontiveros, Steven b: 3/5/61, Tularosa, N.Mex. BR/TR, 6', 180 lbs. Deb: 6/14/85																												
1985	Oak-A	1	3	.250	39	0	0	0	8	75	45	5.4	4	19	2.3	36	4.3	1.92	201	.174	.232	19	16	93	72	-0.9	0	1	1.7
1986	Oak-A	2	2	.500	46	0	0	0	10	73	72	8.9	10	25	3.1	54	6.7	4.68	84	.265	.321	-4	-6	94	93	0.1	0	0	-0.5
1987	Oak-A	10	8	.556	35	22	2	1	1	151	141	8.4	19	50	3.0	97	5.8	3.99	102	.242	.302	8	1	91	90	1.1	0	2	0.3
1988	Oak-A	3	4	.429	10	10	0	0	0	55	57	9.3	4	21	3.4	30	4.9	4.58	81	.265	.324	-4	-5	93	85	-1.1	0	1	-0.3
Total	4	16	17	.485	130	32	2	1	19	354	315	8.0	37	115	2.9	217	5.5	3.79	104	.237	.296	19	6	92	86	-0.8	0	4	1.2
■ **JOSE OQUENDO**	Oquendo, Jose Manuel (Contreras) b: 7/4/63, Rio Piedras, P.R. BB/TR, 5'10", 160 lbs. Deb: 5/02/83																												
1987	StL-N	0	0	—	1	0	0	0	0	1	4	36.0	0	1	9.0	0	0.0	27.00	15	.571	.667	-3	-3	97	82	0.0	0	0	-0.1
1988	StL-N	0	1	.000	1	0	0	0	0	4	4	9.0	0	6	13.5	1	2.3	4.50	80	.267	.476	-0	-0	105	146	-0.4	0	-0	0.0
Total	2	0	1	.000	2	0	0	0	0	5	8	14.4	0	7	12.6	1	1.8	9.00	41	.364	.533	-3	-3	103	133	-0.4	1	-0	-0.1
■ **DON O'RILEY**	O'Riley, Donald Lee b: 3/12/45, Topeka, Kan. BR/TR, 6'3", 205 lbs. Deb: 6/20/69																												
1969	KC-A	1	1	.500	18	0	0	0	1	23	32	12.5	0	15	5.9	10	3.9	7.04	54	.311	.388	-9	-8	104	74	0.1	-0	-0	-0.8
1970	KC-A	0	0	—	9	2	0	0	0	23	26	10.2	5	9	3.5	13	5.1	5.48	68	.277	.340	-4	-5	100	97	0.0	-0	-0	-0.4
Total	2	1	1	.500	27	2	0	0	1	46	58	11.3	5	24	4.7	23	4.5	6.26	60	.294	.366	-13	-13	102	85	0.1	-1	-1	-1.2
■ **JESSE OROSCO**	Orosco, Jesse b: 4/21/57, Santa Barbara, Cal. BR/TL, 6'2", 174 lbs. Deb: 4/05/79																												
1979	NY-N	1	2	.333	18	2	0	0	0	35	33	8.5	4	22	5.7	22	5.7	4.89	74	.260	.370	-4	-5	96	100	-0.1	-1	1	-0.4
1981	NY-N	0	1	.000	8	0	0	0	1	17	13	6.9	2	6	3.2	18	9.5	1.59	225	.213	.275	4	4	103	180	-0.4	-0	0	0.4
1982	NY-N	4	10	.286	54	2	0	0	4	109	92	7.6	7	40	3.3	89	7.3	2.72	132	.230	.297	11	11	100	107	-2.0	-0	0	1.1
1983	NY-N	13	7	.650	62	0	0	0	17	110	76	6.2	3	38	3.1	84	6.9	1.47	247	.197	.266	**26**	**26**	100	121	4.3	1	1	3.0
1984	NY-N	10	6	.625	60	0	0	0	31	87	58	6.0	7	34	3.5	85	8.8	2.59	139	.185	.265	10	10	100	79	1.4	1	-0	1.1
1985	NY-N	8	6	.571	54	0	0	0	17	79	66	7.5	6	34	3.9	68	7.7	2.73	126	.224	.302	8	6	95	107	-0.3	1	-1	0.7
1986	NY-N	8	6	.571	58	0	0	0	21	81	64	7.1	6	35	3.9	62	6.9	2.33	148	.217	.302	13	10	93	126	-1.0	0	-1	1.0
1987	NY-N	3	9	.250	58	0	0	0	16	77	78	9.1	5	31	3.6	78	9.1	4.44	89	.266	.331	-3	-4	97	90	-3.4	-1	0	-0.4
1988	LA-N	3	2	.600	55	0	0	0	9	53	41	7.0	4	30	5.1	43	7.3	2.72	133	.215	.319	4	5	105	124	0.1	-0	0	0.6
Total	9	50	49	.505	427	4	0	0	116	648	521	7.2	44	270	3.8	549	7.6	2.74	132	.221	.299	67	63	98	109	-1.4	1	1	7.1
■ **O'ROURKE**	O'Rourke Deb:7/09/1872																												
1872	Eck-n	0	1	.000	1																								
■ **JIM O'ROURKE**	O'Rourke, James Henry "Orator Jim" b: 8/24/1852, Bridgeport, Conn. d: 1/8/19, Bridgeport, Conn. BR/TR, 5'8", 185 lbs. Deb: 4/26/1872 MH																												
1883	Buf-N	0	0	—	2	0	0	0	1	7	10	12.9	0	1	1.3	1	1.3	6.43	48	.343	.365	-3	-3	99	73	0.0	1	0	-0.1
1884	Buf-N	0	1	.000	4	0	0	0	1	13	7	4.8	0	1	0.7	3	2.1	2.77	113	.166	.185	0	1	105	2	-0.4	2	0	0.0
Total	2	0	1	.000	6	0	0	0	2	20	17	7.6	0	2	0.9	4	1.8	4.05	77	.238	.259	-2	-2	103	27	-0.4	3	0	-0.1
■ **MIKE O'ROURKE**	O'Rourke, Michael J. Deb: 9/01/1890																												
1890	BB-a	1	2	.333	5	5	5	0	0	41	45	9.9	0	10	2.2	8	1.8	3.95	100	.295	.338	-0	0	103	92	0.1	-0	0	0.0
■ **DAVE ORR**	Orr, David L. b: 9/29/1859, New York, N.Y. d: 6/3/15, Brooklyn, N.Y. BL/TR, 5'11", 250 lbs. Deb: 1883 M																												
1885	NY-a	0	0	—	3	0	0	0	0	10	11	9.9	2	5	4.5	1	0.9	7.20	39	.291	.374	-4	-5	86	82	0.0	2	0	-0.3
■ **JOE ORRELL**	Orrell, Forrest Gordon b: 10/6/17, National City, Cal. BR/TR, 6'4", 210 lbs. Deb: 8/12/43																												
1943	Det-A	0	0	—	10	0	0	0	1	19	18	8.5	0	11	5.2	2	0.9	3.79	90	.257	.369	-1	-1	104	105	0.0	0	-0	0.0
1944	Det-A	2	1	.667	10	2	0	0	0	22	26	10.6	0	11	4.5	10	4.1	2.45	145	.286	.365	2	3	104	173	0.3	0	1	0.4
1945	Det-A	2	3	.400	12	5	1	0	0	48	46	8.6	1	24	4.5	14	2.6	3.00	117	.260	.348	2	3	105	126	-0.7	-1	-0	0.2
Total	3	4	4	.500	32	7	1	0	1	89	90	9.1	1	46	4.7	26	2.6	3.03	116	.266	.357	3	5	104	133	-0.4	-1	1	0.6
■ **PHIL ORTEGA**	Ortega, Filomeno Coronado "Kemo" b: 10/7/39, Gilbert, Ariz. BR/TR, 6'2", 170 lbs. Deb: 9/10/60																												
1960	LA-N	0	0	—	3	1	0	0	0	6	12	18.0	1	5	7.5	4	6.0	18.00	24	.400	.459	-9	-9	114	57	0.0	-0	0	-0.7
1961	LA-N	0	2	.000	4	2	1	0	0	13	10	6.9	6	2	1.4	15	10.4	5.54	74	.208	.240	-2	-2	102	85	-0.9	0	0	-0.1
1962	LA-N	0	2	.000	24	3	0	0	1	54	60	10.0	8	39	6.5	30	5.0	6.83	52	.276	.389	-17	-20	91	84	-0.9	-1	-1	-1.9
1963	LA-N	0	0	—	1	0	0	0	0	1	2	18.0	1	0	0.0	1	9.0	18.00	17	.400	.400	-2	-2	94	80	0.0	0	0	-0.1
1964	LA-N	7	9	.438	34	25	4	3	1	157	149	8.5	22	56	3.2	107	6.1	4.01	81	.249	.313	-8	-14	91	101	-0.9	-0	-2	-1.6
1965	Was-A	12	15	.444	35	29	4	2	0	180	176	8.8	33	97	4.8	88	4.4	5.10	69	.262	.354	-33	-31	102	102	0.4	4	-1	-2.8
1966	Was-A	12	12	.500	33	31	5	1	0	197	158	7.2	29	53	2.4	121	5.5	3.93	84	.218	.272	-11	-14	96	79	1.3	-2	-1	-1.7
1967	Was-A	10	10	.500	34	34	5	2	0	220	189	7.7	16	57	2.3	122	5.0	3.03	111	.231	.283	5	8	104	93	0.6	-3	-1	0.5
1968	Was-A	5	12	.294	31	16	1	1	0	116	115	8.9	12	62	4.8	57	4.4	4.97	56	.263	.351	-26	-28	94	93	-2.4	2	-0	-2.8
1969	Cal-A	0	0	—	5	0	0	0	0	8	13	14.6	3	7	7.9	4	4.5	10.13	36	.333	.435	-6	-6	101	94	0.0	0	0	-0.5
Total	10	46	62	.426	204	141	20	9	2	952	884	8.4	131	378	3.6	549	5.2	4.42	75	.246	.318	-109	-117	98	92	-2.8	-1	-6	-11.7
■ **AL ORTH**	Orth, Albert Lewis "Smiling Al" or "The Curveless Wonder" b: 9/5/1872, Tipton, Ind. d: 10/8/48, Lynchburg, Va. BL/TR, 6', 200 lbs. Deb: 8/15/1895 U																												
1895	Phi-N	8	1	.889	11	10	9	0	1	88	103	10.5	0	22	2.3	25	2.6	3.89	121	.313	.356	9	8	98	98	3.3	4	0	1.0
1896	Phi-N	15	10	.600	25	23	19	0	0	196	244	11.2	10	46	2.1	23	1.1	4.41	101	.328	.367	-1	1	102	101	3.4	2	0	0.3
1897	Phi-N	14	19	.424	36	34	29	2	0	282	349	11.1	12	82	2.6	64	2.0	4.63	90	.327	.375	-10	-15	96	96	0.3	8	2	-0.2
1898	Phi-N	15	13	.536	32	28	25	1	0	250	290	10.4	2	53	1.9	52	1.9	3.02	112	.313	.350	16	10	94	118	0.4	8	0	1.8
1899	Phi-N	14	3	.824	21	15	13	3	1	145	149	9.2	0	19	1.2	35	2.2	2.48	148	.289	.314	22	19	95	105	4.8	1	0	1.9
1900	Phi-N	14	14	.500	33	30	24	2	1	262	302	10.4	4	60	2.1	68	2.3	3.78	96	.312	.353	-2	-5	98	97	-1.3	6	2	0.4
1901	Phi-N	20	12	.625	35	33	30	**6**	1	282	250	8.0	3	32	**1.0**	92	2.9	2.27	147	.260	**.290**	33	33	100	93	1.6	6	2	4.4
1902	Was-A	19	18	.514	38	37	36	1	0	324	367	10.2	18	40	**1.1**	76	2.1	3.97	90	.311	.333	-15	-15	100	91	2.9	2	0	-0.9

YEAR	TM/L	W	L	PCT	G	GS	CG	SHO	SV	IP	H	H/G	HR	BB	BB/G	SO	SO/G	ERA	/A	OAVG	OOBP	PR	/A	PF	CPI	WAT	PB	PD	TPI
1903	Was-A	10	22	.313	36	32	30	2	**2**	280	326	10.5	8	62	2.0	88	2.8	4.34	76	.314	.353	-43	-33	111	91	0.0	9	-1	-1.7
1904	Was-A	3	4	.429	10	7	7	0	0	74	88	10.7	2	15	1.8	23	2.8	4.74	54	.320	.355	-18	-18	99	84	0.9	0	0	-1.7
	NY-A	11	6	.647	20	18	11	2	0	138	122	8.0	0	19	1.2	47	3.1	2.67	107	.259	.288	-1	3	111	77	0.9	2	1	0.8
	Yr	14	10	.583	30	25	18	2	0	212	210	8.9	2	34	1.4	70	3.0	3.40	82	.282	.313	-19	-15	107	77	1.8	0	1	-0.9
1905	NY-A	18	16	.529	40	37	26	6	0	305	273	8.1	8	61	1.8	121	3.6	2.86	95	.263	.304	-7	-5	103	90	2.2	-0	-0	-0.5
1906	NY-A	**27**	17	.614	45	39	**36**	3	0	**339**	317	8.4	2	66	1.8	133	3.5	2.34	136	.272	.311	13	**32**	118	107	1.3	5	-1	**4.5**
1907	NY-A	14	21	.400	36	33	21	2	0	249	244	8.8	2	53	1.9	78	2.8	2.60	107	.281	.322	-2	5	110	103	-3.3	7	2	2.0
1908	NY-A	2	13	.133	21	17	8	1	0	139	134	8.7	4	30	1.9	22	1.4	3.43	70	.255	.300	-16	-16	101	84	-4.6	5	-1	-1.2
1909	NY-A	0	0	—	1	1	0	0	0	3	6	18.0	0	1	3.0	1	3.0	12.00	21	.429	.467	-3	-3	99	66	0.0	0	-0	-0.2
Total	15	204	189	.519	440	394	324	31	6	3356	3564	9.6	75	661	1.8	948	2.5	3.37	101	.295	.332	-24	14	103	97	12.8	65	6	10.7
■ **BABY ORTIZ**	Ortiz, Oliverio (Nunez) b: 12/5/19, Camaguey, Cuba d: 3/27/84, Central Senado, Camaguey, Cuba BR/TR, 6', 190 lbs. Deb: 9/23/44																												
1944	Was-A	0	2	.000	2	2	1	0	0	13	13	9.0	0	6	4.2	4	2.8	6.23	50	.255	.328	-4	-5	91	51	-0.9	-0	-1	-0.4
■ **OSSIE ORWOLL**	Orwoll, Oswald Christian b: 11/17/1900, Portland, Ore. d: 5/8/67, Decorah, Iowa BL/TL, 6', 174 lbs. Deb: 4/13/28																												
1928	Phi-A	6	5	.545	27	8	3	0	2	106	110	9.3	7	50	4.2	53	4.5	4.58	87	.274	.342	-6	-7	99	95	-0.8	7	-0	-0.6
1929	Phi-A	0	2	.000	12	0	0	0	1	30	32	9.6	6	6	1.8	12	3.6	4.80	92	.278	.304	-2	-1	104	97	-0.9	1	0	0.0
Total	2	6	7	.462	39	8	3	0	3	136	142	9.4	13	56	3.7	65	4.3	4.63	88	.275	.334	-8	-8	100	96	-1.7	7	-0	-0.6
■ **OZZIE OSBORN**	Osborn, Danny Leon b: 6/19/46, Springfield, Mo. BR/TR, 6'2", 195 lbs. Deb: 4/26/75																												
1975	Chi-A	3	0	1.000	24	0	0	0	0	58	57	8.8	2	37	5.7	38	5.9	4.50	87	.265	.372	-5	-4	104	97	1.5	0	-1	-0.4
■ **BOB OSBORN**	Osborn, John Bode b: 4/17/03, San Diego, Tex. d: 4/19/60, Paris, Ark. BR/TR, 6'1", 175 lbs. Deb: 9/16/25																												
1925	Chi-N	0	0	—	1	0	0	0	0	2	6	27.0	0	0	0.0	0	0.0	0.00	—	.600	.545	1	1	98	0	0.0	0	0	0.1
1926	Chi-N	6	5	.545	31	15	6	0	1	136	157	10.4	3	58	3.8	43	2.8	3.64	110	.301	.355	3	5	105	124	0.2	-3	2	0.5
1927	Chi-N	5	5	.500	24	12	2	0	0	108	125	10.4	2	48	4.0	45	3.8	4.17	93	.294	.359	-3	-4	99	105	-0.4	-0	-1	-0.3
1929	Chi-N	0	0	—	3	1	0	0	0	9	8	8.0	0	2	2.0	1	1.0	3.00	154	.242	.278	2	2	98	79	0.0	0	-0	0.1
1930	Chi-N	10	6	.625	35	13	3	0	1	127	147	10.4	9	53	3.8	42	3.0	4.96	103	.300	.357	0	2	103	101	0.9	-5	2	0.0
1931	Pit-N	6	1	.857	27	2	0	0	0	65	85	11.8	3	20	2.8	9	1.2	4.98	79	.316	.359	-8	-8	102	100	2.6	-0	-1	-0.8
Total	6	27	17	.614	121	43	11	0	2	447	528	10.6	17	181	3.6	140	2.8	4.31	100	.302	.357	-5	-1	102	108	3.3	-8	3	-0.4
■ **PAT OSBORN**	Osborn, Larry Patrick b: 5/4/49, Murray, Ky. BL/TL, 6'4", 195 lbs. Deb: 4/13/74																												
1974	Cin-N	0	0	—	6	0	0	0	0	9	11	11.0	2	4	4.0	4	4.0	8.00	44	.297	.357	-4	-5	96	74	0.0	-0	0	-0.3
1975	Mil-A	0	1	.000	6	1	0	0	0	12	19	14.3	2	9	6.8	1	0.8	5.25	73	.404	.492	-2	-2	101	188	-0.4	0	0	-0.1
Total	2	0	1	.000	12	1	0	0	0	21	30	12.9	4	13	5.6	5	2.1	6.43	57	.357	.437	-6	-6	99	139	-0.4	-0	1	-0.4
■ **TINY OSBORNE**	Osborne, Earnest Preston b: 4/9/1893, Porterdale, Ga. d: 1/5/69, Atlanta, Ga. BL/TR, 6'4.5", 215 lbs. Deb: 4/15/22																												
1922	Chi-N	9	5	.643	41	14	7	1	3	184	183	9.0	7	95	4.6	81	4.0	4.50	87	.271	.356	-8	-12	96	93	1.9	-3	-3	-1.6
1923	Chi-N	8	15	.348	37	25	8	1	1	180	174	8.7	14	89	4.4	69	3.5	4.55	91	.255	.334	-11	-8	103	84	-4.4	-2	-1	-0.9
1924	Chi-N	0	0	—	2	0	0	0	1	3	3	9.0	0	2	6.0	2	6.0	3.00	130	.300	.385	0	0	101	170	0.0	0	0	0.0
	Bro-N	6	5	.545	21	13	6	0	0	104	123	10.6	1	54	4.7	52	4.5	5.11	74	.298	.375	-14	-15	98	92	-0.4	1	-1	-1.4
	Yr	6	5	.545	23	13	6	0	1	107	126	10.6	1	56	4.7	54	4.5	5.05	75	.298	.375	-14	-15	98	92	-0.4	0	-1	-1.4
1925	Bro-N	8	15	.348	41	22	10	0	1	175	210	10.8	9	75	3.9	59	3.0	4.94	82	.304	.365	-13	-17	95	99	-2.7	2	-2	-1.5
Total	4	31	40	.437	142	74	31	2	6	646	693	9.7	31	315	4.4	263	3.7	4.72	85	.280	.356	-46	-52	98	92	-5.6	-3	-6	-5.4
■ **FRED OSBORNE**	Osborne, Frederick W. b: Hampton, Iowa Deb: 7/14/1890																												
1890	Pit-N	0	5	.000	8	5	5	0	0	58	82	12.7	6	45	7.0	14	2.2	8.38	40	.350	.455	-31	-32	95	85	-2.4	1	0	-2.4
■ **WAYNE OSBORNE**	Osborne, Wayne Harold "Ossie" or "Fish Hook" b: 10/11/12, Watsonville, Cal. d: 3/13/87, Camas, Wash. BL/TR, 6'2.5", 172 lbs. Deb: 4/18/35																												
1935	Pit-N	0	0	—	2	0	0	0	0	1	1	9.0	0	0	0.0	1	9.0	9.00	47	.250	.200	-1	-1	105	21	0.0	0	0	0.0
1936	Bos-N	1	1	.500	5	3	0	0	0	20	31	13.9	1	9	4.0	8	3.6	5.85	66	.352	.408	-4	-4	96	111	0.1	0	0	-0.3
Total	2	1	1	.500	7	3	0	0	0	21	32	13.7	1	9	3.9	9	3.9	6.00	65	.348	.398	-5	-5	97	107	0.1	0	0	-0.3
■ **CHARLIE OSGOOD**	Osgood, Charles Benjamin b: 11/23/26, Somerville, Mass. BR/TR, 5'10", 180 lbs. Deb: 6/18/44																												
1944	Bro-N	0	0	—	1	0	0	0	0	3	2	6.0	0	3	9.0	0	0.0	3.00	123	.222	.462	0	0	102	179	0.0	0	0	0.0
■ **DAN OSINSKI**	Osinski, Daniel b: 11/17/33, Chicago, Ill. BR/TR, 6'1.5", 190 lbs. Deb: 4/11/62																												
1962	KC-A	0	0	—	4	0	0	0	0	5	8	14.4	1	8	14.4	4	7.2	16.20	25	.381	.533	-7	-7	101	72	0.0	0	0	-0.5
	LA-A	6	4	.600	33	0	0	0	4	54	45	7.5	3	30	5.0	44	7.3	2.83	143	.223	.315	7	7	102	111	0.8	-1	0	0.7
	Yr	6	4	.600	37	0	0	0	4	59	53	8.1	4	38	5.8	48	7.3	3.97	102	.237	.340	0	1	102	111	0.8	0	0	0.2
1963	LA-A	8	8	.500	47	16	4	1	0	159	145	8.2	15	80	4.5	100	5.7	3.28	102	.242	.328	6	1	92	117	1.0	-2	-1	-0.1
1964	LA-A	3	3	.500	47	4	1	1	2	93	87	8.4	8	39	3.8	88	8.5	3.48	92	.244	.318	1	-3	89	101	0.0	-1	1	-0.2
1965	Mil-N	0	3	.000	61	0	0	0	6	83	81	8.8	4	40	4.3	54	5.9	2.82	129	.261	.339	7	8	103	140	-1.4	-0	0	0.8
1966	Bos-A	4	3	.571	44	1	0	0	2	67	68	9.1	8	28	3.8	44	5.9	3.63	105	.274	.340	-1	1	110	130	0.8	0	-0	0.1
1967	Bos-A	3	1	.750	34	0	0	0	2	64	61	8.6	5	14	2.0	38	5.3	2.53	144	.243	.280	5	8	113	114	0.9	1	-0	1.0
1969	Chi-A	5	5	.500	51	0	0	0	2	61	56	8.3	3	23	3.4	27	4.0	3.54	112	.251	.312	1	3	110	94	0.7	-0	2	0.5
1970	Hou-N	0	1	.000	3	0	0	0	0	4	5	11.3	0	2	4.5	1	2.3	9.00	42	.357	.389	-2	-2	94	69	-0.4	0	-0	-0.1
Total	8	29	28	.509	324	21	5	2	18	590	556	8.5	47	264	4.0	400	6.1	3.34	108	.250	.324	16	17	100	115	2.4	-3	1	2.2
■ **CLAUDE OSTEEN**	Osteen, Claude Wilson b: 8/9/39, Caney Springs, Tenn. BL/TL, 5'11", 160 lbs. Deb: 7/06/57 C																												
1957	Cin-N	0	0	—	3	0	0	0	0	4	4	9.0	0	3	6.8	3	6.8	2.25	183	.250	.368	1	1	106	167	0.0	-0	0	0.1
1959	Cin-N	0	0	—	2	0	0	0	0	8	11	12.4	1	9	10.1	3	3.4	6.75	60	.333	.455	-2	-2	103	122	0.0	-0	0	-0.2
1960	Cin-N	0	1	.000	20	3	0	0	0	48	53	9.9	5	30	5.6	15	2.8	5.06	74	.293	.387	-7	-7	99	112	-0.4	-1	0	-0.7
1961	Cin-N	0	0	—	1	0	0	0	0	⅓	0	0.0	0	0	0.0	0	0.0	0.00	—	.000	.000	0	0	103	0	0.0	0	0	0.0
	Was-A	1	1	.500	3	3	0	0	0	18	14	7.0	3	9	4.5	14	7.0	5.00	78	.219	.316	-2	-2	97	80	0.2	-0	0	-0.1
1962	Was-A	8	13	.381	28	22	7	2	1	150	140	8.4	12	47	2.8	59	3.5	3.66	111	.246	.305	5	7	102	91	0.2	1	0	0.8
1963	Was-A	9	14	.391	40	29	8	2	0	212	222	9.4	23	60	2.5	109	4.6	3.35	109	.270	.314	7	7	101	120	0.9	1	-1	0.7
1964	Was-A	15	13	.536	37	36	13	0	0	257	256	9.0	20	64	2.2	133	4.7	3.33	113	.259	.302	9	12	103	101	4.0	1	2	1.6
1965	LA-N	15	15	.500	40	40	9	1	0	287	253	7.9	19	78	2.4	162	5.1	2.79	114	.236	.286	24	13	90	102	-2.8	-1	6	1.8
1966	LA-N	17	14	.548	39	38	8	3	0	240	238	8.9	6	65	2.4	137	5.1	2.85	120	.261	.303	20	15	95	107	-1.1	5	1	2.3
1967	LA-N	17	17	.500	39	39	14	5	0	288	298	9.3	19	52	1.6	152	4.8	3.22	93	.270	.297	5	-7	89	106	1.9	6	0	-0.1
1968	LA-N	12	18	.400	39	36	5	3	0	254	267	9.5	14	54	1.9	119	4.2	3.08	88	.275	.310	-3	-10	91	114	-2.5	2	1	-0.8
1969	LA-N	20	15	.571	41	41	16	7	0	321	293	8.2	17	74	2.1	183	5.1	2.66	132	.245	.289	33	30	97	107	2.1	5	3	4.1
1970	LA-N	16	14	.533	37	37	11	4	0	259	280	9.7	24	52	1.8	114	4.0	3.82	94	.276	.310	7	-6	89	102	-0.1	5	-0	-0.2
1971	LA-N	14	11	.560	38	38	11	4	0	259	262	9.1	25	63	2.2	109	3.8	3.51	97	.266	.306	-1	-3	98	104	0.3	2	6	0.4
1972	LA-N	20	11	.645	33	33	14	4	0	252	232	8.3	16	69	2.5	100	3.6	2.64	122	.245	.295	23	16	93	113	3.9	10	-0	2.8
1973	LA-N	16	11	.593	33	33	12	3	0	237	227	8.6	20	61	2.3	86	3.3	3.30	110	.258	.302	10	9	99	103	0.1	-1	2	1.0
1974	Hou-N	9	9	.500	23	21	7	2	0	138	158	10.3	8	47	3.1	45	2.9	3.72	95	.292	.344	-1	-3	98	116	0.0	3	0	0.0
	StL-N	0	2	.000	8	2	0	0	0	23	26	10.2	1	11	4.3	6	2.3	4.30	87	.286	.356	-2	-1	103	101	-0.9	-1	0	-0.1
	Yr	9	11	.450	31	23	7	2	0	161	184	10.3	9	58	3.2	51	2.9	3.80	94	.288	.343	-3	-4	98	101	-0.9	3	0	-0.1
1975	Chi-A	7	16	.304	37	37	5	0	0	204	237	10.5	16	92	4.1	63	2.8	4.37	90	.294	.360	-13	-10	104	110	-4.3	0	1	-0.8
Total	18	196	195	.501	541	488	140	40	1	3459	3471	9.0	249	940	2.4	1612	4.2	3.30	104	.263	.309	111	56	96	107	1.5	36	20	12.6
■ **DARRELL OSTEEN**	Osteen, Milton Darrell b: 2/14/43, Oklahoma City, Okla BR/TR, 6'1", 170 lbs. Deb: 9/02/65																												
1965	Cin-N	0	0	—	3	0	0	0	0	3	2	6.0	0	4	12.0	1	3.0	0.00	—	.200	.429	1	1	102	0	0.0	0	0	0.1
1966	Cin-N	0	2	.000	13	0	0	0	1	15	26	15.6	3	9	5.4	17	10.2	12.00	34	.371	.443	-14	-13	114	72	-0.9	0	-0	-1.2
1967	Cin-N	0	2	.000	10	0	0	0	2	14	10	6.4	1	13	8.4	13	8.4	6.43	57	.196	.382	-5	-4	109	66	-0.9	-0	0	-0.3
1970	Oak-A	1	0	1.000	3	1	0	0	0	6	9	13.5	0	3	4.5	3	4.5	6.00	59	.346	.414	-2	-2	96	98	0.5	-0	0	-0.1
Total	4	1	4	.200	29	1	0	0	3	38	47	11.1	4	29	6.9	34	8.1	8.05	47	.299	.416	-19	-18	108	68	-1.3	-0	0	-1.5

YEAR	TM/L	W	L	PCT	G	GS	CG	SHO	SV	IP	H	H/G	HR	BB	BB/G	SO	SO/G	ERA	/A	OAVG	OOBP	PR	/A	PF	CPI	WAT	PB	PD	TPI
■ **FRED OSTENDORF**	Ostendorf, Frederick K. b: 8/5/1890, Baltimore, Md. d: 3/2/65, Keoughtan, Va. BL/TL, 6'.5 ", 169 lbs. Deb: 7/16/14																												
1914	Ind-F	0	0	—	1	0	0	0	0	2	5	22.5	0	2	9.0	0	0.0	22.50	15	.505	.588	-4	-4	108	55	0.0	-0	0	-0.3
■ **BILL OSTER**	Oster, William Charles b: 1/2/33, New York, N.Y. BL/TL, 6'3", 198 lbs. Deb: 8/23/54																												
1954	Phi-A	0	1	.000	8	1	0	0	0	16	19	10.7	2	12	6.8	5	2.8	6.19	63	.311	.413	-4	-4	105	105	-0.4	0	0	-0.3
■ **FRITZ OSTERMUELLER**	Ostermueller, Frederick Raymond b: 9/15/07, Quincy, Ill. d: 12/17/57, Quincy, Ill. BL/TL, 5'11", 175 lbs. Deb: 4/21/34																												
1934	Bos-A	10	13	.435	33	23	10	0	3	199	200	9.0	7	99	4.5	75	3.4	3.48	136	.262	.341	22	28	105	116	-1.6	-1	3	2.8
1935	Bos-A	7	8	.467	22	19	10	0	1	138	135	8.8	0	78	5.1	41	2.7	3.91	123	.257	.351	8	14	108	98	-0.6	1	-0	1.5
1936	Bos-A	10	16	.385	43	23	7	1	2	181	210	10.4	8	84	4.2	90	4.5	4.87	109	.288	.360	3	9	106	99	-2.9	0	2	1.1
1937	Bos-A	3	7	.300	25	7	2	0	1	87	101	10.4	2	44	4.6	29	3.0	4.97	95	.286	.363	-3	-2	102	91	-2.1	3	0	0.1
1938	Bos-A	13	5	.722	31	18	10	1	2	177	199	10.1	15	58	2.9	46	2.3	4.58	105	.275	.327	4	4	100	92	3.2	2	-0	0.5
1939	Bos-A	11	7	.611	34	20	8	0	4	159	173	9.8	6	58	3.3	61	3.5	4.25	116	.277	.332	7	12	107	97	0.5	-2	-0	0.9
1940	Bos-A	5	9	.357	31	16	5	0	0	144	166	10.4	7	70	4.4	80	5.0	4.94	89	.284	.356	-9	-9	100	94	-2.4	4	-1	-0.4
1941	StL-A	0	3	.000	15	2	0	0	0	46	45	8.8	3	23	4.5	20	3.9	4.50	93	.257	.340	-2	-2	101	91	-1.4	0	0	0.0
1942	StL-A	3	1	.750	10	4	2	0	0	44	46	9.4	4	17	3.5	21	4.3	3.68	102	.266	.330	-0	0	102	112	0.9	-0	-1	0.0
1943	StL-A	0	2	.000	11	3	0	0	0	29	36	11.2	1	13	4.0	4	1.2	4.97	67	.321	.386	-5	-5	101	107	-0.9	0	0	-0.4
	Bro-N	1	1	.500	7	1	0	0	0	27	21	7.0	0	12	4.0	15	5.0	3.33	100	.212	.295	0	0	99	64	0.0	-1	-0	-0.1
1944	Bro-N	2	1	.667	10	4	3	0	1	42	46	9.9	3	12	2.6	17	3.6	3.21	114	.267	.309	2	2	102	113	0.7	-0	-0	0.1
	Pit-N	11	7	.611	28	24	14	1	1	205	201	8.8	7	65	2.9	80	3.5	2.72	137	.260	.311	20	23	104	123	0.6	2	-1	2.7
	Yr	13	8	.619	38	28	17	1	2	247	247	9.0	10	77	2.8	97	3.5	2.81	133	.261	.310	22	25	103	123	1.3	-0	-1	2.8
1945	Pit-N	5	4	.556	14	11	4	1	0	81	74	8.2	6	37	4.1	29	3.2	4.56	85	.236	.314	-7	-6	102	75	0.2	3	0	-0.2
1946	Pit-N	13	10	.565	27	25	16	2	0	193	193	9.0	5	56	2.6	57	2.7	2.84	127	.263	.311	12	16	106	110	3.4	6	-2	2.4
1947	Pit-N	12	10	.545	26	24	12	3	0	183	181	8.9	18	68	3.3	66	3.2	3.84	108	.254	.317	5	6	102	97	3.0	0	-2	0.5
1948	Pit-N	8	11	.421	23	22	10	2	0	134	143	9.6	13	41	2.8	43	2.9	4.43	93	.262	.310	-7	-5	104	85	-2.2	-0	-1	-0.5
Total	15	114	115	.498	390	246	113	11	15	2069	2170	9.4	105	835	3.6	774	3.4	3.99	109	.268	.332	51	87	104	101	-1.6	16	-3	11.0
■ **JOE OSTROWSKI**	Ostrowski, Joseph Paul "Professor" or "Specs" b: 11/15/16, W.Wyoming, Pa. BL/TL, 6', 180 lbs. Deb: 7/18/48																												
1948	StL-A	4	6	.400	26	9	3	0	3	78	108	12.5	6	17	2.0	20	2.3	6.00	78	.333	.360	-15	-12	109	92	0.1	1	2	-0.7
1949	StL-A	8	8	.500	40	13	4	0	2	141	185	11.8	16	27	1.7	34	2.2	4.79	91	.307	.334	-9	-7	104	99	2.1	3	-1	-0.4
1950	StL-A	2	4	.333	9	7	2	0	0	57	57	9.0	2	7	1.1	15	2.4	2.53	201	.251	.270	13	16	111	96	-0.3	2	-1	1.8
	NY-A	1	1	.500	21	4	1	0	3	44	50	10.2	11	15	3.1	15	3.1	5.11	86	.294	.351	-3	-4	96	118	-0.1	-0	0	-0.2
	Yr	3	5	.375	30	11	3	0	3	101	107	9.5	13	22	2.0	30	2.7	3.65	131	.270	.306	10	13	104	118	-0.4	2	-1	1.6
1951	NY-A	6	4	.600	34	3	2	0	5	95	103	9.8	4	18	1.7	30	2.8	3.51	104	.279	.308	6	1	88	102	-0.2	-2	-0	0.0
1952	NY-A	2	2	.500	20	1	0	0	2	40	56	12.6	5	14	3.1	17	3.8	5.62	62	.327	.374	-9	-10	95	106	-0.3	-1	-1	-1.0
Total	5	23	25	.479	150	37	12	0	15	455	559	11.1	44	98	1.9	131	2.6	4.55	94	.300	.331	-16	-14	101	101	1.3	2	-1	-0.5
■ **BILL OTEY**	Otey, William Tilford "Steamboat Bill" b: 12/16/1886, Dayton, Ohio d: 4/23/31, Dayton, Ohio BL/TL, 6'2", 181 lbs. Deb: 9/27/07																												
1907	Pit-N	0	1	.000	3	2	1	0	0	16	23	12.9	1	4	2.3	5	2.8	4.50	56	.375	.422	-4	-4	102	123	-0.4	0	-0	-0.3
1910	Was-A	0	1	.000	9	1	1	0	0	35	40	10.3	1	6	1.5	12	3.1	3.34	77	.301	.336	-3	-3	102	111	-0.4	2	-1	-0.4
1911	Was-A	1	3	.250	12	2	0	0	0	50	68	12.2	2	15	2.7	16	2.9	6.30	53	.333	.387	-16	-17	99	82	-0.7	-2	1	-1.4
Total	3	1	5	.167	24	5	2	0	0	101	131	11.7	4	25	2.2	33	2.9	4.99	59	.329	.376	-23	-23	101	98	-1.5	0	-1	-2.1
■ **HARRY OTIS**	Otis, Harry George "Cannonball" b: 10/5/1886, W.New York, N.J. d: 1/29/76, Teaneck, N.J. TL , 6' ", 180 lbs. Deb: 9/05/09																												
1909	Cle-A	2	2	.500	5	3	0	0	0	26	26	9.0	0	18	6.2	6	2.1	1.38	184	.283	.416	3	3	103	331	0.1	-0	0	0.4
■ **DENNIS O'TOOLE**	O'Toole, Dennis Joseph b: 3/13/49, Chicago, Ill. BR/TR, 6'3", 195 lbs. Deb: 9/08/69																												
1969	Chi-A	0	0	—	2	0	0	0	0	4	5	11.3	0	2	4.5	4	9.0	6.75	59	.333	.389	-1	-1	110	80	0.0	0	0	0.0
1970	Chi-A	0	0	—	3	0	0	0	0	3	5	15.0	0	2	6.0	3	9.0	3.00	134	.357	.412	0	0	108	225	0.0	0	0	0.0
1971	Chi-A	0	0	—	1	0	0	0	0	2	0	0.0	0	1	4.5	2	9.0	0.00	—	.000	.143	1	1	97	0	0.0	0	0	0.1
1972	Chi-A	0	0	—	3	0	0	0	0	5	10	18.0	0	2	3.6	5	9.0	5.40	60	.417	.462	-1	-1	106	148	0.0	0	0	0.0
1973	Chi-A	0	0	—	6	0	0	0	0	16	23	12.9	3	3	1.7	8	4.5	5.63	70	.329	.351	-3	-3	103	104	0.0	0	0	-0.2
Total	5	0	0	—	15	0	0	0	0	30	43	12.9	3	10	3.0	22	6.6	5.10	75	.333	.373	-5	-4	104	114	0.0	0	0	-0.1
■ **JIM O'TOOLE**	O'Toole, James Jerome b: 1/10/37, Chicago, Ill. BB/TL, 6', 190 lbs. Deb: 9/26/58																												
1958	Cin-N	0	1	.000	1	1	0	0	0	7	4	5.1	0	5	6.4	4	5.1	1.29	326	.154	.290	2	2	106	88	-0.4	-0	-0	0.2
1959	Cin-N	5	8	.385	28	19	3	1	0	129	144	10.0	14	73	5.1	68	4.7	5.16	79	.287	.373	-17	-16	103	103	-1.3	-0	0	-1.4
1960	Cin-N	12	12	.500	34	31	7	2	1	196	198	9.1	14	66	3.0	124	5.7	3.81	98	.263	.321	-1	-2	99	98	1.6	-3	-3	-0.7
1961	Cin-N	19	9	.679	39	35	11	3	2	253	229	8.1	16	93	3.3	178	6.3	3.09	134	.240	.306	26	29	103	100	3.1	-1	-0	2.9
1962	Cin-N	16	13	.552	36	34	11	3	0	252	222	7.9	20	87	3.1	170	6.1	3.50	113	.238	.302	12	13	100	91	-1.4	-4	-2	0.6
1963	Cin-N	17	14	.548	33	32	12	5	0	234	208	8.0	13	57	2.2	146	5.6	2.88	118	.239	.281	10	13	103	93	0.7	-1	-3	1.1
1964	Cin-N	17	7	.708	30	30	9	3	0	220	194	7.9	8	51	2.1	145	5.9	2.66	135	.235	.276	21	23	102	91	4.3	-1	-2	2.2
1965	Cin-N	3	10	.231	29	22	2	0	1	128	154	10.8	14	47	3.3	71	5.0	5.91	61	.294	.349	-34	-33	102	84	-3.8	-2	-1	-3.4
1966	Cin-N	5	7	.417	25	24	2	0	0	142	139	8.8	16	49	3.1	96	6.1	3.55	116	.254	.315	1	9	114	106	-0.7	-2	-1	0.7
1967	Chi-A	4	3	.571	15	10	1	1	0	54	53	8.8	4	18	3.0	37	6.2	2.83	106	.251	.309	2	1	93	122	0.2	-1	-0	0.0
Total	10	98	84	.538	270	238	58	18	4	1615	1545	8.6	119	546	3.0	1039	5.8	3.57	106	.251	.310	24	40	102	96	2.3	-16	-12	2.2
■ **MARTY O'TOOLE**	O'Toole, Martin James b: 11/27/1888, Wm.Penn, Pa. d: 2/18/49, Aberdeen, Wash. BR/TR, 5'11", 175 lbs. Deb: 9/21/08																												
1908	Cin-N	1	0	1.000	3	2	1	0	0	15	15	9.0	0	7	4.2	5	3.0	2.40	102	.289	.374	-0	0	104	143	0.5	-0	0	0.0
1911	Pit-N	3	2	.600	5	5	3	0	0	38	28	6.6	1	20	4.7	34	8.1	2.37	140	.215	.320	4	4	97	113	0.3	2	0	0.6
1912	Pit-N	15	17	.469	37	36	17	5	0	275	237	7.8	4	159	5.2	150	4.9	2.72	120	.235	.340	21	16	95	106	-4.5	2	1	1.8
1913	Pit-N	6	8	.429	26	15	7	0	1	145	148	9.2	3	55	3.4	58	3.6	3.29	92	.271	.331	-1	-4	94	107	-1.3	-2	-0	-0.6
1914	Pit-N	1	8	.111	19	9	1	0	1	92	92	9.0	3	47	4.6	36	3.5	4.70	55	.270	.345	-20	-22	93	80	-3.3	1	-1	-2.1
	NY-N	1	1	.500	10	5	2	0	0	34	34	9.0	0	12	3.2	13	3.4	4.24	62	.262	.319	-5	-6	94	67	0.0	1	-0	-0.5
	Yr	2	9	.182	29	14	3	0	1	126	126	9.0	3	59	4.2	49	3.5	4.57	57	.268	.338	-25	-28	93	67	-3.3	1	-1	-2.6
Total	5	27	36	.429	100	72	31	5	2	599	554	8.3	11	300	4.5	296	4.4	3.22	95	.251	.337	-1	-12	95	101	-8.3	2	0	-0.8
■ **JIM OTTEN**	Otten, James Edward b: 7/1/51, Lewiston, Mont. BR/TR, 6'2", 195 lbs. Deb: 7/31/74																												
1974	Chi-A	0	1	.000	5	1	0	0	0	16	22	12.4	0	12	6.8	11	6.2	5.63	66	.324	.432	-4	-3	102	106	-0.4	0	0	-0.3
1975	Chi-A	0	0	—	2	0	0	0	0	5	4	7.2	1	7	12.6	3	5.4	7.20	55	.235	.423	-2	-2	104	98	0.0	0	0	-0.1
1976	Chi-A	0	0	—	2	0	0	0	0	6	9	13.5	0	2	3.0	3	4.5	4.50	79	.333	.379	-1	-1	101	113	0.0	0	-0	0.0
1980	StL-N	0	5	.000	31	4	0	0	0	55	71	11.6	3	26	4.3	38	6.2	5.56	66	.323	.388	-12	-11	102	101	-2.4	-0	1	-1.0
1981	StL-N	1	0	1.000	24	0	0	0	0	36	44	11.0	3	20	5.0	20	5.0	5.25	67	.321	.403	-7	-7	101	113	0.5	-0	-1	-0.7
Total	5	1	6	.143	64	5	0	0	0	118	150	11.4	7	67	5.1	75	5.7	5.49	66	.320	.400	-25	-24	102	106	-2.3	-0	-0	-2.1
■ **DAVE OTTO**	Otto, David Alan b: 11/12/64, Chicago, Ill. BL/TL, 6'7", 210 lbs. Deb: 9/08/87																												
1987	Oak-A	0	0	—	3	0	0	0	0	6	7	10.5	1	1	1.5	3	4.5	9.00	45	.304	.333	-3	-3	91	58	0.0	0	0	-0.2
1988	Oak-A	0	0	—	3	2	0	0	0	10	9	8.1	0	6	5.4	7	6.3	1.80	206	.243	.349	2	2	93	193	0.0	0	0	0.2
Total	2	0	0	—	6	2	0	0	0	16	16	9.0	1	7	3.9	10	5.6	4.50	85	.267	.343	-1	-1	92	142	0.0	0	0	0.0
■ **ORVAL OVERALL**	Overall, Orval b: 2/2/1881, Visalia, Cal. d: 7/14/47, Fresno, Cal. BB/TR, 6'2", 214 lbs. Deb: 4/16/05																												
1905	Cin-N	18	23	.439	42	39	32	2	0	318	290	8.2	4	147	4.2	173	4.9	2.86	107	.272	.367	5	8	103	116	-3.9	-2	-2	0.6
1906	Cin-N	4	5	.444	13	10	6	0	0	82	77	8.5	1	46	5.0	33	3.6	4.28	71	.279	.390	-15	-11	116	85	0.2	0	-1	-1.2
	Chi-N	12	3	.800	18	14	13	2	1	144	116	7.3	1	51	3.2	94	5.9	1.88	139	.248	.327	12	12	99	124	1.3	-1	0	1.4
	Yr	16	8	.667	31	24	19	2	1	226	193	7.7	2	97	3.9	127	5.1	2.75	101	.258	.346	-3	1	105	124	1.5	0	-1	0.2
1907	Chi-N	23	7	.767	35	29	25	**8**	3	265	199	6.8	3	69	2.3	139	4.7	1.70	148	.237	.303	23	24	102	105	3.8	4	1	3.0
1908	Chi-N	15	11	.577	37	27	16	4	4	225	165	6.6	3	78	3.1	167	**6.7**	1.92	125	.231	.308	11	12	102	100	-1.5	-1	-1	1.3
1909	Chi-N	20	11	.645	38	32	23	**9**	3	285	204	6.4	1	80	2.5	**205**	**6.5**	1.42	174	**.198**	.262	37	33	95	90	-0.9	8	1	3.9
1910	Chi-N	12	6	.667	23	21	11	4	1	145	106	6.6	2	54	3.4	92	5.7	2.67	109	.212	.291	6	4	96	73	0.0	-1	1	0.5
1913	Chi-N	4	5	.444	11	9	6	1	0	68	73	9.7	1	26	3.4	30	4.0	3.31	94	.284	.338	-1	-2	97	116	-1.0	2	1	0.1

YEAR	TM/L	W	L	PCT	G	GS	CG	SHO	SV	IP	H	H/G	HR	BB	BB/G	SO	SO/G	ERA	/A	OAVG	OOBP	PR	/A	PF	CPI	WAT	PB	PD	TPI
Total	7	108	71	.603	217	181	132	30	12	1532	1230	7.2	16	551	3.2	933	5.5	2.24	121	.239	.317	77	80	101	102	-2.0	10	1	9.6
■ **STUBBY OVERMIRE**	Overmire, Frank b: 5/16/19, Moline, Mich. d: 3/3/77, Lakeland, Fla. BR/TL, 5'7", 170 lbs. Deb: 4/25/43 C																												
1943	Det-A	7	6	.538	29	18	8	3	1	147	135	8.3	5	38	2.3	48	2.9	3.18	108	.243	.288	2	4	104	84	0.5	0	-1	0.4
1944	Det-A	11	11	.500	32	28	11	3	1	200	214	9.6	2	41	1.8	57	2.6	3.06	116	.271	.304	8	11	104	99	-1.5	1	2	1.4
1945	Det-A	9	9	.500	31	22	9	0	4	162	189	10.5	6	42	2.3	36	2.0	3.89	91	.294	.333	-9	-7	105	104	-1.2	0	0	-0.5
1946	Det-A	5	7	.417	24	13	3	0	1	97	106	9.8	6	29	2.7	34	3.2	4.64	80	.274	.320	-12	-10	106	79	-1.8	-1	1	-0.9
1947	Det-A	11	5	.688	28	17	7	3	0	141	142	9.1	9	44	2.8	33	2.1	3.77	101	.259	.312	-1	1	103	91	2.6	-1	-0	0.0
1948	Det-A	3	4	.429	37	4	0	0	3	66	89	12.1	5	31	4.2	14	1.9	6.00	69	.326	.383	-13	-14	97	100	-0.5	-1	1	-1.2
1949	Det-A	1	3	.250	14	1	0	0	0	17	29	15.4	2	9	4.8	3	1.6	10.06	44	.377	.438	-11	-11	106	81	-1.0	0	0	-0.8
1950	StL-A	9	12	.429	31	19	8	2	0	161	200	11.2	11	45	2.5	39	2.2	4.19	121	.298	.341	7	16	111	107	1.0	1	-2	1.4
1951	StL-A	1	6	.143	8	7	3	0	0	53	61	10.4	5	21	3.6	13	2.2	3.57	126	.281	.343	3	6	109	127	-2.0	-1	-1	0.4
	NY-A	1	1	.500	15	4	1	0	0	45	50	10.0	2	18	3.6	14	2.8	4.60	79	.287	.354	-2	-5	88	98	-0.1	0	0	-0.3
	Yr	2	7	.222	23	11	4	0	0	98	111	10.2	7	39	3.6	27	2.5	4.04	102	.284	.348	1	1	100	98	-2.1	-1	-1	0.1
1952	StL-A	0	3	.000	17	4	0	0	0	41	44	9.7	3	7	1.5	10	2.2	3.73	98	.270	.297	-0	-0	100	90	-1.4	0	1	0.0
Total	10	58	67	.464	266	137	50	11	10	1130	1259	10.0	56	325	2.6	301	2.4	3.97	98	.280	.325	-29	-10	104	97	-5.4	-0	1	-0.1
■ **MIKE OVERY**	Overy, Harry Michael b: 1/27/51, Clinton, Ill. BR/TR, 6'2", 190 lbs. Deb: 8/14/76																												
1976	Cal-A	0	2	.000	5	0	0	0	0	7	6	7.7	1	3	3.9	8	10.3	6.43	51	.214	.313	-2	-2	93	53	-0.9	0	0	-0.1
■ **ERNIE OVITZ**	Ovitz, Ernest Gayheart b: 10/7/1885, Mineral Point, Wis. d: 9/11/80, Green Bay, Wis. 5'8.5", 156 lbs. Deb: 6/22/11																												
1911	Chi-N	0	0	—	1	0	0	0	0	2	3	13.5	0	3	13.5	0	0.0	4.50	71	.375	.545	-0	-0	94	210	0.0	0	0	0.0
■ **BOB OWCHINKO**	Owchinko, Robert Dennis b: 1/1/55, Detroit, Mich. BL/TL, 6'2", 190 lbs. Deb: 9/25/76																												
1976	SD-N	0	2	.000	2	2	0	0	0	4	11	24.8	0	3	6.8	4	9.0	18.00	17	.478	.519	-6	-7	90	69	-0.9	-0	0	-0.5
1977	SD-N	9	12	.429	30	28	3	2	0	170	191	10.1	20	67	3.5	101	5.3	4.45	79	.287	.347	-10	-18	89	108	0.1	-2	-2	-2.0
1978	SD-N	10	13	.435	36	33	4	1	0	202	198	8.8	14	78	3.5	94	4.2	3.56	93	.263	.325	0	-6	93	107	-2.0	1	-1	-0.5
1979	SD-N	6	12	.333	42	20	2	0	0	149	144	8.7	16	55	3.3	66	4.0	3.74	97	.259	.319	-0	-2	97	105	-2.0	-0	-0	-0.2
1980	Cle-A	2	9	.182	29	14	1	1	0	114	138	10.9	13	47	3.7	66	5.2	5.29	79	.301	.362	-16	-14	103	98	-3.5	0	0	-1.3
1981	Oak-A	4	3	.571	29	0	0	0	2	39	34	7.8	2	19	4.4	26	6.0	3.23	108	.245	.329	2	1	95	112	0.0	0	-0	0.1
1982	Oak-A	2	4	.333	54	0	0	0	3	102	111	9.8	11	52	4.6	67	5.9	5.21	76	.275	.352	-13	-14	96	91	-0.5	0	-1	-1.4
1983	Pit-N	0	0	—	1	0	0	0	0	0	2	—	1	0	—	0	—	∞	—	1.000	1.000	-1	-1	103	194	0.0	0	0	0.0
1984	Cin-N	3	5	.375	49	4	0	0	2	94	91	8.7	10	39	3.7	60	5.7	4.12	94	.253	.319	-5	-3	107	95	-0.5	1	-1	-0.2
1986	Mon-N	1	0	1.000	3	3	0	0	0	15	17	10.2	1	3	1.8	6	3.6	3.60	102	.288	.323	0	0	98	109	0.5	0	-0	0.0
Total	10	37	60	.381	275	104	10	4	7	889	937	9.5	88	363	3.7	490	5.0	4.29	85	.274	.338	-49	-63	96	103	-8.8	0	-4	-6.0
■ **FRANK OWEN**	Owen, Frank Malcolm "Yip" b: 12/23/1879, Ypsilanti, Mich. d: 11/24/42, Dearborn, Mich. TR , Deb: 4/29/01																												
1901	Det-A	1	3	.250	8	5	3	0	0	56	70	11.3	1	30	4.8	17	2.7	4.34	92	.327	.410	-4	-2	109	116	-1.0	-2	2	0.0
1903	Chi-A	8	12	.400	26	20	15	1	1	167	167	9.0	1	44	2.4	66	3.6	3.50	79	.282	.332	-10	-14	94	87	-0.9	-1	4	-0.9
1904	Chi-A	21	15	.583	37	36	34	4	1	315	243	6.9	2	61	1.7	103	2.9	1.94	129	.234	.276	23	20	97	88	0.3	5	6	3.0
1905	Chi-A	21	13	.618	42	38	32	3	0	334	276	7.4	6	56	1.5	125	3.4	2.10	117	.248	.284	20	13	93	99	0.7	-3	3	1.9
1906	Chi-A	22	13	.629	42	36	27	7	0	293	289	8.9	4	54	1.7	66	2.0	2.33	103	.283	.319	12	2	89	120	0.7	-1	4	0.6
1907	Chi-A	2	3	.400	11	4	2	0	0	47	43	8.2	1	13	2.5	15	2.9	2.49	103	.267	.322	0	0	101	107	-0.7	0	1	0.1
1908	Chi-A	6	7	.462	25	14	5	1	0	140	142	9.1	2	37	2.4	48	3.1	3.41	65	.260	.310	-16	-19	93	88	-1.3	1	2	-1.7
1909	Chi-A	1	1	.500	3	2	1	0	0	16	19	10.7	0	3	1.7	3	1.7	4.50	53	.279	.319	-4	-4	97	65	0.0	-0	0	-0.3
Total	8	82	67	.550	194	155	119	16	2	1368	1249	8.2	17	298	2.0	443	2.9	2.55	99	.263	.307	21	-3	94	99	-2.2	-2	21	2.7
■ **JIM OWENS**	Owens, James Philip "Bear" b: 1/16/34, Gifford, Pa. BR/TR, 5'11", 180 lbs. Deb: 4/19/55 C																												
1955	Phi-N	0	2	.000	3	2	0	0	0	9	13	13.0	2	7	7.0	6	6.0	8.00	51	.382	.465	-4	-4	102	117	-0.9	-0	0	-0.3
1956	Phi-N	0	4	.000	10	5	0	0	0	30	35	10.5	3	22	6.6	22	6.6	7.20	50	.313	.418	-11	-12	95	89	-1.9	0	0	-1.0
1958	Phi-N	1	0	1.000	1	1	0	0	0	7	4	5.1	1	5	6.4	3	3.9	2.57	154	.154	.290	1	1	100	87	0.5	0	0	0.1
1959	Phi-N	12	12	.500	31	30	11	1	1	221	203	8.3	14	73	3.0	135	5.5	3.22	125	.244	.303	18	20	102	97	2.0	-1	-1	1.9
1960	Phi-N	4	14	.222	31	22	6	0	0	150	182	10.9	21	64	3.8	83	5.0	5.04	82	.299	.360	-21	-15	110	109	-4.0	-3	-1	-1.8
1961	Phi-N	5	10	.333	20	17	3	0	0	107	119	10.0	8	32	2.7	38	3.2	4.46	88	.287	.330	-5	-6	98	95	0.3	-1	-2	-0.8
1962	Phi-N	2	4	.333	23	12	1	0	0	70	90	11.6	12	33	4.2	21	2.7	6.30	60	.318	.383	-18	-20	95	100	-0.9	0	-1	-1.9
1963	Cin-N	0	2	.000	19	3	0	0	4	42	42	9.0	6	24	5.1	29	6.2	5.36	63	.259	.344	-10	-9	103	88	-0.9	0	0	-0.8
1964	Hou-N	8	7	.533	48	11	0	0	6	118	115	8.8	7	32	2.4	88	6.7	3.28	106	.262	.301	3	3	98	105	1.7	-1	-1	0.0
1965	Hou-N	6	5	.545	50	0	0	0	8	71	64	8.1	4	29	3.7	53	6.7	3.30	98	.238	.304	2	-1	91	95	1.4	-0	-0	0.0
1966	Hou-N	4	7	.364	40	0	0	0	2	50	53	9.5	5	17	3.1	32	5.8	4.68	76	.273	.324	-6	-6	99	89	-1.0	-0	1	-0.5
1967	Hou-N	0	1	.000	10	0	0	0	0	11	12	9.8	1	2	1.6	6	4.9	4.09	79	.308	.326	-1	-1	95	112	-0.4	0	-0	-0.1
Total	12	42	68	.382	286	103	21	1	21	886	932	9.5	84	340	3.5	516	5.2	4.31	88	.273	.332	-52	-51	100	99	-4.1	-7	-5	-5.2
■ **RICK OWNBEY**	Ownbey, Richard Wayne b: 10/20/57, Corona, Cal. BR/TR, 6'3", 185 lbs. Deb: 8/17/82																												
1982	NY-N	1	2	.333	8	8	2	0	0	50	44	7.9	3	43	7.7	28	5.0	3.78	95	.242	.375	-1	-1	100	120	-0.2	1	-1	0.0
1983	NY-N	1	3	.250	10	4	0	0	0	35	31	8.0	4	21	5.4	19	4.9	4.63	78	.240	.349	-4	-4	100	91	-0.7	-0	0	-0.3
1984	StL-N	0	3	.000	4	4	0	0	0	19	23	10.9	1	8	3.8	11	5.2	4.74	75	.303	.352	-2	-3	99	102	-1.4	-0	-0	-0.2
1986	StL-N	1	3	.250	17	3	0	0	0	43	47	9.8	4	19	4.0	25	5.2	3.77	102	.294	.368	-0	0	103	136	-0.9	-1	-1	0.0
Total	4	3	11	.214	39	19	2	0	0	147	145	8.9	12	91	5.6	83	5.1	4.10	90	.265	.364	-7	-7	101	115	-3.2	-1	-1	-0.5
■ **DOC OZMER**	Ozmer, Horace Robert b: 5/25/01, Atlanta, Ga. d: 12/28/70, Atlanta, Ga. BR/TR, 5'10.5", 185 lbs. Deb: 5/11/23																												
1923	Phi-A	0	0	—	1	0	0	0	0	2	1	4.5	0	1	4.5	1	4.5	4.50	90	.167	.250	-0	-0	102	37	0.0	0	0	0.0
■ **CHARLIE PABOR**	Pabor, Charles Henry b: 9/24/1849, New York, N.Y. d: 4/22/13, New Haven, Conn. TL , 5'8", 155 lbs. Deb: 5/04/1871 M																												
1871	Cle-n	0	1	.000	1																								
1872	Cle-n	1	0	1.000	1																								
1875	Atl-n	0	0	—	2																								
Total	3 n	1	1	.500	4																								
■ **JOHN PACELLA**	Pacella, John Lewis b: 9/15/56, Brooklyn, N.Y. BR/TR, 6'3", 195 lbs. Deb: 9/15/77																												
1977	NY-N	0	0	—	3	0	0	0	0	4	2	4.5	0	2	4.5	1	2.3	0.00	—	.133	.235	2	2	97	0	0.0	0	-0	0.1
1979	NY-N	0	2	.000	4	3	0	0	0	16	16	9.0	0	4	2.3	12	6.8	4.50	80	.246	.290	-1	-2	96	49	-0.9	-0	0	-0.1
1980	NY-N	3	4	.429	32	15	0	0	0	84	89	9.5	5	59	6.3	68	7.3	5.14	68	.280	.387	-14	-15	97	99	0.1	-1	-0	-1.6
1982	NY-A	0	1	.000	3	1	0	0	0	10	13	11.7	0	9	8.1	2	1.8	7.20	55	.342	.451	-3	-4	97	100	-0.4	0	-0	-0.3
	Min-A	1	2	.333	21	1	0	0	2	52	61	10.6	14	37	6.4	20	3.5	7.27	57	.299	.402	-18	-18	102	100	-0.1	0	-1	-1.8
	Yr	1	3	.250	24	2	0	0	2	62	74	10.7	14	46	6.7	22	3.2	7.26	57	.301	.407	-22	-22	101	100	-0.5	0	-1	-2.1
1984	Bal-A	0	1	.000	6	1	0	0	0	15	15	9.0	2	9	5.4	8	4.8	6.60	57	.268	.364	-4	-5	94	77	-0.4	0	-0	-0.4
1986	Det-A	0	0	—	5	0	0	0	1	11	10	8.2	0	13	10.6	5	4.1	4.09	97	.294	.451	0	-0	95	161	0.0	0	1	0.1
Total	6	4	10	.286	74	21	0	0	3	192	206	9.7	21	133	6.2	116	5.4	5.72	66	.282	.386	-40	-42	98	95	-1.7	-1	-2	-4.0
■ **PAT PACILLO**	Pacillo, Patrick Michael b: 7/23/63, Jersey City, N.J. BR/TR, 6'2", 205 lbs. Deb: 5/23/87																												
1987	Cin-N	3	3	.500	12	7	0	0	0	40	41	9.2	7	19	4.3	23	5.2	6.07	69	.270	.347	-9	-8	103	85	0.0	0	-0	-0.7
1988	Cin-N	1	0	1.000	6	0	0	0	0	11	14	11.5	2	4	3.3	11	9.0	4.91	74	.318	.367	-2	-2	105	126	0.5	-0	-0	-0.1
Total	2	4	3	.571	18	7	0	0	0	51	55	9.7	9	23	4.1	34	6.0	5.82	70	.281	.351	-11	-10	103	94	0.5	-0	-0	-0.8
■ **GENE PACKARD**	Packard, Eugene Milo b: 7/13/1887, Colorado Springs Colorado d: 5/19/59, Riverside, Cal. BL/TL, 5'10", 155 lbs. Deb: 9/27/12																												
1912	Cin-N	1	0	1.000	1	1	1	0	0	9	7	7.0	0	4	4.0	2	2.0	3.00	106	.206	.289	0	0	93	50	0.5	1	0	0.1
1913	Cin-N	7	11	.389	39	21	9	2	0	191	208	9.8	2	64	3.0	73	3.4	2.97	112	.286	.339	5	8	104	127	-0.6	-1	-1	0.6
1914	KC-F	20	14	.588	42	34	24	4	5	302	282	8.4	5	88	2.6	154	4.6	2.89	106	.247	.306	11	6	96	92	5.3	4	10	2.1
1915	KC-F	20	12	.625	42	31	21	5	2	282	250	8.0	3	74	2.4	108	3.4	2.68	109	.242	.298	11	8	97	94	3.9	3	10	2.2
1916	Chi-N	10	6	.625	37	15	5	2	5	155	154	8.9	4	38	2.2	36	2.1	2.79	110	.256	.294	-3	5	117	99	2.9	-2	5	1.1

YEAR	TM/L	W	L	PCT	G	GS	CG	SHO	SV	IP	H	H/G	HR	BB	BB/G	SO	SO/G	ERA	/A	OAVG	OOBP	PR	/A	PF	CPI	WAT	PB	PD	TPI
1917	Chi-N	0	0	—	2	0	0	0	0	2	3	13.5	1	0	0.0	1	4.5	9.00	32	.375	.375	-1	-1	105	100	0.0	0	0	0.0
	StL-N	9	6	.600	34	11	6	0	2	153	138	8.1	4	25	1.5	44	2.6	2.47	112	.246	.273	4	5	102	95	1.1	3	-0	0.9
	Yr	9	6	.600	36	11	6	0	2	155	141	8.2	5	25	1.5	45	2.6	2.55	109	.247	.274	3	4	102	95	1.1	0	-0	0.9
1918	StL-N	12	12	.500	30	23	10	1	2	182	184	9.1	6	33	1.6	46	2.3	3.51	75	.266	.298	-15	-18	95	83	2.5	-0	-1	-2.0
1919	Phi-N	6	8	.429	21	16	10	1	1	134	167	11.2	3	30	2.0	24	1.6	4.16	76	.321	.353	-19	-15	109	108	1.0	-2	-0	-1.6
Total	8	85	69	.552	248	152	86	15	17	1410	1393	8.9	28	356	2.3	488	3.1	3.01	100	.262	.308	-7	-1	101	98	16.6	6	23	3.4
JOE PACTWA Pactwa, Joseph Martin b: 6/2/48, Hammond, Ind. BL/TL, 5'11", 185 lbs. Deb: 9/15/75																													
1975	Cal-A	1	0	1.000	4	3	0	0	0	16	23	12.9	0	10	5.6	3	1.7	3.94	92	.343	.418	-0	-1	96	155	0.5	0	-0	0.0
DAVE PAGAN Pagan, David Percy b: 9/15/49, Nipawin, Sask., Can. BR/TR, 6'2", 175 lbs. Deb: 7/01/73																													
1973	NY-A	0	0	—	4	1	0	0	0	13	16	11.1	1	1	0.7	9	6.2	2.77	138	.320	.333	2	2	100	161	0.0	0	0	0.2
1974	NY-A	1	3	.250	16	6	1	0	0	49	49	9.0	1	28	5.1	39	7.2	5.14	67	.265	.360	-8	-9	95	76	-1.0	0	-0	-0.9
1975	NY-A	0	0	—	13	0	0	0	1	31	30	8.7	2	13	3.8	18	5.2	4.06	91	.256	.333	-1	-1	98	93	0.0	0	-0	-0.1
1976	NY-A	1	1	.500	7	2	1	0	0	24	18	6.8	0	4	1.5	13	4.9	2.25	153	.222	.253	3	3	97	80	-0.1	0	-0	0.3
	Bal-A	1	4	.200	20	5	0	0	1	47	54	10.3	2	23	4.4	34	6.5	5.94	58	.298	.366	-13	-13	97	82	-1.5	0	-1	-1.3
	Yr	2	5	.286	27	7	1	0	1	71	72	9.1	2	27	3.4	47	6.0	4.69	73	.273	.333	-9	-10	97	82	-1.6	0	-1	-1.0
1977	Sea-A	1	1	.500	24	4	1	1	2	66	86	11.7	3	26	3.5	30	4.1	6.14	65	.323	.380	-15	-16	98	87	0.2	0	-0	-1.4
	Pit-N	0	0	—	1	0	0	0	0	3	1	3.0	0	0	0.0	4	12.0	0.00	—	.100	.100	1	1	102	0	0.0	0	0	0.2
Total	5	4	9	.308	85	18	3	1	4	233	254	9.8	9	95	3.7	147	5.7	4.94	74	.285	.350	-31	-33	97	87	-2.4	0	-2	-3.0
JOE PAGE Page, Joseph Francis "Fireman" b: 10/28/17, Cherry Valley, Pa. d: 4/21/80, Latrobe, Pa. BL/TL, 6'3", 200 lbs. Deb: 4/19/44																													
1944	NY-A	5	7	.417	19	16	4	0	0	103	100	8.7	3	52	4.5	63	5.5	4.54	79	.258	.342	-13	-11	105	83	-1.3	-0	-1	-1.1
1945	NY-A	6	3	.667	20	9	4	0	0	102	95	8.4	1	46	4.1	50	4.4	2.82	126	.246	.322	6	8	106	108	1.3	1	-2	0.8
1946	NY-A	9	8	.529	31	17	6	1	3	136	126	8.3	7	72	4.8	77	5.1	3.57	96	.252	.344	-1	-2	98	107	-0.5	0	-1	-0.2
1947	NY-A	14	8	.636	56	2	0	0	**17**	141	105	6.7	5	72	4.6	116	7.4	2.49	137	.208	.305	**19**	**15**	92	104	0.2	2	-1	1.6
1948	NY-A	7	8	.467	**55**	1	0	0	16	108	116	9.7	6	66	5.5	77	6.4	4.25	97	.275	.364	0	-2	96	113	-1.8	3	-1	0.1
1949	NY-A	13	8	.619	**60**	0	0	0	**27**	135	103	6.9	8	75	5.0	99	6.6	2.60	157	.215	.320	**24**	**22**	97	122	-0.1	-1	-2	1.9
1950	NY-A	3	7	.300	37	0	0	0	13	55	66	10.8	8	31	5.1	33	5.4	5.07	87	.295	.375	-3	-4	96	114	-2.6	1	-1	-0.3
1954	Pit-N	0	0	—	7	0	0	0	0	10	16	14.4	4	7	6.3	4	3.6	10.80	38	.364	.444	-7	-7	102	96	0.0	0	0	-0.6
Total	8	57	49	.538	285	45	14	1	76	790	727	8.3	42	421	4.8	519	5.9	3.53	106	.247	.337	25	20	98	107	-4.8	5	-7	2.2
PHIL PAGE Page, Philippe Rausac b: 8/23/05, Springfield, Mass. d: 7/27/58, Springfield, Mass BR/TL, 6'2", 175 lbs. Deb: 9/18/28 C																													
1928	Det-A	2	0	1.000	3	2	2	0	0	22	21	8.6	1	10	4.1	3	1.2	2.45	165	.256	.333	4	4	100	148	1.0	-0	1	0.4
1929	Det-A	0	2	.000	10	4	1	0	0	25	29	10.4	1	19	6.8	6	2.2	8.28	50	.296	.389	-11	-12	97	68	-0.9	-1	-1	-1.1
1930	Det-A	0	1	.000	12	0	0	0	0	12	23	17.3	1	9	6.8	2	1.5	9.75	50	.434	.500	-7	-6	106	109	-0.4	0	0	-0.4
1934	Bro-N	1	0	1.000	6	0	0	0	0	10	13	11.7	1	6	5.4	4	3.6	5.40	72	.342	.413	-1	-2	95	129	0.5	-0	1	0.0
Total	4	3	3	.500	31	6	3	0	0	69	86	11.2	4	44	5.7	15	2.0	6.26	67	.317	.398	-16	-16	99	109	0.2	-1	1	-1.1
SAM PAGE Page, Samuel Walter b: 2/11/16, Woodruff, S.C. BL/TR, 6', 172 lbs. Deb: 9/11/39																													
1939	Phi-A	0	3	.000	4	3	1	0	0	22	34	13.9	1	15	6.1	11	4.5	6.95	68	.343	.426	-6	-5	102	101	-1.4	1	1	-0.2
VANCE PAGE Page, Vance Linwood b: 9/15/05, Elm City, N.C. d: 7/14/51, Wilson, N.C. BR/TR, 6', 180 lbs. Deb: 8/06/38																													
1938	Chi-N	5	4	.556	13	9	3	0	1	68	90	11.9	4	13	1.7	18	2.4	3.84	101	.323	.349	-0	0	103	128	-0.1	-1	3	0.2
1939	Chi-N	7	7	.500	27	17	8	1	1	139	169	10.9	8	37	2.4	43	2.8	3.88	101	.298	.334	0	0	100	112	-0.5	3	1	0.4
1940	Chi-N	1	3	.250	30	1	0	0	2	59	65	9.9	1	26	4.0	22	3.4	4.42	86	.271	.327	-4	-4	99	88	-0.9	2	0	-0.1
1941	Chi-N	2	2	.500	25	3	1	0	1	48	48	9.0	2	30	5.6	17	3.2	4.31	79	.254	.359	-4	-5	94	96	0.2	1	0	-0.3
Total	4	15	16	.484	95	30	12	1	5	314	372	10.7	15	106	3.0	100	2.9	4.04	94	.292	.340	-7	-8	99	108	-1.3	4	4	0.2
PAT PAIGE Paige, George Lynn "Piggy" b: 5/5/1883, Paw Paw, Mich. d: 6/8/39, Berlin, Wis. BL/TR, 5'10", 175 lbs. Deb: 5/20/11																													
1911	Cle-A	1	0	1.000	2	1	1	0	0	16	21	11.8	0	7	3.9	6	3.4	4.50	77	.339	.406	-2	-2	103	116	0.5	-0	1	0.0
SATCHEL PAIGE Paige, Leroy Robert b: 7/7/06, Mobile, Ala. d: 6/8/82, Kansas City, Mo. BR/TR, 6'3.5", 180 lbs. Deb: 7/09/48 CH																													
1948	Cle-A	6	1	.857	21	7	3	2	1	73	61	7.5	2	25	3.1	45	5.5	2.47	163	.228	.292	15	13	94	109	2.2	-2	0	1.0
1949	Cle-A	4	7	.364	31	5	1	0	5	83	70	7.6	4	33	3.6	54	5.9	3.04	133	.230	.299	11	9	96	95	-2.0	-1	-1	0.7
1951	StL-A	3	4	.429	23	3	0	0	5	62	67	9.7	6	29	4.2	48	7.0	4.79	94	.276	.349	-5	-2	109	98	0.5	-2	-1	-0.3
1952	StL-A	12	10	.545	46	6	3	2	10	138	116	7.6	5	57	3.7	91	5.9	3.07	119	.226	.302	9	9	100	88	2.8	-2	0	0.8
1953	StL-A	3	9	.250	57	4	0	0	11	117	114	8.8	12	39	3.0	51	3.9	3.54	125	.257	.315	6	11	111	108	-1.7	-3	-2	0.7
1965	KC-A	0	0	—	1	1	0	0	0	3	1	3.0	0	0	0.0	1	3.0	0.00	—	.100	.100	1	1	100	0	0.0	-0	0	0.1
Total	6	28	31	.475	179	26	7	4	32	476	429	8.1	29	183	3.5	290	5.5	3.29	124	.241	.309	37	42	102	98	1.8	-10	-3	3.0
PHIL PAINE Paine, Phillips Steere "Flip" b: 6/8/30, Chepachet, R.I. d: 2/19/78, Lebanon, Pa. BR/TR, 6'2", 180 lbs. Deb: 7/14/51																													
1951	Bos-N	2	0	1.000	21	0	0	0	0	35	36	9.3	2	20	5.1	17	4.4	3.09	124	.271	.380	3	3	97	155	1.0	-1	-0	0.2
1954	Mil-N	1	0	1.000	11	0	0	0	0	14	14	9.0	1	12	7.7	11	7.1	3.86	96	.292	.422	0	-0	91	159	0.5	0	-0	0.0
1955	Mil-N	2	0	1.000	15	0	0	0	0	25	20	7.2	2	14	5.0	26	9.4	2.52	147	.225	.312	4	3	92	136	1.0	0	0	0.4
1956	Mil-N	0	0	—	1	0	0	0	0	0	3	—	0	0	—	0	—	∞	—	1.000	1.000	-2	-2	96	82	0.0	0	0	-0.1
1957	Mil-N	0	0	—	1	0	0	0	0	2	1	4.5	0	3	13.5	2	9.0	0.00	—	.143	.400	1	1	88	0	0.0	0	0	0.1
1958	StL-N	5	1	.833	46	0	0	0	1	73	70	8.6	7	31	3.8	45	5.5	3.58	119	.256	.338	3	6	108	113	2.1	0	0	0.6
Total	6	10	1	.909	95	0	0	0	1	149	144	8.7	12	80	4.8	101	6.1	3.38	119	.260	.356	10	10	101	130	4.6	-0	0	1.2
VICENTE PALACIOS Palacios, Vicente (Hernandez) b: 7/19/63, Verzcruz, Mex. BR/TR, 6'3", 165 lbs. Deb: 9/04/87																													
1987	Pit-N	2	1	.667	6	4	0	0	0	29	27	8.4	1	9	2.8	13	4.0	4.34	98	.250	.308	-1	-0	105	72	0.5	-0	-1	0.0
1988	Pit-N	1	2	.333	7	3	0	0	0	24	28	10.5	3	15	5.6	15	5.6	6.75	50	.295	.381	-9	-9	97	86	-0.5	-0	0	-0.8
Total	2	3	3	.500	13	7	0	0	0	53	55	9.3	4	24	4.1	28	4.8	5.43	71	.271	.343	-10	-9	101	79	0.0	-1	-0	-0.8
MIKE PALAGYI Palagyi, Michael Raymond b: 7/4/17, Conneaut, Ohio BR/TR, 6'2", 185 lbs. Deb: 8/18/39																													
1939	Was-A	0	0	—	1	0	0	0	0	0	0	—	0	3	—	0	—	∞	—	—	1.000	-3	-3	91	41	0.0	0	0	-0.1
ERV PALICA Palica, Ervin Martin (born Ervin Martin Pavliecivich) b: 2/9/28, Lomita, Cal. d: 5/29/82, Huntington Beach, Cal. BR/TR, 6'1.5", 180 lbs. Deb: 4/21/45																													
1947	Bro-N	0	1	.000	3	0	0	0	0	3	2	6.0	0	2	6.0	1	3.0	3.00	139	.182	.333	0	0	103	96	-0.4	0	0	0.0
1948	Bro-N	6	6	.500	41	10	3	0	3	125	111	8.0	13	58	4.2	74	5.3	4.46	91	.239	.324	-7	-6	103	86	-0.4	0	-1	-0.5
1949	Bro-N	8	9	.471	49	1	0	0	6	97	93	8.6	6	49	4.5	44	4.1	3.62	109	.261	.346	5	3	98	116	-2.2	0	0	0.4
1950	Bro-N	13	8	.619	43	19	10	2	1	201	176	7.9	13	98	4.4	131	5.9	3.58	121	.237	.325	13	17	104	96	1.2	2	-4	1.5
1951	Bro-N	2	6	.250	19	8	0	0	0	53	55	9.3	10	20	3.4	15	2.5	4.75	79	.259	.323	-5	-6	95	95	-2.3	0	1	-0.4
1953	Bro-N	0	0	—	4	0	0	0	0	6	10	15.0	1	8	12.0	3	4.5	12.00	36	.370	.514	-5	-5	100	87	0.0	0	0	-0.3
1954	Bro-N	3	3	.500	25	3	0	0	0	68	77	10.2	9	31	4.1	25	3.3	5.29	77	.285	.350	-9	-9	101	94	-0.4	1	-2	-0.9
1955	Bal-A	5	11	.313	33	25	5	1	0	170	165	8.7	10	83	4.4	68	3.6	4.13	90	.260	.337	-3	-8	94	95	-1.3	3	-1	-0.6
1956	Bal-A	4	11	.267	29	14	2	0	0	116	117	9.1	10	50	3.9	62	4.8	4.50	89	.264	.328	-4	-6	97	90	-3.1	-2	-0	-0.7
Total	9	41	55	.427	246	80	20	3	10	839	806	8.6	72	399	4.3	423	4.5	4.23	95	.255	.334	-16	-20	99	95	-8.9	5	-7	-1.5
DONN PALL Pall, Donn Steven b: 1/11/62, Chicaho, Ill. BR/TR, 6'1", 180 lbs. Deb: 8/01/88																													
1988	Chi-A	0	2	.000	17	0	0	0	0	29	39	12.1	1	8	2.5	16	5.0	3.41	115	.328	.362	2	2	99	150	-0.9	0	1	0.2
MIKE PALM Palm, Richard Paul b: 2/13/25, Boston, Mass. BR/TR, 6'3.5", 190 lbs. Deb: 7/11/48																													
1948	Bos-A	0	0	—	3	0	0	0	0	3	6	18.0	0	5	15.0	1	3.0	6.00	69	.400	.550	-1	-1	97	191	0.0	-0	0	0.0
PALMER Palmer b:St.Louis, Mo. Deb: 1885																													
1885	StL-N	0	4	.000	4	4	4	0	0	34	46	12.2	2	20	5.3	9	2.4	3.44	79	.335	.419	-2	-3	97	177	-1.9	-0	0	-0.2
DAVID PALMER Palmer, David William b: 10/19/57, Glens Falls, N.Y. BR/TR, 6'1", 195 lbs. Deb: 9/09/78																													
1978	Mon-N	0	1	.000	5	1	0	0	0	10	9	8.1	1	2	1.8	7	6.3	2.70	127	.243	.282	1	1	96	111	-0.4	-0	1	0.1
1979	Mon-N	10	2	.833	36	11	2	1	2	123	110	8.0	10	30	2.2	72	5.3	2.63	143	.237	.283	15	16	101	105	3.7	-3	-0	1.3

YEAR	TM/L	W	L	PCT	G	GS	CG	SHO	SV	IP	H	H/G	HR	BB	BB/G	SO	SO/G	ERA	/A	OAVG	OOBP	PR	/A	PF	CPI	WAT	PB	PD	TPI
1980	Mon-N	8	6	.571	24	19	3	1	0	130	124	8.6	11	30	2.1	73	5.1	2.98	119	.255	.295	9	8	98	110	0.3	1	1	1.1
1982	Mon-N	6	4	.600	13	13	1	0	0	74	60	7.3	3	36	4.4	46	5.6	3.16	119	.224	.314	4	5	104	94	0.8	-2	0	0.3
1984	Mon-N	7	3	.700	20	19	1	1	0	105	101	8.7	5	44	3.8	66	5.7	3.86	85	.256	.327	-3	-7	91	93	2.2	1	1	-0.5
1985	Mon-N	7	10	.412	24	23	0	0	0	136	128	8.5	5	67	4.4	106	7.0	3.71	91	.250	.337	-2	-5	94	97	-1.9	-1	2	-0.4
1986	Atl-N	11	10	.524	35	35	2	0	0	210	181	7.8	17	102	4.4	170	7.3	3.64	106	.234	.324	2	5	103	97	1.6	2	2	0.9
1987	Atl-N	8	11	.421	28	28	0	0	0	152	169	10.0	17	64	3.8	111	6.6	4.91	91	.281	.349	-14	-8	109	98	-0.1	-1	1	-0.6
1988	Phi-N	7	9	.438	22	22	1	1	0	129	129	9.0	8	48	3.3	85	5.9	4.47	80	.261	.321	-14	-13	103	84	0.5	5	-1	-0.8
Total	9	64	56	.533	207	171	10	4	2	1069	1011	8.5	77	423	3.6	736	6.2	3.71	100	.251	.320	-2	1	101	97	6.7	2	6	1.4

■ **JIM PALMER** Palmer, James Alvin b: 10/15/45, New York, N.Y. BR/TR, 6'3", 190 lbs. Deb: 4/17/65

YEAR	TM/L	W	L	PCT	G	GS	CG	SHO	SV	IP	H	H/G	HR	BB	BB/G	SO	SO/G	ERA	/A	OAVG	OOBP	PR	/A	PF	CPI	WAT	PB	PD	TPI
1965	Bal-A	5	4	.556	27	6	0	0	1	92	75	7.3	6	56	5.5	75	7.3	3.72	92	.229	.338	-3	-3	99	99	-0.1	1	0	0.0
1966	Bal-A	15	10	.600	30	30	6	0	0	208	176	7.6	21	91	3.9	147	6.4	3.46	98	.231	.308	-1	-2	99	100	-0.1	-2	-1	-0.4
1967	Bal-A	3	1	.750	9	9	2	1	0	49	34	6.2	6	20	3.7	23	4.2	2.94	103	.199	.278	2	0	94	97	1.1	0	0	0.1
1969	Bal-A	16	4	**.800**	26	23	11	6	0	181	131	6.5	11	64	3.2	123	6.1	2.34	156	.200	.271	26	26	100	88	4.2	2	-3	2.8
1970	Bal-A	20	10	.667	39	39	17	**5**	0	**305**	263	7.8	21	100	3.0	199	5.9	2.71	129	.231	.290	**34**	27	94	101	0.0	-1	0	2.7
1971	Bal-A	20	9	.690	37	37	20	3	0	282	231	7.4	19	106	3.4	184	5.9	2.68	129	.221	.293	25	25	100	99	2.4	1	0	3.0
1972	Bal-A	21	10	.677	36	36	18	3	0	274	219	7.2	21	70	2.3	184	6.0	2.07	143	.217	.265	30	27	96	109	5.9	4	-1	3.6
1973	Bal-A	22	9	.710	38	37	19	6	1	296	225	6.8	16	113	3.4	158	4.8	**2.40**	**167**	.211	.287	47	**53**	105	99	5.0	0	-1	**5.7**
1974	Bal-A	7	12	.368	26	26	5	2	0	179	176	8.8	12	69	3.5	84	4.2	3.27	102	.257	.322	7	1	92	109	-3.4	0	2	0.3
1975	Bal-A	**23**	11	.676	39	38	25	**10**	1	323	253	7.0	20	80	2.2	193	5.4	**2.09**	**162**	.216	.264	**61**	**46**	89	103	**5.1**	0	2	**5.3**
1976	Bal-A	**22**	13	.629	40	40	23	6	0	**315**	255	7.3	20	84	2.4	159	4.5	2.51	136	.224	.276	35	32	97	100	4.0	0	1	3.7
1977	Bal-A	**20**	11	.645	39	39	**22**	3	0	**319**	263	7.4	24	99	2.8	193	5.4	2.91	130	.229	.288	41	30	92	97	2.0	0	0	3.1
1978	Bal-A	21	12	.636	38	38	19	6	0	**296**	246	7.5	19	97	2.9	138	4.2	2.46	139	.227	.287	43	31	91	106	3.5	0	1	3.4
1979	Bal-A	10	6	.625	23	22	7	0	0	156	144	8.3	12	43	2.5	67	3.9	3.29	123	.246	.293	16	13	96	94	-0.1	0	0	1.3
1980	Bal-A	16	10	.615	34	33	4	0	0	224	238	9.6	26	74	3.0	109	4.4	3.98	101	.275	.328	2	1	99	108	0.0	0	1	0.2
1981	Bal-A	7	8	.467	22	22	5	0	0	127	117	8.3	14	46	3.3	35	2.5	3.76	97	.247	.310	-1	-2	99	98	-1.3	0	1	0.0
1982	Bal-A	15	5	**.750**	36	32	8	2	1	227	195	7.7	22	63	2.5	103	4.1	3.13	129	.231	**.285**	24	23	99	94	4.4	0	1	2.5
1983	Bal-A	5	4	.556	14	11	0	0	0	77	86	10.1	11	19	2.2	34	4.0	4.21	96	.281	.316	-1	-2	99	106	-0.3	0	-1	-0.1
1984	Bal-A	0	3	.000	5	3	0	0	0	18	22	11.0	2	17	8.5	4	2.0	9.00	42	.319	.438	-10	-10	94	80	-1.4	0	0	-0.8
Total	19	268	152	.638	558	521	211	53	4	3948	3349	7.6	303	1311	3.0	2212	5.0	2.86	125	.230	.292	378	318	96	101	30.9	7	5	36.4

■ **LOWELL PALMER** Palmer, Lowell Raymond b: 8/18/47, Sacramento, Cal. BR/TR, 6'1", 190 lbs. Deb: 6/21/69

YEAR	TM/L	W	L	PCT	G	GS	CG	SHO	SV	IP	H	H/G	HR	BB	BB/G	SO	SO/G	ERA	/A	OAVG	OOBP	PR	/A	PF	CPI	WAT	PB	PD	TPI
1969	Phi-N	2	8	.200	26	9	1	1	0	90	91	9.1	12	47	4.7	68	6.8	5.20	69	.264	.354	-16	-16	100	93	-2.4	1	-0	-1.5
1970	Phi-N	1	2	.333	38	5	0	0	0	102	98	8.6	15	55	4.9	85	7.5	5.47	72	.255	.350	-16	-17	98	88	-0.3	1	-0	-1.6
1971	Phi-N	0	0	—	3	1	0	0	0	15	13	7.8	3	13	7.8	6	3.6	6.00	60	.236	.411	-4	-4	105	103	0.0	-0	-0	-0.3
1972	StL-N	0	3	.000	16	2	0	0	0	35	30	7.7	2	26	6.7	25	6.4	3.86	94	.244	.368	-2	-1	105	113	-1.4	-1	0	-0.1
	Cle-A	0	0	—	1	0	0	0	0	2	2	9.0	0	2	9.0	3	13.5	4.50	74	.222	.364	-0	-0	108	76	0.0	0	0	0.0
1974	SD-N	2	5	.286	22	8	1	0	0	73	68	8.4	9	59	7.3	52	6.4	5.67	62	.256	.391	-17	-17	97	96	-0.7	-1	-1	-1.8
Total	5	5	18	.217	106	25	2	1	0	317	302	8.6	41	202	5.7	239	6.8	5.28	70	.255	.366	-55	-56	99	95	-4.8	-0	-1	-5.3

■ **EMILIO PALMERO** Palmero, Emilio Antonio "Pal" b: 6/13/1895, Guanabacoa, Cuba d: 7/15/70, Toledo, Ohio BL/TL, 5'11", 157 lbs. Deb: 9/21/15

YEAR	TM/L	W	L	PCT	G	GS	CG	SHO	SV	IP	H	H/G	HR	BB	BB/G	SO	SO/G	ERA	/A	OAVG	OOBP	PR	/A	PF	CPI	WAT	PB	PD	TPI
1915	NY-N	0	2	.000	3	2	1	0	0	12	10	7.5	0	9	6.8	8	6.0	3.00	85	.233	.393	-0	-1	92	137	-0.9	0	0	0.0
1916	NY-N	0	3	.000	4	1	0	0	0	16	17	9.6	2	8	4.5	8	4.5	7.88	31	.288	.366	-9	-10	94	66	-1.4	-0	1	-0.8
1921	StL-A	4	7	.364	24	9	4	0	0	90	109	10.9	1	49	4.9	26	2.6	5.00	86	.319	.396	-7	-7	101	109	-1.7	1	1	-0.3
1926	Was-A	2	2	.500	7	3	0	0	0	17	22	11.6	1	15	7.9	6	3.2	4.76	82	.344	.447	-1	-2	97	156	-0.1	0	-0	-0.1
1928	Bos-N	0	1	.000	3	1	0	0	0	7	14	18.0	0	2	2.6	0	0.0	5.14	79	.452	.471	-1	-1	101	170	-0.4	-0	-0	0.0
Total	5	6	15	.286	41	16	5	0	0	142	172	10.9	4	83	5.3	48	3.0	5.13	76	.319	.403	-19	-20	99	115	-4.5	1	2	-1.2

■ **ED PALMQUIST** Palmquist, Edwin Lee b: 6/10/33, Los Angeles, Cal. BR/TR, 6'3", 195 lbs. Deb: 6/10/60

YEAR	TM/L	W	L	PCT	G	GS	CG	SHO	SV	IP	H	H/G	HR	BB	BB/G	SO	SO/G	ERA	/A	OAVG	OOBP	PR	/A	PF	CPI	WAT	PB	PD	TPI
1960	LA-N	0	1	.000	22	0	0	0	0	39	34	7.8	6	16	3.7	23	5.3	2.54	169	.243	.315	5	8	114	165	-0.4	-1	0	0.7
1961	LA-N	0	1	.000	5	0	0	0	1	9	10	10.0	0	7	7.0	5	5.0	6.00	68	.333	.442	-2	-2	102	115	-0.4	0	-0	-0.1
	Min-A	1	1	.500	9	2	0	0	0	21	33	14.1	7	13	5.6	13	5.6	9.43	46	.359	.445	-13	-12	107	103	0.1	-0	0	-1.0
Total	2	1	3	.250	36	2	0	0	1	69	77	10.0	13	36	4.7	41	5.3	5.09	84	.294	.378	-9	-6	110	139	-0.7	-1	0	-0.4

■ **JIM PANTHER** Panther, James Edward b: 3/1/45, Burlington, Iowa BR/TR, 6'1", 190 lbs. Deb: 4/05/71

YEAR	TM/L	W	L	PCT	G	GS	CG	SHO	SV	IP	H	H/G	HR	BB	BB/G	SO	SO/G	ERA	/A	OAVG	OOBP	PR	/A	PF	CPI	WAT	PB	PD	TPI
1971	Oak-A	0	1	.000	4	0	0	0	0	6	10	15.0	1	5	7.5	4	6.0	10.50	33	.385	.455	-5	-5	97	88	-0.4	-0	0	-0.4
1972	Tex-A	5	9	.357	58	4	0	0	0	94	101	9.7	8	46	4.4	44	4.2	4.12	72	.277	.360	-11	-12	97	112	0.1	0	0	-1.2
1973	Atl-N	2	3	.400	23	0	0	0	0	31	45	13.1	3	9	2.6	8	2.3	7.55	55	.363	.388	-13	-12	113	85	-0.3	0	-1	-1.2
Total	3	7	13	.350	85	4	0	0	0	131	156	10.7	12	60	4.1	56	3.8	5.22	62	.303	.372	-29	-29	101	104	-0.6	-0	-1	-2.8

■ **JOHN PAPA** Papa, John Paul b: 12/5/40, Bridgeport, Conn. BR/TR, 5'11", 190 lbs. Deb: 4/11/61

YEAR	TM/L	W	L	PCT	G	GS	CG	SHO	SV	IP	H	H/G	HR	BB	BB/G	SO	SO/G	ERA	/A	OAVG	OOBP	PR	/A	PF	CPI	WAT	PB	PD	TPI
1961	Bal-A	0	0	—	2	0	0	0	0	1	2	18.0	1	3	27.0	3	27.0	18.00	21	.400	.625	-2	-2	96	126	0.0	0	0	0.0
1962	Bal-A	0	0	—	1	0	0	0	0	1	3	27.0	0	1	9.0	0	0.0	27.00	14	.600	.571	-3	-3	95	62	0.0	0	0	-0.1
Total	2	0	0	—	3	0	0	0	0	2	5	22.5	1	4	18.0	3	13.5	22.50	17	.500	.600	-4	-4	95	94	0.0	0	0	-0.1

■ **AL PAPAI** Papai, Alfred Thomas b: 5/7/19, Divernon, Ill. BR/TR, 6'3", 185 lbs. Deb: 4/24/48

YEAR	TM/L	W	L	PCT	G	GS	CG	SHO	SV	IP	H	H/G	HR	BB	BB/G	SO	SO/G	ERA	/A	OAVG	OOBP	PR	/A	PF	CPI	WAT	PB	PD	TPI
1948	StL-N	0	1	.000	10	0	0	0	0	16	14	7.9	3	7	3.9	8	4.5	5.06	77	.241	.313	-2	-2	99	88	-0.4	-0	0	-0.1
1949	StL-A	4	11	.267	42	15	6	0	2	142	175	11.1	8	81	5.1	31	2.0	5.07	86	.298	.380	-14	-11	104	101	-1.7	-2	3	-0.9
1950	Bos-A	4	2	.667	16	3	2	0	2	51	61	10.8	5	28	4.9	19	3.4	6.71	76	.293	.374	-12	-9	111	79	0.4	-0	-1	-0.8
	StL-N	1	0	1.000	13	0	0	0	0	19	21	9.9	0	14	6.6	7	3.3	5.21	82	.300	.402	-2	-2	103	103	0.5	-0	0	-0.1
1955	Chi-A	0	0	—	7	0	0	0	0	12	10	7.5	1	8	6.0	5	3.8	3.75	103	.244	.346	0	0	98	116	0.0	-0	1	0.1
Total	4	9	14	.391	88	18	8	0	4	240	281	10.5	17	138	5.2	70	2.6	5.36	83	.291	.375	-30	-24	105	96	-1.2	-3	4	-1.8

■ **LARRY PAPE** Pape, Laurence Albert b: 7/21/1883, Norwood, Ohio d: 7/21/18, Swissvale, Pa. BR/TR, 5'11", 175 lbs. Deb: 7/06/09

YEAR	TM/L	W	L	PCT	G	GS	CG	SHO	SV	IP	H	H/G	HR	BB	BB/G	SO	SO/G	ERA	/A	OAVG	OOBP	PR	/A	PF	CPI	WAT	PB	PD	TPI
1909	Bos-A	2	0	1.000	11	3	2	1	2	58	46	7.1	0	12	1.9	18	2.8	2.02	133	.218	.276	3	4	108	76	1.0	-1	-2	0.2
1911	Bos-A	10	8	.556	27	19	10	1	0	176	167	8.5	3	63	3.2	49	2.5	2.45	134	.264	.335	17	16	99	130	0.9	-1	4	2.0
1912	Bos-A	1	1	.500	13	2	1	0	1	49	74	13.6	0	16	2.9	17	3.1	4.96	69	.366	.418	-9	-8	102	123	-0.2	1	0	-0.7
Total	3	13	9	.591	51	24	13	2	3	283	287	9.1	3	91	2.9	84	2.7	2.80	114	.275	.339	12	13	101	118	1.7	-1	2	1.5

■ **FRANK PAPISH** Papish, Frank Richard "Pap" b: 10/21/17, Pueblo, Colo. d: 8/30/65, Pueblo, Colo. BR/TL, 6'2", 192 lbs. Deb: 5/08/45

YEAR	TM/L	W	L	PCT	G	GS	CG	SHO	SV	IP	H	H/G	HR	BB	BB/G	SO	SO/G	ERA	/A	OAVG	OOBP	PR	/A	PF	CPI	WAT	PB	PD	TPI
1945	Chi-A	4	4	.500	19	5	3	0	1	84	75	8.0	3	40	4.3	45	4.8	3.75	86	.241	.319	-4	-5	96	86	0.2	1	1	-0.2
1946	Chi-A	7	5	.583	31	15	6	2	0	138	122	8.0	7	63	4.1	66	4.3	2.74	125	.243	.325	12	10	97	121	1.3	-0	0	1.1
1947	Chi-A	12	12	.500	38	26	6	1	3	199	185	8.4	6	98	4.4	79	3.6	3.26	112	.245	.327	10	9	99	102	1.2	-5	-1	0.3
1948	Chi-A	2	8	.200	32	14	2	0	4	95	97	9.2	7	75	7.1	41	3.9	5.02	85	.265	.386	-8	-8	100	104	-2.0	-1	-1	-0.8
1949	Cle-A	1	0	1.000	25	3	1	0	1	62	54	7.8	2	39	5.7	23	3.3	3.19	126	.240	.343	7	6	96	114	0.5	0	0	0.6
1950	Pit-N	0	0	—	4	1	0	0	0	2	8	36.0	1	4	18.0	1	4.5	31.50	14	.533	.632	-6	-6	106	79	0.0	0	0	-0.4
Total	6	26	29	.473	149	64	18	3	9	580	541	8.4	26	319	5.0	255	4.0	3.58	103	.249	.340	11	6	98	106	1.2	-5	1	0.6

■ **JOHN PAPPALAU** Pappalau, John Joseph b: 4/3/1875, Albany, N.Y. d: 5/12/44, Albany, N.Y. 6', 175 lbs. Deb: 6/09/1897

YEAR	TM/L	W	L	PCT	G	GS	CG	SHO	SV	IP	H	H/G	HR	BB	BB/G	SO	SO/G	ERA	/A	OAVG	OOBP	PR	/A	PF	CPI	WAT	PB	PD	TPI
1897	Cle-N	0	1	.000	2	1	1	0	0	12	22	16.5	0	6	4.5	3	2.3	10.50	45	.418	.478	-8	-8	110	73	-0.4	-0	0	-0.5

■ **MILT PAPPAS** Pappas, Milton Stephen "Gimpy" (born Miltiades Stergios Papastegios) b: 5/11/39, Detroit, Mich. BR/TR, 6'3", 190 lbs. Deb: 8/10/57

YEAR	TM/L	W	L	PCT	G	GS	CG	SHO	SV	IP	H	H/G	HR	BB	BB/G	SO	SO/G	ERA	/A	OAVG	OOBP	PR	/A	PF	CPI	WAT	PB	PD	TPI
1957	Bal-A	0	0	—	4	0	0	0	0	9	6	6.0	0	3	3.0	3	3.0	1.00	351	.200	.265	3	3	93	175	0.0	-0	0	0.3
1958	Bal-A	10	10	.500	31	21	3	0	0	135	135	9.0	8	48	3.2	72	4.8	4.07	88	.262	.322	-4	-7	95	89	0.4	-0	1	-0.5
1959	Bal-A	15	9	.625	33	27	15	4	3	209	175	7.5	8	75	3.2	120	5.2	3.27	116	.226	.296	14	12	98	81	3.8	-3	-0	0.8
1960	Bal-A	15	11	.577	30	27	11	3	0	206	184	8.0	15	83	3.6	126	5.5	3.36	116	.243	.316	12	12	101	102	0.0	-5	1	0.8
1961	Bal-A	13	9	.591	26	23	11	4	1	178	134	6.8	16	78	3.9	89	4.5	3.03	127	.208	.298	20	16	96	95	0.1	1	2	2.0
1962	Bal-A	12	10	.545	35	32	9	1	0	205	200	8.8	31	75	3.3	130	5.7	4.04	93	.257	.317	-2	-6	95	106	1.7	-0	2	-0.4
1963	Bal-A	16	9	.640	34	32	11	4	0	217	186	7.7	21	69	2.9	120	5.0	3.03	112	.233	.293	15	9	93	105	3.3	-0	3	1.1
1964	Bal-A	16	7	.696	37	36	13	7	0	252	225	8.0	21	48	1.7	157	5.6	2.96	126	.239	.279	19	22	103	94	3.1	-2	-1	2.1

YEAR	TM/L	W	L	PCT	G	GS	CG	SHO	SV	IP	H	H/G	HR	BB	BB/G	SO	SO/G	ERA	/A	OAVG	OOBP	PR	/A	PF	CPI	WAT	PB	PD	TPI
1965	Bal-A	13	9	.591	34	34	9	3	0	221	192	7.8	22	52	2.1	127	5.2	2.61	131	.233	.277	21	20	99	110	0.3	-3	-3	1.5
1966	Cin-N	12	11	.522	33	32	6	2	0	210	224	9.6	23	39	1.7	133	5.7	4.29	96	.275	.304	-16	-4	114	89	1.2	-3	0	-0.5
1967	Cin-N	16	13	.552	34	32	5	3	0	218	218	9.0	19	38	**1.6**	129	5.3	3.34	110	.259	.292	1	8	109	98	0.6	-2	0	0.7
1968	Cin-N	2	5	.286	15	11	0	0	0	63	70	10.0	9	10	1.4	43	6.1	5.57	59	.275	.306	-18	-16	111	72	-1.5	-1	-0	-1.7
	Atl-N	10	8	.556	22	19	3	1	0	121	111	8.3	8	22	1.6	75	5.6	2.38	117	.246	.280	8	6	94	117	1.1	2	-1	0.8
	Yr	12	13	.480	37	30	3	1	0	184	181	8.9	17	32	1.6	118	5.8	3.47	85	.255	.287	-10	-10	99	117	-0.4	-1	-1	-0.9
1969	Atl-N	6	10	.375	26	24	1	0	0	144	149	9.3	14	44	2.8	72	4.5	3.63	102	.267	.320	-0	1	103	109	-2.9	2	-0	0.4
1970	Atl-N	2	2	.500	11	3	1	0	0	36	44	11.0	6	7	1.8	25	6.3	6.00	71	.293	.331	-8	-7	105	83	0.1	-1	0	-0.7
	Chi-N	10	8	.556	21	20	6	2	0	145	135	8.4	14	36	2.2	80	5.0	2.67	180	.248	.289	22	34	119	124	0.8	4	-1	4.3
	Yr	12	10	.545	32	23	7	2	0	181	179	8.9	20	43	2.1	105	5.2	3.33	141	.256	.295	15	27	116	124	0.9	-1	-1	3.6
1971	Chi-N	17	14	.548	35	35	14	**5**	0	261	279	9.6	25	62	2.1	99	3.4	3.52	108	.274	.315	-1	8	110	109	1.4	-1	-2	0.7
1972	Chi-N	17	7	.708	29	28	10	3	0	195	187	8.6	18	29	**1.3**	80	3.7	2.77	140	.251	.283	15	24	112	111	4.7	2	0	3.1
1973	Chi-N	7	12	.368	30	29	1	1	0	162	192	10.7	20	40	2.2	48	2.7	4.28	93	.299	.340	-11	-5	109	111	-2.3	-3	-0	-0.7
Total	17	209	164	.560	520	465	129	43	4	3187	3046	8.6	298	858	2.4	1728	4.9	3.40	111	.252	.301	87	131	103	102	15.9	-15	1	14.1

■ **JIM PARK** Park, James b: 11/10/1892, Richmond, Ky. d: 12/17/70, Lexington, Ky. BR/TR, 6'2", 175 lbs. Deb: 9/07/15

YEAR	TM/L	W	L	PCT	G	GS	CG	SHO	SV	IP	H	H/G	HR	BB	BB/G	SO	SO/G	ERA	/A	OAVG	OOBP	PR	/A	PF	CPI	WAT	PB	PD	TPI
1915	StL-A	2	0	1.000	3	3	1	0	0	23	18	7.0	1	9	3.5	5	2.0	1.17	248	.214	.290	5	4	99	189	1.0	1	-1	0.6
1916	StL-A	1	4	.200	26	6	1	0	0	79	69	7.9	2	25	2.8	26	3.0	2.62	102	.244	.307	2	0	94	101	-1.4	-1	-1	-0.2
1917	StL-A	1	1	.500	13	0	0	0	0	20	27	12.1	1	12	5.4	9	4.0	6.75	39	.333	.419	-9	-9	98	87	0.2	-0	0	-0.9
Total	3	4	5	.444	42	9	2	0	0	122	114	8.4	4	46	3.4	40	3.0	3.02	89	.254	.325	-3	-4	96	115	-0.2	-0	-2	-0.5

■ **DOC PARKER** Parker, Harley Park b: 6/14/1872, Theresa, N.Y. d: 3/3/41, Chicago, Ill. BR/TR, 6'2", 200 lbs. Deb: 7/11/1893

YEAR	TM/L	W	L	PCT	G	GS	CG	SHO	SV	IP	H	H/G	HR	BB	BB/G	SO	SO/G	ERA	/A	OAVG	OOBP	PR	/A	PF	CPI	WAT	PB	PD	TPI
1893	Chi-N	0	0	—	1	0	0	0	1	2	5	22.5	0	1	4.5	0	0.0	13.50	36	.488	.533	-2	-2	104	83	0.0	-0	0	-0.1
1895	Chi-N	4	2	.667	7	6	5	1	0	51	65	11.5	1	9	1.6	9	1.6	3.71	133	.331	.360	6	7	103	115	0.8	1	0	0.7
1896	Chi-N	1	5	.167	9	7	7	0	0	73	100	12.3	3	27	3.3	15	1.8	6.16	77	.350	.406	-15	-12	108	87	-2.0	0	0	-0.8
1901	Cin-N	0	1	.000	1	1	1	0	0	8	26	29.3	1	2	2.3	0	0.0	15.75	21	.560	.579	-11	-11	100	95	-0.4	-0	0	-0.6
Total	4	5	8	.385	18	14	13	1	1	134	196	13.2	5	39	2.6	24	1.6	5.91	80	.364	.407	-21	-18	106	98	-1.6	0	0	-0.8

■ **HARRY PARKER** Parker, Harry William b: 9/14/47, Highland, Ill. BR/TR, 6'3", 190 lbs. Deb: 8/08/70

YEAR	TM/L	W	L	PCT	G	GS	CG	SHO	SV	IP	H	H/G	HR	BB	BB/G	SO	SO/G	ERA	/A	OAVG	OOBP	PR	/A	PF	CPI	WAT	PB	PD	TPI
1970	StL-N	1	1	.500	7	4	0	0	0	22	24	9.8	0	15	6.1	9	3.7	3.27	131	.276	.371	2	3	106	137	0.1	0	0	0.3
1971	StL-N	0	0	—	4	0	0	0	0	5	6	10.8	2	2	3.6	2	3.6	7.20	48	.286	.348	-2	-2	100	95	0.0	0	-0	-0.1
1973	NY-N	8	4	.667	38	9	0	0	5	97	79	7.3	7	36	3.3	63	5.8	3.34	110	.217	.288	4	4	100	77	2.0	-0	-0	0.3
1974	NY-N	4	12	.250	40	16	1	0	4	131	145	10.0	10	46	3.2	58	4.0	3.92	93	.281	.337	-4	-4	100	107	-3.5	-4	-1	-0.9
1975	NY-N	2	3	.400	18	1	0	0	2	35	37	9.5	2	19	4.9	22	5.7	4.37	79	.272	.352	-3	-4	95	98	-0.4	1	-0	-0.2
	StL-N	0	1	.000	14	0	0	0	1	19	21	9.9	3	10	4.7	13	6.2	6.16	61	.288	.356	-5	-5	103	88	-0.4	0	1	-0.3
	Yr	2	4	.333	32	1	0	0	3	54	58	9.7	5	29	4.8	35	5.8	5.00	71	.278	.354	-8	-9	98	88	-0.8	1	1	-0.5
1976	Cle-A	0	0	—	3	0	0	0	0	7	3	3.9	0	0	0.0	5	6.4	0.00	—	.136	.136	3	3	100	0	0.0	0	0	0.3
Total	6	15	21	.417	124	30	1	0	12	316	315	9.0	24	128	3.6	172	4.9	3.84	96	.258	.325	-6	-6	100	95	-2.2	-3	-1	-0.6

■ **CLAY PARKER** Parker, James Clayton b: 12/19/62, Columbia, La. BR/TR, 6'1", 185 lbs. Deb: 9/14/87

YEAR	TM/L	W	L	PCT	G	GS	CG	SHO	SV	IP	H	H/G	HR	BB	BB/G	SO	SO/G	ERA	/A	OAVG	OOBP	PR	/A	PF	CPI	WAT	PB	PD	TPI
1987	Sea-A	0	0	—	3	1	0	0	0	8	15	16.9	2	4	4.5	8	9.0	10.13	45	.405	.465	-5	-5	103	103	0.0	0	0	-0.3

■ **JAY PARKER** Parker, Jay b: 7/8/1874, Theresa, N.Y. d: 6/8/35, Hartford, Mich. BR/TR, 5'11", 185 lbs. Deb: 9/27/1899

YEAR	TM/L	W	L	PCT	G	GS	CG	SHO	SV	IP	H	H/G	HR	BB	BB/G	SO	SO/G	ERA	/A	OAVG	OOBP	PR	/A	PF	CPI	WAT	PB	PD	TPI
1899	Pit-N	0	0	—	1	1	0	0	0	0	0	—	0	2	—	0	—	∞	—	—	1.000	-2	-2	98	31	0.0	0	0	-0.1

■ **ROY PARKER** Parker, Roy W. b: 1897, BR/TR, 6'2", 185 lbs. Deb: 9/10/19

YEAR	TM/L	W	L	PCT	G	GS	CG	SHO	SV	IP	H	H/G	HR	BB	BB/G	SO	SO/G	ERA	/A	OAVG	OOBP	PR	/A	PF	CPI	WAT	PB	PD	TPI
1919	StL-N	0	0	—	2	0	0	0	0	2	6	27.0	0	1	4.5	0	0.0	31.50	9	.333	.400	-6	-6	97	26	0.0	0	0	-0.5

■ **SLICKER PARKS** Parks, Vernon Henry b: 11/10/1895, Dallas, Mich. d: 2/21/78, Royal Oak, Mich. BR/TR, 5'10", 158 lbs. Deb: 7/11/21

YEAR	TM/L	W	L	PCT	G	GS	CG	SHO	SV	IP	H	H/G	HR	BB	BB/G	SO	SO/G	ERA	/A	OAVG	OOBP	PR	/A	PF	CPI	WAT	PB	PD	TPI
1921	Det-A	3	2	.600	10	1	0	0	0	25	33	11.9	2	16	5.8	10	3.6	5.76	71	.306	.397	-4	-5	96	98	0.7	-1	-1	-0.5

■ **BILL PARKS** Parks, William Robert b: 6/4/1849, Easton, Pa. d: 10/10/11, Easton, Pa. 5'8", 150 lbs. Deb: 4/26/1875

YEAR	TM/L	W	L	PCT	G	GS	CG	SHO	SV	IP	H	H/G	HR	BB	BB/G	SO	SO/G	ERA	/A	OAVG	OOBP	PR	/A	PF	CPI	WAT	PB	PD	TPI
1875	Nat-n	3	9	.250	12																								

■ **ROY PARMELEE** Parmelee, Le Roy Earl "Tarzan" b: 4/25/07, Lambertville, Mich d: 8/31/81, Monroe, Mich. BR/TR, 6'1", 190 lbs. Deb: 9/28/29

YEAR	TM/L	W	L	PCT	G	GS	CG	SHO	SV	IP	H	H/G	HR	BB	BB/G	SO	SO/G	ERA	/A	OAVG	OOBP	PR	/A	PF	CPI	WAT	PB	PD	TPI
1929	NY-N	1	0	1.000	2	1	0	0	0	7	13	16.7	1	3	3.9	1	1.3	9.00	51	.481	.500	-3	-3	97	126	0.5	0	0	-0.2
1930	NY-N	0	1	.000	11	1	0	0	0	21	18	7.7	3	26	11.1	19	8.1	9.43	50	.228	.415	-10	-11	96	61	-0.4	1	0	-0.8
1931	NY-N	2	2	.500	13	5	4	0	0	59	47	7.2	1	33	5.0	30	4.6	3.66	99	.223	.333	1	-0	93	85	-0.2	-0	0	0.0
1932	NY-N	0	3	.000	8	3	0	0	0	25	25	9.0	0	14	5.0	23	8.3	3.96	96	.250	.345	-0	-0	98	91	-1.4	1	0	0.1
1933	NY-N	13	8	.619	32	32	14	3	0	218	191	7.9	9	77	3.2	132	5.4	3.18	101	.232	.305	4	1	96	88	0.6	4	0	0.5
1934	NY-N	10	6	.625	22	20	7	2	0	153	134	**7.9**	6	60	3.5	83	4.9	3.41	113	**.238**	.313	11	7	95	94	0.4	2	2	1.1
1935	NY-N	14	10	.583	34	31	13	0	0	226	214	8.5	20	97	3.9	79	3.1	4.22	90	.249	.326	-5	-10	95	93	-0.2	3	2	-0.5
1936	StL-N	11	11	.500	37	28	9	0	2	221	226	9.2	13	107	4.4	79	3.2	4.56	83	.270	.353	-13	-19	95	97	-1.3	0	-1	-1.8
1937	Chi-N	7	8	.467	33	18	8	0	0	146	165	10.2	13	79	4.9	55	3.4	5.12	77	.286	.374	-20	-19	100	102	-1.7	0	1	-1.7
1939	Phi-A	1	6	.143	14	5	0	0	1	45	42	8.4	2	35	7.0	13	2.6	6.40	74	.235	.364	-9	-8	102	65	-2.1	-1	0	-0.7
Total	10	59	55	.518	206	144	55	5	3	1121	1075	8.6	68	531	4.3	514	4.1	4.27	88	.253	.338	-44	-64	96	92	-5.8	10	5	-4.0

■ **MEL PARNELL** Parnell, Melvin Lloyd "Dusty" b: 6/13/22, New Orleans, La. BL/TL, 6', 180 lbs. Deb: 4/20/47

YEAR	TM/L	W	L	PCT	G	GS	CG	SHO	SV	IP	H	H/G	HR	BB	BB/G	SO	SO/G	ERA	/A	OAVG	OOBP	PR	/A	PF	CPI	WAT	PB	PD	TPI
1947	Bos-A	2	3	.400	15	5	1	0	0	51	60	10.6	1	27	4.8	23	4.1	6.35	62	.296	.379	-15	-14	107	75	-0.6	-2	-1	-1.5
1948	Bos-A	15	8	.652	35	27	16	1	0	212	205	8.7	7	90	3.8	77	3.3	3.14	132	.252	.326	27	24	97	112	1.1	-4	2	2.2
1949	Bos-A	**25**	7	.781	39	33	**27**	4	2	**295**	258	7.9	8	134	4.1	122	3.7	2.78	156	.237	.320	**47**	**51**	103	110	**7.6**	2	-1	**5.6**
1950	Bos-A	18	10	.643	40	31	21	2	3	249	244	8.8	17	106	3.8	93	3.4	3.61	141	.259	.334	27	41	111	110	1.4	-2	4	4.5
1951	Bos-A	18	11	.621	36	29	11	3	2	221	229	9.3	11	77	3.1	77	3.1	3.26	135	.272	.329	21	28	106	**119**	2.2	4	0	**3.4**
1952	Bos-A	12	12	.500	33	29	15	3	2	214	207	8.7	13	89	3.7	107	4.5	3.62	109	.255	.327	1	8	107	101	0.2	-4	1	0.6
1953	Bos-A	21	8	.724	38	34	12	5	0	241	217	8.1	15	116	4.3	136	5.1	3.06	141	.239	.325	25	34	108	112	6.4	1	-2	3.5
1954	Bos-A	3	7	.300	19	15	4	1	0	92	104	10.2	7	35	3.4	38	3.7	3.72	101	.287	.342	0	0	101	118	-1.6	-2	0	0.0
1955	Bos-A	2	3	.400	13	9	0	0	1	46	62	12.1	12	25	4.9	18	3.5	7.83	62	.318	.388	-20	-15	122	92	-0.6	1	0	-1.2
1956	Bos-A	7	6	.538	21	20	6	1	0	131	129	8.9	13	59	4.1	41	2.8	3.78	112	.256	.332	6	7	102	105	0.0	-2	-1	0.4
Total	10	123	75	.621	289	232	113	20	10	1752	1715	8.8	104	758	3.9	732	3.8	3.50	124	.257	.331	118	163	106	109	16.1	-7	4	17.5

■ **RUBE PARNHAM** Parnham, James Arthur b: 2/1/1894, Heidelberg, Pa. d: 11/25/63, Mc Keesport, Pa. BR/TR, 6'3", 185 lbs. Deb: 9/20/16

YEAR	TM/L	W	L	PCT	G	GS	CG	SHO	SV	IP	H	H/G	HR	BB	BB/G	SO	SO/G	ERA	/A	OAVG	OOBP	PR	/A	PF	CPI	WAT	PB	PD	TPI
1916	Phi-A	2	1	.667	4	3	2	0	0	25	27	9.7	0	13	4.7	8	2.9	3.96	75	.300	.388	-3	-3	105	111	0.9	1	1	0.0
1917	Phi-A	0	1	.000	2	2	0	0	0	11	12	9.8	1	9	7.4	4	3.3	4.09	63	.316	.447	-2	-2	97	152	-0.4	-0	0	-0.1
Total	2	2	2	.500	6	5	2	0	0	36	39	9.8	1	22	5.5	12	3.0	4.00	71	.305	.407	-5	-5	103	123	0.5	0	1	-0.1

■ **JEFF PARRETT** Parrett, Jeffrey Dale b: 8/26/61, Indianapolis, Ind. BR/TR, 6'4", 185 lbs. Deb: 4/11/86

YEAR	TM/L	W	L	PCT	G	GS	CG	SHO	SV	IP	H	H/G	HR	BB	BB/G	SO	SO/G	ERA	/A	OAVG	OOBP	PR	/A	PF	CPI	WAT	PB	PD	TPI
1986	Mon-N	0	1	.000	12	0	0	0	0	20	19	8.5	3	13	5.8	21	9.4	4.95	74	.247	.352	-3	-3	98	95	-0.4	0	0	-0.2
1987	Mon-N	7	6	.538	45	0	0	0	6	62	53	7.7	8	30	4.4	56	8.1	4.21	103	.229	.311	-1	1	106	88	-0.2	-1	0	0.0
1988	Mon-N	12	4	.750	61	0	0	0	6	92	66	6.5	8	45	4.4	62	6.1	2.64	137	.214	.304	8	10	105	126	4.2	0	-1	1.0
Total	3	19	11	.633	118	0	0	0	12	174	138	7.1	19	88	4.6	139	7.2	3.47	112	.224	.312	5	8	105	109	3.6	0	-1	0.8

■ **MIKE PARROTT** Parrott, Michael Everett Arch b: 12/6/54, Oxnard, Cal. BR/TR, 6'4", 210 lbs. Deb: 9/05/77

YEAR	TM/L	W	L	PCT	G	GS	CG	SHO	SV	IP	H	H/G	HR	BB	BB/G	SO	SO/G	ERA	/A	OAVG	OOBP	PR	/A	PF	CPI	WAT	PB	PD	TPI
1977	Bal-A	0	0	—	3	0	0	0	0	4	4	9.0	0	2	4.5	2	4.5	2.25	167	.250	.333	1	1	92	136	0.0	0	0	0.1
1978	Sea-A	1	5	.167	27	10	0	0	1	82	108	11.9	8	32	3.5	41	4.5	5.16	76	.316	.368	-13	-11	104	106	-1.5	0	0	-1.0
1979	Sea-A	14	12	.538	38	30	13	2	0	229	231	9.1	17	86	3.4	127	5.0	3.77	113	.267	.332	12	13	101	106	3.2	0	2	1.5
1980	Sea-A	1	16	.059	27	16	1	0	3	94	136	13.0	16	42	4.0	53	5.1	7.28	58	.348	.405	-34	-32	105	98	-7.1	0	3	-2.6
1981	Sea-A	3	6	.333	24	12	0	0	1	85	102	10.8	3	28	3.0	43	4.6	5.08	73	.299	.347	-13	-13	101	86	-0.7	0	0	-1.2
Total	5	19	39	.328	119	68	14	2	5	494	581	10.6	44	190	3.5	266	4.8	4.88	84	.297	.355	-47	-42	102	101	-6.1	0	6	-3.2

■ **TOM PARROTT** Parrott, Thomas William "Tacky Tom" b: 4/10/1868, Portland, Ore. d: 1/1/32, Dundee, Ore. BR/TR, 5'10.5", 170 lbs. Deb: 6/18/1893

YEAR	TM/L	W	L	PCT	G	GS	CG	SHO	SV	IP	H	H/G	HR	BB	BB/G	SO	SO/G	ERA	/A	OAVG	OOBP	PR	/A	PF	CPI	WAT	PB	PD	TPI
1893	Chi-N	0	3	.000	4	3	2	0	0	27	35	11.7	1	17	5.7	7	2.3	6.67	73	.330	.423	-6	-5	104	88	-1.4	-0	0	-0.3

YEAR	TM/L	W	L	PCT	G	GS	CG	SHO	SV	IP	H	H/G	HR	BB	BB/G	SO	SO/G	ERA	/A	OAVG	OOBP	PR	/A	PF	CPI	WAT	PB	PD	TPI
	Cin-N	10	7	.588	22	17	11	1	0	154	174	10.2	1	70	4.1	33	1.9	4.44	107	.301	.376	4	6	102	97	1.6	-3	0	0.2
	Yr	10	10	.500	26	20	13	1	0	181	209	10.4	2	87	4.3	40	2.0	4.77	100	.305	.384	-2	0	102	97	0.2	-0	0	-0.1
1894	Cin-N	17	19	.472	41	36	31	1	1	309	402	11.7	19	126	3.7	61	1.8	5.62	96	.338	.401	-10	-7	102	95	2.1	9	4	0.9
1895	Cin-N	11	18	.379	41	31	23	0	**3**	263	382	13.1	8	76	2.6	57	2.0	5.48	94	.361	.403	-20	-10	107	102	-4.3	10	3	1.0
1896	StL-N	1	1	.500	7	2	2	0	0	42	62	13.3	4	18	3.9	8	1.7	6.21	69	.367	.428	-9	-9	98	104	0.3	1	0	-0.6
Total	4	39	48	.448	115	89	69	2	4	795	1055	11.9	33	307	3.5	166	1.9	5.41	95	.340	.399	-40	-25	103	98	-1.7	18	7	1.2

■ JIGGS PARSON Parson, William Edwin b: 12/28/1885, Parker, S.Dak. d: 5/19/67, Los Angeles, Cal. BR/TR, 6'2", 180 lbs. Deb: 5/16/10

YEAR	TM/L	W	L	PCT	G	GS	CG	SHO	SV	IP	H	H/G	HR	BB	BB/G	SO	SO/G	ERA	/A	OAVG	OOBP	PR	/A	PF	CPI	WAT	PB	PD	TPI
1910	Bos-N	0	2	.000	10	4	0	0	0	35	35	9.0	2	26	6.7	7	1.8	3.86	93	.278	.409	-3	-1	118	130	-0.9	-1	0	-0.1
1911	Bos-N	0	1	.000	7	0	0	0	0	25	36	13.0	2	15	5.4	7	2.5	6.48	57	.375	.478	-9	-8	109	122	-0.4	-0	-1	-0.7
Total	2	0	3	.000	17	4	0	0	0	60	71	10.7	4	41	6.2	14	2.1	4.95	74	.320	.439	-12	-9	114	127	-1.3	-2	-1	-0.8

■ CHARLIE PARSONS Parsons, Charles James b: 7/18/1863, Cherry Flats, Pa. d: 3/24/36, Mansfield, Pa. TL, 5'10", 160 lbs. Deb: 5/29/1886

YEAR	TM/L	W	L	PCT	G	GS	CG	SHO	SV	IP	H	H/G	HR	BB	BB/G	SO	SO/G	ERA	/A	OAVG	OOBP	PR	/A	PF	CPI	WAT	PB	PD	TPI
1886	Bos-N	0	2	.000	2	2	2	0	0	16	20	11.3	0	4	2.3	5	2.8	3.94	81	.320	.361	-1	-1	97	107	-0.9	1	0	0.0
1887	NY-a	1	1	.500	4	4	4	0	0	34	51	13.5	0	6	1.6	5	1.3	4.50	88	.361	.387	-1	-2	92	121	0.3	-0	0	-0.1
1890	Cle-N	0	1	.000	2	1	0	0	0	9	12	12.0	0	6	6.0	2	2.0	6.00	58	.337	.433	-2	-3	97	94	-0.4	1	0	0.0
Total	3	1	4	.200	8	7	6	0	0	59	83	12.7	0	16	2.4	12	1.8	4.58	81	.347	.388	-4	-6	94	113	-1.0	2	0	-0.1

■ TOM PARSONS Parsons, Thomas Anthony b: 9/13/39, Lakeville, Conn. BR/TR, 6'7", 210 lbs. Deb: 9/05/63

YEAR	TM/L	W	L	PCT	G	GS	CG	SHO	SV	IP	H	H/G	HR	BB	BB/G	SO	SO/G	ERA	/A	OAVG	OOBP	PR	/A	PF	CPI	WAT	PB	PD	TPI
1963	Pit-N	0	1	.000	1	1	0	0	0	4	7	15.8	1	2	4.5	2	4.5	9.00	36	.368	.409	-3	-3	99	97	-0.4	-0	0	-0.2
1964	NY-N	1	2	.333	4	2	1	0	0	19	20	9.5	1	6	2.8	10	4.7	4.26	82	.274	.321	-2	-2	98	89	0.0	-1	-0	-0.2
1965	NY-N	1	10	.091	35	11	1	1	1	91	108	10.7	17	17	1.7	58	5.7	4.65	79	.290	.320	-11	-10	104	105	-3.9	-1	1	-0.9
Total	3	2	13	.133	40	14	2	1	1	114	135	10.7	19	25	2.0	70	5.5	4.74	77	.291	.324	-15	-14	103	102	-4.3	-2	1	-1.3

■ BILL PARSONS Parsons, William Raymond b: 8/17/48, Riverside, Cal. BR/TR, 6'6", 195 lbs. Deb: 4/13/71

YEAR	TM/L	W	L	PCT	G	GS	CG	SHO	SV	IP	H	H/G	HR	BB	BB/G	SO	SO/G	ERA	/A	OAVG	OOBP	PR	/A	PF	CPI	WAT	PB	PD	TPI
1971	Mil-A	13	17	.433	36	35	12	4	0	245	219	8.0	19	93	3.4	139	5.1	3.20	113	.241	.309	7	11	104	102	0.2	3	0	1.6
1972	Mil-A	13	13	.500	33	30	10	2	0	214	194	8.2	27	68	2.9	111	4.7	3.91	76	.240	.297	-20	-22	97	86	2.2	0	-3	-2.6
1973	Mil-A	3	6	.333	20	17	0	0	0	60	59	8.9	6	67	10.1	30	4.5	6.75	54	.257	.420	-20	-21	96	86	-1.2	0	-0	-1.9
1974	Oak-A	0	0	—	4	0	0	0	0	2	1	4.5	0	3	13.5	2	9.0	0.00	—	.143	.400	1	1	99	0	0.0	0	0	0.1
Total	4	29	36	.446	93	82	22	6	0	521	473	8.2	52	231	4.0	282	4.9	3.89	86	.242	.320	-31	-31	100	93	1.2	3	-3	-2.8

■ STAN PARTENHEIMER Partenheimer, Stanwood Wendell "Party" b: 10/21/22, Chicopee Falls, Mass. BR/TL, 5'11", 175 lbs. Deb: 5/27/44

YEAR	TM/L	W	L	PCT	G	GS	CG	SHO	SV	IP	H	H/G	HR	BB	BB/G	SO	SO/G	ERA	/A	OAVG	OOBP	PR	/A	PF	CPI	WAT	PB	PD	TPI
1944	Bos-A	0	0	—	1	1	0	0	0	1	3	27.0	0	2	18.0	0	0.0	18.00	18	.500	.625	-2	-2	97	95	0.0	-0	0	-0.1
1945	StL-N	0	0	—	8	2	0	0	0	13	12	8.3	2	16	11.1	6	4.2	6.23	59	.250	.424	-4	-4	97	106	0.0	-0	0	-0.3
Total	2	0	0	—	9	3	0	0	0	14	15	9.6	2	18	11.6	6	3.9	7.07	52	.278	.446	-5	-5	97	105	0.0	-1	0	-0.4

■ BILL PASCHALL Paschall, William Herbert b: 4/22/54, Norfolk, Va. BR/TR, 6', 175 lbs. Deb: 9/20/78

YEAR	TM/L	W	L	PCT	G	GS	CG	SHO	SV	IP	H	H/G	HR	BB	BB/G	SO	SO/G	ERA	/A	OAVG	OOBP	PR	/A	PF	CPI	WAT	PB	PD	TPI
1978	KC-A	0	1	.000	2	0	0	0	1	8	6	6.8	0	0	0.0	5	5.6	3.38	113	.207	.226	0	0	101	31	-0.4	0	-0	0.0
1979	KC-A	0	1	.000	7	0	0	0	0	14	18	11.6	2	5	3.2	3	1.9	6.43	69	.300	.368	-3	-3	105	87	-0.4	0	-0	-0.2
1981	KC-A	0	0	—	2	0	0	0	0	2	2	9.0	0	0	0.0	1	4.5	4.50	81	.286	.286	-0	-0	99	64	0.0	0	0	0.0
Total	3	0	2	.000	11	0	0	0	1	24	26	9.8	2	5	1.9	9	3.4	5.25	79	.271	.321	-3	-3	103	66	-0.8	0	-0	-0.2

■ CAMILO PASCUAL Pascual, Camilo Alberto (Lus) "Little Potato" b: 1/20/34, Havana, Cuba BR/TR, 5'11", 170 lbs. Deb: 4/15/54 C

YEAR	TM/L	W	L	PCT	G	GS	CG	SHO	SV	IP	H	H/G	HR	BB	BB/G	SO	SO/G	ERA	/A	OAVG	OOBP	PR	/A	PF	CPI	WAT	PB	PD	TPI
1954	Was-A	4	7	.364	48	4	1	0	3	119	126	9.5	7	61	4.6	60	4.5	4.24	87	.276	.358	-7	-7	99	105	-0.8	-1	3	-0.4
1955	Was-A	2	12	.143	43	16	1	0	3	129	158	11.0	5	70	4.9	82	5.7	6.14	61	.311	.387	-31	-34	94	88	-4.2	0	2	-3.0
1956	Was-A	6	18	.250	39	27	6	0	2	189	194	9.2	33	89	4.2	162	7.7	5.86	76	.261	.341	-36	-30	107	82	-4.5	-2	1	-2.8
1957	Was-A	8	17	.320	29	26	8	2	0	176	168	8.6	11	76	3.9	113	5.8	4.09	94	.258	.328	-6	-5	102	93	-1.4	-2	2	-0.4
1958	Was-A	8	12	.400	31	27	6	2	0	177	166	8.4	14	60	3.1	146	**7.4**	3.15	120	.248	.309	12	12	100	107	0.1	-1	0	1.3
1959	Was-A	17	10	.630	32	30	**17**	**6**	0	239	202	7.6	10	69	2.6	185	7.0	2.64	149	.226	.278	33	34	102	93	**5.7**	6	5	**5.0**
1960	Was-A	12	8	.600	26	22	8	3	2	152	139	8.2	11	53	3.1	143	8.5	3.02	131	.240	.304	14	16	102	101	2.7	3	0	2.0
1961	Min-A	15	16	.484	35	33	15	**8**	0	252	205	7.3	26	100	3.6	**221**	7.9	3.46	125	.217	.292	16	24	107	84	1.6	-1	1	2.5
1962	Min-A	20	11	.645	34	33	**18**	**5**	0	258	236	8.2	25	59	2.1	**206**	7.2	3.31	124	.241	.282	19	23	104	92	3.5	8	0	3.4
1963	Min-A	21	9	.700	31	31	**18**	3	0	248	205	7.4	21	81	2.9	**202**	7.3	2.47	144	.224	.286	32	30	98	115	5.3	6	-1	4.0
1964	Min-A	15	12	.556	36	36	14	1	0	267	245	8.3	30	98	3.3	213	7.2	3.30	110	.241	.305	10	9	100	105	2.1	4	0	1.4
1965	Min-A	9	3	.750	27	27	5	1	0	156	126	7.3	12	63	3.6	96	5.5	3.35	102	.217	.294	2	1	98	84	2.1	3	2	0.6
1966	Min-A	8	6	.571	21	19	2	0	0	103	113	9.9	9	30	2.6	56	4.9	4.89	77	.278	.324	-17	-13	110	85	0.4	1	2	-0.9
1967	Was-A	12	10	.545	28	27	5	1	0	165	147	8.0	15	43	2.3	106	5.8	3.27	102	.237	.287	-1	1	104	93	1.7	1	-0	0.3
1968	Was-A	13	12	.520	31	31	8	4	0	201	181	8.1	11	59	2.6	111	5.0	2.69	104	.239	.294	7	2	94	107	2.8	1	1	0.5
1969	Was-A	2	5	.286	14	13	0	0	0	55	49	8.0	12	38	6.2	34	5.6	6.87	51	.239	.371	-20	-21	96	79	-1.6	0	0	-1.9
	Cin-N	0	0	—	5	1	0	0	0	7	14	18.0	2	4	5.1	3	3.9	9.00	39	.424	.486	-4	-4	99	123	0.0	0	-0	-0.4
1970	LA-N	0	0	—	10	0	0	0	0	14	12	7.7	2	5	3.2	8	5.1	2.57	140	.231	.305	2	2	89	145	0.0	0	0	0.2
1971	Cle-A	2	2	.500	9	1	0	0	0	23	17	6.7	0	11	4.3	20	7.8	3.13	120	.205	.299	1	2	108	68	0.4	1	1	0.4
Total	18	174	170	.506	529	404	132	36	10	2930	2703	8.3	256	1069	3.3	2167	6.7	3.63	103	.244	.309	26	41	101	96	15.9	29	18	11.8

■ CARLOS PASCUAL Pascual, Carlos Alberto (Lus) b: 3/13/31, Havana, Cuba BR/TR, 5'6", 165 lbs. Deb: 9/24/50

YEAR	TM/L	W	L	PCT	G	GS	CG	SHO	SV	IP	H	H/G	HR	BB	BB/G	SO	SO/G	ERA	/A	OAVG	OOBP	PR	/A	PF	CPI	WAT	PB	PD	TPI
1950	Was-A	1	1	.500	2	2	2	0	0	17	12	6.4	0	8	4.2	3	1.6	2.12	218	.194	.296	5	5	101	92	0.1	-0	-1	0.4

■ LARRY PASHNICK Pashnick, Larry John b: 4/25/56, Lincoln Park, Mich. BR/TR, 6'3", 205 lbs. Deb: 4/10/82

YEAR	TM/L	W	L	PCT	G	GS	CG	SHO	SV	IP	H	H/G	HR	BB	BB/G	SO	SO/G	ERA	/A	OAVG	OOBP	PR	/A	PF	CPI	WAT	PB	PD	TPI
1982	Det-A	4	4	.500	28	13	1	0	0	94	110	10.5	17	25	2.4	19	1.8	4.02	101	.297	.337	1	1	100	132	0.0	0	-1	0.0
1983	Det-A	1	3	.250	12	6	0	0	0	38	48	11.4	5	18	4.3	17	4.0	5.21	74	.308	.381	-5	-6	95	115	-1.0	0	1	-0.4
1984	Min-A	2	1	.667	13	1	0	0	0	38	38	9.0	3	11	2.6	10	2.4	3.55	119	.260	.319	2	3	106	103	0.5	0	0	0.3
Total	3	7	8	.467	53	20	1	0	0	170	196	10.4	25	54	2.9	46	2.4	4.18	97	.292	.344	-2	-2	100	122	-0.5	0	0	-0.1

■ CLAUDE PASSEAU Passeau, Claude William b: 4/9/09, Wayensboro, Miss. BR/TR, 6'3", 198 lbs. Deb: 9/29/35

YEAR	TM/L	W	L	PCT	G	GS	CG	SHO	SV	IP	H	H/G	HR	BB	BB/G	SO	SO/G	ERA	/A	OAVG	OOBP	PR	/A	PF	CPI	WAT	PB	PD	TPI
1935	Pit-N	0	1	.000	1	1	0	0	0	3	7	21.0	0	2	6.0	1	3.0	12.00	35	.500	.563	-3	-3	105	99	-0.4	-0	0	-0.1
1936	Phi-N	11	15	.423	49	21	8	2	3	217	247	10.2	7	55	2.3	85	3.5	3.48	128	.280	.320	13	23	111	105	1.7	4	1	2.9
1937	Phi-N	14	18	.438	50	34	18	1	2	**292**	348	10.7	16	79	2.4	135	4.2	4.35	100	.296	.339	-14	-1	111	101	1.3	-0	-0	0.0
1938	Phi-N	11	18	.379	44	33	15	0	1	239	281	10.6	8	93	3.5	100	3.8	4.52	89	.287	.349	-19	-14	106	96	2.0	-3	3	-1.2
1939	Phi-N	2	4	.333	8	8	4	1	0	53	54	9.2	1	25	4.2	29	4.9	4.25	92	.263	.339	-2	-2	99	87	0.2	-0	0	-0.1
	Chi-N	13	9	.591	34	27	13	1	3	221	215	8.8	8	48	2.0	108	4.4	3.05	128	.254	.292	21	21	100	94	1.3	-1	1	2.2
	Yr	15	13	.536	42	35	17	2	3	274	269	8.8	9	73	2.4	**137**	4.5	3.28	119	.255	.301	19	19	100	94	1.5	-0	1	2.1
1940	Chi-N	20	13	.606	46	31	20	4	5	281	259	8.3	8	59	1.9	124	4.0	2.50	**152**	.237	.275	42	41	99	98	4.6	6	1	**5.1**
1941	Chi-N	14	14	.500	34	30	20	3	0	231	262	10.2	10	52	**2.0**	80	3.1	3.35	102	.281	.317	7	1	94	111	1.4	5	-1	0.5
1942	Chi-N	19	14	.576	35	34	24	3	0	278	284	9.2	13	74	2.4	89	2.9	2.69	120	.260	.307	19	17	98	121	**4.7**	0	1	2.0
1943	Chi-N	15	12	.556	35	31	18	1	1	257	245	8.6	10	66	2.3	93	3.3	2.91	114	.249	.293	13	12	98	99	2.2	1	1	1.5
1944	Chi-N	15	9	.625	34	27	18	2	3	227	234	9.3	8	50	2.0	89	3.5	2.89	125	.266	.302	18	18	100	111	3.6	-1	0	1.9
1945	Chi-N	17	9	.654	34	27	19	**5**	1	227	205	8.1	4	59	2.3	98	3.9	2.46	147	.238	.285	34	**29**	95	102	0.7	2	3	**3.5**
1946	Chi-N	9	8	.529	21	21	10	2	0	129	118	8.2	5	42	2.9	47	3.3	3.14	101	.237	.295	4	1	93	81	0.0	3	1	0.4
1947	Chi-N	2	6	.250	19	6	1	1	2	63	97	13.9	7	24	3.4	26	3.7	6.29	67	.353	.395	-16	-14	104	108	-1.7	-2	-1	-1.5
Total	13	162	150	.519	444	331	188	26	21	2718	2856	9.5	105	728	2.4	1104	3.7	3.32	113	.267	.311	119	127	101	102	21.6	13	9	17.1

■ FRANK PASTORE Pastore, Frank Enrico b: 8/21/57, Alhambra, Cal. BR/TR, 6'2", 188 lbs. Deb: 4/04/79

YEAR	TM/L	W	L	PCT	G	GS	CG	SHO	SV	IP	H	H/G	HR	BB	BB/G	SO	SO/G	ERA	/A	OAVG	OOBP	PR	/A	PF	CPI	WAT	PB	PD	TPI
1979	Cin-N	6	7	.462	30	9	2	1	4	95	102	9.7	8	23	2.2	63	6.0	4.26	85	.271	.310	-6	-7	96	85	-1.1	-0	0	-0.7
1980	Cin-N	13	7	.650	27	27	9	2	0	185	161	7.8	13	42	2.0	110	5.4	3.26	112	.233	.273	7	8	101	78	2.5	-1	-1	0.7
1981	Cin-N	4	9	.308	22	22	2	1	0	132	125	8.5	11	35	2.4	81	5.5	4.02	87	.247	.293	-8	-8	101	79	-3.3	-2	-2	-1.0
1982	Cin-N	8	13	.381	31	29	3	2	0	188	210	10.1	13	57	2.7	94	4.5	3.97	94	.286	.334	-8	-5	104	106	0.1	1	-2	-0.5
1983	Cin-N	9	12	.429	36	29	4	1	0	184	207	10.1	20	64	3.1	93	4.5	4.89	77	.290	.344	-26	-23	104	96	-0.6	2	-1	-2.2
1984	Cin-N	3	8	.273	24	16	1	0	0	98	110	10.1	10	40	3.7	53	4.9	6.52	59	.285	.350	-32	-29	107	73	-2.0	-2	0	-2.9
1985	Cin-N	2	1	.667	17	6	1	0	0	54	60	10.0	1	16	2.7	29	4.8	3.83	99	.287	.332	-1	-0	105	100	0.4	-0	0	0.0
1986	Min-A	3	1	.750	33	1	0	0	2	49	54	9.9	4	24	4.4	18	3.3	4.04	113	.283	.350	1	3	109	117	1.1	0	-1	0.2

YEAR	TM/L	W	L	PCT	G	GS	CG	SHO	SV	IP	H	H/G	HR	BB	BB/G	SO	SO/G	ERA	/A	OAVG	OOBP	PR	/A	PF	CPI	WAT	PB	PD	TPI
Total	8	48	58	.453	220	139	22	7	6	985	1029	9.4	80	301	2.8	541	4.9	4.29	87	.270	.320	-72	-61	103	90	-2.9	-2	-5	-6.4
■ **JIM PASTORIUS**	Pastorius, James W. "Sunny Jim" b: 7/12/1881, Pittsburgh, Pa. d: 5/10/41, Pittsburgh, Pa. BL/TL, 5'9", 165 lbs. Deb: 4/15/06																												
1906	Bro-N	10	14	.417	29	24	16	3	0	212	225	9.6	4	69	2.9	58	2.5	3.61	65	.301	.363	-23	-29	90	98	-0.5	0	-1	-3.1
1907	Bro-N	16	12	.571	28	26	20	4	0	222	218	8.8	2	77	3.1	70	2.8	2.35	101	.287	.358	3	0	96	131	3.9	2	-1	0.0
1908	Bro-N	4	20	.167	28	25	16	2	0	214	171	7.2	5	74	3.1	54	2.3	2.44	95	.248	.327	-2	-3	99	98	-6.6	-0	0	-0.3
1909	Bro-N	1	9	.100	12	9	5	0	0	80	91	10.2	4	58	6.5	23	2.6	5.74	47	.313	.429	-28	-27	103	99	-3.6	-1	1	-2.5
Total	4	31	55	.360	97	84	57	9	0	728	705	8.7	15	278	3.4	205	2.5	3.12	77	.284	.360	-50	-59	96	108	-6.8	1	-1	-5.9
■ **JOE PATE**	Pate, Joseph William b: 6/6/1892, Alice, Tex. d: 12/26/48, Fort Worth, Tex. BL/TL, 5'10", 184 lbs. Deb: 4/15/26																												
1926	Phi-A	9	0	1.000	47	2	0	0	6	113	109	8.7	3	51	4.1	24	1.9	2.71	172	.262	.331	**16**	**24**	116	133	4.5	-1	3	2.8
1927	Phi-A	0	3	.000	32	0	0	0	6	54	67	11.2	3	21	3.5	14	2.3	5.17	76	.318	.357	-6	-7	95	101	-1.4	1	0	-0.5
Total	2	9	3	.750	79	2	0	0	12	167	176	9.5	6	72	3.9	38	2.0	3.50	126	.281	.340	10	17	109	123	3.1	0	4	2.3
■ **CASE PATTEN**	Patten, Case Lyman "Casey" b: 5/7/1876, Westport, N.Y. d: 5/31/35, Rochester, N.Y. BB/TL, 6', 175 lbs. Deb: 5/04/01																												
1901	Was-A	18	10	.643	32	30	26	4	0	254	285	10.1	8	74	2.6	109	3.9	3.93	93	.304	.355	-8	-7	100	97	5.6	-5	-1	-0.6
1902	Was-A	17	16	.515	36	34	33	1	1	300	331	9.9	11	89	2.7	92	2.8	4.05	88	.305	.358	-16	-16	100	94	2.5	-9	-1	-1.5
1903	Was-A	11	22	.333	36	34	32	0	1	300	313	9.4	11	80	2.4	133	4.0	3.60	91	.291	.340	-22	-11	111	98	0.6	-7	0	-1.0
1904	Was-A	14	23	.378	45	39	37	2	**3**	358	367	9.2	2	79	2.0	150	3.8	3.07	84	.289	.330	-19	-20	99	99	3.9	-6	-0	-2.0
1905	Was-A	14	22	.389	42	36	29	2	0	310	300	8.7	3	86	2.5	113	3.3	3.14	89	.278	.332	-17	-12	106	96	-1.8	-4	-3	-1.4
1906	Was-A	19	16	.543	38	32	28	7	0	283	253	8.0	2	79	2.5	96	3.1	2.16	117	.263	.319	17	12	94	118	5.9	-4	-1	1.1
1907	Was-A	12	16	.429	36	29	20	1	0	237	272	10.3	3	63	2.4	58	2.2	3.57	67	.314	.360	-27	-31	94	103	2.6	-3	-5	-3.6
1908	Was-A	0	2	.000	4	3	1	0	0	18	25	12.5	0	6	3.0	6	3.0	3.50	66	.333	.383	-2	-2	97	144	-0.9	-0	-0	-0.2
	Bos-A	0	1	.000	1	1	0	0	0	3	8	24.0	0	1	3.0	0	0.0	15.00	15	.533	.563	-4	-4	97	81	-0.4	-0	0	-0.3
	Yr	0	3	.000	5	4	1	0	0	21	33	14.1	0	7	3.0	6	2.6	5.14	45	.367	.412	-6	-7	97	81	-1.3	-0	-0	-0.5
Total	8	105	128	.451	270	238	206	17	5	2063	2154	9.4	40	557	2.4	757	3.3	3.36	88	.292	.342	-98	-92	101	101	18.0	-37	-11	-9.5
■ **DARYL PATTERSON**	Patterson, Daryl Alan b: 11/21/43, Coalinga, Cal. BL/TR, 6'4", 192 lbs. Deb: 4/10/68																												
1968	Det-A	2	3	.400	38	1	0	0	7	68	53	7.0	3	27	3.6	49	6.5	2.12	145	.213	.297	7	7	103	121	-0.8	-1	-0	0.7
1969	Det-A	0	2	.000	18	0	0	0	0	22	15	6.1	2	19	7.8	12	4.9	2.86	129	.205	.358	2	2	102	142	-0.9	-0	-1	0.1
1970	Det-A	7	1	.875	43	0	0	0	2	78	81	9.3	9	39	4.5	55	6.3	4.85	80	.269	.356	-10	-9	104	98	3.1	-1	-1	-1.0
1971	Det-A	0	1	.000	12	0	0	0	0	9	14	14.0	1	6	6.0	5	5.0	5.00	66	.359	.438	-2	-2	95	157	-0.4	0	0	-0.1
	Oak-A	0	0	—	4	0	0	0	0	6	5	7.5	2	4	6.0	2	3.0	7.50	46	.238	.385	-3	-3	99	87	0.0	-0	-0	-0.2
	Yr	0	1	.000	16	0	0	0	0	15	19	11.4	3	10	6.0	7	4.2	6.00	56	.311	.405	-4	-4	96	87	-0.4	0	-0	-0.3
	StL-N	0	1	.000	13	2	0	0	1	27	20	6.7	3	15	5.0	11	3.7	4.33	80	.211	.313	-3	-3	100	77	-0.4	-0	-0	-0.3
1974	Pit-N	2	1	.667	14	0	0	0	1	21	35	15.0	3	9	3.9	8	3.4	7.29	48	.376	.423	-9	-9	97	106	0.4	-0	0	-0.8
Total	5	11	9	.550	142	3	0	0	11	231	223	8.7	23	119	4.6	142	5.5	4.09	86	.256	.346	-17	-15	102	109	1.0	-3	-2	-1.6
■ **DAVE PATTERSON**	Patterson, David Glenn b: 7/25/56, Springfield, Mo. BR/TR, 6', 170 lbs. Deb: 6/09/79																												
1979	LA-N	4	1	.800	36	0	0	0	6	53	62	10.5	5	22	3.7	34	5.8	5.26	71	.292	.353	-9	-9	99	91	1.5	-0	0	-0.9
■ **GIL PATTERSON**	Patterson, Gilbert Thomas b: 9/5/55, Philadelphia, Pa. BR/TR, 6'1", 185 lbs. Deb: 4/19/77																												
1977	NY-A	1	2	.333	10	6	0	0	1	33	38	10.4	3	20	5.5	29	7.9	5.45	72	.290	.391	-5	-6	97	101	-0.6	0	1	-0.4
■ **KEN PATTERSON**	Patterson, Kenneth Brian b: 7/8/64, Costa Mesa, Cal. BL/TL, 6'4", 210 lbs. Deb: 7/09/88																												
1988	Chi-A	0	2	.000	9	2	0	0	1	21	25	10.7	2	7	3.0	8	3.4	4.71	83	.294	.348	-2	-2	99	101	-0.9	0	-0	-0.1
■ **REGGIE PATTERSON**	Patterson, Reginald Allen b: 11/7/58, Birmingham, Ala. BR/TR, 6'4", 180 lbs. Deb: 8/13/81																												
1981	Chi-A	0	1	.000	6	1	0	0	0	7	14	18.0	1	6	7.7	2	2.6	14.14	26	.412	.500	-8	-8	99	74	-0.4	0	0	-0.7
1983	Chi-N	1	2	.333	5	2	0	0	0	19	17	8.1	3	6	2.8	10	4.7	4.74	78	.246	.321	-2	-2	101	88	-0.3	-1	0	-0.2
1984	Chi-N	0	1	.000	3	1	0	0	0	6	10	15.0	1	2	3.0	5	7.5	10.50	37	.357	.400	-5	-4	109	69	-0.4	-0	0	-0.3
1985	Chi-N	3	0	1.000	8	5	1	0	0	39	36	8.3	2	10	2.3	17	3.9	3.00	140	.250	.293	3	5	117	100	1.5	-0	-0	0.5
Total	4	4	4	.500	22	9	1	0	0	71	77	9.8	7	24	3.0	34	4.3	5.20	77	.280	.338	-12	-10	110	91	0.4	-1	0	-0.7
■ **BOB PATTERSON**	Patterson, Robert Chandler b: 5/16/59, Jacksonville, Fla. BR/TR, 6'2", 185 lbs. Deb: 9/02/85																												
1985	SD-N	0	0	—	3	0	0	0	0	4	13	29.3	2	3	6.8	1	2.3	24.75	15	.565	.615	-9	-9	101	80	0.0	0	-0	-0.8
1986	Pit-N	2	3	.400	11	5	0	0	0	36	49	12.3	0	5	1.3	20	5.0	5.00	75	.322	.340	-5	-5	101	85	0.0	-0	1	-0.4
1987	Pit-N	1	4	.200	15	7	0	0	0	43	49	10.3	5	22	4.6	27	5.7	6.70	64	.290	.358	-12	-12	105	80	-1.4	-1	-0	-1.1
Total	3	3	7	.300	29	12	0	0	0	83	111	12.0	7	30	3.3	48	5.2	6.83	59	.323	.368	-27	-26	103	82	-1.4	-1	0	-2.3
■ **ROY PATTERSON**	Patterson, Roy Lewis "Boy Wonder" b: 12/17/1876, Stoddard, Wis. d: 4/14/53, St.Croix Falls, Wis. BR/TR, 6', 185 lbs. Deb: 4/24/01																												
1901	Chi-A	20	16	.556	41	35	30	4	0	312	345	10.0	11	62	1.8	127	3.7	3.37	104	.301	.337	10	5	96	104	-2.0	1	0	0.5
1902	Chi-A	19	14	.576	34	30	26	2	0	268	262	8.8	5	67	2.3	61	2.0	3.06	110	.280	.328	15	9	94	96	1.1	-2	1	1.0
1903	Chi-A	15	15	.500	34	30	26	2	1	293	275	8.4	5	69	2.1	89	2.7	2.70	103	.270	.316	8	2	94	102	2.1	-5	2	0.4
1904	Chi-A	9	9	.500	22	17	14	4	0	165	148	8.1	1	24	1.3	64	3.5	2.29	109	.262	.292	6	4	97	96	-1.3	-3	-1	0.3
1905	Chi-A	4	6	.400	13	9	7	1	0	89	73	7.4	0	16	1.6	29	2.9	1.82	135	.246	.285	8	6	93	106	-1.7	2	1	0.8
1906	Chi-A	10	7	.588	21	18	12	3	1	142	119	7.5	1	17	1.1	45	2.9	2.09	115	.251	.277	9	5	89	87	-0.3	-4	0	0.6
1907	Chi-A	4	6	.400	19	13	4	1	0	96	105	9.8	0	18	1.7	27	2.5	2.63	98	.303	.338	-1	-1	101	118	-1.5	-3	1	0.0
Total	7	81	73	.526	184	152	119	17	2	1365	1327	8.7	23	273	1.8	442	2.9	2.75	107	.277	.316	56	30	95	100	-3.6	-14	4	3.6
■ **MARTY PATTIN**	Pattin, Martin William b: 4/6/43, Charleston, Ill. BR/TR, 5'11", 180 lbs. Deb: 5/14/68																												
1968	Cal-A	4	4	.500	52	4	0	0	3	84	67	7.2	7	37	4.0	66	7.1	2.79	103	.221	.303	2	1	96	112	0.6	-1	-1	0.0
1969	Sea-A	7	12	.368	34	27	2	1	0	159	166	9.4	29	71	4.0	126	7.1	5.60	65	.268	.342	-35	-35	100	88	-0.6	-1	-1	-3.6
1970	Mil-A	14	12	.538	37	29	11	0	0	233	204	7.9	20	71	2.7	161	6.2	3.40	109	.235	.294	8	8	100	88	3.4	-2	2	0.8
1971	Mil-A	14	14	.500	36	36	9	5	0	265	225	7.6	29	73	2.5	169	5.7	3.12	116	.235	.286	10	14	104	99	2.1	-3	-1	1.1
1972	Bos-A	17	13	.567	38	35	13	4	0	253	232	8.3	19	65	2.3	168	6.0	3.24	100	.243	.293	-5	-0	105	91	0.7	0	1	0.1
1973	Bos-A	15	15	.500	34	30	11	2	1	219	238	9.8	31	69	2.8	119	4.9	4.32	93	.277	.333	-12	-8	105	105	-1.5	0	1	-0.6
1974	KC-A	3	7	.300	25	11	2	0	0	117	121	9.3	10	28	2.2	50	3.8	4.00	96	.264	.304	-5	-2	106	86	-1.8	0	-1	-0.2
1975	KC-A	10	10	.500	44	15	5	1	5	177	173	8.8	13	45	2.3	89	4.5	3.25	118	.253	.299	11	11	101	96	-1.1	0	-1	1.1
1976	KC-A	8	14	.364	44	15	4	1	5	141	114	7.3	9	38	2.4	65	4.1	2.49	139	.216	.270	16	15	99	90	-4.1	0	-0	1.6
1977	KC-A	10	3	.769	31	10	4	0	0	128	115	8.1	16	37	2.6	55	3.9	3.59	112	.242	.291	7	6	99	96	2.6	0	-1	0.5
1978	KC-A	3	3	.500	32	5	2	0	4	79	72	8.2	8	25	2.8	30	3.4	3.30	116	.248	.304	4	5	101	106	-0.3	0	-2	0.3
1979	KC-A	5	2	.714	31	7	1	0	3	94	109	10.4	11	21	2.0	41	3.9	4.60	97	.293	.325	-4	-2	105	99	1.4	0	-1	-0.1
1980	KC-A	4	0	1.000	37	0	0	0	4	89	97	9.8	7	23	2.3	40	4.0	3.64	108	.277	.320	4	3	97	105	2.0	0	-1	0.2
Total	13	114	109	.511	475	224	64	14	25	2038	1933	8.5	209	603	2.7	1179	5.2	3.62	102	.250	.304	2	18	102	96	3.4	-7	-5	1.2
■ **JIMMY PATTISON**	Pattison, James Wells b: 12/18/08, New York, N.Y. BL/TL, 6', 185 lbs. Deb: 4/18/29																												
1929	Bro-N	0	1	.000	6	0	0	0	0	12	9	6.8	1	4	3.0	5	3.8	4.50	101	.231	.295	0	0	96	75	-0.4	0	-0	0.0
■ **HARRY PATTON**	Patton, Harry Claude b: 6/29/1884, Gillespie, Ill. d: 6/9/30, St.Louis, Mo. Deb: 8/22/10																												
1910	StL-N	0	0	—	1	0	0	0	0	4	4	9.0	0	2	4.5	2	4.5	2.25	125	.267	.353	0	0	93	153	0.0	0	0	0.1
■ **MIKE PAUL**	Paul, Michael George b: 4/18/45, Detroit, Mich. BL/TL, 6', 175 lbs. Deb: 5/27/68 C																												
1968	Cle-A	5	8	.385	36	7	0	0	3	92	72	7.0	11	35	3.4	87	8.5	3.91	77	.213	.292	-10	-9	101	79	-1.8	0	-1	-1.0
1969	Cle-A	5	10	.333	47	12	0	0	2	117	104	8.0	12	54	4.2	98	7.5	3.62	97	.241	.322	0	-2	96	103	-1.0	-3	-1	-0.5
1970	Cle-A	2	8	.200	30	15	1	0	0	88	91	9.3	13	45	4.6	70	7.2	4.81	89	.271	.349	-11	-5	115	102	-2.8	-1	-1	-0.6
1971	Cle-A	2	7	.222	17	12	1	0	0	62	78	11.3	8	14	2.0	33	4.8	5.95	63	.318	.358	-17	-15	108	91	-1.8	-1	-1	-1.6
1972	Tex-A	8	9	.471	49	20	2	1	1	162	149	8.3	4	52	2.9	108	6.0	2.17	137	.246	.301	16	15	97	**128**	1.7	1	-1	1.6
1973	Tex-A	5	4	.556	36	10	1	0	2	87	104	10.8	9	36	3.7	49	5.1	4.97	77	.295	.362	-11	-11	100	101	1.5	0	1	-0.9
	Chi-N	0	1	.000	11	1	0	0	0	18	17	8.5	2	9	4.5	6	3.0	3.50	114	.258	.342	0	1	109	122	-0.4	-1	0	0.1
1974	Chi-N	0	1	.000	2	0	0	0	0	1	4	36.0	1	1	9.0	1	9.0	36.00	10	.500	.556	-4	-4	102	68	-0.4	0	0	-0.2

YEAR	TM/L	W	L	PCT	G	GS	CG	SHO	SV	IP	H	H/G	HR	BB	BB/G	SO	SO/G	ERA	/A	OAVG	OOBP	PR	/A	PF	CPI	WAT	PB	PD	TPI
Total	7	27	48	.360	228	77	5	1	8	627	619	8.9	60	246	3.5	452	6.5	3.92	89	.260	.327	-35	-31	102	105	-5.0	-5	-4	-3.1
■ GENE PAULETTE	Paulette, Eugene Edward b: 5/26/1891, Centralia, Ill. d: 2/8/66, Little Rock, Ark. BR/TR, 6', 150 lbs. Deb: 6/16/11																												
1918	StL-N	0	0	—	1	0	0	0	0	⅓	1	27.0	0	0	0.0	0	0.0	0.00	—	.500	.500	0	0	95	102	0.5	0	0	0.4
■ GIL PAULSEN	Paulsen, Guilford Paul Hans b: 11/14/02, Graettinger, Iowa BR/TR, 6'2.5", 190 lbs. Deb: 10/03/25																												
1925	StL-N	0	0	—	1	0	0	0	0	2	1	4.5	0	0	0.0	1	4.5	0.00	—	.125	.125	1	1	101	0	0.0	0	0	0.1
■ JOHN PAWLOWSKI	Pawlowski, John b: 9/6/63, Johnson City, N.Y. BR/TR, 6'2", 175 lbs. Deb: 9/19/87																												
1987	Chi-A	0	0	—	2	0	0	0	0	4	7	15.8	0	3	6.8	2	4.5	4.50	108	.438	.500	-0	0	109	211	0.0	0	0	0.0
1988	Chi-A	1	0	1.000	6	0	0	0	0	14	20	12.9	2	3	1.9	10	6.4	8.36	47	.328	.354	-7	-7	99	69	0.5	0	0	-0.6
Total	2	1	0	1.000	8	0	0	0	0	18	27	13.5	2	6	3.0	12	6.0	7.50	55	.351	.388	-7	-7	101	101	0.5	0	0	-0.6
■ MIKE PAXTON	Paxton, Michael De Wayne b: 9/3/53, Memphis, Tenn. BR/TR, 5'11", 190 lbs. Deb: 5/25/77																												
1977	Bos-A	10	5	.667	29	12	2	1	0	108	134	11.2	7	25	2.1	58	4.8	3.83	123	.311	.347	3	11	116	122	1.3	0	-0	1.0
1978	Cle-A	12	11	.522	33	27	5	2	1	191	179	8.4	13	63	3.0	96	4.5	3.86	92	.247	.310	-2	-7	94	83	2.0	0	-1	-0.7
1979	Cle-A	8	8	.500	33	24	3	0	0	160	210	11.8	14	52	2.9	70	3.9	5.91	76	.315	.360	-30	-25	106	88	0.0	0	0	-2.3
1980	Cle-A	0	0	—	4	0	0	0	0	8	13	14.6	4	6	6.8	6	6.8	12.38	34	.394	.475	-7	-7	103	96	0.0	0	0	-0.6
Total	4	30	24	.556	99	63	10	3	1	467	536	10.3	38	146	2.8	230	4.4	4.70	88	.289	.340	-36	-29	103	94	3.3	0	-1	-2.6
■ GEORGE PAYNE	Payne, George Washington b: 5/23/1890, Mt.Vernon, Ky. d: 1/24/59, Bellflower, Cal. BR/TR, 5'11", 172 lbs. Deb: 5/08/20																												
1920	Chi-A	1	1	.500	12	0	0	0	0	30	39	11.7	2	9	2.7	7	2.1	5.40	66	.312	.358	-5	-6	94	85	-0.1	-0	-1	-0.6
■ HARLEY PAYNE	Payne, Harley Fenwick "Lady" b: 1/9/1868, Windsor, Ont., Can. d: 12/29/35, Orwell, Ohio BB/TL, 6', 160 lbs. Deb: 4/18/1896																												
1896	Bro-N	14	16	.467	34	28	24	2	0	242	284	10.6	4	58	2.2	52	1.9	3.38	114	.315	.357	26	12	88	113	0.8	1	3	1.3
1897	Bro-N	14	17	.452	40	38	30	1	0	280	350	11.3	8	71	2.3	86	2.8	4.63	95	.329	.371	-10	-7	102	93	-0.4	-1	2	-0.4
1898	Bro-N	1	0	1.000	1	1	1	0	0	9	11	11.0	0	3	3.0	2	2.0	4.00	87	.324	.379	-0	-1	96	104	0.5	1	0	0.1
1899	Pit-N	1	3	.250	5	5	2	0	0	26	33	11.4	2	4	1.4	8	2.8	3.81	99	.334	.360	0	-0	98	117	-0.9	-1	0	0.0
Total	4	30	36	.455	80	72	57	3	0	557	678	11.0	14	136	2.2	148	2.4	4.04	102	.323	.364	16	5	96	103	0.0	1	5	1.0
■ MIKE PAYNE	Payne, Michael Earl b: 11/15/61, Woonsocket, R.I. BR/TR, 5'11", 165 lbs. Deb: 8/22/84																												
1984	Atl-N	0	1	.000	3	1	0	0	0	6	7	10.5	0	3	4.5	3	4.5	6.00	66	.333	.400	-2	-1	110	91	-0.4	-0	0	0.0
■ MIKE PAZIK	Pazik, Michael Joseph b: 1/26/50, Lynn, Mass. BL/TL, 6'2", 195 lbs. Deb: 5/11/75																												
1975	Min-A	0	4	.000	5	3	0	0	0	20	28	12.6	5	10	4.5	8	3.6	8.10	50	.329	.396	-10	-9	107	90	-1.9	0	-1	-0.8
1976	Min-A	0	0	—	5	0	0	0	0	9	13	13.0	0	4	4.0	6	6.0	7.00	49	.342	.419	-3	-4	98	84	0.0	0	-0	-0.3
1977	Min-A	1	0	1.000	3	3	0	0	0	18	18	9.0	1	6	3.0	6	3.0	2.50	166	.265	.312	3	3	102	142	0.5	0	0	0.4
Total	3	1	4	.200	13	6	0	0	0	47	59	11.3	6	20	3.8	20	3.8	5.74	69	.309	.370	-10	-9	103	109	-1.4	0	-1	-0.7
■ FRANK PEARCE	Pearce, Frank b: Louisville, Ky. Deb: 10/04/1876																												
1876	Lou-N	0	0	—	1	0	0	0	0	4	5	11.3	0	1	2.3	1	2.3	4.50	54	.310	.351	-1	-1	106	74	0.0	-0	0	0.0
■ FRANK PEARCE	Pearce, Franklin Thomas b: 8/31/05, Middletown, Ky. d: 9/3/50, Van Buren, N.Y. BR/TR, 6', 170 lbs. Deb: 4/20/33																												
1933	Phi-N	5	4	.556	20	7	3	1	0	82	78	8.6	5	29	3.2	18	2.0	3.62	112	.251	.307	-3	4	121	90	1.3	-1	0	0.4
1934	Phi-N	0	2	.000	7	1	0	0	0	20	25	11.2	4	5	2.3	4	1.8	7.20	62	.301	.341	-7	-6	111	77	-0.9	1	-1	-0.4
1935	Phi-N	0	0	—	5	0	0	0	0	13	22	15.2	0	6	4.2	7	4.8	8.31	57	.361	.412	-6	-5	117	79	0.0	1	-0	-0.3
Total	3	5	6	.455	32	8	3	1	0	115	125	9.8	9	40	3.1	29	2.3	4.77	88	.275	.327	-16	-7	119	87	0.4	1	-0	-0.3
■ GEORGE PEARCE	Pearce, George Thomas "Filbert" b: 1/10/1888, Aurora, Ill. d: 10/11/35, Joliet, Ill. BL/TL, 5'10.5", 175 lbs. Deb: 4/16/12																												
1912	Chi-N	0	0	—	3	2	0	0	0	15	15	9.0	0	12	7.2	9	5.4	5.40	64	.172	.273	-3	-3	102	11	0.0	-0	1	-0.1
1913	Chi-N	13	5	.722	25	21	15	3	0	163	137	7.6	4	59	3.3	73	4.0	2.32	134	.234	.300	16	14	97	112	3.4	-3	-0	1.1
1914	Chi-N	9	12	.429	30	16	4	0	1	141	122	7.8	3	65	4.1	78	5.0	3.51	78	.239	.314	-11	-12	99	80	-1.7	-3	2	-1.3
1915	Chi-N	13	9	.591	36	20	8	2	0	176	158	8.1	1	77	3.9	96	4.9	3.32	85	.244	.318	-11	-10	103	87	2.7	1	-0	-0.9
1916	Chi-N	0	0	—	4	1	0	0	0	4	6	13.5	0	1	2.3	0	0.0	2.25	137	.300	.304	0	0	117	169	0.0	0	0	0.0
1917	StL-N	1	1	.500	5	0	0	0	0	10	7	6.3	0	3	2.7	4	3.6	3.60	77	.184	.244	-1	-1	102	31	0.0	-1	0	0.0
Total	6	36	27	.571	103	60	27	5	1	509	445	7.9	8	217	3.8	260	4.6	3.11	94	.236	.308	-11	-11	100	90	4.4	-6	2	-1.2
■ JIM PEARCE	Pearce, James Madison b: 6/9/25, Zebulon, N.C. BR/TR, 6'6", 180 lbs. Deb: 9/08/49																												
1949	Was-A	0	1	.000	2	1	0	0	0	5	9	16.2	1	5	9.0	1	1.8	9.00	45	.375	.467	-3	-3	96	111	-0.4	-0	1	-0.1
1950	Was-A	2	1	.667	20	3	1	0	0	57	58	9.2	2	37	5.8	18	2.8	6.00	77	.270	.372	-9	-9	101	77	0.6	-1	-0	-0.8
1953	Was-A	0	1	.000	4	1	0	0	0	9	15	15.0	3	6	6.0	0	0.0	8.00	46	.405	.488	-4	-4	93	135	-0.4	-0	-0	-0.3
1954	Cin-N	1	0	1.000	2	1	1	0	0	11	7	5.7	0	5	4.1	3	2.5	0.00	—	.194	.302	5	5	104	0	0.5	-0	0	0.6
1955	Cin-N	0	1	.000	2	1	0	0	0	3	8	24.0	0	0	0.0	0	0.0	12.00	35	.471	.444	-3	-3	104	82	-0.4	0	-0	-0.1
Total	5	3	4	.429	30	7	2	0	0	85	97	10.3	6	53	5.6	22	2.3	5.82	76	.295	.388	-13	-13	100	75	-0.1	-2	0	-0.7
■ FRANK PEARS	Pears, Frank H. b: 8/30/1866, Kentucky d: 11/29/23, St.Louis, Mo. TR, Deb: 10/06/1889																												
1889	KC-a	0	2	.000	3	2	2	0	0	22	21	8.6	2	9	3.7	5	2.0	4.91	85	.266	.341	-3	-2	109	77	-0.9	-1	0	-0.2
1893	StL-N	0	0	—	1	0	0	0	0	4	9	20.3	0	2	4.5	0	0.0	13.50	35	.461	.511	-4	-4	100	74	0.0	-0	0	-0.2
Total	2	0	2	.000	4	2	2	0	0	26	30	10.4	2	11	3.8	5	1.7	6.23	68	.305	.375	-7	-6	107	77	-0.9	-2	0	-0.4
■ ALEX PEARSON	Pearson, Alexander Franklin b: 3/7/1877, Greensboro, Pa. d: 10/30/66, Rochester, Pa. BR/TR, 5'10.5", 160 lbs. Deb: 8/01/02																												
1902	StL-N	2	6	.250	11	10	8	0	0	82	90	9.9	0	22	2.4	24	2.6	3.95	70	.302	.350	-11	-11	99	81	-1.6	1	-0	-1.0
1903	Cle-A	1	2	.333	4	3	2	0	0	30	34	10.2	1	3	0.9	12	3.6	3.60	78	.308	.327	-2	-3	95	97	-0.5	-1	0	-0.2
Total	2	3	8	.273	15	13	10	0	0	112	124	10.0	1	25	2.0	36	2.9	3.86	72	.304	.344	-13	-14	98	85	-2.1	-0	-0	-1.2
■ IKE PEARSON	Pearson, Issac Overton b: 3/1/17, Grenada, Miss. d: 3/17/85, Sarasota, Fla. BR/TR, 6'1", 180 lbs. Deb: 6/06/39																												
1939	Phi-N	2	13	.133	26	13	4	0	0	125	144	10.4	15	56	4.0	29	2.1	5.76	68	.296	.360	-26	-26	99	93	-4.2	-3	1	-2.6
1940	Phi-N	3	14	.176	29	20	5	1	1	145	160	9.9	13	57	3.5	43	2.7	5.46	72	.275	.340	-26	-25	102	82	-4.1	1	1	-2.1
1941	Phi-N	4	14	.222	46	10	0	0	6	136	139	9.2	8	70	4.6	38	2.5	3.57	104	.266	.352	1	2	103	123	-1.9	-2	0	0.0
1942	Phi-N	1	6	.143	35	7	0	0	0	85	87	9.2	4	50	5.3	21	2.2	4.55	74	.271	.369	-12	-11	101	101	-1.6	-2	-0	-1.4
1946	Phi-N	1	0	1.000	5	2	1	1	0	14	16	10.3	1	8	5.1	6	3.9	3.86	87	.271	.362	-1	-1	98	117	0.5	1	0	0.0
1948	Chi-A	2	3	.400	23	2	0	0	1	53	62	10.5	8	27	4.6	12	2.0	4.92	87	.292	.371	-4	-4	100	118	0.2	-0	1	-0.2
Total	6	13	50	.206	164	54	10	2	8	558	608	9.8	49	268	4.3	149	2.4	4.84	79	.279	.355	-67	-64	101	102	-11.1	-6	2	-6.3
■ MONTE PEARSON	Pearson, Montgomery Marcellus "Hoot" b: 9/2/09, Oakland, Cal. d: 1/27/78, Fresno, Cal. BR/TR, 6', 175 lbs. Deb: 4/22/32																												
1932	Cle-A	0	0	—	8	0	0	0	0	8	10	11.3	1	11	12.4	5	5.6	10.13	47	.323	.488	-5	-5	107	89	0.0	0	1	-0.2
1933	Cle-A	10	5	.667	19	16	10	0	0	135	111	7.4	5	55	3.7	54	3.6	2.33	193	.221	.296	29	32	105	118	2.7	1	-1	3.4
1934	Cle-A	18	13	.581	39	33	19	0	2	255	257	9.1	16	130	4.6	140	4.9	4.52	99	.260	.342	-1	-1	100	93	1.2	6	1	0.6
1935	Cle-A	8	13	.381	30	24	10	1	0	182	199	9.8	9	103	5.1	90	4.5	4.90	90	.279	.363	-9	-10	99	97	-3.3	0	2	-0.6
1936	NY-A	19	7	**.731**	33	31	15	1	1	223	191	**7.7**	13	135	5.4	118	4.8	3.71	122	**.233**	.341	33	20	90	106	2.9	6	1	2.4
1937	NY-A	9	3	.750	22	20	7	1	1	145	145	9.0	6	64	4.0	71	4.4	3.17	142	.261	.337	23	21	97	121	1.7	1	-0	2.0
1938	NY-A	16	7	.696	28	27	17	1	0	202	198	8.8	12	113	5.0	98	4.4	3.97	123	.258	.350	18	20	102	109	1.7	-0	1	2.1
1939	NY-A	12	5	.706	22	20	8	0	0	146	151	9.3	9	70	4.3	76	4.7	4.50	88	.272	.347	2	-9	85	100	0.1	7	1	-0.1
1940	NY-A	7	5	.583	16	16	7	1	0	110	108	8.8	8	44	3.6	43	3.5	3.68	114	.262	.328	9	6	96	111	0.2	-1	2	0.7
1941	Cin-N	1	3	.250	7	4	1	0	0	24	22	8.3	3	15	5.6	8	3.0	5.25	68	.242	.343	-4	-5	98	84	-1.0	-1	-0	-0.5
Total	10	100	61	.621	224	191	94	5	4	1430	1392	8.8	82	740	4.7	703	4.4	4.00	111	.256	.342	96	72	97	105	6.2	19	8	9.8
■ MARV PEASLEY	Peasley, Marvin Warren b: 7/16/1888, Jonesport, Me. d: 12/27/48, San Francisco, Cal BL/TL, 6'1", 175 lbs. Deb: 9/27/10																												
1910	Det-A	0	1	.000	2	1	0	0	0	10	13	11.7	0	11	9.9	4	3.6	8.10	31	.295	.446	-6	-6	100	76	-0.4	0	0	-0.5
■ GEORGE PECHINEY	Pechiney, George Adolphe "Pisch" b: 9/20/1861, Cincinnati, Ohio d: 7/14/43, Cincinnati, Ohio BR/TR, 5'9", 184 lbs. Deb: 1885																												
1885	Cin-a	7	4	.636	11	11	11	1	0	98	95	8.7	1	30	2.8	49	4.5	2.02	165	.266	.323	13	14	103	161	1.0	-2	0	1.2
1886	Cin-a	15	21	.417	40	40	35	2	0	330	355	9.7	5	133	3.6	110	3.0	4.15	80	.285	.354	-26	-31	96	99	-2.6	0	-2	-2.8

YEAR	TM/L	W	L	PCT	G	GS	CG	SHO	SV	IP	H	H/G	HR	BB	BB/G	SO	SO/G	ERA	/A	OAVG	OOBP	PR	/A	PF	CPI	WAT	PB	PD	TPI
1887	Cle-a	1	9	.100	10	10	10	0	0	86	118	12.3	8	44	4.6	24	2.5	7.12	62	.341	.415	-27	-26	103	90	-3.3	-0	0	-1.8
Total	3	23	34	.404	61	61	56	3	0	514	568	9.9	14	207	3.6	183	3.2	4.24	82	.292	.360	-39	-43	98	109	-4.9	-2	-2	-3.4
■ STEVE PEEK	Peek, Stephen George b: 7/30/14, Springfield, Mass BB/TR, 6'2", 195 lbs. Deb: 4/16/41																												
1941	NY-A	4	2	.667	17	8	2	0	0	80	85	9.6	6	39	4.4	18	2.0	5.06	78	.276	.354	-8	-10	95	91	0.1	-3	0	-1.1
■ RED PEERY	Peery, George Allan b: 8/15/06, Payson, Utah d: 5/6/85, Salt Lake City, Ut. BL/TL, 5'11", 160 lbs. Deb: 9/22/27																												
1927	Pit-N	0	0	—	1	0	0	0	0	1	0	0.0	0	1	9.0	0	0.0	0.00	—	.000	.200	0	0	99	0	0.0	0	0	0.1
1929	Bos-N	0	1	.000	9	1	0	0	0	44	53	10.8	1	9	1.8	3	0.6	5.11	90	.305	.332	-2	-3	97	81	-0.4	1	-0	-0.1
Total	2	0	1	.000	10	1	0	0	0	45	53	10.6	1	10	2.0	3	0.6	5.00	91	.298	.328	-2	-2	97	80	-0.4	1	-0	0.0
■ HEINIE PEITZ	Peitz, Henry Clement b: 11/28/1870, St.Louis, Mo. d: 10/23/43, Cincinnati, Ohio BR/TR, 5'11", 165 lbs. Deb: 10/15/1892 C																												
1894	StL-N	0	0	—	1	0	0	0	0	3	7	21.0	0	2	6.0	0	0.0	9.00	61	.478	.540	-1	-1	103	121	0.0	0	0	0.0
1897	Cin-N	0	1	.000	2	1	1	0	0	8	9	10.1	0	4	4.5	0	0.0	7.88	58	.306	.389	-3	-3	107	53	-0.4	0	0	-0.1
1899	Cin-N	0	0	—	1	0	0	0	0	5	6	10.8	0	1	1.8	3	5.4	5.40	75	.322	.356	-1	-1	105	68	0.0	0	0	0.0
Total	3	0	1	.000	4	1	1	0	0	16	22	12.4	0	7	3.9	3	1.7	7.31	63	.351	.416	-5	-5	106	70	-0.4	1	0	-0.1
■ BARNEY PELTY	Pelty, Barney b: 9/10/1880, Farmington, Mo. d: 5/24/39, Farmington, Mo. BR/TR, 5'9", 175 lbs. Deb: 03																												
1903	StL-A	3	3	.500	7	6	5	0	1	49	49	9.0	1	15	2.8	20	3.7	2.39	118	.282	.340	3	2	96	138	0.2	0	-1	0.1
1904	StL-A	15	18	.455	39	35	31	2	0	301	270	8.1	7	77	2.3	126	3.8	2.84	89	.262	.313	-8	-10	98	93	1.0	-7	-1	-1.2
1905	StL-A	14	14	.500	31	28	27	1	0	259	222	7.7	3	68	2.4	114	4.0	2.75	90	.255	.309	-3	-8	93	89	3.7	-3	3	-0.5
1906	StL-A	16	11	.593	34	30	25	4	2	261	189	**6.5**	1	59	2.0	92	3.2	1.59	**164**	**.225**	.275	**32**	29	97	97	2.7	-3	5	4.0
1907	StL-A	12	21	.364	36	31	29	5	1	273	234	7.7	1	64	2.1	85	2.8	2.57	97	.254	.303	-1	-2	98	83	-3.9	-1	2	0.0
1908	StL-A	7	4	.636	20	13	7	2	0	122	104	7.7	0	32	2.4	36	2.7	1.99	122	.241	.309	5	6	102	133	1.2	-3	1	0.8
1909	StL-A	11	11	.500	27	23	17	5	0	199	158	7.1	2	53	2.4	88	4.0	2.31	102	.222	.281	4	1	95	75	2.0	1	4	0.5
1910	StL-A	5	11	.313	27	18	12	3	0	165	157	8.6	3	70	3.8	48	2.6	3.49	73	.263	.348	-18	-18	101	98	0.1	-4	4	-1.8
1911	StL-A	7	15	.318	28	22	18	1	0	197	197	9.0	4	69	3.2	59	2.7	2.97	112	.265	.331	8	8	100	106	0.4	-3	1	0.5
1912	StL-A	1	5	.167	6	6	2	0	0	39	43	9.9	0	15	3.5	10	2.3	5.54	62	.297	.374	-9	-9	103	78	-1.5	-2	0	-0.7
	Was-A	1	4	.200	11	4	1	0	0	44	40	8.2	0	10	2.0	15	3.1	3.27	99	.250	.310	0	-0	97	82	-1.6	0	-1	0.0
	Yr	2	9	.182	17	10	3	0	0	83	83	9.0	0	25	2.7	25	2.7	4.34	77	.269	.332	-9	-9	100	82	-3.1	-2	-1	-0.7
Total	10	92	117	.440	266	216	174	23	4	1909	1663	7.8	22	532	2.5	693	3.3	2.63	100	.251	.310	13	-1	97	95	4.3	-25	15	1.7
■ ALEJANDRO PENA	Pena, Alejandro (Vasquez) b: 6/25/59, Cambiaso, D.R. BR/TR, 5'11", 165 lbs. Deb: 9/14/81																												
1981	LA-N	1	1	.500	14	0	0	0	2	25	18	6.5	2	11	4.0	14	5.0	2.88	116	.194	.279	2	1	96	76	0.0	-1	0	0.1
1982	LA-N	0	2	.000	29	0	0	0	0	36	37	9.3	2	21	5.3	20	5.0	4.75	71	.272	.369	-5	-6	94	96	-0.9	0	1	-0.4
1983	LA-N	12	9	.571	34	26	4	3	1	177	152	7.7	7	51	2.6	120	6.1	2.75	132	.229	.279	18	17	100	85	0.3	-2	2	1.8
1984	LA-N	12	6	.667	28	28	8	**4**	0	199	186	8.4	7	46	2.1	135	6.1	**2.49**	**150**	.246	.289	**24**	**28**	104	108	3.4	-1	-1	2.8
1985	LA-N	0	1	.000	2	1	0	0	0	4	7	15.8	1	3	6.8	2	4.5	9.00	37	.350	.435	-2	-3	92	99	-0.4	-0	0	-0.2
1986	LA-N	1	2	.333	24	10	0	0	1	70	74	9.5	6	30	3.9	46	5.9	4.89	72	.270	.340	-9	-11	95	87	-0.3	0	-1	-1.1
1987	LA-N	2	7	.222	37	7	0	0	11	87	82	8.5	9	37	3.8	76	7.9	3.52	107	.251	.321	5	2	92	113	-2.2	-1	-2	0.0
1988	LA-N	6	7	.462	60	0	0	0	12	94	75	7.2	4	27	2.6	83	7.9	1.91	189	.218	.272	16	18	105	121	-1.4	-1	-0	1.9
Total	8	34	35	.493	228	72	12	7	27	692	631	8.2	38	226	2.9	496	6.5	3.02	121	.241	.299	49	48	100	101	-1.5	-5	-2	4.9
■ HIPOLITO PENA	Pena, Hipolito (Concepcion) b: 1/30/64, Fantino, D.R. BL/TL, 6'3", 165 lbs. Deb: 9/01/86																												
1986	Pit-N	0	3	.000	10	1	0	0	1	8	7	7.9	3	3	3.4	6	6.8	9.00	42	.206	.289	-5	-5	101	50	-1.4	0	0	-0.4
1987	Pit-N	0	3	.000	16	1	0	0	1	26	16	5.5	2	26	9.0	16	5.5	4.50	95	.184	.365	-1	-1	105	86	-1.4	-0	0	0.0
1988	NY-A	1	1	.500	16	0	0	0	0	14	10	6.4	1	9	5.8	10	6.4	2.57	148	.192	.306	2	2	96	107	0.0	0	0	0.2
Total	3	1	7	.125	42	2	0	0	2	48	33	6.2	6	38	7.1	32	6.0	4.69	86	.191	.335	-4	-3	101	86	-2.8	-0	0	-0.2
■ JOSE PENA	Pena, Jose (Gutierrez) b: 12/3/42, Ciudad Juarez, Mex. BR/TR, 6'2", 190 lbs. Deb: 6/01/69																												
1969	Cin-N	1	1	.500	6	0	0	0	0	5	10	18.0	0	5	9.0	3	5.4	18.00	20	.400	.500	-8	-8	99	52	0.0	0	0	-0.7
1970	LA-N	4	3	.571	29	0	0	0	4	57	51	8.1	8	29	4.6	31	4.9	4.42	82	.241	.331	-2	-5	89	98	0.2	0	1	-0.3
1971	LA-N	2	0	1.000	21	0	0	0	1	43	32	6.7	7	18	3.8	44	9.2	3.56	95	.211	.290	-0	-1	98	95	1.0	1	-0	0.0
1972	LA-N	0	0	—	5	0	0	0	0	7	13	16.7	1	6	7.7	4	5.1	9.00	36	.371	.452	-4	-5	93	101	0.0	0	0	-0.4
Total	4	7	4	.636	61	0	0	0	5	112	106	8.5	16	58	4.7	82	6.6	4.98	70	.250	.337	-15	-18	93	95	1.2	1	0	-1.4
■ ORLANDO PENA	Pena, Orlando Gregorio (Quevara) b: 11/17/33, Victoria De Las Tunas, Cuba BR/TR, 5'11", 154 lbs. Deb: 8/24/58																												
1958	Cin-N	1	0	1.000	9	0	0	0	3	15	10	6.0	0	4	2.4	11	6.6	0.60	698	.185	.233	6	6	106	144	0.5	0	-0	0.6
1959	Cin-N	5	9	.357	46	8	1	0	5	136	150	9.9	26	39	2.6	76	5.0	4.76	85	.280	.322	-12	-11	103	102	-1.8	-0	-1	-1.1
1960	Cin-N	0	1	.000	4	0	0	0	0	9	8	8.0	0	3	3.0	9	9.0	3.00	124	.222	.282	1	1	99	63	-0.4	-0	-0	0.0
1962	KC-A	6	4	.600	13	12	6	1	0	90	71	7.1	9	27	2.7	56	5.6	3.00	134	.213	.270	10	10	101	86	1.5	-0	-1	0.9
1963	KC-A	12	20	.375	35	33	9	3	0	217	218	9.0	24	53	2.2	128	5.3	3.69	107	.260	.302	-1	6	109	101	-3.1	-0	-2	0.5
1964	KC-A	12	14	.462	40	32	5	0	0	219	231	9.5	40	73	3.0	184	7.6	4.44	88	.268	.327	-20	-13	108	106	2.5	0	-2	-1.4
1965	KC-A	0	6	.000	12	5	0	0	0	35	42	10.8	4	13	3.3	24	6.2	6.94	50	.302	.361	-14	-14	100	76	-2.9	-0	-0	-1.3
	Det-A	4	6	.400	30	0	0	0	4	57	54	8.5	5	20	3.2	55	8.7	2.53	143	.252	.314	6	7	104	143	-1.3	1	-1	0.7
	Yr	4	12	.250	42	5	0	0	4	92	96	9.4	9	33	3.2	79	7.7	4.21	84	.270	.327	-8	-7	102	143	-4.2	-0	-1	-0.6
1966	Det-A	4	2	.667	54	0	0	0	7	108	105	8.8	16	35	2.9	79	6.6	3.08	114	.252	.309	4	5	102	134	0.8	-1	2	0.7
1967	Det-A	0	1	.000	2	0	0	0	0	2	5	22.5	0	0	0.0	2	9.0	13.50	23	.500	.500	-2	-2	98	86	-0.4	0	-0	-0.2
	Cle-A	0	3	.000	48	1	0	0	8	88	67	6.9	8	22	2.3	72	7.4	3.38	97	.208	.254	-1	-3	101	69	-1.4	-1	-0	-0.1
	Yr	0	4	.000	50	1	0	0	8	90	72	7.2	8	22	2.2	74	7.4	3.60	91	.216	.260	-4	-3	101	69	-1.8	0	-0	-0.3
1970	Pit-N	2	1	.667	23	0	0	0	2	38	38	9.0	6	7	1.7	25	5.9	4.74	82	.268	.303	-3	-4	96	89	0.4	-1	1	-0.3
1971	Bal-A	0	1	.000	5	0	0	0	0	15	16	9.6	0	5	3.0	4	2.4	3.00	116	.281	.328	1	1	100	116	-0.4	-0	0	0.0
1973	Bal-A	1	1	.500	11	2	0	0	1	45	36	7.2	10	8	1.6	23	4.6	4.00	100	.218	.260	-1	0	105	83	-0.1	0	0	0.0
	StL-N	4	4	.500	42	0	0	0	6	62	60	8.7	3	14	2.0	38	5.5	2.18	152	.251	.286	10	8	90	127	0.0	-0	0	0.8
1974	StL-N	5	2	.714	42	0	0	0	1	45	45	9.0	0	20	4.0	23	4.6	2.60	144	.269	.338	5	6	103	139	1.4	0	-0	0.6
	Cal-A	0	0	—	4	0	0	0	3	8	6	6.8	0	1	1.1	5	5.6	0.00	—	.214	.241	3	3	93	0	0.0	0	0	0.4
1975	Cal-A	0	2	.000	7	0	0	0	0	13	13	9.0	0	8	5.5	4	2.8	2.08	175	.283	.382	2	2	96	214	-0.9	0	-0	0.2
Total	14	56	77	.421	427	93	21	4	40	1202	1175	8.8	151	352	2.6	818	6.1	3.71	102	.255	.306	-7	10	103	105	-5.6	-3	-4	1.0
■ RUSTY PENCE	Pence, Russell William b: 3/11/1900, Marine, Ill. d: 8/11/71, Hot Srpings, Ark. BR/TR, 6', 185 lbs. Deb: 5/13/21																												
1921	Chi-A	0	0	—	4	0	0	0	0	5	6	10.8	0	7	12.6	2	3.6	9.00	49	.286	.452	-3	-3	102	78	0.0	-0	0	-0.1
■ KEN PENNER	Penner, Kenneth William b: 4/24/1896, Booneville, Ind. d: 5/28/59, Sacramento, Cal. BL/TR, 5'11.5", 170 lbs. Deb: 9/11/16																												
1916	Cle-A	1	0	1.000	4	2	0	0	0	13	14	9.7	0	4	2.8	5	3.5	4.15	68	.304	.360	-2	-2	99	94	0.5	-0	1	-0.1
1929	Chi-N	0	1	.000	5	0	0	0	0	13	14	9.7	1	6	4.2	3	2.1	2.77	167	.280	.345	3	3	98	166	-0.4	0	0	0.2
Total	2	1	1	.500	9	2	0	0	0	26	28	9.7	1	10	3.5	8	2.8	3.46	107	.292	.352	1	1	99	130	0.1	-0	1	0.1
■ KEWPIE PENNINGTON	Pennington, George Louis b: 9/24/1896, New York, N.Y. d: 5/3/53, Newark, N.J. BR/TR, 5'8.5", 168 lbs. Deb: 4/14/17																												
1917	StL-A	0	0	—	1	0	0	0	0	1	1	9.0	0	0	0.0	0	0.0	0.00	—	.250	.250	0	0	98	0	0.0	0	0	0.0
■ HERB PENNOCK	Pennock, Herbert Jefferis "The Knight Of Kennett Square" b: 2/19/1894, Kennett Square, Pa d: 1/30/48, New York, N.Y. BB/TL, 6', 160 lbs. Deb: 5/14/12 CH																												
1912	Phi-A	1	2	.333	17	2	1	0	2	50	48	8.6	1	30	5.4	38	6.8	4.50	72	.262	.375	-6	-7	97	92	-0.6	-1	0	-0.5
1913	Phi-A	2	1	.667	14	3	1	0	0	33	30	8.2	4	22	6.0	17	4.6	5.18	52	.221	.329	-8	-9	93	65	0.2	-0	-0	-0.8
1914	Phi-A	11	4	.733	28	14	8	3	3	152	136	8.1	1	65	3.8	90	5.3	2.78	91	.248	.330	-1	-4	93	103	1.9	2	-1	-0.4
1915	Phi-A	3	6	.333	11	8	3	1	1	44	46	9.4	2	29	5.9	24	4.9	5.32	57	.266	.377	-12	-11	103	82	0.3	1	1	-0.9
	Bos-A	0	0	—	5	1	0	0	0	14	23	14.8	0	10	6.4	7	4.5	9.64	29	.390	.478	-10	-11	96	80	0.0	0	-1	-1.0
	Yr	3	6	.333	16	9	3	1	1	58	69	10.7	2	39	6.1	31	4.8	6.36	47	.295	.396	-22	-22	101	80	0.3	1	-0	-1.9
1916	Bos-A	0	2	.000	9	2	0	0	1	27	23	7.7	0	8	2.7	12	4.0	3.00	87	.245	.311	-1	-1	92	84	-0.9	-0	-0	-0.1
1917	Bos-A	5	5	.500	24	5	4	1	1	101	90	8.0	2	23	2.0	35	3.1	3.30	85	.243	.292	-7	-5	106	69	-0.7	1	-0	-0.3
1919	Bos-A	16	8	.667	32	26	16	5	0	219	223	9.2	2	48	2.0	70	2.9	2.71	108	.274	.316	12	6	91	107	4.8	1	-2	0.3

YEAR	TM/L	W	L	PCT	G	GS	CG	SHO	SV	IP	H	H/G	HR	BB	BB/G	SO	SO/G	ERA	/A	OAVG	OOBP	PR	/A	PF	CPI	WAT	PB	PD	TPI
1920	Bos-A	16	13	.552	37	31	19	4	2	242	244	9.1	9	61	2.3	68	2.5	3.68	100	.264	.312	3	-0	97	80	2.6	4	-2	0.1
1921	Bos-A	12	14	.462	32	32	15	1	0	223	268	10.8	7	59	2.4	91	3.7	4.04	106	.307	.340	6	6	100	106	-0.7	2	1	0.9
1922	Bos-A	10	17	.370	32	26	15	1	1	202	230	10.2	7	74	3.3	59	2.6	4.32	93	.297	.345	-6	-7	99	99	-0.9	-3	0	-0.9
1923	NY-A	19	6	**.760**	35	27	21	1	3	238	235	8.9	11	68	2.6	93	3.5	3.14	128	.261	.308	22	23	101	100	4.6	0	1	2.4
1924	NY-A	21	9	.700	40	34	25	4	3	286	302	9.5	13	64	2.0	101	3.2	2.83	145	.273	.306	45	40	97	117	4.8	-2	-1	3.7
1925	NY-A	16	17	.485	47	31	21	2	2	**277**	267	8.7	11	71	2.3	88	2.9	2.96	144	.254	**.297**	**44**	**40**	97	97	1.4	-3	-4	3.2
1926	NY-A	23	11	.676	40	33	19	1	2	266	294	9.9	11	43	**1.5**	78	2.6	3.62	108	.282	**.303**	12	8	97	93	4.3	3	1	1.1
1927	NY-A	19	8	.704	34	26	18	1	2	210	225	9.6	5	48	2.1	51	2.2	3.00	129	.283	.313	27	21	94	118	-0.1	-0	-2	1.7
1928	NY-A	17	6	.739	28	24	18	**5**	3	211	215	9.2	2	40	1.7	53	2.3	2.56	140	.267	.296	35	24	89	113	3.1	-0	2	2.4
1929	NY-A	9	11	.450	27	23	8	1	2	157	205	11.8	11	28	1.6	49	2.8	4.93	83	.318	.337	-12	-14	97	97	-2.3	-1	-1	-1.4
1930	NY-A	11	7	.611	25	19	11	1	0	156	194	11.2	8	20	**1.2**	46	2.7	4.33	94	.301	.317	6	-5	87	97	1.2	-1	-2	-0.7
1931	NY-A	11	6	.647	25	25	12	1	0	189	247	11.8	7	30	**1.4**	65	3.1	4.29	96	.315	.337	2	-4	94	110	0.8	1	-1	-0.3
1932	NY-A	9	5	.643	22	21	9	1	0	147	191	11.7	8	38	2.3	54	3.3	4.59	89	.310	.345	-2	-8	91	107	-0.5	0	-0	-0.7
1933	NY-A	7	4	.636	23	5	2	1	4	65	96	13.3	4	21	2.9	22	3.0	5.54	68	.342	.382	-9	-13	88	111	0.4	0	-0	-1.1
1934	Bos-A	2	0	1.000	30	2	1	0	1	62	68	9.9	2	16	2.3	16	2.3	3.05	155	.276	.317	**10**	**12**	105	121	1.0	-0	-1	1.0
Total	22	240	162	.597	617	420	247	35	33	3571	3900	9.8	128	916	2.3	1227	3.1	3.60	106	.281	.321	149	81	96	101	24.7	3	-12	7.7
■ **PAUL PENSON**	Penson, Paul Eugene b: 7/12/31, Kansas City, Kan. BR/TR, 6'1", 185 lbs. Deb: 4/21/54																												
1954	Phi-N	1	1	.500	5	3	0	0	0	16	14	7.9	1	14	7.9	3	1.7	4.50	88	.237	.368	-1	-1	98	96	0.0	-1	-1	-0.1
■ **GENE PENTZ**	Pentz, Eugene David b: 6/21/53, Johnstown, Pa. BR/TR, 6'1", 200 lbs. Deb: 7/29/75																												
1975	Det-A	0	4	.000	13	0	0	0	0	25	27	9.7	0	20	7.2	21	7.6	3.24	124	.293	.398	2	2	106	161	-1.9	0	-0	0.2
1976	Hou-N	3	3	.500	40	0	0	0	5	64	62	8.7	5	31	4.4	36	5.1	2.95	103	.259	.337	4	1	87	138	0.0	0	1	0.2
1977	Hou-N	5	2	.714	41	4	0	0	2	87	76	7.9	8	44	4.6	51	5.3	3.83	94	.236	.323	1	-2	92	94	1.5	-1	0	-0.3
1978	Hou-N	0	0	—	10	0	0	0	0	15	12	7.2	1	13	7.8	8	4.8	6.00	57	.214	.356	-4	-4	95	67	0.0	-0	1	-0.3
Total	4	8	9	.471	104	4	0	0	7	191	177	8.3	14	108	5.1	116	5.5	3.63	95	.250	.341	2	-4	92	115	-0.4	-1	1	-0.2
■ **JIMMY PEOPLES**	Peoples, James Elsworth b: 10/8/1863, Big Beaver, Mich. d: 8/29/20, Detroit, Mich. TR , 5'8", 200 lbs. Deb: 5/29/1884																												
1885	Cin-a	0	2	.000	2	2	1	0	0	15	30	18.0	0	2	1.2	4	2.4	12.00	28	.428	.443	-15	-14	103	65	-0.8	-0	0	-1.2
■ **LAURIN PEPPER**	Pepper, Hugh Mc Laurin b: 1/18/31, Vaughan, Miss. BR/TR, 5'11", 190 lbs. Deb: 7/04/54																												
1954	Pit-N	1	5	.167	14	8	0	0	0	51	63	11.1	4	43	7.6	17	3.0	7.94	52	.315	.417	-22	-22	102	82	-1.5	0	1	-1.7
1955	Pit-N	0	1	.000	14	1	0	0	0	20	30	13.5	5	25	11.2	7	3.1	10.35	39	.370	.514	-14	-14	101	105	-0.4	-0	-0	-1.3
1956	Pit-N	1	1	.500	11	7	0	0	0	30	30	9.0	1	25	7.5	12	3.6	3.00	130	.256	.385	3	3	103	147	0.1	-0	-1	0.2
1957	Pit-N	0	1	.000	5	1	0	0	0	9	11	11.0	1	5	5.0	4	4.0	8.00	46	.297	.372	-4	-4	96	68	-0.4	0	-0	-0.3
Total	4	2	8	.200	44	17	0	0	0	110	134	11.0	11	98	8.0	40	3.3	7.04	57	.308	.425	-38	-37	101	102	-2.2	-0	0	-3.1
■ **BOB PEPPER**	Pepper, Robert Ernest b: 5/3/1895, Rosston, Pa. d: 4/8/68, Fort Cliff, Pa. BR/TR, 6'2", 178 lbs. Deb: 7/23/15																												
1915	Phi-A	0	0	—	1	0	0	0	0	5	6	10.8	0	4	7.2	0	0.0	1.80	169	.333	.478	1	1	103	369	0.0	-0	0	0.0
■ **HARRISON PEPPERS**	Peppers, Harrison (born William Harrison Pepper) b: 9/1866, Kentucky d: 11/5/03, Webb City, Mo. BL , Deb: 6/30/1894																												
1894	Lou-N	0	1	.000	2	1	0	0	0	8	10	11.3	0	4	4.5	0	0.0	6.75	72	.329	.407	-1	-2	91	73	-0.4	-1	0	-0.1
■ **LUIS PERAZA**	Peraza, Luis (Rios) b: 6/17/42, Rio Piedras, P.R. BR/TR, 5'11", 185 lbs. Deb: 4/09/69																												
1969	Phi-N	0	0	—	8	0	0	0	0	9	12	12.0	1	2	2.0	7	7.0	6.00	60	.364	.368	-2	-2	100	105	0.0	-0	0	-0.2
■ **OSWALD PERAZA**	Peraza, Oswald Jose b: 10/19/62, Puerto Cabello, Venez. BR/TR, 6'4", 172 lbs. Deb: 4/04/88																												
1988	Bal-A	5	7	.417	19	15	1	0	0	86	98	10.3	10	37	3.9	61	6.4	5.55	70	.282	.349	-15	-16	97	88	0.8	0	0	-1.4
■ **HUB PERDUE**	Perdue, Herbert Rodney "The Gallatin Squash" b: 6/7/1882, Bethpage, Tenn. d: 10/31/68, Gallatin, Tex. BR/TR, 5'10.5", 192 lbs. Deb: 4/19/11																												
1911	Bos-N	6	10	.375	24	19	9	0	1	137	180	11.8	10	41	2.7	40	2.6	4.99	74	.321	.372	-24	-19	109	104	1.0	-1	-0	-1.8
1912	Bos-N	13	16	.448	37	30	20	1	3	249	295	10.7	11	54	2.0	101	3.7	3.80	99	.293	.331	-11	-1	110	95	2.8	-6	-4	-0.9
1913	Bos-N	16	13	.552	38	32	16	3	1	212	201	8.5	7	39	1.7	91	3.9	3.27	94	.249	.278	-2	-5	96	75	3.0	-4	-7	-1.6
1914	Bos-N	2	5	.286	9	9	2	0	0	51	60	10.6	5	11	1.9	13	2.3	5.82	49	.311	.349	-17	-17	102	80	-1.8	-0	0	-1.5
	StL-N	8	8	.500	22	19	12	0	1	153	160	9.4	3	35	2.1	43	2.5	2.82	102	.290	.323	-1	1	104	124	-0.4	-1	-4	-0.3
	Yr	10	13	.435	31	28	14	0	1	204	220	9.7	8	46	2.0	56	2.5	3.57	80	.295	.326	-18	-16	103	124	-2.2	-0	-4	-1.8
1915	StL-N	6	12	.333	31	13	5	1	1	115	141	11.0	7	19	1.5	29	2.3	4.23	65	.311	.329	-19	-19	101	102	-2.8	-1	-1	-2.1
Total	5	51	64	.443	161	122	64	5	7	917	1037	10.2	43	199	2.0	317	3.1	3.86	85	.290	.325	-73	-61	104	97	1.8	-14	-15	-8.2
■ **GEORGE PEREZ**	Perez, George Thomas b: 12/29/37, San Fernando, Cal. BR/TR, 6'2.5", 200 lbs. Deb: 4/17/58																												
1958	Pit-N	0	1	.000	4	0	0	0	1	8	9	10.1	1	4	4.5	2	2.3	5.63	66	.300	.371	-1	-2	94	97	-0.4	-0	-0	-0.1
■ **MELIDO PEREZ**	Perez, Melido Turpen Gross (born Melido Turpen Gross (Perez)) b: 2/15/66, San Cristobal, D.R. BR/TR, 6'4", 180 lbs. Deb: 9/04/87																												
1987	KC-A	1	1	.500	3	3	0	0	0	10	18	16.2	2	5	4.5	5	4.5	8.10	57	.375	.434	-4	-4	104	107	0.0	0	-0	-0.3
1988	Chi-A	12	10	.545	32	32	3	1	0	197	186	8.5	26	72	3.3	138	6.3	3.79	103	.248	.311	4	3	99	104	2.3	0	-2	0.1
Total	2	13	11	.542	35	35	3	1	0	207	204	8.9	28	77	3.3	143	6.2	4.00	99	.256	.318	-0	-1	99	104	2.3	0	-2	-0.2
■ **PASCUAL PEREZ**	Perez, Pascual Gross (born Pascual Gross (Perez)) b: 5/17/57, San Cristobal, D.R. BR/TR, 6'2", 162 lbs. Deb: 5/07/80																												
1980	Pit-N	0	1	.000	2	2	0	0	0	12	15	11.3	0	2	1.5	7	5.3	3.75	99	.341	.373	-0	-0	103	138	-0.4	0	0	0.0
1981	Pit-N	2	7	.222	17	13	2	0	0	86	92	9.6	5	34	3.6	46	4.8	3.98	84	.273	.339	-5	-6	96	102	-2.3	-0	0	-0.5
1982	Atl-N	4	4	.500	16	11	0	0	0	79	85	9.7	4	17	1.9	29	3.3	3.08	125	.276	.306	5	7	107	113	-0.3	1	0	0.9
1983	Atl-N	15	8	.652	33	33	7	1	0	215	213	8.9	20	51	2.1	144	6.0	3.43	111	.260	.301	5	9	104	102	3.1	-1	1	1.0
1984	Atl-N	14	8	.636	30	30	4	1	0	212	208	8.8	26	51	2.2	145	6.2	3.74	106	.260	.303	-3	5	110	101	3.4	-2	3	0.7
1985	Atl-N	1	13	.071	22	22	0	0	0	95	115	10.9	10	57	5.4	57	5.4	6.16	63	.297	.382	-27	-24	108	91	-5.8	-0	-1	-2.4
1987	Mon-N	7	0	1.000	10	10	2	0	0	70	52	6.7	5	16	2.1	58	7.5	2.31	187	.206	.253	14	16	106	89	3.5	-2	1	1.6
1988	Mon-N	12	8	.600	27	27	4	2	0	188	133	6.4	15	44	2.1	131	6.3	2.44	149	.196	**.248**	21	25	105	82	2.2	-3	2	2.7
Total	8	55	49	.529	157	148	19	4	0	957	913	8.6	85	272	2.6	617	5.8	3.52	108	.252	.303	9	31	106	97	3.4	-7	7	4.0
■ **CECIL PERKINS**	Perkins, Cecil Boyce b: 12/1/40, Baltimore, Md. BR/TR, 6', 175 lbs. Deb: 7/05/67																												
1967	NY-A	0	1	.000	2	1	0	0	0	5	6	10.8	1	2	3.6	1	1.8	9.00	34	.316	.381	-3	-3	96	70	-0.4	-0	0	-0.2
■ **CHARLIE PERKINS**	Perkins, Charles Sullivan "Lefty" b: 9/9/05, Ensley, Ala. d: 5/25/88, Salem, Ore. BR/TL, 6'1", 175 lbs. Deb: 5/01/30																												
1930	Phi-A	0	0	—	8	1	0	0	0	24	25	9.4	0	15	5.6	15	5.6	6.38	70	.313	.392	-5	-5	96	90	0.0	-1	0	-0.4
1934	Bro-N	0	3	.000	11	2	0	0	0	24	37	13.9	3	14	5.3	5	1.9	8.63	45	.336	.414	-12	-13	95	84	-1.4	0	-1	-1.1
Total	2	0	3	.000	19	3	0	0	0	48	62	11.6	3	29	5.4	20	3.8	7.50	56	.326	.404	-17	-18	96	87	-1.4	-1	-1	-1.5
■ **JOHN PERKOVICH**	Perkovich, John Joseph "Perky" b: 3/10/24, Chicago, Ill. BR/TR, 5'11", 170 lbs. Deb: 5/06/50																												
1950	Chi-A	0	0	—	1	0	0	0	0	5	7	12.6	3	1	1.8	3	5.4	7.20	63	.318	.348	-1	-1	99	124	0.0	-0	-0	-0.1
■ **HARRY PERKOWSKI**	Perkowski, Harry Walter b: 9/6/22, Dante, Va. BL/TL, 6'2.5", 196 lbs. Deb: 9/13/47																												
1947	Cin-N	0	0	—	3	1	0	0	0	7	12	15.4	1	3	3.9	2	2.6	3.86	97	.375	.429	0	-0	92	205	0.0	0	0	0.0
1949	Cin-N	1	1	.500	5	3	2	0	0	24	21	7.9	2	14	5.3	3	1.1	4.50	88	.236	.333	-1	-1	98	85	0.2	1	-1	0.0
1950	Cin-N	0	0	—	22	0	0	0	0	34	36	9.5	6	23	6.1	19	5.0	5.29	83	.286	.377	-4	-3	106	118	0.0	1	1	0.0
1951	Cin-N	3	6	.333	35	7	1	0	1	102	96	8.5	2	46	4.1	56	4.9	2.82	144	.251	.329	13	14	103	119	-1.1	-3	1	1.2
1952	Cin-N	12	10	.545	33	24	11	1	0	194	197	9.1	9	89	4.1	86	4.0	3.80	98	.265	.339	-2	-1	100	105	2.2	-0	1	0.0
1953	Cin-N	12	11	.522	33	25	7	2	2	193	204	9.5	26	62	2.9	70	3.3	4.52	95	.271	.325	-5	-5	100	97	1.9	2	-0	-0.2
1954	Cin-N	2	8	.200	28	12	3	1	0	96	100	9.4	16	62	5.8	32	3.0	6.09	70	.276	.376	-22	-20	104	91	-2.9	0	-1	-1.8
1955	Chi-N	3	4	.429	25	4	0	0	2	48	53	9.9	3	25	4.7	28	5.3	5.25	78	.283	.363	-6	-6	101	88	-0.2	-0	1	-0.4
Total	8	33	40	.452	184	76	24	4	5	698	719	9.3	65	324	4.2	296	3.8	4.37	93	.269	.344	-27	-23	101	103	0.1	1	2	-1.2
■ **JON PERLMAN**	Perlman, Jonathan Samuel b: 12/13/56, Dallas, Tex. BL/TR, 6'3", 185 lbs. Deb: 9/06/85																												
1985	Chi-N	1	0	1.000	6	0	0	0	0	9	10	10.0	3	8	8.0	4	4.0	11.00	38	.313	.429	-7	-7	117	78	0.5	-0	0	-0.6
1987	SF-N	0	0	—	10	0	0	0	0	11	11	9.0	1	4	3.3	3	2.5	4.09	95	.256	.320	-0	-0	95	96	0.0	0	-0	0.0

YEAR	TM/L	W	L	PCT	G	GS	CG	SHO	SV	IP	H	H/G	HR	BB	BB/G	SO	SO/G	ERA	/A	OAVG	OOBP	PR	/A	PF	CPI	WAT	PB	PD	TPI
1988	Cle-A	0	2	.000	10	0	0	0	0	20	25	11.2	0	11	4.9	10	4.5	5.40	75	.309	.383	-3	-3	102	93	-0.9	0	1	-0.1
Total	3	1	2	.333	26	0	0	0	0	40	46	10.3	4	23	5.2	17	3.8	6.30	64	.295	.376	-11	-10	103	91	-0.4	-0	1	-0.7

■ **LEN PERME** Perme, Leonard John b: 11/25/17, Cleveland, Ohio BL/TL, 6', 170 lbs. Deb: 9/08/42

YEAR	TM/L	W	L	PCT	G	GS	CG	SHO	SV	IP	H	H/G	HR	BB	BB/G	SO	SO/G	ERA	/A	OAVG	OOBP	PR	/A	PF	CPI	WAT	PB	PD	TPI
1942	Chi-A	0	1	.000	4	1	1	0	0	13	5	3.5	0	4	2.8	4	2.8	1.38	265	.119	.208	3	3	100	18	-0.4	0	0	0.4
1946	Chi-A	0	0	—	4	0	0	0	0	4	6	13.5	0	7	15.8	2	4.5	9.00	38	.316	.500	-2	-2	97	94	0.0	0	0	-0.1
Total	2	0	1	.000	8	1	1	0	0	17	11	5.8	0	11	5.8	6	3.2	3.18	113	.180	.311	1	1	100	36	-0.4	0	0	0.3

■ **HUB PERNOLL** Pernoll, Henry Hubbard b: 3/14/1888, Grant'S Pass, Ore. d: 2/18/44, Grant'S Pass, Ore. BR/TL, 5'8", 175 lbs. Deb: 4/25/10

YEAR	TM/L	W	L	PCT	G	GS	CG	SHO	SV	IP	H	H/G	HR	BB	BB/G	SO	SO/G	ERA	/A	OAVG	OOBP	PR	/A	PF	CPI	WAT	PB	PD	TPI
1910	Det-A	4	3	.571	11	5	4	0	0	55	54	8.8	1	14	2.3	25	4.1	2.95	85	.270	.333	-3	-3	100	110	0.1	-2	3	-0.1
1912	Det-A	0	0	—	3	0	0	0	0	9	9	9.0	0	4	4.0	3	3.0	6.00	53	.265	.342	-3	-3	96	57	0.0	-0	0	-0.2
Total	2	4	3	.571	14	5	4	0	0	64	63	8.9	1	18	2.5	28	3.9	3.38	77	.269	.335	-5	-5	99	102	0.1	-2	3	-0.3

■ **RON PERRANOSKI** Perranoski, Ronald Peter (born Ronald Peter Perzanowski) b: 4/1/36, Paterson, N.J. BL/TL, 6', 180 lbs. Deb: 4/14/61 C

YEAR	TM/L	W	L	PCT	G	GS	CG	SHO	SV	IP	H	H/G	HR	BB	BB/G	SO	SO/G	ERA	/A	OAVG	OOBP	PR	/A	PF	CPI	WAT	PB	PD	TPI
1961	LA-N	7	5	.583	53	1	0	0	6	92	82	8.0	5	41	4.0	56	5.5	2.64	155	.244	.323	14	15	102	133	0.1	-0	0	1.5
1962	LA-N	6	6	.500	**70**	0	0	0	20	107	103	8.7	1	36	3.0	68	5.7	2.86	125	.255	.309	13	8	91	104	-1.1	-1	-1	0.7
1963	LA-N	16	3	**.842**	**69**	0	0	0	21	129	112	7.8	7	43	3.0	75	5.2	1.67	184	.231	.294	**23**	**20**	94	166	5.9	0	0	2.2
1964	LA-N	5	7	.417	72	0	0	0	14	125	128	9.2	5	46	3.3	79	5.7	3.10	104	.263	.320	6	2	91	115	-0.9	-0	2	0.3
1965	LA-N	6	6	.500	59	0	0	0	17	105	85	7.3	2	40	3.4	53	4.5	2.23	143	.226	.297	15	11	90	119	-1.0	1	-1	1.1
1966	LA-N	6	7	.462	55	0	0	0	7	82	82	9.0	4	31	3.4	50	5.5	3.18	108	.269	.322	4	2	95	119	-1.4	1	2	0.6
1967	LA-N	6	7	.462	**70**	0	0	0	16	110	97	7.9	4	45	3.7	75	6.1	2.45	123	.240	.313	11	7	89	127	0.1	-0	2	0.8
1968	Min-A	8	7	.533	66	0	0	0	6	87	86	8.9	5	38	3.9	65	6.7	3.10	102	.252	.317	-1	0	106	114	0.7	-1	0	0.0
1969	Min-A	9	10	.474	75	0	0	0	**31**	120	85	6.4	4	52	3.9	62	4.7	2.10	173	.205	.285	20	20	100	111	-2.1	-1	1	2.1
1970	Min-A	7	8	.467	67	0	0	0	**34**	111	108	8.8	7	42	3.4	55	4.5	2.43	148	.259	.321	16	14	97	148	-1.7	-2	-1	1.1
1971	Min-A	1	4	.200	36	0	0	0	5	43	60	12.6	2	28	5.9	21	4.4	6.70	54	.337	.417	-15	-15	104	97	-1.3	-0	-0	-1.5
	Det-A	0	1	.000	11	0	0	0	2	18	16	8.0	2	3	1.5	8	4.0	2.50	132	.254	.278	2	2	95	138	-0.4	-0	-0	0.1
	Yr	1	5	.167	47	0	0	0	7	61	76	11.2	4	31	4.6	29	4.3	5.46	64	.309	.372	-13	-13	101	138	-1.7	-0	-0	-1.4
1972	Det-A	0	1	.000	17	0	0	0	0	19	23	10.9	2	8	3.8	10	4.7	7.58	46	.307	.376	-10	-9	112	71	-0.4	-0	-0	-0.9
	LA-N	2	0	1.000	9	0	0	0	0	17	19	10.1	0	8	4.2	5	2.6	2.65	121	.292	.365	2	1	93	160	1.0	0	-0	0.1
1973	Cal-A	0	2	.000	8	0	0	0	0	11	11	9.0	0	7	5.7	5	4.1	4.09	90	.282	.396	-0	-1	96	115	-0.9	0	0	0.0
Total	13	79	74	.516	737	1	0	0	179	1176	1097	8.4	50	468	3.6	687	5.3	2.79	122	.250	.316	100	80	96	125	-3.4	-4	3	8.2

■ **BILL PERRIN** Perrin, William Joseph "Lefty" b: 6/23/10, New Orleans, La. d: 6/30/74, New Orleans, La. BR/TL, 5'11", 172 lbs. Deb: 9/30/34

YEAR	TM/L	W	L	PCT	G	GS	CG	SHO	SV	IP	H	H/G	HR	BB	BB/G	SO	SO/G	ERA	/A	OAVG	OOBP	PR	/A	PF	CPI	WAT	PB	PD	TPI
1934	Cle-A	0	1	.000	1	1	0	0	0	5	13	23.4	0	2	3.6	3	5.4	14.40	31	.520	.533	-6	-6	100	91	-0.4	-0	0	-0.3

■ **GEORGE PERRING** Perring, George Wilson b: 8/13/1884, Sharon, Wis. d: 8/20/60, Beloit, Wis. BR/TR, 6', 190 lbs. Deb: 4/30/08

YEAR	TM/L	W	L	PCT	G	GS	CG	SHO	SV	IP	H	H/G	HR	BB	BB/G	SO	SO/G	ERA	/A	OAVG	OOBP	PR	/A	PF	CPI	WAT	PB	PD	TPI
1914	KC-F	0	0	—	1	0	0	0	0	1	2	18.0	0	1	9.0	0	0.0	9.00	34	.449	.550	-1	-1	96	111	0.0	0	0	0.0

■ **POL PERRITT** Perritt, William Dayton b: 8/30/1892, Arcadia, La. d: 10/15/47, Shreveport, La. BR/TR, 6'2", 168 lbs. Deb: 9/07/12

YEAR	TM/L	W	L	PCT	G	GS	CG	SHO	SV	IP	H	H/G	HR	BB	BB/G	SO	SO/G	ERA	/A	OAVG	OOBP	PR	/A	PF	CPI	WAT	PB	PD	TPI
1912	StL-N	1	1	.500	6	3	1	0	0	31	25	7.3	0	10	2.9	13	3.8	3.19	109	.229	.294	1	1	103	62	0.2	-0	0	0.1
1913	StL-N	6	14	.300	36	21	8	0	0	175	205	10.5	9	64	3.3	64	3.3	5.25	59	.300	.358	-40	-42	97	87	-1.2	-1	0	-4.0
1914	StL-N	16	13	.552	41	32	18	3	2	286	248	7.8	7	93	2.9	115	3.6	2.36	122	.245	.306	14	17	104	116	0.8	-3	-2	1.3
1915	NY-N	12	18	.400	35	30	16	4	0	220	226	9.2	6	59	2.4	91	3.7	2.66	96	.266	.315	2	-3	92	121	-2.1	-0	-5	-0.9
1916	NY-N	18	11	.621	40	28	17	5	2	251	243	8.7	11	56	2.0	115	4.1	2.62	94	.257	.297	0	-5	94	111	2.2	-4	-2	-1.1
1917	NY-N	17	7	.708	35	26	14	5	1	215	186	7.8	3	45	1.9	72	3.0	1.88	134	.237	.278	20	15	93	118	2.7	-2	1	1.5
1918	NY-N	18	13	.581	35	31	19	6	0	233	212	8.2	5	38	1.5	60	2.3	2.74	97	.246	.270	1	-2	96	81	0.4	-1	-3	-0.6
1919	NY-N	1	1	.500	11	3	0	0	1	19	27	12.8	0	12	5.7	2	0.9	7.11	40	.386	.446	-9	-9	96	103	-0.1	-1	0	-0.9
1920	NY-N	0	0	—	8	0	0	0	2	15	9	5.4	0	4	2.4	3	1.8	1.80	168	.167	.224	2	2	97	8	0.0	-1	0	0.2
1921	NY-N	2	0	1.000	5	1	0	0	0	12	17	12.8	0	2	1.5	5	3.8	3.75	95	.321	.339	0	-0	94	106	1.0	-0	-0	0.0
	Det-A	1	0	1.000	4	2	0	0	0	13	18	12.5	0	7	4.8	3	2.1	4.85	85	.383	.441	-1	-1	96	148	0.5	0	-0	0.0
Total	10	92	78	.541	256	177	93	23	8	1470	1416	8.7	41	390	2.4	543	3.3	2.89	94	.259	.306	-10	-27	96	105	4.4	-12	-10	-4.4

■ **GAYLORD PERRY** Perry, Gaylord Jackson b: 9/15/38, Williamston, N.C. BR/TR, 6'4", 205 lbs. Deb: 4/14/62

YEAR	TM/L	W	L	PCT	G	GS	CG	SHO	SV	IP	H	H/G	HR	BB	BB/G	SO	SO/G	ERA	/A	OAVG	OOBP	PR	/A	PF	CPI	WAT	PB	PD	TPI
1962	SF-N	3	1	.750	13	7	1	0	0	43	54	11.3	3	14	2.9	20	4.2	5.23	74	.310	.349	-6	-6	99	93	0.7	0	-0	-0.6
1963	SF-N	1	6	.143	31	4	0	0	2	76	84	9.9	10	29	3.4	52	6.2	4.03	77	.279	.338	-6	-8	94	117	-2.5	1	-0	-0.7
1964	SF-N	12	11	.522	44	19	5	2	5	206	179	7.8	16	43	1.9	155	6.8	2.75	127	.232	.273	18	17	99	98	-0.7	-3	-1	1.4
1965	SF-N	8	12	.400	47	26	6	0	1	196	194	8.9	21	70	3.2	170	7.8	4.18	92	.256	.318	-14	-7	109	94	-3.4	-1	3	-0.3
1966	SF-N	21	8	.724	36	35	13	3	0	256	242	8.5	15	40	1.4	201	7.1	2.99	117	.247	.277	18	14	97	88	5.7	0	1	1.6
1967	SF-N	15	17	.469	39	37	18	3	1	293	231	7.1	20	84	2.6	230	7.1	2.61	128	.214	.271	25	24	99	90	-3.1	-2	4	3.0
1968	SF-N	16	15	.516	39	38	19	3	1	291	240	7.4	10	59	1.8	173	5.4	2.44	118	.222	.261	18	14	96	81	-0.8	-2	4	1.8
1969	SF-N	19	14	.576	40	39	26	3	0	**325**	290	8.0	23	91	2.5	233	6.5	2.49	145	.237	.291	40	40	100	117	0.9	-2	3	4.7
1970	SF-N	**23**	13	.639	41	41	23	**5**	0	**329**	292	8.0	27	84	2.3	214	5.9	3.20	121	.237	.287	31	25	96	94	5.0	-3	5	2.6
1971	SF-N	16	12	.571	37	37	14	2	0	280	255	8.2	20	67	2.2	158	5.1	2.76	124	.242	.285	22	21	99	102	0.6	-3	0	1.9
1972	Cle-A	**24**	16	.600	41	40	**29**	5	1	343	253	6.6	17	82	2.2	234	6.1	1.92	**173**	.205	.258	**44**	**53**	108	96	**6.4**	0	3	**7.2**
1973	Cle-A	19	19	.500	41	41	**29**	7	0	344	315	8.2	34	115	3.0	238	6.2	3.38	112	.246	.309	17	16	99	102	2.6	0	1	1.8
1974	Cle-A	21	13	.618	37	37	28	4	0	322	230	6.4	25	99	2.8	216	6.0	2.52	**146**	.204	.265	40	**41**	101	90	5.4	0	1	**4.7**
1975	Cle-A	6	9	.400	15	15	10	1	0	122	120	8.9	16	34	2.5	85	6.3	3.54	107	.256	.305	3	3	100	105	-1.5	0	1	0.4
	Tex-A	12	8	.600	22	22	15	4	0	184	157	7.7	12	36	1.8	148	7.2	3.03	125	.227	.265	15	15	100	74	2.4	0	-0	1.5
	Yr	18	17	.514	37	37	25	5	0	306	277	8.1	28	70	2.1	233	6.9	3.24	117	.238	.280	19	18	100	74	0.9	0	1	1.9
1976	Tex-A	15	14	.517	32	32	21	2	0	250	232	8.4	14	52	1.9	143	5.1	3.24	111	.247	.283	8	10	103	85	1.6	0	-3	0.8
1977	Tex-A	15	12	.556	34	34	13	4	0	238	239	9.0	21	56	2.1	177	6.7	3.37	125	.262	.304	19	22	104	104	-0.6	0	-1	2.2
1978	SD-N	**21**	6	**.778**	37	37	5	2	0	261	241	8.3	9	66	2.3	154	5.3	2.72	122	.248	.293	25	17	93	103	**7.9**	-3	0	1.4
1979	SD-N	12	11	.522	32	32	10	0	0	233	225	8.7	12	67	2.6	140	5.4	3.05	119	.257	.307	18	15	97	105	2.2	-2	1	1.5
1980	Tex-A	6	9	.400	24	24	6	2	0	155	159	9.2	12	46	2.7	107	6.2	3.43	118	.268	.324	11	11	100	111	-1.1	0	1	1.2
	NY-A	4	4	.500	10	8	0	0	0	51	65	11.5	2	18	3.2	28	4.9	4.41	90	.320	.367	-2	-3	98	115	-0.8	0	0	-0.2
	Yr	10	13	.435	34	32	6	2	0	206	224	9.8	14	64	2.8	135	5.9	3.67	110	.278	.327	9	8	100	115	-1.9	0	1	1.0
1981	Atl-N	8	9	.471	23	23	3	0	0	151	182	10.8	9	24	**1.4**	60	3.6	3.93	89	.304	.326	-7	-7	100	109	0.0	3	-1	-0.5
1982	Sea-A	10	12	.455	32	32	6	0	0	217	245	10.2	27	54	2.2	116	4.8	4.40	102	.287	.328	-8	2	110	103	-0.3	0	1	0.2
1983	Sea-A	3	10	.231	16	16	2	0	0	102	116	10.2	18	23	2.0	42	3.7	4.94	84	.286	.325	-10	-9	101	100	-2.5	0	0	-0.8
	KC-A	4	4	.500	14	14	1	1	0	84	98	10.5	6	26	2.8	40	4.3	4.29	97	.292	.334	-2	-1	102	104	0.1	0	0	0.0
	Yr	7	14	.333	30	30	3	1	0	186	214	10.4	24	49	2.4	82	4.0	4.65	89	.286	.326	-12	-10	102	104	-2.4	0	1	-0.8
Total	22	314	265	.542	777	690	303	53	11	5352	4938	8.3	399	1379	2.3	3534	5.9	3.10	117	.245	.293	315	320	100	98	24.2	-16	23	36.8

■ **SCOTT PERRY** Perry, Herbert Scott b: 4/17/1891, Dennison, Tex. d: 10/27/59, Kansas City, Mo. BR/TR, 6'1", 195 lbs. Deb: 5/13/15

YEAR	TM/L	W	L	PCT	G	GS	CG	SHO	SV	IP	H	H/G	HR	BB	BB/G	SO	SO/G	ERA	/A	OAVG	OOBP	PR	/A	PF	CPI	WAT	PB	PD	TPI
1915	StL-A	0	0	—	1	1	0	0	0	2	5	22.5	0	1	4.5	0	0.0	13.50	22	.455	.538	-2	-2	99	88	0.0	0	0	-0.1
1916	Chi-N	2	1	.667	4	3	2	1	0	28	30	9.6	0	3	1.0	10	3.2	2.57	120	.291	.289	0	2	117	119	0.6	1	0	0.3
1917	Cin-N	0	0	—	4	1	0	0	0	13	17	11.8	0	8	5.5	4	2.8	6.92	36	.321	.400	-6	-6	93	81	0.0	-1	-0	-0.6
1918	Phi-A	20	19	.513	44	36	**30**	3	2	**332**	295	8.0	1	111	3.0	81	2.2	1.98	151	.247	.304	29	37	108	**124**	4.7	-7	1	3.8
1919	Phi-A	4	17	.190	25	21	12	0	1	184	193	9.4	4	72	3.5	38	1.9	3.57	101	.282	.352	-7	1	112	103	-3.0	-3	6	0.5
1920	Phi-A	11	25	.306	42	34	20	1	1	264	310	10.6	14	65	2.2	79	2.7	3.61	104	.300	.345	5	4	99	113	-0.4	-3	0	0.0
1921	Phi-A	3	6	.333	12	8	5	0	1	70	77	9.9	4	24	3.1	19	2.4	4.11	111	.288	.331	1	4	107	102	-0.1	-4	1	0.1
Total	7	40	68	.370	132	104	69	5	5	893	927	9.3	23	284	2.9	231	2.3	3.07	113	.277	.331	20	40	106	114	1.8	-17	9	4.0

■ **JIM PERRY** Perry, James Evan b: 10/30/36, Williamston, N.C. BB/TR, 6'4", 190 lbs. Deb: 4/23/59

YEAR	TM/L	W	L	PCT	G	GS	CG	SHO	SV	IP	H	H/G	HR	BB	BB/G	SO	SO/G	ERA	/A	OAVG	OOBP	PR	/A	PF	CPI	WAT	PB	PD	TPI
1959	Cle-A	12	10	.545	44	13	8	2	4	153	122	7.2	10	55	3.2	79	4.6	2.65	138	.225	.291	21	17	95	110	-0.6	3	0	2.1
1960	Cle-A	**18**	10	**.643**	41	36	10	**4**	1	261	257	8.9	35	91	3.1	120	4.1	3.62	105	.260	.319	7	5	98	113	**4.7**	3	0	0.8
1961	Cle-A	10	17	.370	35	35	6	1	0	224	238	9.6	28	87	3.5	90	3.6	4.70	83	.273	.337	-17	-20	97	97	-3.5	-1	-0	-2.0
1962	Cle-A	12	12	.500	35	27	7	3	0	194	213	9.9	21	59	2.7	74	3.4	4.13	95	.285	.335	-3	-5	99	110	0.2	0	1	-0.3
1963	Cle-A	0	0	—	5	0	0	0	0	10	12	10.8	0	2	1.8	7	6.3	5.40	66	.293	.304	-2	-2	98	65	0.0	-0	0	-0.1

YEAR	TM/L	W	L	PCT	G	GS	CG	SHO	SV	IP	H	H/G	HR	BB	BB/G	SO	SO/G	ERA	/A	OAVG	OOBP	PR	/A	PF	CPI	WAT	PB	PD	TPI
	Min-A	9	9	.500	35	25	5	1	1	168	167	8.9	17	57	3.1	65	3.5	3.75	95	.256	.313	-2	-4	98	100	-1.1	3	-1	-0.1
	Yr	9	9	.500	40	25	5	1	1	178	179	9.1	17	59	3.0	72	3.6	3.84	92	.258	.313	-4	-6	98	100	-1.1	-0	-1	-0.2
1964	Min-A	6	3	.667	42	1	0	0	2	65	61	8.4	7	23	3.2	55	7.6	3.46	105	.245	.305	1	1	100	101	1.6	-0	0	0.1
1965	Min-A	12	7	.632	36	19	4	2	0	168	142	7.6	18	47	2.5	88	4.7	2.63	130	.232	.283	16	15	98	118	0.1	1	-1	1.6
1966	Min-A	11	7	.611	33	25	8	1	0	184	149	7.3	17	53	2.6	122	6.0	2.54	149	.222	.279	18	25	110	112	1.4	4	-2	3.3
1967	Min-A	8	7	.533	37	11	3	2	0	131	123	8.5	8	50	3.4	94	6.5	3.02	113	.255	.321	3	6	106	121	-0.3	1	-1	0.6
1968	Min-A	8	6	.571	32	18	3	2	1	139	113	7.3	8	26	1.7	69	4.5	2.27	139	.219	.259	11	14	106	94	1.2	2	1	1.9
1969	Min-A	20	6	.769	46	36	12	3	0	262	244	8.4	18	66	2.3	153	5.3	2.82	129	.247	.296	24	24	100	108	6.1	2	-2	2.5
1970	Min-A	**24**	12	.667	40	40	13	4	0	279	258	8.3	20	57	1.8	168	5.4	3.03	118	.243	.284	21	17	97	92	3.5	6	1	2.5
1971	Min-A	17	17	.500	40	39	8	0	1	270	263	8.8	39	102	3.4	126	4.2	4.23	85	.259	.323	-23	-19	104	99	1.5	1	0	-1.7
1972	Min-A	13	16	.448	35	35	5	2	0	218	191	7.9	14	60	2.5	85	3.5	3.34	98	.236	.288	-7	-1	107	83	-1.7	-1	-1	-0.2
1973	Det-A	14	13	.519	35	34	7	1	0	203	225	10.0	22	55	2.4	66	2.9	4.03	96	.282	.328	-5	-4	101	104	-0.1	0	-0	-0.3
1974	Cle-A	17	12	.586	36	36	8	3	0	252	242	8.6	11	64	2.3	71	2.5	2.96	124	.254	.298	19	20	101	99	3.6	0	-1	2.0
1975	Cle-A	1	6	.143	8	6	0	0	0	38	46	10.9	8	18	4.3	11	2.6	6.63	57	.309	.376	-12	-12	100	95	-2.4	0	0	-1.0
	Oak-A	3	4	.429	15	11	2	1	0	68	61	8.1	7	26	3.4	33	4.4	4.63	75	.237	.318	-6	-9	91	77	-1.0	0	-1	-0.9
	Yr	4	10	.286	23	17	2	1	0	106	107	9.1	15	44	3.7	44	3.7	5.35	67	.264	.339	-18	-21	94	77	-3.4	0	-1	-1.9
Total	17	215	174	.553	630	447	109	32	10	3287	3127	8.6	308	998	2.7	1576	4.3	3.44	106	.252	.306	63	71	101	102	13.2	24	-6	10.8

■ **PAT PERRY** Perry, William Patrick b: 2/4/59, Taylorsville, Ill. BL/TL, 6'1", 170 lbs. Deb: 9/12/85

YEAR	TM/L	W	L	PCT	G	GS	CG	SHO	SV	IP	H	H/G	HR	BB	BB/G	SO	SO/G	ERA	/A	OAVG	OOBP	PR	/A	PF	CPI	WAT	PB	PD	TPI
1985	StL-N	1	0	1.000	6	0	0	0	0	12	3	2.3	0	3	2.3	6	4.5	0.00	—	.077	.143	5	4	93	0	0.5	0	-0	0.5
1986	StL-N	2	3	.400	46	0	0	0	2	69	59	7.7	5	34	4.4	29	3.8	3.78	102	.239	.323	-0	0	103	95	-0.4	-1	1	0.0
1987	StL-N	4	2	.667	45	0	0	0	1	66	54	7.4	7	21	2.9	33	4.5	4.36	91	.222	.286	-2	-3	97	68	0.6	-0	0	-0.2
	Cin-N	1	0	1.000	12	0	0	0	1	15	6	3.6	0	4	2.4	6	3.6	0.00	—	.122	.200	7	7	103	0	0.5	0	0	0.7
	Yr	5	2	.714	57	0	0	0	2	81	60	6.7	7	25	2.8	39	4.3	3.56	113	.203	.265	5	4	98	0	1.1	-0	1	0.5
1988	Cin-N	2	2	.500	12	0	0	0	0	21	21	9.0	4	9	3.9	11	4.7	5.57	65	.262	.323	-5	-5	105	88	-0.1	-0	-0	-0.4
	Chi-N	2	2	.500	35	0	0	0	1	38	40	9.5	5	7	1.7	24	5.7	3.32	109	.270	.304	1	1	105	122	0.1	1	-0	0.3
	Yr	4	4	.500	47	0	0	0	1	59	61	9.3	9	16	2.4	35	5.3	4.12	88	.264	.311	-4	-3	105	122	0.0	-0	-0	-0.1
Total	4	12	9	.571	156	0	0	0	5	221	183	7.5	21	78	3.2	109	4.4	3.58	107	.227	.293	5	6	101	79	1.2	1	1	0.9

■ **PARSON PERRYMAN** Perryman, Emmett Key b: 10/24/1888, Everett Springs, Ga. d: 9/12/66, Starke, Fla. BR/TR, 6'4.5", 193 lbs. Deb: 4/14/15

YEAR	TM/L	W	L	PCT	G	GS	CG	SHO	SV	IP	H	H/G	HR	BB	BB/G	SO	SO/G	ERA	/A	OAVG	OOBP	PR	/A	PF	CPI	WAT	PB	PD	TPI
1915	StL-A	2	4	.333	24	3	0	0	0	50	52	9.4	2	16	2.9	19	3.4	3.96	74	.281	.342	-6	-6	99	95	-0.5	-1	1	-0.5

■ **BILL PERTICA** Pertica, William Andrew b: 3/5/1897, Santa Barbara, Cal. d: 12/28/67, Los Angeles, Cal. BR/TR, 5'9", 165 lbs. Deb: 8/07/18

YEAR	TM/L	W	L	PCT	G	GS	CG	SHO	SV	IP	H	H/G	HR	BB	BB/G	SO	SO/G	ERA	/A	OAVG	OOBP	PR	/A	PF	CPI	WAT	PB	PD	TPI
1918	Bos-A	0	0	—	1	0	0	0	0	3	3	9.0	0	0	0.0	1	3.0	3.00	86	.273	.273	-0	-0	93	71	0.0	-0	0	0.0
1921	StL-N	14	10	.583	38	31	15	2	2	208	212	9.2	9	70	3.0	67	2.9	3.38	104	.267	.326	9	3	93	102	0.5	-3	-3	-0.2
1922	StL-N	8	8	.500	34	14	2	0	0	117	153	11.8	5	65	5.0	30	2.3	5.92	70	.333	.406	-24	-23	100	100	-0.7	-0	1	-2.0
1923	StL-N	0	0	—	1	1	0	0	0	2	2	9.0	0	3	13.5	0	0.0	4.50	80	.250	.462	-0	-0	90	159	0.0	-0	0	0.0
Total	4	22	18	.550	74	46	17	2	2	330	370	10.1	14	138	3.8	98	2.7	4.28	87	.291	.357	-14	-21	95	102	-0.2	-3	-2	-2.2

■ **STAN PERZANOWSKI** Perzanowski, Stanley b: 8/25/50, East Chicago, Ind. BB/TR, 6'2", 170 lbs. Deb: 6/20/71

YEAR	TM/L	W	L	PCT	G	GS	CG	SHO	SV	IP	H	H/G	HR	BB	BB/G	SO	SO/G	ERA	/A	OAVG	OOBP	PR	/A	PF	CPI	WAT	PB	PD	TPI
1971	Chi-A	0	1	.000	5	0	0	0	1	6	14	21.0	1	3	4.5	5	7.5	12.00	28	.412	.447	-6	-6	97	84	-0.4	-0	0	-0.5
1974	Chi-A	0	0	—	2	1	0	0	0	2	8	36.0	1	2	9.0	2	9.0	22.50	16	.533	.588	-4	-4	102	96	0.0	0	0	-0.3
1975	Tex-A	3	3	.500	12	8	1	0	0	66	59	8.0	1	25	3.4	26	3.5	3.00	126	.246	.325	6	6	100	104	0.1	0	1	0.7
1976	Tex-A	0	0	—	5	0	0	0	0	12	20	15.0	3	4	3.0	6	4.5	9.75	37	.385	.441	-8	-8	103	93	0.0	0	0	-0.7
1978	Min-A	2	7	.222	13	7	1	0	1	57	59	9.3	1	26	4.1	31	4.9	5.21	68	.276	.353	-9	-10	94	78	-2.2	0	1	-0.9
Total	5	5	11	.313	37	16	2	0	2	143	160	10.1	7	60	3.8	70	4.4	5.10	72	.288	.361	-21	-23	98	92	-2.5	-0	2	-1.7

■ **GARY PETERS** Peters, Gary Charles b: 4/21/37, Grove City, Pa. BL/TL, 6'2", 200 lbs. Deb: 9/10/59

YEAR	TM/L	W	L	PCT	G	GS	CG	SHO	SV	IP	H	H/G	HR	BB	BB/G	SO	SO/G	ERA	/A	OAVG	OOBP	PR	/A	PF	CPI	WAT	PB	PD	TPI
1959	Chi-A	0	0	—	2	0	0	0	0	1	2	18.0	0	2	18.0	1	9.0	0.00	—	.400	.571	0	0	95	0	0.0	0	0	0.0
1960	Chi-A	0	0	—	2	0	0	0	0	3	4	12.0	0	1	3.0	4	12.0	3.00	128	.286	.333	0	0	99	114	0.0	0	0	0.0
1961	Chi-A	0	0	—	3	0	0	0	1	10	10	9.0	0	2	1.8	6	5.4	1.80	220	.270	.293	2	2	99	167	0.0	0	1	0.4
1962	Chi-A	0	1	.000	5	0	0	0	0	6	8	12.0	0	1	1.5	4	6.0	6.00	62	.308	.345	-1	-2	94	72	-0.4	0	0	0.0
1963	Chi-A	19	8	.704	41	30	13	4	1	243	192	7.1	9	68	2.5	189	7.0	**2.33**	**159**	.216	.274	**35**	**37**	102	95	4.5	8	-1	**5.1**
1964	Chi-A	**20**	8	.714	37	36	11	3	0	274	217	7.1	20	104	3.4	205	6.7	2.50	135	.219	.294	34	27	93	111	4.4	8	0	3.8
1965	Chi-A	10	12	.455	33	30	1	0	0	176	181	9.3	19	63	3.2	95	4.9	3.63	86	.265	.325	-3	-10	91	113	-2.7	2	0	-0.7
1966	Chi-A	12	10	.545	30	27	11	4	0	205	156	6.8	11	45	2.0	129	5.7	**1.98**	**162**	.212	**.255**	**33**	28	93	107	0.9	6	1	4.0
1967	Chi-A	16	11	.593	38	36	11	3	0	260	187	**6.5**	15	91	3.1	215	7.4	2.28	132	**.199**	.273	27	21	93	97	1.5	7	3	3.4
1968	Chi-A	4	13	.235	31	25	6	1	1	163	146	8.1	7	60	3.3	110	6.1	3.75	81	.242	.311	-14	-13	102	84	-3.8	7	0	-0.6
1969	Chi-A	10	15	.400	36	32	7	3	0	219	238	9.8	21	78	3.2	140	5.8	4.52	88	.283	.339	-22	-13	110	99	-0.6	2	-2	-1.2
1970	Bos-A	16	11	.593	34	34	10	4	0	222	221	9.0	20	83	3.4	155	6.3	4.05	101	.257	.324	-8	1	110	93	1.9	6	-1	0.7
1971	Bos-A	14	11	.560	34	32	9	1	1	214	241	10.1	25	70	2.9	100	4.2	4.37	83	.288	.342	-22	-17	105	106	1.1	9	-2	-1.0
1972	Bos-A	3	3	.500	33	4	0	0	1	85	91	9.6	10	38	4.0	67	7.1	4.34	74	.279	.349	-12	-11	105	109	-0.2	1	-0	-1.0
Total	14	124	103	.546	359	286	79	23	5	2081	1894	8.2	157	706	3.1	1420	6.1	3.25	107	.243	.306	51	51	100	101	6.6	57	-0	12.9

■ **JOHN PETERS** Peters, John Paul b: 4/8/1850, Louisiana, Mo. d: 1/4/24, St.Louis, Mo. BR/TR, 180 lbs. Deb: 5/23/1874

YEAR	TM/L	W	L	PCT	G	GS	CG	SHO	SV	IP	H	H/G	HR	BB	BB/G	SO	SO/G	ERA	/A	OAVG	OOBP	PR	/A	PF	CPI	WAT	PB	PD	TPI
1876	Chi-N	0	0	—	1	0	0	0	1	1	1	9.0	0	1	9.0	0	0.0	0.00	—	.265	.418	0	0	113	0	0.0	0	0	0.0

■ **RUBE PETERS** Peters, Oscar C. b: 3/15/1886, Grand Fork, Ill. BR/TR, 6'1", 195 lbs. Deb: 4/13/12

YEAR	TM/L	W	L	PCT	G	GS	CG	SHO	SV	IP	H	H/G	HR	BB	BB/G	SO	SO/G	ERA	/A	OAVG	OOBP	PR	/A	PF	CPI	WAT	PB	PD	TPI
1912	Chi-A	5	6	.455	28	11	4	0	0	109	134	11.1	2	33	2.7	39	3.2	4.13	80	.309	.366	-9	-10	99	109	-0.5	-1	4	-0.5
1914	Bro-F	2	2	.500	11	3	1	0	0	38	52	12.3	1	16	3.8	13	3.1	3.79	85	.358	.422	-2	-2	101	143	0.0	-1	0	-0.2
Total	2	7	8	.467	39	14	5	0	0	147	186	11.4	3	49	3.0	52	3.2	4.04	82	.321	.380	-12	-12	100	118	-0.5	-1	4	-0.7

■ **RAY PETERS** Peters, Raymond James b: 8/27/46, Buffalo, N.Y. BR/TR, 6'5.5", 210 lbs. Deb: 6/04/70

YEAR	TM/L	W	L	PCT	G	GS	CG	SHO	SV	IP	H	H/G	HR	BB	BB/G	SO	SO/G	ERA	/A	OAVG	OOBP	PR	/A	PF	CPI	WAT	PB	PD	TPI
1970	Mil-A	0	2	.000	2	2	0	0	0	2	7	31.5	0	5	22.5	1	4.5	31.50	12	.583	.667	-6	-6	100	69	-0.9	0	0	-0.4

■ **STEVE PETERS** Peters, Steven Bradley b: 11/14/62, Oklahoma City, Okla BL/TL, 5'10", 170 lbs. Deb: 8/11/87

YEAR	TM/L	W	L	PCT	G	GS	CG	SHO	SV	IP	H	H/G	HR	BB	BB/G	SO	SO/G	ERA	/A	OAVG	OOBP	PR	/A	PF	CPI	WAT	PB	PD	TPI
1987	StL-N	0	0	—	12	0	0	0	1	15	17	10.2	1	6	3.6	11	6.6	1.80	221	.298	.359	4	4	97	269	0.0	-0	1	0.4
1988	StL-N	3	3	.500	44	0	0	0	0	45	57	11.4	8	22	4.4	30	6.0	6.40	57	.313	.371	-15	-14	105	99	0.2	-0	-1	-1.5
Total	2	3	3	.500	56	0	0	0	1	60	74	11.1	9	28	4.2	41	6.2	5.25	71	.310	.368	-11	-10	103	142	0.2	-1	0	-1.1

■ **ADAM PETERSON** Peterson, Adam Charles b: 12/11/65, Long Beach, Cal. BR/TR, 6'3", 190 lbs. Deb: 9/19/87

YEAR	TM/L	W	L	PCT	G	GS	CG	SHO	SV	IP	H	H/G	HR	BB	BB/G	SO	SO/G	ERA	/A	OAVG	OOBP	PR	/A	PF	CPI	WAT	PB	PD	TPI
1987	Chi-A	0	0	—	1	1	0	0	0	4	8	18.0	1	3	6.8	1	2.3	13.50	36	.444	.500	-4	-4	109	89	0.0	0	0	-0.2
1988	Chi-A	0	1	.000	2	2	0	0	0	6	6	9.0	0	6	9.0	5	7.5	13.50	29	.240	.387	-6	-6	99	31	-0.4	0	-0	-0.5
Total	2	0	1	.000	3	3	0	0	0	10	14	12.6	1	9	8.1	6	5.4	13.50	32	.326	.434	-10	-10	103	54	-0.4	0	-0	-0.7

■ **FRITZ PETERSON** Peterson, Fritz Fred (born Fred Ingels Peterson) b: 2/8/42, Chicago, Ill. BB/TL, 6', 185 lbs. Deb: 4/15/66

YEAR	TM/L	W	L	PCT	G	GS	CG	SHO	SV	IP	H	H/G	HR	BB	BB/G	SO	SO/G	ERA	/A	OAVG	OOBP	PR	/A	PF	CPI	WAT	PB	PD	TPI
1966	NY-A	12	11	.522	34	32	11	2	0	215	196	8.2	15	40	1.7	96	4.0	3.31	97	.241	.272	3	-2	94	84	1.9	4	-0	0.1
1967	NY-A	8	14	.364	36	30	6	1	0	181	179	8.9	11	43	2.1	102	5.1	3.48	89	.256	.298	-5	-8	96	93	-2.1	1	1	-0.5
1968	NY-A	12	11	.522	36	27	6	2	0	212	187	7.9	13	29	**1.2**	115	4.9	2.63	114	.241	.264	8	9	101	98	0.3	-2	4	1.3
1969	NY-A	17	16	.515	37	37	16	4	0	272	228	7.5	15	43	**1.4**	150	5.0	2.55	136	.229	**.257**	33	28	96	86	0.7	-0	2	3.2
1970	NY-A	20	11	.645	39	37	8	2	0	260	247	8.6	24	40	**1.4**	127	4.4	2.91	117	.248	**.276**	23	14	91	100	3.1	5	2	2.2
1971	NY-A	15	13	.536	37	35	16	4	1	274	269	8.8	25	42	**1.4**	139	4.6	3.05	110	.258	.285	13	9	97	102	1.0	-3	2	0.8
1972	NY-A	17	15	.531	35	35	12	3	0	250	270	9.7	17	44	**1.6**	100	3.6	3.24	87	.276	.306	-5	-12	92	107	0.9	4	1	-0.8
1973	NY-A	8	15	.348	31	31	6	0	0	184	207	10.1	18	49	2.4	59	2.9	3.96	97	.286	.333	-3	-3	100	108	-3.7	0	0	-0.2
1974	NY-A	0	0	—	3	1	0	0	0	8	13	14.6	1	2	2.3	5	5.6	4.50	77	.361	.395	-1	-1	95	147	0.0	0	0	0.0
	Cle-A	9	14	.391	29	29	3	0	0	153	187	11.0	16	37	2.2	52	3.1	4.35	84	.305	.344	-12	-12	101	109	-2.2	0	1	-1.0
	Yr	9	14	.391	32	30	3	0	0	161	200	11.2	17	39	2.2	57	3.2	4.36	84	.308	.347	-13	-13	101	109	-2.2	0	1	-1.0
1975	Cle-A	14	8	.636	25	25	6	2	0	146	154	9.5	15	40	2.5	47	2.9	3.95	96	.275	.328	-3	-3	100	104	3.4	0	1	-0.1
1976	Cle-A	0	3	.000	9	9	0	0	0	47	59	11.3	3	10	1.9	19	3.6	5.55	63	.309	.338	-11	-11	100	80	-1.4	0	0	-1.0
	Tex-A	1	0	1.000	4	2	0	0	0	15	21	12.6	0	7	4.2	4	2.4	3.60	100	.344	.406	-0	0	103	158	0.5	0	0	0.0

YEAR	TM/L	W	L	PCT	G	GS	CG	SHO	SV	IP	H	H/G	HR	BB	BB/G	SO	SO/G	ERA	/A	OAVG	OOBP	PR	/A	PF	CPI	WAT	PB	PD	TPI
	Yr	1	3	.250	13	11	0	0	0	62	80	11.6	3	17	2.5	23	3.3	5.08	70	.316	.355	-11	-11	100	158	-0.9	0	0	-1.0
Total	11	133	131	.504	355	330	90	20	1	2217	2217	9.0	173	426	1.7	1015	4.1	3.30	101	.261	.295	41	9	96	99	2.4	9	15	4.0
■ **JIM PETERSON**	Peterson, James Niels b: 8/18/08, Philadelphia, Pa. d: 4/8/75, Palm Beach, Fla. BR/TR, 6'0.5", 200 lbs. Deb: 7/09/31																												
1931	Phi-A	0	1	.000	6	1	1	0	0	13	18	12.5	0	4	2.8	7	4.8	6.23	71	.321	.367	-3	-3	101	80	-0.4	1	0	-0.1
1933	Phi-A	2	5	.286	32	5	0	0	0	91	114	11.3	6	36	3.6	18	1.8	4.95	79	.305	.355	-7	-10	92	105	-1.5	-0	2	-0.7
1937	Bro-N	0	0	—	3	0	0	0	0	6	8	12.0	3	2	3.0	4	6.0	7.50	56	.333	.385	-2	-2	107	120	0.0	0	1	-0.1
Total	3	2	6	.250	41	6	1	0	0	110	140	11.5	9	42	3.4	29	2.4	5.24	76	.308	.358	-12	-15	93	103	-1.9	1	3	-0.9
■ **KENT PETERSON**	Peterson, Kent Franklin "Pete" b: 12/21/25, Goshen, Utah BR/TL, 5'10", 170 lbs. Deb: 7/15/44																												
1944	Cin-N	0	0	—	1	0	0	0	0	1	0	0.0	0	0	0.0	0	0.0	0.00	—	.000	.000	0	0	95	0	0.0	0	0	0.0
1947	Cin-N	6	13	.316	37	17	3	1	2	152	156	9.2	8	62	3.7	78	4.6	4.26	88	.265	.334	-3	-9	92	90	-3.4	-3	-2	-1.3
1948	Cin-N	2	15	.118	43	17	2	0	1	137	146	9.6	10	59	3.9	64	4.2	4.60	91	.271	.345	-10	-6	106	95	-6.2	-2	0	-0.7
1949	Cin-N	4	5	.444	30	7	2	0	0	66	66	9.0	8	46	6.3	28	3.8	6.27	63	.261	.375	-16	-17	98	84	0.3	-2	-1	-1.7
1950	Cin-N	0	3	.000	9	2	0	0	0	20	25	11.2	4	17	7.6	6	2.7	7.20	61	.305	.424	-7	-6	106	101	-1.4	0	-1	-0.5
1951	Cin-N	1	1	.500	9	0	0	0	0	10	13	11.7	0	8	7.2	5	4.5	6.30	64	.317	.440	-3	-2	103	98	0.1	-0	0	-0.1
1952	Phi-N	0	0	—	3	0	0	0	2	7	2	2.6	0	2	2.6	7	9.0	0.00	—	.091	.167	3	3	99	0	0.0	-0	-0	0.3
1953	Phi-N	0	1	.000	15	0	0	0	0	27	26	8.7	3	21	7.0	20	6.7	6.67	63	.252	.375	-7	-7	98	76	-0.4	-1	-0	-0.7
Total	8	13	38	.255	147	43	7	1	5	420	434	9.3	33	215	4.6	208	4.5	4.95	81	.266	.352	-43	-44	99	89	-11.0	-8	-4	-4.7
■ **SID PETERSON**	Peterson, Sidney Herbert b: 1/31/18, Havelock, N.Dak. BR/TR, 6'3", 200 lbs. Deb: 5/04/43																												
1943	StL-A	2	0	1.000	3	0	0	0	0	10	15	13.5	0	3	2.7	0	0.0	2.70	123	.341	.396	1	1	101	206	1.0	-0	0	0.0
■ **DAN PETRY**	Petry, Daniel Joseph b: 11/13/58, Palo Alto, Cal. BR/TR, 6'4", 185 lbs. Deb: 7/08/79																												
1979	Det-A	6	5	.545	15	15	2	0	0	98	90	8.3	11	33	3.0	43	3.9	3.95	103	.254	.317	3	1	96	100	0.2	0	-1	0.0
1980	Det-A	10	9	.526	27	25	4	3	0	165	156	8.5	9	83	4.5	88	4.8	3.93	108	.253	.335	2	6	105	95	0.2	0	2	0.7
1981	Det-A	10	9	.526	23	22	7	2	0	141	115	7.3	10	57	3.6	79	5.0	3.00	128	.224	.297	10	13	105	97	-0.4	0	2	1.6
1982	Det-A	15	9	.625	35	35	8	1	0	246	220	8.0	15	100	3.7	132	4.8	3.22	127	.241	.314	24	23	100	103	3.1	0	4	2.9
1983	Det-A	19	11	.633	38	38	9	2	0	266	256	8.7	37	99	3.3	122	4.1	3.92	98	.256	.324	4	-2	95	108	2.7	0	3	0.1
1984	Det-A	18	8	.692	35	35	7	2	0	233	231	8.9	21	66	2.5	144	5.6	3.24	116	.259	.310	20	14	94	111	2.1	0	3	1.7
1985	Det-A	15	13	.536	34	34	8	0	0	239	190	7.2	24	81	3.1	109	4.1	3.35	131	.217	.285	21	28	106	85	0.5	0	1	2.9
1986	Det-A	5	10	.333	20	20	2	0	0	116	122	9.5	15	53	4.1	56	4.3	4.66	85	.268	.346	-6	-9	95	101	-2.9	0	1	-0.7
1987	Det-A	9	7	.563	30	21	0	0	0	135	148	9.9	22	76	5.1	93	6.2	5.60	76	.279	.373	-17	-20	96	102	-0.5	0	1	-1.7
1988	Cal-A	3	9	.250	22	22	4	1	0	140	139	8.9	18	59	3.8	64	4.1	4.37	86	.263	.338	-6	-9	95	105	-2.8	0	2	-0.6
Total	10	110	90	.550	279	267	51	11	0	1779	1667	8.4	182	707	3.6	930	4.7	3.80	106	.250	.321	55	45	99	101	2.2	0	19	6.9
■ **JAY PETTIBONE**	Pettibone, Harry Jonathan b: 6/21/57, Mt.Clemens, Mich. BR/TR, 6'4", 182 lbs. Deb: 9/11/83																												
1983	Min-A	0	4	.000	4	4	1	0	0	27	28	9.3	8	8	2.7	10	3.3	5.33	81	.280	.342	-4	-3	106	114	-1.9	0	0	-0.2
■ **PAUL PETTIT**	Pettit, George William Paul "Lefty" b: 11/29/31, Los Angeles, Cal. BL/TL, 6'2", 195 lbs. Deb: 5/04/51																												
1951	Pit-N	0	0	—	2	0	0	0	0	3	2	6.0	1	1	3.0	0	0.0	3.00	144	.200	.273	0	0	110	146	0.0	-0	0	0.0
1953	Pit-N	1	2	.333	10	5	0	0	0	28	33	10.6	1	20	6.4	14	4.5	7.71	59	.297	.405	-11	-10	106	71	0.0	1	0	-0.7
Total	2	1	2	.333	12	5	0	0	0	31	35	10.2	2	21	6.1	14	4.1	7.26	62	.289	.394	-10	-9	107	78	0.0	1	0	-0.7
■ **LEON PETTIT**	Pettit, Leon Arthur "Lefty" b: 6/23/02, Waynesburg, Pa. d: 11/21/74, Columbia, Tenn. BL/TL, 5'10.5", 165 lbs. Deb: 4/18/35																												
1935	Was-A	8	5	.615	41	7	1	0	3	109	129	10.7	6	58	4.8	45	3.7	4.95	83	.301	.381	-6	-10	93	110	2.2	0	-0	-0.8
1937	Phi-N	0	1	.000	3	1	0	0	0	4	6	13.5	1	4	9.0	0	0.0	11.25	38	.353	.476	-3	-3	111	85	-0.4	0	0	-0.2
Total	2	8	6	.571	44	8	1	0	3	113	135	10.8	7	62	4.9	45	3.6	5.18	80	.303	.385	-9	-13	93	109	1.8	0	-0	-1.0
■ **BOB PETTIT**	Pettit, Robert Henry b: 7/19/1861, Williamstown, Mass. d: 11/1/10, Derby, Conn. BL/TR, 5'9", 160 lbs. Deb: 9/03/1887																												
1887	Chi-N	0	0	—	1	0	0	0	1	1	3	27.0	0	2	18.0	0	0.0	0.00	—	.533	.655	0	1	115	0	0.0	0	0	0.0
■ **CHARLIE PETTY**	Petty, Charles E. b: 6/28/1866, Nashville, Tenn. TR , Deb: 7/30/1889																												
1889	Cin-a	2	3	.400	5	5	5	0	0	44	44	9.0	3	20	4.1	10	2.0	5.52	72	.275	.356	-8	-8	103	72	-0.6	1	0	-0.4
1893	NY-N	5	2	.714	9	6	4	0	0	54	66	11.0	0	28	4.7	12	2.0	3.33	144	.317	.398	8	9	103	146	1.5	2	0	1.0
1894	Was-N	3	8	.273	16	12	8	0	0	103	156	13.6	4	32	2.8	14	1.2	5.59	95	.372	.417	-3	-3	100	107	-1.1	-2	0	-0.3
	Cle-N	0	2	.000	4	3	2	0	0	27	42	14.0	4	14	4.7	4	1.3	8.67	68	.379	.448	-10	-8	111	88	-0.9	-2	0	-0.6
	Yr	3	10	.231	20	15	10	0	0	130	198	13.7	8	46	3.2	18	1.2	6.23	87	.374	.424	-13	-11	102	88	-2.0	-2	0	-0.9
Total	3	10	15	.400	34	26	19	0	0	228	308	12.2	11	94	3.7	40	1.6	5.41	93	.343	.405	-13	-10	102	107	-1.1	-1	0	-0.3
■ **JESSE PETTY**	Petty, Jesse Lee "The Silver Fox" b: 11/23/1894, Orr, Okla. d: 10/23/71, St.Paul, Minn. BR/TL, 6', 195 lbs. Deb: 4/14/21																												
1921	Cle-A	0	0	—	4	0	0	0	0	9	10	10.0	0	0	0.0	0	0.0	2.00	206	.345	.286	2	2	96	220	0.0	-0	1	0.2
1925	Bro-N	9	9	.500	28	22	7	0	0	153	188	11.1	15	47	2.8	39	2.3	4.88	83	.304	.348	-10	-14	95	100	1.0	-2	-2	-1.6
1926	Bro-N	17	17	.500	38	33	23	1	1	276	246	**8.0**	9	79	2.6	101	3.3	2.84	136	**.240**	.285	30	31	101	91	1.4	-3	-4	2.4
1927	Bro-N	13	18	.419	42	33	19	2	1	272	263	8.7	13	53	1.8	101	3.3	2.98	137	.254	.281	28	33	104	96	-0.2	-7	-3	2.4
1928	Bro-N	15	15	.500	40	31	15	2	1	234	264	10.2	18	56	2.2	74	2.8	4.04	97	.289	.324	-1	-3	99	100	0.0	-5	-4	-1.1
1929	Pit-N	11	10	.524	36	25	12	1	0	184	197	9.6	12	42	2.1	58	2.8	3.72	129	.277	.305	20	22	102	101	-1.0	-6	-2	1.3
1930	Pit-N	1	6	.143	10	7	0	0	1	41	67	14.7	8	13	2.9	16	3.5	8.34	58	.362	.402	-15	-16	98	92	-2.5	-1	0	-1.3
	Chi-N	1	3	.250	9	3	0	0	0	39	51	11.8	2	6	1.4	18	4.2	3.00	171	.317	.331	9	9	103	152	-1.1	-0	0	0.8
	Yr	2	9	.182	19	10	0	0	1	80	118	13.3	10	19	2.1	34	3.8	5.74	87	.339	.364	-7	-7	100	152	-3.6	-1	0	-0.5
Total	7	67	78	.462	207	154	76	6	4	1208	1286	9.6	77	296	2.2	407	3.0	3.68	113	.275	.309	63	65	100	100	-2.4	-26	-14	3.1
■ **PRETZEL PEZZULLO**	Pezzullo, John b: 12/10/10, Bridgeport, Conn. BL/TL, 5'11.5", 180 lbs. Deb: 4/18/35																												
1935	Phi-N	3	5	.375	41	7	2	0	1	84	115	12.3	5	45	4.8	24	2.6	6.43	73	.321	.397	-22	-16	117	95	-0.3	0	-2	-1.5
1936	Phi-N	0	0	—	1	0	0	0	0	2	1	4.5	0	6	27.0	0	0.0	4.50	99	.167	.583	-0	-0	111	198	0.0	0	0	0.0
Total	2	3	5	.375	42	7	2	0	1	86	116	12.1	5	51	5.3	24	2.5	6.38	74	.319	.402	-23	-16	117	98	-0.3	0	-2	-1.5
■ **JEFF PFEFFER**	Pfeffer, Edward Joseph b: 3/4/1888, Seymour, Ill. d: 8/15/72, Chicago, Ill. BR/TR, 6'3", 210 lbs. Deb: 4/16/11																												
1911	StL-A	0	0	—	2	0	0	0	0	10	11	9.9	0	4	3.6	4	3.6	7.20	46	.297	.366	-4	-4	100	55	0.0	-1	-0	-0.3
1913	Bro-N	0	1	.000	5	2	1	0	0	24	28	10.5	0	13	4.9	13	4.9	3.38	99	.311	.395	-0	-0	105	157	-0.4	-1	0	0.0
1914	Bro-N	23	12	.657	43	34	27	3	4	315	264	7.5	9	91	2.6	135	3.9	1.97	143	.232	.285	29	29	101	113	6.8	-0	-4	2.8
1915	Bro-N	19	14	.576	40	34	26	6	3	292	243	7.5	8	76	2.3	84	2.6	2.10	134	.231	.285	21	23	102	112	2.1	5	-4	2.6
1916	Bro-N	25	11	.694	41	37	30	6	1	329	274	7.5	5	63	1.7	128	3.5	1.91	137	.230	.273	26	26	100	104	4.8	7	-5	3.5
1917	Bro-N	11	15	.423	30	30	24	3	0	266	225	7.6	4	66	2.2	115	3.9	2.23	127	.234	.284	14	18	105	105	-1.2	-5	-2	1.3
1918	Bro-N	1	0	1.000	1	1	1	1	0	9	2	2.0	0	3	3.0	1	1.0	0.00	—	.071	.161	3	3	104	0	0.5	0	0	0.5
1919	Bro-N	17	13	.567	30	30	26	4	0	267	270	9.1	7	49	1.7	92	3.1	2.66	102	.267	.301	7	2	94	113	2.7	2	1	0.4
1920	Bro-N	16	9	.640	30	28	20	2	0	215	225	9.4	5	45	1.9	80	3.3	3.01	113	.273	.306	3	9	108	96	1.3	0	-3	0.8
1921	Bro-N	1	5	.167	6	5	2	0	0	32	36	10.1	0	9	2.5	8	2.3	4.50	88	.310	.341	-3	-2	105	92	-1.9	-2	0	-0.2
	StL-N	9	3	.750	18	13	7	1	0	99	115	10.5	3	28	2.5	22	2.0	4.27	82	.305	.347	-5	-8	93	100	2.6	-1	-2	-0.9
	Yr	10	8	.556	24	18	9	1	0	131	151	10.4	3	37	2.5	30	2.1	4.33	83	.306	.344	-8	-10	96	100	0.7	-2	-1	-1.1
1922	StL-N	19	12	.613	44	32	19	1	2	261	286	9.9	12	58	2.0	83	2.9	3.59	115	.279	.316	15	15	100	97	2.6	3	1	1.8
1923	StL-N	8	9	.471	26	18	7	1	0	152	171	10.1	8	40	2.4	32	1.9	4.03	89	.287	.330	-0	-7	90	99	-0.7	-3	-1	-1.1
1924	StL-N	4	5	.444	16	12	3	0	0	78	102	11.8	3	30	3.5	20	2.3	5.31	75	.318	.373	-12	-12	103	95	0.2	-3	-1	-1.3
	Pit-N	5	3	.625	15	4	1	0	0	59	68	10.4	3	17	2.6	19	2.9	3.05	132	.293	.337	5	6	104	135	0.4	-0	-1	0.5
	Yr	9	8	.529	31	16	4	0	0	137	170	11.2	6	47	3.1	39	2.6	4.34	92	.307	.356	-7	-5	103	135	0.6	-3	-2	-0.8
Total	13	158	112	.585	347	280	194	28	10	2408	2320	8.7	67	592	2.2	836	3.1	2.77	114	.258	.303	98	100	100	106	19.8	2	-19	10.4
■ **BIG JEFF PFEFFER**	Pfeffer, Francis Xavier b: 3/31/1882, Champaign, Ill. d: 12/19/54, Kankakee, Ill. BR/TR, 6'1", 185 lbs. Deb: 4/15/05																												
1905	Chi-N	4	4	.500	15	11	9	0	0	101	84	7.5	2	36	3.2	56	5.0	2.50	120	.254	.334	6	6	100	107	-0.6	1	-0	0.5
1906	Bos-N	13	22	.371	35	35	33	4	0	302	270	8.0	4	114	3.4	158	4.7	2.95	94	.270	.354	-11	-6	106	100	1.6	1	1	0.0
1907	Bos-N	6	8	.429	19	16	12	1	0	144	129	8.1	3	61	3.8	65	4.1	3.00	81	.271	.362	-9	-9	99	101	0.5	3	-1	-1.0

YEAR	TM/L	W	L	PCT	G	GS	CG	SHO	SV	IP	H	H/G	HR	BB	BB/G	SO	SO/G	ERA	/A	OAVG	OOBP	PR	/A	PF	CPI	WAT	PB	PD	TPI
1908	Bos-N	0	0	—	4	0	0	0	0	10	18	16.2	1	8	7.2	3	2.7	12.60	20	.423	.514	-11	-11	106	72	0.0	-0	-0	-1.0
1910	Chi-N	1	0	1.000	13	1	1	0	0	41	43	9.4	1	16	3.5	11	2.4	3.29	89	.281	.353	-1	-2	96	114	0.5	1	-0	-0.1
1911	Bos-N	7	5	.583	26	6	4	1	2	97	116	10.8	3	57	5.3	24	2.2	4.73	78	.301	.391	-14	-11	109	105	2.6	1	0	-0.8
Total	6	31	39	.443	112	69	59	6	2	695	660	8.5	14	292	3.8	317	4.1	3.30	87	.276	.362	-41	-33	103	102	4.6	7	-1	-2.4
■ FRED PFEFFER	Pfeffer, Nathaniel Frederick "Fritz" or "Dandelion" b: 3/17/1860, Louisville, Ky. d: 4/10/32, Chicago, Ill. BR/TR, 5'10.5", 184 lbs. Deb: 5/01/1882 M																												
1884	Chi-N	0	0	—	1	0	0	0	0	1	3	27.0	0	1	9.0	0	0.0	9.00	35	.525	.596	-1	-1	105	164	0.0	0	0	0.0
1885	Chi-N	2	1	.667	5	2	2	0	**2**	32	26	7.3	1	8	2.3	13	3.7	2.53	117	.232	.283	1	2	106	89	-0.1	1	0	0.2
1892	Lou-N	0	0	—	1	0	0	0	0	5	4	7.2	0	5	9.0	0	0.0	1.80	170	.231	.403	1	1	93	215	0.0	0	0	0.1
1894	Lou-N	0	0	—	1	0	0	0	0	7	8	10.3	0	6	7.7	0	0.0	2.57	188	.309	.439	2	2	91	208	0.0	0	0	0.1
Total	4	2	1	.667	8	2	2	0	2	45	41	8.2	1	20	4.0	13	2.6	2.60	128	.255	.337	3	4	102	123	-0.1	2	0	0.4
■ JACK PFIESTER	Pfiester, John Albert "Jack The Giant Killer" (born John Albert Hagenbush) b: 5/24/1878, Cincinnati, Ohio d: 9/3/53, Loveland, Ohio BR/TL, 5'11", 180 lbs. Deb: 03																												
1903	Pit-N	0	3	.000	3	3	2	0	0	19	26	12.3	0	10	4.7	15	7.1	6.16	54	.362	.453	-6	-6	101	91	-1.4	-1	-0	-0.4
1904	Pit-N	1	1	.500	3	2	1	0	0	20	28	12.6	0	9	4.0	6	2.7	7.20	37	.357	.423	-10	-10	98	74	0.0	1	0	-0.8
1906	Chi-N	20	8	.714	31	29	20	4	0	242	173	6.4	3	63	2.3	153	5.7	1.56	167	.228	.298	29	28	99	111	-1.0	-7	0	3.3
1907	Chi-N	14	9	.609	30	22	13	3	0	195	143	6.6	1	48	2.2	90	4.2	**1.15**	**218**	.231	.292	28	29	102	**135**	-1.7	-3	-2	3.3
1908	Chi-N	12	10	.545	33	29	18	3	0	252	204	7.3	1	70	2.5	117	4.2	2.00	120	.251	.319	10	11	102	106	-1.8	-4	-2	1.0
1909	Chi-N	17	6	.739	29	25	13	5	0	197	179	8.2	1	49	2.2	73	3.3	2.42	102	.240	.291	4	1	95	90	2.4	1	3	0.4
1910	Chi-N	6	3	.667	14	13	5	2	0	100	82	7.4	0	26	2.3	34	3.1	1.80	162	.225	.279	14	12	96	97	0.0	-2	-0	1.0
1911	Chi-N	1	4	.200	6	5	3	0	0	34	34	9.0	0	18	4.8	15	4.0	3.97	80	.262	.360	-2	-3	94	92	-1.6	0	1	-0.1
Total	8	71	44	.617	149	128	75	17	0	1059	869	7.4	6	293	2.5	503	4.3	2.04	127	.243	.307	66	64	99	107	-5.1	-15	-2	7.7
■ DAN PFISTER	Pfister, Daniel Albin b: 12/20/36, Plainfield, N.J. BR/TR, 6', 187 lbs. Deb: 9/09/61																												
1961	KC-A	0	0	—	2	0	0	0	0	2	5	22.5	2	4	18.0	3	13.5	18.00	23	.417	.563	-3	-3	104	118	0.0	0	0	-0.2
1962	KC-A	4	14	.222	41	25	2	0	1	196	175	8.0	27	106	4.9	123	5.6	4.55	88	.238	.335	-13	-11	101	94	-4.7	-1	1	-1.0
1963	KC-A	1	0	1.000	3	1	0	0	0	9	8	8.0	1	3	3.0	9	9.0	2.00	197	.229	.300	2	2	109	167	0.5	-0	0	0.2
1964	KC-A	1	5	.167	19	3	0	0	0	41	50	11.0	10	29	6.4	21	4.6	6.59	59	.311	.423	-13	-12	108	117	-1.5	-0	-0	-1.2
Total	4	6	19	.240	65	29	2	0	1	248	238	8.6	40	142	5.2	156	5.7	4.90	82	.252	.353	-28	-25	103	100	-5.7	-2	1	-2.2
■ BILL PFLANN	Pflann, William F. b: Brooklyn, N.Y. 6', 205 lbs. Deb: 6/16/1894																												
1894	Cin-N	0	1	.000	1	1	0	0	0	3	10	30.0	1	4	12.0	0	0.0	27.00	20	.566	.646	-7	-7	102	75	-0.4	-0	0	-0.4
■ LEE PFUND	Pfund, Le Roy Herbert b: 10/10/18, Oak Park, Ill. BR/TR, 6'1", 185 lbs. Deb: 4/21/45																												
1945	Bro-N	3	2	.600	15	10	2	0	0	62	69	10.0	4	35	5.1	27	3.9	5.23	69	.274	.366	-10	-11	95	91	0.2	1	1	-0.9
■ BILL PHEBUS	Phebus, Raymond William b: 8/9/09, Cherryvale, Kan. BR/TR, 5'9", 170 lbs. Deb: 9/06/36																												
1936	Was-A	0	0	—	2	1	0	0	0	7	4	5.1	1	4	5.1	4	5.1	2.57	188	.114	.225	2	2	96	36	0.0	0	-0	0.2
1937	Was-A	3	2	.600	6	5	4	1	1	41	33	7.2	2	24	5.3	12	2.6	2.20	201	.232	.343	11	10	96	176	0.6	1	-1	1.0
1938	Was-A	0	0	—	5	0	0	0	1	6	9	13.5	1	7	10.5	2	3.0	12.00	38	.346	.457	-5	-5	96	78	0.0	-0	0	-0.3
Total	3	3	2	.600	13	6	4	1	2	54	46	7.7	4	35	5.8	18	3.0	3.33	135	.227	.340	8	7	96	147	0.6	1	-1	0.9
■ RAY PHELPS	Phelps, Raymond Clifford b: 12/11/03, Dunlap, Tenn. d: 7/7/71, Fort Pierce, Fla. BR/TR, 6'2", 200 lbs. Deb: 4/23/30																												
1930	Bro-N	14	7	.667	36	24	11	2	0	180	198	9.9	21	52	2.6	64	3.2	4.10	119	.280	.325	17	16	99	107	2.9	-2	2	1.4
1931	Bro-N	7	9	.438	28	26	3	2	0	149	184	11.1	3	44	2.7	50	3.0	5.01	78	.306	.353	-19	-18	101	89	-1.3	-1	0	-1.8
1932	Bro-N	4	5	.444	20	8	4	1	0	79	101	11.5	5	27	3.1	21	2.4	5.92	63	.323	.371	-18	-19	96	93	-0.6	-1	0	-1.8
1935	Chi-A	4	8	.333	27	17	4	0	1	125	126	9.1	10	55	4.0	38	2.7	4.82	101	.262	.335	-5	1	109	87	-1.9	-4	2	0.0
1936	Chi-A	4	6	.400	15	4	2	0	0	69	91	11.9	9	42	5.5	17	2.2	6.00	83	.331	.414	-7	-8	99	121	-1.2	1	1	-0.4
Total	5	33	35	.485	126	79	24	5	1	602	700	10.5	48	220	3.3	190	2.8	4.93	91	.294	.351	-32	-29	101	98	-2.1	-8	5	-2.6
■ DEACON PHILLIPPE	Phillippe, Charles Louis b: 5/23/1872, Rural Retreat, Va. d: 3/30/52, Avalon, Pa. BR/TR, 6'0.5", 180 lbs. Deb: 4/21/1899																												
1899	Lou-N	21	17	.553	42	38	33	2	1	321	331	9.3	10	64	1.8	68	1.9	3.17	125	.290	.327	24	28	103	97	2.8	-2	0	2.5
1900	Pit-N	20	13	.606	38	33	29	1	0	279	274	8.8	7	42	1.4	75	2.4	2.84	131	.279	.309	27	28	101	94	1.8	-4	-2	2.1
1901	Pit-N	22	12	.647	37	32	30	1	2	296	274	8.3	7	38	1.2	103	3.1	2.22	143	.269	.302	**36**	32	96	110	0.0	5	2	3.5
1902	Pit-N	20	9	.690	31	30	29	5	0	272	265	8.8	1	26	**0.9**	122	4.0	2.05	133	.279	.300	22	20	98	108	-1.1	2	-2	2.0
1903	Pit-N	25	9	.735	36	33	31	4	2	289	269	8.4	4	29	**0.9**	123	3.8	2.43	136	.271	**.294**	27	28	101	88	5.1	2	-2	2.6
1904	Pit-N	10	10	.500	21	19	17	3	1	167	183	9.9	1	26	1.4	82	4.4	3.23	82	.305	.337	-9	-11	98	97	-1.3	-3	-0	-1.0
1905	Pit-N	19	13	.594	38	33	25	5	0	279	235	7.6	0	48	**1.5**	133	4.3	2.19	139	.256	.300	25	26	102	94	-1.0	-5	-1	2.7
1906	Pit-N	15	10	.600	33	24	19	3	0	219	216	8.9	3	26	**1.1**	90	3.7	2.47	107	.286	.311	4	4	101	103	-0.1	3	-1	0.4
1907	Pit-N	14	11	.560	35	26	17	1	2	214	214	9.0	2	36	**1.5**	61	2.6	2.61	97	.291	.328	-3	-2	102	102	-0.7	1	-2	-0.4
1908	Pit-N	0	0	—	5	0	0	0	0	12	20	15.0	0	3	2.3	1	0.8	11.25	19	.404	.438	-12	-12	92	54	0.0	0	-1	-1.2
1909	Pit-N	8	3	.727	22	12	7	1	0	132	121	8.3	2	14	1.0	38	2.6	2.32	111	.253	.280	4	4	99	97	0.1	-3	-2	0.2
1910	Pit-N	14	2	.875	31	8	5	1	4	122	111	8.2	4	9	0.7	30	2.2	2.29	146	.239	.258	10	14	110	78	5.9	1	-3	1.3
1911	Pit-N	0	0	—	3	0	0	0	0	6	5	7.5	0	2	3.0	3	4.5	7.50	44	.238	.304	-3	-3	97	33	0.0	1	0	0.0
Total	13	188	109	.633	372	288	242	27	12	2608	2518	8.7	41	363	1.3	929	3.2	2.58	121	.276	.307	152	157	101	98	11.5	-1	-14	14.7
■ BUZ PHILLIPS	Phillips, Albert Abernathy b: 5/25/04, Newton, N.C. d: 11/6/64, Baltimore, Md. BR/TR, 5'11.5", 185 lbs. Deb: 8/05/30																												
1930	Phi-N	0	0	—	14	1	0	0	0	44	68	13.9	6	18	3.7	9	1.8	7.98	68	.354	.403	-15	-12	109	90	0.0	3	-1	-0.8
■ RED PHILLIPS	Phillips, Clarence Lemuel b: 11/3/08, Pauls Valley, Okla. BR/TR, 6'3.5", 195 lbs. Deb: 7/24/34																												
1934	Det-A	2	0	1.000	7	1	1	0	1	23	31	12.1	1	16	6.3	3	1.2	6.26	67	.316	.412	-5	-5	94	98	1.0	1	-1	-0.3
1936	Det-A	2	4	.333	22	6	3	0	0	87	124	12.8	12	22	2.3	15	1.6	6.52	73	.332	.366	-14	-17	95	96	-1.1	2	-0	-1.2
Total	2	4	4	.500	29	7	4	0	1	110	155	12.7	13	38	3.1	18	1.5	6.46	72	.329	.376	-19	-22	94	97	-0.1	3	-1	-1.5
■ JACK PHILLIPS	Phillips, Jack Dorn "Stretch" b: 9/6/21, Clarence, N.Y. BR/TR, 6'4", 193 lbs. Deb: 8/22/47																												
1950	Pit-N	0	0	—	1	0	0	0	0	5	7	12.6	0	1	1.8	2	3.6	7.20	61	.333	.364	-2	-2	106	67	0.0	0	0	0.0
■ JACK PHILLIPS	Phillips, John Stephen b: 5/24/19, St.Louis, Mo. d: 6/16/58, St.Louis, Mo. BR/TR, 6'1", 185 lbs. Deb: 7/13/45																												
1945	NY-N	0	0	—	1	0	0	0	0	4	5	11.3	1	5	11.3	0	0.0	11.25	34	.313	.500	-3	-3	100	86	0.0	0	0	-0.2
■ ED PHILLIPS	Phillips, Norman Edwin b: 9/20/44, Ardmore, Okla. BR/TR, 6'1", 190 lbs. Deb: 4/09/70																												
1970	Bos-A	0	2	.000	18	0	0	0	0	24	29	10.9	4	10	3.8	23	8.6	5.25	78	.312	.383	-4	-3	110	117	-0.9	-0	-0	-0.3
■ TOM PHILLIPS	Phillips, Thomas Gerald b: 4/5/1889, Phillipsburg, Pa. d: 4/12/29, Phillipsburg, Pa. BR/TR, 6'2", 190 lbs. Deb: 9/13/15																												
1915	StL-A	1	3	.250	5	4	1	0	0	27	28	9.3	0	12	4.0	5	1.7	3.00	97	.283	.372	-0	-0	99	134	-0.7	-1	-1	-0.1
1919	Cle-A	3	2	.600	22	3	2	0	0	55	55	9.0	2	34	5.6	18	2.9	2.95	114	.272	.385	**2**	**3**	104	146	0.0	1	-1	0.2
1921	Was-A	1	0	1.000	1	1	1	0	0	9	9	9.0	0	3	3.0	2	2.0	2.00	212	.290	.343	2	2	99	195	0.5	-1	-0	0.1
1922	Was-A	3	7	.300	17	7	2	1	0	70	72	9.3	2	22	2.8	19	2.4	4.89	77	.273	.328	-7	-9	93	73	-1.6	-1	-1	-0.9
Total	4	8	12	.400	45	15	6	1	0	161	164	9.2	4	71	4.0	44	2.5	3.75	94	.275	.356	-3	-4	98	115	-1.8	-1	-3	-0.7
■ BILL PHILLIPS	Phillips, William Corcoran "Whoa Bill" or "Silver Bill" b: 11/9/1868, Allenport, Pa. d: 10/25/41, Charleroi, Pa. BR/TR, 5'11", 180 lbs. Deb: 8/11/1890 M																												
1890	Pit-N	1	9	.100	10	10	9	0	0	82	123	13.5	8	29	3.2	25	2.7	7.57	45	.364	.414	-37	-38	95	83	-2.0	1	0	-2.8
1895	Cin-N	6	7	.462	18	9	6	0	2	109	126	10.4	6	44	3.6	15	1.2	6.03	85	.310	.377	-15	-11	107	76	-0.6	1	0	-0.6
1899	Cin-N	17	9	.654	33	27	18	1	1	228	234	9.2	3	71	2.8	43	1.7	3.32	122	.289	.346	14	19	105	97	3.4	-5	0	1.3
1900	Cin-N	9	11	.450	29	24	17	3	0	208	229	9.9	5	67	2.9	51	2.2	4.28	80	.303	.359	-13	-20	93	87	0.1	-3	0	-2.0
1901	Cin-N	14	18	.438	37	36	29	1	0	281	364	11.7	7	67	2.1	109	3.5	4.64	71	.340	.384	-41	-42	100	99	2.0	1	5	-3.3
1902	Cin-N	16	16	.500	33	33	30	0	0	269	267	8.9	3	55	1.8	85	2.8	2.51	120	.284	.330	8	15	108	108	0.0	10	3	3.2
1903	Cin-N	7	6	.538	16	13	11	1	0	118	134	10.2	0	30	2.3	46	3.5	3.36	104	.316	.371	-1	2	107	107	0.1	-1	2	0.4
Total	7	70	76	.479	176	152	120	6	3	1295	1477	10.3	32	363	2.5	374	2.6	4.09	87	.311	.363	-86	-74	102	96	3.0	4	10	-3.8
■ TAYLOR PHILLIPS	Phillips, William Taylor "Tay" b: 6/18/33, Atlanta, Ga. BL/TL, 5'11", 185 lbs. Deb: 6/08/56																												
1956	Mil-N	5	3	.625	23	6	3	0	2	88	69	7.1	6	33	3.4	36	3.7	2.25	161	.223	.305	15	13	96	130	0.3	-2	2	1.4

YEAR	TM/L	W	L	PCT	G	GS	CG	SHO	SV	IP	H	H/G	HR	BB	BB/G	SO	SO/G	ERA	/A	OAVG	OOBP	PR	/A	PF	CPI	WAT	PB	PD	TPI
1957	Mil-N	3	2	.600	27	6	0	0	2	73	82	10.1	3	40	4.9	36	4.4	5.55	61	.300	.380	-14	-17	88	91	0.0	-1	1	-1.7
1958	Chi-N	7	10	.412	39	27	5	1	1	170	178	9.4	22	79	4.2	102	5.4	4.76	84	.266	.346	-15	-15	101	95	-1.0	-4	1	-1.7
1959	Chi-N	0	2	.000	7	2	0	0	0	17	22	11.6	3	11	5.8	5	2.6	7.41	53	.319	.417	-7	-7	99	97	-0.9	-0	0	-0.6
	Phi-N	1	4	.200	32	3	1	0	1	63	72	10.3	4	31	4.4	35	5.0	5.00	80	.303	.381	-7	-7	102	106	-1.2	-1	0	-0.6
	Yr	1	6	.143	39	5	1	0	1	80	94	10.6	7	42	4.7	40	4.5	5.51	72	.303	.384	-14	-14	101	106	-2.1	-0	1	-1.2
1960	Phi-N	0	1	.000	10	1	0	0	0	14	21	13.5	2	4	2.6	6	3.9	8.36	50	.356	.388	-7	-7	110	84	-0.4	-0	0	-0.6
1963	Chi-A	0	0	—	9	0	0	0	0	14	16	10.3	2	13	8.4	13	8.4	10.29	36	.302	.429	-10	-10	102	70	0.0	-0	0	-0.9
Total	6	16	22	.421	147	45	9	1	6	439	460	9.4	42	211	4.3	233	4.8	4.82	79	.275	.356	-45	-49	98	102	-3.2	-9	4	-4.7
■ **TOM PHOEBUS**	Phoebus, Thomas Harold b: 4/7/42, Baltimore, Md. BR/TR, 5'8", 185 lbs. Deb: 9/15/66																												
1966	Bal-A	2	1	.667	3	3	2	2	0	22	16	6.5	0	6	2.5	17	7.0	1.23	276	.213	.268	5	5	99	159	0.2	0	-0	0.6
1967	Bal-A	14	9	.609	33	33	7	4	0	208	177	7.7	16	114	4.9	179	7.7	3.33	91	.227	.323	-2	-7	94	103	3.3	1	-2	-0.8
1968	Bal-A	15	15	.500	36	36	9	3	0	241	186	6.9	10	105	3.9	193	7.2	2.61	115	.212	.297	10	10	101	97	-1.9	3	-0	1.5
1969	Bal-A	14	7	.667	35	33	6	2	0	202	180	8.0	23	87	3.9	117	5.2	3.52	103	.241	.319	2	3	100	106	0.0	2	-1	0.3
1970	Bal-A	5	5	.500	27	21	3	0	0	135	106	7.1	11	62	4.1	72	4.8	3.07	114	.219	.307	10	6	94	101	-1.2	-0	0	0.7
1971	SD-N	3	11	.214	29	21	2	0	0	133	144	9.7	14	64	4.3	80	5.4	4.47	76	.280	.356	-15	-16	98	107	-3.1	1	-1	-1.5
1972	SD-N	0	1	.000	1	1	0	0	0	6	3	4.5	2	6	9.0	8	12.0	7.50	42	.150	.346	-3	-3	91	67	-0.4	-0	0	-0.2
	Chi-N	3	3	.500	37	1	0	0	6	83	76	8.2	9	45	4.9	59	6.4	3.80	102	.247	.340	-3	1	112	110	-0.2	-1	1	0.1
	Yr	3	4	.429	38	2	0	0	6	89	79	8.0	11	51	5.2	67	6.8	4.04	95	.241	.340	-6	-2	111	110	-0.6	-0	1	-0.1
Total	7	56	52	.519	201	149	29	11	6	1030	888	7.8	85	489	4.3	725	6.3	3.33	100	.233	.319	5	-0	99	104	-3.3	5	-2	0.7
■ **BILL PHYLE**	Phyle, William Joseph b: 6/25/1875, Duluth, Minn. d: 8/6/53, Los Angeles, Cal. TR , Deb: 9/17/1898																												
1898	Chi-N	2	1	.667	3	3	3	2	0	23	24	9.4	0	6	2.3	4	1.6	0.78	469	.290	.338	7	7	102	393	0.4	-0	0	0.8
1899	Chi-N	1	8	.111	10	9	9	0	1	84	92	9.9	2	29	3.1	10	1.1	4.29	86	.302	.363	-4	-6	96	87	-3.5	-2	0	-0.6
1901	NY-N	7	10	.412	24	19	16	0	1	169	208	11.1	2	54	2.9	62	3.3	4.26	74	.328	.385	-18	-21	95	103	0.5	-1	1	-1.7
Total	3	10	19	.345	37	31	28	2	2	276	324	10.6	4	89	2.9	76	2.5	3.98	85	.317	.375	-14	-19	96	122	-2.6	-3	1	-1.5
■ **WILEY PIATT**	Piatt, Wiley Harold "Iron Man" b: 7/13/1874, Blue Creek, Ohio d: 9/20/46, Cincinnati, Ohio BL/TL, 5'10", 175 lbs. Deb: 4/22/1898																												
1898	Phi-N	24	14	.632	39	37	33	**6**	0	306	285	8.4	2	97	2.9	121	3.6	3.18	107	.267	.329	15	7	94	86	5.4	4	-2	0.8
1899	Phi-N	23	15	.605	39	38	31	2	0	305	323	9.5	6	86	2.5	89	2.6	3.45	106	.295	.346	14	7	95	97	-0.4	4	-4	0.6
1900	Phi-N	9	10	.474	22	20	16	1	0	161	194	10.8	5	71	4.0	47	2.6	4.70	77	.322	.393	-18	-19	98	99	-1.3	1	0	-1.5
1901	Phi-A	5	12	.294	18	16	15	0	1	140	176	11.3	4	60	3.9	45	2.9	4.63	79	.328	.396	-15	-15	100	105	-4.1	1	-4	-1.5
	Chi-A	4	2	.667	7	6	4	1	0	52	42	7.3	2	14	2.4	19	3.3	2.77	127	.239	.295	5	4	96	80	0.5	-1	-1	0.3
	Yr	9	14	.391	25	22	19	1	1	192	218	10.2	6	74	3.5	64	3.0	4.13	88	.306	.372	-10	-11	99	80	-3.6	1	-5	-1.2
1902	Chi-A	12	12	.500	32	30	22	2	0	246	263	9.6	3	66	2.4	96	3.5	3.51	95	.298	.347	2	-4	94	96	-1.3	1	-4	-0.7
1903	Bos-N	9	14	.391	25	23	18	0	0	181	198	9.8	5	61	3.0	100	5.0	3.18	101	.305	.368	2	1	98	117	-0.8	1	-3	-0.1
Total	6	86	79	.521	182	170	139	12	1	1391	1481	9.6	27	455	2.9	517	3.3	3.60	97	.296	.355	4	-19	96	97	-2.0	12	-17	-2.1
■ **RON PICHE**	Piche, Ronald Jacques b: 5/22/35, Verdun, Que., Canada BR/TR, 5'11", 165 lbs. Deb: 5/30/60 C																												
1960	Mil-N	3	5	.375	37	0	0	0	9	48	48	9.0	3	23	4.3	38	7.1	3.56	94	.258	.339	1	-1	89	114	-1.3	-0	-1	-0.1
1961	Mil-N	2	2	.500	12	1	1	0	1	23	20	7.8	1	16	6.3	16	6.3	3.52	104	.238	.346	1	0	91	109	0.0	-1	0	0.0
1962	Mil-N	3	2	.600	14	8	2	0	0	52	54	9.3	6	29	5.0	28	4.8	4.85	80	.273	.366	-5	-6	98	104	0.4	-1	1	-0.5
1963	Mil-N	1	1	.500	37	1	0	0	0	53	53	9.0	4	25	4.2	40	6.8	3.40	97	.256	.331	-1	-1	100	113	0.0	-1	1	0.0
1965	Cal-A	0	3	.000	14	1	0	0	0	20	20	9.0	5	12	5.4	14	6.3	6.75	50	.267	.360	-7	-7	98	87	-1.4	-0	0	-0.7
1966	StL-N	1	3	.250	20	0	0	0	2	25	21	7.6	4	18	6.5	21	7.6	4.32	83	.214	.336	-2	-2	100	95	-0.9	-0	-0	-0.2
Total	6	10	16	.385	134	11	3	0	12	221	216	8.8	23	123	5.0	157	6.4	4.19	84	.255	.346	-13	-16	96	106	-3.2	-3	2	-1.5
■ **CHARLIE PICKETT**	Pickett, Charles Albert b: 3/1/1883, Delaware, Ohio d: 5/20/69, Springfield, Ohio BR/TR, 6'1", 175 lbs. Deb: 6/21/10																												
1910	StL-N	0	0	—	2	0	0	0	0	6	7	10.5	0	2	3.0	2	3.0	1.50	188	.280	.333	1	1	93	217	0.0	0	0	0.1
■ **CLARENCE PICKREL**	Pickrel, Clarence Douglas b: 3/28/11, Grenta, Va. d: 11/4/83, Rocky Mount, Va. BR/TR, 6'1", 180 lbs. Deb: 4/22/33																												
1933	Phi-N	1	0	1.000	9	0	0	0	0	14	20	12.9	0	3	1.9	6	3.9	3.86	105	.357	.393	-1	0	121	144	0.5	-0	-1	0.0
1934	Bos-N	0	0	—	10	1	0	0	0	16	24	13.5	0	7	3.9	9	5.1	5.06	69	.333	.392	-2	-3	86	110	0.0	-0	-1	-0.2
Total	2	1	0	1.000	19	1	0	0	0	30	44	13.2	0	10	3.0	15	4.5	4.50	85	.344	.393	-3	-2	102	126	0.5	-0	-1	-0.2
■ **JEFF PICO**	Pico, Jeffrey Mark b: 2/12/66, Antioch, Cal. BR/TR, 6'1", 190 lbs. Deb: 5/31/88																												
1988	Chi-N	6	7	.462	29	13	3	2	1	113	108	8.6	6	37	2.9	57	4.5	4.14	87	.252	.307	-9	-7	105	80	-0.1	-0	0	-0.6
■ **MARIO PICONE**	Picone, Mario Peter "Babe" b: 7/5/26, Brooklyn, N.Y. BR/TR, 5'11", 180 lbs. Deb: 9/27/47																												
1947	NY-N	0	0	—	2	1	0	0	0	7	10	12.9	1	2	2.6	1	1.3	7.71	52	.345	.387	-3	-3	99	83	0.0	1	0	-0.1
1952	NY-N	0	1	.000	2	1	0	0	0	9	11	11.0	2	5	5.0	3	3.0	7.00	54	.306	.390	-3	-3	101	95	-0.4	-0	0	-0.2
1954	NY-N	0	0	—	5	0	0	0	0	14	13	8.4	1	11	7.1	6	3.9	5.14	81	.283	.400	-2	-2	102	108	0.0	0	-0	-0.1
	Cin-N	0	1	.000	4	1	0	0	0	10	9	8.1	3	7	6.3	1	0.9	6.30	67	.243	.356	-2	-2	104	92	-0.4	0	0	-0.1
	Yr	0	1	.000	9	1	0	0	0	24	22	8.3	4	18	6.8	7	2.6	5.63	74	.265	.381	-4	-4	103	92	-0.4	0	0	-0.2
Total	3	0	2	.000	13	3	0	0	0	40	43	9.7	7	25	5.6	11	2.5	6.30	65	.291	.384	-10	-10	102	97	-0.8	1	1	-0.5
■ **AL PIECHOTA**	Piechota, Aloysius Edward "Pie" b: 1/19/14, Chicago, Ill. BR/TR, 6', 195 lbs. Deb: 5/07/40																												
1940	Bos-N	2	5	.286	21	8	2	0	0	61	68	10.0	6	41	6.0	18	2.7	5.75	68	.278	.377	-13	-13	101	93	-1.1	1	-0	-1.1
1941	Bos-N	0	0	—	1	0	0	0	0	1	0	0.0	0	1	9.0	0	0.0	0.00	—	.000	.250	0	0	96	0	0.0	0	0	0.0
Total	2	2	5	.286	22	8	2	0	0	62	68	9.9	6	42	6.1	18	2.6	5.66	69	.274	.375	-13	-12	101	92	-1.1	1	-0	-1.1
■ **CY PIEH**	Pieh, Edwin John b: 9/29/1886, Waunakee, Wis. d: 9/12/45, Jacksonville, Fla BR/TR, 6'2", 190 lbs. Deb: 9/06/13																												
1913	NY-A	1	0	1.000	4	0	0	0	0	10	10	9.0	0	7	6.3	6	5.4	4.50	67	.250	.362	-2	-2	104	76	0.5	0	1	0.0
1914	NY-A	4	4	.500	18	4	1	0	0	62	68	9.9	6	29	4.2	24	3.5	5.08	54	.289	.367	-16	-16	100	92	0.3	0	-1	-1.7
1915	NY-A	4	5	.444	21	8	3	2	0	94	78	7.5	2	39	3.7	46	4.4	2.87	101	.234	.324	1	0	99	98	0.0	-3	0	-0.2
Total	3	9	9	.500	43	12	4	2	0	166	156	8.5	8	75	4.1	76	4.1	3.80	75	.257	.343	-17	-17	99	95	0.8	-3	-0	-1.9
■ **RAY PIERCE**	Pierce, Raymond Lester "Lefty" b: 6/6/1897, Emporia, Kan. d: 5/4/63, Denver, Colo. BL/TL, 5'7", 156 lbs. Deb: 5/12/24																												
1924	Chi-N	0	0	—	6	0	0	0	0	7	7	9.0	2	4	5.1	2	2.6	7.71	51	.269	.333	-3	-3	101	79	0.0	0	-0	-0.2
1925	Phi-N	5	4	.556	23	8	4	0	0	90	134	13.4	7	24	2.4	18	1.8	5.50	91	.356	.388	-12	-5	118	113	0.9	-1	0	-0.3
1926	Phi-N	2	7	.222	37	7	1	0	0	85	128	13.6	3	35	3.7	18	1.9	5.61	73	.348	.392	-17	-14	107	108	-1.9	-2	-1	-1.5
Total	3	7	11	.389	66	15	5	0	0	182	269	13.3	12	63	3.1	38	1.9	5.64	80	.349	.388	-32	-22	112	109	-1.0	-2	-1	-2.0
■ **TONY PIERCE**	Pierce, Tony Michael b: 1/29/46, Brunswick, Ga. BR/TL, 6'1", 190 lbs. Deb: 4/14/67																												
1967	KC-A	3	4	.429	49	6	0	0	7	98	79	7.3	6	30	2.8	61	5.6	3.03	108	.221	.285	2	3	102	88	0.3	-2	-1	0.0
1968	Oak-A	1	2	.333	17	3	0	0	1	33	39	10.6	3	10	2.7	16	4.4	3.82	76	.295	.342	-3	-3	98	122	-0.4	-1	1	-0.3
Total	2	4	6	.400	66	9	0	0	8	131	118	8.1	9	40	2.7	77	5.3	3.23	99	.241	.300	-1	-1	101	97	-0.1	-3	-1	-0.3
■ **BILLY PIERCE**	Pierce, Walter William b: 4/2/27, Detroit, Mich. BL/TL, 5'10", 160 lbs. Deb: 6/01/45																												
1945	Det-A	0	0	—	5	0	0	0	0	10	6	5.4	1	10	9.0	10	9.0	1.80	196	.182	.378	2	2	105	237	0.0	-0	0	0.2
1948	Det-A	3	0	1.000	22	5	0	0	0	55	47	7.7	5	51	8.3	36	5.9	6.38	65	.234	.384	-13	-14	97	78	1.5	2	0	-1.0
1949	Chi-A	7	15	.318	32	26	8	0	0	172	145	7.6	11	112	5.9	95	5.0	3.87	108	.228	.338	6	6	99	93	-2.7	-1	1	0.6
1950	Chi-A	12	16	.429	33	29	15	1	1	219	189	7.8	11	137	5.6	118	4.8	3.99	114	.228	.335	14	13	99	87	1.1	3	-2	1.4
1951	Chi-A	15	14	.517	37	28	18	1	2	240	237	8.9	14	73	2.7	113	4.2	3.04	130	.258	.309	29	24	96	113	-0.2	0	-1	2.3
1952	Chi-A	15	12	.556	33	32	14	4	1	255	214	7.6	12	79	2.8	144	5.1	2.58	141	.227	.284	31	30	99	98	1.0	0	0	3.3
1953	Chi-A	18	12	.600	40	33	19	7	3	271	216	**7.2**	20	102	3.4	**186**	**6.2**	2.72	**152**	**.218**	.288	**38**	**43**	104	100	1.0	-5	-2	3.8
1954	Chi-A	9	10	.474	36	26	12	4	3	189	179	8.5	15	86	4.1	148	**7.0**	3.48	107	.249	.328	5	5	100	105	-2.3	0	-2	0.3
1955	Chi-A	15	10	.600	33	26	16	6	1	206	162	7.1	16	64	2.8	157	6.9	**1.97**	**197**	.213	**.274**	**46**	44	98	**120**	0.3	-0	-1	4.5
1956	Chi-A	20	9	.690	35	33	**21**	1	1	276	261	8.5	24	100	3.3	192	6.3	3.33	127	.249	.312	26	28	102	104	**5.1**	-5	-3	2.1
1957	Chi-A	**20**	12	.625	37	34	**16**	4	2	257	228	8.0	18	71	2.5	171	6.0	3.26	112	.234	.282	15	11	97	82	1.9	-2	0	1.0
1958	Chi-A	17	11	.607	35	32	**19**	3	2	245	204	7.5	33	66	2.4	144	5.3	2.68	137	.227	.276	30	27	98	114	2.6	2	-3	2.8

YEAR	TM/L	W	L	PCT	G	GS	CG	SHO	SV	IP	H	H/G	HR	BB	BB/G	SO	SO/G	ERA	/A	OAVG	OOBP	PR	/A	PF	CPI	WAT	PB	PD	TPI
1959	Chi-A	14	15	.483	34	33	12	2	0	224	217	8.7	26	62	2.5	114	4.6	3.62	102	.253	.302	6	1	95	101	-3.5	3	0	0.4
1960	Chi-A	14	7	.667	32	30	8	1	0	196	201	9.2	24	46	2.1	108	5.0	3.63	106	.266	.304	5	4	99	104	2.7	1	-1	0.4
1961	Chi-A	10	9	.526	39	28	5	1	3	180	190	9.5	17	54	2.7	106	5.3	3.80	104	.275	.321	4	3	99	108	0.0	-2	-0	0.1
1962	SF-N	16	6	.727	30	23	7	2	1	162	147	8.2	19	35	1.9	76	4.2	3.50	111	.239	.282	8	7	99	88	3.3	2	-1	0.7
1963	SF-N	3	11	.214	38	13	3	1	8	99	106	9.6	12	20	1.8	52	4.7	4.27	72	.272	.302	-11	-13	94	91	-4.3	-0	0	-1.3
1964	SF-N	3	0	1.000	34	1	0	0	4	49	40	7.3	6	10	1.8	29	5.3	2.20	159	.222	.256	7	7	99	124	1.5	1	-1	0.8
Total	18	211	169	.555	585	432	193	38	32	3305	2989	8.1	284	1178	3.2	1999	5.4	3.27	119	.240	.303	249	228	99	101	9.0	0	-14	22.4

■ **BILL PIERCY** Piercy, William Benton "Wild Bill" b: 5/2/1896, El Monte, Cal. d: 8/28/51, Long Beach, Cal. BR/TR, 6'1.5", 170 lbs. Deb: 10/03/17

YEAR	TM/L	W	L	PCT	G	GS	CG	SHO	SV	IP	H	H/G	HR	BB	BB/G	SO	SO/G	ERA	/A	OAVG	OOBP	PR	/A	PF	CPI	WAT	PB	PD	TPI
1917	NY-A	0	1	.000	1	1	1	0	0	9	9	9.0	0	2	2.0	4	4.0	3.00	95	.257	.297	-0	-0	107	78	-0.4	0	0	0.0
1921	NY-A	5	4	.556	14	10	5	1	0	82	82	9.0	4	28	3.1	35	3.8	2.96	143	.263	.331	12	12	99	121	-0.5	0	-0	1.1
1922	Bos-A	3	9	.250	29	12	7	1	0	121	140	10.4	2	62	4.6	24	1.8	4.69	85	.304	.375	-9	-9	99	104	-2.2	-1	2	-0.7
1923	Bos-A	8	17	.320	30	24	11	0	0	187	193	9.3	5	73	3.5	51	2.5	3.42	123	.277	.344	12	16	106	116	-2.8	-3	3	1.7
1924	Bos-A	5	7	.417	23	18	3	0	0	121	156	11.6	4	66	4.9	20	1.5	5.95	75	.335	.408	-23	-20	105	103	-0.2	-2	1	-1.8
1926	Chi-N	6	5	.545	19	5	1	0	0	90	96	9.6	1	37	3.7	31	3.1	4.50	89	.280	.347	-7	-5	105	89	0.2	1	0	-0.3
Total	6	27	43	.386	116	70	28	2	0	610	676	10.0	16	268	4.0	165	2.4	4.26	98	.292	.362	-15	-6	103	107	-5.9	-6	7	0.0

■ **MARINO PIERETTI** Pieretti, Marino Paul "Chick" b: 9/23/20, Lucca, Italy d: 1/30/81, San Francisco, Cal BR/TR, 5'7", 153 lbs. Deb: 4/19/45

YEAR	TM/L	W	L	PCT	G	GS	CG	SHO	SV	IP	H	H/G	HR	BB	BB/G	SO	SO/G	ERA	/A	OAVG	OOBP	PR	/A	PF	CPI	WAT	PB	PD	TPI
1945	Was-A	14	13	.519	44	27	14	3	2	233	235	9.1	3	91	3.5	66	2.5	3.32	93	.257	.321	1	-6	92	96	-1.2	2	1	-0.3
1946	Was-A	2	2	.500	30	2	1	0	0	62	70	10.2	9	40	5.8	20	2.9	5.95	55	.292	.385	-17	-18	94	99	0.0	0	1	-1.7
1947	Was-A	2	4	.333	23	10	2	1	0	83	97	10.5	3	47	5.1	32	3.5	4.23	88	.287	.371	-5	-5	101	112	-0.5	-0	-0	-0.4
1948	Was-A	0	2	.000	8	1	0	0	0	12	18	13.5	1	7	5.3	6	4.5	10.50	44	.375	.446	-8	-8	107	75	-0.9	-0	0	-0.6
	Chi-A	8	10	.444	21	18	4	0	1	120	117	8.8	6	52	3.9	28	2.1	4.95	86	.262	.328	-9	-9	100	80	1.6	-1	1	-0.8
	Yr	8	12	.400	29	19	4	0	1	132	135	9.2	7	59	4.0	34	2.3	5.45	79	.273	.339	-17	-17	100	80	0.7	-0	1	-1.4
1949	Chi-A	4	6	.400	39	9	0	0	4	116	131	10.2	10	54	4.2	25	1.9	5.51	76	.289	.358	-17	-17	99	87	0.0	1	2	-1.4
1950	Cle-A	0	1	.000	29	1	0	0	1	47	45	8.6	2	30	5.7	11	2.1	4.21	104	.253	.354	2	1	95	98	-0.4	0	1	0.2
Total	6	30	38	.441	194	68	21	4	8	673	713	9.5	34	321	4.3	188	2.5	4.53	81	.272	.346	-53	-63	96	94	-1.4	2	5	-5.0

■ **AL PIEROTTI** Pierotti, Albert Felix b: 10/24/1895, Boston, Mass. d: 2/12/64, Everett, Mass. BR/TR, 5'10.5", 195 lbs. Deb: 8/09/20

YEAR	TM/L	W	L	PCT	G	GS	CG	SHO	SV	IP	H	H/G	HR	BB	BB/G	SO	SO/G	ERA	/A	OAVG	OOBP	PR	/A	PF	CPI	WAT	PB	PD	TPI
1920	Bos-N	1	1	.500	6	2	2	0	0	25	23	8.3	2	9	3.2	12	4.3	2.88	108	.250	.314	1	1	99	109	0.2	-0	-0	0.0
1921	Bos-N	0	1	.000	2	0	0	0	0	2	3	13.5	0	3	13.5	1	4.5	18.00	19	.375	.500	-3	-3	92	52	-0.4	-0	0	-0.2
Total	2	1	2	.333	8	2	2	0	0	27	26	8.7	2	12	4.0	13	4.3	4.00	79	.260	.333	-2	-3	99	104	-0.2	-0	-0	-0.2

■ **BILL PIERRO** Pierro, William Leonard "Wild Bill" b: 4/15/26, Brooklyn, N.Y. BR/TR, 6'1", 155 lbs. Deb: 7/17/50

YEAR	TM/L	W	L	PCT	G	GS	CG	SHO	SV	IP	H	H/G	HR	BB	BB/G	SO	SO/G	ERA	/A	OAVG	OOBP	PR	/A	PF	CPI	WAT	PB	PD	TPI
1950	Pit-N	0	2	.000	12	3	0	0	0	29	33	10.2	2	28	8.7	13	4.0	10.55	41	.289	.432	-21	-20	106	60	-0.9	-0	-1	-1.7

■ **DAVE PIERSON** Pierson, David P. b: 8/20/1855, Wilkes-Barre, Pa. d: 11/11/22, Trenton, N.J. BR/TR, 5'7", 142 lbs. Deb: 4/25/1876

YEAR	TM/L	W	L	PCT	G	GS	CG	SHO	SV	IP	H	H/G	HR	BB	BB/G	SO	SO/G	ERA	/A	OAVG	OOBP	PR	/A	PF	CPI	WAT	PB	PD	TPI
1876	Cin-N	0	1	.000	1	1	0	0	0	0	2	—	1	0	—	0	—	∞	—	1.000	1.000	-2	-2	100	96	-0.4	-0	0	-0.1

■ **WILLIAM PIERSON** Pierson, William Morris b: 6/14/1899, Atlantic City, N.J. d: 2/20/59, Atlantic City, N.J BL/TL, 6'2", 180 lbs. Deb: 7/04/18

YEAR	TM/L	W	L	PCT	G	GS	CG	SHO	SV	IP	H	H/G	HR	BB	BB/G	SO	SO/G	ERA	/A	OAVG	OOBP	PR	/A	PF	CPI	WAT	PB	PD	TPI
1918	Phi-A	0	1	.000	8	1	0	0	0	22	20	8.2	0	20	8.2	6	2.5	3.27	91	.286	.452	-1	-1	108	162	-0.4	-0	-1	-0.1
1919	Phi-A	0	0	—	2	1	0	0	0	8	9	10.1	0	8	9.0	4	4.5	3.38	107	.333	.486	-0	0	112	193	0.0	0	0	0.1
1924	Phi-A	0	0	—	1	0	0	0	0	3	3	9.0	0	3	9.0	0	0.0	3.00	142	.300	.462	0	0	101	202	0.0	0	0	0.0
Total	3	0	1	.000	11	2	0	0	0	33	32	8.7	0	31	8.5	10	2.7	3.27	100	.299	.461	-1	-0	108	173	-0.4	0	-0	0.0

■ **GEORGE PIKTUZIS** Piktuzis, George Richard b: 1/3/32, Chicago, Ill. BR/TL, 6'2", 200 lbs. Deb: 4/25/56

YEAR	TM/L	W	L	PCT	G	GS	CG	SHO	SV	IP	H	H/G	HR	BB	BB/G	SO	SO/G	ERA	/A	OAVG	OOBP	PR	/A	PF	CPI	WAT	PB	PD	TPI
1956	Chi-N	0	0	—	2	0	0	0	0	5	6	10.8	1	2	3.6	3	5.4	7.20	53	.333	.381	-2	-2	101	92	0.0	0	-0	-0.1

■ **DUANE PILLETTE** Pillette, Duane Xavier "Dee" b: 7/24/22, Detroit, Mich. BR/TR, 6'3", 195 lbs. Deb: 7/19/49

YEAR	TM/L	W	L	PCT	G	GS	CG	SHO	SV	IP	H	H/G	HR	BB	BB/G	SO	SO/G	ERA	/A	OAVG	OOBP	PR	/A	PF	CPI	WAT	PB	PD	TPI
1949	NY-A	2	4	.333	12	3	2	0	0	37	43	10.5	6	19	4.6	9	2.2	4.38	93	.299	.373	-1	-1	97	133	-1.3	-1	1	-0.1
1950	NY-A	0	0	—	4	0	0	0	0	7	9	11.6	0	3	3.9	4	5.1	1.29	341	.321	.375	3	2	96	398	0.0	-0	-0	0.2
	StL-A	3	5	.375	24	7	1	0	2	74	104	12.6	6	44	5.4	18	2.2	7.05	72	.337	.417	-20	-16	111	95	0.0	-1	-0	-1.5
	Yr	3	5	.375	28	7	1	0	2	81	113	12.6	6	47	5.2	22	2.4	6.56	76	.335	.413	-18	-14	110	95	0.0	-1	-0	-1.3
1951	StL-A	6	14	.300	35	24	6	1	0	191	205	9.7	14	115	5.4	65	3.1	4.99	90	.276	.373	-19	-10	109	98	-1.2	-4	-1	-1.3
1952	StL-A	10	13	.435	30	30	9	1	0	205	222	9.7	14	55	2.4	62	2.7	3.60	102	.274	.323	2	1	100	106	0.4	1	-2	0.0
1953	StL-A	7	13	.350	31	25	5	1	0	167	181	9.8	16	62	3.3	58	3.1	4.47	99	.277	.337	-9	-1	111	98	0.0	-1	-1	-0.2
1954	Bal-A	10	14	.417	25	25	11	1	0	179	158	7.9	9	67	3.4	66	3.3	3.12	118	.234	.298	12	11	99	89	1.4	-1	3	1.4
1955	Bal-A	0	3	.000	7	5	0	0	0	21	31	13.3	0	14	6.0	13	5.6	6.43	58	.344	.429	-6	-6	94	98	-1.4	0	0	-0.5
1956	Phi-N	0	0	—	20	0	0	0	0	23	32	12.5	2	12	4.7	10	3.9	6.65	54	.330	.386	-7	-8	95	91	0.0	-0	-0	-0.7
Total	8	38	66	.365	188	119	34	4	2	904	985	9.8	67	391	3.9	305	3.0	4.40	93	.277	.347	-45	-29	104	101	-2.1	-8	-1	-2.7

■ **HERMAN PILLETTE** Pillette, Herman Polycarp "Old Folks" b: 12/26/1895, St.Paul, Ore. d: 4/30/60, Sacramento, Cal. BR/TR, 6'2", 190 lbs. Deb: 7/30/17

YEAR	TM/L	W	L	PCT	G	GS	CG	SHO	SV	IP	H	H/G	HR	BB	BB/G	SO	SO/G	ERA	/A	OAVG	OOBP	PR	/A	PF	CPI	WAT	PB	PD	TPI
1917	Cin-N	0	0	—	1	0	0	0	0	1	4	36.0	0	0	0.0	0	0.0	18.00	14	.571	.571	-2	-2	93	92	0.0	0	0	-0.1
1922	Det-A	19	12	.613	40	37	18	4	1	275	270	8.8	6	95	3.1	71	2.3	2.85	138	.258	.321	37	33	97	111	3.8	-3	3	3.3
1923	Det-A	14	19	.424	47	36	14	0	1	250	280	10.1	7	83	3.0	64	2.3	3.85	98	.288	.339	4	-2	95	101	-4.1	4	4	0.5
1924	Det-A	1	1	.500	19	3	1	0	1	38	46	10.9	1	14	3.3	13	3.1	4.74	88	.297	.352	-2	-2	99	93	0.0	1	0	0.0
Total	4	34	32	.515	107	76	33	4	3	564	600	9.6	14	192	3.1	148	2.4	3.45	113	.275	.332	36	27	96	105	-0.3	2	7	3.7

■ **SQUIZ PILLION** Pillion, Cecil Randolph b: 4/13/1894, Hartford, Conn. d: 9/30/62, Pittsburgh, Pa. TL, 6', 178 lbs. Deb: 8/20/15

YEAR	TM/L	W	L	PCT	G	GS	CG	SHO	SV	IP	H	H/G	HR	BB	BB/G	SO	SO/G	ERA	/A	OAVG	OOBP	PR	/A	PF	CPI	WAT	PB	PD	TPI
1915	Phi-A	0	0	—	2	0	0	0	0	5	10	18.0	0	2	3.6	0	0.0	7.20	42	.400	.464	-2	-2	103	115	0.0	-0	0	-0.1

■ **HORACIO PINA** Pina, Horacio (Garcia) b: 3/12/45, Coahuila, Mexico BR/TR, 6'2", 177 lbs. Deb: 8/14/68

YEAR	TM/L	W	L	PCT	G	GS	CG	SHO	SV	IP	H	H/G	HR	BB	BB/G	SO	SO/G	ERA	/A	OAVG	OOBP	PR	/A	PF	CPI	WAT	PB	PD	TPI
1968	Cle-A	1	1	.500	12	3	0	0	2	31	24	7.0	0	15	4.4	24	7.0	1.74	172	.218	.313	4	4	101	148	0.0	-1	0	0.4
1969	Cle-A	4	2	.667	31	4	0	0	1	47	44	8.4	6	27	5.2	32	6.1	5.17	68	.256	.365	-8	-9	96	95	1.4	1	0	-0.7
1970	Was-A	5	3	.625	61	0	0	0	6	71	66	8.4	4	35	4.4	41	5.2	2.79	129	.250	.337	7	6	97	134	1.4	-0	1	0.7
1971	Was-A	1	1	.500	56	0	0	0	2	58	47	7.3	2	31	4.8	38	5.9	3.57	91	.227	.328	-1	-2	94	90	0.2	-0	1	0.0
1972	Tex-A	2	7	.222	60	0	0	0	15	76	61	7.2	3	43	5.1	60	7.1	3.20	93	.228	.344	-1	-2	97	109	-1.6	0	3	0.1
1973	Oak-A	6	3	.667	47	0	0	0	8	88	58	5.9	8	34	3.5	41	4.2	2.76	118	.193	.286	10	5	86	94	1.0	0	3	0.8
1974	Chi-N	3	4	.429	34	0	0	0	4	47	49	9.4	4	28	5.4	32	6.1	4.02	92	.268	.364	-2	-2	102	115	0.1	-0	1	0.0
	Cal-A	1	2	.333	11	0	0	0	0	12	9	6.8	1	3	2.3	6	4.5	2.25	150	.209	.261	2	1	93	95	-0.2	0	1	0.2
1978	Phi-N	0	0	—	2	0	0	0	0	2	0	0.0	0	0	0.0	4	18.0	0.00	—	.000	.000	1	1	104	0	0.0	-0	0	0.1
Total	8	23	23	.500	314	7	0	0	38	432	358	7.5	28	216	4.5	278	5.8	3.25	103	.231	.329	13	4	95	109	2.3	0	9	1.6

■ **ED PINKHAM** Pinkham, Edward b: 1849, Brooklyn, N.Y. TL, 5'7", 142 lbs. Deb: 5/08/1871

YEAR	TM/L	W	L	PCT	G	GS	CG	SHO	SV	IP	H	H/G	HR	BB	BB/G	SO	SO/G	ERA	/A	OAVG	OOBP	PR	/A	PF	CPI	WAT	PB	PD	TPI
1871	Chi-n	1	0	1.000	1																								

■ **GEORGE PINKNEY** Pinkney, George Burton b: 1/11/1862, Orange Prairie, Ill. d: 11/10/26, Peoria, Ill. BR/TR, 5'7", 160 lbs. Deb: 8/16/1884

YEAR	TM/L	W	L	PCT	G	GS	CG	SHO	SV	IP	H	H/G	HR	BB	BB/G	SO	SO/G	ERA	/A	OAVG	OOBP	PR	/A	PF	CPI	WAT	PB	PD	TPI
1886	Bro-a	0	0	—	1	0	0	0	0	2	2	9.0	0	0	0.0	0	0.0	4.50	77	.271	.271	-0	-0	100	55	0.0	0	0	0.0

■ **ED PINNANCE** Pinnance, Edward D. "Peanuts" b: 10/22/1879, Walpole Island, Ont., Canada d: 12/12/44, Walpole Island, Ontario, Canada BL/TR, 6'1", 180 lbs. Deb: 03

YEAR	TM/L	W	L	PCT	G	GS	CG	SHO	SV	IP	H	H/G	HR	BB	BB/G	SO	SO/G	ERA	/A	OAVG	OOBP	PR	/A	PF	CPI	WAT	PB	PD	TPI
1903	Phi-A	0	0	—	2	1	0	0	1	7	5	6.4	0	2	2.6	2	2.6	2.57	117	.219	.282	0	0	102	63	0.0	-0	-0	0.0

■ **LERTON PINTO** Pinto, William Lerton b: 4/8/1899, Chillcothe, Ohio d: 5/13/83, Oxnard, Cal. BL/TL, 6', 190 lbs. Deb: 5/23/22

YEAR	TM/L	W	L	PCT	G	GS	CG	SHO	SV	IP	H	H/G	HR	BB	BB/G	SO	SO/G	ERA	/A	OAVG	OOBP	PR	/A	PF	CPI	WAT	PB	PD	TPI
1922	Phi-N	0	1	.000	9	0	0	0	0	25	31	11.2	1	14	5.0	4	1.4	5.04	95	.320	.391	-3	-1	117	108	-0.4	-1	-0	-0.1
1924	Phi-N	0	0	—	3	0	0	0	0	4	7	15.8	1	0	0.0	1	2.3	9.00	48	.467	.467	-2	-2	111	108	0.0	-0	0	-0.1
Total	2	0	1	.000	12	0	0	0	0	29	38	11.8	2	14	4.3	5	1.6	5.59	84	.339	.400	-5	-3	116	108	-0.4	-1	-0	-0.2

■ **ED PIPGRAS** Pipgras, Edward John b: 6/15/04, Schleswig, Iowa d: 4/13/64, Currie, Minn. BR/TR, 6'2.5", 175 lbs. Deb: 8/25/32

YEAR	TM/L	W	L	PCT	G	GS	CG	SHO	SV	IP	H	H/G	HR	BB	BB/G	SO	SO/G	ERA	/A	OAVG	OOBP	PR	/A	PF	CPI	WAT	PB	PD	TPI
1932	Bro-N	0	1	.000	5	1	0	0	0	10	16	14.4	2	6	5.4	5	4.5	5.40	69	.348	.423	-2	-2	96	148	-0.4	-0	0	-0.1

■ **GEORGE PIPGRAS** Pipgras, George William b: 12/20/1899, Ida Grove, Iowa d: 10/19/86, Gainesville, Fla. BR/TR, 6'1.5", 185 lbs. Deb: 6/09/23 U

YEAR	TM/L	W	L	PCT	G	GS	CG	SHO	SV	IP	H	H/G	HR	BB	BB/G	SO	SO/G	ERA	/A	OAVG	OOBP	PR	/A	PF	CPI	WAT	PB	PD	TPI
1923	NY-A	1	3	.250	8	2	2	0	0	33	34	9.3	2	25	6.8	12	3.3	6.00	67	.276	.392	-7	-7	101	85	-1.1	-1	-0	-0.7
1924	NY-A	0	1	.000	9	1	0	0	1	15	20	12.0	0	18	10.8	4	2.4	10.20	40	.351	.525	-10	-10	97	85	-0.4	0	1	-0.7

YEAR	TM/L	W	L	PCT	G	GS	CG	SHO	SV	IP	H	H/G	HR	BB	BB/G	SO	SO/G	ERA	/A	OAVG	OOBP	PR	/A	PF	CPI	WAT	PB	PD	TPI
1927	NY-A	10	3	.769	29	21	9	1	0	166	148	8.0	2	77	4.2	81	4.4	4.12	94	.247	.321	0	-4	94	77	1.3	2	-1	-0.3
1928	NY-A	**24**	13	.649	46	38	22	4	3	**301**	314	9.4	4	103	3.1	139	4.2	3.38	106	.272	.324	22	7	89	104	-0.2	-3	-4	-0.1
1929	NY-A	18	12	.600	39	33	13	3	0	225	229	9.2	16	95	3.8	125	5.0	4.24	97	.264	.333	0	-3	97	93	1.2	-4	-3	-0.9
1930	NY-A	15	15	.500	44	30	15	**3**	4	221	230	9.4	9	70	2.9	111	4.5	4.11	99	.263	.316	13	-1	87	89	-1.8	-1	-2	-0.6
1931	NY-A	7	6	.538	36	14	6	1	3	138	134	8.7	8	58	3.8	59	3.8	3.78	108	.251	.320	9	5	94	100	-0.8	-5	-2	-0.2
1932	NY-A	16	9	.640	32	27	14	2	0	219	235	9.7	15	87	3.6	111	4.6	4.19	97	.269	.334	7	-3	91	103	-1.1	1	-2	-0.3
1933	NY-A	2	2	.500	4	4	3	0	0	33	32	8.7	1	12	3.3	14	3.8	3.27	116	.252	.308	4	2	88	103	-0.3	-1	1	0.2
	Bos-A	9	8	.529	22	17	9	2	1	128	140	9.8	5	45	3.2	56	3.9	4.08	107	.276	.334	3	4	102	100	1.7	-0	-2	0.1
	Yr	11	10	.524	26	21	12	2	1	161	172	9.6	6	57	3.2	70	3.9	3.91	109	.271	.329	7	6	99	100	1.4	-1	-1	0.3
1934	Bos-A	0	0	—	2	1	0	0	0	3	4	12.0	1	3	9.0	0	0.0	9.00	53	.308	.438	-2	-1	105	99	0.0	-0	0	0.0
1935	Bos-A	0	1	.000	5	1	0	0	0	5	9	16.2	3	5	9.0	2	3.6	14.40	34	.391	.500	-6	-5	108	99	-0.4	0	0	-0.4
Total	11	102	73	.583	276	189	93	16	12	1487	1529	9.3	66	598	3.6	714	4.3	4.09	97	.266	.331	34	-18	93	95	-1.9	-12	-14	-3.9

■ **COTTON PIPPEN** Pippen, Henry Harold b: 4/2/11, Cisco, Tex. d: 2/15/81, Williams, Cal. BR/TR, 6'2", 180 lbs. Deb: 8/28/36

YEAR	TM/L	W	L	PCT	G	GS	CG	SHO	SV	IP	H	H/G	HR	BB	BB/G	SO	SO/G	ERA	/A	OAVG	OOBP	PR	/A	PF	CPI	WAT	PB	PD	TPI
1936	StL-N	0	2	.000	6	3	0	0	0	21	37	15.9	5	8	3.4	8	3.4	7.71	49	.402	.448	-9	-9	95	125	-0.9	0	1	-0.7
1939	Phi-A	4	11	.267	25	17	5	0	1	119	169	12.8	13	40	3.0	33	2.5	5.97	79	.329	.371	-18	-17	102	102	-2.0	-2	1	-1.5
	Det-A	0	1	.000	3	2	0	0	0	14	18	11.6	1	6	3.9	5	3.2	7.07	72	.310	.348	-4	-3	110	77	-0.4	0	-0	-0.2
	Yr	4	12	.250	28	19	5	0	1	133	187	12.7	14	46	3.1	38	2.6	6.09	78	.326	.367	-22	-20	103	77	-2.4	-2	1	-1.7
1940	Det-A	1	2	.333	4	3	0	0	0	21	29	12.4	3	10	4.3	9	3.9	6.86	69	.326	.392	-6	-5	109	98	-0.6	-1	0	-0.4
Total	3	5	16	.238	38	25	5	0	1	175	253	13.0	22	64	3.3	55	2.8	6.38	73	.336	.381	-36	-34	103	102	-3.9	-3	2	-2.8

■ **GERRY PIRTLE** Pirtle, Gerald Eugene b: 12/3/47, Tulsa, Okla. BR/TR, 6'1", 185 lbs. Deb: 7/02/78

YEAR	TM/L	W	L	PCT	G	GS	CG	SHO	SV	IP	H	H/G	HR	BB	BB/G	SO	SO/G	ERA	/A	OAVG	OOBP	PR	/A	PF	CPI	WAT	PB	PD	TPI
1978	Mon-N	0	2	.000	19	0	0	0	0	26	33	11.4	5	23	8.0	14	4.8	5.88	58	.314	.433	-7	-7	96	131	-0.9	0	0	-0.6

■ **SKIP PITLOCK** Pitlock, Lee Patrick Thomas b: 11/6/47, Hillside, Ill. BL/TL, 6'2", 180 lbs. Deb: 6/12/70

YEAR	TM/L	W	L	PCT	G	GS	CG	SHO	SV	IP	H	H/G	HR	BB	BB/G	SO	SO/G	ERA	/A	OAVG	OOBP	PR	/A	PF	CPI	WAT	PB	PD	TPI
1970	SF-N	5	5	.500	18	15	1	0	0	87	92	9.5	13	48	5.0	56	5.8	4.66	83	.274	.365	-6	-8	96	115	-0.2	-0	0	-0.6
1974	Chi-A	3	3	.500	40	5	0	0	1	106	103	8.7	7	55	4.7	68	5.8	4.42	84	.257	.350	-9	-8	102	92	0.0	0	-1	-0.9
1975	Chi-A	0	0	—	1	0	0	0	0	0	1	—	0	0	—	0	—	—	—	1.000	1.000	0	0	104	0	0.0	0	0	0.0
Total	3	8	8	.500	59	20	1	0	1	193	196	9.1	20	103	4.8	124	5.8	4.52	84	.266	.358	-15	-16	99	102	-0.2	-0	-1	-1.5

■ **TOGIE PITTINGER** Pittinger, Charles Reno b: 1871, Greencastle, Pa. d: 1/14/09, Greencastle, Pa. BL/TR, 6'2", Deb: 4/26/00

YEAR	TM/L	W	L	PCT	G	GS	CG	SHO	SV	IP	H	H/G	HR	BB	BB/G	SO	SO/G	ERA	/A	OAVG	OOBP	PR	/A	PF	CPI	WAT	PB	PD	TPI
1900	Bos-N	2	9	.182	18	13	8	0	0	114	135	10.7	7	54	4.3	27	2.1	5.13	87	.318	.395	-18	-9	120	94	-3.4	-5	0	-1.0
1901	Bos-N	13	16	.448	34	33	27	1	0	281	288	9.2	7	76	2.4	129	4.1	3.01	124	.289	.343	10	22	112	110	-1.7	-9	3	2.6
1902	Bos-N	27	15	.643	46	40	36	7	0	389	360	8.3	4	128	3.0	174	4.0	2.52	104	.271	.341	11	4	94	109	6.5	-7	-2	0.2
1903	Bos-N	18	22	.450	44	39	35	0	1	352	396	10.1	12	143	3.7	140	3.6	3.48	92	.313	.390	-8	-10	98	121	1.4	-8	-3	-1.2
1904	Bos-N	15	21	.417	38	38	35	5	0	335	298	8.0	1	144	3.9	146	3.9	2.66	104	.264	.355	3	4	102	110	2.0	-9	4	0.9
1905	Phi-N	23	14	.622	**46**	37	29	4	2	337	311	8.3	3	104	2.8	136	3.6	3.10	99	.275	.344	-4	-2	102	95	3.9	-4	-3	-0.4
1906	Phi-N	8	10	.444	20	16	9	2	0	130	128	8.9	2	50	3.5	43	3.0	3.39	72	.293	.380	-11	-14	93	104	-0.3	-2	-2	-1.5
1907	Phi-N	9	5	.643	16	12	8	1	0	102	101	8.9	3	35	3.1	37	3.3	3.00	85	.291	.364	-6	-5	103	111	1.4	-1	-1	-0.6
Total	8	115	112	.507	262	228	187	20	3	2040	2017	8.9	39	734	3.2	832	3.7	3.10	98	.286	.360	-24	-12	102	108	9.8	-45	-4	-1.0

■ **STAN PITULA** Pitula, Stanley b: 3/23/31, Hackensack, N.J. d: 8/15/65, Hackensack, N.J. BR/TR, 5'10", 170 lbs. Deb: 4/24/57

YEAR	TM/L	W	L	PCT	G	GS	CG	SHO	SV	IP	H	H/G	HR	BB	BB/G	SO	SO/G	ERA	/A	OAVG	OOBP	PR	/A	PF	CPI	WAT	PB	PD	TPI
1957	Cle-A	2	2	.500	23	5	1	0	0	60	67	10.1	8	32	4.8	17	2.6	4.95	78	.296	.380	-8	-7	102	115	0.0	0	-0	-0.7

■ **JUAN PIZARRO** Pizarro, Juan Ramon (Cordova) b: 2/7/37, Santurce, P.R. BL/TL, 5'11", 170 lbs. Deb: 5/04/57

YEAR	TM/L	W	L	PCT	G	GS	CG	SHO	SV	IP	H	H/G	HR	BB	BB/G	SO	SO/G	ERA	/A	OAVG	OOBP	PR	/A	PF	CPI	WAT	PB	PD	TPI
1957	Mil-N	5	6	.455	24	10	3	0	0	99	99	9.0	16	51	4.6	68	6.2	4.64	73	.261	.343	-8	-14	88	103	-1.4	3	-1	-1.1
1958	Mil-N	6	4	.600	16	10	7	1	1	97	75	7.0	12	47	4.4	84	7.8	2.69	127	.212	.309	14	8	87	120	0.0	3	1	1.1
1959	Mil-N	6	2	.750	29	14	6	2	0	134	117	7.9	13	70	4.7	126	8.5	3.76	98	.237	.337	3	-1	93	104	1.8	-0	0	-0.1
1960	Mil-N	6	7	.462	21	17	3	0	0	115	105	8.2	13	72	5.6	88	6.9	4.54	74	.244	.352	-10	-15	89	98	-1.2	3	-1	-1.2
1961	Chi-A	14	7	.667	39	25	12	1	2	195	164	7.6	17	89	4.1	188	**8.7**	3.05	130	.226	.309	21	20	99	106	3.3	5	-1	2.4
1962	Chi-A	12	14	.462	36	32	9	1	1	203	182	8.1	16	97	4.3	173	**7.7**	3.81	98	.236	.315	4	-2	94	90	-1.7	0	-1	-0.3
1963	Chi-A	16	8	.667	32	28	10	3	1	215	177	7.4	14	63	2.6	163	6.8	2.39	155	.224	.278	30	32	102	109	2.8	2	-2	3.5
1964	Chi-A	19	9	.679	33	33	11	4	0	239	193	7.3	23	55	2.1	162	6.1	2.56	132	.219	.264	28	22	93	96	3.0	5	-1	2.7
1965	Chi-A	6	3	.667	18	18	2	1	0	97	96	8.9	9	37	3.4	65	6.0	3.43	91	.254	.320	0	-3	91	108	0.9	3	0	0.0
1966	Chi-A	8	6	.571	34	9	1	0	3	89	91	9.2	9	39	3.9	42	4.2	3.74	86	.269	.339	-3	-5	93	120	0.9	0	1	-0.4
1967	Pit-N	8	10	.444	50	9	1	1	9	107	99	8.3	10	52	4.4	96	8.1	3.95	86	.245	.330	-7	-7	100	97	-1.0	2	-1	-0.6
1968	Pit-N	1	1	.500	12	0	0	0	0	11	14	11.5	2	10	8.2	6	4.9	3.27	91	.311	.424	-0	-0	100	233	0.0	-0	-0	0.0
	Bos-A	6	8	.429	19	12	6	0	2	108	97	8.1	15	44	3.7	84	7.0	3.58	84	.242	.311	-7	-7	101	108	-1.3	1	2	-0.4
1969	Bos-A	0	1	.000	6	0	0	0	2	9	14	14.0	2	6	6.0	4	4.0	6.00	63	.359	.435	-2	-2	105	141	-0.4	0	0	-0.1
	Cle-A	3	3	.500	48	4	1	0	4	83	67	7.3	6	49	5.3	44	4.8	3.14	111	.229	.332	4	3	96	116	0.6	0	0	0.4
	Oak-A	1	1	.500	3	0	0	0	1	8	3	3.4	1	3	3.4	4	4.5	2.25	147	.125	.214	1	1	91	68	0.0	0	0	0.1
	Yr	4	5	.444	57	4	1	0	7	100	84	7.6	9	58	5.2	52	4.7	3.33	105	.230	.331	3	2	97	68	0.2	1	1	0.4
1970	Chi-N	0	0	—	12	0	0	0	1	16	16	9.0	2	9	5.1	14	7.9	4.50	107	.262	.356	-1	1	119	110	0.0	-0	0	0.1
1971	Chi-N	7	6	.538	16	14	6	3	0	101	78	7.0	10	40	3.6	67	6.0	3.48	110	.209	.286	-0	4	110	77	0.4	1	0	0.6
1972	Chi-N	4	5	.444	16	7	1	0	1	59	66	10.1	7	32	4.9	24	3.7	3.97	98	.293	.375	-3	-1	112	137	-0.8	-1	1	0.0
1973	Chi-N	0	1	.000	2	0	0	0	0	4	6	13.5	1	1	2.3	3	6.8	11.25	35	.353	.381	-3	-3	109	71	-0.4	-0	0	-0.2
	Hou-N	2	2	.500	15	1	0	0	0	23	28	11.0	1	11	4.3	10	3.9	6.65	52	.301	.367	-8	-8	95	74	0.0	-0	1	-0.7
	Yr	2	3	.400	17	1	0	0	0	27	34	11.3	2	12	4.0	13	4.3	7.33	48	.304	.362	-11	-11	97	74	-0.4	-0	1	-0.9
1974	Pit-N	1	1	.500	7	2	0	0	0	24	20	7.5	2	11	4.1	7	2.6	1.88	187	.220	.295	5	4	97	153	0.0	0	-0	0.5
Total	18	131	105	.555	488	245	79	17	28	2036	1807	8.0	201	888	3.9	1522	6.7	3.43	103	.237	.315	56	27	96	104	5.5	28	-4	6.3

■ **GORDIE PLADSON** Pladson, Gordon Cecil b: C., Canada BR/TR, 6'4", 210 lbs. Deb: 9/07/79

YEAR	TM/L	W	L	PCT	G	GS	CG	SHO	SV	IP	H	H/G	HR	BB	BB/G	SO	SO/G	ERA	/A	OAVG	OOBP	PR	/A	PF	CPI	WAT	PB	PD	TPI
1979	Hou-N	0	0	—	4	0	0	0	0	4	9	20.3	1	2	4.5	2	4.5	4.50	75	.450	.500	-0	-0	90	260	0.0	0	0	0.0
1980	Hou-N	0	4	.000	12	6	0	0	0	41	38	8.3	3	16	3.5	13	2.9	4.39	80	.244	.309	-4	-4	97	75	-1.9	-1	0	-0.4
1981	Hou-N	0	0	—	2	0	0	0	0	4	9	20.3	0	3	6.8	3	6.8	9.00	34	.429	.500	-2	-3	87	111	0.0	0	0	-0.2
1982	Hou-N	0	0	—	2	0	0	0	0	1	10	90.0	0	2	18.0	0	0.0	72.00	5	.769	.750	-8	-8	100	71	0.0	0	0	-0.6
Total	4	0	4	.000	20	6	0	0	0	50	66	11.9	4	23	4.1	18	3.2	6.12	56	.314	.376	-14	-15	96	92	-1.9	-1	0	-1.2

■ **EMIL PLANETA** Planeta, Emil Joseph b: 1/31/09, Higganum, Conn. d: 2/2/63, Rocky Hill, Conn. BR/TR, 6', 190 lbs. Deb: 9/20/31

YEAR	TM/L	W	L	PCT	G	GS	CG	SHO	SV	IP	H	H/G	HR	BB	BB/G	SO	SO/G	ERA	/A	OAVG	OOBP	PR	/A	PF	CPI	WAT	PB	PD	TPI
1931	NY-N	0	0	—	2	0	0	0	0	5	7	12.6	0	4	7.2	0	0.0	10.80	33	.292	.393	-4	-4	93	47	0.0	-0	-0	-0.3

■ **ED PLANK** Plank, Edward Arthur b: 4/9/52, Chicago, Ill. BR/TR, 6'1", 205 lbs. Deb: 9/06/78

YEAR	TM/L	W	L	PCT	G	GS	CG	SHO	SV	IP	H	H/G	HR	BB	BB/G	SO	SO/G	ERA	/A	OAVG	OOBP	PR	/A	PF	CPI	WAT	PB	PD	TPI
1978	SF-N	0	0	—	5	0	0	0	0	7	6	7.7	1	2	2.6	1	1.3	3.86	85	.273	.320	-0	-0	91	117	0.0	0	-0	0.0
1979	SF-N	0	0	—	4	0	0	0	0	4	9	20.3	0	2	4.5	1	2.3	6.75	52	.450	.500	-1	-1	93	145	0.0	0	-0	-0.1
Total	2	0	0	—	9	0	0	0	0	11	15	12.3	1	4	3.3	2	1.6	4.91	68	.357	.404	-2	-2	92	127	0.0	0	-0	-0.1

■ **EDDIE PLANK** Plank, Edward Stewart "Gettysburg Eddie" b: 8/31/1875, Gettysburg, Pa. d: 2/24/26, Gettysburg, Pa. BL/TL, 5'11.5", 175 lbs. Deb: 5/13/01 H

YEAR	TM/L	W	L	PCT	G	GS	CG	SHO	SV	IP	H	H/G	HR	BB	BB/G	SO	SO/G	ERA	/A	OAVG	OOBP	PR	/A	PF	CPI	WAT	PB	PD	TPI
1901	Phi-A	17	13	.567	33	32	28	1	0	261	254	8.8	2	68	2.3	90	3.1	3.31	110	.275	.324	10	10	100	84	0.9	-4	-2	0.7
1902	Phi-A	20	15	.571	36	32	31	1	0	300	319	9.6	5	61	1.8	107	3.2	3.30	115	.297	.335	9	16	106	97	-1.4	6	-2	2.1
1903	Phi-A	23	16	.590	**43**	40	33	3	0	336	317	8.5	5	65	1.7	176	4.7	2.38	126	.271	.309	21	23	102	111	2.0	-1	-2	2.3
1904	Phi-A	26	16	.619	43	43	37	7	0	357	309	7.8	2	86	2.2	201	5.1	2.14	122	.255	.305	18	19	101	107	4.9	3	-1	2.0
1905	Phi-A	24	12	.667	41	41	**35**	4	0	347	287	7.4	3	75	1.9	210	5.4	2.26	125	.248	.294	15	21	106	95	2.7	2	-3	2.1
1906	Phi-A	19	6	**.760**	26	25	21	5	0	212	173	7.3	1	51	2.2	108	4.6	2.25	111	.246	.297	10	6	93	91	**6.6**	2	-2	0.4
1907	Phi-A	24	16	.600	43	40	33	**8**	0	344	282	7.4	5	85	2.2	183	4.8	2.20	121	.246	.298	13	17	104	94	-0.2	2	-1	1.9
1908	Phi-A	14	16	.467	34	28	21	4	1	245	202	7.4	1	46	1.7	135	5.0	2.17	121	.224	.269	6	12	110	87	0.7	-1	-5	0.9
1909	Phi-A	19	10	.655	34	33	24	3	0	265	215	7.3	1	62	2.1	132	4.5	1.77	136	.224	.277	21	19	97	94	1.6	4	1	2.3
1910	Phi-A	16	10	.615	38	32	22	1	2	250	218	7.8	3	55	2.0	123	4.4	2.02	121	.237	.286	14	12	97	104	-1.4	-3	-3	0.6
1911	Phi-A	23	8	.742	40	30	24	**6**	**4**	257	237	8.3	2	77	2.7	149	5.2	2.10	141	.255	.322	35	24	88	**133**	4.1	-0	1	2.4
1912	Phi-A	26	6	.813	37	30	23	5	2	260	234	8.1	1	83	2.9	110	3.8	2.22	147	.245	.309	33	30	97	120	9.6	4	-2	2.9

YEAR	TM/L	W	L	PCT	G	GS	CG	SHO	SV	IP	H	H/G	HR	BB	BB/G	SO	SO/G	ERA	/A	OAVG	OOBP	PR	/A	PF	CPI	WAT	PB	PD	TPI
1913	Phi-A	18	10	.643	41	30	18	7	4	243	211	7.8	3	57	2.1	151	5.6	2.59	105	.234	.283	9	3	93	76	0.7	-0	-1	0.2
1914	Phi-A	15	7	.682	34	22	12	4	3	185	178	8.7	2	42	2.0	110	5.4	2.87	88	.266	.315	-3	-7	93	99	1.1	0	-3	-0.9
1915	StL-F	21	11	.656	42	31	23	6	3	268	212	7.1	1	54	**1.8**	147	4.9	2.08	**149**	.218	**.262**	28	30	102	79	4.0	5	-0	4.0
1916	StL-A	16	15	.516	37	26	17	3	3	236	203	7.7	2	67	2.6	88	3.4	2.33	115	.237	.297	13	9	94	98	0.1	0	-3	0.6
1917	StL-A	5	6	.455	20	14	8	1	1	131	105	7.2	2	38	2.6	26	1.8	1.79	147	.225	.287	13	12	98	110	0.8	-1	-2	1.0
Total	17	326	193	.628	622	529	410	69	23	4497	3956	7.9	41	1072	2.1	2246	4.5	2.35	122	.249	.299	266	260	100	99	36.8	17	-29	25.5

■ BILL PLEIS Pleis, William b: 8/5/37, St.Louis, Mo. BL/TL, 5'10", 170 lbs. Deb: 4/16/61

YEAR	TM/L	W	L	PCT	G	GS	CG	SHO	SV	IP	H	H/G	HR	BB	BB/G	SO	SO/G	ERA	/A	OAVG	OOBP	PR	/A	PF	CPI	WAT	PB	PD	TPI
1961	Min-A	4	2	.667	37	0	0	0	2	56	59	9.5	4	34	5.5	32	5.1	4.98	87	.266	.363	-6	-4	107	93	1.3	-1	-1	-0.5
1962	Min-A	2	5	.286	21	4	0	0	3	45	46	9.2	7	14	2.8	31	6.2	4.40	93	.264	.311	-2	-1	104	99	-1.7	1	-1	0.0
1963	Min-A	6	2	.750	36	4	1	0	0	68	67	8.9	10	16	2.1	37	4.9	4.37	81	.258	.293	-6	-6	98	88	1.7	0	-0	-0.5
1964	Min-A	4	1	.800	47	0	0	0	4	51	43	7.6	6	31	5.5	42	7.4	3.88	93	.232	.336	-1	-1	100	105	1.5	0	0	0.0
1965	Min-A	4	4	.500	41	2	0	0	4	51	49	8.6	3	27	4.8	33	5.8	3.00	113	.250	.332	3	2	98	125	-0.8	-1	-0	0.1
1966	Min-A	1	2	.333	8	0	0	0	0	9	5	5.0	1	4	4.0	9	9.0	2.00	189	.152	.237	1	2	110	76	-0.5	0	-0	0.2
Total	6	21	16	.568	190	10	1	0	13	280	269	8.6	31	126	4.1	184	5.9	4.08	93	.251	.324	-11	-9	101	100	1.5	0	-2	-0.7

■ DAN PLESAC Plesac, Daniel Thomas b: 2/4/62, Gary, Ind. BL/TL, 6'5", 205 lbs. Deb: 4/11/86

YEAR	TM/L	W	L	PCT	G	GS	CG	SHO	SV	IP	H	H/G	HR	BB	BB/G	SO	SO/G	ERA	/A	OAVG	OOBP	PR	/A	PF	CPI	WAT	PB	PD	TPI
1986	Mil-A	10	7	.588	51	0	0	0	14	91	81	8.0	5	29	2.9	75	7.4	2.97	145	.240	.292	12	14	103	100	2.0	0	-0	1.3
1987	Mil-A	5	6	.455	57	0	0	0	23	79	63	7.2	8	23	2.6	89	10.1	2.62	174	.213	.274	16	17	102	99	-1.0	0	0	1.6
1988	Mil-A	1	2	.333	50	0	0	0	30	52	46	8.0	2	12	2.1	52	9.0	2.42	168	.234	.275	9	10	103	99	-0.5	0	-0	1.0
Total	3	16	15	.516	158	0	0	0	67	222	190	7.7	15	64	2.6	216	8.8	2.72	160	.229	.281	38	40	103	100	0.5	0	-0	3.9

■ NORMAN PLITT Plitt, Norman William b: 2/21/1893, York, Pa. d: 2/1/54, New York, N.Y. BR/TR, 5'11", 180 lbs. Deb: 4/26/18

YEAR	TM/L	W	L	PCT	G	GS	CG	SHO	SV	IP	H	H/G	HR	BB	BB/G	SO	SO/G	ERA	/A	OAVG	OOBP	PR	/A	PF	CPI	WAT	PB	PD	TPI
1918	Bro-N	0	0	—	1	0	0	0	0	2	3	13.5	0	1	4.5	0	0.0	4.50	64	.429	.500	-0	-0	104	166	0.0	0	0	0.0
1927	Bro-N	2	6	.250	19	8	1	0	0	62	73	10.6	3	36	5.2	9	1.3	4.94	83	.303	.382	-7	-6	104	107	-1.6	-0	0	-0.5
	NY-N	1	0	1.000	3	0	0	0	0	7	9	11.6	0	1	1.3	0	0.0	3.86	100	.310	.355	0	-0	98	110	0.5	-0	0	0.0
	Yr	3	6	.333	22	8	1	0	0	69	82	10.7	3	37	4.8	9	1.2	4.83	84	.303	.376	-7	-6	103	110	-1.1	-0	1	-0.5
Total	2	3	6	.333	23	8	1	0	0	71	85	10.8	3	38	4.8	9	1.1	4.82	83	.307	.382	-7	-6	103	109	-1.1	-0	1	-0.5

■ TIM PLODINEC Plodinec, Timothy Alfred b: 1/27/47, Aliquippa, Pa. BR/TR, 6'4", 190 lbs. Deb: 6/02/72

YEAR	TM/L	W	L	PCT	G	GS	CG	SHO	SV	IP	H	H/G	HR	BB	BB/G	SO	SO/G	ERA	/A	OAVG	OOBP	PR	/A	PF	CPI	WAT	PB	PD	TPI
1972	StL-N	0	0	—	1	0	0	0	0	⅓	3	81.0	0	0	0.0	0	0.0	27.00	—	.750	.750	-1	-1	105	138	0.0	0	0	0.0

■ ERIC PLUNK Plunk, Eric Vaughn b: 9/3/63, Wilmington, Cal. BR/TR, 6'5", 210 lbs. Deb: 5/12/86

YEAR	TM/L	W	L	PCT	G	GS	CG	SHO	SV	IP	H	H/G	HR	BB	BB/G	SO	SO/G	ERA	/A	OAVG	OOBP	PR	/A	PF	CPI	WAT	PB	PD	TPI
1986	Oak-A	4	7	.364	26	15	0	0	0	120	91	6.8	14	102	7.7	98	7.4	5.33	74	.214	.369	-15	-19	94	84	-1.2	0	-2	-1.9
1987	Oak-A	4	6	.400	32	11	0	0	2	95	91	8.6	8	62	5.9	90	8.5	4.74	86	.253	.359	-3	-7	91	95	-1.0	0	-1	-0.7
1988	Oak-A	7	2	.778	49	0	0	0	5	78	62	7.2	6	39	4.5	79	9.1	3.00	123	.217	.308	8	6	93	104	1.8	0	-1	0.5
Total	3	15	15	.500	107	26	0	0	7	293	244	7.5	28	203	6.2	267	8.2	4.52	87	.228	.350	-10	-20	93	93	-0.4	0	-4	-2.1

■ RAY POAT Poat, Raymond Willis b: 12/19/17, Chicago, Ill. BR/TR, 6'2", 200 lbs. Deb: 4/15/42

YEAR	TM/L	W	L	PCT	G	GS	CG	SHO	SV	IP	H	H/G	HR	BB	BB/G	SO	SO/G	ERA	/A	OAVG	OOBP	PR	/A	PF	CPI	WAT	PB	PD	TPI
1942	Cle-A	1	3	.250	4	4	1	1	0	18	24	12.0	1	9	4.5	8	4.0	5.50	62	.296	.374	-4	-4	93	93	-0.9	-0	0	-0.3
1943	Cle-A	2	5	.286	17	4	1	0	0	45	44	8.8	3	20	4.0	31	6.2	4.40	67	.259	.330	-6	-7	90	88	-1.6	-0	0	-0.7
1944	Cle-A	4	8	.333	36	6	1	0	1	81	82	9.1	9	37	4.1	40	4.4	5.11	68	.265	.339	-15	-15	101	85	-1.7	-2	-0	-1.7
1947	NY-N	4	3	.571	7	7	5	0	0	60	53	8.0	8	13	2.0	25	3.8	2.55	159	.238	.276	10	10	99	125	0.4	2	-0	1.2
1948	NY-N	11	10	.524	39	24	7	3	0	158	162	9.2	21	67	3.8	57	3.2	4.33	90	.262	.332	-7	-8	98	103	0.4	-1	-2	-1.0
1949	NY-N	0	0	—	2	0	0	0	0	2	8	36.0	0	1	4.5	0	0.0	22.50	18	.615	.600	-4	-4	101	85	0.0	0	0	-0.3
	Pit-N	0	1	.000	11	2	0	0	0	36	52	13.0	6	15	3.8	17	4.3	6.25	66	.335	.387	-9	-8	102	108	-0.4	-1	-0	-0.8
	Yr	0	1	.000	13	2	0	0	0	38	60	14.2	6	16	3.8	17	4.0	7.11	58	.357	.404	-13	-13	102	108	-0.4	0	-0	-1.1
Total	6	22	30	.423	116	47	15	4	1	400	425	9.6	48	162	3.6	178	4.0	4.55	82	.271	.336	-34	-37	98	101	-3.8	-3	-3	-3.6

■ BUD PODBIELAN Podbielan, Clarence Anthony b: 3/6/24, Curlew, Wash. d: 10/26/82, Syracuse, N.Y. BR/TR, 6'1.5", 170 lbs. Deb: 4/25/49

YEAR	TM/L	W	L	PCT	G	GS	CG	SHO	SV	IP	H	H/G	HR	BB	BB/G	SO	SO/G	ERA	/A	OAVG	OOBP	PR	/A	PF	CPI	WAT	PB	PD	TPI
1949	Bro-N	0	1	.000	7	1	0	0	0	12	9	6.8	1	9	6.8	5	3.8	3.75	105	.205	.352	0	0	98	99	-0.4	-0	1	0.0
1950	Bro-N	5	4	.556	20	10	2	0	1	73	93	11.5	10	29	3.6	28	3.5	5.30	82	.307	.371	-9	-8	104	107	-0.1	-1	1	-0.7
1951	Bro-N	2	2	.500	27	5	1	0	0	80	67	7.5	9	36	4.0	26	2.9	3.49	107	.233	.316	4	2	95	106	-0.3	1	0	0.4
1952	Bro-N	0	0	—	3	0	0	0	0	2	4	18.0	1	3	13.5	1	4.5	18.00	20	.444	.538	-3	-3	98	88	0.0	0	-0	-0.2
	Cin-N	4	5	.444	24	7	4	1	1	87	78	8.1	8	26	2.7	22	2.3	2.79	134	.245	.297	9	9	100	123	0.0	0	-1	0.9
	Yr	4	5	.444	27	7	4	1	1	89	82	8.3	9	29	2.9	23	2.3	3.13	119	.251	.305	6	6	100	123	0.0	0	-1	0.7
1953	Cin-N	6	16	.273	36	24	8	1	1	186	214	10.4	21	67	3.2	74	3.6	4.74	91	.290	.353	-9	-9	100	105	-4.5	-3	-0	-1.1
1954	Cin-N	7	10	.412	27	24	4	0	0	131	157	10.8	20	58	4.0	42	2.9	5.36	79	.300	.364	-19	-16	104	103	-1.2	-1	-2	-1.7
1955	Cin-N	1	2	.333	17	2	0	0	0	42	36	7.7	4	11	2.4	26	5.6	3.21	131	.234	.281	4	5	104	92	-0.4	1	0	0.6
1957	Cin-N	0	1	.000	5	3	1	0	0	16	18	10.1	4	4	2.3	13	7.3	6.19	66	.290	.328	-4	-4	106	89	-0.4	-1	-1	-0.4
1959	Cle-A	0	1	.000	6	0	0	0	0	12	17	12.8	1	2	1.5	5	3.8	6.00	61	.354	.358	-3	-3	95	98	-0.4	-0	0	-0.2
Total	9	25	42	.373	172	76	20	2	3	641	693	9.7	79	245	3.4	242	3.4	4.49	92	.279	.342	-30	-27	101	106	-7.7	-4	-2	-2.4

■ JOHNNY PODGAJNY Podgajny, John Sigmund "Specs" b: 6/10/20, Chester, Pa. d: 3/2/71, Chester, Pa. BR/TR, 6'2", 173 lbs. Deb: 9/15/40

YEAR	TM/L	W	L	PCT	G	GS	CG	SHO	SV	IP	H	H/G	HR	BB	BB/G	SO	SO/G	ERA	/A	OAVG	OOBP	PR	/A	PF	CPI	WAT	PB	PD	TPI
1940	Phi-N	1	3	.250	4	4	3	0	0	35	33	8.5	0	1	0.3	12	3.1	2.83	139	.250	.259	4	4	102	78	-0.4	-0	0	0.5
1941	Phi-N	9	12	.429	34	24	8	0	0	181	191	9.5	8	70	3.5	53	2.6	4.62	81	.270	.334	-20	-18	103	85	2.4	-3	1	-1.9
1942	Phi-N	6	14	.300	43	23	6	0	0	187	191	9.2	9	63	3.0	40	1.9	3.90	86	.268	.331	-12	-11	101	99	0.3	-1	-1	-1.3
1943	Phi-N	4	4	.500	13	5	3	0	0	64	77	10.8	4	16	2.3	13	1.8	4.22	76	.310	.338	-6	-7	96	110	0.6	1	1	-0.4
	Pit-N	0	4	.000	15	5	0	0	0	34	37	9.8	1	13	3.4	7	1.9	4.76	73	.266	.318	-5	-5	103	73	-1.9	-0	1	-0.3
	Yr	4	8	.333	28	10	3	0	0	98	114	10.5	5	29	2.7	20	1.8	4.41	75	.295	.331	-11	-12	98	73	-1.3	1	3	-0.7
1946	Cle-A	0	0	—	6	0	0	0	0	9	13	13.0	0	2	2.0	4	4.0	5.00	63	.302	.333	-1	-2	90	75	0.0	0	0	-0.1
Total	5	20	37	.351	115	61	20	0	0	510	542	9.6	22	165	2.9	129	2.3	4.20	84	.273	.328	-41	-39	101	91	1.0	-3	2	-3.5

■ JOHNNY PODRES Podres, John Joseph b: 9/30/32, Witherbee, N.Y. BL/TL, 5'11", 170 lbs. Deb: 4/17/53 C

YEAR	TM/L	W	L	PCT	G	GS	CG	SHO	SV	IP	H	H/G	HR	BB	BB/G	SO	SO/G	ERA	/A	OAVG	OOBP	PR	/A	PF	CPI	WAT	PB	PD	TPI
1953	Bro-N	9	4	.692	33	18	3	1	0	115	126	9.9	12	64	5.0	82	6.4	4.23	101	.282	.369	1	0	100	122	0.2	2	-0	0.2
1954	Bro-N	11	7	.611	29	21	6	2	0	152	147	8.7	13	53	3.1	79	4.7	4.26	96	.255	.314	-3	-3	101	82	0.3	5	-2	0.1
1955	Bro-N	9	10	.474	27	24	5	2	0	159	160	9.1	15	57	3.2	114	6.5	3.96	103	.259	.323	1	2	101	96	-2.6	-0	-1	0.0
1957	Bro-N	12	9	.571	31	27	10	**6**	3	196	168	7.7	15	44	2.0	109	5.0	**2.66**	**166**	.230	**.272**	26	39	114	94	0.7	1	-0	4.3
1958	LA-N	13	15	.464	39	31	10	2	1	210	208	8.9	27	78	3.3	143	6.1	3.73	113	.261	.324	5	11	106	109	0.1	-4	-2	0.6
1959	LA-N	14	9	.609	34	29	6	2	0	195	192	8.9	23	74	3.4	145	6.7	4.11	97	.261	.327	-3	-3	101	101	1.4	4	1	0.3
1960	LA-N	14	12	.538	34	33	8	1	0	228	217	8.6	25	71	2.8	159	6.3	3.08	139	.250	.304	17	30	114	117	0.2	-2	-2	3.0
1961	LA-N	18	5	**.783**	32	29	6	1	0	183	192	9.4	27	51	2.5	124	6.1	3.74	109	.271	.320	6	7	102	116	**6.0**	2	-1	0.7
1962	LA-N	15	13	.536	40	40	8	0	0	255	270	9.5	20	71	2.5	178	6.3	3.81	94	.272	.318	4	-7	91	100	-2.1	1	-4	-0.9
1963	LA-N	14	12	.538	37	34	10	5	1	198	196	8.9	16	64	2.9	134	6.1	3.55	87	.257	.311	-6	-10	94	100	-1.7	1	-1	-1.0
1964	LA-N	0	2	.000	2	2	0	0	0	3	5	15.0	1	3	9.0	0	0.0	15.00	22	.417	.500	-4	-4	91	79	-0.9	0	-0	-0.3
1965	LA-N	7	6	.538	27	22	2	1	1	134	126	8.5	17	39	2.6	63	4.2	3.43	93	.247	.298	2	-4	90	106	-0.6	1	-2	-0.5
1966	LA-N	0	0	—	1	0	0	0	0	2	2	9.0	0	1	4.5	1	4.5	0.00	—	.400	.375	1	1	95	0	0.0	0	0	0.1
	Det-A	4	5	.444	36	13	2	1	4	108	106	8.8	12	34	2.8	53	4.4	3.42	102	.259	.307	0	1	102	115	-0.8	2	-1	0.3
1967	Det-A	3	1	.750	21	8	0	0	1	63	58	8.3	12	11	1.6	34	4.9	3.86	82	.244	.279	-4	-5	98	97	0.9	-1	-1	-0.6
1969	SD-N	5	6	.455	17	9	1	0	0	65	66	9.1	7	28	3.9	17	2.4	4.29	84	.264	.331	-5	-5	100	99	1.1	-1	-1	-0.6
Total	15	148	116	.561	440	340	77	24	11	2266	2239	8.9	242	743	3.0	1435	5.7	3.67	105	.259	.314	38	50	101	104	2.2	11	-15	5.7

■ JOE POETZ Poetz, Joseph Frank "Bull Montana" b: 6/22/1900, St.Louis, Mo. d: 2/7/42, St.Louis, Mo. BR/TR, 5'10.5", 175 lbs. Deb: 9/14/26

YEAR	TM/L	W	L	PCT	G	GS	CG	SHO	SV	IP	H	H/G	HR	BB	BB/G	SO	SO/G	ERA	/A	OAVG	OOBP	PR	/A	PF	CPI	WAT	PB	PD	TPI
1926	NY-N	0	1	.000	2	1	0	0	0	8	5	5.6	2	8	9.0	0	0.0	3.38	111	.192	.389	0	0	98	169	-0.4	0	0	0.0

■ BOOTS POFFENBERGER Poffenberger, Cletus Elwood b: 7/1/15, Williamsport, Md. BR/TR, 5'10", 178 lbs. Deb: 6/11/37

YEAR	TM/L	W	L	PCT	G	GS	CG	SHO	SV	IP	H	H/G	HR	BB	BB/G	SO	SO/G	ERA	/A	OAVG	OOBP	PR	/A	PF	CPI	WAT	PB	PD	TPI
1937	Det-A	10	5	.667	29	16	5	0	3	137	147	9.7	8	79	5.2	35	2.3	4.66	107	.277	.368	-1	5	108	104	1.7	-1	1	0.5
1938	Det-A	6	7	.462	25	15	8	1	1	125	147	10.6	8	66	4.8	28	2.0	4.82	98	.297	.378	-0	-1	99	111	-1.0	-1	-2	-0.2
1939	Bro-N	0	0	—	3	1	0	0	0	5	7	12.6	1	4	7.2	2	3.6	5.40	77	.318	.423	-1	-1	106	138	0.0	-0	0	0.0
Total	3	16	12	.571	57	32	13	1	4	267	301	10.1	17	149	5.0	65	2.2	4.75	102	.287	.374	-2	3	104	108	0.7	-2	-0	0.3

YEAR	TM/L	W	L	PCT	G	GS	CG	SHO	SV	IP	H	H/G	HR	BB	BB/G	SO	SO/G	ERA	/A	OAVG	OOBP	PR	/A	PF	CPI	WAT	PB	PD	TPI
■ **TOM POHOLSKY** Poholsky, Thomas George b: 8/26/29, Detroit, Mich. BR/TR, 6'3", 205 lbs. Deb: 4/20/50																													
1950	StL-N	0	0	—	5	1	0	0	0	15	16	9.6	2	3	1.8	2	1.2	3.60	118	.281	.317	1	1	103	120	0.0	-0	-0	0.1
1951	StL-N	7	13	.350	38	26	10	1	1	195	204	9.4	15	68	3.1	70	3.2	4.43	90	.271	.328	-10	-10	101	89	-3.6	0	1	-0.7
1954	StL-N	5	7	.417	25	13	4	0	0	106	101	8.6	11	20	1.7	55	4.7	3.06	133	.254	.288	12	12	100	107	-0.6	-1	0	1.2
1955	StL-N	9	11	.450	30	24	8	2	0	151	143	8.5	26	35	2.1	66	3.9	3.81	108	.244	.288	4	5	102	93	0.2	-1	-1	0.4
1956	StL-N	9	14	.391	33	29	7	2	0	203	210	9.3	27	44	2.0	95	4.2	3.59	104	.268	.306	4	3	99	108	-2.6	-1	0	0.3
1957	Chi-N	1	7	.125	28	11	1	0	0	84	117	12.5	9	22	2.4	28	3.0	4.93	77	.330	.364	-10	-11	98	114	-2.7	-1	0	-1.0
Total	6	31	52	.373	159	104	30	5	1	754	791	9.4	90	192	2.3	316	3.8	3.93	101	.270	.313	1	2	100	101	-9.3	-3	2	0.3
■ **JENNINGS POINDEXTER** Poindexter, Chester Jennings "Jinx" b: 9/30/10, Pauls Valley, Okla. d: 3/3/83, Norman, Okla. BL/TL, 5'10", 165 lbs. Deb: 9/15/36																													
1936	Bos-A	0	2	.000	3	3	0	0	0	11	13	10.6	0	16	13.1	2	1.6	6.55	81	.302	.483	-2	-1	106	118	-0.9	-1	0	-0.1
1939	Phi-N	0	0	—	11	1	0	0	0	30	29	8.7	0	15	4.5	12	3.6	4.20	93	.250	.328	-1	-1	99	76	0.0	-0	-0	0.0
Total	2	0	2	.000	14	4	0	0	0	41	42	9.2	0	31	6.8	14	3.1	4.83	88	.264	.376	-3	-3	101	87	-0.9	-1	-0	-0.1
■ **LOU POLCHOW** Polchow, Louis William b: 3/14/1881, Mankato, Minn. d: 8/15/12, Good Thunder, Minn 5'9", Deb: 9/14/02																													
1902	Cle-A	0	1	.000	1	1	1	0	0	8	9	10.1	0	4	4.5	2	2.3	5.63	61	.309	.393	-2	-2	96	75	-0.4	-1	0	-0.1
■ **DICK POLE** Pole, Richard Henry b: 10/13/50, Trout Creek, Mich. BR/TR, 6'3", 200 lbs. Deb: 8/03/73 C																													
1973	Bos-A	3	2	.600	12	7	0	0	0	55	70	11.5	4	18	2.9	24	3.9	5.56	72	.318	.370	-11	-10	105	91	0.3	0	-0	-0.9
1974	Bos-A	1	1	.500	15	2	0	0	1	45	55	11.0	6	13	2.6	32	6.4	4.20	92	.304	.348	-3	-2	106	120	0.0	0	1	0.0
1975	Bos-A	4	6	.400	18	11	2	1	0	90	102	10.2	11	32	3.2	42	4.2	4.40	93	.290	.345	-6	-3	108	109	-1.6	0	0	-0.2
1976	Bos-A	6	5	.545	31	15	1	0	0	121	131	9.7	8	48	3.6	49	3.6	4.31	90	.279	.343	-11	-6	110	98	0.4	0	-1	-0.7
1977	Sea-A	7	12	.368	25	24	3	0	0	122	127	9.4	16	57	4.2	51	3.8	5.16	78	.270	.351	-15	-16	98	92	-0.6	0	-3	-1.7
1978	Sea-A	4	11	.267	21	18	2	0	0	99	122	11.1	16	41	3.7	41	3.7	6.45	61	.306	.368	-29	-28	104	89	-1.8	0	-1	-2.6
Total	6	25	37	.403	122	77	8	1	1	532	607	10.3	61	209	3.5	239	4.0	5.04	79	.290	.353	-74	-63	105	98	-3.3	0	-5	-6.1
■ **KEN POLIVKA** Polivka, Kenneth Lyle "Soup" b: 1/21/21, Chicago, Ill. d: 7/23/88, Aurora, Ill. BL/TL, 5'10.5", 175 lbs. Deb: 4/18/47																													
1947	Cin-N	0	0	—	2	0	0	0	0	3	3	9.0	0	3	9.0	1	3.0	3.00	125	.250	.400	0	0	92	151	0.0	0	0	0.0
■ **HOWIE POLLET** Pollet, Howard Joseph b: 6/26/21, New Orleans, La. d: 8/8/74, Houston, Tex. BL/TL, 6'1.5", 175 lbs. Deb: 8/20/41 C																													
1941	StL-N	5	2	.714	9	8	6	2	0	70	55	7.1	1	27	3.5	37	4.8	1.93	202	.212	.281	13	15	107	114	0.8	-0	1	1.8
1942	StL-N	7	5	.583	27	13	5	2	0	109	102	8.4	7	39	3.2	42	3.5	2.89	118	.242	.307	5	6	103	110	-0.9	3	-2	0.8
1943	StL-N	8	4	.667	16	14	12	5	0	118	83	6.3	2	32	2.4	61	4.7	1.75	193	.200	.257	21	21	100	93	0.0	-1	-2	2.2
1946	StL-N	**21**	10	.677	40	32	22	4	5	**266**	228	7.7	12	86	2.9	107	3.6	**2.10**	**168**	.234	.295	**39**	**42**	103	127	2.5	-0	1	**4.9**
1947	StL-N	9	11	.450	37	24	9	0	2	176	195	10.0	11	87	4.4	73	3.7	4.35	97	.286	.364	-5	-3	104	109	-2.4	2	0	0.0
1948	StL-N	13	8	.619	36	26	11	0	0	186	216	10.5	10	67	3.2	80	3.9	4.55	86	.289	.345	-12	-13	99	97	1.8	-3	1	-1.3
1949	StL-N	20	9	.690	39	28	17	**5**	1	231	228	8.9	9	59	2.3	108	4.2	2.77	157	.256	.300	33	**41**	108	112	3.0	1	-2	**4.3**
1950	StL-N	14	13	.519	37	30	14	2	2	232	228	8.8	19	68	2.6	117	4.5	3.30	129	.256	.305	22	25	103	106	0.3	-2	0	2.3
1951	StL-N	0	3	.000	6	2	0	0	1	12	10	7.5	1	8	6.0	10	7.5	4.50	89	.208	.321	-1	-1	101	67	-1.4	1	0	0.0
	Pit-N	6	10	.375	21	21	4	1	0	129	149	10.4	24	51	3.6	47	3.3	5.02	86	.294	.354	-15	-10	110	112	-0.8	-1	-0	-0.9
	Yr	6	13	.316	27	23	4	1	1	141	159	10.1	25	59	3.8	57	3.6	4.98	86	.287	.351	-16	-11	109	112	-2.2	1	-0	-0.9
1952	Pit-N	7	16	.304	31	30	9	1	0	214	217	9.1	22	71	3.0	90	3.8	4.12	95	.266	.322	-9	-5	105	99	0.6	2	1	-0.1
1953	Pit-N	1	1	.500	5	2	0	0	0	13	27	18.7	2	6	4.2	8	5.5	10.38	44	.482	.500	-9	-8	106	111	0.3	0	-0	-0.7
	Chi-N	5	6	.455	25	16	2	0	1	111	120	9.7	6	44	3.6	45	3.6	4.14	110	.271	.333	2	5	106	96	0.3	-1	-1	0.3
	Yr	6	7	.462	30	18	2	0	1	124	147	10.7	8	50	3.6	53	3.8	4.79	95	.295	.353	-7	-3	106	96	0.6	0	-1	-0.4
1954	Chi-N	8	10	.444	20	20	4	2	0	128	131	9.2	4	54	3.8	58	4.1	3.59	115	.263	.329	7	8	102	96	0.5	2	0	1.1
1955	Chi-N	4	3	.571	24	7	1	1	5	61	62	9.1	11	27	4.0	27	4.0	5.61	73	.265	.333	-11	-10	101	85	0.7	3	1	-0.5
1956	Chi-A	3	1	.750	11	4	0	0	0	26	27	9.3	2	11	3.8	14	4.8	4.15	102	.252	.319	0	0	102	82	0.9	1	0	0.1
	Pit-N	0	4	.000	19	0	0	0	3	23	18	7.0	3	8	3.1	10	3.9	3.13	124	.212	.271	2	2	103	86	-1.9	0	0	0.2
Total	14	131	116	.530	403	277	116	25	20	2105	2096	9.0	146	745	3.2	934	4.0	3.51	114	.260	.319	81	115	104	106	4.3	6	0	14.5
■ **LOU POLLI** Polli, Louis Americo "Crip" b: 7/9/01, Barre, Vt. BR/TR, 5'10.5", 165 lbs. Deb: 4/18/32																													
1932	StL-A	0	0	—	5	0	0	0	0	7	13	16.7	0	3	3.9	5	6.4	5.14	89	.406	.457	-1	-0	103	161	0.0	0	-0	0.0
1944	NY-N	0	2	.000	19	0	0	0	3	36	42	10.5	3	20	5.0	6	1.5	4.50	85	.294	.373	-4	-3	105	117	-0.9	-1	-0	-0.3
Total	2	0	2	.000	24	0	0	0	3	43	55	11.5	3	23	4.8	11	2.3	4.60	85	.314	.388	-4	-3	105	124	-0.9	-1	-1	-0.3
■ **JOHN POLONI** Poloni, John Paul b: 2/28/54, Dearborn, Mich. BL/TL, 6'5", 210 lbs. Deb: 9/16/77																													
1977	Tex-A	1	0	1.000	2	1	0	0	0	7	8	10.3	1	1	1.3	5	6.4	6.43	66	.286	.310	-2	-2	104	65	0.5	0	-0	-0.1
■ **JOHN POMORSKI** Pomorski, John Leon b: 12/30/05, Brooklyn, N.Y. d: 12/6/77, Brampton, Ont., Can. BR/TR, 6', 178 lbs. Deb: 4/17/34																													
1934	Chi-A	0	0	—	3	0	0	0	0	2	1	4.5	0	2	9.0	0	0.0	4.50	103	.143	.333	-0	0	103	49	0.0	0	0	0.0
■ **ARLIE POND** Pond, Erasmus Arlington b: 1/19/1872, Rutland, Vt. d: 9/19/30, Cebu, Philippines TR, 5'10", 160 lbs. Deb: 7/04/1895																													
1895	Bal-N	0	1	.000	6	1	1	0	2	14	10	6.4	0	12	7.7	13	8.4	6.43	77	.217	.379	-3	-2	104	50	-0.4	1	0	0.0
1896	Bal-N	16	8	.667	28	26	21	2	0	214	232	9.8	4	57	2.4	80	3.4	3.49	123	.298	.346	21	19	99	100	-0.5	0	0	1.7
1897	Bal-N	18	9	.667	32	28	23	0	0	248	267	9.7	3	72	2.6	59	2.1	3.52	113	.297	.349	22	12	92	97	-0.5	3	1	1.3
1898	Bal-N	1	1	.500	3	2	1	1	0	20	8	3.6	0	9	4.0	4	1.8	0.45	797	.136	.250	7	7	100	102	-0.1	1	0	0.8
Total	4	35	19	.648	69	57	46	3	2	496	517	9.4	7	150	2.7	156	2.8	3.47	119	.290	.345	47	36	95	97	-1.5	4	1	3.8
■ **ELMER PONDER** Ponder, Charles Elmer b: 6/26/1893, Reed, Okla. d: 4/20/74, Albuquerque, N.Mex BR/TR, 6', 178 lbs. Deb: 9/18/17																													
1917	Pit-N	1	1	.500	3	2	1	1	0	21	12	5.1	0	6	2.6	11	4.7	1.71	162	.167	.237	2	2	103	44	0.3	-1	-1	0.1
1919	Pit-N	0	5	.000	9	5	0	0	0	47	55	10.5	0	6	1.1	6	1.1	4.02	76	.297	.314	-6	-5	105	88	-2.4	-1	-1	-0.6
1920	Pit-N	11	15	.423	33	23	13	2	0	196	182	8.4	3	40	1.8	62	2.8	2.62	121	.246	.279	11	12	101	79	-2.5	-4	1	1.0
1921	Pit-N	2	0	1.000	8	1	1	0	0	25	29	10.4	1	3	1.1	3	1.1	2.16	178	.305	.317	5	5	102	174	1.0	-2	0	0.3
	Chi-N	3	6	.333	16	11	5	0	0	89	117	11.8	7	17	1.7	31	3.1	4.75	86	.321	.348	-10	-6	108	100	-0.9	-3	2	-0.6
	Yr	5	6	.455	24	12	6	0	0	114	146	11.5	8	20	1.6	34	2.7	4.18	97	.317	.341	-5	-2	107	100	0.1	-2	2	-0.3
Total	4	17	27	.386	69	42	20	3	0	378	395	9.4	11	72	1.7	113	2.7	3.21	106	.271	.301	3	8	104	90	-4.5	-10	1	0.2
■ **ED POOLE** Poole, Edward I. b: 9/7/1874, Canton, Ohio d: 3/11/19, Malvern, Ohio TR, 5'10", 175 lbs. Deb: 10/06/00																													
1900	Pit-N	1	0	1.000	1	0	0	0	0	7	4	5.1	0	0	0.0	3	3.9	1.29	290	.184	.184	2	2	101	3	0.5	1	0	0.2
1901	Pit-N	5	4	.556	12	10	8	1	0	80	78	8.8	3	30	3.4	26	2.9	3.60	88	.284	.369	-2	-4	96	101	-0.6	1	0	-0.3
1902	Pit-N	0	0	—	1	0	0	0	0	8	7	7.9	0	3	3.4	2	2.3	1.13	242	.257	.331	1	1	98	218	0.0	0	-0	0.1
	Cin-N	12	4	.750	16	16	16	2	0	138	129	8.4	2	54	3.5	55	3.6	2.15	140	.270	.344	10	13	108	135	4.2	-4	-0	1.4
	Yr	12	4	.750	17	16	16	2	0	146	136	8.4	2	57	3.5	57	3.5	2.10	143	.269	.343	11	15	108	135	4.2	0	-0	1.5
1903	Cin-N	7	13	.350	25	21	18	1	0	184	188	9.2	4	77	3.8	73	3.6	3.28	107	.294	.380	-0	5	107	112	-3.7	0	2	0.6
1904	Bro-N	8	14	.364	25	23	19	1	1	178	178	9.0	4	74	3.7	67	3.4	3.39	79	.288	.371	-13	-14	98	106	0.0	-3	3	-1.1
Total	5	33	35	.485	80	70	61	5	1	595	584	8.8	13	238	3.6	226	3.4	3.04	101	.283	.365	-3	3	103	114	0.4	-5	5	0.9
■ **TOM POORMAN** Poorman, Thomas Iverson b: 10/14/1857, Lock Haven, Pa. d: 2/18/05, Lock Haven, Pa. BL/TR, 5'10.5", 170 lbs. Deb: 5/05/1880																													
1880	Buf-N	1	8	.111	11	9	9	0	1	85	117	12.4	3	19	2.0	13	1.4	4.13	55	.336	.371	-17	-18	96	116	-2.8	-2	0	-1.9
	Chi-N	2	0	1.000	2	1	0	0	0	15	12	7.2	0	8	4.8	0	0.0	2.40	97	.228	.329	-0	-0	98	105	1.0	0	0	0.0
	Yr	3	8	.273	13	10	9	0	1	100	129	11.6	3	27	2.4	13	1.2	3.87	59	.322	.365	-17	-18	96	105	-1.8	-2	0	-1.9
1884	Tol-a	0	1	.000	1	1	1	0	0	9	13	13.0	1	2	2.0	0	0.0	3.00	114	.347	.380	0	0	105	213	-0.4	0	0	0.0
1887	Phi-a	0	0	—	1	0	0	0	0	1	5	45.0	0	1	9.0	1	9.0	63.00	7	.653	.693	-7	-7	100	40	0.0	0	0	-0.3
Total	3	3	9	.250	15	11	10	0	1	110	147	12.0	4	30	2.5	14	1.1	4.34	55	.330	.372	-23	-24	97	122	-2.2	-2	0	-2.2
■ **BILL POPP** Popp, William Peter b: 6/7/1877, St.Louis, Mo. d: 9/5/09, St.Louis, Mo. TR, Deb: 4/19/02																													
1902	StL-N	2	6	.250	9	7	5	0	0	60	87	13.1	2	26	3.9	20	3.0	4.95	56	.364	.427	-14	-15	99	114	-1.6	-2	1	-1.3
■ **ED PORRAY** Porray, Edmund Joseph b: 12/5/1888, At Sea On Atlantic Ocean d: 7/13/54, Lackawaxen, Pa. BR/TR, 5'11", 170 lbs. Deb: 4/17/14																													
1914	Buf-F	0	1	.000	3	3	0	0	0	10	18	16.2	2	7	6.3	0	0.0	4.50	74	.423	.505	-1	-1	104	215	-0.4	-1	0	-0.1

YEAR	TM/L	W	L	PCT	G	GS	CG	SHO	SV	IP	H	H/G	HR	BB	BB/G	SO	SO/G	ERA	/A	OAVG	OOBP	PR	/A	PF	CPI	WAT	PB	PD	TPI
■ CHUCK PORTER	Porter, Charles William b: 1/12/56, Baltimore, Md. BR/TR, 6'3", 187 lbs. Deb: 9/14/81																												
1981	Mil-A	0	0	—	3	0	0	0	0	4	6	13.5	0	1	2.3	1	2.3	4.50	78	.316	.350	-0	-0	95	95	0.0	0	-0	0.0
1982	Mil-A	0	0	—	3	0	0	0	0	4	3	6.8	0	1	2.3	3	6.8	4.50	84	.250	.308	-0	-0	92	67	0.0	0	0	0.0
1983	Mil-A	7	9	.438	25	21	6	1	0	134	162	10.9	9	38	2.6	76	5.1	4.50	82	.298	.339	-6	-12	91	100	-1.5	0	0	-1.0
1984	Mil-A	6	4	.600	17	12	1	0	0	81	92	10.2	8	12	1.3	48	5.3	3.89	95	.284	.307	1	-2	93	100	1.6	0	0	-0.1
1985	Mil-A	0	0	—	6	1	0	0	0	14	15	9.6	1	2	1.3	8	5.1	1.93	227	.273	.293	3	4	106	179	0.0	0	-0	0.4
Total	5	13	13	.500	54	34	7	1	0	237	278	10.6	18	54	2.1	136	5.2	4.14	90	.291	.326	-2	-10	93	104	0.1	0	0	-0.7
■ HENRY PORTER	Porter, Henry b: 6/1858, Vergennes, Vt. d: 12/30/06, Brockton, Mass. BR/TR, Deb: 9/27/1884																												
1884	Mil-U	3	3	.500	6	6	6	1	0	51	32	5.6	1	9	1.6	71	12.5	3.00	100	.185	.225	0	0	100	41	-1.1	1	0	0.1
1885	Bro-a	33	21	.611	54	54	53	2	0	482	427	8.0	11	107	2.0	197	3.7	2.78	122	.249	.293	25	33	105	97	11.0	-3	1	3.1
1886	Bro-a	27	19	.587	48	48	48	1	0	424	439	9.3	8	120	2.5	163	3.5	3.42	101	.277	.328	2	2	100	105	2.4	-9	-2	-0.7
1887	Bro-a	15	24	.385	40	40	38	1	0	340	416	11.0	6	96	2.5	74	2.0	4.21	101	.316	.362	3	1	99	106	-3.6	-2	-3	-0.2
1888	KC-a	18	37	.327	55	54	53	4	0	474	527	10.0	16	120	2.3	145	2.8	4.16	82	.295	.339	-58	-38	112	93	0.1	-13	4	-3.8
1889	KC-a	0	3	.000	4	4	3	0	0	23	52	20.3	0	14	5.5	9	3.5	12.52	33	.462	.521	-22	-21	109	81	-1.4	-1	0	-1.5
Total	6	96	107	.473	207	206	201	9	0	1794	1893	9.5	42	466	2.3	659	3.3	3.70	97	.283	.330	-50	-20	104	98	7.4	-27	2	-3.0
■ NED PORTER	Porter, Ned Swindell b: 7/6/05, Apalachicola, Fla. d: 6/30/68, Gainesville, Fla. BR/TR, 6', 173 lbs. Deb: 8/07/26																												
1926	NY-N	0	0	—	2	0	0	0	0	2	2	9.0	1	0	0.0	1	4.5	4.50	83	.250	.250	-0	-0	98	121	0.0	0	0	0.0
1927	NY-N	0	0	—	1	0	0	0	0	2	3	13.5	0	1	4.5	0	0.0	0.00	—	.333	.400	1	1	98	0	0.0	0	-0	0.1
Total	2	0	0	—	3	0	0	0	0	4	5	11.3	1	1	2.3	1	2.3	2.25	168	.294	.333	1	1	98	60	0.0	0	-0	0.1
■ ODIE PORTER	Porter, Odie Oscar b: 5/24/1877, Borden, Ind. d: 5/2/03, Borden, Ind. Deb: 6/16/02																												
1902	Phi-A	0	1	.000	1	1	1	0	0	8	12	13.5	0	5	5.6	2	2.3	3.38	112	.374	.458	0	0	106	191	-0.4	-0	0	0.1
■ BOB PORTERFIELD	Porterfield, Erwin Coolidge b: 8/10/23, Newport, Va. d: 4/12/80, Sealy, Tex. BR/TR, 6', 190 lbs. Deb: 8/08/48																												
1948	NY-A	5	3	.625	16	12	2	1	0	78	85	9.8	5	34	3.9	30	3.5	4.50	92	.273	.341	-2	-3	96	95	0.2	0	-1	-0.3
1949	NY-A	2	5	.286	12	8	3	0	0	58	53	8.2	3	29	4.5	25	3.9	4.03	101	.251	.335	1	0	97	94	-1.9	-2	-0	-0.1
1950	NY-A	1	1	.500	10	2	0	0	1	20	28	12.6	2	8	3.6	9	4.0	8.55	51	.341	.396	-9	-9	96	75	-0.1	0	0	-0.7
1951	NY-A	0	0	—	2	0	0	0	0	3	5	15.0	0	3	9.0	2	6.0	15.00	24	.385	.500	-4	-4	88	58	0.0	0	0	-0.2
	Was-A	9	8	.529	19	19	10	3	0	133	109	7.4	8	54	3.7	53	3.6	3.25	123	.224	.297	13	11	97	90	2.0	-3	-0	0.8
	Yr	9	8	.529	21	19	10	3	0	136	114	7.5	8	57	3.8	55	3.6	3.51	114	.228	.303	9	7	97	90	2.0	0	0	0.6
1952	Was-A	13	14	.481	31	29	15	3	0	231	222	8.6	7	85	3.3	80	3.1	2.73	135	.254	.320	24	25	100	120	-0.7	0	-3	2.4
1953	Was-A	**22**	10	.688	34	32	**24**	**9**	0	255	243	8.6	19	73	2.6	77	2.7	3.35	111	.257	.306	18	10	93	104	**6.9**	9	2	2.1
1954	Was-A	13	15	.464	32	31	**21**	2	0	244	249	9.2	14	77	2.8	82	3.0	3.32	111	.266	.318	11	10	99	106	1.1	-4	3	1.0
1955	Was-A	10	17	.370	30	27	8	2	0	178	197	10.0	14	54	2.7	74	3.7	4.45	84	.282	.329	-10	-14	94	92	0.6	1	-1	-1.3
1956	Bos-A	3	12	.200	25	18	4	1	0	126	127	9.1	21	64	4.6	53	3.8	5.14	82	.260	.345	-14	-13	102	92	-4.8	4	-1	-0.9
1957	Bos-A	4	4	.500	28	9	3	1	1	102	107	9.4	8	30	2.6	28	2.5	4.06	102	.272	.317	-3	1	109	94	-0.2	-0	1	0.2
1958	Bos-A	0	0	—	2	0	0	0	0	4	3	6.8	1	0	0.0	1	2.3	4.50	88	.214	.200	-0	-0	105	67	0.0	0	-0	0.0
	Pit-N	4	6	.400	37	6	2	1	5	88	78	8.0	7	19	1.9	39	4.0	3.27	113	.241	.278	7	4	94	85	-1.3	-1	0	0.3
1959	Pit-N	0	0	—	6	0	0	0	0	5	6	10.8	1	2	3.6	1	1.8	1.80	227	.286	.333	1	1	104	296	0.0	0	-0	0.1
	Chi-N	0	0	—	4	0	0	0	0	6	14	21.0	1	3	4.5	0	0.0	12.00	32	.424	.472	-5	-5	99	88	0.0	-0	0	-0.4
	Pit-N	1	2	.333	30	0	0	0	1	36	45	11.3	2	17	4.3	18	4.5	4.75	86	.321	.383	-3	-3	104	116	-0.4	-0	1	-0.1
	Yr	1	2	.333	40	0	0	0	1	47	65	12.4	4	22	4.2	19	3.6	5.36	76	.335	.392	-7	-7	103	116	-0.4	-0	1	-0.4
Total	12	87	97	.473	318	193	92	23	8	1567	1571	9.0	113	552	3.2	572	3.3	3.79	102	.263	.322	26	12	98	101	1.4	5	1	2.9
■ AL PORTO	Porto, Alfred "Lefty" b: 6/27/26, Heilwood, Pa. BL/TL, 5'11", 176 lbs. Deb: 4/22/48																												
1948	Phi-N	0	0	—	3	0	0	0	0	4	2	4.5	0	1	2.3	1	2.3	0.00	—	.143	.200	2	2	97	0	0.0	0	-0	0.2
■ ARNIE PORTOCARRERO	Portocarrero, Arnold Mario b: 7/5/31, New York, N.Y. d: 6/21/86, Kansas City, Kan. BR/TR, 6'3", 196 lbs. Deb: 4/18/54																												
1954	Phi-A	9	18	.333	34	33	16	1	0	248	233	8.5	25	114	4.1	132	4.8	4.06	96	.249	.324	-9	-5	105	95	0.1	-2	-4	-1.0
1955	KC-A	5	9	.357	24	20	4	1	0	111	109	8.8	12	67	5.4	34	2.8	4.78	88	.259	.356	-10	-7	106	97	-0.9	-2	-1	-0.8
1956	KC-A	0	1	.000	3	1	0	0	0	8	9	10.1	2	7	7.9	2	2.3	10.13	43	.300	.421	-5	-5	105	75	-0.4	-0	0	-0.4
1957	KC-A	4	9	.308	33	17	1	0	0	115	103	8.1	10	34	2.7	42	3.3	3.91	98	.240	.295	-2	-1	102	80	-1.3	-1	-1	-0.2
1958	Bal-A	15	11	.577	32	27	10	3	2	205	173	7.6	17	57	2.5	90	4.0	3.25	110	.229	.282	12	8	95	86	2.7	0	-3	0.5
1959	Bal-A	2	7	.222	27	14	1	0	0	90	107	10.7	10	32	3.2	23	2.3	6.80	56	.294	.346	-29	-30	98	73	-2.4	-2	1	-2.9
1960	Bal-A	3	2	.600	13	5	1	0	0	41	44	9.7	6	9	2.0	15	3.3	4.39	89	.275	.312	-2	-2	101	95	0.1	-1	-1	-0.3
Total	7	38	57	.400	166	117	33	5	2	818	778	8.6	82	320	3.5	338	3.7	4.31	89	.252	.318	-46	-42	101	88	-2.1	-9	-9	-5.1
■ MARK PORTUGAL	Portugal, Mark Steven b: 10/30/62, Los Angeles, Cal. BR/TR, 6', 170 lbs. Deb: 8/14/85																												
1985	Min-A	1	3	.250	6	4	0	0	0	24	24	9.0	3	14	5.3	12	4.5	5.63	77	.270	.362	-4	-3	104	91	-0.9	0	1	-0.1
1986	Min-A	6	10	.375	27	15	3	0	1	113	112	8.9	10	50	4.0	67	5.3	4.30	106	.265	.339	-1	3	109	99	-1.2	0	-0	0.3
1987	Min-A	1	3	.250	13	7	0	0	0	44	58	11.9	13	24	4.9	28	5.7	7.77	55	.326	.407	-16	-17	96	101	-1.0	0	0	-1.4
1988	Min-A	3	3	.500	26	0	0	0	3	58	60	9.3	11	17	2.6	31	4.8	4.50	93	.274	.322	-3	-2	105	109	-0.2	0	-2	-0.3
Total	4	11	19	.367	72	26	3	0	4	239	254	9.6	37	105	4.0	138	5.2	5.12	86	.280	.351	-25	-19	105	101	-3.3	0	-1	-1.5
■ BILL POSEDEL	Posedel, William John "Sailor Bill" or "Barnacle Bill" b: 8/2/06, San Francisco, Cal. BR/TR, 5'11", 175 lbs. Deb: 4/23/38 C																												
1938	Bro-N	8	9	.471	33	17	6	1	1	140	178	11.4	14	46	3.0	49	3.2	5.66	64	.311	.359	-29	-32	96	94	0.1	1	-1	-3.0
1939	Bos-N	15	13	.536	33	29	18	5	0	221	221	9.0	8	78	3.2	73	3.0	3.91	93	.268	.323	0	-6	93	93	3.3	-3	-1	-1.0
1940	Bos-N	12	17	.414	35	32	18	0	1	233	263	10.2	16	81	3.1	86	3.3	4.13	94	.288	.342	-7	-6	101	110	-0.5	1	-0	-0.5
1941	Bos-N	4	4	.500	18	9	3	0	0	57	61	9.6	6	30	4.7	10	1.6	4.89	71	.279	.364	-8	-9	96	102	0.7	2	-0	-0.6
1946	Bos-N	2	0	1.000	19	0	0	0	4	28	34	10.9	4	13	4.2	9	2.9	7.07	45	.304	.370	-11	-12	94	78	1.0	-0	-0	-1.2
Total	5	41	43	.488	138	87	45	6	6	679	757	10.0	48	248	3.3	227	3.0	4.56	81	.286	.343	-56	-65	97	99	4.6	1	-3	-6.3
■ BOB POSER	Poser, John Falk b: 3/16/10, Columbus, Wis. BL/TR, 6', 173 lbs. Deb: 4/17/32																												
1932	Chi-A	0	0	—	1	0	0	0	0	1	3	27.0	0	2	18.0	1	9.0	18.00	23	.600	.714	-2	-2	91	112	0.0	-0	0	0.0
1935	StL-A	1	1	.500	4	1	0	0	0	14	26	16.7	0	4	2.6	1	0.6	9.00	54	.400	.435	-7	-6	110	83	0.1	0	-0	-0.5
Total	2	1	1	.500	5	1	0	0	0	15	29	17.4	0	6	3.6	2	1.2	9.60	50	.414	.461	-9	-8	109	85	0.1	0	-0	-0.5
■ LOU POSSEHL	Possehl, Louis Thomas b: 4/12/26, Chicago, Ill. BR/TR, 6'2", 180 lbs. Deb: 8/25/46																												
1946	Phi-N	1	2	.333	4	4	0	0	0	14	19	12.2	0	10	6.4	4	2.6	5.79	58	.339	.441	-4	-4	98	110	-0.3	-0	0	-0.3
1947	Phi-N	0	0	—	2	0	0	0	0	4	5	11.3	0	0	0.0	1	2.3	4.50	92	.385	.375	-0	-0	102	135	0.0	0	0	0.1
1948	Phi-N	1	1	.500	3	2	1	0	0	15	17	10.2	3	4	2.4	7	4.2	4.80	80	.304	.350	-1	-2	97	119	0.1	0	0	-0.1
1951	Phi-N	0	1	.000	2	1	0	0	0	6	9	13.5	0	3	4.5	6	9.0	6.00	64	.333	.400	-1	-1	97	93	-0.4	-0	0	0.0
1952	Phi-N	0	1	.000	4	1	0	0	0	13	12	8.3	3	7	4.8	4	2.8	4.85	76	.235	.328	-2	-2	99	97	-0.4	-0	-0	-0.1
Total	5	2	5	.286	15	8	1	0	0	52	62	10.7	6	24	4.2	22	3.8	5.19	71	.305	.379	-8	-9	98	109	-1.0	-0	0	-0.4
■ NELLIE POTT	Pott, Nelson Adolph "Lefty" b: 7/16/1899, Cincinnati, Ohio d: 12/3/63, Cincinnati, Ohio BL/TL, 6', 185 lbs. Deb: 4/19/22																												
1922	Cle-A	0	0	—	2	0	0	0	0	2	7	31.5	1	2	9.0	0	0.0	31.50	13	.583	.600	-6	-6	103	69	0.0	0	0	-0.4
■ DYKES POTTER	Potter, Maryland Dykes b: 9/7/10, Ashland, Ky. BR/TR, 6', 185 lbs. Deb: 4/26/38																												
1938	Bro-N	0	0	—	2	0	0	0	0	2	4	18.0	1	0	0.0	1	4.5	4.50	81	.400	.400	-0	-0	96	236	0.0	0	0	0.0
■ NELS POTTER	Potter, Nelson Thomas "Nellie" b: 8/23/11, Mt.Morris, Ill. BL/TR, 5'11", 180 lbs. Deb: 4/25/36																												
1936	StL-N	0	0	—	1	0	0	0	0	1	0	0.0	0	0	0.0	0	0.0	0.00	—	.000	.000	0	0	95	0	0.0	0	0	0.0
1938	Phi-A	2	12	.143	35	9	4	0	5	111	139	11.3	15	49	4.0	43	3.5	6.49	77	.306	.368	-21	-18	105	91	-4.2	1	-1	-1.5
1939	Phi-A	8	12	.400	41	25	9	0	2	196	258	11.8	26	88	4.0	60	2.8	6.61	71	.321	.381	-43	-41	102	97	0.7	-1	-0	-3.6
1940	Phi-A	9	14	.391	31	25	13	0	0	201	213	9.5	18	71	3.2	73	3.3	4.43	98	.269	.325	-1	-2	99	95	0.8	2	-0	0.0
1941	Phi-A	1	1	.500	10	3	1	0	2	23	35	13.7	3	16	6.3	7	2.7	9.39	45	.337	.421	-13	-13	103	79	0.1	0	0	-1.1
	Bos-A	2	0	1.000	10	0	0	0	0	20	21	9.4	0	16	7.2	6	2.7	4.50	93	.284	.402	-1	-1	101	116	1.0	-0	-0	0.0
	Yr	3	1	.750	20	3	1	0	2	43	56	11.7	3	32	6.7	13	2.7	7.12	60	.315	.413	-14	-14	102	116	1.1	0	-0	-1.1

YEAR	TM/L	W	L	PCT	G	GS	CG	SHO	SV	IP	H	H/G	HR	BB	BB/G	SO	SO/G	ERA	/A	OAVG	OOBP	PR	/A	PF	CPI	WAT	PB	PD	TPI
1943	StL-A	10	5	.667	33	13	8	0	1	168	146	7.8	11	54	2.9	80	4.3	2.79	119	.235	.294	10	10	101	106	2.9	-1	1	1.1
1944	StL-A	19	7	.731	32	29	16	3	0	232	211	8.2	6	70	2.7	91	3.5	2.83	121	.244	.295	15	15	100	97	5.3	-2	2	1.7
1945	StL-A	15	11	.577	32	32	21	3	0	255	212	7.5	10	68	2.4	129	4.6	2.47	156	.226	.273	25	39	114	93	1.3	3	-1	5.0
1946	StL-A	8	9	.471	23	19	10	0	0	145	152	9.4	9	59	3.7	72	4.5	3.72	94	.268	.334	-4	-4	100	104	0.7	3	-1	-0.1
1947	StL-A	4	10	.286	32	10	3	0	2	123	130	9.5	13	44	3.2	65	4.8	4.02	97	.277	.333	-4	-2	106	110	-1.8	3	1	0.3
1948	StL-A	1	1	.500	2	2	0	0	0	10	11	9.9	1	4	3.6	4	3.6	5.40	86	.262	.347	-1	-1	109	84	0.2	1	1	0.0
	Phi-A	2	2	.500	8	0	0	0	1	18	17	8.5	1	5	2.5	13	6.5	4.00	109	.250	.293	1	1	102	80	-0.1	0	-0	0.1
	Yr	3	3	.500	10	2	0	0	1	28	28	9.0	2	9	2.9	17	5.5	4.50	99	.250	.298	-1	-0	104	80	0.1	1	0	0.1
	Bos-N	5	2	.714	18	7	3	0	2	85	77	8.2	4	8	0.8	47	5.0	2.33	168	.245	.256	15	15	99	106	1.1	3	1	2.0
1949	Bos-N	6	11	.353	41	3	1	0	7	97	99	9.2	6	30	2.8	57	5.3	4.18	94	.265	.311	-1	-3	97	88	-2.4	-0	1	-0.2
Total	12	92	97	.487	349	177	89	6	22	1685	1721	9.2	123	582	3.1	747	4.0	4.00	100	.265	.321	-24	-3	103	98	5.6	11	3	3.7
SQUIRE POTTER Potter, Squire b: 3/18/02, Flatwoods, Ky. d: 1/27/83, Ashland, Ky. BR/TR, 6'1", 185 lbs. Deb: 8/07/23																													
1923	Was-A	0	0	—	1	0	0	0	0	3	11	33.0	0	4	12.0	1	3.0	21.00	18	.688	.750	-6	-6	95	104	0.0	0	-0	-0.3
BILL POUNDS Pounds, Jeared Wells b: 3/11/1878, Paterson, N.J. d: 7/7/36, Paterson, N.J. BR/TR, 5'10.5", 178 lbs. Deb: 5/02/03																													
1903	Cle-A	0	0	—	1	0	0	0	0	5	8	14.4	0	0	0.0	2	3.6	10.80	26	.386	.386	-4	-4	95	49	0.0	0	0	-0.3
	Bro-N	0	0	—	1	0	0	0	0	6	8	12.0	1	2	3.0	2	3.0	6.00	55	.346	.398	-2	-2	102	98	0.0	1	0	0.0
ABNER POWELL Powell, Charles Abner "Ab" b: 12/15/1860, Shenandoah, Pa. d: 8/7/53, New Orleans, La. BR/TR, 5'7", 160 lbs. Deb: 8/04/1884																													
1884	Was-U	6	12	.333	18	17	14	1	0	134	135	9.1	3	19	1.3	78	5.2	3.43	86	.267	.293	-6	-7	98	88	-2.0	3	0	-0.5
1886	Bal-a	2	5	.286	7	7	7	0	0	60	66	9.9	2	26	3.9	15	2.3	5.10	64	.290	.363	-11	-12	94	87	-0.7	-0	0	-1.0
	Cin-a	0	1	.000	4	1	1	0	0	15	16	9.6	0	9	5.4	4	2.4	4.80	69	.283	.382	-2	-2	96	94	-0.4	0	0	-0.1
	Yr	2	6	.250	11	8	8	0	0	75	82	9.8	2	35	4.2	19	2.3	5.04	65	.289	.367	-13	-15	94	94	-1.1	-0	0	-1.1
Total	2	8	18	.308	29	25	22	1	0	209	217	9.3	5	54	2.3	97	4.2	4.00	77	.275	.321	-19	-22	97	88	-3.1	3	0	-1.6
DENNIS POWELL Powell, Dennis Clay b: 8/13/63, Moultrie, Ga. BR/TL, 6'3", 175 lbs. Deb: 7/07/85																													
1985	LA-N	1	1	.500	16	2	0	0	1	29	30	9.3	7	13	4.0	19	5.9	5.28	63	.263	.331	-5	-6	92	101	0.0	-0	0	-0.6
1986	LA-N	2	7	.222	27	6	0	0	0	65	65	9.0	5	25	3.5	31	4.3	4.29	82	.272	.335	-4	-6	95	98	-2.2	1	-1	-0.4
1987	Sea-A	1	3	.250	16	3	0	0	0	34	32	8.5	3	15	4.0	17	4.5	3.18	145	.250	.320	5	5	103	121	-0.9	0	0	0.5
1988	Sea-A	1	3	.250	12	2	0	0	0	19	29	13.7	2	11	5.2	15	7.1	8.53	50	.363	.442	-10	-9	108	92	-0.7	0	0	-0.8
Total	4	5	14	.263	71	13	0	0	1	147	156	9.6	17	64	3.9	82	5.0	4.78	80	.278	.346	-14	-16	98	103	-3.8	1	0	-1.3
GROVER POWELL Powell, Grover David b: 10/10/40, Sayre, Pa. d: 5/21/85, Raleigh, N.C. BL/TL, 5'10", 175 lbs. Deb: 7/13/63																													
1963	NY-N	1	1	.500	20	4	1	1	0	50	37	6.7	2	32	5.8	39	7.0	2.70	126	.202	.321	3	4	104	103	0.3	1	0	0.5
JACK POWELL Powell, John Joseph "Red" b: 7/9/1874, Bloomington, Ill. d: 10/17/44, Chicago, Ill. BR/TR, 5'11", 195 lbs. Deb: 6/23/1897																													
1897	Cle-N	15	10	.600	27	26	24	2	0	225	245	9.8	2	62	2.5	61	2.4	3.16	150	.299	.348	29	39	110	108	2.3	-5	0	3.3
1898	Cle-N	23	15	.605	42	41	36	**6**	0	342	328	8.6	8	112	2.9	93	2.4	3.00	114	.273	.335	23	16	95	101	3.3	-6	-2	0.7
1899	StL-N	23	19	.548	48	43	**40**	2	0	373	433	10.4	15	85	2.1	87	2.1	3.52	117	.315	.354	14	25	107	109	-0.4	-2	-2	2.0
1900	StL-N	17	16	.515	38	37	28	3	0	288	325	10.2	9	77	2.4	77	2.4	4.44	78	.308	.355	-24	-32	93	85	2.0	10	1	-1.9
1901	StL-N	19	19	.500	**45**	37	33	2	**3**	338	351	9.3	14	50	1.3	133	3.5	3.54	89	.291	.323	-8	-15	95	89	-1.9	1	-5	-1.8
1902	StL-A	22	17	.564	42	39	36	3	**2**	328	320	8.8	12	93	2.6	137	3.8	3.21	113	.279	.334	13	16	102	98	-0.3	3	-5	1.0
1903	StL-A	15	19	.441	38	34	33	4	**2**	306	294	8.6	11	58	1.7	169	5.0	2.91	97	.274	.312	1	-3	96	99	-1.1	2	-1	-0.4
1904	NY-A	23	19	.548	47	45	38	3	0	390	340	7.8	15	92	2.1	202	4.7	2.45	117	.257	.305	6	19	111	105	-2.7	-4	-6	1.5
1905	NY-A	8	13	.381	37	23	13	1	1	203	214	9.5	4	57	2.5	84	3.7	3.50	77	.296	.347	-19	-18	103	101	-2.3	1	-6	-2.4
	StL-A	2	1	.667	3	3	3	0	0	28	22	7.1	0	5	1.6	12	3.9	1.61	154	.238	.278	3	3	93	110	0.7	-0	-1	0.2
	Yr	10	14	.417	40	26	16	1	1	231	236	9.2	4	62	2.4	96	3.7	3.27	82	.289	.340	-16	-15	101	110	-1.6	1	-7	-2.2
1906	StL-A	13	14	.481	28	26	25	3	1	244	196	7.2	2	55	2.0	132	4.9	1.77	147	.243	.291	25	22	97	111	-0.8	3	-4	2.1
1907	StL-A	13	16	.448	32	31	27	4	1	256	229	8.1	4	62	2.2	96	3.4	2.67	93	.263	.311	-4	-5	98	91	-0.1	-3	-3	-0.8
1908	StL-A	16	13	.552	33	32	23	5	1	256	208	7.3	1	47	1.7	85	3.0	2.11	115	.231	.274	8	9	102	97	0.2	2	-6	0.3
1909	StL-A	12	16	.429	34	27	18	4	3	239	221	8.3	1	42	1.6	82	3.1	2.11	111	.250	.287	10	6	95	98	0.6	0	-4	0.2
1910	StL-A	7	11	.389	21	18	8	3	0	129	121	8.4	0	28	2.0	52	3.6	2.30	110	.250	.292	3	3	101	97	1.2	-2	-4	-0.1
1911	StL-A	8	19	.296	31	27	18	1	1	208	224	9.7	7	44	1.9	52	2.3	3.29	101	.262	.304	1	1	100	82	0.0	-3	-5	-0.6
1912	StL-A	9	16	.360	32	27	19	0	0	235	248	9.5	5	52	2.0	67	2.6	3.10	111	.276	.318	6	9	103	106	0.4	-0	-5	0.4
Total	16	245	253	.492	578	516	422	46	15	4388	4319	8.9	110	1021	2.1	1621	3.3	2.97	106	.275	.320	88	93	100	99	1.1	-1	-58	3.7
JACK POWELL Powell, Reginald Bertrand b: 8/17/1891, Holcomb, Mo. d: 3/12/30, Memphis, Tenn. TR, 6'2", Deb: 6/14/13																													
1913	StL-A	0	0	—	2	0	0	0	0	2	1	4.5	0	2	9.0	0	0.0	0.00	—	.143	.333	1	1	98	0	0.0	0	1	0.1
BILL POWELL Powell, William Burris "Big Bill" b: 5/8/1885, Richmond, Va. d: 9/28/67, E.Liverpool, Ohio BR/TR, 6'2.5", 182 lbs. Deb: 09																													
1909	Pit-N	0	1	.000	3	1	0	0	0	7	7	9.0	0	6	7.7	2	2.6	3.86	67	.292	.452	-1	-1	99	142	-0.4	0	0	0.0
1910	Pit-N	4	6	.400	12	9	4	2	0	75	65	7.8	0	34	4.1	23	2.8	2.40	139	.242	.338	5	8	110	120	-1.4	1	1	1.1
1912	Chi-N	0	0	—	1	0	0	0	0	2	2	9.0	0	1	4.5	0	0.0	9.00	39	.250	.333	-1	-1	102	31	0.0	0	0	0.0
1913	Cin-N	0	1	.000	1	1	0	0	0	⅓	2	54.0	0	2	54.0	0	0.0	54.00	—	1.000	.800	-2	-2	104	86	-0.4	0	0	-0.1
Total	4	4	8	.333	17	11	4	2	0	84	76	8.1	0	43	4.6	25	2.7	2.89	113	.251	.354	1	4	109	120	-2.2	1	2	1.0
TED POWER Power, Ted Henry b: 1/31/55, Guthrie, Okla. BR/TR, 6'4", 215 lbs. Deb: 9/09/81																													
1981	LA-N	1	3	.250	5	2	0	0	0	14	16	10.3	0	7	4.5	7	4.5	3.21	104	.286	.364	0	0	96	135	-1.0	-0	-0	0.0
1982	LA-N	1	1	.500	12	4	0	0	0	34	38	10.1	4	23	6.1	15	4.0	6.62	51	.288	.381	-11	-12	94	85	0.0	-1	0	-1.2
1983	Cin-N	5	6	.455	49	6	1	0	2	111	120	9.7	10	49	4.0	57	4.6	4.54	83	.286	.354	-11	-9	104	104	0.0	-1	-2	-1.2
1984	Cin-N	9	7	.563	**78**	0	0	0	11	109	93	7.7	4	46	3.8	81	6.7	2.81	137	.237	.305	10	13	107	109	2.0	-0	0	1.3
1985	Cin-N	8	6	.571	64	0	0	0	27	80	65	7.3	2	45	5.1	42	4.7	2.70	140	.227	.325	8	10	105	116	0.3	0	-2	0.8
1986	Cin-N	10	6	.625	56	10	0	0	1	129	115	8.0	13	52	3.6	95	6.6	3.70	105	.245	.313	0	3	104	101	1.7	0	-0	0.3
1987	Cin-N	10	13	.435	34	34	2	1	0	204	213	9.4	28	71	3.1	133	5.9	4.50	94	.267	.324	-9	-7	103	97	-2.0	0	-3	-0.8
1988	KC-A	5	6	.455	22	12	2	2	0	80	98	11.0	7	30	3.4	44	4.9	5.96	68	.305	.364	-18	-17	103	88	-0.7	0	-0	-1.6
	Det-A	1	1	.500	4	2	0	0	0	19	23	10.9	1	8	3.8	13	6.2	5.68	66	.307	.373	-4	-4	94	89	0.0	0	0	-0.3
	Yr	6	7	.462	26	14	2	2	0	99	121	11.0	8	38	3.5	57	5.2	5.91	68	.300	.359	-21	-21	101	89	-0.7	0	-0	-1.9
Total	8	50	49	.505	324	70	5	3	41	780	781	9.0	69	331	3.8	487	5.6	4.20	93	.265	.333	-35	-24	103	101	0.3	-2	-8	-2.7
JIM POWERS Powers, James T. b: 1868, New York, N.Y. 5'10", 150 lbs. Deb: 4/18/1890																													
1890	BB-a	1	2	.333	4	2	2	0	0	30	38	11.4	1	16	4.8	3	0.9	5.70	70	.325	.407	-6	-6	103	97	0.1	-1	0	-0.4
IKE POWERS Powers, John Lloyd b: 3/13/06, Hancock, Md. d: 12/22/68, Hancock, Md. BR/TR, 6'0.5", 188 lbs. Deb: 7/26/27																													
1927	Phi-A	1	1	.500	11	1	0	0	0	26	26	9.0	1	7	2.4	3	1.0	4.50	87	.271	.300	-1	-2	95	76	-0.1	1	-0	0.0
1928	Phi-A	1	0	1.000	9	0	0	0	2	12	8	6.0	1	10	7.5	4	3.0	4.50	89	.222	.373	-1	-1	99	107	0.5	0	1	0.0
Total	2	2	1	.667	20	1	0	0	2	38	34	8.1	2	17	4.0	7	1.7	4.50	88	.258	.323	-2	-2	96	86	0.4	1	1	0.0
WILLIE PRALL Prall, Wilfred Anthony b: 4/20/50, Hackensack, N.J. BL/TL, 6'3", 200 lbs. Deb: 9/03/75																													
1975	Chi-N	0	2	.000	3	3	0	0	0	15	21	12.6	1	8	4.8	7	4.2	8.40	46	.339	.408	-8	-8	105	74	-0.9	-0	0	-0.6
AL PRATT Pratt, Albert George "Uncle Al" b: 11/19/1848, Allegheny, Pa. d: 11/21/37, Pittsburgh, Pa. 5'7", 140 lbs. Deb: 5/04/1871 M																													
1871	Cle-n	10	18	.357	28																								
1872	Cle-n	3	9	.250	13																								
Total	2 n	13	27	.325	41																								
JOHN PREGENZER Pregenzer, John Arthur b: 8/2/35, Burlington, Wis. BR/TR, 6'5", 220 lbs. Deb: 4/20/63																													
1963	SF-N	0	0	—	6	0	0	0	1	9	8	8.0	0	8	8.0	5	5.0	5.00	62	.242	.395	-2	-2	94	89	0.0	0	0	-0.1
1964	SF-N	2	0	1.000	13	0	0	0	0	18	21	10.5	1	11	5.5	8	4.0	5.00	70	.296	.384	-3	-3	99	108	1.0	0	-0	-0.2
Total	2	2	0	1.000	19	0	0	0	1	27	29	9.7	1	19	6.3	13	4.3	5.00	67	.279	.388	-5	-5	97	102	1.0	0	0	-0.3

YEAR	TM/L	W	L	PCT	G	GS	CG	SHO	SV	IP	H	H/G	HR	BB	BB/G	SO	SO/G	ERA	/A	OAVG	OOBP	PR	/A	PF	CPI	WAT	PB	PD	TPI
■ JIM PRENDERGAST	Prendergast, James Bartholomew b: 8/23/17, Brooklyn, N.Y. BL/TL, 6'1", 208 lbs. Deb: 4/25/48																												
1948	Bos-N	1	1	.500	10	2	0	0	1	17	30	15.9	1	5	2.6	3	1.6	10.06	39	.380	.417	-12	-12	99	71	-0.1	-1	0	-1.0
■ MIKE PRENDERGAST	Prendergast, Michael Thomas b: 12/15/1888, Arlington, Ill. d: 11/18/67, Omaha, Neb. BR/TR, 5'9.5", 165 lbs. Deb: 4/26/14																												
1914	Chi-F	5	9	.357	30	19	7	1	0	136	131	8.7	6	40	2.6	71	4.7	2.38	120	.255	.313	12	7	89	129	-2.6	-2	-1	0.4
1915	Chi-F	14	12	.538	42	30	16	3	0	254	220	7.8	6	67	2.4	95	3.4	2.48	116	.240	.295	16	11	95	103	-0.6	-7	1	0.5
1916	Chi-N	6	11	.353	35	10	4	2	2	152	127	7.5	5	23	1.4	56	3.3	2.31	133	.228	.253	5	13	117	79	-1.7	-2	-1	1.3
1917	Chi-N	3	6	.333	35	8	1	0	1	99	112	10.2	6	21	1.9	43	3.9	3.36	84	.302	.324	-7	-6	105	123	-1.3	1	-0	-0.5
1918	Phi-N	13	14	.481	33	30	20	0	1	252	257	9.2	6	46	1.6	41	1.5	2.89	106	.273	.295	-4	5	111	103	1.1	-8	-2	-0.4
1919	Phi-N	0	1	.000	5	0	0	0	0	15	20	12.0	0	10	6.0	5	3.0	8.40	38	.351	.413	-9	-9	109	77	-0.4	0	0	-0.7
Total	6	41	53	.436	180	97	48	6	4	908	867	8.6	29	207	2.1	311	3.1	2.75	109	.258	.297	13	24	104	105	-5.5	-17	-3	0.6
■ GEORGE PRENTISS	Prentiss, George Pepper (a.k.a. George Pepper Wilson 1901) b: 6/10/1876, Wilmington, Del. d: 9/8/02, Wilmington, Del. BB, 5'11", 175 lbs. Deb: 9/23/01																												
1901	Bos-A	1	0	1.000	2	1	1	0	0	10	7	6.3	0	6	5.4	0	0.0	1.80	192	.214	.336	2	2	94	128	0.5	1	0	0.2
1902	Bos-A	2	2	.500	7	4	3	0	0	41	55	12.1	0	10	2.2	9	2.0	5.27	67	.348	.387	-8	-8	98	87	-0.1	1	0	-0.6
	Bal-A	0	1	.000	2	2	0	0	0	7	14	18.0	1	5	6.4	1	1.3	10.29	36	.443	.519	-5	-5	104	100	-0.4	-1	-0	-0.4
	Yr	2	3	.400	9	6	3	0	0	48	69	12.9	1	15	2.8	10	1.9	6.00	59	.364	.410	-13	-13	99	100	-0.5	1	-0	-1.0
Total	2	3	3	.500	11	7	4	0	0	58	76	11.8	1	21	3.3	10	1.6	5.28	67	.342	.398	-11	-11	98	96	0.0	1	-0	-0.8
■ JOE PRESKO	Presko, Joseph Edward "Little Joe" b: 10/7/28, Kansas City, Mo. BR/TR, 5'9.5", 165 lbs. Deb: 5/03/51																												
1951	StL-N	7	4	.636	15	12	5	0	2	89	86	8.7	9	20	2.0	38	3.8	3.44	116	.251	.294	5	5	101	96	1.4	-1	-1	0.3
1952	StL-N	7	10	.412	28	18	5	1	0	147	140	8.6	15	57	3.5	63	3.9	4.04	90	.247	.314	-5	-7	97	92	-2.5	-2	-1	-0.9
1953	StL-N	6	13	.316	34	25	4	0	1	162	165	9.2	19	65	3.6	56	3.1	5.00	86	.261	.332	-13	-12	101	86	-4.1	1	-1	-1.1
1954	StL-N	4	9	.308	37	6	1	1	0	72	97	12.1	14	41	5.1	36	4.5	6.88	59	.327	.413	-22	-22	100	104	-2.3	0	-0	-2.1
1957	Det-A	1	1	.500	7	0	0	0	0	11	10	8.2	0	4	3.3	3	2.5	1.64	248	.278	.326	3	3	107	243	0.0	-0	-0	0.3
1958	Det-A	0	0	—	7	0	0	0	2	11	13	10.6	0	1	0.8	6	4.9	3.27	119	.317	.326	1	1	103	119	0.0	0	-0	0.1
Total	6	25	37	.403	128	61	15	2	5	492	511	9.3	57	188	3.4	202	3.7	4.59	87	.267	.333	-32	-33	100	96	-7.5	-1	-4	-3.4
■ TOT PRESSNELL	Pressnell, Forest Charles b: 8/8/06, Findlay, Ohio BR/TR, 5'10", 175 lbs. Deb: 4/21/38																												
1938	Bro-N	11	14	.440	43	19	6	1	3	192	209	9.8	11	56	2.6	57	2.7	3.56	102	.276	.327	5	1	96	111	-0.6	-1	-1	0.0
1939	Bro-N	9	7	.563	31	18	10	2	2	157	171	9.8	8	33	1.9	43	2.5	4.01	104	.273	.306	-2	2	106	85	0.3	-1	0	0.2
1940	Bro-N	6	5	.545	24	4	1	1	2	68	58	7.7	4	17	2.3	21	2.8	3.71	111	.221	.270	1	3	106	66	-0.2	-2	-1	0.0
1941	Chi-N	5	3	.625	29	1	0	0	1	70	69	8.9	2	23	3.0	27	3.5	3.09	110	.253	.319	**4**	2	94	105	1.3	0	-1	0.2
1942	Chi-N	1	1	.500	27	0	0	0	4	39	40	9.2	5	5	1.2	9	2.1	5.54	58	.260	.298	-10	-10	98	69	0.1	1	-0	-0.8
Total	5	32	30	.516	154	42	17	4	12	526	547	9.4	30	134	2.3	157	2.7	3.80	100	.264	.310	-1	-1	100	94	0.9	-3	-2	-0.4
■ JOE PRICE	Price, Joseph Walter b: 11/29/56, Inglewood, Cal. BR/TL, 6'4", 220 lbs. Deb: 6/14/80																												
1980	Cin-N	7	3	.700	24	13	2	0	0	111	95	7.7	10	37	3.0	44	3.6	3.57	102	.236	.297	1	1	101	89	1.7	-2	-1	-0.1
1981	Cin-N	6	1	.857	41	0	0	0	4	54	42	7.0	3	18	3.0	41	6.8	2.50	140	.222	.278	6	6	101	105	2.3	-0	1	0.7
1982	Cin-N	3	4	.429	59	1	0	0	3	73	73	9.0	7	32	3.9	71	8.8	2.84	132	.263	.343	6	7	104	150	0.3	0	-1	0.7
1983	Cin-N	10	6	.625	21	21	5	0	0	144	118	7.4	12	46	2.9	83	5.2	2.88	131	.225	.282	12	14	104	95	2.7	-1	-0	1.4
1984	Cin-N	7	13	.350	30	30	3	1	0	172	176	9.2	19	61	3.2	129	6.8	4.19	92	.261	.320	-11	-6	107	95	-2.0	-1	-3	-0.9
1985	Cin-N	2	2	.500	26	8	0	0	1	65	59	8.2	10	23	3.2	52	7.2	3.88	97	.242	.299	-2	-1	105	98	-0.1	-1	-1	-0.2
1986	Cin-N	1	2	.333	25	2	0	0	0	42	49	10.5	5	22	4.7	30	6.4	5.36	72	.293	.366	-8	-7	104	100	-0.5	0	-1	-0.7
1987	SF-N	2	2	.500	20	0	0	0	1	35	19	4.9	5	13	3.3	42	10.8	2.57	150	.154	.241	6	5	95	69	-0.1	-0	-0	0.5
1988	SF-N	1	6	.143	38	3	0	0	4	62	59	8.6	5	27	3.9	49	7.1	3.92	82	.249	.323	-3	-5	93	96	-2.5	-0	-0	-0.5
Total	9	39	39	.500	284	78	10	1	13	758	690	8.2	76	279	3.3	541	6.4	3.54	105	.243	.307	7	15	103	99	1.8	-5	-6	0.9
■ WILLIAM PRICE	Price, William b: Philadelphia, Pa. Deb: 4/27/1890																												
1890	Phi-a	1	0	1.000	1	1	1	0	0	9	6	6.0	0	7	7.0	1	1.0	2.00	196	.202	.355	2	2	101	149	0.5	-0	0	0.2
■ BOB PRIDDY	Priddy, Robert Simpson b: 12/10/39, Pittsburgh, Pa. BR/TR, 6'1", 200 lbs. Deb: 9/20/62																												
1962	Pit-N	1	0	1.000	2	0	0	0	0	3	4	12.0	0	1	3.0	1	3.0	3.00	133	.308	.357	0	0	101	141	0.5	0	0	0.0
1964	Pit-N	1	2	.333	19	0	0	0	1	34	35	9.3	2	15	4.0	23	6.1	3.97	90	.282	.347	-2	-2	101	115	-0.4	0	-1	-0.2
1965	SF-N	1	0	1.000	8	0	0	0	0	10	6	5.4	1	2	1.8	7	6.3	1.80	215	.176	.211	2	2	109	89	0.5	-0	0	0.2
1966	SF-N	6	3	.667	38	3	0	0	1	91	88	8.7	8	28	2.8	51	5.0	3.96	88	.259	.314	-4	-5	97	93	1.0	0	-1	-0.5
1967	Was-A	3	7	.300	46	8	1	0	4	110	98	8.0	12	33	2.7	57	4.7	3.44	98	.240	.292	-3	-1	104	98	-1.8	1	1	0.2
1968	Chi-A	3	11	.214	35	18	2	0	0	114	106	8.4	14	41	3.2	66	5.2	3.63	84	.244	.309	-8	-8	102	103	-3.4	-1	-2	-1.0
1969	Chi-A	0	0	—	4	0	0	0	0	8	10	11.3	2	2	2.3	5	5.6	4.50	88	.303	.333	-1	-0	110	129	0.0	0	0	0.0
	Cal-A	0	1	.000	15	0	0	0	0	26	24	8.3	4	7	2.4	15	5.2	4.85	76	.242	.287	-4	-3	101	73	-0.4	0	0	-0.3
	Yr	0	1	.000	19	0	0	0	0	34	34	9.0	6	9	2.4	20	5.3	4.76	78	.258	.299	-4	-4	103	73	-0.4	0	0	-0.3
	Atl-N	0	0	—	1	0	0	0	0	2	1	4.5	0	1	4.5	1	4.5	0.00	—	.143	.250	1	1	103	0	0.0	0	0	0.1
1970	Atl-N	5	5	.500	41	0	0	0	8	73	75	9.2	9	24	3.0	32	3.9	5.42	78	.269	.326	-11	-10	105	81	0.3	0	1	-0.8
1971	Atl-N	4	9	.308	40	0	0	0	4	64	71	10.0	8	44	6.2	36	5.1	4.22	91	.289	.388	-5	-3	111	136	-2.6	0	1	-0.1
Total	9	24	38	.387	249	29	3	0	18	535	518	8.7	60	198	3.3	294	4.9	4.00	88	.257	.320	-34	-28	103	100	-6.3	1	-1	-2.4
■ RAY PRIM	Prim, Raymond Lee "Pop" b: 12/30/06, Salitpa, Ala. BR/TL, 6', 178 lbs. Deb: 9/24/33																												
1933	Was-A	0	1	.000	2	1	0	0	0	14	13	8.4	0	2	1.3	6	3.9	3.21	124	.232	.254	2	1	93	58	-0.4	-1	1	0.1
1934	Was-A	0	2	.000	8	1	0	0	0	15	19	11.4	1	8	4.8	3	1.8	6.60	70	.339	.403	-4	-3	102	100	-0.9	-0	0	-0.2
1935	Phi-N	3	4	.429	29	6	1	0	0	73	110	13.6	4	15	1.8	27	3.3	5.79	81	.340	.362	-14	-9	117	95	0.1	-3	-0	-1.0
1943	Chi-N	4	3	.571	29	5	0	0	1	60	67	10.1	2	14	2.1	27	4.1	2.55	130	.282	.314	5	5	98	139	0.6	-0	2	0.7
1945	Chi-N	13	8	.619	34	19	9	3	2	165	142	**7.7**	9	23	**1.3**	88	4.8	**2.40**	**151**	**.228**	**.253**	26	22	95	90	-0.2	3	-1	2.5
1946	Chi-N	2	3	.400	14	2	0	0	1	23	28	11.0	5	10	3.9	10	3.9	5.87	54	.289	.352	-6	-7	93	95	-0.5	0	1	-0.5
Total	6	22	21	.512	116	34	10	3	4	350	379	9.7	21	72	1.9	161	4.1	3.57	107	.272	.303	9	9	100	99	-1.3	-1	3	1.6
■ DON PRINCE	Prince, Donald Mark b: 4/5/38, Clarkton, N.C. BR/TR, 6'4", 200 lbs. Deb: 9/21/62																												
1962	Chi-N	0	0	—	1	0	0	0	0	1	0	0.0	0	1	9.0	0	0.0	0.00	—	.000	.500	0	0	109	0	0.0	0	0	0.1
■ JIM PROCTOR	Proctor, James Arthur b: 9/9/35, Brandywine, Md. BR/TR, 6', 165 lbs. Deb: 9/14/59																												
1959	Det-A	0	1	.000	2	1	0	0	0	3	8	24.0	0	3	9.0	0	0.0	15.00	29	.533	.579	-4	-4	111	95	-0.4	0	0	-0.2
■ RED PROCTOR	Proctor, Noah Richard b: 10/27/1900, Williamsburg, Va. d: 12/17/54, Richmond, Va. BR/TR, 6'1", 165 lbs. Deb: 8/06/23																												
1923	Chi-A	0	0	—	2	0	0	0	0	4	11	24.8	0	2	4.5	0	0.0	13.50	29	.550	.565	-4	-4	99	100	0.0	0	-0	-0.3
■ GEORGE PROESER	Proeser, George "Yatz" b: 5/30/1864, Cincinnati, Ohio d: 10/13/41, New Burlington, O. BL/TL, 5'10", 190 lbs. Deb: 1888																												
1888	Cle-a	3	4	.429	7	7	7	1	0	59	53	8.1	4	30	4.6	20	3.1	3.81	81	.253	.346	-5	-5	100	99	0.3	2	0	-0.2
■ MIKE PROLY	Proly, Michael James b: 12/15/50, Jamaica, N.Y. BR/TR, 6', 185 lbs. Deb: 4/10/76																												
1976	StL-N	1	0	1.000	14	0	0	0	0	17	21	11.1	0	6	3.2	4	2.1	3.71	99	.328	.365	-0	-0	105	132	0.5	0	0	0.0
1978	Chi-A	5	2	.714	14	6	2	0	1	66	63	8.6	4	12	1.6	19	2.6	2.73	141	.250	.282	8	8	102	99	1.8	0	-1	0.8
1979	Chi-A	3	8	.273	38	6	0	0	9	88	89	9.1	6	40	4.1	32	3.3	3.89	112	.260	.336	3	4	103	100	-2.2	0	1	0.5
1980	Chi-A	5	10	.333	62	3	0	0	8	147	136	8.3	7	58	3.6	56	3.4	3.06	129	.253	.319	16	15	98	113	-1.8	0	2	1.6
1981	Phi-N	2	1	.667	35	2	0	0	2	63	66	9.4	6	19	2.7	19	2.7	3.86	101	.282	.328	-3	0	112	112	0.4	-1	1	0.1
1982	Chi-N	5	3	.625	44	1	0	0	1	82	77	8.5	5	22	2.4	24	2.6	2.30	162	.257	.305	12	13	104	145	1.3	1	0	1.6
1983	Chi-N	1	5	.167	60	0	0	0	1	83	79	8.6	5	38	4.1	31	3.4	3.58	103	.259	.336	1	1	101	108	-1.8	-0	0	0.1
Total	7	22	29	.431	267	18	2	0	22	546	531	8.8	33	195	3.2	185	3.0	3.23	121	.261	.321	37	42	102	114	-1.8	-0	3	4.7
■ BILL PROUGH	Prough, Herschel Clinton "Clint" b: 11/28/1887, Markle, Ind. d: 12/29/36, Richmond, Ind. BR/TR, 6'3", 185 lbs. Deb: 4/27/12																												
1912	Cin-N	0	0	—	1	0	0	0	0	3	7	21.0	0	1	3.0	0	0.0	6.00	53	.500	.533	-1	-1	93	176	0.0	-0	-0	0.0
■ AUGIE PRUDHOMME	Prudhomme, John Olgus b: 11/20/02, Frierson, La. BR/TR, 6'2", 186 lbs. Deb: 4/19/29																												
1929	Det-A	1	6	.143	34	6	2	0	1	94	119	11.4	7	53	5.1	26	2.5	6.22	66	.322	.389	-21	-22	97	97	-2.3	1	1	-1.7

YEAR	TM/L	W	L	PCT	G	GS	CG	SHO	SV	IP	H	H/G	HR	BB	BB/G	SO	SO/G	ERA	/A	OAVG	OOBP	PR	/A	PF	CPI	WAT	PB	PD	TPI
■ HUB PRUETT	Pruett, Hubert Shelby "Shucks" b: 9/1/1900, Malden, Mo. d: 1/28/82, Ladue, Mo. BL/TL, 5'10.5", 165 lbs. Deb: 4/26/22																												
1922	StL-A	7	7	.500	39	8	4	0	7	120	99	7.4	2	59	4.4	70	5.3	2.33	177	.235	.320	23	24	102	132	-1.2	-1	2	2.5
1923	StL-A	4	7	.364	32	8	3	0	2	104	109	9.4	3	64	5.5	59	5.1	4.33	96	.279	.372	-4	-2	105	105	-1.4	-1	1	0.0
1924	StL-A	3	4	.429	33	1	0	0	0	65	64	8.9	1	42	5.8	27	3.7	4.57	100	.270	.374	-2	-0	108	97	-0.3	-1	1	0.0
1927	Phi-N	7	17	.292	31	28	12	1	1	186	238	11.5	6	89	4.3	90	4.4	6.05	65	.314	.385	-44	-44	100	88	-1.6	1	3	-3.6
1928	Phi-N	2	4	.333	13	9	4	0	0	71	78	9.9	2	49	6.2	35	4.4	4.56	95	.291	.390	-5	-2	109	112	0.2	-0	0	-0.1
1930	NY-N	5	4	.556	45	8	1	0	3	136	152	10.1	11	63	4.2	49	3.2	4.76	100	.287	.360	3	-0	96	102	0.0	-1	1	0.0
1932	Bos-N	1	5	.167	18	7	4	0	0	63	76	10.9	3	30	4.3	27	3.9	5.14	70	.308	.382	-9	-11	93	106	-1.9	-1	2	-0.8
Total	7	29	48	.377	211	69	28	1	13	745	816	9.9	28	396	4.8	357	4.3	4.63	91	.286	.368	-38	-34	101	104	-6.2	-3	9	-2.0
■ TEX PRUIETT	Pruiett, Charles Le Roy b: 4/10/1883, Osgood, Ind. d: 3/6/53, Ventura, Cal. BL/TR, Deb: 4/26/07																												
1907	Bos-A	3	11	.214	35	17	6	2	3	174	166	8.6	1	59	3.1	54	2.8	3.10	84	.275	.340	-11	-9	103	93	-3.3	-1	1	-0.8
1908	Bos-A	1	7	.125	13	6	1	1	2	59	55	8.4	1	21	3.2	28	4.3	1.98	117	.259	.338	3	2	97	172	-2.9	-1	0	0.3
Total	2	4	18	.182	48	23	7	3	5	233	221	8.5	2	80	3.1	82	3.2	2.82	90	.271	.339	-8	-7	102	113	-6.2	-2	2	-0.5
■ TROY PUCKETT	Puckett, Troy Levi b: 12/10/1889, Winchester, Ind. d: 4/13/71, Winchester, Ind. BL/TR, 6'2", 186 lbs. Deb: 10/04/11																												
1911	Phi-N	0	0	—	1	0	0	0	0	2	4	18.0	0	2	9.0	1	4.5	13.50	27	.444	.583	-2	-2	108	89	0.0	0	0	-0.1
■ MIGUEL PUENTE	Puente, Miguel Antonio (Aguilar) b: 5/8/48, San Luis Potosi, Mex BR/TR, 6', 160 lbs. Deb: 5/03/70																												
1970	SF-N	1	3	.250	6	4	1	0	0	19	25	11.8	5	11	5.2	14	6.6	8.05	48	.325	.387	-8	-9	96	95	-1.0	-1	0	-0.8
■ CHARLIE PULEO	Puleo, Charles Michael b: 2/7/55, Glen Ridge, N.J. BR/TR, 6'2", 190 lbs. Deb: 9/16/81																												
1981	NY-N	0	0	—	4	1	0	0	0	13	8	5.5	0	8	5.5	8	5.5	0.00	—	.182	.302	5	5	103	0	0.0	-0	0	0.6
1982	NY-N	9	9	.500	36	24	1	1	1	171	179	9.4	13	90	4.7	98	5.2	4.47	81	.275	.357	-16	-16	100	102	1.6	-1	3	-1.4
1983	Cin-N	6	12	.333	27	24	0	0	0	144	145	9.1	18	91	5.7	71	4.4	4.88	77	.269	.371	-20	-18	104	105	-2.5	-2	-2	-2.0
1984	Cin-N	1	2	.333	5	4	0	0	0	22	27	11.0	2	15	6.1	6	2.5	5.73	67	.297	.393	-5	-5	107	99	-0.2	0	-1	-0.4
1986	Atl-N	1	2	.333	5	3	1	0	0	24	13	4.9	4	12	4.5	18	6.8	3.00	128	.160	.268	2	2	103	89	-0.3	0	-0	0.3
1987	Atl-N	6	8	.429	35	16	1	0	0	123	122	8.9	11	40	2.9	99	7.2	4.24	105	.262	.315	-2	3	109	92	0.0	1	-2	0.2
1988	Atl-N	5	5	.500	53	3	0	0	1	106	101	8.6	9	47	4.0	70	5.9	3.48	106	.251	.327	-0	2	107	112	1.3	0	-0	0.2
Total	7	28	38	.424	165	75	3	1	2	603	595	8.9	57	303	4.5	370	5.5	4.24	91	.261	.344	-37	-26	104	99	-0.1	-1	-1	-2.5
■ ALFONSO PULIDO	Pulido, Alfonso (Manzo) b: 1/23/57, Veracruz, Mexico BL/TL, 5'11", 170 lbs. Deb: 9/05/83																												
1983	Pit-N	0	0	—	1	1	0	0	0	2	4	18.0	2	1	4.5	1	4.5	9.00	42	.400	.455	-1	-1	103	174	0.0	0	0	0.0
1984	Pit-N	0	0	—	1	0	0	0	0	2	3	13.5	0	1	4.5	2	9.0	9.00	37	.333	.400	-1	-1	94	62	0.0	0	0	0.0
1986	NY-A	1	1	.500	10	3	0	0	1	31	38	11.0	8	9	2.6	13	3.8	4.65	92	.306	.348	-2	-1	103	134	0.0	0	0	0.0
Total	3	1	1	.500	12	4	0	0	1	35	45	11.6	10	11	2.8	16	4.1	5.14	82	.315	.359	-4	-4	102	132	0.0	0	0	0.0
■ SPENCER PUMPELLY	Pumpelly, Spencer Armstrong b: 4/11/1893, Owego, N.Y. d: 12/5/73, Sayre, Pa. Deb: 7/11/25																												
1925	Was-A	0	0	—	1	0	0	0	0	1	1	9.0	1	1	9.0	0	0.0	9.00	46	.333	.500	-1	-1	95	162	0.0	0	0	0.0
■ BLONDIE PURCELL	Purcell, William Aloysius b: Paterson, N.J. 5'9.5", 159 lbs. Deb: 5/01/1879 M																												
1879	Syr-N	4	15	.211	22	17	15	0	0	180	245	12.3	1	19	0.9	28	1.4	3.75	63	.330	.347	-25	-28	95	106	-3.7	3	0	-2.3
	Cin-N	0	2	.000	2	2	2	0	0	18	27	13.5	0	2	1.0	3	1.5	4.00	59	.352	.368	-3	-3	94	116	-0.9	-0	0	-0.2
	Yr	4	17	.190	24	19	17	0	0	198	272	12.4	1	21	1.0	31	1.4	3.77	63	.332	.349	-28	-31	95	116	-4.6	3	0	-2.5
1880	Cin-N	3	17	.150	25	21	21	0	0	196	235	10.8	1	32	1.5	47	2.2	3.21	77	.306	.334	-18	-16	105	109	-4.9	4	0	-1.4
1881	Buf-N	4	1	.800	9	5	5	0	0	62	62	9.0	2	9	1.3	15	2.2	2.76	102	.272	.300	0	0	101	93	1.4	1	0	-1.5
1882	Buf-N	2	1	.667	6	3	2	0	0	31	44	12.8	2	4	1.2	9	2.6	4.94	60	.342	.362	-7	-7	103	103	0.4	1	0	-0.5
1883	Phi-N	2	6	.250	11	9	7	0	0	80	110	12.4	0	12	1.3	30	3.4	4.39	71	.335	.358	-11	-11	99	101	0.4	2	0	-0.8
1884	Phi-N	0	0	—	1	0	0	0	0	4	3	6.8	1	0	0.0	1	2.3	2.25	129	.217	.217	0	0	97	119	0.0	0	0	0.0
1885	Phi-a	0	1	.000	1	0	0	0	0	6	11	16.5	0	2	3.0	3	4.5	6.00	55	.406	.447	-2	-2	102	126	-0.4	0	0	0.0
1886	Bal-a	0	0	—	1	0	0	0	0	1	1	9.0	0	0	0.0	0	0.0	9.00	36	.271	.271	-1	-1	94	28	0.0	0	0	0.0
1887	Bal-a	0	0	—	1	0	0	0	0	4	8	18.0	0	4	9.0	2	4.5	15.75	26	.430	.531	-5	-5	94	65	0.0	0	0	-0.3
Total	9	15	43	.259	79	57	52	0	0	582	746	11.5	7	84	1.3	138	2.1	3.73	70	.320	.343	-72	-72	100	105	-7.7	12	0	-7.0
■ JOHN PURDIN	Purdin, John Nolan b: 7/16/42, Lynx, Ohio BR/TR, 6'2", 185 lbs. Deb: 9/16/64																												
1964	LA-N	2	0	1.000	3	2	1	1	0	16	6	3.4	1	6	3.4	8	4.5	0.56	575	.115	.207	5	5	91	98	1.0	0	-0	0.5
1965	LA-N	2	1	.667	11	2	0	0	0	23	26	10.2	8	13	5.1	16	6.3	6.65	48	.283	.368	-8	-9	90	105	0.3	-0	-1	-0.9
1968	LA-N	2	3	.400	35	1	0	0	2	56	42	6.8	2	21	3.4	38	6.1	3.05	89	.206	.273	-0	-2	91	67	-0.3	1	-0	0.0
1969	LA-N	0	0	—	9	0	0	0	0	16	19	10.7	7	12	6.8	6	3.4	6.19	57	.292	.392	-5	-5	97	136	0.0	-0	0	-0.4
Total	4	6	4	.600	58	5	1	1	2	111	93	7.5	18	52	4.2	68	5.5	3.89	77	.225	.306	-8	-11	92	89	1.0	1	-1	-0.8
■ BOB PURKEY	Purkey, Robert Thomas b: 7/14/29, Pittsburgh, Pa. BR/TR, 6'2", 175 lbs. Deb: 4/14/54																												
1954	Pit-N	3	8	.273	36	11	0	0	0	131	145	10.0	3	62	4.3	38	2.6	5.08	81	.293	.368	-15	-14	102	90	-1.1	-1	5	-0.9
1955	Pit-N	2	7	.222	14	10	2	0	1	68	77	10.2	5	25	3.3	24	3.2	5.29	77	.287	.349	-9	-9	101	84	-1.9	2	1	-0.6
1956	Pit-N	0	0	—	2	0	0	0	0	4	2	4.5	1	0	0.0	1	2.3	2.25	173	.143	.143	1	1	103	46	0.0	0	0	0.1
1957	Pit-N	11	14	.440	48	21	6	1	2	180	194	9.7	10	38	1.9	51	2.6	3.85	97	.278	.314	1	-3	96	95	0.9	0	-0	-0.2
1958	Cin-N	17	11	.607	37	34	17	3	0	250	259	9.3	25	49	1.8	70	2.5	3.60	116	.268	.300	10	16	106	98	**3.7**	-2	2	1.7
1959	Cin-N	13	18	.419	38	33	9	1	1	218	241	9.9	25	43	1.8	78	3.2	4.25	95	.279	.313	-7	-5	103	96	-2.3	3	-0	-0.1
1960	Cin-N	17	11	.607	41	33	11	1	0	253	259	9.2	23	59	2.1	97	3.5	3.59	104	.265	.307	5	4	99	103	4.9	-1	2	0.4
1961	Cin-N	16	12	.571	36	34	13	1	1	246	245	9.0	27	51	1.9	116	4.2	3.73	111	.255	.293	8	11	103	91	-0.8	-4	6	1.4
1962	Cin-N	23	5	**.821**	37	37	18	2	0	288	260	8.1	28	64	2.0	141	4.4	2.81	141	.240	.286	36	**36**	100	109	**8.3**	-2	3	3.9
1963	Cin-N	6	10	.375	21	21	4	1	0	137	143	9.4	12	33	2.2	55	3.6	3.55	96	.272	.312	-4	-2	103	107	-2.4	-1	1	-0.1
1964	Cin-N	11	9	.550	34	25	9	2	1	196	181	8.3	16	49	2.3	78	3.6	3.03	119	.246	.293	11	12	102	106	-0.3	-4	2	1.1
1965	StL-N	10	9	.526	32	17	3	1	2	124	148	10.7	20	33	2.4	39	2.8	5.81	65	.294	.342	-31	-28	106	89	0.6	-3	1	-2.9
1966	Pit-N	0	1	.000	10	0	0	0	1	20	16	7.2	0	4	1.8	5	2.3	1.35	264	.235	.267	5	5	99	162	-0.4	-0	1	0.6
Total	13	129	115	.529	386	276	92	13	9	2115	2170	9.2	195	510	2.2	793	3.4	3.79	103	.266	.309	9	25	102	99	9.2	-13	20	4.4
■ OSCAR PURNER	Purner, Oscar E. b: 1873, Washington, D.C. Deb: 9/02/1895																												
1895	Was-N	0	0	—	1	0	0	0	0	2	4	18.0	1	3	13.5	0	0.0	9.00	56	.437	.576	-1	-1	105	169	0.0	-0	0	0.0
■ AMBROSE PUTTMANN	Puttmann, Ambrose Nicholas "Putty" or "Brose" b: 9/9/1880, Cincinnati, Ohio d: 6/21/36, Jamaica, N.Y. TL, 6'4", 185 lbs. Deb: 03																												
1903	NY-A	2	0	1.000	3	2	1	0	0	19	16	7.6	0	4	1.9	8	3.8	0.95	311	.249	.293	4	4	100	218	1.0	-0	1	0.6
1904	NY-A	2	0	1.000	9	3	2	1	0	49	40	7.3	0	17	3.1	26	4.8	2.76	104	.244	.315	-1	1	111	84	1.0	2	0	0.1
1905	NY-A	2	7	.222	17	9	5	1	1	86	79	8.3	2	37	3.9	39	4.1	4.29	63	.268	.350	-16	-15	103	77	-2.4	3	-0	-1.5
1906	StL-N	2	2	.500	4	4	0	0	0	19	23	10.9	2	9	4.3	12	5.7	5.21	52	.338	.430	-5	-5	104	108	0.5	0	0	-0.4
Total	4	8	9	.471	33	18	8	2	1	173	158	8.2	4	67	3.5	85	4.4	3.59	78	.267	.344	-18	-15	105	98	0.1	5	1	-1.2
■ JOHN PYECHA	Pyecha, John Nicholas b: 11/25/31, Aliquippa, Pa. BR/TR, 6'5", 200 lbs. Deb: 4/24/54																												
1954	Chi-N	0	1	.000	1	0	0	0	0	3	4	12.0	1	2	6.0	2	6.0	9.00	46	.333	.429	-2	-2	102	94	-0.4	-0	0	-0.1
■ HARLAN PYLE	Pyle, Harlan Albert "Firpo" b: 11/29/05, Burchard, Neb. BR/TR, 6'2", 180 lbs. Deb: 9/21/28																												
1928	Cin-N	0	0	—	2	1	0	0	0	1	1	9.0	0	4	36.0	1	9.0	27.00	14	.143	.455	-3	-3	97	19	0.0	-0	0	-0.2
■ SHADOW PYLE	Pyle, Harry Thomas b: 10/30/1861, Reading, Pa. d: 11/26/08, Reading, Pa. 5'8", 136 lbs. Deb: 10/15/1884																												
1884	Phi-N	0	1	.000	1	1	1	0	0	9	9	9.0	0	6	6.0	4	4.0	4.00	72	.269	.381	-1	-1	97	97	-0.4	-1	0	0.0
1887	Chi-N	1	3	.250	4	4	3	0	0	27	32	10.7	1	21	7.0	5	1.7	5.00	93	.310	.427	-3	-1	115	114	-1.1	-0	0	0.0
Total	2	1	4	.200	5	5	4	0	0	36	41	10.3	1	27	6.8	9	2.3	4.75	88	.300	.416	-4	-2	111	110	-1.5	-1	0	0.0
■ EWALD PYLE	Pyle, Herbert Ewald "Lefty" b: 8/27/10, St.Louis, Mo. BL/TL, 6'0.5", 175 lbs. Deb: 4/23/39																												
1939	StL-A	0	2	.000	6	1	0	0	0	8	17	19.1	3	11	12.4	5	5.6	13.50	36	.405	.509	-8	-8	105	103	-0.9	-0	1	-0.6
1942	StL-A	0	0	—	2	0	0	0	0	5	6	10.8	0	4	7.2	1	1.8	7.20	52	.286	.400	-2	-2	102	71	0.0	-0	-0	-0.1
1943	Was-A	4	8	.333	18	11	2	1	1	73	70	8.6	0	45	5.5	25	3.1	4.07	83	.254	.349	-6	-6	102	91	-2.4	-1	-1	-0.7

YEAR	TM/L	W	L	PCT	G	GS	CG	SHO	SV	IP	H	H/G	HR	BB	BB/G	SO	SO/G	ERA	/A	OAVG	OOBP	PR	/A	PF	CPI	WAT	PB	PD	TPI
1944	NY-N	7	10	.412	31	21	3	0	0	164	152	8.3	12	68	3.7	79	4.3	4.34	88	.241	.317	-13	-10	105	80	-0.4	-1	0	-0.9
1945	NY-N	0	0	—	6	1	0	0	0	6	16	24.0	0	4	6.0	2	3.0	18.00	21	.457	.513	-9	-9	100	63	0.0	-0	1	-0.8
	Bos-N	0	1	.000	4	2	0	0	0	14	16	10.3	1	18	11.6	10	6.4	7.07	61	.302	.466	-5	-4	113	106	-0.4	1	-0	-0.3
	Yr	0	1	.000	10	3	0	0	0	20	32	14.4	1	22	9.9	12	5.4	10.35	40	.364	.482	-15	-14	109	106	-0.4	-0	0	-1.1
Total	5	11	21	.344	67	36	5	1	1	270	277	9.2	16	150	5.0	122	4.1	5.03	74	.262	.351	-44	-39	105	84	-4.1	-2	0	-3.4

■ TOM QUALTERS Qualters, Thomas Francis "Money Bags" b: 4/1/35, Mc Keesport, Pa. BR/TR, 6'0.5", 190 lbs. Deb: 9/13/53

YEAR	TM/L	W	L	PCT	G	GS	CG	SHO	SV	IP	H	H/G	HR	BB	BB/G	SO	SO/G	ERA	/A	OAVG	OOBP	PR	/A	PF	CPI	WAT	PB	PD	TPI
1953	Phi-N	0	0	—	1	0	0	0	0	⅓	4	108.0	1	1	27.0	0	0.0	162.00	—	.800	.857	-6	-6	98	57	0.0	0	0	-0.4
1957	Phi-N	0	0	—	6	0	0	0	0	7	12	15.4	0	4	5.1	6	7.7	7.71	50	.400	.457	-3	-3	99	101	0.0	0	0	-0.2
1958	Phi-N	0	0	—	1	0	0	0	0	2	2	9.0	0	1	4.5	0	0.0	4.50	88	.222	.300	-0	-0	100	40	0.0	0	0	0.0
	Chi-A	0	0	—	26	0	0	0	0	43	45	9.4	1	20	4.2	14	2.9	4.19	88	.281	.353	-2	-2	98	100	0.0	0	1	0.0
Total	3	0	0	—	34	0	0	0	0	52	63	10.9	2	26	4.5	20	3.5	5.71	65	.309	.381	-11	-12	98	97	0.0	0	1	-0.6

■ BILL QUARLES Quarles, William H. b: 1869, Petersburg, Va. d: 3/25/1897, Petersburg, Va. 6'3", Deb: 5/21/1891

YEAR	TM/L	W	L	PCT	G	GS	CG	SHO	SV	IP	H	H/G	HR	BB	BB/G	SO	SO/G	ERA	/A	OAVG	OOBP	PR	/A	PF	CPI	WAT	PB	PD	TPI
1891	Was-a	1	1	.500	3	2	2	0	0	22	32	13.1	1	12	4.9	10	4.1	8.18	46	.355	.431	-11	-11	101	75	0.3	-2	0	-0.8
1893	Bos-N	2	1	.667	3	3	3	0	0	27	31	10.3	2	5	1.7	6	2.0	4.67	101	.304	.337	0	0	101	89	0.0	-0	0	0.0
Total	2	3	2	.600	6	5	5	0	0	49	63	11.6	3	17	3.1	16	2.9	6.24	68	.328	.383	-11	-11	101	83	0.3	-2	0	-0.8

■ MEL QUEEN Queen, Melvin Douglas b: 3/26/42, Johnson City, N.Y. BL/TR, 6'1", 189 lbs. Deb: 4/13/64 C

YEAR	TM/L	W	L	PCT	G	GS	CG	SHO	SV	IP	H	H/G	HR	BB	BB/G	SO	SO/G	ERA	/A	OAVG	OOBP	PR	/A	PF	CPI	WAT	PB	PD	TPI
1966	Cin-N	0	0	—	7	0	0	0	1	7	11	14.1	0	6	7.7	9	11.6	6.43	64	.367	.459	-2	-2	114	117	0.0	0	0	-0.1
1967	Cin-N	14	8	.636	31	24	6	2	0	196	155	7.1	17	52	2.4	154	7.1	2.76	133	.215	.270	14	20	109	90	2.6	3	-2	2.5
1968	Cin-N	0	1	.000	5	4	0	0	0	18	25	12.5	7	6	3.0	20	10.0	6.00	55	.333	.373	-6	-5	111	133	-0.4	-0	0	-0.5
1969	Cin-N	1	0	1.000	2	2	0	0	0	12	7	5.3	2	3	2.3	7	5.3	2.25	158	.163	.234	2	2	99	85	0.5	-0	-0	0.2
1970	Cal-A	3	6	.333	34	3	0	0	9	60	58	8.7	5	28	4.2	44	6.6	4.20	81	.261	.343	-3	-5	92	102	-1.6	1	-1	-0.5
1971	Cal-A	2	2	.500	44	0	0	0	4	66	49	6.7	3	29	4.0	53	7.2	1.77	194	.212	.313	12	12	99	161	0.1	-1	-1	1.2
1972	Cal-A	0	0	—	17	0	0	0	0	31	31	9.0	2	19	5.5	19	5.5	4.35	63	.265	.371	-4	-6	90	106	0.0	0	-0	-0.5
Total	7	20	17	.541	140	33	6	2	14	390	336	7.8	36	143	3.3	306	7.1	3.14	112	.233	.306	12	16	103	107	1.2	3	-4	2.3

■ MEL QUEEN Queen, Melvin Joseph b: 3/4/18, Maxwell, Pa. d: 4/4/82, Fort Smith, Ark. BR/TR, 6'0.5", 204 lbs. Deb: 4/18/42

YEAR	TM/L	W	L	PCT	G	GS	CG	SHO	SV	IP	H	H/G	HR	BB	BB/G	SO	SO/G	ERA	/A	OAVG	OOBP	PR	/A	PF	CPI	WAT	PB	PD	TPI
1942	NY-A	1	0	1.000	4	0	0	0	0	6	6	9.0	0	3	4.5	0	0.0	0.00	—	.300	.440	2	2	94	0	0.5	0	0	0.3
1944	NY-A	6	3	.667	10	10	4	1	0	82	68	7.5	7	34	3.7	30	3.3	3.29	110	.227	.300	1	3	105	96	1.3	0	-2	0.1
1946	NY-A	1	1	.500	14	3	1	0	0	30	40	12.0	2	21	6.3	26	7.8	6.60	52	.315	.401	-10	-11	98	91	0.0	-0	-0	-1.0
1947	NY-A	0	0	—	5	0	0	0	0	7	9	11.6	2	4	5.1	2	2.6	9.00	38	.321	.424	-4	-4	92	89	0.0	-0	-0	-0.4
	Pit-N	3	7	.300	14	12	2	0	0	74	70	8.5	8	51	6.2	34	4.1	4.01	104	.244	.356	0	1	102	110	-1.2	-2	-1	-0.1
1948	Pit-N	4	4	.500	25	8	0	0	1	66	82	11.2	8	40	5.5	34	4.6	6.68	62	.308	.396	-20	-19	104	94	-0.2	-2	-1	-1.9
1950	Pit-N	5	14	.263	33	21	4	1	0	120	135	10.1	18	73	5.5	76	5.7	6.00	73	.284	.374	-25	-22	106	94	-3.0	-3	-1	-2.3
1951	Pit-N	7	9	.438	39	21	4	1	0	168	149	8.0	21	99	5.3	123	**6.6**	4.45	97	.233	.336	-9	-2	110	90	0.3	-3	-3	-0.7
1952	Pit-N	0	2	.000	2	2	0	0	0	3	8	24.0	2	4	12.0	3	9.0	33.00	12	.381	.480	-10	-10	105	48	-0.9	0	0	-0.7
Total	8	27	40	.403	146	77	15	3	1	556	567	9.2	68	329	5.3	328	5.3	5.10	81	.262	.357	-74	-61	105	94	-3.2	-11	-8	-6.7

■ EDDIE QUICK Quick, Edward b: Baltimore, Md. d: 5/19/13, Rocky Ford, Colo. 5'11", Deb: 03

YEAR	TM/L	W	L	PCT	G	GS	CG	SHO	SV	IP	H	H/G	HR	BB	BB/G	SO	SO/G	ERA	/A	OAVG	OOBP	PR	/A	PF	CPI	WAT	PB	PD	TPI
1903	NY-A	0	0	—	1	1	0	0	0	4	5	11.3	0	1	2.3	1	2.3	4.50	66	.330	.371	-1	-1	100	94	0.0	-0	0	0.0

■ TAD QUINN Quinn, Clarence Carr b: 9/21/1882, Torrington, Conn. d: 8/6/46, Waterbury, Conn. TR , Deb: 9/27/02

YEAR	TM/L	W	L	PCT	G	GS	CG	SHO	SV	IP	H	H/G	HR	BB	BB/G	SO	SO/G	ERA	/A	OAVG	OOBP	PR	/A	PF	CPI	WAT	PB	PD	TPI
1902	Phi-A	0	1	.000	1	1	1	0	0	8	12	13.5	1	1	1.1	3	3.4	4.50	84	.374	.393	-1	-1	106	133	-0.4	-0	-0	0.0
1903	Phi-A	0	0	—	2	0	0	0	0	9	11	11.0	0	5	5.0	1	1.0	5.00	60	.325	.412	-2	-2	102	99	0.0	1	0	-0.1
Total	2	0	1	.000	3	1	1	0	0	17	23	12.2	1	6	3.2	4	2.1	4.76	71	.349	.403	-3	-3	104	115	-0.4	1	0	-0.1

■ FRANK QUINN Quinn, Frank William b: 11/27/27, Springfield, Mass. BR/TR, 6'2", 180 lbs. Deb: 5/29/49

YEAR	TM/L	W	L	PCT	G	GS	CG	SHO	SV	IP	H	H/G	HR	BB	BB/G	SO	SO/G	ERA	/A	OAVG	OOBP	PR	/A	PF	CPI	WAT	PB	PD	TPI
1949	Bos-A	0	0	—	8	0	0	0	0	22	18	7.4	2	9	3.7	4	1.6	2.86	151	.222	.304	3	4	103	108	0.0	-0	0	0.3
1950	Bos-A	0	0	—	1	0	0	0	0	2	2	9.0	0	1	4.5	0	0.0	9.00	57	.250	.333	-1	-1	111	35	0.0	0	0	0.0
Total	2	0	0	—	9	0	0	0	0	24	20	7.5	2	10	3.8	4	1.5	3.38	130	.225	.307	2	3	104	102	0.0	-0	0	0.3

■ JACK QUINN Quinn, John Picus (born John Quinn Picus) b: 7/5/1883, Janesville, Pa. d: 4/17/46, Pottsville, Pa. BR/TR, 6' ", 196 lbs. Deb: 4/15/09

YEAR	TM/L	W	L	PCT	G	GS	CG	SHO	SV	IP	H	H/G	HR	BB	BB/G	SO	SO/G	ERA	/A	OAVG	OOBP	PR	/A	PF	CPI	WAT	PB	PD	TPI
1909	NY-A	9	5	.643	23	11	8	0	1	119	110	8.3	1	24	1.8	36	2.7	1.97	125	.252	.297	7	7	99	116	2.2	0	3	1.1
1910	NY-A	18	12	.600	35	31	20	0	0	236	214	8.2	2	58	2.2	82	3.1	2.36	113	.247	.299	4	8	106	100	0.8	4	7	2.1
1911	NY-A	8	10	.444	40	16	7	0	2	175	203	10.4	2	41	2.1	71	3.7	3.75	99	.297	.341	-8	-1	111	97	-1.0	-1	3	0.2
1912	NY-A	5	7	.417	18	11	7	0	0	103	139	12.1	4	23	2.0	47	4.1	5.77	61	.325	.365	-28	-26	105	84	0.8	-0	2	-2.1
1913	Bos-N	4	3	.571	8	7	6	1	0	56	55	8.8	1	7	1.1	33	5.3	2.41	127	.261	.283	5	4	96	104	0.8	2	2	0.8
1914	Bal-F	26	14	.650	46	42	27	4	1	343	335	8.8	3	65	1.7	164	4.3	2.60	122	.266	.307	23	22	99	109	5.7	9	3	3.8
1915	Bal-F	9	22	.290	44	31	21	0	1	274	289	9.5	9	63	2.1	118	3.9	3.45	98	.278	.325	-13	-2	111	102	-0.8	4	7	1.2
1918	Chi-A	5	1	.833	6	5	5	0	0	51	38	6.7	0	7	1.2	22	3.9	2.29	121	.216	.237	3	3	100	51	2.1	1	0	0.5
1919	NY-A	15	14	.517	38	31	18	4	0	264	242	8.3	8	65	2.2	97	3.3	2.63	128	.244	.295	18	21	104	89	-1.7	1	1	2.5
1920	NY-A	18	10	.643	41	32	17	2	3	253	271	9.6	8	48	**1.7**	101	3.6	3.20	117	.273	.308	17	15	99	92	1.1	-5	2	1.2
1921	NY-A	8	7	.533	33	13	6	0	0	119	158	11.9	2	32	2.4	44	3.3	3.78	112	.327	.360	7	6	99	129	-1.3	1	0	0.7
1922	Bos-A	13	16	.448	40	32	16	4	0	256	263	9.2	9	59	2.1	67	2.4	3.48	115	.267	.297	16	15	99	88	1.5	-5	5	1.5
1923	Bos-A	13	17	.433	42	28	16	1	7	243	302	11.2	6	53	2.0	71	2.6	3.89	108	.316	.343	3	8	106	113	1.0	-0	-1	0.8
1924	Bos-A	12	13	.480	44	25	13	2	7	229	241	9.5	10	52	2.0	64	2.5	3.26	136	.273	.312	25	30	105	106	1.2	-4	4	2.9
1925	Bos-A	7	8	.467	19	15	8	0	0	105	140	12.0	3	26	2.2	24	2.1	4.37	100	.315	.351	0	-0	99	102	1.9	-2	2	0.0
	Phi-A	6	3	.667	18	14	4	0	0	100	119	10.7	3	16	1.4	19	1.7	3.87	115	.296	.319	6	6	101	96	1.0	-3	1	0.5
	Yr	13	11	.542	37	29	12	0	0	205	259	11.4	6	42	1.8	43	1.9	4.13	107	.305	.332	6	6	100	96	2.9	-2	3	0.5
1926	Phi-A	10	11	.476	31	21	8	3	1	164	191	10.5	4	36	2.0	58	3.2	3.40	136	.296	.323	11	23	116	111	-1.6	-1	1	2.4
1927	Phi-A	15	10	.600	34	25	11	3	1	201	211	9.4	8	37	**1.7**	43	1.9	3.27	120	.278	.305	19	15	95	104	0.3	-6	-1	0.6
1928	Phi-A	18	7	.720	31	28	18	4	1	211	239	10.2	3	34	1.5	43	1.8	2.90	138	.286	.312	27	26	99	119	3.2	-3	1	2.3
1929	Phi-A	11	9	.550	35	18	7	0	2	161	182	10.2	8	39	2.2	41	2.3	3.97	111	.290	.323	5	8	104	100	-2.2	-5	0	0.3
1930	Phi-A	9	7	.563	35	7	0	0	6	90	109	10.9	6	22	2.2	28	2.8	4.40	102	.302	.332	**3**	**1**	96	108	-1.2	1	2	0.3
1931	Bro-N	5	4	.556	39	1	0	0	**15**	64	65	9.1	1	24	3.4	25	3.5	2.67	146	.266	.323	8	9	101	132	0.4	0	1	1.0
1932	Bro-N	3	7	.300	42	0	0	0	**8**	87	102	10.6	1	24	2.5	28	2.9	3.31	112	.296	.336	**5**	**4**	96	122	-2.1	0	0	0.4
1933	Cin-N	0	1	.000	14	0	0	0	1	16	20	11.3	0	5	2.8	3	1.7	3.94	86	.323	.352	-1	-1	102	118	-0.4	-0	1	0.0
Total	23	247	218	.531	756	444	243	28	57	3920	4238	9.7	102	860	2.0	1329	3.1	3.29	114	.280	.317	161	204	103	103	11.7	-13	45	25.0

■ WIMPY QUINN Quinn, Wellington Hunt b: 5/12/18, Birmingham, Ala. d: 9/1/54, Santa Monica, Cal. BR/TR, 6'2", 187 lbs. Deb: 6/08/41

YEAR	TM/L	W	L	PCT	G	GS	CG	SHO	SV	IP	H	H/G	HR	BB	BB/G	SO	SO/G	ERA	/A	OAVG	OOBP	PR	/A	PF	CPI	WAT	PB	PD	TPI
1941	Chi-N	0	0	—	3	0	0	0	0	5	3	5.4	0	3	5.4	2	3.6	7.20	47	.158	.273	-2	-2	94	15	0.0	0	0	-0.1

■ LUIS QUINTANA Quintana, Luis Joaquin (Santos) b: 12/25/51, Vega Baja, P.R. BL/TL, 6'2", 175 lbs. Deb: 7/09/74

YEAR	TM/L	W	L	PCT	G	GS	CG	SHO	SV	IP	H	H/G	HR	BB	BB/G	SO	SO/G	ERA	/A	OAVG	OOBP	PR	/A	PF	CPI	WAT	PB	PD	TPI
1974	Cal-A	2	1	.667	18	0	0	0	0	13	17	11.8	0	14	9.7	11	7.6	4.15	81	.327	.456	-1	-1	93	164	0.6	0	-0	0.0
1975	Cal-A	0	2	.000	4	0	0	0	0	7	13	16.7	2	6	7.7	5	6.4	6.43	56	.394	.487	-2	-2	96	167	-0.9	0	-0	-0.1
Total	2	2	3	.400	22	0	0	0	0	20	30	13.5	2	20	9.0	16	7.2	4.95	70	.353	.467	-3	-3	94	165	-0.3	0	-0	-0.1

■ ART QUIRK Quirk, Arthur Lincoln b: 4/11/38, Providence, R.I. BR/TL, 5'11", 170 lbs. Deb: 4/17/62

YEAR	TM/L	W	L	PCT	G	GS	CG	SHO	SV	IP	H	H/G	HR	BB	BB/G	SO	SO/G	ERA	/A	OAVG	OOBP	PR	/A	PF	CPI	WAT	PB	PD	TPI
1962	Bal-A	2	2	.500	7	5	0	0	0	27	36	12.0	3	18	6.0	18	6.0	6.00	63	.308	.400	-6	-7	95	102	0.1	0	1	-0.5
1963	Was-A	1	0	1.000	7	3	0	0	0	21	23	9.9	3	8	3.4	12	5.1	4.29	86	.280	.333	-2	-1	101	113	0.5	0	-0	-0.1
Total	2	3	2	.600	14	8	0	0	0	48	59	11.1	6	26	4.9	30	5.6	5.25	71	.296	.373	-8	-8	98	107	0.6	0	1	-0.6

■ DAN QUISENBERRY Quisenberry, Daniel Raymond b: 2/7/53, Santa Monica, Cal. BR/TR, 6'2", 170 lbs. Deb: 7/08/79

YEAR	TM/L	W	L	PCT	G	GS	CG	SHO	SV	IP	H	H/G	HR	BB	BB/G	SO	SO/G	ERA	/A	OAVG	OOBP	PR	/A	PF	CPI	WAT	PB	PD	TPI
1979	KC-A	3	2	.600	32	0	0	0	5	40	42	9.4	5	7	1.6	13	2.9	3.15	141	.278	.301	5	6	105	129	0.4	0	1	0.6
1980	KC-A	12	7	.632	**75**	0	0	0	**33**	128	129	9.1	5	27	1.9	37	2.6	3.09	127	.265	.297	14	12	97	100	0.9	0	3	1.5
1981	KC-A	1	4	.200	40	0	0	0	18	62	59	8.6	1	15	2.2	20	2.9	1.74	208	.258	.295	13	13	99	168	-1.4	0	3	1.7
1982	KC-A	9	7	.563	72	0	0	0	**35**	137	126	8.3	12	12	0.8	46	3.0	2.56	159	.252	.261	23	23	100	114	0.1	0	6	2.9
1983	KC-A	5	3	.625	**69**	0	0	0	**45**	139	118	7.6	6	11	0.7	48	3.1	1.94	214	.229	.241	**33**	**34**	102	99	1.1	0	2	3.7

YEAR	TM/L	W	L	PCT	G	GS	CG	SHO	SV	IP	H	H/G	HR	BB	BB/G	SO	SO/G	ERA	/A	OAVG	OOBP	PR	/A	PF	CPI	WAT	PB	PD	TPI
1984	KC-A	6	3	.667	72	0	0	0	**44**	129	121	8.4	10	12	0.8	41	2.9	2.65	150	.247	.263	19	19	99	99	1.4	0	3	2.2
1985	KC-A	8	9	.471	**84**	0	0	0	**37**	129	142	9.9	8	16	1.1	54	3.8	2.37	177	.280	.299	25	26	101	150	-1.4	0	1	2.7
1986	KC-A	3	7	.300	62	0	0	0	12	81	92	10.2	2	24	2.7	36	4.0	2.78	151	.291	.338	13	13	100	148	-1.8	0	2	1.5
1987	KC-A	4	1	.800	47	0	0	0	8	49	58	10.7	3	10	1.8	17	3.1	2.76	168	.287	.321	9	10	104	143	1.5	0	2	1.1
1988	KC-A	0	1	.000	20	0	0	0	1	25	32	11.5	0	5	1.8	9	3.2	3.60	113	.305	.336	1	1	103	109	-0.4	0	1	0.2
	StL-N	2	0	1.000	33	0	0	0	0	38	54	12.8	4	6	1.4	19	4.5	6.16	59	.344	.357	-11	-11	105	94	1.0	0	0	-1.0
Total	10	53	44	.546	606	0	0	0	238	957	973	9.2	56	145	1.4	340	3.2	2.70	151	.266	.289	144	146	101	120	1.4	0	22	17.1
■ CHARLIE RABE	Rabe, Charles Henry b: 5/6/32, Boyce, Tex. BL/TL, 6'1", 180 lbs. Deb: 9/21/57																												
1957	Cin-N	0	1	.000	2	1	0	0	0	8	5	5.6	2	0	0.0	6	6.8	2.25	183	.167	.167	1	2	106	65	-0.4	-0	-0	0.1
1958	Cin-N	0	3	.000	9	1	0	0	0	19	25	11.8	3	9	4.3	10	4.7	4.26	98	.321	.391	-1	-0	106	146	-1.4	-1	0	0.0
Total	2	0	4	.000	11	2	0	0	0	27	30	10.0	5	9	3.0	16	5.3	3.67	114	.278	.333	1	1	106	122	-1.8	-1	0	0.1
■ STEVE RACHUNOK	Rachunok, Stephen Stepanovich "The Mad Russian" b: 12/5/16, Rittman, Ohio BR/TR, 6'4.5", 205 lbs. Deb: 9/17/40																												
1940	Bro-N	0	1	.000	2	1	1	0	0	10	9	8.1	0	5	4.5	10	9.0	4.50	91	.243	.326	-1	-0	106	73	-0.4	0	0	0.0
■ DICK RADATZ	Radatz, Richard Raymond "The Monster" b: 4/2/37, Detroit, Mich. BR/TR, 6'6", 230 lbs. Deb: 4/10/62																												
1962	Bos-A	9	6	.600	**62**	0	0	0	**24**	125	95	6.8	9	40	2.9	144	10.4	2.23	183	.211	.275	**24**	**26**	103	111	1.9	-2	-2	2.3
1963	Bos-A	15	6	.714	66	0	0	0	25	132	94	6.4	9	51	3.5	162	11.0	1.98	196	.201	.277	**24**	**28**	107	124	5.2	-2	-2	2.6
1964	Bos-A	16	9	.640	79	0	0	0	**29**	157	103	5.9	13	58	3.3	181	10.4	2.29	163	.186	.265	23	25	103	92	4.9	-0	-2	2.5
1965	Bos-A	9	11	.450	63	0	0	0	22	124	104	7.5	11	53	3.8	121	8.8	3.92	96	.227	.308	-6	-2	109	83	1.2	1	-1	0.0
1966	Bos-A	0	2	.000	16	0	0	0	4	19	24	11.4	3	11	5.2	19	9.0	4.74	80	.304	.380	-3	-2	110	131	-0.9	-0	-1	-0.2
	Cle-A	0	3	.000	39	0	0	0	10	57	49	7.7	6	34	5.4	49	7.7	4.58	76	.233	.340	-7	-7	102	91	-1.4	-0	-1	-0.8
	Yr	0	5	.000	55	0	0	0	14	76	73	8.6	9	45	5.3	68	8.1	4.62	77	.253	.351	-10	-9	104	91	-2.3	-0	-1	-1.0
1967	Cle-A	0	0	—	3	0	0	0	0	3	5	15.0	1	2	6.0	1	3.0	6.00	54	.357	.438	-1	-1	101	159	0.0	0	0	0.0
	Chi-N	1	0	1.000	20	0	0	0	5	23	12	4.7	4	24	9.4	18	7.0	6.65	51	.154	.369	-8	-8	100	69	0.5	0	-0	-0.8
1969	Det-A	2	2	.500	11	0	0	0	0	19	14	6.6	3	5	2.4	18	8.5	3.32	112	.212	.257	1	1	102	89	-0.1	-0	0	0.1
	Mon-N	0	4	.000	22	0	0	0	3	35	32	8.2	6	18	4.6	32	8.2	5.66	66	.244	.336	-8	-8	103	80	-1.9	0	-0	-0.7
Total	7	52	43	.547	381	0	0	0	122	694	532	6.9	65	296	3.8	745	9.7	3.13	122	.212	.295	39	52	105	100	9.4	-3	-8	5.0
■ CHARLEY RADBOURN	Radbourn, Charles Gardner "Old Hoss" b: 12/11/1854, Rochester, N.Y. d: 2/5/1897, Bloomington, Ill. BR/TR, 5'9", 168 lbs. Deb: 5/05/1880 H																												
1881	Pro-N	25	11	**.694**	41	36	34	3	0	325	309	8.6	1	64	1.8	117	3.2	2.44	105	.262	.300	12	4	92	92	7.8	-0	3	0.4
1882	Pro-N	33	20	.623	55	52	51	**5**	0	474	429	8.1	6	51	1.0	**201**	3.8	2.09	**142**	.249	.270	**42**	**46**	103	98	0.7	-3	1	**4.3**
1883	Pro-N	**48**	25	.658	**76**	68	66	4	1	632	563	8.0	7	56	0.8	315	4.5	2.05	147	.246	**.264**	**76**	**68**	96	90	15.7	15	6	**8.2**
1884	Pro-N	**60**	12	**.833**	**75**	73	**73**	11	1	**679**	528	7.0	18	98	1.3	**441**	5.8	**1.38**	**207**	.223	.254	**121**	**111**	96	111	**21.0**	5	-3	**10.7**
1885	Pro-N	28	21	.571	49	49	49	2	0	446	423	8.5	4	83	1.7	154	3.1	2.20	119	.261	.297	31	21	93	117	6.7	11	3	3.6
1886	Bos-N	27	31	.466	58	58	57	3	0	509	521	9.2	18	111	2.0	218	3.9	3.01	107	.278	.318	17	11	97	109	-1.4	8	2	1.9
1887	Bos-N	24	23	.511	50	50	48	1	0	425	505	10.7	20	133	2.8	87	1.8	4.55	86	.311	.363	-24	-29	97	99	0.5	2	-4	-2.5
1888	Bos-N	7	16	.304	24	24	24	1	0	207	187	8.1	8	45	2.0	64	2.8	2.87	104	.254	.297	-1	2	105	91	-5.2	0	0	0.4
1889	Bos-N	20	11	.645	33	31	28	1	0	277	282	9.2	14	72	2.3	99	3.2	3.67	108	.279	.327	11	9	98	93	0.0	-1	0	0.8
1890	Bos-P	27	12	.692	41	38	36	1	0	343	352	9.2	8	100	2.6	80	2.1	3.31	133	.277	.330	35	42	104	92	4.5	0	4	3.9
1891	Cin-N	11	13	.458	26	24	23	2	0	218	236	9.7	13	62	2.6	54	2.2	4.25	73	.290	.340	-22	-27	93	83	1.2	-0	0	-2.3
Total	11	310	195	.614	528	503	489	34	2	4535	4335	8.6	117	875	1.7	1830	3.6	2.68	119	.263	.300	299	256	97	100	51.5	39	12	29.4
■ GEORGE RADBOURN	Radbourn, George B. "Dordy" b: 4/8/1856, Bloomington, Ill. d: 1/1/04, Bloomington, Ill. Deb: 5/30/1883																												
1883	Det-N	1	2	.333	3	3	2	0	0	22	38	15.5	1	7	2.9	2	0.8	6.55	45	.387	.428	-8	-9	94	108	-0.2	-1	0	-0.6
■ ROY RADEBAUGH	Radebaugh, Roy b: 2/22/1884, Champaign, Ill. d: 1/17/45, Cedar Rapids, Iowa BR/TR, 5'7", 160 lbs. Deb: 9/22/11																												
1911	StL-N	0	0	—	2	1	0	0	0	10	6	5.4	0	4	3.6	1	0.9	2.70	129	.176	.263	1	1	102	43	0.0	-0	0	0.1
■ DREW RADER	Rader, Drew Leon "Lefty" b: 5/14/01, Elmira, N.Y. d: 6/5/75, Catskill, N.Y. BR/TL, 6'2", 187 lbs. Deb: 7/18/21																												
1921	Pit-N	0	0	—	1	0	0	0	0	2	2	9.0	0	0	0.0	0	0.0	0.00	—	.286	.286	1	1	102	0	0.0	-0	0	0.1
■ PAUL RADFORD	Radford, Paul Revere "Shorty" b: 10/14/1861, Roxbury, Mass. d: 2/21/45, Boston, Mass. BR/TR, 5'6", 148 lbs. Deb: 5/01/1883																												
1884	Pro-N	0	2	.000	2	2	1	0	0	13	27	18.7	0	3	2.1	2	1.4	7.62	37	.434	.460	-7	-7	96	105	-0.9	0	0	-0.4
1885	Pro-N	0	2	.000	3	2	2	0	0	18	34	17.0	1	8	4.0	3	1.5	8.00	33	.413	.465	-10	-11	93	104	-0.9	1	0	-0.8
1887	NY-a	0	0	—	2	0	0	0	0	5	15	27.0	1	3	5.4	4	7.2	18.00	22	.531	.576	-8	-8	92	87	0.0	1	0	-0.5
1890	Cle-P	0	0	—	1	0	0	0	0	5	7	12.6	1	1	1.8	3	5.4	3.60	110	.343	.374	0	0	94	167	0.0	0	0	0.0
1891	Bos-a	0	0	—	1	0	0	0	0	1	0	0.0	0	0	0.0	0	0.0	0.00	—	.000	.000	0	0	94	0	0.0	0	0	0.0
1893	Was-N	0	0	—	1	0	0	0	0	1	2	18.0	2	2	18.0	1	9.0	18.00	24	.432	.604	-1	-2	92	156	0.0	0	0	0.0
Total	6	0	4	.000	10	4	3	0	0	43	85	17.8	5	17	3.6	13	2.7	8.58	36	.424	.469	-25	-26	94	109	-1.8	2	0	-1.7
■ HAL RAETHER	Raether, Harold Herman "Bud" b: 10/10/32, Lake Mills, Wis. BR/TR, 6'1", 185 lbs. Deb: 7/04/54																												
1954	Phi-A	0	0	—	1	0	0	0	0	2	1	4.5	0	4	18.0	0	0.0	4.50	87	.200	.556	-0	-0	105	158	0.0	0	0	0.0
1957	KC-A	0	0	—	1	0	0	0	0	2	2	9.0	1	0	0.0	0	0.0	9.00	43	.250	.250	-1	-1	102	61	0.0	0	0	0.0
Total	2	0	0	—	2	0	0	0	0	4	3	6.8	1	4	9.0	0	0.0	6.75	57	.231	.412	-1	-1	103	109	0.0	0	0	0.0
■ KEN RAFFENSBERGER	Raffensberger, Kenneth David b: 8/8/17, York, Pa. BR/TL, 6'2", 185 lbs. Deb: 4/25/39																												
1939	StL-N	0	0	—	1	0	0	0	0	1	2	18.0	0	0	0.0	1	9.0	0.00	—	.400	.400	0	0	103	0	0.0	0	0	0.0
1940	Chi-N	7	9	.438	43	10	3	0	3	115	120	9.4	10	29	2.3	55	4.3	3.37	113	.271	.315	6	6	99	120	-0.8	-1	-1	0.4
1941	Chi-N	0	1	.000	10	1	0	0	0	18	17	8.5	0	7	3.5	5	2.5	4.50	76	.262	.329	-2	-2	94	75	-0.4	-1	1	-0.1
1943	Phi-N	0	1	.000	1	1	1	0	0	8	7	7.9	0	2	2.3	3	3.4	1.13	287	.241	.273	2	2	96	212	-0.4	-0	0	0.2
1944	Phi-N	13	20	.394	37	31	18	3	0	259	257	8.9	9	45	**1.6**	136	4.7	3.06	121	.252	.279	16	19	103	88	-0.1	-4	-3	1.3
1945	Phi-N	0	3	.000	5	4	1	0	0	24	28	10.5	3	14	5.3	6	2.3	4.50	86	.283	.362	-2	-2	102	118	-1.4	-1	0	-0.2
1946	Phi-N	8	15	.348	39	23	14	2	**6**	196	203	9.3	10	39	1.8	73	3.4	3.63	92	.265	.297	-5	-6	98	84	-2.8	-0	-3	-0.9
1947	Phi-N	2	6	.250	10	7	3	1	0	41	50	11.0	4	8	1.8	16	3.5	5.49	75	.307	.335	-6	-6	102	87	-1.5	0	1	-0.4
	Cin-N	6	5	.545	19	15	7	0	1	107	132	11.1	11	29	2.4	38	3.2	4.12	91	.305	.341	-1	-4	92	119	0.8	-1	-1	-0.5
	Yr	8	11	.421	29	22	10	1	1	148	182	11.1	15	37	2.3	54	3.3	4.50	86	.305	.338	-7	-11	95	119	-0.7	0	0	-0.9
1948	Cin-N	11	12	.478	40	24	7	4	0	180	187	9.4	15	37	1.9	57	2.8	3.85	109	.259	.291	2	7	106	86	1.4	-3	-2	0.2
1949	Cin-N	18	17	.514	41	38	20	**5**	0	284	289	9.2	23	80	2.5	103	3.3	3.39	117	.264	.312	20	18	98	109	4.0	1	-3	1.6
1950	Cin-N	14	19	.424	38	35	18	4	0	239	271	10.2	34	40	**1.5**	87	3.3	4.26	103	.279	.305	-3	4	106	98	-0.2	-2	-3	0.0
1951	Cin-N	16	17	.485	42	33	14	5	5	249	232	8.4	30	38	**1.4**	81	2.9	3.43	118	.246	**.274**	15	17	103	92	1.6	-3	-4	1.0
1952	Cin-N	17	13	.567	38	33	18	**6**	1	247	247	9.0	18	45	1.6	93	3.4	2.81	133	.261	.292	25	26	100	117	3.8	-2	-2	2.3
1953	Cin-N	7	14	.333	26	26	9	1	0	174	200	10.3	23	33	1.7	47	2.4	3.93	109	.289	.317	7	7	100	**115**	-2.8	-1	1	0.7
1954	Cin-N	0	2	.000	6	1	0	0	0	10	15	13.5	2	3	2.7	5	4.5	8.10	52	.333	.360	-4	-4	104	79	-0.9	0	-0	-0.3
Total	15	119	154	.436	396	282	133	31	16	2152	2257	9.4	192	449	1.9	806	3.4	3.60	109	.267	.301	71	80	101	101	0.3	-17	-18	5.3
■ AL RAFFO	Raffo, Albert Martin b: 11/27/41, San Francisco, Cal. BR/TR, 6'5", 210 lbs. Deb: 4/29/69																												
1969	Phi-N	1	3	.250	45	0	0	0	1	72	81	10.1	6	25	3.1	38	4.8	4.13	87	.286	.347	-4	-4	100	110	-0.6	0	1	-0.3
■ PAT RAGAN	Ragan, Don Carlos Patrick b: 11/15/1888, Blanchard, Iowa d: 9/4/56, Los Angeles, Cal. BR/TR, 5'10.5", 185 lbs. Deb: 09 C																												
1909	Cin-N	0	1	.000	2	0	0	0	0	8	7	7.9	0	4	4.5	2	2.3	3.38	72	.259	.355	-1	-1	94	99	-0.4	0	-0	0.0
	Chi-N	0	0	—	2	0	0	0	0	4	4	9.0	0	1	2.3	2	4.5	2.25	110	.286	.333	0	0	95	145	0.0	-0	0	0.0
	Yr	0	1	.000	4	0	0	0	0	12	11	8.3	0	5	3.8	4	3.0	3.00	82	.268	.348	-1	-1	94	145	-0.4	0	-0	0.0
1911	Bro-N	4	3	.571	22	7	5	2	1	94	81	7.8	0	31	3.0	39	3.7	2.11	160	.252	.321	14	13	99	137	0.9	-1	-1	1.1
1912	Bro-N	7	18	.280	36	26	12	1	1	208	211	9.1	7	65	2.8	101	4.4	3.63	91	.259	.317	-5	-7	97	79	-3.6	-7	-2	-1.5
1913	Bro-N	15	18	.455	44	32	14	0	0	265	284	9.6	10	64	2.2	109	3.7	3.77	89	.281	.316	-17	-12	105	94	0.7	-2	2	-1.2
1914	Bro-N	10	15	.400	38	26	14	1	3	208	214	9.3	5	85	3.7	106	4.6	2.99	94	.270	.335	-5	-4	101	115	-2.5	-3	0	-0.7
1915	Bro-N	1	0	1.000	5	0	0	0	0	20	11	4.9	0	8	3.6	7	3.1	0.90	312	.164	.247	4	4	102	102	0.5	-0	0	0.4
	Bos-N	16	12	.571	33	26	13	3	0	227	208	8.2	2	59	2.3	81	3.2	2.46	109	.255	.301	7	6	97	112	0.9	-1	-3	0.1

YEAR	TM/L	W	L	PCT	G	GS	CG	SHO	SV	IP	H	H/G	HR	BB	BB/G	SO	SO/G	ERA	/A	OAVG	OOBP	PR	/A	PF	CPI	WAT	PB	PD	TPI
	Yr	17	12	.586	38	26	13	3	0	247	219	8.0	2	67	2.4	88	3.2	2.33	115	.248	.297	12	10	98	112	1.4	-0	-2	0.5
1916	Bos-N	9	9	.500	28	23	14	3	0	182	143	7.1	3	47	2.3	94	4.6	2.08	115	.218	.265	11	6	91	85	-1.4	3	1	1.1
1917	Bos-N	6	9	.400	30	13	5	1	1	148	138	8.4	6	35	2.1	61	3.7	2.92	90	.250	.285	-3	-5	97	93	-1.1	-1	0	-0.6
1918	Bos-N	8	17	.320	30	25	15	2	0	206	212	9.3	4	54	2.4	68	3.0	3.23	81	.270	.311	-11	-14	95	97	-3.6	-1	0	-1.6
1919	Bos-N	0	2	.000	4	3	0	0	0	13	16	11.1	0	3	2.1	3	2.1	6.92	42	.281	.311	-6	-6	100	45	-0.9	0	0	-0.5
	NY-N	1	0	1.000	7	1	1	0	0	23	19	7.4	0	14	5.5	7	2.7	1.57	179	.247	.337	3	3	96	223	0.5	1	0	0.5
	Yr	1	2	.333	11	4	1	0	0	36	35	8.8	0	17	4.3	10	2.5	3.50	81	.261	.327	-2	-3	98	223	-0.4	0	0	0.0
	Chi-A	0	0	—	1	0	0	0	0	1	1	9.0	0	0	0.0	0	0.0	0.00	—	.250	.250	0	0	102	0	0.0	0	0	0.1
1923	Phi-N	0	0	—	1	0	0	0	0	3	6	18.0	1	0	0.0	0	0.0	6.00	79	.400	.400	-1	-0	118	151	0.0	0	-0	0.0
Total	11	77	104	.425	283	182	93	13	6	1610	1555	8.7	38	470	2.6	680	3.8	2.99	97	.259	.308	-8	-18	98	101	-10.0	-12	-2	-2.8
■ **FRANK RAGLAND**	Ragland, Frank Roland b: 5/26/04, Water Valley, Miss d: 7/28/59, Paris, Miss. BR/TR, 6'1", 186 lbs. Deb: 4/17/32																												
1932	Was-A	1	0	1.000	12	1	0	0	0	38	54	12.8	5	21	5.0	11	2.6	7.34	60	.346	.426	-12	-13	98	105	0.5	1	0	-0.9
1933	Phi-N	0	4	.000	11	5	0	0	0	38	51	12.1	1	10	2.4	4	0.9	6.87	59	.317	.354	-15	-12	121	67	-1.9	-0	1	-1.0
Total	2	1	4	.200	23	6	0	0	0	76	105	12.4	6	31	3.7	15	1.8	7.11	60	.331	.391	-27	-24	109	86	-1.4	0	1	-1.9
■ **ERIC RAICH**	Raich, Eric James b: 11/1/51, Detroit, Mich. BR/TR, 6'4", 225 lbs. Deb: 5/24/75																												
1975	Cle-A	7	8	.467	18	17	2	0	0	93	118	11.4	12	31	3.0	34	3.3	5.52	68	.320	.361	-18	-18	100	102	-0.4	0	-1	-1.7
1976	Cle-A	0	0	—	1	0	0	0	0	3	7	21.0	1	0	0.0	1	3.0	15.00	23	.467	.467	-4	-4	100	77	0.0	0	0	-0.2
Total	2	7	8	.467	19	17	2	0	0	96	125	11.7	13	31	2.9	35	3.3	5.81	65	.326	.365	-22	-22	100	101	-0.4	0	-1	-1.9
■ **CHUCK RAINEY**	Rainey, Charles David b: 7/14/54, San Diego, Cal. BR/TR, 5'11", 220 lbs. Deb: 4/08/79																												
1979	Bos-A	8	5	.615	20	16	4	1	1	104	97	8.4	7	41	3.5	41	3.5	3.81	118	.250	.323	5	8	106	93	0.8	0	1	0.8
1980	Bos-A	8	3	.727	16	13	2	1	0	87	92	9.5	7	41	4.2	43	4.4	4.86	85	.273	.352	-8	-7	102	90	2.5	0	-1	-0.7
1981	Bos-A	0	1	.000	11	2	0	0	0	40	39	8.8	2	13	2.9	20	4.5	2.70	143	.252	.304	4	5	106	116	-0.4	0	1	0.6
1982	Bos-A	7	5	.583	27	25	3	3	0	129	146	10.2	14	63	4.4	57	4.0	5.02	89	.294	.368	-13	-8	110	106	0.5	0	1	-0.6
1983	Chi-N	14	13	.519	34	34	1	1	0	191	219	10.3	17	74	3.5	84	4.0	4.48	82	.295	.354	-18	-17	101	107	2.2	1	-3	-1.3
1984	Chi-N	5	7	.417	17	16	0	0	0	88	102	10.4	4	38	3.9	45	4.6	4.30	91	.290	.356	-7	-4	109	105	-1.8	-1	1	-0.3
	Oak-A	1	1	.500	16	0	0	0	1	31	43	12.5	2	17	4.9	10	2.9	6.68	55	.333	.397	-9	-10	92	93	0.0	1	-0	-0.9
Total	6	43	35	.551	141	106	10	6	2	670	738	9.9	53	287	3.9	300	4.0	4.50	90	.284	.352	-46	-33	105	102	3.8	-0	5	-2.4
■ **DAVE RAJSICH**	Rajsich, David Christopher b: 9/28/51, Youngstown, Ohio BL/TL, 6'5", 175 lbs. Deb: 7/02/78																												
1978	NY-A	0	0	—	4	2	0	0	0	13	16	11.1	0	6	4.2	9	6.2	4.15	88	.320	.379	-1	-1	97	119	0.0	0	-0	0.0
1979	Tex-A	1	3	.250	27	3	0	0	0	54	56	9.3	7	18	3.0	32	5.3	3.50	120	.267	.323	4	4	99	119	-0.9	0	1	0.5
1980	Tex-A	2	1	.667	24	1	0	0	2	48	56	10.5	7	22	4.1	35	6.6	6.00	68	.295	.367	-10	-10	100	92	0.6	0	0	-0.9
Total	3	3	4	.429	55	6	0	0	2	115	128	10.0	14	46	3.6	76	5.9	4.62	88	.284	.348	-7	-7	99	108	-0.3	0	1	-0.4
■ **ED RAKOW**	Rakow, Edward Charles "Rock" b: 5/30/36, Pittsburgh, Pa. BB/TR, 5'11", 178 lbs. Deb: 4/22/60																												
1960	LA-N	0	1	.000	9	2	0	0	0	22	30	12.3	5	11	4.5	9	3.7	7.36	58	.323	.387	-9	-8	114	95	-0.4	0	0	-0.6
1961	KC-A	2	8	.200	45	11	1	0	1	125	131	9.4	14	49	3.5	81	5.8	4.75	88	.269	.338	-10	-8	104	94	-2.3	-2	1	-0.8
1962	KC-A	14	17	.452	42	35	11	2	1	235	232	8.9	31	98	3.8	159	6.1	4.25	95	.260	.332	-7	-6	101	103	0.2	-5	2	-0.8
1963	KC-A	9	10	.474	34	26	7	1	0	174	173	8.9	18	61	3.2	104	5.4	3.93	100	.261	.324	-6	0	109	102	0.4	-2	1	0.0
1964	Det-A	8	9	.471	42	13	1	0	3	152	155	9.2	14	59	3.5	96	5.7	3.73	93	.266	.336	-2	-5	95	111	-0.9	-3	2	-0.6
1965	Det-A	0	0	—	6	0	0	0	0	13	14	9.7	2	11	7.6	10	6.9	6.23	58	.280	.391	-4	-4	104	99	0.0	-0	-1	-0.3
1967	Atl-N	3	2	.600	17	3	0	0	0	39	36	8.3	4	15	3.5	25	5.8	5.31	67	.240	.310	-8	-8	105	66	0.6	-1	-0	-0.9
Total	7	36	47	.434	195	90	20	3	5	760	771	9.1	88	304	3.6	484	5.7	4.33	90	.264	.334	-46	-37	103	101	-2.4	-13	4	-4.0
■ **JOHN RALEIGH**	Raleigh, John Austin b: 4/21/1890, Elkhorn, Wis. d: 8/24/55, Escondido, Cal. BR/TL, Deb: 09																												
1909	StL-N	1	10	.091	15	10	3	0	0	81	85	9.4	0	21	2.3	26	2.9	3.78	68	.285	.339	-11	-11	99	89	-4.1	-2	0	-1.0
1910	StL-N	0	0	—	3	1	0	0	0	5	8	14.4	0	0	0.0	2	3.6	9.00	31	.364	.364	-3	-3	93	54	0.0	-0	0	-0.2
Total	2	1	10	.091	18	11	3	0	0	86	93	9.7	0	21	2.2	28	2.9	4.08	64	.291	.340	-14	-14	99	87	-4.1	-2	0	-1.2
■ **PEP RAMBERT**	Rambert, Elmer Donald b: 8/1/16, Cleveland, Ohio d: 11/16/74, W.Palm Beach, Fla. BR/TR, 6', 175 lbs. Deb: 9/23/39																												
1939	Pit-N	0	0	—	2	0	0	0	0	4	7	15.8	0	1	2.3	4	9.0	9.00	44	.389	.421	-2	-2	101	75	0.0	0	0	-0.1
1940	Pit-N	0	1	.000	3	1	0	0	0	8	12	13.5	0	4	4.5	0	0.0	7.88	46	.333	.432	-4	-4	95	87	-0.4	0	0	-0.3
Total	2	0	1	.000	5	1	0	0	0	12	19	14.3	0	5	3.8	4	3.0	8.25	45	.352	.429	-6	-6	97	83	-0.4	0	0	-0.4
■ **PETE RAMBO**	Rambo, Warren Dawson b: 11/1/06, Thoroughfare, N.J. BR/TR, 5'9", 150 lbs. Deb: 9/16/26																												
1926	Phi-N	0	0	—	1	0	0	0	0	4	6	13.5	0	4	9.0	4	9.0	13.50	30	.353	.476	-4	-4	107	56	0.0	0	0	-0.2
■ **ALLAN RAMIREZ**	Ramirez, Daniel Allan b: 5/1/57, Victoria, Tex. BR/TR, 5'10", 180 lbs. Deb: 6/08/83																												
1983	Bal-A	4	4	.500	11	10	1	0	0	57	46	7.3	6	30	4.7	20	3.2	3.47	116	.229	.326	4	4	99	109	-0.6	0	0	0.4
■ **PEDRO RAMOS**	Ramos, Pedro (Guerra) "Pete" b: 4/28/35, Pinar Del Rio, Cuba BB/TR, 6', 175 lbs. Deb: 4/11/55																												
1955	Was-A	5	11	.313	45	9	3	1	5	130	121	8.4	13	39	2.7	34	2.4	3.88	96	.253	.312	1	-2	94	97	-0.7	-2	-1	-0.5
1956	Was-A	12	10	.545	37	18	4	0	0	152	178	10.5	23	76	4.5	54	3.2	5.27	84	.299	.372	-19	-14	107	109	3.2	0	-0	-1.3
1957	Was-A	12	16	.429	43	30	7	1	0	231	251	9.8	43	69	2.7	91	3.5	4.79	80	.271	.323	-26	-24	102	97	1.9	-1	-0	-2.4
1958	Was-A	14	18	.438	43	37	10	4	3	259	277	9.6	38	77	2.7	132	4.6	4.24	89	.273	.323	-14	-13	100	104	1.4	1	-1	-1.2
1959	Was-A	13	19	.406	37	35	11	0	0	234	233	9.0	29	52	2.0	95	3.7	4.15	94	.257	.301	-8	-6	102	90	0.0	-1	-1	-0.6
1960	Was-A	11	18	.379	43	36	14	1	2	**274**	254	8.3	24	99	3.3	160	5.3	3.45	115	.245	.310	13	16	102	99	-3.3	-2	0	1.4
1961	Min-A	11	20	.355	42	34	9	3	2	264	265	9.0	39	79	2.7	174	5.9	3.95	109	.258	.310	2	11	107	102	-3.4	1	-3	1.0
1962	Cle-A	10	12	.455	37	27	7	2	1	201	189	8.5	28	85	3.8	96	4.3	3.72	105	.246	.320	6	4	99	110	-0.9	2	0	0.6
1963	Cle-A	9	8	.529	36	22	5	0	0	185	156	7.6	29	41	2.0	169	8.2	3.11	114	.226	**.269**	11	9	98	101	0.8	1	-1	0.9
1964	Cle-A	7	10	.412	36	19	3	1	0	133	144	9.7	18	26	1.8	98	6.6	5.14	73	.273	.306	-22	-21	103	79	-1.4	2	-1	-1.9
	NY-A	1	0	1.000	13	0	0	0	8	22	13	5.3	1	0	0.0	21	8.6	1.23	297	.183	.176	6	6	101	72	0.5	-1	-1	0.5
	Yr	8	10	.444	49	19	3	1	8	155	157	9.1	19	26	1.5	119	6.9	4.59	81	.259	.285	-17	-15	103	72	-0.9	2	-1	-1.4
1965	NY-A	5	5	.500	65	0	0	0	19	92	80	7.8	7	27	2.6	68	6.7	2.93	119	.237	.289	5	6	101	102	0.2	-1	-1	0.5
1966	NY-A	3	9	.250	52	1	0	0	13	90	98	9.8	10	18	1.8	58	5.8	3.60	89	.283	.310	-2	-4	94	118	-2.6	-0	-0	-0.4
1967	Phi-N	0	0	—	6	0	0	0	0	8	14	15.8	1	8	9.0	1	1.1	9.00	39	.412	.522	-5	-5	104	122	0.0	-0	1	-0.4
1969	Pit-N	0	1	.000	5	0	0	0	0	6	8	12.0	2	0	0.0	4	6.0	6.00	56	.320	.308	-2	-2	94	105	-0.4	-0	0	-0.1
	Cin-N	4	3	.571	38	0	0	0	2	66	73	10.0	8	24	3.3	40	5.5	5.18	68	.284	.341	-12	-12	99	94	0.2	-1	0	-1.2
	Yr	4	4	.500	43	0	0	0	2	72	81	10.1	10	24	3.0	44	5.5	5.25	67	.287	.338	-13	-14	98	94	-0.2	-0	0	-1.3
1970	Was-A	0	0	—	4	0	0	0	0	8	10	11.3	2	4	4.5	10	11.3	7.88	46	.294	.359	-4	-4	97	79	0.0	0	0	-0.3
Total	15	117	160	.422	582	268	73	13	55	2355	2364	9.0	315	724	2.8	1305	5.0	4.08	95	.261	.314	-68	-57	101	100	-4.5	-1	-8	-5.4
■ **WILLIE RAMSDELL**	Ramsdell, James Willard "The Knuck" b: 4/4/16, Williamsburg, Kan. d: 10/8/69, Wichita, Kan. BR/TR, 5'11", 165 lbs. Deb: 9/24/47																												
1947	Bro-N	1	1	.500	2	0	0	0	0	3	4	12.0	0	3	9.0	3	9.0	6.00	70	.333	.471	-1	-1	103	132	-0.1	0	0	0.0
1948	Bro-N	4	4	.500	27	1	0	0	4	50	48	8.6	6	41	7.4	34	6.1	5.22	78	.251	.382	-7	-6	103	102	-0.2	-1	1	-0.5
1950	Bro-N	1	2	.333	5	0	0	0	1	6	7	10.5	0	2	3.0	2	3.0	3.00	144	.292	.370	1	1	104	146	-0.5	-0	0	0.1
	Cin-N	7	12	.368	27	22	8	1	0	157	151	8.7	17	75	4.3	83	4.8	3.73	118	.255	.339	7	12	106	114	-1.5	1	-1	1.1
	Yr	8	14	.364	32	22	8	1	1	163	158	8.7	17	77	4.3	85	4.7	3.70	119	.256	.339	8	12	106	114	-2.0	-0	-1	1.2
1951	Cin-N	9	17	.346	31	31	10	1	0	196	204	9.4	18	70	3.2	88	4.0	4.04	100	.266	.329	-2	0	103	100	-3.1	-1	-2	-0.1
1952	Chi-N	2	3	.400	19	4	0	0	0	67	41	5.5	5	24	3.2	30	4.0	2.42	159	.173	.258	10	11	103	77	-0.4	-1	-1	1.0
Total	5	24	39	.381	111	58	18	2	5	479	455	8.5	46	215	4.0	240	4.5	3.83	108	.250	.331	8	17	104	103	-5.8	-3	-2	1.6
■ **TOAD RAMSEY**	Ramsey, Thomas A. b: 8/8/1864, Indianapolis, Ind. d: 3/27/06, Indianapolis, Ind. BR/TL, Deb: 1885																												
1885	Lou-a	3	6	.333	9	9	9	0	0	79	44	5.0	1	28	3.2	83	9.5	1.94	173	.172	.254	12	12	103	70	-1.3	-3	0	1.0
1886	Lou-a	38	27	.585	67	67	**66**	3	0	**589**	447	**6.8**	3	207	3.2	499	7.6	2.46	151	**.220**	.292	65	82	108	93	**10.2**	-3	-3	7.3
1887	Lou-a	37	27	.578	65	64	61	0	0	561	544	8.7	9	167	2.7	**355**	**5.7**	3.43	132	.268	.323	54	69	106	94	2.5	-11	-7	4.5
1888	Lou-a	8	30	.211	40	40	37	1	0	342	362	9.5	10	86	2.3	228	6.0	3.42	83	.285	.330	-14	-22	93	104	-9.2	-6	-3	-2.7

YEAR	TM/L	W	L	PCT	G	GS	CG	SHO	SV	IP	H	H/G	HR	BB	BB/G	SO	SO/G	ERA	/A	OAVG	OOBP	PR	/A	PF	CPI	WAT	PB	PD	TPI
1889	Lou-a	1	16	.059	18	18	15	0	0	140	175	11.3	7	71	4.6	60	3.9	5.59	70	.322	.400	-27	-26	102	93	-6.1	-0	0	-1.9
	StL-a	3	1	.750	5	3	3	0	0	41	44	9.7	0	10	2.2	33	7.2	3.95	106	.289	.333	-0	1	109	82	0.5	1	0	0.2
	Yr	4	17	.190	23	21	18	0	0	181	219	10.9	7	81	4.0	93	4.6	5.22	76	.315	.386	-28	-25	104	82	-5.6	-0	0	-1.7
1890	StL-a	24	17	.585	44	40	34	1	0	349	325	8.4	10	102	2.6	257	**6.6**	3.69	120	.262	.318	7	29	115	86	0.8	-2	-6	2.2
Total	6	114	124	.479	248	241	225	5	0	2101	1941	8.3	40	671	2.9	1515	6.5	3.30	119	.258	.318	96	143	105	93	-2.6	-24	-19	10.6
■ RIBS RANEY	Raney, Frank Robert Donald (born Frank Robert Donald Raniszewski) b: 2/16/23, Detroit, Mich. BR/TR, 6'4", 190 lbs. Deb: 9/18/49																												
1949	StL-A	1	2	.333	3	3	1	0	0	16	23	12.9	2	12	6.8	5	2.8	7.88	55	.333	.427	-7	-6	104	91	0.0	-1	-0	-0.5
1950	StL-A	0	1	.000	1	0	0	0	0	2	2	9.0	0	2	9.0	2	9.0	4.50	113	.250	.400	0	0	111	101	-0.4	-0	0	0.0
Total	2	1	3	.250	4	3	1	0	0	18	25	12.5	2	14	7.0	7	3.5	7.50	59	.325	.424	-7	-6	105	93	-0.4	-1	0	-0.5
■ VIC RASCHI	Raschi, Victor John Angelo b: 3/28/19, W.Springfield, Mass. d: 10/18/88, Groveland, N.Y. BR/TR, 6'1", 205 lbs. Deb: 9/23/46																												
1946	NY-A	2	0	1.000	2	2	2	0	0	16	14	7.9	0	5	2.8	11	6.2	3.94	87	.230	.284	-1	-1	98	52	1.0	0	0	0.0
1947	NY-A	7	2	.778	15	14	6	1	0	105	89	7.6	11	38	3.3	51	4.4	3.86	89	.226	.294	-2	-5	92	80	1.9	2	-0	-0.3
1948	NY-A	19	8	.704	36	31	18	6	1	223	208	8.4	15	74	3.0	124	5.0	3.83	108	.247	.307	11	7	96	89	3.7	2	-1	0.8
1949	NY-A	21	10	.677	38	37	21	3	0	275	247	8.1	16	138	4.5	124	4.1	3.34	122	.241	.330	26	23	97	105	2.4	1	1	2.4
1950	NY-A	21	8	**.724**	33	32	17	2	1	257	232	8.1	19	116	4.1	155	5.4	3.99	110	.243	.324	17	11	96	91	4.1	1	-3	0.9
1951	NY-A	21	10	.677	35	34	15	4	0	258	233	8.1	20	103	3.6	**164**	5.7	3.28	111	.242	.315	24	10	88	108	2.1	-1	-3	0.5
1952	NY-A	16	6	.727	31	31	13	4	0	223	174	7.0	13	91	3.7	127	5.1	2.78	125	.216	.297	22	17	95	97	3.5	2	-3	1.6
1953	NY-A	13	6	.684	28	26	7	4	1	181	150	7.5	11	55	2.7	76	3.8	3.33	106	.224	**.279**	13	4	88	76	0.9	-2	-2	0.0
1954	StL-N	8	9	.471	30	29	6	2	0	179	182	9.2	24	71	3.6	73	3.7	4.73	86	.268	.331	-13	-13	100	92	0.1	-2	1	-1.2
1955	StL-N	0	1	.000	1	1	0	0	0	2	5	22.5	0	1	4.5	1	4.5	18.00	23	.556	.545	-3	-3	102	72	-0.4	0	0	-0.2
	KC-A	4	6	.400	20	18	1	0	0	101	132	11.8	10	35	3.1	38	3.4	5.44	77	.312	.361	-17	-14	106	95	0.0	-0	1	-1.1
Total	10	132	66	.667	269	255	106	26	3	1820	1666	8.2	139	727	3.6	944	4.7	3.72	105	.244	.315	78	36	95	94	19.3	3	-9	3.4
■ DENNIS RASMUSSEN	Rasmussen, Dennis Lee b: 4/18/59, Los Angles, Cal. BL/TL, 6'7", 230 lbs. Deb: 9/16/83																												
1983	SD-N	0	0	—	4	1	0	0	0	14	10	6.4	1	8	5.1	13	8.4	1.93	187	.200	.310	3	3	99	142	0.0	-0	1	0.3
1984	NY-A	9	6	.600	24	24	1	0	0	148	127	7.7	16	60	3.6	110	6.7	4.56	82	.234	.310	-9	-14	93	77	1.1	0	-1	-1.4
1985	NY-A	3	5	.375	22	16	2	0	0	102	97	8.6	10	42	3.7	63	5.6	3.97	98	.255	.326	2	-1	94	102	-1.5	0	0	0.0
1986	NY-A	18	6	.750	31	31	3	1	0	202	160	7.1	28	74	3.3	131	5.8	3.88	111	.217	.288	7	9	103	82	5.7	0	-1	0.8
1987	NY-A	9	7	.563	26	25	2	0	0	146	145	8.9	31	55	3.4	89	5.5	4.75	92	.260	.325	-4	-6	97	104	0.3	0	-0	-0.5
	Cin-N	4	1	.800	7	7	0	0	0	45	39	7.8	5	12	2.4	39	7.8	4.00	105	.229	.278	0	1	103	74	1.5	-1	0	0.0
1988	Cin-N	2	6	.250	11	11	1	1	0	56	68	10.9	8	22	3.5	27	4.3	5.79	63	.300	.361	-15	-13	105	96	-2.1	1	0	-1.2
	SD-N	14	4	.778	20	20	6	0	0	148	131	8.0	9	36	2.2	85	5.2	2.55	131	.238	.282	15	13	97	110	5.1	2	2	1.9
	Yr	16	10	.615	31	31	7	1	0	204	199	8.8	17	58	2.6	112	4.9	3.44	100	.254	.303	0	-0	99	110	3.0	1	2	0.7
Total	6	59	35	.628	145	135	15	2	0	861	777	8.1	108	309	3.2	557	5.8	4.02	98	.242	.307	-1	-8	98	94	10.1	2	0	-0.1
■ ERIC RASMUSSEN	Rasmussen, Eric Ralph (Born Harold Ralph Rasmussen) b: 3/22/52, Racine, Wis. BR/TR, 6'3", 205 lbs. Deb: 7/21/75																												
1975	StL-N	5	5	.500	14	13	2	1	0	81	86	9.6	8	20	2.2	59	6.6	3.78	99	.264	.305	-1	-0	103	92	0.0	-0	-0	0.0
1976	StL-N	6	12	.333	43	17	2	1	0	150	139	8.3	10	54	3.2	76	4.6	3.54	103	.247	.309	-1	2	105	93	-2.4	-1	3	0.4
1977	StL-N	11	17	.393	34	34	11	3	0	233	223	8.6	24	63	2.4	120	4.6	3.48	107	.254	.302	11	6	95	101	-3.7	1	-1	0.5
1978	StL-N	2	5	.286	10	10	2	1	0	60	61	9.2	4	20	3.0	32	4.8	4.20	82	.270	.318	-4	-5	96	91	-1.1	-1	0	-0.5
	SD-N	12	10	.545	27	24	3	2	0	146	154	9.5	16	43	2.7	59	3.6	4.07	81	.277	.323	-8	-12	93	104	0.7	-1	1	-1.2
	Yr	14	15	.483	37	34	5	3	0	206	215	9.4	20	63	2.8	91	4.0	4.11	81	.274	.321	-12	-17	93	104	-0.4	-1	1	-1.7
1979	SD-N	6	9	.400	45	20	5	3	3	157	142	8.1	9	42	2.4	54	3.1	3.27	111	.244	.286	8	6	97	87	-0.3	-2	-0	0.4
1980	SD-N	4	11	.267	40	14	0	0	1	111	130	10.5	9	33	2.7	50	4.1	4.38	77	.295	.340	-9	-12	94	104	-3.1	-1	-0	-1.3
1982	StL-N	1	2	.333	8	3	0	0	0	18	21	10.5	2	8	4.0	15	7.5	4.50	82	.288	.349	-2	-2	102	108	-0.5	-0	0	-0.1
1983	StL-N	0	0	—	6	0	0	0	1	8	16	18.0	1	4	4.5	6	6.8	11.25	32	.444	.500	-7	-7	98	90	0.0	0	0	-0.6
	KC-A	3	6	.333	11	9	2	1	0	53	61	10.4	4	22	3.7	18	3.1	4.75	88	.289	.352	-4	-3	102	98	-1.4	0	-0	-0.3
Total	8	50	77	.394	238	144	27	12	5	1017	1033	9.1	87	309	2.7	489	4.3	3.85	94	.266	.315	-16	-27	98	97	-11.8	-5	2	-2.7
■ HANS RASMUSSEN	Rasmussen, Henry Florian b: 4/18/1895, Chicago, Ill. d: 1/1/49, Chicago, Ill. BR/TR, 6'6", 220 lbs. Deb: 8/11/15																												
1915	Chi-F	0	0	—	2	0	0	0	0	2	3	13.5	0	2	9.0	2	9.0	13.50	21	.379	.504	-2	-2	95	56	0.0	-0	0	-0.2
■ FRED RATH	Rath, Frederick Helsher b: 9/1/43, Little Rock, Ark. BR/TR, 6'3", 200 lbs. Deb: 9/10/68																												
1968	Chi-A	0	0	—	5	0	0	0	0	11	8	6.5	0	3	2.5	3	2.5	1.64	186	.182	.245	2	2	102	57	0.0	0	0	0.2
1969	Chi-A	0	2	.000	3	2	0	0	0	12	11	8.3	4	8	6.0	4	3.0	7.50	53	.256	.365	-5	-5	110	86	-0.9	-0	0	-0.4
Total	2	0	2	.000	8	2	0	0	0	23	19	7.4	4	11	4.3	7	2.7	4.70	75	.218	.307	-4	-3	106	72	-0.9	-0	0	-0.2
■ STEVE RATZER	Ratzer, Steven Wayne b: 9/9/53, Paterson, N.J. BR/TR, 6'1", 192 lbs. Deb: 10/05/80																												
1980	Mon-N	0	0	—	1	1	0	0	0	4	9	20.3	0	2	4.5	0	0.0	11.25	32	.450	.500	-3	-3	98	87	0.0	-0	0	-0.2
1981	Mon-N	1	1	.500	12	0	0	0	0	17	23	12.2	2	7	3.7	4	2.1	6.35	54	.311	.366	-5	-6	98	87	0.0	-0	1	-0.4
Total	2	1	1	.500	13	1	0	0	0	21	32	13.7	2	9	3.9	4	1.7	7.29	47	.340	.394	-9	-9	98	87	0.0	-0	1	-0.6
■ DOUG RAU	Rau, Douglas James b: 12/15/48, Columbus, Tex. BL/TL, 6'2", 175 lbs. Deb: 9/02/72																												
1972	LA-N	2	2	.500	7	3	2	0	0	33	18	4.9	1	11	3.0	19	5.2	2.18	147	.159	.231	5	4	93	46	-0.1	1	0	0.5
1973	LA-N	4	2	.667	31	3	0	0	3	64	64	9.0	5	28	3.9	51	7.2	3.94	92	.259	.332	-2	-2	99	98	0.6	-1	0	-0.2
1974	LA-N	13	11	.542	36	35	3	1	0	198	191	8.7	20	70	3.2	126	5.7	3.73	87	.251	.313	-2	-10	90	96	-1.8	-0	-0	-1.1
1975	LA-N	15	9	.625	38	38	8	2	0	258	227	7.9	18	61	2.1	151	5.3	3.10	109	.236	.278	15	8	93	84	2.4	2	-1	0.9
1976	LA-N	16	12	.571	34	32	8	3	0	231	221	8.6	18	69	2.7	98	3.8	2.57	135	.258	.313	24	23	99	**139**	0.1	1	-0	2.6
1977	LA-N	14	8	.636	32	32	4	2	0	212	232	9.8	15	49	2.1	126	5.3	3.44	111	.282	.320	11	9	98	114	1.0	-0	-1	0.7
1978	LA-N	15	9	.625	30	30	7	2	0	199	219	9.9	17	68	3.1	95	4.3	3.26	107	.284	.336	7	5	97	**135**	1.3	-1	-2	0.1
1979	LA-N	1	5	.167	11	11	1	1	0	56	73	11.7	3	22	3.5	28	4.5	5.30	70	.320	.381	-10	-10	99	102	-1.9	1	0	-0.8
1981	Cal-A	1	2	.333	3	3	0	0	0	10	14	12.6	2	4	3.6	3	2.7	9.00	42	.341	.400	-6	-6	104	78	-0.3	0	-0	-0.5
Total	9	81	60	.574	222	187	33	11	3	1261	1259	9.0	99	382	2.7	697	5.0	3.35	104	.262	.314	42	20	96	110	1.3	2	-5	2.2
■ BOB RAUCH	Rauch, Robert John b: 6/16/49, Brookings, S.D. BR/TR, 6'4", 200 lbs. Deb: 6/29/72																												
1972	NY-N	0	1	.000	19	0	0	0	1	27	27	9.0	3	21	7.0	23	7.7	5.00	66	.273	.381	-5	-5	96	109	-0.4	-0	0	-0.4
■ LANCE RAUTZHAN	Rautzhan, Clarence George b: 8/20/52, Pottsville, Pa. BR/TL, 6'1", 195 lbs. Deb: 7/23/77																												
1977	LA-N	4	1	.800	25	0	0	0	2	21	25	10.7	0	7	3.0	13	5.6	4.29	89	.313	.360	-1	-1	98	104	1.3	-0	0	0.0
1978	LA-N	2	1	.667	43	0	0	0	4	61	61	9.0	1	19	2.8	25	3.7	2.95	118	.263	.314	4	4	97	109	0.3	-0	2	0.5
1979	LA-N	0	2	.000	12	0	0	0	1	10	9	8.1	0	11	9.9	5	4.5	7.20	52	.273	.447	-4	-4	99	82	-0.9	0	0	-0.2
	Mil-A	0	0	—	3	0	0	0	0	3	3	9.0	0	10	30.0	2	6.0	9.00	47	.300	.650	-2	-2	99	140	0.0	0	0	-0.1
Total	3	6	4	.600	83	0	0	0	7	95	98	9.3	1	47	4.5	45	4.3	3.88	93	.276	.355	-2	-3	97	106	0.7	-1	2	0.3
■ SHANE RAWLEY	Rawley, Shane William b: 7/27/55, Racine, Wis. BR/TL, 6', 170 lbs. Deb: 4/06/78																												
1978	Sea-A	4	9	.308	52	2	0	0	4	111	114	9.2	7	51	4.1	66	5.4	4.14	95	.275	.352	-4	-2	104	105	-0.7	0	1	-0.1
1979	Sea-A	5	9	.357	48	3	0	0	11	84	88	9.4	2	40	4.3	48	5.1	3.86	111	.278	.354	3	4	101	108	-0.9	0	1	0.4
1980	Sea-A	7	7	.500	59	0	0	0	13	114	103	8.1	3	63	5.0	68	5.4	3.32	128	.257	.349	9	12	105	119	1.6	0	2	1.4
1981	Sea-A	4	6	.400	46	0	0	0	8	68	64	8.5	1	38	5.0	35	4.6	3.97	93	.257	.349	-2	-2	101	95	0.0	0	0	-0.1
1982	NY-A	11	10	.524	47	17	3	0	3	164	165	9.1	10	54	3.0	111	6.1	4.06	97	.267	.316	0	-2	97	93	0.8	0	1	0.0
1983	NY-A	14	14	.500	34	33	13	2	1	238	246	9.3	19	79	3.0	124	4.7	3.78	106	.269	.325	8	6	98	105	-1.7	0	0	0.5
1984	NY-A	2	3	.400	11	10	0	0	0	42	46	9.9	0	27	5.8	24	5.1	6.21	60	.272	.369	-10	-12	93	67	-0.6	0	-0	-1.0
	Phi-N	10	6	.625	18	18	3	0	0	120	117	8.8	13	27	2.0	58	4.3	3.83	95	.257	.295	-3	-2	101	92	2.2	-2	-1	-0.4
1985	Phi-N	13	8	.619	36	31	6	2	0	199	188	8.5	16	81	3.7	106	4.8	3.30	111	.249	.319	7	8	102	109	3.4	0	1	1.0
1986	Phi-N	11	7	.611	23	23	7	1	0	158	166	9.5	13	50	2.8	73	4.2	3.53	110	.270	.322	3	6	104	110	1.6	0	-0	0.6
1987	Phi-N	17	11	.607	36	36	4	1	0	230	250	9.8	23	86	3.4	123	4.8	4.38	98	.279	.339	-8	-3	105	103	3.6	-0	-1	-0.3
1988	Phi-N	8	16	.333	32	32	4	1	0	198	220	10.0	27	78	3.5	87	4.0	4.18	85	.286	.346	-16	-14	103	122	-2.3	-1	-0	-1.5
Total	11	106	106	.500	442	205	40	7	40	1726	1767	9.2	134	674	3.5	923	4.8	3.92	100	.269	.333	-13	-1	102	105	7.0	-3	3	0.5

YEAR	TM/L	W	L	PCT	G	GS	CG	SHO	SV	IP	H	H/G	HR	BB	BB/G	SO	SO/G	ERA	/A	OAVG	OOBP	PR	/A	PF	CPI	WAT	PB	PD	TPI
CARL RAY	Ray, Carl Grady b: 1/31/1889, Danbury, N.C. d: 4/3/70, Walnut Cove, N.C. BL/TL, 5'11", 170 lbs. Deb: 9/25/15																												
1915	Phi-A	0	1	.000	2	1	0	0	0	7	11	14.1	0	6	7.7	6	7.7	5.14	59	.333	.488	-2	-2	103	158	-0.4	-0	-0	-0.1
1916	Phi-A	0	1	.000	3	1	0	0	0	9	9	9.0	0	14	14.0	5	5.0	5.00	60	.257	.480	-2	-2	105	129	-0.4	-0	-0	-0.2
Total	2	0	2	.000	5	2	0	0	0	16	20	11.3	0	20	11.3	11	6.2	5.06	59	.294	.484	-4	-4	104	142	-0.8	-0	-0	-0.3
JIM RAY	Ray, James Francis "Sting" b: 12/1/44, Rock Hill, S.C. BR/TR, 6'1", 185 lbs. Deb: 9/16/65																												
1965	Hou-N	0	2	.000	3	2	0	0	0	8	11	12.4	1	6	6.8	7	7.9	10.13	32	.355	.447	-6	-6	91	77	-0.9	-0	0	-0.5
1966	Hou-N	0	0	—	1	0	0	0	0	0	0	—	0	1	—	0	—	∞	—	—	1.000	-1	-1	99	31	0.0	0	0	0.0
1968	Hou-N	2	3	.400	41	2	1	0	1	81	65	7.2	5	25	2.8	71	7.9	2.67	112	.220	.273	3	3	100	93	-0.2	-1	-1	0.1
1969	Hou-N	8	2	.800	40	13	0	0	0	115	105	8.2	11	48	3.8	115	9.0	3.91	93	.245	.317	-4	-3	101	94	3.1	-1	-1	-0.4
1970	Hou-N	6	3	.667	52	2	0	0	5	105	97	8.3	13	49	4.2	67	5.7	3.26	117	.251	.330	9	6	94	131	1.6	-0	0	0.5
1971	Hou-N	10	4	.714	47	1	0	0	3	98	72	6.6	3	31	2.8	46	4.2	2.11	152	.211	.275	15	12	92	101	3.3	0	-2	1.1
1972	Hou-N	10	9	.526	54	0	0	0	8	90	77	7.7	10	44	4.4	50	5.0	4.30	85	.227	.316	-8	-7	105	82	-0.3	-1	-1	-0.9
1973	Hou-N	6	4	.600	42	0	0	0	6	69	65	8.5	5	38	5.0	25	3.3	4.43	78	.253	.346	-6	-7	95	92	1.0	0	-0	-0.7
1974	Det-A	1	3	.250	28	0	0	0	2	52	49	8.5	4	29	5.0	26	4.5	4.50	87	.254	.345	-5	-3	108	91	-0.8	0	0	-0.2
Total	9	43	30	.589	308	20	1	0	25	618	541	7.9	52	271	3.9	407	5.9	3.61	97	.238	.315	-3	-6	99	99	6.8	-3	-5	-1.0
FARMER RAY	Ray, Robert Henry b: 9/17/1886, Ft.Lyon, Colo. d: 3/11/63, Electra, Tex. BL/TR, 5'11", 160 lbs. Deb: 6/13/10																												
1910	StL-A	4	10	.286	21	16	11	0	0	141	146	9.3	3	49	3.1	35	2.2	3.57	71	.285	.356	-17	-16	101	106	-0.4	0	-4	-2.0
CURT RAYDON	Raydon, Curtis Lowell b: 11/18/33, Bloomington, Ill. BR/TR, 6'4", 190 lbs. Deb: 4/15/58																												
1958	Pit-N	8	4	.667	31	20	2	1	1	134	118	7.9	18	61	4.1	85	5.7	3.63	102	.236	.321	5	1	94	105	1.7	-2	-3	-0.3
BUGS RAYMOND	Raymond, Arthur Lawrence b: 2/24/1882, Chicago, Ill. d: 9/7/12, Chicago, Ill. BR/TR, 5'10", 180 lbs. Deb: 9/23/04																												
1904	Det-A	0	1	.000	5	2	1	0	0	15	14	8.4	0	6	3.6	7	4.2	3.00	85	.270	.345	-1	-1	98	101	-0.4	-1	1	0.1
1907	StL-N	2	4	.333	8	6	6	1	0	65	56	7.8	3	21	2.9	34	4.7	1.66	149	.260	.329	6	6	100	162	0.0	-0	0	0.7
1908	StL-N	15	25	.375	48	37	23	5	2	324	236	6.6	2	95	2.6	145	4.0	2.03	115	.232	.306	11	11	100	88	2.2	1	3	1.6
1909	NY-N	18	12	.600	39	31	18	2	0	270	239	8.0	7	87	2.9	121	4.0	2.47	109	.245	.311	4	6	103	110	0.0	-0	2	0.9
1910	NY-N	4	11	.267	19	11	6	0	0	99	106	9.6	2	40	3.6	55	5.0	3.82	73	.280	.362	-9	-11	92	102	-4.2	-0	2	-0.9
1911	NY-N	6	4	.600	17	9	4	1	0	82	73	8.0	1	33	3.6	39	4.3	3.29	102	.248	.328	1	1	99	92	-0.3	-0	1	0.1
Total	6	45	57	.441	136	96	58	9	2	855	724	7.6	15	282	3.0	401	4.2	2.48	105	.247	.320	13	12	100	103	-2.7	-0	9	2.5
HARRY RAYMOND	Raymond, Harry H. "Jack" b: 2/20/1862, Utica, N.Y. d: 3/21/25, San Diego, Cal. 5'9", 179 lbs. Deb: 1888																												
1889	Lou-a	1	0	1.000	1	1	1	0	0	9	8	8.0	0	11	11.0	1	1.0	1.00	393	.252	.445	3	3	102	503	0.5	-0	0	0.3
CLAUDE RAYMOND	Raymond, Joseph Claude Marc "Frenchy" b: 5/7/37, St.Jean, Que., Canada BR/TR, 5'10", 175 lbs. Deb: 4/15/59																												
1959	Chi-A	0	0	—	3	0	0	0	0	4	5	11.3	2	2	4.5	1	2.3	9.00	41	.333	.368	-2	-2	95	105	0.0	0	0	-0.1
1961	Mil-N	1	0	1.000	13	0	0	0	2	20	22	9.9	2	9	4.0	13	5.8	4.05	91	.275	.352	-0	-1	91	113	0.5	-0	0	0.0
1962	Mil-N	5	5	.500	26	0	0	0	10	43	37	7.7	5	15	3.1	40	8.4	2.72	142	.236	.307	6	5	98	129	-0.2	-1	-1	0.4
1963	Mil-N	4	6	.400	45	0	0	0	5	53	57	9.7	12	27	4.6	44	7.5	5.43	60	.268	.358	-13	-13	100	103	-1.1	2	1	-0.9
1964	Hou-N	5	5	.500	38	0	0	0	0	80	64	7.2	3	22	2.5	56	6.3	2.81	124	.229	.283	6	6	98	94	0.8	-0	1	0.7
1965	Hou-N	7	4	.636	33	7	2	0	5	96	87	8.2	6	16	1.5	79	7.4	2.91	111	.244	.279	7	3	91	99	2.3	-0	-0	0.3
1966	Hou-N	7	5	.583	62	0	0	0	16	92	85	8.3	10	25	2.4	73	7.1	3.13	114	.242	.295	5	4	99	105	1.6	-0	-2	0.2
1967	Hou-N	0	4	.000	21	0	0	0	5	31	31	9.0	5	7	2.0	17	4.9	3.19	101	.256	.305	1	0	95	126	-1.9	-0	-0	0.0
	Atl-N	4	1	.800	28	0	0	0	5	34	33	8.7	2	11	2.9	14	3.7	2.65	133	.260	.308	3	3	105	132	1.6	-0	-0	0.4
	Yr	4	5	.444	49	0	0	0	10	65	64	8.9	7	18	2.5	31	4.3	2.91	116	.255	.299	3	3	100	132	-0.3	0	-0	0.4
1968	Atl-N	3	5	.375	36	0	0	0	10	60	56	8.4	4	18	2.7	37	5.6	2.85	98	.256	.304	1	-0	94	119	-0.9	-0	0	0.0
1969	Atl-N	2	2	.500	33	0	0	0	1	48	56	10.5	4	13	2.4	15	2.8	5.25	70	.298	.340	-9	-8	103	88	-0.2	0	-1	-0.8
	Mon-N	1	2	.333	15	0	0	0	1	22	21	8.6	2	8	3.3	11	4.5	4.09	91	.256	.323	-1	-1	103	97	0.0	-0	1	0.0
	Yr	3	4	.429	48	0	0	0	2	70	77	9.9	6	21	2.7	26	3.3	4.89	76	.281	.328	-10	-9	103	97	-0.2	0	-0	-0.8
1970	Mon-N	6	7	.462	59	0	0	0	23	83	76	8.2	13	27	2.9	68	7.4	4.45	93	.240	.297	-4	-3	102	85	0.1	-1	-1	-0.4
1971	Mon-N	1	7	.125	37	0	0	0	0	54	81	13.5	5	25	4.2	29	4.8	4.67	74	.373	.426	-7	-7	100	154	-2.8	-0	1	-0.6
Total	12	46	53	.465	449	7	2	0	83	720	711	8.9	75	225	2.8	497	6.2	3.66	95	.261	.316	-8	-13	98	108	-0.2	-2	0	-0.8
BARRY RAZIANO	Raziano, Barry John b: 2/5/47, New Orleans, La. BB/TR, 5'10", 175 lbs. Deb: 8/18/73																												
1973	KC-A	0	0	—	2	0	0	0	0	5	6	10.8	1	1	1.8	0	0.0	5.40	77	.316	.364	-1	-1	109	115	0.0	0	0	0.0
1974	Cal-A	1	2	.333	13	0	0	0	1	17	15	7.9	1	8	4.2	9	4.8	6.35	53	.246	.333	-5	-6	93	55	-0.2	0	-0	-0.5
Total	2	1	2	.333	15	0	0	0	1	22	21	8.6	2	9	3.7	9	3.7	6.14	58	.262	.341	-6	-6	97	69	-0.2	0	0	-0.5
RIP REAGAN	Reagan, Arthur (born Arthur Edgar Ragan) b: 6/5/1878, Lincoln, Ill. d: 6/8/53, Kansas City, Mo. BR/TR, 5'11", 170 lbs. Deb: 03																												
1903	Cin-N	0	2	.000	3	2	2	0	0	18	40	20.0	0	7	3.5	7	3.5	6.00	58	.474	.520	-5	-5	107	156	-0.9	0	0	-0.4
JIM REARDON	Reardon, James Matthew b: 1866, Hoosick Falls, N.Y. d: 2/25/1891, Hoosick Falls, N.Y Deb: 7/17/1886																												
1886	StL-N	0	1	.000	1	1	1	0	0	8	10	11.3	1	5	5.6	0	0.0	6.75	48	.320	.413	-3	-3	98	92	-0.4	0	0	-0.2
	Cin-a	0	1	.000	1	1	0	0	0	2	5	22.5	0	4	18.0	0	0.0	18.00	18	.481	.625	-3	-3	96	87	-0.4	-1	0	-0.2
JEFF REARDON	Reardon, Jeffrey James b: 10/1/55, Dalton, Mass. BR/TR, 6', 190 lbs. Deb: 8/25/79																												
1979	NY-N	1	2	.333	18	0	0	0	2	21	12	5.1	2	9	3.9	10	4.3	1.71	210	.174	.259	5	4	96	125	-0.1	0	-0	0.4
1980	NY-N	8	7	.533	61	0	0	0	6	110	96	7.9	10	47	3.8	101	8.3	2.62	134	.231	.301	12	11	97	122	1.7	-1	-2	0.8
1981	NY-N	1	0	1.000	18	0	0	0	2	29	27	8.4	2	12	3.7	28	8.7	3.41	105	.245	.323	0	1	103	102	0.5	-0	-0	0.0
	Mon-N	2	0	1.000	25	0	0	0	6	42	21	4.5	3	9	1.9	21	4.5	1.29	266	.148	.200	10	10	98	59	1.0	-0	-1	0.9
	Yr	3	0	1.000	43	0	0	0	8	71	48	6.1	5	21	2.7	49	6.2	2.15	162	.189	.251	11	10	100	59	1.5	-0	-1	0.9
1982	Mon-N	7	4	.636	75	0	0	0	26	109	87	7.2	6	36	3.0	86	7.1	2.06	182	.221	.282	19	21	104	123	1.3	-0	-1	2.0
1983	Mon-N	7	9	.438	66	0	0	0	21	92	87	8.5	7	44	4.3	78	7.6	3.03	121	.250	.328	6	7	101	123	-1.1	-0	-2	0.4
1984	Mon-N	7	7	.500	68	0	0	0	23	87	70	7.2	5	37	3.8	79	8.2	2.90	113	.220	.303	7	4	91	99	0.2	-1	-2	0.1
1985	Mon-N	2	8	.200	63	0	0	0	**41**	88	68	7.0	7	26	2.7	67	6.9	3.17	106	.209	.267	4	2	94	71	-3.1	0	-0	0.2
1986	Mon-N	7	9	.438	62	0	0	0	35	89	83	8.4	12	26	2.6	67	6.8	3.94	93	.251	.299	-2	-3	98	96	-0.8	-0	-0	-0.2
1987	Min-A	8	8	.500	63	0	0	0	31	80	70	7.9	14	28	3.1	83	9.3	4.50	95	.232	.300	-0	-2	96	85	-0.3	0	-1	-0.2
1988	Min-A	2	4	.333	63	0	0	0	42	73	68	8.4	6	15	1.8	56	6.9	2.47	170	.245	.284	12	14	105	125	-1.1	0	-2	1.2
Total	10	52	58	.473	582	0	0	0	235	820	689	7.6	74	289	3.2	676	7.4	2.93	125	.227	.292	73	68	98	104	-1.8	-2	-12	5.6
FRANK REBERGER	Reberger, Frank Beall "Crane" b: 6/7/44, Caldwell, Idaho BL/TR, 6'5", 200 lbs. Deb: 6/06/68																												
1968	Chi-N	0	1	.000	3	1	0	0	0	6	9	13.5	1	2	3.0	3	4.5	4.50	75	.346	.393	-1	-1	112	149	-0.4	0	0	0.0
1969	SD-N	1	2	.333	67	0	0	0	6	88	83	8.5	6	41	4.2	65	6.6	3.58	101	.258	.336	0	0	100	111	0.0	0	2	0.2
1970	SF-N	7	8	.467	45	18	3	0	2	152	178	10.5	13	98	5.8	117	6.9	5.57	70	.293	.389	-26	-29	96	101	-0.9	1	0	-2.6
1971	SF-N	3	0	1.000	13	7	0	0	0	44	37	7.6	5	19	3.9	21	4.3	3.89	88	.228	.312	-2	-2	99	89	1.5	0	0	-0.1
1972	SF-N	3	4	.429	20	11	2	0	0	99	97	8.8	10	37	3.4	52	4.7	4.00	86	.257	.326	-6	-6	100	99	0.0	2	1	-0.2
Total	5	14	15	.483	148	37	5	0	8	389	404	9.3	35	197	4.6	258	6.0	4.51	81	.270	.354	-34	-37	98	102	0.2	4	4	-2.7
JOHN RECCIUS	Reccius, John b: 6/7/1862, Louisville, Ky. d: 9/1/30, Louisville, Ky. 5'6.5", Deb: 5/02/1882																												
1882	Lou-a	4	6	.400	13	10	9	1	0	95	106	10.0	3	22	2.1	31	2.9	3.03	80	.288	.328	-4	-7	90	119	-1.2	3	0	-0.5
1883	Lou-a	0	0	—	1	0	0	0	0	4	10	22.5	0	0	0.0	0	0.0	2.25	138	.475	.475	0	0	94	442	0.0	-0	0	0.0
Total	2	4	6	.400	14	10	9	1	0	99	116	10.5	3	22	2.0	31	2.8	3.00	81	.298	.335	-3	-6	90	132	-1.2	3	0	-0.5
PHIL RECCIUS	Reccius, Phillip b: 6/7/1862, Louisville, Ky. d: 2/15/03, Louisville, Ky. 5'9", 163 lbs. Deb: 9/25/1882																												
1884	Lou-a	6	7	.462	18	11	11	0	0	129	118	8.2	4	19	1.3	46	3.2	2.72	103	.252	.281	7	1	87	106	-1.8	3	0	0.1
1885	Lou-a	0	4	.000	7	5	4	0	1	40	46	10.3	0	11	2.5	10	2.3	3.82	88	.300	.347	-3	-2	103	105	-1.9	1	0	-0.1
1886	Lou-a	0	1	.000	1	1	0	0	0	3	7	21.0	0	3	9.0	0	0.0	9.00	41	.464	.553	-2	-2	108	133	-0.4	0	0	0.0
1887	Cle-a	0	0	—	1	0	0	0	0	7	8	10.3	0	5	6.4	0	0.0	7.71	57	.301	.412	-3	-3	103	67	0.0	-0	0	-0.3
Total	4	6	12	.333	27	17	15	0	1	179	179	9.0	4	38	1.9	56	2.8	3.27	92	.270	.309	0	-5	91	105	-4.1	4	0	-0.3

YEAR	TM/L	W	L	PCT	G	GS	CG	SHO	SV	IP	H	H/G	HR	BB	BB/G	SO	SO/G	ERA	/A	OAVG	OOBP	PR	/A	PF	CPI	WAT	PB	PD	TPI
■ **PHIL REDDING**	Redding, Philip Hayden b: 1/25/1890, Crystal Springs, Miss. d: 3/30/29, Greenwood, Miss. BL/TR, 5'11.5", 190 lbs. Deb: 9/14/12																												
1912	StL-N	2	1	.667	3	3	2	0	0	25	31	11.2	2	11	4.0	9	3.2	5.04	69	.307	.375	-5	-4	103	97	0.7	-1	-0	-0.4
1913	StL-N	0	0	—	1	0	0	0	0	3	2	6.0	0	1	3.0	1	3.0	6.00	52	.286	.300	-1	-1	97	63	0.0	-0	0	0.0
Total	2	2	1	.667	4	3	2	0	0	28	33	10.6	2	12	3.9	10	3.2	5.14	67	.306	.369	-5	-5	102	93	0.7	-1	-0	-0.4
■ **PETE REDFERN**	Redfern, Peter Irvine b: 8/25/54, Glendale, Cal. BR/TR, 6'2", 195 lbs. Deb: 5/15/76																												
1976	Min-A	8	8	.500	23	23	1	1	0	118	105	8.0	6	63	4.8	74	5.6	3.51	98	.241	.337	0	-1	98	102	-0.3	0	-1	-0.1
1977	Min-A	6	9	.400	30	28	1	0	0	137	164	10.8	13	66	4.3	73	4.8	5.19	80	.304	.378	-17	-16	102	105	-1.8	0	1	-1.4
1978	Min-A	0	2	.000	3	2	0	0	0	10	10	9.0	2	6	5.4	4	3.6	6.30	57	.294	.364	-3	-3	94	99	-0.9	0	0	-0.2
1979	Min-A	7	3	.700	40	6	0	0	1	108	106	8.8	8	35	2.9	85	7.1	3.50	131	.258	.312	9	13	108	101	2.0	0	-1	1.2
1980	Min-A	7	7	.500	23	16	2	0	2	105	117	10.0	11	33	2.8	73	6.3	4.54	97	.283	.330	-6	-1	109	95	0.3	0	-1	-0.1
1981	Min-A	9	8	.529	24	23	3	0	0	142	140	8.9	12	52	3.3	77	4.9	4.06	96	.261	.323	-6	-2	107	95	2.4	0	-1	-0.3
1982	Min-A	5	11	.313	27	13	2	0	0	94	122	11.7	16	51	4.9	40	3.8	6.61	63	.322	.397	-26	-26	102	101	-1.3	0	0	-2.3
Total	7	42	48	.467	170	111	9	1	3	714	764	9.6	68	306	3.9	426	5.4	4.54	90	.278	.346	-49	-37	104	100	0.4	0	-2	-3.2
■ **HOWIE REED**	Reed, Howard Dean "Diz" b: 12/21/36, Dallas, Tex. d: 12/7/84, Corpus Christi, Tex. BR/TR, 6'1", 195 lbs. Deb: 9/13/58																												
1958	KC-A	1	0	1.000	3	1	1	0	0	10	5	4.5	0	4	3.6	5	4.5	0.90	448	.132	.214	3	3	107	34	0.5	0	-0	0.4
1959	KC-A	0	3	.000	6	3	0	0	0	21	26	11.1	3	10	4.3	11	4.7	7.29	54	.313	.371	-8	-8	103	83	-1.4	-0	-0	-0.7
1960	KC-A	0	0	—	1	0	0	0	0	2	2	9.0	1	0	0.0	1	4.5	0.00	—	.286	.286	1	1	101	0	0.0	0	0	0.1
1964	LA-N	3	4	.429	26	7	0	0	1	90	79	7.9	4	36	3.6	52	5.2	3.20	101	.236	.305	3	0	91	94	-0.4	-0	1	0.1
1965	LA-N	7	5	.583	38	5	0	0	1	78	73	8.4	6	27	3.1	47	5.4	3.12	102	.243	.308	4	1	90	107	-0.1	0	1	0.1
1966	LA-N	0	0	—	1	0	0	0	0	2	1	4.5	0	0	0.0	0	0.0	0.00	—	.167	.167	1	1	95	0	0.0	-0	0	0.1
	Cal-A	0	1	.000	19	1	0	0	1	43	39	8.2	5	15	3.1	17	3.6	2.93	117	.247	.305	2	2	100	128	-0.4	-1	-0	0.1
1967	Hou-N	1	1	.500	4	2	0	0	0	18	19	9.5	0	2	1.0	9	4.5	3.50	92	.268	.284	-0	-1	95	74	0.1	-0	-0	0.0
1969	Mon-N	6	7	.462	31	15	2	1	1	106	119	10.1	7	50	4.2	59	5.0	4.84	77	.290	.362	-15	-13	103	98	1.4	1	2	-0.9
1970	Mon-N	6	5	.545	57	1	0	0	5	89	81	8.2	7	40	4.0	42	4.2	3.13	131	.252	.334	9	10	102	128	1.0	-0	0	1.0
1971	Mon-N	2	3	.400	43	0	0	0	0	57	66	10.4	8	24	3.8	25	3.9	4.26	81	.296	.356	-5	-5	100	123	-0.1	-0	0	-0.4
Total	10	26	29	.473	229	35	3	1	9	516	510	8.9	41	208	3.6	268	4.7	3.72	96	.261	.328	-5	-9	98	106	0.6	-1	3	-0.1
■ **JERRY REED**	Reed, Jerry Maxwell b: 10/8/55, Bryson City, N.C. BR/TR, 6'1", 190 lbs. Deb: 9/11/81																												
1981	Phi-N	0	1	.000	4	0	0	0	0	5	7	12.6	0	6	10.8	5	9.0	7.20	54	.333	.481	-2	-2	112	104	-0.4	0	0	-0.1
1982	Phi-N	1	0	1.000	7	0	0	0	0	9	11	11.0	0	3	3.0	1	1.0	5.00	67	.324	.395	-1	-2	94	101	0.5	0	-0	-0.1
	Cle-A	1	1	.500	6	1	0	0	0	16	15	8.4	1	3	1.7	10	5.6	3.38	122	.250	.286	1	1	101	85	0.0	0	0	0.1
1983	Cle-A	0	0	—	7	0	0	0	0	21	26	11.1	4	9	3.9	11	4.7	7.29	59	.310	.368	-7	-7	106	85	0.0	0	1	-0.5
1985	Cle-A	3	5	.375	33	5	0	0	8	72	67	8.4	12	19	2.4	37	4.6	4.13	96	.245	.296	0	-1	95	95	0.0	0	1	0.0
1986	Sea-A	4	0	1.000	11	4	0	0	0	35	38	9.8	3	13	3.3	16	4.1	3.09	144	.273	.336	4	5	106	134	2.0	0	-0	0.5
1987	Sea-A	1	2	.333	39	1	0	0	7	82	79	8.7	7	24	2.6	51	5.6	3.40	135	.255	.312	10	11	103	107	-0.4	0	-0	1.0
1988	Sea-A	1	1	.500	46	0	0	0	1	86	82	8.6	8	33	3.5	48	5.0	3.98	108	.256	.322	-0	3	108	100	0.1	0	1	0.4
Total	7	11	10	.524	153	11	0	0	16	326	325	9.0	35	110	3.0	179	4.9	4.03	106	.262	.322	5	9	103	103	1.8	0	2	1.3
■ **RICHARD REED**	Reed, Richard Allen b: 8/16/64, Huntington, W.Va. BR/TR, 6', 195 lbs. Deb: 8/08/88																												
1988	Pit-N	1	0	1.000	2	2	0	0	0	12	10	7.5	1	2	1.5	6	4.5	3.00	112	.233	.255	1	0	97	89	0.5	-0	0	0.0
■ **BOB REED**	Reed, Robert Edward b: 1/12/45, Boston, Mass. BR/TR, 5'10", 175 lbs. Deb: 9/05/69																												
1969	Det-A	0	0	—	8	1	0	0	0	15	9	5.4	0	8	4.8	9	5.4	1.80	206	.184	.293	3	3	102	110	0.0	0	0	0.4
1970	Det-A	2	4	.333	16	4	0	0	2	46	54	10.6	5	14	2.7	26	5.1	4.89	79	.292	.338	-6	-5	104	93	-0.9	-1	-1	-0.6
Total	2	2	4	.333	24	5	0	0	2	61	63	9.3	5	22	3.2	35	5.2	4.13	93	.269	.328	-3	-2	103	97	-0.9	-0	-0	-0.2
■ **RON REED**	Reed, Ronald Lee b: 11/2/42, La Porte, Ind. BR/TR, 6'6", 215 lbs. Deb: 9/26/66																												
1966	Atl-N	1	1	.500	2	2	0	0	0	8	7	7.9	1	4	4.5	6	6.8	2.25	156	.226	.314	1	1	97	153	0.0	-0	-0	0.1
1967	Atl-N	1	1	.500	3	3	0	0	0	21	21	9.0	1	3	1.3	11	4.7	3.00	118	.262	.292	1	1	105	107	0.0	-1	1	0.1
1968	Atl-N	11	10	.524	35	28	6	1	0	202	189	8.4	10	49	2.2	111	4.9	3.34	84	.246	.291	-8	-12	94	85	0.6	1	0	-1.2
1969	Atl-N	18	10	.643	36	33	7	1	0	241	227	8.5	24	56	2.1	160	6.0	3.47	106	.246	.288	3	6	103	92	2.6	-2	-1	0.3
1970	Atl-N	7	10	.412	21	18	6	0	0	135	140	9.3	16	39	2.6	68	4.5	4.40	96	.266	.316	-5	-2	105	93	-1.0	-2	1	-0.3
1971	Atl-N	13	14	.481	32	32	8	1	0	222	221	9.0	26	54	2.2	129	5.2	3.73	103	.261	.299	-6	3	111	98	-0.7	-3	-1	0.0
1972	Atl-N	11	15	.423	31	30	11	1	0	213	222	9.4	18	60	2.5	111	4.7	3.93	93	.270	.315	-11	-6	106	98	-1.0	-1	1	-0.5
1973	Atl-N	4	11	.267	20	19	2	0	1	116	133	10.3	7	31	2.4	64	5.0	4.42	94	.287	.329	-10	-4	113	90	-3.3	-0	1	-0.1
1974	Atl-N	10	11	.476	28	28	6	2	0	186	171	8.3	16	41	2.0	78	3.8	3.39	111	.243	.283	5	8	104	85	-1.4	-3	-2	0.2
1975	Atl-N	4	5	.444	10	10	1	0	0	75	93	11.2	1	16	1.9	40	4.8	4.20	84	.304	.332	-5	-6	97	92	0.2	2	-0	-0.4
	StL-N	9	8	.529	24	24	7	2	0	176	181	9.3	4	37	1.9	99	5.1	3.22	117	.263	.300	8	10	103	90	0.4	-0	-1	1.0
	Yr	13	13	.500	34	34	8	2	0	251	274	9.8	5	53	1.9	139	5.0	3.51	105	.275	.310	3	5	101	90	0.6	2	-1	0.6
1976	Phi-N	8	7	.533	59	4	1	0	14	128	88	6.2	8	32	2.3	96	6.8	2.46	149	.193	.244	15	17	105	70	-1.1	-0	-1	1.7
1977	Phi-N	7	5	.583	60	3	0	0	15	124	101	7.3	9	37	2.7	84	6.1	2.76	139	.223	.279	16	15	98	92	-0.3	-0	-0	1.4
1978	Phi-N	3	4	.429	66	0	0	0	17	109	87	7.2	6	23	1.9	85	7.0	2.23	167	.223	.271	16	18	104	106	-0.7	-0	-2	1.7
1979	Phi-N	13	8	.619	61	0	0	0	5	102	110	9.7	9	32	2.8	58	5.1	4.15	88	.278	.328	-5	-6	97	99	2.4	1	-0	-0.4
1980	Phi-N	7	5	.583	55	0	0	0	9	91	88	8.7	4	30	3.0	54	5.3	4.05	95	.253	.307	-5	-2	106	78	0.3	1	1	0.0
1981	Phi-N	5	3	.625	39	0	0	0	8	61	54	8.0	6	17	2.5	40	5.9	3.10	126	.237	.287	3	5	112	99	0.7	1	-1	0.7
1982	Phi-N	5	5	.500	57	2	0	0	14	98	85	7.8	4	24	2.2	57	5.2	2.66	127	.235	.279	10	8	94	96	-0.4	2	2	1.2
1983	Phi-N	9	1	.900	61	0	0	0	8	96	89	8.3	5	34	3.2	73	6.8	3.47	105	.248	.308	2	2	100	91	3.9	-0	-2	0.0
1984	Chi-A	0	6	.000	51	0	0	0	12	73	67	8.3	7	14	1.7	57	7.0	3.08	144	.248	.280	7	11	111	102	-2.9	0	0	1.1
Total	19	146	140	.510	751	236	55	8	103	2477	2374	8.6	182	633	2.3	1481	5.4	3.46	107	.252	.297	34	66	103	92	-1.7	-6	-2	6.6
■ **BILL REEDER**	Reeder, William Edgar b: 2/20/22, Dike, Texas BR/TR, 6'5", 205 lbs. Deb: 4/23/49																												
1949	StL-N	1	1	.500	21	1	0	0	0	34	33	8.7	2	30	7.9	21	5.6	5.03	87	.270	.405	-4	-3	108	111	-0.1	-0	0	-0.2
■ **STAN REES**	Rees, Stanley Milton "Nellie" b: 2/25/1899, Cynthiana, Ky. d: 8/30/37, Lexington, Ky. BL/TL, 6'3", 190 lbs. Deb: 6/12/18																												
1918	Was-A	1	0	1.000	2	0	0	0	0	2	3	13.5	0	4	18.0	1	4.5	0.00	—	.500	.700	1	1	103	0	0.5	0	0	0.1
■ **BOBBY REEVES**	Reeves, Robert Edwin "Gunner" b: 6/24/04, Hill City, Tenn. BR/TR, 5'11", 170 lbs. Deb: 6/09/26																												
1931	Bos-A	0	0	—	1	0	0	0	0	7	6	7.7	0	1	1.3	0	0.0	3.86	110	.214	.241	0	0	97	35	0.0	0	0	0.0
■ **MIKE REGAN**	Regan, Michael Joseph b: 11/19/1887, Phoenix, N.Y. d: 5/22/61, Albany, N.Y. BR/TR, 5'11", 165 lbs. Deb: 5/13/17																												
1917	Cin-N	11	10	.524	32	26	16	1	0	216	228	9.5	4	41	1.7	50	2.1	2.71	93	.273	.300	0	-5	93	113	0.4	2	2	-0.1
1918	Cin-N	5	5	.500	22	6	4	3	2	80	77	8.7	0	29	3.3	15	1.7	3.26	82	.262	.315	-4	-5	96	92	-0.2	2	-1	-0.4
1919	Cin-N	0	0	—	1	0	0	0	0	2	1	4.5	0	0	0.0	1	4.5	0.00	—	.143	.125	1	1	101	0	0.0	0	0	0.0
Total	3	16	15	.516	55	32	20	4	2	298	306	9.2	4	70	2.1	66	2.0	2.84	90	.269	.303	-4	-9	94	106	0.2	4	2	-0.5
■ **PHIL REGAN**	Regan, Philip Raymond "The Vulture" b: 4/6/37, Otsego, Mich. BR/TR, 6'3", 200 lbs. Deb: 7/19/60 C																												
1960	Det-A	0	4	.000	17	7	0	0	1	68	70	9.3	11	25	3.3	38	5.0	4.50	88	.267	.329	-5	-4	102	102	-1.9	-1	-1	-0.5
1961	Det-A	10	7	.588	32	16	6	0	2	120	134	10.1	19	41	3.1	46	3.5	5.25	72	.281	.335	-16	-20	94	92	-0.4	-2	-3	-2.2
1962	Det-A	11	9	.550	35	23	6	0	0	171	169	8.9	23	64	3.4	87	4.6	4.05	108	.254	.316	-2	6	110	99	0.5	0	-2	0.6
1963	Det-A	15	9	.625	38	27	5	1	1	189	179	8.5	33	59	2.8	115	5.5	3.86	97	.245	.302	-5	-2	104	105	3.6	-1	-3	-0.4
1964	Det-A	5	10	.333	32	21	2	0	1	147	162	9.9	21	49	3.0	91	5.6	5.02	69	.282	.336	-23	-26	95	95	-2.8	5	0	-2.0
1965	Det-A	1	5	.167	16	7	1	0	0	52	57	9.9	6	20	3.5	37	6.4	5.02	72	.282	.338	-9	-8	104	93	-2.0	-0	0	-0.8
1966	LA-N	14	1	.933	65	0	0	0	**21**	117	85	6.5	6	24	1.8	88	6.8	1.62	212	.207	.245	**26**	**24**	95	112	6.4	0	1	2.6
1967	LA-N	6	9	.400	55	3	0	0	6	96	108	10.1	2	32	3.0	53	5.0	3.00	100	.284	.330	4	0	89	130	-0.8	-0	1	0.1
1968	LA-N	2	0	1.000	5	0	0	0	0	8	10	11.3	1	1	1.1	7	7.9	3.38	81	.313	.324	-0	-1	91	141	1.0	-0	-0	0.0
	Chi-N	10	5	.667	68	0	0	0	25	127	109	7.7	9	24	1.7	60	4.3	2.20	153	.232	.266	11	16	112	113	2.5	0	0	2.0
	Yr	12	5	.706	73	0	0	0	**25**	135	119	7.9	10	25	1.7	67	4.5	2.27	146	.237	.269	11	16	111	113	3.5	-0	-0	2.0
1969	Chi-N	12	6	.667	71	0	0	0	17	112	120	9.6	6	35	2.8	56	4.5	3.70	102	.282	.330	-1	1	105	109	2.3	0	0	0.2

YEAR	TM/L	W	L	PCT	G	GS	CG	SHO	SV	IP	H	H/G	HR	BB	BB/G	SO	SO/G	ERA	/A	OAVG	OOBP	PR	/A	PF	CPI	WAT	PB	PD	TPI
1970	Chi-N	5	9	.357	54	0	0	0	12	76	81	9.6	8	32	3.8	31	3.7	4.74	101	.287	.352	-6	1	119	105	-2.2	-1	2	0.1
1971	Chi-N	5	5	.500	48	1	0	0	6	73	84	10.4	4	33	4.1	28	3.5	3.95	97	.301	.365	-4	-1	110	124	0.0	-1	1	0.0
1972	Chi-N	0	1	.000	5	0	0	0	0	4	6	13.5	0	2	4.5	2	4.5	2.25	173	.400	.471	1	1	112	319	-0.4	0	0	0.1
	Chi-A	0	1	.000	10	0	0	0	0	13	18	12.5	1	6	4.2	4	2.8	4.15	78	.346	.410	-2	-1	106	154	-0.4	0	0	0.0
Total	13	96	81	.542	551	105	20	1	92	1373	1392	9.1	150	447	2.9	743	4.9	3.83	98	.265	.318	-30	-14	103	107	5.4	0	-3	-0.2
■ EARL REID	Reid, Earl Percy b: 6/8/13, Bangor, Ala. d: 5/11/84, Cullman, Ala. BL/TR, 6'3", 190 lbs. Deb: 5/08/46																												
1946	Bos-N	1	0	1.000	2	0	0	0	0	3	4	12.0	0	3	9.0	2	6.0	3.00	107	.308	.438	0	0	94	202	0.5	0	0	0.0
■ BILL REIDY	Reidy, William Joseph b: 10/9/1873, Cleveland, Ohio d: 10/14/15, Cleveland, Ohio BR/TR, 5'10", 175 lbs. Deb: 7/21/1896																												
1896	NY-N	0	1	.000	2	1	1	0	0	13	24	16.6	0	2	1.4	1	0.7	7.62	56	.420	.440	-5	-5	99	89	-0.4	-1	0	-0.3
1899	Bro-N	1	0	1.000	2	1	1	0	1	7	9	11.6	0	2	2.6	2	2.6	2.57	153	.337	.383	1	1	102	167	0.5	-1	0	0.1
1901	Mil-A	16	20	.444	37	33	28	2	0	301	364	10.9	14	62	1.9	50	1.5	4.22	85	.320	.355	-19	-21	98	98	3.4	-6	-4	-2.1
1902	StL-A	3	5	.375	12	9	7	0	0	95	111	10.5	0	13	1.2	16	1.5	4.45	82	.317	.342	-9	-9	102	77	-1.3	-0	1	-0.6
1903	StL-A	1	4	.200	5	5	5	1	0	43	53	11.1	1	7	1.5	8	1.7	3.98	71	.327	.354	-5	-6	96	103	-1.4	-1	-1	-0.6
	Bro-N	6	7	.462	15	13	11	0	0	104	130	11.3	0	14	1.2	21	1.8	3.46	96	.337	.369	-2	-2	102	110	-0.6	1	-1	-0.2
1904	Bro-N	0	4	.000	6	4	2	0	1	38	49	11.6	0	6	1.4	11	2.6	4.50	59	.343	.378	-7	-8	98	92	-1.9	-0	-1	-0.7
Total	6	27	41	.397	79	66	55	3	2	601	740	11.1	15	106	1.6	109	1.6	4.18	83	.327	.359	-46	-48	99	97	-1.7	-9	-6	-4.4
■ ART REINHART	Reinhart, Arthur Conrad b: 5/29/1899, Ackley, Iowa d: 11/11/46, Houston, Tex. BL/TL, 6'1", 170 lbs. Deb: 4/26/19																												
1919	StL-N	0	0	—	1	0	0	0	0	0	0	—	0	0	—	0	—	—	—	—	1.000	0	0	97	0	0.0	0	0	0.0
1925	StL-N	11	5	.688	20	16	15	1	0	145	149	9.2	7	47	2.9	26	1.6	3.04	142	.278	.328	20	20	101	129	3.2	5	-0	2.5
1926	StL-N	10	5	.667	27	11	9	0	0	143	159	10.0	5	47	3.0	26	1.6	4.22	91	.295	.337	-6	-6	100	101	1.7	5	1	0.0
1927	StL-N	5	2	.714	21	9	4	2	1	82	82	9.0	5	36	4.0	15	1.6	4.17	99	.267	.339	-2	-0	106	95	1.0	2	-1	0.1
1928	StL-N	4	6	.400	23	9	3	1	2	75	80	9.6	3	27	3.2	12	1.4	2.88	134	.272	.325	9	8	97	123	-1.7	-0	-0	0.7
Total	5	30	18	.625	92	45	31	4	3	445	470	9.5	20	157	3.2	79	1.6	3.60	112	.280	.333	20	22	101	113	4.2	11	-1	3.3
■ JACK REIS	Reis, Harrie Crane b: 6/14/1890, Cincinnati, Ohio d: 7/20/39, Cincinnati, Ohio BR/TR, 5'10.5", 160 lbs. Deb: 9/09/11																												
1911	StL-N	0	0	—	3	0	0	0	0	9	5	5.0	0	8	8.0	4	4.0	1.00	348	.156	.325	2	2	102	185	0.0	-0	0	0.2
■ LAURIE REIS	Reis, Lawrence P. b: 11/20/1858, Illinois d: 1/24/21, Chicago, Ill. BR/TR, 160 lbs. Deb: 10/01/1877																												
1877	Chi-N	3	1	.750	4	4	4	1	0	36	29	7.3	1	6	1.5	11	2.8	0.75	370	.228	.263	8	8	99	199	1.1	-1	0	0.6
1878	Chi-N	1	3	.250	4	4	4	0	0	36	55	13.8	0	4	1.0	8	2.0	3.25	75	.361	.378	-4	-3	106	138	-0.9	-1	0	-0.3
Total	2	4	4	.500	8	8	8	1	0	72	84	10.5	1	10	1.3	19	2.4	2.00	131	.301	.325	4	5	102	169	0.2	-2	0	0.3
■ BOBBY REIS	Reis, Robert Joseph Thomas b: 1/2/09, Woodside, N.Y. d: 5/1/73, St.Paul, Minn. BR/TR, 6'1", 175 lbs. Deb: 9/19/31																												
1935	Bro-N	3	2	.600	14	2	1	0	2	41	46	10.1	0	24	5.3	7	1.5	2.85	134	.277	.366	5	4	95	152	0.7	1	1	0.4
1936	Bos-N	6	5	.545	35	5	3	0	0	139	152	9.8	7	74	4.8	25	1.6	4.47	87	.283	.363	-7	-9	96	107	0.9	1	4	-0.4
1937	Bos-N	0	0	—	4	0	0	0	0	5	3	5.4	0	5	9.0	0	0.0	1.80	195	.158	.333	1	1	90	121	0.0	1	0	0.1
1938	Bos-N	1	6	.143	16	2	1	0	0	58	61	9.5	5	41	6.4	20	3.1	4.97	68	.271	.387	-8	-10	89	109	-2.4	-0	1	-0.9
Total	4	10	13	.435	69	9	5	0	2	243	262	9.7	12	144	5.3	52	1.9	4.26	88	.277	.369	-8	-14	94	115	-0.8	3	5	-0.8
■ TOMMY REIS	Reis, Thomas Edward b: 8/6/14, Newport, Ky. BR/TR, 6'2", 180 lbs. Deb: 4/27/38																												
1938	Phi-N	0	1	.000	4	0	0	0	0	5	8	14.4	0	8	14.4	2	3.6	18.00	22	.364	.516	-8	-8	106	54	-0.4	-0	0	-0.6
	Bos-N	0	0	—	4	0	0	0	0	6	8	12.0	1	1	1.5	4	6.0	7.50	45	.296	.321	-2	-3	89	64	0.0	0	-0	-0.2
	Yr	0	1	.000	8	0	0	0	0	11	16	13.1	1	9	7.4	6	4.9	12.27	30	.327	.424	-10	-11	96	64	-0.4	-0	0	-0.8
■ BUGS REISIGL	Reisigl, Jacob b: 12/12/1887, Brooklyn, N.Y. d: 2/24/57, Amsterdam, N.Y. BR/TR, 5'10.5", 175 lbs. Deb: 9/20/11																												
1911	Cle-A	0	1	.000	2	1	1	0	0	13	13	9.0	1	3	2.1	6	4.2	6.23	55	.271	.314	-4	-4	103	54	-0.4	-1	-0	-0.3
■ DOC REISLING	Reisling, Frank Carl b: 7/25/1874, Martins Ferry, O. d: 3/4/55, Tulsa, Okla. BR/TR, 5'10", 180 lbs. Deb: 9/10/04																												
1904	Bro-N	3	4	.429	7	7	6	1	0	51	45	7.9	0	10	1.8	19	3.4	2.12	126	.274	.349	3	3	98	123	0.4	-0	0	0.4
1905	Bro-N	0	1	.000	2	0	0	0	0	3	3	9.0	0	4	12.0	2	6.0	3.00	101	.287	.484	-0	0	102	199	-0.4	0	0	0.0
1909	Was-A	2	4	.333	10	6	6	1	0	67	70	9.4	0	17	2.3	22	3.0	2.42	98	.270	.315	0	-0	96	112	0.2	0	-1	-0.1
1910	Was-A	10	10	.500	30	20	13	2	1	191	185	8.7	3	44	2.1	57	2.7	2.54	101	.264	.312	-1	0	102	111	1.3	1	-0	0.2
Total	4	15	19	.441	49	33	25	4	1	312	303	8.7	3	75	2.2	100	2.9	2.45	104	.267	.321	3	3	100	114	1.5	2	-1	0.5
■ WIN REMMERSWAAL	Remmerswaal, Wilhelmus Abraham b: 3/8/54, The Hague, Holland BR/TR, 6'2", 160 lbs. Deb: 8/03/79																												
1979	Bos-A	1	0	1.000	8	0	0	0	0	20	26	11.7	1	12	5.4	16	7.2	7.20	62	.317	.402	-7	-6	106	81	0.5	0	-0	-0.5
1980	Bos-A	2	1	.667	14	0	0	0	0	35	39	10.0	4	9	2.3	20	5.1	4.63	89	.295	.333	-2	-2	102	100	0.5	0	-1	-0.2
Total	2	3	1	.750	22	0	0	0	0	55	65	10.6	5	21	3.4	36	5.9	5.56	76	.304	.361	-9	-8	103	93	1.0	0	-1	-0.7
■ ALEX REMNEAS	Remneas, Alexander Norman b: 2/21/1886, Minneapolis, Minn. d: 8/27/75, Phoenix, Ariz. BR/TR, 6'1", 180 lbs. Deb: 4/15/12																												
1912	Det-A	0	0	—	1	0	0	0	0	2	5	22.5	0	0	0.0	0	0.0	22.50	14	.455	.455	-4	-4	96	41	0.0	0	0	-0.2
1915	StL-A	0	0	—	2	0	0	0	0	6	3	4.5	0	3	4.5	5	7.5	1.50	194	.136	.269	1	1	99	41	0.0	-0	0	0.1
Total	2	0	0	—	3	0	0	0	0	8	8	9.0	0	3	3.4	5	5.6	6.75	44	.242	.324	-3	-3	98	41	0.0	0	0	-0.1
■ ERWIN RENFER	Renfer, Erwin Arthur b: 12/11/1891, Elgin, Ill. d: 10/26/57, Sycamore, Ill. BR/TR, 6', 180 lbs. Deb: 9/18/13																												
1913	Det-A	0	1	.000	1	1	0	0	0	6	5	7.5	0	3	4.5	1	1.5	6.00	49	.227	.346	-2	-2	101	48	-0.4	-0	0	-0.1
■ MARSHALL RENFROE	Renfroe, Marshall Daniel b: 5/25/36, Century, Fla. d: 12/10/70, Pensacola, Fla. BL/TL, 6', 180 lbs. Deb: 9/27/59																												
1959	SF-N	0	0	—	1	1	0	0	0	2	3	13.5	1	3	13.5	3	13.5	27.00	14	.333	.500	-5	-5	94	45	0.0	-0	0	-0.3
■ HAL RENIFF	Reniff, Harold Eugene "Porky" b: 7/2/38, Warren, Ohio BR/TR, 6', 215 lbs. Deb: 6/08/61																												
1961	NY-A	2	0	1.000	25	0	0	0	2	45	31	6.2	1	31	6.2	21	4.2	2.60	144	.197	.326	7	6	93	107	1.0	-1	-1	0.5
1962	NY-A	0	0	—	2	0	0	0	0	4	6	13.5	0	5	11.3	1	2.3	6.75	54	.400	.500	-1	-1	92	151	0.0	0	-0	-0.1
1963	NY-A	4	3	.571	48	0	0	0	18	89	63	6.4	3	42	4.2	56	5.7	2.63	135	.202	.293	10	9	98	93	-0.3	-1	3	1.1
1964	NY-A	6	4	.600	41	0	0	0	9	69	47	6.1	3	30	3.9	38	5.0	3.13	117	.199	.279	4	4	101	73	0.0	-1	0	0.4
1965	NY-A	3	4	.429	51	0	0	0	3	85	74	7.8	4	48	5.1	74	7.8	3.81	92	.232	.338	-3	-3	101	91	-0.3	-0	-0	-0.3
1966	NY-A	3	7	.300	56	0	0	0	9	95	80	7.6	2	49	4.6	79	7.5	3.22	100	.229	.325	2	-0	94	99	-1.6	1	-1	0.0
1967	NY-A	0	2	.000	24	0	0	0	0	40	40	9.0	0	14	3.1	24	5.4	4.27	72	.256	.322	-5	-5	96	76	-0.9	-0	-0	-0.5
	NY-N	3	3	.500	29	0	0	0	4	43	42	8.8	1	23	4.8	21	4.4	3.35	103	.266	.346	0	0	102	121	0.6	-0	-1	0.0
Total	7	21	23	.477	276	0	0	0	45	470	383	7.3	14	242	4.6	314	6.0	3.27	106	.225	.319	14	10	98	94	-1.5	-2	0	1.1
■ JIM RENINGER	Reninger, James David b: 3/7/13, Aurora, Ill. BR/TR, 6'3", 210 lbs. Deb: 9/17/38																												
1938	Phi-A	0	2	.000	4	4	1	0	0	23	28	11.0	3	14	5.5	9	3.5	7.04	71	.295	.382	-6	-5	105	84	-0.9	-0	0	-0.4
1939	Phi-A	0	2	.000	4	2	0	0	0	16	24	13.5	3	12	6.8	3	1.7	7.88	60	.369	.439	-6	-6	102	115	-0.9	-0	0	-0.4
Total	2	0	4	.000	8	6	1	0	0	39	52	12.0	6	26	6.0	12	2.8	7.38	66	.325	.406	-12	-11	104	97	-1.8	-1	0	-0.8
■ STEVE RENKO	Renko, Steven b: 12/10/44, Kansas City, Kan. BR/TR, 6'5", 230 lbs. Deb: 6/27/69																												
1969	Mon-N	6	7	.462	18	15	4	0	0	103	94	8.2	14	50	4.4	68	5.9	4.02	92	.243	.328	-5	-4	103	102	1.4	1	-1	-0.3
1970	Mon-N	13	11	.542	41	33	7	1	1	223	203	8.2	27	104	4.2	142	5.7	4.32	95	.241	.325	-7	-5	102	92	2.3	2	-0	-0.2
1971	Mon-N	15	14	.517	40	37	9	3	0	276	256	8.3	24	135	4.4	129	4.2	3.75	93	.247	.330	-9	-8	100	101	2.3	5	-2	-0.5
1972	Mon-N	1	10	.091	30	12	0	0	0	97	96	8.9	11	67	6.2	66	6.1	5.20	69	.262	.371	-19	-17	104	95	-4.3	1	1	-1.5
1973	Mon-N	15	11	.577	36	34	9	0	1	250	201	7.2	26	108	3.9	164	5.9	2.81	137	.218	.297	24	29	105	106	2.6	8	-2	3.9
1974	Mon-N	12	16	.429	37	35	8	1	0	228	222	8.8	17	81	3.2	138	5.4	4.03	94	.257	.316	-10	-6	104	87	-2.0	3	3	0.1
1975	Mon-N	6	12	.333	31	25	3	1	1	170	175	9.3	20	76	4.0	99	5.2	4.08	97	.265	.336	-8	-2	109	105	-2.6	5	0	0.3
1976	Mon-N	0	1	.000	5	1	0	0	0	13	15	10.4	2	3	2.1	4	2.8	5.54	65	.288	.321	-3	-3	103	84	-0.4	0	-0	-0.2
	Chi-N	8	11	.421	28	27	4	1	0	163	164	9.1	12	43	2.4	112	6.2	3.87	101	.258	.302	-7	0	111	85	-0.9	-4	-1	-0.3
	Yr	8	12	.400	33	28	4	1	0	176	179	9.2	14	46	2.4	116	5.9	3.99	97	.260	.303	-9	-2	110	85	-1.3	0	-2	-0.5
1977	Chi-N	2	2	.500	13	8	0	0	1	51	51	9.0	10	21	3.7	34	6.0	4.59	98	.258	.329	-4	-1	115	101	0.0	0	-1	0.0
	Chi-A	5	0	1.000	8	8	0	0	0	53	55	9.3	3	17	2.9	36	6.1	3.57	113	.274	.327	3	3	99	107	2.5	0	0	0.3

YEAR	TM/L	W	L	PCT	G	GS	CG	SHO	SV	IP	H	H/G	HR	BB	BB/G	SO	SO/G	ERA	/A	OAVG	OOBP	PR	/A	PF	CPI	WAT	PB	PD	TPI
1978	Oak-A	6	12	.333	27	25	3	1	0	151	152	9.1	10	67	4.0	89	5.3	4.29	90	.265	.335	-9	-7	103	92	-2.0	0	0	-0.7
1979	Bos-A	11	9	.550	27	27	4	1	0	171	174	9.2	22	53	2.8	99	5.2	4.11	109	.260	.314	2	7	106	96	-0.3	0	-1	0.6
1980	Bos-A	9	9	.500	32	23	1	0	0	165	180	9.8	17	56	3.1	90	4.9	4.20	98	.281	.335	-3	-1	102	104	-0.3	0	-1	-0.1
1981	Cal-A	8	4	.667	22	15	0	0	1	102	93	8.2	7	42	3.7	50	4.4	3.44	110	.250	.321	3	4	104	105	2.4	0	-2	0.2
1982	Cal-A	11	6	.647	31	23	4	0	0	156	163	9.4	17	51	2.9	81	4.7	4.44	91	.269	.323	-6	-7	99	93	1.6	0	-2	-0.8
1983	KC-A	6	11	.353	25	17	1	0	1	121	144	10.7	9	36	2.7	54	4.0	4.31	96	.293	.336	-3	-2	102	102	-2.4	0	-1	-0.2
Total	15	134	146	.479	451	365	57	9	6	2493	2438	8.8	248	1010	3.6	1455	5.3	4.00	98	.256	.324	-59	-20	104	98	-0.1	21	-8	0.6

■ ANDY REPLOGLE Replogle, Andrew David b: 10/7/53, South Bend, Ind. BR/TR, 6'5", 205 lbs. Deb: 4/11/78

YEAR	TM/L	W	L	PCT	G	GS	CG	SHO	SV	IP	H	H/G	HR	BB	BB/G	SO	SO/G	ERA	/A	OAVG	OOBP	PR	/A	PF	CPI	WAT	PB	PD	TPI
1978	Mil-A	9	5	.643	32	18	3	2	0	149	177	10.7	14	47	2.8	41	2.5	3.93	100	.301	.349	-2	0	104	120	1.2	0	-2	-0.2
1979	Mil-A	0	0	—	3	0	0	0	0	8	13	14.6	0	2	2.3	2	2.3	5.63	75	.382	.417	-1	-1	99	114	0.0	0	0	0.0
Total	2	9	5	.643	35	18	3	2	0	157	190	10.9	14	49	2.8	43	2.5	4.01	98	.305	.352	-4	-1	104	120	1.2	0	-2	-0.2

■ XAVIER RESCIGNO Rescigno, Xavier Frederick "Mr. X" b: 10/13/13, New York, N.Y. BR/TR, 5'10.5", 175 lbs. Deb: 4/22/43

YEAR	TM/L	W	L	PCT	G	GS	CG	SHO	SV	IP	H	H/G	HR	BB	BB/G	SO	SO/G	ERA	/A	OAVG	OOBP	PR	/A	PF	CPI	WAT	PB	PD	TPI
1943	Pit-N	6	9	.400	37	14	5	1	2	133	125	8.5	6	45	3.0	41	2.8	2.98	117	.252	.310	6	7	103	109	-1.8	0	-2	0.6
1944	Pit-N	10	8	.556	48	6	2	0	5	124	146	10.6	9	34	2.5	45	3.3	4.35	86	.291	.330	-10	-8	104	99	-0.5	-1	-0	-0.8
1945	Pit-N	3	5	.375	44	1	0	0	9	79	95	10.8	6	34	3.9	29	3.3	5.70	68	.303	.367	-17	-16	102	90	-1.1	-0	-0	-1.5
Total	3	19	22	.463	129	21	7	1	16	336	366	9.8	21	113	3.0	115	3.1	4.13	89	.279	.332	-21	-17	103	101	-3.4	-1	-3	-1.7

■ GEORGE RETTGER Rettger, George Edward b: 7/29/1868, Cleveland, Ohio d: 6/5/21, Lakewood, Ohio TR, 5'11", 175 lbs. Deb: 8/13/1891

YEAR	TM/L	W	L	PCT	G	GS	CG	SHO	SV	IP	H	H/G	HR	BB	BB/G	SO	SO/G	ERA	/A	OAVG	OOBP	PR	/A	PF	CPI	WAT	PB	PD	TPI
1891	StL-a	7	3	.700	14	12	10	1	1	93	85	8.2	4	51	4.9	49	4.7	3.39	122	.257	.356	3	8	112	102	1.1	-4	0	0.5
1892	Cle-N	1	3	.250	6	5	3	0	0	38	32	7.6	2	31	7.3	12	2.8	4.26	78	.240	.384	-4	-4	101	93	-1.1	-0	0	-0.3
	Cin-N	1	0	1.000	1	1	1	0	0	9	8	8.0	0	10	10.0	1	1.0	4.00	85	.250	.429	-1	-1	103	115	0.5	-0	0	0.0
	Yr	2	3	.400	7	6	4	0	0	47	40	7.7	2	41	7.9	13	2.5	4.21	79	.242	.393	-5	-5	101	115	-0.6	-0	0	-0.3
Total	2	9	6	.600	21	18	14	1	1	140	125	8.0	6	92	5.9	62	4.0	3.66	105	.252	.369	-1	3	108	100	0.5	-4	0	0.2

■ OTTO RETTIG Rettig, Adolph John b: 1/29/1894, New York, N.Y. d: 6/16/77, Stuart, Fla. BR/TR, 5'11", 165 lbs. Deb: 7/19/22

YEAR	TM/L	W	L	PCT	G	GS	CG	SHO	SV	IP	H	H/G	HR	BB	BB/G	SO	SO/G	ERA	/A	OAVG	OOBP	PR	/A	PF	CPI	WAT	PB	PD	TPI
1922	Phi-A	1	2	.333	4	4	1	0	0	18	18	9.0	0	12	6.0	3	1.5	5.00	86	.265	.356	-2	-1	106	82	-0.2	-1	0	-0.1

■ ED REULBACH Reulbach, Edward Marvin "Big Ed" b: 12/1/1882, Detroit, Mich. d: 7/17/61, Glens Falls, N.Y. BR/TR, 6'1", 190 lbs. Deb: 5/16/05

YEAR	TM/L	W	L	PCT	G	GS	CG	SHO	SV	IP	H	H/G	HR	BB	BB/G	SO	SO/G	ERA	/A	OAVG	OOBP	PR	/A	PF	CPI	WAT	PB	PD	TPI
1905	Chi-N	18	14	.563	34	29	28	5	1	292	208	**6.4**	2	73	2.3	152	4.7	1.42	211	**.227**	.297	51	51	100	124	-1.2	-5	-1	5.7
1906	Chi-N	19	4	**.826**	33	24	20	6	3	218	129	**5.3**	2	92	3.8	94	3.9	1.65	158	**.197**	.308	24	23	99	95	3.4	-2	3	3.1
1907	Chi-N	17	4	**.810**	27	22	16	4	0	192	147	6.9	1	64	3.0	96	4.5	1.69	149	.241	.322	17	18	102	120	4.1	0	1	2.2
1908	Chi-N	24	7	**.774**	46	35	25	7	1	298	227	6.9	4	106	3.2	133	4.0	2.02	118	.240	.324	11	12	102	107	6.5	6	-1	1.3
1909	Chi-N	19	10	.655	35	32	23	6	0	263	194	6.6	1	82	2.8	105	3.6	1.78	139	.212	.285	24	20	95	102	-0.5	-1	4	2.8
1910	Chi-N	12	8	.600	24	23	14	1	0	173	162	8.4	1	49	2.5	56	2.9	3.12	94	.251	.313	-2	-4	96	84	-1.2	-3	1	-0.6
1911	Chi-N	16	9	.640	33	29	15	2	0	222	191	7.7	3	103	4.2	79	3.2	2.96	108	.236	.325	11	6	94	96	1.5	-0	3	0.7
1912	Chi-N	10	6	.625	39	19	8	0	4	169	161	8.6	7	60	3.2	75	4.0	3.78	92	.252	.323	-7	-6	102	79	0.4	-3	4	-0.4
1913	Chi-N	1	3	.250	10	2	1	0	0	39	41	9.5	1	21	4.8	10	2.3	4.38	71	.281	.362	-5	-6	97	98	-1.0	0	0	-0.4
	Bro-N	7	6	.538	15	12	8	2	0	110	77	6.3	3	34	2.8	46	3.8	2.05	164	.202	.264	14	16	105	86	1.3	-0	-1	1.7
	Yr	8	9	.471	25	14	9	2	0	149	118	7.1	4	55	3.3	56	3.4	2.66	124	.223	.290	9	10	103	86	0.3	0	-1	1.3
1914	Bro-N	11	18	.379	44	29	14	3	3	256	228	8.0	5	83	2.9	119	4.2	2.64	107	.242	.301	4	5	101	96	-3.7	-0	1	0.6
1915	New-F	21	10	.677	33	30	23	4	1	270	233	7.8	3	69	2.3	117	3.9	2.23	127	.236	.287	24	18	94	102	5.7	-0	3	2.3
1916	Bos-N	7	6	.538	21	11	6	0	0	109	99	8.2	1	41	3.4	47	3.9	2.48	96	.251	.320	2	-1	91	120	-0.5	-1	5	0.3
1917	Bos-N	0	1	.000	5	2	0	0	0	22	21	8.6	0	15	6.1	9	3.7	2.86	91	.256	.359	-0	-1	97	137	-0.4	1	1	0.1
Total	13	182	106	.632	399	299	201	40	13	2633	2118	7.2	34	892	3.0	1138	3.9	2.28	123	.233	.307	167	153	98	102	14.4	-8	23	19.4

■ PAUL REUSCHEL Reuschel, Paul Richard b: 1/12/47, Quincy, Ill. BR/TR, 6'4", 225 lbs. Deb: 7/25/75

YEAR	TM/L	W	L	PCT	G	GS	CG	SHO	SV	IP	H	H/G	HR	BB	BB/G	SO	SO/G	ERA	/A	OAVG	OOBP	PR	/A	PF	CPI	WAT	PB	PD	TPI
1975	Chi-N	1	3	.250	28	0	0	0	5	36	44	11.0	1	13	3.3	12	3.0	3.50	109	.312	.363	1	1	105	135	-0.8	-0	0	0.1
1976	Chi-N	4	2	.667	50	2	0	0	3	87	94	9.7	12	33	3.4	55	5.7	4.55	85	.278	.340	-10	-6	111	103	1.2	-0	1	-0.4
1977	Chi-N	5	6	.455	69	0	0	0	4	107	105	8.8	9	40	3.4	62	5.2	4.37	102	.262	.321	-5	1	115	87	-0.4	-2	2	0.2
1978	Chi-N	2	0	1.000	16	0	0	0	0	28	29	9.3	4	13	4.2	13	4.2	5.14	77	.269	.352	-5	-4	111	93	1.0	-0	0	-0.3
	Cle-A	2	4	.333	18	6	1	0	0	90	95	9.5	5	22	2.2	24	2.4	3.10	114	.271	.312	7	4	94	112	-0.6	0	1	0.5
1979	Cle-A	2	1	.667	17	1	0	0	1	45	73	14.6	7	11	2.2	22	4.4	8.00	56	.365	.396	-19	-18	106	88	0.5	0	1	-1.5
Total	5	16	16	.500	198	9	1	0	13	393	440	10.1	38	132	3.0	188	4.3	4.51	90	.286	.339	-32	-21	107	101	0.9	-2	5	-1.4

■ RICK REUSCHEL Reuschel, Rickey Eugene b: 5/16/49, Quincy, Ill. BR/TR, 6'3", 215 lbs. Deb: 6/19/72

YEAR	TM/L	W	L	PCT	G	GS	CG	SHO	SV	IP	H	H/G	HR	BB	BB/G	SO	SO/G	ERA	/A	OAVG	OOBP	PR	/A	PF	CPI	WAT	PB	PD	TPI
1972	Chi-N	10	8	.556	21	18	5	4	0	129	127	8.9	3	29	2.0	87	6.1	2.93	132	.259	.300	8	14	112	99	0.2	-1	-0	1.4
1973	Chi-N	14	15	.483	36	36	7	3	0	237	244	9.3	15	62	2.4	168	6.4	3.00	133	.263	.310	18	26	109	111	0.2	-3	4	2.9
1974	Chi-N	13	12	.520	41	38	8	2	0	241	262	9.8	18	83	3.1	160	6.0	4.29	86	.276	.331	-18	-16	102	94	2.7	2	5	-0.9
1975	Chi-N	11	17	.393	38	37	6	0	1	234	244	9.4	17	67	2.6	155	6.0	3.73	103	.268	.316	-3	2	105	98	-2.4	2	3	0.8
1976	Chi-N	14	12	.538	38	37	9	2	1	260	260	9.0	17	64	2.2	146	5.1	3.46	112	.265	.308	1	12	111	101	2.1	4	3	2.3
1977	Chi-N	20	10	.667	39	37	8	4	1	252	233	8.3	13	74	2.6	166	5.9	2.79	161	.247	.303	32	**47**	115	108	5.7	2	3	**5.9**
1978	Chi-N	14	15	.483	35	35	9	1	0	243	235	8.7	16	54	2.0	115	4.3	3.41	117	.254	.292	5	15	111	92	-0.1	-1	2	1.9
1979	Chi-N	18	12	.600	36	36	5	1	0	239	251	9.5	16	75	2.8	125	4.7	3.62	116	.274	.329	3	16	112	108	3.7	1	5	2.3
1980	Chi-N	11	13	.458	38	38	6	0	0	257	281	9.8	13	76	2.7	140	4.9	3.40	114	.286	.330	6	14	108	**119**	1.4	-1	5	2.0
1981	Chi-N	4	7	.364	13	13	1	0	0	86	87	9.1	4	23	2.4	53	5.5	3.45	108	.267	.318	0	3	106	102	0.0	-2	2	0.3
	NY-A	4	4	.500	12	11	3	0	0	71	75	9.5	4	10	1.3	22	2.8	2.66	136	.280	.305	8	8	99	132	-0.3	0	1	0.9
1983	Chi-N	1	1	.500	4	4	0	0	0	21	18	7.7	1	10	4.3	9	3.9	3.86	95	.234	.318	-1	-0	101	80	0.1	-0	1	0.0
1984	Chi-N	5	5	.500	19	14	1	0	0	92	123	12.0	7	23	2.3	43	4.2	5.18	75	.339	.368	-16	-13	109	109	-0.8	2	1	-0.9
1985	Pit-N	14	8	.636	31	26	9	1	1	194	153	7.1	7	52	2.4	138	6.4	2.27	165	.215	.269	29	32	104	90	5.2	2	4	4.3
1986	Pit-N	9	16	.360	35	34	4	2	0	216	232	9.7	20	57	2.4	125	5.2	3.96	95	.274	.319	-6	-5	101	102	-1.2	0	3	-0.1
1987	Pit-N	8	6	.571	25	25	9	3	0	177	163	8.3	12	35	1.8	80	4.1	2.75	156	.246	.285	26	30	105	108	1.2	1	1	3.5
	SF-N	5	3	.625	9	8	3	1	0	50	44	7.9	1	7	1.3	27	4.9	4.32	90	.230	.259	-1	-3	95	45	0.7	-0	0	-0.1
	Yr	13	9	.591	34	33	**12**	**4**	0	227	207	8.2	13	42	**1.7**	107	4.2	3.09	135	.239	.273	25	**27**	102	45	1.9	1	1	3.4
1988	SF-N	19	11	.633	36	36	7	2	0	245	242	8.9	11	42	1.5	92	3.4	3.12	103	.260	.290	9	3	93	99	4.3	-1	-2	-0.1
Total	16	194	175	.526	506	483	100	26	4	3244	3274	9.1	195	843	2.3	1851	5.1	3.38	115	.264	.309	100	184	106	102	22.7	7	38	26.4

■ JERRY REUSS Reuss, Jerry b: 6/19/49, St.Louis, Mo. BL/TL, 6'5", 200 lbs. Deb: 9/27/69

YEAR	TM/L	W	L	PCT	G	GS	CG	SHO	SV	IP	H	H/G	HR	BB	BB/G	SO	SO/G	ERA	/A	OAVG	OOBP	PR	/A	PF	CPI	WAT	PB	PD	TPI
1969	StL-N	1	0	1.000	1	1	0	0	0	7	2	2.6	0	3	3.9	3	3.9	0.00	—	.091	.259	3	3	99	0	0.5	0	0	0.4
1970	StL-N	7	8	.467	20	20	5	2	0	127	132	9.4	9	49	3.5	74	5.2	4.11	105	.271	.332	-1	3	106	100	0.0	-3	-0	0.0
1971	StL-N	14	14	.500	36	35	7	2	0	211	228	9.7	15	109	4.6	131	5.6	4.78	73	.279	.361	-31	-31	100	96	-1.6	1	-2	-3.2
1972	Hou-N	9	13	.409	33	30	4	1	1	192	177	8.3	14	83	3.9	174	8.2	4.17	87	.246	.325	-15	-11	105	87	-3.0	-2	-1	-1.3
1973	Hou-N	16	13	.552	41	40	12	3	0	279	271	8.7	17	117	3.8	177	5.7	3.74	93	.256	.326	-2	-8	95	96	1.6	-1	-2	-1.1
1974	Pit-N	16	11	.593	35	35	14	1	0	260	259	9.0	20	101	3.5	105	3.6	3.50	100	.261	.321	4	0	97	106	1.7	-0	-2	-0.2
1975	Pit-N	18	11	.621	32	32	15	6	0	237	224	8.5	10	78	3.0	131	5.0	2.54	139	.253	.307	29	26	98	**122**	2.0	2	2	3.3
1976	Pit-N	14	9	.609	31	29	11	3	2	209	209	9.0	16	51	2.2	108	4.7	3.53	99	.256	.298	-1	-1	99	92	1.2	6	-1	0.3
1977	Pit-N	10	13	.435	33	33	8	2	0	208	225	9.7	11	71	3.1	116	5.0	4.11	97	.280	.336	-5	-3	102	97	-3.3	1	1	0.0
1978	Pit-N	3	2	.600	23	12	3	1	0	83	97	10.5	5	23	2.5	42	4.6	4.88	77	.297	.341	-12	-10	105	90	0.3	0	-0	-1.0
1979	LA-N	7	14	.333	39	21	4	1	3	160	178	10.0	4	60	3.4	83	4.7	3.54	105	.282	.338	4	3	99	109	-3.5	1	1	0.5
1980	LA-N	18	6	.750	37	29	10	**6**	3	229	193	7.6	12	40	1.6	111	4.4	2.52	137	.227	.257	28	24	96	84	5.6	-1	1	2.6
1981	LA-N	10	4	.714	22	22	8	2	0	153	138	8.1	6	27	1.6	51	3.0	2.29	146	.243	.278	20	18	96	111	2.5	0	3	2.4
1982	LA-N	18	11	.621	39	37	8	4	0	255	232	8.2	11	50	1.8	138	4.9	3.11	109	.240	.274	14	8	94	78	2.9	3	2	1.3
1983	LA-N	12	11	.522	32	31	7	0	0	223	233	9.4	12	50	2.0	143	5.8	2.95	123	.271	.305	17	17	100	116	-0.8	5	4	2.8
1984	LA-N	5	7	.417	30	15	2	0	1	99	102	9.3	4	31	2.8	44	4.0	3.82	98	.266	.311	-2	-1	104	90	-0.8	1	-1	0.0
1985	LA-N	14	10	.583	34	33	5	3	0	213	210	8.9	13	58	2.5	84	3.5	2.92	113	.260	.307	16	9	92	116	0.0	-1	-2	0.6
1986	LA-N	2	6	.250	19	13	0	0	1	74	96	11.7	13	17	2.1	29	3.5	5.84	60	.313	.347	-17	-19	95	96	-1.7	2	1	-1.6
1987	LA-N	0	0	—	1	0	0	0	0	2	2	9.0	0	0	0.0	2	9.0	4.50	84	.333	.250	-0	-0	92	93	0.0	0	0	0.0

YEAR	TM/L	W	L	PCT	G	GS	CG	SHO	SV	IP	H	H/G	HR	BB	BB/G	SO	SO/G	ERA	/A	OAVG	OOBP	PR	/A	PF	CPI	WAT	PB	PD	TPI
	Cin-N	0	5	.000	7	7	0	0	0	35	52	13.4	2	12	3.1	10	2.6	7.71	55	.351	.399	-14	-14	103	81	-2.4	0	-1	-1.2
	Yr	0	5	.000	8	7	0	0	0	37	54	13.1	2	12	2.9	12	2.9	7.54	56	.348	.392	-14	-14	103	81	-2.4	0	-1	-1.2
	Cal-A	4	5	.444	17	16	1	1	0	82	112	12.3	16	17	1.9	37	4.1	5.27	84	.327	.356	-7	-7	100	118	-0.1	0	1	-0.5
1988	Chi-A	13	9	.591	32	29	2	0	0	183	183	9.0	15	43	2.1	73	3.6	3.44	114	.263	.305	11	10	99	105	3.3	0	0	1.0
Total	20	211	182	.537	594	520	126	38	11	3521	3555	9.1	225	1090	2.8	1866	4.8	3.58	101	.263	.315	38	14	98	100	4.4	15	6	5.1

■ **ALLIE REYNOLDS** Reynolds, Allie Pierce "Superchief" b: 2/10/15, Bethany, Okla. BR/TR, 6', 195 lbs. Deb: 9/17/42

YEAR	TM/L	W	L	PCT	G	GS	CG	SHO	SV	IP	H	H/G	HR	BB	BB/G	SO	SO/G	ERA	/A	OAVG	OOBP	PR	/A	PF	CPI	WAT	PB	PD	TPI
1942	Cle-A	0	0	—	2	0	0	0	0	5	5	9.0	0	4	7.2	2	3.6	0.00	—	.250	.375	2	2	93	0	0.0	-0	-0	0.1
1943	Cle-A	11	12	.478	34	21	11	3	3	199	140	**6.3**	3	109	4.9	**151**	**6.8**	2.98	99	**.202**	.313	7	-1	90	85	-1.3	-1	-0	-0.2
1944	Cle-A	11	8	.579	28	21	5	1	1	158	141	8.0	2	91	5.2	84	4.8	3.30	105	.240	.342	2	3	101	102	2.2	-3	-1	0.0
1945	Cle-A	18	12	.600	44	30	16	2	4	247	227	8.3	7	130	4.7	112	4.1	3.21	103	.247	.337	4	3	98	109	3.5	-7	-1	-0.5
1946	Cle-A	11	15	.423	31	28	9	3	0	183	180	8.9	10	108	5.3	107	5.3	3.89	82	.259	.355	-8	-15	90	105	-0.5	2	-1	-1.4
1947	NY-A	19	8	**.704**	34	30	17	4	2	242	207	7.7	23	123	4.6	129	4.8	3.20	107	.227	.320	14	6	92	108	3.1	-1	-2	0.2
1948	NY-A	16	7	.696	39	31	11	1	3	236	240	9.2	17	111	4.2	101	3.9	3.78	109	.268	.349	13	9	96	117	2.8	0	-3	0.6
1949	NY-A	17	6	.739	35	31	4	2	1	214	200	8.4	15	123	5.2	105	4.4	4.00	102	.250	.349	5	2	97	102	3.8	5	-0	0.7
1950	NY-A	16	12	.571	35	29	14	2	2	241	215	8.0	12	138	5.2	160	6.0	3.73	118	.242	.345	23	18	96	103	-1.6	1	-1	1.6
1951	NY-A	17	8	.680	40	26	16	**7**	7	221	171	**7.0**	12	100	4.1	126	5.1	3.05	119	**.213**	.302	26	14	88	91	1.8	1	-3	1.1
1952	NY-A	20	8	.714	35	29	24	**6**	6	244	194	7.2	10	97	3.6	**160**	5.9	**2.07**	**168**	.218	.298	**44**	38	95	125	4.1	-1	-1	4.0
1953	NY-A	13	7	.650	41	15	5	1	13	145	140	8.7	9	61	3.8	86	5.3	3.41	103	.253	.329	9	2	88	108	0.0	1	-2	0.0
1954	NY-A	13	4	.765	36	18	5	4	7	157	133	7.6	13	66	3.8	100	5.7	3.32	106	.233	.309	7	3	94	98	2.7	-1	-0	0.2
Total	13	182	107	.630	434	309	137	36	49	2492	2193	7.9	133	1261	4.6	1423	5.1	3.30	109	.238	.329	148	84	94	105	20.6	-4	-15	6.4

■ **ARCHIE REYNOLDS** Reynolds, Archie Edward b: 1/3/46, Glendale, Cal. BR/TR, 6'2", 205 lbs. Deb: 8/15/68

YEAR	TM/L	W	L	PCT	G	GS	CG	SHO	SV	IP	H	H/G	HR	BB	BB/G	SO	SO/G	ERA	/A	OAVG	OOBP	PR	/A	PF	CPI	WAT	PB	PD	TPI
1968	Chi-N	0	1	.000	7	1	0	0	0	13	14	9.7	1	7	4.8	6	4.2	6.92	48	.259	.355	-6	-5	112	61	-0.4	1	-0	-0.4
1969	Chi-N	0	1	.000	2	2	0	0	0	7	11	14.1	1	7	9.0	4	5.1	2.57	147	.379	.474	1	1	105	364	-0.4	0	0	0.2
1970	Chi-N	0	2	.000	7	1	0	0	0	15	17	10.2	2	9	5.4	9	5.4	6.60	73	.298	.403	-4	-3	119	93	-0.9	0	-0	-0.2
1971	Cal-A	0	3	.000	15	1	0	0	0	27	32	10.7	2	18	6.0	15	5.0	4.67	74	.305	.397	-4	-4	99	121	-1.4	-0	0	-0.3
1972	Mil-A	0	1	.000	5	2	0	0	0	19	26	12.3	2	8	3.8	13	6.2	7.11	42	.338	.391	-9	-9	97	86	-0.4	1	-1	-0.8
Total	5	0	8	.000	36	7	0	0	0	81	100	11.1	8	49	5.4	47	5.2	5.78	62	.311	.397	-21	-20	105	119	-3.5	2	-0	-1.5

■ **CHARLIE REYNOLDS** Reynolds, Charles E. b: 7/31/1857, Allegany, N.Y. d: 5/1/13, Buffalo, N.Y. Deb: 5/18/1882

YEAR	TM/L	W	L	PCT	G	GS	CG	SHO	SV	IP	H	H/G	HR	BB	BB/G	SO	SO/G	ERA	/A	OAVG	OOBP	PR	/A	PF	CPI	WAT	PB	PD	TPI
1882	Phi-a	1	1	.500	2	2	1	0	0	12	18	13.5	0	3	2.3	4	3.0	5.25	57	.352	.388	-3	-3	111	101	0.0	-1	0	-0.2

■ **CRAIG REYNOLDS** Reynolds, Gordon Craig b: 12/27/52, Houston, Tex. BL/TR, 6'1", 175 lbs. Deb: 8/01/75

YEAR	TM/L	W	L	PCT	G	GS	CG	SHO	SV	IP	H	H/G	HR	BB	BB/G	SO	SO/G	ERA	/A	OAVG	OOBP	PR	/A	PF	CPI	WAT	PB	PD	TPI
1986	Hou-N	0	0	—	1	0	0	0	0	1	3	27.0	0	2	18.0	1	9.0	27.00	14	.500	.625	-3	-3	102	64	0.0	0	0	-0.1

■ **KEN REYNOLDS** Reynolds, Kenneth Lee b: 1/4/47, Trevose, Pa. BL/TL, 6', 180 lbs. Deb: 9/05/70

YEAR	TM/L	W	L	PCT	G	GS	CG	SHO	SV	IP	H	H/G	HR	BB	BB/G	SO	SO/G	ERA	/A	OAVG	OOBP	PR	/A	PF	CPI	WAT	PB	PD	TPI
1970	Phi-N	0	0	—	4	0	0	0	0	2	3	13.5	0	4	18.0	1	4.5	0.00	—	.333	.538	1	1	98	0	0.0	0	0	0.1
1971	Phi-N	5	9	.357	35	25	2	1	0	162	163	9.1	11	82	4.6	81	4.5	4.50	81	.269	.354	-19	-16	105	96	-0.9	2	-1	-1.4
1972	Phi-N	2	15	.118	33	23	2	0	0	154	149	8.7	17	60	3.5	87	5.1	4.27	80	.258	.322	-14	-15	99	93	-6.0	1	-0	-1.3
1973	Mil-A	0	1	.000	2	1	0	0	0	7	5	6.4	1	10	12.9	3	3.9	7.71	48	.200	.444	-3	-3	96	79	-0.4	0	1	-0.1
1975	StL-N	0	1	.000	10	0	0	0	0	17	12	6.4	0	11	5.8	7	3.7	1.59	237	.214	.338	4	4	103	186	-0.4	-0	1	0.5
1976	SD-N	0	3	.000	19	2	0	0	1	32	38	10.7	0	29	8.2	18	5.1	6.47	49	.309	.432	-11	-12	90	92	-1.4	-1	-0	-1.2
Total	6	7	29	.194	103	51	4	1	1	374	370	8.9	29	196	4.7	197	4.7	4.48	78	.265	.352	-41	-40	101	98	-9.1	2	0	-3.4

■ **BOB REYNOLDS** Reynolds, Robert Allen b: 1/21/47, Seattle, Wash. BR/TR, 6', 205 lbs. Deb: 9/19/69

YEAR	TM/L	W	L	PCT	G	GS	CG	SHO	SV	IP	H	H/G	HR	BB	BB/G	SO	SO/G	ERA	/A	OAVG	OOBP	PR	/A	PF	CPI	WAT	PB	PD	TPI
1969	Mon-N	0	0	—	1	1	0	0	0	1	3	27.0	0	3	27.0	2	18.0	27.00	14	.429	.545	-3	-3	103	65	0.0	0	0	-0.1
1971	StL-N	0	0	—	4	0	0	0	0	7	15	19.3	2	6	7.7	4	5.1	10.29	34	.441	.537	-5	-5	100	125	0.0	-0	0	-0.4
	Mil-A	0	1	.000	3	0	0	0	0	6	4	6.0	0	3	4.5	4	6.0	3.00	120	.222	.318	0	0	104	97	-0.4	-0	0	0.0
1972	Bal-A	0	0	—	3	0	0	0	0	10	8	7.2	0	7	6.3	5	4.5	1.80	164	.258	.385	1	1	96	228	0.0	-0	-0	0.1
1973	Bal-A	7	5	.583	42	1	0	0	9	111	88	7.1	3	31	2.5	77	6.2	1.95	206	.219	.269	23	26	105	104	-0.1	0	-2	2.4
1974	Bal-A	7	5	.583	54	0	0	0	7	69	75	9.8	4	14	1.8	43	5.6	2.74	122	.278	.310	7	5	92	128	0.3	0	-0	0.4
1975	Bal-A	0	1	.000	7	0	0	0	0	6	11	16.5	1	1	1.5	1	1.5	9.00	38	.423	.414	-3	-4	89	96	-0.4	0	-0	-0.3
	Det-A	0	2	.000	21	0	0	0	3	35	40	10.3	8	14	3.6	26	6.7	4.63	87	.288	.350	-3	-2	106	123	-0.9	0	0	-0.1
	Cle-A	0	2	.000	5	0	0	0	2	10	11	9.9	0	3	2.7	5	4.5	4.50	84	.289	.341	-1	-1	100	82	-0.9	0	0	0.0
	Yr	0	5	.000	33	0	0	0	5	51	62	10.9	9	18	3.2	32	5.6	5.12	76	.301	.352	-8	-7	103	82	-2.2	0	0	-0.4
Total	6	14	16	.467	140	2	0	0	21	255	255	9.0	18	82	2.9	167	5.9	3.14	119	.264	.317	16	17	101	117	-2.4	-0	-2	2.0

■ **ROSS REYNOLDS** Reynolds, Ross Ernest "Doc" b: 8/20/1887, Barksdale, Tex. d: 6/23/70, Ada, Okla. BR/TR, 6'2", 185 lbs. Deb: 5/02/14

YEAR	TM/L	W	L	PCT	G	GS	CG	SHO	SV	IP	H	H/G	HR	BB	BB/G	SO	SO/G	ERA	/A	OAVG	OOBP	PR	/A	PF	CPI	WAT	PB	PD	TPI
1914	Det-A	5	3	.625	26	7	3	1	0	78	62	7.2	0	39	4.5	31	3.6	2.08	134	.230	.340	6	6	102	135	0.9	-2	-1	0.6
1915	Det-A	0	1	.000	4	2	0	0	0	11	17	13.9	0	5	4.1	2	1.6	6.55	47	.378	.451	-4	-4	105	104	-0.4	-0	0	-0.3
Total	2	5	4	.556	30	9	3	1	0	89	79	8.0	0	44	4.4	33	3.3	2.63	108	.251	.355	1	2	102	131	0.5	-3	-0	0.3

■ **FLINT RHEM** Rhem, Charles Flint "Shad" b: 1/24/01, Rhems, S.C. d: 7/30/69, Columbia, S.C. BR/TR, 6'2", 180 lbs. Deb: 9/06/24

YEAR	TM/L	W	L	PCT	G	GS	CG	SHO	SV	IP	H	H/G	HR	BB	BB/G	SO	SO/G	ERA	/A	OAVG	OOBP	PR	/A	PF	CPI	WAT	PB	PD	TPI
1924	StL-N	2	2	.500	6	3	3	0	1	32	31	8.7	1	17	4.8	20	5.6	4.50	88	.254	.343	-2	-2	103	79	0.3	-0	0	-0.1
1925	StL-N	8	13	.381	30	23	8	1	1	170	204	10.8	16	58	3.1	66	3.5	4.92	88	.299	.352	-12	-12	101	98	-2.7	1	0	-0.8
1926	StL-N	**20**	7	.741	34	34	20	1	0	258	241	8.4	12	75	2.6	72	2.5	3.21	119	.250	.297	18	17	100	93	5.8	-2	1	1.7
1927	StL-N	10	12	.455	27	26	9	2	0	169	189	10.1	6	54	2.9	51	2.7	4.42	94	.285	.335	-9	-5	106	89	-2.9	-6	-3	-1.2
1928	StL-N	11	8	.579	28	22	9	0	3	170	199	10.5	13	71	3.8	47	2.5	4.13	94	.296	.360	-3	-5	97	114	-0.6	-1	2	-0.4
1930	StL-N	12	8	.600	26	19	9	0	0	140	173	11.1	11	37	2.4	47	3.0	4.44	114	.306	.340	8	10	102	109	0.1	-1	-3	0.5
1931	StL-N	11	10	.524	33	26	10	2	1	207	214	9.3	17	60	2.6	72	3.1	3.57	112	.268	.314	7	10	103	107	-2.3	-4	-1	0.4
1932	StL-N	4	2	.667	6	6	5	1	0	50	48	8.6	3	10	1.8	18	3.2	3.06	128	.257	.293	5	5	101	102	1.2	0	0	0.5
	Phi-N	11	7	.611	26	20	10	0	1	169	177	9.4	13	49	2.6	35	1.9	3.73	116	.269	.315	3	11	111	101	2.1	-5	-0	0.7
	Yr	15	9	.625	32	26	15	1	1	219	225	9.2	16	59	2.4	53	2.2	3.58	118	.266	.310	7	16	109	101	3.3	0	-0	1.2
1933	Phi-N	5	14	.263	28	19	3	0	2	125	182	13.1	10	33	2.4	27	1.9	6.62	61	.340	.373	-46	-36	121	86	-3.4	-4	-0	-3.8
1934	StL-N	1	0	1.000	5	1	0	0	1	16	26	14.6	0	7	3.9	6	3.4	4.50	100	.394	.446	-1	0	111	164	0.5	-0	0	0.0
	Bos-N	8	8	.500	25	20	5	2	0	153	164	9.6	5	38	2.2	56	3.3	3.59	98	.273	.311	8	-1	86	98	-0.2	-4	1	-0.4
	Yr	9	8	.529	30	21	5	2	1	169	190	10.1	5	45	2.4	62	3.3	3.67	98	.285	.325	7	-1	89	98	0.3	-0	1	-0.4
1935	Bos-N	0	5	.000	10	6	0	0	0	40	61	13.7	4	11	2.5	10	2.3	5.40	75	.341	.369	-6	-6	100	113	-2.4	-1	0	-0.6
1936	StL-N	2	1	.667	10	4	0	0	0	27	49	16.3	2	9	3.0	7	2.3	6.67	57	.405	.436	-8	-9	95	122	0.4	-0	-0	-0.8
Total	12	105	97	.520	294	229	91	9	10	1726	1958	10.2	113	529	2.8	534	2.8	4.20	97	.287	.334	-39	-21	102	100	-4.1	-29	-3	-4.3

■ **BILLY RHINES** Rhines, William Pearl "Bunker" b: 3/14/1869, Ridgway, Pa. d: 1/30/22, Ridgway, Pa. 5'11", 168 lbs. Deb: 4/22/1890

YEAR	TM/L	W	L	PCT	G	GS	CG	SHO	SV	IP	H	H/G	HR	BB	BB/G	SO	SO/G	ERA	/A	OAVG	OOBP	PR	/A	PF	CPI	WAT	PB	PD	TPI
1890	Cin-N	28	17	.622	46	45	45	6	0	401	337	7.6	6	113	2.5	182	4.1	**1.95**	**194**	.243	**.300**	**72**	**81**	106	113	3.0	-6	1	7.5
1891	Cin-N	17	24	.415	48	43	40	1	1	373	364	8.8	4	124	3.0	138	3.3	2.87	109	.269	.330	20	10	93	96	0.3	-7	4	0.5
1892	Cin-N	4	7	.364	12	10	8	0	0	84	113	12.1	0	36	3.9	12	1.3	5.14	66	.336	.400	-17	-16	103	97	-1.8	1	0	-1.3
1893	Lou-N	1	4	.200	5	5	3	0	0	31	49	14.2	3	19	5.5	0	0.0	8.71	53	.376	.455	-14	-14	98	88	-1.2	-1	0	-1.1
1895	Cin-N	19	10	.655	38	33	25	0	0	268	322	10.8	4	76	2.6	72	2.4	4.84	106	.318	.366	-1	9	107	86	5.1	-4	0	0.6
1896	Cin-N	8	6	.571	19	17	11	3	0	143	128	**8.1**	1	48	3.0	32	2.0	**2.45**	**184**	**.260**	**.326**	30	33	103	108	-0.3	-3	0	2.8
1897	Cin-N	21	15	.583	41	32	26	1	0	289	311	9.7	4	86	2.7	65	2.0	4.08	113	.297	.350	8	17	107	84	0.4	-7	-1	0.9
1898	Pit-N	12	16	.429	31	29	27	2	0	258	289	10.1	0	61	2.1	48	1.7	3.52	101	.305	.347	2	1	98	96	-1.9	-4	5	0.2
1899	Pit-N	4	4	.500	9	9	4	0	0	54	59	9.8	3	13	2.2	6	1.0	6.00	63	.302	.345	-13	-13	98	61	0.0	4	0	-0.7
Total	9	114	103	.525	249	223	189	13	1	1901	1972	9.3	25	576	2.7	555	2.6	3.48	114	.286	.341	86	103	102	96	3.6	-29	9	9.4

■ **BOB RHOADS** Rhoads, Robert Barton "Dusty" b: 10/4/1879, Wooster, Ohio d: 2/12/67, San Bernardino, Cal. TR, 6'1", 215 lbs. Deb: 4/19/02

YEAR	TM/L	W	L	PCT	G	GS	CG	SHO	SV	IP	H	H/G	HR	BB	BB/G	SO	SO/G	ERA	/A	OAVG	OOBP	PR	/A	PF	CPI	WAT	PB	PD	TPI
1902	Chi-N	4	8	.333	16	12	12	1	1	118	131	10.0	1	42	3.2	43	3.3	3.20	83	.305	.367	-6	-7	95	112	-2.0	0	-0	-0.7
1903	StL-N	5	8	.385	17	13	12	1	0	129	154	10.7	3	47	3.3	52	3.6	4.60	72	.324	.388	-19	-18	102	93	0.7	-2	-2	-1.7
	Cle-A	2	3	.400	5	5	5	0	0	41	55	12.1	2	3	0.7	21	4.6	5.27	53	.346	.358	-11	-11	95	87	-0.6	-1	-0	-0.9
1904	Cle-A	10	9	.526	22	19	18	0	0	175	175	9.0	1	48	2.5	72	3.7	2.88	88	.284	.335	-6	-7	98	106	-0.7	0	-1	-0.7

YEAR	TM/L	W	L	PCT	G	GS	CG	SHO	SV	IP	H	H/G	HR	BB	BB/G	SO	SO/G	ERA	/A	OAVG	OOBP	PR	/A	PF	CPI	WAT	PB	PD	TPI
1905	Cle-A	16	9	.640	28	26	24	4	0	235	219	8.4	4	55	2.1	61	2.3	2.83	94	.271	.317	-5	-5	100	98	4.1	4	-0	-0.4
1906	Cle-A	22	10	.688	38	34	31	7	0	315	259	7.4	5	92	2.6	89	2.5	1.80	148	.247	.308	31	30	99	**128**	4.8	-3	-2	3.3
1907	Cle-A	15	14	.517	35	31	23	5	1	275	258	8.4	0	84	2.7	76	2.5	2.29	103	.272	.331	8	2	93	117	-1.2	-1	-1	0.1
1908	Cle-A	18	12	.600	37	30	20	1	0	270	229	7.6	2	73	2.4	62	2.1	1.77	140	.239	.298	19	21	103	142	0.7	3	2	2.7
1909	Cle-A	5	9	.357	20	15	9	2	0	133	124	8.4	1	50	3.4	46	3.1	2.91	88	.281	.361	-6	-5	103	121	-1.6	-0	0	-0.5
Total	8	97	82	.542	218	185	154	21	2	1691	1604	8.5	19	494	2.6	522	2.8	2.61	100	.272	.330	5	0	99	117	4.2	1	-4	1.2
■ RICK RHODEN	Rhoden, Richard Alan b: 5/16/53, Boynton Beach, Fla. BR/TR, 6'3", 195 lbs. Deb: 7/05/74																												
1974	LA-N	1	0	1.000	4	0	0	0	0	9	5	5.0	1	4	4.0	7	7.0	2.00	163	.161	.257	2	1	90	92	0.5	0	0	0.2
1975	LA-N	3	3	.500	26	11	1	0	0	99	94	8.5	8	32	2.9	40	3.6	3.09	110	.253	.306	6	3	93	109	-0.1	-2	0	0.1
1976	LA-N	12	3	.800	27	26	10	3	0	181	165	8.2	17	53	2.6	77	3.8	2.98	116	.242	.294	11	10	99	107	4.2	7	-2	1.5
1977	LA-N	16	10	.615	31	31	4	1	0	216	223	9.3	20	63	2.6	122	5.1	3.75	102	.270	.318	4	2	98	103	0.4	5	-2	0.4
1978	LA-N	10	8	.556	30	23	6	3	0	165	160	8.7	13	51	2.8	79	4.3	3.65	95	.255	.307	-1	-3	97	95	-0.4	-0	-1	-0.4
1979	Pit-N	0	1	.000	1	1	0	0	0	5	5	9.0	0	2	3.6	2	3.6	7.20	54	.263	.333	-2	-2	104	45	-0.4	0	0	0.0
1980	Pit-N	7	5	.583	20	19	2	0	0	127	133	9.4	9	40	2.8	70	5.0	3.83	97	.273	.328	-3	-2	103	102	0.9	6	0	0.5
1981	Pit-N	9	4	.692	21	21	4	2	0	136	147	9.7	6	53	3.5	76	5.0	3.90	86	.283	.344	-6	-8	96	107	3.1	1	1	-0.6
1982	Pit-N	11	14	.440	35	35	6	1	0	230	239	9.4	14	70	2.7	128	5.0	4.15	96	.267	.316	-14	-5	110	86	-2.1	8	2	0.7
1983	Pit-N	13	13	.500	36	35	7	2	1	244	256	9.4	13	68	2.5	153	5.6	3.10	121	.276	.322	15	17	103	**119**	-0.4	-2	1	1.7
1984	Pit-N	14	9	.609	33	33	6	3	0	238	216	8.2	13	62	2.3	136	5.1	2.72	124	.243	.290	23	17	94	105	3.5	10	2	3.1
1985	Pit-N	10	15	.400	35	35	2	0	0	213	254	10.7	18	69	2.9	128	5.4	4.48	84	.296	.349	-21	-17	104	104	1.0	1	-0	-1.5
1986	Pit-N	15	12	.556	34	34	12	1	0	254	211	7.5	17	76	2.7	159	5.6	2.83	132	.228	.285	25	26	101	96	4.1	10	1	3.9
1987	NY-A	16	10	.615	30	29	4	0	0	182	184	9.1	22	61	3.0	107	5.3	3.86	113	.268	.325	12	10	97	113	2.2	0	0	0.9
1988	NY-A	12	12	.500	30	30	5	1	0	197	206	9.4	20	56	2.6	94	4.3	4.20	90	.269	.319	-5	-9	96	97	-0.6	0	-0	-0.9
Total	15	149	119	.556	393	363	69	17	1	2496	2498	9.0	191	760	2.7	1378	5.0	3.56	104	.263	.315	45	41	100	103	15.9	45	1	9.6
■ CHARLIE RHODES	Rhodes, Charles Anderson "Dusty" b: 4/7/1885, Caney, Kan. d: 10/26/18, Caney, Kan. BR/TR, 5'7", 180 lbs. Deb: 7/26/06																												
1906	StL-N	3	4	.429	9	6	3	0	0	45	37	7.4	0	20	4.0	32	6.4	3.40	80	.260	.374	-4	-3	104	85	0.5	-0	0	-0.2
1908	Cin-N	0	0	—	1	0	0	0	0	4	1	2.3	0	2	4.5	4	9.0	0.00	—	.102	.312	1	1	104	0	0.0	-0	0	0.2
	StL-N	1	2	.333	4	4	3	0	0	33	23	6.3	2	12	3.3	15	4.1	3.00	78	.223	.310	-2	-2	100	74	0.0	1	1	-0.1
	Yr	1	2	.333	5	4	3	0	0	37	24	5.8	2	14	3.4	19	4.6	2.68	88	.211	.303	-1	-1	100	74	0.0	-0	1	0.1
1909	StL-N	3	5	.375	12	10	4	0	0	61	55	8.1	0	33	4.9	25	3.7	3.98	65	.256	.360	-9	-9	99	86	0.1	1	2	-0.7
Total	3	7	11	.389	26	20	10	0	0	143	116	7.3	2	67	4.2	76	4.8	3.46	74	.247	.353	-15	-14	101	81	0.6	1	3	-0.8
■ GORDON RHODES	Rhodes, John Gordon "Dusty" b: 8/11/07, Winnemucca, Nev. d: 3/24/60, Long Beach, Cal. BR/TR, 6', 187 lbs. Deb: 4/29/29																												
1929	NY-A	0	4	.000	10	4	0	0	0	43	57	11.9	3	16	3.3	13	2.7	4.81	85	.333	.385	-3	-3	97	122	-1.9	1	-1	-0.2
1930	NY-A	0	0	—	3	0	0	0	0	2	3	13.5	0	4	18.0	1	4.5	9.00	45	.500	.700	-1	-1	87	155	0.0	0	0	0.0
1931	NY-A	6	3	.667	18	11	4	0	0	87	82	8.5	3	52	5.4	36	3.7	3.41	120	.235	.327	9	7	94	102	0.6	1	0	0.7
1932	NY-A	1	2	.333	10	2	1	0	0	24	25	9.4	0	21	7.9	15	5.6	7.88	52	.275	.393	-9	-10	91	67	-0.7	0	1	-0.6
	Bos-A	1	8	.111	12	11	4	0	0	79	79	9.0	5	31	3.5	22	2.5	5.13	89	.261	.323	-6	-5	102	78	-2.7	-2	-0	-0.6
	Yr	2	10	.167	22	13	5	0	0	103	104	9.1	5	52	4.5	37	3.2	5.77	77	.264	.341	-15	-15	100	78	-3.4	0	1	-1.2
1933	Bos-A	12	15	.444	34	29	14	0	0	232	242	9.4	13	93	3.6	85	3.3	4.03	108	.265	.330	6	9	102	100	0.6	5	-1	1.2
1934	Bos-A	12	12	.500	44	31	10	0	2	219	247	10.2	10	98	4.0	79	3.2	4.56	104	.285	.351	-2	4	105	101	0.0	-3	0	0.1
1935	Bos-A	2	10	.167	34	19	1	0	2	146	195	12.0	14	60	3.7	44	2.7	5.42	89	.324	.379	-16	-10	108	111	-4.0	-4	-1	-1.2
1936	Phi-A	9	20	.310	35	28	13	1	1	216	266	11.1	26	102	4.3	61	2.5	5.75	92	.304	.371	-17	-11	105	103	-1.7	-2	-3	-1.2
Total	8	43	74	.368	200	135	47	1	5	1048	1196	10.3	74	477	4.1	356	3.1	4.85	96	.286	.354	-37	-21	103	101	-8.8	-6	-3	-1.8
■ BILL RHODES	Rhodes, William Clarence b: Pottstown, Pa. Deb: 6/14/1893																												
1893	Lou-N	5	12	.294	20	19	17	0	0	152	244	14.4	10	66	3.9	22	1.3	7.64	60	.379	.437	-50	-52	98	93	-2.4	-4	0	-4.0
■ DENNIS RIBANT	Ribant, Dennis Joseph b: 9/20/41, Detroit, Mich. BR/TR, 5'11", 165 lbs. Deb: 8/09/64																												
1964	NY-N	1	5	.167	14	7	1	1	1	58	65	10.1	8	9	1.4	35	5.4	5.12	68	.281	.306	-10	-11	98	82	-1.4	-0	-1	-1.1
1965	NY-N	1	3	.250	19	1	0	0	3	35	29	7.5	5	6	1.5	13	3.3	3.86	95	.228	.257	-1	-1	104	77	-0.3	-1	-0	-0.1
1966	NY-N	11	9	.550	39	26	10	1	3	188	184	8.8	20	40	1.9	84	4.0	3.21	109	.254	.289	8	6	97	103	2.6	1	0	0.7
1967	Pit-N	9	8	.529	38	22	2	0	0	172	186	9.7	16	40	2.1	75	3.9	4.08	83	.280	.319	-13	-13	100	100	0.6	5	2	-0.6
1968	Det-A	2	2	.500	14	0	0	0	1	24	20	7.5	1	10	3.8	7	2.6	2.25	137	.217	.295	2	2	103	115	-0.3	0	-0	0.2
	Chi-A	0	2	.000	17	0	0	0	1	31	42	12.2	3	17	4.9	20	5.8	6.10	50	.318	.396	-11	-11	102	101	-0.9	-1	0	-1.1
	Yr	2	4	.333	31	0	0	0	2	55	62	10.1	4	27	4.4	27	4.4	4.42	69	.276	.351	-9	-8	103	101	-1.2	0	-0	-0.9
1969	StL-N	0	0	—	1	0	0	0	0	1	4	36.0	1	1	9.0	0	0.0	18.00	20	.571	.556	-2	-2	99	149	0.0	0	0	-0.1
	Cin-N	0	0	—	7	0	0	0	0	8	6	6.8	1	3	3.4	7	7.9	1.13	315	.188	.257	2	2	99	175	0.0	0	-0	0.2
	Yr	0	0	—	8	0	0	0	0	9	10	10.0	2	4	4.0	7	7.0	3.00	118	.250	.318	1	1	99	175	0.0	0	-0	0.1
Total	6	24	29	.453	149	56	13	2	9	517	536	9.3	55	126	2.2	241	4.2	3.88	88	.267	.307	-25	-26	99	99	0.3	5	0	-1.9
■ FRANK RICCELLI	Riccelli, Frank Joseph b: 2/24/53, Syracuse, N.Y. BL/TL, 6'3", 205 lbs. Deb: 9/11/76																												
1976	SF-N	1	1	.500	4	3	0	0	0	16	16	9.0	1	5	2.8	11	6.2	5.63	65	.258	.309	-4	-4	104	60	0.1	-0	-0	-0.3
1978	Hou-N	0	0	—	2	0	0	0	0	3	1	3.0	0	0	0.0	1	3.0	0.00	—	.100	.100	1	1	95	0	0.0	0	0	0.1
1979	Hou-N	2	2	.500	11	2	0	0	0	22	22	9.0	0	18	7.4	20	8.2	4.09	83	.262	.388	-1	-2	90	107	-0.1	-1	1	0.0
Total	3	3	3	.500	17	5	0	0	0	41	39	8.6	1	23	5.0	32	7.0	4.39	80	.250	.343	-3	-4	96	80	0.0	-1	0	-0.2
■ SAM RICE	Rice, Edgar Charles b: 2/20/1890, Morocco, Ind. d: 10/13/74, Rossmor, Md. BL/TR, 5'9", 150 lbs. Deb: 8/07/15 H																												
1915	Was-A	1	0	1.000	4	2	1	0	0	18	13	6.5	0	9	4.5	9	4.5	2.00	146	.213	.314	2	2	99	116	0.5	1	0	0.3
1916	Was-A	0	1	.000	5	1	0	0	0	21	18	7.7	0	10	4.3	3	1.3	3.00	94	.237	.326	-0	-0	100	89	-0.4	2	-0	0.0
Total	2	1	1	.500	9	3	1	0	0	39	31	7.2	0	19	4.4	12	2.8	2.54	113	.226	.321	1	1	100	101	0.1	2	0	0.3
■ WOODY RICH	Rich, Woodrow Earl b: 3/9/16, Morganton, N.C. d: 4/18/83, Morganton, N.C. BL/TR, 6'2", 185 lbs. Deb: 4/22/39																												
1939	Bos-A	4	3	.571	21	12	3	0	1	77	78	9.1	2	35	4.1	24	2.8	4.91	100	.264	.343	-2	0	107	84	0.0	0	1	0.2
1940	Bos-A	1	0	1.000	3	1	1	0	0	12	9	6.8	2	1	0.8	8	6.0	0.75	584	.214	.227	5	5	100	369	0.5	-1	-0	0.4
1941	Bos-A	0	0	—	2	1	0	0	0	4	8	18.0	1	2	4.5	4	9.0	15.75	27	.421	.476	-5	-5	101	69	0.0	0	-0	-0.3
1944	Bos-N	1	1	.500	7	2	1	0	0	25	32	11.5	3	12	4.3	6	2.2	5.76	60	.327	.402	-6	-6	96	114	0.1	-0	0	-0.6
Total	4	6	4	.600	33	16	5	0	1	118	127	9.7	8	50	3.8	42	3.2	5.03	90	.280	.352	-9	-7	104	119	0.6	-1	2	-0.3
■ J. R. RICHARD	Richard, James Rodney b: 3/7/50, Vienna, La. BR/TR, 6'8", 222 lbs. Deb: 9/05/71																												
1971	Hou-N	2	1	.667	4	4	1	0	0	21	17	7.3	1	16	6.9	29	12.4	3.43	93	.215	.344	0	-1	92	98	0.5	-1	0	0.0
1972	Hou-N	1	0	1.000	4	1	0	0	0	6	10	15.0	0	8	12.0	8	12.0	13.50	27	.385	.556	-7	-7	105	77	0.5	0	0	-0.5
1973	Hou-N	6	2	.750	16	10	2	1	0	72	54	6.8	2	38	4.8	75	9.4	4.00	87	.210	.313	-3	-4	95	65	2.0	-0	-1	-0.5
1974	Hou-N	2	3	.400	15	9	0	0	0	65	58	8.0	3	36	5.0	42	5.8	4.15	85	.243	.342	-4	-4	98	86	-0.4	0	-1	-0.4
1975	Hou-N	12	10	.545	33	31	7	1	0	203	178	7.9	8	138	6.1	176	7.8	4.39	78	.238	.354	-17	-21	95	85	3.0	4	-2	-1.9
1976	Hou-N	20	15	.571	39	39	14	3	0	291	221	**6.8**	14	151	4.7	214	6.6	2.75	110	**.212**	.309	24	9	87	101	3.3	1	-1	0.8
1977	Hou-N	18	12	.600	36	36	13	3	0	267	212	7.1	18	104	3.5	214	7.2	2.97	122	.218	.289	28	19	92	88	3.5	6	3	2.9
1978	Hou-N	18	11	.621	36	36	16	3	0	275	192	**6.3**	12	141	4.6	**303**	**9.9**	3.11	109	**.196**	.294	14	9	95	75	5.0	1	2	1.2
1979	Hou-N	18	13	.581	38	38	19	4	0	292	220	**6.8**	13	98	3.0	**313**	**9.6**	**2.71**	125	**.209**	.273	**33**	22	90	78	1.3	0	-1	2.1
1980	Hou-N	10	4	.714	17	17	4	4	0	114	65	5.1	2	40	3.2	119	9.4	1.89	185	.166	.240	22	20	97	54	2.5	1	-1	2.3
Total	10	107	71	.601	238	221	76	19	0	1606	1227	6.9	73	770	4.3	1493	8.4	3.15	107	.212	.302	92	42	92	82	21.2	11	1	6.0
■ DUANE RICHARDS	Richards, Duane Lee b: 12/16/36, Spartanburg, Ind. BR/TR, 6'3", 200 lbs. Deb: 9/25/60																												
1960	Cin-N	0	0	—	2	0	0	0	0	3	5	15.0	0	2	6.0	2	6.0	9.00	41	.385	.438	-2	-2	99	85	0.0	0	0	-0.1
■ HARDY RICHARDSON	Richardson, Abram Harding "Old True Blue" b: 4/21/1855, Clarksboro, N.J. d: 1/14/31, Utica, N.Y. BR/TR, 5'9.5", 170 lbs. Deb: 5/01/1879																												
1885	Buf-N	0	0	—	1	0	0	0	0	4	5	11.3	0	3	6.8	1	2.3	2.25	132	.317	.427	0	0	105	248	0.0	0	0	0.0
1886	Det-N	3	0	1.000	4	0	0	0	0	12	11	8.3	1	10	7.5	5	3.8	4.50	76	.256	.397	-2	-1	103	107	1.5	2	0	0.0
Total	2	3	0	1.000	5	0	0	0	0	16	16	9.0	1	13	7.3	6	3.4	3.94	84	.273	.405	-1	-1	104	142	1.5	3	0	0.0

YEAR	TM/L	W	L	PCT	G	GS	CG	SHO	SV	IP	H	H/G	HR	BB	BB/G	SO	SO/G	ERA	/A	OAVG	OOBP	PR	/A	PF	CPI	WAT	PB	PD	TPI
DANNY RICHARDSON	Richardson, Daniel b: 1/25/1863, Elmira, N.Y. d: 9/12/26, New York, N.Y. BR/TR, 5'8", 165 lbs. Deb: 5/22/1884 M																												
1885	NY-N	7	1	.875	9	8	7	1	0	75	58	7.0	0	18	2.2	21	2.5	2.40	120	.223	.274	3	4	102	74	2.0	2	0	0.4
1886	NY-N	0	2	.000	5	1	1	0	0	25	33	11.9	1	11	4.0	17	6.1	5.76	49	.332	.398	-7	-8	85	94	-0.9	1	0	-0.6
1887	NY-N	0	0	—	1	0	0	0	0	0	0	—	0	1	—	0	—	—	—	—	1.000	0	0	106	0	0.0	0	0	0.0
Total	3	7	3	.700	15	9	8	1	0	100	91	8.2	1	30	2.7	38	3.4	3.24	89	.253	.311	-3	-4	98	79	1.1	3	0	-0.2
GORDIE RICHARDSON	Richardson, Gordon Clark b: 7/19/38, Colquitt, Ga. BR/TL, 6', 185 lbs. Deb: 7/26/64																												
1964	StL-N	4	2	.667	19	6	1	0	1	47	40	7.7	2	15	2.9	28	5.4	2.30	171	.231	.292	6	9	111	119	0.7	-0	-1	0.8
1965	NY-N	2	2	.500	35	0	0	0	2	52	41	7.1	5	16	2.8	43	7.4	3.81	97	.224	.286	-2	-1	104	80	0.6	-1	-0	-0.1
1966	NY-N	0	2	.000	15	1	0	0	1	19	24	11.4	7	6	2.8	15	7.1	9.00	39	.312	.349	-11	-12	97	80	-0.9	-0	0	-1.1
Total	3	6	6	.500	69	7	1	0	4	118	105	8.0	14	37	2.8	86	6.6	4.04	93	.242	.300	-6	-4	106	95	0.4	-1	-2	-0.4
JACK RICHARDSON	Richardson, John William b: 10/3/1891, Central City, Ill. d: 1/18/70, Marion, Ill. BB/TR, 6'3", 197 lbs. Deb: 9/17/15																												
1915	Phi-A	0	1	.000	3	3	2	0	0	24	21	7.9	0	14	5.3	11	4.1	2.63	116	.253	.367	1	1	103	137	-0.4	-1	-0	0.0
1916	Phi-A	0	0	—	1	0	0	0	0	1	2	18.0	0	1	9.0	1	9.0	27.00	11	.667	.750	-3	-3	105	50	0.0	0	0	-0.2
Total	2	0	1	.000	4	3	2	0	0	25	23	8.3	0	15	5.4	12	4.3	3.60	84	.267	.382	-2	-2	103	134	-0.4	-1	-0	-0.2
PETE RICHERT	Richert, Peter Gerard b: 10/29/39, Floral Park, N.Y. BL/TL, 5'11", 165 lbs. Deb: 4/12/62																												
1962	LA-N	5	4	.556	19	12	1	0	0	81	77	8.6	6	45	5.0	75	8.3	3.89	92	.249	.344	0	-3	91	101	-0.4	-1	1	-0.3
1963	LA-N	5	3	.625	20	12	1	0	0	78	80	9.2	7	28	3.2	54	6.2	4.50	68	.262	.324	-11	-12	94	85	0.2	1	-1	-1.2
1964	LA-N	2	3	.400	8	6	1	1	0	35	38	9.8	2	18	4.6	25	6.4	4.11	79	.271	.358	-2	-3	91	108	-0.4	-0	1	-0.2
1965	Was-A	15	12	.556	34	29	6	0	0	194	146	6.8	18	84	3.9	161	7.5	2.60	136	.210	.292	19	20	102	110	3.4	-0	-0	2.1
1966	Was-A	14	14	.500	36	34	7	0	0	246	196	7.2	36	69	2.5	195	7.1	3.37	98	.215	.268	2	-2	96	89	1.6	2	-2	-0.1
1967	Was-A	2	6	.250	11	10	1	1	0	54	49	8.2	5	15	2.5	41	6.8	4.67	72	.237	.284	-9	-8	104	66	-1.8	-1	-1	-1.0
	Bal-A	7	10	.412	26	19	5	1	2	132	107	7.3	11	41	2.8	90	6.1	3.00	101	.220	.275	3	0	94	90	-1.1	-1	1	0.0
	Yr	9	16	.360	37	29	6	2	2	186	156	7.5	16	56	2.7	131	6.3	3.48	90	.223	.277	-5	-8	97	90	-2.9	-1	-0	-1.0
1968	Bal-A	6	3	.667	36	0	0	0	6	62	51	7.4	7	12	1.7	47	6.8	3.48	86	.225	.267	-3	-3	101	80	1.1	0	1	-0.2
1969	Bal-A	7	4	.636	44	0	0	0	12	57	42	6.6	7	14	2.2	54	8.5	2.21	165	.202	.249	9	9	100	102	-0.2	-0	-0	0.9
1970	Bal-A	7	2	.778	50	0	0	0	13	55	36	5.9	5	24	3.9	66	10.8	1.96	178	.194	.282	11	9	94	132	1.6	-0	0	1.0
1971	Bal-A	3	5	.375	35	0	0	0	4	36	26	6.5	3	22	5.5	35	8.8	3.50	99	.205	.318	-0	-0	100	90	-1.6	-0	0	0.0
1972	LA-N	2	3	.400	37	0	0	0	6	52	42	7.3	3	18	3.1	38	6.6	2.25	143	.219	.286	7	6	93	111	-0.6	1	-0	0.7
1973	LA-N	3	3	.500	39	0	0	0	7	51	44	7.8	5	19	3.4	31	5.5	3.18	114	.234	.296	3	3	99	102	-0.4	0	1	0.3
1974	StL-N	0	0	—	13	0	0	0	1	11	10	8.2	1	11	9.0	4	3.3	2.45	152	.244	.382	1	2	103	209	0.0	0	-0	0.1
	Phi-N	2	1	.667	21	0	0	0	0	20	15	6.7	0	4	1.8	9	4.0	2.25	167	.205	.244	3	3	104	54	0.5	0	0	0.3
	Yr	2	1	.667	34	0	0	0	1	31	25	7.3	1	15	4.4	13	3.8	2.32	162	.216	.301	5	5	103	54	0.5	0	-0	0.4
Total	13	80	73	.523	429	122	22	3	51	1164	959	7.4	116	424	3.3	925	7.2	3.19	105	.223	.290	33	21	97	97	1.9	-0	-2	2.4
LEW RICHIE	Richie, Lewis A. b: 8/23/1883, Ambler, Pa. d: 8/15/36, South Montain, Pa. BR/TR, 5'8", 165 lbs. Deb: 5/08/06																												
1906	Phi-N	9	11	.450	33	22	14	3	0	206	170	7.4	3	79	3.5	65	2.8	2.40	102	.252	.336	5	1	93	107	-0.2	-2	-3	-0.2
1907	Phi-N	6	6	.500	25	12	9	2	0	117	88	6.8	0	38	2.9	40	3.1	1.77	144	.237	.316	9	10	103	106	-0.6	-0	-1	1.0
1908	Phi-N	7	10	.412	25	15	13	2	1	158	125	7.1	1	49	2.8	58	3.3	1.82	126	.247	.320	9	8	98	117	-2.1	2	-1	0.9
1909	Phi-N	1	1	.500	11	1	0	0	1	45	40	8.0	0	18	3.6	11	2.2	2.00	138	.263	.349	3	4	106	164	0.0	1	-0	0.4
	Bos-N	7	7	.500	22	13	9	2	2	132	118	8.0	2	44	3.0	42	2.9	2.32	114	.247	.312	4	5	102	115	2.2	-2	-3	0.1
	Yr	8	8	.500	33	14	9	2	3	177	158	8.0	2	62	3.2	53	2.7	2.24	119	.250	.318	7	9	103	**115**	2.2	1	-4	0.5
1910	Bos-N	0	3	.000	4	2	0	0	0	16	20	11.3	0	9	5.1	7	3.9	2.81	128	.317	.403	0	1	118	177	-1.4	-1	1	0.1
	Chi-N	11	4	.733	30	11	8	3	4	130	117	8.1	1	51	3.5	52	3.6	2.70	108	.257	.336	5	3	96	114	1.5	3	1	0.7
	Yr	11	7	.611	34	13	8	3	4	146	137	8.4	1	60	3.7	59	3.6	2.71	110	.264	.344	5	5	99	114	0.1	-1	1	0.8
1911	Chi-N	15	11	.577	36	28	18	4	1	253	213	7.6	6	103	3.7	78	2.8	2.31	138	.235	.315	31	25	94	119	-0.4	-2	0	2.2
1912	Chi-N	16	8	.667	39	27	15	4	0	238	222	8.4	5	74	2.8	69	2.6	2.95	118	.249	.310	12	14	102	87	2.1	-4	-2	0.8
1913	Chi-N	2	4	.333	16	6	0	0	0	65	77	10.7	3	30	4.2	15	2.1	5.82	53	.304	.366	-19	-20	97	83	-1.2	-0	-1	-1.9
Total	8	74	65	.532	241	137	86	20	9	1360	1190	7.9	21	495	3.3	437	2.9	2.53	114	.250	.325	60	52	98	110	-0.1	-6	-11	4.1
BERYL RICHMOND	Richmond, Beryl Justice b: 8/24/07, Glen Easton, W.Va. BB/TL, 6'1", 185 lbs. Deb: 4/21/33																												
1933	Chi-N	0	0	—	4	0	0	0	0	5	10	18.0	0	2	3.6	2	3.6	1.80	176	.455	.480	1	1	95	503	0.0	-0	-0	0.0
1934	Cin-N	1	2	.333	6	2	1	0	0	19	23	10.9	0	10	4.7	9	4.3	3.79	112	.303	.371	1	1	105	128	0.0	-1	-0	0.0
Total	2	1	2	.333	10	2	1	0	0	24	33	12.4	0	12	4.5	11	4.1	3.38	119	.337	.395	1	2	103	206	0.0	-1	-0	0.0
LEE RICHMOND	Richmond, J. Lee b: 5/5/1857, Sheffield, Ohio d: 10/1/29, Toledo, Ohio TL, 5'10", 142 lbs. Deb: 5/01/1879																												
1879	Bos-N	1	0	1.000	1	1	1	0	0	9	4	4.0	0	1	1.0	11	11.0	2.00	126	.139	.167	0	1	101	29	0.5	0	0	0.1
1880	Wor-N	32	32	.500	**74**	66	57	5	**3**	591	541	8.2	7	74	1.1	243	3.7	2.15	123	.252	.277	15	33	111	95	4.4	-5	-5	2.7
1881	Wor-N	25	26	.490	53	52	50	3	0	462	547	10.7	7	68	1.3	156	3.0	3.39	88	.307	.332	-31	-21	107	99	**8.7**	-1	2	-1.4
1882	Wor-N	14	33	.298	48	46	44	0	0	411	525	11.5	11	88	1.9	123	2.7	3.74	83	.318	.353	-39	-30	107	116	5.0	8	3	-1.3
1883	Pro-N	3	7	.300	12	12	8	0	0	92	122	11.9	2	27	2.6	13	1.3	3.33	91	.327	.372	-2	-3	96	142	-2.5	4	0	-0.2
1886	Cin-a	0	2	.000	3	2	1	0	0	18	24	12.0	0	11	5.5	6	3.0	8.00	41	.331	.419	-9	-9	96	73	-0.9	0	0	-0.6
Total	6	75	100	.429	191	179	161	8	3	1583	1763	10.0	27	269	1.5	552	3.1	3.06	95	.291	.321	-66	-28	108	104	15.2	7	1	-0.7
RAY RICHMOND	Richmond, Raymond Sinclair b: 6/15/1896, Fillmore, Ill. d: 10/21/69, De Soto, Mo. BR/TR, 6', 175 lbs. Deb: 9/25/20																												
1920	StL-A	2	0	1.000	2	2	1	0	0	17	18	9.5	0	9	4.8	4	2.1	6.35	66	.273	.360	-5	-4	111	57	1.0	-0	0	-0.3
1921	StL-A	0	1	.000	6	2	0	0	0	14	21	13.5	1	13	8.4	6	3.9	11.57	37	.362	.474	-11	-11	101	75	-0.4	-1	0	-0.9
Total	2	2	1	.667	8	4	1	0	0	31	39	11.3	1	22	6.4	10	2.9	8.71	49	.315	.418	-16	-15	106	65	0.6	-1	0	-1.2
REGGIE RICHTER	Richter, Emil Henry b: 9/14/1888, Dusseldorf, Germany d: 8/2/34, Winfield, Ill. BR/TR, 6'2", 180 lbs. Deb: 5/30/11																												
1911	Chi-N	1	3	.250	22	5	0	0	2	55	62	10.1	1	20	3.3	34	5.6	3.11	103	.307	.378	**2**	**1**	94	148	-1.1	-1	-0	0.0
DICK RICKETTS	Ricketts, Richard James b: 12/4/33, Pottstown, Pa. d: 3/6/88, Rochester, N.Y. BL/TR, 6'7", 215 lbs. Deb: 6/14/59																												
1959	StL-N	1	6	.143	12	9	0	0	0	56	68	10.9	7	30	4.8	25	4.0	5.79	73	.301	.378	-11	-10	106	97	-2.3	-2	-2	-1.2
ELMER RIDDLE	Riddle, Elmer Ray b: 7/31/14, Columbus, Ga. d: 5/14/84, Columbus, Ga. BR/TR, 5'11.5", 170 lbs. Deb: 10/01/39																												
1939	Cin-N	0	0	—	1	0	0	0	0	2	1	4.5	0	0	0.0	0	0.0	0.00	—	.143	.143	1	1	100	0	0.0	0	0	0.1
1940	Cin-N	1	2	.333	15	1	1	0	2	34	30	7.9	0	17	4.5	9	2.4	1.85	203	.250	.331	8	7	98	192	-0.6	0	0	0.7
1941	Cin-N	19	4	**.826**	33	22	15	4	1	217	180	7.5	8	59	2.4	80	3.3	**2.24**	159	.224	.276	34	32	98	107	**7.3**	3	-0	3.7
1942	Cin-N	7	11	.389	29	19	7	1	0	158	157	8.9	7	79	4.5	78	4.4	3.70	91	.260	.343	-7	-6	102	107	-2.1	2	-1	-0.3
1943	Cin-N	**21**	11	.656	36	33	19	5	3	260	235	8.1	6	107	3.7	69	2.4	2.63	126	.245	.317	21	20	98	117	4.0	1	-1	2.2
1944	Cin-N	2	2	.500	4	4	2	0	0	27	25	8.3	0	12	4.0	6	2.0	4.00	85	.250	.327	-1	-2	95	80	-0.2	-0	1	0.0
1945	Cin-N	1	4	.200	12	3	0	0	0	30	39	11.7	4	27	8.1	5	1.5	8.10	46	.333	.452	-14	-15	97	96	-1.2	1	0	-1.2
1947	Cin-N	1	0	1.000	16	3	0	0	0	30	42	12.6	5	31	9.3	8	2.4	8.40	45	.333	.465	-14	-16	92	101	0.5	0	-1	-1.4
1948	Pit-N	12	10	.545	28	27	12	3	1	191	184	8.7	20	81	3.8	63	3.0	3.49	118	.250	.324	10	14	104	113	0.2	1	0	1.5
1949	Pit-N	1	8	.111	16	12	1	0	1	74	81	9.9	9	45	5.5	24	2.9	5.35	77	.281	.381	-11	-10	102	103	-3.4	-1	-2	-1.1
Total	10	65	52	.556	190	124	57	13	8	1023	974	8.6	59	458	4.0	342	3.0	3.40	106	.252	.329	26	25	100	112	4.5	7	-3	4.2
DENNY RIDDLEBERGER	Riddleberger, Dennis Michael b: 11/22/45, Clifton Forge, Va. BR/TL, 6'3", 195 lbs. Deb: 9/15/70																												
1970	Was-A	0	0	—	8	0	0	0	0	9	7	7.0	1	2	2.0	5	5.0	1.00	361	.219	.257	3	3	97	258	0.0	0	-0	0.2
1971	Was-A	3	1	.750	57	0	0	0	1	70	67	8.6	9	32	4.1	56	7.2	3.21	101	.260	.338	2	0	94	135	1.2	0	0	0.0
1972	Cle-A	1	3	.250	38	0	0	0	0	54	45	7.5	5	22	3.7	34	5.7	2.50	133	.237	.314	3	5	108	139	-0.8	-0	0	0.5
Total	3	4	4	.500	103	0	0	0	1	133	119	8.1	15	56	3.8	95	6.4	2.77	120	.248	.323	8	8	100	145	0.4	-0	-0	0.7
DORSEY RIDDLEMOSER	Riddlemoser, Dorsey Lee b: 3/25/1875, Frederick, Md. d: 5/11/54, Frederick, Md. BR/TR, Deb: 8/22/1899																												
1899	Was-N	0	0	—	1	0	0	0	0	2	7	31.5	0	2	9.0	0	0.0	18.00	21	.580	.640	-3	-3	98	95	0.0	-0	0	-0.2
JACK RIDGWAY	Ridgway, Jacob A. b: 7/23/1889, Philadelphia, Pa. d: 2/23/28, Philadelphia, Pa. BL/TR, 5'11", 174 lbs. Deb: 5/20/14																												
1914	Bal-F	0	1	.000	4	1	0	0	0	9	20	20.0	1	3	3.0	2	2.0	11.00	29	.475	.510	-8	-8	99	92	-0.4	-0	0	-0.6

YEAR	TM/L	W	L	PCT	G	GS	CG	SHO	SV	IP	H	H/G	HR	BB	BB/G	SO	SO/G	ERA	/A	OAVG	OOBP	PR	/A	PF	CPI	WAT	PB	PD	TPI
■ **STEVE RIDZIK**	Ridzik, Stephen George b: 4/29/29, Yonkers, N.Y. BR/TR, 5'11", 170 lbs. Deb: 9/04/50																												
1950	Phi-N	0	0	—	1	0	0	0	0	3	3	9.0	1	1	3.0	2	6.0	6.00	66	.300	.364	-1	-1	96	114	0.0	0	0	0.0
1952	Phi-N	4	2	.667	24	9	2	0	0	93	74	7.2	10	37	3.6	43	4.2	3.00	123	.218	.294	8	7	99	104	0.7	0	-2	0.5
1953	Phi-N	9	6	.600	42	12	1	0	0	124	119	8.6	15	48	3.5	53	3.8	3.77	111	.256	.327	7	6	98	112	1.1	2	-1	0.7
1954	Phi-N	4	5	.444	35	6	0	0	0	81	72	8.0	7	44	4.9	45	5.0	4.11	97	.233	.323	-0	-1	98	82	-0.3	1	0	0.0
1955	Phi-N	0	1	.000	3	1	0	0	0	11	7	5.7	1	8	6.5	6	4.9	2.45	168	.179	.353	2	2	102	145	-0.4	-1	0	0.1
	Cin-N	0	3	.000	13	2	0	0	0	30	35	10.5	4	14	4.2	6	1.8	4.50	94	.299	.373	-2	-1	104	123	-1.4	-0	-0	-0.1
	Yr	0	4	.000	16	3	0	0	0	41	42	9.2	5	22	4.8	12	2.6	3.95	106	.264	.351	0	1	104	123	-1.8	-1	-0	0.0
1956	NY-N	6	2	.750	41	5	1	1	0	92	80	7.8	7	65	6.4	53	5.2	3.82	98	.240	.362	-0	-1	99	110	2.3	1	-0	0.0
1957	NY-N	0	2	.000	15	0	0	0	0	27	19	6.3	3	19	6.3	13	4.3	4.67	86	.213	.357	-2	-2	103	90	-0.9	-0	0	-0.1
1958	Cle-A	0	2	.000	6	0	0	0	0	9	9	9.0	1	5	5.0	6	6.0	2.00	176	.257	.341	2	2	93	219	-0.9	-0	0	0.2
1963	Was-A	5	6	.455	20	10	0	0	1	90	82	8.2	16	35	3.5	47	4.7	4.80	76	.240	.314	-12	-11	101	88	1.0	0	0	-1.1
1964	Was-A	5	5	.500	49	3	0	0	2	112	96	7.7	10	31	2.5	60	4.8	2.89	129	.236	.293	9	11	103	109	1.0	1	-1	1.1
1965	Was-A	6	4	.600	63	0	0	0	8	110	108	8.8	18	43	3.5	72	5.9	4.01	88	.257	.329	-7	-6	102	113	1.5	0	0	-0.5
1966	Phi-N	0	0	—	2	0	0	0	0	2	5	22.5	0	1	4.5	0	0.0	9.00	40	.455	.462	-1	-1	100	115	0.0	0	0	0.0
Total	12	39	38	.506	314	48	4	1	11	784	709	8.1	93	351	4.0	406	4.7	3.79	101	.243	.325	2	4	100	106	3.7	4	-4	0.8
■ **ELMER RIEGER**	Rieger, Elmer Jay b: 2/25/1889, Perris, Cal. d: 10/21/59, Los Angeles, Cal. BB/TR, 6', 175 lbs. Deb: 4/20/10																												
1910	StL-N	0	2	.000	13	2	0	0	0	21	26	11.1	1	7	3.0	9	3.9	5.57	51	.325	.386	-6	-6	93	90	-0.9	0	0	-0.5
■ **DAVE RIGHETTI**	Righetti, David Allan b: 11/28/58, San Jose, Cal. BL/TL, 6'2", 170 lbs. Deb: 9/16/79																												
1979	NY-A	0	1	.000	3	3	0	0	0	17	10	5.3	2	10	5.3	13	6.9	3.71	108	.182	.299	1	1	95	83	-0.4	0	0	0.1
1981	NY-A	8	4	.667	15	15	2	0	0	105	75	6.4	1	38	3.3	89	7.6	2.06	176	.196	.268	19	18	99	77	1.7	0	-1	1.9
1982	NY-A	11	10	.524	33	27	4	0	1	183	155	7.6	11	108	5.3	163	**8.0**	3.79	104	.229	.335	6	3	97	94	0.8	0	-1	0.1
1983	NY-A	14	8	.636	31	31	7	2	0	217	194	8.0	12	67	2.8	169	7.0	3.44	116	.237	.292	15	13	98	84	2.1	0	-1	1.2
1984	NY-A	5	6	.455	64	0	0	0	31	96	79	7.4	5	37	3.5	90	8.4	2.34	159	.223	.290	18	15	93	112	-0.8	0	0	1.5
1985	NY-A	12	7	.632	74	0	0	0	29	107	96	8.1	5	45	3.8	92	7.7	2.78	141	.241	.312	16	13	94	118	0.8	0	-1	1.3
1986	NY-A	8	8	.500	74	0	0	0	**46**	107	88	7.4	4	35	2.9	83	7.0	2.44	176	.226	.287	21	22	103	106	-0.8	0	-1	2.1
1987	NY-A	8	6	.571	60	0	0	0	31	95	95	9.0	9	44	4.2	77	7.3	3.51	124	.262	.337	10	9	97	124	0.4	0	-0	0.8
1988	NY-A	5	4	.556	60	0	0	0	25	87	86	8.9	5	37	3.8	70	7.2	3.52	108	.257	.329	4	3	96	106	0.3	0	-1	0.2
Total	9	71	54	.568	414	76	13	2	163	1014	878	7.8	54	421	3.7	846	7.5	3.10	128	.233	.307	110	97	97	99	4.1	0	-6	9.2
■ **JOHNNY RIGNEY**	Rigney, John Dungan b: 10/28/14, Oak Park, Ill. d: 10/21/84, Lombard, Ill. BR/TR, 6'2", 190 lbs. Deb: 4/21/37																												
1937	Chi-A	2	5	.286	22	4	0	0	1	91	107	10.6	10	46	4.5	38	3.8	4.95	95	.290	.364	-3	-2	102	108	-1.7	-0	-1	-0.2
1938	Chi-A	9	9	.500	38	12	7	1	1	167	164	8.8	16	72	3.9	84	4.5	3.56	132	.256	.327	23	21	98	117	1.1	-3	0	1.8
1939	Chi-A	15	8	.652	35	29	11	2	0	219	208	8.5	10	84	3.5	119	4.9	3.70	133	.247	.311	22	30	106	91	2.9	-1	-2	2.6
1940	Chi-A	14	18	.438	39	33	19	2	3	281	240	7.7	22	90	2.9	141	4.5	3.11	145	.230	.288	40	43	103	97	-3.3	0	-1	4.3
1941	Chi-A	13	13	.500	30	29	18	3	0	237	224	8.5	21	92	3.5	119	4.5	3.84	101	.249	.316	8	1	94	97	0.0	2	0	0.2
1942	Chi-A	3	3	.500	7	7	6	0	0	59	40	6.1	2	16	2.4	34	5.2	3.20	114	.185	.244	3	3	100	43	0.3	-2	0	0.2
1946	Chi-A	5	5	.500	15	11	3	2	0	83	76	8.2	6	35	3.8	51	5.5	4.01	85	.240	.317	-5	-6	97	81	0.2	-1	-1	-0.6
1947	Chi-A	2	3	.400	11	7	2	0	0	51	42	7.4	3	15	2.6	19	3.4	1.94	189	.228	.281	10	10	99	136	-0.2	-2	1	1.0
Total	8	63	64	.496	197	132	66	10	5	1188	1101	8.3	90	450	3.4	605	4.6	3.58	121	.244	.310	98	100	100	98	-0.7	-6	-3	9.3
■ **JOSE RIJO**	Rijo, Jose Antonio (Abreu) b: 5/13/65, San Cristobal, D.R. BR/TR, 6'1", 160 lbs. Deb: 4/05/84																												
1984	NY-A	2	8	.200	24	5	0	0	2	62	74	10.7	5	33	4.8	47	6.8	4.79	78	.298	.374	-5	-7	93	110	-3.1	0	1	-0.6
1985	Oak-A	6	4	.600	12	9	0	0	0	64	57	8.0	6	28	3.9	65	9.1	3.52	110	.239	.316	5	2	93	104	1.2	0	-1	0.2
1986	Oak-A	9	11	.450	39	26	4	0	1	194	172	8.0	24	108	5.0	176	8.2	4.64	85	.237	.332	-10	-15	94	89	-0.4	0	-1	-1.5
1987	Oak-A	2	7	.222	21	14	1	0	0	82	106	11.6	10	41	4.5	67	7.4	5.93	69	.305	.378	-13	-17	91	97	-2.5	0	0	-1.4
1988	Cin-N	13	8	.619	49	19	0	0	0	162	120	6.7	7	63	3.5	160	8.9	2.39	152	.209	.285	19	22	105	104	2.0	-2	0	2.3
Total	5	32	38	.457	145	73	5	0	3	564	529	8.4	52	273	4.4	515	8.2	4.07	95	.248	.330	-5	-14	96	98	-2.8	-2	-1	-1.0
■ **GEORGE RILEY**	Riley, George Michael b: 10/6/56, Philadelphia, Pa. BL/TL, 6'2", 210 lbs. Deb: 9/15/79																												
1979	Chi-N	0	1	.000	4	1	0	0	0	13	16	11.1	1	6	4.2	5	3.5	5.54	76	.320	.407	-3	-2	112	108	-0.4	-0	0	-0.1
1980	Chi-N	0	4	.000	22	0	0	0	0	36	41	10.3	2	20	5.0	18	4.5	5.75	67	.293	.380	-9	-7	108	88	-1.9	-0	1	-0.6
1984	SF-N	1	0	1.000	5	4	0	0	0	29	39	12.1	1	7	2.2	12	3.7	4.03	87	.315	.358	-1	-2	98	117	0.5	-0	-0	-0.2
1986	Mon-N	0	0	—	10	0	0	0	0	9	7	7.0	0	8	8.0	5	5.0	4.00	92	.212	.372	-0	-0	98	92	0.0	0	-0	0.0
Total	4	1	5	.167	41	5	0	0	0	87	103	10.7	4	41	4.2	40	4.1	4.97	76	.297	.376	-13	-11	104	101	-1.8	-1	1	-0.9
■ **ANDY RINCON**	Rincon, Andrew John b: 3/5/59, Monterey Park, Cal. BR/TR, 6'3", 195 lbs. Deb: 9/15/80																												
1980	StL-N	3	1	.750	4	4	1	0	0	31	23	6.7	1	7	2.0	22	6.4	2.61	141	.215	.259	3	4	102	76	1.1	0	0	0.5
1981	StL-N	3	1	.750	5	5	1	1	0	36	27	6.8	0	5	1.3	13	3.3	1.75	201	.214	.256	7	7	101	92	0.8	1	-0	0.9
1982	StL-N	2	3	.400	11	6	1	0	0	40	35	7.9	1	25	5.6	11	2.5	4.72	78	.241	.349	-5	-5	102	76	-0.7	-0	-0	-0.4
Total	3	8	5	.615	20	15	3	1	0	107	85	7.1	2	37	3.1	46	3.9	3.11	117	.225	.295	5	6	102	81	1.2	1	-0	1.0
■ **JEFF RINEER**	Rineer, Jeffrey Alan b: 7/3/55, Lancaster, Pa. BL/TL, 6'4", 205 lbs. Deb: 9/30/79																												
1979	Bal-A	0	0	—	1	0	0	0	0	1	0	0.0	0	0	0.0	0	0.0	0.00	—	.000	.000	0	0	96	0	0.0	0	0	0.0
■ **JIMMY RING**	Ring, James Joseph b: 2/15/1895, Brooklyn, N.Y. d: 7/6/65, New York, N.Y. BR/TR, 6'1", 170 lbs. Deb: 4/13/17																												
1917	Cin-N	3	7	.300	24	7	3	0	2	88	90	9.2	2	35	3.6	33	3.4	4.40	57	.272	.336	-16	-18	93	82	-2.0	-2	0	-2.1
1918	Cin-N	9	5	.643	21	18	13	4	0	142	130	8.2	5	48	3.0	26	1.6	2.85	93	.247	.307	-1	-3	96	102	1.8	-3	-3	-0.9
1919	Cin-N	10	9	.526	32	18	12	2	3	183	150	7.4	1	51	2.5	61	3.0	2.26	130	.232	.286	13	14	101	99	-2.4	-5	3	1.4
1920	Cin-N	17	16	.515	42	33	18	1	1	267	268	9.0	4	92	3.1	73	2.5	3.54	78	.264	.319	-12	-23	88	84	-0.7	0	1	-2.3
1921	Phi-N	10	19	.345	34	30	21	0	1	246	258	9.4	8	88	3.2	88	3.2	4.24	95	.274	.328	-13	-5	107	84	0.4	-4	3	-0.5
1922	Phi-N	12	18	.400	40	33	17	0	1	249	292	10.6	19	103	3.7	116	4.2	4.59	104	.297	.356	-14	5	117	102	0.8	-5	4	0.5
1923	Phi-N	18	16	.529	39	36	23	0	0	304	336	9.9	13	115	3.4	112	3.3	3.88	122	.283	.339	4	28	118	103	6.1	-11	3	2.2
1924	Phi-N	10	12	.455	32	31	16	1	0	215	236	9.9	9	108	4.5	72	3.0	3.98	108	.286	.361	-3	7	111	113	1.8	-0	2	1.0
1925	Phi-N	14	16	.467	38	37	21	1	0	270	325	10.8	14	119	4.0	93	3.1	4.37	115	.297	.359	-3	20	118	106	0.7	-9	2	1.4
1926	NY-N	11	10	.524	39	23	5	0	2	183	207	10.2	12	74	3.6	76	3.7	4.57	82	.290	.347	-15	-17	98	98	0.8	-3	-1	-2.0
1927	StL-N	0	4	.000	13	3	1	0	0	33	39	10.6	3	17	4.6	13	3.5	6.55	63	.300	.365	-10	-9	106	82	-1.9	1	1	-0.5
1928	Phi-N	4	17	.190	35	25	4	0	1	173	214	11.1	14	103	5.4	72	3.7	6.40	68	.316	.395	-46	-39	109	91	-3.7	-2	1	-3.6
Total	12	118	149	.442	389	294	154	9	11	2353	2545	9.7	104	953	3.6	835	3.2	4.13	95	.281	.342	-115	-52	107	97	1.7	-43	15	-5.4
■ **ALLEN RIPLEY**	Ripley, Allen Stevens b: 10/18/52, Norwood, Mass. BR/TR, 6'3", 190 lbs. Deb: 4/10/78																												
1978	Bos-A	2	5	.286	15	11	1	0	0	73	92	11.3	10	22	2.7	26	3.2	5.55	72	.311	.359	-14	-13	106	97	-1.8	0	-1	-1.2
1979	Bos-A	3	1	.750	16	3	0	0	1	65	77	10.7	9	25	3.5	34	4.7	5.12	88	.295	.360	-6	-5	106	103	0.9	0	-1	-0.5
1980	SF-N	9	10	.474	23	20	2	0	0	113	119	9.5	10	36	2.9	65	5.2	4.14	84	.274	.327	-7	-8	96	99	0.2	-0	0	-0.8
1981	SF-N	4	4	.500	19	14	1	0	0	91	103	10.2	5	27	2.7	47	4.6	4.05	90	.289	.336	-6	-4	105	104	0.0	-1	1	-0.4
1982	Chi-N	5	7	.417	28	19	0	0	0	123	130	9.5	12	38	2.8	57	4.2	4.17	90	.285	.332	-8	-6	104	106	-0.4	-2	1	-0.6
Total	5	23	27	.460	101	67	4	0	1	465	521	10.1	46	148	2.9	229	4.4	4.49	85	.289	.340	-41	-35	103	102	-1.1	-3	-0	-3.5
■ **WALT RIPLEY**	Ripley, Walter Franklin b: 11/26/16, Worcester, Mass. BR/TR, 6', 168 lbs. Deb: 8/17/35																												
1935	Bos-A	0	0	—	2	0	0	0	0	4	7	15.8	0	3	6.8	0	0.0	9.00	54	.412	.476	-2	-2	108	100	0.0	0	-0	-0.1
■ **RAY RIPPELMEYER**	Rippelmeyer, Raymond Roy b: 7/9/33, Valmeyer, Ill. BR/TR, 6'3", 200 lbs. Deb: 4/14/62 C																												
1962	Was-A	1	2	.333	18	1	0	0	0	39	47	10.8	7	17	3.9	17	3.9	5.54	73	.294	.358	-7	-6	102	101	-0.1	2	2	-0.1
■ **CHARLIE RIPPLE**	Ripple, Charles Dawson b: 12/1/21, Bolton, N.C. d: 5/6/79, Wilmington, N.C. BL/TL, 6'2", 210 lbs. Deb: 9/25/44																												
1944	Phi-N	0	0	—	1	1	0	0	0	2	6	27.0	0	4	18.0	2	9.0	18.00	21	.500	.625	-3	-3	103	96	0.0	0	0	-0.1
1945	Phi-N	0	1	.000	4	0	0	0	0	8	7	7.9	0	10	11.3	5	5.6	6.75	58	.241	.425	-3	-3	102	78	-0.4	-0	0	-0.2
1946	Phi-N	1	0	1.000	6	0	0	0	0	3	5	15.0	0	6	18.0	3	9.0	12.00	28	.385	.579	-3	-3	98	94	0.5	0	0	-0.2

YEAR	TM/L	W	L	PCT	G	GS	CG	SHO	SV	IP	H	H/G	HR	BB	BB/G	SO	SO/G	ERA	/A	OAVG	OOBP	PR	/A	PF	CPI	WAT	PB	PD	TPI
Total	3	1	1	.500	11	1	0	0	0	13	18	12.5	0	20	13.8	10	6.9	9.69	38	.333	.507	-9	-9	101	84	0.1	0	0	-0.5
■ **JAY RITCHIE**	Ritchie, Jay Seay b: 11/20/36, Salisbury, N.C. BR/TR, 6'4", 175 lbs. Deb: 8/04/64																												
1964	Bos-A	1	1	.500	21	0	0	0	0	46	43	8.4	4	14	2.7	35	6.8	2.74	137	.249	.292	5	5	103	121	0.1	-1	0	0.5
1965	Bos-A	1	2	.333	44	0	0	0	2	71	83	10.5	3	26	3.3	55	7.0	3.17	119	.302	.354	2	5	109	146	-0.1	0	0	0.6
1966	Atl-N	0	1	.000	22	0	0	0	4	35	32	8.2	3	12	3.1	33	8.5	4.11	85	.241	.293	-2	-2	97	77	-0.4	1	0	0.0
1967	Atl-N	4	6	.400	52	0	0	0	2	82	75	8.2	6	29	3.2	57	6.3	3.18	111	.245	.308	2	3	105	108	-0.7	1	1	0.6
1968	Cin-N	2	3	.400	28	2	0	0	0	57	68	10.7	7	13	2.1	32	5.1	4.58	72	.293	.327	-10	-8	111	99	-0.5	-1	-1	-1.0
Total	5	8	13	.381	167	2	0	0	8	291	301	9.3	23	94	2.9	212	6.6	3.49	103	.269	.319	-3	3	106	114	-1.6	1	0	0.7
■ **WALLY RITCHIE**	Ritchie, Wallace Reid b: 7/12/65, Glendale, Cal. BL/TL, 6'2", 180 lbs. Deb: 5/01/87																												
1987	Phi-N	3	2	.600	49	0	0	0	3	62	60	8.7	8	29	4.2	45	6.5	3.77	113	.254	.330	2	3	105	115	0.5	0	-0	0.3
1988	Phi-N	0	0	—	19	0	0	0	0	26	19	6.6	1	17	5.9	8	2.8	3.12	114	.207	.322	1	1	103	102	0.0	0	-0	0.1
Total	2	3	2	.600	68	0	0	0	3	88	79	8.1	9	46	4.7	53	5.4	3.58	113	.241	.327	3	5	104	111	0.5	0	-0	0.4
■ **REGGIE RITTER**	Ritter, Reggie Blake b: 1/23/60, Malvern, Ark. BL/TR, 6'2", 195 lbs. Deb: 5/17/86																												
1986	Cle-A	0	0	—	5	0	0	0	0	10	14	12.6	1	4	3.6	6	5.4	6.30	65	.341	.396	-2	-2	98	105	0.0	0	0	-0.1
1987	Cle-A	1	1	.500	14	0	0	0	0	27	33	11.0	5	16	5.3	11	3.7	6.00	78	.300	.377	-5	-4	105	105	0.2	0	0	-0.3
Total	2	1	1	.500	19	0	0	0	0	37	47	11.4	6	20	4.9	17	4.1	6.08	74	.311	.382	-7	-6	103	105	0.2	0	1	-0.4
■ **HANK RITTER**	Ritter, William Herbert b: 10/12/1893, Mc Coysville, Pa. d: 9/3/64, Akron, Ohio BR/TR, 6', 180 lbs. Deb: 8/03/12																												
1912	Phi-N	0	0	—	3	0	0	0	0	6	5	7.5	0	5	7.5	1	1.5	4.50	76	.185	.313	-1	-1	101	29	0.0	-0	-0	0.0
1914	NY-N	1	0	1.000	1	0	0	0	0	8	4	4.5	0	4	4.5	4	4.5	1.13	232	.160	.267	1	1	94	105	0.5	-0	-0	0.1
1915	NY-N	2	1	.667	22	2	0	0	2	58	66	10.2	4	15	2.3	35	5.4	4.66	55	.291	.333	-12	-14	92	92	0.6	-1	-0	-1.5
1916	NY-N	1	0	1.000	3	0	0	0	0	5	3	5.4	0	0	0.0	3	5.4	0.00	—	.200	.235	1	1	94	0	0.5	0	0	0.2
Total	4	4	1	.800	29	2	0	0	2	77	78	9.1	4	24	2.8	43	5.0	3.97	66	.265	.320	-10	-12	93	82	1.6	-1	-1	-1.2
■ **JIM RITTWAGE**	Rittwage, James Michael b: 10/23/44, Cleveland, Ohio BR/TR, 6'3", 190 lbs. Deb: 9/07/70																												
1970	Cle-A	1	1	.500	8	3	1	0	0	26	18	6.2	0	21	7.3	16	5.5	4.15	103	.194	.336	-1	0	115	65	0.1	1	0	0.2
■ **TINK RIVIERE**	Riviere, Arthur Bernard b: 8/2/1899, Liberty, Tex. d: 9/27/65, Liberty, Tex. BR/TR, 5'10", 167 lbs. Deb: 4/15/21																												
1921	StL-N	1	0	1.000	18	2	0	0	0	38	45	10.7	2	20	4.7	15	3.6	6.16	57	.280	.362	-10	-11	93	69	0.5	2	-2	-1.0
1925	Chi-A	0	0	—	3	0	0	0	0	5	6	10.8	0	7	12.6	1	1.8	12.60	33	.429	.583	-5	-5	95	85	0.0	-0	1	-0.3
Total	2	1	0	1.000	21	2	0	0	0	43	51	10.7	2	27	5.7	16	3.3	6.91	52	.291	.388	-15	-16	93	71	0.5	2	-1	-1.3
■ **EPPA RIXEY**	Rixey, Eppa "Jeptha" b: 5/3/1891, Culpeper, Va. d: 2/28/63, Cincinnati, Ohio BR/TL, 6'5", 210 lbs. Deb: 6/21/1912 H																												
1912	Phi-N	10	10	.500	23	20	10	3	0	162	147	8.2	2	54	3.0	59	3.3	2.50	137	.247	.312	16	17	101	102	0.4	-1	-1	1.4
1913	Phi-N	9	5	.643	35	19	9	2	2	156	148	8.5	4	56	3.2	75	4.3	3.12	114	.258	.319	2	8	111	104	1.1	-1	1	0.9
1914	Phi-N	2	11	.154	24	15	2	0	0	103	124	10.8	0	45	3.9	41	3.6	4.37	64	.313	.373	-18	-18	101	104	-4.4	-1	0	-1.8
1915	Phi-N	11	12	.478	29	22	10	2	1	177	163	8.3	2	64	3.3	88	4.5	2.39	120	.250	.312	7	10	104	120	-2.4	-0	0	1.1
1916	Phi-N	22	10	.688	38	33	20	3	0	287	239	7.5	2	74	2.3	134	4.2	1.85	133	.229	.277	25	19	94	109	4.4	-1	3	2.4
1917	Phi-N	16	21	.432	39	36	23	4	1	281	249	8.0	1	67	2.1	121	3.9	2.27	126	.241	.282	14	19	106	100	-5.4	-2	4	2.4
1919	Phi-N	6	12	.333	23	18	11	1	0	154	160	9.4	4	50	2.9	63	3.7	3.97	80	.278	.327	-18	-14	109	92	-0.2	-2	2	-1.3
1920	Phi-N	11	22	.333	41	33	25	1	2	284	288	9.1	5	69	2.2	109	3.5	3.49	101	.274	.307	-11	1	112	85	-3.5	1	3	0.6
1921	Cin-N	19	18	.514	40	36	21	2	1	301	324	9.7	1	66	2.0	76	2.3	2.78	138	.282	.313	**34**	35	101	113	2.4	-6	3	3.4
1922	Cin-N	**25**	13	.658	40	38	26	2	0	**313**	337	9.7	13	45	1.3	80	2.3	3.54	109	.275	.296	20	11	94	85	5.3	-1	-0	0.9
1923	Cin-N	20	15	.571	42	37	23	3	1	309	334	9.7	3	65	1.9	97	2.8	2.80	138	.280	.311	41	36	96	116	-0.6	-4	2	3.2
1924	Cin-N	15	14	.517	35	29	15	4	1	238	219	8.3	3	47	1.8	57	2.2	2.76	139	.246	.277	29	28	99	85	-0.7	1	-0	3.0
1925	Cin-N	21	11	.656	39	36	22	2	1	287	302	9.5	8	47	1.5	69	2.2	2.89	143	.273	.300	44	39	97	108	5.3	-1	-2	3.5
1926	Cin-N	14	8	.636	37	29	14	3	0	233	231	8.9	12	58	2.2	61	2.4	3.40	105	.265	.303	11	4	93	98	2.1	1	-2	0.2
1927	Cin-N	12	10	.545	34	29	11	1	1	220	240	9.8	3	43	1.8	42	1.7	3.48	113	.287	.313	11	11	100	101	1.4	3	-1	1.3
1928	Cin-N	19	18	.514	43	37	17	3	2	291	317	9.8	4	67	2.1	58	1.8	3.43	112	.288	.317	18	14	97	103	0.0	-1	-0	1.2
1929	Cin-N	10	13	.435	35	24	11	0	1	201	235	10.5	6	60	2.7	37	1.7	4.16	114	.296	.341	12	13	101	103	0.1	-0	-1	1.1
1930	Cin-N	9	13	.409	32	21	5	0	0	164	207	11.4	11	47	2.6	37	2.0	5.10	91	.317	.355	-2	-9	93	103	0.5	-1	-0	-0.8
1931	Cin-N	4	7	.364	22	17	4	0	0	127	143	10.1	4	30	2.1	22	1.6	3.90	97	.291	.319	-0	-2	98	100	-0.1	-1	3	0.1
1932	Cin-N	5	5	.500	25	11	6	2	0	112	108	8.7	3	16	1.3	14	1.1	2.65	145	.254	.279	15	15	99	103	1.0	1	1	1.7
1933	Cin-N	6	3	.667	16	12	5	1	0	94	118	11.3	1	12	1.1	10	1.0	3.16	107	.298	.312	2	2	102	111	2.1	2	1	0.6
Total	21	266	251	.515	692	552	290	39	14	4494	4633	9.3	92	1082	2.2	1350	2.7	3.15	116	.272	.309	250	248	100	102	8.8	-14	16	25.1
■ **JOHN ROACH**	Roach, John F. b: Farrensville, Pa. d: 3/1/15, Sandusky, Ohio TL, 5'9", 175 lbs. Deb: 5/14/1887																												
1887	NY-N	0	1	.000	1	1	1	0	0	8	18	20.3	0	4	4.5	3	3.4	11.25	38	.461	.511	-6	-6	106	90	-0.4	-0	0	-0.3
■ **SKELL ROACH**	Roach, Skell (born Rudolph C. Weichbrodt) b: 10/20/1871, Germany d: 3/9/58, Oak Park, Ill. BR/TR, Deb: 8/09/1899																												
1899	Chi-N	1	0	1.000	1	1	1	0	0	9	13	13.0	0	1	1.0	0	0.0	3.00	123	.363	.381	1	1	96	153	0.5	-1	0	0.0
■ **BRUCE ROBBINS**	Robbins, Bruce Duane b: 9/10/59, Portland, Ind. BL/TL, 6'1", 190 lbs. Deb: 7/28/79																												
1979	Det-A	3	3	.500	10	8	0	0	0	46	45	8.8	3	21	4.1	22	4.3	3.91	104	.265	.340	2	1	96	104	-0.1	0	-0	0.0
1980	Det-A	4	2	.667	15	6	0	0	0	52	60	10.4	12	28	4.8	23	4.0	6.58	64	.287	.365	-15	-14	105	91	0.9	0	0	-1.2
Total	2	7	5	.583	25	14	0	0	0	98	105	9.6	15	49	4.5	45	4.1	5.33	78	.277	.354	-13	-13	101	97	0.8	0	-0	-1.2
■ **BERT ROBERGE**	Roberge, Bertrand Roland b: 10/3/54, Lewiston, Maine BR/TR, 6'4", 190 lbs. Deb: 5/28/79																												
1979	Hou-N	3	0	1.000	26	0	0	0	4	32	20	5.6	0	17	4.8	13	3.7	1.69	200	.196	.308	7	6	90	137	1.5	-0	-0	0.6
1980	Hou-N	2	0	1.000	14	0	0	0	0	24	24	9.0	2	10	3.8	9	3.4	6.00	58	.261	.340	-6	-7	97	69	1.0	-0	0	-0.6
1982	Hou-N	1	2	.333	22	0	0	0	3	26	29	10.0	0	6	2.1	18	6.2	4.15	87	.284	.318	-2	-2	100	81	-0.4	-0	0	-0.1
1984	Chi-A	3	3	.500	21	0	0	0	0	41	36	7.9	2	15	3.3	25	5.5	3.73	119	.240	.314	1	3	111	87	0.2	0	1	0.4
1985	Mon-N	3	3	.500	42	0	0	0	2	68	58	7.7	5	22	2.9	34	4.5	3.44	98	.232	.293	1	-1	94	86	0.0	-0	0	0.0
1986	Mon-N	0	4	.000	21	0	0	0	1	29	33	10.2	2	10	3.1	20	6.2	6.21	59	.295	.344	-8	-8	98	75	-1.9	-0	0	-0.8
Total	6	12	12	.500	146	0	0	0	10	220	200	8.2	11	80	3.3	119	4.9	3.97	92	.248	.314	-6	-8	98	90	0.4	-1	2	-0.5
■ **DALE ROBERTS**	Roberts, Dale "Mountain Man" b: 4/12/42, Owenton, Ky. BR/TL, 6'4", 180 lbs. Deb: 9/09/67																												
1967	NY-A	0	0	—	2	0	0	0	0	2	3	13.5	0	2	9.0	0	0.0	9.00	34	.429	.583	-1	-1	96	133	0.0	0	0	0.0
■ **DAVE ROBERTS**	Roberts, David Arthur b: 9/11/44, Gallipolis, Ohio BL/TL, 6'3", 195 lbs. Deb: 7/06/69																												
1969	SD-N	0	3	.000	22	5	0	0	1	49	65	11.9	5	19	3.5	19	3.5	4.78	75	.322	.382	-6	-6	100	122	-1.4	1	0	-0.5
1970	SD-N	8	14	.364	43	21	3	2	1	182	182	9.0	16	43	2.1	102	5.0	3.81	103	.261	.300	5	2	97	94	-0.7	1	0	0.3
1971	SD-N	14	17	.452	37	34	14	2	0	270	238	7.9	9	61	2.0	135	4.5	2.10	162	.240	.280	41	39	98	**120**	2.2	2	0	4.7
1972	Hou-N	12	7	.632	35	28	7	3	2	192	227	10.6	18	57	2.7	111	5.2	4.50	81	.296	.341	-22	-18	105	102	1.9	5	-0	-1.4
1973	Hou-N	17	11	.607	39	36	12	6	0	249	264	9.5	15	62	2.2	119	4.3	2.86	122	.271	.311	23	17	95	122	3.3	-2	-1	1.4
1974	Hou-N	10	12	.455	34	30	8	2	1	204	216	9.5	6	65	2.9	72	3.2	3.40	104	.276	.326	5	3	98	106	-1.0	4	2	1.0
1975	Hou-N	8	14	.364	32	27	7	0	1	198	182	8.3	16	73	3.3	101	4.6	4.27	81	.244	.306	-14	-18	95	77	-1.0	-0	1	-1.7
1976	Det-A	16	17	.485	36	36	18	4	0	252	254	9.1	16	63	2.3	79	2.8	4.00	92	.264	.306	-13	-9	105	85	1.0	0	2	-0.7
1977	Det-A	4	10	.286	22	22	5	0	0	129	143	10.0	20	41	2.9	46	3.2	5.16	83	.274	.326	-16	-13	105	87	-2.7	0	-0	-1.2
	Chi-N	1	1	.500	17	6	1	0	1	53	55	9.3	1	12	2.0	23	3.9	3.23	139	.275	.306	4	7	115	103	0.0	-2	2	0.8
1978	Chi-N	6	8	.429	35	20	2	1	1	142	159	10.1	17	56	3.5	54	3.4	5.26	76	.288	.348	-26	-20	111	93	-0.8	7	1	-1.1
1979	SF-N	0	2	.000	26	1	0	0	3	42	42	9.0	3	18	3.9	23	4.9	2.57	136	.262	.335	5	4	93	152	-0.9	-1	0	0.4
	Pit-N	5	2	.714	21	3	0	0	1	39	47	10.8	1	12	2.8	15	3.5	3.23	120	.318	.353	2	3	104	147	1.0	-1	1	0.3
	Yr	5	4	.556	47	4	0	0	4	81	89	9.9	4	30	3.3	38	4.2	2.89	128	.287	.341	8	7	99	147	0.1	-1	1	0.7
1980	Pit-N	0	1	.000	2	0	0	0	0	2	2	9.0	0	1	4.5	1	4.5	4.50	83	.250	.333	-0	-0	103	69	-0.4	0	0	0.0
	Sea-A	2	3	.400	37	4	0	0	3	80	86	9.7	7	27	3.0	47	5.3	4.39	97	.270	.321	-3	-1	105	89	0.1	0	-1	-0.2
1981	NY-N	0	3	.000	7	4	0	0	0	15	26	15.6	5	5	3.0	10	6.0	9.60	37	.366	.408	-10	-10	103	92	-1.4	0	0	-0.9
Total	13	103	125	.452	445	277	77	20	15	2098	2188	9.4	155	615	2.6	957	4.1	3.78	98	.270	.317	-26	-20	101	102	-0.8	15	8	1.2

YEAR	TM/L	W	L	PCT	G	GS	CG	SHO	SV	IP	H	H/G	HR	BB	BB/G	SO	SO/G	ERA	/A	OAVG	OOBP	PR	/A	PF	CPI	WAT	PB	PD	TPI
■ JIM ROBERTS	Roberts, James Newson "Big Jim" b: 10/13/1895, Artesia, Miss. d: 6/24/84, Columbus, Miss. BR/TR, 6'3", 205 lbs. Deb: 7/27/24																												
1924	Bro-N	0	3	.000	11	5	0	0	0	25	41	14.8	1	8	2.9	10	3.6	7.56	50	.360	.408	-10	-10	95	85	-1.4	-0	0	-0.9
1925	Bro-N	0	0	—	1	0	0	0	0	1	1	9.0	0	0	0.0	0	0.0	0.00	—	.500	.250	0	0	95	0	0.0	0	0	0.0
Total	2	0	3	.000	12	5	0	0	0	26	42	14.5	1	8	2.8	10	3.5	7.27	52	.362	.403	-10	-10	98	82	-1.4	-0	0	-0.9
■ LEON ROBERTS	Roberts, Leon Kauffman b: 1/22/51, Vicksburg, Mich. BR/TR, 6'3", 200 lbs. Deb: 9/03/74																												
1984	KC-A	0	0	—	1	0	0	0	0	1	4	36.0	1	1	9.0	1	9.0	27.00	15	.571	.625	-3	-3	99	100	0.0	0	0	-0.1
■ RAY ROBERTS	Roberts, Raymond b: 8/25/1895, Cruger, Miss. d: 1/30/62, Cruger, Miss. BL/TR, 5'11", 180 lbs. Deb: 9/12/19																												
1919	Phi-A	0	2	.000	3	2	0	0	0	14	21	13.5	0	3	1.9	2	1.3	7.71	47	.368	.400	-7	-6	112	71	-0.9	-0	-0	-0.5
■ ROBIN ROBERTS	Roberts, Robin Evan b: 9/30/26, Springfield, Ill. BB/TR, 6', 190 lbs. Deb: 6/18/48 H																												
1948	Phi-N	7	9	.438	20	20	9	0	0	147	148	9.1	10	61	3.7	84	5.1	3.18	120	.278	.353	13	10	97	142	0.1	5	-2	1.3
1949	Phi-N	15	15	.500	43	31	11	3	4	227	229	9.1	15	75	3.0	95	3.8	3.69	110	.273	.331	9	10	101	111	-0.8	-3	-3	0.3
1950	Phi-N	20	11	.645	40	39	21	**5**	1	304	282	8.3	29	77	2.3	146	4.3	3.02	131	.248	.294	**38**	32	96	110	2.5	-3	0	2.8
1951	Phi-N	21	15	.583	44	39	22	6	2	**315**	284	8.1	20	64	1.8	127	3.6	3.03	127	.237	.276	33	28	97	85	4.6	5	-3	3.2
1952	Phi-N	**28**	7	.800	39	37	**30**	3	2	**330**	292	8.0	22	45	**1.2**	148	4.0	2.59	142	.234	.261	**42**	**40**	99	93	**10.6**	2	-3	4.3
1953	Phi-N	**23**	16	.590	44	41	**33**	5	2	**347**	324	8.4	30	61	**1.6**	**198**	5.1	2.75	153	.242	.274	59	**56**	98	103	2.8	2	-1	5.8
1954	Phi-N	**23**	15	.605	45	38	**29**	4	4	**337**	289	7.7	35	56	**1.5**	**185**	4.9	2.96	134	.231	**.263**	41	38	98	86	**5.4**	-3	-4	3.2
1955	Phi-N	**23**	14	.622	41	38	**26**	1	3	**305**	292	8.6	41	53	1.6	160	4.7	3.28	126	.246	**.276**	26	**28**	102	96	5.5	13	-5	3.9
1956	Phi-N	19	18	.514	43	37	**22**	1	3	297	328	9.9	46	40	**1.2**	157	4.8	4.45	81	.282	.301	-23	-28	95	93	2.3	4	-0	-2.4
1957	Phi-N	10	22	.313	39	32	14	2	2	250	246	8.9	40	43	1.5	128	4.6	4.07	94	.252	.281	-5	-6	99	86	-6.8	0	0	-0.5
1958	Phi-N	17	14	.548	35	34	21	1	0	270	270	9.0	30	51	1.7	130	4.3	3.23	122	.259	.289	22	22	100	103	3.4	4	-2	2.4
1959	Phi-N	15	17	.469	35	35	19	2	0	257	267	9.4	34	35	1.2	137	4.8	4.27	94	.263	.286	-9	-7	102	83	1.8	3	-0	-0.3
1960	Phi-N	12	16	.429	35	33	13	2	1	237	256	9.7	31	34	1.3	122	4.6	4.03	103	.275	.297	-7	3	110	98	1.2	-1	-3	0.0
1961	Phi-N	1	10	.091	26	18	2	0	0	117	154	11.8	19	23	1.8	54	4.2	5.85	67	.326	.350	-24	-25	98	99	-3.8	-2	-1	-2.6
1962	Bal-A	10	9	.526	27	25	6	0	0	191	176	8.3	17	41	1.9	102	4.8	2.78	136	.244	.286	25	21	95	111	1.0	2	-1	2.3
1963	Bal-A	14	13	.519	35	35	9	2	0	251	230	8.2	35	40	1.4	124	4.4	3.33	102	.240	.269	8	1	93	94	-0.3	2	-2	0.2
1964	Bal-A	13	7	.650	31	31	8	4	0	204	203	9.0	18	52	2.3	109	4.8	2.91	129	.261	.305	16	19	103	121	1.4	-1	-2	1.8
1965	Bal-A	5	7	.417	20	15	5	1	0	115	110	8.6	17	20	1.6	63	4.9	3.37	102	.252	.279	1	1	99	105	-1.7	1	-1	0.1
	Hou-N	5	2	.714	10	10	3	2	0	76	61	7.2	1	10	1.2	34	4.0	1.89	170	.216	.242	14	11	91	79	1.9	3	-2	1.4
1966	Hou-N	3	5	.375	13	12	1	1	1	64	79	11.1	7	10	1.4	26	3.7	3.80	94	.307	.328	-1	-2	99	123	-0.6	-1	-1	-0.2
	Chi-N	2	3	.400	11	9	1	0	0	48	62	11.6	8	11	2.1	28	5.3	6.19	60	.313	.348	-14	-13	103	88	0.1	1	0	-1.1
	Yr	5	8	.385	24	21	2	1	1	112	141	11.3	15	21	1.7	54	4.3	4.82	75	.307	.335	-15	-15	100	88	-0.5	-1	-0	-1.3
Total	19	286	245	.539	676	609	305	45	25	4689	4582	8.8	505	902	1.7	2357	4.5	3.40	113	.255	.289	264	239	99	99	30.6	33	-35	25.9
■ CHARLIE ROBERTSON	Robertson, Charles Culbertson b: 1/31/1896, Dexter, Tex. d: 8/23/84, Fort Worth, Tex. BL/TR, 6', 175 lbs. Deb: 5/13/19																												
1919	Chi-A	0	1	.000	1	1	0	0	0	2	5	22.5	0	0	0.0	1	4.5	9.00	36	.556	.556	-1	-1	102	124	-0.4	0	0	0.0
1922	Chi-A	14	15	.483	37	34	21	3	0	272	294	9.7	9	89	2.9	83	2.7	3.64	112	.286	.332	12	13	101	107	-0.5	-2	-4	0.7
1923	Chi-A	13	18	.419	38	34	18	1	0	255	262	9.2	8	104	3.7	91	3.2	3.81	104	.272	.335	5	4	99	98	-1.1	0	-2	0.2
1924	Chi-A	4	10	.286	17	14	5	0	0	97	108	10.0	2	54	5.0	29	2.7	5.01	83	.293	.365	-8	-9	98	92	-2.4	-1	-2	-1.0
1925	Chi-A	8	12	.400	24	23	6	2	0	137	181	11.9	8	47	3.1	27	1.8	5.26	79	.327	.365	-13	-16	95	101	-2.4	0	-2	-1.5
1926	StL-A	1	2	.333	8	7	1	0	0	28	38	12.2	4	21	6.8	13	4.2	8.36	50	.333	.430	-13	-13	103	89	-0.2	1	0	-1.0
1927	Bos-N	7	17	.292	28	22	6	0	0	154	188	11.0	2	46	2.7	49	2.9	4.73	79	.308	.343	-14	-17	95	93	-3.3	1	-1	-1.7
1928	Bos-N	2	5	.286	13	7	3	0	1	59	73	11.1	5	16	2.4	17	2.6	5.34	76	.308	.342	-9	-8	101	87	-0.4	-1	-1	-0.9
Total	8	49	80	.380	166	142	60	6	1	1004	1149	10.3	38	377	3.4	310	2.8	4.45	90	.296	.347	-42	-48	99	98	-10.7	-2	-12	-5.2
■ JERRY ROBERTSON	Robertson, Jerry Lee b: 10/13/43, Winchester, Kan. BB/TR, 6'2", 205 lbs. Deb: 4/08/69																												
1969	Mon-N	5	16	.238	38	27	3	0	1	180	186	9.3	17	81	4.1	133	6.7	3.95	94	.272	.344	-7	-5	103	113	-2.9	-3	-3	-1.0
1970	Det-A	0	0	—	11	0	0	0	0	15	19	11.4	1	5	3.0	11	6.6	3.60	107	.306	.348	0	0	104	131	0.0	0	-0	0.0
Total	2	5	16	.238	49	27	3	0	1	195	205	9.5	18	86	4.0	144	6.6	3.92	95	.274	.344	-7	-4	103	114	-2.9	-3	-3	-1.0
■ DICK ROBERTSON	Robertson, Preston b: 1891, Washington, D.C. d: 10/2/44, New Orleans, La. BR/TR, 5'9", 160 lbs. Deb: 9/16/13																												
1913	Cin-N	0	1	.000	2	1	1	0	0	10	13	11.7	0	9	8.1	1	0.9	7.20	46	.342	.468	-4	-4	104	93	-0.4	-0	-0	-0.4
1918	Bro-N	3	6	.333	13	9	7	1	0	87	87	9.0	0	28	2.9	18	1.9	2.59	111	.272	.325	2	3	104	122	-1.1	2	-0	0.5
1919	Was-A	0	1	.000	7	4	0	0	0	28	25	8.0	1	9	2.9	7	2.3	2.25	142	.253	.315	3	3	99	127	-0.4	-1	0	0.2
Total	3	3	8	.273	22	14	8	1	0	125	125	9.0	1	46	3.3	26	1.9	2.88	104	.274	.336	0	1	103	121	-1.9	0	-0	0.3
■ RICH ROBERTSON	Robertson, Richard Paul b: 10/14/44, Albany, Cal. BR/TR, 6'2", 210 lbs. Deb: 9/10/66																												
1966	SF-N	0	0	—	1	0	0	0	0	2	3	13.5	0	2	9.0	2	9.0	9.00	39	.300	.417	-1	-1	97	64	0.0	0	0	0.0
1967	SF-N	0	0	—	1	0	0	0	0	2	3	13.5	0	0	0.0	1	4.5	4.50	74	.333	.333	-0	-0	99	94	0.0	0	0	0.0
1968	SF-N	2	0	1.000	3	1	0	0	0	9	9	9.0	0	3	3.0	8	8.0	6.00	48	.265	.316	-3	-3	96	52	1.0	0	0	-0.2
1969	SF-N	1	3	.250	17	7	1	1	0	44	53	10.8	4	21	4.3	20	4.1	5.52	65	.298	.362	-9	-9	100	94	-1.0	-1	0	-0.9
1970	SF-N	8	9	.471	41	26	6	0	1	184	199	9.7	22	96	4.7	121	5.9	4.84	80	.277	.357	-16	-20	96	104	-1.0	-0	-0	-1.9
1971	SF-N	2	2	.500	23	6	1	0	1	61	66	9.7	5	31	4.6	32	4.7	4.57	75	.267	.350	-7	-8	99	94	-0.1	-1	-1	-0.9
Total	6	13	14	.481	86	40	8	1	2	302	333	9.9	31	153	4.6	184	5.5	4.95	75	.278	.355	-37	-41	97	98	-1.1	-2	-1	-3.9
■ DEWEY ROBINSON	Robinson, Dewey Everett b: 4/28/55, Evanston, Ill. BR/TR, 6', 180 lbs. Deb: 4/06/79																												
1979	Chi-A	0	1	.000	11	0	0	0	0	14	11	7.1	1	9	5.8	5	3.2	6.43	67	.212	.328	-3	-3	103	49	-0.4	0	-0	-0.2
1980	Chi-A	1	1	.500	15	0	0	0	0	35	26	6.7	2	16	4.1	28	7.2	3.09	128	.215	.298	4	3	98	91	0.1	0	0	0.3
1981	Chi-A	1	0	1.000	4	0	0	0	0	4	5	11.3	1	3	6.8	2	4.5	4.50	80	.357	.444	-0	-0	99	193	0.5	0	0	0.0
Total	3	2	2	.500	30	0	0	0	0	53	42	7.1	4	28	4.8	35	5.9	4.08	99	.225	.318	-0	-0	99	87	0.2	0	-0	0.1
■ DON ROBINSON	Robinson, Don Allen b: 6/8/57, Ashland, Ky. BR/TR, 6'4", 225 lbs. Deb: 4/10/78																												
1978	Pit-N	14	6	.700	35	32	9	1	1	228	203	8.0	20	57	2.3	135	5.3	3.47	108	.236	.281	3	7	105	82	3.7	2	-1	0.9
1979	Pit-N	8	8	.500	29	25	4	0	0	161	171	9.6	12	52	2.9	96	5.4	3.86	101	.277	.332	-2	1	104	105	-1.4	1	-3	0.0
1980	Pit-N	7	10	.412	29	24	3	2	1	160	157	8.8	14	45	2.5	103	5.8	3.99	93	.257	.308	-7	-5	103	89	-1.7	6	0	0.1
1981	Pit-N	0	3	.000	16	2	0	0	2	38	47	11.1	4	23	5.4	17	4.0	5.92	57	.313	.385	-10	-11	96	102	-1.4	1	1	-0.9
1982	Pit-N	15	13	.536	38	30	6	0	0	227	213	8.4	26	103	4.1	165	6.5	4.28	93	.250	.327	-17	-8	110	94	0.6	8	-2	0.0
1983	Pit-N	2	2	.500	9	6	0	0	0	36	43	10.8	5	21	5.3	28	7.0	4.50	83	.297	.381	-3	-3	103	127	0.0	1	0	-0.1
1984	Pit-N	5	6	.455	51	1	0	0	10	122	99	7.3	6	49	3.6	110	8.1	3.02	111	.226	.296	8	5	94	93	0.0	4	1	1.0
1985	Pit-N	5	11	.313	44	6	0	0	3	95	95	9.0	6	42	4.0	65	6.2	3.88	97	.255	.333	-3	-1	104	95	-0.9	2	-0	0.1
1986	Pit-N	3	4	.429	50	0	0	0	14	69	61	8.0	5	27	3.5	53	6.9	3.39	110	.237	.305	3	3	101	96	0.2	2	0	0.5
1987	Pit-N	6	6	.500	42	0	0	0	12	65	66	9.1	6	22	3.0	53	7.3	3.88	110	.267	.319	2	3	105	103	0.1	0	0	0.3
	SF-N	5	1	.833	25	0	0	0	7	43	39	8.2	1	18	3.8	26	5.4	2.72	142	.239	.310	7	5	95	107	1.9	2	-1	0.7
	Yr	11	7	.611	67	0	0	0	19	108	105	8.8	7	40	3.3	79	6.6	3.42	120	.255	.315	8	8	101	107	2.0	0	-1	1.0
1988	SF-N	10	5	.667	51	19	3	2	6	177	152	7.7	11	49	2.5	122	6.2	2.44	132	.231	.281	20	15	93	113	2.5	3	-2	1.7
Total	11	80	75	.516	419	145	25	5	56	1421	1346	8.5	116	508	3.2	973	6.2	3.65	102	.251	.312	-2	10	102	97	3.6	32	-5	4.3
■ HUMBERTO ROBINSON	Robinson, Humberto Valentino b: 6/25/30, Colon, Panama BR/TR, 6'1", 155 lbs. Deb: 4/20/55																												
1955	Mil-N	3	1	.750	13	2	1	0	2	38	31	7.3	1	25	5.9	19	4.5	3.08	120	.235	.366	4	3	92	127	0.9	-1	0	0.1
1956	Mil-N	0	0	—	1	0	0	0	0	2	1	4.5	0	2	9.0	0	0.0	0.00	—	.167	.333	1	1	96	0	0.0	0	0	0.1
1958	Mil-N	2	4	.333	19	0	0	0	1	42	30	6.4	4	13	2.8	26	5.6	3.00	114	.203	.271	4	2	87	79	-1.3	1	1	0.3
1959	Cle-A	1	0	1.000	5	0	0	0	0	9	9	9.0	0	4	4.0	6	6.0	4.00	92	.281	.351	-0	-0	95	101	0.5	0	0	0.0
	Phi-N	2	4	.333	31	4	1	0	1	73	70	8.6	6	24	3.0	32	3.9	3.33	121	.251	.303	5	6	102	101	-0.5	1	0	0.7
1960	Phi-N	0	4	.000	33	1	0	0	0	50	48	8.6	6	22	4.0	31	5.6	3.42	121	.255	.326	2	4	110	122	-1.9	-0	0	0.4
Total	5	8	13	.381	102	7	2	0	4	214	189	7.9	17	90	3.8	114	4.8	3.24	119	.241	.316	16	15	99	105	-2.3	0	1	1.6
■ JEFF ROBINSON	Robinson, Jeffrey Daniel b: 12/13/60, Santa Ana, Cal. BR/TR, 6'4", 195 lbs. Deb: 4/07/84																												
1984	SF-N	7	15	.318	34	33	1	1	0	172	195	10.2	12	52	2.7	102	5.3	4.55	77	.288	.339	-18	-20	98	95	-2.6	-2	0	-2.1

YEAR	TM/L	W	L	PCT	G	GS	CG	SHO	SV	IP	H	H/G	HR	BB	BB/G	SO	SO/G	ERA	/A	OAVG	OOBP	PR	/A	PF	CPI	WAT	PB	PD	TPI
1985	SF-N	0	0	—	8	0	0	0	0	12	16	12.0	2	10	7.5	8	6.0	5.25	65	.333	.441	-2	-2	95	147	0.0	0	-0	-0.2
1986	SF-N	6	3	.667	64	1	0	0	8	104	92	8.0	8	32	2.8	90	7.8	3.38	104	.234	.290	4	2	95	85	1.5	-1	-0	0.0
1987	SF-N	6	8	.429	63	0	0	0	10	97	69	6.4	10	48	4.5	82	7.6	2.78	139	.207	.299	14	12	95	115	-1.6	-1	1	1.2
	Pit-N	2	1	.667	18	0	0	0	4	27	20	6.7	1	6	2.0	19	6.3	3.00	142	.215	.260	3	4	105	70	0.5	1	0	0.5
	Yr	8	9	.471	81	0	0	0	14	124	89	6.5	11	54	3.9	101	7.3	2.83	140	.206	.289	17	16	97	70	-1.1	-1	1	1.7
1988	Pit-N	11	5	.688	75	0	0	0	9	125	113	8.1	6	39	2.8	87	6.3	3.02	111	.244	.302	6	5	97	103	2.9	0	0	0.6
Total	5	32	32	.500	262	34	1	1	31	537	505	8.5	39	187	3.1	388	6.5	3.59	100	.251	.313	7	-1	97	99	0.7	-2	1	0.0
■ **JEFF ROBINSON**	Robinson, Jeffrey Mark b: 12/14/61, Ventura, Cal. BR/TR, 6'6", 210 lbs. Deb: 4/12/87																												
1987	Det-A	9	6	.600	29	21	2	1	0	127	132	9.4	16	54	3.8	98	6.9	5.39	79	.262	.339	-13	-16	96	83	0.0	0	-1	-1.5
1988	Det-A	13	6	.684	24	23	6	2	0	172	121	**6.3**	19	72	3.8	114	6.0	2.98	125	**.197**	.281	19	14	94	91	3.2	0	0	1.5
Total	2	22	12	.647	53	44	8	3	0	299	253	7.6	35	126	3.8	212	6.4	4.00	99	.226	.307	6	-1	95	88	3.2	0	-1	0.0
■ **JACK ROBINSON**	Robinson, John Edward b: 2/20/21, Orange, N.J. BR/TR, 6', 175 lbs. Deb: 5/04/49																												
1949	Bos-A	0	0	—	3	0	0	0	0	4	4	9.0	0	1	2.3	1	2.3	2.25	193	.267	.353	1	1	103	165	0.0	0	0	0.1
■ **HANK ROBINSON**	Robinson, John Henry "Rube" (born John Henry Roberson) b: 8/16/1889, Floyd, Ark. d: 7/3/65, N.Little Rock, Ark BR/TL, 5'11.5", 160 lbs. Deb: 9/02/11																												
1911	Pit-N	0	1	.000	5	0	0	0	0	13	13	9.0	0	5	3.5	8	5.5	2.77	120	.283	.365	1	1	97	143	-0.4	-0	1	0.1
1912	Pit-N	12	7	.632	33	16	11	0	2	175	146	7.5	3	30	1.5	79	4.1	2.26	144	.230	.276	22	19	95	79	0.4	2	-0	2.1
1913	Pit-N	14	9	.609	43	23	8	1	0	196	184	8.4	1	41	1.9	50	2.3	2.39	126	.255	.293	18	14	94	108	2.4	-1	-2	1.2
1914	StL-N	7	8	.467	26	16	6	1	0	126	128	9.1	1	32	2.3	30	2.1	3.00	96	.274	.311	-3	-2	104	101	-0.9	-1	2	0.0
1915	StL-N	7	8	.467	32	15	6	1	0	143	128	8.1	1	35	2.2	57	3.6	2.45	113	.245	.291	5	5	101	101	0.0	-2	1	0.4
1918	NY-A	2	4	.333	11	3	1	0	0	48	47	8.8	0	16	3.0	14	2.6	3.00	87	.269	.328	-1	-2	94	104	-0.9	-2	0	-0.4
Total	6	42	37	.532	150	73	32	3	2	701	646	8.3	6	159	2.0	238	3.1	2.53	118	.252	.296	41	35	97	99	0.6	-3	2	3.4
■ **RON ROBINSON**	Robinson, Ronald Dean b: 3/24/62, Exeter, Cal. BR/TR, 6'4", 200 lbs. Deb: 8/14/84																												
1984	Cin-N	1	2	.333	12	5	1	0	0	40	35	7.9	3	13	2.9	24	5.4	2.70	143	.232	.289	4	5	107	105	-0.2	-1	0	0.5
1985	Cin-N	7	7	.500	33	12	0	0	1	108	107	8.9	11	32	2.7	76	6.3	4.00	94	.259	.309	-5	-3	105	92	-0.6	-1	1	-0.2
1986	Cin-N	10	3	.769	70	0	0	0	14	117	110	8.5	10	43	3.3	117	9.0	3.23	120	.253	.318	6	8	104	114	3.4	-1	1	0.9
1987	Cin-N	7	5	.583	48	18	0	0	4	154	148	8.6	14	43	2.5	99	5.8	3.68	114	.256	.301	7	9	103	96	0.9	0	-2	0.7
1988	Cin-N	3	7	.300	17	16	0	0	0	79	88	10.0	5	26	3.0	38	4.3	4.10	88	.285	.334	-6	-4	105	105	-2.2	1	-0	-0.3
Total	5	28	24	.538	180	51	1	0	19	498	488	8.8	43	157	2.8	354	6.4	3.63	108	.259	.311	7	16	104	102	1.3	-2	0	1.6
■ **BILL ROBINSON**	Robinson, William (born William Anderson) b: Taylorsville, Ky. Deb: 8/12/1889																												
1889	Lou-a	0	1	.000	1	1	1	0	0	8	10	11.3	2	6	6.8	2	2.3	10.13	39	.322	.432	-6	-6	102	73	-0.4	0	0	-0.3
■ **YANK ROBINSON**	Robinson, William H. b: 9/19/1859, Philadelphia, Pa. d: 8/25/1894, St.Louis, Mo. BR/TR, 5'6.5", 170 lbs. Deb: 8/24/1882																												
1882	Det-N	0	0	—	1	0	0	0	0	2	0	0.0	0	1	4.5	0	0.0	0.00	—	.000	.155	1	1	104	0	0.0	-0	0	0.1
1884	Bal-U	3	3	.500	11	3	3	0	0	75	96	11.5	1	18	2.2	61	7.3	3.48	95	.316	.355	-4	-1	110	131	-0.2	2	0	0.0
1886	StL-a	0	1	.000	1	1	1	0	0	9	10	10.0	0	7	7.0	1	1.0	3.00	122	.292	.412	0	1	106	174	-0.4	0	0	0.1
1887	StL-a	0	0	—	1	0	0	0	1	3	3	9.0	0	3	9.0	0	0.0	3.00	150	.274	.430	0	0	105	174	0.0	0	0	0.0
Total	4	3	4	.429	14	4	4	0	1	89	109	11.0	1	29	2.9	62	6.3	3.34	101	.308	.360	-2	0	109	134	-0.6	2	0	0.2
■ **CHICK ROBITAILLE**	Robitaille, Joseph Anthony b: 3/2/1879, Whitehall, N.Y. d: 7/30/47, Waterford, N.Y. BR/TR, Deb: N/A.																												
1904	Pit-N	4	3	.571	9	8	8	0	0	66	52	7.1	1	13	1.8	34	4.6	1.91	140	.239	.285	6	6	98	94	0.0	-2	-1	0.5
1905	Pit-N	8	5	.615	17	12	10	0	0	120	126	9.4	1	28	2.1	32	2.4	2.93	104	.299	.347	1	2	102	112	0.0	-2	-0	0.1
Total	2	12	8	.600	26	20	18	0	0	186	178	8.6	2	41	2.0	66	3.2	2.56	113	.279	.326	7	7	100	106	0.0	-4	-1	0.6
■ **ARMANDO ROCHE**	Roche, Armando (Baez) b: 12/7/26, Havana, Cuba BR/TR, 6', 190 lbs. Deb: 5/10/45																												
1945	Was-A	0	0	—	2	0	0	0	0	6	10	15.0	0	2	3.0	0	0.0	6.00	52	.400	.429	-2	-2	92	117	0.0	-0	0	-0.1
■ **MIKE ROCHFORD**	Rochford, Michael Joseph b: 3/14/63, Methuen, Mass. BL/TL, 6'4", 205 lbs. Deb: 9/03/88																												
1988	Bos-A	0	0	—	2	0	0	0	0	2	4	18.0	0	1	4.5	1	4.5	0.00	—	.364	.417	1	1	108	0	0.0	0	0	0.1
■ **RICH RODAS**	Rodas, Richard Martin b: 11/7/59, Roseville, Cal. BL/TL, 6'1", 180 lbs. Deb: 9/06/83																												
1983	LA-N	0	0	—	7	0	0	0	0	5	4	7.2	0	3	5.4	5	9.0	1.80	201	.222	.333	1	1	100	157	0.0	-0	0	0.1
1984	LA-N	0	0	—	3	0	0	0	0	5	5	9.0	2	1	1.8	1	1.8	5.40	69	.250	.286	-1	-1	104	100	0.0	-0	0	0.0
Total	2	0	0	—	10	0	0	0	0	10	9	8.1	2	4	3.6	6	5.4	3.60	102	.237	.310	0	0	102	128	0.0	-0	0	0.1
■ **EDUARDO RODRIGUEZ**	Rodriguez, Eduardo (Reyes) b: 3/6/52, Barceloneta, P.R. BR/TR, 6', 180 lbs. Deb: 6/20/73																												
1973	Mil-A	9	7	.563	30	6	2	0	5	76	71	8.4	6	47	5.6	49	5.8	3.32	111	.247	.351	4	3	96	123	1.7	1	-0	0.4
1974	Mil-A	7	4	.636	43	6	0	0	4	112	97	7.8	7	51	4.1	58	4.7	3.62	103	.240	.322	0	1	103	95	1.8	0	0	0.1
1975	Mil-A	7	0	1.000	43	1	0	0	7	88	77	7.9	9	44	4.5	65	6.6	3.48	110	.235	.328	3	4	101	107	3.5	0	-2	0.2
1976	Mil-A	5	13	.278	45	12	3	0	8	136	124	8.2	10	65	4.3	77	5.1	3.64	97	.249	.329	-2	-2	100	105	-3.0	0	-1	-0.2
1977	Mil-A	5	6	.455	42	5	1	1	4	143	126	7.9	15	56	3.5	104	6.5	4.34	91	.236	.307	-4	-7	97	78	0.4	0	-1	-0.7
1978	Mil-A	5	5	.500	32	8	0	0	2	105	107	9.2	9	26	2.2	51	4.4	3.94	100	.262	.301	-2	-0	104	87	-0.6	0	-0	0.0
1979	KC-A	4	1	.800	29	1	1	0	2	74	79	9.6	9	34	4.1	26	3.2	4.86	91	.276	.352	-5	-3	105	100	1.5	0	-1	-0.4
Total	7	42	36	.538	264	39	7	1	32	734	681	8.4	65	323	4.0	430	5.3	3.89	99	.248	.324	-6	-4	101	97	5.3	1	-5	-0.6
■ **FREDDY RODRIGUEZ**	Rodriguez, Fernando Pedro (Borrego) b: 4/29/24, Havana, Cuba BR/TR, 6', 180 lbs. Deb: 4/18/58																												
1958	Chi-N	0	0	—	7	0	0	0	2	7	8	10.3	2	5	6.4	5	6.4	7.71	52	.267	.389	-3	-3	101	85	0.0	-0	-0	-0.2
1959	Phi-N	0	0	—	1	0	0	0	0	2	4	18.0	1	0	0.0	1	4.5	13.50	30	.400	.455	-2	-2	102	88	0.0	-0	0	-0.1
Total	2	0	0	—	8	0	0	0	2	9	12	12.0	3	5	5.0	6	6.0	9.00	44	.300	.404	-5	-5	101	85	0.0	-0	-0	-0.3
■ **RICK RODRIGUEZ**	Rodriguez, Ricardo b: 9/21/60, Oakland, Cal. BR/TR, 6'3", 190 lbs. Deb: 9/17/86																												
1986	Oak-A	1	2	.333	3	3	0	0	0	16	17	9.6	4	7	3.9	2	1.1	6.75	58	.262	.333	-5	-5	94	77	-0.3	0	0	-0.3
1987	Oak-A	1	0	1.000	15	0	0	0	0	24	32	12.0	1	15	5.6	9	3.4	3.00	136	.337	.429	4	3	91	219	0.5	0	1	0.3
1988	Cle-A	1	2	.333	10	5	0	0	0	33	43	11.7	4	17	4.6	9	2.5	7.09	57	.323	.391	-11	-11	102	90	-0.4	0	1	-0.9
Total	3	3	4	.429	28	8	0	0	0	73	92	11.3	9	39	4.8	20	2.5	5.67	71	.314	.391	-12	-13	97	129	-0.2	0	2	-0.9
■ **ROBERTO RODRIQUEZ**	Rodriquez, Roberto (Munoz) b: 11/29/41, Caracas, Venez. BR/TR, 6'3", 185 lbs. Deb: 5/13/67																												
1967	KC-A	1	1	.500	15	5	0	0	2	40	42	9.4	4	14	3.1	29	6.5	3.60	91	.268	.324	-2	-1	102	116	0.2	-1	-0	-0.2
1970	Oak-A	0	0	—	6	0	0	0	0	12	10	7.5	2	3	2.3	8	6.0	3.00	118	.227	.271	1	1	96	108	0.0	-0	0	0.1
	SD-N	0	0	—	10	0	0	0	3	16	26	14.6	1	5	2.8	8	4.5	6.75	58	.366	.403	-5	-5	97	99	0.0	-0	0	-0.4
	Chi-N	3	2	.600	26	0	0	0	2	43	50	10.5	6	15	3.1	46	9.6	5.86	82	.289	.337	-9	-5	119	85	0.4	1	0	-0.3
	Yr	3	2	.600	36	0	0	0	5	59	76	11.6	7	20	3.1	54	8.2	6.10	75	.311	.356	-13	-10	113	85	0.4	-0	0	-0.7
Total	2	4	3	.571	57	5	0	0	7	111	128	10.4	13	37	3.0	91	7.4	4.86	82	.288	.336	-14	-11	107	100	0.6	-1	-0	-0.8
■ **PREACHER ROE**	Roe, Elwin Charles b: 2/26/15, Ash Flat, Ark. BR/TL, 6'2", 170 lbs. Deb: 8/22/38																												
1938	StL-N	0	0	—	1	0	0	0	0	3	6	18.0	0	2	6.0	1	3.0	12.00	35	.429	.500	-3	-3	111	78	0.0	-0	0	-0.2
1944	Pit-N	13	11	.542	39	25	7	1	1	185	182	8.9	7	59	2.9	88	4.3	3.11	120	.253	.306	10	13	104	101	-1.0	-2	-1	1.0
1945	Pit-N	14	13	.519	33	31	15	3	1	235	228	8.7	11	46	1.8	**148**	**5.7**	2.87	135	.259	.294	24	26	102	108	-0.3	-3	1	2.5
1946	Pit-N	3	8	.273	21	10	1	0	2	70	83	10.7	5	25	3.2	28	3.6	5.14	70	.294	.349	-13	-12	106	88	-1.8	-1	-0	-1.2
1947	Pit-N	4	15	.211	38	22	4	1	2	144	156	9.8	19	63	3.9	59	3.7	5.25	79	.276	.345	-19	-18	102	90	-4.7	-2	-1	-1.9
1948	Bro-N	12	8	.600	34	22	8	2	2	178	156	7.9	14	33	**1.7**	86	4.3	2.63	155	.233	.268	26	28	103	100	1.4	-2	-1	2.7
1949	Bro-N	15	6	**.714**	30	27	13	3	1	213	201	8.5	25	44	1.9	109	4.6	2.79	141	.252	.290	30	27	98	**126**	2.7	-2	-2	2.4
1950	Bro-N	19	11	.633	36	32	16	2	1	251	245	8.8	34	66	2.4	125	4.5	3.30	131	.257	.307	24	29	104	118	2.4	-3	-2	2.4
1951	Bro-N	22	3	**.880**	34	33	19	2	0	258	247	8.6	30	64	2.2	113	3.9	3.03	124	.258	.302	26	20	95	**122**	**9.0**	-4	-1	1.5
1952	Bro-N	11	2	.846	27	25	8	2	0	159	163	9.2	16	39	2.2	83	4.7	3.11	118	.270	.315	11	10	98	**128**	4.0	-3	-1	0.5
1953	Bro-N	11	3	.786	25	24	9	1	0	157	171	9.8	27	40	2.3	85	4.9	4.36	98	.278	.321	-1	-2	100	108	2.4	-4	1	-0.4
1954	Bro-N	3	4	.429	15	10	1	0	0	63	69	9.9	11	23	3.3	31	4.4	5.00	82	.279	.335	-6	-6	101	97	-0.9	-0	-0	-0.5
Total	12	127	84	.602	333	261	101	17	10	1916	1907	9.0	199	504	2.4	956	4.5	3.43	116	.261	.307	108	114	101	111	13.2	-27	-8	8.8

YEAR	TM/L	W	L	PCT	G	GS	CG	SHO	SV	IP	H	H/G	HR	BB	BB/G	SO	SO/G	ERA	/A	OAVG	OOBP	PR	/A	PF	CPI	WAT	PB	PD	TPI
■ CLAY ROE	Roe, James Clay "Shad" b: 1/7/04, Green Briar, Tenn. d: 4/4/56, Cleveland, Miss. BL/TL, 6'1", 180 lbs. Deb: 10/03/23																												
1923	Was-A	0	1	.000	1	1	0	0	0	2	0	0.0	0	6	27.0	2	9.0	0.00	—	.000	.500	1	1	95	0	-0.4	0	0	0.1
■ ED ROEBUCK	Roebuck, Edward Jack b: 7/3/31, East Millsboro, Pa. BR/TR, 6'2", 185 lbs. Deb: 4/18/55																												
1955	Bro-N	5	6	.455	47	0	0	0	12	84	96	10.3	14	24	2.6	33	3.5	4.71	86	.288	.334	-6	-6	101	105	-1.6	-1	1	-0.5
1956	Bro-N	5	4	.556	43	0	0	0	1	89	83	8.4	15	29	2.9	60	6.1	3.94	96	.251	.307	-2	-2	100	102	-0.3	2	1	0.1
1957	Bro-N	8	2	.800	44	1	0	0	8	96	70	6.6	9	46	4.3	73	6.8	2.72	163	.205	.299	12	**18**	114	105	2.9	2	3	2.5
1958	LA-N	0	1	.000	32	0	0	0	5	44	45	9.2	9	15	3.1	26	5.3	3.48	121	.271	.330	2	4	106	143	-0.4	1	-0	0.4
1960	LA-N	8	3	.727	58	0	0	0	8	117	109	8.4	13	38	2.9	77	5.9	2.77	155	.256	.311	13	20	114	139	2.4	-0	2	2.3
1961	LA-N	2	0	1.000	5	0	0	0	0	9	12	12.0	1	2	2.0	9	9.0	5.00	82	.324	.359	-1	-1	102	107	1.0	-0	0	0.0
1962	LA-N	10	2	.833	64	0	0	0	9	119	102	7.7	11	54	4.1	72	5.4	3.10	115	.232	.316	11	6	91	113	3.5	1	0	0.7
1963	LA-N	2	4	.333	29	0	0	0	0	40	54	12.1	4	21	4.7	26	5.8	4.27	72	.321	.391	-4	-5	94	144	-1.3	0	1	-0.4
	Was-A	2	1	.667	26	0	0	0	4	57	63	9.9	5	29	4.6	25	3.9	3.32	111	.284	.363	2	2	101	150	0.7	0	1	0.3
1964	Was-A	0	0	—	2	0	0	0	0	1	0	0.0	0	2	18.0	0	0.0	9.00	42	.000	.333	-1	-1	103	2	0.0	0	0	0.0
	Phi-N	5	3	.625	60	0	0	0	12	77	55	6.4	7	25	2.9	42	4.9	2.22	156	.196	.268	11	11	98	105	0.6	-1	1	1.2
1965	Phi-N	5	3	.625	44	0	0	0	3	50	55	9.9	2	15	2.7	29	5.2	3.42	98	.288	.338	1	-0	95	127	0.9	-0	-1	-0.1
1966	Phi-N	0	2	.000	6	0	0	0	0	6	9	13.5	0	2	3.0	5	7.5	6.00	60	.333	.355	-2	-2	100	84	-0.9	0	-0	-0.1
Total	11	52	31	.627	460	1	0	0	62	789	753	8.6	90	302	3.4	477	5.4	3.35	115	.254	.321	37	44	102	119	7.5	3	7	6.4
■ OSCAR ROETTGER	Roettger, Oscar Frederick Louis "Okkie" b: 2/19/1900, St.Louis, Mo. d: 7/4/86, St.Louis, Mo. BR/TR, 6', 170 lbs. Deb: 7/07/23																												
1923	NY-A	0	0	—	5	0	0	0	1	12	16	12.0	3	12	9.0	7	5.3	8.25	49	.340	.468	-6	-6	101	111	0.0	-0	0	-0.4
1924	NY-A	0	0	—	1	0	0	0	0	0	1	—	0	2	—	0	—	—	—	1.000	1.000	0	0	97	0	0.0	0	0	0.0
Total	2	0	0	—	6	0	0	0	1	12	17	12.8	3	14	10.5	7	5.3	8.25	49	.354	.492	-6	-6	101	111	0.0	-0	0	-0.4
■ JOE ROGALSKI	Rogalski, Joseph Anthony b: 7/15/12, Ashland, Wis. d: 11/20/51, Ashland, Wis. BR/TR, 6'2", 187 lbs. Deb: 9/14/38																												
1938	Det-A	0	0	—	2	0	0	0	0	7	12	15.4	0	0	0.0	2	2.6	2.57	185	.400	.400	2	2	99	257	0.0	-0	-0	0.1
■ LEE ROGERS	Rogers, Lee Otis "Buck" b: 10/8/13, Tuscaloosa, Ala. BR/TL, 5'11", 170 lbs. Deb: 4/27/38																												
1938	Bos-A	1	1	.500	14	2	0	0	0	28	32	10.3	4	18	5.8	7	2.3	6.43	75	.302	.385	-5	-5	100	100	-0.1	-0	1	-0.3
	Bro-N	0	2	.000	12	2	0	0	0	24	23	8.6	0	10	3.8	11	4.1	5.63	65	.256	.327	-5	-5	96	60	-0.9	0	1	-0.3
■ BUCK ROGERS	Rogers, Orlin Woodrow "Lefty" b: 11/5/12, Spring Garden, Va. BR/TL, 5'8.5", 164 lbs. Deb: 9/15/35																												
1935	Was-A	0	1	.000	2	1	0	0	0	10	16	14.4	0	6	5.4	7	6.3	7.20	57	.340	.415	-3	-3	93	87	-0.4	-0	-0	-0.3
■ STEVE ROGERS	Rogers, Stephen Douglas b: 10/26/49, Jefferson City, Mo. BR/TR, 6'2", 175 lbs. Deb: 7/18/73																												
1973	Mon-N	10	5	.667	17	17	7	3	0	134	93	6.2	5	49	3.3	64	4.3	1.54	248	.199	.271	32	34	105	127	2.8	-1	1	4.1
1974	Mon-N	15	22	.405	38	38	11	1	0	254	255	9.0	19	80	2.8	154	5.5	4.46	85	.265	.320	-24	-19	104	82	-3.9	-1	2	-1.7
1975	Mon-N	11	12	.478	35	35	12	3	0	252	248	8.9	13	88	3.1	137	4.9	3.29	121	.260	.318	10	19	109	105	0.4	1	1	2.3
1976	Mon-N	7	17	.292	33	32	8	4	1	230	212	8.3	10	69	2.7	150	5.9	3.21	113	.250	.302	8	10	103	96	-1.8	-2	5	1.5
1977	Mon-N	17	16	.515	40	40	17	4	0	302	272	8.1	16	81	2.4	206	6.1	3.10	125	.242	.290	27	26	99	91	2.0	-5	4	2.6
1978	Mon-N	13	10	.565	30	29	11	1	1	219	186	7.6	12	64	2.6	126	5.2	2.47	139	.235	.289	27	23	96	113	2.4	-2	1	2.4
1979	Mon-N	13	12	.520	37	37	13	**5**	0	249	232	8.4	14	78	2.8	143	5.2	3.00	126	.251	.304	21	21	101	107	-1.7	0	3	2.6
1980	Mon-N	16	11	.593	37	37	**14**	4	0	281	247	7.9	16	85	2.7	147	4.7	2.98	119	.238	.291	20	18	98	96	1.3	1	-1	1.9
1981	Mon-N	12	8	.600	22	22	7	3	0	161	149	8.3	7	41	2.3	87	4.9	3.41	100	.248	.294	1	0	98	84	1.2	-1	-1	-0.1
1982	Mon-N	19	8	.704	35	35	14	4	0	277	245	8.0	12	65	2.1	179	5.8	**2.40**	**156**	.237	.282	**37**	**42**	104	107	5.6	0	0	**4.7**
1983	Mon-N	17	12	.586	36	36	13	**5**	0	273	258	8.5	14	78	2.6	146	4.8	3.23	114	.252	.303	12	14	101	96	2.8	-1	-2	1.1
1984	Mon-N	6	15	.286	31	28	1	0	0	169	171	9.1	12	78	4.2	64	3.4	4.31	76	.267	.343	-14	-19	91	97	-4.6	1	0	-1.8
1985	Mon-N	2	4	.333	8	7	1	0	0	38	51	12.1	1	20	4.7	18	4.3	5.68	59	.329	.397	-9	-10	94	100	-1.0	0	1	-0.8
Total	13	158	152	.510	399	393	129	37	2	2839	2619	8.3	151	876	2.8	1621	5.1	3.17	116	.248	.302	149	159	101	99	5.5	-9	15	18.8
■ TOM ROGERS	Rogers, Thomas Andrew "Shotgun" b: 2/12/1892, Sparta, Tenn. d: 3/7/36, Nashville, Tenn. BR/TR, 6'0.5", 180 lbs. Deb: 4/14/17																												
1917	StL-A	3	6	.333	24	8	3	0	0	109	112	9.2	2	44	3.6	27	2.2	3.88	68	.277	.352	-15	-15	98	93	-0.4	-1	-0	-1.7
1918	StL-A	8	10	.444	29	16	11	0	2	154	148	8.6	3	49	2.9	29	1.7	3.27	84	.267	.319	-9	-9	100	94	-0.6	2	2	-0.5
1919	StL-A	0	1	.000	2	0	0	0	0	1	7	63.0	0	0	0.0	1	9.0	27.00	12	.700	.700	-3	-3	98	116	-0.4	0	0	-0.2
	Phi-A	4	12	.250	23	18	7	1	0	140	152	9.8	9	60	3.9	37	2.4	4.31	84	.292	.369	-17	-11	112	103	-0.1	-0	4	-0.6
	Yr	4	13	.235	25	18	7	1	0	141	159	10.1	9	60	3.8	38	2.4	4.47	81	.300	.374	-20	-13	112	103	-0.5	0	4	-0.8
1921	NY-A	0	1	.000	5	0	0	0	1	11	12	9.8	1	9	7.4	0	0.0	7.36	58	.300	.415	-4	-4	99	87	-0.4	0	1	-0.2
Total	4	15	30	.333	83	42	21	1	3	415	431	9.3	15	162	3.5	94	2.0	3.95	77	.282	.350	-47	-42	104	97	-1.9	1	6	-3.2
■ CLINT ROGGE	Rogge, Francis Clinton b: 7/19/1889, Memphis, Mich. d: 1/6/69, Mt.Clemens, Mich. BL/TR, 5'10", 185 lbs. Deb: 4/11/15																												
1915	Pit-F	17	11	.607	37	31	17	5	0	254	240	8.5	6	93	3.3	93	3.3	2.55	122	.257	.330	14	16	102	129	1.7	-0	5	2.3
1921	Cin-N	1	2	.333	6	3	0	0	0	35	43	11.1	2	9	2.3	12	3.1	4.11	93	.307	.342	-1	-1	101	104	-0.3	0	0	0.0
Total	2	18	13	.581	43	34	17	5	0	289	283	8.8	8	102	3.2	105	3.3	2.74	117	.264	.332	12	15	102	126	1.4	0	5	2.3
■ GARRY ROGGENBURK	Roggenburk, Garry Earl b: 4/16/40, Cleveland, Ohio BR/TL, 6'6", 195 lbs. Deb: 4/20/63																												
1963	Min-A	2	4	.333	36	2	0	0	4	50	47	8.5	3	22	4.0	24	4.3	2.16	164	.253	.338	8	8	98	183	-1.2	0	1	0.9
1965	Min-A	1	0	1.000	12	0	0	0	2	21	21	9.0	1	12	5.1	6	2.6	3.43	99	.266	.347	0	-0	98	124	0.5	-0	-0	0.0
1966	Min-A	1	2	.333	12	0	0	0	1	12	14	10.5	4	10	7.5	3	2.3	6.00	63	.292	.400	-3	-3	110	132	-0.5	0	0	-0.2
	Bos-A	0	0	—	1	0	0	0	0	⅓	1	27.0	0	1	27.0	0	0.0	0.00	—	.500	.667	0	0	110	0	0.0	0	0	0.0
	Yr	1	2	.333	13	0	0	0	1	12	15	11.3	4	11	8.3	3	2.3	6.00	63	.300	.413	-3	-3	110	0	-0.5	0	0	-0.2
1968	Bos-A	0	0	—	4	0	0	0	0	8	9	10.1	0	3	3.4	4	4.5	2.25	133	.257	.316	1	1	101	130	0.0	0	-0	0.1
1969	Bos-A	0	1	.000	7	0	0	0	0	10	13	11.7	1	5	4.5	8	7.2	8.10	47	.342	.422	-5	-5	105	83	-0.4	-0	0	-0.4
	Sea-A	2	2	.500	7	4	1	0	0	24	27	10.1	6	11	4.1	11	4.1	4.50	81	.276	.351	-2	-2	100	127	0.4	-0	0	-0.2
	Yr	2	3	.400	14	4	1	0	0	34	40	10.6	7	16	4.2	19	5.0	5.56	66	.292	.365	-7	-7	102	127	0.0	-0	0	-0.6
Total	5	6	9	.400	79	6	1	0	7	125	132	9.5	15	64	4.6	56	4.0	3.67	97	.272	.356	-2	-2	100	146	-1.2	-0	0	0.2
■ SAUL ROGOVIN	Rogovin, Saul Walter b: 3/24/22, Brooklyn, N.Y. BR/TR, 6'2", 205 lbs. Deb: 4/28/49																												
1949	Det-A	0	1	.000	5	0	0	0	0	6	13	19.5	1	7	10.5	2	3.0	13.50	33	.464	.571	-6	-6	106	98	-0.4	0	-0	-0.5
1950	Det-A	2	1	.667	11	5	1	0	0	40	39	8.8	5	26	5.8	11	2.5	4.50	96	.258	.368	0	-1	95	113	0.2	0	-1	0.0
1951	Det-A	1	1	.500	5	4	0	0	0	24	23	8.6	4	7	2.6	5	1.9	5.25	84	.247	.300	-3	-2	107	74	0.0	1	0	0.0
	Chi-A	11	7	.611	22	22	17	3	0	193	166	7.7	11	67	3.1	77	3.6	2.47	159	.234	.297	35	31	96	121	1.8	-0	-1	3.2
	Yr	12	8	.600	27	26	17	3	0	217	189	7.8	15	74	3.1	82	3.4	**2.78**	**143**	.235	.297	32	**29**	97	121	1.8	1	-0	3.2
1952	Chi-A	14	9	.609	33	30	12	3	1	232	224	8.7	14	79	3.1	121	4.7	3.84	95	.255	.312	-4	-5	99	89	2.3	3	-0	-0.2
1953	Chi-A	7	12	.368	22	19	4	1	1	131	151	10.4	17	48	3.3	62	4.3	5.22	79	.289	.345	-18	-16	104	95	-3.6	-0	0	-1.4
1955	Bal-A	1	8	.111	14	12	1	0	0	71	79	10.0	5	27	3.4	35	4.4	4.56	81	.288	.347	-5	-7	94	98	-3.1	-1	-0	-0.8
	Phi-N	5	3	.625	12	11	5	2	0	73	60	7.4	3	17	2.1	27	3.3	3.08	133	.230	.273	8	8	102	76	1.0	2	-1	1.0
1956	Phi-N	7	6	.538	22	18	3	0	0	107	122	10.3	22	27	2.3	48	4.0	4.96	72	.282	.321	-14	-16	95	97	1.0	-2	-1	-1.8
1957	Phi-N	0	0	—	4	0	0	0	0	8	11	12.4	1	3	3.4	0	0.0	9.00	43	.333	.368	-5	-5	99	68	0.0	0	-0	-0.4
Total	8	48	48	.500	150	121	43	9	2	885	888	9.0	83	308	3.1	388	3.9	4.06	96	.262	.320	-11	-18	98	98	-0.8	2	-3	-0.9
■ LES ROHR	Rohr, Leslie Norvin b: 3/5/46, Lowestoft, England BL/TL, 6'5", 205 lbs. Deb: 9/19/67																												
1967	NY-N	2	1	.667	3	3	0	0	0	17	13	6.9	1	9	4.8	15	7.9	2.12	162	.224	.310	2	2	102	156	0.7	-1	-1	0.1
1968	NY-N	0	2	.000	2	1	0	0	0	6	9	13.5	0	7	10.5	5	7.5	4.50	68	.333	.471	-1	-1	103	164	-0.9	0	0	0.0
1969	NY-N	0	0	—	1	0	0	0	0	1	5	45.0	0	1	9.0	0	0.0	27.00	13	.625	.600	-3	-3	99	89	0.0	0	0	-0.1
Total	3	2	3	.400	6	4	0	0	0	24	27	10.1	1	17	6.4	20	7.5	3.75	89	.290	.383	-1	-1	102	156	-0.2	-0	-1	0.0
■ BILLY ROHR	Rohr, William Joseph b: 7/1/45, San Diego, Cal. BL/TL, 6'3", 170 lbs. Deb: 4/14/67																												
1967	Bos-A	2	3	.400	10	8	2	1	0	42	43	9.2	4	22	4.7	16	3.4	5.14	71	.256	.344	-9	-7	113	84	-0.7	-1	-0	-0.7
1968	Cle-A	1	0	1.000	17	0	0	0	1	18	18	9.0	5	10	5.0	5	2.5	7.00	43	.265	.346	-8	-8	101	85	0.5	-0	0	-0.8
Total	2	3	3	.500	27	8	2	1	1	60	61	9.2	9	32	4.8	21	3.2	5.70	60	.258	.344	-17	-15	109	84	-0.2	-1	-0	-1.5

YEAR	TM/L	W	L	PCT	G	GS	CG	SHO	SV	IP	H	H/G	HR	BB	BB/G	SO	SO/G	ERA	/A	OAVG	OOBP	PR	/A	PF	CPI	WAT	PB	PD	TPI
■ **MINNIE ROJAS**	Rojas, Minervino Alejandro (Landin) b: 11/26/38, Remidios, Las Villas, Cuba BR/TR, 6'1", 170 lbs. Deb: 5/30/66																												
1966	Cal-A	7	4	.636	47	2	0	0	10	84	83	8.9	9	15	1.6	37	4.0	2.89	118	.262	.293	5	5	100	125	1.6	-0	-1	0.4
1967	Cal-A	12	9	.571	72	0	0	0	**27**	122	106	7.8	7	38	2.8	83	6.1	2.51	124	.232	.287	10	8	96	114	1.2	-1	-2	0.6
1968	Cal-A	4	3	.571	38	0	0	0	6	55	55	9.0	11	15	2.5	33	5.4	4.25	67	.252	.298	-8	-9	96	98	1.0	-0	-1	-1.0
Total	3	23	16	.590	157	2	0	0	43	261	244	8.4	27	68	2.3	153	5.3	3.00	105	.246	.291	7	4	97	114	3.8	-2	-4	0.0
■ **COOKIE ROJAS**	Rojas, Octavio Victor (Rivas) b: 3/6/39, Havana, Cuba BR/TR, 5'10", 160 lbs. Deb: 4/10/62 MC																												
1967	Phi-N	0	0	—	1	0	0	0	0	1	1	9.0	0	0	0.0	0	0.0	0.00	—	.200	.200	0	0	104	0	0.0	0	0	0.0
■ **JIM ROLAND**	Roland, James Ivan b: 12/14/42, Franklin, N.C. BR/TL, 6'3", 175 lbs. Deb: 9/20/62																												
1962	Min-A	0	0	—	1	0	0	0	0	2	1	4.5	0	0	0.0	1	4.5	0.00	—	.143	.143	1	1	104	0	0.0	0	0	0.1
1963	Min-A	4	1	.800	10	7	2	1	0	49	32	5.9	4	27	5.0	34	6.2	2.57	138	.185	.291	6	5	98	98	1.4	-2	0	0.4
1964	Min-A	2	6	.250	30	13	1	0	3	94	76	7.3	12	55	5.3	63	6.0	4.12	88	.218	.326	-5	-5	100	91	-1.9	-1	-1	-0.6
1966	Min-A	0	0	—	1	0	0	0	0	2	0	0.0	0	0	0.0	1	4.5	0.00	—	.000	.000	1	1	110	0	0.0	0	0	0.1
1967	Min-A	0	1	.000	25	0	0	0	2	36	33	8.3	3	17	4.3	16	4.0	3.00	114	.244	.318	1	2	106	125	-0.4	-0	-0	0.1
1968	Min-A	4	1	.800	28	4	1	0	0	62	55	8.0	3	24	3.5	36	5.2	3.48	90	.238	.309	-3	-2	106	89	1.5	-1	1	-0.1
1969	Oak-A	5	1	.833	39	3	2	0	1	86	59	6.2	2	46	4.8	48	5.0	2.20	151	.197	.309	14	11	91	114	1.9	-1	0	1.0
1970	Oak-A	3	3	.500	28	2	0	0	2	43	28	5.9	2	23	4.8	26	5.4	2.72	131	.181	.282	5	4	96	71	-0.2	-0	1	0.4
1971	Oak-A	1	3	.250	31	0	0	0	1	45	34	6.8	4	19	3.8	30	6.0	3.20	107	.214	.305	1	1	99	98	-1.1	-0	-0	0.0
1972	Oak-A	0	0	—	2	0	0	0	0	2	5	22.5	0	0	0.0	0	0.0	4.50	64	.455	.417	-0	-0	95	198	0.0	0	0	0.0
	NY-A	0	1	.000	16	0	0	0	0	25	27	9.7	3	16	5.8	13	4.7	5.04	56	.287	.379	-5	-6	92	110	-0.4	-0	0	-0.6
	Tex-A	0	0	—	5	0	0	0	0	3	7	21.0	1	2	6.0	4	12.0	9.00	33	.412	.500	-2	-2	97	142	0.0	0	0	-0.1
	Yr	0	1	.000	23	0	0	0	0	30	39	11.7	4	18	5.4	17	5.1	5.40	53	.317	.392	-8	-9	92	142	-0.4	-0	0	-0.7
Total	10	19	17	.528	216	29	6	1	9	449	357	7.2	34	229	4.6	272	5.5	3.23	106	.218	.314	12	9	98	98	0.8	-5	0	0.7
■ **JOSE ROMAN**	Roman, Jose Rafael (Sarita) b: 5/21/63, Santo Domingo, D.R. BR/TR, 6', 175 lbs. Deb: 9/05/84																												
1984	Cle-A	0	2	.000	3	2	0	0	0	6	9	13.5	1	11	16.5	3	4.5	18.00	24	.391	.541	-9	-9	106	68	-0.9	0	-0	-0.7
1985	Cle-A	0	4	.000	5	3	0	0	0	16	13	7.3	3	14	7.9	12	6.8	6.75	59	.200	.342	-5	-5	95	62	-1.9	0	0	-0.4
1986	Cle-A	1	2	.333	6	5	0	0	0	22	23	9.4	3	17	7.0	9	3.7	6.55	63	.280	.390	-6	-6	98	93	-0.4	0	-1	-0.5
Total	3	1	8	.111	14	10	0	0	0	44	45	9.2	7	42	8.6	24	4.9	8.18	50	.265	.398	-20	-20	98	78	-3.2	0	-1	-1.6
■ **RON ROMANICK**	Romanick, Ronald James b: 11/6/60, Burley, Idaho BR/TR, 6'4", 195 lbs. Deb: 4/05/84																												
1984	Cal-A	12	12	.500	33	33	8	2	0	230	240	9.4	23	61	2.4	87	3.4	3.76	108	.270	.313	6	8	101	105	0.0	0	-2	0.6
1985	Cal-A	14	9	.609	31	31	6	1	0	195	210	9.7	29	62	2.9	64	3.0	4.11	102	.280	.332	1	1	101	117	1.6	0	-3	-0.1
1986	Cal-A	5	8	.385	18	18	1	1	0	106	124	10.5	13	44	3.7	38	3.2	5.52	72	.297	.357	-16	-18	95	95	-2.1	0	-1	-1.7
Total	3	31	29	.517	82	82	15	4	0	531	574	9.7	65	167	2.8	189	3.2	4.24	96	.279	.329	-9	-9	100	107	-0.5	0	-6	-1.2
■ **JIM ROMANO**	Romano, James King b: 4/6/27, Brooklyn, N.Y. BR/TR, 6'4", 190 lbs. Deb: 9/21/50																												
1950	Bro-N	0	0	—	3	1	0	0	0	6	8	12.0	0	2	3.0	8	12.0	6.00	72	.296	.333	-1	-1	104	66	0.0	-0	0	0.0
■ **DUTCH ROMBERGER**	Romberger, Allen Isaiah b: 5/26/27, Klingerstown, Pa. d: 5/26/83, Weikert, Pa. BR/TR, 6', 185 lbs. Deb: 5/31/54																												
1954	Phi-A	1	1	.500	10	0	0	0	0	16	28	15.8	3	12	6.8	6	3.4	11.25	35	.406	.482	-13	-13	105	88	0.3	0	-0	-1.2
■ **RAMON ROMERO**	Romero, Ramon (De Los Santos) b: 1/8/59, San Pedro De Macoris, D.R. BL/TL, 6'4", 170 lbs. Deb: 9/18/84																												
1984	Cle-A	0	0	—	1	0	0	0	0	3	0	0.0	0	0	0.0	3	9.0	0.00	—	.000	.111	1	1	106	0	0.0	0	0	0.1
1985	Cle-A	2	3	.400	19	10	0	0	0	64	69	9.7	13	38	5.3	38	5.3	6.61	60	.276	.380	-17	-19	95	91	0.1	0	-1	-1.8
Total	2	2	3	.400	20	10	0	0	0	67	69	9.3	13	38	5.1	41	5.5	6.31	63	.267	.372	-16	-17	96	87	0.1	0	-1	-1.7
■ **EDDIE ROMMEL**	Rommel, Edwin Americus b: 9/13/1897, Baltimore, Md. d: 8/26/70, Baltimore, Md. BR/TR, 6'2", 197 lbs. Deb: 4/19/20 CU																												
1920	Phi-A	7	7	.500	33	12	8	2	1	174	165	8.5	5	43	2.2	43	2.2	2.84	132	.259	.309	18	17	99	100	2.1	0	5	2.2
1921	Phi-A	16	23	.410	46	32	20	0	3	285	312	9.9	21	87	2.7	71	2.2	3.95	116	.284	.325	11	20	107	102	2.5	-3	3	1.9
1922	Phi-A	**27**	13	.675	**51**	33	22	3	2	294	294	9.0	21	63	1.9	54	1.7	3.28	131	.267	.301	25	33	106	102	**10.2**	-3	3	3.4
1923	Phi-A	18	19	.486	**56**	31	19	3	5	298	306	9.2	14	108	3.3	76	2.3	3.26	125	.271	.322	24	27	102	112	1.4	1	6	**3.4**
1924	Phi-A	18	15	.545	43	34	21	3	1	278	302	9.8	8	94	3.0	72	2.3	3.95	108	.284	.337	9	10	101	98	3.0	-6	8	1.1
1925	Phi-A	**21**	10	.677	52	28	14	1	3	261	285	9.8	10	95	3.3	67	2.3	3.69	120	.281	.335	20	22	101	106	4.3	-1	5	2.5
1926	Phi-A	11	11	.500	37	26	12	3	0	219	225	9.2	10	54	2.2	52	2.1	3.08	151	.268	.303	23	38	116	105	-1.1	-5	2	3.8
1927	Phi-A	11	3	.786	30	17	8	2	1	147	166	10.2	6	48	2.9	33	2.0	4.35	90	.286	.338	-3	-7	95	91	3.5	-2	3	-0.5
1928	Phi-A	13	5	.722	43	11	6	0	4	174	177	9.2	11	26	**1.3**	37	1.9	3.05	131	.266	.289	19	18	99	104	2.3	3	2	2.4
1929	Phi-A	12	2	.857	32	6	4	0	4	114	135	10.7	10	34	2.7	25	2.0	2.84	155	.294	.338	18	20	104	159	3.9	-1	1	1.9
1930	Phi-A	9	4	.692	35	9	5	0	3	130	142	9.8	11	27	1.9	35	2.4	4.29	104	.277	.309	5	3	96	94	0.6	3	1	0.7
1931	Phi-A	7	5	.583	25	10	8	1	0	118	136	10.4	5	27	2.1	18	1.4	2.97	149	.291	.329	18	19	101	142	-1.0	2	-0	2.1
1932	Phi-A	1	2	.333	17	0	0	0	2	65	84	11.6	6	18	2.5	16	2.2	5.54	89	.315	.349	-8	-4	111	98	-0.6	2	2	0.0
Total	13	171	119	.590	500	249	147	18	29	2557	2729	9.6	138	724	2.5	599	2.1	3.54	122	.277	.321	180	217	103	107	31.1	-8	41	24.9
■ **ENRIQUE ROMO**	Romo, Enrique (Navarro) b: 7/15/47, Santa Rosalia, Mex BR/TR, 5'11", 185 lbs. Deb: 4/07/77																												
1977	Sea-A	8	10	.444	58	3	0	0	16	114	93	7.3	8	39	3.1	105	8.3	2.84	141	.227	.297	16	15	98	103	0.8	0	1	1.6
1978	Sea-A	11	7	.611	56	0	0	0	10	107	88	7.4	12	39	3.3	62	5.2	3.70	106	.227	.297	1	3	104	87	3.9	0	-1	0.1
1979	Pit-N	10	5	.667	84	0	0	0	5	129	122	8.5	11	43	3.0	106	7.4	3.00	130	.253	.313	11	13	104	118	1.3	-0	2	1.5
1980	Pit-N	5	5	.500	74	0	0	0	11	124	117	8.5	10	28	2.0	82	6.0	3.27	114	.252	.288	5	6	103	97	0.0	3	1	1.1
1981	Pit-N	1	3	.250	33	0	0	0	9	42	47	10.1	5	18	3.9	23	4.9	4.50	75	.288	.349	-5	-5	96	110	-0.8	-0	-0	-0.6
1982	Pit-N	9	3	.750	45	0	0	0	1	87	81	8.4	11	36	3.7	58	6.0	4.34	91	.245	.316	-7	-4	110	88	3.0	1	-0	-0.2
Total	6	44	33	.571	350	3	0	0	52	603	548	8.2	57	203	3.0	436	6.5	3.45	112	.245	.305	20	28	103	100	8.2	4	2	3.5
■ **VICENTE ROMO**	Romo, Vicente (Navarro) "Huevo" b: 4/12/43, Santa Rosalia, Mex. BR/TR, 6'1", 180 lbs. Deb: 4/11/68																												
1968	LA-N	0	0	—	1	0	0	0	0	1	1	9.0	0	0	0.0	0	0.0	0.00	—	.250	.200	0	0	91	0	0.0	0	0	0.0
	Cle-A	5	3	.625	40	1	0	0	12	83	43	4.7	5	32	3.5	54	5.9	1.63	184	.154	.240	12	13	101	83	0.8	-0	0	1.4
1969	Cle-A	1	1	.500	3	0	0	0	0	8	7	7.9	0	3	3.4	7	7.9	2.25	155	.233	.286	1	1	96	107	0.2	0	-0	0.1
	Bos-A	7	9	.438	52	11	4	1	11	127	116	8.2	14	50	3.5	89	6.3	3.19	119	.247	.313	6	9	105	117	-1.5	-1	0	0.9
	Yr	8	10	.444	55	11	4	1	11	135	123	8.2	14	53	3.5	96	6.4	3.13	121	.246	.311	7	10	104	117	-1.3	0	0	1.0
1970	Bos-A	7	3	.700	48	10	0	0	6	108	115	9.6	14	43	3.6	71	5.9	4.08	100	.273	.336	-4	0	110	109	1.8	0	1	0.1
1971	Chi-A	1	7	.125	45	2	0	0	5	72	52	6.5	5	37	4.6	48	6.0	3.38	100	.202	.295	1	-0	97	77	-2.9	1	1	0.3
1972	Chi-A	3	0	1.000	28	0	0	0	1	52	47	8.1	5	18	3.1	46	8.0	3.29	99	.246	.306	-1	-0	106	105	1.5	-1	1	0.0
1973	SD-N	2	3	.400	49	1	0	0	7	88	85	8.7	11	46	4.7	51	5.2	3.68	96	.260	.341	-0	-1	97	122	0.1	-0	0	-0.1
1974	SD-N	5	5	.500	54	1	0	0	9	71	78	9.9	6	37	4.7	26	3.3	4.56	77	.290	.361	-7	-8	97	110	1.1	-1	2	-0.7
1982	LA-N	1	2	.333	15	6	0	0	1	36	25	6.3	1	14	3.5	24	6.0	3.00	112	.195	.279	2	1	94	66	-0.5	0	1	0.2
Total	8	32	33	.492	335	32	4	1	52	646	569	7.9	61	280	3.9	416	5.8	3.36	106	.239	.313	10	14	102	103	0.6	-1	5	2.2
■ **JOHN ROMONOSKY**	Romonosky, John b: 7/7/29, Harrisburg, Ill. BR/TR, 6'2", 195 lbs. Deb: 9/06/53																												
1953	StL-N	0	0	—	2	2	0	0	0	8	9	10.1	1	4	4.5	3	3.4	4.50	96	.281	.378	-0	-0	101	120	0.0	-0	-0	0.0
1958	Was-A	2	4	.333	18	5	1	0	0	55	52	8.5	6	28	4.6	38	6.2	6.55	58	.243	.324	-17	-17	100	59	-0.4	2	0	-1.3
1959	Was-A	1	0	1.000	12	2	0	0	0	38	36	8.5	4	19	4.5	22	5.2	3.32	118	.254	.349	2	3	102	134	0.5	0	0	0.3
Total	3	3	4	.429	32	9	1	0	0	101	97	8.6	11	51	4.5	63	5.6	5.17	75	.250	.338	-15	-14	101	92	0.1	2	0	-1.0
■ **GILBERT RONDON**	Rondon, Gilbert b: 11/18/53, Bronx, N.Y. BR/TR, 6'2", 200 lbs. Deb: 4/10/76																												
1976	Hou-N	2	2	.500	19	7	0	0	0	54	70	11.7	6	39	6.5	21	3.5	5.67	54	.315	.413	-13	-16	87	114	0.0	1	-1	-1.5
1979	Chi-A	0	0	—	4	0	0	0	0	10	11	9.9	2	6	5.4	3	2.7	3.60	120	.282	.370	1	1	103	164	0.0	0	-0	0.1
Total	2	2	2	.500	23	7	0	0	0	64	81	11.4	8	45	6.3	24	3.4	5.34	60	.310	.406	-12	-15	89	122	0.0	1	-1	-1.4
■ **JIM ROOKER**	Rooker, James Phillip b: 9/23/41, Lakeview, Ore. BR/TL, 6', 195 lbs. Deb: 6/30/68																												
1968	Det-A	0	0	—	2	0	0	0	0	5	4	7.2	0	1	1.8	4	7.2	3.60	85	.235	.278	-0	-0	103	61	0.0	-0	0	0.0
1969	KC-A	4	16	.200	28	22	8	1	0	158	136	7.7	13	73	4.2	108	6.2	3.76	100	.229	.309	-2	0	104	85	-5.5	8	-1	0.8

YEAR	TM/L	W	L	PCT	G	GS	CG	SHO	SV	IP	H	H/G	HR	BB	BB/G	SO	SO/G	ERA	/A	OAVG	OOBP	PR	/A	PF	CPI	WAT	PB	PD	TPI
1970	KC-A	10	15	.400	38	29	6	3	1	204	190	8.4	11	102	4.5	117	5.2	3.53	105	.252	.333	4	4	100	105	0.0	3	-0	0.7
1971	KC-A	2	7	.222	20	7	1	1	0	54	59	9.8	2	24	4.0	31	5.2	5.33	64	.284	.350	-11	-12	98	79	-2.6	-0	-1	-1.3
1972	KC-A	5	6	.455	18	10	4	2	0	72	78	9.8	3	24	3.0	44	5.5	4.38	70	.280	.332	-10	-11	100	87	-0.4	-1	1	-1.1
1973	Pit-N	10	6	.625	41	18	6	3	5	170	143	7.6	12	52	2.8	122	6.5	2.86	118	.229	.284	15	10	92	94	2.2	3	1	1.3
1974	Pit-N	15	11	.577	33	33	15	1	0	263	228	7.8	11	83	2.8	139	4.8	2.77	126	.238	.295	25	21	97	99	1.1	10	1	3.5
1975	Pit-N	13	11	.542	28	28	7	1	0	197	177	8.1	16	76	3.5	102	4.7	2.97	119	.238	.305	15	13	98	106	-0.6	-3	0	1.0
1976	Pit-N	15	8	.652	30	29	10	1	1	199	201	9.1	12	72	3.3	92	4.2	3.35	104	.263	.323	4	3	99	109	2.5	3	-1	0.6
1977	Pit-N	14	9	.609	30	30	7	2	0	204	196	8.6	24	64	2.8	89	3.9	3.09	129	.253	.304	19	20	102	118	0.5	0	-2	2.0
1978	Pit-N	9	11	.450	28	28	1	0	0	163	160	8.8	13	81	4.5	76	4.2	4.25	88	.259	.340	-12	-9	105	97	-1.9	-0	1	-0.7
1979	Pit-N	4	7	.364	19	17	1	0	0	104	106	9.2	11	39	3.4	44	3.8	4.59	85	.266	.327	-10	-8	104	88	-2.2	-1	-0	-0.9
1980	Pit-N	2	2	.500	4	4	0	0	0	18	16	8.0	0	12	6.0	8	4.0	3.50	106	.262	.373	0	0	103	119	0.0	1	0	0.1
Total	13	103	109	.486	319	255	66	15	7	1811	1694	8.4	128	703	3.5	976	4.9	3.46	105	.249	.315	35	32	99	100	-6.9	22	-1	6.0
■ **CHARLIE ROOT**	Root, Charles Henry "Chinski" b: 3/17/1899, Middletown, Ohio d: 11/5/70, Hollister, Cal. BR/TR, 5'10.5", 190 lbs. Deb: 4/18/23 C																												
1923	StL-A	0	4	.000	27	2	0	0	0	60	68	10.2	4	18	2.7	27	4.1	5.70	73	.302	.350	-11	-10	105	84	-1.9	-1	-0	-1.0
1926	Chi-N	18	17	.514	42	32	21	2	2	271	267	8.9	10	62	2.1	127	4.2	2.82	142	.264	.302	30	35	105	111	-0.7	-5	-1	3.1
1927	Chi-N	**26**	15	.634	**48**	36	21	4	2	**309**	296	8.6	16	117	3.4	145	4.2	3.76	103	.254	.321	5	4	99	91	4.7	3	-3	0.2
1928	Chi-N	14	18	.438	40	30	13	1	2	237	214	8.1	15	73	2.8	122	4.6	3.57	104	.242	.296	11	3	93	82	-4.8	0	-3	0.0
1929	Chi-N	19	6	**.760**	43	31	19	4	5	272	286	9.5	12	83	2.7	124	4.1	3.47	133	.275	.321	37	35	98	110	4.6	0	-4	2.8
1930	Chi-N	16	14	.533	37	30	15	**4**	3	220	247	10.1	17	63	2.6	124	5.1	4.34	118	.281	.328	16	19	103	95	-1.5	4	-3	1.9
1931	Chi-N	17	14	.548	39	31	19	3	2	251	240	8.6	7	71	2.5	131	4.7	3.48	104	.252	.305	11	4	94	87	0.1	4	-3	0.4
1932	Chi-N	15	10	.600	39	23	11	0	3	216	211	8.8	10	55	2.3	96	4.0	3.58	111	.253	.298	7	10	103	86	0.6	-2	-2	0.5
1933	Chi-N	15	10	.600	35	30	20	2	0	242	232	8.6	14	61	2.3	86	3.2	2.60	122	.252	.301	20	15	95	120	1.4	-4	-3	0.8
1934	Chi-N	4	7	.364	34	9	2	0	0	118	141	10.8	8	53	4.0	46	3.5	4.27	92	.298	.370	-3	-5	97	121	-2.0	1	-0	-0.3
1935	Chi-N	15	8	.652	38	18	11	1	2	201	193	8.6	15	47	2.1	94	4.2	3.09	124	.252	.294	21	16	95	106	0.1	2	-3	1.5
1936	Chi-N	3	6	.333	33	4	0	0	1	74	81	9.9	3	20	2.4	32	3.9	4.14	99	.280	.327	-1	-0	102	93	-1.8	1	-1	0.0
1937	Chi-N	13	5	.722	43	15	5	0	5	179	173	8.7	18	32	1.6	74	3.7	3.37	116	.253	.287	11	11	100	99	2.9	0	-0	1.1
1938	Chi-N	8	7	.533	44	11	5	0	8	161	163	9.1	10	30	1.7	70	3.9	2.85	136	.258	.290	17	19	103	109	-0.6	-0	-2	1.7
1939	Chi-N	8	8	.500	35	16	8	0	4	167	189	10.2	11	34	1.8	65	3.5	4.04	97	.286	.317	-2	-2	100	97	-0.6	2	-3	-0.2
1940	Chi-N	2	4	.333	36	8	1	0	1	112	118	9.5	9	33	2.7	50	4.0	3.86	98	.265	.310	-0	-1	99	99	-0.9	-1	-0	-0.1
1941	Chi-N	8	7	.533	19	15	6	0	0	107	133	11.2	8	37	3.1	46	3.9	5.38	63	.306	.351	-21	-24	94	92	1.2	2	-1	-2.1
Total	17	201	160	.557	632	341	177	21	40	3197	3252	9.2	187	889	2.5	1459	4.1	3.59	110	.264	.312	147	128	99	99	0.8	8	-33	10.3
■ **CHUCK ROSE**	Rose, Charles Alfred b: 9/1/1885, Macon, Mo. d: 8/4/61, Salina, Kan. BL/TL, 5'8.5", 158 lbs. Deb: 9/13/09																												
1909	StL-A	1	2	.333	3	3	3	0	0	25	32	11.5	1	7	2.5	6	2.2	5.40	43	.330	.393	-8	-8	95	93	-0.2	-1	-1	-0.8
■ **DON ROSE**	Rose, Donald Gary b: 3/19/47, Covina, Cal. BR/TR, 6'3", 195 lbs. Deb: 9/15/71																												
1971	NY-N	0	0	—	1	0	0	0	0	2	2	9.0	0	0	0.0	1	4.5	0.00	—	.286	.286	1	1	96	0	0.0	0	0	0.1
1972	Cal-A	1	4	.200	16	4	0	0	0	43	49	10.3	9	19	4.0	39	8.2	4.19	66	.283	.351	-5	-7	90	130	-1.4	1	-0	-0.6
1974	SF-N	0	0	—	2	0	0	0	0	1	4	36.0	0	1	9.0	0	0.0	9.00	44	.667	.714	-1	-1	109	237	0.0	0	0	0.0
Total	3	1	4	.200	19	4	0	0	0	46	55	10.8	9	20	3.9	40	7.8	4.11	68	.296	.361	-5	-7	90	126	-1.4	1	-0	-0.5
■ **STEVE ROSENBERG**	Rosenberg, Steven Allen b: 10/31/64, Brooklyn, N.Y. BL/TL, 6', 185 lbs. Deb: 6/04/88																												
1988	Chi-A	0	1	.000	33	0	0	0	1	46	53	10.4	5	19	3.7	28	5.5	4.30	91	.298	.355	-2	-2	99	121	-0.4	0	-0	-0.1
■ **ZEKE ROSEBRAUGH**	Rosebraugh, Eli Ezekiel b: 9/1875, Coles County, Ill. d: 1936, California TL Deb: 9/21/1898																												
1898	Pit-N	0	2	.000	4	2	2	0	0	22	23	9.4	0	9	3.7	6	2.5	3.27	108	.291	.363	1	1	98	107	-0.9	1	0	0.1
1899	Pit-N	0	1	.000	2	2	0	0	0	6	14	21.0	0	3	4.5	2	3.0	9.00	42	.480	.528	-3	-3	98	112	-0.4	-0	0	-0.2
Total	2	0	3	.000	6	4	2	0	0	28	37	11.9	0	12	3.9	8	2.6	4.50	80	.342	.407	-3	-3	98	108	-1.3	1	0	-0.1
■ **CHIEF ROSEMAN**	Roseman, James John b: 1856, New York, N.Y. d: 7/4/38, Brooklyn, N.Y. BR/TR, 5'7", 167 lbs. Deb: 5/01/1882 M																												
1885	NY-a	0	1	.000	1	1	0	0	0	1	3	27.0	0	2	18.0	0	0.0	27.00	10	.528	.651	-3	-3	86	67	-0.4	0	0	-0.1
1886	NY-a	0	0	—	1	0	0	0	0	7	6	7.7	0	0	0.0	0	0.0	5.14	71	.241	.241	-1	-1	106	34	0.0	0	0	0.0
1887	NY-a	0	0	—	2	0	0	0	0	8	11	12.4	0	5	5.6	1	1.1	7.88	50	.341	.430	-3	-3	92	77	0.0	-0	0	-0.4
Total	3	0	1	.000	4	1	0	0	0	16	20	11.3	0	7	3.9	1	0.6	7.88	48	.319	.387	-7	-7	98	58	-0.4	0	0	-0.5
■ **STEVE ROSER**	Roser, Emerson Corey b: 1/25/18, Rome, N.Y. BR/TR, 6'4", 220 lbs. Deb: 5/05/44																												
1944	NY-A	4	3	.571	16	6	1	0	1	84	80	8.6	3	34	3.6	34	3.6	3.86	94	.256	.324	-4	-2	105	88	0.3	-2	-0	-0.4
1945	NY-A	0	0	—	11	0	0	0	0	27	27	9.0	1	8	2.7	11	3.7	3.67	97	.262	.313	-1	-0	106	89	0.0	-0	0	0.0
1946	NY-A	1	1	.500	4	1	0	0	0	3	7	21.0	0	4	12.0	1	3.0	18.00	19	.438	.550	-5	-5	98	67	0.0	0	0	-0.4
	Bos-N	1	1	.500	14	1	0	0	1	35	33	8.5	1	18	4.6	18	4.6	3.60	89	.250	.333	-1	-2	94	94	0.0	-1	0	-0.1
Total	3	6	5	.545	45	8	1	0	2	149	147	8.9	5	64	3.9	64	3.9	4.05	87	.261	.331	-10	-9	103	89	0.3	-3	-0	-0.9
■ **BUSTER ROSS**	Ross, Chester Franklin b: 3/11/03, Kuttawa, Ky. d: 4/24/82, Mayfield, Ky. BL/TL, 6'1", 195 lbs. Deb: 6/15/24																												
1924	Bos-A	4	3	.571	30	2	1	1	1	93	109	10.5	3	30	2.9	16	1.5	3.48	127	.307	.342	8	10	105	128	0.9	-0	-1	0.8
1925	Bos-A	3	8	.273	33	8	0	0	0	94	119	11.4	9	40	3.8	15	1.4	6.22	70	.313	.367	-19	-19	99	89	-0.6	-1	-1	-1.9
1926	Bos-A	0	1	.000	1	0	0	0	0	3	5	15.0	0	4	12.0	0	0.0	15.00	28	.385	.500	-4	-4	106	63	-0.4	-0	0	-0.2
Total	3	7	12	.368	64	10	1	1	1	190	233	11.0	12	74	3.5	31	1.5	5.02	88	.311	.358	-15	-13	102	108	-0.1	-2	-2	-1.3
■ **CLIFF ROSS**	Ross, Clifford Davis b: 8/3/28, Philadelphia, Pa. BL/TL, 6'4", 195 lbs. Deb: 9/11/54																												
1954	Cin-N	0	0	—	4	0	0	0	1	3	0	0.0	0	0	0.0	1	3.0	0.00	—	.000	.000	1	1	104	0	0.0	0	0	0.2
■ **ERNIE ROSS**	Ross, Ernest Bertram "Curly" b: 3/31/1880, Toronto, Ont., Can. d: 3/28/50, Toronto, Ont., Can. 5'8", 150 lbs. Deb: 9/17/02																												
1902	Bal-A	1	1	.500	2	2	2	0	0	17	20	10.6	0	12	6.4	2	1.1	7.41	50	.319	.428	-7	-7	104	68	0.2	-1	-1	-0.5
■ **BOB ROSS**	Ross, Floyd Robert b: 11/2/28, Fullerton, Cal. BR/TL, 6', 165 lbs. Deb: 6/16/50																												
1950	Was-A	0	1	.000	6	2	0	0	0	13	15	10.4	1	15	10.4	2	1.4	8.31	56	.300	.435	-5	-5	101	86	-0.4	-0	0	-0.4
1951	Was-A	0	1	.000	11	1	0	0	0	32	36	10.1	3	21	5.9	23	6.5	6.47	62	.295	.388	-8	-9	97	89	-0.4	-0	-1	-0.8
1956	Phi-N	0	0	—	3	0	0	0	0	3	4	12.0	1	2	6.0	4	12.0	9.00	40	.333	.375	-2	-2	95	94	0.0	0	0	0.0
Total	3	0	2	.000	20	3	0	0	0	48	55	10.3	5	38	7.1	29	5.4	7.13	58	.299	.401	-15	-16	98	88	-0.8	-1	-0	-1.2
■ **GARY ROSS**	Ross, Gary Douglas b: 9/16/47, Mc Keesport, Pa. BR/TR, 6'1", 185 lbs. Deb: 6/28/68																												
1968	Chi-N	1	1	.500	13	5	1	0	0	41	44	9.7	1	25	5.5	31	6.8	4.17	80	.288	.373	-5	-4	112	112	0.0	-1	0	-0.4
1969	Chi-N	0	0	—	2	1	0	0	0	2	1	4.5	0	2	9.0	2	9.0	13.50	28	.143	.333	-2	-2	105	15	0.0	0	0	-0.1
	SD-N	3	12	.200	46	7	0	0	3	110	104	8.5	5	56	4.6	58	4.7	4.17	86	.252	.342	-7	-7	100	91	-2.9	-2	2	-0.7
	Yr	3	12	.200	48	8	0	0	3	112	105	8.4	5	58	4.7	60	4.8	4.34	83	.250	.342	-9	-9	100	91	-2.9	0	2	-0.8
1970	SD-N	2	3	.400	33	2	0	0	1	62	72	10.5	8	36	5.2	39	5.7	5.23	75	.305	.394	-8	-9	97	118	0.0	2	1	-0.6
1971	SD-N	1	3	.250	13	0	0	0	0	24	27	10.1	0	11	4.1	13	4.9	3.00	113	.300	.358	1	1	98	150	-0.6	-0	0	0.1
1972	SD-N	4	3	.571	60	0	0	0	3	92	87	8.5	2	49	4.8	46	4.5	2.45	128	.261	.350	10	7	91	161	1.1	-0	1	0.9
1973	SD-N	4	4	.500	58	0	0	0	0	76	93	11.0	8	33	3.9	44	5.2	5.45	65	.304	.369	-15	-16	97	98	0.9	-0	0	-1.6
1974	SD-N	0	0	—	9	0	0	0	0	18	23	11.5	1	6	3.0	11	5.5	4.50	78	.315	.354	-2	-2	97	108	0.0	-0	0	-0.1
1975	Cal-A	0	1	.000	1	1	0	0	0	5	6	10.8	1	1	1.8	4	7.2	5.40	67	.273	.304	-1	-1	96	79	-0.4	0	-0	0.0
1976	Cal-A	8	16	.333	34	31	7	2	0	225	224	9.0	12	58	2.3	100	4.0	3.00	109	.258	.303	13	7	93	107	-3.8	0	5	1.3
1977	Cal-A	2	4	.333	14	12	0	0	0	58	83	12.9	10	11	1.7	30	4.7	5.59	69	.337	.369	-10	-11	95	111	-0.7	0	1	-0.9
Total	10	25	47	.347	283	59	8	2	7	713	764	9.6	48	288	3.6	378	4.8	3.93	88	.278	.344	-25	-37	96	113	-6.4	-2	10	-2.1
■ **GEORGE ROSS**	Ross, George Sidney b: 6/27/1892, San Rafael, Cal. d: 4/22/35, Amityville, N.Y. BL/TL, 5'10.5", 175 lbs. Deb: 6/27/18																												
1918	NY-N	0	0	—	1	0	0	0	1	2	2	9.0	0	3	13.5	2	9.0	0.00	—	.222	.417	1	1	96	0	0.0	-0	0	0.1
■ **BUCK ROSS**	Ross, Lee Ravon b: 2/2/15, Norwood, N.C. d: 11/23/78, Charlotte, N.C. BR/TR, 6'2", 170 lbs. Deb: 5/07/36																												
1936	Phi-A	9	14	.391	30	27	12	1	0	201	253	11.3	17	83	3.7	47	2.1	5.82	91	.304	.362	-18	-12	105	93	0.9	-2	-2	-1.2

YEAR	TM/L	W	L	PCT	G	GS	CG	SHO	SV	IP	H	H/G	HR	BB	BB/G	SO	SO/G	ERA	/A	OAVG	OOBP	PR	/A	PF	CPI	WAT	PB	PD	TPI
1937	Phi-A	5	10	.333	28	22	7	1	0	147	183	11.2	12	63	3.9	37	2.3	4.90	91	.306	.368	-5	-7	96	109	-0.5	-3	0	-0.9
1938	Phi-A	9	16	.360	29	28	10	0	0	184	218	10.7	23	80	3.9	54	2.6	5.33	94	.289	.351	-11	-7	105	98	0.3	-1	-0	-0.5
1939	Phi-A	6	14	.300	29	28	6	1	0	174	216	11.2	17	95	4.9	43	2.2	6.00	79	.302	.373	-27	-25	102	96	-1.8	-1	-2	-2.3
1940	Phi-A	5	10	.333	24	19	10	0	1	156	160	9.2	15	60	3.5	43	2.5	4.38	99	.256	.319	-0	-1	99	89	-0.3	-2	-1	-0.3
1941	Phi-A	0	1	.000	1	1	0	0	0	4	10	22.5	2	2	4.5	0	0.0	18.00	24	.435	.480	-6	-6	103	78	-0.4	-0	0	-0.4
	Chi-A	3	8	.273	20	11	7	0	0	108	99	8.3	6	43	3.6	30	2.5	3.17	123	.239	.308	12	9	94	101	-2.5	1	-2	0.8
	Yr	3	9	.250	21	12	7	0	0	112	109	8.8	8	45	3.6	30	2.4	3.70	105	.249	.316	6	3	94	101	-2.9	-0	-2	0.4
1942	Chi-A	5	7	.417	22	14	4	2	1	113	118	9.4	6	39	3.1	37	2.9	5.02	73	.264	.321	-17	-17	100	73	-0.3	-0	-2	-1.8
1943	Chi-A	11	7	.611	21	21	7	1	0	149	140	8.5	6	56	3.4	41	2.5	3.20	104	.253	.316	2	2	101	105	1.7	-1	-1	0.0
1944	Chi-A	2	7	.222	20	9	2	0	0	90	97	9.7	7	35	3.5	20	2.0	5.20	67	.280	.344	-18	-17	102	84	-2.3	-2	-2	-2.0
1945	Chi-A	1	1	.500	13	2	0	0	0	37	51	12.4	3	17	4.1	8	1.9	5.84	55	.327	.393	-10	-11	96	100	0.0	-0	-0	-1.1
Total	10	56	95	.371	237	182	65	6	2	1363	1545	10.2	114	573	3.8	360	2.4	4.95	88	.283	.346	-98	-92	101	95	-5.2	-11	-13	-9.7

■ MARK ROSS Ross, Mark Joseph b: 8/8/54, Galveston, Tex. BR/TR, 6', 195 lbs. Deb: 9/12/82

YEAR	TM/L	W	L	PCT	G	GS	CG	SHO	SV	IP	H	H/G	HR	BB	BB/G	SO	SO/G	ERA	/A	OAVG	OOBP	PR	/A	PF	CPI	WAT	PB	PD	TPI
1982	Hou-N	0	0	—	4	0	0	0	0	6	3	4.5	0	0	0.0	4	6.0	1.50	240	.143	.143	1	1	100	49	0.0	0	0	0.1
1984	Hou-N	1	0	1.000	2	0	0	0	0	2	1	4.5	0	0	0.0	1	4.5	0.00	—	.125	.125	1	1	92	0	0.5	0	0	0.1
1985	Hou-N	0	2	.000	8	0	0	0	1	13	12	8.3	2	2	1.4	3	2.1	4.85	71	.240	.269	-2	-2	96	65	-0.9	-0	0	-0.1
1987	Pit-N	0	0	—	1	0	0	0	0	1	1	9.0	1	0	0.0	0	0.0	9.00	47	.250	.250	-1	-1	105	104	0.0	0	0	0.0
1988	Tor-A	0	0	—	3	0	0	0	0	7	5	6.4	0	4	5.1	4	5.1	5.14	76	.185	.281	-1	-1	99	32	0.0	0	-0	0.0
Total	5	1	2	.333	18	0	0	0	1	29	22	6.8	3	6	1.9	12	3.7	4.03	89	.200	.239	-1	-1	97	50	-0.4	-0	0	0.1

■ FRANK ROSSO Rosso, Francis James b: 3/1/21, Agawam, Mass. d: 1/26/80, Ulrichsville, O. BR/TR, 5'11", 180 lbs. Deb: 9/15/44

YEAR	TM/L	W	L	PCT	G	GS	CG	SHO	SV	IP	H	H/G	HR	BB	BB/G	SO	SO/G	ERA	/A	OAVG	OOBP	PR	/A	PF	CPI	WAT	PB	PD	TPI
1944	NY-N	0	0	—	2	0	0	0	0	4	11	24.8	0	3	6.8	1	2.3	9.00	42	.550	.583	-2	-2	105	158	0.0	0	0	-0.1

■ MARV ROTBLATT Rotblatt, Marvin "Rotty" b: 10/18/27, Chicago, Ill. BB/TL, 5'7", 160 lbs. Deb: 7/04/48

YEAR	TM/L	W	L	PCT	G	GS	CG	SHO	SV	IP	H	H/G	HR	BB	BB/G	SO	SO/G	ERA	/A	OAVG	OOBP	PR	/A	PF	CPI	WAT	PB	PD	TPI
1948	Chi-A	0	1	.000	7	2	0	0	0	18	19	9.5	0	23	11.5	4	2.0	8.00	53	.271	.453	-7	-7	100	78	-0.4	-0	-1	-0.7
1950	Chi-A	0	0	—	2	0	0	0	0	9	11	11.0	2	5	5.0	6	6.0	6.00	76	.344	.421	-1	-1	99	131	0.0	-0	0	0.0
1951	Chi-A	4	2	.667	26	2	0	0	2	48	44	8.3	4	23	4.3	20	3.8	3.38	117	.244	.332	4	3	96	114	0.9	-2	1	0.2
Total	3	4	3	.571	35	4	0	0	2	75	74	8.9	6	51	6.1	30	3.6	4.80	85	.262	.376	-5	-6	97	107	0.5	-2	1	-0.5

■ JACK ROTHROCK Rothrock, John Houston b: 3/14/05, Long Beach, Cal. d: 2/2/80, San Bernardino, Cal BB/TR, 5'11.5", 165 lbs. Deb: 7/28/25

YEAR	TM/L	W	L	PCT	G	GS	CG	SHO	SV	IP	H	H/G	HR	BB	BB/G	SO	SO/G	ERA	/A	OAVG	OOBP	PR	/A	PF	CPI	WAT	PB	PD	TPI
1928	Bos-A	0	0	—	1	0	0	0	0	1	0	0.0	0	0	0.0	0	0.0	0.00	—	.000	.000	0	0	101	81	-0.4	0	0	-0.2

■ LARRY ROTHSCHILD Rothschild, Lawrence Lee b: 3/12/54, Chicago, Ill. BL/TR, 6'2", 180 lbs. Deb: 9/11/81

YEAR	TM/L	W	L	PCT	G	GS	CG	SHO	SV	IP	H	H/G	HR	BB	BB/G	SO	SO/G	ERA	/A	OAVG	OOBP	PR	/A	PF	CPI	WAT	PB	PD	TPI
1981	Det-A	0	0	—	5	0	0	0	1	6	4	6.0	0	6	9.0	1	1.5	1.50	256	.200	.370	1	2	105	243	0.0	0	0	0.2
1982	Det-A	0	0	—	2	0	0	0	0	3	4	12.0	1	2	6.0	0	0.0	12.00	34	.333	.429	-3	-3	100	72	0.0	0	0	-0.2
Total	2	0	0	—	7	0	0	0	1	9	8	8.0	1	8	8.0	1	1.0	5.00	78	.250	.390	-1	-1	103	186	0.0	0	0	0.0

■ GENE ROUNSAVILLE Rounsaville, Virle Gene b: 9/27/44, Konawa, Okla. BR/TR, 6'3", 205 lbs. Deb: 4/07/70

YEAR	TM/L	W	L	PCT	G	GS	CG	SHO	SV	IP	H	H/G	HR	BB	BB/G	SO	SO/G	ERA	/A	OAVG	OOBP	PR	/A	PF	CPI	WAT	PB	PD	TPI
1970	Chi-A	0	1	.000	8	0	0	0	0	6	10	15.0	1	2	3.0	3	4.5	10.50	38	.357	.387	-5	-4	108	68	-0.4	0	0	-0.3

■ JACK ROWAN Rowan, John Albert b: 6/16/1887, New Castle, Pa. d: 9/29/66, Dayton, Ohio BR/TR, 6'1", 210 lbs. Deb: 9/06/06

YEAR	TM/L	W	L	PCT	G	GS	CG	SHO	SV	IP	H	H/G	HR	BB	BB/G	SO	SO/G	ERA	/A	OAVG	OOBP	PR	/A	PF	CPI	WAT	PB	PD	TPI
1906	Det-A	0	1	.000	1	1	1	0	0	9	15	15.0	0	6	6.0	0	0.0	11.00	27	.400	.483	-8	-8	110	67	-0.4	0	-0	-0.5
1908	Cin-N	3	3	.500	8	7	4	1	0	49	46	8.4	0	16	2.9	24	4.4	1.84	133	.277	.340	3	3	104	149	0.2	-1	1	0.5
1909	Cin-N	11	12	.478	38	23	14	0	0	226	185	7.4	0	104	4.1	81	3.2	2.79	87	.233	.324	-5	-9	94	94	-0.6	-1	-5	-1.4
1910	Cin-N	14	13	.519	42	30	18	4	1	261	242	8.3	4	105	3.6	108	3.7	2.93	106	.254	.334	3	5	102	105	1.0	2	-4	0.3
1911	Phi-N	2	4	.333	12	6	2	0	0	45	59	11.8	3	20	4.0	17	3.4	4.80	76	.316	.385	-7	-6	108	111	-1.0	-1	1	-0.5
	Chi-N	0	0	—	1	0	0	0	0	2	1	4.5	0	2	9.0	0	0.0	4.50	71	.143	.400	-0	-0	94	73	0.0	-0	0	0.0
	Yr	2	4	.333	13	6	2	0	0	47	60	11.5	3	22	4.2	17	3.3	4.79	76	.308	.381	-7	-6	107	73	-1.0	-1	1	-0.5
1913	Cin-N	0	4	.000	5	5	5	0	0	39	37	8.5	0	9	2.1	21	4.8	3.00	111	.264	.303	1	1	104	95	-1.9	1	-0	0.2
1914	Cin-N	1	3	.250	12	2	0	0	2	39	38	8.8	1	10	2.3	16	3.7	3.46	86	.262	.300	-3	-2	107	81	-0.6	-1	-1	-0.3
Total	7	31	40	.437	119	74	44	5	3	670	623	8.4	8	272	3.7	267	3.6	3.08	93	.257	.334	-17	-16	100	102	-3.3	0	-8	-1.7

■ DAVE ROWE Rowe, David E. b: 2/1856, Jacksonville, Ill. BR , 5'9", 180 lbs. Deb: 5/30/1877 M

YEAR	TM/L	W	L	PCT	G	GS	CG	SHO	SV	IP	H	H/G	HR	BB	BB/G	SO	SO/G	ERA	/A	OAVG	OOBP	PR	/A	PF	CPI	WAT	PB	PD	TPI
1877	Chi-N	0	1	.000	1	1	0	0	0	1	3	27.0	0	2	18.0	0	0.0	18.00	15	.524	.647	-2	-2	99	95	-0.4	0	0	0.0
1882	Cle-N	0	1	.000	1	1	1	0	0	9	29	29.0	3	7	7.0	0	0.0	12.00	22	.541	.594	-9	-9	90	151	-0.4	0	0	-0.5
1883	Bal-a	0	0	—	1	0	0	0	0	4	12	27.0	1	2	4.5	1	2.3	20.25	18	.521	.559	-8	-7	113	78	0.0	0	0	-0.4
1884	StL-U	1	0	1.000	1	1	1	0	0	9	10	10.0	0	0	0.0	2	2.0	2.00	148	.287	.287	1	1	98	148	0.5	0	0	0.1
Total	4	1	2	.333	4	3	2	0	0	23	54	21.1	4	11	4.3	3	1.2	9.78	30	.460	.507	-17	-18	98	135	-0.3	1	0	-0.8

■ DON ROWE Rowe, Donald Howard b: 4/3/36, Brawley, Cal. BL/TL, 6', 180 lbs. Deb: 4/09/63 C

YEAR	TM/L	W	L	PCT	G	GS	CG	SHO	SV	IP	H	H/G	HR	BB	BB/G	SO	SO/G	ERA	/A	OAVG	OOBP	PR	/A	PF	CPI	WAT	PB	PD	TPI
1963	NY-N	0	0	—	26	1	0	0	0	55	59	9.7	6	21	3.4	27	4.4	4.25	80	.280	.342	-6	-5	104	107	0.0	0	-1	-0.5

■ KEN ROWE Rowe, Kenneth Darrell b: 12/31/33, Ferndale, Mich. BR/TR, 6'2", 185 lbs. Deb: 4/14/63 C

YEAR	TM/L	W	L	PCT	G	GS	CG	SHO	SV	IP	H	H/G	HR	BB	BB/G	SO	SO/G	ERA	/A	OAVG	OOBP	PR	/A	PF	CPI	WAT	PB	PD	TPI
1963	LA-N	1	1	.500	14	0	0	0	1	28	28	9.0	2	11	3.5	12	3.9	2.89	106	.264	.328	1	1	94	136	-0.1	-0	-0	0.0
1964	Bal-A	1	0	1.000	6	0	0	0	0	4	10	22.5	1	1	2.3	4	9.0	9.00	42	.455	.440	-2	-2	103	129	0.5	-0	0	-0.1
1965	Bal-A	0	0	—	6	0	0	0	0	13	17	11.8	0	2	1.4	3	2.1	3.46	99	.321	.317	-0	-0	99	121	0.0	-0	-1	0.0
Total	3	2	1	.667	26	0	0	0	1	45	55	11.0	3	14	2.8	19	3.8	3.60	90	.304	.338	-1	-2	96	131	0.4	-0	-0	-0.1

■ SCHOOLBOY ROWE Rowe, Lynwood Thomas b: 1/11/10, Waco, Tex. d: 1/8/61, El Dorado, Ark. BR/TR, 6'4.5", 210 lbs. Deb: 4/15/33 C

YEAR	TM/L	W	L	PCT	G	GS	CG	SHO	SV	IP	H	H/G	HR	BB	BB/G	SO	SO/G	ERA	/A	OAVG	OOBP	PR	/A	PF	CPI	WAT	PB	PD	TPI
1933	Det-A	7	4	.636	19	15	8	1	0	123	129	9.4	7	31	2.3	75	5.5	3.59	127	.269	.309	10	13	107	105	1.7	-0	2	1.5
1934	Det-A	24	8	.750	45	30	20	3	1	266	259	8.8	12	81	2.7	149	5.0	3.45	122	.256	.307	31	23	94	99	5.2	12	-0	3.2
1935	Det-A	19	13	.594	42	34	21	**6**	3	276	272	8.9	11	68	2.2	140	4.6	3.68	112	.255	.298	24	13	93	85	-0.6	13	-2	2.3
1936	Det-A	19	10	.655	41	35	19	4	3	245	266	9.8	15	64	2.4	115	4.2	4.52	106	.275	.317	14	7	95	89	4.3	8	2	1.4
1937	Det-A	1	4	.200	10	2	1	0	0	31	49	14.2	7	9	2.6	6	1.7	8.71	57	.350	.388	-14	-13	108	86	-1.6	-0	0	-1.0
1938	Det-A	0	2	.000	4	3	0	0	0	21	20	8.6	1	11	4.7	4	1.7	3.00	158	.256	.333	4	4	99	137	-0.9	0	1	0.4
1939	Det-A	10	12	.455	28	24	8	1	0	164	192	10.5	17	61	3.3	51	2.8	4.99	101	.291	.347	-7	1	110	101	-1.6	2	0	0.4
1940	Det-A	16	3	**.842**	27	23	11	1	0	169	170	9.1	15	43	2.3	61	3.2	3.46	138	.259	.303	17	24	109	105	6.2	5	-0	3.0
1941	Det-A	8	6	.571	27	14	4	0	1	139	155	10.0	6	33	2.1	54	3.5	4.14	107	.278	.314	0	5	107	89	1.2	5	1	1.1
1942	Det-A	1	0	1.000	2	1	0	0	0	10	9	8.1	0	2	1.8	7	6.3	0.00		.220	.256	4	5	113	0	0.5	-1	0	0.5
	Bro-N	1	0	1.000	9	2	0	0	0	30	36	10.8	2	12	3.6	6	1.8	5.40	60	.288	.353	-7	-7	97	85	0.5	0	0	-0.6
1943	Phi-N	14	8	.636	27	25	11	3	1	199	194	8.8	7	29	**1.3**	52	2.4	2.94	110	.247	.274	10	6	96	82	4.6	17	0	0.7
1946	Phi-N	11	4	.733	17	16	9	2	0	136	112	7.4	3	21	1.4	51	3.4	2.12	158	.224	.258	20	18	98	85	**4.1**	2	-2	2.1
1947	Phi-N	14	10	.583	31	28	15	1	1	196	232	10.7	22	45	**2.1**	74	3.4	4.32	96	.292	.329	-5	-4	102	105	4.1	9	-1	0.4
1948	Phi-N	10	10	.500	30	20	8	0	2	148	167	10.2	5	31	1.9	46	2.8	4.07	94	.281	.314	-2	-4	97	89	1.4	2	1	-0.1
1949	Phi-N	3	7	.300	23	6	2	0	0	65	68	9.4	2	17	2.4	22	3.0	4.85	84	.300	.337	-6	-6	101	91	-2.1	2	1	-0.2
Total	15	158	101	.610	382	278	137	22	12	2218	2330	9.5	132	558	2.3	913	3.7	3.88	109	.268	.310	92	86	99	93	27.0	77	1	15.1

■ MIKE ROWLAND Rowland, Michael Evan b: 1/31/53, Chicago, Ill. BR/TR, 6'3", 205 lbs. Deb: 7/25/80

YEAR	TM/L	W	L	PCT	G	GS	CG	SHO	SV	IP	H	H/G	HR	BB	BB/G	SO	SO/G	ERA	/A	OAVG	OOBP	PR	/A	PF	CPI	WAT	PB	PD	TPI
1980	SF-N	1	1	.500	19	0	0	0	0	27	20	6.7	2	8	2.7	8	2.7	2.33	149	.206	.266	4	3	96	97	0.1	0	-0	0.3
1981	SF-N	0	1	.000	9	1	0	0	0	16	13	7.3	1	6	3.4	8	4.5	3.38	109	.232	.303	0	1	105	95	-0.4	0	0	0.1
Total	2	1	2	.333	28	1	0	0	0	43	33	6.9	3	14	2.9	16	3.3	2.72	130	.216	.280	4	4	100	96	-0.3	0	-0	0.4

■ CHARLIE ROY Roy, Charles Robert b: 6/22/1884, Beaulieu, Minn. d: 2/10/50, Blackfoot, Idaho 5'10", 190 lbs. Deb: 6/27/06

YEAR	TM/L	W	L	PCT	G	GS	CG	SHO	SV	IP	H	H/G	HR	BB	BB/G	SO	SO/G	ERA	/A	OAVG	OOBP	PR	/A	PF	CPI	WAT	PB	PD	TPI
1906	Phi-N	0	1	.000	7	1	0	0	0	18	24	12.0	0	5	2.5	6	3.0	5.00	49	.355	.408	-5	-5	93	94	-0.4	-1	-0	-0.5

■ EMILE ROY Roy, Emile Arthur b: 5/26/07, Brighton, Mass. BR/TR, 5'11", 180 lbs. Deb: 9/30/33

YEAR	TM/L	W	L	PCT	G	GS	CG	SHO	SV	IP	H	H/G	HR	BB	BB/G	SO	SO/G	ERA	/A	OAVG	OOBP	PR	/A	PF	CPI	WAT	PB	PD	TPI
1933	Phi-A	0	1	.000	1	1	0	0	0	2	4	18.0	0	4	18.0	3	13.5	31.50	12	.364	.533	-6	-6	92	36	-0.4	0	0	-0.4

■ JEAN-PIERRE ROY Roy, Jean-Pierre b: 6/26/20, Montreal, Que., Can. BB/TR, 5'10", 160 lbs. Deb: 5/05/46

YEAR	TM/L	W	L	PCT	G	GS	CG	SHO	SV	IP	H	H/G	HR	BB	BB/G	SO	SO/G	ERA	/A	OAVG	OOBP	PR	/A	PF	CPI	WAT	PB	PD	TPI
1946	Bro-N	0	0	—	3	1	0	0	0	6	5	7.5	2	5	7.5	6	9.0	10.50	33	.200	.333	-5	-5	100	47	0.0	-0	-0	-0.4

YEAR	TM/L	W	L	PCT	G	GS	CG	SHO	SV	IP	H	H/G	HR	BB	BB/G	SO	SO/G	ERA	/A	OAVG	OOBP	PR	/A	PF	CPI	WAT	PB	PD	TPI
■ **LUTHER ROY**	Roy, Luther Franklin b: 7/29/02, Ooltewah, Tenn. d: 7/24/63, Grand Rapids, Mich. BR/TR, 5'10.5", 161 lbs. Deb: 6/12/24																												
1924	Cle-A	0	5	.000	16	5	2	0	0	49	62	11.4	3	31	5.7	14	2.6	7.71	53	.318	.396	-19	-20	97	76	-2.4	-0	1	-1.6
1925	Cle-A	0	0	—	6	1	0	0	0	10	14	12.6	1	11	9.9	1	0.9	3.60	130	.368	.500	1	1	107	249	0.0	-0	-0	0.0
1927	Chi-N	3	1	.750	11	0	0	0	0	20	14	6.3	0	11	4.9	5	2.3	2.25	172	.209	.317	4	4	99	120	0.9	0	0	0.4
1929	Phi-N	3	6	.333	21	12	1	0	0	89	137	13.9	11	37	3.7	16	1.6	8.39	63	.350	.402	-36	-31	112	84	-1.2	2	1	-2.3
	Bro-N	0	0	—	2	0	0	0	0	4	4	9.0	0	2	4.5	0	0.0	4.50	101	.286	.353	0	0	96	99	0.0	-0	0	0.0
	Yr	3	6	.333	23	12	1	0	0	93	141	13.6	11	39	3.8	16	1.5	8.23	64	.346	.394	-36	-31	111	99	-1.2	2	1	-2.3
Total	4	6	12	.333	56	18	3	0	0	172	231	12.1	15	92	4.8	36	1.9	7.12	66	.328	.397	-51	-46	105	95	-2.7	2	1	-3.5
■ **NORMIE ROY**	Roy, Norman Brooks "Jumbo" b: 11/15/28, Newton, Mass. BR/TR, 6', 200 lbs. Deb: 4/23/50																												
1950	Bos-N	4	3	.571	19	6	2	0	1	60	72	10.8	7	39	5.8	25	3.8	5.10	69	.305	.405	-6	-10	85	122	0.3	0	0	-0.9
■ **DICK ROZEK**	Rozek, Richard Louis b: 3/27/27, Cedar Rapids, Iowa BL/TL, 6'0.5", 190 lbs. Deb: 4/29/50																												
1950	Cle-A	0	0	—	12	2	0	0	0	25	28	10.1	3	19	6.8	14	5.0	5.04	87	.283	.395	-1	-2	95	115	0.0	-1	-1	-0.2
1951	Cle-A	0	0	—	7	1	0	0	0	15	18	10.8	1	11	6.6	5	3.0	3.00	127	.286	.390	2	1	93	185	0.0	0	-0	0.1
1952	Cle-A	1	0	1.000	10	1	0	0	0	13	11	7.6	0	13	9.0	5	3.5	4.85	67	.224	.387	-2	-2	88	81	0.5	-0	0	-0.2
1953	Phi-A	0	0	—	2	0	0	0	0	11	8	6.5	3	9	7.4	2	1.6	4.91	86	.222	.370	-1	-1	105	120	0.0	-0	-0	0.0
1954	Phi-A	0	0	—	2	0	0	0	0	1	0	0.0	0	3	27.0	0	0.0	9.00	43	.000	.444	-1	-1	105	88	0.0	0	0	0.0
Total	5	1	0	1.000	33	4	0	0	0	65	65	9.0	7	55	7.6	26	3.6	4.57	87	.260	.390	-3	-4	95	125	0.5	-1	-1	-0.3
■ **DAVE ROZEMA**	Rozema, David Scott b: 8/5/56, Grand Rapids, Mich. BR/TR, 6'4", 185 lbs. Deb: 4/11/77																												
1977	Det-A	15	7	.682	28	28	16	1	0	218	222	9.2	25	34	**1.4**	92	3.8	3.10	138	.265	.296	24	29	105	116	**5.0**	0	0	3.0
1978	Det-A	9	12	.429	28	28	11	2	0	209	205	8.8	17	41	1.8	57	2.5	3.14	129	.260	.292	15	21	107	103	-2.2	0	-1	2.1
1979	Det-A	4	4	.500	16	16	4	1	0	97	101	9.4	12	30	2.8	33	3.1	3.53	115	.270	.323	8	6	96	123	-0.1	0	0	0.6
1980	Det-A	6	9	.400	42	13	2	1	4	145	152	9.4	11	49	3.0	49	3.0	3.91	108	.277	.332	2	5	105	106	-1.7	0	1	0.6
1981	Det-A	5	5	.500	28	9	2	2	3	104	99	8.6	12	25	2.2	46	4.0	3.63	106	.256	.303	0	2	105	101	-0.4	0	-1	0.2
1982	Det-A	3	0	1.000	8	2	0	0	1	28	17	5.5	2	7	2.3	15	4.8	1.61	254	.179	.234	8	8	100	104	1.5	0	1	0.9
1983	Det-A	8	3	.727	29	16	1	0	2	105	100	8.6	10	29	2.5	63	5.4	3.43	112	.248	.295	8	5	95	97	2.1	0	1	0.6
1984	Det-A	7	6	.538	29	16	0	0	0	101	110	9.8	13	18	1.6	48	4.3	3.74	101	.274	.306	3	0	94	107	-1.0	0	1	0.1
1985	Tex-A	3	7	.300	34	4	0	0	7	88	100	10.2	10	22	2.3	42	4.3	4.19	109	.287	.332	-0	4	110	109	-1.1	0	1	0.4
1986	Tex-A	0	0	—	6	0	0	0	0	11	19	15.5	1	3	2.5	3	2.5	5.73	70	.404	.423	-2	-2	95	138	0.0	0	0	-0.1
Total	10	60	53	.531	248	132	36	7	17	1106	1125	9.2	113	258	2.1	448	3.6	3.47	118	.266	.307	64	78	103	108	2.1	0	3	8.4
■ **JORGE RUBIO**	Rubio, Jorge Jesus (Chavez) b: 4/23/45, Mexicali, Mexico BR/TR, 6'3", 200 lbs. Deb: 4/21/66																												
1966	Cal-A	2	1	.667	7	4	1	1	0	27	22	7.3	2	16	5.3	27	9.0	3.00	114	.220	.325	1	1	100	117	0.5	-1	-0	0.0
1967	Cal-A	0	2	.000	3	3	0	0	0	15	18	10.8	2	9	5.4	4	2.4	3.60	86	.316	.443	-1	-1	96	197	-0.9	1	0	0.0
Total	2	2	3	.400	10	7	1	1	0	42	40	8.6	4	25	5.4	31	6.6	3.21	103	.255	.368	1	0	98	145	-0.4	-0	-0	0.0
■ **DAVE RUCKER**	Rucker, David Michael b: 9/1/57, San Bernardino, Cal BL/TL, 6'1", 185 lbs. Deb: 4/12/81																												
1981	Det-A	0	0	—	2	0	0	0	0	4	3	6.8	0	1	2.3	2	4.5	6.75	57	.188	.278	-1	-1	105	20	0.0	0	0	0.0
1982	Det-A	5	6	.455	27	4	1	0	0	64	62	8.7	4	23	3.2	31	4.4	3.38	121	.251	.318	5	5	100	101	-0.6	0	0	0.5
1983	Det-A	1	2	.333	4	3	0	0	0	9	18	18.0	2	8	8.0	6	6.0	17.00	23	.419	.519	-13	-13	95	69	-0.5	0	0	-1.0
	StL-N	5	3	.625	34	0	0	0	0	37	36	8.8	1	18	4.4	22	5.4	2.68	134	.263	.348	4	4	98	142	1.1	-0	0	0.4
1984	StL-N	2	3	.400	50	0	0	0	0	73	62	7.6	0	34	4.2	38	4.7	2.10	169	.237	.319	12	12	99	140	-0.5	-0	-1	1.1
1985	Phi-N	3	2	.600	39	3	0	0	1	79	83	9.5	6	40	4.6	41	4.7	4.33	85	.279	.357	-6	-6	102	108	0.7	2	0	-0.3
1986	Phi-N	0	2	.000	19	0	0	0	0	25	34	12.2	4	14	5.0	14	5.0	5.76	67	.340	.403	-6	-5	104	124	-0.9	0	0	-0.4
1988	Pit-N	0	2	.000	31	0	0	0	0	28	39	12.5	2	9	2.9	16	5.1	4.82	70	.328	.366	-4	-5	97	115	-0.9	-0	-0	-0.4
Total	7	16	20	.444	206	10	1	0	1	319	337	9.5	19	147	4.1	170	4.8	3.98	93	.276	.350	-9	-10	100	117	-1.6	1	1	-0.1
■ **NAP RUCKER**	Rucker, George Napoleon b: 9/30/1884, Crabapple, Ga. d: 12/19/70, Alpharetta, Ga. BR/TL, 5'11", 190 lbs. Deb: 4/15/07																												
1907	Bro-N	15	13	.536	37	30	26	4	0	275	242	7.9	3	80	2.6	131	4.3	2.06	115	.266	.330	12	9	96	119	2.9	-1	-1	0.9
1908	Bro-N	17	19	.472	42	35	30	6	1	333	265	7.2	1	125	3.4	199	5.4	2.08	111	.249	.339	10	8	99	113	4.3	-0	4	1.4
1909	Bro-N	13	19	.406	38	33	28	6	1	309	245	7.1	6	101	2.9	201	5.9	2.24	119	.228	.303	12	15	103	106	1.4	-5	-3	1.4
1910	Bro-N	17	18	.486	41	39	**27**	6	0	**320**	293	8.2	5	84	2.4	147	4.1	2.59	114	.251	.306	16	13	98	100	2.6	-1	-2	1.1
1911	Bro-N	22	18	.550	48	33	23	5	4	316	255	7.3	12	110	3.1	190	5.4	2.71	125	.226	.300	24	24	99	93	5.4	2	1	2.7
1912	Bro-N	18	21	.462	45	34	23	**6**	4	298	272	8.2	6	72	2.2	151	4.6	2.20	150	.242	.289	40	37	97	96	3.3	2	2	4.1
1913	Bro-N	14	15	.483	41	33	16	4	3	260	236	8.2	3	67	2.3	111	3.8	2.87	117	.249	.296	10	14	105	91	1.5	2	-4	1.3
1914	Bro-N	7	6	.538	16	16	5	0	0	104	113	9.8	3	27	2.3	35	3.0	3.38	83	.275	.316	-7	-7	101	92	0.7	2	0	-0.3
1915	Bro-N	9	4	.692	19	15	7	1	1	123	134	9.8	3	28	2.0	38	2.8	2.41	116	.279	.315	5	5	102	138	2.4	1	1	0.9
1916	Bro-N	2	1	.667	9	4	1	0	0	37	34	8.3	0	7	1.7	14	3.4	1.70	154	.241	.282	4	4	100	119	0.2	-1	0	0.3
Total	10	134	134	.500	336	272	186	38	14	2375	2089	7.9	41	701	2.7	1217	4.6	2.42	119	.247	.309	126	123	100	104	24.7	1	-0	13.8
■ **ERNIE RUDOLPH**	Rudolph, Ernest William b: 2/13/10, Black River Falls Wis. BL/TR, 5'8", 165 lbs. Deb: 6/16/45																												
1945	Bro-N	1	0	1.000	7	0	0	0	0	9	12	12.0	1	7	7.0	3	3.0	5.00	72	.333	.422	-1	-1	95	145	0.5	1	0	0.0
■ **DON RUDOLPH**	Rudolph, Frederick Donald b: 8/16/31, Baltimore, Md. d: 9/12/68, Granada Hills, Cal BL/TL, 5'11", 195 lbs. Deb: 9/21/57																												
1957	Chi-A	1	0	1.000	5	0	0	0	0	12	6	4.5	2	2	1.5	2	1.5	2.25	162	.146	.186	2	2	97	52	0.5	1	-0	0.2
1958	Chi-A	1	0	1.000	7	0	0	0	1	7	4	5.1	0	5	6.4	2	2.6	2.57	143	.190	.346	1	1	98	114	0.5	0	0	0.1
1959	Chi-A	0	0	—	4	0	0	0	1	3	4	12.0	0	2	6.0	0	0.0	0.00	—	.333	.429	1	1	95	0	0.0	0	0	0.2
	Cin-N	0	0	—	5	0	0	0	0	7	13	16.7	1	3	3.9	8	10.3	5.14	79	.394	.444	-1	-1	103	166	0.0	-0	0	0.0
1962	Cle-A	0	0	—	1	0	0	0	0	⅓	1	27.0	0	0	0.0	0	0.0	0.00	—	1.000	1.000	0	0	99	0	0.0	0	0	0.0
	Was-A	8	10	.444	37	23	6	2	0	176	187	9.6	13	42	2.1	68	3.5	3.63	112	.274	.312	7	8	102	104	1.1	1	-1	0.9
	Yr	8	10	.444	38	23	6	2	0	176	188	9.6	13	42	2.1	68	3.5	3.63	112	.275	.313	7	8	102	104	1.1	0	-1	0.9
1963	Was-A	7	19	.269	37	26	4	0	1	174	189	9.8	28	36	1.9	70	3.6	4.55	81	.275	.310	-18	-17	101	97	-3.2	2	-1	-1.5
1964	Was-A	1	3	.250	28	8	0	0	0	70	81	10.4	10	12	1.5	32	4.1	4.11	91	.290	.316	-4	-3	103	108	-0.6	-1	-0	-0.3
Total	6	18	32	.360	124	57	10	2	3	449	485	9.7	54	102	2.0	182	3.6	4.01	96	.276	.313	-12	-8	102	101	-1.7	3	-1	-0.4
■ **DICK RUDOLPH**	Rudolph, Richard "Baldy" b: 8/25/1887, New York, N.Y. d: 10/20/49, Bronx, N.Y. BR/TR, 5'9.5", 160 lbs. Deb: 9/30/10 C																												
1910	NY-N	0	1	.000	3	1	1	0	2	12	21	15.8	0	2	1.5	9	6.8	7.50	37	.350	.371	-6	-6	92	69	-0.4	0	-0	-0.5
1911	NY-N	0	0	—	1	0	0	0	0	2	2	9.0	0	0	0.0	0	0.0	9.00	37	.250	.250	-1	-1	99	18	0.0	0	0	0.0
1913	Bos-N	14	13	.519	33	22	17	1	0	249	258	9.3	4	59	2.1	109	3.9	2.93	105	.276	.309	8	4	96	109	1.8	5	4	1.3
1914	Bos-N	**27**	10	.730	42	36	31	6	0	336	288	7.7	9	61	1.6	138	3.7	2.36	120	.238	.271	16	18	102	87	6.7	-2	2	2.1
1915	Bos-N	22	19	.537	44	43	30	3	1	341	304	8.0	4	64	1.7	147	3.9	2.38	113	.242	.275	14	12	97	92	-0.4	5	0	1.9
1916	Bos-N	19	12	.613	41	38	27	4	3	312	266	7.7	7	38	**1.1**	133	3.8	2.16	110	.235	**.255**	16	8	91	86	1.3	1	6	1.5
1917	Bos-N	13	13	.500	31	30	22	5	0	243	252	9.3	1	54	2.0	96	3.6	3.41	77	.272	.307	-19	-21	97	88	0.9	2	1	-1.9
1918	Bos-N	9	10	.474	21	20	15	3	0	154	144	8.4	2	30	1.8	48	2.8	2.57	102	.255	.283	3	1	95	96	0.9	-1	1	0.1
1919	Bos-N	13	18	.419	37	32	24	2	2	274	282	9.3	2	54	1.8	76	2.5	2.17	134	.276	.302	23	23	100	**142**	0.3	3	0	3.0
1920	Bos-N	4	8	.333	18	12	3	0	0	89	104	10.5	4	24	2.4	24	2.4	4.04	77	.294	.335	-9	-9	99	95	-1.1	0	0	-0.9
1922	Bos-N	0	2	.000	3	3	1	0	0	16	22	12.4	2	5	2.8	3	1.7	5.06	79	.328	.365	-2	-2	98	112	-0.9	0	0	0.0
1923	Bos-N	1	2	.333	4	4	1	0	0	19	27	12.8	0	10	4.7	3	1.4	3.79	108	.333	.409	0	1	102	150	0.0	-1	0	0.0
1927	Bos-N	0	0	—	1	0	0	0	0	1	1	9.0	0	1	9.0	0	0.0	0.00	—	.200	.333	0	0	95	0	0.0	0	0	0.0
Total	13	122	108	.530	279	241	172	25	8	2048	1971	8.7	35	402	1.8	786	3.5	2.66	104	.258	.290	44	25	97	99	9.1	13	15	6.6
■ **DUTCH RUETHER**	Ruether, Walter Henry b: 9/13/1893, Alameda, Cal. d: 5/16/70, Phoenix, Ariz. BL/TL, 6'1.5", 180 lbs. Deb: 4/13/17																												
1917	Chi-N	2	0	1.000	10	4	1	0	0	36	37	9.3	0	12	3.0	23	5.8	2.50	114	.285	.340	1	1	105	152	1.0	2	1	0.2
	Cin-N	1	2	.333	7	4	1	1	0	36	43	10.8	0	14	3.5	12	3.0	3.50	72	.323	.383	-3	-4	93	139	-0.4	2	-0	-0.3
	Yr	3	2	.600	17	8	2	1	0	72	80	10.0	0	26	3.3	35	4.4	3.00	89	.301	.352	-2	-3	99	139	0.6	2	0	-0.1
1918	Cin-N	0	1	.000	2	2	1	0	0	10	10	9.0	0	3	2.7	10	9.0	2.70	98	.244	.298	0	-0	96	93	-0.4	-0	0	0.0
1919	Cin-N	19	6	**.760**	33	29	20	3	0	243	195	7.2	1	83	3.1	78	2.9	1.81	162	.223	.290	30	30	101	120	3.4	5	-2	3.9

YEAR	TM/L	W	L	PCT	G	GS	CG	SHO	SV	IP	H	H/G	HR	BB	BB/G	SO	SO/G	ERA	/A	OAVG	OOBP	PR	/A	PF	CPI	WAT	PB	PD	TPI
1920	Cin-N	16	12	.571	37	33	23	5	3	266	235	8.0	2	96	3.2	99	3.3	2.47	112	.247	.313	20	9	88	106	1.3	0	0	0.8
1921	Bro-N	10	13	.435	36	27	12	1	2	211	247	10.5	7	67	2.9	78	3.3	4.27	93	.299	.343	-11	-7	105	97	-1.8	11	-0	0.5
1922	Bro-N	21	12	.636	35	35	26	2	0	267	290	9.8	11	92	3.1	89	3.0	3.54	110	.282	.335	17	11	95	109	**5.5**	6	-0	1.5
1923	Bro-N	15	14	.517	34	34	20	0	0	275	308	10.1	11	86	2.8	87	2.8	4.22	92	.287	.336	-7	-10	98	93	0.8	4	-2	-0.6
1924	Bro-N	8	13	.381	30	21	13	2	3	168	190	10.2	4	45	2.4	63	3.4	3.91	97	.282	.325	-1	-2	98	92	-4.1	2	1	0.1
1925	Was-A	18	7	.720	30	29	16	1	0	223	241	9.7	5	105	4.2	68	2.7	3.87	108	.281	.355	13	8	95	107	3.3	6	-3	1.4
1926	Was-A	12	6	.667	23	23	9	0	0	169	214	11.4	5	66	3.5	48	2.6	4.85	81	.311	.364	-15	-18	97	99	2.7	4	-2	-1.5
	NY-A	2	3	.400	5	5	1	0	0	36	32	8.0	0	18	4.5	8	2.0	3.50	111	.248	.331	2	2	97	93	-0.7	-2	-1	0.2
	Yr	14	9	.609	28	28	10	0	0	205	246	10.8	5	84	3.7	56	2.5	4.61	85	.300	.354	-13	-16	97	93	2.0	4	-3	-1.3
1927	NY-A	13	6	.684	27	26	12	3	0	184	202	9.9	9	52	2.5	45	2.2	3.38	115	.287	.332	16	10	94	**120**	-0.4	5	0	1.4
Total	11	137	95	.591	309	272	155	18	8	2124	2244	9.5	55	739	3.1	708	3.0	3.50	104	.277	.333	60	31	97	106	10.2	45	-8	7.6
■ BRUCE RUFFIN	Ruffin, Bruce Wayne b: 10/4/63, Lubbock, Tex BR/TL, 6'2", 205 lbs. Deb: 6/28/86																												
1986	Phi-N	9	4	.692	21	21	6	0	0	146	138	8.5	6	44	2.7	70	4.3	2.47	157	.251	.305	20	23	104	125	2.3	-3	-1	2.0
1987	Phi-N	11	14	.440	35	35	3	1	0	205	236	10.4	17	73	3.2	93	4.1	4.35	98	.298	.352	-6	-2	105	112	-1.5	-5	-1	-0.6
1988	Phi-N	6	10	.375	55	15	3	0	3	144	151	9.4	7	80	5.0	82	5.1	4.44	80	.275	.362	-16	-14	103	103	-0.5	-0	1	-1.3
Total	3	26	28	.481	111	71	12	1	3	495	525	9.5	30	197	3.6	245	4.5	3.82	103	.278	.342	-1	7	104	113	0.3	-8	-1	0.1
■ RED RUFFING	Ruffing, Charles Herbert b: 5/3/04, Granville, Ill. d: 2/17/86, Mayfield Hts., O. BR/TR, 6'1.5", 205 lbs. Deb: 5/31/24 CH																												
1924	Bos-A	0	0	—	8	2	0	0	0	23	29	11.3	0	9	3.5	10	3.9	6.65	67	.333	.402	-6	-6	105	83	0.0	-0	-0	-0.5
1925	Bos-A	9	18	.333	37	27	13	3	1	217	253	10.5	10	75	3.1	64	2.7	5.02	87	.299	.345	-15	-16	99	88	0.6	0	-1	-1.4
1926	Bos-A	6	15	.286	37	22	6	0	2	166	169	9.2	4	68	3.7	58	3.1	4.39	97	.274	.334	-7	-3	106	87	-0.5	-0	-1	-0.3
1927	Bos-A	5	13	.278	26	18	10	0	2	158	160	9.1	7	87	5.0	77	4.4	4.67	88	.277	.357	-9	-10	99	96	-1.5	2	0	-0.7
1928	Bos-A	10	25	.286	42	34	**25**	1	2	289	303	9.4	8	96	3.0	118	3.7	3.89	105	.275	.328	5	7	101	96	-4.8	12	-3	1.5
1929	Bos-A	9	22	.290	35	30	18	1	1	244	280	10.3	17	118	4.4	109	4.0	4.87	92	.297	.360	-17	-11	105	103	-4.1	5	-1	-0.3
1930	Bos-A	0	3	.000	4	3	1	0	0	24	32	12.0	1	6	2.3	14	5.3	6.38	70	.323	.342	-5	-5	96	83	-1.4	1	-1	-0.3
	NY-A	15	5	.750	34	25	12	2	1	198	200	9.1	10	62	2.8	117	5.3	4.14	98	.260	.312	11	-2	87	87	4.7	17	-3	1.0
	Yr	15	8	.652	38	28	13	2	1	222	232	9.4	11	68	2.8	131	5.3	4.38	94	.267	.315	7	-7	88	87	3.3	1	-3	0.7
1931	NY-A	16	14	.533	37	30	19	1	2	237	240	9.1	11	87	3.3	132	5.0	4.41	93	.256	.320	-1	-8	94	83	-2.3	10	-3	0.0
1932	NY-A	18	7	.720	35	29	22	3	2	259	219	7.6	16	115	4.0	**190**	**6.6**	3.09	132	**.226**	.307	40	28	91	105	1.2	13	-2	3.7
1933	NY-A	9	14	.391	35	28	18	0	3	235	230	8.8	7	93	3.6	122	4.7	3.91	97	.258	.325	10	-3	88	95	-4.4	8	-0	0.3
1934	NY-A	19	11	.633	36	31	19	5	0	256	232	8.2	18	104	3.7	149	**5.2**	3.94	106	.236	.306	16	7	93	84	1.1	6	-3	0.8
1935	NY-A	16	11	.593	30	29	19	2	0	222	201	8.1	17	76	3.1	81	3.3	3.12	129	.239	.301	33	22	90	103	0.0	13	-2	3.1
1936	NY-A	20	12	.625	33	33	25	3	0	271	274	9.1	22	90	3.0	102	3.4	3.85	118	.263	.319	36	20	90	106	-1.1	15	2	3.3
1937	NY-A	20	7	.741	31	31	22	4	0	256	242	8.5	17	68	2.4	131	4.6	2.99	150	.247	.294	46	43	97	104	3.6	2	-4	4.0
1938	NY-A	**21**	7	**.750**	31	31	22	3	0	247	246	9.0	16	82	3.0	127	4.6	3.32	147	.258	.314	**40**	**42**	102	110	4.6	9	-2	**4.8**
1939	NY-A	21	7	.750	28	28	22	**5**	0	233	211	8.2	15	75	2.9	95	3.7	2.94	134	.240	.298	44	26	85	109	2.7	10	-2	3.1
1940	NY-A	15	12	.556	30	30	20	3	0	226	218	8.7	24	76	3.0	97	3.9	3.38	124	.252	.311	25	21	96	114	-0.4	-3	-3	1.4
1941	NY-A	15	6	.714	23	23	13	2	0	186	177	8.6	13	54	2.6	60	2.9	3.53	111	.252	.301	13	8	95	96	2.0	11	-3	1.6
1942	NY-A	14	7	.667	24	24	16	4	0	194	183	8.5	10	41	1.9	80	3.7	3.20	107	.250	.290	10	5	94	93	0.0	6	-2	1.0
1945	NY-A	7	3	.700	11	11	8	1	0	87	85	8.8	2	20	2.1	24	2.5	2.90	123	.251	.291	5	6	106	91	1.9	0	-2	0.6
1946	NY-A	5	1	.833	8	8	4	2	0	61	37	5.5	2	23	3.4	19	2.8	1.77	193	.171	.247	12	11	98	66	1.9	-1	-1	1.1
1947	Chi-A	3	5	.375	9	9	1	0	0	53	63	10.7	7	16	2.7	11	1.9	6.11	60	.290	.336	-14	-14	99	78	-0.6	-0	-0	-1.3
Total	22	273	225	.548	624	536	335	45	16	4342	4284	8.9	254	1541	3.2	1987	4.1	3.80	109	.258	.317	271	173	95	97	3.2	135	-34	26.5
■ VERN RUHLE	Ruhle, Vernon Gerald b: 1/25/51, Coleman, Mich. BR/TR, 6'1", 185 lbs. Deb: 9/09/74																												
1974	Det-A	2	0	1.000	5	3	1	0	0	33	35	9.5	1	6	1.6	10	2.7	2.73	143	.273	.304	3	4	108	116	1.0	0	-1	0.4
1975	Det-A	11	12	.478	32	31	8	3	0	190	199	9.4	17	65	3.1	67	3.2	4.03	100	.266	.327	-5	0	106	96	2.4	0	-2	-0.2
1976	Det-A	9	12	.429	32	32	5	1	0	200	227	10.2	19	59	2.7	88	4.0	3.92	94	.288	.335	-9	-5	105	113	-0.7	0	-0	-0.5
1977	Det-A	3	5	.375	14	10	0	0	0	66	83	11.3	9	15	2.0	27	3.7	5.73	75	.305	.344	-12	-11	105	89	-0.6	0	-1	-1.0
1978	Hou-N	3	3	.500	13	10	2	2	0	68	57	7.5	0	20	2.6	27	3.6	2.12	160	.224	.280	11	10	95	94	0.2	-1	-1	0.9
1979	Hou-N	2	6	.250	13	10	2	2	0	66	64	8.7	9	8	1.1	33	4.5	4.09	83	.249	.275	-3	-5	90	77	-2.1	-1	-1	-0.6
1980	Hou-N	12	4	.750	28	22	6	2	0	159	148	8.4	7	29	1.6	55	3.1	2.38	147	.251	.282	22	20	97	116	3.5	4	-1	2.4
1981	Hou-N	4	6	.400	20	15	1	0	1	102	97	8.6	6	20	1.8	39	3.4	2.91	104	.250	.286	7	1	87	98	-1.4	3	-2	0.3
1982	Hou-N	9	13	.409	31	21	3	2	1	149	169	10.2	12	24	1.4	56	3.4	3.93	92	.289	.315	-5	-5	100	102	-1.6	-1	-1	-0.7
1983	Hou-N	8	5	.615	41	9	0	0	3	115	107	8.4	13	36	2.8	43	3.4	3.68	89	.249	.304	-1	-5	90	98	1.3	0	1	-0.4
1984	Hou-N	1	9	.100	40	6	0	0	2	90	112	11.2	5	29	2.9	60	6.0	4.60	72	.309	.356	-10	-13	92	105	-3.9	0	1	-1.2
1985	Cle-A	2	10	.167	42	16	1	0	3	125	139	10.0	16	30	2.2	54	3.9	4.32	92	.283	.321	-2	-5	95	104	-3.3	0	-0	-0.4
1986	Cal-A	1	3	.250	16	3	0	0	1	48	46	8.6	5	7	1.3	23	4.3	4.13	97	.247	.274	0	-1	95	73	-1.0	0	1	0.0
Total	13	67	88	.432	327	188	29	12	11	1411	1483	9.5	119	348	2.2	582	3.7	3.73	97	.270	.313	-4	-15	98	101	-6.2	5	-7	-1.0
■ ANDY RUSH	Rush, Jesse Howard b: 12/26/1889, Longton, Kan. d: 3/16/69, Fresno, Cal. BR/TR, 6'3", 180 lbs. Deb: 4/16/25																												
1925	Bro-N	0	1	.000	4	2	0	0	0	10	16	14.4	3	5	4.5	4	3.6	9.00	45	.364	.412	-5	-5	95	98	-0.4	-0	0	-0.4
■ BOB RUSH	Rush, Robert Ransom b: 12/21/25, Battle Creek, Mich BR/TR, 6'4", 205 lbs. Deb: 4/22/48																												
1948	Chi-N	5	11	.313	36	16	4	0	0	133	153	10.4	8	37	2.5	72	4.9	3.92	96	.287	.330	0	-3	95	106	-2.1	-1	1	-0.2
1949	Chi-N	10	18	.357	35	27	9	1	4	201	197	8.8	10	79	3.5	80	3.6	4.07	97	.255	.321	-1	-3	97	86	-1.5	-7	1	-0.8
1950	Chi-N	13	20	.394	39	34	19	1	1	255	261	9.2	11	93	3.3	93	3.3	3.71	120	.265	.329	12	21	107	100	-1.1	-1	2	2.2
1951	Chi-N	11	12	.478	37	29	12	2	2	211	212	9.0	16	68	2.9	129	5.5	3.84	103	.254	.308	3	3	100	89	1.7	-0	1	0.4
1952	Chi-N	17	13	.567	34	32	17	4	0	250	205	7.4	14	81	2.9	157	5.7	2.70	143	.216	.280	29	32	103	88	2.4	7	2	**4.7**
1953	Chi-N	9	14	.391	29	28	8	1	0	167	177	9.5	17	66	3.6	84	4.5	4.53	101	.270	.339	-4	1	106	97	-0.9	-3	1	0.0
1954	Chi-N	13	15	.464	33	32	11	0	0	236	213	8.1	12	103	3.9	124	4.7	3.78	110	.243	.319	8	10	102	85	1.4	7	3	2.1
1955	Chi-N	13	11	.542	33	33	14	3	0	234	204	7.8	19	73	2.8	130	5.0	3.50	117	.234	.291	14	15	101	83	1.9	-4	1	1.4
1956	Chi-N	13	10	.565	32	32	13	1	0	240	210	7.9	30	59	2.2	104	3.9	3.19	119	.233	.277	16	16	101	92	3.7	-3	-2	1.2
1957	Chi-N	6	16	.273	31	29	5	0	0	205	211	9.3	16	66	2.9	103	4.5	4.39	86	.265	.315	-12	-14	98	84	-3.8	2	-2	-1.3
1958	Mil-N	10	6	.625	28	20	5	2	0	147	142	8.7	13	31	1.9	84	5.1	3.43	100	.253	.290	9	-0	87	90	0.6	2	-2	0.0
1959	Mil-N	5	6	.455	31	9	1	1	0	101	102	9.1	5	23	2.0	64	5.7	2.41	153	.257	.295	17	14	93	124	-0.9	0	-1	1.4
1960	Mil-N	2	0	1.000	10	0	0	0	1	15	24	14.4	2	5	3.0	8	4.8	4.20	80	.369	.397	-1	-1	89	174	1.0	1	0	0.0
	Chi-A	0	0	—	9	0	0	0	0	14	16	10.3	4	5	3.2	12	7.7	5.79	66	.302	.344	-3	-3	99	111	0.0	1	0	-0.1
Total	13	127	152	.455	417	321	118	16	8	2409	2327	8.7	177	789	2.9	1244	4.6	3.65	109	.251	.308	87	87	100	92	2.4	0	6	11.0
■ AMOS RUSIE	Rusie, Amos Wilson "The Hoosier Thunderbolt" b: 5/30/1871, Mooresville, Ind. d: 12/6/42, Seattle, Wash. BR/TR, 6'1", 200 lbs. Deb: 5/09/1889 H																												
1889	Ind-N	12	10	.545	33	22	19	1	0	225	246	9.8	12	116	4.6	109	4.4	5.32	83	.294	.380	-32	-22	110	85	2.4	-4	0	-2.0
1890	NY-N	29	34	.460	67	63	56	4	1	549	436	**7.1**	3	289	4.7	**341**	**5.6**	2.56	132	**.232**	.335	61	49	94	101	-2.4	12	6	6.1
1891	NY-N	33	20	.623	61	57	52	**6**	1	500	391	**7.0**	7	262	4.7	**337**	**6.1**	2.56	122	**.228**	.330	44	31	93	92	7.2	5	3	3.4
1892	NY-N	31	31	.500	64	61	58	2	0	532	405	6.9	7	267	4.5	288	4.9	2.88	112	.222	.322	24	21	98	83	2.8	-0	6	2.4
1893	NY-N	33	21	.611	**56**	52	**50**	**4**	1	**482**	451	**8.4**	15	218	4.1	**208**	**3.9**	3.23	**149**	**.263**	.346	**78**	**85**	103	108	8.0	2	5	**8.1**
1894	NY-N	**36**	13	.735	54	50	45	**3**	1	444	426	**8.6**	10	200	4.1	**195**	**4.0**	**2.78**	**189**	**.273**	.356	**126**	**122**	98	124	7.1	3	9	**11.1**
1895	NY-N	23	23	.500	49	47	42	**4**	0	393	384	8.8	9	159	3.6	**201**	**4.6**	3.73	121	.275	.349	46	34	94	93	-0.2	-4	4	2.7
1897	NY-N	28	10	.737	38	37	35	2	0	322	314	8.8	6	87	2.4	135	3.8	**2.54**	164	.277	.328	63	58	96	114	**6.8**	2	3	5.8
1898	NY-N	20	11	.645	37	36	33	4	1	300	288	8.6	6	103	3.1	114	3.4	3.03	112	.273	.338	19	12	94	101	4.9	-0	0	1.0
1901	Cin-N	0	1	.000	3	2	2	0	0	22	43	17.6	1	3	1.2	6	2.5	8.59	39	.434	.451	-13	-13	100	88	-0.4	-1	0	-0.9
Total	10	245	174	.585	462	427	392	30	5	3769	3384	8.1	76	1704	4.1	1934	4.6	3.07	129	.256	.341	417	372	97	100	36.2	14	35	37.7
■ ALLAN RUSSELL	Russell, Allan E. "Rubberarm" b: 7/31/1893, Baltimore, Md. d: 10/20/72, Baltimore, Md. BB/TR, 5'11", 165 lbs. Deb: 9/13/15																												
1915	NY-A	1	2	.333	5	3	1	0	0	27	21	7.0	1	21	7.0	21	7.0	2.67	109	.228	.377	1	1	99	144	-0.3	0	-0	0.0
1916	NY-A	6	10	.375	34	18	8	1	6	171	138	7.3	8	75	3.9	104	5.5	3.21	89	.232	.324	-7	-7	101	93	-2.3	-3	0	-0.9
1917	NY-A	7	8	.467	25	10	6	0	2	104	89	7.7	3	39	3.4	55	4.8	2.25	127	.236	.319	5	7	107	120	0.0	3	-1	1.1

YEAR	TM/L	W	L	PCT	G	GS	CG	SHO	SV	IP	H	H/G	HR	BB	BB/G	SO	SO/G	ERA	/A	OAVG	OOBP	PR	/A	PF	CPI	WAT	PB	PD	TPI
1918	NY-A	7	11	.389	27	18	7	2	4	141	139	8.9	6	73	4.7	54	3.4	3.26	80	.267	.352	-8	-10	94	118	-2.0	-1	-1	-1.2
1919	NY-A	5	5	.500	23	9	4	1	1	91	89	8.8	6	32	3.2	50	4.9	3.46	97	.251	.317	-2	-1	104	88	-0.6	0	0	0.0
	Bos-A	10	4	.714	21	11	9	1	4	121	105	7.8	0	39	2.9	63	4.7	2.53	116	.246	.310	9	6	91	96	3.3	-1	-1	0.3
	Yr	15	9	.625	44	20	13	2	**5**	212	194	8.2	6	71	3.0	113	4.8	2.93	106	.248	.311	7	4	97	96	2.7	0	-0	0.3
1920	Bos-A	5	6	.455	16	10	7	0	1	108	100	8.3	3	38	3.2	53	4.4	3.00	122	.251	.321	10	8	97	97	-0.1	-2	1	0.7
1921	Bos-A	7	11	.389	39	13	7	0	3	173	204	10.6	10	77	4.0	60	3.1	4.11	104	.303	.368	3	3	100	**122**	-1.9	-5	0	-0.1
1922	Bos-A	6	7	.462	34	11	1	0	2	126	152	10.9	6	57	4.1	34	2.4	5.00	80	.314	.373	-13	-14	99	104	0.8	-3	2	-1.3
1923	Was-A	10	7	.588	52	5	4	0	**9**	181	177	8.8	9	77	3.8	67	3.3	3.03	125	.270	.332	19	15	95	128	1.8	2	-3	1.3
1924	Was-A	5	1	.833	37	0	0	0	8	82	83	9.1	1	45	4.9	17	1.9	4.39	93	.282	.356	-1	-3	96	100	1.8	2	-0	-0.1
1925	Was-A	2	4	.333	32	2	0	0	2	69	85	11.1	6	37	4.8	25	3.3	5.74	73	.315	.384	-10	-12	95	100	-1.4	-1	2	-0.9
Total	11	71	76	.483	345	110	54	5	42	1394	1382	8.9	59	610	3.9	603	3.9	3.52	99	.269	.343	4	-6	98	109	-0.9	-10	-0	-1.1
■ LEFTY RUSSELL	Russell, Clarence Dickson b: 7/8/1890, Baltimore, Md. d: 1/22/62, Baltimore, Md. BL/TL, 6'1", 165 lbs. Deb: 10/01/10																												
1910	Phi-A	1	0	1.000	1	1	1	1	0	9	8	8.0	0	2	2.0	5	5.0	0.00	—	.258	.303	3	2	97	0	0.5	-0	0	0.3
1911	Phi-A	0	3	.000	7	2	0	0	0	32	45	12.7	1	18	5.1	7	2.0	7.59	39	.357	.456	-15	-16	88	89	-1.4	1	1	-1.3
1912	Phi-A	0	2	.000	5	2	1	0	0	17	18	9.5	1	14	7.4	9	4.8	7.41	44	.265	.412	-8	-8	97	72	-0.9	-0	0	-0.6
Total	3	1	5	.167	13	5	2	1	0	58	71	11.0	2	34	5.3	21	3.3	6.36	47	.316	.423	-20	-22	92	70	-1.8	1	1	-1.6
■ REB RUSSELL	Russell, Ewell Albert b: 4/12/1889, Jackson, Miss. d: 9/30/73, Indianapolis, Ind BL/TL, 5'11", 185 lbs. Deb: 4/18/13																												
1913	Chi-A	22	16	.579	**52**	36	26	8	4	317	250	7.1	2	79	2.2	122	3.5	1.90	147	.219	.273	36	31	95	86	3.3	2	-5	2.8
1914	Chi-A	8	12	.400	38	23	8	1	1	167	168	9.1	3	33	1.8	79	4.3	2.91	99	.268	.308	-3	-1	105	97	-1.3	3	0	0.3
1915	Chi-A	11	10	.524	41	25	10	3	2	229	215	8.4	0	47	1.8	90	3.5	2.59	106	.249	.292	9	4	94	88	-1.5	5	-2	0.7
1916	Chi-A	18	11	.621	56	25	16	5	3	264	207	7.1	1	42	**1.4**	112	3.8	2.42	124	.220	**.254**	12	17	106	60	1.8	-4	-1	1.3
1917	Chi-A	15	5	**.750**	35	24	11	5	3	189	170	8.1	1	32	**1.5**	54	2.6	1.95	127	.245	.279	15	11	93	101	3.2	5	-1	1.8
1918	Chi-A	7	5	.583	19	15	10	2	0	125	117	8.4	0	33	2.4	38	2.7	2.59	107	.252	.296	2	2	100	90	1.5	-1	-1	0.0
1919	Chi-A	0	0	—	1	0	0	0	0	0	1	—	0	1	—	0	—	—	—	1.000	1.000	0	0	102	0	0.0	0	0	0.0
Total	7	81	59	.579	242	148	81	24	13	1291	1128	7.9	7	267	1.9	495	3.5	2.34	120	.238	.281	71	65	99	85	7.0	10	-10	6.9
■ JACK RUSSELL	Russell, Jack Erwin b: 10/24/05, Paris, Tex. BR/TR, 6'1.5", 178 lbs. Deb: 5/05/26																												
1926	Bos-A	0	5	.000	36	5	1	0	0	98	94	8.6	2	24	2.2	17	1.6	3.58	119	.268	.305	5	7	106	88	-2.4	-0	4	1.1
1927	Bos-A	4	9	.308	34	15	4	1	0	147	172	10.5	5	40	2.4	25	1.5	4.10	100	.298	.334	1	-0	99	102	-0.4	-3	1	-0.1
1928	Bos-A	11	14	.440	32	26	10	2	0	201	233	10.4	6	41	1.8	27	1.2	3.85	106	.294	.323	4	6	101	101	1.6	-0	1	0.6
1929	Bos-A	6	18	.250	35	32	13	0	0	227	263	10.4	12	40	**1.6**	37	1.5	3.93	114	.290	.313	8	13	105	97	-4.4	-5	4	1.2
1930	Bos-A	9	20	.310	35	30	15	0	0	230	302	11.8	11	53	2.1	35	1.4	5.44	82	.321	.349	-20	-25	96	95	-1.3	-2	2	-2.2
1931	Bos-A	10	18	.357	36	31	13	0	0	232	298	11.6	7	65	2.5	45	1.7	5.16	82	.310	.351	-20	-24	97	94	-2.0	0	3	-1.8
1932	Bos-A	1	7	.125	11	6	1	0	0	40	61	13.7	2	15	3.4	7	1.6	6.75	68	.343	.392	-10	-10	102	93	-2.2	-1	0	-0.8
	Cle-A	5	7	.417	18	11	6	0	1	113	146	11.6	5	27	2.2	27	2.2	4.70	102	.310	.345	-3	1	107	103	-1.6	2	1	0.5
	Yr	6	14	.300	29	17	7	0	1	153	207	12.2	7	42	2.5	34	2.0	5.24	90	.319	.358	-13	-8	106	103	-3.8	-1	2	-0.3
1933	Was-A	12	6	.667	50	3	2	0	**13**	124	119	8.6	3	32	2.3	28	2.0	2.69	149	.255	.300	**22**	18	93	119	0.4	-1	4	2.0
1934	Was-A	5	10	.333	**54**	9	3	0	**7**	158	179	10.2	6	56	3.2	38	2.2	4.16	111	.287	.342	6	8	102	105	-1.8	2	2	1.2
1935	Was-A	4	9	.308	43	7	2	0	3	126	170	12.1	10	37	2.6	30	2.1	5.71	72	.324	.362	-18	-22	93	97	-2.0	1	3	-1.6
1936	Was-A	3	2	.600	18	5	1	0	3	50	66	11.9	3	25	4.5	6	1.1	6.30	77	.317	.382	-7	-8	96	94	0.4	-2	1	-0.7
	Bos-A	0	3	.000	23	2	0	0	0	40	57	12.8	2	16	3.6	9	2.0	5.62	95	.345	.390	-3	-1	106	115	-1.4	0	2	0.1
	Yr	3	5	.375	41	7	1	0	3	90	123	12.3	5	41	4.1	15	1.5	6.00	84	.330	.386	-10	-9	100	115	-1.0	-2	3	-0.6
1937	Det-A	2	5	.286	25	0	0	0	4	40	63	14.2	4	20	4.5	10	2.3	7.65	65	.362	.429	-13	-12	108	99	-1.7	-1	1	-0.9
1938	Chi-N	6	1	.857	42	0	0	0	3	102	100	8.8	1	30	2.6	29	2.6	3.35	116	.258	.306	5	6	103	92	2.3	1	3	1.0
1939	Chi-N	4	3	.571	39	0	0	0	3	69	78	10.2	3	24	3.1	32	4.2	3.65	107	.282	.331	**2**	2	100	108	0.2	-2	2	0.1
1940	StL-N	3	4	.429	26	0	0	0	1	54	53	8.8	1	26	4.3	16	2.7	2.50	156	.252	.326	8	8	101	141	-0.7	-2	1	0.8
Total	15	85	141	.376	557	182	71	3	38	2051	2454	10.8	83	571	2.5	418	1.8	4.46	97	.299	.338	-33	-32	100	100	-17.0	-11	35	0.5
■ JEFF RUSSELL	Russell, Jeffrey Lee b: 9/2/61, Cincinnati, Ohio BR/TR, 6'4", 200 lbs. Deb: 8/13/83																												
1983	Cin-N	4	5	.444	10	10	2	0	0	68	58	7.7	7	22	2.9	40	5.3	3.04	124	.233	.284	4	6	104	101	0.0	1	-0	0.7
1984	Cin-N	6	18	.250	33	30	4	2	0	182	186	9.2	15	65	3.2	101	5.0	4.25	91	.263	.324	-13	-8	107	91	-5.4	-0	1	-0.6
1985	Tex-A	3	6	.333	13	13	0	0	0	62	85	12.3	10	27	3.9	44	6.4	7.55	60	.324	.386	-23	-21	110	87	-0.5	0	1	-1.7
1986	Tex-A	5	2	.714	37	0	0	0	2	82	74	8.1	11	31	3.4	54	5.9	3.40	117	.244	.314	7	5	95	114	1.4	0	2	0.7
1987	Tex-A	5	4	.556	52	2	0	0	3	97	109	10.1	9	52	4.8	56	5.2	4.45	104	.285	.369	0	2	104	114	0.8	0	1	0.3
1988	Tex-A	10	9	.526	34	24	5	0	0	189	183	8.7	15	66	3.1	88	4.2	3.81	107	.257	.323	3	5	102	100	1.7	0	2	0.7
Total	6	33	44	.429	179	79	11	2	5	680	695	9.2	67	263	3.5	383	5.1	4.24	97	.266	.332	-21	-10	104	100	-2.0	1	6	0.1
■ JOHN RUSSELL	Russell, John Albert b: 10/20/1894, San Mateo, Cal. d: 11/19/30, Ely, Nev. BL/TL, 6'2", 195 lbs. Deb: 7/04/17																												
1917	Bro-N	0	1	.000	5	1	1	0	0	16	12	6.8	1	6	3.4	1	0.6	4.50	63	.222	.295	-3	-3	105	60	-0.4	0	-0	-0.2
1918	Bro-N	0	0	—	1	0	0	0	0	1	2	18.0	0	1	9.0	0	0.0	18.00	16	.500	.500	-2	-2	104	63	0.0	0	0	-0.1
1921	Chi-A	2	5	.286	11	9	4	0	0	66	82	11.2	3	35	4.8	15	2.0	5.32	82	.314	.386	-8	-7	102	101	-0.9	3	-1	-0.3
1922	Chi-A	0	1	.000	4	1	0	0	1	7	7	9.0	0	4	5.1	3	3.9	6.43	64	.280	.355	-2	-2	101	65	-0.4	-0	0	-0.1
Total	4	2	7	.222	21	11	5	0	1	90	103	10.3	4	46	4.6	19	1.9	5.40	75	.299	.371	-14	-13	103	90	-1.7	3	-1	-0.7
■ MARIUS RUSSO	Russo, Marius Ugo "Lefty" b: 7/19/14, Brooklyn, N.Y. BR/TL, 6'1", 190 lbs. Deb: 6/06/39																												
1939	NY-A	8	3	.727	21	11	9	2	2	116	86	6.7	6	41	3.2	55	4.3	2.41	164	.210	.277	29	20	85	107	0.5	2	2	2.2
1940	NY-A	14	8	.636	30	24	15	0	1	189	181	8.6	17	55	2.6	87	4.1	3.29	128	.249	.302	23	19	96	106	1.9	2	3	2.4
1941	NY-A	14	10	.583	28	27	17	3	1	210	195	8.4	8	87	3.7	105	4.5	3.09	127	.247	.319	25	20	95	109	-1.4	2	2	2.3
1942	NY-A	4	1	.800	9	5	2	0	0	45	41	8.2	2	14	2.8	15	3.0	2.80	123	.244	.304	4	3	94	111	1.0	1	0	0.4
1943	NY-A	5	10	.333	24	14	5	1	1	102	89	7.9	7	45	4.0	42	3.7	3.71	83	.235	.316	-5	-7	94	89	-3.7	1	0	-0.5
1946	NY-A	0	2	.000	8	3	0	0	0	19	26	12.3	1	11	5.2	7	3.3	4.26	80	.333	.416	-2	-2	98	143	-0.9	-1	0	-0.1
Total	6	45	34	.570	120	84	48	6	5	681	618	8.2	41	253	3.3	311	4.1	3.13	123	.242	.309	74	54	93	106	-2.6	8	8	6.7
■ RUST	Rust b:Louisville, Ky. Deb: 7/04/1882																												
1882	Bal-a	0	1	.000	1	1	0	0	0	5	10	18.0	0	1	1.8	0	0.0	7.20	38	.420	.443	-3	-2	102	106	-0.4	0	0	-0.1
■ DICK RUSTECK	Rusteck, Richard Frank b: 7/12/41, Chicago, Ill. BR/TL, 6'1", 175 lbs. Deb: 6/10/66																												
1966	NY-N	1	2	.333	8	3	1	1	0	24	24	9.0	1	8	3.0	9	3.4	3.00	116	.276	.333	2	1	97	126	-0.2	-1	-0	0.1
■ BABE RUTH	Ruth, George Herman "The Bambino" or "The Sultan Of Swat" b: 2/6/1895, Baltimore, Md. d: 8/16/48, New York, N.Y. BL/TL, 6'2", 215 lbs. Deb: 7/11/14 CH																												
1914	Bos-A	2	1	.667	4	3	1	0	0	23	21	8.2	1	7	2.7	3	1.2	3.91	67	.236	.292	-3	-3	96	60	0.3	0	-0	-0.2
1915	Bos-A	18	8	.692	32	28	16	1	0	218	166	6.9	3	85	3.5	112	4.6	2.44	116	.212	.294	12	9	96	84	1.1	15	1	2.8
1916	Bos-A	23	12	.657	44	41	23	**9**	1	324	230	**6.4**	0	118	3.3	170	4.7	**1.75**	149	**.201**	.280	**39**	31	92	90	3.5	14	1	**5.3**
1917	Bos-A	24	13	.649	41	38	**35**	6	2	326	244	6.7	2	108	3.0	128	3.5	2.02	140	.211	.284	23	29	106	85	3.2	15	2	5.8
1918	Bos-A	13	7	.650	20	19	18	1	0	166	125	6.8	1	49	2.7	40	2.2	2.22	116	.214	.267	10	6	93	73	1.6	12	4	0.7
1919	Bos-A	9	5	.643	17	15	12	0	1	133	148	10.0	2	58	3.9	30	2.0	2.98	99	.290	.365	4	-1	91	133	2.3	14	0	0.0
1920	NY-A	1	0	1.000	1	1	0	0	0	4	3	6.8	0	2	4.5	0	0.0	4.50	83	.200	.294	-0	-0	99	35	0.5	1	0	0.0
1921	NY-A	2	0	1.000	2	1	0	0	0	9	14	14.0	1	9	9.0	2	2.0	9.00	47	.350	.469	-5	-5	99	92	1.0	2	0	-0.3
1930	NY-A	1	0	1.000	1	1	1	0	0	9	11	11.0	0	2	2.0	3	3.0	3.00	135	.306	.333	2	1	87	142	0.5	1	1	0.1
1933	NY-A	1	0	1.000	1	1	1	0	0	9	12	12.0	0	3	3.0	0	0.0	5.00	76	.308	.357	-1	-1	88	92	0.5	1	-0	0.0
Total	10	94	46	.671	163	148	107	17	4	1221	974	7.2	10	441	3.3	488	3.6	2.28	122	.221	.295	81	68	96	89	14.5	75	8	14.2
■ JOHNNY RUTHERFORD	Rutherford, John William "Doc" b: 5/5/25, Belleville, Ont., Canada BL/TR, 5'10.5", 170 lbs. Deb: 4/30/52																												
1952	Bro-N	7	7	.500	22	11	4	0	2	97	97	9.0	9	29	2.7	29	2.7	4.27	86	.262	.314	-6	-7	98	90	-1.4	2	1	-0.3
■ DICK RUTHVEN	Ruthven, Richard David b: 3/27/51, Sacramento, Cal. BR/TR, 6'3", 190 lbs. Deb: 4/17/73																												
1973	Phi-N	6	9	.400	25	23	3	1	1	128	125	8.8	10	75	5.3	98	6.9	4.22	95	.257	.357	-8	-3	109	101	-0.6	-1	1	-0.3
1974	Phi-N	9	13	.409	35	35	6	0	0	213	182	7.7	11	116	4.9	153	6.5	4.01	94	.231	.326	-9	-6	104	81	-2.0	-1	-1	-0.7

YEAR	TM/L	W	L	PCT	G	GS	CG	SHO	SV	IP	H	H/G	HR	BB	BB/G	SO	SO/G	ERA	/A	OAVG	OOBP	PR	/A	PF	CPI	WAT	PB	PD	TPI
1975	Phi-N	2	2	.500	11	7	0	0	0	41	37	8.1	2	22	4.8	26	5.7	4.17	88	.243	.339	-2	-2	101	85	0.0	-0	-0	-0.2
1976	Atl-N	14	17	.452	36	36	8	4	0	240	255	9.6	14	90	3.4	142	5.3	4.20	94	.275	.339	-19	-7	112	97	0.7	-1	2	-0.4
1977	Atl-N	7	13	.350	25	23	6	2	0	151	158	9.4	14	62	3.7	84	5.0	4.23	107	.267	.332	-5	5	115	97	-0.7	3	-2	0.7
1978	Atl-N	2	6	.250	13	13	2	1	0	81	78	8.7	8	28	3.1	45	5.0	4.11	99	.257	.310	-5	-0	114	91	-1.6	-2	-0	-0.1
	Phi-N	13	5	.722	20	20	9	2	0	151	136	8.1	13	28	1.7	75	4.5	2.98	125	.248	.277	10	12	104	102	3.6	4	-0	1.8
	Yr	15	11	.577	33	33	11	3	0	232	214	8.3	21	56	2.2	120	4.7	3.38	114	.250	.289	5	12	107	102	2.0	-2	-0	1.7
1979	Phi-N	7	5	.583	20	20	3	2	0	122	121	8.9	10	37	2.7	58	4.3	4.28	85	.256	.309	-7	-9	97	80	0.9	0	-2	-1.0
1980	Phi-N	17	10	.630	33	33	6	1	0	223	241	9.7	9	74	3.0	86	3.5	3.55	108	.283	.337	1	7	106	111	2.4	4	-0	1.1
1981	Phi-N	12	7	.632	23	22	5	0	0	147	162	9.9	10	54	3.3	80	4.9	5.14	76	.281	.338	-27	-20	112	83	2.0	-1	-0	-2.0
1982	Phi-N	11	11	.500	33	31	8	2	0	204	189	8.3	18	59	2.6	115	5.1	3.79	89	.246	.299	-4	-10	94	87	-1.0	-2	-2	-1.4
1983	Phi-N	1	3	.250	7	7	0	0	0	34	46	12.2	5	10	2.6	26	6.9	5.56	65	.333	.368	-7	-7	100	108	-1.0	-0	0	-0.6
	Chi-N	12	9	.571	25	25	5	2	0	149	156	9.4	17	28	1.7	73	4.4	4.11	90	.269	.300	-8	-7	101	90	2.8	2	2	-0.2
	Yr	13	12	.520	32	32	5	2	0	183	202	9.9	22	38	1.9	99	4.9	4.38	84	.279	.314	-15	-14	101	90	1.8	-0	2	-0.8
1984	Chi-N	6	10	.375	23	22	0	0	0	127	154	10.9	14	41	2.9	55	3.9	5.03	78	.302	.354	-20	-16	109	101	-3.1	0	-0	-1.5
1985	Chi-N	4	7	.364	20	15	0	0	0	87	103	10.7	6	37	3.8	26	2.7	4.55	92	.299	.357	-9	-3	117	107	-1.3	-0	-1	-0.4
1986	Chi-N	0	0	—	6	0	0	0	0	11	12	9.8	4	6	4.9	3	2.5	4.91	82	.293	.383	-1	-1	108	150	0.0	-0	-0	-0.1
Total	14	123	127	.492	355	332	61	17	1	2109	2155	9.2	165	767	3.3	1145	4.9	4.14	93	.267	.327	-121	-68	106	95	1.1	6	-4	-5.3

■ **CYCLONE RYAN** Ryan, Daniel R. b: 1866, Capperwhite, Ireland d: 1/30/17, Medfield, Mass. TR , 6', Deb: 8/08/1887

YEAR	TM/L	W	L	PCT	G	GS	CG	SHO	SV	IP	H	H/G	HR	BB	BB/G	SO	SO/G	ERA	/A	OAVG	OOBP	PR	/A	PF	CPI	WAT	PB	PD	TPI
1887	NY-a	0	1	.000	2	1	0	0	0	2	5	22.5	1	6	27.0	0	0.0	27.00	15	.485	.675	-5	-5	92	82	-0.4	0	0	-0.3
1891	Bos-N	0	0	—	1	0	0	0	0	3	2	6.0	0	1	3.0	0	0.0	0.00	—	.201	.274	1	1	109	0	0.0	-0	0	0.1
Total	2	0	1	.000	3	1	0	0	0	5	7	12.6	1	7	12.6	0	0.0	10.80	35	.345	.513	-4	-4	102	33	-0.4	-0	0	-0.2

■ **JACK RYAN** Ryan, Jack "Gulfport" b: 9/19/1884, Lawrenceville, Ill. d: 10/16/49, Hondsboro, Miss. TR , 5'10", 165 lbs. Deb: 7/02/08

YEAR	TM/L	W	L	PCT	G	GS	CG	SHO	SV	IP	H	H/G	HR	BB	BB/G	SO	SO/G	ERA	/A	OAVG	OOBP	PR	/A	PF	CPI	WAT	PB	PD	TPI
1908	Cle-A	1	1	.500	8	1	1	0	1	36	27	6.8	3	2	0.5	7	1.8	2.25	110	.220	.238	1	1	103	92	0.0	0	0	0.1
1909	Bos-A	4	3	.571	13	8	2	0	0	61	65	9.6	0	20	3.0	24	3.5	3.25	83	.281	.349	-5	-4	108	104	0.0	0	-0	-0.4
1911	Bro-N	0	1	.000	3	1	0	0	0	6	9	13.5	1	4	6.0	1	1.5	3.00	113	.375	.483	0	0	99	295	-0.4	-0	0	0.0
Total	3	5	5	.500	24	10	3	0	1	103	101	8.8	4	26	2.3	32	2.8	2.88	92	.267	.324	-4	-3	106	111	-0.4	0	-0	-0.3

■ **JIMMY RYAN** Ryan, James Edward "Pony" b: 2/11/1863, Clinton, Mass. d: 10/26/23, Chicago, Ill. BR/TL, 5'9", 162 lbs. Deb: 1885

YEAR	TM/L	W	L	PCT	G	GS	CG	SHO	SV	IP	H	H/G	HR	BB	BB/G	SO	SO/G	ERA	/A	OAVG	OOBP	PR	/A	PF	CPI	WAT	PB	PD	TPI
1886	Chi-N	0	0	—	5	0	0	0	1	23	19	7.4	2	13	5.1	15	5.9	4.70	77	.237	.343	-4	-3	110	77	0.0	1	0	-0.1
1887	Chi-N	2	1	.667	8	3	2	0	0	45	53	10.6	3	17	3.4	14	2.8	4.20	111	.309	.371	-1	2	115	114	0.3	2	0	0.2
1888	Chi-N	4	0	1.000	8	2	1	0	0	38	47	11.1	3	12	2.8	11	2.6	3.08	97	.318	.369	-1	-0	106	157	2.0	5	0	0.0
1891	Chi-N	0	0	—	2	0	0	0	1	6	11	16.5	0	2	3.0	2	3.0	1.50	234	.409	.450	1	1	105	464	0.0	1	0	0.1
1893	Chi-N	0	0	—	1	0	0	0	0	5	3	5.4	0	0	0.0	1	1.8	0.00	—	.186	.186	3	3	104	0	0.0	0	0	0.2
Total	5	6	1	.857	24	5	3	0	2	117	133	10.2	8	44	3.4	43	3.3	3.62	107	.301	.364	-2	3	110	134	2.3	9	0	0.4

■ **JOHNNY RYAN** Ryan, John Joseph b: Philadelphia, Pa. d: 3/22/02, Philadelphia, Pa. 5'7.5", 150 lbs. Deb: 8/19/1873

YEAR	TM/L	W	L	PCT	G	GS	CG	SHO	SV	IP	H	H/G	HR	BB	BB/G	SO	SO/G	ERA	/A	OAVG	OOBP	PR	/A	PF	CPI	WAT	PB	PD	TPI
1875	NH-n	1	5	.167	6																								
1876	Lou-N	0	0	—	1	0	0	0	0	8	22	24.8	0	0	0.0	1	1.1	5.63	44	.497	.497	-3	-3	106	174	0.0	-0	0	-0.1

■ **JOHN RYAN** Ryan, John M. b: Hamilton, Ohio Deb: 4/19/1884

YEAR	TM/L	W	L	PCT	G	GS	CG	SHO	SV	IP	H	H/G	HR	BB	BB/G	SO	SO/G	ERA	/A	OAVG	OOBP	PR	/A	PF	CPI	WAT	PB	PD	TPI
1884	Bal-U	3	2	.600	6	6	5	0	0	51	61	10.8	1	16	2.8	33	5.8	3.35	99	.302	.353	-2	-0	110	131	0.3	-3	0	-0.1

■ **NOLAN RYAN** Ryan, Lynn Nolan b: 1/31/47, Refugio, Tex. BR/TR, 6'2", 170 lbs. Deb: 9/11/66

YEAR	TM/L	W	L	PCT	G	GS	CG	SHO	SV	IP	H	H/G	HR	BB	BB/G	SO	SO/G	ERA	/A	OAVG	OOBP	PR	/A	PF	CPI	WAT	PB	PD	TPI
1966	NY-N	0	1	.000	2	1	0	0	0	3	5	15.0	1	3	9.0	6	18.0	15.00	23	.357	.471	-4	-4	97	69	-0.4	0	0	-0.3
1968	NY-N	6	9	.400	21	18	3	0	0	134	93	6.2	12	75	5.0	133	8.9	3.09	99	.200	.308	-2	-0	103	99	-0.8	-1	-2	-0.3
1969	NY-N	6	3	.667	25	10	2	0	1	89	60	6.1	3	53	5.4	92	9.3	3.54	101	.189	.304	1	0	99	66	0.6	-1	-2	-0.2
1970	NY-N	7	11	.389	27	19	5	2	1	132	86	5.9	10	97	6.6	125	8.5	3.41	123	.188	.328	9	11	103	96	-2.3	-1	-1	1.0
1971	NY-N	10	14	.417	30	26	3	0	0	152	125	7.4	8	116	6.9	137	8.1	3.97	84	.219	.363	-8	-11	96	95	-2.4	-0	-1	-1.2
1972	Cal-A	19	16	.543	39	39	20	**9**	0	284	166	**5.3**	14	157	5.0	**329**	**10.4**	2.28	120	**.171**	.289	25	15	90	88	2.5	1	-2	1.4
1973	Cal-A	21	16	.568	41	39	26	4	1	326	238	6.6	18	162	4.5	**383**	**10.6**	2.87	128	.203	.300	34	29	96	88	3.6	0	-2	2.9
1974	Cal-A	22	16	.579	42	41	26	3	0	**333**	221	**6.0**	18	202	5.5	**367**	**9.9**	2.89	116	**.190**	.310	27	17	93	89	6.3	0	1	2.0
1975	Cal-A	14	12	.538	28	28	10	5	0	198	152	6.9	13	132	6.0	186	8.5	3.45	105	.213	.337	7	4	96	98	2.5	0	-1	0.2
1976	Cal-A	17	18	.486	39	39	21	**7**	0	284	193	**6.1**	13	183	5.8	**327**	**10.4**	3.36	98	**.195**	.319	5	-3	93	83	0.7	0	0	-0.2
1977	Cal-A	19	16	.543	37	37	**22**	4	0	299	198	**6.0**	12	204	6.1	**341**	**10.3**	2.77	139	**.193**	.323	**43**	36	95	103	3.4	0	0	3.8
1978	Cal-A	10	13	.435	31	31	14	3	0	235	183	7.0	12	148	5.7	**260**	**10.0**	3.71	103	.220	.331	2	3	101	89	-2.4	0	1	0.4
1979	Cal-A	16	14	.533	34	34	17	**5**	0	223	169	**6.8**	15	114	4.6	**223**	**9.0**	3.59	108	**.212**	.308	16	7	92	82	-0.2	0	-0	0.6
1980	Hou-N	11	10	.524	35	35	4	2	0	234	205	7.9	10	98	3.8	200	7.7	3.35	105	.236	.312	7	4	97	90	-0.9	-1	-1	0.0
1981	Hou-N	11	5	.688	21	21	5	3	0	149	99	**6.0**	2	68	4.1	140	8.5	**1.69**	**179**	**.188**	.278	**30**	22	87	104	2.7	3	-1	2.8
1982	Hou-N	16	12	.571	35	35	10	3	0	250	196	7.1	20	109	3.9	245	8.8	3.17	113	**.213**	.298	12	12	100	89	3.0	-2	-0	1.0
1983	Hou-N	14	9	.609	29	29	5	2	0	196	134	**6.2**	9	101	4.6	183	8.4	2.98	110	**.195**	.297	14	6	90	80	2.3	-3	-0	0.2
1984	Hou-N	12	11	.522	30	30	5	2	0	184	143	7.0	12	69	3.4	197	9.6	3.03	109	.211	.284	11	5	92	82	0.7	-1	-3	0.1
1985	Hou-N	10	12	.455	35	35	4	0	0	232	205	8.0	12	95	3.7	209	8.1	3.80	91	.239	.314	-5	-9	96	86	-1.3	-1	-3	-1.3
1986	Hou-N	12	8	.600	30	30	1	0	0	178	119	6.0	14	82	4.1	194	9.8	3.34	113	.188	.281	8	9	102	69	0.2	-3	-1	0.5
1987	Hou-N	8	16	.333	34	34	0	0	0	212	154	**6.5**	14	87	3.7	**270**	**11.5**	**2.76**	138	**.199**	.281	**31**	25	93	84	-3.8	-3	-1	2.1
1988	Hou-N	12	11	.522	33	33	4	1	0	220	186	7.6	18	87	3.6	**228**	**9.3**	3.52	92	.227	.301	-2	-7	93	91	0.4	-3	-3	-1.3
Total	22	273	253	.519	678	644	207	55	3	4547	3330	6.6	260	2442	4.8	4775	9.5	3.15	111	.205	.308	263	172	95	88	14.4	-16	-21	14.2

■ **ROSY RYAN** Ryan, Wilfred Patrick Dolan b: 3/15/1898, Worcester, Mass. d: 12/10/80, Scottsdale, Ariz. BL/TR, 6', 185 lbs. Deb: 9/07/19

YEAR	TM/L	W	L	PCT	G	GS	CG	SHO	SV	IP	H	H/G	HR	BB	BB/G	SO	SO/G	ERA	/A	OAVG	OOBP	PR	/A	PF	CPI	WAT	PB	PD	TPI
1919	NY-N	1	2	.333	4	3	1	0	0	20	20	9.0	0	9	4.0	7	3.1	3.15	89	.260	.341	-1	-1	96	107	-0.6	-1	-0	-0.1
1920	NY-N	0	1	.000	3	1	1	0	0	15	14	8.4	1	4	2.4	5	3.0	1.80	168	.259	.295	2	2	97	169	-0.4	-1	0	0.2
1921	NY-N	7	10	.412	36	16	5	0	3	147	140	8.6	6	32	2.0	58	3.6	3.73	95	.255	.290	1	-3	94	72	-2.9	1	-1	-0.3
1922	NY-N	17	12	.586	46	20	12	1	3	192	194	9.1	5	74	3.5	75	3.5	3.00	137	.269	.330	23	24	100	116	-0.4	1	-1	2.2
1923	NY-N	16	5	.762	**45**	15	7	0	4	173	169	8.8	8	46	2.4	58	3.0	3.49	113	.257	.300	10	9	99	87	4.3	0	0	0.9
1924	NY-N	8	6	.571	37	9	2	0	5	125	137	9.9	1	37	2.7	36	2.6	4.25	80	.285	.329	-5	-12	88	86	-0.4	-1	-2	-1.4
1925	Bos-N	2	8	.200	37	7	1	0	2	123	152	11.1	7	52	3.8	48	3.5	6.29	65	.303	.360	-28	-30	95	76	-2.8	3	-1	-2.5
1926	Bos-N	0	2	.000	7	2	0	0	0	19	29	13.7	1	7	3.3	1	0.5	7.58	44	.392	.409	-8	-9	88	95	-0.9	-0	-0	-0.8
1928	NY-A	0	0	—	3	0	0	0	0	6	17	25.5	1	1	1.5	5	7.5	16.50	22	.486	.500	-8	-9	89	77	0.0	-1	-0	-0.7
1933	Bro-N	1	1	.500	30	0	0	0	2	61	69	10.2	3	16	2.4	22	3.2	4.57	72	.276	.319	-8	-9	98	80	0.1	0	-0	-0.8
Total	10	52	47	.525	248	73	29	1	19	881	941	9.6	33	278	2.8	315	3.2	4.14	91	.277	.325	-22	-38	96	91	-4.0	1	-5	-3.3

■ **MIKE RYBA** Ryba, Dominic Joseph b: 6/9/03, De Lancey, Pa. d: 12/13/71, Brookline Station Mo. BR/TR, 5'11.5", 180 lbs. Deb: 9/22/35 C

YEAR	TM/L	W	L	PCT	G	GS	CG	SHO	SV	IP	H	H/G	HR	BB	BB/G	SO	SO/G	ERA	/A	OAVG	OOBP	PR	/A	PF	CPI	WAT	PB	PD	TPI
1935	StL-N	1	1	.500	2	1	1	0	0	16	15	8.4	0	1	0.6	6	3.4	3.38	120	.242	.250	1	1	100	55	-0.1	1	0	0.2
1936	StL-N	5	1	.833	14	0	0	0	0	45	55	11.0	3	16	3.2	25	5.0	5.40	70	.294	.346	-7	-8	95	87	1.9	-0	-1	-0.8
1937	StL-N	9	6	.600	38	8	5	0	0	135	152	10.1	8	40	2.7	57	3.8	4.13	94	.284	.331	-3	-4	100	100	1.3	4	0	0.1
1938	StL-N	1	1	.500	3	0	0	0	0	5	8	14.4	0	1	1.8	0	0.0	5.40	78	.348	.360	-1	-1	111	99	0.1	0	0	0.0
1941	Bos-A	7	3	.700	40	3	0	0	6	121	143	10.6	14	42	3.1	54	4.0	4.46	94	.297	.346	-4	-4	101	115	1.8	1	2	0.0
1942	Bos-A	3	3	.500	18	0	0	0	3	44	49	10.0	5	13	2.7	16	3.3	3.89	94	.278	.325	-1	-1	100	114	-0.5	1	1	0.1
1943	Bos-A	7	5	.583	40	8	4	1	2	144	142	8.9	4	57	3.6	50	3.1	3.25	106	.262	.328	1	3	104	108	1.6	-0	-1	0.3
1944	Bos-A	12	7	.632	42	7	2	0	2	138	119	7.8	7	39	2.5	50	3.3	3.33	100	.233	.284	2	-0	97	78	2.7	-0	3	0.2
1945	Bos-A	7	6	.538	34	9	4	1	2	123	122	8.9	5	33	2.4	44	3.2	2.49	130	.259	.301	12	10	96	127	1.0	2	-1	1.3
1946	Bos-A	0	1	.000	9	0	0	0	1	13	12	8.3	1	5	3.5	5	3.5	3.46	112	.261	.321	0	1	111	110	-0.4	1	-0	0.1
Total	10	52	34	.605	240	36	16	2	16	784	817	9.4	47	247	2.8	307	3.5	3.66	99	.269	.320	-1	-2	100	103	9.4	9	3	1.5

■ **GARY RYERSON** Ryerson, Gary Lawrence b: 6/7/48, Los Angeles, Cal. BR/TL, 6'1", 175 lbs. Deb: 6/28/72

YEAR	TM/L	W	L	PCT	G	GS	CG	SHO	SV	IP	H	H/G	HR	BB	BB/G	SO	SO/G	ERA	/A	OAVG	OOBP	PR	/A	PF	CPI	WAT	PB	PD	TPI
1972	Mil-A	3	8	.273	20	14	4	1	0	102	119	10.5	9	21	1.9	45	4.0	3.62	82	.290	.317	-6	-7	97	111	-1.9	-1	-1	-1.0
1973	Mil-A	0	1	.000	9	4	0	0	0	23	32	12.5	0	7	2.7	10	3.9	7.83	47	.327	.358	-10	-11	96	60	-0.4	0	0	-0.9
Total	2	3	9	.250	29	18	4	1	0	125	151	10.9	9	28	2.0	55	4.0	4.39	71	.297	.325	-16	-18	97	101	-2.3	-1	-1	-1.9

YEAR	TM/L	W	L	PCT	G	GS	CG	SHO	SV	IP	H	H/G	HR	BB	BB/G	SO	SO/G	ERA	/A	OAVG	OOBP	PR	/A	PF	CPI	WAT	PB	PD	TPI
■ BRET SABERHAGEN	Saberhagen, Bret William b: 4/11/64, Chicago Heights, Ill. BR/TR, 6'1", 160 lbs. Deb: 4/04/84																												
1984	KC-A	10	11	.476	38	18	2	1	1	158	138	7.9	13	36	2.1	73	4.2	3.47	114	.237	.278	9	9	99	82	-0.9	0	0	0.9
1985	KC-A	20	6	.769	32	32	10	1	0	235	211	8.1	19	38	1.5	158	6.1	2.87	146	.241	**.269**	33	35	101	98	6.7	0	2	3.9
1986	KC-A	7	12	.368	30	25	4	2	0	156	165	9.5	15	29	1.7	112	6.5	4.15	101	.268	.301	1	1	100	87	-2.1	0	1	0.2
1987	KC-A	18	10	.643	33	33	15	4	0	257	246	8.6	27	53	1.9	163	5.7	3.36	138	.252	.291	32	37	104	102	4.3	0	0	3.7
1988	KC-A	14	16	.467	35	35	9	0	0	261	271	9.3	18	59	2.0	171	5.9	3.79	107	.269	.307	5	8	103	95	-1.8	0	0	0.8
Total	5	69	55	.556	168	143	40	8	1	1067	1031	8.7	92	215	1.8	677	5.7	3.49	121	.254	.290	80	89	102	94	6.2	0	4	9.5
■ RAY SADECKI	Sadecki, Raymond Michael b: 12/26/40, Kansas City, Kan. BL/TL, 5'11", 180 lbs. Deb: 5/19/60																												
1960	StL-N	9	9	.500	26	26	7	1	0	157	148	8.5	15	86	4.9	95	5.4	3.78	107	.249	.341	-0	5	108	109	-1.0	-0	-2	0.4
1961	StL-N	14	10	.583	31	31	13	0	0	223	196	7.9	28	102	4.1	114	4.6	3.71	122	.238	.317	8	20	113	103	1.8	2	-5	1.9
1962	StL-N	6	8	.429	22	17	4	1	1	102	121	10.7	13	43	3.8	50	4.4	5.56	76	.296	.358	-18	-15	107	95	-1.2	-2	-2	-1.7
1963	StL-N	10	10	.500	36	28	4	1	1	193	198	9.2	25	78	3.6	136	6.3	4.10	85	.266	.336	-17	-14	106	108	-1.3	-1	-3	-1.7
1964	StL-N	20	11	.645	37	32	9	2	1	220	232	9.5	16	60	2.5	119	4.9	3.68	107	.273	.313	-4	6	111	104	3.1	2	-3	0.6
1965	StL-N	6	15	.286	36	28	4	0	1	173	192	10.0	26	64	3.3	122	6.3	5.20	72	.284	.340	-32	-28	106	96	-4.7	2	-2	-2.7
1966	StL-N	2	1	.667	5	3	1	0	0	24	16	6.0	2	9	3.4	21	7.9	2.25	160	.188	.260	4	4	100	91	0.5	2	0	0.6
	SF-N	3	7	.300	26	19	3	1	0	105	125	10.7	20	39	3.3	62	5.3	5.40	65	.293	.353	-21	-22	97	102	-2.4	6	-2	-1.7
	Yr	5	8	.385	31	22	4	1	0	129	141	9.8	22	48	3.3	83	5.8	4.81	73	.276	.337	-17	-19	97	102	-1.9	2	-2	-1.1
1967	SF-N	12	6	.667	35	24	10	2	0	188	165	7.9	8	58	2.8	145	6.9	2.78	121	.238	.293	13	12	99	103	2.4	4	-0	1.7
1968	SF-N	12	18	.400	38	36	13	6	0	254	225	8.0	14	70	2.5	206	7.3	2.91	99	.237	.287	2	-1	96	94	-4.5	-1	-2	-0.4
1969	SF-N	5	8	.385	29	17	4	3	0	138	137	8.9	18	53	3.5	104	6.8	4.24	85	.259	.322	-10	-10	100	98	-2.0	2	2	-0.6
1970	NY-N	8	4	.667	28	19	4	0	0	139	134	8.7	18	52	3.4	89	5.8	3.88	108	.255	.314	3	5	103	105	2.0	1	-2	0.3
1971	NY-N	7	7	.500	34	20	5	2	0	163	139	7.7	10	44	2.4	120	6.6	2.93	114	.229	.282	10	7	96	86	-0.1	1	-2	0.7
1972	NY-N	2	1	.667	34	2	0	0	0	76	73	8.6	3	31	3.7	38	4.5	3.08	108	.257	.323	3	2	96	114	0.4	-0	-1	0.0
1973	NY-N	5	4	.556	31	11	1	0	1	117	109	8.4	11	41	3.2	87	6.7	3.38	109	.248	.309	4	4	100	102	0.4	1	-2	0.2
1974	NY-N	8	8	.500	34	10	3	1	0	103	107	9.3	7	35	3.1	46	4.0	3.41	107	.274	.327	3	3	100	116	1.0	1	-0	0.3
1975	StL-N	1	0	1.000	8	0	0	0	0	11	13	10.6	0	7	5.7	8	6.5	3.27	115	.289	.364	0	1	103	138	0.5	0	-0	0.0
	Atl-N	2	3	.400	25	5	0	0	1	66	73	10.0	3	21	2.9	24	3.3	4.23	83	.286	.337	-4	-5	97	97	0.0	0	-1	-0.5
	Yr	3	3	.500	33	5	0	0	1	77	86	10.1	3	28	3.3	32	3.7	4.09	87	.285	.341	-4	-5	98	97	0.5	0	-1	-0.5
	KC-A	1	0	1.000	5	0	0	0	0	3	5	15.0	0	3	9.0	0	0.0	3.00	128	.333	.444	0	0	101	230	0.5	0	0	0.0
1976	KC-A	0	0	—	3	0	0	0	0	5	7	12.6	0	3	5.4	1	1.8	0.00	—	.368	.455	2	2	99	0	0.0	0	-0	0.2
	Mil-A	2	0	1.000	36	0	0	0	1	37	38	9.2	2	20	4.9	27	6.6	4.38	81	.262	.363	-4	-4	100	97	1.0	0	-1	-0.4
	Yr	2	0	1.000	39	0	0	0	1	42	45	9.6	2	23	4.9	28	6.0	3.86	91	.274	.374	-2	-2	100	97	1.0	0	-1	-0.2
1977	NY-N	0	1	.000	4	0	0	0	0	3	3	9.0	1	3	9.0	0	0.0	6.00	63	.300	.429	-1	-1	97	143	-0.4	0	0	0.0
Total	18	135	131	.508	563	328	85	20	7	2500	2456	8.8	240	922	3.3	1614	5.8	3.78	97	.258	.320	-60	-31	103	101	-4.0	19	-28	-2.8
■ JIM SADOWSKI	Sadowski, James Michael b: 8/7/51, Pittsburgh, Pa. BR/TR, 6'3", 195 lbs. Deb: 4/27/74																												
1974	Pit-N	0	1	.000	4	0	0	0	0	9	7	7.0	1	9	9.0	1	1.0	6.00	58	.233	.372	-2	-2	97	87	-0.4	0	1	-0.1
■ BOB SADOWSKI	Sadowski, Robert b: 2/19/38, Pittsburgh, Pa. BR/TR, 6'2", 195 lbs. Deb: 6/19/63																												
1963	Mil-N	5	7	.417	19	18	5	1	0	117	99	7.6	8	30	2.3	72	5.5	2.62	125	.231	.285	9	9	100	105	-1.2	-2	1	0.8
1964	Mil-N	9	10	.474	51	18	5	0	5	167	159	8.6	18	56	3.0	96	5.2	4.10	83	.251	.314	-10	-13	96	93	-1.3	0	2	-1.0
1965	Mil-N	5	9	.357	34	13	3	0	3	123	117	8.6	11	35	2.6	78	5.7	4.32	84	.250	.303	-11	-9	103	79	-2.3	-2	-1	-1.1
1966	Bos-A	1	1	.500	11	5	0	0	0	33	41	11.2	4	9	2.5	11	3.0	5.45	70	.311	.342	-7	-6	110	98	0.1	-1	0	-0.6
Total	4	20	27	.426	115	54	13	1	8	440	416	8.5	41	130	2.7	257	5.3	3.87	90	.250	.306	-20	-20	100	93	-4.7	-4	2	-1.9
■ TED SADOWSKI	Sadowski, Theodore b: 4/1/36, Pittsburgh, Pa. BR/TR, 6'1.5", 190 lbs. Deb: 9/02/60																												
1960	Was-A	1	0	1.000	9	1	0	0	1	17	17	9.0	4	9	4.8	12	6.4	5.29	75	.258	.351	-3	-3	102	102	0.5	-0	-0	-0.2
1961	Min-A	0	2	.000	15	1	0	0	0	33	49	13.4	6	11	3.0	12	3.3	6.82	63	.348	.389	-10	-9	107	103	-0.9	-1	1	-0.8
1962	Min-A	1	1	.500	19	0	0	0	0	34	37	9.8	6	11	2.9	15	4.0	5.03	82	.301	.353	-4	-3	104	112	0.0	1	0	-0.2
Total	3	2	3	.400	43	2	0	0	1	84	103	11.0	16	31	3.3	39	4.2	5.79	72	.312	.367	-17	-15	105	107	-0.4	-0	1	-1.2
■ JOHNNY SAIN	Sain, John Franklin b: 9/25/17, Havana, Ark. BR/TR, 6'2", 185 lbs. Deb: 4/24/42 C																												
1942	Bos-N	4	7	.364	40	3	0	0	6	97	79	7.3	8	63	5.8	68	6.3	3.90	83	.228	.348	-6	-7	98	103	-0.4	-2	1	-0.7
1946	Bos-N	20	14	.588	37	34	**24**	3	2	265	225	7.6	8	87	3.0	129	4.4	2.21	145	.230	.289	36	29	94	109	2.6	6	3	4.3
1947	Bos-N	21	12	.636	38	35	22	3	1	266	265	9.0	19	79	2.7	132	4.5	3.52	110	.255	.308	16	11	95	96	3.5	12	1	2.3
1948	Bos-N	**24**	15	.615	42	39	**28**	4	1	**315**	297	8.5	19	83	2.4	137	3.9	2.60	150	.245	.293	**47**	**46**	99	115	1.3	2	-1	**4.9**
1949	Bos-N	10	17	.370	37	36	16	1	0	243	285	10.6	15	75	2.8	73	2.7	4.81	81	.291	.340	-21	-24	97	91	-3.6	1	-2	-2.4
1950	Bos-N	20	13	.606	37	37	25	3	0	278	294	9.5	34	70	2.3	96	3.1	3.95	89	.269	.311	6	-13	85	101	2.9	5	-2	-1.1
1951	Bos-N	5	13	.278	26	22	6	1	1	160	195	11.0	16	45	2.5	63	3.5	4.22	91	.299	.342	-5	-7	97	113	-4.1	2	0	-0.3
	NY-A	2	1	.667	7	4	1	0	1	37	41	10.0	5	8	1.9	21	5.1	4.14	88	.281	.316	-0	-2	88	106	0.1	1	1	0.0
1952	NY-A	11	6	.647	35	16	8	0	7	148	149	9.1	15	38	2.3	57	3.5	3.47	100	.261	.305	3	0	95	105	0.7	6	-1	0.5
1953	NY-A	14	7	.667	40	19	10	1	9	189	189	9.0	16	45	2.1	84	4.0	3.00	117	.262	.304	21	11	88	118	0.4	5	0	1.5
1954	NY-A	6	6	.500	45	0	0	0	**22**	77	66	7.7	11	15	1.8	33	3.9	3.16	111	.229	.261	5	3	94	90	-1.5	2	-0	0.5
1955	NY-A	0	0	—	3	0	0	0	0	5	6	10.8	4	1	1.8	5	9.0	7.20	52	.300	.318	-2	-2	94	137	0.0	-0	0	-0.1
	KC-A	2	5	.286	25	0	0	0	1	45	54	10.8	10	10	2.0	12	2.4	5.40	78	.297	.325	-7	-6	106	99	-1.0	-1	-1	-0.7
	Yr	2	5	.286	28	0	0	0	1	50	60	10.8	14	11	2.0	17	3.1	5.58	75	.297	.324	-9	-8	105	99	-1.0	-0	-1	-0.8
Total	11	139	116	.545	412	245	140	16	51	2125	2145	9.1	180	619	2.6	910	3.9	3.49	105	.261	.311	94	39	94	105	0.9	39	-2	8.7
■ RANDY ST. CLAIRE	St.Claire, Randy Anthony b: 8/23/60, Glens Falls, N.Y. BR/TR, 6'3", 180 lbs. Deb: 9/11/84																												
1984	Mon-N	0	0	—	4	0	0	0	0	8	11	12.4	0	2	2.3	4	4.5	4.50	73	.344	.368	-1	-1	91	122	0.0	0	0	0.0
1985	Mon-N	5	3	.625	42	0	0	0	0	69	69	9.0	3	26	3.4	25	3.3	3.91	86	.265	.327	-2	-4	94	94	0.9	1	0	-0.2
1986	Mon-N	2	0	1.000	11	0	0	0	1	19	13	6.2	2	6	2.8	21	9.9	2.37	155	.186	.250	3	3	98	79	1.0	-0	1	0.3
1987	Mon-N	3	3	.500	44	0	0	0	7	67	64	8.6	9	20	2.7	43	5.8	4.03	107	.249	.301	0	2	106	92	-0.2	0	-0	0.2
1988	Mon-N	0	0	—	6	0	0	0	0	7	11	14.1	2	5	6.4	6	7.7	6.43	56	.344	.421	-2	-2	105	138	0.0	0	0	-0.1
	Cin-N	1	0	1.000	10	0	0	0	0	14	13	8.4	3	5	3.2	8	5.1	2.57	141	.241	.300	1	2	105	167	0.5	-0	0	0.2
	Yr	1	0	1.000	16	0	0	0	0	21	24	10.3	5	10	4.3	14	6.0	3.86	94	.276	.347	-1	-1	105	167	0.5	0	0	0.1
Total	5	11	6	.647	117	0	0	0	8	184	181	8.9	19	64	3.1	107	5.2	3.82	99	.257	.315	-1	-1	100	100	2.2	1	1	0.4
■ JIM ST. VRAIN	St.Vrain, James Marcellin b: 6/6/1871, Ralls County, Mo. d: 6/12/37, Butte, Montana BR/TL, 5'9", 175 lbs. Deb: 4/20/02																												
1902	Chi-N	4	6	.400	12	11	10	1	0	95	88	8.3	0	25	2.4	51	4.8	2.08	127	.268	.320	7	6	95	114	-0.9	-2	0	0.7
■ LUIS SALAZAR	Salazar, Luis Ernesto (Garcia) b: 5/19/56, Barcelona, Venez. BR/TR, 6', 185 lbs. Deb: 8/15/80																												
1987	SD-N	0	0	—	2	0	0	0	0	2	2	9.0	0	1	4.5	0	0.0	4.50	89	.250	.333	-0	-0	98	70	0.0	0	0	0.0
■ FREDDY SALE	Sale, Frederick Link b: 5/2/02, Chester, S.C. d: 5/27/56, Hermosa Beach, Cal BR/TR, 5'9", 160 lbs. Deb: 6/30/24																												
1924	Pit-N	0	0	—	1	0	0	0	0	1	2	18.0	0	0	0.0	0	0.0	0.00	—	.500	.500	0	0	104	0	0.0	0	0	0.0
■ HARRY SALISBURY	Salisbury, Henry H. b: 5/15/1855, Providence, R.I. d: 3/29/33, Chicago, Ill. BL , Deb: 8/28/1879																												
1879	Tro-N	4	6	.400	10	10	9	0	0	89	103	10.4	0	11	1.1	31	3.1	2.22	112	.295	.317	3	3	100	**134**	1.1	-4	0	0.0
1882	Pit-a	20	18	.526	38	38	38	1	0	335	315	8.5	1	37	1.0	135	**3.6**	2.63	99	.254	.275	2	-1	97	83	1.9	-5	-3	-0.9
Total	2	24	24	.500	48	48	47	1	0	424	418	8.9	1	48	1.0	166	3.5	2.55	101	.263	.285	5	1	97	94	3.0	-10	-3	-0.9
■ SOLLY SALISBURY	Salisbury, William Ansel b: 11/12/1876, Algona, Iowa d: 1/17/52, Rowena, Ore BR/TR, 5'8.5", 165 lbs. Deb: 4/19/02																												
1902	Phi-N	0	0	—	2	1	0	0	0	6	15	22.5	1	2	3.0	0	0.0	13.50	22	.497	.528	-7	-7	109	85	0.0	-0	-0	-0.6
■ SLIM SALLEE	Sallee, Harry Franklin "Scatter" b: 2/3/1885, Higginsport, Ohio d: 3/23/50, Higginsport, Ohio BL/TL, 6'3", 180 lbs. Deb: 4/16/08																												
1908	StL-N	3	8	.273	25	12	7	1	0	129	144	10.0	1	36	2.5	39	2.7	3.14	74	.315	.368	-11	-11	100	115	-0.7	-3	-0	-1.2
1909	StL-N	10	11	.476	32	27	12	1	0	219	223	9.2	3	59	2.4	55	2.3	2.42	107	.264	.315	4	4	99	119	2.2	-2	-0	0.4
1910	StL-N	7	8	.467	18	13	9	1	2	115	112	8.8	4	24	1.9	46	3.6	2.97	95	.251	.290	1	-2	93	82	0.8	-2	0	-0.3

YEAR	TM/L	W	L	PCT	G	GS	CG	SHO	SV	IP	H	H/G	HR	BB	BB/G	SO	SO/G	ERA	/A	OAVG	OOBP	PR	/A	PF	CPI	WAT	PB	PD	TPI
1911	StL-N	15	9	.625	36	30	18	1	3	245	234	8.6	6	64	2.4	74	2.7	2.76	126	.257	.309	18	20	102	105	3.3	-2	-3	1.5
1912	StL-N	16	17	.485	48	32	20	3	**6**	294	289	8.8	6	72	2.2	108	3.3	2.60	134	.257	.305	26	29	103	98	2.5	-4	-2	2.3
1913	StL-N	19	15	.559	50	31	18	3	5	276	257	8.4	11	60	2.0	106	3.5	2.71	115	.255	.290	15	12	97	105	**6.6**	2	0	1.5
1914	StL-N	18	17	.514	46	30	18	3	**6**	282	252	8.0	5	72	2.3	105	3.4	2.11	137	.246	.289	21	24	104	116	-0.5	2	-1	2.8
1915	StL-N	13	17	.433	46	33	17	2	3	275	245	8.0	6	57	1.9	91	3.0	2.85	97	.238	.270	-3	-2	101	77	-1.3	-3	-1	-0.7
1916	StL-N	5	5	.500	16	7	4	2	1	70	75	9.6	2	23	3.0	28	3.6	3.47	76	.290	.342	-7	-7	100	113	0.9	-0	-1	-0.8
	NY-N	9	4	.692	15	11	7	2	0	112	96	7.7	2	10	0.8	35	2.8	1.37	179	.234	.249	16	13	94	123	2.0	2	-3	1.5
	Yr	14	9	.609	31	18	11	4	1	182	171	8.5	4	33	1.6	63	3.1	2.18	116	.255	.284	9	7	96	123	2.9	-0	-4	0.7
1917	NY-N	18	7	.720	34	24	18	1	**4**	216	199	8.3	4	34	1.4	54	2.3	2.17	116	.249	.272	13	9	93	107	3.3	1	-4	0.6
1918	NY-N	8	8	.500	18	16	12	1	2	132	122	8.3	3	12	**0.8**	33	2.3	2.25	118	.241	**.252**	8	6	96	82	-1.0	-2	-2	0.2
1919	Cin-N	21	7	.750	29	28	22	4	0	228	221	8.7	4	20	0.8	24	0.9	2.05	143	.258	.271	22	23	101	115	3.4	1	-5	2.2
1920	Cin-N	5	6	.455	21	12	6	0	2	116	129	10.0	4	16	1.2	13	1.0	3.34	83	.293	.305	-3	-7	88	99	-0.8	-0	-3	-1.1
	NY-N	1	0	1.000	5	1	1	0	0	17	16	8.5	0	0	0.0	2	1.1	1.59	191	.239	.239	3	3	97	68	0.5	0	-0	0.3
	Yr	6	6	.500	26	13	7	0	2	133	145	9.8	4	16	1.1	15	1.0	3.11	90	.284	.293	0	-5	89	68	-0.3	-0	-3	-0.8
1921	NY-N	6	4	.600	37	0	0	0	2	96	115	10.8	7	14	1.3	23	2.2	3.66	97	.307	.319	1	-1	94	113	0.0	2	-2	0.0
Total	14	174	143	.549	476	307	189	25	36	2822	2729	8.7	68	573	1.8	836	2.7	2.56	114	.258	.293	124	112	99	104	21.2	-8	-26	9.2
■ ROGER SALMON	Salmon, Roger Elliott b: 5/11/1891, Newark, N.J. d: 6/17/74, Belfast, Me. BL/TL, 6'2", 170 lbs. Deb: 5/03/12																												
1912	Phi-A	1	0	1.000	2	1	0	0	0	5	7	12.6	0	4	7.2	5	9.0	9.00	36	.318	.423	-3	-3	97	65	0.5	-0	-0	-0.2
■ GUS SALVE	Salve, Augustus William b: 12/29/1885, Boston, Mass. d: 3/29/71, Providence, R.I. TL, 6', 190 lbs. Deb: 9/14/08																												
1908	Phi-A	0	1	.000	2	1	1	0	0	15	17	10.2	1	9	5.4	6	3.6	4.20	62	.266	.365	-3	-3	110	110	-0.4	-1	-1	-0.2
■ JACK SALVESON	Salveson, John Theodore b: 1/5/14, Fullerton, Cal. d: 12/28/74, Norwalk, Cal. BR/TR, 6'0.5", 180 lbs. Deb: 6/03/33																												
1933	NY-N	0	2	.000	8	2	2	0	0	31	30	8.7	4	14	4.1	8	2.3	3.77	85	.252	.328	-2	-2	96	108	-0.9	-1	0	-0.1
1934	NY-N	3	1	.750	12	4	0	0	0	38	43	10.2	2	13	3.1	18	4.3	3.55	108	.281	.333	2	1	95	116	0.7	0	1	0.2
1935	Pit-N	0	1	.000	5	0	0	0	0	7	11	14.1	1	5	6.4	2	2.6	9.00	47	.306	.405	-4	-4	105	76	-0.4	-0	1	-0.2
	Chi-A	1	2	.333	20	2	2	0	1	67	79	10.6	6	23	3.1	22	3.0	4.84	101	.298	.346	-3	0	109	103	-0.4	2	-0	0.2
1943	Cle-A	5	3	.625	23	11	4	3	3	86	87	9.1	5	26	2.7	24	2.5	3.35	88	.266	.322	-1	-4	90	108	0.8	2	0	-0.1
1945	Cle-A	0	0	—	19	0	0	0	0	44	52	10.6	3	6	1.2	11	2.3	3.68	90	.294	.317	-2	-2	98	107	0.0	3	1	0.2
Total	5	9	9	.500	87	19	8	3	4	273	302	10.0	21	87	2.9	85	2.8	3.99	91	.280	.332	-8	-11	98	107	-0.2	6	2	0.2
■ MANNY SALVO	Salvo, Manuel "Gyp" b: 6/30/13, Sacramento, Cal. BR/TR, 6'4", 210 lbs. Deb: 4/22/39																												
1939	NY-N	4	10	.286	32	18	4	0	1	136	150	9.9	11	75	5.0	69	4.6	4.63	83	.285	.367	-11	-12	99	109	-3.1	-2	1	-1.1
1940	Bos-N	10	9	.526	21	20	14	**5**	0	161	151	8.4	9	43	2.4	60	3.4	3.07	126	.248	.296	14	15	101	104	1.8	-3	-1	1.1
1941	Bos-N	7	16	.304	35	27	11	2	0	195	192	8.9	9	93	4.3	67	3.1	4.06	85	.255	.335	-9	-13	96	93	-3.1	-0	-0	-1.3
1942	Bos-N	7	8	.467	25	14	6	1	0	131	129	8.9	7	41	2.8	25	1.7	3.02	107	.260	.312	4	3	98	117	0.9	-1	-1	0.1
1943	Bos-N	0	1	.000	1	1	0	0	0	5	5	9.0	0	6	10.8	1	1.8	7.20	51	.250	.423	-2	-2	109	71	-0.4	2	-0	0.0
	Phi-N	0	0	—	1	0	0	0	0	⅓	2	54.0	0	1	27.0	0	0.0	27.00	—	.667	.750	-1	-1	96	116	0.0	0	0	0.0
	Bos-N	5	6	.455	20	13	5	1	0	94	94	9.0	6	25	2.4	25	2.4	3.26	113	.261	.308	1	4	109	104	0.1	0	-0	0.5
	Yr	5	7	.417	22	14	5	1	0	99	101	9.2	6	32	2.9	26	2.4	3.55	103	.264	.319	-2	1	109	104	-0.3	2	-1	0.5
Total	5	33	50	.398	135	93	40	9	1	722	723	9.0	42	284	3.5	247	3.1	3.69	98	.261	.327	-4	-5	100	104	-3.8	-4	-2	-0.7
■ JOE SAMBITO	Sambito, Joseph Charles b: 6/28/52, Brooklyn, N.Y. BL/TL, 6'1", 185 lbs. Deb: 7/20/76																												
1976	Hou-N	3	2	.600	20	4	1	1	1	53	45	7.6	4	14	2.4	26	4.4	3.57	85	.237	.285	-0	-3	87	81	0.5	1	1	-0.1
1977	Hou-N	5	5	.500	54	1	0	0	7	89	77	7.8	6	24	2.4	67	6.8	2.33	155	.235	.283	16	13	92	116	0.0	-0	1	1.3
1978	Hou-N	4	9	.308	62	0	0	0	11	88	85	8.7	5	32	3.3	96	9.8	3.07	111	.260	.315	5	3	95	116	-2.1	0	1	0.5
1979	Hou-N	8	7	.533	63	0	0	0	22	91	80	7.9	8	23	2.3	83	8.2	1.78	190	.235	.285	**20**	16	90	163	-0.1	2	1	2.0
1980	Hou-N	8	4	.667	64	0	0	0	17	90	65	6.5	3	22	2.2	75	7.5	2.20	159	.200	.251	14	13	97	72	1.4	-1	0	1.3
1981	Hou-N	5	5	.500	49	0	0	0	10	64	43	6.0	4	22	3.1	41	5.8	1.83	166	.192	.263	12	9	87	111	-0.4	-1	1	0.9
1982	Hou-N	0	0	—	9	0	0	0	4	13	7	4.8	0	2	1.4	7	4.8	0.69	519	.159	.191	4	4	100	34	0.0	-0	0	0.5
1984	Hou-N	0	0	—	32	0	0	0	0	48	39	7.3	5	16	3.0	26	4.9	3.00	110	.228	.288	3	2	92	104	0.0	-0	-1	0.0
1985	NY-N	0	0	—	8	0	0	0	0	11	21	17.2	1	8	6.5	3	2.5	12.27	28	.420	.483	-11	-11	95	79	0.0	0	0	-0.9
1986	Bos-A	2	0	1.000	53	0	0	0	12	45	54	10.8	4	16	3.2	30	6.0	4.80	86	.298	.360	-3	-3	99	103	1.0	0	0	-0.2
1987	Bos-A	2	6	.250	47	0	0	0	0	38	46	10.9	8	16	3.8	35	8.3	6.87	64	.301	.363	-10	-10	99	88	-1.9	0	-0	-0.9
Total	11	37	38	.493	461	5	1	1	84	630	562	8.0	48	195	2.8	489	7.0	3.03	115	.241	.296	50	31	93	107	-1.6	2	4	4.4
■ JOE SAMUELS	Samuels, Joseph Jonas "Skabotch" b: 3/21/05, Scranton, Pa. BR/TR, 6'1.5", 196 lbs. Deb: 4/23/30																												
1930	Det-A	0	0	—	2	0	0	0	0	6	10	15.0	1	6	9.0	1	1.5	16.50	30	.417	.516	-8	-8	106	67	0.0	-0	-0	-0.5
■ ROGER SAMUELS	Samuels, Roger Howard b: 1/5/61, San Jose, Cal. BL/TL, 6'5", 210 lbs. Deb: 7/20/88																												
1988	SF-N	1	2	.333	15	0	0	0	0	23	17	6.7	4	7	2.7	22	8.6	3.52	92	.202	.272	-0	-1	93	87	-0.4	-0	0	0.0
■ ISRAEL SANCHEZ	Sanchez, Israel (Matos) b: 8/20/63, Falcon Lasvias, Cuba BL/TL, 5'9", 170 lbs. Deb: 7/07/88																												
1988	KC-A	3	2	.600	19	1	0	0	1	36	36	9.0	0	18	4.5	14	3.5	4.50	91	.265	.344	-2	-2	103	83	0.4	0	0	-0.1
■ LUIS SANCHEZ	Sanchez, Luis Mercedes (born Mercedes Escoba (Sanchez)) b: 8/24/53, Cariaco, Sucre, Ven. BR/TR, 6'2", 170 lbs. Deb: 4/10/81																												
1981	Cal-A	0	2	.000	17	0	0	0	2	34	39	10.3	4	11	2.9	13	3.4	2.91	130	.287	.340	3	3	104	160	-0.9	0	-0	0.3
1982	Cal-A	7	4	.636	46	0	0	0	5	93	89	8.6	3	34	3.3	58	5.6	3.19	126	.259	.335	9	9	99	114	0.9	0	1	0.9
1983	Cal-A	10	8	.556	56	1	0	0	7	98	92	8.4	6	40	3.7	49	4.5	3.67	107	.254	.325	4	3	96	102	2.1	0	2	0.4
1984	Cal-A	9	7	.563	49	0	0	0	11	84	84	9.0	10	33	3.5	62	6.6	3.32	122	.268	.334	6	7	101	134	1.1	0	-0	0.7
1985	Cal-A	2	0	1.000	26	0	0	0	2	61	67	9.9	9	27	4.0	34	5.0	5.75	72	.283	.354	-11	-11	101	91	1.0	0	0	-0.9
Total	5	28	21	.571	194	1	0	0	27	370	371	9.0	32	145	3.5	216	5.3	3.75	107	.267	.336	12	11	99	116	4.2	0	3	1.4
■ RAUL SANCHEZ	Sanchez, Raul Guadalupe (Rodriguez) b: 12/12/30, Marianao, Cuba BR/TR, 6', 150 lbs. Deb: 4/17/52																												
1952	Was-A	1	1	.500	3	2	1	1	0	13	13	9.0	0	7	4.8	6	4.2	3.46	106	.260	.351	0	0	100	104	0.0	-1	0	0.0
1957	Cin-N	3	2	.600	38	0	0	0	5	62	61	8.9	7	25	3.6	37	5.4	4.79	86	.262	.333	-6	-5	106	90	0.4	1	1	-0.3
1960	Cin-N	1	0	1.000	8	0	0	0	0	15	12	7.2	1	11	6.6	5	3.0	4.80	78	.226	.382	-2	-2	99	94	0.5	0	0	0.0
Total	3	5	3	.625	49	2	1	1	5	90	86	8.6	8	43	4.3	48	4.8	4.60	87	.256	.344	-8	-6	104	92	0.9	0	1	-0.3
■ BEN SANDERS	Sanders, Alexander Bennett b: 2/16/1865, Catharpen, Va. d: 8/29/30, Memphis, Tenn. BR/TR, 6', 210 lbs. Deb: 1888																												
1888	Phi-N	19	10	.655	31	29	28	4	0	275	240	7.9	3	33	**1.1**	121	4.0	1.90	**169**	.248	.272	29	40	113	104	4.6	4	0	5.6
1889	Phi-N	19	18	.514	44	39	34	1	1	350	406	10.4	9	96	2.5	123	3.2	3.55	119	.306	.353	19	26	105	112	0.9	7	-2	2.9
1890	Phi-P	19	18	.514	43	40	37	2	1	347	412	10.7	13	69	1.8	107	2.8	3.76	114	.307	.341	18	20	101	98	-0.2	10	3	2.9
1891	Phi-a	11	5	.688	19	18	15	0	0	145	157	9.7	3	37	2.3	40	2.5	3.79	101	.291	.336	-1	1	103	87	3.0	2	0	0.0
1892	Lou-N	12	19	.387	31	31	30	3	0	268	281	9.4	6	62	2.1	77	2.6	3.22	95	.283	.325	2	-5	93	97	-1.2	10	0	1.0
Total	5	80	70	.533	168	157	144	10	2	1385	1496	9.7	34	297	1.9	468	3.0	3.24	117	.289	.328	66	84	103	101	7.1	33	1	12.4
■ DEE SANDERS	Sanders, Dee Wilma b: 4/8/21, Quitman, Tex. BR/TR, 6'3", 195 lbs. Deb: 8/12/45																												
1945	StL-A	0	0	—	2	0	0	0	0	1	7	63.0	0	1	9.0	1	9.0	54.00	7	.700	.667	-6	-6	114	63	0.0	0	0	-0.4
■ KEN SANDERS	Sanders, Kenneth George "Daffy" b: 7/8/41, St.Louis, Mo. BR/TR, 5'11", 168 lbs. Deb: 8/06/64																												
1964	KC-A	0	2	.000	21	0	0	0	1	27	23	7.7	2	17	5.7	18	6.0	3.67	106	.232	.342	-0	1	108	105	-0.9	0	1	0.2
1966	Bos-A	3	6	.333	24	0	0	0	2	47	36	6.9	2	28	5.4	33	6.3	3.83	99	.214	.325	-2	-0	110	84	-1.1	-0	0	0.0
	KC-A	3	4	.429	38	1	0	0	1	65	59	8.2	7	48	6.6	41	5.7	3.74	88	.250	.370	-2	-3	95	132	-0.2	0	1	-0.2
	Yr	6	10	.375	62	1	0	0	3	112	95	7.6	9	76	6.1	74	5.9	3.78	92	.233	.347	-4	-4	102	132	-1.3	-0	1	-0.2
1968	Oak-A	0	1	.000	7	0	0	0	0	11	8	6.5	1	8	6.5	6	4.9	3.27	89	.229	.356	-0	-0	98	131	-0.4	0	0	0.0
1970	Mil-A	5	2	.714	50	0	0	0	13	92	64	6.3	1	25	2.4	64	6.3	1.76	211	.201	.261	20	20	100	97	1.9	1	1	2.4
1971	Mil-A	7	12	.368	**83**	0	0	0	**31**	136	111	7.3	9	34	2.3	80	5.3	1.92	188	.227	.276	**23**	**26**	104	131	-1.4	-1	2	2.9
1972	Mil-A	2	9	.182	62	0	0	0	17	92	88	8.6	10	31	3.0	51	5.0	3.13	95	.245	.305	-1	-2	97	109	-3.1	0	1	0.0
1973	Min-A	2	4	.333	27	0	0	0	8	44	53	10.8	4	21	4.3	19	3.9	6.14	64	.299	.367	-11	-11	103	85	-0.9	0	0	-0.9

YEAR	TM/L	W	L	PCT	G	GS	CG	SHO	SV	IP	H	H/G	HR	BB	BB/G	SO	SO/G	ERA	/A	OAVG	OOBP	PR	/A	PF	CPI	WAT	PB	PD	TPI
	Cle-A	5	1	.833	15	0	0	0	5	27	18	6.0	2	9	3.0	14	4.7	1.67	227	.188	.252	6	6	99	107	2.1	0	0	0.7
	Yr	7	5	.583	42	0	0	0	13	71	71	9.0	6	30	3.8	33	4.2	4.44	87	.255	.322	-5	-4	102	107	1.2	0	0	-0.2
1974	Cle-A	0	1	.000	9	0	0	0	1	11	21	17.2	5	5	4.1	4	3.3	9.82	37	.404	.448	-8	-8	101	114	-0.4	0	0	-0.7
	Cal-A	0	0	—	9	0	0	0	1	10	10	9.0	0	3	2.7	4	3.6	2.70	125	.278	.310	1	1	93	125	0.0	0	1	0.1
	Yr	0	1	.000	18	0	0	0	2	21	31	13.3	5	8	3.4	8	3.4	6.43	55	.352	.390	-7	-7	97	125	-0.4	0	1	-0.6
1975	NY-N	1	1	.500	29	0	0	0	5	43	31	6.5	2	14	2.9	8	1.7	2.30	150	.205	.262	6	5	95	88	0.0	-0	0	0.5
1976	NY-N	1	2	.333	31	0	0	0	1	47	39	7.5	4	12	2.3	16	3.1	2.87	111	.231	.277	3	2	91	99	-0.5	-0	1	0.2
	KC-A	0	0	—	3	0	0	0	0	3	3	9.0	0	3	9.0	2	6.0	0.00	—	.273	.429	1	1	99	0	0.0	0	0	0.1
Total	10	29	45	.392	408	1	0	0	86	655	564	7.7	49	258	3.5	360	4.9	2.98	117	.235	.306	38	38	100	109	-4.9	-0	7	5.3
■ **ROY SANDERS**	Sanders, Roy Garvin "Butch" or "Pepe" b: 8/1/1892, Stafford, Kan. d: 1/17/50, Kansas City, Mo. BR/TR, 6'0.5", 195 lbs. Deb: 4/16/17																												
1917	Cin-N	0	1	.000	2	2	1	0	0	14	12	7.7	0	16	10.3	3	1.9	4.50	56	.273	.446	-3	-3	93	128	-0.4	-1	1	-0.2
1918	Pit-N	7	9	.438	28	14	6	2	1	156	135	7.8	1	52	3.0	55	3.2	2.60	111	.239	.293	3	5	105	95	-1.3	-1	2	0.7
Total	2	7	10	.412	30	16	7	2	1	170	147	7.8	1	68	3.6	58	3.1	2.75	104	.241	.307	0	2	104	97	-1.7	-2	2	0.5
■ **ROY SANDERS**	Sanders, Roy L. "Simon" b: 1894, BR/TR, 6', 185 lbs. Deb: 8/06/18																												
1918	NY-A	0	2	.000	6	2	0	0	0	26	28	9.7	0	16	5.5	8	2.8	4.15	63	.301	.407	-4	-4	94	115	-0.9	-1	-1	-0.6
1920	StL-A	1	1	.500	8	1	0	0	0	17	20	10.6	1	17	9.0	2	1.1	5.29	80	.313	.463	-3	-2	111	127	0.0	-1	-1	-0.2
Total	2	1	3	.250	14	3	0	0	0	43	48	10.0	1	33	6.9	10	2.1	4.60	69	.306	.431	-7	-7	101	120	-0.9	-2	-1	-0.8
■ **WAR SANDERS**	Sanders, Warren Williams b: 8/2/1877, Maynardville, Tenn. d: 8/3/62, Chattanooga, Tenn. BR/TL, 5'10", 160 lbs. Deb: 4/18/03																												
1903	StL-N	1	6	.143	8	6	3	0	0	40	48	10.8	0	21	4.7	9	2.0	6.07	55	.327	.418	-12	-12	102	76	-1.9	-2	-1	-1.0
1904	StL-N	1	2	.333	4	3	1	0	0	19	25	11.8	1	1	0.5	11	5.2	4.74	57	.348	.366	-4	-4	99	93	-0.4	-1	0	-0.3
Total	2	2	8	.200	12	9	4	0	0	59	73	11.1	1	22	3.4	20	3.1	5.64	55	.334	.402	-17	-17	101	82	-2.3	-2	-0	-1.3
■ **SCOTT SANDERSON**	Sanderson, Scott Douglas b: 7/22/56, Dearborn, Mich. BR/TR, 6'5", 195 lbs. Deb: 8/06/78																												
1978	Mon-N	4	2	.667	10	9	1	1	0	61	52	7.7	3	21	3.1	50	7.4	2.51	136	.232	.295	7	6	96	111	1.1	-1	-1	0.5
1979	Mon-N	9	8	.529	34	24	5	3	1	168	148	7.9	16	54	2.9	138	7.4	3.43	110	.236	.295	6	6	101	90	-0.9	-0	-2	0.4
1980	Mon-N	16	11	.593	33	33	7	3	0	211	206	8.8	18	56	2.4	125	5.3	3.11	114	.257	.303	12	10	98	111	1.3	-3	-2	0.5
1981	Mon-N	9	7	.563	22	22	4	1	0	137	122	8.0	10	31	2.0	77	5.1	2.96	116	.236	.275	8	7	98	90	0.1	2	-2	0.8
1982	Mon-N	12	12	.500	32	32	7	0	0	224	212	8.5	24	58	2.3	158	6.3	3.46	109	.251	.296	4	8	104	99	-0.7	1	-3	0.5
1983	Mon-N	6	7	.462	18	16	0	0	1	81	98	10.9	12	20	2.2	55	6.1	4.67	79	.303	.341	-9	-9	101	108	-0.5	-0	-1	-1.0
1984	Chi-N	8	5	.615	24	24	3	0	0	141	140	8.9	5	24	1.5	76	4.9	3.13	125	.264	.291	7	12	109	96	0.3	-1	1	1.3
1985	Chi-N	5	6	.455	19	19	2	0	0	121	100	7.4	13	27	2.0	80	6.0	3.12	134	.228	.265	6	14	117	89	-0.2	-2	1	1.5
1986	Chi-N	9	11	.450	37	28	1	1	1	170	165	8.7	21	37	2.0	124	6.6	4.18	96	.255	.293	-9	-3	108	85	0.3	-3	-1	-0.7
1987	Chi-N	8	9	.471	32	22	0	0	2	145	156	9.7	23	50	3.1	106	6.6	4.28	97	.274	.331	-3	-2	102	110	0.0	-1	-1	-0.3
1988	Chi-N	1	2	.333	11	0	0	0	0	15	13	7.8	1	3	1.8	6	3.6	5.40	67	.232	.258	-3	-3	105	47	-0.4	0	-0	-0.3
Total	11	87	80	.521	272	229	30	9	5	1474	1412	8.6	146	381	2.3	995	6.1	3.51	108	.253	.297	26	47	104	98	0.4	-9	-11	3.2
■ **FRED SANFORD**	Sanford, John Frederick b: 8/9/19, Garfield, Utah BB/TR, 6'1", 200 lbs. Deb: 5/05/43																												
1943	StL-A	0	0	—	3	0	0	0	0	9	7	7.0	0	4	4.0	2	2.0	2.00	166	.219	.297	1	1	101	120	0.0	0	0	0.2
1946	StL-A	2	1	.667	3	3	2	2	0	22	19	7.8	0	9	3.7	8	3.3	2.05	171	.235	.308	4	4	100	125	0.6	1	0	0.5
1947	StL-A	7	16	.304	34	23	9	0	4	187	186	9.0	17	76	3.7	62	3.0	3.71	105	.261	.326	-0	4	106	108	-2.6	-0	-1	0.2
1948	StL-A	12	21	.364	42	33	9	1	2	227	250	9.9	19	91	3.6	79	3.1	4.64	101	.279	.344	-9	1	109	98	-1.1	-3	1	0.0
1949	NY-A	7	3	.700	29	11	3	0	0	95	100	9.5	9	57	5.4	51	4.8	3.88	105	.270	.363	3	2	97	121	1.0	-2	-0	0.0
1950	NY-A	5	4	.556	26	12	2	0	0	113	103	8.2	9	79	6.3	54	4.3	4.54	97	.252	.364	0	-2	96	103	-0.5	1	3	0.1
1951	NY-A	0	3	.000	11	2	0	0	0	27	15	5.0	2	25	8.3	10	3.3	3.67	99	.169	.342	1	-0	88	93	-1.4	-0	1	0.0
	Was-A	2	3	.400	7	7	0	0	0	37	51	12.4	5	27	6.6	12	2.9	6.57	61	.329	.429	-10	-11	97	110	0.0	-1	-1	-1.0
	StL-A	2	4	.333	9	7	1	0	0	27	37	12.3	6	23	7.7	7	2.3	10.33	44	.308	.420	-19	-17	109	73	0.0	1	-0	-1.4
	Yr	4	10	.286	27	16	1	0	0	91	103	10.2	13	75	7.4	29	2.9	6.82	59	.283	.403	-27	-28	98	73	-1.4	-2	-0	-2.4
Total	7	37	55	.402	164	98	26	3	6	744	768	9.3	67	391	4.7	285	3.4	4.45	95	.268	.351	-28	-18	103	105	-4.0	-5	2	-1.4
■ **JACK SANFORD**	Sanford, John Stanley b: 5/18/29, Wellesley Hills, Mass. BR/TR, 6', 190 lbs. Deb: 9/16/56 C																												
1956	Phi-N	1	0	1.000	3	1	0	0	0	13	7	4.8	0	13	9.0	6	4.2	1.38	260	.184	.389	3	3	95	272	0.5	0	0	0.4
1957	Phi-N	19	8	.704	33	33	15	3	0	237	194	**7.4**	22	94	3.6	**188**	7.1	3.08	125	**.221**	.294	21	20	99	95	**6.1**	-1	-1	1.9
1958	Phi-N	10	13	.435	38	27	7	2	0	186	197	9.5	15	81	3.9	106	5.1	4.45	89	.274	.343	-10	-10	100	95	-0.3	1	-1	-1.0
1959	SF-N	15	12	.556	36	31	10	0	1	222	198	8.0	22	70	2.8	132	5.4	3.16	117	.235	.295	19	13	94	99	0.6	-0	-1	1.1
1960	SF-N	12	14	.462	37	34	11	**6**	0	219	199	8.2	11	99	4.1	125	5.1	3.82	87	.243	.319	-1	-12	89	88	-1.4	2	-1	-1.1
1961	SF-N	13	9	.591	38	33	6	0	0	217	203	8.4	22	87	3.6	112	4.6	4.23	92	.249	.320	-5	-9	96	89	1.1	5	-0	-0.3
1962	SF-N	24	7	.774	39	38	13	2	0	265	233	7.9	23	92	3.1	147	5.0	3.43	113	.234	.298	15	13	99	89	7.0	-0	2	1.5
1963	SF-N	16	13	.552	42	42	11	0	0	284	273	8.7	21	76	2.4	158	5.0	3.52	88	.251	.299	-7	-13	94	91	0.3	3	3	-0.8
1964	SF-N	5	7	.417	18	17	3	1	1	106	91	7.7	7	37	3.1	64	5.4	3.31	106	.228	.295	3	2	99	88	-1.5	1	1	0.4
1965	SF-N	4	5	.444	23	16	0	0	2	91	92	9.1	11	30	3.0	43	4.3	3.96	98	.256	.321	-4	-1	109	102	-1.0	-1	-0	-0.1
	Cal-A	1	2	.333	9	5	0	0	1	29	35	10.9	2	10	3.1	13	4.0	4.66	73	.324	.366	-4	-4	98	114	-0.3	-0	1	-0.3
1966	Cal-A	13	7	.650	50	6	0	0	5	108	108	9.0	11	27	2.3	54	4.5	3.83	89	.271	.311	-5	-5	100	107	3.4	1	1	-0.3
1967	Cal-A	3	2	.600	12	9	0	0	1	48	53	9.9	6	7	1.3	21	3.9	4.50	69	.288	.306	-7	-7	96	95	0.4	1	1	-0.5
	KC-A	1	2	.333	10	1	0	0	0	22	24	9.8	1	14	5.7	13	5.3	6.55	50	.296	.392	-8	-8	102	84	-0.1	-0	1	-0.7
	Yr	4	4	.500	22	10	0	0	1	70	77	9.9	7	21	2.7	34	4.4	5.14	61	.288	.336	-15	-15	98	84	0.3	1	2	-1.2
Total	12	137	101	.576	388	293	76	14	11	2047	1907	8.4	174	737	3.2	1182	5.2	3.69	98	.247	.311	10	-17	97	95	14.8	11	3	0.2
■ **JOSE SANTIAGO**	Santiago, Jose Guillermo (Guzman) "Pants" b: 9/4/28, Coamo, P.R. BR/TR, 5'10", 175 lbs. Deb: 4/17/54																												
1954	Cle-A	0	0	—	1	0	0	0	0	2	0	0.0	0	2	9.0	1	4.5	0.00	—	.000	.250	1	1	101	0	0.0	0	-0	0.1
1955	Cle-A	2	0	1.000	17	0	0	0	0	33	31	8.5	1	14	3.8	19	5.2	2.45	165	.256	.342	6	6	102	157	1.0	1	0	0.7
1956	KC-A	1	2	.333	9	5	0	0	0	22	36	14.7	8	17	7.0	9	3.7	8.18	53	.387	.496	-10	-9	105	139	0.0	0	0	-0.7
Total	3	3	2	.600	27	5	0	0	0	57	67	10.6	9	33	5.2	29	4.6	4.58	91	.306	.406	-3	-3	103	144	1.0	2	0	0.1
■ **JOSE SANTIAGO**	Santiago, Jose Rafael (Alfonso) b: 8/15/40, Juana Diaz, P.R. BR/TR, 6'2", 185 lbs. Deb: 9/09/63																												
1963	KC-A	1	0	1.000	4	0	0	0	0	7	8	10.3	4	2	2.6	6	7.7	9.00	44	.276	.323	-4	-4	109	85	0.5	0	0	-0.3
1964	KC-A	0	6	.000	34	8	0	0	0	84	84	9.0	9	35	3.8	64	6.9	4.71	83	.258	.331	-10	-8	108	87	-2.9	-2	-1	-0.9
1965	KC-A	0	0	—	4	0	0	0	0	5	8	14.4	1	4	7.2	8	14.4	9.00	38	.364	.429	-3	-3	100	99	0.0	0	0	-0.2
1966	Bos-A	12	13	.480	35	28	7	1	2	172	155	8.1	17	58	3.0	119	6.2	3.66	104	.238	.297	-4	2	110	91	0.9	0	-1	0.3
1967	Bos-A	12	4	.750	50	11	2	0	5	145	138	8.6	14	47	2.9	109	6.8	3.60	101	.251	.309	-6	1	113	101	3.6	2	0	0.4
1968	Bos-A	9	4	.692	18	18	7	2	0	124	96	7.0	9	42	3.0	86	6.2	2.25	133	.215	.284	10	10	101	116	2.4	1	-0	1.3
1969	Bos-A	0	0	—	10	0	0	0	0	8	11	12.4	2	4	4.5	4	4.5	3.38	113	.324	.385	0	0	105	211	0.0	0	-0	0.0
1970	Bos-A	0	2	.000	8	0	0	0	1	11	18	14.7	0	8	6.5	8	6.5	10.64	38	.353	.441	-8	-8	110	64	-0.9	1	-0	-0.6
Total	8	34	29	.540	163	65	16	3	8	556	518	8.4	56	200	3.2	404	6.5	3.74	96	.246	.310	-26	-9	108	100	3.6	2	-1	-0.0
■ **AL SANTORINI**	Santorini, Alan Joel b: 5/19/48, Irvington, N.J. BR/TR, 6', 190 lbs. Deb: 9/10/68																												
1968	Atl-N	0	1	.000	1	1	0	0	0	3	4	12.0	1	0	0.0	0	0.0	0.00	—	.286	.286	1	1	94	0	-0.4	0	0	0.1
1969	SD-N	8	14	.364	32	30	2	1	0	185	194	9.4	11	73	3.6	111	5.4	3.94	91	.270	.337	-7	-7	100	102	0.8	-1	1	-0.7
1970	SD-N	1	8	.111	21	12	0	0	1	76	91	10.8	11	43	5.1	41	4.9	6.04	65	.294	.381	-17	-18	97	97	-3.2	-2	-1	-1.9
1971	SD-N	0	2	.000	18	3	0	0	0	38	43	10.2	4	11	2.6	21	5.0	3.79	90	.285	.327	-1	-2	98	113	-0.9	1	-1	-0.1
	StL-N	0	2	.000	19	5	0	0	2	50	51	9.2	2	19	3.4	21	3.8	3.78	92	.270	.335	-2	-2	100	99	-0.9	1	-0	-0.1
	Yr	0	4	.000	37	8	0	0	2	88	94	9.6	6	30	3.1	42	4.3	3.78	91	.275	.332	-3	-3	99	99	-1.8	1	-1	-0.2
1972	StL-N	8	11	.421	30	19	3	3	0	134	136	9.1	6	46	3.1	72	4.8	4.10	89	.263	.322	-10	-7	105	84	-1.2	-2	-1	-0.9
1973	StL-N	0	0	—	6	0	0	0	0	8	14	15.8	1	2	2.3	2	2.3	5.63	59	.400	.425	-2	-2	90	145	0.0	-0	-0	-0.1
Total	6	17	38	.309	127	70	5	4	3	494	533	9.7	36	194	3.5	268	4.9	4.28	85	.276	.341	-37	-36	101	97	-5.8	-4	-3	-3.7

YEAR	TM/L	W	L	PCT	G	GS	CG	SHO	SV	IP	H	H/G	HR	BB	BB/G	SO	SO/G	ERA	/A	OAVG	OOBP	PR	/A	PF	CPI	WAT	PB	PD	TPI
■ **MANNY SARMIENTO**	Sarmiento, Manuel Eduardo (Aponte) b: 2/2/56, Cagua, Venez. BR/TR, 6', 170 lbs. Deb: 7/30/76																												
1976	Cin-N	5	1	.833	22	0	0	0	0	44	36	7.4	1	12	2.5	20	4.1	2.05	171	.222	.277	7	7	100	105	1.7	-1	-1	0.6
1977	Cin-N	0	0	—	24	0	0	0	1	40	28	6.3	6	11	2.5	23	5.2	2.47	157	.196	.247	6	6	99	97	0.0	-0	-1	0.5
1978	Cin-N	9	7	.563	63	4	0	0	5	127	109	7.7	16	54	3.8	72	5.1	4.39	83	.234	.305	-11	-10	102	83	0.0	-2	-1	-1.2
1979	Cin-N	0	4	.000	23	1	0	0	0	39	47	10.8	2	7	1.6	23	5.3	4.62	78	.311	.335	-4	-4	96	95	-1.9	-1	-0	-0.5
1980	Sea-A	0	1	.000	9	0	0	0	1	15	14	8.4	2	6	3.6	15	9.0	3.60	118	.255	.317	1	1	105	114	-0.4	0	-0	0.1
1982	Pit-N	9	4	.692	35	17	4	0	1	165	153	8.3	7	46	2.5	81	4.4	3.38	117	.246	.294	4	11	110	83	2.5	0	-2	1.0
1983	Pit-N	3	5	.375	52	0	0	0	4	84	74	7.9	8	36	3.9	49	5.3	3.00	125	.243	.309	6	7	103	121	-1.0	-1	-1	0.6
Total	7	26	22	.542	228	22	4	0	12	514	461	8.1	42	172	3.0	283	5.0	3.48	109	.242	.298	9	17	104	94	0.9	-4	-5	1.1
■ **KEVIN SAUCIER**	Saucier, Kevin Andrew b: 8/9/56, Pensacola, Fla. BR/TL, 6'1", 190 lbs. Deb: 10/01/78																												
1978	Phi-N	0	1	.000	1	0	0	0	0	2	4	18.0	0	1	4.5	2	9.0	18.00	21	.400	.500	-3	-3	104	52	-0.4	0	0	-0.2
1979	Phi-N	1	4	.200	29	2	0	0	1	62	68	9.9	4	33	4.8	21	3.0	4.21	86	.291	.375	-3	-4	97	119	-1.5	-1	0	-0.3
1980	Phi-N	7	3	.700	40	0	0	0	0	50	50	9.0	2	20	3.6	25	4.5	3.42	112	.281	.357	1	2	106	127	1.6	-1	0	0.2
1981	Det-A	4	2	.667	38	0	0	0	13	49	26	4.8	1	21	3.9	23	4.2	1.65	232	.160	.275	11	12	105	96	0.8	0	0	1.3
1982	Det-A	3	1	.750	31	1	0	0	5	40	35	7.9	0	29	6.5	23	5.2	3.15	129	.254	.382	4	4	100	137	1.0	0	0	0.4
Total	5	15	11	.577	139	3	0	0	19	203	183	8.1	7	104	4.6	94	4.2	3.33	115	.253	.352	10	11	102	118	1.5	-2	1	1.4
■ **DENNIS SAUNDERS**	Saunders, Dennis James b: 1/4/49, Alhambra, Cal. BB/TR, 6'3", 195 lbs. Deb: 5/21/70																												
1970	Det-A	1	1	.500	8	0	0	0	1	14	16	10.3	1	5	3.2	8	5.1	3.21	120	.286	.344	1	1	104	138	0.0	-1	1	0.1
■ **RICH SAUVEUR**	Sauveur, Richard Daniel b: 11/23/63, Arlington, Va. BL/TL, 6'4", 163 lbs. Deb: 7/01/86																												
1986	Pit-N	0	0	—	3	3	0	0	0	12	17	12.8	3	6	4.5	6	4.5	6.00	62	.354	.439	-3	-3	101	142	0.0	0	1	-0.1
1988	Mon-N	0	0	—	4	0	0	0	0	3	3	9.0	1	2	6.0	3	9.0	6.00	60	.250	.357	-1	-1	105	104	0.0	0	0	0.0
Total	2	0	0	—	7	3	0	0	0	15	20	12.0	4	8	4.8	9	5.4	6.00	62	.333	.423	-4	-4	101	135	0.0	0	1	-0.1
■ **JACK SAVAGE**	Savage, John Joseph b: 4/22/64, Louisville, Ky. BR/TR, 6'3", 190 lbs. Deb: 9/14/87																												
1987	LA-N	0	0	—	3	0	0	0	0	3	4	12.0	0	0	0.0	0	0.0	3.00	125	.286	.286	0	0	92	87	0.0	0	0	0.0
■ **BOB SAVAGE**	Savage, John Robert b: 12/1/21, Manchester, N.H. BR/TR, 6'2", 180 lbs. Deb: 6/24/42																												
1942	Phi-A	0	1	.000	8	3	0	0	0	31	24	7.0	0	31	9.0	10	2.9	3.19	116	.220	.390	2	2	101	129	-0.4	0	-0	0.2
1946	Phi-A	3	15	.167	40	19	7	1	2	164	164	9.0	5	93	5.1	78	4.3	4.06	93	.259	.347	-10	-5	107	94	-4.5	1	-3	-0.7
1947	Phi-A	8	10	.444	44	8	2	1	2	146	135	8.3	8	55	3.4	56	3.5	3.76	98	.245	.309	-1	-1	100	85	-1.1	-4	-2	-0.6
1948	Phi-A	5	1	.833	33	1	1	0	5	75	98	11.8	9	33	4.0	26	3.1	6.24	70	.318	.379	-16	-16	102	97	1.9	-1	-1	-1.5
1949	StL-A	0	0	—	4	0	0	0	0	7	12	15.4	1	3	3.9	1	1.3	6.43	68	.400	.429	-2	-2	104	133	0.0	-0	0	-0.1
Total	5	16	27	.372	129	31	10	2	9	423	433	9.2	23	215	4.6	171	3.6	4.32	89	.265	.345	-28	-22	103	95	-4.1	-4	-6	-2.7
■ **DON SAVIDGE**	Savidge, Donald Snyder b: 8/28/08, Berwick, Pa. d: 3/22/83, Santa Barbara, Cal BR/TR, 6'1", 180 lbs. Deb: 8/06/29																												
1929	Was-A	0	0	—	3	0	0	0	0	6	12	18.0	1	2	3.0	2	3.0	9.00	47	.414	.438	-3	-3	100	104	0.0	0	0	-0.2
■ **RALPH SAVIDGE**	Savidge, Ralph Austin "The Human Whipcord" b: 2/3/1879, Jerseytown, Pa. d: 7/22/59, Berwick, Pa. BR/TR, 6'2", 210 lbs. Deb: 9/22/08																												
1908	Cin-N	0	1	.000	4	1	1	0	0	21	18	7.7	0	8	3.4	7	3.0	2.57	95	.259	.335	-1	-0	104	97	-0.4	-1	-1	0.0
1909	Cin-N	0	0	—	1	0	0	0	0	4	10	22.5	1	3	6.8	2	4.5	22.50	11	.588	.667	-9	-9	94	72	0.0	-0	0	-0.6
Total	2	0	1	.000	5	1	1	0	0	25	28	10.1	1	11	4.0	9	3.2	5.76	42	.323	.406	-9	-9	102	93	-0.4	-1	-1	-0.6
■ **MOE SAVRANSKY**	Savransky, Morris b: 1/13/29, Cleveland, Ohio BL/TL, 5'11", 175 lbs. Deb: 4/23/54																												
1954	Cin-N	0	2	.000	16	0	0	0	0	24	23	8.6	6	8	3.0	7	2.6	4.88	87	.247	.314	-2	-2	104	95	-0.9	1	1	0.0
■ **RICK SAWYER**	Sawyer, Richard Clyde b: 4/7/48, Bakersfield, Cal. BR/TR, 6'2", 205 lbs. Deb: 4/28/74																												
1974	NY-A	0	0	—	1	0	0	0	0	2	2	9.0	0	1	4.5	1	4.5	13.50	26	.500	.375	-2	-2	95	56	0.0	0	0	-0.1
1975	NY-A	0	0	—	4	0	0	0	0	6	7	10.5	0	2	3.0	3	4.5	3.00	123	.304	.360	1	0	98	139	0.0	0	-0	0.0
1976	SD-N	5	3	.625	13	11	4	2	0	82	84	9.2	2	38	4.2	33	3.6	2.52	124	.272	.347	9	6	90	156	1.3	1	-0	0.7
1977	SD-N	7	6	.538	56	9	0	0	0	111	136	11.0	15	55	4.5	45	3.6	5.84	60	.316	.390	-24	-29	89	106	1.4	1	1	-2.6
Total	4	12	9	.571	74	20	4	2	0	201	229	10.3	17	96	4.3	82	3.7	4.48	75	.299	.372	-16	-25	90	127	2.7	2	1	-2.0
■ **WILL SAWYER**	Sawyer, Willard Newton b: 7/29/1864, Brimfield, Ohio d: 1/5/36, Kent, Ohio BL/TL, Deb: 7/21/1883																												
1883	Cle-N	4	10	.286	17	15	15	0	0	141	119	**7.6**	1	47	3.0	76	4.9	2.36	138	**.236**	.301	12	14	104	95	-3.6	-7	0	0.7
■ **BILL SAYLES**	Sayles, William Nisbeth b: 7/27/17, Portland, Ore. BR/TR, 6'2", 175 lbs. Deb: 7/17/39																												
1939	Bos-A	0	0	—	5	0	0	0	0	14	14	9.0	1	13	8.4	9	5.8	7.07	70	.264	.403	-4	-3	107	79	0.0	-1	0	-0.2
1943	NY-N	1	3	.250	18	3	1	0	0	53	60	10.2	1	23	3.9	38	6.5	4.75	70	.284	.346	-8	-8	99	86	-0.5	1	-0	-0.7
	Bro-N	0	0	—	5	0	0	0	0	12	13	9.8	0	10	7.5	5	3.8	7.50	44	.271	.397	-6	-6	99	62	0.0	0	-0	-0.5
	Yr	1	3	.250	23	3	1	0	0	65	73	10.1	1	33	4.6	43	6.0	5.26	63	.282	.356	-14	-14	99	62	-0.5	1	-0	-1.2
Total	2	1	3	.250	28	3	1	0	0	79	87	9.9	2	46	5.2	52	5.9	5.58	65	.279	.364	-17	-17	100	81	-0.5	1	-0	-1.4
■ **PHIL SAYLOR**	Saylor, Philip Andrew "Lefty" b: 1/2/1871, Van Wert Co., Ohio d: 7/23/37, W.Alexandria, O. TL , Deb: 7/11/1891																												
1891	Phi-N	0	0	—	1	0	0	0	0	3	2	6.0	1	0	0.0	0	0.0	6.00	53	.201	.201	-1	-1	95	46	0.0	-0	0	0.0
■ **FRANK SCANLAN**	Scanlan, Frank Aloysius b: 4/28/1890, Syracuse, N.Y. d: 4/9/69, Brooklyn, N.Y. 6'1.5", 175 lbs. Deb: 09																												
1909	Phi-N	0	0	—	6	0	0	0	1	11	8	6.5	0	5	4.1	5	4.1	1.64	169	.211	.302	1	1	106	125	0.0	-1	-0	0.1
■ **DOC SCANLAN**	Scanlan, William Dennis b: 3/7/1881, Syracuse, N.Y. d: 5/29/49, Brooklyn, N.Y. BL/TR, 5'8", 165 lbs. Deb: 03																												
1903	Pit-N	0	1	.000	1	1	1	0	0	9	5	5.0	0	6	6.0	0	0.0	4.00	83	.181	.327	-1	-1	101	43	-0.4	0	-0	0.0
1904	Pit-N	1	3	.250	4	3	1	0	0	22	21	8.6	0	20	8.2	10	4.1	4.91	54	.282	.446	-5	-5	98	96	-1.0	-0	-0	-0.5
	Bro-N	6	6	.500	13	12	11	3	0	104	94	8.1	0	40	3.5	40	3.5	2.16	123	.266	.343	7	6	98	129	1.4	-1	-2	0.4
	Yr	7	9	.438	17	15	12	3	0	126	115	8.2	0	60	4.3	50	3.6	2.64	101	.267	.359	1	0	98	129	0.4	-0	-2	-0.1
1905	Bro-N	14	12	.538	33	28	22	2	0	250	220	7.9	4	104	3.7	135	4.9	2.92	104	.264	.351	2	3	102	104	4.8	-2	-2	0.1
1906	Bro-N	18	13	.581	38	33	28	6	2	288	230	7.2	5	127	4.0	120	3.8	3.19	74	.246	.339	-18	-27	90	81	4.7	3	-8	-3.5
1907	Bro-N	6	8	.429	17	15	10	2	0	107	90	7.6	1	61	5.1	59	5.0	3.20	74	.257	.371	-9	-10	96	95	-0.1	5	-2	-1.2
1909	Bro-N	8	7	.533	19	17	12	2	0	141	125	8.0	2	65	4.1	72	4.6	2.94	91	.252	.343	-5	-4	103	110	2.2	5	-1	-0.5
1910	Bro-N	9	11	.450	34	25	14	0	2	217	175	7.3	1	116	4.8	103	4.3	2.61	113	.234	.341	10	8	98	112	0.7	1	-2	0.8
1911	Bro-N	3	10	.231	22	15	3	0	1	114	101	8.0	2	69	5.4	45	3.6	3.63	93	.256	.374	-3	-3	99	109	-3.0	-2	-1	-0.5
Total	8	65	71	.478	181	149	102	15	5	1252	1061	7.6	15	608	4.4	584	4.2	3.00	92	.252	.351	-22	-33	97	102	9.3	8	-18	-4.9
■ **PAT SCANTLEBURY**	Scantlebury, Patrico Athelstan b: 11/11/25, Gatun, Canal Zone BL/TL, 6'1", 180 lbs. Deb: 4/19/56																												
1956	Cin-N	0	1	.000	6	2	0	0	0	19	24	11.4	5	5	2.4	10	4.7	6.63	60	.293	.333	-6	-6	106	83	-0.4	-0	0	-0.5
■ **RANDY SCARBERY**	Scarbery, Randy James b: 6/22/52, Fresno, Cal. BB/TR, 6'1", 185 lbs. Deb: 4/16/79																												
1979	Chi-A	2	8	.200	45	5	0	0	4	101	102	9.1	9	34	3.0	45	4.0	4.63	94	.262	.319	-5	-3	103	82	-2.8	0	0	-0.2
1980	Chi-A	1	2	.333	15	0	0	0	2	29	24	7.4	1	7	2.2	18	5.6	4.03	98	.238	.284	0	-0	98	69	-0.3	0	-0	0.0
Total	2	3	10	.231	60	5	0	0	6	130	126	8.7	10	41	2.8	63	4.4	4.50	94	.257	.312	-4	-4	101	79	-3.1	0	-0	-0.2
■ **RAY SCARBOROUGH**	Scarborough, Ray Wilson (born Rae Wilson Scarborough) b: 7/23/17, Mt.Gilead, N.C. d: 7/1/82, Mount Olive, N.C. BR/TR, 6', 185 lbs. Deb: 6/26/42 C																												
1942	Was-A	2	1	.667	17	5	1	1	0	63	68	9.7	2	32	4.6	16	2.3	4.14	87	.272	.352	-3	-4	99	101	0.7	0	1	-0.2
1943	Was-A	4	4	.500	24	6	2	0	3	86	93	9.7	2	46	4.8	43	4.5	2.83	119	.273	.354	4	5	102	145	-0.3	2	0	0.8
1946	Was-A	7	11	.389	32	20	6	1	1	156	176	10.2	8	74	4.3	46	2.7	4.04	82	.286	.361	-9	-13	94	110	-2.0	-2	2	-1.2
1947	Was-A	6	13	.316	33	18	8	2	0	161	165	9.2	5	67	3.7	63	3.5	3.41	109	.267	.335	5	6	101	109	-2.4	-3	-0	0.2
1948	Was-A	15	8	.652	31	26	9	0	1	185	166	8.1	10	72	3.5	76	3.7	2.82	162	.233	.305	30	36	107	108	**5.7**	-0	1	3.9
1949	Was-A	13	11	.542	34	27	11	1	0	200	204	9.2	10	88	4.0	81	3.6	4.59	88	.265	.339	-9	-12	96	85	4.3	0	1	-1.0
1950	Was-A	3	5	.375	8	8	4	2	0	58	62	9.6	1	22	3.4	24	3.7	4.03	115	.276	.336	3	4	101	96	-0.5	-1	1	0.3
	Chi-A	10	13	.435	27	23	8	1	1	150	160	9.6	10	62	3.7	70	4.2	5.28	86	.274	.343	-12	-12	99	81	1.0	-1	-1	-1.2
	Yr	13	18	.419	35	31	12	3	1	208	222	9.6	11	84	3.6	94	4.1	4.93	92	.273	.339	-8	-9	100	81	0.5	-1	-0	-0.9
1951	Bos-A	12	9	.571	37	22	8	0	0	184	201	9.8	21	61	3.0	71	3.5	5.09	86	.275	.340	-20	-14	106	90	0.2	-2	1	-1.4

YEAR	TM/L	W	L	PCT	G	GS	CG	SHO	SV	IP	H	H/G	HR	BB	BB/G	SO	SO/G	ERA	/A	OAVG	OOBP	PR	/A	PF	CPI	WAT	PB	PD	TPI
1952	Bos-A	1	5	.167	28	8	1	1	4	77	79	9.2	8	35	4.1	29	3.4	4.79	82	.266	.345	-10	-7	107	93	-1.9	0	0	-0.6
	NY-A	5	1	.833	9	4	1	0	0	34	27	7.1	4	15	4.0	13	3.4	2.91	119	.223	.309	3	2	95	119	1.7	2	-0	0.4
	Yr	6	6	.500	37	12	2	1	4	111	106	8.6	12	50	4.1	42	3.4	4.22	90	.251	.326	-7	-5	103	119	-0.2	0	0	-0.2
1953	NY-A	2	2	.500	25	1	0	0	0	55	52	8.5	4	26	4.3	20	3.3	3.27	108	.250	.342	4	2	88	121	-0.4	-0	0	0.2
	Det-A	0	2	.000	13	0	0	0	2	21	34	14.6	3	11	4.7	12	5.1	8.14	50	.354	.432	-10	-10	102	96	-0.9	-0	-0	-0.9
	Yr	2	4	.333	38	1	0	0	2	76	86	10.2	7	37	4.4	32	3.8	4.62	79	.279	.359	-5	-8	92	96	-1.3	-0	0	-0.7
Total	10	80	85	.485	318	168	59	9	12	1430	1487	9.4	88	611	3.8	564	3.5	4.13	97	.267	.340	-22	-19	100	101	5.2	-6	4	-0.7
■ MAC SCARCE	Scarce, Guerrant McCurdy b: 4/8/49, Danville, Va. BL/TL, 6'3", 180 lbs. Deb: 7/10/72																												
1972	Phi-N	1	2	.333	31	0	0	0	4	37	30	7.3	6	20	4.9	40	9.7	3.41	100	.222	.325	0	0	99	119	-0.1	-1	1	0.0
1973	Phi-N	1	8	.111	52	0	0	0	12	71	54	6.8	3	47	6.0	57	7.2	2.41	166	.220	.340	10	13	109	140	-3.3	-1	-1	1.1
1974	Phi-N	3	8	.273	58	0	0	0	5	70	72	9.3	6	35	4.5	50	6.4	5.01	75	.275	.354	-11	-10	104	91	-2.5	-1	-1	-1.1
1975	NY-N	0	0	—	1	0	0	0	0	0	1	—	0	0	—	0	—	—	—	1.000	1.000	0	0	95	0	0.0	0	0	0.0
1978	Min-A	1	1	.500	17	0	0	0	0	32	35	9.8	5	15	4.2	17	4.8	3.94	91	.292	.371	-1	-1	94	144	0.1	0	-1	-0.1
Total	5	6	19	.240	159	0	0	0	21	210	192	8.2	20	117	5.0	164	7.0	3.69	102	.251	.348	-1	1	103	121	-5.8	-2	-2	-0.1
■ AL SCHACHT	Schacht, Alexander b: 11/11/1892, New York, N.Y. d: 7/14/84, Waterbury, Conn. BR/TR, 5'11", 142 lbs. Deb: 9/18/19 C																												
1919	Was-A	2	0	1.000	2	2	1	0	0	15	14	8.4	0	4	2.4	4	2.4	2.40	133	.233	.281	1	1	99	69	1.0	0	-0	0.1
1920	Was-A	6	4	.600	22	11	5	1	1	99	130	11.8	2	30	2.7	19	1.7	4.45	82	.319	.367	-7	-9	96	101	1.5	1	2	-0.5
1921	Was-A	6	6	.500	29	5	2	0	1	83	110	11.9	2	27	2.9	15	1.6	4.88	87	.332	.370	-6	-6	99	107	-0.2	1	-3	-0.7
Total	3	14	10	.583	53	18	8	1	2	197	254	11.6	4	61	2.8	38	1.7	4.48	86	.318	.362	-11	-13	98	101	2.3	2	-2	-1.1
■ SID SCHACHT	Schacht, Sidney b: 2/3/18, Bogota, N.J. BR/TR, 5'11", 170 lbs. Deb: 4/23/50																												
1950	StL-A	0	0	—	8	1	0	0	0	11	24	19.6	5	14	11.5	7	5.7	15.55	33	.429	.543	-13	-13	111	96	0.0	-0	-0	-1.0
1951	StL-A	0	0	—	6	0	0	0	1	6	14	21.0	1	5	7.5	4	6.0	21.00	21	.452	.528	-11	-11	109	59	0.0	0	-0	-0.9
	Bos-N	0	2	.000	5	0	0	0	0	5	6	10.8	0	2	3.6	1	1.8	1.80	213	.300	.364	1	1	97	240	-0.9	0	-0	0.1
Total	2	0	2	.000	19	1	0	0	1	22	44	18.0	6	21	8.6	12	4.9	13.91	33	.411	.508	-23	-23	107	118	-0.9	-0	-0	-1.8
■ HAL SCHACKER	Schacker, Harold b: 4/6/25, Brooklyn, N.Y. BR/TR, 6', 190 lbs. Deb: 5/09/45																												
1945	Bos-N	0	1	.000	6	0	0	0	0	15	14	8.4	2	9	5.4	6	3.6	5.40	79	.241	.333	-3	-2	113	81	-0.4	-0	-0	-0.1
■ GERMANY SCHAEFER	Schaefer, Herman A. b: 2/4/1877, Chicago, Ill. d: 5/16/19, Saranac Lake, N.Y. BR/TR, 5'9", 175 lbs. Deb: 10/05/01																												
1912	Was-A	0	0	—	1	0	0	0	0	1	1	9.0	0	0	0.0	0	0.0	0.00	—	.333	.333	0	0	97	0	0.0	0	0	0.0
1913	Was-A	0	0	—	1	0	0	0	0	⅓	2	54.0	1	0	0.0	0	0.0	54.00	—	.667	.667	-2	-2	105	86	0.0	0	0	-0.1
Total	2	0	0	—	2	0	0	0	0	1	3	27.0	1	0	0.0	0	0.0	18.00	18	.500	.500	-2	-2	97	0	0.0	0	0	-0.1
■ HARRY SCHAEFFER	Schaeffer, Harry Edward "Lefty" b: 6/23/24, Reading, Pa. BL/TL, 6'2.5", 175 lbs. Deb: 7/28/52																												
1952	NY-A	0	1	.000	5	2	0	0	0	17	18	9.5	2	18	9.5	15	7.9	5.29	66	.265	.419	-3	-3	95	114	-0.4	-0	0	-0.2
■ MARK SCHAEFFER	Schaeffer, Mark Philip b: 6/5/48, Santa Monica, Cal. BL/TL, 6'5", 215 lbs. Deb: 4/18/72																												
1972	SD-N	2	0	1.000	41	0	0	0	1	41	52	11.4	3	28	6.1	25	5.5	4.61	68	.319	.412	-5	-7	91	136	1.0	-0	1	-0.6
■ JOE SCHAFFERNOTH	Schaffernoth, Joseph Arthur b: 8/6/37, Trenton, N.J. BR/TR, 6'4.5", 195 lbs. Deb: 4/15/59																												
1959	Chi-N	1	0	1.000	5	1	0	0	0	8	11	12.4	1	4	4.5	3	3.4	7.88	49	.355	.417	-3	-4	99	90	0.5	-0	0	-0.3
1960	Chi-N	2	3	.400	33	0	0	0	3	55	46	7.5	2	17	2.8	33	5.4	2.78	136	.235	.290	6	6	101	100	0.0	0	0	0.7
1961	Chi-N	0	4	.000	21	0	0	0	0	38	43	10.2	7	18	4.3	23	5.4	6.39	64	.293	.365	-10	-10	102	90	-1.9	-1	0	-0.9
	Cle-A	0	1	.000	15	0	0	0	0	17	16	8.5	2	14	7.4	9	4.8	4.76	81	.242	.378	-1	-2	97	104	-0.4	-0	1	0.0
Total	3	3	8	.273	74	1	0	0	3	118	116	8.8	12	53	4.0	68	5.2	4.58	85	.264	.338	-9	-9	100	97	-1.8	-1	1	-0.5
■ ART SCHALLOCK	Schallock, Arthur Lawrence b: 4/25/24, Mill Valley, Cal. BL/TL, 5'9", 160 lbs. Deb: 7/16/51																												
1951	NY-A	3	1	.750	11	6	1	0	0	46	50	9.8	3	20	3.9	19	3.7	3.91	93	.272	.343	1	-1	88	108	0.6	1	0	0.0
1952	NY-A	0	0	—	2	0	0	0	0	2	3	13.5	0	2	9.0	1	4.5	9.00	39	.375	.500	-1	-1	95	90	0.0	0	0	0.0
1953	NY-A	0	0	—	7	1	0	0	1	21	30	12.9	2	15	6.4	13	5.6	3.00	117	.345	.442	2	1	88	246	0.0	0	0	0.1
1954	NY-A	0	1	.000	6	1	1	0	0	17	20	10.6	3	11	5.8	9	4.8	4.24	83	.282	.386	-1	-1	94	138	-0.4	-0	-0	-0.1
1955	NY-A	0	0	—	2	0	0	0	0	3	4	12.0	1	1	3.0	2	6.0	6.00	62	.333	.385	-1	-1	94	126	0.0	0	0	0.0
	Bal-A	3	5	.375	30	6	1	0	0	80	92	10.3	2	42	4.7	33	3.7	4.16	89	.294	.374	-2	-4	94	112	0.0	-1	-1	-0.5
	Yr	3	5	.375	32	6	1	0	0	83	96	10.4	3	43	4.7	35	3.8	4.23	88	.295	.374	-2	-5	94	112	0.0	0	-1	-0.5
Total	5	6	7	.462	58	14	3	0	1	169	199	10.6	11	91	4.8	77	4.1	4.05	90	.295	.378	-1	-8	92	130	0.2	1	-1	-0.5
■ CHARLEY SCHANZ	Schanz, Charley Murrell b: 6/8/19, Anacortes, Wash. BR/TR, 6'3.5", 215 lbs. Deb: 4/20/44																												
1944	Phi-N	13	16	.448	40	30	13	2	3	241	231	8.6	6	103	3.8	84	3.1	3.32	111	.254	.327	8	10	103	105	1.4	-1	0	1.0
1945	Phi-N	4	15	.211	35	21	5	1	5	145	165	10.2	5	87	5.4	56	3.5	4.34	89	.285	.379	-9	-7	102	114	-3.0	-0	1	-0.6
1946	Phi-N	6	6	.500	32	15	4	0	4	116	130	10.1	8	71	5.5	47	3.6	5.82	57	.286	.385	-31	-32	98	87	0.6	-2	1	-3.3
1947	Phi-N	2	4	.333	34	6	1	0	2	102	107	9.4	7	47	4.1	42	3.7	4.15	100	.295	.372	-1	-0	102	122	-0.4	-1	0	0.0
1950	Bos-A	3	2	.600	14	0	0	0	0	23	25	9.8	3	24	9.4	14	5.5	8.22	62	.281	.435	-9	-8	111	83	0.0	-1	0	-0.7
Total	5	28	43	.394	155	72	23	3	14	627	658	9.4	29	332	4.8	243	3.5	4.33	88	.275	.362	-42	-38	102	106	-1.4	-5	1	-3.6
■ JOHN SCHAPPERT	Schappert, John b: Brooklyn, N.Y. d: 7/29/16, Rockaway Beach, N.Y. BR/TR, 5'10", 170 lbs. Deb: 5/03/1882																												
1882	StL-a	8	7	.533	15	14	13	0	0	128	131	9.2	2	32	2.3	38	2.7	3.52	80	.270	.315	-12	-10	104	88	1.2	0	0	-0.8
■ BILL SCHARDT	Schardt, Wilburt "Big Bill" b: 1/20/1886, Cleveland, Ohio d: 7/20/64, Vermilion, Ohio BR/TR, 6'4", 210 lbs. Deb: 4/14/11																												
1911	Bro-N	5	15	.250	39	22	10	1	4	195	190	8.8	3	91	4.2	77	3.6	3.60	94	.266	.355	-4	-5	99	103	-4.4	-0	0	-0.4
1912	Bro-N	0	1	.000	7	0	0	0	1	21	25	10.7	1	6	2.6	7	3.0	4.29	77	.301	.363	-2	-2	97	101	-0.4	-1	2	0.0
Total	2	5	16	.238	46	22	10	1	5	216	215	9.0	4	97	4.0	84	3.5	3.67	92	.269	.356	-6	-7	99	103	-4.8	-1	2	-0.4
■ JEFF SCHATTINGER	Schattinger, Jeffrey Charles b: 10/25/55, Fresno, Cal. BL/TR, 6'5", 200 lbs. Deb: 9/21/81																												
1981	KC-A	0	0	—	1	0	0	0	0	3	2	6.0	0	1	3.0	1	3.0	0.00	—	.182	.357	1	1	99	0	0.0	0	0	0.1
■ DAN SCHATZEDER	Schatzeder, Daniel Ernest b: 12/1/54, Elmhurst, Ill. BL/TL, 6', 185 lbs. Deb: 9/04/77																												
1977	Mon-N	2	1	.667	6	3	1	1	0	22	16	6.5	0	13	5.3	14	5.7	2.45	158	.203	.312	4	3	99	94	0.6	0	0	0.4
1978	Mon-N	7	7	.500	29	18	2	0	0	144	108	6.8	10	68	4.3	69	4.3	3.06	112	.213	.304	8	6	96	95	0.4	3	-2	0.8
1979	Mon-N	10	5	.667	32	21	3	0	1	162	136	7.6	17	59	3.3	106	5.9	2.83	**133**	.225	.290	16	17	101	105	1.5	4	-3	1.9
1980	Det-A	11	13	.458	32	26	9	2	0	193	178	8.3	23	58	2.7	94	4.4	4.01	106	.246	.301	1	5	105	87	-1.5	0	-2	0.3
1981	Det-A	6	8	.429	17	14	1	0	0	71	74	9.4	13	29	3.7	20	2.5	6.08	63	.265	.330	-19	-18	105	79	-1.6	0	-0	-1.7
1982	SF-N	1	4	.200	13	3	0	0	0	33	47	12.8	3	12	3.3	18	4.9	7.36	46	.333	.381	-14	-15	94	79	-1.5	-0	0	-1.3
	Mon-N	0	2	.000	26	1	0	0	0	36	37	9.3	1	12	3.0	15	3.8	3.50	107	.276	.336	0	1	104	110	-0.9	1	-0	0.2
	Yr	1	6	.143	39	4	0	0	0	69	84	11.0	4	24	3.1	33	4.3	5.35	67	.304	.358	-13	-14	99	110	-2.4	-0	0	-1.1
1983	Mon-N	5	2	.714	58	2	0	0	2	87	88	9.1	3	25	2.6	48	5.0	3.21	115	.265	.320	4	5	101	106	1.5	0	-1	0.4
1984	Mon-N	7	7	.500	36	14	1	1	1	136	112	7.4	13	36	2.4	89	5.9	2.71	121	.224	.274	13	9	91	100	0.2	5	-3	1.1
1985	Mon-N	3	5	.375	24	15	1	0	0	104	101	8.7	13	31	2.7	64	5.5	3.81	89	.259	.306	-2	-5	94	102	-1.1	3	0	-0.1
1986	Mon-N	3	2	.600	30	1	0	0	1	59	53	8.1	6	19	2.9	33	5.0	3.20	114	.240	.295	3	3	98	102	0.6	6	-1	0.9
	Phi-N	3	3	.500	25	0	0	0	1	29	28	8.7	3	16	5.0	14	4.3	3.41	113	.252	.336	1	1	104	124	-0.1	0	-0	0.2
	Yr	6	5	.545	55	1	0	0	2	88	81	8.3	9	35	3.6	47	4.8	3.27	114	.243	.309	4	4	100	124	0.5	6	-1	1.1
1987	Phi-N	3	1	.750	26	0	0	0	0	38	40	9.5	4	14	3.3	28	6.6	4.03	106	.278	.329	0	1	105	111	1.0	0	-1	0.0
	Min-A	3	1	.750	30	1	0	0	0	44	64	13.1	8	18	3.7	30	6.1	6.34	68	.342	.399	-9	-10	96	113	1.0	0	-0	-0.9
1988	Cle-A	0	2	.000	15	0	0	0	3	16	26	14.6	6	2	1.1	10	5.6	9.56	42	.351	.377	-10	-10	102	87	-0.9	0	-0	-0.9
	Min-A	0	1	.000	10	0	0	0	0	10	8	7.2	1	5	4.5	7	6.3	1.80	233	.216	.318	2	3	105	195	-0.4	0	0	0.3
	Yr	0	3	.000	25	0	0	0	3	26	34	11.8	7	7	2.4	17	5.9	6.58	62	.304	.347	-8	-7	103	195	-1.3	0	-0	-0.6
Total	12	64	64	.500	409	119	18	4	9	1184	1116	8.5	124	417	3.2	659	5.0	3.77	99	.250	.311	-0	-5	99	99	-1.2	23	-12	1.6
■ RUBE SCHAUER	Schauer, Alexander John (born Dimitri Ivanovich Dimitrihoff) b: 3/19/1891, Odessa, Russia d: 4/15/57, Minneapolis, Minn. BR/TR, 6'2", 192 lbs. Deb: 8/27/13																												
1913	NY-N	0	1	.000	3	1	1	0	0	12	14	10.5	0	9	6.8	7	5.3	7.50	43	.292	.397	-6	-6	100	65	-0.4	-0	0	-0.5

YEAR	TM/L	W	L	PCT	G	GS	CG	SHO	SV	IP	H	H/G	HR	BB	BB/G	SO	SO/G	ERA	/A	OAVG	OOBP	PR	/A	PF	CPI	WAT	PB	PD	TPI
1914	NY-N	0	0	—	6	0	0	0	0	22	16	6.5	2	8	3.3	6	2.5	3.27	80	.205	.270	-1	-2	94	68	0.0	-0	-0	-0.2
1915	NY-N	2	8	.200	32	7	4	0	0	105	101	8.7	4	35	3.0	65	5.6	3.51	72	.258	.309	-9	-11	92	91	-2.8	-2	-0	-1.4
1916	NY-N	1	4	.200	19	3	1	0	0	46	44	8.6	0	16	3.1	24	4.7	2.93	83	.257	.320	-2	-2	94	101	-1.5	0	-0	-0.2
1917	Phi-A	7	16	.304	33	21	10	0	1	215	209	8.7	6	69	2.9	62	2.6	3.14	82	.263	.324	-11	-13	97	97	-1.9	-2	0	-1.6
Total	5	10	29	.256	93	32	16	0	1	400	384	8.6	12	137	3.1	164	3.7	3.35	77	.259	.319	-29	-35	95	93	-6.6	-4	-1	-3.9
■ OWEN SCHEETZ	Scheetz, Owen Franklin b: 12/24/13, New Bedford, Ohio BR/TR, 6', 190 lbs. Deb: 4/22/43																												
1943	Was-A	0	0	—	6	0	0	0	1	9	16	16.0	0	4	4.0	5	5.0	7.00	48	.381	.435	-4	-4	102	101	0.0	-0	0	-0.3
■ LEFTY SCHEGG	Schegg, Gilbert Eugene (born Gilbert Eugene Price) b: 8/28/1889, Leesville, Ohio d: 2/27/63, Niles, Ohio TL , 5'11", 180 lbs. Deb: 8/20/12																												
1912	Was-A	0	0	—	2	1	0	0	0	5	7	12.6	0	4	7.2	3	5.4	3.60	90	.333	.440	-0	-0	97	176	0.0	-0	-0	0.0
■ CARL SCHEIB	Scheib, Carl Alvin b: 1/1/27, Gratz, Pa. BR/TR, 6'1", 192 lbs. Deb: 9/06/43																												
1943	Phi-A	0	1	.000	6	0	0	0	0	19	24	11.4	4	3	1.4	3	1.4	4.26	82	.308	.329	-2	-2	106	132	-0.4	-1	-1	-0.2
1944	Phi-A	0	0	—	15	0	0	0	0	36	36	9.0	1	11	2.8	13	3.3	4.25	82	.257	.327	-3	-3	102	79	0.0	1	1	0.0
1945	Phi-A	0	0	—	4	0	0	0	0	9	6	6.0	0	4	4.0	2	2.0	3.00	108	.207	.294	0	0	96	77	0.0	-0	0	0.0
1947	Phi-A	4	6	.400	21	12	6	2	0	116	121	9.4	11	55	4.3	26	2.0	5.04	73	.274	.352	-17	-17	100	91	-1.0	-2	-2	-2.0
1948	Phi-A	14	8	.636	32	24	15	1	0	199	219	9.9	14	76	3.4	44	2.0	3.93	110	.286	.346	8	9	102	117	2.5	7	0	2.1
1949	Phi-A	9	12	.429	38	23	11	2	0	183	191	9.4	16	118	5.8	43	2.1	5.11	81	.275	.379	-19	-20	99	98	-2.1	3	-3	-1.8
1950	Phi-A	3	10	.231	43	8	1	0	3	106	138	11.7	13	70	5.9	37	3.1	7.22	59	.317	.405	-31	-35	93	90	-2.1	2	-1	-2.9
1951	Phi-A	1	12	.077	46	11	3	0	10	143	132	8.3	7	71	4.5	49	3.1	4.47	98	.250	.341	-6	-2	106	87	-5.4	8	4	1.1
1952	Phi-A	11	7	.611	30	19	8	1	2	158	153	8.7	21	50	2.8	42	2.4	4.39	94	.253	.310	-12	-5	112	88	2.0	-1	0	-0.3
1953	Phi-A	3	7	.300	28	8	3	0	2	96	99	9.3	9	29	2.7	25	2.3	4.88	86	.261	.319	-9	-7	105	79	-1.0	-1	-0	-0.7
1954	Phi-A	0	1	.000	1	1	0	0	0	2	5	22.5	0	1	4.5	1	4.5	22.50	17	.500	.583	-4	-4	105	58	-0.4	0	0	-0.3
	StL-N	0	1	.000	3	1	0	0	0	5	6	10.8	3	5	9.0	5	9.0	10.80	38	.300	.440	-4	-4	100	97	-0.4	-0	0	-0.3
Total	11	45	65	.409	267	107	47	6	17	1072	1130	9.5	99	493	4.1	290	2.4	4.88	85	.274	.351	-100	-87	103	95	-8.3	16	0	-5.3
■ FRANK SCHEIBECK	Scheibeck, Frank S. b: 6/28/1865, Detroit, Mich. d: 10/22/56, Detroit, Mich. BR/TR, 5'7", 145 lbs. Deb: 5/09/1887																												
1887	Cle-a	0	1	.000	1	1	1	0	0	9	17	17.0	1	4	4.0	3	3.0	12.00	37	.416	.468	-8	-8	103	75	-0.4	0	0	-0.4
■ JACK SCHEIBLE	Scheible, John G. b: 2/16/1866, Youngstown, Ohio d: 8/9/1897, Youngstown, Ohio TL , Deb: 9/08/1893																												
1893	Cle-N	1	1	.500	2	2	2	1	0	18	15	7.5	0	11	5.5	1	0.5	2.00	240	.241	.355	5	6	103	160	0.0	-0	0	0.5
1894	Phi-N	0	1	.000	1	1	0	0	0	⅓	6	162.0	0	2	54.0	0	0.0	189.00	—	1.000	1.000	-7	-7	94	57	-0.4	0	0	-0.3
Total	2	1	2	.333	3	3	2	1	0	18	21	10.5	0	13	6.5	1	0.5	5.50	87	.307	.418	-2	-1	103	160	-0.4	-0	0	0.2
■ JIM SCHELLE	Schelle, Gerard Anthony b: 4/13/17, Baltimore, Md. BR/TR, 6'3", 204 lbs. Deb: 7/23/39																												
1939	Phi-A	0	0	—	1	0	0	0	0	0	1	—	0	2	—	0	—	—	—	1.000	1.000	0	0	102	0	0.0	0	0	0.0
■ FRED SCHEMANSKE	Schemanske, Frederick George "Buck" b: 4/28/03, Detroit, Mich. d: 2/18/60, Detroit, Mich. BR/TR, 6'2", 190 lbs. Deb: 9/15/23																												
1923	Was-A	0	0	—	1	0	0	0	0	1	3	27.0	0	0	0.0	0	0.0	27.00	14	.600	.500	-3	-3	95	52	0.0	1	0	-0.1
■ BILL SCHENCK	Schenck, William G. b: Brooklyn, N.Y. 5'7", 171 lbs. Deb: 5/29/1882																												
1882	Lou-a	1	0	1.000	2	1	1	0	0	10	6	5.4	0	1	0.9	4	3.6	0.90	268	.178	.202	2	2	90	52	0.5	0	0	0.2
■ JOHN SCHENEBERG	Scheneberg, John Bluford b: 11/20/1887, Guyandotte, W.Va. d: 9/26/50, Huntington, W.Va. BB/TR, 6'1", 180 lbs. Deb: 9/23/13																												
1913	Pit-N	0	1	.000	1	1	0	0	0	6	10	15.0	0	2	3.0	1	1.5	6.00	50	.400	.414	-2	-2	94	116	-0.4	0	0	0.0
1920	StL-A	0	0	—	1	0	0	0	0	2	7	31.5	0	1	4.5	0	0.0	27.00	16	.583	.615	-5	-5	111	61	0.0	0	-0	-0.3
Total	2	0	1	.000	2	1	0	0	0	8	17	19.1	0	3	3.4	1	1.1	11.25	29	.459	.476	-7	-7	98	102	-0.4	0	0	-0.3
■ FRED SCHERMAN	Scherman, Frederick John b: 7/25/44, Dayton, Ohio BL/TL, 6'1", 195 lbs. Deb: 4/26/69																												
1969	Det-A	1	0	1.000	4	0	0	0	0	4	6	13.5	2	0	0.0	3	6.8	6.75	55	.333	.333	-1	-1	102	118	0.5	0	0	0.0
1970	Det-A	4	4	.500	48	0	0	0	1	70	61	7.8	5	28	3.6	58	7.5	3.21	120	.237	.310	4	5	104	100	0.1	-0	0	0.5
1971	Det-A	11	6	.647	69	1	1	0	20	113	91	7.2	11	49	3.9	46	3.7	2.71	122	.226	.313	10	7	95	123	1.8	2	1	1.0
1972	Det-A	7	3	.700	57	3	0	0	12	94	91	8.7	5	53	5.1	53	5.1	3.64	95	.269	.363	-6	-2	112	121	1.7	-1	-1	-0.3
1973	Det-A	2	2	.500	34	0	0	0	1	62	59	8.6	6	30	4.4	28	4.1	4.21	92	.258	.346	-3	-2	101	101	0.0	0	-1	-0.3
1974	Hou-N	2	5	.286	53	0	0	0	4	61	67	9.9	5	26	3.8	35	5.2	4.13	86	.284	.362	-3	-4	98	116	-1.4	-0	-0	-0.4
1975	Hou-N	0	1	.000	16	0	0	0	0	16	21	11.8	4	4	2.3	13	7.3	5.06	68	.318	.351	-3	-3	95	126	-0.4	-0	0	-0.2
	Mon-N	4	3	.571	34	7	0	0	0	76	84	9.9	3	41	4.9	43	5.1	3.55	112	.283	.369	1	4	109	129	0.7	-1	1	0.4
	Yr	4	4	.500	50	7	0	0	0	92	105	10.3	7	45	4.4	56	5.5	3.82	102	.288	.364	-2	1	107	129	0.3	-0	1	0.2
1976	Mon-N	2	2	.500	31	0	0	0	1	40	42	9.4	5	14	3.1	18	4.0	4.95	73	.261	.326	-6	-6	103	84	0.5	0	-0	-0.6
Total	8	33	26	.559	346	11	1	0	39	536	522	8.8	46	245	4.1	297	5.0	3.66	99	.260	.342	-8	-2	103	114	3.5	-1	-1	0.1
■ BILL SCHERRER	Scherrer, William Joseph b: 1/20/58, Tonawanda, N.Y. BL/TL, 6'4", 170 lbs. Deb: 9/07/82																												
1982	Cin-N	0	1	.000	5	2	0	0	0	17	17	9.0	0	0	0.0	7	3.7	2.65	142	.250	.246	2	2	104	65	-0.4	1	-0	0.3
1983	Cin-N	2	3	.400	73	0	0	0	10	92	73	7.1	6	33	3.2	57	5.6	2.74	138	.225	.286	9	11	104	101	-0.2	-0	1	1.1
1984	Cin-N	1	1	.500	36	0	0	0	1	52	64	11.1	6	15	2.6	35	6.1	5.02	77	.300	.341	-8	-7	107	97	0.1	-0	0	-0.6
	Det-A	1	0	1.000	18	0	0	0	0	19	14	6.6	1	8	3.8	16	7.6	1.89	199	.206	.286	4	4	94	126	0.5	0	-0	0.4
1985	Det-A	3	2	.600	48	0	0	0	0	66	62	8.5	10	41	5.6	46	6.3	4.36	101	.248	.348	-2	0	106	110	0.4	0	1	0.1
1986	Det-A	0	1	.000	13	0	0	0	0	21	19	8.1	3	22	9.4	16	6.9	7.29	54	.244	.408	-7	-8	95	81	-0.4	0	0	-0.6
1987	Cin-N	1	1	.500	23	0	0	0	0	33	43	11.7	3	16	4.4	24	6.5	4.36	97	.328	.391	-1	-1	103	140	0.0	-0	-0	0.0
1988	Bal-A	0	1	.000	4	0	0	0	0	4	8	18.0	2	3	6.8	3	6.8	13.50	29	.400	.478	-4	-4	97	94	-0.4	0	0	-0.3
	Phi-N	0	0	—	8	0	0	0	0	7	7	9.0	0	2	2.6	3	3.9	5.14	69	.269	.321	-1	-1	103	63	0.0	0	0	0.0
Total	7	8	10	.444	228	2	0	0	11	311	307	8.9	31	140	4.1	207	6.0	4.08	97	.260	.332	-8	-4	103	104	-0.4	-0	1	0.4
■ DUTCH SCHESLER	Schesler, Charles b: 6/1/1900, Frankfurt, Germany d: 11/19/53, Harrisburg, Pa. BR/TR, 6'2", 185 lbs. Deb: 4/16/31																												
1931	Phi-N	0	0	—	17	0	0	0	0	38	65	15.4	4	18	4.3	14	3.3	7.34	57	.385	.448	-15	-13	109	114	0.0	-0	0	-1.2
■ LOU SCHETTLER	Schettler, Louis Martin b: 6/12/1886, Pittsburgh, Pa. d: 5/1/60, Youngstown, Ohio BR/TR, 5'11", 160 lbs. Deb: 4/25/10																												
1910	Phi-N	2	6	.250	27	7	3	0	1	107	96	8.1	2	51	4.3	62	5.2	3.20	90	.247	.337	-2	-4	95	96	-2.0	-1	-1	-0.5
■ CURT SCHILLING	Schilling, Curtis Montague b: 11/14/66, Anchorage, Al. BR/TR, 6'4", 205 lbs. Deb: 9/07/88																												
1988	Bal-A	0	3	.000	4	4	0	0	0	15	22	13.2	3	10	6.0	4	2.4	9.60	40	.355	.434	-9	-10	97	88	-1.4	0	-1	-0.8
■ RED SCHILLINGS	Schillings, Elbert Isaiah b: 3/29/1900, Deport, Tex. d: 1/7/54, Oklahoma City, Okla BR/TR, 5'10", 180 lbs. Deb: 9/11/22																												
1922	Phi-A	0	0	—	4	0	0	0	0	8	10	11.3	1	11	12.4	4	4.5	6.75	64	.313	.467	-2	-2	106	121	0.0	-0	-0	-0.2
■ CALVIN SCHIRALDI	Schiraldi, Calvin Drew b: 6/16/62, Houston, Tex. BR/TR, 6'4", 200 lbs. Deb: 9/01/84																												
1984	NY-N	0	2	.000	5	3	0	0	0	17	20	10.6	3	10	5.3	16	8.5	5.82	62	.286	.375	-4	-4	100	99	-0.9	-0	0	-0.3
1985	NY-N	2	1	.667	10	4	0	0	0	26	43	14.9	4	11	3.8	21	7.3	9.00	38	.368	.435	-16	-16	95	89	0.2	-0	0	-1.5
1986	Bos-A	4	2	.667	25	0	0	0	9	51	36	6.4	5	15	2.6	55	9.7	1.41	292	.201	.263	16	15	99	171	0.6	0	-1	1.5
1987	Bos-A	8	5	.615	62	1	0	0	6	84	75	8.0	15	40	4.3	93	10.0	4.39	101	.240	.321	1	0	99	100	1.8	0	0	0.0
1988	Chi-N	9	13	.409	29	27	2	1	1	166	166	9.0	13	63	3.4	140	7.6	4.39	82	.257	.322	-17	-14	105	86	-1.6	-2	-2	-1.8
Total	5	23	23	.500	131	35	2	1	16	344	340	8.9	40	139	3.6	325	8.5	4.37	89	.257	.327	-21	-18	102	103	0.1	-3	-2	-2.1
■ BIFF SCHLITZER	Schlitzer, Victor Joseph b: 12/4/1884, Rochester, N.Y. d: 1/4/48, Wellesley Hills, Mass. BR/TR, 5'11", 175 lbs. Deb: 4/17/08																												
1908	Phi-A	6	8	.429	24	18	11	2	0	131	110	7.6	1	45	3.1	57	3.9	3.16	83	.234	.303	-11	-8	110	80	-0.2	-1	-2	-1.1
1909	Phi-A	0	3	.000	4	3	0	0	0	13	13	9.0	0	7	4.8	6	4.2	5.54	43	.245	.365	-4	-5	97	62	-1.4	0	1	-0.3
	Bos-A	4	4	.500	13	8	5	0	1	70	68	8.7	0	17	2.2	23	3.0	3.47	77	.234	.279	-8	-6	108	48	-0.5	-0	1	-0.5
	Yr	4	7	.364	17	11	5	0	1	83	81	8.8	0	24	2.6	29	3.1	3.80	69	.234	.286	-12	-11	106	48	-1.9	0	2	-0.8
1914	Buf-F	0	0	—	3	0	0	0	0	3	7	21.0	3	2	6.0	1	3.0	18.00	19	.487	.550	-5	-5	104	102	0.0	0	0	-0.3
Total	3	10	15	.400	44	29	16	2	1	217	198	8.2	4	71	2.9	87	3.6	3.61	73	.239	.304	-28	-23	108	69	-2.1	-0	-1	-2.2

YEAR	TM/L	W	L	PCT	G	GS	CG	SHO	SV	IP	H	H/G	HR	BB	BB/G	SO	SO/G	ERA	/A	OAVG	OOBP	PR	/A	PF	CPI	WAT	PB	PD	TPI
■ **GEORGE SCHMEES**	Schmees, George Edward "Rocky" b: 9/6/24, Cincinnati, Ohio BL/TL, 6', 190 lbs. Deb: 4/15/52																												
1952	Bos-A	0	0	—	2	1	0	0	0	6	9	13.5	0	2	3.0	2	3.0	3.00	131	.346	.393	0	1	107	183	0.0	0	0	-0.1
■ **AL SCHMELZ**	Schmelz, Alan George b: 11/12/43, Whittier, Cal. BR/TR, 6'4", 210 lbs. Deb: 9/07/67																												
1967	NY-N	0	0	—	2	0	0	0	0	3	4	12.0	1	1	3.0	2	6.0	3.00	115	.364	.417	0	0	102	278	0.0	0	0	0.0
■ **BUTCH SCHMIDT**	Schmidt, Charles John "Butcher Boy" b: 7/19/1886, Baltimore, Md. d: 9/4/52, Baltimore, Md. BL/TL, 6'1.5", 200 lbs. Deb: 5/11/09																												
1909	NY-A	0	0	—	1	0	0	0	0	5	10	18.0	0	1	1.8	2	3.6	7.20	34	.435	.458	-3	-3	99	106	0.0	-0	-0	-0.2
■ **DAVE SCHMIDT**	Schmidt, David Joseph b: 4/22/57, Niles, Mich. BR/TR, 6'1", 185 lbs. Deb: 5/01/81																												
1981	Tex-A	0	1	.000	14	1	0	0	1	32	31	8.7	1	11	3.1	13	3.7	3.09	106	.258	.326	2	1	90	109	-0.4	0	0	0.1
1982	Tex-A	4	6	.400	33	8	0	0	6	110	118	9.7	5	25	2.0	69	5.6	3.19	121	.279	.320	11	8	94	118	0.0	0	-0	0.8
1983	Tex-A	3	3	.500	31	0	0	0	2	46	42	8.2	3	14	2.7	29	5.7	3.91	105	.241	.298	1	1	101	78	0.1	0	0	0.1
1984	Tex-A	6	6	.500	43	0	0	0	12	70	69	8.9	3	20	2.6	46	5.9	2.57	157	.262	.304	11	11	101	129	0.8	0	1	1.3
1985	Tex-A	7	6	.538	51	4	1	1	5	86	81	8.5	6	22	2.3	46	4.8	3.14	145	.246	.289	10	14	110	97	1.7	0	1	1.5
1986	Chi-A	3	6	.333	49	1	0	0	8	92	94	9.2	10	27	2.6	67	6.6	3.33	128	.264	.320	9	9	101	121	-1.1	0	-1	0.8
1987	Bal-A	10	5	.667	35	14	2	2	1	124	128	9.3	13	26	1.9	70	5.1	3.77	118	.263	.301	10	9	99	96	3.4	0	-1	0.8
1988	Bal-A	8	5	.615	41	9	0	0	2	130	129	8.9	14	38	2.6	67	4.6	3.39	114	.262	.314	8	7	97	117	2.9	0	2	0.8
Total	8	41	38	.519	297	37	3	3	37	690	692	9.0	55	183	2.4	407	5.3	3.33	124	.262	.309	61	60	100	110	7.4	0	2	6.2
■ **FREDDY SCHMIDT**	Schmidt, Frederick Albert b: 2/9/16, Hartford, Conn. BR/TR, 6'1", 185 lbs. Deb: 4/25/44																												
1944	StL-N	7	3	.700	37	9	3	2	5	114	94	7.4	5	58	4.6	58	4.6	3.16	109	.222	.314	6	4	95	94	0.3	0	-1	0.3
1946	StL-N	1	0	1.000	16	0	0	0	0	27	27	9.0	0	15	5.0	14	4.7	3.33	106	.276	.372	0	1	103	129	0.5	-0	0	0.1
1947	StL-N	0	0	—	2	0	0	0	0	4	5	11.3	1	1	2.3	2	4.5	2.25	187	.333	.375	1	1	104	302	0.0	0	-0	0.1
	Phi-N	5	8	.385	29	5	0	0	0	77	76	8.9	4	43	5.0	24	2.8	4.68	89	.285	.382	-5	-5	102	108	-0.2	-2	-1	-0.6
	Chi-N	0	0	—	1	1	0	0	0	3	4	12.0	0	5	15.0	0	0.0	9.00	47	.333	.474	-2	-2	104	98	0.0	-0	-0	-0.1
	Yr	5	8	.385	32	6	0	0	0	84	85	9.1	5	49	5.3	26	2.8	4.71	88	.285	.375	-6	-5	102	98	-0.2	-2	-1	-0.6
Total	3	13	11	.542	85	15	3	2	5	225	206	8.2	10	122	4.9	98	3.9	3.76	99	.252	.348	-0	-1	99	106	0.6	-2	-1	-0.2
■ **PETE SCHMIDT**	Schmidt, Friedrich Christoph Herman b: 7/23/1890, Lowden, Iowa d: 3/11/73, Pembroke, Ont., Can BR/TR, 5'11", 175 lbs. Deb: 7/14/13																												
1913	StL-A	0	0	—	1	0	0	0	1	2	3	13.5	0	2	9.0	0	0.0	4.50	64	.333	.455	-0	-0	98	150	0.0	0	0	0.0
■ **HENRY SCHMIDT**	Schmidt, Henry Martin b: 6/26/1873, Brownsville, Tex. d: 4/23/26, Nashville, Tenn. 5'11", 170 lbs. Deb: 4/17/03																												
1903	Bro-N	22	13	.629	40	36	29	5	2	301	321	9.6	5	120	3.6	96	2.9	3.83	87	.303	.385	-19	-17	102	100	5.1	3	6	-1.0
■ **WILLARD SCHMIDT**	Schmidt, Willard Raymond b: 5/29/28, Hays, Kan. BR/TR, 6'1", 187 lbs. Deb: 4/19/52																												
1952	StL-N	2	3	.400	18	3	0	0	1	35	36	9.3	6	18	4.6	30	7.7	5.14	70	.267	.354	-5	-6	97	102	-0.7	-0	1	-0.4
1953	StL-N	0	2	.000	6	2	0	0	0	18	21	10.5	1	13	6.5	11	5.5	9.00	48	.288	.393	-9	-9	101	61	-0.9	-1	0	-0.8
1955	StL-N	7	6	.538	20	15	8	1	0	130	89	6.2	7	57	3.9	86	6.0	2.77	149	.197	.285	18	20	102	83	1.2	-3	1	1.8
1956	StL-N	6	8	.429	33	21	2	0	1	148	131	8.0	18	78	4.7	52	3.2	3.83	98	.246	.334	-1	-1	99	108	-0.9	2	1	0.2
1957	StL-N	10	3	.769	40	8	1	0	0	117	146	11.2	13	49	3.8	63	4.8	4.77	81	.312	.374	-12	-12	99	116	3.2	0	1	-1.0
1958	Cin-N	3	5	.375	41	2	0	0	0	69	60	7.8	8	33	4.3	41	5.3	2.87	146	.235	.311	8	10	106	127	-0.9	-1	1	1.1
1959	Cin-N	3	2	.600	36	4	0	0	0	71	80	10.1	4	30	3.8	40	5.1	3.93	103	.296	.362	0	1	103	121	0.6	0	1	0.3
Total	7	31	29	.517	194	55	11	1	2	588	563	8.6	57	278	4.3	323	4.9	3.92	101	.258	.336	-1	2	101	106	1.6	-2	6	1.2
■ **CRAZY SCHMIT**	Schmit, Frederick M. "Germany" b: 2/13/1866, Chicago, Ill. d: 10/5/40, Chicago, Ill. BL/TL, 5'10.5", 165 lbs. Deb: 4/21/1890																												
1890	Pit-N	1	9	.100	11	10	9	1	0	83	108	11.7	3	42	4.6	35	3.8	5.86	58	.331	.408	-21	-23	95	90	-2.0	-3	0	-2.0
1892	Bal-N	1	4	.200	6	6	6	0	0	47	37	7.1	0	26	5.0	17	3.3	3.26	103	.228	.335	0	1	102	78	-0.8	-1	0	0.0
1893	Bal-N	3	2	.600	9	6	4	0	0	49	67	12.3	1	22	4.0	10	1.8	6.61	76	.342	.409	-11	-9	108	84	0.7	-0	0	-0.6
	NY-N	0	2	.000	4	4	1	0	0	21	30	12.9	0	17	7.3	5	2.1	7.71	62	.352	.460	-7	-7	103	87	-0.9	1	0	-0.3
	Yr	3	4	.429	13	10	5	0	0	70	97	12.5	1	39	5.0	15	1.9	6.94	71	.345	.425	-18	-15	106	87	-0.2	-0	0	-0.9
1899	Cle-N	2	17	.105	20	19	16	0	0	138	197	12.8	3	62	4.0	24	1.6	5.87	63	.361	.426	-31	-33	96	96	-1.9	-2	0	-2.9
1901	Bal-A	0	2	.000	4	3	1	0	0	23	25	9.8	0	16	6.3	2	0.8	1.96	200	.297	.409	4	5	107	231	-0.9	0	1	0.6
Total	5	7	36	.163	54	48	37	1	0	361	464	11.6	7	185	4.6	93	2.3	5.48	70	.332	.410	-65	-66	99	99	-5.8	-5	1	-5.2
■ **JOHNNY SCHMITZ**	Schmitz, John Albert "Bear Tracks" b: 11/27/20, Wausau, Wis. BR/TL, 6', 170 lbs. Deb: 9/06/41																												
1941	Chi-N	2	0	1.000	5	3	1	0	0	21	12	5.1	0	9	3.9	11	4.7	1.29	265	.182	.278	5	5	94	157	1.0	2	1	0.9
1942	Chi-N	3	7	.300	23	10	1	1	2	87	70	7.2	3	45	4.7	51	5.3	3.41	95	.230	.324	-1	-2	98	97	-1.6	-1	4	0.2
1946	Chi-N	11	11	.500	41	31	14	2	2	224	184	7.4	6	94	3.8	**135**	5.4	2.61	122	**.221**	.296	20	14	93	92	-0.8	-1	2	1.5
1947	Chi-N	13	18	.419	38	28	10	3	4	207	209	9.1	8	80	3.5	97	4.2	3.22	131	.262	.326	20	23	104	110	-1.1	-2	2	2.3
1948	Chi-N	18	13	.581	34	30	18	2	1	242	186	**6.9**	11	97	3.6	100	3.7	2.64	142	**.215**	.289	35	30	95	99	5.1	-2	5	3.4
1949	Chi-N	11	13	.458	36	31	9	3	3	207	227	9.9	11	92	4.0	75	3.3	4.35	91	.287	.357	-7	-9	97	106	1.4	-1	5	-0.4
1950	Chi-N	10	16	.385	39	27	8	3	0	193	217	10.1	23	91	4.2	75	3.5	4.99	89	.284	.358	-18	-12	107	101	-1.1	-4	5	-0.8
1951	Chi-N	1	2	.333	8	3	0	0	0	18	22	11.0	1	15	7.5	6	3.0	8.00	49	.301	.407	-8	-8	100	75	-0.2	-0	1	-0.6
	Bro-N	1	4	.200	16	7	0	0	0	56	55	8.8	4	28	4.5	20	3.2	5.30	71	.259	.347	-8	-10	95	79	-1.6	2	1	-0.6
	Yr	2	6	.250	24	10	0	0	0	74	77	9.4	5	43	5.2	26	3.2	5.96	64	.270	.363	-16	-18	96	79	-1.8	-0	2	-1.2
1952	Bro-N	1	1	.500	10	3	1	0	0	33	29	7.9	3	18	4.9	11	3.0	4.36	84	.238	.336	-2	-3	98	90	-0.1	-0	1	-0.1
	NY-A	1	1	.500	5	2	1	0	1	15	15	9.0	0	9	5.4	3	1.8	3.60	97	.263	.373	0	-0	95	112	-0.1	2	0	0.2
	Cin-N	1	0	1.000	3	0	0	0	0	5	3	5.4	0	3	5.4	3	5.4	0.00	—	.188	.300	2	2	100	0	0.5	0	0	0.2
1953	NY-A	0	0	—	3	0	0	0	2	4	2	4.5	1	3	6.8	0	0.0	2.25	157	.143	.294	1	1	88	147	0.0	0	0	0.1
	Was-A	2	7	.222	24	13	5	0	4	108	118	9.8	9	37	3.1	39	3.3	3.67	101	.286	.341	4	1	93	124	-2.5	-3	1	-0.2
	Yr	2	7	.222	27	13	5	0	6	112	120	9.6	10	40	3.2	39	3.1	3.62	103	.282	.340	5	1	93	124	-2.5	0	1	-0.1
1954	Was-A	11	8	.579	29	23	12	2	1	185	176	8.6	6	64	3.1	56	2.7	2.92	127	.255	.315	17	16	99	108	2.7	-3	2	1.6
1955	Was-A	7	10	.412	32	21	6	1	1	165	187	10.2	8	54	2.9	49	2.7	3.71	101	.291	.343	5	0	94	115	1.0	0	2	0.3
1956	Bos-A	0	0	—	2	0	0	0	0	4	5	11.3	0	4	9.0	0	0.0	0.00	—	.278	.409	2	2	102	0	0.0	-0	0	0.2
	Bal-A	0	3	.000	18	3	0	0	0	38	49	11.6	3	14	3.3	15	3.6	4.03	100	.318	.366	1	-0	97	133	-1.4	-1	1	0.0
	Yr	0	3	.000	20	3	0	0	0	42	54	11.6	3	18	3.9	15	3.2	3.64	111	.314	.371	2	2	97	133	-1.4	-0	1	0.2
Total	13	93	114	.449	366	235	86	17	21	1812	1766	8.8	97	757	3.8	746	3.7	3.55	107	.258	.329	66	49	98	104	1.2	-14	34	8.2
■ **CHARLIE SCHMUTZ**	Schmutz, Charles Otto "King" b: 1/1/1890, San Diego, Cal. d: 6/27/62, Seattle, Wash. BR/TR, 6'1.5", 195 lbs. Deb: 5/13/14																												
1914	Bro-N	1	3	.250	18	5	1	0	0	57	57	9.0	1	13	2.1	21	3.3	3.32	85	.265	.302	-3	-3	101	84	-0.9	1	0	-0.2
1915	Bro-N	0	0	—	1	0	0	0	0	4	7	15.8	0	1	2.3	1	2.3	6.75	42	.438	.444	-2	-2	102	113	0.0	-0	0	-0.1
Total	2	1	3	.250	19	5	1	0	0	61	64	9.4	1	14	2.1	22	3.2	3.54	79	.277	.312	-5	-5	101	86	-0.9	0	1	-0.3
■ **FRANK SCHNEIBERG**	Schneiberg, Frank Frederick b: 3/12/1882, Milwaukee, Wis. d: 5/18/48, Milwaukee, Wis. TR , Deb: 6/08/10																												
1910	Bro-N	0	0	—	1	0	0	0	0	1	5	45.0	0	4	36.0	0	0.0	63.00	5	.625	.750	-7	-7	98	52	0.0	0	0	-0.4
■ **DAN SCHNEIDER**	Schneider, Daniel Louis b: 8/29/42, Evansville, Ind. BL/TL, 6'3", 170 lbs. Deb: 5/12/63																												
1963	Mil-N	1	0	1.000	30	3	0	0	0	44	36	7.4	2	20	4.1	19	3.9	3.07	107	.225	.304	1	1	100	93	0.5	-1	-1	0.0
1964	Mil-N	1	2	.333	13	5	0	0	0	36	38	9.5	6	13	3.3	14	3.5	5.50	62	.270	.321	-8	-8	96	85	-0.5	-1	1	-0.8
1966	Atl-N	0	0	—	14	0	0	0	0	26	35	12.1	1	5	1.7	11	3.8	3.46	101	.324	.350	0	0	97	137	0.0	1	-0	0.1
1967	Hou-N	0	2	.000	54	0	0	0	2	53	60	10.2	5	27	4.6	39	6.6	4.92	65	.296	.369	-9	-10	95	108	-0.9	0	1	-0.8
1969	Hou-N	0	1	.000	6	0	0	0	0	7	16	20.6	2	5	6.4	3	3.9	14.14	26	.485	.488	-8	-8	101	95	-0.4	-0	0	-0.7
Total	5	2	5	.286	117	8	0	0	2	166	185	10.0	16	70	3.8	86	4.7	4.72	71	.287	.347	-24	-25	97	103	-1.3	-0	1	-2.2
■ **JEFF SCHNEIDER**	Schneider, Jeffrey Theodore b: 12/6/52, Bremerton, Wash. BB/TL, 6'3", 195 lbs. Deb: 8/12/81																												
1981	Bal-A	0	0	—	11	0	0	0	1	24	27	10.1	4	12	4.5	17	6.4	4.88	74	.290	.367	-3	-3	99	117	0.0	0	-0	-0.3
■ **PETE SCHNEIDER**	Schneider, Peter Joseph b: 8/20/1895, Los Angeles, Cal. d: 6/1/57, Los Angeles, Cal. BR/TR, 6'1", 194 lbs. Deb: 6/20/14																												
1914	Cin-N	5	13	.278	29	20	11	1	1	144	143	8.9	1	56	3.5	62	3.9	2.81	106	.269	.332	-0	3	107	119	-2.7	1	-1	0.3
1915	Cin-N	14	19	.424	48	35	16	5	2	276	254	8.3	4	104	3.4	108	3.5	2.48	116	.251	.317	8	12	104	121	-1.5	5	-1	1.9

YEAR	TM/L	W	L	PCT	G	GS	CG	SHO	SV	IP	H	H/G	HR	BB	BB/G	SO	SO/G	ERA	/A	OAVG	OOBP	PR	/A	PF	CPI	WAT	PB	PD	TPI
1916	Cin-N	10	19	.345	44	31	16	2	1	274	259	8.5	4	82	2.7	117	3.8	2.69	98	.255	.311	-2	-2	101	108	-2.0	2	-3	-0.2
1917	Cin-N	20	19	.513	46	42	24	0	0	334	311	8.4	4	117	3.2	138	3.7	2.10	119	.255	.317	23	15	93	**145**	0.3	1	-5	1.1
1918	Cin-N	10	15	.400	33	30	17	2	0	217	213	8.8	2	117	4.9	51	2.1	3.53	75	.272	.361	-18	-21	96	113	-3.5	6	-3	-1.9
1919	NY-A	0	1	.000	7	4	0	0	0	29	19	5.9	1	22	6.8	11	3.4	3.41	98	.192	.355	-1	-0	104	85	-0.4	-1	-1	-0.1
Total	6	59	86	.407	207	162	84	10	4	1274	1199	8.5	16	498	3.5	487	3.4	2.66	102	.257	.326	9	7	99	122	-9.8	14	-13	1.1
■ **KARL SCHNELL**	Schnell, Karl Otto b: 9/20/1899, Los Angeles, Cal. BR/TR, 6'1", 176 lbs. Deb: 4/24/22																												
1922	Cin-N	0	0	—	10	0	0	0	0	20	21	9.4	0	18	8.1	5	2.3	2.70	143	.300	.424	3	3	94	209	0.0	0	0	0.3
1923	Cin-N	0	0	—	1	0	0	0	0	1	2	18.0	0	2	18.0	0	0.0	36.00	11	.667	.800	-4	-4	96	47	0.0	0	0	-0.2
Total	2	0	0	—	11	0	0	0	0	21	23	9.9	0	20	8.6	5	2.1	4.29	90	.315	.443	-0	-1	94	201	0.0	0	0	0.1
■ **GERRY SCHOEN**	Schoen, Gerald Thomas b: 1/15/47, New Orleans, La. BR/TR, 6'3", 215 lbs. Deb: 9/14/68																												
1968	Was-A	0	1	.000	1	1	0	0	0	4	6	13.5	1	1	2.3	1	2.3	6.75	41	.400	.438	-2	-2	94	124	-0.4	-0	-0	-0.1
■ **JUMBO SCHOENECK**	Schoeneck, Louis N. b: 3/3/1862, Chicago, Ill. d: 1/20/30, Chicago, Ill. BR/TR, 6'3", 223 lbs. Deb: 4/20/1884																												
1888	Ind-N	0	0	—	2	0	0	0	0	4	5	11.3	0	1	2.3	1	2.3	0.00	—	.320	.361	1	1	98	0	0.0	0	0	0.1
■ **MIKE SCHOOLER**	Schooler, Michael Ralph b: 8/10/62, Anaheim, Cal. BR/TR, 6'3", 220 lbs. Deb: 6/10/88																												
1988	Sea-A	5	8	.385	40	0	0	0	15	48	45	8.4	4	24	4.5	54	10.1	3.56	121	.245	.327	2	4	108	108	-0.5	0	-0	0.4
■ **ED SCHORR**	Schorr, Edward Walter b: 2/14/1891, Bremen, Ohio d: 9/12/69, Atlantic City, N.J. BR/TR, 6'2.5", 180 lbs. Deb: 4/26/15																												
1915	Chi-N	0	0	—	2	0	0	0	0	6	9	13.5	0	5	7.5	3	4.5	7.50	38	.409	.483	-3	-3	103	109	0.0	0	0	-0.2
■ **GENE SCHOTT**	Schott, Eugene Arthur b: 7/14/13, Batavia, Ohio BR/TR, 6'2", 185 lbs. Deb: 4/16/35																												
1935	Cin-N	8	11	.421	33	19	9	1	0	159	153	8.7	5	64	3.6	49	2.8	3.91	98	.253	.320	2	-1	95	88	-0.5	1	3	0.2
1936	Cin-N	11	11	.500	31	22	8	0	1	180	184	9.2	7	73	3.7	65	3.3	3.80	103	.262	.327	4	2	97	97	0.5	6	1	0.9
1937	Cin-N	4	13	.235	37	17	7	2	1	154	150	8.8	2	48	2.8	56	3.3	2.98	122	.253	.304	16	11	93	100	-3.1	-1	1	1.1
1938	Cin-N	5	5	.500	31	4	0	0	2	83	89	9.7	8	32	3.5	21	2.3	4.45	82	.279	.340	-6	-7	96	102	-0.4	-1	1	-0.7
1939	Phi-N	0	1	.000	4	0	0	0	0	11	14	11.5	0	5	4.1	1	0.8	4.91	79	.326	.389	-1	-1	99	117	-0.3	1	-0	-0.5
Total	5	28	41	.406	136	62	24	3	4	587	590	9.0	22	222	3.4	192	2.9	3.73	101	.261	.322	15	3	95	97	-3.8	6	6	1.0
■ **BARNEY SCHREIBER**	Schreiber, David Henry b: 5/8/1882, Waverly, Ohio d: 10/6/64, Chillicothe, Ohio BL/TL, 6', 185 lbs. Deb: 5/15/11																												
1911	Cin-N	0	0	—	3	0	0	0	1	10	19	17.1	2	2	1.8	5	4.5	5.40	58	.413	.438	-2	-3	92	165	0.0	-0	-0	-0.2
■ **PAUL SCHREIBER**	Schreiber, Paul Frederick "Von" b: 10/8/02, Jacksonville, Fla. d: 2/21/82, York, Pa. BR/TR, 6'2", 180 lbs. Deb: 9/02/22 C																												
1922	Bro-N	0	0	—	1	0	0	0	0	1	2	18.0	0	0	0.0	0	0.0	0.00	—	.500	.500	0	0	95	0	0.0	0	0	0.1
1923	Bro-N	0	0	—	9	0	0	0	1	15	16	9.6	1	8	4.8	4	2.4	4.20	93	.276	.366	-0	-0	98	113	0.0	-0	-0	0.0
1945	NY-A	0	0	—	2	0	0	0	0	4	4	9.0	0	2	4.5	1	2.3	4.50	79	.267	.333	-1	-0	106	82	0.0	-0	1	0.0
Total	3	0	0	—	12	0	0	0	1	20	22	9.9	1	10	4.5	5	2.3	4.05	95	.286	.366	-0	-0	99	101	0.0	-0	1	0.1
■ **AL SCHROLL**	Schroll, Albert Bringhurst "Bull" b: 3/22/32, New Orleans, La. BR/TR, 6'2", 210 lbs. Deb: 4/20/58																												
1958	Bos-A	0	0	—	5	0	0	0	0	10	6	5.4	1	4	3.6	7	6.3	4.50	88	.176	.256	-1	-1	105	47	0.0	0	0	0.0
1959	Phi-N	1	1	.500	3	0	0	0	0	9	12	12.0	1	6	6.0	4	4.0	9.00	45	.353	.429	-5	-5	102	82	0.1	0	-0	-0.3
	Bos-A	1	4	.200	14	5	1	0	0	46	47	9.2	3	22	4.3	26	5.1	4.70	87	.269	.345	-4	-3	105	91	-1.4	0	-0	-0.2
1960	Chi-N	0	0	—	2	0	0	0	0	3	3	9.0	1	5	15.0	2	6.0	9.00	42	.273	.500	-2	-2	101	108	0.0	0	0	0.0
1961	Min-A	4	4	.500	11	8	2	0	0	50	53	9.5	5	27	4.9	24	4.3	5.22	83	.266	.360	-7	-5	107	88	0.5	2	-0	-0.2
Total	4	6	9	.400	35	13	3	0	0	118	121	9.2	11	64	4.9	63	4.8	5.34	78	.267	.356	-19	-16	106	86	-0.8	4	-0	-0.7
■ **KEN SCHROM**	Schrom, Kenneth Marvin b: 11/23/54, Grangeville, Idaho BR/TR, 6'2", 195 lbs. Deb: 8/08/80																												
1980	Tor-A	1	0	1.000	17	0	0	0	1	31	32	9.3	2	19	5.5	13	3.8	5.23	78	.274	.364	-4	-4	101	89	0.5	0	0	-0.3
1982	Tor-A	1	0	1.000	6	0	0	0	0	15	13	7.8	3	15	9.0	8	4.8	6.00	74	.232	.394	-3	-3	109	95	0.5	0	-0	-0.2
1983	Min-A	15	8	.652	33	28	6	1	0	196	196	9.0	14	80	3.7	80	3.7	3.72	116	.266	.338	8	13	106	112	4.9	0	-3	1.0
1984	Min-A	5	11	.313	25	21	3	0	0	137	156	10.2	15	41	2.7	49	3.2	4.47	95	.285	.332	-7	-4	106	99	-3.1	0	-2	-0.5
1985	Min-A	9	12	.429	29	26	6	0	0	161	164	9.2	28	59	3.3	74	4.1	4.98	87	.272	.328	-15	-12	104	99	-1.1	0	1	-1.0
1986	Cle-A	14	7	.667	34	33	3	1	0	206	217	9.5	34	49	2.1	87	3.8	4.54	90	.271	.315	-8	-10	98	99	3.5	0	-3	-1.2
1987	Cle-A	6	13	.316	32	29	4	1	0	154	185	10.8	29	57	3.3	61	3.6	6.49	72	.298	.353	-34	-31	105	89	-1.6	0	-2	-2.9
Total	7	51	51	.500	176	137	22	3	1	900	963	9.6	125	320	3.2	372	3.7	4.81	90	.276	.335	-64	-50	103	100	3.6	0	-10	-5.1
■ **RON SCHUELER**	Schueler, Ronald Richard b: 4/14/48, Catherine, Kan. BR/TR, 6'4", 205 lbs. Deb: 4/16/72 C																												
1972	Atl-N	5	8	.385	37	18	3	0	2	145	122	7.6	16	60	3.7	96	6.0	3.66	100	.227	.302	-3	0	106	89	-1.0	0	-1	0.0
1973	Atl-N	8	7	.533	39	20	4	2	2	186	179	8.7	24	66	3.2	124	6.0	3.87	107	.255	.315	-4	5	113	101	0.9	-1	-1	0.5
1974	Phi-N	11	16	.407	44	27	5	0	1	203	202	9.0	17	98	4.3	109	4.8	3.72	101	.264	.345	-2	1	104	113	-2.6	-2	-2	-0.4
1975	Phi-N	4	4	.500	46	6	1	0	0	93	88	8.5	6	40	3.9	69	6.7	5.23	70	.258	.330	-16	-16	101	72	-0.1	-0	1	-1.5
1976	Phi-N	1	0	1.000	35	0	0	0	3	50	44	7.9	4	16	2.9	43	7.7	2.88	127	.243	.305	3	4	105	116	0.5	-0	-0	0.4
1977	Min-A	8	7	.533	52	7	0	0	3	135	131	8.7	16	61	4.1	77	5.1	4.40	94	.260	.337	-5	-4	102	100	0.2	0	2	-0.1
1978	Chi-A	3	5	.375	30	7	0	0	0	82	76	8.3	10	39	4.3	39	4.3	4.28	90	.251	.338	-5	-4	102	101	-0.5	0	0	-0.3
1979	Chi-A	0	1	.000	8	1	0	0	0	20	19	8.5	3	13	5.8	6	2.7	7.20	60	.264	.378	-7	-6	103	77	-0.4	0	-0	-0.5
Total	8	40	48	.455	291	86	13	2	11	914	861	8.5	96	393	3.9	563	5.5	4.08	95	.253	.328	-39	-19	105	99	-3.0	-4	-2	-1.9
■ **DAVE SCHULER**	Schuler, David Paul b: 10/4/53, Framingham, Mass. BR/TL, 6'4", 210 lbs. Deb: 9/17/79																												
1979	Cal-A	0	0	—	1	0	0	0	0	2	2	9.0	1	0	0.0	0	0.0	9.00	43	.333	.286	-1	-1	92	89	0.0	0	0	0.0
1980	Cal-A	0	1	.000	8	0	0	0	0	13	13	9.0	3	2	1.4	7	4.8	3.46	113	.271	.283	1	1	97	133	-0.4	0	-0	0.0
1985	Atl-N	0	0	—	9	0	0	0	0	11	19	15.5	4	3	2.5	10	8.2	6.55	59	.404	.440	-4	-3	108	151	0.0	0	-0	-0.3
Total	3	0	1	.000	18	0	0	0	0	26	34	11.8	8	5	1.7	17	5.9	5.19	75	.337	.355	-4	-4	101	137	-0.4	0	-0	-0.3
■ **BUDDY SCHULTZ**	Schultz, Charles Budd b: 9/19/50, Cleveland, Ohio BR/TL, 6', 170 lbs. Deb: 9/03/75																												
1975	Chi-N	2	0	1.000	6	0	0	0	0	6	11	16.5	0	5	7.5	4	6.0	6.00	64	.367	.457	-2	-1	105	128	1.0	0	0	-0.1
1976	Chi-N	1	1	.500	29	0	0	0	2	24	37	13.9	3	9	3.4	15	5.6	6.00	65	.356	.397	-7	-6	111	114	0.1	-1	1	-0.5
1977	StL-N	6	1	.857	40	3	0	0	1	85	76	8.0	5	24	2.5	66	7.0	2.33	160	.245	.292	15	13	95	128	2.5	0	-0	1.3
1978	StL-N	2	4	.333	62	0	0	0	6	83	68	7.4	6	36	3.9	70	7.6	3.80	90	.226	.303	-2	-3	96	80	-0.6	1	-1	-0.3
1979	StL-N	4	3	.571	31	0	0	0	3	42	40	8.6	7	14	3.0	38	8.1	4.50	87	.256	.303	-4	-3	104	93	0.3	0	-0	-0.3
Total	5	15	9	.625	168	3	0	0	12	240	232	8.7	21	88	3.3	193	7.2	3.68	100	.257	.315	1	-0	99	104	3.3	0	-1	0.1
■ **BARNEY SCHULTZ**	Schultz, George Warren b: 8/15/26, Beverly, N.J. BR/TR, 6'2", 200 lbs. Deb: 4/12/55 C																												
1955	StL-N	1	2	.333	19	0	0	0	4	30	28	8.4	5	15	4.5	19	5.7	7.80	53	.259	.353	-13	-12	102	66	-0.3	-1	1	-1.0
1959	Det-A	1	2	.333	13	0	0	0	0	18	17	8.5	1	14	7.0	17	8.5	4.50	95	.254	.376	-1	-0	111	106	-0.4	1	-0	0.0
1961	Chi-N	7	6	.538	41	0	0	0	7	67	57	7.7	6	25	3.4	59	7.9	2.69	153	.228	.301	10	11	102	117	1.5	-1	-0	1.0
1962	Chi-N	5	5	.500	51	0	0	0	5	78	66	7.6	7	23	2.7	58	6.7	3.81	112	.231	.292	1	4	109	79	1.1	-0	0	0.4
1963	Chi-N	1	0	1.000	15	0	0	0	2	27	25	8.3	5	9	3.0	18	6.0	3.67	94	.263	.312	-1	-1	105	126	0.5	-0	0	0.0
	StL-N	2	0	1.000	24	0	0	0	1	35	36	9.3	5	8	2.1	26	6.7	3.60	96	.263	.305	-1	-0	106	112	1.0	0	-0	0.0
	Yr	3	0	1.000	39	0	0	0	3	62	61	8.9	10	17	2.5	44	6.4	3.63	96	.263	.308	-2	-1	105	112	1.5	-0	0	0.0
1964	StL-N	1	3	.250	30	0	0	0	14	49	35	6.4	1	11	2.0	29	5.3	1.65	238	.201	.242	10	12	111	94	-1.0	-0	-1	1.3
1965	StL-N	2	2	.500	34	0	0	0	2	42	39	8.4	8	11	2.4	38	8.1	3.86	97	.242	.286	-1	-0	106	100	0.0	-0	0	0.0
Total	7	20	20	.500	227	0	0	0	35	346	303	7.9	38	116	3.0	264	6.9	3.64	109	.237	.300	4	13	106	98	2.4	-2	0	1.7
■ **BOB SCHULTZ**	Schultz, Robert Duffy b: 11/27/23, Louisville, Ky. d: 3/31/79, Nashville, Tenn. BR/TL, 6'3", 200 lbs. Deb: 4/20/51																												
1951	Chi-N	3	6	.333	17	10	2	0	0	77	75	8.8	9	51	6.0	27	3.2	5.26	75	.251	.361	-11	-11	100	88	-0.7	-1	-1	-1.2
1952	Chi-N	6	3	.667	29	5	1	0	0	74	63	7.7	3	51	6.2	31	3.8	4.01	96	.232	.352	-2	-1	103	95	1.6	1	-2	-0.2
1953	Chi-N	0	2	.000	7	2	0	0	0	12	13	9.8	2	11	8.3	4	3.0	5.25	87	.289	.424	-1	-1	106	135	-0.9	-0	-1	-0.1
	Pit-N	0	2	.000	11	2	0	0	0	19	26	12.3	3	10	4.7	5	2.4	8.05	57	.321	.409	-8	-7	106	85	-0.9	0	-0	-0.6
	Yr	0	4	.000	18	4	0	0	0	31	39	11.3	5	21	6.1	9	2.6	6.97	65	.307	.408	-9	-8	106	85	-1.8	-0	-1	-0.7
1955	Det-A	0	0	—	1	0	0	0	0	1	2	18.0	0	2	18.0	0	0.0	27.00	14	.333	.500	-3	-3	95	36	0.0	0	0	-0.1

YEAR	TM/L	W	L	PCT	G	GS	CG	SHO	SV	IP	H	H/G	HR	BB	BB/G	SO	SO/G	ERA	/A	OAVG	OOBP	PR	/A	PF	CPI	WAT	PB	PD	TPI
Total	4	9	13	.409	65	19	3	0	0	183	179	8.8	17	125	6.1	67	3.3	5.16	78	.255	.368	-25	-23	102	93	-0.9	-1	-3	-2.2
■ **WEBB SCHULTZ**	Schultz, Webb Carl b: 1/31/1898, Wautoma, Wis. d: 7/26/86, Delavan, Wis. BR/TR, 5'11", 172 lbs. Deb: 8/03/24																												
1924	Chi-A	0	0	—	1	0	0	0	0	1	1	9.0	0	0	0.0	0	0.0	9.00	46	.250	.250	-1	-1	98	17	0.0	0	0	0.0
■ **MIKE SCHULTZ**	Schultz, William Michael b: 12/17/20, Syracuse, N.Y. BL/TL, 6'1", 175 lbs. Deb: 4/20/47																												
1947	Cin-N	0	0	—	1	0	0	0	0	2	4	18.0	0	2	9.0	0	0.0	4.50	83	.444	.545	-0	-0	92	237	0.0	0	0	0.0
■ **JOHN SCHULTZE**	Schultze, John F. b: Burlington, N.J. 6'0.5", 165 lbs. Deb: 5/06/1891																												
1891	Phi-N	0	1	.000	6	1	0	0	0	15	18	10.8	1	11	6.6	4	2.4	6.60	48	.311	.422	-5	-6	95	82	-0.4	0	0	-0.4
■ **AL SCHULZ**	Schulz, Albert Christopher b: 5/12/1889, Toledo, Ohio d: 12/13/31, Gallipolis, Ohio BR/TL, 6', 182 lbs. Deb: 9/25/12																												
1912	NY-A	1	1	.500	3	1	1	0	0	16	11	6.2	0	11	6.2	8	4.5	2.25	157	.183	.310	2	2	105	83	0.3	-0	1	0.3
1913	NY-A	7	13	.350	38	22	9	0	0	193	197	9.2	4	69	3.2	77	3.6	3.73	81	.266	.333	-17	-15	104	86	-0.7	-0	-1	-1.6
1914	NY-A	1	3	.250	6	4	1	0	0	28	27	8.7	0	10	3.2	18	5.8	4.82	57	.237	.310	-6	-6	100	48	-0.8	-0	1	-0.5
	Buf-F	9	12	.429	27	23	10	0	2	171	160	8.4	3	77	4.1	87	4.6	3.37	99	.259	.343	-3	-1	104	102	-2.2	-0	3	0.3
1915	Buf-F	21	14	.600	42	38	25	5	0	310	264	7.7	8	149	4.3	160	4.6	3.08	100	.238	.332	-2	-0	101	102	4.7	-2	4	0.2
1916	Cin-N	8	19	.296	44	22	10	0	2	215	208	8.7	4	93	3.9	95	4.0	3.14	84	.268	.340	-12	-12	101	114	-3.7	-3	0	-1.6
Total	5	47	62	.431	160	110	56	5	4	933	867	8.4	19	409	3.9	445	4.3	3.32	91	.254	.335	-39	-32	102	100	-2.4	-7	8	-2.9
■ **WALT SCHULZ**	Schulz, Walter Frederick b: 4/16/1900, St.Louis, Mo. d: 2/27/28, Prescott, Ark. BR/TR, 6', 170 lbs. Deb: 9/24/20																												
1920	StL-N	0	0	—	2	0	0	0	0	6	10	15.0	0	2	3.0	0	0.0	6.00	51	.370	.400	-2	-2	98	99	0.0	-0	0	-0.1
■ **DON SCHULZE**	Schulze, Donald Arthur b: 9/27/62, Roselle, Ill. BR/TR, 6'3", 215 lbs. Deb: 9/13/83																												
1983	Chi-N	0	1	.000	4	3	0	0	0	14	19	12.2	1	7	4.5	8	5.1	7.07	52	.322	.403	-5	-5	101	83	-0.4	0	0	-0.4
1984	Chi-N	0	0	—	1	1	0	0	0	3	8	24.0	0	1	3.0	2	6.0	12.00	33	.571	.563	-3	-3	109	109	0.0	0	0	-0.1
	Cle-A	3	6	.333	19	14	2	0	0	86	105	11.0	9	27	2.8	39	4.1	4.81	88	.302	.347	-8	-6	106	102	-1.2	0	-0	-0.5
1985	Cle-A	4	10	.286	19	18	1	0	0	94	128	12.3	10	19	1.8	37	3.5	6.03	66	.322	.352	-20	-22	95	90	-1.6	0	1	-1.9
1986	Cle-A	4	4	.500	19	13	1	0	0	85	88	9.3	9	34	3.6	33	3.5	4.98	82	.266	.342	-7	-8	98	88	-0.1	0	-1	-0.8
1987	NY-N	1	2	.333	5	4	0	0	0	22	24	9.8	4	6	2.5	5	2.0	6.14	65	.296	.341	-5	-5	97	89	-0.5	0	1	-0.3
Total	5	12	23	.343	67	53	4	0	0	304	372	11.0	33	94	2.8	124	3.7	5.51	74	.302	.352	-48	-49	100	92	-3.8	1	0	-4.0
■ **HAL SCHUMACHER**	Schumacher, Harold Henry "Prince Hal" b: 11/23/10, Hinckley, N.Y. BR/TR, 6', 190 lbs. Deb: 4/15/31																												
1931	NY-N	1	1	.500	8	2	1	0	1	18	31	15.5	3	14	7.0	11	5.5	11.00	33	.387	.474	-14	-15	93	86	0.0	-0	1	-1.2
1932	NY-N	5	6	.455	27	13	2	1	0	101	119	10.6	3	39	3.5	38	3.4	3.56	106	.288	.349	4	3	98	120	-0.1	1	2	0.5
1933	NY-N	19	12	.613	35	33	21	7	1	259	199	**6.9**	9	84	2.9	96	3.3	2.15	149	**.214**	.276	34	30	96	100	0.7	1	3	3.9
1934	NY-N	23	10	.697	41	36	18	2	0	297	299	9.1	16	89	2.7	112	3.4	3.18	121	.259	.311	29	22	95	108	4.5	10	3	3.4
1935	NY-N	19	9	.679	33	33	19	3	0	262	235	8.1	11	70	2.4	79	2.7	2.89	132	.238	.289	33	27	95	96	3.4	2	7	3.6
1936	NY-N	11	13	.458	35	30	9	3	1	215	234	9.8	15	69	2.9	75	3.1	3.47	114	.280	.330	13	11	98	**120**	-3.1	2	4	1.7
1937	NY-N	13	12	.520	38	29	10	1	1	218	222	9.2	11	89	3.7	100	4.1	3.59	106	.264	.330	8	6	98	107	-2.3	3	1	0.9
1938	NY-N	13	8	.619	28	28	12	4	0	185	178	8.7	12	50	2.4	54	2.6	3.50	110	.248	.297	6	7	102	89	1.8	4	2	1.4
1939	NY-N	13	10	.565	29	27	8	1	0	182	199	9.8	14	89	4.4	58	2.9	4.80	81	.276	.351	-18	-19	99	94	1.5	1	-0	-1.7
1940	NY-N	13	13	.500	34	30	12	1	1	227	218	8.6	14	96	3.8	123	4.9	3.25	119	.251	.322	15	15	100	114	0.8	3	4	2.3
1941	NY-N	12	10	.545	30	26	12	3	1	206	187	8.2	11	79	3.5	63	2.8	3.36	112	.243	.314	6	9	104	98	1.5	-1	-1	0.8
1942	NY-N	12	13	.480	29	29	12	3	0	216	208	8.7	12	82	3.4	49	2.0	3.04	110	.251	.316	7	7	101	113	-2.0	1	2	1.1
1946	NY-N	4	4	.500	24	13	2	0	1	97	95	8.8	8	52	4.8	48	4.5	3.90	90	.255	.341	-5	-4	103	102	0.7	-2	2	-0.3
Total	13	158	121	.566	391	329	138	29	7	2483	2424	8.8	139	902	3.3	906	3.3	3.36	111	.255	.317	117	102	99	104	7.4	23	30	16.4
■ **HACK SCHUMANN**	Schumann, Carl J. b: 8/13/1884, Buffalo, N.Y. d: 3/25/46, Millgrove, N.Y. TR, 6'2", 230 lbs. Deb: 9/19/06																												
1906	Phi-A	0	2	.000	4	2	1	0	0	18	21	10.5	0	8	4.0	9	4.5	4.00	62	.318	.392	-3	-3	93	107	-0.9	-1	-0	-0.2
■ **FERDIE SCHUPP**	Schupp, Ferdinand Maurice b: 1/16/1891, Louisville, Ky. d: 12/16/71, Los Angeles, Cal. BR/TR, 5'10", 150 lbs. Deb: 4/19/13																												
1913	NY-N	0	0	—	5	1	0	0	0	12	10	7.5	0	3	2.3	2	1.5	0.75	425	.244	.289	3	3	100	316	0.0	1	0	0.4
1914	NY-N	0	0	—	8	0	0	0	1	17	19	10.1	0	9	4.8	9	4.8	5.82	45	.306	.405	-6	-6	94	83	0.0	-0	-0	-0.6
1915	NY-N	1	0	1.000	23	1	0	0	0	55	57	9.3	1	29	4.7	28	4.6	5.07	50	.281	.363	-14	-15	92	84	0.5	0	0	-1.5
1916	NY-N	9	3	.750	30	11	8	4	1	140	79	5.1	1	37	2.4	86	5.5	0.90	272	.167	.230	27	24	94	81	2.7	-2	-3	2.2
1917	NY-N	21	7	**.750**	36	32	25	6	0	272	202	**6.7**	7	70	2.3	147	4.9	1.95	129	**.209**	.259	23	17	93	88	5.0	1	-3	1.7
1918	NY-N	0	1	.000	10	2	1	0	0	33	42	11.5	1	27	7.4	22	6.0	7.64	35	.328	.436	-18	-18	96	85	-0.4	-0	0	-1.8
1919	NY-N	1	3	.250	9	4	0	0	1	32	32	9.0	2	18	5.1	17	4.8	5.63	50	.269	.352	-10	-10	96	76	-1.1	0	-1	-1.0
	StL-N	4	4	.500	10	9	6	0	0	70	55	7.1	2	30	3.9	37	4.8	3.73	75	.221	.299	-6	-7	97	68	0.7	-0	-1	-0.8
	Yr	5	7	.417	19	13	6	0	1	102	87	7.7	4	48	4.2	54	4.8	4.32	65	.236	.316	-16	-17	96	68	-0.4	0	-1	-1.8
1920	StL-N	16	13	.552	38	37	17	0	0	251	246	8.8	5	127	4.6	119	4.3	3.51	87	.265	.349	-11	-13	98	101	2.2	5	-2	-0.9
1921	StL-N	2	0	1.000	9	4	1	0	1	37	42	10.2	5	21	5.1	22	5.4	4.14	85	.276	.361	-1	-3	93	120	1.0	0	-0	-0.2
	Bro-N	3	4	.429	20	7	1	0	2	61	75	11.1	2	27	4.0	26	3.8	4.57	87	.310	.373	-5	-4	105	105	-0.5	-1	0	-0.4
	Yr	5	4	.556	29	11	2	0	3	98	117	10.7	7	48	4.4	48	4.4	4.41	86	.295	.364	-7	-7	100	105	0.5	0	-0	-0.6
1922	Chi-A	4	4	.500	18	12	3	1	0	74	79	9.6	4	66	8.0	38	4.6	6.08	67	.284	.412	-17	-16	101	92	0.0	1	-0	-1.4
Total	10	61	39	.610	216	120	62	11	6	1054	938	8.0	30	464	4.0	553	4.7	3.32	87	.244	.322	-35	-49	96	93	10.1	5	-9	-4.3
■ **WAYNE SCHURR**	Schurr, Wayne Allen b: 8/6/37, Garrett, Ind. BR/TR, 6'4", 185 lbs. Deb: 4/15/64																												
1964	Chi-N	0	0	—	26	0	0	0	0	48	57	10.7	3	11	2.1	29	5.4	3.75	100	.298	.332	-1	0	106	115	0.0	-0	-0	0.0
■ **DON SCHWALL**	Schwall, Donald Bernard b: 3/2/36, Wilkes-Barre, Pa. BR/TR, 6'6", 200 lbs. Deb: 5/21/61																												
1961	Bos-A	15	7	.682	25	25	10	2	0	179	167	8.4	8	110	5.5	91	4.6	3.22	128	.255	.360	16	18	103	**131**	4.8	-0	0	1.9
1962	Bos-A	9	15	.375	33	32	5	1	0	182	180	8.9	18	121	6.0	89	4.4	4.95	83	.260	.371	-20	-17	103	100	-2.8	-2	0	-1.8
1963	Pit-N	6	12	.333	33	24	3	2	0	168	158	8.5	13	74	4.0	86	4.6	3.32	98	.255	.331	-1	-1	99	**118**	-2.5	-0	2	0.0
1964	Pit-N	4	3	.571	15	9	0	0	0	50	53	9.5	1	15	2.7	36	6.5	4.32	82	.269	.318	-4	-4	101	77	0.6	2	0	-0.2
1965	Pit-N	9	6	.600	43	1	0	0	4	77	77	9.0	5	30	3.5	55	6.4	2.92	119	.269	.335	5	5	98	140	0.8	-2	2	0.5
1966	Pit-N	3	2	.600	11	4	0	0	0	42	31	6.6	3	21	4.5	24	5.1	2.14	166	.209	.308	7	7	99	136	0.2	-0	0	0.7
	Atl-N	3	3	.500	11	8	0	0	0	45	44	8.8	2	19	3.8	27	5.4	4.40	80	.256	.332	-4	-4	97	81	0.0	-1	-0	-0.5
	Yr	6	5	.545	22	12	0	0	0	87	75	7.8	5	40	4.1	51	5.3	3.31	107	.234	.318	3	2	98	81	0.2	-0	-0	0.2
1967	Atl-N	0	0	—	1	0	0	0	0	1	0	0.0	0	1	9.0	0	0.0	0.00	—	.000	.500	0	0	105	0	0.0	0	0	0.0
Total	7	49	48	.505	172	103	18	5	4	744	710	8.6	50	391	4.7	408	4.9	3.71	101	.257	.347	-0	2	101	115	1.1	-5	4	0.6
■ **BLACKIE SCHWAMB**	Schwamb, Ralph Richard b: 8/6/26, Los Angeles, Cal. BR/TR, 6'5.5", 198 lbs. Deb: 7/25/48																												
1948	StL-A	1	1	.500	12	5	0	0	0	32	44	12.4	3	21	5.9	7	2.0	8.44	55	.331	.417	-15	-13	109	81	0.2	1	0	-1.0
■ **RUDY SCHWENCK**	Schwenck, Rudolph Christian b: 4/6/1884, Louisville, Ky. d: 11/27/41, Anchorage, Ky. 6', 174 lbs. Deb: 09																												
1909	Chi-N	1	1	.500	3	2	0	0	0	4	16	36.0	0	3	6.8	3	6.8	13.50	18	.308	.357	-5	-5	95	54	-0.2	0	1	-0.3
■ **HAL SCHWENK**	Schwenk, Harold Edward b: 8/23/1890, Schuylkill Haven, Pa. d: 9/3/55, Kansas City, Mo. BL/TL, 6', 185 lbs. Deb: 9/04/13																												
1913	StL-A	1	0	1.000	1	1	1	0	0	11	12	9.8	0	4	3.3	3	2.5	3.27	87	.333	.400	-0	-1	98	144	0.5	1	-0	0.0
■ **JIM SCOGGINS**	Scoggins, Lynn J. "Lefty" b: 7/19/1891, Killeen, Tex. d: 8/16/23, Columbia, S.C. BL/TL, 5'11", 165 lbs. Deb: 8/26/13																												
1913	Chi-A	0	1	.000	1	1	0	0	0	0	0	—	0	1	—	0	—	—	—	.000	.500	0	0	95	0	-0.4	0	0	0.0
■ **HERB SCORE**	Score, Herbert Jude b: 6/7/33, Rosedale, N.Y. BL/TL, 6'2", 185 lbs. Deb: 4/15/55																												
1955	Cle-A	16	10	.615	33	32	11	2	0	227	158	6.3	18	154	6.1	**245**	**9.7**	2.85	142	.194	.320	28	30	102	104	0.5	-4	-4	2.3
1956	Cle-A	20	9	.690	35	33	16	**5**	0	249	162	**5.9**	18	129	4.7	**263**	**9.5**	2.53	**163**	**.186**	**.287**	**45**	**44**	99	93	4.6	1	-4	4.3
1957	Cle-A	2	1	.667	5	5	3	1	0	36	18	4.5	0	26	6.5	39	9.8	2.00	194	.149	.300	7	7	102	82	0.5	-0	0	0.8
1958	Cle-A	2	3	.400	12	5	2	1	3	41	29	6.4	1	34	7.5	48	10.5	3.95	89	.197	.346	-1	-2	93	78	-0.4	-0	-1	-0.2
1959	Cle-A	9	11	.450	30	25	9	1	0	161	123	**6.9**	28	115	6.4	147	**8.2**	4.70	78	**.210**	.336	-15	-19	95	91	-2.4	-3	-3	-2.3
1960	Chi-A	5	10	.333	23	22	5	1	0	114	91	7.2	10	87	6.9	78	6.2	3.71	103	.226	.356	2	2	99	112	-3.2	-0	-1	0.0

YEAR	TM/L	W	L	PCT	G	GS	CG	SHO	SV	IP	H	H/G	HR	BB	BB/G	SO	SO/G	ERA	/A	OAVG	OOBP	PR	/A	PF	CPI	WAT	PB	PD	TPI
1961	Chi-A	1	2	.333	8	5	1	0	0	24	22	8.3	3	24	9.0	14	5.3	6.75	59	.259	.387	-7	-7	99	88	-0.5	-1	0	-0.7
1962	Chi-A	0	0	—	4	0	0	0	0	6	6	9.0	1	4	6.0	3	4.5	4.50	83	.261	.370	-0	-1	94	118	0.0	0	0	0.0
Total	8	55	46	.545	150	127	47	11	3	858	609	6.4	79	573	6.0	837	8.8	3.36	117	.200	.322	59	54	99	97	-0.9	-7	-11	4.2
■ DICK SCOTT	Scott, Amos Richard b: 2/5/1883, Bethel, Ohio d: 1/18/11, Chicago, Ill. BR/TR, 6', 180 lbs. Deb: 6/26/01																												
1901	Cin-N	0	2	.000	3	2	2	0	0	21	26	11.1	2	9	3.9	7	3.0	5.14	64	.340	.429	-4	-4	100	110	-0.9	-1	-1	-0.3
■ ED SCOTT	Scott, Edward b: 8/12/1870, Walbridge, Ohio d: 11/1/33, Toledo, Ohio BR/TR, 6'3", Deb: 4/19/00																												
1900	Cin-N	17	21	.447	43	36	32	0	1	323	380	10.6	9	66	1.8	92	2.6	3.82	90	.317	.352	-4	-14	93	100	0.1	-4	10	-0.7
1901	Cle-A	7	6	.538	17	16	11	0	1	125	149	10.7	2	38	2.7	23	1.7	4.39	81	.317	.368	-10	-11	97	93	1.6	0	1	-0.8
Total	2	24	27	.471	60	52	43	0	2	448	529	10.6	11	104	2.1	115	2.3	3.98	87	.317	.357	-14	-25	94	98	1.7	-3	11	-1.5
■ GEORGE SCOTT	Scott, George William b: 11/17/1896, Trenton, Mo. BR/TR, 6'1", 175 lbs. Deb: 9/13/20																												
1920	StL-N	0	0	—	2	0	0	0	0	6	10	15.0	0	2	3.0	0	0.0	6.00	51	.370	.400	-2	-2	98	99	0.0	-0	0	-0.1
■ JIM SCOTT	Scott, James "Death Valley Jim" b: 4/23/1888, Deadwood, S.Dak. d: 4/7/57, Palm Springs, Cal. BR/TR, 6'1", 235 lbs. Deb: 4/25/09																												
1909	Chi-A	12	12	.500	36	29	20	4	0	250	194	7.0	0	93	3.3	135	4.9	2.30	104	.223	.310	5	2	97	93	-0.3	-2	-1	0.1
1910	Chi-A	8	18	.308	41	23	14	2	1	230	182	7.1	5	86	3.4	135	5.3	2.43	99	.226	.303	2	-1	95	96	-4.4	1	3	0.3
1911	Chi-A	14	11	.560	39	26	14	3	0	222	195	7.9	3	81	3.3	128	5.2	2.39	133	.240	.311	23	19	95	104	1.5	-2	-3	1.4
1912	Chi-A	2	2	.500	6	4	2	1	0	38	36	8.5	0	15	3.6	23	5.4	2.13	156	.265	.342	5	5	99	159	0.0	-2	0	0.5
1913	Chi-A	20	20	.500	48	38	25	4	1	312	252	7.3	2	86	2.5	158	4.6	1.90	146	.221	.281	36	31	95	93	-0.6	-6	-1	3.3
1914	Chi-A	14	18	.438	43	33	12	2	1	253	228	8.1	5	75	2.7	138	4.9	2.85	101	.246	.306	-3	1	105	90	-0.6	-1	3	0.4
1915	Chi-A	24	11	.686	48	35	23	**7**	2	296	256	7.8	3	78	2.4	120	3.6	2.04	135	.238	.292	30	24	94	111	4.4	-4	2	2.4
1916	Chi-A	7	14	.333	32	21	8	1	3	165	155	8.5	3	53	2.9	71	3.9	2.73	110	.258	.321	2	5	106	109	-4.7	-4	-0	0.1
1917	Chi-A	6	7	.462	24	17	6	2	1	125	126	9.1	0	42	3.0	37	2.7	1.87	133	.272	.341	11	9	93	172	-1.9	-1	0	0.8
Total	9	107	113	.486	317	226	124	26	9	1891	1624	7.7	21	609	2.9	945	4.5	2.30	120	.238	.305	111	95	97	105	-6.6	-20	3	9.3
■ JACK SCOTT	Scott, John William b: 4/18/1892, Ridgeway, N.C. d: 11/30/59, Durham, N.C. BL/TR, 6'2.5", 199 lbs. Deb: 9/06/16																												
1916	Pit-N	0	0	—	1	0	0	0	0	5	5	9.0	1	3	5.4	4	7.2	10.80	26	.278	.381	-5	-4	107	52	0.0	0	0	-0.3
1917	Bos-N	1	2	.333	7	3	3	0	0	40	36	8.1	0	5	1.1	21	4.7	1.80	145	.255	.278	4	4	97	138	-0.3	-1	-1	0.2
1919	Bos-N	6	6	.500	19	12	7	0	1	104	109	9.4	3	39	3.4	44	3.8	3.12	94	.275	.335	-2	-2	100	118	1.0	-1	-3	-0.6
1920	Bos-N	10	21	.323	44	32	22	3	1	291	308	9.5	6	85	2.6	94	2.9	3.53	88	.277	.327	-13	-13	99	93	-3.8	0	-4	-1.8
1921	Bos-N	15	13	.536	**47**	29	16	2	3	234	258	9.9	9	57	2.2	83	3.2	3.69	95	.283	.323	2	-5	92	95	0.7	11	-1	0.3
1922	Cin-N	0	0	—	1	0	0	0	0	1	2	18.0	0	1	9.0	0	0.0	9.00	43	.500	.500	-1	-1	94	131	0.0	-0	0	0.0
	NY-N	8	2	.800	17	10	5	0	2	80	83	9.3	7	23	2.6	37	4.2	4.39	94	.265	.314	-3	-2	100	80	2.6	1	-1	-0.2
	Yr	8	2	.800	18	10	5	0	2	81	85	9.4	7	24	2.7	37	4.1	4.44	93	.268	.317	-3	-3	100	80	2.6	-0	-1	-0.2
1923	NY-N	16	7	.696	40	25	9	3	1	220	223	9.1	15	65	2.7	79	3.2	3.89	101	.267	.314	3	1	99	92	2.6	7	-2	0.6
1925	NY-N	14	15	.483	36	28	18	2	3	240	251	9.4	10	55	2.1	87	3.3	3.15	133	.269	.305	30	28	98	103	-2.4	5	2	3.4
1926	NY-N	13	15	.464	**50**	22	13	0	5	226	242	9.6	13	53	2.1	82	3.3	4.34	86	.276	.311	-13	-15	98	83	-0.8	9	-1	-0.6
1927	Phi-N	9	21	.300	**48**	25	17	1	1	233	304	11.7	15	69	2.7	69	2.7	5.10	77	.330	.361	-31	-30	100	106	-1.6	9	-0	-2.0
1928	NY-N	4	1	.800	16	3	3	0	1	50	59	10.6	3	11	2.0	17	3.1	3.60	110	.295	.332	2	2	99	113	1.3	1	0	0.3
1929	NY-N	7	6	.538	30	6	2	0	1	92	89	8.7	12	27	2.6	40	3.9	3.52	130	.260	.304	12	11	97	115	-0.1	3	1	1.3
Total	12	103	109	.486	356	195	115	11	19	1816	1969	9.8	94	493	2.4	657	3.3	3.85	96	.281	.323	-13	-28	98	98	-0.8	43	-8	0.6
■ LEFTY SCOTT	Scott, Marshall b: 7/15/15, Roswell, N.Mex. d: 3/3/64, Houston, Tex. BR/TL, 6'0.5", 165 lbs. Deb: 6/15/45																												
1945	Phi-N	0	2	.000	8	2	0	0	0	22	29	11.9	1	12	4.9	5	2.0	4.50	86	.312	.380	-2	-2	102	121	-0.9	-0	-0	-0.1
■ MIKE SCOTT	Scott, Michael Warren b: 4/26/55, Santa Monica, Cal. BR/TR, 6'2", 210 lbs. Deb: 4/18/79																												
1979	NY-N	1	3	.250	18	9	0	0	0	52	59	10.2	4	20	3.5	21	3.6	5.37	67	.289	.345	-9	-10	96	83	-0.6	-1	-0	-1.1
1980	NY-N	1	1	.500	6	6	1	1	0	29	40	12.4	1	8	2.5	13	4.0	4.34	81	.331	.364	-2	-3	97	117	0.1	0	0	-0.2
1981	NY-N	5	10	.333	23	23	1	0	0	136	130	8.6	11	34	2.3	54	3.6	3.90	92	.261	.299	-6	-5	103	90	-1.3	-2	3	-0.3
1982	NY-N	7	13	.350	37	22	1	0	3	147	185	11.3	13	60	3.7	63	3.9	5.14	70	.321	.369	-25	-25	100	109	-1.3	1	3	-2.1
1983	Hou-N	10	6	.625	24	24	2	2	0	145	143	8.9	8	46	2.9	73	4.5	3.72	88	.258	.317	-1	-7	90	91	1.8	1	0	-0.6
1984	Hou-N	5	11	.313	31	29	0	0	0	154	179	10.5	7	43	2.5	83	4.9	4.68	70	.293	.333	-19	-24	92	89	-3.0	0	0	-2.3
1985	Hou-N	18	8	.692	36	35	4	2	0	222	194	7.9	20	80	3.2	137	5.6	3.28	105	.235	.300	8	4	96	97	5.3	2	-2	0.5
1986	Hou-N	18	10	.643	37	37	7	**5**	0	**275**	182	**6.0**	17	72	2.4	**306**	**10.0**	**2.23**	**170**	**.186**	**.240**	**46**	**48**	102	70	2.0	-2	2	**5.4**
1987	Hou-N	16	13	.552	36	36	8	3	0	248	199	7.2	21	79	2.9	233	8.5	3.23	118	.217	**.279**	24	16	93	81	2.7	-1	0	1.4
1988	Hou-N	14	8	.636	32	32	8	5	0	219	162	6.7	19	53	2.2	190	7.8	2.92	111	.204	.255	13	8	93	78	3.2	-2	-1	0.4
Total	10	95	83	.534	280	253	32	18	3	1627	1473	8.1	121	495	2.7	1173	6.5	3.52	100	.242	.296	27	1	96	86	8.9	-5	7	1.1
■ MILT SCOTT	Scott, Milton Parker "Mikado Milt" b: 1/17/1866, Chicago, Ill. d: 11/3/38, Baltimore, Md. 5'9", 160 lbs. Deb: 9/30/1882																												
1886	Bal-a	0	0	—	1	0	0	0	0	3	2	6.0	0	2	6.0	0	0.0	3.00	108	.198	.331	0	0	94	89	0.0	-0	0	0.0
■ MICKEY SCOTT	Scott, Ralph Robert b: 7/25/47, Weimar, Germany BL/TL, 6'1", 155 lbs. Deb: 5/06/72																												
1972	Bal-A	0	1	.000	15	0	0	0	0	23	23	9.0	2	5	2.0	11	4.3	2.74	108	.277	.315	1	1	96	142	-0.4	1	-0	0.1
1973	Bal-A	0	0	—	1	0	0	0	0	2	2	9.0	1	2	9.0	2	9.0	4.50	89	.286	.444	-0	-0	105	210	0.0	0	0	0.0
	Mon-N	1	2	.333	22	0	0	0	0	24	27	10.1	3	9	3.4	11	4.1	5.25	73	.287	.352	-4	-4	105	95	-0.4	-0	0	-0.3
1975	Cal-A	4	2	.667	50	0	0	0	1	68	59	7.8	8	18	2.4	31	4.1	3.31	110	.233	.276	4	2	96	92	1.2	0	-0	0.2
1976	Cal-A	3	0	1.000	33	0	0	0	3	39	47	10.8	3	12	2.8	10	2.3	3.23	101	.307	.343	1	0	93	148	1.5	0	-0	0.0
1977	Cal-A	0	2	.000	12	0	0	0	0	16	19	10.7	1	4	2.3	5	2.8	5.63	69	.302	.329	-3	-3	95	78	-0.9	0	0	-0.2
Total	5	8	7	.533	133	0	0	0	4	172	177	9.3	18	50	2.6	70	3.7	3.72	95	.271	.315	-1	-4	96	112	1.0	0	-1	-0.2
■ DICK SCOTT	Scott, Richard Lewis b: 3/15/33, Portsmouth, N.H. BR/TL, 6'2", 185 lbs. Deb: 5/08/63																												
1963	LA-N	0	0	—	9	0	0	0	2	12	17	12.8	6	3	2.3	6	4.5	6.75	46	.340	.370	-5	-5	94	131	0.0	0	0	-0.4
1964	Chi-N	0	0	—	3	0	0	0	0	4	10	22.5	2	1	2.3	1	2.3	13.50	28	.417	.440	-4	-4	106	93	0.0	0	0	-0.3
Total	2	0	0	—	12	0	0	0	2	16	27	15.2	8	4	2.3	7	3.9	8.44	38	.365	.392	-9	-9	97	122	0.0	0	0	-0.7
■ ROD SCURRY	Scurry, Rodney Grant b: 3/17/56, Sacramento, Cal. BL/TL, 6'2", 180 lbs. Deb: 4/17/80																												
1980	Pit-N	0	2	.000	20	0	0	0	0	38	23	5.4	2	17	4.0	28	6.6	2.13	174	.176	.275	6	7	103	90	-0.9	0	0	0.7
1981	Pit-N	4	5	.444	27	7	0	0	7	74	74	9.0	6	40	4.9	65	7.9	3.77	89	.261	.356	-2	-3	96	115	0.0	0	-1	-0.3
1982	Pit-N	4	5	.444	76	0	0	0	14	104	79	6.8	3	64	5.5	94	8.1	1.73	229	.212	.328	22	**26**	110	173	-0.6	1	-0	2.8
1983	Pit-N	4	9	.308	61	0	0	0	7	68	63	8.3	6	53	7.0	67	8.9	5.56	67	.249	.379	-15	-14	103	86	-2.7	-1	-0	-1.4
1984	Pit-N	5	6	.455	43	0	0	0	4	46	28	5.5	1	22	4.3	48	9.4	2.54	133	.175	.269	5	4	94	64	0.0	-0	0	0.5
1985	Pit-N	0	1	.000	30	0	0	0	2	48	42	7.9	4	28	5.3	43	8.1	3.19	118	.236	.333	2	3	104	118	-0.4	-0	0	0.3
	NY-A	1	0	1.000	5	0	0	0	1	13	5	3.5	2	10	6.9	17	11.8	2.77	141	.125	.294	2	2	94	103	0.5	0	0	0.2
1986	NY-A	1	2	.333	31	0	0	0	2	39	38	8.8	1	22	5.1	36	8.3	3.69	116	.252	.350	2	3	103	103	-0.5	0	0	0.3
1988	Sea-A	0	2	.000	39	0	0	0	2	31	32	9.3	6	18	5.2	33	9.6	4.06	106	.258	.360	-0	1	108	136	-0.9	0	0	0.1
Total	8	19	32	.373	332	7	0	0	39	461	384	7.5	31	274	5.3	431	8.4	3.24	117	.227	.335	23	28	103	117	-5.5	0	0	3.2
■ JOHNNIE SEALE	Seale, Johnny Ray "Durango Kid" b: 11/14/38, Edgewater, Colo. BL/TL, 5'10", 155 lbs. Deb: 9/20/64																												
1964	Det-A	1	0	1.000	4	0	0	0	0	10	6	5.4	1	4	3.6	5	4.5	3.60	96	.171	.250	0	-0	95	52	0.5	-0	1	0.0
1965	Det-A	0	0	—	4	0	0	0	0	3	7	21.0	1	2	6.0	3	9.0	12.00	30	.500	.500	-3	-3	104	118	0.0	0	0	-0.2
Total	2	1	0	1.000	8	0	0	0	0	13	13	9.0	2	6	4.2	8	5.5	5.54	63	.265	.328	-3	-3	97	67	0.5	-0	1	-0.2
■ KIM SEAMAN	Seaman, Kim Michael b: 5/6/57, Pascagoula, Miss. BL/TL, 6'4", 205 lbs. Deb: 9/28/79																												
1979	StL-N	0	0	—	1	0	0	0	0	2	0	0.0	0	2	9.0	3	13.5	0.00	—	.000	.250	1	1	104	0	0.0	0	0	0.1
1980	StL-N	3	2	.600	26	0	0	0	4	24	16	6.0	2	13	4.9	10	3.8	3.38	109	.188	.293	1	1	102	74	0.7	-0	-0	0.1
Total	2	3	2	.600	27	0	0	0	4	26	16	5.5	2	15	5.2	13	4.5	3.12	119	.176	.290	1	2	103	68	0.7	-0	-0	0.2
■ STEVE SEARCY	Searcy, William Steven b: 6/4/64, Knoxville, Tenn. BL/TL, 6'1", 185 lbs. Deb: 8/29/88																												
1988	Det-A	0	2	.000	2	2	0	0	0	8	3	9.0	3	4	4.5	5	5.6	5.63	66	.242	.324	-1	-2	94	103	-0.9	0	0	-0.1

YEAR	TM/L	W	L	PCT	G	GS	CG	SHO	SV	IP	H	H/G	HR	BB	BB/G	SO	SO/G	ERA	/A	OAVG	OOBP	PR	/A	PF	CPI	WAT	PB	PD	TPI
■ **RAY SEARAGE**	Searage, Raymond Mark b: 5/1/55, Freeport, N.Y. BL/TL, 6'1", 180 lbs. Deb: 6/11/81																												
1981	NY-N	1	0	1.000	26	0	0	0	1	37	34	8.3	2	17	4.1	16	3.9	3.65	98	.252	.327	-1	-0	103	100	0.5	0	-0	0.0
1984	Mil-A	2	1	.667	21	0	0	0	6	38	20	4.7	0	16	3.8	29	6.9	0.71	521	.155	.248	14	13	93	135	0.7	0	-0	1.3
1985	Mil-A	1	4	.200	33	0	0	0	1	38	54	12.8	2	24	5.7	36	8.5	5.92	74	.338	.413	-7	-6	106	111	-1.3	0	-1	-0.6
1986	Mil-A	0	1	.000	17	0	0	0	1	22	29	11.9	6	9	3.7	10	4.1	6.95	62	.315	.379	-7	-6	103	101	-0.4	0	0	-0.5
	Chi-A	1	0	1.000	29	0	0	0	0	29	15	4.7	1	19	5.9	26	8.1	0.62	684	.156	.291	11	12	101	318	0.5	0	0	1.2
	Yr	1	1	.500	46	0	0	0	1	51	44	7.8	7	28	4.9	36	6.4	3.35	127	.233	.327	5	5	102	318	0.1	0	0	0.7
1987	Chi-A	2	3	.400	58	0	0	0	2	56	56	9.0	9	24	3.9	33	5.3	4.18	116	.264	.338	2	4	109	115	-0.3	0	0	0.4
Total	5	7	9	.438	184	0	0	0	11	220	208	8.5	20	109	4.5	150	6.1	3.60	117	.252	.335	12	15	103	140	-0.3	0	-1	1.8
■ **TOM SEATON**	Seaton, Thomas Gordon b: 8/30/1887, Blair, Neb. d: 4/10/40, El Paso, Tex. BB/TR, 6', 175 lbs. Deb: 4/20/12																												
1912	Phi-N	16	12	.571	44	27	16	2	2	255	246	8.7	8	106	3.7	118	4.2	3.28	105	.255	.334	4	4	101	95	2.9	0	-2	0.2
1913	Phi-N	**27**	12	.692	52	35	21	6	1	**322**	262	7.3	6	136	3.8	**168**	4.7	2.60	137	.226	.308	22	34	111	98	6.3	-6	2	3.3
1914	Bro-F	25	14	.641	44	38	26	7	2	303	299	8.9	6	102	3.0	172	5.1	3.03	107	.259	.326	6	7	101	104	6.7	4	2	1.3
1915	Bro-F	12	11	.522	32	23	13	0	3	189	199	9.5	6	99	4.7	86	4.1	4.57	65	.300	.391	-32	-33	98	93	1.5	4	0	-2.9
	New-F	2	6	.250	12	10	7	0	1	75	61	7.3	1	21	2.5	28	3.4	2.28	125	.248	.308	6	5	94	97	-2.1	0	0	0.5
	Yr	14	17	.452	44	33	20	0	4	264	260	8.9	7	120	4.1	114	3.9	3.92	75	.286	.369	-26	-29	97	97	-0.6	4	0	-2.4
1916	Chi-N	6	6	.500	31	14	4	0	1	121	108	8.0	3	43	3.2	45	3.3	3.27	94	.246	.308	-9	-3	117	88	0.7	-0	1	-0.1
1917	Chi-N	5	4	.556	16	9	3	1	1	75	60	7.2	0	23	2.8	27	3.2	2.52	113	.227	.285	2	3	105	85	0.7	1	1	0.5
Total	6	93	65	.589	231	156	90	16	11	1340	1235	8.3	30	530	3.6	644	4.3	3.14	104	.253	.327	-2	17	104	96	16.7	3	3	2.8
■ **TOM SEATS**	Seats, Thomas Edward b: 9/24/11, Farmington, N.C. BB/TL, 5'11", 190 lbs. Deb: 5/04/40																												
1940	Det-A	2	2	.500	26	2	0	0	1	56	67	10.8	4	21	3.4	25	4.0	4.66	102	.290	.344	-2	1	109	100	-0.2	-1	0	0.0
1945	Bro-N	10	7	.588	31	18	6	2	0	122	127	9.4	8	37	2.7	44	3.2	4.35	83	.261	.318	-7	-10	95	83	0.5	1	0	-0.9
Total	2	12	9	.571	57	20	6	2	1	178	194	9.8	12	58	2.9	69	3.5	4.45	89	.271	.326	-9	-10	99	88	0.3	-1	0	-0.9
■ **TOM SEAVER**	Seaver, George Thomas "Tom Terrific" b: 11/17/44, Fresno, Cal. BR/TR, 6'1", 195 lbs. Deb: 4/13/67																												
1967	NY-N	16	13	.552	35	34	18	2	0	251	224	8.0	19	78	2.8	170	6.1	2.76	124	.241	.298	17	19	102	114	4.7	2	-0	2.4
1968	NY-N	16	12	.571	36	35	14	5	1	278	224	7.3	15	48	1.6	205	6.6	2.20	139	.222	.257	24	27	103	96	3.6	0	2	3.5
1969	NY-N	**25**	7	**.781**	36	35	18	5	0	273	202	**6.7**	24	82	2.7	208	6.9	2.21	162	**.207**	.267	42	41	99	110	**7.7**	0	2	5.0
1970	NY-N	18	12	.600	37	36	19	2	0	291	230	7.1	21	83	2.6	**283**	**8.8**	**2.81**	**149**	.214	.270	**40**	44	103	86	3.2	3	2	**5.4**
1971	NY-N	20	10	.667	36	35	21	4	0	286	210	6.6	18	61	1.9	**289**	**9.1**	**1.76**	**189**	.206	**.249**	**54**	**50**	96	106	5.4	4	1	**6.5**
1972	NY-N	21	12	.636	35	35	13	3	0	262	215	7.4	23	77	2.6	249	**8.6**	2.92	114	.224	.280	16	12	96	94	4.4	4	2	1.9
1973	NY-N	19	10	.655	36	36	**18**	3	0	290	219	**6.8**	23	64	2.0	**251**	**7.8**	**2.08**	**177**	**.206**	**.250**	**51**	**51**	100	93	4.9	2	0	**6.2**
1974	NY-N	11	11	.500	32	32	12	5	0	236	199	7.6	19	75	2.9	201	**7.7**	3.20	114	.230	.290	11	12	100	88	1.4	-2	3	1.2
1975	NY-N	**22**	9	.710	36	36	15	5	0	280	217	7.0	11	88	2.8	**243**	7.8	2.38	145	.214	.277	39	33	95	90	**7.2**	3	2	4.1
1976	NY-N	14	11	.560	35	34	13	5	0	271	211	7.0	14	77	2.6	**235**	**7.8**	2.59	123	.213	.271	**28**	18	91	84	0.9	-2	1	1.8
1977	NY-N	7	3	.700	13	13	5	3	0	96	79	7.4	7	28	2.6	72	6.8	3.00	126	.221	.274	10	8	97	80	2.6	-0	1	0.9
	Cin-N	14	3	.824	20	20	14	4	0	165	120	6.5	12	38	2.1	124	6.8	2.35	165	.201	.246	29	28	99	77	5.4	4	-1	3.4
	Yr	21	6	.778	33	33	19	**7**	0	261	199	**6.9**	19	66	2.3	196	6.8	2.59	149	**.208**	**.257**	39	36	98	77	**8.0**	-0	-1	4.3
1978	Cin-N	16	14	.533	36	36	8	1	0	260	218	7.5	26	89	3.1	226	7.8	2.87	128	.227	.286	20	23	102	103	-1.1	-0	-2	2.3
1979	Cin-N	16	6	**.727**	32	32	9	**5**	0	215	187	7.8	16	61	2.6	131	5.5	3.14	115	.236	.286	14	11	96	90	**4.6**	2	0	1.3
1980	Cin-N	10	8	.556	26	26	5	1	0	168	140	7.5	24	59	3.2	101	5.4	3.64	100	.225	.289	-1	0	101	90	0.1	1	1	0.2
1981	Cin-N	**14**	2	.875	23	23	6	1	0	166	120	6.5	10	66	3.6	87	4.7	2.55	138	.205	.282	17	18	101	96	**5.7**	4	-1	2.3
1982	Cin-N	5	13	.278	21	21	0	0	0	111	136	11.0	14	44	3.6	62	5.0	5.51	68	.302	.365	-23	-22	104	97	-2.5	-1	-1	-2.1
1983	NY-N	9	14	.391	34	34	5	2	0	231	201	7.8	18	86	3.4	135	5.3	3.55	102	.235	.302	2	2	100	88	-0.8	2	-1	0.3
1984	Chi-A	15	11	.577	34	33	10	4	0	237	216	8.2	27	61	2.3	131	5.0	3.95	112	.240	.285	1	13	111	81	3.3	0	1	1.5
1985	Chi-A	16	11	.593	35	33	6	1	0	239	223	8.4	22	69	2.6	134	5.0	3.16	131	.248	.302	26	26	100	110	2.2	0	2	2.9
1986	Chi-A	2	6	.250	12	12	1	0	0	72	66	8.3	9	27	3.4	31	3.9	4.38	97	.242	.317	-2	-1	101	88	-1.7	0	-1	-0.1
	Bos-A	5	7	.417	16	16	1	0	0	104	114	9.9	8	29	2.5	72	6.2	3.81	108	.278	.322	4	4	99	106	-1.8	0	-0	0.3
	Yr	7	13	.350	28	28	2	0	0	176	180	9.2	17	56	2.9	103	5.3	4.04	103	.261	.314	3	3	100	106	-3.5	0	-1	0.2
Total	20	311	205	.603	656	647	231	61	1	4782	3971	7.5	380	1390	2.6	3640	6.9	2.86	127	.226	.281	422	415	100	94	59.4	28	13	51.2
■ **BOB SEBRA**	Sebra, Robert Bush b: 12/11/61, Ridgewood, N.J. BR/TR, 6'2", 200 lbs. Deb: 6/26/85																												
1985	Tex-A	0	2	.000	7	4	0	0	0	20	26	11.7	4	14	6.3	13	5.8	7.65	60	.306	.402	-8	-7	110	92	-0.9	0	-0	-0.6
1986	Mon-N	5	5	.500	17	13	3	1	0	91	82	8.1	9	25	2.5	66	6.5	3.56	103	.239	.292	2	1	98	89	0.2	1	-1	0.1
1987	Mon-N	6	15	.286	36	27	4	1	0	177	184	9.4	15	67	3.4	156	7.9	4.42	98	.272	.332	-7	-2	106	96	-5.4	-0	-1	-0.2
1988	Phi-N	1	2	.333	3	3	0	0	0	11	15	12.3	0	10	8.2	7	5.7	8.18	43	.333	.417	-6	-6	103	83	-0.2	-1	-0	-0.5
Total	4	12	24	.333	63	47	7	2	0	299	307	9.2	28	116	3.5	242	7.3	4.52	91	.267	.330	-19	-14	104	93	-6.3	0	-1	-1.2
■ **DOC SECHRIST**	Sechrist, Theodore O'Hara b: 2/10/1876, Williamstown, Ky. d: 4/2/50, Louisville, Ky. BR/TR, 5'9", 160 lbs. Deb: 4/28/1899																												
1899	NY-N	0	0	—	1	0	0	0	0	0	0	—	0	2	—	0	—	—	—	—	1.000	0	0	99	0	0.0	0	0	0.0
■ **DON SECRIST**	Secrist, Donald Laverne b: 2/26/44, Seattle, Wash. BL/TL, 6'2", 195 lbs. Deb: 4/11/69																												
1969	Chi-A	0	1	.000	19	0	0	0	0	40	35	7.9	7	14	3.1	23	5.2	6.07	66	.227	.294	-11	-9	110	58	-0.4	0	0	-0.8
1970	Chi-A	0	0	—	9	0	0	0	0	15	19	11.4	2	12	7.2	9	5.4	5.40	74	.333	.437	-3	-2	108	135	0.0	0	0	-0.2
Total	2	0	1	.000	28	0	0	0	0	55	54	8.8	9	26	4.3	32	5.2	5.89	68	.256	.336	-14	-12	109	79	-0.4	0	0	-1.0
■ **DUKE SEDGWICK**	Sedgwick, Henry Kenneth b: 6/1/1898, Martins Ferry, O. d: 12/4/82, Clearwater, Fla. BR/TR, 6', 175 lbs. Deb: 7/12/21																												
1921	Phi-N	1	3	.250	16	5	1	0	0	71	81	10.3	3	32	4.1	21	2.7	4.94	82	.283	.350	-9	-7	107	84	-0.4	-1	-1	-0.8
1923	Was-A	0	1	.000	5	2	1	0	0	16	27	15.2	1	6	3.4	4	2.3	7.88	48	.415	.446	-7	-7	95	102	-0.4	-1	1	-0.6
Total	2	1	4	.200	21	7	2	0	0	87	108	11.2	4	38	3.9	25	2.6	5.48	73	.308	.368	-16	-14	105	87	-0.8	-2	-1	-1.4
■ **CHARLIE SEE**	See, Charles Henry "Chad" b: 10/13/1896, Pleasantville, N.Y d: 7/19/48, Bridgeport, Conn. BL/TR, 5'10.5", 175 lbs. Deb: 8/06/19																												
1920	Cin-N	0	0	—	1	0	0	0	0	6	6	9.0	0	4	6.0	3	4.5	6.00	46	.286	.345	-2	-2	88	72	0.0	0	0	-0.1
■ **CHUCK SEELBACH**	Seelbach, Charles Frederick b: 3/20/48, Lakewood, Ohio BR/TR, 6', 180 lbs. Deb: 6/29/71																												
1971	Det-A	0	0	—	5	0	0	0	0	4	6	13.5	2	7	15.8	1	2.3	13.50	24	.375	.583	-4	-5	95	108	0.0	0	-0	-0.4
1972	Det-A	9	8	.529	61	3	0	0	14	112	96	7.7	6	39	3.1	76	6.1	2.89	119	.238	.303	2	7	112	103	-0.3	1	-1	0.9
1973	Det-A	1	0	1.000	5	0	0	0	0	7	7	9.0	1	2	2.6	2	2.6	3.86	100	.250	.290	-0	0	101	92	0.5	0	1	0.1
1974	Det-A	0	0	—	4	0	0	0	0	8	9	10.1	2	3	3.4	0	0.0	4.50	87	.300	.382	-1	-1	108	143	0.0	0	0	0.0
Total	4	10	8	.556	75	3	0	0	14	131	118	8.1	11	51	3.5	79	5.4	3.37	104	.247	.320	-3	2	111	105	0.2	1	0	0.6
■ **EMMETT SEERY**	Seery, John Emmett b: 2/13/1861, Princeville, Ill. BL/TR, Deb: 4/17/1884																												
1886	StL-N	0	0	—	2	0	0	0	0	7	8	10.3	1	3	3.9	2	2.6	7.71	42	.301	.371	-3	-3	98	68	0.0	0	0	-0.2
■ **HERMAN SEGELKE**	Segelke, Herman Neils b: 4/24/58, San Mateo, Cal. BR/TR, 6'4", 200 lbs. Deb: 4/07/82																												
1982	Chi-N	0	0	—	3	0	0	0	0	4	6	13.5	1	6	13.5	4	9.0	9.00	42	.316	.480	-2	-2	104	108	0.0	0	0	-0.1
■ **DIEGO SEGUI**	Segui, Diego Pablo (Gonzalez) b: 8/17/37, Holguin, Cuba BR/TR, 6', 190 lbs. Deb: 4/12/62																												
1962	KC-A	8	5	.615	37	13	2	0	6	117	89	6.8	16	46	3.5	71	5.5	3.85	105	.211	.286	2	2	101	82	2.1	2	0	0.5
1963	KC-A	9	6	.600	38	23	4	1	0	167	173	9.3	17	73	3.9	116	6.3	3.77	105	.267	.336	-3	3	109	115	2.2	1	1	0.6
1964	KC-A	8	17	.320	40	35	5	2	0	217	219	9.1	30	94	3.9	155	6.4	4.56	86	.260	.332	-23	-16	108	95	-1.2	-0	2	-1.3
1965	KC-A	5	15	.250	40	25	5	1	0	163	166	9.2	18	67	3.7	119	6.6	4.64	74	.261	.330	-21	-22	100	89	-3.3	2	-1	-2.0
1966	Was-A	3	7	.300	21	13	1	1	0	72	82	10.3	8	24	3.0	54	6.8	5.00	66	.291	.340	-13	-14	96	96	-1.6	-0	-0	-1.4
1967	KC-A	3	4	.429	36	3	0	0	1	70	62	8.0	4	31	4.0	52	6.7	3.09	106	.238	.315	1	2	102	110	0.3	-1	-0	0.0
1968	Oak-A	6	5	.545	52	0	0	0	6	83	51	5.5	7	32	3.5	72	7.8	2.39	122	.173	.252	5	5	98	75	0.5	-0	-1	0.5
1969	Sea-A	12	6	.667	66	8	2	0	12	142	127	8.0	14	61	3.9	113	7.2	3.36	108	.238	.311	4	4	100	104	4.3	-0	1	0.5
1970	Oak-A	10	10	.500	47	19	3	2	2	162	130	7.2	9	68	3.8	95	5.3	**2.56**	139	.222	.299	21	18	96	108	-0.9	-2	-1	1.5
1971	Oak-A	10	8	.556	26	21	5	0	0	146	122	7.5	13	63	3.9	81	5.0	3.14	109	.229	.311	5	5	99	103	-1.0	-1	-1	0.3

YEAR	TM/L	W	L	PCT	G	GS	CG	SHO	SV	IP	H	H/G	HR	BB	BB/G	SO	SO/G	ERA	/A	OAVG	OOBP	PR	/A	PF	CPI	WAT	PB	PD	TPI
1972	Oak-A	0	1	.000	7	3	0	0	0	23	25	9.8	2	7	2.7	11	4.3	3.52	82	.287	.337	-1	-2	95	120	-0.4	-0	-0	-0.1
	StL-N	3	1	.750	33	0	0	0	9	56	47	7.6	2	32	5.1	54	8.7	3.05	119	.229	.324	3	4	105	104	1.0	0	1	0.5
1973	StL-N	7	6	.538	65	0	0	0	17	100	78	7.0	6	53	4.8	93	8.4	2.79	118	.211	.305	10	6	90	98	0.5	-1	-1	0.4
1974	Bos-A	6	8	.429	58	0	0	0	10	108	106	8.8	9	49	4.1	76	6.3	4.00	96	.257	.331	-5	-2	106	96	-1.2	0	-0	-0.2
1975	Bos-A	2	5	.286	33	1	1	0	6	71	71	9.0	10	43	5.5	45	5.7	4.82	85	.270	.361	-8	-6	108	106	-1.8	0	-0	-0.6
1977	Sea-A	0	7	.000	40	7	0	0	2	111	108	8.8	20	43	3.5	91	7.4	5.68	71	.251	.316	-20	-21	98	75	-3.4	0	0	-1.9
Total	15	92	111	.453	639	171	28	7	71	1808	1656	8.2	185	786	3.9	1298	6.5	3.81	96	.243	.318	-42	-33	101	98	-3.9	-0	-2	-2.7
■ **JOSE SEGURA**	Segura, Jose Altagracia (Mota) b: 1/26/63, Fundacion, D.R. BR/TR, 5'11", 180 lbs. Deb: 4/10/88																												
1988	Chi-A	0	0	—	4	0	0	0	0	9	19	19.0	1	8	8.0	2	2.0	13.00	30	.432	.519	-9	-9	99	86	0.0	0	0	-0.7
■ **SOCKS SEIBOLD**	Seibold, Harry b: 4/3/1896, Philadelphia, Pa. d: 9/21/65, Philadelphia, Pa. BR/TR, 5'8.5", 162 lbs. Deb: 9/18/15																												
1916	Phi-A	1	2	.333	3	2	1	1	0	22	22	9.0	0	9	3.7	5	2.0	4.09	73	.272	.344	-3	-3	105	82	0.2	-0	1	-0.1
1917	Phi-A	4	16	.200	33	15	9	1	1	160	141	7.9	1	85	4.8	55	3.1	3.94	66	.243	.343	-23	-24	97	76	-4.7	2	-1	-2.4
1919	Phi-A	2	3	.400	14	4	1	0	0	46	58	11.3	2	26	5.1	19	3.7	5.28	68	.322	.419	-11	-9	112	107	0.5	-1	0	-0.8
1929	Bos-N	12	17	.414	33	27	16	1	1	206	228	10.0	17	80	3.5	54	2.4	4.72	97	.285	.344	-0	-3	97	98	1.4	4	-1	0.0
1930	Bos-N	15	16	.484	36	33	20	1	2	251	288	10.3	16	85	3.0	70	2.5	4.12	119	.290	.338	24	22	99	107	1.0	0	-3	1.7
1931	Bos-N	10	18	.357	33	29	10	3	0	206	226	9.9	12	65	2.8	50	2.2	4.67	84	.279	.328	-19	-17	102	86	-2.2	-4	0	-1.9
1932	Bos-N	3	10	.231	28	20	6	1	0	137	173	11.4	12	41	2.7	33	2.2	4.66	78	.309	.352	-12	-16	93	109	-3.5	-1	2	-1.4
1933	Bos-N	1	4	.200	11	5	1	0	1	37	43	10.5	0	14	3.4	10	2.4	3.65	88	.295	.348	-1	-2	96	111	-1.5	0	0	-0.1
Total	8	48	86	.358	191	135	64	8	5	1065	1179	10.0	60	405	3.4	296	2.5	4.42	90	.284	.344	-44	-50	99	96	-8.8	0	-2	-5.0
■ **EPP SELL**	Sell, Lester Elwood b: 4/26/1897, Llewellyn, Pa. d: 2/19/61, Reading, Pa. BR/TR, 6', 175 lbs. Deb: 9/01/22																												
1922	StL-N	4	2	.667	7	5	0	0	0	33	47	12.8	2	6	1.6	5	1.4	6.82	60	.338	.369	-10	-10	100	77	0.8	1	1	-0.6
1923	StL-N	0	1	.000	5	1	0	0	0	15	16	9.6	1	8	4.8	2	1.2	6.00	60	.291	.369	-3	-4	90	81	-0.4	-1	-0	-0.4
Total	2	4	3	.571	12	6	0	0	0	48	63	11.8	3	14	2.6	7	1.3	6.56	60	.325	.369	-13	-14	97	79	0.4	0	-0	-1.0
■ **JEFF SELLERS**	Sellers, Jeffrey Doyle b: 5/11/64, Compton, Cal. BR/TR, 6'1", 175 lbs. Deb: 9/15/85																												
1985	Bos-A	2	0	1.000	4	4	1	0	0	22	24	9.8	1	7	2.9	6	2.5	3.68	114	.273	.320	1	1	102	101	1.0	0	0	0.1
1986	Bos-A	3	7	.300	14	13	1	0	0	82	90	9.9	13	40	4.4	51	5.6	4.94	84	.282	.363	-7	-7	99	110	-2.4	0	0	-0.6
1987	Bos-A	7	8	.467	25	22	4	2	0	140	161	10.4	10	61	3.9	99	6.4	5.27	84	.298	.363	-12	-13	99	96	-0.2	0	0	-1.1
1988	Bos-A	1	7	.125	18	12	1	0	0	86	89	9.3	9	56	5.9	70	7.3	4.81	89	.268	.377	-8	-5	108	106	-3.0	0	-0	-0.4
Total	4	13	22	.371	61	51	7	2	0	330	364	9.9	33	164	4.5	226	6.2	4.96	87	.285	.364	-26	-24	101	103	-4.6	0	0	-2.0
■ **FRANK SELLMAN**	Sellman, Frank C. (Also Played Under Name Of Frank C. Williams 1871-74) b: Baltimore, Md. Deb: 5/04/1871																												
1873	Mar-n	0	1	.000	1																								
■ **DAVE SELLS**	Sells, David Wayne b: 9/18/46, Vacaville, Cal. BR/TR, 5'11", 175 lbs. Deb: 8/02/72																												
1972	Cal-A	2	0	1.000	10	0	0	0	0	16	11	6.2	0	5	2.8	2	1.1	2.81	98	.196	.258	0	-0	90	50	1.0	0	0	0.0
1973	Cal-A	7	2	.778	51	0	0	0	10	68	72	9.5	2	35	4.6	25	3.3	3.71	99	.277	.364	1	-0	96	117	2.6	0	0	0.0
1974	Cal-A	2	3	.400	20	0	0	0	2	39	48	11.1	3	16	3.7	14	3.2	3.69	91	.312	.374	-0	-1	93	145	0.0	0	0	0.0
1975	Cal-A	0	0	—	4	0	0	0	0	8	9	10.1	3	8	9.0	7	7.9	9.00	40	.250	.386	-5	-5	96	79	0.0	0	0	-0.3
	LA-N	0	2	.000	5	0	0	0	0	7	6	7.7	2	3	3.9	1	1.3	3.86	88	.222	.300	-0	-0	93	113	-0.9	0	0	0.0
Total	4	11	7	.611	90	0	0	0	12	138	146	9.5	10	67	4.4	49	3.2	3.91	88	.274	.355	-4	-7	94	115	2.7	0	1	-0.3
■ **DICK SELMA**	Selma, Richard Jay b: 11/4/43, Santa Ana, Cal. BR/TR, 5'11", 160 lbs. Deb: 9/02/65																												
1965	NY-N	2	1	.667	4	4	1	1	0	27	22	7.3	2	9	3.0	26	8.7	3.67	100	.229	.296	-0	0	104	84	0.8	0	1	0.1
1966	NY-N	4	6	.400	30	7	0	0	1	81	84	9.3	11	39	4.3	58	6.4	4.22	83	.274	.355	-6	-7	97	117	0.0	1	2	-0.4
1967	NY-N	2	4	.333	38	4	0	0	2	81	71	7.9	3	36	4.0	52	5.8	2.78	124	.241	.320	5	6	102	119	-0.3	-1	1	0.6
1968	NY-N	9	10	.474	33	23	4	3	0	170	148	7.8	11	54	2.9	117	6.2	2.75	111	.233	.294	4	6	103	104	0.4	2	2	1.1
1969	SD-N	2	2	.500	4	3	1	0	0	22	19	7.8	3	9	3.7	20	8.2	4.09	88	.229	.304	-1	-1	100	85	0.5	0	0	0.0
	Chi-N	10	8	.556	36	25	4	2	1	169	137	7.3	13	72	3.8	161	8.6	3.62	105	.222	.303	-0	3	105	83	-0.1	-0	-1	0.3
	Yr	12	10	.545	40	28	5	2	1	191	156	7.4	16	81	3.8	181	8.5	3.68	102	.223	.303	-2	2	105	83	0.4	0	-0	0.3
1970	Phi-N	8	9	.471	73	0	0	0	22	134	108	7.3	8	59	4.0	153	10.3	2.75	144	.226	.310	**19**	18	98	116	0.3	0	2	2.0
1971	Phi-N	0	2	.000	17	0	0	0	1	25	21	7.6	2	8	2.9	15	5.4	3.24	112	.231	.304	1	1	105	95	-0.9	0	0	0.2
1972	Phi-N	2	9	.182	46	10	1	0	3	99	91	8.3	13	73	6.6	58	5.3	5.55	62	.249	.368	-23	-23	99	90	-2.9	1	1	-2.2
1973	Phi-N	1	1	.500	6	0	0	0	0	8	6	6.8	1	5	5.6	4	4.5	5.63	71	.240	.344	-2	-1	109	81	0.1	0	1	0.0
1974	Cal-A	2	2	.500	18	0	0	0	1	23	22	8.6	2	17	6.7	15	5.9	5.09	66	.272	.392	-4	-4	93	103	0.3	0	1	-0.3
	Mil-A	0	0	—	2	0	0	0	0	2	5	22.5	0	0	0.0	2	9.0	22.50	17	.455	.462	-4	-4	103	46	0.0	0	0	-0.3
	Yr	2	2	.500	20	0	0	0	1	25	27	9.7	2	17	6.1	17	6.1	6.48	52	.290	.391	-8	-9	94	46	0.3	0	1	-0.6
Total	10	42	54	.438	307	76	11	6	31	841	734	7.9	69	381	4.1	681	7.3	3.62	98	.238	.321	-10	-7	101	101	-1.8	3	8	1.1
■ **CARROLL SEMBERA**	Sembera, Carroll William b: 7/26/41, Shiner, Tex. BR/TR, 6', 155 lbs. Deb: 9/28/65																												
1965	Hou-N	0	1	.000	2	1	0	0	0	7	5	6.4	0	3	3.9	4	5.1	3.86	83	.185	.267	-0	-0	91	33	-0.4	-0	0	0.0
1966	Hou-N	1	2	.333	24	0	0	0	1	33	36	9.8	3	16	4.4	21	5.7	3.00	119	.288	.361	2	2	99	162	-0.3	-0	0	0.2
1967	Hou-N	2	6	.250	45	0	0	0	3	60	66	9.9	7	19	2.9	48	7.2	4.80	67	.269	.320	-9	-11	95	86	-1.6	-0	1	-0.9
1969	Mon-N	0	2	.000	23	0	0	0	2	33	28	7.6	1	24	6.5	15	4.1	3.55	105	.246	.370	0	1	103	121	-0.9	0	-0	0.1
1970	Mon-N	0	0	—	5	0	0	0	0	7	14	18.0	2	11	14.1	6	7.7	18.00	23	.424	.565	-11	-11	102	80	0.0	0	0	-0.9
Total	5	3	11	.214	99	1	0	0	6	140	149	9.6	13	73	4.7	94	6.0	4.69	74	.274	.356	-18	-19	98	109	-3.2	-0	1	-1.5
■ **RAY SEMPROCH**	Semproch, Roman Anthony "Baby" b: 1/7/31, Cleveland, Ohio BR/TR, 5'11", 180 lbs. Deb: 4/15/58																												
1958	Phi-N	13	11	.542	36	30	12	2	0	204	211	9.3	25	58	2.6	92	4.1	3.93	101	.264	.315	1	1	100	99	2.3	-5	-1	-0.4
1959	Phi-N	3	10	.231	30	18	2	0	3	112	119	9.6	12	59	4.7	54	4.3	5.38	75	.277	.360	-18	-17	102	91	-2.9	-0	1	-1.5
1960	Det-A	3	0	1.000	17	0	0	0	0	27	29	9.7	2	16	5.3	9	3.0	4.00	98	.269	.360	-0	-0	102	110	1.5	-0	1	0.1
1961	LA-A	0	0	—	2	0	0	0	0	1	1	9.0	0	3	27.0	1	9.0	9.00	50	.333	.571	-1	-0	112	139	0.0	0	0	0.0
Total	4	19	21	.475	85	48	14	2	3	344	360	9.4	39	136	3.6	156	4.1	4.42	90	.269	.335	-18	-17	101	97	0.9	-5	1	-1.8
■ **STEVE SENTENEY**	Senteney, Steve Leonard b: 8/7/57, Indianapolis, Ind. BR/TR, 6'2", 205 lbs. Deb: 6/06/82																												
1982	Tor-A	0	0	—	11	0	0	0	0	22	23	9.4	5	6	2.5	20	8.2	4.91	91	.247	.290	-2	-1	109	82	0.0	0	-0	0.0
■ **MANNY SEOANE**	Seoane, Manuel Modesto b: 6/26/55, Tampa, Fla. BR/TR, 6'3", 187 lbs. Deb: 9/18/77																												
1977	Phi-N	0	0	—	2	1	0	0	0	6	11	16.5	0	3	4.5	4	6.0	6.00	64	.407	.467	-1	-1	98	133	0.0	0	-0	0.0
1978	Chi-N	1	0	1.000	7	1	0	0	0	8	11	12.4	0	6	6.8	5	5.6	5.63	71	.297	.395	-2	-1	111	91	0.5	0	-0	-0.1
Total	2	1	0	1.000	9	2	0	0	0	14	22	14.1	0	9	5.8	9	5.8	5.79	68	.344	.425	-3	-3	106	109	0.5	0	-0	-0.1
■ **BILLY SERAD**	Serad, William I. b: 1863, Philadelphia, Pa. d: 11/1/25, Chester, Pa. BR/TR, 5'7", 156 lbs. Deb: 5/05/1884																												
1884	Buf-N	16	20	.444	37	37	34	2	0	308	373	10.9	21	111	3.2	150	4.4	4.27	73	.309	.367	-44	-39	105	108	-5.4	-7	-3	-3.9
1885	Buf-N	7	21	.250	30	29	27	0	0	241	299	11.2	5	80	3.0	90	3.4	4.11	72	.316	.369	-35	-31	105	110	-4.4	-6	0	-3.1
1887	Cin-a	10	11	.476	22	21	20	2	1	187	201	9.7	7	80	3.9	34	1.6	4.09	112	.288	.362	4	10	106	105	-2.4	-5	0	0.5
1888	Cin-a	2	3	.400	6	5	5	0	0	51	62	10.9	1	19	3.4	4	0.7	3.53	86	.314	.374	-3	-3	99	130	-0.7	-1	0	-0.3
Total	4	35	55	.389	95	92	86	4	1	787	935	10.7	34	290	3.3	278	3.2	4.13	83	.307	.367	-77	-63	105	109	-12.9	-18	-3	-6.8
■ **GARY SERUM**	Serum, Gary Wayne b: 10/24/56, Fargo, N.D. BR/TR, 6'1", 180 lbs. Deb: 7/22/77																												
1977	Min-A	0	0	—	8	0	0	0	0	23	22	8.6	4	10	3.9	14	5.5	4.30	97	.268	.351	-1	-0	102	121	0.0	0	-0	0.0
1978	Min-A	9	9	.500	34	23	6	1	1	184	188	9.2	14	44	2.2	80	3.9	4.11	87	.266	.304	-7	-11	94	84	0.9	0	0	-1.0
1979	Min-A	1	3	.250	20	5	0	0	0	64	93	13.1	10	20	2.8	31	4.4	6.61	69	.354	.394	-17	-14	108	104	-0.9	0	0	-1.3
Total	3	10	12	.455	62	28	6	1	1	271	303	10.1	28	74	2.5	125	4.2	4.72	82	.288	.330	-24	-26	98	92	0.0	0	-0	-2.3
■ **SCOTT SERVICE**	Service, Scott David b: 2/26/67, Cincinnati, Ohio BR/TR, 6'6", 225 lbs. Deb: 9/05/88																												
1988	Phi-N	0	0	—	5	0	0	0	0	5	7	12.6	0	1	1.8	6	10.8	1.80	198	.333	.391	1	1	103	298	0.0	0	0	0.1

YEAR	TM/L	W	L	PCT	G	GS	CG	SHO	SV	IP	H	H/G	HR	BB	BB/G	SO	SO/G	ERA	/A	OAVG	OOBP	PR	/A	PF	CPI	WAT	PB	PD	TPI
■ MERLE SETTLEMIRE	Settlemire, Edgar Merle "Lefty" b: 1/19/03, Santa Fe, Ohio d: 6/12/88, Russell's Point, Ohio BL/TL, 5'9", 156 lbs. Deb: 4/13/28																												
1928	Bos-A	0	6	.000	30	9	0	0	0	82	116	12.7	2	34	3.7	12	1.3	5.49	75	.345	.394	-13	-13	101	111	-2.9	-1	2	-1.0
■ AL SEVERINSEN	Severinsen, Albert Henry b: 11/9/44, Brooklyn, N.Y. BR/TR, 6'3", 220 lbs. Deb: 7/01/69																												
1969	Bal-A	1	1	.500	12	0	0	0	0	20	14	6.3	2	10	4.5	13	5.8	2.25	162	.206	.293	3	3	100	137	-0.2	0	0	0.4
1971	SD-N	2	5	.286	59	0	0	0	8	70	77	9.9	4	30	3.9	31	4.0	3.47	98	.292	.354	-0	-1	98	133	-0.8	-0	1	0.1
1972	SD-N	0	1	.000	17	0	0	0	1	21	13	5.6	1	7	3.0	9	3.9	2.57	122	.173	.259	2	1	91	59	-0.4	-0	0	0.2
Total	3	3	7	.300	88	0	0	0	9	111	104	8.4	7	47	3.8	53	4.3	3.08	110	.256	.326	5	4	97	119	-1.4	0	2	0.7
■ ED SEWARD	Seward, Edward William (born Edward William Sourhardt) b: 6/29/1867, Cleveland, Ohio d: 7/30/47, Cleveland, Ohio TR, 5'7", 175 lbs. Deb: 1885																												
1885	Pro-N	0	0	—	1	0	0	0	0	6	2	3.0	0	0	0.0	1	1.5	0.00	—	.110	.110	2	2	93	0	0.0	-0	0	0.1
1887	Phi-a	25	25	.500	55	52	52	3	0	471	445	8.5	7	140	2.7	155	3.0	4.13	104	.263	.319	9	8	100	75	1.4	-4	-4	0.0
1888	Phi-a	35	19	.648	57	57	57	**6**	0	519	388	6.7	4	127	2.2	**272**	4.7	2.01	148	.219	.272	61	55	97	91	4.3	-4	4	5.3
1889	Phi-a	21	15	.583	39	38	35	3	0	320	353	9.9	8	101	2.8	102	2.9	3.97	93	.295	.350	-4	-9	96	95	1.1	6	-0	-0.1
1890	Phi-a	5	12	.294	21	19	15	1	0	154	165	9.6	4	72	4.2	55	3.2	4.73	83	.290	.370	-15	-14	101	91	-2.5	-2	0	-1.2
1891	Cle-N	2	1	.667	3	3	0	0	0	16	16	9.0	0	1	0.6	4	2.3	3.94	90	.274	.286	-1	-1	106	52	0.6	0	0	0.0
Total	6	88	72	.550	176	169	159	13	0	1486	1369	8.3	23	441	2.7	589	3.6	3.40	107	.258	.315	51	40	98	86	4.9	-4	-0	4.1
■ FRANK SEWARD	Seward, Frank Martin b: 4/7/21, Pennsauken, N.J. BR/TR, 6'3", 200 lbs. Deb: 9/28/43																												
1943	NY-N	0	1	.000	1	1	1	0	0	9	12	12.0	0	5	5.0	2	2.0	3.00	111	.324	.405	0	0	99	181	-0.4	-1	-0	0.0
1944	NY-N	3	2	.600	25	7	2	0	0	78	98	11.3	8	32	3.7	16	1.8	5.42	70	.306	.367	-16	-14	105	100	0.7	-2	-1	-1.6
Total	2	3	3	.500	26	8	3	0	0	87	110	11.4	8	37	3.8	18	1.9	5.17	73	.308	.371	-15	-14	105	108	0.3	-2	-2	-1.6
■ RIP SEWELL	Sewell, Truett Banks b: 5/11/07, Decatur, Ala. BL/TR, 6'1", 180 lbs. Deb: 6/14/32 C																												
1932	Det-A	0	0	—	5	0	0	0	0	11	19	15.5	2	8	6.5	2	1.6	12.27	37	.388	.458	-10	-9	102	80	0.0	0	0	-0.7
1938	Pit-N	0	1	.000	17	0	0	0	1	38	41	9.7	3	21	5.0	17	4.0	4.26	88	.275	.364	-2	-2	99	114	-0.4	-1	1	-0.1
1939	Pit-N	10	9	.526	52	12	5	1	2	176	177	9.1	10	73	3.7	69	3.5	4.09	96	.265	.329	-3	-3	101	95	1.6	1	3	0.1
1940	Pit-N	16	5	.762	33	23	14	2	1	190	169	8.0	6	67	3.2	60	2.8	2.79	131	.238	.303	22	18	95	108	5.8	2	2	2.3
1941	Pit-N	14	17	.452	39	32	18	2	2	249	225	8.1	18	84	3.0	76	2.7	3.72	99	.235	.296	-2	-1	102	82	-2.5	-0	2	0.1
1942	Pit-N	17	15	.531	40	33	18	5	2	248	259	9.4	13	72	2.6	69	2.5	3.41	99	.265	.312	-3	-1	102	102	2.9	-2	-0	-0.2
1943	Pit-N	**21**	9	.700	35	31	**25**	2	3	265	267	9.1	6	75	2.5	65	2.2	2.55	136	.260	.309	24	27	103	121	**6.4**	6	1	3.9
1944	Pit-N	21	12	.636	38	33	24	3	2	286	263	8.3	15	99	3.1	87	2.7	3.18	118	.240	.300	14	18	104	94	2.4	3	-1	2.1
1945	Pit-N	11	9	.550	33	24	9	1	1	188	212	10.1	9	91	4.4	60	2.9	4.07	95	.279	.353	-6	-4	102	108	0.4	6	-0	0.2
1946	Pit-N	8	12	.400	25	20	11	2	0	149	140	8.5	6	53	3.2	33	2.0	3.68	98	.245	.303	-4	-1	106	78	-0.2	0	-1	-0.1
1947	Pit-N	6	4	.600	24	12	4	1	0	121	121	9.0	11	36	2.7	36	2.7	3.57	116	.263	.317	7	8	102	107	1.7	-1	1	0.8
1948	Pit-N	13	3	.813	21	17	7	0	0	122	126	9.3	9	37	2.7	36	2.7	3.47	119	.262	.314	7	9	104	105	5.0	1	-0	1.0
1949	Pit-N	6	1	.857	28	6	2	1	1	76	82	9.7	8	32	3.8	26	3.1	3.91	106	.280	.345	1	2	102	120	2.6	-0	-1	0.1
Total	13	143	97	.596	390	243	137	20	15	2119	2101	8.9	116	748	3.2	636	2.7	3.48	107	.256	.316	45	61	102	101	25.7	16	6	9.5
■ ELMER SEXAUER	Sexauer, Elmer George b: 5/21/26, St.Louis Co., Mo. BR/TR, 6'4", 220 lbs. Deb: 9/06/48																												
1948	Bro-N	0	0	—	2	0	0	0	0	1	0	0.0	0	2	18.0	0	0.0	9.00	45	.000	.500	-1	-1	103	53	0.0	0	0	0.0
■ FRANK SEXTON	Sexton, Frank Joseph b: 7/8/1872, Brockton, Mass. d: 1/4/38, Brighton, Mass. Deb: 6/21/1895																												
1895	Bos-N	1	5	.167	7	5	4	0	0	49	59	10.8	2	22	4.0	14	2.6	5.69	86	.319	.391	-5	-4	102	85	-2.0	-1	0	-0.3
■ GORDON SEYFRIED	Seyfried, Gordon Clay b: 7/4/37, Long Beach, Cal. BR/TR, 6', 185 lbs. Deb: 9/13/63																												
1963	Cle-A	0	1	.000	3	1	0	0	0	7	9	11.6	0	3	3.9	1	1.3	1.29	276	.300	.353	2	2	98	340	-0.4	-0	0	0.2
1964	Cle-A	0	0	—	2	0	0	0	0	2	4	18.0	0	0	0.0	0	0.0	0.00	—	.444	.400	1	1	103	0	0.0	0	0	0.1
Total	2	0	1	.000	5	1	0	0	0	9	13	13.0	0	3	3.0	1	1.0	1.00	359	.333	.364	3	3	99	264	-0.4	-0	0	0.3
■ JAKE SEYMOUR	Seymour, Jacob (born Jacob Semer) b: 1854, Pittsburgh, Pa. d: 8/1/1897, Allegheny, Pa. Deb: 9/23/1882																												
1882	Pit-a	0	1	.000	1	1	1	0	0	8	16	18.0	0	2	2.3	2	2.3	7.88	33	.420	.449	-5	-5	97	99	-0.4	-1	0	-0.3
■ CY SEYMOUR	Seymour, James Bentley b: 12/9/1872, Albany, N.Y. d: 9/20/19, New York, N.Y. BL/TL, 6', 200 lbs. Deb: 4/22/1896																												
1896	NY-N	2	4	.333	11	8	4	0	0	70	75	9.6	8	51	6.6	33	4.2	6.43	67	.296	.414	-16	-17	99	84	-0.9	-1	0	-1.3
1897	NY-N	18	14	.563	38	33	28	2	1	278	254	**8.2**	4	164	5.3	149	**4.8**	3.37	124	**.264**	.371	29	25	96	103	-2.2	1	9	3.0
1898	NY-N	25	19	.568	45	43	39	4	0	357	313	7.9	4	213	5.4	**239**	**6.0**	3.18	107	.256	.366	17	9	94	103	3.4	8	9	2.8
1899	NY-N	14	18	.438	32	32	31	0	0	268	247	8.3	5	170	5.7	142	**4.8**	3.56	107	.267	.381	9	7	99	102	1.3	7	5	2.2
1900	NY-N	2	2	.500	13	7	3	0	0	57	60	9.5	4	60	9.5	19	3.0	6.63	55	.293	.453	-19	-19	99	89	0.2	1	0	-1.4
1902	Cin-N	0	0	—	1	0	0	0	0	3	4	12.0	0	3	9.0	2	6.0	9.00	33	.345	.480	-2	-2	108	71	0.0	0	0	-0.1
Total	6	61	57	.517	140	123	105	6	1	1033	953	8.3	25	661	5.8	584	5.1	3.76	101	.266	.380	18	3	97	101	1.8	16	22	5.2
■ JOHN SHAFFER	Shaffer, John W. "Cannon Ball" b: 2/18/1864, Lock Haven, Pa. d: 11/21/26, Endicott, N.Y. Deb: 9/13/1886																												
1886	NY-a	5	3	.625	8	8	8	1	0	69	40	5.2	0	29	3.8	36	4.7	1.96	187	.177	.271	11	13	106	79	1.6	0	0	1.3
1887	NY-a	2	11	.154	13	13	13	0	0	112	148	11.9	3	53	4.3	22	1.8	6.19	64	.332	.403	-24	-28	92	90	-3.5	-2	0	-2.2
Total	2	7	14	.333	21	21	21	1	0	181	188	9.3	3	82	4.1	58	2.9	4.57	84	.280	.358	-12	-14	97	86	-1.9	-2	0	-0.9
■ GUS SHALLIX	Shallix, August (born August Schallick) b: 3/29/1858, Paderborn, Westphalia, Germany d: 10/28/37, Cincinnati, Ohio BR/TR, 5'11", 165 lbs. Deb: 6/22/1884																												
1884	Cin-a	11	10	.524	23	23	23	0	0	200	163	7.3	7	53	2.4	78	3.5	3.69	90	.230	.284	-10	-8	103	75	-1.9	-11	0	-1.5
1885	Cin-a	6	4	.600	13	12	7	0	0	91	95	9.4	1	33	3.3	15	1.5	3.26	102	.281	.344	-0	1	103	116	0.5	-2	0	0.0
Total	2	17	14	.548	36	35	30	0	0	291	258	8.0	8	86	2.7	93	2.9	3.56	94	.247	.304	-10	-7	103	88	-1.4	-13	0	-1.5
■ GREG SHANAHAN	Shanahan, Paul Gregory b: 12/11/47, Eureka, Cal. BR/TR, 6'2", 190 lbs. Deb: 9/04/73																												
1973	LA-N	0	0	—	7	0	0	0	0	16	14	7.9	2	4	2.3	11	6.2	3.38	108	.230	.273	1	0	99	85	0.0	0	0	0.1
1974	LA-N	0	0	—	4	0	0	0	0	7	7	9.0	1	5	6.4	2	2.6	3.86	85	.259	.353	-0	-0	90	132	0.0	0	0	0.0
Total	2	0	0	—	11	0	0	0	1	23	21	8.2	3	9	3.5	13	5.1	3.52	100	.239	.300	0	-0	96	99	0.0	0	0	0.1
■ HARVEY SHANK	Shank, Harvey Tillman b: 7/29/46, Toronto, Ont., Can. BR/TR, 6'4", 220 lbs. Deb: 5/16/70																												
1970	Cal-A	0	0	—	1	0	0	0	0	3	2	6.0	0	2	6.0	1	3.0	0.00	—	.182	.308	1	1	92	0	0.0	0	0	0.1
■ BILL SHANNER	Shanner, Wilfred William b: 11/4/1894, Oakland City, Ind. d: 12/18/86, Evansville, Ind. BL/TR, Deb: 10/01/20																												
1920	Phi-A	0	0	—	1	0	0	0	0	4	6	13.5	2	1	2.3	1	2.3	6.75	56	.353	.389	-1	-1	99	134	0.0	-0	0	0.0
■ BOBBY SHANTZ	Shantz, Robert Clayton b: 9/26/25, Pottstown, Pa. BR/TL, 5'6", 139 lbs. Deb: 5/01/49																												
1949	Phi-A	6	8	.429	33	7	4	1	2	127	100	7.1	9	74	5.2	58	4.1	3.40	122	.221	.330	11	10	99	101	-1.3	1	4	1.5
1950	Phi-A	8	14	.364	36	23	6	1	0	215	251	10.5	18	85	3.6	93	3.9	4.60	93	.294	.358	-1	-8	93	107	0.5	0	4	-0.3
1951	Phi-A	18	10	.643	32	25	13	3	0	205	213	9.4	15	70	3.1	77	3.4	3.95	111	.270	.331	4	10	106	102	5.5	2	3	1.5
1952	Phi-A	**24**	7	**.774**	33	33	27	5	0	280	230	7.4	21	63	**2.0**	152	4.9	2.48	166	.225	**.269**	37	**51**	112	101	**9.2**	1	2	**6.3**
1953	Phi-A	5	9	.357	16	16	6	0	0	106	107	9.1	10	26	2.2	58	4.9	4.08	103	.263	.304	-1	1	105	88	-0.4	1	2	0.5
1954	Phi-A	1	0	1.000	2	1	0	0	0	8	12	13.5	2	3	3.4	3	3.4	7.88	49	.364	.421	-4	-4	105	105	0.5	0	0	-0.2
1955	KC-A	5	10	.333	23	17	4	1	0	125	124	8.9	8	66	4.8	58	4.2	4.54	93	.264	.347	-8	-5	106	92	-1.4	-2	1	-0.4
1956	KC-A	2	7	.222	45	2	1	0	9	101	95	8.5	12	37	3.3	67	6.0	4.37	100	.248	.318	-2	-0	105	86	-1.5	-1	1	0.0
1957	NY-A	11	5	.688	30	21	9	1	5	173	157	8.2	15	40	2.1	72	3.7	**2.45**	140	.248	.295	26	19	90	**131**	1.2	3	6	2.9
1958	NY-A	7	6	.538	33	13	3	0	0	126	127	9.1	8	35	2.5	80	5.7	3.36	111	.262	.309	6	5	99	103	-0.6	2	3	1.1
1959	NY-A	7	3	.700	33	4	2	2	3	95	64	6.1	4	33	3.1	66	6.3	2.37	150	.189	.258	16	12	92	73	2.0	2	1	1.6
1960	NY-A	5	4	.556	42	0	0	0	11	68	57	7.5	5	24	3.2	54	7.1	2.78	128	.235	.296	8	6	92	112	-0.5	-0	1	0.7
1961	Pit-N	6	3	.667	43	6	2	1	2	89	91	9.2	5	26	2.6	61	6.2	3.34	120	.271	.321	7	6	99	113	1.6	3	2	1.1
1962	Hou-N	1	1	.500	3	3	1	0	0	21	15	6.4	1	5	2.1	14	6.0	1.29	290	.208	.256	6	6	95	156	0.2	-1	2	0.6
	StL-N	5	3	.625	28	0	0	0	4	58	45	7.0	7	20	3.1	47	7.3	2.17	194	.211	.280	11	13	107	128	0.9	-0	1	1.4
	Yr	6	4	.600	31	3	1	0	4	79	60	6.8	8	25	2.8	61	6.9	1.94	211	.210	.274	18	19	104	128	1.1	-1	3	2.0
1963	StL-N	6	4	.600	55	0	0	0	11	79	55	6.3	6	17	1.9	70	8.0	2.62	133	.192	.237	6	7	106	64	0.3	0	3	1.2
1964	StL-N	1	3	.250	16	0	0	0	0	17	14	7.4	2	7	3.7	12	6.4	3.18	124	.226	.292	1	1	111	106	-1.0	0	1	0.3

YEAR	TM/L	W	L	PCT	G	GS	CG	SHO	SV	IP	H	H/G	HR	BB	BB/G	SO	SO/G	ERA	/A	OAVG	OOBP	PR	/A	PF	CPI	WAT	PB	PD	TPI
	Chi-N	0	1	.000	20	0	0	0	1	11	15	12.3	2	6	4.9	12	9.8	5.73	66	.319	.382	-3	-2	106	117	-0.4	0	0	-0.1
	Phi-N	1	1	.500	14	0	0	0	0	32	23	6.5	1	6	1.7	18	5.1	2.25	154	.204	.234	5	4	98	71	0.0	-0	2	0.7
	Yr	2	5	.286	50	0	0	0	1	60	52	7.8	5	19	2.9	42	6.3	3.15	116	.233	.283	3	3	103	71	-1.4	0	4	0.9
Total	16	119	99	.546	537	171	78	15	48	1936	1795	8.3	151	643	3.0	1072	5.0	3.38	119	.248	.308	125	137	101	102	14.8	11	39	20.4
■ **GEORGE SHARROTT**	Sharrott, George Oscar b: 11/2/1869, W.New Brighton, S.I., N.Y. d: 1/6/32, Jamaica, N.Y. BL/TL, Deb: 7/27/1893																												
1893	Bro-N	4	6	.400	13	10	10	0	1	95	114	10.8	3	58	5.5	24	2.3	5.87	73	.313	.408	-13	-17	91	90	-1.0	0	0	-1.2
1894	Bro-N	0	1	.000	2	2	1	0	0	9	7	7.0	0	5	5.0	2	2.0	7.00	72	.234	.343	-2	-2	94	38	-0.4	0	0	0.0
Total	2	4	7	.364	15	12	11	0	1	104	121	10.5	3	63	5.5	26	2.3	5.97	72	.307	.403	-14	-19	91	85	-1.4	0	0	-1.2
■ **JACK SHARROTT**	Sharrott, John Henry b: 8/13/1869, Bangor, Me. d: 12/31/27, Los Angeles, Cal. BR/TR, 5'9", 165 lbs. Deb: 4/22/1890																												
1890	NY-N	11	10	.524	25	20	18	0	0	184	162	7.9	3	88	4.3	84	4.1	2.89	117	.251	.341	14	10	94	103	1.0	-2	0	0.6
1891	NY-N	5	5	.500	10	9	6	0	1	69	47	6.1	2	35	4.6	41	5.3	2.61	119	.204	.309	6	4	93	73	-0.3	4	0	0.7
1892	NY-N	0	0	—	1	0	0	0	0	2	2	9.0	0	1	4.5	1	4.5	4.50	72	.273	.360	-0	-0	98	77	0.0	-0	0	0.0
1893	Phi-N	4	2	.667	12	4	2	0	0	56	53	8.5	1	33	5.3	11	1.8	4.50	102	.265	.369	1	1	98	85	0.8	1	0	0.0
Total	4	20	17	.541	48	33	26	0	1	311	264	7.6	6	157	4.5	137	4.0	3.13	113	.244	.340	20	14	95	93	1.5	2	0	1.3
■ **JOE SHAUTE**	Shaute, Joseph Benjamin "Lefty" b: 8/1/1899, Peckville, Pa. d: 2/21/70, Scranton, Pa. BL/TL, 6', 190 lbs. Deb: 7/06/22																												
1922	Cle-A	0	0	—	2	0	0	0	0	4	7	15.8	2	3	6.8	3	6.8	18.00	23	.389	.476	-6	-6	103	65	0.0	-0	-0	-0.4
1923	Cle-A	10	8	.556	33	16	7	0	0	172	176	9.2	4	53	2.8	61	3.2	3.51	112	.275	.320	9	8	99	99	0.4	-4	-2	0.3
1924	Cle-A	20	17	.541	46	34	21	2	2	283	317	10.1	8	83	2.6	68	2.2	3.75	110	.287	.332	15	12	97	101	4.2	9	-2	1.8
1925	Cle-A	4	12	.250	26	17	10	1	4	131	160	11.0	6	44	3.0	34	2.3	5.43	86	.304	.347	-15	-11	107	83	-3.7	3	-2	-0.8
1926	Cle-A	14	10	.583	34	25	15	1	1	207	215	9.3	9	65	2.8	47	2.0	3.52	111	.278	.331	11	9	97	107	0.4	4	-5	0.8
1927	Cle-A	9	16	.360	45	28	14	0	2	230	255	10.0	9	75	2.9	63	2.5	4.23	97	.286	.331	-2	-4	99	94	-2.3	6	-2	0.0
1928	Cle-A	13	17	.433	36	31	21	1	2	254	295	10.5	9	68	2.4	81	2.9	4.04	109	.299	.338	0	10	108	106	0.9	2	1	1.4
1929	Cle-A	8	8	.500	26	24	8	0	0	162	211	11.7	6	52	2.9	43	2.4	4.28	100	.320	.361	-1	-0	101	116	-0.4	3	-3	0.0
1930	Cle-A	0	0	—	4	0	0	0	0	5	8	14.4	0	4	7.2	2	3.6	14.40	34	.333	.429	-5	-5	105	46	0.0	0	0	-0.3
1931	Bro-N	11	8	.579	25	19	6	0	0	129	162	11.3	9	32	2.2	50	3.5	4.81	81	.305	.343	-14	-13	101	96	1.3	-1	0	-1.2
1932	Bro-N	7	7	.500	34	9	1	0	4	117	147	11.3	8	21	1.6	32	2.5	4.54	82	.301	.329	-9	-11	96	96	-0.3	1	-1	-1.0
1933	Bro-N	3	4	.429	41	4	0	0	2	108	125	10.4	4	31	2.6	26	2.2	3.50	94	.287	.329	-2	-3	98	111	0.0	1	1	0.0
1934	Cin-N	0	2	.000	8	1	0	0	1	17	19	10.1	1	3	1.6	2	1.1	4.24	100	.268	.297	-0	0	105	76	-0.9	0	-1	0.0
Total	13	99	109	.476	360	208	103	5	18	1819	2097	10.4	75	534	2.6	512	2.5	4.15	98	.293	.336	-18	-14	100	101	-0.4	26	-15	0.6
■ **JEFF SHAVER**	Shaver, Jeffrey Thomas b: 7/30/63, Beaver Falls, Pa. BR/TR, 6'3", 185 lbs. Deb: 7/06/88																												
1988	Oak-A	0	0	—	1	0	0	0	0	1	0	0.0	0	0	0.0	0	0.0	0.00	—	.000	.250	0	0	93	0	0.0	0	0	0.0
■ **DON SHAW**	Shaw, Donald Wellington b: 2/23/44, Pittsburgh, Pa. BL/TL, 6', 180 lbs. Deb: 4/11/67																												
1967	NY-N	4	5	.444	40	0	0	0	3	51	40	7.1	5	23	4.1	44	7.8	3.00	115	.219	.292	2	2	102	105	0.5	0	-0	0.2
1968	NY-N	0	0	—	7	0	0	0	0	12	3	2.3	1	5	3.8	11	8.3	0.75	408	.086	.195	3	3	103	78	0.0	0	0	0.4
1969	Mon-N	2	5	.286	35	1	0	0	1	66	61	8.3	9	37	5.0	45	6.1	5.18	72	.254	.348	-12	-11	103	91	-0.3	-1	1	-1.0
1971	StL-N	7	2	.778	45	0	0	0	2	51	45	7.9	1	31	5.5	19	3.4	2.65	131	.237	.339	5	5	100	127	2.3	-0	-0	0.5
1972	StL-N	0	1	.000	8	0	0	0	0	3	5	15.0	1	3	9.0	0	0.0	9.00	40	.417	.500	-2	-2	105	131	-0.4	-0	0	-0.1
	Oak-A	0	1	.000	3	0	0	0	0	5	12	21.6	2	2	3.6	4	7.2	18.00	16	.500	.483	-8	-8	95	77	-0.4	0	0	-0.7
Total	5	13	14	.481	138	1	0	0	6	188	166	7.9	19	101	4.8	123	5.9	4.02	87	.243	.331	-12	-11	102	104	1.7	-0	0	-0.7
■ **DUPEE SHAW**	Shaw, Frederick Lander b: 5/31/1859, Charlestown, Mass. d: 6/11/38, Everett, Mass. BL/TL, 5'8", 165 lbs. Deb: 6/11/1883																												
1883	Det-N	10	15	.400	26	25	23	1	0	227	238	9.4	3	44	1.7	73	2.9	2.50	118	.277	.313	16	11	94	119	-0.2	-2	0	0.6
1884	Det-N	9	18	.333	28	28	25	0	0	228	219	8.6	8	72	2.8	142	5.6	3.04	97	.261	.320	-2	-2	99	98	1.9	-2	2	-0.1
	Bos-U	21	15	.583	39	38	35	5	0	316	227	**6.5**	1	37	1.1	309	**8.8**	1.77	166	**.206**	.232	44	41	98	78	2.8	1	0	3.8
1885	Pro-N	23	26	.469	49	49	47	6	0	400	343	7.7	7	99	2.2	194	4.4	2.57	102	.242	.291	11	3	93	92	-1.0	-9	-3	-0.9
1886	Was-N	13	31	.295	45	44	43	1	0	386	384	9.0	12	91	2.1	177	4.1	3.33	99	.272	.316	-1	-1	100	94	2.7	-10	-2	-1.1
1887	Was-N	7	13	.350	21	20	20	0	0	181	263	13.1	8	46	2.3	47	2.3	6.46	62	.356	.393	-49	-49	99	88	-0.7	-1	0	-3.9
1888	Was-N	0	3	.000	3	3	3	0	0	25	36	13.0	1	7	2.5	8	2.9	6.48	44	.352	.394	-10	-10	101	84	-1.4	-1	0	-0.8
Total	6	83	121	.407	211	207	196	13	0	1763	1710	8.7	40	396	2.0	950	4.8	3.10	99	.264	.307	10	-8	97	94	4.1	-24	-3	-2.4
■ **JIM SHAW**	Shaw, James Aloysius "Grunting Jim" b: 8/19/1893, Pittsburgh, Pa. d: 1/27/62, Washington, D.C. BR/TR, 6', 180 lbs. Deb: 9/15/13																												
1913	Was-A	0	1	.000	2	1	0	0	0	13	8	5.5	0	7	4.8	14	9.7	2.08	148	.205	.340	1	1	105	126	-0.4	-0	1	0.3
1914	Was-A	15	17	.469	48	31	15	5	**4**	257	198	6.9	3	137	4.8	164	5.7	2.70	101	.216	.324	1	1	100	92	-2.0	-3	1	0.2
1915	Was-A	6	11	.353	25	18	7	1	1	133	102	6.9	2	76	5.1	78	5.3	2.50	117	.220	.333	7	6	99	111	-3.2	1	-1	0.7
1916	Was-A	3	8	.273	26	9	5	2	1	106	86	7.3	1	50	4.2	44	3.7	2.63	108	.227	.320	2	2	100	97	-2.5	-0	-3	0.0
1917	Was-A	15	14	.517	47	31	15	2	1	266	233	7.9	1	123	4.2	118	4.0	3.21	77	.242	.328	-16	-22	93	85	1.1	-1	-3	-2.8
1918	Was-A	16	12	.571	41	30	14	4	1	241	201	7.5	2	90	3.4	129	4.8	2.43	117	.228	.296	9	11	103	87	0.4	-5	-4	0.3
1919	Was-A	17	17	.500	**45**	37	23	3	**5**	**307**	274	8.0	5	101	3.0	128	3.8	2.73	117	.244	.309	17	16	99	91	3.6	-1	-6	0.9
1920	Was-A	11	18	.379	38	32	17	0	1	236	285	10.9	12	87	3.3	88	3.4	4.27	86	.314	.376	-12	-16	96	113	-2.5	0	-4	-1.8
1921	Was-A	1	0	1.000	15	4	0	0	3	40	59	13.3	2	17	3.8	4	0.9	7.42	57	.345	.394	-14	-14	99	81	0.5	2	0	-1.0
Total	9	84	98	.462	287	193	96	17	17	1599	1446	8.1	28	688	3.9	767	4.3	3.07	97	.247	.328	-5	-14	98	95	-5.0	-7	-18	-3.2
■ **BOB SHAW**	Shaw, Robert John b: 6/29/33, Bronx, N.Y. BR/TR, 6'2", 195 lbs. Deb: 8/11/57 C																												
1957	Det-A	0	1	.000	7	0	0	0	0	10	11	9.9	2	7	6.3	4	3.6	7.20	56	.289	.391	-4	-3	107	88	-0.4	-0	0	-0.3
1958	Det-A	1	2	.333	11	2	0	0	0	27	32	10.7	2	13	4.3	17	5.7	5.00	78	.302	.363	-4	-3	103	103	-0.4	1	1	-0.1
	Chi-A	4	2	.667	29	3	0	0	1	64	67	9.4	8	28	3.9	18	2.5	4.64	79	.271	.346	-6	-7	98	100	0.9	-1	2	-0.5
	Yr	5	4	.556	40	5	0	0	1	91	99	9.8	10	41	4.1	35	3.5	4.75	79	.280	.351	-10	-10	99	100	0.5	-1	2	-0.6
1959	Chi-A	18	6	**.750**	47	26	8	3	3	231	217	8.5	15	54	2.1	89	3.5	2.69	137	.249	.292	30	25	95	115	4.8	-2	1	2.5
1960	Chi-A	13	13	.500	36	32	7	1	0	193	221	10.3	16	62	2.9	46	2.1	4.06	94	.292	.340	-4	-5	99	110	-1.7	-0	-1	-0.5
1961	Chi-A	3	4	.429	14	10	3	0	0	71	85	10.8	11	20	2.5	31	3.9	3.80	104	.302	.341	2	1	99	139	-0.6	-1	-0	0.0
	KC-A	9	10	.474	26	24	6	0	0	150	165	9.9	13	58	3.5	60	3.6	4.32	97	.281	.342	-5	-2	104	105	1.6	-1	-0	-0.2
	Yr	12	14	.462	40	34	9	0	0	221	250	10.2	24	78	3.2	91	3.7	4.15	99	.286	.341	-3	-1	102	105	1.0	-1	-0	-0.2
1962	Mil-N	15	9	.625	38	29	12	3	2	225	223	8.9	20	44	**1.8**	124	5.0	2.80	138	.260	.300	29	27	98	**123**	2.7	0	-0	2.8
1963	Mil-N	7	11	.389	48	16	3	3	13	159	144	8.2	10	55	3.1	105	5.9	2.66	123	.243	.306	11	11	100	120	-2.4	-0	-1	1.1
1964	SF-N	7	6	.538	61	1	0	0	11	93	105	10.2	5	31	3.0	57	5.5	3.77	93	.286	.342	-2	-3	99	115	-0.1	-1	-1	-0.5
1965	SF-N	16	9	.640	42	33	6	1	2	235	213	8.2	17	53	2.0	148	5.7	2.64	146	.236	.278	23	32	109	102	1.9	-3	1	3.3
1966	SF-N	1	4	.200	13	6	0	0	0	32	45	12.7	9	7	2.0	21	5.9	6.19	56	.324	.351	-9	-10	97	107	-1.6	-1	-0	-1.0
	NY-N	11	10	.524	26	25	7	2	0	168	171	9.2	12	42	2.3	104	5.6	3.91	89	.261	.310	-6	-8	97	88	2.3	3	1	-0.3
	Yr	12	14	.462	39	31	7	2	0	200	216	9.7	21	49	2.2	125	5.6	4.28	82	.272	.317	-15	-17	97	88	0.7	-1	0	-1.3
1967	NY-N	3	9	.250	23	13	3	1	0	99	105	9.5	9	28	2.5	49	4.5	4.27	80	.273	.321	-10	-9	102	94	-2.0	-2	-1	-1.2
	Chi-N	0	2	.000	9	3	0	0	0	22	33	13.5	0	9	3.7	7	2.9	6.14	55	.351	.414	-7	-7	100	104	-0.9	0	-1	-0.6
	Yr	3	11	.214	32	16	3	1	0	121	138	10.3	9	37	2.8	56	4.2	4.61	74	.286	.337	-17	-16	102	104	-2.9	-2	-2	-1.8
Total	11	108	98	.524	430	223	55	14	32	1779	1837	9.3	149	511	2.6	880	4.5	3.52	106	.267	.317	38	40	100	109	4.1	-8	-1	4.5
■ **SAM SHAW**	Shaw, Samuel E. b: 5/1864, Baltimore, Md. BR/TR, 5'5", 140 lbs. Deb: 1888																												
1888	Bal-a	2	4	.333	6	6	6	0	0	53	65	11.0	2	15	2.5	22	3.7	3.40	88	.316	.362	-2	-2	98	134	-0.5	-1	0	-0.2
1893	Chi-N	1	0	1.000	2	2	1	0	0	16	12	6.8	2	13	7.3	1	0.6	5.63	87	.222	.373	-2	-1	104	76	0.5	-0	0	0.0
Total	2	3	4	.429	8	8	7	0	0	69	77	10.0	4	28	3.7	23	3.0	3.91	87	.296	.365	-4	-4	99	120	0.0	-1	0	-0.2
■ **BOB SHAWKEY**	Shawkey, James Robert b: 12/4/1890, Sigel, Pa. d: 12/31/80, Syracuse, N.Y. BR/TR, 5'11", 168 lbs. Deb: 7/16/13 M																												
1913	Phi-A	6	5	.545	18	15	8	1	0	111	92	7.5	2	50	4.1	52	4.2	2.35	115	.207	.291	7	4	93	73	-0.7	-1	1	0.6
1914	Phi-A	16	8	.667	38	31	18	5	2	237	223	8.5	4	75	2.8	89	3.4	2.73	93	.262	.323	0	-5	93	109	0.6	2	-2	-0.7
1915	Phi-A	6	6	.500	17	13	7	1	0	100	103	9.3	3	38	3.4	56	5.0	4.05	75	.278	.346	-12	-11	103	92	1.9	-1	-0	-1.1
	NY-A	4	7	.364	16	9	5	1	0	86	78	8.2	2	35	3.7	31	3.2	3.24	90	.265	.347	-3	-3	99	109	-1.1	2	-1	-0.2

YEAR	TM/L	W	L	PCT	G	GS	CG	SHO	SV	IP	H	H/G	HR	BB	BB/G	SO	SO/G	ERA	/A	OAVG	OOBP	PR	/A	PF	CPI	WAT	PB	PD	TPI
	Yr	10	13	.435	33	22	12	2	0	186	181	8.8	5	73	3.5	87	4.2	3.68	81	.272	.345	-15	-15	101	109	0.8	-1	-1	-1.3
1916	NY-A	24	14	.632	53	27	21	4	8	277	204	6.6	4	81	2.6	122	4.0	2.21	129	.209	.273	19	20	101	76	5.5	-1	0	2.1
1917	NY-A	13	15	.464	32	26	16	2	0	236	207	7.9	2	72	2.7	97	3.7	2.44	117	.243	.306	6	11	107	99	0.0	-1	3	1.6
1918	NY-A	1	1	.500	3	2	1	1	0	16	7	3.9	0	10	5.6	3	1.7	1.13	231	.143	.288	3	3	94	107	0.0	2	0	0.6
1919	NY-A	20	11	.645	41	27	22	3	5	261	218	7.5	7	92	3.2	122	4.2	2.72	123	.231	.303	14	18	104	85	3.1	-1	-1	1.8
1920	NY-A	20	13	.606	38	31	20	5	2	268	246	8.3	10	85	2.9	126	4.2	2.45	153	.248	.308	40	39	99	111	-0.3	-0	-3	3.6
1921	NY-A	18	12	.600	38	31	18	3	2	245	245	9.0	15	86	3.2	124	4.6	4.08	104	.263	.321	6	5	99	87	-1.1	4	-4	0.4
1922	NY-A	20	12	.625	39	34	22	3	1	300	286	8.6	16	98	2.9	130	3.9	2.91	138	.256	.306	38	36	99	109	0.8	-3	0	3.4
1923	NY-A	16	11	.593	36	31	17	1	1	259	232	8.1	17	102	3.5	125	4.3	3.51	114	.246	.314	14	15	101	94	-1.2	-3	-0	1.1
1924	NY-A	16	11	.593	38	25	10	1	0	208	226	9.8	11	74	3.2	114	4.9	4.11	100	.286	.341	3	-0	97	102	0.3	8	-1	0.5
1925	NY-A	6	14	.300	33	20	9	1	0	186	209	10.1	12	67	3.2	67	3.2	4.11	104	.294	.350	6	3	97	110	-3.5	-1	-0	-0.1
1926	NY-A	8	7	.533	29	10	3	1	0	104	102	8.8	8	37	3.2	63	5.5	3.63	107	.263	.317	4	3	97	102	-0.7	2	-0	0.4
1927	NY-A	2	3	.400	19	2	0	0	4	44	44	9.0	1	16	3.3	23	4.7	2.86	135	.262	.321	6	5	94	116	-1.0	-1	0	0.7
Total	15	196	150	.566	488	334	197	33	28	2938	2722	8.3	114	1018	3.1	1360	4.2	3.09	114	.251	.314	151	143	99	97	2.6	3	-9	14.4

■ SPEC SHEA
Shea, Francis Joseph "The Naugatuck Nugget" (born Francis Joseph O'Shea) b: 10/2/20, Naugatuck, Conn. BR/TR, 6', 195 lbs. Deb: 4/19/47

YEAR	TM/L	W	L	PCT	G	GS	CG	SHO	SV	IP	H	H/G	HR	BB	BB/G	SO	SO/G	ERA	/A	OAVG	OOBP	PR	/A	PF	CPI	WAT	PB	PD	TPI
1947	NY-A	14	5	.737	27	23	13	3	1	179	127	6.4	10	89	4.5	89	4.5	3.07	111	.200	.300	13	7	92	84	3.0	2	-3	0.6
1948	NY-A	9	10	.474	28	22	8	1	1	156	117	6.7	10	87	5.0	71	4.1	3.40	121	.208	.311	15	12	96	90	-2.3	0	-2	1.0
1949	NY-A	1	1	.500	20	3	0	0	1	52	48	8.3	5	43	7.4	22	3.8	5.37	76	.250	.381	-7	-7	97	92	-0.1	1	-0	-0.6
1951	NY-A	5	5	.500	25	11	2	2	0	96	112	10.5	11	50	4.7	38	3.6	4.31	84	.300	.385	-2	-7	88	133	-1.1	1	-0	-0.6
1952	Was-A	11	7	.611	22	21	12	2	0	169	144	7.7	6	92	4.9	65	3.5	2.93	126	.231	.329	14	14	100	109	2.1	2	-1	1.6
1953	Was-A	12	7	.632	23	23	11	1	0	165	151	8.2	11	75	4.1	38	2.1	3.93	95	.244	.326	1	-4	93	91	2.8	-0	-1	-0.5
1954	Was-A	2	9	.182	23	11	1	0	0	71	97	12.3	9	34	4.3	22	2.8	6.21	59	.340	.398	-20	-20	99	107	-3.2	-2	1	-1.9
1955	Was-A	2	2	.500	27	4	1	1	2	56	53	8.5	4	27	4.3	16	2.6	4.02	93	.251	.329	-0	-2	94	94	0.5	2	-1	0.0
Total	8	56	46	.549	195	118	48	12	5	944	849	8.1	66	497	4.7	361	3.4	3.79	98	.243	.335	14	-6	95	98	1.8	6	-7	-0.4

■ JOHN SHEA
Shea, John Michael Joseph "Lefty" b: 12/27/04, Everett, Mass. d: 11/30/56, Malden, Mass. BL/TL, 5'10.5", 171 lbs. Deb: 6/30/28

| 1928 | Bos-A | 0 | 0 | — | 1 | 0 | 0 | 0 | 0 | 1 | 1 | 9.0 | 0 | 1 | 9.0 | 0 | 0.0 | 18.00 | 23 | .250 | .400 | -2 | -2 | 101 | 25 | 0.0 | 0 | 0 | 0.0 |

■ MIKE SHEA
Shea, Michael J. b: 3/10/1867, New Orleans, La. 5'10", 170 lbs. Deb: 4/20/1887

| 1887 | Cin-a | 1 | 1 | .500 | 2 | 1 | 1 | 0 | 0 | 17 | 26 | 13.8 | 0 | 10 | 5.3 | 0 | 0.0 | 7.41 | 62 | .366 | .444 | -6 | -5 | 106 | 91 | -0.1 | -0 | 0 | -0.3 |

■ RED SHEA
Shea, Patrick Henry b: 11/29/1898, Ware, Mass. d: 11/17/81, Stafford Springs, Conn. BR/TR, 6', 165 lbs. Deb: 5/06/18

1918	Phi-A	0	0	—	3	0	0	0	0	9	14	14.0	1	2	2.0	2	2.0	4.00	75	.378	.410	-1	-1	108	142	0.0	-0	-0	-0.1
1921	NY-N	5	2	.714	9	2	1	0	0	32	28	7.9	2	2	0.6	10	2.8	3.09	115	.239	.264	2	2	94	73	0.9	-1	-1	0.0
1922	NY-N	0	3	.000	11	2	0	0	0	23	22	8.6	1	11	4.3	5	2.0	4.70	88	.256	.327	-2	-1	100	81	-1.4	-1	1	-0.1
Total	3	5	5	.500	23	4	1	0	0	64	64	9.0	4	15	2.1	17	2.4	3.80	97	.267	.309	-0	-1	98	86	-0.5	-2	0	-0.2

■ STEVE SHEA
Shea, Steven Francis b: 12/5/42, Worcester, Mass. BR/TR, 6'3", 215 lbs. Deb: 7/14/68

1968	Hou-N	4	4	.500	30	0	0	0	6	35	27	6.9	0	11	2.8	15	3.9	3.34	90	.229	.295	-1	-1	100	76	0.4	-1	1	-0.1
1969	Mon-N	0	0	—	10	0	0	0	0	16	18	10.1	2	8	4.5	11	6.2	2.81	132	.300	.366	1	2	103	197	0.0	0	0	0.2
Total	2	4	4	.500	40	0	0	0	6	51	45	7.9	2	19	3.4	26	4.6	3.18	101	.253	.319	-0	-0	101	114	0.4	-1	1	0.1

■ AL SHEALY
Shealy, Albert Berley b: 3/20/1900, Chapin, S.C. d: 3/7/67, Hagerstown, Md. BR/TR, 5'11", 175 lbs. Deb: 4/13/28

1928	NY-A	8	6	.571	23	12	3	0	2	96	124	11.6	4	42	3.9	39	3.7	5.06	71	.308	.369	-11	-16	89	98	-0.9	2	0	-1.2
1930	Chi-N	0	0	—	24	0	0	0	0	27	37	12.3	2	14	4.7	14	4.7	8.00	64	.327	.398	-9	-9	103	76	0.0	1	-0	-0.6
Total	2	8	6	.571	47	12	3	0	2	123	161	11.8	6	56	4.1	53	3.9	5.71	68	.313	.375	-20	-25	92	93	-0.9	4	-0	-1.8

■ JOHN SHEARON
Shearon, John M. b: 1870, Pittsburgh, Pa. d: 2/1/23, Bradford, Pa. Deb: 7/28/1891

| 1891 | Cle-N | 1 | 3 | .250 | 6 | 5 | 4 | 0 | 0 | 46 | 57 | 11.2 | 1 | 24 | 4.7 | 19 | 3.7 | 3.52 | 101 | .318 | .399 | -1 | 0 | 106 | 138 | -0.8 | -0 | 0 | 0.0 |

■ GEORGE SHEARS
Shears, George Penfield b: 4/13/1890, Marshall, Mo. d: 11/12/78, Loveland, Colo. BR/TL, 6'3", 180 lbs. Deb: 4/24/12

| 1912 | NY-A | 0 | 0 | — | 4 | 0 | 0 | 0 | 0 | 15 | 24 | 14.4 | 1 | 11 | 6.6 | 9 | 5.4 | 5.40 | 65 | .364 | .455 | -3 | -3 | 105 | 142 | 0.0 | 0 | 0 | -0.2 |

■ TOM SHEEHAN
Sheehan, Thomas Clancy b: 3/31/1894, Grand Ridge, Ill. d: 10/29/82, Chillicothe, Ohio BR/TR, 6'2.5", 190 lbs. Deb: 7/14/15 MC

1915	Phi-A	9	3	.308	15	13	8	1	0	102	131	11.6	1	38	3.4	22	1.9	4.15	73	.335	.395	-14	-13	103	123	0.2	-3	-1	-1.5
1916	Phi-A	1	16	.059	38	17	8	0	0	188	197	9.4	2	94	4.5	54	2.6	3.69	81	.287	.374	-18	-15	105	112	-6.5	-2	3	-1.4
1921	NY-N	1	0	1.000	12	1	0	0	1	33	43	11.7	1	19	5.2	7	1.9	5.45	78	.326	.409	-4	-4	99	106	0.5	2	2	0.0
1924	Cin-N	9	11	.450	39	16	8	2	1	167	170	9.2	5	54	2.9	52	2.8	3.23	119	.269	.319	12	11	99	107	-1.8	4	-2	1.3
1925	Cin-N	1	0	1.000	10	3	1	0	1	29	37	11.5	3	12	3.7	5	1.6	8.07	51	.298	.360	-12	-13	97	61	0.5	1	-1	-1.0
	Pit-N	1	1	.500	23	0	0	0	2	57	63	9.9	2	13	2.1	13	2.1	2.68	157	.286	.314	10	10	99	136	-0.1	-1	0	0.2
	Yr	2	1	.667	33	3	1	0	3	86	100	10.5	5	25	2.6	18	1.9	4.50	93	.291	.331	-2	-3	98	136	0.4	1	-1	-0.2
1926	Pit-N	0	2	.000	9	4	1	0	0	31	36	10.5	0	12	3.5	16	4.6	6.68	64	.298	.360	-10	-8	111	65	-0.9	-1	-0	-0.8
Total	6	17	39	.304	146	54	26	3	5	607	677	10.0	14	242	3.6	169	2.5	4.00	88	.294	.358	-36	-31	102	109	-8.1	-0	1	-2.6

■ ROLLIE SHELDON
Sheldon, Roland Frank b: 12/17/36, Putnam, Conn. BR/TR, 6'4", 185 lbs. Deb: 4/23/61

1961	NY-A	11	5	.688	35	21	6	2	0	163	149	8.2	17	55	3.0	84	4.6	3.59	105	.246	.307	8	3	99	99	0.4	-2	1	0.2
1962	NY-A	7	8	.467	34	16	2	0	1	118	136	10.4	12	28	2.1	54	4.1	5.49	66	.289	.322	-20	-24	92	80	-1.6	-0	-2	-2.4
1964	NY-A	5	2	.714	19	12	3	0	1	102	92	8.1	18	18	1.6	57	5.0	3.62	101	.243	.274	0	0	101	98	1.0	-2	1	0.0
1965	NY-A	0	0	—	3	0	0	0	0	6	5	7.5	0	1	1.5	7	10.5	1.50	233	.238	.250	1	1	101	142	0.0	-0	0	0.2
	KC-A	10	8	.556	32	29	4	1	0	187	180	8.7	22	56	2.7	105	5.1	3.95	87	.251	.308	-10	-11	100	94	2.9	-2	-0	-1.3
	Yr	10	8	.556	35	29	4	1	0	193	185	8.6	22	57	2.7	112	5.2	3.87	89	.251	.307	-9	-9	100	94	2.9	-0	0	-1.1
1966	KC-A	4	7	.364	14	13	1	1	0	69	73	9.5	3	26	3.4	26	3.4	3.13	105	.275	.331	2	1	95	129	-1.1	-1	0	0.0
	Bos-A	1	6	.143	23	10	1	0	2	80	106	11.9	15	23	2.6	38	4.3	4.95	77	.320	.363	-13	-10	110	124	-2.3	-1	1	-1.0
	Yr	5	13	.278	37	23	2	1	2	149	179	10.8	18	49	3.0	64	3.9	4.11	87	.297	.347	-11	-9	103	124	-3.4	-1	1	-1.0
Total	5	38	36	.514	160	101	17	4	2	725	741	9.2	87	207	2.6	371	4.6	4.08	88	.266	.314	-32	-38	98	100	-0.7	-9	0	-4.3

■ FRANK SHELLENBACK
Shellenback, Frank Victor b: 12/16/1898, Joplin, Mo. d: 8/17/69, Newton, Mass. BR/TR, 6'2", 192 lbs. Deb: 5/08/18 C

1918	Chi-A	9	12	.429	28	21	10	2	2	183	180	8.9	1	74	3.6	47	2.3	2.66	104	.263	.331	2	2	100	116	-0.7	-1	-5	-0.3
1919	Chi-A	1	3	.250	8	4	2	0	0	35	40	10.3	1	16	4.1	10	2.6	5.14	64	.303	.378	-7	-7	102	87	-1.1	-0	-0	-0.7
Total	2	10	15	.400	36	25	12	2	2	218	220	9.1	2	90	3.7	57	2.4	3.06	93	.269	.339	-5	-5	100	111	-1.8	-2	-5	-1.0

■ JIM SHELLENBACK
Shellenback, James Philip b: 11/18/43, Riverside, Cal. BL/TL, 6'2", 200 lbs. Deb: 9/15/66 C

1966	Pit-N	0	0	—	2	0	0	0	0	3	3	9.0	2	3	9.0	0	0.0	9.00	40	.300	.462	-2	-2	99	124	0.0	0	0	-0.1
1967	Pit-N	1	1	.500	6	2	1	0	0	23	23	9.0	1	12	4.7	11	4.3	2.74	123	.250	.343	2	2	100	134	0.9	-0	0	0.2
1969	Pit-N	0	0	—	8	0	0	0	0	17	14	7.4	1	4	2.1	7	3.7	3.18	106	.233	.269	1	0	94	83	0.4	-0	1	0.0
	Was-A	4	7	.364	30	11	2	0	0	85	87	9.2	4	48	5.1	50	5.3	4.02	87	.268	.357	-4	-5	96	114	-1.7	-0	2	-0.2
1970	Was-A	6	7	.462	39	14	2	1	0	117	107	8.2	6	51	3.9	57	4.4	3.69	98	.246	.320	0	-1	97	90	0.4	-2	-1	-0.3
1971	Was-A	3	11	.214	40	15	3	1	0	120	123	9.2	10	49	3.7	47	3.5	3.53	96	.267	.334	-1	-4	94	115	-3.3	-1	1	-1.0
1972	Tex-A	2	4	.333	22	6	0	0	0	57	46	7.3	6	16	2.5	30	4.7	3.47	86	.221	.281	-3	-3	97	91	-0.1	-0	-0	-0.4
1973	Tex-A	0	0	—	2	0	0	0	0	2	2	9.0	1	1	4.5	3	13.5	0.00	—	.000	.000	1	1	100	9	0.0	0	0	0.0
1974	Tex-A	0	0	—	11	0	0	0	0	25	30	10.8	5	12	4.3	14	5.0	5.76	60	.306	.384	-6	-6	96	108	0.0	-1	-0	-0.1
1977	Min-A	0	0	—	5	0	0	0	0	6	10	15.0	1	5	7.5	3	4.5	7.50	55	.385	.469	-2	-2	102	125	0.0	0	0	-0.1
Total	9	16	30	.348	165	48	8	2	2	455	443	8.8	40	200	4.0	222	4.4	3.80	89	.258	.332	-13	-20	96	103	-4.7	-2	3	-1.3

■ BERT SHEPARD
Shepard, Robert Earl b: 6/28/20, Dana, Ind. BL/TL, 5'11", 185 lbs. Deb: 8/04/45

| 1945 | Was-A | 0 | 0 | — | 1 | 0 | 0 | 0 | 0 | 5 | 3 | 5.4 | 0 | 3 | 5.4 | 2 | 3.6 | 1.80 | 172 | .167 | .250 | 1 | 1 | 92 | 50 | 0.0 | -0 | 0 | 0.0 |

■ BILL SHERDEL
Sherdel, William Henry "Wee Willie" b: 8/15/1896, Mc Sherrystown, Pa d: 11/14/68, Mc Sherrystown, Pa BL/TL, 5'10", 160 lbs. Deb: 4/22/18

| 1918 | StL-N | 6 | 12 | .333 | 35 | 17 | 9 | 1 | 0 | 182 | 174 | 8.6 | 9 | 49 | 2.4 | 40 | 2.0 | 2.72 | 97 | .259 | .304 | 1 | -2 | 95 | 105 | -1.5 | 4 | -2 | 0.0 |
| 1919 | StL-N | 5 | 9 | .357 | 36 | 10 | 7 | 0 | 1 | 137 | 137 | 9.0 | 3 | 42 | 2.8 | 52 | 3.4 | 3.48 | 81 | .270 | .319 | -9 | -10 | 97 | 96 | -0.6 | 2 | 1 | -0.7 |

YEAR	TM/L	W	L	PCT	G	GS	CG	SHO	SV	IP	H	H/G	HR	BB	BB/G	SO	SO/G	ERA	/A	OAVG	OOBP	PR	/A	PF	CPI	WAT	PB	PD	TPI
1920	StL-N	11	10	.524	43	7	4	0	**6**	170	183	9.7	1	40	2.1	74	3.9	3.28	93	.297	.336	-3	-4	98	111	0.9	2	2	0.0
1921	StL-N	9	8	.529	38	8	5	1	1	144	137	8.6	7	38	2.4	57	3.6	3.19	110	.247	.291	10	5	93	82	-0.6	-2	1	0.3
1922	StL-N	17	13	.567	47	31	15	3	2	242	298	11.1	12	62	2.3	79	2.9	3.87	106	.303	.336	6	7	100	109	0.6	-0	-4	0.3
1923	StL-N	15	13	.536	39	26	14	0	2	225	270	10.8	15	59	2.4	78	3.1	4.32	83	.296	.335	-8	-18	90	98	0.7	9	-3	-1.2
1924	StL-N	8	9	.471	35	10	6	0	1	169	188	10.0	9	38	2.0	57	3.0	3.41	117	.291	.325	9	11	103	**118**	0.8	1	-2	1.1
1925	StL-N	15	6	**.714**	32	21	17	2	1	200	216	9.7	8	42	1.9	53	2.4	3.11	139	.277	.312	26	27	101	109	4.8	2	-1	2.7
1926	StL-N	16	12	.571	34	29	17	3	0	235	255	9.8	15	49	1.9	59	2.3	3.49	110	.278	.311	9	9	100	104	-0.1	3	-3	0.8
1927	StL-N	17	12	.586	39	28	18	0	**6**	232	241	9.3	17	48	1.9	59	2.3	3.53	117	.269	.301	10	16	106	98	-0.3	1	-4	1.3
1928	StL-N	21	10	.677	38	27	20	0	**5**	249	251	9.1	17	56	2.0	72	2.6	2.86	135	.261	.297	31	28	97	109	2.9	5	-5	2.8
1929	StL-N	10	15	.400	33	22	11	1	0	196	278	12.8	14	58	2.7	69	3.2	5.92	78	.337	.371	-26	-28	98	98	-3.1	2	-2	-2.5
1930	StL-N	3	2	.600	13	7	1	0	0	64	86	12.1	5	13	1.8	29	4.1	4.64	109	.325	.352	2	3	102	112	0.0	-1	-1	0.1
	Bos-N	6	5	.545	21	14	7	0	1	119	131	9.9	10	30	2.3	26	2.0	4.76	103	.283	.315	3	2	99	87	1.0	-4	-1	-0.1
	Yr	9	7	.563	34	21	8	0	1	183	217	10.7	15	43	2.1	55	2.7	4.72	105	.298	.327	5	5	100	87	1.0	-1	-1	0.0
1931	Bos-N	6	10	.375	27	16	8	0	0	138	163	10.6	13	35	2.3	34	2.2	4.24	93	.294	.329	-6	-5	102	106	-0.8	3	-2	-0.3
1932	Bos-N	0	0	—	1	0	0	0	0	2	3	13.5	0	1	4.5	0	0.0	0.00	—	.375	.444	1	1	93	0	0.0	0	0	0.1
	StL-N	0	0	—	3	0	0	0	0	6	7	10.5	0	1	1.5	1	1.5	4.50	87	.304	.320	-0	-0	101	87	0.0	1	0	0.1
	Yr	0	0	—	4	0	0	0	0	8	10	11.3	0	2	2.3	1	1.1	3.38	114	.323	.353	0	0	99	87	0.0	0	0	0.2
Total	15	165	146	.531	514	273	159	11	26	2710	3018	10.0	149	661	2.2	839	2.8	3.72	103	.285	.322	55	38	99	103	4.7	27	-25	4.8

■ **ROY SHERID** Sherid, Royden Richard b: 1/25/07, Norristown, Pa. d: 2/28/82, Parker Ford, Pa. BR/TR, 6'2", 185 lbs. Deb: 5/11/29

YEAR	TM/L	W	L	PCT	G	GS	CG	SHO	SV	IP	H	H/G	HR	BB	BB/G	SO	SO/G	ERA	/A	OAVG	OOBP	PR	/A	PF	CPI	WAT	PB	PD	TPI
1929	NY-A	6	6	.500	33	15	9	0	1	155	165	9.6	6	55	3.2	51	3.0	3.60	114	.277	.337	11	9	97	109	-0.7	-1	-1	0.6
1930	NY-A	12	13	.480	37	21	8	0	4	184	214	10.5	13	87	4.3	59	2.9	5.23	78	.289	.361	-12	-24	87	97	-1.9	-5	-1	-2.6
1931	NY-A	5	5	.500	17	8	3	0	2	74	94	11.4	4	24	2.9	39	4.7	5.72	72	.306	.361	-11	-13	94	89	-0.9	2	0	-0.9
Total	3	23	24	.489	87	44	20	0	7	413	473	10.3	23	166	3.6	149	3.2	4.71	87	.288	.352	-12	-28	92	100	-3.5	-4	-2	-2.9

■ **JOE SHERMAN** Sherman, Joel Powers b: 11/4/1890, Yarmouth, Mass. BR/TR, 6', 165 lbs. Deb: 9/24/15

YEAR	TM/L	W	L	PCT	G	GS	CG	SHO	SV	IP	H	H/G	HR	BB	BB/G	SO	SO/G	ERA	/A	OAVG	OOBP	PR	/A	PF	CPI	WAT	PB	PD	TPI
1915	Phi-A	1	0	1.000	2	1	1	0	0	15	15	9.0	0	1	0.6	5	3.0	2.40	126	.259	.295	1	1	103	102	0.5	1	-0	0.1

■ **DAN SHERMAN** Sherman, Lester Daniel "Babe" b: 5/9/1890, Hubbardsville, N.Y. d: 9/16/55, Highland Park, Mich. BR/TR, 5'6", 145 lbs. Deb: 6/04/14

YEAR	TM/L	W	L	PCT	G	GS	CG	SHO	SV	IP	H	H/G	HR	BB	BB/G	SO	SO/G	ERA	/A	OAVG	OOBP	PR	/A	PF	CPI	WAT	PB	PD	TPI
1914	Chi-F	0	1	.000	1	1	0	0	0	⅓	0	0.0	0	2	54.0	0	0.0	0.00	—	—	1.000	0	0	89	0	-0.4	0	0	0.0

■ **FRED SHERRY** Sherry, Fred Peter (born Fred Peter Schuerholz) b: 1/13/1889, Honesdale, Pa. d: 7/27/75, Honesdale, Pa. BR/TR, 6', 170 lbs. Deb: 4/25/11

YEAR	TM/L	W	L	PCT	G	GS	CG	SHO	SV	IP	H	H/G	HR	BB	BB/G	SO	SO/G	ERA	/A	OAVG	OOBP	PR	/A	PF	CPI	WAT	PB	PD	TPI
1911	Was-A	0	4	.000	10	3	2	0	0	52	63	10.9	1	19	3.3	20	3.5	4.33	77	.310	.369	-6	-6	99	101	-1.9	-1	0	-0.5

■ **LARRY SHERRY** Sherry, Lawrence b: 7/25/35, Los Angeles, Cal. BR/TR, 6'2", 180 lbs. Deb: 4/17/58 C

YEAR	TM/L	W	L	PCT	G	GS	CG	SHO	SV	IP	H	H/G	HR	BB	BB/G	SO	SO/G	ERA	/A	OAVG	OOBP	PR	/A	PF	CPI	WAT	PB	PD	TPI
1958	LA-N	0	0	—	5	0	0	0	0	4	10	22.5	0	7	15.8	2	4.5	13.50	31	.476	.621	-4	-4	106	113	0.0	0	0	-0.3
1959	LA-N	7	2	.778	23	9	1	1	3	94	75	7.2	9	43	4.1	72	6.9	2.20	181	.218	.306	18	19	101	141	2.3	3	-1	2.2
1960	LA-N	14	10	.583	57	3	1	0	7	142	125	7.9	14	82	5.2	114	7.2	3.80	113	.238	.342	-1	8	114	107	1.5	0	1	1.0
1961	LA-N	4	4	.500	53	1	0	0	15	95	90	8.5	10	39	3.7	79	7.5	3.88	105	.252	.329	2	2	102	102	-0.5	0	-2	0.0
1962	LA-N	7	3	.700	58	0	0	0	11	90	81	8.1	8	44	4.4	71	7.1	3.20	112	.241	.332	7	4	91	120	1.1	-0	-0	0.3
1963	LA-N	2	6	.250	36	3	0	0	3	80	82	9.2	8	24	2.7	47	5.3	3.71	83	.265	.315	-4	-6	94	106	-2.3	1	-0	-0.5
1964	Det-A	7	5	.583	38	0	0	0	11	66	52	7.1	7	37	5.0	58	7.9	3.68	94	.216	.321	-0	-2	95	95	0.8	-2	-0	-0.3
1965	Det-A	3	6	.333	39	0	0	0	5	78	71	8.2	5	40	4.6	46	5.3	3.12	116	.254	.335	3	4	104	128	-1.7	2	0	0.7
1966	Det-A	8	5	.615	55	0	0	0	20	78	66	7.6	8	36	4.2	63	7.3	3.81	92	.232	.317	-3	-3	102	98	1.1	2	-1	0.0
1967	Det-A	0	1	.000	20	0	0	0	1	28	35	11.3	3	7	2.3	20	6.4	6.43	49	.289	.323	-10	-10	98	70	-0.4	-0	0	-1.0
	Hou-N	1	2	.333	29	0	0	0	6	41	53	11.6	4	13	2.9	32	7.0	4.83	67	.327	.358	-7	-7	95	117	-0.2	-0	1	-0.7
1968	Cal-A	0	0	—	3	0	0	0	0	3	7	21.0	2	2	6.0	2	6.0	6.00	48	.467	.529	-1	-1	96	266	0.0	0	0	0.0
Total	11	53	44	.546	416	16	2	1	82	799	747	8.4	78	374	4.2	606	6.8	3.67	101	.249	.331	0	3	101	112	1.7	5	-2	1.4

■ **BEN SHIELDS** Shields, Benjamin Cowan "Big Ben" or "Lefty" b: 6/17/03, Huntersville, N.C d: 1/24/82, Woodruff, S.C. BB/TL, 6'1.5", 195 lbs. Deb: 4/17/24

YEAR	TM/L	W	L	PCT	G	GS	CG	SHO	SV	IP	H	H/G	HR	BB	BB/G	SO	SO/G	ERA	/A	OAVG	OOBP	PR	/A	PF	CPI	WAT	PB	PD	TPI
1924	NY-A	0	0	—	2	0	0	0	0	2	6	27.0	0	2	9.0	3	13.5	27.00	15	.545	.615	-5	-5	97	58	0.0	0	0	-0.3
1925	NY-A	3	0	1.000	4	2	2	0	0	24	24	9.0	2	12	4.5	5	1.9	4.88	87	.267	.362	-1	-2	97	91	1.5	-1	-1	-0.2
1930	Bos-A	0	0	—	3	0	0	0	0	10	16	14.4	0	6	5.4	1	0.9	9.00	50	.400	.458	-5	-5	96	91	0.0	-1	0	-0.4
1931	Phi-N	1	0	1.000	4	0	0	0	0	5	9	16.2	1	7	12.6	0	0.0	16.20	26	.391	.500	-7	-7	109	72	0.5	-0	0	-0.5
Total	4	4	0	1.000	13	2	2	0	0	41	55	12.1	3	27	5.9	9	2.0	8.34	52	.335	.424	-18	-18	98	87	2.0	-2	-0	-1.4

■ **CHARLIE SHIELDS** Shields, Charles S. b: 12/10/1879, Jackson, Tenn. d: 8/27/53, Memphis, Tenn. BL/TL, Deb: 4/23/02

YEAR	TM/L	W	L	PCT	G	GS	CG	SHO	SV	IP	H	H/G	HR	BB	BB/G	SO	SO/G	ERA	/A	OAVG	OOBP	PR	/A	PF	CPI	WAT	PB	PD	TPI
1902	Bal-A	4	11	.267	23	15	10	1	1	142	201	12.7	7	32	2.0	28	1.8	4.25	88	.360	.395	-11	-8	104	124	-2.1	-1	-4	-1.1
	StL-A	3	0	1.000	4	4	3	0	0	30	37	11.1	1	7	2.1	6	1.8	3.30	110	.329	.368	1	1	102	129	1.5	2	-0	0.1
	Yr	7	11	.389	27	19	13	1	1	172	238	12.5	8	39	2.0	34	1.8	4.08	91	.355	.390	-10	-7	104	129	-0.6	-1	-5	-1.0
1907	StL-N	0	2	.000	3	2	0	0	0	7	12	15.4	0	7	9.0	1	1.3	9.00	27	.441	.579	-5	-5	100	101	-0.9	-0	0	-0.4
Total	2	7	13	.350	30	21	13	1	1	179	250	12.6	8	46	2.3	35	1.8	4.27	86	.358	.400	-15	-12	104	124	-1.5	1	-5	-1.4

■ **STEVE SHIELDS** Shields, Stephen Mack b: 11/30/58, Gasden, Ala. BR/TR, 6'5", 220 lbs. Deb: 6/01/85

YEAR	TM/L	W	L	PCT	G	GS	CG	SHO	SV	IP	H	H/G	HR	BB	BB/G	SO	SO/G	ERA	/A	OAVG	OOBP	PR	/A	PF	CPI	WAT	PB	PD	TPI
1985	Atl-N	1	2	.333	23	6	0	0	0	68	86	11.4	9	32	4.2	29	3.8	5.16	75	.320	.383	-12	-10	108	118	-0.2	-1	-1	-1.0
1986	Atl-N	0	0	—	6	0	0	0	0	13	13	9.0	4	7	4.8	6	4.2	6.92	56	.271	.364	-5	-4	103	91	0.0	-0	-0	-0.4
	KC-A	0	0	—	3	0	0	0	0	9	3	3.0	1	4	4.0	2	2.0	2.00	210	.111	.212	2	2	100	69	0.0	0	0	0.2
1987	Sea-A	2	0	1.000	20	0	0	0	3	30	43	12.9	7	12	3.6	22	6.6	6.60	70	.333	.382	-7	-7	103	108	1.0	0	0	-0.5
1988	NY-A	5	5	.500	39	0	0	0	0	82	96	10.5	8	30	3.3	55	6.0	4.39	86	.298	.354	-4	-5	96	115	-0.2	0	0	-0.5
Total	4	8	7	.533	91	6	0	0	3	202	241	10.7	29	85	3.8	114	5.1	5.03	79	.303	.364	-25	-24	102	112	0.6	-1	-1	-2.2

■ **VINCE SHIELDS** Shields, Vincent William b: 11/18/1900, Fredericton, N.B., Canada d: 10/17/52, Plaster Rock, N.B. Canada BL/TR, 5'11", 185 lbs. Deb: 9/20/24

YEAR	TM/L	W	L	PCT	G	GS	CG	SHO	SV	IP	H	H/G	HR	BB	BB/G	SO	SO/G	ERA	/A	OAVG	OOBP	PR	/A	PF	CPI	WAT	PB	PD	TPI
1924	StL-N	1	1	.500	2	1	0	0	0	12	10	7.5	1	3	2.3	4	3.0	3.00	132	.227	.314	1	1	103	108	0.1	0	-0	0.1

■ **GARLAND SHIFFLETT** Shifflett, Garland Jessie "Duck" b: 3/28/35, Elkton, Va. BR/TR, 5'10.5", 165 lbs. Deb: 4/22/57

YEAR	TM/L	W	L	PCT	G	GS	CG	SHO	SV	IP	H	H/G	HR	BB	BB/G	SO	SO/G	ERA	/A	OAVG	OOBP	PR	/A	PF	CPI	WAT	PB	PD	TPI
1957	Was-A	0	0	—	6	1	0	0	0	8	6	6.8	0	10	11.3	2	2.3	10.13	38	.222	.410	-6	-6	102	48	0.0	0	-0	-0.5
1964	Min-A	0	2	.000	10	0	0	0	1	18	22	11.0	1	7	3.5	8	4.0	4.50	80	.297	.357	-2	-2	100	105	-0.9	-0	0	-0.1
Total	2	0	2	.000	16	1	0	0	1	26	28	9.7	1	17	5.9	10	3.5	6.23	59	.277	.374	-7	-7	100	87	-0.9	-0	0	-0.6

■ **RAY SHINES** Shines, Anthony Raymond b: 7/18/56, Durham, N.C. BB/TR, 6'1", 210 lbs. Deb: 9/09/83

YEAR	TM/L	W	L	PCT	G	GS	CG	SHO	SV	IP	H	H/G	HR	BB	BB/G	SO	SO/G	ERA	/A	OAVG	OOBP	PR	/A	PF	CPI	WAT	PB	PD	TPI
1985	Mon-N	0	0	—	1	0	0	0	0	1	1	9.0	0	0	0.0	0	0.0	0.00	—	.250	.250	0	0	94	0	0.0	-0	0	0.0

■ **DAVE SHIPANOFF** Shipanoff, David Noel b: 11/13/59, Edmonton, Alb., Can. BR/TR, 6'2", 185 lbs. Deb: 8/09/85

YEAR	TM/L	W	L	PCT	G	GS	CG	SHO	SV	IP	H	H/G	HR	BB	BB/G	SO	SO/G	ERA	/A	OAVG	OOBP	PR	/A	PF	CPI	WAT	PB	PD	TPI
1985	Phi-N	1	2	.333	26	0	0	0	3	36	33	8.3	3	16	4.0	26	6.5	3.25	113	.231	.309	1	2	102	97	-0.3	-0	0	0.1

■ **JOE SHIPLEY** Shipley, Joseph Clark "Moses" b: 5/9/35, Morristown, Tenn. BR/TR, 6'4", 210 lbs. Deb: 7/14/58

YEAR	TM/L	W	L	PCT	G	GS	CG	SHO	SV	IP	H	H/G	HR	BB	BB/G	SO	SO/G	ERA	/A	OAVG	OOBP	PR	/A	PF	CPI	WAT	PB	PD	TPI
1958	SF-N	0	0	—	1	0	0	0	0	1	3	27.0	0	3	27.0	0	0.0	45.00	9	.429	.667	-5	-5	100	51	0.0	0	0	-0.3
1959	SF-N	0	0	—	10	1	0	0	0	18	16	8.0	2	17	8.5	11	5.5	4.50	82	.239	.391	-1	-2	94	115	0.0	-0	-0	-0.1
1960	SF-N	0	0	—	15	0	0	0	0	20	20	9.0	2	9	4.0	9	4.0	5.40	62	.274	.368	-4	-5	89	93	0.0	0	1	-0.3
1963	Chi-A	0	1	.000	3	0	0	0	0	5	9	16.2	0	6	10.8	3	5.4	5.40	69	.409	.536	-1	-1	102	184	-0.4	-0	0	0.0
Total	4	0	1	.000	29	1	0	0	0	44	48	9.8	4	35	7.2	23	4.7	5.93	60	.284	.416	-10	-12	92	111	-0.4	-1	0	-0.7

■ **DUKE SHIREY** Shirey, Clair Lee b: 6/20/1898, Jersey Shore, Pa. d: 9/1/62, Hagerstown, Pa. BR , 6'1", 175 lbs. Deb: 9/28/20

YEAR	TM/L	W	L	PCT	G	GS	CG	SHO	SV	IP	H	H/G	HR	BB	BB/G	SO	SO/G	ERA	/A	OAVG	OOBP	PR	/A	PF	CPI	WAT	PB	PD	TPI
1920	Was-A	0	1	.000	2	1	0	0	0	4	5	11.3	0	2	4.5	0	0.0	6.75	54	.313	.421	-1	-1	96	80	-0.4	-0	-0	-0.1

■ **TEX SHIRLEY** Shirley, Alvis Newman b: 4/25/18, Birthright, Tex. BB/TR, 6'1", 175 lbs. Deb: 9/06/41

YEAR	TM/L	W	L	PCT	G	GS	CG	SHO	SV	IP	H	H/G	HR	BB	BB/G	SO	SO/G	ERA	/A	OAVG	OOBP	PR	/A	PF	CPI	WAT	PB	PD	TPI
1941	Phi-A	0	1	.000	5	0	0	0	1	7	8	10.3	1	6	7.7	1	1.3	2.57	166	.286	.400	1	1	103	249	-0.4	-0	0	0.1
1942	Phi-A	0	1	.000	15	1	0	0	1	36	37	9.3	0	22	5.5	10	2.5	5.25	70	.272	.377	-6	-6	101	84	-0.4	-1	-1	-0.7
1944	StL-A	5	4	.556	23	11	2	1	0	80	59	6.6	4	64	7.2	35	3.9	4.16	82	.203	.344	-7	-7	100	80	-0.1	-1	-1	-0.9
1945	StL-A	8	12	.400	32	24	10	2	0	184	191	9.3	8	93	4.5	77	3.8	3.62	106	.274	.353	-5	5	114	117	-2.7	1	-1	0.7
1946	StL-A	6	12	.333	27	18	7	0	0	140	148	9.5	7	105	6.8	45	2.9	4.95	71	.273	.387	-23	-23	100	98	-2.1	0	-1	-2.2
Total	5	19	30	.388	102	54	19	3	2	447	443	8.9	20	290	5.8	168	3.4	4.25	86	.261	.365	-39	-29	106	104	-5.7	-1	-3	-3.0

YEAR	TM/L	W	L	PCT	G	GS	CG	SHO	SV	IP	H	H/G	HR	BB	BB/G	SO	SO/G	ERA	/A	OAVG	OOBP	PR	/A	PF	CPI	WAT	PB	PD	TPI
■ BOB SHIRLEY	Shirley, Robert Charles b: 6/25/54, Cushing, Okla. BR/TL, 5'11", 180 lbs. Deb: 4/10/77																												
1977	SD-N	12	18	.400	39	35	1	0	0	214	215	9.0	22	100	4.2	146	6.1	3.70	94	.259	.336	5	-5	89	112	-1.0	-2	1	-0.6
1978	SD-N	8	11	.421	50	20	2	0	5	166	164	8.9	10	61	3.3	102	5.5	3.69	90	.262	.322	-2	-7	93	100	-1.9	0	2	-0.5
1979	SD-N	8	16	.333	49	25	4	1	0	205	196	8.6	15	59	2.6	117	5.1	3.38	108	.257	.310	8	6	97	102	-2.8	-2	0	0.4
1980	SD-N	11	12	.478	59	12	3	0	7	137	143	9.4	12	54	3.5	67	4.4	3.55	95	.276	.337	1	-2	94	120	0.7	-2	2	-0.2
1981	StL-N	6	4	.600	28	11	1	0	1	79	78	8.9	6	34	3.9	36	4.1	4.10	86	.260	.330	-5	-5	101	95	0.3	-1	-1	-0.6
1982	Cin-N	8	13	.381	41	20	1	0	0	153	138	8.1	17	73	4.3	89	5.2	3.59	104	.248	.331	0	3	104	113	0.1	-1	1	0.3
1983	NY-A	5	8	.385	25	17	1	1	0	108	122	10.2	10	36	3.0	53	4.4	5.08	78	.293	.338	-12	-13	98	93	-2.1	0	1	-1.1
1984	NY-A	3	3	.500	41	7	1	0	0	114	119	9.4	8	38	3.0	48	3.8	3.39	110	.274	.329	8	4	93	117	-0.1	0	0	0.4
1985	NY-A	5	5	.500	48	8	2	0	2	109	103	8.5	5	26	2.1	55	4.5	2.64	148	.251	.289	18	15	94	113	-0.8	0	-1	1.5
1986	NY-A	0	4	.000	39	6	0	0	3	105	108	9.3	13	40	3.4	64	5.5	5.06	85	.271	.333	-10	-9	103	90	-1.9	0	1	-0.7
1987	NY-A	1	0	1.000	12	1	0	0	0	34	36	9.5	4	16	4.2	12	3.2	4.50	97	.277	.342	-0	-1	97	108	0.5	0	-1	0.0
	KC-A	0	0	—	3	0	0	0	0	7	10	12.9	5	6	7.7	1	1.3	15.43	30	.323	.432	-9	-8	104	76	0.0	0	-0	-0.6
	Yr	1	0	1.000	15	1	0	0	0	41	46	10.1	9	22	4.8	13	2.9	6.37	69	.275	.360	-9	-9	98	76	0.5	0	-1	-0.6
Total	11	67	94	.416	434	162	16	2	18	1431	1432	9.0	127	543	3.4	790	5.0	3.82	96	.264	.327	2	-22	96	106	-9.0	-7	6	-1.7
■ STEVE SHIRLEY	Shirley, Steven Brian b: 10/12/56, San Francsico, Cal. BL/TL, 6', 185 lbs. Deb: 6/21/82																												
1982	LA-N	1	1	.500	11	0	0	0	0	13	15	10.4	0	7	4.8	8	5.5	4.15	81	.300	.379	-1	-1	94	112	0.0	0	0	0.0
■ GEORGE SHOCH	Shoch, George Quintus b: 1/6/1859, Philadelphia, Pa. d: 9/30/37, Philadelphia, Pa. BR/TR, Deb: 9/10/1886																												
1888	Was-N	0	0	—	1	0	0	0	0	3	2	6.0	0	1	3.0	0	0.0	0.00	—	.201	.274	1	1	101	0	0.0	0	0	0.1
■ URBAN SHOCKER	Shocker, Urban James (born Urbain Jacques Shockcor) b: 8/22/1890, Cleveland, Ohio d: 9/9/28, Denver, Colo. BR/TR, 5'10", 170 lbs. Deb: 4/24/16																												
1916	NY-A	4	3	.571	12	9	4	1	0	82	67	7.4	2	32	3.5	43	4.7	2.63	109	.230	.319	2	2	101	102	0.4	1	-0	0.3
1917	NY-A	8	5	.615	26	13	7	0	1	145	124	7.7	5	46	2.9	68	4.2	2.61	110	.241	.303	1	4	107	97	2.0	-1	2	0.6
1918	StL-A	6	5	.545	14	9	7	0	2	95	69	6.5	0	40	3.8	33	3.1	1.80	154	.209	.292	10	10	100	101	0.8	4	1	1.7
1919	StL-A	13	11	.542	30	25	14	5	0	211	193	8.2	6	55	2.3	86	3.7	2.69	117	.244	.296	13	11	98	88	1.6	-0	-1	0.9
1920	StL-A	20	10	.667	38	28	22	5	**5**	246	224	8.2	10	70	2.6	107	3.9	2.71	**156**	.248	.305	30	41	111	100	5.8	2	-0	4.4
1921	StL-A	**27**	12	.692	47	38	30	4	4	327	345	9.5	21	86	2.4	132	3.6	3.55	122	.270	.312	27	28	101	97	8.2	6	3	3.5
1922	StL-A	24	17	.585	48	38	29	2	3	348	365	9.4	22	57	**1.5**	**149**	3.9	2.97	138	.272	.296	41	44	102	108	-0.7	2	-3	4.4
1923	StL-A	20	12	.625	43	35	24	3	5	277	292	9.5	12	49	**1.6**	109	3.5	3.41	122	.272	**.298**	18	23	105	91	5.1	2	-3	2.2
1924	StL-A	16	13	.552	40	33	17	4	1	246	270	9.9	11	52	1.9	88	3.2	4.21	108	.277	.307	1	10	108	80	2.2	5	-2	1.3
1925	NY-A	12	12	.500	41	30	15	2	2	244	278	10.3	17	58	2.1	74	2.7	3.65	117	.294	.328	20	17	97	114	1.3	5	-2	1.8
1926	NY-A	19	11	.633	41	32	18	0	2	258	272	9.5	13	71	2.5	59	2.1	3.38	115	.269	.311	18	15	97	98	1.9	1	-2	1.3
1927	NY-A	18	6	.750	31	27	13	2	0	200	207	9.3	8	41	1.8	35	1.6	2.84	137	.268	.297	29	23	94	110	1.7	3	-2	2.3
1928	NY-A	0	0	—	1	0	0	0	0	2	3	13.5	0	0	0.0	0	0.0	0.00	—	.429	.429	1	1	89	0	0.0	0	0	0.1
Total	13	187	117	.615	412	317	200	28	25	2681	2709	9.1	127	657	2.2	983	3.3	3.17	124	.265	.306	210	230	102	99	30.3	29	-9	24.8
■ MILT SHOFFNER	Shoffner, Milburn James b: 11/13/05, Sherman, Tex. d: 1/19/78, Madison, Ohio BL/TL, 6'1.5", 184 lbs. Deb: 7/20/29																												
1929	Cle-A	2	3	.400	11	3	1	0	0	45	46	9.2	4	22	4.4	15	3.0	5.00	85	.284	.360	-4	-4	101	101	-0.5	-3	0	-0.5
1930	Cle-A	3	4	.429	24	10	1	0	0	85	129	13.7	8	50	5.3	17	1.8	7.94	62	.362	.429	-31	-29	105	98	-0.6	1	-0	-2.3
1931	Cle-A	2	3	.400	12	4	1	0	0	41	55	12.1	4	26	5.7	12	2.6	7.24	64	.320	.411	-13	-12	106	93	-0.4	-1	-0	-1.1
1937	Bos-N	3	1	.750	6	5	3	1	1	43	38	8.0	1	9	1.9	13	2.7	2.51	140	.239	.276	7	5	90	100	1.0	1	1	0.6
1938	Bos-N	8	7	.533	26	15	9	1	1	140	147	9.4	7	36	2.3	49	3.2	3.54	95	.270	.311	4	-3	89	101	0.4	3	-2	-0.1
1939	Bos-N	4	6	.400	25	11	7	0	1	132	133	9.1	4	42	2.9	51	3.5	3.14	116	.265	.313	11	8	93	109	-0.1	-0	0	0.7
	Cin-N	2	2	.500	10	3	0	0	0	38	43	10.2	3	11	2.6	6	1.4	3.32	118	.289	.335	3	3	100	134	-0.3	-1	-0	0.2
	Yr	6	8	.429	35	14	7	0	1	170	176	9.3	7	53	2.8	57	3.0	3.18	117	.270	.317	14	10	95	134	-0.4	-0	0	0.9
1940	Cin-N	1	0	1.000	20	0	0	0	0	54	56	9.3	3	18	3.0	17	2.8	5.67	66	.268	.319	-11	-11	98	68	0.5	-1	-0	-1.2
Total	7	25	26	.490	134	51	22	2	3	578	647	10.1	34	214	3.3	180	2.8	4.58	85	.287	.342	-34	-45	96	101	0.0	-0	-2	-3.7
■ ERNIE SHORE	Shore, Ernest Grady b: 3/24/1891, East Bend, N.C. d: 9/24/80, Winston-Salem, N.C. BR/TR, 6'4", 220 lbs. Deb: 6/20/12																												
1912	NY-N	0	0	—	1	0	0	0	0	1	8	72.0	1	1	9.0	1	9.0	27.00	13	.667	.692	-3	-3	99	165	0.0	0	0	-0.1
1914	Bos-A	10	4	.714	20	16	10	1	1	140	103	6.6	1	34	2.2	51	3.3	1.99	132	.204	.261	12	10	96	66	2.2	-3	2	1.3
1915	Bos-A	19	8	.704	38	32	17	4	0	247	207	7.5	3	66	2.4	102	3.7	1.64	172	.228	.283	36	33	96	123	1.7	-3	4	3.7
1916	Bos-A	16	10	.615	38	28	10	3	1	226	221	8.8	1	49	2.0	62	2.5	2.63	99	.259	.302	5	-1	92	97	0.9	-4	5	0.0
1917	Bos-A	13	10	.565	29	27	14	1	1	227	201	8.0	1	55	2.2	57	2.3	2.22	127	.240	.297	11	15	106	99	-0.5	-2	3	1.9
1919	NY-A	5	8	.385	20	13	3	0	0	95	105	9.9	4	44	4.2	24	2.3	4.17	80	.288	.366	-10	-9	104	100	-2.2	-2	0	-0.9
1920	NY-A	2	2	.500	14	5	2	0	1	44	61	12.5	1	21	4.3	12	2.5	4.91	76	.333	.405	-5	-6	99	112	-0.3	0	1	-0.4
Total	7	65	42	.607	160	121	56	9	5	980	906	8.3	12	270	2.5	309	2.8	2.47	115	.247	.304	46	40	98	100	1.8	-14	15	5.5
■ RAY SHORE	Shore, Raymond Everett b: 6/9/21, Cincinnati, Ohio BR/TR, 6'3", 210 lbs. Deb: 9/21/46 C																												
1946	StL-A	0	0	—	1	0	0	0	0	1	3	27.0	0	1	9.0	1	9.0	18.00	19	.500	.571	-2	-2	100	80	0.0	0	0	-0.1
1948	StL-A	1	2	.333	17	4	0	0	0	38	40	9.5	2	35	8.3	12	2.8	6.39	73	.270	.416	-9	-7	109	90	-0.1	-2	0	-0.7
1949	StL-A	0	1	.000	13	0	0	0	0	23	27	10.6	3	31	12.1	13	5.1	10.96	40	.297	.480	-17	-17	104	74	-0.4	-1	1	-1.5
Total	3	1	3	.250	31	4	0	0	0	62	70	10.2	5	67	9.7	26	3.8	8.27	55	.286	.444	-28	-26	107	84	-0.5	-2	1	-2.3
■ BILL SHORES	Shores, William David b: 5/26/04, Abilene, Tex. d: 2/19/84, Purcell, Okla. BR/TR, 6', 185 lbs. Deb: 4/11/28																												
1928	Phi-A	1	1	.500	3	2	1	0	0	14	13	8.4	0	7	4.5	5	3.2	3.21	124	.250	.328	1	1	99	101	-0.1	-1	-0	0.0
1929	Phi-A	11	6	.647	39	13	5	1	7	153	150	8.8	9	59	3.5	49	2.9	3.59	123	.262	.325	11	14	104	104	-0.5	-2	-1	1.1
1930	Phi-A	12	4	.750	31	19	7	1	0	159	169	9.6	11	70	4.0	48	2.7	4.19	107	.276	.346	8	5	96	110	2.2	-2	0	0.3
1931	Phi-A	0	3	.000	6	2	0	0	0	16	26	14.6	3	10	5.6	2	1.1	5.06	87	.361	.434	-1	-1	101	171	-1.4	0	0	0.0
1933	NY-N	2	1	.667	8	3	1	0	0	37	41	10.0	4	14	3.4	20	4.9	3.89	82	.291	.346	-2	-3	96	123	0.3	1	1	0.0
1936	Chi-A	0	0	—	9	0	0	0	0	17	26	13.8	1	8	4.2	5	2.6	9.53	52	.356	.405	-8	-9	99	74	0.0	-0	0	-0.6
Total	6	26	15	.634	96	39	14	2	7	396	425	9.7	28	168	3.8	129	2.9	4.16	104	.279	.344	9	8	100	109	0.5	-4	1	0.8
■ CHRIS SHORT	Short, Christopher Joseph b: 9/19/37, Milford, Del. BR/TL, 6'4", 205 lbs. Deb: 4/19/59																												
1959	Phi-N	0	0	—	3	2	0	0	0	14	19	12.2	3	10	6.4	8	5.1	8.36	48	.317	.417	-7	-7	102	89	0.0	-1	0	-0.6
1960	Phi-N	6	9	.400	42	10	2	0	3	107	101	8.5	8	52	4.4	54	4.5	3.95	105	.249	.334	-2	2	110	98	0.2	-3	0	0.0
1961	Phi-N	6	12	.333	39	16	1	0	1	127	157	11.1	12	71	5.0	80	5.7	5.95	66	.304	.384	-27	-28	98	94	0.4	-1	-1	-2.7
1962	Phi-N	11	9	.550	47	12	4	0	3	142	149	9.4	13	56	3.5	91	5.8	3.42	110	.272	.343	8	5	95	127	1.1	1	0	0.6
1963	Phi-N	9	12	.429	38	27	6	3	0	198	185	8.4	12	69	3.1	160	7.3	2.95	113	.248	.310	7	9	102	111	-2.3	-2	4	1.1
1964	Phi-N	17	9	.654	42	31	12	4	2	221	174	7.1	10	51	2.1	181	7.4	2.20	157	.217	.264	33	31	98	98	3.0	-1	-1	3.2
1965	Phi-N	18	11	.621	47	40	15	5	2	297	260	7.9	18	89	2.7	237	7.2	2.82	119	.235	.291	24	18	95	102	3.3	-2	-3	1.4
1966	Phi-N	20	10	.667	42	39	19	4	0	272	257	8.5	28	68	2.3	177	5.9	3.54	102	.250	.299	2	2	100	96	4.8	1	0	0.4
1967	Phi-N	9	11	.450	29	26	8	2	1	199	163	7.4	9	74	3.3	142	6.4	2.40	146	.225	.295	22	25	104	113	-1.1	-2	0	2.6
1968	Phi-N	19	13	.594	42	36	9	2	1	270	236	7.9	25	81	2.7	202	6.7	2.93	100	.236	.296	2	0	99	107	4.4	0	-1	0.0
1969	Phi-N	0	0	—	2	2	0	0	0	10	11	9.9	2	4	3.6	5	4.5	7.20	50	.282	.356	-4	-4	100	78	0.0	-0	0	-0.3
1970	Phi-N	9	16	.360	36	34	7	2	1	199	211	9.5	13	66	3.0	133	6.0	4.30	92	.272	.328	-5	-7	98	93	-2.8	-5	-2	-1.4
1971	Phi-N	7	14	.333	31	26	5	2	1	173	182	9.5	22	63	3.3	95	4.9	3.85	94	.274	.333	-7	-4	105	115	-2.2	-2	-0	-0.6
1972	Phi-N	1	1	.500	19	0	0	0	1	23	24	9.4	3	8	3.1	20	7.8	3.91	87	.267	.320	-1	-1	99	107	0.2	0	-0	-0.1
1973	Mil-A	3	5	.375	42	7	0	0	2	72	86	10.8	5	44	5.5	44	5.5	5.13	72	.299	.393	-10	-12	96	104	-0.6	0	-1	-1.1
Total	15	135	132	.506	501	308	88	24	18	2324	2215	8.6	183	806	3.1	1629	6.3	3.43	103	.252	.314	33	29	100	104	8.4	-17	-3	2.5
■ BILL SHORT	Short, William Ross b: 11/27/37, Kingston, N.Y. BL/TL, 5'9", 170 lbs. Deb: 4/23/60																												
1960	NY-A	3	5	.375	10	10	2	0	0	47	49	9.4	5	30	5.7	14	2.7	4.79	75	.282	.381	-5	-6	92	111	-1.6	1	-0	-0.5
1962	Bal-A	0	0	—	5	0	0	0	0	4	8	18.0	0	6	13.5	3	6.8	15.75	24	.381	.536	-5	-5	95	69	0.0	-0	0	-0.4
1966	Bal-A	2	3	.400	6	6	1	1	0	38	34	8.1	2	10	2.4	27	6.4	2.84	119	.239	.284	3	2	99	99	-0.8	-1	1	0.2
	Bos-A	0	0	—	8	0	0	0	0	8	10	11.3	1	2	2.3	2	2.3	4.50	84	.294	.333	-1	-1	110	105	0.0	-0	0	0.0
	Yr	2	3	.400	14	6	1	1	0	46	44	8.6	3	12	2.3	29	5.7	3.13	110	.247	.293	2	2	101	105	-0.8	-1	1	0.2

YEAR	TM/L	W	L	PCT	G	GS	CG	SHO	SV	IP	H	H/G	HR	BB	BB/G	SO	SO/G	ERA	/A	OAVG	OOBP	PR	/A	PF	CPI	WAT	PB	PD	TPI
1967	Pit-N	0	0	—	6	0	0	0	1	2	1	4.5	0	1	4.5	1	4.5	4.50	75	.143	.222	-0	-0	100	16	0.0	-0	0	0.0
1968	NY-N	0	3	.000	34	0	0	0	1	30	24	7.2	0	14	4.2	24	7.2	4.80	64	.220	.305	-6	-6	103	52	-1.4	-0	1	-0.5
1969	Cin-N	0	0	—	4	0	0	0	0	2	4	18.0	0	1	4.5	0	0.0	18.00	20	.400	.455	-3	-3	99	44	0.0	-0	0	-0.2
Total	6	5	11	.313	73	16	3	1	2	131	130	8.9	8	64	4.4	71	4.9	4.74	72	.262	.341	-18	-19	98	90	-3.8	-1	2	-1.4
■ **CLYDE SHOUN**	Shoun, Clyde Mitchell "Hardrock" b: 3/20/12, Mountain City, Tenn. d: 3/20/68, Mountain Home, Tenn. BL/TL, 6'1", 188 lbs. Deb: 8/07/35																												
1935	Chi-N	1	0	1.000	5	1	0	0	0	13	14	9.7	2	5	3.5	5	3.5	2.77	138	.298	.358	2	2	95	202	0.5	-0	-0	0.1
1936	Chi-N	0	0	—	4	0	0	0	0	4	3	6.8	0	6	13.5	1	2.3	13.50	30	.200	.429	-4	-4	102	35	0.0	0	0	-0.3
1937	Chi-N	7	7	.500	37	9	2	0	0	93	118	11.4	9	45	4.4	43	4.2	5.61	70	.309	.372	-18	-17	100	100	-1.2	-1	-1	-1.7
1938	StL-N	6	6	.500	40	12	3	0	1	117	130	10.0	8	43	3.3	37	2.8	4.15	101	.283	.342	-5	1	111	105	0.4	0	-1	0.0
1939	StL-N	3	1	.750	**53**	2	0	0	**9**	103	98	8.6	4	42	3.7	50	4.4	3.76	107	.248	.316	2	**3**	103	87	0.8	-1	-1	0.2
1940	StL-N	13	11	.542	**54**	19	13	1	5	197	193	8.8	13	46	2.1	82	3.7	3.93	99	.255	.295	-2	-1	101	85	-0.1	-1	-0	-0.1
1941	StL-N	3	5	.375	26	6	0	0	0	70	98	12.6	9	20	2.6	34	4.4	5.66	69	.337	.369	-16	-14	107	108	-1.6	0	1	-1.1
1942	StL-N	0	0	—	2	0	0	0	0	2	1	4.5	0	0	0.0	0	0.0	0.00	—	.167	.143	1	1	103	0	0.0	0	0	0.1
	Cin-N	1	3	.250	34	0	0	0	0	72	55	6.9	2	24	3.0	32	4.0	2.25	149	.216	.277	9	9	102	101	-0.9	1	1	1.2
	Yr	1	3	.250	36	0	0	0	0	74	56	6.8	2	24	2.9	32	3.9	2.19	154	.215	.274	9	10	102	101	-0.9	0	1	1.3
1943	Cin-N	14	5	.737	45	5	2	0	7	147	131	8.0	5	46	2.8	61	3.7	3.06	108	.241	.295	5	4	98	90	4.1	3	1	0.9
1944	Cin-N	13	10	.565	38	21	12	1	2	203	193	8.6	10	42	1.9	55	2.4	3.01	113	.248	.285	13	9	95	94	-0.2	1	-3	0.7
1946	Cin-N	1	6	.143	27	5	0	0	0	79	87	9.9	3	26	3.0	20	2.3	4.10	87	.292	.341	-6	-5	105	100	-2.3	-1	-2	-0.8
1947	Cin-N	0	0	—	10	0	0	0	0	14	16	10.3	2	5	3.2	7	4.5	5.14	73	.320	.386	-2	-2	92	119	0.0	0	0	-0.1
	Bos-N	5	3	.625	26	3	1	1	1	74	73	8.9	6	21	2.6	23	2.8	4.38	89	.254	.301	-3	-4	95	76	0.6	-1	-1	-0.5
	Yr	5	3	.625	36	3	1	1	1	88	89	9.1	8	26	2.7	30	3.1	4.50	86	.263	.312	-4	-6	95	76	0.6	0	-1	-0.6
1948	Bos-N	5	1	.833	36	2	1	0	4	74	77	9.4	7	20	2.4	25	3.0	4.01	97	.267	.313	-0	-1	99	96	1.8	0	-2	-0.2
1949	Bos-N	0	0	—	1	0	0	0	0	1	1	9.0	0	0	0.0	0	0.0	0.00	—	.250	.250	0	0	97	0	0.0	0	0	0.0
	Chi-A	1	1	.500	16	0	0	0	0	23	37	14.5	1	13	5.1	8	3.1	5.87	71	.370	.431	-4	-4	99	123	0.2	0	0	-0.3
Total	14	73	59	.553	454	85	34	3	29	1286	1325	9.3	81	404	2.8	483	3.4	3.91	96	.267	.318	-27	-24	101	95	2.1	1	-8	-1.9
■ **ERIC SHOW**	Show, Eric Vaughn b: 5/19/56, Riverside, Cal. BR/TR, 6'1", 185 lbs. Deb: 9/02/81																												
1981	SD-N	1	3	.250	15	0	0	0	3	23	17	6.7	2	9	3.5	22	8.6	3.13	106	.213	.293	1	0	95	93	-0.6	0	0	0.0
1982	SD-N	10	6	.625	47	14	2	2	3	150	117	7.0	10	48	2.9	88	5.3	2.64	125	.217	.278	16	11	92	97	2.2	-1	2	1.2
1983	SD-N	15	12	.556	35	33	4	2	0	201	201	9.0	25	74	3.3	120	5.4	4.16	87	.263	.328	-12	-13	99	101	1.8	0	-2	-1.3
1984	SD-N	15	9	.625	32	32	3	1	0	207	175	7.6	18	88	3.8	104	4.5	3.39	104	.234	.310	5	3	98	101	1.8	7	-1	0.9
1985	SD-N	12	11	.522	35	35	5	2	0	233	212	8.2	27	87	3.4	141	5.4	3.09	118	.243	.311	13	14	101	119	0.3	-2	-2	1.1
1986	SD-N	9	5	.643	24	22	2	0	0	136	109	7.2	11	69	4.6	94	6.2	2.98	120	.225	.320	11	9	96	115	2.5	1	-1	0.8
1987	SD-N	8	16	.333	34	34	5	3	0	206	188	8.2	26	85	3.7	117	5.1	3.84	104	.241	.318	6	3	98	101	-2.2	-4	-1	-0.1
1988	SD-N	16	11	.593	32	32	13	1	0	235	201	7.7	22	53	2.0	144	5.5	3.26	103	.231	.278	5	3	97	89	2.5	-0	-4	-0.1
Total	8	86	73	.541	254	202	34	11	6	1391	1220	7.9	141	513	3.3	830	5.4	3.37	106	.238	.306	45	31	98	103	8.3	1	-10	2.5
■ **LEV SHREVE**	Shreve, Leven Lawrence b: 1/14/1869, Louisville, Ky. d: 10/18/42, Detroit, Mich. TR , 5'11", 150 lbs. Deb: 5/02/1887																												
1887	Bal-a	3	1	.750	5	5	4	1	0	38	33	7.8	0	19	4.5	13	3.1	3.79	107	.247	.340	2	1	94	83	0.9	-1	0	0.0
	Ind-N	5	9	.357	14	14	14	1	0	122	141	10.4	5	65	4.8	22	1.6	4.72	87	.305	.391	-9	-8	101	104	0.7	0	0	-0.5
1888	Ind-N	11	24	.314	35	35	34	1	0	298	352	10.6	23	93	2.8	101	3.1	4.65	59	.308	.360	-60	-62	98	98	-3.3	-0	0	-5.6
1889	Ind-N	0	3	.000	3	3	1	0	0	16	25	14.1	3	12	6.8	5	2.8	14.63	30	.373	.468	-19	-18	110	58	-1.4	-1	0	-1.2
Total	3	19	37	.339	57	57	53	3	0	474	551	10.5	31	189	3.6	141	2.7	4.94	66	.305	.371	-86	-88	99	97	-3.1	-2	0	-7.3
■ **HARRY SHRIVER**	Shriver, Harry Graydon "Pop" b: 9/2/1896, Wadestown, W.Va. d: 1/21/70, Morgantown, W.Va. BR/TR, 6'2", 180 lbs. Deb: 4/14/22																												
1922	Bro-N	4	6	.400	25	14	4	2	0	108	114	9.5	5	48	4.0	38	3.2	3.00	130	.287	.350	13	11	95	146	-0.9	-3	-2	0.5
1923	Bro-N	0	0	—	1	1	0	0	0	4	8	18.0	0	0	0.0	1	2.3	6.75	58	.444	.421	-1	-1	98	115	0.0	-0	-0	0.0
Total	2	4	6	.400	26	15	4	2	0	112	122	9.8	5	48	3.9	39	3.1	3.13	125	.294	.353	12	10	95	145	-0.9	-3	-2	0.5
■ **TOOTS SHULTZ**	Shultz, Wallace Luther b: 10/10/1888, Homestead, Pa. d: 1/30/59, Mc Keesport, Pa. BR/TR, 5'10", 175 lbs. Deb: 5/05/11																												
1911	Phi-N	0	3	.000	5	3	2	0	0	25	30	10.8	5	15	5.4	9	3.2	9.36	39	.300	.412	-17	-16	108	72	-1.4	0	0	-1.2
1912	Phi-N	1	4	.200	22	4	1	0	1	59	75	11.4	2	35	5.3	20	3.1	4.58	75	.316	.411	-8	-8	101	118	-1.4	0	0	-0.6
Total	2	1	7	.125	27	7	3	0	1	84	105	11.3	7	50	5.4	29	3.1	6.00	58	.312	.411	-24	-23	103	104	-2.8	0	1	-1.8
■ **HARRY SHUMAN**	Shuman, Harry b: 3/5/16, Philadelphia, Pa. BR/TR, 6'2", 195 lbs. Deb: 9/14/42																												
1942	Pit-N	0	0	—	1	0	0	0	0	2	0	0.0	0	1	4.5	1	4.5	0.00	—	.000	.167	1	1	102	0	0.0	0	0	0.1
1943	Pit-N	0	0	—	11	0	0	0	0	22	30	12.3	0	8	3.3	5	2.0	5.32	65	.337	.388	-5	-5	103	103	0.0	-0	0	-0.4
1944	Phi-N	0	0	—	18	0	0	0	0	27	26	8.7	1	11	3.7	4	1.3	4.00	93	.245	.314	-1	-1	103	78	0.0	-0	0	0.0
Total	3	0	0	—	30	0	0	0	0	51	56	9.9	1	20	3.5	10	1.8	4.41	81	.280	.344	-5	-5	103	86	0.0	-0	0	-0.3
■ **PAUL SIEBERT**	Siebert, Paul Edward b: 6/5/53, Minneapolis, Minn. BL/TL, 6'2", 205 lbs. Deb: 9/07/74																												
1974	Hou-N	1	1	.500	5	5	1	1	0	25	21	7.6	3	11	4.0	10	3.6	3.60	98	.236	.305	0	-0	98	102	0.0	-1	1	0.0
1975	Hou-N	0	2	.000	7	2	0	0	2	18	20	10.0	0	6	3.0	6	3.0	3.00	115	.294	.351	1	1	95	134	-0.9	-0	0	0.1
1976	Hou-N	0	2	.000	19	0	0	0	0	26	29	10.0	0	18	6.2	10	3.5	3.12	97	.296	.387	1	-0	87	163	-0.9	-0	-1	0.0
1977	SD-N	0	0	—	4	0	0	0	0	4	3	6.8	1	4	9.0	1	2.3	2.25	155	.214	.368	1	1	89	255	0.0	0	-0	0.0
	NY-N	2	1	.667	25	0	0	0	0	28	27	8.7	0	13	4.2	20	6.4	3.86	98	.257	.333	0	-0	97	88	0.7	-0	-0	0.0
	Yr	2	1	.667	29	0	0	0	0	32	30	8.4	1	17	4.8	21	5.9	3.66	103	.250	.338	1	0	96	88	0.7	0	-0	0.0
1978	NY-N	0	2	.000	27	0	0	0	1	28	30	9.6	2	21	6.8	12	3.9	5.14	69	.283	.400	-5	-5	99	106	-0.9	-0	0	-0.4
Total	5	3	8	.273	87	7	1	1	3	129	130	9.1	6	73	5.1	59	4.1	3.77	92	.271	.358	-1	-4	95	121	-2.0	-2	1	-0.3
■ **SONNY SIEBERT**	Siebert, Wilfred Charles b: 1/14/37, St.Mary'S, Mo. BR/TR, 6'3", 190 lbs. Deb: 4/26/64																												
1964	Cle-A	7	9	.438	41	14	3	1	3	156	142	8.2	15	57	3.3	144	8.3	3.23	115	.243	.308	7	9	103	107	-0.8	5	-1	1.3
1965	Cle-A	16	8	.667	39	27	4	1	1	189	139	6.6	14	46	2.2	191	9.1	2.43	139	.206	.256	22	20	97	88	3.8	-2	1	2.1
1966	Cle-A	16	8	**.667**	34	32	11	1	1	241	193	7.2	25	62	2.3	163	6.1	2.80	125	.221	.273	17	18	102	102	4.4	-2	2	2.0
1967	Cle-A	10	12	.455	34	26	7	1	4	185	136	6.6	17	54	2.6	136	6.6	2.38	137	.202	.264	17	18	101	100	-0.1	1	-2	2.0
1968	Cle-A	12	10	.545	31	30	8	4	0	206	145	6.3	12	88	3.8	146	6.4	2.97	101	.198	.286	0	1	101	80	0.3	1	1	0.3
1969	Cle-A	0	1	.000	2	2	0	0	0	14	10	6.4	1	8	5.1	6	3.9	3.21	109	.196	.300	1	0	96	81	-0.4	0	0	0.0
	Bos-A	14	10	.583	43	22	2	0	5	163	151	8.3	21	68	3.8	127	7.0	3.81	100	.245	.319	-3	-0	105	102	1.4	1	2	0.3
	Yr	14	11	.560	45	24	2	0	5	177	161	8.2	22	76	3.9	133	6.8	3.76	100	.241	.318	-3	0	104	102	1.0	0	2	0.3
1970	Bos-A	15	8	.652	33	33	7	2	0	223	207	8.4	29	60	2.4	142	5.7	3.43	119	.248	.298	7	16	110	104	3.2	-2	0	1.6
1971	Bos-A	16	10	.615	32	32	12	4	0	235	220	8.4	20	60	2.3	131	5.0	2.91	125	.245	.290	15	19	105	103	2.9	10	0	3.5
1972	Bos-A	12	12	.500	32	30	7	3	0	196	204	9.4	17	59	2.7	123	5.6	3.81	85	.264	.317	-16	-13	105	97	-1.1	6	1	-0.5
1973	Bos-A	0	1	.000	2	0	0	0	0	2	5	22.5	1	1	4.5	5	22.5	9.00	45	.417	.462	-1	-1	105	144	-0.4	0	0	0.0
	Tex-A	7	11	.389	25	20	1	1	2	120	120	9.0	11	37	2.8	76	5.7	3.98	96	.258	.313	-2	-2	100	90	0.6	0	2	0.0
	Yr	7	12	.368	27	20	1	1	2	122	125	9.2	12	38	2.8	81	6.0	4.06	94	.262	.317	-3	-3	100	90	0.2	0	2	0.0
1974	StL-N	8	8	.500	28	20	5	3	0	134	150	10.1	8	51	3.4	68	4.6	3.83	98	.288	.348	-3	-1	103	114	-0.5	-2	-1	-0.3
1975	SD-N	3	2	.600	6	6	0	0	0	27	37	12.3	2	10	3.3	10	3.3	4.33	85	.330	.381	-2	-2	101	131	0.7	2	0	0.0
	Oak-A	4	4	.500	17	13	0	0	0	61	60	8.9	4	31	4.6	44	6.5	3.69	94	.252	.331	1	-2	91	100	-0.6	0	-1	-0.2
Total	12	140	114	.551	399	307	67	21	16	2152	1919	8.0	197	692	2.9	1512	6.3	3.21	110	.238	.298	58	80	103	99	13.4	19	6	12.1
■ **DWIGHT SIEBLER**	Siebler, Dwight Leroy b: 8/5/37, Columbus, Neb. BR/TR, 6'2", 184 lbs. Deb: 8/26/63																												
1963	Min-A	2	1	.667	7	5	2	0	0	39	25	5.8	6	12	2.8	22	5.1	2.77	128	.182	.253	4	3	98	88	0.4	-0	-1	0.2
1964	Min-A	0	0	—	9	0	0	0	0	11	10	8.2	1	6	4.9	10	8.2	4.91	74	.256	.348	-2	-2	100	88	0.0	0	-0	-0.1
1965	Min-A	0	0	—	7	1	0	0	0	15	11	6.6	2	11	6.6	15	9.0	4.20	81	.193	.324	-1	-1	98	80	0.0	-0	0	-0.1
1966	Min-A	2	2	.500	23	2	0	0	1	50	47	8.5	6	14	2.5	24	4.3	3.42	111	.253	.295	0	2	110	111	-0.1	-1	-1	0.1
1967	Min-A	0	0	—	2	0	0	0	0	3	4	12.0	0	1	3.0	0	0.0	3.00	114	.364	.385	0	0	106	193	0.0	0	0	0.0
Total	5	4	3	.571	48	8	2	0	1	118	97	7.4	15	44	3.4	71	5.4	3.43	106	.226	.294	1	3	103	99	0.3	-1	-2	0.1

YEAR	TM/L	W	L	PCT	G	GS	CG	SHO	SV	IP	H	H/G	HR	BB	BB/G	SO	SO/G	ERA	/A	OAVG	OOBP	PR	/A	PF	CPI	WAT	PB	PD	TPI
■ **CANDY SIERRA**	Sierra, Ulises (Pizarro) b: 3/27/67, Rio Piedras, P.R. BR/TR, 6'2", 190 lbs. Deb: 4/06/88																												
1988	SD-N	0	1	.000	15	0	0	0	0	24	36	13.5	2	11	4.1	20	7.5	5.63	60	.379	.431	-6	-6	97	131	-0.4	-0	-0	-0.6
	Cin-N	0	0	—	1	0	0	0	0	4	5	11.3	0	1	2.3	4	9.0	4.50	80	.294	.333	-0	-0	105	84	0.0	-0	0	0.0
	Yr	0	1	.000	16	0	0	0	0	28	41	13.2	2	12	3.9	24	7.7	5.46	62	.363	.417	-6	-6	98	84	-0.4	-0	-0	-0.6
■ **ED SIEVER**	Siever, Edward T. b: 4/2/1877, Goodard, Kan. d: 2/4/20, Detroit, Mich. BL/TL, 5'11.5", 190 lbs. Deb: 4/26/01																												
1901	Det-A	18	15	.545	38	33	30	2	0	289	334	10.4	9	65	2.0	85	2.6	3.24	124	.310	.349	14	25	109	117	0.0	-6	-1	2.2
1902	Det-A	8	11	.421	25	23	17	4	1	188	166	7.9	0	32	1.5	36	1.7	**1.91**	**187**	.260	.295	35	35	101	109	0.6	-3	-4	3.1
1903	StL-A	13	14	.481	31	27	24	1	0	254	245	8.7	6	39	1.4	90	3.2	2.48	114	.275	.306	13	10	96	109	0.4	-4	2	1.2
1904	StL-A	10	15	.400	29	24	19	2	0	217	235	9.7	3	65	2.7	77	3.2	2.65	95	.300	.354	-1	-3	98	136	-0.9	-2	1	-0.2
1906	Det-A	14	11	.560	30	25	20	1	0	223	240	9.7	5	45	1.8	71	2.9	2.70	110	.301	.338	-0	7	110	124	2.3	-4	-3	0.4
1907	Det-A	18	11	.621	39	33	22	3	1	275	256	8.4	1	52	1.7	88	2.9	2.16	115	.270	.308	12	10	98	109	0.3	-3	-4	0.7
1908	Det-A	2	6	.250	11	9	4	1	0	62	74	10.7	0	13	1.9	23	3.3	3.48	68	.302	.337	-8	-8	99	109	-2.3	-1	-1	-0.8
Total	7	83	83	.500	203	174	136	14	2	1508	1550	9.3	24	311	1.9	470	2.8	2.60	117	.288	.327	64	73	102	117	0.4	-22	-10	6.6
■ **WALTER SIGNER**	Signer, Walter Donald Aloysius b: 10/12/10, New York, N.Y. d: 7/23/74, Greenwich, Conn. BR/TR, 6', 185 lbs. Deb: 9/18/43																												
1943	Chi-N	2	1	.667	4	2	1	0	0	25	24	8.6	3	4	1.4	5	1.8	2.88	115	.245	.269	1	1	98	105	0.5	0	0	0.2
1945	Chi-N	0	0	—	6	0	0	0	1	8	11	12.4	1	5	5.6	0	0.0	3.38	107	.256	.333	0	0	95	121	0.0	-0	-0	0.0
Total	2	2	1	.667	10	2	1	0	1	33	35	9.5	4	9	2.5	5	1.4	3.00	113	.248	.289	2	1	97	109	0.5	0	-0	0.2
■ **SETH SIGSBY**	Sigsby, Seth De Witt (born Seth De Witt) b: 4/30/1874, Cobleskill, N.Y. d: 9/15/53, Schenectady, N.Y 6', 175 lbs. Deb: 6/27/1893																												
1893	NY-N	0	0	—	1	0	0	0	0	3	1	3.0	0	4	12.0	2	6.0	9.00	53	.113	.388	-1	-1	103	30	0.0	-0	0	0.0
■ **AL SIMA**	Sima, Albert b: 10/7/21, Mahwah, N.J. BR/TL, 6', 190 lbs. Deb: 6/28/50																												
1950	Was-A	4	5	.444	17	9	1	0	0	77	89	10.4	9	26	3.0	23	2.7	4.79	96	.291	.339	-2	-1	101	102	0.1	-2	-1	-0.4
1951	Was-A	3	7	.300	18	8	1	0	0	77	79	9.2	5	41	4.8	26	3.0	4.79	83	.261	.345	-6	-7	97	86	-1.2	1	-0	-0.5
1953	Was-A	2	3	.400	31	5	1	0	1	68	63	8.3	7	31	4.1	25	3.3	3.44	108	.249	.333	4	2	93	118	-0.4	-1	1	0.2
1954	Chi-A	0	1	.000	5	1	0	0	1	7	11	14.1	1	2	2.6	1	1.3	5.14	72	.393	.394	-1	-1	100	149	-0.4	-0	-0	0.0
	Phi-A	2	5	.286	29	7	1	0	2	79	101	11.5	9	32	3.6	36	4.1	5.24	74	.309	.367	-13	-12	105	102	-0.4	-2	-1	-1.4
	Yr	2	6	.250	34	8	1	0	3	86	112	11.7	10	34	3.6	37	3.9	5.23	74	.315	.370	-14	-13	104	102	-0.8	-0	-1	-1.4
Total	4	11	21	.344	100	30	4	0	4	308	343	10.0	31	132	3.9	111	3.2	4.62	88	.282	.348	-18	-19	99	103	-2.3	-5	-1	-2.1
■ **CURT SIMMONS**	Simmons, Curtis Thomas b: 5/19/29, Egypt, Pa. BL/TL, 5'11", 175 lbs. Deb: 9/28/47																												
1947	Phi-N	1	0	1.000	1	1	1	0	0	9	5	5.0	0	6	6.0	9	9.0	1.00	414	.161	.297	3	3	102	167	0.5	0	-0	0.4
1948	Phi-N	7	13	.350	31	22	7	0	0	170	169	8.9	8	108	5.7	86	4.6	4.87	78	.266	.368	-17	-20	97	94	-2.0	-1	0	-1.9
1949	Phi-N	4	10	.286	38	14	2	0	1	131	133	9.1	7	55	3.8	83	5.7	4.60	88	.275	.343	-8	-8	101	92	-3.3	-1	-0	-0.7
1950	Phi-N	17	8	.680	31	27	11	2	1	215	178	7.5	19	88	3.7	146	6.1	3.39	117	.223	.299	18	14	96	90	3.1	-1	-0	1.2
1952	Phi-N	14	8	.636	28	28	15	**6**	0	201	170	7.6	11	70	3.1	141	6.3	2.82	131	.227	.290	20	19	99	97	2.1	2	-3	2.0
1953	Phi-N	16	13	.552	32	30	19	4	0	238	211	8.0	17	82	3.1	138	5.2	3.21	131	.236	.298	28	26	98	96	0.5	-3	-3	2.0
1954	Phi-N	14	15	.483	34	33	21	3	1	253	226	8.0	14	98	3.5	125	4.4	2.81	142	.239	.306	35	33	98	106	-0.1	-1	-3	2.9
1955	Phi-N	8	8	.500	25	22	3	0	0	130	148	10.2	15	50	3.5	58	4.0	4.92	84	.290	.351	-13	-12	102	99	0.0	-1	-1	-1.2
1956	Phi-N	15	10	.600	33	27	14	0	0	198	186	8.5	17	65	3.0	88	4.0	3.36	107	.248	.305	9	5	95	97	3.7	4	-0	0.8
1957	Phi-N	12	11	.522	32	29	9	2	0	212	214	9.1	11	50	2.1	92	3.9	3.44	112	.264	.301	10	9	99	95	0.6	3	-3	1.0
1958	Phi-N	7	14	.333	29	27	7	1	1	168	196	10.5	11	40	2.1	78	4.2	4.39	90	.293	.329	-8	-8	100	94	-2.9	0	-1	-0.8
1959	Phi-N	0	0	—	7	0	0	0	0	10	16	14.4	2	0	0.0	4	3.6	4.50	89	.400	.405	-1	-1	102	175	0.0	0	0	0.0
1960	Phi-N	0	0	—	4	2	0	0	0	4	13	29.3	3	6	13.5	4	9.0	18.00	23	.542	.613	-6	-6	110	130	0.0	0	1	-0.4
	StL-N	7	4	.636	23	17	3	1	0	152	149	8.8	11	31	1.8	63	3.7	2.66	152	.257	.292	19	24	108	120	1.0	1	0	2.8
	Yr	7	4	.636	27	19	3	1	0	156	162	9.3	14	37	2.1	67	3.9	3.06	133	.269	.307	12	17	108	**120**	1.0	0	1	2.4
1961	StL-N	9	10	.474	30	29	6	2	0	196	203	9.3	14	64	2.9	99	4.5	3.12	**145**	.269	.323	20	**31**	113	**123**	-0.8	6	-0	**3.9**
1962	StL-N	10	10	.500	31	22	9	4	0	154	167	9.8	18	32	1.9	74	4.3	3.51	120	.280	.315	7	12	107	118	-0.3	0	-1	1.2
1963	StL-N	15	9	.625	32	32	11	6	0	233	209	8.1	13	48	1.9	127	4.9	2.47	140	.239	.279	21	26	106	106	1.7	1	-4	2.7
1964	StL-N	18	9	.667	34	34	12	3	0	244	233	8.6	24	49	1.8	104	3.8	3.43	115	.249	.285	3	14	111	94	3.4	-4	-1	1.1
1965	StL-N	9	15	.375	34	32	5	0	0	203	229	10.2	19	54	2.4	96	4.3	4.08	92	.283	.326	-12	-7	106	105	-3.2	-5	-2	-1.3
1966	StL-N	1	1	.500	10	5	1	0	0	33	35	9.5	3	14	3.8	14	3.8	4.64	78	.269	.333	-4	-4	100	89	0.0	0	-1	-0.3
	Chi-N	4	7	.364	19	10	3	1	0	77	79	9.2	7	21	2.5	24	2.8	4.09	90	.268	.314	-4	-3	103	92	0.0	-0	2	-0.2
	Yr	5	8	.385	29	15	4	1	0	110	114	9.3	10	35	2.9	38	3.1	4.25	86	.268	.320	-8	-7	102	92	0.0	0	1	-0.5
1967	Chi-N	3	7	.300	17	14	3	0	0	82	100	11.0	10	23	2.5	31	3.4	4.94	68	.300	.338	-14	-14	100	101	-2.2	-1	-0	-1.5
	Cal-A	2	1	.667	14	4	1	1	1	35	44	11.3	1	9	2.3	13	3.3	2.57	120	.321	.369	3	2	96	191	0.5	1	-1	0.2
Total	20	193	183	.513	569	461	163	36	5	3348	3313	8.9	255	1063	2.9	1697	4.6	3.54	110	.259	.313	109	137	102	102	2.3	2	-20	13.9
■ **PAT SIMMONS**	Simmons, Patrick Clement (born Patrick Clement Simoni) b: 11/29/08, Watervliet, N.Y. d: 7/3/68, Albany, N.Y. BR/TR, 5'11", 172 lbs. Deb: 4/18/28																												
1928	Bos-A	0	2	.000	31	3	0	0	1	69	69	9.0	4	38	5.0	16	2.1	4.04	101	.271	.361	0	0	101	110	-0.9	-1	-0	0.0
1929	Bos-A	0	0	—	2	0	0	0	1	7	6	7.7	0	3	3.9	2	2.6	0.00	—	.231	.310	3	3	105	0	0.0	-0	0	0.3
Total	2	0	2	.000	33	3	0	0	2	76	75	8.9	4	41	4.9	18	2.1	3.67	113	.267	.357	3	4	102	100	-0.9	-1	-0	0.3
■ **JOE SIMPSON**	Simpson, Joe Allen b: 12/31/51, Purcell, Okla. BL/TL, 6'3", 175 lbs. Deb: 9/02/75																												
1983	KC-A	0	0	—	2	0	0	0	0	3	4	12.0	0	2	6.0	1	3.0	3.00	139	.308	.400	0	0	102	176	0.0	1	0	0.0
■ **STEVE SIMPSON**	Simpson, Steven Edward b: 8/30/48, St.Joseph, Mo. BR/TR, 6'3", 200 lbs. Deb: 9/10/72																												
1972	SD-N	0	2	.000	9	0	0	0	2	11	10	8.2	0	8	6.5	9	7.4	4.91	64	.238	.353	-2	-2	91	71	-0.9	0	0	-0.1
■ **DUKE SIMPSON**	Simpson, Thomas Leo b: 9/15/27, Columbus, Ohio BR/TR, 6'1.5", 190 lbs. Deb: 5/06/53																												
1953	Chi-N	1	2	.333	30	1	0	0	0	45	60	12.0	8	25	5.0	21	4.2	8.00	57	.314	.387	-19	-17	106	83	-0.2	0	-0	-1.5
■ **WAYNE SIMPSON**	Simpson, Wayne Kirby b: 12/2/48, Los Angeles, Cal. BR/TR, 6'3", 220 lbs. Deb: 4/09/70																												
1970	Cin-N	14	3	.824	26	26	10	2	0	176	125	**6.4**	15	81	4.1	119	6.1	3.02	139	**.198**	.295	20	23	103	91	4.7	-4	2	2.2
1971	Cin-N	4	7	.364	22	21	1	0	0	117	106	8.2	9	77	5.9	61	4.7	4.77	70	.244	.352	-17	-19	96	87	-1.4	-2	2	-1.8
1972	Cin-N	8	5	.615	24	22	1	0	0	130	124	8.6	17	49	3.4	70	4.8	4.15	76	.247	.315	-10	-14	91	91	0.0	-3	-3	-2.0
1973	KC-A	3	4	.429	16	10	1	0	0	60	66	9.9	1	35	5.3	29	4.3	5.70	73	.284	.374	-13	-10	109	78	-0.7	0	-0	-0.9
1975	Phi-N	1	0	1.000	7	5	0	0	0	31	31	9.0	1	11	3.2	19	5.5	3.19	115	.263	.326	2	2	101	107	0.5	0	0	0.3
1977	Cal-A	6	12	.333	27	23	0	0	0	122	154	11.4	14	62	4.6	55	4.1	5.83	66	.308	.387	-24	-27	95	100	-2.5	0	-1	-2.6
Total	6	36	31	.537	122	107	13	2	0	636	606	8.6	57	315	4.5	353	5.0	4.37	85	.251	.338	-41	-46	98	92	0.6	-8	0	-4.8
■ **PETE SIMS**	Sims, Clarence b: 5/24/1891, Crown City, Ohio d: 12/2/68, Dallas, Tex. BR/TR, 5'11.5", 165 lbs. Deb: 9/16/15																												
1915	StL-A	1	0	1.000	3	2	0	0	0	8	6	6.8	0	6	6.8	4	4.5	4.50	65	.214	.353	-1	-1	99	66	0.5	1	-0	0.0
■ **BERT SINCOCK**	Sincock, Herbert Sylvester b: 9/8/1887, Barkerville, B.C. Canada d: 8/1/46, Houghton, Mich. 5'10.5", 165 lbs. Deb: 6/25/08																												
1908	Cin-N	0	0	—	1	0	0	0	0	5	3	5.4	0	0	0.0	1	1.8	3.60	68	.196	.196	-1	-1	104	5	0.0	-0	0	0.0
■ **BILL SINGER**	Singer, William Robert "The Singer Throwing Machine" b: 4/24/44, Los Angeles, Cal. BR/TR, 6'4", 184 lbs. Deb: 9/24/64																												
1964	LA-N	0	1	.000	2	2	0	0	0	14	11	7.1	0	12	7.7	3	1.9	3.21	101	.216	.359	1	0	91	108	-0.4	0	0	0.0
1965	LA-N	0	0	—	2	0	0	0	0	1	2	18.0	0	2	18.0	1	9.0	0.00	—	.400	.571	0	0	90	0	0.0	0	0	0.0
1966	LA-N	0	0	—	3	0	0	0	0	4	4	9.0	0	2	4.5	4	9.0	0.00	—	.286	.375	2	2	95	0	0.0	0	0	0.2
1967	LA-N	12	8	.600	32	29	7	3	0	204	185	8.2	5	61	2.7	169	7.5	2.65	114	.239	.297	17	8	89	102	3.0	-2	1	0.6
1968	LA-N	13	17	.433	37	36	12	6	0	256	227	8.0	14	78	2.7	227	**8.0**	2.88	94	.237	.292	3	-5	91	97	-1.3	3	0	-0.1
1969	LA-N	20	12	.625	41	40	16	2	1	316	244	6.9	22	74	2.1	247	7.0	2.34	150	.210	.260	44	41	97	90	4.0	-4	-2	3.8
1970	LA-N	8	5	.615	16	16	5	3	0	106	79	6.7	10	32	2.7	93	7.9	3.14	115	.203	.264	11	5	89	75	1.1	-0	-0	0.4
1971	LA-N	10	17	.370	31	31	8	1	0	203	195	8.6	19	71	3.1	144	6.4	4.17	81	.252	.313	-16	-18	98	86	-4.9	-1	-1	-1.9
1972	LA-N	6	16	.273	26	25	4	3	0	169	148	7.9	8	60	3.2	101	5.4	3.67	87	.237	.301	-4	-9	93	80	-5.8	-2	1	-1.1
1973	Cal-A	20	14	.588	40	40	19	2	0	316	280	8.0	15	130	3.7	241	6.9	3.22	114	.235	.311	21	16	96	91	4.0	0	-2	1.5
1974	Cal-A	7	4	.636	14	14	8	0	0	109	102	8.4	3	43	3.6	77	6.4	2.97	113	.250	.316	8	5	93	104	2.1	0	0	0.5

YEAR	TM/L	W	L	PCT	G	GS	CG	SHO	SV	IP	H	H/G	HR	BB	BB/G	SO	SO/G	ERA	/A	OAVG	OOBP	PR	/A	PF	CPI	WAT	PB	PD	TPI
1975	Cal-A	7	15	.318	29	27	8	0	1	179	171	8.6	18	81	4.1	78	3.9	4.98	73	.257	.335	-24	-27	96	83	-3.4	0	-1	-2.6
1976	Tex-A	4	1	.800	10	10	2	1	0	65	56	7.8	4	27	3.7	34	4.7	3.46	104	.239	.321	0	1	103	100	1.6	0	-0	0.1
	Min-A	9	9	.500	26	26	5	3	0	172	177	9.3	9	69	3.6	63	3.3	3.77	91	.274	.342	-5	-6	98	108	-0.4	0	-2	-0.7
	Yr	13	10	.565	36	36	7	4	0	237	233	8.8	13	96	3.6	97	3.7	3.68	95	.262	.331	-4	-5	99	108	1.2	0	-2	-0.6
1977	Tor-A	2	8	.200	13	12	0	0	0	60	71	10.7	5	39	5.8	33	5.0	6.75	63	.296	.389	-18	-17	105	82	-2.0	0	0	-1.5
Total	14	118	127	.482	322	308	94	24	2	2174	1952	8.1	132	781	3.2	1515	6.3	3.39	100	.240	.306	41	-3	95	92	-2.4	-7	-6	-0.8
■ **ELMER SINGLETON**	Singleton, Bert Elmer "Smoky" b: 6/26/18, Ogden, Utah BR/TR, 6'2", 174 lbs. Deb: 8/20/45																												
1945	Bos-N	1	4	.200	7	5	1	0	0	37	35	8.5	1	14	3.4	14	3.4	4.86	88	.248	.316	-4	-2	113	66	-1.3	-2	0	-0.3
1946	Bos-N	0	1	.000	15	2	0	0	1	34	27	7.1	3	21	5.6	17	4.5	3.71	86	.221	.336	-1	-2	94	96	-0.4	-1	0	-0.2
1947	Pit-N	2	2	.500	36	3	0	0	1	67	70	9.4	9	39	5.2	24	3.2	6.31	66	.267	.359	-17	-16	102	79	0.3	1	0	-1.3
1948	Pit-N	4	6	.400	38	5	1	0	2	92	90	8.8	11	40	3.9	53	5.2	4.99	83	.253	.324	-11	-9	104	83	-1.3	-2	1	-0.8
1950	Was-A	1	2	.333	21	1	0	0	0	36	39	9.8	4	17	4.3	19	4.8	5.25	88	.291	.357	-3	-3	101	101	-0.3	1	1	0.0
1957	Chi-N	0	1	.000	5	2	0	0	0	13	20	13.8	3	2	1.4	6	4.2	6.92	55	.333	.355	-4	-5	98	92	-0.4	-0	0	-0.3
1958	Chi-N	1	0	1.000	2	0	0	0	0	5	1	1.8	0	1	1.8	2	3.6	0.00	—	.071	.133	2	2	101	0	0.5	-0	0	0.2
1959	Chi-N	2	1	.667	21	1	0	0	0	43	40	8.4	2	12	2.5	25	5.2	2.72	143	.252	.289	6	6	99	112	0.5	-1	1	0.6
Total	8	11	17	.393	145	19	2	0	4	327	322	8.9	33	146	4.0	160	4.4	4.84	84	.258	.331	-32	-28	102	86	-2.4	-3	3	-2.1
■ **JOHN SINGLETON**	Singleton, John Edward "Sheriff" b: 11/27/1896, Gallipolis, Ohio d: 10/23/37, Dayton, Ohio BR/TR, 5'11", 171 lbs. Deb: 6/08/22																												
1922	Phi-N	1	10	.091	22	9	3	1	0	93	127	12.3	6	38	3.7	27	2.6	5.90	81	.346	.394	-19	-12	117	104	-4.1	-3	-1	-1.2
■ **DOUG SISK**	Sisk, Douglas Randall b: 9/26/57, Benton, Wash. BR/TR, 6'2", 210 lbs. Deb: 9/06/82																												
1982	NY-N	0	1	.000	8	0	0	0	1	9	5	5.0	1	4	4.0	4	4.0	1.00	361	.172	.294	3	3	100	270	-0.4	0	0	0.3
1983	NY-N	5	4	.556	67	0	0	0	11	104	88	7.6	1	59	5.1	33	2.9	2.25	161	.235	.338	16	16	100	145	1.1	1	-1	1.7
1984	NY-N	1	3	.250	50	0	0	0	15	78	57	6.6	1	54	6.2	32	3.7	2.08	173	.215	.347	13	13	100	160	-1.0	-0	0	1.4
1985	NY-N	4	5	.444	42	0	0	0	2	73	86	10.6	3	40	4.9	26	3.2	5.30	65	.291	.375	-14	-15	95	91	-1.1	-1	1	-1.5
1986	NY-N	4	2	.667	41	0	0	0	1	71	77	9.8	0	31	3.9	31	3.9	3.04	114	.282	.362	5	3	93	136	0.0	-0	-1	0.2
1987	NY-N	3	1	.750	55	0	0	0	3	78	83	9.6	5	22	2.5	37	4.3	3.46	114	.270	.319	5	4	97	109	0.9	-0	1	0.5
1988	Bal-A	3	3	.500	52	0	0	0	0	94	109	10.4	3	45	4.3	26	2.5	3.73	104	.306	.380	3	1	97	137	0.8	0	0	0.2
Total	7	20	19	.513	315	0	0	0	33	507	505	9.0	14	255	4.5	189	3.4	3.21	114	.266	.353	31	26	97	133	0.3	-1	1	2.8
■ **TOMMIE SISK**	Sisk, Tommie Wayne b: 4/12/42, Ardmore, Okla. BR/TR, 6'3", 195 lbs. Deb: 7/19/62																												
1962	Pit-N	0	2	.000	5	3	1	0	0	18	18	9.0	1	8	4.0	6	3.0	4.00	100	.257	.342	-0	-0	101	94	-0.9	-0	-0	0.0
1963	Pit-N	1	3	.250	57	4	1	0	1	108	85	7.1	6	45	3.8	73	6.1	2.92	112	.222	.300	4	4	99	97	-0.8	-0	1	0.5
1964	Pit-N	1	4	.200	42	1	0	0	0	61	91	13.4	4	29	4.3	35	5.2	6.20	57	.364	.418	-18	-18	101	114	-1.4	-1	2	-1.7
1965	Pit-N	7	3	.700	38	12	1	1	0	111	103	8.4	6	50	4.1	66	5.4	3.41	102	.248	.323	2	1	98	104	1.7	-2	-1	-0.1
1966	Pit-N	10	5	.667	34	23	4	1	1	150	146	8.8	14	52	3.1	60	3.6	4.14	86	.256	.320	-9	-10	99	90	1.8	-1	0	-1.0
1967	Pit-N	13	13	.500	37	31	11	2	1	208	196	8.5	6	78	3.4	85	3.7	3.33	102	.253	.318	1	1	100	98	0.0	-2	1	0.0
1968	Pit-N	5	5	.500	33	11	0	0	1	96	101	9.5	3	35	3.3	41	3.8	3.28	91	.282	.344	-3	-3	100	121	0.1	-1	0	-0.3
1969	SD-N	2	13	.133	53	13	1	0	6	143	160	10.1	11	48	3.0	59	3.7	4.78	75	.285	.333	-19	-19	100	89	-4.5	0	0	-1.8
1970	Chi-A	1	1	.500	17	1	0	0	0	33	37	10.1	6	13	3.5	16	4.4	5.45	73	.276	.333	-6	-5	108	90	0.2	0	1	-0.4
Total	9	40	49	.449	316	99	19	4	10	928	937	9.1	57	358	3.5	441	4.3	3.92	88	.266	.330	-48	-49	100	99	-3.8	-7	3	-4.8
■ **DAVE SISLER**	Sisler, David Michael b: 10/16/31, St.Louis, Mo. BR/TR, 6'4", 200 lbs. Deb: 4/21/56																												
1956	Bos-A	9	8	.529	39	14	3	0	3	142	120	7.6	13	72	4.6	93	5.9	4.63	92	.227	.321	-7	-6	102	75	-0.2	-2	0	-0.7
1957	Bos-A	7	8	.467	22	19	5	0	1	122	135	10.0	15	61	4.5	55	4.1	4.72	87	.280	.357	-13	-8	109	105	-0.9	-1	1	-0.6
1958	Bos-A	8	9	.471	30	25	4	1	0	149	157	9.5	22	79	4.8	71	4.3	4.95	80	.276	.356	-20	-17	105	104	-0.7	1	-1	-1.6
1959	Bos-A	0	0	—	3	0	0	0	0	7	9	11.6	3	1	1.3	3	3.9	6.43	63	.310	.333	-2	-2	105	112	0.0	0	-0	-0.1
	Det-A	1	3	.250	32	0	0	0	7	52	46	8.0	4	36	6.2	29	5.0	3.98	108	.242	.358	-1	2	111	109	-0.9	-0	-1	0.1
	Yr	1	3	.250	35	0	0	0	7	59	55	8.4	7	37	5.6	32	4.9	4.27	100	.251	.355	-3	-0	110	109	-0.9	0	-1	0.0
1960	Det-A	7	5	.583	41	0	0	0	6	80	56	6.3	3	45	5.1	47	5.3	2.47	159	.199	.308	12	13	102	103	1.4	-0	1	1.4
1961	Was-A	2	8	.200	45	1	0	0	11	60	55	8.3	6	48	7.2	30	4.5	4.20	93	.251	.384	-1	-2	97	122	-2.3	0	0	0.0
1962	Cin-N	4	3	.571	35	0	0	0	1	44	44	9.0	4	26	5.3	27	5.5	3.89	102	.270	.357	0	0	100	122	-0.1	0	-0	0.0
Total	7	38	44	.463	247	59	12	1	29	656	622	8.5	70	368	5.0	355	4.9	4.34	94	.253	.346	-31	-19	104	101	-3.7	-2	1	-1.5
■ **GEORGE SISLER**	Sisler, George Harold "Georgeous George" b: 3/24/1893, Manchester, Ohio d: 3/26/73, Richmond Heights, Mo. BL/TL, 5'11", 170 lbs. Deb: 6/28/15 MCH																												
1915	StL-A	4	4	.500	15	8	6	0	0	70	62	8.0	0	38	4.9	41	5.3	2.83	103	.247	.355	1	1	99	118	0.6	3	0	0.1
1916	StL-A	1	2	.333	3	3	3	1	0	27	18	6.0	0	6	2.0	12	4.0	1.00	266	.198	.255	5	5	94	125	-0.4	1	1	0.6
1918	StL-A	0	0	—	2	1	0	0	1	8	10	11.3	0	4	4.5	4	4.5	4.50	61	.286	.366	-2	-2	100	92	0.0	1	0	-0.1
1920	StL-A	0	0	—	1	0	0	0	1	1	0	0.0	0	0	0.0	2	18.0	0.00	—	.000	.000	0	0	111	0	0.0	1	0	0.0
1925	StL-A	0	0	—	1	0	0	0	0	2	1	4.5	0	1	4.5	1	4.5	0.00	—	.167	.286	1	1	108	0	0.0	0	0	0.1
1926	StL-A	0	0	—	1	0	0	0	1	2	0	0.0	0	2	9.0	3	13.5	0.00	—	.000	.286	1	1	103	0	0.0	0	0	0.1
1928	Bos-N	0	0	—	1	0	0	0	0	1	0	0.0	0	1	9.0	0	0.0	0.00	—	.000	.333	0	0	101	0	0.0	0	0	0.0
Total	7	5	6	.455	24	12	9	1	3	111	91	7.4	0	52	4.2	63	5.1	2.35	124	.231	.329	8	7	98	111	0.2	7	1	0.8
■ **CARL SITTON**	Sitton, Carl Vetter b: 9/22/1882, Pendleton, S.C. d: 9/11/31, Valdosta, Ga. TR, 5'10.5", 170 lbs. Deb: 4/24/09																												
1909	Cle-A	3	2	.600	14	5	3	0	0	50	50	9.0	1	16	2.9	16	2.9	2.88	89	.263	.327	-2	-2	103	103	0.7	0	-1	-0.2
■ **PETE SIVESS**	Sivess, Peter b: 9/23/13, South River, N.J. BR/TR, 6'3.5", 195 lbs. Deb: 6/13/36																												
1936	Phi-N	3	4	.429	17	6	2	0	0	65	84	11.6	6	36	5.0	22	3.0	4.57	97	.310	.385	-4	-1	111	128	0.4	-2	-1	-0.3
1937	Phi-N	1	1	.500	6	2	1	0	0	23	30	11.7	5	11	4.3	4	1.6	7.04	61	.330	.398	-8	-7	111	101	0.2	-1	-1	-0.7
1938	Phi-N	3	6	.333	39	8	2	0	3	116	143	11.1	12	69	5.4	32	2.5	5.51	73	.306	.389	-22	-19	106	108	0.2	-1	-1	-1.9
Total	3	7	11	.389	62	16	5	0	3	204	257	11.3	23	116	5.1	58	2.6	5.38	78	.310	.389	-34	-27	108	113	0.8	-4	-3	-2.9
■ **JIM SIWY**	Siwy, James b: 9/20/58, Central Falls, R.I BR/TR, 6'4", 200 lbs. Deb: 8/20/82																												
1982	Chi-A	0	0	—	2	1	0	0	0	7	10	12.9	1	5	6.4	3	3.9	10.29	38	.385	.469	-5	-5	97	84	0.0	0	-0	-0.4
1984	Chi-A	0	0	—	1	0	0	0	0	4	3	6.8	0	2	4.5	1	2.3	2.25	197	.231	.294	1	1	111	137	0.0	0	0	0.1
Total	2	0	0	—	3	1	0	0	0	11	13	10.6	1	7	5.7	4	3.3	7.36	56	.333	.408	-4	-4	102	103	0.0	0	-0	-0.3
■ **DAVE SKAUGSTAD**	Skaugstad, David Wendell b: 1/10/40, Algona, Iowa BL/TL, 6'1", 179 lbs. Deb: 9/25/57																												
1957	Cin-N	0	0	—	2	0	0	0	0	6	4	6.0	0	6	9.0	4	6.0	1.50	274	.190	.370	2	2	106	215	0.0	0	0	0.2
■ **DAVE SKEELS**	Skeels, David b: 12/29/1892, Washington State d: 12/2/26, Spokane, Wash. BL/TR, 6'1", 187 lbs. Deb: 9/14/10																												
1910	Det-A	0	0	—	1	1	0	0	0	6	9	13.5	0	4	6.0	2	3.0	12.00	21	.333	.438	-6	-6	100	53	0.0	-0	0	-0.4
■ **CRAIG SKOK**	Skok, Craig Richard b: 9/1/47, Dobbs Ferry, N.Y. BR/TL, 6', 190 lbs. Deb: 5/04/73																												
1973	Bos-A	0	1	.000	11	0	0	0	1	29	35	10.9	2	11	3.4	22	6.8	6.21	65	.304	.357	-8	-7	105	77	-0.4	0	-0	-0.6
1976	Tex-A	0	1	.000	9	0	0	0	0	5	13	23.4	2	3	5.4	5	9.0	12.60	29	.481	.533	-5	-5	103	117	-0.4	0	0	-0.4
1978	Atl-N	3	2	.600	43	0	0	0	2	62	64	9.3	8	27	3.9	28	4.1	4.35	94	.266	.333	-5	-2	114	101	0.8	0	-0	-0.1
1979	Atl-N	1	3	.250	44	0	0	0	2	54	58	9.7	7	17	2.8	30	5.0	4.00	103	.282	.336	-2	1	110	116	-0.7	-0	0	0.1
Total	4	4	7	.364	107	0	0	0	5	150	170	10.2	19	58	3.5	85	5.1	4.86	84	.289	.348	-20	-13	110	103	-0.7	0	-0	-1.0
■ **JOHN SKOPEC**	Skopec, John S. "Buckshot" b: 5/8/1880, Chicago, Ill. d: 10/12/12, Chicago.Ill. BR/TL, 5'10", 190 lbs. Deb: 4/25/01																												
1901	Chi-A	6	3	.667	9	9	6	0	0	68	62	8.2	1	45	6.0	24	3.2	3.18	111	.262	.380	4	3	96	115	0.7	3	3	0.5
1903	Det-A	2	2	.500	6	5	3	0	0	39	46	10.6	0	13	3.0	14	3.2	3.46	82	.317	.373	-2	-3	96	119	0.1	-0	0	-0.2
Total	2	8	5	.615	15	14	9	0	0	107	108	9.1	1	58	4.9	38	3.2	3.28	100	.283	.377	1	-0	96	116	0.8	3	3	0.3
■ **JOHN SLAGLE**	Slagle, John A. b: Lawrence, Ind. BL/TR, Deb: 4/30/1891																												
1891	CM-a	0	0	—	1	0	0	0	1	1	3	27.0	0	1	9.0	1	9.0	0.00	—	.532	.602	0	0	113	0	0.0	-0	0	0.0
■ **ROGER SLAGLE**	Slagle, Roger Lee b: 11/4/53, Wichita, Kan. BB/TR, 6'3", 190 lbs. Deb: 9/07/79																												
1979	NY-A	0	0	—	1	0	0	0	0	2	0	0.0	0	0	0.0	2	9.0	0.00	—	.000	.000	1	1	95	0	0.0	0	0	0.1

YEAR TM/L	W	L	PCT	G	GS	CG	SHO	SV	IP	H	H/G	HR	BB	BB/G	SO	SO/G	ERA	/A	OAVG	OOBP	PR	/A	PF	CPI	WAT	PB	PD	TPI
■ WALT SLAGLE	Slagle, Walter Jennings b: 12/15/1878, Kenton, Ohio d: 6/17/74, San Gabriel, Cal. BB/TR, 6', 165 lbs. Deb: 5/04/10																											
1910 Cin-N	0	0	—	1	0	0	0	0	1	0	0.0	0	3	27.0	0	0.0	9.00	34	.000	.571	-1	-1	102	85	0.0	0	0	0.0
■ CY SLAPNICKA	Slapnicka, Cyril Charles b: 3/23/1886, Cedar Rapids, Iowa d: 10/20/79, Cedar Rapids, Iowa BB/TR, 5'10", 165 lbs. Deb: 9/26/11																											
1911 Chi-N	0	2	.000	3	2	1	0	0	24	21	7.9	0	7	2.6	10	3.8	3.38	95	.236	.313	0	-0	94	75	-0.9	0	1	0.0
1918 Pit-N	1	4	.200	7	6	4	0	1	49	50	9.2	2	22	4.0	3	0.6	4.78	61	.269	.350	-11	-10	105	84	-1.5	-1	-0	-1.1
Total 2	1	6	.143	10	8	5	0	1	73	71	8.8	2	29	3.6	13	1.6	4.32	70	.258	.339	-11	-11	101	81	-2.4	-1	1	-1.1
■ JOHN SLAPPEY	Slappey, John Henry b: 8/8/1898, Albany, Ga. d: 6/10/57, Marietta, Ga. BL/TL, 6'4", 170 lbs. Deb: 8/23/20																											
1920 Phi-A	0	1	.000	3	1	0	0	0	6	15	22.5	0	4	6.0	1	1.5	7.50	50	.441	.500	-2	-3	99	139	-0.4	1	-0	-0.1
■ JIM SLATON	Slaton, James Michael b: 6/19/50, Long Beach, Cal. BR/TR, 6', 185 lbs. Deb: 4/14/71																											
1971 Mil-A	10	8	.556	26	23	5	4	0	148	140	8.5	16	71	4.3	63	3.8	3.77	96	.253	.336	-5	-3	104	107	2.2	-1	-2	-0.6
1972 Mil-A	1	6	.143	9	8	0	0	0	44	50	10.2	3	21	4.3	17	3.5	5.52	54	.287	.356	-12	-12	97	84	-2.2	-1	1	-1.2
1973 Mil-A	13	15	.464	38	38	13	3	0	276	266	8.7	30	99	3.2	134	4.4	3.72	99	.251	.313	3	-1	96	97	0.2	0	-3	-0.4
1974 Mil-A	13	16	.448	40	35	10	3	0	250	255	9.2	22	102	3.7	126	4.5	3.92	95	.268	.336	-8	-6	103	104	-0.7	0	0	-0.5
1975 Mil-A	11	18	.379	37	33	10	3	0	217	238	9.9	28	90	3.7	119	4.9	4.52	85	.276	.340	-18	-16	101	102	-1.6	0	1	-1.5
1976 Mil-A	14	15	.483	38	38	12	2	0	293	287	8.8	14	94	2.9	138	4.2	3.44	103	.259	.313	3	3	100	98	2.1	0	-0	0.2
1977 Mil-A	10	14	.417	32	31	7	1	0	221	223	9.1	25	77	3.1	104	4.2	3.58	110	.266	.330	12	9	97	**118**	0.1	0	0	0.8
1978 Det-A	17	11	.607	35	34	11	2	0	234	235	9.0	27	85	3.3	92	3.5	4.12	98	.263	.327	-9	-2	107	99	2.7	0	-1	-0.2
1979 Mil-A	15	9	.625	32	31	12	3	0	213	229	9.7	15	54	2.3	80	3.4	3.63	116	.278	.319	14	13	99	106	1.2	0	1	1.4
1980 Mil-A	1	1	.500	3	3	0	0	0	16	17	9.6	3	5	2.8	4	2.3	4.50	84	.270	.324	-1	-1	93	102	0.0	0	0	0.0
1981 Mil-A	5	7	.417	24	21	0	0	0	117	120	9.2	10	50	3.8	47	3.6	4.38	80	.273	.344	-9	-12	95	100	-1.6	0	-0	-1.1
1982 Mil-A	10	6	.625	39	7	0	0	6	118	117	8.9	14	41	3.1	59	4.5	3.28	115	.264	.322	11	6	92	127	0.8	0	-0	0.6
1983 Mil-A	14	6	.700	46	0	0	0	5	112	112	9.0	12	56	4.5	38	3.1	4.34	85	.272	.349	-3	-8	91	112	3.8	0	-0	-0.7
1984 Cal-A	7	10	.412	32	22	5	1	0	163	192	10.6	22	56	3.1	67	3.7	4.97	82	.295	.346	-18	-17	101	102	-1.5	0	0	-1.5
1985 Cal-A	6	10	.375	29	24	1	0	1	148	162	9.9	22	63	3.8	60	3.6	4.38	95	.284	.352	-4	-3	101	120	-2.7	0	0	-0.3
1986 Cal-A	4	6	.400	14	12	0	0	0	73	84	10.4	9	29	3.6	31	3.8	5.67	70	.295	.356	-12	-14	95	92	-1.4	0	1	-1.1
Det-A	0	0	—	22	0	0	0	2	40	46	10.3	5	11	2.5	12	2.7	4.05	98	.287	.333	1	-0	95	115	0.0	0	0	0.0
Yr	4	6	.400	36	12	0	0	2	113	130	10.4	14	40	3.2	43	3.4	5.10	78	.287	.344	-11	-14	95	115	-1.4	0	1	-1.1
Total 16	151	158	.489	496	360	86	22	14	2683	2773	9.3	277	1004	3.4	1191	4.0	4.03	95	.270	.332	-55	-63	99	105	1.4	-2	-4	-6.1
■ PHIL SLATTERY	Slattery, Philip Ryan b: 2/25/1893, Harper, Iowa d: 3/2/68, Long Beach, Cal. BR/TL, 5'11", 160 lbs. Deb: 9/16/15																											
1915 Pit-N	0	0	—	3	0	0	0	0	8	5	5.6	0	1	1.1	1	1.1	0.00	—	.185	.258	2	2	98	0	0.0	-0	-0	0.2
■ BARNEY SLAUGHTER	Slaughter, Byron Atkins b: 10/6/1884, Smyrna, Del. d: 5/17/61, Philadelphia, Pa. BR/TR, 5'11.5", 165 lbs. Deb: 8/09/10																											
1910 Phi-N	0	1	.000	8	1	0	0	1	18	21	10.5	0	11	5.5	7	3.5	5.50	52	.318	.416	-5	-5	95	93	-0.4	0	0	-0.4
■ STERLING SLAUGHTER	Slaughter, Sterling Feore b: 11/18/41, Danville, Ill. BR/TR, 5'11", 165 lbs. Deb: 4/19/64																											
1964 Chi-N	2	4	.333	20	6	1	0	0	52	64	11.1	8	32	5.5	32	5.5	5.71	66	.305	.389	-13	-11	106	109	-0.8	-0	-1	-1.2
■ BILL SLAYBACK	Slayback, William Grover b: 2/21/48, Hollywood, Cal. BR/TR, 6'4", 200 lbs. Deb: 6/26/72																											
1972 Det-A	5	6	.455	23	13	3	1	0	82	74	8.1	4	25	2.7	65	7.1	3.18	108	.239	.294	-1	2	112	85	-0.9	-0	1	0.3
1973 Det-A	0	0	—	3	0	0	0	0	2	5	22.5	0	0	0.0	1	4.5	4.50	86	.417	.462	-0	-0	101	203	0.0	0	0	0.0
1974 Det-A	1	3	.250	16	4	0	0	0	55	57	9.3	1	26	4.3	23	3.8	4.75	82	.273	.350	-7	-5	108	83	-0.8	0	-0	-0.5
Total 3	6	9	.400	42	17	3	1	0	139	136	8.8	5	51	3.3	89	5.8	3.82	95	.256	.321	-8	-3	110	86	-1.7	-0	0	-0.2
■ STEVE SLAYTON	Slayton, Foster Herbert b: 4/26/02, Barre, Vt. d: 12/20/84, Manchester, N.H. BR/TR, 6', 163 lbs. Deb: 7/21/28																											
1928 Bos-A	0	0	—	3	0	0	0	0	7	6	7.7	0	3	3.9	2	2.6	3.86	106	.240	.310	0	0	101	74	0.0	-0	-0	0.0
■ LOU SLEATER	Sleater, Louis Mortimer b: 9/8/26, St.Louis, Mo. BL/TL, 5'10", 185 lbs. Deb: 4/25/50																											
1950 StL-A	0	0	—	1	0	0	0	0	1	0	0.0	0	0	0.0	1	9.0	0.00	—	.000	.000	1	1	111	0	0.0	0	0	0.1
1951 StL-A	1	9	.100	20	8	4	0	1	81	88	9.8	7	53	5.9	33	3.7	5.11	88	.271	.380	-9	-5	109	99	-3.5	0	-1	-0.5
1952 StL-A	0	1	.000	4	2	0	0	0	9	9	9.0	1	5	5.0	1	1.0	7.00	52	.265	.350	-3	-3	100	66	-0.4	-0	0	-0.3
Was-A	4	2	.667	14	9	3	1	0	57	56	8.8	4	30	4.7	22	3.5	3.63	101	.260	.355	0	0	100	117	1.0	-2	-1	-0.2
Yr	4	3	.571	18	11	3	1	0	66	65	8.9	5	35	4.8	23	3.1	4.09	90	.261	.354	-3	-3	100	117	0.6	-0	-1	-0.5
1955 KC-A	1	1	.500	16	1	0	0	0	26	33	11.4	3	21	7.3	11	3.8	7.62	55	.324	.425	-11	-10	106	91	0.2	-1	-0	-0.9
1956 Mil-N	2	2	.500	25	1	0	0	0	46	42	8.2	6	27	5.3	32	6.3	3.13	116	.240	.330	3	3	96	129	-0.2	2	1	0.6
1957 Det-A	3	3	.500	41	0	0	0	2	69	61	8.0	9	28	3.7	43	5.6	3.78	107	.237	.304	0	2	107	97	0.0	3	-0	0.6
1958 Det-A	0	0	—	4	0	0	0	0	5	3	5.4	2	6	10.8	4	7.2	7.20	54	.158	.360	-2	-2	103	80	0.0	1	0	0.0
Bal-A	1	0	1.000	6	0	0	0	0	7	14	18.0	0	2	2.6	5	6.4	12.86	28	.438	.457	-7	-7	95	65	0.5	-1	0	-0.7
Yr	1	0	1.000	10	0	0	0	0	12	17	12.8	2	8	6.0	9	6.8	10.50	35	.333	.417	-9	-9	98	65	0.5	1	0	-0.7
Total 7	12	18	.400	131	21	7	1	5	301	306	9.1	32	172	5.1	152	4.5	4.69	86	.263	.356	-28	-22	104	103	-2.4	3	-1	-1.3
■ LEFTY SLOAT	Sloat, Dwain Clifford b: 12/1/18, Nokomis, Ill. BR/TL, 6', 168 lbs. Deb: 4/24/48																											
1948 Bro-N	0	1	.000	4	1	0	0	0	7	7	9.0	0	8	10.3	1	1.3	6.43	63	.280	.441	-2	-2	103	94	-0.4	-0	1	0.0
1949 Chi-N	0	0	—	5	1	0	0	0	9	14	14.0	0	3	3.0	3	3.0	7.00	56	.400	.405	-3	-3	97	101	0.0	0	0	-0.2
Total 2	0	1	.000	9	2	0	0	0	16	21	11.8	0	11	6.2	4	2.3	6.75	59	.350	.421	-5	-5	100	93	-0.4	-0	1	-0.2
■ WALT SMALLWOOD	Smallwood, Walter Clayton b: 4/24/1893, Dayton, Md. d: 4/29/67, Baltimore, Md. BR/TR, 6'2", 190 lbs. Deb: 9/19/17																											
1917 NY-A	0	0	—	2	0	0	0	0	2	1	4.5	0	1	4.5	1	4.5	0.00	—	.167	.286	1	1	107	0	0.0	0	0	0.1
1919 NY-A	0	0	—	6	0	0	0	0	22	20	8.2	1	9	3.7	6	2.5	4.91	68	.263	.356	-4	-4	104	76	0.0	-1	-0	-0.4
Total 2	0	0	—	8	0	0	0	0	24	21	7.9	1	10	3.8	7	2.6	4.50	74	.256	.351	-4	-3	104	69	0.0	-1	-0	-0.3
■ JOHN SMILEY	Smiley, John Patrick b: 3/17/65, Phoenixville, Pa. BL/TL, 6'4", 180 lbs. Deb: 9/01/86																											
1986 Pit-N	1	0	1.000	12	0	0	0	0	12	4	3.0	2	4	3.0	9	6.8	3.75	100	.105	.190	-0	-0	101	28	0.5	0	0	0.0
1987 Pit-N	5	5	.500	63	0	0	0	4	75	69	8.3	7	50	6.0	58	7.0	5.76	74	.244	.354	-14	-12	105	74	0.1	0	0	-1.1
1988 Pit-N	13	11	.542	34	32	5	1	0	205	185	8.1	15	46	2.0	129	5.7	3.25	103	.241	.280	5	2	97	91	0.3	-2	-0	0.0
Total 3	19	16	.543	109	32	5	1	4	292	258	8.0	24	100	3.1	196	6.0	3.91	92	.237	.298	-9	-10	99	84	0.9	-2	-0	-1.1
■ SMITH	Smith Deb:6/09/1884																											
1884 Bal-U	0	0	—	1	1	0	0	0	6	12	18.0	0	2	3.0	2	3.0	9.00	37	.420	.457	-4	-4	110	92	0.0	-0	0	-0.2
■ AL SMITH	Smith, Alfred John b: 10/12/07, Belleville, Ill. d: 4/28/77, Brownsville, Tex. BL/TL, 5'11", 180 lbs. Deb: 5/05/34																											
1934 NY-N	3	5	.375	30	5	0	0	5	67	70	9.4	2	21	2.8	27	3.6	4.30	90	.266	.315	-2	-3	95	80	-1.5	1	0	-0.2
1935 NY-N	10	8	.556	40	10	4	1	5	124	125	9.1	6	32	2.3	44	3.2	3.41	112	.263	.315	8	5	95	105	-0.6	-0	-0	0.4
1936 NY-N	14	13	.519	43	30	9	4	2	209	217	9.3	16	69	3.0	89	3.8	3.79	104	.274	.333	5	4	98	110	-2.0	-2	-1	0.1
1937 NY-N	5	4	.556	33	9	2	0	0	86	91	9.5	8	30	3.1	41	4.3	4.19	91	.275	.335	-3	-3	98	104	-0.4	-2	-1	-0.5
1938 Phi-N	1	4	.200	37	1	0	0	1	86	115	12.0	7	40	4.2	46	4.8	6.28	64	.320	.383	-24	-22	106	92	-0.8	-2	0	-2.2
1939 Phi-N	0	0	—	5	0	0	0	0	9	11	11.0	1	5	5.0	2	2.0	4.00	97	.314	.429	-0	-0	99	166	0.0	-0	0	0.0
1940 Cle-A	15	7	.682	31	24	11	1	2	183	187	9.2	12	55	2.7	46	2.3	3.44	117	.270	.326	19	12	92	117	3.0	7	2	1.9
1941 Cle-A	12	13	.480	29	27	13	2	0	207	204	8.9	12	75	3.3	76	3.3	3.83	109	.256	.317	7	8	101	94	-0.1	2	1	1.1
1942 Cle-A	10	15	.400	30	24	7	1	0	168	163	8.7	9	71	3.8	66	3.5	3.96	86	.251	.322	-6	-11	93	91	-2.5	3	-0	-0.8
1943 Cle-A	17	7	.708	29	27	14	3	1	208	186	8.0	7	72	3.1	72	3.1	2.55	116	.239	.299	17	9	90	110	4.9	4	-0	1.3
1944 Cle-A	7	13	.350	28	26	7	1	0	182	197	9.7	6	69	3.4	44	2.2	3.41	101	.280	.340	0	1	101	116	-2.7	-2	2	0.1
1945 Cle-A	5	12	.294	21	19	8	3	1	134	141	9.5	8	48	3.2	34	2.3	3.83	86	.275	.332	-7	-8	98	104	-3.7	4	2	-0.1
Total 12	99	101	.495	356	202	75	16	17	1663	1707	9.2	94	587	3.2	587	3.2	3.72	99	.267	.327	17	-8	96	105	-6.4	13	5	1.1
■ AL SMITH	Smith, Alfred Kendricks b: 12/13/03, Norristown, Pa. BR/TR, 6', 170 lbs. Deb: 6/18/26																											
1926 NY-N	0	0	—	1	0	0	0	0	2	4	18.0	0	2	9.0	0	0.0	9.00	42	.444	.545	-1	-1	98	118	0.0	0	0	0.0

YEAR TM/L	W	L	PCT	G	GS	CG	SHO	SV	IP	H	H/G	HR	BB	BB/G	SO	SO/G	ERA	/A	OAVG	OOBP	PR	/A	PF	CPI	WAT	PB	PD	TPI
■ **ART SMITH**	Smith, Arthur Laird b: 6/21/06, Boston, Mass. BR/TR, 6', 175 lbs. Deb: 6/09/32																											
1932 Chi-A	0	1	.000	3	2	0	0	0	7	17	21.9	1	4	5.1	1	1.3	11.57	35	.500	.538	-6	-6	91	115	-0.4	-0	1	-0.4
■ **BILLY SMITH**	Smith, Billy Lavern b: 9/13/54, La Marque, Tex. BR/TR, 6'7", 200 lbs. Deb: 6/09/81																											
1981 Hou-N	1	1	.500	10	1	0	0	1	21	20	8.6	3	3	1.3	3	1.3	3.00	101	.263	.284	1	0	87	125	0.0	-0	0	0.0
■ **BRYN SMITH**	Smith, Bryn Nelson b: 8/11/55, Marietta, Ga. BR/TR, 6'2", 200 lbs. Deb: 9/08/81																											
1981 Mon-N	1	0	1.000	7	0	0	0	0	13	14	9.7	1	3	2.1	9	6.2	2.77	123	.280	.321	1	1	98	140	0.5	-0	-0	0.0
1982 Mon-N	2	4	.333	47	1	0	0	3	79	81	9.2	5	23	2.6	50	5.7	4.22	89	.264	.310	-5	-4	104	82	-1.0	-0	0	-0.3
1983 Mon-N	6	11	.353	49	12	5	3	3	155	142	8.2	13	43	2.5	101	5.9	2.50	147	.248	.299	20	20	101	132	-2.7	0	0	2.2
1984 Mon-N	12	13	.480	28	28	4	2	0	179	178	8.9	15	51	2.6	101	5.1	3.32	99	.259	.309	5	-1	91	107	0.0	1	2	0.1
1985 Mon-N	18	5	.783	32	32	4	2	0	222	193	7.8	12	41	1.7	127	5.1	2.92	116	.232	.264	17	11	94	80	6.7	3	-1	1.4
1986 Mon-N	10	8	.556	30	30	1	0	0	187	182	8.8	15	63	3.0	105	5.1	3.95	93	.251	.311	-5	-6	98	88	1.4	1	3	-0.1
1987 Mon-N	10	9	.526	26	26	2	0	0	150	164	9.8	16	31	1.9	94	5.6	4.38	99	.274	.306	-5	-1	106	89	-0.6	-0	-0	0.0
1988 Mon-N	12	10	.545	32	32	1	0	0	198	179	8.1	15	32	**1.5**	122	5.5	3.00	121	.243	.279	10	14	105	99	1.1	-1	-1	1.2
Total 8	71	60	.542	251	161	17	7	6	1183	1133	8.6	92	287	2.2	709	5.4	3.37	108	.251	.295	38	34	99	97	5.4	4	3	4.5
■ **CHARLIE SMITH**	Smith, Charles Edwin b: 4/20/1880, Cleveland, Ohio d: 1/3/29, Wickliffe, Ohio BR/TR, 6'1", 185 lbs. Deb: 8/06/02																											
1902 Cle-A	2	1	.667	3	3	2	1	0	20	23	10.3	0	5	2.3	5	2.3	4.05	85	.314	.358	-1	-1	96	90	0.5	-0	0	0.0
1906 Was-A	9	16	.360	33	22	17	2	0	235	250	9.6	2	75	2.9	105	4.0	2.91	87	.298	.356	-6	-10	94	121	-0.2	-0	-3	-1.2
1907 Was-A	10	20	.333	36	31	21	3	0	259	254	8.8	0	51	1.8	119	4.1	2.61	92	.281	.319	-2	-6	94	99	0.2	-3	3	-0.3
1908 Was-A	9	13	.409	26	23	13	1	1	184	166	8.1	2	60	2.9	83	4.1	2.40	96	.247	.311	-0	-2	97	118	-0.8	-2	-1	-0.2
1909 Was-A	3	12	.200	23	15	7	1	0	146	140	8.6	4	37	2.3	72	4.4	3.27	73	.250	.303	-13	-14	96	76	-2.1	-1	0	-1.5
Bos-A	3	0	1.000	3	3	2	0	0	25	23	8.3	2	2	0.7	11	4.0	2.16	124	.237	.260	1	1	108	96	1.5	0	0	0.2
Yr	6	12	.333	26	18	9	1	0	171	163	8.6	6	39	2.1	83	4.4	3.11	78	.247	.290	-12	-13	98	96	-0.6	-1	0	-1.3
1910 Bos-A	11	6	.647	24	18	11	0	1	156	141	8.1	4	35	2.0	53	3.1	2.31	106	.248	.294	4	3	97	105	2.3	-2	-2	-0.1
1911 Bos-A	0	0	—	1	1	0	0	0	2	2	9.0	1	1	4.5	0	0.0	9.00	37	.250	.333	-1	-1	99	74	0.0	0	0	0.0
Chi-N	3	2	.600	7	5	3	1	0	38	31	7.3	0	7	1.7	11	2.6	1.42	225	.228	.271	8	7	94	127	0.0	-1	-1	0.6
1912 Chi-N	7	4	.636	20	5	1	0	1	94	92	8.8	2	31	3.0	47	4.5	4.21	83	.254	.318	-8	-8	102	65	0.4	1	1	-0.4
1913 Chi-N	7	9	.438	20	17	8	1	0	138	138	9.0	2	34	2.2	47	3.1	2.54	122	.274	.313	10	9	97	127	-2.0	-3	0	0.5
1914 Chi-N	2	4	.333	16	5	1	0	0	54	49	8.2	3	15	2.5	17	2.8	3.83	72	.251	.300	-6	-6	99	75	-1.0	-1	-1	-0.8
Total 10	66	87	.431	212	148	86	10	3	1351	1309	8.7	22	353	2.4	570	3.8	2.81	93	.266	.316	-15	-30	96	104	-1.2	-12	-3	-3.2
■ **POP SMITH**	Smith, Charles Marvin b: 10/12/1856, Digby, N.S., Canada d: 4/18/27, Boston, Mass. BR/TR, 5'11", 170 lbs. Deb: 5/01/1880																											
1883 Col-a	0	0	—	3	0	0	0	0	6	10	15.0	0	0	0.0	0	0.0	7.50	40	.376	.376	-3	-3	91	77	0.0	1	0	-0.2
■ **POP-BOY SMITH**	Smith, Clarence Ossie b: 5/23/1892, Newport, Tenn. d: 2/16/24, Sweetwater, Tex. BR/TR, 6'1", 176 lbs. Deb: 4/19/13																											
1913 Chi-A	0	1	.000	15	2	0	0	0	32	31	8.7	0	11	3.1	13	3.7	3.38	83	.261	.338	-2	-2	95	92	-0.4	-1	1	0.0
1916 Cle-A	1	2	.333	5	3	0	0	1	26	25	8.7	1	11	3.8	4	1.4	3.81	74	.253	.333	-3	-3	99	86	-0.4	0	-0	-0.2
1917 Cle-A	0	1	.000	6	0	0	0	0	9	14	14.0	0	4	4.0	3	3.0	8.00	38	.368	.442	-5	-5	113	81	-0.4	-0	1	-0.3
Total 3	1	4	.200	26	5	0	0	1	67	70	9.4	1	26	3.5	20	2.7	4.16	68	.273	.352	-10	-10	99	88	-1.2	-1	2	-0.5
■ **CLAY SMITH**	Smith, Clay Jamieson b: 9/11/14, Cambridge, Kan. BR/TR, 6'2", 190 lbs. Deb: 9/13/38																											
1938 Cle-A	0	0	—	4	0	0	0	0	11	18	14.7	1	2	1.6	3	2.5	6.55	71	.367	.392	-2	-2	98	103	0.0	-0	0	-0.1
1940 Det-A	1	1	.500	14	1	0	0	0	28	32	10.3	3	13	4.2	14	4.5	5.14	93	.283	.359	-2	-1	109	99	0.0	-1	1	0.0
Total 2	1	1	.500	18	1	0	0	0	39	50	11.5	4	15	3.5	17	3.9	5.54	86	.309	.369	-5	-3	106	100	0.0	-1	1	-0.1
■ **DAVE SMITH**	Smith, David Merwin b: 12/17/14, Sellers, S.C. BR/TR, 5'10", 170 lbs. Deb: 6/16/38																											
1938 Phi-A	2	1	.667	21	0	0	0	0	44	50	10.2	0	28	5.7	13	2.7	5.11	98	.284	.382	-2	-1	105	93	0.7	-1	0	-0.1
1939 Phi-A	0	0	—	1	0	0	0	0	0	1	—	0	2	—	0	—	—	—	1.000	1.000	0	0	102	0	0.0	0	0	0.0
Total 2	2	1	.667	22	0	0	0	0	44	51	10.4	0	30	6.1	13	2.7	5.11	98	.288	.390	-2	-1	105	93	0.7	-1	0	-0.1
■ **DAVE SMITH**	Smith, David Stanley b: 1/21/55, Richmond, Cal. BR/TR, 6'1", 195 lbs. Deb: 4/11/80																											
1980 Hou-N	7	5	.583	57	0	0	0	10	103	90	7.9	1	32	2.8	85	7.4	1.92	182	.237	.299	19	18	97	134	0.2	-1	-1	1.7
1981 Hou-N	5	3	.625	42	0	0	0	8	75	54	6.5	2	23	2.8	52	6.2	2.76	110	.198	.259	6	2	87	61	0.7	0	-0	0.2
1982 Hou-N	5	4	.556	49	1	0	0	11	63	69	9.9	4	31	4.4	28	4.0	3.86	93	.285	.350	-2	-2	100	120	0.7	-0	-1	-0.2
1983 Hou-N	3	1	.750	42	0	0	0	6	73	72	8.9	2	36	4.4	41	5.1	3.08	106	.258	.334	5	2	90	116	1.0	-0	-2	0.0
1984 Hou-N	5	4	.556	53	0	0	0	5	77	60	7.0	5	20	2.3	45	5.3	2.22	148	.214	.266	12	9	92	101	0.6	-0	-0	0.9
1985 Hou-N	9	5	.643	64	0	0	0	27	79	69	7.9	3	17	1.9	40	4.6	2.28	151	.235	.276	12	10	96	106	2.0	0	-1	0.9
1986 Hou-N	4	7	.364	54	0	0	0	33	56	39	6.3	5	22	3.5	46	7.4	2.73	138	.200	.278	6	7	102	94	-2.1	-0	0	0.7
1987 Hou-N	2	3	.400	50	0	0	0	24	60	39	5.8	0	21	3.2	73	10.9	1.65	230	.182	.254	16	14	93	76	-0.3	1	-0	1.5
1988 Hou-N	4	5	.444	51	0	0	0	27	57	60	9.5	1	19	3.0	38	6.0	2.68	120	.268	.321	5	3	93	130	-0.5	-0	-0	0.3
Total 9	44	37	.543	462	1	0	0	151	643	552	7.7	23	221	3.1	448	6.3	2.53	135	.232	.294	79	64	94	105	2.3	-2	-6	6.0
■ **DAVE SMITH**	Smith, David Wayne b: 8/30/57, Tomball, Tex. BR/TR, 6'1", 190 lbs. Deb: 9/18/84																											
1984 Cal-A	0	0	—	1	0	0	0	0	1	4	36.0	1	0	0.0	0	0.0	18.00	23	.571	.571	-2	-2	101	134	0.0	0	0	0.0
1985 Cal-A	0	0	—	4	0	0	0	0	5	5	9.0	1	1	1.8	3	5.4	7.20	58	.278	.300	-2	-2	101	68	0.0	0	0	-0.1
Total 2	0	0	—	5	0	0	0	0	6	9	13.5	2	1	1.5	3	4.5	9.00	46	.360	.370	-3	-3	101	79	0.0	0	0	-0.1
■ **DOUG SMITH**	Smith, Douglass Weldon b: 5/25/1892, Millers Falls, Mass. d: 9/18/73, Greenfield, Mass. BL/TL, 5'10", 168 lbs. Deb: 7/10/12																											
1912 Bos-A	0	0	—	1	0	0	0	0	3	4	12.0	0	0	0.0	1	3.0	3.00	114	.364	.364	0	0	102	160	0.0	0	-0	0.0
■ **EDDIE SMITH**	Smith, Edgar b: 12/14/13, Columbus, N.J. BB/TL, 5'10", 174 lbs. Deb: 9/20/36																											
1936 Phi-A	1	1	.500	2	2	2	0	0	19	22	10.4	3	8	3.8	7	3.3	1.89	280	.275	.341	7	7	105	266	0.2	-1	0	0.7
1937 Phi-A	4	17	.190	38	23	14	1	5	197	178	8.1	18	90	4.1	79	3.6	3.93	113	.242	.321	15	11	96	96	-5.2	2	-2	1.1
1938 Phi-A	3	10	.231	43	7	0	0	4	131	151	10.4	13	76	5.2	78	5.4	5.91	85	.287	.376	-16	-13	105	93	-2.2	2	0	-0.8
1939 Phi-A	1	0	1.000	3	0	0	0	0	4	7	15.8	0	2	4.5	3	6.8	9.00	52	.412	.450	-2	-2	102	93	0.5	0	0	-0.1
Chi-A	9	11	.450	29	22	7	1	0	177	161	8.2	11	90	4.6	67	3.4	3.66	134	.247	.335	19	25	106	110	-2.0	-2	-2	2.1
Yr	10	11	.476	32	22	7	1	0	181	168	8.4	11	92	4.6	70	3.5	3.78	130	.251	.338	17	23	106	110	-1.5	0	-2	2.0
1940 Chi-A	14	9	.609	32	28	12	0	0	207	179	7.8	16	95	4.1	119	5.2	3.22	140	.228	.311	27	29	103	103	2.1	2	-1	3.1
1941 Chi-A	13	17	.433	34	33	21	1	1	263	243	8.3	13	114	3.9	111	3.8	3.18	122	.246	.322	28	21	94	112	-2.3	4	0	2.5
1942 Chi-A	7	20	.259	29	28	18	2	1	215	223	9.3	17	86	3.6	78	3.3	3.98	92	.269	.335	-8	-7	100	107	-6.2	-2	2	-0.7
1943 Chi-A	11	11	.500	25	25	14	2	0	188	197	9.4	2	76	3.6	66	3.2	3.69	91	.277	.343	-8	-7	101	105	-0.7	-1	1	-0.7
1946 Chi-A	8	11	.421	24	21	3	1	1	145	135	8.4	9	60	3.7	59	3.7	2.86	119	.246	.317	10	9	97	118	-1.2	0	-0	0.9
1947 Chi-A	1	3	.250	15	5	0	0	0	33	40	10.9	1	24	6.5	12	3.3	7.36	50	.299	.386	-13	-14	99	73	-0.8	-0	-1	-1.3
Bos-A	1	3	.250	8	3	0	0	0	17	18	9.5	3	18	9.5	15	7.9	7.41	53	.269	.419	-7	-7	107	89	-1.0	0	-0	-0.6
Yr	2	6	.250	23	8	0	0	0	50	58	10.4	4	42	7.6	27	4.9	7.38	51	.289	.397	-20	-20	102	89	-1.8	-0	-1	-1.9
Total 10	73	113	.392	282	197	91	8	12	1596	1554	8.8	106	739	4.2	694	3.9	3.82	108	.256	.334	52	51	100	107	-18.8	5	-2	6.2
■ **EDGAR SMITH**	Smith, Edgar Eugene b: 6/12/1862, Providence, R.I. d: 11/3/1892, Providence, R.I. BR/TR, 5'10", 160 lbs. Deb: 5/25/1883																											
1883 Phi-N	0	1	.000	1	1	0	0	0	7	18	23.1	0	3	3.9	2	2.6	15.43	20	.485	.523	-10	-10	99	74	-0.3	1	0	-0.5
1884 Was-a	0	2	.000	3	2	2	0	0	22	27	11.0	0	5	2.0	4	1.6	4.91	62	.311	.348	-4	-5	93	91	-0.9	-1	0	-0.3
1885 Pro-N	1	0	1.000	1	1	1	0	0	9	9	9.0	0	0	0.0	1	1.0	1.00	263	.271	.271	2	2	93	225	0.5	0	0	0.2
1890 Cle-N	1	4	.200	6	6	5	0	0	44	42	8.6	1	10	2.0	11	2.3	4.30	81	.267	.311	-4	-4	97	62	-0.9	2	0	-0.1
Total 4	2	7	.222	11	10	8	0	0	82	96	10.5	1	18	2.0	18	2.0	5.05	64	.305	.343	-15	-17	96	89	-1.6	2	0	-0.7
■ **MIKE SMITH**	Smith, Elmer Ellsworth b: 3/23/1868, Pittsburgh, Pa. d: 11/5/45, Pittsburgh, Pa. BL/TL, 5'11", 178 lbs. Deb: 5/31/1886																											
1886 Cin-a	4	5	.444	10	10	9	0	0	82	65	7.1	1	54	5.9	41	4.5	3.73	88	.227	.350	-3	-4	96	90	-0.2	4	0	0.0
1887 Cin-a	34	17	.667	52	52	49	3	0	447	400	**8.1**	5	126	2.5	176	3.5	**2.94**	**156**	**.252**	.307	68	**81**	106	94	6.2	3	-6	6.9
1888 Cin-a	22	17	.564	40	40	37	5	0	348	309	8.0	1	89	2.3	154	4.0	2.74	111	.250	.301	12	11	99	92	-1.4	6	-5	1.2
1889 Cin-a	9	12	.429	29	22	16	0	0	203	253	11.2	11	101	4.5	104	4.6	4.88	81	.321	.398	-23	-20	103	107	-2.5	5	0	-1.1

YEAR	TM/L	W	L	PCT	G	GS	CG	SHO	SV	IP	H	H/G	HR	BB	BB/G	SO	SO/G	ERA	/A	OAVG	OOBP	PR	/A	PF	CPI	WAT	PB	PD	TPI
1892	Pit-N	6	7	.462	17	13	12	1	0	134	140	9.4	2	58	3.9	51	3.4	3.63	85	.282	.357	-5	-8	94	100	-0.7	7	0	-0.6
1894	Pit-N	0	0	—	1	0	0	0	0	4	6	13.5	0	1	2.3	0	0.0	4.50	112	.370	.407	0	0	95	122	0.0	1	0	0.0
1898	Cin-N	0	0	—	1	0	0	0	0	1	2	18.0	0	3	27.0	0	0.0	18.00	21	.439	.662	-2	-2	107	85	0.0	0	0	0.0
Total	7	75	58	.564	150	137	123	9	0	1219	1175	8.7	20	432	3.2	526	3.9	3.35	112	.266	.332	48	56	102	96	1.4	26	-11	6.4
■ **FRANK SMITH**	Smith, Frank Elmer "Nig" or "Piano Mover" (born Frank Elmer Schmidt) b: 10/28/1879, Pittsburgh, Pa. d: 11/3/52, Pittsburgh, Pa. BR/TR, 5'10.5", 194 lbs. Deb: 4/22/04																												
1904	Chi-A	16	9	.640	26	23	22	4	0	202	157	7.0	0	58	2.6	107	4.8	2.09	120	.235	.296	11	9	97	93	2.1	4	-2	0.8
1905	Chi-A	19	13	.594	39	31	27	4	0	292	215	6.6	0	107	3.3	171	5.3	2.13	116	.227	.305	17	11	93	96	-0.3	6	0	1.2
1906	Chi-A	5	5	.500	20	13	8	1	1	122	124	9.1	3	37	2.7	53	3.9	3.39	71	.289	.345	-10	-14	89	99	-0.9	5	1	-1.2
1907	Chi-A	23	10	.697	41	37	29	3	0	310	280	8.1	3	111	3.2	139	4.0	2.47	104	.264	.334	2	3	101	111	5.6	4	4	0.8
1908	Chi-A	16	17	.485	41	35	24	3	1	298	213	6.4	2	73	2.2	129	3.9	2.02	109	.203	.256	12	6	93	75	-3.2	2	3	1.1
1909	Chi-A	25	17	.595	**51**	40	**37**	7	1	**365**	278	6.9	1	70	1.7	**177**	4.4	1.80	133	.214	.257	**27**	24	97	70	4.6	5	10	**4.6**
1910	Chi-A	4	9	.308	19	15	9	3	0	129	91	6.3	1	40	2.8	50	3.5	2.02	119	.204	.272	7	5	95	76	-2.0	2	4	1.2
	Bos-A	1	2	.333	4	3	2	0	0	28	22	7.1	0	11	3.5	8	2.6	4.82	51	.234	.321	-7	-7	97	52	-0.5	-0	0	-0.6
	Yr	5	11	.313	23	18	11	3	0	157	113	6.5	1	51	2.9	58	3.3	2.52	95	.208	.277	-0	-2	96	52	-2.5	2	4	0.6
1911	Bos-A	0	0	—	1	1	0	0	0	2	2	9.0	1	1	4.5	0	0.0	9.00	37	.250	.333	-1	-1	99	74	0.0	0	0	0.0
	Cin-N	10	14	.417	34	18	10	0	1	176	198	10.1	1	55	2.8	67	3.4	3.99	79	.289	.345	-11	-17	92	94	-1.2	3	4	-0.9
1912	Cin-N	1	1	.500	7	3	1	0	0	23	34	13.3	1	15	5.9	5	2.0	6.26	51	.351	.438	-7	-8	93	105	0.0	-0	-0	-0.7
1914	Bal-F	10	8	.556	39	22	9	1	2	175	180	9.3	8	47	2.4	83	4.3	2.98	106	.259	.306	4	4	99	100	0.2	2	3	0.8
1915	Bal-F	4	4	.500	17	9	2	0	0	89	108	10.9	5	31	3.1	37	3.7	4.65	73	.330	.388	-16	-13	111	102	1.2	1	0	-1.1
	Bro-F	5	2	.714	15	5	4	1	0	63	69	9.9	2	18	2.6	24	3.4	3.14	95	.308	.360	-1	-1	98	120	1.7	1	0	0.0
	Yr	9	6	.600	32	14	6	1	0	152	177	10.5	7	49	2.9	61	3.6	4.03	80	.321	.377	-17	-14	106	120	2.9	1	0	-1.1
Total	11	139	111	.556	354	255	184	27	6	2274	1971	7.8	28	674	2.7	1050	4.2	2.58	100	.245	.305	28	2	96	90	7.3	34	27	6.0
■ **FRANK SMITH**	Smith, Frank Thomas b: 4/4/28, Pierrepont Manor, N.Y. BR/TR, 6'3", 195 lbs. Deb: 4/18/50																												
1950	Cin-N	2	7	.222	38	4	0	0	3	91	73	7.2	12	39	3.9	55	5.4	3.86	114	.216	.306	3	5	106	89	-2.2	-2	-1	0.3
1951	Cin-N	5	5	.500	50	0	0	0	11	76	65	7.7	7	22	2.6	34	4.0	3.20	127	.230	.289	6	7	103	95	0.6	-1	0	0.7
1952	Cin-N	12	11	.522	53	2	1	0	7	122	109	8.0	13	41	3.0	77	5.7	3.76	99	.242	.306	-0	-0	100	97	1.8	0	-2	-0.1
1953	Cin-N	8	1	.889	50	1	0	0	2	84	89	9.5	15	25	2.7	42	4.5	5.46	79	.272	.321	-11	-11	100	88	3.6	-1	1	-0.9
1954	Cin-N	5	8	.385	50	0	0	0	20	81	60	6.7	15	29	3.2	51	5.7	2.67	159	.211	.280	13	14	104	127	-1.3	1	0	1.5
1955	StL-N	3	1	.750	28	0	0	0	1	39	27	6.2	3	23	5.3	17	3.9	3.23	128	.205	.327	3	4	102	108	1.1	-1	-0	0.3
1956	Cin-N	0	0	—	2	0	0	0	0	3	3	9.0	2	2	6.0	1	3.0	12.00	33	.300	.385	-3	-3	106	84	0.0	0	0	-0.2
Total	7	35	33	.515	271	7	1	0	44	496	426	7.7	67	181	3.3	277	5.0	3.81	108	.234	.304	11	17	103	99	3.6	-3	-2	1.6
■ **FRED SMITH**	Smith, Frederick b: 11/24/1878, New Diggins, Wis. d: 2/4/64, Los Angeles, Cal. BL/TR, 6', 186 lbs. Deb: 6/14/07																												
1907	Cin-N	2	7	.222	18	9	5	0	1	85	90	9.5	3	24	2.5	19	2.0	2.86	82	.305	.365	-4	-5	95	124	-2.2	-2	0	-0.4
■ **FRED SMITH**	Smith, Frederick C. b: 3/25/1863, Greene, N.Y. d: 1/9/41, Syracuse, N.Y. BL/TR, 5'11", 156 lbs. Deb: 4/18/1890																												
1890	Tol-a	19	13	.594	35	34	31	2	0	286	273	8.6	13	90	2.8	116	3.7	3.27	121	.267	.326	19	21	102	106	3.3	-2	0	1.8
■ **GEORGE SMITH**	Smith, George Allen "Columbia George" b: 5/31/1892, Byram, Conn. d: 1/7/65, Greenwich, Conn. BR/TR, 6'2", 163 lbs. Deb: 8/09/16																												
1916	NY-N	3	0	1.000	9	1	0	0	0	21	14	6.0	0	6	2.6	9	3.9	2.57	95	.197	.256	0	-0	94	57	1.5	-0	0	0.0
1917	NY-N	0	3	.000	14	1	1	0	0	38	38	9.0	1	11	2.6	16	3.8	2.84	89	.270	.314	-1	-1	93	117	-1.4	-1	0	-0.2
1918	Cin-N	2	3	.400	10	6	4	1	0	55	71	11.6	3	11	1.8	19	3.1	4.09	65	.329	.343	-8	-9	96	116	-0.5	-2	1	-1.0
	NY-N	2	3	.400	5	2	1	0	0	27	26	8.7	0	6	2.0	4	1.3	4.00	66	.255	.297	-4	-4	96	63	-0.7	0	-1	-0.4
	Bro-N	4	1	.800	8	5	4	0	0	50	43	7.7	0	5	0.9	18	3.2	2.34	123	.249	.270	2	3	104	91	1.6	0	1	0.5
	Yr	8	7	.533	23	13	9	1	0	132	140	9.5	3	22	1.5	41	2.8	3.41	80	.285	.307	-9	-10	99	91	0.4	-2	0	-0.9
1919	NY-N	0	2	.000	3	2	0	0	0	11	18	14.7	1	4	3.3	0	0.0	5.73	49	.383	.423	-3	-4	96	127	-0.9	-0	-0	-0.4
	Phi-N	5	11	.313	31	20	11	1	0	185	194	9.4	7	46	2.2	42	2.0	3.21	98	.278	.316	-6	-1	109	110	-0.7	-3	-0	-0.4
	Yr	5	13	.278	34	22	11	1	0	196	212	9.7	8	50	2.3	42	1.9	3.35	94	.285	.322	-10	-5	108	110	-1.6	-0	-1	-0.8
1920	Phi-N	13	18	.419	43	28	10	2	2	251	265	9.5	10	51	1.8	51	1.8	3.44	102	.283	.311	-9	2	112	96	0.5	-6	-2	-0.5
1921	Phi-N	4	20	.167	39	28	12	1	1	221	303	12.3	12	52	2.1	45	1.8	4.76	85	.335	.360	-24	-18	107	107	-6.4	-8	-2	-2.5
1922	Phi-N	5	14	.263	42	18	6	1	0	194	250	11.6	16	35	1.6	44	2.0	4.78	100	.316	.343	-15	-0	117	98	-3.0	-8	-2	-0.7
1923	Bro-N	3	6	.333	25	7	3	0	1	91	99	9.8	3	28	2.8	15	1.5	3.66	107	.278	.329	3	2	98	100	-1.4	-1	-2	0.0
Total	8	41	81	.336	229	118	52	6	4	1144	1321	10.4	53	255	2.0	263	2.1	3.89	94	.298	.329	-63	-31	107	101	-11.4	-31	-7	-5.6
■ **HEINIE SMITH**	Smith, George Henry b: 10/24/1871, Pittsburgh, Pa. d: 6/25/39, Buffalo, N.Y. BR/TR, 5'9.5", 160 lbs. Deb: 9/08/1897 M																												
1901	NY-N	0	1	.000	2	1	1	0	0	13	24	16.6	0	5	3.5	5	3.5	8.31	38	.452	.531	-7	-7	95	99	-0.4	0	-0	-0.5
■ **GERMANY SMITH**	Smith, George J. b: 4/21/1863, Pittsburgh, Pa. d: 12/1/27, Altoona, Pa. BR/TR, 6', 175 lbs. Deb: 4/17/1884																												
1884	Alt-U	0	0	—	1	0	0	0	0	1	3	27.0	0	0	0.0	1	9.0	9.00	36	.520	.520	-1	-1	109	136	0.0	0	0	0.0
■ **GEORGE SMITH**	Smith, George Shelby b: 10/27/01, Louisville, Ky. d: 5/26/81, Richmond, Va. BR/TR, 6'1", 175 lbs. Deb: 4/21/26																												
1926	Det-A	1	2	.333	23	1	0	0	0	44	55	11.3	3	33	6.8	15	3.1	6.95	56	.318	.419	-14	-15	98	91	-0.4	-0	-1	-1.4
1927	Det-A	4	1	.800	29	0	0	0	0	71	62	7.9	3	50	6.3	32	4.1	3.93	113	.240	.358	2	4	107	100	1.4	3	-0	0.6
1928	Det-A	1	1	.500	39	2	0	0	3	106	103	8.7	3	50	4.2	54	4.6	4.42	92	.263	.335	-4	-4	100	85	0.1	-2	-2	-0.7
1929	Det-A	3	2	.600	14	2	1	0	0	36	42	10.5	1	36	9.0	13	3.3	5.75	72	.307	.438	-6	-6	97	112	0.7	2	1	-0.2
1930	Bos-A	1	2	.333	27	2	0	0	0	74	92	11.2	7	49	6.0	21	2.6	6.57	68	.317	.399	-16	-17	96	101	0.0	2	0	-1.3
Total	5	10	8	.556	132	7	1	0	3	331	354	9.6	17	218	5.9	135	3.7	5.27	80	.283	.379	-39	-39	100	95	1.8	4	-2	-3.0
■ **HAL SMITH**	Smith, Harold Laverne b: 6/30/02, Creston, Iowa BR/TR, 6'3", 195 lbs. Deb: 9/14/32																												
1932	Pit-N	1	0	1.000	2	1	1	1	0	12	9	6.8	0	2	1.5	4	3.0	0.75	515	.209	.239	4	4	100	187	0.5	-0	0	0.4
1933	Pit-N	8	7	.533	28	19	8	2	1	145	149	9.2	5	31	1.9	40	2.5	2.86	110	.261	.302	8	4	94	105	-0.4	-1	-2	0.1
1934	Pit-N	3	4	.429	20	5	1	0	0	50	72	13.0	3	18	3.2	15	2.7	7.20	59	.343	.390	-17	-16	105	87	-0.4	-2	-0	-1.6
1935	Pit-N	0	0	—	1	0	0	0	0	3	2	6.0	0	1	3.0	0	0.0	3.00	141	.200	.273	0	0	105	64	0.0	0	-0	0.0
Total	4	12	11	.522	51	25	10	3	1	210	232	9.9	8	52	2.2	59	2.5	3.77	91	.279	.322	-5	-8	97	105	-0.3	-4	-2	-1.1
■ **HARRY SMITH**	Smith, Harrison Morton b: 8/15/1889, Union, Neb. d: 7/26/64, Dunbar, Neb. BR/TR, 5'9", 160 lbs. Deb: 10/06/12																												
1912	Chi-A	1	0	1.000	1	1	0	0	0	5	6	10.8	0	0	0.0	1	1.8	1.80	184	.333	.333	1	1	99	222	0.5	-0	0	0.1
■ **JACK SMITH**	Smith, Jack Hatfield b: 11/15/35, Pikeville, Ky. BR/TR, 6', 185 lbs. Deb: 9/10/62																												
1962	LA-N	0	0	—	8	0	0	0	1	10	10	9.0	0	4	3.6	7	6.3	4.50	79	.263	.326	-1	-1	91	73	0.0	-0	-0	-0.1
1963	LA-N	0	0	—	4	0	0	0	0	8	10	11.3	2	2	2.3	5	5.6	7.88	39	.303	.359	-4	-4	94	83	0.0	-0	0	-0.3
1964	Mil-N	2	2	.500	22	0	0	0	0	31	28	8.1	3	11	3.2	19	5.5	3.77	90	.237	.295	-1	-1	96	87	-0.1	0	1	0.0
Total	3	2	2	.500	34	0	0	0	1	49	48	8.8	5	17	3.1	31	5.7	4.59	74	.254	.313	-6	-7	95	83	-0.1	-0	1	-0.4
■ **JAKE SMITH**	Smith, Jacob G. b: Dubois, Pa. Deb: 10/03/11																												
1911	Phi-N	0	0	—	2	0	0	0	0	5	3	5.4	0	2	3.6	1	1.8	0.00	—	.176	.263	2	2	108	0	0.0	-0	0	0.2
■ **PHENOMENAL SMITH**	Smith, John Francis (born John Francis Gammon) b: 12/12/1864, Philadelphia, Pa. d: 4/3/52, Manchester, N.H. BL/TL, 5'6.5", 161 lbs. Deb: 4/18/1884																												
1884	Bal-U	3	4	.429	9	8	5	0	0	62	86	12.5	2	17	2.5	13	1.9	3.48	95	.334	.375	-3	-1	110	153	-0.7	-3	0	-0.2
	Phi-a	0	1	.000	1	1	1	0	0	9	14	14.0	0	1	1.0	3	3.0	4.00	91	.364	.380	-1	-0	113	145	-0.4	-0	0	0.0
	Pit-a	0	1	.000	1	1	1	0	0	8	11	12.4	0	2	2.3	4	4.5	9.00	36	.336	.374	-5	-5	101	59	-0.4	-1	0	-0.3
	Yr	0	2	.000	2	2	2	0	0	17	25	13.2	0	3	1.6	7	3.7	6.35	55	.351	.377	-6	-5	107	59	-0.8	-0	0	-0.3
1885	Bro-a	0	1	.000	1	1	1	0	0	8	12	13.5	0	6	6.8	2	2.3	12.38	27	.359	.457	-8	-8	105	57	-0.4	0	0	-0.4
	Phi-a	0	1	.000	1	1	0	0	0	4	7	15.8	0	4	9.0	7	15.8	9.00	37	.395	.507	-3	-3	102	100	-0.4	-0	0	-0.1
	Yr	0	2	.000	2	2	1	0	0	12	19	14.3	0	10	7.5	9	6.8	11.25	30	.372	.474	-11	-11	104	100	-0.8	0	0	-0.5
1886	Det-N	1	1	.500	3	3	3	0	0	25	16	5.8	0	8	2.9	15	5.4	2.16	158	.194	.265	3	3	103	63	-0.2	-1	0	0.3
1887	Bal-a	25	30	.455	58	55	54	1	0	491	526	9.6	7	176	3.2	206	3.8	3.79	107	.288	.350	28	14	94	103	-8.2	8	-0	1.7
1888	Bal-a	14	19	.424	35	32	31	0	0	292	249	7.7	5	137	4.2	152	4.7	3.61	83	.243	.332	-18	-20	98	85	0.3	8	0	-1.0
	Phi-a	2	1	.667	3	3	3	0	0	22	21	8.6	0	10	4.1	19	7.8	2.86	104	.264	.346	0	0	97	118	0.2	1	0	0.1

YEAR	TM/L	W	L	PCT	G	GS	CG	SHO	SV	IP	H	H/G	HR	BB	BB/G	SO	SO/G	ERA	/A	OAVG	OOBP	PR	/A	PF	CPI	WAT	PB	PD	TPI
	Yr	16	20	.444	38	35	34	0	0	314	270	7.7	5	147	4.2	171	4.9	3.55	84	.244	.333	-17	-20	98	118	0.5	8	0	-0.9
1889	Phi-a	2	3	.400	5	5	5	0	0	43	53	11.1	2	25	5.2	12	2.5	4.40	84	.319	.408	-3	-3	96	121	-0.6	0	0	-0.2
1890	Phi-N	8	12	.400	24	20	19	1	0	204	209	9.2	5	89	3.9	81	3.6	4.28	89	.281	.358	-16	-11	107	85	-3.5	3	0	-0.4
	Pit-N	1	3	.250	5	5	5	0	0	44	39	8.0	0	13	2.7	15	3.1	3.07	110	.252	.311	2	1	95	77	0.2	2	0	0.3
	Yr	9	15	.375	29	25	24	1	0	248	248	9.0	5	102	3.7	96	3.5	4.06	92	.276	.350	-14	-9	105	77	-3.3	3	0	-0.1
1891	Phi-N	1	1	.500	3	2	0	0	0	19	20	9.5	1	8	3.8	3	1.4	4.26	75	.284	.357	-2	-2	95	87	0.0	1	0	0.0
Total	8	57	78	.422	149	137	128	2	0	1231	1263	9.2	22	496	3.6	532	3.9	3.87	94	.279	.350	-25	-32	99	97	-14.1	19	-0	-0.2
■ CHICK SMITH	Smith, John William (born Jan Smadt) b: 12/2/1892, Dayton, Ky. d: 10/11/35, Dayton, Ohio BL/TL, 5'8", 165 lbs. Deb: 4/12/13																												
1913	Cin-N	0	1	.000	5	1	0	0	0	18	15	7.5	1	11	5.5	11	5.5	3.50	95	.238	.338	-1	-0	104	103	-0.4	-1	0	0.0
■ LEE SMITH	Smith, Lee Arthur b: 12/4/57, Shreveport, La. BR/TR, 6'5", 220 lbs. Deb: 9/01/80																												
1980	Chi-N	2	0	1.000	18	0	0	0	0	22	21	8.6	0	14	5.7	17	7.0	2.86	135	.259	.361	2	2	108	135	1.0	0	0	0.2
1981	Chi-N	3	6	.333	40	1	0	0	1	67	57	7.7	2	31	4.2	50	6.7	3.49	106	.239	.318	-0	2	106	92	-0.4	-1	-0	0.0
1982	Chi-N	2	5	.286	72	5	0	0	17	117	105	8.1	5	37	2.8	99	7.6	2.69	139	.245	.302	12	14	104	112	-1.2	-0	-1	1.3
1983	Chi-N	4	10	.286	66	0	0	0	**29**	103	70	6.1	5	41	3.6	91	8.0	1.66	221	.194	.271	23	23	101	123	-2.5	-0	-1	2.4
1984	Chi-N	9	7	.563	69	0	0	0	33	101	98	8.7	6	35	3.1	86	7.7	3.65	107	.255	.311	-1	3	109	93	-0.4	-1	0	0.2
1985	Chi-N	7	4	.636	65	0	0	0	33	98	87	8.0	9	32	2.9	112	10.3	3.03	139	.242	.302	6	13	117	109	1.7	-0	-1	1.2
1986	Chi-N	9	9	.500	66	0	0	0	31	90	69	6.9	7	42	4.2	93	9.3	3.10	130	.215	.298	6	9	108	95	1.1	-1	0	0.9
1987	Chi-N	4	10	.286	62	0	0	0	36	84	84	9.0	4	32	3.4	96	10.3	3.11	134	.259	.322	9	10	102	114	-2.8	-0	-0	0.9
1988	Bos-A	4	5	.444	64	0	0	0	29	84	72	7.7	7	37	4.0	96	10.3	2.79	154	.225	.303	11	14	108	112	-0.8	0	-1	1.3
Total	9	44	56	.440	522	6	0	0	209	766	663	7.8	45	301	3.5	740	8.7	2.90	136	.235	.304	68	90	107	108	-4.3	-3	-3	8.4
■ ROY SMITH	Smith, Le Roy Purdy b: 9/6/61, Mt.Vernon, N.Y. BR/TR, 6'3", 200 lbs. Deb: 6/23/84																												
1984	Cle-A	5	5	.500	22	14	0	0	0	86	91	9.5	14	40	4.2	55	5.8	4.60	92	.270	.346	-6	-4	106	107	0.4	0	-1	-0.4
1985	Cle-A	1	4	.200	12	11	1	0	0	62	84	12.2	8	17	2.5	28	4.1	5.37	74	.321	.358	-8	-10	95	106	-1.1	0	-1	-0.9
1986	Min-A	0	2	.000	5	0	0	0	0	10	13	11.7	1	5	4.5	8	7.2	7.20	64	.295	.380	-3	-3	109	75	-0.9	0	0	-0.2
1987	Min-A	1	0	1.000	7	1	0	0	0	16	20	11.3	3	6	3.4	8	4.5	5.06	85	.290	.359	-1	-1	96	112	0.5	0	-0	0.0
1988	Min-A	3	0	1.000	9	4	0	0	0	37	29	7.1	3	12	2.9	17	4.1	2.68	157	.210	.276	5	6	105	93	1.5	0	-1	0.6
Total	5	10	11	.476	55	30	1	0	0	211	237	10.1	29	80	3.4	116	4.9	4.65	90	.279	.341	-13	-11	102	103	0.4	0	-3	-0.9
■ MARK SMITH	Smith, Mark Christopher b: 11/23/55, Arlington, Va. BR/TR, 6'2", 215 lbs. Deb: 8/12/83																												
1983	Oak-A	1	0	1.000	8	1	0	0	0	15	24	14.4	0	6	3.6	10	6.0	6.60	59	.387	.443	-4	-4	96	109	0.5	0	-0	-0.4
■ MIKE SMITH	Smith, Michael Anthony b: 2/23/61, Hinds, Miss. BB/TR, 6', 175 lbs. Deb: 4/06/84																												
1984	Cin-N	1	0	1.000	8	0	0	0	0	10	12	10.8	1	5	4.5	7	6.3	5.40	71	.286	.362	-2	-2	107	91	0.5	0	-0	-0.1
1985	Cin-N	0	0	—	2	0	0	0	0	3	2	6.0	2	1	3.0	2	6.0	6.00	63	.167	.231	-1	-1	105	90	0.0	0	0	0.0
1986	Cin-N	0	0	—	2	1	0	0	0	3	7	21.0	0	1	3.0	1	3.0	15.00	26	.412	.444	-4	-4	104	56	0.0	0	0	-0.3
1988	Mon-N	0	0	—	5	0	0	0	1	9	6	6.0	0	5	5.0	4	4.0	3.00	121	.207	.314	0	1	105	91	0.0	-0	-0	0.0
Total	4	1	0	1.000	17	1	0	0	1	25	27	9.7	3	12	4.3	14	5.0	5.76	65	.270	.345	-6	-6	106	86	0.5	-0	-0	-0.4
■ PETE SMITH	Smith, Peter John b: 2/27/66, Abington, Mass. BR/TR, 6'2", 185 lbs. Deb: 9/08/87																												
1987	Atl-N	1	2	.333	6	6	0	0	0	32	39	11.0	3	14	3.9	11	3.1	4.78	93	.307	.371	-2	-1	109	113	-0.2	-1	-1	-0.2
1988	Atl-N	7	15	.318	32	32	5	3	0	195	183	8.4	15	88	4.1	124	5.7	3.69	100	.250	.325	-5	0	107	103	-0.6	-2	-2	-0.3
Total	2	8	17	.320	38	38	5	3	0	227	222	8.8	18	102	4.0	135	5.4	3.85	99	.258	.332	-8	-1	107	105	-0.8	-2	-3	-0.5
■ PETE SMITH	Smith, Peter Luke b: 3/19/40, Natick, Mass. BR/TR, 6'2", 190 lbs. Deb: 9/13/62																												
1962	Bos-A	0	1	.000	1	1	0	0	0	4	7	15.8	3	2	4.5	1	2.3	18.00	23	.438	.474	-6	-6	103	80	-0.4	-0	0	-0.4
1963	Bos-A	0	0	—	6	1	0	0	0	15	11	6.6	2	6	3.6	6	3.6	3.60	107	.212	.283	0	0	107	89	0.0	-0	0	0.0
Total	2	0	1	.000	7	2	0	0	0	19	18	8.5	5	8	3.8	7	3.3	6.63	59	.265	.329	-6	-6	106	87	-0.4	-0	0	-0.4
■ REGGIE SMITH	Smith, Reginald b: Louisville, Ky. Deb: 7/11/1886																												
1886	Phi-a	0	1	.000	1	1	1	0	0	9	15	15.0	0	5	5.0	4	4.0	7.00	51	.382	.452	-4	-3	103	105	-0.4	-1	0	-0.2
■ ED SMITH	Smith, Rhesa Edward b: 2/21/1879, Mentone, Ind. d: 3/20/55, Tarpon Springs, Fla. BR/TR, 5'11", 170 lbs. Deb: 4/27/06																												
1906	StL-A	8	11	.421	19	18	13	0	0	155	153	8.9	3	53	3.1	45	2.6	3.72	70	.283	.347	-18	-19	97	88	-1.8	2	1	-1.8
■ BOB SMITH	Smith, Robert Ashley b: 7/19/1890, Hardwick, Vt. BR/TR, 5'11", 160 lbs. Deb: 4/19/13																												
1913	Chi-A	0	0	—	1	0	0	0	0	2	3	13.5	1	3	13.5	1	4.5	13.50	21	.273	.429	-2	-2	95	73	0.0	0	0	-0.1
1915	Buf-F	0	0	—	1	0	0	0	0	1	1	9.0	0	2	18.0	0	0.0	18.00	17	.289	.549	-2	-2	101	44	0.0	0	0	-0.1
Total	2	0	0	—	2	0	0	0	0	3	4	12.0	1	5	15.0	1	3.0	15.00	19	.277	.462	-4	-4	97	63	0.0	0	0	-0.2
■ BOB SMITH	Smith, Robert Eldridge b: 4/22/1895, Rogersville, Tenn. d: 7/19/87, Waycross, Ga. BR/TR, 5'10", 175 lbs. Deb: 4/19/23																												
1925	Bos-N	5	3	.625	13	10	6	0	0	93	110	10.6	6	36	3.5	19	1.8	4.45	91	.304	.356	-2	-4	95	108	1.3	2	0	-0.3
1926	Bos-N	10	13	.435	33	23	14	4	1	201	199	8.9	10	75	3.4	44	2.0	3.76	89	.269	.324	1	-9	88	100	0.0	7	2	0.0
1927	Bos-N	10	18	.357	41	32	16	1	3	261	297	10.2	9	75	2.6	81	2.8	3.76	99	.301	.337	5	-1	95	114	-1.3	4	2	0.5
1928	Bos-N	13	17	.433	38	25	14	0	2	244	274	10.1	11	74	2.7	59	2.2	3.87	104	.289	.331	3	5	101	102	2.8	3	2	0.9
1929	Bos-N	11	17	.393	34	29	19	1	3	231	256	10.0	20	71	2.8	65	2.5	4.68	98	.285	.332	1	-2	97	94	0.8	-0	1	-0.1
1930	Bos-N	10	14	.417	38	24	14	2	5	220	247	10.1	25	85	3.5	84	3.4	4.25	116	.290	.346	18	16	99	117	-1.1	-1	1	1.5
1931	Chi-N	15	12	.556	36	29	18	2	2	240	239	9.0	10	62	2.3	63	2.4	3.23	112	.256	.301	17	11	94	95	0.4	2	1	1.3
1932	Chi-N	4	3	.571	34	11	4	1	2	119	148	11.2	4	36	2.7	35	2.6	4.61	86	.303	.348	-10	-8	103	98	0.0	2	1	-0.5
1933	Cin-N	4	4	.500	16	6	4	0	0	74	75	9.1	3	11	1.3	18	2.2	2.19	155	.260	.284	9	10	102	125	0.8	0	-0	1.1
	Bos-N	4	3	.571	14	4	3	1	1	59	68	10.4	3	7	1.1	16	2.4	3.20	100	.296	.309	1	-0	96	117	0.3	0	1	0.1
	Yr	8	7	.533	30	10	7	1	1	133	143	9.7	6	18	1.2	34	2.3	2.64	125	.276	.295	10	10	99	117	1.1	0	1	1.2
1934	Bos-N	6	9	.400	39	5	3	0	5	122	133	9.8	9	36	2.7	26	1.9	4.65	75	.277	.321	-8	-16	86	87	-1.7	1	1	-1.2
1935	Bos-N	8	18	.308	46	20	8	2	5	203	232	10.3	13	61	2.7	58	2.6	3.95	102	.285	.331	2	2	100	108	1.2	2	-1	0.3
1936	Bos-N	6	7	.462	35	11	5	2	8	136	142	9.4	3	35	2.3	36	2.4	3.77	102	.264	.306	4	1	96	84	0.0	0	1	0.2
1937	Bos-N	0	1	.000	18	0	0	0	3	44	52	10.6	6	6	1.2	14	2.9	4.09	86	.295	.324	-1	-3	90	115	-0.4	0	-1	-0.2
Total	13	106	139	.433	435	229	128	16	40	2247	2472	9.9	132	670	2.7	618	2.5	3.94	100	.283	.327	40	1	96	103	3.1	23	12	3.6
■ BOB SMITH	Smith, Robert Gilchrist b: 2/1/31, Woodsville, N.H. BR/TL, 6'1.5", 190 lbs. Deb: 4/29/55																												
1955	Bos-A	0	0	—	1	0	0	0	0	2	1	4.5	0	1	4.5	1	4.5	0.00	—	.200	.333	1	1	122	0	0.0	0	0	0.1
1957	StL-N	0	0	—	6	0	0	0	1	10	12	10.8	0	6	5.4	11	9.9	4.50	86	.267	.358	-1	-1	99	87	0.0	-0	0	0.0
	Pit-N	2	4	.333	20	4	2	0	0	55	48	7.9	2	25	4.1	35	5.7	3.11	120	.229	.312	5	4	96	89	-0.4	-1	-1	0.2
	Yr	2	4	.333	26	4	2	0	1	65	60	8.3	2	31	4.3	46	6.4	3.32	113	.234	.317	4	3	96	89	-0.4	-0	-1	0.2
1958	Pit-N	2	2	.500	35	4	0	0	1	61	61	9.0	6	31	4.6	24	3.5	4.43	84	.262	.343	-3	-5	94	97	-0.1	-1	1	-0.4
1959	Pit-N	0	0	—	20	0	0	0	0	28	32	10.3	1	17	5.5	12	3.9	3.54	116	.291	.377	1	2	104	138	0.0	-0	-0	0.1
	Det-A	0	3	.000	9	0	0	0	0	11	20	16.4	5	3	2.5	10	8.2	8.18	52	.417	.434	-5	-5	111	136	-1.4	-0	0	-0.4
Total	4	4	9	.308	91	8	2	0	2	167	174	9.4	14	83	4.5	93	5.0	4.04	95	.267	.347	-2	-4	98	102	-1.9	-2	-0	-0.4
■ BOB SMITH	Smith, Robert Walkay "Riverboat" b: 5/13/28, Clarence, Mo. BB/TL, 6', 185 lbs. Deb: 4/22/58																												
1958	Bos-A	4	3	.571	17	7	1	0	0	67	61	8.2	4	45	6.0	43	5.8	3.76	105	.248	.357	0	1	105	111	0.4	-1	1	0.1
1959	Chi-N	0	0	—	1	0	0	0	0	1	5	45.0	0	2	18.0	0	0.0	54.00	7	.833	.778	-6	-6	99	59	0.0	-0	0	-0.3
	Cle-A	0	1	.000	12	3	0	0	0	29	31	9.6	2	12	3.7	17	5.3	5.28	69	.282	.333	-5	-5	95	84	-0.4	-1	0	-0.5
Total	2	4	4	.500	30	10	1	0	0	97	97	9.0	6	59	5.5	60	5.6	4.73	82	.268	.359	-10	-9	102	102	0.0	-2	1	-0.7
■ RUFUS SMITH	Smith, Rufus Frazier "Shirt" b: 1/24/05, Guilford College, N.C. d: 8/21/84, Aiken, S.C. BR/TL, 5'8", 165 lbs. Deb: 10/02/27																												
1927	Det-A	0	0	—	1	1	0	0	0	8	8	9.0	0	3	3.4	2	2.3	3.38	132	.242	.324	1	1	107	79	0.0	-1	-0	0.0
■ SHERRY SMITH	Smith, Sherrod Malone b: 2/18/1891, Monticello, Ga. d: 9/12/49, Reidsville, Ga. BR/TL, 6'1", 170 lbs. Deb: 5/11/11																												
1911	Pit-N	0	0	—	1	0	0	0	0	1	4	36.0	0	1	9.0	0	0.0	36.00	9	.667	.714	-4	-4	97	60	0.0	0	0	-0.2
1912	Pit-N	0	0	—	3	0	0	0	1	4	6	13.5	0	1	2.3	3	6.8	6.75	48	.600	.636	-1	-2	95	138	0.0	0	-0	-0.1

YEAR	TM/L	W	L	PCT	G	GS	CG	SHO	SV	IP	H	H/G	HR	BB	BB/G	SO	SO/G	ERA	/A	OAVG	OOBP	PR	/A	PF	CPI	WAT	PB	PD	TPI
1915	Bro-N	14	8	.636	29	20	11	2	2	174	169	8.7	3	42	2.2	52	2.7	2.59	108	.264	.303	3	4	102	116	2.9	3	-0	0.7
1916	Bro-N	14	10	.583	36	23	15	4	1	219	193	7.9	5	45	1.8	67	2.8	2.34	112	.239	.274	7	7	100	95	-0.5	6	1	1.5
1917	Bro-N	12	12	.500	38	23	15	0	3	211	210	9.0	5	51	2.2	58	2.5	3.33	85	.265	.301	-14	-11	105	90	1.0	3	4	-0.5
1919	Bro-N	7	12	.368	30	19	13	2	1	173	181	9.4	3	29	1.5	40	2.1	2.24	122	.278	.304	13	9	94	141	-2.6	-2	3	1.2
1920	Bro-N	11	9	.550	33	12	6	2	3	136	134	8.9	1	27	1.8	33	2.2	1.85	183	.264	.295	19	23	108	135	-0.9	1	5	3.5
1921	Bro-N	7	11	.389	35	17	9	0	4	175	232	11.9	4	34	1.7	36	1.9	3.91	101	.319	.340	-2	1	105	108	-2.2	1	5	0.7
1922	Bro-N	4	8	.333	28	9	3	1	2	109	128	10.6	6	35	2.9	15	1.2	4.54	86	.309	.353	-5	-8	95	106	-2.0	2	1	-0.3
	Cle-A	1	0	1.000	2	2	1	0	0	16	18	10.1	0	3	1.7	4	2.3	3.38	123	.295	.323	1	1	103	102	0.5	1	0	0.2
1923	Cle-A	9	6	.600	30	16	10	1	1	124	129	9.4	4	37	2.7	23	1.7	3.27	120	.269	.319	10	9	99	101	1.1	1	2	1.2
1924	Cle-A	12	14	.462	39	27	20	2	1	248	267	9.7	5	42	**1.5**	34	1.2	3.01	137	.277	.304	34	31	97	105	0.7	-1	3	3.1
1925	Cle-A	11	14	.440	31	30	**22**	1	1	237	296	11.2	11	48	**1.8**	30	1.1	4.86	97	.306	.333	-12	-4	107	87	-0.4	6	-0	0.2
1926	Cle-A	11	10	.524	27	24	16	1	0	188	214	10.2	8	31	1.5	25	1.2	3.73	105	.292	.316	6	4	97	99	-0.9	2	3	0.8
1927	Cle-A	1	4	.200	11	2	1	0	1	38	53	12.6	2	14	3.3	8	1.9	5.45	75	.342	.383	-6	-6	99	107	-1.3	-0	0	-0.5
Total	14	114	118	.491	373	224	142	16	21	2053	2234	9.8	57	440	1.9	428	1.9	3.32	107	.282	.314	48	56	101	106	-4.6	23	26	11.5

■ **TOM SMITH** Smith, Thomas E. b: 12/5/1871, Boston, Mass. d: 3/2/29, Dorchester, Mass. BR/TR, 180 lbs. Deb: 6/06/1894

YEAR	TM/L	W	L	PCT	G	GS	CG	SHO	SV	IP	H	H/G	HR	BB	BB/G	SO	SO/G	ERA	/A	OAVG	OOBP	PR	/A	PF	CPI	WAT	PB	PD	TPI
1894	Bos-N	0	0	—	2	0	0	0	1	6	8	12.0	2	6	9.0	2	3.0	15.00	40	.343	.478	-6	-6	111	61	0.0	-0	0	-0.3
1895	Phi-N	2	3	.400	11	7	4	0	0	68	76	10.1	1	53	7.0	21	2.8	6.88	68	.303	.424	-16	-16	98	75	-0.7	-0	0	-1.2
1896	Lou-N	2	3	.400	11	5	4	0	0	55	73	11.9	2	25	4.1	14	2.3	5.40	82	.342	.411	-6	-6	102	99	0.4	-0	0	-0.4
1898	StL-N	0	1	.000	1	1	1	0	0	9	9	9.0	0	5	5.0	1	1.0	2.00	198	.282	.379	2	2	110	184	-0.4	1	0	0.3
Total	4	4	7	.364	25	13	9	0	1	138	166	10.8	5	89	5.8	38	2.5	6.33	73	.319	.419	-27	-26	101	91	-0.7	-0	0	-1.6

■ **BILL SMITH** Smith, William E. d: 10/28/1897, Guelph, Ont., Can. 151 lbs. Deb: 7/06/1886

YEAR	TM/L	W	L	PCT	G	GS	CG	SHO	SV	IP	H	H/G	HR	BB	BB/G	SO	SO/G	ERA	/A	OAVG	OOBP	PR	/A	PF	CPI	WAT	PB	PD	TPI
1886	Det-N	5	4	.556	9	9	9	0	0	77	81	9.5	0	30	3.5	36	4.2	4.09	83	.283	.351	-7	-6	103	89	-0.9	-1	0	-0.5

■ **BILL SMITH** Smith, William Garland b: 6/8/34, Washington, D.C. BL/TL, 6', 190 lbs. Deb: 9/13/58

YEAR	TM/L	W	L	PCT	G	GS	CG	SHO	SV	IP	H	H/G	HR	BB	BB/G	SO	SO/G	ERA	/A	OAVG	OOBP	PR	/A	PF	CPI	WAT	PB	PD	TPI
1958	StL-N	0	1	.000	2	1	0	0	0	10	12	10.8	0	4	3.6	4	3.6	6.30	68	.324	.381	-3	-2	108	78	-0.4	-0	0	-0.1
1959	StL-N	0	0	—	6	0	0	0	1	8	11	12.4	0	3	3.4	4	4.5	1.13	373	.333	.389	3	3	106	461	0.0	-0	0	0.3
1962	Phi-N	1	5	.167	24	5	0	0	0	50	59	10.6	8	10	1.8	26	4.7	4.32	87	.295	.323	-2	-3	95	112	-1.9	1	-0	-0.2
Total	3	1	6	.143	32	6	0	0	1	68	82	10.9	8	17	2.3	34	4.5	4.24	92	.304	.339	-2	-3	99	148	-2.3	1	-0	0.0

■ **WILLIE SMITH** Smith, Willie b: 2/11/39, Anniston, Ala. BL/TL, 6', 182 lbs. Deb: 6/18/63

YEAR	TM/L	W	L	PCT	G	GS	CG	SHO	SV	IP	H	H/G	HR	BB	BB/G	SO	SO/G	ERA	/A	OAVG	OOBP	PR	/A	PF	CPI	WAT	PB	PD	TPI
1963	Det-A	1	0	1.000	11	2	0	0	2	22	24	9.8	2	13	5.3	16	6.5	4.50	84	.300	.374	-2	-2	104	124	0.5	-0	0	-0.1
1964	LA-A	1	4	.200	15	1	0	0	0	32	34	9.6	5	10	2.8	20	5.6	2.81	114	.293	.336	3	1	89	184	-1.4	6	0	0.2
1968	Cle-A	0	0	—	2	0	0	0	0	5	2	3.6	0	1	1.8	1	1.8	0.00	—	.125	.176	2	2	101	0	0.0	0	0	0.2
	Chi-N	0	0	—	1	0	0	0	0	3	0	0.0	0	0	0.0	2	6.0	0.00	—	.000	.000	1	1	112	0	0.0	0	0	0.1
Total	3	2	4	.333	29	3	0	0	2	62	60	8.7	7	24	3.5	39	5.7	3.05	112	.273	.329	3	2	96	139	-0.9	6	1	0.4

■ **ZANE SMITH** Smith, Zane William b: 12/28/60, Madison, Wis. BL/TL, 6'2", 185 lbs. Deb: 9/10/84

YEAR	TM/L	W	L	PCT	G	GS	CG	SHO	SV	IP	H	H/G	HR	BB	BB/G	SO	SO/G	ERA	/A	OAVG	OOBP	PR	/A	PF	CPI	WAT	PB	PD	TPI
1984	Atl-N	1	0	1.000	3	3	0	0	0	20	16	7.2	1	13	5.8	16	7.2	2.25	175	.219	.333	3	4	110	147	0.5	2	0	0.7
1985	Atl-N	9	10	.474	42	18	2	2	0	147	135	8.3	4	80	4.9	85	5.2	3.80	103	.254	.345	-3	2	108	100	1.2	-1	2	0.4
1986	Atl-N	8	16	.333	38	32	3	1	1	205	209	9.2	8	105	4.6	139	6.1	4.04	95	.275	.359	-7	-4	103	108	-3.3	-3	3	-0.4
1987	Atl-N	15	10	.600	36	36	9	3	0	242	245	9.1	19	91	3.4	130	4.8	4.09	109	.266	.329	-0	10	109	98	4.2	-1	1	1.2
1988	Atl-N	5	10	.333	23	22	3	0	0	140	159	10.2	8	44	2.8	59	3.8	4.31	86	.292	.338	-13	-10	107	102	0.0	0	3	-0.5
Total	5	38	46	.452	142	111	17	6	1	754	764	9.1	40	333	4.0	429	5.1	4.01	100	.270	.342	-21	1	107	103	2.6	-2	9	1.4

■ **MIKE SMITHSON** Smithson, Billy Mike b: 1/21/55, Centerville, Tenn. BL/TR, 6'8", 215 lbs. Deb: 8/27/82

YEAR	TM/L	W	L	PCT	G	GS	CG	SHO	SV	IP	H	H/G	HR	BB	BB/G	SO	SO/G	ERA	/A	OAVG	OOBP	PR	/A	PF	CPI	WAT	PB	PD	TPI
1982	Tex-A	3	4	.429	8	8	3	0	0	47	51	9.8	5	13	2.5	24	4.6	4.98	77	.282	.337	-5	-6	94	90	0.2	0	-1	-0.5
1983	Tex-A	10	14	.417	33	33	10	0	0	223	233	9.4	14	71	2.9	135	5.4	3.91	105	.269	.325	4	5	101	98	-1.6	0	1	0.6
1984	Min-A	15	13	.536	36	36	10	1	0	252	246	8.8	35	54	1.9	144	5.1	3.68	115	.252	.294	9	15	106	98	1.2	0	-1	1.5
1985	Min-A	15	14	.517	37	37	8	3	0	257	264	9.2	25	78	2.7	127	4.4	4.34	99	.270	.328	-6	-1	104	98	1.4	0	-2	-0.2
1986	Min-A	13	14	.481	34	33	8	1	0	198	234	10.6	26	57	2.6	114	5.2	4.77	96	.294	.347	-13	-4	109	106	1.2	0	1	-0.3
1987	Min-A	4	7	.364	21	20	0	0	0	109	126	10.4	17	38	3.1	53	4.4	5.94	72	.286	.350	-18	-20	96	88	-1.7	0	-1	-1.8
1988	Bos-A	9	6	.600	31	18	1	0	0	127	149	10.6	25	37	2.6	73	5.2	5.95	72	.292	.342	-28	-23	108	92	0.9	0	-1	-2.3
Total	7	69	72	.489	200	185	40	5	0	1213	1303	9.7	147	348	2.6	670	5.0	4.53	94	.274	.328	-56	-34	104	97	1.6	0	-3	-3.0

■ **LEFTY SMOLL** Smoll, Clyde Hetrick b: 4/17/14, Quakertown, Pa. d: 8/31/85, Quakertown, Pa. BB/TL, 5'10", 175 lbs. Deb: 4/26/40

YEAR	TM/L	W	L	PCT	G	GS	CG	SHO	SV	IP	H	H/G	HR	BB	BB/G	SO	SO/G	ERA	/A	OAVG	OOBP	PR	/A	PF	CPI	WAT	PB	PD	TPI
1940	Phi-N	2	8	.200	33	9	0	0	0	109	145	12.0	6	36	3.0	31	2.6	5.37	73	.322	.370	-18	-17	102	102	-1.9	-1	-2	-1.9

■ **JOHN SMOLTZ** Smoltz, John Andrew b: 5/15/67, Detroit, Mich. BR/TR, 6'3", 180 lbs. Deb: 7/23/88

YEAR	TM/L	W	L	PCT	G	GS	CG	SHO	SV	IP	H	H/G	HR	BB	BB/G	SO	SO/G	ERA	/A	OAVG	OOBP	PR	/A	PF	CPI	WAT	PB	PD	TPI
1988	Atl-N	2	7	.222	12	12	0	0	0	64	74	10.4	10	33	4.6	37	5.2	5.48	67	.285	.367	-14	-13	107	101	-1.5	-0	-1	-1.3

■ **HARRY SMYTHE** Smythe, William Henry b: 10/24/04, Augusta, Ga. d: 8/28/80, Augusta, Ga. BL/TL, 5'10.5", 179 lbs. Deb: 7/21/29

YEAR	TM/L	W	L	PCT	G	GS	CG	SHO	SV	IP	H	H/G	HR	BB	BB/G	SO	SO/G	ERA	/A	OAVG	OOBP	PR	/A	PF	CPI	WAT	PB	PD	TPI
1929	Phi-N	4	6	.400	19	7	2	0	1	69	94	12.3	3	15	2.0	12	1.6	5.22	101	.330	.358	-4	0	112	99	-0.6	-1	1	0.1
1930	Phi-N	0	3	.000	25	3	0	0	2	50	84	15.1	3	31	5.6	9	1.6	7.74	70	.368	.445	-15	-13	109	101	-1.4	-0	-1	-1.0
1934	NY-A	0	2	.000	8	0	0	0	1	15	24	14.4	1	8	4.8	7	4.2	7.80	53	.381	.432	-6	-6	93	101	-0.9	-0	1	-0.4
	Bro-N	1	1	.500	8	0	0	0	0	21	30	12.9	3	8	3.4	5	2.1	6.00	65	.337	.390	-5	-5	95	112	0.1	1	1	-0.2
Total	3	5	12	.294	60	10	2	0	4	155	232	13.5	10	62	3.6	33	1.9	6.39	78	.349	.401	-29	-24	107	101	-2.8	0	2	-1.5

■ **NAT SNELL** Snell, Nathaniel b: 9/2/52, Orangeburg, S.C. BR/TR, 6'4", 190 lbs. Deb: 9/20/84

YEAR	TM/L	W	L	PCT	G	GS	CG	SHO	SV	IP	H	H/G	HR	BB	BB/G	SO	SO/G	ERA	/A	OAVG	OOBP	PR	/A	PF	CPI	WAT	PB	PD	TPI
1984	Bal-A	1	1	.500	5	0	0	0	0	8	8	9.0	1	1	1.1	7	7.9	2.25	167	.258	.273	2	1	94	148	0.0	0	0	0.1
1985	Bal-A	3	2	.600	43	0	0	0	5	100	100	9.0	4	30	2.7	41	3.7	2.70	151	.260	.311	16	15	98	124	0.4	0	1	1.7
1986	Bal-A	2	1	.667	34	0	0	0	0	72	69	8.6	9	22	2.8	29	3.6	3.88	107	.257	.310	2	2	99	102	0.6	0	1	0.3
1987	Det-A	1	2	.333	22	2	0	0	0	39	39	9.0	5	19	4.4	19	4.4	3.92	109	.267	.345	2	2	96	122	-0.6	0	-1	0.1
Total	4	7	6	.538	104	2	0	0	5	219	216	8.9	19	72	3.0	96	3.9	3.29	126	.260	.316	23	20	98	117	0.4	0	1	2.2

■ **FRANK SNOOK** Snook, Frank Walter b: 3/28/49, Somerville, N.J. BR/TR, 6'2", 180 lbs. Deb: 7/13/73

YEAR	TM/L	W	L	PCT	G	GS	CG	SHO	SV	IP	H	H/G	HR	BB	BB/G	SO	SO/G	ERA	/A	OAVG	OOBP	PR	/A	PF	CPI	WAT	PB	PD	TPI
1973	SD-N	0	2	.000	18	0	0	0	1	27	19	6.3	4	18	6.0	13	4.3	3.67	97	.200	.314	0	-0	97	100	-0.9	-0	1	0.0

■ **COLONEL SNOVER** Snover, Colonel Lester "Bosco" b: 5/16/1895, Hallstead, Pa. d: 4/30/69, Rochester, N.Y. BL/TL, 6'0.5", 200 lbs. Deb: 9/18/19

YEAR	TM/L	W	L	PCT	G	GS	CG	SHO	SV	IP	H	H/G	HR	BB	BB/G	SO	SO/G	ERA	/A	OAVG	OOBP	PR	/A	PF	CPI	WAT	PB	PD	TPI
1919	NY-N	0	1	.000	2	1	0	0	0	9	7	7.0	0	3	3.0	4	4.0	1.00	281	.212	.289	2	2	96	205	-0.4	0	-0	0.2

■ **BRIAN SNYDER** Snyder, Brian Robert b: 2/20/58, Flemington, N.J. BL/TL, 6'3", 185 lbs. Deb: 5/25/85

YEAR	TM/L	W	L	PCT	G	GS	CG	SHO	SV	IP	H	H/G	HR	BB	BB/G	SO	SO/G	ERA	/A	OAVG	OOBP	PR	/A	PF	CPI	WAT	PB	PD	TPI
1985	Sea-A	1	2	.333	15	6	0	0	1	35	44	11.3	2	19	4.9	23	5.9	6.43	62	.306	.386	-9	-10	95	85	-0.3	0	1	-0.8

■ **GENE SNYDER** Snyder, Gene Walter b: 3/31/31, York, Pa. BR/TL, 5'11", 175 lbs. Deb: 4/26/59

YEAR	TM/L	W	L	PCT	G	GS	CG	SHO	SV	IP	H	H/G	HR	BB	BB/G	SO	SO/G	ERA	/A	OAVG	OOBP	PR	/A	PF	CPI	WAT	PB	PD	TPI
1959	LA-N	1	1	.500	11	2	0	0	0	26	32	11.1	1	20	6.9	20	6.9	5.54	72	.299	.406	-5	-4	101	100	0.0	-0	-0	-0.4

■ **GEORGE SNYDER** Snyder, George T. b: 1849, Philadelphia, Pa. d: 8/2/05, Philadelphia, Pa. Deb: 9/30/1882

YEAR	TM/L	W	L	PCT	G	GS	CG	SHO	SV	IP	H	H/G	HR	BB	BB/G	SO	SO/G	ERA	/A	OAVG	OOBP	PR	/A	PF	CPI	WAT	PB	PD	TPI
1882	Phi-a	1	0	1.000	1	1	1	0	0	9	4	4.0	0	2	2.0	0	0.0	0.00	—	.139	.194	3	3	111	0	0.5	0	0	0.3

■ **BILL SNYDER** Snyder, William Nicholas b: 1/28/1898, Mansfield, Ohio d: 10/8/34, Vicksburg, Mich. BR/TR, Deb: 9/04/19

YEAR	TM/L	W	L	PCT	G	GS	CG	SHO	SV	IP	H	H/G	HR	BB	BB/G	SO	SO/G	ERA	/A	OAVG	OOBP	PR	/A	PF	CPI	WAT	PB	PD	TPI
1919	Was-A	0	1	.000	2	1	0	0	0	8	6	6.8	0	3	3.4	5	5.6	1.13	283	.200	.273	2	2	99	107	-0.4	-0	0	0.1
1920	Was-A	2	1	.667	16	4	1	0	1	54	59	9.8	1	28	4.7	17	2.8	4.17	88	.280	.380	-2	-3	96	102	0.6	1	-1	-0.2
Total	2	2	2	.500	18	5	1	0	1	62	65	9.4	1	31	4.5	22	3.2	3.77	95	.270	.367	-0	-1	97	102	0.2	1	-1	-0.1

■ **RAY SOFF** Soff, Raymond John b: 10/31/58, Adrian, Mich. BR/TR, 6', 185 lbs. Deb: 7/17/86

YEAR	TM/L	W	L	PCT	G	GS	CG	SHO	SV	IP	H	H/G	HR	BB	BB/G	SO	SO/G	ERA	/A	OAVG	OOBP	PR	/A	PF	CPI	WAT	PB	PD	TPI
1986	StL-N	4	2	.667	30	0	0	0	0	38	37	8.8	4	13	3.1	22	5.2	3.32	116	.255	.309	2	2	103	113	1.1	-0	1	0.3
1987	StL-N	1	0	1.000	12	0	0	0	0	15	18	10.8	3	5	3.0	9	5.4	6.60	60	.295	.353	-4	-4	97	87	0.5	-0	0	-0.3
Total	2	5	2	.714	42	0	0	0	0	53	55	9.3	7	18	3.1	31	5.3	4.25	92	.267	.322	-2	-2	102	105	1.6	-0	1	0.0

■ **JULIO SOLANO** Solano, Julio Cesar b: 1/8/60, Aqua Blanca, D.R. BR/TR, 6'1", 160 lbs. Deb: 4/05/83

YEAR	TM/L	W	L	PCT	G	GS	CG	SHO	SV	IP	H	H/G	HR	BB	BB/G	SO	SO/G	ERA	/A	OAVG	OOBP	PR	/A	PF	CPI	WAT	PB	PD	TPI
1983	Hou-N	0	2	.000	4	0	0	0	0	6	5	7.5	1	4	6.0	3	4.5	6.00	55	.217	.333	-2	-2	90	67	-0.9	0	0	-0.1

YEAR	TM/L	W	L	PCT	G	GS	CG	SHO	SV	IP	H	H/G	HR	BB	BB/G	SO	SO/G	ERA	/A	OAVG	OOBP	PR	/A	PF	CPI	WAT	PB	PD	TPI
1984	Hou-N	1	3	.250	31	0	0	0	0	51	31	5.5	3	18	3.2	33	5.8	1.94	170	.179	.249	9	8	92	90	-0.9	0	-1	0.7
1985	Hou-N	2	2	.500	20	0	0	0	0	34	34	9.0	5	13	3.4	17	4.5	3.44	100	.262	.326	1	0	96	126	0.0	-0	-1	0.0
1986	Hou-N	3	1	.750	16	1	0	0	0	32	39	11.0	5	22	6.2	21	5.9	7.59	50	.310	.413	-14	-14	102	90	0.8	-1	-0	-1.3
1987	Hou-N	0	0	—	11	0	0	0	0	20	25	11.2	5	9	4.0	12	5.4	7.65	50	.298	.362	-8	-9	93	82	0.0	-0	0	-0.7
1988	Sea-A	0	0	—	17	0	0	0	3	22	22	9.0	3	12	4.9	10	4.1	4.09	105	.268	.347	-0	1	108	123	0.0	0	0	0.1
Total	6	6	8	.429	99	1	0	0	3	165	156	8.5	22	78	4.3	96	5.2	4.47	81	.252	.331	-14	-16	97	100	-1.0	-1	-2	-1.3

■ **MARCELINO SOLIS** Solis, Marcelino b: 7/19/30, San Luis Potosi, Mexico BL/TL, 6'1", 185 lbs. Deb: 7/16/58

YEAR	TM/L	W	L	PCT	G	GS	CG	SHO	SV	IP	H	H/G	HR	BB	BB/G	SO	SO/G	ERA	/A	OAVG	OOBP	PR	/A	PF	CPI	WAT	PB	PD	TPI
1958	Chi-N	3	3	.500	15	4	0	0	0	52	74	12.8	5	20	3.5	15	2.6	6.06	66	.339	.402	-12	-12	101	104	0.2	1	0	-1.0

■ **EDDIE SOLOMON** Solomon, Eddie "Buddy" b: 2/9/51, Perry, Ga. d: 1/12/86, Macon, Ga. BR/TR, 6'2" 185 lbs. Deb: 9/02/73

YEAR	TM/L	W	L	PCT	G	GS	CG	SHO	SV	IP	H	H/G	HR	BB	BB/G	SO	SO/G	ERA	/A	OAVG	OOBP	PR	/A	PF	CPI	WAT	PB	PD	TPI
1973	LA-N	0	0	—	4	0	0	0	0	6	10	15.0	3	4	6.0	6	9.0	7.50	48	.357	.455	-3	-3	99	148	0.0	-0	0	-0.2
1974	LA-N	0	0	—	4	0	0	0	1	6	5	7.5	1	2	3.0	2	3.0	1.50	217	.217	.280	1	1	90	204	0.0	0	0	0.2
1975	Chi-N	0	0	—	6	0	0	0	0	7	7	9.0	1	6	7.7	3	3.9	1.29	298	.269	.382	2	2	105	450	0.0	0	0	0.2
1976	StL-N	1	1	.500	26	2	0	0	0	37	45	10.9	2	16	3.9	19	4.6	4.86	75	.306	.365	-6	-5	105	103	0.1	1	1	-0.2
1977	Atl-N	6	6	.500	18	16	0	0	0	89	110	11.1	10	34	3.4	54	5.5	4.55	99	.305	.362	-6	-0	115	116	1.3	-1	-0	0.0
1978	Atl-N	4	6	.400	37	8	0	0	2	106	98	8.3	12	50	4.2	64	5.4	4.08	100	.247	.327	-6	0	114	98	-0.2	-1	-0	0.0
1979	Atl-N	7	14	.333	31	30	4	0	0	186	184	8.9	19	51	2.5	96	4.6	4.21	98	.254	.304	-10	-2	110	82	-2.2	1	-1	-0.1
1980	Pit-N	7	3	.700	26	12	2	0	0	100	96	8.6	8	37	3.3	35	3.2	2.70	138	.253	.320	10	11	103	135	2.0	1	-0	1.3
1981	Pit-N	8	6	.571	22	17	2	0	1	127	133	9.4	10	27	1.9	38	2.7	3.12	108	.278	.313	5	3	96	**124**	1.7	-1	-1	0.2
1982	Pit-N	2	6	.250	11	10	0	0	0	47	69	13.2	9	18	3.4	18	3.4	6.70	59	.347	.398	-16	-14	110	106	-2.0	-1	-1	-1.5
	Chi-A	1	0	1.000	6	0	0	0	0	7	7	9.0	1	2	2.6	2	2.6	3.86	102	.241	.290	0	0	97	85	0.5	0	-0	0.0
Total	10	36	42	.462	191	95	8	0	4	718	764	9.6	76	247	3.1	337	4.2	4.00	98	.274	.331	-27	-6	107	111	1.2	-1	-3	-0.1

■ **JOE SOMMER** Sommer, Joseph John b: 11/20/1858, Covington, Ky. d: 1/16/38, Cincinnati, Ohio BR/TR, Deb: 7/08/1880

YEAR	TM/L	W	L	PCT	G	GS	CG	SHO	SV	IP	H	H/G	HR	BB	BB/G	SO	SO/G	ERA	/A	OAVG	OOBP	PR	/A	PF	CPI	WAT	PB	PD	TPI
1883	Cin-a	0	0	—	1	0	0	0	0	5	9	16.2	0	1	1.8	2	3.6	5.40	60	.395	.420	-1	-1	98	130	0.0	0	0	0.0
1885	Bal-a	0	0	—	2	0	0	0	1	3	6	18.0	0	0	0.0	0	0.0	9.00	39	.428	.428	-2	-2	109	83	0.0	0	0	-0.1
1886	Bal-a	0	0	—	1	0	0	0	0	4	14	31.5	0	3	6.8	1	2.3	18.00	18	.565	.612	-6	-7	94	95	0.0	-0	0	-0.4
1887	Bal-a	0	0	—	1	0	0	0	0	1	2	18.0	0	1	9.0	0	0.0	9.00	45	.430	.531	-1	-1	94	114	0.0	0	0	0.0
1890	Cle-N	0	0	—	1	0	0	0	0	1	2	18.0	1	2	18.0	0	0.0	0.00	—	.433	.604	0	0	97	0	0.0	0	0	0.0
Total	5	0	0	—	6	0	0	0	1	14	33	21.2	1	7	4.5	3	1.9	9.64	35	.465	.513	-10	-10	99	100	0.0	1	0	-0.5

■ **RUDY SOMMERS** Sommers, Rudolph b: 10/30/1888, Cincinnati, Ohio d: 3/18/49, Louisville, Ky. BB/TL, 5'11", 165 lbs. Deb: 9/08/12

YEAR	TM/L	W	L	PCT	G	GS	CG	SHO	SV	IP	H	H/G	HR	BB	BB/G	SO	SO/G	ERA	/A	OAVG	OOBP	PR	/A	PF	CPI	WAT	PB	PD	TPI
1912	Chi-N	0	1	.000	1	0	0	0	0	3	4	12.0	0	2	6.0	2	6.0	3.00	116	.308	.400	0	0	102	164	-0.4	0	0	0.0
1914	Bro-F	2	7	.222	23	8	2	0	2	82	88	9.7	2	34	3.7	40	4.4	4.06	80	.282	.358	-8	-8	101	99	-2.5	2	0	-0.5
1926	Bos-A	0	0	—	2	0	0	0	0	2	3	13.5	0	3	13.5	0	0.0	13.50	32	.333	.500	-2	-2	106	61	0.0	0	0	-0.1
1927	Bos-A	0	0	—	7	0	0	0	0	14	18	11.6	2	14	9.0	2	1.3	8.36	49	.353	.464	-7	-7	99	102	0.0	0	1	-0.4
Total	4	2	8	.200	33	8	2	0	2	101	113	10.1	4	53	4.7	44	3.9	4.81	70	.294	.380	-16	-16	101	101	-2.9	2	1	-1.0

■ **ANDY SOMMERVILLE** Sommerville, Andrew Henry (born Henry Travers Summersgill) b: 2/6/1876, Brooklyn, N.Y. d: 6/16/31, Richmond Hill, N.Y. Deb: 8/08/1894

YEAR	TM/L	W	L	PCT	G	GS	CG	SHO	SV	IP	H	H/G	HR	BB	BB/G	SO	SO/G	ERA	/A	OAVG	OOBP	PR	/A	PF	CPI	WAT	PB	PD	TPI
1894	Bro-N	0	1	.000	1	1	0	0	0	⅓	1	27.0	0	5	135.0	0	0.0	162.00	—	1.000	1.000	-6	-6	94	35	-0.4	0	0	-0.3

■ **DON SONGER** Songer, Donald C. b: 1/31/1900, Walnut, Kan. d: 10/3/62, Kansas City, Mo. BL/TL, 6', 165 lbs. Deb: 9/21/24

YEAR	TM/L	W	L	PCT	G	GS	CG	SHO	SV	IP	H	H/G	HR	BB	BB/G	SO	SO/G	ERA	/A	OAVG	OOBP	PR	/A	PF	CPI	WAT	PB	PD	TPI
1924	Pit-N	0	0	—	4	1	0	0	1	9	14	14.0	1	3	3.0	3	3.0	7.00	57	.333	.378	-3	-3	104	84	0.0	-0	0	-0.2
1925	Pit-N	0	1	.000	8	0	0	0	0	12	14	10.5	0	8	6.0	4	3.0	2.25	187	.298	.386	3	3	99	219	-0.4	-0	0	0.2
1926	Pit-N	7	8	.467	35	14	5	1	2	126	118	8.4	4	52	3.7	27	1.9	3.14	135	.252	.331	10	15	111	110	-1.1	-3	0	1.4
1927	Pit-N	0	0	—	2	0	0	0	0	5	10	18.0	0	4	7.2	1	1.8	10.80	36	.526	.556	-4	-4	99	114	0.0	-0	0	-0.3
	NY-N	3	5	.375	22	1	0	0	1	50	48	8.6	4	31	5.6	9	1.6	2.88	133	.261	.351	6	5	98	158	-1.4	1	1	0.7
	Yr	3	5	.375	24	1	0	0	1	55	58	9.5	4	35	5.7	10	1.6	3.60	107	.284	.369	2	1	98	158	-1.4	-0	1	0.4
Total	4	10	14	.417	71	16	5	1	4	202	204	9.1	9	98	4.4	44	2.0	3.39	122	.268	.348	11	17	106	127	-2.9	-2	2	1.8

■ **LARY SORENSEN** Sorensen, Lary Alan b: 10/4/55, Detroit, Mich. BR/TR, 6'2", 200 lbs. Deb: 6/07/77

YEAR	TM/L	W	L	PCT	G	GS	CG	SHO	SV	IP	H	H/G	HR	BB	BB/G	SO	SO/G	ERA	/A	OAVG	OOBP	PR	/A	PF	CPI	WAT	PB	PD	TPI
1977	Mil-A	7	10	.412	23	20	9	0	0	142	147	9.3	10	36	2.3	57	3.6	4.37	90	.270	.310	-5	-7	97	82	0.0	0	1	-0.5
1978	Mil-A	18	12	.600	37	36	17	3	1	281	277	8.9	14	50	1.6	78	2.5	3.20	123	.259	.289	18	23	104	91	1.1	0	0	2.4
1979	Mil-A	15	14	.517	34	34	16	2	0	235	250	9.6	30	42	1.6	63	2.4	3.98	105	.275	.306	6	6	99	101	-2.0	0	1	0.6
1980	Mil-A	12	10	.545	35	29	8	2	1	196	242	11.1	13	45	2.1	54	2.5	3.67	103	.311	.344	8	2	93	**126**	0.4	0	1	0.3
1981	StL-N	7	7	.500	23	23	3	1	0	140	149	9.6	3	26	1.7	52	3.3	3.28	107	.271	.304	3	4	101	93	-1.0	-3	0	0.1
1982	Cle-A	10	15	.400	32	30	6	1	0	189	251	12.0	19	55	2.6	62	3.0	5.62	73	.322	.364	-32	-32	101	97	-2.3	0	-1	-3.0
1983	Cle-A	12	11	.522	36	34	8	1	0	223	238	9.6	21	65	2.6	76	3.1	4.24	102	.276	.324	-4	2	106	98	2.1	0	2	0.3
1984	Oak-A	6	13	.316	46	21	2	0	1	183	240	11.8	21	44	2.2	63	3.1	4.92	75	.317	.355	-19	-25	92	108	-3.4	0	-1	-2.5
1985	Chi-N	3	7	.300	45	3	0	0	0	82	86	9.4	8	24	2.6	34	3.7	4.28	98	.274	.321	-6	-1	117	97	-1.8	-0	0	0.0
1987	Mon-N	3	4	.429	23	5	0	0	1	48	56	10.5	7	12	2.3	21	3.9	4.69	92	.286	.330	-3	-2	106	102	-0.8	-1	-1	-0.2
1988	SF-N	0	0	—	12	0	0	0	2	17	24	12.7	1	3	1.6	9	4.8	4.76	68	.329	.346	-2	-3	93	106	0.0	-0	-0	-0.2
Total	11	93	103	.474	346	235	69	10	6	1736	1960	10.2	147	402	2.1	569	2.9	4.15	96	.287	.324	-36	-32	100	100	-7.7	-4	2	-2.7

■ **VIC SORRELL** Sorrell, Victor Garland b: 4/9/01, Morrisville, N.C. d: 5/4/72, Raleigh, N.C. BR/TR, 5'10", 180 lbs. Deb: 4/22/28

YEAR	TM/L	W	L	PCT	G	GS	CG	SHO	SV	IP	H	H/G	HR	BB	BB/G	SO	SO/G	ERA	/A	OAVG	OOBP	PR	/A	PF	CPI	WAT	PB	PD	TPI
1928	Det-A	8	11	.421	29	23	8	0	0	171	182	9.6	9	83	4.4	67	3.5	4.79	85	.277	.351	-14	-14	100	92	-0.4	-4	-3	-1.9
1929	Det-A	14	15	.483	36	31	13	1	1	226	270	10.8	15	106	4.2	81	3.2	5.18	80	.302	.366	-23	-26	97	98	0.9	-5	-1	-2.9
1930	Det-A	16	11	.593	35	30	14	2	1	233	245	9.5	13	106	4.1	97	3.7	3.86	127	.274	.344	20	27	106	115	3.2	-3	-3	1.9
1931	Det-A	13	14	.481	35	32	19	1	1	245	267	9.8	8	114	4.2	99	3.6	4.15	113	.278	.348	6	14	107	107	2.2	-5	1	1.1
1932	Det-A	14	14	.500	32	31	13	1	0	234	234	9.0	11	77	3.0	84	3.2	4.04	113	.259	.314	11	13	102	91	0.0	-3	-2	0.8
1933	Det-A	11	15	.423	36	28	13	1	1	233	233	9.0	18	78	3.0	75	2.9	3.79	121	.260	.313	13	20	107	104	-1.9	-3	-0	1.7
1934	Det-A	6	9	.400	28	19	6	1	2	130	146	10.1	13	45	3.1	46	3.2	4.78	88	.283	.341	-4	-8	94	99	-3.0	-1	2	-0.6
1935	Det-A	4	3	.571	12	6	4	0	0	51	65	11.5	2	25	4.4	22	3.9	4.06	102	.319	.391	2	0	93	141	-0.2	-3	0	-0.1
1936	Det-A	6	7	.462	30	14	5	1	3	131	153	10.5	9	64	4.4	37	2.5	5.29	90	.294	.367	-4	-8	95	100	-0.9	1	2	-0.3
1937	Det-A	0	2	.000	7	2	0	0	1	17	25	13.2	3	8	4.2	11	5.8	9.00	55	.338	.398	-8	-8	108	80	-0.9	-1	0	-0.6
Total	10	92	101	.477	280	216	95	8	10	1671	1820	9.8	101	706	3.8	619	3.3	4.43	102	.279	.344	-0	12	102	102	-1.0	-27	-4	-0.9

■ **ELIAS SOSA** Sosa, Elias (Martinez) b: 6/10/50, La Vega, D.R. BR/TR, 6'2", 186 lbs. Deb: 9/08/72

YEAR	TM/L	W	L	PCT	G	GS	CG	SHO	SV	IP	H	H/G	HR	BB	BB/G	SO	SO/G	ERA	/A	OAVG	OOBP	PR	/A	PF	CPI	WAT	PB	PD	TPI
1972	SF-N	0	1	.000	8	0	0	0	3	16	10	5.6	0	12	6.8	10	5.6	2.25	153	.189	.328	2	2	100	118	-0.4	-0	0	0.2
1973	SF-N	10	4	.714	71	1	0	0	18	107	95	8.0	7	41	3.4	70	5.9	3.28	117	.241	.312	5	7	104	99	2.8	-0	-1	0.6
1974	SF-N	9	7	.563	68	0	0	0	6	101	94	8.4	8	45	4.0	48	4.3	3.48	114	.252	.322	2	5	109	108	1.8	-1	-1	0.3
1975	StL-N	0	3	.000	14	1	0	0	0	27	22	7.3	3	14	4.7	15	5.0	4.00	94	.227	.319	-1	-1	103	91	-1.4	-0	0	-0.1
	Atl-N	2	2	.500	43	0	0	0	2	62	70	10.2	3	29	4.2	31	4.5	4.50	78	.294	.366	-6	-7	97	105	0.3	-0	0	-0.6
	Yr	2	5	.286	57	1	0	0	2	89	92	9.3	6	43	4.3	46	4.7	4.35	83	.271	.349	-7	-7	99	105	-1.1	-0	0	-0.6
1976	Atl-N	4	4	.500	21	0	0	0	3	35	41	10.5	3	13	3.3	32	8.2	5.40	73	.287	.342	-7	-6	112	84	0.5	-0	-0	-0.6
	LA-N	2	4	.333	24	0	0	0	1	34	30	7.9	0	12	3.2	20	5.3	3.44	101	.242	.298	0	0	99	77	-1.2	0	0	0.0
	Yr	6	8	.429	45	0	0	0	4	69	71	9.3	3	25	3.3	52	6.8	4.43	83	.263	.318	-7	-6	106	77	-0.7	-0	-0	-0.6
1977	LA-N	2	2	.500	44	0	0	0	1	64	42	5.9	7	12	1.7	47	6.6	1.97	194	.189	.230	14	13	98	93	-0.3	0	0	1.4
1978	Oak-A	8	2	.800	68	0	0	0	14	109	106	8.8	5	44	3.6	61	5.0	2.64	147	.264	.329	14	15	103	139	3.3	0	0	1.6
1979	Mon-N	8	7	.533	62	0	0	0	18	97	77	7.1	2	37	3.4	59	5.5	1.95	194	.219	.293	19	20	101	120	-0.7	0	-1	1.8
1980	Mon-N	9	6	.600	67	0	0	0	9	94	104	10.0	5	19	1.8	58	5.6	3.06	116	.286	.315	6	5	98	123	0.8	-1	-0	0.4
1981	Mon-N	1	2	.333	32	0	0	0	3	39	46	10.6	3	8	1.8	18	4.2	3.69	93	.297	.324	-1	-1	98	117	-0.5	1	0	0.0
1982	Det-A	3	3	.500	38	0	0	0	4	61	64	9.4	11	18	2.7	24	3.5	4.43	92	.270	.323	-2	-2	100	106	0.0	0	1	-0.1
1983	SD-N	1	4	.200	41	1	0	0	1	72	72	9.0	7	30	3.8	45	5.6	4.38	82	.268	.334	-6	-6	99	98	-1.4	-0	-1	-0.7
Total	12	59	51	.536	601	3	0	0	83	918	873	8.6	64	334	3.3	538	5.3	3.32	113	.255	.316	38	44	102	109	3.6	-3	-2	4.3

■ **JOSE SOSA** Sosa, Jose Ynocencio (born Jose Ynocencio (Sosa)) b: 12/28/52, Santo Domingo, D.R. BR/TR, 5'11", 158 lbs. Deb: 7/22/75

YEAR	TM/L	W	L	PCT	G	GS	CG	SHO	SV	IP	H	H/G	HR	BB	BB/G	SO	SO/G	ERA	/A	OAVG	OOBP	PR	/A	PF	CPI	WAT	PB	PD	TPI
1975	Hou-N	1	3	.250	25	2	0	0	1	47	51	9.8	5	23	4.4	31	5.9	4.02	86	.291	.364	-2	-3	95	127	-0.7	2	-1	-0.2

YEAR	TM/L	W	L	PCT	G	GS	CG	SHO	SV	IP	H	H/G	HR	BB	BB/G	SO	SO/G	ERA	/A	OAVG	OOBP	PR	/A	PF	CPI	WAT	PB	PD	TPI
1976	Hou-N	0	0	—	9	0	0	0	0	12	16	12.0	0	6	4.5	5	3.8	6.75	45	.340	.417	-4	-5	87	94	0.0	0	1	-0.3
Total	2	1	3	.250	34	2	0	0	1	59	67	10.2	5	29	4.4	36	5.5	4.58	73	.302	.376	-6	-8	93	121	-0.7	2	-1	-0.5

■ **ALLEN SOTHORON** Sothoron, Allen Sutton b: 4/27/1893, Bradford, Ohio d: 6/17/39, St.Louis, Mo. BB/TR, 5'11", 182 lbs. Deb: 9/17/14 MC

YEAR	TM/L	W	L	PCT	G	GS	CG	SHO	SV	IP	H	H/G	HR	BB	BB/G	SO	SO/G	ERA	/A	OAVG	OOBP	PR	/A	PF	CPI	WAT	PB	PD	TPI
1914	StL-A	0	0	—	1	0	0	0	0	6	6	9.0	0	4	6.0	3	4.5	6.00	45	.261	.370	-2	-2	100	62	0.0	-0	-0	-0.1
1915	StL-A	0	1	.000	3	1	0	0	0	4	8	18.0	0	5	11.3	2	4.5	6.75	43	.400	.520	-2	-2	99	149	-0.4	-0	0	-0.1
1917	StL-A	14	19	.424	48	32	17	3	4	277	259	8.4	2	96	3.1	85	2.8	2.83	93	.251	.320	-5	-6	98	95	1.8	3	-1	-0.4
1918	StL-A	12	12	.500	29	24	14	2	0	209	152	**6.5**	3	67	2.9	71	3.1	1.94	143	**.205**	.267	19	19	100	79	0.7	-2	-3	1.6
1919	StL-A	20	13	.606	40	30	21	3	3	270	256	8.5	4	87	2.9	106	3.5	2.20	143	.246	.311	31	28	98	113	4.8	-2	-7	2.0
1920	StL-A	8	15	.348	36	26	12	1	2	218	263	10.9	6	89	3.7	81	3.3	4.71	90	.307	.376	-22	-12	111	97	-3.8	-1	-2	-1.4
1921	StL-A	1	2	.333	5	4	1	0	0	28	33	10.6	0	8	2.6	9	2.9	5.14	84	.314	.344	-3	-3	101	86	-0.5	-1	0	-0.2
	Bos-A	0	2	.000	2	2	0	0	0	6	15	22.5	0	5	7.5	2	3.0	13.50	32	.455	.513	-6	-6	100	85	-0.9	1	0	-0.4
	Cle-A	12	4	.750	22	16	10	2	0	145	146	9.1	0	58	3.6	61	3.8	3.23	127	.279	.340	17	14	96	119	3.1	2	-2	1.3
	Yr	13	8	.619	29	22	11	2	0	179	194	9.8	0	71	3.6	72	3.6	3.87	107	.293	.348	8	6	97	119	1.7	-0	-2	0.7
1922	Cle-A	1	3	.250	6	4	2	0	0	25	26	9.4	1	14	5.0	8	2.9	6.48	64	.274	.359	-7	-6	103	68	-0.9	1	-0	-0.4
1924	StL-N	10	16	.385	29	28	16	4	0	197	209	9.5	9	84	3.8	62	2.8	3.56	111	.275	.343	7	9	103	115	-1.3	-2	-3	0.4
1925	StL-N	10	10	.500	28	23	8	2	0	156	173	10.0	7	63	3.6	67	3.9	4.04	107	.280	.346	4	5	101	102	0.0	-1	-4	0.0
1926	StL-N	3	3	.500	15	4	1	0	0	43	37	7.7	2	16	3.3	19	4.0	4.19	91	.247	.299	-2	-2	100	77	-0.3	0	-1	-0.2
Total	11	91	100	.476	264	194	102	17	9	1584	1583	9.0	34	596	3.4	576	3.3	3.31	106	.264	.330	29	35	101	100	2.3	-3	-24	2.1

■ **MARIO SOTO** Soto, Mario Melvin b: 7/12/56, Bani, D.R. BR/TR, 6', 174 lbs. Deb: 7/21/77

YEAR	TM/L	W	L	PCT	G	GS	CG	SHO	SV	IP	H	H/G	HR	BB	BB/G	SO	SO/G	ERA	/A	OAVG	OOBP	PR	/A	PF	CPI	WAT	PB	PD	TPI
1977	Cin-N	2	6	.250	12	10	2	1	0	61	60	8.9	12	26	3.8	44	6.5	5.31	73	.258	.335	-9	-10	99	91	-2.1	-0	0	-0.9
1978	Cin-N	1	0	1.000	5	1	0	0	0	18	13	6.5	1	13	6.5	13	6.5	2.50	147	.197	.329	2	2	102	117	0.5	-0	-0	0.2
1979	Cin-N	3	2	.600	25	0	0	0	0	37	33	8.0	2	30	7.3	32	7.8	5.35	67	.243	.379	-7	-7	96	82	0.2	2	-1	-0.5
1980	Cin-N	10	8	.556	53	12	3	1	4	190	126	**6.0**	11	84	4.0	182	**8.6**	3.08	119	**.187**	.273	11	12	101	66	0.1	-4	0	0.8
1981	Cin-N	12	9	.571	25	25	10	3	0	175	142	7.3	13	61	3.1	151	7.8	3.29	107	.220	.287	4	4	101	81	-0.7	-4	-1	0.0
1982	Cin-N	14	13	.519	35	34	13	2	0	258	202	**7.0**	19	71	2.5	274	**9.6**	2.79	134	.215	**.268**	23	27	104	85	3.5	1	-1	3.0
1983	Cin-N	17	13	.567	34	34	**18**	3	0	274	207	6.8	28	95	3.1	242	7.9	2.69	140	.208	.276	29	33	104	95	3.6	-2	-1	3.2
1984	Cin-N	18	7	.720	33	33	**13**	0	0	237	181	6.9	26	87	3.3	185	7.0	3.53	109	.209	.281	2	8	107	79	6.9	3	-2	1.0
1985	Cin-N	12	15	.444	36	36	9	1	0	257	196	6.9	30	104	3.6	214	7.5	3.57	106	.211	.286	1	6	105	83	-3.0	-2	-1	0.4
1986	Cin-N	5	10	.333	19	19	1	1	0	105	113	9.7	15	46	3.9	67	5.7	4.71	82	.280	.347	-12	-10	104	106	-2.9	-1	-0	-1.0
1987	Cin-N	3	2	.600	6	6	0	0	0	32	34	9.6	7	12	3.4	11	3.1	5.06	83	.279	.333	-3	-3	103	106	0.4	-1	0	-0.3
1988	Cin-N	3	7	.300	14	14	3	1	0	87	88	9.1	8	28	2.9	34	3.5	4.66	78	.267	.322	-12	-10	105	87	-2.2	-1	-1	-1.1
Total	12	100	92	.521	297	224	72	13	4	1731	1395	7.3	172	657	3.4	1449	7.5	3.47	108	.220	.291	29	54	104	85	4.3	-10	-7	4.8

■ **MARK SOUZA** Souza, Kenneth Mark b: 2/1/55, Redwood City, Cal. BL/TL, 6', 180 lbs. Deb: 4/22/80

YEAR	TM/L	W	L	PCT	G	GS	CG	SHO	SV	IP	H	H/G	HR	BB	BB/G	SO	SO/G	ERA	/A	OAVG	OOBP	PR	/A	PF	CPI	WAT	PB	PD	TPI
1980	Oak-A	0	0	—	5	0	0	0	0	7	9	11.6	1	5	6.4	2	2.6	7.71	49	.310	.412	-3	-3	94	84	0.0	0	-0	-0.2

■ **JOHN SOWDERS** Sowders, John b: 12/10/1866, Louisville, Ky. d: 7/29/08, Indianapolis, Ind BR/TL, Deb: 6/28/1887

YEAR	TM/L	W	L	PCT	G	GS	CG	SHO	SV	IP	H	H/G	HR	BB	BB/G	SO	SO/G	ERA	/A	OAVG	OOBP	PR	/A	PF	CPI	WAT	PB	PD	TPI
1887	Ind-N	0	0	—	1	0	0	0	0	3	11	33.0	0	5	15.0	0	0.0	21.00	20	.582	.669	-6	-6	101	98	0.0	-0	0	-0.3
1889	KC-a	6	16	.273	25	23	20	0	1	185	204	9.9	9	105	5.1	104	5.1	4.82	87	.295	.388	-20	-13	109	97	-3.9	-2	0	-1.0
1890	Bro-P	19	16	.543	39	37	28	1	0	309	358	10.4	3	161	4.7	91	2.7	3.82	117	.302	.386	14	22	105	111	-1.2	-5	0	1.5
Total	3	25	32	.439	65	60	48	1	1	497	573	10.4	12	271	4.9	195	3.5	4.29	102	.302	.390	-11	4	107	106	-5.1	-7	0	0.2

■ **BILL SOWDERS** Sowders, William Jefferson "Little Bill" b: 11/29/1864, Louisville, Ky. d: 2/2/51, Indianapolis, Ind. BR/TR, 6', Deb: 1888

YEAR	TM/L	W	L	PCT	G	GS	CG	SHO	SV	IP	H	H/G	HR	BB	BB/G	SO	SO/G	ERA	/A	OAVG	OOBP	PR	/A	PF	CPI	WAT	PB	PD	TPI
1888	Bos-N	19	15	.559	36	35	34	2	0	317	278	7.9	3	73	2.1	132	3.7	2.07	143	.249	.295	27	32	105	110	1.7	-5	1	2.9
1889	Bos-N	1	2	.333	7	4	3	0	2	42	53	11.4	3	23	4.9	10	2.1	5.14	77	.324	.408	-5	-6	98	109	-0.6	0	0	-0.4
	Pit-N	6	5	.545	13	11	9	0	0	53	94	16.0	1	29	4.9	33	5.6	7.47	48	.403	.469	-20	-23	90	103	0.9	2	0	-1.6
	Yr	7	7	.500	20	15	12	0	**2**	95	147	13.9	4	52	4.9	43	4.1	6.44	59	.371	.444	-25	-28	94	103	0.3	0	0	-2.0
1890	Pit-N	3	8	.273	15	11	9	0	0	106	117	9.9	1	24	2.0	30	2.5	4.42	76	.296	.336	-10	-12	95	75	0.7	-2	0	-1.2
Total	3	29	30	.492	71	61	55	2	2	518	542	9.4	8	149	2.6	205	3.6	3.35	96	.284	.336	-9	-7	101	102	2.7	-4	1	-0.3

■ **BOB SPADE** Spade, Robert b: 1/4/1877, Akron, Ohio d: 9/7/24, Cincinnati, Ohio BR/TR, 5'10", 190 lbs. Deb: 9/22/07

YEAR	TM/L	W	L	PCT	G	GS	CG	SHO	SV	IP	H	H/G	HR	BB	BB/G	SO	SO/G	ERA	/A	OAVG	OOBP	PR	/A	PF	CPI	WAT	PB	PD	TPI
1907	Cin-N	1	2	.333	3	3	3	1	0	27	21	7.0	0	9	3.0	7	2.3	1.00	234	.243	.321	4	4	95	201	-0.2	1	-1	0.4
1908	Cin-N	17	12	.586	35	28	22	3	1	249	230	8.3	2	85	3.1	74	2.7	2.75	89	.275	.345	-11	-9	104	103	3.6	1	-4	-1.4
1909	Cin-N	5	5	.500	14	13	8	0	0	98	91	8.4	0	39	3.6	31	2.8	2.85	86	.236	.313	-3	-4	94	86	0.0	4	-4	-0.8
1910	Cin-N	1	2	.333	3	3	1	0	0	17	35	18.5	1	9	4.8	1	0.5	6.88	45	.479	.542	-7	-7	102	153	-0.4	-1	0	-0.6
	StL-A	1	3	.250	7	5	2	1	0	35	34	8.7	1	17	4.4	8	2.1	4.37	58	.270	.361	-7	-7	101	87	-0.3	1	-1	-0.7
Total	4	25	24	.510	62	52	36	5	1	426	411	8.7	4	159	3.4	121	2.6	2.96	83	.273	.347	-24	-23	101	106	2.7	7	-9	-3.1

■ **WARREN SPAHN** Spahn, Warren Edward b: 4/23/21, Buffalo, N.Y. BL/TL, 6', 172 lbs. Deb: 4/19/42 CH

YEAR	TM/L	W	L	PCT	G	GS	CG	SHO	SV	IP	H	H/G	HR	BB	BB/G	SO	SO/G	ERA	/A	OAVG	OOBP	PR	/A	PF	CPI	WAT	PB	PD	TPI
1942	Bos-N	0	0	—	4	2	1	0	0	16	25	14.1	0	11	6.2	7	3.9	5.63	58	.368	.456	-4	-4	98	127	0.0	-0	-0	-0.4
1946	Bos-N	8	5	.615	24	16	8	0	1	126	107	7.6	6	36	2.6	67	4.8	2.93	109	.228	.280	4	4	94	80	1.3	-0	-2	0.1
1947	Bos-N	21	10	.677	40	35	22	**7**	3	**290**	245	7.6	15	84	2.6	123	3.8	**2.33**	**167**	.226	**.281**	**56**	**50**	95	106	4.9	1	-2	**5.0**
1948	Bos-N	15	12	.556	36	35	16	3	1	257	237	8.3	19	77	2.7	114	4.0	3.71	105	.242	.296	7	6	99	84	-1.0	1	0	0.7
1949	Bos-N	**21**	14	.600	38	38	**25**	4	0	**302**	283	8.4	27	86	2.6	**151**	4.5	3.07	127	.245	.296	33	28	97	106	**4.7**	-0	-2	2.6
1950	Bos-N	**21**	17	.553	41	39	25	1	1	293	248	7.6	22	111	3.4	**191**	5.9	3.16	111	.227	.296	32	12	85	93	0.7	5	0	1.5
1951	Bos-N	22	14	.611	39	36	**26**	**7**	0	311	278	8.0	20	109	3.2	**164**	4.7	2.98	129	.238	.301	34	30	97	102	5.1	4	-2	3.3
1952	Bos-N	14	19	.424	40	35	19	5	3	290	263	8.2	19	73	2.3	**183**	5.7	2.98	121	.240	.287	24	20	97	98	0.2	2	1	2.5
1953	Mil-N	**23**	7	.767	35	32	24	5	3	266	211	**7.1**	14	70	2.4	148	5.0	**2.10**	**187**	**.217**	**.267**	**65**	54	92	108	**7.1**	4	2	**6.3**
1954	Mil-N	21	12	.636	39	34	23	1	3	283	262	8.3	24	86	2.7	136	4.3	3.15	118	.245	.297	29	18	91	98	2.8	6	1	2.4
1955	Mil-N	17	14	.548	39	32	16	1	1	246	249	9.1	25	65	2.4	110	4.0	3.26	113	.265	.308	21	12	92	115	0.0	5	0	1.7
1956	Mil-N	20	11	.645	39	35	20	3	3	281	249	8.0	25	52	1.7	128	4.1	2.79	130	.238	.273	**31**	**26**	96	95	2.2	5	-1	3.2
1957	Mil-N	**21**	11	.656	39	35	**18**	4	3	271	241	8.0	23	78	2.6	111	3.7	2.69	126	.237	.289	**36**	21	88	109	2.0	2	0	2.3
1958	Mil-N	**22**	11	**.667**	38	36	**23**	2	1	**290**	257	8.0	29	76	2.4	150	4.7	3.07	112	.237	.285	28	11	87	95	3.5	17	4	3.2
1959	Mil-N	**21**	15	.583	40	36	21	**4**	0	**292**	282	8.7	21	70	2.2	143	4.4	2.96	124	.253	.293	32	23	93	105	1.6	6	-1	2.9
1960	Mil-N	**21**	10	.677	40	33	**18**	4	2	268	254	8.5	24	74	2.5	154	5.2	3.49	96	.250	.299	8	-4	89	96	4.5	3	3	0.0
1961	Mil-N	**21**	13	.618	38	34	**21**	**4**	0	263	236	8.1	24	64	2.2	115	3.9	**3.01**	122	.243	**.286**	**30**	19	91	103	3.6	10	3	3.2
1962	Mil-N	18	14	.563	34	34	**22**	0	0	269	248	8.3	25	55	1.8	118	3.9	3.04	127	.246	.281	27	25	98	100	1.3	4	1	3.1
1963	Mil-N	23	7	.767	33	33	**22**	7	0	260	241	8.3	23	49	1.7	102	3.5	2.60	126	.248	.280	20	20	100	115	8.5	5	4	3.3
1964	Mil-N	6	13	.316	38	25	4	1	4	174	204	10.6	23	52	2.7	78	4.0	5.28	64	.297	.340	-34	-36	96	95	-4.2	2	-1	-3.5
1965	NY-N	4	12	.250	20	19	5	0	0	126	140	10.0	18	35	2.5	56	4.0	4.36	84	.281	.326	-11	-9	104	106	-1.6	1	0	-0.8
	SF-N	3	4	.429	16	11	3	0	0	72	70	8.8	8	21	2.6	34	4.3	3.38	115	.256	.304	1	4	109	112	-0.9	-0	1	0.5
	Yr	7	16	.304	36	30	8	0	0	198	210	9.5	26	56	2.5	90	4.1	4.00	94	.271	.316	-10	-6	106	112	-2.5	1	1	-0.3
Total	21	363	245	.597	750	665	382	63	29	5246	4830	8.3	434	1434	2.5	2583	4.4	3.08	118	.244	.293	471	331	94	101	46.3	82	9	43.1

■ **AL SPALDING** Spalding, Albert Goodwill b: 9/2/1850, Byron, Ill. d: 9/9/15, San Diego, Cal. BR/TR, 6'1", 170 lbs. Deb: 5/05/1871 MH

YEAR	TM/L	W	L	PCT	G	GS	CG	SHO	SV	IP	H	H/G	HR	BB	BB/G	SO	SO/G	ERA	/A	OAVG	OOBP	PR	/A	PF	CPI	WAT	PB	PD	TPI
1871	Bos-n	20	10	.667	31																								
1872	Bos-n	37	8	.822	48																								
1873	Bos-n	41	15	.732	57																								
1874	Bos-n	52	18	.743	71																								
1875	Bos-n	57	5	.919	66																								
1876	Chi-N	**47**	12	**.797**	61	60	53	8	0	529	542	9.2	6	26	0.4	39	0.7	1.75	149	.269	.279	33	51	113	102	8.5	7	5	6.3
1877	Chi-N	1	0	1.000	4	1	0	0	1	11	17	13.9	0	0	0.0	2	1.6	3.27	85	.362	.362	-1	-1	99	135	0.5	0	0	0.0
Total	5 n	207	56	.787	273																								
Total	2	48	12	.800	65	61	53	8	1	540	559	9.3	6	26	0.4	41	0.7	1.78	147	.271	.281	32	50	113	103	9.0	7	5	6.3

■ **BILL SPANSWICK** Spanswick, William Henry b: 7/8/38, Springfield, Mass. BL/TL, 6'3", 195 lbs. Deb: 4/18/64

YEAR	TM/L	W	L	PCT	G	GS	CG	SHO	SV	IP	H	H/G	HR	BB	BB/G	SO	SO/G	ERA	/A	OAVG	OOBP	PR	/A	PF	CPI	WAT	PB	PD	TPI
1964	Bos-A	2	3	.400	29	7	0	0	0	65	75	10.4	9	44	6.1	55	7.6	6.92	54	.306	.405	-24	-23	103	93	-0.2	1	1	-2.0

YEAR	TM/L	W	L	PCT	G	GS	CG	SHO	SV	IP	H	H/G	HR	BB	BB/G	SO	SO/G	ERA	/A	OAVG	OOBP	PR	/A	PF	CPI	WAT	PB	PD	TPI
■ **TULLY SPARKS**	Sparks, Thomas Frank b: 12/12/1874, Aetna, Ga. d: 7/15/37, Anniston, Ala. BR/TR, Deb: 9/15/1897																												
1897	Phi-N	0	1	.000	1	1	1	0	0	8	12	13.5	0	4	4.5	0	0.0	10.13	41	.370	.439	-5	-5	96	59	-0.4	-1	0	-0.3
1899	Pit-N	8	6	.571	28	17	8	0	0	170	180	9.5	1	82	4.3	53	2.8	3.86	98	.295	.379	-0	-2	98	98	1.0	-1	0	-0.2
1901	Mil-A	7	16	.304	29	26	18	0	0	210	228	9.8	5	93	4.0	62	2.7	3.51	102	.297	.373	3	2	98	114	-1.7	-2	-1	0.1
1902	NY-N	4	11	.267	15	13	11	0	1	115	123	9.6	2	40	3.1	40	3.1	3.76	77	.297	.359	-13	-11	104	92	-1.9	-1	3	-0.8
	Bos-A	7	9	.438	17	15	15	1	0	143	151	9.5	4	40	2.5	37	2.3	3.46	101	.296	.347	2	1	98	100	-1.8	-1	0	0.1
1903	Phi-N	11	15	.423	28	28	27	0	0	248	248	9.0	3	56	2.0	88	3.2	2.72	113	.287	.336	15	10	94	105	1.5	-5	-2	0.8
1904	Phi-N	7	16	.304	26	25	19	3	0	201	208	9.3	1	43	1.9	67	3.0	2.64	100	.293	.338	2	-0	97	114	-1.4	-4	-4	-0.4
1905	Phi-N	14	11	.560	34	26	20	3	1	260	217	7.5	2	73	2.5	98	3.4	2.18	140	.254	.319	23	25	102	109	0.5	-3	-6	2.1
1906	Phi-N	19	16	.543	42	37	29	6	3	317	244	6.9	4	62	1.8	114	3.2	2.16	113	.240	.290	17	10	93	82	3.2	1	-5	0.6
1907	Phi-N	22	8	.733	33	31	24	3	1	265	221	7.5	2	51	1.7	90	3.1	2.00	127	.255	.302	14	16	103	96	**6.6**	-8	-5	1.2
1908	Phi-N	16	15	.516	33	31	24	2	2	263	251	8.6	3	51	1.7	85	2.9	2.60	89	.282	.327	-7	-9	98	101	-0.7	-5	-2	-1.1
1909	Phi-N	6	11	.353	24	16	6	1	0	122	126	9.3	4	32	2.4	40	3.0	2.95	94	.280	.332	-5	-2	106	118	-2.4	-1	-1	-0.3
1910	Phi-N	0	2	.000	3	3	0	0	0	15	22	13.2	2	2	1.2	4	2.4	6.00	48	.324	.361	-5	-5	95	90	-0.9	-1	0	-0.5
Total	12	121	137	.469	313	269	202	19	8	2337	2231	8.6	33	629	2.4	778	3.0	2.79	104	.277	.333	41	30	99	101	1.6	-31	-22	1.3
■ **JOE SPARMA**	Sparma, Joseph Blase b: 2/4/42, Massillon, Ohio d: 5/14/86, Columbus, Ohio BR/TR, 6'1", 190 lbs. Deb: 5/20/64																												
1964	Det-A	5	6	.455	21	11	3	2	0	84	62	6.6	4	45	4.8	71	7.6	3.00	115	.207	.311	6	4	95	92	-0.7	1	1	0.7
1965	Det-A	13	8	.619	30	28	6	0	0	167	142	7.7	13	75	4.0	127	6.8	3.18	113	.228	.309	5	8	104	101	1.8	-1	-1	0.7
1966	Det-A	2	7	.222	29	13	0	0	0	92	103	10.1	14	52	5.1	61	6.0	5.28	66	.288	.376	-19	-18	102	109	-2.6	1	-1	-1.9
1967	Det-A	16	9	.640	37	37	11	5	0	218	186	7.7	20	85	3.5	153	6.3	3.76	84	.227	.303	-13	-14	98	86	2.6	-4	-3	-2.2
1968	Det-A	10	10	.500	34	31	7	1	0	182	169	8.4	14	77	3.8	110	5.4	3.71	83	.246	.324	-15	-13	103	98	-2.3	-1	-2	-1.7
1969	Det-A	6	8	.429	23	16	3	2	0	93	78	7.5	5	77	7.5	41	4.0	4.74	78	.231	.371	-12	-11	102	87	-1.6	-1	-1	-1.2
1970	Mon-N	0	4	.000	9	6	1	0	0	29	34	10.6	7	25	7.8	23	7.1	7.14	58	.296	.418	-10	-10	102	106	-1.9	-0	-0	-0.9
Total	7	52	52	.500	183	142	31	10	0	865	774	8.1	77	436	4.5	586	6.1	3.94	86	.239	.329	-57	-54	101	95	-4.7	-6	-7	-6.5
■ **TRIS SPEAKER**	Speaker, Tristram E "The Grey Eagle" b: 4/4/1888, Hubbard, Tex. d: 12/8/58, Lake Whitney, Tex. BL/TL, 5'11.5", 193 lbs. Deb: 9/14/07 MH																												
1914	Bos-A	0	0	—	1	0	0	0	0	1	2	18.0	0	0	0.0	0	0.0	9.00	29	.500	.500	-1	-1	96	95	0.0	1	0	0.0
■ **CLIFF SPECK**	Speck, Robert Clifford b: 8/8/56, Portland, Ore. BR/TR, 6'4", 195 lbs. Deb: 7/30/86																												
1986	Atl-N	2	1	.667	13	1	0	0	0	28	25	8.0	2	15	4.8	21	6.8	4.18	92	.238	.333	-1	-1	103	88	0.6	-0	0	0.0
■ **BY SPEECE**	Speece, Byron Franklin b: 1/6/1897, West Baden, Ind. d: 9/29/74, Elgin, Ore. BR/TR, 5'11", 170 lbs. Deb: 4/21/24																												
1924	Was-A	2	1	.667	21	1	0	0	0	54	60	10.0	0	27	4.5	15	2.5	2.67	152	.303	.369	**9**	**8**	96	178	0.3	-1	1	0.8
1925	Cle-A	3	5	.375	28	3	3	0	1	90	106	10.6	0	28	2.8	26	2.6	4.30	109	.297	.338	1	4	107	92	-0.6	-2	0	0.2
1926	Cle-A	0	0	—	2	0	0	0	0	3	1	3.0	0	2	6.0	1	3.0	0.00	—	.125	.300	1	1	97	0	0.0	0	0	0.2
1930	Phi-N	0	0	—	11	0	0	0	0	20	41	18.4	1	4	1.8	9	4.0	13.05	42	.432	.429	-18	-17	109	67	0.0	0	0	-1.3
Total	4	5	6	.455	62	4	3	0	1	167	208	11.2	1	61	3.3	51	2.7	4.74	96	.316	.360	-6	-3	103	115	-0.3	-2	2	-0.1
■ **FLOYD SPEER**	Speer, Floyd Vernie b: 1/27/13, Booneville, Ark. d: 3/22/69, Little Rock, Ark. BR/TR, 6', 180 lbs. Deb: 4/25/43																												
1943	Chi-A	0	0	—	1	0	0	0	0	1	1	9.0	0	2	18.0	1	9.0	9.00	37	.250	.500	-1	-1	101	82	0.0	0	0	0.0
1944	Chi-A	0	0	—	2	0	0	0	0	2	4	18.0	0	0	0.0	1	4.5	9.00	39	.500	.444	-1	-1	102	98	0.0	0	0	0.0
Total	2	0	0	—	3	0	0	0	0	3	5	15.0	0	2	6.0	2	6.0	9.00	38	.417	.467	-2	-2	102	93	0.0	0	0	0.0
■ **KID SPEER**	Speer, George Nathan b: 6/16/1886, Corning, Mo. d: 1/13/46, Edmonton, Alberta, Canada BL/TL, Deb: 4/24/09																												
1909	Det-A	4	4	.500	12	8	4	0	1	76	88	10.4	2	13	1.5	12	1.4	2.84	93	.293	.331	-3	-2	106	121	-0.8	-1	1	0.0
■ **HACK SPENCER**	Spencer, Fred Calvin b: 4/25/1885, St.Cloud, Minn. d: 2/5/69, St.Anthony, Minn. BR/TR, 5'10.5", 172 lbs. Deb: 4/18/12																												
1912	StL-A	0	0	—	1	0	0	0	0	2	2	9.0	0	0	0.0	0	0.0	0.00	—	.286	.286	1	1	103	0	0.0	0	0	0.1
■ **GEORGE SPENCER**	Spencer, George Elwell b: 7/7/26, Columbus, Ohio BR/TR, 6'1", 215 lbs. Deb: 8/17/50																												
1950	NY-N	1	0	1.000	10	1	1	0	0	25	12	4.3	3	7	2.5	5	1.8	2.52	159	.141	.202	5	4	97	43	0.5	-1	0	0.4
1951	NY-N	10	4	.714	57	4	2	0	6	132	125	8.5	21	56	3.8	36	2.5	3.75	105	.254	.328	3	3	99	118	1.8	-1	1	0.3
1952	NY-N	3	5	.375	35	4	0	0	3	60	57	8.6	13	21	3.2	27	4.1	5.55	68	.251	.316	-12	-12	101	85	-1.4	0	0	-1.1
1953	NY-N	0	0	—	1	0	0	0	0	2	3	13.5	0	2	9.0	1	4.5	9.00	47	.300	.417	-1	-1	98	65	0.0	0	0	0.0
1954	NY-N	1	0	1.000	6	0	0	0	0	12	9	6.8	1	8	6.0	4	3.0	3.75	110	.209	.327	0	1	102	87	0.5	-0	1	0.1
1955	NY-N	0	0	—	1	0	0	0	0	2	1	4.5	1	3	13.5	0	0.0	4.50	88	.167	.444	-0	-0	98	187	0.0	0	0	0.0
1958	Det-A	1	0	1.000	7	0	0	0	0	10	11	9.9	1	4	3.6	5	4.5	2.70	144	.289	.341	1	1	103	177	0.5	0	0	0.2
1960	Det-A	0	1	.000	5	0	0	0	0	8	10	11.3	1	5	5.6	4	4.5	3.38	117	.323	.405	0	1	102	192	-0.4	-0	0	0.0
Total	8	16	10	.615	122	9	3	0	9	251	228	8.2	41	106	3.8	82	2.9	4.05	96	.245	.319	-4	-4	100	106	1.5	-2	2	-0.1
■ **GLENN SPENCER**	Spencer, Glenn Edward b: 9/11/05, Corning, N.Y. d: 12/30/58, Binghamton, N.Y. BR/TR, 5'11", 155 lbs. Deb: 4/11/28																												
1928	Pit-N	0	0	—	4	0	0	0	0	6	4	6.0	0	3	4.5	2	3.0	1.50	278	.200	.280	2	2	105	140	0.0	-0	-0	0.1
1930	Pit-N	8	9	.471	41	10	5	0	4	157	185	10.6	16	63	3.6	60	3.4	5.39	90	.305	.358	-7	-9	98	100	-0.8	-4	-2	-1.3
1931	Pit-N	11	12	.478	38	18	11	1	3	187	180	8.7	8	65	3.1	51	2.5	3.42	115	.260	.319	9	11	102	104	-0.1	-3	-0	0.7
1932	Pit-N	4	8	.333	39	13	5	1	1	138	167	10.9	10	44	2.9	35	2.3	4.96	78	.288	.337	-17	-17	100	88	-2.4	-1	-1	-1.7
1933	NY-N	0	2	.000	17	3	1	0	0	47	52	10.0	3	26	5.0	14	2.7	5.17	62	.284	.366	-10	-10	96	93	-0.9	-0	0	-0.9
Total	5	23	31	.426	139	44	22	2	8	535	588	9.9	37	201	3.4	162	2.7	4.53	91	.282	.339	-22	-24	99	98	-4.2	-9	-3	-3.1
■ **BOB SPICER**	Spicer, Robert Oberton b: 4/11/25, Richmond, Va. BL/TR, 5'10", 173 lbs. Deb: 4/17/55																												
1955	KC-A	0	0	—	2	0	0	0	0	3	9	27.0	2	4	12.0	2	6.0	30.00	14	.529	.636	-9	-9	106	73	0.0	-0	0	-0.6
1956	KC-A	0	0	—	2	0	0	0	0	2	6	27.0	1	1	4.5	0	0.0	22.50	19	.545	.615	-4	-4	105	86	0.0	0	0	-0.2
Total	2	0	0	—	4	0	0	0	0	5	15	27.0	3	5	9.0	2	3.6	27.00	16	.536	.629	-13	-13	106	78	0.0	-0	0	-0.8
■ **DAN SPILLNER**	Spillner, Daniel Ray b: 11/27/51, Casper, Wyo. BR/TR, 6'1", 190 lbs. Deb: 5/21/74																												
1974	SD-N	9	11	.450	30	25	5	2	0	148	153	9.3	15	70	4.3	95	5.8	4.01	88	.267	.342	-6	-8	97	106	1.4	-4	-1	-1.3
1975	SD-N	5	13	.278	37	25	3	0	1	167	194	10.5	14	63	3.4	104	5.6	4.26	86	.293	.347	-12	-11	101	108	-3.4	1	-0	-1.0
1976	SD-N	2	11	.154	32	14	0	0	0	107	120	10.1	11	55	4.6	57	4.8	5.05	62	.291	.362	-18	-23	90	102	-4.3	-1	1	-2.2
1977	SD-N	7	6	.538	76	0	0	0	6	123	130	9.5	12	60	4.4	74	5.4	3.73	94	.280	.352	2	-3	89	127	1.4	1	-2	-0.4
1978	SD-N	1	0	1.000	17	0	0	0	0	26	32	11.1	2	7	2.4	16	5.5	4.50	74	.317	.355	-3	-3	93	111	0.5	0	-0	-0.3
	Cle-A	3	1	.750	36	0	0	0	3	56	54	8.7	2	21	3.4	48	7.7	3.70	96	.254	.315	1	-1	94	87	1.1	0	-1	-0.1
1979	Cle-A	9	5	.643	49	13	3	0	1	158	153	8.7	16	64	3.6	97	5.5	4.61	97	.256	.324	-7	-2	106	86	2.1	0	-1	-0.2
1980	Cle-A	16	11	.593	34	30	7	1	0	194	225	10.4	23	74	3.4	100	4.6	5.29	79	.288	.349	-27	-24	103	91	3.0	0	-2	-2.5
1981	Cle-A	4	4	.500	32	5	1	0	7	97	86	8.0	3	39	3.6	59	5.5	3.15	108	.240	.305	5	3	93	94	0.0	0	0	0.3
1982	Cle-A	12	10	.545	65	0	0	0	21	134	117	7.9	9	45	3.0	90	6.0	2.49	166	.235	.291	**24**	24	101	119	1.5	0	-2	2.2
1983	Cle-A	2	9	.182	60	0	0	0	8	92	117	11.4	7	38	3.7	48	4.7	5.09	85	.315	.376	-10	-8	106	108	-3.2	0	-1	-0.8
1984	Cle-A	0	5	.000	14	8	0	0	1	51	70	12.4	3	22	3.9	23	4.1	5.65	75	.332	.382	-9	-8	106	102	-2.4	0	1	-0.6
	Chi-A	1	0	1.000	22	0	0	0	1	48	51	9.6	7	14	2.6	26	4.9	4.13	108	.276	.325	-1	2	111	110	0.5	0	-0	0.1
	Yr	1	5	.167	36	8	0	0	2	99	121	11.0	10	36	3.3	49	4.5	4.91	88	.301	.356	-10	-6	108	110	-1.9	0	1	-0.5
1985	Chi-A	4	3	.571	52	3	0	0	1	92	83	8.1	10	33	3.2	41	4.0	3.42	121	.245	.307	7	7	100	108	0.4	0	-3	0.5
Total	12	75	89	.457	556	123	19	3	50	1493	1585	9.6	134	605	3.6	878	5.3	4.21	92	.275	.338	-53	-57	99	104	-1.4	-3	-11	-6.3
■ **SCIPIO SPINKS**	Spinks, Scipio Ronald b: 7/12/47, Chicago, Ill. BR/TR, 6'1", 183 lbs. Deb: 9/16/69																												
1969	Hou-N	0	0	—	1	0	0	0	0	2	1	4.5	0	1	4.5	4	18.0	0.00	—	.143	.250	1	1	101	0	0.0	0	0	0.1
1970	Hou-N	0	1	.000	5	2	0	0	0	14	17	10.9	5	9	5.8	6	3.9	9.64	39	.293	.388	-9	-9	94	78	-0.4	-0	-0	-0.8
1971	Hou-N	1	0	1.000	5	3	1	0	0	29	22	6.8	2	13	4.0	26	8.1	3.72	86	.210	.298	-1	-2	92	72	0.5	0	0	-0.1
1972	StL-N	5	5	.500	16	16	6	0	0	118	96	7.3	5	59	4.5	93	7.1	2.67	136	.221	.316	10	13	105	107	0.2	-1	1	1.4
1973	StL-N	1	5	.167	8	8	0	0	0	39	39	9.0	4	25	5.8	25	5.8	4.85	68	.269	.368	-5	-7	90	101	-1.9	1	1	-0.4
Total	5	7	11	.389	35	29	7	0	0	202	175	7.8	16	107	4.8	154	6.9	3.70	96	.234	.329	-3	-4	100	98	-1.6	0	1	0.2

YEAR	TM/L	W	L	PCT	G	GS	CG	SHO	SV	IP	H	H/G	HR	BB	BB/G	SO	SO/G	ERA	/A	OAVG	OOBP	PR	/A	PF	CPI	WAT	PB	PD	TPI
■ PAUL SPLITTORFF Splittorff, Paul William b: 10/8/46, Evansville, Ind. BL/TL, 6'3", 205 lbs. Deb: 9/23/70																													
1970	KC-A	0	1	.000	2	1	0	0	0	9	16	16.0	1	5	5.0	10	10.0	7.00	53	.390	.457	-3	-3	100	119	-0.4	0	0	-0.2
1971	KC-A	8	9	.471	22	22	6	3	0	144	129	8.1	4	35	2.2	80	5.0	2.69	127	.243	.288	12	11	98	96	-0.9	-1	2	1.3
1972	KC-A	12	12	.500	35	33	12	2	0	216	189	7.9	11	67	2.8	140	5.8	3.13	98	.241	.297	-1	-2	100	92	0.2	4	4	0.6
1973	KC-A	20	11	.645	38	38	12	3	0	262	279	9.6	19	78	2.7	110	3.8	3.98	105	.272	.324	-5	5	109	94	4.1	0	1	0.6
1974	KC-A	13	19	.406	36	36	8	1	0	226	252	10.0	23	75	3.0	90	3.6	4.10	94	.285	.333	-12	-6	106	107	-2.7	0	0	-0.5
1975	KC-A	9	10	.474	35	23	6	3	1	159	156	8.8	10	56	3.2	76	4.3	3.17	121	.257	.315	11	12	101	109	-1.6	0	2	1.4
1976	KC-A	11	8	.579	26	23	5	1	0	159	169	9.6	11	59	3.3	59	3.3	3.96	88	.277	.337	-8	-9	99	104	0.6	0	1	-0.7
1977	KC-A	16	6	**.727**	37	37	6	2	0	229	243	9.6	11	83	3.3	99	3.9	3.69	109	.278	.335	10	8	99	108	3.2	0	-0	0.8
1978	KC-A	19	13	.594	39	38	13	2	0	262	244	8.4	22	60	2.1	76	2.6	3.40	112	.247	.287	11	12	101	89	1.2	0	1	1.3
1979	KC-A	15	17	.469	36	35	11	0	0	240	248	9.3	25	77	2.9	77	2.9	4.24	105	.268	.322	-0	5	105	96	-2.0	0	-2	0.3
1980	KC-A	14	11	.560	34	33	4	0	0	204	236	10.4	17	43	1.9	53	2.3	4.15	95	.296	.325	-2	-5	97	103	-0.8	0	0	-0.4
1981	KC-A	5	5	.500	21	15	1	0	0	99	111	10.1	12	23	2.1	48	4.4	4.36	83	.294	.322	-8	-8	99	106	0.2	0	1	-0.6
1982	KC-A	10	10	.500	29	28	0	0	0	162	166	9.2	14	57	3.2	74	4.1	4.28	95	.266	.327	-4	-4	100	93	-1.0	0	0	-0.3
1983	KC-A	13	8	.619	27	27	4	0	0	156	159	9.2	9	52	3.0	61	3.5	3.63	114	.262	.318	8	9	102	99	3.0	0	0	0.9
1984	KC-A	1	3	.250	12	3	0	0	0	28	47	15.1	3	10	3.2	4	1.3	7.71	51	.376	.413	-12	-12	99	96	-0.9	0	1	-0.9
Total	15	166	143	.537	429	392	88	17	1	2555	2644	9.3	192	780	2.7	1057	3.7	3.81	101	.270	.319	-3	15	102	99	2.2	3	10	3.6
■ CARL SPONGBERG Spongberg, Carl Gustav b: 5/21/1884, Idaho Falls, Idaho d: 7/21/38, Los Angeles, Cal. BR/TR, 6'2", 208 lbs. Deb: 8/01/08																													
1908	Chi-N	0	0	—	1	0	0	0	0	7	9	11.6	1	6	7.7	4	5.1	9.00	27	.372	.528	-5	-5	102	87	0.0	1	0	-0.3
■ KARL SPOONER Spooner, Karl Benajmin b: 6/23/31, Oriskany Falls, N.Y. d: 4/10/84, Vero Beach, Fla. BR/TL, 6', 185 lbs. Deb: 9/22/54																													
1954	Bro-N	2	0	1.000	2	2	2	2	0	18	7	3.5	0	6	3.0	27	13.5	0.00	—	.113	.191	8	8	101	0	1.0	0	-0	1.1
1955	Bro-N	8	6	.571	29	14	2	1	2	99	79	7.2	8	41	3.7	78	7.1	3.64	112	.215	.298	4	5	101	76	-0.7	3	-0	0.7
Total	2	10	6	.625	31	16	4	3	2	117	86	6.6	8	47	3.6	105	8.1	3.08	132	.200	.283	13	13	101	64	0.3	3	-0	1.8
■ HOMER SPRAGINS Spragins, Homer Franklin b: 11/9/20, Grenada, Miss. BR/TR, 6'1", 190 lbs. Deb: 9/13/47																													
1947	Phi-N	0	0	—	4	0	0	0	0	5	3	5.4	0	3	5.4	3	5.4	7.20	58	.158	.273	-2	-2	102	13	0.0	0	0	-0.1
■ CHARLIE SPRAGUE Sprague, Charles Wellington b: 10/10/1864, Cleveland, Ohio d: 12/31/12, Des Moines, Iowa 5'11", 150 lbs. Deb: 9/17/1887																													
1887	Chi-N	1	0	1.000	3	3	2	0	0	22	24	9.8	1	13	5.3	9	3.7	4.91	95	.293	.390	-2	-1	115	97	0.5	-1	0	0.0
1889	Cle-N	0	2	.000	2	2	2	0	0	17	27	14.3	0	10	5.3	8	4.2	8.47	50	.377	.453	-8	-8	104	80	-0.9	-0	0	-0.5
1890	Tol-a	9	5	.643	19	12	9	0	0	123	111	8.1	0	78	5.7	59	4.3	3.88	102	.256	.369	-0	1	102	97	2.0	3	0	0.1
Total	3	10	7	.588	24	17	13	0	0	162	162	9.0	1	101	5.6	76	4.2	4.50	90	.276	.382	-11	-8	104	95	1.6	1	0	-0.4
■ ED SPRAGUE Sprague, Edward Nelson b: 9/16/45, Boston, Mass. BR/TR, 6'4", 195 lbs. Deb: 4/10/68																													
1968	Oak-A	3	4	.429	47	1	0	0	4	69	51	6.7	5	34	4.4	34	4.4	3.26	89	.209	.309	-2	-3	98	90	-0.5	-1	1	-0.2
1969	Oak-A	1	1	.500	27	0	0	0	2	46	47	9.2	4	31	6.1	20	3.9	4.50	74	.267	.381	-4	-6	91	109	0.0	0	2	-0.3
1971	Cin-N	1	0	1.000	7	0	0	0	0	11	8	6.5	0	1	0.8	7	5.7	0.00	—	.195	.209	4	4	96	0	0.5	-0	-0	0.4
1972	Cin-N	3	3	.500	33	1	0	0	0	57	55	8.7	6	26	4.1	25	3.9	4.11	77	.261	.343	-4	-6	91	106	-0.5	-1	-1	-0.7
1973	Cin-N	1	3	.250	28	0	0	0	1	39	35	8.1	3	22	5.1	19	4.4	5.08	66	.246	.343	-6	-7	92	80	-1.1	-0	0	-0.6
	StL-N	0	0	—	8	0	0	0	0	8	8	9.0	1	4	4.5	2	2.3	2.25	147	.276	.353	1	1	90	217	0.0	0	0	0.1
	Yr	1	3	.250	36	0	0	0	1	47	43	8.2	4	26	5.0	21	4.0	4.60	73	.247	.335	-5	-6	91	217	-1.1	-0	1	-0.5
	Mil-A	0	1	.000	7	0	0	0	1	10	13	11.7	0	14	12.6	3	2.7	9.00	41	.317	.492	-6	-6	96	89	-0.4	0	0	-0.5
1974	Mil-A	7	2	.778	20	10	3	0	0	94	94	9.0	3	31	3.0	57	5.5	2.39	155	.266	.327	13	14	103	145	2.7	0	-1	1.4
1975	Mil-A	1	7	.125	18	11	0	0	1	67	81	10.9	5	40	5.4	21	2.8	4.70	82	.297	.384	-7	-6	101	113	-2.8	0	-1	-0.6
1976	Mil-A	0	2	.000	3	0	0	0	0	8	14	15.8	0	3	3.4	0	0.0	6.75	52	.438	.459	-3	-3	100	119	-0.9	0	1	-0.1
Total	8	17	23	.425	198	23	3	0	9	409	406	8.9	27	206	4.5	188	4.1	3.83	89	.263	.350	-14	-19	97	110	-3.0	-1	2	-1.1
■ JACK SPRING Spring, Jack Russell b: 3/11/33, Spokane, Wash. BR/TL, 6'1", 175 lbs. Deb: 4/16/55																													
1955	Phi-N	0	1	.000	2	0	0	0	0	3	2	6.0	2	1	3.0	2	6.0	6.00	69	.200	.273	-1	-1	102	114	-0.4	-0	0	0.0
1957	Bos-A	0	0	—	1	0	0	0	0	1	0	0.0	0	0	0.0	2	18.0	0.00	—	.000	.000	0	0	109	0	0.0	0	0	0.0
1958	Was-A	0	0	—	3	1	0	0	0	7	16	20.6	1	7	9.0	1	1.3	14.14	27	.457	.535	-8	-8	100	89	0.0	-0	0	-0.6
1961	LA-A	3	0	1.000	18	4	0	0	0	38	35	8.3	4	15	3.6	27	6.4	4.26	106	.243	.319	-1	1	112	89	1.5	-1	0	0.0
1962	LA-A	4	2	.667	57	0	0	0	6	65	66	9.1	7	30	4.2	31	4.3	4.02	101	.270	.343	-0	0	102	116	0.9	-1	1	0.0
1963	LA-A	3	0	1.000	45	0	0	0	2	38	40	9.5	3	9	2.1	13	3.1	3.08	109	.268	.304	2	1	92	117	1.5	0	1	0.2
1964	LA-A	1	0	1.000	6	0	0	0	0	3	3	9.0	1	3	9.0	0	0.0	3.00	107	.273	.400	0	0	89	261	0.5	0	0	0.0
	Chi-N	0	0	—	7	0	0	0	0	6	4	6.0	0	2	3.0	1	1.5	6.00	63	.200	.250	-2	-1	106	31	0.0	0	0	0.0
	StL-N	0	0	—	2	0	0	0	0	3	8	24.0	1	1	3.0	0	0.0	3.00	131	.471	.450	0	0	111	448	0.0	0	0	0.0
	Yr	0	0	—	9	0	0	0	0	9	12	12.0	1	3	3.0	1	1.0	5.00	76	.316	.341	-1	-1	108	448	0.0	0	0	0.0
1965	Cle-A	1	2	.333	14	0	0	0	0	22	21	8.6	2	10	4.1	9	3.7	3.68	91	.259	.330	-1	-1	97	111	-0.5	0	-0	0.0
Total	8	12	5	.706	155	5	0	0	8	186	195	9.4	21	78	3.8	86	4.2	4.26	91	.273	.338	-9	-8	102	113	3.5	-2	1	-0.4
■ BRAD SPRINGER Springer, Bradford Louis b: 5/9/04, Detroit, Mich. d: 1/4/70, Birmingham, Mich. BL/TL, 6', 155 lbs. Deb: 5/01/25																													
1925	StL-A	0	0	—	2	0	0	0	0	3	1	3.0	0	7	21.0	0	0.0	3.00	158	.200	.533	0	1	108	303	0.0	0	0	0.1
1926	Cin-N	0	0	—	1	0	0	0	0	1	2	18.0	0	2	18.0	1	9.0	9.00	40	.286	.500	-1	-1	93	114	0.0	-0	0	0.0
Total	2	0	0	—	3	0	0	0	0	4	3	6.8	0	9	20.3	1	2.3	4.50	98	.250	.520	-0	-0	104	255	0.0	-0	0	0.1
■ ED SPRINGER Springer, Edward H. b: 2/9/1861, California d: 4/24/26, Los Angeles Co., Cal. 6'2", 187 lbs. Deb: 7/12/1889																													
1889	Lou-a	0	1	.000	1	1	1	0	0	5	8	14.4	0	2	3.6	1	1.8	9.00	44	.378	.432	-3	-3	102	70	-0.4	-0	0	-0.1
■ CHARLIE SPROULL Sproull, Charles William b: 1/9/19, Taylorsville, Ga. d: 1/13/80, Rockford, Ill. BR/TR, 6'3", 185 lbs. Deb: 4/19/45																													
1945	Phi-N	4	10	.286	34	19	2	0	1	130	158	10.9	10	80	5.5	47	3.3	5.95	65	.298	.383	-31	-30	102	92	-0.2	-2	-1	-3.0
■ BOB SPROUT Sprout, Robert Samiel b: 12/5/41, Florin, Pa. BL/TL, 6', 165 lbs. Deb: 9/27/61																													
1961	LA-A	0	0	—	1	1	0	0	0	4	4	9.0	0	3	6.8	2	4.5	4.50	100	.267	.389	-0	0	112	98	0.0	0	-0	0.0
■ BOBBY SPROWL Sprowl, Robert John b: 4/14/56, Sandusky, Ohio BL/TL, 6'2", 190 lbs. Deb: 9/05/78																													
1978	Bos-A	0	2	.000	3	3	0	0	0	13	12	8.3	3	10	6.9	10	6.9	6.23	64	.245	.373	-4	-3	106	89	-0.9	0	-0	-0.2
1979	Hou-N	0	0	—	3	0	0	0	0	4	1	2.3	0	2	4.5	3	6.8	0.00	—	.083	.214	2	2	90	0	0.0	0	0	0.1
1980	Hou-N	0	0	—	1	0	0	0	0	1	1	9.0	0	1	9.0	3	27.0	0.00	—	.250	.400	0	0	97	0	0.0	0	0	0.0
1981	Hou-N	0	1	.000	15	1	0	0	0	29	40	12.4	1	14	4.3	18	5.6	5.90	51	.333	.391	-8	-9	87	98	-0.4	-0	-0	-0.9
Total	4	0	3	.000	22	4	0	0	0	47	54	10.3	4	27	5.2	34	6.5	5.36	62	.292	.375	-9	-11	93	85	-1.3	-0	-0	-1.0
■ MIKE SQUIRES Squires, Michael Lynn b: 3/5/52, Kalamazoo, Mich. BL/TL, 5'11", 185 lbs. Deb: 9/01/75																													
1984	Chi-A	0	0	—	1	0	0	0	0	⅓	0	0.0	0	0	0.0	0	0.0	0.00	—	.000	.000	0	0	111	0	0.0	0	0	0.0
■ GEORGE STABLEIN Stablein, George Charles b: 10/29/57, Inglewood, Cal. BR/TR, 6'4", 185 lbs. Deb: 9/20/80																													
1980	SD-N	0	1	.000	4	2	0	0	0	12	16	12.0	0	3	2.3	4	3.0	3.00	113	.340	.373	1	1	94	166	-0.4	-0	-0	0.0
■ EDDIE STACK Stack, William Edward b: 10/24/1887, Chicago, Ill. d: 8/28/58, Chicago, Ill. BR/TR, 6', 175 lbs. Deb: 6/07/10																													
1910	Phi-N	6	7	.462	20	16	8	1	0	117	115	8.8	7	34	2.6	48	3.7	4.00	72	.266	.326	-13	-14	95	85	-0.6	-2	-1	-1.7
1911	Phi-N	5	5	.500	13	10	5	1	0	78	67	7.7	3	41	4.7	36	4.2	3.58	102	.234	.342	-2	1	108	92	-0.1	-2	0	0.0
1912	Bro-N	7	5	.583	28	17	4	0	1	142	139	8.8	3	55	3.5	45	2.9	3.36	99	.257	.336	1	-1	97	92	2.1	-3	-1	-0.4
1913	Bro-N	4	4	.500	23	9	4	1	0	87	79	8.2	0	32	3.3	34	3.5	2.38	141	.250	.316	8	9	105	117	0.5	-1	-2	0.7
	Chi-N	4	2	.667	11	7	3	1	1	51	56	9.9	1	15	2.6	28	4.9	4.24	73	.280	.332	-6	-6	97	84	0.7	-1	-1	-0.7
	Yr	8	6	.571	34	16	7	2	1	138	135	8.8	1	47	3.1	62	4.0	3.07	106	.261	.321	2	3	102	84	1.2	-1	-3	0.0
1914	Chi-N	0	1	.000	7	1	0	0	0	16	13	7.3	0	11	6.2	9	5.1	5.06	54	.220	.320	-4	-4	99	54	-0.4	-0	0	-0.3
Total	5	26	24	.520	102	60	24	4	2	491	469	8.6	14	188	3.4	200	3.7	3.52	92	.256	.330	-15	-16	100	93	2.2	-9	-4	-2.4
■ GENERAL STAFFORD Stafford, James Joseph "Jamsey" b: 7/9/1868, Webster, Mass. d: 9/11/23, Worcester, Mass. BR/TR, 5'8", 165 lbs. Deb: 8/27/1890																													
1890	Buf-P	3	9	.250	12	12	11	0	0	98	123	11.3	8	43	3.9	21	1.9	5.14	80	.319	.388	-10	-11	97	98	-0.4	-1	0	-0.9

YEAR	TM/L	W	L	PCT	G	GS	CG	SHO	SV	IP	H	H/G	HR	BB	BB/G	SO	SO/G	ERA	/A	OAVG	OOBP	PR	/A	PF	CPI	WAT	PB	PD	TPI
■ JOHN STAFFORD	Stafford, John Henry "Doc" b: 4/8/1870, Dudley, Mass. d: 7/3/40, Worcester, Mass. BR/TR, 5'10", 170 lbs. Deb: 6/15/1893																												
1893	Cle-N	0	1	.000	2	0	0	0	0	7	12	15.4	1	7	9.0	4	5.1	14.14	34	.395	.508	-7	-7	103	69	-0.4	-1	0	-0.5
■ BILL STAFFORD	Stafford, William Charles b: 8/13/39, Catskill, N.Y. BR/TR, 6'1", 188 lbs. Deb: 4/17/60																												
1960	NY-A	3	1	.750	11	8	2	1	0	60	50	7.5	3	18	2.7	36	5.4	2.25	159	.226	.280	11	9	92	109	0.7	-2	1	0.8
1961	NY-A	14	9	.609	36	25	8	3	2	195	168	7.8	13	59	2.7	101	4.7	2.68	140	.232	.291	29	23	93	106	-1.2	2	-1	2.4
1962	NY-A	14	9	.609	35	33	7	2	0	213	188	7.9	23	77	3.3	109	4.6	3.68	99	.233	.299	7	-1	92	90	0.5	3	-1	0.0
1963	NY-A	4	8	.333	28	14	0	0	3	90	104	10.4	16	42	4.2	52	5.2	6.00	59	.287	.361	-24	-24	98	93	-2.9	3	-0	-2.1
1964	NY-A	5	0	1.000	31	1	0	0	4	61	50	7.4	4	22	3.2	39	5.8	2.66	137	.231	.301	7	7	101	115	2.5	-1	0	0.7
1965	NY-A	3	8	.273	22	15	1	0	0	111	93	7.5	16	31	2.5	71	5.8	3.57	98	.229	.281	-1	-1	101	92	-2.3	-3	0	-0.3
1966	KC-A	0	4	.000	9	8	0	0	0	40	42	9.4	2	12	2.7	31	7.0	4.95	66	.273	.322	-7	-7	95	78	-1.9	-1	-1	-0.8
1967	KC-A	0	1	.000	14	0	0	0	0	16	12	6.8	0	9	5.1	10	5.6	1.69	195	.214	.313	3	3	102	161	-0.4	-0	0	0.3
Total	8	43	40	.518	186	104	18	6	9	786	707	8.1	77	270	3.1	449	5.1	3.52	103	.240	.303	24	9	95	99	-5.0	0	-1	1.0
■ CHICK STAHL	Stahl, Charles Sylvester b: 1/10/1873, Avila, Ind. d: 3/28/07, W.Baden, Ind. BL/TL, 5'10", 160 lbs. Deb: 4/19/1897 M																												
1899	Bos-N	0	0	—	1	0	0	0	0	2	2	9.0	0	3	13.5	0	0.0	9.00	44	.283	.497	-1	-1	103	70	0.0	1	0	0.0
■ GERRY STALEY	Staley, Gerald Lee b: 8/21/20, Brush Prairie, Wash. BR/TR, 6', 195 lbs. Deb: 4/20/47																												
1947	StL-N	1	0	1.000	18	1	1	0	0	29	33	10.2	2	8	2.5	14	4.3	2.79	151	.287	.333	4	5	104	151	0.5	-1	1	0.5
1948	StL-N	4	4	.500	31	3	0	0	0	52	61	10.6	5	21	3.6	23	4.0	6.92	56	.288	.346	-17	-17	99	69	-0.3	1	1	-1.4
1949	StL-N	10	10	.500	45	17	5	2	6	171	154	**8.1**	7	41	2.2	55	2.9	2.74	159	**.238**	.283	25	31	108	95	-2.1	-1	3	3.5
1950	StL-N	13	13	.500	42	22	7	1	3	170	201	10.6	14	61	3.2	62	3.3	4.98	85	.300	.361	-16	-14	103	101	-0.2	-1	3	-1.0
1951	StL-N	19	13	.594	42	30	10	4	3	227	244	9.7	14	74	2.9	67	2.7	3.81	105	.275	.334	4	5	101	105	2.8	-2	2	0.6
1952	StL-N	17	14	.548	35	33	15	0	0	240	238	8.9	21	52	2.0	93	3.5	3.26	111	.256	.298	12	10	97	105	-0.7	-1	3	1.1
1953	StL-N	18	9	.667	40	32	10	1	4	230	243	9.5	31	54	2.1	88	3.4	3.99	108	.269	.320	8	8	101	107	4.3	-5	2	0.5
1954	StL-N	7	13	.350	48	20	3	1	2	156	198	11.4	21	47	2.7	50	2.9	5.25	78	.308	.353	-20	-20	100	100	-2.7	-0	2	-1.6
1955	Cin-N	5	8	.385	30	18	2	0	0	120	146	10.9	22	28	2.1	40	3.0	4.65	91	.309	.341	-8	-6	104	119	-1.4	-4	1	-0.7
	NY-A	0	0	—	2	0	0	0	0	2	5	22.5	1	1	4.5	0	0.0	13.50	28	.417	.462	-2	-2	94	96	0.0	0	0	-0.1
1956	NY-A	0	0	—	1	0	0	0	0	⅓	4	108.0	0	0	0.0	1	27.0	108.00	—	.800	.800	-4	-4	95	48	0.0	-0	0	-0.2
	Chi-A	8	3	.727	26	10	5	0	0	102	98	8.6	11	20	1.8	25	2.2	2.91	145	.251	.295	14	15	102	115	2.2	-2	1	1.3
	Yr	8	3	.727	27	10	5	0	0	102	102	9.0	11	20	1.8	26	2.3	3.26	130	.258	.301	10	11	102	115	2.2	-0	1	1.1
1957	Chi-A	5	1	.833	47	0	0	0	7	105	95	8.1	7	27	2.3	44	3.8	2.06	178	.244	.288	**20**	**19**	97	141	1.8	-1	2	2.1
1958	Chi-A	4	5	.444	50	0	0	0	8	85	81	8.6	10	24	2.5	27	2.9	3.18	116	.259	.301	6	5	98	120	-0.7	-1	3	0.7
1959	Chi-A	8	5	.615	**67**	0	0	0	14	116	111	8.6	5	25	1.9	54	4.2	2.25	163	.259	.289	**21**	**18**	95	138	0.1	0	-0	1.9
1960	Chi-A	13	8	.619	64	0	0	0	10	115	94	7.4	8	25	2.0	52	4.1	2.43	158	.227	.265	**18**	**18**	99	103	1.5	1	3	2.2
1961	Chi-A	0	3	.000	16	0	0	0	0	18	17	8.5	3	5	2.5	8	4.0	5.00	79	.246	.293	-2	-2	99	76	-1.4	0	0	-0.1
	KC-A	1	1	.500	23	0	0	0	2	30	32	9.6	4	10	3.0	16	4.8	3.60	117	.278	.333	1	2	104	132	0.2	0	1	0.3
	Det-A	1	1	.500	13	0	0	0	2	13	15	10.4	1	6	4.2	8	5.5	3.46	109	.288	.350	1	0	94	137	-0.1	-0	0	0.1
	Yr	2	5	.286	52	0	0	0	4	61	64	9.4	8	21	3.1	32	4.7	3.98	101	.267	.318	0	0	100	137	-1.3	0	1	0.3
Total	15	134	111	.547	640	186	58	9	61	1981	2070	9.4	187	529	2.4	727	3.3	3.70	108	.270	.317	65	68	100	109	3.8	-16	28	9.7
■ HARRY STALEY	Staley, Henry E. b: 11/3/1866, Jacksonville, Ill. d: 1/12/10, Battle Creek, Mich BR/TR, 5'10", 175 lbs. Deb: 1888																												
1888	Pit-N	12	12	.500	25	24	24	2	0	207	185	8.0	6	53	2.3	89	3.9	2.70	100	.252	.303	3	0	95	96	0.2	-4	0	-0.3
1889	Pit-N	21	26	.447	49	47	46	1	1	420	433	9.3	11	116	2.5	159	3.4	3.51	103	.282	.332	24	5	90	95	-1.1	-5	2	0.0
1890	Pit-P	21	25	.457	46	46	44	3	0	388	392	9.1	6	74	**1.7**	145	3.4	3.22	121	.274	**.310**	43	29	92	81	-0.8	1	-0	2.3
1891	Pit-N	4	5	.444	9	7	6	0	0	72	77	9.6	4	11	1.4	25	3.1	2.88	119	.287	.315	4	4	102	107	0.3	1	0	0.5
	Bos-N	20	8	.714	31	30	26	1	0	252	236	8.4	11	69	2.5	114	4.1	2.50	146	.261	.313	24	32	109	106	3.8	-2	0	3.0
	Yr	24	13	.649	40	37	32	1	0	324	313	8.7	15	80	2.2	139	3.9	2.58	139	.267	.314	27	37	108	106	4.1	1	0	3.5
1892	Bos-N	22	10	.688	37	35	31	3	0	300	273	8.2	10	97	2.9	93	2.8	3.03	120	.255	.317	9	20	111	92	0.5	-7	-1	1.3
1893	Bos-N	18	10	.643	36	31	23	0	0	263	344	11.8	22	81	2.8	61	2.1	5.13	92	.332	.381	-13	-12	101	104	-0.5	4	0	-0.6
1894	Bos-N	12	10	.545	27	21	18	0	0	209	305	13.1	15	61	2.6	32	1.4	6.85	87	.364	.407	-35	-21	111	87	-1.6	-0	-3	-1.5
1895	StL-N	6	13	.316	23	16	13	0	0	159	223	12.6	8	39	2.2	28	1.6	5.26	93	.353	.390	-8	-6	102	101	0.3	-6	0	-0.9
Total	8	136	119	.533	283	257	231	10	1	2270	2468	9.8	93	601	2.4	746	3.0	3.81	105	.292	.339	50	51	100	95	1.1	-18	-2	3.8
■ TRACY STALLARD	Stallard, Evan Tracy b: 8/31/37, Coeburn, Va. BR/TR, 6'5", 204 lbs. Deb: 9/24/60																												
1960	Bos-A	0	0	—	4	0	0	0	0	4	0	0.0	0	2	4.5	6	13.5	0.00	—	.000	.133	2	2	105	0	0.0	0	0	0.2
1961	Bos-A	2	7	.222	43	14	1	0	2	133	110	7.4	15	96	6.5	109	7.4	4.87	85	.229	.353	-13	-11	103	88	-2.3	-3	-2	-1.4
1962	Bos-A	0	0	—	1	0	0	0	0	1	0	0.0	0	0	0.0	0	0.0	0.00	—	.000	.000	0	0	103	0	0.0	0	0	0.0
1963	NY-N	6	17	.261	39	23	5	0	1	155	156	9.1	23	77	4.5	110	6.4	4.70	73	.262	.342	-24	-22	104	99	-2.1	-3	-1	-2.6
1964	NY-N	10	20	.333	36	34	11	2	0	226	213	8.5	20	73	2.9	118	4.7	3.78	92	.252	.309	-6	-8	98	96	0.2	2	-3	-0.8
1965	StL-N	11	8	.579	40	26	4	1	0	194	172	8.0	25	70	3.2	99	4.6	3.39	111	.235	.301	3	8	106	106	1.7	-4	-2	0.3
1966	StL-N	1	5	.167	20	7	0	0	1	52	65	11.3	9	25	4.3	35	6.1	5.71	63	.305	.377	-12	-12	100	106	-1.9	-2	0	-1.3
Total	7	30	57	.345	183	104	21	3	4	765	716	8.4	92	343	4.0	477	5.6	4.16	88	.248	.326	-50	-43	102	98	-4.4	-9	-6	-5.6
■ CHARLEY STANCEU	Stanceu, Charles b: 1/9/16, Canton, Ohio d: 4/3/69, Canton, Ohio BR/TR, 6'2", 190 lbs. Deb: 4/16/41																												
1941	NY-A	3	3	.500	22	2	0	0	0	48	58	10.9	3	35	6.6	21	3.9	5.63	70	.296	.390	-8	-9	95	103	-0.6	-2	-1	-1.0
1946	NY-A	0	0	—	3	0	0	0	0	4	6	13.5	0	5	11.3	3	6.8	9.00	38	.316	.458	-2	-2	98	78	0.0	0	0	-0.1
	Phi-N	2	4	.333	14	11	1	0	0	70	71	9.1	4	39	5.0	23	3.0	4.24	79	.270	.358	-6	-7	98	100	-0.7	-2	-1	-0.9
Total	2	5	7	.417	39	13	1	0	0	122	135	10.0	7	79	5.8	47	3.5	4.94	72	.282	.376	-17	-19	97	101	-1.3	-3	-1	-2.0
■ PETE STANDRIDGE	Standridge, Alfred Peter b: 4/25/1891, Black Diamond, Wash. d: 8/2/63, San Francisco, Cal. BR/TR, 5'10.5", 165 lbs. Deb: 9/19/11																												
1911	StL-N	0	0	—	2	0	0	0	0	5	10	18.0	0	4	7.2	3	5.4	9.00	39	.435	.536	-3	-3	102	115	0.0	-0	0	-0.2
1915	Chi-N	4	1	.800	29	3	2	0	0	112	120	9.6	2	36	2.9	42	3.4	3.62	78	.274	.322	-11	-10	103	94	1.6	3	0	-0.7
Total	2	4	1	.800	31	3	2	0	0	117	130	10.0	2	40	3.1	45	3.5	3.85	74	.282	.334	-14	-13	103	95	1.6	2	0	-0.9
■ AL STANEK	Stanek, Albert Wilfred "Lefty" b: 12/24/43, Springfield, Mass. BL/TL, 5'11.5", 190 lbs. Deb: 4/26/63																												
1963	SF-N	0	0	—	11	0	0	0	0	13	10	6.9	1	12	8.3	5	3.5	4.85	64	.217	.361	-2	-3	94	88	0.0	-0	1	-0.1
■ KEVIN STANFIELD	Stanfield, Kevin Bruce b: 12/19/55, Huron, S.Dak. BL/TL, 6', 190 lbs. Deb: 9/14/79																												
1979	Min-A	0	0	—	3	0	0	0	0	3	2	6.0	0	0	0.0	0	0.0	6.00	76	.200	.200	-1	-0	108	15	0.0	0	0	0.0
■ LEE STANGE	Stange, Albert Lee b: 10/27/36, Chicago, Ill. BR/TR, 5'10", 170 lbs. Deb: 4/15/61 C																												
1961	Min-A	1	0	1.000	7	0	0	0	0	12	15	11.3	1	10	7.5	10	7.5	3.00	144	.294	.410	1	2	107	198	0.5	-0	0	0.2
1962	Min-A	4	3	.571	44	6	1	0	3	95	98	9.3	14	39	3.7	70	6.6	4.45	92	.271	.334	-5	-4	104	106	0.1	-1	-0	-0.4
1963	Min-A	12	5	.706	32	20	7	2	0	165	145	7.9	21	43	2.3	100	5.5	2.62	136	.233	.279	19	17	98	121	3.0	-1	-0	1.7
1964	Min-A	3	6	.333	14	11	2	0	0	80	78	8.8	13	19	2.1	54	6.1	4.72	77	.255	.294	-10	-10	100	81	-1.4	-1	1	-0.9
	Cle-A	4	8	.333	23	14	0	0	0	92	98	9.6	14	31	3.0	78	7.6	4.11	91	.270	.324	-5	-4	103	108	-1.9	-1	-0	-0.4
	Yr	7	14	.333	37	25	2	0	0	172	176	9.2	27	50	2.6	132	6.9	4.40	84	.262	.311	-15	-14	102	108	-3.3	-1	1	-1.3
1965	Cle-A	8	4	.667	41	12	4	2	0	132	122	8.3	13	26	1.8	80	5.5	3.34	101	.247	.280	2	0	97	93	1.8	1	-2	0.0
1966	Cle-A	1	0	1.000	8	2	1	0	0	16	17	9.6	1	3	1.7	8	4.5	2.81	124	.279	.318	1	1	102	138	0.5	0	-0	0.1
	Bos-A	7	9	.438	28	19	8	2	0	153	140	8.2	17	43	2.5	77	4.5	3.35	113	.246	.290	1	7	110	104	0.0	-4	-1	0.4
	Yr	8	9	.471	36	21	9	2	0	169	157	8.4	18	46	2.4	85	4.5	3.30	114	.248	.291	3	9	110	104	0.5	0	-1	0.5
1967	Bos-A	8	10	.444	35	24	6	2	1	182	171	8.5	14	32	1.6	101	5.0	2.77	132	.246	.279	9	18	113	106	-2.0	-3	-2	1.4
1968	Bos-A	5	5	.500	50	2	1	0	12	103	89	7.8	10	25	2.2	53	4.6	3.93	76	.237	.275	-11	-11	101	77	-0.2	0	-1	-1.2
1969	Bos-A	6	9	.400	41	15	2	0	3	137	137	9.0	14	56	3.7	59	3.9	3.68	103	.256	.330	-1	2	105	107	-2.0	-2	-1	0.0
1970	Bos-A	2	2	.500	20	0	0	0	2	27	34	11.3	5	12	4.0	14	4.7	5.67	72	.301	.364	-6	-5	110	105	0.0	-0	0	-0.4
	Chi-A	1	0	1.000	16	0	0	0	0	22	28	11.5	5	5	2.0	14	5.7	5.32	75	.295	.327	-4	-3	108	99	0.5	-0	-0	-0.3
	Yr	3	2	.600	36	0	0	0	2	49	62	11.4	10	17	3.1	28	5.1	5.51	74	.291	.339	-10	-8	109	99	0.5	-0	-0	-0.7
Total	10	62	61	.504	359	125	32	8	21	1216	1172	8.7	142	344	2.5	718	5.3	3.56	102	.252	.300	-8	12	104	104	-1.1	-12	-8	0.2

YEAR	TM/L	W	L	PCT	G	GS	CG	SHO	SV	IP	H	H/G	HR	BB	BB/G	SO	SO/G	ERA	/A	OAVG	OOBP	PR	/A	PF	CPI	WAT	PB	PD	TPI
■ **DON STANHOUSE**	Stanhouse, Donald Joseph b: 2/12/51, Du Quoin, Ill. BR/TR, 6'2.5", 185 lbs. Deb: 4/19/72																												
1972	Tex-A	2	9	.182	24	16	1	0	0	105	83	7.1	8	73	6.3	78	6.7	3.77	79	.223	.342	-8	-9	97	98	-2.7	-0	2	-0.8
1973	Tex-A	1	7	.125	21	5	1	0	1	70	70	9.0	5	44	5.7	42	5.4	4.76	80	.262	.366	-7	-7	100	94	-2.5	0	2	-0.4
1974	Tex-A	1	1	.500	18	0	0	0	0	31	38	11.0	4	17	4.9	26	7.5	4.94	71	.302	.385	-5	-5	96	117	0.0	0	1	-0.4
1975	Mon-N	0	0	—	4	3	0	0	0	13	19	13.2	1	11	7.6	5	3.5	8.31	48	.345	.448	-7	-6	109	89	0.0	0	0	-0.5
1976	Mon-N	9	12	.429	34	26	8	1	1	184	182	8.9	7	92	4.5	79	3.9	3.77	96	.263	.346	-5	-3	103	104	1.6	3	2	0.2
1977	Mon-N	10	10	.500	47	16	1	1	10	158	147	8.4	12	84	4.8	89	5.1	3.42	114	.251	.341	9	8	99	117	0.8	1	-1	0.8
1978	Bal-A	6	9	.400	56	0	0	0	24	75	60	7.2	0	52	6.2	42	5.0	2.88	119	.230	.344	7	4	91	116	-2.2	0	0	0.5
1979	Bal-A	7	3	.700	52	0	0	0	21	73	49	6.0	4	51	6.3	34	4.2	2.84	143	.202	.329	11	10	96	117	0.9	0	1	1.0
1980	LA-N	2	2	.500	21	0	0	0	7	25	30	10.8	4	16	5.8	5	1.8	5.04	69	.306	.393	-4	-4	96	126	-0.1	0	1	-0.3
1982	Bal-A	0	1	.000	17	0	0	0	0	27	29	9.7	3	15	5.0	8	2.7	5.33	76	.276	.368	-4	-4	99	97	-0.4	0	0	-0.3
Total	10	38	54	.413	294	66	11	2	64	761	707	8.4	48	455	5.4	408	4.8	3.83	95	.252	.351	-12	-17	99	108	-4.6	4	8	-0.2
■ **JOE STANKA**	Stanka, Joe Donald b: 7/23/31, Hammon, Okla. BR/TR, 6'5", 201 lbs. Deb: 9/02/59																												
1959	Chi-A	1	0	1.000	2	0	0	0	0	5	2	3.6	1	4	7.2	3	5.4	3.60	102	.111	.273	0	0	95	60	0.5	0	-0	0.0
■ **BUCK STANLEY**	Stanley, John Leonard b: 11/13/1889, Washington, D.C. d: 8/13/40, Norfolk, Va. BL/TL, 5'10", 160 lbs. Deb: 9/12/11																												
1911	Phi-N	0	0	—	4	0	0	0	0	11	14	11.5	0	9	7.4	5	4.1	6.55	56	.326	.442	-4	-4	108	93	0.0	-1	-1	-0.3
■ **JOE STANLEY**	Stanley, Joseph Bernard b: 4/2/1881, Washington, D.C. d: 9/13/67, Detroit, Mich. BB/TR, 5'9.5", 150 lbs. Deb: 9/11/1897																												
1897	Was-N	0	0	—	1	0	0	0	0	1	0	0.0	0	0	0.0	0	0.0	0.00	—	.000	.000	0	0	102	0	0.0	-0	0	0.0
1903	Bos-N	0	0	—	1	0	0	0	0	4	4	9.0	0	4	9.0	4	9.0	9.00	36	.306	.498	-3	-3	98	62	0.0	0	-0	-0.1
1906	Was-A	0	0	—	1	0	0	0	0	3	7	21.0	1	2	6.0	1	3.0	18.00	14	.483	.545	-5	-5	94	73	0.0	0	-0	-0.3
Total	3	0	0	—	3	0	0	0	0	8	11	12.4	1	6	6.8	5	5.6	11.25	27	.365	.485	-7	-7	97	58	0.0	0	-0	-0.4
■ **BOB STANLEY**	Stanley, Robert William b: 11/10/54, Portland, Maine BR/TR, 6'4", 210 lbs. Deb: 4/16/77																												
1977	Bos-A	8	7	.533	41	13	3	1	3	151	176	10.5	10	43	2.6	44	2.6	3.99	118	.294	.341	1	12	116	108	-0.8	0	3	1.6
1978	Bos-A	15	2	.882	52	3	0	0	10	142	142	9.0	5	34	2.2	38	2.4	2.60	154	.266	.306	19	22	106	122	6.1	0	2	2.6
1979	Bos-A	16	12	.571	40	30	9	4	1	217	250	10.4	14	44	1.8	56	2.3	3.98	113	.294	.326	6	12	106	104	0.1	0	2	1.3
1980	Bos-A	10	8	.556	52	17	5	1	14	175	186	9.6	11	52	2.7	71	3.7	3.39	121	.278	.332	13	14	102	117	0.8	0	3	1.8
1981	Bos-A	10	8	.556	35	1	0	0	0	99	110	10.0	3	38	3.5	28	2.5	3.82	101	.294	.358	-2	1	106	118	0.2	0	3	0.4
1982	Bos-A	12	7	.632	48	0	0	0	14	168	161	8.6	11	50	2.7	83	4.4	3.11	**144**	.255	.310	18	26	110	110	1.9	0	4	3.1
1983	Bos-A	8	10	.444	64	0	0	0	33	145	145	9.0	7	38	2.4	65	4.0	2.86	145	.266	.309	20	21	102	123	-0.7	0	-1	2.0
1984	Bos-A	9	10	.474	57	0	0	0	22	107	113	9.5	9	23	1.9	52	4.4	3.53	124	.267	.303	6	10	110	100	-1.0	0	2	1.3
1985	Bos-A	6	6	.500	48	0	0	0	10	88	76	7.8	7	30	3.1	46	4.7	2.86	147	.237	.300	13	13	102	115	0.0	0	0	1.3
1986	Bos-A	6	6	.500	66	1	0	0	16	82	109	12.0	9	22	2.4	54	5.9	4.39	94	.322	.358	-2	-2	99	125	-0.9	0	1	-0.1
1987	Bos-A	4	15	.211	34	20	4	1	0	153	198	11.6	17	42	2.5	67	3.9	5.00	88	.321	.357	-9	-10	99	111	-5.5	0	1	-0.8
1988	Bos-A	6	4	.600	57	0	0	0	5	102	90	7.9	6	29	2.6	57	5.0	3.18	135	.242	.301	9	13	108	102	0.6	0	-0	1.2
Total	12	110	95	.537	594	85	21	7	128	1629	1756	9.7	109	445	2.5	661	3.7	3.57	120	.280	.326	91	132	106	112	0.8	0	21	15.7
■ **MIKE STANTON**	Stanton, Michael Thomas b: 9/25/52, Phenix City, Ala. BB/TR, 6'2", 205 lbs. Deb: 7/09/75																												
1975	Hou-N	0	2	.000	7	2	0	0	1	17	20	10.6	1	20	10.6	16	8.5	7.41	46	.290	.449	-7	-7	95	88	-0.9	0	0	-0.6
1980	Cle-A	1	3	.250	51	0	0	0	5	86	98	10.3	5	44	4.6	74	7.7	5.44	77	.297	.377	-13	-12	103	93	-0.9	0	1	-1.0
1981	Cle-A	3	3	.500	24	0	0	0	2	43	43	9.0	4	18	3.8	34	7.1	4.40	78	.262	.330	-3	-5	93	92	0.0	0	-1	-0.4
1982	Sea-A	2	4	.333	56	1	0	0	7	71	70	8.9	5	21	2.7	49	6.2	4.18	107	.260	.301	-1	2	110	84	-0.8	0	1	0.4
1983	Sea-A	2	3	.400	50	0	0	0	7	65	65	9.0	3	28	3.9	47	6.5	3.32	124	.273	.343	5	6	101	126	0.1	0	-0	0.5
1984	Sea-A	4	4	.500	54	0	0	0	8	61	55	8.1	3	22	3.2	55	8.1	3.54	116	.241	.309	3	4	103	88	0.3	0	-1	0.3
1985	Sea-A	1	2	.333	24	0	0	0	1	29	32	9.9	4	21	6.5	17	5.3	5.28	75	.278	.400	-4	-4	95	114	-0.3	0	1	-0.3
	Chi-A	0	1	.000	11	0	0	0	0	12	15	11.3	2	8	6.0	12	9.0	9.00	46	.294	.383	-6	-6	100	69	-0.4	0	0	-0.5
	Yr	1	3	.250	35	0	0	0	1	41	47	10.3	6	29	6.4	29	6.4	6.37	63	.278	.380	-10	-11	97	69	-0.7	0	1	-0.8
Total	7	13	22	.371	277	3	0	0	31	384	398	9.3	27	182	4.3	304	7.1	4.62	88	.272	.348	-26	-23	102	96	-2.9	0	2	-1.6
■ **DAVE STAPLETON**	Stapleton, David Earl b: 10/16/61, Miami, Arizona BL/TL, 6'1", 185 lbs. Deb: 9/14/87																												
1987	Mil-A	2	0	1.000	4	0	0	0	0	15	13	7.8	0	3	1.8	14	8.4	1.80	253	.241	.276	4	5	102	131	1.0	0	0	0.5
1988	Mil-A	0	0	—	6	0	0	0	0	14	20	12.9	1	9	5.8	6	3.9	5.79	71	.339	.435	-3	-3	103	120	0.0	0	0	-0.2
Total	2	2	0	1.000	10	0	0	0	0	29	33	10.2	1	12	3.7	20	6.2	3.72	116	.292	.362	2	2	102	126	1.0	0	0	0.3
■ **CON STARKEL**	Starkel, Conrad b: 11/16/1880, Germany d: 1/19/33, Tacoma, Wash. BR/TR, 6', 200 lbs. Deb: 4/19/06																												
1906	Was-A	0	0	—	1	0	0	0	0	3	7	21.0	1	2	6.0	1	3.0	18.00	14	.483	.545	-5	-5	94	73	0.0	0	-0	-0.3
■ **RAY STARR**	Starr, Raymond Francis "Iron Man" b: 4/23/06, Nowata, Okla. d: 2/9/63, Baylis, Ill. BR/TR, 6'1", 178 lbs. Deb: 9/11/32																												
1932	StL-N	1	1	.500	3	2	1	1	0	20	19	8.5	2	10	4.5	6	2.7	2.70	145	.284	.380	3	3	101	195	0.1	0	1	0.3
1933	NY-N	0	1	.000	6	2	0	0	0	13	19	13.2	0	10	6.9	2	1.4	5.54	58	.339	.435	-3	-3	96	121	-0.4	-0	0	-0.3
	Bos-N	0	1	.000	9	1	0	0	0	28	32	10.3	4	9	2.9	15	4.8	3.86	83	.296	.347	-2	-2	96	133	-0.4	0	0	-0.1
	Yr	0	2	.000	15	3	0	0	0	41	51	11.2	4	19	4.2	17	3.7	4.39	73	.309	.374	-5	-5	96	133	-0.8	-0	0	-0.4
1941	Cin-N	3	2	.600	7	4	3	2	0	34	28	7.4	1	6	1.6	11	2.9	2.65	134	.219	.257	4	3	98	72	0.2	-0	0	0.3
1942	Cin-N	15	13	.536	37	33	17	4	0	277	228	7.4	10	106	3.4	83	2.7	2.66	126	.226	.297	20	22	102	102	1.2	-5	-1	1.7
1943	Cin-N	11	10	.524	36	33	9	2	1	217	201	8.3	9	91	3.8	42	1.7	3.65	91	.248	.322	-7	-8	98	93	-0.8	-4	0	-1.2
1944	Pit-N	6	5	.545	27	12	5	0	3	90	116	11.6	6	36	3.6	25	2.5	5.00	75	.314	.370	-14	-13	104	106	-0.3	1	-1	-1.1
1945	Pit-N	0	2	.000	4	0	0	0	0	7	10	12.9	0	4	5.1	0	0.0	9.00	43	.370	.424	-4	-4	102	76	-0.9	1	0	-0.2
	Chi-N	1	0	1.000	9	1	0	0	0	13	17	11.8	1	7	4.8	5	3.5	7.62	47	.298	.375	-6	-6	95	69	0.5	0	0	-0.4
	Yr	1	2	.333	13	1	0	0	0	20	27	12.1	1	11	4.9	5	2.3	8.10	46	.321	.392	-10	-10	98	69	-0.4	1	0	-0.6
Total	7	37	35	.514	138	88	35	9	4	699	670	8.6	33	279	3.6	189	2.4	3.53	97	.255	.323	-9	-8	100	101	-0.8	-7	-1	-1.0
■ **DICK STARR**	Starr, Richard Eugene b: 3/2/21, Kittanning, Pa. BR/TR, 6'3", 190 lbs. Deb: 9/05/47																												
1947	NY-A	1	0	1.000	4	1	1	0	0	12	12	9.0	1	8	6.0	1	0.8	1.50	228	.250	.351	3	3	92	283	0.5	1	0	0.3
1948	NY-A	0	0	—	1	0	0	0	0	2	0	0.0	0	2	9.0	2	9.0	4.50	92	.000	.250	-0	-0	96	7	0.0	0	0	0.0
1949	StL-A	1	7	.125	30	8	1	1	0	83	96	10.4	6	48	5.2	44	4.8	4.34	101	.292	.382	-1	0	104	118	-2.5	-1	-1	-0.1
1950	StL-A	7	5	.583	32	16	4	1	2	124	140	10.2	11	74	5.4	30	2.2	5.01	101	.287	.384	-6	1	111	108	2.1	-3	-1	-0.1
1951	StL-A	2	5	.286	15	9	0	0	0	62	66	9.6	10	42	6.1	26	3.8	7.40	61	.273	.385	-23	-20	109	77	-0.5	0	-1	-1.8
	Was-A	1	7	.125	11	11	1	0	0	61	76	11.2	12	24	3.5	17	2.5	5.61	71	.304	.364	-10	-11	97	107	-2.7	1	-1	-1.1
	Yr	3	12	.200	26	20	1	0	0	123	142	10.4	22	66	4.8	43	3.1	6.51	65	.287	.371	-33	-31	103	107	-3.2	0	-2	-2.9
Total	5	12	24	.333	93	45	7	2	2	344	390	10.2	40	198	5.2	120	3.1	5.26	86	.286	.378	-37	-28	106	110	-3.1	-3	-4	-2.8
■ **HERMAN STARRETTE**	Starrette, Herman Paul b: 11/20/38, Statesville, N.C. BR/TR, 6', 175 lbs. Deb: 7/01/63 C																												
1963	Bal-A	0	1	.000	18	0	0	0	0	26	26	9.0	1	7	2.4	13	4.5	3.46	98	.271	.321	0	-0	93	108	-0.4	0	1	0.1
1964	Bal-A	1	0	1.000	5	0	0	0	0	11	9	7.4	0	6	4.9	5	4.1	1.64	229	.250	.333	2	3	103	219	0.5	-0	-0	0.2
1965	Bal-A	0	0	—	4	0	0	0	0	9	8	8.0	0	3	3.0	3	3.0	1.00	342	.258	.306	2	2	99	312	0.0	-0	0	0.3
Total	3	1	1	.500	27	0	0	0	0	46	43	8.4	1	16	3.1	21	4.1	2.54	137	.264	.321	5	5	97	174	0.1	-0	1	0.6
■ **ED STAUFFER**	Stauffer, Charles Edward b: 1/10/1898, Emsworth, Pa. d: 7/2/79, St.Petersburg, Fla BR/TR, 5'11", 185 lbs. Deb: 4/26/23																												
1923	Chi-N	0	0	—	1	0	0	0	0	2	5	22.5	0	1	4.5	0	0.0	13.50	31	.556	.500	-2	-2	103	95	0.0	0	0	-0.1
1925	StL-A	0	1	.000	20	1	0	0	0	30	34	10.2	1	21	6.3	13	3.9	5.40	88	.283	.390	-3	-2	108	88	-0.4	-0	-1	-0.2
Total	2	0	1	.000	21	1	0	0	0	32	39	11.0	1	22	6.2	13	3.7	5.91	79	.302	.399	-5	-4	107	89	-0.4	-0	-1	-0.3
■ **BILL STEARNS**	Stearns, William b: 3/20/1853, Washington, D.C. d: 12/30/1898, Washington, D.C. Deb: 6/26/1871																												
1871	Oly-n	2	0	1.000	2																								
1872	Nat-n	0	11	.000	11																								
1873	Nat-n	7	24	.226	31																								
1874	Har-n	2	16	.111	18																								

YEAR	TM/L	W	L	PCT	G	GS	CG	SHO	SV	IP	H	H/G	HR	BB	BB/G	SO	SO/G	ERA	/A	OAVG	OOBP	PR	/A	PF	CPI	WAT	PB	PD	TPI
1875	Nat-n	1	14	.067	16																								
Total	5 n	12	65	.156	78																								
■ **CHARLIE STECHER**	Stecher, Charles b: Bordentown, N.J. Deb: 9/06/1890																												
1890	Phi-a	0	10	.000	10	10	9	0	0	68	111	14.7	1	60	7.9	18	2.4	10.32	38	.383	.489	-49	-48	101	79	-4.9	1	0	-3.4
■ **ELMER STEELE**	Steele, Elmer Rae b: 5/17/1886, Muitzeskill, N.Y. d: 3/9/66, Rhinebeck, N.Y. BB/TR, 5'11", 200 lbs. Deb: 9/12/07																												
1907	Bos-A	0	1	.000	4	1	0	0	0	11	11	9.0	0	1	0.8	10	8.2	1.64	160	.285	.303	1	1	103	146	-0.4	-1	0	0.2
1908	Bos-A	5	7	.417	16	13	9	1	0	118	85	6.5	1	13	1.0	37	2.8	1.83	127	.209	.239	7	6	97	76	-0.8	-4	-1	0.6
1909	Bos-A	4	4	.500	16	8	2	0	1	76	75	8.9	1	15	1.8	32	3.8	2.84	94	.255	.294	-3	-1	108	80	-0.5	1	0	0.0
1910	Pit-N	0	3	.000	3	3	2	0	0	24	19	7.1	0	3	1.1	7	2.6	2.25	148	.221	.247	2	3	110	56	-1.4	-1	1	0.4
1911	Pit-N	9	9	.500	31	16	7	2	2	166	153	8.3	5	31	1.7	52	2.8	2.60	127	.256	.297	15	13	97	107	-0.8	-0	2	1.4
	Bro-N	0	0	—	5	2	0	0	0	23	24	9.4	0	5	2.0	9	3.5	3.13	108	.258	.296	1	1	99	78	0.0	-1	0	0.0
	Yr	9	9	.500	36	18	7	2	2	189	177	8.4	5	36	1.7	61	2.9	2.67	124	.255	.292	15	14	98	78	-0.8	-0	2	1.4
Total	5	18	24	.429	75	43	20	3	3	418	367	7.9	7	68	1.5	147	3.2	2.41	121	.242	.278	23	23	100	90	-3.9	-5	2	2.6
■ **BOB STEELE**	Steele, Robert Wesley b: 1/5/1894, Cassburn, Ont., Can. d: 1/27/62, Ocala, Fla. BB/TL, 5'10.5", 175 lbs. Deb: 4/17/16																												
1916	StL-N	5	15	.250	29	22	7	1	0	148	156	9.5	6	42	2.6	67	4.1	3.41	77	.285	.325	-13	-13	100	110	-3.9	-1	-3	-1.7
1917	StL-N	1	3	.250	12	6	1	0	0	42	33	7.1	1	19	4.1	23	4.9	3.21	86	.223	.301	-2	-2	102	80	-1.0	2	-1	0.0
	Pit-N	5	11	.313	27	19	13	1	1	180	158	7.9	0	53	2.7	82	4.1	2.75	101	.237	.289	-1	1	103	84	-0.4	1	-2	0.0
	Yr	6	14	.300	39	25	14	1	1	222	191	7.7	1	72	2.9	105	4.3	2.84	98	.235	.291	-3	-1	102	84	-1.4	2	-2	0.0
1918	Pit-N	2	3	.400	10	4	2	1	1	49	44	8.1	2	17	3.1	21	3.9	3.31	87	.240	.301	-3	-2	105	86	-0.5	-0	-0	-0.2
	NY-N	3	5	.375	12	7	5	1	1	66	56	7.6	1	11	1.5	24	3.3	2.59	102	.226	.259	1	0	96	68	-1.3	2	-2	0.0
	Yr	5	8	.385	22	11	7	2	2	115	100	7.8	3	28	2.2	45	3.5	2.90	95	.231	.273	-2	-2	100	68	-1.8	-0	-3	-0.2
1919	NY-N	0	1	.000	1	0	0	0	0	3	3	9.0	0	2	6.0	0	0.0	6.00	47	.250	.333	-1	-1	96	59	-0.4	-0	-0	0.0
Total	4	16	38	.296	91	58	28	4	3	488	450	8.3	10	144	2.7	217	4.0	3.04	90	.249	.299	-19	-17	101	90	-7.5	3	-8	-1.9
■ **BILL STEELE**	Steele, William Mitchell "Big Bill" b: 10/5/1885, Milford, Pa. d: 10/19/49, Overland, Pa. BR/TR, 5'11", 200 lbs. Deb: 9/10/10																												
1910	StL-N	4	4	.500	9	8	8	0	1	72	71	8.9	1	24	3.0	25	3.1	3.25	87	.264	.338	-2	-3	93	100	0.6	2	1	-0.1
1911	StL-N	18	19	.486	43	34	23	1	3	287	287	9.0	8	113	3.5	115	3.6	3.73	93	.269	.345	-10	-8	102	98	-0.7	4	3	0.0
1912	StL-N	9	13	.409	40	25	7	0	2	194	245	11.4	5	66	3.1	67	3.1	4.69	75	.307	.366	-27	-26	103	92	0.0	1	4	-1.9
1913	StL-N	4	4	.500	12	9	2	0	0	54	58	9.7	3	18	3.0	10	1.7	5.00	62	.286	.343	-11	-11	97	83	1.0	-1	-1	-1.2
1914	StL-N	1	2	.333	17	2	0	0	0	53	55	9.3	3	7	1.2	16	2.7	2.72	106	.274	.297	0	1	104	115	-0.5	2	1	0.4
	Bro-N	1	1	.500	8	1	0	0	1	16	17	9.6	1	7	3.9	3	1.7	5.63	50	.258	.324	-5	-5	101	60	0.0	1	-0	-0.4
	Yr	2	3	.400	25	3	0	0	1	69	72	9.4	4	14	1.8	19	2.5	3.39	85	.267	.294	-5	-4	103	60	-0.5	2	1	0.0
Total	5	37	43	.463	129	79	40	1	7	676	733	9.8	21	235	3.1	236	3.1	4.02	83	.282	.346	-55	-53	101	96	0.4	8	7	-3.2
■ **BILL STEEN**	Steen, William John b: 11/11/1887, Pittsburgh, Pa. d: 3/13/79, Signal Hill, Cal. BR/TR, 6'0.5", 180 lbs. Deb: 4/15/12																												
1912	Cle-A	9	8	.529	26	16	6	1	0	143	163	10.3	3	45	2.8	61	3.8	3.78	90	.298	.352	-7	-6	101	109	0.7	2	-1	-0.7
1913	Cle-A	4	5	.444	22	13	7	2	2	128	113	7.9	3	49	3.4	57	4.0	2.46	124	.237	.313	7	8	104	105	-0.9	-0	-0	0.8
1914	Cle-A	9	14	.391	30	22	13	1	0	201	201	9.0	0	68	3.0	97	4.3	2.60	112	.272	.337	3	7	106	123	1.2	1	0	0.7
1915	Cle-A	1	4	.200	10	7	2	0	0	45	51	10.2	1	15	3.0	22	4.4	5.00	63	.290	.352	-10	-9	106	79	-1.1	-0	2	-0.7
	Det-A	5	1	.833	20	7	3	0	4	79	83	9.5	0	22	2.5	28	3.2	2.73	113	.269	.319	2	3	105	108	1.6	-1	2	0.4
	Yr	6	5	.545	30	14	5	0	4	124	134	9.7	1	37	2.7	50	3.6	3.56	87	.275	.328	-8	-6	105	108	0.5	-0	4	-0.3
Total	4	28	32	.467	108	65	31	4	6	596	611	9.2	7	199	3.0	265	4.0	3.05	101	.272	.334	-5	3	104	110	1.5	1	2	0.5
■ **MILT STEENGRAFE**	Steengrafe, Milton Henry b: 5/26/1900, San Francisco, Cal d: 6/2/77, BR/TR, 6', 170 lbs. Deb: 5/05/24																												
1924	Chi-A	0	0	—	3	0	0	0	0	6	15	22.5	0	4	6.0	3	4.5	12.00	35	.484	.528	-5	-5	98	98	0.0	-0	0	-0.4
1926	Chi-A	1	1	.500	13	1	0	0	0	38	43	10.2	1	19	4.5	10	2.4	4.03	90	.295	.366	-0	-2	90	117	0.0	-2	-1	-0.3
Total	2	1	1	.500	16	1	0	0	0	44	58	11.9	1	23	4.7	13	2.7	5.11	72	.328	.393	-5	-7	91	114	0.0	-2	-0	-0.7
■ **MORRIE STEEVENS**	Steevens, Morris Dale b: 10/7/40, Salem, Ill. BL/TL, 6'2", 175 lbs. Deb: 4/13/62																												
1962	Chi-N	0	1	.000	12	1	0	0	0	15	10	6.0	0	11	6.6	5	3.0	2.40	178	.196	.328	3	3	109	122	-0.4	-0	0	0.3
1964	Phi-N	0	0	—	4	0	0	0	0	3	5	15.0	0	1	3.0	3	9.0	3.00	115	.385	.429	0	0	98	224	0.0	0	0	0.0
1965	Phi-N	0	1	.000	6	0	0	0	0	3	5	15.0	1	4	12.0	3	9.0	15.00	22	.417	.563	-4	-4	95	85	-0.4	0	0	-0.3
Total	3	0	2	.000	22	1	0	0	0	21	20	8.6	1	16	6.9	11	4.7	4.29	94	.263	.381	-1	-1	105	131	-0.8	-0	0	0.0
■ **ED STEIN**	Stein, Edward F. b: 9/5/1869, Detroit, Mich. d: 5/10/28, Detroit, Mich. BR/TR, 5'11", 170 lbs. Deb: 7/24/1890																												
1890	Chi-N	12	6	.667	20	18	14	1	0	161	147	8.2	9	83	4.6	65	3.6	3.80	100	.258	.353	-4	0	107	93	1.4	-3	0	0.0
1891	Chi-N	7	6	.538	14	10	9	1	0	101	99	8.8	7	57	5.1	38	3.4	3.74	94	.270	.368	-4	-3	105	103	-0.7	-2	0	-0.2
1892	Bro-N	27	16	.628	48	42	38	6	1	377	310	7.4	5	150	3.6	190	4.5	2.84	115	.236	.314	19	18	99	84	0.8	3	3	2.2
1893	Bro-N	19	15	.559	37	34	28	1	0	298	294	8.9	4	119	3.6	81	2.4	3.78	113	.273	.345	30	16	91	92	2.3	-2	3	1.3
1894	Bro-N	27	14	.659	45	41	38	2	1	359	396	9.9	10	171	4.3	84	2.1	4.54	111	.302	.382	32	19	94	95	7.1	5	1	1.8
1895	Bro-N	15	13	.536	32	27	24	1	1	255	282	10.0	9	93	3.3	55	1.9	4.73	95	.300	.364	2	-7	94	86	-0.1	0	2	-0.3
1896	Bro-N	3	6	.333	17	10	6	0	0	90	130	13.0	6	51	5.1	16	1.6	4.90	78	.362	.441	-5	-11	88	132	-1.1	1	0	-0.8
1898	Bro-N	0	2	.000	3	2	2	0	0	23	39	15.3	0	9	3.5	6	2.3	5.48	63	.399	.450	-5	-5	96	121	-0.9	1	0	-0.2
Total	8	110	78	.585	216	184	159	12	3	1664	1697	9.2	50	733	4.0	535	2.9	3.96	105	.281	.359	63	33	96	93	8.8	4	8	3.8
■ **IRV STEIN**	Stein, Irvin Michael b: 5/21/11, Madisonville, La. d: 1/7/81, Covington, La. BR/TR, 6'2", 170 lbs. Deb: 7/07/32																												
1932	Phi-A	0	0	—	1	0	0	0	0	3	7	21.0	2	1	3.0	0	0.0	12.00	41	.500	.500	-3	-2	111	137	0.0	-0	0	-0.1
■ **RANDY STEIN**	Stein, William Randolph b: 3/7/53, Pomona, Cal. BR/TR, 6'4", 210 lbs. Deb: 4/17/78																												
1978	Mil-A	3	2	.600	31	1	0	0	1	73	78	9.6	5	39	4.8	42	5.2	5.30	74	.280	.368	-12	-11	104	89	0.2	0	0	-1.0
1979	Sea-A	2	3	.400	23	1	0	0	0	41	48	10.5	7	27	5.9	39	8.6	5.93	72	.291	.386	-8	-8	101	103	0.0	0	-1	-0.7
1981	Sea-A	0	1	.000	5	0	0	0	0	9	18	18.0	1	8	8.0	6	6.0	11.00	34	.429	.510	-7	-7	101	97	-0.4	0	0	-0.6
1982	Chi-N	0	0	—	6	0	0	0	0	10	7	6.3	2	7	6.3	6	5.4	3.60	104	.200	.326	0	0	104	117	0.0	0	-0	0.0
Total	4	5	6	.455	65	2	0	0	1	133	151	10.2	15	81	5.5	93	6.3	5.75	70	.290	.382	-27	-26	103	96	-0.2	0	-1	-2.3
■ **RAY STEINEDER**	Steineder, Raymond J. b: 11/13/1895, Salem, N.J. BR/TR, 6'0.5", 160 lbs. Deb: 7/16/23																												
1923	Pit-N	2	0	1.000	15	2	1	0	0	55	58	9.5	3	18	2.9	23	3.8	4.75	80	.278	.335	-5	-6	95	82	1.0	3	-1	-0.3
1924	Pit-N	0	1	.000	5	0	0	0	0	3	6	18.0	0	5	15.0	0	0.0	12.00	33	.400	.524	-3	-3	104	94	-0.4	0	0	-0.2
	Phi-N	1	1	.500	9	0	0	0	0	29	29	9.0	1	16	5.0	11	3.4	4.34	98	.266	.352	-2	-0	111	92	0.2	0	0	0.0
	Yr	1	2	.333	14	0	0	0	0	32	35	9.8	1	21	5.9	11	3.1	5.06	84	.282	.376	-4	-3	110	92	-0.2	0	0	-0.2
Total	2	3	2	.600	29	2	1	0	0	87	93	9.6	4	39	4.0	34	3.5	4.86	82	.279	.351	-9	-9	101	86	0.8	3	-1	-0.5
■ **RICK STEIRER**	Steirer, Ricky Francis b: 8/27/56, Baltimore, Md. BR/TR, 6'4", 200 lbs. Deb: 8/05/82																												
1982	Cal-A	1	0	1.000	10	1	0	0	0	26	25	8.7	2	11	3.8	14	4.8	3.81	106	.243	.316	1	1	99	90	0.5	0	0	0.1
1983	Cal-A	3	2	.600	19	5	0	0	0	62	77	11.2	3	18	2.6	25	3.6	4.79	82	.302	.348	-5	-6	96	96	0.8	0	1	-0.5
1984	Cal-A	0	1	.000	1	1	0	0	0	3	6	18.0	0	2	6.0	2	6.0	15.00	27	.500	.571	-4	-4	101	73	-0.4	0	0	-0.2
Total	3	4	3	.571	30	7	0	0	0	91	108	10.7	5	31	3.1	41	4.1	4.85	82	.292	.346	-8	-9	97	93	0.9	0	1	-0.6
■ **BILL STELLBERGER**	Stellberger, William F. b: 4/22/1865, Detroit, Mich. d: 11/9/36, Detroit, Mich. BL/TL, Deb: 1885																												
1885	Pro-N	0	1	.000	1	1	1	0	0	8	14	15.8	0	4	4.5	0	0.0	7.88	33	.394	.456	-4	-5	93	94	-0.4	-1	0	-0.3
■ **JEFF STEMBER**	Stember, Jeffrey Alan b: 3/2/58, Elizabeth, N.J. BR/TR, 6'5", 220 lbs. Deb: 8/05/80																												
1980	SF-N	0	0	—	1	1	0	0	0	3	2	6.0	1	2	6.0	0	0.0	3.00	116	.167	.286	0	0	96	125	0.0	-0	0	0.0
■ **BILL STEMMEYER**	Stemmeyer, William "Cannon Ball" b: 5/6/1865, Cleveland, Ohio d: 5/3/45, Cleveland, Ohio BR/TR, 6'2", 190 lbs. Deb: 1885																												
1885	Bos-N	1	1	.500	2	2	2	1	0	11	7	5.7	0	11	9.0	8	6.5	0.00	—	.191	.378	3	3	95	0	0.2	1	0	0.5
1886	Bos-N	22	18	.550	41	41	41	0	0	349	300	7.7	11	144	3.7	239	**6.2**	3.02	106	.244	.324	11	7	97	98	3.9	9	-3	1.2
1887	Bos-N	6	8	.429	15	14	14	0	1	119	138	10.4	4	41	3.1	41	3.1	5.22	75	.306	.364	-15	-17	97	83	-1.1	2	0	-1.1
1888	Cle-a	0	2	.000	2	2	2	0	0	16	37	20.8	0	9	5.1	7	3.9	9.00	34	.465	.520	-11	-11	100	116	-0.9	1	0	-0.6

YEAR	TM/L	W	L	PCT	G	GS	CG	SHO	SV	IP	H	H/G	HR	BB	BB/G	SO	SO/G	ERA	/A	OAVG	OOBP	PR	/A	PF	CPI	WAT	PB	PD	TPI
Total	4	29	29	.500	60	59	59	1	1	495	482	8.8	15	205	3.7	295	5.4	3.67	92	.268	.343	-11	-17	97	93	2.1	13	-3	0.0
■ **DAVE STENHOUSE**	Stenhouse, David Rotchford b: 9/12/33, Westerly, R.I. BR/TR, 6', 195 lbs. Deb: 4/18/62																												
1962	Was-A	11	12	.478	34	26	9	2	0	197	169	7.7	24	90	4.1	123	5.6	3.65	111	.234	.314	7	9	102	103	2.2	-5	1	0.6
1963	Was-A	3	9	.250	16	16	2	1	0	87	90	9.3	12	45	4.7	47	4.9	4.55	81	.260	.343	-9	-9	101	101	-1.7	-1	0	-0.9
1964	Was-A	2	7	.222	26	14	1	0	1	88	80	8.2	12	39	4.0	44	4.5	4.81	78	.239	.316	-12	-10	103	79	-1.9	2	-0	-0.8
Total	3	16	28	.364	76	56	12	3	1	372	339	8.2	48	174	4.2	214	5.2	4.14	94	.241	.322	-14	-10	102	97	-1.4	-4	1	-1.1
■ **BUZZ STEPHEN**	Stephen, Louis Roberts b: 7/13/44, Porterville, Cal. BR/TR, 6'4", 205 lbs. Deb: 9/20/68																												
1968	Min-A	1	1	.500	2	2	0	0	0	11	11	9.0	0	7	5.7	4	3.3	4.91	64	.275	.388	-2	-2	106	93	0.0	-0	0	-0.2
■ **BRYAN STEPHENS**	Stephens, Bryan Maris b: 7/14/20, Fayetteville, Ark BR/TR, 6'4", 175 lbs. Deb: 5/15/47																												
1947	Cle-A	5	10	.333	31	5	1	0	1	92	79	7.7	6	39	3.8	34	3.3	4.01	87	.230	.306	-3	-5	94	77	-2.8	-2	-1	-0.8
1948	StL-A	3	6	.333	43	12	2	0	3	123	141	10.3	14	67	4.9	35	2.6	6.00	78	.289	.372	-23	-18	109	92	-0.5	-1	-1	-1.7
Total	2	8	16	.333	74	17	3	0	4	215	220	9.2	20	106	4.4	69	2.9	5.15	80	.264	.345	-27	-24	103	85	-3.3	-3	-2	-2.5
■ **CLARENCE STEPHENS**	Stephens, Clarence Wright b: 8/19/1863, Cincinnati, Ohio d: 2/28/45, Cincinnati, Ohio TR Deb:10/08/1886																												
1886	Cin-a	1	0	1.000	1	1	1	0	0	8	9	10.1	0	5	5.6	6	6.8	5.63	59	.294	.394	-2	-2	96	86	0.5	1	0	0.0
1891	Cin-N	0	1	.000	1	1	1	0	0	8	9	10.1	1	3	3.4	3	3.4	7.88	40	.298	.361	-4	-4	93	57	-0.4	-0	0	-0.3
1892	Cin-N	0	1	.000	1	1	0	0	0	7	12	15.4	0	4	5.1	1	1.3	1.29	264	.392	.462	2	2	103	561	-0.4	-0	0	0.1
Total	3	1	2	.333	3	3	2	0	0	23	30	11.7	1	12	4.7	10	3.9	5.09	64	.328	.406	-4	-5	97	221	-0.3	0	0	-0.2
■ **BEN STEPHENS**	Stephens, George Benjamin b: 9/28/1867, Romeo, Mich. d: 8/5/1896, Armada, Mich. 5'10.5", 170 lbs. Deb: 8/05/1892																												
1892	Bal-N	1	1	.500	5	2	2	0	1	29	37	11.5	2	9	2.8	7	2.2	2.79	121	.324	.373	2	2	102	173	0.3	-2	0	0.0
1893	Was-N	0	6	.000	9	6	6	0	0	64	83	11.7	1	31	4.4	14	2.0	5.91	73	.330	.404	-9	-11	92	89	-2.9	-3	0	-1.1
1894	Was-N	0	0	—	3	2	1	1	0	11	19	15.5	1	8	6.5	1	0.8	4.91	108	.404	.490	1	0	100	176	0.0	-0	0	0.0
Total	3	1	7	.125	17	10	9	1	1	104	139	12.0	4	48	4.2	22	1.9	4.93	84	.337	.406	-7	-9	96	122	-2.6	-5	0	-1.1
■ **EARL STEPHENSON**	Stephenson, Chester Earl b: 7/31/47, Benson, N.C. BL/TL, 6'3", 175 lbs. Deb: 4/07/71																												
1971	Chi-N	1	0	1.000	16	0	0	0	1	20	24	10.8	1	11	4.9	11	4.9	4.50	85	.316	.389	-2	-2	110	121	0.5	-0	0	-0.1
1972	Mil-A	3	5	.375	35	8	1	0	0	80	79	8.9	5	33	3.7	33	3.7	3.26	91	.262	.333	-2	-3	97	116	-0.3	-2	0	-0.4
1977	Bal-A	0	0	—	1	0	0	0	0	3	5	15.0	1	0	0.0	2	6.0	9.00	42	.357	.357	-2	-2	92	83	0.0	0	0	-0.1
1978	Bal-A	0	0	—	2	0	0	0	0	10	10	9.0	0	5	4.5	4	3.6	2.70	127	.294	.375	1	1	91	164	0.0	0	-0	0.0
Total	4	4	5	.444	54	8	1	0	1	113	118	9.4	7	49	3.9	50	4.0	3.58	89	.277	.348	-4	-5	98	120	0.2	-2	0	-0.6
■ **JERRY STEPHENSON**	Stephenson, Jerry Joseph b: 10/6/43, Detroit, Mich. BL/TR, 6'2", 185 lbs. Deb: 4/14/63																												
1963	Bos-A	0	0	—	1	1	0	0	0	2	5	22.5	0	2	9.0	3	13.5	9.00	43	.556	.538	-1	-1	107	157	0.0	-0	0	0.0
1965	Bos-A	1	5	.167	15	8	0	0	0	52	62	10.7	7	33	5.7	49	8.5	6.23	61	.287	.379	-16	-14	109	90	-1.6	1	0	-1.2
1966	Bos-A	2	5	.286	15	11	1	0	0	66	68	9.3	6	44	6.0	50	6.8	5.86	65	.264	.367	-18	-15	110	83	-1.2	-1	0	-1.5
1967	Bos-A	3	1	.750	8	6	0	0	1	40	32	7.2	4	16	3.6	24	5.4	3.82	95	.227	.304	-3	-1	113	89	0.9	0	0	0.0
1968	Bos-A	2	8	.200	23	7	2	0	0	69	81	10.6	4	42	5.5	51	6.7	5.61	53	.295	.381	-20	-20	101	93	-3.1	2	1	-1.8
1969	Sea-A	0	0	—	2	0	0	0	0	3	6	18.0	0	3	9.0	1	3.0	9.00	40	.429	.556	-2	-2	100	122	0.0	-0	0	-0.1
1970	LA-N	0	0	—	3	0	0	0	0	7	11	14.1	0	5	6.4	6	7.7	9.00	40	.379	.471	-4	-4	89	85	0.0	-0	-0	-0.3
Total	7	8	19	.296	67	33	3	0	1	239	265	10.0	21	145	5.5	184	6.9	5.69	62	.281	.373	-63	-57	107	90	-5.0	2	1	-4.9
■ **JOHN STERLING**	Sterling, John A. b: Philadelphia, Pa. Deb: 10/12/1890																												
1890	Phi-a	0	1	.000	1	1	1	0	0	5	16	28.8	1	4	7.2	1	1.8	21.60	18	.549	.604	-10	-10	101	79	-0.4	-0	0	-0.6
■ **RANDY STERLING**	Sterling, Randall Wayne b: 4/21/51, Key West, Fla. BB/TR, 6'2", 195 lbs. Deb: 9/16/74																												
1974	NY-N	1	1	.500	3	2	0	0	0	9	13	13.0	0	3	3.0	2	2.0	5.00	73	.351	.386	-1	-1	100	116	0.1	0	0	0.0
■ **JIM STEVENS**	Stevens, James Arthur "Steve" b: 8/25/1889, Williamsburg, Md. d: 9/25/66, Baltimore, Md. BR/TR, 5'11", 180 lbs. Deb: 8/24/14																												
1914	Was-A	0	0	—	2	0	0	0	0	3	4	12.0	0	2	6.0	0	0.0	9.00	30	.364	.500	-2	-2	100	82	0.0	-0	-0	-0.1
■ **DAVE STEWART**	Stewart, David Keith b: 2/19/57, Oakland, Cal. BR/TR, 6'2", 200 lbs. Deb: 9/22/78																												
1978	LA-N	0	0	—	1	0	0	0	0	2	1	4.5	0	0	0.0	1	4.5	0.00	—	.167	.167	1	1	97	0	0.0	0	0	0.1
1981	LA-N	4	3	.571	32	0	0	0	6	43	40	8.4	3	14	2.9	29	6.1	2.51	133	.250	.293	5	4	96	132	0.0	2	0	0.6
1982	LA-N	9	8	.529	45	14	0	0	1	146	137	8.4	14	49	3.0	80	4.9	3.82	88	.249	.305	-3	-7	94	92	-0.1	1	-1	-0.7
1983	LA-N	5	2	.714	46	1	0	0	8	76	67	7.9	4	33	3.9	54	6.4	2.96	122	.237	.311	6	6	100	106	1.3	-0	-0	0.5
	Tex-A	5	2	.714	8	8	2	0	0	59	50	7.6	2	17	2.6	24	3.7	2.14	193	.233	.291	13	13	101	125	1.6	0	0	1.4
1984	Tex-A	7	14	.333	32	27	3	0	0	192	193	9.0	26	87	4.1	119	5.6	4.73	85	.258	.335	-16	-15	101	93	-2.5	0	-1	-1.5
1985	Tex-A	0	6	.000	42	5	0	0	4	81	86	9.6	13	37	4.1	64	7.1	5.44	84	.273	.346	-12	-8	110	94	-2.9	0	0	-0.7
	Phi-N	0	0	—	4	0	0	0	0	4	5	11.3	0	4	9.0	2	4.5	6.75	54	.278	.409	-1	-1	102	77	0.0	0	-0	-0.1
1986	Phi-N	0	0	—	8	0	0	0	0	12	15	11.3	1	4	3.0	9	6.8	6.75	57	.306	.339	-4	-4	104	73	0.0	0	-0	-0.3
	Oak-A	9	5	.643	29	17	4	1	0	149	137	8.3	15	65	3.9	102	6.2	3.74	105	.241	.318	7	3	94	98	2.4	0	-0	0.3
1987	Oak-A	**20**	13	.606	37	37	8	1	0	261	224	7.7	24	105	3.6	205	7.1	3.69	110	.229	.304	23	11	91	88	4.2	0	-3	0.7
1988	Oak-A	21	12	.636	37	37	**14**	2	0	**276**	240	7.8	14	110	3.6	192	6.3	3.23	115	.234	.305	23	14	93	95	-0.1	0	-3	1.1
Total	9	80	65	.552	321	146	31	4	19	1301	1195	8.3	116	525	3.6	881	6.1	3.76	103	.243	.314	41	17	96	96	3.9	2	-8	1.4
■ **FRANK STEWART**	Stewart, Frank "Stewy" b: 9/8/06, Minneapolis, Minn. BR/TR, 6'1.5", 180 lbs. Deb: 10/02/27																												
1927	Chi-A	0	1	.000	1	1	0	0	0	4	5	11.3	0	4	9.0	0	0.0	9.00	47	.357	.474	-2	-2	103	84	-0.4	-0	1	-0.1
■ **JOE STEWART**	Stewart, Joseph Lawrence "Ace" b: 3/11/1879, Monroe, N.C. d: 2/9/13, Youngstown, Ohio TR, 5'11", 175 lbs. Deb: 9/13/04																												
1904	Bos-N	0	0	—	2	0	0	0	0	9	12	12.0	0	4	4.0	1	1.0	10.00	28	.356	.440	-7	-7	102	53	0.0	-0	-0	-0.6
■ **SAMMY STEWART**	Stewart, Samuel Lee b: 10/28/54, Asheville, N.C. BR/TR, 6'3", 200 lbs. Deb: 9/01/78																												
1978	Bal-A	1	1	.500	2	2	0	0	0	11	10	8.2	0	3	2.5	11	9.0	3.27	104	.238	.283	1	0	91	66	0.0	0	0	0.0
1979	Bal-A	8	5	.615	31	3	1	0	1	118	96	7.3	11	71	5.4	71	5.4	3.51	115	.232	.345	9	7	96	115	-0.2	0	3	0.9
1980	Bal-A	7	7	.500	33	3	2	0	3	119	103	7.8	9	60	4.5	78	5.9	3.55	113	.235	.325	6	6	99	98	-1.3	0	-0	0.6
1981	Bal-A	4	8	.333	29	3	0	0	4	112	89	7.2	8	57	4.6	57	4.6	2.33	**156**	.225	.322	17	16	99	**144**	-2.5	0	0	1.7
1982	Bal-A	10	9	.526	38	12	1	1	5	139	140	9.1	9	62	4.0	69	4.5	4.14	98	.263	.336	-1	-2	99	96	-0.9	0	1	0.0
1983	Bal-A	9	4	.692	58	1	0	0	7	144	138	8.6	7	67	4.2	95	5.9	3.63	111	.253	.331	7	6	99	101	1.5	0	-0	0.6
1984	Bal-A	7	4	.636	60	0	0	0	13	93	81	7.8	7	47	4.5	56	5.4	3.29	114	.241	.327	7	5	94	113	1.4	0	0	0.5
1985	Bal-A	5	7	.417	56	1	0	0	9	130	117	8.1	15	66	4.6	77	5.3	3.60	113	.246	.330	8	7	98	117	-1.1	0	-1	0.6
1986	Bos-A	4	1	.800	27	0	0	0	0	64	64	9.0	7	48	6.8	47	6.6	4.36	95	.266	.380	-1	-2	99	120	1.3	0	-0	-0.1
1987	Cle-A	4	2	.667	25	0	0	0	3	27	25	8.3	4	21	7.0	25	8.3	5.67	83	.234	.362	-4	-3	105	83	1.4	0	0	-0.2
Total	10	59	48	.551	359	25	4	1	45	957	863	8.1	77	502	4.7	586	5.5	3.59	111	.245	.335	50	41	98	110	-0.4	0	2	4.6
■ **BUNKY STEWART**	Stewart, Veston Goff b: 1/7/31, Jasper, N.C. BL/TL, 6', 154 lbs. Deb: 5/04/52																												
1952	Was-A	0	0	—	1	0	0	0	0	1	2	18.0	0	1	9.0	1	9.0	18.00	20	.500	.600	-2	-2	100	65	0.0	0	0	0.0
1953	Was-A	0	2	.000	2	2	1	0	0	15	17	10.2	1	11	6.6	3	1.8	4.80	77	.283	.403	-1	-2	93	114	-0.9	-0	-0	-0.1
1954	Was-A	0	2	.000	29	2	0	0	1	51	67	11.8	3	27	4.8	27	4.8	7.59	49	.324	.390	-22	-22	99	78	-0.9	0	1	-2.0
1955	Was-A	0	0	—	7	1	0	0	0	15	18	10.8	0	6	3.6	10	6.0	4.20	89	.295	.348	-0	-1	94	97	0.0	-0	0	0.0
1956	Was-A	5	7	.417	33	9	1	0	2	105	111	9.5	15	82	7.0	36	3.1	5.57	80	.276	.395	-16	-13	107	106	0.4	-0	1	-1.1
Total	5	5	11	.313	72	14	2	0	3	187	215	10.3	19	127	6.1	77	3.7	6.02	68	.293	.392	-42	-40	102	98	-1.4	-0	2	-3.2
■ **LEFTY STEWART**	Stewart, Walter Cleveland b: 9/23/1900, Sparta, Tenn. d: 9/26/74, Knoxville, Tenn. BR/TL, 5'10", 160 lbs. Deb: 4/20/21																												
1921	Det-A	0	0	—	5	0	0	0	1	9	20	20.0	0	5	5.0	4	4.0	12.00	34	.455	.481	-8	-8	96	84	0.0	-0	0	-0.6
1927	StL-A	8	11	.421	27	19	11	0	1	156	187	10.8	7	43	2.5	43	2.5	4.27	106	.310	.344	-2	4	109	107	0.6	2	1	0.8
1928	StL-A	7	9	.438	29	17	7	1	3	143	173	10.9	5	32	2.0	25	1.6	4.66	89	.310	.339	-10	-8	103	95	-1.5	3	-0	-0.4
1929	StL-A	9	6	.600	23	18	8	1	0	150	137	8.2	11	49	2.9	47	2.8	3.24	130	.246	.303	17	16	100	101	1.4	-3	-0	1.2
1930	StL-A	20	12	.625	35	33	23	1	0	271	281	9.3	21	70	2.3	79	2.6	3.45	148	.268	.309	36	50	110	112	6.6	2	0	5.2

YEAR	TM/L	W	L	PCT	G	GS	CG	SHO	SV	IP	H	H/G	HR	BB	BB/G	SO	SO/G	ERA	/A	OAVG	OOBP	PR	/A	PF	CPI	WAT	PB	PD	TPI
1931	StL-A	14	17	.452	36	33	20	1	0	258	287	10.0	17	85	3.0	89	3.1	4.40	105	.277	.330	-0	-0	105	98	1.4	6	0	1.3
1932	StL-A	15	19	.441	41	32	18	2	1	260	269	9.3	22	99	3.4	86	3.0	4.60	100	.270	.332	-4	-0	103	96	1.2	-1	-1	-0.1
1933	Was-A	15	6	.714	34	31	11	1	0	231	227	8.8	19	60	2.3	69	2.7	3.82	105	.256	.301	12	4	93	95	2.1	1	1	0.5
1934	Was-A	7	11	.389	24	22	7	1	0	152	184	10.9	8	36	2.1	36	2.1	4.03	114	.303	.337	8	10	102	113	-1.0	-2	-0	0.7
1935	Was-A	0	1	.000	1	1	0	0	0	3	8	24.0	1	2	6.0	1	3.0	12.00	34	.533	.556	-3	-3	93	136	-0.4	-0	0	-0.1
	Cle-A	6	6	.500	24	10	2	1	2	91	122	12.1	6	17	1.7	24	2.4	5.44	81	.312	.337	-10	-11	99	87	-0.3	-1	-1	-1.1
	Yr	6	7	.462	25	11	2	1	2	94	130	12.4	7	19	1.8	25	2.4	5.65	78	.320	.346	-12	-13	99	87	-0.7	-0	-1	-1.2
Total	10	101	98	.508	279	216	107	9	8	1724	1895	9.9	117	498	2.6	503	2.6	4.19	108	.281	.326	37	61	103	101	10.1	7	0	7.4
■ **MACK STEWART**	Stewart, William Macklin b: 9/23/14, Stevenson, Ala. d: 3/21/60, Macon, Ga. BR/TR, 6', 167 lbs. Deb: 7/07/44																												
1944	Chi-N	0	0	—	8	0	0	0	0	12	11	8.3	1	4	3.0	3	2.3	1.50	241	.239	.300	3	3	100	210	0.0	-0	-0	0.3
1945	Chi-N	0	1	.000	16	1	0	0	0	28	37	11.9	0	14	4.5	9	2.9	4.82	75	.322	.392	-3	-4	95	109	-0.4	0	0	-0.2
Total	2	0	1	.000	24	1	0	0	0	40	48	10.8	1	18	4.0	12	2.7	3.82	95	.298	.367	-0	-1	97	140	-0.4	0	0	0.1
■ **DAVE STIEB**	Stieb, David Andrew b: 7/22/57, Santa Ana, Cal. BR/TR, 6', 185 lbs. Deb: 6/29/79																												
1979	Tor-A	8	8	.500	18	18	7	1	0	129	139	9.7	11	48	3.3	52	3.6	4.33	103	.276	.339	-1	2	106	99	2.2	0	3	0.4
1980	Tor-A	12	15	.444	34	32	14	4	0	243	232	8.6	12	83	3.1	108	4.0	3.70	110	.260	.320	9	10	101	95	0.8	0	6	1.6
1981	Tor-A	11	10	.524	25	25	11	2	0	184	148	7.2	10	61	3.0	89	4.4	3.18	130	.223	.294	10	20	113	86	3.3	0	2	2.4
1982	Tor-A	17	14	.548	38	38	**19**	**5**	0	**288**	271	8.5	27	75	2.3	141	4.4	3.25	137	.248	.296	27	**38**	109	101	2.4	0	4	**4.5**
1983	Tor-A	17	12	.586	36	36	14	4	0	278	223	7.2	21	93	3.0	187	6.1	3.04	144	.219	.289	32	**42**	108	91	1.4	0	0	**4.4**
1984	Tor-A	16	8	.667	35	35	11	2	0	**267**	215	**7.2**	19	88	3.0	198	6.7	2.83	143	**.221**	.289	35	36	101	97	3.5	0	1	3.9
1985	Tor-A	14	13	.519	36	36	8	2	0	265	206	**7.0**	22	96	3.3	167	5.7	**2.48**	**166**	**.213**	.286	**49**	**48**	99	112	-2.4	0	5	**5.7**
1986	Tor-A	7	12	.368	37	34	1	1	1	205	239	10.5	29	87	3.8	127	5.6	4.74	92	.297	.371	-13	-8	104	119	-3.1	0	2	-0.6
1987	Tor-A	13	9	.591	33	31	3	1	0	185	164	8.0	16	87	4.2	115	5.6	4.09	109	.239	.327	8	7	99	92	0.0	0	1	0.8
1988	Tor-A	16	8	.667	32	31	8	4	0	207	157	6.8	15	79	3.4	147	6.4	3.04	129	.210	.295	21	20	99	91	3.8	0	1	2.2
Total	10	131	109	.546	324	316	96	26	1	2251	1994	8.0	182	797	3.2	1331	5.3	3.37	126	.239	.308	177	216	104	99	11.9	0	23	25.3
■ **FRED STIELY**	Stiely, Fred Warren "Lefty" b: 6/1/01, Pillow, Pa. d: 1/6/81, Valley View, Pa. BB/TL, 5'8", 170 lbs. Deb: 10/06/29																												
1929	StL-A	1	0	1.000	1	1	1	0	0	9	11	11.0	0	3	3.0	2	2.0	0.00	—	.297	.366	4	4	100	0	0.5	1	0	0.7
1930	StL-A	0	1	.000	4	2	1	0	0	19	27	12.8	4	8	3.8	5	2.4	8.53	60	.346	.383	-8	-7	110	91	-0.4	1	-0	-0.4
1931	StL-A	0	0	—	4	0	0	0	0	7	7	9.0	0	3	3.9	2	2.6	6.43	71	.269	.367	-2	-1	105	67	0.0	0	-0	-0.1
Total	3	1	1	.500	9	3	2	0	0	35	45	11.6	4	14	3.6	9	2.3	5.91	81	.319	.376	-6	-4	106	63	0.1	3	-0	0.2
■ **DICK STIGMAN**	Stigman, Richard Lewis b: 1/24/36, Nimrod, Minn. BR/TL, 6'3", 200 lbs. Deb: 4/22/60																												
1960	Cle-A	5	11	.313	41	18	3	0	9	134	118	7.9	13	87	5.8	104	7.0	4.50	85	.238	.343	-9	-10	98	90	-3.0	2	-2	-0.9
1961	Cle-A	2	5	.286	22	6	0	0	0	64	65	9.1	9	25	3.5	48	6.8	4.64	84	.264	.323	-4	-5	97	95	-1.4	-1	0	-0.5
1962	Min-A	12	5	.706	40	15	6	0	3	143	122	7.7	19	64	4.0	116	7.3	3.65	113	.233	.315	5	7	104	104	3.0	-4	-2	0.1
1963	Min-A	15	15	.500	33	33	15	3	0	241	210	7.8	32	81	3.0	193	7.2	3.25	109	.231	.292	10	8	98	103	-2.0	-1	-4	0.2
1964	Min-A	6	15	.286	32	29	5	1	0	190	160	7.6	31	70	3.3	159	7.5	4.03	90	.225	.296	-8	-9	100	88	-4.6	-3	-3	-1.3
1965	Min-A	4	2	.667	33	8	0	0	4	70	59	7.6	14	33	4.2	70	9.0	4.37	78	.227	.311	-7	-8	98	94	0.3	-0	-1	-0.8
1966	Bos-A	2	1	.667	34	10	1	1	0	81	85	9.4	15	46	5.1	65	7.2	5.44	70	.268	.357	-18	-15	110	100	0.6	-1	-1	-1.6
Total	7	46	54	.460	235	119	30	5	16	923	819	8.0	133	406	4.0	755	7.4	4.03	92	.237	.314	-32	-31	100	97	-7.1	-8	-12	-4.8
■ **ROLLIE STILES**	Stiles, Rolland Mays "Lena" b: 11/17/06, Ratcliff, Ark. BR/TR, 6'1.5", 180 lbs. Deb: 6/19/30																												
1930	StL-A	3	6	.333	20	7	3	0	0	102	136	12.0	10	41	3.6	25	2.2	5.91	87	.337	.379	-14	-9	110	110	-0.8	0	-1	-0.7
1931	StL-A	3	1	.750	34	2	0	0	0	81	112	12.4	2	60	6.7	32	3.6	7.22	64	.352	.451	-26	-24	105	102	1.2	-2	-0	-2.2
1933	StL-A	3	7	.300	31	9	6	1	1	115	154	12.1	4	47	3.7	29	2.3	5.01	100	.327	.382	-9	0	117	115	-0.8	-4	-1	-0.3
Total	3	9	14	.391	85	18	9	1	1	298	402	12.1	16	148	4.5	86	2.6	5.92	84	.337	.400	-49	-32	112	110	-0.4	-6	-2	-3.2
■ **ARCHIE STIMMEL**	Stimmel, Archibald May "Lumbago" b: 5/30/1873, Woodsboro, Md. d: 8/18/58, Frederick, Md. BR/TR, 6', 175 lbs. Deb: 7/03/00																												
1900	Cin-N	1	1	.500	2	1	1	0	0	13	18	12.5	1	4	2.8	2	1.4	6.92	50	.353	.400	-5	-5	93	79	0.1	-0	0	-0.3
1901	Cin-N	4	14	.222	20	18	14	1	0	153	170	10.0	10	44	2.6	55	3.2	4.12	80	.309	.371	-14	-14	100	102	-3.9	-4	-3	-1.5
1902	Cin-N	0	4	.000	4	3	3	0	0	26	37	12.8	1	12	4.2	7	2.4	3.46	87	.360	.427	-2	-1	108	162	-1.9	-0	-0	-0.1
Total	3	5	19	.208	26	22	18	1	0	192	225	10.5	12	60	2.8	64	3.0	4.22	78	.320	.381	-20	-20	100	109	-5.7	-5	-3	-1.9
■ **CARL STIMSON**	Stimson, Carl Remus b: 7/18/1894, Hamburg, Iowa d: 11/9/36, Omaha, Neb. BB/TR, 6'5", 190 lbs. Deb: 6/06/23																												
1923	Bos-A	0	0	—	2	0	0	0	0	4	12	27.0	0	5	11.3	1	2.3	22.50	19	.750	.750	-8	-8	106	92	0.0	-0	0	-0.6
■ **HARRY STINE**	Stine, Harry C. b: 2/20/1864, Shenandoah, Pa. d: 6/5/24, Niagara Falls, N.Y TL , 5'6", 150 lbs. Deb: 7/22/1890																												
1890	Phi-a	0	1	.000	1	1	1	0	0	8	17	19.1	0	4	4.5	1	1.1	9.00	44	.447	.500	-5	-5	101	105	-0.4	-0	0	-0.2
■ **LEE STINE**	Stine, Lee Elbert b: 11/17/13, Stillwater, Okla. BR/TR, 5'11", 185 lbs. Deb: 4/17/34																												
1934	Chi-A	0	0	—	4	0	0	0	0	11	11	9.0	2	10	8.2	8	6.5	8.18	57	.268	.423	-5	-4	103	83	0.0	0	-0	-0.3
1935	Chi-A	0	0	—	1	0	0	0	0	2	2	9.0	1	3	13.5	1	4.5	9.00	54	.286	.500	-1	-1	109	123	0.0	0	1	0.0
1936	Cin-N	3	8	.273	40	13	5	0	2	122	157	11.6	6	41	3.0	26	1.9	5.02	78	.318	.369	-14	-15	97	105	-2.4	3	1	-1.0
1938	NY-A	0	0	—	4	0	0	0	0	9	9	9.0	0	1	1.0	4	4.0	1.00	486	.333	.345	4	4	102	484	0.0	-0	-0	0.4
Total	4	3	8	.273	49	13	5	0	2	144	179	11.2	9	55	3.4	39	2.4	5.06	80	.315	.374	-15	-17	98	127	-2.4	3	2	-0.9
■ **JACK STIVETTS**	Stivetts, John Elmer "Happy Jack" b: 3/31/1868, Ashland, Pa. d: 4/18/30, Ashland, Pa. BR/TR, 6'2", 185 lbs. Deb: 6/26/1889																												
1889	StL-a	12	7	.632	26	20	18	2	1	192	153	**7.2**	4	68	3.2	143	**6.7**	**2.25**	**186**	**.232**	**.304**	34	41	109	103	-0.5	-1	0	3.8
1890	StL-a	27	21	.563	54	46	41	3	0	419	399	8.6	14	179	3.8	289	6.2	3.52	126	.266	.344	16	42	115	104	-0.6	15	4	6.5
1891	StL-a	33	22	.600	**64**	56	40	3	1	440	357	7.3	15	232	4.7	**259**	5.3	2.86	145	.235	.336	42	**63**	112	98	-1.7	11	3	**7.9**
1892	Bos-N	35	16	.686	53	48	45	3	1	415	346	7.5	12	171	3.7	180	3.9	3.04	120	.239	.319	12	28	111	86	0.8	15	8	5.8
1893	Bos-N	20	12	.625	37	33	29	1	1	284	315	10.0	17	115	3.6	61	1.9	4.40	107	.297	.366	9	10	101	101	-1.2	9	-1	1.7
1894	Bos-N	26	14	.650	45	39	30	0	0	338	429	11.4	27	127	3.4	76	2.0	4.90	121	.332	.392	16	39	111	107	1.6	10	-2	4.6
1895	Bos-N	17	17	.500	38	34	30	0	0	291	341	10.5	15	89	2.8	111	3.4	4.64	105	.313	.365	5	8	102	94	-1.6	-6	-0	0.1
1896	Bos-N	21	14	.600	42	36	31	2	0	329	353	9.7	20	99	2.7	71	1.9	4.10	114	.296	.350	10	20	107	94	1.9	11	-3	3.4
1897	Bos-N	11	4	.733	18	15	10	0	0	129	147	10.3	5	43	3.0	27	1.9	3.42	131	.309	.366	13	15	103	118	0.8	7	0	1.3
1898	Bos-N	0	1	.000	2	1	1	0	0	12	17	12.8	2	7	5.3	1	0.8	8.25	44	.357	.439	-6	-6	101	86	-0.4	0	0	-0.4
1899	Cle-N	0	4	.000	7	4	3	0	0	38	48	11.4	0	25	5.9	5	1.2	5.68	65	.333	.432	-8	-8	96	92	-1.9	1	0	-0.6
Total	11	202	132	.605	386	332	278	14	4	2887	2905	9.1	131	1155	3.6	1223	3.8	3.74	121	.279	.350	142	255	108	99	-2.8	71	9	34.1
■ **CHUCK STOBBS**	Stobbs, Charles Klein b: 7/2/29, Wheeling, W.Va. BL/TL, 6'1", 185 lbs. Deb: 9/15/47																												
1947	Bos-A	0	1	.000	4	1	0	0	0	9	10	10.0	0	10	10.0	5	5.0	6.00	66	.294	.444	-2	-2	107	103	-0.4	-0	-0	-0.1
1948	Bos-A	0	0	—	6	0	0	0	0	7	9	11.6	0	7	9.0	4	5.1	6.43	65	.321	.457	-2	-2	97	105	0.0	-0	0	-0.1
1949	Bos-A	11	6	.647	26	19	10	0	0	152	145	8.6	10	75	4.4	70	4.1	4.03	108	.254	.340	3	5	103	97	0.6	0	-1	0.5
1950	Bos-A	12	7	.632	32	21	6	0	1	169	158	8.4	17	88	4.7	78	4.2	5.11	100	.250	.340	-10	-0	111	83	0.6	3	1	0.4
1951	Bos-A	10	9	.526	34	25	6	0	0	170	180	9.5	15	74	3.9	75	4.0	4.76	92	.271	.344	-12	-7	106	93	-0.6	-2	-2	-0.9
1952	Chi-A	7	12	.368	38	17	2	0	1	135	118	7.9	9	72	4.8	73	4.9	3.13	116	.237	.334	8	8	99	116	-3.0	-1	1	0.7
1953	Was-A	11	8	.579	27	20	8	0	0	153	146	8.6	11	44	2.6	67	3.9	3.29	113	.246	.298	12	7	93	94	1.7	1	-0	0.8
1954	Was-A	11	11	.500	31	24	10	3	0	182	189	9.3	6	67	3.3	67	3.3	4.10	90	.270	.326	-8	-8	99	87	1.6	0	1	-0.7
1955	Was-A	4	14	.222	41	16	2	0	3	140	169	10.9	13	57	3.7	60	3.9	5.01	74	.302	.358	-16	-20	94	101	-3.3	2	1	-1.6
1956	Was-A	15	15	.500	37	33	15	1	1	240	264	9.9	29	54	**2.0**	97	3.6	3.60	123	.279	.311	15	22	107	114	3.4	-2	1	2.1
1957	Was-A	8	20	.286	42	31	5	2	1	212	235	10.0	28	80	3.4	114	4.8	5.35	72	.279	.338	-37	-35	102	87	-3.2	1	-2	-3.5
1958	Was-A	2	6	.250	19	8	0	0	0	57	87	13.7	7	16	2.5	23	3.6	6.00	63	.369	.392	-14	-14	100	117	-1.4	-2	0	-1.4
	StL-N	1	3	.250	17	0	0	0	1	40	40	9.0	4	14	3.1	25	5.6	3.60	119	.261	.316	2	3	108	105	-0.8	0	1	0.4
1959	Was-A	1	8	.111	41	7	0	0	7	91	82	8.1	13	24	2.4	50	4.9	2.97	132	.238	.282	9	10	102	116	-3.2	-1	0	0.8
1960	Was-A	12	7	.632	40	13	1	1	2	119	115	8.7	13	38	2.9	72	5.4	3.33	119	.252	.306	7	8	102	108	3.1	-2	-2	0.5
1961	Min-A	2	3	.400	24	3	0	0	2	45	56	11.2	8	15	3.0	17	3.4	7.40	58	.311	.360	-17	-15	107	80	-0.1	1	-1	-1.3
Total	15	107	130	.451	459	238	65	7	19	1921	2003	9.4	183	735	3.4	897	4.2	4.29	95	.269	.331	-62	-43	102	99	-5.0	-2	-3	-3.4

YEAR	TM/L	W	L	PCT	G	GS	CG	SHO	SV	IP	H	H/G	HR	BB	BB/G	SO	SO/G	ERA	/A	OAVG	OOBP	PR	/A	PF	CPI	WAT	PB	PD	TPI
■ WES STOCK	Stock, Wesley Gay b: 4/10/34, Longview, Wash. BR/TR, 6'2", 188 lbs. Deb: 4/19/59 C																												
1959	Bal-A	0	0	—	7	0	0	0	1	13	16	11.1	1	2	1.4	8	5.5	3.46	110	.302	.327	1	0	98	124	0.0	-0	-0	0.0
1960	Bal-A	2	2	.500	17	0	0	0	2	34	26	6.9	2	14	3.7	23	6.1	2.91	134	.218	.299	4	4	101	97	-0.2	-1	1	0.4
1961	Bal-A	5	0	1.000	35	1	0	0	3	72	58	7.3	3	27	3.4	47	5.9	3.00	129	.225	.297	8	7	96	92	2.5	-1	2	0.8
1962	Bal-A	3	2	.600	53	0	0	0	3	65	50	6.9	7	36	5.0	34	4.7	4.43	85	.217	.318	-3	-5	95	81	0.6	-0	3	-0.1
1963	Bal-A	7	0	1.000	47	0	0	0	1	75	69	8.3	11	31	3.7	55	6.6	3.96	86	.246	.313	-3	-5	93	103	3.5	-1	1	-0.5
1964	Bal-A	2	0	1.000	14	0	0	0	0	21	17	7.3	5	8	3.4	14	6.0	3.86	97	.233	.298	-1	-0	103	115	1.0	-0	0	0.0
	KC-A	6	3	.667	50	0	0	0	5	93	69	6.7	10	34	3.3	101	9.8	1.94	202	.213	.288	17	20	108	155	2.3	0	-1	2.2
	Yr	8	3	.727	64	0	0	0	5	114	86	6.8	15	42	3.3	115	9.1	2.29	169	.216	.290	17	20	107	155	3.3	-0	-0	2.2
1965	KC-A	0	4	.000	62	2	0	0	4	100	96	8.6	18	40	3.6	52	4.7	5.22	66	.251	.321	-20	-20	100	85	-1.9	-1	2	-1.9
1966	KC-A	2	2	.500	35	0	0	0	3	44	30	6.1	3	21	4.3	31	6.3	2.66	123	.199	.298	4	3	95	108	0.1	-0	-0	0.3
1967	KC-A	0	0	—	1	0	0	0	0	1	3	27.0	0	2	18.0	0	0.0	18.00	18	.500	.625	-2	-2	102	95	0.0	0	0	0.0
Total	9	27	13	.675	321	3	0	0	22	518	434	7.5	60	215	3.7	365	6.3	3.60	102	.231	.308	6	3	99	106	7.9	-4	7	1.2
■ OTIS STOCKSDALE	Stocksdale, Otis Hinkley "Old Gray Fox" b: 8/7/1871, Near Arcadia, Md. d: 3/15/33, Pennsville, N.J. BL/TR, 5'10.5", 180 lbs. Deb: 7/24/1893																												
1893	Was-N	2	8	.200	11	11	7	0	0	69	111	14.5	4	32	4.2	12	1.6	8.22	52	.380	.441	-27	-30	92	86	-1.8	2	0	-2.0
1894	Was-N	5	9	.357	18	14	11	0	0	117	176	13.5	10	42	3.2	10	0.8	5.08	105	.371	.422	3	3	100	127	0.2	1	0	0.3
1895	Was-N	6	11	.353	20	17	11	0	1	136	199	13.2	7	52	3.4	23	1.5	6.09	83	.362	.417	-20	-16	105	99	0.2	2	0	-0.9
	Bos-N	2	2	.500	4	4	1	0	0	23	31	12.1	2	8	3.1	2	0.8	5.87	83	.344	.397	-3	-3	102	96	-0.1	-0	0	-0.1
	Yr	8	13	.381	24	21	12	0	1	159	230	13.0	9	60	3.4	25	1.4	6.06	83	.360	.415	-22	-18	105	96	0.1	2	0	-1.0
1896	Bal-N	0	1	.000	1	0	0	0	0	2	4	18.0	0	2	9.0	1	4.5	22.50	19	.440	.541	-4	-4	99	44	-0.4	1	0	-0.2
Total	4	15	31	.326	54	46	30	0	1	347	521	13.5	23	136	3.5	48	1.2	6.25	80	.368	.423	-50	-49	100	105	-1.9	5	0	-2.9
■ BOB STODDARD	Stoddard, Robert Lyle b: 3/8/57, San Jose, Cal. BR/TR, 6'1", 190 lbs. Deb: 9/04/81																												
1981	Sea-A	2	1	.667	5	5	1	0	0	35	35	9.0	3	9	2.3	22	5.7	2.57	144	.269	.319	4	4	101	149	0.7	0	0	0.5
1982	Sea-A	3	3	.500	9	9	2	1	0	67	48	6.4	7	18	2.4	24	3.2	2.42	186	.205	.266	12	15	110	106	0.2	0	0	1.8
1983	Sea-A	9	17	.346	35	23	2	1	0	176	182	9.3	29	58	3.0	87	4.4	4.40	94	.274	.330	-6	-5	101	109	-0.9	0	3	-0.2
1984	Sea-A	2	3	.400	27	6	0	0	0	79	86	9.8	10	37	4.2	39	4.4	5.13	80	.278	.355	-10	-9	103	96	-0.2	0	1	-0.7
1985	Det-A	0	0	—	8	0	0	0	1	13	15	10.4	3	5	3.5	11	7.6	6.92	63	.268	.328	-4	-4	106	73	0.0	0	1	-0.2
1986	SD-N	1	0	1.000	18	0	0	0	1	23	20	7.8	1	11	4.3	17	6.7	2.35	152	.227	.314	4	3	96	127	0.5	-0	-0	0.3
1987	KC-A	1	3	.250	17	2	0	0	1	40	51	11.5	3	22	4.9	23	5.2	4.27	109	.313	.400	1	2	104	139	-0.9	0	1	0.3
Total	7	18	27	.400	119	45	5	2	3	433	437	9.1	56	160	3.3	223	4.6	4.03	103	.266	.331	1	7	103	112	-0.6	-0	5	1.8
■ TIM STODDARD	Stoddard, Timothy Paul b: 1/24/53, E.Chicago, Ind. BR/TR, 6'7", 230 lbs. Deb: 9/07/75																												
1975	Chi-A	0	0	—	1	0	0	0	0	1	2	18.0	1	0	0.0	0	0.0	9.00	44	.400	.400	-1	-1	104	158	0.0	0	0	0.0
1978	Bal-A	0	1	.000	8	0	0	0	0	18	22	11.0	3	8	4.0	14	7.0	6.00	57	.301	.381	-4	-5	91	99	-0.4	0	0	-0.4
1979	Bal-A	3	1	.750	29	0	0	0	3	58	44	6.8	3	19	2.9	47	7.3	1.71	237	.212	.276	16	15	96	131	0.6	0	0	1.5
1980	Bal-A	5	3	.625	64	0	0	0	26	86	72	7.5	2	38	4.0	64	6.7	2.51	160	.233	.315	15	14	99	115	0.1	0	-1	1.4
1981	Bal-A	4	2	.667	31	0	0	0	7	37	38	9.2	6	18	4.4	32	7.8	3.89	93	.268	.358	-1	-1	99	130	0.8	0	0	0.0
1982	Bal-A	3	4	.429	50	0	0	0	12	56	53	8.5	4	29	4.7	42	6.8	4.02	101	.249	.333	0	0	99	96	-0.8	0	-0	0.0
1983	Bal-A	4	3	.571	47	0	0	0	9	58	65	10.1	10	29	4.5	50	7.8	6.05	67	.293	.365	-13	-13	99	97	-0.1	0	0	-1.2
1984	Chi-N	10	6	.625	58	0	0	0	7	92	77	7.5	9	57	5.6	87	8.5	3.82	102	.236	.339	-2	1	109	108	0.6	-1	-1	0.0
1985	SD-N	1	6	.143	44	0	0	0	1	60	63	9.4	3	37	5.6	42	6.3	4.65	78	.269	.358	-7	-7	101	95	-2.5	-1	-1	-0.7
1986	SD-N	1	3	.250	30	0	0	0	0	45	33	6.6	6	34	6.8	47	9.4	3.80	94	.200	.330	-0	-1	96	98	-0.8	1	0	0.0
	NY-A	4	1	.800	24	0	0	0	0	49	41	7.5	6	23	4.2	34	6.2	3.86	111	.232	.308	2	2	103	97	1.4	0	0	0.2
1987	NY-A	4	3	.571	57	0	0	0	8	93	83	8.0	13	30	2.9	78	7.5	3.48	125	.235	.293	10	9	97	99	0.2	0	-1	0.8
1988	NY-A	2	2	.500	28	0	0	0	3	55	62	10.1	5	27	4.4	33	5.4	6.38	59	.286	.360	-15	-16	96	79	0.0	0	0	-1.4
Total	12	41	35	.539	471	0	0	0	76	708	655	8.3	71	349	4.4	570	7.2	3.98	100	.248	.331	0	-1	100	104	-0.9	-0	-2	0.2
■ ART STOKES	Stokes, Arthur Milton b: 9/13/1896, Emmitsburg, Md. d: 6/3/62, Titusville, Pa. BR/TR, 5'10.5", 155 lbs. Deb: 5/05/25																												
1925	Phi-A	1	1	.500	12	0	0	0	0	24	24	9.0	0	10	3.8	7	2.6	4.13	108	.270	.350	1	1	101	90	0.0	-0	-0	0.0
■ DICK STONE	Stone, Charles Richard b: 12/5/11, Oklahoma City, Okla d: 2/18/1880, Oklahoma City, Okla. BL/TL, 5'9", 153 lbs. Deb: 8/26/45																												
1945	Was-A	0	0	—	3	0	0	0	0	5	6	10.8	0	2	3.6	0	0.0	0.00	—	.316	.364	2	2	92	0	0.0	0	0	0.2
■ DEAN STONE	Stone, Darrah Dean b: 9/1/30, Moline, Ill. BL/TL, 6'4", 205 lbs. Deb: 9/13/53																												
1953	Was-A	0	1	.000	3	1	0	0	0	9	13	13.0	0	5	5.0	5	5.0	8.00	46	.361	.419	-4	-4	93	82	-0.4	-0	0	-0.3
1954	Was-A	12	10	.545	31	23	10	2	0	179	161	8.1	7	69	3.5	87	4.4	3.22	115	.240	.307	10	9	99	90	2.5	-0	-3	0.6
1955	Was-A	6	13	.316	43	24	5	1	1	180	180	9.0	14	114	5.7	84	4.2	4.15	90	.267	.365	-4	-8	94	113	-0.8	-3	-2	-1.3
1956	Was-A	5	7	.417	41	21	2	0	3	132	148	10.1	10	93	6.3	86	5.9	6.27	71	.282	.390	-31	-27	107	85	0.4	-1	-1	-2.6
1957	Was-A	0	0	—	3	0	0	0	0	3	5	15.0	0	2	6.0	3	9.0	9.00	43	.357	.412	-2	-2	102	75	0.0	0	0	-0.1
	Bos-A	1	3	.250	17	8	0	0	1	51	56	9.9	5	35	6.2	32	5.6	5.12	81	.284	.381	-8	-6	109	105	-1.0	-1	1	-0.5
	Yr	1	3	.250	20	8	0	0	1	54	61	10.2	5	37	6.2	35	5.8	5.33	77	.288	.383	-9	-7	108	105	-1.0	0	1	-0.6
1959	StL-N	0	1	.000	18	1	0	0	1	30	30	9.0	4	16	4.8	17	5.1	4.20	100	.273	.348	-1	-0	106	119	-0.4	-0	-0	0.0
1962	Hou-N	3	2	.600	15	7	2	2	0	52	61	10.6	4	20	3.5	31	5.4	4.50	83	.295	.355	-3	-4	95	105	0.9	1	0	-0.3
	Chi-A	1	0	1.000	27	0	0	0	5	30	28	8.4	3	9	2.7	23	6.9	3.30	113	.255	.304	2	1	94	114	0.5	1	-0	0.2
1963	Bal-A	1	2	.333	17	0	0	0	1	19	23	10.9	0	10	4.7	12	5.7	5.21	65	.307	.371	-3	-4	93	93	-0.5	0	0	-0.3
Total	8	29	39	.426	215	85	19	5	12	685	705	9.3	47	373	4.9	380	5.0	4.48	87	.269	.354	-43	-45	100	99	1.2	-6	-4	-4.6
■ DWIGHT STONE	Stone, Dwight Ely b: 8/2/1886, Holt Co., Neb. d: 6/3/76, Glendale, Cal. BR/TR, 6'1.5", 170 lbs. Deb: 4/13/13																												
1913	StL-A	2	6	.250	18	7	4	1	0	91	94	9.3	0	46	4.5	37	3.7	3.56	80	.267	.363	-6	-7	98	102	-1.3	2	1	-0.5
1914	KC-F	8	14	.364	39	22	6	0	0	187	205	9.9	8	77	3.7	88	4.2	4.33	71	.281	.356	-23	-26	96	95	-2.2	-2	2	-2.6
Total	2	10	20	.333	57	29	10	1	0	278	299	9.7	8	123	4.0	125	4.0	4.08	74	.276	.358	-30	-33	96	97	-3.5	-1	3	-3.1
■ ARNIE STONE	Stone, Edwin Arnold b: 10/9/1892, North Creek, N.Y. d: 7/29/48, Hudson Falls, N.Y BR/TL, 6', 180 lbs. Deb: 8/07/23																												
1923	Pit-N	0	1	.000	9	0	0	0	0	12	19	14.3	0	4	3.0	2	1.5	8.25	46	.352	.397	-6	-6	95	68	-0.4	-0	-0	-0.5
1924	Pit-N	4	2	.667	26	2	1	0	0	64	57	8.0	0	15	2.1	7	1.0	2.95	136	.259	.289	6	8	104	96	0.6	-1	0	0.6
Total	2	4	3	.571	35	2	1	0	0	76	76	9.0	0	19	2.3	9	1.1	3.79	105	.277	.309	1	2	102	91	0.2	-1	-0	0.1
■ GEORGE STONE	Stone, George Heard b: 7/9/46, Ruston, La. BL/TL, 6'3", 205 lbs. Deb: 9/15/67																												
1967	Atl-N	0	0	—	2	1	0	0	0	7	8	10.3	0	1	1.3	5	6.4	5.14	69	.267	.290	-1	-1	105	50	0.0	-0	0	0.0
1968	Atl-N	7	4	.636	17	10	2	0	0	75	63	7.6	9	19	2.3	52	6.2	2.76	101	.222	.269	2	0	94	98	1.6	3	-1	0.2
1969	Atl-N	13	10	.565	36	20	3	0	3	165	166	9.1	20	48	2.6	102	5.6	3.65	101	.260	.312	-1	1	103	107	-0.1	1	-1	0.1
1970	Atl-N	11	11	.500	35	30	9	2	0	207	218	9.5	27	50	2.2	131	5.7	3.87	110	.267	.308	4	9	105	106	0.7	4	3	1.6
1971	Atl-N	6	8	.429	27	24	4	2	0	173	186	9.7	19	35	1.8	110	5.7	3.59	107	.274	.308	-2	5	111	108	-1.1	-1	0	0.5
1972	Atl-N	6	11	.353	31	16	2	1	1	111	143	11.6	18	44	3.6	63	5.1	5.51	67	.315	.374	-25	-23	106	109	-2.0	2	1	-1.9
1973	NY-N	12	3	.800	27	20	2	0	1	148	157	9.5	16	31	1.9	77	4.7	2.80	131	.274	.303	14	14	100	135	4.6	2	1	1.9
1974	NY-N	2	7	.222	15	13	1	0	0	77	103	12.0	10	21	2.5	29	3.4	5.03	73	.322	.355	-12	-12	100	109	-2.2	-1	0	-1.2
1975	NY-N	3	3	.500	13	11	1	0	0	57	75	11.8	3	21	3.3	21	3.3	5.05	68	.323	.368	-9	-10	95	102	0.0	0	1	-0.8
Total	9	60	57	.513	203	145	24	5	5	1020	1119	9.9	122	270	2.4	590	5.2	3.89	96	.278	.320	-31	-17	103	110	1.5	10	4	0.4
■ ROCKY STONE	Stone, John Vernon b: 8/23/18, Redding, Cal. d: 11/12/86, Fountain Valley, Cal. BR/TR, 6', 200 lbs. Deb: 5/02/43																												
1943	Cin-N	0	1	.000	13	0	0	0	0	25	23	8.3	0	8	2.9	11	4.0	4.32	77	.237	.295	-3	-3	98	54	-0.4	0	-0	-0.2
■ STEVE STONE	Stone, Steven Michael b: 7/14/47, Euclid, Ohio BR/TR, 5'10", 175 lbs. Deb: 4/08/71																												
1971	SF-N	5	9	.357	24	19	2	2	0	111	110	8.9	9	55	4.5	63	5.1	4.14	83	.259	.346	-8	-9	99	99	-2.5	-2	2	-0.9
1972	SF-N	6	8	.429	27	16	4	1	0	124	97	7.0	11	49	3.6	85	6.2	2.98	116	.218	.292	7	6	100	98	-0.2	-1	0	0.6
1973	Chi-A	6	11	.353	36	22	3	0	1	176	163	8.3	11	82	4.2	138	7.1	4.24	93	.245	.332	-8	-6	103	83	-2.3	0	0	-0.5
1974	Chi-N	8	6	.571	38	23	1	0	0	170	185	9.8	19	64	3.4	90	4.8	4.13	90	.278	.336	-9	-8	102	108	2.1	-3	1	-0.9
1975	Chi-N	12	8	.600	33	32	6	1	0	214	198	8.3	24	80	3.4	139	5.8	3.95	97	.245	.311	-8	-3	105	91	2.8	-2	0	-0.4

YEAR	TM/L	W	L	PCT	G	GS	CG	SHO	SV	IP	H	H/G	HR	BB	BB/G	SO	SO/G	ERA	/A	OAVG	OOBP	PR	/A	PF	CPI	WAT	PB	PD	TPI
1976	Chi-N	3	6	.333	17	15	1	1	0	75	70	8.4	6	21	2.5	33	4.0	4.08	95	.250	.301	-5	-2	111	82	-1.2	-1	-1	-0.3
1977	Chi-A	15	12	.556	31	31	8	0	0	207	228	9.9	25	80	3.5	124	5.4	4.52	89	.281	.341	-10	-12	99	104	0.0	0	-0	-1.1
1978	Chi-A	12	12	.500	30	30	6	1	0	212	196	8.3	19	84	3.6	118	5.0	4.37	88	.247	.315	-14	-12	102	80	1.5	0	-1	-1.3
1979	Bal-A	11	7	.611	32	32	3	0	0	186	173	8.4	31	73	3.5	96	4.6	3.77	107	.248	.316	9	6	96	111	-0.4	0	1	0.6
1980	Bal-A	**25**	7	**.781**	37	37	9	1	0	251	224	8.0	22	101	3.6	149	5.3	3.23	124	.240	.316	23	22	99	106	**7.7**	0	-2	2.0
1981	Bal-A	4	7	.364	15	12	0	0	0	63	63	9.0	7	27	3.9	30	4.3	4.57	79	.266	.337	-6	-7	99	95	-2.0	0	0	-0.6
Total	11	107	93	.535	320	269	43	7	1	1789	1707	8.6	184	716	3.6	1065	5.4	3.96	97	.253	.322	-30	-23	101	97	5.5	-9	0	-2.8
■ TIGE STONE	Stone, William Arthur b: 9/18/01, Macon, Ga. d: 1/1/60, Jacksonville, Fla. 5'8", 145 lbs. Deb: 8/23/23																												
1923	StL-N	0	0	—	1	0	0	0	0	3	5	15.0	1	3	9.0	1	3.0	12.00	30	.455	.571	-3	-3	90	106	0.0	0	0	-0.1
■ BILL STONEMAN	Stoneman, William Hambly b: 4/7/44, Oak Park, Ill. BR/TR, 5'10", 170 lbs. Deb: 7/16/67																												
1967	Chi-N	2	4	.333	28	2	0	0	4	63	51	7.3	7	22	3.1	52	7.4	3.29	103	.223	.283	1	1	100	93	-1.1	-1	-1	-0.1
1968	Chi-N	0	1	.000	18	0	0	0	0	29	35	10.9	6	14	4.3	18	5.6	5.59	60	.310	.382	-8	-7	112	115	-0.4	-0	-0	-0.8
1969	Mon-N	11	19	.367	42	36	8	5	0	236	233	8.9	26	123	4.7	185	7.1	4.39	85	.261	.352	-21	-18	103	105	1.2	-3	-1	-2.1
1970	Mon-N	7	15	.318	40	30	5	3	0	208	209	9.0	26	109	4.7	176	7.6	4.59	90	.263	.358	-12	-11	102	106	-3.5	-2	-1	-1.3
1971	Mon-N	17	16	.515	39	39	20	3	0	295	243	7.4	20	146	4.5	251	7.7	3.14	111	.225	.317	11	11	100	100	2.7	-1	0	1.1
1972	Mon-N	12	14	.462	36	35	13	4	0	251	213	7.6	15	102	3.7	171	6.1	2.98	120	.229	.303	13	17	104	98	0.4	-5	0	1.4
1973	Mon-N	4	8	.333	29	17	0	0	1	97	120	11.1	12	55	5.1	48	4.5	6.77	57	.310	.392	-33	-32	105	90	-1.9	-1	0	-3.1
1974	Cal-A	1	8	.111	13	11	0	0	0	59	78	11.9	8	31	4.7	33	5.0	6.10	55	.322	.399	-16	-18	93	103	-3.3	0	0	-1.6
Total	8	54	85	.388	245	170	46	15	5	1238	1182	8.6	120	602	4.4	934	6.8	4.08	90	.253	.339	-66	-57	102	101	-5.9	-13	-3	-6.5
■ LIL STONER	Stoner, Ulysses Simpson Grant b: 2/28/1899, Bowie, Tex. d: 6/26/66, Enid, Okla. BR/TR, 5'9.5", 180 lbs. Deb: 4/15/22																												
1922	Det-A	4	4	.500	17	7	2	0	0	63	76	10.9	3	35	5.0	18	2.6	7.00	56	.315	.394	-21	-21	97	79	0.0	-1	1	-1.9
1924	Det-A	11	11	.500	36	25	10	1	0	216	271	11.3	13	65	2.7	66	2.8	4.71	89	.316	.356	-11	-13	99	105	-1.2	1	-1	-1.1
1925	Det-A	10	9	.526	34	18	8	0	1	152	166	9.8	6	53	3.1	51	3.0	4.26	101	.283	.343	2	1	98	95	0.0	4	-3	0.1
1926	Det-A	7	10	.412	32	22	7	0	0	160	179	10.1	11	63	3.5	57	3.2	5.46	72	.291	.348	-26	-27	98	83	-1.7	-1	-0	-2.6
1927	Det-A	10	13	.435	38	24	13	0	5	215	251	10.5	9	77	3.2	63	2.6	3.98	112	.301	.350	4	11	107	114	-2.4	-7	-2	0.3
1928	Det-A	5	8	.385	36	11	4	0	4	126	151	10.8	16	42	3.0	29	2.1	4.36	93	.296	.344	-4	-4	100	115	-0.8	-1	-2	-0.6
1929	Det-A	3	3	.500	24	3	1	0	4	53	57	9.7	2	31	5.3	12	2.0	5.26	78	.288	.372	-6	-7	97	94	0.3	-2	2	-0.5
1930	Pit-N	0	0	—	5	0	0	0	0	6	7	10.5	2	3	4.5	1	1.5	4.50	108	.318	.400	0	0	98	174	0.0	0	0	0.0
1931	Phi-N	0	0	—	7	1	0	0	0	14	22	14.1	0	5	3.2	2	1.3	6.43	65	.373	.409	-4	-3	109	101	0.0	-1	0	-0.3
Total	9	50	58	.463	229	111	45	1	14	1005	1180	10.6	62	374	3.3	299	2.7	4.76	88	.301	.354	-66	-64	100	101	-5.8	-7	-5	-6.6
■ MEL STOTTLEMYRE	Stottlemyre, Melvin Leon b: 11/13/41, Hazelton, Mo. BR/TR, 6'1", 178 lbs. Deb: 8/12/64 C																												
1964	NY-A	9	3	.750	13	12	5	2	0	96	77	7.2	3	35	3.3	49	4.6	2.06	177	.219	.292	17	17	101	116	2.2	2	1	2.3
1965	NY-A	20	9	.690	37	37	**18**	4	0	**291**	250	7.7	18	88	2.7	155	4.8	2.63	133	.233	.290	27	28	101	108	**6.6**	0	6	3.9
1966	NY-A	12	20	.375	37	35	9	3	1	251	239	8.6	18	82	2.9	146	5.2	3.80	85	.253	.309	-10	-16	94	92	-2.8	1	4	-1.1
1967	NY-A	15	15	.500	36	36	10	4	0	255	235	8.3	20	88	3.1	151	5.3	2.96	104	.248	.306	8	4	96	117	1.8	-3	6	0.6
1968	NY-A	21	12	.636	36	36	19	6	0	279	243	7.8	21	65	2.1	140	4.5	2.45	123	.234	.277	16	17	101	111	4.9	1	2	2.4
1969	NY-A	20	14	.588	39	39	**24**	3	0	303	267	7.9	19	97	2.9	113	3.4	2.82	123	.239	.297	27	22	96	105	3.7	5	8	3.7
1970	NY-A	15	13	.536	37	37	14	0	0	271	262	8.7	23	84	2.8	126	4.2	3.09	110	.255	.310	19	9	91	**113**	-1.0	9	2	2.1
1971	NY-A	16	12	.571	35	35	19	7	0	270	234	7.8	16	69	2.3	132	4.4	2.87	117	.233	.281	18	15	97	89	2.2	2	3	2.1
1972	NY-A	14	18	.438	36	36	9	7	0	260	250	8.7	13	85	2.9	110	3.8	3.22	88	.254	.312	-4	-12	92	99	-2.7	4	3	-0.6
1973	NY-A	16	16	.500	38	38	19	4	0	273	259	8.5	13	79	2.6	95	3.1	3.07	125	.253	.306	23	23	100	101	0.2	0	2	2.6
1974	NY-A	6	7	.462	16	15	6	0	0	113	119	9.5	7	37	2.9	40	3.2	3.58	96	.272	.330	1	-2	95	106	-1.0	0	-1	-0.2
Total	11	164	139	.541	360	356	152	40	1	2662	2435	8.2	171	809	2.7	1257	4.2	2.97	112	.245	.300	140	105	97	104	14.1	20	35	17.8
■ TODD STOTTLEMYRE	Stottlemyre, Todd Vernon b: 5/20/65, Sunnyside, Wash. BL/TR, 6'3", 185 lbs. Deb: 4/06/88																												
1988	Tor-A	4	8	.333	28	16	0	0	0	98	109	10.0	15	46	4.2	67	6.2	5.69	69	.283	.359	-19	-19	99	95	-2.3	0	-0	-1.8
■ ALLYN STOUT	Stout, Allyn Mc Clelland "Fish Hook" b: 10/31/04, Peoria, Ill. d: 12/22/74, Sikestown, Mo. BR/TR, 5'10", 167 lbs. Deb: 5/16/31																												
1931	StL-N	6	0	1.000	30	3	1	0	3	73	87	10.7	2	34	4.2	40	4.9	4.19	95	.305	.375	-3	-2	103	118	3.0	-2	1	-0.1
1932	StL-N	4	5	.444	36	3	1	0	1	74	87	10.6	5	28	3.4	32	3.9	4.38	89	.305	.362	-4	-4	101	118	-0.1	-1	1	-0.4
1933	StL-N	0	0	—	1	0	0	0	0	2	1	4.5	0	1	4.5	1	4.5	0.00	—	.167	.286	1	1	100	0	0.0	0	0	0.1
	Cin-N	2	3	.400	23	5	2	0	0	71	85	10.8	3	26	3.3	29	3.7	3.80	89	.295	.350	-4	-3	102	114	0.1	-0	-1	-0.3
	Yr	2	3	.400	24	5	2	0	0	73	86	10.6	3	27	3.3	30	3.7	3.70	92	.293	.349	-3	-3	102	114	0.1	0	-1	-0.2
1934	Cin-N	6	8	.429	41	16	4	0	1	141	170	10.9	10	47	3.0	51	3.3	4.85	88	.297	.349	-12	-9	105	98	1.0	-0	-0	-0.8
1935	NY-N	1	4	.200	40	2	0	0	5	88	99	10.1	7	37	3.8	29	3.0	4.91	78	.289	.354	-9	-11	95	100	-1.6	0	-1	-1.0
1943	Bos-N	1	0	1.000	9	0	0	0	1	9	17	17.0	1	4	4.0	3	3.0	7.00	52	.378	.429	-4	-3	109	114	0.5	-0	0	-0.3
Total	6	20	20	.500	180	29	8	0	11	458	546	10.7	28	177	3.5	185	3.6	4.54	86	.299	.358	-34	-32	101	107	2.9	-3	-0	-2.8
■ JESSE STOVALL	Stovall, Jesse Cramer "Scout" b: 7/24/1875, Independence, Mo. d: 7/12/55, San Diego, Cal. BL/TR, 6', 175 lbs. Deb: 8/31/03																												
1903	Cle-A	5	1	.833	6	6	6	2	0	57	44	6.9	0	21	3.3	12	1.9	2.05	137	.233	.310	6	5	95	105	1.9	-2	-1	0.5
1904	Det-A	3	13	.188	22	17	13	1	0	147	170	10.4	3	45	2.8	41	2.5	4.41	58	.314	.367	-30	-30	98	92	-4.4	0	0	-3.0
Total	2	8	14	.364	28	23	19	3	0	204	214	9.4	3	66	2.9	53	2.3	3.75	70	.293	.352	-24	-26	97	95	-2.5	-2	-1	-2.5
■ HARRY STOVEY	Stovey, Harry Duffield (born Harry Duffield Stowe) b: 12/20/1856, Philadelphia, Pa. d: 9/20/37, New Bedford, Mass BR/TR, 5'11.5", 175 lbs. Deb: 5/01/1880 M																												
1880	Wor-N	0	0	—	2	0	0	0	0	6	8	12.0	0	3	4.5	3	4.5	4.50	59	.329	.403	-1	-1	111	113	0.0	0	0	0.0
1883	Phi-a	0	0	—	1	0	0	0	0	3	5	15.0	0	0	0.0	4	12.0	9.00	36	.376	.376	-2	-2	99	64	0.0	0	0	-0.1
1886	Phi-a	0	0	—	1	0	0	0	0	⅓	2	54.0	0	0	0.0	0	0.0	27.00	—	1.000	1.000	-1	-1	103	112	0.0	0	0	0.0
Total	3	0	0	—	4	0	0	0	0	9	15	15.0	0	3	3.0	7	7.0	7.00	41	.379	.423	-4	-4	107	97	0.0	1	0	-0.1
■ HAL STOWE	Stowe, Harold Rudolph b: 8/29/37, Gastonia, N.C. BL/TL, 6', 170 lbs. Deb: 9/30/60																												
1960	NY-A	0	0	—	1	0	0	0	0	1	0	0.0	0	1	9.0	0	0.0	9.00	40	.000	.250	-1	-1	92	48	0.0	0	0	0.0
■ MIKE STRAHLER	Strahler, Michael Wayne b: 3/14/47, Chicago, Ill. BR/TR, 6'4", 180 lbs. Deb: 9/12/70																												
1970	LA-N	1	1	.500	6	0	0	0	1	19	13	6.2	1	10	4.7	11	5.2	1.42	254	.194	.299	6	5	89	176	0.0	0	0	0.5
1971	LA-N	0	0	—	6	0	0	0	0	13	10	6.9	1	8	5.5	7	4.8	2.77	122	.217	.327	1	1	98	122	0.0	-0	-0	0.1
1972	LA-N	1	2	.333	19	2	1	0	0	47	42	8.0	5	22	4.2	25	4.8	3.26	99	.237	.314	1	-0	93	112	-0.5	1	-0	0.0
1973	Det-A	4	5	.444	22	11	1	0	0	80	84	9.4	7	39	4.4	37	4.2	4.39	88	.273	.354	-5	-5	101	101	-0.6	0	-1	-0.4
Total	4	6	8	.429	53	13	2	0	1	159	149	8.4	14	79	4.5	80	4.5	3.57	101	.249	.334	3	1	97	115	-1.1	1	-1	0.2
■ DICK STRAHS	Strahs, Richard Bernard b: 12/4/24, Evanston, Ill. BL/TR, 6', 192 lbs. Deb: 7/24/54																												
1954	Chi-A	0	0	—	9	0	0	0	1	14	16	10.3	0	8	5.1	8	5.1	5.79	64	.271	.353	-3	-3	100	65	0.0	-0	0	-0.2
■ LES STRAKER	Straker, Lester Paul (Bolnalda) b: 10/10/59, Ciudad Bolivar, Ven BR/TR, 6'1", 193 lbs. Deb: 4/11/87																												
1987	Min-A	8	10	.444	31	26	1	0	0	154	150	8.8	24	59	3.4	76	4.4	4.38	98	.257	.322	2	-2	96	101	-1.4	0	-2	-0.2
1988	Min-A	2	5	.286	16	14	1	1	1	83	86	9.3	8	25	2.7	23	2.5	3.90	107	.276	.326	1	3	105	108	-1.7	0	0	0.3
Total	2	10	15	.400	47	40	2	1	1	237	236	9.0	32	84	3.2	99	3.8	4.22	101	.264	.323	2	1	99	103	-3.1	0	-1	0.1
■ BOB STRAMPE	Strampe, Robert Edwin b: 6/13/50, Janesville, Wis. BB/TR, 6'1", 185 lbs. Deb: 5/10/72																												
1972	Det-A	0	0	—	7	0	0	0	0	5	6	10.8	0	7	12.6	4	7.2	10.80	32	.300	.481	-4	-4	112	64	0.0	0	-0	-0.4
■ PAUL STRAND	Strand, Paul Edward b: 12/19/1893, Carbonado, Wash. d: 7/2/74, Salt Lake City, Utah BR/TL, 6'0.5", 190 lbs. Deb: 5/15/13																												
1913	Bos-N	0	0	—	7	0	0	0	0	17	22	11.6	1	12	6.4	6	3.2	2.12	145	.393	.486	2	2	96	363	0.0	-0	0	0.2
1914	Bos-N	5	2	.714	16	3	1	0	0	55	47	7.7	1	23	3.8	33	5.4	2.45	116	.235	.309	2	2	102	105	0.9	2	-0	0.5
1915	Bos-N	1	1	.500	6	2	2	0	1	23	26	10.2	0	3	1.2	13	5.1	2.35	114	.295	.312	1	1	97	139	0.0	-0	-1	0.1
Total	3	6	3	.667	29	5	3	0	1	95	95	9.0	2	38	3.6	52	4.9	2.37	120	.276	.341	5	5	100	159	0.9	2	-1	0.8
■ SCOTT STRATTON	Stratton, C. Scott b: 10/2/1869, Campbellsburg, Ky. d: 3/8/39, Louisville, Ky. BL/TR, 6', 180 lbs. Deb: 1888																												
1888	Lou-a	10	17	.370	33	28	28	2	0	270	287	9.6	7	53	1.8	97	3.2	3.63	79	.286	.321	-17	-23	93	94	0.4	5	0	-2.0

YEAR	TM/L	W	L	PCT	G	GS	CG	SHO	SV	IP	H	H/G	HR	BB	BB/G	SO	SO/G	ERA	/A	OAVG	OOBP	PR	/A	PF	CPI	WAT	PB	PD	TPI
1889	Lou-a	3	13	.188	19	17	13	0	1	134	157	10.5	5	42	2.8	42	2.8	3.22	122	.308	.361	9	11	102	130	-0.3	4	0	0.9
1890	Lou-a	34	14	**.708**	50	49	44	4	0	431	398	8.3	3	61	**1.3**	207	4.3	**2.36**	**170**	.260	**.289**	**72**	**79**	104	107	4.4	14	7	**10.1**
1891	Pit-N	0	2	.000	2	2	2	0	0	18	16	8.0	0	5	2.5	5	2.5	2.50	137	.251	.305	2	2	102	84	-0.9	-1	0	0.1
	Lou-a	6	13	.316	20	20	20	1	0	172	204	10.7	10	34	**1.8**	52	2.7	4.08	84	.310	.344	-7	-12	92	96	-2.0	2	0	-0.8
1892	Lou-N	21	19	.525	42	40	39	2	0	352	342	8.7	1	70	**1.8**	93	2.4	2.91	105	.267	.305	15	6	93	86	4.8	9	2	2.0
1893	Lou-N	12	24	.333	38	36	35	1	0	324	451	12.5	8	104	2.9	44	1.2	5.47	84	.346	.395	-29	-32	98	98	-3.8	2	6	-1.7
1894	Lou-N	1	5	.167	7	5	4	0	0	43	72	15.1	3	13	2.7	3	0.6	8.37	58	.396	.436	-15	-17	91	84	-1.1	2	0	-0.9
	Chi-N	8	5	.615	15	12	11	0	0	119	198	15.0	5	40	3.0	23	1.7	6.05	95	.395	.439	-9	-4	108	113	2.3	7	0	0.6
	Yr	9	10	.474	22	17	15	0	0	162	270	15.0	8	53	2.9	26	1.4	6.67	83	.395	.439	-24	-21	103	113	1.2	2	0	-0.3
1895	Chi-N	2	3	.400	5	5	3	0	0	30	51	15.3	1	14	4.2	4	1.2	9.60	51	.398	.457	-16	-16	103	76	-0.6	1	0	-1.0
Total	8	97	115	.458	231	214	199	10	1	1893	2176	10.3	43	436	2.1	570	2.7	3.88	99	.304	.344	5	-10	98	100	3.2	45	16	7.3

■ MONTY STRATTON Stratton, Monty Franklin Pierce "Gander" b: 5/21/12, Celeste, Tex. d: 9/29/82, Greenville, Tex. BR/TR, 6'5", 180 lbs. Deb: 6/02/34 C

YEAR	TM/L	W	L	PCT	G	GS	CG	SHO	SV	IP	H	H/G	HR	BB	BB/G	SO	SO/G	ERA	/A	OAVG	OOBP	PR	/A	PF	CPI	WAT	PB	PD	TPI
1934	Chi-A	0	0	—	1	0	0	0	0	3	4	12.0	0	1	3.0	0	0.0	6.00	77	.333	.385	-1	-0	103	89	0.0	-0	-0	0.0
1935	Chi-A	1	2	.333	5	5	2	0	0	38	40	9.5	0	9	2.1	8	1.9	4.03	121	.274	.321	2	4	109	86	-0.4	-1	0	0.3
1936	Chi-A	5	7	.417	16	14	3	0	0	95	117	11.1	8	46	4.4	37	3.5	5.21	95	.305	.378	-2	-3	99	110	-1.3	2	2	0.0
1937	Chi-A	15	5	.750	22	21	14	5	0	165	142	7.7	6	37	**2.0**	69	3.8	2.40	**196**	.234	**.278**	41	42	102	105	4.7	-1	1	4.3
1938	Chi-A	15	9	.625	26	22	17	0	2	186	186	9.0	18	56	2.7	82	4.0	4.02	117	.255	.312	16	14	98	95	4.5	6	0	1.9
Total	5	36	23	.610	70	62	36	5	2	487	489	9.0	32	149	2.8	196	3.6	3.71	129	.261	.317	56	57	100	100	7.5	5	2	6.5

■ ED STRATTON Stratton, William Edward b: Baltimore, Md. Deb: 5/14/1873

YEAR	TM/L	W	L	PCT	G	GS	CG	SHO	SV	IP	H	H/G	HR	BB	BB/G	SO	SO/G	ERA	/A	OAVG	OOBP	PR	/A	PF	CPI	WAT	PB	PD	TPI
1873	Mar-n	0	2	.000	2																								

■ JOE STRAUSS Strauss, Josef "Dutch" or "The Socker" b: 3/17/1844, Gecse, Hungary d: 6/25/06, Cincinnati, Ohio BR/TR, Deb: 7/27/1884

YEAR	TM/L	W	L	PCT	G	GS	CG	SHO	SV	IP	H	H/G	HR	BB	BB/G	SO	SO/G	ERA	/A	OAVG	OOBP	PR	/A	PF	CPI	WAT	PB	PD	TPI
1886	Lou-a	0	0	—	2	0	0	0	**1**	4	6	13.5	0	3	6.8	0	0.0	4.50	83	.357	.455	-0	-0	108	158	0.0	-0	0	-0.1

■ OSCAR STREIT Streit, Oscar William b: 7/7/1873, Florence, Ala. d: 10/10/35, Birmingham, Ala. BL/TL, 6'5", 190 lbs. Deb: 4/21/1899

YEAR	TM/L	W	L	PCT	G	GS	CG	SHO	SV	IP	H	H/G	HR	BB	BB/G	SO	SO/G	ERA	/A	OAVG	OOBP	PR	/A	PF	CPI	WAT	PB	PD	TPI
1899	Bos-N	1	0	1.000	2	1	1	0	0	15	15	9.0	1	15	9.0	0	0.0	7.20	55	.283	.442	-6	-5	103	75	0.5	-1	0	-0.4
1902	Cle-A	0	7	.000	8	7	4	0	0	52	72	12.5	3	25	4.3	10	1.7	5.19	66	.355	.426	-9	-10	96	114	-3.4	1	-1	-0.9
Total	2	1	7	.125	10	8	5	0	0	67	87	11.7	4	40	5.4	10	1.3	5.64	63	.340	.429	-15	-16	98	105	-2.9	-0	-1	-1.3

■ ED STRELECKI Strelecki, Edward Henry b: 4/10/05, Newark, N.J. d: 1/9/68, Newark, N.J. BR/TR, 5'11.5", 180 lbs. Deb: 4/16/28

YEAR	TM/L	W	L	PCT	G	GS	CG	SHO	SV	IP	H	H/G	HR	BB	BB/G	SO	SO/G	ERA	/A	OAVG	OOBP	PR	/A	PF	CPI	WAT	PB	PD	TPI
1928	StL-A	0	2	.000	22	2	1	0	1	50	49	8.8	4	17	3.1	8	1.4	4.32	96	.269	.313	-2	-1	103	93	-0.9	0	-0	0.0
1929	StL-A	1	1	.500	7	0	0	0	0	11	12	9.8	1	6	4.9	2	1.6	4.91	86	.279	.365	-1	-1	100	103	0.0	-0	0	0.0
1931	Cin-N	0	0	—	13	0	0	0	0	24	37	13.9	2	9	3.4	3	1.1	9.38	40	.394	.434	-15	-15	98	85	0.0	0	0	-1.2
Total	3	1	3	.250	42	2	1	0	1	85	98	10.4	7	32	3.4	13	1.4	5.82	70	.307	.356	-17	-17	101	92	-0.9	0	1	-1.2

■ PHIL STREMMEL Stremmel, Philip b: 4/16/1880, Zanesville, Ohio d: 12/26/47, Chicago, Ill. BR/TR, 6', 175 lbs. Deb: 9/16/09

YEAR	TM/L	W	L	PCT	G	GS	CG	SHO	SV	IP	H	H/G	HR	BB	BB/G	SO	SO/G	ERA	/A	OAVG	OOBP	PR	/A	PF	CPI	WAT	PB	PD	TPI
1909	StL-A	0	2	.000	2	2	2	0	0	18	20	10.0	0	4	2.0	6	3.0	4.50	52	.308	.357	-4	-4	95	83	-0.9	-1	0	-0.3
1910	StL-A	0	2	.000	5	2	2	0	0	29	31	9.6	0	16	5.0	7	2.2	3.72	68	.287	.379	-4	-4	101	110	-0.9	-0	2	-0.1
Total	2	0	4	.000	7	4	4	0	0	47	51	9.8	0	20	3.8	13	2.5	4.02	61	.295	.371	-8	-8	98	100	-1.8	-1	2	-0.4

■ CUB STRICKER Stricker, John A. (born John A. Streaker) b: 2/15/1860, Philadelphia, Pa. d: 11/19/37, Philadelphia, Pa. BR/TR, 5'3", 138 lbs. Deb: 5/02/1882 M

YEAR	TM/L	W	L	PCT	G	GS	CG	SHO	SV	IP	H	H/G	HR	BB	BB/G	SO	SO/G	ERA	/A	OAVG	OOBP	PR	/A	PF	CPI	WAT	PB	PD	TPI
1882	Phi-a	1	0	1.000	2	0	0	0	0	7	3	3.9	0	1	1.3	2	2.6	1.29	232	.134	.171	1	1	111	20	0.5	-0	0	0.1
1884	Phi-a	0	0	—	1	0	0	0	0	3	6	18.0	0	1	3.0	1	3.0	6.00	61	.424	.462	-1	-1	113	145	0.0	0	0	0.0
1887	Cle-a	0	0	—	3	0	0	0	1	6	5	7.5	0	7	10.5	2	3.0	3.00	147	.239	.430	1	1	103	161	0.0	0	0	0.1
1888	Cle-a	1	0	1.000	2	0	0	0	0	12	16	12.0	0	2	1.5	5	3.8	4.50	68	.334	.361	-2	-2	100	99	0.5	0	0	-0.1
Total	4	2	0	1.000	8	0	0	0	1	28	30	9.6	0	11	3.5	10	3.2	3.54	96	.285	.352	-1	-0	105	97	1.0	1	0	0.1

■ JIM STRICKLAND Strickland, James Michael b: 6/12/46, Los Angeles, Cal. BL/TL, 6', 175 lbs. Deb: 5/19/71

YEAR	TM/L	W	L	PCT	G	GS	CG	SHO	SV	IP	H	H/G	HR	BB	BB/G	SO	SO/G	ERA	/A	OAVG	OOBP	PR	/A	PF	CPI	WAT	PB	PD	TPI
1971	Min-A	1	0	1.000	24	0	0	0	1	31	20	5.8	2	18	5.2	21	6.1	1.45	249	.183	.301	7	7	104	173	0.5	0	0	0.9
1972	Min-A	3	1	.750	25	0	0	0	3	36	28	7.0	7	19	4.8	30	7.5	2.50	132	.214	.309	2	3	107	154	1.0	1	0	0.4
1973	Min-A	0	1	.000	7	0	0	0	0	5	11	19.8	0	5	9.0	6	10.8	12.60	31	.440	.516	-5	-5	103	85	-0.4	0	0	-0.4
1975	Cle-A	0	0	—	4	0	0	0	1	5	4	7.2	0	2	3.6	3	5.4	1.80	210	.222	.333	1	1	100	156	0.0	0	-0	0.1
Total	4	4	2	.667	60	0	0	0	5	77	63	7.4	9	44	5.1	60	7.0	2.69	130	.223	.326	5	7	105	158	1.1	1	0	1.0

■ BILL STRICKLAND Strickland, William Goss b: 3/29/08, Nashville, Ga. BR/TR, 6'2", 170 lbs. Deb: 9/16/37

YEAR	TM/L	W	L	PCT	G	GS	CG	SHO	SV	IP	H	H/G	HR	BB	BB/G	SO	SO/G	ERA	/A	OAVG	OOBP	PR	/A	PF	CPI	WAT	PB	PD	TPI
1937	StL-A	0	0	—	9	0	0	0	0	21	28	12.0	2	15	6.4	6	2.6	6.00	80	.341	.450	-3	-3	103	127	0.0	-0	-0	-0.2

■ ELMER STRICKLETT Stricklett, Elmer Griffin "Spitball" b: 8/29/1876, Glasco, Kan. d: 6/7/64, Santa Cruz, Cal. TR , 5'6", 140 lbs. Deb: 4/22/04

YEAR	TM/L	W	L	PCT	G	GS	CG	SHO	SV	IP	H	H/G	HR	BB	BB/G	SO	SO/G	ERA	/A	OAVG	OOBP	PR	/A	PF	CPI	WAT	PB	PD	TPI
1904	Chi-A	0	1	.000	1	1	0	0	0	7	12	15.4	0	2	2.6	3	3.9	10.29	24	.404	.442	-6	-6	97	64	-0.4	-0	0	-0.4
1905	Bro-N	9	18	.333	33	28	25	1	1	237	259	9.8	0	71	2.7	77	2.9	3.34	91	.310	.374	-9	-8	102	111	0.4	-2	8	0.1
1906	Bro-N	14	18	.438	41	35	28	5	5	292	273	8.4	2	77	2.4	88	2.7	2.71	87	.276	.331	-3	-12	90	99	0.1	5	9	-0.2
1907	Bro-N	12	14	.462	29	26	25	4	0	230	211	8.3	1	65	2.5	69	2.7	2.27	104	.274	.337	5	3	96	114	0.6	1	7	1.1
Total	4	35	51	.407	104	90	78	10	6	766	755	8.9	3	215	2.5	237	2.8	2.84	90	.288	.348	-13	-23	95	107	0.7	4	24	0.6

■ JOHN STRIKE Strike, John b: 1865, Pennsylvania Deb: 5/18/1882

YEAR	TM/L	W	L	PCT	G	GS	CG	SHO	SV	IP	H	H/G	HR	BB	BB/G	SO	SO/G	ERA	/A	OAVG	OOBP	PR	/A	PF	CPI	WAT	PB	PD	TPI
1886	Phi-N	1	1	.500	2	2	1	0	0	15	19	11.4	1	7	4.2	11	6.6	4.80	66	.323	.395	-2	-3	96	113	-0.1	-1	0	-0.2

■ JAKE STRIKER Striker, Wilbur Scott b: 10/23/33, New Washington, O. BL/TL, 6'2", 200 lbs. Deb: 9/25/59

YEAR	TM/L	W	L	PCT	G	GS	CG	SHO	SV	IP	H	H/G	HR	BB	BB/G	SO	SO/G	ERA	/A	OAVG	OOBP	PR	/A	PF	CPI	WAT	PB	PD	TPI
1959	Cle-A	1	0	1.000	1	1	0	0	0	7	8	10.3	0	4	5.1	5	6.4	2.57	142	.296	.375	1	1	95	184	0.5	1	0	0.2
1960	Chi-A	0	0	—	2	0	0	0	0	4	5	11.3	1	1	2.3	1	2.3	4.50	85	.357	.438	-0	-0	99	177	0.0	0	-0	0.0
Total	2	1	0	1.000	3	1	0	0	0	11	13	10.6	1	5	4.1	6	4.9	3.27	114	.317	.396	1	1	96	181	0.5	1	-0	0.2

■ NICK STRINCEVICH Strincevich, Nicholas Mihailovich "Jumbo" b: 3/1/15, Gary, Ind. BR/TR, 6'1", 180 lbs. Deb: 4/23/40

YEAR	TM/L	W	L	PCT	G	GS	CG	SHO	SV	IP	H	H/G	HR	BB	BB/G	SO	SO/G	ERA	/A	OAVG	OOBP	PR	/A	PF	CPI	WAT	PB	PD	TPI
1940	Bos-N	4	8	.333	32	14	5	0	1	129	142	9.9	17	63	4.4	54	3.8	5.51	71	.278	.363	-24	-23	101	96	-1.3	-2	-2	-2.5
1941	Bos-N	0	0	—	3	0	0	0	0	3	7	21.0	0	6	18.0	1	3.0	12.00	29	.412	.583	-3	-3	96	118	0.0	0	0	-0.2
	Pit-N	1	2	.333	12	3	0	1	0	31	35	10.2	4	13	3.8	12	3.5	5.23	71	.280	.343	-5	-5	102	94	-0.5	1	0	-0.3
	Yr	1	2	.333	15	3	0	1	0	34	42	11.1	4	19	5.0	13	3.4	5.82	63	.294	.371	-8	-8	101	94	-0.5	0	0	-0.5
1942	Pit-N	0	0	—	7	1	0	0	0	22	19	7.8	2	9	3.7	10	4.1	2.86	118	.229	.312	1	1	102	116	0.0	-1	0	0.1
1944	Pit-N	14	7	.667	40	26	11	0	2	190	190	9.0	5	37	1.8	47	2.2	3.08	122	.257	.288	11	14	104	93	2.3	-1	5	1.9
1945	Pit-N	16	10	.615	36	29	18	1	2	228	235	9.3	7	49	1.9	74	2.9	3.32	117	.260	.297	12	14	102	91	2.7	0	-2	1.4
1946	Pit-N	10	15	.400	32	22	11	3	1	176	185	9.5	7	44	2.3	49	2.5	3.58	101	.268	.313	-3	1	106	90	-0.2	1	-2	0.0
1947	Pit-N	1	6	.143	32	7	1	0	0	89	111	11.2	9	37	3.7	22	2.2	5.26	79	.316	.378	-12	-11	102	108	-2.2	-2	-0	-1.1
1948	Pit-N	0	0	—	3	0	0	0	0	4	8	18.0	0	2	4.5	1	2.3	9.00	46	.444	.500	-2	-2	104	104	0.0	0	-0	-0.1
	Phi-N	0	1	.000	6	1	0	0	0	17	26	13.8	1	10	5.3	4	2.1	9.00	42	.347	.419	-10	-10	97	76	-0.4	-0	-0	-0.9
	Yr	0	1	.000	9	1	0	0	0	21	34	14.6	1	12	5.1	5	2.1	9.00	43	.366	.434	-12	-12	98	76	-0.4	0	-0	-1.0
Total	8	46	49	.484	203	103	46	5	6	889	958	9.7	52	270	2.7	274	2.8	4.05	94	.273	.324	-34	-24	103	94	0.4	-4	0	-1.7

■ JOHN STROHMAYER Strohmayer, John Emery b: 10/13/46, Belle Fourche, S.D. BR/TR, 6'1", 181 lbs. Deb: 4/29/70

YEAR	TM/L	W	L	PCT	G	GS	CG	SHO	SV	IP	H	H/G	HR	BB	BB/G	SO	SO/G	ERA	/A	OAVG	OOBP	PR	/A	PF	CPI	WAT	PB	PD	TPI
1970	Mon-N	3	1	.750	42	0	0	0	0	76	85	10.1	7	39	4.6	74	8.8	4.86	85	.279	.361	-7	-6	102	100	1.1	-0	-0	-0.6
1971	Mon-N	7	5	.583	27	14	2	0	1	114	124	9.8	16	31	2.4	56	4.4	4.34	80	.281	.329	-11	-11	100	104	1.6	1	-1	-1.1
1972	Mon-N	1	2	.333	48	0	0	0	3	77	73	8.5	6	31	3.6	50	5.8	3.51	102	.256	.325	-0	1	104	107	-0.3	-0	1	0.2
1973	Mon-N	0	1	.000	17	3	0	0	0	35	34	8.7	4	22	5.7	15	3.9	5.14	75	.260	.365	-6	-5	105	92	-0.4	0	-0	-0.4
	NY-N	0	0	—	7	0	0	0	0	10	13	11.7	2	4	3.6	5	4.5	8.10	45	.310	.370	-5	-5	100	74	0.0	0	-0	-0.4
	Yr	0	1	.000	24	3	0	0	0	45	47	9.4	6	26	5.2	20	4.0	5.80	66	.270	.361	-11	-10	104	74	-0.4	0	-0	-0.8
1974	NY-N	0	0	—	1	0	0	0	0	1	0	0.0	0	1	9.0	0	0.0	0.00	—	.000	.250	0	0	100	0	0.0	0	0	0.0
Total	5	11	9	.550	142	17	2	0	4	313	329	9.5	35	128	3.7	200	5.8	4.46	83	.272	.342	-28	-26	102	101	2.0	1	-0	-2.3

■ BRENT STROM Strom, Brent Terry b: 10/14/48, San Diego, Cal. BR/TL, 6'3", 189 lbs. Deb: 7/31/72

YEAR	TM/L	W	L	PCT	G	GS	CG	SHO	SV	IP	H	H/G	HR	BB	BB/G	SO	SO/G	ERA	/A	OAVG	OOBP	PR	/A	PF	CPI	WAT	PB	PD	TPI
1972	NY-N	0	3	.000	11	5	0	0	0	30	34	10.2	7	15	4.5	20	6.0	6.90	48	.296	.366	-11	-12	96	90	-1.4	-1	-1	-1.2
1973	Cle-A	2	10	.167	27	18	2	0	0	123	134	9.8	18	47	3.4	91	6.7	4.61	82	.278	.341	-11	-11	99	103	-3.7	0	1	-1.0

YEAR	TM/L	W	L	PCT	G	GS	CG	SHO	SV	IP	H	H/G	HR	BB	BB/G	SO	SO/G	ERA	/A	OAVG	OOBP	PR	/A	PF	CPI	WAT	PB	PD	TPI
1975	SD-N	8	8	.500	18	16	6	2	0	120	103	7.7	6	33	2.5	56	4.2	2.55	144	.233	.283	14	15	101	100	1.0	-1	0	1.6
1976	SD-N	12	16	.429	36	33	8	1	0	211	188	8.0	15	73	3.1	103	4.4	3.28	96	.239	.300	5	-3	90	94	-0.7	-2	0	-0.5
1977	SD-N	0	2	.000	8	3	0	0	0	17	23	12.2	5	12	6.4	8	4.2	12.18	29	.329	.412	-16	-16	89	67	-0.9	0	0	-1.4
Total	5	22	39	.361	100	75	16	3	0	501	482	8.7	51	180	3.2	278	5.0	3.95	87	.254	.315	-18	-28	95	96	-5.7	-3	1	-2.5
■ **FLOYD STROMME** Stromme, Floyd Marvin "Rock" b: 8/1/16, Copperstown, N.Dak. BR/TR, 5'11", 170 lbs. Deb: 7/05/39																													
1939	Cle-A	0	1	.000	5	0	0	0	0	13	13	9.0	1	13	9.0	4	2.8	4.85	92	.265	.406	-0	-1	96	122	-0.4	0	-0	0.0
■ **SAILOR STROUD** Stroud, Ralph Vivian b: 5/15/1885, Ironia, N.J. d: 4/11/70, Stockton, Cal. BR/TR, 6', 160 lbs. Deb: 4/29/10																													
1910	Det-A	5	9	.357	28	15	7	3	1	130	123	8.5	9	41	2.8	63	4.4	3.25	77	.257	.325	-11	-11	100	103	-2.6	-4	-4	-1.9
1915	NY-N	12	9	.571	32	22	8	0	1	184	194	9.5	3	35	1.7	62	3.0	2.79	91	.281	.312	-1	-5	92	118	2.5	-1	0	-0.6
1916	NY-N	3	2	.600	10	4	0	0	1	47	47	9.0	1	9	1.7	16	3.1	2.68	91	.266	.294	-0	-1	94	106	0.2	-1	-0	-0.2
Total	3	20	20	.500	70	41	15	3	3	361	364	9.1	13	85	2.1	141	3.5	2.94	86	.271	.314	-12	-17	95	111	0.1	-5	-4	-2.7
■ **STEAMBOAT STRUSS** Struss, Clarence Herbert b: 2/24/09, Riverdale, Ill. d: 9/12/85, Grand Rapids, Mich. BR/TR, 5'11", 163 lbs. Deb: 9/30/34																													
1934	Pit-N	0	1	.000	1	1	0	0	0	7	7	9.0	0	6	7.7	3	3.9	6.43	66	.250	.382	-2	-2	105	66	-0.4	0	0	0.0
■ **DUTCH STRYKER** Stryker, Sterling Alpa b: 7/29/1895, Atlantic Highlands, N.J. d: 11/5/64, Red Bank, N.J. BR/TR, 5'11.5", 180 lbs. Deb: 4/16/24																													
1924	Bos-N	3	8	.273	20	10	2	0	0	73	90	11.1	4	22	2.7	22	2.7	6.04	63	.314	.356	-18	-18	99	80	-1.1	-0	2	-1.4
1926	Bro-N	0	0	—	2	0	0	0	0	2	8	36.0	0	1	4.5	0	0.0	27.00	14	.571	.600	-5	-5	101	67	0.0	0	0	-0.4
Total	2	3	8	.273	22	10	2	0	0	75	98	11.8	4	23	2.8	22	2.6	6.60	58	.326	.367	-23	-23	99	79	-1.1	-0	2	-1.8
■ **JOHNNY STUART** Stuart, John Davis "Stud" b: 4/27/01, Clinton, Tenn. d: 5/13/70, Charleston, W.Va. BR/TR, 5'11", 170 lbs. Deb: 7/27/22																													
1922	StL-N	0	0	—	2	1	0	0	0	2	2	9.0	0	2	9.0	1	4.5	9.00	46	.222	.417	-1	-1	100	49	0.0	0	0	0.0
1923	StL-N	9	5	.643	37	10	7	1	3	150	139	8.3	11	70	4.2	55	3.3	4.26	84	.252	.336	-4	-11	90	90	2.0	1	-1	-1.1
1924	StL-N	9	11	.450	28	22	13	0	0	159	167	9.5	12	60	3.4	54	3.1	4.75	84	.273	.334	-16	-14	103	86	0.6	-1	-3	-1.7
1925	StL-N	2	2	.500	15	1	1	0	0	47	52	10.0	6	24	4.6	14	2.7	6.13	70	.278	.359	-10	-9	101	81	0.0	1	-0	-0.7
Total	4	20	18	.526	82	34	21	1	3	358	360	9.1	29	156	3.9	124	3.1	4.75	81	.265	.339	-31	-35	97	87	2.6	1	-4	-3.5
■ **MARLIN STUART** Stuart, Marlin Henry b: 8/8/18, Paragould, Ark. BL/TR, 6'2", 185 lbs. Deb: 4/26/49																													
1949	Det-A	0	2	.000	14	2	0	0	0	30	39	11.7	3	35	10.5	14	4.2	9.00	49	.348	.503	-16	-15	106	95	-0.9	1	0	-1.2
1950	Det-A	3	1	.750	19	1	0	0	2	44	59	12.1	6	22	4.5	19	3.9	5.52	78	.330	.400	-5	-6	95	121	0.7	-1	0	-0.5
1951	Det-A	4	6	.400	29	15	5	0	1	124	119	8.6	9	71	5.2	46	3.3	3.77	116	.258	.358	5	9	107	119	-0.7	1	0	1.0
1952	Det-A	3	2	.600	30	9	2	0	1	91	91	9.0	8	48	4.7	32	3.2	4.95	76	.265	.351	-13	-12	103	91	1.0	-1	-0	-1.2
	StL-A	1	2	.333	12	2	0	0	1	26	26	9.0	3	9	3.1	13	4.5	4.15	88	.260	.310	-1	-1	100	95	-0.2	-0	-1	-0.2
	Yr	4	4	.500	42	11	2	0	2	117	117	9.0	11	57	4.4	45	3.5	4.77	79	.262	.336	-14	-13	102	95	0.8	-1	-1	-1.4
1953	StL-A	8	2	.800	60	2	0	0	7	114	136	10.7	6	44	3.5	46	3.6	3.95	112	.300	.356	1	6	111	119	3.5	-1	-0	0.5
1954	Bal-A	1	2	.333	22	0	0	0	2	38	46	10.9	2	15	3.6	13	3.1	4.50	82	.303	.356	-3	-3	99	107	0.0	-0	0	-0.3
	NY-A	3	0	1.000	10	0	0	0	1	18	28	14.0	0	12	6.0	2	1.0	5.50	64	.350	.421	-4	-4	94	118	1.5	0	0	-0.2
	Yr	4	2	.667	32	0	0	0	3	56	74	11.9	2	27	4.3	15	2.4	4.82	75	.316	.371	-7	-7	97	118	1.5	-0	1	-0.5
Total	6	23	17	.575	196	31	7	0	15	485	544	10.1	37	256	4.8	185	3.4	4.66	89	.289	.370	-36	-27	104	110	4.9	-1	0	-2.1
■ **GEORGE STUELAND** Stueland, George Anton b: 3/2/1899, Algona, Iowa d: 9/9/64, Onawa, Iowa BB/TR, 6'1.5", 174 lbs. Deb: 9/15/21																													
1921	Chi-N	0	1	.000	2	1	0	0	0	11	11	9.0	0	7	5.7	4	3.3	5.73	72	.282	.367	-2	-2	108	76	-0.4	0	0	-0.1
1922	Chi-N	9	4	.692	35	12	4	0	0	113	129	10.3	9	49	3.9	44	3.5	5.81	67	.297	.365	-22	-24	96	84	2.5	-2	-1	-2.4
1923	Chi-N	0	1	.000	6	0	0	0	0	8	11	12.4	0	5	5.6	2	2.3	5.63	74	.478	.533	-1	-1	103	158	-0.4	0	0	0.0
1925	Chi-N	0	0	—	2	0	0	0	0	3	2	6.0	0	3	9.0	2	6.0	3.00	140	.182	.357	0	0	98	90	0.0	0	0	0.1
Total	4	9	6	.600	45	13	4	0	0	135	153	10.2	9	64	4.3	52	3.5	5.73	69	.301	.374	-25	-27	97	88	1.7	-1	-1	-2.4
■ **PAUL STUFFEL** Stuffel, Paul Harrington "Stu" b: 3/22/27, Canton, Ohio BR/TR, 6'2", 185 lbs. Deb: 9/16/50																													
1950	Phi-N	0	0	—	3	0	0	0	0	5	4	7.2	0	1	1.8	3	5.4	1.80	220	.211	.286	1	1	96	105	0.0	0	0	0.1
1952	Phi-N	1	0	1.000	2	1	0	0	0	6	5	7.5	0	7	10.5	3	4.5	3.00	123	.217	.387	0	0	99	142	0.5	-0	0	0.1
1953	Phi-N	0	0	—	2	0	0	0	0	0	0	—	0	4	—	0	—	∞	—	—	1.000	-4	-4	98	31	0.0	0	0	-0.3
Total	3	1	0	1.000	7	1	0	0	0	11	9	7.4	0	12	9.8	6	4.9	5.73	67	.214	.393	-2	-2	97	125	0.5	-0	0	-0.1
■ **GEORGE STULTZ** Stultz, George Irvin b: 6/30/1873, Louisville, Ky. d: 3/19/55, Louisville, Ky. 5'10", 150 lbs. Deb: 9/22/1894																													
1894	Bos-N	1	0	1.000	1	1	1	0	0	9	4	4.0	0	5	5.0	1	1.0	0.00	—	.148	.281	5	6	111	0	0.5	-0	0	0.6
■ **JIM STUMP** Stump, James Gilbert b: 2/10/32, Lansing, Mich. BR/TR, 6', 188 lbs. Deb: 8/29/57																													
1957	Det-A	1	0	1.000	6	0	0	0	0	13	11	7.6	0	8	5.5	2	1.4	2.08	196	.220	.311	2	3	107	127	0.5	0	0	0.4
1959	Det-A	0	0	—	5	0	0	0	0	11	12	9.8	1	4	3.3	6	4.9	2.45	175	.279	.333	2	2	111	178	0.0	1	0	0.3
Total	2	1	0	1.000	11	0	0	0	0	24	23	8.6	1	12	4.5	8	3.0	2.25	185	.247	.321	4	5	109	150	0.5	1	0	0.7
■ **JOHN STUPER** Stuper, John Anton b: 5/9/57, Butler, Pa. BR/TR, 6'2", 200 lbs. Deb: 6/01/82																													
1982	StL-N	9	7	.563	23	21	2	0	0	137	137	9.0	8	55	3.6	53	3.5	3.35	110	.266	.332	4	5	102	114	0.0	-1	-3	0.2
1983	StL-N	12	11	.522	40	30	6	1	1	198	202	9.2	15	71	3.2	81	3.7	3.68	97	.265	.325	-1	-2	98	102	0.9	-0	-1	-0.4
1984	StL-N	3	5	.375	15	12	0	0	1	61	73	10.8	4	20	3.0	19	2.8	5.31	67	.297	.349	-12	-12	99	86	-1.0	-1	0	-1.2
1985	Cin-N	8	5	.615	33	13	1	0	0	99	116	10.5	8	37	3.4	38	3.5	4.55	83	.303	.354	-10	-8	105	108	1.0	-0	0	-0.8
Total	4	32	28	.533	111	76	9	1	1	495	528	9.6	35	183	3.3	191	3.5	3.96	92	.277	.336	-19	-17	101	105	0.9	-3	-4	-2.2
■ **TOM STURDIVANT** Sturdivant, Thomas Virgil "Snake" b: 4/28/30, Gordon, Kan. BL/TR, 6'0.5", 170 lbs. Deb: 4/14/55																													
1955	NY-A	1	3	.250	33	1	0	0	0	68	48	6.4	6	42	5.6	48	6.4	3.18	118	.203	.323	6	4	94	103	-1.1	-1	-0	0.3
1956	NY-A	16	8	.667	32	17	6	2	5	158	134	7.6	15	52	3.0	110	6.3	3.30	119	.224	.290	15	11	95	85	1.4	4	-2	1.3
1957	NY-A	16	6	**.727**	28	28	7	2	0	202	170	7.6	14	80	3.6	118	5.3	2.54	134	.232	.307	28	20	90	121	3.1	1	-2	2.0
1958	NY-A	3	6	.333	15	10	0	0	0	71	77	9.8	6	38	4.8	41	5.2	4.18	89	.274	.363	-3	-4	99	112	-2.0	0	-2	-0.4
1959	NY-A	0	2	.000	7	3	0	0	0	25	20	7.2	4	9	3.2	16	5.8	5.04	70	.222	.282	-3	-4	92	70	-0.9	-1	0	-0.4
	KC-A	2	6	.250	36	3	0	0	5	72	70	8.8	9	34	4.3	57	7.1	4.63	86	.258	.341	-6	-5	103	100	-1.6	-2	1	-0.5
	Yr	2	8	.200	43	6	0	0	5	97	90	8.4	13	43	4.0	73	6.8	4.73	82	.249	.326	-9	-9	100	100	-2.5	-1	1	-0.9
1960	Bos-A	3	3	.500	40	3	0	0	1	101	106	9.4	16	45	4.0	67	6.0	4.99	82	.279	.345	-13	-10	105	102	0.4	-1	-0	-1.0
1961	Was-A	2	6	.250	15	10	1	1	0	80	67	7.5	6	40	4.5	39	4.4	4.61	85	.233	.324	-5	-6	97	78	-1.3	-1	1	-0.6
	Pit-N	5	2	.714	13	11	6	1	1	86	81	8.5	6	17	1.8	45	4.7	2.83	141	.249	.284	12	11	99	103	1.6	1	-1	1.1
1962	Pit-N	9	5	.643	49	12	2	1	2	125	120	8.6	12	39	2.8	76	5.5	3.74	107	.260	.313	3	3	101	101	1.2	-0	0	0.4
1963	Pit-N	0	0	—	3	0	0	0	0	8	8	9.0	1	4	4.5	6	6.8	6.75	48	.267	.333	-3	-3	99	69	0.0	-0	0	-0.2
	Det-A	1	2	.333	28	0	0	0	2	55	43	7.0	7	24	3.9	36	5.9	3.76	100	.221	.294	-1	-0	104	93	-0.4	-1	1	0.0
	KC-A	1	2	.333	17	3	0	0	0	53	47	8.0	3	17	2.9	26	4.4	3.74	106	.237	.297	-1	1	109	79	-0.3	-1	0	0.0
	Yr	2	4	.333	45	3	0	0	2	108	90	7.5	10	41	3.4	62	5.2	3.75	103	.226	.293	-1	1	106	79	-0.7	-1	1	0.0
1964	KC-A	0	0	—	3	0	0	0	0	4	4	9.0	0	1	2.3	1	2.3	9.00	43	.308	.438	-2	-2	108	61	0.0	0	-0	-0.1
	NY-N	0	0	—	16	0	0	0	1	29	34	10.6	2	7	2.2	18	5.6	5.90	59	.306	.344	-8	-8	98	81	0.0	-0	-0	-0.8
Total	10	59	51	.536	335	101	22	7	17	1137	1029	8.1	107	449	3.6	704	5.6	3.74	102	.244	.315	18	9	98	99	0.1	-2	-3	1.1
■ **DICK SUCH** Such, Richard Stanley b: 10/15/44, Sanford, N.C. BL/TR, 6'4", 190 lbs. Deb: 4/06/70 C																													
1970	Was-A	1	5	.167	21	5	0	0	0	50	48	8.6	8	45	8.1	41	7.4	7.56	48	.258	.402	-21	-22	97	79	-1.8	1	0	-2.0
■ **CHARLEY SUCHE** Suche, Charles Morris b: 8/15/15, Cranes Mill, Tex. d: 2/11/84, San Antonio, Tex. BR/TL, 6'2", 190 lbs. Deb: 9/18/38																													
1938	Cle-A	0	0	—	1	0	0	0	0	1	4	36.0	0	3	27.0	1	9.0	36.00	13	.571	.700	-3	-3	98	70	0.0	1	0	-0.1
■ **JIM SUCHECKI** Suchecki, James Joseph b: 8/25/27, Chicago, Ill. BR/TR, 6', 185 lbs. Deb: 5/20/50																													
1950	Bos-A	0	0	—	4	0	0	0	0	4	3	6.8	0	4	9.0	3	6.8	4.50	113	.231	.389	0	0	111	103	0.0	0	0	0.0
1951	StL-A	0	6	.000	29	6	0	0	0	90	113	11.3	8	42	4.2	47	4.7	5.40	83	.299	.364	-13	-9	109	97	-2.9	-2	-1	-1.0
1952	Pit-N	0	0	—	5	0	0	0	0	10	14	12.6	1	4	3.6	6	5.4	5.40	73	.326	.388	-2	-2	105	114	0.0	0	0	-0.1
Total	3	0	6	.000	38	6	0	0	0	104	130	11.3	9	50	4.3	56	4.8	5.37	83	.300	.368	-15	-10	109	98	-2.9	-2	-1	-1.1

YEAR	TM/L	W	L	PCT	G	GS	CG	SHO	SV	IP	H	H/G	HR	BB	BB/G	SO	SO/G	ERA	/A	OAVG	OOBP	PR	/A	PF	CPI	WAT	PB	PD	TPI
■ WILLIE SUDHOFF	Sudhoff, John William "Wee Willie" b: 9/17/1874, St.Louis, Mo. d: 5/25/17, St.Louis, Mo. TR, 5'7", 165 lbs. Deb: 8/20/1897																												
1897	StL-N	2	7	.222	11	9	9	0	0	93	126	12.2	8	21	2.0	19	1.8	4.55	93	.347	.383	-2	-3	99	114	0.0	-1	0	-0.2
1898	StL-N	11	27	.289	41	38	35	0	1	315	355	10.1	11	102	2.9	65	1.9	4.34	91	.306	.363	-26	-14	110	90	1.0	-7	8	-0.9
1899	Cle-N	3	8	.273	11	10	8	0	0	86	131	13.7	3	25	2.6	10	1.0	7.01	53	.376	.418	-30	-32	96	82	1.0	-2	0	-2.6
	StL-N	13	10	.565	26	24	18	0	0	189	203	9.7	6	67	3.2	33	1.6	3.62	114	.298	.361	5	11	107	102	0.3	-0	0	1.0
	Yr	16	18	.471	37	34	26	0	0	275	334	10.9	9	92	3.0	43	1.4	4.68	85	.324	.380	-25	-21	103	102	1.3	-2	0	-1.6
1900	StL-N	6	8	.429	16	14	13	2	0	127	128	9.1	2	37	2.6	29	2.1	2.76	125	.284	.339	13	10	93	113	-0.5	0	0	0.9
1901	StL-N	17	11	.607	38	26	25	1	2	276	281	9.2	4	92	3.0	78	2.5	3.52	89	.290	.362	-6	-12	95	99	2.4	3	2	-0.8
1902	StL-A	12	12	.500	30	25	20	0	0	220	213	8.7	6	67	2.7	42	1.7	2.86	127	.278	.336	17	19	102	108	-1.7	-2	3	2.1
1903	StL-A	21	15	.583	38	35	30	5	0	294	262	8.0	4	56	1.7	104	3.2	2.27	124	.260	.299	22	18	96	104	4.9	-0	2	2.2
1904	StL-A	8	15	.348	27	24	20	1	0	222	232	9.4	8	54	2.2	63	2.6	3.77	67	.293	.338	-29	-31	98	91	-2.3	-1	5	-2.5
1905	StL-A	10	20	.333	32	30	23	1	0	244	222	8.2	8	78	2.9	70	2.6	2.99	83	.266	.329	-9	-14	93	101	-0.9	2	4	-1.0
1906	Was-A	0	2	.000	9	5	0	0	0	20	30	13.5	1	9	4.0	7	3.1	9.00	28	.375	.438	-14	-14	94	70	-0.9	1	1	-1.3
Total	10	103	135	.433	279	240	201	10	3	2086	2183	9.4	61	608	2.6	520	2.2	3.57	92	.293	.348	-59	-65	99	100	3.3	-7	25	-3.1
■ JOE SUGDEN	Sugden, Joseph b: 7/31/1870, Philadelphia, Pa. d: 6/28/59, Philadelphia, Pa. BB/TR, 5'10", 180 lbs. Deb: 7/20/1893 C																												
1902	StL-A	0	0	—	1	0	0	0	0	1	1	9.0	0	0	0.0	0	0.0	0.00	—	.284	.284	0	0	102	0	0.0	0	0	0.0
■ GEORGE SUGGS	Suggs, George Franklin b: 7/7/1882, Kinston, N.C. d: 4/4/49, Kinston, N.C. BR/TR, 5'7.5", 168 lbs. Deb: 4/21/08																												
1908	Det-A	1	1	.500	6	1	1	0	1	27	32	10.7	0	2	0.7	8	2.7	1.67	142	.299	.312	2	2	99	200	-0.1	1	-1	0.1
1909	Det-A	1	3	.250	9	4	2	0	1	44	34	7.0	1	10	2.0	18	3.7	2.05	129	.228	.290	2	3	106	102	-1.1	-1	-0	0.3
1910	Cin-N	20	12	.625	35	30	23	3	3	266	248	8.4	7	48	**1.6**	91	3.1	2.40	129	.253	.297	19	21	102	106	5.1	1	1	2.5
1911	Cin-N	15	13	.536	36	29	17	1	0	261	258	8.9	3	79	2.7	91	3.1	3.00	104	.268	.330	12	4	92	110	2.4	7	3	1.3
1912	Cin-N	19	16	.543	42	36	25	5	3	303	320	9.5	6	56	1.7	104	3.1	2.94	108	.269	.308	16	8	93	93	2.3	-0	1	0.7
1913	Cin-N	8	15	.348	36	22	9	2	2	199	220	9.9	6	35	1.6	73	3.3	4.03	83	.292	.318	-18	-16	104	90	-2.1	2	3	-1.0
1914	Bal-F	24	14	.632	46	38	26	6	4	319	322	9.1	6	57	1.6	132	3.7	2.91	109	.266	.304	11	9	99	99	4.5	4	7	2.2
1915	Bal-F	11	17	.393	35	25	12	0	3	233	288	11.1	13	68	2.6	71	2.7	4.13	82	.318	.370	-29	-20	111	120	2.1	1	4	-1.3
Total	8	99	91	.521	245	185	115	17	17	1652	1722	9.4	42	355	1.9	588	3.2	3.11	102	.275	.319	14	14	100	104	13.1	15	18	4.8
■ ED SUKLA	Sukla, Edward Anthony b: 3/3/43, Long Beach, Cal. BR/TR, 5'11", 170 lbs. Deb: 9/17/64																												
1964	LA-A	0	1	.000	2	0	0	0	0	3	2	6.0	1	1	3.0	3	9.0	6.00	54	.200	.273	-1	-1	89	72	-0.4	0	0	0.0
1965	Cal-A	2	3	.400	25	0	0	0	3	32	32	9.0	3	10	2.8	15	4.2	4.50	76	.264	.316	-4	-4	98	87	-0.2	0	1	-0.2
1966	Cal-A	1	1	.500	12	0	0	0	1	17	18	9.5	4	6	3.2	8	4.2	6.35	54	.281	.338	-6	-6	100	88	0.0	-0	-0	-0.5
Total	3	3	5	.375	39	0	0	0	4	52	52	9.0	8	17	2.9	26	4.5	5.19	65	.267	.321	-10	-10	98	86	-0.6	-0	0	-0.7
■ CHARLIE SULLIVAN	Sullivan, Charles Edward b: 5/23/03, Yadkin Valley, N.C d: 5/28/35, Maiden, N.C. BL/TR, 6'1", 185 lbs. Deb: 4/21/28																												
1928	Det-A	0	2	.000	3	2	0	0	0	12	18	13.5	1	6	4.5	2	1.5	6.75	60	.360	.407	-4	-4	100	105	-0.9	-1	0	-0.3
1930	Det-A	1	5	.167	40	3	2	0	5	94	112	10.7	9	53	5.1	38	3.6	6.51	76	.311	.383	-19	-17	106	95	-1.9	1	1	-1.2
1931	Det-A	3	2	.600	31	4	2	0	0	95	109	10.3	6	46	4.4	28	2.7	4.93	95	.288	.359	-6	-3	107	102	0.9	-1	-0	-0.3
Total	3	4	9	.308	74	9	4	0	5	201	239	10.7	16	105	4.7	68	3.0	5.78	82	.303	.374	-29	-23	106	99	-1.9	-0	1	-1.8
■ FLEURY SULLIVAN	Sullivan, Florence P. b: 1862, E.St.Louis, Ill. d: 2/15/1897, E.St.Louis, Ill. Deb: 5/03/1884																												
1884	Pit-a	16	35	.314	51	51	51	2	0	441	496	10.1	15	96	2.0	189	3.9	4.20	78	.292	.330	-47	-45	101	99	2.3	-9	-0	-4.7
■ FRANK SULLIVAN	Sullivan, Franklin Leal b: 1/23/30, Hollywood, Cal. BR/TR, 6'6.5", 215 lbs. Deb: 7/31/53																												
1953	Bos-A	1	1	.500	14	0	0	0	0	26	24	8.3	3	11	3.8	17	5.9	5.54	78	.264	.346	-4	-4	108	82	0.0	-0	0	-0.3
1954	Bos-A	15	12	.556	36	26	11	3	1	206	185	8.1	18	66	2.9	124	5.4	3.15	119	.240	.300	13	14	101	100	3.1	-2	1	1.4
1955	Bos-A	**18**	13	.581	35	35	16	3	0	**260**	235	8.1	23	100	3.5	129	4.5	2.91	167	.241	.310	30	**56**	122	116	1.5	-6	1	**5.8**
1956	Bos-A	14	7	.667	34	33	12	1	0	242	253	9.4	22	82	3.0	116	4.3	3.42	124	.268	.327	20	22	102	117	3.1	-5	0	1.8
1957	Bos-A	14	11	.560	31	30	14	3	0	241	206	7.7	16	48	**1.8**	127	4.7	2.73	**151**	.230	**.272**	28	37	109	90	0.9	-2	2	**4.3**
1958	Bos-A	13	9	.591	32	29	10	2	3	199	216	9.8	12	49	2.2	103	4.7	3.57	111	.278	.321	4	8	105	105	2.0	-1	-1	0.7
1959	Bos-A	9	11	.450	30	26	5	2	1	178	172	8.7	17	67	3.4	107	5.4	3.94	103	.258	.328	-2	2	105	102	-0.8	-1	-1	0.1
1960	Bos-A	6	16	.273	40	22	4	0	1	154	164	9.6	12	52	3.0	98	5.7	5.08	80	.269	.327	-21	-17	105	76	-4.2	-1	-1	-1.8
1961	Phi-N	3	16	.158	49	18	1	1	6	159	161	9.1	19	55	3.1	114	6.5	4.30	91	.262	.322	-5	-6	98	95	-4.8	0	1	-0.4
1962	Phi-N	0	2	.000	19	0	0	0	0	23	38	14.9	2	12	4.7	12	4.7	6.26	60	.396	.452	-6	-6	95	134	-0.9	0	0	-0.5
	Min-A	4	1	.800	21	0	0	0	5	33	33	9.0	3	13	3.5	10	2.7	3.27	126	.258	.317	3	3	104	117	1.4	-0	0	0.3
1963	Min-A	0	1	.000	10	0	0	0	1	11	15	12.3	1	4	3.3	2	1.6	5.73	62	.349	.388	-3	-3	98	110	-0.4	0	0	-0.1
Total	11	97	100	.492	351	219	73	15	18	1732	1702	8.8	148	559	2.9	959	5.0	3.60	115	.257	.315	59	107	106	102	0.9	-18	2	11.3
■ HARRY SULLIVAN	Sullivan, Harry Andrew b: 4/12/1888, Rockford, Ill. d: 9/22/19, Rockford, Ill. BL/TL, Deb: 09																												
1909	StL-N	0	0	—	2	1	0	0	0	1	4	36.0	1	2	18.0	1	9.0	36.00	7	.500	.600	-4	-4	99	77	0.0	-0	0	-0.3
■ JIM SULLIVAN	Sullivan, James E. b: 4/25/1869, Charlestown, Mass. d: 11/30/01, Roxbury, Mass. BR/TR, 5'10", 155 lbs. Deb: 4/22/1891																												
1891	Bos-N	0	0	—	1	0	0	0	0	⅓	2	54.0	0	5	135.0	0	0.0	81.00	—	1.000	1.000	-3	-3	109	89	0.0	0	0	-0.1
	Col-a	0	1	.000	1	1	1	0	0	9	10	10.0	1	5	5.0	1	1.0	4.00	84	.296	.387	-0	-1	90	124	-0.4	-1	0	0.0
1895	Bos-N	11	9	.550	21	19	16	0	0	179	236	11.9	10	58	2.9	46	2.3	4.83	101	.339	.389	-1	1	102	107	0.2	-5	0	-0.2
1896	Bos-N	11	12	.478	31	26	21	1	1	225	268	10.7	12	68	2.7	33	1.3	4.04	115	.318	.369	8	16	107	108	-2.0	-3	0	1.2
1897	Bos-N	4	5	.444	13	9	8	1	2	89	91	9.2	1	26	2.6	17	1.7	3.94	113	.286	.340	4	5	103	80	-1.6	-3	0	0.2
Total	4	26	27	.491	67	55	46	2	3	502	607	10.9	24	162	2.9	97	1.7	4.36	108	.321	.374	8	18	104	103	-3.8	-11	0	1.1
■ JIM SULLIVAN	Sullivan, James Richard b: 4/5/1894, Mine Run, Va. d: 2/12/72, Burtonsville, Md. BR/TR, 5'11", 165 lbs. Deb: 9/27/21																												
1921	Phi-A	0	2	.000	2	2	2	0	0	17	20	10.6	0	7	3.7	8	4.2	3.18	144	.294	.342	2	3	107	127	-0.9	-1	0	0.1
1922	Phi-A	0	2	.000	20	2	1	0	0	51	76	13.4	3	25	4.4	15	2.6	5.47	79	.373	.416	-8	-7	106	129	-0.9	-1	-0	-0.6
1923	Cle-A	0	1	.000	3	0	0	0	0	5	10	18.0	0	5	9.0	4	7.2	14.40	27	.476	.571	-6	-6	99	82	-0.4	-0	0	-0.4
Total	3	0	5	.000	25	4	3	0	0	73	106	13.1	3	37	4.6	27	3.3	5.55	78	.362	.412	-12	-10	106	125	-2.2	-2	-0	-0.9
■ JOHN SULLIVAN	Sullivan, John Jeremiah "Lefty" b: 5/31/1894, Chicago, Ill. d: 7/7/58, Chicago, Ill. BL/TL, 5'11", 165 lbs. Deb: 7/18/19																												
1919	Chi-A	0	1	.000	4	2	1	0	0	15	24	14.4	0	8	4.8	9	5.4	4.20	78	.364	.440	-2	-2	102	155	-0.4	-0	-1	-0.1
■ JOE SULLIVAN	Sullivan, Joe b: 9/26/10, Mason City, Ill. d: 4/8/85, Sequim, Wash. BL/TL, 5'11", 175 lbs. Deb: 4/20/35																												
1935	Det-A	6	6	.500	25	12	5	0	0	126	119	8.5	4	71	5.1	53	3.8	3.50	118	.244	.341	13	9	93	105	-1.1	-1	-1	0.7
1936	Det-A	2	5	.286	26	4	1	0	1	80	111	12.5	4	40	4.5	32	3.6	6.75	71	.331	.401	-15	-18	95	94	-1.6	-1	-1	-1.5
1939	Bos-N	6	9	.400	31	11	7	0	2	114	114	9.0	3	50	3.9	46	3.6	3.63	101	.266	.335	4	0	93	104	-0.2	3	0	0.3
1940	Bos-N	10	14	.417	36	22	7	0	1	177	157	8.0	9	89	4.5	64	3.3	3.56	109	.240	.332	6	6	101	105	-0.3	-1	0	0.6
1941	Bos-N	2	2	.500	16	2	0	0	0	52	60	10.4	3	26	4.5	11	1.9	4.15	84	.290	.368	-3	-4	96	119	0.3	-1	1	-0.3
	Pit-N	4	1	.800	16	4	0	0	1	39	40	9.2	2	22	5.1	10	2.3	3.00	123	.258	.348	3	3	102	135	1.5	1	0	0.4
	Yr	6	3	.667	32	6	0	0	1	91	100	9.9	5	48	4.7	21	2.1	3.66	97	.275	.355	-0	-1	98	135	1.8	-1	1	0.1
Total	5	30	37	.448	150	55	20	0	5	588	601	9.2	25	298	4.6	216	3.3	4.01	99	.265	.349	7	-3	96	106	-1.4	1	0	0.2
■ MARTY SULLIVAN	Sullivan, Martin C. b: 10/20/1862, Lowell, Mass. d: 1/6/1894, Lowell, Mass. BR/TR, Deb: 4/30/1887																												
1887	Chi-N	0	0	—	1	0	0	0	0	2	6	27.0	0	1	4.5	1	4.5	9.00	52	.533	.571	-1	-1	115	154	0.0	0	0	0.0
■ MIKE SULLIVAN	Sullivan, Michael Joseph "Big Mike" b: 10/23/1866, Boston, Mass. d: 6/14/06, Boston, Mass. BL, 6'1", 210 lbs. Deb: 6/17/1889																												
1889	Was-N	0	3	.000	9	3	3	0	0	41	47	10.3	2	32	7.0	15	3.3	7.24	53	.304	.423	-15	-15	96	76	-1.4	-2	0	-1.3
1890	Chi-N	5	6	.455	12	12	10	0	0	96	108	10.1	3	58	5.4	33	3.1	4.59	83	.300	.397	-11	-8	107	101	-1.4	-3	0	-0.9
1891	Phi-a	0	2	.000	2	2	2	0	0	18	17	8.5	2	10	5.0	7	3.5	3.50	109	.263	.362	0	1	103	118	-0.9	-1	0	0.0
	NY-N	1	2	.333	3	3	3	0	0	24	24	9.0	0	8	3.0	11	4.1	3.38	92	.274	.334	-0	-1	93	83	-0.5	-0	0	0.0
1892	Cin-N	12	4	.750	21	16	15	0	0	166	179	9.7	8	74	4.0	56	3.0	3.09	110	.288	.364	4	6	103	**132**	3.8	-3	0	0.3
1893	Cin-N	8	11	.421	27	18	14	0	1	184	200	9.8	5	103	5.0	40	2.0	5.09	94	.293	.385	-8	-7	102	89	-1.8	-3	0	-0.7
1894	Was-N	2	10	.167	20	12	11	0	1	118	166	12.7	10	74	5.6	21	1.6	6.64	80	.355	.443	-17	-17	100	101	-3.1	-4	0	-1.5
	Cle-N	6	5	.545	13	11	9	0	0	91	128	12.7	4	47	4.6	19	1.9	6.43	92	.355	.430	-11	-5	111	94	0.2	-0	0	-0.3

YEAR	TM/L	W	L	PCT	G	GS	CG	SHO	SV	IP	H	H/G	HR	BB	BB/G	SO	SO/G	ERA	/A	OAVG	OOBP	PR	/A	PF	CPI	WAT	PB	PD	TPI
	Yr	8	15	.348	33	23	20	0	1	209	294	12.7	14	121	5.2	40	1.7	6.55	85	.355	.437	-28	-23	104	94	-2.9	-4	0	-1.8
1895	Cle-N	1	2	.333	4	3	2	0	0	31	42	12.2	1	16	4.6	5	1.5	8.42	54	.345	.421	-13	-13	95	68	-0.6	-1	0	-1.0
1896	NY-N	10	13	.435	25	22	18	0	0	185	188	9.1	3	71	3.5	42	2.0	4.67	92	.285	.355	-6	-8	99	74	-1.4	-4	0	-0.8
1897	NY-N	8	7	.533	23	16	11	1	2	149	183	11.1	6	71	4.3	35	2.1	5.13	81	.325	.401	-14	-16	96	96	-1.2	0	0	-1.2
1898	Bos-N	0	1	.000	3	2	0	0	0	12	19	14.3	1	9	6.8	1	0.8	12.00	30	.383	.478	-11	-11	101	64	-0.4	0	0	-0.8
1899	Bos-N	1	0	1.000	1	1	1	0	0	9	10	10.0	1	4	4.0	1	1.0	5.00	79	.305	.381	-1	-1	103	95	0.5	0	0	0.0
Total	11	54	66	.450	163	121	99	1	4	1124	1311	10.5	46	577	4.6	286	2.3	5.14	85	.310	.393	-103	-97	101	95	-8.2	-22	0	-8.2
■ PAT SULLIVAN	Sullivan, Patrick B. b: 12/22/1862, Milwaukee, Wis. TR, 5'11", 165 lbs. Deb: 8/30/1884																												
1884	KC-U	0	1	.000	1	1	0	0	0	7	15	19.3	1	5	6.4	1	1.3	11.57	24	.436	.508	-7	-7	92	96	-0.4	-0	0	-0.4
■ LEFTY SULLIVAN	Sullivan, Paul Thomas b: 9/7/16, Nashville, Tenn. BL/TL, 6'3", 204 lbs. Deb: 5/06/39																												
1939	Cle-A	0	1	.000	7	1	0	0	0	13	9	6.2	0	9	6.2	4	2.8	4.15	107	.214	.352	1	0	96	89	-0.4	-0	-1	0.0
■ SUTER SULLIVAN	Sullivan, Suter G. b: 10/14/1872, Baltimore, Md. d: 4/19/25, Baltimore, Md. Deb: 7/24/1898																												
1898	StL-N	0	0	—	1	0	0	0	0	6	10	15.0	0	4	6.0	3	4.5	1.50	263	.395	.478	1	2	110	483	0.0	-0	0	0.2
■ TOM SULLIVAN	Sullivan, Thomas b: 3/1/1860, New York, N.Y. d: 4/12/47, Cincinnati, Ohio Deb: 9/27/1884																												
1884	Col-a	2	2	.500	4	4	4	0	0	31	42	12.2	2	3	0.9	12	3.5	4.06	76	.332	.348	-3	-3	96	129	-0.3	-1	0	-0.3
1886	Lou-a	2	7	.222	9	9	8	0	0	75	94	11.3	5	33	4.0	27	3.2	3.96	94	.317	.386	-4	-2	108	139	-2.4	-2	0	-0.2
1888	KC-a	8	16	.333	24	24	24	0	0	215	227	9.5	2	68	2.8	84	3.5	3.39	101	.284	.340	-8	1	112	106	0.2	-6	0	-0.3
1889	KC-a	2	8	.200	10	10	10	0	0	87	111	11.5	3	48	5.0	24	2.5	5.69	73	.326	.410	-18	-15	109	94	-2.5	-1	0	-1.1
Total	4	14	33	.298	47	47	46	0	0	408	474	10.5	12	152	3.4	147	3.2	4.04	90	.304	.365	-33	-19	109	111	-5.0	-10	0	-1.9
■ TOM SULLIVAN	Sullivan, Thomas Augustin b: 10/18/1895, Boston, Mass. d: 9/23/62, Boston, Mass. BL/TL, 5'11", 178 lbs. Deb: 5/15/22																												
1922	Phi-N	0	0	—	3	0	0	0	0	8	16	18.0	0	5	5.6	2	2.3	11.25	42	.410	.489	-6	-6	117	79	0.0	1	0	-0.3
■ SLEEPER SULLIVAN	Sullivan, Thomas Jefferson "Old Iron Hands" b: St.Louis, Mo. d: 9/25/1899, Camden, N.J. TR, 175 lbs. Deb: 5/03/1881																												
1882	StL-a	0	1	.000	1	1	1	0	0	9	15	15.0	0	1	1.0	0	0.0	8.00	35	.376	.391	-5	-5	104	72	-0.4	-0	0	-0.3
1884	StL-U	1	0	1.000	1	1	0	0	0	6	10	15.0	0	0	0.0	3	4.5	4.50	66	.376	.376	-1	-1	98	126	0.5	-0	0	0.0
Total	2	1	1	.500	2	2	1	0	0	15	25	15.0	0	1	0.6	3	1.8	6.60	43	.376	.385	-6	-6	102	94	0.1	-1	0	-0.3
■ BILL SULLIVAN	Sullivan, William T. Deb: 4/19/1890																												
1890	Syr-a	1	4	.200	6	6	4	0	0	42	51	10.9	2	27	5.8	13	2.8	7.93	45	.316	.414	-19	-20	92	72	-1.3	-2	0	-1.6
■ ED SUMMERS	Summers, Oron Edgar "Kickapoo Ed" or "Chief" b: 12/5/1884, Ladoga, Ind. d: 5/12/53, Indianapolis, Ind. BB/TR, 6'2", 180 lbs. Deb: 4/16/08																												
1908	Det-A	24	12	.667	40	32	23	5	1	301	271	8.1	3	55	1.6	103	3.1	1.64	143	.242	.290	25	24	99	**148**	4.2	-6	-1	2.7
1909	Det-A	19	9	.679	35	32	24	3	1	282	243	7.8	4	52	1.7	107	3.4	2.23	118	.227	.269	8	13	106	72	1.6	-5	1	1.6
1910	Det-A	13	12	.520	30	25	18	1	0	220	211	8.6	8	60	2.5	82	3.4	2.54	99	.254	.308	-0	-1	100	111	-0.9	0	1	0.0
1911	Det-A	11	11	.500	30	20	13	0	1	179	189	9.5	3	51	2.6	65	3.3	3.67	98	.274	.334	-7	-2	107	89	-1.6	1	-1	0.0
1912	Det-A	1	1	.500	3	3	1	0	0	17	16	8.5	1	3	1.6	5	2.6	4.76	67	.250	.284	-3	-3	96	57	0.1	1	0	-0.2
Total	5	68	45	.602	138	112	79	9	3	999	930	8.4	19	221	2.0	362	3.3	2.42	111	.246	.296	23	30	103	106	3.4	-9	-0	4.1
■ BILLY SUNDAY	Sunday, William Ashley "Parson" or "The Evangelist" b: 11/9/1862, Ames, Iowa d: 11/6/35, Chicago, Ill. BL, 5'10", 160 lbs. Deb: 5/22/1883																												
1890	Pit-N	0	0	—	1	0	0	0	0	0	2	—	0	0	—	0	—	∞	—	1.000	1.000	-2	-2	95	55	0.0	0	0	-0.1
■ GORDIE SUNDIN	Sundin, Gordon Vincent b: 10/10/37, Minneapolis, Minn. BR/TR, 6'4", 215 lbs. Deb: 9/19/56																												
1956	Bal-A	0	0	—	1	0	0	0	0	0	0	—	0	2	—	0	—	∞	—	—	1.000	-1	-1	97	62	0.0	0	0	0.0
■ STEVE SUNDRA	Sundra, Stephen Richard "Smokey" b: 3/27/10, Luxor, Pa. d: 3/23/52, Cleveland, Ohio BB/TR, 6'1", 185 lbs. Deb: 4/17/36																												
1936	NY-A	0	0	—	1	0	0	0	0	2	2	9.0	0	2	9.0	1	4.5	0.00	—	.286	.444	1	1	90	0	0.0	-0	0	0.1
1938	NY-A	6	4	.600	25	8	3	0	0	94	107	10.2	7	43	4.1	33	3.2	4.79	102	.291	.361	0	1	102	105	-0.3	1	1	0.3
1939	NY-A	11	1	.917	24	11	8	1	0	121	110	8.2	7	56	4.2	27	2.0	2.75	143	.240	.319	25	16	85	128	4.4	4	1	1.9
1940	NY-A	4	6	.400	27	8	2	0	2	99	121	11.0	11	42	3.8	26	2.4	5.55	76	.299	.359	-13	-15	96	98	-1.5	-1	0	-1.3
1941	Was-A	9	13	.409	28	23	11	0	0	168	203	10.9	11	61	3.3	50	2.7	5.30	77	.294	.349	-22	-23	99	88	-1.2	2	-1	-1.9
1942	Was-A	1	3	.250	6	4	2	0	0	34	43	11.4	1	15	4.0	5	1.3	5.56	65	.305	.373	-7	-7	99	90	-0.7	-0	0	-0.6
	StL-A	8	3	.727	20	13	6	0	0	111	122	9.9	2	29	2.4	26	2.1	3.81	98	.275	.317	-2	-1	102	90	2.3	3	-0	0.2
	Yr	9	6	.600	26	17	8	0	0	145	165	10.2	3	44	2.7	31	1.9	4.22	88	.282	.330	-9	-8	101	90	1.6	-0	-0	-0.4
1943	StL-A	15	11	.577	32	29	13	3	0	208	212	9.2	10	66	2.9	44	1.9	3.25	102	.266	.314	1	2	101	109	3.0	1	0	0.3
1944	StL-A	2	0	1.000	3	3	2	0	0	19	15	7.1	1	4	1.9	1	0.5	1.42	241	.211	.253	4	4	100	128	1.0	-0	-0	0.4
1946	StL-A	0	0	—	2	0	0	0	0	4	9	20.3	0	3	6.8	1	2.3	11.25	31	.409	.462	-3	-3	100	83	0.0	0	-0	-0.2
Total	9	56	41	.577	168	99	47	4	2	860	944	9.9	50	321	3.4	214	2.2	4.17	94	.277	.335	-15	-24	98	103	7.0	10	1	-0.8
■ TOM SUNKEL	Sunkel, Thomas Jacob "Lefty" b: 8/9/12, Paris, Ill. BL/TL, 6'1", 190 lbs. Deb: 8/26/37																												
1937	StL-N	0	0	—	9	1	0	0	1	29	24	7.4	0	11	3.4	9	2.8	2.79	139	.214	.280	4	4	100	70	0.0	-1	-0	0.3
1939	StL-N	4	4	.500	20	11	2	1	0	85	79	8.4	4	56	5.9	54	5.7	4.24	95	.242	.347	-3	-2	103	90	-0.6	2	-1	0.0
1941	NY-N	1	1	.500	2	2	1	1	0	15	7	4.2	0	12	7.2	14	8.4	3.00	126	.140	.313	1	1	104	64	0.0	0	-0	0.2
1942	NY-N	3	6	.333	19	11	3	0	0	64	65	9.1	5	41	5.8	29	4.1	4.78	70	.269	.371	-10	-10	101	100	-1.8	-1	-2	-1.3
1943	NY-N	0	1	.000	1	1	0	0	0	3	4	12.0	1	3	9.0	0	0.0	9.00	37	.308	.438	-2	-2	99	97	-0.4	0	0	-0.1
1944	Bro-N	1	3	.250	12	3	0	0	1	24	39	14.6	1	10	3.8	6	2.3	7.50	49	.368	.415	-10	-10	102	91	-0.7	-1	-1	-1.0
Total	6	9	15	.375	63	29	6	2	2	220	218	8.9	11	133	5.4	112	4.6	4.54	82	.256	.353	-21	-19	102	89	-3.5	0	-4	-1.9
■ RICK SURHOFF	Surhoff, Richard Clifford b: 10/3/62, Bronx, N.Y. BR/TR, 6'3", 210 lbs. Deb: 9/08/85																												
1985	Phi-N	1	0	1.000	2	0	0	0	0	1	2	18.0	0	0	0.0	1	9.0	0.00	—	.500	.500	0	0	102	0	0.5	0	0	0.0
	Tex-A	0	1	.000	7	0	0	0	2	8	12	13.5	2	3	3.4	8	9.0	7.88	58	.343	.385	-3	-3	110	96	-0.4	0	-0	-0.2
■ MAX SURKONT	Surkont, Matthew Constantine b: 6/16/22, Central Falls, R.I. d: 10/8/86, Largo, Fla. BR/TR, 6'1", 195 lbs. Deb: 4/19/49																												
1949	Chi-A	3	5	.375	44	2	0	0	4	96	92	8.6	9	60	5.6	38	3.6	4.78	87	.255	.356	-6	-6	99	95	-0.3	-1	-1	-0.8
1950	Bos-N	5	2	.714	9	6	2	0	0	56	63	10.1	5	20	3.2	21	3.4	3.21	110	.285	.346	6	2	85	143	1.4	5	-0	0.6
1951	Bos-N	12	16	.429	37	33	11	2	1	237	230	8.7	21	89	3.4	110	4.2	3.99	96	.252	.319	-1	-4	97	93	-2.1	-0	-2	-0.6
1952	Bos-N	12	13	.480	31	29	12	3	0	215	201	8.4	19	76	3.2	125	5.2	3.77	96	.245	.306	-1	-4	97	92	1.6	-1	-0	-0.5
1953	Mil-N	11	5	.688	28	24	11	2	0	170	168	8.9	22	64	3.4	83	4.4	4.18	94	.255	.317	2	-5	92	97	1.9	6	1	0.2
1954	Pit-N	9	18	.333	33	29	11	0	0	208	216	9.3	25	78	3.4	78	3.4	4.41	94	.268	.325	-8	-6	102	95	-0.4	0	0	-0.5
1955	Pit-N	7	14	.333	35	22	5	0	2	166	194	10.5	23	78	4.2	84	4.6	5.58	73	.298	.369	-29	-28	101	99	-1.6	-1	-2	-2.8
1956	Pit-N	0	0	—	1	0	0	0	0	2	2	9.0	0	3	13.5	1	4.5	4.50	87	.333	.455	-0	-0	103	181	0.0	0	0	0.0
	StL-N	0	0	—	5	0	0	0	0	6	10	15.0	3	2	3.0	5	7.5	9.00	42	.417	.444	-3	-4	99	125	0.0	-0	-0	-0.3
	NY-N	2	2	.500	8	4	1	0	1	32	24	6.8	5	9	2.5	18	5.1	4.78	78	.202	.256	-4	-4	99	50	0.2	-0	-0	-0.3
	Yr	2	2	.500	14	4	1	0	1	40	36	8.1	8	14	3.1	24	5.4	5.40	70	.240	.299	-7	-7	100	50	0.2	-0	-0	-0.6
1957	NY-N	0	1	.000	5	0	0	0	0	6	9	13.5	2	2	3.0	8	12.0	10.50	38	.321	.367	-4	-4	103	69	-0.4	0	0	-0.3
Total	9	61	76	.445	236	149	53	7	8	1194	1209	9.1	134	481	3.6	571	4.3	4.38	89	.262	.329	-48	-63	97	96	0.3	8	-5	-5.3
■ GEORGE SUSCE	Susce, George Daniel b: 9/13/31, Pittsburgh, Pa. BR/TR, 6'1", 180 lbs. Deb: 4/15/55																												
1955	Bos-A	9	7	.563	29	15	6	1	1	144	123	7.7	12	49	3.1	60	3.8	3.06	158	.232	.301	14	29	122	101	0.3	-3	-0	2.8
1956	Bos-A	2	4	.333	21	6	0	0	0	70	71	9.1	14	44	5.7	26	3.3	6.17	69	.262	.367	-16	-15	102	90	-1.1	2	-0	-1.2
1957	Bos-A	7	3	.700	29	5	0	0	1	88	93	9.5	6	41	4.2	40	4.1	4.30	96	.274	.351	-5	-2	109	101	1.9	-1	-1	-0.2
1958	Bos-A	0	0	—	2	0	0	0	0	2	6	27.0	1	1	4.5	0	0.0	18.00	22	.600	.583	-3	-3	105	106	0.0	0	0	-0.2
	Det-A	4	3	.571	27	10	2	0	1	91	90	8.9	7	26	2.6	42	4.2	3.66	106	.259	.309	1	2	103	97	0.5	-1	-2	0.0
	Yr	4	3	.571	29	10	2	0	1	93	96	9.3	8	27	2.6	42	4.1	3.97	98	.268	.317	-2	-1	103	97	0.5	0	-2	-0.2
1959	Det-A	0	0	—	9	0	0	0	0	15	24	14.4	4	9	5.4	9	5.4	12.60	34	.358	.438	-15	-14	111	72	0.0	-0	-0	-1.2
Total	5	22	17	.564	117	36	8	1	3	410	407	8.9	44	170	3.7	177	3.9	4.41	99	.260	.334	-23	-3	111	97	1.6	-3	-3	-0.0

YEAR	TM/L	W	L	PCT	G	GS	CG	SHO	SV	IP	H	H/G	HR	BB	BB/G	SO	SO/G	ERA	/A	OAVG	OOBP	PR	/A	PF	CPI	WAT	PB	PD	TPI
■ **RICK SUTCLIFFE** Sutcliffe, Richard Lee b: 6/21/56, Independence, Mo. BL/TR, 6'7", 215 lbs. Deb: 9/29/76																													
1976	LA-N	0	0	—	1	1	0	0	0	5	2	3.6	0	1	1.8	3	5.4	0.00	—	.125	.176	2	2	99	0	0.0	-0	-0	0.2
1978	LA-N	0	0	—	2	0	0	0	0	2	2	9.0	0	1	4.5	0	0.0	0.00	—	.286	.444	1	1	97	0	0.0	0	0	0.1
1979	LA-N	17	10	.630	39	30	5	1	0	242	217	8.1	16	97	3.6	117	4.4	3.46	108	.243	.311	8	7	99	95	4.3	5	-2	1.0
1980	LA-N	3	9	.250	42	10	1	1	5	110	122	10.0	10	55	4.5	59	4.8	5.56	62	.285	.363	-24	-26	96	87	-3.4	-0	-1	-2.6
1981	LA-N	2	2	.500	14	6	0	0	0	47	41	7.9	5	20	3.8	16	3.1	4.02	83	.238	.320	-3	-3	96	92	-0.2	1	0	-0.2
1982	Cle-A	14	8	.636	34	27	6	1	1	216	174	**7.3**	16	98	4.1	142	5.9	**2.96**	139	**.226**	.311	**27**	28	101	110	3.6	0	1	3.0
1983	Cle-A	17	11	.607	36	35	10	2	0	243	251	9.3	23	102	3.8	160	5.9	4.30	101	.268	.338	-6	1	106	101	4.9	0	2	0.2
1984	Cle-A	4	5	.444	15	15	2	0	0	94	111	10.6	7	46	4.4	58	5.6	5.17	82	.298	.371	-12	-10	106	99	-0.1	0	-0	-0.9
	Chi-N	16	1	**.941**	20	20	7	3	0	150	123	7.4	9	39	2.3	155	9.3	2.70	145	.220	.271	15	20	109	84	**7.4**	3	2	2.9
1985	Chi-N	8	8	.500	20	20	6	3	0	130	119	8.2	12	44	3.0	102	7.1	3.18	132	.240	.302	6	15	117	103	0.4	2	1	2.1
1986	Chi-N	5	14	.263	28	27	4	1	0	177	166	8.4	18	96	4.9	122	6.2	4.63	87	.252	.344	-18	-12	108	92	-4.0	3	1	-0.7
1987	Chi-N	**18**	10	.643	34	34	6	1	0	237	223	8.5	24	106	4.0	174	6.6	3.68	113	.252	.329	11	12	102	110	**5.1**	3	4	1.9
1988	Chi-N	13	14	.481	32	32	12	2	0	226	232	9.2	18	70	2.8	144	5.7	3.86	94	.269	.317	-10	-6	105	102	0.2	3	1	-0.1
Total	12	117	92	.560	317	257	59	15	6	1879	1783	8.5	158	775	3.7	1252	6.0	3.83	104	.253	.324	-4	29	104	99	18.2	18	9	6.9
■ **HARRY SUTER** Suter, Harry Richard "Handsome Harry" or "Rube" b: 9/15/1887, Independence, Mo. d: 7/24/71, Topeka, Kan. BL/TL, 5'10", 190 lbs. Deb: 4/16/09																													
1909	Chi-A	2	3	.400	18	7	3	1	1	87	72	7.4	2	28	2.9	53	5.5	2.48	96	.199	.264	-0	-1	97	45	-0.5	-1	-1	-0.1
■ **DARRELL SUTHERLAND** Sutherland, Darrell Wayne b: 11/14/41, Glendale, Cal. BR/TR, 6'4", 169 lbs. Deb: 6/28/64																													
1964	NY-N	0	3	.000	10	4	0	0	0	27	32	10.7	1	12	4.0	9	3.0	7.67	45	.302	.362	-12	-13	98	65	-1.4	0	1	-1.0
1965	NY-N	3	1	.750	18	2	0	0	0	48	33	6.2	4	17	3.2	16	3.0	2.81	131	.199	.283	4	5	104	94	1.3	0	2	0.7
1966	NY-N	2	0	1.000	31	0	0	0	1	44	60	12.3	6	25	5.1	23	4.7	4.91	71	.339	.420	-6	-7	97	143	1.0	1	1	-0.4
1968	Cle-A	0	0	—	3	0	0	0	0	3	6	18.0	0	4	12.0	2	6.0	9.00	33	.375	.500	-2	-2	101	108	0.0	0	0	-0.1
Total	4	5	4	.556	62	6	0	0	1	122	131	9.7	11	58	4.3	50	3.7	4.80	74	.282	.361	-17	-17	100	105	0.9	1	4	-0.8
■ **SUDS SUTHERLAND** Sutherland, Harvey Scott b: 2/20/1894, Beaverton, Ore. d: 5/11/72, Portland, Ore. BR/TR, 6', 180 lbs. Deb: 4/14/21																													
1921	Det-A	6	2	.750	13	8	3	0	0	58	80	12.4	1	18	2.8	18	2.8	4.97	83	.328	.362	-4	-6	96	98	2.2	3	2	0.0
■ **DIZZY SUTHERLAND** Sutherland, Howard Alvin b: 4/9/23, Washington, D.C. d: 8/26/79, Washington, D.C. BL/TL, 6', 200 lbs. Deb: 9/20/49																													
1949	Was-A	0	1	.000	1	1	0	0	0	1	2	18.0	0	6	54.0	0	0.0	45.00	9	.400	.727	-5	-5	96	52	-0.4	0	0	-0.3
■ **BRUCE SUTTER** Sutter, Howard Bruce b: 1/8/53, Lancaster, Pa. BR/TR, 6'2", 190 lbs. Deb: 5/09/76																													
1976	Chi-N	6	3	.667	52	0	0	0	10	83	63	6.8	4	26	2.8	73	7.9	2.71	143	.209	.268	7	11	111	77	1.8	-1	-0	1.1
1977	Chi-N	7	3	.700	62	0	0	0	31	107	69	5.8	5	23	1.9	129	10.9	1.35	333	.183	.226	31	**37**	115	88	2.1	-0	1	4.0
1978	Chi-N	8	10	.444	64	0	0	0	27	99	82	7.5	10	34	3.1	106	9.6	3.18	125	.220	.283	4	9	111	87	-0.8	-0	0	0.9
1979	Chi-N	6	6	.500	62	0	0	0	**37**	101	67	6.0	3	32	2.9	110	9.8	2.23	189	.186	.246	17	**22**	112	59	0.1	1	1	2.5
1980	Chi-N	5	8	.385	60	0	0	0	**28**	102	90	7.9	5	34	3.0	76	6.7	2.65	147	.242	.296	11	14	108	113	-0.1	-1	0	1.4
1981	StL-N	3	5	.375	48	0	0	0	**25**	82	64	7.0	5	24	2.6	57	6.3	2.63	134	.218	.271	8	8	101	91	-1.4	-1	-1	0.7
1982	StL-N	9	8	.529	70	0	0	0	**36**	102	88	7.8	8	34	3.0	61	5.4	2.91	127	.235	.295	8	9	102	106	-0.5	-0	0	0.9
1983	StL-N	9	10	.474	60	0	0	0	21	89	90	9.1	8	30	3.0	64	6.5	4.25	84	.262	.315	-6	-7	98	88	-0.2	-1	2	-0.5
1984	StL-N	5	7	.417	71	0	0	0	**45**	123	109	8.0	9	23	1.7	77	5.6	1.54	231	.245	.279	**28**	**27**	99	189	-1.2	-1	1	2.9
1985	Atl-N	7	7	.500	58	0	0	0	23	88	91	9.3	13	29	3.0	52	5.3	4.50	87	.267	.322	-9	-6	108	98	1.2	-0	0	-0.6
1986	Atl-N	2	0	1.000	16	0	0	0	3	19	17	8.1	3	9	4.3	16	7.6	4.26	90	.243	.325	-1	-1	103	100	1.0	-0	0	0.0
1988	Atl-N	1	4	.200	38	0	0	0	14	45	49	9.8	4	11	2.2	40	8.0	4.80	77	.275	.316	-7	-6	107	83	-0.9	0	0	-0.5
Total	12	68	71	.489	661	0	0	0	300	1040	879	7.6	77	309	2.7	861	7.5	2.84	136	.230	.282	91	118	106	102	1.1	-5	5	12.8
■ **JACK SUTTHOFF** Sutthoff, John Gerhard "Sunny Jack" b: 6/29/1873, Cincinnati, Ohio d: 8/3/42, Cincinnati, Ohio BL/TR, 5'9", 175 lbs. Deb: 9/15/1898																													
1898	Was-N	0	0	—	2	1	0	0	0	8	16	18.0	1	8	9.0	3	3.4	13.50	28	.439	.540	-9	-9	105	80	0.0	0	0	-0.5
1899	StL-N	0	2	.000	2	2	1	0	0	13	19	13.2	0	10	6.9	4	2.8	10.38	40	.366	.469	-9	-9	107	63	-0.9	-1	0	-0.7
1901	Cin-N	1	6	.143	10	4	4	0	0	70	82	10.5	2	39	5.0	12	1.5	5.53	60	.318	.414	-17	-17	100	89	-2.1	-2	-1	-1.6
1903	Cin-N	16	9	.640	30	27	21	3	0	225	207	8.3	2	79	3.2	76	3.0	2.80	125	.273	.354	12	17	107	104	3.3	-3	-1	1.6
1904	Cin-N	5	6	.455	12	10	8	0	0	90	83	8.3	1	43	4.3	27	2.7	2.30	132	.271	.366	4	7	111	142	-1.1	-0	-2	0.6
	Phi-N	6	13	.316	19	18	17	0	0	164	172	9.4	2	71	3.9	46	2.5	3.68	72	.299	.384	-17	-19	97	104	-0.7	-0	-2	-1.9
	Yr	11	19	.367	31	28	25	0	0	254	255	9.0	3	114	4.0	73	2.6	3.19	87	.288	.375	-13	-11	102	104	-1.8	-0	-4	-1.3
1905	Phi-N	3	4	.429	13	6	4	1	0	78	82	9.5	2	36	4.2	26	3.0	3.81	80	.302	.391	-7	-7	102	108	-0.7	-1	0	-0.6
Total	6	31	40	.437	88	68	55	4	0	648	661	9.2	10	286	4.0	194	2.7	3.65	86	.293	.381	-44	-36	104	107	-2.2	-7	-6	-3.1
■ **DON SUTTON** Sutton, Donald Howard b: 4/2/45, Clio, Ala. BR/TR, 6'1", 185 lbs. Deb: 4/14/66																													
1966	LA-N	12	12	.500	37	35	6	2	0	226	192	7.6	19	52	2.1	209	8.3	2.99	115	.228	.270	16	11	95	86	-1.9	1	-0	1.2
1967	LA-N	11	15	.423	37	34	11	3	1	233	223	8.6	18	57	2.2	169	6.5	3.94	76	.250	.297	-15	-24	89	81	-0.8	0	-2	-2.7
1968	LA-N	11	15	.423	35	27	7	2	1	208	179	7.7	6	59	2.6	162	7.0	2.60	105	.232	.283	9	3	91	92	-1.4	1	-1	0.2
1969	LA-N	17	18	.486	41	41	11	4	0	293	269	8.3	25	91	2.8	217	6.7	3.47	101	.242	.296	4	1	97	91	-1.5	-1	0	0.0
1970	LA-N	15	13	.536	38	38	10	4	0	260	251	8.7	38	78	2.7	201	7.0	4.08	88	.249	.306	-1	-14	89	96	0.0	4	-1	-1.1
1971	LA-N	17	12	.586	38	37	12	4	1	265	231	7.8	10	55	1.9	194	6.6	2.55	133	.238	.275	27	25	98	95	1.4	3	-1	3.0
1972	LA-N	19	9	.679	33	33	18	**9**	0	273	186	**6.1**	13	63	2.1	207	6.8	2.08	155	**.189**	**.238**	42	34	93	66	4.6	-1	0	3.7
1973	LA-N	18	10	.643	33	33	14	3	0	256	196	6.9	18	56	2.0	200	7.0	2.43	150	.209	.255	35	34	99	81	2.1	-2	-0	3.5
1974	LA-N	19	9	.679	40	40	10	5	0	276	241	7.9	23	80	2.6	179	5.8	3.23	101	.229	.285	12	1	90	84	2.2	1	-1	0.0
1975	LA-N	16	13	.552	35	35	11	4	0	254	202	7.2	17	62	2.2	175	6.2	2.87	118	.213	**.259**	22	15	93	70	0.3	-1	-1	1.2
1976	LA-N	21	10	.677	35	34	15	4	0	268	231	7.8	22	82	2.8	161	5.4	3.06	113	.234	.289	13	12	99	97	4.6	-3	-2	0.7
1977	LA-N	14	8	.636	33	33	9	3	0	240	207	7.8	23	69	2.6	150	5.6	3.19	120	.233	.285	19	17	98	93	1.0	1	-1	1.7
1978	LA-N	15	11	.577	34	34	12	2	0	238	228	8.6	29	54	2.0	154	5.8	3.55	98	.250	.290	1	-2	97	96	-0.2	-3	-2	-0.7
1979	LA-N	12	15	.444	33	32	6	1	1	226	201	8.0	21	61	2.4	146	5.8	3.82	97	.239	.284	-2	-3	99	78	-1.3	-2	-1	-0.5
1980	LA-N	13	5	.722	32	31	4	2	1	212	163	6.9	20	47	2.0	128	5.4	**2.21**	157	.211	**.255**	33	29	96	101	3.5	-4	0	2.8
1981	Hou-N	11	9	.550	23	23	6	3	0	159	132	7.5	6	29	1.6	104	5.9	2.60	116	.230	**.260**	16	7	87	84	0.0	1	0	0.9
1982	Hou-N	13	8	.619	27	27	4	0	0	195	169	7.8	10	46	2.1	139	6.4	3.00	120	.232	.276	13	13	100	81	3.2	-1	-1	1.2
	Mil-A	4	1	.800	7	7	2	1	0	55	55	9.0	8	18	2.9	36	5.9	3.27	115	.263	.320	5	3	92	130	1.3	0	1	0.4
1983	Mil-A	8	13	.381	31	31	4	0	0	220	209	8.6	21	54	2.2	134	5.5	4.09	91	.246	.290	-0	-9	91	78	-3.3	0	-1	-1.0
1984	Mil-A	14	12	.538	33	33	1	0	0	213	224	9.5	24	51	2.2	143	6.0	3.76	98	.266	.305	6	-1	93	100	3.1	0	-2	-0.2
1985	Oak-A	13	8	.619	29	29	1	1	0	194	194	9.0	19	51	2.4	91	4.2	3.90	99	.256	.299	5	-1	93	90	3.2	0	-0	0.0
	Cal-A	2	2	.500	5	5	0	0	0	32	27	7.6	6	8	2.3	16	4.5	3.66	114	.233	.282	2	2	101	101	-0.1	0	-1	0.1
	Yr	15	10	.600	34	34	1	1	0	226	221	8.8	25	59	2.3	107	4.3	3.86	101	.251	.297	7	1	94	101	3.1	0	-1	0.1
1986	Cal-A	15	11	.577	34	34	3	1	0	207	192	8.3	31	49	2.1	116	5.0	3.74	107	.242	.286	10	6	95	92	0.3	0	-3	0.3
1987	Cal-A	11	11	.500	35	34	1	0	0	192	199	9.3	38	41	1.9	99	4.6	4.69	95	.269	.311	-5	-5	100	99	0.9	0	-2	-0.6
1988	LA-N	3	6	.333	16	16	0	0	0	87	91	9.4	7	30	3.1	44	4.6	3.93	92	.270	.321	-5	-3	105	103	-1.9	-1	-1	-0.4
Total	23	324	256	.559	774	756	178	58	5	5282	4692	8.0	472	1343	2.3	3574	6.1	3.26	108	.236	.283	263	151	95	88	19.3	-7	-23	13.7
■ **JOHN SUTTON** Sutton, Johnny Ike b: 11/13/52, Dallas, Tex. BR/TR, 5'11", 185 lbs. Deb: 4/07/77																													
1977	StL-N	2	1	.667	14	0	0	0	0	24	28	10.5	1	9	3.4	9	3.4	2.63	142	.315	.366	3	3	95	189	0.5	-0	0	0.3
1978	Min-A	0	0	—	17	0	0	0	0	44	46	9.4	3	15	3.1	18	3.7	3.48	103	.264	.325	1	0	94	104	0.0	0	-0	0.0
Total	2	2	1	.667	31	0	0	0	0	68	74	9.8	4	24	3.2	27	3.6	3.18	114	.281	.339	5	3	95	134	0.5	-0	0	0.3
■ **BILL SWABACH** Swabach, William Deb: 7/09/1887																													
1887	NY-N	0	2	.000	2	2	2	0	0	16	27	15.2	1	6	3.4	6	3.4	5.06	84	.391	.439	-2	-1	106	145	-0.9	-1	0	-0.1
■ **BILL SWAGGERTY** Swaggerty, William David b: 12/5/56, Sanford, Fla. BR/TR, 6'2", 186 lbs. Deb: 8/13/83																													
1983	Bal-A	1	1	.500	7	2	0	0	0	22	23	9.4	1	6	2.5	7	2.9	2.86	141	.267	.315	3	3	99	120	-0.1	0	1	0.4
1984	Bal-A	3	2	.600	23	6	0	0	0	57	68	10.7	7	21	3.3	18	2.8	5.21	72	.302	.355	-8	-9	94	100	0.4	0	-1	-0.9
1985	Bal-A	0	0	—	1	0	0	0	0	2	3	13.5	0	2	9.0	2	9.0	4.50	91	.375	.500	-0	-0	98	184	0.0	0	0	0.0

YEAR	TM/L	W	L	PCT	G	GS	CG	SHO	SV	IP	H	H/G	HR	BB	BB/G	SO	SO/G	ERA	/A	OAVG	OOBP	PR	/A	PF	CPI	WAT	PB	PD	TPI
1986	Bal-A	0	0	—	1	0	0	0	0	1	6	54.0	0	1	9.0	1	9.0	18.00	23	.750	.778	-2	-2	99	176	0.0	0	0	0.0
Total	4	4	3	.571	32	8	0	0	0	82	100	11.0	8	30	3.3	28	3.1	4.72	81	.306	.359	-6	-8	96	109	0.3	0	0	-0.5
■ **CY SWAIM**	Swaim, John Hillary b: 3/11/1874, Cadwallader, Ohio 6'6", 180 lbs. Deb: 5/03/1897																												
1897	Was-N	10	11	.476	27	20	16	0	0	194	227	10.5	5	61	2.8	55	2.6	4.41	99	.314	.368	-2	-1	102	92	0.3	-3	0	-0.2
1898	Was-N	3	11	.214	16	13	9	0	1	101	119	10.6	4	28	2.5	30	2.7	4.28	88	.316	.363	-8	-6	105	95	-2.6	-3	0	-0.7
Total	2	13	22	.371	43	33	25	0	1	295	346	10.6	9	89	2.7	85	2.6	4.36	96	.315	.366	-9	-6	103	93	-2.3	-6	0	-0.9
■ **CRAIG SWAN**	Swan, Craig Steven b: 11/30/50, Van Nuys, Cal. BR/TR, 6'3", 215 lbs. Deb: 9/03/73																												
1973	NY-N	0	1	.000	3	1	0	0	0	8	16	18.0	2	2	2.3	4	4.5	9.00	41	.432	.429	-5	-5	100	111	-0.4	-0	-0	-0.4
1974	NY-N	1	3	.250	7	5	0	0	0	30	28	8.4	1	21	6.3	10	3.0	4.50	81	.255	.355	-3	-3	100	92	-0.8	1	0	-0.1
1975	NY-N	1	3	.250	6	6	0	0	0	31	38	11.0	4	13	3.8	19	5.5	6.39	54	.302	.366	-9	-10	95	84	-0.9	-1	-1	-1.0
1976	NY-N	6	9	.400	23	22	2	1	0	132	129	8.8	11	44	3.0	89	6.1	3.55	90	.254	.313	-1	-5	91	101	-1.9	-0	-1	-0.6
1977	NY-N	9	10	.474	26	24	2	1	0	147	153	9.4	10	56	3.4	71	4.3	4.22	90	.268	.329	-5	-7	97	91	1.4	-0	-2	-0.9
1978	NY-N	9	6	.600	29	28	5	1	0	207	164	7.1	12	58	2.5	125	5.4	**2.43**	**146**	.219	.274	26	26	99	96	2.6	-0	1	2.9
1979	NY-N	14	13	.519	35	35	10	3	0	251	241	8.6	20	57	2.0	145	5.2	3.30	109	.255	.292	12	8	96	96	3.3	-0	-1	0.6
1980	NY-N	5	9	.357	21	21	4	1	0	128	117	8.2	20	30	2.1	79	5.6	3.59	98	.247	.283	0	-1	97	101	-0.9	2	-2	-0.1
1981	NY-N	0	2	.000	5	3	0	0	0	14	10	6.4	0	1	0.6	9	5.8	3.21	111	.204	.220	0	1	103	31	-0.9	-0	0	0.0
1982	NY-N	11	7	.611	37	21	2	0	1	166	165	8.9	13	37	2.0	67	3.6	3.36	107	.256	.292	5	4	100	94	3.4	3	-1	0.6
1983	NY-N	2	8	.200	27	18	0	0	1	96	112	10.5	14	42	3.9	43	4.0	5.53	66	.299	.363	-20	-20	100	98	-2.6	-2	-1	-2.2
1984	NY-N	1	0	1.000	10	0	0	0	0	19	18	8.5	5	7	3.3	10	4.7	8.05	45	.247	.309	-9	-9	100	59	0.5	0	-0	-0.9
	Cal-A	0	1	.000	2	1	0	0	0	5	8	14.4	3	0	0.0	2	3.6	10.80	38	.348	.348	-4	-4	101	86	-0.4	0	0	-0.2
Total	12	59	72	.450	231	185	25	7	2	1234	1199	8.7	115	368	2.7	673	4.9	3.75	95	.256	.306	-12	-26	97	95	2.4	1	-9	-2.3
■ **DUCKY SWAN**	Swan, Harry Gordon b: 8/11/1887, Lancaster, Pa. d: 5/8/46, Pittsburgh, Pa. BR/TR, 5'10", 165 lbs. Deb: 4/28/14																												
1914	KC-F	0	0	—	1	0	0	0	0	1	0	0.0	0	1	9.0	1	9.0	0.00	—	.000	.289	0	0	96	0	0.0	0	0	0.0
■ **RED SWANSON**	Swanson, Arthur Leonard b: 10/15/36, Baton Rouge, La. BR/TR, 6'1.5", 175 lbs. Deb: 9/10/55																												
1955	Pit-N	0	0	—	1	0	0	0	0	2	2	9.0	1	3	13.5	0	0.0	18.00	23	.286	.500	-3	-3	101	60	0.0	0	0	-0.2
1956	Pit-N	0	0	—	9	0	0	0	0	12	21	15.8	1	8	6.0	5	3.8	9.75	40	.438	.460	-8	-8	103	98	0.0	0	1	-0.6
1957	Pit-N	3	3	.500	32	8	1	0	0	73	68	8.4	9	31	3.8	29	3.6	3.70	101	.248	.324	1	0	96	106	0.5	-1	-1	-0.1
Total	3	3	3	.500	42	8	1	0	0	87	91	9.4	11	42	4.3	34	3.5	4.86	77	.277	.351	-10	-11	97	104	0.5	-1	-0	-0.9
■ **ED SWARTWOOD**	Swartwood, Cyrus Edward b: 1/12/1859, Rockford, Ill. d: 5/15/24, Pittsburgh, Pa. TR , 198 lbs. Deb: 8/11/1881																												
1884	Pit-a	0	0	—	1	0	0	0	0	2	6	27.0	0	1	4.5	0	0.0	13.50	24	.524	.563	-2	-2	101	105	0.0	0	0	-0.1
1890	Tol-a	0	0	—	1	0	0	0	0	3	2	6.0	0	0	0.0	1	3.0	3.00	132	.202	.202	0	0	102	27	0.0	0	0	0.0
Total	2	0	0	—	2	0	0	0	0	5	8	14.4	0	1	1.8	1	1.8	7.20	51	.375	.403	-2	-2	102	58	0.0	1	0	-0.1
■ **BUD SWARTZ**	Swartz, Sherwin Merle b: 6/13/29, Tulsa, Okla. BL/TL, 6'2.5", 180 lbs. Deb: 7/12/47																												
1947	StL-A	0	0	—	5	0	0	0	0	5	9	16.2	1	7	12.6	1	1.8	7.20	54	.360	.500	-2	-2	106	148	0.0	0	-0	-0.1
■ **MONTY SWARTZ**	Swartz, Vernon Monroe "Dazzy" b: 1/1/1897, Farmersville, Ohio d: 1/13/80, Germantown, Ohio BR/TR, 5'11", 182 lbs. Deb: 10/03/20																												
1920	Cin-N	0	1	.000	1	1	1	0	0	12	17	12.8	0	2	1.5	2	1.5	4.50	61	.333	.358	-2	-2	88	95	-0.4	1	0	-0.1
■ **PARK SWARTZEL**	Swartzel, Park B. b: 11/21/1865, Knightstown, Ind. d: 1/3/40, Los Angeles, Cal. BR/TR, Deb: 4/17/1889																												
1889	KC-a	19	27	.413	48	47	45	0	1	410	481	10.6	21	117	2.6	147	3.2	4.32	97	.308	.356	-22	-7	109	98	0.7	-10	12	0.0
■ **CHARLIE SWEENEY**	Sweeney, Charles J. b: 4/13/1863, San Francisco, Cal d: 4/4/02, San Francisco, Cal. BR , 5'10.5", 181 lbs. Deb: 5/11/1882																												
1883	Pro-N	7	7	.500	20	18	14	0	0	147	142	8.7	3	28	1.7	48	2.9	3.12	97	.261	.297	0	-2	96	83	-1.1	-1	0	-0.2
1884	Pro-N	17	8	.680	27	24	22	4	1	221	153	**6.2**	4	29	1.2	145	5.9	1.55	184	**.203**	**.233**	35	32	96	65	-1.4	8	2	4.3
	StL-U	24	7	.774	33	32	31	2	0	271	207	6.9	2	13	**0.4**	192	6.4	1.83	162	.216	.227	36	34	98	79	-1.3	11	6	5.1
1885	StL-N	11	21	.344	35	35	32	2	0	275	276	9.0	6	50	1.6	84	2.7	3.93	70	.272	.306	-34	-36	97	75	0.4	0	-0	-3.2
1886	StL-N	5	6	.455	11	11	11	0	0	93	108	10.5	9	39	3.8	28	2.7	4.16	78	.304	.373	-9	-10	98	120	0.9	1	0	-0.6
1887	Cle-a	0	3	.000	3	3	3	0	0	24	42	15.8	0	13	4.9	8	3.0	8.25	53	.397	.463	-11	-10	103	94	-1.4	0	0	-0.6
Total	5	64	52	.552	129	123	113	8	1	1031	928	8.1	24	172	1.5	505	4.4	2.87	102	.249	.282	18	8	97	79	-3.9	19	7	4.8
■ **BILL SWEENEY**	Sweeney, William J. b: Philadelphia, Pa. d: 4/13/08, Paterson, N.J. Deb: N/A.																												
1882	Phi-a	9	10	.474	20	20	18	0	0	170	178	9.4	4	42	2.2	48	2.5	2.91	103	.275	.319	-4	1	111	112	-1.5	-3	-1	-0.1
1884	Bal-U	**40**	21	.656	**62**	60	**58**	4	0	**538**	522	8.7	13	74	1.2	374	6.3	2.59	128	.260	.286	25	43	110	109	**12.7**	-5	3	3.9
Total	2	49	31	.613	82	80	76	4	0	708	700	8.9	17	116	1.5	422	5.4	2.67	121	.263	.294	21	44	110	110	11.2	-8	2	3.8
■ **LES SWEETLAND**	Sweetland, Lester Leo (Born Leo Sweetland) b: 8/15/01, St.Ignace, Mich. d: 3/4/74, Melbourne, Fla. BB/TL, 5'11.5", 155 lbs. Deb: 7/04/27																												
1927	Phi-N	2	10	.167	21	13	6	0	0	104	147	12.7	3	53	4.6	21	1.8	6.14	64	.348	.411	-26	-26	100	102	-3.0	4	4	-1.6
1928	Phi-N	3	15	.167	37	18	5	0	2	135	163	10.9	15	97	6.5	23	1.5	6.60	66	.306	.414	-39	-34	109	97	-3.9	1	2	-2.7
1929	Phi-N	13	11	.542	43	25	10	2	2	204	255	11.3	23	87	3.8	47	2.1	5.12	103	.316	.378	-9	3	112	116	2.0	3	4	1.0
1930	Phi-N	7	15	.318	34	25	8	1	0	167	271	14.6	24	60	3.2	36	1.9	7.71	71	.373	.411	-51	-42	109	101	-0.6	4	1	-3.0
1931	Chi-N	8	7	.533	26	14	9	0	0	130	156	10.8	3	61	4.2	32	2.2	5.05	72	.297	.369	-17	-21	94	93	-0.1	5	0	-1.4
Total	5	33	58	.363	161	95	38	3	4	740	992	12.1	68	358	4.4	159	1.9	6.11	76	.329	.396	-142	-121	106	103	-5.6	17	11	-7.7
■ **STEVE SWETONIC**	Swetonic, Stephen Albert b: 8/13/03, Mt.Pleasant, Pa. d: 4/22/74, Canonsburg, Pa. BR/TR, 5'11", 185 lbs. Deb: 4/17/29																												
1929	Pit-N	8	10	.444	41	12	3	0	5	144	172	10.8	6	50	3.1	35	2.2	4.81	99	.299	.352	-2	-0	102	96	-2.2	3	1	0.4
1930	Pit-N	6	6	.500	23	6	3	1	5	97	107	9.9	7	27	2.5	35	3.2	4.45	109	.276	.319	6	4	98	86	-0.1	-3	-1	0.1
1931	Pit-N	0	2	.000	14	0	0	0	1	28	28	9.0	0	16	5.1	8	2.6	3.86	102	.264	.358	0	0	102	100	-0.9	-0	-0	0.0
1932	Pit-N	11	6	.647	24	19	11	**4**	0	163	134	**7.4**	11	55	3.0	39	2.2	2.82	137	**.221**	.283	19	19	100	93	1.9	-4	-1	1.4
1933	Pit-N	12	12	.500	31	21	8	3	0	165	166	9.1	10	64	3.5	37	2.0	3.49	90	.260	.326	-3	-7	94	104	-1.5	1	-1	-0.6
Total	5	37	36	.507	133	58	25	8	11	597	607	9.2	34	212	3.2	154	2.3	3.80	106	.262	.322	21	16	98	96	-2.8	-2	-2	1.3
■ **BILL SWIFT**	Swift, William Charles b: 10/27/61, Portland, Maine BR/TR, 6', 170 lbs. Deb: 6/07/85																												
1985	Sea-A	6	10	.375	23	21	0	0	0	121	131	9.7	8	48	3.6	55	4.1	4.76	83	.279	.346	-8	-11	95	93	-1.5	0	0	-0.9
1986	Sea-A	2	9	.182	29	17	1	0	0	115	148	11.6	5	55	4.3	55	4.3	5.48	81	.319	.393	-17	-13	106	102	-3.1	0	1	-1.0
1988	Sea-A	8	12	.400	38	24	6	1	0	175	199	10.2	10	65	3.3	47	2.4	4.58	94	.294	.359	-12	-5	108	103	-0.5	0	2	-0.3
Total	3	16	31	.340	90	62	7	1	0	411	478	10.5	23	168	3.7	157	3.4	4.88	87	.297	.365	-36	-29	104	100	-5.1	0	3	-2.2
■ **BILL SWIFT**	Swift, William Vincent b: 1/10/08, Elmira, N.Y. d: 2/23/69, Bartow, Fla. BR/TR, 6'1.5", 192 lbs. Deb: 4/12/32																												
1932	Pit-N	14	10	.583	39	23	11	0	4	214	205	8.6	15	26	**1.1**	64	2.7	3.62	107	.248	.269	6	6	100	75	0.8	-1	-4	0.1
1933	Pit-N	14	10	.583	37	29	13	2	0	218	214	8.8	11	36	1.5	64	2.6	3.14	100	.251	.279	5	-0	94	85	0.6	3	-2	0.1
1934	Pit-N	11	13	.458	37	24	13	1	0	213	244	10.3	15	46	1.9	81	3.4	3.97	107	.284	.323	2	7	105	103	-0.9	1	-2	0.7
1935	Pit-N	15	8	.652	39	21	11	3	1	204	193	8.5	6	37	1.6	74	3.3	2.69	157	.247	.278	30	35	105	97	2.7	3	-4	3.4
1936	Pit-N	16	16	.500	45	31	17	0	2	262	275	9.4	18	63	2.2	92	3.2	4.02	96	.265	.305	-0	-4	96	88	-1.5	10	-5	0.0
1937	Pit-N	9	10	.474	36	17	9	0	3	164	160	8.8	14	34	1.9	84	4.6	3.95	100	.256	.291	-1	0	101	85	-1.5	-1	-3	-0.2
1938	Pit-N	7	5	.583	36	9	2	0	4	150	155	9.3	9	40	2.4	77	4.6	3.24	115	.271	.314	9	8	99	116	0.2	2	-1	0.9
1939	Pit-N	5	7	.417	36	8	2	1	4	130	150	10.4	6	28	1.9	56	3.9	3.88	102	.293	.324	1	1	101	104	-0.3	1	-3	0.0
1940	Bos-N	1	1	.500	4	0	0	0	1	9	12	12.0	0	7	7.0	7	7.0	3.00	130	.308	.413	1	1	101	192	0.1	-0	0	0.1
1941	Bro-N	3	0	1.000	9	0	0	0	1	22	26	10.6	4	7	2.9	9	3.7	3.27	110	.289	.340	1	1	99	159	1.5	-0	-0	0.0
1943	Chi-A	0	2	.000	18	1	0	0	0	51	48	8.5	5	27	4.8	28	4.9	4.24	79	.246	.354	-5	-5	101	102	-0.9	0	-2	-0.6
Total	11	95	82	.537	336	163	78	7	20	1637	1682	9.2	103	351	1.9	636	3.5	3.58	107	.263	.300	49	48	100	94	0.8	18	-25	4.5
■ **OAD SWIGART**	Swigart, Oadis Vaughn b: 2/13/15, Archie, Mo. BL/TR, 6', 175 lbs. Deb: 9/14/39																												
1939	Pit-N	1	1	.500	3	3	1	1	0	24	27	10.1	1	6	2.3	8	3.0	4.50	88	.293	.330	-2	-1	101	90	0.1	0	-0	-0.1
1940	Pit-N	0	2	.000	7	2	0	0	0	22	27	11.0	1	10	4.1	9	3.7	4.50	81	.297	.363	-2	-2	95	108	-0.9	0	0	-0.1
Total	2	1	3	.250	10	5	1	1	0	46	54	10.6	2	16	3.1	17	3.3	4.50	84	.295	.347	-3	-4	98	99	-0.8	0	0	-0.2

YEAR	TM/L	W	L	PCT	G	GS	CG	SHO	SV	IP	H	H/G	HR	BB	BB/G	SO	SO/G	ERA	/A	OAVG	OOBP	PR	/A	PF	CPI	WAT	PB	PD	TPI
■ AD SWIGLER	Swigler, Adam William "Doc" b: 9/21/1895, Philadelphia, Pa. d: 2/5/75, Philadelphia, Pa. 5'10", 180 lbs. Deb: 9/25/17																												
1917	NY-N	0	1	.000	1	1	0	0	0	6	7	10.5	0	8	12.0	4	6.0	6.00	42	.333	.500	-2	-2	93	126	-0.4	-0	0	-0.1
■ GREG SWINDELL	Swindell, Forrest Gregory b: 1/2/65, Houston, Tex. BR/TL, 6'2", 225 lbs. Deb: 8/21/86																												
1986	Cle-A	5	2	.714	9	9	1	0	0	62	57	8.3	9	15	2.2	46	6.7	4.21	97	.243	.286	-0	-1	98	83	1.5	0	1	0.0
1987	Cle-A	3	8	.273	16	15	4	1	0	102	112	9.9	18	37	3.3	97	8.6	5.12	91	.283	.340	-7	-5	105	102	-1.5	0	-0	-0.4
1988	Cle-A	18	14	.563	33	33	12	4	0	242	234	8.7	18	45	1.7	180	6.7	3.20	127	.252	.283	21	23	102	96	3.0	0	-1	2.3
Total	3	26	24	.520	58	57	17	5	0	406	403	8.9	45	97	2.2	323	7.2	3.83	110	.258	.299	13	17	102	95	3.0	0	-1	1.9
■ JOSH SWINDELL	Swindell, Joshua Ernest b: 7/5/1883, Rose Hill, Kan. d: 3/19/69, Fruita, Colo. TR, 6', 180 lbs. Deb: 9/16/11																												
1911	Cle-A	0	1	.000	4	1	1	0	0	17	19	10.1	0	4	2.1	6	3.2	2.12	163	.257	.304	2	3	103	109	-0.4	-0	-0	0.2
■ LEN SWORMSTEDT	Swormstedt, Leonard Jordan b: 10/6/1878, Cincinnati, Ohio d: 7/19/64, Salem, Mass. BR/TR, 5'11.5", 165 lbs. Deb: 9/29/01																												
1901	Cin-N	2	1	.667	3	3	3	0	0	26	19	6.6	2	5	1.7	13	4.5	1.73	191	.225	.277	5	5	100	121	0.7	-1	0	0.5
1902	Cin-N	0	2	.000	2	2	2	0	0	18	22	11.0	1	5	2.5	3	1.5	4.00	75	.326	.372	-2	-2	108	107	-0.9	-1	-0	-0.1
1906	Bos-A	1	1	.500	3	2	2	0	0	21	17	7.3	0	0	0.0	6	2.6	1.29	217	.245	.245	3	4	104	101	0.3	-1	-1	0.3
Total	3	3	4	.429	8	7	7	0	0	65	58	8.0	3	10	1.4	22	3.0	2.22	138	.262	.297	5	6	103	111	0.1	-3	-1	0.7
■ BOB SYKES	Sykes, Robert Joseph b: 12/11/54, Neptune, N.J. BB/TL, 6'1", 195 lbs. Deb: 4/09/77																												
1977	Det-A	5	7	.417	32	20	3	0	0	133	141	9.5	15	50	3.4	58	3.9	4.40	97	.271	.330	-5	-2	105	97	-0.5	0	-0	-0.1
1978	Det-A	6	6	.500	22	10	3	2	2	94	99	9.5	14	34	3.3	58	5.6	3.93	103	.275	.335	-2	1	107	117	-0.3	0	-2	0.0
1979	StL-N	4	3	.571	13	11	0	0	0	67	86	11.6	11	34	4.6	35	4.7	6.18	63	.315	.390	-18	-17	104	101	0.3	-0	-1	-1.6
1980	StL-N	6	10	.375	27	19	4	3	0	126	134	9.6	12	54	3.9	50	3.6	4.64	80	.277	.345	-14	-13	102	96	-1.5	-2	-2	-1.6
1981	StL-N	2	0	1.000	22	1	0	0	0	37	37	9.0	2	18	4.4	14	3.4	4.62	76	.266	.350	-5	-5	101	89	1.0	0	1	-0.3
Total	5	23	26	.469	116	61	10	5	2	457	497	9.8	54	190	3.7	215	4.2	4.65	85	.280	.346	-44	-35	104	101	-1.0	-2	-4	-3.6
■ LOU SYLVESTER	Sylvester, Louis J. b: 2/14/1855, Springfield, Ill. BR/TR, 5'3", 165 lbs. Deb: 4/18/1884																												
1884	Cin-U	0	1	.000	6	1	1	0	1	33	32	8.7	0	6	1.6	7	1.9	3.55	89	.260	.294	-2	-1	105	78	-0.4	1	0	0.0
■ LEFTY TABER	Taber, Edward Timothy b: 1/11/1900, Rock Island, Ill. d: 11/5/83, Lincoln, Neb. BL/TL, 6', 180 lbs. Deb: 9/04/26																												
1926	Phi-N	0	0	—	6	0	0	0	0	8	8	9.0	0	5	5.6	0	0.0	7.88	52	.242	.375	-4	-3	107	48	0.0	-0	0	-0.2
1927	Phi-N	0	1	.000	3	1	0	0	0	3	8	24.0	0	5	15.0	0	0.0	21.00	19	.533	.560	-6	-6	100	81	-0.4	-0	0	-0.4
Total	2	0	1	.000	9	1	0	0	0	11	16	13.1	0	10	8.2	0	0.0	11.45	35	.333	.446	-9	-9	105	57	-0.4	-0	0	-0.6
■ JOHN TABER	Taber, John Pardon b: 6/28/1868, Acushnet, Mass. d: 2/21/40, Boston, Mass. BR/TR, 5'8", Deb: 4/30/1890																												
1890	Bos-N	0	1	.000	2	1	1	0	1	13	11	7.6	0	8	5.5	3	2.1	4.15	92	.244	.358	-1	-0	108	73	-0.4	-1	0	0.0
■ JOHN TAFF	Taff, John Gallatin b: 6/3/1890, Austin, Tex. d: 5/15/61, Houston, Tex. BR/TR, 6', 170 lbs. Deb: 5/11/13																												
1913	Phi-A	0	1	.000	7	1	0	0	1	18	22	11.0	0	5	2.5	9	4.5	6.50	42	.293	.338	-7	-8	93	54	-0.4	-0	0	-0.6
■ DOUG TAITT	Taitt, Douglas John "Poco" b: 8/3/02, Bay City, Mich. d: 12/12/70, Portland, Ore. BL/TR, 6', 176 lbs. Deb: 4/10/28																												
1928	Bos-A	0	0	—	1	0	0	0	0	1	2	18.0	0	2	18.0	1	9.0	27.00	15	.400	.571	-3	-3	101	46	0.0	0	0	-0.1
■ FRED TALBOT	Talbot, Frederick Lealand "Bubby" b: 6/28/41, Washington, D.C. BR/TR, 6'2", 195 lbs. Deb: 9/28/63																												
1963	Chi-A	0	0	—	1	0	0	0	0	3	2	6.0	0	4	12.0	2	6.0	3.00	124	.222	.462	0	0	102	179	0.0	-0	0	0.0
1964	Chi-A	4	5	.444	17	12	3	2	0	75	83	10.0	7	20	2.4	34	4.1	3.72	91	.288	.338	-1	-3	93	119	-1.1	3	-1	0.0
1965	KC-A	10	12	.455	39	33	2	1	0	198	188	8.5	25	86	3.9	117	5.3	4.14	83	.251	.327	-15	-15	100	100	1.8	3	-1	-1.2
1966	KC-A	4	4	.500	11	11	0	0	0	68	65	8.6	6	28	3.7	37	4.9	4.76	69	.248	.322	-10	-11	95	79	0.3	1	0	-1.0
	NY-A	7	7	.500	23	19	3	0	0	124	123	8.9	16	45	3.3	48	3.5	4.14	78	.262	.325	-10	-13	94	105	0.8	1	-0	-1.2
	Yr	11	11	.500	34	30	3	0	0	192	188	8.8	22	73	3.4	85	4.0	4.36	74	.256	.322	-20	-24	94	105	1.1	1	-0	-2.2
1967	NY-A	6	8	.429	29	22	2	0	0	139	132	8.5	20	54	3.5	61	3.9	4.21	73	.252	.318	-15	-17	96	102	-0.2	3	2	-1.2
1968	NY-A	1	9	.100	29	11	1	0	0	99	89	8.1	6	42	3.8	67	6.1	3.36	89	.241	.316	-4	-4	101	100	-4.0	1	1	-0.2
1969	NY-A	0	0	—	8	0	0	0	0	12	13	9.8	1	6	4.5	7	5.3	5.25	66	.283	.339	-2	-2	96	89	0.0	-0	0	-0.2
	Sea-A	5	8	.385	25	16	1	1	0	115	125	9.8	12	41	3.2	67	5.2	4.15	88	.278	.340	-7	-7	100	106	-0.1	2	0	-0.4
	Oak-A	1	2	.333	12	2	0	0	1	19	22	10.4	2	7	3.3	9	4.3	5.21	64	.297	.354	-3	-4	91	94	-0.5	0	0	-0.3
	Yr	6	10	.375	45	18	1	1	1	146	160	9.9	15	54	3.3	83	5.1	4.38	82	.277	.335	-12	-13	99	94	-0.6	2	0	-0.9
1970	Oak-A	0	1	.000	1	0	0	0	0	2	2	9.0	1	1	4.5	0	0.0	9.00	39	.286	.375	-1	-1	96	90	-0.4	0	0	0.0
Total	8	38	56	.404	195	126	12	4	1	854	844	8.9	96	334	3.5	449	4.7	4.12	80	.260	.328	-68	-77	97	102	-3.4	14	2	-5.7
■ ROY TALCOTT	Talcott, Le Roy Everett b: 1/16/20, Brookline, Mass. BR/TR, 6'1.5", 180 lbs. Deb: 6/24/43																												
1943	Bos-N	0	0	—	1	0	0	0	0	1	1	9.0	0	2	18.0	0	0.0	18.00	20	.333	.600	-2	-2	109	53	0.0	0	0	0.0
■ VITO TAMULIS	Tamulis, Vitautis Casimirus b: 7/11/11, Cambridge, Mass. d: 5/5/74, Nashville, Tenn. BL/TL, 5'9", 170 lbs. Deb: 9/25/34																												
1934	NY-A	1	0	1.000	1	1	1	1	0	9	7	7.0	0	1	1.0	5	5.0	0.00	—	.219	.235	4	4	93	0	0.5	0	0	0.5
1935	NY-A	10	5	.667	30	19	9	3	1	161	178	10.0	7	55	3.1	57	3.2	4.08	98	.280	.333	7	-1	90	101	1.4	4	-1	0.1
1938	StL-A	0	3	.000	3	2	0	0	0	15	26	15.6	2	10	6.0	11	6.6	7.80	63	.366	.444	-5	-5	103	108	-1.4	1	0	-0.2
	Bro-N	12	6	.667	38	18	9	0	2	160	181	10.2	11	40	2.3	70	3.9	3.82	95	.288	.328	-1	-3	96	110	3.7	-2	-2	-0.7
1939	Bro-N	9	8	.529	39	17	8	1	4	159	177	10.0	10	45	2.5	83	4.7	4.36	95	.287	.334	-8	-4	106	98	-0.2	-1	0	-0.3
1940	Bro-N	8	5	.615	41	12	4	1	2	154	147	8.6	5	34	2.0	55	3.2	3.10	132	.244	.286	13	17	106	88	0.7	-1	-1	1.6
1941	Phi-N	0	1	.000	6	1	0	0	0	12	21	15.8	1	7	5.3	5	3.8	9.00	41	.382	.453	-7	-7	103	93	-0.4	-0	0	-0.6
	Bro-N	0	0	—	12	0	0	0	1	22	21	8.6	1	10	4.1	8	3.3	3.68	98	.244	.316	-0	-0	99	90	0.0	-1	0	0.0
	Yr	0	1	.000	18	1	0	0	1	34	42	11.1	2	17	4.5	13	3.4	5.56	66	.296	.364	-7	-7	100	90	-0.4	-0	0	-0.6
Total	6	40	28	.588	170	70	31	6	10	692	758	9.9	37	202	2.6	294	3.8	3.97	101	.278	.326	3	2	100	98	4.3	-1	-2	0.4
■ FRANK TANANA	Tanana, Frank Daryl b: 7/3/53, Detroit, Mich. BL/TL, 6'2", 180 lbs. Deb: 9/09/73																												
1973	Cal-A	2	2	.500	4	4	2	1	0	26	20	6.9	2	8	2.8	22	7.6	3.12	118	.200	.259	2	2	96	57	0.0	0	0	0.2
1974	Cal-A	14	19	.424	39	35	12	4	0	269	262	8.8	27	77	2.6	180	6.0	3.11	108	.255	.308	15	8	93	113	0.2	0	0	0.8
1975	Cal-A	16	9	.640	34	33	16	5	0	257	211	7.4	21	73	2.6	**269**	**9.4**	2.63	138	.226	.283	33	29	96	104	4.8	0	3	3.4
1976	Cal-A	19	10	.655	34	34	23	2	0	288	212	6.6	24	73	2.3	261	8.2	2.44	134	.203	**.257**	35	27	93	87	5.7	0	2	3.2
1977	Cal-A	15	9	.625	31	31	20	**7**	0	241	201	7.5	19	61	2.3	205	7.7	**2.54**	152	.227	.282	41	35	95	106	4.1	0	1	3.9
1978	Cal-A	18	12	.600	33	33	10	4	0	239	239	9.0	26	60	2.3	137	5.2	3.65	105	.258	.304	3	5	101	98	2.4	0	-2	0.2
1979	Cal-A	7	5	.583	18	17	2	1	0	90	93	9.3	9	25	2.5	46	4.6	3.90	99	.264	.314	3	-0	92	96	0.6	0	-1	0.0
1980	Cal-A	11	12	.478	32	31	7	0	0	204	223	9.8	18	45	2.0	113	5.0	4.15	94	.277	.317	-2	-5	97	93	1.6	0	-1	-0.5
1981	Bos-A	4	10	.286	24	23	5	2	0	141	142	9.1	17	43	2.7	78	5.0	4.02	96	.265	.317	-6	-2	106	102	-3.5	0	1	-0.1
1982	Tex-A	7	18	.280	30	30	7	0	0	194	199	9.2	16	55	2.6	87	4.0	4.22	91	.264	.314	-3	-8	94	89	-4.0	0	-0	-0.7
1983	Tex-A	7	9	.438	29	22	3	0	0	159	144	8.2	14	49	2.8	108	6.1	3.17	130	.240	.300	16	17	101	103	-0.6	0	3	2.0
1984	Tex-A	15	15	.500	35	35	9	1	0	246	234	8.6	30	81	3.0	141	5.2	3.26	124	.245	.305	20	21	101	110	2.2	0	1	2.3
1985	Tex-A	2	7	.222	13	13	0	0	0	78	89	10.3	15	23	2.7	52	6.0	5.88	78	.287	.332	-15	-11	110	89	-1.9	0	0	-1.0
	Det-A	10	7	.588	20	20	4	0	0	137	131	8.6	13	34	2.2	107	7.0	3.35	131	.250	.295	12	16	106	101	1.3	0	1	1.7
	Yr	12	14	.462	33	33	4	0	0	215	220	9.2	28	57	2.4	159	6.7	4.27	104	.262	.308	-3	4	107	101	-0.6	0	1	0.7
1986	Det-A	12	9	.571	32	31	3	1	0	188	196	9.4	23	65	3.1	119	5.7	4.16	95	.268	.325	0	-4	95	103	0.9	0	1	-0.2
1987	Det-A	15	10	.600	34	34	5	3	0	219	216	8.9	27	56	2.3	146	6.0	3.90	110	.256	.300	14	9	96	97	0.0	0	1	0.9
1988	Det-A	14	11	.560	32	32	2	0	0	203	213	9.4	25	64	2.8	127	5.6	4.21	89	.267	.321	-5	-11	94	100	0.5	0	1	-0.9
Total	16	188	174	.519	474	458	130	31	0	3179	3025	8.6	326	892	2.5	2198	6.2	3.49	110	.249	.301	164	124	97	100	14.3	0	11	15.2
■ JESSE TANNEHILL	Tannehill, Jesse Niles "Powder" b: 7/14/1874, Dayton, Ky. d: 9/22/56, Dayton, Ky. BB/TL, 5'8", 150 lbs. Deb: 6/17/1894 C																												
1894	Cin-N	1	0	1.000	5	1	1	0	1	29	37	11.5	1	16	5.0	7	2.2	7.14	76	.333	.417	-6	-6	102	76	0.5	-2	0	-0.5
1897	Pit-N	9	9	.500	21	16	11	1	1	142	172	10.9	1	24	1.5	40	2.5	4.25	102	.322	.351	1	1	100	87	0.8	2	0	0.1
1898	Pit-N	25	13	.658	43	38	34	5	2	327	338	9.3	2	63	1.7	93	2.6	2.94	120	.288	.325	24	22	98	98	7.7	7	4	3.4
1899	Pit-N	24	14	.632	40	35	32	3	1	313	354	10.2	4	51	1.5	61	1.8	2.73	138	.309	.338	39	36	98	121	5.8	5	4	4.4
1900	Pit-N	20	6	.769	29	27	23	2	0	234	247	9.5	3	43	1.7	50	1.9	2.88	129	.294	.328	21	22	101	105	6.7	7	0	3.0

YEAR	TM/L	W	L	PCT	G	GS	CG	SHO	SV	IP	H	H/G	HR	BB	BB/G	SO	SO/G	ERA	/A	OAVG	OOBP	PR	/A	PF	CPI	WAT	PB	PD	TPI
1901	Pit-N	18	10	.643	32	30	25	4	1	252	240	8.6	1	36	1.3	118	4.2	**2.18**	146	.275	.310	32	28	96	114	0.0	5	-4	3.1
1902	Pit-N	20	6	.769	26	24	23	2	0	231	203	7.9	0	25	1.0	100	3.9	1.95	140	.261	.293	21	20	98	95	1.7	7	-0	3.6
1903	NY-A	15	15	.500	32	31	22	2	0	240	258	9.7	3	34	1.3	106	4.0	3.26	90	.297	.324	-8	-8	100	97	-1.2	5	2	0.1
1904	Bos-A	21	11	.656	33	31	30	4	0	282	256	8.2	5	33	1.1	116	3.7	2.04	129	.264	.289	17	18	101	111	2.0	3	3	3.0
1905	Bos-A	22	9	.710	37	32	27	6	0	272	238	7.9	7	59	2.0	113	3.7	2.48	107	.259	.303	5	5	100	101	**7.1**	6	2	1.5
1906	Bos-A	13	11	.542	27	26	18	2	0	196	207	9.5	9	39	1.8	82	3.8	3.17	88	.297	.334	-10	-8	104	108	4.4	6	0	-0.1
1907	Bos-A	6	7	.462	18	16	10	2	1	131	131	9.0	3	20	1.4	29	2.0	2.47	106	.285	.314	1	2	103	111	0.8	1	0	0.4
1908	Bos-A	0	0	—	1	1	0	0	0	5	4	7.2	0	3	5.4	2	3.6	3.60	64	.200	.304	-1	-1	97	60	0.0	0	0	0.0
	Was-A	2	4	.333	10	9	5	0	0	72	77	9.6	0	23	2.9	14	1.8	3.75	62	.278	.346	-11	-12	97	98	-0.7	2	1	-1.1
	Yr	2	4	.333	11	10	5	0	0	77	81	9.5	0	26	3.0	16	1.9	3.74	62	.273	.343	-12	-12	97	98	-0.7	0	2	-1.1
1909	Was-A	1	1	.500	3	2	2	1	0	21	19	8.1	1	5	2.1	8	3.4	3.43	69	.268	.325	-2	-2	96	92	0.3	0	1	-0.2
1911	Cin-N	0	0	—	1	0	0	0	0	4	6	13.5	0	3	6.8	1	2.3	6.75	46	.316	.409	-1	-2	92	84	0.0	-0	0	-0.1
Total	15	197	116	.629	358	319	263	34	7	2751	2787	9.1	40	477	1.6	940	3.1	2.79	114	.286	.321	122	117	100	104	35.9	55	13	20.6
■ **BRUCE TANNER** Tanner, Bruce Matthew b: 12/9/61, New Castle, Pa. BL/TR, 6'3", 220 lbs. Deb: 6/12/85																													
1985	Chi-A	1	2	.333	10	4	0	0	0	27	34	11.3	1	13	4.3	9	3.0	5.33	78	.309	.383	-4	-4	100	101	-0.5	0	1	-0.2
■ **AL TATE** Tate, Alvin Walter b: 7/1/18, Coleman, Okla. BR/TR, 6', 180 lbs. Deb: 9/27/46																													
1946	Pit-N	0	1	.000	2	1	1	0	0	9	8	8.0	0	7	7.0	2	2.0	5.00	72	.267	.385	-2	-1	106	90	-0.4	0	0	0.0
■ **RANDY TATE** Tate, Randall Lee b: 10/23/52, Florence, Ala. BR/TR, 6'3", 190 lbs. Deb: 4/14/75																													
1975	NY-N	5	13	.278	26	23	2	0	0	138	121	7.9	8	86	5.6	99	6.5	4.43	78	.240	.350	-12	-15	95	86	-4.2	-4	0	-1.9
■ **KEN TATUM** Tatum, Kenneth Ray b: 4/25/44, Alexandria, La. BR/TR, 6'2", 205 lbs. Deb: 5/28/69																													
1969	Cal-A	7	2	.778	45	0	0	0	22	86	51	5.3	1	39	4.1	65	6.8	1.36	269	.172	.275	**22**	**22**	101	113	2.8	4	-0	2.7
1970	Cal-A	7	4	.636	62	0	0	0	17	89	68	6.9	12	26	2.6	50	5.1	2.93	116	.208	.272	8	5	92	94	1.3	1	0	0.6
1971	Bos-A	2	4	.333	36	1	0	0	9	54	50	8.3	3	25	4.2	21	3.5	4.17	88	.255	.353	-4	-3	105	98	-1.0	2	0	0.0
1972	Bos-A	0	2	.000	22	0	0	0	4	29	32	9.9	3	15	4.7	15	4.7	3.10	104	.283	.368	-0	0	105	162	-0.9	0	-0	0.0
1973	Bos-A	0	0	—	1	0	0	0	0	4	6	13.5	2	3	6.8	0	0.0	9.00	45	.462	.500	-2	-2	105	144	0.0	0	-0	-0.1
1974	Chi-A	0	0	—	10	1	0	0	0	21	23	9.9	3	9	3.9	5	2.1	4.71	79	.274	.340	-3	-2	102	98	0.0	0	1	-0.1
Total	6	16	12	.571	176	2	0	0	52	283	230	7.3	24	117	3.7	156	5.0	2.93	121	.224	.309	20	20	99	108	2.2	7	0	3.1
■ **WALT TAUSCHER** Tauscher, Walter Edward b: 11/22/01, La Salle, Ill. BR/TR, 6'1", 186 lbs. Deb: 4/19/28																													
1928	Pit-N	0	0	—	17	0	0	0	1	29	28	8.7	0	12	3.7	7	2.2	4.97	84	.280	.347	-3	-3	105	82	0.0	-0	-0	-0.2
1931	Was-A	1	0	1.000	6	0	0	0	0	12	24	18.0	2	4	3.0	5	3.8	7.50	57	.429	.452	-4	-4	98	134	0.5	0	2	-0.2
Total	2	1	0	1.000	23	0	0	0	1	41	52	11.4	2	16	3.5	12	2.6	5.71	74	.333	.382	-7	-7	103	98	0.5	-0	1	-0.4
■ **ARLAS TAYLOR** Taylor, Arlas Walter "Lefty" or "Foxy" b: 3/16/1896, Warick County, Ind d: 9/10/58, Dade City, Fla. BR/TL, 5'11", Deb: 9/15/21																													
1921	Phi-A	0	1	.000	1	1	0	0	0	2	7	31.5	1	2	9.0	1	4.5	22.50	20	.636	.600	-4	-4	107	104	-0.4	0	0	-0.2
■ **BEN TAYLOR** Taylor, Benjamin Harrison b: 4/2/1889, Paoli, Ind. d: 11/3/46, Martin County, Ind. TR , 5'11", 163 lbs. Deb: 6/28/12																													
1912	Cin-N	0	0	—	2	0	0	0	0	6	9	13.5	0	3	4.5	2	3.0	3.00	106	.346	.433	0	0	93	205	0.0	0	0	0.0
■ **BRUCE TAYLOR** Taylor, Bruce Bell b: 4/16/53, Holden, Mass. BR/TR, 6', 178 lbs. Deb: 8/05/77																													
1977	Det-A	1	0	1.000	19	0	0	0	2	29	23	7.1	2	10	3.1	19	5.9	3.41	125	.219	.288	2	3	105	78	0.5	0	0	0.3
1978	Det-A	0	0	—	1	0	0	0	0	1	0	0.0	0	0	0.0	0	0.0	0.00	—	.000	.000	0	0	107	0	0.0	0	0	0.0
1979	Det-A	1	2	.333	10	0	0	0	0	19	16	7.6	1	7	3.3	8	3.8	4.74	86	.242	.309	-1	-1	96	75	-0.5	0	0	0.0
Total	3	2	2	.500	30	0	0	0	2	49	39	7.2	3	17	3.1	27	5.0	3.86	109	.224	.292	1	2	102	75	0.0	0	0	0.3
■ **CHUCK TAYLOR** Taylor, Charles Gilbert b: 4/18/42, Murfreesboro, Tenn. BR/TR, 6'2", 195 lbs. Deb: 5/27/69																													
1969	StL-N	7	5	.583	27	13	5	1	0	127	108	7.7	8	30	2.1	62	4.4	2.55	139	.235	.282	15	14	99	108	0.6	1	-2	1.4
1970	StL-N	6	7	.462	56	7	1	1	8	124	116	8.4	5	31	2.3	64	4.6	3.12	138	.256	.298	13	16	106	102	0.0	-1	1	1.6
1971	StL-N	3	1	.750	43	1	0	0	3	71	72	9.1	7	25	3.2	46	5.8	3.55	98	.267	.323	-1	-1	100	113	0.9	0	0	0.0
1972	NY-N	0	0	—	20	0	0	0	2	31	44	12.8	2	9	2.6	9	2.6	5.52	60	.341	.378	-7	-8	96	104	0.0	-0	1	-0.6
	Mil-A	0	0	—	5	0	0	0	1	12	8	6.0	0	3	2.3	5	3.8	1.50	198	.200	.273	2	2	97	112	0.0	0	0	0.3
1973	Mon-N	2	0	1.000	8	0	0	0	0	20	17	7.6	3	2	0.9	10	4.5	1.80	213	.230	.247	4	5	105	151	1.0	-0	1	0.5
1974	Mon-N	6	2	.750	61	0	0	0	11	108	101	8.4	8	25	2.1	43	3.6	2.17	175	.256	.295	18	19	104	151	2.1	1	-0	2.1
1975	Mon-N	2	2	.500	54	0	0	0	6	74	72	8.8	6	24	2.9	29	3.5	3.53	113	.264	.315	1	4	109	106	0.1	-0	0	0.3
1976	Mon-N	2	3	.400	31	0	0	0	0	40	38	8.5	4	13	2.9	14	3.1	4.50	80	.273	.323	-4	-4	103	94	0.2	-0	-0	-0.4
Total	8	28	20	.583	305	21	6	2	31	607	576	8.5	43	162	2.4	282	4.2	3.07	123	.258	.304	40	48	103	115	4.9	0	1	5.2
■ **DORN TAYLOR** Taylor, Donald Clyde b: 8/11/58, Abington, Pa. BR/TR, 6'2", 180 lbs. Deb: 4/30/87																													
1987	Pit-N	2	3	.400	14	8	0	0	0	53	48	8.2	10	28	4.8	37	6.3	5.77	74	.247	.341	-10	-9	105	84	-0.4	-0	-0	-0.8
■ **ED TAYLOR** Taylor, Edgar Reuben "Rube" b: 3/23/1877, Palestine, Tex. d: 1/31/12, Dallas, Tex. Deb: 03																													
1903	StL-N	0	0	—	1	0	0	0	0	3	0	0.0	0	0	0.0	1	3.0	0.00	—	.000	.000	1	1	102	0	0.0	-0	0	0.1
■ **GARY TAYLOR** Taylor, Gary William b: 10/19/45, Detroit, Mich. BR/TR, 6'2", 190 lbs. Deb: 9/02/69																													
1969	Det-A	0	1	.000	7	0	0	0	0	10	10	9.0	2	6	5.4	3	2.7	5.40	69	.244	.340	-2	-2	102	87	-0.4	-0	0	-0.1
■ **HARRY TAYLOR** Taylor, Harry Evans b: 12/2/35, San Angelo, Tex. BR/TR, 6', 185 lbs. Deb: 9/17/57																													
1957	KC-A	0	0	—	2	0	0	0	0	9	11	11.0	0	4	4.0	4	4.0	3.00	128	.314	.400	1	1	102	170	0.0	0	-0	0.1
■ **HARRY TAYLOR** Taylor, James Harry b: 5/20/19, E.Glenn, Ind. BR/TR, 6'1", 175 lbs. Deb: 9/22/46																													
1946	Bro-N	0	0	—	4	0	0	0	1	5	5	9.0	0	1	1.8	6	10.8	3.60	95	.313	.333	-0	-0	100	110	0.0	0	0	0.0
1947	Bro-N	10	5	.667	33	20	10	2	1	162	130	**7.2**	10	83	4.6	58	3.2	3.11	134	**.225**	.324	17	19	103	106	1.2	-2	1	1.8
1948	Bro-N	2	7	.222	17	13	2	0	0	81	90	10.0	8	61	6.8	32	3.6	5.33	76	.288	.403	-12	-11	103	111	-2.6	1	2	-0.7
1950	Bos-A	2	0	1.000	3	2	2	1	0	19	13	6.2	0	8	3.8	8	3.8	1.42	358	.197	.284	7	8	111	136	1.0	0	0	0.9
1951	Bos-A	4	9	.308	31	8	1	0	2	81	100	11.1	6	42	4.7	22	2.4	5.78	76	.307	.378	-15	-13	106	95	-3.0	-3	1	-1.2
1952	Bos-A	1	0	1.000	2	1	1	0	0	10	6	5.4	1	6	5.4	1	0.9	1.80	218	.176	.317	2	2	107	164	0.5	0	0	0.3
Total	6	19	21	.475	90	44	16	3	4	358	344	8.6	25	201	5.1	127	3.2	4.10	103	.258	.354	-1	5	104	108	-2.9	-3	4	1.1
■ **JACK TAYLOR** Taylor, John Budd "Brewery Jack" b: 5/23/1873, W.New Brighton, N.Y. d: 2/7/1900, Staten Island, N.Y. 6'1", 190 lbs. Deb: 9/16/1891																													
1891	NY-N	0	1	.000	1	1	1	0	0	8	4	4.5	1	3	3.4	3	3.4	1.13	276	.159	.248	2	2	93	122	-0.4	0	0	0.2
1892	Phi-N	1	0	1.000	3	3	2	0	0	26	28	9.7	2	10	3.5	7	2.4	1.38	244	.288	.355	5	6	103	297	0.5	-0	0	0.5
1893	Phi-N	10	9	.526	25	16	14	0	1	170	189	10.0	8	77	4.1	41	2.2	4.24	108	.297	.373	8	7	98	106	-0.5	-2	0	0.4
1894	Phi-N	23	13	.639	41	34	31	1	1	298	347	10.5	13	96	2.9	76	2.3	4.08	122	.313	.368	42	30	94	105	4.4	9	3	3.2
1895	Phi-N	26	14	.650	41	37	33	1	1	335	403	10.8	7	83	2.2	93	2.5	4.49	105	.318	.360	11	8	98	92	3.7	7	5	1.7
1896	Phi-N	20	21	.488	45	41	35	1	1	359	459	11.5	17	112	2.8	97	2.4	4.79	93	.334	.384	-17	-13	102	100	0.6	-7	4	-1.2
1897	Phi-N	16	20	.444	40	37	35	2	2	317	376	10.7	5	76	2.2	88	2.5	4.23	98	.317	.359	3	-3	96	91	1.2	2	4	0.2
1898	StL-N	15	29	.341	**50**	47	**42**	0	1	**397**	465	10.5	14	83	1.9	89	2.0	3.90	101	.315	.351	-13	2	110	98	3.3	3	9	1.5
1899	Cin-N	9	10	.474	24	18	15	2	2	168	197	10.6	7	41	2.2	34	1.8	4.13	98	.317	.359	-5	-1	105	96	-1.4	-1	0	0.0
Total	9	120	117	.506	270	234	208	7	9	2078	2468	10.7	74	581	2.5	528	2.3	4.23	104	.317	.364	37	44	101	100	11.4	11	24	6.5
■ **JACK TAYLOR** Taylor, John W. b: 1/14/1874, New Straightsville, Ohio d: 3/4/38, Columbus, Ohio BR/TR, 5'10", 170 lbs. Deb: 9/25/1898																													
1898	Chi-N	5	0	1.000	5	5	5	0	0	41	32	7.0	0	10	2.2	11	2.4	2.20	167	.234	.287	6	7	102	79	2.5	1	0	0.8
1899	Chi-N	18	21	.462	41	39	39	1	0	355	380	9.6	6	84	2.1	67	1.7	3.78	98	.297	.341	3	-4	96	86	-2.2	10	2	0.7
1900	Chi-N	10	17	.370	28	26	25	2	1	222	226	9.2	4	58	2.4	57	2.3	2.55	137	.286	.335	28	23	94	122	-3.1	3	0	2.4
1901	Chi-N	13	19	.406	33	31	30	0	0	276	341	11.1	5	44	1.4	68	2.2	3.36	101	.330	.364	-1	1	103	120	0.8	1	2	0.3
1902	Chi-N	23	11	.676	36	33	33	7	1	325	271	7.5	2	43	1.2	83	2.3	**1.33**	**199**	.250	**.285**	**52**	**48**	95	129	**7.2**	4	4	**6.0**
1903	Chi-N	21	14	.600	37	33	33	1	1	312	277	8.0	2	57	1.6	83	2.4	2.45	125	.262	.303	28	21	94	86	0.3	5	0	2.1
1904	StL-N	20	19	.513	41	39	**39**	2	1	352	297	7.6	5	82	2.1	103	2.6	2.22	121	.254	.310	20	18	99	100	1.3	4	1	2.1

YEAR	TM/L	W	L	PCT	G	GS	CG	SHO	SV	IP	H	H/G	HR	BB	BB/G	SO	SO/G	ERA	/A	OAVG	OOBP	PR	/A	PF	CPI	WAT	PB	PD	TPI
1905	StL-N	15	21	.417	37	34	34	3	1	309	302	8.8	10	85	2.5	102	3.0	3.44	83	.285	.345	-15	-20	95	95	1.5	4	-2	-2.2
1906	StL-N	8	9	.471	17	17	17	1	0	155	133	7.7	3	47	2.7	27	1.6	2.15	127	.261	.332	8	10	104	120	1.8	1	0	1.2
	Chi-N	12	3	.800	17	16	15	2	0	147	116	7.1	1	39	2.4	34	2.1	1.84	142	.245	.310	13	13	99	110	1.3	3	-0	1.4
	Yr	20	12	.625	34	33	32	3	0	302	249	7.4	4	86	2.6	61	1.8	2.00	134	.252	.315	21	23	102	110	3.1	1	0	2.6
1907	Chi-N	7	5	.583	18	13	8	0	0	123	127	9.3	3	33	2.4	22	1.6	3.29	76	.296	.348	-11	-11	102	96	-1.0	0	1	-1.0
Total	10	152	139	.522	310	286	278	19	5	2617	2502	8.6	41	582	2.0	657	2.3	2.67	114	.277	.326	132	108	97	105	10.4	35	7	13.8

■ DUMMY TAYLOR Taylor, Luther Haden b: 2/21/1875, Oskaloosa, Kan. d: 8/22/58, Jacksonville, Ill. BR/TR, 6'1", 160 lbs. Deb: 8/27/00

YEAR	TM/L	W	L	PCT	G	GS	CG	SHO	SV	IP	H	H/G	HR	BB	BB/G	SO	SO/G	ERA	/A	OAVG	OOBP	PR	/A	PF	CPI	WAT	PB	PD	TPI
1900	NY-N	4	3	.571	11	7	6	0	0	62	74	10.7	0	24	3.5	16	2.3	2.47	149	.320	.384	8	8	99	169	0.9	-1	0	0.6
1901	NY-N	18	27	.400	**45**	43	37	4	0	353	377	9.6	8	112	2.9	136	3.5	3.19	99	.298	.362	5	-1	95	116	1.1	-7	0	0.0
1902	Cle-A	1	3	.250	4	4	4	1	0	34	37	9.8	0	8	2.1	8	2.1	1.59	216	.302	.345	7	7	96	207	-0.9	-1	1	0.8
	NY-N	8	15	.348	26	25	18	0	0	201	194	8.7	4	55	2.5	87	3.9	2.28	127	.279	.339	11	14	104	126	-0.1	-5	-1	1.4
1903	NY-N	13	13	.500	33	31	18	1	0	245	306	11.2	6	89	3.3	94	3.5	4.22	80	.333	.394	-26	-23	103	107	-2.6	-2	-1	-2.1
1904	NY-N	21	15	.583	37	36	29	5	0	296	231	7.0	6	75	2.3	138	4.2	2.34	116	.239	.300	13	12	100	86	-3.4	-1	3	1.6
1905	NY-N	16	9	.640	32	28	18	4	0	213	200	8.5	5	51	2.2	91	3.8	2.66	108	.277	.332	8	5	96	109	-0.9	-1	1	0.6
1906	NY-N	17	9	.654	31	27	13	2	0	213	186	7.9	4	57	2.4	91	3.8	2.20	117	.263	.323	10	9	97	114	0.9	1	-2	0.8
1907	NY-N	11	7	.611	28	21	11	3	1	171	145	7.6	1	46	2.4	56	2.9	2.42	106	.257	.317	1	3	104	89	1.6	-1	-1	0.2
1908	NY-N	8	5	.615	27	15	6	1	2	128	127	8.9	5	34	2.4	50	3.5	2.32	101	.290	.347	0	0	100	139	-0.1	2	-0	0.0
Total	9	117	106	.525	274	237	160	21	3	1916	1877	8.8	39	551	2.6	767	3.6	2.75	106	.283	.343	38	34	99	113	-3.5	-16	0	3.9

■ WILEY TAYLOR Taylor, Philip Wiley b: 3/18/1888, Wamego, Kan. d: 7/8/54, Westmoreland, Kan. BR/TR, 6'1", 175 lbs. Deb: 9/06/11

YEAR	TM/L	W	L	PCT	G	GS	CG	SHO	SV	IP	H	H/G	HR	BB	BB/G	SO	SO/G	ERA	/A	OAVG	OOBP	PR	/A	PF	CPI	WAT	PB	PD	TPI
1911	Det-A	0	2	.000	3	2	1	0	0	19	18	8.5	0	10	4.7	9	4.3	3.79	95	.247	.345	-1	-0	107	80	-0.9	-1	-0	0.0
1912	Chi-A	0	1	.000	3	3	0	0	0	20	21	9.4	0	14	6.3	4	1.8	4.95	67	.309	.427	-4	-4	99	107	-0.4	-1	0	-0.2
1913	StL-A	0	2	.000	5	4	1	0	0	32	33	9.3	0	16	4.5	12	3.4	4.78	60	.280	.366	-7	-7	98	79	-0.9	-1	0	-0.5
1914	StL-A	2	5	.286	16	8	2	1	0	50	41	7.4	0	25	4.5	20	3.6	3.42	80	.209	.305	-4	-4	100	56	-1.3	-0	-0	-0.3
Total	4	2	10	.167	27	17	4	1	0	121	113	8.4	0	65	4.8	45	3.3	4.09	73	.248	.346	-15	-15	100	74	-3.5	-3	-0	-1.0

■ RON TAYLOR Taylor, Ronald Wesley b: 12/13/37, Toronto, Ont., Can. BR/TR, 6'1", 195 lbs. Deb: 4/11/62

YEAR	TM/L	W	L	PCT	G	GS	CG	SHO	SV	IP	H	H/G	HR	BB	BB/G	SO	SO/G	ERA	/A	OAVG	OOBP	PR	/A	PF	CPI	WAT	PB	PD	TPI
1962	Cle-A	2	2	.500	8	4	1	0	0	33	36	9.8	6	13	3.5	15	4.1	6.00	65	.281	.347	-7	-8	99	88	0.0	0	-0	-0.6
1963	StL-N	9	7	.563	54	9	2	0	11	133	119	8.1	10	30	2.0	91	6.2	2.84	122	.243	.283	7	9	106	105	-0.1	-3	-2	0.5
1964	StL-N	8	4	.667	63	2	0	0	7	101	109	9.7	15	33	2.9	69	6.1	4.63	85	.274	.324	-12	-8	111	99	1.4	-1	2	-0.6
1965	StL-N	2	1	.667	25	0	0	0	1	44	43	8.8	6	15	3.1	26	5.3	4.50	83	.261	.319	-5	-4	106	94	0.5	1	0	-0.2
	Hou-N	1	5	.167	32	1	0	0	4	58	68	10.6	5	16	2.5	37	5.7	6.36	51	.305	.350	-18	-20	91	79	-1.7	-1	-1	-2.2
	Yr	3	6	.333	57	1	0	0	5	102	111	9.8	11	31	2.7	63	5.6	5.56	62	.283	.335	-23	-24	97	79	-1.2	1	-1	-2.4
1966	Hou-N	2	3	.400	36	1	0	0	0	65	89	12.3	5	10	1.4	29	4.0	5.68	63	.333	.357	-15	-15	99	94	-0.2	0	-1	-1.6
1967	NY-N	4	6	.400	50	0	0	0	8	73	60	7.4	1	23	2.8	46	5.7	2.34	147	.230	.283	8	9	102	105	0.2	-1	0	0.9
1968	NY-N	1	5	.167	58	0	0	0	13	77	64	7.5	4	18	2.1	49	5.7	2.69	114	.228	.270	3	3	103	88	-1.8	-1	1	0.3
1969	NY-N	9	4	.692	59	0	0	0	13	76	61	7.2	7	24	2.8	42	5.0	2.72	131	.228	.287	7	7	99	111	1.4	0	0	0.8
1970	NY-N	5	4	.556	57	0	0	0	13	66	65	8.9	5	16	2.2	28	3.8	3.95	106	.265	.295	1	2	103	92	0.4	-0	0	0.2
1971	NY-N	2	2	.500	45	0	0	0	2	69	71	9.3	7	11	1.4	32	4.2	3.65	91	.269	.295	-1	-2	96	97	0.0	0	-0	-0.2
1972	SD-N	0	0	—	4	0	0	0	0	5	9	16.2	5	0	0.0	0	0.0	12.60	25	.375	.375	-5	-5	91	106	0.0	0	0	-0.4
Total	11	45	43	.511	491	17	3	0	72	800	794	8.9	76	209	2.4	464	5.2	3.93	91	.264	.307	-38	-32	102	97	0.1	-5	-1	-3.1

■ TERRY TAYLOR Taylor, Terry Derrell b: 7/28/64, Crestview, Fla. BR/TR, 6'1", 180 lbs. Deb: 8/19/88

YEAR	TM/L	W	L	PCT	G	GS	CG	SHO	SV	IP	H	H/G	HR	BB	BB/G	SO	SO/G	ERA	/A	OAVG	OOBP	PR	/A	PF	CPI	WAT	PB	PD	TPI
1988	Sea-A	0	1	.000	5	5	0	0	0	23	26	10.2	2	11	4.3	9	3.5	6.26	69	.295	.366	-6	-5	108	83	-0.4	0	-1	-0.4

■ PETE TAYLOR Taylor, Vernon Charles b: 11/26/27, Severn, Md. BR/TR, 6'1", 170 lbs. Deb: 5/02/52

YEAR	TM/L	W	L	PCT	G	GS	CG	SHO	SV	IP	H	H/G	HR	BB	BB/G	SO	SO/G	ERA	/A	OAVG	OOBP	PR	/A	PF	CPI	WAT	PB	PD	TPI
1952	StL-A	0	0	—	1	0	0	0	0	2	4	18.0	0	3	13.5	0	0.0	13.50	27	.500	.636	-2	-2	100	97	0.0	0	0	-0.1

■ BILLY TAYLOR Taylor, William Henry "Bollicky Bill" b: 1855, Washington, D.C. d: 5/14/1900, Jacksonville, Fla. TR, 5'11.5", 204 lbs. Deb: 1881

YEAR	TM/L	W	L	PCT	G	GS	CG	SHO	SV	IP	H	H/G	HR	BB	BB/G	SO	SO/G	ERA	/A	OAVG	OOBP	PR	/A	PF	CPI	WAT	PB	PD	TPI
1881	Wor-N	0	1	.000	1	1	1	0	0	8	15	16.9	0	6	6.8	0	0.0	7.88	38	.412	.495	-5	-4	107	106	-0.3	-0	0	-0.4
	Cle-N	0	0	—	1	0	0	0	0	3	0	0.0	0	1	3.0	2	6.0	0.00	—	.000	.111	1	1	96	0	0.0	-0	0	0.0
	Yr	0	1	.000	2	1	1	0	0	11	15	12.3	0	7	5.7	2	1.6	5.73	51	.338	.428	-4	-3	104	0	-0.3	-0	0	-0.4
1882	Pit-a	0	1	.000	1	0	0	0	0	5	11	19.8	0	4	7.2	1	1.8	16.20	16	.443	.520	-8	-8	97	63	-0.4	0	0	-0.4
1883	Pit-a	4	7	.364	19	9	8	0	0	127	166	11.8	4	34	2.4	41	2.9	5.39	60	.321	.363	-29	-30	98	93	0.4	3	0	-2.4
1884	StL-U	25	4	.862	33	29	29	2	**4**	263	222	7.6	2	40	1.4	154	5.3	1.68	176	.234	.265	39	37	98	127	3.3	19	-1	**5.7**
	Phi-a	18	12	.600	30	30	30	1	0	260	232	8.0	3	44	1.5	130	4.5	2.53	145	.247	.281	21	33	113	107	1.4	2	2	3.7
1885	Phi-a	1	5	.167	6	6	6	0	0	52	68	11.8	0	9	1.6	11	1.9	3.29	101	.328	.356	-0	0	102	137	-1.9	-1	0	0.0
1886	Bal-a	1	6	.143	8	8	8	0	0	72	87	10.9	1	20	2.5	37	4.6	5.75	56	.309	.355	-18	-20	94	77	-2.1	2	0	-1.4
1887	Phi-a	1	0	1.000	1	1	1	0	0	9	10	10.0	1	7	7.0	0	0.0	3.00	143	.295	.416	1	1	100	200	0.5	-0	0	0.1
Total	7	50	36	.581	100	84	83	3	4	799	811	9.1	11	165	1.9	376	4.2	3.18	103	.271	.309	2	10	103	111	0.9	24	1	4.9

■ BUD TEACHOUT Teachout, Arthur John b: 2/27/04, Los Angeles, Cal. d: 5/11/85, Laguna Beach, Cal BR/TL, 6'2", 183 lbs. Deb: 5/12/30

YEAR	TM/L	W	L	PCT	G	GS	CG	SHO	SV	IP	H	H/G	HR	BB	BB/G	SO	SO/G	ERA	/A	OAVG	OOBP	PR	/A	PF	CPI	WAT	PB	PD	TPI
1930	Chi-N	11	4	.733	40	16	6	0	0	153	178	10.5	16	48	2.8	59	3.5	4.06	126	.296	.341	16	18	103	118	2.9	2	-0	1.8
1931	Chi-N	1	2	.333	27	3	1	0	0	61	79	11.7	6	28	4.1	14	2.1	5.75	63	.305	.364	-13	-14	94	94	-0.5	0	1	-1.2
1932	StL-N	0	0	—	1	0	0	0	0	1	2	18.0	0	0	0.0	0	0.0	0.00	—	.400	.400	0	0	101	0	0.0	0	0	0.0
Total	3	12	6	.667	68	19	7	0	0	215	259	10.8	22	76	3.2	73	3.1	4.52	103	.299	.348	3	4	100	111	2.4	2	1	0.6

■ WHITE WINGS TEBEAU Tebeau, George E. b: 12/26/1861, St.Louis, Mo. d: 2/4/23, Denver, Colo. BR/TR, 5'9", 175 lbs. Deb: 4/16/1887

YEAR	TM/L	W	L	PCT	G	GS	CG	SHO	SV	IP	H	H/G	HR	BB	BB/G	SO	SO/G	ERA	/A	OAVG	OOBP	PR	/A	PF	CPI	WAT	PB	PD	TPI
1887	Cin-a	0	1	.000	1	1	1	0	0	8	21	23.6	0	3	3.4	1	1.1	13.50	34	.497	.531	-8	-8	106	86	-0.4	0	0	-0.4
1890	Tol-a	0	0	—	1	0	0	0	0	5	9	16.2	0	5	9.0	0	0.0	9.00	44	.407	.516	-3	-3	102	102	0.0	0	0	-0.1
Total	2	0	1	.000	2	1	1	0	0	13	30	20.8	0	8	5.5	1	0.7	11.77	37	.466	.525	-11	-11	105	92	-0.4	1	0	-0.5

■ PATSY TEBEAU Tebeau, Oliver Wendell b: 12/5/1864, St.Louis, Mo. d: 5/15/18, St.Louis, Mo. BR/TR, 5'8", 163 lbs. Deb: 9/20/1887 M

YEAR	TM/L	W	L	PCT	G	GS	CG	SHO	SV	IP	H	H/G	HR	BB	BB/G	SO	SO/G	ERA	/A	OAVG	OOBP	PR	/A	PF	CPI	WAT	PB	PD	TPI
1896	Cle-N	0	0	—	1	0	0	0	0	0	1	—	0	0	—	0	—	—	—	1.000	1.000	0	0	108	0	0.0	0	0	0.0

■ AL TEDROW Tedrow, Allen Seymour b: 12/14/1891, Westerville, Ohio d: 1/23/58, Westerville, Ohio BR/TL, 6', 180 lbs. Deb: 9/15/14

YEAR	TM/L	W	L	PCT	G	GS	CG	SHO	SV	IP	H	H/G	HR	BB	BB/G	SO	SO/G	ERA	/A	OAVG	OOBP	PR	/A	PF	CPI	WAT	PB	PD	TPI
1914	Cle-A	1	2	.333	4	3	1	0	0	22	19	7.8	0	14	5.7	4	1.6	1.23	236	.235	.367	4	4	106	275	0.0	0	-0	0.5

■ KENT TEKULVE Tekulve, Kenton Charles b: 3/5/47, Cincinnati, Ohio BR/TR, 6'4", 180 lbs. Deb: 5/20/74

YEAR	TM/L	W	L	PCT	G	GS	CG	SHO	SV	IP	H	H/G	HR	BB	BB/G	SO	SO/G	ERA	/A	OAVG	OOBP	PR	/A	PF	CPI	WAT	PB	PD	TPI
1974	Pit-N	1	1	.500	8	0	0	0	0	9	12	12.0	1	5	5.0	6	6.0	6.00	58	.343	.409	-2	-2	97	117	0.0	0	1	-0.1
1975	Pit-N	1	2	.333	34	0	0	0	5	56	43	6.9	2	23	3.7	28	4.5	2.25	157	.215	.289	9	8	98	108	-0.5	-0	2	1.0
1976	Pit-N	5	3	.625	64	0	0	0	9	103	91	8.0	3	25	2.2	68	5.9	2.45	142	.241	.284	12	12	99	103	0.6	-1	2	1.4
1977	Pit-N	10	1	.909	72	0	0	0	7	103	89	7.8	5	33	2.9	59	5.2	3.06	130	.236	.291	10	11	102	91	4.3	0	4	1.5
1978	Pit-N	8	7	.533	**91**	0	0	0	31	135	115	7.7	5	55	3.7	77	5.1	2.33	161	.228	.300	**19**	21	105	116	-0.1	-1	3	2.5
1979	Pit-N	10	8	.556	**94**	0	0	0	31	134	109	7.3	5	49	3.3	75	5.0	2.75	141	.222	.291	15	17	104	89	-0.7	-0	2	1.9
1980	Pit-N	8	12	.400	78	0	0	0	21	93	96	9.3	6	40	3.9	47	4.5	3.39	110	.267	.337	2	3	103	117	-2.3	-1	1	0.3
1981	Pit-N	5	5	.500	45	0	0	0	3	65	61	8.4	1	17	2.4	34	4.7	2.49	135	.250	.295	7	6	96	110	0.5	-0	1	0.8
1982	Pit-N	12	8	.600	**85**	0	0	0	20	129	113	7.9	7	46	3.2	66	4.6	2.86	139	.237	.299	11	16	110	105	1.9	-1	2	1.7
1983	Pit-N	7	5	.583	76	0	0	0	18	99	78	7.1	1	36	3.3	52	4.7	1.64	228	.223	.286	22	23	103	142	0.9	-1	1	2.4
1984	Pit-N	3	9	.250	72	0	0	0	13	88	86	8.8	4	33	3.4	36	3.7	2.66	127	.262	.324	9	7	94	136	-2.8	-1	3	0.9
1985	Pit-N	0	0	—	3	0	0	0	0	3	7	21.0	1	5	15.0	4	12.0	18.00	21	.467	.571	-5	-5	104	90	0.0	0	0	-0.3
	Phi-N	4	10	.286	58	0	0	0	14	72	67	8.4	4	25	3.1	36	4.5	3.00	123	.246	.307	5	5	102	107	-2.7	-0	0	0.6
	Yr	4	10	.286	61	0	0	0	14	75	74	8.9	5	30	3.6	40	4.8	3.60	102	.258	.324	-0	1	102	107	-2.7	0	0	0.3
1986	Phi-N	11	5	.688	73	0	0	0	4	110	99	8.1	2	25	2.0	57	4.7	2.54	153	.240	.278	15	16	104	93	2.8	-0	0	1.7
1987	Phi-N	6	4	.600	**90**	0	0	0	3	105	96	8.2	8	29	2.5	60	5.1	3.09	139	.243	.289	12	14	105	99	1.1	0	1	1.5
1988	Phi-N	3	7	.300	70	0	0	0	4	80	87	9.8	3	22	2.5	43	4.8	3.60	99	.276	.320	-1	-0	103	104	-1.2	-0	1	0.0
Total	15	94	87	.519	1013	0	0	0	183	1384	1249	8.1	58	468	3.0	748	4.9	2.77	136	.242	.301	138	152	103	108	1.8	-7	22	17.8

YEAR	TM/L	W	L	PCT	G	GS	CG	SHO	SV	IP	H	H/G	HR	BB	BB/G	SO	SO/G	ERA	/A	OAVG	OOBP	PR	/A	PF	CPI	WAT	PB	PD	TPI
■ **TOM TELLMANN**	Tellmann, Thomas John b: 3/29/54, Warren, Pa. BR/TR, 6'3", 195 lbs. Deb: 6/09/79																												
1979	SD-N	0	0	—	1	0	0	0	0	3	7	21.0	1	0	0.0	1	3.0	15.00	24	.467	.467	-4	-4	97	77	0.0	-0	0	-0.2
1980	SD-N	3	0	1.000	6	2	2	0	1	22	23	9.4	0	8	3.3	9	3.7	1.64	207	.264	.326	5	4	94	193	1.5	-0	0	0.4
1983	Mil-A	9	4	.692	44	0	0	0	8	100	95	8.6	7	35	3.2	48	4.3	2.79	133	.259	.318	14	10	91	135	2.3	0	3	1.3
1984	Mil-A	6	3	.667	50	0	0	0	4	81	82	9.1	6	31	3.4	28	3.1	2.78	133	.272	.331	11	8	93	150	2.0	0	1	0.9
1985	Oak-A	0	0	—	11	0	0	0	0	21	33	14.1	3	9	3.9	8	3.4	5.14	75	.347	.406	-2	-3	93	140	0.0	0	0	-0.2
Total	5	18	7	.720	112	2	2	0	13	227	240	9.5	17	83	3.3	94	3.7	3.05	121	.277	.335	24	16	92	146	5.8	-0	4	2.2
■ **CHUCK TEMPLETON**	Templeton, Charles Sherman b: 6/1/32, Detroit, Mich. BR/TL, 6'3", 210 lbs. Deb: 9/09/55																												
1955	Bro-N	0	1	.000	4	0	0	0	0	5	5	9.0	2	5	9.0	3	5.4	10.80	38	.294	.458	-4	-4	101	88	-0.4	0	0	-0.3
1956	Bro-N	0	1	.000	6	2	0	0	0	16	20	11.3	2	10	5.6	8	4.5	6.75	56	.294	.375	-5	-5	100	82	-0.4	-0	-0	-0.5
Total	2	0	2	.000	10	2	0	0	0	21	25	10.7	4	15	6.4	11	4.7	7.71	50	.294	.394	-9	-9	100	83	-0.8	-0	-0	-0.8
■ **JOHN TENER**	Tener, John Kinley b: 7/25/1863, County Tyrone, Ireland d: 5/19/46, Pittsburgh, Pa. BR/TR, 6'4", 180 lbs. Deb: 1885																												
1888	Chi-N	7	5	.583	12	12	11	1	0	102	90	7.9	6	25	2.2	39	3.4	2.74	110	.250	.298	1	3	106	100	0.2	-0	0	0.3
1889	Chi-N	15	15	.500	35	30	28	1	0	287	302	9.5	16	105	3.3	105	3.3	3.64	109	.286	.350	12	10	98	108	-0.2	7	3	1.9
1890	Pit-P	3	11	.214	14	14	13	0	0	117	160	12.3	8	70	5.4	30	2.3	7.31	53	.338	.424	-40	-44	92	81	-3.9	1	0	-3.0
Total	3	25	31	.446	61	56	52	2	0	506	552	9.8	30	200	3.6	174	3.1	4.30	88	.292	.360	-26	-30	98	100	-3.9	7	3	-0.8
■ **JIM TENNANT**	Tennant, James Mc Donnell b: 3/3/07, Shepherdstown, W.Va d: 4/16/67, Trumbull, Conn. BR/TR, 6'1", 190 lbs. Deb: 9/28/29																												
1929	NY-N	0	0	—	1	0	0	0	0	1	1	9.0	0	0	0.0	1	9.0	0.00	—	.333	.333	1	1	97	0	0.0	0	0	0.0
■ **FRED TENNEY**	Tenney, Frederick b: 11/26/1871, Georgetown, Mass. d: 7/3/52, Boston, Mass. BL/TL, 5'9", 155 lbs. Deb: 6/16/1894 M																												
1905	Bos-N	0	0	—	1	0	0	0	0	2	5	22.5	0	1	4.5	0	0.0	4.50	68	.501	.547	-0	-0	102	245	0.0	0	0	0.0
■ **FRED TENNEY**	Tenney, Frederick Clay b: 7/9/1859, Marlboro, N.H. d: 6/15/19, Fall River, Mass. Deb: 4/28/1884																												
1884	Bos-U	3	1	.750	4	4	4	0	0	35	31	8.0	0	5	1.3	18	4.6	2.31	127	.242	.271	3	2	98	97	0.9	-2	0	-0.6
	WiL-U	0	1	.000	1	1	1	0	0	8	6	6.8	0	4	4.5	10	11.3	1.13	292	.213	.311	2	2	109	229	-0.4	-1	0	0.1
	Yr	3	2	.600	5	5	5	0	0	43	37	7.7	0	9	1.9	28	5.9	2.09	143	.237	.279	4	4	100	229	0.5	-2	0	-0.5
■ **BOB TERLECKI**	Terlecki, Robert Joseph b: 2/14/45, Trenton, N.J. BR/TR, 5'8", 185 lbs. Deb: 8/16/72																												
1972	Phi-N	0	0	—	9	0	0	0	0	13	16	11.1	2	10	6.9	5	3.5	4.85	70	.308	.400	-2	-2	99	138	0.0	0	0	-0.1
■ **GREG TERLECKY**	Terlecky, Gregory John b: 3/20/52, Culver City, Cal. BR/TR, 6'3", 200 lbs. Deb: 6/12/75																												
1975	StL-N	0	1	.000	20	0	0	0	0	30	38	11.4	4	12	3.6	13	3.9	4.50	83	.306	.355	-3	-2	103	120	-0.4	0	0	-0.1
■ **JEFF TERPKO**	Terpko, Jeffrey Michael b: 10/16/50, Sayre, Pa. BR/TR, 6', 180 lbs. Deb: 9/21/74																												
1974	Tex-A	0	0	—	3	0	0	0	0	7	6	7.7	0	4	5.1	3	3.9	1.29	271	.231	.333	2	2	96	222	0.0	0	-0	0.2
1976	Tex-A	3	3	.500	32	0	0	0	0	53	42	7.1	3	29	4.9	24	4.1	2.38	152	.223	.320	7	7	103	135	0.2	0	0	0.8
1977	Mon-N	0	1	.000	13	0	0	0	0	21	28	12.0	2	15	6.4	14	6.0	5.57	70	.346	.434	-4	-4	99	129	-0.4	-0	-0	-0.3
Total	3	3	4	.429	48	0	0	0	0	81	76	8.4	5	48	5.3	41	4.6	3.11	118	.258	.353	5	5	101	141	-0.2	-0	-1	0.7
■ **WALT TERRELL**	Terrell, Charles Walter b: 5/11/58, Jeffersonville, Ind BL/TR, 6'2", 205 lbs. Deb: 9/08/82																												
1982	NY-N	0	3	.000	3	3	0	0	0	21	22	9.4	2	14	6.0	8	3.4	3.43	105	.268	.371	0	0	100	142	-1.4	1	-0	0.1
1983	NY-N	8	8	.500	21	20	4	2	0	134	123	8.3	7	55	3.7	59	4.0	3.56	102	.251	.321	1	1	100	97	1.2	3	-0	0.4
1984	NY-N	11	12	.478	33	33	3	1	0	215	232	9.7	16	80	3.3	114	4.8	3.52	102	.282	.341	2	2	100	124	-1.7	-4	0	-0.1
1985	Det-A	15	10	.600	34	34	5	3	0	229	221	8.7	9	95	3.7	130	5.1	3.85	114	.255	.326	8	14	106	93	2.4	0	3	1.7
1986	Det-A	15	12	.556	34	33	9	2	0	217	199	8.3	30	98	4.1	93	3.9	4.56	87	.245	.327	-9	-15	95	91	0.6	0	2	-1.2
1987	Det-A	17	10	.630	35	35	10	1	0	245	254	9.3	30	94	3.5	143	5.3	4.04	106	.268	.332	12	6	96	110	1.0	0	-1	0.5
1988	Det-A	7	16	.304	29	29	11	1	0	206	199	8.7	20	78	3.4	84	3.7	3.98	94	.258	.321	-0	-6	94	101	-5.4	0	1	-0.4
Total	7	73	71	.507	189	187	42	10	0	1267	1250	8.9	114	514	3.7	631	4.5	3.94	101	.261	.329	14	4	98	104	-3.3	0	5	1.0
■ **JERRY TERRELL**	Terrell, Jerry Wayne b: 7/13/46, Waseca, Minn. BR/TR, 5'11", 165 lbs. Deb: 4/14/73																												
1979	KC-A	0	0	—	1	0	0	0	0	1	0	0.0	0	0	0.0	0	0.0	0.00	—	.000	.000	0	0	105	0	0.0	0	0	0.0
1980	KC-A	0	0	—	1	0	0	0	0	1	1	9.0	0	1	9.0	0	0.0	0.00	—	.250	.400	0	0	97	0	0.0	0	0	0.0
Total	2	0	0	—	2	0	0	0	0	2	1	4.5	0	1	4.5	0	0.0	0.00	—	.143	.250	1	1	101	0	0.0	0	0	0.0
■ **JOHN TERRY**	Terry, John Burchard b: 11/1/1879, Waterbury, Conn. d: 4/27/33, Kansas City, Mo. Deb: 9/17/02																												
1902	Det-A	0	1	.000	1	1	1	0	0	5	8	14.4	0	1	1.8	0	0.0	3.60	100	.389	.417	-0	-0	101	160	-0.4	-0	-0	0.0
1903	StL-A	1	1	.500	3	1	1	0	0	18	21	10.5	0	4	2.0	2	1.0	2.50	113	.315	.353	1	1	96	150	0.1	-1	-0	0.0
Total	2	1	2	.333	4	2	2	0	0	23	29	11.3	0	5	2.0	2	0.8	2.74	109	.332	.368	1	1	97	152	-0.3	-2	-1	0.0
■ **YANK TERRY**	Terry, Lancelot Yank b: 2/11/11, Bedford, Ind. d: 11/4/79, Bloomington, Ind. BR/TR, 6'1", 180 lbs. Deb: 8/03/40																												
1940	Bos-A	1	0	1.000	4	1	0	0	0	19	24	11.4	2	11	5.2	9	4.3	9.00	49	.304	.372	-10	-10	100	66	0.5	0	0	-0.7
1942	Bos-A	6	5	.545	20	11	3	0	1	85	82	8.7	5	43	4.6	37	3.9	3.92	94	.248	.336	-2	-2	100	97	-0.5	-1	-0	-0.3
1943	Bos-A	7	9	.438	30	22	7	0	1	164	147	8.1	8	63	3.5	63	3.5	3.51	98	.242	.308	-4	-1	104	89	-0.1	-3	0	-0.3
1944	Bos-A	6	10	.375	27	17	3	0	0	133	142	9.6	10	65	4.4	30	2.0	4.20	79	.276	.356	-11	-13	97	108	-2.1	2	0	-1.1
1945	Bos-A	0	4	.000	12	4	1	0	0	57	68	10.7	8	14	2.2	28	4.4	4.11	79	.296	.335	-5	-5	96	117	-1.9	-1	-1	-0.7
Total	5	20	28	.417	93	55	14	0	2	458	463	9.1	33	196	3.9	167	3.3	4.09	85	.263	.334	-32	-32	100	99	-4.1	-4	-0	-3.1
■ **RALPH TERRY**	Terry, Ralph Willard b: 1/9/36, Big Cabin, Okla. BR/TR, 6'3", 195 lbs. Deb: 8/06/56																												
1956	NY-A	1	2	.333	3	3	0	0	0	13	17	11.8	2	11	7.6	8	5.5	9.69	41	.347	.452	-8	-8	95	83	-0.6	-0	-0	-0.7
1957	NY-A	1	1	.500	7	2	1	1	0	21	18	7.7	1	8	3.4	7	3.0	3.00	114	.240	.306	2	1	90	102	-0.1	0	0	0.2
	KC-A	4	11	.267	21	19	3	1	0	131	119	8.2	15	47	3.2	80	5.5	3.37	114	.239	.306	6	7	102	102	-2.4	-2	0	0.5
	Yr	5	12	.294	28	21	4	2	0	152	137	8.1	16	55	3.3	87	5.2	3.32	114	.239	.306	8	8	100	102	-2.5	0	0	0.7
1958	KC-A	11	13	.458	40	33	8	3	2	217	217	9.0	29	61	2.5	134	5.6	4.23	95	.262	.309	-11	-5	107	94	-0.4	-1	-2	-0.6
1959	KC-A	2	4	.333	9	7	2	0	0	46	56	11.0	9	19	3.7	35	6.8	5.28	75	.308	.371	-7	-7	103	117	-0.6	-1	1	-0.5
	NY-A	3	7	.300	24	16	5	1	0	127	130	9.2	7	30	2.1	55	3.9	3.40	104	.270	.306	6	2	92	105	-2.1	-2	-0	0.0
	Yr	5	11	.313	33	23	7	1	0	173	186	9.7	16	49	2.5	90	4.7	3.90	94	.280	.323	-1	-5	95	105	-2.7	-1	0	-0.5
1960	NY-A	10	8	.556	35	23	7	3	1	167	149	8.0	15	52	2.8	92	5.0	3.40	105	.237	.298	9	3	92	90	-1.1	-2	0	0.1
1961	NY-A	16	3	.842	31	27	9	2	0	188	162	7.8	19	42	2.0	86	4.1	3.16	119	.232	.273	18	12	93	90	5.2	2	0	1.5
1962	NY-A	**23**	12	.657	43	39	14	3	2	**299**	257	7.7	40	57	1.7	176	5.3	3.19	114	.231	.266	26	15	92	93	3.4	1	-3	1.2
1963	NY-A	17	15	.531	40	37	**18**	3	1	268	246	8.3	29	39	1.3	114	3.8	3.22	110	.242	.269	12	10	98	91	-3.3	-6	-1	0.3
1964	NY-A	7	11	.389	27	14	2	1	4	115	130	10.2	20	31	2.4	77	6.0	4.54	80	.283	.325	-12	-11	101	105	-3.4	1	0	-0.9
1965	Cle-A	11	6	.647	30	26	6	2	0	166	154	8.3	22	23	**1.2**	84	4.6	3.69	91	.242	.266	-4	-6	97	82	2.2	2	-3	-0.7
1966	KC-A	1	5	.167	15	10	0	0	0	64	65	9.1	7	15	2.1	33	4.6	3.80	86	.263	.300	-3	-4	95	100	-1.8	1	-1	-0.3
	NY-N	0	1	.000	11	1	0	0	1	25	27	9.7	1	11	4.0	14	5.0	4.68	75	.293	.365	-3	-3	97	97	-0.4	-0	-0	-0.3
1967	NY-N	0	0	—	2	0	0	0	0	3	1	3.0	0	0	0.0	5	15.0	0.00	—	.091	.091	1	1	102	0	0.0	0	0	0.1
Total	12	107	99	.519	338	257	75	20	11	1850	1748	8.5	216	446	2.2	1000	4.9	3.62	101	.249	.292	33	9	97	94	-5.4	-5	-10	-0.1
■ **SCOTT TERRY**	Terry, Scott Ray b: 11/11/59, Hobbs, N.Mex. BR/TR, 5'10", 185 lbs. Deb: 4/09/86																												
1986	Cin-N	1	2	.333	28	3	0	0	0	56	66	10.6	8	32	5.1	32	5.1	6.11	63	.300	.380	-15	-14	104	96	-0.5	0	0	-1.3
1987	StL-N	0	0	—	11	0	0	0	0	13	13	9.0	0	8	5.5	9	6.2	3.46	115	.260	.356	1	1	97	111	0.0	-0	0	0.1
1988	StL-N	9	6	.600	51	11	1	0	3	129	119	8.3	5	34	2.4	65	4.5	2.93	124	.247	.292	8	10	105	100	2.0	2	0	1.3
Total	3	10	8	.556	90	14	1	0	3	198	198	9.0	13	74	3.4	106	4.8	3.86	96	.264	.323	-6	-3	104	99	1.5	2	1	0.1
■ **ADONIS TERRY**	Terry, William H. b: 8/7/1864, Westfield, Mass. d: 2/24/15, Milwaukee, Wis. BR/TR, 168 lbs. Deb: 5/01/1884																												
1884	Bro-a	20	35	.364	57	56	55	3	0	485	487	9.0	10	75	1.4	233	4.3	3.49	93	.269	.299	-13	-14	100	94	-2.9	4	-4	-1.1
1885	Bro-a	6	17	.261	25	23	23	0	1	209	213	9.2	9	42	1.8	96	4.1	4.26	80	.276	.313	-24	-20	105	81	-5.7	-3	0	-1.6
1886	Bro-a	18	16	.529	34	34	32	5	0	288	263	8.2	1	115	3.6	162	5.1	3.09	112	.253	.327	11	12	100	103	-0.9	3	0	1.0
1887	Bro-a	16	16	.500	40	35	35	1	**3**	318	331	9.4	9	99	2.8	138	3.9	4.02	106	.282	.338	10	8	99	93	1.9	8	4	0.6
1888	Bro-a	13	8	.619	23	23	20	2	0	195	145	**6.7**	2	67	3.1	138	**6.4**	2.03	153	**.219**	.290	22	24	102	104	-0.1	2	0	2.6

YEAR	TM/L	W	L	PCT	G	GS	CG	SHO	SV	IP	H	H/G	HR	BB	BB/G	SO	SO/G	ERA	/A	OAVG	OOBP	PR	/A	PF	CPI	WAT	PB	PD	TPI
1889	Bro-a	22	15	.595	41	39	35	2	0	326	285	7.9	5	126	3.5	186	5.1	3.29	107	.249	.324	20	9	92	84	-2.9	14	6	2.5
1890	Bro-N	26	16	.619	46	44	38	1	0	370	362	8.8	3	133	3.2	185	4.5	2.94	117	.272	.338	25	20	96	104	-2.0	14	1	1.8
1891	Bro-N	6	16	.273	25	22	18	1	1	194	207	9.6	5	80	3.7	65	3.0	4.22	78	.287	.358	-19	-20	98	84	-4.6	3	0	-1.3
1892	Bal-N	0	1	.000	1	1	1	0	0	9	7	7.0	0	7	7.0	3	3.0	4.00	84	.226	.369	-1	-1	102	78	-0.4	-1	0	0.0
	Pit-N	17	7	.708	30	26	24	2	1	240	185	6.9	3	106	4.0	95	3.6	2.51	122	.225	.313	21	15	94	90	5.2	2	0	1.6
	Yr	17	8	.680	31	27	25	2	1	249	192	6.9	3	113	4.1	98	3.5	2.57	120	.225	.315	20	14	94	90	4.8	-1	0	1.6
1893	Pit-N	12	8	.600	26	19	14	0	0	170	177	9.4	5	99	5.2	52	2.8	4.45	110	.284	.382	4	8	105	98	-0.4	1	0	0.9
1894	Pit-N	0	1	.000	1	1	0	0	0	1	2	18.0	0	4	36.0	0	0.0	108.00	5	.439	.702	-11	-11	95	17	-0.4	0	0	-0.6
	Chi-N	5	11	.313	23	21	16	0	0	163	232	12.8	12	123	6.8	39	2.2	5.85	98	.358	.460	-9	-2	108	120	-2.3	4	0	0.4
	Yr	5	12	.294	24	22	16	0	0	164	234	12.8	12	127	7.0	39	2.1	6.48	89	.359	.463	-21	-13	108	120	-2.7	0	0	-0.2
1895	Chi-N	21	14	.600	38	34	31	0	0	311	346	10.0	4	131	3.8	88	2.5	4.80	103	.302	.373	-0	5	103	85	2.4	-6	3	0.2
1896	Chi-N	15	13	.536	30	28	25	1	0	235	268	10.3	6	88	3.4	74	2.8	4.29	110	.309	.373	2	11	108	96	-0.5	2	0	1.3
1897	Chi-N	0	1	.000	1	1	1	0	0	8	11	12.4	0	6	6.8	1	1.1	10.13	43	.350	.454	-5	-5	101	60	-0.4	-1	0	-0.3
Total	14	197	195	.503	441	407	368	18	6	3522	3521	9.0	74	1301	3.3	1555	4.0	3.74	102	.274	.341	34	33	100	94	-14.0	46	11	8.0
■ DICK TERWILLIGER	Terwilliger, Richard Martin b: 6/27/06, Sand Lake, Mich. d: 1/21/69, Greenville, Mich. BR/TR, 5'11", 178 lbs. Deb: 8/18/32																												
1932	StL-N	0	0	—	1	0	0	0	0	3	1	3.0	0	2	6.0	2	6.0	0.00	—	.143	.333	1	1	101	0	0.0	-0	0	0.2
■ JEFF TESREAU	Tesreau, Charles Monroe b: 3/5/1889, Silver Mine, Mo. d: 9/24/46, Hanover, N.H. BR/TR, 6'2", 218 lbs. Deb: 4/12/12																												
1912	NY-N	17	7	.708	36	28	19	3	1	243	177	**6.6**	2	106	3.9	119	4.4	**1.96**	**172**	**.199**	.292	39	38	99	80	1.2	-2	1	3.8
1913	NY-N	22	13	.629	41	38	17	1	0	282	222	**7.1**	7	119	3.8	167	**5.3**	2.17	147	**.220**	.301	32	32	100	111	-1.1	2	1	3.8
1914	NY-N	26	10	.722	42	40	26	**8**	1	322	238	**6.7**	8	128	3.6	189	5.3	2.38	110	**.209**	.287	15	8	94	83	8.2	6	-2	1.2
1915	NY-N	19	16	.543	43	38	24	8	3	306	235	6.9	4	75	2.2	176	5.2	2.29	111	.215	.263	16	8	92	75	3.5	5	1	1.5
1916	NY-N	14	14	.500	40	33	23	5	2	268	249	8.4	9	65	2.2	113	3.8	2.92	84	.250	.294	-9	-14	94	92	-1.8	2	-0	-1.4
1917	NY-N	13	8	.619	33	20	11	1	2	184	168	8.2	6	58	2.8	85	4.2	3.08	82	.249	.303	-8	-11	93	95	-0.2	2	2	-0.9
1918	NY-N	4	4	.500	12	9	3	1	0	74	61	7.4	1	21	2.6	31	3.8	2.31	115	.227	.275	4	3	96	88	-0.4	2	1	0.6
Total	7	115	72	.615	247	206	123	27	9	1679	1350	7.2	37	572	3.1	880	4.7	2.43	114	.223	.288	89	63	95	89	9.4	16	3	8.6
■ BOB TEWKSBURY	Tewksbury, Robert Alan b: 11/30/60, Concord, N.H. BR/TR, 6'4", 200 lbs. Deb: 4/11/86																												
1986	NY-A	9	5	.643	23	20	2	0	0	130	144	10.0	8	31	2.1	49	3.4	3.32	129	.282	.323	12	14	103	119	1.5	0	2	1.6
1987	NY-A	1	4	.200	8	6	0	0	0	33	47	12.8	5	7	1.9	12	3.3	6.82	64	.338	.369	-9	-9	97	92	-1.5	0	0	-0.7
	Chi-N	0	4	.000	7	3	0	0	0	18	32	16.0	1	13	6.5	10	5.0	6.50	64	.421	.484	-5	-5	102	144	-1.9	-1	-1	-0.5
1988	Chi-N	0	0	—	1	1	0	0	0	3	6	18.0	1	2	6.0	1	3.0	9.00	40	.400	.444	-2	-2	105	124	0.0	-0	0	-0.1
Total	3	10	13	.435	39	30	2	0	0	184	229	11.2	15	53	2.6	72	3.5	4.35	98	.309	.352	-3	-2	102	117	-1.9	-1	2	0.3
■ GRANT THATCHER	Thatcher, Ulysses Grant b: 2/23/1877, Maytown, Pa. d: 3/17/36, Lancaster, Pa. TR , 5'10.5", 180 lbs. Deb: 03																												
1903	Bro-N	3	1	.750	4	4	4	0	0	28	33	10.6	1	7	2.3	9	2.9	2.89	115	.319	.362	1	1	102	135	1.0	0	-0	0.1
1904	Bro-N	1	0	1.000	1	0	0	0	0	9	9	9.0	0	2	2.0	4	4.0	4.00	67	.284	.327	-1	-1	98	69	0.5	0	-0	-0.1
Total	2	4	1	.800	5	4	4	0	0	37	42	10.2	1	9	2.2	13	3.2	3.16	100	.311	.354	-0	-0	101	119	1.5	0	-0	0.0
■ GREG THAYER	Thayer, Gregory Allen b: 10/23/49, Cedar Rapids, Iowa BR/TR, 5'11", 182 lbs. Deb: 4/07/78																												
1978	Min-A	1	1	.500	20	0	0	0	0	45	40	8.0	5	30	6.0	30	6.0	3.80	94	.258	.376	-0	-1	94	132	0.1	0	0	0.0
■ JACK THEIS	Theis, John Louis b: 7/23/1891, Georgetown, Ohio d: 7/6/41, Georgetown, Ohio BR/TR, 6', 190 lbs. Deb: 7/05/20																												
1920	Cin-N	0	0	—	1	0	0	0	0	2	1	4.5	0	3	13.5	0	0.0	0.00	—	.143	.400	1	1	88	0	0.0	0	0	0.1
■ DUANE THEISS	Theiss, Duane Charles b: 11/20/53, Zanesville, Ohio BR/TR, 6'3", 185 lbs. Deb: 8/05/77																												
1977	Atl-N	1	1	.500	17	0	0	0	0	21	26	11.1	1	16	6.9	7	3.0	6.43	70	.338	.422	-6	-4	115	106	0.2	-0	0	-0.4
1978	Atl-N	0	0	—	3	0	0	0	0	6	3	4.5	0	3	4.5	3	4.5	1.50	272	.158	.292	1	2	114	125	0.0	-0	0	0.2
Total	2	1	1	.500	20	0	0	0	0	27	29	9.7	1	19	6.3	10	3.3	5.33	83	.302	.397	-4	-3	115	110	0.2	-0	0	-0.2
■ JUG THESENGA	Thesenga, Arnold Joseph b: 4/27/14, Jefferson, S.Dak. BR/TR, 6', 200 lbs. Deb: 9/01/44																												
1944	Was-A	0	0	—	5	1	0	0	0	12	18	13.5	0	12	9.0	2	1.5	5.25	59	.340	.462	-2	-3	91	136	0.0	-0	0	-0.2
■ BERT THIEL	Thiel, Maynard Bert b: 5/4/26, Marion, Wis. BR/TR, 5'10", 185 lbs. Deb: 4/17/52																												
1952	Bos-N	1	1	.500	4	0	0	0	0	7	11	14.1	1	4	5.1	6	7.7	7.71	47	.344	.436	-3	-3	97	105	0.1	0	0	-0.2
■ HENRY THIELMAN	Thielman, Henry Joseph b: 10/3/1880, St.Cloud, Minn. d: 9/2/42, New York, N.Y. BR/TR, 5'11", 175 lbs. Deb: 4/17/02																												
1902	NY-N	0	1	.000	2	2	0	0	0	6	8	12.0	0	6	9.0	5	7.5	1.50	193	.345	.480	1	1	104	426	-0.4	-0	0	0.1
	Cin-N	9	15	.375	25	23	22	0	1	211	201	8.6	2	78	3.3	49	2.1	3.24	93	.273	.343	-11	-5	108	89	-3.3	-4	-1	-0.6
	Yr	9	16	.360	27	25	22	0	1	217	209	8.7	2	84	3.5	54	2.2	3.19	94	.276	.348	-10	-5	108	89	-3.7	-0	-1	-0.5
1903	Bro-N	0	3	.000	4	3	3	0	0	29	31	9.6	3	14	4.3	10	3.1	4.66	71	.304	.398	-4	-4	102	101	-1.4	1	1	-0.3
Total	2	9	19	.321	31	28	25	0	1	246	240	8.8	5	98	3.6	64	2.3	3.37	91	.279	.354	-14	-9	107	99	-5.1	-3	0	-0.8
■ JAKE THIELMAN	Thielman, John Peter b: 5/20/1879, St.Cloud, Minn. d: 1/28/28, Minneapolis, Minn. BR/TR, 5'11", 175 lbs. Deb: 4/23/05																												
1905	StL-N	15	16	.484	32	29	26	0	0	242	265	9.9	4	62	2.3	87	3.2	3.50	81	.310	.365	-14	-18	95	106	3.2	8	3	-1.4
1906	StL-N	0	1	.000	1	1	0	0	0	5	5	9.0	0	2	3.6	0	0.0	3.60	76	.288	.361	-1	-0	104	91	-0.4	0	0	0.0
1907	Cle-A	11	8	.579	20	18	18	3	0	166	151	8.2	2	34	1.8	56	3.0	2.33	101	.266	.307	4	1	93	101	0.5	1	-3	-0.1
1908	Cle-A	4	3	.571	11	8	5	0	0	62	59	8.6	2	9	1.3	15	2.2	3.63	68	.260	.300	-9	-8	103	81	0.0	4	2	-0.6
	Bos-A	0	0	—	1	0	0	0	0	1	3	27.0	1	0	0.0	0	0.0	27.00	9	.600	.600	-3	-3	97	78	0.0	0	0	-0.2
	Yr	4	3	.571	12	8	5	0	0	63	62	8.9	3	9	1.3	15	2.1	4.00	62	.263	.290	-11	-11	103	78	0.0	4	2	-0.8
Total	4	30	28	.517	65	56	49	3	0	476	483	9.1	9	107	2.0	158	3.0	3.16	83	.289	.338	-22	-28	96	101	3.3	14	2	-2.3
■ DAVE THIES	Thies, David Robert b: 3/21/37, Minneapolis, Minn. BR/TR, 6'4", 205 lbs. Deb: 4/20/63																												
1963	KC-A	0	1	.000	9	2	0	0	0	25	26	9.4	2	12	4.3	9	3.2	4.68	84	.274	.364	-3	-2	109	100	-0.4	1	0	0.0
■ JAKE THIES	Thies, Vernon Arthur b: 4/1/26, St.Louis, Mo. BR/TR, 5'11", 170 lbs. Deb: 4/24/54																												
1954	Pit-N	3	9	.250	33	18	3	1	0	130	120	8.3	13	49	3.4	57	3.9	3.88	107	.244	.308	3	4	102	89	-1.6	-2	0	0.2
1955	Pit-N	0	1	.000	1	1	0	0	0	4	5	11.3	0	3	6.8	0	0.0	4.50	90	.357	.450	-0	-0	101	167	-0.4	0	-0	0.0
Total	2	3	10	.231	34	19	3	1	0	134	125	8.4	13	52	3.5	57	3.8	3.90	106	.248	.313	3	4	102	91	-2.0	-2	0	0.2
■ BOBBY THIGPEN	Thigpen, Robert Thomas b: 7/17/63, Tallahassee, Fla. BR/TR, 6'3", 195 lbs. Deb: 8/06/86																												
1986	Chi-A	2	0	1.000	20	0	0	0	7	36	26	6.5	1	12	3.0	20	5.0	1.75	243	.205	.275	10	10	101	119	1.0	0	0	1.0
1987	Chi-A	7	5	.583	51	0	0	0	16	89	86	8.7	10	24	2.4	52	5.3	2.73	178	.256	.306	17	**21**	109	139	1.3	0	0	2.1
1988	Chi-A	5	8	.385	68	0	0	0	34	90	96	9.6	6	33	3.3	62	6.2	3.30	119	.273	.334	7	6	99	126	-0.8	0	0	0.6
Total	3	14	13	.519	139	0	0	0	57	215	208	8.7	17	69	2.9	134	5.6	2.80	155	.255	.314	34	37	103	130	1.5	0	0	3.7
■ DICK THOENEN	Thoenen, Richard Crispin b: 1/9/44, Mexico, Mo. BR/TR, 6'6", 215 lbs. Deb: 9/16/67																												
1967	Phi-N	0	0	—	1	0	0	0	0	1	2	18.0	0	0	0.0	0	0.0	9.00	39	.500	.400	-1	-1	104	98	0.0	0	0	0.0
■ TOMMY THOMAS	Thomas, Alphonse b: 12/23/1899, Baltimore, Md. d: 4/27/88, Dallastown, Pa. BR/TR, 5'10", 175 lbs. Deb: 4/17/26																												
1926	Chi-A	15	12	.556	44	32	13	2	2	249	225	8.1	7	110	4.0	127	4.6	3.80	96	**.244**	.317	6	-4	90	80	0.9	-0	-3	-0.7
1927	Chi-A	19	16	.543	40	36	24	3	1	**308**	271	7.9	16	94	2.7	107	3.1	2.98	143	.244	.292	40	44	103	98	3.4	-4	-4	3.5
1928	Chi-A	17	16	.515	36	32	24	3	2	283	277	8.8	14	76	2.4	129	4.1	3.08	131	.259	.303	30	30	100	105	1.8	3	-3	3.0
1929	Chi-A	14	18	.438	36	31	**24**	2	1	260	270	9.3	17	60	2.1	62	2.1	3.18	130	.269	.302	31	28	98	108	1.6	3	-3	2.6
1930	Chi-A	5	13	.278	34	27	7	0	0	169	229	12.2	13	44	2.3	58	3.1	5.22	94	.323	.350	-11	-6	105	105	-2.9	-4	0	-0.8
1931	Chi-A	10	14	.417	43	36	11	2	2	245	298	10.9	17	69	2.5	72	2.6	4.74	89	.292	.337	-10	-15	96	97	1.1	1	-1	-1.3
1932	Chi-A	3	3	.500	12	3	1	0	0	44	55	11.3	6	15	3.1	11	2.3	6.14	66	.307	.359	-8	-10	91	94	0.8	-1	-0	-0.9
	Was-A	8	7	.533	18	14	7	1	0	117	114	8.8	5	46	3.5	36	2.8	3.54	124	.255	.319	12	11	98	104	-0.9	1	-2	0.9
	Yr	11	10	.524	30	17	8	1	0	161	169	9.4	11	61	3.4	47	2.6	4.25	101	.270	.329	4	1	96	104	-0.1	-1	-2	0.0
1933	Was-A	7	7	.500	35	14	2	0	3	135	149	9.9	9	49	3.3	35	2.3	4.80	83	.273	.329	-8	-12	93	88	-1.7	2	-2	-1.1
1934	Was-A	8	9	.471	33	18	7	1	1	133	154	10.4	9	58	3.9	42	2.8	5.48	84	.294	.360	-15	-13	102	92	0.6	-1	-2	-1.3

YEAR	TM/L	W	L	PCT	G	GS	CG	SHO	SV	IP	H	H/G	HR	BB	BB/G	SO	SO/G	ERA	/A	OAVG	OOBP	PR	/A	PF	CPI	WAT	PB	PD	TPI
1935	Was-A	0	0	—	1	0	0	0	0	⅓	3	81.0	0	0	0.0	0	0.0	54.00	—	.750	.750	-2	-2	93	70	0.0	0	0	-0.1
	Phi-N	0	1	.000	4	1	0	0	0	12	15	11.3	2	5	3.8	3	2.3	5.25	90	.313	.370	-2	-1	117	117	-0.4	-0	-0	0.0
1936	StL-A	11	9	.550	36	21	8	1	0	180	219	10.9	25	72	3.6	40	2.0	5.25	103	.297	.358	-4	3	107	108	3.1	-3	-3	-0.1
1937	StL-A	0	1	.000	17	2	0	0	0	31	46	13.4	2	10	2.9	10	2.9	6.97	69	.348	.390	-8	-8	103	91	-0.4	-1	0	-0.6
	Bos-A	0	2	.000	9	0	0	0	0	11	16	13.1	2	4	3.3	4	3.3	4.09	116	.340	.396	1	1	102	177	-0.9	-0	0	0.1
	Yr	0	3	.000	26	2	0	0	0	42	62	13.3	4	14	3.0	14	3.0	6.21	77	.344	.387	-7	-7	103	177	-1.3	-1	0	-0.5
Total	12	117	128	.478	398	267	128	15	12	2177	2341	9.7	144	712	2.9	736	3.0	4.11	104	.275	.325	53	43	99	99	6.1	-5	-22	3.2
■ **BLAINE THOMAS**	Thomas, Blaine M. "Baldy" b: 1888, Glendora, Cal. d: 8/21/15, Glendora, Cal. BR/TR, 5'10", 165 lbs. Deb: 8/25/11																												
1911	Bos-A	0	0	—	2	2	0	0	0	5	3	5.4	0	7	12.6	0	0.0	0.00	—	.273	.579	2	2	99	0	0.0	0	0	0.2
■ **CARL THOMAS**	Thomas, Carl Leslie b: 5/28/32, Minneapolis, Minn. BR/TR, 6'5", 245 lbs. Deb: 4/19/60																												
1960	Cle-A	1	0	1.000	4	0	0	0	0	10	8	7.2	1	10	9.0	5	4.5	7.20	53	.229	.404	-4	-4	98	73	0.5	1	0	-0.2
■ **LEFTY THOMAS**	Thomas, Clarence Fletcher b: 10/4/03, Glade Springs, Va. d: 3/21/52, Charlottesville, Va. BL/TL, 6', 183 lbs. Deb: 9/26/25																												
1925	Was-A	0	2	.000	2	2	1	0	0	13	14	9.7	0	7	4.8	10	6.9	2.08	201	.264	.344	3	3	95	165	-0.9	-1	0	0.2
1926	Was-A	0	0	—	6	0	0	0	0	9	8	8.0	0	10	10.0	3	3.0	5.00	78	.267	.409	-1	-1	97	110	0.0	0	-0	-0.1
Total	2	0	2	.000	8	2	1	0	0	22	22	9.0	0	17	7.0	13	5.3	3.27	124	.265	.371	2	2	96	143	-0.9	-1	-0	0.1
■ **CLAUDE THOMAS**	Thomas, Claude Alfred "Lefty" b: 5/15/1890, Stanberry, Mo. d: 3/6/46, Sulphur, Okla. BL/TL, 6'1", 180 lbs. Deb: 9/14/16																												
1916	Was-A	1	2	.333	7	4	1	1	0	28	27	8.7	1	12	3.9	7	2.3	4.18	68	.265	.353	-4	-4	100	89	-0.4	-1	-0	-0.5
■ **FAY THOMAS**	Thomas, Fay Wesley "Scow" b: 10/10/04, Holyrood, Kan. BR/TR, 6'2", 195 lbs. Deb: 6/27/27																												
1927	NY-N	0	0	—	9	0	0	0	0	16	19	10.7	3	4	2.3	11	6.2	3.38	114	.302	.338	1	1	98	163	0.0	-0	-0	0.0
1931	Cle-A	2	4	.333	16	2	1	0	0	49	63	11.6	2	32	5.9	25	4.6	5.14	90	.323	.416	-4	-3	106	124	-1.0	-1	-1	-0.3
1932	Bro-N	0	1	.000	7	2	0	0	0	17	22	11.6	0	8	4.2	9	4.8	7.41	50	.306	.375	-7	-7	96	64	-0.4	-0	0	-0.6
1935	StL-A	7	15	.318	49	19	4	0	1	147	165	10.1	11	89	5.4	67	4.1	4.78	102	.289	.380	-5	2	110	113	-3.1	-3	2	0.1
Total	4	9	20	.310	81	23	5	0	1	229	269	10.6	16	133	5.2	112	4.4	4.95	94	.299	.384	-15	-7	107	115	-4.5	-5	1	-0.8
■ **FROSTY THOMAS**	Thomas, Forrest b: 5/23/1881, Faucett, Mo. d: 3/18/70, St.Joseph, Mo. BR/TR, 6', 185 lbs. Deb: 5/01/05																												
1905	Det-A	0	1	.000	2	1	0	0	0	6	10	15.0	0	3	4.5	5	7.5	7.50	35	.399	.463	-3	-3	100	94	-0.4	-0	0	-0.2
■ **BUD THOMAS**	Thomas, Luther Baxter b: 9/9/10, Faber, Va. BR/TR, 6', 180 lbs. Deb: 9/13/32																												
1932	Was-A	0	0	—	2	0	0	0	0	3	1	3.0	0	2	6.0	1	3.0	0.00	—	.100	.250	1	1	98	0	0.0	0	0	0.1
1933	Was-A	0	0	—	2	0	0	0	0	4	11	24.8	1	2	4.5	1	2.3	15.75	25	.550	.609	-5	-5	93	105	0.0	-0	0	-0.3
1937	Phi-A	8	15	.348	35	26	6	1	0	170	208	11.0	15	52	2.8	54	2.9	4.98	89	.295	.342	-7	-10	96	94	-0.3	-1	-3	-1.2
1938	Phi-A	9	14	.391	42	29	7	1	0	212	259	11.0	23	62	2.6	48	2.0	4.92	102	.299	.342	-3	2	105	102	0.9	-3	-1	-0.1
1939	Phi-A	0	1	.000	2	2	0	0	0	4	8	18.0	2	1	2.3	0	0.0	15.75	30	.421	.429	-5	-5	102	77	-0.4	-0	0	-0.3
	Was-A	0	0	—	4	0	0	0	0	9	11	11.0	0	2	2.0	0	0.0	6.00	70	.306	.333	-1	-2	91	70	0.0	-0	0	-0.1
	Det-A	7	0	1.000	27	0	0	0	1	47	45	8.6	7	20	3.8	14	2.7	4.21	120	.254	.322	2	4	110	107	3.5	-1	0	0.4
	Yr	7	1	.875	33	2	0	0	1	60	64	9.6	9	23	3.5	14	2.1	5.25	94	.276	.332	-4	-2	106	107	3.1	-1	0	0.0
1940	Det-A	0	1	.000	3	0	0	0	0	4	8	18.0	1	3	6.8	0	0.0	9.00	53	.421	.458	-2	-2	109	129	-0.4	0	1	0.0
1941	Det-A	1	3	.250	26	1	0	0	2	73	74	9.1	4	22	2.7	17	2.1	4.19	106	.260	.302	-0	2	107	83	-0.9	-1	2	0.3
Total	7	25	34	.424	143	58	13	2	3	526	625	10.7	53	166	2.8	135	2.3	4.96	95	.292	.339	-20	-14	102	96	2.4	-7	-1	-1.2
■ **MYLES THOMAS**	Thomas, Myles Lewis b: 10/22/1897, State College, Pa. d: 12/12/63, Toledo, Ohio BR/TR, 5'9.5", 170 lbs. Deb: 4/18/26																												
1926	NY-A	6	6	.500	33	13	3	0	0	140	140	9.0	6	65	4.2	38	2.4	4.24	92	.271	.339	-3	-5	97	94	-0.9	-3	1	-0.7
1927	NY-A	7	4	.636	21	9	1	0	0	89	111	11.2	4	43	4.3	25	2.5	4.85	80	.322	.388	-7	-10	94	113	-0.5	2	0	-0.7
1928	NY-A	1	0	1.000	12	1	0	0	0	32	33	9.3	3	9	2.5	10	2.8	3.38	106	.277	.318	2	1	89	122	0.5	1	0	0.1
1929	NY-A	0	2	.000	5	1	0	0	0	15	27	16.2	1	9	5.4	3	1.8	10.80	38	.409	.456	-11	-11	97	82	-0.9	-0	1	-0.9
	Was-A	7	8	.467	22	14	7	0	2	125	139	10.0	3	48	3.5	33	2.4	3.53	121	.288	.340	10	10	100	116	0.0	2	0	1.2
	Yr	7	10	.412	27	15	7	0	2	140	166	10.7	4	57	3.7	36	2.3	4.31	98	.302	.355	-1	-1	100	116	-0.9	-0	1	0.3
1930	Was-A	2	2	.500	12	2	0	0	0	34	49	13.0	3	15	4.0	12	3.2	8.21	56	.358	.398	-13	-14	98	87	-0.3	-1	-1	-1.2
Total	5	23	22	.511	105	40	11	0	2	435	499	10.3	20	189	3.9	121	2.5	4.63	87	.299	.358	-23	-29	97	106	-2.1	0	1	-2.2
■ **ROY THOMAS**	Thomas, Roy Allen b: 3/24/1874, Norristown, Pa. d: 11/20/59, Norristown, Pa. BL/TL, 5'11", 150 lbs. Deb: 4/14/1899																												
1900	Phi-N	0	0	—	1	0	0	0	0	3	4	12.0	0	0	0.0	0	0.0	3.00	121	.345	.345	0	0	98	126	0.0	0	0	0.0
■ **ROY THOMAS**	Thomas, Roy Justin b: 6/22/53, Quantico, Va. BR/TR, 6'5", 215 lbs. Deb: 9/21/77																												
1977	Hou-N	0	0	—	4	0	0	0	0	6	5	7.5	0	3	4.5	4	6.0	3.00	120	.208	.296	1	0	92	61	0.0	0	0	0.0
1978	StL-N	1	1	.500	16	1	0	0	3	28	21	6.8	0	16	5.1	16	5.1	3.86	89	.216	.308	-1	-1	96	71	0.1	0	1	0.0
1979	StL-N	3	4	.429	26	6	0	0	1	77	66	7.7	9	24	2.8	44	5.1	2.92	133	.237	.292	7	8	104	113	-0.6	-1	1	0.9
1980	StL-N	2	3	.400	24	5	0	0	0	55	59	9.7	3	25	4.1	22	3.6	4.75	78	.274	.351	-7	-6	102	90	-0.2	-0	1	-0.5
1983	Sea-A	3	1	.750	43	0	0	0	1	89	95	9.6	3	32	3.2	77	7.8	3.44	120	.275	.334	6	7	101	113	1.2	0	-0	0.6
1984	Sea-A	3	2	.600	21	1	0	0	1	50	52	9.4	8	37	6.7	42	7.6	5.22	79	.280	.399	-7	-6	103	119	0.7	0	0	-0.5
1985	Sea-A	7	0	1.000	40	0	0	0	1	94	66	6.3	8	48	4.6	70	6.7	3.35	118	.202	.301	8	6	95	91	3.5	0	-1	0.5
1987	Sea-A	1	0	1.000	8	0	0	0	0	21	23	9.9	2	11	4.7	14	6.0	5.14	90	.299	.380	-2	-1	103	110	0.5	0	-0	-0.1
Total	8	20	11	.645	182	13	0	0	7	420	387	8.3	33	196	4.2	289	6.2	3.81	104	.250	.331	6	7	100	102	5.2	-1	1	0.9
■ **STAN THOMAS**	Thomas, Stanley Brown b: 7/11/49, Rumford, Me. BR/TR, 6'2", 185 lbs. Deb: 7/05/74																												
1974	Tex-A	0	0	—	12	0	0	0	0	14	22	14.1	1	6	3.9	8	5.1	6.43	54	.379	.424	-4	-5	96	111	0.0	0	0	-0.3
1975	Tex-A	4	4	.500	46	1	0	0	3	81	72	8.0	2	34	3.8	46	5.1	3.11	121	.239	.320	6	6	100	96	0.1	0	0	0.7
1976	Cle-A	4	4	.500	37	7	2	0	6	106	88	7.5	5	41	3.5	54	4.6	2.29	153	.229	.306	14	14	100	127	0.0	0	3	1.9
1977	Sea-A	2	6	.250	13	9	1	0	0	58	74	11.5	8	25	3.9	14	2.2	6.05	66	.310	.375	-13	-13	98	96	-1.4	0	-0	-1.2
	NY-A	1	0	1.000	3	0	0	0	0	6	7	10.5	0	4	6.0	1	1.5	7.50	53	.280	.355	-2	-2	97	58	0.5	0	-0	-0.2
	Yr	3	6	.333	16	9	1	0	0	64	81	11.4	8	29	4.1	15	2.1	6.19	65	.300	.363	-15	-16	98	58	-0.9	0	-0	-1.4
Total	4	11	14	.440	111	17	3	0	9	265	263	8.9	16	110	3.7	123	4.2	3.70	100	.261	.334	1	0	99	108	-0.8	0	3	0.9
■ **TOM THOMAS**	Thomas, Thomas R. "Savage Tom" b: 12/27/1873, Shawnee, Ohio d: 9/23/42, Shawnee, Ohio 6'4", 195 lbs. Deb: 9/30/1899																												
1899	StL-N	1	1	.500	4	2	2	0	0	25	22	7.9	1	4	1.4	8	2.9	2.52	163	.258	.291	4	4	107	90	0.0	0	0	0.4
1900	StL-N	2	2	.500	5	1	1	0	0	26	38	13.2	2	4	1.4	7	2.4	3.81	91	.366	.389	-0	-1	93	143	0.1	-0	0	0.0
Total	2	3	3	.500	9	3	3	0	0	51	60	10.6	3	8	1.4	15	2.6	3.18	119	.317	.345	3	3	100	117	0.1	-0	0	0.4
■ **ERSKINE THOMASON**	Thomason, Melvin Erskine b: 8/13/48, Laurens, S.C. BR/TR, 6'1", 190 lbs. Deb: 9/18/74																												
1974	Phi-N	0	0	—	1	0	0	0	0	1	0	0.0	0	0	0.0	1	9.0	0.00	—	.000	.000	0	0	104	0	0.0	0	0	0.0
■ **ART THOMPSON**	Thompson, Arthur J. Deb: 6/17/1884																												
1884	Was-U	0	1	.000	1	1	1	0	0	8	10	11.3	0	3	3.4	8	9.0	6.75	44	.311	.370	-3	-3	98	69	-0.4	-1	0	-0.2
■ **FORREST THOMPSON**	Thompson, David Forrest b: 3/3/18, Mooresville, N.C. d: 2/26/79, Charlotte, N.C. BL/TL, 5'11", 195 lbs. Deb: 4/26/48																												
1948	Was-A	6	10	.375	46	7	0	0	4	131	134	9.2	9	54	3.7	40	2.7	3.85	119	.262	.325	6	11	107	103	0.1	2	-0	1.3
1949	Was-A	1	3	.250	9	1	1	0	0	16	22	12.4	1	9	5.1	8	4.5	4.50	90	.328	.400	-1	-1	96	138	-0.4	2	0	0.1
Total	2	7	13	.350	55	8	1	0	4	147	156	9.6	10	63	3.9	48	2.9	3.92	115	.270	.334	6	10	106	107	-0.3	4	-0	1.4
■ **JUNIOR THOMPSON**	Thompson, Eugene Earl b: 6/7/17, Latham, Ill. BR/TR, 6'1", 185 lbs. Deb: 4/26/39																												
1939	Cin-N	13	5	.722	42	11	5	3	2	152	130	7.7	6	55	3.3	87	5.2	2.55	154	.236	.301	23	23	100	115	2.5	0	-1	2.3
1940	Cin-N	16	9	.640	33	31	17	3	0	225	197	7.9	10	96	3.8	103	4.1	3.32	113	.233	.310	13	11	98	95	-0.2	3	-1	1.3
1941	Cin-N	6	6	.500	27	15	4	0	1	109	117	9.7	6	57	4.7	46	3.8	4.87	73	.272	.348	-15	-16	98	91	-0.7	1	2	-1.2
1942	Cin-N	4	7	.364	29	10	1	0	0	102	86	7.6	5	53	4.7	35	3.1	3.35	100	.226	.318	-0	0	102	95	-1.5	2	4	0.6
1946	NY-N	4	6	.400	39	1	0	0	4	63	36	5.1	5	40	5.7	31	4.4	1.29	274	.190	.311	15	16	103	247	0.0	0	2	1.9
1947	NY-N	4	2	.667	15	0	0	0	0	36	36	9.0	3	27	6.8	13	3.3	4.25	95	.279	.390	-1	-1	99	131	0.9	-1	1	0.0
Total	6	47	35	.573	185	68	27	6	7	687	602	7.9	35	328	4.3	315	4.1	3.26	113	.239	.321	35	33	99	115	1.0	6	6	4.9

YEAR	TM/L	W	L	PCT	G	GS	CG	SHO	SV	IP	H	H/G	HR	BB	BB/G	SO	SO/G	ERA	/A	OAVG	OOBP	PR	/A	PF	CPI	WAT	PB	PD	TPI
■ FULLER THOMPSON	Thompson, Fuller Weidner b: 5/1/1889, Los Angeles, Cal. d: 2/19/72, Los Angeles, Cal. BR/TR, 5'11.5", 164 lbs. Deb: 8/19/11																												
1911	Bos-N	0	0	—	3	0	0	0	0	5	5	9.0	0	2	3.6	0	0.0	3.60	103	.294	.368	-0	0	109	114	0.0	0	0	0.0
■ HARRY THOMPSON	Thompson, Harold b: 9/9/1889, Nanticoke, Pa. d: 2/14/51, Reno, Nev. BL/TL, 5'8", 150 lbs. Deb: 4/24/19																												
1919	Was-A	0	3	.000	12	2	0	0	1	43	48	10.0	0	8	1.7	10	2.1	3.56	90	.293	.333	-2	-2	99	93	-1.4	1	0	0.0
	Phi-A	0	1	.000	3	0	0	0	0	12	16	12.0	4	3	2.3	1	0.8	6.75	54	.327	.365	-5	-4	112	102	-0.4	-1	0	-0.4
	Yr	0	4	.000	15	2	0	0	1	55	64	10.5	4	11	1.8	11	1.8	4.25	77	.298	.332	-6	-6	102	102	-1.8	1	0	-0.4
■ LEE THOMPSON	Thompson, John Dudley "Lefty" b: 2/26/1898, Smithfield, Utah d: 2/17/63, Santa Barbara, Cal BL/TL, 6'1", 185 lbs. Deb: 9/04/21																												
1921	Chi-A	0	3	.000	4	4	0	0	0	21	32	13.7	0	6	2.6	4	1.7	8.14	54	.333	.362	-9	-9	102	59	-1.4	0	-1	-0.7
■ GUS THOMPSON	Thompson, John Gustav b: 6/22/1877, Humboldt, Iowa d: 3/28/58, Kalispell, Mont. 6'2", 185 lbs. Deb: 03																												
1903	Pit-N	2	2	.500	5	4	3	0	0	43	52	10.9	1	16	3.3	22	4.6	3.56	93	.326	.391	-1	-1	101	123	-0.4	0	-1	-0.1
1906	StL-N	2	11	.154	17	12	8	0	0	103	111	9.7	2	25	2.2	36	3.1	4.28	64	.308	.361	-19	-18	104	82	-3.7	-1	1	-1.7
Total	2	4	13	.235	22	16	11	0	0	146	163	10.0	3	41	2.5	58	3.6	4.07	71	.313	.370	-20	-19	103	94	-4.1	-1	-0	-1.8
■ JOCKO THOMPSON	Thompson, John Samuel b: 1/17/20, Beverly, Mass. d: 2/3/88, Olney, Md. BL/TL, 6', 185 lbs. Deb: 9/21/48																												
1948	Phi-N	1	0	1.000	2	2	1	0	0	13	10	6.9	0	9	6.2	7	4.8	2.77	138	.233	.365	2	2	97	134	0.5	0	-0	0.1
1949	Phi-N	1	3	.250	8	5	1	0	0	31	38	11.0	6	11	3.2	12	3.5	6.97	58	.314	.366	-10	-10	101	88	-1.0	-0	-0	-0.9
1950	Phi-N	0	0	—	2	0	0	0	0	4	1	2.3	0	4	9.0	2	4.5	0.00	—	.077	.294	2	2	96	0	0.0	0	0	0.2
1951	Phi-N	4	8	.333	29	14	3	2	1	119	102	7.7	12	59	4.5	60	4.5	3.86	100	.231	.321	1	-0	97	93	-1.8	-1	-1	-0.1
Total	4	6	11	.353	41	21	5	2	1	167	151	8.1	18	83	4.5	81	4.4	4.26	91	.244	.332	-5	-7	98	93	-2.3	-1	-1	-0.7
■ MIKE THOMPSON	Thompson, Michael Wayne b: 9/6/49, Denver, Colo. BR/TR, 6'3", 190 lbs. Deb: 5/19/71																												
1971	Was-A	1	6	.143	16	12	0	0	0	67	53	7.1	3	54	7.3	41	5.5	4.84	67	.222	.365	-10	-12	94	80	-2.2	0	0	-1.1
1973	StL-N	0	0	—	2	2	0	0	0	4	1	2.3	0	5	11.3	3	6.8	0.00	—	.077	.333	2	1	90	0	0.0	-0	0	0.1
1974	StL-N	0	3	.000	19	4	0	0	0	38	37	8.8	1	35	8.3	25	5.9	5.68	66	.274	.425	-9	-8	103	95	-1.4	-1	0	-0.8
	Atl-N	0	0	—	1	1	0	0	0	4	7	15.8	0	2	4.5	2	4.5	4.50	83	.412	.450	-0	-0	104	174	0.0	0	0	0.0
	Yr	0	3	.000	20	5	0	0	0	42	44	9.4	1	37	7.9	27	5.8	5.57	67	.286	.418	-9	-9	103	174	-1.4	-1	0	-0.8
1975	Atl-N	0	6	.000	16	10	0	0	0	52	60	10.4	2	32	5.5	42	7.3	4.67	75	.305	.383	-6	-7	97	112	-2.9	-1	1	-0.6
Total	4	1	15	.063	54	29	0	0	0	165	158	8.6	6	128	7.0	113	6.2	4.85	71	.263	.386	-24	-25	97	94	-6.5	-1	1	-2.4
■ RICH THOMPSON	Thompson, Richard Neil b: 11/1/58, New York, N.Y. BB/TR, 6'3", 225 lbs. Deb: 4/28/85																												
1985	Cle-A	3	8	.273	57	0	0	0	5	80	95	10.7	8	48	5.4	30	3.4	6.30	63	.303	.393	-19	-21	95	96	-1.4	0	-2	-2.1
■ THOMAS THOMPSON	Thompson, Thomas Carl b: 11/7/1889, Spring City, Tenn. d: 1/16/63, La Jolla, Cal. BR/TR, 5'9.5", 170 lbs. Deb: 6/05/12																												
1912	NY-A	0	2	.000	7	2	1	0	0	33	43	11.7	0	13	3.5	15	4.1	6.00	59	.341	.415	-10	-9	105	93	-0.9	1	-1	-0.8
■ WILL THOMPSON	Thompson, Will McLain b: 8/30/1870, Pittsburgh, Pa. d: 6/9/62, Pittsburgh, Pa. BR/TR, 5'11.5", 190 lbs. Deb: 7/09/1892																												
1892	Pit-N	0	1	.000	1	1	0	0	0	3	3	9.0	0	5	15.0	0	0.0	3.00	103	.273	.501	0	0	94	224	-0.4	0	0	0.0
■ HANK THORMAHLEN	Thormahlen, Herbert Ehler "Lefty" b: 7/5/1896, Jersey City, N.J. d: 2/6/55, Los Angeles, Cal. BL/TL, 6', 180 lbs. Deb: 9/29/17																												
1917	NY-A	0	1	.000	1	1	0	0	0	8	9	10.1	0	4	4.5	5	5.6	2.25	127	.281	.378	0	1	107	182	-0.4	-0	-0	0.0
1918	NY-A	7	3	.700	16	12	5	2	0	113	85	6.8	1	52	4.1	22	1.8	2.47	105	.217	.314	4	2	94	94	2.2	-3	0	-0.1
1919	NY-A	12	10	.545	30	25	13	2	1	189	155	7.4	10	61	2.9	62	3.0	2.62	128	.228	.295	13	15	104	91	-0.6	-1	-1	1.5
1920	NY-A	9	6	.600	29	15	6	0	1	143	178	11.2	5	43	2.7	35	2.2	4.15	90	.312	.362	-6	-6	99	106	-0.1	1	1	-0.3
1921	Bos-A	1	7	.125	23	9	3	0	0	96	101	9.5	3	34	3.2	17	1.6	4.50	95	.277	.337	-2	-2	100	86	-2.9	-1	-0	-0.2
1925	Bro-N	0	3	.000	5	2	0	0	0	16	22	12.4	0	9	5.1	7	3.9	3.94	103	.333	.407	1	0	95	153	-1.4	0	0	0.1
Total	6	29	30	.492	104	64	27	4	2	565	550	8.8	19	203	3.2	148	2.4	3.33	104	.261	.329	9	9	100	98	-3.2	-3	1	1.0
■ PAUL THORMODSGARD	Thormodsgard, Paul Gayton b: 11/10/53, San Francisco, Cal. BR/TR, 6'2", 190 lbs. Deb: 4/10/77																												
1977	Min-A	11	15	.423	37	37	8	1	0	218	236	9.7	25	65	2.7	94	3.9	4.62	90	.280	.328	-13	-11	102	94	-2.7	0	-1	-1.2
1978	Min-A	1	6	.143	12	12	1	0	0	66	81	11.0	7	17	2.3	23	3.1	5.05	71	.308	.346	-9	-11	94	97	-2.3	0	-1	-1.0
1979	Min-A	0	0	—	1	0	0	0	0	1	3	27.0	1	0	0.0	1	9.0	9.00	51	.500	.500	-1	-0	108	213	0.0	0	0	0.0
Total	3	12	21	.364	50	49	9	1	0	285	320	10.1	33	82	2.6	118	3.7	4.74	85	.288	.333	-23	-23	100	95	-5.0	0	-2	-2.2
■ JOHN THORNTON	Thornton, John b: 1870, Washington, D.C. d: 8/31/1893, Pensacola, Fla. 5'10.5", 175 lbs. Deb: 8/14/1889																												
1889	Was-N	0	1	.000	1	1	1	0	0	9	8	8.0	0	7	7.0	3	3.0	5.00	77	.253	.388	-1	-1	96	77	-0.4	-1	0	0.0
1891	Phi-N	15	16	.484	37	32	23	1	2	269	268	9.0	3	115	3.8	52	1.7	3.68	87	.273	.349	-10	-15	95	85	-0.4	-6	0	-1.8
1892	Phi-N	0	2	.000	3	2	1	0	0	12	16	12.0	1	17	12.8	2	1.5	12.75	26	.334	.508	-13	-12	103	65	-0.8	1	0	-1.2
Total	3	15	19	.441	41	35	25	1	2	290	292	9.1	4	139	4.3	57	1.8	4.10	79	.275	.359	-24	-28	96	84	-1.6	-6	0	-3.0
■ WALTER THORNTON	Thornton, Walter Miller b: 2/18/1875, Lewiston, Maine d: 7/14/60, Los Angeles, Cal. TL, 6'1", 180 lbs. Deb: 7/01/1895																												
1895	Chi-N	2	0	1.000	7	2	2	0	1	40	58	13.0	3	31	7.0	13	2.9	6.07	81	.360	.464	-6	-5	103	119	1.0	2	0	-0.1
1896	Chi-N	2	1	.667	5	5	2	0	0	24	30	11.3	1	13	4.9	10	3.8	6.00	79	.329	.413	-4	-3	108	87	0.4	2	0	0.0
1897	Chi-N	6	7	.462	16	16	15	0	0	130	164	11.4	4	51	3.5	55	3.8	4.71	92	.331	.393	-6	-5	101	101	0.2	4	0	-0.3
1898	Chi-N	13	10	.565	28	25	21	2	0	215	226	9.5	4	56	2.3	56	2.3	3.35	110	.292	.340	6	8	102	97	0.0	6	0	0.7
Total	4	23	18	.561	56	48	40	2	1	409	478	10.5	12	151	3.3	134	2.9	4.20	97	.314	.376	-10	-6	102	100	1.6	14	0	0.3
■ BOB THORPE	Thorpe, Robert Joseph b: 1/12/35, San Diego, Cal. d: 3/17/60, San Diego, Cal. BR/TR, 6'1", 170 lbs. Deb: 4/17/55																												
1955	Chi-N	0	0	—	2	0	0	0	0	3	4	12.0	0	0	0.0	0	0.0	3.00	136	.333	.333	0	0	101	137	0.0	0	0	0.1
■ GEORGE THROOP	Throop, George Lynford b: 11/24/50, Pasadena, Cal. BR/TR, 6'7", 205 lbs. Deb: 9/07/75																												
1975	KC-A	0	0	—	7	0	0	0	2	9	8	8.0	1	2	2.0	8	8.0	4.00	96	.250	.278	-0	-0	101	84	0.0	0	0	0.0
1977	KC-A	0	0	—	4	0	0	0	1	5	1	1.8	1	4	7.2	1	1.8	3.60	112	.059	.238	0	0	99	27	0.0	0	0	0.1
1978	KC-A	1	0	1.000	1	0	0	0	0	3	2	6.0	0	3	9.0	2	6.0	0.00	—	.222	.385	1	1	101	0	0.5	0	0	0.2
1979	KC-A	0	0	—	4	0	0	0	0	3	7	21.0	0	5	15.0	1	3.0	12.00	37	.467	.600	-3	-3	105	114	0.0	0	0	-0.1
	Hou-N	1	0	1.000	14	0	0	0	0	22	23	9.4	4	11	4.5	15	6.1	3.27	103	.271	.350	1	0	90	160	0.5	-0	-0	0.0
Total	4	2	0	1.000	30	0	0	0	3	42	41	8.8	6	25	5.4	27	5.8	3.86	95	.259	.353	-0	-1	95	113	1.0	-0	1	0.2
■ LOU THUMAN	Thuman, Louis Charles Frank b: 12/13/16, Baltimore, Md. BR/TR, 6'2", 185 lbs. Deb: 9/08/39																												
1939	Was-A	0	0	—	3	0	0	0	0	4	5	11.3	0	2	4.5	1	2.3	9.00	47	.278	.333	-2	-2	91	44	0.0	0	0	-0.1
1940	Was-A	0	1	.000	2	0	0	0	0	5	10	18.0	0	7	12.6	0	0.0	14.40	29	.400	.515	-6	-6	95	75	-0.4	-0	0	-0.4
Total	2	0	1	.000	5	0	0	0	0	9	15	15.0	0	9	9.0	1	1.0	12.00	35	.349	.444	-8	-8	94	61	-0.4	-0	0	-0.5
■ MARK THURMOND	Thurmond, Mark Anthony b: 9/12/56, Houston, Tex. BL/TL, 6', 180 lbs. Deb: 5/14/83																												
1983	SD-N	7	3	.700	21	18	2	0	0	115	104	8.1	7	33	2.6	49	3.8	2.66	135	.248	.298	12	12	99	117	2.1	-2	1	1.2
1984	SD-N	14	8	.636	32	29	1	1	0	179	174	8.7	12	55	2.8	57	2.9	2.97	118	.256	.305	12	11	98	113	2.0	1	2	1.5
1985	SD-N	7	11	.389	36	23	1	1	2	138	154	10.0	9	44	2.9	57	3.7	3.98	92	.291	.340	-6	-5	101	110	-2.3	-2	1	-0.5
1986	SD-N	3	7	.300	17	15	2	1	0	71	96	12.2	7	27	3.4	32	4.1	6.46	55	.325	.375	-22	-23	96	89	-1.7	1	0	-2.0
	Det-A	4	1	.800	25	4	0	0	3	52	44	7.6	7	17	2.9	17	2.9	1.90	208	.234	.292	13	12	95	184	1.4	0	-1	1.1
1987	Det-A	0	1	.000	48	0	0	0	5	62	83	12.0	5	24	3.5	21	3.0	4.21	102	.331	.382	2	0	96	140	-0.4	-0	-0	0.0
1988	Bal-A	1	8	.111	43	6	0	0	3	75	80	9.6	10	27	3.2	29	3.5	4.56	85	.277	.339	-5	-6	97	104	-3.0	0	-1	-0.6
Total	6	36	39	.480	222	95	6	3	13	692	735	9.6	57	227	3.0	262	3.4	3.68	101	.277	.329	8	2	98	118	-1.9	-1	2	0.7
■ SLOPPY THURSTON	Thurston, Hollis John b: 6/2/1899, Fremont, Neb. d: 9/14/73, Los Angeles, Cal. BR/TR, 5'11", 165 lbs. Deb: 4/19/23																												
1923	StL-A	0	0	—	2	1	0	0	0	4	8	18.0	0	2	4.5	0	0.0	6.75	62	.421	.435	-1	-1	105	126	0.0	0	-0	0.0
	Chi-A	7	8	.467	44	12	8	0	4	192	223	10.5	11	36	1.7	55	2.6	3.05	130	.308	.327	20	19	99	140	0.3	6	-0	2.4
	Yr	7	8	.467	46	13	8	0	4	196	231	10.6	11	38	1.7	55	2.5	3.12	127	.310	.330	19	18	99	**140**	0.3	0	-1	2.4
1924	Chi-A	20	14	.588	38	36	**28**	1	1	291	330	10.2	17	60	1.9	37	1.1	3.80	109	.290	.320	14	11	98	102	5.6	4	0	1.6
1925	Chi-A	10	14	.417	36	25	9	0	1	183	250	12.3	14	47	2.3	35	1.7	5.95	70	.335	.367	-32	-36	95	92	-2.5	6	2	-2.4
1926	Chi-A	6	8	.429	31	13	6	1	3	134	164	11.0	10	36	2.4	35	2.4	5.04	72	.311	.340	-15	-21	90	94	-1.3	6	-1	-1.6
1927	Was-A	13	13	.500	29	28	13	2	0	205	254	11.2	16	60	2.6	38	1.7	4.48	89	.308	.346	-8	-11	96	107	-1.3	9	-1	-0.3

YEAR	TM/L	W	L	PCT	G	GS	CG	SHO	SV	IP	H	H/G	HR	BB	BB/G	SO	SO/G	ERA	/A	OAVG	OOBP	PR	/A	PF	CPI	WAT	PB	PD	TPI
1930	Bro-N	6	4	.600	24	11	5	2	1	106	110	9.3	4	17	1.4	26	2.2	3.40	144	.266	.291	19	18	99	88	0.5	-0	1	1.7
1931	Bro-N	9	9	.500	24	17	11	0	0	143	175	11.0	3	39	2.5	23	1.4	3.97	99	.301	.340	-2	-1	101	106	-0.3	2	-1	0.1
1932	Bro-N	12	8	.600	28	20	10	2	0	153	174	10.2	14	38	2.2	35	2.1	4.06	92	.287	.327	-3	-6	96	106	1.8	6	1	0.0
1933	Bro-N	6	8	.429	32	15	5	0	3	131	171	11.7	4	34	2.3	22	1.5	4.53	72	.319	.357	-17	-18	98	105	0.0	-1	2	-1.7
Total	9	89	86	.509	288	178	95	8	13	1542	1859	10.9	93	369	2.2	306	1.8	4.24	94	.304	.336	-25	-46	97	106	2.8	38	3	-0.2
■ **LUIS TIANT**	Tiant, Luis Clemente (Vega) b: 11/23/40, Marianao, Cuba BR/TR, 6', 180 lbs. Deb: 7/19/64																												
1964	Cle-A	10	4	.714	19	16	9	3	1	127	94	6.7	13	47	3.3	105	7.4	2.83	132	.207	.279	11	13	103	94	3.3	-2	0	1.3
1965	Cle-A	11	11	.500	41	30	10	2	1	196	166	7.6	20	66	3.0	152	7.0	3.54	95	.228	.289	-2	-4	97	87	-0.8	-2	0	-0.5
1966	Cle-A	12	11	.522	46	16	7	**5**	8	155	121	7.0	16	50	2.9	145	8.4	2.79	125	.213	.275	11	12	102	99	0.6	-1	1	1.1
1967	Cle-A	12	9	.571	33	29	9	1	2	214	177	7.4	24	67	2.8	219	**9.2**	2.73	120	.221	.281	12	13	101	107	2.4	5	-2	1.7
1968	Cle-A	21	9	.700	34	32	19	**9**	0	258	152	**5.3**	16	73	2.5	264	9.2	**1.60**	**187**	**.168**	.232	**39**	40	101	79	6.1	-5	-2	4.1
1969	Cle-A	9	20	.310	38	37	9	1	0	250	229	8.2	37	129	4.6	156	5.6	3.71	94	.246	.335	-2	-6	96	118	-3.2	7	-1	0.0
1970	Min-A	7	3	.700	18	17	2	1	0	93	84	8.1	12	41	4.0	50	4.8	3.39	106	.246	.326	3	2	97	118	1.3	6	-0	0.8
1971	Bos-A	1	7	.125	21	10	1	0	0	72	73	9.1	8	32	4.0	59	7.4	4.88	75	.259	.330	-11	-10	105	83	-3.0	-0	-0	-1.0
1972	Bos-A	15	6	.714	43	19	12	6	3	179	128	6.4	7	65	3.3	123	6.2	**1.91**	169	.202	.271	23	26	105	103	4.2	-2	-1	2.8
1973	Bos-A	20	13	.606	35	35	23	0	0	272	217	7.2	32	78	2.6	206	6.8	3.34	120	.219	**.276**	15	20	105	84	2.5	0	-1	2.0
1974	Bos-A	22	13	.629	38	38	25	**7**	0	311	281	8.1	21	82	2.4	176	5.1	2.92	132	.241	.290	24	32	106	96	4.8	0	-3	3.2
1975	Bos-A	18	14	.563	35	35	18	2	0	260	262	9.1	25	72	2.5	142	4.9	4.02	102	.264	.313	-7	2	108	92	-0.9	0	-3	-0.1
1976	Bos-A	21	12	.636	38	38	19	3	0	279	274	8.8	25	64	2.1	131	4.2	3.06	126	.260	.300	14	25	110	113	4.9	0	-2	2.5
1977	Bos-A	12	8	.600	32	32	3	3	0	189	210	10.0	26	51	2.4	124	5.9	4.52	104	.279	.323	-9	4	116	97	0.0	0	-2	0.2
1978	Bos-A	13	8	.619	32	31	12	5	0	212	185	7.9	26	57	2.4	114	4.8	3.31	121	.234	.286	11	16	106	94	0.4	0	-2	1.5
1979	NY-A	13	8	.619	30	30	5	1	0	196	190	8.7	22	53	2.4	104	4.8	3.90	103	.251	.297	7	2	95	88	1.7	0	-0	0.2
1980	NY-A	8	9	.471	25	25	3	0	0	136	139	9.2	10	50	3.3	84	5.6	4.90	81	.265	.323	-13	-14	98	77	-2.3	0	1	-1.2
1981	Pit-N	2	5	.286	9	9	1	0	0	57	54	8.5	3	19	3.0	32	5.1	3.95	85	.243	.302	-3	-4	96	74	-1.2	1	-1	-0.3
1982	Cal-A	2	2	.500	6	5	0	0	0	30	39	11.7	3	8	2.4	30	9.0	5.70	71	.310	.348	-5	-6	99	87	-0.2	0	-1	-0.5
Total	19	229	172	.571	573	484	187	49	15	3486	3075	7.9	346	1104	2.9	2416	6.2	3.30	113	.236	.294	119	164	103	96	20.6	7	-19	17.8
■ **JAY TIBBS**	Tibbs, Jay Lindsey b: 1/4/62, Birmingham, Ala. BR/TR, 6'3", 185 lbs. Deb: 7/15/84																												
1984	Cin-N	6	2	.750	14	14	3	1	0	101	87	7.8	4	33	2.9	40	3.6	2.85	135	.238	.298	8	11	107	100	2.3	-1	-1	1.0
1985	Cin-N	10	16	.385	35	34	5	2	0	218	216	8.9	14	83	3.4	98	4.0	3.92	96	.262	.322	-8	-3	105	94	-4.4	-3	1	-0.5
1986	Mon-N	7	9	.438	35	31	3	2	0	190	181	8.6	12	70	3.3	117	5.5	3.98	92	.256	.319	-5	-7	98	91	-0.8	0	-1	-0.7
1987	Mon-N	4	5	.444	19	12	0	0	0	83	95	10.3	10	34	3.7	54	5.9	4.99	87	.289	.352	-8	-6	106	100	-0.9	0	-1	-0.5
1988	Bal-A	4	15	.211	30	24	1	0	0	159	184	10.4	18	63	3.6	82	4.6	5.38	72	.293	.353	-25	-27	97	95	-3.7	0	0	-2.5
Total	5	31	47	.397	133	115	12	5	0	751	763	9.1	58	283	3.4	391	4.7	4.22	91	.267	.329	-38	-31	102	95	-7.5	-4	-1	-3.2
■ **DICK TIDROW**	Tidrow, Richard William b: 5/14/47, San Francisco, Cal. BR/TR, 6'4", 210 lbs. Deb: 4/18/72																												
1972	Cle-A	14	15	.483	39	34	10	3	0	237	200	7.6	21	70	2.7	123	4.7	2.77	120	.230	.285	8	14	108	103	0.7	-4	-3	0.9
1973	Cle-A	14	16	.467	42	40	13	2	0	275	289	9.5	31	95	3.1	138	4.5	4.42	86	.270	.328	-18	-19	99	95	0.9	0	-1	-2.0
1974	Cle-A	1	3	.250	4	4	0	0	0	19	21	9.9	4	13	6.2	8	3.8	7.11	52	.276	.383	-7	-7	101	87	-0.9	0	0	-0.6
	NY-A	11	9	.550	33	25	5	0	1	191	205	9.7	14	53	2.5	100	4.7	3.86	89	.279	.323	-5	-9	95	101	0.0	0	-2	-1.0
	Yr	12	12	.500	37	29	5	0	1	210	226	9.7	18	66	2.8	108	4.6	4.16	83	.278	.327	-12	-16	96	101	-0.9	0	-1	-1.6
1975	NY-A	6	3	.667	37	0	0	0	5	69	65	8.5	5	31	4.0	38	5.0	3.13	118	.256	.337	5	4	98	125	1.4	0	-1	0.3
1976	NY-A	4	5	.444	47	2	0	0	10	92	80	7.8	5	24	2.3	65	6.4	2.64	130	.233	.280	9	8	97	97	-1.2	0	-1	0.7
1977	NY-A	11	4	.733	49	7	0	0	5	151	143	8.5	20	41	2.4	83	4.9	3.16	125	.250	.298	15	13	97	114	2.4	0	-1	1.2
1978	NY-A	7	11	.389	31	25	4	0	0	185	191	9.3	13	53	2.6	73	3.6	3.84	95	.267	.316	-1	-4	97	93	-3.4	0	-2	-0.5
1979	NY-A	2	1	.667	14	0	0	0	2	23	38	14.9	5	4	1.6	7	2.7	7.83	51	.409	.416	-9	-10	95	109	0.4	0	1	-0.7
	Chi-N	11	5	.688	63	0	0	0	4	103	86	7.5	5	42	3.7	68	5.9	2.71	155	.231	.306	12	17	112	108	3.3	0	1	2.0
1980	Chi-N	6	5	.545	**84**	0	0	0	6	116	97	7.5	10	53	4.1	97	7.5	2.79	139	.229	.313	11	14	108	121	1.4	-1	-0	1.4
1981	Chi-N	3	10	.231	51	0	0	0	9	75	73	8.8	6	30	3.6	39	4.7	5.04	74	.256	.317	-13	-11	106	75	-2.5	-1	-1	-1.2
1982	Chi-N	8	3	.727	65	0	0	0	6	104	106	9.2	6	29	2.5	62	5.4	3.38	111	.265	.313	3	4	104	104	2.9	-1	-2	0.2
1983	Chi-A	2	4	.333	50	1	0	0	7	92	86	8.4	13	34	3.3	66	6.5	4.21	98	.242	.305	-1	-1	102	90	-1.3	0	1	0.0
1984	NY-N	0	0	—	11	0	0	0	0	16	25	14.1	5	7	3.9	8	4.5	9.00	40	.357	.410	-10	-10	100	95	0.0	0	0	-0.8
Total	13	100	94	.515	620	138	32	5	55	1748	1705	8.8	163	579	3.0	975	5.0	3.68	101	.257	.314	-3	7	101	101	4.1	-5	-10	-0.1
■ **BOBBY TIEFENAUER**	Tiefenauer, Bobby Gene b: 10/10/29, Desloge, Mo. BR/TR, 6'2", 185 lbs. Deb: 7/14/52 C																												
1952	StL-N	0	0		6	0	0	0	0	8	12	13.5	1	7	7.9	3	3.4	7.88	46	.343	.442	-4	-4	97	101	0.0	-0	0	-0.3
1955	StL-N	1	4	.200	18	0	0	0	0	33	31	8.5	6	10	2.7	16	4.4	4.36	95	.261	.324	-1	-1	102	109	-1.3	-0	0	0.0
1960	Cle-A	0	1	.000	6	0	0	0	0	9	8	8.0	0	3	3.0	2	2.0	2.00	190	.242	.297	2	2	98	128	-0.4	0	0	0.2
1961	StL-N	0	0	—	3	0	0	0	0	4	9	20.3	0	4	9.0	3	6.8	6.75	67	.450	.542	-1	-1	113	166	0.0	0	-0	0.0
1962	Hou-N	2	4	.333	43	0	0	0	1	85	91	9.6	6	21	2.2	60	6.4	4.34	86	.277	.317	-4	-6	95	88	-0.4	0	-2	-0.6
1963	Mil-N	1	1	.500	12	0	0	0	2	30	20	6.0	1	4	1.2	22	6.6	1.20	273	.194	.218	7	7	100	103	0.0	-0	1	0.9
1964	Mil-N	4	6	.400	46	0	0	0	13	73	61	7.5	6	15	1.8	48	5.9	3.21	106	.225	.267	3	2	96	81	-1.3	-1	-1	0.0
1965	Mil-N	0	1	.000	6	0	0	0	0	7	8	10.3	1	3	3.9	7	9.0	7.71	47	.286	.353	-3	-3	103	71	-0.4	0	0	-0.2
	NY-A	1	1	.500	10	0	0	0	2	20	19	8.5	3	5	2.3	15	6.7	3.60	97	.253	.298	-0	-0	101	109	0.0	0	0	0.0
	Cle-A	0	5	.000	15	0	0	0	4	22	24	9.8	3	10	4.1	13	5.3	4.91	69	.273	.340	-4	-4	97	99	-2.4	-0	-0	-0.3
	Yr	1	6	.143	25	0	0	0	6	42	43	9.2	6	15	3.2	28	6.0	4.29	80	.259	.316	-4	-4	99	99	-2.4	0	-0	-0.3
1967	Cle-A	0	1	.000	5	0	0	0	0	11	9	7.4	0	3	2.5	6	4.9	0.82	400	.225	.273	3	3	101	256	-0.4	0	-0	0.3
1968	Chi-N	0	1	.000	9	0	0	0	1	13	20	13.8	2	2	1.4	9	6.2	6.23	54	.351	.344	-5	-4	112	101	-0.4	-0	-0	-0.4
Total	10	9	25	.265	179	0	0	0	23	315	312	8.9	29	87	2.5	204	5.8	3.86	93	.260	.307	-7	-9	98	100	-7.0	-1	-2	-0.4
■ **VERLE TIEFENTHALER**	Tiefenthaler, Verle Matthew b: 7/11/37, Breda, Iowa BL/TR, 6'1", 190 lbs. Deb: 4/19/62																												
1962	Chi-A	0	0	—	3	0	0	0	0	4	6	13.5	1	7	15.8	1	2.3	9.00	42	.353	.542	-2	-2	94	129	0.0	0	-0	-0.1
■ **EDDIE TIEMEYER**	Tiemeyer, Edward Carl b: 5/9/1885, Cincinnati, Ohio d: 9/27/46, Cincinnati, Ohio BR/TR, 5'11.5", 185 lbs. Deb: 8/19/06																												
1906	Cin-N	0	0	—	1	0	0	0	0	1	1	9.0	0	1	9.0	1	9.0	0.00	—	.288	.447	0	0	116	0	0.0	-0	0	0.0
■ **MIKE TIERNAN**	Tiernan, Michael Joseph "Silent Mike" b: 1/21/1867, Trenton, N.J. d: 11/9/18, New York, N.Y. BL/TL, 5'11", 165 lbs. Deb: 4/30/1887																												
1887	NY-N	1	2	.333	5	0	0	0	1	20	33	14.8	2	7	3.1	3	1.3	9.00	47	.385	.432	-11	-11	106	82	-0.5	1	0	-0.7
■ **LES TIETJE**	Tietje, Leslie William "Toots" b: 9/11/11, Sumner, Iowa BR/TR, 6'0.5", 178 lbs. Deb: 9/18/33																												
1933	Chi-A	2	0	1.000	3	3	1	0	0	22	16	6.5	1	15	6.1	9	3.7	2.45	180	.203	.326	4	5	103	130	1.0	0	0	0.5
1934	Chi-A	5	14	.263	34	22	6	1	0	176	174	8.9	20	96	4.9	81	4.1	4.81	97	.257	.346	-6	-3	103	97	-2.5	-8	2	-0.7
1935	Chi-A	9	15	.375	30	21	9	1	0	170	184	9.7	14	81	4.3	64	3.4	4.29	113	.277	.352	3	11	109	110	-3.0	-2	-2	0.8
1936	Chi-A	0	0	—	2	0	0	0	0	2	6	27.0	0	5	22.5	3	13.5	31.50	16	.462	.611	-6	-6	99	56	0.0	0	0	-0.3
	StL-A	3	5	.375	14	7	2	0	0	50	65	11.7	2	30	5.4	16	2.9	6.66	81	.310	.393	-9	-7	107	88	0.0	-2	1	-0.6
	Yr	3	5	.375	16	7	2	0	0	52	71	12.3	2	35	6.1	19	3.3	7.62	71	.318	.408	-15	-13	107	88	0.0	0	1	-0.9
1937	StL-A	1	2	.333	5	4	2	0	0	30	32	9.6	0	17	5.1	5	1.5	4.20	114	.283	.371	1	2	103	108	0.1	-2	-1	0.0
1938	StL-A	2	5	.286	17	8	2	1	0	62	83	12.0	8	38	5.5	15	2.2	7.55	65	.327	.409	-19	-18	103	92	-0.7	-1	-0	-1.6
Total	6	22	41	.349	105	65	22	3	0	512	560	9.8	45	282	5.0	193	3.4	5.12	94	.279	.364	-31	-17	106	101	-5.1	-13	-0	-1.9
■ **RAY TIFT**	Tift, Raymond Frank b: 6/21/1884, Fitchburg, Mass. d: 3/29/45, Verona, N.J. TR , Deb: 8/07/07																												
1907	NY-A	0	0	—	4	1	0	0	0	19	33	15.6	0	4	1.9	6	2.8	4.74	59	.409	.437	-5	-4	110	133	0.0	-1	-0	-0.4
■ **JOHNNY TILLMAN**	Tillman, John Lawrence "Ducky" b: 10/6/1893, Bridgeport, Conn. d: 4/7/64, Harrisburg, Pa. BB/TR, 5'11", 170 lbs. Deb: 9/20/15																												
1915	StL-A	1	0	1.000	2	1	0	0	0	10	6	5.4	0	4	3.6	6	5.4	0.90	324	.176	.263	2	2	99	127	0.5	-0	0	0.2
■ **THAD TILLOTSON**	Tillotson, Thaddeus Asa b: 12/20/40, Merced, Cal. BR/TR, 6'2.5", 195 lbs. Deb: 4/14/67																												
1967	NY-A	3	9	.250	43	5	1	0	2	98	99	9.1	9	39	3.6	62	5.7	4.04	77	.261	.326	-9	-10	96	100	-2.6	-0	0	-1.0
1968	NY-A	1	0	1.000	7	0	0	0	0	10	11	9.9	0	7	6.3	1	0.9	4.50	67	.282	.367	-2	-2	101	103	0.5	-0	0	-0.1

YEAR	TM/L	W	L	PCT	G	GS	CG	SHO	SV	IP	H	H/G	HR	BB	BB/G	SO	SO/G	ERA	/A	OAVG	OOBP	PR	/A	PF	CPI	WAT	PB	PD	TPI
Total	2	4	9	.308	50	5	1	0	2	108	110	9.2	9	46	3.8	63	5.3	4.08	76	.263	.330	-11	-12	96	101	-2.1	-1	1	-1.1
■ **GARY TIMBERLAKE** Timberlake, Gary Dale b: 8/8/48, Laconia, Ind. BR/TL, 6'2", 205 lbs. Deb: 6/18/69																													
1969	Sea-A	0	0	—	2	2	0	0	0	6	7	10.5	0	9	13.5	4	6.0	7.50	49	.269	.457	-3	-3	100	84	0.0	-0	-0	-0.2
■ **TOM TIMMERMANN** Timmermann, Thomas Henry b: 5/12/40, Breese, Ill. BR/TR, 6'4", 215 lbs. Deb: 6/18/69																													
1969	Det-A	4	3	.571	31	1	1	0	1	56	50	8.0	1	26	4.2	42	6.8	2.73	135	.238	.324	6	6	102	111	0.1	-0	-1	0.5
1970	Det-A	6	7	.462	61	0	0	0	27	85	90	9.5	3	34	3.6	49	5.2	4.13	94	.273	.333	-4	-3	104	92	-0.3	-2	-0	-0.4
1971	Det-A	7	6	.538	52	2	0	0	4	84	82	8.8	6	37	4.0	51	5.5	3.86	85	.262	.337	-4	-5	95	103	-0.2	-1	0	-0.6
1972	Det-A	8	10	.444	34	25	3	2	0	150	121	7.3	12	41	2.5	88	5.3	2.88	120	.216	.272	3	9	112	82	-1.8	-1	-2	0.9
1973	Det-A	1	1	.500	17	1	0	0	1	39	39	9.0	4	11	2.5	21	4.8	3.69	105	.258	.307	1	1	101	95	0.0	0	-0	0.0
	Cle-A	8	7	.533	29	15	4	0	2	124	117	8.5	15	54	3.9	62	4.5	4.94	77	.251	.329	-15	-16	99	81	1.4	0	-0	-1.5
	Yr	9	8	.529	46	16	4	0	3	163	156	8.6	19	65	3.6	83	4.6	4.64	82	.252	.324	-15	-15	100	81	1.4	0	-1	-1.5
1974	Cle-A	1	1	.500	4	0	0	0	0	10	9	8.1	1	5	4.5	2	1.8	5.40	68	.250	.333	-2	-2	101	74	0.0	0	1	0.0
Total	6	35	35	.500	228	44	8	2	35	548	508	8.3	42	208	3.4	315	5.2	3.78	96	.246	.314	-15	-8	103	90	-0.8	-4	-2	-1.1
■ **BEN TINCUP** Tincup, Austin Ben b: 12/14/1890, Adair, Okla. d: 7/5/80, Claremore, Okla. BL/TR, 6'1", 180 lbs. Deb: 5/22/14																													
1914	Phi-N	8	10	.444	28	17	9	3	2	155	165	9.6	0	62	3.6	108	6.3	2.61	108	.286	.351	3	3	101	142	-0.7	-1	1	0.4
1915	Phi-N	0	0	—	10	0	0	0	0	31	26	7.5	1	9	2.6	10	2.9	2.03	141	.263	.302	2	3	104	158	0.0	-1	0	0.2
1918	Phi-N	0	1	.000	8	1	0	0	0	17	24	12.7	0	6	3.2	6	3.2	7.41	42	.329	.366	-9	-8	111	65	-0.4	-0	1	-0.7
1928	Chi-N	0	0	—	2	0	0	0	0	9	14	14.0	0	1	1.0	3	3.0	7.00	53	.378	.366	-3	-3	93	82	0.0	-0	0	-0.2
Total	4	8	11	.421	48	18	9	3	2	212	229	9.7	1	78	3.3	127	5.4	3.10	93	.291	.346	-6	-5	102	135	-1.1	-3	3	-0.3
■ **BUD TINNING** Tinning, Lyle Forrest b: 3/12/06, Pilger, Neb. d: 1/17/61, Evansville, Ind. BB/TR, 5'11", 198 lbs. Deb: 4/20/32																													
1932	Chi-N	5	3	.625	24	7	2	0	0	93	93	9.0	3	24	2.3	30	2.9	2.81	142	.263	.307	11	12	103	117	0.4	-1	0	1.2
1933	Chi-N	13	6	.684	32	21	10	3	1	175	169	8.7	3	60	3.1	59	3.0	3.19	99	.255	.316	3	-0	95	97	3.0	1	-2	-0.2
1934	Chi-N	4	6	.400	39	7	1	1	3	129	134	9.3	9	46	3.2	44	3.1	3.35	117	.269	.323	10	8	97	120	-1.5	-1	-1	0.6
1935	StL-N	0	0	—	4	0	0	0	0	8	9	10.1	1	5	5.6	2	2.3	5.63	72	.300	.405	-1	-1	100	114	0.0	-0	0	0.0
Total	4	22	15	.595	99	35	13	4	4	405	405	9.0	16	135	3.0	135	3.0	3.20	113	.262	.318	23	18	97	109	1.9	-1	-3	1.6
■ **DAN TIPPLE** Tipple, Daniel E. "Big Dan" or "Rusty" b: 2/13/1890, Rockford, Ill. d: 3/26/60, Omaha, Neb. BR/TR, 6', 176 lbs. Deb: 9/18/15																													
1915	NY-A	1	1	.500	3	2	2	0	0	19	14	6.6	1	11	5.2	14	6.6	0.95	307	.203	.313	4	4	99	267	0.1	-1	-1	0.3
■ **JACK TISING** Tising, Johnnie Joseph b: 10/9/03, High Point, Mo. d: 9/5/67, Leadville, Ohio BL/TR, 6'2", 180 lbs. Deb: 4/24/36																													
1936	Pit-N	1	3	.250	10	6	1	0	0	47	52	10.0	5	24	4.6	27	5.2	4.21	92	.272	.347	-1	-2	96	111	-1.0	0	-0	-0.1
■ **CANNONBALL TITCOMB** Titcomb, Ledell b: 8/21/1866, W.Baldwin, Me. d: 6/8/50, Kingston, N.H. BL/TL, 5'6", 157 lbs. Deb: 5/05/1886																													
1886	Phi-N	0	5	.000	5	5	5	0	0	41	43	9.4	1	24	5.3	24	5.3	3.73	85	.283	.381	-2	-3	96	116	-2.4	-2	0	-0.3
1887	Phi-a	1	2	.333	3	3	3	0	0	24	31	11.6	1	19	7.1	16	6.0	6.00	71	.327	.440	-5	-5	100	107	-0.4	-1	0	-0.3
	NY-N	4	3	.571	9	9	9	0	0	72	68	8.5	3	37	4.6	34	4.3	4.13	104	.264	.356	-1	1	106	92	0.2	-4	0	-0.1
1888	NY-N	14	8	.636	23	23	22	4	0	197	149	6.8	5	46	2.1	129	5.9	2.24	112	.222	.272	13	6	89	81	0.0	-3	0	0.2
1889	NY-N	1	2	.333	3	3	3	0	0	26	27	9.3	1	16	5.5	7	2.4	6.58	62	.283	.386	-7	-7	101	67	-0.7	-1	0	-0.6
1890	Roc-a	10	9	.526	20	19	19	1	0	169	168	8.9	6	97	5.2	73	3.9	3.78	94	.275	.374	2	-4	92	114	0.6	-5	0	-0.8
Total	5	30	29	.508	63	62	61	5	0	529	486	8.3	17	239	4.1	283	4.8	3.49	94	.258	.342	0	-13	94	96	-2.7	-16	0	-1.9
■ **DAVE TOBIK** Tobik, David Vance b: 3/2/53, Euclid, Ohio BR/TR, 6'1", 190 lbs. Deb: 8/26/78																													
1978	Det-A	0	0	—	5	0	0	0	0	12	12	9.0	1	3	2.3	11	8.3	3.75	108	.261	.306	0	0	107	90	0.0	0	-0	0.0
1979	Det-A	3	5	.375	37	0	0	0	3	69	59	7.7	12	25	3.3	48	6.3	4.30	94	.231	.293	-1	-2	96	86	-1.1	0	-1	-0.2
1980	Det-A	1	0	1.000	17	1	0	0	0	61	61	9.0	7	21	3.1	34	5.0	3.98	106	.266	.324	0	2	105	103	0.5	0	-0	0.1
1981	Det-A	2	2	.500	27	0	0	0	1	60	47	7.1	7	33	5.0	32	4.8	2.70	142	.215	.310	6	8	105	126	-0.1	0	-1	0.6
1982	Det-A	4	9	.308	51	1	0	0	9	99	86	7.8	8	38	3.5	63	5.7	3.55	115	.241	.308	6	6	100	97	-2.6	0	-1	0.5
1983	Tex-A	2	1	.667	27	0	0	0	9	44	36	7.4	2	13	2.7	30	6.1	3.68	112	.222	.278	2	2	101	65	0.6	0	0	0.2
1984	Tex-A	1	6	.143	24	0	0	0	5	42	44	9.4	5	17	3.6	30	6.4	3.64	111	.265	.333	2	2	101	118	-2.3	0	1	0.2
1985	Sea-A	1	0	1.000	8	0	0	0	1	9	10	10.0	2	3	3.0	8	8.0	6.00	66	.286	.325	-2	-2	95	92	0.5	0	-0	-0.1
Total	8	14	23	.378	196	2	0	0	28	396	355	8.1	44	153	3.5	256	5.8	3.70	110	.242	.308	14	16	101	99	-4.5	0	-3	1.3
■ **JIM TOBIN** Tobin, James Anthony "Abba Dabba" b: 12/27/12, Oakland, Cal. d: 5/19/69, Oakland, Cal. BR/TR, 6', 185 lbs. Deb: 4/30/37																													
1937	Pit-N	6	3	.667	20	8	7	0	1	87	74	7.7	1	28	2.9	37	3.8	3.00	132	.226	.289	9	9	101	77	1.2	7	-2	1.5
1938	Pit-N	14	12	.538	40	33	14	2	0	241	254	9.5	17	66	2.5	70	2.6	3.47	108	.270	.317	8	7	99	109	-0.8	7	-2	1.2
1939	Pit-N	9	9	.500	25	19	8	0	0	145	194	12.0	7	33	2.0	43	2.7	4.53	87	.319	.350	-10	-9	101	106	1.0	5	-1	-0.5
1940	Bos-N	7	3	.700	15	11	9	0	0	96	102	9.6	8	24	2.3	29	2.7	3.84	101	.264	.306	0	0	101	95	2.5	3	-1	0.3
1941	Bos-N	12	12	.500	33	26	20	3	0	238	229	8.7	12	60	2.3	61	2.3	3.10	112	.253	.295	14	10	96	100	2.2	3	4	1.7
1942	Bos-N	12	21	.364	37	33	**28**	1	0	**288**	283	8.8	20	96	3.0	71	2.2	3.97	82	.257	.315	-21	-23	98	91	-1.7	14	6	-0.3
1943	Bos-N	14	14	.500	33	30	24	1	0	250	241	8.7	12	69	2.5	52	1.9	2.66	138	.251	.297	20	28	109	113	1.7	5	2	**4.4**
1944	Bos-N	18	19	.486	43	36	**28**	5	3	299	271	8.2	18	97	2.9	83	2.5	3.01	115	.240	.297	20	15	96	101	2.6	7	7	3.0
1945	Bos-N	9	14	.391	27	25	16	0	0	197	220	10.1	10	56	2.6	38	1.7	3.84	112	.282	.328	-1	10	113	104	-1.4	4	2	1.8
	Det-A	4	5	.444	14	6	2	0	1	58	61	9.5	2	28	4.3	14	2.2	3.57	99	.274	.355	-1	-0	105	119	-1.0	0	1	0.1
Total	9	105	112	.484	287	227	156	12	5	1899	1929	9.1	107	557	2.6	498	2.4	3.44	106	.262	.311	38	46	101	102	6.3	54	16	13.2
■ **PAT TOBIN** Tobin, Marion Brooks b: 1/28/16, Hermitage, Ark. d: 1/21/75, Shreveport, La. BR/TR, 6'1", 198 lbs. Deb: 8/21/41																													
1941	Phi-A	0	0	—	1	0	0	0	0	1	4	36.0	0	2	18.0	0	0.0	36.00	12	.571	.600	-4	-4	103	63	0.0	0	0	-0.2
■ **FRANK TODD** Todd, George Franklin b: 10/18/1869, Aberdeen, Md. d: 8/11/19, Havre De Grace, Md. TL , Deb: 7/14/1898																													
1898	Lou-N	0	2	.000	4	2	0	0	0	11	23	18.8	1	8	6.5	5	4.1	13.91	25	.450	.525	-13	-13	98	73	-0.9	0	0	-0.9
■ **JACKSON TODD** Todd, Jackson A b: 11/20/51, Tulsa, Okla. BR/TR, 6'2", 180 lbs. Deb: 5/05/77																													
1977	NY-N	3	6	.333	19	10	0	0	0	72	78	9.8	8	20	2.5	39	4.9	4.75	80	.273	.321	-7	-8	97	85	-0.6	-1	0	-0.8
1979	Tor-A	0	1	.000	12	1	0	0	0	32	40	11.3	7	7	2.0	14	3.9	5.91	76	.299	.333	-6	-5	106	92	-0.4	0	0	-0.4
1980	Tor-A	5	2	.714	12	12	4	0	0	85	90	9.5	14	30	3.2	44	4.7	4.02	102	.276	.338	0	1	101	119	1.8	0	1	0.2
1981	Tor-A	2	7	.222	21	13	3	0	0	98	94	8.6	10	31	2.8	41	3.8	3.95	105	.251	.311	-3	2	113	92	-1.6	0	1	0.3
Total	4	10	16	.385	64	36	7	0	0	287	302	9.5	39	88	2.8	138	4.3	4.39	93	.270	.324	-16	-10	105	98	-0.8	-1	2	-0.7
■ **JIM TODD** Todd, James Richard b: 9/21/47, Lancaster, Pa. BL/TR, 6'2", 190 lbs. Deb: 4/29/74																													
1974	Chi-N	4	2	.667	43	6	0	0	3	88	82	8.4	7	41	4.2	42	4.3	3.89	95	.252	.336	-3	-2	102	99	1.3	-1	1	-0.2
1975	Oak-A	8	3	.727	58	0	0	0	12	122	104	7.7	4	33	2.4	50	3.7	2.29	151	.234	.286	20	16	91	110	1.8	0	4	2.0
1976	Oak-A	7	8	.467	49	0	0	0	4	83	87	9.4	6	34	3.7	22	2.4	3.80	91	.276	.351	-3	-3	98	116	-1.0	0	2	0.0
1977	Chi-N	1	1	.500	20	0	0	0	0	31	47	13.6	1	19	5.5	17	4.9	9.00	50	.336	.422	-18	-16	115	71	0.0	-0	0	-1.4
1978	Sea-A	3	4	.429	49	2	0	0	3	107	113	9.5	4	61	5.1	37	3.1	3.87	102	.280	.369	-1	1	104	115	0.4	0	0	0.1
1979	Oak-A	2	5	.286	51	0	0	0	2	81	108	12.0	12	51	5.7	26	2.9	6.56	59	.329	.412	-21	-24	91	107	-0.4	0	0	-2.2
Total	6	25	23	.521	270	8	0	0	24	512	541	9.5	34	239	4.2	194	3.4	4.22	88	.277	.354	-24	-28	98	107	2.1	-2	7	-1.7
■ **HAL TOENES** Toenes, William Harrel b: 10/8/17, Mobile, Ala. BR/TR, 5'11.5", 175 lbs. Deb: 9/17/47																													
1947	Was-A	0	1	.000	3	1	0	0	0	7	11	14.1	0	2	2.6	5	6.4	6.43	58	.379	.406	-2	-2	101	99	-0.4	0	-0	-0.1
■ **FREDDIE TOLIVER** Toliver, Freddie Lee b: 2/3/61, Natchez, Miss. BR/TR, 6'1", 165 lbs. Deb: 9/15/84																													
1984	Cin-N	0	0	—	3	1	0	0	0	10	7	6.3	0	7	6.3	4	3.6	0.90	428	.206	.333	3	3	107	323	0.0	-0	-0	0.3
1985	Phi-N	0	4	.000	11	3	0	0	1	25	27	9.7	2	17	6.1	23	8.3	4.68	79	.273	.376	-3	-3	102	105	-1.9	1	0	-0.1
1986	Phi-N	0	2	.000	5	5	0	0	0	26	28	9.7	0	11	3.8	20	6.9	3.46	112	.286	.348	1	1	104	116	-0.9	-0	0	0.2
1987	Phi-N	1	1	.500	10	4	0	0	0	30	34	10.2	2	17	5.1	25	7.5	5.70	75	.291	.374	-5	-5	105	91	0.0	-1	0	-0.4
1988	Min-A	7	6	.538	21	19	0	0	0	115	116	9.1	8	52	4.1	69	5.4	4.23	99	.270	.344	-3	-0	105	102	-0.2	0	0	0.0
Total	5	8	13	.381	50	32	0	0	1	206	212	9.3	12	104	4.5	141	6.2	4.24	96	.272	.353	-8	-4	105	113	-3.0	0	0	0.0

YEAR	TM/L	W	L	PCT	G	GS	CG	SHO	SV	IP	H	H/G	HR	BB	BB/G	SO	SO/G	ERA	/A	OAVG	OOBP	PR	/A	PF	CPI	WAT	PB	PD	TPI
■ DICK TOMANEK	Tomanek, Richard Carl "Bones" b: 1/6/31, Avon Lake, Ohio BL/TL, 6'1", 175 lbs. Deb: 9/25/53																												
1953	Cle-A	1	0	1.000	1	1	1	0	0	9	6	6.0	1	6	6.0	6	6.0	2.00	185	.176	.317	2	2	93	143	0.5	-1	-0	0.1
1954	Cle-A	0	0	—	1	0	0	0	0	2	1	4.5	1	1	4.5	0	0.0	4.50	84	.167	.286	-0	-0	101	124	0.0	0	0	0.0
1957	Cle-A	2	1	.667	34	2	0	0	0	70	67	8.6	13	37	4.8	55	7.1	5.66	68	.248	.339	-15	-14	102	82	0.5	0	0	-1.2
1958	Cle-A	2	3	.400	18	6	2	0	0	58	61	9.5	8	28	4.3	42	6.5	5.59	63	.276	.358	-12	-13	93	90	-0.4	0	0	-1.2
	KC-A	5	5	.500	36	2	1	0	5	72	69	8.6	5	28	3.5	50	6.3	3.63	111	.252	.318	1	3	107	96	0.3	1	-0	0.4
	Yr	7	8	.467	54	8	3	0	5	130	130	9.0	13	56	3.9	92	6.4	4.50	84	.261	.333	-11	-10	101	96	-0.1	0	0	-0.8
1959	KC-A	0	1	.000	16	0	0	0	2	21	27	11.6	6	12	5.1	13	5.6	6.43	62	.310	.394	-6	-6	103	118	-0.4	0	0	-0.4
Total	5	10	10	.500	106	11	4	0	7	232	231	9.0	34	112	4.3	166	6.4	4.93	78	.259	.342	-29	-28	101	94	0.5	1	1	-2.3
■ ANDY TOMASIC	Tomasic, Andrew John b: 12/10/19, Hokendauqua, Pa. BR/TR, 6', 175 lbs. Deb: 4/28/49																												
1949	NY-N	0	1	.000	2	0	0	0	0	5	9	16.2	2	5	9.0	2	3.6	18.00	23	.375	.483	-8	-8	101	64	-0.4	-0	-0	-0.6
■ DAVE TOMLIN	Tomlin, David Allen b: 6/22/49, Maysville, Ky. BL/TL, 6'2", 180 lbs. Deb: 9/02/72																												
1972	Cin-N	0	0	—	3	0	0	0	0	4	7	15.8	2	1	2.3	2	4.5	9.00	35	.412	.400	-2	-3	91	122	0.0	0	0	-0.2
1973	Cin-N	1	2	.333	16	0	0	0	1	28	24	7.7	5	15	4.8	20	6.4	4.82	70	.238	.325	-4	-5	92	91	-0.6	-0	0	-0.4
1974	SD-N	2	0	1.000	47	0	0	0	2	58	59	9.2	4	30	4.7	29	4.5	4.34	81	.271	.349	-5	-5	97	101	1.0	-0	1	-0.4
1975	SD-N	4	2	.667	67	0	0	0	1	83	87	9.4	5	31	3.4	48	5.2	3.25	113	.275	.329	4	4	101	123	1.2	1	3	0.8
1976	SD-N	0	1	.000	49	1	0	0	0	73	62	7.6	4	20	2.5	43	5.3	2.84	111	.235	.286	5	2	90	96	-0.4	-0	2	0.4
1977	SD-N	4	4	.500	76	0	0	0	3	102	98	8.6	3	32	2.8	55	4.9	3.00	117	.259	.311	10	6	89	108	0.5	0	1	0.7
1978	Cin-N	9	1	.900	57	0	0	0	4	62	88	12.8	3	30	4.4	32	4.6	5.81	63	.326	.392	-15	-15	102	100	3.9	0	1	-1.4
1979	Cin-N	2	2	.500	53	0	0	0	1	58	59	9.2	3	18	2.8	30	4.7	2.64	137	.269	.320	7	6	96	137	-0.1	0	0	0.7
1980	Cin-N	3	0	1.000	27	0	0	0	0	26	38	13.2	2	11	3.8	6	2.1	5.54	66	.355	.398	-6	-5	101	118	1.5	0	0	-0.4
1982	Mon-N	0	0	—	1	0	0	0	0	2	1	4.5	0	1	4.5	2	9.0	4.50	84	.167	.286	-0	-0	104	40	0.0	0	0	0.0
1983	Pit-N	0	0	—	5	0	0	0	0	4	6	13.5	0	1	2.3	5	11.3	6.75	55	.316	.350	-1	-1	103	63	0.0	0	0	0.0
1985	Pit-N	0	0	—	1	0	0	0	0	1	1	9.0	0	1	9.0	0	0.0	0.00	—	.333	.500	0	0	104	0	0.0	0	0	0.0
1986	Mon-N	0	0	—	7	0	0	0	0	10	13	11.7	1	7	6.3	6	5.4	5.40	68	.317	.404	-2	-2	98	124	0.0	0	0	-0.1
Total	13	25	12	.676	409	1	0	0	12	511	543	9.6	32	198	3.5	278	4.9	3.82	92	.277	.336	-8	-17	96	109	7.0	1	9	-0.3
■ CHUCK TOMPKINS	Tompkins, Charles Herbert b: 9/1/1889, Prescott, Ark. d: 9/20/75, Prescott, Ark. BR/TR, 6', 185 lbs. Deb: 6/25/12																												
1912	Cin-N	0	0	—	1	0	0	0	0	3	5	15.0	0	0	0.0	1	3.0	0.00	—	.357	.357	1	1	93	0	0.0	0	0	0.2
■ RON TOMPKINS	Tompkins, Ronald Everett "Stretch" b: 11/27/44, San Diego, Cal. BR/TR, 6'4", 198 lbs. Deb: 9/09/65																												
1965	KC-A	0	0	—	5	1	0	0	0	10	9	8.1	0	3	2.7	4	3.6	3.60	96	.237	.302	-0	-0	100	72	0.0	-0	0	0.0
1971	Chi-N	0	2	.000	35	0	0	0	3	40	31	7.0	3	21	4.7	20	4.5	4.05	94	.214	.322	-3	-1	110	78	-0.9	0	1	0.0
Total	2	0	2	.000	40	1	0	0	3	50	40	7.2	3	24	4.3	24	4.3	3.96	94	.219	.318	-3	-1	108	77	-0.9	-0	1	0.0
■ TOMMY TOMS	Toms, Thomas Howard b: 10/15/51, Charlottesville, Va BR/TR, 6'4", 195 lbs. Deb: 5/04/75																												
1975	SF-N	0	1	.000	7	0	0	0	0	10	13	11.7	1	6	5.4	6	5.4	6.30	59	.317	.396	-3	-3	102	95	-0.4	0	0	-0.2
1976	SF-N	0	1	.000	7	0	0	0	1	9	13	13.0	1	1	1.0	4	4.0	6.00	61	.351	.359	-2	-2	104	97	-0.4	0	0	-0.1
1977	SF-N	0	1	.000	4	0	0	0	0	4	7	15.8	0	2	4.5	2	4.5	2.25	182	.333	.391	1	1	105	248	-0.4	0	0	0.1
Total	3	0	3	.000	18	0	0	0	1	23	33	12.9	2	9	3.5	12	4.7	5.48	68	.333	.382	-5	-4	103	122	-1.2	0	0	-0.2
■ FRED TONEY	Toney, Fred Alexandra b: 12/11/1888, Nashville, Tenn. d: 3/11/53, Nashville, Tenn. BR/TR, 6'1", 195 lbs. Deb: 4/15/11																												
1911	Chi-N	1	1	.500	18	4	1	0	0	67	55	7.4	3	35	4.7	27	3.6	2.42	132	.229	.339	7	6	94	135	-0.1	-1	1	0.5
1912	Chi-N	1	2	.333	9	2	0	0	0	24	21	7.9	0	11	4.1	9	3.4	5.25	66	.239	.330	-5	-5	102	50	-0.6	-0	-1	-0.4
1913	Chi-N	2	2	.500	7	5	2	0	0	39	52	12.0	1	22	5.1	12	2.8	6.00	52	.327	.403	-12	-13	97	94	-0.2	1	0	-1.0
1915	Cin-N	17	6	.739	36	23	18	6	2	223	160	6.5	1	73	2.9	108	4.4	1.57	182	.207	.269	29	32	104	109	6.4	-5	1	3.3
1916	Cin-N	14	17	.452	41	38	21	3	1	300	247	7.4	7	78	2.3	146	4.4	2.28	116	.231	.281	11	12	101	98	1.9	-4	-4	0.4
1917	Cin-N	24	16	.600	43	42	31	7	1	340	300	7.9	4	77	2.0	123	3.3	2.20	114	.238	.279	19	12	93	101	4.8	-5	-5	0.0
1918	Cin-N	6	10	.375	21	19	9	1	2	137	148	9.7	2	31	2.0	32	2.1	2.89	92	.282	.313	-2	-4	96	112	-2.5	0	1	-0.2
	NY-N	6	2	.750	11	9	7	1	1	85	55	5.8	1	7	0.7	19	2.0	1.69	156	.192	.208	10	9	96	48	1.7	-1	-1	0.9
	Yr	12	12	.500	32	28	16	2	**3**	222	203	8.2	3	38	1.5	51	2.1	2.43	109	.250	.277	8	6	96	48	-0.8	0	-0	0.7
1919	NY-N	13	6	.684	24	20	14	4	1	181	157	7.8	6	35	1.7	40	2.0	1.84	153	.235	.270	22	19	96	121	1.8	1	-3	2.0
1920	NY-N	21	11	.656	42	37	17	4	1	278	266	8.6	8	57	1.8	81	2.6	2.65	114	.259	.294	15	12	97	98	4.2	3	-2	1.3
1921	NY-N	18	11	.621	42	32	16	1	3	249	274	9.9	14	65	2.3	63	2.3	3.61	98	.289	.325	5	-2	94	107	0.3	2	-1	0.0
1922	NY-N	5	6	.455	13	12	6	0	0	86	91	9.5	5	31	3.2	10	1.0	4.19	98	.277	.335	-1	-1	100	93	-1.3	-3	-2	-0.4
1923	StL-N	11	12	.478	29	28	16	1	0	197	211	9.6	8	61	2.8	48	2.2	3.84	94	.282	.328	4	-5	90	101	-0.9	-4	3	-0.6
Total	12	139	102	.577	336	271	158	28	12	2206	2037	8.3	60	583	2.4	718	2.9	2.69	111	.251	.297	102	75	96	102	15.5	-16	-11	5.8
■ DOC TONKIN	Tonkin, Harry Glenville b: 8/11/1881, Concord, N.H. d: 5/30/59, Miami, Fla. BL/TL, 5'9", 165 lbs. Deb: 8/19/07																												
1907	Was-A	0	0	—	1	0	0	0	0	3	6	18.0	0	5	15.0	0	0.0	6.00	40	.443	.593	-1	-1	94	194	0.0	1	0	0.0
■ STEVE TOOLE	Toole, Stephen John b: 4/9/1859, New Orleans, La. d: 3/28/19, Pittsburgh, Pa. BR/TL, 6', 170 lbs. Deb: 4/20/1886																												
1886	Bro-a	6	6	.500	13	12	11	0	0	104	100	8.7	0	64	5.5	48	4.2	4.41	78	.263	.369	-11	-11	100	91	-0.5	4	0	-0.5
1887	Bro-a	14	10	.583	24	24	22	1	0	194	186	8.6	1	106	4.9	48	2.2	4.31	98	.265	.362	-0	-2	99	88	3.4	-0	0	-0.1
1888	KC-a	5	6	.455	12	10	10	0	0	92	124	12.1	4	50	4.9	35	3.4	6.75	51	.336	.416	-38	-34	112	88	1.1	-0	0	-2.6
1890	BB-a	2	4	.333	6	6	6	0	0	53	47	8.0	0	39	6.6	10	1.7	4.08	97	.252	.382	-1	-1	103	97	0.1	1	0	0.1
Total	4	27	26	.509	55	52	49	1	0	443	457	9.3	5	259	5.3	141	2.9	4.81	81	.279	.378	-50	-46	102	90	4.1	5	0	-3.1
■ RUPE TOPPIN	Toppin, Ruperto b: 12/7/41, Panama City, Panama BR/TR, 6', 185 lbs. Deb: 7/28/62																												
1962	KC-A	0	0	—	2	0	0	0	0	2	1	4.5	0	5	22.5	1	4.5	13.50	30	.167	.545	-2	-2	101	55	0.0	0	0	-0.1
■ RED TORKELSON	Torkelson, Chester Leroy b: 3/19/1894, Chicago, Ill. d: 9/22/64, Chicago, Ill. BR/TR, 6', 175 lbs. Deb: 8/29/17																												
1917	Cle-A	2	1	.667	4	3	0	0	0	22	33	13.5	1	13	5.3	10	4.1	7.77	39	.333	.421	-12	-12	113	80	0.3	-0	0	-1.0
■ PABLO TORREALBA	Torrealba, Pablo Arnoldo (Torrealba) b: 4/28/48, Barquisimento, Ven. BL/TL, 5'10", 173 lbs. Deb: 4/09/75																												
1975	Atl-N	0	1	.000	6	0	0	0	0	7	7	9.0	0	3	3.9	5	6.4	1.29	274	.250	.323	2	2	97	220	-0.4	0	1	0.3
1976	Atl-N	0	2	.000	36	0	0	0	2	53	67	11.4	0	22	3.7	33	5.6	3.57	110	.315	.382	-0	2	112	137	-0.9	-1	1	0.3
1977	Oak-A	4	6	.400	41	10	3	0	2	117	127	9.8	5	38	2.9	51	3.9	2.62	150	.279	.329	19	17	97	146	0.1	0	2	1.9
1978	Chi-A	2	4	.333	25	3	1	1	1	57	69	10.9	6	39	6.2	23	3.6	4.74	81	.301	.404	-6	-6	102	126	-0.7	0	-1	-0.6
1979	Chi-A	0	0	—	3	0	0	0	0	6	5	7.5	1	2	3.0	1	1.5	1.50	289	.250	.292	2	2	103	288	0.0	0	0	0.2
Total	5	6	13	.316	111	13	4	1	5	240	275	10.3	12	104	3.9	113	4.2	3.26	120	.291	.359	16	18	101	145	-1.9	-0	2	2.1
■ ANGEL TORRES	Torres, Angel Rafael (Ruiz) b: 10/24/52, Las Ciengas, Azua, D.R. BL/TL, 5'11", 168 lbs. Deb: 9/12/77																												
1977	Cin-N	0	0	—	5	0	0	0	0	8	7	7.9	2	8	9.0	8	9.0	2.25	172	.233	.385	1	1	99	269	0.0	0	0	0.1
■ GIL TORRES	Torres, Don Gilberto (Nunez) b: 8/23/15, Regla, Cuba d: 1/11/83, Regla, Cuba BR/TR, 6', 155 lbs. Deb: 4/25/40																												
1940	Was-A	0	0	—	2	0	0	0	0	3	3	9.0	0	0	0.0	1	3.0	0.00	—	.273	.273	1	1	95	0	0.0	0	0	0.1
1946	Was-A	0	0	—	3	0	0	0	1	7	9	11.6	0	3	3.9	2	2.6	7.71	43	.310	.375	-3	-3	94	60	0.0	1	-0	-0.2
Total	2	0	0	—	5	0	0	0	1	10	12	10.8	0	3	2.7	3	2.7	5.40	66	.300	.349	-2	-2	94	42	0.0	1	0	-0.1
■ HECTOR TORRES	Torres, Hector Epitacio (Marroquin) b: 9/16/45, Monterrey, Mexico BR/TR, 6', 175 lbs. Deb: 4/10/68																												
1972	Mon-N	0	0	—	1	0	0	0	0	1	5	45.0	0	0	0.0	0	0.0	18.00	20	.714	.714	-2	-2	104	130	0.0	0	0	-0.1
■ MIKE TORREZ	Torrez, Michael Augustine b: 8/28/46, Topeka, Kan. BR/TR, 6'5", 220 lbs. Deb: 9/10/67																												
1967	StL-N	0	1	.000	3	1	0	0	0	6	5	7.5	0	1	1.5	5	7.5	3.00	111	.238	.304	0	0	99	87	-0.4	-0	-0	0.0
1968	StL-N	2	1	.667	5	2	0	0	0	19	20	9.5	1	12	5.7	6	2.8	2.84	98	.286	.379	0	-0	93	178	0.3	0	0	0.0
1969	StL-N	10	4	.714	24	15	3	0	0	108	96	8.0	7	62	5.2	61	5.1	3.58	99	.240	.345	0	-0	99	106	2.8	-2	0	-0.1
1970	StL-N	8	10	.444	30	28	5	1	0	179	168	8.4	12	103	5.2	100	5.0	4.22	102	.248	.344	-3	2	106	96	-0.4	4	-0	0.5
1971	StL-N	1	2	.333	9	6	0	0	0	36	41	10.3	2	30	7.5	8	2.0	6.00	58	.304	.419	-10	-10	100	101	-0.5	1	0	-0.8
	Mon-N	0	0	—	1	0	0	0	0	3	4	12.0	0	1	3.0	2	6.0	0.00	—	.308	.357	1	1	100	0	0.0	0	0	0.2

YEAR	TM/L	W	L	PCT	G	GS	CG	SHO	SV	IP	H	H/G	HR	BB	BB/G	SO	SO/G	ERA	/A	OAVG	OOBP	PR	/A	PF	CPI	WAT	PB	PD	TPI
	Yr	1	2	.333	10	6	0	0	0	39	45	10.4	2	31	7.2	10	2.3	5.54	63	.300	.409	-9	-9	100	0	-0.5	1	1	-0.6
1972	Mon-N	16	12	.571	34	33	13	0	0	243	215	8.0	15	103	3.8	112	4.1	3.33	108	.242	.320	3	7	104	101	3.6	0	2	1.0
1973	Mon-N	9	12	.429	35	34	3	1	0	208	207	9.0	17	115	5.0	90	3.9	4.46	86	.262	.354	-18	-14	105	97	-1.3	-1	2	-1.3
1974	Mon-N	15	8	.652	32	30	6	1	0	186	184	8.9	10	84	4.1	92	4.5	3.58	106	.257	.334	1	4	104	101	4.0	-3	5	0.6
1975	Bal-A	20	9	**.690**	36	36	16	2	0	271	238	7.9	15	133	4.4	119	4.0	3.06	110	.239	.329	22	10	89	111	4.7	0	1	1.1
1976	Oak-A	16	12	.571	39	39	13	4	0	266	231	7.8	15	87	2.9	115	3.9	2.50	138	.235	.296	30	28	98	115	1.1	0	-1	3.1
1977	Oak-A	3	1	.750	4	4	2	0	0	26	23	8.0	3	11	3.8	12	4.2	4.50	87	.242	.315	-1	-2	97	85	1.2	0	0	-0.1
	NY-A	14	12	.538	31	31	15	2	0	217	212	8.8	20	75	3.1	90	3.7	3.82	103	.259	.321	6	3	97	100	-1.8	0	-2	0.1
	Yr	17	13	.567	35	35	17	2	0	243	235	8.7	23	86	3.2	102	3.8	3.89	101	.256	.319	5	1	97	100	-0.6	0	-2	0.0
1978	Bos-A	16	13	.552	36	36	15	2	0	250	272	9.8	19	99	3.6	120	4.3	3.96	101	.281	.343	-5	1	106	108	-1.5	0	-2	0.0
1979	Bos-A	16	13	.552	36	36	12	1	0	252	254	9.1	20	121	4.3	125	4.5	4.50	100	.264	.343	-8	-0	106	94	-0.4	0	-0	0.0
1980	Bos-A	9	16	.360	36	32	6	1	0	207	256	11.1	18	75	3.3	97	4.2	5.09	81	.313	.362	-24	-22	102	102	-4.2	0	2	-1.9
1981	Bos-A	10	3	.769	22	22	2	0	0	127	130	9.2	10	51	3.6	54	3.8	3.69	105	.267	.334	-0	3	106	109	3.4	0	-1	0.1
1982	Bos-A	9	9	.500	31	31	1	0	0	176	196	10.0	20	74	3.8	84	4.3	5.22	86	.282	.353	-22	-14	110	93	-0.8	0	-2	-1.5
1983	NY-N	10	17	.370	39	34	5	0	0	222	227	9.2	16	113	4.6	94	3.8	4.38	83	.271	.351	-18	-18	100	99	-1.8	-5	0	-2.3
1984	NY-N	1	5	.167	9	8	0	0	0	38	55	13.0	3	18	4.3	16	3.8	4.97	72	.369	.429	-6	-6	100	145	-2.0	1	0	-0.4
	Oak-A	0	0	—	2	0	0	0	0	2	9	40.5	0	3	13.5	2	9.0	31.50	12	.563	.632	-6	-6	92	69	0.0	0	0	-0.4
Total	18	185	160	.536	494	458	117	15	0	3042	3043	9.0	223	1371	4.1	1404	4.2	3.96	97	.264	.339	-58	-36	102	103	6.0	-4	4	-2.1
■ **LOU TOST**	Tost, Louis Eugene b: 6/1/11, Cumberland, Wash. d: 2/22/67, Santa Clara, Cal. BL/TL, 6', 175 lbs. Deb: 4/20/42																												
1942	Bos-N	10	10	.500	35	22	5	1	0	148	146	8.9	12	52	3.2	43	2.6	3.53	92	.256	.319	-4	-5	98	105	1.9	0	-1	-0.5
1943	Bos-N	0	1	.000	3	1	0	0	0	7	10	12.9	2	4	5.1	3	3.9	5.14	71	.357	.438	-1	-1	109	167	-0.4	-0	0	0.0
1947	Pit-N	0	0	—	1	0	0	0	0	1	3	27.0	0	0	0.0	0	0.0	9.00	46	.600	.500	-1	-1	102	156	0.0	-0	0	0.0
Total	3	10	11	.476	39	23	5	1	0	156	159	9.2	14	56	3.2	46	2.7	3.63	90	.263	.326	-5	-6	99	108	1.5	0	-1	-0.5
■ **PAUL TOTH**	Toth, Paul Louis b: 6/30/35, McRoberts, Ky. BR/TR, 6'1", 175 lbs. Deb: 4/22/62																												
1962	StL-N	1	0	1.000	6	1	1	0	0	17	18	9.5	1	4	2.1	5	2.6	5.29	80	.295	.324	-3	-2	107	79	0.5	1	-0	-0.1
	Chi-N	3	1	.750	6	4	1	0	0	34	29	7.7	2	10	2.6	11	2.9	4.24	101	.240	.297	-1	0	109	73	1.2	0	-0	0.0
	Yr	4	1	.800	12	5	2	0	0	51	47	8.3	3	14	2.5	16	2.8	4.59	93	.257	.306	-4	-2	108	73	1.7	1	-1	-0.1
1963	Chi-N	5	9	.357	27	14	3	2	0	131	115	7.9	9	35	2.4	66	4.5	3.09	112	.240	.285	3	5	105	94	-2.1	-3	-1	0.1
1964	Chi-N	0	2	.000	4	2	0	0	0	11	15	12.3	2	5	4.1	0	0.0	8.18	46	.341	.400	-6	-5	106	86	-0.9	0	1	-0.3
Total	3	9	12	.429	43	21	5	2	0	193	177	8.3	14	54	2.5	82	3.8	3.78	98	.251	.298	-6	-2	106	89	-1.3	-2	-1	-0.3
■ **CLAY TOUCHSTONE**	Touchstone, Clayland Maffitt b: 1/24/03, Moore, Pa. d: 4/28/49, Beaumont, Tex. BR/TR, 5'9", 175 lbs. Deb: 9/04/28																												
1928	Bos-N	0	0	—	5	0	0	0	0	8	15	16.9	0	2	2.3	1	1.1	4.50	90	.417	.450	-0	-0	101	175	0.0	-0	0	0.0
1929	Bos-N	0	0	—	1	0	0	0	0	3	6	18.0	1	0	0.0	1	3.0	15.00	31	.429	.429	-3	-3	97	68	0.0	-0	0	-0.2
1945	Chi-A	0	0	—	6	0	0	0	0	10	14	12.6	1	6	5.4	4	3.6	5.40	60	.311	.396	-2	-2	96	115	0.0	-0	0	-0.2
Total	3	0	0	—	12	0	0	0	0	21	35	15.0	2	8	3.4	6	2.6	6.43	58	.368	.421	-6	-6	98	131	0.0	-0	0	-0.4
■ **CESAR TOVAR**	Tovar, Cesar Leonardo "Pepito" (born Cesar Leonard Perez (Tovar)) b: 7/3/40, Caracas, Venez. BR/TR, 5'9", 155 lbs. Deb: 4/12/65																												
1968	Min-A	0	0	—	1	1	0	0	0	1	0	0.0	0	1	9.0	1	9.0	0.00	—	.000	.250	0	0	106	86	2.6	0	-3	-2.2
■ **IRA TOWNSEND**	Townsend, Ira Dance "Pat" b: 1/9/1894, Weimar, Tex. d: 7/21/65, Schulenberg, Tex. BR/TR, 6'1", 180 lbs. Deb: 8/25/20																												
1920	Bos-N	0	0	—	4	1	0	0	0	7	10	12.9	0	2	2.6	1	1.3	1.29	242	.370	.433	1	1	99	464	0.0	-0	0	0.1
1921	Bos-N	0	0	—	4	0	0	0	0	7	11	14.1	1	4	5.1	0	0.0	6.43	54	.344	.425	-2	-2	92	121	0.0	-0	0	-0.1
Total	2	0	0	—	8	1	0	0	0	14	21	13.5	1	6	3.9	1	0.6	3.86	86	.356	.429	-1	-1	96	292	0.0	-1	0	0.0
■ **HAPPY TOWNSEND**	Townsend, John b: 4/9/1879, Townsend, Del. d: 12/21/63, Wilmington, Del. BR/TR, 6', 190 lbs. Deb: 4/19/01																												
1901	Phi-N	9	6	.600	19	16	14	2	0	144	118	**7.4**	3	64	4.0	72	4.5	3.44	97	**.246**	.340	-2	-2	100	81	0.1	-4	-2	-0.3
1902	Was-A	9	16	.360	27	26	22	0	0	220	233	9.5	12	89	3.6	71	2.9	4.46	80	.296	.368	-22	-22	100	91	-2.8	4	-1	-2.0
1903	Was-A	2	11	.154	20	13	10	0	0	127	145	10.3	3	48	3.4	54	3.8	4.75	69	.310	.374	-25	-21	111	89	-3.4	-5	0	-1.9
1904	Was-A	5	26	.161	36	34	31	2	0	291	319	9.9	3	100	3.1	143	4.4	3.59	72	.303	.363	-32	-33	99	105	-6.3	-2	-2	-3.5
1905	Was-A	7	16	.304	34	24	22	0	0	263	247	8.5	2	84	2.9	102	3.5	2.63	106	.272	.334	0	5	106	113	-3.5	0	-3	0.2
1906	Cle-A	3	7	.300	17	12	8	1	0	93	92	8.9	1	31	3.0	31	3.0	2.90	92	.283	.346	-2	-2	99	110	-2.4	-1	0	-0.2
Total	6	35	82	.299	153	125	107	5	0	1138	1154	9.1	24	416	3.3	473	3.7	3.59	84	.287	.355	-83	-74	102	100	-18.3	-8	-8	-7.7
■ **LEO TOWNSEND**	Townsend, Leo Alphonse "Lefty" b: 1/15/1891, Mobile, Ala. d: 12/3/76, Mobile, Ala. BL/TL, 5'10", 160 lbs. Deb: 9/08/20																												
1920	Bos-N	2	2	.500	7	1	1	0	0	24	18	6.8	1	2	0.8	0	0.0	1.50	207	.220	.230	4	4	99	95	0.3	-0	0	0.5
1921	Bos-N	0	1	.000	1	1	0	0	0	1	2	18.0	0	3	27.0	0	0.0	36.00	10	.400	.556	-4	-4	92	41	-0.4	0	0	-0.2
Total	2	2	3	.400	8	2	1	0	0	25	20	7.2	1	5	1.8	0	0.0	2.88	109	.230	.260	1	1	99	93	-0.1	-0	0	0.3
■ **BILL TOZER**	Tozer, William Louis b: 7/3/1882, St.Louis, Mo. d: 2/23/55, Belmont, Cal. BR/TR, 6', 200 lbs. Deb: 4/16/08																												
1908	Cin-N	0	0	—	4	0	0	0	0	11	11	9.0	0	4	3.3	5	4.1	1.64	149	.297	.381	1	1	104	208	0.0	-0	0	0.1
■ **FRED TRAUTMAN**	Trautman, Frederick Orlando b: 3/24/1892, Bucyrus, Ohio d: 2/15/64, Bucyrus, Ohio BR/TR, 6'1", 175 lbs. Deb: 4/27/15																												
1915	New-F	0	0	—	1	0	0	0	0	3	4	12.0	0	1	3.0	2	6.0	6.00	47	.351	.404	-1	-1	94	81	0.0	-0	0	0.0
■ **JOHN TRAUTWEIN**	Trautwein, John Howard b: 8/7/62, Lafayette Hills, Pa. BR/TR, 6'3", 195 lbs. Deb: 4/07/88																												
1988	Bos-A	0	1	.000	9	0	0	0	0	16	26	14.6	2	9	5.1	8	4.5	9.00	48	.382	.462	-9	-8	108	94	-0.4	0	0	-0.7
■ **ALLAN TRAVERS**	Travers, Aloysius Joseph "Joe" b: 5/7/1892, Philadelphia, Pa. d: 4/19/68, Philadelphia, Pa. BR/TR, 6'1", 180 lbs. Deb: 5/18/12																												
1912	Det-A	0	1	.000	1	1	1	0	0	8	26	29.3	0	7	7.9	1	1.1	15.75	20	.605	.660	-11	-11	96	110	-0.4	-0	1	-0.6
■ **BILL TRAVERS**	Travers, William Edward b: 10/27/52, Norwood, Mass. BL/TL, 6'4", 187 lbs. Deb: 5/19/74																												
1974	Mil-A	2	3	.400	23	1	0	0	0	53	59	10.0	6	30	5.1	31	5.3	4.92	76	.296	.380	-8	-7	103	112	-0.3	0	0	-0.6
1975	Mil-A	6	11	.353	28	23	5	0	1	136	130	8.6	15	60	4.0	57	3.8	4.30	89	.252	.338	-8	-7	101	96	-1.4	0	-1	-0.7
1976	Mil-A	15	16	.484	34	34	15	3	0	240	211	7.9	21	95	3.6	120	4.5	2.81	125	.237	.312	19	19	100	120	2.3	0	-1	2.0
1977	Mil-A	4	12	.250	19	19	2	1	0	122	140	10.3	13	57	4.2	49	3.6	5.24	75	.291	.366	-16	-18	97	99	-3.3	0	0	-1.6
1978	Mil-A	12	11	.522	28	28	8	3	0	176	184	9.4	20	58	3.0	66	3.4	4.40	89	.268	.326	-12	-9	104	93	-1.1	0	1	-0.8
1979	Mil-A	14	8	.636	30	27	9	2	0	187	196	9.4	33	45	2.2	74	3.6	3.90	108	.270	.311	7	6	99	113	1.4	0	-2	0.4
1980	Mil-A	12	6	.667	29	25	7	1	0	154	147	8.6	20	47	2.7	62	3.6	3.92	96	.249	.308	2	-3	93	94	2.8	0	-1	-0.2
1981	Cal-A	0	1	.000	4	4	0	0	0	10	14	12.6	2	4	3.6	5	4.5	8.10	47	.333	.391	-5	-5	104	84	-0.4	0	0	-0.4
1983	Cal-A	0	3	.000	10	7	0	0	0	43	58	12.1	4	19	4.0	24	5.0	5.86	67	.331	.393	-9	-9	96	107	-1.4	0	0	-0.8
Total	9	65	71	.478	205	168	46	10	1	1121	1139	9.1	134	415	3.3	488	3.9	4.10	94	.265	.330	-29	-32	99	105	-1.4	0	-3	-2.7
■ **HARRY TREKELL**	Trekell, Harry Roy b: 11/18/1892, Breda, Ill. d: 11/4/65, Spokane, Wash. BR/TR, 6'1.5", 170 lbs. Deb: 8/16/13																												
1913	StL-N	0	1	.000	7	1	1	0	0	30	25	7.5	2	8	2.4	15	4.5	4.50	69	.221	.276	-4	-5	97	52	-0.4	-0	-0	-0.4
■ **BILL TREMEL**	Tremel, William Leonard "Mumbles" b: 7/4/29, Lilly, Pa. BR/TR, 5'11", 180 lbs. Deb: 6/12/54																												
1954	Chi-N	1	2	.333	33	0	0	0	4	51	45	7.9	3	28	4.9	21	3.7	4.24	98	.243	.332	-1	-1	102	85	-0.2	0	-1	0.0
1955	Chi-N	3	0	1.000	23	0	0	0	2	39	33	7.6	2	18	4.2	13	3.0	3.69	111	.239	.313	1	2	101	90	1.5	0	-1	0.2
1956	Chi-N	0	0	—	1	0	0	0	0	1	3	27.0	0	0	0.0	0	0.0	9.00	42	.600	.600	-1	-1	101	154	0.0	0	0	0.0
Total	3	4	2	.667	57	0	0	0	6	91	81	8.0	5	46	4.5	34	3.4	4.05	102	.247	.327	-0	1	102	88	1.3	1	-2	0.2
■ **BOB TRICE**	Trice, Robert Lee b: 8/28/28, Newton, Ga. BR/TR, 6'2.5", 190 lbs. Deb: 9/13/53																												
1953	Phi-A	2	1	.667	3	3	1	0	0	23	25	9.8	4	6	2.3	4	1.6	5.48	77	.275	.320	-4	-3	105	83	0.7	0	1	-0.1
1954	Phi-A	7	8	.467	19	18	8	1	0	119	146	11.0	14	48	3.6	22	1.7	5.60	70	.305	.359	-25	-22	105	94	1.6	5	0	-1.6
1955	KC-A	0	0	—	4	0	0	0	0	10	14	12.6	4	6	5.4	2	1.8	9.00	47	.326	.392	-6	-5	106	96	0.0	1	1	-0.3
Total	3	9	9	.500	26	21	9	1	0	152	185	11.0	22	60	3.6	28	1.7	5.80	68	.302	.356	-34	-31	105	92	2.3	5	2	-2.0
■ **JOE TRIMBLE**	Trimble, Joseph Gerard b: 10/12/30, Providence, R.I. BR/TR, 6'1", 190 lbs. Deb: 4/29/55																												
1955	Bos-A	0	0	—	2	0	0	0	0	2	0	0.0	0	3	13.5	1	4.5	0.00	—	.000	.375	1	1	122	0	0.0	0	0	0.1

YEAR	TM/L	W	L	PCT	G	GS	CG	SHO	SV	IP	H	H/G	HR	BB	BB/G	SO	SO/G	ERA	/A	OAVG	OOBP	PR	/A	PF	CPI	WAT	PB	PD	TPI
1957	Pit-N	0	2	.000	5	4	0	0	0	20	23	10.3	7	13	5.8	9	4.0	8.10	46	.291	.389	-9	-10	96	93	-0.9	-0	0	-0.8
Total	2	0	2	.000	7	4	0	0	0	22	23	9.4	7	16	6.5	10	4.1	7.36	52	.274	.388	-9	-9	98	84	-0.9	-0	0	-0.7
■ **KEN TRINKLE**	Trinkle, Kenneth Wayne b: 12/15/19, Paoli, Ind. d: 5/10/76, Paoli, Ind. BR/TR, 6'1.5", 175 lbs. Deb: 4/25/43																												
1943	NY-N	1	5	.167	11	6	1	0	0	46	51	10.0	3	15	2.9	10	2.0	3.72	90	.276	.327	-2	-2	99	106	-1.5	1	1	0.0
1946	NY-N	7	14	.333	**48**	13	2	0	2	151	146	8.7	8	74	4.4	49	2.9	3.87	91	.253	.335	-8	-6	103	93	-1.8	-2	-0	-0.8
1947	NY-N	8	4	.667	**62**	0	0	0	10	94	100	9.6	3	48	4.6	37	3.5	3.73	108	.278	.358	3	3	99	116	1.9	-0	2	0.5
1948	NY-N	4	5	.444	53	0	0	0	7	71	66	8.4	6	41	5.2	20	2.5	3.17	123	.244	.348	6	6	98	131	-0.5	0	1	0.7
1949	Phi-N	1	1	.500	42	0	0	0	2	74	79	9.6	3	30	3.6	14	1.7	4.01	101	.299	.364	0	0	101	122	0.0	-0	1	0.1
Total	5	21	29	.420	216	19	3	0	21	436	442	9.1	23	208	4.3	130	2.7	3.74	101	.267	.346	0	2	101	110	-1.9	-2	5	0.5
■ **RICH TROEDSON**	Troedson, Richard La Monte b: 5/1/50, Palo Alto, Cal. BL/TL, 6'1", 170 lbs. Deb: 4/09/73																												
1973	SD-N	7	9	.438	50	18	2	0	1	152	167	9.9	12	59	3.5	81	4.8	4.26	83	.284	.343	-10	-12	97	103	0.9	-0	2	-1.0
1974	SD-N	1	1	.500	15	1	0	0	1	19	24	11.4	6	8	3.8	11	5.2	8.53	41	.300	.367	-10	-11	97	80	0.2	-0	0	-0.9
Total	2	8	10	.444	65	19	2	0	2	171	191	10.1	18	67	3.5	92	4.8	4.74	75	.286	.346	-20	-23	97	100	1.1	-0	2	-1.9
■ **HAL TROSKY**	Trosky, Harold Arthur Jr. "Hoot" (born Harold Arthur Troyavesky Jr.) b: 9/29/36, Cleveland, Ohio BR/TR, 6'3", 205 lbs. Deb: 9/25/58																												
1958	Chi-A	1	0	1.000	2	0	0	0	0	3	5	15.0	0	2	6.0	1	3.0	6.00	61	.385	.467	-1	-1	98	126	0.5	0	0	0.0
■ **BILL TROTTER**	Trotter, William Felix b: 8/10/08, Cisne, Ill. d: 8/26/84, Arlington, Mass. BR/TR, 6'2", 195 lbs. Deb: 4/23/37																												
1937	StL-A	2	9	.182	34	12	3	0	1	122	150	11.1	14	50	3.7	37	2.7	5.83	82	.304	.368	-16	-14	103	97	-2.1	-3	-2	-1.6
1938	StL-A	0	1	.000	1	1	1	0	0	8	8	9.0	0	0	0.0	1	1.1	5.63	88	.242	.229	-1	-1	103	28	-0.4	-0	1	0.0
1939	StL-A	6	13	.316	41	13	4	0	0	157	205	11.8	16	54	3.1	61	3.5	5.33	91	.318	.370	-12	-8	105	109	0.5	-1	1	-0.7
1940	StL-A	7	6	.538	36	4	1	0	2	98	117	10.7	5	31	2.8	29	2.7	3.77	126	.300	.349	7	**10**	108	125	1.3	-2	1	0.9
1941	StL-A	4	2	.667	29	0	0	0	0	50	68	12.2	2	19	3.4	17	3.1	5.94	71	.332	.385	-10	-10	101	97	1.2	-1	1	-0.8
1942	StL-A	0	1	.000	3	0	0	0	0	2	5	22.5	0	2	9.0	0	0.0	18.00	21	.385	.467	-3	-3	102	55	-0.4	0	0	-0.2
	Was-A	3	1	.750	17	0	0	0	0	41	52	11.4	4	14	3.1	13	2.9	5.71	63	.304	.353	-9	-10	99	90	1.2	-0	0	-0.9
	Yr	3	2	.600	20	0	0	0	0	43	57	11.9	4	16	3.3	13	2.7	6.28	58	.310	.361	-13	-13	99	90	0.8	0	1	-1.1
1944	StL-N	0	1	.000	2	1	0	0	0	6	14	21.0	5	4	6.0	0	0.0	13.50	25	.467	.486	-7	-7	95	129	-0.4	-0	0	-0.5
Total	7	22	34	.393	163	31	9	0	3	484	619	11.5	46	174	3.2	158	2.9	5.39	85	.313	.366	-52	-42	104	105	0.9	-7	1	-3.8
■ **DIZZY TROUT**	Trout, Paul Howard b: 6/29/15, Sandcut, Ind. d: 2/28/72, Harvey, Ill. BR/TR, 6'2.5", 195 lbs. Deb: 4/25/39																												
1939	Det-A	9	10	.474	33	22	6	0	2	162	168	9.3	5	74	4.1	72	4.0	3.61	140	.270	.344	18	26	110	116	-1.0	-1	-1	2.4
1940	Det-A	3	7	.300	33	10	1	0	2	101	125	11.1	4	54	4.8	64	5.7	4.46	107	.307	.388	-1	3	109	124	-2.4	-2	2	0.3
1941	Det-A	9	9	.500	37	18	6	1	2	152	144	8.5	7	84	5.0	88	5.2	3.73	119	.252	.343	7	12	107	107	0.3	0	1	1.4
1942	Det-A	12	18	.400	35	29	13	1	0	223	214	8.6	15	89	3.6	91	3.7	3.43	120	.249	.318	6	17	113	105	-2.7	2	3	2.6
1943	Det-A	**20**	12	.625	44	30	18	**5**	6	247	204	7.4	6	101	3.7	111	4.0	2.48	138	.227	.299	22	26	104	107	4.6	2	4	3.8
1944	Det-A	27	14	.659	49	40	**33**	**7**	0	**352**	314	8.0	9	83	2.1	144	3.7	**2.12**	**167**	.237	.282	**51**	**56**	104	113	5.3	12	7	**8.8**
1945	Det-A	18	15	.545	41	31	18	4	2	246	252	9.2	8	79	2.9	97	3.5	3.15	112	.267	.318	6	10	105	109	-1.0	4	3	2.0
1946	Det-A	17	13	.567	38	32	23	5	3	276	244	8.0	11	97	3.2	151	4.9	2.35	157	.238	.301	35	41	106	119	-0.8	3	4	5.6
1947	Det-A	10	11	.476	32	26	9	2	2	186	186	9.0	6	65	3.1	74	3.6	3.48	109	.261	.319	5	7	103	97	-1.5	3	3	1.4
1948	Det-A	10	14	.417	32	23	11	2	2	184	193	9.4	6	73	3.6	91	4.5	3.42	121	.269	.334	18	15	97	113	-2.3	2	2	1.8
1949	Det-A	3	6	.333	33	0	0	0	3	59	68	10.4	2	21	3.2	19	2.9	4.42	100	.292	.341	-1	0	106	95	-1.8	-0	2	0.2
1950	Det-A	13	5	.722	34	20	11	1	4	185	190	9.2	13	64	3.1	88	4.3	3.75	116	.267	.327	17	12	95	105	2.7	2	3	1.6
1951	Det-A	9	14	.391	42	22	7	0	5	192	172	8.1	13	75	3.5	89	4.2	4.03	109	.240	.311	2	8	107	82	-2.2	4	4	1.7
1952	Det-A	1	5	.167	10	2	0	0	1	27	30	10.0	4	19	6.3	20	6.7	5.33	71	.286	.383	-5	-5	103	110	-1.4	1	1	-0.2
	Bos-A	9	8	.529	26	17	2	0	1	134	133	8.9	3	68	4.6	57	3.8	3.63	108	.263	.345	1	5	107	106	0.7	-1	1	0.5
	Yr	10	13	.435	36	19	2	0	2	161	163	9.1	7	87	4.9	77	4.3	3.91	100	.267	.352	-4	-0	106	106	-0.7	1	2	0.3
1957	Bal-A	0	0	—	2	0	0	0	0	⅓	4	108.0	0	0	0.0	0	0.0	81.00	—	.800	.800	-3	-3	93	64	0.0	0	0	-0.2
Total	15	170	161	.514	521	322	158	28	35	2726	2641	8.7	112	1046	3.5	1256	4.1	3.23	124	.255	.320	177	232	105	108	-3.5	32	38	33.7
■ **STEVE TROUT**	Trout, Steven Russell b: 7/30/57, Detroit, Mich. BL/TL, 6'4", 195 lbs. Deb: 7/01/78																												
1978	Chi-A	3	0	1.000	4	3	1	0	0	22	19	7.8	0	11	4.5	11	4.5	4.09	94	.229	.309	-1	-1	102	63	1.5	0	0	0.0
1979	Chi-A	11	8	.579	34	18	6	2	4	155	165	9.6	10	59	3.4	76	4.4	3.89	111	.273	.338	6	8	103	105	2.4	0	1	0.9
1980	Chi-A	9	16	.360	32	30	7	2	0	200	229	10.3	14	49	2.2	89	4.0	3.69	107	.290	.331	8	6	98	113	-2.4	0	2	0.8
1981	Chi-A	8	7	.533	20	18	3	0	0	125	122	8.8	7	38	2.7	54	3.9	3.46	105	.261	.317	3	2	99	102	0.4	0	0	0.3
1982	Chi-A	6	9	.400	25	19	2	0	0	120	130	9.8	9	50	3.8	62	4.7	4.28	92	.273	.339	-3	-4	97	98	-2.0	0	0	-0.3
1983	Chi-N	10	14	.417	34	32	1	0	0	180	217	10.9	13	59	3.0	80	4.0	4.65	79	.305	.352	-20	-19	101	103	-0.6	1	2	-1.6
1984	Chi-N	13	7	.650	32	31	6	2	0	190	205	9.7	7	59	2.8	81	3.8	3.41	115	.285	.334	4	11	109	117	1.5	-1	4	1.4
1985	Chi-N	9	7	.563	24	24	3	1	0	141	142	9.1	8	63	4.0	44	2.8	3.38	124	.270	.343	3	13	117	122	1.4	-2	2	1.5
1986	Chi-N	5	7	.417	37	25	0	0	0	161	184	10.3	6	78	4.4	69	3.9	4.75	85	.298	.370	-18	-13	108	101	-0.2	1	1	-1.1
1987	Chi-N	6	3	.667	11	11	3	2	0	75	72	8.6	3	27	3.2	32	3.8	3.00	138	.260	.325	9	10	102	118	1.7	-0	0	1.0
	NY-A	0	4	.000	14	9	0	0	0	46	51	10.0	4	37	7.2	27	5.3	6.65	65	.274	.397	-11	-12	97	82	-1.9	0	0	-1.0
1988	Sea-A	4	7	.364	15	13	0	0	0	56	86	13.8	6	31	5.0	14	2.3	7.88	55	.361	.439	-24	-22	108	98	-0.7	0	0	-2.0
Total	11	84	89	.486	282	233	32	9	4	1471	1622	9.9	87	561	3.4	639	3.9	4.13	97	.285	.346	-45	-21	104	107	1.1	-2	13	-0.1
■ **BOB TROWBRIDGE**	Trowbridge, Robert b: 6/27/30, Hudson, N.Y. d: 4/3/80, Hudson, N.Y. BR/TR, 6'1", 180 lbs. Deb: 4/22/56																												
1956	Mil-N	3	2	.600	19	4	1	0	0	51	38	6.7	4	34	6.0	40	7.1	2.65	137	.210	.336	6	6	96	127	0.0	-1	0	0.6
1957	Mil-N	7	5	.583	32	16	3	1	1	126	118	8.4	9	52	3.7	75	5.4	3.64	93	.248	.318	3	-3	88	95	-0.3	-1	-0	-0.5
1958	Mil-N	1	3	.250	27	4	0	0	1	55	53	8.7	4	26	4.3	31	5.1	3.93	87	.252	.331	0	-3	87	94	-1.1	-0	-1	-0.3
1959	Mil-N	1	0	1.000	16	0	0	0	1	30	45	13.5	2	10	3.0	22	6.6	6.00	61	.344	.377	-7	-8	93	99	0.5	-0	-0	-0.7
1960	KC-A	1	3	.250	22	1	0	0	2	68	70	9.3	6	34	4.5	33	4.4	4.63	85	.281	.352	-6	-5	101	103	-0.6	-1	0	-0.5
Total	5	13	13	.500	116	25	4	1	5	330	324	8.8	25	156	4.3	201	5.5	3.95	90	.260	.336	-3	-14	92	102	-1.5	-4	-0	-1.4
■ **BUN TROY**	Troy, Robert b: 8/22/1888, Germany d: 10/7/18, Meuse, France BR/TR, 6'4", 195 lbs. Deb: 9/15/12																												
1912	Det-A	0	1	.000	1	1	1	0	0	7	9	11.6	0	3	3.9	1	1.3	5.14	62	.346	.433	-1	-2	96	116	-0.4	-0	-0	-0.1
■ **VIRGIL TRUCKS**	Trucks, Virgil Oliver "Fire" b: 4/26/19, Birmingham, Ala. BR/TR, 5'11", 198 lbs. Deb: 9/27/41 C																												
1941	Det-A	0	0	—	1	0	0	0	0	2	4	18.0	0	0	0.0	3	13.5	9.00	49	.500	.500	-1	-1	107	104	0.0	0	0	0.0
1942	Det-A	14	8	.636	28	20	8	2	0	168	147	7.9	3	74	4.0	91	4.9	2.73	151	.231	.309	17	26	113	105	3.8	-4	-1	2.3
1943	Det-A	16	10	.615	33	25	10	2	2	203	170	7.5	11	52	2.3	118	5.2	2.84	121	.225	.273	10	13	104	84	3.3	-1	-2	1.1
1945	Det-A	0	0	—	1	1	0	0	0	5	3	5.4	0	2	3.6	3	5.4	1.80	196	.176	.263	1	1	105	74	0.0	-0	0	0.1
1946	Det-A	14	9	.609	32	29	15	2	0	237	217	8.2	23	75	2.8	161	6.1	3.23	114	.241	.297	7	12	106	99	0.4	-1	-1	1.1
1947	Det-A	10	12	.455	36	26	8	2	2	181	186	9.2	14	79	3.9	108	5.4	4.52	84	.263	.334	-16	-14	103	89	-2.1	2	-1	-1.2
1948	Det-A	14	13	.519	43	26	7	0	2	212	190	8.1	14	85	3.6	123	5.2	3.78	110	.240	.307	12	9	97	90	0.4	-3	-1	0.4
1949	Det-A	19	11	.633	41	32	17	**6**	4	275	209	6.8	16	124	4.1	**153**	5.0	2.81	158	.211	.297	42	50	106	94	2.8	-7	-3	4.1
1950	Det-A	3	1	.750	7	7	2	1	0	48	45	8.4	6	21	3.9	25	4.7	3.56	122	.243	.321	5	4	95	110	0.7	-1	1	0.4
1951	Det-A	13	8	.619	37	18	6	1	1	154	153	8.9	9	75	4.4	89	5.2	4.32	102	.262	.343	-3	1	107	96	3.2	-1	2	0.2
1952	Det-A	5	19	.208	35	29	8	3	1	197	190	8.7	12	82	3.7	129	5.9	3.97	95	.251	.325	-7	-4	103	90	-4.7	-0	2	-0.1
1953	StL-A	5	4	.556	16	12	4	2	2	88	83	8.5	4	32	3.3	47	4.8	3.07	144	.249	.318	9	13	111	109	1.5	-1	-1	1.2
	Chi-A	15	6	.714	24	21	13	3	1	176	151	7.7	14	67	3.4	102	5.2	2.86	144	.232	.304	22	25	104	110	3.7	2	1	3.0
	Yr	20	10	.667	40	33	17	5	3	264	234	8.0	18	99	3.4	149	5.1	2.93	144	.237	.305	31	38	106	110	5.2	-1	0	4.2
1954	Chi-A	19	12	.613	40	33	16	**5**	3	265	224	7.6	13	95	3.2	152	5.2	2.78	133	.228	.294	28	27	100	93	0.1	-1	1	2.9
1955	Chi-A	13	8	.619	32	26	7	3	0	175	176	9.1	19	61	3.1	91	4.7	3.96	98	.260	.319	0	-2	98	97	0.8	-3	0	-0.4
1956	Det-A	6	5	.545	22	16	3	1	1	120	104	7.8	15	63	4.7	43	3.2	3.83	103	.239	.336	4	2	95	109	0.2	1	-1	0.1
1957	KC-A	9	7	.563	48	7	0	0	7	116	106	8.2	12	62	4.8	55	4.3	3.03	127	.248	.339	10	11	102	137	2.5	-1	0	1.0
1958	KC-A	0	1	.000	16	0	0	0	3	22	18	7.4	2	15	6.1	15	6.1	2.05	197	.222	.337	4	5	107	183	-0.4	-0	0	0.5
	NY-A	2	1	.667	25	0	0	0	1	40	40	9.0	1	24	5.4	26	5.8	4.50	83	.265	.357	-3	-3	99	94	0.3	0	-0	-0.3
	Yr	2	2	.500	41	0	0	0	4	62	58	8.4	3	39	5.7	41	6.0	3.63	106	.249	.350	1	1	102	94	-0.1	-0	-0	0.2

YEAR	TM/L	W	L	PCT	G	GS	CG	SHO	SV	IP	H	H/G	HR	BB	BB/G	SO	SO/G	ERA	/A	OAVG	OOBP	PR	/A	PF	CPI	WAT	PB	PD	TPI
Total	17	177	135	.567	517	328	124	33	30	2684	2416	8.1	188	1088	3.6	1534	5.1	3.38	117	.240	.312	142	175	103	99	16.5	-20	-4	16.4

■ **MIKE TRUJILLO** Trujillo, Michael Andrew b: 1/12/60, Denver, Colo. BR/TR, 6'1", 180 lbs. Deb: 4/14/85

YEAR	TM/L	W	L	PCT	G	GS	CG	SHO	SV	IP	H	H/G	HR	BB	BB/G	SO	SO/G	ERA	/A	OAVG	OOBP	PR	/A	PF	CPI	WAT	PB	PD	TPI
1985	Bos-A	4	4	.500	27	7	1	0	1	84	112	12.0	7	23	2.5	19	2.0	4.82	87	.320	.364	-6	-6	102	111	0.0	0	2	-0.3
1986	Bos-A	0	0	—	3	0	0	0	0	6	7	10.5	0	6	9.0	4	6.0	9.00	46	.304	.433	-3	-3	99	69	0.0	0	1	-0.2
	Sea-A	3	2	.600	11	4	1	1	1	41	32	7.0	5	15	3.3	19	4.2	2.41	184	.215	.281	8	9	106	123	0.8	0	0	0.9
	Yr	3	2	.600	14	4	1	1	1	47	39	7.5	5	21	4.0	23	4.4	3.26	135	.227	.305	5	6	105	123	0.8	0	1	0.7
1987	Sea-A	4	4	.500	28	7	0	0	1	66	70	9.5	12	26	3.5	36	4.9	6.14	75	.277	.345	-12	-11	103	85	0.2	0	-1	-1.1
1988	Det-A	0	0	—	6	0	0	0	0	12	11	8.3	2	5	3.8	5	3.8	5.25	71	.234	.308	-2	-2	94	73	0.0	0	0	-0.1
Total	4	11	10	.524	75	18	2	1	3	209	232	10.0	26	75	3.2	83	3.6	4.91	89	.282	.342	-15	-13	102	102	1.0	0	2	-0.8

■ **ED TRUMBULL** Trumbull, Edward J. (born Edward J. Trembly) b: 11/3/1860, Chicopee, Mass. Deb: 5/10/1884

YEAR	TM/L	W	L	PCT	G	GS	CG	SHO	SV	IP	H	H/G	HR	BB	BB/G	SO	SO/G	ERA	/A	OAVG	OOBP	PR	/A	PF	CPI	WAT	PB	PD	TPI
1884	Was-a	1	9	.100	10	10	10	0	0	84	108	11.6	4	31	3.3	43	4.6	4.71	64	.321	.378	-14	-16	93	117	-2.5	-2	0	-1.2

■ **JOHN TSITOURIS** Tsitouris, John Philip b: 5/4/36, Monroe, N.C. BR/TR, 6', 175 lbs. Deb: 6/13/57

YEAR	TM/L	W	L	PCT	G	GS	CG	SHO	SV	IP	H	H/G	HR	BB	BB/G	SO	SO/G	ERA	/A	OAVG	OOBP	PR	/A	PF	CPI	WAT	PB	PD	TPI
1957	Det-A	1	0	1.000	2	0	0	0	0	3	8	24.0	0	2	6.0	2	6.0	9.00	45	.500	.556	-2	-2	107	138	0.5	-0	0	-0.1
1958	KC-A	0	0	—	1	1	0	0	0	3	2	6.0	0	2	6.0	1	3.0	3.00	134	.182	.308	0	0	107	65	0.0	-0	0	0.0
1959	KC-A	4	3	.571	24	10	0	0	0	83	90	9.8	3	35	3.8	50	5.4	4.99	79	.271	.340	-10	-9	103	79	0.9	-1	-0	-0.9
1960	KC-A	0	2	.000	14	2	0	0	0	33	38	10.4	3	21	5.7	12	3.3	6.55	60	.297	.406	-10	-10	101	95	-0.9	-1	0	-0.9
1962	Cin-N	1	0	1.000	4	2	1	1	0	21	13	5.6	0	7	3.0	7	3.0	0.86	461	.181	.277	7	7	100	188	0.5	-1	-0	0.7
1963	Cin-N	12	8	.600	30	21	8	3	0	191	167	7.9	20	38	1.8	113	5.3	3.16	107	.232	.278	3	5	103	91	1.6	-4	-3	-0.1
1964	Cin-N	9	13	.409	37	24	6	1	2	175	178	9.2	20	75	3.9	146	7.5	3.81	94	.263	.333	-5	-4	102	114	-3.3	2	-1	-0.2
1965	Cin-N	6	9	.400	31	20	3	0	1	131	134	9.2	18	65	4.5	91	6.3	4.95	73	.265	.351	-20	-20	102	99	-2.1	-2	-1	-2.2
1966	Cin-N	0	0	—	1	0	0	0	0	1	3	27.0	0	1	9.0	0	0.0	18.00	23	.750	.667	-2	-2	114	104	0.0	0	0	-0.1
1967	Cin-N	1	0	1.000	2	1	0	0	0	8	4	4.5	1	6	6.8	4	4.5	3.38	109	.154	.303	0	0	109	86	0.5	0	0	0.1
1968	Cin-N	0	3	.000	3	3	0	0	0	13	16	11.1	6	8	5.5	6	4.2	6.92	48	.302	.403	-6	-5	111	125	-1.4	0	0	-0.4
Total	11	34	38	.472	149	84	18	5	3	662	653	8.9	71	260	3.5	432	5.9	4.13	87	.257	.328	-45	-38	103	101	-3.7	-6	-5	-4.1

■ **TOMMY TUCKER** Tucker, Thomas Joseph "Foghorn" b: 10/28/1863, Holyoke, Mass. d: 10/22/35, Montague, Mass. BB/TR, 5'11", 165 lbs. Deb: 4/16/1887

YEAR	TM/L	W	L	PCT	G	GS	CG	SHO	SV	IP	H	H/G	HR	BB	BB/G	SO	SO/G	ERA	/A	OAVG	OOBP	PR	/A	PF	CPI	WAT	PB	PD	TPI
1888	Bal-a	0	0	—	1	0	0	0	0	2	4	18.0	0	0	0.0	2	9.0	4.50	67	.429	.429	-0	-0	98	162	0.0	0	0	0.0
1891	Bos-N	0	0	—	1	0	0	0	0	1	3	27.0	0	0	0.0	0	0.0	9.00	41	.531	.531	-1	-1	109	132	0.0	0	0	0.0
Total	2	0	0	—	2	0	0	0	0	3	7	21.0	0	0	0.0	2	6.0	6.00	53	.468	.468	-1	-1	102	152	0.0	0	0	0.0

■ **TOM TUCKEY** Tuckey, Thomas H. "Tabasco Tom" b: 10/7/1883, Connecticut d: 10/17/50, New York, N.Y. TL , 6'3", Deb: 8/11/08

YEAR	TM/L	W	L	PCT	G	GS	CG	SHO	SV	IP	H	H/G	HR	BB	BB/G	SO	SO/G	ERA	/A	OAVG	OOBP	PR	/A	PF	CPI	WAT	PB	PD	TPI
1908	Bos-N	3	3	.500	8	8	3	1	0	72	60	7.5	2	20	2.5	26	3.3	2.50	99	.258	.327	-1	-0	106	98	0.5	-2	0	0.0
1909	Bos-N	0	9	.000	17	10	4	0	0	91	104	10.3	1	22	2.2	16	1.6	4.25	62	.295	.342	-17	-16	102	86	-4.4	-1	1	-1.5
Total	2	3	12	.200	25	18	7	1	0	163	164	9.1	3	42	2.3	42	2.3	3.48	74	.280	.336	-18	-16	103	92	-3.9	-3	1	-1.5

■ **JOHN TUDOR** Tudor, John Thomas b: 2/2/54, Schenectady, N.Y. BL/TL, 6', 185 lbs. Deb: 8/16/79

YEAR	TM/L	W	L	PCT	G	GS	CG	SHO	SV	IP	H	H/G	HR	BB	BB/G	SO	SO/G	ERA	/A	OAVG	OOBP	PR	/A	PF	CPI	WAT	PB	PD	TPI
1979	Bos-A	1	2	.333	6	6	1	0	0	28	39	12.5	2	9	2.9	11	3.5	6.43	70	.345	.375	-7	-6	106	93	-0.5	0	1	-0.4
1980	Bos-A	8	5	.615	16	13	5	0	0	92	81	7.9	4	31	3.0	45	4.4	3.03	136	.238	.301	10	11	102	94	1.4	0	2	1.4
1981	Bos-A	4	3	.571	18	11	2	0	1	79	74	8.4	11	28	3.2	44	5.0	4.56	85	.252	.317	-8	-6	106	89	0.2	0	1	-0.5
1982	Bos-A	13	10	.565	32	30	6	1	0	196	215	9.9	20	59	2.7	146	6.7	3.63	124	.280	.333	10	19	110	121	0.5	0	2	2.2
1983	Bos-A	13	12	.520	34	34	7	2	0	242	236	8.8	32	81	3.0	136	5.1	4.09	101	.255	.314	-0	1	102	98	1.1	0	-1	0.0
1984	Pit-N	12	11	.522	32	32	6	1	0	212	200	8.5	19	56	2.4	117	5.0	3.27	103	.248	.292	8	2	94	98	1.4	3	-0	0.5
1985	StL-N	21	8	.724	36	36	14	**10**	0	275	209	6.8	14	49	1.6	169	5.5	1.93	174	.209	**.248**	51	44	93	91	4.5	2	1	5.1
1986	StL-N	13	7	.650	30	30	3	0	0	219	197	8.1	22	53	2.2	107	4.4	2.92	132	.244	.286	20	23	103	109	3.4	-1	1	2.4
1987	StL-N	10	2	.833	16	16	0	0	0	96	100	9.4	11	32	3.0	54	5.1	3.84	103	.272	.328	3	1	97	113	3.7	1	1	0.3
1988	StL-N	6	5	.545	21	21	4	1	0	145	131	8.1	5	31	1.9	55	3.4	2.30	158	.247	.282	19	21	105	121	0.8	-1	1	2.5
	LA-N	4	3	.571	9	9	1	0	0	52	58	10.0	5	10	1.7	32	5.5	2.42	150	.284	.315	6	7	105	169	0.0	-1	0	0.7
	Yr	10	8	.556	30	30	5	1	0	197	189	8.6	10	41	1.9	87	4.0	2.33	155	.255	.290	25	28	105	**169**	0.8	-1	1	3.2
Total	10	105	68	.607	250	238	49	15	1	1636	1540	8.5	145	439	2.4	916	5.0	3.19	120	.250	.298	111	116	101	106	16.5	3	8	14.2

■ **OSCAR TUERO** Tuero, Oscar (Monzon) (born Oscar Tuero Monzon) b: 12/17/1898, Canada d: 10/21/60, Houston, Tex. BR/TR, 5'8.5", 158 lbs. Deb: 5/30/18

YEAR	TM/L	W	L	PCT	G	GS	CG	SHO	SV	IP	H	H/G	HR	BB	BB/G	SO	SO/G	ERA	/A	OAVG	OOBP	PR	/A	PF	CPI	WAT	PB	PD	TPI
1918	StL-N	1	2	.333	11	3	2	0	0	44	32	6.5	0	10	2.0	13	2.7	1.02	258	.208	.259	9	8	95	152	-0.1	0	-0	0.9
1919	StL-N	5	7	.417	**45**	17	4	0	**4**	155	137	8.0	4	42	2.4	45	2.6	3.19	88	.242	.300	-5	-7	97	85	0.2	1	-1	-0.6
1920	StL-N	0	0	—	2	0	0	0	0	1	5	45.0	0	1	9.0	0	0.0	36.00	9	.833	.750	-4	-4	98	79	0.0	0	0	-0.3
Total	3	6	9	.400	58	20	6	0	4	200	174	7.8	4	53	2.4	58	2.6	2.88	96	.240	.296	0	-2	96	100	0.1	1	-1	-0.0

■ **BOB TUFTS** Tufts, Robert Malcolm b: 11/2/55, Medford, Mass. BL/TL, 6'5", 215 lbs. Deb: 8/10/81

YEAR	TM/L	W	L	PCT	G	GS	CG	SHO	SV	IP	H	H/G	HR	BB	BB/G	SO	SO/G	ERA	/A	OAVG	OOBP	PR	/A	PF	CPI	WAT	PB	PD	TPI
1981	SF-N	0	0	—	11	0	0	0	0	15	20	12.0	1	6	3.6	12	7.2	3.60	102	.308	.365	-0	0	105	144	0.0	-0	1	0.1
1982	KC-A	2	0	1.000	10	0	0	0	2	20	24	10.8	3	3	1.3	13	5.8	4.50	90	.293	.314	-1	-1	100	101	1.0	0	-1	-0.1
1983	KC-A	0	0	—	6	0	0	0	0	7	16	20.6	1	5	6.4	3	3.9	7.71	54	.444	.524	-3	-3	102	155	0.0	0	0	-0.2
Total	3	2	0	1.000	27	0	0	0	2	42	60	12.9	5	14	3.0	28	6.0	4.71	84	.328	.376	-4	-4	102	125	1.0	-0	0	-0.2

■ **LEE TUNNELL** Tunnell, Byron Lee b: 10/30/60, Tyler, Tex. BR/TR, 6'1", 180 lbs. Deb: 9/04/82

YEAR	TM/L	W	L	PCT	G	GS	CG	SHO	SV	IP	H	H/G	HR	BB	BB/G	SO	SO/G	ERA	/A	OAVG	OOBP	PR	/A	PF	CPI	WAT	PB	PD	TPI
1982	Pit-N	1	1	.500	5	3	0	0	0	18	17	8.5	1	5	2.5	4	2.0	4.00	99	.254	.320	-1	-0	110	86	0.0	-0	0	0.0
1983	Pit-N	11	6	.647	35	25	5	3	0	178	167	8.4	15	58	2.9	95	4.8	3.64	103	.252	.311	-0	2	103	95	2.5	-1	2	0.3
1984	Pit-N	1	7	.125	26	6	0	0	1	68	81	10.7	6	40	5.3	51	6.8	5.29	64	.298	.382	-13	-15	94	103	-2.9	-1	1	-1.3
1985	Pit-N	4	10	.286	24	23	0	0	0	132	126	8.6	11	57	3.9	74	5.0	4.02	93	.251	.326	-6	-4	104	92	-1.4	-2	1	-0.5
1987	StL-N	4	4	.500	32	9	0	0	0	74	90	10.9	5	34	4.1	49	6.0	4.86	82	.307	.373	-6	-7	97	109	-0.5	1	0	-0.5
Total	5	21	28	.429	122	66	5	3	1	470	481	9.2	38	194	3.7	273	5.2	4.19	89	.268	.337	-26	-24	101	97	-2.3	-4	4	-2.0

■ **GEORGE TURBEVILLE** Turbeville, George Elkins b: 8/24/14, Turbeville, S.C. d: 10/5/83, Salisbury, N.C. BR/TL, 6'1", 175 lbs. Deb: 7/20/35

YEAR	TM/L	W	L	PCT	G	GS	CG	SHO	SV	IP	H	H/G	HR	BB	BB/G	SO	SO/G	ERA	/A	OAVG	OOBP	PR	/A	PF	CPI	WAT	PB	PD	TPI
1935	Phi-A	0	3	.000	19	6	2	0	0	64	74	10.4	2	69	9.7	20	2.8	7.59	60	.312	.457	-22	-22	102	93	-1.4	-2	-1	-2.0
1936	Phi-A	2	5	.286	12	6	2	0	0	44	42	8.6	6	32	6.5	10	2.0	6.34	84	.258	.396	-6	-5	105	93	-0.5	-1	-0	-0.4
1937	Phi-A	0	4	.000	31	3	0	0	0	77	80	9.4	2	56	6.5	17	2.0	4.79	93	.266	.378	-1	-3	96	96	-1.9	0	-1	-0.2
Total	3	2	12	.143	62	15	4	0	0	185	196	9.5	10	157	7.6	47	2.3	6.13	76	.280	.410	-30	-30	100	94	-3.8	-2	-2	-2.6

■ **LUCAS TURK** Turk, Lucas Newton "Harlem" or "Chief" b: 5/2/1898, Homer, Ga. BR/TR, 6', 165 lbs. Deb: 6/07/22

YEAR	TM/L	W	L	PCT	G	GS	CG	SHO	SV	IP	H	H/G	HR	BB	BB/G	SO	SO/G	ERA	/A	OAVG	OOBP	PR	/A	PF	CPI	WAT	PB	PD	TPI
1922	Was-A	0	0	—	5	0	0	0	0	12	16	12.0	0	5	3.8	1	0.8	6.75	55	.340	.396	-4	-4	93	80	0.0	0	-1	-0.3

■ **BOB TURLEY** Turley, Robert Lee "Bullet Bob" b: 9/19/30, Troy, Ill. BR/TR, 6'2", 215 lbs. Deb: 9/29/51 C

YEAR	TM/L	W	L	PCT	G	GS	CG	SHO	SV	IP	H	H/G	HR	BB	BB/G	SO	SO/G	ERA	/A	OAVG	OOBP	PR	/A	PF	CPI	WAT	PB	PD	TPI
1951	StL-A	0	1	.000	1	1	0	0	0	7	11	14.1	0	3	3.9	5	6.4	7.71	58	.355	.412	-3	-2	109	80	-0.4	-0	0	-0.1
1953	StL-A	2	6	.250	10	7	3	1	0	60	39	5.8	4	44	6.6	61	9.2	3.30	134	.184	.328	5	7	111	90	-1.1	1	-1	0.9
1954	Bal-A	14	15	.483	35	35	14	0	0	247	178	**6.5**	7	181	6.6	**185**	6.7	3.46	106	**.203**	.335	7	6	99	86	3.5	-3	-1	0.3
1955	NY-A	17	13	.567	36	34	13	6	1	247	168	**6.1**	16	177	6.4	210	7.7	3.06	122	**.193**	.327	25	18	94	99	-1.6	-0	-2	1.6
1956	NY-A	8	4	.667	27	21	5	1	1	132	138	9.4	13	103	7.0	91	6.2	5.05	78	.273	.395	-13	-16	95	108	0.6	-0	-1	-1.6
1957	NY-A	13	6	.684	32	23	9	4	3	176	120	**6.1**	17	85	4.3	152	**7.8**	2.71	126	**.194**	.296	21	14	90	101	1.4	-1	-0	1.2
1958	NY-A	**21**	7	**.750**	33	31	**19**	6	1	245	178	**6.5**	24	128	4.7	168	6.2	2.98	126	**.206**	.310	22	21	99	105	**6.0**	-1	-2	1.9
1959	NY-A	8	11	.421	33	22	7	3	0	154	141	8.2	15	83	4.9	111	6.5	4.32	82	.245	.335	-8	-13	92	94	-1.8	-1	-1	-1.5
1960	NY-A	9	3	.750	34	24	4	1	5	173	138	7.2	14	87	4.5	87	4.5	3.28	109	.222	.316	11	6	92	99	2.1	-3	-1	0.1
1961	NY-A	3	5	.375	15	12	1	0	0	72	74	9.3	11	51	6.4	48	6.0	5.75	65	.269	.386	-14	-16	93	99	-1.7	-1	-1	-1.6
1962	NY-A	3	3	.500	24	8	0	0	1	69	68	8.9	8	47	6.1	42	5.5	4.57	80	.263	.377	-5	-7	92	114	-0.4	-1	1	-0.7
1963	LA-A	2	7	.222	19	12	3	2	0	87	71	7.3	5	51	5.3	70	7.2	3.31	101	.222	.325	3	0	92	101	-2.2	1	-0	0.1
	Bos-A	1	4	.200	11	7	0	0	0	41	42	9.2	6	28	6.1	35	7.7	6.15	63	.256	.366	-11	-10	107	82	-1.4	-0	-0	-1.0
	Yr	3	11	.214	30	19	3	2	0	128	113	7.9	11	79	5.6	105	7.4	4.22	83	.232	.336	-8	-10	97	82	-3.6	1	-0	-0.9
Total	12	101	85	.543	310	237	78	24	12	1710	1366	7.2	140	1068	5.6	1265	6.7	3.65	101	.220	.334	40	7	96	98	3.0	-11	-8	-0.4

■ **TUCK TURNER** Turner, George A. b: 2/13/1873, W.New Brighton, N.Y. d: 7/16/45, Staten Island, N.Y. BL , Deb: 8/18/1893

YEAR	TM/L	W	L	PCT	G	GS	CG	SHO	SV	IP	H	H/G	HR	BB	BB/G	SO	SO/G	ERA	/A	OAVG	OOBP	PR	/A	PF	CPI	WAT	PB	PD	TPI
1894	Phi-N	0	0	—	1	0	0	0	0	6	9	13.5	1	2	3.0	3	4.5	7.50	67	.370	.418	-1	-2	94	93	0.0	1	0	0.0

YEAR	TM/L	W	L	PCT	G	GS	CG	SHO	SV	IP	H	H/G	HR	BB	BB/G	SO	SO/G	ERA	/A	OAVG	OOBP	PR	/A	PF	CPI	WAT	PB	PD	TPI
■ JIM TURNER	Turner, James Riley "Milkman Jim" b: 8/6/03, Antioch, Tenn. BL/TR, 6', 185 lbs. Deb: 4/30/37 C																												
1937	Bos-N	20	11	.645	33	30	**24**	**5**	1	257	228	8.0	13	52	1.8	69	2.4	**2.38**	**148**	.235	**.272**	**44**	32	90	105	4.8	4	-0	**3.7**
1938	Bos-N	14	18	.438	35	34	22	3	0	268	267	9.0	21	54	1.8	71	2.4	3.46	97	.259	.294	10	-3	89	97	-2.6	4	4	0.4
1939	Bos-N	4	11	.267	25	22	9	0	0	158	181	10.3	10	51	2.9	50	2.8	4.27	85	.293	.341	-6	-11	93	105	-2.8	2	1	-0.7
1940	Cin-N	14	7	.667	24	23	11	0	0	187	187	9.0	9	32	1.5	53	2.6	2.89	130	.264	.292	20	18	98	113	0.5	3	-1	2.2
1941	Cin-N	6	4	.600	23	10	3	0	0	113	120	9.6	5	24	1.9	34	2.7	3.11	114	.277	.312	7	6	98	116	0.4	-1	2	0.7
1942	Cin-N	0	0	—	3	0	0	0	0	3	5	15.0	1	3	9.0	0	0.0	12.00	28	.333	.444	-3	-3	102	81	0.0	-0	0	-0.2
	NY-A	1	1	.500	5	0	0	0	1	7	4	5.1	0	1	1.3	2	2.6	1.29	267	.167	.200	2	2	94	37	-0.2	-0	0	0.2
1943	NY-A	3	0	1.000	18	0	0	0	1	43	44	9.2	1	13	2.7	15	3.1	3.56	87	.260	.311	-1	-2	94	88	1.5	-1	-0	-0.3
1944	NY-A	4	4	.500	35	0	0	0	7	42	42	9.0	3	22	4.7	13	2.8	3.43	105	.264	.339	0	1	105	123	-0.2	0	-1	0.1
1945	NY-A	3	4	.429	30	0	0	0	**10**	54	45	7.5	4	31	5.2	22	3.7	3.67	97	.225	.319	-2	-1	106	92	-0.6	-1	1	0.0
Total	9	69	60	.535	231	119	69	8	20	1132	1123	8.9	67	283	2.3	329	2.6	3.22	110	.260	.301	70	40	94	104	0.8	12	7	6.1
■ KEN TURNER	Turner, Kenneth Charles b: 8/17/43, Framingham, Mass. BR/TL, 6'2", 190 lbs. Deb: 6/11/67																												
1967	Cal-A	1	2	.333	13	1	0	0	0	17	16	8.5	4	4	2.1	6	3.2	4.24	73	.239	.292	-2	-2	96	99	-0.4	-0	0	-0.1
■ TED TURNER	Turner, Theodore Holhot b: 5/4/1892, Lawrenceburg, Ky. d: 2/4/58, Lexington, Ky. BR/TR, 6', 180 lbs. Deb: 4/20/20																												
1920	Chi-N	0	0	—	1	0	0	0	0	1	2	18.0	0	1	9.0	0	0.0	18.00	17	.400	.500	-2	-2	99	51	0.0	-0	0	-0.1
■ TINK TURNER	Turner, Thomas Lovatt b: 2/20/1890, Swarthmore, Pa. d: 2/25/62, Philadelphia, Pa. BR/TR, 6'1", 190 lbs. Deb: 9/24/15																												
1915	Phi-A	0	1	.000	1	1	0	0	0	2	5	22.5	1	3	13.5	0	0.0	22.50	13	.500	.615	-4	-4	103	80	-0.4	0	0	-0.3
■ ELMER TUTWILER	Tutwiler, Elmer Strange b: 11/19/05, Carbon Hill, Ala. d: 5/3/76, Pensacola, Fla. BR/TR, 5'11", 158 lbs. Deb: 8/20/28																												
1928	Pit-N	0	0	—	2	0	0	0	0	4	4	9.0	0	0	0.0	1	2.3	4.50	93	.267	.267	-0	-0	105	48	0.0	-0	0	0.0
■ TWINK TWINING	Twining, Howard Earle "Doc" b: 5/30/1894, Horsham, Pa. d: 6/14/73, Lansdale, Pa. BR/TR, 6', 168 lbs. Deb: 7/09/16																												
1916	Cin-N	0	0	—	1	0	0	0	0	2	4	18.0	1	1	4.5	0	0.0	13.50	20	.444	.545	-2	-2	101	105	0.0	0	0	-0.1
■ LARRY TWITCHELL	Twitchell, Lawrence Grant b: 2/18/1864, Cleveland, Ohio d: 4/23/30, Cleveland, Ohio BR/TR, 6', 185 lbs. Deb: 4/30/1886																												
1886	Det-N	0	2	.000	4	4	2	0	0	25	35	12.6	1	12	4.3	6	2.2	6.48	53	.345	.414	-9	-9	103	91	-0.9	-2	0	-0.7
1887	Det-N	11	1	.917	15	12	11	0	1	112	120	9.6	3	36	2.9	24	1.9	4.34	91	.289	.346	-4	-5	97	87	4.7	5	0	-0.3
1888	Det-N	0	0	—	2	0	0	0	1	4	6	13.5	1	0	0.0	3	6.8	6.75	41	.361	.361	-2	-2	97	97	0.0	0	0	-0.1
1889	Cle-N	0	0	—	1	0	0	0	0	1	0	0.0	0	1	9.0	0	0.0	0.00	—	.000	.276	0	0	104	0	0.0	0	0	0.0
1890	Buf-P	5	7	.417	13	12	12	0	0	104	112	9.7	3	72	6.2	29	2.5	4.59	89	.287	.398	-4	-6	97	97	1.3	1	0	-3.6
1891	Col-a	1	1	.500	6	1	1	0	0	31	29	8.4	1	13	3.8	8	2.3	4.06	82	.262	.339	-1	-2	90	76	0.1	2	0	-0.1
1894	Lou-N	0	0	—	1	0	0	0	0	3	5	15.0	1	1	3.0	0	0.0	6.00	80	.395	.439	-0	-0	91	151	0.0	0	0	0.0
Total	7	17	11	.607	42	29	26	0	2	280	307	9.9	10	135	4.3	70	2.3	4.63	84	.293	.373	-19	-23	97	90	5.2	7	0	-4.8
■ WAYNE TWITCHELL	Twitchell, Wayne Lee b: 3/10/48, Portland, Ore. BR/TR, 6'6", 215 lbs. Deb: 9/07/70																												
1970	Mil-A	0	0	—	2	0	0	0	0	2	3	13.5	0	1	4.5	5	22.5	9.00	41	.333	.400	-1	-1	100	61	0.0	0	0	0.0
1971	Phi-N	1	0	1.000	6	1	0	0	0	16	8	4.5	1	10	5.6	15	8.4	0.00	—	.145	.275	6	6	105	0	0.5	-0	0	0.7
1972	Phi-N	5	9	.357	49	15	1	1	1	140	138	8.9	6	56	3.6	112	7.2	4.05	84	.259	.326	-9	-10	99	87	-0.3	-2	-1	-1.3
1973	Phi-N	13	9	.591	34	28	10	5	0	223	172	6.9	16	99	4.0	169	6.8	2.50	160	.219	.305	29	37	109	121	3.3	-4	-3	3.3
1974	Phi-N	6	9	.400	25	18	2	0	0	112	122	9.8	11	65	5.2	72	5.8	5.22	72	.276	.369	-20	-18	104	95	-1.4	-1	-1	-1.9
1975	Phi-N	5	10	.333	36	20	0	0	0	134	132	8.9	10	78	5.2	101	6.8	4.43	83	.261	.350	-12	-11	101	97	-2.9	-2	-3	-1.5
1976	Phi-N	3	1	.750	26	2	0	0	1	62	55	8.0	3	18	2.6	67	9.7	1.74	211	.241	.299	12	13	105	170	0.7	0	0	1.5
1977	Phi-N	0	5	.000	12	8	0	0	0	46	50	9.8	3	25	4.9	37	7.2	4.50	85	.287	.369	-3	-3	98	108	-2.4	-0	1	-0.2
	Mon-N	6	5	.545	22	22	2	0	0	139	116	7.5	18	49	3.2	93	6.0	4.21	92	.230	.297	-5	-5	99	81	0.9	2	-1	-0.3
	Yr	6	10	.375	34	30	2	0	0	185	166	8.1	21	74	3.6	130	6.3	4.28	90	.244	.316	-8	-8	99	81	-1.5	-0	-0	-0.5
1978	Mon-N	4	12	.250	33	15	0	0	0	112	121	9.7	16	71	5.7	69	5.5	5.38	64	.286	.386	-22	-24	96	108	-3.8	-1	-1	-2.6
1979	NY-N	5	3	.625	33	2	0	0	0	64	55	7.7	6	55	7.7	44	6.2	5.20	69	.243	.388	-10	-11	96	96	1.6	1	-0	-1.0
	Sea-A	0	2	.000	4	2	0	0	0	14	11	7.1	2	10	6.4	5	3.2	5.14	83	.220	.359	-1	-1	101	91	-0.9	0	0	0.0
Total	10	48	65	.425	282	133	15	6	2	1064	983	8.3	92	537	4.5	789	6.7	3.98	94	.250	.337	-37	-30	102	102	-4.7	-7	-9	-3.3
■ JEFF TWITTY	Twitty, Jeffrey Dean b: 11/10/57, Lancaster, S.C. BL/TL, 6'2", 185 lbs. Deb: 7/05/80																												
1980	KC-A	2	1	.667	13	0	0	0	0	22	33	13.5	4	7	2.9	9	3.7	6.14	64	.351	.388	-5	-5	97	113	0.3	0	0	-0.4
■ CY TWOMBLY	Twombly, Edwin Parker b: 6/15/1897, Groveland, Mass. d: 12/3/74, Savannah, Ga. BL/TL, 5'10.5", 170 lbs. Deb: 6/25/21																												
1921	Chi-A	1	2	.333	7	4	0	0	0	28	26	8.4	1	25	8.0	7	2.3	5.79	76	.283	.417	-5	-4	102	100	-0.2	-2	1	-0.4
■ LEFTY TYLER	Tyler, George Albert b: 12/14/1889, Derry, N.H. d: 9/29/53, Lowell, Mass. BL/TL, 6', 175 lbs. Deb: 9/20/10																												
1910	Bos-N	0	0	—	2	0	0	0	0	11	11	9.0	1	6	4.9	6	4.9	2.45	146	.275	.370	1	1	118	183	0.0	1	-0	0.2
1911	Bos-N	7	10	.412	28	20	10	1	0	165	150	8.2	11	109	5.9	90	4.9	5.07	73	.243	.365	-31	-25	109	80	1.6	-0	3	-2.0
1912	Bos-N	12	22	.353	42	29	18	0	0	256	262	9.2	8	126	4.4	144	5.1	4.18	90	.267	.356	-22	-12	110	87	0.4	-2	4	-0.9
1913	Bos-N	16	17	.485	39	34	**28**	4	2	290	245	7.6	2	108	3.4	143	4.4	2.79	110	.235	.306	13	9	96	92	1.1	4	7	2.1
1914	Bos-N	16	14	.533	38	34	21	5	2	271	247	8.2	7	101	3.4	140	4.6	2.69	106	.249	.321	3	5	102	109	-2.3	0	-2	0.4
1915	Bos-N	10	9	.526	32	24	15	1	0	205	182	8.0	6	84	3.7	89	3.9	2.85	94	.243	.315	-2	-4	97	105	-0.3	7	-1	0.2
1916	Bos-N	17	10	.630	34	28	21	6	1	249	200	7.2	6	58	2.1	117	4.2	2.02	118	.226	.270	16	10	91	99	1.7	7	2	2.1
1917	Bos-N	14	12	.538	32	28	22	4	1	239	203	7.6	1	86	3.2	98	3.7	2.52	104	.240	.304	5	2	97	105	2.0	4	3	1.4
1918	Chi-N	19	8	.704	33	30	22	**8**	1	269	218	7.3	1	67	2.2	102	3.4	2.01	135	.226	.272	23	21	98	95	2.5	2	3	3.0
1919	Chi-N	2	2	.500	6	5	3	0	0	30	20	6.0	0	13	3.9	9	2.7	2.10	138	.196	.277	3	3	99	85	0.0	1	1	0.5
1920	Chi-N	11	12	.478	27	27	18	2	0	193	193	9.0	6	57	2.7	57	2.7	3.31	94	.268	.315	-4	-4	99	93	-0.1	5	3	0.4
1921	Chi-N	3	2	.600	10	6	4	0	0	50	59	10.6	2	14	2.5	8	1.4	3.24	127	.294	.338	3	5	108	118	0.8	0	-0	0.5
Total	12	127	118	.518	323	265	182	31	7	2228	1990	8.0	51	829	3.3	1003	4.1	2.95	101	.244	.313	8	7	100	97	7.4	30	22	7.9
■ JIM TYNG	Tyng, James Alexander b: 5/27/1856, Philadelphia, Pa. d: 10/30/31, New York, N.Y. 5'9", 155 lbs. Deb: 9/23/1879																												
1879	Bos-N	1	2	.333	3	3	3	0	0	27	35	11.7	0	6	2.0	7	2.3	5.00	51	.319	.355	-8	-7	101	79	-0.6	1	0	-0.4
1888	Phi-N	0	0	—	1	0	0	0	1	4	8	18.0	0	2	4.5	2	4.5	4.50	71	.430	.485	-1	-1	113	189	0.0	-0	0	0.0
Total	2	1	2	.333	4	3	3	0	1	31	43	12.5	0	8	2.3	9	2.6	4.94	53	.335	.375	-8	-8	103	93	-0.6	1	0	-0.4
■ DAVE TYRIVER	Tyriver, David Burton b: 10/31/37, Oshkosh, Wis. d: 10/28/88, Oshkosh, Wis. BR/TR, 6' ", 175 lbs. Deb: 8/21/62																												
1962	Cle-A	0	0	—	4	0	0	0	0	11	10	8.2	2	7	5.7	7	5.7	4.09	96	.250	.367	-0	-0	99	132	0.0	-0	0	0.0
■ JIMMY UCHRINSCKO	Uchrinscko, James Emerson b: 10/20/1900, W.Newton, Pa. BL/TR, 6', 180 lbs. Deb: 7/20/26																												
1926	Was-A	0	0	—	3	0	0	0	0	8	13	14.6	0	8	9.0	0	0.0	10.13	39	.433	.538	-5	-6	97	96	0.0	-0	0	-0.4
■ GEORGE UHLE	Uhle, George Ernest "The Bull" b: 9/18/1898, Cleveland, Ohio d: 2/26/85, Lakewood, Ohio BR/TR, 6', 190 lbs. Deb: 4/30/19 C																												
1919	Cle-A	10	5	.667	26	12	7	1	0	127	129	9.1	1	43	3.0	50	3.5	2.91	116	.261	.329	4	6	104	101	1.3	3	0	1.0
1920	Cle-A	4	5	.444	27	6	2	0	1	85	98	10.4	3	29	3.1	27	2.9	5.19	73	.296	.367	-13	-13	100	83	-1.3	2	0	-0.9
1921	Cle-A	16	13	.552	41	28	13	2	2	238	288	10.9	9	63	2.4	63	2.4	4.01	103	.306	.341	7	3	96	108	-1.6	4	-3	0.3
1922	Cle-A	22	16	.579	50	40	23	**5**	3	287	328	10.3	6	89	2.8	82	2.6	4.08	102	.290	.340	-1	2	103	95	3.5	8	-3	0.6
1923	Cle-A	**26**	16	.619	54	44	**29**	1	5	**358**	378	9.5	8	102	2.6	109	2.7	3.77	104	.271	.318	8	6	99	87	4.9	17	0	2.3
1924	Cle-A	9	15	.375	28	25	15	0	1	196	238	10.9	6	75	3.4	57	2.6	4.78	86	.306	.365	-12	-14	97	99	-1.9	8	1	-1.2
1925	Cle-A	13	11	.542	29	26	17	1	0	211	218	9.3	5	78	3.3	68	2.9	4.09	115	.268	.329	7	14	107	86	2.2	5	-3	1.7
1926	Cle-A	**27**	11	**.711**	39	36	**32**	3	1	**318**	300	8.5	7	118	3.3	159	4.5	2.83	138	.253	.315	42	38	97	111	**7.4**	4	-0	4.2
1927	Cle-A	8	9	.471	25	22	10	1	1	153	187	11.0	3	59	3.5	69	4.1	4.35	94	.310	.363	-4	-5	99	110	0.7	4	-1	0.0
1928	Cle-A	12	17	.414	31	28	18	2	1	214	252	10.6	8	48	2.0	74	3.1	4.08	107	.300	.330	-1	7	108	104	0.3	6	2	1.7
1929	Det-A	15	11	.577	32	30	23	1	0	249	283	10.2	9	58	2.1	100	3.6	4.08	101	.287	.316	4	1	97	92	3.4	9	-3	0.7
1930	Det-A	12	12	.500	33	29	18	1	3	239	239	9.0	18	75	2.8	117	4.4	3.65	135	.264	.317	27	34	106	108	0.4	8	-3	3.7
1931	Det-A	11	12	.478	29	18	15	2	2	193	190	8.9	10	49	2.3	63	2.9	3.50	134	.255	.301	19	25	107	97	1.8	5	-1	2.9
1932	Det-A	6	6	.500	33	15	6	1	5	147	152	9.3	15	42	2.6	51	3.1	4.47	102	.266	.314	0	1	102	93	0.0	1	-1	0.1

YEAR	TM/L	W	L	PCT	G	GS	CG	SHO	SV	IP	H	H/G	HR	BB	BB/G	SO	SO/G	ERA	/A	OAVG	OOBP	PR	/A	PF	CPI	WAT	PB	PD	TPI
1933	Det-A	0	0	—	1	0	0	0	0	1	2	18.0	1	0	0.0	1	9.0	18.00	25	.500	.500	-2	-1	107	95	0.0	0	0	0.0
	NY-N	1	1	.500	6	1	0	0	0	14	16	10.3	1	6	3.9	4	2.6	7.71	42	.302	.361	-7	-7	96	64	-0.1	-0	0	-0.6
	NY-A	6	1	.857	12	6	4	0	0	61	63	9.3	4	20	3.0	26	3.8	5.16	73	.257	.321	-6	-9	88	72	2.3	4	-1	-0.5
1934	NY-A	2	4	.333	10	2	0	0	0	16	30	16.9	3	7	3.9	10	5.6	10.13	41	.400	.440	-10	-11	93	93	-1.3	2	-0	-0.7
1936	Cle-A	0	1	.000	7	0	0	0	0	13	26	18.0	2	5	3.5	5	3.5	8.31	64	.419	.463	-5	-4	105	119	-0.4	3	-0	-0.3
Total	17	200	166	.546	513	368	232	21	25	3120	3417	9.9	119	966	2.8	1135	3.3	3.99	105	.281	.331	60	73	101	98	21.6	93	-15	15.0
■ BOB UHLE	Uhle, Robert Ellwood "Lefty" b: 9/17/13, San Francisco, Cal. BB/TL, 5'11", 175 lbs. Deb: 5/08/38																												
1938	Chi-A	0	0	—	1	0	0	0	0	2	1	4.5	0	0	0.0	0	0.0	0.00	—	.167	.167	1	1	98	0	0.0	0	0	0.1
1940	Det-A	0	0	—	1	0	0	0	0	0	4	—	0	2	—	0	—	∞	—	1.000	1.000	-4	-4	109	72	0.0	0	0	-0.2
Total	2	0	0	—	2	0	0	0	0	2	5	22.5	0	2	9.0	0	0.0	18.00	26	.500	.583	-3	-3	98	0	0.0	0	0	-0.1
■ JERRY UJDUR	Ujdur, Gerald Raymond b: 3/5/57, Duluth, Minn. BR/TR, 6'1", 195 lbs. Deb: 8/17/80																												
1980	Det-A	1	0	1.000	9	2	0	0	0	21	36	15.4	5	10	4.3	8	3.4	7.71	55	.383	.439	-9	-8	105	117	0.5	0	-1	-0.7
1981	Det-A	0	0	—	4	4	0	0	0	14	19	12.2	2	5	3.2	5	3.2	6.43	60	.322	.369	-4	-4	105	92	0.0	0	0	-0.3
1982	Det-A	10	10	.500	25	25	7	0	0	178	150	7.6	29	69	3.5	86	4.3	3.69	110	.230	.303	8	8	100	102	-0.2	0	-1	0.7
1983	Det-A	0	4	.000	11	6	0	0	0	34	41	10.9	6	20	5.3	13	3.4	7.15	54	.293	.385	-12	-12	95	85	-1.9	0	-1	-1.1
1984	Cle-A	1	2	.333	4	3	0	0	0	14	22	14.1	1	6	3.9	6	3.9	7.07	60	.355	.417	-5	-4	106	99	-0.3	0	-1	-0.4
Total	5	12	16	.429	53	40	7	0	0	261	268	9.2	43	110	3.8	118	4.1	4.79	85	.266	.339	-22	-21	100	100	-1.9	0	-2	-1.8
■ SANDY ULLRICH	Ullrich, Carlos Santiago (Castello) b: 7/25/21, Havana, Cuba BR/TR, 6'1", 180 lbs. Deb: 5/03/44																												
1944	Was-A	0	0	—	3	0	0	0	0	10	17	15.3	2	4	3.6	2	1.8	9.00	35	.386	.449	-6	-7	91	97	0.0	0	0	-0.5
1945	Was-A	3	3	.500	28	6	0	0	1	81	91	10.1	3	34	3.8	26	2.9	4.56	68	.276	.337	-11	-13	92	86	-0.3	1	1	-1.0
Total	2	3	3	.500	31	6	0	0	1	91	108	10.7	5	38	3.8	28	2.8	5.04	61	.289	.350	-17	-20	92	87	-0.3	1	1	-1.5
■ DUTCH ULRICH	Ulrich, Frank W. b: 11/18/1899, Baltimore, Md. d: 2/11/29, Baltimore, Md. BR/TR, 6'2", 195 lbs. Deb: 4/18/25																												
1925	Phi-N	3	3	.500	21	4	2	1	0	65	73	10.1	6	12	1.7	29	4.0	3.05	165	.285	.309	9	14	118	130	0.3	-1	1	1.4
1926	Phi-N	8	13	.381	45	17	8	1	1	148	178	10.8	9	37	2.3	52	3.2	4.07	101	.304	.339	-4	0	107	109	0.0	2	-0	0.2
1927	Phi-N	8	11	.421	32	18	14	1	1	193	201	9.4	6	40	1.9	42	2.0	3.17	124	.271	.299	16	16	100	100	1.4	-5	-2	0.8
Total	3	19	27	.413	98	39	24	3	2	406	452	10.0	21	89	2.0	123	2.7	3.48	119	.286	.316	21	30	106	108	1.7	-5	-2	2.4
■ ARNOLD UMBACH	Umbach, Arnold William b: 12/6/42, Williamsburg, Va. BR/TR, 6'1", 180 lbs. Deb: 10/03/64																												
1964	Mil-N	1	0	1.000	1	1	0	0	0	8	11	12.4	0	4	4.5	7	7.9	3.38	101	.333	.395	0	0	96	165	0.5	0	0	0.0
1966	Atl-N	0	2	.000	22	3	0	0	0	41	40	8.8	1	18	4.0	23	5.0	3.07	114	.256	.335	2	2	97	114	-0.9	0	-0	0.2
Total	2	1	2	.333	23	4	0	0	0	49	51	9.4	1	22	4.0	30	5.5	3.12	112	.270	.346	3	2	97	122	-0.4	0	-0	0.2
■ JIM UMBARGER	Umbarger, James Harold b: 2/17/53, Burbank, Cal. BL/TL, 6'6", 200 lbs. Deb: 4/08/75																												
1975	Tex-A	8	7	.533	56	12	3	2	2	131	134	9.2	11	59	4.1	50	3.4	4.12	92	.276	.348	-5	-5	100	108	0.7	0	1	-0.3
1976	Tex-A	10	12	.455	30	30	10	3	0	197	208	9.5	12	54	2.5	105	4.8	3.15	115	.274	.315	8	10	103	118	-0.3	0	-0	1.0
1977	Oak-A	1	5	.167	12	8	1	0	0	44	62	12.7	3	28	5.7	24	4.9	6.55	60	.354	.441	-12	-13	97	111	-1.6	0	0	-1.1
	Tex-A	1	1	.500	3	2	0	0	0	13	14	9.7	2	4	2.8	5	3.5	5.54	76	.275	.321	-2	-2	104	80	0.0	0	-0	-0.1
	Yr	2	6	.250	15	10	1	0	0	57	76	12.0	5	32	5.1	29	4.6	6.32	63	.326	.401	-14	-15	98	80	-1.6	0	0	-1.2
1978	Tex-A	5	8	.385	32	9	1	0	1	98	116	10.7	9	36	3.3	60	5.5	4.87	74	.299	.356	-12	-14	96	100	-1.9	0	1	-1.2
Total	4	25	33	.431	133	61	15	5	3	483	534	10.0	37	181	3.4	244	4.5	4.14	90	.287	.345	-23	-23	100	110	-3.1	0	2	-1.7
■ JIM UMBRICHT	Umbricht, James b: 9/17/30, Chicago, Ill. d: 4/8/64, Houston, Tex. BR/TR, 6'4", 215 lbs. Deb: 9/26/59																												
1959	Pit-N	0	0	—	1	1	0	0	0	7	7	9.0	3	4	5.1	3	3.9	6.43	64	.259	.355	-2	-2	104	108	0.0	-0	0	-0.1
1960	Pit-N	1	2	.333	17	3	0	0	1	41	40	8.8	5	27	5.9	26	5.7	5.05	72	.270	.372	-6	-6	97	104	-0.6	0	-1	-0.6
1961	Pit-N	0	0	—	1	0	0	0	0	3	5	15.0	0	2	6.0	1	3.0	3.00	133	.333	.412	0	0	99	201	0.0	0	0	0.1
1962	Hou-N	4	0	1.000	34	0	0	0	2	67	51	6.9	3	17	2.3	55	7.4	2.01	185	.213	.266	14	13	95	104	2.0	-0	1	1.3
1963	Hou-N	4	3	.571	35	3	0	0	0	76	52	6.2	6	21	2.5	48	5.7	2.61	120	.195	.249	6	4	95	76	1.0	-0	1	0.5
Total	5	9	5	.643	88	7	0	0	3	194	155	7.2	17	71	3.3	133	6.2	3.06	114	.222	.291	13	9	96	94	2.4	-0	0	1.2
■ WILLIE UNDERHILL	Underhill, Willie Vern b: 9/6/04, Yowell, Tex. d: 10/26/70, Bay City, Tex. BR/TR, 6'2", 185 lbs. Deb: 9/08/27																												
1927	Cle-A	0	2	.000	4	1	0	0	0	8	12	13.5	0	11	12.4	4	4.5	10.13	40	.375	.511	-5	-5	99	91	-0.9	-0	0	-0.4
1928	Cle-A	1	2	.333	11	3	1	0	0	28	33	10.6	0	20	6.4	16	5.1	4.50	97	.306	.397	-1	-0	108	122	-0.2	2	0	0.1
Total	2	1	4	.200	15	4	1	0	0	36	45	11.3	0	31	7.8	20	5.0	5.75	75	.321	.425	-7	-6	106	115	-1.1	1	0	-0.3
■ FRED UNDERWOOD	Underwood, Frederick Theodore b: 10/14/1868, St.Louis Co., Mo. d: 1/26/06, Kansas City, Mo. Deb: 7/18/1894																												
1894	Bro-N	2	4	.333	7	6	5	0	0	47	80	15.3	1	30	5.7	10	1.9	7.85	64	.400	.478	-13	-15	94	99	-1.1	2	0	-0.8
■ PAT UNDERWOOD	Underwood, Patrick John b: 2/9/57, Kokomo, Ind. BL/TL, 6', 175 lbs. Deb: 5/31/79																												
1979	Det-A	6	4	.600	27	15	1	0	0	122	126	9.3	17	29	2.1	83	6.1	4.57	89	.269	.309	-5	-7	96	90	0.8	0	-1	-0.7
1980	Det-A	3	6	.333	49	7	0	0	5	113	121	9.6	12	35	2.8	60	4.8	3.58	118	.277	.328	6	8	105	118	-1.6	0	0	0.8
1982	Det-A	4	8	.333	33	12	2	0	3	99	108	9.8	17	22	2.0	43	3.9	4.73	86	.269	.304	-7	-7	100	89	-2.1	0	1	-0.5
1983	Det-A	0	0	—	4	0	0	0	0	10	11	9.9	1	6	5.4	2	1.8	9.00	43	.289	.386	-5	-6	95	60	0.0	0	-0	-0.5
Total	4	13	18	.419	113	34	3	0	8	344	366	9.6	47	92	2.4	188	4.9	4.42	93	.272	.316	-11	-11	100	98	-2.9	0	-0	-0.9
■ TOM UNDERWOOD	Underwood, Thomas Gerald b: 12/22/53, Kokomo, Ind. BR/TL, 5'11", 170 lbs. Deb: 8/19/74																												
1974	Phi-N	1	0	1.000	7	0	0	0	0	13	15	10.4	1	5	3.5	8	5.5	4.85	78	.313	.364	-2	-2	104	106	0.5	-0	-0	-0.1
1975	Phi-N	14	13	.519	35	35	7	2	0	219	221	9.1	12	84	3.5	123	5.1	4.15	88	.262	.328	-13	-12	101	87	-0.3	-2	-4	-1.7
1976	Phi-N	10	5	.667	33	25	3	0	2	156	154	8.9	9	63	3.6	94	5.4	3.52	104	.260	.327	-0	3	105	104	0.9	-2	-2	0.0
1977	Phi-N	3	2	.600	14	0	0	0	1	33	44	12.0	2	18	4.9	20	5.5	5.18	74	.328	.392	-5	-5	98	115	0.0	-0	-0	-0.4
	StL-N	6	9	.400	19	17	1	0	0	100	104	9.4	7	57	5.1	66	5.9	4.95	75	.278	.366	-12	-14	95	96	-1.7	0	-1	-1.4
	Yr	9	11	.450	33	17	1	0	1	133	148	10.0	9	75	5.1	86	5.8	5.01	75	.290	.373	-16	-19	96	96	-1.7	-0	-1	-1.8
1978	Tor-A	6	14	.300	31	30	7	1	0	198	201	9.1	23	87	4.0	139	6.3	4.09	94	.263	.336	-7	-5	102	104	-1.9	0	-3	-0.7
1979	Tor-A	9	16	.360	33	32	12	1	0	227	213	8.4	23	95	3.8	127	5.0	3.69	121	.253	.329	14	20	106	109	0.7	0	-1	1.9
1980	NY-A	13	9	.591	38	27	2	2	2	187	163	7.8	15	66	3.2	116	5.6	3.66	108	.237	.302	8	6	98	86	-0.8	0	0	0.6
1981	NY-A	1	4	.200	9	6	0	0	0	33	32	8.7	2	13	3.5	29	7.9	4.36	83	.262	.326	-3	-3	99	86	-1.5	0	-0	-0.2
	Oak-A	3	2	.600	16	5	1	0	1	51	37	6.5	4	25	4.4	46	8.1	3.18	110	.202	.300	3	2	95	88	0.1	0	0	0.2
	Yr	4	6	.400	25	11	1	0	1	84	69	7.4	6	38	4.1	75	8.0	3.64	97	.226	.311	0	-1	97	88	-1.4	0	0	0.0
1982	Oak-A	10	6	.625	56	10	2	0	7	153	136	8.0	11	68	4.0	79	4.6	3.29	119	.241	.315	13	11	96	106	3.0	0	-2	0.8
1983	Oak-A	9	7	.563	51	15	0	0	4	145	156	9.7	13	50	3.1	62	3.8	4.03	97	.277	.332	1	-2	96	106	1.7	0	-3	-0.4
1984	Bal-A	1	0	1.000	37	1	0	0	1	72	78	9.8	8	31	3.9	39	4.9	3.50	107	.282	.345	4	2	94	136	0.5	0	1	0.3
Total	11	86	87	.497	379	203	35	6	18	1587	1554	8.8	130	662	3.8	948	5.4	3.88	100	.259	.329	2	2	100	101	1.2	-4	-14	-1.1
■ WOODY UPCHURCH	Upchurch, Jefferson Woodrow b: 4/13/11, Buies Creek, N.C. d: 10/23/71, Buies Creek, N.C. BR/TL, 6', 180 lbs. Deb: 9/14/35																												
1935	Phi-A	0	2	.000	3	3	1	0	0	21	23	9.9	3	12	5.1	2	0.9	5.14	89	.271	.357	-2	-1	102	100	-0.9	0	-0	0.0
1936	Phi-A	0	2	.000	7	2	1	0	0	22	36	14.7	7	14	5.7	6	2.5	9.82	54	.353	.431	-12	-11	105	96	-0.9	-1	-1	-0.9
Total	2	0	4	.000	10	5	2	0	0	43	59	12.3	10	26	5.4	8	1.7	7.53	65	.316	.397	-13	-12	104	98	-1.8	-0	-1	-0.9
■ JOHN UPHAM	Upham, John Leslie b: 12/29/41, Windsor, Ont., Can. BL/TL, 6', 180 lbs. Deb: 4/16/67																												
1967	Chi-N	0	1	.000	5	0	0	0	0	1	4	36.0	1	2	18.0	2	18.0	45.00	8	.571	.600	-5	-5	100	66	-0.4	1	0	-0.3
1968	Chi-N	0	0	—	2	0	0	0	0	7	2	2.6	0	3	3.9	2	2.6	0.00	—	.087	.222	2	3	112	0	0.0	0	0	0.3
Total	2	0	1	.000	7	0	0	0	0	8	6	6.8	1	5	5.6	4	4.5	5.63	60	.200	.324	-2	-2	111	8	-0.4	1	0	0.0
■ BILL UPHAM	Upham, William Lawrence b: 4/4/1888, Akron, Ohio d: 9/14/59, Newark, N.J. BB/TR, 6', 178 lbs. Deb: 4/10/15																												
1915	Bro-F	6	8	.429	33	11	4	2	5	121	129	9.6	0	40	3.0	46	3.4	3.05	98	.274	.331	-0	-1	98	110	-0.4	-2	4	0.1
1918	Bos-N	1	1	.500	3	2	2	0	0	21	28	12.0	2	1	0.4	8	3.4	5.14	51	.326	.322	-6	-6	95	89	0.1	0	0	-0.5
Total	2	7	9	.438	36	13	6	2	5	142	157	10.0	2	41	2.6	54	3.4	3.36	87	.282	.330	-6	-7	98	107	-0.3	-1	4	-0.4

YEAR	TM/L	W	L	PCT	G	GS	CG	SHO	SV	IP	H	H/G	HR	BB	BB/G	SO	SO/G	ERA	/A	OAVG	OOBP	PR	/A	PF	CPI	WAT	PB	PD	TPI
■ **JERRY UPP**	Upp, George Henry b: 12/10/1883, Sandusky, Ohio d: 6/30/37, Sandusky, Ohio TL , Deb: 9/02/09																												
1909	Cle-A	2	1	.667	7	4	2	0	0	27	26	8.7	0	12	4.0	13	4.3	1.67	153	.260	.339	2	3	103	180	0.6	0	1	0.4
■ **CECIL UPSHAW**	Upshaw, Cecil Lee b: 10/22/42, Spearsville, La. BR/TR, 6'6", 205 lbs. Deb: 10/01/66																												
1966	Atl-N	0	0	—	1	0	0	0	0	3	0	0.0	0	3	9.0	2	6.0	0.00	—	.000	.273	1	1	97	0	0.0	0	0	0.2
1967	Atl-N	2	3	.400	30	0	0	0	8	45	42	8.4	4	8	1.6	31	6.2	2.60	136	.247	.292	4	5	105	123	-0.3	1	0	0.6
1968	Atl-N	8	7	.533	52	0	0	0	13	117	98	7.5	6	24	1.8	74	5.7	2.46	113	.229	.270	7	4	94	96	0.5	0	-0	0.5
1969	Atl-N	6	4	.600	62	0	0	0	27	105	102	8.7	7	29	2.5	57	4.9	2.91	127	.259	.302	8	9	103	116	0.3	1	1	1.2
1971	Atl-N	11	6	.647	49	0	0	0	17	82	95	10.4	5	28	3.1	56	6.1	3.51	109	.292	.343	-0	3	111	124	2.6	-2	-0	0.1
1972	Atl-N	3	5	.375	42	0	0	0	13	54	50	8.3	5	19	3.2	23	3.8	3.67	100	.249	.308	-1	0	106	97	-0.6	-0	1	0.0
1973	Atl-N	0	1	.000	5	0	0	0	0	4	8	18.0	0	2	4.5	3	6.8	9.00	46	.444	.476	-2	-2	113	100	-0.4	0	0	-0.1
	Hou-N	2	3	.400	35	0	0	0	1	38	38	9.0	3	15	3.6	21	5.0	4.50	77	.259	.325	-4	-4	95	83	-0.4	-0	1	-0.3
	Yr	2	4	.333	40	0	0	0	1	42	46	9.9	3	17	3.6	24	5.1	4.93	72	.277	.342	-6	-6	97	83	-0.8	0	1	-0.4
1974	Cle-A	0	1	.000	7	0	0	0	0	8	10	11.3	1	4	4.5	7	7.9	3.38	109	.345	.389	0	0	101	196	-0.4	0	0	0.0
	NY-A	1	5	.167	36	0	0	0	6	60	53	8.0	1	24	3.6	27	4.1	3.00	115	.254	.333	4	3	95	112	-2.0	0	1	0.4
	Yr	1	6	.143	43	0	0	0	6	68	63	8.3	2	28	3.7	34	4.5	3.04	114	.262	.341	4	3	96	112	-2.4	0	1	0.4
1975	Chi-A	1	1	.500	29	0	0	0	1	47	49	9.4	5	21	4.0	22	4.2	3.26	121	.271	.356	3	4	104	142	0.1	0	-0	0.3
Total	9	34	36	.486	348	0	0	0	86	563	545	8.7	37	177	2.8	323	5.2	3.13	111	.258	.314	20	22	101	112	-0.6	1	2	2.9
■ **BILL UPTON**	Upton, William Ray b: 7/18/29, Esther, Mo. BR/TR, 6', 167 lbs. Deb: 4/13/54																												
1954	Phi-A	0	0	—	2	0	0	0	1	5	6	10.8	1	1	1.8	2	3.6	1.80	217	.300	.318	1	1	105	288	0.0	0	0	0.1
■ **JACK URBAN**	Urban, Jack Elmer b: 12/5/28, Omaha, Neb. BR/TR, 5'8", 155 lbs. Deb: 6/13/57																												
1957	KC-A	7	4	.636	31	13	3	0	0	129	111	7.7	7	45	3.1	55	3.8	3.35	115	.237	.296	6	7	102	88	2.3	2	1	1.2
1958	KC-A	8	11	.421	30	24	5	1	1	132	150	10.2	17	51	3.5	54	3.7	5.93	68	.286	.345	-32	-28	107	82	-1.1	-2	-1	-2.9
1959	StL-N	0	0	—	8	0	0	0	0	11	18	14.7	1	7	5.7	4	3.3	9.00	47	.409	.472	-6	-6	106	98	0.0	-0	-0	-0.5
Total	3	15	15	.500	69	37	8	1	1	272	279	9.2	25	103	3.4	113	3.7	4.83	82	.269	.328	-32	-27	104	85	1.2	0	-0	-2.2
■ **JOHN URREA**	Urrea, John Godoy b: 2/9/55, Los Angeles, Cal. BR/TR, 6'3", 200 lbs. Deb: 4/10/77																												
1977	StL-N	7	6	.538	41	12	2	1	4	140	126	8.1	13	35	2.3	81	5.2	3.15	118	.244	.287	12	9	95	98	0.4	2	1	1.1
1978	StL-N	4	9	.308	27	12	1	0	0	99	108	9.8	4	47	4.3	61	5.5	5.36	64	.284	.364	-20	-21	96	85	-1.8	-1	0	-2.1
1979	StL-N	0	0	—	3	2	0	0	0	11	13	10.6	0	9	7.4	5	4.1	4.09	95	.310	.431	-0	-0	104	139	0.0	0	0	0.0
1980	StL-N	4	1	.800	30	1	0	0	3	65	57	7.9	2	41	5.7	36	5.0	3.46	107	.239	.348	1	2	102	106	1.6	0	-1	0.1
1981	SD-N	2	2	.500	38	0	0	0	2	49	43	7.9	1	28	5.1	19	3.5	2.39	138	.239	.344	6	5	95	147	0.4	0	-1	0.5
Total	5	17	18	.486	139	27	3	1	9	364	347	8.6	20	160	4.0	202	5.0	3.73	96	.256	.333	-1	-6	97	104	0.6	2	-1	-0.4
■ **BOB VAIL**	Vail, Robert Garfield "Doc" b: 9/24/1881, Linneus, Maine d: 3/22/42, Philadelphia, Pa. 5'10", 165 lbs. Deb: 8/27/08																												
1908	Pit-N	1	2	.333	4	1	0	0	0	15	15	9.0	0	7	4.2	9	5.4	6.00	36	.295	.391	-6	-6	92	60	-0.6	1	-1	-0.6
■ **RENE VALDEZ**	Valdez, Rene Gutierrez (born Rene Gutierrez (Valdez)) b: 6/2/29, Guanabacoa, Cuba BR/TR, 6'3", 175 lbs. Deb: 4/21/57																												
1957	Bro-N	1	1	.500	5	1	0	0	0	13	13	9.0	1	7	4.8	10	6.9	5.54	80	.265	.339	-2	-2	114	78	0.0	0	-0	-0.1
■ **SERGIO VALDEZ**	Valdez, Sergio Sanchez (born Sergio Sanchez (Valdez)) b: 9/7/64, Elias Pina, D.R. BR/TR, 6', 165 lbs. Deb: 9/10/86																												
1986	Mon-N	0	4	.000	5	5	0	0	0	25	39	14.0	2	11	4.0	20	7.2	6.84	54	.361	.425	-9	-9	98	102	-1.9	-0	-0	-0.8
■ **CORKY VALENTINE**	Valentine, Harold Lewis b: 1/4/29, Troy, Ohio BR/TR, 6'1", 203 lbs. Deb: 4/17/54																												
1954	Cin-N	12	11	.522	36	28	7	3	1	194	211	9.8	24	60	2.8	73	3.4	4.45	95	.282	.334	-8	-4	104	100	1.1	-2	-2	-0.7
1955	Cin-N	2	1	.667	10	5	0	0	0	27	29	9.7	5	16	5.3	14	4.7	7.33	57	.276	.362	-10	-9	104	77	0.5	-1	1	-0.8
Total	2	14	12	.538	46	33	7	3	1	221	240	9.8	29	76	3.1	87	3.5	4.81	88	.282	.338	-18	-14	104	97	1.6	-3	-1	-1.5
■ **JOHN VALENTINE**	Valentine, John Gill b: 11/21/1855, Brooklyn, N.Y. d: 10/10/03, Central Islip, N.Y Deb: 5/03/1883																												
1883	Col-a	2	10	.167	13	12	11	0	0	102	130	11.5	0	17	1.5	13	1.1	3.53	85	.316	.343	-3	-6	91	122	-3.1	3	0	-0.2
■ **VITO VALENTINETTI**	Valentinetti, Vito John b: 9/16/28, W.New York, N.J. BR/TR, 6', 195 lbs. Deb: 6/20/54																												
1954	Chi-A	0	0	—	1	0	0	0	0	1	4	36.0	1	2	18.0	1	9.0	54.00	7	.571	.667	-6	-6	100	55	0.0	0	0	-0.3
1956	Chi-N	6	4	.600	42	2	0	0	1	95	84	8.0	10	36	3.4	26	2.5	3.79	100	.243	.305	-0	0	101	93	1.8	-1	-1	-0.2
1957	Chi-N	0	0	—	9	0	0	0	0	12	12	9.0	1	7	5.3	8	6.0	2.25	169	.255	.345	2	2	98	184	0.0	0	-0	0.2
	Cle-A	2	2	.500	11	2	1	0	0	24	26	9.8	3	13	4.9	9	3.4	4.88	79	.289	.367	-3	-3	102	112	0.0	-0	0	-0.2
1958	Det-A	1	0	1.000	15	0	0	0	2	19	18	8.5	4	5	2.4	10	4.7	3.32	117	.257	.312	1	1	103	138	0.5	0	-0	0.1
	Was-A	4	6	.400	23	10	2	0	0	96	106	9.9	16	49	4.6	33	3.1	5.06	75	.286	.368	-14	-14	100	110	0.0	2	2	-0.9
	Yr	5	6	.455	38	10	2	0	2	115	124	9.7	20	54	4.2	43	3.4	4.77	80	.281	.357	-13	-12	101	110	0.5	0	1	-0.8
1959	Was-A	0	2	.000	7	1	0	0	0	11	16	13.1	0	10	8.2	7	5.7	9.82	40	.356	.466	-7	-7	102	78	-0.9	0	0	-0.5
Total	5	13	14	.481	108	15	3	0	3	258	266	9.3	35	122	4.3	94	3.3	4.71	81	.273	.348	-27	-26	101	108	1.4	1	0	-1.8
■ **FERNANDO VALENZUELA**	Valenzuela, Fernando (Anguamea) b: 11/1/60, Navoja, Mexico BL/TL, 5'11", 180 lbs. Deb: 9/15/80																												
1980	LA-N	2	0	1.000	10	0	0	0	1	18	8	4.0	0	5	2.5	16	8.0	0.00	—	.136	.197	7	7	96	0	1.0	-0	0	0.8
1981	LA-N	13	7	.650	25	25	**11**	**8**	0	**192**	140	6.6	11	61	2.9	**180**	8.4	2.48	135	.205	.266	21	19	96	85	2.1	3	2	2.6
1982	LA-N	19	13	.594	37	37	18	4	0	285	247	7.8	13	83	2.6	199	6.3	2.87	117	.236	.287	23	16	94	94	2.1	1	5	2.3
1983	LA-N	15	10	.600	35	35	9	4	0	257	245	8.6	16	99	3.5	189	6.6	3.75	97	.255	.317	-3	-4	100	94	1.3	2	4	0.2
1984	LA-N	12	17	.414	34	34	12	2	0	**261**	218	7.5	14	106	3.7	240	8.3	3.03	123	.229	.302	16	20	104	97	-2.5	4	4	3.1
1985	LA-N	17	10	.630	35	35	14	5	0	272	211	7.0	14	101	3.3	208	6.9	2.45	135	.214	.282	35	26	92	99	1.7	4	2	3.3
1986	LA-N	**21**	11	.656	34	34	**20**	3	0	269	226	7.6	18	85	2.8	242	8.1	3.14	112	.226	.283	17	11	95	85	**6.8**	4	4	2.0
1987	LA-N	14	14	.500	34	34	**12**	1	0	251	254	9.1	25	124	4.4	190	6.8	3.98	95	.262	.342	3	-6	92	110	1.5	0	3	-0.3
1988	LA-N	5	8	.385	23	22	3	0	1	142	142	9.0	11	76	4.8	64	4.1	4.25	85	.268	.348	-13	-10	105	106	-2.2	1	3	-0.5
Total	9	118	90	.567	267	256	99	27	2	1947	1691	7.8	122	740	3.4	1528	7.1	3.17	112	.235	.302	108	80	97	95	11.8	20	26	13.5
■ **CLAY Van ALSTYNE**	Van Alstyne, Clayton Emory "Spike" b: 5/24/1900, Stuyvesant, N.Y. d: 1/5/60, Hudson, N.Y. BR/TR, 5'11", 180 lbs. Deb: 8/20/27																												
1927	Was-A	0	0	—	2	0	0	0	0	3	3	9.0	0	0	0.0	0	0.0	3.00	133	.250	.250	0	0	96	53	0.0	0	-0	0.0
1928	Was-A	0	0	—	4	0	0	0	0	21	26	11.1	0	13	5.6	5	2.1	5.57	74	.329	.408	-4	-3	101	106	0.0	1	1	0.0
Total	2	0	0	—	6	0	0	0	0	24	29	10.9	0	13	4.9	5	1.9	5.25	78	.319	.391	-3	-3	101	100	0.0	1	1	0.0
■ **RUSS Van ATTA**	Van Atta, Russell "Sheriff" b: 6/21/06, Augusta, N.J. d: 10/10/86, Andover, N.J. BL/TL, 6', 184 lbs. Deb: 4/25/33																												
1933	NY-A	12	4	.750	26	22	10	2	1	157	160	9.2	8	63	3.6	76	4.4	4.18	90	.262	.326	2	-7	88	94	3.1	4	0	-0.3
1934	NY-A	3	5	.375	28	9	0	0	0	88	107	10.9	3	46	4.7	39	4.0	6.34	66	.307	.385	-18	-21	93	85	-1.5	1	-1	-1.8
1935	NY-A	0	0	—	5	0	0	0	0	5	5	9.0	0	4	7.2	3	5.4	3.60	111	.263	.391	0	0	90	128	0.0	-0	-0	0.0
	StL-A	9	16	.360	53	17	1	0	3	170	201	10.6	10	86	4.6	87	4.6	5.35	91	.292	.368	-17	-9	110	94	-2.2	-1	-1	-0.9
	Yr	9	16	.360	**58**	17	1	0	3	175	206	10.6	10	90	4.6	90	4.6	5.30	92	.291	.369	-16	-8	109	94	-2.2	-0	-2	-0.9
1936	StL-A	4	7	.364	**52**	9	2	0	2	123	164	12.0	9	68	5.0	59	4.3	6.59	82	.320	.396	-21	-16	107	95	-0.1	-1	1	-1.3
1937	StL-A	1	2	.333	16	6	1	0	0	59	74	11.3	2	32	4.9	34	5.2	5.49	87	.307	.379	-6	-5	103	97	0.1	3	1	0.0
1938	StL-A	4	7	.364	25	12	3	1	0	104	118	10.2	7	61	5.3	35	3.0	6.06	82	.289	.374	-15	-13	103	87	0.0	-2	0	-1.1
1939	StL-A	0	0	—	2	1	0	0	0	7	9	11.6	0	7	9.0	6	7.7	11.57	42	.310	.447	-5	-5	105	60	0.0	-0	-0	-0.4
Total	7	33	41	.446	207	76	17	3	6	713	838	10.6	39	367	4.6	339	4.3	5.59	83	.293	.369	-80	-77	101	92	-0.6	4	-1	-5.8
■ **OZZIE Van BRABANT**	Van Brabant, Camille Oscar b: 9/28/26, Kingsville, Ont., Canada BR/TR, 6'1", 165 lbs. Deb: 4/13/54																												
1954	Phi-A	0	2	.000	9	2	0	0	0	27	35	11.7	3	18	6.0	10	3.3	7.00	56	.347	.435	-10	-9	105	103	-0.9	1	1	-0.7
1955	KC-A	0	0	—	2	0	0	0	0	2	4	18.0	1	2	9.0	1	4.5	18.00	23	.400	.462	-3	-3	106	73	0.0	0	0	-0.2
Total	2	0	2	.000	11	2	0	0	0	29	39	12.1	4	20	6.2	11	3.4	7.76	51	.351	.438	-13	-12	105	101	-0.9	1	1	-0.9
■ **DAZZY VANCE**	Vance, Clarence Arthur b: 3/4/1891, Orient, Iowa d: 2/16/61, Homosassa Springs, Fla. BR/TR, 6'2", 200 lbs. Deb: 4/16/15 H																												
1915	Pit-N	0	1	.000	1	1	0	0	0	3	3	9.0	0	5	15.0	0	0.0	9.00	30	.375	.643	-2	-2	98	110	-0.4	-0	0	-0.1
	NY-A	0	3	.000	8	3	1	0	0	28	23	7.4	1	16	5.1	18	5.8	3.54	82	.232	.350	-2	-2	99	95	-1.4	2	-0	0.0
1918	NY-A	0	0	—	2	0	0	0	0	2	9	40.5	0	2	9.0	0	0.0	18.00	14	.692	.733	-3	-3	94	130	0.0	0	0	-0.3

YEAR	TM/L	W	L	PCT	G	GS	CG	SHO	SV	IP	H	H/G	HR	BB	BB/G	SO	SO/G	ERA	/A	OAVG	OOBP	PR	/A	PF	CPI	WAT	PB	PD	TPI
1922	Bro-N	18	12	.600	36	30	16	**6**	0	246	259	9.5	9	94	3.4	**134**	**4.9**	3.70	106	.276	.338	11	6	95	102	3.7	2	0	0.7
1923	Bro-N	18	15	.545	37	35	21	3	0	280	263	8.5	9	100	3.2	**197**	**6.3**	3.50	111	.250	.315	16	12	98	88	2.1	-3	0	0.9
1924	Bro-N	**28**	6	.824	35	34	**30**	3	0	309	238	**6.9**	11	77	2.2	**262**	**7.6**	**2.16**	**176**	**.213**	**.265**	**59**	**56**	98	88	**10.6**	-2	0	**5.9**
1925	Bro-N	**22**	9	.710	31	31	26	**4**	0	265	247	8.4	8	66	2.2	**221**	**7.5**	3.53	115	.250	.297	22	15	95	80	**8.3**	0	1	1.5
1926	Bro-N	9	10	.474	24	22	12	1	1	169	172	9.2	7	58	3.1	**140**	**7.5**	3.89	99	.271	.324	-1	-1	101	94	0.2	-1	2	0.0
1927	Bro-N	16	15	.516	34	32	**25**	2	1	273	242	**8.0**	12	69	2.3	**184**	**6.1**	2.70	151	**.239**	.282	37	42	104	97	3.0	-2	-2	4.0
1928	Bro-N	22	10	.688	38	32	24	**4**	2	280	226	**7.3**	11	72	2.3	**200**	**6.4**	**2.09**	**188**	**.221**	**.271**	**59**	**57**	99	99	**6.8**	2	1	**6.4**
1929	Bro-N	14	13	.519	31	26	17	1	0	231	244	9.5	15	47	**1.8**	126	4.9	3.90	117	.274	.307	21	17	96	95	1.8	-2	1	1.4
1930	Bro-N	17	15	.531	35	31	20	**4**	0	259	241	**8.4**	15	55	1.9	173	6.0	**2.61**	**188**	.246	.284	**68**	**66**	99	108	-0.9	-5	-1	**5.7**
1931	Bro-N	11	13	.458	30	29	12	2	0	219	221	9.1	12	53	2.2	150	**6.2**	3.37	116	.261	.298	12	13	101	96	-1.5	-2	1	1.2
1932	Bro-N	12	11	.522	27	24	9	1	1	176	171	8.7	10	57	2.9	103	5.3	4.19	89	.256	.309	-6	-9	96	82	0.0	-3	0	-1.2
1933	StL-N	6	2	.750	28	11	2	0	3	99	105	9.5	3	28	2.5	67	6.1	3.55	95	.267	.314	-2	-2	100	92	1.9	-0	-1	-0.3
1934	Cin-N	0	2	.000	6	2	0	0	0	18	28	14.0	1	11	5.5	9	4.5	7.50	57	.350	.430	-7	-7	105	95	-0.9	0	0	-0.5
	StL-N	1	1	.500	19	4	1	0	1	59	62	9.5	4	14	2.1	33	5.0	3.66	123	.271	.315	3	6	111	103	-0.1	-0	-0	0.5
	Yr	1	3	.250	25	6	1	0	1	77	90	10.5	5	25	2.9	42	4.9	4.56	98	.290	.343	-4	-1	110	103	-1.0	0	-0	0.0
1935	Bro-N	3	2	.600	20	0	0	0	2	51	55	9.7	3	16	2.8	28	4.9	4.41	86	.268	.329	-2	-3	95	88	0.7	-2	-0	-0.4
Total	16	197	140	.585	442	347	216	31	11	2967	2809	8.5	131	840	2.5	2045	6.2	3.24	124	.251	.301	281	261	99	94	33.9	-17	2	25.4

■ **SANDY VANCE** Vance, Gene Covington b: 1/5/47, Lamar, Colo. BR/TR, 6'2", 180 lbs. Deb: 4/26/70

YEAR	TM/L	W	L	PCT	G	GS	CG	SHO	SV	IP	H	H/G	HR	BB	BB/G	SO	SO/G	ERA	/A	OAVG	OOBP	PR	/A	PF	CPI	WAT	PB	PD	TPI
1970	LA-N	7	7	.500	20	18	2	0	0	115	109	8.5	9	37	2.9	45	3.5	3.13	115	.248	.304	12	6	89	107	-0.5	1	-2	0.4
1971	LA-N	2	1	.667	10	3	0	0	0	26	38	13.2	1	9	3.1	11	3.8	6.92	49	.355	.388	-10	-10	98	86	0.4	-0	-0	-1.0
Total	2	9	8	.529	30	21	2	0	0	141	147	9.4	10	46	2.9	56	3.6	3.83	93	.269	.321	2	-4	91	103	-0.1	1	-3	-0.6

■ **JOE VANCE** Vance, Joseph Albert "Sandy" b: 9/16/05, Devine, Tex. d: 7/4/78, Devine, Tex. BR/TR, 6'1.5", 190 lbs. Deb: 4/18/35

YEAR	TM/L	W	L	PCT	G	GS	CG	SHO	SV	IP	H	H/G	HR	BB	BB/G	SO	SO/G	ERA	/A	OAVG	OOBP	PR	/A	PF	CPI	WAT	PB	PD	TPI
1935	Chi-A	2	2	.500	10	0	0	0	0	31	36	10.5	1	21	6.1	12	3.5	6.68	73	.295	.388	-8	-6	109	81	0.1	-1	1	-0.5
1937	NY-A	1	0	1.000	2	2	0	0	0	15	11	6.6	2	9	5.4	3	1.8	3.00	150	.204	.317	3	2	97	117	0.5	-1	1	0.2
1938	NY-A	0	0	—	3	1	0	0	0	11	20	16.4	2	4	3.3	2	1.6	7.36	66	.408	.444	-3	-3	102	127	0.0	2	0	0.0
Total	3	3	2	.600	15	3	0	0	0	57	67	10.6	5	34	5.4	17	2.7	5.84	82	.298	.383	-8	-7	105	99	0.6	0	1	-0.3

■ **CHRIS Van CUYK** Van Cuyk, Christian Gerald b: 3/1/27, Kimberly, Wis. BL/TL, 6'6", 215 lbs. Deb: 7/16/50

YEAR	TM/L	W	L	PCT	G	GS	CG	SHO	SV	IP	H	H/G	HR	BB	BB/G	SO	SO/G	ERA	/A	OAVG	OOBP	PR	/A	PF	CPI	WAT	PB	PD	TPI
1950	Bro-N	1	3	.250	12	4	1	0	0	33	33	9.0	3	12	3.3	21	5.7	4.91	88	.266	.329	-3	-2	104	84	-1.0	-1	-1	-0.2
1951	Bro-N	1	2	.333	9	6	0	0	0	29	33	10.2	4	11	3.4	16	5.0	5.59	67	.295	.372	-5	-6	95	100	-0.6	0	0	-0.4
1952	Bro-N	5	6	.455	23	16	4	0	1	98	104	9.6	12	40	3.7	66	6.1	5.14	71	.271	.343	-15	-16	98	91	-1.5	2	-1	-1.4
Total	3	7	11	.389	44	26	5	0	1	160	170	9.6	19	63	3.5	103	5.8	5.17	74	.274	.345	-23	-24	99	91	-3.1	1	-1	-2.0

■ **JOHNNY Van CUYK** Van Cuyk, John Henry b: 7/7/21, Little Chute, Wis. BL/TL, 6'1", 190 lbs. Deb: 9/18/47

YEAR	TM/L	W	L	PCT	G	GS	CG	SHO	SV	IP	H	H/G	HR	BB	BB/G	SO	SO/G	ERA	/A	OAVG	OOBP	PR	/A	PF	CPI	WAT	PB	PD	TPI
1947	Bro-N	0	0	—	2	0	0	0	0	3	5	15.0	0	1	3.0	2	6.0	6.00	70	.357	.375	-1	-1	103	99	0.0	0	0	0.0
1948	Bro-N	0	0	—	3	0	0	0	0	5	4	7.2	1	1	1.8	1	1.8	3.60	113	.200	.238	0	0	103	68	0.0	0	0	0.0
1949	Bro-N	0	0	—	2	0	0	0	0	2	3	13.5	0	1	4.5	0	0.0	9.00	44	.429	.444	-1	-1	98	89	0.0	0	0	0.0
Total	3	0	0	—	7	0	0	0	0	10	12	10.8	1	3	2.7	3	2.7	5.40	75	.293	.326	-2	-1	102	82	0.0	0	0	0.0

■ **ED VANDE BERG** Vande Berg, Edward John b: 10/26/58, Redlands, Cal. BR/TL, 6'2", 175 lbs. Deb: 4/07/82

YEAR	TM/L	W	L	PCT	G	GS	CG	SHO	SV	IP	H	H/G	HR	BB	BB/G	SO	SO/G	ERA	/A	OAVG	OOBP	PR	/A	PF	CPI	WAT	PB	PD	TPI
1982	Sea-A	9	4	.692	**78**	0	0	0	5	76	54	6.4	5	32	3.8	60	7.1	2.37	189	.207	.290	14	18	110	115	2.9	0	2	2.0
1983	Sea-A	2	4	.333	68	0	0	0	5	64	59	8.3	6	22	3.1	49	6.9	3.38	122	.246	.304	5	5	101	104	-0.2	0	0	0.5
1984	Sea-A	8	12	.400	50	17	2	0	7	130	165	11.4	18	50	3.5	71	4.9	4.78	86	.313	.366	-11	-9	103	119	-1.3	0	-0	-0.9
1985	Sea-A	2	1	.667	76	0	0	0	3	68	71	9.4	4	31	4.1	34	4.5	3.71	107	.274	.348	3	2	95	118	0.6	0	1	0.3
1986	LA-N	1	5	.167	60	0	0	0	0	71	83	10.5	8	33	4.2	42	5.3	3.42	103	.290	.360	2	1	95	149	-1.8	-0	1	0.2
1987	Cle-A	1	0	1.000	55	0	0	0	0	72	96	12.0	9	21	2.6	40	5.0	5.13	91	.325	.364	-5	-4	105	113	0.5	0	0	-0.2
1988	Tex-A	2	2	.500	26	0	0	0	2	37	44	10.7	2	11	2.7	18	4.4	4.14	98	.308	.346	-1	-0	102	115	0.2	0	-0	0.0
Total	7	25	28	.472	413	17	2	0	22	518	572	9.9	52	200	3.5	314	5.5	3.93	105	.284	.344	8	12	102	120	0.9	-0	3	1.9

■ **HY VANDENBERG** Vandenberg, Harold Harris b: 3/17/06, Abilene, Kan. BR/TR, 6'2.5", 190 lbs. Deb: 6/08/35

YEAR	TM/L	W	L	PCT	G	GS	CG	SHO	SV	IP	H	H/G	HR	BB	BB/G	SO	SO/G	ERA	/A	OAVG	OOBP	PR	/A	PF	CPI	WAT	PB	PD	TPI
1935	Bos-A	0	0	—	3	0	0	0	0	5	15	27.0	1	4	7.2	2	3.6	21.60	22	.500	.559	-10	-9	108	72	0.0	0	0	-0.6
1937	NY-N	0	1	.000	1	1	1	0	0	8	10	11.3	0	6	6.8	2	2.3	7.88	49	.313	.410	-4	-4	98	73	-0.4	-1	1	-0.2
1938	NY-N	0	1	.000	6	1	0	0	0	18	28	14.0	2	12	6.0	7	3.5	7.50	52	.368	.449	-7	-7	102	107	-0.4	-1	1	-0.5
1939	NY-N	0	0	—	2	1	0	0	0	6	10	15.0	0	6	9.0	3	4.5	6.00	64	.345	.457	-1	-1	99	124	0.0	-0	0	-0.1
1940	NY-N	1	1	.500	13	3	1	0	1	32	27	7.6	2	16	4.5	17	4.8	3.94	98	.227	.317	-0	-0	100	86	0.1	-0	-0	0.0
1944	Chi-N	7	4	.636	35	9	2	0	2	126	123	8.8	8	51	3.6	54	3.9	3.64	99	.255	.321	-0	-0	100	100	1.7	1	0	0.0
1945	Chi-N	7	3	.700	30	7	3	2	2	95	91	8.6	4	33	3.1	35	3.3	3.51	103	.259	.323	3	1	95	104	0.9	-1	0	0.0
Total	7	15	10	.600	90	22	7	2	5	290	304	9.4	17	128	4.0	120	3.7	4.34	85	.271	.343	-19	-21	99	99	1.9	-1	1	-1.4

■ **JOHNNY VANDER MEER** Vander Meer, John Samuel "Double No-Hit" or "The Dutch Master" b: 11/2/14, Prospect Park, N.J. BB/TL, 6'1", 190 lbs. Deb: 4/22/37

YEAR	TM/L	W	L	PCT	G	GS	CG	SHO	SV	IP	H	H/G	HR	BB	BB/G	SO	SO/G	ERA	/A	OAVG	OOBP	PR	/A	PF	CPI	WAT	PB	PD	TPI
1937	Cin-N	3	5	.375	19	9	4	0	0	84	63	6.8	0	69	7.4	52	5.6	3.86	94	.209	.353	1	-2	93	86	0.1	1	2	0.1
1938	Cin-N	15	10	.600	32	29	16	3	0	225	177	**7.1**	12	103	4.1	125	5.0	3.12	116	**.213**	.299	17	13	96	86	1.7	-2	-1	0.9
1939	Cin-N	5	9	.357	30	21	8	0	0	129	128	8.9	7	95	6.6	102	7.1	4.67	84	.264	.379	-11	-11	100	102	-3.1	-1	-1	-1.2
1940	Cin-N	3	1	.750	10	7	2	0	1	48	38	7.1	3	41	7.7	41	7.7	3.75	100	.211	.357	1	0	98	104	0.6	2	0	0.2
1941	Cin-N	16	13	.552	33	32	18	6	0	226	172	**6.8**	8	126	5.0	**202**	**8.0**	2.83	126	.214	.316	20	18	98	105	-0.5	-3	2	1.8
1942	Cin-N	18	12	.600	33	33	21	4	0	244	188	6.9	6	102	3.8	**186**	**6.9**	2.43	138	.208	.286	24	25	102	91	3.6	-1	1	2.9
1943	Cin-N	15	16	.484	36	36	21	3	0	289	228	7.1	5	162	5.0	**174**	**5.4**	2.87	115	.224	.326	16	14	98	106	-2.6	-2	3	1.7
1946	Cin-N	10	12	.455	29	25	11	5	0	204	175	7.7	11	78	3.4	94	4.1	3.18	113	.233	.299	5	9	105	88	0.4	2	-2	1.0
1947	Cin-N	9	14	.391	30	29	9	3	0	186	186	9.0	11	87	4.2	79	3.8	4.40	85	.261	.338	-7	-14	92	89	-2.2	-2	-1	-1.6
1948	Cin-N	17	14	.548	33	33	14	3	0	232	204	7.9	15	124	4.8	120	4.7	3.41	123	.239	.331	14	20	106	108	4.1	-0	-1	2.1
1949	Cin-N	5	10	.333	28	24	7	3	0	160	172	9.7	12	85	4.8	76	4.3	4.89	81	.281	.364	-15	-17	98	99	-1.3	-3	1	-1.6
1950	Chi-N	3	4	.429	32	6	0	0	1	74	60	7.3	10	59	7.2	41	5.0	3.77	118	.221	.358	3	5	107	119	0.1	-0	0	0.5
1951	Cle-A	0	1	.000	1	1	0	0	0	3	8	24.0	0	1	3.0	2	6.0	18.00	21	.500	.529	-5	-5	93	65	-0.4	-0	1	-0.3
Total	13	119	121	.496	346	285	131	30	2	2104	1799	7.7	100	1132	4.8	1294	5.5	3.44	107	.232	.327	63	58	99	98	0.5	-10	4	6.5

■ **BEN Van DYKE** Van Dyke, Benjamin Harrison b: 8/15/1888, Clintonville, Pa. d: 10/22/73, Sarasota, Fla. BR/TL, 6'1", 150 lbs. Deb: 09

YEAR	TM/L	W	L	PCT	G	GS	CG	SHO	SV	IP	H	H/G	HR	BB	BB/G	SO	SO/G	ERA	/A	OAVG	OOBP	PR	/A	PF	CPI	WAT	PB	PD	TPI
1909	Phi-N	0	0	—	2	0	0	0	0	7	7	9.0	0	4	5.1	5	6.4	3.86	72	.269	.367	-1	-1	106	97	0.0	-0	-0	0.0
1912	Bos-A	0	0	—	3	1	0	0	0	14	13	8.4	0	7	4.5	8	5.1	3.21	106	.245	.344	0	0	102	100	0.0	-0	-0	0.0
Total	2	0	0	—	5	1	0	0	0	21	20	8.6	0	11	4.7	13	5.6	3.43	94	.253	.352	-1	-1	104	99	0.0	-0	-1	0.0

■ **ELAM VANGILDER** Vangilder, Elam Russell b: 4/23/1896, Cape Girardeau, Mo d: 4/30/77, Cape Girardeau, Mo BR/TR, 6'1", 192 lbs. Deb: 9/18/19

YEAR	TM/L	W	L	PCT	G	GS	CG	SHO	SV	IP	H	H/G	HR	BB	BB/G	SO	SO/G	ERA	/A	OAVG	OOBP	PR	/A	PF	CPI	WAT	PB	PD	TPI
1919	StL-A	1	0	1.000	3	1	1	0	0	13	15	10.4	0	3	2.1	6	4.2	2.08	151	.306	.346	2	2	98	177	0.5	1	1	0.3
1920	StL-A	3	8	.273	24	13	4	0	0	105	131	11.2	7	40	3.4	25	2.1	5.49	77	.310	.373	-20	-15	111	88	-2.5	-2	-0	-1.5
1921	StL-A	11	12	.478	31	21	10	1	0	180	196	9.8	10	67	3.3	48	2.4	3.95	109	.278	.332	7	7	101	99	-1.1	-2	-0	0.5
1922	StL-A	19	13	.594	43	30	19	3	4	245	248	9.1	13	48	1.8	63	2.3	3.42	121	.270	.303	17	19	102	95	-0.2	14	-2	3.0
1923	StL-A	16	17	.485	41	35	20	4	1	282	276	8.8	11	120	3.8	74	2.4	3.06	136	.266	.332	29	**35**	105	121	0.0	-0	-3	3.2
1924	StL-A	5	10	.333	43	18	5	0	1	145	183	11.4	10	55	3.4	49	3.0	5.65	81	.317	.369	-23	-18	108	95	-2.4	4	1	-1.1
1925	StL-A	14	8	.636	52	16	4	1	6	193	225	10.5	11	92	4.3	61	2.8	4.71	100	.303	.369	-7	0	108	108	2.7	-3	-0	-0.1
1926	StL-A	9	11	.450	42	19	8	1	1	181	196	9.7	12	98	4.9	40	2.0	5.17	80	.285	.360	-23	-20	103	92	0.9	1	-2	-1.9
1927	StL-A	10	12	.455	44	23	12	3	1	203	245	10.9	13	102	4.5	62	2.7	4.79	94	.275	.341	-15	-6	109	87	1.4	2	-4	-0.6
1928	Det-A	11	10	.524	38	11	7	0	5	156	163	9.4	4	67	3.9	43	2.5	3.92	103	.272	.337	2	2	100	99	1.8	2	0	0.4
1929	Det-A	0	1	.000	6	0	0	0	0	11	16	13.1	1	7	5.7	3	2.5	6.55	63	.348	.418	-3	-3	97	109	-0.4	-0	1	-0.1
Total	11	99	102	.493	367	187	90	13	19	1714	1894	9.9	92	699	3.7	474	2.5	4.28	100	.284	.344	-34	3	105	100	0.7	16	-9	2.1

■ **GEORGE Van HALTREN** Van Haltren, George Edward Martin "Rip" b: 3/30/1866, St.Louis, Mo. d: 9/29/45, Oakland, Cal. BL/TL, 5'11", 170 lbs. Deb: 6/27/1887 M

YEAR	TM/L	W	L	PCT	G	GS	CG	SHO	SV	IP	H	H/G	HR	BB	BB/G	SO	SO/G	ERA	/A	OAVG	OOBP	PR	/A	PF	CPI	WAT	PB	PD	TPI
1887	Chi-N	11	7	.611	20	18	18	1	1	161	177	9.9	7	66	3.7	76	4.2	3.86	121	.295	.364	3	15	115	112	0.6	-2	0	1.3
1888	Chi-N	13	13	.500	30	24	24	4	1	246	263	9.6	16	60	2.2	139	5.1	3.51	85	.287	.331	-19	-14	106	105	-1.8	12	0	-1.3

YEAR	TM/L	W	L	PCT	G	GS	CG	SHO	SV	IP	H	H/G	HR	BB	BB/G	SO	SO/G	ERA	/A	OAVG	OOBP	PR	/A	PF	CPI	WAT	PB	PD	TPI
1890	Bro-P	15	10	.600	28	25	23	0	2	223	272	11.0	8	89	3.6	48	1.9	4.28	104	.313	.377	-1	5	105	103	0.9	10	0	0.4
1891	Bal-a	0	1	.000	6	1	0	0	0	23	38	14.9	1	10	3.9	7	2.7	5.09	73	.385	.442	-3	-3	100	134	-0.4	3	0	-0.2
1892	Bal-N	0	0	—	4	0	0	0	0	15	28	16.8	1	7	4.2	5	3.0	9.60	35	.412	.467	-11	-10	102	85	0.0	2	0	-1.2
1895	NY-N	0	0	—	1	0	0	0	0	5	13	23.4	0	2	3.6	1	1.8	12.60	36	.502	.538	-4	-4	94	90	0.0	0	0	-0.2
1896	NY-N	1	0	1.000	2	0	0	0	0	8	5	5.6	1	1	1.1	3	3.4	2.25	191	.197	.227	2	2	99	72	0.5	1	0	0.2
1900	NY-N	0	0	—	1	0	0	0	0	3	1	3.0	0	3	9.0	0	0.0	0.00	—	.116	.345	1	1	99	0	0.0	0	0	0.1
1901	NY-N	0	0	—	1	0	0	0	0	6	12	18.0	0	6	9.0	2	3.0	3.00	105	.456	.571	0	0	95	345	0.0	0	1	0.0
Total	9	40	31	.563	93	68	65	5	4	690	809	10.6	34	244	3.2	281	3.7	4.06	97	.307	.366	-31	-11	107	108	-0.2	26	1	-0.9
■ IKE Van ZANDT	Van Zandt, Charles Isaac b: 1877, Brooklyn, N.Y. d: 9/14/08, Nashua, N.H. BL , Deb: 8/05/01																												
1901	NY-N	0	0	—	2	0	0	0	0	13	16	11.1	0	8	5.5	2	1.4	6.92	46	.332	.437	-5	-5	95	76	0.0	-0	-1	-0.5
1905	StL-A	0	0	—	1	0	0	0	0	7	2	2.6	0	2	2.6	3	3.9	0.00	—	.102	.186	2	2	93	0	0.0	0	0	0.2
Total	2	0	0	—	3	0	0	0	0	20	18	8.1	0	10	4.5	5	2.3	4.50	65	.266	.368	-3	-4	95	49	0.0	-0	-1	-0.3
■ ANDY VARGA	Varga, Andrew William b: 12/11/30, Chicago, Ill. BR/TL, 6'4", 187 lbs. Deb: 9/09/50																												
1950	Chi-N	0	0	—	1	0	0	0	0	1	0	0.0	0	1	9.0	0	0.0	0.00	—	.000	.333	0	0	107	0	0.0	0	0	0.0
1951	Chi-N	0	0	—	2	0	0	0	0	3	2	6.0	0	6	18.0	1	3.0	3.00	132	.200	.471	0	0	100	216	0.0	0	0	0.0
Total	2	0	0	—	3	0	0	0	0	4	2	4.5	0	7	15.8	1	2.3	2.25	181	.167	.450	1	1	102	162	0.0	0	0	0.0
■ ROBERTO VARGAS	Vargas, Roberto Enrique b: 5/29/29, Santurce, P.R. BL/TL, 5'11", 170 lbs. Deb: 4/17/55																												
1955	Mil-N	0	0	—	25	0	0	0	2	25	39	14.0	4	14	5.0	13	4.7	8.64	43	.355	.422	-13	-14	92	89	0.0	0	1	-1.1
■ BILL VARGUS	Vargus, William Fay b: 11/11/1899, N.Scituate, Mass. d: 2/12/79, Hyannis, Mass. BL/TL, 6', 165 lbs. Deb: 6/23/25																												
1925	Bos-N	1	1	.500	11	2	1	0	0	36	45	11.3	1	13	3.3	5	1.3	4.00	102	.302	.355	1	0	95	113	0.1	0	0	0.0
1926	Bos-N	0	0	—	4	0	0	0	0	3	4	12.0	0	1	3.0	0	0.0	3.00	112	.333	.357	0	0	88	168	0.0	0	0	0.0
Total	2	1	1	.500	15	2	1	0	0	39	49	11.3	1	14	3.2	5	1.2	3.92	102	.304	.355	1	0	95	117	0.1	0	0	0.0
■ DIKE VARNEY	Varney, Lawrence Delano b: 8/9/1880, Dover, N.H. d: 4/23/50, Long Island City, N.Y. TL , 6', 165 lbs. Deb: 7/03/02																												
1902	Cle-A	1	1	.500	3	3	0	0	0	15	14	8.4	0	12	7.2	7	4.2	6.00	57	.271	.408	-4	-4	96	68	0.0	-0	0	-0.3
■ CAL VASBINDER	Vasbinder, Moses Calhoun b: 7/19/1880, Scio, Ohio d: 12/22/50, Cadiz, Ohio BR/TR, 6'2", Deb: 4/27/02																												
1902	Cle-A	0	0	—	2	0	0	0	0	5	5	9.0	1	8	14.4	2	3.6	9.00	38	.284	.508	-3	-3	96	91	0.0	0	0	-0.2
■ RAFAEL VASQUEZ	Vasquez, Rafael b: 6/28/58, La Romana, D.R. BR/TR, 6', 160 lbs. Deb: 4/06/79																												
1979	Sea-A	1	0	1.000	9	0	0	0	0	16	23	12.9	4	6	3.4	9	5.1	5.06	84	.354	.411	-1	-1	101	156	0.5	0	-0	-0.1
■ PORTER VAUGHAN	Vaughan, Cecil Porter "Lefty" b: 5/11/19, Stevensville, Va. BR/TL, 6'1", 178 lbs. Deb: 6/16/40																												
1940	Phi-A	2	9	.182	18	15	5	0	2	99	104	9.5	9	61	5.5	46	4.2	5.36	81	.264	.362	-11	-11	99	90	-2.7	0	-1	-1.0
1941	Phi-A	0	2	.000	5	3	1	0	0	23	32	12.5	3	12	4.7	6	2.3	7.83	55	.327	.393	-9	-9	103	84	-0.9	-0	-0	-0.8
1946	Phi-A	0	0	—	1	0	0	0	0	0	1	—	0	1	—	0	—	—	—	1.000	1.000	0	0	107	0	0.0	0	0	0.0
Total	3	2	11	.154	24	18	6	0	2	122	137	10.1	12	74	5.5	52	3.8	5.83	74	.278	.370	-20	-20	100	89	-3.6	-0	-1	-1.8
■ CHARLIE VAUGHAN	Vaughan, Charles Wayne b: 10/6/47, Mercedes, Tex. BR/TL, 6'1.5", 185 lbs. Deb: 9/03/66																												
1966	Atl-N	1	0	1.000	1	1	0	0	0	7	8	10.3	0	3	3.9	6	7.7	2.57	136	.296	.355	1	1	97	164	0.5	0	0	0.1
1969	Atl-N	0	0	—	1	0	0	0	0	1	1	9.0	0	3	27.0	1	9.0	18.00	21	.250	.571	-2	-2	103	56	0.0	0	0	0.0
Total	2	1	0	1.000	2	1	0	0	0	8	9	10.1	0	6	6.8	7	7.9	4.50	78	.290	.395	-1	-1	98	151	0.5	0	0	0.1
■ ROY VAUGHN	Vaughn, Clarence Leroy b: 9/4/11, Sedalia, Mo. d: 3/1/37, Martinsville, Va. BB/TR, 6'0.5", 178 lbs. Deb: 7/01/34																												
1934	Phi-A	0	0	—	2	0	0	0	0	4	3	6.8	1	3	6.8	1	2.3	2.25	197	.176	.300	1	1	98	150	0.0	-0	-0	0.0
■ DE WAYNE VAUGHN	Vaughn, De Wayne Mathew b: 7/22/59, Oklahoma City, Okla BR/TR, 6'1", 175 lbs. Deb: 4/17/88																												
1988	Tex-A	0	0	—	8	0	0	0	0	15	24	14.4	4	4	2.4	8	4.8	7.80	52	.348	.373	-6	-6	102	97	0.0	0	-0	-0.6
■ FARMER VAUGHN	Vaughn, Harry Francis b: 3/1/1864, Rural Dale, Ohio d: 2/21/14, Cincinnati, Ohio BR/TR, 6'3", 177 lbs. Deb: 10/07/1886																												
1891	CM-a	0	0	—	1	0	0	0	0	7	12	15.4	0	1	1.3	0	0.0	3.86	109	.394	.413	-0	0	113	155	0.0	0	0	0.0
■ HIPPO VAUGHN	Vaughn, James Leslie b: 4/9/1888, Weatherford, Tex. d: 5/29/66, Chicago, Ill. BB/TL, 6'4", 215 lbs. Deb: 6/19/08																												
1908	NY-A	0	0	—	2	0	0	0	0	2	1	4.5	0	4	18.0	2	9.0	4.50	54	.167	.500	-0	-0	101	130	0.0	-0	0	0.0
1910	NY-A	13	11	.542	30	25	18	5	1	222	190	7.7	1	58	2.4	107	4.3	1.82	146	.237	.297	17	21	106	121	-0.9	-3	-0	2.3
1911	NY-A	8	10	.444	26	18	11	0	0	146	158	9.7	2	54	3.3	74	4.6	4.38	85	.284	.354	-17	-11	111	85	-1.0	-1	1	-0.9
1912	NY-A	2	8	.200	15	10	5	1	0	63	66	9.4	1	37	5.3	46	6.6	5.14	69	.264	.361	-13	-11	105	75	-1.9	-2	1	-0.9
	Was-A	4	3	.571	12	8	4	0	0	81	75	8.3	0	43	4.8	49	5.4	2.89	112	.253	.356	4	3	97	122	-0.1	-0	2	0.5
	Yr	6	11	.353	27	18	9	1	0	144	141	8.8	1	80	5.0	95	5.9	3.88	87	.258	.357	-8	-8	101	122	-2.0	-2	3	-0.4
1913	Chi-N	5	1	.833	7	6	5	2	0	56	37	5.9	0	27	4.3	36	5.8	1.45	214	.182	.281	11	10	97	98	1.9	-0	0	1.1
1914	Chi-N	21	13	.618	42	35	23	4	1	294	236	7.2	1	109	3.3	165	5.1	2.05	134	.222	.292	24	23	99	99	4.6	-0	-0	2.5
1915	Chi-N	20	12	.625	41	34	18	4	1	270	240	8.0	4	77	2.6	148	4.9	2.87	99	.238	.293	-3	-1	103	84	5.3	1	-1	0.0
1916	Chi-N	17	15	.531	44	35	21	4	1	294	269	8.2	4	67	2.1	144	4.4	2.20	140	.250	.288	14	28	117	114	3.2	-5	1	3.1
1917	Chi-N	23	13	.639	41	39	27	5	0	296	255	7.8	3	91	2.8	195	**5.9**	2.01	142	.235	.292	23	27	105	120	6.6	-0	3	3.6
1918	Chi-N	**22**	10	.688	35	33	27	**8**	0	**290**	216	**6.7**	4	76	2.4	**148**	**4.6**	**1.74**	**156**	**.208**	.261	**33**	**31**	98	91	2.1	4	-1	**4.2**
1919	Chi-N	21	14	.600	38	37	25	4	1	**307**	264	7.7	3	62	1.8	**141**	4.1	1.79	162	.234	.271	**38**	**38**	99	115	3.1	-0	-3	4.1
1920	Chi-N	19	16	.543	40	38	24	4	0	301	301	9.0	8	81	2.4	131	3.9	2.54	122	.264	.311	20	19	99	114	2.4	4	-2	2.2
1921	Chi-N	3	11	.214	17	14	7	0	0	109	153	12.6	8	31	2.6	30	2.5	6.03	68	.341	.378	-27	-23	108	93	-3.5	2	-1	-2.0
Total	13	178	137	.565	390	332	215	41	5	2731	2461	8.1	39	817	2.7	1416	4.7	2.48	121	.244	.300	124	155	104	105	21.8	-2	-1	19.8
■ AL VEACH	Veach, Alvis Lindell b: 8/6/09, Maylene, Ala. BR/TR, 5'11", 178 lbs. Deb: 9/22/35																												
1935	Phi-A	0	2	.000	2	2	1	0	0	10	20	18.0	1	9	8.1	3	2.7	11.70	39	.417	.500	-8	-8	102	91	-0.9	-1	0	-0.6
■ BOBBY VEACH	Veach, Robert Hayes b: 6/29/1888, Island, Ky. d: 8/7/45, Detroit, Mich. BL/TR, 5'11", 160 lbs. Deb: 8/06/12																												
1918	Det-A	0	0	—	1	0	0	0	1	2	2	9.0	0	2	9.0	0	0.0	4.50	61	.286	.444	-0	-0	99	117	0.0	0	0	0.0
■ PEEK-A-BOO VEACH	Veach, William Walter b: 6/15/1862, Indianapolis, Ind d: 11/12/37, Indianapolis, Ind. Deb: 8/24/1884																												
1884	KC-U	3	9	.250	12	12	12	0	0	104	95	8.2	1	10	0.9	62	5.4	2.42	114	.248	.267	7	4	92	96	0.4	-1	0	0.3
1887	Lou-a	0	1	.000	1	1	1	0	0	9	5	5.0	1	8	8.0	2	2.0	4.00	114	.173	.352	0	1	106	88	-0.4	-0	0	0.0
Total	2	3	10	.231	13	13	13	0	0	113	100	8.0	2	18	1.4	64	5.1	2.55	113	.243	.275	7	4	93	96	0.0	-1	0	0.3
■ BOB VEALE	Veale, Robert Andrew b: 10/28/35, Birmingham, Ala. BB/TR, 6'6", 212 lbs. Deb: 4/16/62																												
1962	Pit-N	2	2	.500	11	6	2	0	1	46	39	7.6	2	25	4.9	42	8.2	3.72	107	.235	.328	1	1	101	91	-0.2	1	-0	0.2
1963	Pit-N	5	2	.714	34	7	3	2	3	78	59	6.8	1	40	4.6	68	7.8	1.04	314	.215	.312	19	19	99	254	1.7	-0	0	2.1
1964	Pit-N	18	12	.600	40	38	14	1	0	280	222	7.1	8	124	4.0	**250**	8.0	2.73	130	.217	.301	25	26	101	94	3.7	-0	-1	2.7
1965	Pit-N	17	12	.586	39	37	14	7	0	266	221	7.5	5	119	4.0	276	9.3	2.84	122	.225	.308	21	19	98	96	1.2	-4	-1	1.4
1966	Pit-N	16	12	.571	38	37	12	3	0	268	228	7.7	18	102	3.4	229	7.7	3.02	118	.232	.302	17	16	99	99	0.1	-2	-2	1.3
1967	Pit-N	16	8	.667	33	31	6	1	0	203	184	8.2	12	119	5.3	179	7.9	3.64	93	.245	.346	-6	-6	100	108	4.4	-5	1	-1.0
1968	Pit-N	13	14	.481	36	33	13	4	0	245	187	6.9	13	94	3.5	171	6.3	2.06	145	.211	.284	25	25	100	116	-0.3	-2	-2	2.6
1969	Pit-N	13	14	.481	34	34	9	1	0	226	232	9.2	8	91	3.6	213	8.5	3.23	105	.267	.333	9	4	94	114	-1.7	-5	-0	-0.1
1970	Pit-N	10	15	.400	34	32	5	1	0	202	189	8.4	15	94	4.2	178	7.9	3.92	99	.246	.324	3	-1	96	95	-3.7	1	-2	-0.1
1971	Pit-N	6	0	1.000	37	0	0	0	2	46	59	11.5	5	24	4.7	40	7.8	7.04	48	.314	.381	-18	-19	97	82	3.0	1	-1	-1.9
1972	Pit-N	0	0	—	5	0	0	0	0	9	10	10.0	0	7	7.0	6	6.0	6.00	58	.313	.405	-3	-3	100	94	0.0	-0	-0	-0.2
	Bos-A	2	0	1.000	6	0	0	0	2	8	2	2.3	0	3	3.4	10	11.3	0.00	—	.083	.185	3	3	105	0	1.0	-0	0	0.3
1973	Bos-A	2	3	.400	32	0	0	0	11	36	37	9.3	2	12	3.0	25	6.3	3.50	114	.268	.318	1	2	105	102	-0.6	0	1	0.3
1974	Bos-A	0	1	.000	18	0	0	0	2	13	15	10.4	2	4	2.8	16	11.1	5.54	69	.283	.328	-3	-2	106	83	-0.4	0	-0	-0.2
Total	13	120	95	.558	397	255	78	20	21	1926	1684	7.9	91	858	4.0	1703	8.0	3.07	113	.236	.315	96	86	99	108	8.2	-16	-8	7.4

YEAR	TM/L	W	L	PCT	G	GS	CG	SHO	SV	IP	H	H/G	HR	BB	BB/G	SO	SO/G	ERA	/A	OAVG	OOBP	PR	/A	PF	CPI	WAT	PB	PD	TPI
■ LOU VEDDER	Vedder, Louis Edward b: 4/20/1897, Oakville, Mich. BR/TR, 5'10.5", 175 lbs. Deb: 9/18/20																												
1920	Det-A	0	0	—	1	0	0	0	0	2	0	0.0	0	0	0.0	1	4.5	0.00	—	.000	.000	1	1	106	0	0.0	0	0	0.1
■ AL VEIGEL	Veigel, Allen Francis b: 1/30/17, Dover, Ohio BR/TR, 6'1", 180 lbs. Deb: 9/21/39																												
1939	Bos-N	0	1	.000	2	2	0	0	0	3	3	9.0	0	5	15.0	1	3.0	6.00	61	.250	.444	-1	-1	93	106	-0.4	-0	-0	0.0
■ BUCKY VEIL	Veil, Frederick William b: 8/2/1881, Tyrone, Pa. d: 4/16/31, Altoona, Pa. BR/TR, 5'10", 165 lbs. Deb: 4/19/03																												
1903	Pit-N	5	3	.625	12	6	4	0	0	71	70	8.9	1	36	4.6	20	2.5	3.80	87	.284	.379	-4	-4	101	94	-0.1	-0	-0	-0.3
1904	Pit-N	0	0	—	1	1	0	0	0	5	4	7.2	0	4	7.2	1	1.8	5.40	49	.256	.437	-1	-2	98	73	0.0	0	0	0.0
Total	2	5	3	.625	13	7	4	0	0	76	74	8.8	1	40	4.7	21	2.5	3.91	84	.282	.383	-6	-5	101	93	-0.1	0	-0	-0.3
■ CARLOS VELAZQUEZ	Velazquez, Carlos (Quinones) b: 3/22/48, Loiza, P.R. BR/TR, 5'11", 180 lbs. Deb: 7/20/73																												
1973	Mil-A	2	2	.500	18	0	0	0	2	38	46	10.9	5	10	2.4	12	2.8	2.61	141	.297	.333	5	5	96	181	0.2	0	0	0.5
■ JOE VERBANIC	Verbanic, Joseph Michael b: 4/24/43, Washington, Pa. BR/TR, 6', 155 lbs. Deb: 7/22/66																												
1966	Phi-N	1	1	.500	17	0	0	0	0	14	12	7.7	2	10	6.4	7	4.5	5.14	70	.226	.344	-2	-2	100	83	0.0	0	-0	-0.2
1967	NY-A	4	3	.571	28	6	1	1	2	80	74	8.3	6	21	2.4	39	4.4	2.81	110	.249	.296	4	2	96	117	0.8	-0	2	0.4
1968	NY-A	6	7	.462	40	11	2	1	4	97	104	9.6	6	41	3.8	40	3.7	3.15	95	.284	.355	-2	-2	101	145	-0.6	-1	1	-0.1
1970	NY-A	1	0	1.000	7	0	0	0	0	16	20	11.3	1	12	6.8	8	4.5	4.50	76	.323	.423	-1	-2	91	144	0.5	0	1	0.0
Total	4	12	11	.522	92	17	3	2	6	207	210	9.1	15	84	3.7	94	4.1	3.26	96	.270	.339	-2	-3	98	130	0.7	-1	4	0.1
■ AL VERDEL	Verdel, Albert Alfred "Stumpy" b: 6/10/21, Punxsutawney, Pa. BR/TR, 5'9.5", 186 lbs. Deb: 4/20/44																												
1944	Phi-N	0	0	—	1	0	0	0	0	1	0	0.0	0	0	0.0	0	0.0	0.00	—	.000	.000	0	0	103	0	0.0	0	0	0.0
■ TOMMY VEREKER	Vereker, John James b: 12/2/1893, Baltimore, Md. d: 4/2/74, Baltimore, Md. 5'10", 185 lbs. Deb: 6/17/15																												
1915	Bal-F	0	0	—	2	0	0	0	0	3	3	9.0	1	2	6.0	1	3.0	15.00	23	.289	.404	-4	-4	111	44	0.0	0	0	-0.3
■ JOHN VERHOEVEN	Verhoeven, John C b: 7/3/53, Long Beach, Cal. BR/TR, 6'5", 200 lbs. Deb: 7/06/76																												
1976	Cal-A	0	2	.000	21	0	0	0	4	37	35	8.5	2	14	3.4	23	5.6	3.41	96	.252	.314	0	-1	93	98	-0.9	0	1	0.1
1977	Cal-A	0	2	.000	3	0	0	0	0	5	4	7.2	0	4	7.2	3	5.4	3.60	107	.222	.391	0	0	95	110	-0.9	0	0	0.0
	Chi-A	0	0	—	6	0	0	0	0	10	9	8.1	0	2	1.8	6	5.4	2.70	149	.231	.262	2	1	99	64	0.0	0	1	0.2
	Yr	0	2	.000	9	0	0	0	0	15	13	7.8	0	6	3.6	9	5.4	3.00	132	.224	.292	2	2	97	64	-0.9	0	1	0.2
1980	Min-A	3	4	.429	44	0	0	0	0	100	109	9.8	10	29	2.6	42	3.8	3.96	112	.289	.332	1	5	109	114	-0.3	0	0	0.5
1981	Min-A	0	0	—	25	0	0	0	0	52	57	9.9	4	14	2.4	16	2.8	3.98	98	.288	.327	-2	-0	107	108	0.0	0	0	0.0
Total	4	3	8	.273	99	0	0	0	4	204	214	9.4	16	63	2.8	90	4.0	3.79	106	.278	.326	1	6	105	107	-2.1	0	2	0.8
■ JOE VERNON	Vernon, Joseph Henry b: 11/25/1889, Mansfield, Mass. d: 3/13/55, Philadelphia, Pa. BR/TR, 5'11", 160 lbs. Deb: 7/20/12																												
1912	Chi-N	0	0	—	1	0	0	0	0	4	4	9.0	0	6	13.5	1	2.3	11.25	31	.286	.524	-3	-3	102	66	0.0	-0	-0	-0.2
1914	Bro-F	0	0	—	1	1	0	0	0	3	4	12.0	0	5	15.0	0	0.0	12.00	27	.352	.550	-3	-3	101	71	0.0	-0	0	-0.2
Total	2	0	0	—	2	1	0	0	0	7	8	10.3	0	11	14.1	1	1.3	11.57	29	.315	.535	-6	-6	102	68	0.0	-0	-0	-0.4
■ BOB VESELIC	Veselic, Robert Michael b: 9/27/55, Pittsburgh, Pa. BR/TR, 6', 175 lbs. Deb: 9/18/80																												
1980	Min-A	0	0	—	1	0	0	0	0	4	3	6.8	1	1	2.3	2	4.5	4.50	98	.214	.267	-0	-0	109	81	0.0	0	0	0.0
1981	Min-A	1	1	.500	5	0	0	0	0	23	22	8.6	1	12	4.7	13	5.1	3.13	125	.250	.333	1	2	107	115	0.2	0	-1	0.1
Total	2	1	1	.500	6	0	0	0	0	27	25	8.3	2	13	4.3	15	5.0	3.33	119	.245	.325	1	2	107	110	0.2	0	-1	0.1
■ LEE VIAU	Viau, Leon b: 7/5/1868, Hanover, N.H. d: 12/17/47, Wayne, N.J. BR/TR, 5'4", 160 lbs. Deb: 1888																												
1888	Cin-a	27	14	.659	42	42	42	1	0	388	331	7.7	7	110	2.6	164	3.8	2.64	115	.243	.299	18	17	99	96	4.2	-10	-1	0.5
1889	Cin-a	22	20	.524	47	42	38	1	1	373	379	9.1	8	136	3.3	152	3.7	3.79	105	.278	.344	2	8	103	91	-1.1	-9	-3	-0.2
1890	Cin-N	7	5	.583	13	10	7	1	0	90	97	9.7	8	39	3.9	41	4.1	4.50	84	.291	.365	-9	-7	106	97	0.0	-3	0	-0.7
	Cle-N	4	9	.308	13	13	13	1	0	107	101	8.5	4	42	3.5	30	2.5	3.36	103	.265	.337	2	1	97	95	-0.4	-1	0	0.0
	Yr	11	14	.440	26	23	20	2	0	197	198	9.0	12	81	3.7	71	3.2	3.88	93	.277	.351	-7	-6	101	95	-0.4	-3	0	-0.7
1891	Cle-N	18	17	.514	45	38	31	0	0	344	367	9.6	3	138	3.6	130	3.4	3.01	118	.287	.356	13	20	106	**113**	2.0	-4	2	1.8
1892	Cle-N	0	1	.000	1	1	0	0	0	1	5	45.0	0	1	9.0	0	0.0	36.00	9	.653	.693	-4	-4	101	69	-0.4	0	0	-0.2
	Lou-N	4	11	.267	16	15	14	1	0	131	156	10.7	7	56	3.8	36	2.5	3.98	77	.309	.378	-10	-13	93	116	-2.8	1	0	-1.0
	Bos-N	1	0	1.000	1	1	1	0	0	9	5	5.0	0	4	4.0	1	1.0	0.00	—	.173	.273	3	4	111	0	0.5	-1	0	0.4
	Yr	5	12	.294	18	17	15	1	0	141	166	10.6	7	61	3.9	37	2.4	3.96	78	.307	.377	-10	-13	94	0	-2.7	1	0	-0.8
Total	5	83	77	.519	178	162	146	5	1	1443	1441	9.0	37	526	3.3	554	3.5	3.32	105	.274	.340	16	25	102	100	2.0	-27	-2	0.6
■ RUBE VICKERS	Vickers, Harry Porter b: 5/17/1878, St. Mary's, Ont., Can. d: 12/9/58, Belleville, Mich. BL/TR, 6'2", 225 lbs. Deb: 9/21/02																												
1902	Cin-N	0	3	.000	3	3	3	0	0	21	31	13.3	0	8	3.4	6	2.6	6.00	50	.368	.423	-8	-7	108	89	-1.4	1	-1	-0.6
1903	Bro-N	0	1	.000	4	1	1	0	0	14	27	17.4	0	9	5.8	5	3.2	10.93	30	.441	.519	-12	-12	102	79	-0.4	-1	1	-0.8
1907	Phi-A	2	2	.500	10	4	3	1	0	50	44	7.9	1	12	2.2	21	3.8	3.42	78	.259	.308	-5	-4	104	69	-0.3	-1	0	-0.3
1908	Phi-A	18	19	.486	53	34	21	6	1	317	264	7.5	0	71	2.0	156	4.4	2.21	118	.231	.282	6	14	110	96	1.8	-1	-3	1.2
1909	Phi-A	2	2	.500	18	3	1	0	1	56	60	9.6	0	19	3.1	25	4.0	3.38	71	.274	.338	-6	-6	97	93	-0.3	-1	-1	-0.7
Total	5	22	27	.449	88	45	29	7	2	458	426	8.4	1	119	2.3	213	4.2	2.93	90	.254	.309	-24	-15	107	92	-0.6	-3	-4	-1.2
■ TOM VICKERY	Vickery, Thomas Gill "Vinegar Tom" b: 5/5/1867, Milford, N.J. d: 3/21/21, Burlington, N.J. 6', 170 lbs. Deb: 4/21/1890																												
1890	Phi-N	24	22	.522	46	46	41	1	0	382	405	9.5	8	184	4.3	162	3.8	3.44	111	.288	.370	5	16	107	113	-3.8	-5	-2	0.9
1891	Chi-N	5	5	.500	14	12	7	0	0	80	72	8.1	4	44	4.9	39	4.4	4.05	87	.253	.353	-6	-5	105	81	-0.8	-2	0	-0.5
1892	Bal-N	8	10	.444	24	21	17	0	0	176	189	9.7	3	87	4.4	49	2.5	3.53	95	.288	.371	-5	-3	102	112	1.9	2	0	0.0
1893	Phi-N	4	5	.444	13	11	7	0	0	80	100	11.2	1	37	4.2	15	1.7	5.40	85	.322	.395	-6	-7	98	92	-0.9	1	0	-0.4
Total	4	41	42	.494	97	90	72	1	0	718	766	9.6	16	352	4.4	265	3.3	3.75	100	.288	.371	-12	1	105	107	-3.6	-4	-2	-0.0
■ BOB VINES	Vines, Robert Earl b: 2/25/1897, Waxahachie, Tex. d: 10/18/82, Orlando, Fla. BR/TR, 6'4", 184 lbs. Deb: 9/03/24																												
1924	StL-N	0	0	—	2	0	0	0	0	11	23	18.8	1	0	0.0	0	0.0	9.00	44	.426	.418	-6	-6	103	91	0.0	-1	-0	-0.5
1925	Phi-N	0	0	—	3	0	0	0	0	4	9	20.3	0	3	6.8	0	0.0	11.25	45	.450	.480	-3	-3	118	94	0.0	0	0	-0.2
Total	2	0	0	—	5	0	0	0	0	15	32	19.2	1	3	1.8	0	0.0	9.60	44	.432	.438	-9	-9	107	92	0.0	-1	-0	-0.7
■ DAVE VINEYARD	Vineyard, David Kent b: 2/25/41, Clay, W.Va. BR/TR, 6'3", 195 lbs. Deb: 7/18/64																												
1964	Bal-A	2	5	.286	19	6	1	0	0	54	57	9.5	5	27	4.5	50	8.3	4.17	90	.274	.351	-3	-3	103	109	-1.8	0	-1	-0.2
■ BILL VINTON	Vinton, William Miller b: 4/27/1865, Winthrop, Mass. d: 9/3/1893, Pawtucket, R.I. BR/TR, 6'1", 160 lbs. Deb: 7/03/1884																												
1884	Phi-N	10	10	.500	21	21	20	0	0	182	166	8.2	6	35	1.7	105	5.2	2.23	130	.252	.289	15	14	97	107	2.7	-6	0	0.7
1885	Phi-N	3	6	.333	9	9	8	0	0	77	90	10.5	0	23	2.7	21	2.5	3.04	96	.303	.353	-2	-1	104	129	-1.5	-3	0	-0.3
	Phi-a	4	3	.571	7	7	6	2	0	55	46	7.5	1	15	2.5	34	5.6	2.45	135	.238	.293	5	5	102	104	0.6	-0	0	0.5
Total	2	17	19	.472	37	37	34	2	0	314	302	8.7	7	73	2.1	160	4.6	2.46	121	.263	.307	18	18	100	112	1.8	-9	0	0.9
■ FRANK VIOLA	Viola, Frank John b: 4/19/60, Hempstead, N.Y. BL/TL, 6'4", 200 lbs. Deb: 6/06/82																												
1982	Min-A	4	10	.286	22	22	3	1	0	126	152	10.9	22	38	2.7	84	6.0	5.21	80	.302	.350	-16	-15	102	104	-1.6	0	-1	-1.5
1983	Min-A	7	15	.318	35	34	4	0	0	210	242	10.4	34	92	3.9	127	5.4	5.49	79	.287	.360	-33	-27	106	99	-3.1	0	-1	-2.7
1984	Min-A	18	12	.600	35	35	10	4	0	258	225	7.8	28	73	2.5	149	5.2	3.21	132	.233	.288	23	29	106	96	3.5	0	-3	2.7
1985	Min-A	18	14	.563	36	36	9	0	0	251	262	9.4	26	68	2.4	135	4.8	4.09	106	.268	.314	2	6	104	97	3.2	0	-2	0.4
1986	Min-A	16	13	.552	37	37	7	1	0	246	257	9.4	37	83	3.0	191	7.0	4.50	102	.268	.326	-9	2	109	99	3.4	0	-3	0.0
1987	Min-A	17	10	.630	36	36	7	1	0	252	230	8.2	29	66	2.4	197	7.0	2.89	148	.241	.291	44	39	96	**115**	3.4	0	-1	3.8
1988	Min-A	**24**	7	**.774**	35	35	7	2	0	255	236	8.3	20	54	1.9	193	6.8	2.65	158	.245	.284	38	**44**	105	115	**8.3**	0	-1	4.6
Total	7	104	81	.562	236	235	47	9	0	1598	1604	9.0	196	474	2.7	1076	6.1	3.86	112	.260	.313	49	79	104	104	17.1	0	-12	7.3
■ JAKE VIRTUE	Virtue, Jacob Kitchline "Guesses" b: 3/2/1865, Philadelphia, Pa. d: 2/3/43, Camden, N.J. BB/TR, 5'9.5", 165 lbs. Deb: 7/21/1890																												
1893	Cle-N	0	0	—	1	0	0	0	0	5	3	5.4	0	3	5.4	2	3.6	1.80	267	.186	.313	2	2	103	111	0.0	0	0	0.1
1894	Cle-N	0	0	—	1	0	0	0	0	0	0	—	0	1	—	0	—	—	—	—	1.000	0	0	111	0	0.0	-0	0	0.0
Total	2	0	0	—	2	0	0	0	0	5	3	5.4	0	4	7.2	2	3.6	1.80	267	.186	.348	2	2	103	111	0.0	0	0	0.1

YEAR	TM/L	W	L	PCT	G	GS	CG	SHO	SV	IP	H	H/G	HR	BB	BB/G	SO	SO/G	ERA	/A	OAVG	OOBP	PR	/A	PF	CPI	WAT	PB	PD	TPI
■ **JOE VITELLI**	Vitelli, Antonio Joseph b: 4/12/08, Mckees Rocks, Pa. d: 2/7/67, Pittsburgh, Pa. BR/TR, 6'1", 195 lbs. Deb: 5/30/44																												
1944	Pit-N	0	0	—	4	0	0	0	0	7	5	6.4	1	7	9.0	2	2.6	2.57	146	.185	.361	1	1	104	170	0.0	-0	0	0.1
■ **OLLIE VOIGT**	Voigt, Olen Edward "Ode" b: 1/29/1900, Wheaton, Ill. d: 4/7/70, Scottsdale, Ariz. BL/TR, 6'1", 170 lbs. Deb: 4/19/24																												
1924	StL-A	1	0	1.000	8	1	0	0	0	16	21	11.8	1	13	7.3	4	2.3	5.63	81	.356	.447	-2	-2	108	133	0.5	1	1	0.0
■ **BILL VOISELLE**	Voiselle, William Symmes "Big Bill" or "Ninety-Six" b: 1/29/19, Greenwood, S.C. BR/TR, 6'4", 200 lbs. Deb: 9/01/42																												
1942	NY-N	0	1	.000	2	1	0	0	0	9	6	6.0	1	4	4.0	5	5.0	2.00	168	.176	.263	1	1	101	102	-0.4	0	0	0.2
1943	NY-N	1	2	.333	4	4	3	0	0	31	18	5.2	1	14	4.1	19	5.5	2.03	164	.154	.239	5	5	99	39	0.0	-1	-1	0.4
1944	NY-N	21	16	.568	43	41	25	1	0	**313**	276	7.9	31	118	3.4	**161**	4.6	3.02	126	.232	.300	21	27	105	108	5.3	2	-4	2.8
1945	NY-N	14	14	.500	41	35	14	4	0	232	249	9.7	15	97	3.8	115	4.5	4.50	85	.273	.338	-18	-18	100	94	-0.3	-3	0	-1.9
1946	NY-N	9	15	.375	36	25	10	2	0	178	171	8.6	14	85	4.3	89	4.5	3.74	94	.248	.327	-6	-4	103	95	-0.7	-2	-0	-0.6
1947	NY-N	1	4	.200	11	5	1	0	0	43	44	9.2	4	22	4.6	20	4.2	4.60	88	.284	.370	-3	-3	99	110	-1.5	-1	0	-0.2
	Bos-N	8	7	.533	22	20	7	0	0	131	146	10.0	10	51	3.5	59	4.1	4.33	90	.280	.344	-4	-7	95	100	-0.3	-1	1	-0.6
	Yr	9	11	.450	33	25	8	0	0	174	190	9.8	14	73	3.8	79	4.1	4.40	89	.280	.349	-6	-9	96	100	-1.8	-1	1	-0.8
1948	Bos-N	13	13	.500	37	30	9	2	2	216	226	9.4	18	90	3.8	89	3.7	3.63	108	.272	.339	8	7	99	120	-2.3	-4	-2	0.0
1949	Bos-N	7	8	.467	30	22	5	4	1	169	170	9.1	14	78	4.2	63	3.4	4.05	97	.263	.338	-0	-3	97	104	-0.2	-2	1	-0.3
1950	Chi-N	0	4	.000	19	7	0	0	0	51	64	11.3	7	29	5.1	25	4.4	5.82	76	.303	.387	-10	-8	107	103	-1.9	-1	-1	-0.8
Total	9	74	84	.468	245	190	74	13	3	1373	1370	9.0	115	588	3.9	645	4.2	3.83	100	.258	.329	-6	-1	101	103	-2.3	-10	-6	-1.0
■ **JAKE VOLZ**	Volz, Jacob Phillip "Silent Jake" b: 4/4/1878, San Antonio, Tex. d: 8/11/62, San Antonio, Tex. BR/TR, 5'10", 175 lbs. Deb: 9/28/01																												
1901	Bos-A	1	0	1.000	1	1	1	0	0	7	6	7.7	2	9	11.6	5	6.4	9.00	38	.250	.455	-4	-4	94	80	0.5	-1	-1	-0.3
1905	Bos-N	0	2	.000	3	2	0	0	0	9	12	12.0	0	8	8.0	1	1.0	10.00	31	.360	.496	-7	-7	102	67	-0.9	-0	-1	-0.6
1908	Cin-N	1	2	.333	7	4	1	0	0	23	16	6.3	1	12	4.7	6	2.3	3.52	69	.227	.355	-3	-3	104	76	-0.4	0	-1	-0.3
Total	3	2	4	.333	11	7	2	0	0	39	34	7.8	3	29	6.7	12	2.8	6.00	46	.266	.413	-14	-14	102	74	-0.8	-1	-2	-1.2
■ **TONY Von FRICKEN**	Von Fricken, Anthony b: 5/30/1870, Brooklyn, N.Y. d: 3/22/47, Troy, N.Y. BB/TR, 5'11.5", 160 lbs. Deb: 5/09/1890																												
1890	Bos-N	0	1	.000	1	1	1	0	0	8	23	25.9	0	8	9.0	2	2.3	10.13	38	.523	.596	-6	-6	108	141	-0.4	-1	0	-0.3
■ **BRUCE Von HOFF**	Von Hoff, Bruce Frederick b: 11/17/43, Oakland, Cal. BR/TR, 6', 187 lbs. Deb: 9/28/65																												
1965	Hou-N	0	0	—	3	0	0	0	0	3	3	9.0	0	2	6.0	1	3.0	9.00	36	.250	.357	-2	-2	91	41	0.0	0	0	-0.1
1967	Hou-N	0	3	.000	10	10	0	0	0	50	52	9.4	3	28	5.0	22	4.0	4.86	66	.268	.349	-8	-9	95	89	-1.4	-1	-1	-1.0
Total	2	0	3	.000	13	10	0	0	0	53	55	9.3	3	30	5.1	23	3.9	5.09	63	.267	.350	-10	-11	95	86	-1.4	-1	-1	-1.1
■ **DAVE Von OHLEN**	Von Ohlen, David b: 10/25/58, Flushing, N.Y. BL/TL, 6'2", 200 lbs. Deb: 5/13/83																												
1983	StL-N	3	2	.600	46	0	0	0	2	68	71	9.4	3	25	3.3	21	2.8	3.31	108	.280	.341	2	2	98	123	0.6	0	-0	0.2
1984	StL-N	1	0	1.000	27	0	0	0	1	35	39	10.0	0	8	2.1	19	4.9	3.09	115	.300	.333	2	2	99	125	0.5	0	1	0.4
1985	Cle-A	3	2	.600	26	0	0	0	0	43	47	9.8	3	20	4.2	12	2.5	2.93	135	.288	.342	6	5	95	165	0.9	0	0	0.5
1986	Oak-A	0	3	.000	24	0	0	0	1	15	18	10.8	0	7	4.2	4	2.4	3.60	109	.300	.368	1	1	94	126	-1.4	0	0	0.1
1987	Oak-A	0	0	—	4	0	0	0	0	6	10	15.0	1	1	1.5	3	4.5	7.50	54	.400	.407	-2	-2	91	108	0.0	0	-0	-0.1
Total	5	7	7	.500	127	0	0	0	4	167	185	10.0	7	61	3.3	59	3.2	3.34	111	.293	.345	9	7	97	134	0.6	1	2	1.1
■ **CY VORHEES**	Vorhees, Henry Bert b: 9/30/1874, Lodi, Ohio d: 2/8/10, Perry, Ohio 6'3", 200 lbs. Deb: 4/17/02																												
1902	Phi-N	3	3	.500	10	4	3	1	0	54	63	10.5	1	20	3.3	24	4.0	3.83	79	.315	.378	-6	-5	109	104	0.5	2	-1	-0.5
	Was-A	0	1	.000	1	1	1	0	0	8	10	11.3	0	2	2.3	1	1.1	4.50	79	.332	.374	-1	-1	100	92	-0.4	1	0	0.0
■ **ED VOSBERG**	Vosberg, Edward John b: 9/28/61, Tucson, Ariz. BL/TL, 6'1", 190 lbs. Deb: 9/17/86																												
1986	SD-N	0	1	.000	5	3	0	0	0	14	17	10.9	1	9	5.8	8	5.1	6.43	56	.304	.400	-4	-4	96	88	-0.4	-0	-0	-0.4
■ **ALEX VOSS**	Voss, Alexander b: 1855, Roswell, Ga. d: 8/31/06, Cincinnati, Ohio BR/TR, 6'1", 180 lbs. Deb: 4/17/1884																												
1884	Was-U	5	14	.263	27	20	18	0	0	186	206	10.0	2	32	1.5	112	5.4	3.58	83	.286	.316	-12	-13	98	98	-3.9	-4	0	-1.0
	KC-U	0	6	.000	7	6	6	0	0	53	74	12.6	2	7	1.2	17	2.9	4.25	65	.335	.356	-7	-9	92	118	-2.9	-2	0	-0.6
	Yr	5	20	.200	34	26	24	0	0	239	280	10.5	4	39	1.5	129	4.9	3.73	78	.297	.325	-19	-22	97	118	-6.8	-4	0	-1.6
■ **RIP VOWINKEL**	Vowinkel, John Henry b: 11/18/1884, Oswego, N.Y. d: 7/13/66, Oswego, N.Y. BR/TR, 5'10", 195 lbs. Deb: 9/05/05																												
1905	Cin-N	3	3	.500	6	6	4	0	0	45	52	10.4	2	10	2.0	7	1.4	4.20	73	.319	.362	-6	-6	103	96	0.0	-0	-2	-0.6
■ **PETE VUCKOVICH**	Vuckovich, Peter Dennis b: 10/27/52, Johnstown, Pa. BR/TR, 6'4", 215 lbs. Deb: 8/03/75																												
1975	Chi-A	0	1	.000	4	2	0	0	0	10	17	15.3	0	7	6.3	5	4.5	13.50	29	.386	.462	-11	-11	104	57	-0.4	0	0	-0.8
1976	Chi-A	7	4	.636	33	7	1	0	0	110	122	10.0	3	60	4.9	62	5.1	4.66	77	.287	.372	-14	-13	101	99	2.3	0	0	-1.3
1977	Tor-A	7	7	.500	53	8	3	1	8	148	143	8.7	13	59	3.6	123	7.5	3.47	123	.257	.327	10	13	105	112	1.9	0	1	1.3
1978	StL-N	12	12	.500	45	23	6	2	1	198	187	8.5	9	59	2.7	149	6.8	2.55	135	.253	.303	23	19	96	123	1.8	-1	2	2.1
1979	StL-N	15	10	.600	34	32	9	0	0	233	229	8.8	22	64	2.5	145	5.6	3.59	109	.260	.306	4	8	104	99	2.1	-2	-1	0.5
1980	StL-N	12	9	.571	32	30	7	3	1	222	203	8.2	18	68	2.8	132	5.4	3.41	109	.247	.301	5	7	102	96	2.5	1	-1	0.9
1981	Mil-A	**14**	4	.778	24	23	2	1	0	150	137	8.2	9	57	3.4	84	5.0	3.54	99	.249	.319	2	-1	95	97	**4.8**	0	1	0.0
1982	Mil-A	18	6	**.750**	30	30	9	1	0	224	234	9.4	14	102	4.1	105	4.2	3.33	113	.275	.351	19	11	92	**131**	**5.2**	0	1	1.2
1983	Mil-A	0	2	.000	3	3	0	0	0	15	15	9.0	0	10	6.0	10	6.0	4.80	77	.259	.377	-1	-2	91	86	-0.9	0	-0	-0.1
1985	Mil-A	6	10	.375	22	22	1	0	0	113	134	10.7	16	48	3.8	55	4.4	5.50	80	.298	.370	-17	-14	106	103	-1.2	0	-1	-1.3
1986	Mil-A	2	4	.333	6	6	0	0	0	32	33	9.3	3	11	3.1	12	3.4	3.09	139	.273	.331	4	4	103	141	-0.8	0	0	0.5
Total	11	93	69	.574	286	186	38	8	10	1455	1454	9.0	107	545	3.4	882	5.5	3.66	104	.264	.329	23	22	100	109	17.3	-2	2	3.0
■ **PAUL WACHTEL**	Wachtel, Paul Horine b: 4/30/1888, Myersville, Md. d: 12/15/64, San Antonio, Tex. BR/TR, 5'11", 175 lbs. Deb: 9/18/17																												
1917	Bro-N	0	0	—	2	0	0	0	0	6	9	13.5	0	4	6.0	3	4.5	10.50	27	.375	.433	-5	-5	105	67	0.0	0	-0	-0.4
■ **CHARLIE WACKER**	Wacker, Charles James b: 12/8/1883, Jeffersonville, Ind d: 8/7/48, Evansville, Ind. BL/TL, 5'9", Deb: 09																												
1909	Pit-N	0	0	—	1	0	0	0	0	2	2	9.0	0	1	4.5	0	0.0	0.00	—	.400	.500	1	1	99	0	0.0	0	0	0.1
■ **RUBE WADDELL**	Waddell, George Edward b: 10/13/1876, Bradford, Pa. d: 4/1/14, San Antonio, Tex. BR/TL, 6'1.5", 196 lbs. Deb: 9/08/1897 H																												
1897	Lou-N	0	1	.000	2	1	1	0	0	14	17	10.9	0	6	3.9	5	3.2	3.21	131	.322	.392	2	2	97	137	-0.4	-1	0	0.0
1899	Lou-N	7	2	.778	10	9	9	1	1	79	69	7.9	4	14	1.6	44	5.0	3.08	129	.257	.293	7	8	103	77	2.6	-0	0	0.7
1900	Pit-N	8	13	.381	29	22	16	2	0	209	176	**7.6**	3	55	2.4	**130**	**5.6**	**2.37**	**158**	**.249**	**.303**	31	32	101	94	-3.8	-2	0	2.8
1901	Pit-N	0	2	.000	2	2	0	0	0	8	10	11.3	0	9	10.1	4	4.5	9.00	35	.340	.508	-5	-5	96	77	-0.9	-0	0	-0.3
	Chi-N	14	14	.500	29	28	26	0	0	244	239	8.8	5	66	2.4	168	6.2	2.80	121	.280	.338	14	16	103	110	3.2	6	3	2.0
	Yr	14	16	.467	31	30	26	0	0	252	249	8.9	5	75	2.7	172	6.1	3.00	113	.282	.343	9	11	102	110	2.3	-0	4	1.7
1902	Phi-A	24	7	.774	33	27	26	3	0	276	224	7.3	7	64	2.1	**210**	**6.8**	2.05	185	.244	.293	46	53	106	102	7.5	7	-0	**6.4**
1903	Phi-A	21	16	.568	39	38	**34**	4	0	324	274	7.6	3	85	2.4	**302**	**8.4**	2.44	123	.250	.304	18	20	102	94	0.7	-7	0	2.2
1904	Phi-A	25	19	.568	46	46	39	8	0	383	307	7.2	5	91	2.1	**349**	**8.2**	1.62	**161**	.241	.291	**41**	42	101	125	2.1	-7	1	5.2
1905	Phi-A	**27**	10	**.730**	**46**	34	27	7	0	329	231	**6.3**	5	90	2.5	**287**	**7.9**	**1.48**	**190**	**.219**	.280	**43**	**49**	106	117	6.4	-2	0	**5.8**
1906	Phi-A	15	17	.469	43	34	22	8	0	273	221	7.3	1	92	3.0	**196**	**6.5**	2.21	113	.245	.314	15	9	93	103	-2.4	1	-2	0.8
1907	Phi-A	19	13	.594	44	33	20	7	0	285	234	7.4	2	73	2.3	**232**	**7.3**	2.15	123	.246	.300	12	16	104	95	-0.3	-6	-2	1.6
1908	StL-A	19	14	.576	43	36	25	5	3	286	223	7.0	0	90	2.8	232	**7.3**	1.89	129	.213	.281	16	17	102	102	1.4	-2	-1	1.9
1909	StL-A	11	14	.440	31	28	16	5	0	220	204	8.3	1	57	2.3	141	5.8	2.37	99	.267	.323	3	-1	95	118	0.8	-5	-2	-0.2
1910	StL-A	3	1	.750	10	2	0	0	1	33	31	8.5	1	11	3.0	16	4.4	3.55	71	.242	.307	-4	-4	101	74	1.3	-0	-1	-0.5
Total	13	193	143	.574	407	340	261	50	5	2963	2460	7.5	37	803	2.4	2316	7.0	2.16	136	.245	.302	239	253	101	106	18.2	-19	-3	28.4
■ **TOM WADDELL**	Waddell, Thomas David b: 9/17/58, Dundee, Scotland BR/TR, 6'1", 185 lbs. Deb: 4/15/84																												
1984	Cle-A	7	4	.636	58	0	0	0	6	97	68	6.3	12	37	3.4	59	5.5	3.06	138	.202	.272	10	13	106	93	1.9	0	-0	1.2
1985	Cle-A	8	6	.571	49	9	1	0	9	113	104	8.3	20	39	3.1	53	4.2	4.86	81	.246	.306	-9	-11	95	87	2.4	0	0	-1.0
1987	Cle-A	0	1	.000	6	0	0	0	0	6	7	10.5	1	7	10.5	6	9.0	13.50	35	.292	.469	-6	-6	105	59	-0.4	0	-0	-0.5
Total	3	15	11	.577	113	9	1	0	15	216	179	7.5	33	83	3.5	118	4.9	4.29	96	.229	.297	-5	-4	100	89	3.9	0	-1	-0.3

YEAR	TM/L	W	L	PCT	G	GS	CG	SHO	SV	IP	H	H/G	HR	BB	BB/G	SO	SO/G	ERA	/A	OAVG	OOBP	PR	/A	PF	CPI	WAT	PB	PD	TPI
■ **BEN WADE**	Wade, Benjamin Styron b: 11/26/22, Morehead City, N.C BR/TR, 6'3", 195 lbs. Deb: 4/30/48																												
1948	Chi-N	0	1	.000	2	0	0	0	0	5	4	7.2	0	4	7.2	1	1.8	7.20	52	.211	.348	-2	-2	95	43	-0.4	-0	0	-0.1
1952	Bro-N	11	9	.550	37	24	5	1	3	180	166	8.3	19	94	4.7	118	5.9	3.60	102	.246	.337	3	1	98	115	-1.3	1	-2	0.1
1953	Bro-N	7	5	.583	32	0	0	0	3	90	79	7.9	15	33	3.3	65	6.5	3.80	112	.232	.308	5	5	100	101	-0.8	0	-2	0.3
1954	Bro-N	1	1	.500	23	0	0	0	3	45	62	12.4	9	21	4.2	25	5.0	8.20	50	.339	.388	-21	-21	101	86	-0.1	-1	-1	-2.0
	StL-N	0	0	—	13	0	0	0	0	23	27	10.6	3	15	5.9	19	7.4	5.48	74	.303	.404	-4	-4	100	114	0.0	-0	0	-0.3
	Yr	1	1	.500	36	0	0	0	3	68	89	11.8	12	36	4.8	44	5.8	7.28	56	.319	.393	-24	-24	100	114	-0.1	-1	-0	-2.3
1955	Pit-N	0	1	.000	11	1	0	0	1	28	26	8.4	3	14	4.5	7	2.3	3.21	127	.252	.333	3	3	101	132	-0.4	-0	-0	0.2
Total	5	19	17	.528	118	25	5	1	10	371	364	8.8	49	181	4.4	235	5.7	4.34	90	.259	.341	-16	-18	99	108	-3.0	-0	-4	-1.8
■ **JAKE WADE**	Wade, Jacob Fields "Whistling Jake" b: 4/1/12, Morehead City, N.C. BL/TL, 6'2", 175 lbs. Deb: 4/22/36																												
1936	Det-A	4	5	.444	13	11	4	1	0	78	93	10.7	7	52	6.0	30	3.5	5.31	90	.296	.394	-2	-5	95	113	-0.7	-0	-1	-0.4
1937	Det-A	7	10	.412	33	25	7	1	0	165	160	8.7	13	107	5.8	69	3.8	5.40	92	.257	.363	-14	-8	108	86	-2.6	-2	1	-0.7
1938	Det-A	3	2	.600	27	2	0	0	0	70	73	9.4	9	48	6.2	23	3.0	6.56	72	.268	.372	-14	-14	99	82	0.3	-2	0	-1.3
1939	Bos-A	1	4	.200	20	6	1	0	0	48	68	12.8	1	37	6.9	21	3.9	6.19	80	.358	.449	-8	-7	107	121	-1.6	-2	-0	-0.7
	StL-A	0	2	.000	4	2	1	0	0	16	26	14.6	1	19	10.7	9	5.1	11.25	43	.356	.484	-12	-11	105	80	-0.9	-1	0	-0.9
	Yr	1	6	.143	24	8	2	0	0	64	94	13.2	2	56	7.9	30	4.2	7.45	66	.357	.459	-20	-18	106	80	-2.5	-2	0	-1.6
1942	Chi-A	5	5	.500	15	10	3	0	0	86	84	8.8	2	56	5.9	32	3.3	4.08	90	.255	.360	-4	-4	100	100	0.5	1	1	-0.1
1943	Chi-A	3	7	.300	21	9	3	1	0	84	66	7.1	3	54	5.8	41	4.4	3.00	111	.222	.341	3	3	101	115	-2.2	-0	-1	0.2
1944	Chi-A	2	4	.333	19	5	1	0	2	75	75	9.0	3	41	4.9	35	4.2	4.80	73	.261	.347	-11	-11	102	82	-0.8	1	-2	-1.1
1946	NY-A	2	1	.667	13	1	0	0	1	35	33	8.5	2	14	3.6	22	5.7	2.31	148	.250	.324	5	4	98	147	0.4	-0	0	0.5
	Was-A	0	0	—	6	0	0	0	0	11	12	9.8	1	12	9.8	9	7.4	4.91	67	.279	.436	-2	-2	94	128	0.0	-0	0	-0.1
	Yr	2	1	.667	19	1	0	0	1	46	45	8.8	3	26	5.1	31	6.1	2.93	115	.256	.350	3	2	97	128	0.4	-0	1	0.4
Total	8	27	40	.403	171	71	20	3	3	668	690	9.3	42	440	5.9	291	3.9	5.00	85	.269	.373	-60	-54	102	100	-7.6	-5	-1	-4.6
■ **JACK WADSWORTH**	Wadsworth, John L. b: 12/17/1867, Wellington, Ohio d: 7/8/41, Elyria, Ohio BL/TR, 180 lbs. Deb: 5/01/1890																												
1890	Cle-N	2	16	.111	20	19	19	0	0	170	202	10.7	6	81	4.3	26	1.4	5.24	66	.312	.388	-32	-34	97	89	-6.2	-3	0	-2.9
1893	Bal-N	0	3	.000	3	3	0	0	0	16	37	20.8	0	8	4.5	2	1.1	11.25	45	.468	.517	-12	-11	108	91	-1.4	1	0	-0.6
1894	Lou-N	4	18	.182	22	22	20	0	0	173	261	13.6	10	103	5.4	57	3.0	7.60	64	.371	.452	-43	-53	91	91	-4.1	1	0	-3.7
1895	Lou-N	0	1	.000	2	0	0	0	0	9	24	24.0	0	7	7.0	2	2.0	16.00	30	.509	.572	-11	-11	99	80	-0.4	-0	0	-0.7
Total	4	6	38	.136	47	44	39	0	0	368	524	12.8	16	199	4.9	87	2.1	6.87	62	.355	.431	-98	-108	94	90	-12.1	-1	0	-7.9
■ **CHARLIE WAGNER**	Wagner, Charles Thomas "Broadway" b: 12/3/12, Reading, Pa. BR/TR, 5'11", 170 lbs. Deb: 4/19/38 C																												
1938	Bos-A	1	3	.250	13	6	1	0	0	37	47	11.4	5	24	5.8	14	3.4	8.27	58	.309	.402	-14	-14	100	80	-1.1	-1	-1	-1.2
1939	Bos-A	3	1	.750	9	5	0	0	0	38	49	11.6	3	14	3.3	13	3.1	4.26	116	.320	.371	2	3	107	133	0.8	-2	0	0.1
1940	Bos-A	1	0	1.000	12	1	0	0	0	29	45	14.0	5	8	2.5	13	4.0	5.59	78	.344	.379	-4	-4	100	123	0.5	-0	0	-0.3
1941	Bos-A	12	8	.600	29	25	12	3	0	187	175	8.4	14	85	4.1	51	2.5	3.08	136	.245	.322	22	23	101	120	1.4	-1	-0	2.2
1942	Bos-A	14	11	.560	29	26	17	2	0	205	184	8.1	5	95	4.2	52	2.3	3.29	112	.247	.327	8	9	100	106	-1.1	-5	1	0.5
1946	Bos-A	1	0	1.000	8	4	0	0	0	31	32	9.3	6	19	5.5	14	4.1	5.81	67	.276	.372	-8	-7	111	98	0.5	-1	-0	-0.7
Total	6	32	23	.582	100	67	30	5	0	527	532	9.1	38	245	4.2	157	2.7	3.91	104	.264	.340	6	10	102	111	1.0	-9	-0	0.6
■ **GARY WAGNER**	Wagner, Gary Edward b: 6/28/40, Bridgeport, Ill. BR/TR, 6'4", 185 lbs. Deb: 4/18/65																												
1965	Phi-N	7	7	.500	59	0	0	0	7	105	87	7.5	6	49	4.2	91	7.8	3.00	112	.233	.317	6	4	95	111	-0.3	-0	1	0.5
1966	Phi-N	0	1	.000	5	1	0	0	0	6	8	12.0	1	5	7.5	2	3.0	9.00	40	.333	.433	-4	-4	100	85	-0.4	0	-0	-0.3
1967	Phi-N	0	0	—	1	0	0	0	0	2	1	4.5	0	0	0.0	1	4.5	0.00	—	.167	.167	1	1	104	0	0.0	0	0	0.1
1968	Phi-N	4	4	.500	44	0	0	0	8	78	69	8.0	0	31	3.6	43	5.0	3.00	98	.243	.320	-0	-0	99	98	0.2	-1	1	0.0
1969	Phi-N	0	3	.000	9	2	0	0	0	19	31	14.7	3	7	3.3	8	3.8	8.05	44	.365	.388	-9	-9	100	92	-1.4	-0	-1	-0.9
	Bos-A	1	3	.250	6	1	0	0	0	16	18	10.1	1	15	8.4	9	5.1	6.19	61	.300	.440	-5	-4	105	101	-1.0	-0	0	-0.4
1970	Bos-A	3	1	.750	38	0	0	0	7	40	36	8.1	3	19	4.3	20	4.5	3.37	121	.232	.317	2	3	110	97	0.9	-0	-0	0.3
Total	6	15	19	.441	162	4	0	0	22	266	250	8.5	14	126	4.3	174	5.9	3.72	91	.253	.334	-9	-10	99	102	-2.0	-2	1	-0.7
■ **HONUS WAGNER**	Wagner, John Peter "The Flying Dutchman" b: 2/24/1874, Mansfield, Pa. d: 12/6/55, Carnegie, Pa. BR/TR, 5'11", 200 lbs. Deb: 7/19/1897 MCH																												
1900	Pit-N	0	0	—	1	0	0	0	0	3	3	9.0	0	4	12.0	1	3.0	0.00	—	.283	.479	1	1	101	0	0.0	1	0	0.1
1902	Pit-N	0	0	—	1	0	0	0	0	5	4	7.2	0	2	3.6	5	9.0	0.00	—	.240	.322	2	2	98	0	0.0	0	0	0.2
Total	2	0	0	—	2	0	0	0	0	8	7	7.9	0	6	6.8	6	6.8	0.00	—	.257	.391	3	3	99	0	0.0	1	0	0.3
■ **MARK WAGNER**	Wagner, Mark Duane b: 3/4/54, Conneaut, Ohio BR/TR, 6', 165 lbs. Deb: 8/20/76																												
1984	Oak-A	0	0	—	1	0	0	0	0	2	2	9.0	0	1	4.5	1	4.5	0.00	—	.400	.429	1	1	92	0	0.0	0	0	0.1
■ **BULL WAGNER**	Wagner, William George b: 1/1/1888, Lilley, Mich. d: 10/2/67, Muskegon, Mich. BR/TR, 6'0.5", 225 lbs. Deb: 6/02/13																												
1913	Bro-N	4	2	.667	18	1	0	0	0	71	77	9.8	5	30	3.8	11	1.4	5.45	62	.285	.354	-18	-17	105	82	1.3	0	-1	-1.6
1914	Bro-N	0	1	.000	6	0	0	0	0	12	14	10.5	0	12	9.0	4	3.0	6.75	42	.311	.450	-5	-5	101	92	-0.4	-0	0	-0.5
Total	2	4	3	.571	24	1	0	0	0	83	91	9.9	5	42	4.6	15	1.6	5.64	58	.289	.369	-23	-22	104	83	0.9	0	-1	-2.1
■ **RICK WAITS**	Waits, Michael Richard b: 5/15/52, Atlanta, Ga. BL/TL, 6'3", 194 lbs. Deb: 9/17/73																												
1973	Tex-A	0	0	—	1	0	0	0	1	1	1	9.0	0	1	9.0	0	0.0	9.00	42	.333	.500	-1	-1	100	75	0.0	0	0	0.0
1975	Cle-A	6	2	.750	16	7	3	0	1	70	57	7.3	3	25	3.2	34	4.4	2.96	128	.221	.291	6	6	100	82	2.1	0	0	0.7
1976	Cle-A	7	9	.438	26	22	4	2	0	124	143	10.4	7	54	3.9	65	4.7	3.99	88	.297	.365	-6	-7	100	118	-1.1	0	1	-0.6
1977	Cle-A	9	7	.563	37	16	1	0	2	135	132	8.8	8	64	4.3	62	4.1	4.00	100	.262	.339	1	-0	98	99	1.9	0	0	0.0
1978	Cle-A	13	15	.464	34	33	15	2	0	230	206	8.1	16	86	3.4	97	3.8	3.21	110	.240	.307	15	8	94	96	0.9	0	3	1.2
1979	Cle-A	16	13	.552	34	34	8	3	0	231	230	9.0	26	91	3.5	91	3.5	4.44	101	.264	.331	-5	1	106	95	1.7	0	2	0.2
1980	Cle-A	13	14	.481	33	33	9	2	0	224	231	9.3	18	82	3.3	109	4.4	4.46	93	.270	.329	-10	-7	103	89	-0.3	0	-1	-0.8
1981	Cle-A	8	10	.444	22	21	5	1	0	126	173	12.4	7	44	3.1	51	3.6	4.93	69	.330	.377	-18	-21	93	111	-1.2	0	2	-1.8
1982	Cle-A	2	13	.133	25	21	2	0	0	115	128	10.0	13	57	4.5	44	3.4	5.40	76	.290	.365	-17	-16	101	97	-5.5	0	1	-1.4
1983	Cle-A	0	1	.000	8	0	0	0	0	20	23	10.3	1	9	4.0	13	5.8	4.50	96	.307	.352	-1	-0	106	114	-0.4	0	0	0.0
	Mil-A	0	2	.000	10	2	0	0	0	30	39	11.7	1	11	3.3	20	6.0	5.10	73	.320	.373	-3	-5	91	100	-0.9	0	-0	-0.4
	Yr	0	3	.000	18	2	0	0	0	50	62	11.2	2	20	3.6	33	5.9	4.86	81	.308	.364	-4	-5	97	100	-1.3	0	-0	-0.4
1984	Mil-A	2	4	.333	47	1	0	0	3	73	84	10.4	7	24	3.0	49	6.0	3.58	104	.297	.342	3	1	93	133	-0.5	0	0	0.1
1985	Mil-A	3	2	.600	24	0	0	0	1	47	67	12.8	3	20	3.8	24	4.6	6.51	67	.340	.395	-12	-11	106	95	0.7	0	1	-1.0
Total	12	79	92	.462	317	190	47	10	8	1426	1514	9.6	110	568	3.6	659	4.2	4.25	92	.277	.340	-48	-52	99	100	-2.6	0	8	-3.8
■ **BILL WAKEFIELD**	Wakefield, William Sumner b: 5/24/41, Kansas City, Mo. BR/TR, 6', 175 lbs. Deb: 4/18/64																												
1964	NY-N	3	5	.375	62	4	0	0	2	120	103	7.7	10	61	4.6	61	4.6	3.60	97	.235	.332	-1	-2	98	107	0.3	-0	0	-0.1
■ **RUBE WALBERG**	Walberg, George Elvin b: 7/27/1896, Pine City, Minn. d: 10/27/78, Tempe, Ariz. BL/TL, 6'1.5", 190 lbs. Deb: 4/29/23																												
1923	NY-N	0	0	—	2	0	0	0	0	5	4	7.2	0	1	1.8	1	1.8	1.80	219	.211	.250	1	1	99	63	0.0	-0	0	0.1
	Phi-A	4	8	.333	26	10	4	0	0	115	122	9.5	10	60	4.7	38	3.0	5.32	76	.280	.358	-17	-16	102	88	-1.6	3	0	-1.1
1924	Phi-A	0	0	—	6	2	0	0	0	7	10	12.9	0	10	12.9	3	3.9	12.86	33	.345	.500	-7	-7	101	65	0.0	0	0	-0.5
1925	Phi-A	8	14	.364	53	20	7	0	7	192	197	9.2	11	77	3.6	82	3.8	3.98	111	.269	.333	9	10	101	96	-4.4	-4	1	0.7
1926	Phi-A	12	10	.545	40	19	5	2	2	151	168	10.0	4	60	3.6	72	4.3	2.80	166	.292	.358	20	31	116	154	-0.1	-3	-1	2.8
1927	Phi-A	16	12	.571	46	34	15	0	4	249	257	9.3	18	91	3.3	136	4.9	3.94	100	.271	.327	6	-1	95	100	-0.5	4	-0	0.2
1928	Phi-A	17	12	.586	38	30	15	3	1	236	236	9.0	19	64	2.4	112	4.3	3.55	113	.265	.307	13	12	99	103	-1.4	1	1	1.3
1929	Phi-A	18	11	.621	40	33	20	3	4	268	256	8.6	22	99	3.3	94	3.2	3.59	123	.254	.312	19	24	104	99	-1.7	-1	-2	2.2
1930	Phi-A	13	12	.520	38	30	12	2	1	205	207	9.1	6	85	3.7	100	4.4	4.70	95	.262	.327	-1	-5	96	80	-3.0	-2	-1	-0.7
1931	Phi-A	20	12	.625	44	35	19	1	3	**291**	298	9.2	16	109	3.4	106	3.3	3.74	118	.266	.326	21	22	101	108	-2.1	-6	-1	1.4
1932	Phi-A	17	10	.630	41	34	19	3	1	272	305	10.1	16	103	3.4	96	3.2	4.73	105	.282	.339	-8	7	111	95	0.8	-4	-0	0.4
1933	Phi-A	9	13	.409	40	20	10	1	4	201	224	10.0	12	95	4.3	68	3.0	4.88	80	.278	.348	-13	-21	92	94	-2.6	-1	1	-2.0
1934	Bos-A	6	7	.462	30	10	2	0	1	105	118	10.1	5	41	3.5	38	3.3	4.03	117	.284	.342	5	8	105	110	-0.4	-1	1	0.8
1935	Bos-A	5	9	.357	44	10	4	0	3	143	152	9.6	10	54	3.4	44	2.8	3.90	124	.273	.334	9	15	108	109	-2.1	-2	-1	1.1

YEAR	TM/L	W	L	PCT	G	GS	CG	SHO	SV	IP	H	H/G	HR	BB	BB/G	SO	SO/G	ERA	/A	OAVG	OOBP	PR	/A	PF	CPI	WAT	PB	PD	TPI
1936	Bos-A	5	4	.556	24	9	5	0	0	100	98	8.8	7	36	3.2	49	4.4	4.41	121	.257	.318	7	10	106	89	0.7	-1	0	0.8
1937	Bos-A	5	7	.417	32	11	3	0	1	105	143	12.3	7	46	3.9	46	3.9	5.57	85	.332	.393	-11	-10	102	110	-1.2	-1	-0	-0.9
Total	15	155	141	.524	544	307	140	15	32	2645	2795	9.5	163	1031	3.5	1085	3.7	4.16	107	.273	.334	53	80	102	101	-19.6	-18	-2	6.6
■ **DOC WALDBAUER**	Waldbauer, Albert Charles b: 2/22/1892, Richmond, Va. d: 7/16/69, Yakima, Wash. BR/TR, 6', 172 lbs. Deb: 9/24/17																												
1917	Was-A	0	0	—	2	0	0	0	1	5	10	18.0	0	2	3.6	2	3.6	7.20	34	.476	.522	-3	-3	93	127	0.0	-0	0	-0.2
■ **BOB WALK**	Walk, Robert Vernon b: 11/26/56, Van Nuys, Cal. BR/TR, 6'3", 185 lbs. Deb: 5/26/80																												
1980	Phi-N	11	7	.611	27	27	2	0	0	152	163	9.7	8	71	4.2	94	5.6	4.56	84	.276	.351	-16	-12	106	93	1.1	-0	-1	-1.2
1981	Atl-N	1	4	.200	12	8	0	0	0	43	41	8.6	6	23	4.8	16	3.3	4.60	76	.250	.339	-5	-5	100	95	-1.4	-0	-1	-0.5
1982	Atl-N	11	9	.550	32	27	3	1	0	164	179	9.8	19	59	3.2	84	4.6	4.88	79	.280	.340	-23	-19	107	94	0.0	2	-2	-1.9
1983	Atl-N	0	0	—	1	1	0	0	0	4	7	15.8	0	2	4.5	4	9.0	6.75	56	.412	.450	-1	-1	104	117	0.0	-0	0	0.0
1984	Pit-N	1	1	.500	2	2	0	0	0	10	8	7.2	1	4	3.6	10	9.0	2.70	125	.200	.273	1	1	94	82	0.1	-0	-0	0.0
1985	Pit-N	2	3	.400	9	9	1	1	0	59	60	9.2	3	18	2.7	40	6.1	3.66	103	.265	.315	-0	1	104	95	0.2	-2	-1	-0.1
1986	Pit-N	7	8	.467	44	15	1	1	2	142	129	8.2	14	64	4.1	78	4.9	3.74	100	.251	.331	-0	0	101	108	1.0	1	2	0.2
1987	Pit-N	8	2	.800	39	12	1	1	0	117	107	8.2	11	51	3.9	78	6.0	3.31	129	.245	.323	10	13	105	115	3.1	1	1	1.4
1988	Pit-N	12	10	.545	32	32	1	1	0	213	183	7.7	6	65	2.7	81	3.4	2.70	124	.230	.284	18	15	97	93	0.4	-2	0	1.5
Total	9	53	44	.546	198	133	9	5	2	904	877	8.7	68	357	3.6	485	4.8	3.82	98	.256	.324	-18	-9	102	99	4.5	-1	0	-0.6
■ **ED WALKER**	Walker, Edward Harrison b: 8/11/1874, Cambois, England d: 9/29/47, Akron, Ohio BL/TL, 6'5", 242 lbs. Deb: 9/26/02																												
1902	Cle-A	0	1	.000	1	1	1	0	0	8	11	12.4	0	3	3.4	1	1.1	3.38	102	.353	.410	0	0	96	152	-0.4	0	0	0.0
1903	Cle-A	0	0	—	3	3	0	0	0	12	13	9.8	0	10	7.5	4	3.0	5.25	53	.299	.430	-3	-3	95	96	0.0	-0	-1	-0.3
Total	2	0	1	.000	4	4	1	0	0	20	24	10.8	0	13	5.8	5	2.3	4.50	68	.322	.422	-3	-3	96	118	-0.4	0	-1	-0.3
■ **DIXIE WALKER**	Walker, Ewart Gladstone b: 6/1/1887, Brownsville, Pa. d: 11/14/65, Leeds, Ala. BL/TR, 6', 192 lbs. Deb: 9/17/09																												
1909	Was-A	3	1	.750	4	4	4	0	0	36	31	7.8	0	6	1.5	25	6.3	2.50	95	.217	.248	-0	-0	96	40	1.3	-0	0	0.0
1910	Was-A	11	11	.500	29	26	16	3	0	199	177	8.0	2	68	3.1	84	3.8	3.30	78	.245	.317	-17	-16	102	80	1.4	-3	-2	-2.1
1911	Was-A	8	13	.381	32	24	15	2	0	186	205	9.9	2	50	2.4	65	3.1	3.39	98	.286	.339	-1	-2	99	102	-0.9	4	-2	0.1
1912	Was-A	3	6	.333	9	8	5	0	0	60	72	10.8	2	18	2.7	29	4.3	5.25	62	.300	.359	-13	-13	97	83	-2.0	1	0	-1.1
Total	4	25	31	.446	74	62	40	5	0	481	485	9.1	6	142	2.7	203	3.8	3.52	83	.266	.326	-31	-31	100	86	-0.2	2	-3	-3.1
■ **MYSTERIOUS WALKER**	Walker, Frederick Mitchell b: 3/21/1884, Utica, Neb. d: 2/1/58, Oak Park, Ill. BR/TR, 5'10.5", 185 lbs. Deb: 6/28/10																												
1910	Cin-N	0	0	—	1	0	0	0	0	3	4	12.0	0	4	12.0	1	3.0	3.00	103	.333	.500	0	0	102	253	0.0	-0	0	0.0
1912	Cle-A	0	0	—	1	0	0	0	0	1	0	0.0	0	1	9.0	0	0.0	0.00	—	.000	.200	0	0	101	0	0.0	0	0	0.0
1913	Bro-N	1	3	.250	11	8	3	0	0	58	44	6.8	3	35	5.4	35	5.4	3.57	94	.233	.359	-2	-1	105	107	-0.8	-0	2	0.0
1914	Pit-F	4	16	.200	35	21	12	0	0	169	197	10.5	3	74	3.9	79	4.2	4.31	71	.294	.367	-21	-23	96	100	-5.6	-2	4	-2.0
1915	Bro-F	2	4	.333	13	7	2	0	1	66	61	8.3	3	22	3.0	28	3.8	3.68	81	.242	.303	-5	-5	98	77	-0.8	1	0	-0.4
Total	5	7	23	.233	61	36	17	0	1	297	306	9.3	9	136	4.1	143	4.3	4.00	78	.272	.353	-28	-29	98	97	-7.2	-1	6	-2.4
■ **GEORGE WALKER**	Walker, George A. b: 1863, Hamilton, Ontario, Canada TR , 5'9", 184 lbs. Deb: 1888																												
1888	Bal-a	1	3	.250	4	4	4	1	0	35	36	9.3	2	14	3.6	18	4.6	5.91	51	.279	.349	-11	-11	98	68	-0.7	-1	0	-0.9
■ **LUKE WALKER**	Walker, James Luke b: 9/2/43, De Kalb, Tex. BL/TL, 6'2", 190 lbs. Deb: 9/07/65																												
1965	Pit-N	0	0	—	2	0	0	0	0	5	2	3.6	0	1	1.8	5	9.0	0.00	—	.118	.167	2	2	98	0	0.0	0	0	0.2
1966	Pit-N	0	1	.000	10	1	0	0	0	10	8	7.2	0	15	13.5	7	6.3	4.50	79	.205	.436	-1	-1	99	110	-0.4	-0	-0	0.0
1968	Pit-N	0	3	.000	39	2	0	0	3	62	42	6.1	1	39	5.7	66	9.6	2.03	147	.190	.311	7	7	100	114	-1.4	-1	1	0.8
1969	Pit-N	4	6	.400	31	15	3	1	0	119	98	7.4	5	57	4.3	96	7.3	3.63	93	.226	.314	-0	-3	94	82	-1.3	-3	1	-0.5
1970	Pit-N	15	6	.714	42	19	5	3	3	163	129	7.1	6	89	4.9	124	6.8	3.04	128	.219	.320	18	15	96	100	4.2	-1	0	1.4
1971	Pit-N	10	8	.556	28	24	4	2	0	160	157	8.8	9	53	3.0	86	4.8	3.54	95	.262	.318	-1	-3	97	99	-0.6	-3	-2	-0.8
1972	Pit-N	4	6	.400	26	12	2	0	2	93	98	9.5	4	34	3.3	48	4.6	3.39	102	.278	.331	1	1	100	116	-1.7	-1	-0	0.0
1973	Pit-N	7	12	.368	37	18	2	1	1	122	129	9.5	9	66	4.9	74	5.5	4.65	72	.270	.354	-13	-17	92	94	-2.5	-2	-1	-2.0
1974	Det-A	5	5	.500	28	9	0	0	0	92	100	9.8	9	54	5.3	52	5.1	4.99	78	.278	.371	-14	-11	108	98	0.5	0	-0	-1.1
Total	9	45	47	.489	243	100	16	7	9	826	763	8.3	43	408	4.4	558	6.1	3.64	97	.247	.332	-2	-11	97	98	-3.2	-10	-2	-2.0
■ **ROY WALKER**	Walker, James Roy "Dixie" b: 4/13/1893, Lawrenceburg, Tenn d: 2/10/62, New Orleans, La. BB/TR, 6'1.5", 180 lbs. Deb: 8/22/12																												
1912	Cle-A	0	0	—	1	0	0	0	0	2	0	0.0	0	2	9.0	1	4.5	0.00	—	.000	.250	1	1	101	0	0.0	0	0	0.1
1915	Cle-A	4	9	.308	25	15	4	0	1	131	122	8.4	1	65	4.5	57	3.9	3.98	79	.261	.360	-15	-12	106	91	-1.2	-2	-2	-1.7
1917	Chi-N	0	1	.000	2	1	0	0	0	7	8	10.3	0	5	6.4	4	5.1	3.86	74	.286	.382	-1	-1	105	121	-0.4	-0	-0	0.0
1918	Chi-N	1	3	.250	13	7	2	0	1	43	50	10.5	1	15	3.1	20	4.2	2.72	100	.298	.347	0	-0	98	152	-1.1	-1	0	0.0
1921	StL-N	11	12	.478	38	24	11	0	3	171	194	10.2	10	53	2.8	52	2.7	4.21	83	.293	.339	-8	-13	93	97	-2.0	0	-1	-1.4
1922	StL-N	1	2	.333	12	2	0	0	0	32	34	9.6	1	15	4.2	14	3.9	4.78	86	.293	.353	-2	-2	100	93	-0.5	-0	-1	-0.3
Total	6	17	27	.386	91	49	17	0	5	386	408	9.5	13	155	3.6	148	3.5	3.99	84	.282	.349	-26	-27	99	101	-5.2	-4	-5	-3.3
■ **JERRY WALKER**	Walker, Jerry Allen b: 2/12/39, Ada, Okla. BB/TR, 6'1", 195 lbs. Deb: 7/06/57 C																												
1957	Bal-A	1	0	1.000	13	3	1	1	1	28	24	7.7	1	14	4.5	13	4.2	2.89	121	.245	.333	3	2	93	120	0.5	-1	0	0.1
1958	Bal-A	0	0	—	6	0	0	0	0	10	16	14.4	2	5	4.5	6	5.4	7.20	50	.340	.404	-4	-4	95	102	0.0	-0	-0	-0.3
1959	Bal-A	11	10	.524	30	22	7	2	4	182	160	7.9	13	52	2.6	100	4.9	2.92	130	.240	.292	19	18	98	105	1.0	-1	0	1.8
1960	Bal-A	3	4	.429	29	18	1	0	5	118	107	8.2	15	56	4.3	48	3.7	3.74	104	.247	.331	2	2	101	111	-0.8	5	1	0.7
1961	KC-A	8	14	.364	36	24	4	0	2	168	161	8.6	23	96	5.1	56	3.0	4.82	87	.253	.352	-15	-12	104	98	-0.4	3	0	-0.7
1962	KC-A	8	9	.471	31	21	3	1	0	143	165	10.4	27	78	4.9	57	3.6	5.92	68	.288	.373	-31	-30	101	101	0.4	5	1	-2.2
1963	Cle-A	6	6	.500	39	2	0	0	1	88	92	9.4	15	36	3.7	41	4.2	4.91	72	.265	.332	-13	-13	98	97	0.2	-0	-0	-1.3
1964	Cle-A	0	1	.000	6	0	0	0	0	10	9	8.1	1	4	3.6	5	4.5	4.50	83	.257	.333	-1	-1	103	89	-0.4	-0	-0	0.0
Total	8	37	44	.457	190	90	16	4	13	747	734	8.8	97	341	4.1	326	3.9	4.36	89	.259	.337	-39	-38	100	103	0.5	10	2	-1.9
■ **MARTY WALKER**	Walker, Martin Van Buren "Buddy" b: 3/27/1899, Philadelphia, Pa. d: 4/24/78, Philadelphia, Pa. BL/TL, 6', 170 lbs. Deb: 9/30/28																												
1928	Phi-N	0	1	.000	1	1	0	0	0	0	2	—	0	3	—	0	—	∞	—	1.000	.833	-2	-2	109	102	-0.4	0	0	-0.1
■ **MIKE WALKER**	Walker, Michael Charles b: 10/4/66, Chicago, Ill. BR/TR, 6'1", 175 lbs. Deb: 9/09/88																												
1988	Cle-A	0	1	.000	3	1	0	0	0	9	8	8.0	0	10	10.0	7	7.0	7.00	58	.258	.429	-3	-3	102	77	-0.4	0	0	-0.2
■ **TOM WALKER**	Walker, Robert Thomas b: 11/7/48, Tampa, Fla. BR/TR, 6'1", 188 lbs. Deb: 4/23/72																												
1972	Mon-N	2	2	.500	46	0	0	0	2	75	71	8.5	4	22	2.6	42	5.0	2.88	124	.248	.303	5	6	104	104	0.2	-0	-0	0.6
1973	Mon-N	7	5	.583	54	0	0	0	4	92	95	9.3	7	42	4.1	68	6.7	3.62	106	.274	.338	1	2	105	121	1.2	-1	-0	0.1
1974	Mon-N	4	5	.444	33	8	1	0	2	92	96	9.4	7	28	2.7	70	6.8	3.82	99	.266	.318	-2	-0	104	95	-0.3	0	-1	0.0
1975	Det-A	3	8	.273	36	9	1	0	0	115	116	9.1	16	40	3.1	60	4.7	4.46	90	.261	.319	-9	-5	106	94	-1.3	-0	-2	-0.6
1976	StL-N	1	2	.333	10	0	0	0	3	20	22	9.9	2	3	1.3	11	4.9	4.05	90	.265	.287	-1	-1	105	81	-0.3	1	-1	0.0
1977	Mon-N	1	1	.500	11	0	0	0	0	19	15	7.1	2	7	3.3	10	4.7	4.74	82	.221	.293	-2	-2	99	63	0.1	-0	-0	-0.1
	Cal-A	0	0	—	1	0	0	0	0	2	3	13.5	2	0	0.0	1	4.5	9.00	43	.375	.375	-1	-1	95	145	0.0	0	0	0.0
Total	6	18	23	.439	191	17	2	0	11	415	418	9.1	40	142	3.1	262	5.7	3.86	99	.262	.318	-9	-1	105	100	-0.4	-0	-3	0.0
■ **TOM WALKER**	Walker, Thomas William b: 8/1/1881, Philadelphia, Pa. d: 7/10/44, Woodbury Heights N.J. BR/TR, 5'11", 170 lbs. Deb: 9/27/02																												
1902	Phi-A	0	1	.000	1	1	1	0	0	8	10	11.3	0	0	0.0	2	2.3	5.63	67	.332	.332	-2	-2	106	61	-0.4	-0	1	0.0
1904	Cin-N	15	8	.652	24	24	22	2	0	217	196	8.1	2	53	2.2	64	2.7	2.24	136	.270	.336	12	19	111	118	2.4	-5	-2	1.9
1905	Cin-N	9	7	.563	23	19	12	1	0	145	171	10.6	3	44	2.7	28	1.7	3.23	95	.325	.384	-4	-3	103	132	0.8	-1	-1	-0.2
Total	3	24	16	.600	48	44	35	3	0	370	377	9.2	5	97	2.4	94	2.3	2.70	114	.294	.355	6	15	108	122	2.8	-6	-2	1.7
■ **BILL WALKER**	Walker, William Henry b: 10/7/03, E.St.Louis, Ill. d: 6/14/66, E.St.Louis, Ill. BR/TL, 6', 175 lbs. Deb: 9/13/27																												
1927	NY-N	0	0	—	3	0	0	0	0	4	6	13.5	0	5	11.3	4	9.0	9.00	43	.429	.478	-2	-2	98	111	0.0	0	0	-0.1
1928	NY-N	3	6	.333	22	8	1	0	0	76	79	9.4	9	31	3.7	39	4.6	4.74	84	.275	.336	-6	-7	99	94	-2.0	-2	-0	-0.7
1929	NY-N	14	7	.667	29	23	13	1	0	178	188	9.5	11	57	2.9	65	3.3	**3.08**	148	.274	.324	32	29	97	**129**	2.9	-3	-3	2.1
1930	NY-N	17	15	.531	39	34	13	2	1	245	258	9.5	19	88	3.2	105	3.9	3.93	121	.268	.328	28	23	96	101	-1.1	-1	-1	1.8

YEAR	TM/L	W	L	PCT	G	GS	CG	SHO	SV	IP	H	H/G	HR	BB	BB/G	SO	SO/G	ERA	/A	OAVG	OOBP	PR	/A	PF	CPI	WAT	PB	PD	TPI
1931	NY-N	16	9	.640	37	28	19	**6**	3	239	212	8.0	6	64	2.4	121	4.6	**2.26**	**160**	.231	.282	**43**	**36**	93	101	2.3	-6	-4	2.6
1932	NY-N	8	12	.400	31	22	9	0	2	163	177	9.8	23	55	3.0	74	4.1	4.14	92	.274	.330	-5	-6	98	111	-1.5	-2	1	-0.6
1933	StL-N	9	10	.474	29	20	6	2	0	158	168	9.6	8	67	3.8	41	2.3	3.42	98	.273	.340	-1	-1	100	117	-1.1	-2	1	-0.1
1934	StL-N	12	4	.750	24	19	10	1	0	153	160	9.4	11	66	3.9	76	4.5	3.12	145	.270	.340	16	24	111	**137**	2.9	-5	-1	1.9
1935	StL-N	13	8	.619	37	25	8	2	1	193	222	10.4	7	78	3.6	79	3.7	3.82	106	.288	.352	4	5	100	116	0.0	-4	-0	0.0
1936	StL-N	5	6	.455	21	13	4	2	1	80	106	11.9	5	27	3.0	22	2.5	5.85	65	.318	.360	-16	-18	95	90	-1.0	2	1	-1.4
Total	10	97	77	.557	272	192	83	16	8	1489	1576	9.5	99	538	3.3	626	3.8	3.59	114	.271	.329	93	82	98	112	1.4	-23	-6	5.5

■ JIM WALKUP Walkup, James Elton b: 12/14/09, Havana, Ark. BR/TR, 6'1", 170 lbs. Deb: 9/22/34

YEAR	TM/L	W	L	PCT	G	GS	CG	SHO	SV	IP	H	H/G	HR	BB	BB/G	SO	SO/G	ERA	/A	OAVG	OOBP	PR	/A	PF	CPI	WAT	PB	PD	TPI
1934	StL-A	0	0	—	3	0	0	0	0	8	6	6.8	0	5	5.6	6	6.8	2.25	212	.200	.314	2	2	106	107	0.0	0	-0	0.2
1935	StL-A	6	9	.400	55	20	4	1	0	181	226	11.2	17	104	5.2	44	2.2	6.27	78	.305	.387	-36	-28	110	94	-0.4	-3	-1	-2.8
1936	StL-A	0	3	.000	5	2	0	0	0	16	20	11.3	0	6	3.4	5	2.8	7.88	68	.308	.361	-5	-4	107	61	-1.4	-1	1	-0.3
1937	StL-A	9	12	.429	27	18	6	0	0	150	218	13.1	16	83	5.0	46	2.8	7.38	65	.347	.418	-46	-43	103	97	2.2	-1	2	-3.5
1938	StL-A	1	12	.077	18	13	1	0	0	94	127	12.2	13	53	5.1	28	2.7	6.80	73	.329	.410	-21	-19	103	103	-5.1	-2	0	-1.7
1939	StL-A	0	1	.000	1	0	0	0	0	1	2	18.0	0	1	9.0	0	0.0	0.00	—	.500	.600	1	1	105	0	-0.4	0	0	0.0
	Det-A	0	1	.000	7	0	0	0	0	12	15	11.3	3	8	6.0	5	3.8	7.50	68	.319	.390	-4	-3	110	104	-0.4	0	0	-0.2
	Yr	0	2	.000	8	0	0	0	0	13	17	11.8	3	9	6.2	5	3.5	6.92	73	.333	.406	-3	-3	109	104	-0.8	0	0	-0.2
Total	6	16	38	.296	116	53	11	1	0	462	614	12.0	49	260	5.1	134	2.6	6.74	73	.323	.400	-110	-95	106	96	-5.5	-6	1	-8.3

■ JIM WALKUP Walkup, James Huey b: 11/3/1895, Havana, Ark. BR/TL, 5'8", 150 lbs. Deb: 4/30/27

YEAR	TM/L	W	L	PCT	G	GS	CG	SHO	SV	IP	H	H/G	HR	BB	BB/G	SO	SO/G	ERA	/A	OAVG	OOBP	PR	/A	PF	CPI	WAT	PB	PD	TPI
1927	Det-A	0	0	—	2	0	0	0	0	2	3	13.5	0	0	0.0	0	0.0	4.50	99	.429	.375	-0	-0	107	148	0.0	-0	0	0.0

■ MURRAY WALL Wall, Murray Wesley b: 9/19/26, Dallas, Tex. d: 10/8/71, Lone Oak, Tex. BR/TR, 6'3", 185 lbs. Deb: 7/04/50

YEAR	TM/L	W	L	PCT	G	GS	CG	SHO	SV	IP	H	H/G	HR	BB	BB/G	SO	SO/G	ERA	/A	OAVG	OOBP	PR	/A	PF	CPI	WAT	PB	PD	TPI
1950	Bos-N	0	0	—	1	0	0	0	0	4	5	11.3	0	2	4.5	0	0.0	4.50	78	.313	.368	-0	-0	85	111	0.0	-0	-0	0.0
1957	Bos-A	3	0	1.000	11	0	0	0	1	24	21	7.9	3	2	0.8	13	4.9	3.38	122	.233	.240	1	2	109	76	1.5	0	1	0.4
1958	Bos-A	8	9	.471	52	1	0	0	10	114	109	8.6	14	33	2.6	53	4.2	3.63	109	.255	.305	2	4	105	106	-0.7	-2	3	0.5
1959	Bos-A	1	4	.200	15	0	0	0	3	32	31	8.7	5	15	4.2	8	2.3	5.34	76	.267	.338	-5	-5	105	92	-1.4	-1	1	-0.4
	Was-A	0	0	—	1	0	0	0	0	1	3	27.0	1	0	0.0	0	0.0	9.00	44	.600	.600	-1	-1	102	240	0.0	-0	0	0.0
	Bos-A	1	1	.500	11	0	0	0	0	17	26	13.8	2	11	5.8	6	3.2	5.82	70	.371	.442	-4	-3	105	141	0.0	-0	-0	-0.3
	Yr	2	5	.286	27	0	0	0	3	50	60	10.8	8	26	4.7	14	2.5	5.58	73	.313	.383	-10	-8	105	141	-1.4	-1	1	-0.7
Total	4	13	14	.481	91	1	0	0	14	192	195	9.1	25	63	3.0	80	3.8	4.13	97	.269	.320	-7	-3	105	104	-0.6	-3	5	0.2

■ STAN WALL Wall, Stanley Arthur b: 6/16/51, Butler, Mo. BL/TL, 6'1", 175 lbs. Deb: 7/19/75

YEAR	TM/L	W	L	PCT	G	GS	CG	SHO	SV	IP	H	H/G	HR	BB	BB/G	SO	SO/G	ERA	/A	OAVG	OOBP	PR	/A	PF	CPI	WAT	PB	PD	TPI
1975	LA-N	0	1	.000	10	0	0	0	0	16	12	6.8	0	7	3.9	6	3.4	1.69	201	.222	.303	3	3	93	158	-0.4	0	0	0.3
1976	LA-N	2	2	.500	31	0	0	0	1	50	50	9.0	5	15	2.7	27	4.9	3.60	96	.269	.318	-1	-1	99	113	-0.1	-0	-0	-0.1
1977	LA-N	2	3	.400	25	0	0	0	0	32	36	10.1	3	13	3.7	22	6.2	5.34	72	.279	.345	-5	-5	98	83	-0.8	-0	-1	-0.5
Total	3	4	6	.400	66	0	0	0	1	98	98	9.0	8	35	3.2	55	5.1	3.86	93	.266	.325	-2	-3	98	111	-1.3	-1	-1	-0.3

■ DAVE WALLACE Wallace, David William b: 9/7/47, Waterbury, Conn. BR/TR, 5'10", 185 lbs. Deb: 7/18/73

YEAR	TM/L	W	L	PCT	G	GS	CG	SHO	SV	IP	H	H/G	HR	BB	BB/G	SO	SO/G	ERA	/A	OAVG	OOBP	PR	/A	PF	CPI	WAT	PB	PD	TPI
1973	Phi-N	0	0	—	4	0	0	0	0	4	13	29.3	1	2	4.5	2	4.5	20.25	20	.591	.600	-7	-7	109	87	0.0	0	0	-0.6
1974	Phi-N	0	1	.000	3	0	0	0	0	3	4	12.0	2	3	9.0	3	9.0	9.00	42	.308	.412	-2	-2	104	125	-0.4	0	0	-0.1
1978	Tor-A	0	0	—	6	0	0	0	0	14	12	7.7	1	11	7.1	7	4.5	3.86	100	.245	.371	-0	0	102	117	0.0	0	-0	0.0
Total	3	0	1	.000	13	0	0	0	0	21	29	12.4	4	16	6.9	12	5.1	7.71	50	.345	.433	-9	-9	104	112	-0.4	0	0	-0.7

■ HUCK WALLACE Wallace, Harry Clinton "Lefty" b: 7/27/1882, Richmond, Ind. d: 7/6/51, Cleveland, Ohio BL/TL, 5'6", 160 lbs. Deb: 6/05/12

YEAR	TM/L	W	L	PCT	G	GS	CG	SHO	SV	IP	H	H/G	HR	BB	BB/G	SO	SO/G	ERA	/A	OAVG	OOBP	PR	/A	PF	CPI	WAT	PB	PD	TPI
1912	Phi-N	0	0	—	4	0	0	0	0	5	7	12.6	0	4	7.2	4	7.2	0.00	—	.350	.458	2	2	101	0	0.0	0	0	0.2

■ LEFTY WALLACE Wallace, James Harold b: 8/12/21, Evansville, Ind. d: 7/28/82, Evansville, Ind. BL/TL, 5'11", 160 lbs. Deb: 5/05/42

YEAR	TM/L	W	L	PCT	G	GS	CG	SHO	SV	IP	H	H/G	HR	BB	BB/G	SO	SO/G	ERA	/A	OAVG	OOBP	PR	/A	PF	CPI	WAT	PB	PD	TPI
1942	Bos-N	1	3	.250	19	3	1	0	0	49	39	7.2	3	24	4.4	20	3.7	3.86	84	.217	.311	-3	-3	98	79	-0.7	-0	-1	-0.4
1945	Bos-N	1	0	1.000	5	3	1	0	0	20	18	8.1	1	9	4.0	4	1.8	4.50	95	.240	.326	-2	-0	113	77	0.5	-1	0	0.0
1946	Bos-N	3	3	.500	27	8	2	0	0	75	76	9.1	5	31	3.7	27	3.2	4.20	76	.253	.320	-7	-8	94	82	-0.1	-0	2	-0.7
Total	3	5	6	.455	51	14	4	0	0	144	133	8.3	9	64	4.0	51	3.2	4.13	81	.240	.318	-11	-12	98	80	-0.3	-2	1	-1.1

■ MIKE WALLACE Wallace, Michael Sherman b: 2/3/51, Gastonia, N.C. BL/TL, 6'2", 190 lbs. Deb: 6/27/73

YEAR	TM/L	W	L	PCT	G	GS	CG	SHO	SV	IP	H	H/G	HR	BB	BB/G	SO	SO/G	ERA	/A	OAVG	OOBP	PR	/A	PF	CPI	WAT	PB	PD	TPI
1973	Phi-N	1	1	.500	20	3	1	0	1	33	38	10.4	1	15	4.1	20	5.5	3.82	105	.304	.363	-1	1	109	124	0.1	-0	-0	0.0
1974	Phi-N	1	0	1.000	8	0	0	0	0	8	12	13.5	0	2	2.3	1	1.1	5.63	67	.324	.359	-2	-2	104	80	0.5	0	-0	-0.1
	NY-A	6	0	1.000	23	1	0	0	0	52	42	7.3	3	35	6.1	34	5.9	2.42	142	.222	.339	7	6	95	141	3.0	0	-1	0.5
1975	NY-A	0	0	—	3	0	0	0	0	4	11	24.8	1	1	2.3	2	4.5	15.75	23	.458	.480	-5	-5	98	78	0.0	0	0	-0.4
	StL-N	0	0	—	9	0	0	0	0	9	9	9.0	0	5	5.0	6	6.0	2.00	188	.281	.359	2	2	103	210	0.0	0	0	0.2
1976	StL-N	3	2	.600	49	0	0	0	2	66	66	9.0	3	39	5.3	40	5.5	4.09	90	.264	.356	-4	-3	105	102	0.7	0	0	-0.2
1977	Tex-A	0	0	—	5	0	0	0	0	8	10	11.3	1	10	11.3	2	2.3	7.88	54	.323	.465	-3	-3	104	105	0.0	0	0	-0.2
Total	5	11	3	.786	117	4	1	0	3	180	188	9.4	9	107	5.3	105	5.3	3.95	94	.273	.362	-7	-5	102	121	4.3	0	-0	-0.2

■ BOBBY WALLACE Wallace, Roderick John b: 11/4/1873, Pittsburgh, Pa. d: 11/3/60, Torrance, Cal. BR/TR, 5'8", 170 lbs. Deb: 9/15/1894 MUCH

YEAR	TM/L	W	L	PCT	G	GS	CG	SHO	SV	IP	H	H/G	HR	BB	BB/G	SO	SO/G	ERA	/A	OAVG	OOBP	PR	/A	PF	CPI	WAT	PB	PD	TPI
1894	Cle-N	2	1	.667	4	3	3	0	0	26	28	9.7	1	22	7.6	10	3.5	5.54	106	.297	.430	-1	1	111	95	0.5	-2	0	0.0
1895	Cle-N	12	14	.462	30	28	22	1	1	229	271	10.7	3	87	3.4	63	2.5	4.09	111	.315	.378	18	11	95	106	-4.2	-1	0	0.8
1896	Cle-N	10	7	.588	22	16	13	2	0	145	167	10.4	2	49	3.0	46	2.9	3.35	140	.311	.369	16	22	108	119	-0.5	0	0	1.9
1902	StL-A	0	0	—	1	1	0	0	0	2	3	13.5	0	0	0.0	1	4.5	0.00	—	.374	.374	1	1	102	0	0.0	0	0	0.1
Total	4	24	22	.522	57	48	38	3	1	402	469	10.5	6	158	3.5	120	2.7	3.90	120	.313	.378	34	35	100	109	-4.2	-2	0	2.8

■ TIM WALLACH Wallach, Timothy Charles b: 9/14/57, Huntington Park, Cal. BR/TR, 6'3", 220 lbs. Deb: 9/06/80

YEAR	TM/L	W	L	PCT	G	GS	CG	SHO	SV	IP	H	H/G	HR	BB	BB/G	SO	SO/G	ERA	/A	OAVG	OOBP	PR	/A	PF	CPI	WAT	PB	PD	TPI
1987	Mon-N	0	0	—	1	0	0	0	0	1	1	9.0	0	0	0.0	0	0.0	0.00	—	.333	.333	0	0	106	0	0.0	1	0	0.0

■ RED WALLER Waller, John Francis b: 6/16/1883, Washington, D.C. d: 2/9/15, Secaucus, N.J. Deb: 09

YEAR	TM/L	W	L	PCT	G	GS	CG	SHO	SV	IP	H	H/G	HR	BB	BB/G	SO	SO/G	ERA	/A	OAVG	OOBP	PR	/A	PF	CPI	WAT	PB	PD	TPI
1909	NY-N	0	0	—	1	0	0	0	0	1	3	27.0	0	0	0.0	1	9.0	0.00	—	.429	.500	0	0	103	0	0.0	0	0	0.1

■ AUGIE WALSH Walsh, August Sothley b: 8/9/04, Wilmington, Del. d: 11/12/85, San Rafael, Cal. BR/TR, 6', 175 lbs. Deb: 10/02/27

YEAR	TM/L	W	L	PCT	G	GS	CG	SHO	SV	IP	H	H/G	HR	BB	BB/G	SO	SO/G	ERA	/A	OAVG	OOBP	PR	/A	PF	CPI	WAT	PB	PD	TPI
1927	Phi-N	0	1	.000	1	1	1	0	0	10	12	10.8	3	5	4.5	0	0.0	4.50	87	.333	.405	-1	-1	100	173	-0.4	0	-0	0.0
1928	Phi-N	4	9	.308	38	11	2	0	2	122	160	11.8	13	40	3.0	38	2.8	6.20	70	.321	.366	-30	-25	109	89	0.2	2	-2	-2.2
Total	2	4	10	.286	39	12	3	0	2	132	172	11.7	16	45	3.1	38	2.6	6.07	71	.322	.369	-31	-26	109	95	-0.2	2	-2	-2.2

■ CONNIE WALSH Walsh, Cornelius R. b: 4/23/1882, St.Louis, Mo. d: 4/5/53, St.Louis, Mo. Deb: 9/16/07

YEAR	TM/L	W	L	PCT	G	GS	CG	SHO	SV	IP	H	H/G	HR	BB	BB/G	SO	SO/G	ERA	/A	OAVG	OOBP	PR	/A	PF	CPI	WAT	PB	PD	TPI
1907	Pit-N	0	0	—	1	0	0	0	0	1	1	9.0	0	1	9.0	0	0.0	9.00	28	.289	.448	-1	-1	102	54	0.0	0	0	0.0

■ ED WALSH Walsh, Edward Arthur b: 2/11/05, Meriden, Conn. d: 10/31/37, Meriden, Conn. BR/TR, 6'1", 180 lbs. Deb: 7/04/28

YEAR	TM/L	W	L	PCT	G	GS	CG	SHO	SV	IP	H	H/G	HR	BB	BB/G	SO	SO/G	ERA	/A	OAVG	OOBP	PR	/A	PF	CPI	WAT	PB	PD	TPI
1928	Chi-A	4	7	.364	14	10	3	0	0	78	86	9.9	2	42	4.8	32	3.7	4.96	82	.290	.377	-8	-8	100	97	-1.2	-2	-1	-0.9
1929	Chi-A	6	11	.353	24	20	7	0	0	129	156	10.9	9	64	4.5	31	2.2	5.65	73	.312	.378	-20	-22	98	98	-0.8	2	1	-1.7
1930	Chi-A	1	4	.200	37	4	0	0	0	104	131	11.3	8	30	2.6	37	3.2	5.37	91	.316	.353	-8	-6	105	101	-1.2	0	1	-0.3
1932	Chi-A	0	2	.000	4	4	1	0	0	20	26	11.7	3	13	5.8	7	3.1	8.55	48	.299	.390	-9	-10	91	74	-0.9	0	0	-0.7
Total	4	11	24	.314	79	38	11	0	0	331	399	10.8	22	149	4.1	107	2.9	5.57	78	.307	.371	-45	-45	100	97	-4.1	1	1	-3.6

■ ED WALSH Walsh, Edward Augustine "Big Ed" b: 5/14/1881, Plains, Pa. d: 5/26/59, Pompano Beach, Fla BR/TR, 6'1", 193 lbs. Deb: 5/07/04 MUCH

YEAR	TM/L	W	L	PCT	G	GS	CG	SHO	SV	IP	H	H/G	HR	BB	BB/G	SO	SO/G	ERA	/A	OAVG	OOBP	PR	/A	PF	CPI	WAT	PB	PD	TPI
1904	Chi-A	6	3	.667	18	8	6	1	1	111	90	7.3	1	32	2.6	57	4.6	2.59	97	.243	.303	0	-1	97	84	1.0	3	0	0.0
1905	Chi-A	8	3	.727	22	13	9	1	0	137	121	7.9	0	29	1.9	71	4.7	2.17	114	.260	.304	7	5	93	108	1.8	-0	0	0.5
1906	Chi-A	17	13	.567	41	31	24	**10**	1	278	215	7.0	1	58	1.9	171	5.5	1.88	128	.236	.282	25	16	89	92	-1.4	-1	8	2.7
1907	Chi-A	24	18	.571	**56**	46	**37**	5	**4**	**422**	341	7.3	3	87	1.9	206	4.4	**1.60**	**160**	.243	.288	**44**	**45**	101	115	-0.1	-2	22	**8.1**
1908	Chi-A	**40**	15	**.727**	**66**	49	**42**	**11**	**6**	**464**	343	6.7	2	56	1.1	**269**	5.2	1.42	156	.203	.232	**50**	41	93	81	**12.7**	2	14	**6.6**
1909	Chi-A	15	11	.577	31	28	20	**8**	2	230	166	6.5	0	50	2.0	127	5.0	1.41	170	.203	**.253**	27	**25**	97	75	2.0	4	7	3.9
1910	Chi-A	18	20	.474	**45**	36	33	7	**5**	370	242	5.9	4	61	**1.5**	258	6.3	**1.26**	190	**.187**	**.226**	**52**	47	95	57	1.3	4	10	**7.2**
1911	Chi-A	27	18	.600	**56**	37	33	5	**4**	**369**	327	8.0	4	72	1.8	**255**	6.2	2.22	143	.239	**.280**	46	39	95	88	5.5	-1	15	5.6
1912	Chi-A	27	17	.614	**62**	41	32	6	**10**	**393**	332	7.6	6	94	2.2	254	5.8	2.15	154	.231	.279	52	51	99	97	6.2	5	7	6.1
1913	Chi-A	8	3	.727	16	14	7	1	1	98	91	8.4	1	39	3.6	34	3.1	2.57	108	.243	.321	4	2	95	103	2.5	-1	1	0.3

YEAR	TM/L	W	L	PCT	G	GS	CG	SHO	SV	IP	H	H/G	HR	BB	BB/G	SO	SO/G	ERA	/A	OAVG	OOBP	PR	/A	PF	CPI	WAT	PB	PD	TPI
1914	Chi-A	2	3	.400	8	5	3	1	0	45	33	6.6	0	20	4.0	15	3.0	2.80	103	.212	.305	-0	0	105	73	-0.2	-1	1	0.1
1915	Chi-A	3	0	1.000	3	3	3	1	0	27	19	6.3	0	7	2.3	12	4.0	1.33	207	.202	.257	5	4	94	99	1.5	1	-1	0.5
1916	Chi-A	0	1	.000	2	1	0	0	0	3	4	12.0	0	3	9.0	3	9.0	3.00	100	.286	.412	-0	-0	106	177	-0.4	0	0	0.0
1917	Bos-N	0	1	.000	4	3	1	0	0	18	22	11.0	0	9	4.5	4	2.0	3.50	75	.314	.390	-2	-2	97	143	-0.4	1	0	0.0
Total	14	195	126	.607	430	315	250	57	34	2965	2346	7.1	22	617	1.9	1736	5.3	1.82	145	.224	.269	310	272	96	89	32.0	13	83	41.6
■ JUNIOR WALSH Walsh, James Gerald b: 3/7/19, Newark, N.J. BR/TR, 5'11", 185 lbs. Deb: 9/14/46																													
1946	Pit-N	0	1	.000	4	2	0	0	0	10	9	8.1	0	10	9.0	2	1.8	5.40	67	.237	.408	-2	-2	106	82	-0.4	-1	0	-0.2
1948	Pit-N	1	0	1.000	2	0	0	0	0	4	4	9.0	1	5	11.3	0	0.0	11.25	37	.235	.409	-3	-3	104	59	0.5	-0	0	-0.2
1949	Pit-N	1	4	.200	9	7	1	1	0	43	40	8.4	5	16	3.3	24	5.0	5.02	82	.244	.311	-5	-4	102	73	-1.3	-1	-1	-0.5
1950	Pit-N	1	1	.500	38	2	0	0	2	62	56	8.1	6	34	4.9	33	4.8	5.08	86	.246	.338	-6	-5	106	82	0.2	1	0	-0.3
1951	Pit-N	1	4	.200	36	1	0	0	0	73	92	11.3	9	46	5.7	32	3.9	6.90	63	.304	.390	-24	-21	110	87	-1.2	0	0	-1.9
Total	5	4	10	.286	89	12	1	1	2	192	201	9.4	21	111	5.2	91	4.3	5.91	72	.268	.360	-41	-35	106	81	-2.2	-1	-0	-3.1
■ JIM WALSH Walsh, James Thomas b: 7/10/1894, Roxbury, Mass. d: 5/13/67, Boston, Mass. BL/TL, 5'11", 175 lbs. Deb: 8/25/21																													
1921	Det-A	0	0	—	3	0	0	0	0	4	2	4.5	0	1	2.3	3	6.8	2.25	182	.125	.176	1	1	96	71	0.0	0	-0	0.1
■ DEE WALSH Walsh, Leo Thomas b: 3/28/1890, St.Louis, Mo. d: 7/14/71, St.Louis, Mo. BB/TR, 5'9.5", 165 lbs. Deb: 4/10/13																													
1915	StL-A	0	0	—	1	0	0	0	0	2	2	9.0	0	2	9.0	0	0.0	13.50	22	.222	.364	-2	-2	99	25	0.0	0	0	-0.1
■ JIMMY WALSH Walsh, Michael Timothy "Runt" b: 3/25/1886, Lima, Ohio d: 1/21/47, Baltimore, Md. BR/TR, 5'9", 174 lbs. Deb: 4/25/10																													
1911	Phi-N	0	1	.000	1	0	0	0	0	3	7	21.0	1	1	3.0	1	3.0	12.00	31	.500	.533	-3	-3	108	0	0.0	0	0	0.0
■ GENE WALTER Walter, Gene Winston b: 11/22/60, Chicago, Ill. BL/TL, 6'4", 200 lbs. Deb: 8/09/85																													
1985	SD-N	0	2	.000	15	0	0	0	3	22	12	4.9	0	8	3.3	18	7.4	2.05	178	.158	.233	4	4	101	35	-0.9	0	0	0.5
1986	SD-N	2	2	.500	57	0	0	0	1	98	89	8.2	7	49	4.5	84	7.7	3.86	93	.247	.336	-1	-3	96	100	0.2	1	1	-0.1
1987	NY-N	1	2	.333	21	0	0	0	0	20	18	8.1	1	13	5.8	11	4.9	3.15	126	.243	.360	2	2	97	130	-0.5	0	-0	0.2
1988	NY-N	0	1	.000	19	0	0	0	0	17	21	11.1	0	11	5.8	14	7.4	3.71	82	.309	.400	-0	-1	88	143	-0.4	0	0	-0.1
	Sea-A	1	0	1.000	16	0	0	0	0	26	21	7.3	0	15	5.2	13	4.5	5.19	83	.216	.330	-4	-3	108	55	0.5	0	-0	-0.2
Total	4	4	7	.364	128	0	0	0	4	183	161	7.9	8	96	4.7	140	6.9	3.74	98	.238	.333	0	-1	98	93	-1.1	1	1	0.3
■ BERNIE WALTER Walter, James Bernard b: 8/15/08, Dover, Tenn. BR/TR, 6'1", 175 lbs. Deb: 8/16/30																													
1930	Pit-N	0	0	—	1	0	0	0	0	1	0	0.0	0	0	0.0	1	9.0	0.00	—	.000	.000	1	1	98	0	0.0	0	0	0.1
■ CHARLIE WALTERS Walters, Charles Leonard b: 2/21/47, Minneapolis, Minn. BR/TR, 6'4", 190 lbs. Deb: 4/11/69																													
1969	Min-A	0	0	—	6	0	0	0	0	7	6	7.7	1	3	3.9	2	2.6	5.14	70	.240	.333	-1	-1	100	84	0.0	0	0	0.0
■ MIKE WALTERS Walters, Michael Charles b: BR/TR, 6'5", 203 lbs. Deb: 7/08/83																													
1983	Min-A	1	1	.500	23	0	0	0	2	59	52	7.9	4	20	3.1	21	3.2	4.12	105	.243	.305	-0	1	106	82	0.1	0	0	0.2
1984	Min-A	0	3	.000	23	0	0	0	2	29	31	9.6	1	14	4.3	10	3.1	3.72	113	.287	.365	1	2	106	123	-1.4	0	-0	0.1
Total	2	1	4	.200	46	0	0	0	4	88	83	8.5	5	34	3.5	31	3.2	3.99	108	.258	.325	1	3	106	95	-1.3	0	-0	0.3
■ BUCKY WALTERS Walters, William Henry b: 4/19/09, Philadelphia, Pa. BR/TR, 6'1", 180 lbs. Deb: 9/18/31 MC																													
1934	Phi-N	0	0	—	2	1	0	0	0	7	8	10.3	1	2	2.6	7	9.0	1.29	350	.296	.367	2	2	111	430	0.0	0	1	0.3
1935	Phi-N	9	9	.500	24	22	8	2	0	151	168	10.0	9	68	4.1	40	2.4	4.17	113	.289	.365	-3	9	117	117	1.4	1	2	0.9
1936	Phi-N	11	21	.344	40	33	15	4	0	258	284	9.9	11	115	4.0	66	2.3	4.26	105	.277	.349	-7	6	111	100	-0.3	3	8	2.0
1937	Phi-N	14	15	.483	37	34	15	3	0	246	292	10.7	14	86	3.1	87	3.2	4.76	91	.295	.348	-23	-12	111	96	2.4	4	4	0.1
1938	Phi-N	4	8	.333	12	12	9	1	0	83	91	9.9	8	42	4.6	28	3.0	5.20	77	.276	.362	-13	-11	106	93	0.3	3	0	-0.6
	Cin-N	11	6	.647	27	22	11	2	1	168	168	9.0	5	66	3.5	65	3.5	3.70	98	.255	.321	2	-1	96	91	2.1	-0	3	0.1
	Yr	15	14	.517	39	34	20	3	1	251	259	9.3	13	108	3.9	93	3.3	4.20	90	.261	.332	-11	-12	99	91	2.4	3	3	-0.5
1939	Cin-N	**27**	11	.711	39	36	**31**	2	0	**319**	250	**7.1**	15	109	3.1	**137**	3.9	**2.29**	**171**	**.220**	.284	**58**	**58**	100	111	5.1	13	4	**8.4**
1940	Cin-N	**22**	10	.688	36	36	**29**	3	0	**305**	241	**7.1**	19	92	2.7	115	3.4	**2.48**	152	**.220**	.280	**46**	**43**	98	109	1.9	3	-1	4.9
1941	Cin-N	19	15	.559	37	35	**27**	5	2	**302**	292	8.7	10	88	2.6	129	3.8	2.83	126	.255	.305	27	24	98	111	-0.4	2	2	3.1
1942	Cin-N	15	14	.517	34	32	21	2	0	254	223	7.9	8	73	2.6	109	3.9	2.66	127	.231	.286	19	20	102	94	0.6	6	2	3.2
1943	Cin-N	15	15	.500	34	34	21	5	0	246	244	8.9	8	109	4.0	80	2.9	3.55	93	.264	.336	-5	-7	98	105	-2.0	8	1	0.2
1944	Cin-N	**23**	8	.742	34	32	27	6	1	285	233	**7.4**	10	87	2.7	77	2.4	2.40	142	**.219**	.279	**38**	**32**	95	94	**6.9**	8	1	**4.4**
1945	Cin-N	10	10	.500	22	22	12	3	0	168	166	8.9	6	51	2.7	45	2.4	2.68	138	.259	.310	21	19	97	124	1.9	5	-0	2.5
1946	Cin-N	10	7	.588	22	22	10	2	0	151	146	8.7	9	64	3.8	60	3.6	2.56	140	.258	.333	14	17	105	142	2.5	-2	2	2.0
1947	Cin-N	8	8	.500	20	20	5	2	0	122	137	10.1	15	49	3.6	43	3.2	5.75	65	.278	.344	-23	-27	92	82	0.4	3	-1	-2.3
1948	Cin-N	0	3	.000	7	5	1	0	0	35	42	10.8	6	18	4.6	19	4.9	4.63	91	.316	.382	-3	-2	106	140	-1.4	0	1	0.0
1950	Bos-N	0	0	—	1	0	0	0	0	4	5	11.3	0	2	4.5	0	0.0	4.50	78	.313	.368	-0	-0	85	111	0.0	-0	-0	0.0
Total	16	198	160	.553	428	398	242	42	4	3104	2990	8.7	154	1121	3.3	1107	3.2	3.30	115	.253	.317	151	169	101	106	21.4	58	27	29.2
■ DICK WANTZ Wantz, Richard Carter b: 4/11/40, South Gate, Cal. d: 5/13/65, Inglewood, Cal. BR/TR, 6'5", 175 lbs. Deb: 4/13/65																													
1965	Cal-A	0	0	—	1	0	0	0	0	1	3	27.0	0	0	0.0	2	18.0	18.00	19	.500	.500	-2	-2	98	64	0.0	0	0	-0.1
■ WARD Ward Deb:N/A.																													
1885	Pro-N	0	1	.000	1	1	1	0	0	8	10	11.3	0	1	1.1	3	3.4	4.50	58	.317	.338	-1	-2	93	85	-0.4	-0	0	-0.1
■ COLIN WARD Ward, Colin Norval b: 11/22/60, Los Angeles, Cal. BL/TL, 6'3", 190 lbs. Deb: 9/21/85																													
1985	SF-N	0	0	—	6	2	0	0	0	12	10	7.5	0	7	5.3	8	6.0	4.50	76	.233	.327	-1	-1	95	69	0.0	-0	0	-0.1
■ MONTE WARD Ward, John Montgomery b: 3/3/1860, Bellefonte, Pa. d: 3/4/25, Augusta, Ga. BL/TR, 5'9", 165 lbs. Deb: 7/15/1878 MH																													
1878	Pro-N	22	13	.629	37	37	37	6	0	334	308	8.3	3	34	0.9	116	3.1	**1.51**	**148**	.255	.275	**30**	27	97	107	5.9	2	2	**2.9**
1879	Pro-N	**47**	19	**.712**	70	60	58	2	**1**	587	571	8.8	5	36	0.6	**239**	3.7	2.15	110	.260	.272	23	14	94	91	4.5	16	4	3.3
1880	Pro-N	39	24	.619	70	67	59	**8**	1	595	501	7.6	5	45	0.7	230	3.5	1.74	126	.237	.253	**42**	30	92	87	0.0	1	7	3.4
1881	Pro-N	18	18	.500	39	35	32	3	0	330	326	8.9	2	53	1.4	119	3.2	2.13	120	.270	.301	24	16	92	110	-3.0	4	5	1.5
1882	Pro-N	19	12	.613	33	32	29	4	**1**	278	261	8.4	6	36	1.2	72	2.3	2.59	115	.256	.281	9	12	103	91	-0.1	-1	5	1.1
1883	NY-N	16	13	.552	33	25	24	1	0	277	278	9.0	3	31	1.0	121	3.9	2.70	117	.269	.290	14	14	101	92	2.7	5	4	1.3
1884	NY-N	3	3	.500	9	5	5	0	0	61	72	10.6	2	18	2.7	23	3.4	3.39	85	.303	.352	-3	-4	97	118	-0.2	1	0	-0.2
Total	7	164	102	.617	291	261	244	24	3	2462	2317	8.5	26	253	0.9	920	3.4	2.10	119	.257	.277	138	107	96	95	9.8	29	27	13.3
■ DICK WARD Ward, Richard Ole b: 5/21/09, Herrick, S.Dak. d: 5/30/66, Freeland, Wash. BR/TR, 6'1", 198 lbs. Deb: 5/03/34																													
1934	Chi-N	0	0	—	3	0	0	0	0	6	9	13.5	0	2	3.0	1	1.5	3.00	131	.375	.393	1	1	97	215	0.0	-0	0	0.0
1935	StL-N	0	0	—	1	0	0	0	0	0	0	—	0	1	—	0	—	—	—	—	1.000	0	0	100	0	0.0	0	0	0.0
Total	2	0	0	—	4	0	0	0	0	6	9	13.5	0	3	4.5	1	1.5	3.00	131	.375	.414	1	1	97	215	0.0	-0	0	0.0
■ DUANE WARD Ward, Roy Duane b: 5/28/64, Park View, N.Mex. BR/TR, 6'4", 185 lbs. Deb: 4/12/86																													
1986	Atl-N	0	1	.000	10	0	0	0	0	16	22	12.4	2	8	4.5	8	4.5	7.31	53	.349	.411	-6	-6	103	95	-0.4	-0	1	-0.5
	Tor-A	0	1	.000	2	1	0	0	0	2	3	13.5	0	4	18.0	1	4.5	13.50	32	.300	.533	-2	-2	104	74	-0.4	0	0	-0.1
1987	Tor-A	1	0	1.000	12	1	0	0	0	12	14	10.5	0	12	9.0	10	7.5	6.75	66	.326	.456	-3	-3	99	102	0.5	0	0	-0.2
1988	Tor-A	9	3	.750	64	0	0	0	15	112	101	8.1	5	60	4.8	91	7.3	3.29	119	.245	.341	8	8	99	115	2.9	0	-0	0.7
Total	3	10	5	.667	88	2	0	0	15	142	140	8.9	7	84	5.3	110	7.0	4.18	95	.265	.364	-3	-3	99	111	2.6	-0	0	-0.1
■ JON WARDEN Warden, Jonathan Edgar "Warbler" b: 10/1/46, Columbus, Ohio BB/TL, 6', 205 lbs. Deb: 4/11/68																													
1968	Det-A	4	1	.800	28	0	0	0	3	37	30	7.3	5	15	3.6	25	6.1	3.65	84	.217	.290	-3	-2	103	88	1.1	-0	-1	-0.3
■ CURT WARDLE Wardle, Curtis Ray b: 11/16/60, Downey, Cal. BL/TL, 6'5", 220 lbs. Deb: 8/30/84																													
1984	Min-A	0	0	—	2	0	0	0	0	4	3	6.8	2	0	0.0	5	11.3	4.50	94	.200	.200	-0	-0	106	96	0.0	0	0	0.0
1985	Min-A	1	3	.250	35	0	0	0	1	49	49	9.0	9	28	5.1	47	8.6	5.51	78	.266	.358	-7	-7	104	99	-0.9	0	1	-0.4
	Cle-A	7	6	.538	15	12	0	0	0	66	78	10.6	11	34	4.6	37	5.0	6.68	59	.297	.370	-19	-20	95	89	1.8	0	-1	-1.9
	Yr	8	9	.471	50	12	0	0	1	115	127	9.9	20	62	4.9	84	6.6	6.18	66	.283	.363	-26	-27	99	89	0.9	0	-0	-2.3
Total	2	8	9	.471	52	12	0	0	1	119	130	9.8	22	62	4.7	89	6.7	6.13	67	.281	.361	-26	-27	99	93	0.9	0	0	-2.3

YEAR TM/L	W	L	PCT	G	GS	CG	SHO	SV	IP	H	H/G	HR	BB	BB/G	SO	SO/G	ERA	/A	OAVG	OOBP	PR	/A	PF	CPI	WAT	PB	PD	TPI
■ **JACK WARHOP**	Warhop, John Milton "Chief" or "Crab" (born John Milton Wauhop) b: 7/4/1884, Hinton, W.Va. d: 10/4/60, Freeport, Ill. BR/TR, 5'9.5", 168 lbs. Deb: 9/19/08																											
1908 NY-A	1	2	.333	5	4	3	0	0	36	40	10.0	0	8	2.0	11	2.8	4.50	54	.292	.349	-8	-8	101	86	0.0	-1	0	-0.7
1909 NY-A	13	15	.464	36	23	21	3	2	243	197	7.3	2	81	3.0	95	3.5	2.41	102	.233	.319	2	1	99	101	-0.8	-2	1	0.2
1910 NY-A	14	14	.500	37	27	20	0	2	243	219	8.1	1	79	2.9	75	2.8	3.00	89	.246	.320	-13	-9	106	89	-2.3	-1	-4	-1.4
1911 NY-A	12	13	.480	31	25	17	1	0	210	239	10.2	6	44	1.9	71	3.0	4.16	89	.286	.333	-19	-10	111	84	-0.5	-4	-2	-1.1
1912 NY-A	10	19	.345	39	32	16	0	3	258	256	8.9	3	59	2.1	110	3.8	2.86	123	.266	.319	14	19	105	108	0.4	-1	-3	1.6
1913 NY-A	4	6	.400	15	7	1	0	0	62	69	10.0	1	33	4.8	11	1.6	3.77	80	.292	.406	-6	-5	104	129	0.2	-1	-2	-0.6
1914 NY-A	8	15	.348	37	23	15	0	0	217	182	7.5	8	44	1.8	56	2.3	2.36	116	.235	.286	9	9	100	96	-2.9	-1	-2	0.8
1915 NY-A	7	9	.438	21	19	12	0	0	143	164	10.3	7	52	3.3	34	2.1	3.97	73	.309	.384	-16	-17	99	123	-0.2	-2	-2	-2.0
Total 8	69	93	.426	221	160	105	4	7	1412	1366	8.7	28	400	2.5	463	3.0	3.12	96	.262	.328	-38	-21	104	100	-6.1	-12	-14	-3.2
■ **CY WARMOTH**	Warmoth, Wallace Walter b: 2/2/1893, Bone Gap, Ill. d: 6/20/57, Mt.Carmel, Ill. BL/TL, 5'11", 158 lbs. Deb: 8/31/16																											
1916 StL-N	0	0	—	3	0	0	0	0	5	12	21.6	0	4	7.2	1	1.8	14.40	18	.500	.567	-7	-7	100	87	0.0	-0	-0	-0.6
1922 Was-A	1	0	1.000	5	1	1	0	0	19	15	7.1	0	9	4.3	8	3.8	1.42	263	.205	.293	6	5	93	117	0.5	-0	-0	0.4
1923 Was-A	7	5	.583	21	13	4	0	0	105	103	8.8	4	76	6.5	45	3.9	4.29	88	.261	.374	-4	-6	95	101	1.2	2	0	-0.3
Total 3	8	5	.615	29	14	5	0	0	129	130	9.1	4	89	6.2	54	3.8	4.26	88	.264	.373	-5	-7	95	102	1.7	1	0	-0.5
■ **LON WARNEKE**	Warneke, Lonnie "The Arkansas Hummingbird" b: 3/28/09, Mt.Ida, Ark. d: 6/23/76, Hot Springs, Ark. BR/TR, 6'2", 185 lbs. Deb: 4/18/30 U																											
1930 Chi-N	0	0	—	1	0	0	0	0	1	2	18.0	0	5	45.0	0	0.0	45.00	11	.400	.636	-4	-4	103	46	0.0	0	0	-0.2
1931 Chi-N	2	4	.333	20	7	3	0	0	64	67	9.4	1	37	5.2	27	3.8	3.23	112	.269	.358	4	3	94	131	-1.1	1	-1	0.2
1932 Chi-N	**22**	6	**.786**	35	32	25	**4**	0	277	247	8.0	12	64	2.1	106	3.4	**2.37**	**168**	.237	.280	**46**	**49**	103	108	**7.5**	-1	0	5.3
1933 Chi-N	18	13	.581	36	34	**26**	4	1	287	262	8.2	8	75	2.4	133	4.2	2.01	158	.244	.289	42	37	95	130	1.0	11	3	5.8
1934 Chi-N	22	10	.688	43	35	23	3	3	291	273	8.4	16	66	2.0	143	4.4	3.22	122	.244	.285	27	23	97	88	5.2	-1	0	2.2
1935 Chi-N	20	13	.606	42	30	20	1	4	262	257	8.8	19	50	1.7	120	4.1	3.06	125	.257	.291	28	22	95	107	-1.3	2	-1	2.2
1936 Chi-N	16	13	.552	40	29	13	4	1	240	246	9.2	10	76	2.9	113	4.2	3.45	119	.264	.318	15	17	102	102	-0.3	0	-1	1.7
1937 StL-N	18	11	.621	36	33	18	2	0	239	280	10.5	32	69	2.6	87	3.3	4.52	86	.287	.332	-16	-17	100	105	3.4	5	-3	-1.3
1938 StL-N	13	8	.619	31	26	12	4	0	197	199	9.1	14	64	2.9	89	4.1	3.97	106	.256	.310	-4	5	111	88	3.3	5	-2	0.9
1939 StL-N	13	7	.650	34	21	6	2	2	162	160	8.9	14	49	2.7	59	3.3	3.78	106	.259	.313	3	4	103	96	1.4	1	-0	0.5
1940 StL-N	16	10	.615	33	31	17	1	0	232	235	9.1	17	47	1.8	85	3.3	3.14	124	.257	.294	18	19	101	106	2.2	3	1	2.4
1941 StL-N	17	9	.654	37	30	12	4	0	246	227	8.3	19	82	3.0	83	3.0	3.15	124	.249	.308	13	20	107	111	0.8	-2	-2	1.8
1942 StL-N	6	4	.600	12	12	5	0	0	82	76	8.3	8	15	1.6	31	3.4	3.29	103	.238	.271	0	1	103	85	-0.6	3	-1	0.4
Chi-N	5	7	.417	15	12	8	1	2	99	97	8.8	2	21	1.9	28	2.5	2.27	142	.259	.293	11	11	98	126	-0.3	-0	0	1.1
Yr	11	11	.500	27	24	13	1	2	181	173	8.6	10	36	**1.8**	59	2.9	2.73	121	.249	.283	12	12	100	126	-0.9	3	-1	1.5
1943 Chi-N	4	5	.444	21	10	4	0	0	88	82	8.4	3	18	1.8	30	3.1	3.17	105	.246	.282	2	1	98	81	-0.3	1	1	0.4
1945 Chi-N	0	1	.000	9	1	0	0	0	14	16	10.3	0	1	0.6	6	3.9	3.86	94	.267	.279	-0	-0	95	62	-0.4	0	0	0.0
Total 15	192	121	.613	445	343	192	30	13	2781	2726	8.8	175	739	2.4	1140	3.7	3.18	120	.255	.301	187	192	100	105	20.5	27	-4	23.4
■ **ED WARNER**	Warner, Edward Emory b: 6/20/1889, Fitchburg, Mass. d: 2/5/54, New York, N.Y. BR/TL, 5'10.5", 165 lbs. Deb: 7/02/12																											
1912 Pit-N	1	1	.500	11	3	1	1	0	45	40	8.0	0	18	3.6	13	2.6	3.60	90	.238	.323	-1	-2	95	69	-0.1	-1	1	-0.1
■ **JACK WARNER**	Warner, Jack Dyer b: 7/12/40, Brandywine, W.Va. BR/TR, 5'11", 190 lbs. Deb: 4/10/62																											
1962 Chi-N	0	0	—	7	0	0	0	0	7	9	11.6	3	0	0.0	3	3.9	7.71	55	.321	.310	-3	-3	109	92	0.0	0	0	-0.1
1963 Chi-N	0	1	.000	8	0	0	0	0	23	21	8.2	1	8	3.1	7	2.7	2.74	126	.256	.319	1	2	105	123	-0.4	0	-0	0.2
1964 Chi-N	0	0	—	7	0	0	0	0	9	12	12.0	0	4	4.0	6	6.0	3.00	125	.333	.390	1	1	106	180	0.0	0	0	0.1
1965 Chi-N	0	1	.000	11	0	0	0	0	16	22	12.4	1	9	5.1	7	3.9	8.44	43	.355	.419	-9	-9	103	80	-0.4	-0	0	-0.8
Total 4	0	2	.000	33	0	0	0	0	55	64	10.5	5	21	3.4	23	3.8	5.07	72	.308	.362	-10	-9	105	116	-0.8	0	1	-0.6
■ **MIKE WARREN**	Warren, Michael Bruce b: 3/26/61, Inglewood, Cal. BR/TR, 6'1", 175 lbs. Deb: 6/12/83																											
1983 Oak-A	5	3	.625	12	9	3	1	0	66	51	7.0	4	18	2.5	30	4.1	4.09	96	.215	.267	-0	-1	96	58	1.3	0	-1	-0.1
1984 Oak-A	3	6	.333	24	12	0	0	0	90	104	10.4	11	44	4.4	61	6.1	4.90	75	.291	.367	-9	-12	92	108	-1.3	0	-2	-1.3
1985 Oak-A	1	4	.200	16	6	0	0	0	49	52	9.6	13	38	7.0	48	8.8	6.61	58	.261	.387	-13	-15	93	99	-1.4	0	-1	-1.4
Total 3	9	13	.409	52	27	3	1	0	205	207	9.1	28	100	4.4	139	6.1	5.05	75	.261	.344	-23	-28	94	90	-1.4	0	-4	-2.8
■ **TOMMY WARREN**	Warren, Thomas Gentry b: 7/5/17, Tulsa, Okla. d: 1/2/68, Tulsa, Okla. BB/TL, 6'1", 190 lbs. Deb: 4/18/44																											
1944 Bro-N	1	4	.200	22	4	2	0	0	69	74	9.7	4	40	5.2	18	2.3	4.96	74	.270	.354	-10	-10	102	90	-1.2	1	0	-0.7
■ **DAN WARTHEN**	Warthen, Daniel Dean b: 12/1/52, Omaha, Neb. BB/TL, 6', 200 lbs. Deb: 5/18/75																											
1975 Mon-N	8	6	.571	40	18	2	0	3	168	130	7.0	8	87	4.7	128	6.9	3.11	128	.217	.311	10	16	109	91	1.5	-3	1	1.5
1976 Mon-N	2	10	.167	23	16	2	1	0	90	76	7.6	8	66	6.6	67	6.7	5.30	68	.232	.356	-18	-17	103	79	-3.1	-3	0	-1.9
1977 Mon-N	2	3	.400	12	6	1	0	0	35	33	8.5	7	38	9.8	26	6.7	7.97	49	.262	.413	-16	-16	99	85	-0.2	-0	1	-1.4
Phi-N	0	1	.000	3	0	0	0	0	4	4	9.0	0	5	11.3	1	2.3	0.00	—	.267	.429	2	2	98	0	-0.4	0	0	0.2
Yr	2	4	.333	15	6	1	0	0	39	37	8.5	7	43	9.9	27	6.2	7.15	54	.261	.415	-14	-14	99	0	-0.6	-0	1	-1.2
1978 Hou-N	0	1	.000	5	1	0	0	0	11	10	8.2	3	2	1.6	2	1.6	4.09	83	.250	.279	-1	-1	95	110	-0.4	-0	-0	0.0
Total 4	12	21	.364	83	41	5	1	3	308	253	7.4	26	198	5.8	224	6.5	4.30	89	.228	.339	-23	-16	106	87	-2.6	-6	1	-1.6
■ **GEORGE WASHBURN**	Washburn, George Edward b: 10/6/14, Solon, Me. d: 1/5/79, Baton Rouge, La. BL/TR, 6'1", 175 lbs. Deb: 5/04/41																											
1941 NY-A	0	1	.000	1	1	0	0	0	2	2	9.0	0	5	22.5	1	4.5	13.50	29	.286	.583	-2	-2	95	75	-0.4	-0	0	-0.1
■ **GREG WASHBURN**	Washburn, Gregory James b: 12/3/46, Coal City, Ill. BR/TR, 6', 190 lbs. Deb: 6/07/69																											
1969 Cal-A	0	2	.000	8	2	0	0	0	11	21	17.2	0	5	4.1	4	3.3	8.18	45	.404	.450	-6	-6	101	98	-0.9	0	0	-0.4
■ **LIBE WASHBURN**	Washburn, Libeus b: 6/16/1874, Lyme, N.H. d: 3/22/40, Malone, N.Y. BB/TL, 5'10", 180 lbs. Deb: 5/30/02																											
1903 Phi-N	0	4	.000	4	4	4	0	0	35	44	11.3	0	11	2.8	9	2.3	4.37	71	.333	.384	-4	-5	94	96	-1.9	-0	-1	-0.4
■ **RAY WASHBURN**	Washburn, Ray Clark b: 5/31/38, Pasco, Wash. BR/TR, 6'1", 205 lbs. Deb: 9/20/61																											
1961 StL-N	1	1	.500	3	2	1	0	0	20	10	4.5	1	7	3.1	12	5.4	1.80	252	.152	.240	5	6	113	67	0.0	-1	0	0.6
1962 StL-N	12	9	.571	34	25	2	1	0	176	187	9.6	25	58	3.0	109	5.6	4.09	103	.273	327	-3	2	107	109	1.3	1	1	0.5
1963 StL-N	5	3	.625	11	11	4	2	0	64	50	7.0	5	14	2.0	47	6.6	3.09	112	.212	.258	1	3	106	69	0.5	-1	1	0.3
1964 StL-N	3	4	.429	15	10	0	0	2	60	60	9.0	7	17	2.6	28	4.2	4.05	97	.264	.322	-3	-1	111	104	-0.8	-0	1	0.0
1965 StL-N	9	11	.450	28	16	1	1	2	119	114	8.6	15	28	2.1	67	5.1	3.63	103	.254	.292	-1	2	106	101	-1.0	0	-1	0.2
1966 StL-N	11	9	.550	27	26	4	1	0	170	183	9.7	15	44	2.3	98	5.2	3.76	96	.280	.320	-3	-3	100	107	0.9	-2	1	-0.3
1967 StL-N	10	7	.588	27	27	3	1	0	186	190	9.2	14	42	2.0	98	4.7	3.53	95	.265	.304	-3	-4	99	99	-0.5	-2	2	-0.3
1968 StL-N	14	8	.636	31	30	8	4	0	215	191	8.0	9	47	2.0	124	5.2	2.26	123	.239	.278	17	12	93	111	1.2	0	-2	1.2
1969 StL-N	3	8	.273	28	16	2	0	1	132	133	9.1	9	49	3.3	80	5.5	3.07	116	.261	.322	8	7	99	120	-2.7	-2	1	0.6
1970 Cin-N	4	4	.500	35	3	0	0	0	66	90	12.3	7	48	6.5	37	5.0	6.95	60	.324	.417	-21	-20	103	98	-0.8	-1	1	-1.9
Total 10	72	64	.529	239	166	25	10	5	1208	1208	9.0	107	354	2.6	700	5.2	3.54	101	.261	.311	-3	3	101	104	-1.9	-7	5	0.9
■ **BUCK WASHER**	Washer, William b: 10/11/1882, Akron, Ohio d: 12/8/55, Akron, Ohio TR , 5'10", 175 lbs. Deb: 4/25/05																											
1905 Phi-N	0	0	—	1	0	0	0	0	3	4	12.0	0	5	15.0	0	0.0	6.00	51	.349	.547	-1	-1	102	142	0.0	-0	0	0.0
■ **GARY WASLEWSKI**	Waslewski, Gary Lee b: 7/21/41, Meriden, Conn. BR/TR, 6'4", 190 lbs. Deb: 6/11/67																											
1967 Bos-A	2	2	.500	12	8	0	0	0	42	34	7.3	3	20	4.3	20	4.3	3.21	113	.225	.311	0	2	113	103	-0.1	-1	0	0.2
1968 Bos-A	4	7	.364	34	11	2	0	2	105	108	9.3	9	40	3.4	59	5.1	3.69	81	.269	.338	-8	-8	101	114	-1.7	-2	2	-0.8
1969 StL-N	0	2	.000	12	0	0	0	1	21	19	8.1	3	8	3.4	16	6.9	3.86	92	.244	.315	-1	-1	99	104	-0.9	-0	1	0.0
Mon-N	3	7	.300	30	14	3	1	1	109	102	8.4	5	63	5.2	63	5.2	3.30	112	.252	.357	4	5	103	124	-0.2	-2	0	0.3
Yr	3	9	.250	42	14	3	1	2	130	121	8.4	8	71	4.9	79	5.5	3.39	109	.250	.348	3	4	102	124	-1.1	-0	1	0.3
1970 Mon-N	0	2	.000	6	4	0	0	0	25	23	8.3	3	15	5.4	19	6.8	5.04	82	.247	.349	-3	-3	102	89	-0.9	-0	1	-0.1
NY-A	2	2	.500	26	5	0	0	0	55	42	6.9	4	27	4.4	27	4.4	3.11	109	.219	.319	4	2	91	106	-0.2	-0	1	0.2
1971 NY-A	0	1	.000	24	0	0	0	1	36	28	7.0	2	16	4.0	17	4.3	3.25	103	.214	.298	1	0	97	81	-0.4	-0	0	0.0
1972 Oak-A	0	3	.000	8	0	0	0	0	18	12	6.0	3	8	4.0	8	4.0	2.00	145	.190	.282	2	2	95	147	-1.4	-0	0	0.2
Total 6	11	26	.297	152	42	5	1	5	411	368	8.1	32	197	4.3	229	5.0	3.44	100	.243	.332	-1	-0	101	111	-5.8	-6	4	0.0

YEAR	TM/L	W	L	PCT	G	GS	CG	SHO	SV	IP	H	H/G	HR	BB	BB/G	SO	SO/G	ERA	/A	OAVG	OOBP	PR	/A	PF	CPI	WAT	PB	PD	TPI
■ **STEVE WATERBURY**	Waterbury, Steven Craig b: 4/6/52, Carbondale, Ill. BR/TR, 6'5", 190 lbs. Deb: 9/14/76																												
1976	StL-N	0	0	—	5	0	0	0	0	6	7	10.5	0	3	4.5	4	6.0	6.00	61	.304	.385	-2	-2	105	78	0.0	0	0	-0.1
■ **FRED WATERS**	Waters, Fred Warren b: 2/2/27, Benton, Miss. BL/TL, 5'11", 185 lbs. Deb: 9/20/55																												
1955	Pit-N	0	0	—	2	0	0	0	0	5	7	12.6	1	2	3.6	0	0.0	3.60	113	.318	.375	0	0	101	174	0.0	-0	0	0.0
1956	Pit-N	2	2	.500	23	5	1	0	0	51	48	8.5	3	30	5.3	14	2.5	2.82	138	.258	.353	5	6	103	147	0.3	-1	-1	0.3
Total	2	2	2	.500	25	5	1	0	0	56	55	8.8	4	32	5.1	14	2.3	2.89	135	.264	.355	6	6	103	149	0.3	-2	-1	0.3
■ **BOB WATKINS**	Watkins, Robert Cecil b: 3/12/48, San Francisco, Cal. BR/TR, 6'1", 170 lbs. Deb: 9/06/69																												
1969	Hou-N	0	0	—	5	0	0	0	0	16	13	7.3	1	13	7.3	11	6.2	5.06	72	.241	.382	-3	-3	101	90	0.0	-0	-0	-0.2
■ **DOC WATSON**	Watson, Charles John b: 1/30/1885, Kensington, Ohio d: 12/30/49, San Diego, Cal. BR/TL, 6', 170 lbs. Deb: 9/03/13																												
1913	Chi-N	1	0	1.000	1	1	1	0	0	9	8	8.0	0	6	6.0	1	1.0	1.00	310	.242	.375	2	2	97	369	0.5	0	-0	0.2
1914	Chi-F	9	8	.529	26	18	10	3	1	172	145	7.6	2	49	2.6	69	3.6	2.04	140	.256	.315	22	16	89	113	-0.5	-3	0	1.2
	StL-F	3	4	.429	9	7	4	2	0	56	41	6.6	1	24	3.9	18	2.9	1.93	180	.230	.321	8	10	108	114	0.1	-1	0	1.0
	Yr	12	12	.500	35	25	14	5	1	228	186	7.3	3	73	2.9	87	3.4	2.01	149	.249	.316	30	25	94	114	-0.4	-3	0	2.2
1915	StL-F	9	9	.500	33	20	6	0	0	136	132	8.7	1	58	3.8	45	3.0	3.97	78	.273	.355	-14	-13	102	95	-1.1	-3	-2	-1.8
Total	3	22	21	.512	69	46	21	5	1	373	326	7.9	4	137	3.3	133	3.2	2.70	113	.258	.333	18	14	97	113	-1.0	-7	-3	0.6
■ **MULE WATSON**	Watson, John Reeves b: 10/15/1896, Homer, La. d: 8/25/49, Shreveport, La. BR/TR, 6'1.5", 185 lbs. Deb: 7/04/18																												
1918	Phi-A	7	10	.412	21	19	11	3	0	142	139	8.8	0	44	2.8	30	1.9	3.36	89	.288	.341	-9	-6	108	103	0.1	-3	-2	-1.1
1919	Phi-A	0	1	.000	4	2	0	0	0	14	17	10.9	2	7	4.5	6	3.9	7.07	51	.309	.387	-6	-5	112	79	-0.4	-1	1	-0.4
1920	Bos-N	0	0	—	1	0	0	0	0	3	0	0.0	0	0	0.0	0	0.0	0.00	—	.000	.000	1	1	99	0	0.0	-0	0	0.1
	Pit-N	0	0	—	5	0	0	0	0	11	15	12.3	2	7	5.7	1	0.8	9.00	35	.326	.400	-7	-7	101	75	0.0	-0	0	-0.6
	Bos-N	5	4	.556	12	10	4	2	0	72	79	9.9	0	17	2.1	16	2.0	3.75	83	.298	.328	-5	-5	99	93	1.2	-1	0	-0.6
	Yr	5	4	.556	18	10	4	2	0	86	94	9.8	2	24	2.5	17	1.8	4.29	73	.294	.331	-11	-11	100	93	1.2	-1	0	-1.1
1921	Bos-N	14	13	.519	44	31	15	1	2	259	269	9.3	11	57	2.0	48	1.7	3.86	91	.270	.304	-2	-10	92	81	0.1	-4	-0	-1.4
1922	Bos-N	8	14	.364	41	29	8	1	1	201	262	11.7	9	59	2.6	53	2.4	4.70	85	.317	.357	-13	-16	98	100	0.3	-0	-0	-1.4
1923	Bos-N	1	2	.333	11	4	1	0	1	31	42	12.2	2	20	5.8	10	2.9	5.23	78	.339	.413	-4	-4	102	124	0.0	-0	0	-0.3
	NY-N	8	5	.615	17	15	8	0	0	108	117	9.8	11	21	1.8	26	2.2	3.42	115	.280	.311	7	6	99	113	0.0	-1	-1	0.4
	Yr	9	7	.563	28	19	9	0	1	139	159	10.3	13	41	2.7	36	2.3	3.82	104	.293	.337	3	2	99	113	0.0	-0	-1	0.1
1924	NY-N	7	4	.636	22	16	6	1	0	100	122	11.0	7	24	2.2	18	1.6	3.78	90	.303	.339	1	-4	88	117	0.4	4	-1	-0.1
Total	7	50	53	.485	178	126	53	8	4	941	1062	10.2	44	256	2.4	208	2.0	4.04	89	.293	.333	-38	-48	97	98	1.7	-8	-3	-5.4
■ **MILT WATSON**	Watson, Milton Wilson "Mule" b: 1/10/1890, Flovilla, Ga. d: 4/10/62, Pine Bluff, Ark. BR/TR, 6'1", 180 lbs. Deb: 7/26/16																												
1916	StL-N	4	6	.400	18	13	5	2	0	103	109	9.5	3	33	2.9	27	2.4	3.06	86	.283	.335	-5	-5	100	123	0.1	0	-1	-0.5
1917	StL-N	10	13	.435	41	20	5	3	0	161	149	8.3	3	51	2.9	45	2.5	3.52	79	.252	.313	-14	-13	102	85	-2.4	-4	1	-1.6
1918	Phi-N	5	7	.417	23	11	6	0	0	113	126	10.0	1	36	2.9	29	2.3	3.42	90	.293	.335	-8	-4	111	111	-0.4	-4	-1	-0.9
1919	Phi-N	2	4	.333	8	4	3	0	0	47	51	9.8	3	19	3.6	12	2.3	5.17	61	.282	.343	-12	-11	109	83	0.0	-2	0	-1.1
Total	4	21	30	.412	90	48	19	5	0	424	435	9.2	10	139	3.0	113	2.4	3.57	80	.274	.328	-40	-33	105	101	-2.7	-10	-0	-4.1
■ **MOTHER WATSON**	Watson, Walter L. b: 1/27/1865, Middleport, Ohio d: 11/23/1898, Middleport, Ohio 5'9", 145 lbs. Deb: 5/19/1887																												
1887	Cin-a	0	1	.000	2	2	1	0	0	14	22	14.1	0	6	3.9	1	0.6	5.79	79	.372	.430	-2	-2	106	112	-0.4	-1	0	-0.1
■ **EDDIE WATT**	Watt, Edward Dean b: 4/4/42, Lamoni, Iowa BR/TR, 5'10", 183 lbs. Deb: 4/12/66																												
1966	Bal-A	9	7	.563	43	13	1	0	4	146	123	7.6	11	44	2.7	102	6.3	3.82	89	.230	.289	-6	-7	99	78	-0.5	6	-2	-0.3
1967	Bal-A	3	5	.375	49	0	0	0	8	104	67	5.8	5	37	3.2	93	8.0	2.25	134	.183	.259	11	9	94	79	-0.8	2	0	1.2
1968	Bal-A	5	5	.500	59	0	0	0	11	83	63	6.8	1	35	3.8	72	7.8	2.28	132	.209	.289	6	7	101	96	-0.5	-1	0	0.7
1969	Bal-A	5	2	.714	56	0	0	0	16	71	49	6.2	3	26	3.3	46	5.8	1.65	221	.194	.266	16	16	100	115	0.5	-0	0	1.6
1970	Bal-A	7	7	.500	53	0	0	0	12	55	44	7.2	3	29	4.7	33	5.4	3.27	107	.239	.342	3	1	94	119	-1.8	-0	0	0.1
1971	Bal-A	3	1	.750	35	0	0	0	11	40	39	8.8	1	8	1.8	26	5.8	1.80	193	.260	.290	7	7	100	154	0.6	-0	-0	0.7
1972	Bal-A	2	3	.400	38	0	0	0	7	46	30	5.9	2	20	3.9	23	4.5	2.15	137	.191	.278	5	4	96	100	-0.5	-0	0	0.4
1973	Bal-A	3	4	.429	30	0	0	0	5	71	62	7.9	8	21	2.7	38	4.8	3.30	122	.235	.293	4	6	105	96	-0.9	0	-1	0.5
1974	Phi-N	1	1	.500	42	0	0	0	6	38	39	9.2	3	26	6.2	23	5.4	4.03	93	.275	.379	-2	-1	104	127	0.0	-0	0	0.0
1975	Chi-N	0	1	.000	6	0	0	0	0	6	14	21.0	0	8	12.0	6	9.0	13.50	28	.452	.561	-7	-6	105	94	-0.4	0	0	-0.5
Total	10	38	36	.514	411	13	1	0	80	660	530	7.2	37	254	3.5	462	6.3	2.90	116	.222	.296	38	35	99	99	-4.3	6	-3	4.4
■ **FRANK WATT**	Watt, Frank Marion "Kilo" b: 12/15/02, Washington, D.C. d: 8/31/56, Washington, D.C. BR/TR, 6'1", 205 lbs. Deb: 4/14/31																												
1931	Phi-N	5	5	.500	38	12	5	0	2	123	147	10.8	5	49	3.6	25	1.8	4.83	87	.296	.357	-13	-9	109	95	0.7	0	-2	-0.9
■ **JIM WAUGH**	Waugh, James Elden b: 11/25/33, Lancaster, Ohio BR/TR, 6'3", 185 lbs. Deb: 4/19/52																												
1952	Pit-N	1	6	.143	17	7	1	0	0	52	61	10.6	4	32	5.5	18	3.1	6.40	61	.285	.377	-15	-14	105	81	-1.6	-0	0	-1.3
1953	Pit-N	4	5	.444	29	11	1	0	0	90	108	10.8	21	56	5.6	23	2.3	6.50	70	.295	.386	-22	-19	106	102	0.8	0	-1	-1.8
Total	2	5	11	.313	46	18	2	0	0	142	169	10.7	25	88	5.6	41	2.6	6.46	67	.291	.383	-38	-34	106	94	-0.8	0	-1	-3.1
■ **FRANK WAYENBERG**	Wayenberg, Frank b: 8/27/1898, Franklin, Kan. d: 4/16/75, Zanesville, Ohio BR/TR, 6'0.5", 172 lbs. Deb: 8/25/24																												
1924	Cle-A	0	0	—	2	1	0	0	0	7	7	9.0	0	5	6.4	3	3.9	5.14	80	.259	.382	-1	-1	97	84	0.0	0	0	0.0
■ **HAL WEAFER**	Weafer, Kenneth Albert "Al" b: 2/6/14, Woburn, Mass. BR/TR, 6'0.5", 183 lbs. Deb: 5/29/36																												
1936	Bos-N	0	0	—	1	0	0	0	0	3	6	18.0	1	3	9.0	0	0.0	12.00	32	.375	.474	-3	-3	96	94	0.0	-0	-0	-0.2
■ **FLOYD WEAVER**	Weaver, David Floyd b: 5/12/41, Ben Franklin, Tex. BR/TR, 6'4", 195 lbs. Deb: 9/30/62																												
1962	Cle-A	1	0	1.000	1	1	0	0	0	5	3	5.4	1	0	0.0	8	14.4	1.80	217	.167	.167	1	1	99	74	0.5	0	0	0.2
1965	Cle-A	2	2	.500	32	1	0	0	1	61	61	9.0	10	24	3.5	37	5.5	5.46	62	.265	.336	-14	-14	97	89	0.0	0	0	-1.4
1970	Chi-A	1	2	.333	31	3	0	0	0	62	52	7.5	7	31	4.5	51	7.4	4.35	92	.233	.324	-4	-2	108	87	0.0	-1	-1	-0.3
1971	Mil-A	0	1	.000	21	0	0	0	0	27	33	11.0	3	18	6.0	12	4.0	7.33	49	.320	.406	-12	-11	104	88	-0.4	0	0	-1.0
Total	4	4	5	.444	85	5	0	0	1	155	149	8.7	21	73	4.2	108	6.3	5.23	70	.260	.340	-28	-27	103	87	0.1	-0	-1	-2.5
■ **HARRY WEAVER**	Weaver, Harry Abraham b: 2/26/1892, Clarendon, Pa. d: 5/30/83, Rochester, N.Y. BR/TR, 5'11", 160 lbs. Deb: 9/18/15																												
1915	Phi-A	0	2	.000	2	2	2	0	0	18	18	9.0	1	10	5.0	1	0.5	3.00	101	.290	.397	-0	0	103	163	-0.9	-0	1	0.1
1916	Phi-A	0	0	—	3	0	0	0	0	8	14	15.8	0	5	5.6	2	2.3	10.13	29	.424	.500	-6	-6	105	82	0.0	0	0	-0.5
1917	Chi-N	1	1	.500	4	2	1	0	0	20	17	7.6	0	7	3.1	8	3.6	2.70	105	.230	.293	0	0	105	82	0.0	-0	1	0.1
1918	Chi-N	2	2	.500	8	3	1	1	1	33	27	7.4	1	7	1.9	9	2.5	2.18	124	.227	.262	2	2	98	90	-0.4	0	1	0.3
1919	Chi-N	0	1	.000	2	1	0	0	0	3	6	18.0	0	2	6.0	1	3.0	12.00	24	.375	.474	-3	-3	99	72	-0.4	-0	-0	-0.2
Total	5	3	6	.333	19	8	4	1	1	82	82	9.0	2	31	3.4	21	2.3	3.62	79	.270	.336	-7	-7	102	103	-1.7	0	3	-0.2
■ **JIM WEAVER**	Weaver, James Brian "Fluff" b: 2/19/39, Lancaster, Pa. BL/TL, 6', 178 lbs. Deb: 8/13/67																												
1967	Cal-A	3	0	1.000	13	2	0	0	1	30	26	7.8	2	9	2.7	20	6.0	2.70	115	.232	.293	2	1	96	108	1.5	-1	2	0.3
1968	Cal-A	0	1	.000	14	0	0	0	0	23	22	8.6	4	10	3.9	8	3.1	2.35	122	.259	.330	2	1	96	198	-0.4	-0	-1	0.1
Total	2	3	1	.750	27	2	0	0	1	53	48	8.2	6	19	3.2	28	4.8	2.55	118	.244	.309	3	3	96	147	1.1	-1	1	0.4
■ **JIM WEAVER**	Weaver, James Dement "Big Jim" b: 11/25/03, Obion County, Ky. d: 12/12/83, Lakeland, Fla. BR/TR, 6'6", 230 lbs. Deb: 8/27/28																												
1928	Was-A	0	0	—	3	0	0	0	0	6	2	3.0	0	6	9.0	2	3.0	1.50	273	.143	.391	2	2	101	269	0.0	-0	0	0.2
1931	NY-A	2	1	.667	17	5	2	0	0	58	66	10.2	1	29	4.5	28	4.3	5.28	78	.280	.358	-6	-8	94	84	0.2	-2	0	-0.8
1934	StL-A	2	0	1.000	5	5	2	0	0	20	17	7.6	3	20	9.0	11	4.9	6.30	76	.236	.394	-4	-3	106	91	1.0	-0	1	-0.2
	Chi-N	11	9	.550	27	20	8	1	0	159	163	9.2	5	54	3.1	98	5.5	3.91	100	.263	.321	3	0	97	90	-0.3	-5	-1	-0.4
1935	Pit-N	14	8	.636	33	22	11	**4**	0	176	177	9.1	9	58	3.0	87	4.4	3.43	124	.254	.310	12	16	105	98	2.1	-4	1	1.3
1936	Pit-N	14	8	.636	38	31	11	1	0	226	239	9.5	12	74	2.9	108	4.3	4.30	90	.272	.323	-7	-11	96	89	2.5	-5	-2	-1.6
1937	Pit-N	8	5	.615	32	9	2	1	0	110	106	8.7	2	31	2.5	44	3.6	3.19	124	.255	.300	9	9	101	95	0.9	-0	-2	0.7
1938	StL-A	0	1	.000	1	1	0	0	0	7	9	11.6	0	9	11.6	4	5.1	9.00	55	.321	.462	-3	-3	103	85	-0.4	-0	0	-0.2
	Cin-N	6	4	.600	30	15	2	0	3	129	109	7.6	6	54	3.8	64	4.5	3.14	116	.227	.297	9	7	96	91	0.6	0	-1	0.7
1939	Cin-N	0	0	—	3	0	0	0	0	3	3	9.0	0	1	3.0	3	9.0	3.00	130	.250	.308	0	0	100	89	0.0	-0	0	0.0

YEAR	TM/L	W	L	PCT	G	GS	CG	SHO	SV	IP	H	H/G	HR	BB	BB/G	SO	SO/G	ERA	/A	OAVG	OOBP	PR	/A	PF	CPI	WAT	PB	PD	TPI
Total	8	57	36	.613	189	108	38	7	3	894	891	9.0	38	336	3.4	449	4.5	3.88	102	.258	.320	14	10	99	93	6.6	-17	-3	-0.3
■ MONTE WEAVER	Weaver, Montgomery Morton "Prof" b: 6/15/06, Hilton, N.C. BL/TR, 6', 170 lbs. Deb: 9/20/31																												
1931	Was-A	1	0	1.000	3	1	1	0	0	10	11	9.9	0	6	5.4	6	5.4	4.50	96	.268	.354	-0	-0	98	93	0.5	-0	0	0.0
1932	Was-A	22	10	.688	43	30	13	1	2	234	236	9.1	9	112	4.3	83	3.2	4.08	107	.261	.339	10	8	98	99	4.0	6	-2	1.0
1933	Was-A	10	5	.667	23	21	12	1	0	152	147	8.7	3	53	3.1	45	2.7	3.26	123	.257	.319	17	12	93	107	0.4	-3	-1	0.8
1934	Was-A	11	15	.423	31	31	11	0	0	205	255	11.2	16	63	2.8	51	2.2	4.79	96	.306	.347	-7	-4	102	106	-0.3	-2	-2	-0.7
1935	Was-A	1	1	.500	5	2	0	0	0	12	16	12.0	1	6	4.5	4	3.0	5.25	79	.320	.386	-1	-1	93	114	0.1	0	0	0.0
1936	Was-A	6	4	.600	26	5	3	0	1	91	92	9.1	3	38	3.8	15	1.5	4.35	111	.262	.327	7	5	96	89	0.7	1	-0	0.4
1937	Was-A	12	9	.571	30	26	9	0	0	189	197	9.4	21	70	3.3	44	2.1	4.19	105	.266	.329	9	5	96	101	2.1	1	1	0.5
1938	Was-A	7	6	.538	31	18	7	0	0	139	157	10.2	9	74	4.8	43	2.8	5.24	87	.282	.363	-7	-10	96	94	0.6	3	-1	-0.6
1939	Bos-A	1	0	1.000	9	1	1	0	1	20	26	11.7	0	13	5.8	6	2.7	6.75	73	.321	.404	-5	-4	107	89	0.5	-1	-1	-0.4
Total	9	71	50	.587	201	135	57	2	4	1052	1137	9.7	62	435	3.7	297	2.5	4.36	102	.276	.340	24	10	97	100	8.6	4	-5	1.0
■ ORLIE WEAVER	Weaver, Orville Forest b: 6/4/1886, Newport, Ky. d: 11/28/70, New Orleans, La. BR/TR, 6', 180 lbs. Deb: 9/14/10																												
1910	Chi-N	1	1	.500	7	2	2	0	0	32	34	9.6	2	15	4.2	22	6.2	3.66	80	.270	.352	-2	-3	96	108	-0.2	-1	-1	-0.3
1911	Chi-N	2	2	.500	6	4	1	1	0	44	29	5.9	0	17	3.5	20	4.1	2.05	156	.196	.296	7	6	94	93	-0.2	-1	-0	0.4
	Bos-N	3	12	.200	27	17	4	0	0	121	140	10.4	9	84	6.2	50	3.7	6.47	57	.303	.418	-41	-37	109	90	-2.4	-2	-2	-3.7
	Yr	5	14	.263	33	21	5	1	0	165	169	9.2	9	101	5.5	70	3.8	5.29	68	.275	.384	-35	-31	105	90	-2.6	-1	-3	-3.3
Total	2	6	15	.286	40	23	7	1	0	197	203	9.3	11	116	5.3	92	4.2	5.03	69	.276	.383	-37	-34	104	94	-2.8	-4	-4	-3.6
■ ROGER WEAVER	Weaver, Roger Edward b: 10/6/54, Amsterdam, N.Y. BR/TR, 6'3", 190 lbs. Deb: 6/06/80																												
1980	Det-A	3	4	.429	19	6	0	0	0	64	56	7.9	5	34	4.8	42	5.9	4.08	104	.247	.340	-0	1	105	97	-0.5	0	1	0.2
■ SAM WEAVER	Weaver, Samuel H. b: 7/10/1855, Philadelphia, Pa. d: 2/1/14, Philadelphia, Pa. BR/TR, 185 lbs. Deb: 10/25/1875																												
1875	Phi-n	1	0	1.000	1																								
1878	Mil-N	12	31	.279	45	43	39	1	0	383	371	8.7	2	21	**0.5**	95	2.2	1.95	134	.264	**.275**	15	**29**	114	86	2.7	-3	0	2.8
1882	Phi-a	26	15	.634	42	41	41	2	0	371	374	9.1	6	35	0.8	104	2.5	2.74	109	.267	.285	-2	10	111	94	7.1	1	0	1.3
1883	Lou-a	26	22	.542	48	48	47	4	0	419	468	10.1	3	38	0.8	116	2.5	3.72	83	.288	.304	-19	-29	94	91	0.6	-0	0	-2.6
1884	Phi-U	5	10	.333	17	17	14	0	0	136	206	13.6	3	11	0.7	40	2.6	5.76	50	.354	.366	-42	-44	95	93	0.3	-1	0	-3.5
1886	Phi-a	0	2	.000	2	2	1	0	0	11	30	24.5	0	2	1.6	2	1.6	14.73	24	.503	.519	-14	-14	103	79	-0.9	-1	0	-0.9
Total	5	69	80	.463	154	151	142	7	0	1320	1449	9.9	14	107	0.7	357	2.4	3.23	91	.286	.300	-62	-42	105	90	9.8	-4	1	-2.9
■ LEFTY WEBB	Webb, Cleon Earl b: 3/1/1885, Mt.Gilead, Ohio d: 1/12/58, Circleville, Ohio BB/TL, 5'11", 165 lbs. Deb: 5/23/10																												
1910	Pit-N	2	1	.667	7	3	2	0	0	27	29	9.7	0	9	3.0	6	2.0	5.67	59	.266	.333	-8	-7	110	54	0.4	-0	0	-0.6
■ HANK WEBB	Webb, Henry Gaylon Matthew b: 5/21/50, Copiague, N.Y. BR/TR, 6'3", 175 lbs. Deb: 9/05/72																												
1972	NY-N	0	0	—	6	2	0	0	0	18	18	9.0	1	9	4.5	15	7.5	4.50	74	.261	.342	-2	-2	96	87	0.0	-1	1	-0.2
1973	NY-N	0	0	—	2	0	0	0	0	2	2	9.0	1	2	9.0	1	4.5	9.00	41	.286	.444	-1	-1	100	105	0.0	0	0	0.0
1974	NY-N	0	2	.000	3	2	0	0	0	10	15	13.5	1	10	9.0	8	7.2	7.20	51	.341	.473	-4	-4	100	113	-0.9	-0	-0	-0.3
1975	NY-N	7	6	.538	29	15	3	1	0	115	102	8.0	12	62	4.9	38	3.0	4.07	85	.236	.329	-6	-8	95	91	0.5	2	-1	-0.7
1976	NY-N	0	1	.000	8	0	0	0	0	16	17	9.6	2	7	3.9	7	3.9	4.50	71	.274	.351	-2	-2	91	111	-0.4	0	0	-0.1
1977	LA-N	0	0	—	5	0	0	0	0	8	5	5.6	1	1	1.1	2	2.3	2.25	170	.192	.241	1	1	98	105	0.0	0	0	0.1
Total	6	7	9	.438	53	19	3	1	0	169	159	8.5	18	91	4.8	71	3.8	4.31	80	.248	.341	-13	-16	95	94	-0.8	1	-1	-1.2
■ RED WEBB	Webb, Samuel Henry b: 9/25/24, Washington, D.C. BL/TR, 6', 175 lbs. Deb: 9/15/48																												
1948	NY-N	2	1	.667	5	3	2	0	0	28	27	8.7	2	10	3.2	9	2.9	3.21	121	.248	.306	2	2	98	107	0.5	0	0	0.2
1949	NY-N	1	1	.500	20	0	0	0	0	45	41	8.2	3	21	4.2	9	1.8	4.00	102	.248	.326	0	0	101	94	0.0	2	2	0.4
Total	2	3	2	.600	25	3	2	0	0	73	68	8.4	5	31	3.8	18	2.2	3.70	108	.248	.318	3	2	100	99	0.5	2	2	0.6
■ BILL WEBB	Webb, William Frederick b: 12/12/13, Atlanta, Ga. BR/TR, 6'2", 180 lbs. Deb: 5/15/43																												
1943	Phi-N	0	0	—	1	0	0	0	0	1	1	9.0	1	1	9.0	0	0.0	9.00	36	.333	.500	-1	-1	96	160	0.0	0	0	0.0
■ LES WEBBER	Webber, Lester Elmer b: 5/6/15, Lakeport, Cal. d: 11/13/86, Santa Maria, Cal. BR/TR, 6'0.5", 185 lbs. Deb: 5/17/42																												
1942	Bro-N	3	2	.600	19	3	1	0	1	52	46	8.0	2	22	3.8	23	4.0	2.94	109	.230	.306	2	2	97	95	-0.2	-1	1	0.1
1943	Bro-N	2	2	.500	54	0	0	0	**10**	116	112	8.7	6	69	5.4	24	1.9	3.80	88	.264	.360	-6	-6	99	116	0.0	-1	2	-0.4
1944	Bro-N	7	8	.467	48	9	1	0	3	140	157	10.1	9	64	4.1	42	2.7	4.95	74	.282	.347	-21	-20	102	92	0.8	1	3	-1.5
1945	Bro-N	7	3	.700	17	7	5	0	0	75	69	8.3	3	25	3.0	30	3.6	3.60	100	.237	.298	2	-0	95	78	1.6	-1	-1	-0.1
1946	Bro-N	3	3	.500	11	4	0	0	0	43	34	7.1	5	15	3.1	16	3.3	2.30	148	.225	.287	5	5	100	134	-0.5	-1	-1	0.4
	Cle-A	1	1	.500	4	2	0	0	0	5	13	23.4	0	5	9.0	5	9.0	25.20	13	.464	.529	-12	-12	90	49	0.1	0	0	-0.9
1948	Cle-A	0	0	—	1	0	0	0	0	1	3	27.0	0	1	9.0	1	9.0	27.00	15	.750	.667	-3	-3	94	72	0.0	0	0	-0.1
Total	6	23	19	.548	154	25	7	0	14	432	434	9.0	25	201	4.2	141	2.9	4.19	83	.262	.337	-32	-34	99	100	1.8	-2	5	-2.5
■ CHARLIE WEBER	Weber, Charles P. "Count" b: 10/22/1868, Cincinnati, Ohio d: 6/13/14, Beaumont, Tex. Deb: 7/30/1898																												
1898	Was-N	0	1	.000	1	1	0	0	0	4	9	20.3	0	1	2.3	0	0.0	15.75	24	.469	.495	-5	-5	105	57	-0.4	-0	0	-0.3
■ MIKE WEGENER	Wegener, Michael Denis b: 10/8/46, Denver, Colo. BR/TR, 6'4", 215 lbs. Deb: 4/09/69																												
1969	Mon-N	5	14	.263	32	26	4	1	0	166	150	8.1	10	96	5.2	124	6.7	4.39	84	.243	.342	-15	-13	103	87	-1.8	2	1	-0.8
1970	Mon-N	3	6	.333	25	16	1	0	0	104	100	8.7	16	56	4.8	35	3.0	5.28	78	.252	.347	-14	-13	102	90	-1.1	-2	-1	-1.4
Total	2	8	20	.286	57	42	5	1	0	270	250	8.3	26	152	5.1	159	5.3	4.73	82	.247	.344	-29	-26	102	88	-2.9	0	1	-2.2
■ BILL WEGMAN	Wegman, William Edward b: 12/19/62, Cincinnati, Ohio BR/TR, 6'5", 200 lbs. Deb: 9/14/85																												
1985	Mil-A	2	0	1.000	3	3	0	0	0	18	17	8.5	3	3	1.5	6	3.0	3.50	125	.246	.274	1	2	106	101	1.0	0	-0	0.1
1986	Mil-A	5	12	.294	35	32	2	0	0	198	217	9.9	32	43	2.0	82	3.7	5.14	84	.279	.319	-21	-18	103	89	-3.4	0	-1	-1.8
1987	Mii-A	12	11	.522	34	33	7	0	0	225	229	9.2	31	53	2.1	102	4.1	4.24	108	.265	.308	6	8	102	97	-0.8	0	0	0.7
1988	Mil-A	13	13	.500	32	31	4	1	0	199	207	9.4	24	50	2.3	84	3.8	4.12	99	.265	.308	-3	-1	103	97	-1.0	0	-1	-0.1
Total	4	32	36	.471	104	99	13	1	0	640	670	9.4	90	149	2.1	274	3.9	4.46	97	.269	.311	-17	-9	103	95	-4.2	0	-2	-1.1
■ BIGGS WEHDE	Wehde, Wilbur b: 11/23/06, Holstein, Iowa d: 9/21/70, Sioux Falls, S.Dak. BR/TR, 5'10.5", 180 lbs. Deb: 9/15/30																												
1930	Chi-A	0	0	—	4	0	0	0	0	6	7	10.5	1	7	10.5	3	4.5	10.50	47	.304	.455	-4	-4	105	82	0.0	-0	1	-0.2
1931	Chi-A	1	0	1.000	8	0	0	0	0	16	19	10.7	0	10	5.6	3	1.7	6.75	62	.333	.443	-4	-5	96	98	0.5	-0	1	-0.3
Total	2	1	0	1.000	12	0	0	0	0	22	26	10.6	1	17	7.0	6	2.5	7.77	56	.325	.447	-8	-8	98	93	0.5	-1	1	-0.5
■ HERM WEHMEIER	Wehmeier, Herman Ralph b: 2/18/27, Cincinnati, Ohio d: 5/21/73, Dallas, Tex. BR/TR, 6'2", 185 lbs. Deb: 9/07/45																												
1945	Cin-N	0	1	.000	2	2	0	0	0	5	10	18.0	0	4	7.2	0	0.0	12.60	29	.435	.519	-5	-5	97	78	-0.4	-0	0	-0.3
1947	Cin-N	0	0	—	1	0	0	0	0	1	0	0.0	0	0	0.0	0	0.0	0.00	—	.000	.000	0	0	92	0	0.0	0	0	0.0
1948	Cin-N	11	8	.579	33	24	6	0	0	147	179	11.0	21	75	4.6	56	3.4	5.88	72	.299	.376	-31	-27	106	98	2.9	-4	-0	-2.9
1949	Cin-N	11	12	.478	33	29	11	1	0	213	202	8.5	20	117	4.9	80	3.4	4.69	85	.253	.348	-15	-17	98	93	1.7	3	-2	-1.5
1950	Cin-N	10	18	.357	41	32	12	0	4	230	255	10.0	27	135	5.3	121	4.7	5.67	77	.281	.372	-39	-33	106	93	-2.7	-3	-3	-3.5
1951	Cin-N	7	10	.412	39	22	10	2	2	185	167	8.1	15	89	4.3	93	4.5	3.70	110	.241	.327	5	7	103	99	-0.5	3	-2	1.0
1952	Cin-N	9	11	.450	33	26	6	1	0	190	197	9.3	23	103	4.9	83	3.9	5.16	72	.269	.361	-30	-30	100	96	0.0	2	-4	-3.0
1953	Cin-N	1	6	.143	28	10	2	0	0	82	100	11.0	20	47	5.2	32	3.5	7.13	60	.299	.378	-26	-26	100	93	-2.3	-0	-1	-2.4
1954	Cin-N	0	3	.000	12	3	0	0	2	34	36	9.5	6	21	5.6	13	3.4	6.62	64	.271	.369	-10	-9	104	81	-1.4	-1	1	-0.8
	Phi-N	10	8	.556	25	17	10	2	0	138	117	7.6	10	51	3.3	49	3.2	3.85	103	.231	.295	3	2	98	74	1.3	-2	-0	0.0
	Yr	10	11	.476	37	20	10	2	2	172	153	8.0	16	72	3.8	62	3.2	4.40	92	.238	.310	-6	-7	99	74	-0.1	-1	1	-0.8
1955	Phi-N	10	12	.455	31	29	10	1	0	194	176	8.2	21	67	3.1	85	3.9	4.41	93	.241	.302	-8	-6	102	77	-1.0	3	-1	-0.3
1956	Phi-N	0	2	.000	3	3	0	0	0	20	18	8.1	2	11	4.9	8	3.6	4.05	89	.240	.330	-1	-1	95	93	-0.9	-1	-1	-0.2
	StL-N	12	9	.571	34	19	7	2	1	171	150	7.9	16	71	3.7	68	3.6	3.68	102	.240	.310	2	1	99	92	1.8	4	-1	0.4
	Yr	12	11	.522	37	22	7	2	1	191	168	7.9	18	82	3.9	76	3.6	3.72	100	.240	.313	1	0	99	92	0.9	-1	-1	0.2
1957	StL-N	10	7	.588	36	18	5	0	0	165	165	9.0	25	54	2.9	91	5.0	4.31	89	.253	.309	-8	-8	99	91	0.5	0	0	-0.7
1958	StL-N	0	1	.000	3	3	0	0	0	6	13	19.5	2	2	3.0	4	6.0	13.50	32	.448	.484	-6	-6	108	86	-0.4	1	0	-0.4

YEAR TM/L	W	L	PCT	G	GS	CG	SHO	SV	IP	H	H/G	HR	BB	BB/G	SO	SO/G	ERA	/A	OAVG	OOBP	PR	/A	PF	CPI	WAT	PB	PD	TPI
Det-A	1	0	1.000	7	3	0	0	0	23	21	8.2	2	5	2.0	11	4.3	2.35	165	.241	.280	4	4	103	122	0.5	-1	0	0.4
Total 13	92	108	.460	361	240	79	9	9	1804	1806	9.0	210	852	4.3	794	4.0	4.79	84	.260	.339	-165	-154	101	91	-0.9	5	-14	-14.2

■ **DAVE WEHRMEISTER** Wehrmeister, David Thomas b: 11/9/52, Berwyn, Ill. BR/TR, 6'4", 195 lbs. Deb: 4/16/76

YEAR TM/L	W	L	PCT	G	GS	CG	SHO	SV	IP	H	H/G	HR	BB	BB/G	SO	SO/G	ERA	/A	OAVG	OOBP	PR	/A	PF	CPI	WAT	PB	PD	TPI
1976 SD-N	0	4	.000	7	4	0	0	0	19	27	12.8	0	11	5.2	10	4.7	7.58	41	.333	.404	-9	-9	90	76	-1.9	-1	0	-0.9
1977 SD-N	1	3	.250	30	6	0	0	0	70	81	10.4	8	44	5.7	32	4.1	6.04	58	.293	.389	-17	-20	89	94	-0.7	0	-0	-1.9
1978 SD-N	1	0	1.000	4	0	0	0	0	7	8	10.3	1	5	6.4	2	2.6	6.43	52	.276	.371	-2	-2	93	86	0.5	0	-0	-0.2
1981 NY-A	0	0	—	5	0	0	0	0	7	6	7.7	0	7	9.0	7	9.0	5.14	70	.240	.394	-1	-1	99	87	0.0	0	0	0.0
1984 Phi-N	0	0	—	7	0	0	0	0	15	18	10.8	1	7	4.2	13	7.8	7.20	51	.300	.366	-6	-6	101	72	0.0	-0	0	-0.5
1985 Chi-A	2	2	.500	23	0	0	0	2	39	35	8.1	4	10	2.3	32	7.4	3.46	120	.241	.302	3	3	100	100	0.0	0	-0	0.3
Total 6	4	9	.308	76	10	0	0	2	157	175	10.0	14	84	4.8	96	5.5	5.68	64	.284	.369	-32	-36	94	91	-2.1	-1	0	-3.2

■ **STUMP WEIDMAN** Weidman, George E. b: 2/17/1861, Rochester, N.Y. d: 3/2/05, New York, N.Y. BR/TR, Deb: 8/26/1880

YEAR TM/L	W	L	PCT	G	GS	CG	SHO	SV	IP	H	H/G	HR	BB	BB/G	SO	SO/G	ERA	/A	OAVG	OOBP	PR	/A	PF	CPI	WAT	PB	PD	TPI
1880 Buf-N	0	9	.000	17	13	9	0	0	114	141	11.1	1	9	0.7	25	2.0	3.39	67	.313	.326	-13	-14	96	103	-4.4	-5	0	-1.9
1881 Det-N	8	5	.615	13	13	13	1	0	115	108	8.5	1	12	0.9	26	2.0	**1.80**	**164**	.260	**.281**	12	15	106	109	1.8	0	0	1.5
1882 Det-N	25	20	.556	46	45	43	4	0	411	391	8.6	10	39	0.9	161	3.5	2.63	114	.258	.277	12	17	104	89	4.4	-6	1	1.1
1883 Det-N	20	24	.455	52	47	41	3	**2**	402	435	9.7	8	72	1.6	183	4.1	3.54	83	.284	.316	-18	-27	94	89	2.9	-6	1	-3.2
1884 Det-N	4	21	.160	26	26	24	0	0	213	257	10.9	9	57	2.4	96	4.1	3.72	80	.308	.352	-18	-18	99	111	-5.2	-4	0	-1.5
1885 Det-N	14	24	.368	38	38	37	3	0	330	343	9.4	7	63	1.7	149	4.1	3.14	89	.279	.314	-12	-13	99	100	-0.8	-4	-3	-1.8
1886 KC-N	12	36	.250	51	51	48	1	0	428	549	11.5	11	112	2.4	168	3.5	4.52	83	.325	.367	-58	-36	114	102	0.1	-11	4	-3.3
1887 Det-N	13	7	.650	21	21	20	0	0	183	221	10.9	9	60	3.0	56	2.8	5.36	74	.314	.368	-27	-29	97	87	0.4	-2	0	-2.4
NY-a	4	8	.333	12	12	11	1	0	97	122	11.3	3	25	2.3	37	3.4	4.64	85	.322	.363	-4	-7	92	101	0.0	-1	0	-0.7
NY-N	0	1	.000	1	1	1	0	0	8	10	11.3	0	2	2.3	4	4.5	1.13	380	.322	.363	3	3	106	382	-0.4	0	0	0.3
1888 NY-N	1	1	.500	2	2	2	0	0	18	17	8.5	2	8	4.0	5	2.5	3.50	72	.263	.344	-1	-2	89	114	-0.1	-0	0	-0.1
Total 9	101	156	.393	279	269	249	13	2	2319	2594	10.1	61	459	1.8	910	3.5	3.61	88	.293	.328	-123	-111	101	98	-1.3	-40	1	-12.0

■ **DICK WEIK** Weik, Richard Henry "Legs" b: 11/17/27, Waterloo, Iowa BR/TR, 6'3.5", 184 lbs. Deb: 9/08/48

YEAR TM/L	W	L	PCT	G	GS	CG	SHO	SV	IP	H	H/G	HR	BB	BB/G	SO	SO/G	ERA	/A	OAVG	OOBP	PR	/A	PF	CPI	WAT	PB	PD	TPI
1948 Was-A	1	2	.333	3	3	0	0	0	13	14	9.7	1	22	15.2	8	5.5	5.54	83	.311	.529	-2	-1	107	164	0.0	2	0	0.0
1949 Was-A	3	12	.200	27	14	2	3	1	95	78	7.4	5	103	9.8	58	5.5	5.40	75	.230	.404	-13	-14	96	90	-3.0	-1	1	-1.2
1950 Was-A	1	3	.250	14	5	1	0	0	44	38	7.8	2	47	9.6	26	5.3	4.30	108	.236	.401	1	2	101	115	-0.8	-1	-1	0.0
Cle-A	1	3	.250	11	2	0	0	0	26	18	6.2	1	26	9.0	16	5.5	3.81	115	.205	.381	2	2	95	111	-1.1	0	0	0.2
Yr	2	6	.250	25	7	1	0	0	70	56	7.2	3	73	9.4	42	5.4	4.11	110	.225	.394	4	3	99	111	-1.9	-1	-1	0.2
1953 Det-A	0	1	.000	12	1	0	0	0	19	32	15.2	3	23	10.9	6	2.8	14.21	29	.386	.505	-22	-21	102	73	-0.3	1	0	-2.5
1954 Det-A	0	1	.000	9	1	0	0	0	16	23	12.9	3	16	9.0	9	5.1	7.31	52	.348	.476	-6	-6	101	122	-0.4	-0	-0	-0.6
Total 5	6	22	.214	76	26	3	3	1	213	203	8.6	15	237	10.0	123	5.2	5.92	71	.260	.425	-39	-40	99	103	-5.6	1	0	-4.1

■ **ED WEILAND** Weiland, Edwin Nicholas b: 11/26/14, Evanston, Ill. d: 7/12/71, Chicago, Ill. BL/TR, 5'11", 180 lbs. Deb: 5/01/40

YEAR TM/L	W	L	PCT	G	GS	CG	SHO	SV	IP	H	H/G	HR	BB	BB/G	SO	SO/G	ERA	/A	OAVG	OOBP	PR	/A	PF	CPI	WAT	PB	PD	TPI
1940 Chi-A	0	0	—	5	0	0	0	0	14	15	9.6	5	7	4.5	3	1.9	9.00	50	.263	.338	-7	-7	103	71	0.0	-0	-0	-0.6
1942 Chi-A	0	0	—	5	0	0	0	0	10	18	16.2	0	3	2.7	4	3.6	7.20	51	.383	.412	-4	-4	100	96	0.0	-0	-0	-0.3
Total 2	0	0	—	10	0	0	0	0	24	33	12.4	5	10	3.8	7	2.6	8.25	50	.317	.371	-11	-11	102	81	0.0	-0	-1	-0.9

■ **BOB WEILAND** Weiland, Robert George "Lefty" b: 12/14/05, Chicago, Ill. d: 11/9/88, Chicago, Ill. BL/TL, 6'4", 215 lbs. Deb: 9/30/28

YEAR TM/L	W	L	PCT	G	GS	CG	SHO	SV	IP	H	H/G	HR	BB	BB/G	SO	SO/G	ERA	/A	OAVG	OOBP	PR	/A	PF	CPI	WAT	PB	PD	TPI
1928 Chi-A	1	0	1.000	1	1	1	1	0	9	7	7.0	0	5	5.0	9	9.0	0.00	—	.212	.333	4	4	100	0	0.5	0	0	0.5
1929 Chi-A	2	4	.333	15	9	1	0	1	62	62	9.0	3	43	6.2	25	3.6	5.81	71	.268	.380	-11	-11	98	82	-0.3	-1	-1	-1.1
1930 Chi-A	0	4	.000	14	3	0	0	0	33	38	10.4	1	21	5.7	15	4.1	6.55	75	.297	.391	-7	-6	105	85	-1.9	-1	-0	-0.6
1931 Chi-A	2	7	.222	15	8	3	0	0	75	75	9.0	3	46	5.5	38	4.6	5.16	81	.259	.356	-6	-8	96	87	-1.7	1	1	-0.5
1932 Bos-A	6	16	.273	43	27	7	0	1	196	231	10.6	11	97	4.5	63	2.9	4.50	102	.295	.371	-0	2	102	117	-0.2	-1	3	0.3
1933 Bos-A	8	14	.364	39	27	12	0	3	216	197	8.2	19	100	4.2	97	4.0	3.88	113	.244	.324	10	12	102	103	-1.7	-4	-2	0.6
1934 Bos-A	1	5	.167	11	7	2	0	0	56	63	10.1	4	27	4.3	29	4.7	5.46	87	.293	.356	-6	-5	105	94	-1.9	-1	0	-0.4
Cle-A	1	5	.167	16	7	2	0	0	70	71	9.1	5	30	3.9	42	5.4	4.11	109	.262	.331	3	3	100	99	-2.0	-0	-0	0.2
Yr	2	10	.167	27	14	4	0	0	126	134	9.6	9	57	4.1	71	5.1	4.71	97	.276	.342	-3	-2	102	99	-3.9	-1	-0	-0.2
1935 StL-A	0	2	.000	14	4	0	0	0	32	39	11.0	6	31	8.7	11	3.1	9.56	51	.298	.436	-18	-17	110	78	-0.9	-1	-1	-1.5
1937 StL-N	15	14	.517	41	34	21	2	0	264	283	9.6	14	94	3.2	105	3.6	3.55	110	.276	.333	11	10	100	115	-0.2	1	-2	0.9
1938 StL-N	16	11	.593	35	29	11	1	1	228	248	9.8	14	67	2.6	117	4.6	3.59	117	.272	.322	5	16	111	106	3.6	-4	-1	1.2
1939 StL-N	10	12	.455	32	23	6	3	1	146	146	9.0	4	50	3.1	63	3.9	3.58	112	.264	.323	6	7	103	98	-2.9	-4	-1	0.2
1940 StL-N	0	0	—	1	0	0	0	0	1	3	27.0	1	0	0.0	0	0.0	27.00	14	.600	.600	-3	-3	101	81	0.0	0	0	-0.1
Total 12	62	94	.397	277	179	66	7	7	1388	1463	9.5	85	611	4.0	614	4.0	4.24	101	.272	.343	-13	5	103	103	-9.6	-17	-3	-0.3

■ **CARL WEILMAN** Weilman, Carl Woolworth "Zeke" (born Carl Woolworth Weilenmann) b: 11/29/1889, Hamilton, Ohio d: 5/25/24, Hamilton, Ohio BL/TL, 6'5.5", 187 lbs. Deb: 8/24/12

YEAR TM/L	W	L	PCT	G	GS	CG	SHO	SV	IP	H	H/G	HR	BB	BB/G	SO	SO/G	ERA	/A	OAVG	OOBP	PR	/A	PF	CPI	WAT	PB	PD	TPI
1912 StL-A	2	4	.333	8	6	5	2	1	48	42	7.9	0	3	0.6	24	4.5	2.81	122	.227	.239	3	3	103	45	0.0	-1	0	0.4
1913 StL-A	10	20	.333	39	28	17	2	0	252	262	9.4	2	60	2.1	79	2.8	3.39	84	.281	.328	-13	-15	98	94	-1.8	-3	1	-1.4
1914 StL-A	18	13	.581	44	36	20	3	1	299	260	7.8	1	84	2.5	119	3.6	2.08	131	.237	.298	22	22	100	106	4.0	-1	1	2.5
1915 StL-A	18	19	.486	47	31	19	3	4	296	240	7.3	6	83	2.5	125	3.8	2.34	125	.229	.287	20	19	99	93	3.1	2	-1	2.1
1916 StL-A	17	18	.486	46	31	19	1	2	276	237	7.7	3	76	2.5	91	3.0	2.15	124	.242	.301	21	16	94	113	-1.1	-1	-3	1.3
1917 StL-A	1	2	.333	5	3	0	0	0	19	19	9.0	1	6	2.8	9	4.3	1.89	138	.268	.325	2	2	98	174	-0.1	-1	1	0.2
1919 StL-A	10	6	.625	20	20	12	3	0	148	133	8.1	3	45	2.7	44	2.7	2.07	152	.244	.305	19	18	98	**118**	2.4	0	-0	1.9
1920 StL-A	9	13	.409	30	24	13	1	2	183	201	9.9	6	61	3.0	45	2.2	4.48	94	.291	.351	-14	-5	111	88	-2.1	-3	1	-0.5
Total 8	85	95	.472	239	179	105	15	10	1521	1394	8.2	22	418	2.5	536	3.2	2.67	112	.251	.307	59	56	99	101	4.4	-7	1	6.5

■ **JAKE WEIMER** Weimer, Jacob "Tornado Jake" b: 11/29/1873, Ottumwa, Iowa d: 6/19/28, Chicago, Ill. BR/TL, 5'11", 175 lbs. Deb: 4/17/03

YEAR TM/L	W	L	PCT	G	GS	CG	SHO	SV	IP	H	H/G	HR	BB	BB/G	SO	SO/G	ERA	/A	OAVG	OOBP	PR	/A	PF	CPI	WAT	PB	PD	TPI
1903 Chi-N	20	8	.714	35	33	27	3	0	282	241	**7.7**	4	104	3.3	128	4.1	2.30	133	**.256**	.337	30	24	94	112	4.8	2	-1	2.2
1904 Chi-N	20	14	.588	37	37	31	5	0	307	229	6.7	1	97	2.8	177	5.2	1.91	141	.230	.303	28	27	99	98	-0.6	-2	2	3.2
1905 Chi-N	18	12	.600	33	30	26	2	1	250	212	7.6	1	80	2.9	107	3.9	2.27	132	.258	.333	20	20	100	113	0.0	2	-1	2.1
1906 Cin-N	20	14	.588	41	39	31	6	1	305	263	7.8	0	99	2.9	141	4.2	2.21	138	.262	.336	14	29	116	113	5.8	4	0	3.3
1907 Cin-N	11	14	.440	29	26	19	3	0	209	165	7.1	6	63	2.7	67	2.9	2.41	97	.251	.338	1	-2	95	100	0.2	3	2	0.0
1908 Cin-N	8	7	.533	15	15	9	2	0	117	110	8.5	2	50	3.8	36	2.8	2.38	102	.281	.371	-1	1	104	139	0.9	2	1	0.2
1909 NY-N	0	0	—	1	0	0	0	0	3	7	21.0	0	0	0.0	1	3.0	9.00	30	.467	.500	-2	-2	103	108	0.0	-0	0	-0.1
Total 7	97	69	.584	191	180	143	21	2	1473	1227	7.5	14	493	3.0	657	4.0	2.23	127	.254	.333	91	98	101	110	11.1	11	4	10.9

■ **LEFTY WEINERT** Weinert, Phillip Walter b: 4/21/02, Philadelphia, Pa. d: 4/17/73, Rockledge, Fla. BL/TL, 6'1", 195 lbs. Deb: 9/24/19

YEAR TM/L	W	L	PCT	G	GS	CG	SHO	SV	IP	H	H/G	HR	BB	BB/G	SO	SO/G	ERA	/A	OAVG	OOBP	PR	/A	PF	CPI	WAT	PB	PD	TPI
1919 Phi-N	0	0	—	1	0	0	0	0	4	11	24.8	0	2	4.5	0	0.0	18.00	18	.478	.520	-7	-7	109	65	0.0	1	0	-0.3
1920 Phi-N	1	1	.500	10	2	0	0	0	22	27	11.0	1	19	7.8	10	4.1	6.14	57	.333	.443	-7	-6	112	107	0.2	-1	0	-0.7
1921 Phi-N	1	0	1.000	8	0	0	0	0	12	8	6.0	1	5	3.8	2	1.5	1.50	270	.216	.304	3	3	107	216	0.5	0	-1	0.3
1922 Phi-N	8	11	.421	34	22	10	0	1	167	189	10.2	10	70	3.8	58	3.1	3.40	141	.289	.348	13	26	117	**130**	0.8	-0	-2	2.5
1923 Phi-N	4	17	.190	38	20	8	0	1	156	207	11.9	10	81	4.7	46	2.7	5.42	87	.327	.401	-25	-12	118	110	-4.6	3	-3	-1.0
1924 Phi-N	0	1	.000	8	1	0	0	0	15	10	6.0	0	11	6.6	7	4.2	2.40	178	.204	.328	2	3	111	124	-0.4	-1	0	0.3
1927 Chi-N	1	1	.500	5	3	1	0	0	20	21	9.4	2	6	2.7	5	2.3	4.50	86	.259	.300	-1	-1	99	78	0.0	0	-0	-0.1
1928 Chi-N	1	0	1.000	10	0	0	0	0	17	24	12.7	0	9	4.8	8	4.2	5.29	70	.393	.459	-2	-3	93	137	0.5	-0	-1	-0.3
1931 NY-A	2	2	.500	17	0	0	0	0	25	31	11.2	2	19	6.8	24	8.6	6.12	67	.316	.430	-5	-6	94	119	-0.3	-0	0	-0.4
Total 9	18	33	.353	131	49	19	0	2	438	528	10.8	26	222	4.6	160	3.3	4.58	99	.308	.380	-29	-3	113	120	-3.3	2	-6	0.3

■ **ROY WEIR** Weir, William Franklin "Bill" b: 2/25/11, Portland, Maine BL/TL, 5'8.5", 170 lbs. Deb: 6/25/36

YEAR TM/L	W	L	PCT	G	GS	CG	SHO	SV	IP	H	H/G	HR	BB	BB/G	SO	SO/G	ERA	/A	OAVG	OOBP	PR	/A	PF	CPI	WAT	PB	PD	TPI
1936 Bos-N	4	3	.571	12	7	3	2	0	57	53	8.4	0	24	3.8	29	4.6	2.84	136	.241	.314	7	6	96	99	0.7	2	1	0.9
1937 Bos-N	1	1	.500	10	4	1	0	0	33	27	7.4	0	19	5.2	8	2.2	3.82	92	.227	.329	0	-1	90	79	0.0	-1	1	-0.1
1938 Bos-N	1	0	1.000	5	0	0	0	0	13	14	9.7	4	6	4.2	3	2.1	6.92	49	.269	.339	-5	-5	89	87	0.5	0	0	-0.3
1939 Bos-N	0	0	—	2	0	0	0	0	3	1	3.0	0	1	3.0	2	6.0	0.00	—	.125	.200	1	1	93	0	0.0	-0	0	0.1
Total 4	6	4	.600	29	11	4	2	0	106	95	8.1	4	50	4.2	42	3.6	3.57	103	.238	.319	5	1	93	88	1.2	1	2	0.6

YEAR	TM/L	W	L	PCT	G	GS	CG	SHO	SV	IP	H	H/G	HR	BB	BB/G	SO	SO/G	ERA	/A	OAVG	OOBP	PR	/A	PF	CPI	WAT	PB	PD	TPI
■ **CURT WELCH**	Welch, Curtis Benton b: 2/11/1862, E.Liverpool, Ohio d: 8/29/1896, E.Liverpool, Ohio BR, 5'10", 175 lbs. Deb: 5/01/1884																												
1884	Tol-a	1	0	1.000	1	1	1	1	0	9	5	5.0	0	0	0.0	5	5.0	0.00	—	.170	.170	3	3	105	0	0.5	0	0	0.4
1890	Phi-a	0	0	—	1	0	0	0	0	1	6	54.0	0	0	0.0	1	9.0	54.00	7	.696	.696	-6	-6	101	50	0.0	0	0	-0.3
Total	2	1	0	1.000	2	1	1	1	0	10	11	9.9	0	0	0.0	6	5.4	5.40	64	.289	.289	-2	-2	105	5	0.5	0	0	0.1
■ **TED WELCH**	Welch, Floyd John b: 10/17/1892, Coyville, Kan. d: 1/6/43, Great Bend, Kan. BL/TR, 5'9.5", 160 lbs. Deb: 5/15/14																												
1914	StL-F	0	0	—	3	0	0	0	0	6	6	9.0	0	3	4.5	2	3.0	6.00	58	.289	.379	-2	-2	108	60	0.0	-0	0	-0.1
■ **JOHNNY WELCH**	Welch, John Vernon b: 12/2/06, Washington, D.C. d: 9/2/40, St.Louis, Mo. BL/TR, 6'3", 184 lbs. Deb: 5/22/26																												
1926	Chi-N	0	0	—	3	0	0	0	0	4	5	11.3	0	1	2.3	0	0.0	2.25	178	.357	.375	1	1	105	239	0.0	0	-0	0.1
1927	Chi-N	0	0	—	1	0	0	0	0	1	0	0.0	0	3	27.0	1	9.0	9.00	43	.000	.429	-1	-1	99	56	0.0	0	0	0.0
1928	Chi-N	0	0	—	3	0	0	0	0	4	13	29.3	0	0	0.0	2	4.5	15.75	23	.591	.565	-5	-5	93	93	0.0	0	0	-0.4
1931	Chi-N	2	1	.667	8	3	1	0	0	34	39	10.3	2	10	2.6	7	1.9	3.71	98	.291	.338	1	-0	94	117	0.4	2	0	0.2
1932	Bos-A	4	6	.400	20	8	3	1	0	72	93	11.6	3	38	4.8	26	3.3	5.25	87	.312	.391	-6	-5	102	110	0.9	1	0	-0.2
1933	Bos-A	4	9	.308	47	7	1	0	3	129	142	9.9	6	67	4.7	68	4.7	4.60	95	.283	.360	-5	-3	102	105	-1.8	-1	1	-0.2
1934	Bos-A	13	15	.464	41	22	8	1	0	206	223	9.7	14	76	3.3	91	4.0	4.50	105	.274	.336	-0	5	105	96	-1.1	-1	0	0.5
1935	Bos-A	10	9	.526	31	19	10	1	2	143	155	9.8	4	53	3.3	48	3.0	4.47	108	.273	.338	-0	6	108	87	0.4	-0	-0	0.6
1936	Bos-A	2	1	.667	9	3	1	0	0	33	43	11.7	4	8	2.2	9	2.5	5.45	98	.305	.338	-2	-0	106	96	0.5	1	0	0.0
	Pit-N	0	0	—	9	1	0	0	1	22	22	9.0	3	6	2.5	5	2.0	4.50	86	.265	.304	-1	-2	96	92	0.0	1	-1	0.0
Total	9	35	41	.461	172	63	24	3	6	648	735	10.2	36	262	3.6	257	3.6	4.67	98	.285	.349	-18	-6	104	99	-0.7	3	1	0.6
■ **MICKEY WELCH**	Welch, Michael Francis "Smiling Mickey" b: 7/4/1859, Brooklyn, N.Y. d: 7/30/41, Concord, N.H. BR/TR, 5'8", 160 lbs. Deb: 5/01/1880 H																												
1880	Tro-N	34	30	.531	65	64	64	4	0	574	575	9.0	7	80	1.3	123	1.9	2.54	104	.269	.296	-11	7	112	99	8.3	9	-5	1.4
1881	Tro-N	21	18	.538	40	40	40	3	0	368	371	9.1	7	78	1.9	104	2.5	2.67	105	.274	.313	5	6	101	101	4.5	-3	-6	-0.2
1882	Tro-N	14	16	.467	33	33	30	**5**	0	281	334	10.7	7	62	2.0	53	1.7	3.46	81	.303	.340	-18	-20	98	113	1.8	1	-2	-1.9
1883	NY-N	25	23	.521	54	52	46	4	0	426	431	9.1	11	66	1.4	144	3.0	2.73	116	.270	.299	20	21	101	101	3.6	3	-6	1.7
1884	NY-N	39	21	.650	65	65	62	4	0	557	528	8.5	12	146	2.4	345	5.6	2.50	115	.259	.308	29	23	97	106	11.2	10	-5	2.5
1885	NY-N	44	11	**.800**	56	55	55	7	1	492	372	6.8	4	131	2.4	258	4.7	1.66	173	.220	.276	63	66	102	110	**7.9**	3	-8	6.1
1886	NY-N	33	22	.600	59	59	56	1	0	500	514	9.3	13	163	2.9	272	4.9	2.99	94	.279	.337	18	-9	85	118	-2.3	5	-4	-1.1
1887	NY-N	22	15	.595	40	40	39	2	0	346	339	8.8	7	91	2.4	115	3.0	3.36	127	.271	.321	27	35	106	93	2.4	1	-3	3.0
1888	NY-N	26	19	.578	47	47	47	5	0	425	328	6.9	12	108	2.3	167	3.5	1.93	130	.225	.279	43	28	89	103	-3.1	3	-5	2.4
1889	NY-N	27	12	.692	45	41	39	3	**2**	375	340	8.2	14	149	3.6	125	3.0	3.02	135	.257	.332	42	44	101	104	2.7	-3	-3	3.5
1890	NY-N	17	13	.567	37	37	33	2	0	292	268	8.3	5	122	3.8	97	3.0	2.99	113	.259	.337	19	12	94	100	3.1	-2	0	0.8
1891	NY-N	5	9	.357	22	15	14	0	1	160	176	9.9	7	97	5.5	46	2.6	4.27	73	.293	.391	-16	-21	93	103	-2.4	-3	0	-2.0
1892	NY-N	0	0	—	1	1	0	0	0	5	11	19.8	0	4	7.2	1	1.8	14.40	22	.453	.530	-6	-6	98	71	0.0	0	0	-0.3
Total	13	307	209	.595	564	549	525	40	4	4801	4587	8.6	106	1297	2.4	1850	3.5	2.71	113	.263	.314	213	189	99	105	37.7	21	-47	15.9
■ **BOB WELCH**	Welch, Robert Lynn b: 11/3/56, Detroit, Mich. BR/TR, 6'3", 190 lbs. Deb: 6/20/78																												
1978	LA-N	7	4	.636	23	13	4	3	3	111	92	7.5	6	26	2.1	66	5.4	2.03	171	.229	.271	19	18	97	120	0.7	0	-1	1.8
1979	LA-N	5	6	.455	25	12	1	0	5	81	82	9.1	7	32	3.6	64	7.1	4.00	93	.265	.335	-2	-3	99	101	-0.3	-0	-1	-0.3
1980	LA-N	14	9	.609	32	32	3	2	0	214	190	8.0	15	79	3.3	141	5.9	3.28	105	.242	.306	8	4	96	100	1.3	3	-1	0.7
1981	LA-N	9	5	.643	23	23	2	1	0	141	141	9.0	11	41	2.6	88	5.6	3.45	97	.259	.308	1	-1	96	102	1.3	2	-1	0.0
1982	LA-N	16	11	.593	36	36	9	3	0	236	199	7.6	19	81	3.1	176	6.7	3.36	101	.229	.295	7	0	94	88	1.7	-1	-1	-0.1
1983	LA-N	15	12	.556	31	31	4	3	0	204	164	7.2	13	72	3.2	156	6.9	2.65	137	.222	.289	22	22	100	100	-0.1	-2	-0	2.1
1984	LA-N	13	13	.500	31	29	3	1	0	179	191	9.6	11	58	2.9	126	6.3	3.77	99	.273	.326	-4	-1	104	102	0.4	-3	2	-0.1
1985	LA-N	14	4	.778	23	23	8	3	0	167	141	7.6	16	35	1.9	96	5.2	2.32	142	.225	.270	24	18	92	113	4.4	2	1	2.2
1986	LA-N	7	13	.350	33	33	7	3	0	236	227	8.7	14	55	2.1	183	7.0	3.28	107	.251	.295	12	6	95	93	-2.4	-0	-1	0.5
1987	LA-N	15	9	.625	35	35	6	**4**	0	252	204	7.3	21	86	3.1	196	7.0	3.21	117	.221	.286	24	15	92	88	4.2	2	2	1.8
1988	Oak-A	17	9	.654	36	36	4	2	0	245	237	8.7	22	81	3.0	158	5.8	3.64	102	.257	.317	9	2	93	106	0.5	0	0	0.2
Total	11	132	95	.581	328	303	51	25	8	2066	1868	8.1	155	646	2.8	1450	6.3	3.20	111	.242	.299	120	82	96	100	11.7	3	-1	8.8
■ **DON WELCHEL**	Welchel, Donald Ray b: 2/3/57, Atlanta, Tex. BR/TR, 6'4", 205 lbs. Deb: 9/15/82																												
1982	Bal-A	1	0	1.000	2	0	0	0	0	4	6	13.5	0	2	4.5	3	6.8	9.00	45	.300	.364	-2	-2	99	49	0.5	0	0	-0.1
1983	Bal-A	0	2	.000	11	0	0	0	0	27	33	11.0	1	10	3.3	16	5.3	5.33	76	.297	.347	-4	-4	99	84	-0.9	0	-0	-0.3
Total	2	1	2	.333	13	0	0	0	0	31	39	11.3	1	12	3.5	19	5.5	5.81	69	.298	.349	-6	-6	99	79	-0.4	0	-0	-0.4
■ **DAVID WELLS**	Wells, David Lee b: 5/20/63, Torrance, Cal. BL/TL, 6'3", 187 lbs. Deb: 6/30/87																												
1987	Tor-A	4	3	.571	18	2	0	0	1	29	37	11.5	0	12	3.7	32	9.9	4.03	110	.311	.371	1	1	99	117	0.0	0	0	0.1
1988	Tor-A	3	5	.375	41	0	0	0	4	64	65	9.1	12	31	4.4	56	7.9	4.64	85	.269	.351	-5	-5	99	115	-1.2	0	-0	-0.4
Total	2	7	8	.467	59	2	0	0	5	93	102	9.9	12	43	4.2	88	8.5	4.45	92	.283	.358	-3	-4	99	115	-1.2	0	0	-0.3
■ **ED WELLS**	Wells, Edwin Lee "Satchelfoot" b: 6/7/1900, Ashland, Ohio d: 5/1/86, Birmingham, Ala. BL/TL, 6'1.5", 183 lbs. Deb: 6/16/23																												
1923	Det-A	0	0	—	7	0	0	0	0	10	11	9.9	0	6	5.4	6	5.4	5.40	70	.306	.386	-2	-2	95	91	0.0	-0	-0	-0.1
1924	Det-A	6	8	.429	29	15	5	0	4	102	117	10.3	2	42	3.7	33	2.9	4.06	103	.291	.344	2	1	99	102	-1.7	-1	1	0.2
1925	Det-A	6	9	.400	35	14	5	0	2	134	190	12.8	8	62	4.2	45	3.0	6.25	69	.345	.398	-28	-29	98	100	-1.8	2	0	-2.3
1926	Det-A	12	10	.545	36	26	9	**4**	0	178	201	10.2	7	76	3.8	58	2.9	4.15	95	.297	.359	-2	-4	98	110	0.8	0	-3	-0.6
1927	Det-A	0	1	.000	8	1	0	0	1	20	28	12.6	3	5	2.3	5	2.3	6.75	66	.333	.363	-6	-5	107	88	-0.4	0	1	-0.3
1929	NY-A	13	9	.591	31	23	10	3	0	193	179	8.3	19	81	3.8	78	3.6	4.34	95	.248	.314	-2	-5	97	85	0.6	1	-4	-0.7
1930	NY-A	12	3	.800	27	21	7	0	0	151	185	11.0	11	49	2.9	46	2.7	5.19	78	.302	.351	-9	-19	87	97	4.3	1	-2	-1.8
1931	NY-A	9	5	.643	27	10	6	0	2	117	130	10.0	7	37	2.8	34	2.6	4.31	95	.286	.337	1	-3	94	104	0.6	1	-1	-0.2
1932	NY-A	3	3	.500	22	0	0	0	2	32	38	10.7	1	12	3.4	13	3.7	4.22	97	.302	.347	1	-0	91	115	-0.8	-1	0	0.0
1933	StL-A	6	14	.300	36	22	10	0	1	204	230	10.1	13	63	2.8	58	2.6	4.19	120	.278	.324	2	19	117	100	-1.9	-2	-3	1.5
1934	StL-A	1	7	.125	33	8	2	0	1	92	108	10.6	7	35	3.4	27	2.6	4.79	100	.292	.346	-3	-0	106	100	-2.8	-2	1	0.0
Total	11	68	69	.496	291	140	54	7	13	1233	1417	10.3	78	468	3.4	403	2.9	4.65	93	.291	.346	-45	-47	100	99	-3.1	0	-10	-4.3
■ **JOHN WELLS**	Wells, John Frederick b: 11/25/22, Junction City, Kan BR/TR, 5'11.5", 180 lbs. Deb: 9/14/44																												
1944	Bro-N	0	2	.000	4	2	0	0	0	15	18	10.8	1	11	6.6	7	4.2	5.40	68	.316	.420	-3	-3	102	116	-0.9	0	0	-0.2
■ **CHRIS WELSH**	Welsh, Christopher Charles b: 4/14/55, Wilmington, Del. BL/TL, 6'2", 185 lbs. Deb: 4/12/81																												
1981	SD-N	6	7	.462	22	19	4	2	0	124	122	8.9	9	41	3.0	51	3.7	3.77	88	.264	.320	-4	-6	95	99	1.0	-0	1	-0.5
1982	SD-N	8	8	.500	28	20	3	1	0	139	146	9.5	16	63	4.1	48	3.1	4.92	67	.268	.343	-20	-25	92	91	0.0	4	1	-2.0
1983	SD-N	0	1	.000	7	1	0	0	0	14	13	8.4	2	2	1.3	5	3.2	2.57	140	.236	.254	2	2	99	110	-0.4	-0	-0	0.1
	Mon-N	0	1	.000	16	5	0	0	0	45	46	9.2	5	18	3.6	17	3.4	5.00	74	.267	.349	-7	-7	101	89	-0.4	1	1	-0.3
	Yr	0	2	.000	23	6	0	0	0	59	59	9.0	7	20	3.1	22	3.4	4.42	83	.260	.327	-5	-5	101	89	-0.8	-0	1	-0.2
1985	Tex-A	2	5	.286	25	6	0	0	0	76	101	12.0	11	25	3.0	31	3.7	4.14	110	.316	.370	0	4	110	142	-0.8	0	-1	0.3
1986	Cin-N	6	9	.400	24	24	1	0	0	139	163	10.6	9	40	2.6	40	2.6	4.79	81	.301	.344	-16	-14	104	96	-1.9	0	-0	-1.3
Total	5	22	31	.415	122	75	8	3	0	537	591	9.9	52	189	3.2	192	3.2	4.46	82	.282	.341	-46	-48	99	102	-2.5	5	3	-3.7
■ **DICK WELTEROTH**	Welteroth, Richard John b: 8/3/27, Williamsport, Pa. BR/TR, 5'11", 165 lbs. Deb: 5/16/48																												
1948	Was-A	2	1	.667	33	2	0	0	1	65	73	10.1	6	50	6.9	16	2.2	5.54	83	.286	.399	-9	-7	107	106	0.7	-1	-0	-0.7
1949	Was-A	2	5	.286	52	2	0	0	2	95	107	10.1	6	89	8.4	37	3.5	7.39	55	.296	.425	-34	-35	96	85	-0.3	-1	0	-3.3
1950	Was-A	0	0	—	5	0	0	0	0	6	5	7.5	0	6	9.0	2	3.0	3.00	154	.217	.379	1	1	101	125	0.0	0	0	0.1
Total	3	4	6	.400	90	4	0	0	3	166	185	10.0	12	145	7.9	55	3.0	6.51	66	.290	.413	-42	-41	101	94	0.4	-2	-0	-3.9
■ **TONY WELZER**	Welzer, Anton Frank b: 4/5/1899, Germany d: 3/18/71, Milwaukee, Wis. BR/TR, 5'11", 160 lbs. Deb: 4/13/26																												
1926	Bos-A	4	3	.571	39	6	1	1	0	139	167	10.8	5	53	3.4	29	1.9	4.86	88	.308	.356	-13	-9	106	97	1.4	2	4	-0.3
1927	Bos-A	6	11	.353	37	19	8	0	1	172	214	11.2	10	71	3.7	56	2.9	4.71	87	.318	.372	-11	-12	99	113	0.3	-2	0	-1.2
Total	2	10	14	.417	76	25	9	1	1	311	381	11.0	15	124	3.6	85	2.5	4.77	87	.313	.365	-24	-21	102	106	1.7	-0	4	-1.5

YEAR	TM/L	W	L	PCT	G	GS	CG	SHO	SV	IP	H	H/G	HR	BB	BB/G	SO	SO/G	ERA	/A	OAVG	OOBP	PR	/A	PF	CPI	WAT	PB	PD	TPI
■ **BUTCH WENSLOFF**	Wensloff, Charles William b: 12/3/15, Sausalito, Cal. BR/TR, 5'11", 185 lbs. Deb: 5/02/43																												
1943	NY-A	13	11	.542	29	27	18	1	1	223	179	7.2	7	70	2.8	105	4.2	2.54	121	.219	.276	19	14	94	88	-2.0	0	-1	1.4
1947	NY-A	3	1	.750	11	5	1	0	0	52	41	7.1	3	22	3.8	18	3.1	2.60	132	.217	.296	6	5	92	103	0.7	1	-1	0.5
1948	Cle-A	0	1	.000	1	0	0	0	0	2	2	9.0	1	3	13.5	2	9.0	9.00	45	.286	.500	-1	-1	94	123	-0.4	0	0	0.0
Total	3	16	13	.552	41	32	19	1	1	277	222	7.2	11	95	3.1	125	4.1	2.60	121	.219	.282	24	17	93	91	-1.7	1	-1	1.9
■ **FRED WENZ**	Wenz, Frederick Charles "Fireball" b: 8/26/41, Bound Brook, N.J. BR/TR, 6'3", 214 lbs. Deb: 6/04/68																												
1968	Bos-A	0	0	—	1	0	0	0	0	1	0	0.0	0	2	18.0	3	27.0	0.00	—	.000	.400	0	0	101	0	0.0	0	0	0.0
1969	Bos-A	1	0	1.000	8	0	0	0	0	11	9	7.4	7	10	8.2	11	9.0	5.73	66	.225	.380	-3	-2	105	152	0.5	0	0	-0.1
1970	Phi-N	2	0	1.000	22	0	0	0	1	30	27	8.1	2	13	3.9	24	7.2	4.50	88	.237	.308	-1	-2	98	75	1.0	-1	-1	-0.2
Total	3	3	0	1.000	31	0	0	0	1	42	36	7.7	9	25	5.4	38	8.1	4.71	83	.229	.330	-4	-4	100	93	1.5	-0	-1	-0.3
■ **PERRY WERDEN**	Werden, Percival Wheritt b: 7/21/1865, St.Louis, Mo. d: 1/9/34, Minneapolis, Minn. BR/TR, 6'2", 220 lbs. Deb: 4/24/1884																												
1884	StL-U	12	1	.923	16	16	12	1	0	141	113	7.2	1	22	1.4	51	3.3	1.98	149	.225	.257	16	15	98	98	3.7	-0	0	1.3
■ **BILL WERLE**	Werle, William George "Bugs" b: 12/21/20, Oakland, Cal. BL/TL, 6'2.5", 182 lbs. Deb: 4/22/49																												
1949	Pit-N	12	13	.480	35	29	10	2	0	221	243	9.9	22	51	2.1	106	4.3	4.24	97	.278	.320	-5	-3	102	98	0.5	-3	1	-0.4
1950	Pit-N	8	16	.333	48	22	6	0	8	215	249	10.4	25	65	2.7	78	3.3	4.60	95	.290	.340	-11	-5	106	104	-1.4	1	4	0.0
1951	Pit-N	8	6	.571	59	9	2	0	6	150	181	10.9	20	51	3.1	57	3.4	5.64	77	.304	.358	-28	-22	110	96	2.0	3	3	-1.3
1952	Pit-N	0	0	—	5	0	0	0	0	4	9	20.3	1	1	2.3	1	2.3	9.00	44	.429	.455	-2	-2	105	117	0.0	0	0	-0.1
	StL-N	1	2	.333	19	0	0	0	1	39	40	9.2	6	15	3.5	23	5.3	4.85	75	.268	.335	-5	-5	97	98	-0.5	-0	1	-0.4
	Yr	1	2	.333	24	0	0	0	1	43	49	10.3	7	16	3.3	24	5.0	5.23	70	.288	.349	-7	-8	98	98	-0.5	0	2	-0.5
1953	Bos-A	0	1	.000	5	0	0	0	0	12	7	5.3	1	1	0.8	4	3.0	1.50	288	.179	.190	3	4	108	91	-0.4	-0	1	0.5
1954	Bos-A	0	1	.000	14	0	0	0	0	25	41	14.8	5	10	3.6	14	5.0	4.32	87	.376	.424	-2	-2	101	192	-0.4	-0	-0	-0.1
Total	6	29	39	.426	185	60	18	2	15	666	770	10.4	80	194	2.6	283	3.8	4.69	90	.291	.340	-49	-35	105	103	-0.2	1	10	-1.8
■ **GEORGE WERLEY**	Werley, George William b: 9/8/38, St.Louis, Mo. BR/TR, 6'2", 196 lbs. Deb: 9/29/56																												
1956	Bal-A	0	0	—	1	0	0	0	0	1	1	9.0	0	2	18.0	0	0.0	9.00	45	.250	.500	-1	-1	97	80	0.0	0	0	0.0
■ **JOHNNY WERTZ**	Wertz, Henry Levi b: 4/20/1898, Pomaria, S.C. BR/TR, 5'10", 180 lbs. Deb: 4/14/26																												
1926	Bos-N	11	9	.550	32	23	7	1	0	189	212	10.1	6	47	2.2	65	3.1	3.29	102	.287	.328	11	1	88	117	2.3	4	2	0.7
1927	Bos-N	4	10	.286	42	15	4	0	1	164	204	11.2	5	52	2.9	39	2.1	4.55	82	.315	.356	-12	-15	95	105	-1.9	-0	-1	-1.5
1928	Bos-N	0	2	.000	10	2	0	0	0	18	31	15.5	2	8	4.0	5	2.5	10.50	39	.369	.419	-13	-13	101	70	-0.9	0	0	-1.1
1929	Bos-N	0	0	—	4	0	0	0	1	6	13	19.5	1	4	6.0	2	3.0	10.50	44	.433	.500	-4	-4	97	106	0.0	0	0	-0.2
Total	4	15	21	.417	88	40	11	1	2	377	460	11.0	14	111	2.6	111	2.6	4.30	83	.307	.349	-17	-31	92	109	-0.5	4	1	-2.1
■ **DAVID WEST**	West, David Lee b: 9/1/64, Memphis, Tenn. BL/TL, 6'6", 205 lbs. Deb: 9/24/88																												
1988	NY-N	1	0	1.000	2	1	0	0	0	6	6	9.0	0	3	4.5	3	4.5	3.00	101	.273	.360	0	0	88	132	0.5	1	0	0.1
■ **FRANK WEST**	West, Frank b: 1873, Wilmerding, Pa. Deb: 7/11/1894																												
1894	Bos-N	0	0	—	1	0	0	0	0	3	5	15.0	0	2	6.0	1	3.0	9.00	66	.395	.478	-1	-1	111	83	0.0	-0	0	0.0
■ **HI WEST**	West, James Hiram b: 8/8/1884, Roseville, Ill. d: 5/25/63, Los Angeles, Cal. BR/TR, 6', 185 lbs. Deb: 9/08/05																												
1905	Cle-A	2	2	.500	6	4	4	1	0	33	43	11.7	0	10	2.7	15	4.1	4.09	65	.342	.390	-5	-5	100	114	0.0	-1	-2	-0.6
1911	Cle-A	3	4	.429	13	8	3	0	1	65	84	11.6	1	18	2.5	17	2.4	3.74	92	.343	.395	-3	-2	103	136	-0.6	-2	-1	-0.2
Total	2	5	6	.455	19	12	7	1	1	98	127	11.7	1	28	2.6	32	2.9	3.86	82	.343	.393	-8	-7	102	129	-0.6	-3	-3	-0.8
■ **LEFTY WEST**	West, Weldon Edison b: 9/3/15, Gibsonville, N.C. d: 7/23/79, Hendersonville, N.C. BR/TL, 6', 165 lbs. Deb: 4/30/44																												
1944	StL-A	0	0	—	11	0	0	0	0	24	34	12.8	1	19	7.1	11	4.1	6.38	54	.366	.450	-8	-8	100	120	0.0	-0	-0	-0.8
1945	StL-A	3	4	.429	24	8	1	0	0	74	71	8.6	2	31	3.8	38	4.6	3.65	105	.245	.315	-2	2	114	82	-0.6	-3	-1	-0.2
Total	2	3	4	.429	35	8	1	0	0	98	105	9.6	3	50	4.6	49	4.5	4.32	87	.274	.351	-10	-6	111	91	-0.6	-4	-2	-1.0
■ **HUYLER WESTERVELT**	Westervelt, Huyler b: 10/1/1870, Piermont, N.Y. Deb: 4/21/1894																												
1894	NY-N	7	10	.412	23	18	11	1	0	141	170	10.9	4	76	4.9	35	2.2	5.04	104	.321	.406	5	3	98	99	-3.4	-5	0	-0.1
■ **BUZZ WETZEL**	Wetzel, Charles Edward b: 8/25/1894, Jay, Okla. d: 3/7/41, Globe, Ariz. BR/TR, 6'1", 162 lbs. Deb: 7/25/27																												
1927	Phi-A	0	0	—	2	1	0	0	0	5	8	14.4	0	5	9.0	0	0.0	7.20	54	.400	.520	-2	-2	95	124	0.0	0	0	0.0
■ **SHORTY WETZEL**	Wetzel, George William b: 1868, Philadelphia, Pa. d: 2/25/1899, Dayton, Ohio Deb: 1885																												
1885	Bal-a	0	2	.000	2	2	2	0	0	18	27	13.5	0	9	4.5	6	3.0	8.00	44	.359	.428	-10	-9	109	80	-0.9	-1	0	-0.6
■ **STEFAN WEVER**	Wever, Stefan Matthew b: 4/22/58, Marburg, W.Germ BR/TR, 6'8", 245 lbs. Deb: 9/17/82																												
1982	NY-A	0	1	.000	1	1	0	0	0	3	6	18.0	1	3	9.0	2	6.0	24.00	16	.429	.500	-7	-7	97	53	-0.4	0	0	-0.4
■ **GUS WEYHING**	Weyhing, August "Cannonball" b: 9/29/1866, Louisville, Ky. d: 9/4/55, Louisville, Ky. BR/TR, 5'10", 145 lbs. Deb: 5/02/1887																												
1887	Phi-a	26	28	.481	55	55	53	2	0	466	465	9.0	13	167	3.2	193	3.7	4.27	100	.273	.338	2	0	100	85	0.0	-8	-2	-0.8
1888	Phi-a	28	18	.609	47	47	45	3	0	404	314	7.0	4	111	2.5	204	4.5	2.25	132	.226	.283	36	32	97	93	0.0	5	2	3.6
1889	Phi-a	30	21	.588	54	53	50	4	0	449	382	7.7	15	212	4.2	213	4.3	2.95	126	.244	.334	45	38	96	102	2.2	-14	-4	1.6
1890	Bro-P	30	16	.652	49	46	38	3	0	390	419	9.7	10	179	4.1	177	4.1	3.60	124	.286	.364	27	37	105	105	5.8	-6	-7	2.1
1891	Phi-a	31	20	.608	52	51	51	3	0	450	428	8.6	12	161	3.2	219	4.4	3.18	120	.265	.331	27	32	103	94	6.4	-17	-4	1.0
1892	Phi-N	32	21	.604	59	49	46	6	**3**	470	411	7.9	9	168	3.2	202	3.9	2.66	127	.247	.316	33	37	103	97	3.2	-11	-8	1.7
1893	Phi-N	23	16	.590	42	40	33	2	0	345	399	10.4	10	145	3.8	101	2.6	4.75	97	.306	.375	-3	-6	98	95	1.9	-9	-1	-1.2
1894	Phi-N	16	14	.533	38	34	25	2	1	266	365	12.3	12	116	3.9	81	2.7	5.82	86	.350	.415	-14	-24	94	98	-0.6	-8	-2	-2.5
1895	Phi-N	0	2	.000	2	2	0	0	0	9	23	23.0	0	13	13.0	5	5.0	20.00	24	.498	.608	-15	-15	98	70	-0.9	-1	0	-0.9
	Pit-N	1	0	1.000	1	1	1	0	0	9	10	10.0	0	5	5.0	3	3.0	1.00	461	.301	.393	4	4	96	437	0.5	0	0	0.4
	Lou-N	7	19	.269	28	25	22	1	0	213	285	12.0	9	66	2.8	53	2.2	5.41	87	.342	.390	-15	-16	99	95	0.0	-0	0	-1.2
	Yr	8	21	.276	31	28	23	1	0	231	318	12.4	9	84	3.3	61	2.4	5.81	81	.348	.403	-26	-28	98	95	-0.4	-1	0	-1.7
1896	Lou-N	2	3	.400	5	5	4	0	0	42	62	13.3	6	15	3.2	9	1.9	6.64	67	.367	.418	-11	-10	102	100	0.4	-1	0	-0.8
1898	Was-N	15	26	.366	45	42	39	0	0	361	428	10.7	10	84	2.1	92	2.3	4.51	84	.317	.357	-36	-30	105	87	1.3	-5	-2	-3.2
1899	Was-N	17	21	.447	43	38	34	2	0	335	414	11.1	8	76	2.0	96	2.6	4.54	83	.328	.366	-26	-28	98	90	3.5	-1	-7	-3.0
1900	StL-N	3	2	.600	7	5	3	0	0	47	60	11.5	2	21	4.0	6	1.1	4.79	72	.335	.405	-6	-7	93	106	0.7	-2	0	-0.7
	Bro-N	3	4	.429	8	8	3	0	0	48	66	12.4	1	20	3.8	8	1.5	4.31	91	.351	.414	-3	-2	106	123	-1.0	-0	0	-0.1
	Yr	6	6	.500	15	13	6	0	0	95	126	11.9	3	41	3.9	14	1.3	4.55	81	.343	.409	-9	-9	100	123	-0.3	-2	0	-0.8
1901	Cle-A	0	0	—	2	1	0	0	0	11	20	16.4	0	5	4.1	0	0.0	8.18	44	.414	.469	-6	-6	97	92	0.0	-1	0	-0.4
	Cin-N	0	1	.000	1	1	1	0	0	9	11	11.0	0	2	2.0	3	3.0	3.00	110	.344	.417	0	0	100	150	-0.4	-0	-0	0.0
Total	14	264	232	.532	538	503	448	28	4	4324	4562	9.5	121	1566	3.3	1665	3.5	3.89	102	.287	.351	40	39	100	96	23.0	-79	-35	-4.4
■ **JOHN WEYHING**	Weyhing, John b: 6/24/1869, Louisville, Ky. d: 6/20/1890, Louisville, Ky. BL/TL, 6'2", 185 lbs. Deb: 1888																												
1888	Cin-a	3	4	.429	8	8	7	0	0	66	52	7.1	0	17	2.3	30	4.1	1.23	247	.229	.282	13	13	99	164	-0.9	-1	0	1.2
1889	Col-a	0	0	—	1	0	0	0	0	1	1	9.0	0	4	36.0	0	0.0	27.00	13	.275	.655	-3	-3	92	49	0.0	0	0	-0.1
Total	2	3	4	.429	9	8	7	0	0	67	53	7.1	0	21	2.8	30	4.0	1.61	189	.229	.294	11	11	99	162	-0.9	-1	0	1.1
■ **LEE WHEAT**	Wheat, Leroy William b: 9/15/29, Edwardsville, Ill BR/TR, 6'4", 200 lbs. Deb: 4/21/54																												
1954	Phi-A	0	2	.000	8	1	0	0	0	28	38	12.2	1	9	2.9	7	2.3	5.79	67	.304	.350	-6	-6	105	76	-0.9	-0	-0	-0.5
1955	KC-A	0	0	—	3	0	0	0	0	2	8	36.0	1	3	13.5	1	4.5	22.50	19	.533	.611	-4	-4	106	103	0.0	0	0	-0.3
Total	2	0	2	.000	11	1	0	0	0	30	46	13.8	2	12	3.6	8	2.4	6.90	57	.329	.381	-11	-10	105	78	-0.9	-0	0	-0.8
■ **CHARLIE WHEATLEY**	Wheatley, Charles b: 6/27/1893, Rosedale, Kan. d: 12/10/82, Tulsa, Okla. BR/TR, 5'11", 174 lbs. Deb: 9/06/12																												
1912	Det-A	1	4	.200	5	5	2	0	0	35	45	11.6	1	17	4.4	14	3.6	6.17	52	.331	.413	-11	-12	96	92	-1.3	-2	0	-0.9
■ **WOODY WHEATON**	Wheaton, Elwood Pierce b: 10/3/14, Philadelphia, Pa. BL/TL, 5'8.5", 160 lbs. Deb: 9/28/43																												
1944	Phi-A	0	1	.000	11	1	1	0	0	38	36	8.5	1	20	4.7	15	3.6	3.55	99	.255	.343	-1	-0	102	105	-0.4	0	-1	0.0

YEAR	TM/L	W	L	PCT	G	GS	CG	SHO	SV	IP	H	H/G	HR	BB	BB/G	SO	SO/G	ERA	/A	OAVG	OOBP	PR	/A	PF	CPI	WAT	PB	PD	TPI
■ **RIP WHEELER**	Wheeler, Floyd Clark b: 3/2/1898, Marion, Ky. d: 9/18/68, Marion, Ky. BR/TR, 6', 180 lbs. Deb: 9/30/21																												
1921	Pit-N	0	0	—	1	0	0	0	0	3	6	18.0	0	1	3.0	0	0.0	9.00	43	.500	.533	-2	-2	102	119	0.0	-0	0	-0.1
1922	Pit-N	0	0	—	1	0	0	0	0	1	1	9.0	0	2	18.0	0	0.0	0.00	—	.333	.600	0	0	101	0	0.0	0	0	0.1
1923	Chi-N	1	2	.333	3	3	1	0	0	24	28	10.5	2	5	1.9	5	1.9	4.88	85	.298	.343	-2	-2	103	94	-0.5	-1	1	-0.1
1924	Chi-N	3	6	.333	29	4	0	0	0	101	103	9.2	8	21	1.9	16	1.4	3.92	100	.265	.295	-1	-0	101	85	-1.6	-1	0	0.0
Total	4	4	8	.333	34	7	1	0	0	129	138	9.6	10	29	2.0	21	1.5	4.19	94	.278	.314	-4	-3	101	87	-2.1	-2	2	-0.1
■ **GEORGE WHEELER**	Wheeler, George L. (born George L. Heroux) b: 8/3/1869, Metheun, Mass. d: 3/23/46, Santa Ana, Cal. BB , Deb: 9/18/1896																												
1896	Phi-N	1	1	.500	3	2	2	0	0	16	18	10.1	0	5	2.8	2	1.1	3.94	113	.306	.361	1	1	102	93	0.0	-1	0	0.0
1897	Phi-N	11	10	.524	26	19	17	0	0	191	229	10.8	3	62	2.9	35	1.6	3.96	105	.320	.374	8	4	96	105	2.2	-1	0	0.2
1898	Phi-N	6	8	.429	15	13	10	0	0	112	155	12.5	1	36	2.9	20	1.6	4.18	81	.352	.401	-7	-10	94	119	-1.3	-1	0	-0.9
1899	Phi-N	3	1	.750	6	5	3	0	0	39	44	10.2	1	13	3.0	3	0.7	6.00	61	.308	.366	-9	-10	95	64	0.7	1	0	-0.7
Total	4	21	20	.512	50	39	32	0	0	358	446	11.2	5	116	2.9	60	1.5	4.25	91	.328	.381	-8	-15	96	104	1.6	-1	0	-1.4
■ **HARRY WHEELER**	Wheeler, Harry Eugene b: 3/3/1858, Versailles, Ind. d: 10/9/1900, Cincinnati, Ohio BR/TR, 5'11", 165 lbs. Deb: 6/19/1878 M																												
1878	Pro-N	6	1	.857	7	6	6	0	0	62	70	10.2	1	25	3.6	25	3.6	3.48	64	.295	.362	-8	-9	97	101	2.5	-1	0	-0.7
1879	Cin-N	0	1	.000	1	1	0	0	0	1	6	54.0	0	4	36.0	0	0.0	81.00	3	.685	.784	-9	-9	94	47	-0.4	-0	0	-0.5
1882	Cin-a	1	2	.333	4	1	1	0	0	22	21	8.6	1	12	4.9	10	4.1	5.73	47	.257	.352	-7	-7	100	66	-0.7	1	0	-0.5
1883	Col-a	0	1	.000	1	1	0	0	0	5	13	23.4	0	2	3.6	0	0.0	7.20	42	.485	.521	-2	-2	91	161	-0.4	0	0	-0.1
1884	KC-U	0	1	.000	1	1	1	0	0	8	7	7.9	0	0	0.0	6	6.8	1.13	245	.240	.240	2	1	92	160	-0.3	0	0	0.0
Total	5	7	6	.538	14	10	8	0	0	98	117	10.7	2	43	3.9	41	3.8	4.78	51	.305	.375	-25	-26	97	100	0.7	-0	0	-1.8
■ **GARY WHEELOCK**	Wheelock, Gary Richard b: 11/29/51, Bakersfield, Cal. BR/TR, 6'3", 205 lbs. Deb: 9/17/76																												
1976	Cal-A	0	0	—	2	0	0	0	0	2	6	27.0	0	1	4.5	2	9.0	27.00	12	.500	.571	-5	-5	93	53	0.0	0	0	-0.4
1977	Sea-A	6	9	.400	17	17	2	0	0	88	94	9.6	16	26	2.7	47	4.8	4.91	82	.268	.319	-8	-9	98	91	0.1	0	-1	-0.8
1980	Sea-A	0	0	—	1	1	0	0	0	3	4	12.0	0	1	3.0	1	3.0	6.00	71	.333	.385	-1	-1	105	84	0.0	0	0	0.0
Total	3	6	9	.400	20	18	2	0	0	93	104	10.1	16	28	2.7	50	4.8	5.42	74	.277	.330	-14	-15	98	90	0.1	0	-1	-1.2
■ **JACK WHILLOCK**	Whillock, Jack Franklin b: 11/4/42, Clinton, Ark. BR/TR, 6'3", 195 lbs. Deb: 8/29/71																												
1971	Det-A	0	2	.000	7	0	0	0	1	8	10	11.3	0	2	2.3	6	6.8	5.63	59	.323	.343	-2	-2	95	78	-0.9	-0	0	-0.1
■ **PAT WHITAKER**	Whitaker, William H. b: 11/1864, St.Louis, Mo. d: 7/15/02, St.Louis, Mo. TR , Deb: 1888																												
1888	Bal-a	1	1	.500	2	2	2	0	0	14	13	8.4	0	6	3.9	5	3.2	5.14	58	.259	.338	-3	-3	98	62	0.1	-1	0	-0.3
1889	Bal-a	1	0	1.000	1	1	1	0	0	9	10	10.0	0	4	4.0	1	1.0	2.00	191	.297	.371	2	2	99	199	0.5	-0	0	0.2
Total	2	2	1	.667	3	3	3	0	0	23	23	9.0	0	10	3.9	6	2.3	3.91	85	.274	.351	-1	-2	98	115	0.6	-1	0	-0.1
■ **BILL WHITBY**	Whitby, William Edward b: 7/29/43, Crewe, Va. BR/TR, 6'1", 190 lbs. Deb: 6/17/64																												
1964	Min-A	0	0	—	4	0	0	0	0	6	8	12.0	3	1	1.5	2	3.0	9.00	40	.308	.333	-4	-4	100	85	0.0	-0	0	-0.3
■ **BOB WHITCHER**	Whitcher, Robert Arthur b: 4/29/17, Berlin, N.H. BL/TL, 5'8", 165 lbs. Deb: 8/20/45																												
1945	Bos-N	0	2	.000	6	3	0	0	0	16	12	6.8	1	12	6.8	6	3.4	2.81	152	.235	.369	2	3	113	159	-0.9	0	0	0.3
■ **ABE WHITE**	White, Adel b: 5/16/04, Winder, Ga. d: 10/1/78, Atlanta, Ga. BR/TL, 6', 185 lbs. Deb: 7/10/37																												
1937	StL-N	0	1	.000	5	0	0	0	0	9	14	14.0	1	3	3.0	2	2.0	7.00	56	.341	.386	-3	-3	100	91	-0.4	0	0	-0.2
■ **ERNIE WHITE**	White, Ernest Daniel b: 9/5/16, Pacolet Mills, S.C d: 5/22/74, Augusta, Ga. BR/TL, 5'11.5", 175 lbs. Deb: 5/09/40 C																												
1940	StL-N	1	1	.500	8	1	0	0	0	22	29	11.9	0	14	5.7	15	6.1	4.09	95	.315	.400	-1	-0	101	140	0.0	1	1	0.1
1941	StL-N	17	7	.708	32	25	12	3	2	210	169	7.2	12	70	3.0	117	5.0	2.40	**162**	.217	.283	29	35	107	106	2.8	0	-3	3.5
1942	StL-N	7	5	.583	26	19	7	1	2	128	113	7.9	11	41	2.9	67	4.7	2.53	134	.232	.290	11	12	103	118	-0.9	0	-2	1.2
1943	StL-N	5	5	.500	14	10	5	1	0	79	78	8.9	4	33	3.8	28	3.2	3.76	90	.257	.327	-3	-3	100	96	-1.3	0	-1	-0.3
1946	Bos-N	0	1	.000	12	1	0	0	0	24	22	8.3	1	12	4.5	8	3.0	4.13	78	.256	.343	-2	-2	94	89	-0.4	0	-1	-0.2
1947	Bos-N	0	0	—	1	1	0	0	0	4	1	2.3	0	1	2.3	1	2.3	0.00	—	.083	.154	2	2	95	0	0.0	0	-0	0.2
1948	Bos-N	0	2	.000	15	0	0	0	2	23	13	5.1	0	17	6.7	8	3.1	1.96	200	.167	.306	5	5	99	110	-0.9	-0	-1	0.4
Total	7	30	21	.588	108	57	24	5	6	490	425	7.8	28	188	3.5	244	4.5	2.77	131	.231	.301	41	48	103	108	-0.7	2	-7	4.9
■ **DEKE WHITE**	White, George Frederick b: 9/8/1872, Albany, N.Y. d: 11/5/57, Ilion, N.Y. BB/TL, Deb: 9/14/1895																												
1895	Phi-N	1	0	1.000	3	1	1	0	1	17	17	9.0	1	13	6.9	6	3.2	10.06	47	.280	.407	-10	-10	98	48	0.5	-1	0	-0.7
■ **DOC WHITE**	White, Guy Harris b: 4/9/1879, Washington, D.C. d: 2/19/69, Silver Spring, Md. BL/TL, 6'1", 150 lbs. Deb: 4/22/01																												
1901	Phi-N	14	13	.519	31	27	22	0	0	237	241	9.2	2	56	2.1	132	5.0	3.19	104	.290	.345	3	4	100	99	-1.9	5	2	1.1
1902	Phi-N	16	20	.444	36	35	34	3	1	306	277	8.1	3	72	2.1	185	**5.4**	2.53	120	.266	.319	8	17	109	94	1.4	4	2	3.0
1903	Chi-A	17	16	.515	37	36	29	3	0	300	258	7.7	4	69	2.1	114	3.4	2.13	130	.253	.300	27	21	94	109	2.9	6	3	3.2
1904	Chi-A	16	12	.571	30	30	23	7	0	228	201	7.9	6	68	2.7	115	4.5	1.78	141	.259	.318	21	18	97	**152**	-0.1	0	1	2.3
1905	Chi-A	17	13	.567	36	33	25	4	0	260	204	7.1	2	58	2.0	120	4.2	1.77	140	.238	.287	25	20	93	110	-1.1	0	-0	2.2
1906	Chi-A	18	6	.750	28	24	20	7	0	219	160	6.6	2	38	1.6	95	3.9	**1.52**	158	.226	**.266**	28	21	89	97	4.7	4	2	3.1
1907	Chi-A	**27**	13	.675	46	35	24	6	1	291	270	8.4	3	38	**1.2**	141	4.4	2.26	114	.270	.296	9	10	101	99	5.9	3	5	2.1
1908	Chi-A	18	13	.581	41	37	24	5	0	296	267	8.1	2	69	2.1	126	3.8	2.55	86	.244	.295	-5	-11	93	98	0.1	4	7	0.0
1909	Chi-A	11	9	.550	24	21	14	3	0	178	149	7.5	1	31	1.6	77	3.9	1.72	139	.226	.269	15	13	97	90	0.9	6	-1	1.6
1910	Chi-A	15	13	.536	33	29	20	2	1	237	219	8.3	2	50	1.9	111	4.2	2.66	90	.243	.291	-4	-7	95	82	2.7	2	2	-0.1
1911	Chi-A	10	14	.417	34	29	16	4	2	214	219	9.2	2	35	**1.5**	72	3.0	2.99	106	.271	.309	8	4	95	93	-2.4	3	-1	0.7
1912	Chi-A	8	10	.444	32	19	9	1	0	172	172	9.0	1	47	2.5	57	3.0	3.24	102	.267	.325	2	1	99	98	-1.1	-2	-1	0.0
1913	Chi-A	2	4	.333	19	8	2	0	0	103	106	9.3	1	39	3.4	39	3.4	3.50	80	.278	.353	-6	-8	95	103	-1.0	-1	2	-0.5
Total	13	189	156	.548	427	363	262	45	5	3041	2743	8.1	31	670	2.0	1384	4.1	2.39	113	.256	.304	133	104	97	102	11.0	36	23	18.7
■ **HAL WHITE**	White, Harold George b: 3/18/19, Utica, N.Y. BR/TR, 5'10", 165 lbs. Deb: 4/22/41																												
1941	Det-A	0	0	—	4	0	0	0	0	9	11	11.0	0	6	6.0	2	2.0	6.00	74	.306	.378	-2	-2	107	90	0.0	-0	0	-0.1
1942	Det-A	12	12	.500	34	25	12	4	1	217	212	8.8	6	82	3.4	93	3.9	2.90	142	.252	.320	18	29	113	115	0.7	-2	0	3.1
1943	Det-A	7	12	.368	32	24	7	2	2	178	150	7.6	6	71	3.6	58	2.9	3.39	101	.228	.301	-2	1	104	80	-2.7	-1	1	0.1
1946	Det-A	1	1	.500	11	1	1	0	0	27	34	11.3	5	15	5.0	12	4.0	5.67	65	.312	.392	-6	-6	106	113	-0.1	-1	1	-0.5
1947	Det-A	4	5	.444	35	5	0	0	2	85	91	9.6	5	47	5.0	33	3.5	3.60	106	.279	.368	1	2	103	130	-0.8	0	1	0.4
1948	Det-A	2	1	.667	27	0	0	0	1	43	46	9.6	2	26	5.4	17	3.6	6.07	68	.272	.369	-9	-9	97	77	0.5	0	-1	-0.8
1949	Det-A	1	0	1.000	9	0	0	0	2	12	5	3.8	0	4	3.0	4	3.0	0.00	—	.125	.205	6	6	106	0	0.5	0	1	0.7
1950	Det-A	9	6	.600	42	8	3	1	1	111	96	7.8	7	65	5.3	53	4.3	4.54	95	.239	.336	0	-3	95	86	-0.1	-2	0	-0.3
1951	Det-A	3	4	.429	38	4	0	0	4	76	74	8.8	7	49	5.8	23	2.7	4.74	93	.264	.370	-5	-3	107	105	-0.2	-0	2	0.0
1952	Det-A	1	8	.111	41	0	0	0	5	63	53	7.6	1	39	5.6	18	2.6	3.71	102	.237	.341	-0	0	103	93	-2.9	-0	1	0.1
1953	StL-A	0	0	—	10	0	0	0	0	10	8	7.2	1	3	2.7	2	1.8	2.70	164	.205	.267	1	2	111	89	0.0	0	0	0.2
	StL-N	6	5	.545	49	0	0	0	7	85	84	8.9	5	39	4.1	32	3.4	2.96	145	.272	.344	12	13	101	146	0.1	-2	1	1.1
1954	StL-N	0	0	—	4	0	0	0	0	5	11	19.8	2	4	7.2	2	3.6	19.80	21	.440	.533	-9	-9	100	70	0.0	-0	0	-0.7
Total	12	46	54	.460	336	67	23	7	25	921	875	8.6	47	450	4.4	349	3.4	3.78	106	.253	.336	6	24	104	102	-5.0	-7	7	3.3
■ **DEACON WHITE**	White, James Laurie b: 12/7/1847, Caton, N.Y. d: 7/7/39, Aurora, Ill. BL/TR, 5'11", 175 lbs. Deb: 5/04/1871 M																												
1876	Chi-N	0	0	—	1	0	0	0	1	2	1	4.5	0	0	0.0	3	13.5	0.00	—	.152	.152	1	1	113	0	0.0	0	0	0.1
1890	Buf-P	0	0	—	1	0	0	0	0	8	18	20.3	0	2	2.3	0	0.0	9.00	46	.457	.483	-4	-4	97	99	0.0	0	0	-0.2
Total	2	0	0	—	2	0	0	0	1	10	19	17.1	0	2	1.8	3	2.7	7.20	53	.413	.438	-4	-4	100	79	0.0	0	0	-0.1
■ **LARRY WHITE**	White, Larry David b: 9/25/58, San Fernando, Cal. BR/TR, 6'5", 190 lbs. Deb: 9/20/83																												
1983	LA-N	0	0	—	4	0	0	0	0	7	4	5.1	0	3	3.9	5	6.4	1.29	281	.167	.259	2	2	100	85	0.0	0	0	0.2
1984	LA-N	0	1	.000	7	1	0	0	0	12	9	6.8	2	6	4.5	10	7.5	3.00	125	.209	.300	1	1	104	119	-0.4	-0	-0	0.1
Total	2	0	1	.000	11	1	0	0	0	19	13	6.2	2	9	4.3	15	7.1	2.37	156	.194	.286	3	3	102	107	-0.4	-0	0	0.3
■ **KIRBY WHITE**	White, Oliver Kirby "Red" or "Buck" b: 1/3/1884, Hillsboro, Ohio d: 4/22/43, Hillsboro, Ohio BL/TR, 6', 190 lbs. Deb: 09																												
1909	Bos-N	6	13	.316	23	19	11	0	0	148	134	8.1	5	80	4.9	53	3.2	3.22	82	.245	.343	-10	-10	102	103	0.3	-0	-1	-1.1

YEAR	TM/L	W	L	PCT	G	GS	CG	SHO	SV	IP	H	H/G	HR	BB	BB/G	SO	SO/G	ERA	/A	OAVG	OOBP	PR	/A	PF	CPI	WAT	PB	PD	TPI
1910	Bos-N	1	2	.333	3	3	3	0	0	26	15	5.2	2	12	4.2	6	2.1	1.38	259	.188	.316	5	6	118	193	0.0	1	0	0.9
	Pit-N	10	9	.526	30	21	7	3	2	153	142	8.4	2	75	4.4	42	2.5	3.47	96	.258	.352	-7	-2	110	98	-0.6	3	-3	-0.1
	Yr	11	11	.500	33	24	10	3	2	179	157	7.9	4	87	4.4	48	2.4	3.17	107	.248	.343	-3	4	111	98	-0.6	1	-3	0.8
1911	Pit-N	0	1	.000	2	1	0	0	0	3	3	9.0	1	1	3.0	1	3.0	9.00	37	.250	.308	-2	-2	97	56	-0.4	-0	0	-0.1
Total	3	17	25	.405	58	44	21	3	2	330	294	8.0	10	168	4.6	102	2.8	3.25	94	.247	.345	-15	-8	107	107	-0.7	3	-4	-0.4
■ **STEVE WHITE**	White, Stephen Vincent b: 12/21/1884, Dorchester, Mass. d: 1/29/75, Braintree, Mass. BR/TR, 5'10", 160 lbs. Deb: 5/29/12																												
1912	Was-A	0	0	—	1	0	0	0	0	1	2	18.0	1	0	0.0	1	9.0	0.00	—	.667	.667	0	0	97	0	0.0	0	0	0.0
	Bos-N	0	0	—	3	0	0	0	0	6	9	13.5	0	5	7.5	2	3.0	6.00	63	.391	.517	-2	-1	110	137	0.0	-1	0	-0.1
■ **BILL WHITE**	White, William Dighton b: 5/1/1860, Bridgeport, Ohio d: 12/29/24, Bellaire, Ohio TR , Deb: 5/03/1884																												
1886	Lou-a	0	0	—	1	0	0	0	0	1	2	18.0	0	2	18.0	1	9.0	9.00	41	.426	.597	-1	-1	108	145	0.0	0	0	0.0
■ **WILL WHITE**	White, William Henry "Whoop-La" b: 10/11/1854, Caton, N.Y. d: 8/31/11, Port Carling, Ont. Canada BB/TR, 5'9.5", 175 lbs. Deb: 7/20/1877 M																												
1877	Bos-N	2	1	.667	3	3	3	1	0	27	27	9.0	0	2	0.7	7	2.3	3.00	95	.268	.283	-1	-0	101	66	0.0	-1	0	0.0
1878	Cin-N	30	21	.588	52	52	52	5	0	468	477	9.2	1	45	0.9	169	3.3	1.79	119	.274	.292	27	18	93	112	-6.1	-7	-2	0.6
1879	Cin-N	43	31	.581	**76**	75	**75**	4	0	**680**	676	8.9	10	68	0.9	232	3.1	1.99	118	.265	.284	**39**	27	94	112	**21.5**	-16	-6	0.3
1880	Cin-N	18	42	.300	62	62	58	3	0	517	550	9.6	9	56	1.0	161	2.8	2.14	116	.281	.301	13	20	105	**130**	5.3	-10	-7	0.4
1881	Det-N	0	2	.000	2	2	2	0	0	18	24	12.0	0	2	1.0	5	2.5	5.00	59	.333	.351	-4	-4	106	77	-0.9	-1	0	-0.3
1882	Cin-a	**40**	12	**.769**	54	54	**52**	**8**	0	**480**	411	7.7	4	71	1.3	122	2.3	1.54	174	.237	.266	**61**	**61**	100	**125**	**13.1**	6	13	**7.8**
1883	Cin-a	**43**	22	.662	65	64	64	**6**	0	577	473	7.4	17	104	1.6	141	2.2	**2.09**	155	.229	.266	**78**	**73**	98	111	8.3	3	-3	6.7
1884	Cin-a	34	18	.654	52	52	52	7	0	456	479	9.5	17	74	1.5	118	2.3	3.32	100	.278	.308	-4	1	103	111	3.7	-2	-7	-0.6
1885	Cin-a	18	15	.545	34	34	33	2	0	293	295	9.1	9	64	2.0	80	2.5	3.53	94	.273	.314	-9	-7	103	95	-0.6	-4	-4	-1.1
1886	Cin-a	1	2	.333	3	3	3	0	0	26	28	9.7	1	10	3.5	6	2.1	4.15	79	.285	.352	-2	-2	96	102	-0.3	-1	0	-0.2
Total	10	229	166	.580	403	401	394	36	0	3542	3440	8.7	68	496	1.3	1041	2.6	2.28	121	.262	.289	198	184	99	114	44.0	-32	-16	13.6
■ **JOHN WHITEHEAD**	Whitehead, John Henderson "Silent John" b: 4/27/09, Coleman, Tex. d: 10/20/64, Bonham, Tex. BR/TR, 6'2", 195 lbs. Deb: 4/19/35																												
1935	Chi-A	13	13	.500	28	27	18	1	0	222	209	8.5	17	101	4.1	72	2.9	3.73	130	.250	.329	18	28	109	104	0.4	-6	3	2.5
1936	Chi-A	13	13	.500	34	32	15	1	1	231	254	9.9	9	98	3.8	70	2.7	4.64	107	.276	.345	10	8	99	94	-1.0	2	3	1.2
1937	Chi-A	11	8	.579	26	24	8	4	0	166	191	10.4	14	56	3.0	45	2.4	4.07	116	.294	.351	10	12	102	120	0.5	1	-1	1.1
1938	Chi-A	10	11	.476	32	24	10	2	2	183	218	10.7	12	80	3.9	38	1.9	4.77	99	.299	.363	0	-1	98	108	0.8	-4	-1	-0.4
1939	Chi-A	0	3	.000	7	4	0	0	0	32	60	16.9	4	5	1.4	9	2.5	8.16	60	.408	.411	-13	-12	106	103	-1.4	-1	0	-1.0
	StL-A	1	3	.250	26	4	0	0	1	66	88	12.0	10	17	2.3	9	1.2	5.86	83	.321	.354	-9	-7	105	103	-0.1	-2	1	-0.6
	Yr	1	6	.143	33	8	0	0	1	98	148	13.6	14	22	2.0	18	1.7	6.61	74	.352	.374	-22	-19	105	103	-1.5	-1	1	-1.6
1940	StL-A	1	3	.250	15	4	1	1	0	40	46	10.3	3	14	3.1	11	2.5	5.40	88	.286	.339	-5	-3	108	84	-0.8	-1	-0	-0.3
1942	StL-A	0	0	—	4	0	0	0	0	4	8	18.0	0	1	2.3	0	0.0	6.75	55	.421	.476	-1	-1	102	130	0.0	0	0	0.0
Total	7	49	54	.476	172	119	52	9	4	944	1074	10.2	69	372	3.5	254	2.4	4.60	105	.287	.349	11	25	103	104	-1.6	-11	5	2.5
■ **MILT WHITEHEAD**	Whitehead, Milton P. b: 1862, Canada d: 8/15/01, Highland Township San Bernardino County, Cal. Deb: 4/20/1884																												
1884	StL-U	0	1	.000	1	1	1	0	0	8	14	15.8	0	2	2.3	2	2.3	9.00	33	.387	.420	-5	-5	98	75	-0.3	-0	0	-0.4
■ **EARL WHITEHILL**	Whitehill, Earl Oliver b: 2/7/1900, Cedar Rapids, Iowa d: 10/22/54, Omaha, Neb. BL/TL, 5'9.5", 174 lbs. Deb: 9/15/23 C																												
1923	Det-A	2	0	1.000	8	3	1	0	0	33	22	6.0	2	15	4.1	19	5.2	2.73	139	.188	.288	5	4	95	79	1.0	1	-0	0.5
1924	Det-A	17	9	.654	35	32	16	2	0	233	260	10.0	8	79	3.1	65	2.5	3.86	108	.288	.343	10	8	99	106	3.2	0	-0	0.8
1925	Det-A	11	11	.500	35	33	15	1	2	239	267	10.1	13	88	3.3	83	3.1	4.67	92	.293	.350	-7	-10	98	96	-0.5	0	-1	-0.9
1926	Det-A	16	13	.552	36	34	13	0	0	252	271	9.7	7	79	2.8	109	3.9	4.00	98	.277	.326	1	-2	98	90	1.4	5	-1	0.1
1927	Det-A	16	14	.533	41	31	17	3	3	236	238	9.1	4	105	4.0	95	3.6	3.36	133	.267	.339	21	29	107	110	0.0	-1	-3	2.5
1928	Det-A	11	16	.407	31	30	12	1	0	196	214	9.8	8	78	3.6	93	4.3	4.32	94	.277	.333	-6	-6	100	92	-1.1	-1	1	-0.5
1929	Det-A	14	15	.483	38	28	18	1	1	245	267	9.8	16	96	3.5	103	3.8	4.63	89	.280	.340	-10	-14	97	92	0.9	5	-0	-0.8
1930	Det-A	17	13	.567	34	31	16	0	1	221	248	10.1	8	80	3.3	109	4.4	4.24	116	.285	.342	10	17	106	105	2.8	-4	-2	1.0
1931	Det-A	13	16	.448	34	34	22	0	0	271	287	9.5	22	118	3.9	81	2.7	4.08	114	.274	.343	9	18	107	115	1.5	-5	2	1.5
1932	Det-A	16	12	.571	33	31	17	3	0	244	255	9.4	17	93	3.4	81	3.0	4.54	100	.269	.332	-2	0	102	94	2.3	2	-2	0.1
1933	Was-A	22	8	.733	39	37	19	2	1	270	271	9.0	9	100	3.3	96	3.2	3.33	120	.262	.326	28	20	93	112	4.2	3	-2	1.9
1934	Was-A	14	11	.560	32	31	15	0	0	235	269	10.3	10	94	3.6	96	3.7	4.52	102	.290	.349	-1	2	102	102	3.2	3	-0	0.4
1935	Was-A	14	13	.519	34	34	19	1	0	279	318	10.3	16	104	3.4	102	3.3	4.29	96	.289	.346	5	-5	93	107	2.3	-1	1	-0.4
1936	Was-A	14	11	.560	28	28	14	0	0	212	252	10.7	17	89	3.8	63	2.7	4.88	99	.294	.359	4	-1	96	106	0.8	-0	-1	-0.1
1937	Cle-A	8	8	.500	33	22	6	1	2	147	189	11.6	9	80	4.9	53	3.2	6.49	69	.322	.402	-31	-33	97	94	-0.5	1	1	-2.6
1938	Cle-A	9	8	.529	26	23	4	0	0	160	187	10.5	18	83	4.7	60	3.4	5.57	84	.289	.374	-14	-16	98	99	-0.5	-2	-2	-1.6
1939	Chi-N	4	7	.364	24	11	2	1	1	89	102	10.3	8	50	5.1	42	4.2	5.16	76	.292	.377	-12	-12	100	105	-1.8	-2	-1	-1.3
Total	17	218	185	.541	541	473	226	16	11	3562	3917	9.9	192	1431	3.6	1350	3.4	4.36	100	.282	.345	9	-1	99	102	19.2	5	-10	0.6
■ **CHARLIE WHITEHOUSE**	Whitehouse, Charles Evis "Lefty" b: 1/25/1894, Charleston, Ill. d: 7/19/60, Indianapolis, Ind BB/TL, 6', 152 lbs. Deb: 8/29/14																												
1914	Ind-F	2	0	1.000	8	2	2	0	0	26	34	11.8	0	5	1.7	10	3.5	4.85	71	.348	.379	-5	-4	108	88	1.0	-1	0	-0.4
1915	New-F	2	2	.500	11	3	1	0	0	40	46	10.3	0	17	3.8	18	4.0	4.27	67	.319	.390	-6	-6	94	98	0.0	-1	0	-0.6
1919	Was-A	0	1	.000	6	1	0	0	0	12	13	9.8	1	6	4.5	5	3.8	4.50	71	.283	.365	-2	-2	99	98	-0.4	-0	-0	-0.1
Total	3	4	3	.571	25	6	3	0	0	78	93	10.7	1	28	3.2	33	3.8	4.50	69	.323	.383	-12	-12	99	95	0.6	-2	-0	-1.1
■ **GIL WHITEHOUSE**	Whitehouse, Gilbert Arthur b: 10/15/1893, Somerville, Mass. d: 2/14/26, Brewer, Me. BB/TR, 5'10", 170 lbs. Deb: 6/20/12																												
1915	New-F	0	0	—	1	0	0	0	0	1	0	0.0	0	1	9.0	0	0.0	0.00	—	.000	.289	0	0	94	0	0.0	0	0	0.0
■ **LEN WHITEHOUSE**	Whitehouse, Leonard Joseph b: 9/10/57, Burlington, Vt. BL/TL, 5'11", 175 lbs. Deb: 9/01/81																												
1981	Tex-A	0	1	.000	2	1	0	0	0	3	8	24.0	1	2	6.0	2	6.0	18.00	18	.500	.500	-5	-5	90	83	-0.4	0	0	-0.4
1983	Min-A	7	1	.875	60	0	0	0	2	74	70	8.5	6	44	5.4	44	5.4	4.14	105	.261	.358	-0	2	106	112	3.2	0	-1	0.1
1984	Min-A	2	2	.500	30	0	0	0	1	31	29	8.4	3	17	4.9	18	5.2	3.19	132	.254	.353	3	4	106	140	0.0	0	-0	0.3
1985	Min-A	0	0	—	5	0	0	0	1	7	12	15.4	4	2	2.6	4	5.1	11.57	37	.353	.389	-6	-6	104	88	0.0	0	0	-0.4
Total	4	9	4	.692	97	1	0	0	4	115	119	9.3	14	65	5.1	68	5.3	4.70	91	.275	.364	-8	-5	106	118	2.8	0	-1	-0.4
■ **JESSE WHITING**	Whiting, Jesse W. b: 5/30/1879, Philadelphia, Pa. d: 10/28/37, Philadelphia, Pa. Deb: 9/27/02																												
1902	Phi-N	0	1	.000	1	1	1	0	0	9	13	13.0	0	6	6.0	0	0.0	5.00	61	.363	.455	-2	-2	109	120	-0.4	0	0	-0.1
1906	Bro-N	1	1	.500	3	2	2	1	0	25	26	9.4	0	6	2.2	7	2.5	2.88	82	.299	.352	-1	-1	90	109	0.1	1	1	0.0
1907	Bro-N	0	0	—	1	0	0	0	0	3	3	9.0	0	3	9.0	2	6.0	12.00	20	.289	.448	-3	-3	96	40	0.0	-0	0	-0.2
Total	3	1	2	.333	5	3	3	1	0	37	42	10.2	0	15	3.6	9	2.2	4.14	61	.316	.389	-6	-7	95	106	-0.3	1	1	-0.3
■ **ART WHITNEY**	Whitney, Arthur Wilson b: 1/16/1858, Brockton, Mass. d: 8/15/43, Lowell, Mass. BR/TR, 5'8", 155 lbs. Deb: 5/01/1880																												
1882	Det-N	0	1	.000	3	2	1	0	0	18	31	15.5	1	8	4.0	11	5.5	6.00	50	.386	.442	-6	-6	104	124	-0.3	-1	0	-0.8
1886	Pit-a	0	0	—	1	0	0	0	0	6	7	10.5	0	3	4.5	2	3.0	3.00	103	.302	.382	0	0	90	157	0.0	0	0	0.0
1889	NY-N	0	1	.000	1	0	0	0	0	6	7	10.5	0	3	4.5	3	4.5	3.00	136	.307	.388	1	1	101	148	-0.4	0	0	0.1
Total	3	0	2	.000	5	2	1	0	0	30	45	13.5	1	14	4.2	16	4.8	4.80	68	.357	.421	-5	-5	101	136	-0.7	-1	0	-0.7
■ **JIM WHITNEY**	Whitney, James Evans "Grasshopper Jim" b: 11/10/1857, Conklin, N.Y. d: 5/21/1891, Binghamton, N.Y. BL/TR, 6'2", 172 lbs. Deb: 5/02/1881																												
1881	Bos-N	**31**	33	.484	**66**	63	**57**	6	0	**552**	548	8.9	6	90	1.5	162	2.6	2.48	104	.271	.302	18	7	93	97	5.9	12	-4	1.2
1882	Bos-N	24	21	.533	49	48	46	3	0	420	404	8.7	3	41	0.9	180	3.9	2.64	111	.260	.279	12	14	102	86	-0.1	22	2	4.1
1883	Bos-N	37	21	.638	62	56	54	1	**2**	514	492	8.6	7	35	**0.6**	**345**	**6.0**	2.24	142	.259	.273	51	54	102	96	-0.4	18	1	7.8
1884	Bos-N	23	14	.622	38	37	35	6	0	336	272	7.3	12	27	**0.7**	270	7.2	2.09	133	.230	.247	33	26	93	75	-1.4	10	4	4.2
1885	Bos-N	18	32	.360	51	50	50	2	0	441	503	10.3	14	37	**0.8**	200	4.1	2.98	90	.298	.313	-8	-15	95	115	-5.0	7	5	-0.1
1886	KC-N	12	32	.273	46	44	42	3	0	393	465	10.6	9	55	**1.3**	167	3.8	4.49	84	.308	.332	-52	-32	114	84	1.1	6	5	-0.9
1887	Was-N	24	21	.533	47	47	46	3	0	405	430	9.6	16	42	**0.9**	146	3.2	3.22	124	.287	.307	37	35	99	100	7.8	10	3	4.3
1888	Was-N	18	21	.462	39	39	37	2	0	325	317	8.8	6	54	1.5	79	2.2	3.05	94	.269	.301	-8	-7	101	87	4.2	-1	-2	-0.9
1889	Ind-N	2	7	.222	9	8	7	0	0	70	106	13.6	4	19	2.4	16	2.1	6.81	65	.366	.405	-22	-19	110	87	-2.2	5	0	-0.9
1890	Phi-a	2	2	.500	6	4	3	0	0	40	61	13.7	1	11	2.5	6	1.3	5.17	76	.367	.407	-6	-6	101	116	0.3	-0	0	-0.4

YEAR	TM/L	W	L	PCT	G	GS	CG	SHO	SV	IP	H	H/G	HR	BB	BB/G	SO	SO/G	ERA	/A	OAVG	OOBP	PR	/A	PF	CPI	WAT	PB	PD	TPI
Total	10	191	204	.484	413	396	377	26	2	3496	3598	9.3	78	411	1.1	1571	4.0	2.97	105	.277	.299	57	54	100	94	10.2	88	14	18.4
■ **BILL WHITROCK**	Whitrock, William Franklin b: 3/4/1870, Cincinnati, Ohio d: 7/26/35, Derby, Conn. TR, 5'7.5", 170 lbs. Deb: 5/03/1890																												
1890	StL-a	5	6	.455	16	11	10	0	1	105	104	8.9	2	40	3.4	39	3.3	3.51	126	.274	.343	4	11	115	103	-1.1	-3	0	0.8
1893	Lou-N	2	4	.333	6	6	4	0	0	38	54	12.8	3	14	3.3	7	1.7	8.05	57	.351	.405	-14	-15	98	75	-0.4	1	0	-0.9
1894	Lou-N	0	1	.000	1	1	0	0	0	4	8	18.0	0	2	4.5	0	0.0	9.00	54	.439	.495	-2	-2	91	97	-0.4	-0	0	-0.1
	Cin-N	2	6	.250	10	8	8	0	0	70	110	14.1	7	39	5.0	9	1.2	6.69	81	.381	.455	-11	-10	102	111	-1.6	-2	0	-0.9
	Yr	2	7	.222	11	9	8	0	0	74	118	14.4	7	41	5.0	9	1.1	6.81	79	.384	.457	-12	-12	101	111	-2.0	-0	0	-1.0
1896	Phi-N	0	1	.000	2	1	1	0	0	9	10	10.0	0	3	3.0	1	1.0	3.00	149	.304	.362	1	1	102	122	-0.4	-1	0	0.1
Total	4	9	18	.333	35	27	23	0	1	226	286	11.4	12	98	3.9	56	2.2	5.34	90	.327	.395	-21	-13	107	102	-3.9	-5	0	-1.0
■ **EDDIE WHITSON**	Whitson, Eddie Lee b: 5/19/55, Johnson City, Tenn. BR/TR, 6'3", 195 lbs. Deb: 9/04/77																												
1977	Pit-N	1	0	1.000	5	2	0	0	0	16	11	6.2	0	9	5.1	10	5.6	3.38	118	.204	.303	1	1	102	72	0.5	-1	-0	0.0
1978	Pit-N	5	6	.455	43	0	0	0	4	74	66	8.0	5	37	4.5	64	7.8	3.28	114	.243	.330	2	4	105	112	-0.9	-0	-1	0.3
1979	Pit-N	2	3	.400	19	7	0	0	1	58	53	8.2	6	36	5.6	31	4.8	4.34	90	.238	.342	-4	-3	104	91	-0.8	-1	-0	-0.4
	SF-N	5	8	.385	18	17	2	0	0	100	98	8.8	5	39	3.5	62	5.6	3.96	88	.254	.321	-2	-5	93	86	-0.8	-0	-0	-0.5
	Yr	7	11	.389	37	24	2	0	1	158	151	8.6	11	75	4.3	93	5.3	4.10	89	.248	.328	-6	-8	97	86	-1.6	-1	-1	-0.9
1980	SF-N	11	13	.458	34	34	6	2	0	212	222	9.4	7	56	2.4	90	3.8	3.10	112	.271	.314	12	9	96	110	-0.1	-4	-2	0.3
1981	SF-N	6	9	.400	22	22	2	1	0	123	130	9.5	10	47	3.4	65	4.8	4.02	91	.273	.335	-7	-5	105	103	-1.6	-1	-2	-0.7
1982	Cle-A	4	2	.667	40	9	1	1	2	108	91	7.6	6	58	4.8	61	5.1	3.25	127	.231	.319	10	10	101	103	1.1	0	-2	0.9
1983	SD-N	5	7	.417	31	21	2	0	1	144	143	8.9	23	50	3.1	81	5.1	4.31	84	.256	.314	-11	-11	99	95	-1.0	1	-4	-1.4
1984	SD-N	14	8	.636	31	31	1	0	0	189	181	8.6	16	42	2.0	103	4.9	3.24	109	.255	.292	7	6	98	102	2.0	-4	1	0.3
1985	NY-A	10	8	.556	30	30	2	2	0	159	201	11.4	19	43	2.4	89	5.0	4.87	80	.309	.349	-13	-17	94	108	-0.7	0	-1	-1.7
1986	NY-A	5	2	.714	14	4	0	0	0	37	54	13.1	5	23	5.6	27	6.6	7.54	57	.335	.407	-14	-13	103	93	1.3	0	0	-1.2
	SD-N	1	7	.125	17	12	0	0	0	76	85	10.1	8	37	4.4	46	5.4	5.57	64	.287	.362	-16	-17	96	90	-2.8	-0	0	-1.6
1987	SD-N	10	13	.435	36	34	3	1	0	206	197	8.6	36	64	2.8	135	5.9	4.72	85	.251	.308	-14	-17	98	88	0.7	-1	-2	-1.9
1988	SD-N	13	11	.542	34	33	3	1	0	205	202	8.9	17	45	2.0	118	5.2	3.78	89	.259	.293	-7	-10	97	91	0.8	1	-1	-0.9
Total	12	92	97	.487	374	256	22	8	8	1707	1734	9.1	163	586	3.1	982	5.2	4.04	91	.264	.321	-55	-68	98	98	-2.3	-11	-13	-8.5
■ **WALT WHITTAKER**	Whittaker, Walter Elton "Doc" b: 6/11/1894, Chelsea, Mass. d: 8/9/65, Pembroke, Mass. BL/TR, 5'9.5", 165 lbs. Deb: 7/06/16																												
1916	Phi-A	0	0	—	1	0	0	0	0	2	3	13.5	0	2	9.0	0	0.0	4.50	66	.375	.500	-0	-0	105	174	0.0	0	0	0.0
■ **KEMP WICKER**	Wicker, Kemp Caswell (born Kemp Caswell Whicker) b: 8/13/06, Kernersville, N.C. d: 6/11/73, Kernersville, N.C BR/TL, 5'11", 182 lbs. Deb: 8/14/36																												
1936	NY-A	1	2	.333	7	0	0	0	0	20	31	13.9	2	11	4.9	5	2.3	7.65	59	.356	.420	-6	-7	90	100	-0.7	-0	0	-0.5
1937	NY-A	7	3	.700	16	10	6	1	0	88	107	10.9	8	26	2.7	14	1.4	4.40	102	.296	.338	2	1	97	107	0.6	-3	-2	-0.3
1938	NY-A	1	0	1.000	1	0	0	0	0	1	0	0.0	0	1	9.0	0	0.0	0.00	—	.000	.250	1	1	102	0	0.5	0	0	0.0
1941	Bro-N	1	2	.333	16	2	0	0	1	32	30	8.4	3	14	3.9	8	2.3	3.66	99	.252	.321	-0	-0	99	108	-0.6	0	0	0.0
Total	4	10	7	.588	40	12	6	1	1	141	168	10.7	13	52	3.3	27	1.7	4.66	92	.294	.347	-3	-6	97	105	-0.2	-2	-2	-0.8
■ **BOB WICKER**	Wicker, Robert Kitridge b: 5/24/1878, Bedford, Ind. d: 1/22/55, Evanston, Ill. BR/TR, 6'2", 180 lbs. Deb: 8/11/01																												
1901	StL-N	0	0	—	1	0	0	0	0	3	4	12.0	0	1	3.0	2	6.0	0.00	—	.343	.395	1	1	95	0	0.0	0	0	0.1
1902	StL-N	5	12	.294	22	16	14	1	0	152	159	9.4	1	45	2.7	78	4.6	3.20	86	.293	.350	-7	-8	99	98	-2.7	1	2	-0.4
1903	StL-N	0	0	—	1	0	0	0	0	5	4	7.2	0	3	5.4	3	5.4	0.00	—	.241	.357	2	2	102	0	0.0	-0	1	0.3
	Chi-N	20	9	.690	32	27	24	1	1	247	236	8.6	3	74	2.7	110	4.0	3.02	101	.276	.336	7	1	94	93	4.1	5	-5	-0.3
	Yr	20	9	.690	33	27	24	1	1	252	240	8.6	3	77	2.8	113	4.0	2.96	103	.275	.336	9	3	94	93	4.1	-0	-5	0.0
1904	Chi-N	17	9	.654	30	27	23	4	0	229	201	7.9	6	58	2.3	99	3.9	2.67	101	.259	.313	1	1	99	93	1.8	1	-5	-0.3
1905	Chi-N	13	6	.684	22	22	17	4	0	178	139	7.0	3	47	2.4	86	4.3	2.02	148	.239	.298	19	19	100	101	2.2	-2	-3	1.8
1906	Chi-N	3	5	.375	10	8	5	0	0	72	70	8.8	0	19	2.4	25	3.1	3.00	87	.282	.333	-3	-3	99	92	-2.0	-1	-1	-0.4
	Cin-N	6	11	.353	20	17	14	0	0	150	150	9.0	3	46	2.8	69	4.1	2.70	113	.288	.347	-1	6	116	118	-1.5	1	-4	0.2
	Yr	9	16	.360	30	25	19	0	0	222	220	8.9	3	65	2.6	94	3.8	2.80	104	.286	.343	-4	3	111	118	-3.5	-1	-5	-0.2
Total	6	64	52	.552	138	117	97	10	1	1036	963	8.4	16	293	2.5	472	4.1	2.73	106	.271	.329	19	20	100	98	1.9	5	-15	1.0
■ **DAVE WICKERSHAM**	Wickersham, David Clifford b: 9/27/35, Erie, Pa. BR/TR, 6'3", 188 lbs. Deb: 9/18/60																												
1960	KC-A	0	0	—	5	0	0	0	2	8	4	4.5	0	1	1.1	3	3.4	1.13	349	.148	.179	2	2	101	13	0.0	-0	0	0.3
1961	KC-A	2	1	.667	17	0	0	0	2	21	25	10.7	0	5	2.1	10	4.3	5.14	82	.309	.356	-3	-2	104	85	0.7	1	0	0.0
1962	KC-A	11	4	.733	30	9	3	0	1	110	105	8.6	13	43	3.5	61	5.0	4.17	96	.257	.334	-2	-2	101	103	4.1	-3	1	-0.2
1963	KC-A	12	15	.444	38	34	4	1	1	238	244	9.2	21	79	3.0	118	4.5	4.08	97	.268	.325	-12	-4	109	100	-0.1	-4	1	-0.5
1964	Det-A	19	12	.613	40	36	11	1	1	254	224	7.9	28	81	2.9	164	5.8	3.44	101	.232	.298	5	0	95	92	3.4	-5	-0	-0.5
1965	Det-A	9	14	.391	34	27	8	3	0	195	179	8.3	12	61	2.8	109	5.0	3.78	95	.241	.305	-7	-4	104	82	-3.6	-4	1	-0.6
1966	Det-A	8	3	.727	38	14	3	0	1	141	139	8.9	14	54	3.4	93	5.9	3.19	110	.261	.333	4	5	102	132	2.3	-3	1	0.3
1967	Det-A	4	5	.444	36	4	0	0	4	85	72	7.6	6	33	3.5	44	4.7	2.75	115	.235	.310	5	4	98	122	-0.9	-2	1	0.4
1968	Pit-N	1	0	1.000	11	0	0	0	1	21	21	9.0	0	13	5.6	9	3.9	3.43	87	.276	.358	-1	-1	100	123	0.5	0	0	0.0
1969	KC-A	2	3	.400	34	0	0	0	5	50	58	10.4	6	14	2.5	27	4.9	3.96	95	.294	.341	-2	-1	104	121	-0.1	0	0	0.0
Total	10	68	57	.544	283	124	29	5	18	1123	1071	8.6	100	384	3.1	638	5.1	3.66	100	.252	.317	-11	-2	102	102	6.3	-18	4	-0.8
■ **AL WIDMAR**	Widmar, Albert Joseph b: 3/20/25, Cleveland, Ohio BR/TR, 6'3", 185 lbs. Deb: 4/25/47 C																												
1947	Bos-A	0	0	—	2	0	0	0	0	1	1	9.0	1	2	18.0	1	9.0	18.00	22	.200	.429	-2	-2	107	71	0.0	0	0	-0.1
1948	StL-A	2	6	.250	49	0	0	0	1	83	88	9.5	4	48	5.2	34	3.7	4.45	105	.275	.366	-2	2	109	105	-1.4	1	2	0.4
1950	StL-A	7	15	.318	36	26	8	1	4	195	211	9.7	16	74	3.4	78	3.6	4.75	107	.271	.334	-4	7	111	87	-1.8	-4	1	0.4
1951	StL-A	4	9	.308	26	16	4	0	0	108	157	13.1	19	52	4.3	28	2.3	6.50	69	.344	.407	-29	-24	109	113	-0.5	-1	1	-2.1
1952	Chi-A	0	0	—	1	0	0	0	0	2	4	18.0	1	0	0.0	2	9.0	4.50	81	.444	.444	-0	-0	99	258	0.0	0	0	0.0
Total	5	13	30	.302	114	42	12	1	5	389	461	10.7	41	176	4.1	143	3.3	5.21	93	.294	.363	-36	-17	110	99	-3.7	-4	3	-1.4
■ **WILD BILL WIDNER**	Widner, William Waterfield b: 6/3/1867, Cincinnati, Ohio d: 12/10/08, Cincinnati, Ohio BR/TR, 6', 180 lbs. Deb: 6/08/1887																												
1887	Cin-a	1	0	1.000	1	1	1	0	0	9	11	11.0	2	2	2.0	0	0.0	5.00	91	.315	.352	-1	-0	106	117	0.5	-0	0	0.0
1888	Was-N	5	7	.417	13	13	13	0	0	115	111	8.7	7	22	1.7	33	2.6	2.82	101	.267	.304	0	1	101	107	0.6	-1	0	0.0
1889	Col-a	12	20	.375	41	34	25	2	1	294	368	11.3	11	85	2.6	63	1.9	5.20	68	.322	.369	-44	-54	92	87	-2.7	-1	0	-4.4
1890	Col-a	4	8	.333	13	10	8	1	0	96	103	9.7	3	24	2.3	14	1.3	3.28	113	.290	.335	6	5	96	115	-2.6	-1	0	0.3
1891	CM-a	0	1	.000	1	1	1	0	0	8	13	14.6	0	4	4.5	0	0.0	7.88	53	.381	.446	-4	-3	113	83	-0.4	-0	0	-0.2
Total	5	22	36	.379	69	59	48	3	1	522	606	10.4	23	137	2.4	110	1.9	4.36	79	.306	.351	-42	-52	95	97	-4.6	-3	0	-4.3
■ **TED WIEAND**	Wieand, Franklin Delano Roosevelt b: 4/4/33, Walnutport, Pa. BR/TR, 6'2", 195 lbs. Deb: 9/27/58																												
1958	Cin-N	0	0	—	1	0	0	0	0	2	4	18.0	1	0	0.0	2	9.0	9.00	47	.400	.400	-1	-1	106	115	0.0	0	0	0.0
1960	Cin-N	0	1	.000	5	0	0	0	0	4	4	9.0	2	5	11.3	3	6.8	11.25	33	.250	.429	-3	-3	99	81	-0.4	0	0	-0.2
Total	2	0	1	.000	6	0	0	0	0	6	8	12.0	3	5	7.5	5	7.5	10.50	37	.308	.419	-4	-4	101	92	-0.4	0	0	-0.2
■ **CHARLIE WIEDEMEYER**	Wiedemeyer, Charles John "Chick" b: 1/31/14, Chicago, Ill. d: 10/27/79, Lake Geneva, Fla. BL/TL, 6'3", 180 lbs. Deb: 9/09/34																												
1934	Chi-N	0	0	—	4	1	0	0	0	8	16	18.0	0	4	4.5	2	2.3	10.13	39	.432	.488	-5	-6	97	93	0.0	-0	0	-0.4
■ **JACK WIENEKE**	Wieneke, John b: 3/10/1894, Saltzburg, Pa. d: 3/16/33, Pleasant Ridge, Mich. BR/TL, 6', 182 lbs. Deb: 7/04/21																												
1921	Chi-A	0	1	.000	10	3	0	0	0	25	39	14.0	4	17	6.1	10	3.6	8.28	53	.351	.429	-11	-11	102	95	-0.4	-1	0	-0.9
■ **BOB WIESLER**	Wiesler, Robert George b: 8/13/30, St.Louis, Mo. BB/TL, 6'3", 188 lbs. Deb: 8/03/51																												
1951	NY-A	0	2	.000	4	3	0	0	0	9	13	13.0	0	11	11.0	3	3.0	14.00	26	.361	.500	-10	-10	88	61	-0.9	-0	0	-0.8
1954	NY-A	3	2	.600	6	5	0	0	0	30	28	8.4	0	30	9.0	25	7.5	4.20	84	.259	.420	-2	-2	94	116	-0.2	1	-0	-0.1
1955	NY-A	0	2	.000	16	7	0	0	0	53	39	6.6	1	49	8.3	22	3.7	3.91	96	.212	.377	0	-1	94	97	-0.9	-1	1	0.0
1956	Was-A	3	12	.200	37	21	3	0	0	123	141	10.3	11	112	8.2	49	3.6	6.44	69	.300	.428	-31	-27	107	101	-3.7	-3	1	-2.6
1957	Was-A	1	1	.500	3	2	1	0	0	16	15	8.4	2	11	6.2	9	5.1	4.50	86	.250	.375	-1	-1	102	108	0.2	0	0	0.0
1958	Was-A	0	0	—	4	0	0	0	0	9	14	14.0	2	5	5.0	5	5.0	7.00	54	.359	.435	-3	-3	100	122	0.0	-0	1	-0.2
Total	6	7	19	.269	70	38	4	0	0	240	250	9.4	16	218	8.2	113	4.2	5.78	70	.279	.417	-47	-46	101	101	-5.5	-4	3	-3.7

YEAR	TM/L	W	L	PCT	G	GS	CG	SHO	SV	IP	H	H/G	HR	BB	BB/G	SO	SO/G	ERA	/A	OAVG	OOBP	PR	/A	PF	CPI	WAT	PB	PD	TPI
■ **WHITEY WIETELMANN** Wietelmann, William Frederick b: 3/15/19, Zanesville, Ohio BB/TR, 6', 170 lbs. Deb: 9/06/39 C																													
1945	Bos-N	0	0	—	1	0	0	0	0	1	6	54.0	0	2	18.0	0	0.0	54.00	8	.667	.727	-6	-6	113	59	0.0	0	0	-0.3
1946	Bos-N	0	0	—	3	0	0	0	0	7	9	11.6	1	4	5.1	2	2.6	7.71	41	.310	.378	-3	-4	94	83	0.0	0	-0	-0.2
Total	2	0	0	—	4	0	0	0	0	8	15	16.9	1	6	6.8	2	2.3	13.50	25	.395	.458	-9	-9	96	80	0.0	1	-0	-0.5
■ **JIMMY WIGGS** Wiggs, James Alvin "Big Jim" b: 9/1/1876, Trondheim, Norway d: 1/20/63, Xenia, Ohio BB/TR, 6'4", 200 lbs. Deb: 4/23/03																													
1903	Cin-N	0	1	.000	2	1	0	0	0	5	12	21.6	0	2	3.6	2	3.6	5.40	65	.509	.564	-1	-1	107	197	-0.4	-0	0	0.0
1905	Det-A	3	3	.500	7	7	4	0	0	41	30	6.6	0	29	6.4	37	8.1	3.29	80	.226	.364	-3	-3	100	90	0.0	-0	-0	-0.2
1906	Det-A	0	0	—	4	1	0	0	0	10	11	9.9	1	7	6.3	7	6.3	5.40	55	.305	.419	-3	-3	110	101	0.0	0	0	-0.2
Total	3	3	4	.429	13	9	4	0	0	56	53	8.5	1	38	6.1	46	7.4	3.86	72	.275	.397	-7	-7	103	102	-0.4	-0	0	-0.4
■ **BILL WIGHT** Wight, William Robert "Lefty" b: 4/12/22, Rio Vista, Cal. BL/TL, 6'1", 180 lbs. Deb: 4/17/46																													
1946	NY-A	2	2	.500	14	4	1	0	0	40	44	9.9	1	30	6.7	11	2.5	4.50	76	.289	.397	-4	-5	98	115	-0.1	-1	0	-0.5
1947	NY-A	1	0	1.000	1	1	1	0	0	9	8	8.0	0	2	2.0	3	3.0	1.00	342	.242	.286	3	2	92	233	0.5	0	0	0.4
1948	Chi-A	9	20	.310	34	32	7	1	1	223	238	9.6	9	135	5.4	68	2.7	4.80	89	.278	.370	-13	-13	100	100	-1.2	-7	0	-1.7
1949	Chi-A	15	13	.536	35	33	14	3	1	245	254	9.3	9	96	3.5	78	2.9	3.31	126	.275	.338	24	24	99	118	3.5	-1	0	2.2
1950	Chi-A	10	16	.385	30	28	13	3	0	206	213	9.3	10	79	3.5	62	2.7	3.58	127	.270	.330	23	22	99	109	-0.1	-8	1	1.4
1951	Bos-A	7	7	.500	34	17	4	2	0	118	128	9.8	5	63	4.8	38	2.9	5.11	86	.282	.364	-13	-10	106	90	-0.8	-5	1	-1.1
1952	Bos-A	2	1	.667	10	2	0	0	0	24	14	5.3	3	14	5.3	5	1.9	3.00	131	.169	.293	2	2	107	89	0.5	-0	1	0.3
	Det-A	5	9	.357	23	19	8	3	0	144	167	10.4	7	55	3.4	65	4.1	3.88	97	.291	.349	-3	-2	103	113	0.4	1	2	0.1
	Yr	7	10	.412	33	21	8	3	0	168	181	9.7	10	69	3.7	70	3.8	3.75	101	.275	.340	-1	1	103	113	0.9	-0	2	0.4
1953	Det-A	0	3	.000	13	4	0	0	0	25	35	12.6	4	14	5.0	10	3.6	9.00	45	.333	.392	-14	-14	102	77	-1.4	1	-1	-1.2
	Cle-A	2	1	.667	20	0	0	0	1	27	29	9.7	1	16	5.3	14	4.7	3.67	101	.282	.375	1	0	93	127	0.3	-1	0	0.0
	Yr	2	4	.333	33	4	0	0	1	52	64	11.1	5	30	5.2	24	4.2	6.23	62	.308	.384	-13	-14	97	127	-1.1	1	-0	-1.2
1955	Cle-A	0	0	—	17	0	0	0	1	24	24	9.0	0	9	3.4	9	3.4	2.63	154	.261	.324	4	4	102	118	0.0	0	2	0.6
	Bal-A	6	8	.429	19	14	8	2	2	117	111	8.5	6	39	3.0	54	4.2	2.46	151	.252	.304	20	16	94	130	0.7	-2	2	1.7
	Yr	6	8	.429	36	14	8	2	3	141	135	8.6	6	48	3.1	63	4.0	2.49	151	.254	.308	23	20	95	130	0.7	0	4	2.3
1956	Bal-A	9	12	.429	35	26	7	1	0	175	198	10.2	7	72	3.7	84	4.3	4.01	100	.289	.355	3	0	97	110	-0.4	-1	-1	-0.1
1957	Bal-A	6	6	.500	27	17	2	0	0	121	122	9.1	4	54	4.0	50	3.7	3.64	96	.271	.344	2	-2	93	109	0.0	-3	-1	-0.5
1958	Cin-N	0	1	.000	7	0	0	0	0	7	7	9.0	1	4	5.1	5	6.4	3.86	109	.292	.393	0	0	106	147	-0.4	0	0	0.1
	StL-N	3	0	1.000	28	1	1	0	2	57	64	10.1	7	32	5.1	18	2.8	5.05	84	.290	.365	-7	-5	108	105	1.5	-0	1	-0.4
	Yr	3	1	.750	35	1	1	0	2	64	71	10.0	8	36	5.1	23	3.2	4.92	87	.290	.368	-7	-5	108	105	1.1	0	1	-0.3
Total	12	77	99	.438	347	198	66	15	8	1562	1656	9.5	74	714	4.1	574	3.3	3.95	103	.277	.348	26	21	99	110	3.0	-28	9	1.3
■ **FRED WIGINGTON** Wigington, Fred Thomas b: 12/16/1897, Rogers, Neb. d: 5/8/80, Mesa, Ariz. BR/TR, 5'10", 168 lbs. Deb: 4/20/23																													
1923	StL-N	0	0	—	4	0	0	0	0	8	11	12.4	0	5	5.6	2	2.3	3.38	106	.367	.410	1	0	90	199	0.0	-0	0	0.0
■ **SANDY WIHTOL** Wihtol, Alexander Ames b: 6/1/55, Palo Alto, Cal. BR/TR, 6'1", 195 lbs. Deb: 9/07/79																													
1979	Cle-A	0	0	—	5	0	0	0	0	11	10	8.2	0	3	2.5	6	4.9	3.27	137	.238	.289	1	1	106	68	0.0	0	0	0.2
1980	Cle-A	1	0	1.000	17	0	0	0	1	35	35	9.0	2	14	3.6	20	5.1	3.60	116	.257	.327	2	2	103	101	0.5	0	-1	0.1
1982	Cle-A	0	0	—	6	0	0	0	0	12	9	6.8	1	7	5.3	8	6.0	4.50	91	.220	.340	-1	-1	101	85	0.0	0	-0	0.0
Total	3	1	0	1.000	28	0	0	0	1	58	54	8.4	3	24	3.7	34	5.3	3.72	113	.247	.323	2	3	103	91	0.5	0	-1	0.3
■ **MILT WILCOX** Wilcox, Milton Edward b: 4/20/50, Honolulu, Hawaii BR/TR, 6'2", 185 lbs. Deb: 9/05/70																													
1970	Cin-N	3	1	.750	5	2	1	1	1	22	19	7.8	2	7	2.9	13	5.3	2.45	170	.229	.293	4	4	103	125	0.7	-0	0	0.5
1971	Cin-N	2	2	.500	18	3	0	0	1	43	43	9.0	2	17	3.6	21	4.4	3.35	100	.269	.332	1	-0	96	116	0.0	-1	0	0.0
1972	Cle-A	7	14	.333	32	27	4	2	0	156	145	8.4	18	72	4.2	90	5.2	3.40	97	.251	.332	-6	-2	108	119	-3.1	1	-2	-0.2
1973	Cle-A	8	10	.444	26	19	4	0	0	134	143	9.6	14	68	4.6	82	5.5	5.84	65	.275	.365	-30	-31	99	82	0.1	0	1	-2.8
1974	Cle-A	2	2	.500	41	2	1	0	4	71	74	9.4	10	24	3.0	33	4.2	4.69	78	.271	.333	-8	-8	101	96	0.1	0	1	-0.7
1975	Chi-N	0	1	.000	25	0	0	0	0	38	50	11.8	4	17	4.0	21	5.0	5.68	67	.323	.382	-9	-8	105	103	-0.4	0	0	-0.7
1977	Det-A	6	2	.750	20	13	1	0	0	106	96	8.2	13	37	3.1	82	7.0	3.65	117	.241	.304	5	7	105	95	2.2	0	-0	0.7
1978	Det-A	13	12	.520	29	17	16	2	0	215	208	8.7	22	68	2.8	132	5.5	3.77	107	.255	.313	0	7	107	97	-0.2	0	1	0.8
1979	Det-A	12	10	.545	33	29	7	0	0	197	201	9.2	18	73	3.3	109	5.0	4.34	94	.267	.334	-2	-6	96	97	0.5	0	3	-0.2
1980	Det-A	13	11	.542	32	31	13	1	0	199	201	9.1	24	68	3.1	97	4.4	4.48	95	.262	.322	-10	-5	105	91	0.7	0	1	-0.3
1981	Det-A	12	9	.571	24	24	8	1	0	166	152	8.2	10	52	2.8	79	4.3	3.04	126	.247	.306	12	15	105	107	0.6	0	1	1.7
1982	Det-A	12	10	.545	29	29	9	1	0	194	187	8.7	18	85	3.9	112	5.2	3.62	113	.257	.335	10	10	100	113	0.9	0	3	1.2
1983	Det-A	11	10	.524	26	26	9	2	0	186	164	7.9	19	74	3.6	101	4.9	3.97	97	.237	.312	2	-2	95	89	-0.8	0	3	0.0
1984	Det-A	17	8	.680	33	33	0	0	0	194	183	8.5	13	66	3.1	119	5.5	3.99	94	.252	.316	0	-5	94	88	1.5	0	1	-0.3
1985	Det-A	1	3	.250	8	8	0	0	0	39	51	11.8	6	14	3.2	20	4.6	4.85	91	.315	.367	-3	-2	106	121	-1.0	0	1	0.0
1986	Sea-A	0	8	.000	13	10	0	0	0	56	74	11.9	11	28	4.5	26	4.2	5.46	81	.327	.398	-8	-6	106	128	-3.9	0	0	-0.5
Total	16	119	113	.513	394	273	73	10	6	2016	1991	8.9	204	770	3.4	1137	5.1	4.08	97	.260	.328	-42	-30	101	100	-2.1	0	14	-0.8
■ **RANDY WILES** Wiles, Randall E b: 9/10/51, Fort Belvoir, Va. BL/TL, 6'1", 185 lbs. Deb: 8/07/77																													
1977	Chi-A	1	1	.500	5	0	0	0	0	3	5	15.0	1	3	9.0	0	0.0	9.00	45	.417	.500	-2	-2	99	132	0.0	0	0	-0.1
■ **MARK WILEY** Wiley, Mark Eugene b: 2/28/48, National City, Cal. BR/TR, 6'1", 200 lbs. Deb: 6/17/75 C																													
1975	Min-A	1	3	.250	15	3	1	0	2	39	50	11.5	4	13	3.0	15	3.5	6.00	68	.325	.372	-10	-8	107	93	-0.9	0	-1	-0.8
1978	SD-N	1	0	1.000	4	1	0	0	0	8	11	12.4	1	1	1.1	1	1.1	5.63	59	.324	.343	-2	-2	93	92	0.5	-0	0	-0.1
	Tor-A	0	0	—	2	0	0	0	0	3	3	9.0	0	1	3.0	2	6.0	6.00	64	.273	.333	-1	-1	102	56	0.0	0	0	0.0
Total	2	2	3	.400	21	4	1	0	2	50	64	11.5	5	15	2.7	18	3.2	5.94	66	.322	.365	-12	-11	105	91	-0.4	-0	-1	-0.9
■ **HARRY WILHELM** Wilhelm, Harry Lester b: 4/7/1874, Uniontown, Pa. d: 2/20/44, Republic, Pa. BR/TR, 5'7", 155 lbs. Deb: 8/12/1899																													
1899	Lou-N	1	1	.500	5	3	2	0	0	25	36	13.0	1	3	1.1	6	2.2	6.12	65	.363	.381	-6	-6	103	80	0.0	2	0	-0.3
■ **KAISER WILHELM** Wilhelm, Irvin Key b: 1/26/1874, Wooster, Ohio d: 5/21/36, Rochester, N.Y. BR/TR, 6', 162 lbs. Deb: 4/18/03 MC																													
1903	Pit-N	5	3	.625	12	9	7	1	0	86	88	9.2	0	25	2.6	20	2.1	3.24	102	.292	.352	0	1	101	95	-0.1	-2	1	0.2
1904	Bos-N	14	20	.412	39	36	30	3	0	288	316	9.9	8	74	2.3	73	2.3	3.69	75	.305	.356	-31	-29	102	98	1.7	-8	0	-2.8
1905	Bos-N	3	23	.115	34	27	23	0	0	242	287	10.7	7	75	2.8	76	2.8	4.54	67	.325	.381	-42	-40	102	95	-8.9	-2	2	-3.6
1908	Bro-N	16	22	.421	42	36	33	6	0	332	266	7.2	3	83	2.3	99	2.7	1.87	123	.247	.305	18	16	99	106	2.8	-4	2	2.2
1909	Bro-N	3	13	.188	22	17	14	1	0	163	176	9.7	3	59	3.3	45	2.5	3.26	82	.289	.353	-12	-10	103	117	-3.9	2	1	-0.9
1910	Bro-N	3	7	.300	15	5	0	0	0	68	88	11.6	3	18	2.4	17	2.3	4.76	62	.314	.358	-13	-14	98	93	-1.4	2	1	-1.0
1914	Bal-F	12	17	.414	47	27	11	1	5	244	263	9.7	10	81	3.0	113	4.2	4.02	79	.291	.349	-22	-23	99	101	-4.0	3	4	-1.6
1915	Bal-F	0	0	—	1	0	0	0	0	1	0	0.0	0	0	0.0	0	0.0	0.00	—	.000	.000	0	0	111	0	0.0	0	0	0.0
1921	Phi-N	0	0	—	4	0	0	0	0	8	11	12.4	0	3	3.4	1	1.1	3.38	120	.393	.424	0	1	107	192	0.0	-0	-0	0.0
Total	9	56	105	.348	216	157	118	12	5	1432	1495	9.4	34	418	2.6	444	2.8	3.44	82	.292	.348	-101	-99	101	102	-13.8	-10	12	-7.5
■ **HOYT WILHELM** Wilhelm, James Hoyt b: 7/26/23, Huntersville, N.C. BR/TR, 6', 190 lbs. Deb: 4/19/52 H																													
1952	NY-N	15	3	**.833**	**71**	0	0	0	11	159	127	7.2	12	57	3.2	108	6.1	**2.43**	**155**	.220	.293	23	23	101	119	5.5	0	1	2.5
1953	NY-N	7	8	.467	**68**	0	0	0	15	145	127	7.9	13	77	4.8	71	4.4	3.04	138	.238	.331	**20**	**18**	98	129	0.2	1	-1	1.8
1954	NY-N	12	4	.750	57	0	0	0	7	111	77	6.2	5	52	4.2	64	5.2	2.11	196	.198	.294	**24**	**25**	102	109	2.8	-2	1	2.4
1955	NY-N	4	1	.800	59	0	0	0	0	103	104	9.1	10	40	3.5	71	6.2	3.93	101	.266	.325	1	0	98	104	1.5	-1	3	0.2
1956	NY-N	4	9	.308	64	0	0	0	8	89	97	9.8	7	43	4.3	71	7.2	3.84	98	.280	.352	-1	-1	99	117	-1.9	0	2	0.1
1957	StL-N	1	4	.200	40	0	0	0	11	55	52	8.5	7	21	3.4	29	4.7	4.25	91	.254	.329	-2	-2	99	97	-1.5	-1	-0	-0.3
	Cle-A	1	0	1.000	2	0	0	0	1	4	2	4.5	1	1	2.3	0	0.0	2.25	172	.154	.267	1	1	102	139	0.5	0	-0	0.1
1958	Cle-A	2	7	.222	30	6	1	0	5	90	70	7.0	4	35	3.5	57	5.7	2.50	141	.215	.286	13	10	93	99	-2.5	-1	1	1.0
	Bal-A	1	3	.250	9	4	3	1	0	41	25	5.5	2	10	2.2	35	7.7	1.98	181	.179	.232	8	7	95	70	-0.9	-1	0	0.7
	Yr	3	10	.231	39	10	4	1	5	131	95	6.5	6	45	3.1	92	6.3	2.34	151	.203	.268	21	17	94	70	-3.4	-1	1	1.7
1959	Bal-A	15	11	.577	32	27	13	3	0	226	178	7.1	13	77	3.1	139	5.5	**2.19**	**173**	.224	.294	**42**	**40**	98	**132**	2.8	-6	-1	3.6
1960	Bal-A	11	8	.579	41	11	3	1	7	147	125	7.7	13	39	2.4	107	6.6	3.31	118	.228	.275	9	10	101	80	0.0	-3	1	0.8

YEAR	TM/L	W	L	PCT	G	GS	CG	SHO	SV	IP	H	H/G	HR	BB	BB/G	SO	SO/G	ERA	/A	OAVG	OOBP	PR	/A	PF	CPI	WAT	PB	PD	TPI
1961	Bal-A	9	7	.563	51	1	0	0	18	110	89	7.3	5	41	3.4	87	7.1	2.29	168	.219	.293	21	19	96	111	-0.3	-1	1	1.9
1962	Bal-A	7	10	.412	52	0	0	0	15	93	64	6.2	5	34	3.3	90	8.7	1.94	195	.197	.272	21	19	95	114	-1.1	-0	1	1.9
1963	Chi-A	5	8	.385	55	3	0	0	21	136	106	7.0	8	30	2.0	111	7.3	2.65	140	.215	.257	15	16	102	82	-2.2	-1	1	1.7
1964	Chi-A	12	9	.571	73	0	0	0	27	131	94	6.5	7	30	2.1	95	6.5	1.99	170	.202	.247	24	20	93	91	-0.6	-0	-1	2.0
1965	Chi-A	7	7	.500	66	0	0	0	20	144	88	5.5	11	32	2.0	106	6.6	1.81	173	.177	.224	**26**	21	91	79	-1.0	-1	-1	2.0
1966	Chi-A	5	2	.714	46	0	0	0	6	81	50	5.6	6	17	1.9	61	6.8	1.67	192	.178	.221	16	14	93	89	1.5	0	-1	1.4
1967	Chi-A	8	3	.727	49	0	0	0	12	89	58	5.9	2	34	3.4	76	7.7	1.31	229	.183	.267	**19**	**17**	93	129	2.3	-1	-1	1.7
1968	Chi-A	4	4	.500	72	0	0	0	12	94	69	6.6	4	24	2.3	72	6.9	1.72	176	.205	.258	13	14	102	111	0.6	-0	-1	1.5
1969	Cal-A	5	7	.417	44	0	0	0	10	66	45	6.1	4	18	2.5	53	7.2	2.45	149	.194	.258	9	9	101	77	-0.2	-1	-0	0.8
	Atl-N	2	0	1.000	8	0	0	0	4	12	5	3.8	0	4	3.0	14	10.5	0.75	493	.119	.213	4	4	103	17	1.0	-0	0	0.4
1970	Atl-N	6	4	.600	50	0	0	0	13	78	69	8.0	7	39	4.5	67	7.7	3.12	136	.234	.322	8	10	105	116	1.3	-0	0	1.0
	Chi-N	0	1	.000	3	0	0	0	0	4	4	9.0	1	3	6.8	1	2.3	9.00	53	.286	.389	-2	-2	119	78	-0.4	0	0	0.0
	Yr	6	5	.545	53	0	0	0	13	82	73	8.0	8	42	4.6	68	7.5	3.40	126	.234	.322	6	8	105	78	0.9	-0	1	1.0
1971	Atl-N	0	0	—	3	0	0	0	0	2	6	27.0	2	1	4.5	1	4.5	18.00	21	.500	.538	-3	-3	111	114	0.0	0	0	-0.2
	LA-N	0	1	.000	9	0	0	0	3	18	6	3.0	1	4	2.0	15	7.5	1.00	339	.111	.169	5	5	98	23	-0.4	-0	-0	0.5
	Yr	0	1	.000	12	0	0	0	3	20	12	5.4	3	5	2.3	16	7.2	2.70	127	.182	.236	2	2	99	23	-0.4	0	0	0.3
1972	LA-N	0	1	.000	16	0	0	0	1	25	20	7.2	0	15	5.4	9	3.2	4.68	69	.217	.313	-3	-4	93	57	-0.4	-0	0	-0.3
Total	21	143	122	.540	1070	52	20	5	227	2253	1757	7.0	150	778	3.1	1610	6.4	2.52	146	.216	.283	310	289	98	103	6.6	-20	5	29.2

■ **LEFTY WILKIE** Wilkie, Aldon Jay b: 10/30/14, Zealandia, Sask., Canada BL/TL, 5'11.5", 175 lbs. Deb: 4/22/41

YEAR	TM/L	W	L	PCT	G	GS	CG	SHO	SV	IP	H	H/G	HR	BB	BB/G	SO	SO/G	ERA	/A	OAVG	OOBP	PR	/A	PF	CPI	WAT	PB	PD	TPI
1941	Pit-N	2	4	.333	26	6	2	1	2	79	90	10.3	1	40	4.6	16	1.8	4.56	81	.289	.362	-8	-8	102	99	-1.0	1	1	-0.5
1942	Pit-N	6	7	.462	35	6	3	0	1	107	112	9.4	4	37	3.1	18	1.5	4.21	80	.269	.321	-11	-10	102	87	0.2	2	2	-0.5
1946	Pit-N	0	0	—	7	0	0	0	0	8	13	14.6	0	3	3.4	3	3.4	10.13	36	.382	.432	-6	-6	106	65	0.0	0	-0	-0.5
Total	3	8	11	.421	68	12	5	1	3	194	215	10.0	5	80	3.7	37	1.7	4.59	76	.283	.343	-25	-23	102	91	-0.8	3	3	-1.5

■ **ERIC WILKINS** Wilkins, Eric Lamoine b: 12/9/56, St.Louis, Mo. BR/TR, 6'1", 190 lbs. Deb: 4/11/79

YEAR	TM/L	W	L	PCT	G	GS	CG	SHO	SV	IP	H	H/G	HR	BB	BB/G	SO	SO/G	ERA	/A	OAVG	OOBP	PR	/A	PF	CPI	WAT	PB	PD	TPI
1979	Cle-A	2	4	.333	16	14	0	0	0	70	77	9.9	4	38	4.9	52	6.7	4.37	103	.289	.377	-1	1	106	115	-0.9	0	0	0.1

■ **ROY WILKINSON** Wilkinson, Roy Hamilton b: 5/8/1893, Canandaigua, N.Y. d: 7/2/56, Louisville, Ky. BR/TR, 6'1", 170 lbs. Deb: 4/29/18

YEAR	TM/L	W	L	PCT	G	GS	CG	SHO	SV	IP	H	H/G	HR	BB	BB/G	SO	SO/G	ERA	/A	OAVG	OOBP	PR	/A	PF	CPI	WAT	PB	PD	TPI
1918	Cle-A	0	0	—	1	0	0	0	0	1	0	0.0	0	0	0.0	0	0.0	0.00	—	.000	.000	0	0	107	0	0.0	0	0	0.0
1919	Chi-A	1	1	.500	4	1	1	1	0	22	21	8.6	0	10	4.1	5	2.0	2.05	161	.266	.348	3	3	102	160	-0.1	2	1	0.6
1920	Chi-A	7	9	.438	34	11	8	0	2	145	162	10.1	6	48	3.0	30	1.9	4.03	88	.297	.356	-4	-8	94	103	-2.5	-2	-3	-1.2
1921	Chi-A	4	20	.167	36	23	11	0	3	198	259	11.8	4	78	3.5	50	2.3	5.14	85	.334	.375	-19	-17	102	105	-7.4	-4	5	-1.3
1922	Chi-A	0	1	.000	4	1	0	0	1	14	24	15.4	1	6	3.9	3	1.9	9.00	45	.393	.449	-8	-8	101	88	-0.4	-0	0	-0.6
Total	5	12	31	.279	79	36	20	1	6	380	466	11.0	11	142	3.4	88	2.1	4.67	85	.318	.369	-27	-29	99	107	-10.4	-5	4	-2.5

■ **BILL WILKINSON** Wilkinson, William Carl b: 8/10/64, Greybull, Wyoming BR/TL, 5'10", 160 lbs. Deb: 6/13/85

YEAR	TM/L	W	L	PCT	G	GS	CG	SHO	SV	IP	H	H/G	HR	BB	BB/G	SO	SO/G	ERA	/A	OAVG	OOBP	PR	/A	PF	CPI	WAT	PB	PD	TPI
1985	Sea-A	0	2	.000	2	2	0	0	0	6	8	12.0	2	6	9.0	5	7.5	13.50	29	.333	.467	-6	-6	95	71	-0.9	0	0	-0.4
1987	Sea-A	3	4	.429	56	0	0	0	10	76	61	7.2	8	21	2.5	73	8.6	3.67	125	.223	.271	7	8	103	78	-0.3	0	-1	0.6
1988	Sea-A	2	2	.500	30	0	0	0	2	31	28	8.1	3	15	4.4	25	7.3	3.48	124	.233	.316	2	3	108	101	0.3	0	-0	0.2
Total	3	5	8	.385	88	2	0	0	12	113	97	7.7	13	42	3.3	103	8.2	4.14	108	.232	.296	2	4	104	84	-0.9	0	-1	0.4

■ **TED WILKS** Wilks, Theodore "Cork" b: 11/13/15, Fulton, N.Y. BR/TR, 5'9.5", 178 lbs. Deb: 4/25/44 C

YEAR	TM/L	W	L	PCT	G	GS	CG	SHO	SV	IP	H	H/G	HR	BB	BB/G	SO	SO/G	ERA	/A	OAVG	OOBP	PR	/A	PF	CPI	WAT	PB	PD	TPI
1944	StL-N	17	4	**.810**	36	21	16	4	0	208	173	7.5	12	49	2.1	70	3.0	2.64	130	.227	.272	22	19	95	94	4.6	-1	-4	1.4
1945	StL-N	4	7	.364	18	16	4	1	0	98	103	9.5	9	29	2.7	28	2.6	2.94	125	.270	.319	9	8	97	136	-2.3	-0	-2	0.6
1946	StL-N	8	0	1.000	40	4	0	0	1	95	88	8.3	13	38	3.6	40	3.8	3.41	103	.248	.317	0	1	103	115	4.0	0	-1	0.1
1947	StL-N	4	0	1.000	37	0	0	0	5	50	57	10.3	10	11	2.0	28	5.0	5.04	84	.279	.317	-5	-5	104	96	2.0	0	0	-0.3
1948	StL-N	6	6	.500	57	2	1	0	13	131	113	7.8	5	39	2.7	71	4.9	2.61	150	.235	.287	**20**	**19**	99	105	-0.5	0	-1	1.9
1949	StL-N	10	3	.769	**59**	0	0	0	**9**	118	105	8.0	7	38	2.9	71	5.4	3.74	116	.240	.295	4	8	108	82	2.7	-3	-2	0.3
1950	StL-N	2	0	1.000	18	0	0	0	0	24	27	10.1	4	9	3.4	15	5.6	6.75	63	.287	.349	-7	-7	103	79	1.0	-1	0	-0.6
1951	StL-N	0	0	—	17	0	0	0	1	18	19	9.5	1	5	2.5	5	2.5	3.00	133	.279	.324	2	2	101	129	0.0	-0	-0	0.1
	Pit-N	3	5	.375	48	1	1	0	12	83	69	7.5	6	24	2.6	43	4.7	2.82	154	.231	.286	11	14	110	102	-0.3	-1	1	1.4
	Yr	3	5	.375	**65**	1	1	0	**13**	101	88	7.8	7	29	2.6	48	4.3	2.85	150	.240	.293	12	**16**	108	102	-0.3	-0	0	1.5
1952	Pit-N	5	5	.500	44	0	0	0	4	72	65	8.1	9	31	3.9	24	3.0	3.63	108	.245	.321	1	2	105	113	1.6	-0	-1	0.1
	Cle-A	0	0	—	7	0	0	0	1	12	8	6.0	0	7	5.3	6	4.5	3.75	86	.186	.288	-0	-1	88	51	0.0	0	0	0.0
1953	Cle-A	0	0	—	4	0	0	0	0	4	5	11.3	0	3	6.8	2	4.5	6.75	55	.278	.381	-1	-1	93	66	0.0	0	0	0.0
Total	10	59	30	.663	385	44	22	5	46	913	832	8.2	76	283	2.8	403	4.0	3.26	118	.244	.299	55	59	101	103	12.8	-5	-10	5.0

■ **ED WILLETT** Willett, Robert Edgar b: 3/7/1884, Norfolk, Va. d: 5/10/34, Wellington, Kan. BR/TR, 6', 183 lbs. Deb: 9/05/06

YEAR	TM/L	W	L	PCT	G	GS	CG	SHO	SV	IP	H	H/G	HR	BB	BB/G	SO	SO/G	ERA	/A	OAVG	OOBP	PR	/A	PF	CPI	WAT	PB	PD	TPI
1906	Det-A	0	3	.000	3	3	3	0	0	25	24	8.6	0	8	2.9	16	5.8	3.96	75	.277	.339	-4	-3	110	74	-1.4	-1	1	-0.1
1907	Det-A	1	5	.167	10	6	1	0	0	49	47	8.6	0	20	3.7	27	5.0	3.67	68	.276	.352	-6	-6	98	84	-2.1	-1	1	-0.5
1908	Det-A	15	8	.652	30	22	18	2	1	197	186	8.5	2	60	2.7	77	3.5	2.28	103	.261	.331	2	2	99	143	2.0	-2	4	0.7
1909	Det-A	21	10	.677	41	34	25	3	1	293	239	7.3	5	76	2.3	89	2.7	2.33	113	.221	.281	5	10	106	76	1.8	3	-1	1.0
1910	Det-A	16	11	.593	37	25	18	4	0	224	175	7.0	2	74	3.0	65	2.6	2.37	106	.217	.296	4	4	100	85	1.2	-2	7	0.9
1911	Det-A	13	14	.481	38	27	15	2	1	231	261	10.2	5	80	3.1	86	3.4	3.66	98	.295	.363	-8	-2	107	111	-2.5	6	3	0.8
1912	Det-A	17	15	.531	37	31	28	1	0	284	281	8.9	3	84	2.7	89	2.8	3.30	97	.262	.326	2	-3	96	96	2.8	-1	5	0.2
1913	Det-A	13	14	.481	34	30	19	0	0	242	237	8.8	0	89	3.3	59	2.2	3.09	95	.260	.333	-4	-4	101	97	1.4	7	3	0.7
1914	StL-F	4	16	.200	27	21	14	0	0	175	208	10.7	5	56	2.9	73	3.8	4.22	82	.295	.355	-20	-15	108	99	-5.4	3	6	-0.5
1915	StL-F	2	3	.400	17	2	1	0	2	53	61	10.4	2	18	3.1	19	3.2	4.58	68	.295	.360	-9	-9	102	95	-0.6	1	0	-0.7
Total	10	102	99	.507	274	201	142	12	5	1773	1719	8.7	24	565	2.9	600	3.0	3.08	96	.259	.327	-39	-26	102	98	-2.8	12	29	2.5

■ **CARL WILLEY** Willey, Carlton Francis b: 6/6/31, Cherryfield, Me. BR/TR, 6', 175 lbs. Deb: 4/30/58

YEAR	TM/L	W	L	PCT	G	GS	CG	SHO	SV	IP	H	H/G	HR	BB	BB/G	SO	SO/G	ERA	/A	OAVG	OOBP	PR	/A	PF	CPI	WAT	PB	PD	TPI
1958	Mil-N	9	7	.563	23	19	9	**4**	0	140	110	7.1	14	53	3.4	74	4.8	2.70	127	.215	.288	19	11	87	101	-0.4	-2	-2	0.7
1959	Mil-N	5	9	.357	26	15	5	2	0	117	126	9.7	12	31	2.4	51	3.9	4.15	88	.273	.316	-3	-6	93	96	-2.5	-1	-1	-0.8
1960	Mil-N	6	7	.462	28	21	2	1	0	145	136	8.4	19	65	4.0	109	6.8	4.34	77	.248	.328	-9	-16	89	97	-1.2	1	-1	-1.5
1961	Mil-N	6	12	.333	35	22	4	0	0	160	147	8.3	20	65	3.7	91	5.1	3.82	96	.247	.317	4	-3	91	102	-3.6	-6	3	-0.5
1962	Mil-N	2	5	.286	30	6	0	0	1	73	95	11.7	9	20	2.5	40	4.9	5.42	71	.319	.357	-12	-13	98	100	-1.6	1	-0	-1.1
1963	NY-N	9	14	.391	30	28	7	4	0	183	149	7.3	24	69	3.4	101	5.0	3.10	110	.220	.294	4	6	104	103	1.5	-1	0	0.7
1964	NY-N	0	2	.000	14	3	0	0	0	30	37	11.1	5	8	2.4	14	4.2	3.60	97	.301	.338	-0	-0	98	149	-0.9	-0	-1	-0.1
1965	NY-N	1	2	.333	13	3	1	0	0	28	30	9.6	2	15	4.8	13	4.2	4.18	88	.270	.364	-2	-2	104	111	0.1	-1	-0	-0.1
Total	8	38	58	.396	199	117	28	11	1	876	830	8.5	105	326	3.3	493	5.1	3.76	94	.250	.315	1	-20	94	102	-8.6	-8	-2	-2.7

■ **NICK WILLHITE** Willhite, Jon Nicholas b: 1/27/41, Tulsa, Okla. BL/TL, 6'2", 190 lbs. Deb: 6/16/63

YEAR	TM/L	W	L	PCT	G	GS	CG	SHO	SV	IP	H	H/G	HR	BB	BB/G	SO	SO/G	ERA	/A	OAVG	OOBP	PR	/A	PF	CPI	WAT	PB	PD	TPI
1963	LA-N	2	3	.400	8	8	1	1	0	38	44	10.4	5	10	2.4	28	6.6	3.79	81	.286	.327	-2	-3	94	118	-0.8	1	-1	-0.2
1964	LA-N	2	4	.333	10	7	2	0	0	44	43	8.8	4	13	2.7	24	4.9	3.68	88	.264	.309	-1	-2	91	104	-0.9	-0	1	-0.1
1965	Was-A	0	0	—	5	0	0	0	0	6	10	15.0	2	4	6.0	3	4.5	7.50	47	.345	.424	-3	-3	102	121	0.0	0	0	-0.2
	LA-N	2	2	.500	15	6	0	0	1	42	47	10.1	7	22	4.7	28	6.0	5.36	59	.288	.376	-8	-10	90	108	-0.2	3	0	-0.7
1966	LA-N	0	0	—	6	0	0	0	0	4	3	6.8	0	5	11.3	4	9.0	2.25	152	.214	.421	1	1	95	201	0.0	0	0	0.1
1967	Cal-A	0	2	.000	10	7	0	0	0	39	39	9.0	8	16	3.7	22	5.1	4.38	71	.258	.327	-5	-6	96	110	-0.9	-1	0	-0.6
	NY-N	0	1	.000	4	1	0	0	0	8	9	10.1	1	5	5.6	9	10.1	9.00	38	.257	.350	-5	-5	102	50	-0.4	-0	0	-0.4
Total	5	6	12	.333	58	29	3	1	1	181	195	9.7	27	75	3.7	118	5.9	4.57	70	.275	.342	-23	-28	93	109	-3.2	2	1	-2.1

■ **ALBERT WILLIAMS** Williams, Albert Hamilton (De Souza) b: 5/6/54, Pearl Lagoon, Nic. BR/TR, 6'4", 190 lbs. Deb: 5/07/80

YEAR	TM/L	W	L	PCT	G	GS	CG	SHO	SV	IP	H	H/G	HR	BB	BB/G	SO	SO/G	ERA	/A	OAVG	OOBP	PR	/A	PF	CPI	WAT	PB	PD	TPI
1980	Min-A	6	2	.750	18	9	3	0	1	77	73	8.5	9	30	3.5	35	4.1	3.51	126	.253	.321	5	8	109	110	2.1	0	-1	0.7
1981	Min-A	6	10	.375	23	22	4	0	0	150	160	9.6	11	52	3.1	76	4.6	4.08	96	.276	.333	-7	-3	107	100	0.0	0	-2	-0.5
1982	Min-A	9	7	.563	26	26	3	0	0	154	166	9.7	18	55	3.2	61	3.6	4.21	99	.276	.332	-2	-1	102	105	2.6	0	0	0.0
1983	Min-A	11	14	.440	36	29	4	1	1	193	196	9.1	21	68	3.2	68	3.2	4.15	104	.262	.324	-2	4	106	98	0.2	0	-2	0.2
1984	Min-A	3	5	.375	17	11	1	0	0	69	75	9.8	9	22	2.9	22	2.9	5.74	74	.284	.350	-13	-12	106	86	-0.9	0	0	-1.0
Total	5	35	38	.479	120	97	15	1	2	643	670	9.4	68	227	3.2	262	3.7	4.24	99	.270	.330	-19	-4	106	100	4.0	0	-4	-0.6

YEAR	TM/L	W	L	PCT	G	GS	CG	SHO	SV	IP	H	H/G	HR	BB	BB/G	SO	SO/G	ERA	/A	OAVG	OOBP	PR	/A	PF	CPI	WAT	PB	PD	TPI
■ **AL WILLIAMS**	Williams, Almon Edward b: 5/11/14, Valhermosa Springs, Ala. d: 7/19/49, Groves, Tex. BR/TR, 6'3", 200 lbs. Deb: 4/19/37																												
1937	Phi-A	4	1	.800	16	8	2	0	1	75	88	10.6	0	49	5.9	27	3.2	5.40	82	.300	.395	-6	-8	96	97	1.7	-2	0	-0.8
1938	Phi-A	0	7	.000	30	8	1	0	0	93	128	12.4	6	54	5.2	25	2.4	6.97	72	.324	.401	-23	-20	105	90	-3.4	-3	-0	-1.9
Total	2	4	8	.333	46	16	3	0	1	168	216	11.6	6	103	5.5	52	2.8	6.27	76	.314	.399	-29	-28	101	93	-1.7	-5	0	-2.7
■ **GUS WILLIAMS**	Williams, Augustine H. b: 1870, New York, N.Y. d: 10/14/1890, New York, N.Y. 5'11", 170 lbs. Deb: 4/18/1890																												
1890	BB-a	0	1	.000	2	2	1	0	0	12	13	9.8	0	12	9.0	2	1.5	7.50	53	.292	.442	-5	-5	103	75	-0.4	1	0	-0.2
■ **CHARLIE WILLIAMS**	Williams, Charles Prosek b: 10/11/47, Flushing, N.Y. BR/TR, 6'2", 200 lbs. Deb: 4/23/71																												
1971	NY-N	5	6	.455	31	9	1	0	0	90	92	9.2	7	41	4.1	53	5.3	4.80	69	.267	.339	-13	-15	96	86	-0.6	-1	-1	-1.7
1972	SF-N	0	2	.000	3	2	0	0	0	9	14	14.0	3	3	3.0	3	3.0	9.00	38	.333	.370	-6	-6	100	85	-0.9	-0	-0	-0.5
1973	SF-N	3	0	1.000	12	2	0	0	0	23	32	12.5	2	7	2.7	11	4.3	6.65	58	.330	.358	-8	-7	104	82	1.5	0	0	-0.6
1974	SF-N	1	3	.250	39	7	0	0	0	100	93	8.4	6	31	2.8	48	4.3	2.79	142	.250	.304	9	13	109	114	-0.8	-1	2	1.5
1975	SF-N	5	3	.625	55	2	0	0	3	98	94	8.6	2	66	6.1	45	4.1	3.49	106	.261	.374	2	2	102	122	1.1	0	2	0.4
1976	SF-N	2	0	1.000	48	2	0	0	1	85	80	8.5	4	39	4.1	34	3.6	2.96	123	.256	.332	5	7	104	126	1.0	-0	1	0.8
1977	SF-N	6	5	.545	55	8	1	0	0	119	116	8.8	9	60	4.5	41	3.1	4.01	102	.262	.350	-1	1	105	105	0.9	0	-0	0.1
1978	SF-N	1	3	.250	25	1	0	0	0	48	60	11.3	5	28	5.3	22	4.1	5.44	60	.314	.396	-10	-12	91	111	-1.0	-1	0	-1.2
Total	8	23	22	.511	268	33	2	0	4	572	581	9.1	38	275	4.3	257	4.0	3.98	94	.269	.347	-22	-16	102	109	1.2	-2	3	-1.2
■ **LEFTY WILLIAMS**	Williams, Claude Preston b: 3/9/1893, Aurora, Mo. d: 11/4/59, Laguna Beach, Cal. BR/TL, 5'9", 160 lbs. Deb: 9/17/13																												
1913	Det-A	1	3	.250	5	4	3	0	1	29	34	10.6	0	4	1.2	9	2.8	4.97	59	.286	.315	-7	-7	101	60	-0.8	-0	-1	-0.7
1914	Det-A	0	1	.000	1	1	0	0	0	1	3	27.0	0	2	18.0	0	0.0	0.00	—	.429	.556	0	0	102	0	-0.4	0	0	0.0
1916	Chi-A	13	7	.650	43	26	10	2	1	224	220	8.8	5	65	2.6	138	**5.5**	2.89	103	.267	.327	-2	2	106	110	1.9	-1	-4	-0.1
1917	Chi-A	17	8	.680	45	29	8	1	1	230	221	8.6	3	81	3.2	85	3.3	2.97	84	.252	.321	-8	-12	93	93	1.3	-2	-4	-2.0
1918	Chi-A	6	4	.600	15	14	7	2	1	106	76	6.5	0	47	4.0	30	2.5	2.72	102	.209	.303	1	1	100	74	1.4	-2	-2	-0.3
1919	Chi-A	23	11	.676	41	40	27	5	1	297	265	8.0	8	58	1.8	125	3.8	2.64	125	.244	.289	19	21	102	86	2.8	0	-5	1.8
1920	Chi-A	22	14	.611	39	38	25	0	0	299	302	9.1	15	90	2.7	128	3.9	3.91	91	.271	.332	-4	-12	94	89	-0.4	1	-3	-1.3
Total	7	82	48	.631	189	152	80	10	5	1186	1121	8.5	31	347	2.6	515	3.9	3.13	99	.255	.316	0	-5	99	91	5.8	-4	-20	-2.6
■ **MUTT WILLIAMS**	Williams, David Carter b: 7/31/1891, Ozark, Ark. d: 3/30/62, Fayetteville, Ark. BR/TR, 6'3.5", 195 lbs. Deb: 10/04/13																												
1913	Was-A	1	0	1.000	1	1	0	0	0	4	4	9.0	1	2	4.5	1	2.3	4.50	68	.286	.375	-1	-1	105	130	0.5	0	0	0.0
1914	Was-A	0	0	—	5	0	0	0	1	7	5	6.4	0	4	5.1	3	3.9	5.14	53	.227	.346	-2	-2	100	56	0.0	0	-0	-0.1
Total	2	1	0	1.000	6	1	0	0	1	11	9	7.4	1	6	4.9	4	3.3	4.91	58	.250	.357	-3	-3	102	83	0.5	0	-0	-0.1
■ **DAVE WILLIAMS**	Williams, David Owen b: 1879, Scranton, Pa. d: 4/25/18, Hot Springs, Ark. TL , Deb: 7/02/02																												
1902	Bos-A	0	0	—	3	0	0	0	0	19	22	10.4	0	11	5.2	7	3.3	5.21	67	.315	.408	-3	-4	98	88	0.0	1	-1	-0.3
■ **DON WILLIAMS**	Williams, Donald Fred b: 9/14/31, Floyd, Va. BR/TR, 6'2", 180 lbs. Deb: 9/12/58																												
1958	Pit-N	0	0	—	2	0	0	0	0	4	6	13.5	1	1	2.3	3	6.8	6.75	55	.375	.412	-1	-1	94	117	0.0	0	0	0.0
1959	Pit-N	0	0	—	6	0	0	0	0	12	17	12.8	1	3	2.3	3	2.3	6.75	61	.362	.377	-4	-4	104	93	0.0	1	-0	-0.2
1962	KC-A	0	0	—	3	0	0	0	0	4	6	13.5	0	0	0.0	1	2.3	9.00	45	.353	.368	-2	-2	101	61	0.0	-0	0	-0.1
Total	3	0	0	—	11	0	0	0	0	20	29	13.0	2	4	1.8	7	3.1	7.20	56	.363	.382	-7	-7	101	91	0.0	1	-0	-0.3
■ **DON WILLIAMS**	Williams, Donald Reid "Dino" b: 9/2/35, Los Angeles, Cal. BR/TR, 6'5", 218 lbs. Deb: 8/04/63																												
1963	Min-A	0	0	—	3	0	0	0	0	4	8	18.0	1	6	13.5	2	4.5	11.25	32	.381	.519	-3	-3	98	108	0.0	0	0	-0.2
■ **DALE WILLIAMS**	Williams, Elisha Alphonso b: 10/6/1855, Ludlow, Ky. d: 10/22/39, Covington, Ky. BR/TR, 5'9", 175 lbs. Deb: 8/12/1876																												
1876	Cin-N	1	8	.111	9	9	9	0	0	83	123	13.3	1	4	0.4	9	1.0	4.23	55	.348	.355	-18	-18	100	94	-0.9	-2	0	-1.5
■ **FRANK WILLIAMS**	Williams, Frank Lee b: 2/13/58, Seattle, Wash. BR/TR, 6'1", 180 lbs. Deb: 4/05/84																												
1984	SF-N	9	4	.692	61	1	1	1	3	106	88	7.5	2	51	4.3	91	7.7	3.57	98	.226	.313	0	-1	98	80	3.3	1	4	0.5
1985	SF-N	2	4	.333	49	0	0	0	0	73	65	8.0	5	35	4.3	54	6.7	4.19	81	.242	.333	-5	-6	95	90	-0.3	-0	0	-0.6
1986	SF-N	3	1	.750	36	0	0	0	1	52	35	6.1	0	21	3.6	33	5.7	1.21	291	.212	.309	15	13	95	217	1.0	0	1	1.5
1987	Cin-N	4	0	1.000	85	0	0	0	2	106	101	8.6	5	39	3.3	60	5.1	2.29	184	.254	.318	21	23	103	151	2.0	-1	1	2.3
1988	Cin-N	3	2	.600	60	0	0	0	1	63	59	8.4	6	35	5.0	43	6.1	2.57	141	.252	.348	6	7	105	171	0.3	-0	0	0.8
Total	5	21	11	.656	291	1	1	1	7	400	348	7.8	18	181	4.1	281	6.3	2.88	128	.239	.323	37	36	99	133	6.3	1	5	4.5
■ **JOHNNIE WILLIAMS**	Williams, John Brodie "Honolulu Johnnie" b: 7/16/1889, Honolulu, Hawaii d: 9/8/63, Long Beach, Cal. BR/TR, 6', 180 lbs. Deb: 4/21/14																												
1914	Det-A	0	2	.000	4	3	1	0	0	11	17	13.9	0	5	4.1	4	3.3	6.55	43	.378	.440	-5	-5	102	98	-0.9	-0	-0	-0.4
■ **LEON WILLIAMS**	Williams, Leon Theo "Lefty" b: 12/2/05, Macon, Ga. BL/TL, 5'10.5", 154 lbs. Deb: 6/02/26																												
1926	Bro-N	0	0	—	8	0	0	0	0	8	16	18.0	0	2	2.3	3	3.4	5.63	68	.421	.439	-2	-2	101	141	0.0	0	1	0.0
■ **MARSH WILLIAMS**	Williams, Marshall Mc Diarmid "Cap" b: 2/21/1893, Faison, N.C. d: 2/22/35, Tucson, Ariz. BR/TR, 6', 180 lbs. Deb: 7/07/16																												
1916	Phi-A	0	6	.000	10	4	3	0	0	51	71	12.5	4	31	5.5	17	3.0	7.94	37	.350	.436	-29	-28	105	84	-2.9	-1	-1	-2.7
■ **MATT WILLIAMS**	Williams, Matthew Evan b: 7/25/59, Houston, Tex. BR/TR, 6'1", 200 lbs. Deb: 8/02/83																												
1983	Tor-A	1	1	.500	4	3	0	0	0	8	13	14.6	5	7	7.9	5	5.6	14.63	30	.361	.467	-9	-9	108	87	0.0	0	0	-0.7
1985	Tex-A	2	1	.667	6	3	0	0	0	26	20	6.9	3	10	3.5	22	7.6	2.42	188	.211	.283	5	6	110	120	0.7	0	-1	0.6
Total	2	3	2	.600	10	6	0	0	0	34	33	8.7	8	17	4.5	27	7.1	5.29	85	.252	.338	-4	-3	109	112	0.7	0	-0	-0.1
■ **MITCH WILLIAMS**	Williams, Mitchell Steven b: 11/17/64, Santa Ana, Cal. BL/TL, 6'3", 180 lbs. Deb: 4/09/86																												
1986	Tex-A	8	6	.571	**80**	0	0	0	8	98	69	6.3	8	79	7.3	90	8.3	3.58	111	.202	.366	7	4	95	112	0.6	0	-1	0.3
1987	Tex-A	8	6	.571	85	1	0	0	6	109	63	5.2	9	94	7.8	129	10.7	3.22	144	.175	.350	15	17	104	111	1.5	0	1	1.7
1988	Tex-A	2	7	.222	67	0	0	0	18	68	48	6.4	4	47	6.2	61	8.1	4.63	88	.203	.341	-5	-4	102	77	-2.2	0	0	-0.3
Total	3	18	19	.486	232	1	0	0	32	275	180	5.9	21	220	7.2	280	9.2	3.70	115	.192	.353	17	17	100	103	-0.1	0	0	1.7
■ **STEAMBOAT WILLIAMS**	Williams, Rees Gephardt b: 1/31/1892, Cascade, Mont. d: 6/29/79, Deer River, Minn. BL/TR, 5'11", 170 lbs. Deb: 7/12/14																												
1914	StL-N	0	1	.000	5	1	0	0	0	11	13	10.6	1	6	4.9	2	1.6	6.55	44	.295	.358	-5	-4	104	76	-0.4	-0	0	-0.4
1916	StL-N	6	7	.462	36	8	5	0	1	105	121	10.4	6	27	2.3	25	2.1	4.20	62	.291	.325	-18	-18	100	94	0.8	1	-0	-1.9
Total	2	6	8	.429	41	9	5	0	1	116	134	10.4	7	33	2.6	27	2.1	4.42	60	.291	.329	-23	-23	100	92	0.4	1	-0	-2.3
■ **RICK WILLIAMS**	Williams, Richard Allen b: 11/9/52, Merced, Cal. BR/TR, 6'1", 180 lbs. Deb: 6/12/78																												
1978	Hou-N	1	2	.333	17	1	0	0	0	35	43	11.1	2	10	2.6	17	4.4	4.63	73	.301	.333	-4	-5	95	95	-0.3	-1	0	-0.4
1979	Hou-N	4	7	.364	31	16	2	2	0	121	122	9.1	6	30	2.2	37	2.8	3.27	103	.261	.303	6	1	90	96	-1.8	3	0	0.4
Total	2	5	9	.357	48	17	2	2	0	156	165	9.5	8	40	2.3	54	3.1	3.58	95	.270	.310	2	-3	91	96	-2.1	2	1	0.0
■ **ACE WILLIAMS**	Williams, Robert Fulton b: 3/18/17, Montclair, N.J. BR/TL, 6'2", 174 lbs. Deb: 7/15/40																												
1940	Bos-N	0	0	—	5	0	0	0	0	9	21	21.0	0	12	12.0	5	5.0	16.00	24	.375	.493	-12	-12	101	66	0.0	-0	0	-1.0
1946	Bos-N	0	0	—	1	0	0	0	0	0	1	—	0	1	—	0	—	—	—	1.000	1.000	0	0	94	0	0.0	0	0	0.0
Total	2	0	0	—	6	0	0	0	0	9	22	22.0	0	13	13.0	5	5.0	16.00	24	.386	.507	-12	-12	101	66	0.0	-0	0	-1.0
■ **STAN WILLIAMS**	Williams, Stanley Wilson b: 9/14/36, Enfield, N.H. BR/TR, 6'5", 230 lbs. Deb: 5/17/58 C																												
1958	LA-N	9	7	.563	27	21	3	2	0	119	99	7.5	10	65	4.9	80	6.1	4.01	105	.228	.331	-1	3	106	89	1.6	-3	0	0.0
1959	LA-N	5	5	.500	35	15	2	0	0	125	102	7.3	12	86	6.2	89	6.4	3.96	101	.228	.353	-0	0	101	107	-0.5	1	0	0.2
1960	LA-N	14	10	.583	38	30	9	2	1	207	162	7.0	26	72	3.1	175	7.6	3.00	143	.210	.279	18	29	114	94	1.5	-0	1	3.3
1961	LA-N	15	12	.556	41	35	6	2	0	235	213	8.2	21	108	4.1	205	7.9	3.91	105	.242	.324	3	5	102	94	-0.5	0	-1	0.5
1962	LA-N	14	12	.538	40	28	4	1	1	186	184	8.9	16	98	4.7	108	5.2	4.45	80	.253	.337	-11	-18	91	89	-1.8	-1	-1	-2.0
1963	NY-A	9	8	.529	29	21	6	1	0	146	137	8.4	7	57	3.5	98	6.0	3.21	111	.249	.321	7	6	98	107	-1.6	-1	1	0.6
1964	NY-A	1	5	.167	21	10	1	0	0	82	76	8.3	7	38	4.2	54	5.9	3.84	95	.248	.325	-2	-2	101	97	-2.1	-0	1	-0.1
1965	Cle-A	0	0	—	3	0	0	0	0	4	6	13.5	1	3	6.8	1	2.3	6.75	50	.353	.429	-1	-2	97	130	0.0	0	0	-0.1
1967	Cle-A	6	4	.600	16	8	2	1	1	79	64	7.3	6	24	2.7	75	8.5	2.62	125	.218	.274	5	6	101	98	1.3	-1	-1	0.3
1968	Cle-A	13	11	.542	44	24	6	2	9	194	163	7.6	14	51	2.4	147	6.8	2.51	120	.225	.281	10	11	101	106	0.2	1	-0	1.3

YEAR	TM/L	W	L	PCT	G	GS	CG	SHO	SV	IP	H	H/G	HR	BB	BB/G	SO	SO/G	ERA	/A	OAVG	OOBP	PR	/A	PF	CPI	WAT	PB	PD	TPI
1969	Cle-A	6	14	.300	61	15	3	0	12	178	155	7.8	25	67	3.4	139	7.0	3.94	88	.235	.310	-6	-9	96	95	-2.3	-0	-1	-1.0
1970	Min-A	10	1	.909	68	0	0	0	15	113	85	6.8	8	32	2.5	76	6.1	1.99	180	.208	.268	22	20	97	113	4.3	-2	-1	1.7
1971	Min-A	4	5	.444	46	1	0	0	4	78	63	7.3	7	44	5.1	47	5.4	4.15	87	.220	.334	-6	-5	104	86	-0.1	-1	-1	-0.6
	StL-N	3	0	1.000	10	0	0	0	0	13	13	9.0	0	2	1.4	8	5.5	1.38	251	.265	.309	3	3	100	220	1.5	-0	0	0.4
1972	Bos-A	0	0	—	3	0	0	0	0	4	5	11.3	0	1	2.3	3	6.8	6.75	48	.294	.333	-2	-2	105	53	0.0	0	0	-0.1
Total	14	109	94	.537	482	208	42	11	43	1763	1527	7.8	160	748	3.8	1305	6.7	3.48	107	.232	.312	39	46	101	99	1.5	-9	-3	4.4
■ TED WILLIAMS	Williams, Theodore Samuel "The Kid', "The Thumper" or "The Splendid Splinter" b: 8/30/18, San Diego, Cal. BL/TR, 6'3", 205 lbs. Deb: 4/20/39 MH																												
1940	Bos-A	0	0	—	1	0	0	0	0	2	3	13.5	0	0	0.0	1	4.5	4.50	97	.333	.333	-0	-0	100	99	0.0	1	0	0.0
■ TOM WILLIAMS	Williams, Thomas C. b: 8/19/1870, Minersville, Ohio d: 7/27/40, Columbus, Ohio Deb: 5/01/1892																												
1892	Cle-N	1	0	1.000	2	1	1	0	0	9	9	9.0	1	1	1.0	3	3.0	3.00	110	.273	.295	0	0	101	108	0.5	-1	0	0.0
1893	Cle-N	1	1	.500	5	2	2	0	0	24	33	12.4	1	10	3.8	6	2.3	4.88	99	.343	.405	-1	-0	103	116	0.0	1	0	0.1
Total	2	2	1	.667	7	3	3	0	0	33	42	11.5	2	11	3.0	9	2.5	4.36	101	.326	.379	-0	0	102	114	0.5	-0	0	0.1
■ POP WILLIAMS	Williams, Walter Merrill b: 5/19/1874, Bowdoinham, Me. d: 8/4/59, Topsham, Maine BL/TR, 5'11", 190 lbs. Deb: 9/14/1898																												
1898	Was-N	0	2	.000	2	2	2	0	0	17	32	16.9	0	7	3.7	3	1.6	8.47	45	.425	.473	-9	-9	105	90	-0.9	1	0	-0.5
1902	Chi-N	11	16	.407	31	31	26	1	0	254	259	9.2	2	63	2.2	94	3.3	2.52	105	.289	.340	7	4	95	116	-2.8	2	3	0.7
1903	Chi-N	0	1	.000	1	1	1	0	0	5	9	16.2	0	0	0.0	2	3.6	5.40	57	.417	.417	-1	-1	94	111	-0.4	-0	0	0.0
	Phi-N	1	1	.500	2	2	2	0	0	18	21	10.5	0	6	3.0	8	4.0	3.00	103	.321	.387	1	0	94	132	0.2	0	1	0.1
	Bos-N	4	5	.444	10	10	9	1	0	83	97	10.5	3	37	4.0	20	2.2	4.12	78	.327	.417	-8	-8	98	114	0.2	0	-1	-0.7
	Yr	5	7	.417	13	13	12	1	0	106	127	10.8	3	43	3.7	30	2.5	3.99	80	.330	.410	-8	-9	97	114	0.0	-0	0	-0.6
Total	3	16	25	.390	46	46	40	2	0	377	418	10.0	5	113	2.7	127	3.0	3.20	89	.308	.368	-10	-15	96	115	-3.7	3	3	-0.4
■ WASH WILLIAMS	Williams, Washington J. b: Philadelphia, Pa. d: 1/1890, Philadelphia, Pa. 5'11", 180 lbs. Deb: 8/05/1884																												
1885	Chi-N	0	0	—	1	1	0	0	0	2	2	9.0	0	5	22.5	0	0.0	13.50	22	.271	.566	-2	-2	106	68	0.0	-0	0	-0.1
■ NED WILLIAMSON	Williamson, Edward Nagle b: 10/24/1857, Philadelphia, Pa. d: 3/3/1894, Willow Springs, Ark BR/TR, 5'11", 170 lbs. Deb: 5/01/1878																												
1881	Chi-N	1	1	.500	3	1	1	0	0	18	14	7.0	0	0	0.0	2	1.0	2.00	143	.225	.225	2	2	103	40	-0.2	0	0	0.2
1882	Chi-N	0	0	—	1	0	0	0	0	3	9	27.0	1	1	3.0	0	0.0	6.00	45	.523	.549	-1	-1	95	262	0.0	0	0	0.0
1883	Chi-N	0	0	—	1	0	0	0	0	1	1	9.0	0	1	9.0	1	9.0	9.00	37	.268	.423	-1	-1	107	54	0.0	0	0	0.0
1884	Chi-N	0	0	—	2	0	0	0	0	2	8	36.0	0	2	9.0	0	0.0	18.00	17	.596	.648	-3	-3	105	110	0.0	1	0	-0.2
1885	Chi-N	0	0	—	2	0	0	0	**2**	6	2	3.0	0	0	0.0	3	4.5	0.00	—	.110	.110	2	2	106	0	0.0	0	0	0.2
1886	Chi-N	0	0	—	2	0	0	0	1	3	2	6.0	0	0	0.0	1	3.0	0.00	—	.200	.200	1	1	110	0	0.0	0	0	0.1
1887	Chi-N	0	0	—	1	0	0	0	0	2	2	9.0	0	1	4.5	0	0.0	9.00	52	.275	.363	-1	-1	115	41	0.0	0	0	0.0
Total	7	1	1	.500	12	1	1	0	3	35	38	9.8	1	5	1.3	7	1.8	3.34	92	.288	.314	-2	-1	104	53	-0.2	3	0	0.3
■ MARK WILLIAMSON	Williamson, Mark Alan b: 7/21/59, Corpus Christi, Tex. BR/TR, 6' ", 155 lbs. Deb: 4/08/87																												
1987	Bal-A	8	9	.471	61	2	0	0	3	125	122	8.8	12	41	3.0	73	5.3	4.03	110	.261	.319	6	6	99	98	0.9	0	1	0.6
1988	Bal-A	5	8	.385	37	10	2	0	2	118	125	9.5	14	40	3.1	69	5.3	4.88	79	.272	.329	-12	-13	97	90	0.5	0	-0	-1.3
Total	2	13	17	.433	98	12	2	0	5	243	247	9.1	26	81	3.0	142	5.3	4.44	94	.266	.324	-6	-8	98	94	1.4	0	1	-0.7
■ AL WILLIAMSON	Williamson, Silas Albert b: 2/20/1900, Bucksville, Ark. d: 11/29/78, Hot Springs, Ark. BR/TR, 5'11", 160 lbs. Deb: 4/27/28																												
1928	Chi-A	0	0	—	1	0	0	0	0	2	1	4.5	0	0	0.0	0	0.0	0.00	—	.167	.143	1	1	100	0	0.0	0	0	0.1
■ CARL WILLIS	Willis, Carl Blake b: 12/28/60, Danville, Va. BL/TR, 6'4", 210 lbs. Deb: 6/09/84																												
1984	Det-A	0	2	.000	10	2	0	0	0	16	25	14.1	1	5	2.8	4	2.3	7.31	52	.362	.405	-6	-6	94	88	-0.9	0	0	-0.5
	Cin-N	0	1	.000	7	0	0	0	1	10	8	7.2	1	2	1.8	3	2.7	3.60	107	.222	.256	-0	0	107	71	-0.4	0	0	0.0
1985	Cin-N	1	0	1.000	11	0	0	0	1	14	21	13.5	3	5	3.2	6	3.9	9.00	42	.344	.377	-8	-8	105	79	0.5	0	-0	-0.7
1986	Cin-N	1	3	.250	29	0	0	0	0	52	54	9.3	4	32	5.5	24	4.2	4.50	86	.278	.373	-4	-4	104	111	-1.0	0	1	-0.2
1988	Chi-A	0	0	—	6	0	0	0	0	12	17	12.8	3	7	5.3	6	4.5	8.25	47	.362	.436	-6	-6	99	104	0.0	0	0	-0.5
Total	4	2	6	.250	63	2	0	0	2	104	125	10.8	12	51	4.4	43	3.7	5.88	65	.307	.377	-24	-23	102	99	-1.8	0	1	-1.9
■ LEFTY WILLIS	Willis, Charles William b: 11/4/05, Leetown, W.Va. d: 5/10/62, Bethesda, Md. BL/TL, 6'1", 175 lbs. Deb: 10/03/25																												
1925	Phi-A	0	0	—	1	1	0	0	0	5	9	16.2	2	2	3.6	3	5.4	10.80	41	.409	.440	-4	-4	101	100	0.0	-1	0	-0.2
1926	Phi-A	0	0	—	13	1	0	0	1	32	31	8.7	0	12	3.4	13	3.7	1.41	330	.270	.331	9	12	116	247	0.0	-0	-0	1.1
1927	Phi-A	3	1	.750	15	2	1	0	0	27	32	10.7	2	11	3.7	7	2.3	5.67	69	.308	.352	-5	-5	95	90	0.8	-1	1	-0.4
Total	3	3	1	.750	29	4	1	0	1	64	72	10.1	4	25	3.5	23	3.2	3.94	110	.299	.350	1	3	106	169	0.8	-1	1	0.5
■ DALE WILLIS	Willis, Dale Jerome b: 5/29/38, Calhoun, Ga. BR/TR, 5'11", 165 lbs. Deb: 4/14/63																												
1963	KC-A	0	2	.000	25	0	0	0	1	45	46	9.2	3	25	5.0	47	9.4	5.00	79	.266	.362	-7	-5	109	92	-0.9	-0	1	-0.4
■ JIM WILLIS	Willis, James Gladden b: 3/20/27, Doyline, La. BL/TR, 6'3", 175 lbs. Deb: 4/22/53																												
1953	Chi-N	2	1	.667	13	3	2	0	0	43	37	7.7	1	17	3.6	15	3.1	3.14	145	.228	.311	5	7	106	89	0.6	-1	1	0.7
1954	Chi-N	0	1	.000	14	1	0	0	0	23	22	8.6	1	18	7.0	5	2.0	3.91	106	.256	.394	0	1	102	122	-0.4	-1	1	0.1
Total	2	2	2	.500	27	4	2	0	0	66	59	8.0	2	35	4.8	20	2.7	3.41	129	.238	.342	6	7	105	101	0.2	-2	2	0.8
■ JOE WILLIS	Willis, Joseph Denk b: 4/9/1890, Coal Grove, Ohio d: 12/4/66, Ironton, Ohio BR/TL, 6'1", 185 lbs. Deb: 5/03/11																												
1911	StL-A	0	1	.000	1	1	0	0	0	7	8	10.3	0	3	3.9	0	0.0	5.14	65	.308	.379	-1	-1	100	84	-0.4	0	-0	-0.1
	StL-N	0	1	.000	2	2	1	0	0	15	13	7.8	0	4	2.4	5	3.0	4.20	83	.232	.283	-1	-1	102	47	-0.4	-1	0	-0.1
1912	StL-N	4	9	.308	31	17	4	0	2	130	143	9.9	3	62	4.3	55	3.8	4.43	79	.278	.361	-15	-14	103	87	-1.7	-2	-1	-1.4
1913	StL-N	0	0	—	7	0	0	0	1	10	9	8.1	0	11	9.9	6	5.4	7.20	43	.257	.408	-4	-5	97	70	0.0	-0	0	-0.4
Total	3	4	11	.267	41	20	5	0	3	162	173	9.6	3	80	4.4	66	3.7	4.61	75	.274	.359	-22	-21	102	82	-2.5	-2	-1	-2.0
■ LES WILLIS	Willis, Lester Evans "Wimpy" or "Lefty" b: 1/17/08, Nacogdoches, Tex. d: 1/22/82, Jasper, Tex. BL/TL, 5'9.5", 195 lbs. Deb: 4/28/47																												
1947	Cle-A	0	2	.000	22	2	0	0	1	44	58	11.9	3	24	4.9	10	2.0	3.48	100	.324	.396	1	0	94	171	-0.9	-1	-1	-0.1
■ MIKE WILLIS	Willis, Michael Henry b: 12/26/50, Oklahoma City, Okla BL/TL, 6'2", 205 lbs. Deb: 4/13/77																												
1977	Tor-A	2	6	.250	43	3	0	0	5	107	105	8.8	15	38	3.2	59	5.0	3.95	108	.260	.317	1	4	105	105	-1.0	0	1	0.4
1978	Tor-A	3	7	.300	44	2	1	0	7	101	104	9.3	11	39	3.5	52	4.6	4.54	85	.271	.329	-9	-8	102	93	-0.9	0	0	-0.7
1979	Tor-A	0	3	.000	17	1	0	0	0	27	35	11.7	1	16	5.3	8	2.7	8.33	54	.333	.406	-12	-12	106	74	-1.4	0	0	-1.0
1980	Tor-A	2	1	.667	20	0	0	0	3	26	25	8.7	3	11	3.8	14	4.8	1.73	236	.248	.325	7	7	101	221	0.7	0	0	0.7
1981	Tor-A	0	4	.000	20	0	0	0	0	35	43	11.1	6	20	5.1	16	4.1	5.91	70	.301	.381	-9	-7	113	104	-1.9	0	0	-0.6
Total	5	7	21	.250	144	6	1	0	15	296	312	9.5	36	124	3.8	149	4.5	4.59	90	.274	.339	-22	-16	105	108	-4.5	0	1	-1.2
■ RON WILLIS	Willis, Ronald Earl b: 7/12/43, Willisville, Tenn. d: 11/21/77, Memphis, Tenn. BR/TR, 6'2", 185 lbs. Deb: 9/20/66																												
1966	StL-N	0	0	—	4	0	0	0	1	3	1	3.0	0	1	3.0	2	6.0	0.00	—	.100	.182	1	1	100	0	0.0	0	0	0.1
1967	StL-N	6	5	.545	65	0	0	0	10	81	76	8.4	3	43	4.8	42	4.7	2.67	125	.257	.349	6	6	99	148	-0.7	1	2	1.0
1968	StL-N	2	3	.400	48	0	0	0	4	64	50	7.0	4	28	3.9	39	5.5	3.38	82	.213	.293	-3	-4	93	78	-0.7	-1	1	-0.4
1969	StL-N	1	2	.333	26	0	0	0	0	32	26	7.3	4	19	5.3	23	6.5	4.22	84	.224	.326	-2	-2	99	94	-0.5	0	1	0.0
	Hou-N	0	0	—	3	0	0	0	0	2	3	13.5	0	0	0.0	2	9.0	0.00	—	.300	.273	1	1	101	0	0.0	0	0	0.1
	Yr	1	2	.333	29	0	0	0	0	34	29	7.7	4	19	5.0	25	6.6	3.97	90	.223	.316	-1	-2	99	0	-0.5	0	1	0.1
1970	SD-N	2	2	.500	42	0	0	0	4	56	53	8.5	4	28	4.5	20	3.2	4.02	97	.247	.335	0	-1	97	98	0.4	-1	1	0.0
Total	5	11	12	.478	188	0	0	0	19	238	209	7.9	15	119	4.5	128	4.8	3.33	101	.237	.325	4	1	97	107	-1.5	0	5	0.8
■ VIC WILLIS	Willis, Victor Gazaway b: 4/12/1876, Cecil Co., Md. d: 8/3/47, Elkton, Md. BR/TR, 6'2", 185 lbs. Deb: 4/20/1898																												
1898	Bos-N	25	13	.658	41	38	29	1	0	311	264	7.6	5	148	4.3	160	4.6	2.84	128	.250	.342	27	28	101	100	-0.9	-6	0	2.2
1899	Bos-N	27	8	.771	41	38	35	**5**	2	343	277	**7.3**	6	117	3.1	120	3.1	**2.49**	159	**.242**	.312	52	56	103	90	7.9	-3	1	5.3
1900	Bos-N	10	17	.370	32	29	22	2	0	236	258	9.8	11	106	4.0	53	2.0	4.19	106	.301	.378	-13	6	120	101	-3.5	-8	0	0.1
1901	Bos-N	18	17	.514	38	35	33	**6**	2	305	262	7.7	6	78	2.3	133	3.9	2.36	**158**	.255	.314	33	**46**	112	104	0.7	-1	-1	**4.7**
1902	Bos-N	27	19	.587	**51**	46	**45**	4	**3**	**410**	372	8.2	6	101	2.2	**225**	4.9	2.20	119	.267	.323	27	19	94	112	3.8	-4	4	2.5
1903	Bos-N	12	18	.400	33	32	29	2	0	278	256	8.3	3	88	2.8	125	4.0	2.98	108	.271	.339	9	7	98	92	-0.8	-1	2	0.9

YEAR	TM/L	W	L	PCT	G	GS	CG	SHO	SV	IP	H	H/G	HR	BB	BB/G	SO	SO/G	ERA	/A	OAVG	OOBP	PR	/A	PF	CPI	WAT	PB	PD	TPI
1904	Bos-N	18	25	.419	43	43	**39**	2	0	350	357	9.2	7	109	2.8	196	5.0	2.85	97	.292	.356	-5	-3	102	118	2.7	1	6	0.3
1905	Bos-N	12	29	.293	41	41	36	4	0	342	340	8.9	7	107	2.8	149	3.9	3.21	95	.289	.355	-8	-6	102	105	-3.0	-3	6	0.0
1906	Pit-N	23	13	.639	41	36	32	6	1	322	295	8.2	0	76	2.1	124	3.5	1.73	153	.272	.322	32	33	101	**141**	1.8	-1	5	4.5
1907	Pit-N	21	11	.656	39	37	27	6	1	293	234	7.2	4	69	2.1	107	3.3	2.33	108	.247	.303	4	6	102	82	3.1	-2	1	0.8
1908	Pit-N	23	11	.676	41	38	25	7	0	305	239	7.1	2	69	2.0	97	2.9	2.07	105	.243	.297	9	3	92	88	2.3	-0	-0	0.3
1909	Pit-N	22	11	.667	39	35	24	4	1	290	243	7.5	3	83	2.6	95	2.9	2.23	115	.231	.289	12	11	99	94	-1.5	-2	1	1.3
1910	StL-N	9	12	.429	33	23	12	1	3	212	224	9.5	6	61	2.6	67	2.8	3.35	84	.275	.326	-8	-13	93	98	0.3	-1	2	-1.2
Total	13	247	204	.548	513	471	388	50	13	3997	3621	8.2	66	1212	2.7	1651	3.7	2.63	116	.264	.328	171	187	101	103	12.9	-31	27	21.7

■ CLAUDE WILLOUGHBY Willoughby, Claude William "Flunky" or "Weeping Willie" b: 11/14/1898, Fredonia, Kan. d: 8/14/73, McPherson, Kan. BR/TR, 5'9.5", 165 lbs. Deb: 9/18/25

YEAR	TM/L	W	L	PCT	G	GS	CG	SHO	SV	IP	H	H/G	HR	BB	BB/G	SO	SO/G	ERA	/A	OAVG	OOBP	PR	/A	PF	CPI	WAT	PB	PD	TPI
1925	Phi-N	2	1	.667	3	3	1	0	0	23	26	10.2	0	11	4.3	6	2.3	1.96	257	.295	.373	6	8	118	229	0.6	-1	-0	0.6
1926	Phi-N	8	12	.400	47	18	6	0	1	168	218	11.7	7	71	3.8	37	2.0	5.95	69	.327	.383	-40	-35	107	93	0.3	-1	2	-3.0
1927	Phi-N	3	7	.300	35	6	1	1	2	98	126	11.6	7	53	4.9	14	1.3	6.52	60	.321	.392	-28	-28	100	90	-0.4	-2	-1	-2.8
1928	Phi-N	6	5	.545	35	13	5	1	1	131	180	12.4	6	83	5.7	26	1.8	5.29	82	.340	.420	-19	-14	109	121	2.1	-1	-1	-1.3
1929	Phi-N	15	14	.517	49	34	14	1	4	243	288	10.7	15	108	4.0	50	1.9	5.00	105	.296	.361	-8	7	112	98	1.7	-5	4	0.6
1930	Phi-N	4	17	.190	41	24	5	1	1	153	241	14.2	17	68	4.0	38	2.2	7.59	72	.369	.418	-44	-37	109	99	-4.9	-4	2	-3.1
1931	Pit-N	0	2	.000	9	2	1	0	0	26	32	11.1	4	12	4.2	4	1.4	6.23	63	.305	.367	-7	-7	102	94	-0.9	0	0	-0.5
Total	7	38	58	.396	219	100	33	4	9	842	1111	11.9	56	406	4.3	175	1.9	5.84	81	.326	.390	-140	-106	108	103	-1.5	-15	7	-9.5

■ JIM WILLOUGHBY Willoughby, James Arthur b: 1/31/49, Salinas, Cal. BR/TR, 6'2", 185 lbs. Deb: 9/05/71

YEAR	TM/L	W	L	PCT	G	GS	CG	SHO	SV	IP	H	H/G	HR	BB	BB/G	SO	SO/G	ERA	/A	OAVG	OOBP	PR	/A	PF	CPI	WAT	PB	PD	TPI
1971	SF-N	0	1	.000	2	1	0	0	0	4	8	18.0	0	1	2.3	3	6.8	9.00	38	.400	.429	-2	-2	99	80	-0.4	-0	0	-0.1
1972	SF-N	6	4	.600	11	11	7	0	0	88	72	7.4	8	14	1.4	40	4.1	2.35	146	.222	.252	11	11	100	99	1.5	1	0	1.3
1973	SF-N	4	5	.444	39	12	1	1	1	123	138	10.1	21	37	2.7	60	4.4	4.68	82	.295	.344	-14	-12	104	111	-0.8	1	-1	-1.1
1974	SF-N	1	4	.200	18	4	0	0	0	41	51	11.2	7	9	2.0	12	2.6	4.61	86	.304	.331	-4	-3	109	111	-1.3	-0	1	-0.2
1975	Bos-A	5	2	.714	24	0	0	0	8	48	46	8.6	6	16	3.0	29	5.4	3.56	114	.247	.308	1	3	108	103	1.1	0	0	0.3
1976	Bos-A	3	12	.200	54	0	0	0	10	99	94	8.5	4	31	2.8	37	3.4	2.82	137	.256	.317	8	12	110	121	-4.6	0	1	1.4
1977	Bos-A	6	2	.750	31	0	0	0	2	55	54	8.8	5	18	2.9	33	5.4	4.91	96	.258	.316	-5	-1	116	76	1.5	0	1	0.0
1978	Chi-A	1	6	.143	59	0	0	0	13	93	95	9.2	6	19	1.8	36	3.5	3.87	99	.275	.314	-1	-0	102	94	-2.3	0	2	0.1
Total	8	26	36	.419	238	28	8	1	34	551	558	9.1	57	145	2.4	250	4.1	3.79	103	.267	.314	-7	6	106	104	-5.3	1	5	1.7

■ FRANK WILLS Wills, Frank Lee b: 10/26/58, New Orleans, La. BR/TR, 6'2", 200 lbs. Deb: 7/31/83

YEAR	TM/L	W	L	PCT	G	GS	CG	SHO	SV	IP	H	H/G	HR	BB	BB/G	SO	SO/G	ERA	/A	OAVG	OOBP	PR	/A	PF	CPI	WAT	PB	PD	TPI
1983	KC-A	2	1	.667	6	4	0	0	0	35	35	9.0	2	15	3.9	23	5.9	4.11	101	.259	.329	-0	0	102	91	0.5	0	-0	0.0
1984	KC-A	2	3	.400	10	5	0	0	0	37	39	9.5	3	13	3.2	21	5.1	5.11	78	.271	.323	-5	-5	99	78	-0.5	0	-1	-0.4
1985	Sea-A	5	11	.313	24	18	1	0	1	123	122	8.9	18	68	5.0	67	4.9	6.00	66	.266	.357	-25	-28	95	86	-2.6	0	0	-2.5
1986	Cle-A	4	4	.500	26	0	0	0	4	40	43	9.7	6	16	3.6	32	7.2	4.95	83	.272	.324	-3	-4	98	95	-0.1	0	0	-0.3
1987	Cle-A	0	1	.000	6	0	0	0	1	5	3	5.4	0	7	12.6	4	7.2	5.40	87	.176	.385	-1	-0	105	78	-0.4	0	0	0.0
1988	Tor-A	0	0	—	10	0	0	0	0	21	22	9.4	2	6	2.6	19	8.1	5.14	76	.272	.315	-3	-3	99	78	0.0	0	1	-0.1
Total	6	13	20	.394	82	27	1	0	6	261	264	9.1	31	125	4.3	166	5.7	5.38	75	.266	.341	-37	-39	98	86	-3.1	0	0	-3.3

■ TED WILLS Wills, Theodore Carl b: 2/9/34, Fresno, Cal. BL/TL, 6'2", 200 lbs. Deb: 5/24/59

YEAR	TM/L	W	L	PCT	G	GS	CG	SHO	SV	IP	H	H/G	HR	BB	BB/G	SO	SO/G	ERA	/A	OAVG	OOBP	PR	/A	PF	CPI	WAT	PB	PD	TPI
1959	Bos-A	2	6	.250	9	8	2	0	0	56	68	10.9	9	24	3.9	24	3.9	5.30	77	.302	.366	-9	-8	105	109	-1.9	1	-0	-0.6
1960	Bos-A	1	1	.500	15	0	0	0	1	30	38	11.4	4	16	4.8	28	8.4	7.50	54	.317	.399	-12	-11	105	85	0.1	1	1	-0.9
1961	Bos-A	3	2	.600	17	0	0	0	0	20	24	10.8	2	19	8.5	11	4.9	5.85	71	.304	.426	-4	-4	103	115	0.6	-0	0	-0.3
1962	Bos-A	0	0	—	1	0	0	0	0	⅓	2	54.0	0	1	27.0	0	0.0	27.00	—	1.000	1.000	-1	-1	103	140	0.0	0	0	0.0
	Cin-N	0	2	.000	26	5	0	0	3	61	61	9.0	12	23	3.4	58	8.6	5.31	74	.266	.340	-9	-9	100	95	-0.9	1	-0	-0.7
1965	Chi-A	2	0	1.000	15	0	0	0	1	19	17	8.1	2	14	6.6	12	5.7	2.84	110	.258	.381	1	1	91	182	1.0	0	0	0.1
Total	5	8	11	.421	83	13	2	0	5	186	210	10.2	29	97	4.7	133	6.4	5.52	71	.291	.374	-34	-33	102	109	-1.1	3	1	-2.4

■ WHITEY WILSHERE Wilshere, Vernon Sprague b: 8/3/12, Poplar Ridge, N.Y. d: 5/23/85, Cooperstown, N.Y. BL/TL, 6', 180 lbs. Deb: 6/24/34

YEAR	TM/L	W	L	PCT	G	GS	CG	SHO	SV	IP	H	H/G	HR	BB	BB/G	SO	SO/G	ERA	/A	OAVG	OOBP	PR	/A	PF	CPI	WAT	PB	PD	TPI
1934	Phi-A	0	1	.000	9	2	0	0	0	22	39	16.0	0	15	6.1	19	7.8	11.86	37	.394	.470	-18	-18	98	71	-0.4	-0	-1	-1.5
1935	Phi-A	9	9	.500	27	18	7	3	1	142	136	8.6	8	78	4.9	80	5.1	4.06	112	.253	.351	6	8	102	105	1.8	-4	-0	0.4
1936	Phi-A	1	2	.333	5	3	0	0	0	18	21	10.5	1	19	9.5	4	2.0	7.00	76	.288	.426	-4	-3	105	93	0.0	-0	-0	-0.2
Total	3	10	12	.455	41	23	7	3	1	182	196	9.7	9	112	5.5	103	5.1	5.29	87	.276	.376	-16	-14	102	100	1.4	-4	-1	-1.3

■ TERRY WILSHUSEN Wilshusen, Terry Wayne b: 3/22/49, Atascadero, Cal. BR/TR, 6'2", 210 lbs. Deb: 4/07/73

YEAR	TM/L	W	L	PCT	G	GS	CG	SHO	SV	IP	H	H/G	HR	BB	BB/G	SO	SO/G	ERA	/A	OAVG	OOBP	PR	/A	PF	CPI	WAT	PB	PD	TPI
1973	Cal-A	0	0	—	1	0	0	0	0	⅓	0	0.0	0	2	54.0	0	0.0	81.00	—	.000	.750	-3	-3	96	22	0.0	0	0	-0.2

■ DON WILSON Wilson, Donald Edward b: 2/12/45, Monroe, La. d: 1/5/75, Houston, Tex. BR/TR, 6'2.5", 195 lbs. Deb: 9/29/66

YEAR	TM/L	W	L	PCT	G	GS	CG	SHO	SV	IP	H	H/G	HR	BB	BB/G	SO	SO/G	ERA	/A	OAVG	OOBP	PR	/A	PF	CPI	WAT	PB	PD	TPI
1966	Hou-N	1	0	1.000	1	0	0	0	0	6	5	7.5	1	1	1.5	7	10.5	3.00	119	.238	.273	0	0	99	113	0.5	1	0	0.1
1967	Hou-N	10	9	.526	31	28	7	3	0	184	141	6.9	10	69	3.4	159	7.8	2.79	115	.209	.287	12	9	95	87	1.8	-1	-2	0.5
1968	Hou-N	13	16	.448	33	30	9	3	0	209	187	8.1	9	70	3.0	175	7.5	3.27	92	.236	.295	-7	-6	100	85	0.1	4	-2	-0.4
1969	Hou-N	16	12	.571	34	34	13	1	0	225	210	8.4	16	97	3.9	235	9.4	4.00	91	.245	.323	-10	-9	101	89	2.3	-2	-0	-1.0
1970	Hou-N	11	6	.647	29	27	3	0	0	184	188	9.2	15	66	3.2	94	4.6	3.91	97	.259	.324	3	-2	94	98	2.9	-2	-3	-0.7
1971	Hou-N	16	10	.615	35	34	18	3	0	268	195	**6.5**	15	79	2.7	180	6.0	2.45	131	**.202**	.263	30	22	92	81	3.7	-0	-3	2.0
1972	Hou-N	15	10	.600	33	33	13	3	0	228	196	7.7	16	66	2.6	172	6.8	2.68	135	.233	.285	20	24	105	104	1.7	-3	1	2.5
1973	Hou-N	11	16	.407	37	32	10	3	2	239	187	7.0	21	92	3.5	149	5.6	3.20	109	.213	.289	12	7	95	84	-2.9	1	-2	0.6
1974	Hou-N	11	13	.458	33	27	5	4	0	205	170	7.5	16	100	4.4	112	4.9	3.07	115	.227	.313	13	11	98	106	-1.1	2	-2	1.0
Total	9	104	92	.531	266	245	78	20	2	1748	1479	7.6	119	640	3.3	1283	6.6	3.15	109	.228	.297	74	57	98	91	9.0	-1	-14	4.6

■ DUANE WILSON Wilson, Duane Lewis b: 6/29/34, Wichita, Kan. BL/TL, 6'1", 185 lbs. Deb: 7/03/58

YEAR	TM/L	W	L	PCT	G	GS	CG	SHO	SV	IP	H	H/G	HR	BB	BB/G	SO	SO/G	ERA	/A	OAVG	OOBP	PR	/A	PF	CPI	WAT	PB	PD	TPI
1958	Bos-A	0	0	—	2	2	0	0	0	6	10	15.0	0	7	10.5	3	4.5	6.00	66	.400	.500	-1	-1	105	156	0.0	-0	0	0.0

■ FIN WILSON Wilson, Finis Elbert b: 12/9/1889, East Fork, Ky. d: 3/9/59, Coral Gables, Fla. BL/TL, 6'1", 194 lbs. Deb: 9/26/14

YEAR	TM/L	W	L	PCT	G	GS	CG	SHO	SV	IP	H	H/G	HR	BB	BB/G	SO	SO/G	ERA	/A	OAVG	OOBP	PR	/A	PF	CPI	WAT	PB	PD	TPI
1914	Bro-F	0	1	.000	2	1	1	0	0	7	7	9.0	0	11	14.1	4	5.1	7.71	42	.289	.512	-4	-3	101	85	-0.4	1	0	-0.2
1915	Bro-F	1	8	.111	18	11	5	0	0	102	85	7.5	1	53	4.7	47	4.1	3.79	78	.249	.356	-9	-9	98	93	-3.4	3	1	-0.4
Total	2	1	9	.100	20	12	6	0	0	109	92	7.6	1	64	5.3	51	4.2	4.05	74	.251	.369	-12	-13	98	92	-3.8	3	1	-0.6

■ ZEKE WILSON Wilson, Frank Ealton b: 12/24/1869, Benton, Ala. d: 4/26/28, Montgomery, Ala. BR/TR, 5'10", Deb: 4/23/1895

YEAR	TM/L	W	L	PCT	G	GS	CG	SHO	SV	IP	H	H/G	HR	BB	BB/G	SO	SO/G	ERA	/A	OAVG	OOBP	PR	/A	PF	CPI	WAT	PB	PD	TPI
1895	Bos-N	2	4	.333	6	6	4	0	0	45	54	10.8	1	27	5.4	5	1.0	5.20	94	.318	.411	-2	-2	102	98	-1.1	1	0	0.0
	Cle-N	3	1	.750	8	7	3	0	0	45	63	12.6	3	20	4.0	16	3.2	4.20	108	.352	.417	3	2	95	143	0.6	-2	0	0.0
	Yr	5	5	.500	14	13	7	0	0	90	117	11.7	4	47	4.7	21	2.1	4.70	100	.335	.414	1	0	98	143	-0.5	1	0	0.0
1896	Cle-N	17	9	.654	33	29	20	1	1	240	265	9.9	9	81	3.0	56	2.1	4.01	117	.302	.361	9	18	108	98	1.2	1	7	2.4
1897	Cle-N	16	11	.593	34	30	26	1	0	264	323	11.0	9	83	2.8	69	2.4	4.16	114	.324	.376	5	17	110	105	2.3	-4	2	1.4
1898	Cle-N	13	18	.419	33	31	28	1	0	255	307	10.8	4	51	1.8	45	1.6	3.60	95	.321	.355	0	-5	95	106	-4.1	-3	4	-0.3
1899	StL-N	1	1	.500	5	2	2	0	0	26	30	10.4	0	4	1.4	3	1.0	4.50	92	.313	.341	-2	-1	107	73	0.0	-2	0	-0.1
Total	5	52	44	.542	119	105	83	3	1	875	1042	10.7	26	266	2.7	194	2.0	4.02	107	.318	.369	13	28	104	104	-1.1	-8	13	3.4

■ GARY WILSON Wilson, Gary Steven b: 11/21/54, Camden, Ark. BR/TR, 6'2", 185 lbs. Deb: 4/13/79

YEAR	TM/L	W	L	PCT	G	GS	CG	SHO	SV	IP	H	H/G	HR	BB	BB/G	SO	SO/G	ERA	/A	OAVG	OOBP	PR	/A	PF	CPI	WAT	PB	PD	TPI
1979	Hou-N	0	0	—	6	0	0	0	0	7	15	19.3	2	6	7.7	6	7.7	12.86	26	.441	.500	-7	-7	90	97	0.0	0	-0	-0.6

■ GLENN WILSON Wilson, Glenn Dwight b: 12/22/58, Baytown, Tex. BR/TR, 6'1", 190 lbs. Deb: 4/15/82

YEAR	TM/L	W	L	PCT	G	GS	CG	SHO	SV	IP	H	H/G	HR	BB	BB/G	SO	SO/G	ERA	/A	OAVG	OOBP	PR	/A	PF	CPI	WAT	PB	PD	TPI
1987	Phi-N	0	0	—	1	0	0	0	0	1	0	0.0	0	0	0.0	1	9.0	0.00	—	.000	.000	0	0	105	0	0.0	0	0	0.0

■ TEX WILSON Wilson, Gomer Russell b: 7/8/01, Trenton, Tex. d: 9/15/46, Sulphur Springs, Tex. BR/TL, 5'10", 170 lbs. Deb: 9/02/24

YEAR	TM/L	W	L	PCT	G	GS	CG	SHO	SV	IP	H	H/G	HR	BB	BB/G	SO	SO/G	ERA	/A	OAVG	OOBP	PR	/A	PF	CPI	WAT	PB	PD	TPI
1924	Bro-N	0	0	—	2	0	0	0	0	4	7	15.8	0	1	2.3	1	2.3	13.50	28	.412	.400	-4	-4	98	54	0.0	-0	0	-0.3

■ HIGHBALL WILSON Wilson, Howard Paul b: 8/9/1878, Philadelphia, Pa. d: 10/16/34, Havre-De-Grace, Md TR, Deb: 9/13/1899

YEAR	TM/L	W	L	PCT	G	GS	CG	SHO	SV	IP	H	H/G	HR	BB	BB/G	SO	SO/G	ERA	/A	OAVG	OOBP	PR	/A	PF	CPI	WAT	PB	PD	TPI
1899	Cle-N	0	1	.000	1	1	1	0	0	8	12	13.5	0	5	5.6	1	1.1	9.00	41	.372	.456	-5	-5	96	70	-0.4	0	0	-0.2
1902	Phi-A	7	5	.583	13	10	8	0	0	96	103	9.7	1	19	1.8	18	1.7	2.44	155	.299	.336	12	14	106	131	-0.2	-1	-1	1.3
1903	Was-A	7	18	.280	30	28	25	1	0	242	269	10.0	7	43	1.6	56	2.1	3.31	99	.304	.337	-10	-1	111	108	-1.5	1	-4	-0.4
1904	Was-A	0	3	.000	3	3	3	0	0	25	33	11.9	0	4	1.4	11	4.0	4.68	55	.343	.369	-6	-6	99	92	-1.4	1	0	-0.5

YEAR	TM/L	W	L	PCT	G	GS	CG	SHO	SV	IP	H	H/G	HR	BB	BB/G	SO	SO/G	ERA	/A	OAVG	OOBP	PR	/A	PF	CPI	WAT	PB	PD	TPI
Total	4	14	27	.341	47	42	37	1	0	371	417	10.1	8	71	1.7	86	2.1	3.30	102	.307	.342	-8	3	109	112	-3.5	2	-6	0.2
■ JIM WILSON	Wilson, James Alger b: 2/20/22, San Diego, Cal. d: 9/2/86, Newport Beach, Cal BR/TR, 6'1.5", 200 lbs. Deb: 4/18/45																												
1945	Bos-A	6	8	.429	23	21	8	2	0	144	121	7.6	7	88	5.5	50	3.1	3.31	98	.228	.331	1	-1	96	102	-0.4	2	-2	-0.1
1946	Bos-A	0	0	—	1	0	0	0	0	1	2	18.0	1	0	0.0	0	0.0	18.00	22	.500	.500	-2	-2	111	92	0.0	0	0	-0.1
1948	StL-A	0	0	—	4	0	0	0	0	3	5	15.0	0	5	15.0	1	3.0	12.00	39	.417	.556	-3	-2	109	95	0.0	0	0	-0.1
1949	Phi-A	0	0	—	2	0	0	0	0	5	7	12.6	2	5	9.0	2	3.6	14.40	29	.350	.480	-6	-6	99	73	0.0	-0	-0	-0.4
1951	Bos-N	7	7	.500	20	15	5	0	1	110	131	10.7	14	40	3.3	33	2.7	5.40	71	.294	.356	-18	-19	97	94	0.1	-0	-1	-1.8
1952	Bos-N	12	14	.462	33	33	14	0	0	234	234	9.0	19	90	3.5	104	4.0	4.23	85	.262	.329	-13	-16	97	94	1.1	-0	-1	-1.7
1953	Mil-N	4	9	.308	20	18	5	0	0	114	107	8.4	16	43	3.4	71	5.6	4.34	90	.243	.312	-1	-5	92	89	-3.2	1	1	-0.2
1954	Mil-N	8	2	.800	27	19	6	4	0	128	129	9.1	12	36	2.5	52	3.7	3.52	106	.266	.318	8	3	91	107	2.7	0	1	0.4
1955	Bal-A	12	18	.400	34	31	14	4	0	235	200	7.7	17	87	3.3	96	3.7	3.45	108	.228	.294	13	7	94	82	0.9	-1	-0	0.5
1956	Bal-A	4	2	.667	7	7	1	0	0	48	49	9.2	5	16	3.0	31	5.8	5.06	79	.268	.327	-5	-6	97	81	1.2	2	0	-0.2
	Chi-A	9	12	.429	28	21	6	3	0	160	149	8.4	15	70	3.9	82	4.6	4.05	104	.248	.325	2	3	102	93	-2.5	4	-0	0.7
	Yr	13	14	.481	35	28	7	3	0	208	198	8.6	20	86	3.7	113	4.9	4.28	98	.252	.323	-3	-2	101	93	-1.3	2	0	0.5
1957	Chi-A	15	8	.652	30	29	12	**5**	0	202	189	8.4	22	65	2.9	100	4.5	3.48	105	.249	.306	7	4	97	102	2.1	-0	-1	0.2
1958	Chi-A	9	9	.500	28	23	4	1	1	156	156	9.0	21	63	3.6	70	4.0	4.10	90	.268	.333	-6	-7	98	110	-0.5	-3	-1	-1.1
Total	12	86	89	.491	257	217	75	19	2	1540	1479	8.6	151	608	3.6	692	4.0	4.01	93	.254	.322	-21	-47	96	96	1.5	4	-5	-3.9
■ JACK WILSON	Wilson, John Francis "Black Jack" b: 4/12/12, Portland, Ore. BR/TR, 5'11", 210 lbs. Deb: 9/09/34																												
1934	Phi-A	0	1	.000	2	2	1	0	0	9	15	15.0	1	9	9.0	2	2.0	12.00	37	.405	.511	-8	-8	98	86	-0.4	-0	0	-0.5
1935	Bos-A	3	4	.429	23	6	2	0	1	64	72	10.1	0	36	5.1	19	2.7	4.22	114	.290	.377	2	4	108	113	-0.5	2	1	0.7
1936	Bos-A	6	8	.429	43	9	2	0	3	136	152	10.1	4	86	5.7	74	4.9	4.43	120	.284	.379	9	14	106	115	-0.7	-0	0	1.2
1937	Bos-A	16	10	.615	51	21	14	1	7	221	209	8.5	13	119	4.8	137	5.6	3.71	128	.258	.350	22	25	102	115	2.8	-3	1	2.2
1938	Bos-A	15	15	.500	37	27	11	3	1	195	200	9.2	16	91	4.2	96	4.4	4.29	112	.262	.337	11	11	100	100	-2.7	0	-1	0.9
1939	Bos-A	11	11	.500	36	22	6	0	2	177	198	10.1	10	75	3.8	80	4.1	4.68	105	.281	.344	-1	5	107	96	-1.8	-4	-0	0.1
1940	Bos-A	12	6	.667	41	16	9	0	5	158	170	9.7	17	87	5.0	102	5.8	5.07	86	.270	.360	-12	-12	100	97	2.8	5	-2	-0.8
1941	Bos-A	4	13	.235	27	12	4	1	1	116	140	10.9	7	70	5.4	55	4.3	5.04	83	.300	.388	-12	-11	101	111	-5.0	-1	2	-0.8
1942	Was-A	1	4	.200	12	6	1	0	0	42	57	12.2	2	23	4.9	18	3.9	6.64	54	.322	.397	-14	-14	99	89	-1.2	-1	-0	-1.4
	Det-A	0	0	—	9	0	0	0	0	13	20	13.8	3	5	3.5	7	4.8	4.85	85	.351	.397	-2	-1	113	159	0.0	-0	0	0.0
	Yr	1	4	.200	21	6	1	0	0	55	77	12.6	5	28	4.6	25	4.1	6.22	60	.328	.393	-16	-15	102	159	-1.2	-1	-0	-1.4
Total	9	68	72	.486	281	121	50	5	20	1131	1233	9.8	73	601	4.8	590	4.7	4.59	102	.278	.361	-4	13	103	106	-6.7	-3	1	1.6
■ JOHN WILSON	Wilson, John Nicodemus b: 6/15/1890, Boonsboro, Md. d: 9/23/54, Annapolis, Md. BR/TR, 6'1", 185 lbs. Deb: 6/11/13																												
1913	Was-A	0	0	—	3	0	0	0	0	4	4	9.0	0	3	6.8	1	2.3	4.50	68	.267	.389	-1	-1	105	91	0.0	0	0	0.0
■ JOHN WILSON	Wilson, John Samuel b: 4/25/03, Coal City, Ala. d: 8/27/80, Chattanooga, Tenn. BR/TR, 6'2", 164 lbs. Deb: 5/09/27																												
1927	Bos-A	0	2	.000	5	2	2	0	0	25	31	11.2	1	13	4.7	8	2.9	3.60	114	.326	.389	2	1	99	158	-0.9	-1	-0	0.0
1928	Bos-A	0	0	—	2	0	0	0	0	5	6	10.8	0	6	10.8	1	1.8	9.00	46	.333	.480	-3	-3	101	84	0.0	-0	0	-0.1
Total	2	0	2	.000	7	2	2	0	0	30	37	11.1	1	19	5.7	9	2.7	4.50	91	.327	.406	-1	-1	99	145	-0.9	-1	-0	-0.1
■ MAX WILSON	Wilson, Max b: 6/3/16, Haw River, N.C. d: 1/2/77, Greensboro, N.C. BL/TL, 5'7", 160 lbs. Deb: 9/10/40																												
1940	Phi-N	0	0	—	3	0	0	0	0	7	16	20.6	1	2	2.6	3	3.9	12.86	31	.444	.462	-7	-7	102	82	0.0	-0	0	-0.5
1946	Was-A	0	1	.000	9	0	0	0	0	13	16	11.1	1	9	6.2	8	5.5	6.92	48	.320	.410	-5	-5	94	90	-0.4	0	-0	-0.4
Total	2	0	1	.000	12	0	0	0	0	20	32	14.4	2	11	4.9	11	4.9	9.00	39	.372	.430	-12	-12	97	87	-0.4	-0	0	-0.9
■ PETE WILSON	Wilson, Peter Alex b: 10/9/1885, Springfield, Mass. d: 6/5/57, St.Petersburg, Fla TL , Deb: 9/15/08																												
1908	NY-A	3	3	.500	6	6	4	1	0	39	27	6.2	0	33	7.6	28	6.5	3.46	70	.191	.349	-5	-5	101	83	0.8	-1	-0	-0.4
1909	NY-A	6	5	.545	14	12	7	1	0	94	82	7.9	2	43	4.1	44	4.2	3.16	78	.230	.320	-7	-7	99	80	0.6	-1	-1	-0.8
Total	2	9	8	.529	20	18	11	2	0	133	109	7.4	2	76	5.1	72	4.9	3.25	75	.219	.329	-12	-12	100	81	1.4	-2	-1	-1.2
■ EARL WILSON	Wilson, Robert Earl (Name Changed From Wilson, Earl Lawrence) b: 10/2/34, Ponchatoula, La. BR/TR, 6'3", 216 lbs. Deb: 7/28/59																												
1959	Bos-A	1	1	.500	9	4	0	0	0	24	21	7.9	2	31	11.6	17	6.4	6.00	68	.241	.426	-6	-5	105	100	0.0	2	0	-0.2
1960	Bos-A	3	2	.600	13	9	2	0	0	65	61	8.4	4	48	6.6	40	5.5	4.71	87	.247	.362	-6	-5	105	90	0.8	-0	0	-0.3
1962	Bos-A	12	8	.600	31	28	4	1	0	191	163	7.7	21	111	5.2	137	6.5	3.91	104	.231	.335	1	4	103	101	2.6	3	-1	0.7
1963	Bos-A	11	16	.407	37	34	6	3	0	211	184	7.8	18	105	4.5	123	5.2	3.75	103	.234	.319	-3	3	107	94	-2.1	5	1	0.9
1964	Bos-A	11	12	.478	33	31	5	0	0	202	213	9.5	37	73	3.3	166	7.4	4.50	83	.269	.326	-20	-17	103	105	0.8	9	0	-0.7
1965	Bos-A	13	14	.481	36	36	8	1	0	231	221	8.6	27	77	3.0	164	6.4	3.97	95	.250	.309	-13	-5	109	93	2.5	9	-1	0.3
1966	Bos-A	5	5	.500	15	14	5	1	0	101	88	7.8	14	36	3.2	67	6.0	3.83	99	.235	.301	-4	-0	110	96	0.5	4	-0	0.4
	Det-A	13	6	.684	23	23	8	2	0	163	126	7.0	16	38	2.1	133	7.3	2.60	135	.213	.262	15	16	102	97	3.2	9	2	3.2
	Yr	18	11	.621	38	37	13	3	0	264	214	7.3	30	74	2.5	200	6.8	3.07	118	.220	.276	11	16	105	97	3.7	4	2	3.6
1967	Det-A	**22**	11	.667	39	38	12	0	0	264	216	7.4	34	92	3.1	184	6.3	3.27	97	.224	.287	-1	-3	98	101	4.7	7	1	0.6
1968	Det-A	13	12	.520	34	33	10	3	0	224	192	7.7	20	65	2.6	168	6.8	2.85	108	.231	.283	3	6	103	101	-2.5	10	1	2.0
1969	Det-A	12	10	.545	35	35	5	1	0	215	209	8.7	23	69	2.9	150	6.3	3.31	112	.256	.312	8	9	102	112	-0.1	0	1	1.1
1970	Det-A	4	6	.400	18	16	4	1	0	96	87	8.2	15	32	3.0	74	6.9	4.41	88	.238	.300	-7	-6	104	83	-0.8	2	0	-0.3
	SD-N	1	6	.143	15	9	0	0	0	65	82	11.4	5	19	2.6	29	4.0	4.85	81	.309	.355	-6	-7	97	104	-2.1	0	-1	-0.7
Total	11	121	109	.526	338	310	69	13	0	2052	1863	8.2	236	796	3.5	1452	6.4	3.69	99	.242	.310	-39	-10	104	99	7.5	60	2	7.0
■ ROY WILSON	Wilson, Roy Edward "Lefty" b: 9/13/1896, Foster, Iowa d: 12/3/69, Clarion, Iowa BL/TL, 6', 175 lbs. Deb: 4/18/28																												
1928	Chi-A	0	0	—	1	0	0	0	0	3	2	6.0	0	3	9.0	2	6.0	0.00	—	.167	.333	1	1	100	0	0.0	-0	0	0.2
■ STEVE WILSON	Wilson, Stephen Douglas b: 12/13/64, Victoria, B.C., Can. BL/TL, 6'4", 195 lbs. Deb: 9/16/88																												
1988	Tex-A	0	0	—	3	0	0	0	0	8	7	7.9	1	4	4.5	1	1.1	5.63	72	.259	.355	-1	-1	102	84	0.0	0	-0	-0.1
■ TREVOR WILSON	Wilson, Trevor Kirk b: 6/7/66, Torrance, Cal. BL/TL, 6', 175 lbs. Deb: 9/05/88																												
1988	SF-N	0	2	.000	4	4	0	0	0	22	25	10.2	1	8	3.3	15	6.1	4.09	79	.298	.344	-2	-2	93	112	-0.9	0	-0	-0.1
■ WALTER WILSON	Wilson, Walter Wood b: 11/24/13, Glenn, Ga. BL/TR, 6'4", 190 lbs. Deb: 4/17/45																												
1945	Det-A	1	3	.250	25	4	1	0	0	70	76	9.8	4	35	4.5	28	3.6	4.63	76	.284	.368	-10	-9	105	101	-1.0	-2	1	-0.9
■ WILLY WILSON	Wilson, William b: 1/7/1884, Columbus, Ohio d:10/28/25, Seattle, Wash. BR/TR, Deb: 10/03/06																												
1906	Was-A	0	1	.000	1	1	1	0	0	7	3	3.9	0	2	2.6	1	1.3	2.57	99	.146	.222	0	-0	94	9	-0.4	-0	0	0.0
■ MUTT WILSON	Wilson, William Clarence "Lank" b: 7/20/1896, Kiser, N.C. d: 8/31/62, Wildwood, Fla. BR/TR, 6'3", 167 lbs. Deb: 9/11/20																												
1920	Det-A	1	1	.500	3	2	1	0	0	13	12	8.3	0	5	3.5	4	2.8	3.46	116	.240	.309	0	1	106	66	0.2	-0	-1	0.0
■ BILL WILSON	Wilson, William Donald b: 11/6/28, Central City, Neb. BR/TR, 6'2", 200 lbs. Deb: 9/24/50																												
1955	KC-A	0	0	—	1	0	0	0	0	1	1	9.0	0	1	9.0	1	9.0	0.00	—	.250	.400	0	0	106	0	0.0	0	0	0.0
■ BILL WILSON	Wilson, William Harlan b: 9/21/42, Pomeroy, Ohio BR/TR, 6'2", 195 lbs. Deb: 4/08/69																												
1969	Phi-N	2	5	.286	37	0	0	0	6	62	53	7.7	6	36	5.2	48	7.0	3.34	107	.231	.332	2	2	100	114	-0.9	-0	-1	0.0
1970	Phi-N	1	0	1.000	37	0	0	0	0	58	57	8.8	5	33	5.1	41	6.4	4.81	82	.263	.349	-5	-5	98	94	0.5	0	-0	-0.4
1971	Phi-N	4	6	.400	38	0	0	0	7	59	39	5.9	4	22	3.4	40	6.1	3.05	119	.188	.262	3	4	105	64	-0.1	-1	2	0.5
1972	Phi-N	1	1	.500	23	0	0	0	0	30	26	7.8	1	11	3.3	18	5.4	3.30	103	.234	.296	1	0	99	82	0.2	0	0	0.1
1973	Phi-N	1	3	.250	44	0	0	0	4	49	54	9.9	7	29	5.3	24	4.4	6.61	60	.293	.381	-16	-14	109	86	-0.8	-1	-0	-1.5
Total	5	9	15	.375	179	0	0	0	17	258	229	8.0	23	131	4.6	171	6.0	4.22	89	.241	.326	-16	-14	102	89	-1.1	-1	1	-1.3
■ HOOKS WILTSE	Wiltse, George Leroy b: 9/7/1880, Hamilton, N.Y. d: 1/21/59, Long Beach, N.Y. BR/TL, 6', 185 lbs. Deb: 4/21/04 C																												
1904	NY-N	13	3	.813	24	16	14	2	3	165	150	8.2	8	61	3.3	105	**5.7**	2.84	96	.268	.345	-2	-2	100	112	3.3	3	3	0.0
1905	NY-N	15	6	.714	32	19	18	1	4	197	158	7.2	5	61	2.8	120	5.5	2.47	116	.245	.315	11	9	96	97	1.1	7	5	1.5
1906	NY-N	16	11	.593	38	26	21	4	6	249	227	8.2	3	58	2.1	125	4.5	2.28	113	.270	.320	10	8	97	110	-0.9	2	-1	0.8
1907	NY-N	13	12	.520	33	21	14	3	2	190	171	8.1	3	48	2.3	79	3.7	2.18	117	.270	.326	6	8	104	114	-0.3	-0	2	1.1

YEAR	TM/L	W	L	PCT	G	GS	CG	SHO	SV	IP	H	H/G	HR	BB	BB/G	SO	SO/G	ERA	/A	OAVG	OOBP	PR	/A	PF	CPI	WAT	PB	PD	TPI
1908	NY-N	23	14	.622	44	38	30	7	2	330	266	7.3	4	73	2.0	118	3.2	2.24	105	.249	.303	4	4	100	88	-0.5	6	-0	0.4
1909	NY-N	20	11	.645	37	30	22	4	3	269	228	7.6	9	51	1.7	119	4.0	2.01	134	.233	.275	18	20	103	104	2.1	2	-2	2.0
1910	NY-N	14	12	.538	36	30	18	2	2	235	232	8.9	4	52	2.0	88	3.4	2.72	103	.261	.303	8	2	92	97	-1.3	1	-3	0.0
1911	NY-N	12	9	.571	30	24	11	4	0	187	177	8.5	7	39	1.9	92	4.4	3.27	102	.251	.292	3	2	99	81	-1.3	-1	0	0.0
1912	NY-N	9	6	.600	28	17	5	0	3	134	140	9.4	7	28	1.9	58	3.9	3.16	107	.265	.303	4	3	99	90	-0.9	4	2	0.8
1913	NY-N	0	0	—	17	2	0	0	3	58	53	8.2	1	8	1.2	25	3.9	1.55	205	.237	.264	11	11	100	118	0.0	-0	0	1.2
1914	NY-N	1	1	.500	20	0	0	0	1	38	41	9.7	2	12	2.8	19	4.5	2.84	92	.289	.329	-0	-1	94	136	0.0	1	0	0.1
1915	Bro-F	3	5	.375	18	3	1	0	5	59	49	7.5	1	7	1.1	17	2.6	2.29	130	.226	.257	5	5	98	76	-0.7	-2	0	0.2
Total	12	139	90	.607	357	226	154	27	34	2111	1892	8.1	54	498	2.1	965	4.1	2.47	112	.255	.305	77	69	99	99	0.6	22	6	8.1
■ HAL WILTSE	Wiltse, Harold James "Whitey" b: 8/6/03, Clay City, Ill. d: 11/2/83, Bunkie, La. BL/TL, 5'9", 168 lbs. Deb: 4/13/26																												
1926	Bos-A	8	15	.348	37	29	9	1	0	196	201	9.2	6	99	4.5	59	2.7	4.22	101	.273	.349	-4	1	106	97	0.9	-5	0	-0.3
1927	Bos-A	10	18	.357	36	29	13	1	1	219	276	11.3	5	76	3.1	47	1.9	5.10	80	.321	.363	-23	-24	99	97	0.7	-2	1	-2.2
1928	Bos-A	0	2	.000	2	2	1	0	0	12	16	12.0	1	1	0.8	5	3.8	9.00	46	.314	.364	-7	-7	101	57	-0.9	-1	-0	-0.5
	StL-A	2	5	.286	26	5	0	0	0	72	93	11.6	4	35	4.4	23	2.9	5.25	79	.316	.375	-10	-9	103	106	-1.6	0	0	-0.7
	Yr	2	7	.222	28	7	1	0	0	84	109	11.7	5	36	3.9	28	3.0	5.79	72	.313	.366	-16	-15	103	106	-2.5	-1	0	-1.2
1931	Phi-N	0	0	—	1	0	0	0	0	1	3	27.0	0	0	0.0	0	0.0	9.00	47	.600	.600	-1	-1	109	158	0.0	0	0	0.0
Total	4	20	40	.333	102	65	23	2	1	500	589	10.6	16	211	3.8	134	2.4	4.88	85	.303	.360	-44	-39	102	97	-0.9	-7	2	-3.7
■ SNAKE WILTSE	Wiltse, Lewis De Witt b: 12/5/1871, Bouckville, N.Y. d: 8/25/28, Harrisburg, Pa. BR/TL, Deb: 5/05/01																												
1901	Pit-N	1	4	.200	7	5	3	0	0	44	57	11.7	2	13	2.7	10	2.0	4.30	74	.345	.406	-5	-5	96	118	-1.6	-1	1	-0.3
	Phi-A	13	5	.722	19	19	18	2	0	166	185	10.0	1	35	1.9	40	2.2	3.58	102	.302	.340	2	1	100	94	3.8	9	1	0.2
1902	Phi-A	8	8	.500	19	17	13	0	1	138	182	11.9	7	41	2.7	28	1.8	5.15	74	.344	.391	-24	-21	106	97	-1.5	-2	-1	-1.9
	Bal-A	7	11	.389	19	18	18	0	0	164	215	11.8	4	51	2.8	37	2.0	5.10	73	.343	.392	-28	-25	104	94	0.4	6	-1	-2.2
	Yr	15	19	.441	38	35	31	0	1	302	397	11.8	11	92	2.7	65	1.9	5.13	73	.343	.392	-52	-46	105	94	-1.1	-2	-2	-4.1
1903	NY-A	0	3	.000	4	3	2	0	1	25	35	12.6	1	6	2.2	6	2.2	5.40	55	.355	.392	-7	-7	100	98	-1.4	0	-0	-0.6
Total	3	29	31	.483	68	62	54	2	2	537	674	11.3	15	146	2.4	121	2.0	4.59	79	.332	.378	-62	-57	102	97	-0.3	13	-0	-4.8
■ FRED WINCHELL	Winchell, Frederick Russell (born Frederick Cook) b: 1/23/1882, Arlington, Mass. d: 8/8/58, Toronto, Ont., Can. TR/TR, 5'8", Deb: 9/16/09																												
1909	Cle-A	0	3	.000	4	3	0	0	1	14	16	10.3	0	2	1.3	7	4.5	6.43	40	.296	.321	-6	-6	103	48	-1.4	0	-0	-0.6
■ ED WINEAPPLE	Wineapple, Edward "Lefty" b: 8/10/06, Boston, Mass. BL/TL, 6', 195 lbs. Deb: 9/15/29																												
1929	Was-A	0	0	—	1	0	0	0	0	4	7	15.8	0	3	6.8	1	2.3	4.50	95	.467	.556	-0	-0	100	224	0.0	-0	-0	0.0
■ RALPH WINEGARNER	Winegarner, Ralph Lee b: 10/29/09, Benton, Kan. BR/TR, 6', 182 lbs. Deb: 9/20/30 C																												
1932	Cle-A	1	0	1.000	5	1	1	0	0	17	7	3.7	0	13	6.9	5	2.6	1.06	452	.123	.286	6	7	107	123	0.5	-1	-0	0.6
1934	Cle-A	5	4	.556	22	6	4	0	0	78	91	10.5	1	39	4.5	32	3.7	5.54	81	.289	.363	-9	-9	100	84	0.0	1	0	-0.6
1935	Cle-A	2	2	.500	25	4	2	0	0	67	89	12.0	10	29	3.9	41	5.5	5.78	76	.313	.374	-10	-10	99	106	0.0	4	0	-0.8
1936	Cle-A	0	0	—	9	0	0	0	0	15	18	10.8	0	6	3.6	3	1.8	4.80	110	.295	.353	0	1	105	94	0.0	-1	-0	0.1
1949	StL-A	0	0	—	9	0	0	0	0	17	24	12.7	2	2	1.1	8	4.2	7.41	59	.329	.347	-6	-6	104	71	0.0	2	-0	-0.3
Total	5	8	6	.571	70	11	7	0	0	194	229	10.6	13	89	4.1	89	4.1	5.34	85	.290	.359	-18	-17	101	94	0.5	5	-0	-1.0
■ JIM WINFORD	Winford, James Head "Cowboy" b: 10/9/09, Shelbyville, Tenn. d: 12/16/70, Miami, Okla. BR/TR, 6'1", 180 lbs. Deb: 9/10/32																												
1932	StL-N	1	1	.500	4	1	0	0	0	8	9	10.1	0	5	5.6	4	4.5	6.75	58	.273	.368	-3	-3	101	62	0.1	1	0	0.0
1934	StL-N	0	2	.000	5	1	0	0	0	13	17	11.8	0	6	4.2	3	2.1	7.62	59	.327	.410	-5	-4	111	76	-0.9	0	-0	-0.3
1935	StL-N	0	0	—	2	1	0	0	0	11	13	10.6	1	5	4.1	7	5.7	4.09	99	.283	.353	-0	-0	100	115	0.0	-0	0	0.0
1936	StL-N	11	10	.524	39	23	10	1	3	192	203	9.5	10	68	3.2	72	3.4	3.80	100	.269	.327	5	0	95	101	-0.8	-4	-4	-0.7
1937	StL-N	2	4	.333	16	4	0	0	0	46	56	11.0	2	27	5.3	17	3.3	5.87	66	.311	.386	-10	-10	100	95	-1.0	-1	-0	-1.0
1938	Bro-N	0	1	.000	2	1	0	0	0	6	9	13.5	1	4	6.0	4	6.0	10.50	35	.346	.419	-4	-5	96	74	-0.4	0	-0	-0.3
Total	6	14	18	.438	68	31	10	1	3	276	307	10.0	14	115	3.8	107	3.5	4.57	84	.281	.346	-17	-22	97	98	-3.0	-3	-5	-2.3
■ ERNIE WINGARD	Wingard, Ernest James "Jim" b: 10/17/1900, Prattville, Ala. d: 1/17/77, Prattville, Ala. BL/TL, 6'2", 176 lbs. Deb: 5/01/24																												
1924	StL-A	13	12	.520	36	26	14	0	1	218	215	8.9	6	85	3.5	23	0.9	3.51	130	.262	.322	18	25	108	97	1.0	2	-3	2.4
1925	StL-A	9	10	.474	32	18	8	0	0	145	183	11.4	10	77	4.8	20	1.2	5.52	86	.319	.389	-18	-13	108	104	-1.1	3	2	-0.5
1926	StL-A	5	8	.385	39	16	7	0	3	169	188	10.0	9	76	4.0	30	1.6	3.57	117	.290	.354	9	11	103	**128**	-0.2	1	3	1.5
1927	StL-A	2	13	.133	38	17	7	0	0	156	213	12.3	7	79	4.6	28	1.6	6.58	69	.340	.398	-42	-36	109	93	-5.0	1	1	-2.9
Total	4	29	43	.403	145	77	36	0	4	688	799	10.5	32	317	4.1	101	1.3	4.64	97	.299	.362	-34	-12	107	105	-5.3	8	3	0.5
■ TED WINGFIELD	Wingfield, Frederick Davis b: 8/7/1899, Bedford, Va. d: 7/18/75, Johnson City, Tenn. BR/TR, 5'11", 168 lbs. Deb: 9/23/23																												
1923	Was-A	0	0	—	1	0	0	0	0	1	0	0.0	0	0	0.0	1	9.0	0.00	—	.000	.000	0	0	95	0	0.0	0	0	0.0
1924	Was-A	0	0	—	4	0	0	0	0	7	9	11.6	0	4	5.1	2	2.6	2.57	158	.300	.371	1	1	96	178	0.0	-0	-0	0.1
	Bos-A	0	2	.000	4	3	2	0	0	26	23	8.0	0	8	2.8	4	1.4	2.42	183	.240	.292	5	6	105	96	-0.9	1	0	0.7
	Yr	0	2	.000	8	3	2	0	0	33	32	8.7	0	12	3.3	6	1.6	2.45	178	.254	.312	7	7	103	96	-0.9	-1	0	0.8
1925	Bos-A	12	19	.387	41	26	18	2	2	254	267	9.5	11	92	3.3	30	1.1	3.97	110	.278	.332	12	11	99	99	2.1	2	6	1.8
1926	Bos-A	11	16	.407	43	20	9	1	3	191	220	10.4	11	50	2.4	30	1.4	4.43	96	.298	.327	-9	-4	106	96	2.4	-0	2	-0.2
1927	Bos-A	1	7	.125	20	8	2	0	0	75	105	12.6	2	27	3.2	1	0.1	5.04	81	.357	.390	-7	-8	99	122	-2.4	0	2	-0.4
Total	5	24	44	.353	113	57	31	3	5	554	624	10.1	24	181	2.9	68	1.1	4.18	103	.294	.337	3	7	102	102	1.2	2	10	2.0
■ LAVE WINHAM	Winham, Lafayette Sharkey "Lefty" b: 10/23/1881, Brooklyn, N.Y. d: 9/12/51, Brooklyn, N.Y. BL/TL, 5'11", 200 lbs. Deb: 4/21/02																												
1902	Bro-N	0	0	—	1	0	0	0	0	3	4	12.0	0	2	6.0	1	3.0	0.00	—	.345	.441	1	1	94	0	0.0	-0	0	0.1
1903	Pit-N	3	1	.750	5	4	3	1	0	36	33	8.3	0	21	5.3	22	5.5	2.25	147	.267	.373	4	4	101	145	0.6	-1	-1	0.3
Total	2	3	1	.750	6	4	3	1	0	39	37	8.5	0	23	5.3	23	5.3	2.08	157	.274	.379	5	5	101	134	0.6	-2	-0	0.4
■ GEORGE WINKELMAN	Winkelman, George Edward b: 2/18/1865, Washington, D.C. d: 5/19/60, Washington, D.C. BL/TL, Deb: 8/04/1883																												
1886	Was-N	0	1	.000	1	1	0	0	0	6	12	18.0	0	5	7.5	4	6.0	10.50	32	.429	.516	-5	-5	100	92	-0.4	-0	0	-0.3
■ GEORGE WINN	Winn, George Benjamin "Breezy" or "Lefty" b: 10/26/1897, Perry, Ga. d: 11/1/69, Roberta, Ga. BL/TL, 5'11", 170 lbs. Deb: 4/29/19																												
1919	Bos-A	0	0	—	3	0	0	0	0	5	6	10.8	0	1	1.8	0	0.0	7.20	41	.353	.389	-2	-2	91	66	0.0	-0	-0	-0.2
1922	Cle-A	1	2	.333	8	3	1	0	0	34	44	11.6	2	5	1.3	7	1.9	4.50	92	.317	.333	-2	-1	103	97	-0.4	1	0	0.0
1923	Cle-A	0	0	—	1	0	0	0	0	2	0	0.0	0	1	4.5	0	0.0	0.00	—	.000	.143	1	1	99	0	0.0	0	0	0.1
Total	3	1	2	.333	12	3	1	0	0	41	50	11.0	2	7	1.5	7	1.5	4.61	86	.309	.331	-3	-3	101	89	-0.4	1	-0	-0.1
■ JIM WINN	Winn, James Francis b: 9/23/59, Stockton, Cal. BR/TR, 6'3", 210 lbs. Deb: 4/10/83																												
1983	Pit-N	0	0	—	7	0	0	0	0	11	12	9.8	2	6	4.9	3	2.5	7.36	51	.267	.353	-5	-4	103	68	0.0	0	0	-0.3
1984	Pit-N	1	0	1.000	9	0	0	0	1	19	19	9.0	2	9	4.3	11	5.2	3.79	89	.264	.346	-0	-1	94	115	0.5	-0	0	0.0
1985	Pit-N	3	6	.333	30	7	0	0	0	76	77	9.1	4	31	3.7	22	2.6	5.21	72	.266	.337	-14	-12	104	74	-0.2	-0	2	-1.0
1986	Pit-N	3	5	.375	50	3	0	0	3	88	85	8.7	9	38	3.9	70	7.2	3.58	105	.258	.332	1	2	101	115	-0.1	-0	1	0.2
1987	Chi-A	4	6	.400	56	0	0	0	6	94	95	9.1	10	62	5.9	44	4.2	4.79	101	.271	.386	-3	1	109	113	-0.7	0	3	0.3
1988	Min-A	1	0	1.000	9	0	0	0	0	21	33	14.1	4	10	4.3	9	3.9	6.00	70	.355	.413	-5	-4	105	129	0.5	0	0	-0.3
Total	6	12	17	.414	161	10	0	0	10	309	321	9.3	31	156	4.5	159	4.6	4.66	88	.272	.358	-25	-20	104	104	0.0	-1	6	-1.1
■ TOM WINSETT	Winsett, John Thomas "Long Tom" b: 11/24/09, Mc Kenzie, Tenn. BL/TR, 6'2", 190 lbs. Deb: 4/20/30																												
1937	Bro-N	0	0	—	1	0	0	0	0	1	3	27.0	0	2	18.0	0	0.0	18.00	23	.600	.714	-2	-2	107	109	0.0	0	0	0.0
■ HANK WINSTON	Winston, Henry Rudolph b: 6/15/04, Youngville, N.C. d: 2/4/74, Jacksonville, Fla. BL/TR, 6'3.5", 226 lbs. Deb: 9/30/33																												
1933	Phi-A	0	0	—	1	0	0	0	0	7	7	9.0	0	6	7.7	2	2.6	6.43	61	.280	.406	-2	-2	92	84	0.0	-0	0	-0.1
1936	Bro-N	1	3	.250	14	0	0	0	0	32	40	11.3	2	16	4.5	8	2.3	6.19	69	.301	.370	-8	-7	107	84	-0.8	-1	-0	-0.6
Total	2	1	3	.250	15	0	0	0	0	39	47	10.8	2	22	5.1	10	2.3	6.23	68	.297	.376	-9	-9	104	84	-0.8	-1	0	-0.7
■ GEORGE WINTER	Winter, George Lovington "Sassafras" b: 4/27/1878, New Providence, Pa d: 5/26/51, Franklin Lakes, N.J. TR, 5'8", 155 lbs. Deb: 6/15/01																												
1901	Bos-A	16	12	.571	28	28	26	1	0	241	234	8.7	4	66	2.5	63	2.4	2.80	123	.274	.326	23	17	94	103	-0.2	-3	-1	1.6
1902	Bos-A	11	9	.550	20	20	18	0	0	168	149	8.0	2	53	2.8	51	2.7	3.00	117	.261	.323	11	9	98	87	-0.2	-2	-0	0.9

YEAR	TM/L	W	L	PCT	G	GS	CG	SHO	SV	IP	H	H/G	HR	BB	BB/G	SO	SO/G	ERA	/A	OAVG	OOBP	PR	/A	PF	CPI	WAT	PB	PD	TPI
1903	Bos-A	9	8	.529	24	19	14	0	0	178	182	9.2	4	37	1.9	64	3.2	3.08	103	.287	.326	-3	2	108	102	-1.8	-5	-1	0.1
1904	Bos-A	8	4	.667	20	16	12	1	0	136	126	8.3	4	27	1.8	31	2.1	2.32	114	.268	.308	4	5	101	115	0.8	-2	-2	0.4
1905	Bos-A	16	16	.500	35	27	24	2	0	264	249	8.5	5	54	1.8	119	4.1	2.97	89	.273	.314	-9	-9	100	93	-0.4	3	0	-0.9
1906	Bos-A	6	18	.250	29	22	18	1	2	208	215	9.3	8	38	1.6	72	3.1	4.11	68	.292	.327	-33	-31	104	78	-2.8	2	-1	-3.1
1907	Bos-A	12	15	.444	35	27	21	4	1	257	198	6.9	2	61	2.1	88	3.1	2.07	127	.235	.286	14	16	103	84	1.3	0	-1	1.6
1908	Bos-A	4	14	.222	22	17	8	0	0	148	150	9.1	3	36	2.2	55	3.3	3.04	76	.275	.324	-11	-12	97	111	-5.1	-1	-0	-1.2
	Det-A	1	5	.167	7	6	5	0	1	56	49	7.9	0	7	1.1	25	4.0	1.61	147	.240	.276	5	5	99	132	-2.1	-1	1	0.7
	Yr	5	19	.208	29	23	13	0	1	204	199	8.8	3	43	1.9	80	3.5	2.65	88	.264	.306	-6	-7	98	132	-7.2	-1	1	-0.5
Total	8	83	101	.451	220	182	146	9	4	1656	1552	8.4	32	379	2.1	568	3.1	2.87	101	.269	.315	1	3	101	96	-10.5	-8	-4	0.1
■ CLARENCE WINTERS	Winters, Clarence John b: 9/7/1898, Detroit, Mich. d: 6/29/45, Detroit, Mich. Deb: 8/28/24																												
1924	Bos-A	0	1	.000	4	2	0	0	0	7	22	28.3	0	4	5.1	3	3.9	20.57	22	.512	.542	-13	-13	105	67	-0.4	0	-0	-1.0
■ JESSE WINTERS	Winters, Jesse Franklin "Buck" or "T-Bone" b: 12/22/1893, Stephenville, Tex. d: 6/5/86, Abilene, Texas BR/TR, 6'1", 165 lbs. Deb: 5/03/19																												
1919	NY-N	1	2	.333	16	2	0	0	3	28	39	12.5	1	13	4.2	6	1.9	5.46	51	.339	.410	-8	-8	96	111	-0.6	-0	-0	-0.8
1920	NY-N	0	0	—	21	0	0	0	0	46	37	7.2	1	28	5.5	14	2.7	3.52	86	.233	.354	-2	-3	97	93	0.0	-1	1	-0.2
1921	Phi-N	5	10	.333	18	14	10	0	0	114	142	11.2	4	28	2.2	22	1.7	3.63	111	.310	.342	2	5	107	118	0.0	-3	2	0.4
1922	Phi-N	6	6	.500	34	9	4	0	2	138	176	11.5	8	56	3.7	29	1.9	5.35	89	.319	.371	-19	-9	117	98	1.3	-0	1	-0.6
1923	Phi-N	1	6	.143	21	6	1	0	1	78	116	13.4	7	39	4.5	23	2.7	7.38	64	.348	.411	-29	-23	118	91	-1.9	-1	-0	-2.1
Total	5	13	24	.351	110	31	15	0	6	404	510	11.4	21	164	3.7	94	2.1	5.06	83	.316	.372	-56	-39	110	103	-1.2	-5	2	-3.3
■ ALAN WIRTH	Wirth, Alan Lee b: 12/8/56, Mesa, Ariz. BR/TR, 6'4", 190 lbs. Deb: 4/09/78																												
1978	Oak-A	5	6	.455	16	14	2	1	0	81	72	8.0	6	34	3.8	31	3.4	3.44	112	.252	.328	3	4	103	110	0.3	0	-1	0.3
1979	Oak-A	1	0	1.000	5	1	0	0	0	12	14	10.5	2	8	6.0	7	5.3	6.00	64	.298	.397	-2	-3	91	108	0.5	0	0	-0.2
1980	Oak-A	0	0	—	2	0	0	0	0	2	3	13.5	0	0	0.0	1	4.5	4.50	84	.333	.333	-0	-0	94	91	0.0	0	0	0.0
Total	3	6	6	.500	23	15	2	1	0	95	89	8.4	8	42	4.0	39	3.7	3.79	102	.260	.338	1	1	101	109	0.8	0	-1	0.1
■ ARCHIE WISE	Wise, Archibald Edwin b: 7/31/12, Waxahachie, Tex. d: 2/2/78, Dallas, Tex. BR/TR, 6', 165 lbs. Deb: 7/24/32																												
1932	Chi-A	0	0	—	2	0	0	0	0	7	8	10.3	1	5	6.4	2	2.6	5.14	79	.258	.378	-1	-1	91	106	0.0	-1	0	0.0
■ RICK WISE	Wise, Richard Charles b: 9/13/45, Jackson, Mich. BR/TR, 6'1", 180 lbs. Deb: 4/18/64																												
1964	Phi-N	5	3	.625	25	8	0	0	0	69	78	10.2	7	25	3.3	39	5.1	4.04	86	.277	.339	-4	-4	98	110	0.6	2	-1	-0.3
1966	Phi-N	5	6	.455	22	13	3	0	0	99	100	9.1	5	24	2.2	58	5.3	3.73	97	.262	.305	-1	-1	100	87	-0.8	-4	-1	-0.4
1967	Phi-N	11	11	.500	36	25	6	3	0	181	177	8.8	8	45	2.2	111	5.5	3.28	107	.259	.303	2	5	104	97	-0.1	2	1	0.9
1968	Phi-N	9	15	.375	30	30	7	1	0	182	210	10.4	12	37	1.8	97	4.8	4.55	65	.292	.326	-32	-32	99	89	-2.6	7	1	-2.6
1969	Phi-N	15	13	.536	33	31	14	4	0	220	215	8.8	17	61	2.5	144	5.9	3.23	111	.257	.303	9	9	100	105	3.9	7	1	1.8
1970	Phi-N	13	14	.481	35	34	5	1	0	220	253	10.4	15	65	2.7	113	4.6	4.17	95	.287	.334	-3	-5	98	103	0.8	5	1	0.0
1971	Phi-N	17	14	.548	38	37	17	4	0	272	261	8.6	20	70	2.3	155	5.1	2.88	126	.254	.298	18	23	105	111	4.2	9	0	3.7
1972	StL-N	16	16	.500	35	35	20	2	0	269	250	8.4	16	71	2.4	142	4.8	3.11	117	.251	.296	10	16	105	98	0.7	0	2	2.1
1973	StL-N	16	12	.571	35	34	14	5	0	259	259	9.0	18	59	2.1	144	5.0	3.37	98	.257	.296	9	-2	90	93	2.3	7	-0	0.4
1974	Bos-A	3	4	.429	9	9	1	0	0	49	47	8.6	2	16	2.9	25	4.6	3.86	100	.251	.308	-1	-0	106	79	-0.5	0	-0	0.0
1975	Bos-A	19	12	.613	35	35	17	1	0	255	262	9.2	34	72	2.5	141	5.0	3.95	103	.263	.310	-5	4	108	99	0.9	0	-1	0.2
1976	Bos-A	14	11	.560	34	34	11	4	0	224	218	8.8	18	48	1.9	93	3.7	3.54	109	.255	.292	-0	8	110	90	1.4	0	2	1.0
1977	Bos-A	11	5	.688	26	20	4	2	0	128	151	10.6	19	28	2.0	85	6.0	4.78	99	.291	.330	-10	-1	116	98	1.9	0	1	0.0
1978	Cle-A	9	19	.321	33	31	9	1	0	212	226	9.6	22	59	2.5	106	4.5	4.33	82	.275	.319	-13	-19	94	93	-4.1	0	-0	-1.8
1979	Cle-A	15	10	.600	34	34	9	2	0	232	229	8.9	24	68	2.6	108	4.2	3.72	121	.256	.304	13	20	106	96	2.8	0	4	2.4
1980	SD-N	6	8	.429	27	27	1	0	0	154	172	10.1	14	37	2.2	59	3.4	3.68	92	.285	.321	-1	-5	94	111	-0.3	-1	-1	-0.6
1981	SD-N	4	8	.333	18	18	0	0	0	98	116	10.7	10	19	1.7	27	2.5	3.77	88	.296	.322	-3	-5	95	116	-0.6	-2	0	-0.6
1982	SD-N	0	0	—	1	0	0	0	0	2	3	13.5	0	0	0.0	0	0.0	9.00	37	.333	.333	-1	-1	92	46	0.0	0	0	0.0
Total	18	188	181	.509	506	455	138	30	0	3125	3227	9.3	261	804	2.3	1647	4.7	3.69	100	.267	.310	-14	6	102	99	10.5	34	9	6.2
■ ROY WISE	Wise, Roy Ogden b: 11/18/24, Springfield, Ill. BB/TR, 6'2", 170 lbs. Deb: 5/13/44																												
1944	Pit-N	0	0	—	2	0	0	0	0	3	4	12.0	0	3	9.0	1	3.0	9.00	42	.333	.467	-2	-2	104	78	0.0	0	0	-0.1
■ BILL WISE	Wise, William E. b: 3/15/1861, Washington, D.C. d: 5/5/40, Washington, D.C. Deb: 5/02/1882																												
1882	Bal-a	1	2	.333	3	3	3	0	0	26	30	10.4	0	4	1.4	9	3.1	2.77	99	.295	.321	-0	-0	102	121	0.2	-1	0	0.0
1884	Was-U	23	18	.561	50	41	34	4	0	364	383	9.5	5	60	1.5	268	6.6	3.04	97	.276	.305	-1	-3	98	106	6.9	2	5	0.3
1886	Was-N	0	1	.000	1	1	0	0	0	3	6	18.0	0	2	6.0	0	0.0	9.00	37	.429	.501	-2	-2	100	102	-0.4	-0	0	-0.1
Total	3	24	21	.533	54	45	37	4	0	393	419	9.6	5	66	1.5	277	6.3	3.07	96	.278	.309	-3	-5	99	107	6.7	0	5	0.2
■ JACK WISNER	Wisner, John Henry b: 11/5/1899, Grand Rapids, Mich. d: 12/15/81, Jackson, Mich. BR/TR, 6'3", 195 lbs. Deb: 9/12/19																												
1919	Pit-N	1	0	1.000	4	1	1	0	0	19	12	5.7	0	7	3.3	4	1.9	0.95	323	.185	.270	4	4	105	155	0.5	-1	0	0.4
1920	Pit-N	1	3	.250	17	2	1	0	0	45	46	9.2	1	10	2.0	13	2.6	3.40	93	.274	.308	-1	-1	101	88	-0.9	-1	1	0.0
1925	NY-N	0	0	—	25	0	0	0	0	40	33	7.4	4	14	3.1	13	2.9	3.82	110	.228	.293	2	2	98	81	0.0	-1	0	0.1
1926	NY-N	2	2	.500	5	3	2	0	0	28	21	6.8	4	10	3.2	5	1.6	3.54	106	.208	.274	1	1	98	80	0.0	-0	0	0.0
Total	4	4	5	.444	51	6	4	0	0	132	112	7.6	9	41	2.8	35	2.4	3.20	112	.234	.291	6	6	100	94	-0.4	-3	1	0.5
■ WHITEY WISTERT	Wistert, Francis Michael b: 2/20/12, Chicago, Ill. d: 4/23/85, Painesville, Ohio BR/TR, 6'4", 210 lbs. Deb: 9/11/34																												
1934	Cin-N	0	1	.000	2	1	0	0	0	8	5	5.6	1	5	5.6	1	1.1	1.13	378	.185	.303	3	3	105	292	-0.4	-0	-0	0.2
■ ROY WITHERUP	Witherup, Foster Leroy b: 7/26/1886, N.Washington, Pa. d: 12/23/41, New Bethlehem, Pa. 6', 185 lbs. Deb: 5/14/06																												
1906	Bos-N	0	3	.000	8	3	3	0	0	46	59	11.5	2	19	3.7	14	2.7	6.26	44	.344	.412	-19	-18	106	81	-1.4	-1	-1	-1.7
1908	Was-A	2	4	.333	6	6	4	0	0	48	51	9.6	0	8	1.5	31	5.8	3.00	77	.264	.297	-3	-4	97	91	-0.7	-1	0	-0.3
1909	Was-A	1	5	.167	12	8	5	0	0	68	79	10.5	1	20	2.6	26	3.4	4.24	56	.306	.356	-13	-14	96	91	-1.1	-2	-2	-1.5
Total	3	3	12	.200	26	17	12	0	0	162	189	10.5	3	47	2.6	71	3.9	4.44	56	.303	.354	-35	-36	99	88	-3.2	-3	-2	-3.5
■ RED WITT	Witt, George Adrian b: 11/9/33, Long Beach, Cal. BR/TR, 6'3", 185 lbs. Deb: 9/21/57																												
1957	Pit-N	0	1	.000	1	1	0	0	0	1	4	36.0	1	5	45.0	1	9.0	54.00	7	.500	.692	-6	-6	96	66	-0.4	0	0	-0.3
1958	Pit-N	9	2	.818	18	15	5	3	0	106	78	6.6	2	59	5.0	81	6.9	1.61	230	.209	.314	28	25	94	158	3.4	-1	-0	2.5
1959	Pit-N	0	7	.000	15	11	0	0	0	51	58	10.2	7	32	5.6	30	5.3	6.88	59	.293	.389	-17	-16	104	85	-3.4	-1	-0	-1.5
1960	Pit-N	1	2	.333	10	6	0	0	0	30	33	9.9	3	12	3.6	15	4.5	4.20	87	.300	.352	-1	-2	97	122	-0.6	-1	-0	-0.2
1961	Pit-N	0	1	.000	9	1	0	0	0	16	17	9.6	5	5	2.8	9	5.1	6.19	64	.274	.328	-4	-4	99	92	-0.4	1	-0	-0.3
1962	LA-A	1	1	.500	5	2	0	0	0	10	15	13.5	4	5	4.5	10	9.0	8.10	50	.349	.408	-5	-5	102	113	0.0	0	-0	-0.3
	Hou-N	0	2	.000	8	2	0	0	0	15	20	12.0	2	9	5.4	10	6.0	7.20	52	.339	.411	-5	-6	95	99	-0.9	0	0	-0.4
Total	6	11	16	.407	66	38	5	3	0	229	225	8.8	24	127	5.0	156	6.1	4.32	88	.263	.354	-10	-13	97	126	-2.3	-2	-1	-0.5
■ MIKE WITT	Witt, Michael Atwater b: 7/20/60, Fullerton, Cal. BR/TR, 6'7", 185 lbs. Deb: 4/11/81																												
1981	Cal-A	8	9	.471	22	21	7	1	0	129	123	8.6	9	47	3.3	75	5.2	3.28	116	.251	.326	6	7	104	111	0.1	0	-1	0.7
1982	Cal-A	8	6	.571	33	26	5	1	0	180	177	8.9	8	47	2.3	85	4.3	3.50	115	.260	.309	12	11	99	95	0.0	0	-0	1.0
1983	Cal-A	7	14	.333	43	19	2	0	5	154	173	10.1	14	75	4.4	77	4.5	4.91	80	.293	.372	-14	-17	96	107	-2.6	0	0	-1.6
1984	Cal-A	15	11	.577	34	34	9	2	0	247	227	8.3	17	84	3.1	196	7.1	3.46	117	.244	.306	15	16	101	94	2.3	0	-1	1.6
1985	Cal-A	15	9	.625	35	35	6	1	0	250	228	8.2	22	98	3.5	180	6.5	3.56	117	.243	.315	16	17	101	100	2.1	0	0	1.7
1986	Cal-A	18	10	.643	34	34	14	3	0	269	218	7.3	22	73	2.4	208	7.0	2.84	140	.221	.275	40	34	95	91	2.8	0	2	3.7
1987	Cal-A	16	14	.533	36	36	10	0	0	247	252	9.2	34	84	3.1	192	7.0	4.01	111	.261	.319	13	12	100	105	2.3	0	-0	1.1
1988	Cal-A	13	16	.448	34	34	12	2	0	250	263	9.5	14	87	3.1	133	4.8	4.14	91	.272	.329	-5	-10	95	96	-0.5	0	-0	-1.0
Total	8	100	89	.529	271	239	65	10	5	1726	1661	8.7	140	595	3.1	1146	6.0	3.68	110	.254	.316	82	70	99	99	6.5	0	-0	7.2
■ BOBBY WITT	Witt, Robert Andrew b: 5/11/64, Arlington, Mass. BR/TR, 6'2", 190 lbs. Deb: 4/10/86																												
1986	Tex-A	11	9	.550	31	31	0	0	0	158	130	7.4	18	143	8.1	174	9.9	5.47	73	.223	.372	-23	-26	95	85	0.3	0	0	-2.3
1987	Tex-A	8	10	.444	26	25	1	0	0	143	114	7.2	10	140	8.8	160	10.1	4.91	95	.219	.382	-7	-4	104	92	-0.3	0	0	-0.3
1988	Tex-A	8	10	.444	22	22	13	2	0	174	134	6.9	13	101	5.2	148	7.7	3.93	103	.216	.321	1	3	102	86	0.2	0	-1	0.2

YEAR	TM/L	W	L	PCT	G	GS	CG	SHO	SV	IP	H	H/G	HR	BB	BB/G	SO	SO/G	ERA	/A	OAVG	OOBP	PR	/A	PF	CPI	WAT	PB	PD	TPI
Total	3	27	29	.482	79	78	14	2	0	475	378	7.2	41	384	7.3	482	9.1	4.74	89	.219	.358	-29	-28	100	87	0.2	0	0	-2.4
■ JOHNNIE WITTIG	Wittig, John Carl "Hans" b: 6/16/14, Baltimore, Md. BR/TR, 6', 180 lbs. Deb: 8/04/38																												
1938	NY-N	2	3	.400	13	6	2	0	0	39	41	9.5	4	26	6.0	14	3.2	4.85	80	.263	.366	-5	-4	102	100	-0.6	-1	-1	-0.6
1939	NY-N	0	2	.000	5	2	1	0	0	17	18	9.5	0	14	7.4	4	2.1	7.41	52	.281	.402	-7	-7	99	70	-0.9	-1	0	-0.6
1941	NY-N	3	5	.375	25	9	0	0	0	85	111	11.8	5	45	4.8	47	5.0	5.61	67	.319	.393	-19	-17	104	103	-0.8	-0	-2	-1.8
1943	NY-N	5	15	.250	40	22	4	1	4	164	171	9.4	14	76	4.2	56	3.1	4.23	79	.272	.346	-16	-16	99	103	-3.3	-3	-3	-2.2
1949	Bos-A	0	0	—	1	0	0	0	0	2	2	9.0	0	2	9.0	0	0.0	9.00	48	.286	.444	-1	-1	103	63	0.0	0	0	0.0
Total	5	10	25	.286	84	39	7	1	4	307	343	10.1	23	163	4.8	121	3.5	4.90	73	.285	.366	-46	-46	101	101	-5.6	-6	-6	-5.2
■ PETE WOJEY	Wojey, Peter Paul b: 12/1/19, Stowe, Pa. BR/TR, 5'11", 185 lbs. Deb: 7/02/54																												
1954	Bro-N	1	1	.500	14	1	0	0	1	28	24	7.7	3	14	4.5	21	6.8	3.21	127	.242	.336	3	3	101	127	-0.1	-0	1	0.3
1956	Det-A	0	0	—	2	0	0	0	0	4	2	4.5	0	1	2.3	1	2.3	2.25	176	.167	.214	1	1	95	50	0.0	0	0	0.1
1957	Det-A	0	0	—	2	0	0	0	0	1	1	9.0	0	0	0.0	0	0.0	0.00	—	.200	.167	0	0	107	0	0.0	0	0	0.1
Total	3	1	1	.500	18	1	0	0	1	33	27	7.4	3	15	4.1	22	6.0	3.00	136	.233	.317	4	4	100	114	-0.1	-0	1	0.5
■ ED WOJNA	Wojna, Edward David b: 8/20/60, Bridgeport, Conn. BR/TR, 6'1", 185 lbs. Deb: 6/16/85																												
1985	SD-N	2	4	.333	15	7	0	0	0	42	53	11.4	6	19	4.1	18	3.9	5.79	63	.312	.379	-10	-10	101	105	-1.0	-0	0	-0.9
1986	SD-N	2	2	.500	7	7	1	0	0	39	42	9.7	2	16	3.7	19	4.4	3.23	111	.268	.335	2	1	96	119	0.2	-0	-1	0.1
1987	SD-N	0	3	.000	5	3	0	0	0	18	25	12.5	2	6	3.0	13	6.5	6.00	67	.333	.381	-4	-4	98	103	-1.4	-1	1	-0.3
Total	3	4	9	.308	27	17	1	0	0	99	120	10.9	10	41	3.7	50	4.5	4.82	76	.299	.362	-12	-12	99	110	-2.2	-1	0	-1.1
■ ERNIE WOLF	Wolf, Ernest Adolph b: 2/2/1889, Newark, N.J. d: 5/23/64, Atlantic Highlands, N.J. BR/TR, 5'11", 174 lbs. Deb: 9/10/12																												
1912	Cle-A	0	0	—	1	0	0	0	0	6	8	12.0	0	4	6.0	1	1.5	6.00	57	.348	.444	-2	-2	101	105	0.0	-0	-0	-0.1
■ WALLY WOLF	Wolf, Walter Beck b: 1/5/42, Los Angeles, Cal. BR/TR, 6'0.5", 191 lbs. Deb: 9/27/69																												
1969	Cal-A	0	0	—	2	0	0	0	0	2	3	13.5	1	3	13.5	2	9.0	13.50	27	.333	.500	-2	-2	101	90	0.0	0	0	-0.1
1970	Cal-A	0	0	—	4	0	0	0	0	5	3	5.4	1	4	7.2	5	9.0	5.40	63	.176	.333	-1	-1	92	73	0.0	0	0	0.0
Total	2	0	0	—	6	0	0	0	0	7	6	7.7	2	7	9.0	7	9.0	7.71	45	.231	.394	-3	-3	94	78	0.0	0	0	-0.1
■ LEFTY WOLF	Wolf, Walter Francis b: 6/10/1900, Hartford, Conn. d: 9/25/71, New Orleans, La. BR/TL, 5'10", 163 lbs. Deb: 7/04/21																												
1921	Phi-A	0	0	—	8	0	0	0	0	15	15	9.0	0	16	9.6	11	6.6	7.20	64	.273	.440	-5	-4	107	80	0.0	-0	-0	-0.3
■ CHICKEN WOLF	Wolf, William Van Winkle b: 5/12/1862, Louisville, Ky. d: 5/16/03, Louisville, Ky. BR , 5'9", 190 lbs. Deb: 5/02/1882 M																												
1882	Lou-a	0	0	—	1	0	0	0	0	6	11	16.5	0	3	4.5	1	1.5	9.00	27	.399	.458	-4	-4	90	85	0.0	0	0	-0.2
1885	Lou-a	0	0	—	1	0	0	0	0	1	1	9.0	0	0	0.0	1	9.0	9.00	37	.272	.272	-1	-1	103	28	0.0	0	0	0.0
1886	Lou-a	0	0	—	1	0	0	0	0	3	7	21.0	0	0	0.0	0	0.0	15.00	25	.464	.464	-4	-4	108	61	0.0	0	0	-0.2
Total	3	0	0	—	3	0	0	0	0	10	19	17.1	0	3	2.7	2	1.8	10.80	27	.410	.446	-9	-9	96	72	0.0	1	0	-0.4
■ CHUCK WOLFE	Wolfe, Charles Hunt b: 2/15/1897, Wolfsburg, Pa. d: 11/27/57, Schellsburg, Pa. BL/TR, 5'7", 175 lbs. Deb: 8/02/23																												
1923	Phi-A	0	0	—	3	0	0	0	0	10	6	5.4	1	8	7.2	1	0.9	3.60	113	.194	.350	0	1	102	105	0.0	0	-0	0.0
■ ED WOLFE	Wolfe, Edward Anthony b: 1/2/29, Los Angeles, Cal. BR/TR, 6'3", 185 lbs. Deb: 4/19/52																												
1952	Pit-N	0	0	—	3	0	0	0	0	4	7	15.8	1	5	11.3	1	2.3	6.75	58	.467	.619	-1	-1	105	206	0.0	0	0	0.0
■ BARNEY WOLFE	Wolfe, Wilbert Otto b: 1/9/1876, Independence, Pa. d: 2/27/53, N.Charleroi, Pa. BR/TR, 6'1", Deb: 4/24/03																												
1903	NY-A	6	9	.400	20	16	12	1	0	148	143	8.7	1	26	1.6	48	2.9	2.98	99	.275	.310	-0	-0	100	89	-2.0	-4	-0	0.0
1904	NY-A	0	3	.000	7	3	2	0	0	34	31	8.2	1	4	1.1	8	2.1	3.18	90	.265	.289	-2	-1	111	74	-1.4	-1	0	0.0
	Was-A	6	9	.400	17	16	13	2	0	127	131	9.3	0	22	1.6	44	3.1	3.26	79	.290	.323	-9	-10	99	89	1.6	-1	-2	-1.2
	Yr	6	12	.333	24	19	15	2	0	161	162	9.1	1	26	1.5	52	2.9	3.24	81	.285	.316	-12	-11	102	89	0.2	-1	-2	-1.2
1905	Was-A	9	13	.409	28	23	17	1	1	182	162	8.0	1	37	1.8	52	2.6	2.57	109	.262	.304	2	5	106	93	-0.3	-2	-2	0.2
1906	Was-A	0	3	.000	4	3	2	0	0	20	17	7.6	0	10	4.5	8	3.6	4.05	63	.254	.351	-3	-3	94	71	-1.4	0	0	-0.3
Total	4	21	37	.362	76	61	46	4	1	511	484	8.5	3	99	1.7	160	2.8	2.96	94	.273	.311	-14	-10	102	89	-3.5	-9	-5	-1.3
■ BILL WOLFE	Wolfe, William b: Jersey City, N.J. Deb: 9/10/02																												
1902	Phi-N	0	1	.000	1	1	1	0	0	9	13	13.0	0	6	6.0	0	0.0	5.00	61	.363	.455	-2	-2	109	120	-0.4	0	0	-0.1
■ ROGER WOLFF	Wolff, Roger Francis b: 4/10/11, Evansville, Ill. BR/TR, 6'0.5", 208 lbs. Deb: 9/20/41																												
1941	Phi-A	0	2	.000	2	2	2	0	0	17	15	7.9	0	4	2.1	2	1.1	3.18	134	.231	.275	2	2	103	66	-0.9	-0	-0	0.2
1942	Phi-A	12	15	.444	32	25	15	2	3	214	206	8.7	16	69	2.9	94	4.0	3.32	111	.249	.305	8	9	101	103	2.2	-3	0	0.6
1943	Phi-A	10	15	.400	41	26	13	2	6	221	232	9.4	11	72	2.9	91	3.7	3.54	98	.274	.329	-6	-1	106	109	1.8	-4	-3	-0.7
1944	Was-A	4	15	.211	33	21	5	0	2	155	186	10.8	9	60	3.5	73	4.2	4.99	62	.295	.352	-27	-32	91	93	-4.9	1	2	-2.9
1945	Was-A	20	10	.667	33	29	21	4	2	250	200	7.2	7	53	1.9	108	3.9	2.12	146	.215	**.254**	34	27	92	82	4.1	-4	-1	2.3
1946	Was-A	5	8	.385	21	17	6	0	0	122	115	8.5	8	30	2.2	50	3.7	2.58	128	.249	.296	12	10	94	118	-1.4	-1	-1	0.8
1947	Cle-A	0	0	—	7	2	0	0	0	16	15	8.4	1	10	5.6	5	2.8	3.94	89	.259	.375	-0	-1	94	120	0.0	-0	1	0.0
	Pit-N	1	4	.200	13	6	1	0	0	30	49	14.7	4	18	5.4	7	2.1	8.70	48	.368	.439	-15	-15	102	94	-1.2	-1	-1	-1.4
Total	7	52	69	.430	182	128	63	8	13	1025	1018	8.9	56	316	2.8	430	3.8	3.41	99	.258	.311	8	-2	97	99	-0.3	-12	-3	-1.1
■ MELLIE WOLFGANG	Wolfgang, Meldon John "Red" b: 3/20/1890, Albany, N.Y. d: 6/30/47, Albany, N.Y. BR/TR, 5'9", 160 lbs. Deb: 4/18/14																												
1914	Chi-A	9	5	.643	24	11	9	2	0	119	96	7.3	0	32	2.4	50	3.8	1.89	152	.219	.272	11	13	105	83	2.6	-0	4	1.9
1915	Chi-A	2	2	.500	17	2	0	0	0	54	39	6.5	0	12	2.0	21	3.5	1.83	150	.211	.263	7	6	94	82	-0.3	-1	-1	0.3
1916	Chi-A	4	6	.400	27	14	6	1	0	127	103	7.3	2	42	3.0	36	2.6	1.98	151	.228	.296	12	14	106	113	-1.5	0	1	1.8
1917	Chi-A	0	0	—	5	0	0	0	0	18	18	9.0	1	6	3.0	3	1.5	5.00	50	.305	.379	-5	-5	93	89	0.0	-1	-0	-0.5
1918	Chi-A	0	1	.000	4	0	0	0	0	8	12	13.5	0	3	3.4	1	1.1	5.63	49	.333	.385	-3	-3	100	88	-0.4	0	0	-0.1
Total	5	15	14	.517	77	27	15	3	0	326	268	7.4	3	95	2.6	111	3.1	2.18	132	.229	.289	23	25	103	95	0.4	-2	5	3.4
■ HARRY WOLTER	Wolter, Harry Meigs b: 7/11/1884, Monterey, Cal. d: 7/7/70, Palo Alto, Cal. BL/TL, 5'10", 175 lbs. Deb: 5/14/07																												
1907	Pit-N	0	0	—	1	0	0	0	0	2	3	13.5	0	2	9.0	0	0.0	4.50	56	.379	.504	-0	-0	102	162	0.0	-0	0	0.0
	StL-N	0	2	.000	3	3	1	0	0	23	27	10.6	1	18	7.0	8	3.1	4.30	57	.331	.462	-5	-5	100	132	-0.9	1	-1	-0.4
	Yr	0	2	.000	4	3	1	0	0	25	30	10.8	1	20	7.2	8	2.9	4.32	57	.335	.466	-5	-5	100	132	-0.9	-0	-1	-0.4
1909	Bos-A	4	4	.500	11	6	0	0	0	59	66	10.1	0	30	4.6	21	3.2	3.51	76	.303	.397	-7	-5	108	127	-0.5	2	0	-0.5
Total	2	4	6	.400	15	9	1	0	0	84	96	10.3	1	50	5.4	29	3.1	3.75	70	.312	.418	-12	-11	106	129	-1.4	3	-1	-0.9
■ RYNIE WOLTERS	Wolters, Reinders Albertis b: 12/18/1842 d: 1/3/17, Newark, N.J. TR, 6', 175 lbs. Deb: 5/18/1871 /1871																												
1871	Mut-n	16	16	.500	32																								
1872	Cle-n	2	6	.250	8																								
1873	Res-n	0	1	.000	1																								
Total	3 n	18	23	.439	41																								
■ DOOLEY WOMACK	Womack, Horace Guy b: 8/25/39, Columbia, S.C. BL/TR, 6', 170 lbs. Deb: 4/14/66																												
1966	NY-A	7	3	.700	42	1	0	0	4	75	52	6.2	6	23	2.8	50	6.0	2.64	122	.198	.265	7	5	94	88	2.4	0	2	0.8
1967	NY-A	5	6	.455	65	0	0	0	18	97	80	7.4	6	35	3.2	57	5.3	2.41	128	.230	.296	9	7	96	126	0.1	1	4	1.4
1968	NY-A	3	7	.300	45	0	0	0	2	62	53	7.7	6	29	4.2	27	3.9	3.19	94	.244	.327	-1	-1	101	122	-2.1	0	2	0.1
1969	Hou-N	2	1	.667	30	0	0	0	0	51	49	8.6	1	20	3.5	32	5.6	3.53	103	.259	.332	0	1	101	100	0.5	-0	2	0.3
	Sea-A	2	1	.667	9	0	0	0	0	14	15	9.6	0	3	1.9	8	5.1	2.57	142	.273	.305	2	2	100	115	0.7	-0	0	0.2
1970	Oak-A	0	0	—	2	0	0	0	0	3	4	12.0	2	1	3.0	3	9.0	15.00	24	.308	.357	-4	-4	96	62	0.0	0	0	-0.2
Total	5	19	18	.514	193	1	0	0	24	302	253	7.5	21	111	3.3	177	5.3	2.95	109	.233	.302	12	9	97	110	1.6	1	11	2.6
■ SPADES WOOD	Wood, Charles Asher b: 1/13/09, Spartanburg, S.C. d: 5/18/86, Wichita, Kan. BL/TL, 5'10.5", 150 lbs. Deb: 8/16/30																												
1930	Pit-N	4	3	.571	9	7	4	0	0	58	61	9.5	4	32	5.0	23	3.6	5.12	95	.270	.356	-1	-2	98	87	0.4	1	-2	-0.1
1931	Pit-N	2	6	.250	15	10	2	0	0	64	69	9.7	2	46	6.5	33	4.6	6.05	65	.273	.385	-16	-15	102	78	-1.9	1	-0	-1.3
Total	2	6	9	.400	24	17	6	0	0	122	130	9.6	6	78	5.8	56	4.1	5.61	78	.271	.372	-16	-17	100	82	-1.5	1	-2	-1.4

YEAR	TM/L	W	L	PCT	G	GS	CG	SHO	SV	IP	H	H/G	HR	BB	BB/G	SO	SO/G	ERA	/A	OAVG	OOBP	PR	/A	PF	CPI	WAT	PB	PD	TPI
■ GEORGE WOOD	Wood, George A. "Dandy" b: 11/9/1858, Boston, Mass. d: 4/4/24, Harrisburg, Pa. BL/TR, 5'10.5", 175 lbs. Deb: 5/01/1880 M																												
1883	Det-N	0	0	—	1	0	0	0	0	5	8	14.4	0	3	5.4	0	0.0	7.20	41	.369	.446	-2	-2	94	95	0.0	0	0	-0.1
1885	Det-N	0	0	—	1	0	0	0	0	4	5	11.3	0	1	2.3	1	2.3	0.00	—	.317	.358	1	1	99	0	0.0	0	0	0.1
1888	Phi-N	0	0	—	2	0	0	0	**2**	2	3	13.5	0	1	4.5	0	0.0	4.50	71	.361	.430	-0	-0	113	134	0.0	0	0	0.0
1889	Phi-N	0	0	—	1	0	0	0	0	1	2	18.0	0	0	0.0	2	18.0	18.00	23	.432	.432	-2	-2	105	40	0.0	0	0	0.0
Total	4	0	0	—	5	0	0	0	2	12	18	13.5	0	5	3.8	3	2.3	5.25	58	.358	.416	-3	-3	100	65	0.0	1	0	0.0
■ JOE WOOD	Wood, Howard Ellsworth "Smokey Joe" b: 10/25/1889, Kansas City, Mo. d: 7/27/85, West Haven, Conn BR/TR, 5'11", 180 lbs. Deb: 8/24/08																												
1908	Bos-A	1	1	.500	6	2	1	1	0	23	14	5.5	0	16	6.3	11	4.3	2.35	99	.161	.298	0	-0	97	70	0.0	-1	-0	0.0
1909	Bos-A	11	7	.611	24	19	13	4	0	161	121	6.8	1	43	2.4	88	4.9	2.18	123	.209	.270	5	9	108	64	0.7	-0	-4	0.6
1910	Bos-A	12	13	.480	35	17	14	3	0	199	155	7.0	3	56	2.5	145	6.6	1.67	147	.220	.287	19	17	97	117	-1.3	5	2	2.8
1911	Bos-A	23	17	.575	44	33	25	5	3	276	226	7.4	1	76	2.5	231	**7.5**	2.02	163	.223	.284	40	39	99	88	3.4	8	2	5.1
1912	Bos-A	**34**	5	**.872**	43	38	**35**	**10**	1	344	267	7.0	2	82	2.1	258	6.8	1.91	179	.216	.272	55	58	102	93	**12.8**	11	8	8.5
1913	Bos-A	11	5	.688	23	18	12	1	2	146	120	7.4	0	61	3.8	123	7.6	2.28	132	.229	.319	11	12	103	106	2.9	4	4	1.8
1914	Bos-A	9	3	.750	18	14	11	1	1	113	94	7.5	1	34	2.7	67	5.3	2.63	100	.229	.288	1	0	96	77	2.4	-0	0	0.0
1915	Bos-A	15	5	**.750**	25	16	10	3	2	157	120	6.9	1	44	2.5	63	3.6	**1.49**	**189**	.216	.275	25	23	96	118	2.7	4	1	3.2
1917	Cle-A	0	1	.000	5	1	0	0	1	16	17	9.6	0	7	3.9	2	1.1	3.38	89	.309	.387	-1	-1	113	127	-0.4	-1	0	0.0
1919	Cle-A	0	0	—	1	0	0	0	1	1	0	0.0	0	0	0.0	0	0.0	0.00	—	.000	.000	0	0	104	0	0.0	0	0	0.0
1920	Cle-A	0	0	—	1	0	0	0	0	2	4	18.0	0	2	9.0	1	4.5	22.50	17	.444	.545	-4	-4	100	46	0.0	0	0	-0.2
Total	11	116	57	.671	225	158	121	28	11	1438	1138	7.1	9	421	2.6	989	6.2	2.03	147	.220	.285	152	154	100	95	23.2	31	13	21.8
■ JOHN WOOD	Wood, John B. b: 1871, 5'7", 142 lbs. Deb: 5/09/1896																												
1896	StL-N	0	0	—	1	0	0	0	0	0	1	—	0	2	—	0	—	∞	—	1.000	1.000	-1	-1	98	117	0.0	0	0	0.0
■ JOE WOOD	Wood, Joseph Frank b: 5/20/16, Shoshola, Pa. BR/TR, 6', 190 lbs. Deb: 5/01/44																												
1944	Bos-A	0	1	.000	3	1	0	0	0	10	13	11.7	0	3	2.7	5	4.5	6.30	53	.317	.356	-3	-3	97	71	-0.4	-0	0	-0.2
■ PETE WOOD	Wood, Peter Burke b: 2/1/1857, Hamilton, Ont., Can. d: 3/15/23, Chicago, Ill. TR, 5'7", 185 lbs. Deb: 1885																												
1885	Buf-N	8	15	.348	24	22	21	0	0	199	235	10.6	8	66	3.0	38	1.7	4.48	66	.305	.360	-37	-34	105	98	0.2	-1	0	-2.9
1889	Phi-N	1	1	.500	3	2	2	0	0	19	28	13.3	0	3	1.4	8	3.8	5.21	81	.359	.383	-2	-2	105	96	0.0	-1	0	-0.2
Total	2	9	16	.360	27	24	23	0	0	218	263	10.9	8	69	2.8	46	1.9	4.54	68	.310	.362	-39	-36	105	98	0.2	-2	0	-3.1
■ WILBUR WOOD	Wood, Wilbur Forrester b: 10/22/41, Cambridge, Mass. BR/TL, 6', 180 lbs. Deb: 6/30/61																												
1961	Bos-A	0	0	—	6	1	0	0	0	13	14	9.7	2	7	4.8	7	4.8	5.54	75	.269	.344	-2	-2	103	90	0.0	-0	-0	-0.2
1962	Bos-A	0	0	—	1	1	0	0	0	8	6	6.8	0	3	3.4	3	3.4	3.38	121	.214	.290	1	1	103	64	0.0	-0	0	0.1
1963	Bos-A	0	5	.000	25	6	0	0	0	65	67	9.3	10	13	1.8	28	3.9	3.74	103	.270	.306	-1	1	107	115	-2.4	-2	-0	0.0
1964	Bos-A	0	0	—	4	0	0	0	0	6	13	19.5	1	3	4.5	5	7.5	16.50	23	.433	.471	-9	-9	103	63	0.0	-0	0	-0.7
	Pit-N	0	2	.000	3	2	1	0	0	17	16	8.5	0	11	5.8	7	3.7	3.71	96	.246	.367	-0	-0	101	105	-0.9	-1	-1	0.0
1965	Pit-N	1	1	.500	34	1	0	0	0	51	44	7.8	3	16	2.8	29	5.1	3.18	109	.237	.296	2	2	98	94	0.0	-1	-1	0.0
1967	Chi-A	4	2	.667	51	8	0	0	4	95	95	9.0	2	28	2.7	47	4.5	2.46	122	.260	.307	8	6	93	129	0.8	-0	-0	0.5
1968	Chi-A	13	12	.520	**88**	2	0	0	16	159	127	7.2	8	33	1.9	74	4.2	1.87	163	.222	.260	**20**	**21**	102	119	2.6	-1	-0	2.3
1969	Chi-A	10	11	.476	**76**	0	0	0	15	120	113	8.5	13	40	3.0	73	5.5	3.00	133	.248	.305	8	13	110	119	1.2	-2	1	1.3
1970	Chi-A	9	13	.409	**77**	0	0	0	21	122	118	8.7	7	36	2.7	85	6.3	2.80	143	.258	.308	12	16	108	118	1.2	-1	2	1.9
1971	Chi-A	22	13	.629	44	42	22	7	1	334	272	7.3	21	62	1.7	210	5.7	1.91	176	.222	.259	**58**	54	97	112	5.7	-4	2	**6.0**
1972	Chi-A	**24**	17	.585	49	49	20	8	0	**377**	325	7.8	28	74	1.8	193	4.6	2.51	130	.235	.272	24	31	106	103	1.3	-3	4	3.8
1973	Chi-A	**24**	20	.545	49	48	21	4	0	**359**	381	9.6	25	91	2.3	199	5.0	3.46	114	.270	.313	14	19	103	102	3.8	0	1	2.0
1974	Chi-A	20	19	.513	42	42	22	1	0	320	305	8.6	27	80	2.3	169	4.8	3.60	103	.254	.299	1	4	102	91	0.7	0	3	0.7
1975	Chi-A	16	20	.444	43	43	14	2	0	291	309	9.6	26	92	2.8	140	4.3	4.11	96	.272	.326	-10	-6	104	96	-1.0	0	1	-0.4
1976	Chi-A	4	3	.571	7	7	5	1	0	56	51	8.2	3	11	1.8	31	5.0	2.25	159	.242	.276	8	8	101	114	1.0	0	1	1.0
1977	Chi-A	7	8	.467	24	18	5	1	0	123	139	10.2	10	50	3.7	42	3.1	4.98	81	.293	.363	-12	-13	99	100	-1.2	0	2	-1.0
1978	Chi-A	10	10	.500	28	27	4	0	0	168	187	10.0	23	74	4.0	69	3.7	5.20	74	.285	.351	-26	-25	102	97	1.2	0	2	-2.2
Total	17	164	156	.512	651	297	114	24	57	2684	2582	8.7	209	724	2.4	1411	4.7	3.24	113	.254	.302	95	121	102	105	14.0	-14	15	15.1
■ GENE WOODBURN	Woodburn, Eugene Stewart b: 8/20/1886, Bellaire, Ohio d: 1/18/61, Sandusky, Ohio BR/TR, 6', 175 lbs. Deb: 7/27/11																												
1911	StL-N	1	5	.167	11	6	1	0	0	38	22	5.2	0	40	9.5	23	5.4	5.45	64	.167	.382	-9	-8	102	57	-1.9	1	1	-0.5
1912	StL-N	1	4	.200	20	5	1	0	0	48	60	11.3	0	42	7.9	25	4.7	5.63	62	.305	.436	-12	-11	103	100	-1.2	-2	-1	-1.2
Total	2	2	9	.182	31	11	2	0	0	86	82	8.6	0	82	8.6	48	5.0	5.55	63	.249	.413	-20	-20	102	81	-3.1	-0	0	-1.7
■ FRED WOODCOCK	Woodcock, Fred Wayland b: 5/17/1868, Winchendon, Mass. d: 8/11/43, Ashburnham, Mass. BL/TL, 6'2", 190 lbs. Deb: 5/17/1892																												
1892	Pit-N	1	2	.333	5	4	3	0	0	33	42	11.5	1	17	4.6	8	2.2	3.55	87	.324	.402	-1	-2	94	144	-0.5	1	0	0.0
■ GEORGE WOODEND	Woodend, George Anthony b: 12/9/17, Hartford, Conn. d: 2/6/80, Hartford, Conn. BR/TR, 6', 200 lbs. Deb: 4/22/44																												
1944	Bos-N	0	0	—	3	0	0	0	0	2	5	22.5	0	5	22.5	0	0.0	13.50	26	.556	.667	-2	-2	96	136	0.0	0	0	-0.1
■ HAL WOODESHICK	Woodeshick, Harold Joseph b: 8/24/32, Wilkes-Barre, Pa. BR/TL, 6'3", 200 lbs. Deb: 9/14/56																												
1956	Det-A	0	2	.000	2	2	0	0	0	5	12	21.6	1	3	5.4	1	1.8	14.40	27	.444	.500	-6	-6	95	81	-0.9	0	0	-0.4
1958	Cle-A	6	6	.500	14	9	3	0	0	72	71	8.9	4	25	3.1	27	3.4	3.63	97	.265	.337	1	-1	93	107	0.0	-1	3	0.1
1959	Was-A	2	4	.333	31	3	0	0	0	61	58	8.6	2	36	5.3	30	4.4	3.69	106	.253	.343	1	2	102	107	-0.5	-1	1	0.1
1960	Was-A	4	5	.444	41	14	1	0	4	115	131	10.3	7	60	4.7	46	3.6	4.70	84	.289	.368	-11	-9	102	102	-0.2	-2	2	-0.8
1961	Was-A	3	2	.600	7	6	1	0	0	40	38	8.5	3	24	5.4	24	5.4	4.05	97	.257	.359	-0	-1	97	112	0.9	-1	1	0.0
	Det-A	1	1	.500	12	2	0	0	0	18	25	12.5	3	17	8.5	13	6.5	8.00	47	.316	.429	-8	-8	94	94	-0.1	-0	1	-0.6
	Yr	4	3	.571	19	8	1	0	0	58	63	9.8	6	41	6.4	37	5.7	5.28	73	.273	.373	-8	-9	96	94	0.8	-1	2	-0.6
1962	Hou-N	5	16	.238	31	26	2	1	0	139	161	10.4	3	54	3.5	82	5.3	4.40	85	.290	.346	-7	-10	95	94	-4.5	-1	0	-1.1
1963	Hou-N	11	9	.550	55	0	0	0	10	114	75	5.9	3	42	3.3	94	7.4	1.97	158	.186	.264	17	15	95	86	2.7	-0	3	1.9
1964	Hou-N	2	9	.182	61	0	0	0	**23**	78	73	8.4	3	32	3.7	58	6.7	2.77	126	.249	.329	7	6	98	129	-3.0	-0	2	0.8
1965	Hou-N	3	4	.429	27	0	0	0	3	32	27	7.6	3	18	5.1	22	6.2	3.09	104	.227	.321	2	0	91	116	0.2	0	1	0.1
	StL-N	3	2	.600	51	0	0	0	15	60	47	7.1	1	27	4.1	37	5.6	1.80	208	.221	.311	12	13	106	152	0.5	-1	2	1.5
	Yr	6	6	.500	78	0	0	0	18	92	74	7.2	4	45	4.4	59	5.8	2.25	159	.223	.315	13	13	101	152	0.7	0	2	1.6
1966	StL-N	2	1	.667	59	0	0	0	4	70	57	7.3	5	23	3.0	30	3.9	1.93	187	.224	.287	13	13	100	139	0.5	0	3	1.8
1967	StL-N	2	1	.667	36	0	0	0	2	42	41	8.8	2	28	6.0	20	4.3	5.14	65	.252	.362	-8	-8	99	83	0.2	-0	1	-0.8
Total	11	44	62	.415	427	62	7	1	61	846	816	8.7	40	389	4.1	484	5.1	3.56	101	.254	.334	12	5	98	108	-4.2	-7	18	2.6
■ DAN WOODMAN	Woodman, Daniel Courtenay "Cocoa" b: 7/8/1893, Danvers, Mass. d: 12/14/62, Danvers, Mass. BR/TR, 5'8", 160 lbs. Deb: 7/10/14																												
1914	Buf-F	0	0	—	13	0	0	0	1	34	30	7.9	0	11	2.9	13	3.4	2.38	140	.264	.329	3	4	104	106	0.0	-0	0	0.3
1915	Buf-F	0	0	—	5	1	0	0	0	15	14	8.4	0	9	5.4	1	0.6	4.20	73	.275	.384	-2	-2	101	86	0.0	0	0	-0.1
Total	2	0	0	—	18	1	0	0	1	49	44	8.1	0	20	3.7	14	2.6	2.94	111	.268	.347	1	2	103	100	0.0	-0	0	0.2
■ CLARENCE WOODS	Woods, Clarence Cofield b: 6/11/1892, Woods Ridge, Ohio County, Ind. d: 7/2/69, Rising Sun, Ind. BR/TR, 6'5", 230 lbs. Deb: 8/08/14																												
1914	Ind-F	0	0	—	2	0	0	0	1	2	1	4.5	0	2	9.0	1	4.5	4.50	77	.169	.379	-0	-0	108	56	0.0	0	0	0.0
■ PINKY WOODS	Woods, George Rowland b: 5/22/15, Waterbury, Conn. d: 10/30/82, Los Angeles, Cal. BR/TR, 6'5", 225 lbs. Deb: 6/20/43																												
1943	Bos-A	5	6	.455	23	12	2	0	1	101	109	9.7	6	55	4.9	32	2.9	4.90	70	.284	.368	-18	-16	104	97	0.1	-0	0	-1.7
1944	Bos-A	4	8	.333	38	20	5	1	0	171	171	9.0	4	88	4.6	56	2.9	3.26	102	.266	.354	3	1	97	122	-2.0	-1	2	0.1
1945	Bos-A	4	7	.364	24	12	3	0	2	107	108	9.1	3	63	5.3	36	3.0	4.21	77	.268	.360	-10	-12	96	100	-1.1	1	1	-0.9
Total	3	13	21	.382	85	44	10	1	3	379	388	9.2	13	206	4.9	124	2.9	3.97	84	.272	.359	-25	-27	99	109	-3.0	-1	3	-2.5
■ JOHN WOODS	Woods, John Fulton "Abe" b: 1/18/1898, Princeton, W.Va. d: 10/4/46, Norfolk, Va. BR/TR, 6', 175 lbs. Deb: 9/16/24																												
1924	Bos-A	0	0	—	1	0	0	0	0	1	0	0.0	0	3	27.0	0	0.0	0.00	—	.000	.500	0	0	105	0	0.0	0	0	0.0
■ WALT WOODS	Woods, Walter Sydney b: 4/28/1875, Rye, N.H. d: 10/30/51, Portsmouth, N.H. BR/TR, 5'9.5", 165 lbs. Deb: 4/20/1898																												
1898	Chi-N	9	13	.409	27	22	18	3	0	215	224	9.4	7	59	2.5	26	1.1	3.14	117	.290	.340	11	13	102	107	-3.3	-4	0	0.5

YEAR	TM/L	W	L	PCT	G	GS	CG	SHO	SV	IP	H	H/G	HR	BB	BB/G	SO	SO/G	ERA	/A	OAVG	OOBP	PR	/A	PF	CPI	WAT	PB	PD	TPI
1899	Lou-N	9	13	.409	26	21	17	0	0	186	216	10.5	9	37	1.8	21	1.0	3.29	120	.315	.350	12	14	103	116	-2.0	-3	0	0.8
1900	Pit-N	0	0	—	1	0	0	0	0	3	3	9.0	0	4	12.0	1	3.0	0.00	—	.283	.479	1	1	101	0	0.0	-0	0	0.1
Total	3	18	26	.409	54	43	35	3	0	404	443	9.9	16	100	2.2	48	1.1	3.19	119	.301	.346	24	28	102	110	-5.3	-8	0	1.4
■ DICK WOODSON	Woodson, Richard Lee b: 3/30/45, Oelwein, Iowa BR/TR, 6'5", 205 lbs. Deb: 4/08/69																												
1969	Min-A	7	5	.583	44	10	2	0	1	110	99	8.1	11	49	4.0	66	5.4	3.68	98	.237	.319	-1	-1	100	96	-0.1	-1	1	0.0
1970	Min-A	1	2	.333	21	0	0	0	1	31	29	8.4	2	19	5.5	22	6.4	3.77	95	.244	.340	-0	-1	97	100	-0.6	-0	0	0.0
1972	Min-A	14	14	.500	36	36	9	3	0	252	193	6.9	19	101	3.6	150	5.4	2.71	121	.211	.287	10	16	107	94	0.0	-6	1	1.3
1973	Min-A	10	8	.556	23	23	4	2	0	141	137	8.7	12	68	4.3	53	3.4	3.96	100	.254	.337	-2	-0	103	98	1.1	0	-2	-0.1
1974	Min-A	1	1	.500	5	4	0	0	0	27	30	10.0	5	4	1.3	12	4.0	4.33	84	.273	.304	-2	-2	101	97	0.0	0	1	0.0
	NY-A	1	2	.333	8	3	0	0	0	28	34	10.9	6	12	3.9	12	3.9	5.79	60	.301	.367	-7	-7	95	104	-0.5	0	-1	-0.7
	Yr	2	3	.400	13	7	0	0	0	55	64	10.5	11	16	2.6	24	3.9	5.07	70	.286	.333	-9	-9	98	104	-0.5	0	0	-0.7
Total	5	34	32	.515	137	76	15	5	2	589	522	8.0	55	253	3.9	315	4.8	3.47	103	.236	.313	-2	6	103	96	-0.1	-7	0	0.5
■ FRANK WOODWARD	Woodward, Frank Russell b: 5/17/1894, New Haven, Conn. d: 6/11/61, New Haven, Conn. BR/TR, 5'10", 175 lbs. Deb: 4/17/18																												
1918	Phi-N	0	0	—	2	0	0	0	0	6	6	9.0	0	4	6.0	4	6.0	6.00	51	.250	.357	-2	-2	111	58	0.0	0	0	-0.1
1919	Phi-N	6	9	.400	17	12	6	0	0	101	109	9.7	5	35	3.1	27	2.4	4.72	67	.291	.343	-20	-18	109	91	0.7	1	-2	-1.8
	StL-N	3	5	.375	17	7	2	0	1	72	65	8.1	1	28	3.5	18	2.3	2.63	107	.248	.311	2	1	97	113	-0.1	-2	-0	0.0
	Yr	9	14	.391	34	19	8	0	1	173	174	9.1	6	63	3.3	45	2.3	3.85	78	.271	.323	-18	-16	104	113	0.6	1	-2	-1.8
1921	Was-A	0	0	—	3	1	0	0	0	11	11	9.0	0	3	2.5	4	3.3	5.73	74	.282	.311	-2	-2	99	61	0.0	0	0	0.0
1922	Was-A	0	0	—	1	0	0	0	0	2	3	13.5	0	3	13.5	2	9.0	13.50	28	.375	.500	-2	-2	93	70	0.0	-0	0	-0.1
1923	Chi-A	0	1	.000	2	1	0	0	0	2	5	22.5	0	1	4.5	0	0.0	13.50	29	.500	.500	-2	-2	99	86	-0.4	0	0	-0.1
Total	5	9	15	.375	42	21	8	0	1	194	199	9.2	6	74	3.4	55	2.6	4.22	74	.277	.335	-26	-24	103	96	0.2	-1	-1	-2.1
■ BOB WOODWARD	Woodward, Robert John b: 9/28/62, Hanover, N.H. BR/TR, 6'3", 185 lbs. Deb: 9/05/85																												
1985	Bos-A	1	0	1.000	5	2	0	0	0	27	17	5.7	0	9	3.0	16	5.3	1.67	253	.168	.248	7	8	102	51	0.5	0	-1	0.8
1986	Bos-A	2	3	.400	9	6	0	0	0	36	46	11.5	4	11	2.8	14	3.5	5.25	79	.313	.360	-4	-4	99	102	-0.7	0	0	-0.3
1987	Bos-A	1	1	.500	9	6	0	0	0	37	53	12.9	6	15	3.6	15	3.6	7.05	63	.338	.390	-11	-11	99	97	0.0	0	-1	-1.0
1988	Bos-A	0	0	—	1	0	0	0	0	1	2	18.0	0	1	9.0	0	0.0	9.00	48	.500	.600	-1	-1	108	132	0.0	0	0	0.0
Total	4	4	4	.500	24	14	0	0	0	101	118	10.5	10	36	3.2	45	4.0	4.99	85	.289	.346	-8	-8	100	87	-0.2	0	-1	-0.5
■ FLOYD WOOLDRIDGE	Wooldridge, Floyd Lewis b: 8/25/28, Jerico Springs, Mo BR/TR, 6'1", 185 lbs. Deb: 5/01/55																												
1955	StL-N	2	4	.333	18	8	2	0	0	58	64	9.9	9	27	4.2	14	2.2	4.81	86	.281	.354	-5	-4	102	106	-0.7	0	-1	-0.4
■ JUNIOR WOOTEN	Wooten, Earl Hazwell b: 1/16/24, Pelzer, S.C. BR/TL, 5'11", 160 lbs. Deb: 9/16/47																												
1948	Was-A	0	0	—	1	0	0	0	0	2	2	9.0	0	2	9.0	1	4.5	9.00	51	.250	.400	-1	-1	107	52	0.0	0	0	0.0
■ FRED WORDEN	Worden, Fred B. b: 9/4/1894, St.Louis, Mo. d: 11/9/41, St.Louis, Mo. BR/TR, Deb: 9/28/14																												
1914	Phi-A	0	0	—	1	0	0	0	0	2	8	36.0	0	0	0.0	1	4.5	18.00	14	.615	.615	-3	-3	93	97	0.0	-0	0	-0.2
■ HOGE WORKMAN	Workman, Harry Hall b: 9/25/1899, Huntington, W.Va. d: 5/20/72, Ft.Myers, Fla. BR/TR, 5'11", 170 lbs. Deb: 6/27/24																												
1924	Bos-A	0	0	—	11	0	0	0	0	18	25	12.5	2	11	5.5	7	3.5	8.50	52	.325	.413	-9	-8	105	78	0.0	-0	0	-0.7
■ RALPH WORKS	Works, Ralph Talmadge "Judge" b: 3/16/1888, Payson, Ill. d: 8/8/41, Pasadena, Cal. BL/TR, 6'2.5", 185 lbs. Deb: 5/01/09																												
1909	Det-A	4	1	.800	16	4	4	0	2	64	62	8.7	0	17	2.4	31	4.4	1.97	134	.261	.313	4	5	106	129	1.1	-2	-1	0.5
1910	Det-A	3	6	.333	18	10	5	0	1	86	73	7.6	1	39	4.1	36	3.8	3.56	71	.235	.328	-10	-10	100	77	-1.8	1	-1	-0.9
1911	Det-A	11	5	.688	30	15	9	3	0	167	173	9.3	3	67	3.6	68	3.7	3.88	92	.268	.342	-10	-6	107	87	2.3	-4	-4	-0.9
1912	Det-A	5	10	.333	27	16	9	1	1	157	185	10.6	1	66	3.8	64	3.7	4.24	76	.308	.383	-16	-18	96	110	-2.0	-3	0	-1.6
	Cin-N	1	1	.500	3	1	1	0	0	10	4	3.6	0	5	4.5	5	4.5	2.70	118	.133	.278	1	1	93	36	0.0	-0	-0	0.0
1913	Cin-N	0	1	.000	5	2	0	0	0	15	15	9.0	0	8	4.8	4	2.4	7.80	43	.242	.342	-8	-7	104	43	-0.4	-0	0	-0.6
Total	5	24	24	.500	99	48	28	4	4	499	512	9.2	5	202	3.6	208	3.8	3.79	83	.271	.348	-39	-36	102	95	-0.8	-8	-5	-3.5
■ TODD WORRELL	Worrell, Todd Roland b: 9/28/59, Arcadia, Cal. BR/TR, 6'5", 200 lbs. Deb: 8/28/85																												
1985	StL-N	3	0	1.000	17	0	0	0	5	22	17	7.0	2	7	2.9	17	7.0	2.86	117	.215	.273	2	1	93	91	1.5	-0	-0	0.1
1986	StL-N	9	10	.474	74	0	0	0	**36**	104	86	7.4	9	41	3.5	73	6.3	2.08	185	.229	.298	**19**	**20**	103	154	-0.3	0	-2	2.0
1987	StL-N	8	6	.571	75	0	0	0	33	95	86	8.1	8	34	3.2	92	8.7	2.65	150	.242	.304	15	14	97	126	-0.1	-0	0	1.4
1988	StL-N	5	9	.357	68	0	0	0	32	90	69	6.9	7	34	3.4	78	7.8	3.00	121	.214	.284	5	6	105	92	-1.7	-0	-0	0.6
Total	4	25	25	.500	234	0	0	0	106	311	258	7.5	26	116	3.4	260	7.5	2.58	147	.228	.294	41	42	101	123	-0.6	-0	-2	4.1
■ RICH WORTHAM	Wortham, Richard Cooper b: 10/22/53, Odessa, Tex. BR/TL, 6', 185 lbs. Deb: 5/03/78																												
1978	Chi-A	3	2	.600	8	8	2	0	0	59	59	9.0	1	23	3.5	25	3.8	3.05	126	.267	.331	5	5	102	113	0.7	0	-0	0.5
1979	Chi-A	14	14	.500	34	33	5	0	0	204	195	8.6	21	100	4.4	119	5.3	4.90	89	.255	.335	-15	-13	103	85	1.3	0	-2	-1.3
1980	Chi-A	4	7	.364	41	10	0	0	1	92	102	10.0	4	58	5.7	45	4.4	5.97	66	.285	.379	-20	-20	98	82	-0.9	0	1	-1.8
1983	Oak-A	0	0	—	1	0	0	0	0	0	3	—	0	1	—	0	—	∞	—	1.000	1.000	-1	-1	96	196	0.0	0	0	0.0
Total	4	21	23	.477	84	51	7	0	1	355	359	9.1	26	182	4.6	189	4.8	4.89	85	.266	.348	-31	-29	101	89	1.1	0	-1	-2.6
■ AL WORTHINGTON	Worthington, Allan Fulton "Red" b: 2/5/29, Birmingham, Ala. BR/TR, 6'2", 195 lbs. Deb: 7/06/53 C																												
1953	NY-N	4	8	.333	20	17	5	2	0	102	103	9.1	6	54	4.8	52	4.6	3.44	122	.258	.345	10	8	98	118	-1.6	-2	0	0.6
1954	NY-N	0	2	.000	10	1	0	0	0	18	21	10.5	0	15	7.5	8	4.0	3.50	118	.333	.439	1	1	102	182	-0.9	-1	0	0.1
1956	NY-N	7	14	.333	28	24	4	0	0	166	158	8.6	20	74	4.0	95	5.2	3.96	95	.254	.331	-3	-4	99	103	-2.6	2	2	0.0
1957	NY-N	8	11	.421	55	12	1	1	4	158	140	8.0	19	56	3.2	90	5.1	4.22	95	.237	.304	-6	-4	103	83	-0.5	-2	0	-0.5
1958	SF-N	11	7	.611	54	12	1	0	6	151	152	9.1	17	57	3.4	76	4.5	3.64	108	.255	.317	5	5	100	103	1.9	0	0	0.5
1959	SF-N	2	3	.400	42	3	0	0	2	73	68	8.4	8	37	4.6	45	5.5	3.70	100	.253	.341	2	-0	94	119	-0.6	-1	1	0.0
1960	Bos-A	0	1	.000	6	0	0	0	0	12	17	12.8	1	11	8.3	7	5.3	7.50	54	.340	.452	-5	-5	105	100	-0.4	-0	0	-0.4
	Chi-A	1	1	.500	4	0	0	0	0	5	3	5.4	0	4	7.2	1	1.8	3.60	106	.176	.292	0	0	99	67	0.0	1	0	0.1
	Yr	1	2	.333	10	0	0	0	0	17	20	10.6	1	15	7.9	8	4.2	6.35	63	.299	.407	-5	-4	103	67	-0.4	-0	0	-0.3
1963	Cin-N	4	4	.500	50	0	0	0	10	81	75	8.3	6	31	3.4	55	6.1	3.00	113	.248	.316	3	4	103	118	-0.1	-0	2	0.6
1964	Cin-N	1	0	1.000	6	0	0	0	0	7	14	18.0	0	2	2.6	6	7.7	10.29	35	.400	.425	-5	-5	102	77	0.5	0	-0	-0.4
	Min-A	5	6	.455	41	0	0	0	14	72	47	5.9	4	28	3.5	59	7.4	1.38	263	.183	.256	18	18	100	125	-0.3	-1	1	1.9
1965	Min-A	10	7	.588	62	0	0	0	21	80	57	6.4	4	41	4.6	59	6.6	2.14	159	.207	.303	12	11	98	133	-0.5	0	2	1.4
1966	Min-A	6	3	.667	65	0	0	0	16	91	66	6.5	6	27	2.7	93	9.2	2.47	153	.199	.258	10	13	110	82	1.2	1	1	1.7
1967	Min-A	8	9	.471	59	0	0	0	16	92	77	7.5	6	38	3.7	80	7.8	2.84	120	.229	.303	4	6	106	110	-1.4	-1	0	0.6
1968	Min-A	4	5	.444	54	0	0	0	**18**	76	67	7.9	1	32	3.8	57	6.8	2.72	116	.238	.307	2	4	106	104	-0.3	-1	0	0.3
1969	Min-A	4	1	.800	46	0	0	0	3	61	65	9.6	7	20	3.0	51	7.5	4.57	79	.278	.331	-6	-6	100	94	1.3	-1	-0	-0.7
Total	14	75	82	.478	602	69	11	3	110	1245	1130	8.2	105	527	3.8	834	6.0	3.39	110	.243	.316	41	48	101	106	-4.3	-5	7	5.8
■ GENE WRIGHT	Wright, Clarence Eugene "Big Gene" b: 12/11/1878, Cleveland, Ohio d: 10/29/30, Barberton, Ohio BR/TR, 6'2", 185 lbs. Deb: 10/05/01																												
1901	Bro-N	1	0	1.000	1	1	1	0	0	9	6	6.0	0	1	1.0	6	6.0	1.00	342	.207	.234	2	2	103	85	0.5	0	-0	0.2
1902	Cle-A	7	11	.389	21	18	15	1	1	148	150	9.1	6	75	4.6	52	3.2	3.95	87	.287	.377	-6	-9	96	101	-2.2	-2	-2	-0.9
1903	Cle-A	3	9	.250	15	12	8	0	0	102	122	10.8	1	58	5.1	42	3.7	5.74	49	.320	.410	-32	-33	95	86	-3.3	2	1	-2.8
	StL-A	3	5	.375	8	8	7	1	0	61	73	10.8	2	16	2.4	37	5.5	3.69	76	.320	.365	-5	-6	96	115	-0.7	-1	1	-0.4
	Yr	6	14	.300	23	20	15	1	0	163	195	10.8	3	74	4.1	79	4.4	4.97	57	.320	.394	-37	-39	95	115	-4.0	2	2	-3.2
1904	StL-A	0	1	.000	1	1	0	0	0	4	10	22.5	0	2	4.5	3	6.8	13.50	19	.497	.543	-5	-5	98	82	-0.4	-0	1	-0.3
Total	4	14	26	.350	46	40	31	2	1	324	361	10.0	9	152	4.2	140	3.9	4.50	69	.306	.385	-45	-50	96	98	-6.1	-1	1	-4.2
■ CLYDE WRIGHT	Wright, Clyde b: 2/20/41, Jefferson City, Tenn. BR/TL, 6'1", 180 lbs. Deb: 6/15/66																												
1966	Cal-A	4	7	.364	20	13	3	1	0	91	92	9.1	11	25	2.5	37	3.7	3.76	91	.265	.311	-3	-3	100	108	-1.4	-1	0	-0.4
1967	Cal-A	5	5	.500	20	11	1	0	0	77	76	8.9	5	24	2.8	35	4.1	3.27	95	.260	.313	-0	-1	96	110	-0.1	2	0	0.1
1968	Cal-A	10	6	.625	41	13	2	1	3	126	123	8.8	13	44	3.1	71	5.1	3.93	73	.256	.316	-13	-15	96	97	3.1	2	-1	-1.5
1969	Cal-A	1	8	.111	37	5	0	0	0	64	66	9.3	4	30	4.2	31	4.4	4.08	90	.278	.357	-3	-3	101	108	-3.3	0	0	-0.2
1970	Cal-A	22	12	.647	39	39	7	2	0	261	226	7.8	24	88	3.0	110	3.8	2.83	120	.232	.296	26	17	92	108	5.0	3	-2	1.8

YEAR	TM/L	W	L	PCT	G	GS	CG	SHO	SV	IP	H	H/G	HR	BB	BB/G	SO	SO/G	ERA	/A	OAVG	OOBP	PR	/A	PF	CPI	WAT	PB	PD	TPI
1971	Cal-A	16	17	.485	37	37	10	2	0	277	225	7.3	17	82	2.7	135	4.4	2.99	115	.226	.280	15	14	99	85	0.6	1	5	2.1
1972	Cal-A	18	11	.621	35	35	15	2	0	251	229	8.2	14	80	2.9	87	3.1	2.98	92	.246	.304	3	-6	90	102	4.5	7	3	0.3
1973	Cal-A	11	19	.367	37	36	13	1	0	257	273	9.6	26	76	2.7	65	2.3	3.68	100	.273	.319	4	0	96	108	-4.2	0	4	0.4
1974	Mil-A	9	20	.310	38	32	15	0	0	232	264	10.2	22	54	2.1	64	2.5	4.42	84	.284	.319	-21	-18	103	90	-5.5	0	2	-1.6
1975	Tex-A	4	6	.400	25	14	1	0	0	93	105	10.2	7	47	4.5	32	3.1	4.45	85	.294	.362	-7	-7	100	112	-0.8	0	2	-0.5
Total	10	100	111	.474	329	235	67	9	3	1729	1679	8.7	143	550	2.9	667	3.5	3.50	96	.256	.311	-0	-24	96	100	-2.1	14	13	0.5
■ **DAVE WRIGHT**	Wright, David William b: 8/27/1875, Dennison, Ohio d: 1/18/46, Dennison, Ohio BR/TR, 6', 185 lbs. Deb: 7/22/1895																												
1895	Pit-N	0	0	—	1	0	0	0	0	2	6	27.0	0	1	4.5	0	0.0	27.00	17	.538	.576	-5	-5	96	50	0.0	-0	0	-0.3
1897	Chi-N	1	0	1.000	1	1	1	0	0	7	17	21.9	1	2	2.6	4	5.1	15.43	28	.488	.516	-9	-9	101	72	0.5	-0	0	-0.4
Total	2	1	0	1.000	2	1	1	0	0	9	23	23.0	1	3	3.0	4	4.0	18.00	24	.500	.531	-14	-14	100	67	0.5	0	0	-0.7
■ **GEORGE WRIGHT**	Wright, George b: 1/28/1847, Yonkers, N.Y. d: 8/21/37, Boston, Mass. BR/TR, 5'9.5", 150 lbs. Deb: 5/05/1871 MH																												
1876	Bos-N	0	0	—	1	0	0	0	0	1	1	9.0	0	0	0.0	1	9.0	0.00	—	.265	.265	0	0	94	0	0.0	0	0	0.0
■ **ED WRIGHT**	Wright, Henderson Edward b: 5/15/19, Dyersburg, Tenn. BR/TR, 6'1", 180 lbs. Deb: 7/29/45																												
1945	Bos-N	8	3	.727	15	12	7	1	0	111	104	8.4	7	33	2.7	24	1.9	2.51	170	.254	.305	16	22	113	136	2.9	-3	-1	2.0
1946	Bos-N	12	9	.571	36	21	8	2	0	176	164	8.4	8	71	3.6	44	2.3	3.53	91	.250	.319	-2	-6	94	92	1.1	6	0	0.0
1947	Bos-N	3	3	.500	23	6	1	0	0	65	80	11.1	9	35	4.8	14	1.9	6.37	61	.305	.384	-17	-18	95	94	-0.2	-0	-0	-1.7
1948	Bos-N	0	0	—	3	0	0	0	0	5	9	16.2	0	2	3.6	2	3.6	1.80	217	.474	.500	1	1	99	514	0.0	0	0	0.1
1952	Phi-A	2	1	.667	24	0	0	0	1	41	55	12.1	6	20	4.4	9	2.0	6.59	63	.320	.392	-13	-11	112	98	0.5	-0	-0	-1.1
Total	5	25	16	.610	101	39	16	3	1	398	412	9.3	30	161	3.6	93	2.1	4.00	93	.271	.337	-15	-13	101	110	4.3	3	-2	-0.7
■ **JIM WRIGHT**	Wright, James "Jiggs" b: 9/19/1900, Hyde, England d: 4/10/63, Oakland, Cal. BR/TR, 6'2.5", 195 lbs. Deb: 9/14/27																												
1927	StL-A	1	0	1.000	2	1	1	0	0	12	8	6.0	0	4	3.0	4	3.0	4.50	100	.182	.245	-0	0	109	19	0.5	-0	-0	0.0
1928	StL-A	0	0	—	2	0	0	0	0	2	3	13.5	0	2	9.0	2	9.0	13.50	31	.375	.455	-2	-2	103	61	0.0	0	0	-0.1
Total	2	1	0	1.000	4	1	1	0	0	14	11	7.1	0	6	3.9	6	3.9	5.79	77	.212	.283	-3	-2	108	25	0.5	-0	0	-0.1
■ **JIM WRIGHT**	Wright, James Clifton b: 12/21/50, Reed City, Mich. BR/TR, 6'1", 165 lbs. Deb: 4/15/78																												
1978	Bos-A	8	4	.667	24	16	5	3	0	116	122	9.5	8	24	1.9	56	4.3	3.57	112	.276	.319	3	6	106	104	1.0	0	-1	0.4
1979	Bos-A	1	0	1.000	11	1	0	0	0	23	19	7.4	5	7	2.7	15	5.9	5.09	88	.226	.302	-2	-2	106	82	0.5	0	-0	-0.1
Total	2	9	4	.692	35	17	5	3	0	139	141	9.1	13	31	2.0	71	4.6	3.82	107	.268	.316	1	4	106	101	1.5	0	-2	0.3
■ **JIM WRIGHT**	Wright, James Leon b: 3/3/55, St.Joseph, Mo. BR/TR, 6'5", 205 lbs. Deb: 4/22/81																												
1981	KC-A	2	3	.400	17	4	0	0	0	52	57	9.9	5	21	3.6	27	4.7	3.46	105	.277	.348	1	1	99	129	-0.4	0	-1	0.0
1982	KC-A	0	0	—	7	0	0	0	0	24	32	12.0	3	6	2.3	9	3.4	5.25	77	.320	.352	-3	-3	100	103	0.0	0	-0	-0.3
Total	2	2	3	.400	24	4	0	0	0	76	89	10.5	8	27	3.2	36	4.3	4.03	93	.291	.349	-2	-2	99	121	-0.4	0	-1	-0.3
■ **RICKY WRIGHT**	Wright, James Richard b: 11/22/58, Paris, Tex. BL/TL, 6'3", 175 lbs. Deb: 7/28/82																												
1982	LA-N	2	1	.667	14	5	0	0	0	33	28	7.6	1	20	5.5	24	6.5	3.00	112	.233	.331	2	1	94	113	0.4	0	0	0.2
1983	LA-N	0	0	—	6	0	0	0	0	6	5	7.5	0	2	3.0	5	7.5	3.00	121	.227	.269	0	0	100	72	0.0	0	-0	0.0
	Tex-A	0	0	—	1	0	0	0	0	2	0	0.0	0	1	4.5	2	9.0	0.00	—	.000	.125	1	1	101	0	0.0	0	-0	0.1
1984	Tex-A	0	2	.000	8	1	0	0	0	15	20	12.0	3	11	6.6	6	3.6	6.00	67	.357	.449	-3	-3	101	140	-0.9	0	0	-0.2
1985	Tex-A	0	0	—	5	0	0	0	0	8	5	5.6	0	5	5.6	7	7.9	4.50	101	.185	.313	-0	0	110	51	0.0	0	0	0.0
1986	Tex-A	1	0	1.000	21	1	0	0	0	39	44	10.2	1	21	4.8	23	5.3	5.08	78	.284	.367	-4	-5	95	88	0.5	0	1	-0.3
Total	5	3	3	.500	55	7	0	0	0	103	102	8.9	5	60	5.2	67	5.9	4.28	89	.265	.354	-4	-5	97	98	0.0	0	1	-0.2
■ **KEN WRIGHT**	Wright, Kenneth Warren b: 9/4/46, Pensacola, Fla. BR/TR, 6'2", 210 lbs. Deb: 4/10/70																												
1970	KC-A	1	2	.333	47	0	0	0	3	53	49	8.3	2	29	4.9	30	5.1	5.26	70	.261	.368	-9	-9	100	83	-0.2	-0	-0	-0.9
1971	KC-A	3	6	.333	21	12	1	1	1	78	66	7.6	6	47	5.4	56	6.5	3.69	92	.230	.337	-2	-2	98	99	-1.6	-1	1	-0.2
1972	KC-A	1	2	.333	17	0	0	0	4	18	15	7.5	0	15	7.5	18	9.0	5.00	61	.231	.369	-4	-4	100	76	-0.4	-0	0	-0.4
1973	KC-A	6	5	.545	25	12	1	0	0	81	60	6.7	6	82	9.1	75	8.3	4.89	85	.210	.382	-10	-6	109	87	0.0	0	-1	-0.7
1974	NY-A	0	0	—	3	0	0	0	0	6	5	7.5	0	7	10.5	2	3.0	3.00	115	.227	.414	0	0	95	149	0.0	0	0	0.0
Total	5	11	15	.423	113	24	2	1	8	236	195	7.4	14	180	6.9	181	6.9	4.54	82	.230	.364	-24	-22	102	91	-2.2	-2	-1	-2.2
■ **MEL WRIGHT**	Wright, Melvin James b: 5/11/28, Manila, Ark. d: 5/16/83, Montreal, Que. BR/TR, 6'3", 210 lbs. Deb: 4/17/54 C																												
1954	StL-N	0	0	—	9	0	0	0	0	10	16	14.4	2	11	9.9	4	3.6	10.80	38	.348	.492	-7	-7	100	90	0.0	-0	0	-0.6
1955	StL-N	2	2	.500	29	0	0	0	1	36	44	11.0	4	9	2.3	18	4.5	6.25	66	.308	.338	-9	-8	102	80	0.2	-1	0	-0.8
1960	Chi-N	0	1	.000	9	0	0	0	2	16	17	9.6	1	3	1.7	8	4.5	5.06	75	.279	.299	-2	-2	101	72	-0.4	-0	-0	-0.2
1961	Chi-N	0	1	.000	11	0	0	0	0	21	42	18.0	3	4	1.7	6	2.6	10.71	38	.416	.430	-16	-15	102	81	-0.4	-0	1	-1.3
Total	4	2	4	.333	58	0	0	0	3	83	119	12.9	10	27	2.9	36	3.9	7.70	53	.339	.379	-34	-34	102	80	-0.6	-2	1	-2.9
■ **BOB WRIGHT**	Wright, Robert Cassius b: 12/13/1891, Greensburg, Ind. BR/TR, 6'1.5", 175 lbs. Deb: 9/21/15																												
1915	Chi-N	0	0	—	2	0	0	0	0	4	6	13.5	0	0	0.0	3	6.8	2.25	126	.353	.353	0	0	103	206	0.0	0	0	0.0
■ **ROY WRIGHT**	Wright, Roy Earl b: 9/26/33, Buchtel, Ohio BR/TR, 6'2", 170 lbs. Deb: 9/30/56																												
1956	NY-N	0	1	.000	1	1	0	0	0	3	8	24.0	1	2	6.0	0	0.0	15.00	25	.533	.588	-4	-4	99	105	-0.4	-0	0	-0.2
■ **RASTY WRIGHT**	Wright, Wayne Bromley b: 11/5/1895, Ceredo, W.Va. d: 6/12/48, Columbus, Ohio BR/TR, 5'11", 160 lbs. Deb: 6/22/17																												
1917	StL-A	0	1	.000	16	1	0	0	0	40	48	10.8	0	10	2.3	5	1.1	5.40	49	.300	.345	-12	-12	98	68	-0.4	0	0	-1.1
1918	StL-A	8	2	.800	18	13	6	1	0	111	99	8.0	1	18	1.5	25	2.0	2.51	110	.244	.275	3	3	100	82	3.2	3	-1	0.6
1919	StL-A	0	5	.000	24	5	2	0	0	63	79	11.3	1	20	2.9	14	2.0	5.57	56	.315	.368	-16	-17	98	78	-2.4	-1	0	-1.7
1922	StL-A	9	7	.563	31	16	5	0	5	154	148	8.6	7	50	2.9	44	2.6	2.92	141	.262	.320	19	20	102	118	-0.5	-2	1	1.9
1923	StL-A	7	4	.636	20	8	4	0	0	83	107	11.6	6	34	3.7	26	2.8	6.40	65	.317	.378	-22	-21	105	84	1.7	0	0	-1.7
Total	5	24	19	.558	109	43	17	1	5	451	481	9.6	15	132	2.6	114	2.3	4.05	87	.280	.330	-29	-27	101	93	1.6	1	0	-2.0
■ **HARRY WRIGHT**	Wright, William Henry b: 1/10/1835, Sheffield, England d: 10/3/1895, Atlantic City, N.J. BR/TR, 5'9.5", 157 lbs. Deb: 5/05/1871 MH																												
1871	Bos-n	0	0	—	2																								
1872	Bos-n	2	0	1.000	2																								
1873	Bos-n	2	1	.667	3																								
Total	3 n	4	1	.800	7																								
■ **LUCKY WRIGHT**	Wright, William Simmons "William The Red" or "Deacon" b: 2/21/1880, Tontogany, Ohio d: 7/6/41, Tontogany, Ohio BR/TR, 6', 178 lbs. Deb: 4/18/09																												
1909	Cle-A	0	4	.000	5	4	3	0	0	28	21	6.8	0	7	2.3	5	1.6	3.21	79	.223	.277	-2	-2	103	52	-1.9	-1	0	-0.1
■ **FRANK WURM**	Wurm, Frank James b: 4/27/24, Cambridge, N.Y. BB/TL, 6'1", 175 lbs. Deb: 9/04/44																												
1944	Bro-N	0	0	—	1	1	0	0	0	1	1	9.0	0	5	45.0	1	9.0	36.00	10	.500	.857	-4	-4	102	56	0.0	0	0	-0.2
■ **JOHN WYATT**	Wyatt, John Thomas b: 4/19/35, Chicago, Ill. BR/TR, 5'11.5", 200 lbs. Deb: 9/08/61																												
1961	KC-A	0	0	—	5	0	0	0	1	7	8	10.3	0	4	5.1	6	7.7	2.57	163	.296	.371	1	1	104	199	0.0	0	0	0.1
1962	KC-A	10	7	.588	59	9	0	0	11	125	121	8.7	12	80	5.8	106	7.6	4.46	90	.253	.361	-7	-6	101	102	2.4	-2	-1	-0.8
1963	KC-A	6	4	.600	63	0	0	0	21	92	83	8.1	12	43	4.2	81	7.9	3.13	126	.239	.314	5	8	109	125	1.4	-1	-0	0.7
1964	KC-A	9	8	.529	**81**	0	0	0	20	128	111	7.8	23	52	3.7	74	5.2	3.59	109	.236	.304	1	5	108	113	2.5	-1	-1	0.2
1965	KC-A	2	6	.250	65	0	0	0	18	89	78	7.9	8	53	5.4	70	7.1	3.24	106	.241	.340	2	2	100	128	-1.2	-0	0	0.2
1966	KC-A	0	3	.000	19	0	0	0	2	24	19	7.1	3	16	6.0	25	9.4	5.25	62	.213	.343	-5	-5	95	77	-1.4	0	1	-0.4
	Bos-A	3	4	.429	42	0	0	0	8	72	59	7.4	3	27	3.4	63	7.9	3.13	121	.229	.303	2	5	110	96	0.0	-1	-1	0.3
	Yr	3	7	.300	61	0	0	0	10	96	78	7.3	6	43	4.0	88	8.3	3.66	100	.223	.309	-2	0	107	96	-1.4	0	-1	-0.1
1967	Bos-A	10	7	.588	60	0	0	0	20	93	71	6.9	6	39	3.8	68	6.6	2.61	139	.217	.296	6	11	113	112	0.4	-1	1	1.2
1968	Bos-A	1	2	.333	8	0	0	0	0	11	9	7.4	2	6	4.9	11	9.0	4.09	73	.231	.340	-1	-1	101	113	-0.5	0	0	0.0
	NY-A	0	2	.000	7	0	0	0	0	8	7	7.9	1	9	10.1	6	6.8	2.25	134	.219	.381	1	1	101	224	-0.9	-0	0	0.1
	Det-A	1	0	1.000	22	0	0	0	2	30	26	7.8	2	11	3.3	25	7.5	2.40	128	.236	.304	2	2	103	132	0.5	-0	0	0.2
	Yr	2	4	.333	37	0	0	0	2	49	42	7.7	5	26	4.8	42	7.7	2.76	111	.230	.322	1	2	102	132	-0.9	-0	0	0.3

YEAR	TM/L	W	L	PCT	G	GS	CG	SHO	SV	IP	H	H/G	HR	BB	BB/G	SO	SO/G	ERA	/A	OAVG	OOBP	PR	/A	PF	CPI	WAT	PB	PD	TPI
1969	Oak-A	0	1	.000	4	0	0	0	0	8	8	9.0	0	6	6.8	5	5.6	5.63	59	.250	.400	-2	-2	91	79	-0.4	-0	0	-0.1
Total	9	42	44	.488	435	9	0	0	103	687	600	7.9	72	346	4.5	540	7.1	3.47	108	.237	.325	6	21	106	114	2.8	-7	-2	1.7

■ **WHIT WYATT** Wyatt, John Whitlow b: 9/27/07, Kensington, Ga. BR/TR, 6'1", 185 lbs. Deb: 9/16/29 C

YEAR	TM/L	W	L	PCT	G	GS	CG	SHO	SV	IP	H	H/G	HR	BB	BB/G	SO	SO/G	ERA	/A	OAVG	OOBP	PR	/A	PF	CPI	WAT	PB	PD	TPI
1929	Det-A	0	1	.000	4	4	1	0	0	25	30	10.8	1	18	6.5	14	5.0	6.84	60	.309	.405	-7	-8	97	86	-0.4	-1	1	-0.6
1930	Det-A	4	5	.444	21	7	2	0	2	86	76	8.0	6	35	3.7	68	7.1	3.56	138	.239	.314	10	13	106	100	-0.3	3	0	1.5
1931	Det-A	0	2	.000	4	1	1	0	0	20	30	13.5	2	12	5.4	8	3.6	9.00	52	.361	.439	-10	-10	107	89	-0.9	0	-1	-0.7
1932	Det-A	9	13	.409	43	22	10	0	1	206	228	10.0	12	102	4.5	82	3.6	5.02	91	.286	.360	-12	-11	102	99	-2.2	0	-1	-1.0
1933	Det-A	0	1	.000	10	0	0	0	0	17	20	10.6	1	9	4.8	9	4.8	4.24	108	.377	.463	0	1	107	182	-0.4	-0	0	0.0
	Chi-A	3	4	.429	26	7	2	0	1	88	91	9.3	7	45	4.6	31	3.2	4.60	96	.317	.404	-3	-2	103	133	0.0	0	0	0.0
	Yr	3	5	.375	36	7	2	0	1	105	111	9.5	8	54	4.6	40	3.4	4.54	98	.325	.408	-3	-1	104	133	-0.4	-0	0	0.0
1934	Chi-A	4	11	.267	23	6	2	0	2	68	83	11.0	10	37	4.9	36	4.8	7.15	65	.303	.382	-20	-19	103	86	-1.8	0	0	-1.5
1935	Chi-A	4	3	.571	30	1	0	0	5	52	65	11.3	6	25	4.3	22	3.8	6.75	72	.308	.377	-13	-11	109	88	0.6	1	1	-0.7
1936	Chi-A	0	0	—	3	0	0	0	1	3	3	9.0	0	0	0.0	0	0.0	0.00	—	.273	.273	2	2	99	0	0.0	0	0	0.1
1937	Cle-A	2	3	.400	29	4	2	0	0	73	67	8.3	3	40	4.9	52	6.4	4.44	101	.244	.332	1	0	97	82	-0.6	3	0	0.3
1939	Bro-N	8	3	.727	16	14	6	2	0	109	88	7.3	3	39	3.2	52	4.3	2.31	180	.224	.286	19	22	106	109	2.3	-0	1	2.5
1940	Bro-N	15	14	.517	37	34	16	**5**	0	239	233	8.8	19	62	2.3	124	4.7	3.46	118	.254	.300	10	17	106	101	-1.7	-0	-2	1.5
1941	Bro-N	**22**	10	.688	38	35	23	**7**	1	288	223	7.0	10	82	2.6	176	5.5	2.34	154	**.212**	**.268**	**41**	**40**	99	88	2.1	7	-1	**5.1**
1942	Bro-N	19	7	.731	31	30	16	0	0	217	185	7.7	9	63	2.6	104	4.3	2.74	117	.225	.283	14	12	97	90	2.6	1	-1	1.2
1943	Bro-N	14	5	.737	26	26	13	3	0	181	139	**6.9**	5	43	2.1	80	4.0	2.49	134	**.207**	**.253**	18	17	99	66	4.5	4	-2	2.2
1944	Bro-N	2	6	.250	9	9	1	0	0	38	51	12.1	1	16	3.8	4	0.9	7.11	52	.311	.371	-15	-14	102	71	-1.5	-0	-0	-1.3
1945	Phi-N	0	7	.000	10	10	2	0	0	51	72	12.7	3	14	2.5	10	1.8	5.29	73	.330	.360	-8	-8	102	101	-3.4	0	1	-0.6
Total	16	106	95	.527	360	210	97	17	13	1761	1684	8.6	98	642	3.3	872	4.5	3.79	105	.253	.317	27	40	102	94	-1.1	18	-5	8.0

■ **JOHN WYCKOFF** Wyckoff, John Weldon b: 2/19/1892, Williamsport, Pa. d: 5/8/61, Sheboygan Falls, Wis. BR/TR, 6'1", 175 lbs. Deb: 4/19/13

YEAR	TM/L	W	L	PCT	G	GS	CG	SHO	SV	IP	H	H/G	HR	BB	BB/G	SO	SO/G	ERA	/A	OAVG	OOBP	PR	/A	PF	CPI	WAT	PB	PD	TPI
1913	Phi-A	2	4	.333	17	7	4	0	0	62	56	8.1	1	46	6.7	31	4.5	4.35	62	.233	.363	-10	-11	93	78	-1.3	0	0	-1.0
1914	Phi-A	11	7	.611	32	20	11	0	2	185	153	7.4	2	103	5.0	86	4.2	3.02	84	.228	.334	-6	-10	93	92	-0.5	-0	-5	-1.5
1915	Phi-A	10	22	.313	43	34	20	1	0	276	238	7.8	1	165	5.4	157	5.1	3.52	86	.246	.359	-18	-15	103	97	0.8	-4	1	-1.8
1916	Phi-A	0	1	.000	7	2	1	0	0	21	20	8.6	1	20	8.6	4	1.7	5.57	53	.247	.402	-6	-6	105	84	-0.4	1	0	-0.5
	Bos-A	0	0	—	8	0	0	0	1	23	19	7.4	0	18	7.0	18	7.0	4.70	55	.232	.370	-5	-5	92	73	0.0	-0	-1	-0.6
	Yr	0	1	.000	15	2	1	0	1	44	39	8.0	1	38	7.8	22	4.5	5.11	54	.238	.381	-11	-11	98	73	-0.4	1	-1	-1.1
1917	Bos-A	0	0	—	1	0	0	0	0	5	4	7.2	0	4	7.2	1	1.8	1.80	157	.222	.391	0	1	106	205	0.0	-0	0	0.1
1918	Bos-A	0	0	—	1	0	0	0	0	2	4	18.0	0	1	4.5	2	9.0	0.00	—	.400	.455	1	1	93	0	0.0	-0	0	0.0
Total	6	23	34	.404	109	63	36	1	3	574	494	7.7	5	357	5.6	299	4.7	3.54	79	.239	.355	-43	-47	98	92	-1.4	-4	-4	-5.3

■ **FRANK WYMAN** Wyman, Frank H. b: 5/10/1862, Haverhill, Mass. d: 2/4/16, Everett, Mass. Deb: 6/24/1884

YEAR	TM/L	W	L	PCT	G	GS	CG	SHO	SV	IP	H	H/G	HR	BB	BB/G	SO	SO/G	ERA	/A	OAVG	OOBP	PR	/A	PF	CPI	WAT	PB	PD	TPI
1884	KC-U	0	1	.000	3	1	1	0	0	21	37	15.9	0	3	1.3	9	3.9	6.86	40	.389	.408	-9	-10	92	96	-0.3	-0	0	-1.1

■ **EARLY WYNN** Wynn, Early "Gus" b: 1/6/20, Hartford, Ala. BB/TR, 6', 190 lbs. Deb: 9/13/39 CH

YEAR	TM/L	W	L	PCT	G	GS	CG	SHO	SV	IP	H	H/G	HR	BB	BB/G	SO	SO/G	ERA	/A	OAVG	OOBP	PR	/A	PF	CPI	WAT	PB	PD	TPI
1939	Was-A	0	2	.000	3	3	1	0	0	20	26	11.7	0	10	4.5	1	0.4	5.85	72	.313	.371	-3	-4	91	89	-0.9	0	-1	-0.3
1941	Was-A	3	1	.750	5	5	4	0	0	40	35	7.9	1	10	2.3	15	3.4	1.57	260	.226	.269	11	11	99	135	1.1	-0	0	1.2
1942	Was-A	10	16	.385	30	28	10	1	0	190	246	11.7	6	73	3.5	58	2.7	5.12	70	.314	.370	-31	-32	99	99	-0.9	2	-1	-2.9
1943	Was-A	18	12	.600	37	33	12	3	0	257	232	8.1	15	83	2.9	89	3.1	2.91	116	.240	.296	11	13	102	102	2.1	7	-2	2.1
1944	Was-A	8	17	.320	33	25	19	2	2	208	221	9.6	3	67	2.9	65	2.8	3.38	92	.277	.328	1	-6	91	106	-3.2	2	-2	-0.6
1946	Was-A	8	5	.615	17	12	9	0	0	107	112	9.4	8	33	2.8	36	3.0	3.11	106	.267	.322	5	2	94	119	1.7	6	0	0.9
1947	Was-A	17	15	.531	33	31	22	2	0	247	251	9.1	13	90	3.3	73	2.7	3.64	102	.262	.327	2	2	101	99	3.8	7	-1	0.8
1948	Was-A	8	19	.296	33	31	15	1	0	198	236	10.7	18	94	4.3	49	2.2	5.82	79	.295	.363	-34	-27	107	90	-2.9	2	-2	-2.4
1949	Cle-A	11	7	.611	26	23	6	0	0	165	186	10.1	8	57	3.1	62	3.4	4.15	97	.282	.337	1	-2	96	96	0.8	-1	1	-0.2
1950	Cle-A	18	8	.692	32	28	14	2	0	214	166	**7.0**	20	101	4.2	143	**6.0**	**3.20**	137	**.212**	**.300**	33	28	95	95	3.5	7	0	3.4
1951	Cle-A	20	13	.606	37	34	21	3	1	**274**	227	7.5	18	107	3.5	133	4.4	3.02	126	.225	.296	**33**	24	93	98	0.1	1	-1	2.4
1952	Cle-A	23	12	.657	42	33	19	4	3	286	239	7.5	23	132	4.2	153	4.8	2.90	111	.231	.313	25	11	88	115	2.9	5	-0	1.4
1953	Cle-A	17	12	.586	36	34	16	1	0	252	234	8.4	19	107	3.8	138	4.9	3.93	94	.245	.320	2	-6	93	90	-0.2	9	-1	0.1
1954	Cle-A	**23**	11	.676	40	36	20	3	2	**271**	225	7.5	21	83	2.8	155	5.1	2.72	138	.225	.279	30	31	101	94	-1.2	1	-3	3.2
1955	Cle-A	17	11	.607	32	31	16	6	0	230	207	8.1	19	80	3.1	122	4.8	2.82	144	.240	.301	29	31	102	112	0.1	1	-3	3.2
1956	Cle-A	20	9	.690	38	35	18	4	2	278	233	7.5	19	91	2.9	158	5.1	2.72	151	.228	.288	44	43	99	101	4.6	4	1	**5.0**
1957	Cle-A	14	17	.452	40	37	13	1	1	263	270	9.2	32	104	3.6	**184**	6.3	4.31	90	.265	.331	-15	-13	102	99	-1.6	-2	-0	-1.5
1958	Chi-A	14	16	.467	40	34	11	4	2	240	214	8.0	27	104	3.9	**179**	6.7	4.13	89	.242	.319	-9	-12	98	92	-2.1	3	-2	-1.1
1959	Chi-A	**22**	10	.688	37	37	14	5	0	**256**	202	7.1	20	119	4.2	179	6.3	3.16	116	.216	.307	20	15	95	96	3.8	9	-1	2.3
1960	Chi-A	13	12	.520	36	35	13	**4**	1	237	220	8.4	20	112	4.3	158	6.0	3.49	110	.247	.328	10	9	99	107	-1.1	6	-2	1.3
1961	Chi-A	8	2	.800	17	16	5	0	0	110	88	7.2	11	47	3.8	64	5.2	3.52	113	.220	.298	6	5	99	89	2.9	-0	-2	0.4
1962	Chi-A	7	15	.318	27	26	11	3	0	168	171	9.2	15	56	3.0	91	4.9	4.45	84	.264	.324	-9	-13	94	88	-4.6	0	-2	-1.4
1963	Cle-A	1	2	.333	20	5	1	0	1	55	50	8.2	2	15	2.5	29	4.7	2.29	155	.250	.291	8	8	98	130	-0.4	1	-0	0.9
Total	23	300	244	.551	691	612	290	49	15	4566	4291	8.5	338	1775	3.5	2334	4.6	3.54	107	.248	.316	171	119	97	100	8.3	69	-23	18.2

■ **BILLY WYNNE** Wynne, Billy Vernon b: 7/31/43, Williamston, N.C. BL/TR, 6'3", 205 lbs. Deb: 8/06/67

YEAR	TM/L	W	L	PCT	G	GS	CG	SHO	SV	IP	H	H/G	HR	BB	BB/G	SO	SO/G	ERA	/A	OAVG	OOBP	PR	/A	PF	CPI	WAT	PB	PD	TPI
1967	NY-N	0	0	—	6	1	0	0	0	9	12	12.0	0	2	2.0	4	4.0	3.00	115	.324	.341	0	0	102	150	0.0	-0	-0	0.0
1968	Chi-A	0	0	—	1	0	0	0	0	2	2	9.0	0	2	9.0	1	4.5	4.50	68	.250	.400	-0	-0	102	102	0.0	0	0	0.0
1969	Chi-A	7	7	.500	20	20	6	1	0	129	143	10.0	14	50	3.5	67	4.7	4.05	98	.283	.348	-6	-1	110	114	1.0	-1	0	0.0
1970	Chi-A	1	4	.200	12	9	0	0	0	44	54	11.0	8	22	4.5	19	3.9	5.32	75	.298	.365	-8	-6	108	111	-1.0	-1	1	-0.5
1971	Cal-A	0	0	—	3	0	0	0	0	4	6	13.5	0	2	4.5	6	13.5	4.50	77	.375	.444	-0	-0	99	146	0.0	0	0	0.0
Total	5	8	11	.421	42	30	6	1	0	188	217	10.4	22	78	3.7	97	4.6	4.31	91	.290	.354	-14	-8	109	116	0.0	-2	1	-0.5

■ **BILL WYNNE** Wynne, William Andrew b: 3/27/1869, Neuse, N.C. d: 8/7/51, Raleigh, N.C. BR/TR, 5'11.5", 161 lbs. Deb: 8/31/1894

YEAR	TM/L	W	L	PCT	G	GS	CG	SHO	SV	IP	H	H/G	HR	BB	BB/G	SO	SO/G	ERA	/A	OAVG	OOBP	PR	/A	PF	CPI	WAT	PB	PD	TPI
1894	Was-N	0	1	.000	1	1	1	0	0	8	10	11.3	0	8	9.0	2	2.3	6.75	79	.329	.468	-1	-1	100	93	-0.4	-0	0	0.0

■ **HANK WYSE** Wyse, Henry Washington "Hooks" b: 3/1/18, Lunsford, Ark. BR/TR, 5'11.5", 185 lbs. Deb: 9/07/42

YEAR	TM/L	W	L	PCT	G	GS	CG	SHO	SV	IP	H	H/G	HR	BB	BB/G	SO	SO/G	ERA	/A	OAVG	OOBP	PR	/A	PF	CPI	WAT	PB	PD	TPI
1942	Chi-N	2	1	.667	4	4	1	1	0	28	33	10.6	1	6	1.9	8	2.6	1.93	168	.287	.320	4	4	98	193	0.6	-0	-0	0.4
1943	Chi-N	9	7	.563	38	15	8	2	5	156	160	9.2	4	34	2.0	45	2.6	2.94	113	.266	.303	7	6	98	105	1.3	-3	3	0.7
1944	Chi-N	16	15	.516	41	34	14	3	1	257	277	9.7	9	57	2.0	86	3.0	3.15	115	.278	.315	13	13	100	113	1.1	-1	0	1.3
1945	Chi-N	22	10	.688	38	34	23	2	0	278	272	8.8	17	55	1.8	77	2.5	2.69	135	.256	.291	**34**	29	95	117	2.7	-2	2	2.9
1946	Chi-N	14	12	.538	40	27	12	2	1	201	206	9.2	7	52	2.3	52	2.3	2.69	118	.265	.310	16	11	93	116	0.1	2	2	1.5
1947	Chi-N	6	9	.400	37	19	5	1	1	142	158	10.0	12	64	4.1	53	3.4	4.31	98	.286	.355	-4	-1	104	111	-0.8	-2	1	-0.1
1950	Phi-A	9	14	.391	41	23	4	0	0	171	192	10.1	16	87	4.6	33	1.7	5.84	73	.287	.372	-24	-30	93	89	1.1	-3	0	-2.9
1951	Phi-A	1	2	.333	9	1	0	0	0	15	24	14.4	0	8	4.8	5	3.0	7.80	56	.381	.444	-6	-6	106	92	-0.3	-0	0	-0.5
	Was-A	0	0	—	3	2	0	0	0	9	17	17.0	0	10	10.0	3	3.0	10.00	40	.378	.491	-6	-6	97	93	0.0	-1	0	-0.5
	Yr	1	2	.333	12	3	0	0	0	24	41	15.4	0	18	6.8	8	3.0	8.63	49	.380	.465	-12	-12	103	93	-0.3	-0	0	-1.0
Total	8	79	70	.530	251	159	67	11	8	1257	1339	9.6	66	373	2.7	362	2.6	3.52	104	.274	.324	36	21	97	111	5.8	-11	8	2.8

■ **BIFF WYSONG** Wysong, Harlan b: 4/13/05, Clarksville, Ohio d: 8/8/51, Xenia, Ohio BL/TL, 6'3", 195 lbs. Deb: 8/10/30

YEAR	TM/L	W	L	PCT	G	GS	CG	SHO	SV	IP	H	H/G	HR	BB	BB/G	SO	SO/G	ERA	/A	OAVG	OOBP	PR	/A	PF	CPI	WAT	PB	PD	TPI
1930	Cin-N	0	1	.000	1	1	0	0	0	2	6	27.0	0	3	13.5	1	4.5	22.50	21	.545	.563	-4	-4	93	77	-0.4	0	0	-0.2
1931	Cin-N	0	2	.000	12	2	0	0	0	22	25	10.2	2	23	9.4	5	2.0	7.77	49	.298	.432	-10	-10	98	88	-0.9	0	-1	-0.9
1932	Cin-N	1	0	1.000	7	0	0	0	0	12	13	9.8	0	8	6.0	5	3.8	3.75	102	.277	.362	0	0	99	119	0.5	-0	0	0.0
Total	3	1	3	.250	20	3	0	0	0	36	44	11.0	2	34	8.5	11	2.8	7.25	53	.310	.422	-13	-14	98	98	-0.8	-0	-0	-1.1

■ **RUSTY YARNALL** Yarnall, Waldo William b: 10/22/02, Chicago, Ill. d: 10/9/85, Lowell, Mass. BR/TR, 6', 175 lbs. Deb: 6/30/26

YEAR	TM/L	W	L	PCT	G	GS	CG	SHO	SV	IP	H	H/G	HR	BB	BB/G	SO	SO/G	ERA	/A	OAVG	OOBP	PR	/A	PF	CPI	WAT	PB	PD	TPI
1926	Phi-N	0	1	.000	1	0	0	0	0	1	3	27.0	0	1	9.0	0	0.0	18.00	23	.500	.500	-2	-2	107	80	-0.4	-0	0	0.0

■ **RUBE YARRISON** Yarrison, Byron Wardsworth b: 3/9/1896, Montgomery, Pa. d: 4/22/77, Williamsport, Pa. BR/TR, 5'11", 165 lbs. Deb: 4/13/22

YEAR	TM/L	W	L	PCT	G	GS	CG	SHO	SV	IP	H	H/G	HR	BB	BB/G	SO	SO/G	ERA	/A	OAVG	OOBP	PR	/A	PF	CPI	WAT	PB	PD	TPI
1922	Phi-A	1	2	.333	18	1	0	0	0	34	50	13.2	4	12	3.2	10	2.6	8.21	52	.362	.408	-16	-15	106	85	-0.2	-0	0	-1.3

YEAR	TM/L	W	L	PCT	G	GS	CG	SHO	SV	IP	H	H/G	HR	BB	BB/G	SO	SO/G	ERA	/A	OAVG	OOBP	PR	/A	PF	CPI	WAT	PB	PD	TPI
1924	Bro-N	0	2	.000	3	2	0	0	0	11	12	9.8	0	3	2.5	2	1.6	6.55	58	.267	.314	-3	-3	98	47	-0.9	-0	0	-0.2
Total	2	1	4	.200	21	3	0	0	0	45	62	12.4	4	15	3.0	12	2.4	7.80	54	.339	.385	-19	-18	104	76	-1.1	-0	0	-1.5
■ **EMIL YDE**	Yde, Emil Ogden b: 1/28/1900, Great Lakes, Ill. d: 12/4/68, Leesburg, Fla. BB/TL, 5'11", 165 lbs. Deb: 4/21/24																												
1924	Pit-N	16	3	**.842**	33	22	14	4	0	194	171	7.9	3	62	2.9	53	2.5	2.83	142	.244	.303	22	26	104	98	6.2	1	1	3.0
1925	Pit-N	17	9	.654	33	28	13	0	0	207	254	11.0	11	75	3.3	41	1.8	4.13	102	.309	.361	3	2	99	117	1.3	-1	-1	0.0
1926	Pit-N	8	7	.533	37	22	12	1	0	187	181	8.7	3	81	3.9	34	1.6	3.66	116	.260	.325	3	12	111	94	-0.1	2	-0	1.5
1927	Pit-N	1	3	.250	9	2	0	0	0	30	45	13.5	1	15	4.5	9	2.7	9.60	40	.375	.425	-19	-19	99	75	-1.1	-0	1	-1.6
1929	Det-A	7	3	.700	29	6	4	1	0	87	100	10.3	8	63	6.5	23	2.4	5.28	78	.296	.396	-10	-11	97	110	2.3	3	-1	-0.6
Total	5	49	25	.662	141	80	43	6	0	705	751	9.6	26	296	3.8	160	2.0	4.02	103	.281	.344	0	10	103	103	8.6	5	1	2.3
■ **JOE YEAGER**	Yeager, Joseph F. "Little Joe" b: 8/28/1875, Philadelphia, Pa. d: 7/2/37, Detroit, Mich. BR/TR, Deb: 4/22/1898																												
1898	Bro-N	12	22	.353	36	33	32	0	0	291	333	10.3	4	80	2.5	70	2.2	3.65	95	.310	.357	-1	-6	96	102	-1.0	-3	5	-0.2
1899	Bro-N	2	2	.500	10	4	2	1	1	48	56	10.5	1	16	3.0	6	1.1	4.88	81	.316	.372	-5	-5	102	82	-0.4	-0	0	-0.3
1900	Bro-N	1	1	.500	2	2	2	0	0	17	21	11.1	1	5	2.6	2	1.1	6.88	57	.327	.376	-6	-6	106	66	-0.1	0	0	-0.3
1901	Det-A	12	11	.522	26	25	22	2	1	200	209	9.4	4	46	2.1	38	1.7	2.61	153	.289	.332	23	31	109	121	-0.6	4	2	4.0
1902	Det-A	6	12	.333	19	15	14	0	0	140	171	11.0	5	41	2.6	28	1.8	4.82	74	.327	.376	-19	-19	101	91	-1.3	3	3	-1.6
1903	Det-A	0	1	.000	1	1	1	0	0	9	15	15.0	0	0	0.0	1	1.0	4.00	71	.396	.396	-1	-1	96	141	-0.4	0	0	0.0
Total	6	33	49	.402	94	80	73	3	2	705	805	10.3	15	188	2.4	145	1.9	3.75	98	.309	.356	-10	-6	102	103	-3.8	4	10	1.6
■ **AL YEARGIN**	Yeargin, James Almond b: 10/16/01, Mauldin, S.C. d: 5/8/37, Greenville, S.C. BR/TR, 5'11", 170 lbs. Deb: 10/01/22																												
1922	Bos-N	0	1	.000	1	1	1	0	0	7	5	6.4	1	2	2.6	1	1.3	1.29	312	.192	.250	2	2	98	152	-0.4	-0	0	0.2
1924	Bos-N	1	11	.083	32	12	6	0	0	141	162	10.3	7	42	2.7	34	2.2	5.11	75	.293	.335	-19	-20	99	82	-4.5	-2	4	-1.7
Total	2	1	12	.077	33	13	7	0	0	148	167	10.2	8	44	2.7	35	2.1	4.93	78	.288	.331	-17	-18	99	85	-4.9	-2	4	-1.5
■ **LARRY YELLEN**	Yellen, Lawrence Alan b: 1/4/43, Brooklyn, N.Y. BR/TR, 5'11", 190 lbs. Deb: 9/26/63																												
1963	Hou-N	0	0	—	1	1	0	0	0	5	7	12.6	0	1	1.8	3	5.4	3.60	87	.280	.296	-0	-0	95	82	0.0	-0	0	0.0
1964	Hou-N	0	0	—	13	1	0	0	0	21	27	11.6	4	10	4.3	9	3.9	6.86	51	.297	.359	-8	-8	98	86	0.0	-0	-0	-0.7
Total	2	0	0	—	14	2	0	0	0	26	34	11.8	4	11	3.8	12	4.2	6.23	55	.293	.346	-8	-8	98	85	0.0	-0	-0	-0.7
■ **CHIEF YELLOWHORSE**	Yellowhorse, Moses J. b: 1/28/1898, Pawnee, Okla. d: 4/10/64, Pawnee, Okla. BR/TR, 5'10", 180 lbs. Deb: 4/15/21																												
1921	Pit-N	5	3	.625	10	4	1	0	1	48	45	8.4	1	13	2.4	19	3.6	3.00	128	.254	.297	4	4	102	89	0.4	-2	-2	0.0
1922	Pit-N	3	1	.750	28	5	2	0	0	78	92	10.6	0	20	2.3	24	2.8	4.50	92	.305	.338	-3	-3	101	88	0.9	1	-1	-0.2
Total	2	8	4	.667	38	9	3	0	1	126	137	9.8	1	33	2.4	43	3.1	3.93	103	.286	.323	1	2	101	88	1.3	-2	-2	-0.2
■ **CARROLL YERKES**	Yerkes, Charles Carroll "Lefty" b: 6/13/03, McSherrystown, Pa d: 12/20/50, Oakland, Cal. BR/TL, 5'11", 180 lbs. Deb: 5/31/27																												
1927	Phi-A	0	0	—	1	0	0	0	0	1	0	0.0	0	1	9.0	0	0.0	0.00	—	.000	.250	0	0	95	0	0.0	0	0	0.1
1928	Phi-A	0	1	.000	2	1	1	0	0	9	7	7.0	0	2	2.0	1	1.0	2.00	200	.233	.273	2	2	99	114	-0.4	-0	1	0.2
1929	Phi-A	1	0	1.000	19	2	0	0	1	37	47	11.4	0	13	3.2	11	2.7	4.62	96	.329	.374	-2	-1	104	111	0.5	-2	2	0.0
1932	Chi-N	0	0	—	2	0	0	0	0	9	5	5.0	2	3	3.0	4	4.0	3.00	133	.167	.242	1	1	103	90	0.0	0	-0	0.1
1933	Chi-N	0	0	—	1	0	0	0	0	2	2	9.0	0	1	4.5	0	0.0	4.50	70	.286	.333	-0	-0	95	93	0.0	0	0	0.0
Total	5	1	1	.500	25	3	1	0	1	58	61	9.5	2	20	3.1	16	2.5	3.88	109	.288	.339	2	2	103	105	0.1	-2	3	0.4
■ **STAN YERKES**	Yerkes, Stanley Lewis "Yank" b: 11/28/1874, Cheltenham, Pa. d: 7/28/40, Boston, Mass. 5'10", Deb: 5/03/01																												
1901	Bal-A	0	1	.000	1	1	1	0	0	8	12	13.5	0	2	2.3	4	4.5	6.75	58	.368	.405	-3	-3	107	79	-0.4	0	0	-0.1
	StL-N	3	1	.750	4	4	4	0	0	34	35	9.3	2	6	1.6	15	4.0	3.18	99	.288	.321	1	-0	95	103	0.9	-1	-0	0.0
1902	StL-N	12	21	.364	39	37	27	1	0	273	341	11.2	1	79	2.6	81	2.7	3.66	75	.331	.381	-27	-28	99	111	-2.6	-3	-3	-3.0
1903	StL-N	0	1	.000	1	1	0	0	0	5	8	14.4	0	0	0.0	3	5.4	1.80	185	.388	.388	1	1	102	279	-0.4	-0	-0	0.1
Total	3	15	24	.385	45	43	32	1	0	320	396	11.1	3	87	2.4	103	2.9	3.66	77	.329	.376	-28	-29	99	112	-2.5	-4	-3	-3.0
■ **RICH YETT**	Yett, Richard Martin b: 10/6/62, Pomona, Cal. BR/TR, 6'2", 187 lbs. Deb: 4/13/85																												
1985	Min-A	0	0	—	1	1	0	0	0	⅓	1	27.0	0	2	54.0	0	0.0	27.00	—	.333	.600	-1	-1	104	63	0.0	0	0	0.0
1986	Cle-A	5	3	.625	39	3	1	1	1	79	84	9.6	10	37	4.2	50	5.7	5.13	80	.275	.349	-8	-9	98	94	0.9	0	-1	-0.9
1987	Cle-A	3	9	.250	37	11	2	0	1	98	96	8.8	21	49	4.5	59	5.4	5.23	89	.257	.343	-8	-6	105	100	-2.0	0	-1	-0.6
1988	Cle-A	9	6	.600	23	22	0	0	0	134	146	9.8	11	55	3.7	71	4.8	4.63	88	.275	.342	-10	-9	102	94	1.8	0	-2	-0.9
Total	4	17	18	.486	100	37	3	1	2	311	327	9.5	42	143	4.1	180	5.2	4.98	86	.269	.345	-27	-25	102	96	0.7	0	-4	-2.4
■ **EARL YINGLING**	Yingling, Earl Hershey "Chink" b: 10/29/1888, Chillicothe, Ohio d: 10/2/62, Columbus, Ohio BL/TL, 5'11.5", 180 lbs. Deb: 4/12/11																												
1911	Cle-A	1	0	1.000	4	3	1	0	0	22	30	12.3	1	9	3.7	6	2.5	4.50	77	.326	.392	-3	-3	103	117	0.5	0	0	-0.1
1912	Bro-N	6	11	.353	25	16	12	0	0	163	186	10.3	10	56	3.1	51	2.8	3.59	92	.284	.342	-3	-5	97	107	-0.6	3	-2	-0.3
1913	Bro-N	8	8	.500	26	13	8	2	0	147	158	9.7	2	10	0.6	40	2.4	2.57	130	.280	.290	10	13	105	109	1.0	8	-1	2.2
1914	Cin-N	9	13	.409	34	27	8	3	0	198	207	9.4	6	54	2.5	80	3.6	3.45	87	.274	.316	-15	-10	107	95	0.4	1	-2	-0.9
1918	Was-A	1	2	.333	5	2	2	0	0	38	30	7.1	0	12	2.8	15	3.6	2.13	134	.238	.290	3	3	103	106	-0.5	3	1	0.9
Total	5	25	34	.424	94	61	31	5	0	568	611	9.7	19	141	2.2	192	3.0	3.22	99	.279	.319	-8	-1	103	103	0.8	16	-3	1.8
■ **JOE YINGLING**	Yingling, Joseph Granville b: 7/23/1866, Westminster, Md. d: 10/24/46, Manchester, Md. BR/TL, 5'7.5", 145 lbs. Deb: 5/28/1886																												
1886	Was-N	0	0	—	1	0	0	0	0	3	7	21.0	0	1	3.0	1	3.0	12.00	28	.467	.501	-3	-3	100	82	0.0	-0	0	-0.2
■ **LEN YOCHIM**	Yochim, Leonard Joseph b: 10/16/28, New Orleans, La. BL/TL, 6'2", 200 lbs. Deb: 9/18/51																												
1951	Pit-N	1	1	.500	2	2	0	0	0	9	10	10.0	0	11	11.0	5	5.0	8.00	54	.278	.458	-4	-4	110	78	0.1	-0	0	-0.3
1954	Pit-N	0	1	.000	10	1	0	0	0	20	30	13.5	2	8	3.6	7	3.1	7.20	58	.361	.400	-7	-7	102	95	-0.4	0	1	-0.5
Total	2	1	2	.333	12	3	0	0	0	29	40	12.4	2	19	5.9	12	3.7	7.45	56	.336	.420	-11	-10	104	89	-0.3	-0	1	-0.8
■ **RAY YOCHIM**	Yochim, Raymond Austin Aloysius b: 7/19/22, New Orleans, La. BR/TR, 6'1", 170 lbs. Deb: 5/02/48																												
1948	StL-N	0	0	—	1	0	0	0	0	1	0	0.0	0	3	27.0	1	9.0	0.00	—	.000	.500	0	0	99	0	0.0	0	0	0.0
1949	StL-N	0	0	—	3	0	0	0	0	2	3	13.5	1	4	18.0	3	13.5	18.00	24	.273	.467	-3	-3	108	63	0.0	0	0	-0.2
Total	2	0	0	—	4	0	0	0	0	3	3	9.0	1	7	21.0	4	12.0	12.00	35	.214	.476	-3	-3	105	42	0.0	0	0	-0.2
■ **LEFTY YORK**	York, James Edward b: 11/1/1892, West Fork, Ark. d: 4/9/61, York, Pa. BL/TL, 5'10", 185 lbs. Deb: 9/12/19																												
1919	Phi-A	0	2	.000	2	2	0	0	0	4	13	29.3	0	5	11.3	2	4.5	27.00	13	.500	.581	-11	-10	112	58	-0.9	-0	0	-0.8
1921	Chi-N	5	9	.357	40	10	4	1	1	139	170	11.0	5	63	4.1	57	3.7	4.73	87	.308	.372	-15	-10	108	102	-1.0	-2	-3	-1.4
Total	2	5	11	.313	42	12	4	1	1	143	183	11.5	5	68	4.3	59	3.7	5.35	76	.317	.382	-25	-20	109	100	-1.9	-3	-3	-2.2
■ **JIM YORK**	York, James Harlan b: 8/27/47, Maywood, Cal. BR/TR, 6'3", 200 lbs. Deb: 9/21/70																												
1970	KC-A	1	1	.500	4	0	0	0	0	8	5	5.6	2	2	2.3	6	6.8	3.38	110	.179	.226	0	0	100	82	0.2	-0	-0	0.0
1971	KC-A	5	5	.500	53	0	0	0	3	93	70	6.8	7	44	4.3	103	10.0	2.90	117	.203	.293	6	5	98	88	-0.2	1	-0	0.6
1972	Hou-N	0	1	.000	26	0	0	0	0	36	45	11.3	3	18	4.5	25	6.3	5.25	69	.321	.390	-7	-6	105	111	-0.4	-0	0	-0.6
1973	Hou-N	3	4	.429	41	0	0	0	6	53	65	11.0	4	20	3.4	22	3.7	4.42	79	.305	.358	-4	-6	95	111	-0.5	-0	0	-0.5
1974	Hou-N	2	2	.500	28	0	0	0	1	38	48	11.4	1	19	4.5	15	3.6	3.32	107	.298	.372	1	1	98	141	0.0	-1	0	0.1
1975	Hou-N	4	4	.500	19	4	0	0	0	47	43	8.2	1	25	4.8	17	3.3	3.83	90	.251	.349	-1	-2	95	99	0.7	-0	-1	-0.3
1976	NY-A	1	0	1.000	3	0	0	0	0	10	14	12.6	1	4	3.6	6	5.4	5.40	64	.333	.404	-2	-2	97	116	0.5	0	0	-0.1
Total	7	16	17	.485	174	4	0	0	10	285	290	9.2	19	132	4.2	194	6.1	3.79	92	.264	.341	-7	-10	98	105	0.3	-1	-1	-0.8
■ **GUS YOST**	Yost, Gus 6'5", Deb: 6/12/1893																												
1893	Chi-N	0	1	.000	1	1	0	0	0	3	3	9.0	0	8	24.0	1	3.0	15.00	33	.276	.583	-3	-3	104	65	-0.4	-0	0	-0.2
■ **FLOYD YOUMANS**	Youmans, Floyd Everett b: 5/11/64, Tampa, Fla. BR/TR, 6'2", 180 lbs. Deb: 7/01/85																												
1985	Mon-N	4	3	.571	14	12	0	0	0	77	57	6.7	3	49	5.7	54	6.3	2.45	137	.206	.323	10	8	94	118	0.4	-0	-2	0.6
1986	Mon-N	13	12	.520	33	32	6	2	0	219	145	6.0	14	118	4.8	202	8.3	3.53	104	.188	.295	5	3	98	70	1.0	2	-3	0.1
1987	Mon-N	9	8	.529	23	23	3	3	0	116	112	8.7	13	47	3.6	94	7.3	4.66	93	.251	.317	-7	-4	106	84	-0.4	1	-0	-0.3
1988	Mon-N	3	6	.333	14	13	1	1	0	84	64	6.9	8	41	4.4	54	5.8	3.21	113	.213	.305	2	4	105	100	-1.5	-0	-0	0.4
Total	4	29	29	.500	84	80	10	6	0	496	378	6.9	38	255	4.6	404	7.3	3.57	105	.211	.306	9	10	100	86	-0.5	2	-5	0.8

YEAR	TM/L	W	L	PCT	G	GS	CG	SHO	SV	IP	H	H/G	HR	BB	BB/G	SO	SO/G	ERA	/A	OAVG	OOBP	PR	/A	PF	CPI	WAT	PB	PD	TPI
■ CHARLIE YOUNG	Young, Charles "Cy" b: 1/12/1893, Philadelphia, Pa. d: 5/12/52, Riverside, N.J. BR/TR, 5'10.5", 155 lbs. Deb: 9/05/15																												
1915	Bal-F	2	3	.400	9	5	1	0	0	35	39	10.0	0	21	5.4	13	3.3	5.91	57	.312	.411	-11	-10	111	76	0.4	0	0	-0.9
■ CURT YOUNG	Young, Curtis Allen b: 4/16/60, Saginaw, Mich. BR/TL, 6'1", 175 lbs. Deb: 6/24/83																												
1983	Oak-A	0	1	.000	8	2	0	0	0	9	17	17.0	1	5	5.0	5	5.0	16.00	25	.386	.460	-12	-12	96	55	-0.4	0	-0	-1.0
1984	Oak-A	9	4	.692	20	17	2	1	0	109	118	9.7	9	31	2.6	41	3.4	4.05	91	.274	.331	-1	-4	92	101	2.8	0	-1	-0.4
1985	Oak-A	0	4	.000	19	7	0	0	0	46	57	11.2	15	22	4.3	19	3.7	7.24	53	.300	.374	-16	-17	93	99	-1.9	0	-0	-1.6
1986	Oak-A	13	9	.591	29	27	5	2	0	198	176	8.0	19	57	2.6	116	5.3	3.45	114	.236	.291	16	10	94	91	2.8	0	0	1.0
1987	Oak-A	13	7	.650	31	31	6	0	0	203	194	8.6	38	44	2.0	124	5.5	4.08	100	.252	.291	9	-0	91	99	3.3	0	0	0.0
1988	Oak-A	11	8	.579	26	26	1	0	0	156	162	9.3	23	50	2.9	69	4.0	4.15	89	.275	.332	-3	-8	93	114	-0.9	0	-1	-0.8
Total	6	46	33	.582	133	110	14	3	0	721	724	9.0	105	209	2.6	374	4.7	4.27	91	.261	.314	-6	-31	93	100	5.7	0	-2	-2.8
■ CY YOUNG	Young, Denton True b: 3/29/1867, Gilmore, Ohio d: 11/4/55, Newcomerstown, Ohio BR/TR, 6'2", 210 lbs. Deb: 8/06/1890 MH																												
1890	Cle-N	9	6	.600	17	16	16	0	0	148	145	8.8	6	30	**1.8**	39	2.4	3.47	100	.272	.311	2	-0	97	83	3.2	-5	0	-0.4
1891	Cle-N	27	22	.551	55	46	43	0	2	424	431	9.1	4	140	3.0	147	3.1	2.84	125	.277	.337	24	33	106	104	5.5	-4	0	2.9
1892	Cle-N	36	12	**.750**	53	49	48	**9**	0	453	363	7.2	8	118	2.3	168	3.3	**1.93**	**172**	.231	**.285**	**68**	**70**	101	101	**10.2**	-7	8	**7.1**
1893	Cle-N	**34**	16	.680	53	46	42	1	1	423	442	9.4	10	103	**2.2**	102	2.2	3.36	143	.284	.329	62	68	103	101	**9.0**	-5	6	6.0
1894	Cle-N	26	21	.553	52	47	44	2	1	409	488	10.7	19	106	**2.3**	108	2.4	3.94	150	.319	.363	63	89	111	109	2.0	-11	8	7.3
1895	Cle-N	**35**	10	.778	47	40	36	**4**	0	370	363	8.8	10	75	**1.8**	121	2.9	3.24	140	.276	**.315**	64	53	95	91	10.7	-2	9	5.0
1896	Cle-N	28	15	.651	51	46	42	**5**	**3**	414	477	10.4	7	62	**1.3**	**140**	3.0	3.24	145	.311	.338	52	67	108	107	2.2	6	8	**7.7**
1897	Cle-N	21	19	.525	**46**	38	35	2	0	335	391	10.5	8	49	**1.3**	88	2.4	3.79	125	.314	.340	20	35	110	94	0.0	-6	4	3.2
1898	Cle-N	25	13	.658	46	41	40	1	0	378	387	9.2	6	41	**1.0**	101	2.4	2.52	135	.286	.307	45	38	95	106	5.9	6	7	4.9
1899	StL-N	26	16	.619	44	42	**40**	4	1	369	368	9.0	10	44	**1.1**	111	2.7	2.59	**159**	.283	**.306**	**52**	**63**	107	102	3.9	-1	6	**6.7**
1900	StL-N	19	19	.500	41	35	32	**4**	0	321	337	9.4	7	36	**1.0**	115	3.2	3.00	115	.293	.314	25	16	93	96	1.7	-2	1	1.3
1901	Bos-A	**33**	10	.767	43	41	38	**5**	0	371	324	**7.9**	6	37	**0.9**	**158**	3.8	**1.63**	**212**	**.254**	**.275**	**84**	**75**	94	118	**11.6**	1	1	**7.5**
1902	Bos-A	**32**	11	.744	**45**	43	**41**	3	0	**385**	350	8.2	6	53	1.2	160	3.7	2.15	163	.265	.294	**61**	**58**	98	104	**10.9**	3	-6	5.3
1903	Bos-A	**28**	9	**.757**	40	35	**34**	**7**	**2**	**342**	294	7.7	6	37	**1.0**	176	4.6	2.08	153	.253	.276	33	**42**	108	97	**6.5**	12	-4	**5.8**
1904	Bos-A	26	16	.619	43	41	40	**10**	1	380	327	7.7	6	29	**0.7**	200	4.7	1.97	134	.254	.270	27	28	101	96	0.2	3	-5	2.7
1905	Bos-A	18	19	.486	38	33	31	4	0	321	248	7.0	3	30	**0.8**	210	5.9	1.82	145	.235	**.257**	29	29	100	84	-1.1	-1	-2	3.2
1906	Bos-A	13	21	.382	39	34	28	0	2	288	288	9.0	3	25	**0.8**	140	4.4	3.19	87	.286	.303	-16	-13	104	80	2.0	-2	-2	-1.5
1907	Bos-A	21	15	.583	43	37	33	6	2	343	286	7.5	3	51	1.3	147	3.9	1.99	131	.249	.281	21	24	103	91	6.7	-0	-6	2.0
1908	Bos-A	21	11	.656	36	33	30	3	2	299	230	6.9	1	37	1.1	150	4.5	1.26	183	.213	.240	37	35	97	108	6.1	2	-6	3.5
1909	Cle-A	19	15	.559	35	34	30	3	0	295	267	8.1	4	59	1.8	109	3.3	2.26	113	.250	.294	7	10	103	100	3.7	-0	-2	0.9
1910	Cle-A	7	10	.412	21	20	14	1	0	163	149	8.2	0	27	1.5	58	3.2	2.54	101	.252	.289	-0	0	102	87	-1.0	-0	1	0.1
1911	Cle-A	3	4	.429	7	7	4	0	0	46	54	10.6	2	13	2.5	20	3.9	3.91	88	.298	.349	-3	-2	103	103	-0.6	-2	-0	-0.1
	Bos-N	4	5	.444	11	11	8	2	0	80	83	9.3	4	15	1.7	35	3.9	3.71	100	.268	.308	-3	0	109	85	1.0	-3	0	-0.1
Total	22	511	315	.619	906	815	749	76	17	7357	7092	8.7	139	1217	1.5	2803	3.4	2.63	138	.271	.304	754	810	102	99	100.3	-20	27	81.0
■ HARLEY YOUNG	Young, Harlan Edward "Cy The Third" b: 9/28/1883, Portland, Ind. d: 3/26/75, Jacksonville, Fla. BR/TR, 6'2", Deb: 4/21/08																												
1908	Pit-N	0	2	.000	8	3	0	0	0	48	40	7.5	0	10	1.9	17	3.2	2.25	96	.262	.328	1	-0	92	97	-0.9	-0	1	0.0
	Bos-N	0	1	.000	6	2	1	0	0	27	29	9.7	0	4	1.3	12	4.0	3.33	74	.314	.362	-3	-3	106	96	-0.4	0	0	-0.2
	Yr	0	3	.000	14	5	1	0	0	75	69	8.3	0	14	1.7	29	3.5	2.64	86	.276	.322	-2	-3	97	96	-1.3	-0	1	-0.2
■ IRV YOUNG	Young, Irving Melrose "Young Cy" or "Cy The Second" b: 7/21/1877, Columbia Falls, Maine d: 1/14/35, Brewer, Maine BL/TL, 5'10", 170 lbs. Deb: 4/14/05																												
1905	Bos-N	20	21	.488	43	42	**41**	6	0	**378**	337	8.0	6	71	1.7	156	3.7	2.90	105	.266	.309	4	6	102	83	6.0	-8	4	1.0
1906	Bos-N	16	25	.390	43	41	**37**	4	0	**358**	349	8.8	7	83	2.1	151	3.8	2.92	95	.284	.332	-11	-5	106	99	2.6	-7	2	-0.3
1907	Bos-N	10	23	.303	40	32	22	3	1	245	287	10.5	5	58	2.1	86	3.2	3.97	61	.327	.377	-41	-42	99	97	-4.4	-1	1	-4.2
1908	Bos-N	4	9	.308	16	11	7	1	0	85	94	10.0	2	19	2.0	32	3.4	2.86	87	.313	.357	-5	-4	106	123	-1.6	-1	-1	-0.4
	Pit-N	4	3	.571	16	7	3	1	1	90	73	7.3	1	21	2.1	31	3.1	2.00	108	.253	.314	3	2	92	105	-0.3	1	-1	0.1
	Yr	8	12	.400	32	18	10	2	1	175	167	8.6	3	40	2.1	63	3.2	2.42	96	.282	.333	-1	-2	99	105	-1.9	-1	-2	-0.3
1910	Chi-A	4	8	.333	27	17	7	4	0	136	122	8.1	0	39	2.6	64	4.2	2.71	88	.247	.306	-3	-5	95	89	-1.5	-2	-0	-0.7
1911	Chi-A	5	6	.455	24	11	3	1	2	93	99	9.6	2	25	2.4	40	3.9	4.35	73	.229	.271	-10	-12	95	31	-0.5	-0	1	-1.1
Total	6	63	95	.399	209	161	120	20	4	1385	1361	8.8	23	316	2.1	560	3.6	3.11	87	.278	.327	-63	-60	101	91	0.3	-18	5	-5.6
■ J. B. YOUNG	Young, J. B. b: Mt.Carmel, Pa. Deb: 6/10/1892																												
1892	StL-N	0	0	—	1	0	0	0	0	2	9	40.5	0	2	9.0	1	4.5	22.50	14	.628	.674	-4	-4	97	99	0.0	-0	0	-0.2
■ KIP YOUNG	Young, Kip Lane b: 10/29/54, Georgetown, Ohio BR/TR, 5'11", 175 lbs. Deb: 7/21/78																												
1978	Det-A	6	7	.462	14	13	7	0	0	106	94	8.0	9	30	2.5	49	4.2	2.80	144	.246	.299	12	15	107	116	-0.8	0	-1	1.4
1979	Det-A	2	2	.500	13	7	0	0	0	44	60	12.3	11	11	2.3	22	4.5	6.34	64	.323	.360	-10	-11	96	102	0.0	0	1	-0.9
Total	2	8	9	.471	27	20	7	0	0	150	154	9.2	20	41	2.5	71	4.3	3.84	106	.271	.319	1	4	104	112	-0.8	0	-1	0.5
■ MATT YOUNG	Young, Matthew John b: 8/9/58, Pasadena, Cal. BL/TL, 6'3", 205 lbs. Deb: 4/06/83																												
1983	Sea-A	11	15	.423	33	32	5	2	0	204	178	7.9	17	79	3.5	130	5.7	3.26	126	.236	.310	18	20	101	104	1.3	0	2	2.2
1984	Sea-A	6	8	.429	22	22	1	0	0	113	141	11.2	11	57	4.5	73	5.8	5.73	72	.307	.380	-22	-20	103	97	-0.4	0	1	-1.8
1985	Sea-A	12	19	.387	37	35	5	2	1	218	242	10.0	23	76	3.1	136	5.6	4.91	81	.282	.342	-19	-23	95	95	-2.7	0	-2	-2.3
1986	Sea-A	8	6	.571	65	5	1	0	13	104	108	9.3	9	46	4.0	82	7.1	3.81	117	.272	.354	4	7	106	121	2.0	0	-1	0.6
1987	LA-N	5	8	.385	47	0	0	0	11	54	62	10.3	3	17	2.8	42	7.0	4.50	84	.288	.338	-2	-4	92	93	-0.9	-0	-2	-0.5
Total	5	42	56	.429	204	94	12	4	25	693	731	9.5	63	275	3.6	463	6.0	4.36	94	.272	.341	-20	-21	100	102	-0.7	-0	-2	-1.8
■ CHIEF YOUNGBLOOD	Youngblood, Albert Clyde b: 6/13/1900, Hillsboro, Tex. d: 7/6/68, Amarillo, Tex. BL/TR, 6'3", 202 lbs. Deb: 7/16/22																												
1922	Was-A	0	0	—	2	0	0	0	0	4	9	20.3	0	7	15.8	0	0.0	15.75	24	.429	.563	-5	-5	93	89	0.0	-0	0	-0.4
■ DUCKY YOUNT	Yount, Herbert Macon "Hub" b: 12/7/1885, Iredell Co., N.C. d: 5/9/70, Winston-Salem, N.C. BR/TR, 6'2", 178 lbs. Deb: 5/28/14																												
1914	Bal-F	1	1	.500	13	1	1	0	0	41	44	9.7	2	19	4.2	19	4.2	4.17	76	.304	.385	-4	-5	99	102	0.0	-1	0	-0.5
■ LARRY YOUNT	Yount, Lawrence King b: 2/15/50, Houston, Tex. BR/TR, 6'2", 185 lbs. Deb: 9/15/71																												
1971	Hou-N	0	0	—	1	0	0	0	0	0	0	—	0	0	—	0	—	—	—	—	—	0	0	92	0	0.0	0	0	0.0
■ CARL YOWELL	Yowell, Carl Columbus "Sundown" b: 12/20/02, Madison Va. d: 7/27/85, Jacksonville, Tex. BL/TL, 6'4", 180 lbs. Deb: 9/05/24																												
1924	Cle-A	1	1	.500	4	2	2	0	0	27	37	12.3	1	13	4.3	8	2.7	6.67	62	.343	.400	-7	-8	97	90	0.1	-1	-0	-0.6
1925	Cle-A	2	3	.400	12	4	1	0	0	36	40	10.0	1	17	4.3	12	3.0	4.50	104	.310	.384	-0	1	107	113	-0.2	-1	0	0.0
Total	2	3	4	.429	16	6	3	0	0	63	77	11.0	2	30	4.3	20	2.9	5.43	82	.325	.391	-8	-7	103	103	-0.1	-1	0	-0.6
■ EDDIE YUHAS	Yuhas, John Edward b: 8/5/24, Youngstown, Ohio d: 7/6/86, Winston-Salem, N.C BR/TR, 6'1", 180 lbs. Deb: 4/17/52																												
1952	StL-N	12	2	.857	54	2	0	0	6	99	90	8.2	5	35	3.2	39	3.5	2.73	133	.243	.308	11	10	97	117	4.8	1	-1	1.0
1953	StL-N	0	0	—	2	0	0	0	0	1	3	27.0	0	0	0.0	0	0.0	18.00	24	.500	.500	-2	-2	101	65	0.0	0	0	0.0
Total	2	12	2	.857	56	2	0	0	6	100	93	8.4	5	35	3.2	39	3.5	2.88	126	.247	.311	10	8	97	117	4.8	1	-1	1.0
■ ADRIAN ZABALA	Zabala, Adrian (Rodriguez) b: 8/26/16, San Antonio De Los Banos, Cuba BL/TL, 5'11", 165 lbs. Deb: 8/11/45																												
1945	NY-N	2	4	.333	11	5	1	0	0	43	46	9.6	2	20	4.2	14	2.9	4.81	79	.284	.355	-5	-5	100	94	-1.0	1	0	-0.3
1949	NY-N	2	3	.400	15	4	2	1	1	41	44	9.7	5	10	2.2	13	2.9	5.27	77	.278	.318	-6	-5	101	83	-0.3	-1	-1	-0.6
Total	2	4	7	.364	26	9	3	1	1	84	90	9.6	7	30	3.2	27	2.9	5.04	78	.281	.337	-10	-10	100	88	-1.3	-0	-1	-0.9
■ ZIP ZABEL	Zabel, George Washington b: 2/18/1891, Wetmore, Kan. d: 5/31/70, Beloit, Wis. BR/TR, 6'1.5", 185 lbs. Deb: 10/05/13																												
1913	Chi-N	1	0	1.000	1	1	0	0	0	5	3	5.4	0	1	1.8	0	0.0	0.00	—	.167	.211	2	2	97	0	0.5	0	0	0.2
1914	Chi-N	4	4	.500	29	7	2	0	3	128	104	7.3	5	45	3.2	50	3.5	2.18	126	.235	.298	9	8	99	120	0.0	-1	-1	0.7
1915	Chi-N	7	10	.412	36	17	8	3	0	163	124	6.8	3	84	4.6	60	3.3	3.20	89	.218	.308	-8	-7	103	83	-1.2	-4	3	-0.6
Total	3	12	14	.462	66	25	10	3	3	296	231	7.0	8	130	4.0	110	3.3	2.71	104	.224	.302	2	3	101	98	-0.7	-5	2	0.3
■ CHINK ZACHARY	Zachary, Albert Myron (born Albert Myron Zarski) b: 10/19/17, Brooklyn, N.Y. BR/TR, 5'11", 182 lbs. Deb: 4/23/44																												
1944	Bro-N	0	2	.000	4	2	0	0	0	10	10	9.0	2	7	6.3	3	2.7	9.90	37	.238	.360	-7	-7	102	52	-0.9	-0	-0	-0.6

YEAR	TM/L	W	L	PCT	G	GS	CG	SHO	SV	IP	H	H/G	HR	BB	BB/G	SO	SO/G	ERA	/A	OAVG	OOBP	PR	/A	PF	CPI	WAT	PB	PD	TPI
■ **TOM ZACHARY**				Zachary, Jonathan Thompson Walton (a.k.a. Zach Walton 1918)							b: 5/7/1896, Graham, N.C.					d: 1/24/69, Burlington, N.C.			BL/TL, 6'1", 187 lbs.		Deb: 7/11/18							
1918	Phi-A	2	0	1.000	2	2	0	0	0	8	9	10.1	0	7	7.9	1	1.1	5.63	53	.321	.444	-3	-2	108	103	1.0	1	0	-0.1
1919	Was-A	1	5	.167	17	7	0	0	0	62	68	9.9	0	20	2.9	9	1.3	2.90	110	.292	.350	2	2	99	124	-1.7	2	-1	0.3
1920	Was-A	15	16	.484	44	31	19	3	2	263	289	9.9	7	78	2.7	53	1.8	3.76	97	.285	.339	1	-3	96	96	1.3	6	0	0.1
1921	Was-A	18	16	.529	39	31	17	2	1	250	314	11.3	10	59	2.1	53	1.9	3.96	107	.319	.350	9	8	99	118	0.3	2	-0	0.9
1922	Was-A	15	10	.600	32	25	13	1	1	185	190	9.2	6	43	2.1	37	1.8	3.11	120	.275	.311	19	13	93	108	3.9	6	-0	1.7
1923	Was-A	10	16	.385	35	29	10	0	0	204	270	11.9	9	63	2.8	40	1.8	4.50	84	.321	.360	-12	-16	95	109	-3.1	-0	-1	-1.6
1924	Was-A	15	9	.625	33	27	13	1	2	203	198	8.8	5	53	2.3	45	2.0	2.75	148	.264	.308	33	30	96	113	1.0	4	1	3.4
1925	Was-A	12	15	.444	38	33	11	1	2	218	247	10.2	10	74	3.1	58	2.4	3.84	109	.296	.343	13	8	95	113	-4.5	-2	-0	0.5
1926	StL-A	14	15	.483	34	31	18	3	0	247	264	9.6	14	97	3.5	53	1.9	3.61	115	.288	.342	11	15	103	122	2.3	5	2	2.3
1927	StL-A	4	6	.400	13	12	6	0	0	78	110	12.7	4	27	3.1	13	1.5	4.38	103	.345	.381	-2	1	109	133	0.1	-3	-1	-0.1
	Was-A	4	7	.364	15	14	5	1	0	103	116	10.1	2	30	2.6	13	1.1	3.93	101	.290	.333	2	0	96	98	-1.9	-2	-3	-0.3
	Yr	8	13	.381	28	26	11	1	0	181	226	11.2	6	57	2.8	26	1.3	4.13	102	.314	.354	0	2	102	98	-1.8	-3	-3	-0.4
1928	Was-A	6	9	.400	20	14	5	1	0	103	130	11.4	5	40	3.5	19	1.7	5.42	76	.322	.372	-16	-15	101	98	-1.4	1	1	-1.1
	NY-A	3	3	.500	7	6	3	0	1	46	54	10.6	1	15	2.9	7	1.4	3.91	92	.320	.361	1	-2	89	125	-0.6	-0	1	0.0
	Yr	9	12	.429	27	20	8	1	1	149	184	11.1	6	55	3.3	26	1.6	4.95	80	.321	.367	-15	-17	97	125	-2.0	1	2	-1.1
1929	NY-A	12	0	1.000	26	11	7	2	2	120	131	9.8	5	30	2.3	35	2.6	2.48	166	.277	.318	24	22	97	144	**6.0**	0	-3	1.9
1930	NY-A	1	1	.500	3	3	0	0	0	17	18	9.5	0	9	4.8	1	0.5	6.35	64	.269	.333	-3	-4	87	63	0.0	1	1	-0.2
	Bos-N	11	5	.688	24	22	10	1	0	151	192	11.4	9	50	3.0	57	3.4	4.59	107	.317	.359	6	6	99	112	3.6	2	-1	0.6
1931	Bos-N	11	15	.423	33	28	16	3	2	229	243	9.6	8	53	2.1	64	2.5	3.10	127	.272	.308	19	21	102	109	0.2	-2	2	2.3
1932	Bos-N	12	11	.522	32	24	12	1	0	212	231	9.8	5	55	2.3	67	2.8	3.10	117	.280	.320	18	12	93	117	0.6	6	-2	1.6
1933	Bos-N	7	9	.438	26	20	6	2	2	125	134	9.6	1	35	2.5	22	1.6	3.53	91	.276	.317	-3	-5	96	94	-1.5	-2	0	-0.6
1934	Bos-N	1	2	.333	5	4	2	1	0	24	27	10.1	1	8	3.0	4	1.5	3.38	104	.278	.333	2	0	86	116	-0.4	-1	-0	0.0
	Bro-N	5	6	.455	22	12	4	0	2	102	122	10.8	5	21	1.9	28	2.5	4.41	88	.301	.334	-4	-6	95	99	-0.1	1	-1	-0.5
	Yr	6	8	.429	27	16	6	1	2	126	149	10.6	6	29	2.1	32	2.3	4.21	94	.297	.334	-2	-6	94	99	-0.5	-1	-1	-0.5
1935	Bro-N	7	12	.368	25	21	9	1	4	158	193	11.0	10	35	2.0	33	1.9	3.59	106	.297	.330	8	4	95	121	-2.0	-1	0	0.3
1936	Bro-N	0	0	—	1	0	0	0	0	⅓	2	54.0	0	1	27.0	0	0.0	54.00	—	1.000	.750	-2	-2	107	70	0.0	0	0	-0.1
	Phi-N	0	3	.000	7	2	0	0	0	20	28	12.6	2	11	4.9	8	3.6	8.10	55	.329	.390	-9	-8	111	79	-1.4	1	0	-0.5
	Yr	0	3	.000	8	2	0	0	1	20	30	13.5	2	12	5.4	8	3.6	9.00	49	.345	.404	-11	-10	111	79	-1.4	0	0	-0.6
Total	19	186	191	.493	533	409	186	24	22	3128	3580	10.3	119	914	2.6	720	2.1	3.73	106	.294	.337	117	79	97	112	1.7	25	-3	10.8
■ **CHRIS ZACHARY**				Zachary, William Christopher						b: 2/19/44, Knoxville, Tenn.				BL/TR, 6'2", 200 lbs.			Deb: 4/11/63												
1963	Hou-N	2	2	.500	22	7	0	0	0	57	62	9.8	5	22	3.5	42	6.6	4.89	64	.272	.337	-10	-11	95	87	0.3	-1	1	-1.1

The All-Time Leaders

The All-Time Leaders

This section is divided into two parts: lifetime leaders and single season leaders. Both groups command our attention and convey the pleasures of the game, which lie as much in contemplation of the past as in experiencing the present: Henry Aaron, 755; Babe Ruth, 714; Willie Mays, 660—this is no mere aggregation of names and numbers, as in a telephone directory . . . it comprises the romance and lore of the home run, and of baseball itself. Hoss Radbourn, 60, 1884; Jack Chesbro, 41, 1904; Christy Mathewson, 37, 1908; Lefty Grove, 31, 1931; Denny McLain, 31, 1968 . . . you can fill in the blanks that tell the story of pitching's most glorious seasons.

What follows are the all-time great achievements in 95 categories, both the traditional statistics and the new. For most of these we will give not the top 10 or 20 but the top 100, because some categories would otherwise be dominated by players of a certain era (for example, slugging average by batters of the 1920s and 1930s, earned run average by pitchers of 1900–1919). And for many stats we will offer a second kind of ranking, broken out into the five distinct eras of baseball, with the top 10 or 15 leaders in each. For example, breaking out single-season home runs this way would produce lists topped by these men:

1876–1892: Ned Williamson, 27, 1884
1893–1919: Babe Ruth, 29, 1919
1920–1941: Babe Ruth, 60, 1927
1942–1960: Ralph Kiner, 54, 1949
1961–1988: Roger Maris, 61, 1961

And for single-season Adjusted ERA (normalized to league average and adjusted for home-park factor), we get:

1876–1892: Tim Keefe, 276
  (adjusted from actual 0.80), 1880
1893–1919: Walter Johnson, 285
  (adjusted from actual 1.14), 1913
1920–1941: Lefty Grove, 214
  (adjusted from actual 2.06), 1931
1942–1960: Whitey Ford, 204
  (adjusted from actual 2.01), 1958
1961–1988: Bob Gibson, 253
  (adjusted from actual 1.12), 1968

This is quite a different lineup from the traditional list of ERA leaders (which relegates pre-1900 pitching to the shadows), where of the 15 top spots, 14 are accorded to pitchers active from 1905 to 1918. Is there a baseball fan alive who thinks that all the great pitchers were created in that 14-year span and that the mold was then broken?

But enough expostulation and fulmination. Let's set some ground rules, define some terms that may still be unfamiliar after you've browsed through the Annual Record and Player and Pitcher registers, and get on with the show.

To be eligible for a lifetime pitching category that is stated as an average, a man must have pitched 1,500 or more innings, or 750 or more innings if he is a relief pitcher, in the major leagues; for a counting statistic, he must simply have attained the necessary quantity to crack the list. For a single season category expressed as an average, he must have pitched one inning per league scheduled game or have attained the necessary quantity (wins, strikeouts, saves) to head a counted list.

To be eligible for a lifetime batting category that is stated as an average, a man must have played in 1,000 or more games; for counting stats such as stolen bases, a Vince Coleman can take his place on the list despite his distance from 1,000 games played. And to reach the single-season batting lists, a man must have 3.1 plate appearances per scheduled game.

We provide tables of the top fielding performances, too, sorted by position as you would expect. But we go one step further and rank several *batting* categories by position, thus recognizing and illustrating the greater demands for fielding skill at such positions as shortstop, catcher, and second base, and the comparatively plentiful supply of batting talent in the outfield and at first base. As we establish a 1000-game minimum for inclusion in all but a few batting and baserunning categories, we likewise establish for these positional rankings a minimum of 1000 games played at the position. (This explains why Wade Boggs, for example, places among the leaders in several batting categories but is not to be found in the list of the best hitting third basemen; while he played in 1027 games through 1988, he still fell 48 short of the charmed circle at third base.)

For the three principal categories—Total Player Rating, Total Pitcher Index, and Total Baseball Ranking—we have introduced several variations. For example, TPR and TBR are shown 500 deep for lifetime leaders—sorted first by highest value; then alphabetically so that the reader may find a particular player without scanning 500 names; and last by the above-named eras, the top 25 in each. Total Pitcher Index is also sorted this way, but because far fewer pitchers than position players meet the longevity criteria, the lifetime groupings go 300 and 200 deep rather than 500 and 300. Ties are calculated to as many decimal places as needed to break them, but averages are shown to only three places. When two or more players are tied in an averaged category with a narrow base of data, such as a season's won-lost percentage, the reader can presume a numerical dead heat (and obviously this goes for counting stats, too—one man's 39 doubles are as good as another's). But where there is a tie for batting average, earned run average, or any of the sabermetric measures,

the reader may assume that the man listed above the other(s) has the minutely higher average.

Here are the few stats carried in this section that are not carried in the Annual Record or Registers, with definitions where the terms are not self-explanatory (see Glossary for formulas):

Batting, Baserunning, Fielding

Runs (scored) Per Game
Home Run Percentage   Home runs per 100 at bats
Bases on Balls Percentage   Walks (most) per 100 at bats
At-Bats Per Strikeout
Relative Batting Average   Normalized to league average
Isolated Power   Slugging average minus batting average
Extra Base Hits
Pinch Hits
Pinch Hit Batting Average
Pinch Hit Home Runs
Total Chances Per Game   Broken out by position
Chances Accepted Per Game   Broken out by position
Putouts   Broken out by position
Putouts Per Game   Broken out by position

Assists   Broken out by position
Assists Per Game   Broken out by position
Double Plays   Broken out by position

Pitching

Hit Batsmen
Wins Above League   A pitcher's won-lost record restated by adding his Pitching Wins above the league average to the record that a league-average pitcher would have had with the same number of decisions (for example, Tom Seaver goes 20–10 with 7 Pitching Wins; applying the 7 wins to a 15–15 mark in the same 30 decisions results in a WAL of 22–8).

Percentage of Team Wins
Relief Games
Pitchers' Batting Runs
Pitchers' Fielding Runs
Relief Wins
Relief Losses
Relief Innings Pitched
Relief Points   Relief wins plus saves minus losses

Games

1	Pete Rose	3562
2	Carl Yastrzemski	3308
3	Hank Aaron	3298
4	Ty Cobb	3034
5	Stan Musial	3026
6	Willie Mays	2992
7	Rusty Staub	2951
8	Brooks Robinson	2896
9	Al Kaline	2834
10	Eddie Collins	2826
11	Reggie Jackson	2820
12	Frank Robinson	2808
13	Honus Wagner	2792
14	Tris Speaker	2789
15	Tony Perez	2777
16	Mel Ott	2730
17	Graig Nettles	2700
18	Rabbit Maranville	2670
19	Joe Morgan	2649
20	Lou Brock	2616
21	Luis Aparicio	2599
22	Willie McCovey	2588
23	Darrell Evans	2580
24	Paul Waner	2549
25	Ernie Banks	2528
26	Sam Crawford	2517
27	Babe Ruth	2503
28	Dave Concepcion	2488
	Billy Williams	2488
30	Nap Lajoie	2480
31	Max Carey	2476
32	Rod Carew	2469
	Vada Pinson	2469
34	Ted Simmons	2456
35	Bill Dahlen	2443
36	Ron Fairly	2442
37	Harmon Killebrew	2435
38	Roberto Clemente	2433
39	Willie Davis	2429
40	Luke Appling	2422
41	Bill Buckner	2416
42	Zach Wheat	2410
43	Mickey Vernon	2409
44	Sam Rice	2404
45	Mickey Mantle	2401
46	Eddie Mathews	2391
47	Jake Beckley	2386
48	Bobby Wallace	2382
49	Enos Slaughter	2380
50	Buddy Bell	2371
51	George Davis	2368
	Al Oliver	2368
53	Nellie Fox	2367
54	Mike Schmidt	2362
55	Willie Stargell	2360
56	Jose Cruz	2353
57	Steve Garvey	2332
58	Bert Campaneris	2328
59	Charlie Gehringer	2323
60	Jimmie Foxx	2317
61	Frankie Frisch	2311
62	Harry Hooper	2308
63	Don Baylor	2292
	Ted Williams	2292
65	Goose Goslin	2287
66	Jimmy Dykes	2282
67	Cap Anson	2276
68	Lave Cross	2274
69	Dave Winfield	2269
70	Rogers Hornsby	2259
71	Larry Bowa	2247
72	Ron Santo	2243
73	Fred Clarke	2242
74	Doc Cramer	2239
75	Dwight Evans	2236
76	Chris Speier	2232
77	Red Schoendienst	2216
78	Al Simmons	2215
79	Joe Torre	2209
80	Tommy Corcoran	2200
81	Tony Taylor	2195
82	Richie Ashburn	2189
83	Bill Russell	2181
84	Chris Chambliss	2175
85	Joe Judge	2171
86	Charlie Grimm	2166
	Pee Wee Reese	2166
88	Lou Gehrig	2164
89	Bill Mazeroski	2163
90	Johnny Bench	2158
91	Tommy Leach	2156
92	Toby Harrah	2155
93	Harry Heilmann	2146
94	Duke Snider	2143
95	Bid McPhee	2135
96	Robin Yount	2131
97	Stuffy McInnis	2128
98	Orlando Cepeda	2124
	Joe Cronin	2124
100	Willie Keeler	2123

At Bats

1	Pete Rose	14053
2	Hank Aaron	12364
3	Carl Yastrzemski	11988
4	Ty Cobb	11434
5	Stan Musial	10972
6	Willie Mays	10881
7	Brooks Robinson	10654
8	Honus Wagner	10430
9	Lou Brock	10332
10	Luis Aparicio	10230
11	Tris Speaker	10207
12	Al Kaline	10116
13	Rabbit Maranville	10078
14	Frank Robinson	10006
15	Eddie Collins	9948
16	Reggie Jackson	9864
17	Tony Perez	9778
18	Rusty Staub	9720
19	Vada Pinson	9645
20	Nap Lajoie	9589
21	Sam Crawford	9570
22	Jake Beckley	9526
23	Paul Waner	9459
24	Mel Ott	9456
25	Roberto Clemente	9454
26	Ernie Banks	9421
27	Max Carey	9363
28	Billy Williams	9350
29	Rod Carew	9315
30	Joe Morgan	9277
31	Sam Rice	9269
32	Nellie Fox	9232
33	Bill Buckner	9178
34	Willie Davis	9174
35	Doc Cramer	9140
36	Frankie Frisch	9112
37	Zach Wheat	9106
38	Cap Anson	9101
39	Lave Cross	9068
40	Al Oliver	9049
41	Bill Dahlen	9031
	George Davis	9031
43	Graig Nettles	8986
44	Buddy Bell	8913
45	Charlie Gehringer	8860
46	Luke Appling	8856
47	Steve Garvey	8835
48	Tommy Corcoran	8804
49	Harry Hooper	8785
50	Al Simmons	8759
51	Mickey Vernon	8731
52	Dave Concepcion	8723
53	Darrell Evans	8697
54	Bert Campaneris	8684
55	Ted Simmons	8680
56	Goose Goslin	8656
57	Bobby Wallace	8618
58	Willie Keeler	8591
59	Fred Clarke	8568
60	Eddie Mathews	8537
61	Red Schoendienst	8479
62	Jesse Burkett	8421
	Dave Winfield	8421
64	Larry Bowa	8418
65	Babe Ruth	8399
66	Richie Ashburn	8365
67	Robin Yount	8293
68	Bid McPhee	8291
69	George Sisler	8267
70	Mike Schmidt	8204
71	Don Baylor	8198
72	Willie McCovey	8197
73	Rogers Hornsby	8173
74	Jimmy Ryan	8164
75	Harmon Killebrew	8147
76	Ron Santo	8143
77	Jimmie Foxx	8134
78	Mickey Mantle	8102
79	Pee Wee Reese	8058
80	Jimmy Dykes	8046
81	George Van Haltren	8021
82	Jim Rice	8016
83	Lou Gehrig	8001
84	Joe Kuhel	7984
85	Tommy Leach	7959
86	Enos Slaughter	7946
87	Orlando Cepeda	7927
	Willie Stargell	7927
89	Jose Cruz	7917
	Charlie Grimm	7917
91	Joe Judge	7898
92	Joe Torre	7874
93	Stuffy McInnis	7822
94	Roger Connor	7794
95	Harry Heilmann	7787
96	Lloyd Waner	7772
97	Dwight Evans	7761
98	Bill Mazeroski	7755
99	Billy Herman	7707
100	Ted Williams	7706

Runs

1	Ty Cobb	2245
2	Hank Aaron	2174
	Babe Ruth	2174
4	Pete Rose	2165
5	Willie Mays	2062
6	Stan Musial	1949
7	Lou Gehrig	1888
8	Tris Speaker	1881
9	Mel Ott	1859
10	Frank Robinson	1829
11	Eddie Collins	1819
12	Carl Yastrzemski	1816
13	Ted Williams	1798
14	Charlie Gehringer	1774
15	Jimmie Foxx	1751
16	Honus Wagner	1736
17	Jesse Burkett	1720
18	Cap Anson	1719
	Willie Keeler	1719
20	Billy Hamilton	1690
21	Bid McPhee	1678
22	Mickey Mantle	1677
23	Joe Morgan	1650
24	Jimmy Ryan	1642
25	George Van Haltren	1639
26	Paul Waner	1626
27	Al Kaline	1622
28	Roger Connor	1620
29	Fred Clarke	1619
30	Lou Brock	1610
31	Jake Beckley	1600
32	Ed Delahanty	1599
33	Bill Dahlen	1586
34	Rogers Hornsby	1579
35	Hugh Duffy	1553
36	Reggie Jackson	1551
37	Max Carey	1545
38	George Davis	1539
39	Frankie Frisch	1532
40	Dan Brouthers	1523
41	Tom Brown	1521
42	Sam Rice	1514
43	Eddie Mathews	1509
44	Al Simmons	1507
45	Nap Lajoie	1502
46	Harry Stovey	1492
47	Mike Schmidt	1487
48	Goose Goslin	1483
49	Arlie Latham	1478
50	Herman Long	1456
51	Jim O'Rourke	1446
52	Harry Hooper	1429
53	Dummy Hoy	1426
54	Rod Carew	1424
55	Joe Kelley	1421
56	Roberto Clemente	1416
57	Billy Williams	1410
58	Monte Ward	1408
59	Mike Griffin	1405
60	Sam Crawford	1391
61	Joe DiMaggio	1390
62	Vada Pinson	1366
63	Doc Cramer	1357
	King Kelly	1357
65	Tommy Leach	1355
66	Pee Wee Reese	1338
67	Luis Aparicio	1335
68	Lave Cross	1332
69	George Gore	1327
70	Richie Ashburn	1322
71	Luke Appling	1319
72	Patsy Donovan	1318
73	Dave Winfield	1314
74	Darrell Evans	1313
	Mike Tiernan	1313
76	Ernie Banks	1305
77	Jimmy Sheckard	1296
78	Kiki Cuyler	1295
79	Harry Heilmann	1291
80	Zach Wheat	1289
81	Dwight Evans	1287
	Heinie Manush	1287
83	George Sisler	1284
84	Harmon Killebrew	1283
85	Donie Bush	1280
86	Nellie Fox	1279
87	Fred Tenney	1278
88	Tony Perez	1272
89	Duke Snider	1259
90	Bobby Bonds	1258
91	Sam Thompson	1256
92	Rabbit Maranville	1255
93	Enos Slaughter	1247
94	Stan Hack	1239
	Bob Johnson	1239
96	Don Baylor	1236
	Joe Kuhel	1236
98	Robin Yount	1234
99	George Brett	1233
	Joe Cronin	1233

Runs per Game

1	Billy Hamilton	1.06
2	George Gore	1.01
3	Harry Stovey	1.00
4	King Kelly	.93
5	John McGraw	.93
6	Mike Griffin	.93
7	Dan Brouthers	.91
8	Arlie Latham	.91
9	Hugh Duffy	.89
10	Sam Thompson	.89
11	Mike Tiernan	.89
12	Lou Gehrig	.87
13	Ed Delahanty	.87
14	Babe Ruth	.87
15	Buck Ewing	.86
16	Tom Brown	.85
17	Hardy Richardson	.84
18	Tommy McCarthy	.84
19	Tip O'Neill	.83
20	Cupid Childs	.83
21	Jesse Burkett	.83
22	Denny Lyons	.83
23	Curt Welch	.83
24	George Van Haltren	.83
25	Jimmy Ryan	.82
26	Earle Combs	.82
27	Jim O'Rourke	.82
28	Roger Connor	.81
29	Willie Keeler	.81
30	Pete Browning	.81
31	Red Rolfe	.80
32	Joe DiMaggio	.80
33	Rickey Henderson	.80
34	Dummy Hoy	.79
35	John Reilly	.79
36	Bid McPhee	.79
37	Ted Williams	.78
38	Henry Larkin	.78
39	Herman Long	.78
40	Hughie Jennings	.77
41	Monte Ward	.77
42	Joe Kelley	.77
43	Charlie Gehringer	.76
44	Jimmie Foxx	.76
45	Cap Anson	.76
46	Hank Greenberg	.75
47	George Wood	.75
48	George Pinkney	.75
49	Dom DiMaggio	.75
50	Ed McKean	.74
51	Ty Cobb	.74
52	Mike Smith	.74
53	Ned Hanlon	.73
54	Earl Averill	.73
55	Oyster Burns	.73
56	Jack Rowe	.73
57	Paul Hines	.73
58	Patsy Donovan	.72
59	Fred Clarke	.72
60	Max Bishop	.72
61	Ezra Sutton	.72
62	Charlie Comiskey	.72
63	Lu Blue	.71
64	Sam Wise	.71
65	Paul Molitor	.71
66	Mickey Cochrane	.70
67	Tim Raines	.70
68	Tommy Henrich	.70
69	Mike Hornung	.70
70	Blondie Purcell	.70
71	Rogers Hornsby	.70
72	Mickey Mantle	.70
73	Billy Shindle	.70
74	Paul Radford	.69
75	Billy Nash	.69
76	Wade Boggs	.69
77	Dave Foutz	.69
78	Kiki Cuyler	.69
79	Willie Mays	.69
80	Roy Thomas	.69
81	Jackie Robinson	.69
82	Tommy Dowd	.68
83	Johnny Pesky	.68
84	Mel Ott	.68
85	Bobby Bonds	.68
86	Al Simmons	.68
87	Harlond Clift	.68
88	Billy Werber	.68
89	Tris Speaker	.67
90	Ned Williamson	.67
91	Jake Beckley	.67
92	Ross Youngs	.67
93	Jack Glasscock	.67
94	Chuck Klein	.67
95	Ben Chapman	.67
96	Ron LeFlore	.67
97	Bob Johnson	.67
98	Frankie Frisch	.66
99	Kip Selbach	.66
100	Cub Stricker	.66

Hits

#	Player	Total
1	Pete Rose	4256
2	Ty Cobb	4190
3	Hank Aaron	3771
4	Stan Musial	3630
5	Tris Speaker	3514
6	Carl Yastrzemski	3419
7	Honus Wagner	3415
8	Eddie Collins	3310
9	Willie Mays	3283
10	Nap Lajoie	3242
11	Paul Waner	3152
12	Rod Carew	3053
13	Lou Brock	3023
14	Al Kaline	3007
15	Roberto Clemente	3000
16	Cap Anson	2995
17	Sam Rice	2987
18	Sam Crawford	2961
19	Frank Robinson	2943
20	Willie Keeler	2932
21	Jake Beckley	2930
	Rogers Hornsby	2930
23	Al Simmons	2927
24	Zach Wheat	2884
25	Frankie Frisch	2880
26	Mel Ott	2876
27	Babe Ruth	2873
28	Jesse Burkett	2850
29	Brooks Robinson	2848
30	Charlie Gehringer	2839
31	George Sisler	2812
32	Vada Pinson	2757
33	Luke Appling	2749
34	Al Oliver	2743
35	Goose Goslin	2735
36	Tony Perez	2732
37	Lou Gehrig	2721
38	Rusty Staub	2716
39	Billy Williams	2711
40	Doc Cramer	2705
41	Luis Aparicio	2677
42	Fred Clarke	2672
43	Bill Buckner	2669
44	Max Carey	2665
45	Nellie Fox	2663
46	George Davis	2660
	Harry Heilmann	2660
48	Ted Williams	2654
49	Jimmie Foxx	2646
50	Lave Cross	2644
51	Rabbit Maranville	2605
52	Steve Garvey	2599
53	Ed Delahanty	2597
54	Reggie Jackson	2584
55	Ernie Banks	2583
56	Richie Ashburn	2574
57	Willie Davis	2561
58	George Van Haltren	2532
59	Heinie Manush	2524
60	Joe Morgan	2517
61	Jimmy Ryan	2502
62	Buddy Bell	2499
63	Mickey Vernon	2495
64	Ted Simmons	2472
65	Joe Medwick	2471
66	Roger Connor	2467
67	Harry Hooper	2466
68	Lloyd Waner	2459
69	Bill Dahlen	2457
70	Red Schoendienst	2449
71	Dave Winfield	2421
72	Pie Traynor	2416
73	Mickey Mantle	2415
74	Robin Yount	2407
75	Stuffy McInnis	2405
76	Jim Rice	2403
77	George Brett	2399
78	Enos Slaughter	2383
79	Edd Roush	2376
80	Joe Judge	2352
81	Orlando Cepeda	2351
82	Billy Herman	2345
83	Joe Torre	2342
84	Dave Concepcion	2326
	Jake Daubert	2326
86	Eddie Mathews	2315
87	Jim Bottomley	2313
88	Bobby Wallace	2309
89	Jim O'Rourke	2304
90	Kiki Cuyler	2299
	Charlie Grimm	2299
92	Dan Brouthers	2296
93	Joe Cronin	2285
94	Hugh Duffy	2282
95	Dave Parker	2270
96	Jimmy Dykes	2256
97	Ron Santo	2254
98	Patsy Donovan	2253
99	Tommy Corcoran	2252
100	Jose Cruz	2251

Doubles

#	Player	Total
1	Tris Speaker	793
2	Pete Rose	746
3	Stan Musial	725
4	Ty Cobb	724
5	Nap Lajoie	657
6	Carl Yastrzemski	646
7	Honus Wagner	640
8	Hank Aaron	624
9	Paul Waner	603
10	Charlie Gehringer	574
11	Harry Heilmann	542
12	Rogers Hornsby	541
13	Joe Medwick	540
14	Al Simmons	539
15	Lou Gehrig	534
16	Al Oliver	529
17	Cap Anson	528
	Frank Robinson	528
19	Ted Williams	525
20	Willie Mays	523
21	Ed Delahanty	522
22	Joe Cronin	515
23	Babe Ruth	506
24	Tony Perez	505
25	Goose Goslin	500
26	Rusty Staub	499
27	Al Kaline	498
	Sam Rice	498
29	Bill Buckner	494
30	Heinie Manush	491
31	Mickey Vernon	490
32	George Brett	488
	Mel Ott	488
34	Lou Brock	486
	Billy Herman	486
36	Vada Pinson	485
37	Hal McRae	484
38	Ted Simmons	483
39	Brooks Robinson	482
40	Zach Wheat	476
41	Jake Beckley	473
42	Frankie Frisch	466
43	Jim Bottomley	465
44	Reggie Jackson	463
45	Dan Brouthers	460
46	Sam Crawford	458
	Jimmie Foxx	458
48	Jimmy Dykes	453
49	Jimmy Ryan	451
50	George Davis	450
51	Joe Morgan	449
52	Rod Carew	445
53	George Burns	444
54	Dave Parker	443
	Robin Yount	443
56	Dick Bartell	442
57	Roger Connor	441
58	Luke Appling	440
	Roberto Clemente	440
	Steve Garvey	440
61	Eddie Collins	437
62	Cesar Cedeno	436
	Joe Sewell	436
64	Wally Moses	435
65	Billy Williams	434
66	Joe Judge	433
67	Dwight Evans	429
68	Red Schoendienst	427
69	Sherry Magee	425
	George Sisler	425
71	Willie Stargell	423
72	Buddy Bell	421
73	Max Carey	419
74	Orlando Cepeda	417
75	Keith Hernandez	416
76	Cecil Cooper	415
77	Jim O'Rourke	414
78	Bill Dahlen	413
	Enos Slaughter	413
80	Joe Kuhel	412
	Dave Winfield	412
82	Lave Cross	411
83	Ernie Banks	407
	Ben Chapman	407
85	Earl Averill	401
	Marty McManus	401
	Mike Schmidt	401
88	Babe Herman	399
	Gee Walker	399
90	Chuck Klein	398
91	Doc Cramer	396
	Gabby Hartnett	396
	Bob Johnson	396
94	Willie Davis	395
95	Luis Aparicio	394
	Kiki Cuyler	394
	Charlie Grimm	394
98	Bobby Veach	393
99	Chris Chambliss	392
	Del Pratt	392

Triples

#	Player	Total
1	Sam Crawford	309
2	Ty Cobb	294
3	Honus Wagner	252
4	Jake Beckley	243
5	Roger Connor	233
6	Tris Speaker	223
7	Fred Clarke	220
8	Dan Brouthers	205
9	Joe Kelley	194
10	Paul Waner	190
11	Bid McPhee	188
12	Eddie Collins	186
13	Ed Delahanty	185
14	Sam Rice	184
15	Edd Roush	183
16	Jesse Burkett	182
17	Ed Konetchy	181
18	Buck Ewing	178
19	Rabbit Maranville	177
	Stan Musial	177
21	Harry Stovey	175
22	Goose Goslin	173
23	Tommy Leach	172
	Zach Wheat	172
25	Rogers Hornsby	169
26	Joe Jackson	168
27	Roberto Clemente	166
	Sherry Magee	166
29	Jake Daubert	165
	George Davis	165
31	Elmer Flick	164
	George Sisler	164
	Pie Traynor	164
34	Bill Dahlen	163
	Lou Gehrig	163
	Nap Lajoie	163
37	Mike Tiernan	162
38	George Van Haltren	161
39	Harry Hooper	160
	Heinie Manush	160
	Sam Thompson	160
42	Max Carey	159
	Joe Judge	159
44	Ed McKean	158
45	Kiki Cuyler	157
	Jimmy Ryan	157
47	Tommy Corcoran	155
48	Earle Combs	154
49	Jim Bottomley	151
	Harry Heilmann	151
51	Kip Selbach	149
	Al Simmons	149
53	Wally Pipp	148
	Enos Slaughter	148
55	Bobby Veach	147
56	Harry Davis	146
	Charlie Gehringer	146
58	Willie Keeler	145
59	Bobby Wallace	143
60	Lou Brock	141
61	Willie Mays	140
62	John Reilly	139
63	Tom Brown	138
	Willie Davis	138
	Frankie Frisch	138
	Jimmy Williams	138
67	Babe Ruth	136
	Jimmy Sheckard	136
	Mike Smith	136
70	Lave Cross	135
	Pete Rose	135
72	Shano Collins	133
73	Jim O'Rourke	132
	George Wood	132
75	Joe DiMaggio	131
	Buck Freeman	131
77	Buddy Myer	130
78	Oyster Burns	129
	Larry Gardner	129
80	Earl Averill	128
	Arky Vaughan	128
82	Vada Pinson	127
83	Hardy Richardson	126
84	Jimmie Foxx	125
85	John Anderson	124
	Cap Anson	124
	Hal Chase	124
	Frank Schulte	124
89	Larry Doyle	123
	Duke Farrell	123
	Willie Wilson	123
92	Dummy Hoy	121
93	Mickey Vernon	120
94	Fred Pfeffer	119
95	Joe Cronin	118
	Hugh Duffy	118
	Lloyd Waner	118
98	5 players tied	117

Triples (by era)

1876-1892

#	Player	Total
1	Roger Connor	233
2	Dan Brouthers	205
3	Bid McPhee	188
4	Buck Ewing	178
5	Harry Stovey	175
6	Sam Thompson	160
7	John Reilly	139
8	Tom Brown	138
9	Jim O'Rourke	132
	George Wood	132
11	Oyster Burns	129
12	Hardy Richardson	126
13	Cap Anson	124
14	Fred Pfeffer	119
15	Bill Kuehne	115

1893-1919

#	Player	Total
1	Sam Crawford	309
2	Ty Cobb	294
3	Honus Wagner	252
4	Jake Beckley	243
5	Tris Speaker	223
6	Fred Clarke	220
7	Joe Kelley	194
8	Eddie Collins	186
9	Ed Delahanty	185
10	Jesse Burkett	182
11	Ed Konetchy	181
12	Tommy Leach	172
	Zach Wheat	172
14	Joe Jackson	168
15	Sherry Magee	166

1920-1941

#	Player	Total
1	Paul Waner	190
2	Sam Rice	184
3	Edd Roush	183
4	Rabbit Maranville	177
5	Goose Goslin	173
6	Rogers Hornsby	169
7	George Sisler	164
	Pie Traynor	164
9	Lou Gehrig	163
10	Heinie Manush	160
11	Max Carey	159
	Joe Judge	159
13	Kiki Cuyler	157
14	Earle Combs	154
15	2 players tied	151

1942-1960

#	Player	Total
1	Stan Musial	177
2	Enos Slaughter	148
3	Joe DiMaggio	131
4	Mickey Vernon	120
5	Nellie Fox	112
6	Wally Moses	110
7	Richie Ashburn	109
8	Bill Bruton	102
	Jeff Heath	102
10	Phil Cavarretta	99
11	Dixie Walker	96
12	Bob Elliott	94
13	Bobby Doerr	89
14	Duke Snider	85
15	2 players tied	83

1961-1988

#	Player	Total
1	Roberto Clemente	166
2	Lou Brock	141
3	Willie Mays	140
4	Willie Davis	138
5	Pete Rose	135
6	Vada Pinson	127
7	Willie Wilson	123
8	George Brett	117
9	Rod Carew	112
10	Robin Yount	102
11	Larry Bowa	99
12	Hank Aaron	98
	Garry Templeton	98
14	Joe Morgan	96
15	Jose Cruz	94

Home Runs

1	Hank Aaron	755
2	Babe Ruth	714
3	Willie Mays	660
4	Frank Robinson	586
5	Harmon Killebrew	573
6	Reggie Jackson	563
7	Mike Schmidt	542
8	Mickey Mantle	536
9	Jimmie Foxx	534
10	Willie McCovey	521
	Ted Williams	521
12	Ernie Banks	512
	Eddie Mathews	512
14	Mel Ott	511
15	Lou Gehrig	493
16	Stan Musial	475
	Willie Stargell	475
18	Carl Yastrzemski	452
19	Dave Kingman	442
20	Billy Williams	426
21	Duke Snider	407
22	Darrell Evans	403
23	Al Kaline	399
24	Graig Nettles	390
25	Johnny Bench	389
26	Frank Howard	382
27	Orlando Cepeda	379
	Tony Perez	379
	Jim Rice	379
30	Norm Cash	377
31	Rocky Colavito	374
32	Gil Hodges	370
33	Ralph Kiner	369
34	Joe DiMaggio	361
35	Johnny Mize	359
36	Yogi Berra	358
37	Dave Winfield	357
38	Lee May	354
39	Dick Allen	351
40	George Foster	348
41	Dwight Evans	346
42	Ron Santo	342
43	Boog Powell	339
44	Don Baylor	338
45	Joe Adcock	336
46	Dale Murphy	334
47	Eddie Murray	333
48	Bobby Bonds	332
49	Hank Greenberg	331
50	Willie Horton	325
51	Carlton Fisk	323
52	Roy Sievers	318
53	Ron Cey	316
54	Reggie Smith	314
55	Greg Luzinski	307
	Al Simmons	307
57	Gary Carter	302
58	Rogers Hornsby	301
59	Chuck Klein	300
60	Andre Dawson	298
61	Rusty Staub	292
62	Jim Wynn	291
63	Fred Lynn	289
64	Del Ennis	288
	Bob Johnson	288
	Hank Sauer	288
67	Frank Thomas	286
68	Dave Parker	285
69	Ken Boyer	282
70	Ted Kluszewski	279
71	Rudy York	277
72	Roger Maris	275
73	Steve Garvey	272
74	George Scott	271
75	Joe Morgan	268
	Brooks Robinson	268
	Gorman Thomas	268
78	George Hendrick	267
79	Vic Wertz	266
80	Bobby Thomson	264
81	Bob Allison	256
	Jack Clark	256
	Larry Parrish	256
	Vada Pinson	256
85	George Brett	255
	John Mayberry	255
87	Larry Doby	253
	Joe Gordon	253
	Andy Thornton	253
90	Bobby Murcer	252
	Joe Torre	252
92	Cy Williams	251
93	Goose Goslin	248
	Ted Simmons	248
95	Vern Stephens	247
96	Ken Singleton	246
97	Deron Johnson	245
98	Lance Parrish	244
	Hack Wilson	244
100	4 players tied	242

Home Runs (by era)

1876-1892

1	Roger Connor	137
2	Sam Thompson	127
3	Harry Stovey	121
4	Dan Brouthers	106
5	Cap Anson	97
6	Fred Pfeffer	94
7	Jack Clements	77
8	Jerry Denny	74
9	Buck Ewing	71
10	King Kelly	69
11	Hardy Richardson	68
	George Wood	68
13	John Reilly	67
14	Oyster Burns	65
	Bug Holliday	65

1893-1919

1	Zach Wheat	132
2	Gavvy Cravath	119
3	Ty Cobb	118
	Jimmy Ryan	118
	Tilly Walker	118
6	Tris Speaker	117
7	Hugh Duffy	105
	Mike Tiernan	105
9	Ed Delahanty	101
	Honus Wagner	101
11	Sam Crawford	98
12	Frank Baker	96
13	Frank Schulte	93
14	Herman Long	91
15	Jake Beckley	87

1920-1941

1	Babe Ruth	714
2	Jimmie Foxx	534
3	Mel Ott	511
4	Lou Gehrig	493
5	Hank Greenberg	331
6	Al Simmons	307
7	Rogers Hornsby	301
8	Chuck Klein	300
9	Bob Johnson	288
10	Cy Williams	251
11	Goose Goslin	248
12	Hack Wilson	244
13	Wally Berger	242
14	Dolph Camilli	239
15	Earl Averill	238

1942-1960

1	Mickey Mantle	536
2	Ted Williams	521
3	Eddie Mathews	512
4	Stan Musial	475
5	Duke Snider	407
6	Gil Hodges	370
7	Ralph Kiner	369
8	Joe DiMaggio	361
9	Johnny Mize	359
10	Yogi Berra	358
11	Joe Adcock	336
12	Roy Sievers	318
13	Del Ennis	288
	Hank Sauer	288
15	Frank Thomas	286

1961-1988

1	Hank Aaron	755
2	Willie Mays	660
3	Frank Robinson	586
4	Harmon Killebrew	573
5	Reggie Jackson	563
6	Mike Schmidt	542
7	Willie McCovey	521
8	Ernie Banks	512
9	Willie Stargell	475
10	Carl Yastrzemski	452
11	Dave Kingman	442
12	Billy Williams	426
13	Darrell Evans	403
14	Al Kaline	399
15	Graig Nettles	390

Home Run Percentage

1	Babe Ruth	8.50
2	Ralph Kiner	7.09
3	Harmon Killebrew	7.03
4	Ted Williams	6.76
5	Dave Kingman	6.62
6	Mickey Mantle	6.62
7	Mike Schmidt	6.61
8	Jimmie Foxx	6.57
9	Hank Greenberg	6.37
10	Willie McCovey	6.36
11	Lou Gehrig	6.16
12	Hank Aaron	6.11
13	Willie Mays	6.07
14	Hank Sauer	6.01
15	Eddie Mathews	6.00
16	Willie Stargell	5.99
17	Frank Howard	5.89
18	Frank Robinson	5.86
19	Bob Horner	5.77
20	Roy Campanella	5.76
21	Rocky Colavito	5.75
22	Gus Zernial	5.74
23	Gorman Thomas	5.73
24	Reggie Jackson	5.71
25	Dick Stuart	5.70
26	Duke Snider	5.68
27	Norm Cash	5.62
28	Johnny Mize	5.57
29	Dick Allen	5.54
30	Ernie Banks	5.43
31	Dale Murphy	5.41
32	Mel Ott	5.40
33	Roger Maris	5.39
34	Joe DiMaggio	5.29
35	Gil Hodges	5.26
36	Wally Post	5.24
37	Al Rosen	5.15
38	Jesse Barfield	5.14
39	Hack Wilson	5.13
40	Bob Allison	5.09
41	Joe Adcock	5.09
42	Johnny Bench	5.08
43	Boog Powell	5.07
44	Nate Colbert	5.06
45	Charlie Keller	4.99
46	Roy Sievers	4.98
47	Cliff Johnson	4.97
48	Don Mincher	4.97
49	George Foster	4.96
50	Eddie Murray	4.86
51	Tom Brunansky	4.86
52	Tony Armas	4.84
53	Jack Clark	4.81
54	Andy Thornton	4.78
55	Orlando Cepeda	4.78
56	Leon Wagner	4.77
57	Jim Lemon	4.76
58	Yogi Berra	4.74
59	Don Demeter	4.73
60	Larry Doby	4.73
61	Jim Rice	4.73
62	Lance Parrish	4.73
63	Greg Luzinski	4.72
64	Bobby Bonds	4.71
65	Ted Kluszewski	4.71
66	Rudy York	4.70
67	Pedro Guerrero	4.69
68	Wally Berger	4.69
69	John Mayberry	4.68
70	Kirk Gibson	4.66
71	Lee May	4.65
72	Darrell Evans	4.63
73	Kent Hrbek	4.63
74	Chuck Klein	4.63
75	Gene Tenace	4.58
76	Charlie Maxwell	4.56
77	Billy Williams	4.56
78	Frank Thomas	4.55
79	Fred Lynn	4.53
80	Jim Ray Hart	4.49
81	Carlton Fisk	4.47
82	Gary Roenicke	4.47
83	Dolph Camilli	4.46
84	Reggie Smith	4.46
85	Dwight Evans	4.46
86	Woodie Held	4.45
87	Willie Horton	4.45
88	Oscar Gamble	4.44
89	Joe Gordon	4.43
90	Hal Trosky	4.42
91	Ron Cey	4.41
92	Wes Covington	4.40
93	Jim Wynn	4.37
94	Dale Long	4.37
95	Vic Wertz	4.36
96	Andre Dawson	4.36
97	Graig Nettles	4.34
98	Jeff Burroughs	4.34
99	Jason Thompson	4.33
100	Stan Musial	4.33

Home Run Pctg. (by era)

1876-1892

1	Sam Thompson	2.12
2	Harry Stovey	1.97
3	Jack Clements	1.80
4	Roger Connor	1.76
5	Dan Brouthers	1.58
6	Jerry Denny	1.50
7	Denny Lyons	1.44
8	Charlie Bennett	1.44
9	Fred Pfeffer	1.43
10	John Reilly	1.43
11	Oyster Burns	1.40
12	Ned Williamson	1.38
13	Buck Ewing	1.32
14	George Wood	1.27
15	Tip O'Neill	1.22

1893-1919

1	Gavvy Cravath	3.01
2	Tilly Walker	2.33
3	Buck Freeman	1.95
4	Mike Tiernan	1.78
5	Fred Luderus	1.73
6	Frank Baker	1.60
7	Hugh Duffy	1.49
8	Charlie Hickman	1.48
9	Zach Wheat	1.45
10	Jimmy Ryan	1.45
11	Frank Schulte	1.42
12	Casey Stengel	1.40
13	Ed Delahanty	1.35
14	Mike Donlin	1.32
15	Chief Wilson	1.28

1920-1941

1	Babe Ruth	8.50
2	Jimmie Foxx	6.57
3	Hank Greenberg	6.37
4	Lou Gehrig	6.16
5	Mel Ott	5.40
6	Hack Wilson	5.13
7	Wally Berger	4.69
8	Chuck Klein	4.63
9	Dolph Camilli	4.46
10	Hal Trosky	4.42
11	Bob Johnson	4.16
12	Ken Williams	4.03
13	Earl Averill	3.75
14	Cy Williams	3.70
15	Rogers Hornsby	3.68

1942-1960

1	Ralph Kiner	7.09
2	Ted Williams	6.76
3	Mickey Mantle	6.62
4	Hank Sauer	6.01
5	Eddie Mathews	6.00
6	Roy Campanella	5.76
7	Gus Zernial	5.74
8	Duke Snider	5.68
9	Johnny Mize	5.57
10	Joe DiMaggio	5.29
11	Gil Hodges	5.26
12	Wally Post	5.24
13	Al Rosen	5.15
14	Joe Adcock	5.09
15	Charlie Keller	4.99

1961-1988

1	Harmon Killebrew	7.03
2	Dave Kingman	6.62
3	Mike Schmidt	6.61
4	Willie McCovey	6.36
5	Hank Aaron	6.11
6	Willie Mays	6.07
7	Willie Stargell	5.99
8	Frank Howard	5.89
9	Frank Robinson	5.86
10	Bob Horner	5.77
11	Rocky Colavito	5.75
12	Gorman Thomas	5.73
13	Reggie Jackson	5.71
14	Dick Stuart	5.70
15	Norm Cash	5.62

Total Bases

1	Hank Aaron	6856
2	Stan Musial	6134
3	Willie Mays	6066
4	Ty Cobb	5856
5	Babe Ruth	5793
6	Pete Rose	5752
7	Carl Yastrzemski	5539
8	Frank Robinson	5373
9	Tris Speaker	5104
10	Lou Gehrig	5060
11	Mel Ott	5041
12	Jimmie Foxx	4956
13	Ted Williams	4884
14	Honus Wagner	4862
15	Al Kaline	4852
16	Reggie Jackson	4834
17	Rogers Hornsby	4712
18	Ernie Banks	4706
19	Al Simmons	4685
20	Billy Williams	4599
21	Tony Perez	4532
22	Mickey Mantle	4511
23	Roberto Clemente	4492
24	Nap Lajoie	4474
	Paul Waner	4474
26	Eddie Mathews	4349
	Mike Schmidt	4349
28	Sam Crawford	4331
29	Goose Goslin	4325
30	Brooks Robinson	4270
31	Vada Pinson	4264
32	Eddie Collins	4260
33	Charlie Gehringer	4257
34	Lou Brock	4238
35	Willie McCovey	4219
36	Willie Stargell	4190
37	Rusty Staub	4185
38	Jake Beckley	4150
39	Harmon Killebrew	4143
40	Zach Wheat	4100
41	Al Oliver	4083
42	Cap Anson	4062
43	Jim Rice	4057
44	Harry Heilmann	4053
45	Dave Winfield	4052
46	Rod Carew	3998
47	Joe Morgan	3962
48	Orlando Cepeda	3959
49	Sam Rice	3955
50	Joe DiMaggio	3948
51	Steve Garvey	3941
52	Frankie Frisch	3937
53	George Brett	3886
54	George Sisler	3868
55	Duke Snider	3865
56	Joe Medwick	3852
57	Ted Simmons	3793
58	Ed Delahanty	3792
59	Roger Connor	3785
60	Graig Nettles	3779
	Ron Santo	3779
62	Willie Davis	3778
63	Bill Buckner	3775
64	Darrell Evans	3768
65	Jesse Burkett	3759
66	Mickey Vernon	3741
67	Jim Bottomley	3737
68	Dwight Evans	3713
69	Dave Parker	3708
70	Fred Clarke	3674
71	Heinie Manush	3665
72	George Davis	3659
73	Johnny Bench	3644
74	Yogi Berra	3643
75	Buddy Bell	3635
76	Johnny Mize	3621
	Jimmy Ryan	3621
78	Robin Yount	3615
79	Max Carey	3609
80	Enos Slaughter	3599
81	Don Baylor	3571
82	Willie Keeler	3566
83	Joe Torre	3560
84	Joe Cronin	3546
85	Luke Appling	3528
86	Chuck Klein	3522
87	Luis Aparicio	3504
88	Bob Johnson	3501
89	Lee May	3495
90	Dan Brouthers	3484
91	Lave Cross	3466
92	Bill Dahlen	3448
93	Ken Boyer	3443
94	Reggie Smith	3439
95	Doc Cramer	3430
96	Cecil Cooper	3424
97	Del Ennis	3423
	Rabbit Maranville	3423
99	Gil Hodges	3422
100	Eddie Murray	3421

Runs Batted In

1	Hank Aaron	2297
2	Babe Ruth	2209
3	Lou Gehrig	1990
4	Stan Musial	1951
5	Ty Cobb	1933
6	Jimmie Foxx	1922
7	Willie Mays	1903
8	Cap Anson	1879
9	Mel Ott	1860
10	Carl Yastrzemski	1844
11	Ted Williams	1839
12	Al Simmons	1827
13	Frank Robinson	1812
14	Honus Wagner	1732
15	Reggie Jackson	1702
16	Tony Perez	1652
17	Ernie Banks	1636
18	Goose Goslin	1609
19	Nap Lajoie	1599
20	Rogers Hornsby	1584
	Harmon Killebrew	1584
22	Al Kaline	1583
23	Jake Beckley	1575
24	Mike Schmidt	1567
25	Willie McCovey	1555
26	Willie Stargell	1540
27	Harry Heilmann	1538
28	Joe DiMaggio	1537
29	Tris Speaker	1528
30	Sam Crawford	1525
31	Mickey Mantle	1509
32	Billy Williams	1475
33	Rusty Staub	1466
34	Ed Delahanty	1464
35	Eddie Mathews	1453
36	Dave Winfield	1438
37	George Davis	1435
38	Yogi Berra	1430
39	Charlie Gehringer	1427
40	Joe Cronin	1424
41	Jim Rice	1423
42	Jim Bottomley	1422
43	Ted Simmons	1389
44	Joe Medwick	1383
45	Johnny Bench	1376
46	Orlando Cepeda	1365
47	Brooks Robinson	1357
48	Johnny Mize	1337
49	Duke Snider	1333
50	Ron Santo	1331
51	Al Oliver	1326
52	Roger Connor	1322
53	Darrell Evans	1315
54	Graig Nettles	1314
	Pete Rose	1314
56	Mickey Vernon	1311
57	Paul Waner	1309
58	Steve Garvey	1308
59	Roberto Clemente	1305
60	Enos Slaughter	1304
61	Eddie Collins	1299
	Sam Thompson	1299
63	Del Ennis	1284
64	Bob Johnson	1283
65	Don Baylor	1276
	Hank Greenberg	1276
67	Gil Hodges	1274
68	Pie Traynor	1273
69	Zach Wheat	1248
70	Bobby Doerr	1247
71	Dave Parker	1245
72	Frankie Frisch	1244
	Lee May	1244
74	George Foster	1239
75	Bill Dahlen	1233
76	George Brett	1231
77	Bill Dickey	1210
	Dave Kingman	1210
79	Chuck Klein	1201
80	Bob Elliott	1195
81	Joe Kelley	1194
82	Tony Lazzeri	1191
83	Eddie Murray	1190
84	Bill Buckner	1189
85	Boog Powell	1187
86	Joe Torre	1185
87	Dwight Evans	1183
	Heinie Manush	1183
89	Gabby Hartnett	1179
90	Vic Wertz	1178
91	Sherry Magee	1176
92	George Sisler	1175
93	Vern Stephens	1174
94	Vada Pinson	1170
95	Bobby Veach	1166
96	Earl Averill	1164
97	Willie Horton	1163
98	Rocky Colavito	1159
99	Rudy York	1152
100	Roy Sievers	1147

Runs Batted In (by era)

1876-1892

1	Cap Anson	1879
2	Roger Connor	1322
3	Sam Thompson	1299
4	Fred Pfeffer	1019
5	Jim O'Rourke	1010
6	Buck Ewing	883
7	Monte Ward	867
8	Deacon White	756
9	Tom Burns	733
10	Jerry Denny	667
	Ned Williamson	667
12	Jack Rowe	644
13	John Morrill	643
14	Bug Holliday	617
15	Walt Wilmot	594

1893-1919

1	Ty Cobb	1933
2	Honus Wagner	1732
3	Nap Lajoie	1599
4	Jake Beckley	1575
5	Tris Speaker	1528
6	Sam Crawford	1525
7	Ed Delahanty	1464
8	George Davis	1435
9	Eddie Collins	1299
10	Zach Wheat	1248
11	Bill Dahlen	1233
12	Joe Kelley	1194
13	Sherry Magee	1176
14	Bobby Veach	1166
15	Bobby Wallace	1121

1920-1941

1	Babe Ruth	2209
2	Lou Gehrig	1990
3	Jimmie Foxx	1922
4	Mel Ott	1860
5	Al Simmons	1827
6	Goose Goslin	1609
7	Rogers Hornsby	1584
8	Harry Heilmann	1538
9	Charlie Gehringer	1427
10	Joe Cronin	1424
11	Jim Bottomley	1422
12	Joe Medwick	1383
13	Paul Waner	1309
14	Bob Johnson	1283
15	Hank Greenberg	1276

1942-1960

1	Stan Musial	1951
2	Ted Williams	1839
3	Joe DiMaggio	1537
4	Mickey Mantle	1509
5	Eddie Mathews	1453
6	Yogi Berra	1430
7	Johnny Mize	1337
8	Duke Snider	1333
9	Mickey Vernon	1311
10	Enos Slaughter	1304
11	Del Ennis	1284
12	Gil Hodges	1274
13	Bobby Doerr	1247
14	Bob Elliott	1195
15	Vic Wertz	1178

1961-1988

1	Hank Aaron	2297
2	Willie Mays	1903
3	Carl Yastrzemski	1844
4	Frank Robinson	1812
5	Reggie Jackson	1702
6	Tony Perez	1652
7	Ernie Banks	1636
8	Harmon Killebrew	1584
9	Al Kaline	1583
10	Mike Schmidt	1567
11	Willie McCovey	1555
12	Willie Stargell	1540
13	Billy Williams	1475
14	Rusty Staub	1466
15	Dave Winfield	1438

Runs Batted In per Game

1	Sam Thompson	.92
2	Lou Gehrig	.92
3	Hank Greenberg	.92
4	Joe DiMaggio	.89
5	Babe Ruth	.88
6	Jimmie Foxx	.83
7	Cap Anson	.83
8	Al Simmons	.82
9	Ted Williams	.80
10	Ed Delahanty	.80
11	Hack Wilson	.79
12	Bob Meusel	.76
13	Hal Trosky	.75
14	Rudy York	.72
15	Harry Heilmann	.72
16	Jim Bottomley	.71
17	Johnny Mize	.71
18	Roy Campanella	.70
19	Goose Goslin	.70
20	Rogers Hornsby	.70
21	Jim Rice	.70
22	Earl Averill	.70
23	Joe Medwick	.70
24	Hank Aaron	.70
25	Ralph Kiner	.69
26	Bob Johnson	.69
27	Al Rosen	.69
28	Chuck Klein	.69
29	Tony Lazzeri	.68
30	Vern Stephens	.68
31	Mel Ott	.68
32	Bill Dickey	.68
33	Del Ennis	.67
34	Yogi Berra	.67
35	Bob Horner	.67
36	Buck Ewing	.67
37	Joe Cronin	.67
38	Bobby Doerr	.67
39	Dick Stuart	.67
40	Wally Berger	.67
41	Mike Schmidt	.66
42	Roger Connor	.66
43	Jake Beckley	.66
44	Pie Traynor	.66
45	Eddie Murray	.65
46	Ken Williams	.65
47	Willie Stargell	.65
48	Harmon Killebrew	.65
49	Charlie Keller	.65
50	Chick Hafey	.65
51	Ernie Banks	.65
52	Glenn Wright	.65
53	Jackie Jensen	.65
54	Frank Robinson	.65
55	Nap Lajoie	.64
56	Stan Musial	.64
57	Joe Kelley	.64
58	Orlando Cepeda	.64
59	Babe Herman	.64
60	Jeff Heath	.64
61	Bobby Veach	.64
62	Dick Allen	.64
63	Johnny Bench	.64
64	Dolph Camilli	.64
65	Ty Cobb	.64
66	Willie Mays	.64
67	Irish Meusel	.64
68	Dave Winfield	.63
69	Larry Doby	.63
70	Vic Wertz	.63
71	Patsy Tebeau	.63
72	Rocky Colavito	.63
73	George Kelly	.63
74	Gus Zernial	.63
75	Mickey Mantle	.63
76	George Foster	.63
77	Frank Baker	.63
78	Bill Terry	.63
79	Steve Brodie	.63
80	Hank Sauer	.63
81	Dave Kingman	.62
82	Joe Gordon	.62
83	Duke Snider	.62
84	Honus Wagner	.62
85	Frank McCormick	.62
86	Greg Luzinski	.62
87	Tommy Henrich	.62
88	Joe Vosmik	.62
89	Jack Rowe	.62
90	Gil Hodges	.62
91	Charlie Gehringer	.61
92	Dave Parker	.61
93	George Brett	.61
94	Kent Hrbek	.61
95	Fred Pfeffer	.61
96	Ripper Collins	.61
97	Roy Sievers	.61
98	Eddie Mathews	.61
99	George Davis	.61
100	Sam Mertes	.61

Walks

1	Babe Ruth	2056
2	Ted Williams	2019
3	Joe Morgan	1865
4	Carl Yastrzemski	1845
5	Mickey Mantle	1734
6	Mel Ott	1708
7	Eddie Yost	1614
8	Stan Musial	1599
9	Pete Rose	1566
10	Darrell Evans	1564
11	Harmon Killebrew	1559
12	Lou Gehrig	1508
13	Eddie Collins	1499
14	Mike Schmidt	1486
15	Willie Mays	1464
16	Jimmie Foxx	1452
17	Eddie Mathews	1444
18	Frank Robinson	1420
19	Hank Aaron	1402
20	Tris Speaker	1381
21	Reggie Jackson	1375
22	Willie McCovey	1345
23	Luke Appling	1302
24	Al Kaline	1277
25	Ken Singleton	1263
26	Rusty Staub	1255
27	Ty Cobb	1249
28	Jim Wynn	1224
29	Pee Wee Reese	1210
30	Richie Ashburn	1198
31	Billy Hamilton	1187
32	Charlie Gehringer	1186
33	Dwight Evans	1171
34	Donie Bush	1158
35	Max Bishop	1153
	Toby Harrah	1153
37	Harry Hooper	1136
38	Jimmy Sheckard	1135
39	Ron Santo	1108
40	Lu Blue	1092
	Stan Hack	1092
42	Paul Waner	1091
43	Graig Nettles	1088
44	Bobby Grich	1087
45	Bob Johnson	1075
46	Harlond Clift	1070
47	Bill Dahlen	1064
48	Joe Cronin	1059
49	Ron Fairly	1052
50	Billy Williams	1045
51	Norm Cash	1043
	Eddie Joost	1043
53	Roy Thomas	1042
54	Max Carey	1040
55	Rogers Hornsby	1038
56	Jim Gilliam	1036
57	Sal Bando	1031
58	Jesse Burkett	1029
	Keith Hernandez	1029
60	Rod Carew	1018
	Enos Slaughter	1018
62	Ron Cey	1012
	Willie Randolph	1012
64	Ralph Kiner	1011
65	Dummy Hoy	1004
66	Miller Huggins	1003
67	Roger Connor	1002
68	Boog Powell	1001
69	Eddie Stanky	996
70	Cupid Childs	990
71	Gene Tenace	984
72	Bid McPhee	981
73	Joe Kuhel	980
	Earl Torgeson	980
75	Augie Galan	979
76	Brian Downing	971
	Duke Snider	971
78	Bob Elliott	967
79	Mike Hargrove	965
	Buddy Myer	965
81	Honus Wagner	963
82	Jimmy Dykes	958
83	Mickey Vernon	955
84	Cap Anson	952
	Joe Judge	952
86	Rocky Colavito	951
87	Goose Goslin	948
88	Dolph Camilli	947
89	Gil Hodges	943
90	Elmer Valo	942
91	Gary Matthews	940
92	Willie Stargell	937
	Arky Vaughan	937
94	Dave Winfield	936
95	Roy White	934
96	Rick Ferrell	931
97	Tony Perez	925
98	Rick Monday	924
99	Gene Woodling	921
100	Bobby Bonds	914

Walks Ratio

1	Ted Williams	20.76
2	Max Bishop	20.42
3	Babe Ruth	19.67
4	Eddie Stanky	18.80
5	Ferris Fain	18.70
6	Gene Tenace	18.31
7	Roy Cullenbine	18.03
8	Eddie Yost	18.01
9	Mickey Mantle	17.63
10	John McGraw	17.56
11	Charlie Keller	17.14
12	Joe Morgan	16.74
13	Earl Torgeson	16.47
14	Bernie Carbo	16.45
15	Roy Thomas	16.44
16	Ralph Kiner	16.26
17	Harmon Killebrew	16.06
18	Billy Hamilton	15.92
19	Lou Gehrig	15.86
20	Elmer Valo	15.78
21	Joe Ferguson	15.77
22	Harlond Clift	15.74
23	Eddie Joost	15.69
24	Lu Blue	15.61
25	Jim Wynn	15.54
26	Mike Schmidt	15.34
27	Mel Ott	15.30
28	Miller Huggins	15.29
29	Darrell Evans	15.24
30	Jimmie Foxx	15.15
31	Joe Cunningham	15.12
32	Dolph Camilli	15.03
33	Cupid Childs	14.98
34	Ken Singleton	14.94
35	Rickey Henderson	14.86
36	Elbie Fletcher	14.85
37	Merv Rettenmund	14.83
38	Mike Hargrove	14.78
39	Topsy Hartsel	14.74
40	Dwayne Murphy	14.63
41	Wayne Garrett	14.59
42	Jason Thompson	14.52
43	Eddie Mathews	14.47
44	Mickey Cochrane	14.22
45	Andy Thornton	14.20
46	Wade Boggs	14.19
47	Augie Galan	14.16
48	Gene Woodling	14.15
49	Jack Clark	14.11
50	Willie McCovey	14.10
51	Hank Greenberg	14.09
52	Darrell Porter	14.04
53	Larry Doby	14.01
54	John Mayberry	13.92
55	John Briggs	13.87
56	Bill North	13.85
57	Donie Bush	13.85
58	Wally Schang	13.79
59	Roger Bresnahan	13.74
60	Willie Randolph	13.72
61	Paul Radford	13.71
62	Steve Braun	13.69
63	Norm Siebern	13.64
64	Bob Allison	13.64
65	Bobby Grich	13.63
66	Al Rosen	13.61
67	Toby Harrah	13.48
68	Norm Cash	13.46
69	Mike Jorgensen	13.46
70	Bob Johnson	13.45
71	Brian Downing	13.44
72	Tommy Henrich	13.40
73	Rick Ferrell	13.38
74	Wayne Gross	13.36
75	Carl Yastrzemski	13.34
76	Grady Hatton	13.31
77	Lyn Lary	13.28
78	Ed Bailey	13.21
79	Lee Mazzilli	13.20
80	Jackie Robinson	13.17
81	Jack Graney	13.14
82	Dwight Evans	13.11
83	Eddie Collins	13.10
84	Rick Monday	13.09
85	Don Mincher	13.08
86	Pee Wee Reese	13.06
87	Jeff Burroughs	13.05
88	Stan Hack	13.05
89	Gary Roenicke	13.04
90	Boog Powell	13.03
91	Jimmy Sheckard	12.99
92	Charlie Maxwell	12.98
93	Gorman Thomas	12.97
94	Andy Seminick	12.92
95	Don Buford	12.86
96	Luke Appling	12.82
97	John Milner	12.79
98	Jim Dwyer	12.78
99	Keith Hernandez	12.78
100	Ron Fairly	12.77

Strikeouts

1	Reggie Jackson	2597
2	Willie Stargell	1936
3	Tony Perez	1867
4	Mike Schmidt	1866
5	Dave Kingman	1816
6	Bobby Bonds	1757
7	Lou Brock	1730
8	Mickey Mantle	1710
9	Harmon Killebrew	1699
10	Lee May	1570
11	Dick Allen	1556
12	Willie McCovey	1550
13	Frank Robinson	1532
14	Willie Mays	1526
15	Rick Monday	1513
16	Greg Luzinski	1495
17	Eddie Mathews	1487
18	Dwight Evans	1486
19	Frank Howard	1460
20	Jim Wynn	1427
21	George Foster	1419
22	George Scott	1418
23	Carl Yastrzemski	1393
24	Jim Rice	1384
25	Hank Aaron	1383
26	Darrell Evans	1364
27	Larry Parrish	1359
28	Dale Murphy	1355
29	Ron Santo	1343
30	Gorman Thomas	1339
31	Babe Ruth	1330
32	Deron Johnson	1318
33	Willie Horton	1313
34	Jimmie Foxx	1311
35	Johnny Bench	1278
	Bobby Grich	1278
37	Dave Parker	1246
	Ken Singleton	1246
39	Duke Snider	1237
40	Ernie Banks	1236
41	Ron Cey	1235
42	Roberto Clemente	1230
43	Boog Powell	1226
44	Dave Winfield	1224
45	Graig Nettles	1209
46	Vada Pinson	1196
47	Dave Concepcion	1186
48	Orlando Cepeda	1170
49	Claudell Washington	1157
50	Tony Armas	1153
51	Pete Rose	1143
52	Bert Campaneris	1142
53	Donn Clendenon	1140
54	Gil Hodges	1137
55	Jeff Burroughs	1135
	Leo Cardenas	1135
57	Bob Bailey	1126
58	Gary Matthews	1125
59	Carlton Fisk	1118
60	Jim Fregosi	1097
61	Joe Torre	1094
62	Norm Cash	1091
63	Tony Taylor	1083
64	Tommy Harper	1080
65	Andre Dawson	1072
66	Don Baylor	1069
67	Johnny Callison	1064
68	Joe Adcock	1059
69	Doug Rader	1055
70	Billy Williams	1046
71	Lance Parrish	1044
72	Bob Allison	1033
73	Jose Cruz	1031
74	Reggie Smith	1030
75	Rod Carew	1028
76	Darrell Porter	1025
77	Al Kaline	1020
78	Ken Boyer	1017
79	Joe Morgan	1015
80	George Hendrick	1013
81	Larry Doby	1011
82	Amos Otis	1008
83	Steve Garvey	1003
84	Fred Lynn	1001
85	Gene Tenace	998
86	Brooks Robinson	990
87	Jack Clark	985
88	Chris Speier	979
89	Willie Davis	977
90	Dick McAuliffe	974
91	Dolph Camilli	961
92	Dick Stuart	957
93	Keith Hernandez	956
94	Frank White	951
95	Woodie Held	944
96	Aurelio Rodriguez	943
97	Larry Hisle	941
98	Cesar Cedeno	938
99	Robin Yount	937
100	Clete Boyer	931

At Bats per Strikeout

1	Joe Sewell	62.6
2	Lloyd Waner	44.9
3	Nellie Fox	42.7
4	Tommy Holmes	40.9
5	Andy High	33.8
6	Sam Rice	33.7
7	Frankie Frisch	33.5
8	Dale Mitchell	33.5
9	Johnny Cooney	31.5
10	Frank McCormick	30.3
11	Don Mueller	29.9
12	Billy Southworth	29.5
13	Rip Radcliff	28.9
14	Edd Roush	28.3
15	Pie Traynor	27.2
16	Doc Cramer	26.5
17	Carson Bigbee	26.0
18	Hank Severeid	25.5
19	George Sisler	25.3
20	Paul Waner	25.2
21	Sparky Adams	24.9
22	Lou Finney	24.9
23	Deacon White	24.8
24	Jack Rowe	24.8
25	Irish Meusel	24.6
26	Ezra Sutton	24.6
27	Red Schoendienst	24.5
28	Vic Power	24.5
29	Arky Vaughan	24.0
30	Felix Millan	23.9
31	Mickey Cochrane	23.8
32	Charlie Gehringer	23.8
33	Monte Ward	23.5
34	George Kell	23.4
35	George Cutshaw	23.2
36	Jack Tobin	23.1
37	Taffy Wright	23.1
38	Hughie Critz	23.1
39	Mark Koenig	22.5
40	Ernie Lombardi	22.3
41	Heinie Manush	22.2
42	Bobby Richardson	22.2
43	Jo-Jo Moore	22.0
44	Earl Sheely	21.8
45	Bill Dickey	21.8
46	Johnny Pesky	21.8
47	Rick Ferrell	21.8
48	Glenn Beckert	21.4
49	Dick Siebert	21.2
50	Bill Buckner	20.9
51	Eddie Waitkus	20.9
52	Max Flack	20.8
53	Dixie Walker	20.7
54	Everett Scott	20.7
55	Earle Combs	20.7
56	Paul Hines	20.6
57	Freddy Lindstrom	20.3
58	Mickey Owen	20.2
59	Joe Vosmik	20.1
60	Lou Boudreau	19.5
61	Milt Stock	19.5
62	Willard Marshall	19.3
63	Debs Garms	19.3
64	Charlie Grimm	19.3
65	Harry Rice	19.3
66	Skeeter Newsome	19.2
67	Curt Walker	19.1
68	Peanuts Lowrey	19.1
69	Charlie Jamieson	19.0
70	Muddy Ruel	19.0
71	Tommy Griffith	18.9
72	Tommy Thevenow	18.9
73	Joe Stripp	18.6
74	Joe DiMaggio	18.5
75	Bob Fothergill	18.5
76	Bing Miller	18.3
77	Riggs Stephenson	18.3
78	Yogi Berra	18.2
79	Billy Herman	18.0
80	Lee Magee	18.0
81	Dave Cash	18.0
82	Elmer Valo	17.7
83	Heinie Groh	17.6
84	Luke Sewell	17.5
85	Rich Dauer	17.5
86	Buddy Lewis	17.4
87	Billy Goodman	17.2
88	Jim Gilliam	17.1
89	Harvey Kuenn	17.1
90	Gus Mancuso	17.1
91	Jimmy Wilson	17.1
92	Billy Cox	17.0
93	Ken Williams	16.9
94	George Case	16.9
95	Cecil Travis	16.9
96	Luke Appling	16.8
97	Jackie Hayes	16.8
98	Jackie Robinson	16.8
99	Johnny Ray	16.7
100	Bibb Falk	16.7

Batting Average

1	Ty Cobb	.366
2	Rogers Hornsby	.358
3	Joe Jackson	.356
4	Wade Boggs	.356
5	Ed Delahanty	.346
6	Ted Williams	.344
7	Billy Hamilton	.344
8	Tris Speaker	.344
9	Dan Brouthers	.342
10	Babe Ruth	.342
11	Harry Heilmann	.342
12	Pete Browning	.341
13	Willie Keeler	.341
14	Bill Terry	.341
15	George Sisler	.340
16	Lou Gehrig	.340
17	Jesse Burkett	.338
18	Nap Lajoie	.338
19	Riggs Stephenson	.336
20	Al Simmons	.334
21	John McGraw	.334
22	Paul Waner	.333
23	Eddie Collins	.333
24	Mike Donlin	.333
25	Stan Musial	.331
26	Sam Thompson	.331
27	Heinie Manush	.330
28	Cap Anson	.329
29	Rod Carew	.328
30	Honus Wagner	.327
31	Tip O'Neill	.326
32	Bob Fothergill	.325
33	Jimmie Foxx	.325
34	Earle Combs	.325
35	Joe DiMaggio	.325
36	Babe Herman	.324
37	Hugh Duffy	.324
38	Joe Medwick	.324
39	Edd Roush	.323
40	Sam Rice	.322
41	Ross Youngs	.322
42	Kiki Cuyler	.321
43	Charlie Gehringer	.320
44	Chuck Klein	.320
45	Pie Traynor	.320
46	Mickey Cochrane	.320
47	Ken Williams	.319
48	Earl Averill	.318
49	Arky Vaughan	.318
50	Roberto Clemente	.317
51	Chick Hafey	.317
52	Joe Kelley	.317
53	Zach Wheat	.317
54	Roger Connor	.317
55	Lloyd Waner	.316
56	Frankie Frisch	.316
57	Goose Goslin	.316
58	George Van Haltren	.316
59	Bibb Falk	.314
60	Cecil Travis	.314
61	Hank Greenberg	.313
62	Jack Fournier	.313
63	Elmer Flick	.313
64	Bill Dickey	.313
65	Dale Mitchell	.312
66	Johnny Mize	.312
67	Joe Sewell	.312
68	George Brett	.312
69	Fred Clarke	.312
70	Barney McCosky	.312
71	Bing Miller	.312
72	Hughie Jennings	.311
73	Freddy Lindstrom	.311
74	Jackie Robinson	.311
75	Baby Doll Jacobson	.311
76	Taffy Wright	.311
77	Rip Radcliff	.311
78	Ginger Beaumont	.311
79	Mike Tiernan	.311
80	Denny Lyons	.310
81	Luke Appling	.310
82	Irish Meusel	.310
83	Mike Smith	.310
84	Bobby Veach	.310
85	Jim O'Rourke	.310
86	John Stone	.310
87	Jim Bottomley	.310
88	Sam Crawford	.309
89	Bob Meusel	.309
90	Jack Tobin	.309
91	Spud Davis	.308
92	Richie Ashburn	.308
93	King Kelly	.308
94	Jake Beckley	.308
95	Stuffy McInnis	.307
96	Pedro Guerrero	.307
97	Joe Vosmik	.307
98	Frank Baker	.307
99	George Burns	.307
100	Matty Alou	.307

Batting Average (by era)

1876-1892

1	Dan Brouthers	.342
2	Pete Browning	.341
3	Sam Thompson	.331
4	Cap Anson	.329
5	Tip O'Neill	.326
6	Roger Connor	.317
7	Denny Lyons	.310
8	Jim O'Rourke	.310
9	King Kelly	.308
10	Deacon White	.303
11	Henry Larkin	.303
12	Buck Ewing	.303
13	George Gore	.301
14	Paul Hines	.301
15	Oyster Burns	.300

1893-1919

1	Ty Cobb	.366
2	Joe Jackson	.356
3	Ed Delahanty	.346
4	Billy Hamilton	.344
5	Tris Speaker	.344
6	Willie Keeler	.341
7	Jesse Burkett	.338
8	Nap Lajoie	.338
9	John McGraw	.334
10	Eddie Collins	.333
11	Mike Donlin	.333
12	Honus Wagner	.327
13	Hugh Duffy	.324
14	Zach Wheat	.317
15	Elmer Flick	.313

1920-1941

1	Rogers Hornsby	.358
2	Babe Ruth	.342
3	Harry Heilmann	.342
4	Bill Terry	.341
5	George Sisler	.340
6	Lou Gehrig	.340
7	Riggs Stephenson	.336
8	Al Simmons	.334
9	Paul Waner	.333
10	Heinie Manush	.330
11	Bob Fothergill	.325
12	Jimmie Foxx	.325
13	Earle Combs	.325
14	Babe Herman	.324
15	Joe Medwick	.324

1942-1960

1	Ted Williams	.344
2	Stan Musial	.331
3	Joe DiMaggio	.325
4	Dale Mitchell	.312
5	Johnny Mize	.312
6	Barney McCosky	.312
7	Jackie Robinson	.311
8	Taffy Wright	.311
9	Richie Ashburn	.308
10	Johnny Pesky	.307
11	George Kell	.306
12	Dixie Walker	.306
13	Harvey Kuenn	.303
14	Tommy Holmes	.302
15	Enos Slaughter	.300

1961-1988

1	Wade Boggs	.356
2	Rod Carew	.328
3	Roberto Clemente	.317
4	George Brett	.312
5	Pedro Guerrero	.307
6	Matty Alou	.307
7	Ralph Garr	.306
8	Hank Aaron	.305
9	Tim Raines	.305
10	Bill Madlock	.305
11	Tony Oliva	.304
12	Manny Mota	.304
13	Al Oliver	.303
14	Pete Rose	.303
15	Willie Mays	.302

Batting Average (by position)

First Base

1	Dan Brouthers	.342
2	Bill Terry	.341
3	George Sisler	.340
4	Lou Gehrig	.340
5	Cap Anson	.329
6	Rod Carew	.328
7	Jimmie Foxx	.325
8	Roger Connor	.317
9	Hank Greenberg	.313
10	Jack Fournier	.313

Second Base

1	Rogers Hornsby	.358
2	Nap Lajoie	.338
3	Eddie Collins	.333
4	Charlie Gehringer	.320
5	Frankie Frisch	.316
6	Cupid Childs	.306
7	Billy Herman	.304
8	Buddy Myer	.303
9	Del Pratt	.292
10	Tony Lazzeri	.292

Shortstop

1	Honus Wagner	.327
2	Arky Vaughan	.318
3	Joe Sewell	.312
4	Luke Appling	.310
5	Ed McKean	.303
6	Joe Cronin	.301
7	Lou Boudreau	.295
8	George Davis	.295
9	Glenn Wright	.294
10	Travis Jackson	.291

Third Base

1	Pie Traynor	.320
2	George Brett	.312
3	Denny Lyons	.310
4	Frank Baker	.307
5	George Kell	.306
6	Bill Madlock	.305
7	Stan Hack	.301
8	Pinky Whitney	.295
9	Jimmy Collins	.294
10	Mike Higgins	.292

Outfield

1	Ty Cobb	.366
2	Joe Jackson	.356
3	Ed Delahanty	.346
4	Ted Williams	.344
5	Billy Hamilton	.344
6	Tris Speaker	.344
7	Babe Ruth	.342
8	Harry Heilmann	.342
9	Willie Keeler	.341
10	Jesse Burkett	.338

Catcher

1	Mickey Cochrane	.320
2	Bill Dickey	.313
3	Spud Davis	.308
4	Ernie Lombardi	.306
5	Gabby Hartnett	.297
6	Manny Sanguillen	.296
7	Smoky Burgess	.295
8	Thurman Munson	.292
9	Hank Severeid	.289
10	Jack Clements	.286

Relative Batting Average

1	Wade Boggs	135.4
2	Ty Cobb	134.8
3	Joe Jackson	133.1
4	Pete Browning	131.5
5	Ted Williams	128.1
6	Dan Brouthers	127.8
7	Nap Lajoie	127.3
8	Rod Carew	127.0
9	Rogers Hornsby	126.2
10	Tris Speaker	125.2
11	Tip O'Neill	125.2
12	Willie Keeler	124.6
13	Stan Musial	123.9
14	Mike Donlin	123.6
15	Honus Wagner	123.1
16	Billy Hamilton	122.7
17	Ed Delahanty	122.7
18	Cap Anson	122.7
19	Jesse Burkett	121.7
20	Eddie Collins	121.6
21	Sam Thompson	121.1
22	Roberto Clemente	120.7
23	Tony Oliva	120.4
24	Harry Heilmann	119.4
25	Babe Ruth	119.2
26	George Brett	118.9
27	George Sisler	118.9
28	Sam Crawford	118.9
29	King Kelly	118.2
30	Jim O'Rourke	118.1
31	Matty Alou	117.9
32	Joe Medwick	117.8
33	Paul Waner	117.8
34	Elmer Flick	117.4
35	Roger Connor	117.4
36	Bill Terry	117.3
37	Lou Gehrig	117.2
38	Joe DiMaggio	117.1
39	Ginger Beaumont	117.0
40	Ralph Garr	116.7
41	Pedro Guerrero	116.6
42	Manny Mota	116.4
43	Dale Mitchell	116.3
44	John McGraw	116.2
45	Henry Larkin	116.2
46	Deacon White	116.0
47	Hank Aaron	116.0
48	Paul Hines	115.8
	Tim Raines	115.8
50	George Gore	115.7
51	Jackie Robinson	115.7
52	Pete Rose	115.6
53	Edd Roush	115.5
54	Al Simmons	115.4
55	Frank Baker	115.4
56	Al Kaline	115.4
57	Bill Madlock	115.2
58	Arky Vaughan	115.1
59	Al Oliver	115.1
60	Riggs Stephenson	115.0
61	Mickey Mantle	115.0
62	Johnny Mize	114.9
63	Zach Wheat	114.9
64	Hugh Duffy	114.8
65	George Kell	114.8
66	Barney McCosky	114.7
67	Richie Ashburn	114.6
68	Hardy Richardson	114.6
69	Johnny Pesky	114.5
70	Harvey Kuenn	114.5
71	Rico Carty	114.4
72	Willie Mays	114.3
73	Jim Rice	114.1
74	Fred Clarke	114.0
75	Heinie Manush	114.0
76	Cy Seymour	113.9
77	Jimmie Foxx	113.8
78	Joe Torre	113.8
79	Cecil Cooper	113.5
80	Keith Hernandez	113.4
81	Frank Robinson	113.4
82	Taffy Wright	113.4
83	Tommy Davis	113.4
84	Paul Molitor	113.3
85	Minnie Minoso	113.1
86	Tommy Holmes	113.0
87	Joe Kelley	112.9
88	Orlando Cepeda	112.9
89	Denny Lyons	112.9
90	Mickey Rivers	112.9
91	Bake McBride	112.8
92	Manny Sanguillen	112.8
93	Thurman Munson	112.8
94	Hal Chase	112.7
95	Ken Griffey	112.7
96	Heinie Zimmerman	112.7
97	Ross Youngs	112.7
98	John Reilly	112.6
99	Bobby Veach	112.5
100	Dick Allen	112.5

On Base Percentage

1	Ted Williams	.483
2	Babe Ruth	.474
3	John McGraw	.460
4	Billy Hamilton	.455
5	Wade Boggs	.448
6	Lou Gehrig	.447
7	Rogers Hornsby	.434
8	Ty Cobb	.432
9	Jimmie Foxx	.428
10	Tris Speaker	.427
11	Ferris Fain	.425
12	Eddie Collins	.424
13	Max Bishop	.423
	Dan Brouthers	.423
	Joe Jackson	.423
	Mickey Mantle	.423
17	Mickey Cochrane	.419
18	Stan Musial	.418
19	Cupid Childs	.414
	Mel Ott	.414
21	Jesse Burkett	.413
22	Hank Greenberg	.412
23	Ed Delahanty	.410
	Harry Heilmann	.410
	Charlie Keller	.410
	Jackie Robinson	.410
	Eddie Stanky	.410
28	Roy Cullenbine	.408
	Roy Thomas	.408
30	Denny Lyons	.407
	Riggs Stephenson	.407
32	Joe Cunningham	.406
	Arky Vaughan	.406
34	Charlie Gehringer	.404
	Paul Waner	.404
36	Pete Browning	.403
37	Lu Blue	.402
38	Mike Hargrove	.400
	Rickey Henderson	.400
40	Luke Appling	.399
	Joe Kelley	.399
	Elmer Valo	.399
	Ross Youngs	.399
44	Joe DiMaggio	.398
	Ralph Kiner	.398
46	Richie Ashburn	.397
	Earle Combs	.397
	Roger Connor	.397
	Johnny Mize	.397
	Mike Smith	.397
51	Cap Anson	.395
	Earl Averill	.395
	Rod Carew	.395
	Joe Morgan	.395
	Hack Wilson	.395
	Eddie Yost	.395
57	Stan Hack	.394
	Johnny Pesky	.394
59	Bob Johnson	.393
	Tim Raines	.393
	Wally Schang	.393
	Bill Terry	.393
	Ken Williams	.393
64	Jack Fournier	.392
	George Grantham	.392
	Tip O'Neill	.392
	Frank Robinson	.392
	Mike Tiernan	.392
69	Keith Hernandez	.391
	Minnie Minoso	.391
	Joe Sewell	.391
	Ken Singleton	.391
	Gene Tenace	.391
74	Harlond Clift	.390
	Joe Cronin	.390
	Augie Galan	.390
77	Bernie Carbo	.389
	Buddy Myer	.389
79	Dolph Camilli	.388
	Mike Griffin	.388
	Gene Woodling	.388
82	Larry Doby	.387
	Goose Goslin	.387
	Willie Mays	.387
	Earl Torgeson	.387
	Honus Wagner	.387
87	Kiki Cuyler	.386
	George Gore	.386
	Barney McCosky	.386
	Al Rosen	.386
	Mike Schmidt	.386
92	George Van Haltren	.385
93	Hugh Duffy	.384
	Elbie Fletcher	.384
	Pedro Guerrero	.384
	Dummy Hoy	.384
	Hughie Jennings	.384
	Willie Keeler	.384
	Sam Thompson	.384
100	8 players tied	.383

Slugging Average

1	Babe Ruth	.690
2	Ted Williams	.634
3	Lou Gehrig	.632
4	Jimmie Foxx	.609
5	Hank Greenberg	.605
6	Joe DiMaggio	.579
7	Rogers Hornsby	.577
8	Johnny Mize	.562
9	Stan Musial	.559
10	Willie Mays	.557
11	Mickey Mantle	.557
12	Hank Aaron	.555
13	Ralph Kiner	.548
14	Hack Wilson	.545
15	Chuck Klein	.543
16	Duke Snider	.540
17	Frank Robinson	.537
18	Al Simmons	.535
19	Dick Allen	.534
20	Earl Averill	.534
21	Mel Ott	.533
22	Babe Herman	.532
23	Ken Williams	.530
24	Mike Schmidt	.530
25	Willie Stargell	.529
26	Chick Hafey	.526
27	Hal Trosky	.522
28	Wally Berger	.522
29	Harry Heilmann	.520
30	Dan Brouthers	.519
31	Charlie Keller	.518
32	Joe Jackson	.517
33	Willie McCovey	.515
34	Ty Cobb	.512
35	Eddie Mathews	.509
36	Jeff Heath	.509
37	Harmon Killebrew	.509
38	Pedro Guerrero	.508
39	Jim Rice	.506
40	Bob Johnson	.506
41	Bill Terry	.506
42	George Brett	.505
43	Ed Delahanty	.505
44	Sam Thompson	.505
45	Joe Medwick	.505
46	Jim Bottomley	.500
47	Tris Speaker	.500
48	Eddie Murray	.500
49	Goose Goslin	.500
50	Roy Campanella	.500
51	Ernie Banks	.500
52	Orlando Cepeda	.499
53	Bob Horner	.499
54	Frank Howard	.499
55	Ted Kluszewski	.498
56	Bob Meusel	.497
57	Hank Sauer	.496
58	Al Rosen	.495
59	Fred Lynn	.494
60	Kent Hrbek	.494
61	Dale Murphy	.492
62	Billy Williams	.492
63	Ripper Collins	.492
64	Dolph Camilli	.492
65	Tommy Henrich	.491
66	Larry Doby	.490
67	Reggie Jackson	.490
68	Dick Stuart	.489
69	Reggie Smith	.489
70	Gabby Hartnett	.489
71	Rocky Colavito	.489
72	Norm Cash	.488
73	Andre Dawson	.487
74	Gil Hodges	.487
75	Bill Dickey	.486
76	Gus Zernial	.486
77	Roger Connor	.486
78	Joe Adcock	.485
79	Wally Post	.485
80	Wade Boggs	.485
81	Jesse Barfield	.484
82	Jack Fournier	.483
83	Rudy York	.483
84	Yogi Berra	.482
85	Jack Clark	.482
86	Dave Parker	.482
87	Kirk Gibson	.482
88	Dave Winfield	.481
89	Charlie Gehringer	.480
90	George Foster	.480
91	Al Kaline	.480
92	Heinie Manush	.479
93	Dwight Evans	.478
94	Gavvy Cravath	.478
95	Dave Kingman	.478
96	Mickey Cochrane	.478
97	Greg Luzinski	.478
98	Leon Durham	.477
99	Tony Oliva	.476
100	Roger Maris	.476

Production

1	Babe Ruth	1.163
2	Ted Williams	1.116
3	Lou Gehrig	1.080
4	Jimmie Foxx	1.038
5	Hank Greenberg	1.017
6	Rogers Hornsby	1.010
7	Mickey Mantle	.979
8	Joe DiMaggio	.977
	Stan Musial	.977
10	Johnny Mize	.959
11	Mel Ott	.947
12	Ralph Kiner	.946
13	Ty Cobb	.945
14	Willie Mays	.944
15	Dan Brouthers	.942
16	Joe Jackson	.940
	Hack Wilson	.940
18	Wade Boggs	.933
19	Hank Aaron	.932
20	Harry Heilmann	.930
21	Frank Robinson	.929
22	Earl Averill	.928
	Charlie Keller	.928
24	Tris Speaker	.927
25	Ken Williams	.924
26	Chuck Klein	.922
27	Duke Snider	.921
28	Mike Schmidt	.916
29	Ed Delahanty	.915
	Babe Herman	.915
	Al Simmons	.915
32	Dick Allen	.914
33	Bob Johnson	.899
	Bill Terry	.899
35	Chick Hafey	.898
36	Mickey Cochrane	.897
37	Pedro Guerrero	.892
	Willie McCovey	.892
	Willie Stargell	.892
	Hal Trosky	.892
41	Eddie Mathews	.888
	Sam Thompson	.888
43	George Brett	.887
	Goose Goslin	.887
	Billy Hamilton	.887
	Harmon Killebrew	.887
47	Charlie Gehringer	.884
48	Roger Connor	.883
	Jackie Robinson	.883
50	Al Rosen	.882
51	Wally Berger	.881
52	Dolph Camilli	.880
	Riggs Stephenson	.880
54	Jeff Heath	.879
55	Larry Doby	.877
	Paul Waner	.877
57	Jack Fournier	.875
	Eddie Murray	.875
59	Tommy Henrich	.873
60	John McGraw	.871
61	Pete Browning	.870
62	Jim Bottomley	.869
63	Bill Dickey	.868
64	Joe Medwick	.867
65	Kent Hrbek	.866
66	Norm Cash	.865
67	Jim Rice	.864
68	Fred Lynn	.862
69	Roy Campanella	.861
70	Jesse Burkett	.860
	Kiki Cuyler	.860
72	Jack Clark	.859
	Earle Combs	.859
	Al Kaline	.859
	Reggie Smith	.859
	Arky Vaughan	.859
77	Gabby Hartnett	.858
78	Gavvy Cravath	.857
	Joe Cronin	.857
80	Heinie Manush	.856
	Billy Williams	.856
82	George Grantham	.854
	Mike Tiernan	.854
84	Frank Howard	.853
	Honus Wagner	.853
86	Orlando Cepeda	.852
	Eddie Collins	.852
	Ripper Collins	.852
	Ted Kluszewski	.852
	Bob Meusel	.852
	Dale Murphy	.852
92	Rocky Colavito	.851
	Mike Donlin	.851
	Minnie Minoso	.851
95	Joe Kelley	.850
	Denny Lyons	.850
	Tip O'Neill	.850
98	Dwight Evans	.849
	Bob Nieman	.849
100	2 players tied	.848

Adjusted Production

1	Babe Ruth	209
2	Ted Williams	186
3	Lou Gehrig	181
4	Rogers Hornsby	176
5	Mickey Mantle	173
6	Dan Brouthers	171
7	Ty Cobb	168
	Joe Jackson	168
9	Pete Browning	166
10	Jimmie Foxx	162
11	Johnny Mize	157
	Stan Musial	157
13	Hank Aaron	156
	Joe DiMaggio	156
	Willie Mays	156
	Tris Speaker	156
17	Dick Allen	155
	Ed Delahanty	155
	Hank Greenberg	155
	Mel Ott	155
21	Roger Connor	154
	Charlie Keller	154
	Frank Robinson	154
24	Nap Lajoie	151
25	Wade Boggs	150
	Elmer Flick	150
	Pedro Guerrero	150
	Honus Wagner	150
29	Gavvy Cravath	149
	Harry Heilmann	149
31	Ralph Kiner	148
	Willie McCovey	148
	Mike Schmidt	148
	Willie Stargell	148
	Sam Thompson	148
36	Eddie Mathews	145
	Hack Wilson	145
38	Sam Crawford	144
	Mike Donlin	144
	Harry Stovey	144
41	Frank Howard	143
	Henry Larkin	143
43	George Brett	142
	Jesse Burkett	142
	Eddie Collins	142
	Jack Fournier	142
	Harmon Killebrew	142
	Eddie Murray	142
49	Billy Hamilton	141
	Babe Herman	141
	Denny Lyons	141
	Tip O'Neill	141
53	Jack Clark	140
	Jeff Heath	140
	Reggie Jackson	140
	Bob Johnson	140
	Mike Tiernan	140
58	Cap Anson	139
	Wally Berger	139
	Duke Snider	139
61	Norm Cash	138
	Al Rosen	138
63	Oyster Burns	137
	Sherry Magee	137
	Gene Tenace	137
	Bill Terry	137
67	Larry Doby	136
	King Kelly	136
	John McGraw	136
	Reggie Smith	136
	Arky Vaughan	136
	Dave Winfield	136
73	Frank Baker	135
	Dolph Camilli	135
	Rickey Henderson	135
	Chuck Klein	135
	Ken Williams	135
78	Orlando Cepeda	134
	George Gore	134
	Al Kaline	134
	Jim O'Rourke	134
	Boog Powell	134
83	Frank Chance	133
	Fred Clarke	133
	Rocky Colavito	133
	Chick Hafey	133
	Charlie Hickman	133
	Paul Hines	133
	Joe Morgan	133
	Bob Nieman	133
	Tim Raines	133
	Paul Waner	133
93	Earl Averill	132
	Tommy Henrich	132
	Keith Hernandez	132
	Joe Kelley	132
	Joe Medwick	132
	Bill Nicholson	132
	Ken Singleton	132
100	10 players tied	131

Batting Runs

1	Babe Ruth	1322
2	Ted Williams	1166
3	Ty Cobb	1033
4	Stan Musial	983
5	Lou Gehrig	918
6	Hank Aaron	878
7	Rogers Hornsby	843
8	Tris Speaker	841
9	Willie Mays	827
10	Jimmie Foxx	803
	Mickey Mantle	803
12	Frank Robinson	773
13	Mel Ott	767
14	Honus Wagner	663
15	Dan Brouthers	648
16	Carl Yastrzemski	617
17	Eddie Collins	604
18	Mike Schmidt	594
19	Cap Anson	564
20	Roger Connor	563
21	Nap Lajoie	555
22	Ed Delahanty	544
23	Harmon Killebrew	532
24	Willie McCovey	524
25	Jesse Burkett	522
26	Johnny Mize	520
27	Harry Heilmann	517
28	Al Kaline	513
29	Joe DiMaggio	507
30	Sam Crawford	504
31	Billy Hamilton	491
32	Paul Waner	490
33	Willie Stargell	483
34	Eddie Mathews	480
35	Dick Allen	469
36	Hank Greenberg	468
	Reggie Jackson	468
38	Billy Williams	463
39	George Brett	458
40	Joe Jackson	452
41	Duke Snider	441
42	Joe Morgan	438
43	Rod Carew	431
44	Pete Rose	416
45	Al Simmons	399
46	Ralph Kiner	391
47	Norm Cash	390
48	Joe Kelley	388
49	Fred Clarke	383
50	Reggie Smith	379
51	Charlie Gehringer	376
	Jim Rice	376
	Sam Thompson	376
54	Chuck Klein	375
55	Dwight Evans	373
56	Pete Browning	369
57	Bob Johnson	366
58	Eddie Murray	361
	Arky Vaughan	361
60	Harry Stovey	360
61	Roberto Clemente	353
	Joe Medwick	353
63	Willie Keeler	350
64	Ron Santo	345
65	Goose Goslin	340
66	Wade Boggs	337
	Orlando Cepeda	337
	Dave Winfield	337
69	Elmer Flick	335
70	Earl Averill	334
	Zach Wheat	334
72	Ken Singleton	332
73	Sherry Magee	330
74	Frank Howard	324
75	Keith Hernandez	322
76	King Kelly	321
77	Dolph Camilli	319
78	Rusty Staub	318
	Bill Terry	318
80	Fred Lynn	314
81	Jimmy Ryan	311
82	Mike Tiernan	309
83	Enos Slaughter	306
84	Boog Powell	305
	Hack Wilson	305
86	Babe Herman	304
87	Jim O'Rourke	303
88	Minnie Minoso	299
89	Joe Torre	298
90	George Gore	297
91	Rocky Colavito	296
92	Jake Beckley	292
	Tony Perez	292
94	Greg Luzinski	291
95	Ernie Banks	288
96	Hugh Duffy	286
	Charlie Keller	286
98	Jack Fournier	285
99	Dale Murphy	284
100	John McGraw	282

Adjusted Batting Runs

1	Babe Ruth	1357
2	Ted Williams	1089
3	Ty Cobb	1025
4	Lou Gehrig	963
5	Stan Musial	927
6	Hank Aaron	901
7	Rogers Hornsby	858
8	Mickey Mantle	838
9	Willie Mays	837
10	Tris Speaker	809
11	Mel Ott	772
12	Jimmie Foxx	768
13	Frank Robinson	754
14	Honus Wagner	646
15	Dan Brouthers	634
16	Eddie Collins	620
17	Mike Schmidt	563
18	Ed Delahanty	562
	Nap Lajoie	562
20	Roger Connor	552
21	Willie McCovey	538
22	Eddie Mathews	535
23	Harry Heilmann	534
24	Joe DiMaggio	522
25	Carl Yastrzemski	513
26	Reggie Jackson	507
27	Johnny Mize	505
28	Jesse Burkett	500
29	Harmon Killebrew	498
30	Willie Stargell	486
31	Sam Crawford	485
32	Al Kaline	484
33	Joe Morgan	476
34	Paul Waner	473
35	Cap Anson	466
36	Dick Allen	463
37	Billy Hamilton	442
38	George Brett	441
39	Joe Jackson	439
40	Hank Greenberg	434
41	Rod Carew	419
42	Duke Snider	407
43	Billy Williams	401
44	Bob Johnson	389
45	Eddie Murray	388
46	Pete Browning	387
47	Dave Winfield	386
48	Pete Rose	382
49	Fred Clarke	379
50	Ralph Kiner	373
51	Norm Cash	369
52	Al Simmons	367
53	Sam Thompson	364
54	Roberto Clemente	362
55	Goose Goslin	359
56	Arky Vaughan	357
57	Ken Singleton	350
58	Reggie Smith	349
59	Elmer Flick	345
	Frank Howard	345
61	Charlie Gehringer	342
62	Zach Wheat	341
63	Orlando Cepeda	339
64	Joe Kelley	338
65	Bill Terry	332
66	Rusty Staub	331
67	Keith Hernandez	328
68	Sherry Magee	327
69	Chuck Klein	324
	Mike Tiernan	324
71	Harry Stovey	323
72	Babe Herman	318
73	Joe Medwick	317
74	Wade Boggs	314
75	Jake Beckley	313
76	Hack Wilson	311
77	Willie Keeler	310
78	Dwight Evans	309
	Boog Powell	309
80	Jim Rice	307
81	Joe Torre	304
82	Earl Averill	303
83	Jack Fournier	301
84	Jim O'Rourke	300
85	Minnie Minoso	298
86	Charlie Keller	296
87	Jack Clark	293
88	Rocky Colavito	291
89	Fred Lynn	283
	Jim Wynn	283
91	Ron Santo	282
92	Dolph Camilli	281
93	Larry Doby	276
94	Bobby Bonds	274
	Darrell Evans	274
96	George Van Haltren	273
97	George Davis	272
	Tony Perez	272
99	Greg Luzinski	269
100	John McGraw	267

Batting Wins

1	Babe Ruth	127.5
2	Ted Williams	115.9
3	Ty Cobb	106.6
4	Stan Musial	99.7
5	Hank Aaron	91.1
6	Tris Speaker	85.9
7	Willie Mays	85.5
8	Lou Gehrig	85.4
9	Rogers Hornsby	84.8
10	Mickey Mantle	82.9
11	Frank Robinson	80.7
12	Mel Ott	76.2
13	Jimmie Foxx	75.3
14	Honus Wagner	68.4
15	Carl Yastrzemski	64.3
16	Mike Schmidt	62.0
17	Eddie Collins	62.0
18	Nap Lajoie	57.0
19	Dan Brouthers	56.7
20	Harmon Killebrew	55.8
21	Willie McCovey	54.9
22	Sam Crawford	53.6
23	Al Kaline	53.4
24	Johnny Mize	52.2
25	Willie Stargell	51.0
26	Harry Heilmann	50.8
27	Cap Anson	49.9
28	Dick Allen	49.8
29	Roger Connor	49.3
30	Eddie Mathews	49.2
31	Joe DiMaggio	48.6
32	Billy Williams	48.6
33	Paul Waner	48.5
34	Reggie Jackson	48.1
35	Ed Delahanty	48.0
36	Jesse Burkett	47.9
37	Joe Jackson	47.4
38	George Brett	46.1
39	Joe Morgan	45.9
40	Rod Carew	44.7
41	Hank Greenberg	44.5
42	Duke Snider	44.4
43	Pete Rose	43.9
44	Billy Hamilton	42.8
45	Norm Cash	41.1
46	Reggie Smith	40.3
47	Ralph Kiner	39.1
48	Jim Rice	37.8
49	Dwight Evans	37.6
50	Fred Clarke	37.4
51	Al Simmons	37.4
52	Roberto Clemente	36.7
53	Chuck Klein	36.7
54	Arky Vaughan	36.4
55	Ron Santo	36.3
56	Eddie Murray	36.0
57	Sherry Magee	35.7
58	Joe Kelley	35.7
59	Joe Medwick	35.7
60	Bob Johnson	35.2
61	Charlie Gehringer	35.1
62	Orlando Cepeda	35.1
63	Frank Howard	34.4
64	Zach Wheat	34.4
65	Dave Winfield	34.3
66	Elmer Flick	34.1
67	Ken Singleton	34.0
68	Willie Keeler	33.8
69	Keith Hernandez	33.6
70	Wade Boggs	33.4
71	Rusty Staub	33.3
72	Sam Thompson	32.6
73	Boog Powell	32.4
74	Dolph Camilli	32.2
75	Pete Browning	32.1
76	Goose Goslin	31.8
77	Harry Stovey	31.6
78	Fred Lynn	31.5
79	Joe Torre	31.4
80	Enos Slaughter	30.9
81	Earl Averill	30.8
82	Bill Terry	30.8
83	Rocky Colavito	30.7
84	Tony Perez	30.6
85	Minnie Minoso	30.3
86	Greg Luzinski	30.1
87	Ernie Banks	29.8
88	Dale Murphy	29.7
89	Gavvy Cravath	29.6
90	Hack Wilson	29.5
91	Babe Herman	29.5
92	Tony Oliva	28.9
93	King Kelly	28.8
94	Jack Fournier	28.8
95	Charlie Keller	28.5
96	Jack Clark	28.5
97	Bobby Bonds	28.4
98	Cy Williams	28.4
99	Darrell Evans	28.2
100	Johnny Bench	27.8

Adjusted Batting Wins

1	Babe Ruth	130.9
2	Ted Williams	108.2
3	Ty Cobb	105.7
4	Stan Musial	94.0
5	Hank Aaron	93.4
6	Lou Gehrig	89.6
7	Willie Mays	86.5
8	Mickey Mantle	86.5
9	Rogers Hornsby	86.3
10	Tris Speaker	82.6
11	Frank Robinson	78.7
12	Mel Ott	76.7
13	Jimmie Foxx	72.0
14	Honus Wagner	66.7
15	Eddie Collins	63.6
16	Mike Schmidt	58.8
17	Nap Lajoie	57.7
18	Willie McCovey	56.4
19	Dan Brouthers	55.5
20	Eddie Mathews	54.8
21	Carl Yastrzemski	53.4
22	Harry Heilmann	52.4
23	Harmon Killebrew	52.2
24	Reggie Jackson	52.1
25	Sam Crawford	51.6
26	Willie Stargell	51.3
27	Johnny Mize	50.7
28	Al Kaline	50.4
29	Joe DiMaggio	50.1
30	Joe Morgan	49.9
31	Ed Delahanty	49.6
32	Dick Allen	49.2
33	Roger Connor	48.3
34	Paul Waner	46.8
35	Joe Jackson	46.0
36	Jesse Burkett	45.9
37	George Brett	44.4
38	Rod Carew	43.5
39	Billy Williams	42.1
40	Cap Anson	41.3
41	Hank Greenberg	41.3
42	Duke Snider	41.0
43	Pete Rose	40.3
44	Dave Winfield	39.3
45	Norm Cash	38.9
46	Eddie Murray	38.7
47	Billy Hamilton	38.6
48	Roberto Clemente	37.7
49	Bob Johnson	37.4
50	Ralph Kiner	37.3
51	Reggie Smith	37.1
52	Fred Clarke	37.0
53	Frank Howard	36.7
54	Arky Vaughan	36.0
55	Ken Singleton	35.8
56	Sherry Magee	35.4
57	Orlando Cepeda	35.3
58	Elmer Flick	35.2
59	Zach Wheat	35.1
60	Rusty Staub	34.7
61	Al Simmons	34.4
62	Keith Hernandez	34.2
63	Goose Goslin	33.6
64	Pete Browning	33.6
65	Boog Powell	32.8
66	Bill Terry	32.1
67	Joe Medwick	32.1
68	Joe Torre	32.0
69	Charlie Gehringer	31.9
70	Chuck Klein	31.7
71	Sam Thompson	31.6
72	Dwight Evans	31.1
73	Wade Boggs	31.1
74	Joe Kelley	31.1
75	Jim Rice	30.9
76	Babe Herman	30.9
77	Jack Clark	30.4
78	Jack Fournier	30.4
79	Rocky Colavito	30.2
80	Minnie Minoso	30.2
81	Hack Wilson	30.1
82	Willie Keeler	30.0
83	Jim Wynn	29.9
84	Ron Santo	29.6
85	Charlie Keller	29.5
86	Jake Beckley	28.6
87	Tony Perez	28.5
88	Bobby Bonds	28.4
89	Fred Lynn	28.4
90	Harry Stovey	28.4
91	Dolph Camilli	28.4
92	Darrell Evans	28.2
93	Mike Tiernan	28.1
94	Earl Averill	28.0
95	Greg Luzinski	27.9
96	Larry Doby	27.5
97	Gavvy Cravath	27.5
98	Johnny Bench	27.4
99	Ernie Banks	27.2
100	Jim O'Rourke	26.8

Runs Created

1	Babe Ruth	2841
2	Ty Cobb	2801
3	Stan Musial	2625
4	Hank Aaron	2550
5	Ted Williams	2538
6	Willie Mays	2372
7	Tris Speaker	2320
8	Lou Gehrig	2317
9	Mel Ott	2235
10	Pete Rose	2220
11	Honus Wagner	2203
12	Jimmie Foxx	2190
13	Carl Yastrzemski	2147
14	Frank Robinson	2126
15	Rogers Hornsby	2074
16	Mickey Mantle	2070
17	Eddie Collins	2050
18	Nap Lajoie	1875
19	Paul Waner	1851
20	Al Kaline	1846
21	Ed Delahanty	1821
22	Joe Morgan	1804
23	Jesse Burkett	1785
	Charlie Gehringer	1785
25	Reggie Jackson	1772
26	Al Simmons	1771
27	Cap Anson	1751
28	Mike Schmidt	1741
29	Eddie Mathews	1738
30	Goose Goslin	1702
31	Sam Crawford	1700
32	Billy Hamilton	1698
33	Harry Heilmann	1693
34	Billy Williams	1671
35	Jake Beckley	1654
36	Roger Connor	1645
37	Fred Clarke	1639
38	Willie McCovey	1638
39	Willie Keeler	1633
40	Dan Brouthers	1622
41	Harmon Killebrew	1609
42	Joe DiMaggio	1606
43	George Davis	1605
44	Rod Carew	1595
45	Red Rolfe	1579
46	Roberto Clemente	1557
	George Van Haltren	1557
48	Jimmy Ryan	1549
49	Zach Wheat	1539
50	Rusty Staub	1534
51	Willie Stargell	1531
52	Tony Perez	1523
53	Ernie Banks	1513
54	Lou Brock	1512
55	Joe Kelley	1510
56	Johnny Mize	1502
57	Sam Rice	1497
58	Hugh Duffy	1495
59	Luke Appling	1493
60	George Brett	1492
	George Sisler	1492
62	Duke Snider	1487
63	Bill Dahlen	1473
64	Max Carey	1471
65	Darrell Evans	1466
66	Frankie Frisch	1465
67	Enos Slaughter	1432
68	Joe Cronin	1426
69	Dave Winfield	1424
70	Bob Johnson	1418
71	Dwight Evans	1408
72	Vada Pinson	1394
73	Heinie Manush	1387
	Mickey Vernon	1387
75	Richie Ashburn	1386
76	Jim Bottomley	1384
77	Ron Santo	1379
78	Chuck Klein	1378
79	Joe Medwick	1372
80	Jim Rice	1362
81	Earl Averill	1358
	Brooks Robinson	1358
83	Harry Hooper	1349
84	Al Oliver	1348
85	Orlando Cepeda	1338
86	Kiki Cuyler	1336
87	Bid McPhee	1334
88	Hank Greenberg	1331
89	Arky Vaughan	1323
90	Sherry Magee	1311
91	Joe Judge	1301
92	Sam Thompson	1296
93	Dick Allen	1290
94	Yogi Berra	1284
	Lave Cross	1284
	Ted Simmons	1284
97	Eddie Murray	1279
98	Norm Cash	1278
	Dummy Hoy	1278
100	Reggie Smith	1277

Total Average

1	Babe Ruth	1.421
2	Ted Williams	1.372
3	Lou Gehrig	1.249
4	Billy Hamilton	1.190
5	Jimmie Foxx	1.170
6	John McGraw	1.135
7	Hank Greenberg	1.128
8	Rogers Hornsby	1.118
	Mickey Mantle	1.118
10	Ty Cobb	1.091
11	Stan Musial	1.066
12	Dan Brouthers	1.061
13	Mel Ott	1.049
14	Joe DiMaggio	1.039
	Ralph Kiner	1.039
16	Rickey Henderson	1.035
17	Ed Delahanty	1.031
18	Tris Speaker	1.030
19	Johnny Mize	1.028
20	Joe Jackson	1.027
	Charlie Keller	1.027
22	Willie Mays	1.026
23	Hack Wilson	1.010
24	Frank Robinson	1.007
25	Wade Boggs	1.002
26	Tim Raines	1.000
27	Mike Schmidt	.998
28	Hank Aaron	.983
29	Jackie Robinson	.977
30	Harry Heilmann	.976
	Ken Williams	.976
32	Dick Allen	.974
33	Earl Averill	.972
	Duke Snider	.972
35	Mike Tiernan	.969
36	Eddie Collins	.966
37	Mickey Cochrane	.961
38	Chuck Klein	.956
39	Denny Lyons	.954
40	Joe Kelley	.953
41	Roger Connor	.952
	Babe Herman	.952
43	Bob Johnson	.949
44	Harmon Killebrew	.948
45	Pete Browning	.946
	Dolph Camilli	.946
	Joe Morgan	.946
48	Willie McCovey	.941
49	Eddie Mathews	.940
50	Sam Thompson	.939
	Honus Wagner	.939
52	Jesse Burkett	.937
53	Charlie Gehringer	.930
	Pedro Guerrero	.930
55	Hugh Duffy	.929
56	Larry Doby	.924
57	Al Rosen	.922
	Harry Stovey	.922
59	Al Simmons	.918
60	Goose Goslin	.917
	Chick Hafey	.917
62	Kiki Cuyler	.915
63	Tommy Henrich	.914
	Willie Stargell	.914
65	George Brett	.913
66	Jack Fournier	.909
	Mike Smith	.909
68	Gavvy Cravath	.907
	Mike Donlin	.907
	Bill Terry	.907
	Arky Vaughan	.907
72	Riggs Stephenson	.906
73	Norm Cash	.905
	Mike Griffin	.905
	Paul Waner	.905
76	Roy Cullenbine	.904
77	Hal Trosky	.903
78	Kirk Gibson	.900
79	George Grantham	.898
80	Tip O'Neill	.897
81	Cupid Childs	.896
	Jeff Heath	.896
83	Jack Clark	.895
84	Ferris Fain	.894
	Elmer Flick	.894
	Eddie Murray	.894
87	Minnie Minoso	.892
88	Bobby Bonds	.890
89	Gene Tenace	.888
90	Wally Berger	.886
91	Frank Chance	.884
92	Reggie Jackson	.883
93	Joe Cronin	.881
	Reggie Smith	.881
95	Al Kaline	.880
	George VanHaltren	.880
97	Tony Lazzeri	.879
	Dale Murphy	.879
99	Harlond Clift	.878
100	Fred Lynn	.877

Runs Produced

1	Ty Cobb	4060
2	Hank Aaron	3716
3	Babe Ruth	3669
4	Cap Anson	3501
5	Stan Musial	3425
6	Lou Gehrig	3385
7	Honus Wagner	3367
8	Pete Rose	3319
9	Willie Mays	3305
10	Tris Speaker	3292
11	Mel Ott	3208
	Carl Yastrzemski	3208
13	Jimmie Foxx	3139
14	Ted Williams	3116
15	Jake Beckley	3088
16	Eddie Collins	3071
17	Frank Robinson	3055
18	Al Simmons	3027
19	Nap Lajoie	3018
20	Charlie Gehringer	3017
21	Ed Delahanty	2962
22	George Davis	2901
23	Rogers Hornsby	2862
24	Goose Goslin	2844
25	Paul Waner	2822
26	Sam Crawford	2818
27	Al Kaline	2806
28	Roger Connor	2805
29	Hugh Duffy	2747
30	Bill Dahlen	2735
31	Dan Brouthers	2712
32	Reggie Jackson	2690
33	Frankie Frisch	2671
34	Mickey Mantle	2650
35	Harry Heilmann	2646
36	Jimmy Ryan	2617
37	Jesse Burkett	2597
38	George VanHaltren	2584
39	Fred Clarke	2567
40	Joe DiMaggio	2566
41	Sam Rice	2558
42	Joe Kelley	2550
43	Tony Perez	2545
44	Joe Morgan	2515
45	Mike Schmidt	2512
46	Willie Keeler	2495
47	Joe Cronin	2487
48	Roberto Clemente	2481
49	Billy Williams	2459
50	Eddie Mathews	2450
51	Ernie Banks	2429
52	Sam Thompson	2428
53	Herman Long	2417
54	Jim O'Rourke	2406
55	Zach Wheat	2405
56	Pie Traynor	2398
57	Dave Winfield	2395
58	Luke Appling	2390
59	Billy Hamilton	2386
60	Enos Slaughter	2382
61	Jim Bottomley	2380
62	Joe Medwick	2376
63	Rusty Staub	2363
64	Lou Brock	2361
65	Heinie Manush	2360
66	George Sisler	2358
67	Rod Carew	2347
68	Mickey Vernon	2335
69	Brooks Robinson	2321
70	Al Oliver	2296
71	Harmon Killebrew	2294
72	Tommy Corcoran	2285
73	Vada Pinson	2280
74	Max Carey	2276
75	Jim Rice	2271
76	Willie McCovey	2263
77	Willie Stargell	2260
78	Monte Ward	2249
79	Yogi Berra	2247
80	Bob Johnson	2234
81	Kiki Cuyler	2232
82	Darrell Evans	2225
83	Ted Simmons	2215
84	George Brett	2209
85	Sherry Magee	2205
86	Duke Snider	2185
87	Steve Garvey	2179
88	Don Baylor	2174
89	Harry Hooper	2171
90	Doc Cramer	2162
91	Joe Kuhel	2154
92	Earl Averill	2150
93	Joe Sewell	2145
94	Bobby Wallace	2144
95	Ron Santo	2127
96	Joe Judge	2125
97	Dwight Evans	2124
98	Bobby Doerr	2118
99	Orlando Cepeda	2117
	Graig Nettles	2117

Clutch Hitting Index

1	Cap Anson	139
2	Duffy Lewis	136
	Earl Sheely	136
	Pie Traynor	136
5	Bobby Veach	135
6	Kitty Bransfield	132
7	Tom Burns	131
	Tommy Thevenow	131
9	Tommy Davis	130
	Chick Gandil	130
	Sherry Magee	130
	Sam Mertes	130
	Possum Whitted	130
14	Larry Gardner	129
	Stuffy McInnis	129
	Pinky Whitney	129
	Heinie Zimmerman	129
18	Red Smith	128
19	Frank Chance	127
	Bob Elliott	127
	Ted Simmons	127
	Patsy Tebeau	127
23	Rube Bressler	126
	Harry Steinfeldt	126
	Glenn Wright	126
26	Frank McCormick	125
	Keith Moreland	125
	Fred Pfeffer	125
	Enos Slaughter	125
	Gus Suhr	125
31	Gavvy Cravath	124
	Joe Cronin	124
	George Cutshaw	124
	Bob Fothergill	124
	Hughie Jennings	124
	Frank LaPorte	124
	Cookie Lavagetto	124
	Dots Miller	124
	Red Murray	124
	Billy Nash	124
	Lee Tannehill	124
	Ned Williamson	124
	Taffy Wright	124
44	Frank Baker	123
	Ferris Fain	123
	Art Fletcher	123
	Tom Herr	123
	Jackie Jensen	123
	Luke Sewell	123
	Billy Sullivan	123
	Bobby Wallace	123
	Vic Wertz	123
	Deacon White	123
54	Frank Bowerman	122
	Roy Campanella	122
	Tony Cuccinello	122
	Art Devlin	122
	Del Ennis	122
	Harry Heilmann	122
	Solly Hofman	122
	Willie Kamm	122
	Sam Mele	122
	Willie Montanez	122
	Muddy Ruel	122
	Ray Schalk	122
66	Lou Criger	121
	Ron Fairly	121
	Keith Hernandez	121
	Steve Kemp	121
	Dan McGann	121
	Tony Perez	121
	Boog Powell	121
	Joe Sewell	121
	Riggs Stephenson	121
	Joe Tinker	121
76	Steve Brodie	120
	Tommy Corcoran	120
	Walt Dropo	120
	Kid Elberfeld	120
	Bibb Falk	120
	Carl Furillo	120
	Mike Higgins	120
	George Kelly	120
	Tony Lazzeri	120
	Irish Meusel	120
	Mike Mowrey	120
	Del Pratt	120
	Elmer Smith	120
	Dick Stuart	120
	Honus Wagner	120
	Bob Watson	120
92	Sal Bando	119
	Duke Farrell	119
	Hank Majeski	119
	Frank Malzone	119
	Joe Medwick	119
	Jimmy Wilson	119
	Hack Wilson	119
	Rudy York	119
100	21 players tied	118

Isolated Power

1	Babe Ruth	.348
2	Lou Gehrig	.292
3	Hank Greenberg	.292
4	Ted Williams	.289
5	Jimmie Foxx	.284
6	Ralph Kiner	.269
7	Mike Schmidt	.261
8	Mickey Mantle	.259
9	Willie Mays	.256
10	Joe DiMaggio	.254
11	Harmon Killebrew	.252
12	Johnny Mize	.250
13	Hank Aaron	.250
14	Willie Stargell	.247
15	Willie McCovey	.245
16	Duke Snider	.244
17	Frank Robinson	.243
18	Dave Kingman	.242
19	Dick Allen	.242
20	Eddie Mathews	.238
21	Hack Wilson	.238
22	Charlie Keller	.231
23	Hank Sauer	.230
24	Mel Ott	.229
25	Stan Musial	.228
26	Reggie Jackson	.228
27	Dick Stuart	.225
28	Ernie Banks	.225
29	Frank Howard	.225
30	Roy Campanella	.224
31	Chuck Klein	.223
32	Gorman Thomas	.223
33	Rocky Colavito	.223
34	Bob Horner	.222
35	Wally Berger	.221
36	Gus Zernial	.221
37	Wally Post	.220
38	Hal Trosky	.219
39	Dale Murphy	.219
40	Rogers Hornsby	.218
41	Jesse Barfield	.217
42	Norm Cash	.217
43	Bob Allison	.217
44	Roger Maris	.216
45	Earl Averill	.216
46	Jeff Heath	.216
47	Dolph Camilli	.215
48	Gil Hodges	.214
49	Ken Williams	.211
50	Al Rosen	.210
51	Bob Johnson	.210
52	Tommy Henrich	.209
53	Chick Hafey	.209
54	Jack Clark	.209
55	Johnny Bench	.208
56	Roy Sievers	.208
57	Rudy York	.208
58	Joe Adcock	.208
59	Fred Lynn	.207
60	Nate Colbert	.207
61	Babe Herman	.207
62	Larry Doby	.207
63	Jim Rice	.206
64	Dwight Evans	.206
65	George Foster	.206
66	Eddie Murray	.205
67	Andre Dawson	.204
68	Kirk Gibson	.204
69	Bobby Bonds	.203
70	Orlando Cepeda	.203
71	Billy Williams	.202
72	Greg Luzinski	.202
73	Cliff Johnson	.202
74	Reggie Smith	.202
75	Kent Hrbek	.202
76	Pedro Guerrero	.201
77	Al Simmons	.201
78	Don Mincher	.201
79	Tony Armas	.200
80	Tom Brunansky	.200
81	Ted Kluszewski	.200
82	Leon Durham	.199
83	Jim Lemon	.198
84	Andy Thornton	.198
85	Bill Nicholson	.198
86	Lance Parrish	.198
87	Dale Long	.198
88	Yogi Berra	.198
89	Joe Gordon	.197
90	Boog Powell	.196
91	Ripper Collins	.196
92	Don Demeter	.195
93	Carlton Fisk	.194
94	Dave Winfield	.194
95	George Brett	.193
96	Lee May	.192
97	Vic Wertz	.192
98	Mack Jones	.192
99	Gabby Hartnett	.192
100	Bobby Thomson	.191

Extra Base Hits

1	Hank Aaron	1477
2	Stan Musial	1377
3	Babe Ruth	1356
4	Willie Mays	1323
5	Lou Gehrig	1190
6	Frank Robinson	1186
7	Carl Yastrzemski	1157
8	Ty Cobb	1136
9	Tris Speaker	1133
10	Jimmie Foxx	1117
	Ted Williams	1117
12	Reggie Jackson	1075
13	Mel Ott	1071
14	Pete Rose	1041
15	Rogers Hornsby	1011
16	Ernie Banks	1009
17	Mike Schmidt	1002
18	Al Simmons	995
19	Honus Wagner	993
20	Al Kaline	972
21	Tony Perez	963
22	Willie Stargell	953
23	Mickey Mantle	952
24	Billy Williams	948
25	Eddie Mathews	938
26	Goose Goslin	921
27	Willie McCovey	920
28	Paul Waner	906
29	Charlie Gehringer	904
30	Nap Lajoie	903
31	Harmon Killebrew	887
32	Joe DiMaggio	881
33	Harry Heilmann	876
34	Vada Pinson	868
35	Sam Crawford	865
36	George Brett	860
37	Joe Medwick	858
38	Duke Snider	850
39	Roberto Clemente	846
40	Dave Winfield	843
41	Dwight Evans	841
42	Rusty Staub	838
43	Jim Bottomley	835
44	Al Oliver	825
45	Orlando Cepeda	823
46	Jim Rice	819
47	Brooks Robinson	818
48	Joe Morgan	813
49	Roger Connor	811
50	Johnny Mize	809
51	Ed Delahanty	808
52	Jake Beckley	803
	Joe Cronin	803
54	Dave Parker	798
55	Johnny Bench	794
56	Mickey Vernon	782
57	Hank Greenberg	781
58	Zach Wheat	780
59	Bob Johnson	779
60	Ted Simmons	778
61	Lou Brock	776
62	Ron Santo	774
63	Chuck Klein	772
64	Dan Brouthers	771
65	Earl Averill	767
66	Darrell Evans	761
	Heinie Manush	761
68	Steve Garvey	755
69	Dick Allen	750
70	Cap Anson	749
71	Graig Nettles	746
72	Hal McRae	741
73	Reggie Smith	734
74	Don Baylor	732
	Robin Yount	732
76	Enos Slaughter	730
77	Yogi Berra	728
78	Jimmy Ryan	726
79	Andre Dawson	725
	Lee May	725
81	Sam Rice	716
82	Willie Davis	715
	Del Ennis	715
84	Bill Buckner	714
85	Carlton Fisk	713
	Gil Hodges	713
87	Frankie Frisch	709
	Eddie Murray	709
89	Dave Kingman	707
90	Fred Lynn	704
91	Cecil Cooper	703
92	George Foster	702
93	Bobby Bonds	700
94	Gabby Hartnett	696
95	Cesar Cedeno	695
96	Bobby Doerr	693
97	Babe Herman	690
	George Sisler	690
99	George Davis	688
100	Kiki Cuyler	679

Pinch Hits

1	Manny Mota	150
2	Smoky Burgess	145
3	Greg Gross	136
4	Jose Morales	123
5	Jerry Lynch	116
6	Red Lucas	114
7	Steve Braun	113
8	Terry Crowley	108
9	Gates Brown	107
10	Mike Lum	103
11	Rusty Staub	100
12	Larry Biittner	95
	Vic Davalillo	95
14	Jerry Hairston	93
	Dave Philley	93
16	Jay Johnstone	92
17	Ed Kranepool	90
	Elmer Valo	90
19	Jim Dwyer	86
20	Joel Youngblood	85
21	Jesus Alou	82
	Kurt Bevacqua	82
	Tim McCarver	82
	Denny Walling	82

Pinch Hit Average

1	Tommy Davis	.320
2	Frenchy Bordagaray	.312
3	Frankie Baumholtz	.307
4	Red Schoendienst	.303
5	Bob Fothergill	.300
6	Dave Philley	.299
7	Manny Mota	.297
8	Ted Easterly	.296
9	Harvey Hendrick	.295
10	Thad Bosley	.290
11	Manny Sanquillen	.288
12	Smoky Burgess	.286
13	Rick Miller	.286
14	Johnny Mize	.283
15	Bubba Morton	.281
16	Steve Braun	.281
17	Don Mueller	.280
18	Rusty Staub	.279
19	Mickey Vernon	.279
20	Gene Woodling	.278
21	Bobby Adams	.277
22	Ed Kranepool	.277
23	Jose Moarles	.276
24	Ron Northey	.276
25	Glenn Adams	.276

Pinch Hit Home Runs

1	Cliff Johnson	20
2	Jerry Lynch	18
3	Gates Brown	16
	Smoky Burgess	16
	Willie McCovey	16
6	George Crowe	14
7	Joe Adcock	12
	Bob Cerv	12
	Jose Morales	12
	Graig Nettles	12
11	Jeff Burroughs	11
	Jay Johnstone	11
	Fred Whitfield	11
	Cy Williams	11
15	Mike Lum	10
	Ken McMullen	10
	Don Mincher	10
	Wally Post	10
	Champ Summers	10
	Jerry Turner	10
	Gus Zernial	10

Stolen Bases

1	Lou Brock	938
2	Billy Hamilton	912
3	Ty Cobb	892
4	Rickey Henderson	794
5	Eddie Collins	743
6	Arlie Latham	739
7	Max Carey	738
8	Honus Wagner	722
9	Joe Morgan	689
10	Tom Brown	657
11	Bert Campaneris	649
12	George Davis	616
13	Dummy Hoy	594
14	Maury Wills	586
15	George Van Haltren	583
16	Hugh Duffy	574
17	Bid McPhee	568
18	Willie Wilson	564
19	Davey Lopes	557
20	Cesar Cedeno	550
21	Bill Dahlen	547
22	Tim Raines	544
23	Monte Ward	540
24	Herman Long	534
25	Patsy Donovan	518
26	Jack Doyle	515
27	Harry Stovey	509
28	Luis Aparicio	506
	Fred Clarke	506
30	Willie Keeler	495
31	Clyde Milan	494
32	Omar Moreno	487
33	Mike Griffin	473
34	Tommy McCarthy	468
35	Jimmy Sheckard	465
36	Bobby Bonds	461
37	Ed Delahanty	455
	Ron LeFlore	455
39	Curt Welch	453
40	Joe Kelley	443
41	Sherry Magee	441
42	John McGraw	436
43	Tris Speaker	433
44	Bob Bescher	428
	Mike Tiernan	428
46	Charlie Comiskey	419
	Frankie Frisch	419
48	Jimmy Ryan	418
49	Tommy Harper	408
50	Donie Bush	405
51	Ozzie Smith	403
52	Frank Chance	401
53	Bill Lange	399
54	Willie Davis	398
55	Sam Mertes	396
56	Bill North	395
57	Jesse Burkett	389
58	Tommy Corcoran	387
59	Dave Collins	385
	Tom Daly	385
	Freddie Patek	385
62	George Burns	383
	Hugh Nicol	383
64	Fred Pfeffer	382
65	Nap Lajoie	381
	Walt Wilmot	381
67	Harry Hooper	375
	George Sisler	375
69	Jack Glasscock	372
70	King Kelly	368
71	Sam Crawford	366
	Tommy Dowd	366
73	Hal Chase	363
74	Tommy Leach	361
75	Hughie Jennings	359
	Fielder Jones	359
77	Buck Ewing	354
78	Rod Carew	353
79	Tommy Tucker	352
80	Sam Rice	351
81	George Case	349
82	Paul Radford	346
83	Julio Cruz	343
84	Amos Otis	341
85	John Anderson	338
	Willie Mays	338
87	Joe Tinker	336
88	Kip Selbach	334
89	Elmer Flick	330
90	Jose Cardenal	329
	Ned Hanlon	329
92	Monte Cross	328
	Kiki Cuyler	328
	Kid Gleason	328
95	Johnny Evers	324
	Miller Huggins	324
97	Ed McKean	323
98	Dave Concepcion	321
	Red Murray	321
100	2 players tied	318

Stolen Base Average

(100 or more stolen bases)

1	Tim Raines	87.0
2	Willie Wilson	84.1
3	Davey Lopes	83.0
4	Julio Cruz	81.5
5	Joe Morgan	81.0
6	Rickey Henderson	80.9
7	Ozzie Smith	80.4
8	Mickey Mantle	80.1
9	Andy VanSlyke	79.6
10	Luis Aparicio	78.8
11	Ryne Sandberg	78.6
12	Amos Otis	78.6
13	Paul Molitor	78.5
14	Kirk Gibson	78.2
15	Tommy Harper	77.9
16	Miguel Dilone	77.4
17	Willie McGee	76.8
18	Willie Mays	76.6
19	Bert Campaneris	76.5
20	Ron LeFlore	76.2
21	George Case	76.2
22	Mookie Wilson	76.1
23	Juan Samuel	76.0
24	Willie Randolph	75.4
25	Cesar Cedeno	75.4
26	Lou Brock	75.3
27	Willie Davis	75.2
28	Larry Bowa	75.2
29	Bump Wills	75.1
30	Andre Dawson	75.0
	Tom Herr	75.0
32	Mickey Rivers	74.8
33	Dave Concepcion	74.7
34	Freddie Patek	74.6
35	Lloyd Moseby	74.5
36	Alan Bannister	74.5
37	Johnny Temple	74.5
	John Wathan	74.5
39	Bake McBride	74.4
40	Lonnie Smith	74.1
41	Sandy Alomar	73.9
42	Frank Taveras	73.9
43	Maury Wills	73.8
44	Dave Collins	73.8
45	Gene Richards	73.5
46	Al Bumbry	73.4
47	Bobby Bonds	73.2
48	Jim Landis	73.2
49	Garry Maddox	72.9
50	Omar Moreno	72.8

Stolen Base Runs

1	Rickey Henderson	126
2	Tim Raines	115
3	Joe Morgan	110
4	Willie Wilson	105
5	Davey Lopes	99
6	Lou Brock	97
7	Bert Campaneris	75
8	Luis Aparicio	70
9	Ozzie Smith	62
10	Cesar Cedeno	58
11	Julio Cruz	56
12	Tommy Harper	53
13	Ron LeFlore	51
	Maury Wills	51
15	Amos Otis	47
16	Paul Molitor	43
17	Willie Davis	41
18	Willie Mays	40
19	George Case	39
20	Bobby Bonds	37
	Omar Moreno	37
	Freddie Patek	37
23	Dave Collins	33
	Miguel Dilone	33
25	Larry Bowa	32
	Ryne Sandberg	32
27	Dave Concepcion	31
	Mookie Wilson	31
29	Hank Aaron	28
	Andre Dawson	28
	Willie McGee	28
	Lonnie Smith	28
33	Kirk Gibson	26
	Willie Randolph	26
	Mickey Rivers	26
	Juan Samuel	26
	Frank Taveras	26
38	Andy Van Slyke	25
39	Mickey Mantle	23
40	Lloyd Moseby	22
41	Al Bumbry	21
	Bill North	21
	Gene Richards	21
44	Sandy Alomar	20
	Bump Wills	20
46	Garry Maddox	19
47	Vada Pinson	18
48	Bake McBride	17
49	Tom Herr	16
50	3 players tied	15

Stolen Base Wins

1	Rickey Henderson	12.6
2	Tim Raines	12.0
3	Joe Morgan	11.5
4	Willie Wilson	10.5
5	Davey Lopes	10.2
6	Lou Brock	10.2
7	Bert Campaneris	7.9
8	Luis Aparicio	7.3
9	Ozzie Smith	6.5
10	Cesar Cedeno	6.1
11	Tommy Harper	5.6
12	Julio Cruz	5.6
13	Maury Wills	5.3
14	Ron LeFlore	5.2
15	Amos Otis	4.9
16	Willie Davis	4.3
17	Paul Molitor	4.3
18	Willie Mays	4.1
19	George Case	3.9
20	Freddie Patek	3.8
21	Omar Moreno	3.8
22	Bobby Bonds	3.8
23	Miguel Dilone	3.4
24	Dave Collins	3.4
25	Larry Bowa	3.3
26	Ryne Sandberg	3.3
27	Mookie Wilson	3.2
28	Dave Concepcion	3.2
29	Andre Dawson	2.9
30	Willie McGee	2.9
31	Hank Aaron	2.9
32	Lonnie Smith	2.9
33	Frank Taveras	2.7
34	Juan Samuel	2.7
35	Mickey Rivers	2.7
36	Kirk Gibson	2.6
37	Willie Randolph	2.6
38	Andy Van Slyke	2.6
39	Mickey Mantle	2.4
40	Gene Richards	2.2
41	Lloyd Moseby	2.2
42	Bill North	2.2
43	Al Bumbry	2.1
44	Sandy Alomar	2.1
45	Bump Wills	2.0
46	Garry Maddox	2.0
47	Vada Pinson	1.9
48	Bake McBride	1.8
49	Tom Herr	1.7
50	Jose Cardenal	1.6

Games

First Base
1. Jake Beckley — 2377
2. Mickey Vernon — 2237
3. Lou Gehrig — 2137
4. Charlie Grimm — 2131
5. Joe Judge — 2084
6. Ed Konetchy — 2073
7. Steve Garvey — 2059
8. Cap Anson — 2058
9. Joe Kuhel — 2057
10. Willie McCovey — 2045

Second Base
1. Eddie Collins — 2650
2. Joe Morgan — 2527
3. Nellie Fox — 2295
4. Charlie Gehringer — 2206
5. Bid McPhee — 2125
6. Bill Mazeroski — 2094
7. Nap Lajoie — 2035
8. Frank White — 1939
9. Bobby Doerr — 1852
10. Red Schoendienst — 1834

Shortstop
1. Luis Aparicio — 2581
2. Larry Bowa — 2222
3. Luke Appling — 2218
4. Dave Concepcion — 2176
5. Rabbit Maranville — 2153
6. Bill Dahlen — 2132
7. Bert Campaneris — 2097
8. Tommy Corcoran — 2073
9. Roy McMillan — 2028
10. Pee Wee Reese — 2014

Third Base
1. Brooks Robinson — 2870
2. Graig Nettles — 2412
3. Eddie Mathews — 2181
4. Buddy Bell — 2172
5. Mike Schmidt — 2167
6. Ron Santo — 2130
7. Eddie Yost — 2008
8. Ron Cey — 1989
9. Aurelio Rodriguez — 1983
10. Sal Bando — 1896

Outfield
1. Ty Cobb — 2935
2. Willie Mays — 2843
3. Hank Aaron — 2760
4. Tris Speaker — 2698
5. Lou Brock — 2507
6. Al Kaline — 2488
7. Max Carey — 2421
8. Vada Pinson — 2403
9. Roberto Clemente — 2370
10. Zach Wheat — 2337

Catcher
1. Bob Boone — 2056
2. Al Lopez — 1918
3. Jim Sundberg — 1854
4. Carlton Fisk — 1838
5. Rick Ferrell — 1806
6. Gabby Hartnett — 1793
7. Gary Carter — 1776
8. Ted Simmons — 1772
9. Johnny Bench — 1744
10. Ray Schalk — 1726

Pitcher
1. Hoyt Wilhelm — 1070
2. Kent Tekulve — 1013
3. Lindy McDaniel — 987
4. Rollie Fingers — 944
5. Gene Garber — 931
6. Cy Young — 906
7. Sparky Lyle — 899
8. Jim Kaat — 898
9. Don McMahon — 874
10. Phil Niekro — 864

Fielding Average

First Base
1. Steve Garvey — .996
2. Wes Parker — .996
3. Dan Driessen — .995
4. Jim Spencer — .995
5. Frank McCormick — .995
6. Keith Hernandez — .994
7. Vic Power — .994
8. Joe Adcock — .994
9. Mike Jorgensen — .994
10. Ernie Banks — .994

Second Base
1. Tom Herr — .988
2. Jim Gantner — .985
3. Frank White — .984
4. Bobby Grich — .984
5. Jerry Lumpe — .984
6. Cookie Rojas — .984
7. Dave Cash — .984
8. Nellie Fox — .984
9. Tommy Helms — .983
10. Glenn Hubbard — .983

Shortstop
1. Larry Bowa — .980
2. Ozzie Smith — .978
3. Mark Belanger — .977
4. Bucky Dent — .976
5. Alan Trammell — .976
6. Roger Metzger — .976
7. Tim Foli — .973
8. Dal Maxvill — .973
9. Lou Boudreau — .973
10. Cal Ripken — .972

Third Base
1. Brooks Robinson — .971
2. Ken Reitz — .970
3. George Kell — .969
4. Don Money — .968
5. Don Wert — .968
6. Willie Kamm — .967
7. Heinie Groh — .967
8. Carney Lansford — .966
9. Clete Boyer — .965
10. Gary Gaetti — .965

Outfield
1. Terry Puhl — .993
2. Brett Butler — .992
3. Pete Rose — .991
4. Amos Otis — .991
5. Joe Rudi — .991
6. Mickey Stanley — .991
7. Jim Piersall — .990
8. Jim Landis — .989
9. Ken Berry — .989
10. Tommy Holmes — .989

Catcher
1. Bill Freehan — .993
2. Elston Howard — .993
3. Jim Sundberg — .993
4. Sherm Lollar — .992
5. Johnny Edwards — .992
6. Tom Haller — .992
7. Gary Carter — .991
8. Jerry Grote — .991
9. Ernie Whitt — .991
10. Rick Cerone — .991

Pitcher
1. Don Mossi — .990
2. Gary Nolan — .990
3. Lon Warneke — .988
4. Jim Wilson — .988
5. Woodie Fryman — .988
6. Rick Rhoden — .987
7. Larry Gura — .986
8. Pete Alexander — .985
9. General Crowder — .984
10. Bill Monbouquette — .984

Total Chances per Game

First Base
1. Tom Jones — 11.38
2. George Stovall — 11.30
3. George Kelly — 11.09
4. Candy LaChance — 11.05
5. Wally Pipp — 11.05
6. Ed Konetchy — 11.04
7. George Burns — 10.92
8. Bill Terry — 10.91
9. Cap Anson — 10.84
10. Walter Holke — 10.83

Second Base
1. Fred Pfeffer — 6.95
2. Bid McPhee — 6.71
3. Cub Stricker — 6.53
4. Lou Bierbauer — 6.42
5. Cupid Childs — 6.32
6. Ski Melillo — 6.16
7. Hughie Critz — 6.07
8. Frankie Frisch — 6.05
9. Bucky Harris — 6.00
10. Nap Lajoie — 6.00

Shortstop
1. Dave Bancroft — 6.33
2. Herman Long — 6.32
3. Bill Dahlen — 6.26
4. George Davis — 6.22
5. Rabbit Maranville — 6.10
6. Bobby Wallace — 6.10
7. Tommy Corcoran — 6.09
8. Monte Cross — 6.06
9. Bones Ely — 6.06
10. Honus Wagner — 5.99

Third Base
1. Jerry Denny — 4.20
2. Billy Shindle — 4.15
3. Billy Nash — 4.08
4. Arlie Latham — 4.04
5. Denny Lyons — 4.00
6. Jimmy Collins — 3.89
7. Hick Carpenter — 3.81
8. Jimmy Austin — 3.74
9. Lave Cross — 3.73
10. Frank Baker — 3.64

Outfield
1. Taylor Douthit — 3.16
2. Richie Ashburn — 3.04
3. Dom DiMaggio — 2.99
4. Dwayne Murphy — 2.98
5. Mike Kreevich — 2.95
6. Sam Chapman — 2.91
7. Sam West — 2.88
8. Max Carey — 2.87
9. Fred Schulte — 2.84
10. Lloyd Waner — 2.81

Catcher
1. Johnny Edwards — 6.98
2. John Roseboro — 6.83
3. Bill Freehan — 6.79
4. Tony Pena — 6.54
5. Jerry Grote — 6.53
6. Gary Carter — 6.48
7. Tim McCarver — 6.41
8. Tom Haller — 6.33
9. Bill Killefer — 6.27
10. Earl Battey — 6.21

Pitcher
1. Nick Altrock — 3.72
2. Harry Howell — 3.61
3. Addie Joss — 3.60
4. Ed Walsh — 3.48
5. Nixey Callahan — 3.45
6. Willie Sudhoff — 3.35
7. George Mullin — 3.23
8. Barney Pelty — 3.20
9. Chick Fraser — 3.12
10. Jack Taylor — 3.03

Chances Accepted per Game

First Base
1. Tom Jones — 11.21
2. George Stovall — 11.15
3. George Kelly — 11.00
4. Wally Pipp — 10.96
5. Ed Konetchy — 10.93
6. Candy LaChance — 10.87
7. Bill Terry — 10.82
8. George Burns — 10.77
9. Walter Holke — 10.75
10. Stuffy McInnis — 10.71

Second Base
1. Fred Pfeffer — 6.39
2. Bid McPhee — 6.33
3. Lou Bierbauer — 6.00
4. Ski Melillo — 6.00
5. Cub Stricker — 5.92
6. Hughie Critz — 5.91
7. Frankie Frisch — 5.89
8. Cupid Childs — 5.88
9. Bucky Harris — 5.79
10. Nap Lajoie — 5.78

Shortstop
1. Dave Bancroft — 5.98
2. George Davis — 5.85
3. Rabbit Maranville — 5.81
4. Bill Dahlen — 5.80
5. Herman Long — 5.78
6. Bobby Wallace — 5.73
7. Travis Jackson — 5.67
8. Dick Bartell — 5.64
9. Tommy Corcoran — 5.63
10. Honus Wagner — 5.63

Third Base
1. Jerry Denny — 3.71
2. Billy Shindle — 3.70
3. Billy Nash — 3.66
4. Jimmy Collins — 3.61
5. Denny Lyons — 3.54
6. Arlie Latham — 3.52
7. Lave Cross — 3.50
8. Jimmy Austin — 3.49
9. Frank Baker — 3.43
10. Bill Bradley — 3.37

Outfield
1. Taylor Douthit — 3.07
2. Richie Ashburn — 2.98
3. Dwayne Murphy — 2.95
4. Dom DiMaggio — 2.92
5. Mike Kreevich — 2.89
6. Sam Chapman — 2.83
7. Sam West — 2.83
8. Max Carey — 2.77
9. Fred Schulte — 2.77
10. Lloyd Waner — 2.76

Catcher
1. Johnny Edwards — 6.92
2. John Roseboro — 6.76
3. Bill Freehan — 6.75
4. Jerry Grote — 6.47
5. Tony Pena — 6.46
6. Gary Carter — 6.43
7. Tim McCarver — 6.35
8. Tom Haller — 6.28
9. Earl Battey — 6.15
10. Bill Killefer — 6.12

Pitcher
1. Nick Altrock — 3.59
2. Addie Joss — 3.47
3. Harry Howell — 3.46
4. Ed Walsh — 3.35
5. Nixey Callahan — 3.23
6. Willie Sudhoff — 3.14
7. George Mullin — 3.07
8. Barney Pelty — 3.00
9. Jack Taylor — 2.91
10. Chick Fraser — 2.90

Putouts

First Base

1	Jake Beckley	23709
2	Ed Konetchy	21361
3	Cap Anson	20759
4	Charlie Grimm	20711
5	Stuffy McInnis	20119
6	Mickey Vernon	19808
7	Jake Daubert	19634
8	Lou Gehrig	19510
9	Joe Kuhel	19386
10	Joe Judge	19264

Second Base

1	Bid McPhee	6545
2	Eddie Collins	6526
3	Nellie Fox	6090
4	Joe Morgan	5742
5	Nap Lajoie	5496
6	Charlie Gehringer	5369
7	Bill Mazeroski	4974
8	Bobby Doerr	4928
9	Billy Herman	4780
10	Fred Pfeffer	4714

Shortstop

1	Rabbit Maranville	5139
2	Bill Dahlen	4850
3	Dave Bancroft	4623
4	Honus Wagner	4576
5	Tommy Corcoran	4550
6	Luis Aparicio	4548
7	Luke Appling	4398
8	Herman Long	4228
9	Bobby Wallace	4142
10	Pee Wee Reese	4040

Third Base

1	Brooks Robinson	2697
2	Jimmy Collins	2372
3	Eddie Yost	2356
4	Lave Cross	2304
5	Pie Traynor	2289
6	Billy Nash	2236
7	Frank Baker	2154
8	Willie Kamm	2151
9	Eddie Mathews	2049
10	Willie Jones	2045

Outfield

1	Willie Mays	7095
2	Tris Speaker	6787
3	Max Carey	6363
4	Ty Cobb	6361
5	Richie Ashburn	6089
6	Hank Aaron	5539
7	Willie Davis	5449
8	Doc Cramer	5412
9	Vada Pinson	5097
10	Al Kaline	5035

Catcher

1	Gary Carter	10360
2	Bob Boone	10265
3	Bill Freehan	9941
4	Carlton Fisk	9428
5	Jim Sundberg	9414
6	John Roseboro	9291
7	Johnny Bench	9260
8	Johnny Edwards	8925
9	Ted Simmons	8906
10	Yogi Berra	8729

Pitcher

1	Phil Niekro	390
2	Ferguson Jenkins	363
3	Gaylord Perry	349
4	Don Sutton	329
5	Tom Seaver	328
6	Tony Mullane	327
7	Jim Galvin	324
8	Rick Reuschel	319
9	Robin Roberts	316
10	Chick Fraser	315

Putouts per Game

First Base

1	Tom Jones	10.53
2	Candy LaChance	10.48
3	George Stovall	10.45
4	George Kelly	10.37
5	Wally Pipp	10.33
6	Ed Konetchy	10.31
7	Bill Phillips	10.22
8	Walter Holke	10.20
9	Charlie Comiskey	10.15
10	John Reilly	10.12

Second Base

1	Bid McPhee	3.09
2	Fred Pfeffer	3.07
3	Cub Stricker	2.99
4	Jerry Priddy	2.74
5	Bucky Harris	2.73
6	Nap Lajoie	2.71
7	Bobby Doerr	2.67
8	Lou Bierbauer	2.66
9	Cupid Childs	2.66
10	Nellie Fox	2.66

Shortstop

1	Dave Bancroft	2.47
2	Honus Wagner	2.43
3	Rabbit Maranville	2.39
4	Monte Cross	2.37
5	George Davis	2.36
6	Herman Long	2.36
7	Dick Bartell	2.31
8	Bill Dahlen	2.28
9	Ivy Olson	2.27
10	Bobby Wallace	2.27

Third Base

1	Jerry Denny	1.60
2	Denny Lyons	1.56
3	Billy Nash	1.53
4	Jimmy Austin	1.43
5	Billy Shindle	1.43
6	Jimmy Collins	1.41
7	Frank Baker	1.40
8	Hick Carpenter	1.37
9	Lave Cross	1.34
10	Hans Lobert	1.30

Outfield

1	Taylor Douthit	3.01
2	Richie Ashburn	2.90
3	Dwayne Murphy	2.88
4	Dom DiMaggio	2.82
5	Mike Kreevich	2.81
6	Sam Chapman	2.74
7	Sam West	2.74
8	Fred Schulte	2.70
9	Rickey Henderson	2.68
10	Chet Lemon	2.68
11	Lloyd Waner	2.68

Catcher

1	Johnny Edwards	6.42
2	John Roseboro	6.30
3	Bill Freehan	6.29
4	Jerry Grote	6.00
5	Tim McCarver	5.92
6	Tom Haller	5.85
7	Tony Pena	5.85
8	Gary Carter	5.84
9	Earl Battey	5.69
10	Elston Howard	5.67

Pitcher

1	Dave Foutz	0.79
2	Dan Petry	0.79
3	Nick Altrock	0.78
4	Chick Fraser	0.73
5	Jack Morris	0.72
6	Carl Morton	0.72
7	Ted Breitenstein	0.70
8	Mel Stottlemyre	0.68
9	Larry Corcoran	0.67
10	Guy Hecker	0.67

Assists

First Base

1	Keith Hernandez	1631
2	George Sisler	1529
3	Mickey Vernon	1448
4	Fred Tenney	1363
5	Chris Chambliss	1351
6	Bill Buckner	1332
7	Norm Cash	1317
8	Jake Beckley	1315
9	Joe Judge	1301
10	Ed Konetchy	1292

Second Base

1	Eddie Collins	7630
2	Charlie Gehringer	7068
3	Joe Morgan	6967
4	Bid McPhee	6905
5	Bill Mazeroski	6685
6	Nellie Fox	6373
7	Nap Lajoie	6262
8	Frankie Frisch	6026
9	Bobby Doerr	5710
10	Billy Herman	5681

Shortstop

1	Luis Aparicio	8016
2	Bill Dahlen	7500
3	Rabbit Maranville	7354
4	Luke Appling	7218
5	Tommy Corcoran	7106
6	Larry Bowa	6857
7	Dave Concepcion	6594
8	Dave Bancroft	6561
9	Roger Peckinpaugh	6337
10	Bobby Wallace	6303

Third Base

1	Brooks Robinson	6205
2	Graig Nettles	5279
3	Mike Schmidt	4975
4	Buddy Bell	4913
5	Ron Santo	4581
6	Eddie Mathews	4322
7	Aurelio Rodriguez	4150
8	Ron Cey	4018
9	Sal Bando	3720
10	2 players tied	3701

Outfield

1	Tris Speaker	448
2	Ty Cobb	392
3	Jimmy Ryan	375
4	George Van Haltren	351
5	Tom Brown	348
6	Harry Hooper	344
7	Max Carey	339
8	Jimmy Sheckard	307
9	Clyde Milan	294
10	King Kelly	290

Catcher

1	Deacon McGuire	1859
2	Ray Schalk	1811
3	Steve O'Neill	1698
4	Red Dooin	1590
5	Chief Zimmer	1580
6	Johnny Kling	1552
7	Ivey Wingo	1487
8	Wilbert Robinson	1452
9	Wally Schang	1420
10	Duke Farrell	1417

Pitcher

1	Cy Young	2027
2	Christy Mathewson	1503
3	Pete Alexander	1413
4	Jim Galvin	1390
5	Walter Johnson	1351
6	George Mullin	1261
7	Burleigh Grimes	1252
8	Jack Quinn	1243
9	Ed Walsh	1207
10	Eppa Rixey	1195

Assists per Game

First Base

1	Bill Buckner	0.88
2	Keith Hernandez	0.86
3	Ferris Fain	0.84
4	Vic Power	0.83
5	Eddie Murray	0.78
6	George Sisler	0.78
7	Rudy York	0.77
8	Fred Tenney	0.76
9	Mike Hargrove	0.75
10	Dick Stuart	0.75

Second Base

1	Hughie Critz	3.54
2	Frankie Frisch	3.42
3	Ski Melillo	3.38
4	Glenn Hubbard	3.36
5	Lou Bierbauer	3.34
6	Fred Pfeffer	3.33
7	Rogers Hornsby	3.31
8	Bid McPhee	3.25
9	Tony Cuccinello	3.23
10	Cupid Childs	3.22

Shortstop

1	Germany Smith	3.70
2	Art Fletcher	3.56
3	Bill Dahlen	3.52
4	Ozzie Smith	3.52
5	Dave Bancroft	3.51
6	Bones Ely	3.50
7	Travis Jackson	3.50
8	George Davis	3.49
9	Jack Glasscock	3.46
10	Bobby Wallace	3.46

Third Base

1	Mike Schmidt	2.30
2	Buddy Bell	2.27
3	Billy Shindle	2.27
4	Arlie Latham	2.26
5	Clete Boyer	2.24
6	Jimmy Collins	2.20
7	Graig Nettles	2.19
8	George Brett	2.18
9	Darrell Evans	2.18
10	Brooks Robinson	2.17

Outfield

1	Tommy McCarthy	0.23
2	Pop Corkhill	0.22
3	Chicken Wolf	0.22
4	Sam Thompson	0.21
5	Tom Brown	0.20
6	Jimmy Ryan	0.20
7	George Van Haltren	0.20
8	Curt Welch	0.20
9	Ed Delahanty	0.19
10	George Gore	0.19

Catcher

1	Duke Farrell	1.42
2	Red Dooin	1.34
3	Johnny Kling	1.33
4	Bill Killefer	1.32
5	Oscar Stanage	1.29
6	Chief Zimmer	1.28
7	John Warner	1.27
8	Ivey Wingo	1.21
9	Billy Sullivan	1.18
10	George Gibson	1.17

Pitcher

1	Addie Joss	2.96
2	Harry Howell	2.84
3	Nick Altrock	2.81
4	Ed Walsh	2.81
5	Willie Sudhoff	2.76
6	George Mullin	2.62
7	Nixey Callahan	2.58
8	Ed Willett	2.55
9	Barney Pelty	2.51
10	Jack Taylor	2.49

Double Plays

First Base
1	Mickey Vernon	2044
2	Joe Kuhel	1769
3	Charlie Grimm	1733
4	Chris Chambliss	1687
5	Gil Hodges	1614
6	Keith Hernandez	1604
7	Jim Bottomley	1582
8	Lou Gehrig	1574
9	Jimmie Foxx	1528
10	Joe Judge	1500

Second Base
1	Bill Mazeroski	1706
2	Nellie Fox	1619
3	Bobby Doerr	1507
4	Joe Morgan	1505
5	Charlie Gehringer	1444
6	Red Schoendienst	1368
7	Bobby Grich	1302
8	Frank White	1267
9	Willie Randolph	1241
10	Eddie Collins	1215

Shortstop
1	Luis Aparicio	1553
2	Luke Appling	1424
3	Roy McMillan	1304
4	Dave Concepcion	1290
5	Larry Bowa	1265
6	Pee Wee Reese	1246
7	Dick Groat	1237
8	Phil Rizzuto	1217
9	Bert Campaneris	1186
10	Rabbit Maranville	1183

Third Base
1	Brooks Robinson	618
2	Graig Nettles	470
3	Mike Schmidt	442
4	Buddy Bell	430
5	Aurelio Rodriguez	408
6	Ron Santo	395
7	Eddie Mathews	369
8	Ken Boyer	355
9	Sal Bando	345
	Eddie Yost	345

Outfield
1	Tris Speaker	139
2	Ty Cobb	107
3	Max Carey	86
4	Tom Brown	85
5	Harry Hooper	81
6	Jimmy Sheckard	80
7	Mike Griffin	74
8	Dummy Hoy	72
	Jimmy Ryan	72
10	Fielder Jones	70

Catcher
1	Ray Schalk	226
2	Yogi Berra	175
	Steve O'Neill	175
4	Gabby Hartnett	163
5	Jimmy Wilson	153
6	Wally Schang	149
7	Bob Boone	148
8	Deacon McGuire	142
	Jim Sundberg	142
10	Rollie Hemsley	141
	Ivey Wingo	141

Pitcher
1	Phil Niekro	80
	Warren Spahn	80
3	Freddie Fitzsimmons	79
4	Bob Lemon	78
5	Bucky Walters	76
6	Burleigh Grimes	74
7	Walter Johnson	72
8	Tommy John	69
9	Jim Kaat	65
10	Dizzy Trout	63

Fielding Runs

1	Bill Mazeroski	351
2	Nap Lajoie	300
3	Bill Dahlen	278
4	Bid McPhee	276
5	Ozzie Smith	262
6	Mike Schmidt	241
7	Fred Pfeffer	234
8	George Davis	208
9	Jack Glasscock	200
10	Glenn Hubbard	185
11	Buddy Bell	179
12	Clete Boyer	178
13	Tris Speaker	177
14	Dave Bancroft	176
15	Max Carey	170
	Bobby Wallace	170
17	Bobby Doerr	168
	Joe Tinker	168
19	Richie Ashburn	167
20	Dick Bartell	163
21	Art Fletcher	155
22	Gary Carter	153
23	Manny Trillo	151
24	Frankie Frisch	150
25	Graig Nettles	143
26	Hughie Jennings	142
27	Aurelio Rodriguez	140
28	Bobby Grich	139
29	Lee Tannehill	138
30	Bobby Knoop	135
31	George McBride	134
	Brooks Robinson	134
33	Joe Gerhardt	132
	Jim Sundberg	132
35	Jimmy Collins	131
36	Darrell Evans	129
	Ron Santo	129
38	Keith Hernandez	126
39	Fred Dunlap	125
40	Red Schoendienst	123
41	Lou Bierbauer	122
	Mickey Doolan	122
43	Lou Boudreau	121
44	Bill Freehan	120
45	Ski Melillo	119
46	Danny Richardson	118
47	Mark Belanger	116
48	Gene Alley	115
49	Phil Rizzuto	114
	Roy Smalley	114
51	Roberto Clemente	113
52	Germany Smith	107
53	Thurman Munson	106
54	Luis Aparicio	105
55	Rick Burleson	102
	Fred Tenney	102
57	Lave Cross	101
	Julio Cruz	101
	Johnny Logan	101
	Gil McDougald	101
61	Buck Ewing	100
62	Hobe Ferris	99
63	Luke Appling	98
64	Hughie Critz	97
	Rabbit Maranville	97
66	Willie Mays	96
	Ryne Sandberg	96
68	Del Crandall	94
	Billy Jurges	94
70	Monte Ward	93
71	Bill Buckner	92
	Ron Hansen	92
73	Billy Herman	89
	Del Pratt	89
75	Jerry Denny	88
	Rickey Henderson	88
77	Duke Farrell	87
	Bump Wills	87
79	Carlton Fisk	86
	Dick Groat	86
	Tony Pena	86
	Ted Simmons	86
	Curt Welch	86
84	Billy Shindle	85
	George Sisler	85
	Burgess Whitehead	85
87	Tim Foli	84
88	Bill Bergen	83
	Travis Jackson	83
90	Bob Johnson	81
	Vic Power	81
	Hardy Richardson	81
93	Joe Sewell	80
94	Cupid Childs	78
	Nellie Fox	78
	Roy McMillan	78
	Roger Peckinpaugh	78
	Everett Scott	78
	Jim Wynn	78
100	Maury Wills	75

Fielding Wins

1	Bill Mazeroski	36.5
2	Nap Lajoie	30.8
3	Ozzie Smith	27.4
4	Bill Dahlen	26.5
5	Mike Schmidt	25.2
6	Bid McPhee	24.0
7	Fred Pfeffer	20.4
8	George Davis	19.6
9	Glenn Hubbard	19.2
10	Clete Boyer	18.5
11	Buddy Bell	18.3
12	Tris Speaker	18.1
13	Dave Bancroft	17.9
14	Joe Tinker	17.8
15	Jack Glasscock	17.8
16	Max Carey	17.4
17	Bobby Wallace	17.2
18	Richie Ashburn	16.7
19	Art Fletcher	16.5
20	Bobby Doerr	16.5
21	Dick Bartell	16.0
22	Gary Carter	16.0
23	Manny Trillo	15.7
24	Lee Tannehill	15.0
25	Graig Nettles	14.8
26	Frankie Frisch	14.7
27	Aurelio Rodriguez	14.6
28	Bobby Knoop	14.6
29	George McBride	14.4
30	Bobby Grich	14.2
31	Brooks Robinson	14.1
32	Ron Santo	13.6
33	Jim Sundberg	13.3
34	Darrell Evans	13.3
35	Keith Hernandez	13.2
36	Mickey Doolan	13.1
37	Bill Freehan	12.8
38	Jimmy Collins	12.7
39	Roy Thomas	12.6
40	Hughie Jennings	12.5
41	Red Schoendienst	12.3
42	Gene Alley	12.2
43	Lou Boudreau	12.1
44	Mark Belanger	12.1
45	Roberto Clemente	11.8
46	Joe Gerhardt	11.6
47	Roy Smalley	11.4
48	Phil Rizzuto	11.4
49	Fred Dunlap	11.3
50	Ski Melillo	11.1
51	Thurman Munson	11.0
52	Luis Aparicio	11.0
53	Hobe Ferris	10.5
54	Rick Burleson	10.3
55	Lou Bierbauer	10.3
56	Danny Richardson	10.3
57	Gil McDougald	10.2
58	Johnny Logan	10.2
59	Julio Cruz	10.1
60	Fred Tenney	10.1
61	Ryne Sandberg	10.0
62	Willie Mays	9.9
63	Rabbit Maranville	9.8
64	Ron Hansen	9.7
65	Billy Jurges	9.5
66	Del Crandall	9.5
67	Bill Buckner	9.5
68	Luke Appling	9.4
69	Hughie Critz	9.4
70	Lave Cross	9.3
71	Germany Smith	9.2
72	Del Pratt	9.2
73	Billy Herman	9.0
74	Tony Pena	9.0
75	Ted Simmons	8.9
76	Dick Groat	8.8
77	Bump Wills	8.8
78	Bill Bergen	8.8
79	Rickey Henderson	8.8
80	Tim Foli	8.7
81	Buck Ewing	8.7
82	Carlton Fisk	8.7
83	Burgess Whitehead	8.5
84	George Sisler	8.4
85	Vic Power	8.3
86	Jim Wynn	8.2
87	Monte Ward	8.2
88	Travis Jackson	8.0
89	Everett Scott	7.9
90	Roy McMillan	7.9
91	Roger Peckinpaugh	7.9
92	Nellie Fox	7.9
93	Maury Wills	7.9
94	Jerry Denny	7.8
95	Bob Johnson	7.8
96	Duke Farrell	7.7
97	Doug Rader	7.7
98	Dave Cash	7.6
99	John Stearns	7.6
100	Johnny Evers	7.6

Fielding Wins (by position)

First Base
1	Keith Hernandez	13.2
2	Fred Tenney	10.1
3	Bill Buckner	9.5
4	George Sisler	8.4
5	Vic Power	8.3
6	Bill Terry	6.3
7	Ed Konetchy	6.0
8	Cap Anson	4.8
9	Fred Luderus	4.7
10	Ferris Fain	4.7

Second Base
1	Bill Mazeroski	36.5
2	Nap Lajoie	30.8
3	Bid McPhee	24.0
4	Fred Pfeffer	20.4
5	Glenn Hubbard	19.2
6	Bobby Doerr	16.5
7	Manny Trillo	15.7
8	Frankie Frisch	14.7
9	Bobby Knoop	14.6
10	Bobby Grich	14.2

Shortstop
1	Ozzie Smith	27.4
2	Bill Dahlen	26.5
3	George Davis	19.6
4	Dave Bancroft	17.9
5	Joe Tinker	17.8
6	Jack Glasscock	17.8
7	Bobby Wallace	17.2
8	Art Fletcher	16.5
9	Dick Bartell	16.0
10	George McBride	14.4

Third Base
1	Mike Schmidt	25.2
2	Clete Boyer	18.5
3	Buddy Bell	18.3
4	Graig Nettles	14.8
5	Aurelio Rodriguez	14.6
6	Brooks Robinson	14.1
7	Ron Santo	13.6
8	Darrell Evans	13.3
9	Jimmy Collins	12.7
10	Lave Cross	9.3

Outfield
1	Tris Speaker	18.1
2	Max Carey	17.4
3	Richie Ashburn	16.7
4	Roberto Clemente	11.8
5	Willie Mays	9.9
6	Rickey Henderson	8.8
7	Jim Wynn	8.2
8	Bob Johnson	7.8
9	Curt Welch	7.4
10	Tommy Leach	7.3

Catcher
1	Gary Carter	16.0
2	Jim Sundberg	13.3
3	Bill Freehan	12.8
4	Thurman Munson	11.0
5	Del Crandall	9.5
6	Tony Pena	9.0
7	Ted Simmons	8.9
8	Carlton Fisk	8.7
9	Duke Farrell	7.7
10	Gabby Hartnett	6.8

Total Player Rating

1	Babe Ruth	105.1
2	Ty Cobb	90.6
3	Hank Aaron	90.1
4	Ted Williams	89.8
5	Willie Mays	86.2
6	Nap Lajoie	85.2
7	Tris Speaker	79.9
8	Mike Schmidt	77.9
9	Rogers Hornsby	77.3
10	Honus Wagner	75.6
11	Frank Robinson	71.2
12	Eddie Collins	70.5
13	Stan Musial	70.1
14	Mickey Mantle	69.8
15	Joe Morgan	63.9
16	Lou Gehrig	60.8
17	Mel Ott	60.1
18	Jimmie Foxx	53.2
19	George Davis	48.4
	Eddie Mathews	48.4
21	Bobby Grich	47.4
22	Ed Delahanty	46.1
	Carl Yastrzemski	46.1
24	Al Kaline	45.9
25	Rickey Henderson	44.0
	Reggie Jackson	44.0
27	George Brett	43.8
28	Joe DiMaggio	43.6
29	Charlie Gehringer	43.5
30	Bill Dahlen	43.3
31	Rod Carew	41.0
32	Dan Brouthers	40.4
33	Arky Vaughan	40.3
34	Roberto Clemente	39.6
35	Paul Waner	38.9
36	Roger Connor	38.8
37	Luke Appling	38.5
38	Joe Cronin	38.2
39	Willie McCovey	38.1
	Ron Santo	38.1
41	Ozzie Smith	38.0
42	Bob Johnson	37.8
43	Bid McPhee	37.5
44	Gary Carter	37.4
45	Keith Hernandez	37.3
46	Frankie Frisch	37.2
47	Dave Winfield	36.6
48	Johnny Mize	36.5
49	Joe Jackson	36.1
50	Gabby Hartnett	35.7
51	Dick Allen	35.6
	Bobby Doerr	35.6
53	Yogi Berra	34.8
54	Frank Baker	34.6
55	Jack Glasscock	34.5
56	Bill Mazeroski	34.4
	Ted Simmons	34.4
58	Lou Boudreau	34.3
59	Billy Herman	34.0
	Bobby Wallace	34.0
61	Eddie Murray	33.7
62	Carlton Fisk	33.4
	Reggie Smith	33.4
64	Jackie Robinson	33.3
65	Joe Sewell	33.1
66	Wade Boggs	32.9
67	Harmon Killebrew	32.8
68	Darrell Evans	32.5
69	Willie Stargell	31.6
70	Tim Raines	31.5
71	Robin Yount	31.4
72	Cap Anson	31.3
	Bobby Bonds	31.3
74	Jim Wynn	31.1
75	Bill Dickey	30.6
76	Johnny Bench	30.2
	Jesse Burkett	30.2
	Billy Williams	30.2
79	Joe Torre	29.8
80	Dave Bancroft	29.7
81	Norm Cash	29.6
	Cupid Childs	29.6
83	Rusty Staub	29.4
	Sam Thompson	29.4
85	Bill Freehan	28.9
	Hank Greenberg	28.9
87	Elmer Flick	28.5
	Sherry Magee	28.5
89	Roy Thomas	28.1
90	Fred Clarke	28.0
	Fred Dunlap	28.0
92	Bill Terry	27.8
93	Buck Ewing	27.6
	Joe Gordon	27.6
95	Mickey Cochrane	27.5
96	Richie Ashburn	27.0
	Pete Browning	27.0
	Ralph Kiner	27.0
99	Cal Ripken	26.7
100	Hughie Jennings	26.6

Total Player Rating

101	Willie Randolph	26.5
	Jim Rice	26.5
103	Max Carey	26.1
	Tony Oliva	26.1
105	Hardy Richardson	25.9
106	Stan Hack	25.8
107	Joe Medwick	25.7
108	Buddy Bell	25.6
	Heinie Groh	25.6
110	George Sisler	25.5
111	Jack Clark	25.4
	Harry Heilmann	25.4
113	Dick Bartell	25.2
	Dwight Evans	25.2
	Wally Schang	25.2
116	Thurman Munson	25.1
117	Rocky Colavito	25.0
	Billy Hamilton	25.0
119	Ernie Banks	24.9
120	Pete Rose	24.7
121	Andre Dawson	24.6
122	Chuck Klein	24.3
	Duke Snider	24.3
124	Jake Beckley	24.2
	King Kelly	24.2
	Al Simmons	24.2
127	Graig Nettles	24.1
128	Sam Crawford	23.9
129	Cesar Cedeno	23.8
	Jimmy Collins	23.8
131	Jack Fournier	23.7
	Pedro Guerrero	23.7
133	Minnie Minoso	23.6
	Harry Stovey	23.6
135	Ed Konetchy	23.5
136	Charlie Keller	23.4
	Ernie Lombardi	23.4
138	Brooks Robinson	23.3
139	Joe Kelley	23.1
140	Goose Goslin	22.9
141	Harlond Clift	22.7
	Roy Smalley	22.7
143	Roy Campanella	22.2
	Dave Parker	22.2
145	George Foster	22.1
146	Ron Cey	21.9
147	Del Pratt	21.7
148	Eddie Stanky	21.6
149	Gil McDougald	21.5
150	Fred Lynn	21.3
151	Zach Wheat	21.1
152	Art Fletcher	21.0
	Jim Fregosi	21.0
	Travis Jackson	21.0
	Charley Jones	21.0
156	Fred Pfeffer	20.3
	Ken Singleton	20.3
158	Joe Tinker	20.2
159	Denny Lyons	20.1
160	Frank Howard	20.0
161	Tony Gwynn	19.9
162	Mike Griffin	19.7
163	Ken Williams	19.6
164	Orlando Cepeda	19.5
165	Kiki Cuyler	19.4
166	Gavvy Cravath	19.3
	Darrell Porter	19.3
	Ryne Sandberg	19.3
	Jimmy Sheckard	19.3
170	Darryl Strawberry	19.2
	Lou Whitaker	19.2
	Roy White	19.2
173	Bill Joyce	19.1
	Dale Myer	19.1
175	Miller Huggins	19.0
	Pee Wee Reese	19.0
177	Ken Boyer	18.9
	Jose Cruz	18.9
	Fred Tenney	18.9
180	Roger Bresnahan	18.8
181	Paul Molitor	18.7
182	Bob Elliott	18.5
183	Earl Averill	18.4
	Pie Traynor	18.4
185	Gene Alley	18.3
	Wally Berger	18.3
	Babe Herman	18.3
188	Ferris Fain	18.1
	Chet Lemon	18.1
190	Larry Doby	17.7
	Paul Hines	17.7
	Alan Trammell	17.7
193	Ray Chapman	17.5
194	Rico Carty	17.3
	Roy Cullenbine	17.3
	John McGraw	17.3
197	Dolph Camilli	17.2
	Hal McRae	17.2
	Amos Otis	17.2
200	Art Devlin	16.9

Total Player Rating

201	Charlie Bennett	16.8
	Hack Wilson	16.8
203	Brian Downing	16.7
	Benny Kauff	16.7
205	Johnny Evers	16.6
	Toby Harrah	16.6
207	Duke Farrell	16.2
	Lonny Frey	16.2
209	Frank Chance	16.1
	Deacon McGuire	16.1
	Rudy York	16.1
212	George Gore	16.0
	Bill Nicholson	16.0
	Edd Roush	16.0
	Andy Thornton	16.0
216	Ed Bailey	15.9
	Don Buford	15.9
	Lance Parrish	15.9
219	Jimmy Ryan	15.8
220	Doug DeCinces	15.7
	Jeff Heath	15.7
	Tommy Leach	15.7
	Boog Powell	15.7
224	Smoky Burgess	15.6
	Jim O'Rourke	15.6
226	Mike Hargrove	15.5
227	Phil Rizzuto	15.4
	Vern Stephens	15.4
	Maury Wills	15.4
230	Don Baylor	15.2
	Ben Chapman	15.2
	Billy Nash	15.2
	George Van Haltren	15.2
234	Dave Concepcion	15.1
235	Rick Ferrell	15.0
	Tony Lazzeri	15.0
	Red Schoendienst	15.0
238	Henry Larkin	14.8
239	Sid Gordon	14.7
	Glenn Hubbard	14.7
241	Tommy Henrich	14.6
242	Harry Davis	14.4
	Mike Donlin	14.4
	Mike Tiernan	14.4
245	Enos Slaughter	14.3
246	Andy Seminick	14.2
247	Walker Cooper	14.1
	Gil Hodges	14.1
249	Johnny Logan	14.0
	Roger Peckinpaugh	14.0
251	Kirk Gibson	13.9
	Kip Selbach	13.9
	Richie Zisk	13.9
254	Tony Perez	13.8
	John Titus	13.8
256	Elston Howard	13.7
	Dwayne Murphy	13.7
258	Tony Cuccinello	13.6
259	Bobby Murcer	13.5
	Johnny Pesky	13.5
261	Bob Allison	13.0
	Luis Aparicio	13.0
	Bill Bradley	13.0
	Augie Galan	13.0
265	Roy Sievers	12.9
	Bump Wills	12.9
	Heinie Zimmerman	12.9
268	Willie Kamm	12.8
	Ken Keltner	12.8
	Sixto Lezcano	12.8
	Jim Sundberg	12.8
272	Jack Clements	12.7
	Lave Cross	12.7
	Buddy Myer	12.7
275	Solly Hemus	12.6
	Larry Hisle	12.6
	Cliff Johnson	12.6
	Don Mattingly	12.6
	George Stone	12.6
280	Nellie Fox	12.5
	Chief Zimmer	12.5
282	Bobby Knoop	12.4
283	Tim McCarver	12.3
284	Ron Hunt	12.2
	John Romano	12.2
	Cy Seymour	12.2
287	Charlie Hickman	12.1
	Ed McFarland	12.1
	Al Oliver	12.1
	Bob Watson	12.1
	Jimmy Williams	12.1
292	Ross Youngs	12.0
293	Orator Shaffer	11.9
294	Ron Hansen	11.8
295	Davey Lopes	11.7
296	Dave Johnson	11.6
297	Donie Bush	11.5
298	Del Crandall	11.4
299	Jim Gentile	11.3
	Greg Luzinski	11.3

Total Player Rating

	Tip O'Neill	11.3
	Mike Smith	11.3
	Dixie Walker	11.3
304	Oyster Burns	11.2
	Ken Griffey	11.2
	Stan Spence	11.2
	Sam Wise	11.2
308	Jake Daubert	11.0
309	Jesse Barfield	10.8
	Roger Maris	10.8
	Bill Melton	10.8
	Manny Sanguillen	10.8
	Red Smith	10.8
314	Sal Bando	10.7
	Tommy Holmes	10.7
	Jackie Jensen	10.7
	Whitey Kurowski	10.7
	Al Rosen	10.7
	Chicken Wolf	10.7
320	Johnny Kling	10.6
321	Rick Burleson	10.5
	Harry Danning	10.5
	Larry Doyle	10.5
	Topsy Hartsel	10.5
325	Cecil Cooper	10.4
	Tom Daly	10.4
	Gene Tenace	10.4
328	Kid Elberfeld	10.3
	Bill Madlock	10.3
330	Johnny Callison	10.2
	Jerry Denny	10.2
	Chick Hafey	10.2
	Stan Lopata	10.2
	Jerry Priddy	10.2
335	Oscar Gamble	10.1
	Cecil Travis	10.1
337	Bobby Avila	10.0
	Riggs Stephenson	10.0
339	Ray Boone	9.9
	Dick Groat	9.9
	George Kell	9.9
	George Wood	9.9
343	Dave Cash	9.8
	Spud Davis	9.8
	Curt Welch	9.8
	Vic Wertz	9.8
347	Willie Keeler	9.7
	Ben Oglivie	9.7
349	Bill Lange	9.6
	Mickey Vernon	9.6
	Ned Williamson	9.6
352	Joe Adcock	9.5
	Tony Pena	9.5
	Earl Torgeson	9.5
355	Frankie Hayes	9.4
	Freddie Patek	9.4
	John Stearns	9.4
	Cy Williams	9.4
359	Earle Combs	9.3
	Tom Haller	9.3
	Hank Sauer	9.3
	Gene Woodling	9.3
363	Tony Bernazard	9.2
	Lefty O'Doul	9.2
	Bob O'Farrell	9.2
	Claude Ritchey	9.2
	Snuffy Stirnweiss	9.2
368	Marty McManus	9.1
369	Jimmy Barrett	9.0
	Andy Van Slyke	9.0
371	Johnny Bates	8.9
	Max Bishop	8.9
	Bert Campaneris	8.9
	Phil Cavarretta	8.9
	Freddy Lindstrom	8.9
376	Hugh Duffy	8.7
	Woody English	8.7
	Bob Horner	8.7
379	Hank Gowdy	8.6
	Butch Wynegar	8.6
381	Clete Boyer	8.5
	Joe Ferguson	8.5
	Ken McMullen	8.5
	Mike Mitchell	8.5
385	Fred Luderus	8.4
	Doug Rader	8.4
	Ezra Sutton	8.4
	Hank Thompson	8.4
389	Willie Horton	8.3
	Don Mincher	8.3
	Rico Petrocelli	8.3
392	Elbie Fletcher	8.2
	Don Money	8.2
394	Ripper Collins	8.1
	Dom DiMaggio	8.1
	Joe Harris	8.1
	Garry Templeton	8.1
398	Bernie Carbo	7.9
	George Grantham	7.9
	Sherm Lollar	7.9

Total Player Rating

	Bill Sweeney	7.9
	Billy Werber	7.9
403	George Selkirk	7.7
404	Ginger Beaumont	7.6
	Dan McGann	7.6
	Pete Runnels	7.6
	Lee Tannehill	7.6
	Pinky Whitney	7.6
409	Buck Herzog	7.5
410	Larry Gardner	7.4
	Ossee Schreckengost	7.4
	Deacon White	7.4
413	Marty Marion	7.3
	Pete Reiser	7.3
	Bobby Veach	7.3
416	Mike Grady	7.2
	Heinie Manush	7.2
	Denis Menke	7.2
	Tom Tresh	7.2
420	Mark Belanger	7.1
	Del Ennis	7.1
	Kent Hrbek	7.1
	Johnny Ray	7.1
	Bill Skowron	7.1
425	Julio Cruz	6.9
	Bubbles Hargrave	6.9
	Billy Jurges	6.9
	Sammy Strang	6.9
429	Ival Goodman	6.8
	Jason Thompson	6.8
431	John Mayberry	6.7
	Duke Sims	6.7
	John Stone	6.7
434	Brett Butler	6.6
	Socks Seybold	6.6
436	Abner Dalrymple	6.5
	George Hendrick	6.5
438	Eddie Joost	6.4
	Lyn Lary	6.4
	Buddy Lewis	6.4
441	Matty McIntyre	6.3
	Heinie Peitz	6.3
	Eric Soderholm	6.3
444	Bake McBride	6.2
	Art Wilson	6.2
446	Al Bridwell	6.1
	John Briggs	6.1
	Lou Criger	6.1
	Gary Gaetti	6.1
	Dick McAuliffe	6.1
	Jim McTamany	6.1
	Danny Murphy	6.1
453	Chili Davis	6.0
	Leon Durham	6.0
	Bob Nieman	6.0
456	Odell Hale	5.9
	Harry Steinfeldt	5.9
	Manny Trillo	5.9
	Tim Wallach	5.9
	Glenn Wright	5.9
461	Merv Rettenmund	5.8
	Danny Richardson	5.8
	Mickey Rivers	5.8
464	Hal Chase	5.7
	Mike Epstein	5.7
	Joe Gerhardt	5.7
	Von Hayes	5.7
	Steve Kemp	5.7
	Pepper Martin	5.7
	Gary Matthews	5.7
	Terry Puhl	5.7
	Emmett Seery	5.7
	Pete Ward	5.7
474	Bill Doran	5.6
475	Jim Delahanty	5.5
	Charlie Maxwell	5.5
	Norm Siebern	5.5
478	George Bell	5.4
	Mike Easler	5.4
	Woodie Held	5.4
	Bill White	5.4
482	Dusty Baker	5.3
	Jody Davis	5.3
	Scott Fletcher	5.3
	Ron LeFlore	5.3
	Herman Long	5.3
	Earl Smith	5.3
488	Jiggs Donahue	5.2
	Ted Kluszewski	5.2
	John Reilly	5.2
	Elmer Valo	5.2
	Mookie Wilson	5.2
493	Jeff Burroughs	5.1
	Jack Doyle	5.1
	Monte Ward	5.1
496	6 players tied	5.0

Total Player Rating (alpha.)

Hank Aaron	90.1
Joe Adcock	9.5
Dick Allen	35.6
Gene Alley	18.3
Bob Allison	13.0
Cap Anson	31.3
Luis Aparicio	13.0
Luke Appling	38.5
Richie Ashburn	27.0
Earl Averill	18.4
Bobby Avila	10.0
Ed Bailey	15.9
Frank Baker	34.6
Dusty Baker	5.3
Dave Bancroft	29.7
Sal Bando	10.7
Ernie Banks	24.9
Jesse Barfield	10.8
Jimmy Barrett	9.0
Dick Bartell	25.2
Johnny Bates	8.9
Don Baylor	15.2
Ginger Beaumont	7.6
Jake Beckley	24.2
Mark Belanger	7.1
Buddy Bell	25.6
George Bell	5.4
Johnny Bench	30.2
Charlie Bennett	16.8
Wally Berger	18.3
Tony Bernazard	9.2
Yogi Berra	34.8
Max Bishop	8.9
Wade Boggs	32.9
Bobby Bonds	31.3
Ray Boone	9.9
Lou Boudreau	34.3
Clete Boyer	8.5
Ken Boyer	18.9
Bill Bradley	13.0
Roger Bresnahan	18.8
George Brett	43.8
Al Bridwell	6.1
John Briggs	6.1
Dan Brouthers	40.4
Pete Browning	27.0
Don Buford	15.9
Smoky Burgess	15.6
Jesse Burkett	30.2
Rick Burleson	10.5
Oyster Burns	11.2
Jeff Burroughs	5.1
Donie Bush	11.5
Brett Butler	6.6
Johnny Callison	10.2
Dolph Camilli	17.2
Roy Campanella	22.2
Bert Campaneris	8.9
Bernie Carbo	7.9
Rod Carew	41.0
Max Carey	26.1
Gary Carter	37.4
Rico Carty	17.3
Dave Cash	9.8
Norm Cash	29.6
Phil Cavarretta	8.9
Cesar Cedeno	23.8
Orlando Cepeda	19.5
Ron Cey	21.9
Frank Chance	16.1
Ray Chapman	17.5
Ben Chapman	15.2
Hal Chase	5.7
Cupid Childs	29.6
Jack Clark	25.4
Fred Clarke	28.0
Roberto Clemente	39.6
Jack Clements	12.7
Harlond Clift	22.7
Ty Cobb	90.6
Mickey Cochrane	27.5
Rocky Colavito	25.0
Eddie Collins	70.5
Ripper Collins	8.1
Jimmy Collins	23.8
Earle Combs	9.3
Dave Concepcion	15.1
Roger Connor	38.8
Cecil Cooper	10.4
Walker Cooper	14.1
Del Crandall	11.4
Gavvy Cravath	19.3
Sam Crawford	23.9
Lou Criger	6.1
Joe Cronin	38.2
Lave Cross	12.7
Jose Cruz	18.9
Julio Cruz	6.9
Tony Cuccinello	13.6
Roy Cullenbine	17.3

Total Player Rating (alpha.)

Kiki Cuyler	19.4
Bill Dahlen	43.3
Abner Dalrymple	6.5
Tom Daly	10.4
Harry Danning	10.5
Jake Daubert	11.0
Chili Davis	6.0
George Davis	48.4
Harry Davis	14.4
Jody Davis	5.3
Spud Davis	9.8
Andre Dawson	24.6
Ed Delahanty	46.1
Jim Delahanty	5.5
Jerry Denny	10.2
Art Devlin	16.9
Bill Dickey	30.6
Larry Doby	17.7
Bobby Doerr	35.6
Jiggs Donahue	5.2
Mike Donlin	14.4
Bill Doran	5.6
Brian Downing	16.7
Jack Doyle	5.1
Larry Doyle	10.5
Hugh Duffy	8.7
Fred Dunlap	28.0
Leon Durham	6.0
Doug DeCinces	15.7
Dom DiMaggio	8.1
Joe DiMaggio	43.6
Mike Easler	5.4
Kid Elberfeld	10.3
Bob Elliott	18.5
Woody English	8.7
Del Ennis	7.1
Mike Epstein	5.7
Darrell Evans	32.5
Dwight Evans	25.2
Johnny Evers	16.6
Buck Ewing	27.6
Ferris Fain	18.1
Duke Farrell	16.2
Joe Ferguson	8.5
Rick Ferrell	15.0
Carlton Fisk	33.4
Art Fletcher	21.0
Elbie Fletcher	8.2
Scott Fletcher	5.3
Elmer Flick	28.5
George Foster	22.1
Jack Fournier	23.7
Nellie Fox	12.5
Jimmie Foxx	53.2
Bill Freehan	28.9
Jim Fregosi	21.0
Lonny Frey	16.2
Frankie Frisch	37.2
Gary Gaetti	6.1
Augie Galan	13.0
Oscar Gamble	10.1
Larry Gardner	7.4
Lou Gehrig	60.8
Charlie Gehringer	43.5
Jim Gentile	11.3
Joe Gerhardt	5.7
Kirk Gibson	13.9
Jack Glasscock	34.5
Ival Goodman	6.8
Joe Gordon	27.6
Sid Gordon	14.7
George Gore	16.0
Goose Goslin	22.9
Hank Gowdy	8.6
Mike Grady	7.2
George Grantham	7.9
Hank Greenberg	28.9
Bobby Grich	47.4
Ken Griffey	11.2
Mike Griffin	19.7
Dick Groat	9.9
Heinie Groh	25.6
Pedro Guerrero	23.7
Tony Gwynn	19.9
Stan Hack	25.8
Chick Hafey	10.2
Odell Hale	5.9
Tom Haller	9.3
Billy Hamilton	25.0
Ron Hansen	11.8
Bubbles Hargrave	6.9
Mike Hargrove	15.5
Toby Harrah	16.6
Joe Harris	8.1
Gabby Hartnett	35.7
Topsy Hartsel	10.5
Frankie Hayes	9.4
Von Hayes	5.7
Jeff Heath	15.7
Harry Heilmann	25.4

Total Player Rating (alpha.)

Woodie Held	5.4
Solly Hemus	12.6
Rickey Henderson	44.0
George Hendrick	6.5
Tommy Henrich	14.6
Babe Herman	18.3
Billy Herman	34.0
Keith Hernandez	37.3
Buck Herzog	7.5
Charlie Hickman	12.1
Paul Hines	17.7
Larry Hisle	12.6
Gil Hodges	14.1
Tommy Holmes	10.7
Bob Horner	8.7
Rogers Hornsby	77.3
Willie Horton	8.3
Elston Howard	13.7
Frank Howard	20.0
Kent Hrbek	7.1
Glenn Hubbard	14.7
Miller Huggins	19.0
Ron Hunt	12.2
Joe Jackson	36.1
Reggie Jackson	44.0
Travis Jackson	21.0
Hughie Jennings	26.6
Jackie Jensen	10.7
Cliff Johnson	12.6
Dave Johnson	11.6
Bob Johnson	37.8
Charley Jones	21.0
Eddie Joost	6.4
Bill Joyce	19.1
Billy Jurges	6.9
Al Kaline	45.9
Willie Kamm	12.8
Benny Kauff	16.7
Willie Keeler	9.7
George Kell	9.9
Charlie Keller	23.4
Joe Kelley	23.1
King Kelly	24.2
Ken Keltner	12.8
Steve Kemp	5.7
Harmon Killebrew	32.8
Ralph Kiner	27.0
Chuck Klein	24.3
Johnny Kling	10.6
Ted Kluszewski	5.2
Bobby Knoop	12.4
Ed Konetchy	23.5
Whitey Kurowski	10.7
Nap Lajoie	85.2
Bill Lange	9.6
Henry Larkin	14.8
Lyn Lary	6.4
Tony Lazzeri	15.0
Tommy Leach	15.7
Chet Lemon	18.1
Buddy Lewis	6.4
Sixto Lezcano	12.8
Freddy Lindstrom	8.9
Johnny Logan	14.0
Sherm Lollar	7.9
Ernie Lombardi	23.4
Herman Long	5.3
Stan Lopata	10.2
Davey Lopes	11.7
Fred Luderus	8.4
Greg Luzinski	11.3
Fred Lynn	21.3
Denny Lyons	20.1
Ron LeFlore	5.3
Bill Madlock	10.3
Sherry Magee	28.5
Mickey Mantle	69.8
Heinie Manush	7.2
Marty Marion	7.3
Roger Maris	10.8
Pepper Martin	5.7
Eddie Mathews	48.4
Gary Matthews	5.7
Don Mattingly	12.6
Charlie Maxwell	5.5
John Mayberry	6.7
Willie Mays	86.2
Bill Mazeroski	34.4
Joe Medwick	25.7
Bill Melton	10.8
Denis Menke	7.2
Don Mincher	8.3
Minnie Minoso	23.6
Mike Mitchell	8.5
Johnny Mize	36.5
Paul Molitor	18.7
Don Money	8.2
Joe Morgan	63.9
Thurman Munson	25.1
Bobby Murcer	13.5

Total Player Rating (alpha.)

Dale Murphy	19.1
Danny Murphy	6.1
Dwayne Murphy	13.7
Eddie Murray	33.7
Stan Musial	70.1
Buddy Myer	12.7
Dick McAuliffe	6.1
Bake McBride	6.2
Tim McCarver	12.3
Willie McCovey	38.1
Gil McDougald	21.5
Ed McFarland	12.1
Dan McGann	7.6
John McGraw	17.3
Deacon McGuire	16.1
Matty McIntyre	6.3
Marty McManus	9.1
Ken McMullen	8.5
Bid McPhee	37.5
Hal McRae	17.2
Jim McTamany	6.1
Billy Nash	15.2
Graig Nettles	24.1
Bill Nicholson	16.0
Bob Nieman	6.0
Lefty O'Doul	9.2
Bob O'Farrell	9.2
Tip O'Neill	11.3
Jim O'Rourke	15.6
Ben Oglivie	9.7
Tony Oliva	26.1
Al Oliver	12.1
Amos Otis	17.2
Mel Ott	60.1
Dave Parker	22.2
Lance Parrish	15.9
Freddie Patek	9.4
Roger Peckinpaugh	14.0
Heinie Peitz	6.3
Tony Pena	9.5
Tony Perez	13.8
Johnny Pesky	13.5
Rico Petrocelli	8.3
Fred Pfeffer	20.3
Darrell Porter	19.3
Boog Powell	15.7
Del Pratt	21.7
Jerry Priddy	10.2
Terry Puhl	5.7
Doug Rader	8.4
Tim Raines	31.5
Willie Randolph	26.5
Johnny Ray	7.1
Pee Wee Reese	19.0
John Reilly	5.2
Pete Reiser	7.3
Merv Rettenmund	5.8
Jim Rice	26.5
Hardy Richardson	25.9
Danny Richardson	5.8
Cal Ripken	26.7
Claude Ritchey	9.2
Mickey Rivers	5.8
Phil Rizzuto	15.4
Brooks Robinson	23.3
Frank Robinson	71.2
Jackie Robinson	33.3
John Romano	12.2
Pete Rose	24.7
Al Rosen	10.7
Edd Roush	16.0
Pete Runnels	7.6
Babe Ruth	105.1
Jimmy Ryan	15.8
Ryne Sandberg	19.3
Manny Sanguillen	10.8
Ron Santo	38.1
Hank Sauer	9.3
Wally Schang	25.2
Mike Schmidt	77.9
Red Schoendienst	15.0
Ossee Schreckengost	7.4
Emmett Seery	5.7
Kip Selbach	13.9
George Selkirk	7.7
Andy Seminick	14.2
Joe Sewell	33.1
Socks Seybold	6.6
Cy Seymour	12.2
Orator Shaffer	11.9
Jimmy Sheckard	19.3
Norm Siebern	5.5
Roy Sievers	12.9
Al Simmons	24.2
Ted Simmons	34.4
Duke Sims	6.7
Ken Singleton	20.3
George Sisler	25.5
Bill Skowron	7.1
Enos Slaughter	14.3

Total Player Rating (alpha.)

Roy Smalley	22.7
Reggie Smith	33.4
Earl Smith	5.3
Mike Smith	11.3
Red Smith	10.8
Ozzie Smith	38.0
Duke Snider	24.3
Eric Soderholm	6.3
Tris Speaker	79.9
Stan Spence	11.2
Eddie Stanky	21.6
Willie Stargell	31.6
Rusty Staub	29.4
John Stearns	9.4
Harry Steinfeldt	5.9
Vern Stephens	15.4
Riggs Stephenson	10.0
Snuffy Stirnweiss	9.2
George Stone	12.6
John Stone	6.7
Harry Stovey	23.6
Sammy Strang	6.9
Darryl Strawberry	19.2
Jim Sundberg	12.8
Ezra Sutton	8.4
Bill Sweeney	7.9
Lee Tannehill	7.6
Garry Templeton	8.1
Gene Tenace	10.4
Fred Tenney	18.9
Bill Terry	27.8
Roy Thomas	28.1
Hank Thompson	8.4
Jason Thompson	6.8
Sam Thompson	29.4
Andy Thornton	16.0
Mike Tiernan	14.4
Joe Tinker	20.2
John Titus	13.8
Earl Torgeson	9.5
Joe Torre	29.8
Alan Trammell	17.7
Cecil Travis	10.1
Pie Traynor	18.4
Tom Tresh	7.2
Manny Trillo	5.9
Elmer Valo	5.2
George Van Haltren	15.2
Andy Van Slyke	9.0
Arky Vaughan	40.3
Bobby Veach	7.3
Mickey Vernon	9.6
Honus Wagner	75.6
Dixie Walker	11.3
Bobby Wallace	34.0
Tim Wallach	5.9
Paul Waner	38.9
Monte Ward	5.1
Pete Ward	5.7
Bob Watson	12.1
Curt Welch	9.8
Billy Werber	7.9
Vic Wertz	9.8
Zach Wheat	21.1
Lou Whitaker	19.2
Deacon White	7.4
Roy White	19.2
Bill White	5.4
Pinky Whitney	7.6
Billy Williams	30.2
Cy Williams	9.4
Jimmy Williams	12.1
Ken Williams	19.6
Ted Williams	89.8
Ned Williamson	9.6
Bump Wills	12.9
Maury Wills	15.4
Art Wilson	6.2
Hack Wilson	16.8
Mookie Wilson	5.2
Dave Winfield	36.6
Sam Wise	11.2
Chicken Wolf	10.7
George Wood	9.9
Gene Woodling	9.3
Glenn Wright	5.9
Butch Wynegar	8.6
Jim Wynn	31.1
Carl Yastrzemski	46.1
Rudy York	16.1
Ross Youngs	12.0
Robin Yount	31.4
Chief Zimmer	12.5
Heinie Zimmerman	12.9
Richie Zisk	13.9

Total Player Rating (by era)

1876-1892

1	Dan Brouthers	40.4
2	Roger Connor	38.8
3	Bid McPhee	37.5
4	Jack Glasscock	34.5
5	Cap Anson	31.3
6	Sam Thompson	29.4
7	Fred Dunlap	28.0
8	Buck Ewing	27.6
9	Pete Browning	27.0
10	Hardy Richardson	25.9
11	King Kelly	24.2
12	Harry Stovey	23.6
13	Charley Jones	21.0
14	Fred Pfeffer	20.3
15	Denny Lyons	20.1
16	Mike Griffin	19.7
17	Paul Hines	17.7
18	Charlie Bennett	16.8
19	George Gore	16.0
20	Jim O'Rourke	15.6
21	Billy Nash	15.2
22	Henry Larkin	14.8
23	Jack Clements	12.7
24	Orator Shaffer	11.9
25	Tip O'Neill	11.3

1893-1919

1	Ty Cobb	90.6
2	Nap Lajoie	85.2
3	Tris Speaker	79.9
4	Honus Wagner	75.6
5	Eddie Collins	70.5
6	George Davis	48.4
7	Ed Delahanty	46.1
8	Bill Dahlen	43.3
9	Joe Jackson	36.1
10	Frank Baker	34.6
11	Bobby Wallace	34.0
12	Jesse Burkett	30.2
13	Cupid Childs	29.6
14	Elmer Flick	28.5
	Sherry Magee	28.5
16	Roy Thomas	28.1
17	Fred Clarke	28.0
18	Hughie Jennings	26.6
19	Heinie Groh	25.6
20	Billy Hamilton	25.0
21	Jake Beckley	24.2
22	Sam Crawford	23.9
23	Jimmy Collins	23.8
24	Ed Konetchy	23.5
25	Joe Kelley	23.1

1920-1941

1	Babe Ruth	105.1
2	Rogers Hornsby	77.3
3	Lou Gehrig	60.8
4	Mel Ott	60.1
5	Jimmie Foxx	53.2
6	Charlie Gehringer	43.5
7	Arky Vaughan	40.3
8	Paul Waner	38.9
9	Luke Appling	38.5
10	Joe Cronin	38.2
11	Bob Johnson	37.8
12	Frankie Frisch	37.2
13	Gabby Hartnett	35.7
14	Billy Herman	34.0
15	Joe Sewell	33.1
16	Bill Dickey	30.6
17	Dave Bancroft	29.7
18	Hank Greenberg	28.9
19	Bill Terry	27.8
20	Mickey Cochrane	27.5
21	Max Carey	26.1
22	Stan Hack	25.8
23	Joe Medwick	25.7
24	George Sisler	25.5
25	Harry Heilmann	25.4

Total Player Rating (by era)

1942-1960

1	Ted Williams	89.8
2	Stan Musial	70.1
3	Mickey Mantle	69.8
4	Eddie Mathews	48.4
5	Joe DiMaggio	43.6
6	Johnny Mize	36.5
7	Bobby Doerr	35.6
8	Yogi Berra	34.8
9	Lou Boudreau	34.3
10	Jackie Robinson	33.3
11	Joe Gordon	27.6
12	Richie Ashburn	27.0
	Ralph Kiner	27.0
14	Duke Snider	24.3
15	Minnie Minoso	23.6
16	Charlie Keller	23.4
17	Roy Campanella	22.2
18	Eddie Stanky	21.6
19	Gil McDougald	21.5
20	Pee Wee Reese	19.0
21	Bob Elliott	18.5
22	Ferris Fain	18.1
23	Larry Doby	17.7
24	Roy Cullenbine	17.3
25	Rudy York	16.1

1961-1988

1	Hank Aaron	90.1
2	Willie Mays	86.2
3	Mike Schmidt	77.9
4	Frank Robinson	71.2
5	Joe Morgan	63.9
6	Bobby Grich	47.4
7	Carl Yastrzemski	46.1
8	Al Kaline	45.9
9	Rickey Henderson	44.0
	Reggie Jackson	44.0
11	George Brett	43.8
12	Rod Carew	41.0
13	Roberto Clemente	39.6
14	Willie McCovey	38.1
	Ron Santo	38.1
16	Ozzie Smith	38.0
17	Gary Carter	37.4
18	Keith Hernandez	37.3
19	Dave Winfield	36.6
20	Dick Allen	35.6
21	Bill Mazeroski	34.4
	Ted Simmons	34.4
23	Eddie Murray	33.7
24	Carlton Fisk	33.4
	Reggie Smith	33.4

Wins

1	Cy Young	511
2	Walter Johnson	417
3	Pete Alexander	373
4	Christy Mathewson	372
5	Warren Spahn	363
6	Kid Nichols	362
7	Jim Galvin	361
8	Tim Keefe	342
9	Steve Carlton	329
10	John Clarkson	327
11	Eddie Plank	326
12	Don Sutton	324
13	Phil Niekro	318
14	Gaylord Perry	314
15	Tom Seaver	311
16	Charley Radbourn	310
17	Mickey Welch	307
18	Lefty Grove	300
	Early Wynn	300
20	Tommy John	286
	Robin Roberts	286
22	Tony Mullane	285
23	Ferguson Jenkins	284
24	Jim Kaat	283
25	Red Ruffing	273
	Nolan Ryan	273
27	Burleigh Grimes	270
28	Jim Palmer	268
29	Bob Feller	266
	Eppa Rixey	266
31	Jim McCormick	265
32	Gus Weyhing	264
33	Ted Lyons	260
34	Bert Blyleven	254
	Red Faber	254
36	Carl Hubbell	253
37	Bob Gibson	251
38	Jack Quinn	247
	Vic Willis	247
40	Joe McGinnity	246
41	Jack Powell	245
	Amos Rusie	245
43	Juan Marichal	243
44	Herb Pennock	240
45	Mordecai Brown	239
46	Clark Griffith	237
	Waite Hoyt	237
48	Whitey Ford	236
49	Charlie Buffinton	232
50	Sam Jones	229
	Luis Tiant	229
	Will White	229
53	George Mullin	228
54	Jim Bunning	224
	Jim Hunter	224
56	Paul Derringer	223
	Mel Harder	223
58	Hooks Dauss	222
	Jerry Koosman	222
60	Joe Niekro	221
61	Bob Caruthers	218
	Earl Whitehill	218
63	Freddie Fitzsimmons	217
	Mickey Lolich	217
65	Wilbur Cooper	216
66	Stan Coveleski	215
	Jim Perry	215
68	Chief Bender	212
69	Bobo Newsom	211
	Billy Pierce	211
	Jerry Reuss	211
72	Jesse Haines	210
73	Vida Blue	209
	Don Drysdale	209
	Milt Pappas	209
76	Eddie Cicotte	208
77	Bob Lemon	207
	Carl Mays	207
	Hal Newhouser	207
80	Silver King	204
	Al Orth	204
82	Lew Burdette	203
83	Jack Stivetts	202
84	Rube Marquard	201
	Charlie Root	201
86	George Uhle	200
87	Jack Chesbro	198
	Bucky Walters	198
89	Larry French	197
	Bob Friend	197
	Jesse Tannehill	197
	Adonis Terry	197
	Dazzy Vance	197
94	Claude Osteen	196
	Bob Shawkey	196
96	Joe Bush	195
	Sam Leever	195
	Ed Walsh	195
99	5 players tied	194

Losses

1	Cy Young	315
2	Jim Galvin	307
3	Walter Johnson	279
4	Phil Niekro	274
5	Gaylord Perry	265
6	Don Sutton	256
7	Jack Powell	253
	Nolan Ryan	253
9	Eppa Rixey	251
10	Robin Roberts	245
	Warren Spahn	245
12	Steve Carlton	244
	Early Wynn	244
14	Jim Kaat	237
15	Gus Weyhing	232
16	Bob Friend	230
	Ted Lyons	230
18	Bert Blyleven	226
	Ferguson Jenkins	226
20	Tim Keefe	225
	Red Ruffing	225
22	Tommy John	224
23	Bobo Newsom	222
24	Tony Mullane	220
25	Jack Quinn	218
26	Sam Jones	217
27	Jim McCormick	214
28	Red Faber	213
29	Paul Derringer	212
	Chick Fraser	212
	Burleigh Grimes	212
32	Jerry Koosman	209
	Mickey Welch	209
34	Pete Alexander	208
35	Kid Nichols	207
36	Tom Seaver	205
37	Joe Niekro	204
	Jim Whitney	204
	Vic Willis	204
40	George Mullin	196
41	Claude Osteen	195
	Charley Radbourn	195
	Adonis Terry	195
44	Eddie Plank	193
45	Mickey Lolich	191
	Tom Zachary	191
47	Al Orth	189
48	Christy Mathewson	187
49	Mel Harder	186
50	Earl Whitehill	185
51	Jim Bunning	184
52	Joe Bush	183
	Larry Jackson	183
	Curt Simmons	183
55	Hooks Dauss	182
	Waite Hoyt	182
	Jerry Reuss	182
58	Murry Dickson	181
	Dutch Leonard	181
	Rick Wise	181
61	Lee Meadows	180
62	Bill Dinneen	179
	Pink Hawley	179
	Dolf Luque	179
65	John Clarkson	178
	Wilbur Cooper	178
67	Rube Marquard	177
68	Red Donahue	175
	Tom Hughes	175
	Rick Reuschel	175
71	Bob Gibson	174
	Jim Perry	174
	Amos Rusie	174
	Frank Tanana	174
75	Luis Tiant	172
76	Larry French	171
77	Ted Breitenstein	170
	Camilo Pascual	170
79	Billy Pierce	169
80	Red Ames	167
	Bert Cunningham	167
	Red Ehret	167
83	Don Drysdale	166
	Howard Ehmke	166
	Jim Hunter	166
	George Uhle	166
	Will White	166
88	Mark Baldwin	165
	Bump Hadley	165
	Si Johnson	165
91	Milt Gaston	164
	Win Mercer	164
	Milt Pappas	164
94	Bob Feller	162
	Bill Hutchinson	162
	Herb Pennock	162
97	Vida Blue	161
	Dizzy Trout	161
99	4 players tied	160

Winning Percentage

1	Dave Foutz	.690
2	Whitey Ford	.690
3	Bob Caruthers	.688
4	Lefty Grove	.680
5	Vic Raschi	.667
6	Christy Mathewson	.665
7	Larry Corcoran	.665
8	Sam Leever	.661
9	Sal Maglie	.657
10	Sandy Koufax	.655
11	Johnny Allen	.654
12	Ron Guidry	.651
13	Lefty Gomez	.649
14	Mordecai Brown	.648
15	John Clarkson	.648
16	Dizzy Dean	.644
17	Pete Alexander	.642
18	Jim Palmer	.638
19	Kid Nichols	.636
20	Joe McGinnity	.634
21	Deacon Phillippe	.633
22	Ed Reulbach	.632
23	Juan Marichal	.631
24	Mort Cooper	.631
25	Allie Reynolds	.630
26	Jesse Tannehill	.629
27	Eddie Plank	.628
28	Ray Kremer	.627
29	Firpo Marberry	.627
30	Tommy Bond	.627
31	Chief Bender	.624
32	Don Newcombe	.623
33	Nig Cuppy	.623
34	Addie Joss	.623
35	Fred Goldsmith	.622
36	Doc Crandall	.622
37	Carl Hubbell	.622
	Carl Mays	.622
39	Bob Feller	.621
40	Mel Parnell	.621
41	Clark Griffith	.619
42	Cy Young	.619
43	Bob Lemon	.618
44	John Candelaria	.617
	Monte Ward	.617
46	Urban Shocker	.615
47	Jeff Tesreau	.615
48	Jim Maloney	.615
49	Charley Radbourn	.614
50	Lon Warneke	.613
51	Gary Nolan	.611
52	Schoolboy Rowe	.610
53	Carl Erskine	.610
54	Ed Walsh	.607
55	Charlie Ferguson	.607
56	Dave McNally	.607
57	Hooks Wiltse	.607
58	John Tudor	.607
59	Art Nehf	.605
60	Jack Stivetts	.605
61	Charlie Buffinton	.604
62	Orval Overall	.603
63	Tim Keefe	.603
64	Tom Seaver	.603
65	Stan Coveleski	.602
66	Preacher Roe	.602
67	Wes Ferrell	.601
68	J. R. Richard	.601
69	Jack Chesbro	.600
	Jack Morris	.600
71	Walter Johnson	.599
72	Freddie Fitzsimmons	.598
73	Eddie Lopat	.597
74	Warren Spahn	.597
75	Herb Pennock	.597
76	Rip Sewell	.596
77	Mickey Welch	.595
78	Mike Garcia	.594
79	Pat Malone	.593
80	General Crowder	.592
81	Harry Brecheen	.591
82	Jim Bagby	.591
83	Bob Gibson	.591
84	Dutch Ruether	.591
85	Denny McLain	.590
86	Eddie Rommel	.590
87	Jack Coombs	.590
88	Tiny Bonham	.589
89	Mike Cuellar	.587
90	Bill Bernhard	.586
91	Jeff Pfeffer	.585
92	Ed Stein	.585
93	Lew Burdette	.585
94	Amos Rusie	.585
95	Dazzy Vance	.585
96	Tommy Bridges	.584
97	Ed Morris	.584
98	Noodles Hahn	.583
99	Eddie Cicotte	.583
100	Bob Welch	.581

Games

1	Hoyt Wilhelm	1070
2	Kent Tekulve	1013
3	Lindy McDaniel	987
4	Rollie Fingers	944
5	Gene Garber	931
6	Cy Young	906
7	Sparky Lyle	899
8	Jim Kaat	898
9	Don McMahon	874
10	Phil Niekro	864
11	Roy Face	848
12	Tug McGraw	824
13	Rich Gossage	811
14	Walter Johnson	802
15	Gaylord Perry	777
16	Don Sutton	774
17	Darold Knowles	765
18	Jack Quinn	756
19	Ron Reed	751
20	Tommy John	750
	Warren Spahn	750
22	Tom Burgmeier	745
	Gary Lavelle	745
24	Steve Carlton	741
25	Ron Perranoski	737
26	Ron Kline	736
27	Clay Carroll	731
28	Mike Marshall	723
29	Willie Hernandez	712
30	Johnny Klippstein	711
31	Stu Miller	704
32	Joe Niekro	702
33	Bill Campbell	700
34	Jim Galvin	697
35	Pete Alexander	696
36	Bob Miller	694
37	Grant Jackson	692
	Eppa Rixey	692
39	Early Wynn	691
40	Eddie Fisher	690
41	Charlie Hough	683
42	Ted Abernathy	681
43	Nolan Ryan	678
44	Robin Roberts	676
45	Waite Hoyt	674
46	Red Faber	669
47	Dave Giusti	668
48	Ferguson Jenkins	664
49	Bruce Sutter	661
50	Tom Seaver	656
51	Paul Lindblad	655
52	Wilbur Wood	651
53	Sam Jones	647
	Dave LaRoche	647
55	Dutch Leonard	640
	Gerry Staley	640
57	Diego Segui	639
58	Greg Minton	637
59	Christy Mathewson	634
60	Charlie Root	632
61	Jim Perry	630
62	Lew Burdette	626
63	Murry Dickson	625
	Woodie Fryman	625
65	Red Ruffing	624
66	Eddie Plank	622
67	Kid Nichols	621
68	Dick Tidrow	620
69	Herb Pennock	617
70	Burleigh Grimes	616
	Lefty Grove	616
72	Terry Forster	614
73	Jerry Koosman	612
74	Bert Blyleven	611
75	Dan Quisenberry	606
76	Bob Friend	602
	Al Worthington	602
78	Elias Sosa	601
79	Tim Keefe	600
	Bobo Newsom	600
81	Ted Lyons	594
	Jerry Reuss	594
	Bob Stanley	594
84	Pedro Borbon	593
85	Jim Bunning	591
86	Turk Farrell	590
87	Moe Drabowsky	589
88	Mickey Lolich	586
89	Billy Pierce	585
90	Jim Brewer	584
91	Mel Harder	582
	Pedro Ramos	582
	Jeff Reardon	582
94	Paul Derringer	579
95	Jack Powell	578
96	Bob Locker	576
97	Stan Bahnsen	574
98	Luis Tiant	573
99	Jim Grant	571
100	2 players tied	570

Games Started

1	Cy Young	815
2	Don Sutton	756
3	Phil Niekro	716
4	Steve Carlton	709
5	Tommy John	690
	Gaylord Perry	690
7	Jim Galvin	682
8	Walter Johnson	665
	Warren Spahn	665
10	Tom Seaver	647
11	Nolan Ryan	644
12	Jim Kaat	625
13	Early Wynn	612
14	Robin Roberts	609
15	Bert Blyleven	605
16	Pete Alexander	598
17	Ferguson Jenkins	594
	Tim Keefe	594
19	Kid Nichols	562
20	Eppa Rixey	552
21	Christy Mathewson	551
22	Mickey Welch	549
23	Red Ruffing	536
24	Eddie Plank	529
25	Jerry Koosman	527
26	Jim Palmer	521
27	Jerry Reuss	520
28	Jim Bunning	519
29	John Clarkson	518
30	Jack Powell	516
31	Tony Mullane	505
32	Charley Radbourn	503
	Gus Weyhing	503
34	Joe Niekro	500
35	Bob Friend	497
36	Mickey Lolich	496
37	Burleigh Grimes	495
38	Claude Osteen	488
39	Sam Jones	487
40	Jim McCormick	485
41	Bob Feller	484
	Ted Lyons	484
	Luis Tiant	484
44	Red Faber	483
	Bobo Newsom	483
	Rick Reuschel	483
47	Bob Gibson	482
48	Jim Hunter	476
49	Vida Blue	473
	Earl Whitehill	473
51	Vic Willis	471
52	Don Drysdale	465
	Milt Pappas	465
54	Curt Simmons	461
55	Frank Tanana	458
	Mike Torrez	458
57	Lefty Grove	457
	Juan Marichal	457
59	Rick Wise	455
60	Jim Perry	447
61	Paul Derringer	445
62	Jack Quinn	444
63	Whitey Ford	438
64	Mel Harder	433
65	Billy Pierce	432
66	Doyle Alexander	431
	Carl Hubbell	431
68	Larry Jackson	429
69	George Mullin	428
70	Amos Rusie	427
71	Freddie Fitzsimmons	426
72	Waite Hoyt	423
73	Herb Pennock	420
74	Ken Holtzman	410
75	Tom Zachary	409
76	Wilbur Cooper	408
77	Bob Forsch	407
	Adonis Terry	407
79	Lee Meadows	404
	Camilo Pascual	404
81	Rube Marquard	403
82	Will White	401
83	Bucky Walters	398
84	Charlie Buffinton	396
	Dave McNally	396
	Jim Whitney	396
87	Al Orth	394
88	Steve Rogers	393
89	Paul Splittorff	392
90	Chick Fraser	389
91	Hooks Dauss	388
	Jesse Haines	388
93	Stan Coveleski	385
94	Larry French	384
95	Joe McGinnity	381
96	Bob Knepper	380
97	Mike Cuellar	379
98	Bill Lee	378
99	Burt Hooton	377
100	Dutch Leonard	375

Games Started (by era)

1876-1892

1	Jim Galvin	682
2	Tim Keefe	594
3	Mickey Welch	549
4	John Clarkson	518
5	Tony Mullane	505
6	Charley Radbourn	503
	Gus Weyhing	503
8	Jim McCormick	485
9	Amos Rusie	427
10	Adonis Terry	407
11	Will White	401
12	Charlie Buffinton	396
	Jim Whitney	396
14	Silver King	371
15	Jack Stivetts	332

1893-1919

1	Cy Young	815
2	Walter Johnson	665
3	Kid Nichols	562
4	Christy Mathewson	551
5	Eddie Plank	529
6	Jack Powell	516
7	Vic Willis	471
8	George Mullin	428
9	Wilbur Cooper	408
10	Rube Marquard	403
11	Al Orth	394
12	Chick Fraser	389
13	Hooks Dauss	388
14	Joe McGinnity	381
15	Clark Griffith	372

1920-1941

1	Pete Alexander	598
2	Eppa Rixey	552
3	Red Ruffing	536
4	Burleigh Grimes	495
5	Sam Jones	487
6	Ted Lyons	484
7	Red Faber	483
	Bobo Newsom	483
9	Earl Whitehill	473
10	Lefty Grove	457
11	Paul Derringer	445
12	Jack Quinn	444
13	Mel Harder	433
14	Carl Hubbell	431
15	Freddie Fitzsimmons	426

1942-1960

1	Warren Spahn	665
2	Early Wynn	612
3	Robin Roberts	609
4	Bob Friend	497
5	Bob Feller	484
6	Curt Simmons	461
7	Whitey Ford	438
8	Billy Pierce	432
9	Bucky Walters	398
10	Dutch Leonard	375
11	Hal Newhouser	374
12	Lew Burdette	373
13	Bob Buhl	369
14	Vern Law	364
15	Bob Lemon	350

1961-1988

1	Don Sutton	756
2	Phil Niekro	716
3	Steve Carlton	709
4	Tommy John	690
	Gaylord Perry	690
6	Tom Seaver	647
7	Nolan Ryan	644
8	Jim Kaat	625
9	Bert Blyleven	605
10	Ferguson Jenkins	594
11	Jerry Koosman	527
12	Jim Palmer	521
13	Jerry Reuss	520
14	Jim Bunning	519
15	Joe Niekro	500

Complete Games

1	Cy Young	749
2	Jim Galvin	639
3	Tim Keefe	557
4	Kid Nichols	533
5	Walter Johnson	531
6	Mickey Welch	525
7	Charley Radbourn	489
8	John Clarkson	485
9	Tony Mullane	469
10	Jim McCormick	466
11	Gus Weyhing	448
12	Pete Alexander	438
13	Christy Mathewson	434
14	Jack Powell	422
15	Eddie Plank	410
16	Will White	394
17	Amos Rusie	392
18	Vic Willis	388
19	Warren Spahn	382
20	Jim Whitney	377
21	Adonis Terry	368
22	Ted Lyons	356
23	George Mullin	353
24	Charlie Buffinton	351
25	Chick Fraser	342
26	Clark Griffith	337
27	Red Ruffing	335
28	Silver King	329
29	Al Orth	324
30	Bill Hutchinson	319
31	Burleigh Grimes	314
	Joe McGinnity	314
33	Red Donahue	313
34	Guy Hecker	310
35	Bill Dinneen	306
36	Robin Roberts	305
37	Gaylord Perry	303
38	Ted Breitenstein	300
39	Bob Caruthers	298
	Lefty Grove	298
41	Pink Hawley	297
	Ed Morris	297
43	Mark Baldwin	296
44	Tommy Bond	294
45	Brickyard Kennedy	293
46	Eppa Rixey	290
	Early Wynn	290
48	Bill Donovan	289
	Bobby Mathews	289
50	Bert Cunningham	286
51	Wilbur Cooper	279
	Bob Feller	279
	Sadie McMahon	279
54	Jack Stivetts	278
	Jack Taylor	278
56	Pretzels Getzien	277
57	Red Faber	273
58	Mordecai Brown	271
59	Frank Dwyer	270
	Jouett Meekin	270
61	Ferguson Jenkins	267
62	Icebox Chamberlin	264
	Matt Kilroy	264
64	Jesse Tannehill	263
65	Doc White	262
66	Jack Chesbro	261
	Rube Waddell	261
68	Red Ehret	260
	Carl Hubbell	260
70	Larry Corcoran	256
71	Chief Bender	255
	Bob Gibson	255
73	Steve Carlton	254
74	Frank Killen	253
75	Win Mercer	252
76	Paul Derringer	251
77	Sam Jones	250
	Ed Walsh	250
79	Eddie Cicotte	249
	Stump Weidman	249
81	Herb Pennock	247
82	Bobo Newsom	246
83	George Bradley	245
	Hooks Dauss	245
	Phil Niekro	245
86	Harry Howell	244
	Juan Marichal	244
	Monte Ward	244
89	Jack Quinn	243
90	Deacon Phillippe	242
	Bucky Walters	242
92	Sam Leever	241
93	Kid Gleason	240
94	Addie Joss	234
95	George Uhle	232
96	Bert Blyleven	231
	Carl Mays	231
	Tom Seaver	231
	Harry Staley	231
100	Earl Moore	230

Complete Games (by era)

1876-1892

1	Jim Galvin	639
2	Tim Keefe	557
3	Mickey Welch	525
4	Charley Radbourn	489
5	John Clarkson	485
6	Tony Mullane	469
7	Jim McCormick	466
8	Gus Weyhing	448
9	Will White	394
10	Amos Rusie	392
11	Jim Whitney	377
12	Adonis Terry	368
13	Charlie Buffinton	351
14	Silver King	329
15	Guy Hecker	310

1893-1919

1	Cy Young	749
2	Kid Nichols	533
3	Walter Johnson	531
4	Christy Mathewson	434
5	Jack Powell	422
6	Eddie Plank	410
7	Vic Willis	388
8	George Mullin	353
9	Chick Fraser	342
10	Clark Griffith	337
11	Al Orth	324
12	Bill Hutchinson	319
13	Joe McGinnity	314
14	Red Donahue	313
15	Bill Dinneen	306

1920-1941

1	Pete Alexander	438
2	Ted Lyons	356
3	Red Ruffing	335
4	Burleigh Grimes	314
5	Lefty Grove	298
6	Eppa Rixey	290
7	Red Faber	273
8	Carl Hubbell	260
9	Paul Derringer	251
10	Sam Jones	250
11	Herb Pennock	247
12	Bobo Newsom	246
13	Jack Quinn	243
14	George Uhle	232
15	Carl Mays	231

1942-1960

1	Warren Spahn	382
2	Robin Roberts	305
3	Early Wynn	290
4	Bob Feller	279
5	Bucky Walters	242
6	Hal Newhouser	212
7	Billy Pierce	193
8	Dutch Leonard	192
9	Bob Lemon	188
10	Eddie Lopat	164
11	Bob Friend	163
	Curt Simmons	163
13	Lew Burdette	158
	Dizzy Trout	158
15	Whitey Ford	156

1961-1988

1	Gaylord Perry	303
2	Ferguson Jenkins	267
3	Bob Gibson	255
4	Steve Carlton	254
5	Phil Niekro	245
6	Juan Marichal	244
7	Bert Blyleven	231
	Tom Seaver	231
9	Jim Palmer	211
10	Nolan Ryan	207
11	Mickey Lolich	195
12	Luis Tiant	187
13	Jim Hunter	181
14	Jim Kaat	180
15	Don Sutton	178

Shutouts

1	Walter Johnson	110
2	Pete Alexander	90
3	Christy Mathewson	78
4	Cy Young	76
5	Eddie Plank	69
6	Warren Spahn	63
7	Tom Seaver	61
8	Don Sutton	58
9	Mordecai Brown	57
	Ed Walsh	57
11	Jim Galvin	56
	Bob Gibson	56
13	Bert Blyleven	55
	Steve Carlton	55
	Nolan Ryan	55
16	Jim Palmer	53
	Gaylord Perry	53
18	Juan Marichal	52
19	Rube Waddell	50
	Vic Willis	50
21	Don Drysdale	49
	Ferguson Jenkins	49
	Luis Tiant	49
	Early Wynn	49
25	Kid Nichols	48
26	Tommy John	46
	Jack Powell	46
28	Whitey Ford	45
	Addie Joss	45
	Phil Niekro	45
	Robin Roberts	45
	Red Ruffing	45
	Doc White	45
34	Babe Adams	44
	Bob Feller	44
36	Milt Pappas	43
37	Jim Hunter	42
	Bucky Walters	42
39	Mickey Lolich	41
	Hippo Vaughn	41
41	Chief Bender	40
	Jim Bunning	40
	Larry French	40
	Sandy Koufax	40
	Claude Osteen	40
	Ed Reulbach	40
	Mel Stottlemyre	40
	Mickey Welch	40
49	Tim Keefe	39
	Eppa Rixey	39
51	Stan Coveleski	38
	Sam Leever	38
	Billy Pierce	38
	Jerry Reuss	38
	Nap Rucker	38
56	Vida Blue	37
	John Clarkson	37
	Bill Doak	37
	Larry Jackson	37
	Steve Rogers	37
61	Tommy Bond	36
	Wilbur Cooper	36
	Mike Cuellar	36
	Bob Friend	36
	Carl Hubbell	36
	Sam Jones	36
	Camilo Pascual	36
	Allie Reynolds	36
	Curt Simmons	36
	Will White	36
71	Joe Bush	35
	Jack Chesbro	35
	Eddie Cicotte	35
	Jack Coombs	35
	Bill Donovan	35
	Burleigh Grimes	35
	Lefty Grove	35
	Earl Moore	35
	George Mullin	35
	Herb Pennock	35
81	Charley Radbourn	34
	Jesse Tannehill	34
83	Tommy Bridges	33
	Lew Burdette	33
	Dean Chance	33
	Jerry Koosman	33
	Lefty Leifield	33
	Dutch Leonard	33
	Jim McCormick	33
	Dave McNally	33
	Hal Newhouser	33
	Bob Shawkey	33
	Virgil Trucks	33
94	Mort Cooper	32
	Paul Derringer	32
	Joe McGinnity	32
	Jim Perry	32
98	10 players tied	31

Saves

1	Rollie Fingers	341
2	Rich Gossage	302
3	Bruce Sutter	300
4	Sparky Lyle	238
	Dan Quisenberry	238
6	Jeff Reardon	235
7	Hoyt Wilhelm	227
8	Gene Garber	218
9	Lee Smith	209
10	Roy Face	193
11	Mike Marshall	188
12	Kent Tekulve	183
13	Tug McGraw	180
14	Ron Perranoski	179
15	Lindy McDaniel	172
16	Dave Righetti	163
17	Stu Miller	154
18	Don McMahon	153
19	Dave Smith	151
20	Ted Abernathy	148
21	Dave Giusti	145
22	Clay Carroll	143
	Darold Knowles	143
24	Greg Minton	142
25	Steve Bedrosian	138
26	Gary Lavelle	136
27	Jim Brewer	132
	Willie Hernandez	132
29	Ron Davis	130
30	Bob Stanley	128
31	Terry Forster	127
32	Bill Campbell	126
	Dave LaRoche	126
34	John Hiller	125
35	Jack Aker	123
36	Dick Radatz	122
37	Jesse Orosco	116
38	Tippy Martinez	115
39	Frank Linzy	111
40	Al Worthington	110
41	Fred Gladding	109
42	Wayne Granger	108
	Ron Kline	108
44	Johnny Murphy	107
45	Bill Caudill	106
46	Ron Reed	103
	John Wyatt	103
48	Tom Burgmeier	102
	Ellis Kinder	102
50	Firpo Marberry	101
51	Al Hrabosky	97
52	Clem Labine	96
	Randy Moffitt	96
54	Bob Locker	95
55	Aurelio Lopez	93
56	Tom Hume	92
	Phil Regan	92
58	Bill Henry	90
59	Donnie Moore	89
60	Jim Kern	88
61	Ken Sanders	86
62	Joe Sambito	84
63	Mark Clear	83
	Turk Farrell	83
	Claude Raymond	83
	Elias Sosa	83
67	Larry Sherry	82
68	Eddie Fisher	81
69	Doug Bair	80
	Pedro Borbon	80
	Eddie Watt	80
72	Grant Jackson	79
73	Al Holland	78
74	Don Aase	77
75	Joe Page	76
	Tim Stoddard	76
77	Neil Allen	75
	Ed Farmer	75
79	Jim Konstanty	74
80	Turk Lown	73
81	Ron Taylor	72
82	Diego Segui	71
83	Dick Hall	68
	Skip Lockwood	68
85	Jim Brosnan	67
86	Al Benton	66
	Johnny Klippstein	66
88	Clint Brown	64
	Dennis Eckersley	64
	Paul Lindblad	64
	Tom Morgan	64
	Don Stanhouse	64
93	Don Elston	63
	Joe Heving	63
	Gary Lucas	63
	Al McBean	63
97	Ed Roebuck	62
98	Charlie Hough	61
	Gerry Staley	61
	Hal Woodeshick	61

Innings Pitched

1	Cy Young	7357
2	Jim Galvin	5941
3	Walter Johnson	5925
4	Phil Niekro	5404
5	Gaylord Perry	5352
6	Don Sutton	5282
7	Warren Spahn	5246
8	Steve Carlton	5217
9	Pete Alexander	5189
10	Tim Keefe	5061
	Kid Nichols	5061
12	Mickey Welch	4801
13	Tom Seaver	4782
14	Christy Mathewson	4778
15	Robin Roberts	4689
16	Tommy John	4644
17	Early Wynn	4566
18	Nolan Ryan	4547
19	Tony Mullane	4540
20	John Clarkson	4537
21	Charley Radbourn	4535
22	Jim Kaat	4529
23	Ferguson Jenkins	4498
24	Eddie Plank	4497
25	Eppa Rixey	4494
26	Bert Blyleven	4461
27	Jack Powell	4388
28	Red Ruffing	4342
29	Gus Weyhing	4324
30	Jim McCormick	4276
31	Burleigh Grimes	4181
32	Ted Lyons	4162
33	Red Faber	4086
34	Vic Willis	3997
35	Jim Palmer	3948
36	Lefty Grove	3940
37	Jack Quinn	3920
38	Bob Gibson	3885
39	Sam Jones	3884
40	Jerry Koosman	3839
41	Bob Feller	3828
42	Amos Rusie	3769
43	Waite Hoyt	3763
44	Bobo Newsom	3762
45	Jim Bunning	3759
46	George Mullin	3686
47	Paul Derringer	3646
48	Mickey Lolich	3640
49	Bob Friend	3612
50	Carl Hubbell	3591
51	Joe Niekro	3585
52	Herb Pennock	3571
53	Earl Whitehill	3562
54	Will White	3542
55	Adonis Terry	3522
56	Jerry Reuss	3521
57	Juan Marichal	3506
58	Jim Whitney	3496
59	Luis Tiant	3486
60	Wilbur Cooper	3482
61	Claude Osteen	3459
62	Jim Hunter	3449
63	Joe McGinnity	3441
64	Don Drysdale	3432
65	Mel Harder	3426
66	Charlie Buffinton	3403
67	Hooks Dauss	3391
68	Clark Griffith	3387
69	Al Orth	3356
70	Chick Fraser	3355
71	Curt Simmons	3348
72	Vida Blue	3344
73	Rube Marquard	3309
74	Billy Pierce	3305
75	Jim Perry	3287
76	Larry Jackson	3262
77	Rick Reuschel	3244
78	Freddie Fitzsimmons	3225
79	Eddie Cicotte	3223
80	Dolf Luque	3221
81	Dutch Leonard	3220
82	Jesse Haines	3208
83	Red Ames	3197
	Charlie Root	3197
85	Silver King	3190
86	Milt Pappas	3187
87	Frank Tanana	3179
88	Mordecai Brown	3171
	Whitey Ford	3171
90	Lee Meadows	3160
91	Larry French	3152
92	Doyle Alexander	3144
93	Tom Zachary	3128
94	Rick Wise	3125
95	George Uhle	3120
96	Bucky Walters	3104
97	Joe Bush	3088
98	Stan Coveleski	3081
99	Bill Dinneen	3075
100	Lew Burdette	3067

Innings Pitched (by era)

1876-1892

1	Jim Galvin	5941
2	Tim Keefe	5061
3	Mickey Welch	4801
4	Tony Mullane	4540
5	John Clarkson	4537
6	Charley Radbourn	4535
7	Gus Weyhing	4324
8	Jim McCormick	4276
9	Amos Rusie	3769
10	Will White	3542
11	Adonis Terry	3522
12	Jim Whitney	3496
13	Charlie Buffinton	3403
14	Silver King	3190
15	Guy Hecker	2906

1893-1919

1	Cy Young	7357
2	Walter Johnson	5925
3	Kid Nichols	5061
4	Christy Mathewson	4778
5	Eddie Plank	4497
6	Jack Powell	4388
7	Vic Willis	3997
8	George Mullin	3686
9	Wilbur Cooper	3482
10	Joe McGinnity	3441
11	Hooks Dauss	3391
12	Clark Griffith	3387
13	Al Orth	3356
14	Chick Fraser	3355
15	Rube Marquard	3309

1920-1941

1	Pete Alexander	5189
2	Eppa Rixey	4494
3	Red Ruffing	4342
4	Burleigh Grimes	4181
5	Ted Lyons	4162
6	Red Faber	4086
7	Lefty Grove	3940
8	Jack Quinn	3920
9	Sam Jones	3884
10	Waite Hoyt	3763
11	Bobo Newsom	3762
12	Paul Derringer	3646
13	Carl Hubbell	3591
14	Herb Pennock	3571
15	Earl Whitehill	3562

1942-1960

1	Warren Spahn	5246
2	Robin Roberts	4689
3	Early Wynn	4566
4	Bob Feller	3828
5	Bob Friend	3612
6	Curt Simmons	3348
7	Billy Pierce	3305
8	Dutch Leonard	3220
9	Whitey Ford	3171
10	Bucky Walters	3104
11	Lew Burdette	3067
12	Murry Dickson	3053
13	Hal Newhouser	2993
14	Bob Lemon	2849
15	Dizzy Trout	2726

1961-1988

1	Phil Niekro	5404
2	Gaylord Perry	5352
3	Don Sutton	5282
4	Steve Carlton	5217
5	Tom Seaver	4782
6	Tommy John	4644
7	Nolan Ryan	4547
8	Jim Kaat	4529
9	Ferguson Jenkins	4498
10	Bert Blyleven	4461
11	Jim Palmer	3948
12	Bob Gibson	3885
13	Jerry Koosman	3839
14	Jim Bunning	3759
15	Mickey Lolich	3640

Hits per Game

1	Nolan Ryan	6.59
2	Sandy Koufax	6.79
3	J. R. Richard	6.88
4	Andy Messersmith	6.94
5	Hoyt Wilhelm	7.02
6	Sam McDowell	7.04
7	Ed Walsh	7.12
8	Bob Turley	7.19
9	Orval Overall	7.23
10	Jeff Tesreau	7.24
11	Ed Reulbach	7.24
12	Mario Soto	7.25
13	Addie Joss	7.30
14	Rich Gossage	7.37
15	Jim Maloney	7.39
16	Rube Waddell	7.47
17	Tom Seaver	7.47
18	Walter Johnson	7.48
19	Charlie Hough	7.58
20	Bob Gibson	7.60
21	Don Wilson	7.61
22	Jim Palmer	7.63
23	Sam Jones	7.68
24	Larry Cheney	7.68
25	Mordecai Brown	7.69
26	Bob Feller	7.69
27	Johnny Vander Meer	7.70
28	Jim Hunter	7.72
29	Al Downing	7.72
30	Jim Scott	7.73
31	Bobby Bolin	7.79
32	Stan Williams	7.80
33	Rollie Fingers	7.80
34	Frank Smith	7.80
35	Dean Chance	7.81
36	Fernando Valenzuela	7.82
37	Tug McGraw	7.82
38	Barney Pelty	7.84
39	Whitey Ford	7.85
40	Denny McLain	7.86
41	Bob Veale	7.87
42	Jack Coombs	7.89
43	George McQuillan	7.89
44	Chief Bender	7.89
45	Moe Drabowsky	7.91
46	Vida Blue	7.91
47	Nap Rucker	7.92
48	Tim Keefe	7.92
49	Eddie Plank	7.92
50	Allie Reynolds	7.92
51	Luis Tiant	7.94
52	Christy Mathewson	7.94
53	Rudy May	7.95
54	Ray Culp	7.96
55	Dave Stieb	7.97
56	Bill Donovan	7.98
57	Juan Pizarro	7.99
58	Howie Camnitz	7.99
59	Don Sutton	7.99
60	Gary Bell	8.01
61	Earl Moore	8.02
62	Sonny Siebert	8.03
63	Lefty Tyler	8.04
64	Hal Newhouser	8.04
65	Jack Morris	8.05
66	Claude Hendrix	8.06
67	Steve Carlton	8.06
68	Hooks Wiltse	8.07
69	Willie Mitchell	8.07
70	Larry Corcoran	8.07
71	Amos Rusie	8.08
72	Bill Singer	8.08
73	Bob Lemon	8.08
74	Stu Miller	8.09
75	Gary Nolan	8.09
76	Don Drysdale	8.09
77	Eddie Cicotte	8.09
78	Juan Marichal	8.09
79	Virgil Trucks	8.10
80	Hippo Vaughn	8.11
81	Doc White	8.12
82	Kirby Higbe	8.12
83	Blue Moon Odom	8.13
84	Mort Cooper	8.14
85	Bob Welch	8.14
86	Mike Cuellar	8.14
87	Jim Shaw	8.14
88	Billy Pierce	8.14
89	Mike Scott	8.15
90	Red Ames	8.15
91	Vic Willis	8.15
92	Eddie Fisher	8.17
93	Earl Wilson	8.17
94	Harry Brecheen	8.18
95	Jim Bibby	8.18
96	Steve Barber	8.18
97	Dave Davenport	8.19
98	Lefty Leifield	8.19
99	Gary Peters	8.19
100	Bob Ewing	8.20

Home Runs Allowed

1	Robin Roberts	505
2	Ferguson Jenkins	484
3	Phil Niekro	482
4	Don Sutton	472
5	Warren Spahn	434
6	Steve Carlton	414
7	Gaylord Perry	399
8	Jim Kaat	395
9	Bert Blyleven	384
10	Tom Seaver	380
11	Jim Hunter	374
12	Jim Bunning	372
13	Mickey Lolich	347
14	Luis Tiant	346
15	Early Wynn	338
16	Frank Tanana	326
17	Juan Marichal	320
18	Pedro Ramos	315
19	Jim Perry	308
20	Jim Palmer	303
21	Murry Dickson	302
22	Milt Pappas	298
23	Doyle Alexander	296
	Tommy John	296
25	Jim Grant	292
26	Jerry Koosman	290
27	Lew Burdette	289
28	Bob Friend	286
29	Dennis Eckersley	284
	Billy Pierce	284
31	Don Drysdale	280
32	Jim Slaton	277
33	Joe Niekro	276
34	Floyd Bannister	275
35	Jack Morris	272
36	Vern Law	268
37	Vida Blue	263
38	Rick Wise	261
39	Nolan Ryan	260
40	Larry Jackson	259
41	Bob Gibson	257
42	Camilo Pascual	256
43	Mike McCormick	255
	Curt Simmons	255
45	Charlie Hough	254
	Red Ruffing	254
47	Don Newcombe	252
48	Ken Holtzman	249
	Claude Osteen	249
50	Steve Renko	248
51	Denny McLain	242
	Johnny Podres	242
53	Harvey Haddix	240
	Ray Sadecki	240
55	Bob Buhl	238
56	Earl Wilson	236
57	Scott McGregor	235
58	Joe Coleman	234
59	Jim Lonborg	233
60	Dave McNally	230
61	Mike Flanagan	229
62	Whitey Ford	228
	Dennis Martinez	228
64	Carl Hubbell	227
65	Ron Guidry	226
66	Don Cardwell	225
	Jerry Reuss	225
68	Bob Feller	224
69	Stan Bahnsen	223
	Ted Lyons	223
	Mike Torrez	223
72	Mike Cuellar	222
73	Ray Burris	221
74	Jim Clancy	219
75	Mike Caldwell	218
	Ron Kline	218
77	John Candelaria	217
78	Ralph Terry	216
79	Ned Garver	213
80	Bill Monbouquette	211
81	Herm Wehmeier	210
82	Joe Nuxhall	209
	Marty Pattin	209
	Wilbur Wood	209
85	Gary Bell	206
	Bob Forsch	206
	Bobo Newsom	206
88	Bob Knepper	205
89	Larry Gura	204
	Sandy Koufax	204
	Milt Wilcox	204
92	Johnny Klippstein	203
93	Ross Grimsley	202
	Dennis Leonard	202
95	Juan Pizarro	201
96	Carl Erskine	199
	Rudy May	199
	Preacher Roe	199
99	Dick Donovan	198
100	3 players tied	197

Home Runs Allowed (by era)

1876-1892

1	John Clarkson	161
2	Jack Stivetts	131
3	Jim Galvin	122
4	Gus Weyhing	121
5	Charley Radbourn	117
6	Mickey Welch	106
7	Tony Mullane	96
8	Pretzels Getzien	95
9	Harry Staley	93
10	Charlie Buffinton	87
11	Jim McCormick	86
12	Mark Baldwin	81
	Ad Gumbert	81
14	Jim Whitney	78
15	Amos Rusie	76

1893-1919

1	Kid Nichols	156
2	Cy Young	139
3	Jack Powell	110
4	Frank Dwyer	109
5	Rube Marquard	107
6	Bill Hutchinson	104
7	Wilbur Cooper	103
8	Walter Johnson	97
9	Christy Mathewson	92
10	Brickyard Kennedy	91
11	Hooks Dauss	87
12	Kid Carsey	81
13	Ted Breitenstein	79
14	Bill Dinneen	78
15	2 players tied	75

1920-1941

1	Red Ruffing	254
2	Carl Hubbell	227
3	Ted Lyons	223
4	Bobo Newsom	206
5	Earl Whitehill	192
6	Charlie Root	187
7	Freddie Fitzsimmons	186
8	Tommy Bridges	181
9	Lon Warneke	175
10	George Blaeholder	173
	Syl Johnson	173
12	Bump Hadley	167
13	Jesse Haines	165
14	Pete Alexander	164
	Larry French	164

1942-1960

1	Robin Roberts	505
2	Warren Spahn	434
3	Early Wynn	338
4	Murry Dickson	302
5	Lew Burdette	289
6	Bob Friend	286
7	Billy Pierce	284
8	Vern Law	268
9	Curt Simmons	255
10	Don Newcombe	252
11	Johnny Podres	242
12	Harvey Haddix	240
13	Bob Buhl	238
14	Whitey Ford	228
15	Bob Feller	224

1961-1988

1	Ferguson Jenkins	484
2	Phil Niekro	482
3	Don Sutton	472
4	Steve Carlton	414
5	Gaylord Perry	399
6	Jim Kaat	395
7	Bert Blyleven	384
8	Tom Seaver	380
9	Jim Hunter	374
10	Jim Bunning	372
11	Mickey Lolich	347
12	Luis Tiant	346
13	Frank Tanana	326
14	Juan Marichal	320
15	Pedro Ramos	315

Walks

#	Player	Walks
1	Nolan Ryan	2442
2	Steve Carlton	1833
3	Phil Niekro	1809
4	Early Wynn	1775
5	Bob Feller	1764
6	Bobo Newsom	1732
7	Amos Rusie	1704
8	Gus Weyhing	1566
9	Red Ruffing	1541
10	Bump Hadley	1442
11	Warren Spahn	1434
12	Earl Whitehill	1431
13	Tony Mullane	1409
14	Sam Jones	1396
15	Tom Seaver	1390
16	Gaylord Perry	1379
17	Mike Torrez	1371
18	Walter Johnson	1359
19	Don Sutton	1343
20	Bob Gibson	1336
21	Chick Fraser	1332
22	Sam McDowell	1312
23	Jim Palmer	1311
24	Mark Baldwin	1307
25	Adonis Terry	1301
26	Mickey Welch	1297
27	Burleigh Grimes	1295
28	Kid Nichols	1268
29	Joe Bush	1263
30	Joe Niekro	1262
31	Allie Reynolds	1261
32	Bob Lemon	1251
33	Hal Newhouser	1249
34	George Mullin	1238
35	Tommy John	1237
36	Bert Blyleven	1224
	Tim Keefe	1224
38	Cy Young	1217
39	Red Faber	1213
40	Vic Willis	1212
41	Ted Breitenstein	1203
42	Brickyard Kennedy	1201
43	Jerry Koosman	1198
44	Tommy Bridges	1192
45	John Clarkson	1191
46	Lefty Grove	1187
47	Vida Blue	1185
48	Billy Pierce	1178
49	Charlie Hough	1168
50	Jack Stivetts	1155
51	Johnny Vander Meer	1132
52	Bill Hutchinson	1128
53	Ted Lyons	1121
	Bucky Walters	1121
55	Mel Harder	1118
56	Earl Moore	1108
57	Bob Buhl	1105
58	Luis Tiant	1104
59	Mickey Lolich	1099
60	Lefty Gomez	1095
61	Jerry Reuss	1090
62	Virgil Trucks	1088
63	Whitey Ford	1086
64	Jim Kaat	1083
65	Eppa Rixey	1082
66	Eddie Plank	1072
67	Camilo Pascual	1069
68	Bob Turley	1068
69	Hooks Dauss	1067
70	Icebox Chamberlin	1065
71	Bert Cunningham	1064
72	Curt Simmons	1063
73	Bill Donovan	1059
74	Murry Dickson	1058
	Jouett Meekin	1058
76	Vern Kennedy	1049
77	Dizzy Trout	1046
78	Howard Ehmke	1042
79	Wes Ferrell	1040
80	Tommy Byrne	1037
81	Red Ames	1034
82	Rube Walberg	1031
83	Jack Powell	1021
84	Bob Shawkey	1018
85	Steve Renko	1010
86	Jim Slaton	1004
87	Joe Coleman	1003
	Waite Hoyt	1003
89	Jim Bunning	1000
90	Jim Perry	998
91	Ferguson Jenkins	997
92	Kirby Higbe	979
93	Johnny Klippstein	978
94	Pink Hawley	974
95	Silver King	970
96	George Uhle	966
97	Rudy May	958
98	Lee Meadows	956
99	Jim Hunter	954
100	Jimmy Ring	953

Fewest Walks per Game

#	Player	Avg
1	Tommy Bond	0.58
2	George Bradley	0.67
3	Terry Larkin	0.71
4	Monte Ward	0.92
5	Fred Goldsmith	0.96
6	Jim Whitney	1.06
7	Bobby Mathews	1.11
8	Jim Galvin	1.13
9	Deacon Phillippe	1.25
10	Will White	1.26
11	Babe Adams	1.29
12	Jack Lynch	1.39
13	Addie Joss	1.41
14	Cy Young	1.49
15	Guy Hecker	1.51
16	Lee Richmond	1.53
17	Jesse Tannehill	1.56
18	Jim McCormick	1.58
19	Christy Mathewson	1.58
20	Red Lucas	1.61
21	Nick Altrock	1.62
22	Pete Alexander	1.65
23	Jumbo McGinnis	1.65
24	Tiny Bonham	1.66
25	Ed Morris	1.67
26	Noodles Hahn	1.69
27	Charlie Ferguson	1.72
28	Fritz Peterson	1.73
29	Robin Roberts	1.73
30	Charley Radbourn	1.74
31	Dick Rudolph	1.77
32	Al Orth	1.77
33	Stump Weidman	1.78
34	Pete Donohue	1.80
35	Jess Barnes	1.80
36	Carl Hubbell	1.82
37	Juan Marichal	1.82
38	Slim Sallee	1.83
39	Bill Bernhard	1.83
40	Lew Burdette	1.84
41	Curt Davis	1.85
42	Ed Siever	1.86
43	Larry Corcoran	1.87
44	Ed Walsh	1.87
45	Ken Raffensberger	1.88
46	Paul Derringer	1.88
47	Bob Caruthers	1.90
48	Mordecai Brown	1.91
49	Sherry Smith	1.93
50	Bill Swift	1.93
51	George Suggs	1.93
52	Watty Clark	1.97
53	Jack Quinn	1.97
54	Frank Kitson	1.98
55	Doc White	1.98
56	Sam Leever	1.99
57	Henry Boyle	1.99
58	Ferguson Jenkins	1.99
59	Jack Taylor	2.00
60	Vern Law	2.01
61	Dupee Shaw	2.02
62	Syl Johnson	2.03
63	John Candelaria	2.04
64	Jim Barr	2.04
65	Don Newcombe	2.05
66	Clark Griffith	2.06
67	George Winter	2.06
68	Dutch Leonard	2.06
69	Walter Johnson	2.06
70	Scott Stratton	2.07
71	Hal Brown	2.08
72	Lary Sorensen	2.08
73	Red Donahue	2.09
74	Larry Jansen	2.09
75	Jack Powell	2.09
76	Dizzy Dean	2.10
77	Bill Monbouquette	2.12
78	Hooks Wiltse	2.12
79	Joe McGinnity	2.12
80	Chief Bender	2.12
81	Art Nehf	2.13
82	Pretzels Getzien	2.13
83	Ken Johnson	2.14
84	Jack Chesbro	2.14
85	Eddie Plank	2.15
86	Jim Kaat	2.15
87	Sloppy Thurston	2.15
88	Phil Douglas	2.16
89	Eppa Rixey	2.17
90	Ralph Terry	2.17
91	Bob Purkey	2.17
92	Tim Keefe	2.18
93	Scott McGregor	2.18
94	Bill Gullickson	2.18
95	Carl Mays	2.19
96	Dennis Eckersley	2.19
97	Bill Sherdel	2.20
98	Bill Duggleby	2.20
99	Doc Crandall	2.20
100	Wilbur Cooper	2.20

Strikeouts

#	Player	SO
1	Nolan Ryan	4775
2	Steve Carlton	4136
3	Tom Seaver	3640
4	Don Sutton	3574
5	Gaylord Perry	3534
6	Walter Johnson	3506
7	Bert Blyleven	3431
8	Phil Niekro	3342
9	Ferguson Jenkins	3192
10	Bob Gibson	3117
11	Jim Bunning	2855
12	Mickey Lolich	2832
13	Cy Young	2803
14	Warren Spahn	2583
15	Bob Feller	2581
16	Jerry Koosman	2556
17	Tim Keefe	2527
18	Christy Mathewson	2502
19	Don Drysdale	2486
20	Jim Kaat	2461
21	Sam McDowell	2453
22	Luis Tiant	2416
23	Sandy Koufax	2396
24	Robin Roberts	2357
25	Early Wynn	2334
26	Rube Waddell	2316
27	Juan Marichal	2303
28	Lefty Grove	2266
29	Eddie Plank	2246
30	Tommy John	2227
31	Jim Palmer	2212
32	Pete Alexander	2198
	Frank Tanana	2198
34	Vida Blue	2175
35	Camilo Pascual	2167
36	Bobo Newsom	2082
37	Dazzy Vance	2045
38	Jim Hunter	2012
39	Billy Pierce	1999
40	Red Ruffing	1987
41	John Clarkson	1978
42	Whitey Ford	1956
43	Amos Rusie	1934
44	Kid Nichols	1868
45	Jerry Reuss	1866
46	Rick Reuschel	1851
47	Mickey Welch	1850
48	Charley Radbourn	1830
49	Dennis Eckersley	1810
50	Tony Mullane	1807
51	Jim Galvin	1799
52	Hal Newhouser	1796
53	Charlie Hough	1780
54	Ron Guidry	1778
55	Rudy May	1760
56	Joe Niekro	1747
57	Ed Walsh	1736
58	Bob Friend	1734
59	Joe Coleman	1728
	Milt Pappas	1728
61	Chief Bender	1711
62	Larry Jackson	1709
63	Jim McCormick	1704
64	Jack Morris	1703
	Bob Veale	1703
66	Red Ames	1702
67	Charlie Buffinton	1700
68	Curt Simmons	1697
69	Carl Hubbell	1677
70	Tommy Bridges	1674
71	Gus Weyhing	1665
72	Vic Willis	1651
73	Rick Wise	1647
74	Floyd Bannister	1642
75	Al Downing	1639
76	Mike Cuellar	1632
77	Chris Short	1629
78	Andy Messersmith	1625
79	Jack Powell	1621
	Steve Rogers	1621
81	Ray Sadecki	1614
82	Claude Osteen	1612
83	Hoyt Wilhelm	1610
84	Jim Maloney	1605
85	Ken Holtzman	1601
86	Rube Marquard	1593
87	Woodie Fryman	1587
88	Jim Perry	1576
89	Harvey Haddix	1575
90	Jim Whitney	1571
91	Adonis Terry	1555
92	Dean Chance	1534
	Virgil Trucks	1534
94	Fernando Valenzuela	1528
95	Bill Donovan	1522
	Juan Pizarro	1522
97	Jon Matlack	1516
98	Toad Ramsey	1515
	Bill Singer	1515
100	3 players tied	1512

Strikeouts per Game

#	Player	Avg
1	Nolan Ryan	9.45
2	Sandy Koufax	9.27
3	Sam McDowell	8.86
4	J. R. Richard	8.37
5	Bob Veale	7.96
6	Jim Maloney	7.81
7	Rich Gossage	7.69
8	Mario Soto	7.53
9	Sam Jones	7.53
10	Bob Gibson	7.22
11	Steve Carlton	7.14
12	Fernando Valenzuela	7.06
13	Rube Waddell	7.03
14	Mickey Lolich	7.00
15	Bert Blyleven	6.92
16	Rollie Fingers	6.87
17	Tom Seaver	6.85
18	Jim Bunning	6.84
19	Juan Pizarro	6.73
20	Bobby Bolin	6.71
21	Ray Culp	6.69
22	Ron Guidry	6.69
23	Stan Williams	6.66
24	Bob Turley	6.66
25	Camilo Pascual	6.66
26	Don Wilson	6.61
27	Tug McGraw	6.58
28	Denny Lemaster	6.57
29	Floyd Bannister	6.57
30	Andy Messersmith	6.56
31	Don Drysdale	6.52
32	Al Downing	6.50
33	Toad Ramsey	6.49
34	Mike Scott	6.49
35	Diego Segui	6.46
36	Hoyt Wilhelm	6.43
37	Dean Chance	6.43
38	Ferguson Jenkins	6.39
39	Moe Drabowsky	6.38
40	Earl Wilson	6.37
41	Harvey Haddix	6.34
42	Sonny Siebert	6.32
43	Bob Welch	6.32
44	Chris Short	6.31
45	Bill Singer	6.27
46	Luis Tiant	6.24
47	Frank Tanana	6.22
48	Turk Farrell	6.22
49	Dazzy Vance	6.20
50	Stu Miller	6.18
51	Clay Kirby	6.16
52	Gary Bell	6.15
53	Gary Peters	6.14
54	Denny McLain	6.12
55	Mike Krukow	6.12
56	Don Sutton	6.09
57	Dennis Eckersley	6.07
58	Bob Feller	6.07
59	Frank Viola	6.06
60	Fred Norman	6.05
61	Joe Coleman	6.05
62	Rudy May	6.04
63	Rick Sutcliffe	6.00
64	Jerry Koosman	5.99
65	Mike Witt	5.98
66	Gaylord Perry	5.94
67	Charlie Hough	5.92
68	Woodie Fryman	5.92
69	Juan Marichal	5.91
70	John Montefusco	5.90
71	Steve Barber	5.89
72	Vida Blue	5.85
73	Jack Morris	5.84
74	Danny Darwin	5.81
75	Joey Jay	5.81
76	Ray Sadecki	5.81
77	Jim O'Toole	5.79
78	John Candelaria	5.79
79	Dave Giusti	5.78
80	Jon Matlack	5.77
81	Larry Dierker	5.75
82	Lindy McDaniel	5.72
83	Tony Cloninger	5.70
84	Johnny Podres	5.70
85	Jim Bibby	5.64
86	Billy O'Dell	5.62
87	Gene Garber	5.61
88	Gary Nolan	5.58
89	Phil Niekro	5.57
90	Billy Hoeft	5.55
91	Whitey Ford	5.55
92	Johnny Vander Meer	5.54
93	Pat Dobson	5.53
94	Orval Overall	5.48
95	Billy Pierce	5.44
96	Dennis Leonard	5.44
97	Don Mossi	5.42
98	Vinegar Bend Mizell	5.41
99	Hal Newhouser	5.40
100	Ken Johnson	5.40

Earned Run Average

1	Ed Walsh	1.82
2	Addie Joss	1.89
3	Mordecai Brown	2.06
4	Monte Ward	2.10
5	Christy Mathewson	2.13
6	Rube Waddell	2.16
7	Walter Johnson	2.17
8	Orval Overall	2.24
9	Tommy Bond	2.25
10	Ed Reulbach	2.28
	Will White	2.28
12	Jim Scott	2.30
13	Larry Corcoran	2.35
	Eddie Plank	2.35
15	Eddie Cicotte	2.38
	Ed Killian	2.38
	George McQuillan	2.38
18	Doc White	2.39
19	Nap Rucker	2.42
20	Jim McCormick	2.43
	Jeff Tesreau	2.43
22	Terry Larkin	2.44
23	Chief Bender	2.46
24	Sam Leever	2.47
	Lefty Leifield	2.47
	Hooks Wiltse	2.47
27	Hippo Vaughn	2.48
28	Bob Ewing	2.49
29	George Bradley	2.50
30	Hoyt Wilhelm	2.52
31	Noodles Hahn	2.55
32	Pete Alexander	2.56
	Slim Sallee	2.56
34	Deacon Phillippe	2.58
	Frank Smith	2.58
36	Ed Siever	2.60
37	Bob Rhoads	2.61
38	Tim Keefe	2.62
39	Red Ames	2.63
	Barney Pelty	2.63
	Vic Willis	2.63
	Cy Young	2.63
43	Claude Hendrix	2.65
44	Joe McGinnity	2.66
	Dick Rudolph	2.66
46	Nick Altrock	2.67
	Charlie Ferguson	2.67
	Jack Taylor	2.67
	Carl Weilman	2.67
50	Jack Chesbro	2.68
	Cy Falkenberg	2.68
	Charley Radbourn	2.68
53	Bill Donovan	2.69
	Fred Toney	2.69
55	Larry Cheney	2.70
56	Mickey Welch	2.71
57	Fred Goldsmith	2.73
58	Whitey Ford	2.74
	Harry Howell	2.74
60	Howie Camnitz	2.75
	Dummy Taylor	2.75
62	Babe Adams	2.76
	Sandy Koufax	2.76
	Dutch Leonard	2.76
65	Jeff Pfeffer	2.77
66	Jack Coombs	2.78
	Earl Moore	2.78
68	Tully Sparks	2.79
	Jesse Tannehill	2.79
70	Phil Douglas	2.80
71	John Clarkson	2.81
72	Ray Fisher	2.82
	Ed Morris	2.82
	George Mullin	2.82
75	Bob Caruthers	2.84
	Dave Foutz	2.84
77	Andy Messersmith	2.86
	Jim Palmer	2.86
	Tom Seaver	2.86
80	Jim Galvin	2.87
	George Winter	2.87
82	Willie Mitchell	2.88
83	Wilbur Cooper	2.89
	Stan Coveleski	2.89
	Juan Marichal	2.89
86	Rollie Fingers	2.90
87	Bob Gibson	2.91
88	Harry Brecheen	2.92
	Dean Chance	2.92
	Doc Crandall	2.92
	Rich Gossage	2.92
	Carl Mays	2.92
	Jumbo McGinnis	2.92
94	Dave Davenport	2.93
	Guy Hecker	2.93
96	Don Drysdale	2.95
	Kid Nichols	2.95
	Lefty Tyler	2.95
99	Charlie Buffinton	2.96
	Mort Cooper	2.96

Earned Run Average (by era)

1876-1892

1	Monte Ward	2.10
2	Tommy Bond	2.25
3	Will White	2.28
4	Larry Corcoran	2.35
5	Jim McCormick	2.43
6	Terry Larkin	2.44
7	George Bradley	2.50
8	Tim Keefe	2.62
9	Charlie Ferguson	2.67
10	Charley Radbourn	2.68
11	Mickey Welch	2.71
12	Fred Goldsmith	2.73
13	John Clarkson	2.81
14	Ed Morris	2.82
15	2 players tied	2.84

1893-1919

1	Ed Walsh	1.82
2	Addie Joss	1.89
3	Mordecai Brown	2.06
4	Christy Mathewson	2.13
5	Rube Waddell	2.16
6	Walter Johnson	2.17
7	Orval Overall	2.24
8	Ed Reulbach	2.28
9	Jim Scott	2.30
10	Eddie Plank	2.35
11	Eddie Cicotte	2.38
	Ed Killian	2.38
	George McQuillan	2.38
14	Doc White	2.39
15	Nap Rucker	2.42

1920-1941

1	Pete Alexander	2.56
2	Stan Coveleski	2.89
3	Carl Mays	2.92
4	Carl Hubbell	2.98
5	Dizzy Dean	3.04
6	Lefty Grove	3.06
7	Bob Shawkey	3.09
8	Red Faber	3.15
	Eppa Rixey	3.15
10	Urban Shocker	3.17
11	Lon Warneke	3.18
12	Art Nehf	3.20
13	Jess Barnes	3.21
14	George Mogridge	3.23
15	2 players tied	3.24

1942-1960

1	Hoyt Wilhelm	2.52
2	Whitey Ford	2.74
3	Harry Brecheen	2.92
4	Mort Cooper	2.96
5	Max Lanier	3.01
6	Tiny Bonham	3.06
	Hal Newhouser	3.06
8	Warren Spahn	3.08
9	Sal Maglie	3.15
10	Eddie Lopat	3.21
11	Bob Lemon	3.23
	Dizzy Trout	3.23
13	Stu Miller	3.24
14	Bob Feller	3.25
	Dutch Leonard	3.25

1961-1988

1	Sandy Koufax	2.76
2	Andy Messersmith	2.86
	Jim Palmer	2.86
	Tom Seaver	2.86
5	Juan Marichal	2.89
6	Rollie Fingers	2.90
7	Bob Gibson	2.91
8	Dean Chance	2.92
	Rich Gossage	2.92
10	Don Drysdale	2.95
11	Mel Stottlemyre	2.97
12	Bob Veale	3.07
13	Gary Nolan	3.08
14	Joe Horlen	3.10
	Gaylord Perry	3.10

Adjusted Earned Run Average

1	Lefty Grove	148
2	Walter Johnson	147
3	Hoyt Wilhelm	146
4	Ed Walsh	145
5	Addie Joss	142
6	Mordecai Brown	140
	Kid Nichols	140
8	Cy Young	138
9	Rube Waddell	136
10	Pete Alexander	135
	Christy Mathewson	135
12	John Clarkson	134
13	Harry Brecheen	133
	Whitey Ford	133
	Noodles Hahn	133
16	Sandy Koufax	131
17	Carl Hubbell	130
	Hal Newhouser	130
19	Dizzy Dean	129
	Rich Gossage	129
	Amos Rusie	129
22	Stan Coveleski	127
	Nig Cuppy	127
	Bob Gibson	127
	Tom Seaver	127
26	Tommy Bridges	126
	Tim Keefe	126
	Max Lanier	126
	Sal Maglie	126
	Dave Stieb	126
31	Lefty Gomez	125
	Jim Palmer	125
33	Dave Foutz	124
	Mel Parnell	124
	Urban Shocker	124
	Dizzy Trout	124
	Dazzy Vance	124
38	Mort Cooper	123
	Silver King	123
	Sam Leever	123
	Ed Reulbach	123
42	Eddie Cicotte	122
	Larry Corcoran	122
	Bob Feller	122
	Juan Marichal	122
	Andy Messersmith	122
	Eddie Plank	122
	Eddie Rommel	122
49	Bert Blyleven	121
	Bob Caruthers	121
	Don Drysdale	121
	Clark Griffith	121
	Joe McGinnity	121
	Orval Overall	121
	Deacon Phillippe	121
	Jack Stivetts	121
	Hippo Vaughn	121
	Will White	121
59	Tiny Bonham	120
	Jim Scott	120
	Bob Stanley	120
	John Tudor	120
	Lon Warneke	120
64	Dean Chance	119
	Red Faber	119
	Rollie Fingers	119
	Ron Guidry	119
	Bob Lemon	119
	Dutch Leonard	119
	Carl Mays	119
	Billy Pierce	119
	Charley Radbourn	119
	Toad Ramsey	119
	Nap Rucker	119
	Bobby Shantz	119
	Monte Ward	119
77	Charlie Ferguson	118
	Thornton Lee	118
	Dolf Luque	118
	Ted Lyons	118
	Jim McCormick	118
	Sadie McMahon	118
	Warren Spahn	118
84	Babe Adams	117
	John Candelaria	117
	Wes Ferrell	117
	Gene Garber	117
	Mike Garcia	117
	Firpo Marberry	117
	Tony Mullane	117
	Gary Nolan	117
	Gaylord Perry	117
	Ed Siever	117
	Virgil Trucks	117
95	11 players tied	116

Adjusted ERA (by era)

1876-1892

1	John Clarkson	134
2	Amos Rusie	129
3	Tim Keefe	126
4	Dave Foutz	124
5	Silver King	123
6	Larry Corcoran	122
7	Bob Caruthers	121
	Jack Stivetts	121
	Will White	121
10	Charley Radbourn	119
	Toad Ramsey	119
	Monte Ward	119
13	Charlie Ferguson	118
	Jim McCormick	118
	Sadie McMahon	118

1893-1919

1	Walter Johnson	147
2	Ed Walsh	145
3	Addie Joss	142
4	Mordecai Brown	140
	Kid Nichols	140
6	Cy Young	138
7	Rube Waddell	136
8	Christy Mathewson	135
9	Noodles Hahn	133
10	Nig Cuppy	127
11	Sam Leever	123
	Ed Reulbach	123
13	Eddie Cicotte	122
	Eddie Plank	122
15	5 players tied	121

1920-1941

1	Lefty Grove	148
2	Pete Alexander	135
3	Carl Hubbell	130
4	Dizzy Dean	129
5	Stan Coveleski	127
6	Tommy Bridges	126
7	Lefty Gomez	125
8	Urban Shocker	124
	Dazzy Vance	124
10	Eddie Rommel	122
11	Lon Warneke	120
12	Red Faber	119
	Carl Mays	119
14	3 players tied	118

1942-1960

1	Hoyt Wilhelm	146
2	Harry Brecheen	133
	Whitey Ford	133
4	Hal Newhouser	130
5	Max Lanier	126
	Sal Maglie	126
7	Mel Parnell	124
	Dizzy Trout	124
9	Mort Cooper	123
10	Bob Feller	122
11	Tiny Bonham	120
12	Bob Lemon	119
	Dutch Leonard	119
	Billy Pierce	119
	Bobby Shantz	119

1961-1988

1	Sandy Koufax	131
2	Rich Gossage	129
3	Bob Gibson	127
	Tom Seaver	127
5	Dave Stieb	126
6	Jim Palmer	125
7	Juan Marichal	122
	Andy Messersmith	122
9	Bert Blyleven	121
	Don Drysdale	121
11	Bob Stanley	120
	John Tudor	120
13	Dean Chance	119
	Rollie Fingers	119
	Ron Guidry	119

Pitching Runs

1	Cy Young	754
2	Walter Johnson	705
3	Lefty Grove	595
4	Kid Nichols	533
5	Pete Alexander	484
6	Warren Spahn	471
7	Tom Seaver	422
8	Christy Mathewson	418
9	Amos Rusie	417
10	Tim Keefe	402
11	Carl Hubbell	394
12	Whitey Ford	387
13	Bob Feller	385
14	Jim Palmer	378
15	John Clarkson	369
16	Lefty Gomez	322
17	Gaylord Perry	315
18	Ted Lyons	314
19	Ed Walsh	310
	Hoyt Wilhelm	310
21	Charley Radbourn	299
22	Red Faber	294
23	Mordecai Brown	293
24	Bob Gibson	291
25	Dazzy Vance	281
26	Bert Blyleven	276
27	Red Ruffing	271
28	Dutch Leonard	267
29	Don Drysdale	266
	Eddie Plank	266
31	Robin Roberts	264
32	Nolan Ryan	263
	Don Sutton	263
34	Juan Marichal	262
35	Tommy Bridges	257
	Stan Coveleski	257
37	Hal Newhouser	256
38	Bob Lemon	250
	Eppa Rixey	250
40	Billy Pierce	249
41	Tony Mullane	247
42	Dolf Luque	245
43	Sandy Koufax	244
44	Steve Carlton	240
45	Rube Waddell	239
46	Clark Griffith	233
47	Tommy John	230
48	Carl Mays	217
49	Addie Joss	214
50	Bob Caruthers	213
	Jim McCormick	213
	Mickey Welch	213
53	Waite Hoyt	210
	Urban Shocker	210
55	Silver King	207
56	Ron Guidry	204
57	Nig Cuppy	201
58	Eddie Cicotte	200
59	Will White	198
60	Phil Niekro	196
61	Harry Brecheen	193
62	Mel Harder	190
63	Lon Warneke	187
64	Eddie Lopat	185
65	Dizzy Dean	184
	Joe McGinnity	184
67	Eddie Rommel	180
68	Jim Bunning	179
69	Larry French	178
70	Ed Morris	177
	Dave Stieb	177
	Dizzy Trout	177
73	Spud Chandler	176
74	Mike Garcia	175
75	Freddie Fitzsimmons	174
	Sam Leever	174
	Andy Messersmith	174
78	Sadie McMahon	173
79	Vic Willis	171
	Early Wynn	171
81	Wilbur Cooper	169
	Thornton Lee	169
83	Ed Reulbach	167
84	Frank Tanana	164
85	Babe Adams	161
	Jack Quinn	161
87	Charlie Buffinton	160
	Ferguson Jenkins	160
89	Noodles Hahn	158
90	Jim Galvin	157
91	Vida Blue	155
	Sal Maglie	155
	Firpo Marberry	155
94	Guy Hecker	152
	Deacon Phillippe	152
	Joe Wood	152
97	Bob Shawkey	151
	Bucky Walters	151
99	Herb Pennock	149
	Steve Rogers	149

Adjusted Pitching Runs

1	Cy Young	810
2	Kid Nichols	667
3	Walter Johnson	665
4	Lefty Grove	644
5	Pete Alexander	523
6	John Clarkson	485
7	Tom Seaver	415
8	Christy Mathewson	396
9	Tim Keefe	382
10	Amos Rusie	372
11	Carl Hubbell	354
12	Bob Gibson	338
13	Bert Blyleven	332
14	Warren Spahn	331
15	Gaylord Perry	320
16	Whitey Ford	318
	Jim Palmer	318
18	Hal Newhouser	305
19	Ted Lyons	304
20	Phil Niekro	302
21	Bob Feller	299
22	Tommy Bridges	293
23	Hoyt Wilhelm	289
24	Mordecai Brown	288
25	Ed Walsh	272
26	Steve Carlton	271
27	Stan Coveleski	270
28	Red Faber	266
29	Dazzy Vance	261
30	Eddie Plank	260
31	Clark Griffith	258
	Tony Mullane	258
33	Charley Radbourn	256
34	Ferguson Jenkins	255
	Jack Stivetts	255
36	Silver King	253
	Rube Waddell	253
38	Eppa Rixey	248
39	Juan Marichal	246
40	Nig Cuppy	242
41	Robin Roberts	239
42	Don Drysdale	232
	Dizzy Trout	232
44	Urban Shocker	230
45	Lefty Gomez	229
46	Billy Pierce	228
47	Sandy Koufax	223
48	Dutch Leonard	221
49	Eddie Rommel	217
50	Dave Stieb	216
51	Joe McGinnity	214
52	Jim McCormick	208
53	Harry Brecheen	206
54	Dolf Luque	205
55	Addie Joss	204
	Jack Quinn	204
57	Jim Bunning	200
58	Wes Ferrell	198
59	Dizzy Dean	194
60	Lon Warneke	192
61	Bob Caruthers	190
	Bob Lemon	190
63	Noodles Hahn	189
	Tommy John	189
	Mickey Welch	189
66	Carl Mays	187
	Sadie McMahon	187
	Vic Willis	187
69	Eddie Cicotte	186
70	Rick Reuschel	184
	Will White	184
72	Mel Harder	182
73	Wilbur Cooper	180
74	Waite Hoyt	179
75	Virgil Trucks	175
76	Red Ruffing	173
77	Frank Dwyer	172
	Nolan Ryan	172
79	Ron Guidry	169
	Sam Leever	169
	Bucky Walters	169
82	Thornton Lee	168
83	Larry French	167
84	Luis Tiant	164
85	Mel Parnell	163
86	Steve Rogers	159
87	Sal Maglie	158
88	Babe Adams	157
	Deacon Phillippe	157
90	Larry Jackson	156
91	Hippo Vaughn	155
92	Jim Galvin	154
	Joe Wood	154
94	Andy Messersmith	153
	Ed Reulbach	153
96	Kent Tekulve	152
97	Dave Foutz	151
	Jerry Koosman	151
	Don Sutton	151
100	Charlie Buffinton	150

Pitching Wins

1	Walter Johnson	71.5
2	Cy Young	70.5
3	Lefty Grove	55.5
4	Warren Spahn	47.7
5	Pete Alexander	47.7
6	Kid Nichols	47.5
7	Tom Seaver	44.1
8	Christy Mathewson	43.9
9	Whitey Ford	39.4
10	Jim Palmer	39.4
11	Carl Hubbell	38.6
12	Bob Feller	37.3
13	Amos Rusie	36.1
14	Tim Keefe	36.0
15	Ed Walsh	34.3
16	Gaylord Perry	33.1
17	John Clarkson	32.5
18	Hoyt Wilhelm	31.9
19	Mordecai Brown	31.2
20	Bob Gibson	30.6
21	Lefty Gomez	29.9
22	Ted Lyons	29.6
23	Red Faber	29.0
24	Bert Blyleven	28.5
25	Eddie Plank	28.2
26	Don Drysdale	27.8
27	Nolan Ryan	27.5
28	Don Sutton	27.3
29	Juan Marichal	27.3
30	Dazzy Vance	27.0
31	Robin Roberts	26.8
32	Charley Radbourn	26.6
33	Dutch Leonard	26.4
34	Hal Newhouser	25.8
35	Stan Coveleski	25.7
36	Red Ruffing	25.5
37	Steve Carlton	25.2
38	Rube Waddell	25.2
39	Steve Carlton	25.1
40	Bob Lemon	25.1
41	Sandy Koufax	25.1
42	Billy Pierce	25.0
43	Tommy Bridges	24.2
44	Dolf Luque	23.9
45	Tommy John	23.8
46	Addie Joss	23.2
47	Carl Mays	22.2
48	Tony Mullane	21.6
49	Eddie Cicotte	21.3
50	Clark Griffith	20.8
51	Urban Shocker	20.5
52	Phil Niekro	20.5
53	Ron Guidry	20.4
54	Waite Hoyt	20.2
55	Harry Brecheen	19.5
56	Mickey Welch	19.4
57	Jim McCormick	19.2
58	Joe McGinnity	19.1
59	Lon Warneke	18.8
60	Bob Caruthers	18.7
61	Eddie Lopat	18.7
62	Jim Bunning	18.5
63	Dizzy Dean	18.5
64	Andy Messersmith	18.4
65	Sam Leever	18.1
66	Mel Harder	18.1
67	Will White	18.0
68	Ed Reulbach	18.0
69	Dizzy Trout	17.8
70	Wilbur Cooper	17.7
71	Dave Stieb	17.6
72	Spud Chandler	17.6
73	Silver King	17.6
74	Larry French	17.6
75	Mike Garcia	17.5
76	Vic Willis	17.5
77	Early Wynn	17.3
78	Nig Cuppy	17.1
79	Eddie Rommel	17.1
80	Freddie Fitzsimmons	17.1
81	Babe Adams	16.7
82	Ferguson Jenkins	16.7
83	Frank Tanana	16.6
84	Thornton Lee	16.3
85	Vida Blue	16.2
86	Jack Quinn	16.1
87	Joe Wood	15.9
88	Ed Morris	15.7
89	Steve Rogers	15.6
90	Sal Maglie	15.5
91	Noodles Hahn	15.5
92	Jerry Koosman	15.4
93	Bucky Walters	15.3
94	Deacon Phillippe	15.3
95	Jon Matlack	15.3
96	Bob Shawkey	15.2
97	Rollie Fingers	15.2
98	Rich Gossage	15.1
99	Mel Stottlemyre	15.1
100	Allie Reynolds	15.0

Adjusted Pitching Wins

1	Cy Young	75.8
2	Walter Johnson	67.5
3	Lefty Grove	60.0
4	Kid Nichols	59.4
5	Pete Alexander	51.6
6	Tom Seaver	43.4
7	John Clarkson	42.7
8	Christy Mathewson	41.5
9	Bob Gibson	35.5
10	Carl Hubbell	34.7
11	Bert Blyleven	34.2
12	Tim Keefe	34.2
13	Gaylord Perry	33.7
14	Warren Spahn	33.5
15	Jim Palmer	33.1
16	Whitey Ford	32.4
17	Amos Rusie	32.2
18	Phil Niekro	31.6
19	Hal Newhouser	30.7
20	Mordecai Brown	30.7
21	Ed Walsh	30.1
22	Hoyt Wilhelm	29.7
23	Bob Feller	29.0
24	Ted Lyons	28.6
25	Steve Carlton	28.3
26	Tommy Bridges	27.6
27	Eddie Plank	27.6
28	Stan Coveleski	27.0
29	Rube Waddell	26.6
30	Ferguson Jenkins	26.6
31	Red Faber	26.2
32	Juan Marichal	25.6
33	Dazzy Vance	25.1
34	Eppa Rixey	25.0
35	Robin Roberts	24.3
36	Don Drysdale	24.3
37	Dizzy Trout	23.4
38	Clark Griffith	23.1
39	Billy Pierce	22.9
40	Sandy Koufax	22.9
41	Charley Radbourn	22.8
42	Tony Mullane	22.5
43	Urban Shocker	22.5
44	Joe McGinnity	22.2
45	Addie Joss	22.1
46	Dutch Leonard	21.9
47	Silver King	21.5
48	Dave Stieb	21.5
49	Jack Stivetts	21.3
50	Lefty Gomez	21.3
51	Harry Brecheen	20.8
52	Jim Bunning	20.7
53	Nig Cuppy	20.6
54	Eddie Rommel	20.6
55	Jack Quinn	20.4
56	Dolf Luque	20.0
57	Eddie Cicotte	19.8
58	Tommy John	19.5
59	Dizzy Dean	19.5
60	Lon Warneke	19.3
61	Rick Reuschel	19.2
62	Vic Willis	19.1
63	Carl Mays	19.1
64	Bob Lemon	19.1
65	Wilbur Cooper	18.8
66	Jim McCormick	18.8
67	Noodles Hahn	18.5
68	Wes Ferrell	18.3
69	Nolan Ryan	18.0
70	Virgil Trucks	17.7
71	Sam Leever	17.6
72	Mel Harder	17.3
73	Luis Tiant	17.2
74	Mickey Welch	17.2
75	Waite Hoyt	17.2
76	Bucky Walters	17.2
77	Ron Guidry	16.9
78	Will White	16.8
79	Hippo Vaughn	16.7
80	Bob Caruthers	16.7
81	Steve Rogers	16.6
82	Larry French	16.5
83	Ed Reulbach	16.5
84	Babe Adams	16.3
85	Red Ruffing	16.3
86	Larry Jackson	16.2
87	Andy Messersmith	16.2
88	Thornton Lee	16.2
89	Joe Wood	16.1
90	Mel Parnell	16.1
91	Kent Tekulve	15.9
92	Deacon Phillippe	15.8
93	Sal Maglie	15.8
94	Don Sutton	15.7
95	Jerry Koosman	15.7
96	Sadie McMahon	15.5
97	Rich Gossage	15.2
98	Spud Chandler	14.9
99	John Candelaria	14.9
100	Frank Dwyer	14.6

Opponents' Batting Average

1	Sandy Koufax	.205
	Nolan Ryan	.205
3	Andy Messersmith	.212
	J. R. Richard	.212
5	Sam McDowell	.215
6	Hoyt Wilhelm	.216
7	Mario Soto	.220
	Bob Turley	.220
9	Jeff Tesreau	.223
10	Jim Maloney	.224
11	Ed Walsh	.225
12	Rich Gossage	.226
	Tom Seaver	.226
14	Bob Gibson	.228
	Charlie Hough	.228
	Walter Johnson	.228
	Don Wilson	.228
18	Sam Jones	.230
	Jim Palmer	.230
20	Bobby Bolin	.231
	Bob Feller	.231
	Jim Hunter	.231
23	Al Downing	.232
	Johnny Vander Meer	.232
	Stan Williams	.232
26	Larry Cheney	.233
	Ed Reulbach	.233
28	Dean Chance	.234
	Denny McLain	.234
30	Ray Culp	.235
	Rollie Fingers	.235
	Whitey Ford	.235
	Fernando Valenzuela	.235
34	Moe Drabowsky	.236
	Don Sutton	.236
	Luis Tiant	.236
	Bob Veale	.236
38	Vida Blue	.237
	Juan Marichal	.237
	Tug McGraw	.237
	Juan Pizarro	.237
42	Addie Joss	.238
	Rudy May	.238
	Allie Reynolds	.238
	Jim Scott	.238
	Sonny Siebert	.238
47	Gary Bell	.239
	Don Drysdale	.239
	Jack Morris	.239
	Hal Newhouser	.239
	Gary Nolan	.239
	Dave Stieb	.239
53	Steve Carlton	.240
	Mort Cooper	.240
	Orval Overall	.240
	Billy Pierce	.240
	Bill Singer	.240
	Virgil Trucks	.240
59	Kirby Higbe	.241
	Bob Lemon	.241
61	Harry Brecheen	.242
	Jim Bunning	.242
	Stu Miller	.242
	Mike Scott	.242
	Bob Welch	.242
	Earl Wilson	.242
67	Jim Bibby	.243
	Mike Cuellar	.243
	Larry Dierker	.243
	Eddie Fisher	.243
	Claude Hendrix	.243
	Joe Horlen	.243
	Ferguson Jenkins	.243
	Willie Mitchell	.243
	Gary Peters	.243
	Diego Segui	.243
77	Bert Blyleven	.244
	Jack Coombs	.244
	Lefty Gomez	.244
	Ron Guidry	.244
	Blue Moon Odom	.244
	Camilo Pascual	.244
	Vic Raschi	.244
	Warren Spahn	.244
	Lefty Tyler	.244
	Hippo Vaughn	.244
87	Steve Barber	.245
	Sal Maglie	.245
	Dave McNally	.245
	Van Mungo	.245
	Gaylord Perry	.245
	Mel Stottlemyre	.245
	Rube Waddell	.245
94	Mordecai Brown	.246
	Eddie Cicotte	.246
	Clay Kirby	.246
	Mickey Lolich	.246
	Fred Norman	.246
	Billy O'Dell	.246
	Frank Smith	.246

Opponents' On Base Pctg.

1	Ed Walsh	.270
2	Addie Joss	.272
3	Sandy Koufax	.273
4	Juan Marichal	.274
5	Walter Johnson	.277
6	Babe Adams	.278
	Monte Ward	.278
8	Tom Seaver	.281
9	Pete Alexander	.282
	Tommy Bond	.282
	Jim Hunter	.282
12	Gary Nolan	.283
	Don Sutton	.283
	Hoyt Wilhelm	.283
15	Ferguson Jenkins	.284
	Andy Messersmith	.284
17	George Bradley	.285
18	Tiny Bonham	.286
	Carl Hubbell	.286
20	Christy Mathewson	.287
21	Denny McLain	.288
	Jeff Tesreau	.288
23	Larry Corcoran	.289
	Rollie Fingers	.289
	Robin Roberts	.289
	Will White	.289
27	John Candelaria	.290
	Don Drysdale	.290
	Ron Guidry	.290
	Dick Rudolph	.290
31	Terry Larkin	.291
	Mario Soto	.291
33	Mordecai Brown	.292
	Jim Palmer	.292
	Ralph Terry	.292
36	Mike Cuellar	.293
	Dennis Eckersley	.293
	Ed Morris	.293
	Don Mossi	.293
	Gaylord Perry	.293
	Slim Sallee	.293
	Warren Spahn	.293
43	Jim Bunning	.294
	Dizzy Dean	.294
	Charlie Ferguson	.294
	Eddie Fisher	.294
	Bob Gibson	.294
	Tim Keefe	.294
	Luis Tiant	.294
50	Harry Brecheen	.295
	Phil Douglas	.295
	Jim McCormick	.295
	Don Newcombe	.295
	Fritz Peterson	.295
55	Chief Bender	.296
	Mort Cooper	.296
	Joe Horlen	.296
	George McQuillan	.296
	Mike Scott	.296
60	Bert Blyleven	.297
	Eddie Cicotte	.297
	Claude Hendrix	.297
	Ken Johnson	.297
	Jumbo McGinnis	.297
	Ron Reed	.297
	Fred Toney	.297
	Don Wilson	.297
68	Hal Brown	.298
	Whitey Ford	.298
	Fred Goldsmith	.298
	Bill Gullickson	.298
	Sonny Siebert	.298
	John Tudor	.298
74	Larry Dierker	.299
	Turk Farrell	.299
	Bill Hands	.299
	Larry Jansen	.299
	Eddie Plank	.299
	Charley Radbourn	.299
	Bob Welch	.299
	Jim Whitney	.299
82	Vida Blue	.300
	Dean Chance	.300
	Rich Gossage	.300
	Harvey Haddix	.300
	Bobby Mathews	.300
	Jon Matlack	.300
	Billy O'Dell	.300
	Mel Stottlemyre	.300
	Bill Swift	.300
	Hippo Vaughn	.300
92	10 players tied	.301

Wins Above Team

1	Cy Young	100.3
2	Walter Johnson	90.3
3	Pete Alexander	81.9
4	Christy Mathewson	66.0
5	Lefty Grove	63.2
6	Tom Seaver	59.4
7	Jim McCormick	56.6
8	Jim Galvin	55.8
9	Charley Radbourn	51.5
10	Warren Spahn	46.3
11	Clark Griffith	46.1
12	Whitey Ford	44.7
13	Will White	44.0
14	Juan Marichal	39.1
15	Mickey Welch	37.7
16	Bob Feller	37.5
17	Tony Mullane	37.3
18	Phil Niekro	36.9
19	Eddie Plank	36.8
20	Ted Lyons	36.5
21	Amos Rusie	36.2
22	Kid Nichols	36.0
23	Jesse Tannehill	35.9
24	Wes Ferrell	35.4
25	Steve Carlton	34.9
26	Carl Hubbell	34.7
27	Charlie Buffinton	34.5
28	Dazzy Vance	33.9
29	Joe McGinnity	32.7
30	Ed Walsh	32.0
31	Bob Gibson	31.5
32	Eddie Rommel	31.1
33	Ed Morris	31.0
34	Sandy Koufax	30.9
	Jim Palmer	30.9
36	Robin Roberts	30.6
37	Bob Caruthers	30.5
38	Urban Shocker	30.3
39	Guy Hecker	29.8
	Ferguson Jenkins	29.8
	Sadie McMahon	29.8
42	Ron Guidry	29.7
43	Mordecai Brown	29.5
44	Addie Joss	28.7
45	Dizzy Dean	27.7
46	Bobby Mathews	27.1
47	Schoolboy Rowe	27.0
48	John Candelaria	26.8
49	Sam Leever	26.3
50	Rip Sewell	25.7
51	Tommy John	25.5
52	Jack Chesbro	25.3
53	Frank Killen	25.0
54	Red Lucas	24.7
	Herb Pennock	24.7
	Nap Rucker	24.7
57	Russ Ford	24.4
58	Gaylord Perry	24.2
59	Red Faber	24.1
60	Johnny Allen	23.9
61	Charlie Ferguson	23.6
	Noodles Hahn	23.6
63	Chief Bender	23.2
	Tim Keefe	23.2
	Firpo Marberry	23.2
	Joe Wood	23.2
67	Sal Maglie	23.1
68	Gus Weyhing	23.0
69	John Clarkson	22.9
70	Rick Reuschel	22.7
71	Burleigh Grimes	22.3
72	Carl Mays	22.2
73	Dutch Leonard	21.8
	Hippo Vaughn	21.8
75	Claude Passeau	21.6
	George Uhle	21.6
77	Spud Chandler	21.4
	Jim Maloney	21.4
	Bucky Walters	21.4
80	Hal Newhouser	21.2
	J. R. Richard	21.2
	Slim Sallee	21.2
83	Freddie Fitzsimmons	21.1
84	Vida Blue	21.0
85	Babe Adams	20.9
86	Art Nehf	20.7
87	Allie Reynolds	20.6
	Luis Tiant	20.6
89	Lon Warneke	20.5
90	Ted Breitenstein	20.4
91	Stan Coveleski	20.3
92	Jim Hunter	20.2
93	Ray Kremer	20.1
94	Don Newcombe	20.0
95	Tommy Bridges	19.8
	Jeff Pfeffer	19.8
97	Orel Hershiser	19.6
98	Wilbur Cooper	19.4
99	Vic Raschi	19.3
	Don Sutton	19.3

Wins Above League

1	Cy Young	413.0
2	Walter Johnson	348.0
3	Jim Galvin	334.0
4	Warren Spahn	304.0
5	Phil Niekro	296.0
6	Pete Alexander	290.5
7	Don Sutton	290.0
8	Gaylord Perry	289.5
9	Steve Carlton	286.5
10	Kid Nichols	284.5
11	Tim Keefe	283.5
12	Christy Mathewson	279.5
13	Early Wynn	272.0
14	Robin Roberts	265.5
15	Nolan Ryan	263.0
16	Jim Kaat	260.0
17	Eddie Plank	259.5
18	Eppa Rixey	258.5
19	Tom Seaver	258.5
	Mickey Welch	258.0
21	Ferguson Jenkins	255.0
	Tommy John	255.0
23	John Clarkson	252.5
	Tony Mullane	252.5
	Charley Radbourn	252.5
26	Jack Powell	249.0
	Red Ruffing	249.0
28	Gus Weyhing	248.0
29	Ted Lyons	245.0
30	Burleigh Grimes	241.0
31	Bert Blyleven	240.0
32	Jim McCormick	239.5
33	Red Faber	233.5
34	Jack Quinn	232.5
35	Vic Willis	225.5
36	Sam Jones	223.0
37	Lefty Grove	220.5
38	Paul Derringer	217.5
39	Bobo Newsom	216.5
40	Jerry Koosman	215.5
41	Bob Feller	214.0
42	Bob Friend	213.5
43	Bob Gibson	212.5
	Joe Niekro	212.5
45	George Mullin	212.0
46	Jim Palmer	210.0
47	Waite Hoyt	209.5
	Amos Rusie	209.5
49	Mel Harder	204.5
50	Jim Bunning	204.0
	Mickey Lolich	204.0
52	Carl Hubbell	203.5
53	Hooks Dauss	202.0
54	Earl Whitehill	201.5
55	Herb Pennock	201.0
56	Luis Tiant	200.5
57	Will White	197.5
	Jim Whitney	197.5
59	Wilbur Cooper	197.0
60	Al Orth	196.5
	Jerry Reuss	196.5
62	Adonis Terry	196.0
63	Claude Osteen	195.5
64	Jim Hunter	195.0
65	Jim Perry	194.5
66	Joe McGinnity	194.0
67	Chick Fraser	193.5
68	Juan Marichal	192.5
69	Charlie Buffinton	192.0
70	Clark Griffith	191.5
71	Billy Pierce	190.0
72	Joe Bush	189.0
	Rube Marquard	189.0
74	Larry Jackson	188.5
	Tom Zachary	188.5
76	Curt Simmons	188.0
77	Don Drysdale	187.5
78	Dolf Luque	186.5
	Milt Pappas	186.5
80	Dutch Leonard	186.0
81	Vida Blue	185.0
82	Mordecai Brown	184.5
	Rick Reuschel	184.5
	Rick Wise	184.5
85	Larry French	184.0
	Jesse Haines	184.0
	Lee Meadows	184.0
88	George Uhle	183.0
89	Freddie Fitzsimmons	181.5
90	Frank Tanana	181.0
91	Charlie Root	180.5
92	Bucky Walters	179.0
93	Eddie Cicotte	178.5
	Stan Coveleski	178.5
	Silver King	178.5
	Hal Newhouser	178.5
97	Murry Dickson	176.5
98	Red Ames	175.0
	Bill Dinneen	175.0
100	Lew Burdette	173.5

Relief Games

1	Hoyt Wilhelm	1018
2	Kent Tekulve	1013
3	Gene Garber	922
4	Lindy McDaniel	913
5	Rollie Fingers	907
6	Sparky Lyle	899
7	Don McMahon	872
8	Roy Face	821
9	Tug McGraw	785
10	Rich Gossage	774
11	Darold Knowles	757
12	Tom Burgmeier	742
	Gary Lavelle	742
14	Ron Perranoski	736
15	Clay Carroll	703
16	Willie Hernandez	701
17	Mike Marshall	699
18	Bill Campbell	691
19	Bruce Sutter	661
20	Ted Abernathy	647
21	Dave LaRoche	632
22	Greg Minton	630
23	Eddie Fisher	627
24	Paul Lindblad	623
25	Stu Miller	611
26	Grant Jackson	609
27	Dan Quisenberry	606
28	Elias Sosa	598
29	Bob Miller	595
30	Pedro Borbon	589
31	Jeff Reardon	582
32	Bob Locker	576
33	Terry Forster	575
34	Jim Brewer	549
	Johnny Klippstein	549
36	Al Hrabosky	544
	Tippy Martinez	544
38	Dave Giusti	535
39	Ron Kline	533
	Randy Moffitt	533
	Al Worthington	533
42	Dale Murray	517
43	Lee Smith	516
44	Frank Linzy	514
45	Doug Bair	513
46	Bob Stanley	509
47	John Hiller	502
48	Jack Aker	495
49	Tom Hume	488
50	Bill Henry	483

Relief Wins

1	Hoyt Wilhelm	143
2	Lindy McDaniel	141
3	Rollie Fingers	114
	Ron Kline	114
5	Rich Gossage	110
	Bob Stanley	110
7	Turk Farrell	106
8	Stu Miller	105
9	Roy Face	104
10	Johnny Klippstein	101
11	Dave Giusti	100
	Dick Tidrow	100
13	Sparky Lyle	99
14	Mike Marshall	97
15	Clay Carroll	96
	Gene Garber	96
	Tug McGraw	96
	Phil Regan	96
19	Kent Tekulve	94
20	Dick Hall	93
	Johnny Murphy	93
22	Diego Segui	92
23	Don McMahon	90
24	Moe Drabowsky	88
25	John Hiller	87
26	Grant Jackson	86
27	Eddie Fisher	85
28	Bill Campbell	83
29	Gary Lavelle	80
	Pete Richert	80
31	Tom Burgmeier	79
	Ron Perranoski	79
33	Clem Labine	77
34	Mace Brown	76
	Joe Heving	76
36	Hugh Casey	75
	Dan Spillner	75
	Al Worthington	75
39	Doug Bird	73
	Clyde Shoun	73
41	Mark Clear	71
	Dave Righetti	71
43	Pedro Borbon	69
	Jim Brewer	69
	Bob Miller	69
46	Willie Hernandez	68
	Paul Lindblad	68
	Bruce Sutter	68
49	Al McBean	67
	Tom Morgan	67

Relief Losses

1	Ron Kline	144
2	Hoyt Wilhelm	122
3	Lindy McDaniel	119
4	Rollie Fingers	118
	Johnny Klippstein	118
6	Gene Garber	113
7	Mike Marshall	112
8	Turk Farrell	111
	Diego Segui	111
10	Moe Drabowsky	105
11	Stu Miller	103
12	Rich Gossage	97
	Skip Lockwood	97
14	Roy Face	95
	Bob Stanley	95
16	Dick Tidrow	94
17	Dave Giusti	93
18	Tug McGraw	92
19	Dan Spillner	89
20	Kent Tekulve	87
21	Al Worthington	82
22	Bob Miller	81
	Phil Regan	81
24	Gary Lavelle	77
	Orlando Pena	77
26	John Hiller	76
	Sparky Lyle	76
28	Dick Hall	75
	Grant Jackson	75
30	Darold Knowles	74
	Ron Perranoski	74
32	Clay Carroll	73
	Pete Richert	73
34	Andy Hassler	71
	Tom Hume	71
	Bruce Sutter	71
37	Eddie Fisher	70
38	Ted Abernathy	69
	Neil Allen	69
40	Bill Campbell	68
	Don McMahon	68
42	Jim Brewer	65
	Terry Forster	65
	Joe Gibbon	65
45	Mike Fornieles	64
	Dan Schatzeder	64
47	Paul Lindblad	63
48	Mark Davis	62
	Hal Woodeshick	62
50	3 players tied	61

Relief Innings Pitched

1	Hoyt Wilhelm	2253
2	Lindy McDaniel	2140
3	Ron Kline	2078
4	Johnny Klippstein	1970
5	Diego Segui	1808
6	Dick Tidrow	1748
7	Dave Giusti	1718
8	Turk Farrell	1704
9	Rollie Fingers	1701
10	Stu Miller	1694
11	Moe Drabowsky	1640
12	Bob Stanley	1629
13	Rich Gossage	1578
14	Bob Miller	1552
15	Eddie Fisher	1540
16	Tug McGraw	1516
17	Gene Garber	1509
18	Dan Spillner	1493
19	Sparky Lyle	1391
20	Mike Marshall	1387
21	Kent Tekulve	1384
22	Roy Face	1375
23	Phil Regan	1373
24	Grant Jackson	1359
25	Clay Carroll	1353
26	Don McMahon	1313
27	Clyde Shoun	1286
28	Dick Hall	1259
29	Tom Burgmeier	1258
30	Al Worthington	1245
31	John Hiller	1241
32	Skip Lockwood	1236
33	Bill Campbell	1229
34	Paul Lindblad	1214
35	Doug Bird	1213
36	Orlando Pena	1202
37	Dan Schatzeder	1184
38	Ron Perranoski	1176
39	Pete Richert	1164
40	Mike Fornieles	1156
41	Ted Abernathy	1146
42	Andy Hassler	1122
43	Joe Gibbon	1118
44	Terry Forster	1105
45	Darold Knowles	1091
46	Tom Hume	1086
	Gary Lavelle	1086
48	Clem Labine	1079
49	Mace Brown	1075
50	Ray Moore	1074

Relief Points

1	Rollie Fingers	792
2	Rich Gossage	727
3	Bruce Sutter	665
4	Hoyt Wilhelm	618
5	Sparky Lyle	598
6	Dan Quisenberry	538
7	Jeff Reardon	516
8	Gene Garber	515
9	Lindy McDaniel	507
10	Roy Face	499
11	Kent Tekulve	467
12	Tug McGraw	460
13	Mike Marshall	458
14	Lee Smith	450
15	Ron Perranoski	442
16	Don McMahon	418
17	Stu Miller	415
18	Dave Righetti	414
19	Clay Carroll	405
20	Dave Giusti	397
21	Bob Stanley	381
22	Gary Lavelle	355
23	Ted Abernathy	353
	Dave Smith	353
25	Bill Campbell	350
26	John Hiller	348
27	Johnny Murphy	347
28	Darold Knowles	344
29	Willie Hernandez	339
30	Jim Brewer	337
31	Greg Minton	331
32	Steve Bedrosian	328
33	Dave LaRoche	324
34	Tom Burgmeier	307
35	Dick Radatz	305
36	Ron Davis	301
37	Ron Kline	300
38	Tippy Martinez	298
39	Terry Forster	297
40	Jack Aker	295
	Phil Regan	295
42	Clem Labine	290
43	Frank Linzy	289
44	Al Worthington	288
45	Al Hrabosky	287
46	Jesse Orosco	283
47	Fred Gladding	280
48	Aurelio Lopez	274
49	Turk Farrell	267
50	Bob Locker	265

Relief Ranking

1	Hoyt Wilhelm	371.4
2	Rich Gossage	236.8
3	Kent Tekulve	224.1
4	Bruce Sutter	218.5
5	Dan Quisenberry	214.9
6	John Hiller	186.0
7	Sparky Lyle	185.1
8	Rollie Fingers	177.9
9	Bob Stanley	172.8
10	Lee Smith	161.0
11	Gene Garber	147.7
12	Dave Righetti	142.7
13	Mike Marshall	141.2
14	Gary Lavelle	139.3
15	Jeff Reardon	125.9
16	Clay Carroll	121.2
17	Ron Perranoski	121.1
18	Tug McGraw	120.3
19	Stu Miller	115.2
20	Willie Hernandez	113.5
21	Jesse Orosco	112.0
22	Don McMahon	110.3
23	Dave Smith	106.4
24	Johnny Murphy	102.8
25	Tom Burgmeier	94.7
26	Frank Linzy	93.8
27	Lindy McDaniel	91.7
28	Steve Bedrosian	86.3
29	Dick Radatz	84.6
30	Al Hrabosky	81.5
31	Roy Face	80.9
32	Bill Henry	75.8
33	Bob Locker	71.2
34	Darold Knowles	69.6
35	Dave Schmidt	69.1
36	Terry Forster	68.8
37	Jim Kern	67.4
38	Dick Hall	66.1
39	Greg Minton	66.0
40	Joe Beggs	65.6
41	Clem Labine	64.2
42	Al Worthington	64.0
43	Bill Campbell	61.5
44	Rick Camp	60.4
45	Ted Wilks	58.5
46	Marv Grissom	58.1
47	Elias Sosa	56.4
48	Al Holland	55.8
49	Tom Ferrick	55.2
50	Jim Brewer	53.4

Relievers' Runs

1	Hoyt Wilhelm	310
2	Rollie Fingers	146
	Rich Gossage	146
4	Dan Quisenberry	144
5	Kent Tekulve	138
6	Sparky Lyle	122
7	John Hiller	112
8	Dave Righetti	110
9	Stu Miller	107
10	Ron Perranoski	100
11	Johnny Murphy	98
12	Don McMahon	97
13	Clay Carroll	94
14	Gary Lavelle	93
15	Bob Stanley	91
	Bruce Sutter	91
17	Mike Marshall	85
18	Tug McGraw	83
19	Dave Smith	79
20	Tom Burgmeier	73
	Jeff Reardon	73
22	Lee Smith	68
23	Jesse Orosco	67
24	Willie Hernandez	66
25	Bob Locker	64
26	Greg Minton	61
	Dave Schmidt	61
28	Gene Garber	60
29	Jim Brewer	59
30	Frank Linzy	58
31	Lindy McDaniel	56
32	Joe Beggs	55
	Dick Hall	55
	Jim Konstanty	55
	Ted Wilks	55
36	Darold Knowles	53
	Gary Lucas	53
38	Bill Henry	52
39	Joe Sambito	50
	Sammy Stewart	50
41	Terry Forster	49
	Al Holland	49
	Al Hrabosky	49
	Jim Kern	49
45	Roy Face	48
	Tippy Martinez	48
47	Marv Grissom	47
48	Al McBean	45
49	Wilcy Moore	44
50	Mace Brown	43

Adjusted Relievers' Runs

1	Hoyt Wilhelm	289
2	Kent Tekulve	152
3	Rich Gossage	147
4	Dan Quisenberry	146
5	John Hiller	132
	Bob Stanley	132
7	Sparky Lyle	122
8	Bruce Sutter	118
9	Rollie Fingers	106
10	Dave Righetti	97
11	Gene Garber	94
12	Lee Smith	90
13	Clay Carroll	89
14	Gary Lavelle	88
	Stu Miller	88
16	Tug McGraw	87
17	Mike Marshall	85
18	Tom Burgmeier	83
19	Don McMahon	82
20	Ron Perranoski	80
21	Willie Hernandez	79
22	Lindy McDaniel	72
23	Johnny Murphy	69
24	Jeff Reardon	68
25	Bill Henry	65
26	Dave Smith	64
27	Jesse Orosco	63
28	Dave Schmidt	60
29	Ted Wilks	59
30	Frank Linzy	58
	Bob Locker	58
32	Steve Bedrosian	56
	Joe Beggs	56
	Terry Forster	56
35	Rick Camp	53
	Al Hrabosky	53
37	Dick Radatz	52
38	Roy Face	50
	Dick Hall	50
	Greg Minton	50
41	Marv Grissom	49
	Clem Labine	49
43	Al Holland	48
	Darold Knowles	48
	Chuck Taylor	48
	Al Worthington	48
47	Bill Campbell	46
48	Jim Kern	45
	Andy McGaffigan	45
50	3 players tied	44

Clutch Pitching Index

1	Bob Rhoads	117
	Ed Siever	117
3	Ed Killian	114
	Will White	114
5	Ron Kline	113
	Bill Lee	113
	Dummy Taylor	113
8	Al Benton	112
	Lefty Leifield	112
	Eddie Lopat	112
	Win Mercer	112
	Bob Stanley	112
	Tom Zachary	112
14	Whitey Ford	111
	Preacher Roe	111
16	Steve Blass	110
	Bob Miller	110
	Bill Wight	110
19	Bob Buhl	109
	Max Butcher	109
	Dan Casey	109
	Max Lanier	109
	Sal Maglie	109
	Mel Parnell	109
	Bob Shaw	109
	Gerry Staley	109
	Geoff Zahn	109
28	Steve Barber	108
	Sheriff Blake	108
	Bill Duggleby	108
	Frank Dwyer	108
	Lefty Gomez	108
	Lefty Grove	108
	Mel Harder	108
	Carl Morton	108
	George Mullin	108
	Togie Pittinger	108
	Dizzy Trout	108
	Bob Veale	108
40	Nelson Briles	107
	Lloyd Brown	107
	Larry French	107
	Claude Osteen	107
	Eddie Rommel	107
	Eddie Smith	107
46	Jim Bagby	106
	Roger Craig	106
	Red Faber	106
	Freddie Fitzsimmons	106
	Joe Haynes	106
	Tommy John	106
	Bobby Mathews	106
	Cal McLish	106
	Jeff Pfeffer	106
	Howie Pollet	106
	Dutch Ruether	106
	Sherry Smith	106
	Sloppy Thurston	106
	John Tudor	106
	Rube Waddell	106
	Bucky Walters	106
62	Nixey Callahan	105
	Nig Cuppy	105
	Jack Curtis	105
	Murry Dickson	105
	Red Donahue	105
	Dick Ellsworth	105
	Wes Ferrell	105
	Fred Frankhouse	105
	Gene Garber	105
	Mike Garcia	105
	Guy Hecker	105
	Ken Heintzelman	105
	Johnny Klippstein	105
	Thornton Lee	105
	Dutch Leonard	105
	Ted Lyons	105
	Tug McGraw	105
	Stu Miller	105
	Clarence Mitchell	105
	Shane Rawley	105
	Allie Reynolds	105
	Johnny Sain	105
	Jim Scott	105
	Jim Slaton	105
	Al Smith	105
	Jack Taylor	105
	Hippo Vaughn	105
	Lon Warneke	105
	Mickey Welch	105
	Wilbur Wood	105
92	36 players tied	104

Pitcher Batting Runs

1	Red Ruffing	135
2	Bob Caruthers	112
3	Wes Ferrell	104
4	Walter Johnson	98
5	Red Lucas	97
6	George Uhle	93
7	George Mullin	90
8	Jim Whitney	88
9	Guy Hecker	87
10	Bob Lemon	86
11	Warren Spahn	82
12	Don Newcombe	81
13	Schoolboy Rowe	77
14	Babe Ruth	75
15	Jack Stivetts	71
16	Early Wynn	69
17	Bob Gibson	67
18	Al Orth	65
19	Carl Mays	62
20	Earl Wilson	60
21	Don Drysdale	59
22	Doc Crandall	58
	Bucky Walters	58
24	Gary Peters	57
25	Christy Mathewson	56
26	Jesse Tannehill	55
27	Jim Tobin	54
28	Claude Hendrix	53
29	Charlie Ferguson	52
	Ad Gumbert	52
31	Steve Carlton	51
	Burleigh Grimes	51
33	Tony Mullane	50
34	Bob Forsch	49
35	Joe Bush	48
36	Dave Foutz	46
	Adonis Terry	46
38	Vern Law	45
	Rick Rhoden	45
	Dutch Ruether	45
	Scott Stratton	45
42	Don Larsen	43
	Jack Scott	43
44	Jim Kaat	42
45	Tommy Byrne	40
	Wilbur Cooper	40
	Fred Hutchinson	40
	Frank Killen	40
49	Charley Radbourn	39
	Johnny Sain	39
51	Sloppy Thurston	38
52	Clark Griffith	36
	Mickey McDermott	36
	Claude Osteen	36
	Doc White	36
56	Ken Brett	35
	Jack Coombs	35
	Harvey Haddix	35
	Dolf Luque	35
	Jack Taylor	35
61	Chief Bender	34
	Frank Smith	34
	Rick Wise	34
64	Win Mercer	33
	Art Nehf	33
	Robin Roberts	33
	Ben Sanders	33
68	Ray Caldwell	32
	Hooks Dauss	32
	Al Maul	32
	Jouett Meekin	32
	Don Robinson	32
	Dizzy Trout	32
74	Jim Hunter	31
	Ted Lyons	31
	Joe Wood	31
77	Lefty Tyler	30
78	Charlie Buffinton	29
	Lew Burdette	29
	Brickyard Kennedy	29
	Joe Nuxhall	29
	Camilo Pascual	29
	Urban Shocker	29
	Monte Ward	29
85	Ed Brandt	28
	Eddie Lopat	28
	Jim Maloney	28
	Clarence Mitchell	28
	Juan Pizarro	28
	Tom Seaver	28
91	Frank Kitson	27
	Bill Sherdel	27
	Lon Warneke	27
94	Ned Garver	26
	Johnny Lush	26
	Joe Shaute	26
	Mike Smith	26
98	8 players tied	25

Pitcher Fielding Runs

1	Ed Walsh	83
2	Carl Mays	73
3	Christy Mathewson	65
4	Freddie Fitzsimmons	59
	Bob Lemon	59
6	Burleigh Grimes	58
7	Tommy John	54
8	Harry Gumbert	50
9	Harry Howell	47
10	Jack Quinn	45
11	Bill Doak	42
12	John Clarkson	41
	Eddie Rommel	41
14	Willis Hudlin	40
15	Jim Galvin	39
	Bobby Shantz	39
17	Rick Reuschel	38
	Dizzy Trout	38
19	Hooks Dauss	37
20	Amos Rusie	35
	Jack Russell	35
	Mel Stottlemyre	35
23	Charlie Buffinton	34
	Johnny Schmitz	34
25	Nick Altrock	32
	Howard Ehmke	32
27	John Denny	31
	Murry Dickson	31
	Randy Jones	31
30	Pete Alexander	30
	Red Ames	30
	Tommy Bond	30
	Curt Davis	30
	Hal Schumacher	30
35	Addie Joss	29
	Ed Willett	29
37	Ben Cantwell	28
	George Mullin	28
	Gerry Staley	28
40	Ted Abernathy	27
	Tom Burgmeier	27
	Spud Chandler	27
	Tony Mullane	27
	Phil Niekro	27
	Frank Smith	27
	Bucky Walters	27
	Monte Ward	27
	Vic Willis	27
	Cy Young	27
50	Don Drysdale	26
	Whitey Ford	26
	Sid Hudson	26
	Sherry Smith	26
	Fernando Valenzuela	26
55	Nixey Callahan	25
	Willie Sudhoff	25
57	Mike Caldwell	24
	Larry Jackson	24
	Matt Kilroy	24
	Jack Taylor	24
61	Jean Dubuc	23
	Joe Horlen	23
	Dutch Leonard	23
	Gene Packard	23
	Gaylord Perry	23
	Ed Reulbach	23
	Dave Stieb	23
	Doc White	23
69	Mike Boddicker	22
	Tom Brewer	22
	Frank Corridon	22
	Ned Garvin	22
	Carl Hubbell	22
	Brickyard Kennedy	22
	Lindy McDaniel	22
	Stu Miller	22
	Hal Newhouser	22
	Dan Quisenberry	22
	Kent Tekulve	22
	Lefty Tyler	22
81	Ted Breitenstein	21
	Claude Hendrix	21
	Frank Owen	21
	Bob Stanley	21
85	Elden Auker	20
	Jess Barnes	20
	Joe Bush	20
	Harry Coveleski	20
	Red Donahue	20
	Gene Garber	20
	Darold Knowles	20
	Frank Linzy	20
	Mike Marshall	20
	Dennis Martinez	20
	Wilcy Moore	20
	Claude Osteen	20
	Bob Purkey	20
98	10 players tied	19

Total Pitcher Index

#	Player	Index
1	Walter Johnson	81.5
2	Cy Young	81.0
3	Kid Nichols	65.3
4	Pete Alexander	64.8
5	Lefty Grove	59.9
6	Christy Mathewson	54.6
7	John Clarkson	52.6
8	Tom Seaver	51.2
9	Bob Gibson	46.3
10	Warren Spahn	43.1
11	Ed Walsh	41.6
12	Tim Keefe	38.8
13	Whitey Ford	38.6
	Carl Hubbell	38.6
15	Hal Newhouser	38.5
16	Phil Niekro	38.0
17	Amos Rusie	37.7
18	Gaylord Perry	36.8
19	Jim Palmer	36.4
20	Steve Carlton	35.6
21	Ted Lyons	35.4
22	Bob Lemon	35.2
	Tony Mullane	35.2
24	Mordecai Brown	35.1
25	Carl Mays	34.8
26	Don Drysdale	34.7
27	Bert Blyleven	34.6
28	Jack Stivetts	34.1
29	Dizzy Trout	33.7
30	Ferguson Jenkins	32.1
31	Wes Ferrell	30.9
32	Juan Marichal	30.8
33	Clark Griffith	29.4
	Charley Radbourn	29.4
35	Bob Caruthers	29.2
	Bucky Walters	29.2
	Hoyt Wilhelm	29.2
38	Tommy Bridges	28.5
39	Rube Waddell	28.4
40	Tommy John	27.0
41	Bob Feller	26.9
	Addie Joss	26.9
43	Burleigh Grimes	26.7
44	Red Ruffing	26.5
45	Rick Reuschel	26.4
46	Silver King	26.1
47	Stan Coveleski	26.0
48	Robin Roberts	25.9
49	Dolf Luque	25.8
50	Eddie Plank	25.5
51	Dazzy Vance	25.4
52	Red Faber	25.3
	Dave Stieb	25.3
54	Eppa Rixey	25.1
55	Jack Quinn	25.0
56	Eddie Rommel	24.9
57	Urban Shocker	24.8
58	Nig Cuppy	24.3
59	Harry Brecheen	23.9
60	Lon Warneke	23.4
61	Guy Hecker	23.2
62	Eddie Cicotte	23.0
63	Freddie Fitzsimmons	22.7
	Dutch Leonard	22.7
65	Billy Pierce	22.4
66	Jim McCormick	21.9
67	Joe Wood	21.8
68	Vic Willis	21.7
69	Spud Chandler	21.3
70	Jim Kaat	21.2
71	Joe McGinnity	21.0
72	Wilbur Cooper	20.8
73	Charlie Buffinton	20.7
74	Jesse Tannehill	20.6
75	Bobby Shantz	20.4
76	Larry Jackson	20.1
77	Sandy Koufax	20.0
78	Dizzy Dean	19.9
79	Murry Dickson	19.8
	Hippo Vaughn	19.8
81	Ed Reulbach	19.4
82	Curt Davis	19.3
83	Don Newcombe	19.1
84	Andy Messersmith	19.0
85	Steve Rogers	18.8
86	Jim Bunning	18.7
	Doc White	18.7
88	Jim Whitney	18.4
89	Dave Foutz	18.3
	Lefty Gomez	18.3
91	Early Wynn	18.2
92	Mel Harder	18.0
93	Noodles Hahn	17.9
94	Mel Stottlemyre	17.8
	Kent Tekulve	17.8
	Luis Tiant	17.8
97	Ned Garver	17.7
	Ron Guidry	17.7
99	Babe Adams	17.5
	Eddie Lopat	17.5

Total Pitcher Index

#	Player	Index
	Mel Parnell	17.5
102	Claude Hendrix	17.3
103	Thornton Lee	17.1
	Claude Passeau	17.1
	Dan Quisenberry	17.1
106	Larry French	16.8
107	Waite Hoyt	16.4
	George Mullin	16.4
	Hal Schumacher	16.4
	Virgil Trucks	16.4
111	Frank Dwyer	16.3
112	John Candelaria	16.0
113	Sadie McMahon	15.9
	Mickey Welch	15.9
115	Harry Howell	15.8
116	Max Lanier	15.7
	Sam Leever	15.7
	Bob Stanley	15.7
119	Charlie Ferguson	15.5
120	Larry Corcoran	15.4
121	Charlie Hough	15.2
	Bill Hutchinson	15.2
	Frank Tanana	15.2
124	Schoolboy Rowe	15.1
	Wilbur Wood	15.1
126	Frank Killen	15.0
	George Uhle	15.0
128	Sal Maglie	14.9
129	Orel Hershiser	14.7
	Deacon Phillippe	14.7
131	Mort Cooper	14.6
132	Mike Garcia	14.5
	Howie Pollet	14.5
134	Bob Shawkey	14.4
135	Rich Gossage	14.3
136	Babe Ruth	14.2
	Nolan Ryan	14.2
	John Tudor	14.2
139	Johnny Antonelli	14.1
	Milt Pappas	14.1
141	Jerry Koosman	13.9
	Jim Maloney	13.9
	Curt Simmons	13.9
144	Fred Hutchinson	13.8
	Nap Rucker	13.8
	Jack Taylor	13.8
147	Don Sutton	13.7
148	Dennis Eckersley	13.6
	Will White	13.6
150	Fernando Valenzuela	13.5
151	Jim Galvin	13.4
152	Russ Ford	13.3
	Monte Ward	13.3
154	John Hiller	13.2
	Jack Morris	13.2
	Jim Tobin	13.2
157	Sparky Lyle	13.0
158	Gary Peters	12.9
159	Ted Breitenstein	12.8
	Bruce Sutter	12.8
161	Chief Bender	12.6
	Rollie Fingers	12.6
	Gene Garber	12.6
	Claude Osteen	12.6
165	Tom Burgmeier	12.5
	Jon Matlack	12.5
167	Harvey Haddix	12.4
	Sam McDowell	12.4
	Ben Sanders	12.4
170	Stu Miller	12.3
171	Ewell Blackwell	12.2
	Frank Lary	12.2
	Mike Marshall	12.2
174	Sonny Siebert	12.1
175	Dean Chance	11.9
176	Camilo Pascual	11.8
177	Tex Hughson	11.7
178	Firpo Marberry	11.6
179	Ned Garvin	11.5
	Sherry Smith	11.5
181	Clay Carroll	11.4
	Icebox Chamberlin	11.4
183	Frank Sullivan	11.3
184	Lindy McDaniel	11.0
	Fritz Ostermueller	11.0
	Bob Rush	11.0
187	Tommy Bond	10.9
	Jack Chesbro	10.9
	Van Mungo	10.9
	Jake Weimer	10.9
191	Jim Perry	10.8
	Tom Zachary	10.8
193	Red Ames	10.7
	Al Orth	10.7
195	Al Brazle	10.6
	Ellis Kinder	10.6
	Tug McGraw	10.6
	Toad Ramsey	10.6
199	Mark Baldwin	10.5
	Pink Hawley	10.5

Total Pitcher Index

#	Player	Index
201	Jeff Pfeffer	10.4
202	Bill Hands	10.3
	Red Lucas	10.3
	Charlie Root	10.3
205	Joe Dobson	10.1
	Art Nehf	10.1
207	Harry Coveleski	10.0
208	Ed Morris	9.9
209	Lefty Leifield	9.8
	Gary Nolan	9.8
	Monte Pearson	9.8
212	Johnny Allen	9.7
	Mike Cuellar	9.7
	Hooks Dauss	9.7
	Don Mossi	9.7
	Gerry Staley	9.7
217	Nixey Callahan	9.6
	Charlie Leibrandt	9.6
	Orval Overall	9.6
	Rick Rhoden	9.6
221	Joe Horlen	9.5
	Rip Sewell	9.5
223	Vida Blue	9.4
	Clint Brown	9.4
	Gary Lavelle	9.4
	Billy Rhines	9.4
227	Terry Forster	9.3
	Jim Scott	9.3
229	Mike Boddicker	9.2
	Bill Lee	9.2
	Dave Righetti	9.2
	Slim Sallee	9.2
233	Matt Kilroy	9.1
234	Joe Benz	9.0
	Larry Jansen	9.0
236	Howard Ehmke	8.9
	Willie Hernandez	8.9
	Frank Linzy	8.9
239	Watty Clark	8.8
	Sam Jones	8.8
	Don McMahon	8.8
	Preacher Roe	8.8
	Bob Welch	8.8
244	John Denny	8.7
	Burt Hooton	8.7
	Johnny Sain	8.7
247	Bob Ewing	8.6
	Jeff Tesreau	8.6
249	Bill Lee	8.5
	Bob Locker	8.5
251	Lee Smith	8.4
252	Ray Kremer	8.3
253	Bill Dinneen	8.2
	Vern Law	8.2
	Ron Perranoski	8.2
	Johnny Schmitz	8.2
257	Joe Bush	8.1
	George Mogridge	8.1
	Hooks Wiltse	8.1
260	Jess Barnes	8.0
	Adonis Terry	8.0
	Whit Wyatt	8.0
263	Win Mercer	7.9
	Lefty Tyler	7.9
265	Al Benton	7.8
	Tiny Bonham	7.8
	Paul Derringer	7.8
	Bill Doak	7.8
	Harry Gumbert	7.8
	Willis Hudlin	7.8
271	Bob Friend	7.7
	Darold Knowles	7.7
	Herb Pennock	7.7
274	Dave McNally	7.6
	Dutch Ruether	7.6
276	Bump Hadley	7.5
	Greg Minton	7.5
278	Paul Minner	7.4
	Johnny Murphy	7.4
	Lefty Stewart	7.4
	Bob Veale	7.4
282	Scott Stratton	7.3
	Frank Viola	7.3
284	Jesse Haines	7.2
	Dutch Leonard	7.2
	Al McBean	7.2
	Mike Witt	7.2
288	Doyle Alexander	7.1
	Joe Beggs	7.1
	Lloyd Brown	7.1
	Don Gullett	7.1
	Brickyard Kennedy	7.1
	Mickey McDermott	7.1
	Jesse Orosco	7.1
295	Larry Cheney	7.0
	Dick Donovan	7.0
	Steve Gromek	7.0
	Larry Gura	7.0
	Bill Hoffer	7.0
	Earl Wilson	7.0

Total Pitcher Index (alpha.)

Babe Adams	17.5
Doyle Alexander	7.1
Pete Alexander	64.8
Johnny Allen	9.7
Red Ames	10.7
Johnny Antonelli	14.1
Mark Baldwin	10.5
Jess Barnes	8.0
Joe Beggs	7.1
Chief Bender	12.6
Al Benton	7.8
Joe Benz	9.0
Ewell Blackwell	12.2
Vida Blue	9.4
Bert Blyleven	34.6
Mike Boddicker	9.2
Tommy Bond	10.9
Tiny Bonham	7.8
Al Brazle	10.6
Harry Brecheen	23.9
Ted Breitenstein	12.8
Tommy Bridges	28.5
Clint Brown	9.4
Lloyd Brown	7.1
Mordecai Brown	35.1
Charlie Buffinton	20.7
Jim Bunning	18.7
Tom Burgmeier	12.5
Joe Bush	8.1
Nixey Callahan	9.6
John Candelaria	16.0
Steve Carlton	35.6
Clay Carroll	11.4
Bob Caruthers	29.2
Icebox Chamberlin	11.4
Dean Chance	11.9
Spud Chandler	21.3
Jack Chesbro	10.9
Eddie Cicotte	23.0
Watty Clark	8.8
John Clarkson	52.6
Wilbur Cooper	20.8
Mort Cooper	14.6
Larry Corcoran	15.4
Harry Coveleski	10.0
Stan Coveleski	26.0
Mike Cuellar	9.7
Nig Cuppy	24.3
Hooks Dauss	9.7
Curt Davis	19.3
Dizzy Dean	19.9
John Denny	8.7
Paul Derringer	7.8
Murry Dickson	19.8
Bill Dinneen	8.2
Bill Doak	7.8
Joe Dobson	10.1
Don Drysdale	34.7
Frank Dwyer	16.3
Dennis Eckersley	13.6
Howard Ehmke	8.9
Bob Ewing	8.6
Red Faber	25.3
Bob Feller	26.9
Charlie Ferguson	15.5
Wes Ferrell	30.9
Rollie Fingers	12.6
Freddie Fitzsimmons	22.7
Whitey Ford	38.6
Russ Ford	13.3
Terry Forster	9.3
Dave Foutz	18.3
Larry French	16.8
Bob Friend	7.7
Jim Galvin	13.4
Gene Garber	12.6
Mike Garcia	14.5
Ned Garver	17.7
Ned Garvin	11.5
Bob Gibson	46.3
Lefty Gomez	18.3
Rich Gossage	14.3
Clark Griffith	29.4
Burleigh Grimes	26.7
Lefty Grove	59.9
Ron Guidry	17.7
Don Gullett	7.1
Harry Gumbert	7.8
Harvey Haddix	12.4
Bump Hadley	7.5
Noodles Hahn	17.9
Jesse Haines	7.2
Bill Hands	10.3
Mel Harder	18.0
Pink Hawley	10.5
Guy Hecker	23.2
Claude Hendrix	17.3
Willie Hernandez	8.9
Orel Hershiser	14.7
John Hiller	13.2

Total Pitcher Index (alpha.)

Burt Hooton	8.7
Joe Horlen	9.5
Charlie Hough	15.2
Harry Howell	15.8
Waite Hoyt	16.4
Carl Hubbell	38.6
Willis Hudlin	7.8
Tex Hughson	11.7
Fred Hutchinson	13.8
Bill Hutchinson	15.2
Larry Jackson	20.1
Larry Jansen	9.0
Ferguson Jenkins	32.1
Tommy John	27.0
Walter Johnson	81.5
Sam Jones	8.8
Addie Joss	26.9
Jim Kaat	21.2
Tim Keefe	38.8
Brickyard Kennedy	7.1
Frank Killen	15.0
Matt Kilroy	9.1
Ellis Kinder	10.6
Silver King	26.1
Darold Knowles	7.7
Jerry Koosman	13.9
Sandy Koufax	20.0
Ray Kremer	8.3
Max Lanier	15.7
Frank Lary	12.2
Gary Lavelle	9.4
Vern Law	8.2
Thornton Lee	17.1
Bill Lee	8.5
Bill Lee	9.2
Sam Leever	15.7
Charlie Leibrandt	9.6
Lefty Leifield	9.8
Bob Lemon	35.2
Dutch Leonard	22.7
Dutch Leonard	7.2
Frank Linzy	8.9
Bob Locker	8.5
Eddie Lopat	17.5
Red Lucas	10.3
Dolf Luque	25.8
Sparky Lyle	13.0
Ted Lyons	35.4
Sal Maglie	14.9
Jim Maloney	13.9
Firpo Marberry	11.6
Juan Marichal	30.8
Mike Marshall	12.2
Christy Mathewson	54.6
Jon Matlack	12.5
Carl Mays	34.8
Win Mercer	7.9
Andy Messersmith	19.0
Stu Miller	12.3
Paul Minner	7.4
Greg Minton	7.5
George Mogridge	8.1
Ed Morris	9.9
Jack Morris	13.2
Don Mossi	9.7
Tony Mullane	35.2
George Mullin	16.4
Van Mungo	10.9
Johnny Murphy	7.4
Al McBean	7.2
Jim McCormick	21.9
Lindy McDaniel	11.0
Mickey McDermott	7.1
Sam McDowell	12.4
Joe McGinnity	21.0
Tug McGraw	10.6
Don McMahon	8.8
Sadie McMahon	15.9
Dave McNally	7.6
Art Nehf	10.1
Don Newcombe	19.1
Hal Newhouser	38.5
Kid Nichols	65.3
Phil Niekro	38.0
Gary Nolan	9.8
Jesse Orosco	7.1
Al Orth	10.7
Claude Osteen	12.6
Fritz Ostermueller	11.0
Orval Overall	9.6
Jim Palmer	36.4
Milt Pappas	14.1
Mel Parnell	17.5
Camilo Pascual	11.8
Claude Passeau	17.1
Monte Pearson	9.8
Herb Pennock	7.7
Ron Perranoski	8.2
Gaylord Perry	36.8
Jim Perry	10.8

Total Pitcher Index (alpha.)

Gary Peters	12.9
Jeff Pfeffer	10.4
Deacon Phillippe	14.7
Billy Pierce	22.4
Eddie Plank	25.5
Howie Pollet	14.5
Jack Quinn	25.0
Dan Quisenberry	17.1
Charley Radbourn	29.4
Toad Ramsey	10.6
Ed Reulbach	19.4
Rick Reuschel	26.4
Billy Rhines	9.4
Rick Rhoden	9.6
Dave Righetti	9.2
Eppa Rixey	25.1
Robin Roberts	25.9
Preacher Roe	8.8
Steve Rogers	18.8
Eddie Rommel	24.9
Charlie Root	10.3
Schoolboy Rowe	15.1
Nap Rucker	13.8
Dutch Ruether	7.6
Red Ruffing	26.5
Bob Rush	11.0
Amos Rusie	37.7
Babe Ruth	14.2
Nolan Ryan	14.2
Johnny Sain	8.7
Slim Sallee	9.2
Ben Sanders	12.4
Johnny Schmitz	8.2
Hal Schumacher	16.4
Jim Scott	9.3
Tom Seaver	51.2
Rip Sewell	9.5
Bob Shawkey	14.4
Urban Shocker	24.8
Sonny Siebert	12.1
Curt Simmons	13.9
Lee Smith	8.4
Sherry Smith	11.5
Warren Spahn	43.1
Gerry Staley	9.7
Bob Stanley	15.7
Lefty Stewart	7.4
Dave Stieb	25.3
Jack Stivetts	34.1
Mel Stottlemyre	17.8
Scott Stratton	7.3
Frank Sullivan	11.3
Bruce Sutter	12.8
Don Sutton	13.7
Frank Tanana	15.2
Jesse Tannehill	20.6
Jack Taylor	13.8
Kent Tekulve	17.8
Adonis Terry	8.0
Jeff Tesreau	8.6
Luis Tiant	17.8
Jim Tobin	13.2
Dizzy Trout	33.7
Virgil Trucks	16.4
John Tudor	14.2
Lefty Tyler	7.9
George Uhle	15.0
Fernando Valenzuela	13.5
Dazzy Vance	25.4
Hippo Vaughn	19.8
Bob Veale	7.4
Frank Viola	7.3
Rube Waddell	28.4
Ed Walsh	41.6
Bucky Walters	29.2
Monte Ward	13.3
Lon Warneke	23.4
Jake Weimer	10.9
Mickey Welch	15.9
Bob Welch	8.8
Doc White	18.7
Will White	13.6
Jim Whitney	18.4
Hoyt Wilhelm	29.2
Vic Willis	21.7
Hooks Wiltse	8.1
Mike Witt	7.2
Joe Wood	21.8
Wilbur Wood	15.1
Whit Wyatt	8.0
Early Wynn	18.2
Cy Young	81.0
Tom Zachary	10.8

Total Pitcher Index (by era)

1876-1892

1	John Clarkson	52.6
2	Tim Keefe	38.8
3	Amos Rusie	37.7
4	Tony Mullane	35.2
5	Jack Stivetts	34.1
6	Charley Radbourn	29.4
7	Bob Caruthers	29.2
8	Silver King	26.1
9	Guy Hecker	23.2
10	Jim McCormick	21.9
11	Charlie Buffinton	20.7
12	Jim Whitney	18.4
13	Dave Foutz	18.3
14	Sadie McMahon	15.9
	Mickey Welch	15.9
16	Charlie Ferguson	15.5
17	Larry Corcoran	15.4
18	Will White	13.6
19	Jim Galvin	13.4
20	Monte Ward	13.3
21	Ben Sanders	12.4
22	Icebox Chamberlin	11.4
23	Tommy Bond	10.9
24	Toad Ramsey	10.6
25	Mark Baldwin	10.5

1893-1919

1	Walter Johnson	81.5
2	Cy Young	81.0
3	Kid Nichols	65.3
4	Christy Mathewson	54.6
5	Ed Walsh	41.6
6	Mordecai Brown	35.1
7	Clark Griffith	29.4
8	Rube Waddell	28.4
9	Addie Joss	26.9
10	Eddie Plank	25.5
11	Nig Cuppy	24.3
12	Eddie Cicotte	23.0
13	Joe Wood	21.8
14	Vic Willis	21.7
15	Joe McGinnity	21.0
16	Wilbur Cooper	20.8
17	Jesse Tannehill	20.6
18	Hippo Vaughn	19.8
19	Ed Reulbach	19.4
20	Doc White	18.7
21	Noodles Hahn	17.9
22	Babe Adams	17.5
23	Claude Hendrix	17.3
24	George Mullin	16.4
25	Frank Dwyer	16.3

1920-1941

1	Pete Alexander	64.8
2	Lefty Grove	59.9
3	Carl Hubbell	38.6
4	Ted Lyons	35.4
5	Carl Mays	34.8
6	Wes Ferrell	30.9
7	Tommy Bridges	28.5
8	Burleigh Grimes	26.7
9	Red Ruffing	26.5
10	Stan Coveleski	26.0
11	Dolf Luque	25.8
12	Dazzy Vance	25.4
13	Red Faber	25.3
14	Eppa Rixey	25.1
15	Jack Quinn	25.0
16	Eddie Rommel	24.9
17	Urban Shocker	24.8
18	Lon Warneke	23.4
19	Freddie Fitzsimmons	22.7
20	Dizzy Dean	19.9
21	Curt Davis	19.3
22	Lefty Gomez	18.3
23	Mel Harder	18.0
24	Thornton Lee	17.1
	Claude Passeau	17.1

Total Pitcher Index (by era)

1942-1960

1	Warren Spahn	43.1
2	Whitey Ford	38.6
3	Hal Newhouser	38.5
4	Bob Lemon	35.2
5	Dizzy Trout	33.7
6	Bucky Walters	29.2
	Hoyt Wilhelm	29.2
8	Bob Feller	26.9
9	Robin Roberts	25.9
10	Harry Brecheen	23.9
11	Dutch Leonard	22.7
12	Billy Pierce	22.4
13	Spud Chandler	21.3
14	Bobby Shantz	20.4
15	Murry Dickson	19.8
16	Don Newcombe	19.1
17	Early Wynn	18.2
18	Ned Garver	17.7
19	Eddie Lopat	17.5
	Mel Parnell	17.5
21	Virgil Trucks	16.4
22	Max Lanier	15.7
23	Sal Maglie	14.9
24	Mort Cooper	14.6
25	2 players tied	14.5

1961-1988

1	Tom Seaver	51.2
2	Bob Gibson	46.3
3	Phil Niekro	38.0
4	Gaylord Perry	36.8
5	Jim Palmer	36.4
6	Steve Carlton	35.6
7	Don Drysdale	34.7
8	Bert Blyleven	34.6
9	Ferguson Jenkins	32.1
10	Juan Marichal	30.8
11	Tommy John	27.0
12	Rick Reuschel	26.4
13	Dave Stieb	25.3
14	Jim Kaat	21.2
15	Larry Jackson	20.1
16	Sandy Koufax	20.0
17	Andy Messersmith	19.0
18	Steve Rogers	18.8
19	Jim Bunning	18.7
20	Mel Stottlemyre	17.8
	Kent Tekulve	17.8
	Luis Tiant	17.8
23	Ron Guidry	17.7
24	Dan Quisenberry	17.1
25	John Candelaria	16.0

Total Baseball Ranking

1	Babe Ruth	119.3
2	Ty Cobb	90.6
3	Hank Aaron	90.1
4	Ted Williams	89.8
5	Willie Mays	86.2
6	Nap Lajoie	85.2
7	Walter Johnson	81.5
8	Cy Young	81.0
9	Tris Speaker	79.9
10	Mike Schmidt	77.9
11	Rogers Hornsby	77.3
12	Honus Wagner	75.6
13	Frank Robinson	71.2
14	Eddie Collins	70.5
15	Stan Musial	70.1
16	Mickey Mantle	69.8
17	Kid Nichols	65.3
18	Pete Alexander	64.8
19	Joe Morgan	63.9
20	Lou Gehrig	60.8
21	Mel Ott	60.1
22	Lefty Grove	59.9
23	Christy Mathewson	54.6
24	Jimmie Foxx	53.2
25	John Clarkson	52.6
26	Tom Seaver	51.2
27	George Davis	48.4
	Eddie Mathews	48.4
29	Bobby Grich	47.4
30	Bob Gibson	46.3
31	Ed Delahanty	46.1
	Carl Yastrzemski	46.1
33	Al Kaline	45.9
34	Rickey Henderson	44.0
	Reggie Jackson	44.0
36	George Brett	43.8
37	Joe DiMaggio	43.6
38	Charlie Gehringer	43.5
39	Bill Dahlen	43.3
40	Warren Spahn	43.1
41	Ed Walsh	41.6
42	Rod Carew	41.0
43	Dan Brouthers	40.4
44	Arky Vaughan	40.3
45	Roberto Clemente	39.6
46	Paul Waner	38.9
47	Roger Connor	38.8
	Tim Keefe	38.8
49	Whitey Ford	38.6
	Carl Hubbell	38.6
51	Luke Appling	38.5
	Hal Newhouser	38.5
53	Joe Cronin	38.2
54	Willie McCovey	38.1
	Ron Santo	38.1
56	Ozzie Smith	38.0
	Phil Niekro	38.0
58	Bob Johnson	37.8
59	Amos Rusie	37.7
60	Bid McPhee	37.5
61	Gary Carter	37.4
62	Keith Hernandez	37.3
63	Frankie Frisch	37.2
64	Gaylord Perry	36.8
65	Bobby Wallace	36.7
66	Dave Winfield	36.6
67	Johnny Mize	36.5
68	Jim Palmer	36.4
69	Joe Jackson	36.1
70	Gabby Hartnett	35.7
71	Dick Allen	35.6
	Bobby Doerr	35.6
	Steve Carlton	35.6
	Bob Caruthers	35.6
75	Ted Lyons	35.4
76	Bob Lemon	35.2
	Tony Mullane	35.2
78	Mordecai Brown	35.1
79	Jack Stivetts	35.0
80	Yogi Berra	34.8
	Carl Mays	34.8
82	Don Drysdale	34.7
83	Frank Baker	34.6
	Bert Blyleven	34.6
85	Jack Glasscock	34.5
86	Bill Mazeroski	34.4
	Ted Simmons	34.4
88	Lou Boudreau	34.3
89	Billy Herman	34.0
90	Eddie Murray	33.7
	Dizzy Trout	33.7
92	Carlton Fisk	33.4
	Reggie Smith	33.4
94	Jackie Robinson	33.3
95	Joe Sewell	33.1
96	Wade Boggs	32.9
97	Harmon Killebrew	32.8
98	Darrell Evans	32.5
99	Ferguson Jenkins	32.1
100	Willie Stargell	31.6

Total Baseball Ranking

101	Tim Raines	31.5
102	Robin Yount	31.4
103	Cap Anson	31.3
	Bobby Bonds	31.3
105	Jim Wynn	31.1
106	Wes Ferrell	30.9
107	Juan Marichal	30.8
108	Bill Dickey	30.6
109	Johnny Bench	30.2
	Billy Williams	30.2
111	Joe Torre	29.8
112	Dave Bancroft	29.7
113	Norm Cash	29.6
	Cupid Childs	29.6
115	Rusty Staub	29.4
	Sam Thompson	29.4
	Clark Griffith	29.4
	Charley Radbourn	29.4
119	Hoyt Wilhelm	29.2
120	Bill Freehan	28.9
	Hank Greenberg	28.9
122	Elmer Flick	28.5
	Sherry Magee	28.5
	Tommy Bridges	28.5
125	Rube Waddell	28.4
126	Fred Clarke	28.0
	Fred Dunlap	28.0
128	Jesse Burkett	27.9
129	Bill Terry	27.8
130	Buck Ewing	27.6
	Joe Gordon	27.6
132	Mickey Cochrane	27.5
133	Bucky Walters	27.4
134	Richie Ashburn	27.0
	Pete Browning	27.0
	Ralph Kiner	27.0
	Tommy John	27.0
138	Bob Feller	26.9
	Addie Joss	26.9
140	Cal Ripken	26.7
	Burleigh Grimes	26.7
142	Hughie Jennings	26.6
143	Willie Randolph	26.5
	Jim Rice	26.5
	Red Ruffing	26.5
146	Rick Reuschel	26.4
147	Max Carey	26.1
	Tony Oliva	26.1
	Silver King	26.1
150	Stan Coveleski	26.0
151	Hardy Richardson	25.9
	Robin Roberts	25.9
153	Stan Hack	25.8
	Dolf Luque	25.8
155	Joe Medwick	25.7
156	Buddy Bell	25.6
	Heinie Groh	25.6
158	George Sisler	25.5
	Eddie Plank	25.5
160	Jack Clark	25.4
	Harry Heilmann	25.4
	Dazzy Vance	25.4
163	Red Faber	25.3
	Dave Stieb	25.3
165	Dick Bartell	25.2
	Dwight Evans	25.2
	Wally Schang	25.2
168	Thurman Munson	25.1
	Eppa Rixey	25.1
170	Rocky Colavito	25.0
	Billy Hamilton	25.0
	Jack Quinn	25.0
173	Ernie Banks	24.9
	Eddie Rommel	24.9
175	Urban Shocker	24.8
176	Pete Rose	24.7
177	Andre Dawson	24.6
178	Chuck Klein	24.3
	Duke Snider	24.3
	Nig Cuppy	24.3
181	Jake Beckley	24.2
	King Kelly	24.2
	Al Simmons	24.2
184	Graig Nettles	24.1
185	Guy Hecker	24.0
186	Sam Crawford	23.9
	Harry Brecheen	23.9
188	Cesar Cedeno	23.8
	Jimmy Collins	23.8
190	Jack Fournier	23.7
	Pedro Guerrero	23.7
192	Minnie Minoso	23.6
	Harry Stovey	23.6
194	Ed Konetchy	23.5
195	Charlie Keller	23.4
	Ernie Lombardi	23.4
	Lon Warneke	23.4
198	Brooks Robinson	23.3
199	Joe Kelley	23.1
200	Eddie Cicotte	23.0

Total Baseball Ranking

201	Goose Goslin	22.9
202	Harlond Clift	22.7
	Roy Smalley	22.7
	Freddie Fitzsimmons	22.7
	Dutch Leonard	22.7
206	Billy Pierce	22.4
207	Roy Campanella	22.2
	Dave Parker	22.2
209	George Foster	22.1
210	Roy Thomas	22.0
211	Ron Cey	21.9
	Jim McCormick	21.9
213	Del Pratt	21.7
	Vic Willis	21.7
215	Eddie Stanky	21.6
216	Gil McDougald	21.5
217	Fred Lynn	21.3
	Spud Chandler	21.3
219	Jim Kaat	21.2
220	Zach Wheat	21.1
221	Art Fletcher	21.0
	Jim Fregosi	21.0
	Travis Jackson	21.0
	Charley Jones	21.0
	Joe McGinnity	21.0
226	Wilbur Cooper	20.8
227	Jesse Tannehill	20.6
228	Bobby Shantz	20.4
229	Fred Pfeffer	20.3
	Ken Singleton	20.3
231	Joe Tinker	20.2
232	Denny Lyons	20.1
	Larry Jackson	20.1
234	Frank Howard	20.0
	Sandy Koufax	20.0
236	Tony Gwynn	19.9
	Dizzy Dean	19.9
238	Murry Dickson	19.8
	Hippo Vaughn	19.8
240	Mike Griffin	19.7
241	Ken Williams	19.6
242	Orlando Cepeda	19.5
	Joe Wood	19.5
244	Kiki Cuyler	19.4
	Ed Reulbach	19.4
246	Gavvy Cravath	19.3
	Darrell Porter	19.3
	Ryne Sandberg	19.3
	Jimmy Sheckard	19.3
	Charlie Buffinton	19.3
	Curt Davis	19.3
252	Roger Bresnahan	19.2
	Darryl Strawberry	19.2
	Lou Whitaker	19.2
	Roy White	19.2
256	Bill Joyce	19.1
	Dale Murphy	19.1
	Don Newcombe	19.1
259	Miller Huggins	19.0
	Pee Wee Reese	19.0
	Andy Messersmith	19.0
262	Ken Boyer	18.9
	Jose Cruz	18.9
	Fred Tenney	18.9
265	Steve Rogers	18.8
266	Paul Molitor	18.7
	Jim Bunning	18.7
	Doc White	18.7
269	Bob Elliott	18.5
270	Earl Averill	18.4
	Pie Traynor	18.4
	Monte Ward	18.4
	Jim Whitney	18.4
274	Gene Alley	18.3
	Wally Berger	18.3
	Babe Herman	18.3
	Lefty Gomez	18.3
278	Early Wynn	18.2
279	Ferris Fain	18.1
	Chet Lemon	18.1
281	Mel Harder	18.0
282	Noodles Hahn	17.9
283	Mel Stottlemyre	17.8
	Kent Tekulve	17.8
	Luis Tiant	17.8
286	Larry Doby	17.7
	Paul Hines	17.7
	Mike Smith	17.7
	Alan Trammell	17.7
	Ned Garver	17.7
	Ron Guidry	17.7
292	Ray Chapman	17.5
	Babe Adams	17.5
	Eddie Lopat	17.5
	Mel Parnell	17.5
296	Cy Seymour	17.4
297	Rico Carty	17.3
	Roy Cullenbine	17.3
	John McGraw	17.3
	Claude Hendrix	17.3

Total Baseball Ranking

301	Dolph Camilli	17.2
	Hal McRae	17.2
	Amos Otis	17.2
304	Thornton Lee	17.1
	Claude Passeau	17.1
	Dan Quisenberry	17.1
307	Art Devlin	16.9
308	Charlie Bennett	16.8
	Hack Wilson	16.8
	Larry French	16.8
311	Brian Downing	16.7
	Benny Kauff	16.7
313	Johnny Evers	16.6
	Toby Harrah	16.6
315	Dave Foutz	16.4
	Waite Hoyt	16.4
	George Mullin	16.4
	Hal Schumacher	16.4
	Virgil Trucks	16.4
320	Frank Dwyer	16.3
321	Duke Farrell	16.2
	Lonny Frey	16.2
323	Frank Chance	16.1
	Deacon McGuire	16.1
	Rudy York	16.1
326	George Gore	16.0
	Bill Nicholson	16.0
	Edd Roush	16.0
	Andy Thornton	16.0
	John Candelaria	16.0
331	Ed Bailey	15.9
	Don Buford	15.9
	Lance Parrish	15.9
	Sadie McMahon	15.9
	Mickey Welch	15.9
336	Jimmy Ryan	15.8
	Harry Howell	15.8
338	Doug DeCinces	15.7
	Jeff Heath	15.7
	Tommy Leach	15.7
	Boog Powell	15.7
	Max Lanier	15.7
	Sam Leever	15.7
	Bob Stanley	15.7
345	Smoky Burgess	15.6
	Jim O'Rourke	15.6
347	Mike Hargrove	15.5
	Charlie Ferguson	15.5
349	Phil Rizzuto	15.4
	Vern Stephens	15.4
	Maury Wills	15.4
	Larry Corcoran	15.4
353	Don Baylor	15.2
	Ben Chapman	15.2
	Billy Nash	15.2
	Charlie Hough	15.2
	Bill Hutchinson	15.2
	Frank Tanana	15.2
359	Dave Concepcion	15.1
	Schoolboy Rowe	15.1
	Wilbur Wood	15.1
362	Rick Ferrell	15.0
	Tony Lazzeri	15.0
	Red Schoendienst	15.0
	Frank Killen	15.0
	George Uhle	15.0
367	Sal Maglie	14.9
368	Henry Larkin	14.8
369	Sid Gordon	14.7
	Glenn Hubbard	14.7
	Orel Hershiser	14.7
	Deacon Phillippe	14.7
373	Tommy Henrich	14.6
	Mort Cooper	14.6
375	Mike Garcia	14.5
	Howie Pollet	14.5
377	Harry Davis	14.4
	Mike Donlin	14.4
	Mike Tiernan	14.4
	Bob Shawkey	14.4
381	Enos Slaughter	14.3
	George Van Haltren	14.3
	Rich Gossage	14.3
384	Andy Seminick	14.2
	Nolan Ryan	14.2
	John Tudor	14.2
387	Walker Cooper	14.1
	Gil Hodges	14.1
	Johnny Antonelli	14.1
	Milt Pappas	14.1
391	Johnny Logan	14.0
	Roger Peckinpaugh	14.0
393	Kirk Gibson	13.9
	Kip Selbach	13.9
	Richie Zisk	13.9
	Jerry Koosman	13.9
	Jim Maloney	13.9
	Curt Simmons	13.9
399	Tony Perez	13.8
	Fred Hutchinson	13.8

Total Baseball Ranking

	Nap Rucker	13.8
	Jack Taylor	13.8
403	Elston Howard	13.7
	Dwayne Murphy	13.7
	Don Sutton	13.7
406	Tony Cuccinello	13.6
	Dennis Eckersley	13.6
	Will White	13.6
409	Bobby Murcer	13.5
	Johnny Pesky	13.5
	Fernando Valenzuela	13.5
412	Jim Galvin	13.4
413	Russ Ford	13.3
414	John Hiller	13.2
	Jack Morris	13.2
	Jim Tobin	13.2
417	Bob Allison	13.0
	Luis Aparicio	13.0
	Bill Bradley	13.0
	Augie Galan	13.0
	Sparky Lyle	13.0
422	Roy Sievers	12.9
	Bump Wills	12.9
	Heinie Zimmerman	12.9
	Gary Peters	12.9
426	Willie Kamm	12.8
	Ken Keltner	12.8
	Sixto Lezcano	12.8
	Jim Sundberg	12.8
	Ted Breitenstein	12.8
	Bruce Sutter	12.8
432	Jack Clements	12.7
	Lave Cross	12.7
	Buddy Myer	12.7
435	Solly Hemus	12.6
	Larry Hisle	12.6
	Cliff Johnson	12.6
	Don Mattingly	12.6
	George Stone	12.6
	Chief Bender	12.6
	Rollie Fingers	12.6
	Gene Garber	12.6
	Claude Osteen	12.6
444	Nellie Fox	12.5
	Chief Zimmer	12.5
	Tom Burgmeier	12.5
	Jon Matlack	12.5
448	Bobby Knoop	12.4
	Harvey Haddix	12.4
	Sam McDowell	12.4
	Ben Sanders	12.4
452	Tim McCarver	12.3
	Stu Miller	12.3
454	Ron Hunt	12.2
	John Romano	12.2
	Ewell Blackwell	12.2
	Frank Lary	12.2
	Mike Marshall	12.2
459	Charlie Hickman	12.1
	Ed McFarland	12.1
	Al Oliver	12.1
	Bob Watson	12.1
	Jimmy Williams	12.1
	Sonny Siebert	12.1
465	Ross Youngs	12.0
466	Orator Shaffer	11.9
	Dean Chance	11.9
468	Ron Hansen	11.8
	Camilo Pascual	11.8
470	Davey Lopes	11.7
	Tex Hughson	11.7
472	Dave Johnson	11.6
	Firpo Marberry	11.6
474	Donie Bush	11.5
	Ned Garvin	11.5
	Sherry Smith	11.5
477	Del Crandall	11.4
	John Titus	11.4
	Clay Carroll	11.4
	Icebox Chamberlin	11.4
481	Jim Gentile	11.3
	Greg Luzinski	11.3
	Dixie Walker	11.3
	Frank Sullivan	11.3
485	Oyster Burns	11.2
	Ken Griffey	11.2
	Tip O'Neill	11.2
	Stan Spence	11.2
	Sam Wise	11.2
490	Jake Daubert	11.0
	Lindy McDaniel	11.0
	Fritz Ostermueller	11.0
	Bob Rush	11.0
494	Tommy Bond	10.9
	Jack Chesbro	10.9
	Van Mungo	10.9
	Jake Weimer	10.9
498	7 players tied	10.8

Total Baseball Ranking (alpha.)

Hank Aaron	90.1
Babe Adams	17.5
Pete Alexander	64.8
Dick Allen	35.6
Gene Alley	18.3
Bob Allison	13.0
Cap Anson	31.3
Johnny Antonelli	14.1
Luis Aparicio	13.0
Luke Appling	38.5
Richie Ashburn	27.0
Earl Averill	18.4
Ed Bailey	15.9
Frank Baker	34.6
Dave Bancroft	29.7
Ernie Banks	24.9
Dick Bartell	25.2
Don Baylor	15.2
Jake Beckley	24.2
Buddy Bell	25.6
Johnny Bench	30.2
Chief Bender	12.6
Charlie Bennett	16.8
Wally Berger	18.3
Yogi Berra	34.8
Ewell Blackwell	12.2
Bert Blyleven	34.6
Wade Boggs	32.9
Tommy Bond	10.9
Bobby Bonds	31.3
Lou Boudreau	34.3
Ken Boyer	18.9
Bill Bradley	13.0
Harry Brecheen	23.9
Ted Breitenstein	12.8
Roger Bresnahan	19.2
George Brett	43.8
Tommy Bridges	28.5
Dan Brouthers	40.4
Mordecai Brown	35.1
Pete Browning	27.0
Charlie Buffinton	19.3
Don Buford	15.9
Jim Bunning	18.7
Smoky Burgess	15.6
Tom Burgmeier	12.5
Jesse Burkett	27.9
Oyster Burns	11.2
Donie Bush	11.5
Dolph Camilli	17.2
Roy Campanella	22.2
John Candelaria	16.0
Max Carey	26.1
Rod Carew	41.0
Steve Carlton	35.6
Clay Carroll	11.4
Gary Carter	37.4
Rico Carty	17.3
Bob Caruthers	35.6
Norm Cash	29.6
Cesar Cedeno	23.8
Orlando Cepeda	19.5
Ron Cey	21.9
Icebox Chamberlin	11.4
Frank Chance	16.1
Dean Chance	11.9
Spud Chandler	21.3
Ray Chapman	17.5
Ben Chapman	15.2
Jack Chesbro	10.9
Cupid Childs	29.6
Eddie Cicotte	23.0
Jack Clark	25.4
Fred Clarke	28.0
John Clarkson	52.6
Roberto Clemente	39.6
Jack Clements	12.7
Harland Clift	22.7
Ty Cobb	90.6
Mickey Cochrane	27.5
Rocky Colavito	25.0
Eddie Collins	70.5
Jimmy Collins	23.8
Dave Concepcion	15.1
Roger Connor	38.8
Walker Cooper	14.1
Wilbur Cooper	20.8
Mort Cooper	14.6
Larry Corcoran	15.4
Stan Coveleski	26.0
Del Crandall	11.4
Gavvy Cravath	19.3
Sam Crawford	23.9
Joe Cronin	38.2
Lave Cross	12.7
Jose Cruz	18.9
Tony Cuccinello	13.6
Roy Cullenbine	17.3
Nig Cuppy	24.3
Kiki Cuyler	19.4

Total Baseball Ranking (alpha.)

Bill Dahlen	43.3
Jake Daubert	11.0
George Davis	48.4
Harry Davis	14.4
Curt Davis	19.3
Andre Dawson	24.6
Dizzy Dean	19.9
Ed Delahanty	46.1
Art Devlin	16.9
Bill Dickey	30.6
Murry Dickson	19.8
Larry Doby	17.7
Bobby Doerr	35.6
Mike Donlin	14.4
Brian Downing	16.7
Don Drysdale	34.7
Fred Dunlap	28.0
Frank Dwyer	16.3
Doug DeCinces	15.7
Joe DiMaggio	43.6
Dennis Eckersley	13.6
Bob Elliott	18.5
Darrell Evans	32.5
Dwight Evans	25.2
Johnny Evers	16.6
Buck Ewing	27.6
Red Faber	25.3
Ferris Fain	18.1
Duke Farrell	16.2
Bob Feller	26.9
Charlie Ferguson	15.5
Rick Ferrell	15.0
Wes Ferrell	30.9
Rollie Fingers	12.6
Carlton Fisk	33.4
Freddie Fitzsimmons	22.7
Art Fletcher	21.0
Elmer Flick	28.5
Whitey Ford	38.6
Russ Ford	13.3
George Foster	22.1
Jack Fournier	23.7
Dave Foutz	16.4
Nellie Fox	12.5
Jimmie Foxx	53.2
Bill Freehan	28.9
Jim Fregosi	21.0
Larry French	16.8
Lonny Frey	16.2
Frankie Frisch	37.2
Augie Galan	13.0
Jim Galvin	13.4
Gene Garber	12.6
Mike Garcia	14.5
Ned Garver	17.7
Ned Garvin	11.5
Lou Gehrig	60.8
Charlie Gehringer	43.5
Jim Gentile	11.3
Kirk Gibson	13.9
Bob Gibson	46.3
Jack Glasscock	34.5
Lefty Gomez	18.3
Joe Gordon	27.6
Sid Gordon	14.7
George Gore	16.0
Goose Goslin	22.9
Rich Gossage	14.3
Hank Greenberg	28.9
Bobby Grich	47.4
Ken Griffey	11.2
Mike Griffin	19.7
Clark Griffith	29.4
Burleigh Grimes	26.7
Heinie Groh	25.6
Lefty Grove	59.9
Pedro Guerrero	23.7
Ron Guidry	17.7
Tony Gwynn	19.9
Stan Hack	25.8
Harvey Haddix	12.4
Noodles Hahn	17.9
Billy Hamilton	25.0
Ron Hansen	11.8
Mel Harder	18.0
Mike Hargrove	15.5
Toby Harrah	16.6
Gabby Hartnett	35.7
Jeff Heath	15.7
Guy Hecker	24.0
Harry Heilmann	25.4
Solly Hemus	12.6
Rickey Henderson	44.0
Claude Hendrix	17.3
Tommy Henrich	14.6
Babe Herman	18.3
Billy Herman	34.0
Keith Hernandez	37.3
Orel Hershiser	14.7
Charlie Hickman	12.1

Total Baseball Ranking (alpha.)

John Hiller	13.2
Paul Hines	17.7
Larry Hisle	12.6
Gil Hodges	14.1
Rogers Hornsby	77.3
Charlie Hough	15.2
Elston Howard	13.7
Frank Howard	20.0
Harry Howell	15.8
Waite Hoyt	16.4
Glenn Hubbard	14.7
Carl Hubbell	38.6
Miller Huggins	19.0
Tex Hughson	11.7
Ron Hunt	12.2
Fred Hutchinson	13.8
Bill Hutchinson	15.2
Joe Jackson	36.1
Reggie Jackson	44.0
Travis Jackson	21.0
Larry Jackson	20.1
Ferguson Jenkins	32.1
Hughie Jennings	26.6
Tommy John	27.0
Cliff Johnson	12.6
Dave Johnson	11.6
Bob Johnson	37.8
Walter Johnson	81.5
Charley Jones	21.0
Addie Joss	26.9
Bill Joyce	19.1
Jim Kaat	21.2
Al Kaline	45.9
Willie Kamm	12.8
Benny Kauff	16.7
Tim Keefe	38.8
Charlie Keller	23.4
Joe Kelley	23.1
King Kelly	24.2
Ken Keltner	12.8
Harmon Killebrew	32.8
Frank Killen	15.0
Ralph Kiner	27.0
Silver King	26.1
Chuck Klein	24.3
Bobby Knoop	12.4
Ed Konetchy	23.5
Jerry Koosman	13.9
Sandy Koufax	20.0
Nap Lajoie	85.2
Max Lanier	15.7
Henry Larkin	14.8
Frank Lary	12.2
Tony Lazzeri	15.0
Tommy Leach	15.7
Thornton Lee	17.1
Sam Leever	15.7
Chet Lemon	18.1
Bob Lemon	35.2
Dutch Leonard	22.7
Sixto Lezcano	12.8
Johnny Logan	14.0
Ernie Lombardi	23.4
Eddie Lopat	17.5
Davey Lopes	11.7
Dolf Luque	25.8
Greg Luzinski	11.3
Sparky Lyle	13.0
Fred Lynn	21.3
Denny Lyons	20.1
Ted Lyons	35.4
Sherry Magee	28.5
Sal Maglie	14.9
Jim Maloney	13.9
Mickey Mantle	69.8
Firpo Marberry	11.6
Juan Marichal	30.8
Mike Marshall	12.2
Eddie Mathews	48.4
Christy Mathewson	54.6
Jon Matlack	12.5
Don Mattingly	12.6
Willie Mays	86.2
Carl Mays	34.8
Bill Mazeroski	34.4
Joe Medwick	25.7
Andy Messersmith	19.0
Stu Miller	12.3
Minnie Minoso	23.6
Johnny Mize	36.5
Paul Molitor	18.7
Joe Morgan	63.9
Jack Morris	13.2
Tony Mullane	35.2
George Mullin	16.4
Van Mungo	10.9
Thurman Munson	25.1
Bobby Murcer	13.5
Dale Murphy	19.1
Dwayne Murphy	13.7

Total Baseball Ranking (alpha.)

Eddie Murray	33.7
Stan Musial	70.1
Buddy Myer	12.7
Tim McCarver	12.3
Jim McCormick	21.9
Willie McCovey	38.1
Lindy McDaniel	11.0
Gil McDougald	21.5
Sam McDowell	12.4
Ed McFarland	12.1
Joe McGinnity	21.0
John McGraw	17.3
Deacon McGuire	16.1
Sadie McMahon	15.9
Bid McPhee	37.5
Hal McRae	17.2
Billy Nash	15.2
Graig Nettles	24.1
Don Newcombe	19.1
Hal Newhouser	38.5
Kid Nichols	65.3
Bill Nicholson	16.0
Phil Niekro	38.0
Tip O'Neill	11.2
Jim O'Rourke	15.6
Tony Oliva	26.1
Al Oliver	12.1
Claude Osteen	12.6
Fritz Ostermueller	11.0
Amos Otis	17.2
Mel Ott	60.1
Jim Palmer	36.4
Milt Pappas	14.1
Dave Parker	22.2
Mel Parnell	17.5
Lance Parrish	15.9
Camilo Pascual	11.8
Claude Passeau	17.1
Roger Peckinpaugh	14.0
Tony Perez	13.8
Gaylord Perry	36.8
Johnny Pesky	13.5
Gary Peters	12.9
Fred Pfeffer	20.3
Deacon Phillippe	14.7
Billy Pierce	22.4
Howie Pollet	14.5
Darrell Porter	19.3
Boog Powell	15.7
Del Pratt	21.7
Jack Quinn	25.0
Dan Quisenberry	17.1
Charley Radbourn	29.4
Tim Raines	31.5
Willie Randolph	26.5
Pee Wee Reese	19.0
Ed Reulbach	19.4
Rick Reuschel	26.4
Jim Rice	26.5
Hardy Richardson	25.9
Cal Ripken	26.7
Eppa Rixey	25.1
Phil Rizzuto	15.4
Robin Roberts	25.9
Brooks Robinson	23.3
Frank Robinson	71.2
Jackie Robinson	33.3
Steve Rogers	18.8
John Romano	12.2
Eddie Rommel	24.9
Pete Rose	24.7
Edd Roush	16.0
Schoolboy Rowe	15.1
Nap Rucker	13.8
Red Ruffing	26.5
Bob Rush	11.0
Amos Rusie	37.7
Babe Ruth	119.3
Jimmy Ryan	15.8
Nolan Ryan	14.2
Ryne Sandberg	19.3
Ben Sanders	12.4
Ron Santo	38.1
Wally Schang	25.2
Mike Schmidt	77.9
Red Schoendienst	15.0
Hal Schumacher	16.4
Tom Seaver	51.2
Kip Selbach	13.9
Andy Seminick	14.2
Joe Sewell	33.1
Cy Seymour	17.4
Orator Shaffer	11.9
Bobby Shantz	20.4
Bob Shawkey	14.4
Jimmy Sheckard	19.3
Urban Shocker	24.8
Sonny Siebert	12.1
Roy Sievers	12.9

Total Baseball Ranking (alpha.)

Al Simmons	24.2
Ted Simmons	34.4
Curt Simmons	13.9
Ken Singleton	20.3
George Sisler	25.5
Enos Slaughter	14.3
Roy Smalley	22.7
Reggie Smith	33.4
Mike Smith	17.7
Ozzie Smith	38.0
Sherry Smith	11.5
Duke Snider	24.3
Warren Spahn	43.1
Tris Speaker	79.9
Stan Spence	11.2
Eddie Stanky	21.6
Bob Stanley	15.7
Willie Stargell	31.6
Rusty Staub	15.4
Vern Stephens	15.4
Dave Stieb	25.3
Jack Stivetts	35.0
George Stone	12.6
Mel Stottlemyre	17.8
Harry Stovey	23.6
Darryl Strawberry	19.2
Frank Sullivan	11.3
Jim Sundberg	12.8
Bruce Sutter	12.8
Don Sutton	13.7
Frank Tanana	15.2
Jesse Tannehill	20.6
Jack Taylor	13.8
Kent Tekulve	17.8
Fred Tenney	18.9
Bill Terry	27.8
Roy Thomas	22.0
Sam Thompson	29.4
Andy Thornton	16.0
Luis Tiant	17.8
Mike Tiernan	14.4
Joe Tinker	20.2
John Titus	11.4
Jim Tobin	13.2
Joe Torre	29.8
Alan Trammell	17.7
Pie Traynor	18.4
Dizzy Trout	33.7
Virgil Trucks	16.4
John Tudor	14.2
George Uhle	15.0
Fernando Valenzuela	13.5
George Van Haltren	14.3
Dazzy Vance	25.4
Arky Vaughan	40.3
Hippo Vaughn	19.8
Rube Waddell	28.4
Honus Wagner	75.6
Dixie Walker	11.3
Bobby Wallace	36.7
Ed Walsh	41.6
Bucky Walters	27.4
Paul Waner	38.9
Monte Ward	18.4
Lon Warneke	23.4
Bob Watson	12.1
Jake Weimer	10.9
Mickey Welch	15.9
Zach Wheat	21.1
Lou Whitaker	19.2
Roy White	19.2
Doc White	18.7
Will White	13.6
Jim Whitney	18.4
Hoyt Wilhelm	29.2
Billy Williams	30.2
Jimmy Williams	12.1
Ken Williams	19.6
Ted Williams	89.8
Vic Willis	21.7
Bump Wills	12.9
Maury Wills	15.4
Hack Wilson	16.8
Dave Winfield	36.6
Sam Wise	11.2
Joe Wood	19.5
Wilbur Wood	15.1
Jim Wynn	31.1
Early Wynn	18.2
Carl Yastrzemski	46.1
Rudy York	16.1
Cy Young	81.0
Ross Youngs	12.0
Robin Yount	31.4
Chief Zimmer	12.5
Heinie Zimmerman	12.9
Richie Zisk	13.9

Total Baseball Ranking (by era)

1876-1892

1	John Clarkson	52.6
2	Dan Brouthers	40.4
3	Roger Connor	38.8
	Tim Keefe	38.8
5	Amos Rusie	37.7
6	Bid McPhee	37.5
7	Bob Caruthers	35.6
8	Tony Mullane	35.2
9	Jack Stivetts	35.0
10	Jack Glasscock	34.5
11	Cap Anson	31.3
12	Sam Thompson	29.4
	Charley Radbourn	29.4
14	Fred Dunlap	28.0
15	Buck Ewing	27.6
16	Pete Browning	27.0
17	Silver King	26.1
18	Hardy Richardson	25.9
19	King Kelly	24.2
20	Guy Hecker	24.0
21	Harry Stovey	23.6
22	Jim McCormick	21.9
23	Charley Jones	21.0
24	Fred Pfeffer	20.3
25	Denny Lyons	20.1

1893-1919

1	Ty Cobb	90.6
2	Nap Lajoie	85.2
3	Walter Johnson	81.5
4	Cy Young	81.0
5	Tris Speaker	79.9
6	Honus Wagner	75.6
7	Eddie Collins	70.5
8	Kid Nichols	65.3
9	Christy Mathewson	54.6
10	George Davis	48.4
11	Ed Delahanty	46.1
12	Bill Dahlen	43.3
13	Ed Walsh	41.6
14	Bobby Wallace	36.7
15	Joe Jackson	36.1
16	Mordecai Brown	35.1
17	Frank Baker	34.6
18	Cupid Childs	29.6
19	Clark Griffith	29.4
20	Elmer Flick	28.5
	Sherry Magee	28.5
22	Rube Waddell	28.4
23	Fred Clarke	28.0
24	Jesse Burkett	27.9
25	Addie Joss	26.9

1920-1941

1	Babe Ruth	119.3
2	Rogers Hornsby	77.3
3	Pete Alexander	64.8
4	Lou Gehrig	60.8
5	Mel Ott	60.1
6	Lefty Grove	59.9
7	Jimmie Foxx	53.2
8	Charlie Gehringer	43.5
9	Arky Vaughan	40.3
10	Paul Waner	38.9
11	Carl Hubbell	38.6
12	Luke Appling	38.5
13	Joe Cronin	38.2
14	Bob Johnson	37.8
15	Frankie Frisch	37.2
16	Gabby Hartnett	35.7
17	Ted Lyons	35.4
18	Carl Mays	34.8
19	Billy Herman	34.0
20	Joe Sewell	33.1
21	Wes Ferrell	30.9
22	Bill Dickey	30.6
23	Dave Bancroft	29.7
24	Hank Greenberg	28.9
25	Tommy Bridges	28.5

Total Baseball Ranking (by era)

1942-1960

1	Ted Williams	89.8
2	Stan Musial	70.1
3	Mickey Mantle	69.8
4	Eddie Mathews	48.4
5	Joe DiMaggio	43.6
6	Warren Spahn	43.1
7	Whitey Ford	38.6
8	Hal Newhouser	38.5
9	Johnny Mize	36.5
10	Bobby Doerr	35.6
11	Bob Lemon	35.2
12	Yogi Berra	34.8
13	Lou Boudreau	34.3
14	Dizzy Trout	33.7
15	Jackie Robinson	33.3
16	Hoyt Wilhelm	29.2
17	Joe Gordon	27.6
18	Bucky Walters	27.4
19	Richie Ashburn	27.0
	Ralph Kiner	27.0
21	Bob Feller	26.9
22	Robin Roberts	25.9
23	Duke Snider	24.3
24	Harry Brecheen	23.9
25	Minnie Minoso	23.6

1961-1988

1	Hank Aaron	90.1
2	Willie Mays	86.2
3	Mike Schmidt	77.9
4	Frank Robinson	71.2
5	Joe Morgan	63.9
6	Tom Seaver	51.2
7	Bobby Grich	47.4
8	Bob Gibson	46.3
9	Carl Yastrzemski	46.1
10	Al Kaline	45.9
11	Rickey Henderson	44.0
	Reggie Jackson	44.0
13	George Brett	43.8
14	Rod Carew	41.0
15	Roberto Clemente	39.6
16	Willie McCovey	38.1
	Ron Santo	38.1
18	Ozzie Smith	38.0
	Phil Niekro	38.0
20	Gary Carter	37.4
21	Keith Hernandez	37.3
22	Gaylord Perry	36.8
23	Dave Winfield	36.6
24	Jim Palmer	36.4
25	2 players tied	35.6

At Bats

1	Willie Wilson, 1980	705
2	Juan Samuel, 1984	701
3	Dave Cash, 1975	699
4	Matty Alou, 1969	698
5	Woody Jensen, 1936	696
6	Maury Wills, 1962	695
	Omar Moreno, 1979	695
8	Bobby Richardson, 1962	692
9	Kirby Puckett, 1985	691
10	Lou Brock, 1967	689
	Sandy Alomar, 1971	689
12	Dave Cash, 1974	687
	Tony Fernandez, 1986	687
14	Horace Clarke, 1970	686
15	Lloyd Waner, 1931	681
	Jo-Jo Moore, 1935	681
17	Pete Rose, 1973	680
	Frank Taveras, 1979	680
	Kirby Puckett, 1986	680
20	Harvey Kuenn, 1953	679
	Curt Flood, 1964	679
	Bobby Richardson, 1964	679
23	Dick Groat, 1962	678
24	Matty Alou, 1970	677
	Jim Rice, 1978	677
	Don Mattingly, 1986	677
27	Felix Millan, 1975	676
	Omar Moreno, 1980	676
29	Rennie Stennett, 1974	673
	Bill Buckner, 1985	673
31	Rabbit Maranville, 1922	672
	Tony Oliva, 1964	672
	Sandy Alomar, 1970	672
	Garry Templeton, 1979	672
35	Jack Tobin, 1921	671
36	Al Simmons, 1932	670
	Pete Rose, 1965	670
	Buddy Bell, 1979	670
39	Vada Pinson, 1965	669
	Larry Bowa, 1974	669
41	Buddy Lewis, 1937	668
	Brooks Robinson, 1961	668
	Ralph Garr, 1973	668
44	Carl Furillo, 1951	667
45	Billy Herman, 1935	666
	Zoilo Versalles, 1965	666
	Felipe Alou, 1966	666
	Dave Cash, 1976	666
	Ron LeFlore, 1978	666
	Paul Molitor, 1982	666
51	Tommy Davis, 1962	665
	Pete Rose, 1976	665
53	Taylor Douthit, 1930	664
	Bobby Richardson, 1965	664
	Don Kessinger, 1969	664
	Lou Brock, 1970	664
57	Jake Wood, 1961	663
	Bill Virdon, 1962	663
	Bobby Bonds, 1970	663
	Rick Burleson, 1977	663
	Cal Ripken, 1983	663
	Juan Samuel, 1985	663
	Joe Carter, 1986	663
64	Lloyd Waner, 1929	662
	Hughie Critz, 1930	662
	Richie Ashburn, 1949	662
	Granny Hamner, 1949	662
	Bobby Richardson, 1961	662
	Curt Flood, 1963	662
	Felipe Alou, 1968	662
	Pete Rose, 1975	662
72	Doc Cramer, 1933	661
	Doc Cramer, 1940	661
	Ken Hubbs, 1962	661
	Cecil Cooper, 1983	661
76	Tom Brown, 1892	660
	Doc Cramer, 1941	660
	Lou Brock, 1968	660
	Enos Cabell, 1978	660
80	Lloyd Waner, 1928	659
	Hughie Critz, 1932	659
	Red Schoendienst, 1947	659
	Billy Moran, 1962	659
	Zoilo Versalles, 1964	659
	Luis Aparicio, 1966	659
	Steve Garvey, 1975	659
	Warren Cromartie, 1979	659
88	Heinie Manush, 1933	658
	Doc Cramer, 1938	658
	Bill White, 1963	658
	Dave Cash, 1978	658
	Steve Garvey, 1980	658
	Julio Franco, 1984	658
94	Cesar Tovar, 1971	657
	Bill Buckner, 1982	657
	Jim Rice, 1984	657
	Kirby Puckett, 1988	657
98	9 players tied	656

Runs

1	Billy Hamilton, 1894	192
2	Tom Brown, 1891	177
	Babe Ruth, 1921	177
4	Tip O'Neill, 1887	167
	Lou Gehrig, 1936	167
6	Billy Hamilton, 1895	166
7	Willie Keeler, 1894	165
	Joe Kelley, 1894	165
9	Arlie Latham, 1887	163
	Babe Ruth, 1928	163
	Lou Gehrig, 1931	163
12	Willie Keeler, 1895	162
13	Hugh Duffy, 1890	161
	Hugh Duffy, 1894	161
15	Fred Dunlap, 1884	160
	Jesse Burkett, 1896	160
17	Hughie Jennings, 1895	159
18	Bobby Lowe, 1894	158
	Babe Ruth, 1920	158
	Babe Ruth, 1927	158
	Chuck Klein, 1930	158
22	John McGraw, 1894	156
	Rogers Hornsby, 1929	156
24	King Kelly, 1886	155
	Kiki Cuyler, 1930	155
26	Dan Brouthers, 1887	153
	Jesse Burkett, 1895	153
	Willie Keeler, 1896	153
29	Arlie Latham, 1886	152
	Mike Griffin, 1889	152
	Harry Stovey, 1889	152
	Billy Hamilton, 1896	152
	Billy Hamilton, 1897	152
	Lefty O'Doul, 1929	152
	Woody English, 1930	152
	Al Simmons, 1930	152
	Chuck Klein, 1932	152
38	Babe Ruth, 1923	151
	Jimmie Foxx, 1932	151
	Joe DiMaggio, 1937	151
41	George Gore, 1886	150
	Babe Ruth, 1930	150
	Ted Williams, 1949	150
44	Herman Long, 1893	149
	Bill Dahlen, 1894	149
	Ed Delahanty, 1895	149
	Lou Gehrig, 1927	149
	Babe Ruth, 1931	149
49	Hub Collins, 1890	148
	Jake Stenzel, 1894	148
	Joe Kelley, 1895	148
	Joe Kelley, 1896	148
53	Mike Tiernan, 1889	147
	Hugh Duffy, 1893	147
	Ed Delahanty, 1894	147
	Ty Cobb, 1911	147
57	Darby O'Brien, 1889	146
	Tom Brown, 1890	146
	Hack Wilson, 1930	146
	Rickey Henderson, 1985	146
61	Jesse Burkett, 1893	145
	Cupid Childs, 1893	145
	Ed Delahanty, 1893	145
	Patsy Donovan, 1894	145
	Willie Keeler, 1897	145
	Nap Lajoie, 1901	145
	Harlond Clift, 1936	145
68	Hugh Duffy, 1889	144
	Billy Hamilton, 1889	144
	Ty Cobb, 1915	144
	Kiki Cuyler, 1925	144
	Charlie Gehringer, 1930	144
	Al Simmons, 1932	144
	Charlie Gehringer, 1936	144
	Hank Greenberg, 1938	144
76	Cupid Childs, 1894	143
	John McGraw, 1898	143
	Babe Ruth, 1924	143
	Babe Herman, 1930	143
	Lou Gehrig, 1930	143
	Earle Combs, 1932	143
	Red Rolfe, 1937	143
83	Mike Griffin, 1887	142
	Harry Stovey, 1890	142
	Jesse Burkett, 1901	142
	Paul Waner, 1928	142
	Ted Williams, 1946	142
88	Billy Hamilton, 1891	141
	Rogers Hornsby, 1922	141
	Ted Williams, 1942	141
91	Tom Poorman, 1887	140
	Jimmy Ryan, 1889	140
	Jim McTamany, 1890	140
	Mike Griffin, 1895	140
	Willie Keeler, 1899	140
	John McGraw, 1899	140
	Max Carey, 1922	140
	Earl Averill, 1931	140
99	9 players tied	139

Runs per Game

1	Ross Barnes, 1876	1.91
2	Fred Dunlap, 1884	1.58
3	Billy Hamilton, 1894	1.49
4	George Gore, 1890	1.42
5	Billy Hamilton, 1895	1.35
6	Tip O'Neill, 1887	1.35
7	Billy Hamilton, 1893	1.34
8	Herman Long, 1894	1.32
9	King Kelly, 1886	1.31
10	Tom Brown, 1891	1.29
11	Ed Delahanty, 1894	1.29
12	Hugh Duffy, 1894	1.29
13	Ed Delahanty, 1895	1.28
14	Willie Keeler, 1894	1.28
	Joe Kelley, 1894	1.28
16	George Gore, 1886	1.27
17	John McGraw, 1894	1.26
18	Dan Brouthers, 1887	1.24
19	Willie Keeler, 1895	1.24
20	Bill Dahlen, 1894	1.23
21	Orator Shaffer, 1884	1.23
22	Jimmy Ryan, 1894	1.22
23	Willie Keeler, 1896	1.21
24	Hughie Jennings, 1895	1.21
25	Cupid Childs, 1894	1.21
26	Mike Tiernan, 1889	1.20
27	Harry Stovey, 1890	1.20
28	Jesse Burkett, 1896	1.20
29	Arlie Latham, 1887	1.20
30	Billy Hamilton, 1897	1.20
31	John McGraw, 1899	1.20
32	Harry Stovey, 1884	1.19
33	Bobby Lowe, 1894	1.19
34	George Gore, 1882	1.18
35	George Gore, 1881	1.18
36	Harry Stovey, 1883	1.17
37	Cupid Childs, 1893	1.17
38	Jesse Burkett, 1895	1.17
39	Hugh Duffy, 1890	1.17
40	Babe Ruth, 1921	1.16
41	Herman Long, 1893	1.16
42	Harry Stovey, 1885	1.16
43	Billy Hamilton, 1896	1.16
44	Jesse Burkett, 1893	1.16
45	King Kelly, 1885	1.16
46	Dan Brouthers, 1886	1.15
47	Hub Collins, 1890	1.15
48	John McGraw, 1895	1.15
49	Abner Dalrymple, 1882	1.14
50	George Gore, 1883	1.14
51	Tom Brown, 1890	1.14
52	Mike Griffin, 1894	1.14
53	Hughie Jennings, 1897	1.14
54	Arlie Latham, 1886	1.13
55	Ed Swartwood, 1882	1.13
56	Pete Browning, 1883	1.13
57	Jake Stenzel, 1894	1.13
	Joe Kelley, 1895	1.13
	Joe Kelley, 1896	1.13
60	Willie Keeler, 1897	1.12
61	Hugh Duffy, 1893	1.12
62	Jim McTamany, 1890	1.12
63	Jim O'Rourke, 1877	1.11
64	Dan Brouthers, 1894	1.11
65	Babe Ruth, 1920	1.11
66	Charlie Comiskey, 1887	1.11
67	King Kelly, 1884	1.11
68	Mike Griffin, 1889	1.11
	Harry Stovey, 1889	1.11
70	Nap Lajoie, 1901	1.11
71	Mike Griffin, 1890	1.10
72	Jesse Burkett, 1894	1.10
73	Jim O'Rourke, 1884	1.10
74	Al Simmons, 1930	1.10
75	Sam Thompson, 1895	1.10
76	George Gore, 1889	1.10
77	Ed Delahanty, 1893	1.10
	Patsy Donovan, 1894	1.10
79	Tom Daly, 1894	1.10
80	Bill Dahlen, 1896	1.10
81	Mike Hornung, 1883	1.09
82	Hardy Richardson, 1887	1.09
83	Sam Thompson, 1894	1.09
84	Jack Rowe, 1887	1.09
85	John Reilly, 1884	1.09
86	Jim O'Rourke, 1883	1.09
87	Seery, 1884	1.08
88	Billy Hamilton, 1890	1.08
	Roger Connor, 1890	1.08
90	Lou Gehrig, 1936	1.08
91	Ezra Sutton, 1883	1.07
92	Darby O'Brien, 1889	1.07
93	Curt Welch, 1889	1.07
94	Harry Stovey, 1882	1.07
95	Mike Griffin, 1895	1.07
96	Ed Delahanty, 1896	1.07
97	Dick Burns, 1884	1.06
98	Jim O'Rourke, 1885	1.06
99	Bid McPhee, 1887	1.06
100	2 players tied	%1.06

Hits

1	George Sisler, 1920	257
2	Lefty O'Doul, 1929	254
	Bill Terry, 1930	254
4	Al Simmons, 1925	253
5	Rogers Hornsby, 1922	250
	Chuck Klein, 1930	250
7	Ty Cobb, 1911	248
8	George Sisler, 1922	246
9	Heinie Manush, 1928	241
	Babe Herman, 1930	241
11	Jesse Burkett, 1896	240
	Wade Boggs, 1985	240
13	Willie Keeler, 1897	239
	Rod Carew, 1977	239
15	Ed Delahanty, 1899	238
	Don Mattingly, 1986	238
17	Hugh Duffy, 1894	237
	Harry Heilmann, 1921	237
	Paul Waner, 1927	237
	Joe Medwick, 1937	237
21	Jack Tobin, 1921	236
22	Rogers Hornsby, 1921	235
23	Lloyd Waner, 1929	234
	Kirby Puckett, 1988	234
25	Joe Jackson, 1911	233
26	Nap Lajoie, 1901	232
	Earl Averill, 1936	232
28	Earle Combs, 1927	231
	Freddy Lindstrom, 1928	231
	Freddy Lindstrom, 1930	231
	Matty Alou, 1969	231
32	Stan Musial, 1948	230
	Tommy Davis, 1962	230
	Joe Torre, 1971	230
	Pete Rose, 1973	230
	Willie Wilson, 1980	230
37	Rogers Hornsby, 1929	229
38	Kiki Cuyler, 1930	228
	Stan Musial, 1946	228
40	Nap Lajoie, 1910	227
	Ty Cobb, 1912	227
	Rogers Hornsby, 1924	227
	Jim Bottomley, 1925	227
	Sam Rice, 1925	227
	Billy Herman, 1935	227
	Charlie Gehringer, 1936	227
47	Jesse Burkett, 1901	226
	Joe Jackson, 1912	226
	Bill Terry, 1929	226
	Chuck Klein, 1932	226
51	Tip O'Neill, 1887	225
	Jesse Burkett, 1895	225
	Ty Cobb, 1917	225
	Harry Heilmann, 1925	225
	Johnny Hodapp, 1930	225
	Bill Terry, 1932	225
57	George Sisler, 1925	224
	Joe Medwick, 1935	224
	Tommy Holmes, 1945	224
60	Frankie Frisch, 1923	223
	Lloyd Waner, 1927	223
	Paul Waner, 1928	223
	Chuck Klein, 1933	223
	Joe Medwick, 1936	223
	Hank Aaron, 1959	223
	Kirby Puckett, 1986	223
67	Sam Thompson, 1893	222
	Tris Speaker, 1912	222
	Eddie Collins, 1920	222
	Charlie Jamieson, 1923	222
71	Jesse Burkett, 1899	221
	Zach Wheat, 1925	221
	Lloyd Waner, 1928	221
	Heinie Manush, 1933	221
	Richie Ashburn, 1951	221
76	Pete Browning, 1887	220
	Billy Hamilton, 1894	220
	Kiki Cuyler, 1925	220
	Lou Gehrig, 1930	220
	Stan Musial, 1943	220
81	Ed Delahanty, 1893	219
	Willie Keeler, 1894	219
	Jimmy Williams, 1899	219
	Cy Seymour, 1905	219
	Chuck Klein, 1929	219
	Lefty O'Doul, 1932	219
	Paul Waner, 1937	219
	Ralph Garr, 1971	219
	Cecil Cooper, 1980	219
90	12 players tied	218

Doubles

#	Player	Value
1	Earl Webb, 1931	67
2	George Burns, 1926	64
	Joe Medwick, 1936	64
4	Hank Greenberg, 1934	63
5	Paul Waner, 1932	62
6	Charlie Gehringer, 1936	60
7	Tris Speaker, 1923	59
	Chuck Klein, 1930	59
9	Billy Herman, 1935	57
	Billy Herman, 1936	57
11	Joe Medwick, 1937	56
	George Kell, 1950	56
13	Ed Delahanty, 1899	55
	Gee Walker, 1936	55
15	Hal McRae, 1977	54
16	Tris Speaker, 1912	53
	Al Simmons, 1926	53
	Paul Waner, 1936	53
	Stan Musial, 1953	53
	Don Mattingly, 1986	53
21	Tip O'Neill, 1887	52
	Tris Speaker, 1921	52
	Tris Speaker, 1926	52
	Lou Gehrig, 1927	52
	Johnny Frederick, 1929	52
	Enos Slaughter, 1939	52
27	Hugh Duffy, 1894	51
	Nap Lajoie, 1910	51
	Baby Doll Jacobson, 1926	51
	George Burns, 1927	51
	Johnny Hodapp, 1930	51
	Beau Bell, 1937	51
	Joe Cronin, 1938	51
	Stan Musial, 1944	51
	Mickey Vernon, 1946	51
	Frank Robinson, 1962	51
	Pete Rose, 1978	51
38	Tris Speaker, 1920	50
	Harry Heilmann, 1927	50
	Paul Waner, 1928	50
	Kiki Cuyler, 1930	50
	Chuck Klein, 1932	50
	Charlie Gehringer, 1934	50
	Odell Hale, 1936	50
	Ben Chapman, 1936	50
	Hank Greenberg, 1940	50
	Stan Musial, 1946	50
	Stan Spence, 1946	50
49	Ned Williamson, 1883	49
	Ed Delahanty, 1895	49
	Nap Lajoie, 1904	49
	George Sisler, 1920	49
	Heinie Manush, 1930	49
	Riggs Stephenson, 1932	49
	Hank Greenberg, 1937	49
	Robin Yount, 1980	49
57	Joe Kelley, 1894	48
	Nap Lajoie, 1901	48
	Nap Lajoie, 1906	48
	Tris Speaker, 1922	48
	Joe Sewell, 1927	48
	Babe Herman, 1930	48
	Dick Bartell, 1932	48
	Earl Averill, 1934	48
	Wally Moses, 1937	48
	Joe Medwick, 1939	48
	Stan Musial, 1943	48
	Keith Hernandez, 1979	48
	Don Mattingly, 1985	48
70	Harry Davis, 1905	47
	Ty Cobb, 1911	47
	George Burns, 1923	47
	Lou Gehrig, 1926	47
	Bob Meusel, 1927	47
	Lou Gehrig, 1928	47
	Heinie Manush, 1928	47
	Rogers Hornsby, 1929	47
	Chick Hafey, 1929	47
	Adam Comorosky, 1930	47
	Ed Morgan, 1930	47
	Charlie Gehringer, 1930	47
	Dale Alexander, 1931	47
	Eric McNair, 1932	47
	Joe Vosmik, 1935	47
	Joe Vosmik, 1937	47
	Joe Medwick, 1938	47
	Tommy Holmes, 1945	47
	Vada Pinson, 1959	47
	Wes Parker, 1970	47
	Pete Rose, 1975	47
	Fred Lynn, 1975	47
	Cal Ripken, 1983	47
	Wade Boggs, 1986	47
94	24 players tied	46

Triples

#	Player	Value
1	Chief Wilson, 1912	36
2	Dave Orr, 1886	31
	Heinie Reitz, 1894	31
4	Perry Werden, 1893	29
5	Harry Davis, 1897	28
6	George Davis, 1893	27
	Sam Thompson, 1894	27
	Jimmy Williams, 1899	27
9	John Reilly, 1890	26
	George Treadway, 1894	26
	Joe Jackson, 1912	26
	Sam Crawford, 1914	26
	Kiki Cuyler, 1925	26
14	Roger Connor, 1894	25
	Buck Freeman, 1899	25
	Sam Crawford, 1903	25
	Larry Doyle, 1911	25
	Tom Long, 1915	25
19	Ed McKean, 1893	24
	Ty Cobb, 1911	24
21	Harry Stovey, 1884	23
	Sam Thompson, 1887	23
	Mike Smith, 1893	23
	Dan Brouthers, 1894	23
	Nap Lajoie, 1897	23
	Ty Cobb, 1912	23
	Sam Crawford, 1913	23
	Ty Cobb, 1917	23
	Earle Combs, 1927	23
	Adam Comorosky, 1930	23
	Dale Mitchell, 1949	23
32	Roger Connor, 1887	22
	Bid McPhee, 1890	22
	Jake Beckley, 1890	22
	Joe Visner, 1890	22
	Willie Keeler, 1894	22
	Kip Selbach, 1895	22
	John Anderson, 1898	22
	Honus Wagner, 1900	22
	Tommy Leach, 1902	22
	Sam Crawford, 1902	22
	Bill Bradley, 1903	22
	Elmer Flick, 1906	22
	Mike Mitchell, 1911	22
	Birdie Cree, 1911	22
	Tris Speaker, 1913	22
	Hi Myers, 1920	22
	Jake Daubert, 1922	22
	Paul Waner, 1926	22
	Earle Combs, 1930	22
	Snuffy Stirnweiss, 1945	22
52	Dave Orr, 1885	21
	Mike Tiernan, 1890	21
	Billy Shindle, 1890	21
	Tom Brown, 1891	21
	Ed Delahanty, 1892	21
	Sam Thompson, 1895	21
	Mike Tiernan, 1895	21
	Tom McCreery, 1896	21
	George VanHaltren, 1896	21
	Bobby Wallace, 1897	21
	Jimmy Williams, 1901	21
	Bill Keister, 1901	21
	Jimmy Williams, 1902	21
	Cy Seymour, 1905	21
	Frank Schulte, 1911	21
	Frank Baker, 1912	21
	Sam Crawford, 1912	21
	Vic Saier, 1913	21
	Joe Jackson, 1916	21
	Edd Roush, 1924	21
	Earle Combs, 1928	21
	Willie Wilson, 1985	21
74	36 players tied	20

Triples (by era)

1876-1892

#	Player	Value
1	Dave Orr, 1886	31
2	John Reilly, 1890	26
3	Harry Stovey, 1884	23
	Sam Thompson, 1887	23
5	Roger Connor, 1887	22
	Bid McPhee, 1890	22
	Jake Beckley, 1890	22
	Joe Visner, 1890	22
9	Dave Orr, 1885	21
	Mike Tiernan, 1890	21
	Billy Shindle, 1890	21
	Tom Brown, 1891	21
	Ed Delahanty, 1892	21
14	10 players tied	20

1893-1919

#	Player	Value
1	Chief Wilson, 1912	36
2	Heinie Reitz, 1894	31
3	Perry Werden, 1893	29
4	Harry Davis, 1897	28
5	George Davis, 1893	27
	Sam Thompson, 1894	27
	Jimmy Williams, 1899	27
8	George Treadway, 1894	26
	Joe Jackson, 1912	26
	Sam Crawford, 1914	26
11	Roger Connor, 1894	25
	Buck Freeman, 1899	25
	Sam Crawford, 1903	25
	Larry Doyle, 1911	25
	Tom Long, 1915	25

1920-1941

#	Player	Value
1	Kiki Cuyler, 1925	26
2	Earle Combs, 1927	23
	Adam Comorosky, 1930	23
4	Hi Myers, 1920	22
	Jake Daubert, 1922	22
	Paul Waner, 1926	22
	Earle Combs, 1930	22
8	Edd Roush, 1924	21
	Earle Combs, 1928	21
10	12 players tied	20

1942-1960

#	Player	Value
1	Dale Mitchell, 1949	23
2	Snuffy Stirnweiss, 1945	22
3	Stan Musial, 1943	20
	Stan Musial, 1946	20
	Willie Mays, 1957	20
6	Johnny Barrett, 1944	19
7	Stan Musial, 1948	18
	Minnie Minoso, 1954	18
9	Enos Slaughter, 1942	17
	Jim Gilliam, 1953	17
11	6 players tied	16

1961-1988

#	Player	Value
1	Willie Wilson, 1985	21
2	George Brett, 1979	20
3	Garry Templeton, 1979	19
	Juan Samuel, 1984	19
	Ryne Sandberg, 1984	19
6	Garry Templeton, 1977	18
	Willie McGee, 1985	18
8	Ralph Garr, 1974	17
9	Johnny Callison, 1965	16
	Willie Davis, 1970	16
	Rod Carew, 1977	16
	Paul Molitor, 1979	16
13	11 players tied	15

Home Runs

#	Player	Value
1	Roger Maris, 1961	61
2	Babe Ruth, 1927	60
3	Babe Ruth, 1921	59
4	Jimie Foxx, 1932	58
	Hank Greenberg, 1938	58
6	Hack Wilson, 1930	56
7	Babe Ruth, 1920	54
	Babe Ruth, 1928	54
	Ralph Kiner, 1949	54
	Mickey Mantle, 1961	54
11	Mickey Mantle, 1956	52
	Willie Mays, 1965	52
	George Foster, 1977	52
14	Ralph Kiner, 1947	51
	Johnny Mize, 1947	51
	Willie Mays, 1955	51
17	Jimmie Foxx, 1938	50
18	Babe Ruth, 1930	49
	Lou Gehrig, 1934	49
	Lou Gehrig, 1936	49
	Ted Kluszewski, 1954	49
	Willie Mays, 1962	49
	Harmon Killebrew, 1964	49
	Frank Robinson, 1966	49
	Harmon Killebrew, 1969	49
	Andre Dawson, 1987	49
	Mark McGwire, 1987	49
28	Jimmie Foxx, 1933	48
	Harmon Killebrew, 1962	48
	Frank Howard, 1968	48
	Willie Stargell, 1971	48
	Dave Kingman, 1979	48
	Mike Schmidt, 1980	48
34	Babe Ruth, 1926	47
	Lou Gehrig, 1927	47
	Ralph Kiner, 1950	47
	Eddie Mathews, 1953	47
	Ted Kluszewski, 1955	47
	Ernie Banks, 1958	47
	Willie Mays, 1964	47
	Reggie Jackson, 1969	47
	George Bell, 1987	47
44	Babe Ruth, 1924	46
	Babe Ruth, 1929	46
	Babe Ruth, 1931	46
	Lou Gehrig, 1931	46
	Joe DiMaggio, 1937	46
	Eddie Mathews, 1959	46
	Orlando Cepeda, 1961	46
	Jim Gentile, 1961	46
	Harmon Killebrew, 1961	46
	Jim Rice, 1978	46
54	Ernie Banks, 1959	45
	Rocky Colavito, 1961	45
	Hank Aaron, 1962	45
	Harmon Killebrew, 1963	45
	Willie McCovey, 1969	45
	Johnny Bench, 1970	45
	Mike Schmidt, 1979	45
	Gorman Thomas, 1979	45
62	Jimmie Foxx, 1934	44
	Hank Greenberg, 1946	44
	Ernie Banks, 1955	44
	Hank Aaron, 1957	44
	Hank Aaron, 1963	44
	Willie McCovey, 1963	44
	Hank Aaron, 1966	44
	Harmon Killebrew, 1967	44
	Carl Yastrzemski, 1967	44
	Frank Howard, 1968	44
	Hank Aaron, 1969	44
	Frank Howard, 1970	44
	Willie Stargell, 1973	44
	Dale Murphy, 1987	44
76	Chuck Klein, 1929	43
	Johnny Mize, 1940	43
	Ted Williams, 1949	43
	Al Rosen, 1953	43
	Duke Snider, 1956	43
	Ernie Banks, 1957	43
	Dave Johnson, 1973	43
	Tony Armas, 1984	43
84	Rogers Hornsby, 1922	42
	Mel Ott, 1929	42
	Hal Trosky, 1936	42
	Ralph Kiner, 1951	42
	Duke Snider, 1953	42
	Gus Zernial, 1953	42
	Gil Hodges, 1954	42
	Duke Snider, 1955	42
	Roy Sievers, 1957	42
	Mickey Mantle, 1958	42
	Rocky Colavito, 1959	42
	Harmon Killebrew, 1959	42
	Dick Stuart, 1963	42
	Billy Williams, 1970	42
	Jose Canseco, 1988	42
99	18 players tied	41

Home Runs (by era)

1876-1892

1	Ned Williamson, 1884	27
2	Fred Pfeffer, 1884	25
3	Abner Dalrymple, 1884	22
4	Cap Anson, 1884	21
5	Sam Thompson, 1889	20
6	Billy O'Brien, 1887	19
	Bug Holliday, 1889	19
	Harry Stovey, 1889	19
9	Jerry Denny, 1889	18
10	Roger Connor, 1887	17
	Jimmy Ryan, 1889	17
12	Fred Pfeffer, 1887	16
	Jimmy Ryan, 1888	16
	Harry Stovey, 1891	16
	Mike Tiernan, 1891	16

1893-1919

1	Babe Ruth, 1919	29
2	Buck Freeman, 1899	25
3	Gavvy Cravath, 1915	24
4	Frank Schulte, 1911	21
5	Ed Delahanty, 1893	19
	Gavvy Cravath, 1913	19
	Gavvy Cravath, 1914	19
8	Hugh Duffy, 1894	18
	Sam Thompson, 1895	18
	Fred Luderus, 1913	18
	Vic Saier, 1914	18
12	5 players tied	17

1920-1941

1	Babe Ruth, 1927	60
2	Babe Ruth, 1921	59
3	Jimmie Foxx, 1932	58
	Hank Greenberg, 1938	58
5	Hack Wilson, 1930	56
6	Babe Ruth, 1920	54
	Babe Ruth, 1928	54
8	Jimmie Foxx, 1938	50
9	Babe Ruth, 1930	49
	Lou Gehrig, 1934	49
	Lou Gehrig, 1936	49
12	Jimmie Foxx, 1933	48
13	Babe Ruth, 1926	47
	Lou Gehrig, 1927	47
15	5 players tied	46

1942-1960

1	Ralph Kiner, 1949	54
2	Mickey Mantle, 1956	52
3	Ralph Kiner, 1947	51
	Johnny Mize, 1947	51
	Willie Mays, 1955	51
6	Ted Kluszewski, 1954	49
7	Ralph Kiner, 1950	47
	Eddie Mathews, 1953	47
	Ted Kluszewski, 1955	47
	Ernie Banks, 1958	47
11	Eddie Mathews, 1959	46
12	Ernie Banks, 1959	45
13	Hank Greenberg, 1946	44
	Ernie Banks, 1955	44
	Hank Aaron, 1957	44

1961-1988

1	Roger Maris, 1961	61
2	Mickey Mantle, 1961	54
3	Willie Mays, 1965	52
	George Foster, 1977	52
5	Willie Mays, 1962	49
	Harmon Killebrew, 1964	49
	Frank Robinson, 1966	49
	Harmon Killebrew, 1969	49
	Andre Dawson, 1987	49
	Mark McGwire, 1987	49
11	Harmon Killebrew, 1962	48
	Frank Howard, 1969	48
	Willie Stargell, 1971	48
	Dave Kingman, 1979	48
	Mike Schmidt, 1980	48

Home Run Percentage

1	Babe Ruth, 1920	11.79
2	Babe Ruth, 1927	11.11
3	Babe Ruth, 1921	10.93
4	Mickey Mantle, 1961	10.51
5	Hank Greenberg, 1938	10.43
6	Roger Maris, 1961	10.34
7	Babe Ruth, 1928	10.07
8	Jimmie Foxx, 1932	9.91
9	Ralph Kiner, 1949	9.84
10	Mickey Mantle, 1956	9.76
11	Hack Wilson, 1930	9.57
12	Babe Ruth, 1926	9.49
	Hank Aaron, 1971	9.49
14	Jim Gentile, 1961	9.47
15	Babe Ruth, 1930	9.46
16	Willie Stargell, 1971	9.39
17	Willie Mays, 1965	9.32
18	Babe Ruth, 1929	9.22
19	Boog Powell, 1964	9.20
20	Willie McCovey, 1969	9.16
21	Ted Williams, 1957	9.05
22	Ralph Kiner, 1947	9.03
23	Dave Kingman, 1979	9.02
24	Babe Ruth, 1932	8.97
25	Jimmie Foxx, 1938	8.85
26	Harmon Killebrew, 1969	8.83
27	Mark McGwire, 1987	8.80
28	Willie Mays, 1955	8.79
29	Mike Schmidt, 1980	8.76
30	Mike Schmidt, 1981	8.76
31	Harmon Killebrew, 1963	8.74
32	Johnny Mize, 1947	8.70
33	Babe Ruth, 1924	8.70
	Harmon Killebrew, 1962	8.70
35	Babe Ruth, 1922	8.62
36	Babe Ruth, 1931	8.61
37	Ralph Kiner, 1950	8.59
38	Reggie Jackson, 1969	8.56
39	Ted Kluszewski, 1954	8.55
40	Frank Robinson, 1966	8.51
41	Harmon Killebrew, 1961	8.50
42	Harmon Killebrew, 1964	8.49
43	Lou Gehrig, 1934	8.46
	Lou Gehrig, 1936	8.46
45	George Foster, 1977	8.46
46	Willie Stargell, 1973	8.43
47	Hank Greenberg, 1946	8.41
48	Eddie Mathews, 1954	8.40
49	Rocky Colavito, 1958	8.38
50	Jimmie Foxx, 1933	8.38
51	Joe Adcock, 1956	8.37
52	Jack Clark, 1987	8.35
53	Mike Schmidt, 1979	8.32
54	Eddie Mathews, 1955	8.22
55	Jimmie Foxx, 1934	8.16
56	Willie Mays, 1964	8.13
57	Eddie Mathews, 1953	8.12
58	Ted Williams, 1941	8.11
59	Frank Howard, 1969	8.11
60	Mickey Mantle, 1958	8.09
61	Gorman Thomas, 1979	8.08
62	Lou Gehrig, 1927	8.05
63	Harmon Killebrew, 1967	8.04
	Hank Aaron, 1969	8.04
65	Reggie Jackson, 1980	7.98
66	Mickey Mantle, 1962	7.96
67	Duke Snider, 1956	7.93
68	Darrell Evans, 1985	7.92
69	Ralph Kiner, 1951	7.91
70	Roy Campanella, 1953	7.90
71	Willie Mays, 1962	7.89
	Andre Dawson, 1987	7.89
73	Hank Sauer, 1954	7.88
74	Willie McCovey, 1970	7.88
75	Duke Snider, 1957	7.87
76	Orlando Cepeda, 1961	7.86
77	Babe Ruth, 1923	7.85
78	Roger Maris, 1960	7.82
79	Duke Snider, 1955	7.81
80	Dave Kingman, 1976	7.81
	Eric Davis, 1987	7.81
82	Willie McCovey, 1963	7.80
83	Harmon Killebrew, 1970	7.78
84	Frank Howard, 1970	7.77
	Dale Murphy, 1987	7.77
86	Eddie Mathews, 1959	7.74
87	Rogers Hornsby, 1925	7.74
88	Rocky Colavito, 1961	7.72
89	Mel Ott, 1929	7.71
90	George Bell, 1987	7.70
91	Harmon Killebrew, 1959	7.69
	Norm Cash, 1962	7.69
	Dave Johnson, 1973	7.69
94	Ted Kluszewski, 1955	7.68
95	Cy Williams, 1923	7.66
	Norm Cash, 1961	7.66
97	Ernie Banks, 1959	7.64
98	Dick Allen, 1966	7.63
99	Ernie Banks, 1958	7.62
100	Hank Aaron, 1962	7.60

Home Run Pctg. (by era)

1876-1892

1	Ned Williamson, 1884	6.47
2	Fred Pfeffer, 1884	5.35
3	Cap Anson, 1884	4.42
4	Abner Dalrymple, 1884	4.22
5	Billy O'Brien, 1887	4.19
6	Sam Thompson, 1889	3.75
7	Roger Connor, 1887	3.61
8	Dan Brouthers, 1884	3.52
9	Harry Stovey, 1889	3.42
10	Bug Holliday, 1889	3.37
11	Fred Pfeffer, 1887	3.34
12	Harry Stovey, 1883	3.33
13	Jerry Denny, 1889	3.11
14	Dan Brouthers, 1881	2.96
15	Mike Tiernan, 1891	2.95

1893-1919

1	Babe Ruth, 1919	6.71
2	Bill Joyce, 1894	4.79
3	Gavvy Cravath, 1915	4.60
4	Jack Clements, 1893	4.52
5	Buck Freeman, 1899	4.25
6	Gavvy Cravath, 1914	3.81
7	Jim Canavan, 1894	3.65
8	Frank Schulte, 1911	3.64
9	Gavvy Cravath, 1913	3.62
10	Bill Joyce, 1895	3.59
11	Sherry Magee, 1911	3.37
12	Vic Saier, 1914	3.35
13	Sam Thompson, 1895	3.35
14	Hugh Duffy, 1894	3.34
15	Ed Delahanty, 1893	3.19

1920-1941

1	Babe Ruth, 1920	11.79
2	Babe Ruth, 1927	11.11
3	Babe Ruth, 1921	10.93
4	Hank Greenberg, 1938	10.43
5	Babe Ruth, 1928	10.07
6	Jimmie Foxx, 1932	9.91
7	Hack Wilson, 1930	9.57
8	Babe Ruth, 1926	9.49
9	Babe Ruth, 1930	9.46
10	Babe Ruth, 1929	9.22
11	Babe Ruth, 1932	8.97
12	Jimmie Foxx, 1938	8.85
13	Babe Ruth, 1924	8.70
14	Babe Ruth, 1922	8.62
15	Babe Ruth, 1931	8.61

1942-1960

1	Ralph Kiner, 1949	9.84
2	Mickey Mantle, 1956	9.76
3	Ted Williams, 1957	9.05
4	Ralph Kiner, 1947	9.03
5	Willie Mays, 1955	8.79
6	Johnny Mize, 1947	8.70
7	Ralph Kiner, 1950	8.59
8	Ted Kluszewski, 1954	8.55
9	Hank Greenberg, 1946	8.41
10	Eddie Mathews, 1954	8.40
11	Rocky Colavito, 1958	8.38
12	Joe Adcock, 1956	8.37
13	Eddie Mathews, 1955	8.22
14	Eddie Mathews, 1953	8.12
15	Mickey Mantle, 1958	8.09

1961-1988

1	Mickey Mantle, 1961	10.51
2	Roger Maris, 1961	10.34
3	Hank Aaron, 1971	9.49
4	Jim Gentile, 1961	9.47
5	Willie Stargell, 1971	9.39
6	Willie Mays, 1965	9.32
7	Boog Powell, 1964	9.20
8	Willie McCovey, 1969	9.16
9	Dave Kingman, 1979	9.02
10	Harmon Killebrew, 1969	8.83
11	Mark McGwire, 1987	8.80
12	Mike Schmidt, 1981	8.76
13	Mike Schmidt, 1980	8.76
14	Harmon Killebrew, 1963	8.74
15	Harmon Killebrew, 1962	8.70

Total Bases

1	Babe Ruth, 1921	457
2	Rogers Hornsby, 1922	450
3	Lou Gehrig, 1927	447
4	Chuck Klein, 1930	445
5	Jimmie Foxx, 1932	438
6	Stan Musial, 1948	429
7	Hack Wilson, 1930	423
8	Chuck Klein, 1932	420
9	Lou Gehrig, 1930	419
10	Joe DiMaggio, 1937	418
11	Babe Ruth, 1927	417
12	Babe Herman, 1930	416
13	Lou Gehrig, 1931	410
14	Rogers Hornsby, 1929	409
	Lou Gehrig, 1934	409
16	Joe Medwick, 1937	406
	Jim Rice, 1978	406
18	Chuck Klein, 1929	405
	Hal Trosky, 1936	405
20	Jimmie Foxx, 1933	403
	Lou Gehrig, 1936	403
22	Hank Aaron, 1959	400
23	George Sisler, 1920	399
	Babe Ruth, 1923	399
25	Jimmie Foxx, 1938	398
26	Lefty O'Doul, 1929	397
	Hank Greenberg, 1937	397
28	Al Simmons, 1925	392
	Bill Terry, 1930	392
	Al Simmons, 1930	392
31	Babe Ruth, 1924	391
32	Hank Greenberg, 1935	389
33	Babe Ruth, 1920	388
	George Foster, 1977	388
	Don Mattingly, 1986	388
36	Earl Averill, 1936	385
37	Hank Greenberg, 1940	384
38	Stan Musial, 1949	382
	Willie Mays, 1955	382
	Willie Mays, 1962	382
	Jim Rice, 1977	382
42	Rogers Hornsby, 1925	381
43	Babe Ruth, 1928	380
	Hank Greenberg, 1938	380
	Frank Robinson, 1962	380
46	Babe Ruth, 1930	379
	Ernie Banks, 1958	379
48	Rogers Hornsby, 1921	378
	Duke Snider, 1954	378
50	Willie Mays, 1954	377
51	Mickey Mantle, 1956	376
52	Babe Ruth, 1931	374
	Hal Trosky, 1934	374
	Tony Oliva, 1964	374
55	Rogers Hornsby, 1924	373
	Al Simmons, 1929	373
	Bill Terry, 1932	373
	Billy Williams, 1970	373
59	Hugh Duffy, 1894	372
60	Lou Gehrig, 1932	370
	Duke Snider, 1953	370
	Hank Aaron, 1963	370
	Don Mattingly, 1985	370
64	Kiki Cuyler, 1925	369
	Ripper Collins, 1934	369
	Jimmie Foxx, 1936	369
	Hank Aaron, 1957	369
	Jim Rice, 1979	369
	George Bell, 1987	369
70	Johnny Mize, 1940	368
	Ted Williams, 1949	368
	Ted Kluszewski, 1954	368
73	Ty Cobb, 1911	367
	Ken Williams, 1922	367
	Heinie Manush, 1928	367
	Al Simmons, 1932	367
	Joe Medwick, 1936	367
	Joe DiMaggio, 1936	367
	Tommy Holmes, 1945	367
	Al Rosen, 1953	367
	Frank Robinson, 1966	367
	Robin Yount, 1982	367
83	Lou Gehrig, 1937	366
	Stan Musial, 1946	366
	Willie Mays, 1957	366
	Roger Maris, 1961	366
	Hank Aaron, 1962	366
88	Harry Heilmann, 1921	365
	Babe Ruth, 1926	365
	Chuck Klein, 1933	365
	Joe Medwick, 1935	365
	Kirby Puckett, 1986	365
93	Lou Gehrig, 1928	364
94	Dale Alexander, 1929	363
	Eddie Mathews, 1953	363
	George Brett, 1979	363
97	Jim Bottomley, 1928	362
98	4 players tied	361

Runs Batted In

1	Hack Wilson, 1930	190
2	Lou Gehrig, 1931	184
3	Hank Greenberg, 1937	183
4	Lou Gehrig, 1927	175
	Jimmie Foxx, 1938	175
6	Lou Gehrig, 1930	174
7	Babe Ruth, 1921	171
8	Chuck Klein, 1930	170
	Hank Greenberg, 1935	170
10	Jimmie Foxx, 1932	169
11	Joe DiMaggio, 1937	167
12	Sam Thompson, 1887	166
13	Sam Thompson, 1895	165
	Al Simmons, 1930	165
	Lou Gehrig, 1934	165
16	Babe Ruth, 1927	164
17	Babe Ruth, 1931	163
	Jimmie Foxx, 1933	163
19	Hal Trosky, 1936	162
20	Hack Wilson, 1929	159
	Lou Gehrig, 1937	159
	Ted Williams, 1949	159
	Vern Stephens, 1949	159
24	Al Simmons, 1929	157
25	Jimmie Foxx, 1930	156
26	Ken Williams, 1922	155
	Joe DiMaggio, 1948	155
28	Babe Ruth, 1929	154
	Joe Medwick, 1937	154
30	Babe Ruth, 1930	153
	Tommy Davis, 1962	153
32	Rogers Hornsby, 1922	152
	Lou Gehrig, 1936	152
34	Mel Ott, 1929	151
	Lou Gehrig, 1932	151
	Al Simmons, 1932	151
37	Hank Greenberg, 1940	150
38	Rogers Hornsby, 1929	149
	George Foster, 1977	149
40	Johnny Bench, 1970	148
41	Cap Anson, 1886	147
42	Ed Delahanty, 1893	146
	Babe Ruth, 1926	146
	Hank Greenberg, 1938	146
45	Hugh Duffy, 1894	145
	Chuck Klein, 1929	145
	Ted Williams, 1939	145
	Al Rosen, 1953	145
	Don Mattingly, 1985	145
50	Walt Dropo, 1950	144
	Vern Stephens, 1950	144
52	Hardy Richardson, 1890	143
	Rogers Hornsby, 1925	143
	Earl Averill, 1931	143
	Don Hurst, 1932	143
	Jimmie Foxx, 1936	143
	Ernie Banks, 1959	143
58	Lou Gehrig, 1928	142
	Babe Ruth, 1928	142
	Hal Trosky, 1934	142
	Roy Campanella, 1953	142
	Orlando Cepeda, 1961	142
	Roger Maris, 1961	142
64	Sam Thompson, 1894	141
	Ted Kluszewski, 1954	141
	Jim Gentile, 1961	141
	Willie Mays, 1962	141
68	Joe DiMaggio, 1938	140
	Rocky Colavito, 1961	140
	Harmon Killebrew, 1969	140
71	Harry Heilmann, 1921	139
	Lou Gehrig, 1933	139
	Hank Greenberg, 1934	139
	Jim Rice, 1978	139
	Don Baylor, 1979	139
76	Bob Meusel, 1925	138
	Goose Goslin, 1930	138
	Joe Medwick, 1936	138
	Zeke Bonura, 1936	138
	Johnny Mize, 1947	138
81	Ed Delahanty, 1899	137
	Babe Ruth, 1920	137
	Jim Bottomley, 1929	137
	Dale Alexander, 1929	137
	Chuck Klein, 1932	137
	Babe Ruth, 1932	137
	Johnny Mize, 1940	137
	Ted Williams, 1942	137
	Vern Stephens, 1948	137
	Joe Torre, 1971	137
	Andre Dawson, 1987	137
92	George Kelly, 1924	136
	Jim Bottomley, 1928	136
	Ed Morgan, 1930	136
	Duke Snider, 1955	136
	Frank Robinson, 1962	136
97	5 players tied	135

Runs Batted In per Game

1	Sam Thompson, 1894	1.42
2	Sam Thompson, 1895	1.39
3	Sam Thompson, 1887	1.31
4	Hack Wilson, 1930	1.23
5	Al Simmons, 1930	1.20
6	Hank Greenberg, 1937	1.19
7	Lou Gehrig, 1931	1.19
8	Cap Anson, 1886	1.18
9	Jimmie Foxx, 1938	1.17
10	Hugh Duffy, 1894	1.16
11	Dave Orr, 1890	1.16
12	Ed Delahanty, 1894	1.15
13	Babe Ruth, 1929	1.14
14	Tom Burns, 1884	1.13
15	Lou Gehrig, 1930	1.13
16	Lou Gehrig, 1927	1.13
17	Babe Ruth, 1921	1.13
18	Babe Ruth, 1931	1.12
19	Hank Greenberg, 1935	1.12
20	Ed Delahanty, 1893	1.11
21	Joe DiMaggio, 1937	1.11
22	Hardy Richardson, 1890	1.10
23	Al Simmons, 1929	1.10
24	Jimmie Foxx, 1932	1.10
25	Jimmie Foxx, 1933	1.09
26	Chuck Klein, 1930	1.09
27	Babe Ruth, 1927	1.09
28	Oyster Burns, 1890	1.08
29	Hal Trosky, 1936	1.07
30	Lou Gehrig, 1934	1.07
31	Ed McKean, 1893	1.06
32	Hack Wilson, 1929	1.06
33	Walt Dropo, 1950	1.06
34	Babe Ruth, 1930	1.06
35	Buck Ewing, 1893	1.05
36	Lave Cross, 1894	1.05
37	Joe DiMaggio, 1939	1.05
38	Dan Brouthers, 1894	1.04
39	Rogers Hornsby, 1925	1.04
40	Jim O'Rourke, 1890	1.04
41	George Davis, 1897	1.03
42	Babe Ruth, 1932	1.03
43	Ted Williams, 1949	1.03
	Vern Stephens, 1949	1.03
45	Ed Delahanty, 1896	1.02
46	Steve Brodie, 1895	1.02
	Joe Kelley, 1895	1.02
48	Jimmie Foxx, 1930	1.02
49	Hank Greenberg, 1940	1.01
50	Ken Williams, 1922	1.01
	Joe DiMaggio, 1948	1.01
52	Lou Gehrig, 1937	1.01
53	Cap Anson, 1882	1.01
54	George Decker, 1894	1.01
55	George Brett, 1980	1.01
56	Joe DiMaggio, 1940	1.01
57	Mel Ott, 1929	1.01
58	Nap Lajoie, 1897	1.00
	Al Simmons, 1931	1.00
60	Roger Connor, 1889	.99
61	Tommy McCarthy, 1894	.99
62	Jake Beckley, 1890	.99
63	Dan Brouthers, 1883	.99
64	Joe Medwick, 1937	.99
65	Rogers Hornsby, 1922	.99
66	Roy Campanella, 1953	.99
67	Jimmy Collins, 1897	.99
68	Ed McKean, 1894	.98
69	Bug Holliday, 1894	.98
70	Lou Gehrig, 1936	.98
71	Al Simmons, 1932	.98
72	Walt Wilmot, 1894	.98
73	Cap Anson, 1881	.98
74	Chuck Klein, 1929	.97
	Ted Williams, 1939	.97
76	Heinie Reitz, 1894	.97
77	Lou Gehrig, 1932	.97
78	Vern Stephens, 1950	.97
79	Joe DiMaggio, 1938	.97
80	Babe Ruth, 1920	.96
81	Cap Anson, 1885	.96
82	Hugh Duffy, 1897	.96
83	Sam Thompson, 1893	.96
84	Billy Nash, 1893	.96
85	Babe Ruth, 1926	.96
86	Harry Heilmann, 1929	.96
87	Tommy McCarthy, 1893	.96
88	Rogers Hornsby, 1929	.96
89	Hughie Jennings, 1895	.95
	Nap Lajoie, 1901	.95
91	Don Hurst, 1932	.95
92	Jim Gentile, 1961	.95
93	Jack Doyle, 1894	.95
94	Bill Dickey, 1937	.95
95	Ted Kluszewski, 1954	.95
96	George Kelly, 1924	.94
97	George Foster, 1977	.94
98	Hank Greenberg, 1938	.94
99	Rudy York, 1938	.94
100	Tommy Davis, 1962	.94

Walks

1	Babe Ruth, 1923	170
2	Ted Williams, 1947	162
	Ted Williams, 1949	162
4	Ted Williams, 1946	156
5	Eddie Yost, 1956	151
6	Eddie Joost, 1949	149
7	Babe Ruth, 1920	148
	Eddie Stanky, 1945	148
	Jim Wynn, 1969	148
10	Jimmy Sheckard, 1911	147
11	Mickey Mantle, 1957	146
12	Ted Williams, 1941	145
	Ted Williams, 1942	145
	Harmon Killebrew, 1969	145
15	Babe Ruth, 1921	144
	Babe Ruth, 1926	144
	Eddie Stanky, 1950	144
	Ted Williams, 1951	144
19	Babe Ruth, 1924	142
20	Eddie Yost, 1950	141
21	Babe Ruth, 1927	138
22	Eddie Stanky, 1946	137
	Roy Cullenbine, 1947	137
	Ralph Kiner, 1951	137
	Willie McCovey, 1970	137
26	Jack Crooks, 1892	136
	Babe Ruth, 1930	136
	Ferris Fain, 1949	136
	Ted Williams, 1954	136
	Jack Clark, 1987	136
31	Babe Ruth, 1928	135
	Eddie Yost, 1959	135
33	Ferris Fain, 1950	133
34	Lou Gehrig, 1935	132
	Frank Howard, 1970	132
	Joe Morgan, 1975	132
37	Bob Elliott, 1948	131
	Eddie Yost, 1954	131
	Harmon Killebrew, 1967	131
40	Babe Ruth, 1932	130
	Lou Gehrig, 1936	130
42	Eddie Yost, 1952	129
	Mickey Mantle, 1958	129
44	Max Bishop, 1929	128
	Max Bishop, 1930	128
	Babe Ruth, 1931	128
	Harmon Killebrew, 1970	128
	Carl Yastrzemski, 1970	128
	Mike Schmidt, 1983	128
50	Lu Blue, 1931	127
	Lou Gehrig, 1937	127
	Eddie Stanky, 1951	127
	Jim Wynn, 1976	127
54	Billy Hamilton, 1894	126
	Lu Blue, 1929	126
	Ted Williams, 1948	126
	Eddie Yost, 1951	126
	Mickey Mantle, 1961	126
	Darrell Evans, 1974	126
60	Richie Ashburn, 1954	125
	Eddie Yost, 1960	125
	Gene Tenace, 1977	125
	Wade Boggs, 1988	125
64	John McGraw, 1899	124
	Norm Cash, 1961	124
	Eddie Mathews, 1963	124
	Darrell Evans, 1973	124
68	Bill Joyce, 1890	123
	Eddie Yost, 1953	123
	Ken Singleton, 1973	123
71	Jimmy Sheckard, 1912	122
	Lou Gehrig, 1929	122
	Luke Appling, 1935	122
	Ralph Kiner, 1950	122
	Eddie Joost, 1952	122
	Mickey Mantle, 1962	122
	John Mayberry, 1973	122
78	Jack Crooks, 1893	121
	Topsy Hartsel, 1905	121
	Roy Cullenbine, 1941	121
	Luke Appling, 1949	121
	Willie McCovey, 1969	121
	Darrell Porter, 1979	121
	Von Hayes, 1987	121
85	Cupid Childs, 1893	120
	Eddie Lake, 1947	120
	Joe Morgan, 1974	120
	Mike Schmidt, 1979	120
89	13 players tied	119

Strikeouts

1	Bobby Bonds, 1970	189
2	Bobby Bonds, 1969	187
3	Rob Deer, 1987	186
4	Pete Incaviglia, 1986	185
5	Mike Schmidt, 1975	180
6	Rob Deer, 1986	179
7	Dave Nicholson, 1963	175
	Gorman Thomas, 1979	175
	Jose Canseco, 1986	175
10	Jim Presley, 1986	172
11	Reggie Jackson, 1968	171
12	Gorman Thomas, 1980	170
13	Juan Samuel, 1984	168
	Pete Incaviglia, 1987	168
15	Gary Alexander, 1978	166
	Steve Balboni, 1985	166
	Cory Snyder, 1987	166
18	Donn Clendenon, 1968	163
19	Butch Hobson, 1977	162
	Juan Samuel, 1987	162
21	Dick Allen, 1968	161
	Reggie Jackson, 1971	161
23	Bo Jackson, 1987	158
24	Dan Tartabull, 1986	157
	Jose Canseco, 1987	157
	Jim Presley, 1987	157
27	Tommie Agee, 1970	156
	Dave Kingman, 1982	156
	Reggie Jackson, 1982	156
	Tony Armas, 1984	156
31	Frank Howard, 1967	155
	Jeff Burroughs, 1975	155
33	Willie Stargell, 1971	154
	Larry Parrish, 1987	154
35	Dave Kingman, 1975	153
	Andres Galarraga, 1988	153
	Rob Deer, 1988	153
	Pete Incaviglia, 1988	153
39	George Scott, 1966	152
	Larry Hisle, 1969	152
41	Don Lock, 1963	151
	Greg Luzinski, 1975	151
	Juan Samuel, 1988	151
44	Dick Allen, 1965	150
	Nate Colbert, 1970	150
	Ron Kittle, 1983	150
47	Billy Grabarkewitz, 1970	149
	Mike Schmidt, 1976	149
	Fred McGriff, 1988	149
50	Bobby Bonds, 1973	148
	Mike Schmidt, 1983	148
	Gorman Thomas, 1983	148
53	Deron Johnson, 1971	146
	Nate Colbert, 1973	146
	Steve Balboni, 1986	146
	Jesse Barfield, 1986	146
	Bo Jackson, 1988	146
58	Lee May, 1972	145
	Bobby Darwin, 1972	145
	Dale Murphy, 1978	145
61	Dick Stuart, 1963	144
	Bobby Knoop, 1966	144
	Dick Allen, 1969	144
64	Nelson Mathews, 1964	143
	Byron Browne, 1966	143
	Rick Monday, 1968	143
	Gorman Thomas, 1982	143
	Jesse Barfield, 1985	143
69	Harmon Killebrew, 1962	142
	Donn Clendenon, 1966	142
	Lee May, 1969	142
	Jim Wynn, 1969	142
	Reggie Jackson, 1969	142
	Cito Gaston, 1970	142
	Juan Samuel, 1986	142
76	Jake Wood, 1961	141
	Frank Howard, 1968	141
	Bobby Bonds, 1977	141
	Reggie Jackson, 1984	141
	Dale Murphy, 1985	141
	Juan Samuel, 1985	141
	Dale Murphy, 1986	141
	Darryl Strawberry, 1986	141
	Jesse Barfield, 1987	141
	Jack Clark, 1988	141
86	Dave Kingman, 1972	140
	Greg Luzinski, 1977	140
	Reggie Jackson, 1983	140
89	Larry Hisle, 1970	139
	Ron LeFlore, 1975	139
	Steve Balboni, 1984	139
	Jack Clark, 1987	139
93	Jim Lemon, 1956	138
	Dick Allen, 1964	138
	Mike Schmidt, 1974	138
	George Foster, 1978	138
	Jerry Martin, 1982	138
	Reggie Jackson, 1985	138
99	11 players tied	137

At Bats per Strikeout

1	Mike McGeary, 1876	276.0
2	Cap Anson, 1878	261.0
3	Joe Sewell, 1932	167.7
4	John Peters, 1876	158.0
5	Joe Sewell, 1925	152.0
6	John Clapp, 1876	149.0
7	Joe Sewell, 1929	144.5
8	Jack Doyle, 1894	140.7
9	Joe Start, 1877	135.5
10	Joe Start, 1876	132.0
11	Joe Sewell, 1933	131.0
12	Levi Meyerle, 1876	128.0
13	Jim Holdsworth, 1876	120.5
14	Lon Knight, 1876	120.0
15	Charlie Hollocher, 1922	118.4
16	Ezra Sutton, 1876	118.0
17	Monte Ward, 1893	117.6
18	Bobby Mathews, 1876	109.0
19	Stuffy McInnis, 1922	107.4
20	Paul Hines, 1876	101.7
21	Deacon White, 1876	101.0
22	Willie Keeler, 1894	98.3
23	Al Spalding, 1876	97.3
24	Stuffy McInnis, 1924	96.8
25	Joe Sewell, 1926	96.3
26	Davy Force, 1876	95.7
27	Joe Start, 1878	95.0
28	Joe Quinn, 1895	90.5
29	Monte Ward, 1894	90.0
30	Deacon White, 1877	88.7
31	Cap Anson, 1881	85.8
32	Cap Anson, 1877	85.0
33	Everett Mills, 1876	84.7
34	John Cassidy, 1877	83.7
35	Joe Sewell, 1927	81.3
36	Dan Brouthers, 1889	80.8
37	Joe Start, 1879	79.3
38	Joe Quinn, 1893	78.1
39	Pie Traynor, 1929	77.1
40	Cal McVey, 1876	77.0
41	Lave Cross, 1894	75.6
42	Tom Carey, 1876	72.3
43	Steve Brodie, 1894	71.6
44	Ned Cuthbert, 1876	70.8
45	Tommy Holmes, 1945	70.7
46	Jack Glasscock, 1893	69.7
47	Wes Fisler, 1876	69.5
48	Sam Rice, 1929	68.4
49	Monte Ward, 1889	68.4
50	Emil Verban, 1947	67.5
51	George Hall, 1876	67.0
52	Lave Cross, 1895	66.9
53	Tom York, 1876	65.8
54	Tris Speaker, 1927	65.4
55	Joe Sewell, 1928	65.3
56	Sam Rice, 1925	64.9
57	Stuffy McInnis, 1921	64.9
58	Homer Summa, 1926	64.6
59	Mickey Cochrane, 1929	64.3
60	Jack Glasscock, 1890	64.0
61	Mike Dorgan, 1881	63.5
62	Ed McKean, 1896	63.4
63	Eddie Collins, 1923	63.1
64	Dummy Hoy, 1893	62.7
65	Lloyd Waner, 1933	62.5
66	Patsy Donovan, 1893	62.4
67	Lou Boudreau, 1948	62.2
68	Farmer Vaughn, 1896	61.9
69	Mickey Cochrane, 1927	61.7
70	Frankie Frisch, 1927	61.7
71	Joe Sewell, 1931	60.5
72	Willie Keeler, 1896	60.4
73	Jack Glasscock, 1887	60.4
74	Jimmy Hallinan, 1876	60.0
75	Lave Cross, 1893	59.3
76	Joe Gerhardt, 1876	58.4
77	Lou Bierbauer, 1894	58.3
	Dan Brouthers, 1894	58.3
79	Lou Bierbauer, 1895	58.3
80	Jack Glasscock, 1889	58.2
81	Dale Mitchell, 1949	58.2
82	Sam Dungan, 1893	58.1
83	Jim McCormick, 1880	57.8
84	Jack Manning, 1876	57.6
85	Tommy Holmes, 1944	57.4
86	Freddy Leach, 1931	57.2
87	Eddie Booth, 1876	57.0
88	Pie Traynor, 1928	56.9
89	Roger Connor, 1885	56.9
90	Dale Mitchell, 1952	56.8
91	Nellie Fox, 1958	56.6
92	Jack Farrell, 1880	56.5
93	Lloyd Waner, 1938	56.3
94	Sam Rice, 1921	56.1
95	Tommy Holmes, 1942	55.8
96	George Pinkney, 1893	55.8
97	John Morrill, 1876	55.6
98	Dan Brouthers, 1887	55.6
99	Ivy Olson, 1922	55.1
100	Jimmy Brown, 1942	55.1

Strikeouts per At Bat

1	Rob Deer, 1987	39.24
2	Dave Nicholson, 1963	38.98
3	Rob Deer, 1986	38.41
4	Pete Incaviglia, 1986	34.26
5	Gary Alexander, 1978	33.33
6	Jack Clark, 1987	33.17
7	Pete Incaviglia, 1987	33.01
8	Dick Allen, 1969	32.88
9	Mike Schmidt, 1975	32.03
10	Reggie Jackson, 1970	31.69
11	Larry Hisle, 1969	31.54
12	Gorman Thomas, 1979	31.42
13	Rob Deer, 1988	31.10
14	Reggie Jackson, 1968	30.92
15	Dick Allen, 1968	30.90
16	Dan Tartabull, 1986	30.72
17	Dave Kingman, 1975	30.48
18	Willie Stargell, 1971	30.14
19	Bobby Bonds, 1969	30.06
20	Reggie Jackson, 1985	30.00
21	Frank Howard, 1967	29.87
22	Dave Kingman, 1981	29.75
23	Darryl Strawberry, 1986	29.68
24	Rick Monday, 1968	29.67
25	Dave Kingman, 1972	29.66
26	Willie Mays, 1971	29.50
27	Reggie Jackson, 1982	29.43
28	Gorman Thomas, 1978	29.42
29	Ron Kittle, 1984	29.40
30	Jose Canseco, 1986	29.17
31	Dave Kingman, 1982	29.16
32	Ron Kittle, 1983	28.85
33	Cory Snyder, 1987	28.77
34	Jim Wynn, 1969	28.69
35	Steve Balboni, 1986	28.52
36	Bobby Bonds, 1970	28.51
37	Dave Kingman, 1976	28.48
38	Don Lock, 1963	28.44
39	Jack Clark, 1988	28.43
40	Reggie Jackson, 1971	28.40
41	Eric Davis, 1987	28.27
42	Bobby Darwin, 1972	28.27
43	Gary Pettis, 1985	28.22
44	Billy Grabarkewitz, 1970	28.17
45	Jim Presley, 1986	27.92
46	Donn Clendenon, 1968	27.91
47	Fred McGriff, 1988	27.80
48	Jim Gentile, 1964	27.79
49	Mike Schmidt, 1983	27.72
50	Steve Balboni, 1985	27.67
51	Gorman Thomas, 1983	27.66
52	Larry Parrish, 1987	27.65
53	Nate Colbert, 1973	27.60
54	Reggie Jackson, 1986	27.45
55	Dale Murphy, 1978	27.36
56	Butch Hobson, 1977	27.32
57	Mike Marshall, 1983	27.31
58	Jim Presley, 1987	27.30
59	Gene Tenace, 1977	27.23
60	Mike Epstein, 1970	27.21
61	Gorman Thomas, 1980	27.07
62	Reggie Jackson, 1984	26.86
63	Don Lock, 1964	26.76
64	Bobby Knoop, 1967	26.61
65	Jerry Martin, 1982	26.59
66	Pancho Herrera, 1960	26.56
67	Jesse Barfield, 1985	26.53
68	Jeff Burroughs, 1975	26.50
69	Mike Marshall, 1985	26.45
70	Jack Howell, 1987	26.28
71	Eric Davis, 1988	26.27
72	Nate Colbert, 1970	26.22
73	Tony Armas, 1981	26.14
74	Frank Meinke, 1884	26.10
75	Willie Stargell, 1972	26.06
76	Gorman Thomas, 1985	26.03
77	Bob Allison, 1965	26.03
	Reggie Jackson, 1978	26.03
79	Jack Howell, 1988	26.00
80	Dick Allen, 1966	25.95
81	Bobby Knoop, 1968	25.91
	John Shelby, 1988	25.91
83	Bobby Bonds, 1975	25.90
84	Reggie Jackson, 1969	25.87
85	Billy Cowan, 1964	25.75
86	Harmon Killebrew, 1962	25.72
87	Dick Allen, 1970	25.71
88	Mickey Mantle, 1967	25.68
89	Jim Lemon, 1956	25.65
90	Mike Schmidt, 1976	25.51
91	Gene Tenace, 1975	25.50
92	Mike Schmidt, 1982	25.49
93	Phil Bradley, 1986	25.48
94	Nate Colbert, 1969	25.47
95	Boog Powell, 1966	25.46
96	George Foster, 1971	25.37
97	Greg Luzinski, 1975	25.34
98	Leroy Stanton, 1977	25.33
99	George Scott, 1966	25.29
100	Dick Stuart, 1965	25.28

Batting Average

1	Hugh Duffy, 1894	.440
2	Tip O'Neill, 1887	.435
3	Ross Barnes, 1876	.429
4	Nap Lajoie, 1901	.426
5	Willie Keeler, 1897	.424
6	Rogers Hornsby, 1924	.424
7	George Sisler, 1922	.420
8	Ty Cobb, 1911	.420
9	Fred Dunlap, 1884	.412
10	Ty Cobb, 1912	.410
11	Ed Delahanty, 1899	.410
12	Jesse Burkett, 1896	.410
13	Jesse Burkett, 1895	.409
14	Joe Jackson, 1911	.408
15	Sam Thompson, 1894	.407
16	George Sisler, 1920	.407
17	Ed Delahanty, 1894	.407
18	Ted Williams, 1941	.406
19	Billy Hamilton, 1894	.404
20	Ed Delahanty, 1895	.404
21	Rogers Hornsby, 1925	.403
22	Harry Heilmann, 1923	.403
23	Pete Browning, 1887	.402
24	Rogers Hornsby, 1922	.401
25	Bill Terry, 1930	.401
26	Hughie Jennings, 1896	.401
27	Ty Cobb, 1922	.401
28	Cap Anson, 1881	.399
29	Lefty O'Doul, 1929	.398
30	Harry Heilmann, 1927	.398
31	Rogers Hornsby, 1921	.397
32	Ed Delahanty, 1896	.397
33	Jesse Burkett, 1899	.396
34	Joe Jackson, 1912	.395
35	Harry Heilmann, 1921	.394
36	Babe Ruth, 1923	.393
37	Harry Heilmann, 1925	.393
38	Babe Herman, 1930	.393
39	Joe Kelley, 1894	.393
40	Sam Thompson, 1895	.392
41	John McGraw, 1899	.391
42	Ty Cobb, 1913	.390
43	Fred Clarke, 1897	.390
44	Al Simmons, 1931	.390
45	George Brett, 1980	.390
46	Tris Speaker, 1925	.389
47	Bill Lange, 1895	.389
48	Billy Hamilton, 1895	.389
49	Ty Cobb, 1921	.389
50	Ted Williams, 1957	.388
51	King Kelly, 1886	.388
52	Rod Carew, 1977	.388
53	Luke Appling, 1936	.388
54	Tris Speaker, 1920	.388
55	Deacon White, 1877	.387
56	Al Simmons, 1925	.387
57	Rogers Hornsby, 1928	.387
58	Tris Speaker, 1916	.386
59	Willie Keeler, 1896	.386
60	Chuck Klein, 1930	.386
61	Lave Cross, 1894	.386
	Hughie Jennings, 1895	.386
63	Willie Keeler, 1898	.385
64	Arky Vaughan, 1935	.385
65	Rogers Hornsby, 1923	.384
66	Ty Cobb, 1919	.384
67	Nap Lajoie, 1910	.384
68	Ty Cobb, 1910	.383
69	Jesse Burkett, 1897	.383
70	Tris Speaker, 1912	.383
71	Ty Cobb, 1917	.383
72	Lefty O'Doul, 1930	.383
73	Joe Jackson, 1920	.382
74	Ty Cobb, 1918	.382
75	Honus Wagner, 1900	.381
76	Babe Herman, 1929	.381
77	Joe DiMaggio, 1939	.381
78	Al Simmons, 1930	.381
79	Paul Waner, 1927	.380
80	Rogers Hornsby, 1929	.380
81	Billy Hamilton, 1893	.380
82	Tris Speaker, 1923	.380
83	Goose Goslin, 1928	.379
84	Freddy Lindstrom, 1930	.379
85	Willie Keeler, 1899	.379
86	Lou Gehrig, 1930	.379
87	John Cassidy, 1877	.378
88	Pete Browning, 1882	.378
89	Ty Cobb, 1925	.378
90	Babe Ruth, 1924	.378
91	Sam Crawford, 1911	.378
92	Tris Speaker, 1922	.378
93	Earl Averill, 1936	.378
94	Babe Ruth, 1921	.378
95	Heinie Manush, 1928	.378
96	Heinie Manush, 1926	.378
97	Ed Delahanty, 1897	.377
98	Willie Keeler, 1895	.377
99	Ty Cobb, 1909	.377
100	Cy Seymour, 1905	.377

Batting Average (by era)

1876-1892

1	Tip O'Neill, 1887	.435
2	Ross Barnes, 1876	.429
3	Fred Dunlap, 1884	.412
4	Pete Browning, 1887	.402
5	Cap Anson, 1881	.399
6	King Kelly, 1886	.388
7	Deacon White, 1877	.387
8	John Cassidy, 1877	.378
9	Pete Browning, 1882	.378
10	Dan Brouthers, 1883	.374
11	Pete Browning, 1890	.373
12	Dan Brouthers, 1889	.373
13	Dave Orr, 1890	.373
14	Sam Thompson, 1887	.372
15	Tommy Tucker, 1889	.372

1893-1919

1	Hugh Duffy, 1894	.440
2	Nap Lajoie, 1901	.426
3	Willie Keeler, 1897	.424
4	Ty Cobb, 1911	.420
5	Ty Cobb, 1912	.410
6	Ed Delahanty, 1899	.410
7	Jesse Burkett, 1896	.410
8	Jesse Burkett, 1895	.409
9	Joe Jackson, 1911	.408
10	Sam Thompson, 1894	.407
11	Ed Delahanty, 1894	.407
12	Billy Hamilton, 1894	.404
13	Ed Delahanty, 1895	.404
14	Hughie Jennings, 1896	.401
15	Ed Delahanty, 1896	.397

1920-1941

1	Rogers Hornsby, 1924	.424
2	George Sisler, 1922	.420
3	George Sisler, 1920	.407
4	Ted Williams, 1941	.406
5	Rogers Hornsby, 1925	.403
6	Harry Heilmann, 1923	.403
7	Rogers Hornsby, 1922	.401
8	Bill Terry, 1930	.401
9	Ty Cobb, 1922	.401
10	Lefty O'Doul, 1929	.398
11	Harry Heilmann, 1927	.398
12	Rogers Hornsby, 1921	.397
13	Harry Heilmann, 1921	.394
14	Babe Ruth, 1923	.393
15	Harry Heilmann, 1925	.393

1942-1960

1	Ted Williams, 1957	.388
2	Stan Musial, 1948	.376
3	Ted Williams, 1948	.369
4	Stan Musial, 1946	.365
5	Mickey Mantle, 1957	.365
6	Harry Walker, 1947	.363
7	Dixie Walker, 1944	.357
8	Stan Musial, 1943	.357
9	Ted Williams, 1942	.356
10	Phil Cavarretta, 1945	.355
11	Lou Boudreau, 1948	.355
12	Stan Musial, 1951	.355
13	Hank Aaron, 1959	.355
14	Billy Goodman, 1950	.354
15	Harvey Kuenn, 1959	.353

1961-1988

1	George Brett, 1980	.390
2	Rod Carew, 1977	.388
3	Tony Gwynn, 1987	.370
4	Wade Boggs, 1985	.368
5	Wade Boggs, 1988	.366
6	Rico Carty, 1970	.366
7	Rod Carew, 1974	.364
8	Wade Boggs, 1987	.363
9	Joe Torre, 1971	.363
10	Wade Boggs, 1983	.361
11	Norm Cash, 1961	.361
12	Rod Carew, 1975	.359
13	Roberto Clemente, 1967	.357
14	Wade Boggs, 1986	.357
15	Kirby Puckett, 1988	.356

Batting Average (by position)

First Base

1	George Sisler, 1922	.420
2	George Sisler, 1920	.407
3	Bill Terry, 1930	.401
4	Cap Anson, 1881	.399
5	Rod Carew, 1977	.388
6	Lou Gehrig, 1930	.379
7	Dan Brouthers, 1883	.374
8	Lou Gehrig, 1928	.374
9	Lou Gehrig, 1927	.373
10	Dan Brouthers, 1889	.373

Second Base

1	Ross Barnes, 1876	.429
2	Nap Lajoie, 1901	.426
3	Rogers Hornsby, 1924	.424
4	Fred Dunlap, 1884	.412
5	Rogers Hornsby, 1925	.403
6	Rogers Hornsby, 1922	.401
7	Rogers Hornsby, 1921	.397
8	Rogers Hornsby, 1928	.387
9	Nap Lajoie, 1910	.384
10	Rogers Hornsby, 1929	.380

Shortstop

1	Hughie Jennings, 1896	.401
2	Luke Appling, 1936	.388
3	Hughie Jennings, 1895	.386
4	Arky Vaughan, 1935	.385
5	Honus Wagner, 1905	.363
6	Hughie Jennings, 1897	.355
7	Honus Wagner, 1903	.355
8	Honus Wagner, 1908	.354
9	Honus Wagner, 1907	.350
10	Honus Wagner, 1904	.349

Third Base

1	John McGraw, 1899	.391
2	George Brett, 1980	.390
3	Lave Cross, 1894	.386
4	Freddy Lindstrom, 1930	.379
5	Heinie Zimmerman, 1912	.372
6	John McGraw, 1895	.369
7	Wade Boggs, 1985	.368
8	Denny Lyons, 1887	.367
9	Wade Boggs, 1988	.366
10	Pie Traynor, 1930	.366

Outfield

1	Hugh Duffy, 1894	.440
2	Tip O'Neill, 1887	.435
3	Willie Keeler, 1897	.424
4	Ty Cobb, 1911	.420
5	Ty Cobb, 1912	.410
6	Ed Delahanty, 1899	.410
7	Jesse Burkett, 1896	.410
8	Jesse Burkett, 1895	.409
9	Joe Jackson, 1911	.408
10	Sam Thompson, 1894	.407

Catcher

1	Cal McVey, 1877	.368
2	Mickey Cochrane, 1930	.357
3	Wilbert Robinson, 1894	.353
4	Spud Davis, 1933	.349
5	Mickey Cochrane, 1931	.349
6	Ernie Lombardi, 1938	.342
7	Gabby Hartnett, 1930	.339
8	Mickey Cochrane, 1932	.338
9	Ted Simmons, 1975	.332
10	Bill Dickey, 1937	.332

Relative Batting Average

1	Fred Dunlap, 1884	1.667
2	Ross Barnes, 1876	1.608
3	Tip O'Neill, 1887	1.564
4	Nap Lajoie, 1910	1.537
5	Ty Cobb, 1910	1.534
6	Pete Browning, 1882	1.526
7	Cap Anson, 1881	1.512
8	King Kelly, 1886	1.508
9	Ty Cobb, 1912	1.507
10	Roger Connor, 1885	1.507
11	Tris Speaker, 1916	1.506
12	Ty Cobb, 1917	1.501
13	Nap Lajoie, 1904	1.500
14	Nap Lajoie, 1901	1.500
15	Ty Cobb, 1911	1.494
16	Ty Cobb, 1909	1.492
17	Ted Williams, 1957	1.476
18	Ty Cobb, 1913	1.475
19	Ted Williams, 1941	1.472
20	Ty Cobb, 1918	1.469
21	George Gore, 1880	1.461
22	Rogers Hornsby, 1924	1.461
23	Rod Carew, 1977	1.458
24	Orator Shaffer, 1884	1.455
25	Dan Brouthers, 1885	1.455
26	Joe Jackson, 1911	1.453
27	Joe Jackson, 1912	1.451
28	Dan Brouthers, 1882	1.449
29	Dave Orr, 1884	1.448
30	George Brett, 1980	1.448
31	Ty Cobb, 1915	1.448
32	Pete Browning, 1887	1.446
33	Ty Cobb, 1916	1.445
34	Cap Anson, 1886	1.442
35	Pete Browning, 1885	1.439
36	Dan Brouthers, 1886	1.439
37	Honus Wagner, 1908	1.434
38	George Sisler, 1922	1.433
39	Cap Anson, 1882	1.428
40	Cy Seymour, 1905	1.425
41	Willie Keeler, 1897	1.422
42	Ed Delahanty, 1899	1.414
43	Wade Boggs, 1988	1.413
44	King Kelly, 1884	1.411
45	Joe Jackson, 1913	1.410
46	Rod Carew, 1974	1.408
47	Wade Boggs, 1985	1.407
48	Tris Speaker, 1912	1.406
49	Deacon White, 1877	1.405
50	Dan Brouthers, 1883	1.401
51	Chicken Wolf, 1890	1.401
52	Stan Musial, 1948	1.400
53	George Stone, 1906	1.400
54	Cap Anson, 1888	1.399
55	George Sisler, 1920	1.398
56	Joe Torre, 1971	1.397
57	Hugh Duffy, 1894	1.395
58	Stan Musial, 1946	1.392
59	Ty Cobb, 1919	1.392
60	Rod Carew, 1975	1.391
61	Tommy Tucker, 1889	1.390
62	Nap Lajoie, 1906	1.390
63	John Reilly, 1884	1.389
64	Ed Swartwood, 1883	1.389
65	Harry Heilmann, 1923	1.389
66	Mickey Mantle, 1957	1.388
67	Willie Keeler, 1898	1.387
68	Honus Wagner, 1907	1.387
69	Roberto Clemente, 1967	1.385
70	George Sisler, 1917	1.383
71	Jim O'Rourke, 1884	1.383
72	Pete Browning, 1886	1.382
73	Tris Speaker, 1917	1.380
74	Ezra Sutton, 1884	1.380
75	Ty Cobb, 1907	1.379
76	Hick Carpenter, 1882	1.379
77	Roger Connor, 1886	1.378
78	Jesse Burkett, 1896	1.378
79	Paul Hines, 1879	1.377
80	Tony Gwynn, 1987	1.375
81	Pete Browning, 1884	1.374
82	Tris Speaker, 1913	1.374
83	Kirby Puckett, 1988	1.374
84	John Cassidy, 1877	1.373
85	Honus Wagner, 1905	1.372
86	Dave Orr, 1886	1.372
87	Rico Carty, 1970	1.372
88	George Hall, 1876	1.372
89	Tip O'Neill, 1888	1.371
90	Eddie Collins, 1909	1.370
91	Wade Boggs, 1987	1.370
92	Dan Brouthers, 1889	1.370
93	Ty Cobb, 1922	1.369
94	Norm Cash, 1961	1.368
95	Cap Anson, 1880	1.367
96	Jesse Burkett, 1899	1.367
97	Willie Keeler, 1904	1.366
98	Jesse Burkett, 1901	1.365
99	Hardy Richardson, 1886	1.365
100	Wade Boggs, 1986	1.365

On Base Percentage

1	Ted Williams, 1941	.551
2	John McGraw, 1899	.547
3	Babe Ruth, 1923	.545
4	Babe Ruth, 1920	.530
5	Ted Williams, 1957	.528
6	Billy Hamilton, 1894	.523
7	Ted Williams, 1954	.516
8	Babe Ruth, 1926	.516
9	Mickey Mantle, 1957	.515
10	Babe Ruth, 1924	.513
11	Babe Ruth, 1921	.512
12	Rogers Hornsby, 1924	.507
13	Joe Kelley, 1894	.502
14	Hugh Duffy, 1894	.502
15	Ed Delahanty, 1895	.500
16	Ted Williams, 1942	.499
17	Ted Williams, 1947	.499
18	Rogers Hornsby, 1928	.498
19	Ted Williams, 1946	.497
20	Ted Williams, 1948	.497
21	Bill Joyce, 1894	.496
22	Babe Ruth, 1931	.495
23	Babe Ruth, 1930	.493
24	Arky Vaughan, 1935	.491
25	Ted Williams, 1949	.490
26	Billy Hamilton, 1895	.490
27	Billy Hamilton, 1893	.490
28	Tip O'Neill, 1887	.490
29	Rogers Hornsby, 1925	.489
	Babe Ruth, 1932	.489
31	Norm Cash, 1961	.488
32	Mickey Mantle, 1962	.488
33	Babe Ruth, 1927	.487
34	Ty Cobb, 1915	.486
35	Jesse Burkett, 1895	.486
36	Tris Speaker, 1920	.483
37	King Kelly, 1886	.483
38	Harry Heilmann, 1923	.481
39	Wade Boggs, 1988	.480
40	Billy Hamilton, 1898	.480
41	Tris Speaker, 1925	.479
	Ted Williams, 1956	.479
43	Ed Delahanty, 1894	.478
44	Lou Gehrig, 1936	.478
45	Billy Hamilton, 1896	.477
46	Cupid Childs, 1894	.475
47	Harry Heilmann, 1927	.475
48	John McGraw, 1898	.474
49	Tris Speaker, 1922	.474
50	Lou Gehrig, 1927	.474
51	Luke Appling, 1936	.474
52	Lou Gehrig, 1930	.473
53	Lou Gehrig, 1937	.473
54	Hughie Jennings, 1896	.472
55	Ed Delahanty, 1896	.472
56	John McGraw, 1897	.471
57	Joe Morgan, 1975	.471
58	Dan Brouthers, 1891	.471
59	Tris Speaker, 1916	.470
60	Bill Joyce, 1896	.470
61	Joe Kelley, 1896	.469
62	Tris Speaker, 1923	.469
63	Jimmie Foxx, 1932	.469
64	Jesse Burkett, 1897	.468
65	Ty Cobb, 1925	.468
66	Joe Jackson, 1911	.468
67	Lou Gehrig, 1928	.467
68	Ty Cobb, 1913	.467
69	George Sisler, 1922	.467
70	Mike Griffin, 1894	.467
71	Cupid Childs, 1896	.467
72	Mickey Mantle, 1956	.467
73	Wade Boggs, 1987	.467
74	Ty Cobb, 1911	.467
75	Dan Brouthers, 1890	.466
76	Lou Gehrig, 1935	.466
77	Lou Gehrig, 1934	.465
78	Lefty O'Doul, 1929	.465
79	Jimmie Foxx, 1939	.464
80	Tris Speaker, 1912	.464
81	Pete Browning, 1887	.464
82	Ted Williams, 1951	.464
83	Willie Keeler, 1897	.464
84	Bob Caruthers, 1887	.463
85	Ed Delahanty, 1899	.463
86	Cupid Childs, 1893	.463
87	Jimmie Foxx, 1929	.463
88	Hughie Jennings, 1897	.463
89	Jesse Burkett, 1899	.463
90	Ross Barnes, 1876	.462
	Jimmie Foxx, 1938	.462
	Ted Williams, 1958	.462
93	Dan Brouthers, 1889	.462
94	Ty Cobb, 1922	.462
95	Babe Ruth, 1928	.461
96	Jack Clark, 1987	.461
97	Eddie Collins, 1925	.461
98	Billy Hamilton, 1897	.461
99	Jesse Burkett, 1896	.461
100	Fred Clarke, 1897	.461

Slugging Average

1	Babe Ruth, 1920	.847
2	Babe Ruth, 1921	.846
3	Babe Ruth, 1927	.772
4	Lou Gehrig, 1927	.765
5	Babe Ruth, 1923	.764
6	Rogers Hornsby, 1925	.756
7	Jimmie Foxx, 1932	.749
8	Babe Ruth, 1924	.739
9	Babe Ruth, 1926	.737
10	Ted Williams, 1941	.735
11	Babe Ruth, 1930	.732
12	Ted Williams, 1957	.731
13	Hack Wilson, 1930	.723
14	Rogers Hornsby, 1922	.722
15	Lou Gehrig, 1930	.721
16	Babe Ruth, 1928	.709
17	Al Simmons, 1930	.708
18	Lou Gehrig, 1934	.706
19	Mickey Mantle, 1956	.705
20	Jimmie Foxx, 1938	.704
21	Jimmie Foxx, 1933	.703
22	Stan Musial, 1948	.702
23	Babe Ruth, 1931	.700
24	Babe Ruth, 1929	.697
25	Lou Gehrig, 1936	.696
26	Rogers Hornsby, 1924	.696
27	Jimmie Foxx, 1939	.694
28	Tip O'Neill, 1887	.691
29	Hugh Duffy, 1894	.690
30	Mickey Mantle, 1961	.687
31	Chuck Klein, 1930	.687
32	Sam Thompson, 1894	.686
33	Hank Greenberg, 1938	.683
34	Rogers Hornsby, 1929	.679
35	Babe Herman, 1930	.678
36	Joe DiMaggio, 1937	.673
37	Babe Ruth, 1922	.672
38	Joe DiMaggio, 1939	.671
39	Hank Greenberg, 1940	.670
40	Hank Aaron, 1971	.669
41	Hank Greenberg, 1937	.668
42	Ted Williams, 1946	.667
43	Willie Mays, 1954	.667
44	Mickey Mantle, 1957	.665
45	George Brett, 1980	.664
46	Lou Gehrig, 1931	.662
47	Norm Cash, 1961	.662
48	Babe Ruth, 1932	.661
49	Willie Mays, 1955	.659
50	Ralph Kiner, 1949	.658
51	Chuck Klein, 1929	.657
52	Babe Ruth, 1919	.657
53	Willie McCovey, 1969	.656
54	Sam Thompson, 1895	.654
55	Jimmie Foxx, 1934	.653
56	Chick Hafey, 1930	.652
57	Ted Williams, 1949	.650
58	Bill Joyce, 1894	.648
59	Lou Gehrig, 1928	.648
60	Ted Williams, 1942	.648
61	Duke Snider, 1954	.647
62	Chuck Klein, 1932	.646
63	Jim Gentile, 1961	.646
64	Willie Stargell, 1973	.646
65	Willie Mays, 1965	.645
66	Mike Schmidt, 1981	.644
67	Hal Trosky, 1936	.644
68	Nap Lajoie, 1901	.643
69	Joe DiMaggio, 1941	.643
70	Lou Gehrig, 1937	.643
71	Ted Kluszewski, 1954	.642
72	Al Simmons, 1929	.642
73	Joe Medwick, 1937	.641
74	Al Simmons, 1931	.641
75	Ralph Kiner, 1947	.639
76	Rogers Hornsby, 1921	.639
77	Frank Robinson, 1966	.637
78	Jimmie Foxx, 1930	.637
79	Fred Lynn, 1979	.637
80	Hank Aaron, 1959	.636
81	Johnny Mize, 1940	.636
82	Jimmie Foxx, 1935	.636
83	Mel Ott, 1929	.635
84	Ted Williams, 1954	.635
85	Ted Williams, 1947	.634
86	Chick Hafey, 1929	.632
87	George Sisler, 1920	.632
88	Rogers Hornsby, 1928	.632
89	Harry Heilmann, 1923	.632
	Dick Allen, 1966	.632
91	Ed Delahanty, 1896	.631
92	George Foster, 1977	.631
93	Jimmie Foxx, 1936	.631
94	Gabby Hartnett, 1930	.630
95	Jim Bottomley, 1928	.628
96	Hank Greenberg, 1935	.628
97	Duke Snider, 1955	.628
98	Willie Stargell, 1971	.628
99	Rogers Hornsby, 1923	.627
100	Ken Williams, 1922	.627

Production

1	Babe Ruth, 1920	1.378
2	Babe Ruth, 1921	1.358
3	Babe Ruth, 1923	1.309
4	Ted Williams, 1941	1.286
5	Babe Ruth, 1927	1.259
6	Ted Williams, 1957	1.259
7	Babe Ruth, 1926	1.253
8	Babe Ruth, 1924	1.252
9	Rogers Hornsby, 1925	1.245
10	Lou Gehrig, 1927	1.240
11	Babe Ruth, 1930	1.225
12	Jimmie Foxx, 1932	1.218
13	Rogers Hornsby, 1924	1.203
14	Babe Ruth, 1931	1.195
15	Lou Gehrig, 1930	1.194
16	Hugh Duffy, 1894	1.192
17	Rogers Hornsby, 1922	1.181
18	Tip O'Neill, 1887	1.180
19	Mickey Mantle, 1957	1.179
20	Hack Wilson, 1930	1.177
21	Lou Gehrig, 1936	1.174
22	Mickey Mantle, 1956	1.172
23	Lou Gehrig, 1934	1.172
24	Babe Ruth, 1928	1.170
25	Jimmie Foxx, 1938	1.166
26	Ted Williams, 1946	1.164
27	Jimmie Foxx, 1939	1.158
28	Jimmie Foxx, 1933	1.153
29	Stan Musial, 1948	1.152
30	Ted Williams, 1954	1.151
31	Babe Ruth, 1932	1.150
32	Norm Cash, 1961	1.150
33	Ted Williams, 1942	1.147
34	Sam Thompson, 1894	1.145
35	Bill Joyce, 1894	1.143
36	Ted Williams, 1949	1.141
37	Rogers Hornsby, 1929	1.139
38	Mickey Mantle, 1961	1.138
39	Ted Williams, 1947	1.133
40	Babe Herman, 1930	1.132
41	Al Simmons, 1930	1.130
42	Rogers Hornsby, 1928	1.130
43	Babe Ruth, 1929	1.128
44	George Brett, 1980	1.124
45	Chuck Klein, 1930	1.123
46	Hank Greenberg, 1938	1.122
47	Joe DiMaggio, 1939	1.119
48	Ed Delahanty, 1895	1.117
49	Lou Gehrig, 1937	1.116
50	Lou Gehrig, 1928	1.115
51	Babe Ruth, 1919	1.114
52	Willie McCovey, 1969	1.114
53	Harry Heilmann, 1923	1.113
54	Ted Williams, 1948	1.112
55	Lou Gehrig, 1931	1.108
56	Babe Ruth, 1922	1.106
57	Hank Greenberg, 1937	1.105
58	Joe Kelley, 1894	1.104
59	Hank Greenberg, 1940	1.103
60	Ed Delahanty, 1896	1.103
61	Jimmie Foxx, 1934	1.102
62	Arky Vaughan, 1935	1.098
63	Rogers Hornsby, 1921	1.097
64	Jimmie Foxx, 1935	1.096
65	Nap Lajoie, 1901	1.094
66	Mickey Mantle, 1962	1.093
67	Harry Heilmann, 1927	1.091
68	Ralph Kiner, 1949	1.089
69	Jimmie Foxx, 1929	1.088
70	Ty Cobb, 1911	1.088
71	Lefty O'Doul, 1929	1.087
72	Rogers Hornsby, 1923	1.086
73	Al Simmons, 1931	1.085
74	Joe DiMaggio, 1937	1.085
75	Sam Thompson, 1895	1.085
76	Ted Williams, 1956	1.084
77	Mel Ott, 1929	1.084
78	Joe DiMaggio, 1941	1.083
79	Willie Mays, 1954	1.083
80	Mike Schmidt, 1981	1.083
81	Hank Aaron, 1971	1.082
82	George Sisler, 1920	1.082
83	Tris Speaker, 1922	1.080
84	Ralph Kiner, 1951	1.079
85	Tris Speaker, 1923	1.079
86	Jim Gentile, 1961	1.074
87	Duke Snider, 1954	1.074
88	Lou Gehrig, 1932	1.072
89	Bill Terry, 1930	1.071
90	Jimmie Foxx, 1936	1.071
91	Johnny Mize, 1939	1.070
92	Fred Dunlap, 1884	1.069
93	Jimmie Foxx, 1930	1.066
94	Ty Cobb, 1925	1.066
95	Earl Averill, 1936	1.065
96	Chuck Klein, 1929	1.065
97	Ed Delahanty, 1894	1.063
98	Stan Musial, 1951	1.063
99	Willie Mays, 1955	1.063
100	Fred Lynn, 1979	1.063

Adjusted Production

1	Babe Ruth, 1920	255
2	Fred Dunlap, 1884	249
3	Babe Ruth, 1921	235
4	Mickey Mantle, 1957	234
5	Babe Ruth, 1923	232
6	Babe Ruth, 1919	231
7	Pete Browning, 1882	231
8	Ted Williams, 1941	231
9	Babe Ruth, 1930	230
10	Babe Ruth, 1926	226
11	Babe Ruth, 1927	223
12	Babe Ruth, 1924	222
13	Babe Ruth, 1928	221
14	Lou Gehrig, 1930	221
15	Dave Orr, 1885	220
16	Jimmie Foxx, 1933	219
17	Ted Williams, 1957	219
18	Lou Gehrig, 1927	218
19	Honus Wagner, 1908	217
20	Babe Ruth, 1931	215
21	Ty Cobb, 1917	215
22	Rogers Hornsby, 1924	214
23	Ted Williams, 1954	213
24	Ted Williams, 1942	213
25	Norm Cash, 1961	213
26	Ty Cobb, 1910	211
27	Tip O'Neill, 1887	210
28	Roger Connor, 1886	209
29	Rogers Hornsby, 1925	209
30	Ty Cobb, 1912	209
31	Mickey Mantle, 1956	209
32	George Hall, 1876	208
33	Lou Gehrig, 1934	208
34	George Brett, 1980	207
35	Dan Brouthers, 1885	207
36	Mickey Mantle, 1961	207
37	Lou Gehrig, 1928	207
38	Stan Musial, 1948	207
39	Willie McCovey, 1969	206
40	Mickey Mantle, 1962	205
41	Babe Ruth, 1932	204
42	Rogers Hornsby, 1923	204
43	Nap Lajoie, 1901	203
44	Nap Lajoie, 1904	201
45	Nap Lajoie, 1910	201
46	Willie Stargell, 1973	200
47	Joe DiMaggio, 1939	199
48	Rogers Hornsby, 1928	199
49	Frank Robinson, 1967	199
50	Ted Williams, 1947	198
51	Ross Barnes, 1876	198
52	Harry Lumley, 1906	198
53	Rogers Hornsby, 1922	198
54	Harry Heilmann, 1923	198
55	Rogers Hornsby, 1921	197
56	Reggie Jackson, 1969	197
57	Lou Gehrig, 1936	197
58	Ed Swartwood, 1882	196
59	Orator Shaffer, 1878	196
60	Frank Robinson, 1966	196
61	Orator Shaffer, 1884	195
62	Ty Cobb, 1913	195
63	Ed Delahanty, 1899	195
64	Ted Williams, 1946	195
65	Ty Cobb, 1918	195
66	Ted Williams, 1948	194
67	Joe Jackson, 1912	193
68	Honus Wagner, 1904	193
69	Dave Orr, 1884	193
70	Dan Brouthers, 1882	193
71	Dan Brouthers, 1886	193
72	Pete Browning, 1884	193
73	Roger Connor, 1888	193
74	Tris Speaker, 1916	192
75	Lip Pike, 1876	192
76	Ed Delahanty, 1895	192
77	George Stone, 1906	191
78	Lou Gehrig, 1931	191
79	Ed Delahanty, 1902	191
80	Cupid Childs, 1890	191
81	Pedro Guerrero, 1985	191
82	Dick Allen, 1972	191
83	Cy Seymour, 1905	190
84	Dan Brouthers, 1883	190
85	Ed Swartwood, 1883	190
86	Willie Stargell, 1971	189
87	Joe Jackson, 1911	189
88	Rocky Colavito, 1958	189
89	King Kelly, 1879	189
90	Pete Browning, 1885	189
91	Willie McCovey, 1970	188
92	Ed Delahanty, 1896	188
93	Babe Ruth, 1929	188
94	John Reilly, 1884	188
95	Dan Brouthers, 1891	188
96	Roger Connor, 1882	188
97	Jim Gentile, 1961	188
98	Ty Cobb, 1911	187
99	Ted Williams, 1949	187
100	Joe DiMaggio, 1941	187

Batting Runs

1	Babe Ruth, 1921	119
2	Babe Ruth, 1923	119
3	Babe Ruth, 1920	113
4	Ted Williams, 1941	102
5	Lou Gehrig, 1927	101
6	Babe Ruth, 1924	101
7	Babe Ruth, 1927	101
8	Babe Ruth, 1926	97
9	Jimmie Foxx, 1932	97
10	Ted Williams, 1946	94
11	Rogers Hornsby, 1924	94
12	Ted Williams, 1942	93
13	Babe Ruth, 1931	92
14	Ted Williams, 1947	91
15	Stan Musial, 1948	90
16	Rogers Hornsby, 1922	90
17	Ted Williams, 1957	90
18	Babe Ruth, 1930	90
19	Mickey Mantle, 1957	89
20	Ted Williams, 1949	89
21	Lou Gehrig, 1930	88
22	Tip O'Neill, 1887	88
23	Rogers Hornsby, 1925	87
24	Norm Cash, 1961	86
25	Lou Gehrig, 1934	86
26	Babe Ruth, 1928	84
27	Mickey Mantle, 1956	83
28	Jimmie Foxx, 1933	83
29	Lou Gehrig, 1936	82
30	Lou Gehrig, 1931	80
31	Ty Cobb, 1911	78
32	Jimmie Foxx, 1938	78
33	Hugh Duffy, 1894	77
34	Carl Yastrzemski, 1967	76
35	Mickey Mantle, 1961	76
36	Willie McCovey, 1969	76
37	Lou Gehrig, 1928	76
38	Ted Williams, 1948	76
39	Hack Wilson, 1930	75
40	Ty Cobb, 1917	75
41	Rogers Hornsby, 1921	74
42	Rogers Hornsby, 1929	74
43	Frank Robinson, 1966	74
44	Lou Gehrig, 1937	73
45	George Sisler, 1920	73
46	Tris Speaker, 1912	73
47	Fred Dunlap, 1884	72
48	Rogers Hornsby, 1928	72
49	Stan Musial, 1949	72
50	Arky Vaughan, 1935	72
51	Joe Jackson, 1911	72
52	Carl Yastrzemski, 1970	72
53	Ty Cobb, 1915	72
54	Nap Lajoie, 1901	72
55	Babe Ruth, 1932	71
56	Ted Williams, 1954	71
57	Tris Speaker, 1923	71
58	Stan Musial, 1946	71
59	Ralph Kiner, 1951	71
60	Harry Heilmann, 1923	71
61	Joe Jackson, 1912	70
62	Stan Musial, 1951	70
63	Ralph Kiner, 1949	70
64	Ed Delahanty, 1899	70
65	Chuck Klein, 1933	69
66	Joe Medwick, 1937	69
67	Hank Greenberg, 1940	69
68	Johnny Mize, 1939	69
69	Babe Herman, 1930	69
70	Lou Gehrig, 1932	69
71	Lefty O'Doul, 1929	68
72	Nap Lajoie, 1910	68
73	Chuck Klein, 1932	68
74	Ed Delahanty, 1895	68
75	Ty Cobb, 1910	68
76	Ty Cobb, 1912	68
77	Wade Boggs, 1987	68
78	Chuck Klein, 1930	67
79	Jimmie Foxx, 1935	67
80	Hank Greenberg, 1937	67
81	Rod Carew, 1977	67
82	Frank Robinson, 1962	67
83	Babe Ruth, 1919	66
84	Jimmie Foxx, 1934	66
85	Ed Delahanty, 1896	66
86	Dick Allen, 1972	66
87	Jimmie Foxx, 1939	66
88	Hank Greenberg, 1938	66
89	Dan Brouthers, 1886	66
90	Cy Seymour, 1905	66
91	Wade Boggs, 1988	66
92	Tris Speaker, 1920	66
93	Harmon Killebrew, 1969	66
94	Joe Jackson, 1913	66
95	Stan Musial, 1943	65
96	Hank Aaron, 1971	65
97	Honus Wagner, 1908	65
98	George Brett, 1980	65
99	Willie Mays, 1965	65
100	Tris Speaker, 1916	65

Adjusted Batting Runs

1	Babe Ruth, 1921	117
2	Babe Ruth, 1923	115
3	Babe Ruth, 1920	111
4	Babe Ruth, 1924	102
5	Lou Gehrig, 1927	101
6	Babe Ruth, 1927	101
7	Ted Williams, 1941	100
8	Babe Ruth, 1930	99
9	Lou Gehrig, 1930	99
10	Babe Ruth, 1926	98
11	Mickey Mantle, 1957	93
12	Babe Ruth, 1931	93
13	Rogers Hornsby, 1924	92
14	Babe Ruth, 1928	91
15	Ted Williams, 1942	90
16	Jimmie Foxx, 1933	90
17	Stan Musial, 1948	90
18	Lou Gehrig, 1934	90
19	Norm Cash, 1961	89
20	Rogers Hornsby, 1922	89
21	Lou Gehrig, 1936	88
22	Rogers Hornsby, 1925	86
23	Ted Williams, 1947	85
24	Mickey Mantle, 1956	84
25	Ted Williams, 1957	84
26	Ted Williams, 1946	84
27	Jimmie Foxx, 1932	84
28	Lou Gehrig, 1928	83
29	Ted Williams, 1949	83
30	Lou Gehrig, 1931	82
31	Mickey Mantle, 1961	79
32	Rogers Hornsby, 1921	79
33	Tip O'Neill, 1887	79
34	Ty Cobb, 1917	76
35	Jimmie Foxx, 1938	76
36	Ted Williams, 1948	75
37	Willie McCovey, 1969	75
38	Babe Ruth, 1932	75
39	Rogers Hornsby, 1928	75
40	Harry Heilmann, 1923	73
41	Lou Gehrig, 1932	73
42	Frank Robinson, 1966	73
43	Rogers Hornsby, 1929	73
44	Ed Delahanty, 1899	72
45	Ty Cobb, 1911	72
46	Ty Cobb, 1912	72
47	Babe Ruth, 1919	72
48	Lou Gehrig, 1937	72
49	Nap Lajoie, 1901	71
50	Ted Williams, 1954	71
51	Hack Wilson, 1930	70
52	Tris Speaker, 1923	70
53	Fred Dunlap, 1884	70
54	Joe Jackson, 1911	69
55	Joe Jackson, 1912	69
56	Stan Musial, 1951	69
57	Ralph Kiner, 1949	69
58	Ed Delahanty, 1895	69
59	Jimmie Foxx, 1934	69
60	Nap Lajoie, 1910	69
61	Joe Medwick, 1937	68
62	Wade Boggs, 1987	68
63	Honus Wagner, 1908	68
64	Babe Herman, 1930	68
65	Reggie Jackson, 1969	68
66	Chuck Klein, 1935	68
67	Billy Hamilton, 1894	68
68	Lou Gehrig, 1933	68
69	Jimmie Foxx, 1935	67
70	Tris Speaker, 1912	67
71	Al Rosen, 1953	67
72	Hank Aaron, 1959	67
73	Ty Cobb, 1910	67
74	Arky Vaughan, 1935	67
75	Carl Yastrzemski, 1967	66
76	Stan Musial, 1946	66
77	Joe DiMaggio, 1941	66
78	Hank Greenberg, 1938	66
79	George Brett, 1980	66
80	Ralph Kiner, 1951	66
81	Ty Cobb, 1915	65
82	Willie McCovey, 1970	65
83	Frank Robinson, 1962	65
84	Tris Speaker, 1916	65
85	Al Simmons, 1930	65
86	Johnny Mize, 1939	65
87	Ed Delahanty, 1896	65
88	Rod Carew, 1977	65
89	Rogers Hornsby, 1920	64
90	Harmon Killebrew, 1969	64
91	Duke Snider, 1954	64
92	Cy Seymour, 1905	64
93	Willie Mays, 1955	64
94	Carl Yastrzemski, 1970	64
95	Stan Musial, 1949	63
96	George Sisler, 1920	63
97	Willie Stargell, 1973	63
98	Babe Ruth, 1929	63
99	Rogers Hornsby, 1927	63
100	Tris Speaker, 1920	63

#	Batting Wins		Adjusted Batting Wins		Runs Created		Total Average	
1	Babe Ruth, 1923	11.5	Babe Ruth, 1923	11.2	Babe Ruth, 1921	238	Babe Ruth, 1920	1.843
2	Babe Ruth, 1921	11.2	Babe Ruth, 1921	10.9	Babe Ruth, 1923	223	Babe Ruth, 1921	1.782
3	Babe Ruth, 1920	11.0	Babe Ruth, 1920	10.8	Hugh Duffy, 1894	216	Babe Ruth, 1923	1.746
4	Ted Williams, 1941	9.9	Ted Williams, 1941	9.7	Babe Ruth, 1920	211	Ted Williams, 1941	1.702
5	Ted Williams, 1946	9.9	Mickey Mantle, 1957	9.6	Lou Gehrig, 1927	208	Babe Ruth, 1926	1.634
6	Lou Gehrig, 1927	9.6	Lou Gehrig, 1927	9.6	Jimmie Foxx, 1932	207	Babe Ruth, 1927	1.615
7	Babe Ruth, 1927	9.6	Babe Ruth, 1924	9.6	Ty Cobb, 1911	207	Hugh Duffy, 1894	1.613
8	Babe Ruth, 1924	9.5	Babe Ruth, 1927	9.6	Billy Hamilton, 1894	206	Billy Hamilton, 1894	1.605
9	Ted Williams, 1942	9.5	Babe Ruth, 1926	9.5	Babe Ruth, 1924	205	Ted Williams, 1957	1.602
10	Ted Williams, 1947	9.4	Ted Williams, 1942	9.2	Babe Ruth, 1927	204	John McGraw, 1899	1.601
11	Babe Ruth, 1926	9.4	Rogers Hornsby, 1924	9.1	Ted Williams, 1941	202	Babe Ruth, 1924	1.596
12	Rogers Hornsby, 1924	9.3	Babe Ruth, 1930	9.0	Rogers Hornsby, 1922	200	Lou Gehrig, 1927	1.555
13	Ted Williams, 1957	9.3	Stan Musial, 1948	9.0	Lou Gehrig, 1936	199	Rogers Hornsby, 1925	1.549
14	Mickey Mantle, 1957	9.2	Lou Gehrig, 1930	8.9	Babe Ruth, 1926	196	Mickey Mantle, 1957	1.544
15	Stan Musial, 1948	9.0	Norm Cash, 1961	8.9	Lou Gehrig, 1930	195	Babe Ruth, 1930	1.538
16	Jimmie Foxx, 1932	8.9	Ted Williams, 1947	8.8	Lou Gehrig, 1934	195	Bill Joyce, 1894	1.528
17	Ted Williams, 1949	8.6	Ted Williams, 1946	8.8	Tip O'Neill, 1887	194	Ed Delahanty, 1895	1.517
18	Norm Cash, 1961	8.5	Babe Ruth, 1928	8.8	Ted Williams, 1949	193	Tip O'Neill, 1887	1.514
19	Babe Ruth, 1931	8.5	Babe Ruth, 1931	8.7	Babe Ruth, 1931	192	Joe Kelley, 1894	1.503
20	Rogers Hornsby, 1922	8.5	Ted Williams, 1957	8.7	Babe Ruth, 1930	191	Babe Ruth, 1931	1.499
21	Carl Yastrzemski, 1967	8.4	Jimmie Foxx, 1933	8.5	Stan Musial, 1948	191	Jimmie Foxx, 1932	1.470
22	Ty Cobb, 1917	8.3	Ty Cobb, 1917	8.5	Hack Wilson, 1930	189	Ty Cobb, 1911	1.464
23	Rogers Hornsby, 1925	8.2	Rogers Hornsby, 1922	8.4	Jimmie Foxx, 1938	189	Rogers Hornsby, 1924	1.461
24	Mickey Mantle, 1956	8.1	Lou Gehrig, 1934	8.3	Ted Williams, 1946	188	Ted Williams, 1954	1.452
25	Babe Ruth, 1928	8.1	Mickey Mantle, 1956	8.3	Mickey Mantle, 1956	188	Billy Hamilton, 1895	1.443
26	Babe Ruth, 1930	8.1	Ted Williams, 1949	8.0	Rogers Hornsby, 1925	187	Babe Ruth, 1932	1.439
27	Lou Gehrig, 1930	8.0	Rogers Hornsby, 1925	8.0	Ted Williams, 1947	186	Lou Gehrig, 1936	1.437
28	Willie McCovey, 1969	8.0	Lou Gehrig, 1928	8.0	Rogers Hornsby, 1924	186	Ted Williams, 1946	1.431
29	Lou Gehrig, 1934	8.0	Honus Wagner, 1908	7.9	Chuck Klein, 1930	186	Joe Kelley, 1896	1.430
30	Frank Robinson, 1966	7.9	Willie McCovey, 1969	7.9	Lou Gehrig, 1931	185	Mickey Mantle, 1956	1.429
31	Jimmie Foxx, 1933	7.8	Mickey Mantle, 1961	7.8	Ted Williams, 1942	185	Lou Gehrig, 1930	1.427
32	Ty Cobb, 1911	7.7	Frank Robinson, 1966	7.8	Jimmie Foxx, 1933	184	Babe Ruth, 1928	1.418
33	Ty Cobb, 1915	7.6	Rogers Hornsby, 1921	7.8	Rogers Hornsby, 1929	183	Lou Gehrig, 1934	1.414
34	Nap Lajoie, 1910	7.6	Lou Gehrig, 1936	7.7	Babe Herman, 1930	183	Hack Wilson, 1930	1.411
35	Honus Wagner, 1908	7.6	Jimmie Foxx, 1932	7.7	Babe Ruth, 1928	182	Rogers Hornsby, 1928	1.409
36	Mickey Mantle, 1961	7.6	Lou Gehrig, 1931	7.6	Lou Gehrig, 1937	181	Sam Thompson, 1894	1.409
37	Ty Cobb, 1910	7.5	Nap Lajoie, 1910	7.6	Joe Kelley, 1894	181	Ed Delahanty, 1896	1.405
38	Stan Musial, 1946	7.5	Babe Ruth, 1919	7.5	Lefty O'Doul, 1929	180	Jimmie Foxx, 1938	1.403
39	Dick Allen, 1972	7.5	Ty Cobb, 1910	7.4	Mickey Mantle, 1957	178	Ted Williams, 1942	1.400
40	Lou Gehrig, 1931	7.4	Carl Yastrzemski, 1967	7.3	Norm Cash, 1961	178	Ted Williams, 1947	1.394
41	Carl Yastrzemski, 1970	7.4	Ted Williams, 1948	7.3	Hank Greenberg, 1937	178	Mickey Mantle, 1961	1.387
42	Rogers Hornsby, 1921	7.3	Ted Williams, 1954	7.3	Joe Kelley, 1896	178	Billy Hamilton, 1893	1.386
43	Lou Gehrig, 1928	7.3	Rogers Hornsby, 1928	7.3	Billy Hamilton, 1895	177	Mickey Mantle, 1962	1.385
44	Ted Williams, 1948	7.3	Tris Speaker, 1916	7.2	Willie Keeler, 1897	176	Rogers Hornsby, 1922	1.384
45	Ted Williams, 1954	7.3	Ty Cobb, 1912	7.2	George Sisler, 1920	176	Bill Lange, 1895	1.373
46	Chuck Klein, 1933	7.3	Dick Allen, 1972	7.1	Ed Delahanty, 1895	175	Norm Cash, 1961	1.372
47	Lou Gehrig, 1936	7.3	Reggie Jackson, 1969	7.1	Tris Speaker, 1912	175	Bob Caruthers, 1887	1.368
48	Tris Speaker, 1912	7.3	Harry Heilmann, 1923	7.1	Ed Delahanty, 1899	175	King Kelly, 1886	1.366
49	Ty Cobb, 1909	7.2	Ty Cobb, 1911	7.1	Joe Jackson, 1911	175	Babe Ruth, 1919	1.358
50	Stan Musial, 1949	7.2	Stan Musial, 1946	7.0	Nap Lajoie, 1901	174	Jimmie Foxx, 1933	1.353
51	Tris Speaker, 1916	7.2	Stan Musial, 1951	7.0	Mickey Mantle, 1961	174	Babe Herman, 1930	1.351
52	Tip O'Neill, 1887	7.1	Ty Cobb, 1915	6.9	Ty Cobb, 1912	174	Ted Williams, 1949	1.349
53	Ralph Kiner, 1951	7.1	Babe Ruth, 1932	6.9	Stan Musial, 1949	173	Ted Williams, 1948	1.347
54	George Sisler, 1920	7.1	Joe Jackson, 1912	6.9	Joe DiMaggio, 1937	173	Lou Gehrig, 1937	1.347
55	Rogers Hornsby, 1928	7.1	Rogers Hornsby, 1920	6.9	Benny Kauff, 1914	172	Joe Morgan, 1976	1.346
56	Jimmie Foxx, 1938	7.1	Ralph Kiner, 1949	6.9	Hank Greenberg, 1938	172	Rogers Hornsby, 1929	1.338
57	Joe Jackson, 1911	7.1	Jimmie Foxx, 1938	6.9	Ted Williams, 1948	172	Ty Cobb, 1912	1.328
58	Stan Musial, 1951	7.0	Joe Jackson, 1911	6.8	Chuck Klein, 1932	171	Ty Cobb, 1910	1.321
59	Joe Jackson, 1912	7.0	Joe Medwick, 1937	6.8	Hank Greenberg, 1940	171	Jake Stenzel, 1894	1.320
60	Hank Aaron, 1971	7.0	Nap Lajoie, 1904	6.8	Ed Delahanty, 1896	170	Hank Greenberg, 1938	1.319
61	Stan Musial, 1943	7.0	Tris Speaker, 1923	6.8	Joe Medwick, 1937	170	Arky Vaughan, 1935	1.317
62	Arky Vaughan, 1935	7.0	Hank Aaron, 1963	6.8	Bill Terry, 1930	170	Billy Hamilton, 1896	1.316
63	Joe Jackson, 1913	7.0	Lou Gehrig, 1932	6.8	Stan Musial, 1951	169	Jimmie Foxx, 1934	1.316
64	Babe Ruth, 1919	7.0	Hank Aaron, 1959	6.7	Lou Gehrig, 1928	169	Bill Joyce, 1896	1.315
65	Ralph Kiner, 1949	6.9	Al Rosen, 1953	6.7	Rogers Hornsby, 1921	169	Ty Cobb, 1913	1.314
66	Harmon Killebrew, 1967	6.9	Harmon Killebrew, 1969	6.7	Earl Averill, 1936	168	Jimmie Foxx, 1939	1.313
67	Nap Lajoie, 1904	6.9	Tris Speaker, 1912	6.7	Jimmie Foxx, 1936	168	Tris Speaker, 1912	1.310
68	Harmon Killebrew, 1969	6.9	Joe Torre, 1971	6.6	Lou Gehrig, 1932	168	Joe Jackson, 1911	1.308
69	Johnny Mize, 1939	6.9	Rogers Hornsby, 1929	6.6	Sam Thompson, 1895	167	Joe Morgan, 1975	1.307
70	Tris Speaker, 1923	6.9	Stan Musial, 1943	6.6	Ted Williams, 1957	167	Harry Heilmann, 1923	1.306
71	Cy Seymour, 1905	6.8	Cy Seymour, 1905	6.6	Ed Delahanty, 1893	167	Harry Heilmann, 1927	1.303
72	Willie Mays, 1965	6.8	Carl Yastrzemski, 1970	6.6	Stan Musial, 1953	166	Jimmie Foxx, 1935	1.299
73	Harry Heilmann, 1923	6.8	Willie Stargell, 1973	6.6	Joe Jackson, 1912	166	Stan Musial, 1948	1.298
74	Hank Aaron, 1963	6.8	Lou Gehrig, 1937	6.6	Tris Speaker, 1923	166	Babe Ruth, 1929	1.297
75	Joe Medwick, 1937	6.8	Ralph Kiner, 1951	6.6	Jesse Burkett, 1896	166	Willie McCovey, 1969	1.296
76	Ty Cobb, 1912	6.8	Ed Delahanty, 1899	6.6	Jimmie Foxx, 1934	165	Lou Gehrig, 1931	1.295
77	Chuck Klein, 1932	6.7	George Brett, 1980	6.6	Ralph Kiner, 1951	165	Ed Delahanty, 1894	1.290
78	Rogers Hornsby, 1929	6.7	Carl Yastrzemski, 1968	6.6	Ty Cobb, 1917	165	Joe Kelley, 1895	1.289
79	Lou Gehrig, 1937	6.7	Joe Jackson, 1913	6.6	Jake Stenzel, 1894	165	Mel Ott, 1929	1.287
80	Rogers Hornsby, 1920	6.7	Wade Boggs, 1987	6.5	Jesse Burkett, 1895	164	Lou Gehrig, 1928	1.287
81	Joe Torre, 1971	6.7	Frank Robinson, 1962	6.5	Stan Musial, 1946	164	Nap Lajoie, 1901	1.285
82	Hack Wilson, 1930	6.7	Willie McCovey, 1970	6.5	Ralph Kiner, 1949	163	Hank Greenberg, 1937	1.285
83	Rod Carew, 1977	6.7	Ty Cobb, 1909	6.5	Arky Vaughan, 1935	163	Tris Speaker, 1922	1.284
84	Wade Boggs, 1988	6.7	Arky Vaughan, 1935	6.5	Jimmie Foxx, 1935	163	Jimmie Foxx, 1929	1.282
85	Frank Robinson, 1962	6.6	Johnny Mize, 1939	6.5	Al Simmons, 1930	163	George Brett, 1980	1.278
86	Mickey Mantle, 1958	6.6	Nap Lajoie, 1901	6.4	Johnny Mize, 1939	162	Al Simmons, 1930	1.278
87	Carl Yastrzemski, 1968	6.6	George Stone, 1906	6.4	Chuck Klein, 1933	162	Chuck Klein, 1930	1.274
88	Babe Ruth, 1932	6.6	Mickey Mantle, 1958	6.4	George Sisler, 1922	162	Willie Keeler, 1897	1.271
89	Billy Williams, 1972	6.6	Rod Carew, 1977	6.4	Joe DiMaggio, 1941	162	Sam Thompson, 1895	1.269
90	Joe Morgan, 1976	6.5	Jimmie Foxx, 1934	6.4	Duke Snider, 1954	161	Fred Clarke, 1897	1.269
91	Reggie Jackson, 1969	6.5	Lou Gehrig, 1933	6.4	Hank Greenberg, 1935	161	Babe Ruth, 1922	1.268
92	Hank Greenberg, 1940	6.5	Willie Mays, 1963	6.4	Duke Snider, 1953	161	Ty Cobb, 1915	1.267
93	Johnny Mize, 1940	6.5	Joe DiMaggio, 1941	6.4	Rod Carew, 1977	160	Jack Clark, 1987	1.265
94	George Brett, 1980	6.5	Tip O'Neill, 1887	6.4	Bill Lange, 1895	160	Jesse Burkett, 1895	1.265
95	Nap Lajoie, 1901	6.5	Hank Aaron, 1971	6.4	Denny Lyons, 1887	160	Hughie Jennings, 1896	1.263
96	Wade Boggs, 1987	6.4	Harmon Killebrew, 1967	6.4	Frank Robinson, 1962	160	Billy Hamilton, 1898	1.262
97	Duke Snider, 1954	6.4	Willie Stargell, 1971	6.4	Harry Heilmann, 1923	159	George Sisler, 1922	1.256
98	Ty Cobb, 1916	6.4	Lou Gehrig, 1935	6.3	Billy Hamilton, 1896	159	Ty Cobb, 1917	1.256
99	Tris Speaker, 1920	6.4	Joe Morgan, 1976	6.3	Harry Heilmann, 1921	159	Benny Kauff, 1914	1.256
100	Fred Dunlap, 1884	6.3	Jimmie Foxx, 1935	6.3	Chuck Klein, 1929	158	Ted Williams, 1956	1.255

Runs Produced

1	Lou Gehrig, 1931	301
2	Babe Ruth, 1921	289
3	Hugh Duffy, 1894	288
	Chuck Klein, 1930	288
5	Al Simmons, 1930	281
6	Hughie Jennings, 1895	280
	Hack Wilson, 1930	280
	Hank Greenberg, 1937	280
9	Sam Thompson, 1895	278
10	Lou Gehrig, 1927	277
11	Kiki Cuyler, 1930	276
	Lou Gehrig, 1930	276
13	Billy Hamilton, 1894	275
14	Ed Delahanty, 1894	274
15	Sam Thompson, 1887	273
16	Ed Delahanty, 1893	272
	Joe Kelley, 1895	272
	Joe DiMaggio, 1937	272
19	Joe Kelley, 1894	270
	Lou Gehrig, 1936	270
21	Ty Cobb, 1911	266
	Rogers Hornsby, 1929	266
	Babe Ruth, 1931	266
	Ted Williams, 1949	266
25	Jimmie Foxx, 1938	264
26	Ed Delahanty, 1899	263
27	Babe Ruth, 1927	262
	Jimmie Foxx, 1932	262
29	Al Simmons, 1932	260
	Lou Gehrig, 1937	260
31	Hugh Duffy, 1893	259
	Walt Wilmot, 1894	259
33	Hardy Richardson, 1890	258
34	Dan Brouthers, 1894	256
	Bobby Lowe, 1894	256
	Jake Stenzel, 1894	256
	Nap Lajoie, 1901	256
38	Hack Wilson, 1929	255
	Lou Gehrig, 1932	255
	Hank Greenberg, 1935	255
41	Cap Anson, 1886	254
	Willie Keeler, 1894	254
	Lou Gehrig, 1928	254
	Babe Ruth, 1930	254
45	Harry Stovey, 1889	252
46	Rogers Hornsby, 1922	251
	Babe Ruth, 1928	251
	Earl Averill, 1931	251
	Chuck Klein, 1932	251
50	Charlie Gehringer, 1934	250
51	Hugh Duffy, 1897	248
52	John McGraw, 1894	247
	Mel Ott, 1929	247
54	Hughie Jennings, 1896	246
	Tris Speaker, 1923	246
	Jimmie Foxx, 1930	246
	Zeke Bonura, 1936	246
	Tommy Davis, 1962	246
59	Sam Thompson, 1893	245
	Bill Terry, 1930	245
	Lou Gehrig, 1933	245
	Charlie Gehringer, 1936	245
	Ted Williams, 1939	245
64	Steve Brodie, 1894	244
	Ed Delahanty, 1895	244
	Ed Delahanty, 1896	244
	Ken Williams, 1922	244
	Lou Gehrig, 1934	244
	Hal Trosky, 1936	244
70	Tom Brown, 1891	243
71	Dan Brouthers, 1887	242
	Ed McKean, 1895	242
	Lefty O'Doul, 1929	242
	Ted Williams, 1942	242
75	Lave Cross, 1894	241
	Bill Dahlen, 1894	241
	Babe Ruth, 1920	241
78	Dan Brouthers, 1892	240
	Joe Kelley, 1896	240
	Ty Cobb, 1915	240
	George Sisler, 1920	240
	Babe Ruth, 1923	240
	Joe Cronin, 1930	240
	Jimmie Foxx, 1933	240
85	Hughie Jennings, 1894	239
	Vern Stephens, 1950	239
87	Babe Ruth, 1926	238
	Babe Herman, 1930	238
	Hank Greenberg, 1940	238
90	Rogers Hornsby, 1925	237
	Al Simmons, 1929	237
	Joe DiMaggio, 1938	237
93	Hugh Duffy, 1890	236
	Ed McKean, 1894	236
	Sam Thompson, 1894	236
	Willie Keeler, 1895	236
	George Davis, 1897	236
	Frank Baker, 1912	236
	Tris Speaker, 1920	236
	Rogers Hornsby, 1921	236

Clutch Hitting Index

1	Tom Burns, 1884	229
2	Tom Herr, 1987	200
3	Ed Abbaticchio, 1907	194
4	Bill McClellan, 1878	193
5	George Davis, 1906	179
6	Possum Whitted, 1920	178
7	Sam Crawford, 1910	176
8	Frank LaPorte, 1914	176
9	Jack Barry, 1913	176
10	Heinie Reitz, 1896	176
11	George Stovall, 1911	176
12	Stuffy McInnis, 1914	176
13	John Sullivan, 1943	175
14	Cy Seymour, 1908	175
15	Larry Kopf, 1920	174
16	Cookie Lavagetto, 1941	173
17	Cap Anson, 1893	172
18	Farmer Vaughn, 1893	172
19	Pie Traynor, 1928	172
20	Larry Gardner, 1920	171
21	Cap Anson, 1880	171
22	Heinie Zimmerman, 1917	171
23	Bill Dahlen, 1904	170
	Sherry Magee, 1918	170
25	Ned Williamson, 1885	170
26	Clyde Barnhart, 1925	170
27	Cap Anson, 1881	169
28	Cap Anson, 1885	169
29	Joe Kelley, 1898	169
30	John Gochnauer, 1903	168
31	Cap Anson, 1882	167
32	Jim O'Rourke, 1887	167
33	Maurice VanRobays, 1940	167
34	Monte Ward, 1881	167
35	Mike Higgins, 1938	167
36	Frank LaPorte, 1910	166
37	Bill Hague, 1878	166
38	Ross Youngs, 1921	166
39	Bob Ferguson, 1877	165
40	Deacon White, 1876	165
41	Johnny Berardino, 1941	165
42	Cap Anson, 1896	165
43	King Kelly, 1880	165
44	Larry Gardner, 1921	164
45	Bernie Friberg, 1924	164
46	Fred Pfeffer, 1886	164
47	Russ McKelvy, 1878	164
48	Steve Brodie, 1895	163
49	Tom Burns, 1888	163
50	Harmon Killebrew, 1971	163
51	Earl Sheely, 1931	163
52	Kid Gleason, 1897	163
53	John Ganzel, 1901	162
54	Joe Gerhardt, 1879	162
	Mike Dorgan, 1886	162
	Sam Mertes, 1905	162
57	Art Croft, 1877	162
	Sherry Magee, 1910	162
59	Dixie Walker, 1946	161
60	Joe Tinker, 1906	161
61	Enos Slaughter, 1952	161
62	Ed Konetchy, 1918	160
	Wally Pipp, 1923	160
64	Harry Swacina, 1914	160
65	Amos Otis, 1982	160
66	John Mayberry, 1976	160
67	Bill Brubaker, 1936	160
68	Tommy Corcoran, 1904	159
69	George Davis, 1902	159
70	Fred Pfeffer, 1885	159
	Milt Stock, 1923	159
72	Stuffy McInnis, 1918	159
73	Fred Pfeffer, 1882	159
74	Ed McKean, 1892	159
75	Tommy Corcoran, 1903	158
76	Enos Slaughter, 1950	158
77	Charlie Dexter, 1901	158
78	Jack Burdock, 1883	158
	Rudy York, 1946	158
80	Billy Nash, 1892	158
	Steve Evans, 1910	158
	Bobby Veach, 1915	158
	Irish Meusel, 1924	158
	Roy Schalk, 1945	158
85	Fred Hartman, 1898	158
86	Dixie Walker, 1945	157
87	Del Pratt, 1916	157
88	Glenn Wright, 1927	157
	Bob Elliott, 1945	157
90	Mike Mowrey, 1916	157
	Red Smith, 1918	157
92	Clyde Engle, 1909	157
	Bill Johnson, 1943	157
94	Denis Menke, 1969	157
95	Jim Nealon, 1906	156
96	Bid McPhee, 1896	156
	Gus Bell, 1959	156
	Tommy Davis, 1973	156
99	Art Fletcher, 1915	156
100	Ray Bates, 1917	156

Isolated Power

1	Babe Ruth, 1920	.472
2	Babe Ruth, 1921	.469
3	Babe Ruth, 1927	.417
4	Lou Gehrig, 1927	.392
5	Babe Ruth, 1928	.386
6	Jimmie Foxx, 1932	.385
7	Babe Ruth, 1930	.373
8	Babe Ruth, 1923	.372
9	Mickey Mantle, 1961	.370
10	Hank Greenberg, 1938	.369
11	Hack Wilson, 1930	.368
12	Babe Ruth, 1926	.366
13	Babe Ruth, 1924	.361
14	Babe Ruth, 1922	.357
15	Jimmie Foxx, 1938	.356
16	Rogers Hornsby, 1925	.353
17	Mickey Mantle, 1956	.353
18	Babe Ruth, 1929	.353
19	Roger Maris, 1961	.351
20	Ralph Kiner, 1949	.348
21	Jimmie Foxx, 1933	.347
22	Willie Stargell, 1973	.347
23	Lou Gehrig, 1934	.344
24	Jim Gentile, 1961	.344
25	Ted Williams, 1957	.343
26	Lou Gehrig, 1930	.343
27	Lou Gehrig, 1936	.342
28	Hank Aaron, 1971	.341
29	Willie Mays, 1955	.340
30	Mike Schmidt, 1980	.338
31	Willie McCovey, 1969	.336
32	Babe Ruth, 1919	.336
33	Jimmie Foxx, 1939	.334
34	Reggie Jackson, 1969	.333
35	Willie Stargell, 1971	.333
36	Hank Greenberg, 1937	.332
37	Hank Greenberg, 1940	.330
38	Ted Williams, 1941	.329
39	Mark McGwire, 1987	.329
40	Willie Mays, 1965	.328
41	Babe Ruth, 1931	.328
42	Mike Schmidt, 1981	.328
43	Hank Greenberg, 1946	.327
44	Joe DiMaggio, 1937	.327
45	Al Simmons, 1930	.327
46	Stan Musial, 1948	.326
47	Ralph Kiner, 1947	.326
48	Dave Kingman, 1979	.325
49	Ted Williams, 1946	.325
50	Eddie Mathews, 1953	.325
51	Willie McCovey, 1970	.323
52	Willie Mays, 1954	.322
53	Lou Gehrig, 1931	.321
54	Johnny Mize, 1940	.321
55	Frank Robinson, 1966	.321
56	Rogers Hornsby, 1922	.321
57	Duke Snider, 1955	.320
58	Babe Ruth, 1932	.319
59	Jimmie Foxx, 1934	.319
60	Ralph Kiner, 1951	.318
61	Ralph Kiner, 1950	.318
62	Harmon Killebrew, 1961	.318
63	Rocky Colavito, 1958	.317
64	Chick Hafey, 1930	.316
65	Boog Powell, 1964	.316
66	Ted Kluszewski, 1954	.316
67	Dick Allen, 1966	.315
68	Eddie Mathews, 1954	.313
69	Duke Snider, 1957	.313
70	Eddie Mathews, 1955	.313
71	Johnny Mize, 1947	.312
72	Willie Mays, 1964	.311
73	Willie Mays, 1962	.311
74	George Foster, 1977	.311
75	Mike Schmidt, 1979	.311
76	Jack Clark, 1987	.310
77	Hank Greenberg, 1939	.310
78	Harmon Killebrew, 1969	.308
79	Ted Williams, 1949	.307
80	Hank Aaron, 1969	.307
81	Duke Snider, 1954	.307
82	Mel Ott, 1929	.306
83	Duke Snider, 1956	.306
84	Joe Adcock, 1956	.306
85	Mickey Mantle, 1955	.306
86	Wally Berger, 1930	.305
87	Jim Bottomley, 1928	.304
88	Fred Lynn, 1979	.303
89	Harmon Killebrew, 1962	.303
90	Jimmie Foxx, 1930	.302
91	Chuck Klein, 1929	.302
92	Ernie Banks, 1958	.301
93	Norm Cash, 1961	.301
94	Chuck Klein, 1930	.301
95	Hank Greenberg, 1935	.300
96	Hal Trosky, 1936	.300
97	Ernie Banks, 1955	.300
98	Mike Schmidt, 1977	.300
99	Mickey Mantle, 1957	.300
	Eric Davis, 1987	.300

Extra Base Hits

1	Babe Ruth, 1921	119
2	Lou Gehrig, 1927	117
3	Chuck Klein, 1930	107
4	Chuck Klein, 1932	103
	Hank Greenberg, 1937	103
	Stan Musial, 1948	103
7	Rogers Hornsby, 1922	102
8	Lou Gehrig, 1930	100
	Jimmie Foxx, 1932	100
10	Babe Ruth, 1920	99
	Babe Ruth, 1923	99
	Hank Greenberg, 1940	99
13	Hank Greenberg, 1935	98
14	Babe Ruth, 1927	97
	Hack Wilson, 1930	97
	Joe Medwick, 1937	97
17	Hank Greenberg, 1934	96
	Hal Trosky, 1936	96
	Joe DiMaggio, 1937	96
20	Lou Gehrig, 1934	95
	Joe Medwick, 1936	95
22	Rogers Hornsby, 1929	94
	Chuck Klein, 1929	94
	Babe Herman, 1930	94
	Jimmie Foxx, 1933	94
26	Jim Bottomley, 1928	93
	Al Simmons, 1930	93
	Lou Gehrig, 1936	93
29	Babe Ruth, 1924	92
	Lou Gehrig, 1931	92
	Jimmie Foxx, 1938	92
	Stan Musial, 1953	92
	Hank Aaron, 1959	92
	Frank Robinson, 1962	92
35	Babe Ruth, 1928	91
36	Rogers Hornsby, 1925	90
	Stan Musial, 1949	90
	Willie Mays, 1962	90
	Willie Stargell, 1973	90
40	Hal Trosky, 1934	89
	Duke Snider, 1954	89
42	Joe DiMaggio, 1936	88
43	Tris Speaker, 1923	87
	Kiki Cuyler, 1925	87
	Lou Gehrig, 1928	87
	Ripper Collins, 1934	87
	Charlie Gehringer, 1936	87
	Johnny Mize, 1940	87
	Willie Mays, 1954	87
	Robin Yount, 1982	87
51	George Sisler, 1920	86
	Babe Ruth, 1930	86
	Wally Moses, 1937	86
	Johnny Mize, 1939	86
	Ted Williams, 1939	86
	Stan Musial, 1946	86
	Eddie Mathews, 1953	86
	Reggie Jackson, 1969	86
	Hal McRae, 1977	86
	Jim Rice, 1978	86
	Don Mattingly, 1985	86
	Don Mattingly, 1986	86
63	Tip O'Neill, 1887	85
	Chick Hafey, 1929	85
	Goose Goslin, 1930	85
	Lou Gehrig, 1932	85
	Lou Gehrig, 1933	85
	Earl Averill, 1934	85
	Hank Greenberg, 1938	85
	Rudy York, 1940	85
	Ted Williams, 1949	85
	Stan Musial, 1954	85
	Frank Robinson, 1966	85
	George Foster, 1977	85
	George Brett, 1979	85
76	Hugh Duffy, 1894	84
	Sam Thompson, 1895	84
	Ken Williams, 1922	84
	Al Simmons, 1929	84
	Ed Morgan, 1930	84
	Earl Webb, 1931	84
	Joe DiMaggio, 1941	84
	Duke Snider, 1953	84
	Tony Oliva, 1964	84
	Johnny Bench, 1970	84
	Jim Rice, 1979	84
87	Rogers Hornsby, 1921	83
	Lou Gehrig, 1926	83
	Dale Alexander, 1929	83
	Jimmie Foxx, 1930	83
	Earl Averill, 1932	83
	Lou Gehrig, 1937	83
	Ted Williams, 1946	83
	Ernie Banks, 1957	83
	Hank Aaron, 1961	83
	Jim Rice, 1977	83
	George Bell, 1987	83
98	14 players tied	82

Pinch Hits

1	Jose Morales, 1976	25
2	Dave Philley, 1961	24
	Vic Bavalillo, 1970	24
	Rusty Staub, 1983	24
5	Sam Leslie, 1932	22
	Red Schoendienst, 1962	22
	Wallace Johnson, 1988	22
9	Doc Miller, 1913	21
	Peanuts Lowrey, 1953	21
	Smoky Burgess, 1966	21
	Merv Rettenmund, 1977	21
13	Ed Coleman, 1936	20
	Frenchy Bordagaray, 1938	20
	Joe Frazier, 1954	20
	Smoky Burgess, 1965	20
	Ken Boswell, 1976	20
	Jerry Turner, 1978	20
	Thad Bosley, 1985	20
	Chris Chambliss, 1986	20
21	many players tied	19

Pinch Hit Average

1	Ed Kranepool, 1974	.486
2	Smead Jolley, 1931	.467
3	Frenchy Bordagaray, 1938	.465
4	Rick Miller, 1983	.457
5	Jose Pagan, 1969	.452
6	Elmer Valo, 1955	.452
7	Gates Brown, 1968	.450
8	Ted Easterly, 1912	.433
	Milt Thompson, 1985	.433
	Randy Bush, 1986	.433
11	Joe Cronin, 1943	.429
	Don Dillard, 1961	.429
13	Candy Maldonado, 1986	.425
14	Richie Ashburn, 1962	.419
	Dick Williams, 1962	.419
16	Merritt Ranew, 1963	.415
	Carl Taylor, 1969	.415
18	Kurt Bevacqua, 1983	.412
19	Jerry Turner, 1978	.408
20	Bob Bowman, 1958	.406
	Harry Spilman, 1986	.406
22	Frankie Baumholtz, 1955	.405
23	6 players tied	.400

Pinch Hit Home Runs

1	Johnny Frederick, 1932	6
2	Joe Cronin, 1943	5
	Butch Nieman, 1945	5
	Gene Freese, 1959	5
	Jerry Lynch, 1961	5
	Cliff Johnson, 1974	5
	Lee Lacy, 1978	5
	Jerry Turner, 1978	5
9	Ernie Lombardi, 1946	4
	Del Wilber, 1953	4
	Bill Taylor, 1955	4
	Bob Thurman, 1957	4
	Rip Repulski, 1958	4
	George Crowe, 1959	4
	George Crowe, 1960	4
	Johnny Blanchard, 1961	4
	Carl Sawatski, 1961	4
	Jerry Lynch, 1963	4
	Don Mincher, 1964	4
	Hal Breeden, 1973	4
	Mike Ivie, 1978	4
	Del Unser, 1979	4
	Jeff Burroughs‡ 1982	4
	Danny Heep, 1983	4
	Candy Maldonado, 1986	4

Stolen Bases

1	Hugh Nicol, 1887	138
2	Rickey Henderson, 1982	130
3	Arlie Latham, 1887	129
4	Lou Brock, 1974	118
5	Charlie Comiskey, 1887	117
6	Monte Ward, 1887	111
	Billy Hamilton, 1889	111
	Billy Hamilton, 1891	111
9	Vince Coleman, 1985	110
10	Arlie Latham, 1888	109
	Vince Coleman, 1987	109
12	Rickey Henderson, 1983	108
13	Vince Coleman, 1986	107
14	Tom Brown, 1891	106
15	Maury Wills, 1962	104
16	Pete Browning, 1887	103
	Hugh Nicol, 1888	103
18	Jim Fogarty, 1887	102
	Billy Hamilton, 1890	102
20	Rickey Henderson, 1980	100
21	Jim Fogarty, 1889	99
22	Billy Hamilton, 1894	98
23	Harry Stovey, 1890	97
	Billy Hamilton, 1895	97
	Ron LeFlore, 1980	97
26	Ty Cobb, 1915	96
	Omar Moreno, 1980	96
28	Bid McPhee, 1887	95
	Curt Welch, 1888	95
30	Mike Griffin, 1887	94
	Maury Wills, 1965	94
32	Tommy McCarthy, 1888	93
	Rickey Henderson, 1988	93
34	Darby O'Brien, 1889	91
35	Tim Raines, 1983	90
36	Curt Welch, 1887	89
	Herman Long, 1889	89
38	Tom Poorman, 1887	88
	Blondie Purcell, 1887	88
	Monte Ward, 1892	88
	Clyde Milan, 1912	88
42	Harry Stovey, 1888	87
	Arlie Latham, 1891	87
	Joe Kelley, 1896	87
	Rickey Henderson, 1986	87
46	Cub Stricker, 1887	86
47	Tommy Tucker, 1887	85
	Hub Collins, 1890	85
	Hugh Duffy, 1891	85
50	King Kelly, 1887	84
	Chippy McGarr, 1887	84
	Billy Sunday, 1890	84
	Bill Lange, 1896	84
54	Tommy McCarthy, 1890	83
	Billy Hamilton, 1896	83
	Ty Cobb, 1911	83
	Willie Wilson, 1979	83
58	Dummy Hoy, 1888	82
	John Reilly, 1888	82
60	Eddie Collins, 1910	81
	Bob Bescher, 1911	81
	Vince Coleman, 1988	81
63	Emmett Seery, 1888	80
	Hugh Nicol, 1889	80
	Rickey Henderson, 1985	80
	Eric Davis, 1986	80
67	Tom Brown, 1890	79
	Dave Collins, 1980	79
	Willie Wilson, 1980	79
70	Hugh Duffy, 1890	78
	Tom Brown, 1892	78
	John McGraw, 1894	78
	Ron LeFlore, 1979	78
	Tim Raines, 1982	78
75	Ted Scheffler, 1890	77
	Jimmy Sheckard, 1899	77
	Davey Lopes, 1975	77
	Omar Moreno, 1979	77
	Rudy Law, 1983	77
80	Ed McKean, 1887	76
	Walt Wilmot, 1890	76
	Dusty Miller, 1896	76
	Ty Cobb, 1909	76
84	Yank Robinson, 1887	75
	George VanHaltren, 1891	75
	Benny Kauff, 1914	75
	Bill North, 1976	75
	Tim Raines, 1984	75
89	Frank Fennelly, 1887	74
	Harry Stovey, 1887	74
	Walt Wilmot, 1894	74
	Clyde Milan, 1913	74
	Fritz Maisel, 1914	74
	Lou Brock, 1966	74
95	7 players tied	73

Stolen Base Average

(20 or more stolen bases)

1	Kevin McReynolds, 1988	100.0
2	Max Carey, 1922	96.2
3	Ken Griffey, 1980	95.8
4	Stan Javier, 1988	95.2
5	Amos Otis, 1970	94.3
6	Jack Perconte, 1985	93.9
7	Miguel Dilone, 1984	93.1
	Bob Dernier, 1986	93.1
9	Don Baylor, 1972	92.3
	Oddibe McDowell, 1987	92.3
11	Davey Lopes, 1985	92.2
12	Eric Davis, 1988	92.1
13	Bobby Bonds, 1969	91.8
	Davey Lopes, 1978	91.8
15	Davey Lopes, 1979	91.7
16	Jim Wynn, 1965	91.5
17	Larry Bowa, 1977	91.4
18	Ryne Sandberg, 1987	91.3
	Alan Trammell, 1987	91.3
20	Jerry Mumphrey, 1980	91.2
21	Tom Herr, 1985	91.2
22	Jack Smith, 1925	90.9
	Davey Lopes, 1981	90.9
	Tim Raines, 1987	90.9
25	Willie Wilson, 1984	90.4
26	Bake McBride, 1978	90.3
27	Henry Cotto, 1988	90.0
28	Mitchell Page, 1977	89.4
29	Tommy Harper, 1973	89.3
	Rick Manning, 1981	89.3
	Eric Davis, 1987	89.3
32	Jake Wood, 1962	88.9
	Tommy Harper, 1964	88.9
	Enzo Hernandez, 1972	88.9
	Dusty Baker, 1973	88.9
	Leon Lacy, 1981	88.9
	Rickey Henderson, 1985	88.9
38	Willie Wilson, 1980	88.8
39	Tim Raines, 1985	88.6
	Tim Raines, 1986	88.6
41	Bert Campaneris, 1969	88.6
	Kirk Gibson, 1988	88.6
43	Willie Mays, 1971	88.5
44	Dale Murphy, 1983	88.2
	Tim Raines, 1984	88.2
	Kirk Gibson, 1985	88.2
47	Willie Wilson, 1983	88.1
48	George Case, 1942	88.0
	Frank Robinson, 1961	88.0
	Bobby Bonds, 1972	88.0

Stolen Base Runs

1	Rickey Henderson, 1988 ...	20
2	Tim Raines, 1983	19
3	Rickey Henderson, 1985 ...	18
4	Willie Wilson, 1979	18
	Ron LeFlore, 1980	18
	Willie Wilson, 1980	18
7	Eric Davis, 1986	17
8	Tim Raines, 1984	17
9	Davey Lopes, 1975	16
	Rudy Law, 1983	16
11	Tim Raines, 1985	16
	Tim Raines, 1986	16
13	Rickey Henderson, 1986 ...	15
14	Ron LeFlore, 1979	15
15	Tim Raines, 1981	15
16	Max Carey, 1922	14
	Joe Morgan, 1975	14
18	Bert Campaneris, 1969	14
	Tim Raines, 1982	14
20	Davey Lopes, 1976	13
	Willie Wilson, 1983	13
22	Mickey Rivers, 1975	13
	Joe Morgan, 1976	13
	Jerry Mumphrey, 1980	13
	Juan Samuel, 1984	13
26	Fritz Maisel, 1914	12
	Al Wiggins, 1983	12
	Tim Raines, 1987	12
29	Julio Cruz, 1978	12
	Davey Lopes, 1985	12
	Ozzie Smith, 1988	12
32	Lou Brock, 1966	11
	Lou Brock, 1968	11
	Gary Pettis, 1985	11
	Eric Davis, 1987	11
36	Bobby Bonds, 1969	11
	Tommy Harper, 1969	11
	Joe Morgan, 1973	11
	Davey Lopes, 1978	11
	Dave Collins, 1980	11
	Rod Scott, 1980	11
	Willie Wilson, 1984	11
	Willie Wilson, 1987	11
44	Amos Otis, 1971	11
	Larry Lintz, 1974	11
	Frank Taveras, 1976	11
	Ron LeFlore, 1978	11
	Davey Lopes, 1979	11
49	5 players tied	11

Stolen Base Wins

1	Rickey Henderson, 1988 ...	2.0
2	Tim Raines, 1983	1.9
3	Ron LeFlore, 1980	1.9
4	Eric Davis, 1986	1.8
5	Rickey Henderson, 1985 ...	1.8
6	Willie Wilson, 1980	1.8
7	Tim Raines, 1984	1.7
8	Willie Wilson, 1979	1.7
9	Davey Lopes, 1975	1.7
10	Tim Raines, 1985	1.6
11	Tim Raines, 1986	1.6
12	Rudy Law, 1983	1.6
13	Tim Raines, 1981	1.6
14	Rickey Henderson, 1986 ...	1.5
15	Joe Morgan, 1975	1.5
16	Ron LeFlore, 1979	1.5
17	Tim Raines, 1982	1.4
18	Bert Campaneris, 1969	1.4
19	Davey Lopes, 1976	1.4
20	Joe Morgan, 1976	1.3
21	Jerry Mumphrey, 1980	1.3
22	Max Carey, 1922	1.3
23	Fritz Maisel, 1914	1.3
24	Juan Samuel, 1984	1.3
25	Lou Brock, 1968	1.3
26	Willie Wilson, 1983	1.3
27	Mickey Rivers, 1975	1.3
28	Ozzie Smith, 1988	1.3
29	Al Wiggins, 1983	1.3
30	Davey Lopes, 1985	1.2
31	Julio Cruz, 1978	1.2
32	Lou Brock, 1966	1.2
33	Tim Raines, 1987	1.2
34	Davey Lopes, 1978	1.2
35	Dave Collins, 1980	1.2
	Rod Scott, 1980	1.2
37	Bobby Bonds, 1969	1.2
38	Tommy Harper, 1969	1.2
39	Amos Otis, 1971	1.2
40	Joe Morgan, 1973	1.2
41	Frank Taveras, 1976	1.1
42	Eric Davis, 1987	1.1
43	Gary Pettis, 1985	1.1
44	Larry Lintz, 1974	1.1
45	Willie Wilson, 1984	1.1
46	Davey Lopes, 1979	1.1
47	Ron LeFlore, 1978	1.1
48	Jim Wynn, 1965	1.1
49	Omar Moreno, 1979	1.1
50	George Case, 1943	1.1

Fielding Average

First Base

1	Steve Garvey, 1984	1.000
2	Stuffy McInnis, 1921	.999
3	Frank McCormick, 1946 ...	.999
4	Steve Garvey, 1981	.999
5	Jim Spencer, 1973	.999
6	Wes Parker, 1968	.999
7	Eddie Murray, 1981	.999
8	Jim Spencer, 1976	.998
9	Jim Spencer, 1981	.998
10	Joe Judge, 1930	.998

Second Base

1	Bobby Grich, 1985	.997
2	Rob Wilfong, 1980	.995
3	Bobby Grich, 1973	.995
4	Frank White, 1988	.994
5	Jerry Adair, 1964	.994
6	Ryne Sandberg, 1986	.994
7	Tim Cullen, 1970	.994
8	Manny Trillo, 1982	.994
9	Johnny Ray, 1986	.993
10	Tim Flannery, 1986	.993

Shortstop

1	Larry Bowa, 1979	.991
2	Ed Brinkman, 1972	.990
3	Larry Bowa, 1972	.987
4	Ozzie Smith, 1987	.987
5	Larry Bowa, 1971	.987
6	Larry Bowa, 1978	.986
7	Frank Duffy, 1973	.986
8	Roger Metzger, 1976	.986
9	Dave Concepcion, 1977	.986
10	Tim Foli, 1982	.985

Third Base

1	Don Money, 1974	.989
2	Hank Majeski, 1947	.988
3	Aurelio Rodriguez, 1978	.987
4	Willie Kamm, 1933	.984
5	George Kell, 1946	.983
6	Heinie Groh, 1924	.983
7	Carney Lansford, 1979	.983
8	George Kell, 1950	.982
9	Pinky Whitney, 1937	.982
10	Buddy Bell, 1980	.981

Outfield

1	Danny Litwhiler, 1942	1.000
	Willard Marshall, 1951	1.000
	Sam Mele, 1952	1.000
	Tony Gonzalez, 1962	1.000
	Don Demeter, 1963	1.000
	Rocky Colavito, 1965	1.000
	Curt Flood, 1966	1.000
	Johnny Callison, 1968	1.000
	Mickey Stanley, 1968	1.000
	Ken Harrelson, 1968	1.000
	Ken Berry, 1969	1.000
	Mickey Stanley, 1970	1.000
	Roy White, 1971	1.000
	Al Kaline, 1971	1.000
	Ken Berry, 1972	1.000
	Carl Yastrzemski, 1977	1.000
	Terry Puhl, 1979	1.000
	Gary Roenicke, 1980	1.000
	Ken Landreaux, 1981	1.000
	Terry Puhl, 1981	1.000
	Ken Singleton, 1981	1.000
	Brian Downing, 1982	1.000
	John Lowenstein, 1982	1.000
	Brian Downing, 1984	1.000

Catcher

1	Spud Davis, 1939	1.000
	Buddy Rosar, 1946	1.000
	Lou Berberet, 1957	1.000
	Pete Daley, 1957	1.000
	Yogi Berra, 1958	1.000
	Rick Cerone, 1988	1.000
7	Joe Azcue, 1967	.999
8	Wes Westrum, 1950	.999
9	Thurman Munson, 1971	.998
10	Rick Cerone, 1987	.998

Pitcher (92 or more total chances)

1	Kid Nichols, 1896	1.000
	Frank Owen, 1904	1.000
	Mordecai Brown, 1908	1.000
	Pete Alexander, 1913	1.000
	Walter Johnson, 1913	1.000
	Eppa Rixey, 1917	1.000
	Walter Johnson, 1917	1.000
	Hal Schumacher, 1935	1.000
	Larry Jackson, 1964	1.000
	Randy Jones, 1976	1.000

Total Chances per Game

First Base

1	Joe Gerhardt, 1876	13.28
2	Jiggs Donahue, 1907	12.73
3	Oscar Walker, 1879	12.60
4	Joe Start, 1878	12.54
5	Tim Murnane, 1878	12.52
6	Joe Start, 1879	12.49
7	Jake Goodman, 1878	12.45
8	Herman Dehlman, 1876	12.36
9	Phil Todt, 1926	12.36
10	Joe Start, 1877	12.35

Second Base

1	Thorny Hawkes, 1879	8.44
2	Chick Fulmer, 1879	8.34
3	Jack Burdock, 1878	8.30
4	Ed Somerville, 1876	8.28
5	Joe Gerhardt, 1877	8.12
6	Fred Pfeffer, 1884	8.08
7	Jack Burdock, 1879	7.88
8	Joe Quest, 1878	7.81
9	Pop Smith, 1885	7.74
10	Joe Quest, 1879	7.73

Shortstop

1	Herman Long, 1889	7.27
2	Hughie Jennings, 1895	7.16
3	Dave Bancroft, 1918	7.14
4	George Davis, 1899	7.08
5	Hughie Jennings, 1896	7.07
6	Hughie Jennings, 1897	7.01
7	Bobby Wallace, 1901	6.97
8	Monte Cross, 1897	6.97
9	Bill Dahlen, 1895	6.93
10	Gene DeMontreville, 1897 ..	6.91

Third Base

1	Al Nichols, 1876	5.81
2	Bob Ferguson, 1877	5.61
3	Jumbo Davis, 1888	5.13
4	Cap Anson, 1876	5.03
5	Billy Shindle, 1892	4.93
6	Jack Gleason, 1882	4.90
7	Bill Bradley, 1900	4.87
8	George Bradley, 1880	4.84
9	Will Foley, 1877	4.79
10	Levi Meyerle, 1876	4.78

Outfield

1	Fred Treacey, 1876	4.39
2	Redleg Snyder, 1876	3.84
3	Taylor Douthit, 1928	3.68
4	Mike Mansell, 1879	3.64
5	Richie Ashburn, 1951	3.64
6	Chet Lemon, 1977	3.60
7	Thurman Tucker, 1944	3.58
8	Kirby Puckett, 1984	3.57
9	Irv Noren, 1951	3.53
10	Richie Ashburn, 1949	3.49

Catcher

1	Bill Holbert, 1883	10.63
2	Sam Trott, 1884	10.35
3	Bill Holbert, 1884	9.66
4	Jocko Milligan, 1884	9.40
5	Mert Hackett, 1884	9.35
6	Barney Gilligan, 1884	9.30
7	Mike Hines, 1883	9.27
8	George Baker, 1884	8.99
9	Jocko Milligan, 1885	8.82
10	Lew Brown, 1877	8.65

Pitcher

1	Harry Howell, 1905	5.42
2	Harry Howell, 1904	5.12
3	Will White, 1882	4.76
4	Ed Walsh, 1907	4.75
5	George Mullin, 1904	4.53
6	Tony Mullane, 1882	4.38
7	Red Donahue, 1902	4.37
8	Nick Altrock, 1905	4.37
9	Harry Howell, 1906	4.34
10	Nick Altrock, 1904	4.26

Chances Accepted per Game

First Base
1 Jiggs Donahue, 1907 .... 12.65
2 Joe Gerhardt, 1876 .... 12.54
3 Phil Todt, 1926 .... 12.21
4 Joe Start, 1879 .... 12.15
5 George Burns, 1914 .... 12.10
6 Stuffy McInnis, 1918 .... 12.10
7 George Stovall, 1908 .... 12.08
8 George Kelly, 1920 .... 12.01
9 Joe Start, 1878 .... 12.00
10 Oscar Walker, 1879 .... 11.92

Second Base
1 Jack Burdock, 1878 ...... 7.62
2 Thorny Hawkes, 1879 ...... 7.56
3 Chick Fulmer, 1879 ...... 7.55
4 Fred Pfeffer, 1884 ...... 7.29
5 Joe Gerhardt, 1877 ...... 7.21
6 Ed Somerville, 1876 ...... 7.20
7 Jack Burdock, 1879 ...... 7.18
8 Joe Quest, 1879 ...... 7.16
9 Joe Gerhardt, 1890 ...... 7.14
10 Pop Smith, 1885 .... 7.13

Shortstop
1 Hughie Jennings, 1895 ..... 6.73
2 George Davis, 1899 ...... 6.69
3 Dave Bancroft, 1918 ...... 6.62
4 Hughie Jennings, 1896 ..... 6.56
5 Hughie Jennings, 1897 ..... 6.53
6 Dave Bancroft, 1920 ...... 6.49
7 Rabbit Maranville, 1919 .... 6.48
8 Bobby Wallace, 1901 ...... 6.48
9 Monte Cross, 1897 ...... 6.41
10 Dave Bancroft, 1920 .... 6.40

Third Base
1 Bob Ferguson, 1877 .... 4.71
2 Al Nichols, 1876 .... 4.53
3 Billy Shindle, 1892 .... 4.34
4 Jumbo Davis, 1888 ...... 4.33
5 Bill Bradley, 1900 ...... 4.29
6 Cap Anson, 1876 ...... 4.27
7 Lave Cross, 1899 ...... 4.21
8 Joe Battin, 1883 ...... 4.17
9 Bill Hague, 1878 ...... 4.16
10 George Bradley, 1880 ...... 4.14

Outfield
1 Fred Treacey, 1876 .... 3.70
2 Taylor Douthit, 1928 ...... 3.62
3 Richie Ashburn, 1951 ...... 3.59
4 Thurman Tucker, 1944 ...... 3.55
5 Kirby Puckett, 1984 ...... 3.55
6 Chet Lemon, 1977 ...... 3.52
7 Irv Noren, 1951 .... 3.45
8 Richie Ashburn, 1951 ...... 3.42
9 Carden Gillenwater, 1945 .... 3.39
10 Jim Busby, 1952 .... 3.39

Catcher
1 Bill Holbert, 1883 .... 9.78
2 Sam Trott, 1884 .... 9.63
3 Jocko Milligan, 1884 .... 8.83
4 Bill Holbert, 1884 .... 8.75
5 Mert Hackett, 1884 .... 8.68
6 Barney Gilligan, 1884 ...... 8.63
7 Duffy Dyer, 1972 .... 8.25
8 Jocko Milligan, 1885 .... 8.25
9 Mike Hines, 1883 .... 8.22
10 George Baker, 1884 .... 8.06

Pitcher
1 Harry Howell, 1905 .... 5.24
2 Harry Howell, 1904 .... 4.97
3 Ed Walsh, 1907 .... 4.68
4 Will White, 1882 .... 4.56
5 Nick Altrock, 1905 .... 4.32
6 George Mullin, 1904 .... 4.24
7 Tony Mullane, 1882 .... 4.20
8 Willie Sudhoff, 1904 .... 4.19
9 Red Donahue, 1902 .... 4.14
10 Nick Altrock, 1904 .... 4.13

Putouts

First Base
1 Jiggs Donahue, 1907 1846
2 George Kelly, 1920 1759
3 Phil Todt, 1926 1755
4 Wally Pipp, 1926 1710
5 Jiggs Donahue, 1906 1697
6 Candy LaChance, 1904 1691
7 Tom Jones, 1907 1687
8 Ernie Banks, 1965 1682
9 Wally Pipp, 1922 1667
10 Lou Gehrig, 1927 1662

Second Base
1 Bid McPhee, 1886 529
2 Bobby Grich, 1974 484
3 Bucky Harris, 1922 483
4 Nellie Fox, 1956 478
5 Lou Bierbauer, 1889 472
6 Billy Herman, 1933 466
7 Bill Wambsganss, 1924 463
8 Cub Stricker, 1887 461
9 Buddy Myer, 1935 460
10 Bill Sweeney, 1912 459

Shortstop
1 Hughie Jennings, 1895 425
   Donie Bush, 1914 425
3 Joe Cassidy, 1905 408
4 Rabbit Maranville, 1914 407
5 Dave Bancroft, 1922 405
   Eddie Miller, 1940 405
7 Monte Cross, 1898 404
8 Dave Bancroft, 1921 396
9 Mickey Doolan, 1906 395
10 Buck Weaver, 1913 392

Third Base
1 Denny Lyons, 1887 255
2 Jimmy Williams, 1899 251
   Jimmy Collins, 1900 251
4 Jimmy Collins, 1898 243
   Willie Kamm, 1928 243
6 Willie Kamm, 1927 236
7 Frank Baker, 1913 233
8 Bill Coughlin, 1901 232
9 Ernie Courtney, 1905 229
10 Jimmy Austin, 1911 228

Outfield
1 Taylor Douthit, 1928 547
2 Richie Ashburn, 1951 538
3 Richie Ashburn, 1949 514
4 Chet Lemon, 1977 512
5 Dwayne Murphy, 1980 507
6 Dom DiMaggio, 1948 503
   Richie Ashburn, 1956 503
8 Richie Ashburn, 1957 502
9 Richie Ashburn, 1953 496
10 Richie Ashburn, 1958 495

Catcher
1 Johnny Edwards, 1969 1135
2 Johnny Edwards, 1963 1008
3 Randy Hundley, 1969 978
4 Tony Pena, 1983 976
5 Bill Freehan, 1968 971
6 Gary Carter, 1985 956
7 Gary Carter, 1982 954
8 Bill Freehan, 1967 950
9 Johnny Bench, 1968 942
10 Elston Howard, 1964 939

Pitcher
1 Dave Foutz, 1886 57
2 Tony Mullane, 1882 54
3 George Bradley, 1876 50
   Guy Hecker, 1884 50
5 Mike Boddicker, 1984 49
6 Larry Corcoran, 1884 47
7 Al Spalding, 1876 45
   Ted Breitenstein, 1895 45
9 3 players tied 44

Putouts per Game

First Base
1 Joe Gerhardt, 1876 .... 12.30
2 Joe Start, 1879 .... 11.98
3 Joe Start, 1878 .... 11.79
4 Jiggs Donahue, 1907 ...... 11.76
5 Joe Start, 1877 .... 11.73
6 Herman Dehlman, 1876 ...... 11.72
7 Joe Start, 1880 .... 11.63
8 Jake Goodman, 1878 ...... 11.55
9 George Burns, 1914 ...... 11.53
10 Oscar Walker, 1879 .... 11.50

Second Base
1 Jack Burdock, 1878 ...... 4.08
2 Jack Burdock, 1880 ...... 3.81
3 Bid McPhee, 1886 ...... 3.78
4 Bid McPhee, 1884 ...... 3.71
5 Joe Quest, 1878 ...... 3.68
6 Cub Stricker, 1887 ...... 3.66
7 Lou Bierbauer, 1889 ...... 3.63
8 Joe Gerhardt, 1890 ...... 3.63
9 Jack Burdock, 1879 ...... 3.61
10 Chick Fulmer, 1879 ...... 3.59

Shortstop
1 Hughie Jennings, 1895 ..... 3.24
2 Dave Bancroft, 1918 ...... 2.97
3 Hughie Jennings, 1896 ..... 2.90
4 George Davis, 1898 ...... 2.88
5 George Davis, 1899 ...... 2.88
6 Hughie Jennings, 1897 ..... 2.87
7 Rabbit Maranville, 1919 .... 2.76
8 Honus Wagner, 1913 ...... 2.75
9 Kid Elberfeld, 1901 ...... 2.74
10 Buck Weaver, 1914 .... 2.74

Third Base
1 Al Nichols, 1876 .... 2.16
2 Cap Anson, 1878 .... 2.05
3 Hick Carpenter, 1880 ...... 2.03
4 Bob Ferguson, 1877 ...... 1.95
5 Denny Lyons, 1887 ...... 1.86
6 Patsy Tebeau, 1890 ...... 1.85
7 Cap Anson, 1877 ...... 1.85
8 Joe Battin, 1876 ...... 1.83
9 Jerry Denny, 1883 ...... 1.82
10 Frank Hankinson, 1881 .... 1.80

Outfield
1 Taylor Douthit, 1928 ...... 3.55
2 Fred Treacey, 1876 ...... 3.54
3 Richie Ashburn, 1951 ...... 3.49
4 Thurman Tucker, 1944 ...... 3.45
5 Chet Lemon, 1977 .... 3.44
6 Kirby Puckett, 1984 ...... 3.42
7 Jim Busby, 1952 .... 3.36
8 Richie Ashburn, 1949 ...... 3.34
9 Irv Noren, 1951 .... 3.33
10 Sam West, 1935 .... 3.33

Catcher
1 Sam Trott, 1884 .... 8.18
2 Bill Holbert, 1883 ...... 7.75
3 Duffy Dyer, 1972 ...... 7.58
4 Johnny Edwards, 1969 ...... 7.52
5 Barney Gilligan, 1884 ...... 7.47
6 John Romano, 1964 ...... 7.44
7 Johnny Edwards, 1964 ...... 7.42
8 Joe Azcue, 1967 ...... 7.40
9 John Roseboro, 1960 ...... 7.36
10 Jerry Grote, 1971 .... 7.31

Pitcher
1 Mike Boddicker, 1984 ...... 1.44
2 Oil Can Boyd, 1985 .... 1.20
3 Nick Altrock, 1904 ...... 1.13
4 Snake Wiltse, 1902 ...... 1.11
5 Rube Waddell, 1901 ...... 1.10
6 Dave Foutz, 1887 ...... 1.10
7 Dwight Gooden, 1986 ...... 1.09
8 Dan Petry, 1984 ...... 1.09
9 Nat Hudson, 1888 .... 1.08
   Al Nipper, 1986 .... 1.08

Assists

First Base
1 Bill Buckner, 1985 184
2 Sid Bream, 1986 166
3 Bill Buckner, 1983 161
4 Bill Buckner, 1982 159
5 Bill Buckner, 1986 157
6 Mickey Vernon, 1949 155
7 Fred Tenney, 1905 152
   Eddie Murray, 1985 152
9 Ferris Fain, 1952 150
10 3 players tied 149

Second Base
1 Frankie Frisch, 1927 641
2 Hughie Critz, 1926 588
3 Rogers Hornsby, 1927 582
4 Ski Melillo, 1930 572
5 Ryne Sandberg, 1983 571
6 Rabbit Maranville, 1924 568
7 Frank Parkinson, 1922 562
8 Tony Cuccinello, 1936 559
9 Johnny Hodapp, 1930 557
10 Lou Bierbauer, 1892 555

Shortstop
1 Ozzie Smith, 1980 621
2 Glenn Wright, 1924 601
3 Dave Bancroft, 1920 598
4 Tommy Thevenow, 1926 597
5 Ivan DeJesus, 1977 595
6 Cal Ripken, 1984 583
7 Whitey Wietelmann, 1943 ... 581
8 Dave Bancroft, 1922 579
9 Rabbit Maranville, 1914 574
10 Don Kessinger, 1968 573

Third Base
1 Graig Nettles, 1971 412
2 Graig Nettles, 1973 410
   Brooks Robinson, 1974 410
4 Harland Clift, 1937 405
   Brooks Robinson, 1967 405
6 Mike Schmidt, 1974 404
7 Doug DeCinces, 1982 399
8 Clete Boyer, 1962 396
   Mike Schmidt, 1977 396
   Buddy Bell, 1982 396

Outfield
1 Orator Shaffer, 1879 50
2 Hugh Nicol, 1884 48
3 Hardy Richardson, 1881 45
4 Tommy McCarthy, 1888 44
   Jimmy Bannon, 1894 44
   Chuck Klein, 1930 44
7 Charlie Duffee, 1889 43
8 Jim Fogarty, 1889 42
9 Orator Shaffer, 1883 41
   Jim Lillie, 1884 41

Catcher
1 Bill Rariden, 1915 238
2 Bill Rariden, 1914 215
3 Pat Moran, 1903 214
4 Oscar Stanage, 1911 212
   Art Wilson, 1914 212
6 Gabby Street, 1909 210
7 Frank Snyder, 1915 204
8 George Gibson, 1910 203
9 Bill Bergen, 1909 202
   Claude Berry, 1914 202

Pitcher
1 Ed Walsh, 1907 227
2 Will White, 1882 223
3 Ed Walsh, 1908 190
4 Harry Howell, 1905 178
5 Tony Mullane, 1882 177
6 John Clarkson, 1885 174
7 John Clarkson, 1889 172
8 Matt Kilroy, 1887 167
9 Jack Chesbro, 1904 166
10 George Mullin, 1904 163

Assists per Game

First Base
1	Bill Buckner, 1986	1.14
2	Bill Buckner, 1985	1.14
3	Bill Buckner, 1983	1.12
4	Sid Bream, 1986	1.08
5	Ferris Fain, 1951	1.05
6	Ferris Fain, 1952	1.04
7	Fred Tenney, 1905	1.03
8	Keith Hernandez, 1983	1.02
9	Bob Robertson, 1971	1.02
10	Sid Bream, 1988	1.01

Second Base
1	Joe Gerhardt, 1877	4.28
2	Frankie Frisch, 1927	4.19
3	Thorny Hawkes, 1879	4.13
4	Hughie Critz, 1933	4.07
5	Frank Parkinson, 1922	4.04
6	Joe Quest, 1879	3.99
7	Chick Fulmer, 1879	3.96
8	Ed Somerville, 1876	3.92
9	Ski Melillo, 1930	3.86
10	Glenn Hubbard, 1985	3.85

Shortstop
1	Germany Smith, 1885	4.21
2	Arthur Irwin, 1880	4.13
3	Dave Bancroft, 1920	4.12
4	Art Fletcher, 1919	4.10
5	Bill Dahlen, 1895	4.09
6	Bobby Wallace, 1901	4.04
7	Jack Glasscock, 1887	4.04
8	Germany Smith, 1892	4.04
9	Henry Easterday, 1888	3.99
10	Dave Bancroft, 1920	3.99

Third Base
1	Jumbo Davis, 1888	2.96
2	Buddy Bell, 1981	2.93
3	George Bradley, 1880	2.89
4	Bill Hague, 1878	2.85
5	Billy Shindle, 1892	2.85
6	Bob Ferguson, 1877	2.77
7	Ned Williamson, 1879	2.76
8	Arlie Latham, 1884	2.75
9	Bill Bradley, 1900	2.75
10	Arlie Latham, 1891	2.74

Outfield
1	Orator Shaffer, 1879	0.69
2	Hardy Richardson, 1881	0.57
3	Hugh Nicol, 1884	0.55
4	King Kelly, 1878	0.51
5	John Cassidy, 1878	0.50
	King Kelly, 1880	0.50
7	King Kelly, 1883	0.46
8	Jake Evans, 1882	0.46
9	Orator Shaffer, 1878	0.44
10	Dick Higham, 1878	0.44

Catcher
1	Bill Holbert, 1884	2.41
2	Tom Daly, 1887	2.31
3	Bill Holbert, 1882	2.14
4	Pop Snyder, 1884	2.08
5	Bill Holbert, 1883	2.03
6	Buck Ewing, 1881	2.02
7	Pat Moran, 1903	2.00
8	Charlie Reipschlager, 1885	1.98
9	Connie Mack, 1888	1.92
10	King Kelly, 1888	1.92

Pitcher
1	Harry Howell, 1905	4.68
2	Harry Howell, 1904	4.21
3	Will White, 1882	4.13
4	Ed Walsh, 1907	4.05
5	Willie Sudhoff, 1904	3.85
6	Red Donahue, 1902	3.71
7	George Mullin, 1904	3.62
8	Frank Owen, 1904	3.51
9	Carl Mays, 1918	3.49
10	Nick Altrock, 1905	3.47

Double Plays

First Base
1	Ferris Fain, 1949	194
2	Ferris Fain, 1950	192
3	Donn Clendenon, 1966	182
4	Ron Jackson, 1979	175
5	Gil Hodges, 1951	171
6	Mickey Vernon, 1949	168
7	Ted Kluszewski, 1954	166
8	Rudy York, 1944	163
9	Donn Clendenon, 1965	161
	Rod Carew, 1977	161

Second Base
1	Bill Mazeroski, 1966	161
2	Jerry Priddy, 1950	150
3	Bill Mazeroski, 1961	144
4	Nellie Fox, 1957	141
	Dave Cash, 1974	141
6	Buddy Myer, 1935	138
	Bill Mazeroski, 1962	138
8	Jerry Coleman, 1950	137
	Jackie Robinson, 1951	137
	Red Schoendienst, 1954	137

Shortstop
1	Rick Burleson, 1980	147
2	Roy Smalley, 1979	144
3	Bobby Wine, 1970	137
4	Lou Boudreau, 1944	134
5	Spike Owen, 1986	133
6	Rafael Ramirez, 1982	130
7	Roy McMillan, 1954	129
8	Hod Ford, 1928	128
	Vern Stephens, 1949	128
	Gene Alley, 1966	128

Third Base
1	Graig Nettles, 1971	54
2	Harlond Clift, 1937	50
3	Johnny Pesky, 1949	48
	Paul Molitor, 1982	48
5	Sammy Hale, 1927	46
	Clete Boyer, 1965	46
	Gary Gaetti, 1983	46
8	Eddie Yost, 1950	45
	Frank Malzone, 1961	45
	Darrell Evans, 1974	45

Outfield
1	Happy Felsch, 1919	15
2	Jimmy Sheckard, 1899	14
3	Tom Brown, 1893	13
4	Tom Brown, 1886	12
	Tommy McCarthy, 1888	12
	Jimmy Bannon, 1894	12
	Mike Griffin, 1895	12
	Danny Green, 1899	12
	Cy Seymour, 1905	12
	Ginger Beaumont, 1907	12
	Ty Cobb, 1907	12
	Tris Speaker, 1909	12
	Jimmy Sheckard, 1911	12
	Tris Speaker, 1914	12
	Mel Ott, 1929	12

Catcher
1	Steve O'Neill, 1916	36
2	Frankie Hayes, 1945	29
3	Ray Schalk, 1916	25
	Yogi Berra, 1951	25
5	Jack Lapp, 1915	23
	Muddy Ruel, 1924	23
	Frankie Hayes, 1945	23
	Tom Haller, 1968	23
9	Steve O'Neill, 1914	22
	Bob O'Farrell, 1922	22

Pitcher
1	Bob Lemon, 1953	15
2	Eddie Rommel, 1924	12
	Curt Davis, 1934	12
	Randy Jones, 1976	12
5	Scott Perry, 1919	11
	Tom Rogers, 1919	11
	Art Nehf, 1920	11
	Burleigh Grimes, 1925	11
	Gene Bearden, 1948	11
10	10 players tied	10

Fielding Runs

1	Glenn Hubbard, 1985	56.8
2	Rabbit Maranville, 1914	49.5
3	Danny Richardson, 1892	49.4
4	Frankie Frisch, 1927	48.8
5	Freddie Maguire, 1928	48.2
6	Nap Lajoie, 1908	46.7
7	Bill Mazeroski, 1963	46.6
8	Herman Long, 1889	45.1
9	Danny Richardson, 1891	43.6
10	Dick Bartell, 1936	43.4
11	George Davis, 1899	43.3
12	Ozzie Smith, 1980	42.8
	Ozzie Guillen, 1988	42.8
14	Dave Shean, 1910	42.2
15	Cupid Childs, 1896	41.9
16	Bill Mazeroski, 1966	40.9
17	Bill Mazeroski, 1962	40.7
18	Ryne Sandberg, 1983	40.5
19	Fred Pfeffer, 1884	40.4
	Hughie Critz, 1933	40.4
21	Harlond Clift, 1937	40.1
22	Graig Nettles, 1971	39.6
23	Nap Lajoie, 1907	39.3
24	Cal Ripken, 1984	38.8
25	Bid McPhee, 1889	38.3
26	John Kerins, 1886	37.7
	Everett Scott, 1921	37.7
28	Fred Pfeffer, 1888	37.4
29	Buddy Bell, 1982	37.0
30	Tim Wallach, 1985	36.8
31	Bill Holbert, 1883	36.7
	Germany Smith, 1885	36.7
	Nap Lajoie, 1903	36.7
	Dick Bartell, 1937	36.7
35	Bobby Knoop, 1964	36.6
36	Arlie Latham, 1884	36.5
37	Buck Weaver, 1913	36.4
38	Lou Bierbauer, 1889	36.2
39	Miller Huggins, 1905	36.1
	Ivan DeJesus, 1977	36.1
41	Billy Shindle, 1888	35.9
	Billy Shindle, 1892	35.9
	Manny Trillo, 1977	35.9
44	Joe Cassidy, 1905	35.7
45	Clete Boyer, 1962	35.5
46	Marty Barrett, 1987	35.2
47	Jack Glasscock, 1887	34.6
48	Freddie Patek, 1973	34.5
49	Ollie Beard, 1889	34.4
50	Zoilo Versalles, 1962	34.1
51	Bobby Wallace, 1899	34.0
52	Joe Gerhardt, 1890	33.9
	Manny Trillo, 1978	33.9
	Ozzie Smith, 1982	33.9
55	Glenn Hubbard, 1986	33.8
56	Ski Melillo, 1931	33.7
57	Bill Mazeroski, 1964	33.5
58	Donie Bush, 1914	33.2
59	Harry Steinfeldt, 1900	33.0
	Eddie Collins, 1910	33.0
	Art Fletcher, 1915	33.0
	Chuck Klein, 1930	33.0
	Tony Pena, 1985	33.0
64	Bob Allen, 1890	32.9
	George Davis, 1898	32.9
	Roy Smalley, 1979	32.9
67	Ozzie Smith, 1978	32.7
68	Jerry Priddy, 1950	32.6
69	Bid McPhee, 1893	32.5
70	Bill Dahlen, 1894	32.2
	Tommy Leach, 1904	32.2
	Joe Tinker, 1908	32.2
	Pep Young, 1938	32.2
74	Mike Mowrey, 1913	31.8
75	Germany Smith, 1887	31.6
76	Bid McPhee, 1886	31.5
	Hughie Jennings, 1894	31.5
	George McBride, 1908	31.5
	Bill Mazeroski, 1961	31.5
	Clete Boyer, 1961	31.5
	Ed Brinkman, 1970	31.5
82	Arthur Irwin, 1880	31.4
83	Luis Aparicio, 1960	31.3
84	Pop Smith, 1885	31.2
	Leo Cardenas, 1969	31.2
	Garry Templeton, 1980	31.2
87	Johnny Evers, 1904	31.1
	Ron Santo, 1967	31.1
89	Bid McPhee, 1888	31.0
	Rick Burleson, 1980	31.0
91	Buck Herzog, 1915	30.9
	Bucky Dent, 1979	30.9
	Ozzie Smith, 1984	30.9
94	Tommy McCarthy, 1888	30.7
	Mark Belanger, 1977	30.7
96	Jack Glasscock, 1889	30.6
	Bill Mazeroski, 1965	30.6
98	Buck Herzog, 1914	30.5
99	Hughie Jennings, 1895	30.4
100	2 players tied	30.3

Fielding Runs (by position)

First Base
1	Bill Buckner, 1985	25.0
2	Chick Gandil, 1914	21.4
3	Jiggs Donahue, 1907	20.8
4	Vic Power, 1960	20.7
5	Fred Tenney, 1905	20.3
6	Jake Beckley, 1892	19.7
7	Mickey Vernon, 1949	18.5
8	Rudy York, 1943	18.3
9	Jack Burns, 1931	17.9
10	Keith Hernandez, 1979	17.8

Second Base
1	Glenn Hubbard, 1985	56.8
2	Frankie Frisch, 1927	48.8
3	Freddie Maguire, 1928	48.2
4	Nap Lajoie, 1908	46.7
5	Bill Mazeroski, 1963	46.6
6	Danny Richardson, 1891	43.6
7	Dave Shean, 1910	42.2
8	Cupid Childs, 1896	41.9
9	Bill Mazeroski, 1966	40.9
10	Bill Mazeroski, 1962	40.7

Shortstop
1	Rabbit Maranville, 1914	49.5
2	Herman Long, 1889	45.1
3	Dick Bartell, 1936	43.4
4	George Davis, 1899	43.3
5	Ozzie Smith, 1980	42.8
6	Ozzie Guillen, 1988	42.8
7	Cal Ripken, 1984	38.8
8	Everett Scott, 1921	37.7
9	Germany Smith, 1885	36.7
10	Dick Bartell, 1937	36.7

Third Base
1	Harlond Clift, 1937	40.1
2	Graig Nettles, 1971	39.6
3	Buddy Bell, 1982	37.0
4	Tim Wallach, 1985	36.8
5	Arlie Latham, 1884	36.5
6	Billy Shindle, 1888	35.9
7	Billy Shindle, 1892	35.9
8	Clete Boyer, 1962	35.5
9	Tommy Leach, 1904	32.2
10	Mike Mowrey, 1913	31.8

Outfield
1	Chuck Klein, 1930	33.0
2	Tommy McCarthy, 1888	30.7
3	Dave Parker, 1977	30.0
4	Jim Fogarty, 1887	28.6
5	Richie Ashburn, 1957	27.3
6	Tom Brown, 1893	26.9
7	Ed Delahanty, 1893	26.7
8	Chet Lemon, 1977	26.5
9	Johnny Callison, 1962	25.8
10	Richie Ashburn, 1951	25.5

Catcher
1	Bill Holbert, 1883	36.7
2	Tony Pena, 1985	33.0
3	Gary Carter, 1983	28.7
4	Gary Carter, 1978	25.0
5	Pop Snyder, 1884	24.8
6	Del Crandall, 1959	24.8
7	Johnny Edwards, 1962	24.1
8	John Stearns, 1978	23.9
9	Gary Carter, 1980	23.7
10	Bill Rariden, 1915	23.5

Fielding Wins

1	Glenn Hubbard, 1985	6.0
2	Rabbit Maranville, 1914	5.3
3	Nap Lajoie, 1908	5.3
4	Bill Mazeroski, 1963	5.1
5	Frankie Frisch, 1927	4.8
6	Freddie Maguire, 1928	4.7
7	Danny Richardson, 1892	4.6
8	Ozzie Smith, 1980	4.5
9	Dave Shean, 1910	4.4
10	Nap Lajoie, 1907	4.3
11	Ozzie Guillen, 1988	4.3
12	Bill Mazeroski, 1966	4.3
13	Hughie Critz, 1933	4.3
14	Graig Nettles, 1971	4.3
15	Ryne Sandberg, 1983	4.2
16	Dick Bartell, 1936	4.2
17	Bill Mazeroski, 1962	4.1
18	George Davis, 1899	3.9
19	Joe Cassidy, 1905	3.9
20	Cal Ripken, 1984	3.9
21	Danny Richardson, 1891	3.9
22	Buck Weaver, 1913	3.9
23	Tim Wallach, 1985	3.9
24	Bobby Knoop, 1964	3.8
25	Herman Long, 1889	3.8
26	Nap Lajoie, 1903	3.8
27	Miller Huggins, 1905	3.8
28	Joe Tinker, 1908	3.7
29	Buddy Bell, 1982	3.7
30	Harland Clift, 1937	3.7
31	Fred Pfeffer, 1888	3.7
32	Donie Bush, 1914	3.7
33	Eddie Collins, 1910	3.7
34	Art Fletcher, 1915	3.7
35	Ivan DeJesus, 1977	3.7
36	Dick Bartell, 1937	3.6
37	Manny Trillo, 1977	3.6
38	Fred Pfeffer, 1884	3.6
39	George McBride, 1908	3.6
40	Manny Trillo, 1978	3.6
41	Clete Boyer, 1962	3.6
42	Ozzie Smith, 1982	3.6
43	Cupid Childs, 1896	3.6
44	Bill Mazeroski, 1964	3.5
45	Freddie Patek, 1973	3.5
46	Everett Scott, 1921	3.5
47	Glenn Hubbard, 1986	3.5
48	Horace Clarke, 1968	3.5
49	Tony Pena, 1985	3.5
50	Ozzie Smith, 1978	3.5
51	Buck Herzog, 1915	3.4
52	Zoilo Versalles, 1962	3.4
53	Tommy Leach, 1904	3.4
54	Ron Santo, 1967	3.4
55	Heinie Wagner, 1908	3.4
56	Marty Barrett, 1987	3.4
57	Arlie Latham, 1884	3.3
58	Billy Shindle, 1892	3.3
59	Billy Shindle, 1888	3.3
60	Brooks Robinson, 1967	3.3
61	John Kerins, 1886	3.3
62	Mike Mowrey, 1913	3.3
63	Germany Smith, 1885	3.3
64	Garry Templeton, 1980	3.3
65	Johnny Evers, 1904	3.3
66	Buck Herzog, 1914	3.3
67	Leo Cardenas, 1969	3.3
68	Ed Brinkman, 1970	3.3
69	Al Burch, 1908	3.3
70	Ozzie Smith, 1984	3.2
71	Bid McPhee, 1889	3.2
72	Pep Young, 1938	3.2
73	Bill Mazeroski, 1965	3.2
74	Bill Holbert, 1883	3.2
75	Luis Aparicio, 1968	3.2
76	Rabbit Maranville, 1919	3.2
77	Roy Smalley, 1979	3.2
78	Johnny Evers, 1907	3.2
79	Luis Aparicio, 1969	3.2
80	Luis Aparicio, 1960	3.2
81	Ski Melillo, 1931	3.1
82	Freddie Patek, 1972	3.1
83	Bill Mazeroski, 1961	3.1
84	Clete Boyer, 1961	3.1
85	Dave Cash, 1974	3.1
86	Billy Herman, 1933	3.1
87	Rick Burleson, 1980	3.1
88	Dave Bancroft, 1920	3.1
89	Dave Bancroft, 1917	3.1
90	Bobby Wallace, 1899	3.1
91	George Davis, 1898	3.1
92	Art Devlin, 1906	3.1
93	Lou Bierbauer, 1889	3.1
94	Arthur Irwin, 1880	3.1
95	Jerry Priddy, 1950	3.1
96	Mark Belanger, 1977	3.0
97	Dave Parker, 1977	3.0
98	Roy McMillan, 1956	3.0
99	Harry Steinfeldt, 1900	3.0
100	Bucky Dent, 1979	3.0

Total Player Rating

1	Babe Ruth, 1921	9.9
2	Babe Ruth, 1923	9.0
	Cal Ripken, 1984	9.0
4	Nap Lajoie, 1910	8.9
5	Babe Ruth, 1920	8.8
6	Babe Ruth, 1927	8.5
7	Babe Ruth, 1924	8.3
	Ted Williams, 1942	8.3
9	Lou Gehrig, 1927	8.2
10	Ted Williams, 1947	8.1
	Stan Musial, 1948	8.1
	Mickey Mantle, 1957	8.1
13	Rogers Hornsby, 1920	8.0
	Ted Williams, 1941	8.0
	Joe Morgan, 1975	8.0
16	Nap Lajoie, 1903	7.9
	Ty Cobb, 1917	7.9
18	Babe Ruth, 1926	7.8
	Willie Mays, 1955	7.8
20	George Sisler, 1920	7.7
	Babe Ruth, 1930	7.7
	Ted Williams, 1946	7.7
23	Fred Dunlap, 1884	7.6
	Jimmie Foxx, 1933	7.6
	Mickey Mantle, 1956	7.6
	Norm Cash, 1961	7.6
	Ron Santo, 1966	7.6
28	Ted Williams, 1949	7.5
	Jackie Robinson, 1951	7.5
30	Nap Lajoie, 1901	7.4
	Mike Schmidt, 1980	7.4
	Rickey Henderson, 1985	7.4
33	Nap Lajoie, 1904	7.3
	Tris Speaker, 1912	7.3
35	Rogers Hornsby, 1921	7.2
	Rogers Hornsby, 1922	7.2
	Chuck Klein, 1930	7.2
	Carl Yastrzemski, 1967	7.2
	Mike Schmidt, 1977	7.2
40	Tris Speaker, 1913	7.1
	Babe Ruth, 1919	7.1
	Harland Clift, 1937	7.1
	Rod Carew, 1974	7.1
44	Honus Wagner, 1905	7.0
	Tris Speaker, 1914	7.0
	Babe Ruth, 1928	7.0
	Rogers Hornsby, 1929	7.0
	Stan Musial, 1951	7.0
	Mickey Mantle, 1961	7.0
	Ron Santo, 1967	7.0
	Carl Yastrzemski, 1968	7.0
	Mike Schmidt, 1974	7.0
	George Brett, 1985	7.0
54	Ty Cobb, 1909	6.9
	Joe Jackson, 1912	6.9
	Reggie Jackson, 1969	6.9
57	Nap Lajoie, 1906	6.8
	Honus Wagner, 1908	6.8
	Nap Lajoie, 1908	6.8
	Rogers Hornsby, 1924	6.8
	Lou Gehrig, 1930	6.8
	Lou Boudreau, 1944	6.8
	Mike Schmidt, 1982	6.8
64	Ted Williams, 1957	6.7
	George Brett, 1980	6.7
66	Honus Wagner, 1906	6.6
	Tris Speaker, 1916	6.6
	Snuffy Stirnweiss, 1944	6.6
	Ted Williams, 1948	6.6
	Mike Schmidt, 1981	6.6
	Robin Yount, 1982	6.6
72	Nap Lajoie, 1907	6.5
	Ty Cobb, 1911	6.5
	Joe Jackson, 1911	6.5
	Joe Cronin, 1930	6.5
	Eddie Lake, 1945	6.5
	Frank Robinson, 1966	6.5
	Ryne Sandberg, 1984	6.5
79	Babe Ruth, 1931	6.4
	Charlie Gehringer, 1936	6.4
	Arky Vaughan, 1938	6.4
	Snuffy Stirnweiss, 1945	6.4
	Willie Mays, 1958	6.4
	Willie Mays, 1964	6.4
	Pedro Guerrero, 1985	6.4
86	Ty Cobb, 1910	6.3
	Honus Wagner, 1912	6.3
	Duke Kenworthy, 1914	6.3
	Eddie Collins, 1915	6.3
	Benny Kauff, 1915	6.3
	Frankie Frisch, 1927	6.3
	Hank Aaron, 1959	6.3
	Frank Robinson, 1962	6.3
	Willie Mays, 1965	6.3
	Eric Davis, 1987	6.3
96	14 players tied	6.2

Total Player Rating (alpha.)

Hank Aaron, 1959	6.3
Lou Boudreau, 1944	6.8
George Brett, 1980	6.7
George Brett, 1985	7.0
Rod Carew, 1974	7.1
Norm Cash, 1961	7.6
Harland Clift, 1937	7.1
Ty Cobb, 1909	6.9
Ty Cobb, 1910	6.3
Ty Cobb, 1911	6.5
Ty Cobb, 1917	7.9
Eddie Collins, 1915	6.3
Joe Cronin, 1930	6.5
Eric Davis, 1987	6.3
Fred Dunlap, 1884	7.6
Jimmie Foxx, 1933	7.6
Frankie Frisch, 1927	6.3
Lou Gehrig, 1927	8.2
Lou Gehrig, 1930	6.8
Charlie Gehringer, 1936	6.4
Pedro Guerrero, 1985	6.4
Rickey Henderson, 1985	7.4
Rogers Hornsby, 1920	8.0
Rogers Hornsby, 1921	7.2
Rogers Hornsby, 1922	7.2
Rogers Hornsby, 1924	6.8
Rogers Hornsby, 1929	7.0
Joe Jackson, 1911	6.5
Joe Jackson, 1912	6.9
Reggie Jackson, 1969	6.9
Benny Kauff, 1915	6.3
Duke Kenworthy, 1914	6.3
Chuck Klein, 1930	7.2
Nap Lajoie, 1901	7.4
Nap Lajoie, 1903	7.9
Nap Lajoie, 1904	7.3
Nap Lajoie, 1906	6.8
Nap Lajoie, 1907	6.5
Nap Lajoie, 1908	6.8
Nap Lajoie, 1910	8.9
Eddie Lake, 1945	6.5
Mickey Mantle, 1956	7.6
Mickey Mantle, 1957	8.1
Mickey Mantle, 1961	7.0
Willie Mays, 1955	7.8
Willie Mays, 1958	6.4
Willie Mays, 1964	6.4
Willie Mays, 1965	6.3
Joe Morgan, 1975	8.0
Stan Musial, 1948	8.1
Stan Musial, 1951	7.0
Cal Ripken, 1984	9.0
Jackie Robinson, 1951	7.5
Frank Robinson, 1962	6.3
Frank Robinson, 1966	6.5
Babe Ruth, 1919	7.1
Babe Ruth, 1920	8.8
Babe Ruth, 1921	9.9
Babe Ruth, 1923	9.0
Babe Ruth, 1924	8.3
Babe Ruth, 1926	7.8
Babe Ruth, 1927	8.5
Babe Ruth, 1928	7.0
Babe Ruth, 1930	7.7
Babe Ruth, 1931	6.4
Ryne Sandberg, 1984	6.5
Ron Santo, 1966	7.6
Ron Santo, 1967	7.0
Mike Schmidt, 1974	7.0
Mike Schmidt, 1977	7.2
Mike Schmidt, 1980	7.4
Mike Schmidt, 1981	6.6
Mike Schmidt, 1982	6.8
George Sisler, 1920	7.7
Tris Speaker, 1912	7.3
Tris Speaker, 1913	7.1
Tris Speaker, 1914	7.0
Tris Speaker, 1916	6.6
Snuffy Stirnweiss, 1944	6.6
Snuffy Stirnweiss, 1945	6.4
Arky Vaughan, 1938	6.4
Honus Wagner, 1905	7.0
Honus Wagner, 1906	6.6
Honus Wagner, 1908	6.8
Honus Wagner, 1912	6.3
Ted Williams, 1941	8.0
Ted Williams, 1942	8.3
Ted Williams, 1946	7.7
Ted Williams, 1947	8.1
Ted Williams, 1948	6.6
Ted Williams, 1949	7.5
Ted Williams, 1957	6.7
Carl Yastrzemski, 1967	7.2
Carl Yastrzemski, 1968	7.0
Robin Yount, 1982	6.6

Total Player Rating (by era)

1876-1892

1	Fred Dunlap, 1884	7.6
2	Cupid Childs, 1890	6.1
3	Fred Pfeffer, 1884	5.8
4	Bill Dahlen, 1892	5.5
5	Tip O'Neill, 1887	5.2
6	Dan Brouthers, 1892	5.1
7	Jack Glasscock, 1889	4.9
	Harry Stovey, 1889	4.9
9	Hub Collins, 1888	4.8
10	King Kelly, 1886	4.7
	Bid McPhee, 1886	4.7
	Herman Long, 1889	4.7
13	Sam Barkley, 1884	4.6
14	6 players tied	4.5

1893-1919

1	Nap Lajoie, 1910	8.9
2	Nap Lajoie, 1903	7.9
	Ty Cobb, 1917	7.9
4	Nap Lajoie, 1901	7.4
5	Nap Lajoie, 1904	7.3
	Tris Speaker, 1912	7.3
7	Tris Speaker, 1913	7.1
	Babe Ruth, 1919	7.1
9	Honus Wagner, 1905	7.0
	Tris Speaker, 1914	7.0
11	Ty Cobb, 1909	6.9
	Joe Jackson, 1912	6.9
13	Nap Lajoie, 1906	6.8
	Honus Wagner, 1908	6.8
	Nap Lajoie, 1908	6.8

1920-1941

1	Babe Ruth, 1921	9.9
2	Babe Ruth, 1923	9.0
3	Babe Ruth, 1920	8.8
4	Babe Ruth, 1927	8.5
5	Babe Ruth, 1924	8.3
6	Lou Gehrig, 1927	8.2
7	Rogers Hornsby, 1920	8.0
	Ted Williams, 1941	8.0
9	Babe Ruth, 1926	7.8
10	George Sisler, 1920	7.7
	Babe Ruth, 1930	7.7
12	Jimmie Foxx, 1933	7.6
13	Rogers Hornsby, 1921	7.2
	Rogers Hornsby, 1922	7.2
	Chuck Klein, 1930	7.2

1942-1960

1	Ted Williams, 1942	8.3
2	Ted Williams, 1947	8.1
	Stan Musial, 1948	8.1
	Mickey Mantle, 1957	8.1
5	Willie Mays, 1955	7.8
6	Ted Williams, 1946	7.7
7	Mickey Mantle, 1956	7.6
8	Ted Williams, 1949	7.5
	Jackie Robinson, 1951	7.5
10	Stan Musial, 1951	7.0
11	Lou Boudreau, 1944	6.8
12	Ted Williams, 1957	6.7
13	Snuffy Stirnweiss, 1944	6.6
	Ted Williams, 1948	6.6
15	Eddie Lake, 1945	6.5

1961-1988

1	Cal Ripken, 1984	9.0
2	Joe Morgan, 1975	8.0
3	Norm Cash, 1961	7.6
	Ron Santo, 1966	7.6
5	Mike Schmidt, 1980	7.4
	Rickey Henderson, 1985	7.4
7	Carl Yastrzemski, 1967	7.2
	Mike Schmidt, 1977	7.2
9	Rod Carew, 1974	7.1
10	Mickey Mantle, 1961	7.0
	Ron Santo, 1967	7.0
	Carl Yastrzemski, 1968	7.0
	Mike Schmidt, 1974	7.0
	George Brett, 1985	7.0
15	Reggie Jackson, 1969	6.9

Wins

	Player	Wins
1	Charley Radbourn, 1884	60
2	John Clarkson, 1885	53
3	Guy Hecker, 1884	52
4	John Clarkson, 1889	49
5	Charley Radbourn, 1883	48
	Charlie Buffinton, 1884	48
7	Al Spalding, 1876	47
	Monte Ward, 1879	47
9	Jim Galvin, 1883	46
	Jim Galvin, 1884	46
	Matt Kilroy, 1887	46
12	George Bradley, 1876	45
	Jim McCormick, 1880	45
	Silver King, 1888	45
15	Mickey Welch, 1885	44
	Bill Hutchinson, 1891	44
17	Tommy Bond, 1879	43
	Will White, 1879	43
	Larry Corcoran, 1880	43
	Will White, 1883	43
21	Lady Baldwin, 1886	42
	Tim Keefe, 1886	42
	Bill Hutchinson, 1890	42
24	Tim Keefe, 1883	41
	Dave Foutz, 1886	41
	Ed Morris, 1886	41
	Jack Chesbro, 1904	41
28	Tommy Bond, 1877	40
	Tommy Bond, 1878	40
	Will White, 1882	40
	Bill Sweeney, 1884	40
	Bob Caruthers, 1885	40
	Bob Caruthers, 1889	40
	Ed Walsh, 1908	40
35	Monte Ward, 1880	39
	Mickey Welch, 1884	39
	Ed Morris, 1885	39
38	Toad Ramsey, 1886	38
	John Clarkson, 1887	38
	Kid Gleason, 1890	38
41	Jim Galvin, 1879	37
	Jim Whitney, 1883	37
	Tim Keefe, 1884	37
	Jack Lynch, 1884	37
	Tony Mullane, 1884	37
	Toad Ramsey, 1887	37
	Bill Hutchinson, 1892	37
	Christy Mathewson, 1908	37
49	Jim McCormick, 1882	36
	John Clarkson, 1886	36
	Sadie McMahon, 1890	36
	Cy Young, 1892	36
	Amos Rusie, 1894	36
	Walter Johnson, 1913	36
55	Jim Devlin, 1877	35
	Tony Mullane, 1883	35
	Larry Corcoran, 1884	35
	Tim Keefe, 1887	35
	Tim Keefe, 1888	35
	Ed Seward, 1888	35
	Silver King, 1889	35
	Kid Nichols, 1892	35
	Jack Stivetts, 1892	35
	Cy Young, 1895	35
	Joe McGinnity, 1904	35
66	Mickey Welch, 1880	34
	Larry Corcoran, 1883	34
	Ed Morris, 1884	34
	Will White, 1884	34
	Mike Smith, 1887	34
	Scott Stratton, 1890	34
	Mark Baldwin, 1890	34
	George Haddock, 1891	34
	Sadie McMahon, 1891	34
	Frank Killen, 1893	34
	Kid Nichols, 1893	34
	Cy Young, 1893	34
	Joe Wood, 1912	34
79	Charley Radbourn, 1882	33
	Dave Foutz, 1885	33
	Henry Porter, 1885	33
	Mickey Welch, 1886	33
	Tony Mullane, 1886	33
	John Clarkson, 1888	33
	John Clarkson, 1891	33
	Amos Rusie, 1891	33
	Jack Stivetts, 1891	33
	Amos Rusie, 1893	33
	Jouett Meekin, 1894	33
	Cy Young, 1901	33
	Christy Mathewson, 1904	33
	Walter Johnson, 1912	33
	Pete Alexander, 1916	33
94	9 players tied	32

Wins (by era)

1876-1892

	Player	Wins
1	Charley Radbourn, 1884	60
2	John Clarkson, 1885	53
3	Guy Hecker, 1884	52
4	John Clarkson, 1889	49
5	Charley Radbourn, 1883	48
	Charlie Buffinton, 1884	48
7	Al Spalding, 1876	47
	Monte Ward, 1879	47
9	Jim Galvin, 1883	46
	Jim Galvin, 1884	46
	Matt Kilroy, 1887	46
12	George Bradley, 1876	45
	Jim McCormick, 1880	45
	Silver King, 1888	45
15	2 players tied	44

1893-1919

	Player	Wins
1	Jack Chesbro, 1904	41
2	Ed Walsh, 1908	40
3	Christy Mathewson, 1908	37
4	Amos Rusie, 1894	36
	Walter Johnson, 1913	36
6	Cy Young, 1895	35
	Joe McGinnity, 1904	35
8	Frank Killen, 1893	34
	Kid Nichols, 1893	34
	Cy Young, 1893	34
	Joe Wood, 1912	34
12	6 players tied	33

1920-1941

	Player	Wins
1	Jim Bagby, 1920	31
	Lefty Grove, 1931	31
3	Dizzy Dean, 1934	30
4	Dazzy Vance, 1924	28
	Lefty Grove, 1930	28
	Dizzy Dean, 1935	28
7	Pete Alexander, 1920	27
	Carl Mays, 1921	27
	Urban Shocker, 1921	27
	Eddie Rommel, 1922	27
	Dolf Luque, 1923	27
	George Uhle, 1926	27
	Bucky Walters, 1939	27
	Bob Feller, 1940	27
15	7 players tied	26

[1942-1960]

	Player	Wins
1	Hal Newhouser, 1944	29
2	Robin Roberts, 1952	28
3	Dizzy Trout, 1944	27
	Don Newcombe, 1956	27
5	Hal Newhouser, 1946	26
	Bob Feller, 1946	26
7	Hal Newhouser, 1945	25
	Dave Ferriss, 1946	25
	Mel Parnell, 1949	25
10	Johnny Sain, 1948	24
	Bobby Shantz, 1952	24
12	13 players tied	23

1961-1988

	Player	Wins
1	Denny McLain, 1968	31
2	Sandy Koufax, 1966	27
	Steve Carlton, 1972	27
4	Sandy Koufax, 1965	26
	Juan Marichal, 1968	26
6	12 players tied	25

Losses

	Player	Losses
1	John Coleman, 1883	48
2	Will White, 1880	42
3	Larry McKeon, 1884	41
4	George Bradley, 1879	40
	Jim McCormick, 1879	40
6	Henry Porter, 1888	37
	Kid Carsey, 1891	37
	George Cobb, 1892	37
9	Stump Weidman, 1886	36
	Bill Hutchinson, 1892	36
11	Jim Devlin, 1876	35
	Jim Galvin, 1880	35
	Fleury Sullivan, 1884	35
	Adonis Terry, 1884	35
	Hardie Henderson, 1885	35
	Red Donahue, 1897	35
17	Bobby Mathews, 1876	34
	Bob Barr, 1884	34
	Matt Kilroy, 1886	34
	Al Mays, 1887	34
	Mark Baldwin, 1889	34
	Amos Rusie, 1890	34
23	Harry McCormick, 1879	33
	Jim Whitney, 1881	33
	Lee Richmond, 1882	33
	Frank Mountain, 1883	33
	Jersey Bakely, 1888	33
28	Lee Richmond, 1880	32
	Hardie Henderson, 1883	32
	John Harkins, 1884	32
	Jim Whitney, 1885	32
	Jim Whitney, 1886	32
33	Sam Weaver, 1878	31
	Will White, 1879	31
	Charley Radbourn, 1886	31
	Dupee Shaw, 1886	31
	Billy Crowell, 1887	31
	Ed Beatin, 1890	31
	Amos Rusie, 1892	31
40	Mickey Welch, 1880	30
	Jim McCormick, 1881	30
	Jim McCormick, 1882	30
	Jack Lynch, 1886	30
	Phenomenal Smith, 1887	30
	Toad Ramsey, 1888	30
	John Ewing, 1889	30
	Ted Breitenstein, 1895	30
	Jim Hughey, 1899	30
49	Tommy Bond, 1880	29
	Jim Galvin, 1883	29
	Egyptian Healy, 1887	29
	Hank O'Day, 1888	29
	Bert Cunningham, 1888	29
	Red Ehret, 1889	29
	Silver King, 1891	29
	Bill Hart, 1896	29
	Jack Taylor, 1898	29
	Vic Willis, 1905	29
59	Jim McCormick, 1880	28
	Doc Landis, 1882	28
	Hank O'Day, 1884	28
	Hugh Daily, 1884	28
	Al Mays, 1886	28
	Gus Weyhing, 1887	28
	Mark Baldwin, 1891	28
	Duke Esper, 1893	28
	Bill Hill, 1896	28
68	Jim Galvin, 1879	27
	Tim Keefe, 1881	27
	Tim Keefe, 1883	27
	Jersey Bakely, 1884	27
	Charlie Buffinton, 1885	27
	Tony Mullane, 1886	27
	Toad Ramsey, 1886	27
	Toad Ramsey, 1887	27
	Park Swartzel, 1889	27
	Phil Knell, 1891	27
	Mark Baldwin, 1892	27
	Pink Hawley, 1894	27
	Chick Fraser, 1896	27
	Bill Hart, 1897	27
	Willie Sudhoff, 1898	27
	Bill Carrick, 1899	27
	Dummy Taylor, 1901	27
	George Bell, 1910	27
	Paul Derringer, 1933	27
87	18 players tied	26

Winning Percentage

1	Roy Face, 1959	.947
2	Rick Sutcliffe, 1984	.941
3	Ron Guidry, 1978	.893
4	Freddie Fitzsimmons, 1940	.889
5	Lefty Grove, 1931	.886
6	Preacher Roe, 1951	.880
7	Fred Goldsmith, 1880	.875
	Jim McCormick, 1884	.875
9	Joe Wood, 1912	.872
10	David Cone, 1988	.870
11	Orel Hershiser, 1985	.864
12	Billy Taylor, 1884	.862
	Bill Donovan, 1907	.862
	Whitey Ford, 1961	.862
15	Dwight Gooden, 1985	.857
	Roger Clemens, 1986	.857
17	Chief Bender, 1914	.850
18	Lefty Grove, 1930	.848
19	Tom Hughes, 1916	.842
	Emil Yde, 1924	.842
	Schoolboy Rowe, 1940	.842
	Sandy Consuegra, 1954	.842
	Ralph Terry, 1961	.842
	Ron Perranoski, 1963	.842
25	Lefty Gomez, 1934	.839
26	Bill Hoffer, 1895	.838
	Denny McLain, 1968	.838
28	Walter Johnson, 1913	.837
29	Charley Radbourn, 1884	.833
	King Cole, 1910	.833
	Spud Chandler, 1943	.833
	Sandy Koufax, 1963	.833
33	Ed Reulbach, 1906	.826
	Elmer Riddle, 1941	.826
35	Jim Hughes, 1899	.824
	Jack Chesbro, 1902	.824
	Dazzy Vance, 1924	.824
38	Chief Bender, 1910	.821
	Bob Purkey, 1962	.821
40	Sal Maglie, 1950	.818
41	Joe McGinnity, 1904	.814
42	Mordecai Brown, 1906	.813
	Russ Ford, 1910	.813
	Eddie Plank, 1912	.813
	Carl Hubbell, 1936	.813
46	Dizzy Dean, 1934	.811
47	Ed Reulbach, 1907	.810
	Doc Crandall, 1910	.810
	Johnny Allen, 1932	.810
	Ted Wilks, 1944	.810
	Phil Niekro, 1982	.810
52	General Crowder, 1928	.808
	Bobo Newsom, 1940	.808
	Tiny Bonham, 1942	.808
	Larry Jansen, 1947	.808
	Dave McNally, 1971	.808
	Jim Hunter, 1973	.808
58	Christy Mathewson, 1909	.806
	Howie Camnitz, 1909	.806
	Dave Ferriss, 1946	.806
	Juan Marichal, 1966	.806
62	Eddie Cicotte, 1919	.806
63	Mickey Welch, 1885	.800
	Ed Doheny, 1902	.800
	Sam Leever, 1905	.800
	Bert Humphries, 1913	.800
	Stan Coveleski, 1925	.800
	Firpo Marberry, 1931	.800
	Robin Roberts, 1952	.800
	Eddie Lopat, 1953	.800
	Don Newcombe, 1955	.800
	Jim Palmer, 1969	.800
	John Candelaria, 1977	.800
	Larry Gura, 1978	.800
75	Al Spalding, 1876	.797
76	Christy Mathewson, 1905	.795
77	Don Newcombe, 1956	.794
78	Jocko Flynn, 1886	.793
	Ellis Kinder, 1949	.793
	Sal Maglie, 1951	.793
81	Dutch Leonard, 1914	.792
	Sandy Koufax, 1964	.792
	Wally Bunker, 1964	.792
84	Fred Klobedanz, 1897	.788
	Bill James, 1914	.788
	Joe Bush, 1922	.788
87	Jouett Meekin, 1894	.786
	Lon Warneke, 1932	.786
	Tex Hughson, 1942	.786
	Ron Guidry, 1985	.786
91	Bob Caruthers, 1889	.784
92	George Mullin, 1909	.784
93	Jack Manning, 1876	.783
	Bill Bernhard, 1902	.783
	Tex Hughson, 1944	.783
	Jack Kramer, 1948	.783
	Johnny Podres, 1961	.783
	Bryn Smith, 1985	.783
	Bobby Ojeda, 1986	.783
	Tom Browning, 1988	.783

Winning Percentage (by era)

1876-1892
1. Fred Goldsmith, 1880 ...... .875
   Jim McCormick, 1884 ...... .875
3. Billy Taylor, 1884 .... .862
4. Charley Radbourn, 1884 ..... .833
5. Mickey Welch, 1885 .... .800
6. Al Spalding, 1876 .... .797
7. Jocko Flynn, 1886 .... .793
8. Bob Caruthers, 1889 ...... .784
9. Manning, 1876 .... .783
10. Charlie Sweeney, 1884 ..... .774
11. Will White, 1882 .... .769
    Charlie Ferguson, 1886 .... .769
13. John Clarkson, 1885 ...... .768
14. Lady Baldwin, 1886 .... .764
15. 2 players tied .... .763

1893-1919
1. Joe Wood, 1912 .... .872
2. Bill Donovan, 1907 .... .862
3. Chief Bender, 1914 .... .850
4. Tom Hughes, 1916 .... .842
5. Bill Hoffer, 1895 .... .838
6. Walter Johnson, 1913 ...... .837
7. King Cole, 1910 .... .833
8. Ed Reulbach, 1906 .... .826
9. Jim Hughes, 1899 .... .824
   Jack Chesbro, 1902 .... .824
11. Chief Bender, 1910 ...... .821
12. Joe McGinnity, 1904 ..... .814
13. Mordecai Brown, 1906 ..... .813
    Russ Ford, 1910 .... .813
    Eddie Plank, 1912 .... .813

1920-1941
1. Freddie Fitzsimmons, 1940 . .889
2. Lefty Grove, 1931 .... .886
3. Lefty Grove, 1930 .... .848
4. Emil Yde, 1924 .... .842
   Schoolboy Rowe, 1940 ..... .842
6. Lefty Gomez, 1934 .... .839
7. Elmer Riddle, 1941 ...... .826
8. Dazzy Vance, 1924 .... .824
9. Carl Hubbell, 1936 ...... .813
10. Dizzy Dean, 1934 .... .811
11. Johnny Allen, 1932 ...... .810
12. General Crowder, 1928 .... .808
    Bobo Newsom, 1940 ...... .808
14. Stan Coveleski, 1925 ..... .800
    Firpo Marberry, 1931 ..... .800

1942-1960
1. Roy Face, 1959 .... .947
2. Preacher Roe, 1951 ...... .880
3. Sandy Consuegra, 1954 .... .842
4. Spud Chandler, 1943 ..... .833
5. Sal Maglie, 1950 .... .818
6. Ted Wilks, 1944 .... .810
7. Tiny Bonham, 1942 .... .808
   Larry Jansen, 1947 ...... .808
9. Dave Ferriss, 1946 ...... .806
10. Robin Roberts, 1952 ..... .800
    Eddie Lopat, 1953 ...... .800
    Don Newcombe, 1955 ..... .800
13. Don Newcombe, 1956 ..... .794
14. Ellis Kinder, 1949 ...... .793
    Sal Maglie, 1951 .... .793

1961-1988
1. Rick Sutcliffe, 1984 ...... .941
2. Ron Guidry, 1978 .... .893
3. David Cone, 1988 .... .870
4. Orel Hershiser, 1985 ..... .864
5. Whitey Ford, 1961 .... .862
6. Dwight Gooden, 1985 ..... .857
   Roger Clemens, 1986 ..... .857
8. Ralph Terry, 1961 .... .842
   Ron Perranoski, 1963 ..... .842
10. Denny McLain, 1968 ..... .838
11. Sandy Koufax, 1963 ..... .833
12. Bob Purkey, 1962 .... .821
13. Phil Niekro, 1982 ...... .810
14. Dave McNally, 1971 ...... .808
    Jim Hunter, 1973 .... .808

Games

1. Mike Marshall, 1974 106
2. Kent Tekulve, 1979 94
3. Mike Marshall, 1973 92
4. Kent Tekulve, 1978 91
5. Wayne Granger, 1969 90
   Mike Marshall, 1979 90
   Kent Tekulve, 1987 90
8. Mark Eichhorn, 1987 89
9. Wilbur Wood, 1968 88
10. Rob Murphy, 1987 87
11. Kent Tekulve, 1982 85
    Frank Williams, 1987 85
    Mitch Williams, 1987 85
14. Ted Abernathy, 1965 84
    Enrique Romo, 1979 84
    Dick Tidrow, 1980 84
    Dan Quisenberry, 1985 84
18. Ken Sanders, 1971 83
    Craig Lefferts, 1986 83
20. Eddie Fisher, 1965 82
    Bill Campbell, 1983 82
22. John Wyatt, 1964 81
    Dale Murray, 1976 81
    Jeff Robinson, 1987 81
25. Pedro Borbon, 1973 80
    Willie Hernandez, 1984 80
    Mitch Williams, 1986 80
28. Dick Radatz, 1964 79
29. Hal Woodeshick, 1965 78
    Ted Abernathy, 1968 78
    Bill Campbell, 1976 78
    Rollie Fingers, 1977 78
    Tom Hume, 1980 78
    Kent Tekulve, 1980 78
    Greg Minton, 1982 78
    Ed Vande Berg, 1982 78
    Ted Power, 1984 78
    Tim Burke, 1985 78
    Lance McCullers, 1987 78
40. Bob Locker, 1967 77
    Wilbur Wood, 1970 77
    Charlie Hough, 1976 77
    Butch Metzger, 1976 77
    Rick Camp, 1980 77
    Gary Lavelle, 1984 77
    Mark Davis, 1985 77
    Craig Lefferts, 1987 77
48. Will White, 1879 76
    Jim Galvin, 1883 76
    Charley Radbourn, 1883 ... 76
    Wilbur Wood, 1969 76
    Ron Herbel, 1970 76
    Larry Hardy, 1974 76
    Rollie Fingers, 1974 76
    Dan Spillner, 1977 76
    Dave Tomlin, 1977 76
    Sid Monge, 1979 76
    Rod Scurry, 1982 76
    Tippy Martinez, 1982 76
    Kent Tekulve, 1983 76
    Ed Vande Berg, 1985 76
    Rob Murphy, 1988 76
63. Charley Radbourn, 1884 75
    Guy Hecker, 1884 75
    Bill Hutchinson, 1884 75
    Ron Perranoski, 1969 75
    Rollie Fingers, 1975 75
    Butch Metzger, 1977 75
    Dan Quisenberry, 1980 75
    Willie Hernandez, 1982 75
    Jeff Reardon, 1982 75
    Roger McDowell, 1986 75
    Todd Worrell, 1987 75
    Juan Agosto, 1988 75
    Jeff Robinson, 1988 75
76. Jim McCormick, 1880 74
    Lee Richmond, 1880 74
    Jim Konstanty, 1950 74
    Bob Miller, 1964 74
    Ron Kline, 1965 74
    Dan McGinn, 1969 74
    Bob Lacey, 1978 74
    Enrique Romo, 1980 74
    Willie Hernandez, 1983 74
    Greg Minton, 1984 74
    Scott Garrelts, 1985 74
    Willie Hernandez, 1985 74
    Dave Righetti, 1985 74
    Johnny Franco, 1986 74
    Todd Worrell, 1986 74
    Dave Righetti, 1986 74
    Dale Mohorcic, 1987 74
93. 13 players tied 73

Games (by era)

1876-1892
1. Will White, 1879 76
   Jim Galvin, 1883 76
   Charley Radbourn, 1883 76
4. Charley Radbourn, 1884 75
   Guy Hecker, 1884 75
   Bill Hutchinson, 1892 75
7. Jim McCormick, 1880 74
   Lee Richmond, 1880 74
9. John Clarkson, 1889 73
10. Jim Galvin, 1884 72
11. Bill Hutchinson, 1890 71
12. Monte Ward, 1879 70
    Monte Ward, 1880 70
    John Clarkson, 1885 70
15. Matt Kilroy, 1887 69

1893-1919
1. Ed Walsh, 1908 66
2. Ed Walsh, 1912 62
3. Dave Davenport, 1916 59
4. Amos Rusie, 1893 56
   Ted Breitenstein, 1894 56
   Pink Hawley, 1895 56
   Ed Walsh, 1907 56
   Christy Mathewson, 1908 ... 56
   Ed Walsh, 1911 56
   Reb Russell, 1916 56
11. Frank Killen, 1893 55
    Joe McGinnity, 1903 55
    Jack Chesbro, 1904 55
    Dave Davenport, 1915 55
15. 3 players tied 54

1920-1941
1. Firpo Marberry, 1926 64
2. Clint Brown, 1939 61
3. Garland Braxton, 1927 58
   Russ VanAtta, 1935 58
5. Eddie Rommel, 1923 56
   Firpo Marberry, 1927 56
   Hugh Mulcahy, 1940 56
8. Firpo Marberry, 1925 55
   Bump Hadley, 1931 55
   Jim Walkup, 1935 55
11. George Uhle, 1923 54
    Firpo Marberry, 1932 54
    Jack Russell, 1934 54
    Chubby Dean, 1939 54
    Clyde Shoun, 1940 54

1942-1960
1. Jim Konstanty, 1950 74
2. Hoyt Wilhelm, 1952 71
3. Ace Adams, 1943 70
   Mike Fornieles, 1960 70
5. Ellis Kinder, 1953 69
   Don Elston, 1958 69
7. Hoyt Wilhelm, 1953 68
   Roy Face, 1956 68
   Roy Face, 1960 68
10. Andy Karl, 1945 67
    Turk Lown, 1957 67
    Gerry Staley, 1959 67
13. 6 players tied 65

1961-1988
1. Mike Marshall, 1974 106
2. Kent Tekulve, 1979 94
3. Mike Marshall, 1973 92
4. Kent Tekulve, 1978 91
5. Wayne Granger, 1969 90
   Mike Marshall, 1979 90
   Kent Tekulve, 1987 90
8. Mark Eichhorn, 1987 89
9. Wilbur Wood, 1968 88
10. Rob Murphy, 1987 87
11. Kent Tekulve, 1982 85
    Frank Williams, 1987 85
    Mitch Williams, 1987 85
14. 4 players tied 84

Games Started

1. Will White, 1879 75
   Jim Galvin, 1883 75
3. Jim McCormick, 1880 74
4. Charley Radbourn, 1884 73
   Guy Hecker, 1884 73
6. Jim Galvin, 1884 72
   John Clarkson, 1889 72
8. Bill Hutchinson, 1892 71
9. John Clarkson, 1885 70
10. Matt Kilroy, 1887 69
11. Jim Devlin, 1876 68
    Charley Radbourn, 1883 ... 68
    Tim Keefe, 1883 68
    Matt Kilroy, 1886 68
15. Monte Ward, 1880 67
    Jim McCormick, 1882 67
    Charlie Buffinton, 1884 ... 67
    Toad Ramsey, 1886 67
19. Jim Galvin, 1879 66
    Lee Richmond, 1880 66
    Tony Mullane, 1884 66
    Bill Hutchinson, 1890 66
23. Mickey Welch, 1884 65
    Silver King, 1888 65
25. George Bradley, 1876 64
    Tommy Bond, 1879 64
    Mickey Welch, 1880 64
    Will White, 1883 64
    Tim Keefe, 1886 64
    Toad Ramsey, 1887 64
31. Jim Whitney, 1881 63
    Ed Morris, 1885 63
    Ed Morris, 1886 63
    Amos Rusie, 1890 63
35. Will White, 1880 62
36. Jim Devlin, 1877 61
    John Coleman, 1883 61
    Hardie Henderson, 1885 ... 61
    Jersey Bakely, 1888 61
    Amos Rusie, 1892 61
41. Al Spalding, 1876 60
    Jim McCormick, 1879 60
    Monte Ward, 1879 60
    Larry Corcoran, 1880 60
    Larry McKeon, 1884 60
    Bill Sweeney, 1884 60
47. Tommy Bond, 1878 59
    Frank Mountain, 1883 59
    Larry Corcoran, 1884 59
    Mickey Welch, 1886 59
    John Clarkson, 1887 59
    Mark Baldwin, 1889 59
53. Tommy Bond, 1877 58
    Terry Larkin, 1879 58
    Jim McCormick, 1881 58
    Tim Keefe, 1884 58
    Hugh Daily, 1884 58
    Charley Radbourn, 1886 ... 58
    Bill Hutchinson, 1891 58
    Sadie McMahon, 1891 58
61. Tommy Bond, 1880 57
    Dave Foutz, 1886 57
    Ed Seward, 1888 57
    Sadie McMahon, 1890 57
    Mark Baldwin, 1890 57
    Amos Rusie, 1891 57
67. Bobby Mathews, 1876 56
    Terry Larkin, 1877 56
    Terry Larkin, 1878 56
    Jim Whitney, 1883 56
    Adonis Terry, 1884 56
    Lady Baldwin, 1886 56
    Tony Mullane, 1886 56
    Tim Keefe, 1887 56
    Matt Kilroy, 1889 56
    Silver King, 1890 56
    Jack Stivetts, 1891 56
78. George Derby, 1881 55
    Tony Mullane, 1884 55
    Mickey Welch, 1885 55
    John Clarkson, 1886 55
    Phenomenal Smith, 1887 ... 55
    Gus Weyhing, 1887 55
    Ed Morris, 1888 55
    Kid Gleason, 1890 55
86. George Bradley, 1879 54
    Harry McCormick, 1879 54
    Jim Galvin, 1880 54
    Will White, 1882 54
    Henry Porter, 1885 54
    John Clarkson, 1888 54
    Henry Porter, 1888 54
    Ed Beatin, 1890 54
    Bob Barr, 1890 54
95. 9 players tied 53

Games Started (by era)

1876-1892

1	Will White, 1879	75
	Jim Galvin, 1883	75
3	Jim McCormick, 1880	74
4	Charley Radbourn, 1884	73
	Guy Hecker, 1884	73
6	Jim Galvin, 1884	72
	John Clarkson, 1889	72
8	Bill Hutchinson, 1892	71
9	John Clarkson, 1885	70
10	Matt Kilroy, 1887	69
11	Jim Devlin, 1876	68
	Charley Radbourn, 1883	68
	Tim Keefe, 1883	68
	Matt Kilroy, 1886	68
15	4 players tied	67

1893-1919

1	Amos Rusie, 1893	52
2	Jack Chesbro, 1904	51
3	Ted Breitenstein, 1894	50
	Amos Rusie, 1894	50
	Ted Breitenstein, 1895	50
	Pink Hawley, 1895	50
	Frank Killen, 1896	50
8	Ed Walsh, 1908	49
9	Frank Killen, 1893	48
	Jouett Meekin, 1894	48
	Joe McGinnity, 1903	48
12	Cy Young, 1894	47
	Amos Rusie, 1895	47
	Jack Taylor, 1898	47
15	8 players tied	46

1920-1941

1	George Uhle, 1923	44
2	Pete Alexander, 1920	40
	Stan Coveleski, 1921	40
	George Uhle, 1922	40
	George Caster, 1938	40
	Bobo Newsom, 1938	40
	Bob Feller, 1941	40
8	Red Faber, 1920	39
	Red Faber, 1921	39
	Hooks Dauss, 1923	39
	Howard Ehmke, 1923	39
	George Earnshaw, 1930	39
	General Crowder, 1932	39
	Kirby Higbe, 1941	39
15	24 players tied	38

1942-1960

1	Bob Feller, 1946	42
	Bob Friend, 1956	42
3	Bill Voiselle, 1944	41
	Robin Roberts, 1953	41
5	Dizzy Trout, 1944	40
6	Johnny Sain, 1948	39
	Robin Roberts, 1950	39
	Warren Spahn, 1950	39
	Vern Bickford, 1950	39
	Robin Roberts, 1951	39
	Ron Kline, 1956	39
	Lew Burdette, 1959	39
13	10 players tied	38

1961-1988

1	Wilbur Wood, 1972	49
2	Wilbur Wood, 1973	48
3	Mickey Lolich, 1971	45
4	Phil Niekro, 1979	44
5	Wilbur Wood, 1975	43
	Phil Niekro, 1977	43
7	10 players tied	42

Complete Games

1	Will White, 1879	75
2	Charley Radbourn, 1884	73
3	Jim McCormick, 1880	72
	Jim Galvin, 1883	72
	Guy Hecker, 1884	72
6	Jim Galvin, 1884	71
7	Tim Keefe, 1883	68
	John Clarkson, 1885	68
	John Clarkson, 1889	68
10	Bill Hutchinson, 1892	67
11	Jim Devlin, 1876	66
	Charley Radbourn, 1883	66
	Matt Kilroy, 1886	66
	Toad Ramsey, 1886	66
	Matt Kilroy, 1887	66
16	Jim Galvin, 1879	65
	Jim McCormick, 1882	65
	Tony Mullane, 1884	65
	Bill Hutchinson, 1890	65
20	Mickey Welch, 1880	64
	Will White, 1883	64
	Silver King, 1888	64
23	George Bradley, 1876	63
	Charlie Buffinton, 1884	63
	Ed Morris, 1885	63
	Ed Morris, 1886	63
27	Mickey Welch, 1884	62
	Tim Keefe, 1886	62
29	Jim Devlin, 1877	61
	Toad Ramsey, 1887	61
31	Jersey Bakely, 1888	60
32	Tommy Bond, 1879	59
	Jim McCormick, 1879	59
	Monte Ward, 1880	59
	John Coleman, 1883	59
	Larry McKeon, 1884	59
	Hardie Henderson, 1885	59
38	Tommy Bond, 1877	58
	Monte Ward, 1879	58
	Will White, 1880	58
	Bill Sweeney, 1884	58
	Amos Rusie, 1892	58
43	Tommy Bond, 1878	57
	Terry Larkin, 1879	57
	Larry Corcoran, 1880	57
	Lee Richmond, 1880	57
	Jim McCormick, 1881	57
	Jim Whitney, 1881	57
	Frank Mountain, 1883	57
	Larry Corcoran, 1884	57
	Tim Keefe, 1884	57
	Charley Radbourn, 1886	57
	Ed Seward, 1888	57
54	Terry Larkin, 1878	56
	Hugh Daily, 1884	56
	Mickey Welch, 1886	56
	John Clarkson, 1887	56
	Amos Rusie, 1890	56
	Bill Hutchinson, 1891	56
60	Bobby Mathews, 1876	55
	Terry Larkin, 1877	55
	George Derby, 1881	55
	Adonis Terry, 1884	55
	Mickey Welch, 1885	55
	Lady Baldwin, 1886	55
	Dave Foutz, 1886	55
	Tony Mullane, 1886	55
	Matt Kilroy, 1889	55
	Sadie McMahon, 1890	55
70	Jim Whitney, 1883	54
	Tim Keefe, 1887	54
	Phenomenal Smith, 1887	54
	Ed Morris, 1888	54
	Mark Baldwin, 1889	54
	Kid Gleason, 1890	54
	Mark Baldwin, 1890	54
77	Al Spalding, 1876	53
	George Bradley, 1879	53
	Jack Lynch, 1884	53
	Bob Caruthers, 1885	53
	Henry Porter, 1885	53
	Gus Weyhing, 1887	53
	John Clarkson, 1888	53
	Henry Porter, 1888	53
	Ed Beatin, 1890	53
	Sadie McMahon, 1891	53
87	Will White, 1878	52
	Will White, 1882	52
	Will White, 1884	52
	Ed Seward, 1887	52
	Bob Barr, 1890	52
	Amos Rusie, 1891	52
93	Charley Radbourn, 1882	51
	Tony Mullane, 1882	51
	Larry Corcoran, 1883	51
	Fleury Sullivan, 1884	51
	Guy Hecker, 1885	51
	Tim Keefe, 1888	51
	Gus Weyhing, 1891	51
100	11 players tied	50

Complete Games (by era)

1876-1892

1	Will White, 1879	75
2	Charley Radbourn, 1884	73
3	Jim McCormick, 1880	72
	Jim Galvin, 1883	72
	Guy Hecker, 1884	72
6	Jim Galvin, 1884	71
7	Tim Keefe, 1883	68
	John Clarkson, 1885	68
	John Clarkson, 1889	68
10	Bill Hutchinson, 1892	67
11	Jim Devlin, 1876	66
	Charley Radbourn, 1883	66
	Matt Kilroy, 1886	66
	Toad Ramsey, 1886	66
	Matt Kilroy, 1887	66

1893-1919

1	Amos Rusie, 1893	50
2	Jack Chesbro, 1904	48
3	Ted Breitenstein, 1894	46
	Ted Breitenstein, 1895	46
5	Amos Rusie, 1894	45
	Vic Willis, 1902	45
7	Kid Nichols, 1893	44
	Cy Young, 1894	44
	Pink Hawley, 1895	44
	Frank Killen, 1896	44
	Joe McGinnity, 1903	44
12	7 players tied	42

1920-1941

1	Pete Alexander, 1920	33
	Burleigh Grimes, 1923	33
3	Red Faber, 1921	32
	George Uhle, 1926	32
5	Red Faber, 1922	31
	Wes Ferrell, 1935	31
	Bobo Newsom, 1938	31
	Bucky Walters, 1939	31
	Bob Feller, 1940	31
10	8 players tied	30

1942-1960

1	Bob Feller, 1946	36
2	Dizzy Trout, 1944	33
	Robin Roberts, 1953	33
4	Robin Roberts, 1952	30
5	Hal Newhouser, 1945	29
	Hal Newhouser, 1946	29
	Robin Roberts, 1954	29
8	Jim Tobin, 1942	28
	Jim Tobin, 1944	28
	Johnny Sain, 1948	28
	Bob Lemon, 1952	28
12	Bucky Walters, 1944	27
	Mel Parnell, 1949	27
	Vern Bickford, 1950	27
	Bobby Shantz, 1952	27

1961-1988

1	Juan Marichal, 1968	30
	Ferguson Jenkins, 1971	30
	Steve Carlton, 1972	30
	Jim Hunter, 1975	30
5	Mickey Lolich, 1971	29
	Gaylord Perry, 1972	29
	Gaylord Perry, 1973	29
	Ferguson Jenkins, 1974	29
9	Bob Gibson, 1968	28
	Denny McLain, 1968	28
	Bob Gibson, 1969	28
	Gaylord Perry, 1974	28
	Rick Langford, 1980	28
14	4 players tied	27

Shutouts

1	George Bradley, 1876	16
	Pete Alexander, 1916	16
3	Jack Coombs, 1910	13
	Bob Gibson, 1968	13
5	Tommy Bond, 1879	12
	Jim Galvin, 1884	12
	Ed Morris, 1886	12
	Pete Alexander, 1915	12
9	Charley Radbourn, 1884	11
	Dave Foutz, 1886	11
	Christy Mathewson, 1908	11
	Ed Walsh, 1908	11
	Walter Johnson, 1913	11
	Sandy Koufax, 1963	11
	Dean Chance, 1964	11
16	John Clarkson, 1885	10
	Cy Young, 1904	10
	Ed Walsh, 1906	10
	Joe Wood, 1912	10
	Dave Davenport, 1915	10
	Carl Hubbell, 1933	10
	Mort Cooper, 1942	10
	Bob Feller, 1946	10
	Bob Lemon, 1948	10
	Juan Marichal, 1965	10
	Jim Palmer, 1975	10
	John Tudor, 1985	10
28	Tommy Bond, 1878	9
	George Derby, 1881	9
	Cy Young, 1892	9
	Joe McGinnity, 1904	9
	Mordecai Brown, 1906	9
	Addie Joss, 1906	9
	Mordecai Brown, 1908	9
	Addie Joss, 1908	9
	Orval Overall, 1909	9
	Pete Alexander, 1913	9
	Walter Johnson, 1914	9
	Cy Falkenberg, 1914	9
	Babe Ruth, 1916	9
	Stan Coveleski, 1917	9
	Pete Alexander, 1919	9
	Bill Lee, 1938	9
	Bob Porterfield, 1953	9
	Luis Tiant, 1968	9
	Denny McLain, 1969	9
	Don Sutton, 1972	9
	Nolan Ryan, 1972	9
	Bert Blyleven, 1973	9
	Ron Guidry, 1978	9
51	Al Spalding, 1876	8
	Monte Ward, 1880	8
	Will White, 1882	8
	Charlie Buffinton, 1884	8
	Tony Mullane, 1884	8
	Tim Keefe, 1888	8
	John Clarkson, 1889	8
	Christy Mathewson, 1902	8
	Jack Chesbro, 1902	8
	Rube Waddell, 1904	8
	Christy Mathewson, 1905	8
	Ed Killian, 1905	8
	Lefty Leifield, 1906	8
	Rube Waddell, 1906	8
	Orval Overall, 1907	8
	Christy Mathewson, 1907	8
	Eddie Plank, 1907	8
	Mordecai Brown, 1909	8
	Christy Mathewson, 1909	8
	Ed Walsh, 1909	8
	Mordecai Brown, 1910	8
	Russ Ford, 1910	8
	Walter Johnson, 1910	8
	Reb Russell, 1913	8
	Jeff Tesreau, 1914	8
	Al Mamaux, 1915	8
	Jeff Tesreau, 1915	8
	Joe Bush, 1916	8
	Pete Alexander, 1917	8
	Jim Bagby, 1917	8
	Walter Johnson, 1917	8
	Hippo Vaughn, 1918	8
	Lefty Tyler, 1918	8
	Walter Johnson, 1918	8
	Carl Mays, 1918	8
	Babe Adams, 1920	8
	Hal Newhouser, 1945	8
	Steve Barber, 1961	8
	Camilo Pascual, 1961	8
	Whitey Ford, 1964	8
	Sandy Koufax, 1965	8
	Don Drysdale, 1968	8
	Juan Marichal, 1969	8
	Vida Blue, 1971	8
	Steve Carlton, 1972	8
	Wilbur Wood, 1972	8
	Fernando Valenzuela, 1981	8
	Dwight Gooden, 1985	8
	Orel Hershiser, 1988	8
	Roger Clemens, 1988	8

Saves

1	Dave Righetti, 1986	46
2	Dan Quisenberry, 1983	45
	Bruce Sutter, 1984	45
	Dennis Eckersley, 1988	45
5	Dan Quisenberry, 1984	44
6	Jeff Reardon, 1988	42
7	Jeff Reardon, 1985	41
8	Steve Bedrosian, 1987	40
9	Johnny Franco, 1988	39
10	John Hiller, 1973	38
11	Clay Carroll, 1972	37
	Rollie Fingers, 1978	37
	Bruce Sutter, 1979	37
	Dan Quisenberry, 1985	37
	Doug Jones, 1988	37
16	Bruce Sutter, 1982	36
	Bill Caudill, 1984	36
	Todd Worrell, 1986	36
	Lee Smith, 1987	36
20	Wayne Granger, 1970	35
	Sparky Lyle, 1972	35
	Rollie Fingers, 1977	35
	Dan Quisenberry, 1982	35
	Jeff Reardon, 1986	35
25	Ron Perranoski, 1970	34
	Don Aase, 1986	34
	Tom Henke, 1987	34
	Jim Gott, 1988	34
	Bobby Thigpen, 1988	34
30	Rich Gossage, 1980	33
	Dan Quisenberry, 1980	33
	Bob Stanley, 1983	33
	Lee Smith, 1984	33
	Lee Smith, 1985	33
	Dave Smith, 1986	33
	Todd Worrell, 1987	33
37	Jack Aker, 1966	32
	Mike Marshall, 1979	32
	Willie Hernandez, 1984	32
	Bob James, 1985	32
	Johnny Franco, 1987	32
	Todd Worrell, 1988	32
43	Ted Abernathy, 1965	31
	Ron Perranoski, 1969	31
	Ken Sanders, 1971	31
	Mike Marshall, 1973	31
	Bruce Sutter, 1977	31
	Bill Campbell, 1977	31
	Kent Tekulve, 1978	31
	Kent Tekulve, 1979	31
	Jesse Orosco, 1984	31
	Dave Righetti, 1984	31
	Willie Hernandez, 1985	31
	Donnie Moore, 1985	31
	Lee Smith, 1986	31
	Jeff Reardon, 1987	31
	Dave Righetti, 1987	31
58	Dave Giusti, 1971	30
	Ed Farmer, 1980	30
	Gene Garber, 1982	30
	Greg Minton, 1982	30
	Rich Gossage, 1982	30
	Ron Davis, 1983	30
	Dan Plesac, 1988	30
65	Luis Arroyo, 1961	29
	Dick Radatz, 1964	29
	Ron Kline, 1965	29
	Fred Gladding, 1969	29
	Lindy McDaniel, 1970	29
	Terry Forster, 1972	29
	Jim Kern, 1979	29
	Rollie Fingers, 1982	29
	Lee Smith, 1983	29
	Al Holland, 1984	29
	Ron Davis, 1984	29
	Jay Howell, 1985	29
	Dave Righetti, 1985	29
	Steve Bedrosian, 1986	29
	Johnny Franco, 1986	29
	Lee Smith, 1988	29
81	Roy Face, 1962	28
	Ted Abernathy, 1967	28
	Doug Bair, 1978	28
	Bruce Sutter, 1980	28
	Rollie Fingers, 1981	28
	Steve Bedrosian, 1988	28
	Mark Davis, 1988	28
88	17 players tied	27

Innings Pitched

1	Will White, 1879	680
2	Charley Radbourn, 1884	679
3	Guy Hecker, 1884	671
4	Jim McCormick, 1880	658
5	Jim Galvin, 1883	656
6	Jim Galvin, 1884	636
7	Charley Radbourn, 1883	632
8	Bill Hutchinson, 1892	627
9	John Clarkson, 1885	623
10	Jim Devlin, 1876	622
11	John Clarkson, 1889	620
12	Tim Keefe, 1883	619
13	Bill Hutchinson, 1890	603
14	Jim McCormick, 1882	596
15	Monte Ward, 1880	595
16	Jim Galvin, 1879	593
17	Lee Richmond, 1880	591
18	Toad Ramsey, 1886	589
	Matt Kilroy, 1887	589
20	Monte Ward, 1879	587
	Charlie Buffinton, 1884	587
22	Silver King, 1888	586
23	Matt Kilroy, 1886	583
24	Ed Morris, 1885	581
25	Will White, 1883	577
26	Tony Mullane, 1884	576
27	Mickey Welch, 1880	574
28	George Bradley, 1876	573
29	Toad Ramsey, 1887	561
	Bill Hutchinson, 1891	561
31	Jim Devlin, 1877	559
32	Mickey Welch, 1884	557
33	Tommy Bond, 1879	555
	Ed Morris, 1886	555
35	Jim Whitney, 1881	552
36	Amos Rusie, 1890	549
37	Jim McCormick, 1879	546
38	Tim Keefe, 1886	540
39	Hardie Henderson, 1885	539
40	John Coleman, 1883	538
	Bill Sweeney, 1884	538
42	Larry Corcoran, 1880	536
43	Tommy Bond, 1878	533
	Jersey Bakely, 1888	533
45	Amos Rusie, 1892	532
46	Tony Mullane, 1886	530
47	Al Spalding, 1876	529
48	Jim McCormick, 1881	526
49	John Clarkson, 1887	523
50	Tommy Bond, 1877	521
51	Ed Seward, 1888	519
52	Will White, 1880	517
	Larry Corcoran, 1884	517
54	Bobby Mathews, 1876	516
55	Jim Whitney, 1883	514
	Mark Baldwin, 1889	514
57	Terry Larkin, 1879	513
58	Larry McKeon, 1884	512
59	Charley Radbourn, 1886	509
	Sadie McMahon, 1890	509
61	Terry Larkin, 1878	506
	Kid Gleason, 1890	506
63	Dave Foutz, 1886	504
64	Frank Mountain, 1883	503
	Sadie McMahon, 1891	503
66	Terry Larkin, 1877	501
	Hugh Daily, 1884	501
	Mark Baldwin, 1890	501
69	Mickey Welch, 1886	500
	Amos Rusie, 1891	500
71	George Derby, 1881	495
72	Tommy Bond, 1880	493
	Bob Barr, 1890	493
74	Tim Keefe, 1884	492
	Mickey Welch, 1885	492
76	Phenomenal Smith, 1887	491
77	George Bradley, 1879	487
	Jack Lynch, 1884	487
	Lady Baldwin, 1886	487
80	Adonis Terry, 1884	485
81	John Clarkson, 1888	483
82	Bob Caruthers, 1885	482
	Henry Porter, 1885	482
	Amos Rusie, 1893	482
85	Matt Kilroy, 1889	481
86	Will White, 1882	480
	Guy Hecker, 1885	480
	Ed Morris, 1888	480
89	Tim Keefe, 1887	479
90	Jim Galvin, 1881	474
	Charley Radbourn, 1882	474
	Larry Corcoran, 1883	474
	Henry Porter, 1888	474
	Ed Beatin, 1890	474
95	Ed Seward, 1887	471
96	Gus Weyhing, 1892	470
97	Will White, 1878	468
98	John Clarkson, 1886	467
99	Gus Weyhing, 1887	466
100	Ed Walsh, 1908	464

Innings Pitched (by era)

1876-1892

1	Will White, 1879	680
2	Charley Radbourn, 1884	679
3	Guy Hecker, 1884	671
4	Jim McCormick, 1880	658
5	Jim Galvin, 1883	656
6	Jim Galvin, 1884	636
7	Charley Radbourn, 1883	632
8	Bill Hutchinson, 1892	627
9	John Clarkson, 1885	623
10	Jim Devlin, 1876	622
11	John Clarkson, 1889	620
12	Tim Keefe, 1883	619
13	Bill Hutchinson, 1890	603
14	Jim McCormick, 1882	596
15	Monte Ward, 1880	595

1893-1919

1	Amos Rusie, 1893	482
2	Ed Walsh, 1908	464
3	Jack Chesbro, 1904	455
4	Ted Breitenstein, 1894	447
5	Amos Rusie, 1894	444
	Pink Hawley, 1895	444
7	Joe McGinnity, 1903	434
8	Frank Killen, 1896	432
9	Ted Breitenstein, 1895	430
10	Kid Nichols, 1893	425
11	Cy Young, 1893	423
12	Ed Walsh, 1907	422
13	Frank Killen, 1893	415
14	Cy Young, 1896	414
15	Vic Willis, 1902	410

1920-1941

1	Pete Alexander, 1920	363
2	George Uhle, 1923	358
3	Red Faber, 1922	352
4	Urban Shocker, 1922	348
5	Bob Feller, 1941	343
6	Jim Bagby, 1920	340
7	Carl Mays, 1921	337
8	Red Faber, 1921	331
	Burleigh Grimes, 1928	331
10	Bobo Newsom, 1938	330
11	Wilbur Cooper, 1920	327
	Wilbur Cooper, 1921	327
	Urban Shocker, 1921	327
	Burleigh Grimes, 1923	327
	General Crowder, 1932	327

1942-1960

1	Bob Feller, 1946	371
2	Dizzy Trout, 1944	352
3	Robin Roberts, 1953	347
4	Robin Roberts, 1954	337
5	Robin Roberts, 1952	330
6	Johnny Sain, 1948	315
	Robin Roberts, 1951	315
8	Bob Friend, 1956	314
9	Bill Voiselle, 1944	313
	Hal Newhouser, 1945	313
11	Hal Newhouser, 1944	312
	Vern Bickford, 1950	312
13	Warren Spahn, 1951	311
14	Bob Lemon, 1952	310
15	Robin Roberts, 1955	305

1961-1988

1	Wilbur Wood, 1972	377
2	Mickey Lolich, 1971	376
3	Wilbur Wood, 1973	359
4	Steve Carlton, 1972	346
5	Gaylord Perry, 1973	344
6	Gaylord Perry, 1972	343
7	Phil Niekro, 1979	342
8	Sandy Koufax, 1965	336
	Denny McLain, 1968	336
10	Wilbur Wood, 1971	334
	Phil Niekro, 1978	334
12	Nolan Ryan, 1974	333
13	Phil Niekro, 1977	330
14	Gaylord Perry, 1970	329
15	2 players tied	328

Hits per Game

1	Nolan Ryan, 1972	5.26
2	Luis Tiant, 1968	5.30
3	Ed Reulbach, 1906	5.33
4	Dutch Leonard, 1914	5.56
5	Carl Lundgren, 1907	5.65
6	Sid Fernandez, 1985	5.72
7	Tommy Byrne, 1949	5.74
8	Dave McNally, 1968	5.77
9	Sandy Koufax, 1965	5.79
10	Russ Ford, 1910	5.82
11	Al Downing, 1963	5.83
12	Bob Gibson, 1968	5.84
13	Herb Score, 1956	5.86
14	Sam McDowell, 1965	5.87
15	Ed Walsh, 1910	5.89
16	Mike Scott, 1986	5.96
17	Floyd Youmans, 1986	5.96
18	Nolan Ryan, 1977	5.96
19	Mario Soto, 1980	5.97
20	Nolan Ryan, 1974	5.97
21	Nolan Ryan, 1981	5.98
22	Nolan Ryan, 1986	6.02
23	Vida Blue, 1971	6.03
24	Sam McDowell, 1966	6.03
25	Walter Johnson, 1913	6.03
26	Jim Bibby, 1973	6.05
27	Sam McDowell, 1968	6.06
28	Pete Alexander, 1915	6.06
29	Joe Horlen, 1964	6.06
30	Andy Messersmith, 1969	6.08
31	Tim Keefe, 1880	6.09
32	Stan Coveleski, 1917	6.10
33	Jim Hunter, 1972	6.10
34	Sid Fernandez, 1988	6.11
35	Nolan Ryan, 1976	6.12
36	Bob Turley, 1955	6.12
37	Don Sutton, 1972	6.13
38	Bob Turley, 1957	6.14
39	Ron Guidry, 1978	6.14
40	Nolan Ryan, 1983	6.15
41	Mordecai Brown, 1908	6.17
42	Sandy Koufax, 1963	6.19
43	Sandy Koufax, 1964	6.22
44	Charlie Sweeney, 1884	6.23
45	Roger Nelson, 1972	6.24
46	Cy Morgan, 1909	6.24
47	Herb Score, 1955	6.26
48	Dean Chance, 1964	6.28
49	Christy Mathewson, 1909	6.28
	J. R. Richard, 1978	6.28
51	Art Fromme, 1909	6.29
52	Vean Gregg, 1911	6.32
53	Rube Waddell, 1905	6.32
54	Jack Coombs, 1910	6.32
55	Jeff Robinson, 1988	6.33
56	Allie Reynolds, 1943	6.33
57	Larry Cheney, 1916	6.33
58	Walter Johnson, 1912	6.33
59	Sonny Siebert, 1968	6.33
60	Roger Clemens, 1986	6.34
61	Willie Mitchell, 1913	6.35
62	Pascual Perez, 1988	6.37
63	Harry Krause, 1909	6.38
64	Eddie Cicotte, 1917	6.38
65	Spec Shea, 1947	6.39
66	Babe Ruth, 1916	6.39
67	Dave Boswell, 1966	6.39
68	Wayne Simpson, 1970	6.39
69	Dutch Leonard, 1915	6.39
70	Ed Reulbach, 1905	6.41
71	Addie Joss, 1908	6.42
72	Gaylord Perry, 1974	6.43
73	Frank Smith, 1908	6.43
74	Mordecai Brown, 1906	6.43
	Dwight Gooden, 1985	6.43
76	Jack Pfiester, 1906	6.43
77	Luis Tiant, 1972	6.44
78	Eddie Fisher, 1965	6.44
79	Orval Overall, 1909	6.44
80	Mordecai Brown, 1909	6.45
81	Denny McLain, 1968	6.46
82	Fred Toney, 1915	6.46
83	Ray Caldwell, 1914	6.46
84	Dupee Shaw, 1884	6.47
85	Jim McCormick, 1884	6.47
86	Gary Peters, 1967	6.47
87	Walter Johnson, 1910	6.47
88	Frank Smith, 1910	6.48
89	Bob Turley, 1954	6.49
90	Hecker, 1882	6.49
91	Ed Walsh, 1909	6.50
92	Al Mamaux, 1915	6.50
93	Tom Seaver, 1981	6.51
94	Sam Jones, 1955	6.51
95	Bobby Bolin, 1968	6.51
96	Claude Hendrix, 1914	6.51
	Jim Palmer, 1969	6.51
98	Barney Pelty, 1906	6.52
99	King Cole, 1910	6.53

Hits per Game (by era)

1876-1892

1	Tim Keefe, 1880	6.09
2	Charlie Sweeney, 1884	6.23
3	Dupee Shaw, 1884	6.47
4	Jim McCormick, 1884	6.47
5	Hecker, 1882	6.49
6	Tim Keefe, 1888	6.55
7	Adonis Terry, 1888	6.69
8	Silver King, 1888	6.71
9	Tim Keefe, 1885	6.72
10	Frank Knauss, 1890	6.72
11	Ed Seward, 1888	6.73
12	Tony Mullane, 1892	6.77
13	Larry Corcoran, 1880	6.78
14	Mickey Welch, 1885	6.80
15	Cannonball Titcomb, 1888	6.81

1893-1919

1	Ed Reulbach, 1906	5.33
2	Dutch Leonard, 1914	5.56
3	Carl Lundgren, 1907	5.65
4	Russ Ford, 1910	5.82
5	Ed Walsh, 1910	5.89
6	Walter Johnson, 1913	6.03
7	Pete Alexander, 1915	6.06
8	Stan Coveleski, 1917	6.10
9	Mordecai Brown, 1908	6.17
10	Cy Morgan, 1909	6.24
11	Christy Mathewson, 1909	6.28
12	Art Fromme, 1909	6.29
13	Vean Gregg, 1911	6.32
14	Rube Waddell, 1905	6.32
15	Jack Coombs, 1910	6.32

1920-1941

1	Johnny Vander Meer, 1941	6.85
2	Bob Feller, 1939	6.88
3	Bob Feller, 1940	6.89
4	Hal Schumacher, 1933	6.92
5	Dazzy Vance, 1924	6.93
6	Whit Wyatt, 1941	6.97
7	Bucky Walters, 1939	7.05
8	Johnny Vander Meer, 1938	7.08
9	Bucky Walters, 1940	7.11
10	Lefty Gomez, 1934	7.12
11	Ernie White, 1941	7.24
12	Bump Hadley, 1931	7.25
13	Dazzy Vance, 1928	7.26
14	Dolf Luque, 1920	7.27
15	Bob Feller, 1938	7.28

1942-1960

1	Tommy Byrne, 1949	5.74
2	Herb Score, 1956	5.86
3	Bob Turley, 1955	6.12
4	Bob Turley, 1957	6.14
5	Herb Score, 1955	6.26
6	Allie Reynolds, 1943	6.33
7	Spec Shea, 1947	6.39
8	Bob Turley, 1954	6.49
9	Sam Jones, 1955	6.51
10	Bob Turley, 1958	6.54
11	Hal Newhouser, 1946	6.60
12	Don Larsen, 1956	6.65
13	Whitey Ford, 1955	6.66
14	Johnny Niggeling, 1943	6.67
15	Mort Cooper, 1942	6.68

1961-1988

1	Nolan Ryan, 1972	5.26
2	Luis Tiant, 1968	5.30
3	Sid Fernandez, 1985	5.72
4	Dave McNally, 1968	5.77
5	Sandy Koufax, 1965	5.79
6	Al Downing, 1963	5.83
7	Bob Gibson, 1968	5.84
8	Sam McDowell, 1965	5.87
9	Mike Scott, 1986	5.96
10	Floyd Youmans, 1986	5.96
11	Nolan Ryan, 1977	5.96
12	Mario Soto, 1980	5.97
13	Nolan Ryan, 1974	5.97
14	Nolan Ryan, 1981	5.98
15	Nolan Ryan, 1986	6.02

Home Runs Allowed

1	Bert Blyleven, 1986	50
2	Robin Roberts, 1956	46
	Bert Blyleven, 1987	46
4	Pedro Ramos, 1957	43
5	Denny McLain, 1966	42
6	Robin Roberts, 1955	41
	Phil Niekro, 1979	41
8	Robin Roberts, 1957	40
	Ralph Terry, 1962	40
	Orlando Pena, 1964	40
	Phil Niekro, 1970	40
	Ferguson Jenkins, 1979	40
	Jack Morris, 1986	40
14	Murry Dickson, 1948	39
	Pedro Ramos, 1961	39
	Jim Perry, 1971	39
	Jim Hunter, 1973	39
	Jack Morris, 1987	39
19	Warren Hacker, 1955	38
	Pedro Ramos, 1958	38
	Lew Burdette, 1959	38
	Jim Bunning, 1963	38
	Don Sutton, 1970	38
	Mickey Lolich, 1974	38
	Matt Keough, 1982	38
	Floyd Bannister, 1987	38
	Don Sutton, 1987	38
	Curt Young, 1987	38
29	Jim Bunning, 1959	37
	Earl Wilson, 1964	37
	Luis Tiant, 1969	37
	Ferguson Jenkins, 1975	37
	Jack Morris, 1982	37
	Dan Petry, 1983	37
	Frank Viola, 1986	37
36	Larry Jansen, 1949	36
	Art Mahaffey, 1962	36
	Pete Richert, 1966	36
	Mickey Lolich, 1971	36
	Eddie Whitson, 1987	36
	Charlie Hough, 1987	36
	Tom Browning, 1988	36
43	Larry Corcoran, 1884	35
	Warren Hacker, 1953	35
	Robin Roberts, 1954	35
	Don Newcombe, 1955	35
	Jim Perry, 1960	35
	Roger Craig, 1962	35
	Robin Roberts, 1963	35
	Sammy Ellis, 1966	35
	Denny McLain, 1967	35
	Ferguson Jenkins, 1973	35
	Mickey Lolich, 1973	35
	Mike Caldwell, 1983	35
	Mike Smithson, 1984	35
	Scott McGregor, 1986	35
	Scott Bankhead, 1987	35
	Bruce Hurst, 1987	35
59	Preacher Roe, 1950	34
	Johnny Sain, 1950	34
	Ken Raffensberger, 1950	34
	Robin Roberts, 1959	34
	Paul Foytack, 1959	34
	Juan Marichal, 1962	34
	Dick Ellsworth, 1964	34
	Bill Monbouquette, 1964	34
	Bob Gibson, 1965	34
	Jim Grant, 1965	34
	Earl Wilson, 1967	34
	Jim Hunter, 1969	34
	Mike Cuellar, 1970	34
	Gaylord Perry, 1973	34
	Rick Wise, 1975	34
	Frank Viola, 1983	34
	Danny Darwin, 1985	34
	Scott McGregor, 1985	34
	Ken Schrom, 1986	34
	Don Carman, 1987	34
	Mike Witt, 1987	34
80	Don Newcombe, 1956	33
	Camilo Pascual, 1956	33
	Jim Bunning, 1957	33
	Billy Pierce, 1958	33
	Mike McCormick, 1961	33
	Gene Conley, 1961	33
	Phil Regan, 1963	33
	Phil Ortega, 1965	33
	Jim Merritt, 1969	33
	Lew Krausse, 1970	33
	Jerry Garvin, 1977	33
	Dennis Leonard, 1979	33
	Bill Travers, 1979	33
	Rick Langford, 1982	33
	Ken Dixon, 1986	33
	Bill Gullickson, 1987	33
	Willie Fraser, 1988	33
97	26 players tied	32

Home Runs Allowed (by era)

1876-1892

1	Larry Corcoran, 1884	35
2	Charlie Getzien, 1889	27
3	Bill Hutchinson, 1891	26
4	Charlie Getzien, 1887	24
	Egyptian Healy, 1887	24
6	Jim Galvin, 1884	23
	Mark Baldwin, 1887	23
	Lev Shreve, 1888	23
9	Billy Serad, 1884	21
	John Clarkson, 1885	21
	Park Swartzel, 1889	21
	George Cobb, 1892	21
13	8 players tied	20

1893-1919

1	Frank Dwyer, 1894	27
	Jack Stivetts, 1894	27
3	Kid Nichols, 1894	23
4	Harry Staley, 1893	22
	Kid Carsey, 1894	22
6	Ted Breitenstein, 1894	21
7	Jack Stivetts, 1896	20
8	Tom Parrott, 1894	19
	Cy Young, 1894	19
10	Kid Gleason, 1893	18
	Al Orth, 1902	18
12	5 players tied	17

1920-1941

1	Lon Warneke, 1937	32
2	Phil Collins, 1934	30
	Bobo Newsom, 1938	30
4	Ray Kremer, 1930	29
	Lynn Nelson, 1938	29
6	George Earnshaw, 1932	28
	George Earnshaw, 1934	28
8	Roy Mahaffey, 1932	27
	Carl Hubbell, 1935	27
	Luke Hamlin, 1939	27
	Lynn Nelson, 1939	27
	Johnny Marcum, 1939	27
13	Freddie Fitzsimmons, 1930	26
	Gordon Rhodes, 1936	26
	Nels Potter, 1939	26

1942-1960

1	Robin Roberts, 1956	46
2	Pedro Ramos, 1957	43
3	Robin Roberts, 1955	41
4	Robin Roberts, 1957	40
5	Murry Dickson, 1948	39
6	Warren Hacker, 1955	38
	Pedro Ramos, 1958	38
	Lew Burdette, 1959	38
9	Jim Bunning, 1959	37
10	Larry Jansen, 1949	36
11	Warren Hacker, 1953	35
	Robin Roberts, 1954	35
	Don Newcombe, 1955	35
	Jim Perry, 1960	35
15	5 players tied	34

1961-1988

1	Bert Blyleven, 1986	50
2	Bert Blyleven, 1987	46
3	Denny McLain, 1966	42
4	Phil Niekro, 1979	41
5	Ralph Terry, 1962	40
	Orlando Pena, 1964	40
	Phil Niekro, 1970	40
	Ferguson Jenkins, 1979	40
	Jack Morris, 1986	40
10	Pedro Ramos, 1961	39
	Jim Perry, 1971	39
	Jim Hunter, 1973	39
	Jack Morris, 1987	39
14	7 players tied	38

Walks

1	Amos Rusie, 1890	289
2	Mark Baldwin, 1889	274
3	Amos Rusie, 1892	267
4	Amos Rusie, 1891	262
5	Mark Baldwin, 1890	249
6	Jack Stivetts, 1891	232
7	Mark Baldwin, 1891	227
8	Phil Knell, 1891	226
9	Bob Barr, 1890	219
10	Amos Rusie, 1893	218
11	Cy Seymour, 1898	213
12	Gus Weyhing, 1889	212
13	Ed Crane, 1890	210
14	Bob Feller, 1938	208
15	Toad Ramsey, 1886	207
16	Icebox Chamberlin, 1891	206
17	Mike Morrison, 1887	205
18	Henry Gruber, 1890	204
	Nolan Ryan, 1977	204
20	John Clarkson, 1889	203
21	Nolan Ryan, 1974	202
22	Bert Cunningham, 1890	201
23	Amos Rusie, 1894	200
24	Bill Hutchinson, 1890	199
25	Mark Baldwin, 1892	194
	Bob Feller, 1941	194
27	Bobo Newsom, 1938	192
28	Ted Breitenstein, 1894	191
29	Ed Crane, 1892	189
	Tony Mullane, 1893	189
31	Tony Mullane, 1891	187
	Bill Hutchinson, 1892	187
	Kid Gleason, 1893	187
34	Ed Beatin, 1890	186
35	Sam Jones, 1955	185
36	Tom Vickery, 1890	184
37	Nolan Ryan, 1976	183
38	Matt Kilroy, 1886	182
	Frank Killen, 1893	182
40	Willie McGill, 1893	181
	Bob Harmon, 1911	181
	Bob Turley, 1954	181
43	Jack Stivetts, 1890	179
	Gus Weyhing, 1892	179
	Tommy Byrne, 1949	179
46	Bill Hutchinson, 1891	178
	Ted Breitenstein, 1895	178
48	Bob Turley, 1955	177
49	Phenomenal Smith, 1887	176
	George Hemming, 1893	176
51	Silver King, 1892	174
52	Jack Stivetts, 1892	171
	Jouett Meekin, 1894	171
	Ed Stein, 1894	171
	Bump Hadley, 1932	171
56	Icebox Chamberlin, 1892	170
	Cy Seymour, 1899	170
58	Willie McGill, 1891	168
	Gus Weyhing, 1892	168
	Brickyard Kennedy, 1893	168
	Elmer Myers, 1916	168
62	Toad Ramsey, 1887	167
	Gus Weyhing, 1887	167
	Darby O'Brien, 1889	167
	Kid Gleason, 1890	167
	Bill Daley, 1890	167
	Bobo Newsom, 1937	167
68	Tony Mullane, 1890	166
	Sadie McMahon, 1890	166
	Phil Knell, 1890	166
	Chick Fraser, 1896	166
72	Icebox Chamberlin, 1889	165
	Dan Casey, 1890	165
	Kid Gleason, 1891	165
	John Wyckoff, 1915	165
76	Cy Seymour, 1897	164
	Earl Moore, 1911	164
	Phil Niekro, 1977	164
79	Mickey Welch, 1886	163
	Silver King, 1890	163
	Hank O'Day, 1890	163
	George Haddock, 1892	163
83	Johnny Vander Meer, 1943	162
	Nolan Ryan, 1973	162
85	John Sowders, 1890	161
	Kid Carsey, 1891	161
	Gus Weyhing, 1891	161
88	Tommy Byrne, 1950	160
89	George Hemming, 1894	159
	Amos Rusie, 1895	159
	Marty O'Toole, 1912	159
92	Joe Coleman, 1974	158
93	Matt Kilroy, 1887	157
	Bert Cunningham, 1888	157
	Pink Hawley, 1896	157
	Grover Lowdermilk, 1915	157
	Nolan Ryan, 1972	157
98	5 players tied	156

Fewest Walks per Game

1 George Zettlein, 1876 . . . . . . 0.23
2 Cherokee Fisher, 1876 . . . . . 0.24
3 George Bradley, 1880 . . . . . . 0.28
4 Tommy Bond, 1876 . . . . 0.29
5 Tommy Bond, 1879 . . . . 0.39
6 Bobby Mathews, 1876 . . . . . . 0.42
7 Charlie Sweeney, 1884 . . . . . 0.43
8 Guy Hecker, 1882 . . . . 0.43
9 Dale Williams, 1876 . . . . 0.43
10 Al Spalding, 1876 . . . . 0.44
11 Jim Galvin, 1879 . . . . 0.47
12 George Bradley, 1879 . . . . . . 0.48
13 Sam Weaver, 1878 . . . . 0.49
14 Terry Larkin, 1879 . . . . 0.53
15 Jim Devlin, 1876 . . . . 0.54
16 Denny Driscoll, 1882 . . . . 0.54
17 Terry Larkin, 1878 . . . . 0.55
18 Monte Ward, 1879 . . . . 0.55
19 Tommy Bond, 1878 . . . . 0.56
20 Candy Cummings, 1876 . . . . . 0.58
21 George Bradley, 1876 . . . . . . 0.60
22 Henry Boyle, 1884 . . . . 0.60
   Jim McCormick, 1884 . . . . . . 0.60
24 George Bradley, 1884 . . . . . . 0.61
25 Harry McCormick, 1879 . . . . . 0.61
26 Jim Whitney, 1883 . . . . 0.61
27 Babe Adams, 1920 . . . . 0.62
28 Christy Mathewson, 1913 . . . 0.62
29 John Murphy, 1884 . . . . 0.62
30 Tommy Bond, 1877 . . . . 0.62
31 Jim Galvin, 1880 . . . . 0.63
32 Jim Devlin, 1877 . . . . 0.66
33 Christy Mathewson, 1914 . . . 0.66
34 Tommy Bond, 1884 . . . . 0.67
35 Monte Ward, 1880 . . . . 0.68
36 Jim Galvin, 1883 . . . . 0.69
37 Cy Young, 1904 . . . . 0.69
38 Bobby Mathews, 1882 . . . . . . 0.69
39 Stump Weidman, 1880 . . . . . . 0.71
40 Jim Whitney, 1884 . . . . 0.72
41 Sam Weaver, 1884 . . . . 0.73
42 Bobby Mathews, 1883 . . . . . . 0.73
43 Tricky Nichols, 1878 . . . . 0.73
44 Red Lucas, 1933 . . . . 0.74
45 Candy Cummings, 1877 . . . . . 0.75
46 Guy Hecker, 1884 . . . . 0.75
47 Jim Whitney, 1885 . . . . 0.76
48 Fred Goldsmith, 1880 . . . . . . 0.77
49 Jack Lynch, 1884 . . . . 0.78
50 Cy Young, 1906 . . . . 0.78
51 Babe Adams, 1919 . . . . 0.79
52 Slim Sallee, 1919 . . . . 0.79
   Babe Adams, 1922 . . . . 0.79
54 Charley Radbourn, 1883 . . . . 0.80
55 John Coleman, 1883 . . . . 0.80
56 Jim Galvin, 1882 . . . . 0.81
57 Ed Dugan, 1884 . . . . 0.81
58 Sam Weaver, 1883 . . . . 0.82
59 Slim Sallee, 1918 . . . . 0.82
60 Dory Dean, 1876 . . . . 0.82
61 Tommy Bond, 1880 . . . . 0.82
62 Addie Joss, 1908 . . . . 0.83
63 Foghorn Bradley, 1876 . . . . . 0.83
64 Curry Foley, 1879 . . . . 0.83
65 Cy Young, 1905 . . . . 0.84
66 Fred Goldsmith, 1882 . . . . . . 0.84
67 Sam Weaver, 1882 . . . . 0.85
68 Stump Weidman, 1882 . . . . . . 0.85
69 Lamarr Hoyt, 1985 . . . . 0.86
70 Deacon Phillippe, 1902 . . . . . 0.86
71 Will White, 1878 . . . . 0.87
72 Walter Burke, 1884 . . . . 0.87
73 Jim Galvin, 1881 . . . . 0.87
74 Jim Whitney, 1882 . . . . 0.88
75 Jack Lynch, 1883 . . . . 0.88
76 Pete Alexander, 1923 . . . . . . 0.89
77 Jumbo McGinnis, 1884 . . . . . 0.89
78 George Bradley, 1877 . . . . . . 0.89
79 Jim Galvin, 1884 . . . . 0.89
80 Cy Young, 1901 . . . . 0.90
81 Will White, 1879 . . . . 0.90
82 Deacon Phillippe, 1903 . . . . . 0.90
83 Monte Ward, 1878 . . . . 0.92
84 Fred Goldsmith, 1883 . . . . . . 0.92
85 George Bradley, 1883 . . . . . . 0.93
86 Jim Whitney, 1887 . . . . 0.93
87 Stump Weidman, 1881 . . . . . . 0.94
88 Terry Larkin, 1877 . . . . 0.95
89 Bill Purcell, 1879 . . . . 0.95
90 Tiny Bonham, 1942 . . . . 0.96
91 Christy Mathewson, 1908 . . . 0.97
92 Christy Mathewson, 1915 . . . 0.97
93 Charley Radbourn, 1882 . . . . 0.97
94 Fred Corey, 1880 . . . . 0.97
95 Cy Young, 1903 . . . . 0.97
96 Jesse Tannehill, 1902 . . . . . . 0.97
97 Will White, 1880 . . . . 0.97
98 Cy Young, 1898 . . . . 0.98
99 Bill Burns, 1908 . . . . 0.98
100 Christy Mathewson, 1912 . . . 0.99

Fewest Walks/Game (by era)

1876-1892

1 George Zettlein, 1876 . . . . . . 0.23
2 Cherokee Fisher, 1876 . . . . . 0.24
3 George Bradley, 1880 . . . . . . 0.28
4 Tommy Bond, 1876 . . . . 0.29
5 Tommy Bond, 1879 . . . . 0.39
6 Bobby Mathews, 1876 . . . . . . 0.42
7 Charlie Sweeney, 1884 . . . . . 0.43
8 Guy Hecker, 1882 . . . . 0.43
9 Dale Williams, 1876 . . . . 0.43
10 Al Spalding, 1876 . . . . 0.44
11 Jim Galvin, 1879 . . . . 0.47
12 George Bradley, 1879 . . . . . . 0.48
13 Sam Weaver, 1878 . . . . 0.49
14 Terry Larkin, 1879 . . . . 0.53
15 Jim Devlin, 1876 . . . . 0.54

1893-1919

1 Christy Mathewson, 1913 . . . 0.62
2 Christy Mathewson, 1914 . . . 0.66
3 Cy Young, 1904 . . . . 0.69
4 Cy Young, 1906 . . . . 0.78
5 Babe Adams, 1919 . . . . 0.79
6 Slim Sallee, 1919 . . . . 0.79
7 Slim Sallee, 1918 . . . . 0.82
8 Addie Joss, 1908 . . . . 0.83
9 Cy Young, 1905 . . . . 0.84
10 Deacon Phillippe, 1902 . . . . . 0.86
11 Cy Young, 1901 . . . . 0.90
12 Deacon Phillippe, 1903 . . . . . 0.90
13 Christy Mathewson, 1908 . . . 0.97
14 Christy Mathewson, 1915 . . . 0.97
15 Cy Young, 1903 . . . . 0.97

1920-1941

1 Babe Adams, 1920 . . . . 0.62
2 Red Lucas, 1933 . . . . 0.74
3 Babe Adams, 1922 . . . . 0.79
4 Pete Alexander, 1923 . . . . . . 0.89
5 Babe Adams, 1921 . . . . 1.01
6 Paul Derringer, 1939 . . . . 1.05
7 Carl Hubbell, 1934 . . . . 1.06
8 Bill Swift, 1932 . . . . 1.09
9 Pete Alexander, 1925 . . . . . . 1.11
10 Herb Pennock, 1930 . . . . 1.15
11 Red Lucas, 1932 . . . . 1.17
12 Pete Alexander, 1921 . . . . . . 1.18
13 Watty Clark, 1935 . . . . 1.22
14 Pete Donohue, 1926 . . . . 1.23
15 Pete Alexander, 1922 . . . . . . 1.24

1942-1960

1 Tiny Bonham, 1942 . . . . 0.96
2 Tiny Bonham, 1945 . . . . 1.09
3 Don Newcombe, 1959 . . . . . . 1.09
4 Lew Burdette, 1960 . . . . 1.14
5 Lew Burdette, 1959 . . . . 1.18
6 Robin Roberts, 1956 . . . . 1.21
7 Robin Roberts, 1959 . . . . 1.23
8 Robin Roberts, 1952 . . . . 1.23
9 Hal Brown, 1960 . . . . 1.25
10 Ray Prim, 1945 . . . . 1.25
11 Robin Roberts, 1960 . . . . 1.29
12 Fred Hutchinson, 1951 . . . . . . 1.29
13 Ted Lyons, 1942 . . . . 1.30
14 Schoolboy Rowe, 1943 . . . . . 1.31
15 Vern Law, 1960 . . . . 1.32

1961-1988

1 Lamarr Hoyt, 1985 . . . . 0.86
2 Dennis Eckersley, 1985 . . . . . 1.01
3 Gary Nolan, 1976 . . . . 1.02
4 Ferguson Jenkins, 1971 . . . . 1.02
5 Juan Marichal, 1966 . . . . 1.06
6 Lamarr Hoyt, 1983 . . . . 1.07
7 Lew Burdette, 1961 . . . . 1.09
8 Scott McGregor, 1979 . . . . . . 1.18
9 Jim Merritt, 1967 . . . . 1.18
10 Rick Honeycutt, 1981 . . . . . . 1.20
11 Vern Law, 1966 . . . . 1.21
12 Dick Donovan, 1963 . . . . 1.22
13 Fritz Peterson, 1968 . . . . 1.23
14 Ferguson Jenkins, 1974 . . . . 1.23
15 Gary Nolan, 1975 . . . . 1.24

Strikeouts

1 Matt Kilroy, 1886 513
2 Toad Ramsey, 1886 499
3 Hugh Daily, 1884 483
4 Charley Radbourn, 1884 441
5 Charlie Buffinton, 1884 417
6 Guy Hecker, 1884 385
7 Nolan Ryan, 1973 383
8 Sandy Koufax, 1965 382
9 Bill Sweeney, 1884 374
10 Jim Galvin, 1884 369
11 Mark Baldwin, 1889 368
12 Nolan Ryan, 1974 367
13 Tim Keefe, 1883 361
14 Toad Ramsey, 1887 355
15 Rube Waddell, 1904 349
16 Bob Feller, 1946 348
17 Hardie Henderson, 1884 346
18 Jim Whitney, 1883 345
   Mickey Welch, 1884 345
20 Amos Rusie, 1890 341
   Nolan Ryan, 1977 341
22 Amos Rusie, 1891 337
23 Tim Keefe, 1888 333
24 Tony Mullane, 1884 329
   Nolan Ryan, 1972 329
26 Nolan Ryan, 1976 327
27 Ed Morris, 1886 326
28 Sam McDowell, 1965 325
29 Tim Keefe, 1884 323
   Lady Baldwin, 1886 323
31 Sandy Koufax, 1966 317
32 Bill Hutchinson, 1892 316
33 Charley Radbourn, 1883 315
34 John Clarkson, 1886 313
   Walter Johnson, 1910 313
   J. R. Richard, 1979 313
37 Steve Carlton, 1972 310
38 Dupee Shaw, 1884 309
39 Larry McKeon, 1884 308
   John Clarkson, 1885 308
   Mickey Lolich, 1971 308
42 Sandy Koufax, 1963 306
   Mike Scott, 1986 306
44 Sam McDowell, 1970 304
45 Walter Johnson, 1912 303
   J. R. Richard, 1978 303
47 Ed Morris, 1884 302
   Rube Waddell, 1903 302
49 Vida Blue, 1971 301
50 Ed Morris, 1885 298
51 Tim Keefe, 1886 291
   Sadie McMahon, 1890 291
   Roger Clemens, 1988 291
54 Bill Hutchinson, 1890 289
   Jack Stivetts, 1890 289
   Tom Seaver, 1971 289
57 Amos Rusie, 1892 288
58 Rube Waddell, 1905 287
59 Jack Lynch, 1884 286
   Bobby Mathews, 1884 286
   Bobby Mathews, 1885 286
   Steve Carlton, 1980 286
   Steve Carlton, 1982 286
64 John Clarkson, 1889 284
65 Dave Foutz, 1886 283
   Sam McDowell, 1968 283
   Tom Seaver, 1970 283
68 Denny McLain, 1968 280
69 Jim Galvin, 1883 279
   Sam McDowell, 1969 279
71 Bob Veale, 1965 276
   Dwight Gooden, 1984 276
73 Hal Newhouser, 1946 275
   Steve Carlton, 1983 275
75 Bob Gibson, 1970 274
   Ferguson Jenkins, 1970 274
   Mario Soto, 1982 274
78 Ferguson Jenkins, 1969 273
79 Larry Corcoran, 1884 272
   Mickey Welch, 1886 272
   Ed Seward, 1888 272
82 Mickey Lolich, 1969 271
83 Jim Whitney, 1884 270
   Bob Gibson, 1965 270
   Nolan Ryan, 1987 270
86 Ed Walsh, 1908 269
   Sandy Koufax, 1961 269
   Bob Gibson, 1969 269
   Frank Tanana, 1975 269
90 Larry Corcoran, 1880 268
   Bill Wise, 1884 268
   Jim Bunning, 1965 268
   Bob Gibson, 1968 268
   Dwight Gooden, 1985 268
95 Christy Mathewson, 1903 . . . 267
96 Jim Maloney, 1963 265
97 Bob Emslie, 1884 264
   Luis Tiant, 1968 264
99 3 players tied 263

Strikeouts (by era)

1876-1892

1 Matt Kilroy, 1886 513
2 Toad Ramsey, 1886 499
3 Hugh Daily, 1884 483
4 Charley Radbourn, 1884 441
5 Charlie Buffinton, 1884 417
6 Guy Hecker, 1884 385
7 Bill Sweeney, 1884 374
8 Jim Galvin, 1884 369
9 Mark Baldwin, 1889 368
10 Tim Keefe, 1883 361
11 Toad Ramsey, 1887 355
12 Hardie Henderson, 1884 346
13 Jim Whitney, 1883 345
   Mickey Welch, 1884 345
15 Amos Rusie, 1890 341

1893-1919

1 Rube Waddell, 1904 349
2 Walter Johnson, 1910 313
3 Walter Johnson, 1912 303
4 Rube Waddell, 1903 302
5 Rube Waddell, 1905 287
6 Ed Walsh, 1908 269
7 Christy Mathewson, 1903 . . . 267
8 Christy Mathewson, 1908 . . . 259
9 Ed Walsh, 1910 258
   Joe Wood, 1912 258
11 Ed Walsh, 1911 255
12 Ed Walsh, 1912 254
13 Walter Johnson, 1913 243
14 Pete Alexander, 1915 241

1920-1941

1 Dazzy Vance, 1924 262
2 Bob Feller, 1940 261
3 Bob Feller, 1941 260
4 Bob Feller, 1939 246
5 Bob Feller, 1938 240
6 Van Mungo, 1936 238
7 Bobo Newsom, 1938 226
8 Dazzy Vance, 1925 221
9 Lefty Grove, 1930 209
10 Johnny Vander Meer, 1941 . . 202
11 Dazzy Vance, 1928 200
12 Dizzy Dean, 1933 199
13 Dazzy Vance, 1923 197
14 Dizzy Dean, 1934 195
   Dizzy Dean, 1936 195

1942-1960

1 Bob Feller, 1946 348
2 Hal Newhouser, 1946 275
3 Herb Score, 1956 263
4 Don Drysdale, 1960 246
5 Herb Score, 1955 245
6 Don Drysdale, 1959 242
7 Sam Jones, 1958 225
8 Hal Newhouser, 1945 212
9 Bob Turley, 1955 210
10 Sam Jones, 1959 209
11 Jim Bunning, 1959 201
   Jim Bunning, 1960 201
13 Robin Roberts, 1953 198
   Sam Jones, 1955 198
15 Sandy Koufax, 1960 197

1961-1988

1 Nolan Ryan, 1973 383
2 Sandy Koufax, 1965 382
3 Nolan Ryan, 1974 367
4 Nolan Ryan, 1977 341
5 Nolan Ryan, 1972 329
6 Nolan Ryan, 1976 327
7 Sam McDowell, 1965 325
8 Sandy Koufax, 1966 317
9 J. R. Richard, 1979 313
10 Steve Carlton, 1972 310
11 Mickey Lolich, 1971 308
12 Sandy Koufax, 1963 306
   Mike Scott, 1986 306
14 Sam McDowell, 1970 304
15 J. R. Richard, 1978 303

Strikeouts per Game

1	Nolan Ryan, 1987	11.46
2	Dwight Gooden, 1984	11.39
3	Sam McDowell, 1965	10.71
4	Nolan Ryan, 1973	10.57
5	Sandy Koufax, 1962	10.57
6	Sam McDowell, 1966	10.44
7	Nolan Ryan, 1972	10.43
8	Nolan Ryan, 1976	10.36
9	Nolan Ryan, 1977	10.26
10	Sandy Koufax, 1965	10.23
11	Sandy Koufax, 1960	10.13
12	Mike Scott, 1986	10.01
13	Nolan Ryan, 1978	9.96
14	Roger Clemens, 1988	9.92
15	Nolan Ryan, 1974	9.92
16	J. R. Richard, 1978	9.92
17	Nolan Ryan, 1986	9.81
18	Herb Score, 1955	9.71
19	J. R. Richard, 1979	9.65
20	Nolan Ryan, 1984	9.64
21	Tom Griffin, 1969	9.57
22	Mario Soto, 1982	9.56
23	Jim Maloney, 1963	9.54
24	Sid Fernandez, 1985	9.53
25	Herb Score, 1956	9.51
26	Sam McDowell, 1968	9.47
27	Sandy Koufax, 1961	9.46
28	Frank Tanana, 1975	9.42
29	Don Wilson, 1969	9.40
30	Bob Veale, 1965	9.34
31	Nolan Ryan, 1988	9.33
32	Mark Langston, 1986	9.23
33	Dave Boswell, 1966	9.21
34	Luis Tiant, 1967	9.21
35	Luis Tiant, 1968	9.21
36	Sam McDowell, 1964	9.21
37	Sid Fernandez, 1988	9.10
38	Sonny Siebert, 1965	9.10
39	Tom Seaver, 1971	9.09
40	Dennis Eckersley, 1976	9.05
41	Sandy Koufax, 1964	9.00
	Sam McDowell, 1967	9.00
	Nolan Ryan, 1979	9.00
44	Sam McDowell, 1970	8.97
45	Jim Maloney, 1964	8.92
46	Jose Rijo, 1988	8.89
47	Sandy Koufax, 1963	8.86
48	Sandy Koufax, 1966	8.83
49	Sid Fernandez, 1986	8.82
50	Nolan Ryan, 1982	8.82
51	Sam McDowell, 1969	8.81
52	Dupee Shaw, 1884	8.80
53	Tom Seaver, 1970	8.75
54	Al Downing, 1963	8.74
55	Bob Moose, 1969	8.74
56	Steve Carlton, 1983	8.71
57	Dwight Gooden, 1985	8.71
58	Steve Carlton, 1982	8.70
59	Vida Blue, 1971	8.68
60	Mickey Lolich, 1969	8.68
61	Juan Pizarro, 1961	8.68
62	Hugh Daily, 1884	8.68
63	Mark Langston, 1987	8.67
64	Bob Johnson, 1970	8.66
65	Jim Maloney, 1966	8.64
66	Bruce Hurst, 1986	8.64
67	Mario Soto, 1980	8.62
68	Jim Maloney, 1965	8.61
69	Tom Seaver, 1972	8.55
70	Dick Selma, 1969	8.53
71	Bob Veale, 1969	8.48
72	Steve Carlton, 1981	8.48
73	Steve Carlton, 1980	8.47
74	Nolan Ryan, 1981	8.46
75	Mike Scott, 1987	8.46
76	Nolan Ryan, 1975	8.45
77	Hal Newhouser, 1946	8.45
78	Floyd Bannister, 1985	8.45
79	Bob Feller, 1946	8.44
80	Fernando Valenzuela, 1981	8.44
81	Roger Clemens, 1986	8.43
82	Ed Correa, 1986	8.42
83	Nolan Ryan, 1983	8.40
84	Rube Waddell, 1903	8.39
85	Bob Gibson, 1970	8.39
86	Sam Jones, 1956	8.38
87	Mickey Lolich, 1965	8.34
88	Don Sutton, 1966	8.32
89	Jose DeLeon, 1988	8.32
90	Floyd Youmans, 1986	8.30
91	David Cone, 1988	8.30
92	Jim Bunning, 1965	8.29
93	Fernando Valenzuela, 1984	8.28
94	Teddy Higuera, 1987	8.24
95	Dave Boswell, 1967	8.23
96	Don Drysdale, 1960	8.23
97	Jose DeLeon, 1985	8.23
98	Pedro Ramos, 1963	8.22
99	Herb Score, 1959	8.22
100	Rube Waddell, 1904	8.20

Strikeouts per Game (by era)

1876-1892

1	Dupee Shaw, 1884	8.80
2	Hugh Daily, 1884	8.68
3	Charlie Geggus, 1884	7.93
4	Matt Kilroy, 1886	7.92
5	John Clarkson, 1884	7.78
6	Toad Ramsey, 1886	7.62
7	Jim Whitney, 1884	7.23
8	Mike Dorgan, 1884	7.17
9	Walter Burke, 1884	7.13
10	Hardie Henderson, 1884	7.09
11	Tim Keefe, 1888	6.91
12	Jim McCormick, 1884	6.90
13	Bob Black, 1884	6.80
14	Lady Baldwin, 1885	6.79
15	Jack Stivetts, 1889	6.70

1893-1919

1	Rube Waddell, 1903	8.39
2	Rube Waddell, 1904	8.20
3	Rube Waddell, 1905	7.85
4	Rube Marquard, 1911	7.67
5	Joe Wood, 1911	7.53
6	Walter Johnson, 1910	7.53
7	Walter Johnson, 1912	7.41
8	Rube Waddell, 1907	7.33
9	Rube Waddell, 1908	7.30
10	Dutch Leonard, 1914	7.04
11	Red Ames, 1906	6.92
12	Rube Waddell, 1902	6.85
13	Red Ames, 1905	6.78
14	Joe Wood, 1912	6.75
15	Orval Overall, 1908	6.68

1920-1941

1	Johnny Vander Meer, 1941	8.04
2	Bob Feller, 1938	7.77
3	Dazzy Vance, 1924	7.63
4	Dazzy Vance, 1925	7.51
5	Dazzy Vance, 1926	7.46
6	Bob Feller, 1939	7.45
7	Bob Feller, 1940	7.34
8	Van Mungo, 1936	6.87
9	Bob Feller, 1941	6.82
10	Van Mungo, 1937	6.82
11	Lefty Grove, 1926	6.77
12	Bill Hallahan, 1930	6.72
13	George Earnshaw, 1928	6.66
14	Red Ruffing, 1932	6.60
15	Lefty Grove, 1930	6.46

1942-1960

1	Sandy Koufax, 1960	10.13
2	Herb Score, 1955	9.71
3	Herb Score, 1956	9.51
4	Hal Newhouser, 1946	8.45
5	Bob Feller, 1946	8.44
6	Sam Jones, 1956	8.38
7	Don Drysdale, 1960	8.23
8	Herb Score, 1959	8.22
9	Sam Jones, 1958	8.10
10	Don Drysdale, 1959	8.04
11	Bob Turley, 1957	7.77
12	Camilo Pascual, 1956	7.71
13	Bob Turley, 1955	7.65
14	Stan Williams, 1960	7.61
15	Sam Jones, 1957	7.57

1961-1988

1	Nolan Ryan, 1987	11.46
2	Dwight Gooden, 1984	11.39
3	Sam McDowell, 1965	10.71
4	Nolan Ryan, 1973	10.57
5	Sandy Koufax, 1962	10.57
6	Sam McDowell, 1966	10.44
7	Nolan Ryan, 1972	10.43
8	Nolan Ryan, 1976	10.36
9	Nolan Ryan, 1977	10.26
10	Sandy Koufax, 1965	10.23
11	Mike Scott, 1986	10.01
12	Nolan Ryan, 1978	9.96
13	Roger Clemens, 1988	9.92
14	Nolan Ryan, 1974	9.92
15	J. R. Richard, 1978	9.92

Earned Run Average

1	Tim Keefe, 1880	0.86
2	Dutch Leonard, 1914	0.96
3	Mordecai Brown, 1906	1.04
4	Bob Gibson, 1968	1.12
5	Walter Johnson, 1913	1.14
6	Christy Mathewson, 1909	1.15
7	Jack Pfiester, 1907	1.15
8	Addie Joss, 1908	1.16
9	Carl Lundgren, 1907	1.17
10	Denny Driscoll, 1882	1.21
11	Pete Alexander, 1915	1.22
12	George Bradley, 1876	1.23
13	Cy Young, 1908	1.26
14	Ed Walsh, 1910	1.26
15	Walter Johnson, 1918	1.27
16	Christy Mathewson, 1905	1.27
17	Hecker, 1882	1.30
18	Jack Coombs, 1910	1.30
19	Mordecai Brown, 1909	1.31
20	Jack Taylor, 1902	1.33
21	Walter Johnson, 1910	1.35
22	George Bradley, 1880	1.38
23	Charley Radbourn, 1884	1.38
24	Mordecai Brown, 1907	1.39
25	Walter Johnson, 1912	1.39
26	Harry Krause, 1909	1.39
27	Ed Walsh, 1909	1.41
28	Ed Walsh, 1908	1.42
29	Ed Reulbach, 1905	1.42
30	Orval Overall, 1909	1.42
31	Christy Mathewson, 1908	1.43
32	Fred Anderson, 1917	1.44
33	Mordecai Brown, 1908	1.47
34	Rube Waddell, 1905	1.48
35	Walter Johnson, 1919	1.49
36	Joe Wood, 1915	1.49
37	Monte Ward, 1878	1.51
38	Harry McCormick, 1882	1.51
39	Doc White, 1906	1.52
40	George McQuillan, 1908	1.52
41	Dwight Gooden, 1985	1.53
42	Eddie Cicotte, 1917	1.53
43	Will White, 1882	1.54
44	Jim McCormick, 1884	1.54
45	Cy Morgan, 1910	1.55
46	Charlie Sweeney, 1884	1.55
47	Walter Johnson, 1915	1.55
48	Pete Alexander, 1916	1.55
49	Howie Camnitz, 1908	1.56
50	Jack Pfiester, 1906	1.56
51	Jim Devlin, 1876	1.56
52	Fred Toney, 1915	1.57
53	Eddie Cicotte, 1913	1.58
54	Rube Marquard, 1916	1.58
55	Tim Keefe, 1885	1.58
56	Chief Bender, 1910	1.58
57	Barney Pelty, 1906	1.59
58	Addie Joss, 1904	1.59
59	Ed Walsh, 1907	1.60
60	Luis Tiant, 1968	1.60
61	Joe McGinnity, 1904	1.61
62	Ray Collins, 1910	1.62
63	Rube Waddell, 1904	1.62
64	Howie Camnitz, 1909	1.62
65	Cy Young, 1901	1.63
66	Spud Chandler, 1943	1.64
67	Ernie Shore, 1915	1.64
68	Silver King, 1888	1.64
69	Ed Summers, 1908	1.64
70	Walter Johnson, 1908	1.65
71	Russ Ford, 1910	1.65
72	Dean Chance, 1964	1.65
73	Ed Reulbach, 1906	1.65
74	Chief Bender, 1909	1.66
75	Sam Leever, 1907	1.66
76	Carl Hubbell, 1933	1.66
77	Mickey Welch, 1885	1.66
78	Candy Cummings, 1876	1.67
79	Joe Wood, 1910	1.67
80	Tommy Bond, 1876	1.68
81	Billy Taylor, 1884	1.68
82	Ned Garvin, 1904	1.68
83	Ed Reulbach, 1907	1.69
84	Claude Hendrix, 1914	1.69
85	Bill Burns, 1908	1.69
86	Nolan Ryan, 1981	1.69
87	Jim McCormick, 1878	1.69
88	Orval Overall, 1907	1.70
	Rube Foster, 1914	1.70
90	Addie Joss, 1909	1.70
91	Ed Killian, 1909	1.72
92	Walter Johnson, 1914	1.72
93	Doc White, 1909	1.72
94	Bill Doak, 1914	1.72
95	Addie Joss, 1906	1.72
	Pete Alexander, 1919	1.72
97	Sandy Koufax, 1966	1.73
98	Bob Ewing, 1907	1.73
99	Vic Willis, 1906	1.73
100	Charlie Chech, 1908	1.73

Earned Run Average (by era)

1876-1892

1	Tim Keefe, 1880	0.86
2	Denny Driscoll, 1882	1.21
3	George Bradley, 1876	1.23
4	Guy Hecker, 1882	1.30
5	George Bradley, 1880	1.38
6	Charley Radbourn, 1884	1.38
7	Monte Ward, 1878	1.51
8	Harry McCormick, 1882	1.51
9	Will White, 1882	1.54
10	Jim McCormick, 1884	1.54
11	Charlie Sweeney, 1884	1.55
12	Jim Devlin, 1876	1.56
13	Tim Keefe, 1885	1.58
14	Silver King, 1888	1.64
15	Mickey Welch, 1885	1.66

1893-1919

1	Dutch Leonard, 1914	0.96
2	Mordecai Brown, 1906	1.04
3	Walter Johnson, 1913	1.14
4	Christy Mathewson, 1909	1.15
5	Jack Pfiester, 1907	1.15
6	Addie Joss, 1908	1.16
7	Carl Lundgren, 1907	1.17
8	Pete Alexander, 1915	1.22
9	Cy Young, 1908	1.26
10	Ed Walsh, 1910	1.26
11	Walter Johnson, 1918	1.27
12	Christy Mathewson, 1905	1.27
13	Jack Coombs, 1910	1.30
14	Mordecai Brown, 1909	1.31
15	Jack Taylor, 1902	1.33

1920-1941

1	Carl Hubbell, 1933	1.66
2	Pete Alexander, 1920	1.91
3	Dolf Luque, 1923	1.93
4	Lon Warneke, 1933	2.01
5	Lefty Grove, 1931	2.06
6	Dazzy Vance, 1928	2.09
7	Hal Schumacher, 1933	2.15
8	Dazzy Vance, 1924	2.16
9	Babe Adams, 1920	2.16
10	Burleigh Grimes, 1920	2.22
11	Elmer Riddle, 1941	2.24
12	Bill Walker, 1931	2.26
13	Wilcy Moore, 1927	2.28
14	Bucky Walters, 1939	2.29
15	Carl Hubbell, 1934	2.30

1942-1960

1	Spud Chandler, 1943	1.64
2	Mort Cooper, 1942	1.77
3	Hal Newhouser, 1945	1.81
4	Max Lanier, 1943	1.90
5	Hal Newhouser, 1946	1.94
6	Billy Pierce, 1955	1.97
7	Whitey Ford, 1958	2.01
8	Al Benton, 1945	2.02
9	Allie Reynolds, 1952	2.07
10	Howie Pollet, 1946	2.10
	Warren Spahn, 1953	2.10
12	Ted Lyons, 1942	2.10
13	Spud Chandler, 1946	2.10
14	Dizzy Trout, 1944	2.12
15	Roger Wolff, 1945	2.12

1961-1988

1	Bob Gibson, 1968	1.12
2	Dwight Gooden, 1985	1.53
3	Luis Tiant, 1968	1.60
4	Dean Chance, 1964	1.65
5	Nolan Ryan, 1981	1.69
6	Sandy Koufax, 1966	1.73
7	Sandy Koufax, 1964	1.74
8	Ron Guidry, 1978	1.74
9	Tom Seaver, 1971	1.76
10	Sam McDowell, 1968	1.81
11	Vida Blue, 1971	1.82
12	Phil Niekro, 1967	1.87
13	Joe Horlen, 1964	1.88
14	Sandy Koufax, 1963	1.88
15	Luis Tiant, 1972	1.91

Adjusted Earned Run Average

1	Tim Keefe, 1880	305
2	Dutch Leonard, 1914	278
3	Walter Johnson, 1913	271
4	Mordecai Brown, 1906	270
5	Bob Gibson, 1968	254
6	Pete Alexander, 1915	242
7	Walter Johnson, 1912	238
8	Christy Mathewson, 1909	238
9	Christy Mathewson, 1905	237
10	Dwight Gooden, 1985	229
11	Jack Pfiester, 1907	227
12	Walter Johnson, 1918	227
13	Lefty Grove, 1931	224
14	Carl Lundgren, 1907	223
15	Ed Reulbach, 1905	221
16	Charley Radbourn, 1884	219
17	Cy Young, 1901	219
18	Addie Joss, 1908	218
19	Denny Driscoll, 1882	216
20	Ron Guidry, 1978	214
21	Walter Johnson, 1919	212
22	Jim McCormick, 1884	211
23	Silver King, 1888	207
24	Billy Pierce, 1955	203
25	Dolf Luque, 1923	203
26	Sandy Koufax, 1966	202
27	Mort Cooper, 1942	202
28	Al Maul, 1895	202
29	Lefty Gomez, 1937	202
30	Jack Taylor, 1902	200
31	Hank Aguirre, 1962	200
32	Mordecai Brown, 1909	199
33	Carl Hubbell, 1933	198
34	Clark Griffith, 1898	198
35	Jack Coombs, 1910	198
36	Monty Stratton, 1937	198
37	Hal Newhouser, 1945	197
38	Billy Rhines, 1890	197
39	Lefty Grove, 1939	197
40	Joe Wood, 1915	196
41	Hal Newhouser, 1946	196
42	Rube Waddell, 1905	196
43	Charlie Sweeney, 1884	195
44	Tim Keefe, 1885	195
45	Dean Chance, 1964	195
46	Spud Chandler, 1943	194
47	Guy Hecker, 1882	194
48	Harry McCormick, 1882	193
49	Warren Spahn, 1953	192
50	Whitey Ford, 1958	192
51	Walter Johnson, 1915	192
52	Jack Stivetts, 1889	192
53	Vida Blue, 1971	192
54	Dazzy Vance, 1930	192
55	Amos Rusie, 1894	191
56	Vean Gregg, 1911	191
57	Will White, 1882	190
58	Tom Seaver, 1971	190
59	Lefty Grove, 1936	190
60	Ed Walsh, 1910	189
61	Dazzy Vance, 1928	189
62	Mordecai Brown, 1907	188
63	Walter Johnson, 1910	188
64	Phil Niekro, 1967	188
65	Rube Waddell, 1902	188
66	Lefty Grove, 1926	188
67	Sandy Koufax, 1964	187
68	Joe Wood, 1912	187
69	Luis Tiant, 1968	187
70	Billy Rhines, 1896	187
71	Johnny Antonelli, 1954	186
72	Billy Taylor, 1884	186
73	Eddie Cicotte, 1919	186
74	Cy Young, 1908	186
75	Max Lanier, 1943	186
76	Mickey Welch, 1885	185
77	Lefty Gomez, 1934	185
78	Joe Horlen, 1964	184
79	Ed Siever, 1902	184
80	Orval Overall, 1909	184
81	Russ Ford, 1914	183
82	Juan Marichal, 1965	183
83	Lefty Grove, 1930	182
84	Dave Foutz, 1886	182
85	Nolan Ryan, 1981	182
86	Fred Anderson, 1917	182
87	Wilcy Moore, 1927	181
88	Harry Krause, 1909	181
89	Jeff Tesreau, 1912	180
90	Lefty Grove, 1932	180
91	Jack Pfiester, 1906	180
92	Fred Toney, 1915	179
93	Hnery Boyle, 1884	179
94	Ernie Shore, 1915	179
95	Ted Lyons, 1939	178
96	Lefty Grove, 1935	178
97	John Tudor, 1985	178
98	Joe McGinnity, 1904	178
99	Jim McCormick, 1883	178
100	Kid Nichols, 1890	178

Adjusted ERA (by era)

1876-1892

1	Tim Keefe, 1880	305
2	Charley Radbourn, 1884	219
3	Denny Driscoll, 1882	216
4	Jim McCormick, 1884	211
5	Silver King, 1888	207
6	Billy Rhines, 1890	197
7	Charlie Sweeney, 1884	195
8	Tim Keefe, 1885	195
9	Guy Hecker, 1882	194
10	Harry McCormick, 1882	193
11	Jack Stivetts, 1889	192
12	Will White, 1882	190
13	Billy Taylor, 1884	186
14	Mickey Welch, 1885	185
15	Dave Foutz, 1886	182

1893-1919

1	Dutch Leonard, 1914	278
2	Walter Johnson, 1913	271
3	Mordecai Brown, 1906	270
4	Pete Alexander, 1915	242
5	Walter Johnson, 1912	238
6	Christy Mathewson, 1909	238
7	Christy Mathewson, 1905	237
8	Jack Pfiester, 1907	227
9	Walter Johnson, 1918	227
10	Carl Lundgren, 1907	223
11	Ed Reulbach, 1905	221
12	Cy Young, 1901	219
13	Addie Joss, 1908	218
14	Walter Johnson, 1919	212
15	Al Maul, 1895	202

1920-1941

1	Lefty Grove, 1931	224
2	Dolf Luque, 1923	203
3	Lefty Gomez, 1937	202
4	Carl Hubbell, 1933	198
5	Monty Stratton, 1937	198
6	Lefty Grove, 1939	197
7	Dazzy Vance, 1930	192
8	Lefty Grove, 1936	190
9	Dazzy Vance, 1928	189
10	Lefty Grove, 1926	188
11	Lefty Gomez, 1934	185
12	Lefty Grove, 1930	182
13	Wilcy Moore, 1927	181
14	Lefty Grove, 1932	180
15	Ted Lyons, 1939	178

1942-1960

1	Billy Pierce, 1955	203
2	Mort Cooper, 1942	202
3	Hal Newhouser, 1945	197
4	Hal Newhouser, 1946	196
5	Spud Chandler, 1943	194
6	Warren Spahn, 1953	192
7	Whitey Ford, 1958	192
8	Johnny Antonelli, 1954	186
9	Max Lanier, 1943	186
10	Harry Brecheen, 1948	178
11	Al Benton, 1945	177
12	Mike Garcia, 1949	174
13	Allie Reynolds, 1952	174
14	Gene Bearden, 1948	174
15	Howie Pollet, 1946	173

1961-1988

1	Bob Gibson, 1968	254
2	Dwight Gooden, 1985	229
3	Ron Guidry, 1978	214
4	Sandy Koufax, 1966	202
5	Hank Aguirre, 1962	200
6	Dean Chance, 1964	195
7	Vida Blue, 1971	192
8	Tom Seaver, 1971	190
9	Phil Niekro, 1967	188
10	Sandy Koufax, 1964	187
11	Luis Tiant, 1968	187
12	Joe Horlen, 1964	184
13	Juan Marichal, 1965	183
14	Nolan Ryan, 1981	182
15	John Tudor, 1985	178

Pitching Runs

1	Amos Rusie, 1894	126.1
2	Charley Radbourn, 1884	120.6
3	Guy Hecker, 1884	107.9
4	Silver King, 1888	92.3
5	John Clarkson, 1889	89.5
6	Cy Young, 1901	84.0
7	Matt Kilroy, 1887	80.3
8	Walter Johnson, 1912	79.9
9	Pink Hawley, 1895	79.3
10	Silver King, 1890	78.8
11	Will White, 1883	77.6
12	Amos Rusie, 1893	77.5
13	Charley Radbourn, 1883	76.4
14	Dave Foutz, 1886	75.2
15	Lefty Grove, 1931	74.7
16	Jouett Meekin, 1894	74.4
17	Dolf Luque, 1923	74.2
18	Scott Stratton, 1890	72.2
19	Billy Rhines, 1890	71.8
20	Lefty Gomez, 1937	70.7
21	Jim Galvin, 1884	69.4
22	George Bradley, 1876	69.1
23	Walter Johnson, 1913	68.6
24	Cy Young, 1892	68.5
25	Lefty Grove, 1930	68.5
26	Kid Nichols, 1897	68.5
27	Dazzy Vance, 1930	68.1
28	Lefty Gomez, 1934	67.9
29	Mike Smith, 1887	67.5
30	Sandy Koufax, 1966	67.5
31	John Clarkson, 1885	67.1
32	Red Faber, 1921	66.5
33	Toad Ramsey, 1886	64.8
34	Warren Spahn, 1953	64.7
35	Christy Mathewson, 1905	64.7
36	Kid Nichols, 1890	64.0
37	Pete Alexander, 1915	64.0
38	Cy Young, 1895	63.9
39	Dwight Gooden, 1985	63.8
40	Kid Nichols, 1896	63.5
41	Kid Nichols, 1898	63.5
42	Amos Rusie, 1897	63.4
43	Cy Young, 1894	63.4
44	Bob Gibson, 1968	63.2
45	Mickey Welch, 1885	63.1
46	Ted Breitenstein, 1893	63.1
47	Bob Caruthers, 1885	62.9
48	Bob Feller, 1940	62.8
49	Clark Griffith, 1898	62.6
50	Lefty Grove, 1936	62.6
51	Ron Guidry, 1978	62.0
52	Cy Young, 1893	61.9
53	Ed Morris, 1886	61.8
54	Will White, 1882	61.4
55	Amos Rusie, 1890	61.3
56	Carl Hubbell, 1934	61.3
57	Tim Keefe, 1883	61.0
58	Jim Palmer, 1975	61.0
59	Dean Chance, 1964	61.0
60	Claude Hendrix, 1914	60.9
61	Cy Young, 1902	60.7
62	Hugh Daily, 1884	60.6
63	Ed Seward, 1888	60.5
64	Robin Roberts, 1953	59.2
65	Thornton Lee, 1941	59.2
66	Dazzy Vance, 1928	59.0
67	Dazzy Vance, 1924	58.8
68	Bob Feller, 1939	58.5
69	Charlie Ferguson, 1886	58.3
70	Win Mercer, 1894	58.3
71	Kid Nichols, 1895	58.2
72	Bucky Walters, 1939	57.8
73	Carl Hubbell, 1936	57.8
74	Lady Baldwin, 1886	57.7
75	Bill Hutchinson, 1890	57.7
76	Wilbur Wood, 1971	57.7
77	Ed Morris, 1885	57.7
78	Carl Hubbell, 1933	57.6
79	Jesse Duryea, 1889	57.4
80	Guy Hecker, 1885	57.2
81	Vida Blue, 1971	57.2
82	Tony Mullane, 1883	57.1
83	Steve Carlton, 1972	56.9
84	John Clarkson, 1887	56.5
85	Sandy Koufax, 1965	56.1
86	Warren Spahn, 1947	56.1
87	Walter Johnson, 1919	55.9
88	Bill Hoffer, 1895	55.1
89	Joe Wood, 1912	54.9
90	Kid Nichols, 1893	54.9
91	Tim Keefe, 1885	54.7
92	Bob Feller, 1946	54.4
93	Tom Seaver, 1971	54.3
94	Charlie Buffinton, 1884	54.2
95	Hal Newhouser, 1945	54.0
96	Toad Ramsey, 1887	54.0
97	Walter Johnson, 1918	53.9
98	Mel Harder, 1934	53.4
99	Lefty Grove, 1932	53.3
100	Red Ehret, 1890	53.3

Adjusted Pitching Runs

1	Amos Rusie, 1894	125.0
2	Charley Radbourn, 1884	124.0
3	Silver King, 1888	114.0
4	Dave Foutz, 1886	97.2
5	John Clarkson, 1887	94.8
6	John Clarkson, 1889	94.2
7	John Clarkson, 1885	93.9
8	Jim Devlin, 1877	90.5
9	Cy Young, 1894	89.8
10	Silver King, 1890	87.7
11	Amos Rusie, 1893	86.3
12	Mike Smith, 1887	85.5
13	Scott Stratton, 1890	85.3
14	Will White, 1883	84.8
15	Billy Rhines, 1890	84.1
16	Jim Galvin, 1884	83.3
17	Toad Ramsey, 1886	82.8
18	Kid Nichols, 1890	82.0
19	Lefty Grove, 1931	81.6
20	Guy Hecker, 1884	81.3
21	Kid Nichols, 1897	81.0
22	Bill Hutchinson, 1890	79.4
23	Cy Young, 1901	79.4
24	Walter Johnson, 1912	78.8
25	Tim Keefe, 1883	78.3
26	Charley Radbourn, 1883	77.8
27	Mickey Welch, 1885	77.6
28	Kid Nichols, 1896	77.4
29	Walter Johnson, 1913	75.1
30	John Clarkson, 1886	74.0
31	Will White, 1882	74.0
32	Cy Young, 1892	74.0
33	Lefty Grove, 1932	73.7
34	Jouett Meekin, 1894	73.4
35	Lefty Gomez, 1937	73.3
36	Lady Baldwin, 1886	73.3
37	Toad Ramsey, 1887	72.5
38	Pete Alexander, 1915	72.4
39	Cy Young, 1896	71.4
40	Ed Morris, 1885	71.1
41	Pink Hawley, 1895	71.0
42	Lefty Grove, 1936	70.9
43	Dolf Luque, 1923	70.9
44	Tony Mullane, 1883	70.8
45	Cy Young, 1893	70.4
46	Matt Kilroy, 1887	69.4
47	Kid Nichols, 1898	69.2
48	Dazzy Vance, 1930	68.8
49	Kid Gleason, 1890	68.3
50	Dizzy Dean, 1934	68.0
51	Lefty Grove, 1930	67.6
52	Jack Stivetts, 1891	67.6
53	Al Spalding, 1876	67.1
54	Bill Hoffer, 1895	67.0
55	Clark Griffith, 1898	66.7
56	Nig Cuppy, 1896	66.6
57	Tim Keefe, 1885	66.4
58	Tim Keefe, 1887	66.2
59	Christy Mathewson, 1905	65.9
60	Jesse Duryea, 1889	65.8
61	Tony Mullane, 1887	65.4
62	Red Faber, 1921	65.4
63	Bob Caruthers, 1886	65.3
64	Cy Young, 1899	64.3
65	Lefty Grove, 1935	64.2
66	Red Ehret, 1890	64.2
67	Kid Nichols, 1891	64.0
68	Kid Nichols, 1895	63.9
69	Joe Wood, 1912	63.8
70	Lefty Grove, 1926	63.4
71	Sandy Koufax, 1966	63.4
72	Icebox Chamberlin, 1889	63.4
73	Jim Whitney, 1883	62.6
74	Bucky Walters, 1939	62.0
75	Ed Seward, 1888	61.9
76	Lefty Gomez, 1934	61.7
77	Frank Killen, 1893	61.5
78	Guy Hecker, 1885	61.4
79	Mark Baldwin, 1890	61.3
80	Ted Breitenstein, 1893	61.3
81	Hal Newhouser, 1945	61.0
82	Amos Rusie, 1897	60.9
83	Kid Nichols, 1893	60.9
84	Hugh Daily, 1884	60.6
85	Dwight Gooden, 1985	60.6
86	Ron Guidry, 1978	60.6
87	Hal Newhouser, 1946	60.4
88	Bobo Newsom, 1940	60.1
89	Joe McGinnity, 1899	59.8
90	Cy Young, 1902	59.8
91	Silver King, 1889	59.7
92	Vic Willis, 1899	59.2
93	Carl Hubbell, 1934	58.5
94	Bob Gibson, 1968	58.3
95	Juan Marichal, 1965	58.3
96	Carl Hubbell, 1936	58.3
97	Walter Johnson, 1918	58.2
98	Frank Sullivan, 1955	58.2
99	Charlie Buffinton, 1888	58.1
100	Dizzy Trout, 1944	58.0

Pitching Wins

1. Charley Radbourn, 1884 .... 10.8
2. Guy Hecker, 1884 — 9.9
3. Amos Rusie, 1894 — 9.7
4. Silver King, 1888 — 8.5
5. Walter Johnson, 1912 — 8.0
6. John Clarkson, 1889 — 7.8
7. Cy Young, 1901 — 7.6
8. Walter Johnson, 1913 — 7.3
9. Bob Gibson, 1968 — 7.2
10. Dolf Luque, 1923 — 7.1
11. Pete Alexander, 1915 — 7.1
12. Sandy Koufax, 1966 — 7.1
13. Lefty Grove, 1931 — 7.0
14. Will White, 1883 — 6.8
15. Christy Mathewson, 1905 — 6.7
16. Dwight Gooden, 1985 — 6.7
17. Charley Radbourn, 1883 — 6.7
18. Dave Foutz, 1886 — 6.6
19. Matt Kilroy, 1887 — 6.5
20. Lefty Gomez, 1937 — 6.5
21. Pink Hawley, 1895 — 6.4
22. Dean Chance, 1964 — 6.4
23. Ron Guidry, 1978 — 6.4
24. Billy Rhines, 1890 — 6.4
25. Amos Rusie, 1893 — 6.4
26. Scott Stratton, 1890 — 6.4
27. Cy Young, 1892 — 6.3
28. Claude Hendrix, 1914 — 6.3
29. John Clarkson, 1885 — 6.3
30. Lefty Gomez, 1934 — 6.3
31. Silver King, 1890 — 6.3
32. Warren Spahn, 1953 — 6.2
33. Jim Palmer, 1975 — 6.2
34. Red Faber, 1921 — 6.2
35. Wilbur Wood, 1971 — 6.2
36. Jim Galvin, 1884 — 6.2
37. Lefty Grove, 1930 — 6.2
38. Vida Blue, 1971 — 6.2
39. Steve Carlton, 1972 — 6.1
40. Carl Hubbell, 1933 — 6.1
41. George Bradley, 1876 — 6.1
42. Walter Johnson, 1918 — 6.0
43. Dazzy Vance, 1930 — 6.0
44. Carl Hubbell, 1934 — 6.0
45. Mickey Welch, 1885 — 5.9
46. Bob Feller, 1940 — 5.9
47. Kid Nichols, 1898 — 5.9
48. Sandy Koufax, 1965 — 5.9
49. Kid Nichols, 1897 — 5.9
50. Clark Griffith, 1898 — 5.9
51. Walter Johnson, 1919 — 5.8
52. Dazzy Vance, 1924 — 5.8
53. Tom Seaver, 1971 — 5.8
54. Hal Newhouser, 1945 — 5.8
55. Bucky Walters, 1939 — 5.8
56. Dazzy Vance, 1928 — 5.8
57. Cy Young, 1902 — 5.8
58. Thornton Lee, 1941 — 5.7
59. Ed Walsh, 1910 — 5.7
60. Ed Walsh, 1908 — 5.7
61. Robin Roberts, 1953 — 5.7
62. Jouett Meekin, 1894 — 5.7
63. Bob Feller, 1946 — 5.7
64. Kid Nichols, 1890 — 5.7
65. Toad Ramsey, 1886 — 5.7
66. Bob Caruthers, 1885 — 5.7
67. Will White, 1882 — 5.6
68. Carl Hubbell, 1936 — 5.6
69. Ed Seward, 1888 — 5.6
70. Walter Johnson, 1915 — 5.6
71. Lefty Grove, 1936 — 5.5
72. Warren Spahn, 1947 — 5.5
73. Jack Taylor, 1902 — 5.5
74. Joe Wood, 1912 — 5.5
75. Mike Smith, 1887 — 5.5
76. Amos Rusie, 1890 — 5.5
77. Mordecai Brown, 1906 — 5.4
78. Mordecai Brown, 1909 — 5.4
79. Amos Rusie, 1897 — 5.4
80. Ed Morris, 1886 — 5.4
81. Walter Johnson, 1910 — 5.4
82. Kid Nichols, 1896 — 5.4
83. Bob Feller, 1939 — 5.4
84. Dizzy Trout, 1944 — 5.4
85. Tim Keefe, 1883 — 5.4
86. Joe McGinnity, 1904 — 5.4
87. John Tudor, 1985 — 5.4
88. Hal Newhouser, 1946 — 5.3
89. Tom Seaver, 1973 — 5.3
90. Jack Coombs, 1910 — 5.3
91. Hugh Daily, 1884 — 5.3
92. Ed Reulbach, 1905 — 5.3
93. Pete Alexander, 1920 — 5.3
94. Pete Alexander, 1916 — 5.3
95. Charlie Ferguson, 1886 — 5.3
96. Sandy Koufax, 1963 — 5.3
97. Juan Marichal, 1969 — 5.2
98. Lady Baldwin, 1886 — 5.2
99. Ed Walsh, 1912 — 5.2
100. Bob Gibson, 1969 — 5.2

Adjusted Pitching Wins

1. Charley Radbourn, 1884 .... 11.1
2. Silver King, 1888 — 10.5
3. Amos Rusie, 1894 — 9.6
4. John Clarkson, 1885 — 8.8
5. Dave Foutz, 1886 — 8.5
6. John Clarkson, 1889 — 8.2
7. Jim Devlin, 1877 — 8.1
8. John Clarkson, 1887 — 8.0
9. Pete Alexander, 1915 — 8.0
10. Walter Johnson, 1913 — 8.0
11. Walter Johnson, 1912 — 7.9
12. Lefty Grove, 1931 — 7.6
13. Scott Stratton, 1890 — 7.5
14. Billy Rhines, 1890 — 7.5
15. Will White, 1883 — 7.5
16. Jim Galvin, 1884 — 7.4
17. Guy Hecker, 1884 — 7.4
18. Mickey Welch, 1885 — 7.3
19. Kid Nichols, 1890 — 7.3
20. Toad Ramsey, 1886 — 7.3
21. Cy Young, 1901 — 7.2
22. Amos Rusie, 1893 — 7.1
23. Bill Hutchinson, 1890 — 7.1
24. Silver King, 1890 — 7.0
25. Kid Nichols, 1897 — 6.9
26. Mike Smith, 1887 — 6.9
27. Tim Keefe, 1883 — 6.9
28. Cy Young, 1892 — 6.9
29. Christy Mathewson, 1905 — 6.9
30. Cy Young, 1892 — 6.8
31. Lefty Grove, 1932 — 6.8
32. Dolf Luque, 1923 — 6.8
33. Will White, 1882 — 6.8
34. Charley Radbourn, 1883 — 6.8
35. Lefty Gomez, 1937 — 6.7
36. John Clarkson, 1886 — 6.7
37. Bob Gibson, 1968 — 6.7
38. Sandy Koufax, 1966 — 6.6
39. Lady Baldwin, 1886 — 6.6
40. Dizzy Dean, 1934 — 6.6
41. Kid Nichols, 1896 — 6.6
42. Hal Newhouser, 1945 — 6.5
43. Walter Johnson, 1918 — 6.5
44. Kid Nichols, 1898 — 6.5
45. Ed Morris, 1885 — 6.4
46. Dwight Gooden, 1985 — 6.4
47. Joe Wood, 1912 — 6.4
48. Hal Newhouser, 1946 — 6.3
49. Lefty Grove, 1936 — 6.3
50. Tim Keefe, 1885 — 6.2
51. Ron Guidry, 1978 — 6.2
52. Clark Griffith, 1898 — 6.2
53. Tony Mullane, 1883 — 6.2
54. Vida Blue, 1971 — 6.2
55. Jack Chesbro, 1904 — 6.2
56. Bucky Walters, 1939 — 6.2
57. Juan Marichal, 1965 — 6.2
58. Lefty Grove, 1926 — 6.1
59. Red Faber, 1921 — 6.1
60. Lefty Grove, 1930 — 6.1
61. Dizzy Trout, 1944 — 6.1
62. Kid Gleason, 1890 — 6.1
63. Dazzy Vance, 1930 — 6.1
64. Cy Young, 1896 — 6.1
65. Joe McGinnity, 1904 — 6.0
66. Mordecai Brown, 1906 — 6.0
67. Mort Cooper, 1942 — 6.0
68. Lefty Grove, 1935 — 6.0
69. Gaylord Perry, 1972 — 6.0
70. Carl Hubbell, 1933 — 5.9
71. Al Spalding, 1876 — 5.9
72. Toad Ramsey, 1887 — 5.9
73. Wilbur Wood, 1971 — 5.9
74. Cy Young, 1899 — 5.8
75. Frank Sullivan, 1955 — 5.8
76. Jack Stivetts, 1891 — 5.8
77. Cy Falkenberg, 1914 — 5.8
78. Cy Young, 1893 — 5.8
79. Ed Reulbach, 1905 — 5.8
80. Pink Hawley, 1895 — 5.8
81. Lefty Gomez, 1934 — 5.7
82. Bob Caruthers, 1886 — 5.7
83. Ed Seward, 1888 — 5.7
84. Jim Palmer, 1975 — 5.7
85. Kid Nichols, 1891 — 5.7
86. Charlie Buffinton, 1888 — 5.7
87. Carl Hubbell, 1934 — 5.7
88. Rube Waddell, 1905 — 5.7
89. Dazzy Vance, 1924 — 5.7
90. Carl Hubbell, 1936 — 5.7
91. Walter Johnson, 1915 — 5.7
92. Steve Carlton, 1972 — 5.7
93. Bobo Newsom, 1940 — 5.7
94. Cy Young, 1902 — 5.7
95. Nig Cuppy, 1896 — 5.6
96. Red Ehret, 1890 — 5.6
97. Dazzy Vance, 1928 — 5.6
98. Johnny Antonelli, 1954 — 5.6
99. Walter Johnson, 1919 — 5.6
100. Addie Joss, 1908 — 5.6

Opponents' Batting Average

1. Luis Tiant, 1968 — .168
2. Nolan Ryan, 1972 — .171
3. Sandy Koufax, 1965 — .179
4. Dutch Leonard, 1914 — .180
5. Sid Fernandez, 1985 — .181
6. Dave McNally, 1968 — .182
7. Tommy Byrne, 1949 — .183
8. Al Downing, 1963 — .184
9. Bob Gibson, 1968 — .184
10. Sam McDowell, 1965 — .185
11. Herb Score, 1956 — .186
12. Mike Scott, 1986 — .186
13. Ed Walsh, 1910 — .187
14. Mario Soto, 1980 — .187
15. Walter Johnson, 1913 — .187
16. Nolan Ryan, 1981 — .188
17. Russ Ford, 1910 — .188
18. Nolan Ryan, 1986 — .188
19. Floyd Youmans, 1986 — .188
20. Sam McDowell, 1966 — .188
21. Sandy Koufax, 1963 — .189
22. Sam McDowell, 1968 — .189
23. Don Sutton, 1972 — .189
24. Jim Hunter, 1972 — .189
25. Vida Blue, 1971 — .189
26. Nolan Ryan, 1974 — .190
27. Andy Messersmith, 1969 — .190
28. Joe Horlen, 1964 — .190
29. Sid Fernandez, 1988 — .191
30. Pete Alexander, 1915 — .191
31. Sandy Koufax, 1964 — .191
32. Jim Bibby, 1973 — .192
33. Bob Turley, 1955 — .193
34. Nolan Ryan, 1977 — .193
35. Ron Guidry, 1978 — .193
36. Stan Coveleski, 1917 — .194
37. Bob Turley, 1957 — .194
38. Herb Score, 1955 — .194
39. Nolan Ryan, 1976 — .195
40. Nolan Ryan, 1983 — .195
41. Dean Chance, 1964 — .195
42. Roger Clemens, 1986 — .195
43. Walter Johnson, 1912 — .196
44. Roger Nelson, 1972 — .196
45. J. R. Richard, 1978 — .196
46. Pascual Perez, 1988 — .196
47. Jeff Robinson, 1988 — .197
48. Ed Reulbach, 1906 — .197
49. Dave Boswell, 1967 — .197
50. Sandy Koufax, 1962 — .197
51. Addie Joss, 1908 — .197
52. Sonny Siebert, 1968 — .198
53. Larry Cheney, 1916 — .198
54. Wayne Simpson, 1970 — .198
55. Orval Overall, 1909 — .198
56. Gary Peters, 1967 — .199
57. Jeff Tesreau, 1912 — .199
58. Willie Mitchell, 1913 — .199
59. Tim Keefe, 1880 — .199
60. Nolan Ryan, 1987 — .199
61. Christy Mathewson, 1909 — .200
62. Denny McLain, 1968 — .200
63. Bobby Bolin, 1968 — .200
    Jim Palmer, 1969 — .200
65. Spec Shea, 1947 — .200
66. Art Fromme, 1909 — .201
67. Babe Ruth, 1916 — .201
68. Dwight Gooden, 1985 — .201
69. Hal Newhouser, 1946 — .201
70. Jack Coombs, 1910 — .201
71. Dwight Gooden, 1984 — .202
72. Jim Maloney, 1963 — .202
73. Cy Morgan, 1909 — .202
74. Mordecai Brown, 1909 — .202
75. Allie Reynolds, 1943 — .202
76. Juan Marichal, 1966 — .202
77. Luis Tiant, 1972 — .202
78. Dave Boswell, 1967 — .202
79. Sonny Siebert, 1967 — .202
80. Don Wilson, 1971 — .202
81. Bob Turley, 1954 — .203
82. Eddie Cicotte, 1917 — .203
83. Frank Smith, 1908 — .203
84. Ed Walsh, 1908 — .203
85. Nolan Ryan, 1973 — .203
86. Ed Walsh, 1909 — .203
87. Dick Hughes, 1967 — .203
88. Joe Horlen, 1967 — .203
89. Claude Hendrix, 1914 — .203
90. Frank Tanana, 1976 — .203
91. Charlie Sweeney, 1884 — .203
92. Johnny Niggeling, 1943 — .204
93. Carl Lundgren, 1907 — .204
94. Bob Gibson, 1962 — .204
95. Don Larsen, 1956 — .204
96. Mike Cuellar, 1969 — .204
97. Mike Scott, 1988 — .204
98. Gaylord Perry, 1974 — .204
99. Harry Krause, 1909 — .204
100. Mort Cooper, 1942 — .204

Opponents' On Base Pctg.

1. Walter Johnson, 1913 — .217
2. Guy Hecker, 1882 — .218
3. Addie Joss, 1908 — .218
4. Jim McCormick, 1884 — .221
5. Sandy Koufax, 1965 — .225
6. Ed Walsh, 1910 — .226
7. Charlie Sweeney, 1884 — .227
8. Sandy Koufax, 1963 — .227
9. Pete Alexander, 1915 — .228
10. Juan Marichal, 1966 — .228
11. Christy Mathewson, 1909 — .228
12. Bob Gibson, 1968 — .230
13. Dave McNally, 1968 — .231
14. Dupee Shaw, 1884 — .232
15. Luis Tiant, 1968 — .232
16. Ed Walsh, 1908 — .232
17. Charlie Sweeney, 1884 — .233
18. Roger Nelson, 1972 — .233
19. Babe Adams, 1919 — .235
20. George Bradley, 1880 — .236
21. Henry Boyle, 1884 — .236
22. Tim Keefe, 1880 — .236
23. Juan Marichal, 1965 — .238
24. Jim Hunter, 1972 — .238
25. Sandy Koufax, 1964 — .238
26. Don Sutton, 1972 — .238
27. Denny Driscoll, 1882 — .238
28. Mordecai Brown, 1909 — .239
29. Cy Young, 1908 — .240
30. Mike Scott, 1986 — .240
31. Pete Alexander, 1919 — .241
32. Denny McLain, 1968 — .241
33. Guy Hecker, 1884 — .242
34. George Bradley, 1876 — .242
35. Warren Hacker, 1952 — .244
36. Russ Ford, 1910 — .245
37. Tommy Bond, 1876 — .245
38. Dutch Leonard, 1914 — .246
39. Ron Guidry, 1978 — .246
40. Joe Horlen, 1964 — .247
41. Jim Whitney, 1884 — .247
42. John Tudor, 1985 — .248
43. Silver King, 1888 — .248
44. Eddie Cicotte, 1917 — .248
45. Ed Morris, 1884 — .248
46. Pascual Perez, 1988 — .248
47. Walter Johnson, 1912 — .248
48. Dick Hughes, 1967 — .249
49. Tom Seaver, 1971 — .249
50. Vida Blue, 1971 — .249
51. Pat Jarvis, 1968 — .250
52. Sandy Koufax, 1966 — .250
53. Fred Anderson, 1917 — .250
    Turk Farrell, 1963 — .250
55. Tom Seaver, 1973 — .250
56. Babe Adams, 1920 — .250
57. Roger Clemens, 1986 — .251
58. Claude Hendrix, 1914 — .251
59. Joe Horlen, 1967 — .251
60. Dennis Eckersley, 1985 — .252
61. Eddie Fisher, 1965 — .252
62. Slim Sallee, 1918 — .252
63. Monte Ward, 1880 — .253
64. Dwight Gooden, 1985 — .253
65. Ed Walsh, 1909 — .253
66. Walter Johnson, 1918 — .253
67. Ray Prim, 1945 — .253
68. Whit Wyatt, 1943 — .253
69. Don Drysdale, 1964 — .253
70. Juan Marichal, 1963 — .254
71. Charley Radbourn, 1884 — .254
72. Carl Hubbell, 1933 — .254
73. Roger Wolff, 1945 — .254
74. Russ Ford, 1914 — .254
75. Chief Bender, 1909 — .254
76. Jack Lynch, 1884 — .254
77. Reb Russell, 1916 — .254
78. Don Sutton, 1980 — .255
79. Mort Cooper, 1942 — .255
80. Dick Rudolph, 1916 — .255
81. Tim Keefe, 1885 — .255
82. Jess Barnes, 1919 — .255
83. Gary Peters, 1966 — .255
84. Don Newcombe, 1956 — .255
85. Mike Scott, 1988 — .255
86. Pete Alexander, 1916 — .255
87. Chief Bender, 1910 — .255
88. Lady Baldwin, 1885 — .255
89. Steve Carlton, 1972 — .255
90. Don Sutton, 1973 — .255
91. Addie Joss, 1909 — .255
92. Ron Guidry, 1981 — .256
93. Bobby Bolin, 1968 — .256
94. Jim Merritt, 1967 — .256
95. Frank Smith, 1908 — .256
96. Dean Chance, 1968 — .256
97. Sonny Siebert, 1965 — .256
98. Christy Mathewson, 1908 — .256
99. Jim Hunter, 1974 — .256
100. Bill Burns, 1908 — .257

Wins Above Team

1	George Bradley, 1876	22.5
2	Will White, 1879	21.5
3	Charley Radbourn, 1884	21.0
4	Jim McCormick, 1880	19.4
5	Guy Hecker, 1884	18.0
6	Jim Galvin, 1883	17.6
7	Jim Devlin, 1877	17.5
8	Charley Radbourn, 1883	15.7
9	Matt Kilroy, 1887	15.4
10	Jim Galvin, 1884	15.1
11	Jim Devlin, 1876	15.0
12	Charlie Buffinton, 1884	14.9
13	Tony Mullane, 1884	14.8
14	Walter Johnson, 1913	14.7
15	Jack Chesbro, 1904	14.0
16	Sadie McMahon, 1890	13.6
17	Will White, 1882	13.1
18	Ed Morris, 1885	12.9
19	Joe Wood, 1912	12.8
20	Bill Sweeney, 1884	12.7
	Ed Walsh, 1908	12.7
22	John Clarkson, 1889	12.1
23	Tommy Bond, 1879	12.0
24	Lefty Grove, 1931	11.8
25	Steve Carlton, 1972	11.7
26	Cy Young, 1901	11.6
27	Bill Hutchinson, 1891	11.4
	Denny McLain, 1968	11.4
29	Terry Larkin, 1878	11.2
	Mickey Welch, 1884	11.2
	Bob Caruthers, 1889	11.2
32	Henry Porter, 1885	11.0
	Bill Hoffer, 1895	11.0
	Christy Mathewson, 1908	11.0
35	Cy Young, 1902	10.9
36	Cy Young, 1895	10.7
37	Dazzy Vance, 1924	10.6
	Robin Roberts, 1952	10.6
	Ron Guidry, 1978	10.6
40	Bobby Mathews, 1876	10.5
	Dizzy Dean, 1934	10.5
42	Toad Ramsey, 1886	10.2
	Cy Young, 1892	10.2
	Joe McGinnity, 1904	10.2
	Eddie Rommel, 1922	10.2
46	Lefty Grove, 1930	10.1
47	Ed Morris, 1886	10.0
	Bill Donovan, 1907	10.0
49	Frank Mountain, 1883	9.9
	Eddie Cicotte, 1919	9.9
	Lefty Gomez, 1934	9.9
52	Kid Gleason, 1890	9.8
	Pete Alexander, 1915	9.8
	Hal Newhouser, 1944	9.8
55	Bobby Mathews, 1885	9.7
	Russ Ford, 1910	9.7
	Roger Clemens, 1986	9.7
58	Charlie Ferguson, 1886	9.6
	Pete Conway, 1888	9.6
	Eddie Plank, 1912	9.6
61	Pete Alexander, 1916	9.5
	Carl Hubbell, 1936	9.5
	Dwight Gooden, 1985	9.5
64	Jouett Meekin, 1894	9.4
	Walter Johnson, 1912	9.4
	Claude Hendrix, 1914	9.4
67	Joe McGinnity, 1900	9.3
	Sandy Koufax, 1963	9.3
69	Bert Cunningham, 1898	9.2
	Walter Johnson, 1911	9.2
	Bobby Shantz, 1952	9.2
	Don Newcombe, 1956	9.2
	Juan Marichal, 1966	9.2
	Bob Gibson, 1970	9.2
75	Tim Keefe, 1888	9.1
	Whitey Ford, 1961	9.1
77	Jim McCormick, 1882	9.0
	Cy Young, 1893	9.0
	Preacher Roe, 1951	9.0
80	Frank Killen, 1892	8.9
	Red Faber, 1921	8.9
82	Tim Keefe, 1883	8.8
	Tim Keefe, 1887	8.8
	Christy Mathewson, 1909	8.8
	Dolf Luque, 1923	8.8
86	Lee Richmond, 1881	8.7
	Jim Hughes, 1899	8.7
	Juan Marichal, 1963	8.7
	Juan Marichal, 1968	8.7
90	Jumbo McGinnis, 1882	8.6
	Jim McCormick, 1883	8.6
	Lefty Grove, 1933	8.6
	Bob Feller, 1946	8.6
	Roy Face, 1959	8.6
95	7 players tied	8.5

Wins Above League

1	Charley Radbourn, 1884	47.1
2	Silver King, 1888	43.5
3	Guy Hecker, 1884	43.4
4	John Clarkson, 1885	43.3
5	Charley Radbourn, 1883	43.3
6	John Clarkson, 1889	42.2
7	Jim Galvin, 1884	41.4
8	Tim Keefe, 1883	40.9
9	Bill Hutchinson, 1890	40.6
10	Jim Galvin, 1883	40.2
11	Jim McCormick, 1880	40.0
12	Will White, 1883	40.0
13	Toad Ramsey, 1886	39.8
14	Will White, 1879	39.6
15	Bill Hutchinson, 1892	38.4
16	Matt Kilroy, 1887	38.1
17	Jim Devlin, 1877	38.1
18	Ed Morris, 1885	37.9
19	Toad Ramsey, 1887	37.9
20	Jim Devlin, 1876	37.6
21	John Clarkson, 1887	37.5
22	Dave Foutz, 1886	37.0
23	Tony Mullane, 1884	36.6
24	Charlie Buffinton, 1884	36.5
25	George Bradley, 1876	36.5
26	Amos Rusie, 1890	36.0
27	Bill Hutchinson, 1891	35.7
28	Jim Galvin, 1879	35.5
29	Al Spalding, 1876	35.4
30	Lee Richmond, 1880	35.3
31	Monte Ward, 1879	35.3
32	Tommy Bond, 1879	35.1
33	Monte Ward, 1880	35.0
34	Mickey Welch, 1885	34.8
35	Ed Morris, 1886	34.5
36	Jim Whitney, 1883	34.5
37	Bill Sweeney, 1884	34.3
38	Jim McCormick, 1882	34.3
39	Lady Baldwin, 1886	34.1
40	Amos Rusie, 1894	34.1
41	Amos Rusie, 1893	34.1
42	Mark Baldwin, 1890	33.9
43	Sadie McMahon, 1891	33.6
44	Kid Gleason, 1890	33.6
45	Tommy Bond, 1877	33.4
46	Jack Stivetts, 1891	33.3
47	Hugh Daily, 1884	33.3
48	John Clarkson, 1886	33.2
49	Larry Corcoran, 1884	33.2
50	Tim Keefe, 1886	33.1
51	Silver King, 1890	33.0
52	Amos Rusie, 1892	32.9
53	Will White, 1882	32.8
54	Ed Seward, 1888	32.7
55	Jack Chesbro, 1904	32.7
56	Tim Keefe, 1887	32.6
57	Mickey Welch, 1880	32.5
58	Mike Smith, 1887	32.4
59	Ed Walsh, 1908	32.4
60	Jim Whitney, 1881	32.3
61	Mickey Welch, 1884	32.3
62	Pink Hawley, 1895	32.3
63	Guy Hecker, 1885	32.0
64	Tommy Bond, 1878	31.8
65	Tim Keefe, 1884	31.8
66	Larry Corcoran, 1880	31.7
67	Scott Stratton, 1890	31.5
68	Sadie McMahon, 1890	31.5
69	George Derby, 1881	31.4
70	Matt Kilroy, 1889	31.4
71	Hardie Henderson, 1885	31.3
72	Larry Corcoran, 1883	31.3
73	Tony Mullane, 1883	31.2
74	Will White, 1880	31.1
75	Charley Radbourn, 1882	31.1
76	Bob Caruthers, 1885	31.1
77	Jesse Duryea, 1889	31.1
78	Cy Young, 1892	30.8
79	Cy Young, 1893	30.8
80	Silver King, 1889	30.5
81	Cy Young, 1894	30.4
82	Joe McGinnity, 1903	30.4
83	Walter Johnson, 1912	30.4
84	John Clarkson, 1891	30.3
85	Jim McCormick, 1879	30.3
86	Kid Nichols, 1890	30.3
87	Gus Weyhing, 1892	30.2
88	Matt Kilroy, 1886	30.1
89	Charley Radbourn, 1886	30.0
90	Tony Mullane, 1882	30.0
91	Billy Rhines, 1890	30.0
92	Mark Baldwin, 1889	29.9
93	Henry Porter, 1885	29.9
94	Kid Nichols, 1892	29.6
95	Walter Johnson, 1913	29.5
96	Amos Rusie, 1891	29.4
97	Tony Mullane, 1887	29.3
98	Phil Knell, 1891	29.3
99	Kid Nichols, 1891	29.2
100	Jim McCormick, 1881	29.2

Relief Games

1	Mike Marshall, 1974	106
2	Kent Tekulve, 1979	94
3	Mike Marshall, 1973	92
4	Kent Tekulve, 1978	91
5	Wayne Granger, 1969	90
	Mike Marshall, 1979	90
	Kent Tekulve, 1987	90
8	Mark Eichhorn, 1987	89
9	Wilbur Wood, 1968	88
10	Rob Murphy, 1987	87
11	Kent Tekulve, 1982	85
	Frank Williams, 1987	85
	Mitch Williams, 1987	85
14	Ted Abernathy, 1965	84
	Enrique Romo, 1979	84
	Dick Tidrow, 1980	84
	Dan Quisenberry, 1985	84
18	Ken Sanders, 1971	83
	Craig Lefferts, 1986	83
20	Eddie Fisher, 1965	82
	Bill Campbell, 1983	82
22	John Wyatt, 1964	81
	Dale Murray, 1976	81
	Jeff Robinson, 1987	81
25	Pedro Borbon, 1973	80
	Willie Hernandez, 1984	80
	Mitch Williams, 1986	80
28	Dick Radatz, 1964	79
29	Hal Woodeshick, 1965	78
	Ted Abernathy, 1968	78
	Bill Campbell, 1976	78
	Rollie Fingers, 1977	78
	Tom Hume, 1980	78
	Kent Tekulve, 1980	78
	Greg Minton, 1982	78
	Ed Vande Berg, 1982	78
	Ted Power, 1984	78
	Tim Burke, 1985	78
	Lance McCullers, 1987	78
40	Bob Locker, 1967	77
	Wilbur Wood, 1970	77
	Charlie Hough, 1976	77
	Butch Metzger, 1976	77
	Rick Camp, 1980	77
	Gary Lavelle, 1984	77
	Mark Davis, 1985	77
	Craig Lefferts, 1987	77
48	12 players tied	76

Relief Wins

1	Roy Face, 1959	18
2	John Hiller, 1974	17
	Bill Campbell, 1976	17
4	Jim Konstanty, 1950	16
	Ron Perranoski, 1963	16
	Dick Radatz, 1964	16
	Tom Johnson, 1977	16
8	Mace Brown, 1938	15
	Hoyt Wilhelm, 1952	15
	Joe Black, 1952	15
	Luis Arroyo, 1961	15
	Dick Radatz, 1963	15
	Eddie Fisher, 1965	15
	Mike Marshall, 1974	15
	Dale Murray, 1975	15
	Bob Stanley, 1978	15
17	Joe Page, 1947	14
	Clyde King, 1951	14
	Hersh Freeman, 1956	14
	Lindy McDaniel, 1959	14
	Larry Sherry, 1960	14
	Stu Miller, 1961	14
	Stu Miller, 1965	14
	Phil Regan, 1966	14
	Frank Linzy, 1969	14
	Mike Marshall, 1972	14
	Mike Marshall, 1973	14
	Ron Davis, 1979	14
	Mark Clear, 1982	14
	Jim Slaton, 1983	14
	Roger McDowell, 1986	14
	Mark Eichhorn, 1986	14
33	21 players tied	13

Relief Losses

1	Craig Anderson, 1962	17
2	Gene Garber, 1979	16
3	Fay Thomas, 1935	15
	Mike Marshall, 1979	15
5	Ike Pearson, 1941	14
	Stan Williams, 1969	14
	Darold Knowles, 1970	14
	Mike Caldwell, 1973	14
	John Hiller, 1974	14
	Mike Marshall, 1975	14
	John Hiller, 1977	14
12	Ed Heusser, 1940	13
	Roy Face, 1956	13
	Ryne Duren, 1961	13
	Jack Hamilton, 1966	13
	Tommie Sisk, 1969	13
	Wilbur Wood, 1970	13
	Rollie Fingers, 1978	13
	Skip Lockwood, 1978	13
	John D'Acquisto, 1979	13
	Terry Felton, 1982	13
	Tom Hume, 1984	13
23	Morrie Martin, 1953	12
	Camilo Pascual, 1955	12
	Wally Burnette, 1957	12
	Brooks Lawrence, 1959	12
	Lindy McDaniel, 1959	12
	Ray Narleski, 1959	12
	Roy Face, 1961	12
	Orlando Pena, 1965	12
	Clay Carroll, 1967	12
	Wilbur Wood, 1968	12
	Gary Ross, 1969	12
	Ken Sanders, 1971	12
	Mike Marshall, 1974	12
	Gene Garber, 1975	12
	Jim Willoughby, 1976	12
	Charlie Hough, 1977	12
	Mike Marshall, 1978	12
	Bob Shirley, 1980	12
	Kent Tekulve, 1980	12
	Jim Bibby, 1983	12
	Rick Lysander, 1983	12
	Ed Vande Berg, 1984	12
	Mark Davis, 1985	12
	Ken Howell, 1986	12
47	Hal Elliott, 1930	11
	Red Faber, 1932	11
	Whit Wyatt, 1934	11
	Ace Adams, 1944	11
	Eddie Erautt, 1949	11
	Nels Potter, 1949	11
	Bob Muncrief, 1949	11
	Jim Konstanty, 1951	11
	Sheldon Jones, 1951	11
	Frank Smith, 1952	11
	Jack Meyer, 1955	11
	Pedro Ramos, 1955	11
	Jack Meyer, 1956	11
	Luis Arroyo, 1957	11
	Al Worthington, 1957	11
	Tex Clevenger, 1960	11
	Frank Funk, 1961	11
	Billy Muffett, 1961	11
	Billy Pierce, 1963	11
	Ed Connolly, 1964	11
	Jack Kralick, 1965	11
	Dick Radatz, 1965	11
	Frank Linzy, 1966	11
	Jim Grant, 1969	11
	Wilbur Wood, 1969	11
	Ray Corbin, 1971	11
	Jim Shellenback, 1971	11
	Mike Marshall, 1973	11
	Tug McGraw, 1974	11
	Rollie Fingers, 1976	11
	Rich Gossage, 1978	11
	Dave Heaverlo, 1979	11
	Dave LaRoche, 1979	11
	Eric Rasmussen, 1980	11
81	Cy Young, 1894	30

Relief Innings Pitched

1	Mike Marshall, 1974	208
2	Andy Karl, 1945	181
3	Mike Marshall, 1973	179
4	Stan Williams, 1969	178
5	Stu Miller, 1959	168
	Bill Campbell, 1976	168
7	Eddie Fisher, 1965	165
8	Tom Hume, 1979	163
9	Hoyt Wilhelm, 1952	159
	Bob Heffner, 1964	159
	Wilbur Wood, 1968	159
12	Jack Russell, 1934	158
	Kirby Higbe, 1948	158
	Al Worthington, 1957	158
15	Dick Radatz, 1964	157
	Paul Hartzell, 1978	157
	Mark Eichhorn, 1986	157
18	Morrie Martin, 1953	156
19	Garland Braxton, 1927	155
	Firpo Marberry, 1927	155
	Tom Hall, 1970	155
22	Al Brazle, 1951	154
23	Tom Underwood, 1982	153
24	Jim Konstanty, 1950	152
	Bob Anderson, 1961	152
26	Al Worthington, 1958	151
	Jack Lamabe, 1963	151
	Clay Carroll, 1969	151
29	Lou North, 1922	150
	Bill Werle, 1951	150
	John Hiller, 1974	150
32	Jack Hamilton, 1966	149
	Mike Caldwell, 1973	149
34	Ray Corbin, 1973	148
	Pete Vuckovich, 1977	148
36	Fay Thomas, 1935	147
	Tom Johnson, 1977	147
	Mike Proly, 1980	147
39	Fritz Dorish, 1953	146
40	Hoyt Wilhelm, 1953	145
	Jose Santiago, 1967	145
	Wayne Granger, 1969	145
	Bob Stanley, 1983	145
	Tom Underwood, 1983	145
45	7 players tied	144

Relief Points

1	Dave Righetti, 1986	100
2	Dan Quisenberry, 1983	97
	Dan Quisenberry, 1984	97
4	Dennis Eckersley, 1988	96
5	Bruce Sutter, 1984	93
6	John Hiller, 1973	91
7	Steve Bedrosian, 1987	87
8	Johnny Franco, 1988	84
	Jeff Reardon, 1988	84
10	Luis Arroyo, 1961	83
	Sparky Lyle, 1972	83
	Dan Quisenberry, 1980	83
	Bill Caudill, 1984	83
14	Clay Carroll, 1972	82
	Bruce Sutter, 1982	82
16	Dick Radatz, 1964	81
	Dan Quisenberry, 1982	81
	Dan Quisenberry, 1985	81
19	Bruce Sutter, 1979	80
	Todd Worrell, 1986	80
21	Mike Marshall, 1973	79
	Bill Campbell, 1977	79
	Jim Kern, 1979	79
	Willie Hernandez, 1984	79
25	Jeff Reardon, 1985	78
26	Wayne Granger, 1970	77
	Rollie Fingers, 1977	77
	Lee Smith, 1984	77
29	Jack Aker, 1966	76
	Rich Gossage, 1980	76
	Greg Minton, 1982	76
	Jesse Orosco, 1984	76
	Lee Smith, 1985	76
	Todd Worrell, 1987	76
	Doug Jones, 1988	76
36	Dave Righetti, 1985	75
	Jeff Reardon, 1986	75
	Johnny Franco, 1987	75
39	Dick Radatz, 1963	74
	Ron Perranoski, 1970	74
	Kent Tekulve, 1979	74
	Jim Gott, 1988	74
43	Bruce Sutter, 1977	73
	Sparky Lyle, 1977	73
	Rollie Fingers, 1978	73
	Bob James, 1985	73
	Don Aase, 1986	73
48	4 players tied	72

Relief Ranking

1	Jim Kern, 1979	66.9
2	Mike Marshall, 1979	64.3
3	Rich Gossage, 1977	63.4
4	Mark Eichhorn, 1986	60.3
5	John Hiller, 1973	59.2
6	Bill Caudill, 1982	58.2
7	Ellis Kinder, 1953	56.7
8	Sid Monge, 1979	55.3
9	Bruce Sutter, 1977	55.2
10	Bill Campbell, 1977	54.3
11	Donnie Moore, 1985	53.7
12	Dave Righetti, 1986	51.6
13	Jesse Orosco, 1983	51.2
14	Dick Radatz, 1963	50.8
15	Todd Worrell, 1986	49.4
16	Rich Gossage, 1975	48.8
17	Dan Quisenberry, 1985	48.6
18	Rich Gossage, 1978	47.6
19	Doug Corbett, 1980	47.5
20	Roy Face, 1962	47.4
21	Bruce Sutter, 1984	46.7
22	Mike Marshall, 1972	46.5
23	Bob James, 1985	46.4
24	Luis Arroyo, 1961	45.8
25	Tom Murphy, 1974	45.2
26	Sparky Lyle, 1977	45.2
27	Johnny Franco, 1988	45.0
28	Dick Radatz, 1964	44.9
29	Joe Page, 1949	44.8
30	Al Hrabosky, 1975	44.6
31	Lindy McDaniel, 1960	44.4
32	Ken Sanders, 1971	44.3
33	Willie Hernandez, 1985	44.3
34	Dan Spillner, 1982	43.7
35	Frank Linzy, 1965	42.9
36	Ron Perranoski, 1969	42.8
37	Lee Smith, 1983	42.7
38	Stu Miller, 1965	42.2
39	Dan Quisenberry, 1983	42.2
40	Bruce Sutter, 1979	41.9
41	Marv Grissom, 1954	41.7
42	John Hiller, 1974	41.1
43	Rich Gossage, 1983	41.0
44	Hoyt Wilhelm, 1964	40.8
45	Mark Clear, 1982	39.7
46	Rollie Fingers, 1981	39.5
47	Jim Konstanty, 1950	39.1
48	Gene Garber, 1982	38.8
49	Ted Abernathy, 1967	38.5
50	Hoyt Wilhelm, 1954	38.5

Relievers' Runs

1. Mark Eichhorn, 1986 ...... 43.0
2. Jim Kern, 1979 .... 42.2
3. Rich Gossage, 1977 ...... 33.8
4. John Hiller, 1973 .... 33.1
5. Dan Quisenberry, 1983 .... 33.0
6. Willie Hernandez, 1984 .... 32.2
7. Bob Lee, 1964 .... 32.2
8. Doug Corbett, 1980 ...... 31.1
9. Rich Gossage, 1975 ...... 30.8
10. Bruce Sutter, 1977 .... 30.5
11. Tim Burke, 1987 .... 29.3
12. Sparky Lyle, 1977 .... 29.0
13. Bruce Sutter, 1984 .... 28.1
14. Mike Marshall, 1974 ...... 27.9
15. Rollie Fingers, 1973 ..... 26.9
16. Sid Monge, 1979 .... 26.6
17. Jesse Orosco, 1983 ...... 26.5
18. Hoyt Wilhelm, 1965 ...... 26.3
19. Rich Gossage, 1978 ...... 26.3
20. Phil Regan, 1966 .... 25.9
21. Jim Grant, 1970 .... 25.8
22. Aurelio Lopez, 1979 ...... 25.7
23. Ellis Kinder, 1953 .... 25.5
24. Donnie Moore, 1985 ...... 25.5
25. Dan Quisenberry, 1985 .... 25.5
26. Mike Marshall, 1979 ...... 25.2
27. Jim Konstanty, 1950 ...... 25.0
28. Sparky Lyle, 1974 .... 24.9
29. Joe Black, 1952 .... 24.9
30. Ted Abernathy, 1967 ...... 24.7
31. Bob James, 1985 .... 24.7
32. Greg Minton, 1982 .... 24.3
33. Gary Lavelle, 1977 .... 24.3
34. Dick Radatz, 1963 .... 24.2
35. Hoyt Wilhelm, 1954 ...... 24.2
36. Luis Arroyo, 1961 .... 24.2
37. Dick Radatz, 1962 .... 24.1
38. Joe Page, 1949 .... 24.0
39. Dan Spillner, 1982 ...... 23.8
40. Hoyt Wilhelm, 1964 ...... 23.8
41. Tom Murphy, 1974 .... 23.5
42. Ken Sanders, 1971 ...... 23.4
43. Dick Radatz, 1964 .... 23.2
44. Marv Grissom, 1954 ...... 23.2
45. Bob Reynolds, 1973 ...... 23.2
46. Dan Quisenberry, 1982 .... 23.1
47. Dick Hyde, 1958 .... 23.1
48. Ron Perranoski, 1963 ..... 23.1
49. Hoyt Wilhelm, 1952 ...... 22.9
50. Rollie Fingers, 1981 ...... 22.7

Adjusted Relievers' Runs

1. Mark Eichhorn, 1986 ...... 46.7
2. Jim Kern, 1979 .... 42.1
3. Bruce Sutter, 1977 ...... 37.0
4. Doug Corbett, 1980 ...... 36.3
5. Rich Gossage, 1977 ...... 35.3
6. Dan Quisenberry, 1983 .... 33.8
7. John Hiller, 1973 .... 33.6
8. Rich Gossage, 1975 ...... 32.8
9. Tim Burke, 1987 .... 31.8
10. Mike Marshall, 1979 ...... 30.9
11. Sid Monge, 1979 .... 30.1
12. Willie Hernandez, 1984 .... 29.8
13. Ellis Kinder, 1953 .... 29.6
14. Bill Campbell, 1977 ...... 28.4
15. Ted Abernathy, 1967 ..... 28.3
16. Sparky Lyle, 1977 .... 28.1
17. Bruce Sutter, 1984 .... 27.5
18. Dick Radatz, 1963 .... 27.3
19. Hoyt Wilhelm, 1954 ...... 26.7
20. Ellis Kinder, 1951 .... 26.6
21. Bob Reynolds, 1973 ...... 26.6
22. Dan Quisenberry, 1985 .... 26.5
23. Gary Lavelle, 1977 .... 26.5
24. Rod Scurry, 1982 .... 26.0
25. Marv Grissom, 1954 ...... 26.0
26. Bob Lee, 1964 .... 25.9
27. Donnie Moore, 1985 ...... 25.9
28. Jesse Orosco, 1983 ...... 25.8
29. Joe Black, 1952 .... 25.7
30. Andy McGaffigan, 1987 .... 25.7
31. Rich Gossage, 1978 ...... 25.5
32. Lindy McDaniel, 1960 ..... 25.4
33. Greg Harris, 1985 .... 25.4
34. Dick Radatz, 1962 .... 25.4
35. Joe Pate, 1926 .... 25.3
36. Ken Sanders, 1971 ...... 25.0
37. Tom Burgmeier, 1982 ..... 25.0
38. Tom Murphy, 1974 .... 24.7
39. Bob James, 1985 .... 24.7
40. Tug McGraw, 1980 .... 24.6
41. Hoyt Wilhelm, 1952 ...... 24.5
42. Phil Regan, 1966 .... 24.4
43. Dick Radatz, 1964 .... 24.3
44. Joe Page, 1949 .... 24.2
45. Jim Grant, 1970 .... 24.1
46. Dan Spillner, 1982 ...... 23.9
47. Aurelio Lopez, 1979 ...... 23.6
48. Bill Caudill, 1980 .... 23.5
49. Tom Burgmeier, 1980 ..... 23.3
50. Dan Quisenberry, 1982 .... 23.2

Percent of Team Wins (by era)

1876-1892

1. Will White, 1879 .... 100.0
   Bobby Mathews, 1876 ..... 100.0
   Jim Devlin, 1877 .... 100.0
   Jim Devlin, 1876 .... 100.0
   George Bradley, 1876 ..... 100.0
6. Tommy Bond, 1878 .... 97.6
7. Terry Larkin, 1878 .... 96.7
8. Jim McCormick, 1880 ..... 95.7
9. Tommy Bond, 1877 .... 95.2
10. Terry Larkin, 1877 .... 93.5
11. Al Spalding, 1876 .... 90.4
   Jim Galvin, 1883 .... 88.5
13. Will White, 1880 .... 85.7
   Jim McCormick, 1882 ..... 85.7
15. Mickey Welch, 1880 ..... 82.9

1893-1919

1. Ted Breitenstein, 1895 .... 48.7
2. Amos Rusie, 1893 .... 48.5
3. Ted Breitenstein, 1894 .... 48.2
4. Cy Young, 1893 .... 46.6
5. Ed Walsh, 1908 .... 45.5
   Frank Killen, 1896 .... 45.5
7. Ted Breitenstein, 1896 .... 45.0
8. Jack Chesbro, 1904 ...... 44.6
9. Pink Hawley, 1895 .... 43.7
10. Win Mercer, 1896 .... 43.1
11. Noodles Hahn, 1901 ..... 42.3
12. Frank Killen, 1893 .... 42.0
13. Cy Young, 1901 .... 41.8
14. Cy Young, 1895 .... 41.6
15. Cy Young, 1902 .... 41.6

1920-1941

1. Eddie Rommel, 1922 ..... 41.5
2. Red Faber, 1921 .... 40.3
3. Buck Newsom, 1938 ..... 36.4
4. Jimmy Ring, 1923 .... 36.0
   Pete Alexander, 1920 ..... 36.0
6. Ted Lyons, 1930 .... 35.5
7. Curt Davis, 1934 .... 33.9
8. Urban Shocker, 1921 ..... 33.3
   Bob Feller, 1941 .... 33.3
   Ed Morris, 1928 .... 33.3
11. Howard Ehmke, 1923 ..... 32.8
12. Dazzy Vance, 1925 ...... 32.4
   Paul Derringer, 1935 ..... 32.4
14. Wes Ferrell, 1935 .... 32.1
15. George Uhle, 1923 .... 31.7

1942-1960

1. Ned Garver, 1951 .... 38.5
2. Bob Feller, 1946 .... 38.2
3. Murry Dickson, 1952 ..... 33.3
4. Robin Roberts, 1952 ..... 32.2
5. Bill Voiselle, 1944 .... 31.3
6. Murry Dickson, 1951 ..... 31.3
7. Phil Marchildon, 1942 ..... 30.9
8. Dizzy Trout, 1944 .... 30.7
9. Robin Roberts, 1954 ..... 30.7
10. Bobby Shantz, 1952 ...... 30.4
11. Ewell Blackwell, 1947 ..... 30.1
12. Robin Roberts, 1955 ..... 29.9
13. Johnny Antonelli, 1956 ... 29.9
14. Dave Ferriss, 1945 .... 29.6
15. 2 players tied 29.0

1961-1988

1. Steve Carlton, 1972 ...... 45.8
2. Gaylord Perry, 1972 ...... 33.3
3. Nolan Ryan, 1974 .... 32.4
4. Phil Niekro, 1979 .... 31.8
5. Larry Jackson, 1964 ..... 31.6
6. Wilbur Wood, 1973 ...... 31.2
7. Bob Gibson, 1970 .... 30.3
8. Randy Jones, 1976 ...... 30.1
9. Denny McLain, 1968 ..... 30.1
10. Fergie Jenkins, 1974 ..... 29.8
11. Dave Stieb, 1981 .... 29.7
12. Juan Marichal, 1968 ..... 29.5
13. Sam McDowell, 1969 ..... 29.0
14. Fergie Jenkins, 1971 ..... 28.9
15. Fernando Valenzuela, 1986 . 28.8

Clutch Pitching Index

1. Henry Boyle, 1886 .... 171.4
2. Freddie Fitzsimmons, 1933 . 153.6
3. Ned Garvin, 1904 .... 152.8
4. Mordecai Brown, 1903 .... 152.5
5. Doc White, 1904 .... 151.8
6. Max Lanier, 1943 .... 150.7
7. Carl Lundgren, 1902 ..... 149.8
8. Jim McCormick, 1878 .... 148.3
9. Ed Summers, 1908 ...... 147.9
10. Mike O'Neill, 1904 .... 145.9
11. Pete Schneider, 1917 ..... 145.3
12. Sammy Stewart, 1981 .... 144.3
13. Joe McGinnity, 1908 ..... 144.2
14. Andy Coakley, 1905 ..... 144.0
15. Ed Willett, 1908 .... 143.4
16. Ed Killian, 1907 .... 142.5
17. Bob Rhoads, 1908 .... 141.9
18. Cy Morgan, 1910 .... 141.6
19. Ben Tincup, 1914 .... 141.5
   Dick Rudolph, 1919 ..... 141.5
21. Lefty Gomez, 1931 .... 141.4
22. Sherry Smith, 1919 ...... 141.3
23. Vic Willis, 1906 .... 141.1
24. Fred Olmstead, 1910 ..... 140.9
25. Fred Blanding, 1913 ..... 140.8
26. Bert Humphries, 1915 .... 139.6
   Rick Honeycutt, 1983 .... 139.6
28. Sloppy Thurston, 1923 .... 139.3
29. Doug Rau, 1976 .... 139.2
30. Mal Eason, 1902 .... 139.1
31. Al Benton, 1945 .... 139.0
32. Mordecai Brown, 1906 .... 138.8
33. Al Brazle, 1947 .... 138.7
34. Charlie Hodnett, 1884 .... 138.6
35. Andy Coakley, 1908 ...... 138.0
36. Allan Anderson, 1988 .... 137.5
37. Ed Poole, 1902 .... 137.0
38. Spud Chandler, 1942 ..... 136.4
39. King Cole, 1910 .... 136.2
40. Red Faber, 1917 .... 136.1
41. Ed Siever, 1904 .... 136.0
42. Jack Pfiester, 1907 ...... 135.3
43. Bob Buhl, 1957 .... 135.1
44. Al Maul, 1895 .... 134.8
45. Stu Miller, 1959 .... 134.6
46. Dutch Leonard, 1948 ..... 134.5
   Doug Rau, 1978 .... 134.5
48. Ken Chase, 1940 .... 134.4
49. John Tudor, 1988 .... 134.3
50. Harry Salisbury, 1879 .... 134.0
51. Charlie Chech, 1905 ..... 133.9
52. Mike Marshall, 1973 ..... 133.7
53. Eddie Plank, 1911 .... 133.4
54. Bill Burns, 1909 .... 133.3
   Joe Horlen, 1968 .... 133.3
56. Lon Knight, 1876 .... 133.1
57. Bill Bernhard, 1904 ...... 133.0
58. Art Nehf, 1928 .... 132.9
59. Win Mercer, 1894 .... 132.6
60. Walt Dickson, 1914 ...... 132.5
   Gene Bearden, 1948 ..... 132.5
62. Howie Camnitz, 1908 .... 132.4
63. Harry Moran, 1915 ...... 132.3
   Hoyt Wilhelm, 1959 ..... 132.3
65. Stan Baumgartner, 1924 ... 132.1
66. Hugh Daily, 1887 .... 132.0
67. Bump Hadley, 1939 ...... 131.9
68. Chick Fraser, 1900 ...... 131.8
69. Mike Sullivan, 1892 ..... 131.7
70. Steve Blass, 1972 .... 131.5
71. Don Schwall, 1961 ...... 131.4
72. Jim Pastorius, 1907 ...... 131.2
73. Andy Coakley, 1907 ..... 131.0
74. Bobby Shantz, 1957 ...... 130.9
75. Pete Vuckovich, 1982 .... 130.8
76. George Mullin, 1914 ..... 130.7
77. Ted Lyons, 1942 .... 130.6
78. Bill Lee, 1978 .... 130.5
79. Lon Warneke, 1933 ...... 130.4
80. Hal McKain, 1929 .... 130.3
81. Larry Pape, 1911 .... 130.2
   Vean Gregg, 1913 ...... 130.2
83. Hi Bithorn, 1942 .... 130.1
84. Johnny Lush, 1906 ...... 129.9
85. Will White, 1880 .... 129.8
   George Kaiserling, 1915 ... 129.8
   Rollie Naylor, 1920 ...... 129.8
   Ruben Gomez, 1954 ..... 129.8
89. Earl Moore, 1911 .... 129.6
   Lefty Weinert, 1922 ..... 129.6
91. Tom Hughes, 1912 ...... 129.4
   Bill Walker, 1929 .... 129.4
   Larry McWilliams, 1984 .... 129.4
94. Clint Rogge, 1915 .... 129.3
   Ned Garver, 1948 .... 129.3
96. Carl Lundgren, 1907 ..... 129.2
   Clarence Mitchell, 1929 ... 129.2
   Atley Donald, 1944 ...... 129.2
99. 3 players tied 129.1

Pitcher Batting Runs

1. Guy Hecker, 1884 — 28.9
2. Bob Caruthers, 1886 — 22.5
3. Jim Whitney, 1882 — 21.3
4. Wes Ferrell, 1935 — 21.2
5. Don Drysdale, 1965 — 20.4
6. Bob Caruthers, 1887 — 19.9
7. Don Newcombe, 1955 — 19.9
8. Guy Hecker, 1886 — 18.3
9. Wes Ferrell, 1931 — 17.7
10. Billy Taylor, 1884 — 17.3
11. Tony Mullane, 1882 — 17.1
12. Schoolboy Rowe, 1943 — 17.1
13. Bob Caruthers, 1889 — 17.1
14. Red Ruffing, 1930 — 16.5
15. Jim Whitney, 1883 — 16.4
16. Warren Spahn, 1958 — 16.3
17. Charlie Ferguson, 1887 — 16.2
18. George Uhle, 1923 — 16.1
19. Walter Johnson, 1925 — 16.0
20. Red Lucas, 1930 — 15.6
21. Bob Lemon, 1950 — 15.3
22. Charlie Ferguson, 1885 — 15.2
23. Babe Ruth, 1917 — 15.1
24. Don Newcombe, 1959 — 15.0
25. Bob Lemon, 1949 — 14.8
26. Jack Stivetts, 1890 — 14.8
27. Dave Foutz, 1887 — 14.6
28. Claude Hendrix, 1912 — 14.6
29. Doc Crandall, 1915 — 14.5
30. Jack Bentley, 1923 — 14.5
31. Jim Tobin, 1942 — 14.3
32. Babe Ruth, 1915 — 14.3
33. Red Ruffing, 1936 — 14.2
34. Babe Ruth, 1916 — 14.0
35. Jack Stivetts, 1892 — 14.0
36. Jack Coombs, 1911 — 13.9
37. Red Lucas, 1932 — 13.8
38. Scott Stratton, 1888 — 13.7
39. Pete Conway, 1888 — 13.4
40. Monte Ward, 1879 — 13.4
41. Scott Stratton, 1890 — 13.2
42. Joe Bush, 1924 — 13.1
43. Terry Larkin, 1878 — 13.1
44. Elam Vangilder, 1922 — 13.1
45. Robin Roberts, 1955 — 13.0
46. Adonis Terry, 1890 — 12.9
47. Charley Radbourn, 1883 — 12.9
48. Clark Griffith, 1901 — 12.7
49. Adonis Terry, 1889 — 12.6
50. Red Lucas, 1933 — 12.5
51. Schoolboy Rowe, 1935 — 12.5
52. Bob Lemon, 1948 — 12.4
53. Curt Davis, 1939 — 12.4
54. Red Ruffing, 1935 — 12.4
55. Red Ruffing, 1932 — 12.4
56. Bucky Walters, 1939 — 12.4
57. Ferguson Jenkins, 1971 — 12.3
58. Jim Whitney, 1881 — 12.2
59. Red Ruffing, 1928 — 12.2
60. Pink Hawley, 1895 — 12.1
61. Dave Ferriss, 1945 — 11.9
62. Charlie Ferguson, 1886 — 11.9
63. Dizzy Trout, 1944 — 11.9
64. Al Maul, 1893 — 11.9
65. Johnny Sain, 1947 — 11.8
66. Wes Ferrell, 1936 — 11.8
67. Ad Gumbert, 1889 — 11.8
68. Jim Hunter, 1971 — 11.8
69. Amos Rusie, 1890 — 11.8
70. Babe Ruth, 1918 — 11.7
71. Charley Radbourn, 1885 — 11.7
72. Joe Bowman, 1939 — 11.6
73. Schoolboy Rowe, 1934 — 11.6
74. Bob Gibson, 1970 — 11.6
75. Frank Killen, 1893 — 11.5
76. George Mullin, 1904 — 11.5
77. Charlie Buffinton, 1884 — 11.4
78. Dutch Ruether, 1921 — 11.4
79. Cy Young, 1903 — 11.4
80. Bob Caruthers, 1891 — 11.4
81. Jouett Meekin, 1896 — 11.4
82. Erv Brame, 1929 — 11.4
83. George VanHaltren, 1888 — 11.3
84. Erv Brame, 1930 — 11.3
85. Claude Hendrix, 1915 — 11.1
86. Matt Kilroy, 1887 — 11.1
87. Jack Stivetts, 1896 — 11.1
88. Fred Hutchinson, 1950 — 11.0
89. Red Ruffing, 1941 — 10.8
90. Carl Mays, 1921 — 10.8
91. Jim Whitney, 1887 — 10.8
92. Blue Moon Odom, 1969 — 10.8
93. Red Lucas, 1931 — 10.7
94. Fred Hutchinson, 1947 — 10.5
95. Jack Scott, 1921 — 10.5
96. Dick Burns, 1884 — 10.5
97. Walter Johnson, 1917 — 10.4
98. Ad Gumbert, 1891 — 10.4
99. Lon Warneke, 1933 — 10.4
100. Jack Powell, 1900 — 10.3

Pitcher Fielding Runs

1. Ed Walsh, 1907 — 21.5
2. Harry Howell, 1905 — 17.5
3. Ed Walsh, 1911 — 14.7
4. Ed Walsh, 1908 — 13.7
5. Will White, 1882 — 12.5
6. Park Swartzel, 1889 — 12.3
7. John Clarkson, 1889 — 11.0
8. Tommy Bond, 1880 — 10.2
9. Gene Packard, 1914 — 10.1
10. Frank Smith, 1909 — 10.0
- Carl Mays, 1926 — 10.0
12. Matt Kilroy, 1887 — 9.9
13. Ed Walsh, 1910 — 9.8
14. Sadie McMahon, 1890 — 9.6
- Ed Scott, 1900 — 9.6
- Gene Packard, 1915 — 9.6
17. Tony Mullane, 1882 — 9.5
- Mike Morrison, 1887 — 9.5
- Christy Mathewson, 1908 — 9.5
20. Harry Howell, 1904 — 9.4
21. Nick Cullop, 1915 — 9.3
22. Al Mays, 1887 — 9.2
23. Carl Mays, 1916 — 9.1
24. Charlie Buffinton, 1888 — 9.0
- Amos Rusie, 1894 — 9.0
- Hooks Dauss, 1915 — 9.0
27. Cy Young, 1895 — 8.9
- Carl Mays, 1918 — 8.9
29. Curt Davis, 1934 — 8.7
30. Matt Kilroy, 1889 — 8.6
- Jack Taylor, 1898 — 8.6
32. Cy Seymour, 1897 — 8.5
- Cy Seymour, 1898 — 8.5
- Nick Altrock, 1905 — 8.5
- Elmer Stricklett, 1906 — 8.5
- Claude Hendrix, 1914 — 8.5
- Bob Lemon, 1948 — 8.5
38. Tony Mullane, 1884 — 8.4
- Cy Young, 1896 — 8.4
- Elmer Stricklett, 1905 — 8.4
41. Silver King, 1890 — 8.3
- Gene Krapp, 1915 — 8.3
- Hooks Dauss, 1920 — 8.3
- Wilcy Moore, 1927 — 8.3
- Bucky Walters, 1936 — 8.3
46. John Clarkson, 1887 — 8.2
- Cy Young, 1892 — 8.2
- Addie Joss, 1907 — 8.2
49. Carl Mays, 1924 — 8.1
- Randy Jones, 1976 — 8.1
51. Harry Howell, 1907 — 8.0
- Burleigh Grimes, 1925 — 8.0
53. Carl Mays, 1917 — 7.9
- Fred Newman, 1965 — 7.9
55. Cy Young, 1894 — 7.8
- Eddie Rommel, 1924 — 7.8
- Mel Stottlemyre, 1969 — 7.8
58. Jack Stivetts, 1892 — 7.7
- Freddie Fitzsimmons, 1931 — 7.7
- Mel Harder, 1933 — 7.7
- Harry Gumbert, 1938 — 7.7
- Bob Lemon, 1953 — 7.7
63. Tommy Bond, 1879 — 7.6
- John Clarkson, 1885 — 7.6
- Willie Sudhoff, 1898 — 7.6
- Harry Gumbert, 1937 — 7.6
- Russ Christopher, 1943 — 7.6
- John Denny, 1978 — 7.6
69. George Mullin, 1904 — 7.5
- Ed Walsh, 1906 — 7.5
- Joe Wood, 1912 — 7.5
- Carl Hubbell, 1933 — 7.5
73. Larry Corcoran, 1884 — 7.4
- Jim Galvin, 1884 — 7.4
- George Suggs, 1914 — 7.4
76. Bill Hutchinson, 1892 — 7.3
- Jean Dubuc, 1913 — 7.3
- Gene Krapp, 1913 — 7.3
79. Jim McCormick, 1883 — 7.2
- Scott Stratton, 1890 — 7.2
- Mark Baldwin, 1890 — 7.2
- Red Ames, 1909 — 7.2
- Christy Mathewson, 1911 — 7.2
- Russ Christopher, 1945 — 7.2
85. Monte Ward, 1880 — 7.1
- Jim Galvin, 1887 — 7.1
- Harry Howell, 1906 — 7.1
- Bill Doak, 1915 — 7.1
89. Larry Corcoran, 1880 — 7.0
- Jim Galvin, 1881 — 7.0
- Christy Mathewson, 1901 — 7.0
- Ned Garvin, 1903 — 7.0
- Doc White, 1908 — 7.0
- Ed Walsh, 1912 — 7.0
- Harry Coveleski, 1914 — 7.0
- George McConnell, 1915 — 7.0
- Hal Schumacher, 1935 — 7.0
98. Guy Hecker, 1884 — 6.9
- Eddie Cicotte, 1913 — 6.9
100. 6 players tied — 6.8

Total Pitcher Index

1. Silver King, 1888 — 11.9
2. Amos Rusie, 1894 — 11.1
3. Charley Radbourn, 1884 — 10.7
- Guy Hecker, 1884 — 10.7
5. Bob Caruthers, 1886 — 10.5
6. Dave Foutz, 1886 — 10.3
7. Scott Stratton, 1890 — 10.1
8. John Clarkson, 1887 — 9.8
9. Walter Johnson, 1912 — 9.5
10. Pete Alexander, 1915 — 9.3
11. Jim Devlin, 1877 — 9.2
- Tony Mullane, 1884 — 9.2
13. John Clarkson, 1885 — 9.1
14. John Clarkson, 1889 — 9.0
15. Walter Johnson, 1913 — 8.8
- Dizzy Trout, 1944 — 8.8
17. Joe Wood, 1912 — 8.5
18. Bucky Walters, 1939 — 8.4
19. Walter Johnson, 1918 — 8.3
20. Charley Radbourn, 1883 — 8.2
21. Amos Rusie, 1893 — 8.1
- Ed Walsh, 1907 — 8.1
- Hal Newhouser, 1945 — 8.1
24. Jack Stivetts, 1891 — 7.9
- Dwight Gooden, 1985 — 7.9
26. Will White, 1882 — 7.8
- Jim Whitney, 1883 — 7.8
- Guy Hecker, 1885 — 7.8
29. Kid Nichols, 1890 — 7.7
- Cy Young, 1896 — 7.7
31. Tim Keefe, 1883 — 7.6
- Christy Mathewson, 1905 — 7.6
33. Billy Rhines, 1890 — 7.5
- Cy Young, 1901 — 7.5
- Bob Gibson, 1968 — 7.5
36. Silver King, 1890 — 7.4
- Dolf Luque, 1923 — 7.4
- Lefty Grove, 1931 — 7.4
- Wes Ferrell, 1935 — 7.4
40. Guy Hecker, 1886 — 7.3
- Toad Ramsey, 1886 — 7.3
- Cy Young, 1894 — 7.3
- Pink Hawley, 1895 — 7.3
- Kid Nichols, 1897 — 7.3
45. Charlie Ferguson, 1886 — 7.2
- Ed Walsh, 1910 — 7.2
- Gaylord Perry, 1972 — 7.2
48. Jim Devlin, 1876 — 7.1
- Jim Galvin, 1884 — 7.1
- Charlie Buffinton, 1888 — 7.1
- Bill Hutchinson, 1890 — 7.1
- Carl Hubbell, 1933 — 7.1
53. Cy Young, 1892 — 7.0
- Jack Chesbro, 1904 — 7.0
- Dizzy Dean, 1934 — 7.0
56. Matt Kilroy, 1887 — 6.9
- Mike Smith, 1887 — 6.9
- Walter Johnson, 1915 — 6.9
- Ron Guidry, 1978 — 6.9
60. John Clarkson, 1886 — 6.8
- Nig Cuppy, 1896 — 6.8
- Kid Nichols, 1896 — 6.8
- Red Faber, 1921 — 6.8
- Hal Newhouser, 1946 — 6.8
- Steve Carlton, 1972 — 6.8
66. Will White, 1883 — 6.7
- Lady Baldwin, 1886 — 6.7
- Clark Griffith, 1898 — 6.7
- Kid Nichols, 1898 — 6.7
- Cy Young, 1899 — 6.7
- Claude Hendrix, 1914 — 6.7
- Lefty Grove, 1936 — 6.7
- Juan Marichal, 1965 — 6.7
74. Tony Mullane, 1883 — 6.6
- Ed Walsh, 1908 — 6.6
- Walter Johnson, 1919 — 6.6
- Lefty Grove, 1932 — 6.6
78. Matt Kilroy, 1889 — 6.5
- Jack Stivetts, 1890 — 6.5
- Christy Mathewson, 1909 — 6.5
- Tom Seaver, 1971 — 6.5
82. Frank Killen, 1893 — 6.4
- Rube Waddell, 1902 — 6.4
- Dazzy Vance, 1928 — 6.4
85. Al Spalding, 1876 — 6.3
- Jesse Duryea, 1889 — 6.3
- Walter Johnson, 1914 — 6.3
- Pete Alexander, 1917 — 6.3
- Pete Alexander, 1920 — 6.3
- Burleigh Grimes, 1928 — 6.3
- Lefty Grove, 1935 — 6.3
- Lefty Gomez, 1937 — 6.3
- Bob Lemon, 1948 — 6.3
- Bobby Shantz, 1952 — 6.3
- Warren Spahn, 1953 — 6.3
- Bob Gibson, 1969 — 6.3
97. 7 players tied — 6.2

Total Pitcher Index (alpha.)

Pete Alexander, 1915	9.3
Pete Alexander, 1917	6.3
Pete Alexander, 1920	6.3
Lady Baldwin, 1886	6.7
Charlie Buffinton, 1888	7.1
Steve Carlton, 1972	6.8
Bob Caruthers, 1886	10.5
Jack Chesbro, 1904	7.0
John Clarkson, 1885	9.1
John Clarkson, 1886	6.8
John Clarkson, 1887	9.8
John Clarkson, 1889	9.0
Nig Cuppy, 1896	6.8
Dizzy Dean, 1934	7.0
Jim Devlin, 1876	7.1
Jim Devlin, 1877	9.2
Jesse Duryea, 1889	6.3
Red Faber, 1921	6.8
Charlie Ferguson, 1886	7.2
Wes Ferrell, 1935	7.4
Dave Foutz, 1886	10.3
Jim Galvin, 1884	7.1
Bob Gibson, 1968	7.5
Bob Gibson, 1969	6.3
Lefty Gomez, 1937	6.3
Dwight Gooden, 1985	7.9
Clark Griffith, 1898	6.7
Burleigh Grimes, 1928	6.3
Lefty Grove, 1931	7.4
Lefty Grove, 1932	6.6
Lefty Grove, 1935	6.3
Lefty Grove, 1936	6.7
Ron Guidry, 1978	6.9
Pink Hawley, 1895	7.3
Guy Hecker, 1884	10.7
Guy Hecker, 1885	7.8
Guy Hecker, 1886	7.3
Claude Hendrix, 1914	6.7
Carl Hubbell, 1933	7.1
Bill Hutchinson, 1890	7.1
Walter Johnson, 1912	9.5
Walter Johnson, 1913	8.8
Walter Johnson, 1914	6.3
Walter Johnson, 1915	6.9
Walter Johnson, 1918	8.3
Walter Johnson, 1919	6.6
Tim Keefe, 1883	7.6
Frank Killen, 1893	6.4
Matt Kilroy, 1887	6.9
Matt Kilroy, 1889	6.5
Silver King, 1888	11.9
Silver King, 1890	7.4
Bob Lemon, 1948	6.3
Dolf Luque, 1923	7.4
Juan Marichal, 1965	6.7
Christy Mathewson, 1905	7.6
Christy Mathewson, 1909	6.5
Tony Mullane, 1883	6.6
Tony Mullane, 1884	9.2
Hal Newhouser, 1945	8.1
Hal Newhouser, 1946	6.8
Kid Nichols, 1890	7.7
Kid Nichols, 1896	6.8
Kid Nichols, 1897	7.3
Kid Nichols, 1898	6.7
Gaylord Perry, 1972	7.2
Charley Radbourn, 1883	8.2
Charley Radbourn, 1884	10.7
Toad Ramsey, 1886	7.3
Billy Rhines, 1890	7.5
Amos Rusie, 1893	8.1
Amos Rusie, 1894	11.1
Tom Seaver, 1971	6.5
Bobby Shantz, 1952	6.3
Mike Smith, 1887	6.9
Warren Spahn, 1953	6.3
Al Spalding, 1876	6.3
Jack Stivetts, 1890	6.5
Jack Stivetts, 1891	7.9
Scott Stratton, 1890	10.1
Dizzy Trout, 1944	8.8
Dazzy Vance, 1928	6.4
Rube Waddell, 1902	6.4
Ed Walsh, 1907	8.1
Ed Walsh, 1908	6.6
Ed Walsh, 1910	7.2
Bucky Walters, 1939	8.4
Will White, 1882	7.8
Will White, 1883	6.7
Jim Whitney, 1883	7.8
Joe Wood, 1912	8.5
Cy Young, 1892	7.0
Cy Young, 1894	7.3
Cy Young, 1896	7.7
Cy Young, 1899	6.7
Cy Young, 1901	7.5

Total Pitcher Index (by era)

1876-1892

1	Silver King, 1888	11.9
2	Charley Radbourn, 1884	10.7
	Guy Hecker, 1884	10.7
4	Bob Caruthers, 1886	10.5
5	Dave Foutz, 1886	10.3
6	Scott Stratton, 1890	10.1
7	John Clarkson, 1887	9.8
8	Jim Devlin, 1877	9.2
	Tony Mullane, 1884	9.2
10	John Clarkson, 1885	9.1
11	John Clarkson, 1889	9.0
12	Charley Radbourn, 1883	8.2
13	Jack Stivetts, 1891	7.9
14	3 players tied	7.8

1893-1919

1	Amos Rusie, 1894	11.1
2	Walter Johnson, 1912	9.5
3	Pete Alexander, 1915	9.3
4	Walter Johnson, 1913	8.8
5	Joe Wood, 1912	8.5
6	Walter Johnson, 1918	8.3
7	Amos Rusie, 1893	8.1
	Ed Walsh, 1907	8.1
9	Cy Young, 1896	7.7
10	Christy Mathewson, 1905	7.6
11	Cy Young, 1901	7.5
12	Cy Young, 1894	7.3
	Pink Hawley, 1895	7.3
	Kid Nichols, 1897	7.3
15	Ed Walsh, 1910	7.2

1920-1941

1	Bucky Walters, 1939	8.4
2	Dolf Luque, 1923	7.4
	Lefty Grove, 1931	7.4
	Wes Ferrell, 1935	7.4
5	Carl Hubbell, 1933	7.1
6	Dizzy Dean, 1934	7.0
7	Red Faber, 1921	6.8
8	Lefty Grove, 1936	6.7
9	Lefty Grove, 1932	6.6
10	Dazzy Vance, 1928	6.4
11	Pete Alexander, 1920	6.3
	Burleigh Grimes, 1928	6.3
	Lefty Grove, 1935	6.3
	Lefty Gomez, 1937	6.3
15	Burleigh Grimes, 1920	6.2

1942-1960

1	Dizzy Trout, 1944	8.8
2	Hal Newhouser, 1945	8.1
3	Hal Newhouser, 1946	6.8
4	Bob Lemon, 1948	6.3
	Bobby Shantz, 1952	6.3
	Warren Spahn, 1953	6.3
7	Spud Chandler, 1943	6.1
8	Hal Newhouser, 1944	5.9
	Johnny Antonelli, 1954	5.9
10	Ned Garver, 1950	5.8
	Robin Roberts, 1953	5.8
	Frank Sullivan, 1955	5.8
13	Dizzy Trout, 1946	5.6
	Mel Parnell, 1949	5.6
	Bob Lemon, 1949	5.6

1961-1988

1	Dwight Gooden, 1985	7.9
2	Bob Gibson, 1968	7.5
3	Gaylord Perry, 1972	7.2
4	Ron Guidry, 1978	6.9
5	Steve Carlton, 1972	6.8
6	Juan Marichal, 1965	6.7
7	Tom Seaver, 1971	6.5
8	Bob Gibson, 1969	6.3
9	Ferguson Jenkins, 1971	6.2
	Tom Seaver, 1973	6.2
11	Juan Marichal, 1969	6.1
12	Wilbur Wood, 1971	6.0
	Phil Niekro, 1978	6.0
14	Sandy Koufax, 1966	5.9
	Rick Reuschel, 1977	5.9

Total Baseball Ranking

1	Silver King, 1888	11.9
2	Amos Rusie, 1894	11.1
3	Charley Radbourn, 1884	10.7
	Guy Hecker, 1884	10.7
5	Bob Caruthers, 1886	10.5
6	Dave Foutz, 1886	10.3
7	Scott Stratton, 1890	10.1
8	Babe Ruth, 1921	9.9
9	John Clarkson, 1887	9.8
10	Walter Johnson, 1912	9.5
11	Pete Alexander, 1915	9.3
12	Jim Devlin, 1877	9.2
	Tony Mullane, 1884	9.2
14	John Clarkson, 1885	9.1
15	Babe Ruth, 1923	9.0
	Cal Ripken, 1984	9.0
	John Clarkson, 1889	9.0
18	Nap Lajoie, 1910	8.9
19	Babe Ruth, 1920	8.8
	Walter Johnson, 1913	8.8
	Dizzy Trout, 1944	8.8
22	Babe Ruth, 1927	8.5
	Joe Wood, 1912	8.5
24	Bucky Walters, 1939	8.4
25	Babe Ruth, 1924	8.3
	Ted Williams, 1942	8.3
	Walter Johnson, 1918	8.3
28	Lou Gehrig, 1927	8.2
	Charley Radbourn, 1883	8.2
30	Ted Williams, 1947	8.1
	Stan Musial, 1948	8.1
	Mickey Mantle, 1957	8.1
	Amos Rusie, 1893	8.1
	Ed Walsh, 1907	8.1
	Hal Newhouser, 1945	8.1
36	Rogers Hornsby, 1920	8.0
	Ted Williams, 1941	8.0
	Joe Morgan, 1975	8.0
39	Nap Lajoie, 1903	7.9
	Ty Cobb, 1917	7.9
	Jack Stivetts, 1891	7.9
	Dwight Gooden, 1985	7.9
43	Babe Ruth, 1926	7.8
	Willie Mays, 1955	7.8
	Will White, 1882	7.8
	Jim Whitney, 1883	7.8
	Guy Hecker, 1885	7.8
48	George Sisler, 1920	7.7
	Babe Ruth, 1930	7.7
	Ted Williams, 1946	7.7
	Kid Nichols, 1890	7.7
	Cy Young, 1896	7.7
53	Fred Dunlap, 1884	7.6
	Jimmie Foxx, 1933	7.6
	Mickey Mantle, 1956	7.6
	Norm Cash, 1961	7.6
	Ron Santo, 1966	7.6
	Tim Keefe, 1883	7.6
	Christy Mathewson, 1905	7.6
60	Ted Williams, 1949	7.5
	Jackie Robinson, 1951	7.5
	Billy Rhines, 1890	7.5
	Cy Young, 1901	7.5
	Bob Gibson, 1968	7.5
65	Nap Lajoie, 1901	7.4
	Mike Schmidt, 1980	7.4
	Rickey Henderson, 1985	7.4
	Silver King, 1890	7.4
	Dolf Luque, 1923	7.4
	Lefty Grove, 1931	7.4
	Wes Ferrell, 1935	7.4
72	Nap Lajoie, 1904	7.3
	Tris Speaker, 1912	7.3
	Guy Hecker, 1886	7.3
	Toad Ramsey, 1886	7.3
	Cy Young, 1894	7.3
	Pink Hawley, 1895	7.3
	Kid Nichols, 1897	7.3
79	Rogers Hornsby, 1921	7.2
	Rogers Hornsby, 1922	7.2
	Chuck Klein, 1930	7.2
	Carl Yastrzemski, 1967	7.2
	Mike Schmidt, 1977	7.2
	Charlie Ferguson, 1886	7.2
	Ed Walsh, 1910	7.2
	Gaylord Perry, 1972	7.2
87	Tris Speaker, 1913	7.1
	Babe Ruth, 1919	7.1
	Harlond Clift, 1937	7.1
	Rod Carew, 1974	7.1
	Jim Devlin, 1876	7.1
	Jim Galvin, 1884	7.1
	Charlie Buffinton, 1888	7.1
	Bill Hutchinson, 1890	7.1
	Carl Hubbell, 1933	7.1
96	13 players tied	7.0

Total Baseball Rank (alpha.)

Pete Alexander, 1915	9.3
Charlie Buffinton, 1888	7.1
Rod Carew, 1974	7.1
Bob Caruthers, 1886	10.5
Norm Cash, 1961	7.6
John Clarkson, 1885	9.1
John Clarkson, 1887	9.8
John Clarkson, 1889	9.0
Harlond Clift, 1937	7.1
Ty Cobb, 1917	7.9
Jim Devlin, 1876	7.1
Jim Devlin, 1877	9.2
Fred Dunlap, 1884	7.6
Charlie Ferguson, 1886	7.2
Wes Ferrell, 1935	7.4
Dave Foutz, 1886	10.3
Jimmie Foxx, 1933	7.6
Jim Galvin, 1884	7.1
Lou Gehrig, 1927	8.2
Bob Gibson, 1968	7.5
Dwight Gooden, 1985	7.9
Lefty Grove, 1931	7.4
Pink Hawley, 1895	7.3
Guy Hecker, 1884	10.7
Guy Hecker, 1885	7.8
Guy Hecker, 1886	7.3
Rickey Henderson, 1985	7.4
Rogers Hornsby, 1920	8.0
Rogers Hornsby, 1921	7.2
Rogers Hornsby, 1922	7.2
Carl Hubbell, 1933	7.1
Bill Hutchinson, 1890	7.1
Walter Johnson, 1912	9.5
Walter Johnson, 1913	8.8
Walter Johnson, 1918	8.3
Tim Keefe, 1883	7.6
Silver King, 1888	11.9
Silver King, 1890	7.4
Chuck Klein, 1930	7.2
Nap Lajoie, 1901	7.4
Nap Lajoie, 1903	7.9
Nap Lajoie, 1904	7.3
Nap Lajoie, 1910	8.9
Dolf Luque, 1923	7.4
Mickey Mantle, 1956	7.6
Mickey Mantle, 1957	8.1
Christy Mathewson, 1905	7.6
Willie Mays, 1955	7.8
Joe Morgan, 1975	8.0
Tony Mullane, 1884	9.2
Stan Musial, 1948	8.1
Hal Newhouser, 1945	8.1
Kid Nichols, 1890	7.7
Kid Nichols, 1897	7.3
Gaylord Perry, 1972	7.2
Charley Radbourn, 1883	8.2
Charley Radbourn, 1884	10.7
Toad Ramsey, 1886	7.3
Billy Rhines, 1890	7.5
Cal Ripken, 1984	9.0
Jackie Robinson, 1951	7.5
Amos Rusie, 1893	8.1
Amos Rusie, 1894	11.1
Babe Ruth, 1919	7.1
Babe Ruth, 1920	8.8
Babe Ruth, 1921	9.9
Babe Ruth, 1923	9.0
Babe Ruth, 1924	8.3
Babe Ruth, 1926	7.8
Babe Ruth, 1927	8.5
Babe Ruth, 1930	7.7
Ron Santo, 1966	7.6
Mike Schmidt, 1977	7.2
Mike Schmidt, 1980	7.4
George Sisler, 1920	7.7
Tris Speaker, 1912	7.3
Tris Speaker, 1913	7.1
Jack Stivetts, 1891	7.9
Scott Stratton, 1890	10.1
Dizzy Trout, 1944	8.8
Ed Walsh, 1907	8.1
Ed Walsh, 1910	7.2
Bucky Walters, 1939	8.4
Will White, 1882	7.8
Jim Whitney, 1883	7.8
Ted Williams, 1941	8.0
Ted Williams, 1942	8.3
Ted Williams, 1946	7.7
Ted Williams, 1947	8.1
Ted Williams, 1949	7.5
Joe Wood, 1912	8.5
Carl Yastrzemski, 1967	7.2
Cy Young, 1894	7.3
Cy Young, 1896	7.7
Cy Young, 1901	7.5

Total Baseball Rank (by era)

1876-1892

1	Silver King, 1888	11.9
2	Charley Radbourn, 1884	10.7
	Guy Hecker, 1884	10.7
4	Bob Caruthers, 1886	10.5
5	Dave Foutz, 1886	10.3
6	Scott Stratton, 1890	10.1
7	John Clarkson, 1887	9.8
8	Jim Devlin, 1877	9.2
	Tony Mullane, 1884	9.2
10	John Clarkson, 1885	9.1
11	John Clarkson, 1889	9.0
12	Charley Radbourn, 1883	8.2
13	Jack Stivetts, 1891	7.9
14	3 players tied	7.8

1893-1919

1	Amos Rusie, 1894	11.1
2	Walter Johnson, 1912	9.5
3	Pete Alexander, 1915	9.3
4	Nap Lajoie, 1910	8.9
5	Walter Johnson, 1913	8.8
6	Joe Wood, 1912	8.5
7	Walter Johnson, 1918	8.3
8	Amos Rusie, 1893	8.1
	Ed Walsh, 1907	8.1
10	Nap Lajoie, 1903	7.9
	Ty Cobb, 1917	7.9
12	Cy Young, 1896	7.7
13	Christy Mathewson, 1905	7.6
14	Cy Young, 1901	7.5
15	Nap Lajoie, 1901	7.4

1920-1941

1	Babe Ruth, 1921	9.9
2	Babe Ruth, 1923	9.0
3	Babe Ruth, 1920	8.8
4	Babe Ruth, 1927	8.5
5	Bucky Walters, 1939	8.4
6	Babe Ruth, 1924	8.3
7	Lou Gehrig, 1927	8.2
8	Rogers Hornsby, 1920	8.0
	Ted Williams, 1941	8.0
10	Babe Ruth, 1926	7.8
11	George Sisler, 1920	7.7
	Babe Ruth, 1930	7.7
13	Jimmie Foxx, 1933	7.6
14	3 players tied	7.4

1942-1960

1	Dizzy Trout, 1944	8.8
2	Ted Williams, 1942	8.3
3	Ted Williams, 1947	8.1
	Stan Musial, 1948	8.1
	Mickey Mantle, 1957	8.1
	Hal Newhouser, 1945	8.1
7	Willie Mays, 1955	7.8
8	Ted Williams, 1946	7.7
9	Mickey Mantle, 1956	7.6
10	Ted Williams, 1949	7.5
	Jackie Robinson, 1951	7.5
12	Stan Musial, 1948	7.0
13	Lou Boudreau, 1944	6.8
	Hal Newhouser, 1946	6.8
15	Ted Williams, 1957	6.7

1961-1988

1	Cal Ripken, 1984	9.0
2	Joe Morgan, 1975	8.0
3	Dwight Gooden, 1985	7.9
4	Norm Cash, 1961	7.6
	Ron Santo, 1966	7.6
6	Bob Gibson, 1968	7.5
7	Mike Schmidt, 1980	7.4
	Rickey Henderson, 1985	7.4
9	Carl Yastrzemski, 1967	7.2
	Mike Schmidt, 1977	7.2
	Gaylord Perry, 1972	7.2
12	Rod Carew, 1974	7.1
13	5 players tied	7.0

The Rosters

The Rosters

The Team Roster

The Team Roster, like the three rosters that follow it, is offered as an adjunct to the three principal statistical sections of *Total Baseball:* the Annual Record, the Player Register, and the Pitcher Register. Employed together, these rosters and registers give a thorough accounting of major league baseball records. And as we observe the 120th anniversary of professional baseball, it can be said that these records are the very core of the game, the only imperishable remains of men who strode the fields of play yesterday or a hundred years ago.

The Team Roster lists the regular players, pitchers, key substitutes, and managers for all 2,010 team seasons in the history of professional league play since 1871. It does not contain the name of every man who played for every team in every year, for many teams have employed up to 50 or more players in a single season. The Team Roster allows the reader, by scanning its pages, to find who were the prominent players for a given team in a given year, or to track over time a team's personnel at a particular position (such as the "turnstile" at third base for the New York Mets since their inception). For a complete record of every one of the 13,160 major league players, consult the Player and Pitcher Registers.

Those included in a team roster are

- All managers
- All everyday players at eight positions, plus designated hitters
- Key utility or substitute players (unlimited, provided they have played in at least 60 percent of the scheduled games that year and are not listed as *regulars* at any position—that is, as having played at least 98 games during a 162-game season)
- Starting pitchers (the top five, provided they have pitched at least 60 percent of the innings that together would yield one inning per scheduled game—that is, 98 innings in a 162-game season)
- Relief pitchers (up to two, provided they have pitched at least 30 percent of the innings that would yield a rate of

one inning per scheduled game—50 innings in a 162-game season; and provided that they averaged less than three innings pitched per appearance).

The yearly team rosters are grouped alphabetically by city. At the head of each city's entry is a listing of the leagues and years in which that city was represented in the top rank of baseball. The teams representing that city are grouped by league in the order shown at the head of the entry; the organizing principle is to present the teams in the order of the leagues' demise (excepting, of course, the National and American Leagues). Accordingly, for a city like Chicago, represented in all six major leagues, the teams would be presented in this order:

> National Association (last year, 1875)
> Union Association (last year, 1884)
> Players League (last year, 1890)
> American Association (last year, 1891)
> Federal League (last year, 1915)
> National League (first year, 1876)
> American League (first year, 1901)

The team and league abbreviations used in this section are found on the final page of this book. Other abbreviations used in the Team Roster are these:

M	Manager
1B	First Base
2B	Second Base
SS	Shortstop
3B	Third Base
OF	Outfield
C	Catcher
DH	Designated Hitter
UT	Utility (substitute)
P	Pitcher
RP	Relief Pitcher

Altoona

ALT U 1884

ALT 1884 U

M E. Curtis
1B F. Harris
2B C. Dougherty
SS G. Smith
3B H. Koons
OF F. Shaffer
OF J. Brown
OF J. Murphy
C J. Moore
P J. Murphy

Atlanta

ATL N 1966-1988

ATL 1966 N

M R. Bragan
M W. Hitchcock
1B F. Alou
2B W. Woodward
SS D. Menke
3B E. Mathews
OF H. Aaron
OF R. Carty
OF M. Jones
C J. Torre
P T. Cloninger
P K. Johnson
P D. Lemaster
RP C. Carroll
RP F. Olivo

ATL 1967 N

M W. Hitchcock
M K. Silvestri
1B F. Alou
2B W. Woodward
SS D. Menke
3B C. Boyer
OF H. Aaron
OF M. Jones
OF R. Carty
C J. Torre
P D. Lemaster
P K. Johnson
P P. Niekro
P R. Jarvis
RP R. Kelley
RP C. Carroll

ATL 1968 N

M C. Harris
1B D. Johnson
2B F. Millan
SS R. Jackson
3B C. Boyer
OF F. Alou
OF H. Aaron
OF M. Lum
C J. Torre
UT J. Francona
UT O. Martinez
P P. Niekro
P R. Jarvis
P R. Reed
P K. Johnson
P M. Pappas
RP C. Upshaw
RP J. Britton

ATL 1969 N

M C. Harris
1B O. Cepeda
2B F. Millan
SS R. Jackson
3B C. Boyer
OF H. Aaron
OF F. Alou
OF M. Lum
C R. Didier
UT R. Carty
P P. Niekro
P R. Reed
P R. Jarvis
P G. Stone
P M. Pappas
RP C. Upshaw
RP G. Neibauer

ATL 1970 N

M C. Harris
1B O. Cepeda
2B F. Millan
SS R. Jackson
3B C. Boyer
OF R. Carty
OF H. Aaron
OF A. Gonzalez
C J. Tillman
UT G. Garrido
UT M. Lum
P R. Jarvis
P P. Niekro
P J. Nash
P G. Stone
P R. Reed
RP J. Wilhelm
RP R. Priddy

ATL 1971 N

M C. Harris
1B H. Aaron
2B F. Millan
SS M. Perez
3B D. Evans
OF R. Garr
OF R. Jackson
OF M. Lum
C E. Williams
P P. Niekro
P R. Reed
P G. Stone
P R. Jarvis
P T. Kelley
RP C. Upshaw
RP S. Barber

ATL 1972 N

M C. Harris
M E. Mathews
1B H. Aaron
2B F. Millan
SS M. Perez
3B D. Evans
OF R. Garr
OF J. Baker
OF M. Lum
C E. Williams
P P. Niekro
P R. Reed
P R. Schueler
P T. Kelley
P G. Stone
RP R. Jarvis
RP C. Upshaw

ATL 1973 N

M E. Mathews
1B M. Lum
2B D. Johnson
SS M. Perez
3B D. Evans
OF J. Baker
OF R. Garr
OF H. Aaron
C J. Oates
UT R. Jackson
P C. Morton
P P. Niekro
P R. Schueler
P R. Harrison
P R. Reed
RP T. House

ATL 1974 N

M E. Mathews
M C. King
1B D. Johnson
2B M. Perez
SS C. Robinson
3B D. Evans
OF J. Baker
OF R. Garr
OF R. Office
C J. Oates
UT H. Aaron
UT M. Lum
P P. Niekro
P C. Morton
P L. Capra
P R. Reed
P R. Harrison
RP T. House
RP M. Leon

ATL 1975 N

M C. King
M C. Ryan
1B E. Williams
2B M. Perez
SS L. Blanks
3B D. Evans
OF R. Garr
OF J. Baker
OF R. Office
C V. Correll
UT M. Lum
P C. Morton
P P. Niekro
RP M. Leon
RP T. House

ATL 1976 N

M J. Bristol
1B G. Montanez
2B R. Gilbreath
SS D. Chaney
3B J. Royster
OF J. Wynn
OF K. Henderson
OF R. Office
C V. Correll
UT D. May
UT T. Paciorek
P P. Niekro
P R. Ruthven
P J. Messersmith
P C. Morton
P F. LaCorte
RP R. Moret
RP P. Devine

ATL 1977 N

M J. Bristol
M R. Turner
M V. Benson
M J. Bristol
1B G. Montanez
2B R. Gilbreath
SS P. Rockett
3B A. Moore
OF J. Burroughs
OF G. Matthews
OF R. Office
C B. Pocoroba
UT R. Bonnell
UT J. Royster
P P. Niekro
P R. Ruthven
P L. Capra
P J. Messersmith
RP D. Campbell
RP M. Leon

ATL 1978 N

M R. Cox
1B D. Murphy
2B J. Royster
SS D. Chaney
3B J. Horner
OF J. Burroughs
OF R. Office
OF G. Matthews
C B. Pocoroba
UT R. Beall
UT R. Bonnell
UT R. Gilbreath
P P. Niekro
P P. Hanna
P M. Mahler
P L. McWilliams
RP E. Solomon
RP H. Garber

ATL 1979 N

M R. Cox
1B D. Murphy
2B G. Hubbard
SS J. Frias
3B J. Horner
OF G. Matthews
OF R. Bonnell
OF J. Burroughs
C B. Benedict
UT M. Lum
UT R. Office
UT J. Royster
P P. Niekro
P E. Solomon
P R. Matula
P A. Brizzolara
P M. Mahler
RP H. Garber
RP J. McLaughlin

ATL 1980 N

M R. Cox
1B C. Chambliss
2B G. Hubbard
SS J. Gomez
3B J. Horner
OF D. Murphy
OF G. Matthews
OF J. Burroughs
C B. Benedict
UT J. Royster
P P. Niekro
P D. Alexander
P T. Boggs
P R. Matula
P L. McWilliams
RP R. Camp
RP H. Garber

ATL 1981 N

M R. Cox
1B C. Chambliss
2B G. Hubbard
SS R. Ramirez
3B J. Horner
OF D. Murphy
OF C. Washington
OF R. Linares
C B. Benedict
UT J. Royster
P G. Perry
P T. Boggs
P P. Niekro
P R. Mahler
RP J. Montefusco
RP R. Camp

ATL 1982 N

M J. Torre
1B C. Chambliss
2B G. Hubbard
SS R. Ramirez
3B J. Horner
OF D. Murphy
OF C. Washington
OF B. Butler
C B. Benedict
UT J. Royster
P P. Niekro
P R. Mahler
P R. Camp
P R. Walk
RP S. Bedrosian
RP H. Garber

ATL 1983 N

M J. Torre
1B C. Chambliss
2B G. Hubbard
SS R. Ramirez
3B J. Horner
OF D. Murphy
OF B. Butler
OF C. Washington
C B. Benedict
P J. McMurtry
P P. Perez
P P. Niekro
P R. Camp
P P. Falcone
RP S. Bedrosian
RP T. Forster

ATL 1984 N

M J. Torre
1B C. Chambliss
2B G. Hubbard
SS R. Ramirez
3B R. Johnson
OF D. Murphy
OF C. Washington
OF B. Komminsk
C B. Benedict
UT G. Perry
P R. Mahler
P P. Perez
P J. McMurtry
P R. Camp
P L. Barker
RP H. Garber
RP S. Bedrosian

ATL 1985 N

M G. Haas
M R. Wine
1B J. Horner
2B G. Hubbard
SS R. Ramirez
3B K. Oberkfell
OF D. Murphy
OF T. Harper
OF C. Washington
C R. Cerone
UT C. Chambliss
UT B. Komminsk
UT G. Perry
P R. Mahler
P S. Bedrosian
P Z. Smith
RP R. Camp
RP H. Garber

ATL 1986 N

M C. Tanner
1B J. Horner
2B G. Hubbard
SS A. Thomas
3B K. Oberkfell
OF D. Murphy
OF O. Moreno
OF T. Harper
C O. Virgil
UT C. Chambliss
UT R. Ramirez
P R. Mahler
P D. Palmer
P Z. Smith
P D. Alexander
RP J. Dedmon
RP J. McMurtry

ATL 1987 N

M C. Tanner
1B G. Perry
2B G. Hubbard
SS A. Thomas
3B K. Oberkfell
OF D. Murphy
OF D. James
OF G. Griffey
C O. Virgil
UT G. Nettles
P Z. Smith
P R. Mahler
P D. Palmer
P C. Puleo
P D. Alexander
RP J. Acker
RP J. Dedmon

ATL 1988 N

M C. Tanner
M R. Nixon
1B G. Perry
2B R. Gant
SS A. Thomas
3B K. Oberkfell
OF D. Murphy
OF D. James
OF A. Hall
C O. Virgil
P R. Mahler
P P. Smith
P T. Glavine
P Z. Smith
RP C. Puleo
RP J. Alvarez

Baltimore

MAR n 1873
Marylands
BAL n 1872-1874
Lord Baltimores
BAL U 1884
BAL a 1882-1889
BB a 1890
Combined with
Brooklyn
BAL a 1891
BAL N 1892-1899
BAL A 1901-1902
BAL F 1914-1915
BAL A 1954-1988

MAR 1873 n

M W. Smith
1B W. Lennon
2B M. Simpson
SS L. Say
3B H. Kohler
OF W. Smith
OF J. Smith
OF W. French
C M. Hooper
P W. Stratton
P F. Sellman
P McDoolan

BAL 1872 n

M W. Craver
M E. Mills
1B E. Mills
2B T. Carey
SS J. Radcliff
3B D. Force
OF G. Hall
OF T. York
OF L. Pike
C W. Craver
UT W. Fisher
UT R. Higham
P R. Mathews
P W. Fisher

BAL 1873 n

M C. McVey
M T. Carey
1B E. Mills
2B T. Carey
SS J. Radcliff
3B D. Force
OF T. York
OF L. Pike
OF G. Hall
C W. Craver
UT C. McVey
P W. Cummings
P A. Brainard

BAL 1874 n

M W. White
1B C. Gould
2B J. Manning
SS L. Say
3B W. White
OF J. Ryan
OF C. Dean
OF O. Bielaski
C C. Snyder
P A. Brainard
P J. Manning

BAL 1884 U

M W. Henderson
1B C. Levis
2B J. Phelan
SS L. Say
3B W. Robinson
OF J. Seery
OF E. Cuthbert
OF B. Graham
C E. Fusselback
P W. Sweeney
P T. Lee
P A. Atkinson

BAL 1882 a

M H. Myers
1B C. Householder
2B G. Pierce
SS H. Myers
3B J. Shetzline
OF C. Waitt
OF T. Brown
OF J. Cline
C E. Whiting
P S. Landis
P F. Nichols
P E. Geis

BAL 1883 a

M W. Barnie
1B D. Stearns
2B T. Manning
SS L. Say
3B J. McCormick
OF J. Clinton
OF D. Eggler
OF D. Rowe
C J. Kelly
P J. Henderson
P R. Emslie
P J. Fox

BAL 1884 a

M W. Barnie
1B D. Stearns
2B T. Manning
SS J. Macullar
3B J. Sommer
OF J. Clinton
OF T. York
OF F. Gardner
C S. Trott
P R. Emslie
P J. Henderson

BAL 1885 a

M W. Barnie
1B D. Stearns
2B T. Manning
SS J. Macullar
3B M. Muldoon
OF J. Sommer
OF D. Casey
OF E. Greer
C W. Traffley
UT T. Burns
P J. Henderson
P R. Emslie
P J. Henry

BAL 1886 a

M W. Barnie
1B M. Scott
2B M. Muldoon
SS J. Macullar
3B J. Davis
OF J. Manning
OF J. Sommer
OF P. O'Connell
C C. Fulmer
P M. Kilroy
P G. McGinnis
P J. Henderson

BAL 1887 a

M W. Barnie
1B T. Tucker
2B W. Greenwood
SS T. Burns
3B J. Davis
OF W. Purcell
OF M. Griffin
OF J. Sommer
C S. Trott
P M. Kilroy
P J. Smith

BAL 1888 a

M W. Barnie
1B T. Tucker
2B W. Greenwood
SS J. Farrell
3B W. Shindle
OF M. Griffin
OF W. Purcell
OF T. Burns
C C. Fulmer
P E. Cunningham
P M. Kilroy
P J. Smith

BAL 1889 a

M W. Barnie
1B T. Tucker
2B J. Mack
SS J. Farrell
3B W. Shindle
OF M. Hornung
OF M. Griffin
OF J. Sommer
C E. Tate
P M. Kilroy
P F. Foreman
P E. Cunningham

BB 1890 a

M J. Kennedy
M W. Barnie
1B W. O'Brien
2B J. Gerhardt
SS J. Nelson
3B J. Davis
OF J. Peltz
OF H. Simon
OF E. Daily
C J. Toy
P E. Daily
P C. McCullough
P M. Mattimore
P L. German
P J. McMahon
P C. Murphy

BAL 1891 a

M W. Barnie
1B P. Werden
2B S. Wise
SS G. Van Haltren
3B P. Gilbert
OF W. Johnson
OF C. Welch
OF I. Ray
C W. Robinson
P J. McMahon
P E. Cunningham
P M. Madden
P J. Healy

BAL 1892 N

M G. Van Haltren
M J. Waltz
M E. Hanlon
1B E. Sutcliffe
2B J. Stricker
SS T. O'Rourke
3B W. Shindle
OF G. Van Haltren
OF H. Stovey
OF C. Welch

C W. Robinson
P J. McMahon
P G. Cobb
P T. Vickery
P C. Buffinton

BAL 1893 N

M E. Hanlon
1B H. Taylor
2B H. Reitz
SS J. McGraw
3B W. Shindle
OF J. Kelley
OF G. Treadway
OF J. Long
C W. Robinson
P J. McMahon
P A. Mullane
P W. Hawke
P E. McNabb
P K. Baker

BAL 1894 N

M E. Hanlon
1B D. Brouthers
2B H. Reitz
SS H. Jennings
3B J. McGraw
OF J. Kelley
OF W. Brodie
OF W. Keeler
C W. Robinson
P J. McMahon
P W. Hawke
P W. Gleason
P A. Inks
P A. Mullane

BAL 1895 N

M E. Hanlon
1B G. Carey
2B W. Gleason
SS H. Jennings
3B J. McGraw
OF J. Kelley
OF W. Keeler
OF W. Brodie
C W. Robinson
P W. Hoffer
P G. Hemming
P C. Esper
P A. Clarkson
P J. McMahon

BAL 1896 N

M E. Hanlon
1B J. Doyle
2B H. Reitz
SS H. Jennings
3B J. Donnelly
OF W. Brodie
OF J. Kelley
OF W. Keeler
C W. Robinson
UT W. Clarke
P W. Hoffer
P E. Pond
P G. Hemming
P J. McMahon
P C. Esper

BAL 1897 N

M E. Hanlon
1B J. Doyle
2B H. Reitz
SS H. Jennings
3B J. McGraw
OF J. Stenzel
OF J. Kelley
OF W. Keeler
C W. Clarke
P J. Corbett
P W. Hoffer
P E. Pond
P J. Nops

BAL 1898 N

M E. Hanlon
1B D. McGann
2B De Montreville
SS H. Jennings
3B J. McGraw
OF W. Keeler
OF J. Kelley
OF J. Holmes
C W. Robinson
P J. McJames
P J. Hughes
P A. Maul
P J. Nops

P F. Kitson

BAL 1899 N

M J. McGraw
1B G. LaChance
2B De Montreville
SS W. Keister
3B J. McGraw
OF S. Sheckard
OF J. Holmes
OF W. Brodie
C W. Robinson
P J. McGinnity
P F. Kitson
P J. Nops
P H. Howell

BAL 1901 A

M J. McGraw
1B J. Hart
2B J. Williams
SS W. Keister
3B J. McGraw
OF J. Seymour
OF J. Jackson
OF W. Brodie
C R. Bresnahan
UT M. Donlin
UT J. Dunn
P J. McGinnity
P H. Howell
P F. Foreman
P J. Nops

BAL 1902 A

M J. McGraw
M W. Robinson
1B D. McGann
2B J. Williams
SS W. Gilbert
3B R. Bresnahan
OF A. Selbach
OF J. Seymour
OF H. Arndt
C W. Robinson
P J. McGinnity
P H. Howell
P L. Wiltse
P C. Shields
P J. Katoll

BAL 1914 F

M F. Knabe
1B H. Swacina
2B F. Knabe
SS M. Doolan
3B M. Walsh
OF V. Duncan
OF B. Meyer
OF G. Simmons
C F. Jacklitsch
P J. Quinn
P G. Suggs
P I. Wilhelm
P F. Smith
P W. Bailey

BAL 1915 F

M F. Knabe
1B H. Swacina
2B F. Knabe
SS M. Doolan
3B M. Walsh
OF V. Duncan
OF S. McCandless
OF G. Zinn
C F. Owens
P J. Quinn
P G. Suggs
P W. Bailey
P C. Bender
P A. Johnson

BAL 1954 A

M J. Dykes
1B E. Waitkus
2B R. Young
SS G. Hunter
3B V. Stephens
OF C. Diering
OF C. Abrams
OF J. Fridley
C C. Courtney
UT G. Coan
UT R. Kennedy
UT R. Kryhoski
P R. Turley
P J. Coleman
P D. Larsen
P D. Pillette

P L. Kretlow
RP R. Chakales
RP M. Blyzka

BAL 1955 A

M P. Richards
1B G. Triandos
2B F. Marsh
SS G. Miranda
3B J. Causey
OF C. Diering
OF C. Abrams
OF D. Philley
C H. Smith
P J. Wilson
P E. Palica
P R. Moore
P W. Wight
RP A. Schallock
RP D. Johnson

BAL 1956 A

M P. Richards
1B R. Boyd
2B W. Gardner
SS G. Miranda
3B G. Kell
OF J. Francona
OF R. Nieman
OF R. Williams
C G. Triandos
P R. Moore
P C. Johnson
P W. Wight
P H. Brown
P E. Palica
RP D. Ferrarese
RP G. Zuverink

BAL 1957 A

M P. Richards
1B R. Boyd
2B W. Gardner
SS G. Miranda
3B G. Kell
OF A. Pilarcik
OF R. Nieman
OF J. Busby
C G. Triandos
UT J. Francona
P C. Johnson
P R. Moore
P W. Loes
P H. Brown
P W. O'Dell
RP G. Zuverink
RP K. Lehman

BAL 1958 A

M P. Richards
1B R. Boyd
2B W. Gardner
SS G. Miranda
3B B. Robinson
OF A. Pilarcik
OF E. Woodling
OF J. Busby
C G. Triandos
UT F. Castleman
UT R. Nieman
UT R. Williams
P J. Harshman
P W. O'Dell
P A. Portocarrero
P M. Pappas
P C. Johnson
RP G. Zuverink
RP K. Lehman

BAL 1959 A

M P. Richards
1B R. Boyd
2B W. Gardner
SS A. Carrasquel
3B B. Robinson
OF W. Tasby
OF E. Woodling
OF A. Pilarcik
C G. Triandos
UT W. Klaus
UT R. Nieman
P J. Wilhelm
P M. Pappas
P W. O'Dell
P J. Walker
P H. Brown
RP W. Loes
RP E. Johnson

BAL 1960 A

M P. Richards
1B J. Gentile
2B M. Breeding
SS R. Hansen
3B B. Robinson
OF J. Brandt
OF E. Woodling
OF G. Stephens
C G. Triandos
UT A. Pilarcik
P C. Estrada
P M. Pappas
P J. Fisher
P S. Barber
P H. Brown
RP G. Jones

BAL 1961 A

M P. Richards
M C. Harris
1B J. Gentile
2B K. Adair
SS R. Hansen
3B B. Robinson
OF J. Brandt
OF R. Snyder
OF D. Herzog
C G. Triandos
UT R. Williams
P S. Barber
P C. Estrada
P J. Fisher
P M. Pappas
P H. Brown
RP J. Wilhelm
RP W. Stock

BAL 1962 A

M W. Hitchcock
1B J. Gentile
2B M. Breeding
SS K. Adair
3B B. Robinson
OF J. Brandt
OF R. Snyder
OF J. Powell
C G. Triandos
UT D. Herzog
UT D. Nicholson
P C. Estrada
P M. Pappas
P R. Roberts
P J. Fisher
P S. Barber
RP R. Hall
RP W. Hoeft

BAL 1963 A

M W. Hitchcock
1B J. Gentile
2B K. Adair
SS L. Aparicio
3B B. Robinson
OF J. Brandt
OF R. Snyder
OF J. Powell
C J. Orsino
UT R. Saverine
UT A. Smith
P S. Barber
P R. Roberts
P M. Pappas
P M. McCormick
P D. McNally
RP S. Miller
RP R. Hall

BAL 1964 A

M H. Bauer
1B N. Siebern
2B K. Adair
SS L. Aparicio
3B B. Robinson
OF S. Bowens
OF J. Brandt
OF J. Powell
C R. Brown
P M. Pappas
P W. Bunker
P R. Roberts
P D. McNally
P S. Barber
RP S. Miller
RP H. Haddix

BAL 1965 A

M H. Bauer
1B J. Powell
2B K. Adair

SS L. Aparicio
3B B. Robinson
OF C. Blefary
OF P. Blair
OF R. Snyder
C R. Brown
UT N. Siebern
P M. Pappas
P S. Barber
P D. McNally
P W. Bunker
P R. Roberts
RP S. Miller
RP R. Hall

BAL 1966 A

M H. Bauer
1B J. Powell
2B D. Johnson
SS L. Aparicio
3B B. Robinson
OF F. Robinson
OF P. Blair
OF C. Blefary
C A. Etchebarren
UT R. Snyder
P D. McNally
P J. Palmer
P E. Watt
P W. Bunker
P S. Barber
RP M. Drabowsky
RP S. Miller

BAL 1967 A

M H. Bauer
1B J. Powell
2B D. Johnson
SS L. Aparicio
3B B. Robinson
OF P. Blair
OF F. Robinson
OF C. Blefary
C A. Etchebarren
UT R. Snyder
P T. Phoebus
P P. Richert
P W. Dillman
P D. McNally
P J. Hardin
RP E. Watt
RP M. Drabowsky

BAL 1968 A

M H. Bauer
M E. Weaver
1B J. Powell
2B D. Johnson
SS M. Belanger
3B B. Robinson
OF P. Blair
OF F. Robinson
OF C. Blefary
C A. Etchebarren
UT D. Buford
P D. McNally
P J. Hardin
P T. Phoebus
P D. Leonhard
P E. Brabender
RP E. Watt
RP P. Richert

BAL 1969 A

M E. Weaver
1B J. Powell
2B D. Johnson
SS M. Belanger
3B B. Robinson
OF P. Blair
OF F. Robinson
OF D. Buford
C E. Hendricks
P M. Cuellar
P D. McNally
P T. Phoebus
P J. Palmer
P J. Hardin
RP D. Leonhard
RP E. Watt

BAL 1970 A

M E. Weaver
1B J. Powell
2B D. Johnson
SS M. Belanger
3B B. Robinson
OF D. Buford
OF P. Blair
OF F. Robinson
C E. Hendricks

UT M. Rettenmund
P J. Palmer
P M. Cuellar
P D. McNally
P J. Hardin
P T. Phoebus
RP M. Lopez
RP R. Hall

BAL 1971 A

M E. Weaver
1B J. Powell
2B D. Johnson
SS M. Belanger
3B B. Robinson
OF P. Blair
OF M. Rettenmund
OF D. Buford
C E. Hendricks
UT F. Robinson
P M. Cuellar
P J. Palmer
P P. Dobson
P D. McNally
RP G. Jackson

BAL 1972 A

M E. Weaver
1B J. Powell
2B D. Johnson
SS M. Belanger
3B B. Robinson
OF P. Blair
OF D. Buford
OF M. Rettenmund
C J. Oates
UT D. Baylor
UT T. Crowley
UT R. Grich
P J. Palmer
P P. Dobson
P M. Cuellar
P D. McNally
P D. Alexander
RP R. Harrison

BAL 1973 A

M E. Weaver
1B J. Powell
2B R. Grich
SS M. Belanger
3B B. Robinson
OF P. Blair
OF D. Baylor
OF R. Coggins
C E. Williams
DH H. Davis
UT A. Bumbry
P J. Palmer
P M. Cuellar
P D. McNally
P D. Alexander
P J. Jefferson
RP R. Reynolds
RP G. Jackson

BAL 1974 A

M E. Weaver
1B J. Powell
2B R. Grich
SS M. Belanger
3B B. Robinson
OF P. Blair
OF D. Baylor
OF R. Coggins
C E. Williams
DH H. Davis
P R. Grimsley
P M. Cuellar
P D. McNally
P J. Palmer
P D. Alexander
RP R. Reynolds
RP G. Jackson

BAL 1975 A

M E. Weaver
1B L. May
2B R. Grich
SS M. Belanger
3B B. Robinson
OF K. Singleton
OF P. Blair
OF D. Baylor
C D. Duncan
DH H. Davis
UT A. Bumbry
P J. Palmer
P M. Torrez
P M. Cuellar
P R. Grimsley

P D. Alexander
RP G. Jackson

BAL 1976 A

M E. Weaver
1B A. Muser
2B R. Grich
SS M. Belanger
3B D. DeCinces
OF P. Blair
OF K. Singleton
OF R. Jackson
C D. Duncan
DH L. May
UT A. Bumbry
P J. Palmer
P M. Garland
P R. May
P R. Grimsley
P M. Cuellar
RP D. Miller

BAL 1977 A

M E. Weaver
1B L. May
2B B. Smith
SS M. Belanger
3B D. DeCinces
OF K. Singleton
OF A. Bumbry
OF H. Kelly
C J. Dempsey
DH E. Murray
UT A. Muser
P J. Palmer
P R. May
P M. Flanagan
P R. Grimsley
P J. D. Martinez
RP F. T. Martinez

BAL 1978 A

M E. Weaver
1B E. Murray
2B R. Dauer
SS M. Belanger
3B D. DeCinces
OF K. Singleton
OF L. Harlow
OF C. Lopez
C J. Dempsey
DH L. May
UT H. Kelly
P J. Palmer
P M. Flanagan
P J. D. Martinez
P S. McGregor
RP D. Stanhouse
RP J. Kerrigan

BAL 1979 A

M E. Weaver
1B E. Murray
2B R. Dauer
SS A. Garcia
3B D. DeCinces
OF A. Bumbry
OF K. Singleton
OF G. Roenicke
C J. Dempsey
DH L. May
UT M. Belanger
UT J. Lowenstein
P J. D. Martinez
P M. Flanagan
P S. Stone
P S. McGregor
P J. Palmer
RP F. T. Martinez
RP D. Stanhouse

BAL 1980 A

M E. Weaver
1B E. Murray
2B R. Dauer
SS M. Belanger
3B D. DeCinces
OF A. Bumbry
OF K. Singleton
OF G. Roenicke
C J. Dempsey
DH T. Crowley
UT A. Garcia
UT J. Lowenstein
P S. McGregor
P S. Stone
P M. Flanagan
P J. Palmer
P S. Stewart
RP T. Stoddard
RP F. T. Martinez

BAL 1981 A

M   E. Weaver
1B   E. Murray
2B   R. Dauer
SS   M. Belanger
3B   D. DeCinces
OF   A. Bumbry
OF   G. Roenicke
OF   J. Lowenstein
C   J. Dempsey
DH   T. Crowley
UT   J. Dwyer
UT   K. Singleton
P   J. D. Martinez
P   S. McGregor
P   J. Palmer
P   M. Flanagan
P   S. Stewart
RP   F. T. Martinez
RP   D. Ford

BAL 1982 A

M   E. Weaver
1B   E. Murray
2B   L. Sakata
SS   C. Ripken
3B   R. Dauer
OF   A. Bumbry
OF   G. Roenicke
OF   D. Ford
C   J. Dempsey
DH   K. Singleton
UT   J. Lowenstein
P   J. D. Martinez
P   M. Flanagan
P   J. Palmer
P   S. McGregor
P   S. Stewart
RP   F. T. Martinez
RP   R. Grimsley

BAL 1983 A

M   J. Altobelli
1B   E. Murray
2B   R. Dauer
SS   C. Ripken
3B   T. Cruz
OF   J. Shelby
OF   J. Lowenstein
OF   A. Bumbry
C   J. Dempsey
DH   K. Singleton
UT   J. Dwyer
UT   D. Ford
UT   G. Roenicke
P   S. McGregor
P   G. Davis
P   M. Boddicker
P   J. D. Martinez
P   M. Flanagan
RP   S. Stewart
RP   F. T. Martinez

BAL 1984 A

M   J. Altobelli
1B   E. Murray
2B   R. Dauer
SS   C. Ripken
3B   W. Gross
OF   J. Shelby
OF   G. Roenicke
OF   M. Young
C   J. Dempsey
DH   K. Singleton
UT   A. Bumbry
UT   J. Lowenstein
P   M. Boddicker
P   M. Flanagan
P   G. Davis
P   S. McGregor
P   J. D. Martinez
RP   S. Stewart
RP   F. T. Martinez

BAL 1985 A

M   J. Altobelli
M   C. Ripken
M   E. Weaver
1B   E. Murray
2B   A. Wiggins
SS   C. Ripken
3B   F. Rayford
OF   F. Lynn
OF   L. Lacy
OF   M. Young
C   J. Dempsey
DH   L. Sheets
UT   J. Dwyer
UT   W. Gross
UT   G. Roenicke
P   S. McGregor

P   M. Boddicker
P   J. D. Martinez
P   G. Davis
P   K. Dixon
RP   S. Stewart
RP   N. Snell

BAL 1986 A

M   E. Weaver
1B   E. Murray
2B   J. Bonilla
SS   C. Ripken
3B   F. Rayford
OF   J. Shelby
OF   L. Lacy
OF   F. Lynn
C   J. Dempsey
DH   L. Sheets
UT   J. Beniquez
UT   M. Young
P   M. Boddicker
P   S. McGregor
P   K. Dixon
P   M. Flanagan
P   G. Davis
RP   R. Bordi
RP   D. Aase

BAL 1987 A

M   C. Ripken
1B   E. Murray
2B   W. Ripken
SS   C. Ripken
3B   C. Knight
OF   L. Sheets
OF   F. Lynn
OF   H. Gerhart
C   T. Kennedy
DH   M. Young
P   M. Boddicker
P   E. Bell
P   D. Schmidt
P   J. Habyan
P   K. Dixon
RP   M. Williamson
RP   T. Arnold

BAL 1988 A

M   C. Ripken
M   F. Robinson
1B   E. Murray
2B   W. Ripken
SS   C. Ripken
3B   R. Gonzales
OF   J. Orsulak
OF   H. Gerhart
OF   F. Lynn
C   M. Tettleton
DH   L. Sheets
UT   J. Traber
P   J. Bautista
P   J. Tibbs
P   J. Ballard
P   M. Boddicker
P   D. Schmidt
RP   D. Sisk
RP   M. Thurmond

Boston

BOS n 1871-1875
BOS U 1884
BOS P 1890
BOS a 1891
BOS N 1876-1952
  Moved to
  Milwaukee
BOS A 1901-1988

BOS 1871 n

M   W. Wright
1B   C. Gould
2B   R. Barnes
SS   G. Wright
3B   H. Schafer
OF   W. Wright
OF   D. Birdsall
OF   J. Cone
C   C. McVey
P   A. Spalding

BOS 1872 n

M   W. Wright
1B   C. Gould
2B   R. Barnes
SS   G. Wright
3B   H. Schafer
OF   W. Wright
OF   F. Rogers
OF   A. Leonard
C   C. McVey

P   A. Spalding

BOS 1873 n

M   W. Wright
1B   J. O'Rourke
2B   R. Barnes
SS   G. Wright
3B   H. Schafer
OF   W. Wright
OF   A. Leonard
OF   R. Addy
C   J. White
P   A. Spalding

BOS 1874 n

M   W. Wright
1B   J. O'Rourke
2B   R. Barnes
SS   G. Wright
3B   H. Schafer
OF   C. McVey
OF   A. Leonard
OF   G. Hall
C   J. White
P   A. Spalding

BOS 1875 n

M   W. Wright
1B   C. McVey
2B   R. Barnes
SS   G. Wright
3B   H. Schafer
OF   A. Leonard
OF   J. Manning
OF   J. O'Rourke
C   J. White
P   A. Spalding
P   J. Manning

BOS 1884 U

M   T. Murnane
1B   T. Murnane
2B   T. O'Brien
SS   W. Hackett
3B   J. Irwin
OF   M. Slattery
OF   E. Crane
OF   F. Butler
C   L. Brown
P   W. Burke
P   F. Shaw
P   T. Bond

BOS 1890 P

M   M. Kelly
1B   D. Brouthers
2B   J. Quinn
SS   A. Irwin
3B   W. Nash
OF   T. Brown
OF   A. Richardson
OF   H. Stovey
C   M. Murphy
UT   M. Kelly
P   C. Radbourn
P   A. Gumbert
P   W. Daley
P   M. Kilroy

BOS 1891 a

M   A. Irwin
1B   D. Brouthers
2B   J. Stricker
SS   P. Radford
3B   C. Farrell
OF   T. Brown
OF   H. Duffy
OF   A. Richardson
C   M. Murphy
P   G. Haddock
P   C. Buffinton
P   J. O'Brien
P   W. Daley

BOS 1876 N

M   W. Wright
1B   T. Murnane
2B   J. Morrill
SS   G. Wright
3B   H. Schafer
OF   J. O'Rourke
OF   J. Manning
OF   A. Leonard
C   L. Brown
P   J. Borden
P   G. Bradley

BOS 1877 N

M   W. Wright
1B   J. O'Rourke
2B   G. Wright
SS   E. Sutton
3B   J. Morrill
OF   J. O'Rourke
OF   A. Leonard
OF   T. Murnane
C   L. Brown
P   T. Bond

BOS 1878 N

M   W. Wright
1B   J. Morrill
2B   J. Burdock
SS   G. Wright
3B   E. Sutton
OF   A. Leonard
OF   J. Manning
OF   J. O'Rourke
C   C. Snyder
P   T. Bond

BOS 1879 N

M   W. Wright
1B   E. Cogswell
2B   J. Burdock
SS   E. Sutton
3B   J. Morrill
OF   C. Jones
OF   J. O'Rourke
OF   S. Houck
C   C. Snyder
P   T. Bond

BOS 1880 N

M   W. Wright
1B   J. Morrill
2B   J. Burdock
SS   E. Sutton
3B   J. H. O'Rourke
OF   C. Jones
OF   J. O'Rourke
OF   C. Foley
P   P. Powers
P   T. Bond
P   C. Foley

BOS 1881 N

M   W. Wright
1B   J. Morrill
2B   J. Burdock
SS   R. Barnes
3B   E. Sutton
OF   M. Hornung
OF   W. Crowley
OF   F. Lewis
C   C. Snyder
P   J. Whitney
P   J. Fox

BOS 1882 N

M   J. Morrill
1B   J. Morrill
2B   J. Burdock
SS   S. Wise
3B   E. Sutton
OF   P. Hotaling
OF   M. Hornung
OF   W. Rowen
C   T. Deasley
P   J. Whitney
P   R. Mathews

BOS 1883 N

M   J. Burdock
M   J. Morrill
1B   J. Morrill
2B   J. Burdock
SS   S. Wise
3B   E. Sutton
OF   M. Hornung
OF   P. Radford
OF   C. Buffinton
C   M. Hines
P   J. Whitney

BOS 1884 N

M   J. Morrill
1B   J. Morrill
2B   J. Burdock
SS   S. Wise
3B   E. Sutton
OF   M. Hornung
OF   W. Crowley
OF   J. Manning
C   M. Hackett
P   C. Buffinton
P   J. Whitney

BOS 1885 N

M   J. Morrill
1B   J. Morrill
2B   J. Burdock
SS   S. Wise
3B   E. Sutton
OF   T. Poorman
OF   T. McCarthy
C   T. Gunning
P   J. Whitney
P   C. Buffinton
P   J. Davis

BOS 1886 N

M   J. Morrill
1B   S. Wise
2B   J. Burdock
SS   J. Morrill
3B   W. Nash
OF   R. Johnston
OF   M. Hornung
OF   T. Poorman
C   C. Daily
UT   E. Sutton
P   C. Radbourn
P   W. Stemmeyer

BOS 1887 N

M   M. Kelly
M   J. Morrill
1B   J. Morrill
2B   J. Burdock
SS   S. Wise
3B   W. Nash
OF   R. Johnston
OF   M. Hornung
OF   M. Kelly
C   E. Tate
UT   E. Sutton
P   C. Radbourn
P   M. Madden
P   R. Conway
P   W. Stemmeyer

BOS 1888 N

M   J. Morrill
1B   J. Morrill
2B   J. Quinn
SS   S. Wise
3B   W. Nash
OF   R. Johnston
OF   M. Hornung
OF   T. Brown
C   M. Kelly
P   J. Clarkson
P   W. Sowders
P   C. Radbourn
P   M. Madden

BOS 1889 N

M   J. Hart
1B   D. Brouthers
2B   A. Richardson
SS   J. Quinn
3B   W. Nash
OF   R. Johnston
OF   M. Kelly
OF   T. Brown
C   C. Bennett
P   J. Clarkson
P   C. Radbourn
P   M. Madden

BOS 1890 N

M   F. Selee
1B   T. Tucker
2B   C. Smith
SS   H. Long
3B   J. McGarr
OF   W. Brodie
OF   M. Sullivan
OF   P. Hines
C   C. Bennett
P   C. Nichols
P   J. Clarkson
P   C. Getzien

BOS 1891 N

M   F. Selee
1B   T. Tucker
2B   J. Quinn
SS   H. Long
3B   W. Nash
OF   H. Stovey
OF   W. Brodie
OF   R. Lowe
C   C. Bennett
P   J. Clarkson
P   C. Nichols
P   H. Staley
P   C. Getzien

BOS 1892 N

M   F. Selee
1B   T. Tucker
2B   J. Quinn
SS   H. Long
3B   W. Nash
OF   T. McCarthy
OF   H. Duffy
OF   R. Lowe
C   M. Kelly
P   C. Nichols
P   J. Stivetts
P   H. Staley
P   J. Clarkson

BOS 1893 N

M   F. Selee
1B   T. Tucker
2B   R. Lowe
SS   H. Long
3B   W. Nash
OF   H. Duffy
OF   S. Carroll
OF   T. McCarthy
C   C. Bennett
P   C. Nichols
P   J. Stivetts
P   H. Staley
P   H. Gastright

BOS 1894 N

M   F. Selee
1B   T. Tucker
2B   R. Lowe
SS   H. Long
3B   W. Nash
OF   J. Bannon
OF   T. McCarthy
OF   H. Duffy
C   C. Ganzel
C   C. Nichols
P   J. Stivetts
P   H. Staley
P   T. Lovett

BOS 1895 N

M   F. Selee
1B   T. Tucker
2B   R. Lowe
SS   H. Long
3B   W. Nash
OF   H. Duffy
OF   J. Bannon
OF   T. McCarthy
C   C. Ganzel
P   C. Nichols
P   J. Stivetts
P   P. Dolan
P   J. Sullivan

BOS 1896 N

M   F. Selee
1B   T. Tucker
2B   R. Lowe
SS   H. Long
3B   J. Collins
OF   W. Hamilton
OF   H. Duffy
OF   J. Bannon
C   M. Bergen
UT   F. Tenney
P   C. Nichols
P   J. Stivetts
P   J. Sullivan
P   F. Klobedanz

BOS 1897 N

M   F. Selee
1B   F. Tenney
2B   R. Lowe
SS   H. Long
3B   J. Collins
OF   H. Duffy
OF   W. Hamilton
OF   C. Stahl
C   M. Bergen
P   C. Nichols
P   F. Klobedanz
P   E. Lewis
P   J. Sullivan

BOS 1898 N

M   F. Selee
1B   F. Tenney
2B   R. Lowe
SS   H. Long
3B   J. Collins
OF   H. Duffy
OF   C. Stahl
OF   W. Hamilton
C   M. Bergen
P   C. Nichols
P   E. Lewis
P   V. Willis
P   F. Klobedanz

BOS 1899 N

M   F. Selee
1B   F. Tenney
2B   R. Lowe
SS   H. Long
3B   J. Collins
OF   C. Stahl
OF   H. Duffy
OF   W. Hamilton
C   M. Bergen
P   V. Willis
P   C. Nichols
P   E. Lewis
P   J. Meekin
P   F. Killen

BOS 1900 N

M   F. Selee
1B   F. Tenney
2B   R. Lowe
SS   H. Long
3B   J. Collins
OF   W. Hamilton
OF   C. Stahl
OF   J. Freeman
C   W. Clarke
P   W. Dinneen
P   V. Willis
P   C. Nichols
P   E. Lewis
P   C. Pittinger

BOS 1901 N

M   F. Selee
1B   F. Tenney
2B   De Montreville
SS   H. Long
3B   R. Lowe
OF   W. Hamilton
OF   J. Slagle
OF   D. Cooley
C   M. Kittridge
P   C. Nichols
P   W. Dinneen
P   V. Willis
P   C. Pittinger

BOS 1902 N

M   A. Buckenberger
1B   F. Tenney
2B   De Montreville
SS   H. Long
3B   L. Gremminger
OF   P. Carney
OF   D. Cooley
OF   W. Lush
C   M. Kittridge
P   V. Willis
P   C. Pittinger
P   M. Eason
P   J. Malarkey

BOS 1903 N

M   A. Buckenberger
1B   F. Tenney
2B   E. Abbaticchio
SS   H. Aubrey
3B   L. Gremminger
OF   D. Cooley
OF   C. Dexter
OF   P. Carney
C   P. Moran
UT   J. Stanley
P   C. Pittinger
P   V. Willis
P   J. Malarkey
P   W. Piatt

BOS 1904 N

M   A. Buckenberger
1B   F. Tenney
2B   F. Raymer
SS   E. Abbaticchio
3B   J. Delahanty

OF P. Geier
OF D. Cooley
OF V. Cannell
C T. Needham
UT P. Moran
P V. Willis
P C. Pittinger
P I. Wilhelm
P T. Fisher
P E. McNichol

BOS 1905 N

M F. Tenney
1B F. Tenney
2B F. Raymer
SS E. Abbaticchio
3B H. Wolverton
OF V. Cannell
OF J. Delahanty
OF P. Dolan
C P. Moran
P I. Young
P V. Willis
P C. Fraser
P I. Wilhelm

BOS 1906 N

M F. Tenney
1B F. Tenney
2B A. Strobel
SS A. Bridwell
3B D. Brain
OF P. Dolan
OF J. Bates
OF G. Howard
C T. Needham
P I. Young
P V. Lindaman
P F. Pfeffer
P A. Dorner

BOS 1907 N

M F. Tenney
1B F. Tenney
2B C. Ritchey
SS A. Bridwell
3B D. Brain
OF C. Beaumont
OF J. Bates
OF N. Randall
C T. Needham
P A. Dorner
P V. Lindaman
P I. Young
P P. Flaherty
P F. Pfeffer

BOS 1908 N

M J. Kelley
1B D. McGann
2B C. Ritchey
SS W. Dahlen
3B W. Sweeney
OF G. Browne
OF C. Beaumont
OF J. Bates
C F. Bowerman
P V. Lindaman
P P. Flaherty
P A. Dorner
P G. Ferguson
P T. McCarthy

BOS 1909 N

M F. Bowerman
M H. Smith
1B F. Stem
2B D. Shean
SS J. Coffey
3B W. Sweeney
OF D. Becker
OF C. Beaumont
OF R. Thomas
C G. Graham
UT F. Beck
P A. Mattern
P G. Ferguson
P O. White
P L. Richie
P C. Brown

BOS 1910 N

M F. Lake
1B B. Sharpe
2B D. Shean
SS W. Sweeney
3B C. Herzog
OF W. Collins
OF F. Beck
OF R. Miller
C G. Graham
P A. Mattern
P C. Brown
P S. Frock
P C. Curtis
P G. Ferguson

BOS 1911 N

M F. Tenney
1B F. Tenney
2B W. Sweeney
SS C. Herzog
3B W. Ingerton
OF R. Miller
OF A. Kaiser
OF M. Donlin
C J. Kling
P C. Brown
P A. Mattern
P G. Tyler
P H. Perdue
P O. Weaver

BOS 1912 N

M J. Kling
1B B. Houser
2B W. Sweeney
SS J. O'Rourke
3B E. McDonald
OF A. Campbell
OF G. Jackson
OF J. Titus
C J. Kling
UT A. Devlin
UT J. Kirke
P G. Tyler
P O. Hess
P H. Perdue
P W. Dickson
P E. Donnelly

BOS 1913 N

M G. Stallings
1B R. Myers
2B W. Sweeney
SS W. Maranville
3B A. Devlin
OF J. Connolly
OF L. Mann
OF J. Titus
C W. Rariden
P G. Tyler
P R. Rudolph
P O. Hess
P H. Perdue
P W. James

BOS 1914 N

M G. Stallings
1B C. Schmidt
2B J. Evers
SS W. Maranville
3B C. Deal
OF L. Mann
OF J. Connolly
OF L. Gilbert
C H. Gowdy
P R. Rudolph
P W. James
P G. Tyler
P R. Crutcher

BOS 1915 N

M G. Stallings
1B C. Schmidt
2B J. Evers
SS W. Maranville
3B J. Smith
OF S. Magee
OF J. Moran
OF J. Connolly
C H. Gowdy
UT E. Fitzpatrick
P R. Rudolph
P T. Hughes
P D. Ragan
P G. Tyler

BOS 1916 N

M G. Stallings
1B E. Konetchy
2B J. Evers
SS W. Maranville
3B J. Smith
OF S. Magee
OF F. Snodgrass
OF J. Wilhoit
C H. Gowdy
P R. Rudolph
P G. Tyler
P D. Ragan
P J. Barnes
P T. Hughes

BOS 1917 N

M G. Stallings
1B E. Konetchy
2B J. Rawlings
SS W. Maranville
3B J. Smith
OF J. Kelly
OF R. Powell
OF W. Rehg
C W. Tragesser
P J. Barnes
P R. Rudolph
P G. Tyler
P A. Nehf
P D. Ragan

BOS 1918 N

M G. Stallings
1B E. Konetchy
2B C. Herzog
SS J. Rawlings
3B J. Smith
OF A. Wickland
OF R. Powell
OF R. Massey
C A. Wilson
P A. Nehf
P D. Ragan
P R. Rudolph
P B. Hearn
P D. Fillingim

BOS 1919 N

M G. Stallings
1B W. Holke
2B C. Herzog
SS W. Maranville
3B N. Boeckel
OF R. Powell
OF W. Cruise
OF J. Riggert
C H. Gowdy
UT J. Smith
P R. Rudolph
P D. Fillingim
P A. Nehf
P R. Keating
P A. Demaree

BOS 1920 N

M G. Stallings
1B W. Holke
2B C. Pick
SS W. Maranville
3B N. Boeckel
OF R. Powell
OF L. Mann
OF W. Cruise
C G. O'Neil
P J. Oeschger
P J. Scott
P D. Fillingim
P H. McQuillan

BOS 1921 N

M F. Mitchell
1B W. Holke
2B H. Ford
SS W. Barbare
3B N. Boeckel
OF R. Powell
OF W. Southworth
OF W. Cruise
C G. O'Neil
P J. Oeschger
P J. Watson
P H. McQuillan
P D. Fillingim
P J. Scott

BOS 1922 N

M F. Mitchell
1B W. Holke
2B W. Kopf
SS H. Ford
3B N. Boeckel
OF R. Powell
OF W. Cruise
OF A. Nixon
C G. O'Neil
UT W. Barbare
P J. Watson
P F. Miller
P R. Marquard
P J. Oeschger
P H. McQuillan
RP T. McNamara
RP E. Braxton

BOS 1923 N

M F. Mitchell
1B J. McInnis
2B H. Ford
SS R. Smith
3B N. Boeckel
OF W. Southworth
OF A. Felix
OF R. Powell
C G. O'Neil
P R. Marquard
P J. Genewich
P J. Barnes
P J. Oeschger
P T. McNamara
RP D. Fillingim

BOS 1924 N

M D. Bancroft
1B J. McInnis
2B J. Tierney
SS R. Smith
3B E. Padgett
OF C. Stengel
OF W. Cunningham
OF F. Wilson
C G. O'Neil
P J. Barnes
P J. Genewich
P J. Cooney
P T. McNamara
P J. Yeargin

BOS 1925 N

M D. Bancroft
1B M. Burrus
2B W. Gautreau
SS D. Bancroft
3B W. Marriott
OF J. Welsh
OF A. Felix
OF D. Harris
C F. Gibson
UT B. Neis
P J. Cooney
P J. Barnes
P L. Benton
P J. Genewich
P K. Graham
RP R. Marquard
RP A. Kamp

BOS 1926 N

M D. Bancroft
1B M. Burrus
2B W. Gautreau
SS D. Bancroft
3B A. High
OF E. Brown
OF J. Welsh
OF J. Smith
C J. Taylor
P L. Benton
P J. Genewich
P R. Smith
P H. Wertz
P G. Mogridge

BOS 1927 N

M D. Bancroft
1B J. Fournier
2B W. Gautreau
SS D. Bancroft
3B A. High
OF E. Brown
OF J. Welsh
OF L. Richbourg
C J. Hogan
UT E. Farrell
UT G. Moore
P R. Smith
P K. Greenfield
P J. Genewich
P H. Wertz
P C. Robertson
RP G. Mogridge

BOS 1928 N

M J. Slattery
M R. Hornsby
1B G. Sisler
2B R. Hornsby
SS E. Farrell
3B L. Bell
OF L. Richbourg
OF E. Brown
OF J. Smith
C J. Taylor
P R. Smith
P E. Brandt
P A. Delaney
P K. Greenfield
RP F. Edwards

BOS 1929 N

M E. Fuchs
1B G. Sisler
2B F. Maguire
SS W. Maranville
3B L. Bell
OF L. Richbourg
OF G. Harper
OF B. Clark
C A. Spohrer
P R. Smith
P H. Seibold
P P. Jones
P E. Brandt
P B. Cantwell

BOS 1930 N

M W. McKechnie
1B G. Sisler
2B F. Maguire
SS W. Maranville
3B C. Chatham
OF W. Berger
OF L. Richbourg
OF J. Welsh
C A. Spohrer
P H. Seibold
P R. Smith
P B. Cantwell
P J. Zachary
P E. Brandt
RP B. Cunningham

BOS 1931 N

M W. McKechnie
1B E. Sheely
2B F. Maguire
SS W. Maranville
3B W. Urbanski
OF W. Berger
OF R. Worthington
OF E. Schulmerich
C A. Spohrer
UT L. Richbourg
P E. Brandt
P J. Zachary
P H. Seibold
P B. Cantwell
P W. Sherdel
RP H. Haid

BOS 1932 N

M W. McKechnie
1B C. Shires
2B W. Maranville
SS W. Urbanski
3B W. Knothe
OF W. Berger
OF R. Worthington
OF E. Schulmerich
C A. Spohrer
UT R. Moore
P E. Brandt
P W. Betts
P R. Brown
P J. Zachary
P B. Cantwell
RP F. Frankhouse
RP B. Cunningham

BOS 1933 N

M W. McKechnie
1B B. Jordan
2B W. Maranville
SS W. Urbanski
3B A. Whitney
OF W. Berger
OF R. Moore
OF H. Lee
C J. Hogan
P E. Brandt
P B. Cantwell
P F. Frankhouse
P W. Betts
P J. Zachary

BOS 1934 N

M W. McKechnie
1B B. Jordan
2B M. McManus
SS W. Urbanski
3B A. Whitney
OF W. Berger
OF H. Lee
OF R. Thompson
C A. Spohrer
UT J. Hogan
UT R. Moore
P E. Brandt
P F. Frankhouse
P W. Betts
P C. Rhem
P B. Cantwell

BOS 1935 N

M W. McKechnie
1B B. Jordan
2B L. Mallon
SS W. Urbanski
3B A. Whitney
OF W. Berger
OF H. Lee
OF R. Thompson
C A. Spohrer
UT R. Moore
P F. Frankhouse
P B. Cantwell
P R. Smith
P E. Brandt
P W. Betts
RP L. Benton

BOS 1936 N

M W. McKechnie
1B B. Jordan
2B A. Cuccinello
SS W. Urbanski
3B J. Coscarart
OF E. Moore
OF H. Lee
OF W. Berger
C A. Lopez
UT R. Thompson
P D. Mac Fayden
P J. Chaplin
P J. Lanning
P R. Reis
P R. Smith

BOS 1937 N

M W. McKechnie
1B E. Fletcher
2B A. Cuccinello
SS H. Warstler
3B G. English
OF E. Moore
OF V. DiMaggio
OF D. Garms
C A. Lopez
P L. Fette
P J. Turner
P D. Mac Fayden
P G. Bush
P J. Lanning
RP I. Hutchinson

BOS 1938 N

M C. Stengel
1B E. Fletcher
2B A. Cuccinello
SS H. Warstler
3B J. Stripp
OF V. DiMaggio
OF J. Cooney
OF M. West
C R. Mueller
UT D. Garms
P J. Turner
P L. Fette
P D. Mac Fayden
P I. Hutchinson
P M. Shoffner

BOS 1939 N

M C. Stengel
1B J. Hassett
2B A. Cuccinello
SS E. Miller
3B H. Majeski
OF M. West
OF J. Cooney
OF D. Garms
C A. Lopez
UT A. Simmons
UT H. Warstler
P W. Posedel
P D. Mac Fayden
P J. Turner
P L. Fette
P M. Shoffner

BOS 1940 N

M C. Stengel
1B J. Hassett
2B C. Rowell
SS E. Miller
3B S. Sisti
OF C. Ross
OF M. West
OF J. Cooney
C R. Berres
UT E. Moore
P R. Errickson
P W. Posedel
P J. Sullivan
P M. Salvo
P N. Strincevich
RP A. Javery
RP A. Piechota

BOS 1941 N

M C. Stengel
1B J. Hassett
2B C. Rowell
SS E. Miller
3B S. Sisti
OF M. West
OF J. Cooney
OF E. Moore
C R. Berres
UT P. Waner
P J. Tobin
P M. Salvo
P A. Johnson
P R. Errickson
P A. Javery
RP J. Hutchings
RP F. Lamanna

BOS 1942 N

M C. Stengel
1B M. West
2B S. Sisti
SS E. Miller
3B F. Fernandez
OF T. Holmes
OF P. Waner
OF C. Ross
C E. Lombardi
P J. Tobin
P A. Javery
P L. Tost
P M. Salvo
P T. Earley
RP J. Sain
RP W. Donovan

BOS 1943 N

M R. Coleman
M C. Stengel
1B J. McCarthy
2B C. Ryan
SS W. Wietelmann
3B E. Joost
OF T. Holmes
OF C. Workman
OF E. Nieman
C P. Masi
UT C. Ross
P A. Javery
P N. Andrews
P C. Barrett
P J. Tobin
P M. Salvo
RP D. Odom

BOS 1944 N

M R. Coleman
1B C. Etchison
2B C. Ryan
SS W. Wietelmann
3B D. Phillips
OF T. Holmes
OF E. Nieman
OF C. Workman
C P. Masi
UT M. Macon
P J. Tobin
P N. Andrews
P A. Javery
P C. Barrett
P I. Hutchinson

BOS 1945 N

M R. Coleman
M A. Bissonette
1B V. Shupe
2B W. Wietelmann
SS R. Culler
3B C. Workman
OF T. Holmes
OF C. Gillenwater
OF E. Nieman
C P. Masi

P J. Tobin
P R. Logan
P J. Hutchings
P N. Andrews
P H. Wright
RP D. Hendrickson

BOS 1946 N

M W. Southworth
1B R. Sanders
2B C. Ryan
SS R. Culler
3B F. Fernandez
OF T. Holmes
OF C. Rowell
OF C. Gillenwater
C P. Masi
UT J. Hopp
P J. Sain
P M. Cooper
P H. Wright
P W. Lee
P S. Johnson
RP J. Wallace

BOS 1947 N

M W. Southworth
1B C. Torgeson
2B C. Ryan
SS R. Culler
3B R. Elliott
OF T. Holmes
OF J. Hopp
OF C. Rowell
C P. Masi
P W. Spahn
P J. Sain
P C. Barrett
P W. Voiselle
P S. Johnson
RP C. Shoun
RP H. Wright

BOS 1948 N

M W. Southworth
1B C. Torgeson
2B E. Stanky
SS A. Dark
3B R. Elliott
OF T. Holmes
OF J. Heath
OF M. McCormick
C P. Masi
P J. Sain
P W. Spahn
P W. Voiselle
P V. Bickford
P C. Barrett
RP R. Hogue
RP C. Shoun

BOS 1949 N

M W. Southworth
M J. Cooney
1B E. Fletcher
2B E. Stanky
SS A. Dark
3B R. Elliott
OF J. Russell
OF T. Holmes
OF M. Rickert
C W. Salkeld
UT S. Sisti
P W. Spahn
P J. Sain
P V. Bickford
P W. Voiselle
P J. Antonelli
RP N. Potter
RP R. Hall

BOS 1950 N

M W. Southworth
1B C. Torgeson
2B R. Hartsfield
SS J. Kerr
3B R. Elliott
OF S. Jethroe
OF S. Gordon
OF T. Holmes
C W. Cooper
UT W. Marshall
P V. Bickford
P W. Spahn
P J. Sain
P R. Chipman
RP R. Hogue
RP J. Antonelli

BOS 1951 N

M W. Southworth
M T. Holmes
1B C. Torgeson
2B R. Hartsfield
SS J. Kerr
3B R. Elliott
OF S. Jethroe
OF W. Marshall
OF S. Gordon
C W. Cooper
UT S. Sisti
P W. Spahn
P M. Surkont
P V. Bickford
P J. Sain
P C. Nichols
RP D. Cole
RP G. Estock

BOS 1952 N

M T. Holmes
M C. Grimm
1B C. Torgeson
2B J. Dittmer
SS J. Logan
3B E. Mathews
OF S. Jethroe
OF S. Gordon
OF H. Daniels
C W. Cooper
P W. Spahn
P J. Wilson
P M. Surkont
P V. Bickford
P S. Burdette
RP S. Jones

BOS 1901 A

M J. Collins
1B J. Freeman
2B A. Ferris
SS F. Parent
3B J. Collins
OF T. Dowd
OF C. Hemphill
OF C. Stahl
C Schreckengost
P D. Young
P E. Lewis
P G. Winter
P F. Mitchell
P G. Cuppy

BOS 1902 A

M J. Collins
1B G. LaChance
2B A. Ferris
SS F. Parent
3B J. Collins
OF J. Freeman
OF C. Stahl
OF P. Dougherty
C L. Criger
P D. Young
P W. Dinneen
P G. Winter
P T. Sparks

BOS 1903 A

M J. Collins
1B G. LaChance
2B A. Ferris
SS F. Parent
3B J. Collins
OF J. Freeman
OF P. Dougherty
OF C. Stahl
C L. Criger
UT J. O'Brien
P D. Young
P W. Dinneen
P N. Gibson
P G. Winter

BOS 1904 A

M J. Collins
1B G. LaChance
2B A. Ferris
SS F. Parent
3B J. Collins
OF C. Stahl
OF J. Freeman
OF A. Selbach
C L. Criger
P D. Young
P W. Dinneen
P J. Tannehill
P N. Gibson

P G. Winter

BOS 1905 A

M J. Collins
1B M. Grimshaw
2B A. Ferris
SS F. Parent
3B J. Collins
OF J. Burkett
OF C. Stahl
OF A. Selbach
C L. Criger
UT J. Freeman
P D. Young
P J. Tannehill
P G. Winter
P W. Dinneen
P N. Gibson

BOS 1906 A

M J. Collins
C C. Stahl
1B M. Grimshaw
2B A. Ferris
SS F. Parent
3B J. Morgan
OF C. Stahl
OF J. Hoey
OF J. Hayden
C C. Armbruster
UT J. Freeman
P D. Young
P J. Harris
P W. Dinneen
P G. Winter
P J. Tannehill

BOS 1907 A

M D. Young
M G. Huff
M R. Unglaub
M J. McGuire
1B R. Unglaub
2B A. Ferris
SS C. Wagner
3B J. Knight
OF D. Sullivan
OF W. Congalton
OF J. Barrett
C L. Criger
UT F. Parent
P D. Young
P G. Winter
P D. Glaze
P C. Pruiett
P J. Tannehill

BOS 1908 A

M J. McGuire
M F. Lake
1B G. Stahl
2B A. McConnell
SS C. Wagner
3B H. Lord
OF H. Gessler
OF J. Thoney
OF D. Sullivan
C L. Criger
UT C. Cravath
P D. Young
P E. Cicotte
P H. Morgan
P F. Burchell
P G. Winter

BOS 1909 A

M F. Lake
1B G. Stahl
2B A. McConnell
SS C. Wagner
3B H. Lord
OF T. Speaker
OF H. Niles
OF H. Gessler
C W. Carrigan
P F. Arellanes
P H. Wood
P E. Cicotte
P C. Chech

BOS 1910 A

M P. Donovan
1B G. Stahl
2B W. Gardner
SS C. Wagner
3B H. Lord
OF H. Hooper
OF G. Lewis
OF T. Speaker
C W. Carrigan

UT A. Engle
UT E. Cicotte
P R. Collins
P H. Wood
P C. Hall
P E. Karger

BOS 1911 A

M P. Donovan
1B A. Engle
2B C. Wagner
SS S. Yerkes
3B W. Gardner
OF T. Speaker
OF H. Hooper
OF G. Lewis
C W. Carrigan
UT A. Williams
P H. Wood
P E. Cicotte
P R. Collins
P L. Pape
P C. Hall

BOS 1912 A

M G. Stahl
1B G. Stahl
2B S. Yerkes
SS C. Wagner
3B W. Gardner
OF G. Lewis
OF T. Speaker
OF H. Hooper
C W. Carrigan
P H. Wood
P T. O'Brien
P H. Bedient
P R. Collins
P C. Hall

BOS 1913 A

M G. Stahl
M W. Carrigan
1B A. Engle
2B S. Yerkes
SS C. Wagner
3B W. Gardner
OF H. Hooper
OF G. Lewis
OF T. Speaker
C W. Carrigan
P H. Leonard
P H. Bedient
P R. Collins
P H. Wood
P E. Moseley

BOS 1914 A

M W. Carrigan
1B R. Hoblitzel
2B S. Yerkes
SS L. Scott
3B W. Gardner
OF T. Speaker
OF G. Lewis
OF H. Hooper
C W. Carrigan
UT H. Janvrin
P R. Collins
P H. Leonard
P G. Foster
P H. Bedient
P E. Shore

BOS 1915 A

M W. Carrigan
1B R. Hoblitzel
2B C. Wagner
SS L. Scott
3B W. Gardner
OF G. Lewis
OF T. Speaker
OF H. Hooper
C C. Thomas
UT H. Janvrin
P G. Foster
P E. Shore
P G. Ruth
P H. Leonard
P H. Wood

BOS 1916 A

M W. Carrigan
1B R. Hoblitzel
2B J. Barry
SS L. Scott
3B W. Gardner
OF G. Lewis
OF H. Hooper
OF C. Walker

C C. Thomas
UT H. Janvrin
P G. Ruth
P H. Leonard
P C. Mays
P E. Shore
P G. Foster

BOS 1917 A

M J. Barry
1B R. Hoblitzel
2B J. Barry
SS L. Scott
3B W. Gardner
OF H. Hooper
OF G. Lewis
OF C. Walker
C S. Agnew
P G. Ruth
P H. Leonard
P C. Mays
P E. Shore
P G. Foster

BOS 1918 A

M E. Barrow
1B J. McInnis
2B D. Shean
SS L. Scott
3B F. Thomas
OF H. Hooper
OF A. Strunk
OF G. Whiteman
C S. Agnew
UT G. Ruth
UT W. Schang
P C. Mays
P L. Bush
P S. Jones
P H. Leonard

BOS 1919 A

M E. Barrow
1B J. McInnis
2B M. Shannon
SS L. Scott
3B O. Vitt
OF H. Hooper
OF G. Ruth
OF R. Roth
C W. Schang
P S. Jones
P H. Pennock
P C. Mays
P A. Russell
P W. Hoyt

BOS 1920 A

M E. Barrow
1B J. McInnis
2B M. McNally
SS L. Scott
3B E. Foster
OF M. Menosky
OF H. Hooper
OF T. Hendryx
C A. Walters
UT W. Schang
P S. Jones
P L. Bush
P H. Pennock
P H. Harper
P W. Hoyt

BOS 1921 A

M H. Duffy
1B J. McInnis
2B D. Pratt
SS L. Scott
3B E. Foster
OF J. Collins
OF M. Menosky
OF H. Leibold
C H. Ruel
P S. Jones
P L. Bush
P H. Pennock
P A. Russell
P E. Myers

BOS 1922 A

M H. Duffy
1B G. Burns
2B D. Pratt
SS J. Mitchell
3B J. Dugan
OF J. Collins
OF M. Menosky
OF J. Harris
C H. Ruel

P J. Quinn
P H. Collins
P H. Pennock
P J. Ferguson
P B. Karr
RP C. Fullerton

BOS 1923 A

M F. Chance
1B G. Burns
2B W. Fewster
SS J. Mitchell
3B H. Shanks
OF J. Harris
OF I. Flagstead
OF R. Reichle
C V. Picinich
UT J. Collins
UT N. McMillan
P H. Ehmke
P J. Quinn
P J. Ferguson
P W. Piercy
P G. Murray
RP F. O'Doul

BOS 1924 A

M L. Fohl
1B J. Harris
2B W. Wambsganss
SS E. Lee
3B D. Clark
OF I. Flagstead
OF R. Veach
OF I. Boone
C S. O'Neill
P H. Ehmke
P J. Ferguson
P J. Quinn
P C. Fullerton
P W. Piercy
RP G. Murray

BOS 1925 A

M L. Fohl
1B P. Todt
2B W. Wambsganss
SS E. Lee
3B J. Prothro
OF I. Flagstead
OF I. Boone
OF R. Carlyle
C V. Picinich
UT E. Vache
P H. Ehmke
P F. Wingfield
P C. Ruffing
P P. Zahniser
P J. Quinn
RP C. Ross
RP O. Fuhr

BOS 1926 A

M L. Fohl
1B P. Todt
2B W. Regan
SS E. Rigney
3B F. Haney
OF W. Jacobson
OF I. Flagstead
OF S. Rosenthal
C A. Gaston
P H. Wiltse
P F. Wingfield
P P. Zahniser
P C. Ruffing
P A. Welzer
RP J. Russell

BOS 1927 A

M W. Carrigan
1B P. Todt
2B W. Regan
SS C. Myer
3B W. Rogell
OF I. Flagstead
OF W. Shaner
OF J. Tobin
C G. Hartley
UT H. Carlyle
UT J. Rothrock
P H. Wiltse
P W. Harriss
P A. Welzer
P D. Mac Fayden
P C. Ruffing

BOS 1928 A

M W. Carrigan
1B P. Todt

2B W. Regan
SS W. Gerber
3B C. Myer
OF D. Taitt
OF I. Flagstead
OF K. Williams
C F. Hofmann
UT W. Rogell
UT J. Rothrock
P C. Ruffing
P W. Morris
P J. Russell
P D. Mac Fayden
P W. Harriss
RP E. Settlemire
RP P. Simmons

BOS 1929 A

M W. Carrigan
1B P. Todt
2B W. Regan
SS H. Rhyne
3B R. Reeves
OF R. Scarritt
OF J. Rothrock
OF W. Barrett
C C. Berry
UT E. Bigelow
UT W. Narleski
P C. Ruffing
P N. Gaston
P J. Russell
P D. Mac Fayden
P W. Morris
RP E. Carroll

BOS 1930 A

M C. Wagner
1B P. Todt
2B W. Regan
SS H. Rhyne
3B O. Miller
OF T. Oliver
OF W. Webb
OF R. Scarritt
C C. Berry
UT C. Durst
P N. Gaston
P D. Mac Fayden
P H. Lisenbee
P J. Russell
P E. Durham
RP G. Smith

BOS 1931 A

M J. Collins
1B W. Sweeney
2B H. Warstler
SS H. Rhyne
3B O. Miller
OF W. Webb
OF T. Oliver
OF J. Rothrock
C C. Berry
UT U. Pickering
UT A. Van Camp
P J. Russell
P D. Mac Fayden
P W. Moore
P H. Lisenbee
P E. Durham

BOS 1932 A

M J. Collins
M M. McManus
1B D. Alexander
2B M. Olson
SS H. Warstler
3B U. Pickering
OF S. Jolley
OF T. Oliver
OF R. Johnson
C H. Tate
UT J. Watwood
P R. Weiland
P E. Durham
P R. Kline
P I. Andrews
RP W. Moore
RP J. Michaels

BOS 1933 A

M M. McManus
1B D. Alexander
2B U. Hodapp
SS H. Warstler
3B M. McManus
OF R. Johnson
OF A. Cooke
OF S. Jolley
C R. Ferrell

UT W. Werber
P J. Rhodes
P R. Weiland
P L. Brown
P H. Johnson
P I. Andrews
RP J. Welch
RP R. Kline

BOS 1934 A

M S. Harris
1B E. Morgan
2B C. Cissell
SS L. Lary
3B W. Werber
OF R. Johnson
OF C. Reynolds
OF J. Solters
C R. Ferrell
UT M. Bishop
P J. Rhodes
P J. Welch
P F. Ostermueller
P W. Ferrell
P H. Johnson
RP H. Pennock

BOS 1935 A

M J. Cronin
1B E. Dahlgren
2B O. Melillo
SS J. Cronin
3B W. Werber
OF M. Almada
OF R. Johnson
OF A. Cooke
C R. Ferrell
P W. Ferrell
P R. Grove
P J. Rhodes
P J. Welch
P G. Walberg
RP J. Wilson
RP G. Hockette

BOS 1936 A

M J. Cronin
1B J. Foxx
2B O. Melillo
SS D. McNair
3B W. Werber
OF R. Cramer
OF A. Cooke
OF M. Almada
C R. Ferrell
P W. Ferrell
P R. Grove
P F. Ostermueller
P J. Marcum
P J. Wilson

BOS 1937 A

M J. Cronin
1B J. Foxx
2B D. McNair
SS J. Cronin
3B M. Higgins
OF R. Cramer
OF C. Mills
OF W. Chapman
C E. Desautels
P R. Grove
P J. Wilson
P L. Newsom
P J. Marcum
P A. McKain

BOS 1938 A

M J. Cronin
1B J. Foxx
2B R. Doerr
SS J. Cronin
3B M. Higgins
OF R. Cramer
OF J. Vosmik
OF W. Chapman
C E. Desautels
P J. Bagby
P J. Wilson
P F. Ostermueller
P R. Grove
P G. Dickman
RP A. McKain

BOS 1939 A

M J. Cronin
1B J. Foxx
2B R. Doerr
SS J. Cronin
3B J. Tabor
OF T. Williams
OF J. Vosmik
OF R. Cramer
C J. Peacock
UT L. Finney
P R. Grove
P J. Wilson
P F. Ostermueller
P E. Auker
P D. Galehouse
RP G. Dickman
RP J. Heving

BOS 1940 A

M J. Cronin
1B J. Foxx
2B R. Doerr
SS J. Cronin
3B J. Tabor
OF R. Cramer
OF T. Williams
OF D. DiMaggio
C E. Desautels
UT L. Finney
P J. Bagby
P J. Wilson
P R. Grove
P F. Ostermueller
P H. Hash
RP G. Dickman

BOS 1941 A

M J. Cronin
1B J. Foxx
2B R. Doerr
SS J. Cronin
3B J. Tabor
OF D. DiMaggio
OF T. Williams
OF L. Finney
C F. Pytlak
P H. Newsome
P M. Harris
P C. Wagner
P R. Grove
P J. Dobson

BOS 1942 A

M J. Cronin
1B U. Lupien
2B R. Doerr
SS J. Pesky
3B J. Tabor
OF D. DiMaggio
OF T. Williams
OF L. Finney
C W. Conroy
P C. Hughson
P C. Wagner
P J. Dobson
P H. Newsome
P T. Judd
RP M. Brown

BOS 1943 A

M J. Cronin
1B U. Lupien
2B R. Doerr
SS L. Newsome
3B J. Tabor
OF E. Fox
OF D. Culberson
OF G. Metkovich
C R. Partee
P C. Hughson
P L. Terry
P J. Dobson
P T. Judd
P H. Newsome
RP M. Brown

BOS 1944 A

M J. Cronin
1B L. Finney
2B R. Doerr
SS L. Newsome
3B J. Tabor
OF R. Johnson
OF E. Fox
OF G. Metkovich
C R. Partee
P C. Hughson
P G. Woods
P J. Bowman
P R. O'Neill
P D. Ryba
RP F. Barrett

BOS 1945 A

M J. Cronin
1B G. Metkovich
2B L. Newsome
SS E. Lake
3B J. Tobin
OF R. Johnson
OF D. Culberson
OF T. McBride
C R. Garbark
UT J. Lazor
P D. Ferriss
P J. Wilson
P R. O'Neill
P C. Hausmann
P D. Ryba
RP F. Barrett

BOS 1946 A

M J. Cronin
1B P. York
2B R. Doerr
SS J. Pesky
3B G. Russell
OF T. Williams
OF D. DiMaggio
OF G. Metkovich
C H. Wagner
P C. Hughson
P D. Ferriss
P M. Harris
P J. Dobson
P J. Bagby
RP E. Johnson
RP R. Klinger

BOS 1947 A

M J. Cronin
1B J. Jones
2B R. Doerr
SS J. Pesky
3B S. Dente
OF T. Williams
OF D. DiMaggio
OF S. Mele
C G. Tebbetts
P J. Dobson
P D. Ferriss
P C. Hughson
P D. Galehouse
P E. Johnson
RP J. Murphy
RP W. Zuber

BOS 1948 A

M J. McCarthy
1B W. Goodman
2B R. Doerr
SS V. Stephens
3B J. Pesky
OF D. DiMaggio
OF T. Williams
OF S. Spence
C G. Tebbetts
P J. Dobson
P M. Parnell
P J. Kramer
P E. Kinder
P D. Galehouse
RP E. Johnson

BOS 1949 A

M J. McCarthy
1B W. Goodman
2B R. Doerr
SS V. Stephens
3B J. Pesky
OF T. Williams
OF D. DiMaggio
OF A. Zarilla
C G. Tebbetts
P M. Parnell
P E. Kinder
P J. Dobson
P C. Stobbs
P J. Kramer
RP C. Hughson
RP E. Johnson

BOS 1950 A

M J. McCarthy
M S. O'Neill
1B W. Dropo
2B R. Doerr
SS V. Stephens
3B J. Pesky
OF D. DiMaggio
OF A. Zarilla
OF T. Williams
C G. Tebbetts
UT W. Goodman
P M. Parnell
P E. Kinder
P J. Dobson
P C. Stobbs
P M. McDermott

BOS 1951 A

M S. O'Neill
1B W. Dropo
2B R. Doerr
SS J. Pesky
3B V. Stephens
OF T. Williams
OF D. DiMaggio
OF C. Vollmer
C J. Moss
UT W. Goodman
P M. Parnell
P R. Scarborough
P M. McDermott
P C. Stobbs
P W. Nixon
RP E. Kinder
RP J. Taylor

BOS 1952 A

M L. Boudreau
1B R. Gernert
2B W. Goodman
SS J. Lipon
3B G. Kell
OF D. DiMaggio
OF W. Evers
OF M. Throneberry
C S. White
P M. Parnell
P M. McDermott
P P. Trout
P S. Hudson
P R. Brodowski
RP I. Delock
RP R. Scarborough

BOS 1953 A

M L. Boudreau
1B R. Gernert
2B W. Goodman
SS M. Bolling
3B G. Kell
OF J. Piersall
OF T. Umphlett
OF W. Evers
C S. White
P M. Parnell
P M. McDermott
P H. Brown
P S. Hudson
P W. Nixon
RP E. Kinder
RP B. Flowers

BOS 1954 A

M L. Boudreau
1B H. Agganis
2B T. Lepcio
SS M. Bolling
3B G. Hatton
OF J. Jensen
OF J. Piersall
OF T. Williams
C S. White
UT W. Goodman
UT K. Olson
P F. Sullivan
P W. Nixon
P T. Brewer
P L. Kiely
P W. Henry
RP H. Brown
RP E. Kinder

BOS 1955 A

M M. Higgins
1B N. Zauchin
2B W. Goodman
SS W. Klaus
3B G. Hatton
OF J. Jensen
OF J. Piersall
OF T. Williams
C S. White
UT G. Stephens
P F. Sullivan
P W. Nixon
P T. Brewer
P G. Susce
P I. Delock
RP L. Kiely
RP T. Hurd

BOS 1956 A

M M. Higgins
1B J. Vernon
2B W. Goodman
SS D. Buddin
3B W. Klaus
OF J. Piersall
OF J. Jensen
OF T. Williams
C S. White
UT R. Gernert
UT G. Stephens
P T. Brewer
P F. Sullivan
P W. Nixon
P D. Sisler
P M. Parnell
RP I. Delock
RP T. Hurd

BOS 1957 A

M M. Higgins
1B R. Gernert
2B T. Lepcio
SS W. Klaus
3B F. Malzone
OF J. Piersall
OF J. Jensen
OF T. Williams
C S. White
UT G. Stephens
UT J. Vernon
P F. Sullivan
P T. Brewer
P W. Nixon
P J. Fornieles
P D. Sisler
RP I. Delock

BOS 1958 A

M M. Higgins
1B R. Gernert
2B J. Runnels
SS D. Buddin
3B F. Malzone
OF J. Jensen
OF J. Piersall
OF T. Williams
C S. White
UT G. Stephens
P T. Brewer
P F. Sullivan
P I. Delock
P D. Sisler
P J. Fornieles
RP M. Wall
RP L. Kiely

BOS 1959 A

M M. Higgins
M P. York
M W. Jurges
1B R. Gernert
2B J. Runnels
SS D. Buddin
3B F. Malzone
OF J. Jensen
OF G. Geiger
OF G. Stephens
C S. White
UT R. Keough
UT V. Wertz
UT T. Williams
P T. Brewer
P J. Casale
P F. Sullivan
P Monbouquette
P I. Delock
RP J. Fornieles
RP L. Kiely

BOS 1960 A

M W. Jurges
M D. Baker
M M. Higgins
1B V. Wertz
2B J. Runnels
SS D. Buddin
3B F. Malzone
OF W. Tasby
OF L. Clinton
OF T. Williams
C R. Nixon
UT E. Green
P Monbouquette
P T. Brewer
P F. Sullivan
P I. Delock
P B. Muffett
RP J. Fornieles
RP T. Sturdivant

BOS 1961 A

M M. Higgins
1B J. Runnels
2B C. Schilling
SS D. Buddin
3B F. Malzone
OF C. Yastrzemski
OF G. Geiger
OF J. Jensen
C J. Pagliaroni
P Monbouquette
P D. Conley
P D. Schwall
P I. Delock
P E. Stallard
RP J. Fornieles
RP B. Muffett

BOS 1962 A

M M. Higgins
1B J. Runnels
2B C. Schilling
SS E. Bressoud
3B F. Malzone
OF C. Yastrzemski
OF G. Geiger
OF C. Hardy
C J. Pagliaroni
UT L. Clinton
P D. Conley
P Monbouquette
P R. Wilson
P D. Schwall
RP R. Radatz
RP J. Fornieles

BOS 1963 A

M J. Pesky
1B R. Stuart
2B C. Schilling
SS E. Bressoud
3B F. Malzone
OF C. Yastrzemski
OF L. Clinton
OF G. Geiger
C J. Tillman
UT R. Mejias
UT R. Nixon
P Monbouquette
P R. Wilson
P D. Morehead
P R. Heffner
RP J. Lamabe
RP R. Radatz

BOS 1964 A

M J. Pesky
M W. Herman
1B R. Stuart
2B J. Jones
SS E. Bressoud
3B F. Malzone
OF C. Yastrzemski
OF J. Thomas
OF A. Conigliaro
C J. Tillman
UT F. Mantilla
P Monbouquette
P R. Wilson
P J. Lamabe
P D. Morehead
RP R. Heffner
RP R. Radatz

BOS 1965 A

M W. Herman
1B J. Thomas
2B F. Mantilla
SS A. Petrocelli
3B F. Malzone
OF A. Conigliaro
OF C. Yastrzemski
OF L. Green
C J. Tillman
UT E. Bressoud
UT J. Jones
P R. Wilson
P Monbouquette
P D. Morehead
P J. Lonborg
P D. Bennett
RP R. Radatz
RP A. Earley

BOS 1966 A

M W. Herman
M J. Runnels
1B G. Scott
2B G. Smith
SS A. Petrocelli
3B J. Foy
OF C. Yastrzemski
OF A. Conigliaro
OF D. Demeter
C M. Ryan
UT J. Jones
P J. Lonborg
P J. Santiago
P D. Brandon
P A. Stange
P R. Wilson
RP R. Stigman
RP D. McMahon

BOS 1967 A

M R. Williams
1B G. Scott
2B M. Andrews
SS A. Petrocelli
3B J. Foy
OF C. Yastrzemski
OF C. Smith
OF A. Conigliaro
C M. Ryan
UT J. Tartabull
P J. Lonborg
P A. Stange
P G. Bell
P D. Brandon
RP J. Santiago
RP J. Wyatt

BOS 1968 A

M R. Williams
1B G. Scott
2B M. Andrews
SS A. Petrocelli
3B J. Foy
OF C. Yastrzemski
OF C. Smith
OF K. Harrelson
C J. Gibson
UT J. Jones
P R. Culp
P G. Bell
P R. Ellsworth
P J. Santiago
P J. Lonborg
RP A. Stange
RP A. Lyle

BOS 1969 A

M R. Williams
M E. Popowski
1B J. Jones
2B M. Andrews
SS A. Petrocelli
3B G. Scott
OF C. Yastrzemski
OF C. Smith
OF A. Conigliaro
C J. Gibson
UT J. Lahoud
UT S. O'Brien
P R. Culp
P M. Nagy
P W. Siebert
P J. Lonborg
P A. Stange
RP V. Romo
RP A. Lyle

BOS 1970 A

M E. Kasko
1B C. Yastrzemski
2B M. Andrews
SS A. Petrocelli
3B G. Scott
OF A. Conigliaro
OF C. Smith
OF W. Conigliaro
C G. Moses
P R. Culp
P W. Siebert
P G. Peters
P K. Brett
P M. Nagy
RP V. Romo
RP A. Lyle

BOS 1971 A

M E. Kasko
1B G. Scott
2B D. Griffin
SS L. Aparicio
3B A. Petrocelli
OF C. Smith
OF C. Yastrzemski
OF W. Conigliaro
C D. Josephson
UT J. Lahoud

P R. Culp
P W. Siebert
P G. Peters
P J. Lonborg
RP W. Lee
RP B. Bolin

BOS 1972 A

M E. Kasko
1B D. Cater
2B D. Griffin
SS L. Aparicio
3B A. Petrocelli
OF T. Harper
OF C. Smith
OF C. Yastrzemski
C C. Fisk
UT B. Oglivie
P M. Pattin
P W. Siebert
P L. Tiant
P J. Curtis
P L. McGlothen
RP G. Peters
RP W. Lee

BOS 1973 A

M E. Kasko
M E. Popowski
1B C. Yastrzemski
2B D. Griffin
SS L. Aparicio
3B A. Petrocelli
OF T. Harper
OF R. Miller
OF D. Evans
C C. Fisk
DH O. Cepeda
UT C. Smith
P W. Lee
P L. Tiant
P J. Curtis
P M. Pattin
P R. Moret
RP B. Bolin

BOS 1974 A

M D. Johnson
1B C. Yastrzemski
2B D. Griffin
SS M. Guerrero
3B A. Petrocelli
OF D. Evans
OF R. Miller
OF J. Beniquez
C R. Montgomery
DH T. Harper
UT R. Burleson
UT B. Carbo
UT C. Cooper
UT R. McAuliffe
P L. Tiant
P W. Lee
P R. Cleveland
P R. Drago
P R. Moret
RP D. Segui

BOS 1975 A

M D. Johnson
1B C. Yastrzemski
2B D. Griffin
SS R. Burleson
3B A. Petrocelli
OF F. Lynn
OF D. Evans
OF J. Rice
C C. Fisk
DH C. Cooper
UT B. Carbo
P L. Tiant
P W. Lee
P R. Wise
P R. Cleveland
P R. Moret
RP R. Drago
RP D. Segui

BOS 1976 A

M D. Johnson
M D. Zimmer
1B C. Yastrzemski
2B R. Doyle
SS R. Burleson
3B C. Hobson
OF D. Evans
OF F. Lynn
OF J. Rice
C C. Fisk
DH C. Cooper
UT R. Miller
P L. Tiant
P R. Wise
P F. Jenkins
P R. Cleveland
P R. Pole
RP J. Willoughby
RP T. Murphy

BOS 1977 A

M D. Zimmer
1B G. Scott
2B R. Doyle
SS R. Burleson
3B C. Hobson
OF C. Yastrzemski
OF F. Lynn
OF R. Miller
C C. Fisk
DH J. Rice
P F. Jenkins
P R. Cleveland
P L. Tiant
P R. Stanley
P R. Wise
RP W. Campbell
RP J. Willoughby

BOS 1978 A

M D. Zimmer
1B G. Scott
2B G. Remy
SS R. Burleson
3B C. Hobson
OF F. Lynn
OF D. Evans
OF C. Yastrzemski
C C. Fisk
DH J. Rice
P D. Eckersley
P M. Torrez
P L. Tiant
P W. Lee
P J. Wright
RP R. Stanley
RP R. Drago

BOS 1979 A

M D. Zimmer
1B R. Watson
2B G. Remy
SS R. Burleson
3B C. Hobson
OF D. Evans
OF F. Lynn
OF J. Rice
C G. Allenson
DH C. Yastrzemski
P M. Torrez
P D. Eckersley
P R. Stanley
P S. Renko
P C. Rainey
RP R. Drago
RP T. Burgmeier

BOS 1980 A

M D. Zimmer
M J. Pesky
1B A. Perez
2B D. Stapleton
SS R. Burleson
3B G. Hoffman
OF D. Evans
OF F. Lynn
OF J. Rice
C C. Fisk
DH C. Yastrzemski
P M. Torrez
P D. Eckersley
P R. Stanley
P S. Renko
P R. Drago
RP T. Burgmeier

BOS 1981 A

M R. Houk
1B A. Perez
2B G. Remy
SS G. Hoffman
3B C. Lansford
OF J. Rice
OF D. Evans
OF R. Miller
C R. Gedman
DH C. Yastrzemski
UT D. Stapleton
P D. Eckersley
P F. Tanana
P M. Torrez
P J. Tudor
P R. Ojeda
RP R. Stanley
RP M. Clear

BOS 1982 A

M R. Houk
1B D. Stapleton
2B G. Remy
SS G. Hoffman
3B C. Lansford
OF D. Evans
OF J. Rice
OF R. Miller
C G. Allenson
DH C. Yastrzemski
UT W. Boggs
P D. Eckersley
P J. Tudor
P M. Torrez
P R. Stanley
P C. Rainey
RP M. Clear
RP T. Burgmeier

BOS 1983 A

M R. Houk
1B D. Stapleton
2B G. Remy
SS G. Hoffman
3B W. Boggs
OF J. Rice
OF A. Armas
OF D. Evans
C G. Allenson
DH C. Yastrzemski
UT R. Miller
UT T. Nichols
P J. Tudor
P B. Hurst
P D. Eckersley
P R. Ojeda
P M. Brown
RP R. Stanley
RP M. Clear

BOS 1984 A

M R. Houk
1B W. Buckner
2B M. Barrett
SS J. Gutierrez
3B W. Boggs
OF D. Evans
OF J. Rice
OF A. Armas
C R. Gedman
DH M. Easler
P B. Hurst
P R. Ojeda
P D. Boyd
P A. Nipper
P W. Clemens
RP R. Stanley
RP M. Clear

BOS 1985 A

M J. McNamara
1B W. Buckner
2B M. Barrett
SS J. Gutierrez
3B W. Boggs
OF D. Evans
OF J. Rice
OF S. Lyons
C R. Gedman
DH M. Easler
UT A. Armas
P D. Boyd
P B. Hurst
P A. Nipper
P R. Ojeda
RP S. Crawford
RP R. Stanley

BOS 1986 A

M J. McNamara
1B W. Buckner
2B M. Barrett
SS E. Romero
3B W. Boggs
OF J. Rice
OF D. Evans
OF A. Armas
C R. Gedman
DH D. Baylor
P W. Clemens
P D. Boyd
P B. Hurst
P A. Nipper
P G. Seaver
RP R. Stanley
RP S. Stewart

BOS 1987 A

M J. McNamara
1B D. Evans
2B M. Barrett
SS S. Owen
3B W. Boggs
OF E. Burks
OF J. Rice
OF M. Greenwell
C M. Sullivan
DH D. Baylor
P W. Clemens
P B. Hurst
P A. Nipper
P R. Stanley
P J. Sellers
RP W. Gardner
RP C. Schiraldi

BOS 1988 A

M J. McNamara
M J. Morgan
1B T. Benzinger
2B M. Barrett
SS J. Reed
3B W. Boggs
OF M. Greenwell
OF E. Burks
OF D. Evans
C R. Gedman
DH J. Rice
P W. Clemens
P B. Hurst
P W. Gardner
P D. Boyd
P B. Smithson
RP R. Stanley
RP L. Smith

Brooklyn

ECK n 1872
Eckfords
ATL n 1872-1875
Atlantics
BRO a 1884-1889
BB a 1890
Combined with Baltimore
BRO P 1890
BRO F 1914-1915
BRO N 1890-1957
Moved to Los Angeles

ECK 1872 n

M J. Clinton
M J. Wood
1B A. Allison
2B J. Nelson
SS J. Snyder
3B F. Fleet
OF A. Gedney
OF D. Patterson
OF J. Snyder
C D. Allison
UT J. Clinton
P A. Martin
P G. Zettlein
P J. McDermott
P Malone

ATL 1872 n

M R. Ferguson
1B H. Dehlman
2B J. Hall
SS J. Burdock
3B R. Ferguson
OF J. Remsen
OF A. Thake
OF D. McDonald
C T. Barlow
P J. Britt

ATL 1873 n

M R. Ferguson
1B H. Dehlman
2B J. Burdock
SS R. Pearce
3B R. Ferguson
OF C. Pabor
OF J. Remsen
OF W. Boyd
C T. Barlow
P J. Britt

ATL 1874 n

M R. Ferguson
1B H. Dehlman
2B J. Farrow
SS R. Pearce
3B R. Ferguson
OF J. Chapman
OF E. Booth
OF R. Clack
C J. Knowdell
P T. Bond

ATL 1875 n

M C. Pabor
M W. Boyd
1B F. Crane
2B W. Boyd
SS H. Kessler
3B A. Nichols
OF C. Pabor
OF R. Clack
OF P. McGee
C J. Knowdell
P J. Cassidy
P J. Clinton
P O'Neill

BRO 1884 a

M G. Taylor
1B C. Householder
2B W. Greenwood
SS W. Geer
3B F. Warner
OF J. Cassidy
OF J. Remsen
OF O. Walker
C J. Corcoran
P W. Terry
P S. Kimber
P J. Conway

BRO 1885 a

M C. Hackett
M C. Byrne
1B W. Phillips
2B G. Pinkney
SS G. Smith
3B W. McClellan
OF C. Swartwood
OF P. Hotaling
OF J. Cassidy
C J. Hayes
UT W. Terry
P H. Porter
P J. Harkins

BRO 1886 a

M C. Byrne
1B W. Phillips
2B W. McClellan
SS G. Smith
3B G. Pinkney
OF C. Swartwood
OF E. Burch
OF J. McTamany
C J. Peoples
P H. Porter
P J. Harkins
P W. Terry
P J. Henderson
P S. Toole

BRO 1887 a

M C. Byrne
1B W. Phillips
2B W. McClellan
SS G. Smith
3B G. Pinkney
OF J. McTamany
OF C. Swartwood
OF E. Greer
C J. Peoples
UT W. Terry
P H. Porter
P J. Harkins
P S. Toole
P J. Henderson

BRO 1888 a

M W. McGunnigle
1B D. Orr
2B J. Burdock
SS G. Smith
3B G. Pinkney
OF W. O'Brien
OF P. Radford
OF D. Foutz
C A. Bushong
UT R. Caruthers
P M. Hughes
P W. Terry
P A. Mays

BRO 1889 a

M W. McGunnigle
1B D. Foutz
2B G. Collins
SS G. Smith
3B G. Pinkney
OF J. Corkhill
OF W. O'Brien
OF T. Burns
C J. Visner
P R. Caruthers
P W. Terry
P T. Lovett
P M. Hughes

BB 1890 a

M J. Kennedy
M W. Barnie
1B W. O'Brien
2B J. Gerhardt
SS J. Nelson
3B J. Davis
OF J. Peltz
OF H. Simon
OF E. Daily
C J. Toy
P E. Daily
P C. McCullough
P M. Mattimore
P L. German
P J. McMahon
P C. Murphy

BRO 1890 P

M J. Ward
1B D. Orr
2B L. Bierbauer
SS J. Ward
3B W. Joyce
OF J. Seery
OF J. McGeachey
OF G. Andrews
C T. Kinslow
UT G. Van Haltren
P A. Weyhing
P J. Sowders
P C. Murphy
P G. Hemming

BRO 1914 F

M W. Bradley
1B R. Myers
2B A. Hofman
SS E. Gagnier
3B G. Wisterzil
OF L. Evans
OF A. Shaw
OF C. Cooper
C G. Land
UT G. Anderson
P T. Seaton
P E. Lafitte
P J. Finneran

BRO 1915 F

M L. Magee
M J. Ganzel
1B R. Myers
2B L. Magee
SS F. Smith
3B A. Halt
OF B. Kauff
OF G. Anderson
OF C. Cooper
C G. Land
P J. Finneran
P D. Marion
P T. Seaton
P J. Bluejacket
P W. Upham

BRO 1890 N

M W. McGunnigle
1B D. Foutz
2B G. Collins
SS G. Smith
3B G. Pinkney
OF T. Burns
OF W. O'Brien
OF W. Terry
C T. Daly
P T. Lovett

BRO 1891 N

M J. Ward
1B D. Foutz
2B G. Collins
SS J. Ward
3B G. Pinkney
OF M. Griffin
OF T. Burns
OF W. O'Brien
C T. Kinslow
P T. Lovett
P R. Caruthers
P G. Hemming
P W. Terry
P A. Inks

BRO 1892 N

M J. Ward
1B D. Brouthers
2B J. Ward
SS T. Corcoran
3B W. Joyce
OF T. Burns
OF M. Griffin
OF W. O'Brien
C C. Daily
UT T. Daly
P G. Haddock
P E. Stein
P W. Hart
P W. Kennedy

BRO 1893 N

M D. Foutz
1B D. Brouthers
2B T. Daly
SS T. Corcoran
3B G. Shoch
OF T. Burns
OF M. Griffin
OF D. Foutz
C T. Kinslow
P W. Kennedy
P E. Stein
P G. Haddock
P D. Daub
P T. Lovett

BRO 1894 N

M D. Foutz
1B D. Foutz
2B T. Daly
SS T. Corcoran
3B W. Shindle
OF T. Burns
OF G. Treadway
OF M. Griffin
C T. Kinslow
P W. Kennedy
P E. Stein
P D. Daub
P H. Gastright

BRO 1895 N

M D. Foutz
1B G. LaChance
2B T. Daly
SS T. Corcoran
3B W. Shindle
OF M. Griffin
OF J. Anderson
OF G. Treadway
C J. Grim
P W. Kennedy
P E. Stein
P A. Gumbert
P D. Daub
P C. Lucid

BRO 1896 N

M D. Foutz
1B G. LaChance
2B T. Daly
SS T. Corcoran
3B W. Shindle
OF M. Griffin
OF T. McCarthy
OF F. Jones
C J. Grim
UT J. Anderson
P W. Kennedy
P H. Payne
P D. Daub
P B. Abbey
P E. Stein

BRO 1897 N

M W. Barnie
1B G. LaChance
2B G. Shoch
SS G. Smith
3B W. Shindle
OF F. Jones
OF M. Griffin
OF J. Anderson
C J. Grim

P W. Kennedy
P H. Payne
P J. Dunn
P C. Fisher
P D. Daub

BRO 1898 N

M W. Barnie
M M. Griffin
M C. Ebbets
1B G. LaChance
2B W. Hallman
SS G. Magoon
3B W. Shindle
OF F. Jones
OF M. Griffin
OF S. Sheckard
C J. Ryan
P W. Kennedy
P J. Dunn
P J. Yeager
P R. Miller
P J. McKenna

BRO 1899 N

M E. Hanlon
1B D. McGann
2B T. Daly
SS W. Dahlen
3B J. Casey
OF J. Kelley
OF W. Keeler
OF F. Jones
C C. Farrell
UT J. Anderson
P J. Dunn
P J. Hughes
P W. Kennedy
P J. McJames

BRO 1900 N

M E. Hanlon
1B H. Jennings
2B T. Daly
SS W. Dahlen
3B L. Cross
OF W. Keeler
OF F. Jones
OF S. Sheckard
C C. Farrell
UT J. Kelley
P J. McGinnity
P W. Kennedy
P F. Kitson
P H. Howell

BRO 1901 N

M E. Hanlon
1B J. Kelley
2B T. Daly
SS W. Dahlen
3B C. Irwin
OF W. Keeler
OF S. Sheckard
OF T. McCreery
C J. McGuire
P W. Donovan
P F. Kitson
P J. Hughes
P E. Newton
P J. McJames

BRO 1902 N

M E. Hanlon
1B T. McCreery
2B T. Flood
SS W. Dahlen
3B C. Irwin
OF P. Dolan
OF W. Keeler
OF S. Sheckard
C H. Hearne
P W. Donovan
P E. Newton
P F. Kitson
P J. Hughes
P R. Evans

BRO 1903 N

M E. Hanlon
1B J. Doyle
2B T. Flood
SS W. Dahlen
3B S. Strang
OF S. Sheckard
OF J. Dobbs
OF W. McCredie
C L. Ritter
P O. Jones
P H. Schmidt

P V. Garvin
P R. Evans
P W. Reidy

BRO 1904 N

M E. Hanlon
1B F. Dillon
2B A. Jordan
SS C. Babb
3B M. McCormick
OF H. Lumley
OF S. Sheckard
OF J. Dobbs
C W. Bergen
UT H. Gessler
P O. Jones
P J. Cronin
P V. Garvin
P E. Poole
P W. Scanlan

BRO 1905 N

M E. Hanlon
1B H. Gessler
2B C. Malay
SS P. Lewis
3B E. Batch
OF S. Sheckard
OF H. Lumley
OF J. Dobbs
C L. Ritter
P J. McIntire
P W. Scanlan
P E. Stricklett
P M. Eason
P O. Jones

BRO 1906 N

M P. Donovan
1B T. Jordan
2B C. Alperman
SS P. Lewis
3B J. Casey
OF W. Maloney
OF H. Lumley
OF J. McCarthy
C W. Bergen
UT J. Hummel
P E. Stricklett
P W. Scanlan
P J. McIntire
P M. Eason
P J. Pastorius

BRO 1907 N

M P. Donovan
1B T. Jordan
2B C. Alperman
SS P. Lewis
3B J. Casey
OF W. Maloney
OF H. Lumley
OF E. Batch
C L. Ritter
UT J. Hummel
P G. Rucker
P G. Bell
P E. Stricklett
P J. Pastorius
P J. McIntire

BRO 1908 N

M P. Donovan
1B T. Jordan
2B H. Pattee
SS P. Lewis
3B T. Sheehan
OF H. Lumley
OF A. Burch
OF W. Maloney
C W. Bergen
UT J. Hummel
P G. Rucker
P I. Wilhelm
P J. McIntire
P J. Pastorius
P G. Bell

BRO 1909 N

M H. Lumley
1B T. Jordan
2B C. Alperman
SS T. McMillan
3B J. Lennox
OF A. Burch
OF W. Clement
OF H. Lumley
C W. Bergen
UT J. Hummel
P G. Rucker

P G. Bell
P J. McIntire
P I. Wilhelm
P W. Scanlan

BRO 1910 N

M W. Dahlen
1B J. Daubert
2B J. Hummel
SS A. Smith
3B J. Lennox
OF Z. Wheat
OF W. Davidson
OF T. Dalton
C W. Bergen
UT A. Burch
P G. Rucker
P G. Bell
P E. Barger
P W. Scanlan
P E. Knetzer
RP F. Dessau

BRO 1911 N

M W. Dahlen
1B J. Daubert
2B J. Hummel
SS A. Tooley
3B E. Zimmerman
OF R. Coulson
OF Z. Wheat
OF W. Davidson
C W. Bergen
P G. Rucker
P E. Barger
P E. Knetzer
P W. Schardt
P W. Scanlan

BRO 1912 N

M W. Dahlen
1B J. Daubert
2B G. Cutshaw
SS A. Tooley
3B J. Smith
OF J. Moran
OF Z. Wheat
OF H. Northen
C L. Miller
UT J. Hummel
P G. Rucker
P D. Ragan
P E. Yingling
P W. Stack
P E. Knetzer

BRO 1913 N

M W. Dahlen
1B J. Daubert
2B G. Cutshaw
SS R. Fisher
3B J. Smith
OF Z. Wheat
OF J. Moran
OF C. Stengel
C L. Miller
P D. Ragan
P G. Rucker
P F. Allen
P C. Curtis
P E. Yingling

BRO 1914 N

M W. Robinson
1B J. Daubert
2B G. Cutshaw
SS R. Egan
3B J. Smith
OF Z. Wheat
OF C. Stengel
OF T. Dalton
C G. McCarty
P E. Pfeffer
P E. Reulbach
P D. Ragan
P R. Aitchison
P F. Allen

BRO 1915 N

M W. Robinson
1B J. Daubert
2B G. Cutshaw
SS O. O'Mara
3B G. Getz
OF H. Myers
OF Z. Wheat
OF C. Stengel
C L. Miller
P E. Pfeffer
P W. Dell

P J. Coombs
P S. Smith
P E. Appleton

BRO 1916 N

M W. Robinson
1B J. Daubert
2B G. Cutshaw
SS I. Olson
3B H. Mowrey
OF Z. Wheat
OF C. Stengel
OF H. Myers
C J. Meyers
UT J. Johnston
P E. Pfeffer
P L. Cheney
P S. Smith
P R. Marquard
P J. Coombs

BRO 1917 N

M W. Robinson
1B J. Daubert
2B G. Cutshaw
SS I. Olson
3B H. Mowrey
OF C. Stengel
OF D. Hickman
OF Z. Wheat
C L. Miller
UT J. Johnston
UT H. Myers
P E. Pfeffer
P L. Cadore
P R. Marquard
P S. Smith
P L. Cheney

BRO 1918 N

M W. Robinson
1B J. Daubert
2B M. Doolan
SS I. Olson
3B O. O'Mara
OF H. Myers
OF Z. Wheat
OF J. Johnston
C L. Miller
P B. Grimes
P R. Marquard
P L. Cheney
P J. Coombs
P P. Robertson

BRO 1919 N

M W. Robinson
1B E. Konetchy
2B J. Johnston
SS I. Olson
3B L. Malone
OF Z. Wheat
OF H. Myers
OF T. Griffith
C E. Krueger
P E. Pfeffer
P L. Cadore
P A. Mamaux
P B. Grimes
P S. Smith

BRO 1920 N

M W. Robinson
1B E. Konetchy
2B P. Kilduff
SS I. Olson
3B J. Johnston
OF H. Myers
OF Z. Wheat
OF T. Griffith
C L. Miller
UT B. Neis
P B. Grimes
P L. Cadore
P E. Pfeffer
P A. Mamaux
P R. Marquard

BRO 1921 N

M W. Robinson
1B R. Schmandt
2B P. Kilduff
SS I. Olson
3B J. Johnston
OF Z. Wheat
OF H. Myers
OF T. Griffith
C L. Miller
UT B. Neis
P B. Grimes

P L. Cadore
P W. Ruether
P C. Mitchell
P S. Smith

BRO 1922 N

M W. Robinson
1B R. Schmandt
2B I. Olson
SS J. Johnston
3B A. High
OF Z. Wheat
OF H. Myers
OF T. Griffith
C J. DeBerry
UT B. Griffith
P W. Ruether
P B. Grimes
P C. Vance
P L. Cadore
P S. Smith
RP A. Mamaux

BRO 1923 N

M W. Robinson
1B J. Fournier
2B J. Johnston
SS M. Berg
3B A. High
OF T. Griffith
OF B. Neis
OF A. Bailey
C J. Taylor
UT Z. Wheat
P B. Grimes
P C. Vance
P W. Ruether
P L. Dickerman
P F. Henry
RP A. Decatur

BRO 1924 N

M W. Robinson
1B J. Fournier
2B A. High
SS J. Mitchell
3B M. Stock
OF Z. Wheat
OF T. Griffith
OF E. Brown
C J. Taylor
P B. Grimes
P C. Vance
P W. Ruether
P W. Doak
P A. Decatur

BRO 1925 N

M W. Robinson
1B J. Fournier
2B M. Stock
SS J. Mitchell
3B J. Johnston
OF E. Brown
OF Z. Wheat
OF E. Cox
C J. Taylor
P C. Vance
P B. Grimes
P W. Ehrhardt
P E. Osborne
P J. Petty
RP W. Hubbell

BRO 1926 N

M W. Robinson
1B F. Herman
2B W. Fewster
SS J. Butler
3B W. Marriott
OF A. Felix
OF E. Cox
OF Z. Wheat
C G. O'Neil
UT M. Jacobson
P J. Petty
P B. Grimes
P D. McWeeny
P R. McGraw
P C. Vance
RP W. Ehrhardt

BRO 1927 N

M W. Robinson
1B F. Herman
2B J. Partridge
SS J. Butler
3B R. Barrett
OF M. Carey
OF A. Statz

OF A. Felix
C J. DeBerry
UT H. Hendrick
P C. Vance
P J. Petty
P J. Elliott
P D. McWeeny
P W. Doak
RP W. Ehrhardt
RP W. Clark

BRO 1928 N

M W. Robinson
1B D. Bissonette
2B D. Flowers
SS D. Bancroft
3B H. Hendrick
OF R. Bressler
OF F. Herman
OF M. Carey
C J. DeBerry
P C. Vance
P D. McWeeny
P J. Petty
P W. Clark
P J. Elliott
RP R. Moss
RP W. Ehrhardt

BRO 1929 N

M W. Robinson
1B D. Bissonette
2B G. Moore
SS D. Bancroft
3B W. Gilbert
OF J. Frederick
OF F. Herman
OF R. Bressler
C V. Picinich
UT H. Hendrick
P W. Clark
P C. Vance
P R. Moss
P E. Dudley
P D. McWeeny
RP W. Moore
RP N. Ballou

BRO 1930 N

M W. Robinson
1B D. Bissonette
2B C. Finn
SS F. Wright
3B W. Gilbert
OF F. Herman
OF J. Frederick
OF R. Bressler
C A. Lopez
P C. Vance
P W. Clark
P A. Luque
P J. Elliott
P R. Phelps

BRO 1931 N

M W. Robinson
1B D. Bissonette
2B C. Finn
SS G. Slade
3B W. Gilbert
OF F. Herman
OF J. Frederick
OF F. O'Doul
C A. Lopez
P W. Clark
P C. Vance
P R. Phelps
P H. Thurston
P F. Heimach
RP J. Quinn
RP W. Moore

BRO 1932 N

M M. Carey
1B G. Kelly
2B A. Cuccinello
SS F. Wright
3B J. Stripp
OF F. O'Doul
OF L. Wilson
OF D. Taylor
C A. Lopez
UT J. Frederick
P W. Clark
P V. Mungo
P C. Vance
P F. Heimach
P H. Thurston
RP J. Quinn
RP W. Moore

BRO 1933 N

M M. Carey
1B S. Leslie
2B A. Cuccinello
SS F. Wright
3B J. Stripp
OF J. Frederick
OF D. Taylor
OF L. Wilson
C A. Lopez
P W. Beck
P V. Mungo
P R. Benge
P O. Carroll
P H. Thurston
RP J. Shaute
RP W. Ryan

BRO 1934 N

M C. Stengel
1B S. Leslie
2B A. Cuccinello
SS L. Frey
3B J. Stripp
OF L. Koenecke
OF R. Boyle
OF D. Taylor
C A. Lopez
UT J. Frederick
UT J. Jordan
P V. Mungo
P R. Benge
P E. Leonard
P J. Babich
P J. Zachary
RP O. Carroll
RP W. Beck

BRO 1935 N

M C. Stengel
1B S. Leslie
2B A. Cuccinello
SS L. Frey
3B J. Stripp
OF R. Boyle
OF S. Bordagaray
OF D. Taylor
C A. Lopez
UT J. Bucher
UT J. Jordan
UT L. Koenecke
P V. Mungo
P W. Clark
P G. Earnshaw
P J. Zachary
P J. Babich
RP L. Munns
RP C. Vance

BRO 1936 N

M C. Stengel
1B J. Hassett
2B J. Jordan
SS L. Frey
3B J. Stripp
OF J. Cooney
OF G. Watkins
OF S. Bordagaray
C R. Berres
UT J. Bucher
UT E. Phelps
P V. Mungo
P F. Frankhouse
P E. Brandt
P A. Butcher
P W. Clark
RP G. Jeffcoat
RP T. Baker

BRO 1937 N

M B. Grimes
1B J. Hassett
2B H. Lavagetto
SS E. English
3B J. Stripp
OF H. Manush
OF J. Cooney
OF J. Winsett
C E. Phelps
UT G. Brack
UT J. Bucher
P A. Butcher
P L. Hamlin
P F. Frankhouse
P W. Hoyt
P V. Mungo
RP G. Jeffcoat

BRO 1938 N

M B. Grimes

1B A. Camilli
2B J. Hudson
SS L. Durocher
3B H. Lavagetto
OF E. Koy
OF G. Rosen
OF J. Hassett
C E. Phelps
P L. Hamlin
P F. Fitzsimmons
P F. Pressnell
P V. Tamulis
P W. Posedel

BRO 1939 N

M L. Durocher
1B A. Camilli
2B P. Coscarart
SS L. Durocher
3B H. Lavagetto
OF E. Koy
OF E. Moore
OF A. Parks
C E. Phelps
UT J. Hudson
P H. Hamlin
P H. Casey
P V. Tamulis
P F. Pressnell
P F. Fitzsimmons
RP I. Hutchinson
RP R. Evans

BRO 1940 N

M L. Durocher
1B A. Camilli
2B P. Coscarart
SS H. Reese
3B H. Lavagetto
OF F. Walker
OF J. Medwick
OF J. Vosmik
C E. Phelps
P J. Wyatt
P L. Hamlin
P V. Tamulis
P H. Casey
P J. Carleton
RP F. Pressnell

BRO 1941 N

M L. Durocher
1B A. Camilli
2B W. Herman
SS H. Reese
3B H. Lavagetto
OF F. Walker
OF H. Reiser
OF J. Medwick
C A. Owen
UT J. Wasdell
P W. Higbe
P J. Wyatt
P H. Casey
P C. Davis
P L. Hamlin

BRO 1942 N

M L. Durocher
1B A. Camilli
2B W. Herman
SS H. Reese
3B J. Vaughan
OF J. Medwick
OF H. Reiser
OF F. Walker
C A. Owen
P W. Higbe
P J. Wyatt
P C. Davis
P L. French
P E. Head
RP H. Casey
RP L. Webber

BRO 1943 N

M L. Durocher
1B A. Camilli
2B W. Herman
SS J. Vaughan
3B S. Bordagaray
OF F. Walker
OF A. Galan
OF P. Waner
C A. Owen
P W. Higbe
P J. Wyatt
P E. Head
P C. Davis
P L. Newsom
RP L. Webber

BRO 1944 N

M L. Durocher
1B H. Schultz
2B E. Stanky
SS R. Bragan
3B S. Bordagaray
OF A. Galan
OF F. Walker
OF G. Rosen
C A. Owen
UT L. Olmo
P H. Gregg
P C. Davis
P R. Melton
RP L. Webber

BRO 1945 N

M L. Durocher
1B A. Galan
2B E. Stanky
SS E. Basinski
3B S. Bordagaray
OF F. Walker
OF G. Rosen
OF L. Olmo
C M. Sandlock
P H. Gregg
P V. Lombardi
P C. Davis
P A. Herring
P T. Seats
RP C. King
RP C. Buker

BRO 1946 N

M L. Durocher
1B E. Stevens
2B E. Stanky
SS H. Reese
3B H. Lavagetto
OF F. Walker
OF C. Furillo
OF H. Reiser
C H. Edwards
UT A. Galan
UT D. Whitman
P J. Hatten
P W. Higbe
P V. Lombardi
P H. Behrman
P H. Gregg
RP H. Casey
RP A. Herring

BRO 1947 N

M C. Sukeforth
M B. Shotton
1B J. Robinson
2B E. Stanky
SS H. Reese
3B J. Jorgensen
OF F. Walker
OF C. Furillo
OF H. Reiser
C H. Edwards
P R. Branca
P J. Hatten
P V. Lombardi
P J. Taylor
RP H. Gregg
RP H. Behrman

BRO 1948 N

M L. Durocher
M F. Blades
M B. Shotton
1B G. Hodges
2B J. Robinson
SS H. Reese
3B W. Cox
OF E. Hermanski
OF C. Furillo
OF M. Rackley
C R. Campanella
UT C. Edwards
P R. Barney
P R. Branca
P J. Hatten
P E. Roe
P E. Palica
RP H. Behrman
RP P. Minner

BRO 1949 N

M B. Shotton
1B G. Hodges
2B J. Robinson
SS H. Reese
3B W. Cox
OF E. Snider

OF C. Furillo
OF E. Hermanski
C R. Campanella
P D. Newcombe
P E. Roe
P J. Hatten
P R. Branca
P J. Banta
RP E. Palica
RP P. Minner

BRO 1950 N

M B. Shotton
1B G. Hodges
2B J. Robinson
SS H. Reese
3B W. Cox
OF C. Furillo
OF E. Snider
OF E. Hermanski
C R. Campanella
P D. Newcombe
P E. Roe
P E. Palica
P R. Branca
P D. Bankhead

BRO 1951 N

M C. Dressen
1B G. Hodges
2B J. Robinson
SS H. Reese
3B W. Cox
OF C. Furillo
OF E. Snider
OF A. Pafko
C R. Campanella
P D. Newcombe
P E. Roe
P R. Branca
P C. Erskine
RP C. King
RP C. Podbielan

BRO 1952 N

M C. Dressen
1B G. Hodges
2B J. Robinson
SS H. Reese
3B W. Cox
OF E. Snider
OF A. Pafko
OF C. Furillo
C R. Campanella
UT G. Shuba
P C. Erskine
P W. Loes
P B. Wade
P E. Roe
P C. Van Cuyk
RP J. Black

BRO 1953 N

M C. Dressen
1B G. Hodges
2B J. Gilliam
SS H. Reese
3B W. Cox
OF E. Snider
OF C. Furillo
OF D. Thompson
C R. Campanella
UT J. Robinson
P C. Erskine
P R. Meyer
P W. Loes
P E. Roe
P R. Milliken
RP C. Labine
RP B. Wade

BRO 1954 N

M W. Alston
1B G. Hodges
2B J. Gilliam
SS H. Reese
3B D. Hoak
OF C. Furillo
OF E. Snider
OF J. Robinson
C R. Campanella
P C. Erskine
P R. Meyer
P J. Podres
P W. Loes
P D. Newcombe
RP C. Labine
RP J. Hughes

BRO 1955 N

M W. Alston
1B G. Hodges
2B J. Gilliam
SS H. Reese
3B J. Robinson
OF E. Snider
OF C. Furillo
OF E. Amoros
C R. Campanella
UT D. Hoak
P D. Newcombe
P C. Erskine
P J. Podres
P W. Loes
P K. Spooner
RP C. Labine
RP E. Roebuck

BRO 1956 N

M W. Alston
1B G. Hodges
2B J. Gilliam
SS H. Reese
3B R. Jackson
OF E. Snider
OF C. Furillo
OF E. Amoros
C R. Campanella
UT J. Robinson
P D. Newcombe
P R. Craig
P S. Maglie
P C. Erskine
P D. Drysdale
RP C. Labine
RP E. Roebuck

BRO 1957 N

M W. Alston
1B G. Hodges
2B J. Gilliam
SS C. Neal
3B H. Reese
OF G. Cimoli
OF E. Snider
OF C. Furillo
C R. Campanella
UT E. Amoros
P D. Drysdale
P D. Newcombe
P J. Podres
P D. McDevitt
P R. Craig
RP C. Labine
RP E. Roebuck

Buffalo

BUF N 1879-1885
BUF P 1890
BUF F 1914-1915

BUF 1879 N

M J. Clapp
1B O. Walker
2B C. Fulmer
SS D. Force
3B A. Richardson
OF D. Eggler
OF M. Hornung
OF W. Crowley
C J. Clapp
P J. Galvin

BUF 1880 N

M S. Crane
1B T. Esterbrook
2B D. Force
SS M. Moynahan
3B A. Richardson
OF W. Crowley
OF M. Hornung
OF D. Stearns
C J. Rowe
P J. Galvin
P G. Weidman
P T. Poorman

BUF 1881 N

M J. O'Rourke
1B D. Brouthers
2B D. Force
SS J. Peters
3B J. O'Rourke
OF A. Richardson
OF C. Foley
OF J. White
C J. Rowe

P J. Galvin
P J. Lynch

BUF 1882 N

M J. O'Rourke
1B D. Brouthers
2B A. Richardson
SS D. Force
3B J. White
OF C. Foley
OF C. Rowe
OF J. O'Rourke
C J. Rowe
P J. Galvin
P H. Daily

BUF 1883 N

M J. O'Rourke
1B D. Brouthers
2B A. Richardson
SS D. Force
3B J. White
OF J. O'Rourke
OF J. Lillie
C J. Rowe
P J. Galvin
P G. Derby

BUF 1884 N

M J. O'Rourke
1B D. Brouthers
2B A. Richardson
SS D. Force
3B J. White
OF J. Lillie
OF J. O'Rourke
OF D. Eggler
C J. Rowe
UT G. Myers
P J. Galvin
P W. Serad

BUF 1885 N

M J. Galvin
M J. Chapman
1B D. Brouthers
2B D. Force
SS J. Rowe
3B J. White
OF J. Lillie
OF W. Crowley
OF A. Richardson
C G. Myers
P J. Galvin
P W. Serad
P P. Conway
P P. Wood

BUF 1890 P

M J. Rowe
M J. Faatz
M J. Rowe
1B J. White
2B S. Wise
SS J. Rowe
3B J. Irwin
OF E. Beecher
OF W. Hoy
OF W. Halligan
C C. Mack
P G. Haddock
P E. Cunningham
P G. Keefe
P J. Stafford

BUF 1914 F

M H. Schlafly
1B J. Agler
2B T. Downey
SS W. Louden
3B F. Smith
OF C. Hanford
OF F. Delahanty
OF C. McDonald
C W. Blair
P J. Anderson
P E. Krapp
P R. Ford
P E. Moore
P A. Schulz

BUF 1915 F

M H. Schlafly
M W. Blair
M H. Lord
1B H. Chase
2B W. Louden
SS W. Roach

3B H. Lord
OF T. Dalton
OF A. Engle
OF B. Meyer
C W. Blair
UT A. Hofman
P A. Schulz
P H. Bedient
P J. Anderson
P E. Krapp
P R. Ford
RP R. Marshall

California

CAL A 1965-1988

CAL 1965 A

M W. Rigney
1B V. Power
2B R. Knoop
SS J. Fregosi
3B P. Schaal
OF J. Cardenal
OF W. Smith
OF A. Pearson
C R. Rodgers
UT J. Adcock
P F. Newman
P W. Chance
P M. Lopez
P G. Brunet
P B. May
RP R. Lee
RP A. Gatewood

CAL 1966 A

M W. Rigney
1B N. Siebern
2B R. Knoop
SS J. Fregosi
3B P. Schaal
OF J. Cardenal
OF E. Kirkpatrick
OF F. Reichardt
C R. Rodgers
UT T. Satriano
P W. Chance
P G. Brunet
P M. Lopez
P F. Newman
RP J. Sanford
RP R. Lee

CAL 1967 A

M W. Rigney
1B D. Mincher
2B R. Knoop
SS J. Fregosi
3B P. Schaal
OF F. Reichardt
OF J. Hall
OF J. Cardenal
C R. Rodgers
P G. Brunet
P J. McGlothlin
P R. Clark
P J. Hamilton
RP M. Rojas
RP W. Kelso

CAL 1968 A

M W. Rigney
1B D. Mincher
2B R. Knoop
SS J. Fregosi
3B A. Rodriguez
OF F. Reichardt
OF R. Repoz
OF V. Davalillo
C R. Rodgers
UT C. Hinton
UT T. Satriano
P G. Brunet
P J. McGlothlin
P S. Ellis
P C. Wright
P T. Murphy
RP M. Pattin
RP J. Messersmith

CAL 1969 A

M W. Rigney
M H. Phillips
1B J. Spencer
2B S. Alomar
SS J. Fregosi
3B A. Rodriguez
OF J. Johnstone
OF F. Reichardt

OF W. Voss
C J. Azcue
UT R. Repoz
P J. Messersmith
P T. Murphy
P J. McGlothlin
P R. May
P G. Brunet
RP E. Fisher
RP K. Tatum

CAL 1970 A

M H. Phillips
1B J. Spencer
2B S. Alomar
SS J. Fregosi
3B K. McMullen
OF A. Johnson
OF R. Repoz
OF J. Johnstone
C J. Azcue
P C. Wright
P T. Murphy
P R. May
P J. Messersmith
RP E. Fisher
RP K. Tatum

CAL 1971 A

M H. Phillips
1B J. Spencer
2B S. Alomar
SS J. Fregosi
3B K. McMullen
OF A. Berry
OF R. Repoz
OF A. Gonzalez
C J. Stephenson
P C. Wright
P J. Messersmith
P T. Murphy
P R. May
RP E. Fisher
RP L. Allen

CAL 1972 A

M D. Rice
1B R. Oliver
2B S. Alomar
SS L. Cardenas
3B K. McMullen
OF V. Pinson
OF L. Stanton
OF A. Berry
C A. Kusnyer
P L. Ryan
P C. Wright
P R. May
P J. Messersmith
P R. Clark
RP L. Allen
RP E. Fisher

CAL 1973 A

M B. Winkles
1B M. Epstein
2B S. Alomar
SS R. Meoli
3B A. Gallagher
OF A. Berry
OF V. Pinson
OF L. Stanton
C J. Torborg
DH F. Robinson
UT T. McCraw
UT R. Oliver
P L. Ryan
P W. Singer
P C. Wright
P R. May
RP S. Barber
RP D. Sells

CAL 1974 A

M B. Winkles
M D. Herzog
M R. Williams
1B J. Doherty
2B D. Doyle
SS D. Chalk
3B P. Schaal
OF J. Rivers
OF L. Stanton
OF J. Lahoud
C E. Rodriguez
DH F. Robinson
UT R. Oliver
UT R. Valentine
P L. Ryan
P F. Tanana
P A. Hassler

P R. Lange
P W. Singer
RP C. Lockwood

CAL 1975 A
M R. Williams
1B B. Bochte
2B G. Remy
SS M. Miley
3B D. Chalk
OF J. Rivers
OF L. Stanton
OF M. Nettles
C E. Rodriguez
DH T. Harper
P F. Tanana
P E. Figueroa
P L. Ryan
P W. Singer
P A. Hassler
RP D. Kirkwood
RP R. Scott

CAL 1976 A
M R. Williams
M N. Sherry
1B B. Bochte
2B G. Remy
SS D. Chalk
3B B. Jackson
OF R. Torres
OF B. Bonds
OF D. Collins
C A. Etchebarren
DH H. Davis
UT W. Melton
P F. Tanana
P L. Ryan
P G. Ross
P P. Hartzell
P D. Kirkwood
RP R. Drago

CAL 1977 A
M N. Sherry
M D. Garcia
1B T. Solaita
2B G. Remy
SS S. Mulliniks
3B D. Chalk
OF B. Bonds
OF G. Flores
OF J. Rudi
C T. Humphrey
DH D. Baylor
UT R. Jackson
P L. Ryan
P F. Tanana
P P. Hartzell
P K. Brett
P W. Simpson
RP D. Miller
RP D. LaRoche

CAL 1978 A
M D. Garcia
M J. Fregosi
1B R. Fairly
2B R. Grich
SS D. Chalk
3B C. Lansford
OF L. Bostock
OF R. Miller
OF J. Rudi
C B. Downing
DH D. Baylor
UT R. Jackson
P F. Tanana
P L. Ryan
P R. Knapp
P D. Aase
P K. Brett
RP P. Hartzell
RP D. LaRoche

CAL 1979 A
M J. Fregosi
1B R. Carew
2B R. Grich
SS D. Campaneris
3B C. Lansford
OF D. Ford
OF R. Miller
OF D. Baylor
C B. Downing
DH W. Aikens
P C. Frost
P L. Ryan
P J. Barr
P D. Aase
P R. Knapp

RP M. Clear
RP D. LaRoche

CAL 1980 A
M J. Fregosi
1B R. Carew
2B R. Grich
SS F. Patek
3B C. Lansford
OF R. Miller
OF L. Harlow
OF J. Rudi
C T. Donohue
DH J. Thompson
P F. Tanana
P D. Aase
P A. Martinez
P R. Knapp
RP D. LaRoche
RP M. Clear

CAL 1981 A
M J. Fregosi
M G. Mauch
M G. Mauch
1B R. Carew
2B R. Grich
SS R. Burleson
3B C. Hobson
OF D. Ford
OF F. Lynn
OF B. Downing
C N. Ott
DH D. Baylor
P G. Zahn
P K. Forsch
P M. Witt
P S. Renko
RP J. Jefferson
RP A. Hassler

CAL 1982 A
M G. Mauch
1B R. Carew
2B R. Grich
SS T. Foli
3B D. DeCinces
OF B. Downing
OF R. Jackson
OF F. Lynn
C B. Boone
DH D. Baylor
UT J. Beniquez
UT R. Clark
P G. Zahn
P K. Forsch
P M. Witt
P S. Renko
P B. Kison
RP L. Sanchez
RP A. Hassler

CAL 1983 A
M J. McNamara
1B R. Carew
2B R. Grich
SS T. Foli
3B D. DeCinces
OF F. Lynn
OF E. Valentine
OF B. Downing
C B. Boone
DH R. Jackson
UT R. Jackson
UT D. Sconiers
P T. John
P K. Forsch
P G. Zahn
P M. Witt
P B. Kison
RP L. Sanchez
RP J. Curtis

CAL 1984 A
M J. McNamara
1B R. Carew
2B R. Wilfong
SS R. Schofield
3B D. DeCinces
OF F. Lynn
OF G. Pettis
OF B. Downing
C B. Boone
DH R. Jackson
UT J. Beniquez
UT R. Grich
P M. Witt
P R. Romanick
P G. Zahn
P T. John
P J. Slaton

RP D. Corbett
RP L. Sanchez

CAL 1985 A
M G. Mauch
1B R. Carew
2B R. Grich
SS R. Schofield
3B D. DeCinces
OF G. Pettis
OF B. Downing
OF R. Jackson
C R. Boone
DH R. Jones
UT J. Beniquez
P M. Witt
P R. Romanick
P K. McCaskill
P J. Slaton
RP D. Moore
RP S. Cliburn

CAL 1986 A
M G. Mauch
1B W. Joyner
2B R. Wilfong
SS R. Schofield
3B D. DeCinces
OF G. Pettis
OF B. Downing
OF R. Jones
C B. Boone
DH R. Jackson
UT R. Grich
UT J. Hendrick
P M. Witt
P K. McCaskill
P D. Sutton
P R. Romanick
RP D. Corbett
RP D. Moore

CAL 1987 A
M G. Mauch
1B W. Joyner
2B M. McLemore
SS R. Schofield
3B D. DeCinces
OF D. White
OF G. Pettis
OF J. Howell
C B. Boone
DH B. Downing
P M. Witt
P D. Sutton
P W. Fraser
P J. Lazorko
P J. Candelaria
RP D. Buice
RP C. Finley

CAL 1988 A
M O. Rojas
M L. Stubing
1B W. Joyner
2B J. Ray
SS R. Schofield
3B J. Howell
OF C. Davis
OF D. White
OF A. Armas
C B. Boone
DH B. Downing
P M. Witt
P W. Fraser
P C. Finley
P K. McCaskill
P D. Petry
RP S. Cliburn
RP G. Minton

Chicago

CHI n 1871
CHI n 1874-1875
CP U 1884
  Combined with
  Pittsburgh
CHI P 1890
CHI F 1914-1915
CHI A 1901-1988
CHI N 1876-1988

CHI 1871 n
M J. Wood
1B M. McAtee
2B J. Wood
SS E. Duffy
3B E. Pinkham
OF F. Treacey
OF J. Simmons

OF T. Foley
C C. Hodes
UT M. King
P G. Zettlein

CHI 1874 n
M F. Malone
M J. Wood
1B J. Glenn
2B L. Meyerle
SS J. Peters
3B D. Force
OF E. Cuthbert
OF P. Hines
OF F. Treacey
C F. Malone
P G. Zettlein

CHI 1875 n
M J. Wood
1B J. Devlin
2B R. Hugham
SS J. Peters
3B W. White
OF O. Bielaski
OF J. Glenn
OF P. Hines
C W. Hastings
P G. Zettlein
P J. Devlin
P M. Golden

CP 1884 U
M E. Hengle
M J. Battin
M J. Ellick
1B L. Schoeneck
2B E. Hengle
SS S. Matthias
3B C. Householder
OF J. Ellick
OF C. Briggs
OF H. Wheeler
C W. Krieg
P H. Daily
P A. Atkinson
P J. Horan

CHI 1890 P
M C. Comiskey
1B C. Comiskey
2B N. Pfeffer
SS C. Bastian
3B E. Williamson
OF J. O'Neill
OF H. Duffy
OF J. Ryan
C C. Farrell
UT J. Boyle
P M. Baldwin
P C. King
P C. Bartson

CHI 1914 F
M J. Tinker
1B F. Beck
2B J. Farrell
SS J. Tinker
3B R. Zeider
OF A. Wickland
OF E. Zwilling
OF M. Flack
C A. Wilson
P C. Hendrix
P M. Fiske
P E. Lange
P C. Watson
P M. Prendergast

CHI 1915 F
M J. Tinker
1B F. Beck
2B R. Zeider
SS J. Smith
3B H. Fritz
OF E. Zwilling
OF M. Flack
OF L. Mann
C A. Wilson
UT W. Fischer
P G. McConnell
P C. Hendrix
P M. Prendergast
P M. Brown
P D. Black

CHI 1901 A
M C. Griffith

1B W. Isbell
2B S. Mertes
SS F. Shugarts
3B F. Hartman
OF F. Jones
OF H. McFarland
OF W. Hoy
C W. Sullivan
P R. Patterson
P C. Griffith
P J. Callahan
P J. Katoll
P E. Harvey

CHI 1902 A
M C. Griffith
1B W. Isbell
2B T. Daly
SS G. Davis
3B S. Strang
OF F. Jones
OF E. Green
OF S. Mertes
C W. Sullivan
P J. Callahan
P R. Patterson
P W. Piatt
P C. Griffith
P V. Garvin

CHI 1903 A
M J. Callahan
1B W. Isbell
2B G. Magoon
SS L. Tannehill
3B J. Callahan
OF F. Jones
OF E. Green
OF J. Holmes
C J. Slattery
P G. White
P P. Flaherty
P R. Patterson
P F. Owen

CHI 1904 A
M J. Callahan
M F. Jones
1B J. Donahue
2B A. Dundon
SS G. Davis
3B L. Tannehill
OF F. Jones
OF E. Green
OF J. Callahan
C W. Sullivan
UT W. Isbell
P F. Owen
P N. Altrock
P G. White
P F. Smith
P R. Patterson

CHI 1905 A
M F. Jones
1B J. Donahue
2B A. Dundon
SS G. Davis
3B L. Tannehill
OF F. Jones
OF E. Green
OF J. Callahan
C W. Sullivan
P F. Owen
P N. Altrock
P F. Smith
P G. White
P E. Walsh

CHI 1906 A
M F. Jones
1B J. Donahue
2B W. Isbell
SS G. Davis
3B L. Tannehill
OF F. Jones
OF W. Hahn
OF W. O'Neill
C W. Sullivan
P F. Owen
P N. Altrock
P E. Walsh
P G. White
P R. Patterson

CHI 1907 A
M F. Jones
1B J. Donahue
2B W. Isbell
SS G. Davis

3B G. Rohe
OF W. Hahn
OF F. Jones
OF P. Dougherty
C W. Sullivan
P E. Walsh
P F. Smith
P G. White
P N. Altrock
P R. Patterson

CHI 1908 A
M F. Jones
1B J. Donahue
2B G. Davis
SS F. Parent
3B L. Tannehill
OF F. Jones
OF P. Dougherty
OF W. Hahn
C W. Sullivan
UT J. Anderson
P E. Walsh
P F. Smith
P G. White
P F. Owen
P N. Altrock

CHI 1909 A
M W. Sullivan
1B W. Isbell
2B J. Atz
SS F. Parent
3B L. Tannehill
OF P. Dougherty
OF W. Hahn
OF D. Altizer
C W. Sullivan
UT W. Purtell
P F. Smith
P J. Scott
P E. Walsh
P W. Burns

CHI 1910 A
M H. Duffy
1B C. Gandil
2B R. Zeider
SS R. Blackburne
3B W. Purtell
OF P. Dougherty
OF J. Collins
OF P. Meloan
C F. Payne
P E. Walsh
P G. White
P J. Scott
P F. Olmstead
P I. Young

CHI 1911 A
M H. Duffy
1B J. Collins
2B A. McConnell
SS L. Tannehill
3B H. Lord
OF M. McIntyre
OF F. Bodie
OF J. Callahan
C W. Sullivan
P E. Walsh
P J. Scott
P G. White
P F. Lange
P F. Olmstead

CHI 1912 A
M J. Callahan
1B R. Zeider
2B M. Rath
SS G. Weaver
3B H. Lord
OF F. Bodie
OF J. Callahan
OF J. Collins
C W. Kuhn
P E. Walsh
P J. Benz
P G. White
P F. Lange
P E. Cicotte

CHI 1913 A
M J. Callahan
1B H. Chase
2B M. Rath
SS G. Weaver
3B H. Lord
OF J. Collins
OF F. Bodie

OF W. Mattick
C R. Schalk
P E. Russell
P J. Scott
P E. Cicotte
P J. Benz
P G. White

CHI 1914 A
M J. Callahan
1B J. Fournier
2B R. Blackburne
SS G. Weaver
3B J. Breton
OF J. Collins
OF C. Demmitt
OF F. Bodie
C R. Schalk
P J. Benz
P E. Cicotte
P J. Scott
P U. Faber
P E. Russell
RP W. Lathrop

CHI 1915 A
M C. Rowland
1B J. Fournier
2B E. Collins
SS G. Weaver
3B R. Blackburne
OF O. Felsch
OF J. Collins
OF J. Murphy
C R. Schalk
P U. Faber
P J. Scott
P J. Benz
P E. Russell
P E. Cicotte

CHI 1916 A
M C. Rowland
1B J. Fournier
2B E. Collins
SS Z. Terry
3B G. Weaver
OF J. Jackson
OF O. Felsch
OF J. Collins
C R. Schalk
P E. Russell
P C. Williams
P U. Faber
P E. Cicotte
P J. Scott

CHI 1917 A
M C. Rowland
1B C. Gandil
2B E. Collins
SS C. Risberg
3B G. Weaver
OF O. Felsch
OF J. Jackson
OF H. Leibold
C R. Schalk
P E. Cicotte
P U. Faber
P C. Williams
P E. Russell
P D. Danforth

CHI 1918 A
M C. Rowland
1B C. Gandil
2B E. Collins
SS G. Weaver
3B F. McMullin
OF H. Leibold
OF J. Collins
OF J. Murphy
C R. Schalk
UT C. Risberg
P E. Cicotte
P F. Shellenback
P J. Benz
P D. Danforth
P E. Russell

CHI 1919 A
M W. Gleason
1B C. Gandil
2B E. Collins
SS C. Risberg
3B G. Weaver
OF J. Jackson
OF O. Felsch
OF H. Leibold
C R. Schalk

P E. Cicotte
P C. Williams
P R. Kerr
P U. Faber
P G. Lowdermilk
RP D. Danforth

CHI 1920 A
M W. Gleason
1B J. Collins
2B E. Collins
SS C. Risberg
3B G. Weaver
OF J. Jackson
OF O. Felsch
OF H. Leibold
C R. Schalk
P U. Faber
P E. Cicotte
P C. Williams
P R. Kerr
P R. Wilkinson

CHI 1921 A
M W. Gleason
1B E. Sheely
2B E. Collins
SS E. Johnson
3B E. Mulligan
OF B. Falk
OF A. Strunk
OF H. Hooper
C R. Schalk
UT J. Mostil
P U. Faber
P R. Kerr
P R. Wilkinson
P C. Hodge
P D. McWeeny

CHI 1922 A
M W. Gleason
1B E. Sheely
2B E. Collins
SS E. Johnson
3B E. Mulligan
OF H. Hooper
OF B. Falk
OF J. Mostil
C R. Schalk
P U. Faber
P C. Robertson
P G. Leverett
P C. Hodge
P T. Blankenship

CHI 1923 A
M W. Gleason
1B E. Sheely
2B E. Collins
SS H. McClellan
3B W. Kamm
OF J. Mostil
OF H. Hooper
OF B. Falk
C R. Schalk
P C. Robertson
P U. Faber
P M. Cvengros
P T. Blankenship
P G. Leverett

CHI 1924 A
M J. Evers
M E. Walsh
M E. Collins
M J. Evers
1B E. Sheely
2B E. Collins
SS W. Barrett
3B W. Kamm
OF B. Falk
OF H. Hooper
OF J. Mostil
C C. Crouse
UT M. Archdeacon
P H. Thurston
P T. Lyons
P U. Faber
P G. Connally
P T. Blankenship

CHI 1925 A
M E. Collins
1B E. Sheely
2B E. Collins
SS I. Davis
3B W. Kamm
OF J. Mostil
OF B. Falk

OF H. Hooper
C R. Schalk
P T. Lyons
P U. Faber
P T. Blankenship
P H. Thurston
P C. Robertson
RP G. Connally

CHI 1926 A
M E. Collins
1B E. Sheely
2B E. Collins
SS W. Hunnefield
3B W. Kamm
OF B. Falk
OF J. Mostil
OF W. Barrett
C R. Schalk
P T. Lyons
P A. Thomas
P T. Blankenship
P U. Faber
P J. Edwards

CHI 1927 A
M R. Schalk
1B J. Clancy
2B A. Ward
SS W. Hunnefield
3B W. Kamm
OF W. Barrett
OF B. Falk
OF A. Metzler
C H. McCurdy
P A. Thomas
P T. Lyons
P T. Blankenship
P G. Connally
P U. Faber
RP W. Jacobs
RP A. Cole

CHI 1928 A
M R. Schalk
M R. Blackburne
1B J. Clancy
2B W. Hunnefield
SS C. Cissell
3B W. Kamm
OF A. Metzler
OF J. Mostil
OF B. Falk
C C. Crouse
P A. Thomas
P T. Lyons
P G. Adkins
P U. Faber
P T. Blankenship
RP G. Connally

CHI 1929 A
M R. Blackburne
1B C. Shires
2B J. Kerr
SS C. Cissell
3B W. Kamm
OF A. Metzler
OF C. Reynolds
OF C. Hoffman
C M. Berg
UT J. Clancy
P A. Thomas
P T. Lyons
P U. Faber
P H. McKain
P G. Adkins

CHI 1930 A
M O. Bush
1B J. Watwood
2B C. Cissell
SS M. Mulleavy
3B W. Kamm
OF S. Jolley
OF C. Reynolds
OF E. Barnes
C H. Tate
P T. Lyons
P C. Caraway
P A. Thomas
P U. Faber
P F. Henry
RP E. Walsh
RP H. McKain

CHI 1931 A
M O. Bush
1B L. Blue
2B J. Kerr

SS C. Cissell
3B W. Sullivan
OF C. Reynolds
OF J. Watwood
OF L. Fonseca
C H. Tate
UT L. Appling
UT R. Fothergill
P V. Frasier
P A. Thomas
P C. Caraway
P U. Faber
P H. McKain
RP J. Moore
RP E. Braxton

CHI 1932 A
M L. Fonseca
1B L. Blue
2B M. Hayes
SS L. Appling
3B C. Selph
OF E. Funk
OF R. Seeds
OF R. Fothergill
C F. Grube
UT R. Kress
UT W. Sullivan
P T. Lyons
P S. Jones
P N. Gaston
P V. Frasier
P P. Gregory
RP U. Faber

CHI 1933 A
M L. Fonseca
1B R. Kress
2B M. Hayes
SS L. Appling
3B J. Dykes
OF G. Haas
OF A. Simmons
OF E. Swanson
C F. Grube
P T. Lyons
P S. Jones
P N. Gaston
P E. Durham
P W. Miller
RP J. Heving
RP U. Faber

CHI 1934 A
M L. Fonseca
M J. Dykes
1B H. Bonura
2B M. Hayes
SS L. Appling
3B J. Dykes
OF A. Simmons
OF E. Swanson
OF G. Haas
C E. Madjeski
P G. Earnshaw
P T. Lyons
P N. Gaston
P S. Jones
P L. Tietje
RP J. Heving
RP J. Wyatt

CHI 1935 A
M J. Dykes
1B H. Bonura
2B M. Hayes
SS L. Appling
3B J. Dykes
OF R. Radcliff
OF A. Simmons
OF G. Haas
C J. Sewell
UT S. Washington
P J. Whitehead
P L. Kennedy
P T. Lyons
P L. Tietje
P S. Jones
RP J. Wyatt

CHI 1936 A
M J. Dykes
1B H. Bonura
2B M. Hayes
SS L. Appling
3B J. Dykes
OF M. Kreevich
OF R. Radcliff
OF G. Haas
C J. Sewell
UT A. Piet

P L. Kennedy
P J. Whitehead
P M. Cain
P T. Lyons
P M. Stratton
RP C. Brown
RP R. Evans

CHI 1937 A
M J. Dykes
1B H. Bonura
2B M. Hayes
SS L. Appling
3B A. Piet
OF F. Walker
OF R. Radcliff
OF M. Kreevich
C J. Sewell
P L. Kennedy
P T. Lee
P T. Lyons
P J. Whitehead
P M. Stratton
RP C. Brown

CHI 1938 A
M J. Dykes
1B J. Kuhel
2B M. Hayes
SS L. Appling
3B M. Owen
OF M. Kreevich
OF G. Walker
OF H. Steinbacher
C J. Sewell
UT L. Berger
UT R. Radcliff
P T. Lee
P T. Lyons
P M. Stratton
P J. Whitehead
P J. Rigney

CHI 1939 A
M J. Dykes
1B J. Kuhel
2B A. Bejma
SS L. Appling
3B D. McNair
OF G. Walker
OF M. Kreevich
OF L. Rosenthal
C M. Tresh
UT R. Radcliff
P T. Lee
P J. Rigney
P E. Smith
P T. Lyons
P J. Knott
RP C. Brown

CHI 1940 A
M J. Dykes
1B J. Kuhel
2B J. Webb
SS L. Appling
3B R. Kennedy
OF T. Wright
OF M. Kreevich
OF J. Solters
C M. Tresh
UT L. Rosenthal
P J. Rigney
P T. Lee
P E. Smith
P T. Lyons
P J. Knott
RP C. Brown
RP P. Appleton

CHI 1941 A
M J. Dykes
1B J. Kuhel
W.
2B Knickerbocker
SS L. Appling
3B D. Lodigiani
OF T. Wright
OF M. Kreevich
OF M. Hoag
C M. Tresh
P T. Lee
P E. Smith
P J. Rigney
P T. Lyons
P W. Dietrich

CHI 1942 A
M J. Dykes
1B J. Kuhel

2B D. Kolloway
SS L. Appling
3B R. Kennedy
OF W. Moses
OF M. Hoag
OF T. Wright
C M. Tresh
P J. Humphries
P E. Smith
P T. Lyons
P W. Dietrich
P L. Ross
RP J. Haynes

CHI 1943 A
M J. Dykes
1B J. Kuhel
2B D. Kolloway
SS L. Appling
3B E. Hodgin
OF W. Moses
OF T. Tucker
OF G. Curtwright
C M. Tresh
P O. Grove
P E. Smith
P J. Humphries
P W. Dietrich
P L. Ross
RP G. Maltzberger
RP W. Swift

CHI 1944 A
M J. Dykes
1B H. Trosky
2B L. Schalk
SS J. Webb
3B E. Hodgin
OF W. Moses
OF T. Tucker
OF E. Carnett
C M. Tresh
P W. Dietrich
P O. Grove
P E. Lopat
P J. Humphries
P J. Haynes
RP G. Maltzberger

CHI 1945 A
M J. Dykes
1B M. Farrell
2B L. Schalk
SS C. Michaels
3B A. Cuccinello
OF W. Moses
OF J. Dickshot
OF O. Hockett
C M. Tresh
UT G. Curtwright
P T. Lee
P O. Grove
P E. Lopat
P J. Humphries
P W. Dietrich
RP J. Johnson

CHI 1946 A
M J. Dykes
M T. Lyons
1B H. Trosky
2B D. Kolloway
SS L. Appling
3B D. Lodigiani
OF T. Tucker
OF T. Wright
OF R. Kennedy
C M. Tresh
P E. Lopat
P O. Grove
P J. Haynes
P E. Smith
P F. Papish
RP E. Caldwell
RP R. Hamner

CHI 1947 A
M T. Lyons
1B P. York
2B D. Kolloway
SS L. Appling
3B F. Baker
OF D. Philley
OF R. Kennedy
OF T. Wright
C M. Tresh
UT C. Michaels
P E. Lopat
P F. Papish
P J. Haynes
P O. Grove

P R. Gillespie
RP E. Harrist
RP P. Gebrian

CHI 1948 A
M T. Lyons
1B U. Lupien
2B D. Kolloway
SS C. Michaels
3B L. Appling
OF D. Philley
OF T. Wright
OF J. Seerey
C A. Robinson
UT F. Baker
UT E. Hodgin
P W. Wight
P J. Haynes
P A. Gettel
P M. Pieretti
P R. Gumpert
RP H. Judson
RP F. Papish

CHI 1949 A
M J. Onslow
1B C. Kress
2B C. Michaels
SS L. Appling
3B F. Baker
OF D. Philley
OF G. Metkovich
OF H. Adams
C D. Wheeler
P W. Wight
P R. Gumpert
P W. Pierce
P R. Kuzava
P H. Judson
RP M. Pieretti
RP M. Surkont

CHI 1950 A
M J. Onslow
M J. Corriden
1B W. Robinson
2B J. Fox
SS A. Carrasquel
3B H. Majeski
OF D. Philley
OF G. Zernial
OF M. Rickert
C P. Masi
P W. Pierce
P W. Wight
P R. Cain
P R. Gumpert
P R. Scarborough
RP H. Judson
RP L. Aloma

CHI 1951 A
M P. Richards
1B W. Robinson
2B J. Fox
SS A. Carrasquel
3B R. Dillinger
OF J. Busby
OF A. Zarilla
OF S. Minoso
C P. Masi
UT E. Stewart
P W. Pierce
P S. Rogovin
P K. Holcombe
P J. Dobson
P R. Gumpert
RP L. Aloma
RP M. Rotblatt

CHI 1952 A
M P. Richards
1B W. Robinson
2B J. Fox
SS A. Carrasquel
3B H. Rodriguez
OF S. Minoso
OF S. Mele
OF R. Coleman
C J. Lollar
P W. Pierce
P S. Rogovin
P J. Dobson
P M. Grissom
P C. Stobbs
RP H. Dorish
RP W. Kennedy

CHI 1953 A
M P. Richards

1B F. Fain
2B J. Fox
SS A. Carrasquel
3B R. Elliott
OF M. Rivera
OF S. Minoso
OF S. Mele
C J. Lollar
P W. Pierce
P V. Trucks
P J. Fornieles
P S. Rogovin
P S. Consuegra
RP H. Dorish
RP H. Bearden

CHI 1954 A
M P. Richards
M M. Marion
1B F. Fain
2B J. Fox
SS A. Carrasquel
3B C. Michaels
OF S. Minoso
OF M. Rivera
OF J. Groth
C J. Lollar
P V. Trucks
P B. Keegan
P W. Pierce
P J. Harshman
P S. Consuegra
RP H. Dorish
RP M. Martin

CHI 1955 A
M M. Marion
1B W. Dropo
2B J. Fox
SS A. Carrasquel
3B G. Kell
OF M. Rivera
OF S. Minoso
OF J. Busby
C J. Lollar
UT W. Nieman
P W. Pierce
P J. Donovan
P J. Harshman
P V. Trucks
P C. Johnson
RP S. Consuegra
RP M. Howell

CHI 1956 A
M M. Marion
1B W. Dropo
2B J. Fox
SS L. Aparicio
3B F. Hatfield
OF S. Minoso
OF L. Doby
OF M. Rivera
C J. Lollar
P W. Pierce
P R. Donovan
P J. Harshman
P J. Wilson
P R. Keegan
RP M. Howell

CHI 1957 A
M A. Lopez
1B C. Torgeson
2B J. Fox
SS L. Aparicio
3B J. Phillips
OF S. Minoso
OF L. Doby
OF J. Landis
C J. Lollar
UT S. Esposito
UT M. Rivera
P W. Pierce
P R. Donovan
P J. Wilson
P J. Harshman
P R. Keegan
RP G. Staley
RP M. Howell

CHI 1958 A
M A. Lopez
1B C. Torgeson
2B J. Fox
SS L. Aparicio
3B W. Goodman
OF J. Landis
OF A. Smith
OF M. Rivera
C J. Lollar

UT S. Esposito
P R. Donovan
P W. Pierce
P E. Wynn
P J. Wilson
P R. Moore
RP G. Staley
RP R. Shaw

CHI 1959 A

M A. Lopez
1B C. Torgeson
2B J. Fox
SS L. Aparicio
3B J. Phillips
OF J. Landis
OF A. Smith
OF M. Rivera
C J. Lollar
UT W. Goodman
P E. Wynn
P R. Shaw
P W. Pierce
P R. Donovan
P A. Latman
RP G. Staley
RP O. Lown

CHI 1960 A

M A. Lopez
1B R. Sievers
2B J. Fox
SS L. Aparicio
3B E. Freese
OF S. Minoso
OF J. Landis
OF A. Smith
C J. Lollar
P E. Wynn
P W. Pierce
P R. Shaw
P F. Baumann
P R. Kemmerer
RP G. Staley
RP R. Donovan

CHI 1961 A

M A. Lopez
1B R. Sievers
2B J. Fox
SS L. Aparicio
3B A. Smith
OF S. Minoso
OF J. Landis
OF F. Robinson
C J. Lollar
UT J. Martin
P J. Pizarro
P F. Baumann
P W. Pierce
P C. McLish
P R. Herbert
RP O. Lown
RP R. Kemmerer

CHI 1962 A

M A. Lopez
1B J. Cunningham
2B J. Fox
SS L. Aparicio
3B A. Smith
OF F. Robinson
OF J. Landis
OF N. Hershberger
C C. Carreon
P R. Herbert
P J. Pizarro
P E. Fisher
P E. Wynn
P J. Buzhardt
RP D. Zanni
RP O. Lown

CHI 1963 A

M A. Lopez
1B T. McCraw
2B J. Fox
SS R. Hansen
3B P. Ward
OF F. Robinson
OF J. Landis
OF D. Nicholson
C J. Martin
UT C. Carreon
UT N. Hershberger
UT A. Weis
P G. Peters
P R. Herbert
P J. Pizarro
P J. Buzhardt
P J. Horlen
RP J. Wilhelm
RP J. Brosnan

CHI 1964 A

M A. Lopez
1B T. McCraw
2B A. Weis
SS R. Hansen
3B P. Ward
OF F. Robinson
OF N. Hershberger
OF J. Landis
C J. Martin
UT D. Buford
UT D. Nicholson
P G. Peters
P J. Pizarro
P J. Horlen
P J. Buzhardt
P R. Herbert
RP J. Wilhelm
RP E. Fisher

CHI 1965 A

M A. Lopez
1B W. Skowron
2B D. Buford
SS R. Hansen
3B P. Ward
OF A. Berry
OF F. Robinson
OF D. Cater
C J. Martin
UT T. McCraw
UT J. Romano
UT A. Weis
P J. Horlen
P J. Buzhardt
P T. John
P G. Peters
P B. Howard
RP E. Fisher
RP J. Wilhelm

CHI 1966 A

M E. Stanky
1B T. McCraw
2B A. Weis
SS L. Elia
3B D. Buford
OF T. Agee
OF A. Berry
OF F. Robinson
C J. Romano
UT K. Adair
UT W. Skowron
P T. John
P J. Horlen
P G. Peters
P J. Buzhardt
P B. Howard
RP R. Locker
RP D. Higgins

CHI 1967 A

M E. Stanky
1B T. McCraw
2B J. Causey
SS R. Hansen
3B D. Buford
OF T. Agee
OF A. Berry
OF P. Ward
C J. Martin
UT W. Williams
P G. Peters
P J. Horlen
P T. John
P B. Howard
RP R. Locker
RP W. Wood

CHI 1968 A

M E. Stanky
M J. Moss
M A. Lopez
M J. Moss
M A. Lopez
1B T. McCraw
2B S. Alomar
SS L. Aparicio
3B P. Ward
OF A. Berry
OF H. Davis
OF C. Bradford
C D. Josephson
P J. Horlen
P J. Fisher
P T. John
P G. Peters
P F. Carlos
RP W. Wood
RP J. Wilhelm

CHI 1969 A

M A. Lopez
M D. Gutteridge
1B G. Hopkins
2B R. Knoop
SS L. Aparicio
3B W. Melton
OF A. Berry
OF W. Williams
OF C. May
C E. Herrmann
UT P. Ward
P J. Horlen
P T. John
P G. Peters
P B. Wynne
RP W. Wood
RP D. Osinski

CHI 1970 A

M D. Gutteridge
M M. Adair
M C. Tanner
1B G. Hopkins
2B R. Knoop
SS L. Aparicio
3B W. Melton
OF C. May
OF A. Berry
OF W. Williams
C E. Herrmann
UT T. McCraw
UT S. O'Brien
P T. John
P G. Janeski
P J. Horlen
RP W. Wood
RP J. Crider

CHI 1971 A

M C. Tanner
1B C. May
2B M. Andrews
SS L. Alvarado
3B W. Melton
OF F. Reichardt
OF J. Johnstone
OF W. Williams
C E. Herrmann
UT C. McKinney
P W. Wood
P T. Bradley
P T. John
P C. Johnson
P J. Horlen
RP S. Kealey
RP V. Romo

CHI 1972 A

M C. Tanner
1B R. Allen
2B M. Andrews
SS R. Morales
3B E. Spiezio
OF C. May
OF H. Kelly
OF J. Johnstone
C E. Herrmann
UT L. Alvarado
UT F. Reichardt
P W. Wood
P T. Bradley
P S. Bahnsen
P D. Lemonds
RP T. Forster
RP R. Gossage

CHI 1973 A

M C. Tanner
1B A. Muser
2B J. Orta
SS E. Leon
3B W. Melton
OF H. Kelly
OF J. Jeter
OF W. Sharp
C E. Herrmann
DH C. May
P W. Wood
P S. Bahnsen
P S. Stone
P T. Forster
P E. Fisher
RP C. Acosta
RP R. Gossage

CHI 1974 A

M C. Tanner
1B R. Allen
2B J. Orta
SS R. Dent
3B W. Melton
OF K. Henderson
OF C. May
OF W. Sharp
C E. Herrmann
DH H. Kelly
UT B. Downing
UT A. Muser
UT R. Santo
P W. Wood
P J. Kaat
P S. Bahnsen
P C. Johnson
RP T. Forster
RP L. Pitlock

CHI 1975 A

M C. Tanner
1B C. May
2B J. Orta
SS R. Dent
3B W. Melton
OF K. Henderson
OF H. Kelly
OF N. Nyman
C B. Downing
DH D. Johnson
P J. Kaat
P W. Wood
P C. Osteen
P J. Jefferson
RP R. Gossage
RP D. Hamilton

CHI 1976 A

M P. Richards
1B J. Spencer
2B J. Brohamer
SS R. Dent
3B K. Bell
OF C. Lemon
OF R. Garr
OF J. Orta
C B. Downing
DH H. Kelly
UT W. Stein
P R. Gossage
P C. Johnson
P K. Brett
P F. Barrios
P T. Forster
RP D. Hamilton
RP C. Carroll

CHI 1977 A

M R. Lemon
1B J. Spencer
2B J. Orta
SS A. Bannister
3B E. Soderholm
OF C. Lemon
OF R. Garr
OF R. Zisk
C J. Essian
DH O. Gamble
UT L. Johnson
P F. Barrios
P S. Stone
P K. Kravec
P R. Knapp
P W. Wood
RP L. LaGrow
RP D. Hamilton

CHI 1978 A

M R. Lemon
M L. Doby
1B L. Johnson
2B J. Orta
SS D. Kessinger
3B E. Soderholm
OF R. Garr
OF C. Lemon
OF C. Washington
C W. Nahorodny
DH R. Molinaro
P S. Stone
P K. Kravec
P F. Barrios
P W. Wood
RP J. Willoughby
RP L. LaGrow

CHI 1979 A

M D. Kessinger
M A. LaRussa
1B M. Squires
2B A. Bannister
SS G. Pryor
3B K. Bell
OF C. Lemon
OF C. Washington
OF R. Torres
C M. May
DH J. Orta
UT R. Garr
UT L. Johnson
P K. Kravec
P R. Wortham
P R. Baumgarten
P S. Trout
RP R. Scarbery
RP M. Proly

CHI 1980 A

M A. LaRussa
1B M. Squires
2B J. Morrison
SS T. Cruz
3B K. Bell
OF C. Lemon
OF H. Baines
OF W. Nordhagen
C B. Kimm
DH L. Johnson
UT R. Molinaro
UT G. Pryor
P R. Burns
P S. Trout
P R. Dotson
P R. Baumgarten
P D. Hoyt
RP M. Proly
RP E. Farmer

CHI 1981 A

M A. LaRussa
1B M. Squires
2B A. Bernazard
SS W. Almon
3B J. Morrison
OF C. Lemon
OF R. LeFlore
OF H. Baines
C C. Fisk
DH G. Luzinski
UT R. Kuntz
UT W. Nordhagen
P R. Burns
P R. Dotson
P D. Lamp
P S. Trout
P R. Baumgarten
RP D. Hoyt
RP E. Farmer

CHI 1982 A

M A. LaRussa
1B M. Squires
2B A. Bernazard
SS W. Almon
3B A. Rodriguez
OF H. Baines
OF S. Kemp
OF R. Law
C C. Fisk
DH G. Luzinski
UT V. Law
UT T. Paciorek
P D. Hoyt
P R. Dotson
P D. Lamp
P J. Koosman
P R. Burns
RP S. Barojas
RP K. Hickey

CHI 1983 A

M A. LaRussa
1B M. Squires
2B J. Cruz
SS J. Dybzinski
3B V. Law
OF H. Baines
OF R. Kittle
OF R. Law
C C. Fisk
DH G. Luzinski
UT S. Fletcher
UT J. Hairston
UT T. Paciorek
UT G. Walker
P D. Hoyt
P R. Dotson
P F. Bannister
P R. Burns
P J. Koosman
RP D. Lamp
RP R. Tidrow

CHI 1984 A

M A. LaRussa
1B G. Walker
2B J. Cruz
SS S. Fletcher
3B V. Law
OF H. Baines
OF R. Law
OF R. Kittle
C C. Fisk
DH G. Luzinski
UT J. Hairston
UT T. Paciorek
UT M. Squires
P R. Dotson
P G. Seaver
P D. Hoyt
P F. Bannister
P R. Burns
RP R. Reed
RP J. Agosto

CHI 1985 A

M A. LaRussa
1B G. Walker
2B J. Cruz
SS O. Guillen
3B T. Hulett
OF H. Baines
OF R. Law
OF D. Boston
C C. Fisk
DH R. Kittle
UT S. Fletcher
UT L. Salazar
P G. Seaver
P R. Burns
P F. Bannister
P W. Nelson
RP R. James
RP D. Spillner

CHI 1986 A

M A. LaRussa
M D. Rader
M J. Fregosi
1B G. Walker
2B J. Cruz
SS O. Guillen
3B T. Hulett
OF H. Baines
OF J. Cangelosi
OF T. Nichols
C C. Fisk
DH R. Kittle
UT J. Hairston
P R. Dotson
P F. Bannister
P J. Cowley
P N. Allen
P J. Davis
RP W. Nelson
RP W. Dawley

CHI 1987 A

M J. Fregosi
1B G. Walker
2B F. Manrique
SS O. Guillen
3B T. Hulett
OF I. Calderon
OF G. Redus
OF K. Williams
C C. Fisk
DH H. Baines
UT D. Boston
UT D. Hill
P F. Bannister
P R. Dotson
P J. DeLeon
P W. Long
RP J. Winn
RP R. Thigpen

CHI 1988 A

M J. Fregosi
1B G. Walker
2B F. Manrique
SS O. Guillen
3B S. Lyons
OF D. Pasqua
OF D. Gallagher
OF D. Boston
C C. Fisk
DH H. Baines
P M. Perez
P J. Reuss
P W. Long
P D. LaPoint
P J. McDowell
RP R. Horton
RP R. Thigpen

CHI 1876 N

M A. Spalding
1B C. McVey
2B R. Barnes
SS J. Peters
3B A. Anson
OF P. Hines
OF J. Glenn
OF O. Bielaski
C J. White
P A. Spalding

CHI 1877 N

M A. Spalding
1B A. Spalding
2B R. Barnes
SS J. Peters
3B A. Anson
OF P. Hines
OF J. Glenn
OF D. Eggler
C C. McVey
P G. Bradley
P L. Reis

CHI 1878 N

M R. Ferguson
1B J. Start
2B W. McClellan
SS R. Ferguson
3B F. Hankinson
OF J. Cassidy
OF J. Remsen
OF A. Anson
C W. Harbidge
P F. Larkin
P L. Reis

CHI 1879 N

M A. Anson
M F. Flint
M L. Brown
M F. Flint
1B A. Anson
2B J. Quest
SS J. Peters
3B E. Williamson
OF G. Shaffer
OF A. Dalrymple
OF G. Gore
C F. Flint
P F. Larkin
P F. Hankinson

CHI 1880 N

M A. Anson
1B A. Anson
2B J. Quest
SS T. Burns
3B E. Williamson
OF A. Dalrymple
OF G. Gore
OF M. Kelly
C F. Flint
P L. Corcoran
P F. Goldsmith

CHI 1881 N

M A. Anson
1B A. Anson
2B J. Quest
SS T. Burns
3B E. Williamson
OF A. Dalrymple
OF M. Kelly
OF G. Gore
C F. Flint
P L. Corcoran
P F. Goldsmith

CHI 1882 N

M A. Anson
1B A. Anson
2B T. Burns
SS M. Kelly
3B E. Williamson
OF G. Gore
OF A. Dalrymple
OF H. Nicol
C F. Flint
P F. Goldsmith
P L. Corcoran

CHI 1883 N
M A. Anson
1B A. Anson
2B N. Pfeffer
SS T. Burns
3B E. Williamson
OF G. Gore
OF M. Kelly
OF A. Dalrymple
C F. Flint
P L. Corcoran
P F. Goldsmith

CHI 1884 N
M A. Anson
1B A. Anson
2B N. Pfeffer
SS T. Burns
3B E. Williamson
OF A. Dalrymple
OF G. Gore
OF M. Kelly
C F. Flint
P L. Corcoran
P F. Goldsmith
P J. Clarkson

CHI 1885 N
M A. Anson
1B A. Anson
2B N. Pfeffer
SS T. Burns
3B E. Williamson
OF A. Dalrymple
OF G. Gore
OF M. Kelly
C F. Flint
P J. Clarkson
P J. McCormick
P T. Kennedy

CHI 1886 N
M A. Anson
1B A. Anson
2B N. Pfeffer
SS E. Williamson
3B T. Burns
OF G. Gore
OF A. Dalrymple
OF J. Ryan
C F. Flint
UT M. Kelly
P J. Clarkson
P J. McCormick
P J. Flynn

CHI 1887 N
M A. Anson
1B A. Anson
2B N. Pfeffer
SS E. Williamson
3B T. Burns
OF J. Ryan
OF M. Sullivan
OF W. Sunday
C T. Daly
P J. Clarkson
P M. Baldwin

CHI 1888 N
M A. Anson
1B A. Anson
2B N. Pfeffer
SS E. Williamson
3B T. Burns
OF J. Ryan
OF M. Sullivan
OF H. Duffy
C T. Daly
P A. Krock
P M. Baldwin
P J. Tener

CHI 1889 N
M A. Anson
1B A. Anson
2B N. Pfeffer
SS E. Williamson
3B T. Burns
OF G. Van Haltren
OF H. Duffy
OF J. Ryan
C C. Farrell
P W. Hutchinson
P J. Tener
P J. Dwyer
P A. Gumbert

CHI 1890 N
M A. Anson
1B A. Anson
2B R. Glenalvin
SS J. Cooney
3B T. Burns
OF W. Wilmot
OF S. Carroll
OF J. Andrews
C M. Kittridge
UT H. Earl
P W. Hutchinson
P J. Luby
P E. Stein
P M. Sullivan
P W. Coughlin

CHI 1891 N
M A. Anson
1B A. Anson
2B N. Pfeffer
SS J. Cooney
3B W. Dahlen
OF S. Carroll
OF W. Wilmot
OF J. Ryan
C M. Kittridge
P W. Hutchinson
P A. Gumbert
P J. Luby
P E. Stein

CHI 1892 N
M A. Anson
1B A. Anson
2B J. Canavan
SS W. Dahlen
3B W. Parrott
OF J. Ryan
OF S. Dungan
OF W. Wilmot
C W. Schriver
P W. Hutchinson
P A. Gumbert
P J. Luby

CHI 1893 N
M A. Anson
1B A. Anson
2B W. Lange
SS W. Dahlen
3B W. Parrott
OF S. Dungan
OF W. Wilmot
OF J. Ryan
C M. Kittridge
UT G. Decker
P W. Hutchinson
P W. McGill
P A. Mauck

CHI 1894 N
M A. Anson
1B A. Anson
2B W. Parrott
SS W. Dahlen
3B C. Irwin
OF W. Wilmot
OF W. Lange
OF J. Ryan
C W. Schriver
UT G. Decker
P W. Hutchinson
P C. Griffith
P W. McGill
P W. Terry
P C. Stratton

CHI 1895 N
M A. Anson
1B A. Anson
2B A. Stewart
SS W. Dahlen
3B W. Everett
OF W. Lange
OF W. Wilmot
OF J. Ryan
C T. Donahue
P C. Griffith
P W. Terry
P W. Hutchinson

CHI 1896 N
M A. Anson
1B A. Anson
2B N. Pfeffer
SS W. Dahlen
3B W. Everett
OF J. Ryan
OF W. Lange
OF G. Decker
C M. Kittridge
P C. Griffith
P D. Friend
P W. Terry
P H. Briggs

CHI 1897 N
M A. Anson
1B A. Anson
2B J. Connor
SS W. Dahlen
3B W. Everett
OF J. Ryan
OF W. Lange
OF G. Decker
C M. Kittridge
UT J. Callahan
UT W. McCormick
P C. Griffith
P D. Friend
P H. Briggs
P R. Denzer

CHI 1898 N
M T. Burns
1B W. Everett
2B J. Connor
SS W. Dahlen
3B W. McCormick
OF J. Ryan
OF W. Lange
OF S. Mertes
C T. Donahue
P C. Griffith
P J. Callahan
P W. Woods
P M. Kilroy

CHI 1899 N
M T. Burns
1B W. Everett
2B W. McCormick
SS De Montreville
3B H. Wolverton
OF J. Ryan
OF E. Green
OF S. Mertes
C T. Donahue
UT W. Lange
P J. Taylor
P C. Griffith
P J. Callahan
P V. Garvin

CHI 1900 N
M T. Loftus
1B J. Ganzel
2B C. Childs
SS W. McCormick
3B W. Bradley
OF J. McCarthy
OF J. Ryan
OF E. Green
C T. Donahue
UT S. Mertes
P J. Callahan
P C. Griffith
P V. Garvin
P J. Taylor
P J. Menefee

CHI 1901 N
M T. Loftus
1B J. Doyle
2B C. Childs
SS W. McCormick
3B F. Raymer
OF T. Hartsel
OF E. Green
OF F. Chance
C J. Kling
UT C. Dexter
P T. Hughes
P J. Taylor
P G. Waddell
P M. Eason

CHI 1902 N
M F. Selee
1B F. Chance
2B R. Lowe
SS J. Tinker
3B H. Schaefer
OF J. Slagle
OF D. Jones
OF J. Dobbs
C J. Kling
P J. Taylor
P W. Williams
P C. Lundgren
P R. Rhoads
P J. St. Vrain

CHI 1903 N
M F. Selee
1B F. Chance
2B J. Evers
SS J. Tinker
3B J. Casey
OF J. Slagle
OF D. Jones
OF R. Harley
C J. Kling
P J. Taylor
P J. Weimer
P R. Wicker
P C. Lundgren
P J. Menefee

CHI 1904 N
M F. Selee
1B F. Chance
2B J. Evers
SS J. Tinker
3B J. Casey
OF J. Slagle
OF J. McCarthy
OF D. Jones
C J. Kling
P J. Weimer
P H. Briggs
P C. Lundgren
P R. Wicker
P M. Brown

CHI 1905 N
M F. Selee
M F. Chance
1B F. Chance
2B J. Evers
SS J. Tinker
3B J. Casey
OF J. Slagle
OF W. Maloney
OF F. Schulte
C J. Kling
P E. Reulbach
P J. Weimer
P M. Brown
P R. Wicker
P C. Lundgren

CHI 1906 N
M F. Chance
1B F. Chance
2B J. Evers
SS J. Tinker
3B H. Steinfeldt
OF S. Sheckard
OF F. Schulte
OF J. Slagle
C J. Kling
P M. Brown
P J. Pfiester
P E. Reulbach
P C. Lundgren
P J. Taylor

CHI 1907 N
M F. Chance
1B F. Chance
2B J. Evers
SS J. Tinker
3B H. Steinfeldt
OF S. Sheckard
OF J. Slagle
OF F. Schulte
C J. Kling
UT A. Hofman
P O. Overall
P M. Brown
P C. Lundgren
P J. Pfiester
P E. Reulbach

CHI 1908 N
M F. Chance
1B F. Chance
2B J. Evers
SS J. Tinker
3B H. Steinfeldt
OF S. Sheckard
OF F. Schulte
OF J. Slagle
C J. Kling
UT A. Hofman
P M. Brown
P E. Reulbach
P J. Pfiester
P O. Overall
P C. Fraser

CHI 1909 N
M F. Chance
1B F. Chance
2B J. Evers
SS J. Tinker
3B H. Steinfeldt
OF A. Hofman
OF S. Sheckard
OF F. Schulte
C J. Archer
P M. Brown
P O. Overall
P E. Reulbach
P J. Pfiester
P F. Kroh

CHI 1910 N
M F. Chance
1B F. Chance
2B J. Evers
SS J. Tinker
3B H. Steinfeldt
OF F. Schulte
OF S. Sheckard
OF A. Hofman
C J. Kling
UT J. Archer
UT H. Zimmerman
P M. Brown
P L. Cole
P J. McIntire
P E. Reulbach
P O. Overall

CHI 1911 N
M F. Chance
1B V. Saier
2B H. Zimmerman
SS J. Tinker
3B J. Doyle
OF S. Sheckard
OF F. Schulte
OF A. Hofman
C J. Archer
P M. Brown
P L. Richie
P E. Reulbach
P L. Cole
P J. McIntire
RP E. Richter

CHI 1912 N
M F. Chance
1B V. Saier
2B J. Evers
SS J. Tinker
3B H. Zimmerman
OF S. Sheckard
OF F. Schulte
OF T. Leach
C J. Archer
P L. Cheney
P J. Lavender
P L. Richie
P E. Reulbach
P C. Smith

CHI 1913 N
M J. Evers
1B V. Saier
2B J. Evers
SS A. Bridwell
3B H. Zimmerman
OF F. Schulte
OF T. Leach
OF M. Mitchell
C J. Archer
P L. Cheney
P J. Lavender
P A. Humphries
P G. Pearce
P C. Smith

CHI 1914 N
M H. O'Day
1B V. Saier
2B W. Sweeney
SS J. Corriden
3B H. Zimmerman
OF W. Good
OF T. Leach
OF F. Schulte
C R. Bresnahan
P L. Cheney
P J. Vaughn
P J. Lavender
P A. Humphries
P G. Pearce
RP K. Hageman

CHI 1915 N
M R. Bresnahan
1B V. Saier
2B H. Zimmerman
SS R. Fisher
3B A. Phelan
OF F. Williams
OF F. Schulte
OF W. Good
C J. Archer
P J. Vaughn
P J. Lavender
P G. Pearce
P A. Humphries
P G. Zabel

CHI 1916 N
M J. Tinker
1B V. Saier
2B F. Knabe
SS W. Wortman
3B H. Zimmerman
OF M. Flack
OF F. Williams
OF L. Mann
C J. Archer
UT R. Zeider
P J. Vaughn
P C. Hendrix
P J. Lavender
P G. McConnell
P E. Packard

CHI 1917 N
M F. Mitchell
1B F. Merkle
2B L. Doyle
SS W. Wortman
3B C. Deal
OF F. Williams
OF M. Flack
OF L. Mann
C A. Wilson
UT H. Wolter
UT R. Zeider
P J. Vaughn
P P. Douglas
P C. Hendrix
P A. Demaree
P P. Carter
RP M. Prendergast

CHI 1918 N
M F. Mitchell
1B F. Merkle
2B R. Zeider
SS C. Hollocher
3B C. Deal
OF L. Mann
OF G. Paskert
OF M. Flack
C W. Killefer
P J. Vaughn
P G. Tyler
P C. Hendrix
P P. Douglas

CHI 1919 N
M F. Mitchell
1B F. Merkle
2B C. Pick
SS C. Hollocher
3B C. Deal
OF M. Flack
OF G. Paskert
OF L. Mann
C W. Killefer
P J. Vaughn
P G. Alexander
P C. Hendrix
P E. Martin
P P. Douglas

CHI 1920 N
M F. Mitchell
1B F. Merkle
2B Z. Terry
SS C. Hollocher
3B C. Deal
OF G. Paskert
OF D. Robertson
OF M. Flack
C R. O'Farrell
UT T. Barber
P G. Alexander
P J. Vaughn
P C. Hendrix
P G. Tyler
P E. Martin

CHI 1921 N
M J. Evers
M W. Killefer
1B O. Grimes
2B Z. Terry
SS C. Hollocher
3B C. Deal
OF M. Flack
OF T. Barber
OF G. Maisel
C R. O'Farrell
UT J. Kelleher
P G. Alexander
P E. Martin
P A. Freeman
P V. Cheeves
P J. York

CHI 1922 N
M W. Killefer
1B O. Grimes
2B Z. Terry
SS C. Hollocher
3B M. Krug
OF L. Miller
OF A. Statz
OF B. Friberg
C R. O'Farrell
P V. Aldridge
P G. Alexander
P E. Osborne
P V. Cheeves
P P. Jones

CHI 1923 N
M W. Killefer
1B O. Grimes
2B G. Grantham
SS E. Adams
3B B. Friberg
OF A. Statz
OF L. Miller
OF C. Heathcote
C R. O'Farrell
P G. Alexander
P V. Aldridge
P A. Kaufmann
P E. Osborne
P H. Keen
RP F. Fussell

CHI 1924 N
M W. Killefer
1B H. Cotter
2B G. Grantham
SS E. Adams
3B B. Friberg
OF A. Statz
OF D. Grigsby
OF C. Heathcote
C C. Hartnett
P V. Aldridge
P H. Keen
P A. Kaufmann
P W. Jacobs
P G. Alexander

CHI 1925 N
M W. Killefer
M W. Maranville
M G. Gibson
1B C. Grimm
2B E. Adams
SS W. Maranville
3B H. Freigau
OF C. Heathcote
OF J. Brooks
OF T. Griffith
C C. Hartnett
P G. Alexander
P J. Blake
P A. Cooper
P A. Kaufmann
P G. Bush
RP H. Keen

CHI 1926 N
M J. McCarthy
1B C. Grimm
2B E. Adams
SS J. Cooney
3B H. Freigau
OF L. Wilson
OF C. Heathcote
OF J. Stephenson
C C. Hartnett

P C. Root
P J. Blake
A. Kaufmann
P P. Jones
P G. Bush

CHI 1927 N

M J. McCarthy
1B C. Grimm
2B C. Beck
SS E. English
3B E. Adams
OF L. Wilson
OF J. Stephenson
OF W. Webb
C C. Hartnett
P C. Root
P J. Blake
P G. Bush
P H. Carlson
P J. Brillheart

CHI 1928 N

M J. McCarthy
1B C. Grimm
2B F. Maguire
SS E. English
3B C. Beck
OF L. Wilson
OF J. Stephenson
OF H. Cuyler
C C. Hartnett
P P. Malone
P J. Blake
P C. Root
P G. Bush
P A. Nehf
RP H. Carlson

CHI 1929 N

M J. McCarthy
1B C. Grimm
2B R. Hornsby
SS E. English
3B N. McMillan
OF L. Wilson
OF J. Stephenson
OF H. Cuyler
C J. Taylor
P C. Root
P G. Bush
P P. Malone
P J. Blake
P A. Nehf
RP M. Cvengros

CHI 1930 N

M J. McCarthy
M R. Hornsby
1B C. Grimm
2B C. Blair
SS E. English
3B L. Bell
OF H. Cuyler
OF L. Wilson
OF J. Stephenson
C C. Hartnett
P P. Malone
P G. Bush
P C. Root
P J. Blake
P A. Teachout
RP L. Nelson

CHI 1931 N

M R. Hornsby
1B C. Grimm
2B R. Hornsby
SS E. English
3B L. Bell
OF H. Cuyler
OF L. Wilson
OF D. Taylor
C C. Hartnett
P C. Root
P R. Smith
P P. Malone
P G. Bush
P L. Sweetland
RP F. May
RP A. Teachout

CHI 1932 N

M R. Hornsby
M C. Grimm
1B C. Grimm
2B W. Herman
SS W. Jurges
3B E. English
OF J. Stephenson

OF J. Moore
OF H. Cuyler
C C. Hartnett
P L. Warneke
P G. Bush
P P. Malone
P C. Root
P B. Grimes
RP F. May

CHI 1933 N

M C. Grimm
1B C. Grimm
2B W. Herman
SS W. Jurges
3B E. English
OF J. Demaree
OF F. Herman
OF J. Stephenson
C C. Hartnett
P L. Warneke
P G. Bush
P C. Root
P P. Malone
P L. Tinning

CHI 1934 N

M C. Grimm
1B C. Grimm
2B W. Herman
SS W. Jurges
3B S. Hack
OF H. Cuyler
OF F. Herman
OF C. Klein
C C. Hartnett
UT E. English
UT G. Stainback
P L. Warneke
P W. Lee
P G. Bush
P P. Malone
P J. Weaver

CHI 1935 N

M C. Grimm
1B P. Cavaretta
2B W. Herman
SS W. Jurges
3B S. Hack
OF A. Galan
OF C. Klein
OF J. Demaree
C C. Hartnett
P L. Warneke
P W. Lee
P L. French
P C. Root
P J. Carleton
RP F. Kowalik

CHI 1936 N

M C. Grimm
1B P. Cavaretta
2B W. Herman
SS W. Jurges
3B S. Hack
OF J. Demaree
OF A. Galan
OF E. Allen
C C. Hartnett
P W. Lee
P L. French
P L. Warneke
P J. Carleton
P C. Davis
RP C. Root
RP C. Bryant

CHI 1937 N

M C. Grimm
1B J. Collins
2B W. Herman
SS W. Jurges
3B S. Hack
OF J. Demaree
OF A. Galan
OF J. Marty
C C. Hartnett
UT P. Cavaretta
P W. Lee
P L. French
P J. Carleton
P C. Root
P L. Parmelee
RP C. Shoun

CHI 1938 N

M C. Grimm
M C. Hartnett

1B J. Collins
2B W. Herman
SS W. Jurges
3B S. Hack
OF C. Reynolds
OF J. Demaree
OF A. Galan
C C. Hartnett
P W. Lee
P C. Bryant
P L. French
P J. Carleton
P C. Root
RP J. Russell

CHI 1939 N

M C. Hartnett
1B G. Russell
2B W. Herman
SS R. Bartell
3B S. Hack
OF A. Galan
OF H. Leiber
OF J. Gleeson
C C. Hartnett
P W. Lee
P C. Passeau
P L. French
P C. Root
P V. Page
RP J. Russell
RP R. Lillard

CHI 1940 N

M C. Hartnett
1B P. Cavaretta
2B W. Herman
SS R. Mattick
3B S. Hack
OF W. Nicholson
OF J. Gleeson
OF H. Leiber
C A. Todd
UT N. Dallessandro
P C. Passeau
P L. French
P W. Lee
P V. Olsen
P J. Mooty
RP K. Raffensberger
RP V. Page

CHI 1941 N

M J. Wilson
1B E. Dahlgren
2B L. Stringer
SS R. Sturgeon
3B S. Hack
OF W. Nicholson
OF N. Dallessandro
OF P. Cavaretta
C C. McCullough
P C. Passeau
P V. Olsen
P W. Lee
P J. Mooty
P P. Erickson
RP F. Pressnell
RP V. Page

CHI 1942 N

M J. Wilson
1B P. Cavaretta
2B L. Stringer
SS L. Merullo
3B S. Hack
OF W. Nicholson
OF L. Novikoff
OF N. Dallessandro
C C. McCullough
UT G. Russell
P C. Passeau
P W. Lee
P H. Bithorn
P V. Olsen
P L. Fleming

CHI 1943 N

M J. Wilson
1B P. Cavaretta
2B E. Stanky
SS L. Merullo
3B S. Hack
OF W. Nicholson
OF H. Lowrey
OF L. Novikoff
C C. McCullough
P C. Passeau
P H. Bithorn
P S. Derringer

P H. Wyse
P E. Hanyzewski
RP R. Prim

CHI 1944 N

M J. Wilson
M R. Johnson
M C. Grimm
1B P. Cavaretta
2B D. Johnson
SS L. Merullo
3B S. Hack
OF W. Nicholson
OF A. Pafko
OF N. Dallessandro
C D. Williams
UT H. Hughes
P H. Wyse
P C. Passeau
P S. Derringer
P L. Fleming
P R. Chipman

CHI 1945 N

M C. Grimm
1B P. Cavaretta
2B D. Johnson
SS L. Merullo
3B S. Hack
OF W. Nicholson
OF A. Pafko
OF H. Lowrey
C T. Livingston
P H. Wyse
P C. Passeau
P S. Derringer
P R. Prim
P H. Borowy
RP R. Chipman

CHI 1946 N

M C. Grimm
1B E. Waitkus
2B D. Johnson
SS W. Jurges
3B S. Hack
OF H. Lowrey
OF M. Rickert
OF P. Cavaretta
C C. McCullough
UT W. Nicholson
UT R. Sturgeon
P J. Schmitz
P H. Wyse
P H. Borowy
P P. Erickson
P E. Kush

CHI 1947 N

M C. Grimm
1B E. Waitkus
2B D. Johnson
SS L. Merullo
3B H. Lowrey
OF W. Nicholson
OF A. Pafko
OF P. Cavaretta
C R. Scheffing
P J. Schmitz
P D. Lade
P H. Borowy
P P. Erickson
P H. Wyse
RP E. Kush
RP R. Meers

CHI 1948 N

M C. Grimm
1B E. Waitkus
2B H. Schenz
SS R. Smalley
3B A. Pafko
OF W. Nicholson
OF H. Jeffcoat
OF H. Lowrey
C R. Scheffing
UT P. Cavaretta
P J. Schmitz
P R. Meyer
P R. McCall
P R. Rush
P H. Borowy
RP A. Dobernic
RP E. Kush

CHI 1949 N

M C. Grimm
M F. Frisch

1B H. Reich
2B E. Verban
SS R. Smalley
3B F. Gustine
OF H. Jeffcoat
OF A. Pafko
OF H. Sauer
C A. Owen
UT P. Cavaretta
P J. Schmitz
P R. Rush
P E. Leonard
P W. Dubiel
P D. Lade
RP R. Chipman
RP J. Adkins

CHI 1950 N

M F. Frisch
1B P. Ward
2B W. Terwilliger
SS R. Smalley
3B W. Serena
OF A. Pafko
OF H. Sauer
OF R. Borkowski
C A. Owen
P R. Rush
P J. Schmitz
P P. Minner
P F. Hiller
P W. Dubiel
RP J. Vander Meer
RP E. Leonard

CHI 151 N

M F. Frisch
M P. Cavaretta
1B K. Connors
2B E. Miksis
SS R. Smalley
3B R. Jackson
OF F. Baumholtz
OF H. Sauer
OF H. Jeffcoat
C F. Burgess
P R. Rush
P P. Minner
P C. McLish
P F. Hiller
P O. Lown
RP E. Leonard
RP W. Dubiel

CHI 1952 N

M P. Cavarretta
1B D. Fondy
2B E. Miksis
SS R. Smalley
3B R. Jackson
OF H. Sauer
OF F. Baumholtz
OF H. Jeffcoat
C M. Atwell
UT E. Hermanski
UT W. Serena
P R. Rush
P J. Klippstein
P W. Hacker
P P. Minner
P O. Lown
RP R. Schultz
RP E. Leonard

CHI 1953 N

M P. Cavarretta
1B D. Fondy
2B E. Miksis
SS R. Smalley
3B R. Jackson
OF F. Baumholtz
OF R. Kiner
OF H. Sauer
C C. McCullough
UT H. Jeffcoat
P W. Hacker
P P. Minner
P J. Klippstein
P R. Rush
P O. Lown
RP E. Leonard

CHI 1954 N

M S. Hack
1B D. Fondy
2B E. Baker
SS E. Banks
3B R. Jackson
OF R. Kiner

OF H. Sauer
OF R. Talbot
C J. Garagiola
P R. Rush
P P. Minner
P W. Hacker
P J. Klippstein
P H. Pollet
RP J. Davis
RP H. Jeffcoat

CHI 1955 N

M S. Hack
1B D. Fondy
2B E. Baker
SS E. Banks
3B R. Jackson
OF E. Miksis
OF J. King
OF H. Sauer
C H. Chiti
UT F. Baumholtz
UT R. Speake
P S. Jones
P R. Rush
P W. Hacker
P P. Minner
P J. Davis
RP H. Jeffcoat
RP H. Pollet

CHI 1956 N

M S. Hack
1B D. Fondy
2B E. Baker
SS E. Banks
3B D. Hoak
OF W. Moryn
OF M. Irvin
OF T. Whisenant
C H. Landrith
UT J. King
UT E. Miksis
P R. Rush
P S. Jones
P W. Hacker
P C. Kaiser
P J. Brosnan
RP J. Davis
RP O. Lown

CHI 1957 N

M R. Scheffing
1B R. Long
2B R. Morgan
SS E. Banks
3B R. Adams
OF W. Moryn
OF C. Tanner
C C. Neeman
UT J. Bolger
UT R. Speake
P M. Drabowsky
P R. Drott
P R. Rush
P D. Elston
P D. Hillman
RP J. Brosnan
RP O. Lown

CHI 1958 N

M R. Scheffing
1B R. Long
2B A. Taylor
SS E. Banks
3B A. Dark
OF R. Thomson
OF W. Moryn
OF R. Walls
C S. Taylor
P W. Phillips
P G. Hobbie
P R. Drott
P D. Hillman
P M. Drabowsky
RP D. Elston
RP W. Henry

CHI 1959 N

M R. Scheffing
1B R. Long
2B A. Taylor
SS E. Banks
3B A. Dark
OF G. Altman
OF R. Walls
OF R. Thomson
C S. Taylor

UT R. Marshall
UT W. Moryn
P R. Anderson
P G. Hobbie
P D. Hillman
P M. Drabowsky
P A. Ceccarelli
RP W. Henry
RP D. Elston

CHI 1960 N

M C. Grimm
M L. Boudreau
1B E. Bouchee
2B G. Kindall
SS E. Banks
3B R. Santo
OF D. Ashburn
OF R. Will
OF G. Altman
C M. Thacker
UT F. Thomas
UT D. Zimmer
P G. Hobbie
P R. Anderson
P R. Ellsworth
P D. Cardwell
RP D. Elston
RP S. Morehead

CHI 1961 N

M A. Himsl
M H. Craft
M A. Himsl
M E. Tappe
M H. Craft
M A. Himsl
M E. Tappe
M L. Klein
M E. Tappe
1B E. Bouchee
2B D. Zimmer
SS E. Banks
3B R. Santo
OF B. Williams
OF G. Altman
OF A. Heist
C R. Bertell
UT D. Ashburn
UT G. Kindall
P D. Cardwell
P G. Hobbie
P R. Ellsworth
P J. Curtis
RP R. Anderson
RP R. Drott

CHI 1962 N

M E. Tappe
M L. Klein
M C. Metro
1B E. Banks
2B K. Hubbs
SS K. Rodgers
3B R. Santo
OF B. Williams
OF G. Altman
OF L. Brock
C R. Bertell
P R. Buhl
P R. Ellsworth
P D. Cardwell
P C. Koonce
P G. Hobbie
RP R. Anderson
RP G. Schultz

CHI 1963 N

M R. Kennedy
1B E. Banks
2B K. Hubbs
SS K. Rodgers
3B R. Santo
OF B. Williams
OF L. Brock
OF E. Burton
C R. Bertell
P R. Ellsworth
P L. Jackson
P R. Buhl
P G. Hobbie
P P. Toth
RP L. McDaniel
RP D. Elston

CHI 1964 N

M R. Kennedy
1B E. Banks
2B J. Amalfitano

SS K. Rodgers
3B R. Santo
OF B. Williams
OF B. Cowan
OF L. Gabrielson
C R. Bertell
UT J. Stewart
P L. Jackson
P R. Ellsworth
P R. Buhl
P S. Burdette
P E. Broglio
RP L. McDaniel
RP D. Elston

CHI 1965 N
M R. Kennedy
M L. Klein
1B E. Banks
2B G. Beckert
SS D. Kessinger
3B R. Santo
OF B. Williams
OF D. Landrum
OF D. Clemens
C V. Roznovsky
UT J. Stewart
P L. Jackson
P R. Ellsworth
P R. Buhl
P C. Koonce
RP T. Abernathy
RP L. McDaniel

CHI 1966 N
M L. Durocher
1B E. Banks
2B G. Beckert
SS D. Kessinger
3B R. Santo
OF B. Williams
OF B. Browne
OF A. Phillips
C C. Hundley
P R. Ellsworth
P K. Holtzman
P F. Jenkins
P W. Hands
RP C. Koonce
RP C. Hendley

CHI 1967 N
M L. Durocher
1B E. Banks
2B G. Beckert
SS D. Kessinger
3B R. Santo
OF B. Williams
OF A. Phillips
OF T. Savage
C C. Hundley
P F. Jenkins
P R. Nye
P J. Niekro
P R. Culp
P W. Hands
RP C. Hartenstein
RP W. Stoneman

CHI 1968 N
M L. Durocher
1B E. Banks
2B G. Beckert
SS D. Kessinger
3B R. Santo
OF B. Williams
OF A. Phillips
OF J. Hickman
C C. Hundley
UT G. Hiser
UT P. Popovich
P F. Jenkins
P B. Hooton
P R. Reuschel
P M. Pappas
P W. Bonham
RP R. Locker
RP B. Burris

CHI 1969 N
M L. Durocher
1B E. Banks
2B G. Beckert
SS D. Kessinger
3B R. Santo
OF B. Williams
OF J. Hickman
OF D. Young
C C. Hundley
UT W. Smith
P F. Jenkins
P W. Hands
P K. Holtzman

P R. Selma
RP P. Regan
RP T. Abernathy

CHI 1970 N
M L. Durocher
1B J. Hickman
2B G. Beckert
SS D. Kessinger
3B R. Santo
OF B. Williams
OF J. Callison
OF C. James
C C. Hundley
P F. Jenkins
P K. Holtzman
P W. Hands
P M. Pappas
P G. Decker
RP P. Regan
RP J. Colborn

CHI 1971 N
M L. Durocher
1B J. Pepitone
2B G. Beckert
SS D. Kessinger
3B R. Santo
OF B. Williams
OF B. Davis
OF J. Callison
C C. Cannizzaro
UT J. Hickman
P F. Jenkins
P M. Pappas
P W. Hands
P K. Holtzman
P J. Pizarro
RP P. Regan
RP W. Bonham

CHI 1972 N
M L. Durocher
M C. Lockman
1B J. Hickman
2B G. Beckert
SS D. Kessinger
3B R. Santo
OF B. Williams
OF J. Cardenal
OF R. Monday
C C. Hundley
P F. Jenkins
P B. Hooton
P M. Pappas
P W. Hands
P R. Reuschel
RP T. Phoebus
RP J. Aker

CHI 1973 N
M C. Lockman
1B J. Hickman
2B G. Beckert
SS D. Kessinger
3B R. Santo
OF B. Williams
OF R. Monday
OF J. Cardenal
OF B. Williams
C C. Hundley
UT G. Hiser
UT P. Popovich
P F. Jenkins
P B. Hooton
P R. Reuschel
P M. Pappas
P W. Bonham
RP R. Locker
RP B. Burris

CHI 1974 N
M C. Lockman
M R. Marshall
1B A. Thornton
2B V. Harris
SS D. Kessinger
3B B. Madlock
OF J. Morales
OF R. Monday
OF J. Cardenal
C S. Swisher
UT B. Williams
P W. Bonham
P R. Reuschel
P B. Hooton
P S. Stone
RP K. Frailing
RP D. LaRoche

CHI 1975 N
M R. Marshall
1B A. Thornton
2B J. Trillo
SS D. Kessinger
3B B. Madlock
OF J. Morales
OF J. Cardenal
OF R. Monday
C S. Swisher
UT R. LaCock
P B. Burris
P R. Reuschel
P W. Bonham
P S. Stone
RP D. Knowles
RP T. Dettore

CHI 1976 N
M R. Marshall
1B R. LaCock
2B J. Trillo
SS M. Kelleher
3B B. Madlock
OF J. Morales
OF J. Cardenal
OF R. Monday
C S. Swisher
UT G. Mitterwald
UT H. Wallis
P R. Reuschel
P B. Burris
P W. Bonham
P S. Renko
RP P. Reuschel
RP H. Sutter

CHI 1977 N
M H. Franks
1B W. Buckner
2B J. Trillo
SS I. DeJesus
3B S. Ontiveros
OF B. Murcer
OF J. Morales
OF G. Gross
C G. Mitterwald
UT L. Biittner
UT J. Cardenal
UT E. Clines
P R. Reuschel
P B. Burris
P W. Bonham
P M. Krukow
RP G. Hernandez
RP H. Sutter

CHI 1978 N
M H. Franks
1B W. Buckner
2B J. Trillo
SS I. DeJesus
3B S. Ontiveros
OF B. Murcer
OF G. Gross
OF D. Kingman
C R. Rader
UT L. Biittner
UT E. Clines
P R. Reuschel
P D. Lamp
P B. Burris
P D. Roberts
P M. Krukow
RP D. Moore
RP H. Sutter

CHI 1979 N
M H. Franks
M J. Amalfitano
1B W. Buckner
2B T. Sizemore
SS I. DeJesus
3B S. Ontiveros
OF J. Martin
OF D. Kingman
OF V. Thompson
C B. Foote
UT L. Biittner
P R. Reuschel
P L. McGlothen
P D. Lamp
P M. Krukow
P K. Holtzman
RP R. Tidrow
RP H. Sutter

CHI 1980 N
M P. Gomez
M J. Amalfitano
1B W. Buckner
2B M. Tyson
SS I. DeJesus
3B L. Randle
OF J. Martin
OF M. Vail
OF V. Thompson
C T. Blackwell
UT L. Biittner
UT S. Dillard
UT J. Figueroa
UT M. Kelleher
P R. Reuschel
P M. Krukow
P D. Lamp
P L. McGlothen
RP W. Caudill
RP R. Tidrow

CHI 1981 N
M J. Amalfitano
1B W. Buckner
2B M. Tyson
SS I. DeJesus
3B K. Reitz
OF L. Durham
OF S. Henderson
OF J. Morales
C J. Davis
P M. Krukow
P R. Martz
P R. Reuschel
P K. Kravec
P J. Bird
RP R. Tidrow
RP W. Caudill

CHI 1982 N
M L. Elia
1B W. Buckner
2B B. Wills
SS L. Bowa
3B R. Sandberg
OF L. Durham
OF G. Woods
OF B. Moreland
C J. Davis
UT J. Johnstone
UT J. Kennedy
P F. Jenkins
P J. Bird
P D. Noles
P R. Martz
P A. Ripley
RP L. Smith
RP R. Tidrow

CHI 1983 N
M L. Elia
M C. Fox
1B W. Buckner
2B R. Sandberg
SS L. Bowa
3B R. Cey
OF B. Moreland
OF M. Hall
OF L. Durham
C J. Davis
P C. Rainey
P S. Trout
P F. Jenkins
P R. Ruthven
P D. Noles
RP W. Campbell
RP L. Smith

CHI 1984 N
M J. Frey
1B L. Durham
2B R. Sandberg
SS L. Bowa
3B R. Cey
OF G. Matthews
OF R. Dernier
OF B. Moreland
C J. Davis
UT H. Cotto
P S. Trout
P D. Eckersley
P R. Sutcliffe
P S. Sanderson
P R. Ruthven
RP L. Smith
RP T. Stoddard

CHI 1985 N
M J. Frey
1B L. Durham
2B R. Sandberg
SS S. Dunston
3B R. Cey
1B W. Buckner
OF B. Dernier
OF G. Matthews
C J. Davis
UT T. Bosley
UT D. Lopes
UT C. Speier
P D. Eckersley
P S. Fontenot
P S. Trout
P R. Sutcliffe
P S. Sanderson
RP L. Smith
RP L. Sorensen

CHI 1986 N
M J. Frey
M J. Vukovich
M E. Michael
1B L. Durham
2B R. Sandberg
SS S. Dunston
3B R. Cey
OF B. Moreland
OF G. Matthews
OF R. Dernier
C J. Davis
UT J. Mumphrey
P D. Eckersley
P R. Sutcliffe
P S. Sanderson
P S. Trout
P E. Lynch
RP L. Smith
RP G. Hoffman

CHI 1987 N
M E. Michael
M F. Lucchesi
1B L. Durham
2B R. Sandberg
SS S. Dunston
3B B. Moreland
OF A. Dawson
OF D. Martinez
OF J. Mumphrey
C J. Davis
UT B. Dayett
UT J. Trillo
P R. Sutcliffe
P J. Moyer
P G. Maddux
P S. Sanderson
P L. Lancaster
RP E. Lynch
RP L. Smith

CHI 1988 N
M D. Zimmer
1B M. Grace
2B R. Sandberg
SS S. Dunston
3B V. Law
OF R. Palmeiro
OF A. Dawson
OF D. Jackson
C D. Berryhill
P G. Maddux
P R. Sutcliffe
P J. Moyer
P C. Schiraldi
P J. Pico
RP F. DiPino
RP L. Lancaster

Cincinnati

CIN N 1876-1880
CIN U 1884
CIN a 1882-1889
CM a 1891
   Combined with
   Milwaukee
CIN N 1890-1988

CIN 1876 N
M C. Gould
1B C. Gould
2B C. Sweasy
SS H. Kessler
3B W. Foley
OF C. Jones
OF E. Snyder
OF D. Pearson
C A. Booth
P C. Dean
P W. Fisher
P E. Williams

CIN 1877 N
M L. Pike
1B L. Pike
2B J. McPhee
3B R. Cey

M R. Addy
1B C. Gould
2B J. Hallinan
SS J. Manning
3B W. Foley
OF R. Addy
OF L. Pike
OF C. Jones
C W. Hastings
UT A. Booth
P W. Cummings
P R. Mathews
P R. Mitchell

CIN 1878 N
M C. McVey
1B J. Sullivan
2B J. Gerhardt
SS W. Geer
3B C. McVey
OF C. Jones
OF M. Kelly
OF L. Pike
C J. White
P W. White
P R. Mitchell

CIN 1879 N
M J. White
M C. McVey
1B C. McVey
2B J. Gerhardt
SS R. Barnes
3B M. Kelly
OF L. Dickerson
OF P. Hotaling
OF W. Foley
C J. White
P W. White

CIN 1880 N
M J. Clapp
1B J. Reilly
2B C. Smith
SS L. Say
3B W. Carpenter
OF W. Purcell
OF M. Mansell
OF J. Manning
C J. Clapp
P W. White

CIN 1884 U
M D. O'Leary
M S. Crane
1B M. Powell
2B S. Crane
SS R. Jones
3B C. Barber
OF L. Sylvester
OF W. Harbidge
OF W. Hawes
C J. Kelly
UT R. Burns
P G. Bradley
P J. McCormick

CIN 1882 a
M C. Snyder
1B D. Stearns
2B J. McPhee
SS C. Fulmer
3B W. Carpenter
OF J. Sommer
OF J. Macullar
OF H. Wheeler
C C. Snyder
P W. White
P P. McCormick

CIN 1883 a
M C. Snyder
1B J. Reilly
2B J. McPhee
SS C. Fulmer
3B W. Carpenter
OF J. Sommer
OF C. Jones
OF J. Corkhill
C C. Snyder
P W. White
P L. Deagle
P P. McCormick

CIN 1884 a
M W. White
M C. Snyder
1B J. Reilly
2B J. McPhee
SS J. Peoples
3B W. Carpenter
OF C. Jones
OF J. Corkhill
OF T. Mansell
C C. Snyder
P W. White
P W. Mountjoy
P A. Shallix

CIN 1885 a
M O. Caylor
1B J. Reilly
2B J. McPhee
SS F. Fennelly
3B W. Carpenter
OF C. Jones
OF J. Corkhill
OF J. Clinton
C C. Snyder
P W. White
P L. McKeon
P W. Mountjoy
P G. Pechiney
P A. Shallix

CIN 1886 a
M O. Caylor
1B J. Reilly
2B J. McPhee
SS F. Fennelly
3B W. Carpenter
OF C. Jones
OF J. Corkhill
OF F. Lewis
C C. Baldwin
P A. Mullane
P G. Pechiney
P L. McKeon

CIN 1887 a
M G. Schmelz
1B J. Reilly
2B J. McPhee
SS F. Fennelly
3B W. Carpenter
OF J. Corkhill
OF H. Nicol
OF G. Tebeau
C C. Baldwin
P E. Smith
P A. Mullane
P W. Serad

CIN 1888 a
M G. Schmelz
1B J. Reilly
2B J. McPhee
SS F. Fennelly
3B W. Carpenter
OF H. Nicol
OF G. Tebeau
OF J. Corkhill
C L. Keenan
P L. Viau
P A. Mullane
P E. Smith

CIN 1889 a
M G. Schmelz
1B J. Reilly
2B J. McPhee
SS O. Beard
3B W. Carpenter
OF J. Holliday
OF G. Tebeau
OF H. Nicol
C L. Keenan
P J. Duryea
P L. Viau
P A. Mullane
P E. Smith

CM 1891 a
M M. Kelly
M C. Cushman
1B J. Carney
2B W. Robinson
SS J. Canavan
3B A. Whitney
OF R. Johnston
OF J. Seery
OF G. Andrews
C M. Kelly
UT H. Vaughn
P J. Dwyer
P E. Crane
P W. Mains
P G. Davies
P F. Killen

CIN 1890 N

M T. Loftus
1B J. Reilly
2B J. McPhee
SS O. Beard
3B C. Marr
OF J. Holliday
OF J. Knight
OF H. Nicol
C J. Harrington
P W. Rhines
P J. Duryea
P F. Foreman
P L. Viau

CIN 1891 N

M T. Loftus
1B J. Reilly
2B J. McPhee
SS G. Smith
3B W. Latham
OF J. Holliday
OF C. Marr
OF W. Halligan
C J. Harrington
P A. Mullane
P W. Rhines
P C. Radbourn
P E. Crane

CIN 1892 N

M C. Comiskey
1B C. Comiskey
2B J. McPhee
SS G. Smith
3B W. Latham
OF J. Holliday
OF J. O'Neill
OF L. Browning
C M. Murphy
P E. Chamberlin
P A. Mullane
P J. Dwyer
P M. Sullivan

CIN 1893 N

M C. Comiskey
1B C. Comiskey
2B J. McPhee
SS G. Smith
3B W. Latham
OF J. Holliday
OF J. Canavan
OF J. McCarthy
C H. Vaughn
P J. Dwyer
P E. Chamberlin
P M. Sullivan
P T. Parrott
P A. Mullane

CIN 1894 N

M C. Comiskey
1B C. Comiskey
2B J. McPhee
SS G. Smith
3B W. Latham
OF W. Hoy
OF J. Holliday
OF J. Canavan
C M. Murphy
P J. Dwyer
P T. Parrott
P E. Chamberlin
P C. Fisher

CIN 1895 N

M W. Ewing
1B W. Ewing
2B J. McPhee
SS G. Smith
3B W. Latham
OF C. Miller
OF W. Hoy
OF G. Hogriever
C H. Vaughn
P J. Dwyer
P W. Rhines
P T. Parrott
P F. Foreman
P W. Phillips

CIN 1896 N

M W. Ewing
1B W. Ewing
2B J. McPhee
SS G. Smith
3B C. Irwin
OF C. Miller
OF E. Burke
OF W. Hoy
C H. Peitz
UT H. Vaughn
P J. Dwyer
P P. Ehret
P F. Foreman
P C. Fisher
P W. Rhines

CIN 1897 N

M W. Ewing
1B J. Beckley
2B J. McPhee
SS C. Ritchey
3B C. Irwin
OF W. Hoy
OF C. Miller
OF E. Burke
C H. Peitz
UT T. Corcoran
P T. Breitenstein
P W. Rhines
P J. Dwyer
P P. Ehret
P W. Damman

CIN 1898 N

M W. Ewing
1B J. Beckley
2B J. McPhee
SS T. Corcoran
3B C. Irwin
OF C. Miller
OF E. Smith
OF A. McBride
C H. Peitz
P E. Hawley
P T. Breitenstein
P W. Hill
P J. Dwyer
P W. Damman

CIN 1899 N

M W. Ewing
1B J. Beckley
2B J. McPhee
SS T. Corcoran
3B C. Irwin
OF A. Selbach
OF E. Smith
OF C. Miller
C H. Peitz
UT H. Steinfeldt
P F. Hahn
P E. Hawley
P W. Phillips
P T. Breitenstein
P J. Taylor

CIN 1900 N

M R. Allen
1B J. Beckley
2B J. Quinn
SS T. Corcoran
3B H. Steinfeldt
OF J. Barrett
OF A. McBride
OF S. Crawford
C H. Peitz
P E. Scott
P F. Hahn
P E. Newton
P W. Phillips
P T. Breitenstein

CIN 1901 N

M J. McPhee
1B J. Beckley
2B H. Steinfeldt
SS G. Magoon
3B C. Irwin
OF R. Harley
OF S. Crawford
OF J. Dobbs
C W. Bergen
P F. Hahn
P W. Phillips
P E. Newton
P A. Stimmel

CIN 1902 N

M J. McPhee
M F. Bancroft
M J. Kelley
1B J. Beckley
2B H. Peitz
SS T. Corcoran
3B H. Steinfeldt
OF S. Crawford
OF W. Hoy
OF J. Dobbs
C W. Bergen
P F. Hahn
P W. Phillips
P H. Thielman
P E. Poole
P G. Ewing

CIN 1903 N

M J. Kelley
1B J. Beckley
2B T. Daly
SS T. Corcoran
3B H. Steinfeldt
OF J. Seymour
OF M. Donlin
OF P. Dolan
C H. Peitz
UT J. Kelley
P F. Hahn
P G. Ewing
P J. Sutthoff
P E. Poole
P C. Harper

CIN 1904 N

M J. Kelley
1B J. Kelley
2B M. Huggins
SS T. Corcoran
3B H. Steinfeldt
OF J. Seymour
OF F. Odwell
OF P. Dolan
C G. Schlei
P F. Hahn
P C. Harper
P W. Kellum
P T. Walker
P G. Ewing

CIN 1905 N

M J. Kelley
1B J. Barry
2B M. Huggins
SS T. Corcoran
3B H. Steinfeldt
OF J. Seymour
OF F. Odwell
OF J. Kelley
C G. Schlei
P O. Overall
P G. Ewing
P C. Chech
P C. Harper
P T. Walker

CIN 1906 N

M E. Hanlon
1B J. Deal
2B M. Huggins
SS T. Corcoran
3B J. Delahanty
OF J. Kelley
OF F. Jude
OF J. Seymour
C G. Schlei
P J. Weimer
P G. Ewing
P C. Fraser
P R. Wicker
P C. Hall

CIN 1907 N

M E. Hanlon
1B J. Ganzel
2B M. Huggins
SS J. Lobert
3B H. Mowrey
OF M. Mitchell
OF A. Kruger
OF F. Odwell
C J. McLean
P G. Ewing
P A. Coakley
P J. Weimer
P R. Hitt
P A. Mason

CIN 1908 N

M J. Ganzel
1B J. Ganzel
2B M. Huggins
SS R. Hulswitt
3B J. Lobert
OF J. Kane
OF M. Mitchell
OF G. Paskert
C G. Schlei
UT J. McLean
P G. Ewing
P R. Spade
P A. Coakley
P W. Campbell
P J. Weimer

CIN 1909 N

M C. Griffith
1B R. Hoblitzel
2B R. Egan
SS T. Downey
3B J. Lobert
OF M. Mitchell
OF R. Bescher
OF E. Oakes
C J. McLean
UT G. Paskert
P A. Fromme
P H. Gaspar
P J. Rowan
P G. Ewing
P W. Campbell

CIN 1910 N

M C. Griffith
1B R. Hoblitzel
2B R. Egan
SS T. McMillan
3B J. Lobert
OF R. Bescher
OF M. Mitchell
OF G. Paskert
C J. McLean
UT T. Downey
P H. Gaspar
P G. Suggs
P J. Rowan
P F. Beebe
P W. Burns

CIN 1911 N

M C. Griffith
1B R. Hoblitzel
2B R. Egan
SS T. Downey
3B E. Grant
OF R. Bescher
OF J. Bates
OF M. Mitchell
C J. McLean
P G. Suggs
P H. Gaspar
P R. Keefe
P A. Fromme
P F. Smith

CIN 1912 N

M H. O'Day
1B R. Hoblitzel
2B R. Egan
SS J. Esmond
3B A. Phelan
OF M. Mitchell
OF R. Bescher
OF A. Marsans
C J. McLean
UT E. Grant
P G. Suggs
P J. Benton
P A. Fromme
P A. Humphrieee

CIN 1913 N

M J. Tinker
1B R. Hoblitzel
2B H. Groh
SS J. Tinker
3B J. Dodge
OF R. Bescher
OF J. Bates
OF A. Marsans
C T. Clarke
P G. Johnson
P G. Suggs
P E. Packard
P L. Ames
P M. Brown
RP F. Harter

CIN 1914 N

M C. Herzog
1B R. Hoblitzel
2B H. Groh
SS C. Herzog
3B J. Niehoff
OF J. Moran
OF B. Daniels
OF G. Twombly
C T. Clarke
UT M. Gonzalez
P L. Ames
P J. Benton
P P. Douglas
P E. Yingling
P P. Schneider

CIN 1915 N

M C. Herzog
1B F. Mollwitz
2B W. Rodgers
SS C. Herzog
3B H. Groh
OF T. Griffith
OF W. Killefer
OF T. Leach
C I. Wingo
P E. Dale
P P. Schneider
P F. Toney
P J. Benton
P C. Lear

CIN 1916 N

M C. Herzog
M I. Wingo
M C. Mathewson
1B H. Chase
2B W. Louden
SS C. Herzog
3B H. Groh
OF T. Griffith
OF A. Neale
OF E. Roush
C I. Wingo
P F. Toney
P P. Schneider
P A. Schulz
P C. Mitchell
P E. Knetzer

CIN 1917 N

M C. Mathewson
1B H. Chase
2B D. Shean
SS W. Kopf
3B H. Groh
OF E. Roush
OF A. Neale
OF T. Griffith
C I. Wingo
P F. Toney
P P. Schneider
P M. Regan
P C. Mitchell
P H. Eller

CIN 1918 N

M C. Mathewson
M H. Groh
1B H. Chase
2B L. Magee
SS R. Blackburne
3B H. Groh
OF T. Griffith
OF E. Roush
OF A. Neale
C I. Wingo
UT S. Magee
P H. Eller
P P. Schneider
P J. Ring
P F. Toney
P R. Bressler

CIN 1919 N

M P. Moran
1B J. Daubert
2B M. Rath
SS W. Kopf
3B H. Groh
OF A. Neale
OF E. Roush
OF R. Bressler
C I. Wingo
P H. Eller
P W. Ruether
P H. Sallee
P J. Ring
P R. Fisher

CIN 1920 N

M P. Moran
1B J. Daubert
2B M. Rath
SS W. Kopf
3B H. Groh
OF L. Duncan
OF A. Neale
OF E. Roush
C I. Wingo
P J. Ring
P W. Ruether
P H. Eller
P A. Luque
P R. Fisher

CIN 1921 N

M P. Moran
1B J. Daubert
2B S. Bohne
SS W. Kopf
3B H. Groh
OF L. Duncan
OF E. Roush
OF R. Bressler
C I. Wingo
P A. Luque
P E. Rixey
P R. Marquard
P P. Donohue
RP S. Napier

CIN 1922 N

M P. Moran
1B J. Daubert
2B S. Bohne
SS J. Caveney
3B R. Pinelli
OF G. Burns
OF L. Duncan
OF G. Harper
C E. Hargrave
P E. Rixey
P J. Couch
P A. Luque
P P. Donohue
P F. Keck
RP J. Gillespie

CIN 1923 N

M P. Moran
1B J. Daubert
2B S. Bohne
SS J. Caveney
3B R. Pinelli
OF G. Burns
OF L. Duncan
OF E. Roush
C E. Hargrave
P A. Luque
P E. Rixey
P P. Donohue
P J. Benton
RP F. Keck

CIN 1924 N

M J. Hendricks
1B J. Daubert
2B H. Critz
SS J. Caveney
3B R. Pinelli
OF E. Roush
OF W. Walker
OF G. Burns
C E. Hargrave
UT S. Bohne
UT R. Bressler
UT L. Duncan
P E. Rixey
P C. Mays
P P. Donohue
P A. Luque
P T. Sheehan
RP F. May

CIN 1925 N

M J. Hendricks
1B W. Holke
2B H. Critz
SS J. Caveney
3B R. Pinelli
OF W. Walker
OF E. Roush
OF W. Zitzmann
C E. Hargrave
UT R. Bressler
UT E. Smith
P P. Donohue
P A. Luque
P E. Rixey
P J. Benton
P F. May
RP H. Biemiller

CIN 1926 N

M J. Hendricks
1B W. Pipp
2B H. Critz
SS F. Emmer
3B C. Dressen
OF W. Walker
OF E. Roush
OF W. Christensen
C E. Hargrave
P P. Donohue
P C. Mays
P A. Luque
P E. Rixey
P F. May

CIN 1927 N

M J. Hendricks
1B W. Pipp
2B H. Critz
SS H. Ford
3B C. Dressen
OF W. Walker
OF R. Bressler
OF E. Allen
C E. Hargrave
P C. Lucas
P F. May
P A. Luque
P E. Rixey
P P. Donohue

CIN 1928 N

M J. Hendricks
1B G. Kelly
2B H. Critz
SS H. Ford
3B C. Dressen
OF E. Allen
OF W. Walker
OF W. Zitzmann
C V. Picinich
UT W. Pipp
P E. Rixey
P A. Luque
P R. Kolp
P C. Lucas
P P. Donohue
RP P. Appleton

CIN 1929 N

M J. Hendricks
1B G. Kelly
2B H. Critz
SS H. Ford
3B C. Dressen
OF E. Swanson
OF W. Walker
OF E. Allen
C J. Gooch
P C. Lucas
P E. Rixey
P F. May
P P. Donohue
P A. Luque
RP K. Ash
RP W. Ehrhardt

CIN 1930 N

M D. Howley
1B J. Stripp
2B H. Ford
SS L. Durocher
3B A. Cuccinello
OF W. Walker
OF R. Meusel
OF H. Heilmann
C C. Sukeforth
UT E. Swanson
P B. Frey
P C. Lucas
P L. Benton
P R. Kolp
P E. Rixey
RP S. Johnson
RP A. Campbell

CIN 1931 N

M D. Howley
1B H. Hendrick
2B A. Cuccinello
SS L. Durocher
3B J. Stripp
OF E. Crabtree
OF T. Douthit
OF E. Roush
C C. Sukeforth
UT H. Cullop
P S. Johnson
P C. Lucas
P L. Benton
P B. Frey
P E. Rixey

CIN 1932 N

M D. Howley
1B H. Hendrick
2B G. Grantham
SS L. Durocher
3B W. Gilbert
OF F. Herman
OF E. Crabtree
OF W. Roettger
C E. Lombardi
UT T. Douthit
P C. Lucas
P S. Johnson
P O. Carroll
P L. Benton
P R. Kolp
RP J. Ogden

CIN 1933 N

M O. Bush
1B J. Bottomley
2B J. Morrissey
SS O. Bluege
3B E. Adams
OF C. Hafey
OF H. Rice
OF J. Moore
C E. Lombardi
P S. Derringer
P C. Lucas
P S. Johnson
P L. Benton
P R. Kolp

CIN 1934 N

M R. O'Farrell
M B. Shotton
M C. Dressen
1B J. Bottomley
2B A. Piet
SS G. Slade
3B M. Koenig
OF C. Hafey
OF A. Comorosky
OF H. Pool
C E. Lombardi
P S. Derringer
P B. Frey
P S. Johnson
P A. Freitas
P A. Stout
RP J. Brennan
RP R. Kolp

CIN 1935 N

M C. Dressen
1B J. Bottomley
2B A. Kampouris
SS W. Myers
3B L. Riggs
OF I. Goodman
OF S. Byrd
OF F. Herman
C E. Lombardi
P S. Derringer
P A. Hollingsworth
P E. Schott
P A. Freitas
P S. Johnson

CIN 1936 N

M C. Dressen
1B L. Scarsella
2B A. Kampouris
SS W. Myers
3B L. Riggs
OF H. Cuyler
OF I. Goodman
OF F. Herman
C E. Lombardi
UT C. Chapman
UT T. Thevenow
P S. Derringer
P A. Hollingsworth
P E. Schott
P W. Hallahan
P B. Frey
RP J. Brennan

CIN 1937 N

M C. Dressen
M R. Wallace
1B B. Jordan
2B A. Kampouris
SS W. Myers
3B L. Riggs
OF I. Goodman
OF H. Cuyler
OF C. Hafey
C E. Lombardi
UT L. Scarsella
P L. Grissom
P S. Derringer
P R. Davis
P A. Hollingsworth
P E. Schott

CIN 1938 N

M W. McKechnie
1B F. McCormick
2B L. Frey
SS W. Myers
3B L. Riggs
OF H. Craft
OF I. Goodman
OF W. Berger
C E. Lombardi
P S. Derringer
P J. Vander Meer
P W. Walters
P R. Davis
P J. Weaver
RP E. Schott
RP J. Cascarella

CIN 1939 N

M W. McKechnie
1B F. McCormick
2B L. Frey
SS W. Myers
3B W. Werber
OF H. Craft
OF I. Goodman
OF W. Berger
C E. Lombardi
P W. Walters
P S. Derringer
P L. Moore
P L. Grissom
P E. Thompson

CIN 1940 N

M W. McKechnie
1B F. Mc Cormick
2B L. Frey
SS W. Myers
3B W. Werber
OF I. Goodman
OF H. Craft
OF M. Mc Cormick
C E. Lombardi
P W. Walters
P S. Derringer
P E. Thompson
P J. Turner
P L. Moore
RP J. Beggs
RP M. Shoffner

CIN 1941 N

M W. McKechnie
1B F. Mc Cormick
2B L. Frey
SS E. Joost
3B W. Werber
OF H. Craft
OF M. Mc Cormick
OF J. Gleeson
C E. Lombardi
P W. Walters
P S. Derringer
P J. Vander Meer
P E. Riddle
P J. Turner
RP L. Moore
RP J. Beggs

CIN 1942 N

M W. McKechnie
1B F. McCormick
2B L. Frey
SS E. Joost
3B B. Haas
OF M. Marshall
OF G. Walker
OF E. Tipton
C R. Lamanno
P R. Starr
P W. Walters
P J. Vander Meer
P S. Derringer
P E. Riddle
RP J. Beggs
RP C. Shoun

CIN 1943 N

M W. McKechnie
1B F. McCormick
2B L. Frey
SS E. Miller
3B S. Mesner
OF E. Tipton
OF M. Marshall
OF G. Walker
C R. Mueller
UT E. Crabtree
UT B. Haas
P J. Vander Meer
P E. Riddle
P W. Walters
P R. Starr
P C. Shoun
RP J. Beggs

CIN 1944 N

M W. McKechnie
1B F. McCormick
2B W. Williams
SS E. Miller
3B S. Mesner
OF E. Tipton
OF G. Walker
OF D. Clay
C R. Mueller
P W. Walters
P C. Shoun
P E. Heusser
P T. DeLa Cruz
P H. Gumbert

CIN 1945 N

M W. McKechnie
1B F. McCormick
2B W. Williams
SS E. Miller
3B S. Mesner
OF D. Clay
OF A. Libke
OF E. Tipton
C A. Lakeman
UT G. Walker
P E. Heusser
P J. Bowman
P W. Walters
P H. Fox
P L. Kennedy
RP H. Lisenbee

CIN 1946 N

M W. McKechnie
M H. Gowdy
1B B. Haas
2B R. Adams
SS E. Miller
3B G. Hatton
OF D. Clay
OF A. Libke
OF E. Lukon
C R. Mueller
UT L. Frey
P J. Vander Meer
P E. Blackwell
P J. Beggs
P E. Heusser
P W. Walters
RP C. Shoun
RP R. Malloy

CIN 1947 N

M J. Neun
1B N. Young
2B B. Zientara
SS E. Miller
3B G. Hatton
OF F. Baumholtz
OF A. Galan
OF B. Haas
C R. Lamanno
P E. Blackwell
P J. Vander Meer
P K. Peterson
P E. Lively
P W. Walters
RP J. Hetki
RP H. Gumbert

CIN 1948 N

M J. Neun
M W. Walters
1B T. Kluszewski
2B R. Adams
SS T. Stallcup
3B G. Hatton
OF H. Sauer
OF J. Wyrostek
OF F. Baumholtz
C R. Lamanno
UT D. Litwhiler
P J. Vander Meer
P K. Raffensberger
P H. Fox
P H. Wehmeier
P E. Blackwell
RP H. Gumbert
RP W. Cress

CIN 1949 N

M W. Walters
M J. Sewell
1B T. Kluszewski
2B J. Bloodworth
SS T. Stallcup
3B G. Hatton
OF J. Wyrostek
OF L. Merriman
OF D. Litwhiler
C W. Cooper
UT R. Adams
P K. Raffensberger
P H. Fox
P H. Wehmeier
P J. Vander Meer
P E. Lively
RP E. Erautt
RP E. Blackwell

CIN 1950 N

M J. Sewell
1B T. Kluszewski
2B C. Ryan
SS T. Stallcup
3B G. Hatton
OF J. Wyrostek
OF R. Usher
OF L. Merriman
C H. Howell
UT R. Adams
UT J. Adcock
P E. Blackwell
P K. Raffensberger
P H. Wehmeier
P H. Fox
P J. Ramsdell
RP F. Smith
RP E. Erautt

CIN 1951 N

M J. Sewell
1B T. Kluszewski
2B C. Ryan
SS T. Stallcup
3B G. Hatton
OF J. Wyrostek
OF J. Adcock
OF L. Merriman
C H. Howell
UT R. Adams
UT R. Usher
P K. Raffensberger
P E. Blackwell
P H. Fox
P J. Ramsdell
P H. Wehmeier
RP H. Perkowski
RP F. Smith

CIN 1952 N

M J. Sewell
M E. Brucker
M R. Hornsby
1B T. Kluszewski
2B G. Hatton
SS R. McMillan
3B R. Adams
OF W. Marshall
OF R. Borkowski
OF J. Adcock
C A. Seminick
P K. Raffensberger
P H. Perkowski
P H. Wehmeier
P E. Church
P F. Hiller
RP F. Smith
RP J. Nuxhall

CIN 1953 N

M R. Hornsby
M C. Mills
1B T. Kluszewski
2B E. Bridges
SS R. McMillan
3B R. Adams
OF J. Greengrass
OF D. Bell
OF W. Marshall
C A. Seminick
UT R. Borkowski
P H. Perkowski
P C. Podbielan
P K. Raffensberger
P J. Nuxhall
P F. Baczewski
RP F. Smith
RP H. Wehmeier

CIN 1954 N

M G. Tebbetts
1B T. Kluszewski
2B J. Temple
SS R. McMillan
3B R. Adams
OF D. Bell
OF J. Greengrass
OF W. Post
C A. Seminick
UT C. Harmon
P J. Fowler
P H. Valentine
P J. Nuxhall
P C. Podbielan
P F. Baczewski
RP H. Judson
RP F. Smith

CIN 1955 N

M G. Tebbetts
1B T. Kluszewski
2B J. Temple
SS R. McMillan
3B E. Bridges
OF W. Post
OF D. Bell
OF S. Palys
C F. Burgess
UT C. Harmon
P J. Nuxhall
P J. Fowler
P J. Klippstein
P J. Collum
P G. Staley
RP R. Minarcin
RP H. Freeman

CIN 1956 N

M G. Tebbetts
1B T. Kluszewski
2B J. Temple
SS R. McMillan
3B R. Jablonski
OF F. Robinson
OF D. Bell
OF W. Post
C L. Bailey
P B. Lawrence
P J. Klippstein
P J. Nuxhall
P J. Fowler
P H. Jeffcoat
RP H. Freeman
RP T. Acker

CIN 1957 N

M G. Tebbetts
1B G. Crowe
2B J. Temple
SS R. McMillan
3B D. Hoak
OF F. Robinson
OF W. Post
OF D. Bell
C L. Bailey
P B. Lawrence
P H. Jeffcoat
P J. Nuxhall
P D. Gross
P J. Klippstein
RP T. Acker
RP J. Fowler

CIN 1958 N

M G. Tebbetts
M J. Dykes
1B G. Crowe
2B J. Temple
SS R. McMillan
3B D. Hoak
OF F. Robinson
OF D. Bell
OF G. Lynch
C L. Bailey
UT F. Burgess
UT A. Grammas
UT R. Thurman
P R. Purkey
P H. Haddix
P B. Lawrence
P J. Nuxhall
P D. Newcombe
RP H. Jeffcoat
RP W. Schmidt

CIN 1959 N

M E. Smith
M F. Hutchinson
1B F. Robinson
2B J. Temple
SS E. Kasko
3B W. Jones
OF V. Pinson
OF D. Bell
OF G. Lynch
C L. Bailey
UT F. Thomas
P D. Newcombe
P R. Purkey
P J. Nuxhall
P J. O'Toole
RP O. Pena
RP B. Lawrence

CIN 1960 N

M F. Hutchinson
1B F. Robinson
2B A. Martin
SS R. McMillan
3B E. Kasko
OF V. Pinson
OF D. Bell
OF W. Post
C L. Bailey
UT G. Lynch
P R. Purkey
P J. Hook
P J. O'Toole
P C. McLish
RP J. Nuxhall
RP J. Brosnan

CIN 1961 N

M F. Hutchinson
1B G. Coleman
2B D. Blasingame
SS E. Kasko
3B E. Freese
OF V. Pinson
OF F. Robinson
OF W. Post
C G. Zimmerman
UT D. Bell
UT G. Lynch
P J. O'Toole
P J. Jay
P R. Purkey
P K. Hunt
P J. Maloney
RP J. Brosnan
RP J. Hook

CIN 1962 N

M F. Hutchinson
1B G. Coleman
2B D. Blasingame
SS L. Cardenas
3B E. Kasko
OF F. Robinson
OF V. Pinson
OF W. Post
C J. Edwards
UT R. Keough
UT G. Lynch
P R. Purkey
P J. Jay
P J. O'Toole
P J. Maloney
RP J. Klippstein
RP J. Brosnan

CIN 1963 N

M F. Hutchinson
1B G. Coleman
2B P. Rose
SS L. Cardenas
3B E. Freese
OF V. Pinson
OF F. Robinson
OF T. Harper
C J. Edwards
P J. Maloney
P J. O'Toole
P J. Nuxhall
P J. Tsitouris
P J. Jay
RP A. Worthington
RP W. Henry

CIN 1964 N

M F. Hutchinson
M R. Sisler
M F. Hutchinson
M R. Sisler
1B D. Johnson
2B P. Rose
SS L. Cardenas
3B S. Boros
OF F. Robinson
OF V. Pinson
OF T. Harper
C J. Edwards
UT R. Keough
P J. O'Toole
P J. Maloney
P R. Purkey
P J. Jay
P J. Tsitouris
RP S. Ellis
RP W. McCool

CIN 1965 N

M R. Sisler
1B A. Perez
2B P. Rose
SS L. Cardenas
3B D. Johnson
OF V. Pinson
OF T. Harper
OF F. Robinson
C J. Edwards
UT G. Coleman
P S. Ellis
P J. Maloney
P J. Jay
P J. Nuxhall
P J. Tsitouris
RP W. McCool
RP T. Davidson

CIN 1966 N

M D. Heffner
M J. Bristol
1B A. Perez
2B P. Rose
SS L. Cardenas
3B T. Helms
OF V. Pinson
OF T. Harper
OF D. Johnson
C J. Edwards
P J. Maloney
P S. Ellis
P M. Pappas
P J. O'Toole
P J. Nuxhall
RP D. Nottebart
RP W. McCool

CIN 1967 N

M J. Bristol
1B L. May
2B T. Helms
SS L. Cardenas
3B A. Perez
OF V. Pinson
OF P. Rose
OF T. Harper
C J. Edwards
UT D. Johnson
UT H. Ruiz
P G. Nolan
P M. Pappas
P M. Queen
P J. Maloney
P S. Ellis
RP T. Abernathy
RP D. Nottebart

CIN 1968 N

M J. Bristol
1B L. May
2B T. Helms
SS L. Cardenas
3B A. Perez
OF P. Rose
OF A. Johnson
OF V. Pinson
C J. Bench
UT M. Jones
P G. Culver
P J. Maloney
P G. Arrigo
P G. Nolan
RP T. Abernathy
RP C. Carroll

CIN 1969 N

M J. Bristol
1B L. May
2B T. Helms
SS W. Woodward
3B A. Perez
OF P. Rose
OF R. Tolan
OF A. Johnson

C   J. Bench
UT J. Stewart
P   J. Merritt
P   T. Cloninger
P   J. Maloney
P   J. Fisher
P   G. Nolan
RP C. Carroll
RP W. Granger

CIN 1970 N
M   G. Anderson
1B L. May
2B T. Helms
SS D. Concepcion
3B A. Perez
OF P. Rose
OF R. Tolan
OF B. Carbo
C   J. Bench
UT J. Stewart
UT W. Woodward
P   G. Nolan
P   J. Merritt
P   J. McGlothlin
P   W. Simpson
P   T. Cloninger
RP C. Carroll
RP W. Granger

CIN 1971 N
M   G. Anderson
1B L. May
2B T. Helms
SS D. Concepcion
3B A. Perez
OF P. Rose
OF G. Foster
OF H. McRae
C   J. Bench
UT B. Carbo
UT W. Woodward
P   G. Nolan
P   D. Gullett
P   J. McGlothlin
P   R. Grimsley
P   W. Simpson
RP W. Granger
RP C. Carroll

CIN 1972 N
M   G. Anderson
1B A. Perez
2B J. Morgan
SS D. Concepcion
3B D. Menke
OF P. Rose
OF R. Tolan
OF C. Geronimo
C   J. Bench
P   J. Billingham
P   R. Grimsley
P   G. Nolan
P   J. McGlothlin
P   D. Gullett
RP T. Hall
RP P. Borbon

CIN 1973 N
M   G. Anderson
1B A. Perez
2B J. Morgan
SS D. Concepcion
3B D. Menke
OF P. Rose
OF C. Geronimo
OF R. Tolan
C   J. Bench
UT D. Chaney
UT D. Driessen
P   J. Billingham
P   R. Grimsley
P   D. Gullett
P   F. Norman
RP P. Borbon
RP T. Hall

CIN 1974 N
M   G. Anderson
1B A. Perez
2B J. Morgan
SS D. Concepcion
3B D. Driessen
OF P. Rose
OF C. Geronimo
OF G. Foster
C   J. Bench
UT D. Chaney
P   D. Gullett
P   C. Kirby
P   J. Billingham

P   F. Norman
RP P. Borbon
RP C. Carroll

CIN 1975 N
M   G. Anderson
1B A. Perez
2B J. Morgan
SS D. Concepcion
3B P. Rose
OF C. Geronimo
OF G. Foster
OF G. Griffey
C   J. Bench
P   G. Nolan
P   J. Billingham
P   F. Norman
P   D. Gullett
P   P. Darcy
RP P. Borbon
RP C. Carroll

CIN 1976 N
M   G. Anderson
1B A. Perez
2B J. Morgan
SS D. Concepcion
3B P. Rose
OF C. Geronimo
OF G. Griffey
OF D. Collins
C   J. Bench
UT D. Driessen
P   G. Nolan
P   P. Zachry
P   F. Norman
P   J. Billingham
P   S. Alcala
RP P. Borbon
RP R. Eastwick

CIN 1977 N
M   G. Anderson
1B D. Driessen
2B J. Morgan
SS D. Concepcion
3B P. Rose
OF G. Foster
OF G. Griffey
OF C. Geronimo
C   J. Bench
P   F. Norman
P   G. Seaver
P   J. Billingham
P   P. Moskau
P   D. Capilla
RP P. Borbon
RP D. Murray

CIN 1978 N
M   G. Anderson
1B D. Driessen
2B J. Morgan
SS D. Concepcion
3B P. Rose
OF G. Foster
OF G. Griffey
OF C. Geronimo
C   J. Bench
P   J. Billingham
P   R. Grimsley
P   G. Nolan
P   J. McGlothlin
P   D. Gullett
RP T. Hall
RP P. Borbon

CIN 1979 N
M   J. McNamara
1B D. Driessen
2B J. Morgan
SS D. Concepcion
3B C. Knight
OF C. Geronimo
OF G. Foster
OF G. Griffey
C   J. Bench
UT D. Collins
P   G. Seaver
P   M. LaCoss
P   F. Norman
P   W. Bonham
P   P. Moskau
RP T. Hume
RP C. Bair

CIN 1980 N
M   J. McNamara
1B D. Driessen

2B J. Kennedy
SS D. Concepcion
3B C. Knight
OF G. Foster
OF D. Collins
OF G. Griffey
C   J. Bench
UT C. Geronimo
UT R. Oester
P   M. Soto
P   F. Pastore
P   C. Leibrandt
P   M. LaCoss
P   G. Seaver
RP T. Hume
RP C. Bair

CIN 1981 N
M   J. McNamara
1B D. Driessen
2B R. Oester
SS D. Concepcion
3B C. Knight
OF G. Foster
OF G. Griffey
OF D. Collins
C   J. Nolan
P   M. Soto
P   G. Seaver
P   F. Pastore
P   B. Berenyi
P   M. LaCoss
RP T. Hume
RP P. Moskau

CIN 1982 N
M   J. McNamara
M   R. Nixon
1B D. Driessen
2B R. Oester
SS D. Concepcion
3B J. Bench
OF P. Householder
OF C. Cedeno
OF E. Milner
C   A. Trevino
UT L. Biittner
P   M. Soto
P   B. Berenyi
P   F. Pastore
P   R. Shirley
P   G. Seaver
RP G. Harris
RP J. Kern

CIN 1983 N
M   R. Nixon
1B D. Driessen
2B R. Oester
SS D. Concepcion
3B N. Esasky
OF E. Milner
OF G. Redus
OF P. Householder
C   D. Bilardello
UT J. Bench
UT C. Cedeno
UT D. Walker
P   M. Soto
P   B. Berenyi
P   F. Pastore
P   C. Puleo
P   J. Price
RP T. Power
RP W. Scherrer

CIN 1984 N
M   V. Rapp
M   P. Rose
1B D. Driessen
2B R. Oester
SS D. Concepcion
3B N. Esasky
OF D. Parker
OF G. Redus
OF E. Milner
C   B. Gulden
UT C. Cedeno
UT T. Foley
UT W. Krenchicki
P   M. Soto
P   J. Russell
P   J. Price
P   J. Tibbs
P   F. Pastore
RP T. Hume
RP T. Power

CIN 1985 N
M   P. Rose
1B P. Rose

2B R. Oester
SS D. Concepcion
3B D. Bell
OF D. Parker
OF E. Milner
OF G. Redus
C   D. Van Gorder
UT N. Esasky
P   T. Browning
P   M. Soto
P   J. Tibbs
P   R. Robinson
P   J. Stuper
RP J. Franco
RP T. Power

CIN 1986 N
M   P. Rose
1B N. Esasky
2B R. Oester
SS K. Stillwell
3B D. Bell
OF D. Parker
OF E. Milner
OF E. Davis
C   B. Diaz
UT W. Venable
P   W. Gullickson
P   T. Browning
P   J. Denny
P   C. Welsh
P   M. Soto
RP T. Power
RP R. Robinson

CIN 1987 N
M   P. Rose
1B N. Esasky
2B R. Oester
SS B. Larkin
3B D. Bell
OF D. Parker
OF E. Davis
OF T. Jones
C   B. Diaz
UT D. Concepcion
UT K. Daniels
UT T. Francona
UT K. Stillwell
P   T. Power
P   T. Browning
P   W. Gullickson
P   G. Hoffman
P   R. Robinson
RP F. Williams
RP R. Murphy

CIN 1988 N
M   P. Rose
M   T. Helms
1B N. Esasky
2B H. Treadway
SS B. Larkin
3B C. Sabo
OF K. Daniels
OF E. Davis
OF P. O'Neill
C   B. Diaz
UT D. Collins
UT D. Concepcion
UT T. Jones
UT L. McClendon
UT T. McGriff
UT R. Oester
UT J. Reed
UT H. Winningham
P   D. Jackson
P   T. Browning
P   J. Rijo
P   M. Soto
P   R. Robinson
RP J. Franco
RP R. Murphy

Cleveland

CLE n 1871-1872
CLE N 1879-1884
CLE a 1887-1888
CLE P 1890
CLE N 1889-1899
CLE A 1901-1988

CLE 1871 n
M   C. Pabor
1B J. Carleton
2B E. Kimball
SS J. Bass
3B E. Sutton
OF A. Allison
OF C. Pabor
OF E. White

C   J. White
P   A. Pratt

CLE 1872 n
M   W. Hastings
M   J. White
1B J. Simmons
2B C. Sweasy
SS J. Holdsworth
3B E. Sutton
OF C. Pabor
OF A. Allison
OF R. Wolters
C   J. White
UT W. Hastings
P   A. Pratt
P   R. Wolters

CLE 1879 N
M   J. McCormick
1B W. Phillips
2B J. Glasscock
SS T. Carey
3B F. Warner
OF C. Eden
OF G. Strief
OF W. Riley
C   M. Kennedy
UT A. Gilligan
P   J. McCormick
P   R. Mitchell

CLE 1880 N
M   J. McCormick
1B W. Phillips
2B F. Dunlap
SS J. Glasscock
3B J. Hankinson
OF G. Shaffer
OF P. Hotaling
OF E. Hanlon
C   M. Kennedy
P   J. McCormick
P   F. Gardner

CLE 1881 N
M   M. McGeary
M   J. McCormick
1B W. Phillips
2B F. Dunlap
SS J. Glasscock
3B G. Bradley
OF G. Shaffer
OF J. Remsen
OF M. Moynahan
C   J. Clapp
P   J. McCormick
P   E. Nolan

CLE 1882 N
M   J. McCormick
M   F. Dunlap
1B W. Phillips
2B F. Dunlap
SS J. Glasscock
3B M. Muldoon
OF G. Shaffer
OF T. Esterbrook
OF J. Richmond
C   C. Briody
P   J. McCormick
P   G. Bradley

CLE 1883 N
M   F. Bancroft
1B W. Phillips
2B F. Dunlap
SS J. Glasscock
3B M. Muldoon
OF T. York
OF P. Hotaling
OF J. Evans
C   A. Bushong
P   H. Daily
P   J. McCormick
P   W. Sawyer

CLE 1884 N
M   C. Hackett
1B W. Phillips
2B G. Smith
SS J. Glasscock
3B M. Muldoon
OF P. Hotaling
OF J. Evans
OF W. Murphy
C   A. Bushong
P   J. Harkins
P   J. McCormick

CLE 1887 a
M   J. Williams
1B J. Toy
2B J. Stricker
SS E. McKean
3B P. Reccius
OF P. Hotaling
OF M. Allen
OF F. Mann
C   C. Snyder
P   W. Crowell
P   M. Morrison
P   H. Daily
P   R. Gilks
P   G. Pechiney

CLE 1888 a
M   J. Williams
M   T. Loftus
1B J. Faatz
2B J. Stricker
SS E. McKean
3B A. Alberts
OF P. Hotaling
OF R. Gilks
OF R. Hogan
C   C. Zimmer
P   E. Bakely
P   J. O'Brien
P   W. Crowell

CLE 1890 P
M   H. Larkin
M   O. Tebeau
1B H. Larkin
2B J. Stricker
SS E. Delahanty
3B O. Tebeau
OF L. Browning
OF J. McAleer
OF P. Radford
C   E. Sutcliffe
P   H. Gruber
P   E. Bakely
P   J. O'Brien
P   W. McGill

CLE 1889 N
M   T. Loftus
1B J. Faatz
2B J. Stricker
SS E. McKean
3B O. Tebeau
OF P. Radford
OF L. Twitchell
OF J. McAleer
C   C. Zimmer
P   J. O'Brien
P   E. Beatin
P   E. Bakely
P   H. Gruber

CLE 1890 N
M   G. Schmelz
M   R. Leadley
1B W. Veach
2B J. Ardner
SS E. McKean
3B W. Smalley
OF G. Davis
OF R. Gilks
OF V. Dailey
C   C. Zimmer
P   E. Beatin
P   J. Wadsworth
P   D. Young
P   E. Lincoln
P   L. Viau

CLE 1891 N
M   R. Leadley
M   O. Tebeau
1B J. Virtue
2B C. Childs
SS E. McKean
3B O. Tebeau
OF J. McAleer
OF G. Davis
OF J. Johnson
C   C. Zimmer
P   D. Young
P   H. Gruber
P   L. Viau

CLE 1892 N
M   O. Tebeau
1B J. Virtue
2B C. Childs
SS E. McKean

3B G. Davis
OF J. McAleer
OF J. Burkett
OF J. O'Connor
C   C. Zimmer
P   D. Young
P   G. Cuppy
P   J. Clarkson
P   G. Davies

CLE 1893 N
M   O. Tebeau
1B J. Virtue
2B C. Childs
SS E. McKean
3B J. McGarr
OF J. Burkett
OF W. Ewing
OF J. McAleer
C   C. Zimmer
UT J. O'Connor
UT J. O'Connor
P   D. Young
P   J. Clarkson
P   G. Cuppy
P   C. Hastings

CLE 1894 N
M   O. Tebeau
1B O. Tebeau
2B C. Childs
SS E. McKean
3B J. McGarr
OF J. Burkett
OF H. Blake
OF J. McAleer
C   C. Zimmer
UT J. O'Connor
P   D. Young
P   G. Cuppy
P   J. Clarkson
P   M. Sullivan

CLE 1895 N
M   O. Tebeau
1B O. Tebeau
2B C. Childs
SS E. McKean
3B J. McGarr
OF J. McAleer
OF J. Burkett
OF H. Blake
C   C. Zimmer
UT J. O'Connor
UT G. Tebeau
P   D. Young
P   G. Cuppy
P   R. Wallace
P   P. Knell

CLE 1896 N
M   O. Tebeau
1B O. Tebeau
2B C. Childs
SS E. McKean
3B J. McGarr
OF J. Burkett
OF J. McAleer
OF H. Blake
C   C. Zimmer
P   D. Young
P   G. Cuppy
P   F. Wilson

CLE 1897 N
M   O. Tebeau
1B O. Tebeau
2B C. Childs
SS R. Wallace
3B J. Burkett
OF L. Sockalexis
OF J. O'Connor
C   C. Zimmer
P   D. Young
P   F. Wilson
P   J. Powell
P   G. Cuppy

CLE 1898 N
M   O. Tebeau
1B O. Tebeau
2B C. Childs
SS E. McKean
3B R. Wallace
OF J. Burkett
OF H. Blake
OF J. McAleer
C   L. Criger
UT J. O'Connor

P D. Young
P J. Powell
P F. Wilson
P G. Cuppy

CLE 1899 N

M L. Cross
M J. Quinn
1B T. Tucker
2B J. Quinn
SS R. Lochhead
3B S. Sullivan
OF T. Dowd
OF R. Harley
OF L. McAllister
C J. Sugden
P J. Hughey
P C. Knepper
P C. Bates
P F. Schmit
P J. Colliflower

CLE 1901 A

M J. McAleer
1B G. LaChance
2B E. Beck
SS F. Scheibeck
3B W. Bradley
OF O. Pickering
OF J. O'Brien
OF J. McCarthy
C R. Wood
P H. Dowling
P E. Moore
P W. Hart
P E. Scott
P J. Bracken

CLE 1902 A

M W. Armour
1B C. Hickman
2B N. Lajoie
SS J. Gochnauer
3B W. Bradley
OF E. Flick
OF H. Bay
OF J. McCarthy
C H. Bemis
P E. Moore
P A. Joss
P W. Bernhard
P C. Wright

CLE 1903 A

M W. Armour
1B C. Hickman
2B N. Lajoie
SS J. Gochnauer
3B W. Bradley
OF E. Flick
OF H. Bay
OF J. McCarthy
C H. Bemis
P A. Joss
P E. Moore
P W. Bernhard
P F. Donahue
P C. Wright

CLE 1904 A

M W. Armour
1B C. Hickman
2B N. Lajoie
SS T. Turner
3B W. Bradley
OF E. Flick
OF W. Lush
OF H. Bay
C H. Bemis
P W. Bernhard
P F. Donahue
P E. Moore
P A. Joss
P R. Rhoads

CLE 1905 A

M N. Lajoie
M W. Bradley
M N. Lajoie
1B C. Carr
2B N. Lajoie
SS T. Turner
3B W. Bradley
OF H. Bay
OF E. Flick
OF J. Jackson
C F. Buelow
UT G. Stovall
P A. Joss
P E. Moore

P R. Rhoads
P W. Bernhard
P F. Donahue

CLE 1906 A

M N. Lajoie
1B C. Rossman
2B N. Lajoie
SS T. Turner
3B W. Bradley
OF E. Flick
OF W. Congalton
OF J. Jackson
C H. Bemis
UT G. Stovall
P O. Hess
P R. Rhoads
P A. Joss
P W. Bernhard
P J. Townsend

CLE 1907 A

M N. Lajoie
1B G. Stovall
2B N. Lajoie
SS T. Turner
3B W. Bradley
OF W. Hinchman
OF E. Flick
OF J. Birmingham
C J. Clarke
P A. Joss
P G. Liebhardt
P R. Rhoads
P J. Thielman

CLE 1908 A

M N. Lajoie
1B G. Stovall
2B N. Lajoie
SS G. Perring
3B W. Bradley
OF J. B. Clarke
OF J. Birmingham
OF W. Hinchman
C J. A. Clarke
P A. Joss
P R. Rhoads
P G. Liebhardt
P C. Berger
P C. Chech

CLE 1909 A

M N. Lajoie
M J. McGuire
1B G. Stovall
2B N. Lajoie
SS C. Ball
3B W. Bradley
OF W. Hinchman
OF J. Birmingham
OF W. Good
C T. Easterly
P D. Young
P C. Berger
P A. Joss
P F. Falkenberg
P R. Rhoads

CLE 1910 A

M J. McGuire
1B G. Stovall
2B N. Lajoie
SS T. Turner
3B W. Bradley
OF J. Graney
OF J. Birmingham
OF A. Kruger
C T. Easterly
P F. Falkenberg
P W. Mitchell
P D. Young
P E. Koestner
P F. Harkness

CLE 1911 A

M J. McGuire
M G. Stovall
1B G. Stovall
2B C. Ball
SS I. Olson
3B T. Turner
OF J. Jackson
OF J. Graney
OF J. Birmingham
C A. Fisher
UT T. Easterly
P S. Gregg
P E. Krapp
P W. Mitchell

P F. Blanding
P G. Kahler

CLE 1912 A

M H. Davis
M J. Birmingham
1B A. Griggs
2B N. Lajoie
SS R. Peckinpaugh
3B T. Turner
OF J. Jackson
OF J. Birmingham
OF J. Ryan
C S. O'Neill
UT I. Olson
P S. Gregg
P F. Blanding
P G. Kahler
P W. Mitchell
P W. Steen

CLE 1913 A

M J. Birmingham
1B W. Johnston
2B N. Lajoie
SS R. Chapman
3B I. Olson
OF J. Jackson
OF J. Graney
OF H. Leibold
C S. O'Neill
UT T. Turner
P S. Gregg
P F. Falkenberg
P W. Mitchell
P F. Blanding
P W. Steen

CLE 1914 A

M J. Birmingham
1B W. Johnston
2B N. Lajoie
SS R. Chapman
3B T. Turner
OF J. Graney
OF J. Jackson
OF H. Leibold
C S. O'Neill
P W. Mitchell
P W. Steen
P Z. Hagerman
P G. Morton
P F. Blanding

CLE 1915 A

M J. Birmingham
M L. Fohl
1B J. Kirke
2B W. Wambsganss
SS R. Chapman
3B W. Barbare
OF E. Smith
OF J. Graney
OF H. Leibold
C S. O'Neill
P G. Morton
P W. Mitchell
P Z. Hagerman
P S. Jones
P J. Walker
RP O. Harstad

CLE 1916 A

M L. Fohl
1B C. Gandil
2B I. Howard
SS W. Wambsganss
3B T. Turner
OF J. Graney
OF T. Speaker
OF R. Roth
C S. O'Neill
UT R. Chapman
P J. Bagby
P S. Coveleski
P G. Morton
P E. Klepfer
P F. Coumbe

CLE 1917 A

M L. Fohl
1B J. Harris
2B W. Wambsganss
SS R. Chapman
3B J. Evans
OF J. Graney
OF T. Speaker
OF R. Roth
C S. O'Neill
P J. Bagby

P S. Coveleski
P E. Klepfer
P G. Morton
P F. Coumbe

CLE 1918 A

M L. Fohl
1B W. Johnston
2B W. Wambsganss
SS R. Chapman
3B J. Evans
OF T. Speaker
OF R. Roth
OF H. Wood
C S. O'Neill
P S. Coveleski
P J. Bagby
P G. Morton
P F. Coumbe
P J. Enzmann

CLE 1919 A

M L. Fohl
M T. Speaker
1B W. Johnston
2B W. Wambsganss
SS R. Chapman
3B W. Gardner
OF T. Speaker
OF J. Graney
OF E. Smith
C S. O'Neill
P S. Coveleski
P J. Bagby
P G. Morton
P E. Myers
P G. Uhle
RP T. Phillips

CLE 1920 A

M T. Speaker
1B W. Johnston
2B W. Wambsganss
SS R. Chapman
3B W. Gardner
OF T. Speaker
OF E. Smith
OF C. Jamieson
C S. O'Neill
P J. Bagby
P S. Coveleski
P R. Caldwell
P G. Morton

CLE 1921 A

M T. Speaker
1B W. Johnston
2B W. Wambsganss
SS J. Sewell
3B W. Gardner
OF C. Jamieson
OF T. Speaker
OF E. Smith
C S. O'Neill
P S. Coveleski
P G. Uhle
P J. Mails
P J. Bagby
P R. Caldwell

CLE 1922 A

M T. Speaker
1B J. McInnis
2B W. Wambsganss
SS J. Sewell
3B W. Gardner
OF C. Jamieson
OF H. Wood
OF T. Speaker
C S. O'Neill
P G. Uhle
P S. Coveleski
P G. Morton
P J. Mails
P J. Bagby
RP J. Lindsey

CLE 1923 A

M T. Speaker
1B F. Brower
2B W. Wambsganss
SS J. Sewell
3B W. Lutzke
OF C. Jamieson
OF T. Speaker
OF H. Summa
C S. O'Neill
P G. Uhle
P S. Coveleski
P J. Edwards

P J. Shaute
P G. Morton
RP G. Metivier
RP J. Boone

CLE 1924 A

M T. Speaker
1B G. Burns
2B W. Fewster
SS J. Sewell
3B W. Lutzke
OF C. Jamieson
OF T. Speaker
OF H. Summa
C G. Myatt
UT P. McNulty
P J. Shaute
P S. Smith
P S. Coveleski
P G. Uhle
RP G. Metivier

CLE 1925 A

M T. Speaker
1B G. Burns
2B W. Fewster
SS J. Sewell
3B W. Lutzke
OF C. Jamieson
OF J. Graney
OF T. Speaker
C S. O'Neill
UT F. Spurgeon
P S. Smith
P G. Uhle
P B. Karr
P W. Miller
P G. Buckeye

CLE 1926 A

M T. Speaker
1B G. Burns
2B F. Spurgeon
SS J. Sewell
3B W. Lutzke
OF H. Summa
OF T. Speaker
OF C. Jamieson
C J. L. Sewell
P G. Uhle
P E. Levsen
P J. Shaute
P S. Smith
P G. Buckeye

CLE 1927 A

M J. McCallister
1B G. Burns
2B L. Fonseca
SS J. Sewell
3B W. Lutzke
OF H. Summa
OF C. Jamieson
OF F. Eichrodt
C J. L. Sewell
P G. Hudlin
P J. Shaute
P G. Buckeye
P W. Miller
P G. Uhle

CLE 1928 A

M R. Peckinpaugh
1B L. Fonseca
2B H. Lind
SS J. Sewell
3B U. Hodapp
OF H. Summa
OF C. Jamieson
OF E. Langford
C J. L. Sewell
P J. Shaute
P G. Hudlin
P G. Uhle
P W. Miller
P G. Grant
RP W. Bayne
RP M. Harder

CLE 1929 A

M R. Peckinpaugh
1B L. Fonseca
2B U. Hodapp
SS J. Tavener
3B J. Sewell
OF H. Averill
OF B. Falk
OF C. Jamieson
C J. L. Sewell
UT E. Morgan

P G. Hudlin
P W. Ferrell
P W. Miller
P J. Shaute
P J. Miljus

CLE 1930 A

M R. Peckinpaugh
1B E. Morgan
2B U. Hodapp
SS J. Goldman
3B J. Sewell
OF H. Averill
OF R. Porter
OF C. Jamieson
C J. Sewell
P J. Shaute
P S. Smith
P S. Coveleski
P G. Uhle
RP G. Metivier

CLE 1931 A

M R. Peckinpaugh
1B E. Morgan
2B U. Hodapp
SS E. Montague
3B W. Kamm
OF H. Averill
OF J. Vosmik
OF R. Porter
C J. Sewell
UT J. Burnett
P W. Ferrell
P G. Hudlin
P C. Brown
P M. Harder
RP P. Appleton

CLE 1932 A

M R. Peckinpaugh
1B E. Morgan
2B C. Cissell
SS J. Burnett
3B W. Kamm
OF J. Vosmik
OF H. Averill
OF R. Porter
C J. Sewell
P W. Ferrell
P C. Brown
P M. Harder
P G. Hudlin
P O. Hildebrand

CLE 1933 A

M R. Peckinpaugh
M B. Falk
M W. Johnson
1B E. Boss
2B A. Hale
SS Knickerbocker
3B W. Kamm
OF H. Averill
OF R. Porter
OF J. Vosmik
C R. Spencer
UT C. Cissell
P M. Harder
P O. Hildebrand
P W. Ferrell
P C. Brown
P G. Hudlin
RP G. Connally
RP B. Bean

CLE 1934 A

M W. Johnson
1B H. Trosky
2B A. Hale
SS Knickerbocker
3B W. Kamm
OF H. Averill
OF J. Vosmik
OF E. Rice
C F. Pytlak
P M. Pearson
P M. Harder
P O. Hildebrand
P G. Hudlin
P L. Brown
RP B. Bean
RP C. Brown

CLE 1935 A

M W. Johnson
M S. O'Neill
1B H. Trosky
2B L. Berger
SS Knickerbocker

3B A. Hale
OF J. Vosmik
OF H. Averill
OF M. Galatzer
C E. Phillips
P M. Harder
P G. Hudlin
P M. Pearson
P T. Lee
P O. Hildebrand
RP L. Brown
RP R. Winegarner

CLE 1936 A

M S. O'Neill
1B H. Trosky
2B R. Hughes
SS Knickerbocker
3B A. Hale
OF H. Averill
OF J. Vosmik
OF C. Weatherly
C W. Sullivan
P J. Allen
P M. Harder
P O. Hildebrand
P D. Galehouse
P L. Brown
RP T. Lee
RP G. Hudlin

CLE 1937 A

M S. O'Neill
1B H. Trosky
2B J. Kroner
SS L. Lary
3B A. Hale
OF H. Averill
OF J. Solters
OF B. Campbell
C F. Pytlak
UT R. Hughes
P M. Harder
P D. Galehouse
P G. Hudlin
P R. Feller
RP L. Brown
RP J. Wyatt

CLE 1938 A

M O. Vitt
1B H. Trosky
2B A. Hale
SS L. Lary
3B K. Keltner
OF H. Averill
OF J. Heath
OF B. Campbell
C F. Pytlak
P R. Feller
P M. Harder
P J. Allen
P E. Whitehill
P G. Hudlin
RP J. Humphries
RP A. Milnar

CLE 1939 A

M O. Vitt
1B H. Trosky
2B A. Hale
SS J. Webb
3B K. Keltner
OF W. Chapman
OF B. Campbell
OF J. Heath
C R. Hemsley
UT O. Grimes
UT C. Weatherly
P R. Feller
P A. Milnar
P M. Harder
P J. Allen
P G. Hudlin
RP J. Dobson

CLE 1940 A

M O. Vitt
1B H. Trosky
2B R. Mack
SS L. Boudreau
3B K. Keltner
OF W. Chapman
OF C. Weatherly
OF R. Bell
C R. Hemsley
UT J. Heath
P R. Feller
P A. Milnar
P M. Harder

P A. Smith
P J. Allen
RP J. Dobson
RP H. Eisenstat

CLE 1941 A

M R. Peckinpaugh
1B H. Trosky
2B R. Mack
SS L. Boudreau
3B K. Keltner
OF J. Heath
OF G. Walker
OF C. Weatherly
C R. Hemsley
UT C. Campbell
P R. Feller
P A. Milnar
P A. Smith
P J. Bagby
RP C. Brown
RP J. Heving

CLE 1942 A

M L. Boudreau
1B L. Fleming
2B R. Mack
SS L. Boudreau
3B K. Keltner
OF J. Heath
OF O. Hockett
OF C. Weatherly
C O. Denning
P J. Bagby
P M. Harder
P A. Dean
P A. Smith
P A. Milnar
RP T. Ferrick
RP H. Eisenstat

CLE 1943 A

M L. Boudreau
1B M. Rocco
2B R. Mack
SS L. Boudreau
3B K. Keltner
OF O. Hockett
OF R. Cullenbine
OF J. Heath
C W. Rosar
P J. Bagby
P A. Smith
P A. Reynolds
P L. Kennedy
P M. Harder
RP J. Heving
RP M. Naymick

CLE 1944 A

M L. Boudreau
1B M. Rocco
2B R. Mack
SS L. Boudreau
3B K. Keltner
OF R. Cullenbine
OF O. Hockett
OF J. Seerey
C W. Rosar
P S. Gromek
P M. Harder
P A. Smith
P E. Klieman
P A. Reynolds
RP J. Heving
RP R. Poat

CLE 1945 A

M L. Boudreau
1B M. Rocco
2B L. Meyer
SS L. Boudreau
3B D. Ross
OF J. Seerey
OF F. Mackiewicz
OF J. Heath
C F. Hayes
UT A. Cihocki
P S. Gromek
P A. Reynolds
P J. Bagby
P A. Smith
P E. Klieman
RP M. Center
RP J. Salveson

CLE 1946 A

M L. Boudreau
1B L. Fleming
2B L. Meyer
SS L. Boudreau
3B K. Keltner
OF H. Edwards
OF G. Case
OF J. Seerey
C J. Hegan
P R. Feller
P C. Embree
P A. Reynolds
P S. Gromek
RP R. Lemon
RP J. Krakauskas

CLE 1947 A

M L. Boudreau
1B W. Robinson
2B J. Gordon
SS L. Boudreau
3B K. Keltner
OF G. Metkovich
OF L. Mitchell
OF H. Edwards
C J. Hegan
UT L. Fleming
UT H. Peck
P R. Feller
P D. Black
P R. Lemon
P C. Embree
P A. Gettel
RP B. Stephens
RP E. Klieman

CLE 1948 A

M L. Boudreau
1B W. Robinson
2B J. Gordon
SS L. Boudreau
3B K. Keltner
OF L. Mitchell
OF L. Doby
OF T. Tucker
C J. Hegan
P R. Lemon
P R. Feller
P H. Bearden
P S. Gromek
P S. Zoldak
RP E. Klieman
RP R. Christopher

CLE 1949 A

M L. Boudreau
1B J. Vernon
2B J. Gordon
SS L. Boudreau
3B K. Keltner
OF L. Mitchell
OF L. Doby
OF R. Kennedy
C J. Hegan
P R. Lemon
P R. Feller
P E. Garcia
P E. Wynn
P J. Benton
RP L. Paige
RP F. Papish

CLE 1950 A

M L. Boudreau
1B L. Easter
2B J. Gordon
SS R. Boone
3B A. Rosen
OF R. Kennedy
OF L. Doby
OF L. Mitchell
C J. Hegan
P R. Lemon
P R. Feller
P E. Wynn
P E. Garcia
P S. Gromek
RP S. Zoldak
RP J. Benton

CLE 1951 A

M A. Lopez
1B L. Easter
2B R. Avila
SS R. Boone
3B A. Rosen
OF L. Doby
OF L. Mitchell
OF R. Kennedy
C J. Hegan
UT S. Chapman
UT H. Simpson
P E. Wynn
P R. Lemon
P E. Garcia
P R. Feller
P S. Gromek
RP L. Brissie

CLE 1952 A

M A. Lopez
1B L. Easter
2B R. Avila
SS R. Boone
3B A. Rosen
OF L. Doby
OF L. Mitchell
OF H. Simpson
C J. Hegan
P R. Lemon
P E. Garcia
P E. Wynn
P R. Feller
P S. Gromek
RP L. Brissie
RP M. Harris

CLE 1953 A

M A. Lopez
1B W. Glynn
2B R. Avila
SS G. Strickland
3B A. Rosen
OF L. Doby
OF L. Mitchell
OF R. Kennedy
C J. Hegan
P R. Lemon
P E. Garcia
P E. Wynn
P R. Feller
P D. Hoskins
RP R. Hooper

CLE 1954 A

M A. Lopez
1B W. Glynn
2B R. Avila
SS G. Strickland
3B A. Rosen
OF L. Doby
OF D. Philley
OF A. Smith
C J. Hegan
UT V. Wertz
P E. Wynn
P E. Garcia
P R. Lemon
P A. Houtteman
P R. Feller
RP D. Mossi
RP R. Narleski

CLE 1955 A

M A. Lopez
1B V. Wertz
2B R. Avila
SS G. Strickland
3B A. Rosen
OF L. Doby
OF A. Smith
OF R. Kiner
C J. Hegan
P E. Wynn
P H. Score
P R. Lemon
P E. Garcia
P A. Houtteman
RP R. Narleski
RP D. Mossi

CLE 1956 A

M A. Lopez
1B V. Wertz
2B R. Avila
SS A. Carrasquel
3B A. Rosen
OF J. Busby
OF A. Smith
OF R. Colavito
C J. Hegan
UT E. Woodling
P E. Wynn
P R. Lemon
P H. Score
P E. Garcia
RP D. Mossi
RP C. McLish

CLE 1957 A

M M. Farrell
1B V. Wertz
2B R. Avila
SS A. Carrasquel
3B A. Smith
OF R. Colavito
OF E. Woodling
OF R. Maris
C J. Hegan
UT L. Raines
P E. Wynn
P E. Garcia
P D. Mossi
P R. Narleski
P C. McLish
RP L. Daley
RP R. Tomanek

CLE 1958 A

M R. Bragan
M J. Gordon
1B J. Vernon
2B R. Avila
SS G. Hunter
3B W. Harrell
OF S. Minoso
OF R. Colavito
OF L. Doby
C R. Nixon
UT W. Moran
P C. McLish
P J. Grant
P R. Narleski
P G. Bell
P D. Ferrarese
RP D. Mossi

CLE 1959 A

M J. Gordon
1B V. Power
2B A. Martin
SS W. Held
3B G. Strickland
OF R. Colavito
OF S. Minoso
OF J. Piersall
C R. Nixon
UT J. Francona
P C. McLish
P G. Bell
P J. Grant
P H. Score
P J. Perry
RP E. Garcia

CLE 1960 A

M J. Gordon
M J. White
M J. Dykes
1B V. Power
2B K. Aspromonte
SS W. Held
3B J. Phillips
OF J. Francona
OF J. Piersall
OF H. Kuenn
C J. Romano
UT J. Temple
P J. Perry
P J. Grant
P G. Bell
P A. Latman
P R. Stigman
RP J. Klippstein
RP D. Newcombe

CLE 1961 A

M J. Dykes
M M. Harder
1B V. Power
2B J. Temple
SS W. Held
3B J. Phillips
OF W. Kirkland
OF J. Francona
OF J. Piersall
C J. Romano
P J. Grant
P G. Bell
P J. Perry
P A. Latman
P W. Hawkins
RP L. Locke
RP F. Funk

CLE 1962 A

M F. McGaha
M M. Harder
1B J. Francona
2B G. Kindall
SS W. Held
3B J. Phillips
OF W. Kirkland
OF T. Cline
OF C. Essegian
C J. Romano
UT A. Luplow
P R. Donovan
P P. Ramos
P J. Perry
P A. Latman
P J. Grant
RP G. Bell
RP F. Funk

CLE 1963 A

M G. Tebbetts
1B F. Whitfield
2B W. Held
SS G. Kindall
3B R. Alvis
OF J. Francona
OF W. Kirkland
OF V. Davalillo
C J. Azcue
UT J. Adcock
UT A. Luplow
P J. Grant
P R. Donovan
P J. Kralick
P P. Ramos
P A. Latman
RP G. Bell
RP J. Walker

CLE 1964 A

M G. Strickland
M G. Tebbetts
1B R. Chance
2B L. Brown
SS R. Howser
3B R. Alvis
OF L. Wagner
OF V. Davalillo
OF J. Francona
C J. Romano
UT W. Held
UT F. Whitfield
P J. Kralick
P S. McDowell
P R. Donovan
P W. Siebert
P P. Ramos
RP G. Bell
RP D. McMahon

CLE 1965 A

M G. Tebbetts
1B F. Whitfield
2B P. Gonzalez
SS L. Brown
3B R. Alvis
OF R. Colavito
OF L. Wagner
OF V. Davalillo
C J. Azcue
UT C. Hinton
UT R. Howser
P S. McDowell
P L. Tiant
P W. Siebert
P R. Terry
P A. Stange
RP G. Bell
RP J. Kralick

CLE 1966 A

M G. Tebbetts
M G. Strickland
1B F. Whitfield
2B P. Gonzalez
SS L. Brown
3B R. Alvis
OF R. Colavito
OF L. Wagner
OF V. Davalillo
C J. Azcue
UT C. Hinton
UT R. Salmon
P G. Bell
P W. Siebert
P S. McDowell
P S. Hargan
P L. Tiant
RP J. Kralick
RP R. Radatz

CLE 1967 A

M J. Adcock
1B A. Horton
2B P. Gonzalez
SS L. Brown
3B R. Alvis
OF C. Hinton
OF V. Davalillo
OF L. Wagner
C J. Azcue
UT A. Maye
UT F. Whitfield
P S. McDowell
P S. Hargan
P L. Tiant
P W. Siebert
P J. O'Donoghue
RP O. Pena
RP G. Culver

CLE 1968 A

M A. Dark
1B A. Horton
2B V. Fuller
SS L. Brown
3B R. Alvis
OF J. Cardenal
OF T. Harper
OF A. Maye
C J. Azcue
UT R. Salmon
UT D. Sims
P S. McDowell
P L. Tiant
P W. Siebert
P S. Williams
P S. Hargan
RP E. Fisher
RP M. Paul

CLE 1969 A

M A. Dark
1B A. Horton
2B V. Fuller
SS L. Brown
3B R. Alvis
OF K. Harrelson
OF J. Cardenal
OF R. Snyder
C D. Sims
UT R. Scheinblum
P S. McDowell
P L. Tiant
P S. Hargan
P R. Ellsworth
RP S. Williams
RP M. Paul

CLE 1970 A

M A. Dark
1B A. Horton
2B E. Leon
SS J. Heidemann
3B G. Nettles
OF V. Pinson
OF T. Uhlaender
OF R. Foster
C R. Fosse
UT C. Hinton
UT D. Sims
P S. McDowell
P R. Hand
P W. Chance
P S. Hargan
RP D. Higgins
RP M. Paul

CLE 1971 A

M A. Dark
M J. Lipon
1B C. Chambliss
2B E. Leon
SS J. Heidemann
3B G. Nettles
OF V. Pinson
OF T. Uhlaender
OF R. Foster
C R. Fosse
P S. McDowell
P S. Dunning
P A. Foster
P R. Lamb
P S. Hargan
RP V. Colbert
RP P. Hennigan

CLE 1972 A

M K. Aspromonte
1B C. Chambliss
2B J. Brohamer
SS F. Duffy
3B G. Nettles
OF D. Bell
OF D. Unser
OF A. Johnson
C R. Fosse
UT T. McCraw
P G. Perry
P R. Tidrow
P M. Wilcox
P R. Lamb
P S. Dunning
RP P. Hennigan
RP E. Farmer

CLE 1973 A

M K. Aspromonte
1B C. Chambliss
2B J. Brohamer
SS F. Duffy
3B D. Bell
OF R. Torres
OF L. Spikes
OF G. Hendrick
C D. Duncan
DH O. Gamble
UT J. Ellis
UT J. Lowenstein
UT W. Williams
P G. Perry
P R. Tidrow
P M. Wilcox
P T. Timmermann
P B. Strom
RP T. Hilgendorf
RP R. Lamb

CLE 1974 A

M K. Aspromonte
1B J. Ellis
2B J. Brohamer
SS F. Duffy
3B D. Bell
OF L. Spikes
OF G. Hendrick
OF J. Lowenstein
C D. Duncan
DH O. Gamble
UT R. Torres
P G. Perry
P J. Perry
P F. Peterson
P R. Bosman
RP T. Buskey
RP F. Beene

CLE 1975 A

M F. Robinson
1B J. Powell
2B D. Kuiper
SS F. Duffy
3B D. Bell
OF G. Hendrick
OF R. Manning
OF L. Spikes
C A. Ashby
DH R. Carty
UT O. Gamble
P D. Eckersley
P F. Peterson
P D. Hood
P R. Harrison
P G. Perry
RP D. LaRoche
RP T. Buskey

CLE 1976 A

M F. Robinson
1B J. Powell
2B D. Kuiper
SS F. Duffy
3B D. Bell
OF G. Hendrick
OF R. Manning
OF L. Spikes
C A. Ashby
DH R. Carty
UT L. Blanks
P P. Dobson
P D. Eckersley
P J. Brown
P J. Bibby
P M. Waits
RP J. Kern
RP S. Thomas

CLE 1977 A

M F. Robinson
M J. Torborg
1B A. Thornton
2B D. Kuiper
SS F. Duffy
3B D. Bell
OF J. Norris
OF L. Dade
OF B. Bochte
C F. Kendall
DH R. Carty
UT L. Blanks

P	M. Garland
P	D. Eckersley
P	J. Bibby
P	M. Waits
P	A. Fitzmorris
RP	D. Hood
RP	J. Kern

CLE 1978 A
M J. Torborg
1B A. Thornton
2B D. Kuiper
SS T. Veryzer
3B D. Bell
OF R. Manning
OF J. Grubb
OF L. Dade
C G. Alexander
DH B. Carbo
UT J. Norris
P M. Waits
P R. Wise
P M. Paxton
P D. Hood
P D. Clyde
RP J. Kern
RP I. Monge

CLE 1979 A
M J. Torborg
M D. Garcia
1B A. Thornton
2B D. Kuiper
SS T. Veryzer
3B C. Harrah
OF R. Manning
OF B. Bonds
OF J. Norris
C G. Alexander
DH C. Johnson
UT D. Hargrove
P R. Wise
P M. Waits
P M. Paxton
P D. Spillner
P L. Barker
RP I. Monge
RP V. Cruz

CLE 1980 A
M D. Garcia
1B D. Hargrove
2B J. Brohamer
SS T. Veryzer
3B C. Harrah
OF R. Manning
OF J. Orta
OF M. Dilone
C R. Hassey
DH J. Charboneau
UT J. Dybzinski
P L. Barker
P M. Waits
P D. Spillner
P M. Garland
P R. Owchinko
RP I. Monge
RP M. Stanton

CLE 1981 A
M D. Garcia
1B D. Hargrove
2B D. Kuiper
SS T. Veryzer
3B C. Harrah
OF R. Manning
OF J. Orta
OF M. Dilone
C R. Hassey
DH A. Thornton
UT A. Bannister
P R. Blyleven
P L. Barker
P J. Denny
P M. Waits
P D. Spillner
RP I. Monge
RP M. Stanton

CLE 1982 A
M D. Garcia
1B D. Hargrove
2B J. Perconte
SS M. Fischlin
3B C. Harrah
OF R. Manning
OF V. Hayes
OF M. Dilone
C R. Hassey
DH A. Thornton
UT A. Bannister

P L. Barker
P R. Sutcliffe
P L. Sorensen
P J. Denny
P M. Waits
RP D. Spillner
RP E. Whitson

CLE 1983 A
M M. Ferraro
M P. Corrales
1B D. Hargrove
2B J. Trillo
SS J. Franco
3B C. Harrah
OF G. Vukovich
OF J. Thomas
OF A. Bannister
C R. Hassey
DH A. Thornton
UT P. Tabler
P R. Sutcliffe
P L. Sorensen
P R. Blyleven
P L. Barker
P N. Heaton
RP D. Spillner
RP K. Anderson

CLE 1984 A
M P. Corrales
1B D. Hargrove
2B A. Bernazard
SS J. Franco
3B B. Jacoby
OF B. Butler
OF G. Vukovich
OF M. Castillo
C G. Willard
DH A. Thornton
UT P. Tabler
P R. Blyleven
P N. Heaton
P S. Comer
P S. Farr
RP E. Camacho
RP T. Waddell

CLE 1985 A
M P. Corrales
1B P. Tabler
2B A. Bernazard
SS J. Franco
3B B. Jacoby
OF B. Butler
OF G. Vukovich
OF J. Carter
C G. Willard
DH A. Thornton
UT D. Hargrove
UT O. Nixon
P N. Heaton
P R. Blyleven
RP V. Ruhle
RP T. Waddell

CLE 1986 A
M P. Corrales
1B P. Tabler
2B A. Bernazard
SS J. Franco
3B B. Jacoby
OF B. Butler
OF M. Hall
OF J. Carter
C A. Allanson
DH A. Thornton
UT O. Nixon
UT J. Snyder
P T. Candiotti
P P. Niekro
P K. Schrom
RP S. Bailes
RP R. Yett

CLE 1987 A
M P. Corrales
M H. Edwards
1B J. Carter
2B A. Bernazard
SS J. Franco
3B B. Jacoby
OF J. Snyder
OF B. Butler
OF M. Hall
C C. Bando
DH P. Tabler
P T. Candiotti
P K. Schrom
P P. Niekro
P S. Bailes

P S. Carlton
RP R. Yett
RP D. Jones

CLE 1988 A
M H. Edwards
1B W. Upshaw
2B J. Franco
SS J. Bell
3B B. Jacoby
OF J. Carter
OF J. Snyder
OF M. Hall
C A. Allanson
DH R. Kittle
P F. Swindell
P T. Candiotti
P J. Farrell
P S. Bailes
P R. Yett
RP D. Jones

Columbus

COL a 1883-1884
COL a 1889-1891

COL 1883 a
M H. Phillips
1B J. Field
2B C. Smith
SS J. Richmond
3B W. Kuehne
OF T. Brown
OF H. Wheeler
OF F. Mann
C R. Kemler
P F. Mountain
P E. Dundon
P J. Valentine

COL 1884 a
M G. Schmelz
1B J. Field
2B C. Smith
SS J. Richmond
3B W. Kuehne
OF T. Brown
OF F. Mann
OF J. Cahill
C R. Kemler
UT F. Carroll
P E. Morris
P F. Mountain

COL 1889 a
M A. Buckenberger
1B D. Orr
2B W. Greenwood
SS H. Easterday
3B C. Marr
OF J. McTamany
OF E. Daily
OF J. Johnson
C J. O'Connor
P M. Baldwin
P W. Widner
P H. Gastright
P A. Mays

COL 1890 a
M A. Buckenberger
M G. Schmelz
M J. Sullivan
1B M. Lehane
2B C. Crooks
SS H. Easterday
3B C. Reilly
OF J. Johnson
OF J. Sneed
OF J. McTamany
C J. O'Connor
P H. Gastright
P F. Knauss
P J. Easton
P E. Chamberlin
P W. Widner

COL 1891 a
M G. Schmelz
1B M. Lehane
2B C. Crooks
SS W. Wheelock
3B W. Kuehne
OF C. Duffee
OF J. Sneed
OF J. McTamany
C J. Donahue

P P. Knell
P H. Gastright
P J. Dolan
P J. Easton

Detroit

DET N 1881-1888
DET A 1901-1988

DET 1881 N
M F. Bancroft
1B M. Powell
2B J. Gerhardt
SS S. Houck
3B A. Whitney
OF A. Knight
OF G. Wood
OF E. Hanlon
C C. Bennett
P G. Derby
P G. Weidman
P F. Mountain

DET 1882 N
M F. Bancroft
1B M. Powell
2B J. Troy
SS M. McGeary
3B J. Farrell
OF G. Wood
OF A. Knight
OF E. Hanlon
C C. Bennett
P G. Weidman
P G. Derby

DET 1883 N
M J. Chapman
1B M. Powell
2B S. Trott
SS S. Houck
3B J. Farrell
OF G. Wood
OF E. Hanlon
OF G. Weidman
C C. Bennett
P G. Weidman
P F. Shaw
P D. Jones

DET 1884 N
M J. Chapman
1B M. Scott
2B W. Geis
SS F. Meinke
3B J. Farrell
OF G. Wood
OF E. Hanlon
OF G. Weidman
C C. Bennett
P F. Shaw
P C. Getzien
P F. Brill

DET 1885 N
M C. Morton
M W. Watkins
1B W. McQuery
2B S. Crane
SS M. Phillips
3B J. Donnelly
OF E. Hanlon
OF G. Wood
OF S. Thompson
C C. Bennett
P G. Weidman
P C. Getzien
P C. Baldwin
P D. Casey

DET 1886 N
M W. Watkins
1B D. Brouthers
2B F. Dunlap
SS J. Rowe
3B J. White
OF E. Hanlon
OF S. Thompson
OF A. Richardson
C C. Bennett
P C. Baldwin
P C. Getzien
P P. Conway
P W. Smith

DET 1887 N
M W. Watkins

1B D. Brouthers
2B F. Dunlap
SS J. Rowe
3B J. White
OF S. Thompson
OF E. Hanlon
OF A. Richardson
C C. Ganzel
P C. Getzien
P C. Baldwin
P G. Weidman
P P. Conway

DET 1888 N
M W. Watkins
M R. Leadley
1B D. Brouthers
2B A. Richardson
SS J. Rowe
3B J. White
OF L. Twitchell
OF E. Hanlon
OF C. Campau
C C. Bennett
C C. Ganzel
UT C. Ganzel
P C. Getzien
P P. Conway
P H. Gruber
P E. Beatin

DET 1901 A
M G. Stallings
1B F. Dillon
2B W. Gleason
SS N. Elberfeld
3B J. Casey
OF J. Barrett
OF W. Nance
OF J. Holmes
C F. Buelow
UT L. McAllister
P R. Miller
P E. Siever
P J. Cronin
P J. Yeager

DET 1902 A
M J. Dwyer
1B F. Dillon
2B W. Gleason
SS N. Elberfeld
3B J. Casey
OF J. Barrett
OF R. Harley
OF J. Holmes
C J. McGuire
P G. Mercer
P G. Mullin
P E. Siever
P R. Miller
P J. Yeager

DET 1903 A
M E. Barrow
1B C. Carr
2B G. Smith
SS L. McAllister
3B J. Yeager
OF S. Crawford
OF J. Barrett
OF W. Lush
C J. McGuire
P G. Mullin
P W. Donovan
P F. Kitson
P C. Kisinger

DET 1904 A
M E. Barrow
M R. Lowe
1B C. Carr
2B R. Lowe
SS C. O'Leary
3B L. Gremminger
OF J. Barrett
OF M. McIntyre
OF S. Crawford
C L. Drill
UT C. Robinson
P G. Mullin
P E. Killian
P W. Donovan
P F. Kitson
P J. Stovall

DET 1905 A
M W. Armour
1B C. Lindsay
2B H. Schaefer
SS C. O'Leary

1B D. Brouthers
2B F. Dunlap
SS J. Rowe
3B J. White
OF S. Thompson
OF E. Hanlon
OF A. Richardson
C C. Ganzel
P C. Baldwin
P C. Getzien
P G. Weidman
P P. Conway

DET 1906 A
M W. Armour
1B C. Lindsay
2B H. Schaefer
SS C. O'Leary
3B W. Coughlin
OF M. McIntyre
OF S. Crawford
OF D. Cooley
C L. Drill
P L. Drill
P G. Mullin
P E. Killian
P W. Donovan
P F. Kitson

DET 1906 A
M W. Armour
1B C. Lindsay
2B H. Schaefer
SS C. O'Leary
3B W. Coughlin
OF M. McIntyre
OF S. Crawford
OF D. Jones
C C. Schmidt
P G. Mullin
P F. Donahue
P E. Siever
P W. Donovan
P E. Killian

DET 1907 A
M H. Jennings
1B C. Rossman
2B J. Downs
SS C. O'Leary
3B W. Coughlin
OF T. Cobb
OF S. Crawford
OF D. Jones
C C. Schmidt
UT H. Schaefer
P G. Mullin
P E. Killian
P E. Siever
P W. Donovan

DET 1908 A
M H. Jennings
1B C. Rossman
2B J. Downs
SS H. Schaefer
3B W. Coughlin
OF M. McIntyre
OF T. Cobb
OF S. Crawford
C C. Schmidt
P O. Summers
P G. Mullin
P W. Donovan
P R. Willett
P E. Killian

DET 1909 A
M H. Jennings
1B C. Rossman
2B J. Downs
SS O. Bush
3B G. Moriarty
OF T. Cobb
OF S. Crawford
OF M. McIntyre
C C. Schmidt
P G. Mullin
P R. Willett
P O. Summers
P E. Killian
P W. Donovan

DET 1910 A
M H. Jennings
1B T. Jones
2B J. Delahanty
SS O. Bush
3B G. Moriarty
OF S. Crawford
OF D. Jones
C O. Stanage
P G. Mullin
P R. Willett
P O. Summers
P W. Donovan
P R. Stroud

DET 1911 A
M H. Jennings
1B J. Delahanty
2B C. O'Leary
SS O. Bush
3B G. Moriarty
OF S. Crawford
OF T. Cobb
OF D. Jones
C O. Stanage

UT D. Drake
P G. Mullin
P R. Willett
P O. Summers
P E. Lafitte
P W. Donovan

DET 1912 A
M H. Jennings
1B G. Moriarty
2B W. Louden
SS O. Bush
3B C. Deal
OF S. Crawford
OF T. Cobb
OF D. Jones
C O. Stanage
P R. Willett
P J. Dubuc
P G. Mullin
P J. Lake
P R. Works

DET 1913 A
M H. Jennings
1B D. Gainer
2B O. Vitt
SS O. Bush
3B G. Moriarty
OF S. Crawford
OF R. Veach
OF T. Cobb
C O. Stanage
P J. Dubuc
P R. Willett
P R. Dauss
P M. Hall
P J. Lake
RP W. House

DET 1914 A
M H. Jennings
1B G. Burns
2B M. Kavanagh
SS O. Bush
3B G. Moriarty
OF S. Crawford
OF R. Veach
OF T. Cobb
C O. Stanage
P H. Coveleski
P R. Dauss
P J. Dubuc
P T. Cavet
P M. Main

DET 1915 A
M H. Jennings
1B G. Burns
2B R. Young
SS O. Bush
3B O. Vitt
OF S. Crawford
OF R. Veach
OF T. Cobb
C O. Stanage
UT M. Kavanagh
P H. Coveleski
P R. Dauss
P J. Dubuc
P B. Boland

DET 1916 A
M H. Jennings
1B G. Burns
2B R. Young
SS O. Bush
3B O. Vitt
OF R. Veach
OF T. Cobb
OF S. Crawford
C O. Stanage
UT H. Heilmann
P H. Coveleski
P R. Dauss
P J. Dubuc
P W. James
P G. Cunningham
RP B. Boland

DET 1917 A
M H. Jennings
1B G. Burns
2B R. Young
SS O. Bush
3B O. Vitt
OF R. Veach
OF T. Cobb
OF H. Heilmann
C O. Stanage

P G. Dauss
P B. Boland
P H. Ehmke
P W. James
P W. Mitchell

DET 1918 A

M H. Jennings
1B H. Heilmann
2B R. Young
SS O. Bush
3B O. Vitt
OF R. Veach
OF T. Cobb
OF G. Harper
C A. Yelle
P G. Dauss
P B. Boland
P R. Kallio
P G. Cunningham
P W. James

DET 1919 A

M H. Jennings
1B H. Heilmann
2B R. Young
SS O. Bush
3B R. Jones
OF R. Veach
OF T. Cobb
OF I. Flagstead
C E. Ainsmith
UT C. Shorten
P G. Dauss
P H. Ehmke
P B. Boland
P H. Leonard
P Y. Ayers
RP G. Cunningham

DET 1920 A

M H. Jennings
1B H. Heilmann
2B R. Young
SS O. Bush
3B R. Pinelli
OF R. Veach
OF T. Cobb
OF C. Shorten
C O. Stanage
UT I. Flagstead
P G. Dauss
P H. Ehmke
P J. Oldham
P Y. Ayers
P H. Leonard

DET 1921 A

M T. Cobb
1B L. Blue
2B R. Young
SS O. Bush
3B R. Jones
OF R. Veach
OF H. Heilmann
OF T. Cobb
C J. Bassler
P H. Leonard
P G. Dauss
P J. Oldham
P H. Ehmke
P C. Holling

DET 1922 A

M T. Cobb
1B L. Blue
2B G. Cutshaw
SS E. Rigney
3B R. Jones
OF R. Veach
OF T. Cobb
OF H. Heilmann
C J. Bassler
P H. Ehmke
P H. Pillette
P G. Dauss
P J. Oldham
P A. Olsen

DET 1923 A

M T. Cobb
1B L. Blue
2B F. Haney
SS E. Rigney
3B R. Jones
OF T. Cobb
OF H. Heilmann
OF R. Veach
C J. Bassler
UT R. Fothergill

UT H. Manush
UT D. Pratt
P G. Dauss
P H. Pillette
P K. Holloway
P S. Johnson
P A. Cole
RP R. Francis

DET 1924 A

M T. Cobb
1B L. Blue
2B D. Pratt
SS E. Rigney
3B R. Jones
OF T. Cobb
OF H. Heilmann
OF H. Manush
C J. Bassler
P E. Whitehill
P U. Stoner
P H. Collins
P K. Holloway
P G. Dauss

DET 1925 A

M T. Cobb
1B L. Blue
2B J. O'Rourke
SS J. Tavener
3B F. Haney
OF H. Heilmann
OF A. Wingo
OF T. Cobb
C J. Bassler
UT H. Manush
P E. Whitehill
P G. Dauss
P K. Holloway
P U. Stoner
P H. Collins
RP J. Doyle

DET 1926 A

M T. Cobb
1B L. Blue
2B C. Gehringer
SS J. Tavener
3B J. Warner
OF H. Heilmann
OF H. Manush
OF R. Fothergill
C C. Manion
UT J. Neun
UT J. O'Rourke
UT A. Wingo
P E. Whitehill
P S. Gibson
P E. Wells
P U. Stoner
P K. Holloway

DET 1927 A

M G. Moriarty
1B L. Blue
2B C. Gehringer
SS J. Tavener
3B J. Warner
OF H. Manush
OF R. Fothergill
OF H. Heilmann
C C. Woodall
UT M. McManus
P E. Whitehill
P U. Stoner
P S. Gibson
P K. Holloway
P H. Collins
RP G. Smith

DET 1928 A

M G. Moriarty
1B W. Sweeney
2B C. Gehringer
SS J. Tavener
3B M. McManus
OF H. Rice
OF H. Heilmann
OF R. Fothergill
C W. Hargrave
P O. Carroll
P E. Whitehill
P V. Sorrell
P E. Vangilder
P U. Stoner
RP G. Smith

DET 1929 A

M S. Harris
1B D. Alexander

2B C. Gehringer
SS H. Schuble
3B M. McManus
OF M. Johnson
OF H. Rice
OF H. Heilmann
C E. Phillips
UT R. Fothergill
P G. Uhle
P E. Whitehill
P V. Sorrell
P O. Carroll
RP J. Prudhomme
RP U. Stoner

DET 1930 A

M S. Harris
1B D. Alexander
2B C. Gehringer
SS M. Koenig
3B M. McManus
OF E. Funk
OF R. Johnson
OF J. Stone
C R. Hayworth
P G. Uhle
P V. Sorrell
P E. Whitehill
P E. Hogsett
P W. Hoyt
RP C. Sullivan

DET 1931 A

M S. Harris
1B D. Alexander
2B C. Gehringer
SS W. Rogell
3B M. McManus
OF R. Johnson
OF J. Stone
OF H. Walker
C R. Hayworth
UT M. Koenig
UT M. Owen
P E. Whitehill
P V. Sorrell
P G. Uhle
P T. Bridges
P A. Herring

DET 1932 A

M S. Harris
1B H. Davis
2B C. Gehringer
SS W. Rogell
3B H. Schuble
OF J. Stone
OF G. Walker
OF W. Webb
C R. Hayworth
P E. Whitehill
P V. Sorrell
P J. Wyatt
P T. Bridges
P E. Hogsett

DET 1933 A

M S. Harris
1B H. Greenberg
2B C. Gehringer
SS W. Rogell
3B M. Owen
OF J. Stone
OF E. Fox
OF G. Walker
C R. Hayworth
P F. Marberry
P V. Sorrell
P T. Bridges
P C. Fischer
P L. Rowe
RP E. Hogsett
RP A. Herring

DET 1934 A

M G. Cochrane
1B H. Greenberg
2B C. Gehringer
SS W. Rogell
3B M. Owen
OF L. Goslin
OF E. Fox
OF J. White
C G. Cochrane
UT G. Walker
P T. Bridges
P L. Rowe
P E. Auker
P F. Marberry
P V. Sorrell

RP E. Hogsett

DET 1935 A

M G. Cochrane
1B H. Greenberg
2B C. Gehringer
SS W. Rogell
3B M. Owen
OF L. Goslin
OF E. Fox
OF J. White
OF G. Cochrane
UT G. Walker
P L. Rowe
P T. Bridges
P A. Crowder
P E. Auker
P J. Sullivan
RP E. Hogsett

DET 1936 A

M G. Cochrane
1B J. Burns
2B C. Gehringer
SS W. Rogell
3B M. Owen
OF L. Goslin
OF A. Simmons
OF G. Walker
C R. Hayworth
P T. Bridges
P L. Rowe
P E. Auker
P V. Sorrell
P A. Lawson
RP C. Kimsey

DET 1937 A

M G. Cochrane
M D. Baker
M G. Cochrane
M D. Baker
M R. Perkins
1B H. Greenberg
2B C. Gehringer
SS W. Rogell
3B M. Owen
OF G. Walker
OF E. Fox
OF J. White
C P. York
P E. Auker
P T. Bridges
P A. Lawson
P J. Wade
P C. Poffenberger

DET 1938 A

M G. Cochrane
M D. Baker
1B H. Greenberg
2B C. Gehringer
SS W. Rogell
3B D. Ross
OF E. Fox
OF F. Walker
OF C. Morgan
C P. York
UT M. Christman
P L. Kennedy
P G. Gill
P E. Auker
P T. Bridges
P A. Lawson
RP G. Coffman
RP J. Wade

DET 1939 A

M D. Baker
1B H. Greenberg
2B C. Gehringer
SS F. Croucher
3B M. Higgins
OF W. McCosky
OF E. Fox
OF H. Averill
C G. Tebbetts
UT P. York
P L. Newsom
P T. Bridges
P L. Rowe
P P. Trout
P J. Benton
RP L. Thomas

DET 1940 A

M D. Baker
1B P. York
2B C. Gehringer
SS R. Bartell

3B M. Higgins
OF H. Greenberg
OF W. McCosky
OF E. Fox
C G. Tebbetts
UT B. Campbell
P L. Newsom
P T. Bridges
P L. Rowe
P J. Gorsica
P H. Newhouser
RP J. Benton
RP T. Seats

DET 1941 A

M D. Baker
1B P. York
2B C. Gehringer
SS F. Croucher
3B M. Higgins
OF B. Campbell
OF W. McCosky
OF R. Radcliff
C G. Tebbetts
UT G. Stainback
P L. Newsom
P H. Newhouser
P J. Gorsica
P J. Benton
P P. Trout
RP L. Thomas

DET 1942 A

M D. Baker
1B P. York
2B J. Bloodworth
SS W. Hitchcock
3B M. Higgins
OF W. McCosky
OF R. Cramer
OF R. Harris
C G. Tebbetts
P J. Benton
P P. Trout
P H. White
P H. Newhouser
P T. Bridges
RP R. Henshaw
RP J. Gorsica

DET 1943 A

M S. O'Neill
1B P. York
2B J. Bloodworth
SS J. Hoover
3B M. Higgins
OF R. Wakefield
OF R. Cramer
OF R. Harris
C P. Richards
P P. Trout
P V. Trucks
P H. Newhouser
P T. Bridges
P H. White
RP J. Gorsica
RP R. Henshaw

DET 1944 A

M S. O'Neill
1B P. York
2B E. Mayo
SS J. Hoover
3B M. Higgins
OF R. Cramer
OF J. Outlaw
OF R. Wakefield
C P. Richards
P P. Trout
P H. Newhouser
P J. Gentry
P F. Overmire
P J. Gorsica
RP W. Beck

DET 1945 A

M S. O'Neill
1B P. York
2B E. Mayo
SS J. Webb
3B R. Maier
OF R. Cullenbine
OF R. Cramer
OF J. Outlaw
C R. Swift
P H. Newhouser
P P. Trout
P J. Benton
P F. Overmire
P L. Mueller
RP W. Wilson

RP G. Caster

DET 1946 A

M S. O'Neill
1B H. Greenberg
2B J. Bloodworth
SS E. Lake
3B G. Kell
OF R. Wakefield
OF R. Cullenbine
OF W. Evers
C G. Tebbetts
P H. Newhouser
P P. Trout
P V. Trucks
P F. Hutchinson
P J. Benton

DET 1947 A

M S. O'Neill
1B R. Cullenbine
2B E. Mayo
SS E. Lake
3B G. Kell
OF W. Evers
OF P. Mullin
OF R. Wakefield
C R. Swift
UT V. Wertz
P H. Newhouser
P F. Hutchinson
P P. Trout
P V. Trucks
P F. Overmire
RP H. White
RP J. Gorsica

DET 1948 A

M S. O'Neill
1B G. Vico
2B E. Mayo
SS J. Lipon
3B G. Kell
OF W. Evers
OF P. Mullin
OF V. Wertz
C R. Swift
UT R. Wakefield
P H. Newhouser
P F. Hutchinson
P V. Trucks
P P. Trout
P A. Houtteman
RP F. Overmire
RP W. Pierce

DET 1949 A

M R. Rolfe
1B P. Campbell
2B C. Berry
SS J. Lipon
3B G. Kell
OF V. Wertz
OF W. Evers
OF J. Groth
C A. Robinson
UT D. Kolloway
UT E. Lake
UT P. Mullin
P H. Newhouser
P V. Trucks
P A. Houtteman
P T. Gray
P F. Hutchinson
RP P. Trout

DET 1950 A

M R. Rolfe
1B D. Kolloway
2B G. Priddy
SS J. Lipon
3B G. Kell
OF J. Groth
OF V. Wertz
OF W. Evers
C A. Robinson
P A. Houtteman
P F. Hutchinson
P H. Newhouser
P P. Trout
P T. Gray
RP H. White
RP P. Calvert

DET 1951 A

M R. Rolfe
1B R. Kryhoski
2B G. Priddy
SS J. Lipon
3B G. Kell

OF V. Wertz
OF J. Groth
OF W. Evers
C M. Ginsberg
UT P. Mullin
P T. Gray
P P. Trout
P F. Hutchinson
P V. Trucks
P R. Cain
RP H. Bearden
RP H. White

DET 1952 A

M R. Rolfe
M F. Hutchinson
1B W. Dropo
2B G. Priddy
SS C. Berry
3B F. Hatfield
OF J. Groth
OF V. Wertz
OF P. Mullin
C M. Ginsberg
P T. Gray
P A. Houtteman
P V. Trucks
P H. Newhouser
P W. Wight
RP H. White
RP R. Littlefield

DET 1953 A

M F. Hutchinson
1B W. Dropo
2B J. Pesky
SS H. Kuenn
3B R. Boone
OF R. Nieman
OF J. Delsing
OF D. Lund
C M. Batts
UT F. Hatfield
P W. Hoeft
P N. Garver
P T. Gray
P S. Gromek
P R. Branca
RP R. Marlowe
RP R. Herbert

DET 1954 A

M F. Hutchinson
1B W. Dropo
2B F. Bolling
SS H. Kuenn
3B R. Boone
OF W. Tuttle
OF A. Kaline
OF J. Delsing
C H. House
P S. Gromek
P N. Garver
P G. Zuverink
P W. Hoeft
P A. Aber
RP R. Marlowe
RP R. Herbert

DET 1955 A

M S. Harris
1B C. Torgeson
2B F. Hatfield
SS H. Kuenn
3B R. Boone
OF W. Tuttle
OF A. Kaline
OF J. Delsing
C H. House
UT J. Phillips
P F. Lary
P N. Garver
P W. Hoeft
P S. Gromek
RP W. Birrer
RP A. Aber

DET 1956 A

M S. Harris
1B C. Torgeson
2B F. Bolling
SS H. Kuenn
3B R. Boone
OF A. Kaline
OF W. Tuttle
OF C. Maxwell
C H. House
P F. Lary
P P. Foytack
P W. Hoeft
P S. Gromek

P   V. Trucks
RP D. Maas
RP A. Aber

DET 1957 A

M   J. Tighe
1B R. Boone
2B F. Bolling
SS H. Kuenn
3B R. Bertoia
OF A. Kaline
OF C. Maxwell
OF W. Tuttle
C   H. House
P   J. Bunning
P   F. Lary
P   D. Maas
P   P. Foytack
P   W. Hoeft
RP L. Sleater
RP H. Byrd

DET 1958 A

M   J. Tighe
M   H. Norman
1B B. Harris
2B F. Bolling
SS A. Martin
3B R. Bertoia
OF A. Kaline
OF H. Kuenn
OF C. Maxwell
C   R. Wilson
P   F. Lary
P   P. Foytack
P   J. Bunning
P   W. Hoeft
P   H. Moford
RP H. Aguirre
RP T. Morgan

DET 1959 A

M   H. Norman
M   J. Dykes
1B B. Harris
2B F. Bolling
SS E. Bridges
3B E. Yost
OF H. Kuenn
OF C. Maxwell
OF A. Kaline
C   L. Berberet
P   J. Bunning
P   P. Foytack
P   D. Mossi
P   F. Lary
RP R. Narleski
RP T. Morgan

DET 1960 A

M   J. Dykes
M   W. Hitchcock
M   J. Gordon
1B N. Cash
2B F. Bolling
SS H. Fernandez
3B E. Yost
OF R. Colavito
OF A. Kaline
OF C. Maxwell
C   L. Berberet
UT B. Chrisley
P   F. Lary
P   J. Bunning
P   D. Mossi
P   R. Bruce
P   P. Burnside
RP H. Aguirre
RP D. Sisler

DET 1961 A

M   R. Scheffing
1B N. Cash
2B J. Wood
SS H. Fernandez
3B S. Boros
OF R. Colavito
OF W. Bruton
OF A. Kaline
C   R. Brown
P   F. Lary
P   J. Bunning
P   D. Mossi
P   P. Foytack
P   P. Regan
RP T. Fox
RP H. Aguirre

DET 1962 A

M   R. Scheffing
1B N. Cash
2B J. Wood
SS H. Fernandez
3B S. Boros
OF R. Colavito
OF W. Bruton
OF A. Kaline
C   R. Brown
UT R. McAuliffe
P   J. Bunning
P   H. Aguirre
P   D. Mossi
P   P. Regan
P   P. Foytack
P   S. Jones
RP R. Kline

DET 1963 A

M   R. Scheffing
M   C. Dressen
1B N. Cash
2B J. Wood
SS R. McAuliffe
3B J. Phillips
OF R. Colavito
OF A. Kaline
OF W. Bruton
C   G. Triandos
UT W. Freehan
P   J. Bunning
P   H. Aguirre
P   P. Regan
P   M. Lolich
P   D. Mossi
RP T. Fox
RP R. Anderson

DET 1964 A

M   C. Dressen
1B N. Cash
2B J. Lumpe
SS R. McAuliffe
3B D. Wert
OF A. Kaline
OF W. Brown
OF G. Thomas
C   W. Freehan
UT W. Bruton
UT D. Demeter
P   D. Wickersham
P   M. Lolich
P   H. Aguirre
P   E. Rakow
P   P. Regan
RP F. Gladding
RP L. Sherry

DET 1965 A

M   R. Swift
M   C. Dressen
1B N. Cash
2B J. Lumpe
SS R. McAuliffe
3B D. Wert
OF W. Horton
OF A. Kaline
OF D. Demeter
C   W. Freehan
P   M. Lolich
P   D. McLain
P   H. Aguirre
P   D. Wickersham
P   J. Sparma
RP L. Sherry
RP T. Fox

DET 1966 A

M   C. Dressen
M   R. Swift
M   F. Skaff
1B N. Cash
2B J. Lumpe
SS R. McAuliffe
3B D. Wert
OF W. Horton
OF A. Kaline
OF J. Northrup
C   W. Freehan
UT J. Wood
P   D. McLain
P   M. Lolich
P   R. Wilson
P   D. Wickersham
P   J. Podres
RP O. Pena
RP L. Sherry

DET 1967 A

M   E. Smith
1B N. Cash
2B R. McAuliffe
SS R. Oyler
3B D. Wert
OF J. Northrup
OF A. Kaline
OF M. Stanley
C   W. Freehan
UT W. Horton
P   R. Wilson
P   D. McLain
P   J. Sparma
P   M. Lolich
RP D. Wickersham
RP F. Gladding

DET 1968 A

M   E. Smith
1B N. Cash
2B R. McAuliffe
SS R. Oyler
3B D. Wert
OF J. Northrup
OF W. Horton
OF M. Stanley
C   W. Freehan
UT A. Kaline
P   D. McLain
P   R. Wilson
P   M. Lolich
P   J. Sparma
P   J. Hiller
RP P. Dobson
RP D. Patterson

DET 1969 A

M   E. Smith
1B N. Cash
2B R. McAuliffe
SS T. Tresh
3B D. Wert
OF J. Northrup
OF W. Horton
OF A. Kaline
C   W. Freehan
UT M. Stanley
P   D. McLain
P   M. Lolich
P   R. Wilson
P   M. Kilkenny
RP P. Dobson
RP J. Hiller

DET 1970 A

M   E. Smith
1B N. Cash
2B R. McAuliffe
SS C. Gutierrez
3B D. Wert
OF J. Northrup
OF M. Stanley
OF W. Horton
C   W. Freehan
UT A. Kaline
UT E. Maddox
P   M. Lolich
P   J. Niekro
P   L. Cain
P   M. Kilkenny
P   R. Wilson
RP J. Hiller
RP T. Timmermann

DET 1971 A

M   A. Martin
1B N. Cash
2B R. McAuliffe
SS E. Brinkman
3B A. Rodriguez
OF M. Stanley
OF A. Kaline
OF W. Horton
C   W. Freehan
UT J. Northrup
P   M. Lolich
P   J. Coleman
P   L. Cain
P   J. Niekro
RP F. Scherman
RP W. Chance

DET 1972 A

M   A. Martin
1B N. Cash
2B R. McAuliffe
SS E. Brinkman
3B A. Rodriguez
OF M. Stanley
OF J. Northrup
OF W. Horton
C   W. Freehan
UT W. Brown
UT A. Kaline
P   M. Lolich
P   J. Coleman
P   T. Timmermann
P   W. Fryman
RP C. Seelbach
RP F. Scherman

DET 1973 A

M   A. Martin
M   J. Schultz
1B N. Cash
2B R. McAuliffe
SS E. Brinkman
3B A. Rodriguez
OF M. Stanley
OF J. Northrup
OF W. Horton
C   W. Freehan
DH W. Brown
P   M. Lolich
P   J. Coleman
P   J. Perry
P   W. Fryman
RP J. Hiller
RP F. Scherman

DET 1974 A

M   R. Houk
1B W. Freehan
2B G. Sutherland
SS E. Brinkman
3B A. Rodriguez
OF J. Northrup
OF M. Stanley
OF W. Horton
C   G. Moses
DH A. Kaline
P   M. Lolich
P   J. Coleman
P   L. LaGrow
P   W. Fryman
RP J. Hiller
RP J. Ray

DET 1975 A

M   R. Houk
1B L. Pierce
2B G. Sutherland
SS T. Veryzer
3B A. Rodriguez
OF R. LeFlore
OF L. Roberts
OF B. Oglivie
C   W. Freehan
DH W. Horton
UT D. Meyer
P   M. Lolich
P   J. Coleman
P   V. Ruhle
P   L. LaGrow
P   R. Bare
RP J. Hiller

DET 1976 A

M   R. Houk
1B J. Thompson
2B P. Garcia
SS T. Veryzer
3B A. Rodriguez
OF R. LeFlore
OF D. Staub
OF A. Johnson
C   B. Kimm
DH W. Horton
UT D. Meyer
UT B. Oglivie
P   D. Roberts
P   M. Fidrych
P   V. Ruhle
P   R. Bare
P   J. Crawford
RP J. Hiller
RP S. Grilli

DET 1977 A

M   R. Houk
1B J. Thompson
2B R. Fuentes
SS T. Veryzer
3B A. Rodriguez
OF R. LeFlore
OF S. Kemp
OF B. Oglivie
C   M. May
DH D. Staub
P   D. Rozema
P   F. Arroyo
P   R. Sykes
P   D. Roberts
P   J. Crawford
RP J. Hiller
RP S. Foucault

DET 1978 A

M   R. Houk
1B J. Thompson
2B L. Whitaker
SS A. Trammell
3B A. Rodriguez
OF S. Kemp
OF R. LeFlore
OF T. Corcoran
C   M. May
DH D. Staub
P   J. Slaton
P   M. Wilcox
P   D. Rozema
P   J. Billingham
P   K. Young
RP J. Hiller

DET 1979 A

M   J. Moss
M   R. Tracewski
M   G. Anderson
1B J. Thompson
2B L. Whitaker
SS A. Trammell
3B A. Rodriguez
OF S. Kemp
OF J. Morales
OF R. LeFlore
C   L. Parrish
DH D. Staub
P   J. Morris
P   M. Wilcox
P   J. Billingham
P   P. Underwood
P   D. Petry
RP A. Lopez
RP J. Hiller

DET 1980 A

M   G. Anderson
1B R. Hebner
2B L. Whitaker
SS A. Trammell
3B T. Brookens
OF R. Peters
OF A. Cowens
OF S. Kemp
C   L. Parrish
DH J. Summers
UT J. Wockenfuss
P   J. Morris
P   M. Wilcox
P   D. Schatzeder
P   D. Petry
P   D. Rozema
RP A. Lopez
RP P. Underwood

DET 1981 A

M   G. Anderson
1B R. Hebner
2B L. Whitaker
SS A. Trammell
3B T. Brookens
OF S. Kemp
OF A. Cowens
OF K. Gibson
C   L. Parrish
DH J. Wockenfuss
UT L. Jones
P   J. Morris
P   M. Wilcox
P   D. Petry
P   D. Rozema
P   D. Schatzeder
RP A. Lopez
RP D. Tobik

DET 1982 A

M   G. Anderson
1B E. Cabell
2B L. Whitaker
SS A. Trammell
3B T. Brookens
OF L. Herndon
OF C. Lemon
OF G. Wilson
C   L. Parrish
DH M. Ivie
P   J. Morris
P   D. Petry
P   M. Wilcox
P   G. Ujdur
P   P. Underwood
RP D. Tobik
RP D. Rucker

DET 1983 A

M   G. Anderson
1B E. Cabell
2B L. Whitaker
SS A. Trammell
3B T. Brookens
OF C. Lemon
OF G. Wilson
OF L. Herndon
C   L. Parrish
DH K. Gibson
UT R. Leach
P   J. Morris
P   D. Petry
P   M. Wilcox
P   J. Berenguer
P   D. Rozema
RP A. Lopez
RP H. Bailey

DET 1984 A

M   G. Anderson
1B D. Bergman
2B L. Whitaker
SS A. Trammell
3B H. Johnson
OF C. Lemon
OF K. Gibson
OF L. Herndon
C   L. Parrish
DH D. Evans
UT T. Brookens
UT B. Garbey
P   J. Morris
P   D. Petry
P   M. Wilcox
P   J. Berenguer
P   D. Rozema
RP G. Hernandez
RP A. Lopez

DET 1985 A

M   G. Anderson
1B D. Evans
2B L. Whitaker
SS A. Trammell
3B T. Brookens
OF C. Lemon
OF K. Gibson
OF L. Herndon
C   L. Parrish
DH J. Grubb
P   J. Morris
P   D. Petry
P   C. Terrell
P   F. Tanana
RP G. Hernandez
RP A. Lopez

DET 1986 A

M   G. Anderson
1B D. Evans
2B L. Whitaker
SS A. Trammell
3B D. Coles
OF C. Lemon
OF K. Gibson
OF D. Collins
C   L. Parrish
DH J. Grubb
UT T. Brookens
UT L. Herndon
UT P. Sheridan
P   J. Morris
P   C. Terrell
P   F. Tanana
P   E. King
P   R. O'Neal
RP G. Hernandez
RP W. Campbell

DET 1987 A

M   G. Anderson
1B D. Evans
2B L. Whitaker
SS A. Trammell
3B T. Brookens
OF C. Lemon
OF P. Sheridan
OF K. Gibson
C   M. Nokes
DH B. Madlock
P   J. Morris
P   C. Terrell
P   F. Tanana
P   D. Petry
P   J. Robinson
RP E. King
RP M. Henneman

DET 1988 A

M   G. Anderson
1B D. Bergman
2B L. Whitaker
SS A. Trammell
3B T. Brookens
OF C. Lemon
OF G. Pettis
OF P. Sheridan
C   M. Nokes
DH D. Evans
UT C. Knight
UT L. Salazar
P   J. Morris
P   D. Alexander
P   C. Terrell
P   F. Tanana
P   J. Robinson
RP P. Gibson
RP M. Henneman

Elizabeth

RES n 1873
Resolutes

RES n 1873

M   J. Benjamin
1B M. Campbell
2B B. Laughlin
SS F. Wordsworth
3B Nevins
OF H. Austin
OF A. Allison
OF E. Booth
C   D. Allison
UT F. Fleet
P   H. Campbell

Fort Wayne

KEK n 1871
Kekiongas

KEK 1871 n

M   W. Lennon
M   J. Deane
1B J. Foran
2B T. Carey
SS W. Goldsmith
3B F. Sellman
OF W. Kelley
OF S. Armstrong
OF E. Mincher
C   W. Lennon
P   R. Mathews

Hartford

HAR n 1874-1875
HAR N 1876-1877
Played in Brooklyn 1877

HAR 1874 n

M   L. Pike
1B E. Mills
2B R. Addy
SS T. Barlow
3B W. Boyd
OF J. Tipper
OF L. Pike
OF W. Boyd
C   W. Hastings
UT W. Barnie
P   W. Fisher
P   W. Stearns

HAR 1875 n

M   R. Ferguson
1B E. Mills
2B J. Burdock
SS T. Carey
3B R. Ferguson
OF T. York
OF J. Remsen
OF A. Allison
C   D. Allison
P   W. Cummings
P   T. Bond

HAR 1876 N

M   R. Ferguson
1B E. Mills
2B J. Burdock
SS T. Carey
3B R. Ferguson
OF J. Remsen

OF T. York
OF R. Higham
C D. Allison
P T. Bond
P W. Cummings

HAR 1877 N

M R. Ferguson
1B J. Start
2B J. Burdock
SS T. Carey
3B R. Ferguson
OF J. Cassidy
OF T. York
OF J. Holdsworth
C W. Harbidge
P F. Larkin

Houston

HOU N 1962-1988

HOU 1962 N

M H. Craft
1B N. Larker
2B J. Amalfitano
SS R. Lillis
3B R. Aspromonte
OF R. Mejias
OF C. Warwick
OF A. Spangler
C H. Smith
UT J. Pendleton
P R. Farrell
P K. Johnson
P R. Bruce
P J. Golden
P H. Woodeshick
RP B. Tiefenauer
RP D. McMahon

HOU 1963 N

M H. Craft
1B D. Staub
2B E. Fazio
SS R. Lillis
3B R. Aspromonte
OF C. Warwick
OF H. Goss
OF A. Spangler
C J. Bateman
UT J. Runnels
UT J. Temple
P K. Johnson
P R. Farrell
P D. Nottebart
P R. Bruce
P H. Brown
RP H. Woodeshick
RP D. McMahon

HOU 1964 N

M H. Craft
M C. Harris
1B W. Bond
2B J. Fox
SS E. Kasko
3B R. Aspromonte
OF A. Spangler
OF A. Gaines
OF J. White
C G. Grote
UT R. Lillis
P K. Johnson
P R. Bruce
P R. Farrell
P D. Nottebart
P H. Brown
RP J. Owens
RP J. Raymond

HOU 1965 N

M C. Harris
1B W. Bond
2B J. Morgan
SS R. Lillis
3B R. Aspromonte
OF J. Wynn
OF D. Staub
OF A. Maye
C R. Brand
UT A. Gaines
P R. Bruce
P R. Farrell
P D. Nottebart
P L. Dierker
P D. Giusti
RP J. Raymond
RP J. Owens

HOU 1966 N

M G. Hatton
1B C. Harrison
2B J. Morgan
SS R. Jackson
3B R. Aspromonte
OF D. Staub
OF J. Wynn
OF A. Maye
C J. Bateman
UT D. Nicholson
P M. Cuellar
P D. Giusti
P L. Dierker
P R. Farrell
P R. Bruce
RP J. Raymond
RP R. Taylor

HOU 1967 N

M G. Hatton
1B E. Mathews
2B J. Morgan
SS R. Jackson
3B R. Aspromonte
OF J. Wynn
OF D. Staub
OF R. Davis
C J. Bateman
P M. Cuellar
P D. Giusti
P D. Wilson
P R. Belinsky
P L. Dierker
RP A. Latman
RP C. Sembera

HOU 1968 N

M G. Hatton
M H. Walker
1B D. Staub
2B D. Menke
SS H. Torres
3B D. Rader
OF J. Wynn
OF N. Miller
OF R. Davis
C J. Bateman
UT R. Aspromonte
P D. Giusti
P L. Dierker
P D. Lemaster
P D. Wilson
P M. Cuellar
RP J. Buzhardt
RP J. Ray

HOU 1969 N

M H. Walker
1B C. Blefary
2B J. Morgan
SS D. Menke
3B D. Rader
OF J. Wynn
OF N. Miller
OF J. Alou
C J. Edwards
P L. Dierker
P D. Lemaster
P D. Wilson
P T. Griffin
RP J. Ray
RP J. Billingham

HOU 1970 N

M H. Walker
1B R. Watson
2B J. Morgan
SS D. Menke
3B D. Rader
OF J. Wynn
OF J. Alou
OF C. Cedeno
C J. Edwards
P L. Dierker
P J. Billingham
P D. Wilson
P D. Lemaster
P T. Griffin
RP J. Ray
RP R. Cook

HOU 1971 N

M H. Walker
1B D. Menke
2B J. Morgan
SS R. Metzger
3B D. Rader
OF C. Cedeno
OF J. Wynn
OF J. Alou
C J. Edwards
UT R. Watson
P D. Wilson
P J. Billingham
P K. Forsch
P L. Dierker
P W. Blasingame
RP J. Ray
RP G. Culver

HOU 1972 N

M H. Walker
M F. Parker
M L. Durocher
1B L. May
2B T. Helms
SS R. Metzger
3B D. Rader
OF J. Wynn
OF R. Watson
OF C. Cedeno
C J. Edwards
P D. Wilson
P L. Dierker
P D. Roberts
P J. Reuss
P K. Forsch
RP G. Culver
RP T. Griffin

HOU 1973 N

M L. Durocher
1B L. May
2B T. Helms
SS R. Metzger
3B D. Rader
OF R. Watson
OF C. Cedeno
OF J. Wynn
C A. Jutze
P J. Reuss
P D. Roberts
P D. Wilson
P K. Forsch
P T. Griffin
RP J. Crawford
RP J. Ray

HOU 1974 N

M P. Gomez
1B L. May
2B T. Helms
SS R. Metzger
3B D. Rader
OF C. Cedeno
OF G. Gross
OF R. Watson
C M. May
UT R. Gallagher
UT L. Milbourne
P L. Dierker
P T. Griffin
P D. Wilson
P D. Roberts
P C. Osteen
RP K. Forsch
RP M. Cosgrove

HOU 1975 N

M P. Gomez
M W. Virdon
1B R. Watson
2B R. Andrews
SS R. Metzger
3B D. Rader
OF C. Cedeno
OF G. Gross
OF W. Howard
C M. May
UT E. Cabell
UT J. Cruz
UT C. Johnson
P L. Dierker
P J. Richard
P D. Roberts
P D. Konieczny
P K. Forsch
RP J. Niekro
RP J. Crawford

HOU 1976 N

M W. Virdon
1B R. Watson
2B R. Andrews
SS R. Metzger
3B E. Cabell
OF C. Cedeno
OF J. Cruz
OF G. Gross
C E. Herrmann
UT C. Johnson
P J. Richard
P L. Dierker
P J. Andujar
P J. Niekro
RP K. Forsch
RP E. Pentz

HOU 1977 N

M W. Virdon
1B R. Watson
2B A. Howe
SS R. Metzger
3B E. Cabell
OF J. Cruz
OF C. Cedeno
OF W. Howard
C J. Ferguson
UT J. Gonzalez
P J. Richard
P M. Lemongello
P J. Niekro
P J. Andujar
P F. Bannister
RP J. Sambito
RP E. Pentz

HOU 1978 N

M W. Virdon
1B R. Watson
2B A. Howe
SS J. Sexton
3B E. Cabell
OF J. Cruz
OF T. Puhl
OF D. Walling
C L. Pujols
UT D. Bergman
P J. Richard
P M. Lemongello
P J. Niekro
P T. Dixon
P J. Andujar
RP K. Forsch
RP J. Sambito

HOU 1979 N

M W. Virdon
1B C. Cedeno
2B R. Landestoy
SS G. Reynolds
3B E. Cabell
OF J. Cruz
OF T. Puhl
OF J. Leonard
C A. Ashby
UT A. Howe
P J. Richard
P J. Niekro
P J. Andujar
P K. Forsch
P R. Williams
RP J. Sambito
RP R. Niemann

HOU 1980 N

M W. Virdon
1B A. Howe
2B J. Morgan
SS G. Reynolds
3B E. Cabell
OF J. Cruz
OF C. Cedeno
OF T. Puhl
C A. Ashby
UT R. Landestoy
UT D. Walling
P J. Niekro
P L. Ryan
P K. Forsch
P V. Ruhle
P J. Andujar
RP D. Smith
RP J. Sambito

HOU 1981 N

M W. Virdon
1B C. Cedeno
2B J. Pittman
SS G. Reynolds
3B A. Howe
OF J. Cruz
OF T. Puhl
OF A. Scott
C A. Ashby
P J. Niekro
P D. Sutton
P R. Knepper
P L. Ryan
P V. Ruhle
RP D. Smith
RP J. Sambito

HOU 1982 N

M W. Virdon
M R. Lillis
1B C. Knight
2B P. Garner
SS R. Thon
3B A. Howe
OF J. Cruz
OF T. Puhl
OF A. Scott
C A. Ashby
P J. Niekro
P L. Ryan
P D. Sutton
P R. Knepper
P V. Ruhle
RP M. LaCoss
RP F. LaCorte

HOU 1983 N

M R. Lillis
1B C. Knight
2B W. Doran
SS R. Thon
3B P. Garner
OF J. Cruz
OF T. Puhl
OF O. Moreno
C A. Ashby
UT D. Walling
P J. Niekro
P R. Knepper
P L. Ryan
P M. Scott
P M. LaCoss
RP V. Ruhle
RP W. Dawley

HOU 1984 N

M R. Lillis
1B E. Cabell
2B W. Doran
SS G. Reynolds
3B P. Garner
OF J. Cruz
OF J. Mumphrey
OF T. Puhl
C J. Bailey
UT K. Bass
P J. Niekro
P R. Knepper
P L. Ryan
P M. Scott
P M. LaCoss
RP W. Dawley
RP V. Ruhle

HOU 1985 N

M R. Lillis
1B G. Davis
2B W. Doran
SS G. Reynolds
3B P. Garner
OF K. Bass
OF J. Cruz
OF J. Mumphrey
C J. Bailey
UT D. Walling
P R. Knepper
P L. Ryan
P M. Scott
P J. Niekro
RP W. Dawley
RP D. Smith

HOU 1986 N

M H. Lanier
1B G. Davis
2B W. Doran
SS R. Thon
3B D. Walling
OF K. Bass
OF J. Cruz
OF W. Hatcher
C A. Ashby
UT P. Garner
UT G. Reynolds
P M. Scott
P R. Knepper
P L. Ryan
P J. Deshaies
RP C. Kerfeld
RP A. Lopez

HOU 1987 N

M H. Lanier
1B G. Davis
2B W. Doran
SS G. Reynolds
3B D. Walling
OF K. Bass
OF W. Hatcher
OF J. Cruz
C A. Ashby
P M. Scott
P L. Ryan
P D. Darwin
P R. Knepper
P J. Deshaies
RP L. Andersen
RP D. Smith

HOU 1988 N

M H. Lanier
1B G. Davis
2B W. Doran
SS R. Ramirez
3B D. Bell
OF K. Bass
OF G. Young
OF W. Hatcher
C A. Trevino
UT T. Puhl
P L. Ryan
P M. Scott
P J. Deshaies
P D. Darwin
P R. Knepper
RP J. Agosto
RP L. Andersen

Indianapolis

IND N 1878
IND a 1884
IND N 1887-1889
IND F 1914

IND 1878 N

M J. Clapp
1B A. Croft
2B J. Quest
SS F. Warner
3B E. Williamson
OF G. Shaffer
OF R. McKelvy
OF J. Clapp
C F. Flint
P E. Nolan
P J. McCormick
P T. Healey

IND 1884 a

M J. Gifford
M W. Watkins
1B J. Kerins
2B E. Merrill
SS M. Phillips
3B P. Callahan
OF J. Peltz
OF J. Weihe
OF J. Morrison
C J. Keenan
P L. McKeon
P R. Barr
P J. Aydelott
P A. McCauley

IND 1887 N

M G. Burnham
M F. Thomas
M H. Fogel
1B O. Schomberg
2B C. Bassett
SS J. Glasscock
3B J. Denny
OF J. Seery
OF J. McGeachey
OF J. Canill
C G. Myers
P J. Healy
P H. Boyle
P L. Shreve

IND 1888 N

M H. Spence
1B T. Esterbrook
2B C. Bassett
SS J. Glasscock
3B J. Denny
OF J. Seery
OF P. Hines
OF J. McGeachey
C R. Buckley
P H. Boyle
P J. Healy
P L. Shreve
P W. Burdick

IND 1889 N

M F. Bancroft
M J. Glasscock
1B P. Hines
2B C. Bassett
SS J. Glasscock
3B J. Denny
OF J. McGeachey
OF J. Seery
OF M. Sullivan
C R. Buckley
P H. Boyle
P C. Getzien
P A. Rusie

IND 1914 F

M W. Phillips
1B C. Carr
2B F. LaPorte
SS J. Esmond
3B W. McKechnie
OF B. Kauff
OF A. Campbell
OF A. Scheer
C W. Rariden
P F. Falkenberg
P E. Moseley
P G. Kaiserling
P G. Mullin
P H. Billiard

Kansas City

KC U 1884
KC N 1886
KC a 1888-1889
KC F 1914-1915
KC A 1955-1967
Moved to Oakland
KC A 1969-1988

KC 1884 U

M H. Wheeler
M M. Porter
M T. Sullivan
1B J. Sweeney
2B C. Berry
SS C. Cross
3B P. Sullivan
OF F. Shaffer
OF F. Wyman
OF B. McLaughlin
C C. Baldwin
P E. Hickman

KC 1886 N

M D. Rowe
1B W. McQuery
2B J. Myers
SS C. Bassett
3B J. Donnelly
OF J. Lillie
OF P. Radford
OF D. Rowe
C C. Briody
P G. Weidman
P J. Whitney

KC 1888 a

M D. Rowe
M S. Barkley
M W. Watkins
1B W. Phillips
2B S. Barkley
SS H. Easterday
3B J. Davis
OF J. McTamany
OF J. Cline
OF W. Hamilton
C J. Donahue
P H. Porter
P T. Sullivan
P W. Fagan
P F. Hoffman
P S. Toole

KC 1889 a

M W. Watkins
1B D. Stearns
2B S. Barkley
SS H. Long
3B J. Davis
OF W. Hamilton
OF J. Burns
OF J. Manning
C C. Hoover
P P. Swartzel
P J. Conway
P J. Sowders
P J. McCarty

P   T. Sullivan

KC 1914 F
M   G. Stovall
1B   G. Stovall
2B   W. Kenworthy
SS   C. Goodwin
3B   G. Perring
OF   C. Chadbourne
OF   E. Gilmore
OF   A. Kruger
C   T. Easterly
P   E. Packard
P   N. Cullop
P   D. Stone
P   B. Harris
P   E. Henning

KC 1915 F
M   G. Stovall
1B   G. Stovall
2B   W. Kenworthy
SS   J. Rawlings
3B   G. Perring
OF   C. Chadbourne
OF   A. Shaw
OF   E. Gilmore
C   T. Easterly
P   N. Cullop
P   E. Packard
P   G. Johnson
P   M. Main
P   E. Henning

KC 1955 A
M   L. Boudreau
1B   V. Power
2B   J. Finigan
SS   J. DeMaestri
3B   H. Lopez
OF   G. Zernial
OF   H. Simpson
OF   W. Wilson
C   J. Astroth
UT   W. Renna
UT   E. Slaughter
UT   E. Valo
P   A. Ditmar
P   A. Kellner
P   R. Shantz
P   A. Ceccarelli
P   A. Portocarrero
RP   T. Gorman
RP   W. Harrington

KC 1956 A
M   L. Boudreau
1B   V. Power
2B   J. Finigan
SS   J. DeMaestri
3B   H. Lopez
OF   H. Simpson
OF   J. Groth
OF   L. Skizas
C   C. Thompson
UT   G. Zernial
P   A. Ditmar
P   T. Gorman
P   W. Burnette
P   L. Kretlow
P   W. Herriage
RP   J. Crimian
RP   R. Shantz

KC 1957 A
M   L. Boudreau
M   H. Craft
1B   V. Power
2B   G. Hunter
SS   J. DeMaestri
3B   H. Lopez
OF   G. Zernial
OF   W. Held
OF   R. Cerv
C   H. Smith
UT   L. Skizas
P   N. Garver
P   T. Morgan
P   A. Kellner
P   R. Terry
P   J. Urban
RP   V. Trucks
RP   W. Burnette

KC 1958 A
M   H. Craft
1B   V. Power
2B   H. Hunter
SS   J. DeMaestri
3B   H. Smith

OF   W. Tuttle
OF   R. Cerv
OF   R. Maris
C   H. Chiti
UT   R. Martyn
P   R. Terry
P   N. Garver
P   R. Herbert
P   J. Urban
P   R. Grim
RP   T. Gorman
RP   R. Tomanek

KC 1959 A
M   H. Craft
1B   K. Hadley
2B   W. Terwilliger
SS   J. DeMaestri
3B   R. Williams
OF   W. Tuttle
OF   R. Cerv
OF   R. Maris
C   H. House
UT   J. Lumpe
UT   H. Smith
P   L. Daley
P   N. Garver
P   R. Herbert
P   J. Kucks
P   R. Grim
RP   W. Coleman
RP   T. Sturdivant

KC 1960 A
M   R. Elliott
1B   M. Throneberry
2B   J. Lumpe
SS   K. Hamlin
3B   A. Carey
OF   W. Tuttle
OF   R. Snyder
OF   N. Siebern
C   P. Daley
UT   H. Bauer
UT   R. Williams
P   R. Herbert
P   L. Daley
P   R. Hall
P   N. Garver
P   J. Kucks
RP   K. Johnson
RP   M. Kutyna

KC 1961 A
M   J. Gordon
M   H. Bauer
1B   N. Siebern
2B   J. Lumpe
SS   R. Howser
3B   J. Causey
OF   L. Posada
OF   R. Del Greco
OF   J. Hankins
C   H. Sullivan
P   J. Archer
P   N. Bass
P   J. Walker
P   R. Shaw
P   J. Nuxhall
RP   E. Rakow
RP   W. Kunkel

KC 1962 A
M   H. Bauer
1B   N. Siebern
2B   J. Lumpe
SS   R. Howser
3B   E. Charles
OF   G. Cimoli
OF   R. Del Greco
OF   M. Jimenez
C   H. Sullivan
UT   J. Causey
UT   J. Tartabull
P   E. Rakow
P   D. Pfister
P   J. Walker
P   W. Fischer
P   D. Segui
RP   J. Wyatt
RP   D. McDevitt

KC 1963 A
M   E. Lopat
1B   N. Siebern
2B   J. Lumpe
SS   J. Causey
3B   E. Charles
OF   G. Cimoli
OF   R. Del Greco
OF   J. Tartabull

C   H. Edwards
UT   C. Essegian
P   D. Wickersham
P   O. Pena
P   E. Rakow
P   M. Drabowsky
P   D. Segui
RP   E. Bowsfield
RP   W. Fischer

KC 1964 A
M   E. Lopat
M   F. McGaha
1B   J. Gentile
2B   R. Green
SS   J. Causey
3B   E. Charles
OF   R. Colavito
OF   N. Mathews
OF   J. Tartabull
C   H. Edwards
UT   G. Alusik
P   O. Pena
P   D. Segui
P   J. O'Donoghue
P   M. Drabowsky
RP   J. Wyatt
RP   E. Bowsfield

KC 1965 A
M   F. McGaha
M   H. Sullivan
1B   K. Harrelson
2B   R. Green
SS   D. Campaneris
3B   E. Charles
OF   N. Hershberger
OF   J. Landis
OF   T. Reynolds
C   W. Bryan
UT   J. Causey
P   F. Talbot
P   R. Sheldon
P   J. O'Donoghue
P   D. Segui
P   J. Hunter
RP   W. Stock
RP   J. Wyatt

KC 1966 A
M   A. Dark
1B   K. Harrelson
2B   R. Green
SS   D. Campaneris
3B   E. Charles
OF   N. Hershberger
OF   L. Stahl
OF   J. Nossek
C   P. Roof
UT   D. Cater
UT   R. Repoz
P   L. Krausse
P   J. Hunter
P   J. Nash
P   P. Lindblad
RP   J. Aker
RP   K. Sanders

KC 1967 A
M   A. Dark
M   L. Appling
1B   R. Webster
2B   J. Donaldson
SS   D. Campaneris
3B   R. Green
OF   N. Hershberger
OF   R. Monday
OF   J. Gosger
C   P. Roof
UT   D. Cater
P   J. Hunter
P   J. Nash
P   C. Dobson
P   L. Krausse
P   J. Odom
RP   P. Lindblad
RP   T. Pierce

KC 1969 A
M   J. Gordon
1B   M. Fiore
2B   K. Adair
SS   J. Hernandez
3B   J. Foy
OF   L. Piniella
OF   H. Kelly
OF   R. Oliver
C   E. Rodriguez
UT   E. Kirkpatrick
P   W. Bunker
P   R. Drago

P   W. Butler
P   R. Nelson
P   J. Rooker
RP   M. Drabowsky
RP   T. Burgmeier

KC 1970 A
M   C. Metro
M   R. Lemon
1B   R. Oliver
2B   O. Rojas
SS   J. Hernandez
3B   P. Schaal
OF   A. Otis
OF   L. Piniella
OF   H. Kelly
C   E. Kirkpatrick
P   R. Drago
P   R. Johnson
P   J. Rooker
P   W. Butler
P   D. Morehead
RP   A. Fitzmorris
RP   T. Burgmeier

KC 1971 A
M   R. Lemon
1B   G. Hopkins
2B   O. Rojas
SS   F. Patek
3B   P. Schaal
OF   A. Otis
OF   L. Piniella
OF   J. Keough
C   J. May
UT   E. Kirkpatrick
UT   R. Oliver
P   R. Drago
P   M. Hedlund
P   P. Splittorff
P   J. Dal Canton
P   A. Fitzmorris
RP   J. York
RP   T. Burgmeier

KC 1972 A
M   R. Lemon
1B   J. Mayberry
2B   O. Rojas
SS   F. Patek
3B   P. Schaal
OF   L. Piniella
OF   A. Otis
OF   R. Scheinblum
C   E. Kirkpatrick
UT   S. Hovley
P   R. Drago
P   P. Splittorff
P   R. Nelson
P   J. Dal Canton
P   M. Hedlund
RP   A. Fitzmorris
RP   T. Abernathy

KC 1973 A
M   J. McKeon
1B   J. Mayberry
2B   O. Rojas
SS   F. Patek
3B   P. Schaal
OF   A. Otis
OF   L. Piniella
OF   E. Kirkpatrick
C   F. Healy
DH   H. McRae
UT   K. Bevacqua
UT   S. Hovley
P   P. Splittorff
P   S. Busby
P   R. Drago
P   H. Garber
P   J. Dal Canton
RP   J. Bird
RP   S. Mingori

KC 1974 A
M   J. McKeon
1B   J. Mayberry
2B   O. Rojas
SS   F. Patek
3B   G. Brett
OF   A. Otis
OF   J. Wohlford
OF   V. Pinson
C   F. Healy
DH   H. McRae
UT   A. Cowens
UT   F. White
P   S. Busby
P   P. Splittorff
P   A. Fitzmorris

P   J. Dal Canton
P   M. Pattin
RP   L. McDaniel
RP   J. Bird

KC 1975 A
M   J. McKeon
M   D. Herzog
1B   J. Mayberry
2B   O. Rojas
SS   J. Hernandez
3B   G. Brett
OF   A. Otis
OF   L. Piniella
OF   H. Kelly
C   E. Kirkpatrick
P   R. Drago
P   R. Johnson
P   J. Rooker
P   W. Butler
P   D. Morehead
RP   A. Fitzmorris
RP   T. Burgmeier

KC 1976 A
M   D. Herzog
1B   J. Mayberry
2B   F. White
SS   F. Patek
3B   G. Brett
OF   A. Otis
OF   A. Cowens
OF   T. Poquette
C   J. Martinez
DH   H. McRae
UT   J. Wohlford
P   D. Leonard
P   A. Fitzmorris
P   J. Bird
P   P. Splittorff
P   M. Pattin
RP   M. Littell
RP   S. Mingori

KC 1977 A
M   D. Herzog
1B   J. Mayberry
2B   F. White
SS   F. Patek
3B   G. Brett
OF   A. Cowens
OF   A. Otis
OF   T. Poquette
C   D. Porter
DH   H. McRae
UT   J. Zdeb
P   D. Leonard
P   J. Colborn
P   P. Splittorff
P   A. Hassler
P   M. Pattin
RP   J. Bird
RP   L. Gura

KC 1978 A
M   D. Herzog
1B   R. LaCock
2B   F. White
SS   F. Patek
3B   G. Brett
OF   A. Otis
OF   A. Cowens
OF   W. Wilson
C   D. Porter
DH   H. McRae
UT   R. Hurdle
P   L. Gura
P   H. Black
P   P. Splittorff
P   S. Renko
RP   D. Quisenberry
RP   M. Armstrong

KC 1979 A
M   D. Herzog
1B   R. LaCock
2B   F. White
SS   F. Patek
3B   G. Brett
OF   W. Wilson
OF   A. Otis
OF   A. Cowens
C   D. Porter
DH   H. McRae
UT   U. Washington
P   P. Splittorff
P   D. Leonard

P   J. Dal Canton
P   M. Pattin
RP   L. McDaniel
RP   J. Bird

KC 1980 A
M   J. Frey
1B   W. Aikens
2B   F. White
SS   U. Washington
3B   G. Brett
OF   W. Wilson
OF   C. Hurdle
OF   A. Otis
C   D. Porter
DH   H. McRae
UT   R. LaCock
UT   J. Wathan
P   L. Gura
P   D. Leonard
P   P. Splittorff
P   R. Gale
P   D. Martin
RP   D. Quisenberry
RP   M. Pattin

KC 1981 A
M   J. Frey
M   R. Howser
1B   W. Aikens
2B   F. White
SS   U. Washington
3B   G. Brett
OF   W. Wilson
OF   A. Otis
OF   C. Geronimo
C   J. Wathan
DH   H. McRae
P   D. Leonard
P   L. Gura
P   R. Gale
P   P. Splittorff
P   M. Jones
RP   D. Quisenberry
RP   D. Martin

KC 1982 A
M   R. Howser
1B   W. Aikens
2B   F. White
SS   U. Washington
3B   G. Brett
OF   J. Martin
OF   W. Wilson
OF   A. Otis
C   J. Wathan
DH   H. McRae
P   L. Gura
P   V. Blue
P   P. Splittorff
P   D. Leonard
RP   D. Quisenberry
RP   M. Armstrong

KC 1983 A
M   R. Howser
1B   W. Aikens
2B   F. White
SS   U. Washington
3B   G. Brett
OF   W. Wilson
OF   P. Sheridan
OF   A. Otis
C   J. Wathan
DH   H. McRae
P   L. Gura
P   H. Black
P   P. Splittorff
P   S. Renko
RP   D. Quisenberry
RP   M. Armstrong

KC 1984 A
M   R. Howser
1B   S. Balboni
2B   F. White
SS   O. Concepcion
3B   G. Pryor
OF   D. Motley
OF   P. Sheridan
OF   W. Wilson
C   D. Slaught
DH   H. McRae
UT   G. Brett
UT   J. Orta
UT   J. Wathan
P   H. Black
P   M. Gubicza
P   L. Gura
P   B. Saberhagen
P   C. Leibrandt

P   L. Gura
P   R. Gale
RP   E. Rodriguez
RP   A. Hrabosky

KC 1985 A
M   R. Howser
1B   S. Balboni
2B   F. White
SS   O. Concepcion
3B   G. Brett
OF   W. Wilson
OF   L. Smith
OF   D. Motley
C   J. Sundberg
DH   H. McRae
UT   L. Jones
UT   J. Orta
P   C. Leibrandt
P   B. Saberhagen
P   D. Jackson
P   H. Black
P   M. Gubicza
RP   D. Quisenberry
RP   T. Beckwith

KC 1986 A
M   R. Howser
M   M. Ferraro
1B   S. Balboni
2B   F. White
SS   A. Salazar
3B   G. Brett
OF   W. Wilson
OF   L. Smith
OF   R. Law
C   J. Sundberg
DH   J. Orta
UT   R. Biancalana
UT   H. McRae
P   C. Leibrandt
P   D. Leonard
P   D. Jackson
P   M. Gubicza
P   B. Saberhagen
RP   H. Black
RP   S. Farr

KC 1987 A
M   W. Gardner
M   J. Wathan
1B   G. Brett
2B   F. White
SS   A. Salazar
3B   K. Seitzer
OF   D. Tartabull
OF   W. Wilson
OF   V. Jackson
C   J. Quirk
DH   S. Balboni
P   B. Saberhagen
P   C. Leibrandt
P   D. Jackson
P   H. Black
RP   S. Farr
RP   J. Gleaton

KC 1988 A
M   J. Wathan
1B   G. Brett
2B   F. White
SS   K. Stillwell
3B   K. Seitzer
OF   W. Wilson
OF   D. Tartabull
OF   V. Jackson
C   J. Quirk
DH   W. Buckner
P   M. Gubicza
P   B. Saberhagen
P   C. Leibrandt
P   F. Bannister
RP   S. Farr
RP   J. Montgomery

Keokuk

WES n 1875
Westerns

WES 1875 n
M   J. Simmons
1B   J. Carbine
2B   J. Miller
SS   J. Hallinan
3B   W. Goldsmith
OF   C. Jones
OF   J. Simmons
OF   W. Barnie
C   J. Quinn
P   M. Golden

Los Angeles

LA A 1961-1964
Moved to California
LA N 1958-1988

LA 1961 A
M W. Rigney
1B S. Bilko
2B K. Aspromonte
SS J. Koppe
3B E. Yost
OF K. Hunt
OF L. Wagner
OF A. Pearson
C E. Averill
UT T. Kluszewski
UT J. Thomas
P K. McBride
P E. Grba
P E. Bowsfield
P R. Moeller
P R. Kline
RP J. Donohue
RP R. Duren

LA 1962 A
M W. Rigney
1B J. Thomas
2B W. Moran
SS J. Koppe
3B F. Torres
OF A. Pearson
OF L. Wagner
OF G. Thomas
C R. Rodgers
P W. Chance
P R. Belinsky
P E. Grba
P D. Lee
P K. McBride
RP J. Fowler
RP R. Duren

LA 1963 A
M W. Rigney
1B J. Thomas
2B W. Moran
SS J. Fregosi
3B F. Torres
OF A. Pearson
OF L. Wagner
OF M. Perry
C R. Rodgers
P K. McBride
P W. Chance
P D. Osinski
P D. Lee
RP J. Navarro
RP J. Fowler

LA 1964 A
M W. Rigney
1B J. Adcock
2B R. Knoop
SS J. Fregosi
3B F. Torres
OF W. Smith
OF L. Clinton
OF J. Piersall
C R. Rodgers
UT A. Pearson
UT T. Satriano
P W. Chance
P F. Newman
P A. Latman
P R. Belinsky
P K. McBride
RP R. Lee
RP D. Osinski

LA 1958 N
M W. Alston
1B G. Hodges
2B C. Neal
SS D. Zimmer
3B R. Gray
OF C. Furillo
OF G. Cimoli
OF E. Snider
C J. Roseboro
UT J. Gilliam
UT N. Larker
P D. Drysdale
P J. Podres
P S. Koufax
P S. Williams
P C. Erskine
RP C. Labine
RP F. Kipp

LA 1959 N
M W. Alston
1B G. Hodges
2B C. Neal
SS D. Zimmer
3B J. Gilliam
OF W. Moon
OF D. Demeter
OF E. Snider
C J. Roseboro
UT R. Fairly
UT N. Larker
P D. Drysdale
P J. Podres
P S. Koufax
P R. Craig
P D. McDevitt
RP C. Labine
RP J. Fowler

LA 1960 N
M W. Alston
1B N. Larker
2B C. Neal
SS M. Wills
3B J. Gilliam
OF W. Moon
OF F. Howard
OF H. T. Davis
C J. Roseboro
UT G. Hodges
UT E. Snider
P D. Drysdale
P J. Podres
P S. Williams
P S. Koufax
P R. Craig
RP L. Sherry
RP E. Roebuck

LA 1961 N
M W. Alston
1B G. Hodges
2B C. Neal
SS M. Wills
3B J. Gilliam
OF W. Moon
OF W. Davis
OF H. T. Davis
C J. Roseboro
UT R. Fairly
UT N. Larker
P S. Koufax
P D. Drysdale
P S. Williams
P J. Podres
RP R. Craig
RP L. Sherry

LA 1962 N
M W. Alston
1B R. Fairly
2B L. Burright
SS M. Wills
3B J. Gilliam
OF W. Davis
OF H. T. Davis
OF F. Howard
C J. Roseboro
P D. Drysdale
P J. Podres
P S. Williams
P S. Koufax
RP E. Roebuck
RP R. Perranoski

LA 1963 N
M W. Alston
1B R. Fairly
2B J. Gilliam
SS M. Wills
3B K. McMullen
OF W. Davis
OF H. T. Davis
OF F. Howard
C J. Roseboro
UT W. Moon
UT R. Tracewski
P D. Drysdale
P S. Koufax
P J. Podres
P R. Miller
RP R. Perranoski
RP L. Sherry

LA 1964 N
M W. Alston
1B R. Fairly
2B N. Oliver
SS M. Wills
3B J. Gilliam
OF W. Davis
OF H. T. Davis
OF F. Howard
C J. Roseboro
UT M. Parker
UT R. Tracewski
P D. Drysdale
P S. Koufax
P F. Ortega
P J. Moeller
RP R. Miller
RP R. Perranoski

LA 1965 N
M W. Alston
1B M. Parker
2B J. Lefebvre
SS M. Wills
3B J. Kennedy
OF R. Fairly
OF W. Davis
OF L. Johnson
C J. Roseboro
UT J. Gilliam
P S. Koufax
P D. Drysdale
P C. Osteen
P J. Podres
RP R. Perranoski
RP R. Miller

LA 1966 N
M W. Alston
1B M. Parker
2B J. Lefebvre
SS M. Wills
3B J. Kennedy
OF W. Davis
OF L. Johnson
OF R. Fairly
C J. Roseboro
UT H. T. Davis
P S. Koufax
P D. Drysdale
P C. Osteen
P D. Sutton
RP P. Regan
RP R. Miller

LA 1967 N
M W. Alston
1B M. Parker
2B R. Hunt
SS E. Michael
3B J. Lefebvre
OF W. Davis
OF R. Fairly
OF A. Ferrara
C J. Roseboro
UT R. Bailey
UT L. Johnson
P C. Osteen
P D. Drysdale
P D. Sutton
P W. Singer
P J. Brewer
RP R. Perranoski
RP P. Regan

LA 1968 N
M W. Alston
1B M. Parker
2B P. Popovich
SS Z. Versalles
3B R. Bailey
OF W. Davis
OF R. Fairly
OF L. Gabrielson
C T. Haller
UT J. Fairey
P W. Singer
P C. Osteen
P D. Drysdale
P D. Sutton
P M. Kekich
RP J. Grant
RP J. Brewer

LA 1969 N
M W. Alston
1B M. Parker
2B T. Sizemore
SS M. Wills
3B W. Sudakis
OF W. Davis
OF W. Crawford
OF A. Kosco
C T. Haller
UT W. Russell
P C. Osteen
P W. Singer
P D. Sutton
P A. Foster
RP J. Brewer
RP P. Mikkelsen

LA 1970 N
M W. Alston
1B M. Parker
2B T. Sizemore
SS M. Wills
3B B. Grabarkewitz
OF W. Davis
OF M. Mota
OF W. Crawford
C T. Haller
UT J. Lefebvre
P D. Sutton
P C. Osteen
P A. Foster
P J. Moeller
P G. Vance
RP J. Brewer
RP F. Norman

LA 1971 N
M W. Alston
1B M. Parker
2B J. Lefebvre
SS M. Wills
3B S. Garvey
OF W. Davis
OF W. Crawford
OF W. Buckner
C D. Sims
UT R. Allen
UT R. Valentine
P D. Sutton
P A. Downing
P C. Osteen
P W. Singer
RP J. Brewer
RP P. Mikkelsen

LA 1972 N
M W. Alston
1B M. Parker
2B L. Lacy
SS W. Russell
3B S. Garvey
OF W. Davis
OF M. Mota
OF F. Robinson
C C. Cannizzaro
UT W. Buckner
UT W. Crawford
UT R. Valentine
P D. Sutton
P C. Osteen
P A. Downing
P T. John
P W. Singer
RP J. Brewer
RP P. Mikkelsen

LA 1973 N
M W. Alston
1B W. Buckner
2B D. Lopes
SS W. Russell
3B R. Cey
OF W. Davis
OF W. Crawford
OF T. Paciorek
C J. Ferguson
UT S. Garvey
P D. Sutton
P J. Messersmith
P C. Osteen
P T. John
P A. Downing
RP C. Hough
RP J. Brewer

LA 1974 N
M W. Alston
1B S. Garvey
2B D. Lopes
SS W. Russell
3B R. Cey
OF J. Wynn
OF W. Buckner
OF W. Crawford
C S. Yeager
UT J. Ferguson
P J. Messersmith
P D. Sutton
P D. Rau
P T. John
P A. Downing
RP M. Marshall
RP C. Hough

LA 1975 N
M W. Alston
1B S. Garvey
2B D. Lopes
SS W. Russell
3B R. Cey
OF J. Wynn
OF W. Crawford
OF W. Buckner
C S. Yeager
UT L. Lacy
P J. Messersmith
P D. Rau
P D. Sutton
P B. Hooton
P R. Rhoden
RP M. Marshall
RP C. Hough

LA 1976 N
M W. Alston
M T. Lasorda
1B S. Garvey
2B D. Lopes
SS W. Russell
3B R. Cey
OF W. Buckner
OF J. Baker
OF C. Smith
C S. Yeager
P D. Sutton
P D. Rau
P B. Hooton
P T. John
P R. Rhoden
RP C. Hough
RP M. Marshall

LA 1977 N
M T. Lasorda
1B S. Garvey
2B D. Lopes
SS W. Russell
3B R. Cey
OF J. Baker
OF C. Smith
OF R. Monday
C S. Yeager
P D. Sutton
P B. Hooton
P T. John
P R. Rhoden
P D. Rau
RP C. Hough
RP E. Sosa

LA 1978 N
M T. Lasorda
1B S. Garvey
2B D. Lopes
SS W. Russell
3B R. Cey
OF J. Baker
OF C. Smith
OF W. North
C S. Yeager
UT L. Lacy
UT R. Monday
P D. Sutton
P B. Hooton
P T. John
P D. Rau
P R. Rhoden
RP C. Hough
RP T. Forster

LA 1979 N
M T. Lasorda
1B S. Garvey
2B D. Lopes
SS W. Russell
3B R. Cey
OF J. Baker
OF D. Thomas
OF G. Thomasson
C S. Yeager
UT J. Ferguson
P R. Sutcliffe
P D. Sutton
P B. Hooton
P J. Reuss
P C. Hough
RP D. Patterson

LA 1980 N
M T. Lasorda
1B S. Garvey
2B D. Lopes
SS W. Russell
3B R. Cey
OF J. Baker
OF R. Law
OF C. Smith
C S. Yeager
UT J. Johnstone
UT D. Thomas
P J. Reuss
P R. Welch
P D. Sutton
P B. Hooton
P D. Goltz
RP R. Sutcliffe
RP R. Castillo

LA 1981 N
M T. Lasorda
1B S. Garvey
2B D. Lopes
SS W. Russell
3B R. Cey
OF J. Baker
OF K. Landreaux
OF P. Guerrero
C M. Scioscia
UT D. Thomas
P F. Valenzuela
P J. Reuss
P B. Hooton
P R. Welch
RP D. Goltz
RP S. Howe

LA 1982 N
M T. Lasorda
1B S. Garvey
2B S. Sax
SS W. Russell
3B R. Cey
OF J. Baker
OF P. Guerrero
OF K. Landreaux
C M. Scioscia
UT R. Monday
UT R. Roenicke
P F. Valenzuela
P J. Reuss
P R. Welch
P D. Stewart
P B. Hooton
RP S. Howe
RP T. Forster

LA 1983 N
M T. Lasorda
1B G. Brock
2B S. Sax
SS W. Russell
3B P. Guerrero
OF J. Baker
OF K. Landreaux
OF M. Marshall
C S. Yeager
UT D. Thomas
P F. Valenzuela
P J. Reuss
P R. Welch
P A. Pena
P B. Hooton
RP T. Niedenfuer
RP D. Stewart

LA 1984 N
M T. Lasorda
1B G. Brock
2B S. Sax
SS D. Anderson
3B G. Rivera
OF K. Landreaux
OF M. Marshall
OF C. Maldonado
C M. Scioscia
UT P. Guerrero
P F. Valenzuela
P A. Pena
P O. Hershiser
P F. Honeycutt
P R. Welch
RP B. Hooton
RP P. Zachry

LA 1985 N
M T. Lasorda
1B G. Brock
2B S. Sax
SS M. Duncan
3B D. Anderson
OF K. Landreaux
OF M. Marshall
OF C. Maldonado
C M. Scioscia
UT P. Guerrero
P F. Valenzuela
P O. Hershiser
P J. Reuss
P R. Welch
P F. Honeycutt
RP T. Niedenfuer
RP K. Howell

LA 1986 N
M T. Lasorda
1B G. Brock
2B S. Sax
SS M. Duncan
3B B. Madlock
OF R. Williams
OF F. Stubbs
OF M. Marshall
C M. Scioscia
UT E. Cabell
UT K. Landreaux
UT W. Russell
P F. Valenzuela
P R. Welch
P O. Hershiser
P F. Honeycutt
RP K. Howell
RP T. Niedenfuer

LA 1987 N
M T. Lasorda
1B F. Stubbs
2B S. Sax
SS M. Duncan
3B M. Hatcher
OF J. Shelby
OF P. Guerrero
OF M. Marshall
C M. Scioscia
UT D. Anderson
UT K. Landreaux
P O. Hershiser
P R. Welch
P F. Valenzuela
P F. Honeycutt
RP T. Leary
RP A. Pena

LA 1988 N
M T. Lasorda
1B F. Stubbs
2B S. Sax
SS A. Griffin
3B J. Hamilton
OF K. Gibson
OF J. Shelby
OF M. Marshall
C M. Scioscia
UT D. Anderson
UT M. Davis
P O. Hershiser
P T. Leary
P T. Belcher
P F. Valenzuela
RP A. Pena
RP B. Holton

Louisville

LOU N 1876-1877
LOU a 1882-1891
LOU N 1892-1899

LOU 1876 N
M J. Chapman
1B J. Gerhardt
2B E. Somerville
SS C. Fulmer
3B J. Hague
OF W. Hastings
OF J. Ryan
OF A. Allison
C C. Snyder
P J. Devlin

LOU 1877 N
M J. Chapman
1B G. Latham
2B J. Gerhardt
SS W. Craver
3B J. Hague
OF G. Hall
OF G. Shaffer
OF W. Crowley
C C. Snyder
P J. Devlin

LOU 1882 a
M D. Mack
1B G. Hecker
2B L. Browning
SS D. Mack
3B W. Schenck
OF S. Maskrey
OF W. Wolf
OF J. Reccius
C D. Sullivan
P A. Mullane

LOU 1883 a
M J. Gerhardt
1B G. Latham
2B J. Gerhardt
SS J. Leary
3B J. Gleason
OF S. Maskrey
OF W. Wolf
OF L. Browning
C E. Whiting
P G. Hecker
P S. Weaver

LOU 1884 a
M M. Walsh
1B G. Latham
2B J. Gerhardt
SS T. McLaughlin
3B L. Browning
OF S. Maskrey
OF W. Wolf
OF J. Cline
C D. Sullivan
UT P. Reccius
P G. Hecker
P J. Driscoll
P L. Deagle

LOU 1885 a
M J. Hart
1B J. Kerins
2B T. McLaughlin
SS J. Miller
3B P. Reccius
OF L. Browning
OF W. Wolf
OF S. Maskrey
C J. Crotty
P G. Hecker
P N. Baker
P A. Mays
P T. Ramsey

LOU 1886 a
M J. Hart
1B J. Kerins
2B J. Mack
SS W. White
3B J. Werrick
OF W. Wolf
OF L. Browning
OF J. Strauss
C A. Cross
P T. Ramsey
P G. Hecker

LOU 1887 a
M J. Kelly
1B J. Kerins
2B J. Mack
SS W. White
3B J. Werrick
OF L. Browning
OF W. Wolf
OF G. Collins
C P. Cook
UT G. Hecker
P T. Ramsey
P E. Chamberlin

LOU 1888 a
M J. Kelly
M M. Davidson
M J. Kerins
M M. Davidson
1B S. Smith
2B J. Mack
SS W. Wolf
3B J. Werrick
OF L. Browning
OF J. Kerins
OF G. Collins
C P. Cook
P T. Ramsey
P E. Chamberlin
P J. Ewing

LOU 1889 a
M T. Esterbrook
M W. Wolf
M D. Shannon
M J. Chapman
1B G. Hecker
2B D. Shannon
SS P. Tomney
3B H. Raymond
OF W. Weaver
OF W. Wolf
OF L. Browning
C P. Cook
UT H. Vaughn
P P. Ehret
P J. Ewing
P T. Ramsey
P M. McDermott

LOU 1890 a
M J. Chapman
1B H. Taylor
2B T. Shinnick
SS P. Tomney
3B H. Raymond
OF C. Hamburg
OF W. Weaver
OF W. Wolf
C J. Ryan
P C. Stratton
P P. Ehret
P G. Meakim
P H. Goodall
P E. Daily

LOU 1891 a
M J. Chapman
1B H. Taylor
2B T. Shinnick
SS H. Jennings
3B O. Beard
OF W. Wolf
OF W. Weaver
OF P. Donovan
C J. Ryan
UT T. Cahill
P J. Fitzgerald
P J. Meekin
P P. Ehret
P C. Stratton
P J. Doran

LOU 1892 N
M J. Chapman
M N. Pfeffer
1B L. Whistler
2B N. Pfeffer
SS H. Jennings
3B W. Kuehne
OF T. Brown
OF W. Weaver
OF H. Taylor
C J. Grim
P C. Stratton
P A. Sanders
P F. Clausen
P J. Meekin
P A. Jones

LOU 1893 N
M W. Barnie
1B W. Brown
2B N. Pfeffer
SS T. O'Rourke
3B G. Pinkney
OF T. Brown
OF W. Weaver
OF L. Browning
C J. Grim
P J. Hemming
P C. Stratton
P W. Rhodes
P J. Menefee

LOU 1894 N
M W. Barnie
1B C. Lutenberg
2B N. Pfeffer
SS D. Richardson
3B J. Denny
OF T. Brown
OF F. Clarke
OF L. Twitchell
C J. Grim
P G. Hemming
P P. Knell
P J. Menefee
P J. Wadsworth

LOU 1895 N
M J. McCloskey
1B H. Spies
2B J. O'Brien
SS F. Shugarts
3B J. Collins
OF F. Clarke
OF T. Gettinger
OF J. Wright
C J. Warner
P E. Cunningham
P A. Weyhing
P M. McDermott
P A. Inks

LOU 1896 N
M J. McCloskey
M W. McGunnigle
1B J. Rogers
2B J. O'Brien
SS J. Dolan
3B W. Clingman
OF F. Clarke
OF T. McCreery
OF C. Dexter
C G. Miller
P C. Fraser
P W. Hill
P E. Cunningham
P A. Herman

LOU 1897 N
M J. Rogers
M F. Clarke
1B P. Werden
2B J. Rogers
SS J. Stafford
3B W. Clingman
OF F. Clarke
OF T. McCreery
OF O. Pickering
C W. Wilson
P C. Fraser
P E. Cunningham
P W. Hill
P W. Magee

LOU 1898 N
M F. Clarke
1B J. Wagner
2B G. Smith
SS C. Ritchey
3B W. Clingman
OF F. Clarke
OF W. Hoy
OF C. Dexter
C M. Kittridge
P E. Cunningham
P W. Magee
P H. Dowling
P C. Fraser

LOU 1899 N
M F. Clarke
1B M. Kelley
2B C. Ritchey
SS W. Clingman
3B T. Leach
OF W. Hoy
OF F. Clarke
OF C. Dexter
C C. Zimmer
UT J. Wagner
P E. Cunningham
P C. Phillippe
P H. Dowling
P W. Woods

Middletown

MAN n 1872
Mansfields

MAN 1872 n
M J. Clapp
1B T. Murnane
2B E. Booth
SS J. O'Rourke
3B G. Fields
OF F. McCarton
OF J. Tipper
OF H. Allen
C J. Clapp
P C. Bentley
P F. Buttery

Milwaukee

MIL N 1878
MIL U 1884
CM a 1891
  Combined with
  Cincinnati
MIL A 1901
MIL N 1953-1965
  Moved to Atlanta
MIL A 1970-1988

MIL 1878 N
M J. Chapman
1B J. Goodman
2B J. Peters
SS W. Redmond
3B W. Foley
OF A. Dalrymple
OF M. Golden
OF W. Holbert
C C. Bennett
UT G. Creamer
P S. Weaver

MIL 1884 U
M T. Loftus
1B T. Griffin
2B J. Myers
SS T. Sexton
3B T. Morrissey
OF R. Hogan
OF S. Behel
OF C. Baldwin
C C. Broughton
P H. Porter
P E. Cushman

CM 1891 a
M M. Kelly
M C. Cushman
1B J. Carney
2B W. Robinson
SS J. Canavan
3B A. Whitney
OF R. Johnston
OF J. Seery
OF G. Andrews
C M. Kelly
P J. Dwyer
P E. Crane
P W. Mains
P G. Davies
P F. Killen

MIL 1901 A
M H. Duffy
1B J. Anderson
2B W. Gilbert
SS W. Conroy
3B J. Burke
OF W. Hallman
OF H. Duffy
OF I. Waldron
C W. Maloney
UT W. Friel
P W. Reidy
P V. Garvin
P B. Husting
P T. Sparks
P E. Hawley

MIL 1953 N
M C. Grimm
1B J. Adcock
2B J. Dittmer
SS J. Logan
3B E. Mathews
OF W. Bruton
OF A. Pafko
OF S. Gordon
C D. Crandall
UT J. Pendleton
P W. Spahn
P S. Burdette
P J. Antonelli
P M. Surkont
P R. Buhl
RP E. Johnson
RP V. Bickford

MIL 1954 N
M C. Grimm
1B J. Adcock
2B D. O'Connell
SS J. Logan
3B E. Mathews
OF W. Bruton
OF A. Pafko
OF H. Aaron
C D. Crandall
P W. Spahn
P S. Burdette
P R. Buhl
P J. Jay
P J. Pizarro
RP D. McMahon

MIL 1955 N
M C. Grimm
1B G. Crowe
2B D. O'Connell
SS J. Logan
3B E. Mathews
OF W. Bruton
OF H. Aaron
OF R. Thomson
C D. Crandall
P W. Spahn
P S. Burdette
P D. Conley
P J. Wilson
P C. Nichols
RP D. Jolly
RP E. Johnson

MIL 1956 N
M C. Grimm
M F. Haney
1B J. Adcock
2B D. O'Connell
SS J. Logan
3B E. Mathews
OF H. Aaron
OF W. Bruton
OF R. Thomson
C D. Crandall
UT F. Torre
P W. Spahn
P S. Burdette
P R. Buhl
P C. Willey
P D. Nottebart
RP D. McMahon

MIL 1957 N
M F. Haney
1B F. Torre
2B A. Schoendienst
SS J. Logan
3B E. Mathews
OF H. Aaron
OF J. Covington
OF W. Bruton
C D. Crandall
P W. Spahn
P S. Burdette
P R. Buhl
P D. Conley
P R. Trowbridge
RP W. Phillips
RP E. Johnson

MIL 1958 N
M F. Haney
1B F. Torre
2B A. Schoendienst
SS J. Logan
3B E. Mathews
OF H. Aaron
OF W. Bruton
OF A. Pafko
C D. Crandall
UT J. Adcock
P W. Spahn
P S. Burdette
P R. Rush
P C. Willey
P J. Pizarro
RP D. Conley
RP D. McMahon

MIL 1959 N
M F. Haney
1B J. Adcock
2B F. Mantilla
SS J. Logan
3B E. Mathews
OF H. Aaron
OF W. Bruton
OF J. Covington
C D. Crandall
UT F. Torre
P W. Spahn
P S. Burdette
P R. Buhl
P J. Jay
P J. Pizarro
RP D. McMahon

MIL 1960 N
M C. Dressen
1B J. Adcock
2B C. Cottier
SS J. Logan
3B E. Mathews
OF H. Aaron
OF W. Bruton
OF A. Spangler
C D. Crandall
UT J. Covington
P S. Burdette
P W. Spahn
P R. Buhl
P C. Willey
P J. Jay
RP D. McMahon
RP G. Brunet

MIL 1961 N
M C. Dressen
M G. Tebbetts
1B J. Adcock
2B F. Bolling
SS R. McMillan
3B E. Mathews
OF H. Aaron
OF F. Thomas
OF A. Maye
C J. Torre
P S. Burdette
P W. Spahn
P R. Buhl
P C. Willey
P D. Nottebart
RP D. McMahon

MIL 1962 N
M G. Tebbetts
1B J. Adcock
2B F. Bolling
SS R. McMillan
3B E. Mathews
OF H. Aaron
OF A. Maye
OF M. Jones
C D. Crandall
UT T. Aaron
P W. Spahn
P R. Shaw
P C. Hendley
P S. Burdette
P T. Cloninger
RP J. Curtis
RP C. Willey

MIL 1963 N
M R. Bragan
1B E. Oliver
2B F. Bolling
SS R. McMillan
3B E. Mathews
OF H. Aaron
OF A. Maye
OF M. Jones
C J. Torre
P W. Spahn
P D. Lemaster
P C. Hendley
P R. Shaw
P T. Cloninger
RP H. Fischer
RP J. Raymond

MIL 1964 N
M R. Bragan
1B E. Oliver
2B F. Bolling
SS D. Menke
3B E. Mathews
OF H. Aaron
OF A. Maye
OF R. Carty
C J. Torre
UT F. Alou
UT T. Cline
P T. Cloninger
P D. Lemaster
P W. Spahn
P H. Fischer
P R. Sadowski
RP B. Tiefenauer
RP W. Hoeft

MIL 1965 N
M R. Bragan
1B E. Oliver
2B F. Bolling
SS W. Woodward
3B E. Mathews
OF H. Aaron
OF M. Jones
OF F. Alou
C J. Torre
UT T. Cline
P T. Cloninger
P W. Blasingame
P K. Johnson
P D. Lemaster
P R. Sadowski
RP W. O'Dell
RP D. Osinski

MIL 1970 A
M J. Bristol
1B J. Hegan
2B T. Kubiak
SS R. Pena
3B T. Harper
OF D. Walton
OF R. Snyder
OF D. May
C P. Roof
UT G. McNertney
UT T. Savage
P M. Pattin
P L. Krausse
P C. Lockwood
P B. Bolin
P E. Brabender
RP K. Sanders
RP J. Gelnar

MIL 1971 A
M J. Bristol
1B R. Pena
2B R. Theobald
SS F. Auerbach
3B T. Harper
OF D. May
OF J. Briggs
OF W. Voss
C E. Rodriguez
UT A. Kosco
P M. Pattin
P W. Parsons
P C. Lockwood
P L. Krausse
P J. Slaton
RP K. Sanders
RP J. Morris

MIL 1972 A
M J. Bristol
M R. McMillan
M D. Crandall
1B G. Scott
2B R. Theobald
SS F. Auerbach
3B M. Ferraro
OF D. May
OF J. Briggs
OF J. Lahoud
C E. Rodriguez
UT R. Heise
P J. Lonborg
P W. Parsons
P C. Lockwood
P J. Colborn
P K. Brett

RP K. Sanders
RP C. Stephenson

MIL 1973 A

M D. Crandall
1B G. Scott
2B P. Garcia
SS T. Johnson
3B D. Money
OF D. May
OF J. Briggs
OF R. Coluccio
C D. Porter
DH O. Brown
P J. Colborn
P J. Slaton
P J. Bell
P C. Lockwood
P B. Champion
RP E. Rodriguez
RP C. Short

MIL 1974 A

M D. Crandall
1B G. Scott
2B P. Garcia
SS R. Yount
3B D. Money
OF J. Briggs
OF R. Coluccio
OF D. May
C D. Porter
DH R. Mitchell
UT A. Berry
P J. Slaton
P C. Wright
P J. Colborn
P K. Kobel
P B. Champion
RP T. Murphy
RP E. Rodriguez

MIL 1975 A

M D. Crandall
M H. Kuenn
1B G. Scott
2B P. Garcia
SS R. Yount
3B D. Money
OF S. Lezcano
OF W. Sharp
OF J. Thomas
C D. Porter
DH H. Aaron
UT K. Bevacqua
P P. Broberg
P J. Slaton
P J. Colborn
P W. Travers
P T. Hausman
RP E. Rodriguez
RP T. Murphy

MIL 1976 A

M A. Grammas
1B G. Scott
2B T. Johnson
SS R. Yount
3B D. Money
OF S. Lezcano
OF V. Joshua
OF J. Thomas
C D. Porter
DH H. Aaron
P J. Slaton
P W. Travers
P J. Colborn
P G. Augustine
P E. Rodriguez
RP W. Castro
RP D. Frisella

MIL 1977 A

M A. Grammas
1B C. Cooper
2B D. Money
SS R. Yount
3B S. Bando
OF V. Joshua
OF J. Wohlford
OF S. Lezcano
C C. Moore
DH J. Quirk
P J. Slaton
P G. Augustine
P B. Haas
P E. Rodriguez
P L. Sorensen
RP S. Hinds
RP R. McClure

MIL 1978 A

M G. Bamberger
1B C. Cooper
2B P. Molitor
SS R. Yount
3B S. Bando
OF J. Thomas
OF S. Lezcano
OF B. Oglivie
C C. Moore
DH L. Hisle
UT D. Money
P R. Caldwell
P D. Sutton
P B. Haas
P G. Augustine
P W. Travers
P A. Replogle
RP W. Stein
RP R. McClure

MIL 1979 A

M G. Bamberger
1B C. Cooper
2B P. Molitor
SS R. Yount
3B S. Bando
OF J. Thomas
OF S. Lezcano
OF B. Oglivie
C C. Moore
DH R. Davis
P L. Sorensen
P R. Caldwell
P J. Slaton
P W. Travers
P B. Haas
RP G. Augustine
RP R. Cleveland

MIL 1980 A

M R. Rodgers
M G. Bamberger
M R. Rodgers
1B C. Cooper
2B P. Molitor
SS R. Yount
3B J. Gantner
OF J. Thomas
OF B. Oglivie
OF S. Lezcano
C C. Moore
DH R. Davis
P B. Haas
P R. Caldwell
P L. Sorensen
P W. Travers
P R. Cleveland
RP R. McClure
RP W. Castro

MIL 1981 A

M R. Rodgers
1B C. Cooper
2B J. Gantner
SS R. Yount
3B D. Money
OF B. Oglivie
OF J. Thomas
OF M. Brouhard
C T. Simmons
DH L. Hisle
UT R. Howell
P P. Vuckovich
P R. Caldwell
P B. Haas
P J. Slaton
P R. Lerch
RP R. Fingers
RP R. Cleveland

MIL 1982 A

M R. Rodgers
M H. Kuenn
1B C. Cooper
2B J. Gantner
SS R. Yount
3B P. Molitor
OF B. Oglivie
OF J. Thomas
OF C. Moore
C T. Simmons
DH R. Howell
P R. Caldwell
P P. Vuckovich
P B. Haas
P R. McClure
P J. Slaton
RP R. Fingers
RP D. Bernard

MIL 1983 A

M H. Kuenn
1B C. Cooper
2B J. Gantner
SS R. Yount
3B P. Molitor
OF C. Moore
OF B. Oglivie
OF R. Manning
C T. Simmons
DH R. Howell
P R. Caldwell
P D. Sutton
P B. Haas
P R. McClure
P C. Porter
RP J. Slaton
RP T. Tellmann

MIL 1984 A

M R. Lachemann
1B C. Cooper
2B J. Gantner
SS R. Yount
3B E. Romero
OF B. Oglivie
OF D. James
OF R. Manning
C J. Sundberg
DH T. Simmons
P D. Sutton
P B. Haas
P J. Cocanower
P R. McClure
P R. Caldwell
RP P. Ladd
RP T. Tellmann

MIL 1985 A

M G. Bamberger
1B C. Cooper
2B J. Gantner
SS E. Riles
3B P. Molitor
OF R. Yount
OF B. Oglivie
OF P. Householder
C C. Moore
DH T. Simmons
P D. Darwin
P T. Higuera
P B. Burris
P B. Haas
P J. Cocanower
RP R. Gibson
RP R. McClure

MIL 1986 A

M G. Bamberger
M T. Trebelhorn
1B C. Cooper
2B J. Gantner
SS E. Riles
3B P. Molitor
OF R. Yount
OF R. Deer
OF R. Manning
C C. Moore
DH B. Oglivie
P T. Higuera
P W. Wegman
P T. Leary
P J. Nieves
P D. Darwin
RP D. Plesac
RP M. Clear

MIL 1987 A

M T. Trebelhorn
1B G. Brock
2B J. Castillo
SS D. Sveum
3B E. Riles
OF R. Yount
OF R. Deer
OF G. Braggs
C W. Surhoff
DH C. Cooper
UT M. Felder
UT R. Manning
UT P. Molitor
P T. Higuera
P W. Wegman
P J. Nieves
P C. Bosio
RP C. Crim
RP D. Plesac

MIL 1988 A

M T. Trebelhorn
1B G. Brock
2B J. Gantner
SS D. Sveum
3B P. Molitor
OF R. Yount
OF R. Deer
OF J. Leonard
C W. Surhoff
DH T. Meyer
P T. Higuera
P W. Wegman
P C. Bosio
P D. August
P M. Birkbeck
RP C. Crim
RP O. Jones

Minnesota

MIN
A 1961-1988

MIN 1961 A

M H. Lavagetto
M S. Mele
M H. Lavagetto
M S. Mele
1B H. Killebrew
2B A. Martin
SS Z. Versalles
3B W. Tuttle
OF L. Green
OF W. Allison
OF J. Lemon
C E. Battey
P P. Ramos
P C. Pascual
P J. Kralick
P J. Kaat
P D. Lee
RP W. Pleis
RP R. Moore

MIN 1962 A

M S. Mele
1B V. Power
2B B. Allen
SS Z. Versalles
3B R. Rollins
OF L. Green
OF H. Killebrew
OF W. Allison
C E. Battey
UT W. Tuttle
P J. Kaat
P C. Pascual
P J. Kralick
P R. Stigman
P J. Bonikowski
RP A. Stange
RP G. Maranda

MIN 1963 A

M S. Mele
1B V. Power
2B B. Allen
SS Z. Versalles
3B R. Rollins
OF W. Allison
OF J. Hall
OF H. Killebrew
C E. Battey
UT L. Green
P C. Pascual
P R. Stigman
P J. Kaat
P J. Perry
P A. Stange
RP W. Dailey
RP W. Pleis

MIN 1964 A

M S. Mele
1B W. Allison
2B B. Allen
SS Z. Versalles
3B R. Rollins
OF P. Oliva
OF H. Killebrew
OF J. Hall
C E. Battey
UT D. Mincher
P C. Pascual
P J. Kaat
P R. Stigman
P J. Grant
RP G. Arrigo
RP A. Worthington

MIN 1965 A

M S. Mele
1B D. Mincher
2B G. Kindall
SS Z. Versalles
3B R. Rollins
OF P. Oliva
OF J. Hall
OF W. Allison
C E. Battey
UT H. Killebrew
UT H. Valdespino
P J. Grant
P J. Kaat
P J. Perry
P C. Pascual
P D. Boswell
RP A. Worthington
RP J. Klippstein

MIN 1966 A

M S. Mele
1B D. Mincher
2B B. Allen
SS Z. Versalles
3B H. Killebrew
OF P. Oliva
OF J. Hall
OF T. Uhlaender
C E. Battey
UT C. Tovar
P J. Kaat
P J. Grant
P J. Perry
P D. Boswell
P J. Merritt
RP A. Worthington
RP P. Cimino

MIN 1967 A

M S. Mele
M C. Ermer
1B H. Killebrew
2B R. Carew
SS Z. Versalles
3B R. Rollins
OF P. Oliva
OF W. Allison
OF T. Uhlaender
C G. Zimmerman
UT C. Tovar
P W. Chance
P J. Kaat
P J. Merritt
P D. Boswell
P J. Perry
RP A. Worthington
RP R. Kline

MIN 1968 A

M C. Ermer
1B R. Reese
2B R. Carew
SS J. Hernandez
3B C. Tovar
OF T. Uhlaender
OF P. Oliva
OF W. Allison
C J. Roseboro
UT R. Clark
UT H. Killebrew
UT F. Quilici
P W. Chance
P J. Merritt
P J. Kaat
P D. Boswell
P J. Perry
RP R. Perranoski
RP A. Worthington

MIN 1969 A

M A. Martin
1B R. Reese
2B R. Carew
SS L. Cardenas
3B H. Killebrew
OF P. Oliva
OF T. Uhlaender
OF C. Tovar
C J. Roseboro
UT F. Quilici
P J. Perry
P D. Boswell
P J. Kaat
P T. Hall
RP R. Perranoski
RP R. Miller

MIN 1970 A

M W. Rigney
1B R. Reese
2B D. Thompson
SS L. Cardenas
3B H. Killebrew
OF P. Oliva
OF C. Tovar
OF J. Holt
C G. Mitterwald
UT F. Quilici
P J. Perry
P J. Kaat
P R. Blyleven
P W. Zepp
RP T. Hall
RP S. Williams

MIN 1971 A

M W. Rigney
1B R. Reese
2B R. Carew
SS L. Cardenas
3B S. Braun
OF C. Tovar
OF P. Oliva
OF J. Holt
C G. Mitterwald
UT H. Killebrew
P R. Blyleven
P J. Perry
P J. Kaat
RP A. Corbin
RP T. Hall

MIN 1972 A

M W. Rigney
M F. Quilici
1B H. Killebrew
2B R. Carew
SS D. Thompson
3B E. Soderholm
OF A. Darwin
OF C. Tovar
OF S. Brye
C P. Roof
UT S. Braun
UT J. Nettles
UT R. Reese
P R. Blyleven
P R. Woodson
P J. Perry
P A. Corbin
P J. Kaat
RP D. LaRoche
RP W. Granger

MIN 1973 A

M F. Quilici
1B J. Lis
2B R. Carew
SS D. Thompson
3B S. Braun
OF L. Hisle
OF A. Darwin
OF J. Holt
C G. Mitterwald
DH P. Oliva
UT J. Terrell
P R. Blyleven
P J. Kaat
P G. Decker
P W. Hands
P R. Woodson
RP A. Corbin
RP E. Bane

MIN 1974 A

M F. Quilici
1B C. Kusick
2B R. Carew
SS D. Thompson
3B E. Soderholm
OF A. Darwin
OF L. Hisle
OF S. Brye
C G. Borgmann
DH P. Oliva
UT S. Braun
UT H. Killebrew
UT J. Terrell
P R. Blyleven
P G. Decker
P D. Goltz
P V. Albury
P W. Hands
RP W. Campbell
RP T. Burgmeier

MIN 1975 A

M F. Quilici
1B C. Kusick
2B R. Carew
SS D. Thompson
3B E. Soderholm
OF D. Ford
OF S. Braun
OF L. Bostock
C G. Borgmann
DH P. Oliva
UT J. Terrell
P R. Blyleven
P J. Hughes
P D. Goltz
P V. Albury
RP W. Campbell
RP T. Burgmeier

MIN 1976 A

M G. Mauch
1B R. Carew
2B R. Randall
SS R. Smalley
3B M. Cubbage
OF L. Hisle
OF D. Ford
OF L. Bostock
C H. Wynegar
DH C. Kusick
UT S. Braun
P D. Goltz
P J. Hughes
P W. Singer
P S. Luebber
P P. Redfern
RP W. Campbell
RP T. Burgmeier

MIN 1977 A

M G. Mauch
1B R. Carew
2B R. Randall
SS R. Smalley
3B M. Cubbage
OF L. Bostock
OF D. Ford
OF L. Hisle
C H. Wynegar
DH C. Kusick
UT R. Chiles
P D. Goltz
P P. Thormodsgard
P G. Zahn
P P. Redfern
RP T. Johnson
RP R. Schueler

MIN 1978 A

M G. Mauch
1B R. Carew
2B R. Randall
SS R. Smalley
3B M. Cubbage
OF D. Ford
OF H. Powell
OF W. Norwood
C H. Wynegar
DH G. Adams
UT J. Morales
UT J. Rivera
P R. Erickson
P G. Zahn
P D. Goltz
P G. Serum
RP M. Marshall

MIN 1979 A

M G. Mauch
1B R. Jackson
2B R. Wilfong
SS R. Smalley
3B J. Castino
OF K. Landreaux
OF J. Rivera
OF H. Powell
C H. Wynegar
DH J. Morales
UT G. Adams
P J. Koosman
P D. Goltz
P G. Zahn
P P. Hartzell
P R. Erickson
RP M. Marshall
RP P. Redfern

MIN 1980 A

M G. Mauch
M J. Goryl
1B R. Jackson
2B R. Wilfong
SS R. Smalley
3B J. Castino
OF H. Powell

OF R. Sofield
OF K. Landreaux
C H. Wynegar
DH M. Morales
UT G. Adams
UT M. Cubbage
UT P. Mackanin
P J. Koosman
P G. Zahn
P R. Erickson
P D. Jackson
P P. Redfern
RP D. Corbett
RP J. Verhoeven

MIN 1981 A

M J. Goryl
M W. Gardner
1B D. Goodwin
2B R. Wilfong
SS R. Smalley
3B J. Castino
OF M. Hatcher
OF G. Ward
OF R. Engle
C S. Butera
DH G. Adams
UT P. Mackanin
UT H. Powell
P A. Williams
P P. Redfern
P F. Arroyo
P J. Koosman
P R. Erickson
RP D. Corbett
RP D. Cooper

MIN 1982 A

M W. Gardner
1B K. Hrbek
2B J. Castino
SS R. Washington
3B G. Gaetti
OF G. Ward
OF T. Brunansky
OF R. Mitchell
C T. Laudner
DH R. Johnson
P R. Castillo
P B. Havens
P A. Williams
P F. Viola
P J. O'Connor
RP T. Felton
RP R. Davis

MIN 1983 A

M W. Gardner
1B K. Hrbek
2B J. Castino
SS R. Washington
3B G. Gaetti
OF G. Ward
OF T. Brunansky
OF D. Brown
C R. Engle
DH R. Bush
UT M. Hatcher
P F. Viola
P K. Schrom
P A. Williams
P R. Castillo
RP R. Lysander
RP R. Davis

MIN 1984 A

M W. Gardner
1B K. Hrbek
2B T. Teufel
SS A. Jimenez
3B G. Gaetti
OF T. Brunansky
OF K. Puckett
OF M. Hatcher
C R. Engle
DH R. Bush
P F. Viola
P B. Smithson
P J. Butcher
P K. Schrom
P E. Hodge
RP W. Filson
RP R. Davis

MIN 1985 A

M W. Gardner
M R. Miller
1B K. Hrbek
2B T. Teufel
SS G. Gagne
3B G. Gaetti

OF K. Puckett
OF T. Brunansky
OF M. Hatcher
C M. Salas
DH R. Smalley
UT R. Bush
P B. Smithson
P F. Viola
P J. Butcher
P K. Schrom
P R. Blyleven
RP W. Filson
RP R. Davis

MIN 1986 A

M R. Miller
M J. Kelly
1B K. Hrbek
2B S. Lombardozzi
SS G. Gagne
3B G. Gaetti
OF K. Puckett
OF T. Brunansky
OF R. Bush
C M. Salas
DH R. Smalley
UT M. Hatcher
P R. Blyleven
P F. Viola
P B. Smithson
P N. Heaton
P M. Portugal
RP K. Atherton
RP R. Jackson

MIN 1987 A

M J. Kelly
1B K. Hrbek
2B S. Lombardozzi
SS G. Gagne
3B G. Gaetti
OF K. Puckett
OF T. Brunansky
OF C. Gladden
C T. Laudner
DH R. Smalley
UT R. Bush
UT J. Davidson
UT A. Newman
P R. Blyleven
P F. Viola
P L. Straker
P B. Smithson
P J. Niekro
RP J. Berenguer
RP G. Frazier

MIN 1988 A

M J. Kelly
1B K. Hrbek
2B S. Lombardozzi
SS G. Gagne
3B G. Gaetti
OF K. Puckett
OF C. Gladden
OF R. Bush
C T. Laudner
DH E. Larkin
UT J. Davidson
UT J. Moses
UT A. Newman
P F. Viola
P R. Blyleven
P A. Anderson
P C. Lea
P F. Toliver
RP J. Berenguer
RP K. Atherton

Montreal

MON N 1969-1988

MON 1969 N

M G. Mauch
1B R. Bailey
2B G. Sutherland
SS R. Wine
3B J. Laboy
OF D. Staub
OF M. Jones
OF A. Phillips
C R. Brand
UT T. Cline
P W. Stoneman
P J. Robertson
P M. Wegener
P G. Waslewski
P H. Reed
RP D. McGinn
RP D. Shaw

MON 1970 N

M G. Mauch
1B R. Fairly
2B G. Sutherland
SS R. Wine
3B J. Laboy
OF D. Staub
OF M. Jones
OF A. Phillips
C J. Bateman
UT R. Bailey
UT M. Staehle
P C. Morton
P S. Renko
P W. Stoneman
P M. Wegener
RP D. McGinn
RP H. Reed

MON 1971 N

M G. Mauch
1B R. Fairly
2B R. Hunt
SS R. Wine
3B R. Bailey
OF D. Staub
OF C. Day
OF J. Fairey
C J. Bateman
UT G. Sutherland
P W. Stoneman
P S. Renko
P C. Morton
P E. McAnally
P J. Strohmayer
RP M. Marshall
RP D. McGinn

MON 1972 N

M G. Mauch
1B M. Jorgensen
2B R. Hunt
SS T. Foli
3B R. Bailey
OF K. Singleton
OF C. Day
OF C. Mashore
C J. Boccabella
UT R. Fairly
UT R. Woods
P W. Stoneman
P M. Torrez
P C. Morton
P E. McAnally
P B. Moore
RP M. Marshall
RP J. Strohmayer

MON 1973 N

M G. Mauch
1B M. Jorgensen
2B R. Hunt
SS T. Foli
3B R. Bailey
OF K. Singleton
OF R. Fairly
OF R. Woods
C J. Boccabella
UT H. Breeden
UT C. Day
UT J. Frias
P S. Renko
P M. Torrez
P B. Moore
P E. McAnally
P S. Rogers
RP M. Marshall
RP R. Walker

MON 1974 N

M G. Mauch
1B M. Jorgensen
2B J. Cox
SS T. Foli
3B R. Hunt
OF W. Davis
OF K. Singleton
OF R. Bailey
C B. Foote
UT R. Fairly
UT L. Lintz
P S. Rogers
P S. Renko
P M. Torrez
P D. Blair
P E. McAnally
RP C. Taylor
RP R. Walker

MON 1975 N

M G. Mauch
1B M. Jorgensen
2B P. Mackanin
SS T. Foli
3B L. Parrish
OF J. Mangual
OF L. Biittner
OF G. Carter
C B. Foote
UT R. Bailey
P S. Rogers
P S. Renko
P D. Warthen
P D. Blair
P W. Fryman
RP D. Murray
RP D. DeMola

MON 1976 N

M K. Kuehl
M C. Fox
1B M. Jorgensen
2B P. Mackanin
SS T. Foli
3B L. Parrish
OF J. White
OF E. Valentine
OF D. Unser
C B. Foote
UT J. Morales
P S. Rogers
P W. Fryman
P D. Stanhouse
P D. Carrithers
RP D. Murray
RP S. Dunning

MON 1977 N

M R. Williams
1B A. Perez
2B D. Cash
SS C. Speier
3B L. Parrish
OF W. Cromartie
OF A. Dawson
OF E. Valentine
C G. Carter
UT D. Unser
P S. Rogers
P J. Brown
P D. Stanhouse
P W. Twitchell
P S. Bahnsen
RP J. Kerrigan
RP W. McEnaney

MON 1978 N

M R. Williams
1B A. Perez
2B D. Cash
SS C. Speier
3B L. Parrish
OF W. Cromartie
OF A. Dawson
OF E. Valentine
C G. Carter
UT D. Unser
P J. Grimsley
P S. Rogers
P D. Schatzeder
P R. May
P W. Twitchell
RP S. Bahnsen
RP D. Knowles

MON 1979 N

M R. Williams
1B A. Perez
2B R. Scott
SS C. Speier
3B L. Parrish
OF W. Cromartie
OF A. Dawson
OF E. Valentine
C G. Carter
P S. Rogers
P W. Lee
P S. Sanderson
P D. Schatzeder
P R. Grimsley
RP E. Sosa
RP R. May

MON 1980 N

M R. Williams
1B W. Cromartie
2B R. Scott
SS C. Speier
3B L. Parrish

OF A. Dawson
OF R. LeFlore
OF R. Office
C G. Carter
UT J. White
P S. Rogers
P S. Sanderson
P W. Gullickson
P D. Palmer
P W. Lee
RP F. Norman
RP E. Sosa

MON 1981 N

M R. Williams
M W. Fanning
1B W. Cromartie
2B R. Scott
SS C. Speier
3B L. Parrish
OF A. Dawson
OF T. Raines
OF J. White
C G. Carter
P S. Rogers
P S. Renko
P D. Blair
P W. Fryman
RP W. Lee
RP S. Bahnsen

MON 1982 N

M W. Fanning
1B A. Oliver
2B R. Flynn
SS C. Speier
3B T. Wallach
OF A. Dawson
OF W. Cromartie
OF T. Raines
C G. Carter
P S. Rogers
P W. Gullickson
P S. Sanderson
P C. Lea
P B. Burris
RP J. Reardon
RP B. Smith

MON 1983 N

M W. Virdon
1B A. Oliver
2B R. Flynn
SS C. Speier
3B T. Wallach
OF A. Dawson
OF T. Raines
OF W. Cromartie
C G. Carter
UT T. Francona
UT R. Little
P S. Rogers
P W. Gullickson
P C. Lea
P B. Smith
P B. Burris
RP J. Reardon
RP D. Schatzeder

MON 1984 N

M W. Virdon
M W. Fanning
1B T. Francona
2B R. Flynn
SS A. Salazar
3B T. Wallach
OF T. Raines
OF A. Dawson
OF J. Wohlford
C G. Carter
UT D. Thomas
P W. Gullickson
P C. Lea
P B. Smith
P S. Rogers
P D. Schatzeder
RP R. James
RP J. Reardon

MON 1985 N

M R. Rodgers
1B D. Driessen
2B V. Law
SS H. Brooks
3B T. Wallach
OF T. Raines
OF A. Dawson
OF H. Winningham
C M. Fitzgerald
UT T. Francona

P B. Smith
P W. Gullickson
P J. Hesketh
P D. Palmer
P D. Schatzeder
RP T. Burke
RP J. Reardon

MON 1986 N

M R. Rodgers
1B A. Galarraga
2B V. Law
SS H. Brooks
3B T. Wallach
OF T. Raines
OF M. Webster
OF A. Dawson
C D. Bilardello
UT W. Krenchicki
P F. Youmans
P J. Tibbs
P B. Smith
P J. Martinez
RP A. McGaffigan
RP T. Burke

MON 1987 N

M R. Rodgers
1B A. Galarraga
2B V. Law
SS H. Brooks
3B T. Wallach
OF M. Webster
OF T. Raines
OF H. Winningham
C M. Fitzgerald
UT C. Candaele
UT T. Foley
P N. Heaton
P R. Sebra
P B. Smith
P J. Martinez
P F. Youmans
RP A. McGaffigan
RP T. Burke

MON 1988 N

M R. Rodgers
1B A. Galarraga
2B T. Foley
SS L. Rivera
3B T. Wallach
OF H. Brooks
OF T. Raines
OF O. Nixon
C N. Santovenia
P J. Martinez
P B. Smith
P P. Perez
P J. Dopson
P B. Holman
RP J. Parrett
RP A. McGaffigan

Newark

NEW F 1915

NEW 1915 F

M W. Phillips
M W. McKechnie
1B E. Huhn
2B F. LaPorte
SS J. Esmond
3B W. McKechnie
OF A. Scheer
OF E. Roush
OF A. Campbell
C W. Rariden
P E. Reulbach
P E. Moseley
P G. Kaiserling
P H. Moran
P F. Falkenberg

New Haven

NH n 1875

NH 1875 n

M C. Gould
M G. Latham
M C. Pabor
1B C. Gould
2B E. Somerville
SS S. Wright
3B H. Luff
OF J. Tipper
OF J. McKelvey

OF J. Ryan
C T. McGinley
UT W. Geer
P F. Nichols

New York

MUT n 1871-1875
   Mutuals
NY N 1876
NY a 1883-1887
NY P 1890
NY N 1883-1957
   Moved to San
   Francisco
NY N 1962-1988
NY A 1903-1988

MUT 1871 n

M R. Ferguson
1B J. Start
2B R. Higham
SS R. Pearce
3B R. Ferguson
OF D. Eggler
OF D. Patterson
OF J. Hatfield
C C. Mills
P R. Wolters

MUT 1872 n

M R. Pearce
1B J. Start
2B J. Hatfield
SS R. Pearce
3B W. Boyd
OF D. Eggler
OF J. McMullin
OF G. Bechtel
C N. Hicks
UT C. Fulmer
P W. Cummings

MUT 1873 n

M J. Hatfield
M J. Start
1B J. Start
2B J. Nelson
SS J. Holdsworth
3B J. Hatfield
OF A. Gedney
OF D. Eggler
OF A. Martin
C N. Hicks
UT R. Higham
P R. Mathews

MUT 1874 n

M T. Carey
M R. Higham
1B J. Start
2B J. Nelson
SS T. Carey
3B J. Burdock
OF J. Remsen
OF J. Hatfield
OF D. Allison
C R. Higham
P R. Mathews

MUT 1875 n

M N. Hicks
1B J. Start
2B J. Nelson
SS J. Hallinan
3B J. Gerhardt
OF A. Gedney
OF E. Booth
OF J. Holdsworth
C N. Hicks
P R. Mathews

NY 1876 N

M W. Cammeyer
1B J. Start
2B W. Craver
SS J. Hallinan
3B A. Nichols
OF F. Treacey
OF E. Booth
OF J. Holdsworth
C N. Hicks
P R. Mathews

NY 1883 a

M J. Mutrie
1B S. Brady
2B S. Crane
SS J. Nelson

3B T. Esterbrook
OF E. Kennedy
OF J. Roseman
OF J. O'Rourke
C W. Holbert
P T. Keefe
P J. Lynch

NY 1884 a

M J. Mutrie
1B D. Orr
2B J. Troy
SS J. Nelson
3B T. Esterbrook
OF S. Brady
OF J. Roseman
OF E. Kennedy
C W. Holbert
P T. Keefe
P J. Lynch

NY 1885 a

M J. Gifford
1B D. Orr
2B T. Forster
SS J. Nelson
3B F. Hankinson
OF S. Brady
OF J. Roseman
OF E. Kennedy
C C. Reipschlager
P J. Lynch
P E. Cushman
P D. Crothers
P E. Begley
P J. Becannon

NY 1886 a

M J. Gifford
M R. Ferguson
1B D. Orr
2B T. Forster
SS J. Nelson
3B F. Hankinson
OF J. Roseman
OF S. Brady
OF S. Behel
C C. Reipschlager
P J. Lynch
P A. Mays
P E. Cushman

NY 1887 a

M R. Ferguson
M D. Orr
M O. Caylor
1B D. Orr
2B J. Gerhardt
SS P. Radford
3B F. Hankinson
OF W. O'Brien
OF C. Jones
OF J. Roseman
C W. Holbert
P A. Mays
P E. Cushman
P J. Lynch
P J. Shaffer
P G. Weidman

NY 1890 P

M W. Ewing
1B R. Connor
2B D. Shannon
SS D. Richardson
3B A. Whitney
OF J. O'Rourke
OF M. Slattery
OF G. Gore
C W. Ewing
P E. Crane
P H. O'Day
P J. Ewing
P T. Keefe

NY 1883 N

M J. Clapp
1B R. Connor
2B J. Troy
SS E. Caskin
3B F. Hankinson
OF J. Gillespie
OF M. Dorgan
OF J. Ward
C W. Ewing
P M. Welch
P J. O'Neill

NY 1884 N

M J. Price
M J. Ward
1B A. McKinnon
2B R. Connor
SS E. Caskin
3B F. Hankinson
OF P. Gillespie
OF M. Dorgan
OF J. Ward
C W. Ewing
UT D. Richardson
P M. Welch
P E. Begley

NY 1885 N

M J. Mutrie
1B R. Connor
2B J. Gerhardt
SS J. Ward
3B T. Esterbrook
OF J. O'Rourke
OF P. Gillespie
OF M. Dorgan
C W. Ewing
P M. Welch
P T. Keefe

NY 1886 N

M J. Mutrie
1B R. Connor
2B J. Gerhardt
SS J. Ward
3B T. Esterbrook
OF M. Dorgan
OF P. Gillespie
OF D. Richardson
C W. Ewing
UT J. O'Rourke
P T. Keefe
P M. Welch

NY 1887 N

M J. Mutrie
1B R. Connor
2B D. Richardson
SS J. Ward
3B W. Ewing
OF G. Gore
OF M. Tiernan
OF P. Gillespie
C W. Brown
UT J. O'Rourke
P T. Keefe
P M. Welch
P W. George

NY 1888 N

M J. Mutrie
1B R. Connor
2B D. Richardson
SS J. Ward
3B A. Whitney
OF M. Tiernan
OF M. Slattery
OF J. O'Rourke
C W. Ewing
P T. Keefe
P M. Welch
P L. Titcomb
P E. Crane

NY 1889 N

M J. Mutrie
1B R. Connor
2B D. Richardson
SS J. Ward
3B A. Whitney
OF J. O'Rourke
OF M. Tiernan
OF G. Gore
C W. Ewing
P M. Welch
P T. Keefe
P E. Crane
P H. O'Day

NY 1890 N

M J. Mutrie
1B L. Whistler
2B C. Bassett
SS J. Glasscock
3B J. Denny
OF M. Tiernan
OF J. Burkett
OF M. Hornung
C R. Buckley
UT A. Clarke
P A. Rusie

P M. Welch
P J. Sharrott

NY 1891 N

M J. Mutrie
1B R. Connor
2B D. Richardson
SS J. Glasscock
3B C. Bassett
OF M. Tiernan
OF G. Gore
OF J. O'Rourke
C R. Buckley
P A. Rusie
P J. Ewing
P M. Welch

NY 1892 N

M P. Powers
1B W. Ewing
2B E. Burke
SS W. Fuller
3B D. Lyons
OF M. Tiernan
OF J. O'Rourke
OF H. Lyons
C J. Boyle
P A. Rusie
P C. King
P E. Crane

NY 1893 N

M J. Ward
1B R. Connor
2B J. Ward
SS W. Fuller
3B G. Davis
OF E. Burke
OF M. Tiernan
OF J. Stafford
C J. Doyle
P A. Rusie
P M. Baldwin
P L. German

NY 1894 N

M J. Ward
1B J. Doyle
2B J. Ward
SS W. Fuller
3B G. Davis
OF G. Van Haltren
OF E. Burke
OF M. Tiernan
C C. Farrell
P A. Rusie
P J. Meekin
P H. Westervelt
P L. German
P W. Clark

NY 1895 N

M G. Davis
M J. Doyle
M H. Watkins
1B J. Doyle
2B J. Stafford
SS W. Fuller
3B G. Davis
OF G. Van Haltren
OF M. Tiernan
OF E. Burke
C C. Farrell
P A. Rusie
P W. Clark
P J. Meekin
P L. German

NY 1896 N

M A. Irwin
M W. Joyce
1B W. Clark
2B W. Gleason
SS F. Connaughton
3B G. Davis
OF G. Van Haltren
OF M. Tiernan
OF J. Stafford
C P. Wilson
P W. Clark
P J. Meekin
P M. Sullivan
P E. Doheny

NY 1897 N

M W. Joyce
1B W. Clark
2B W. Gleason
SS G. Davis

3B W. Joyce
OF G. Van Haltren
OF M. Tiernan
OF J. Holmes
C J. Warner
P A. Rusie
P J. Meekin
P J. Seymour
P M. Sullivan
P E. Doheny

NY 1898 N

M W. Joyce
M A. Anson
M J. Joyce
1B W. Joyce
2B W. Gleason
SS G. Davis
3B F. Hartman
OF G. Van Haltren
OF M. Tiernan
OF J. Doyle
C J. Warner
P J. Seymour
P J. Meekin
P A. Rusie
P E. Doheny

NY 1899 N

M J. Day
M F. Hoey
1B J. Doyle
2B W. Gleason
SS G. Davis
3B F. Hartman
OF G. Van Haltren
OF T. O'Brien
OF C. Foster
C J. Warner
UT P. Wilson
P W. Carrick
P J. Seymour
P E. Doheny
P J. Meekin
P C. Gettig

NY 1900 N

M W. Ewing
M G. Davis
1B J. Doyle
2B W. Gleason
SS G. Davis
3B C. Hickman
OF G. Van Haltren
OF A. Selbach
OF E. Smith
C F. Bowerman
P W. Carrick
P E. Hawley
P G. Mercer
P E. Doheny

NY 1901 N

M G. Davis
1B J. Ganzel
2B R. Nelson
SS G. Davis
3B S. Strang
OF G. Van Haltren
OF A. Selbach
OF A. McBride
C J. Warner
UT C. Hickman
P L. Taylor
P C. Mathewson
P W. Phyle

NY 1902 N

M H. Fogel
M G. Smith
M J. McGraw
1B D. McGann
2B G. Smith
SS J. Bean
3B W. Lauder
OF W. Brodie
OF J. Jones
OF G. Browne
C F. Bowerman
UT J. Dunn
P C. Mathewson
P L. Taylor
P R. Evans
P J. McGinnity
P T. Sparks

NY 1903 N

M J. McGraw
1B D. McGann
2B D. Gilbert

SS C. Babb
3B W. Lauder
OF G. Browne
OF S. Mertes
OF R. Bresnahan
C J. Warner
P J. McGinnity
P C. Mathewson
P L. Taylor
P J. Cronin
P R. Miller

NY 1904 N

M J. McGraw
1B D. McGann
2B W. Gilbert
SS W. Dahlen
3B A. Devlin
OF G. Browne
OF S. Mertes
OF R. Bresnahan
C J. Warner
P J. McGinnity
P C. Mathewson
P L. Taylor
P G. Wiltse
P L. Ames

NY 1905 N

M J. McGraw
1B D. McGann
2B W. Gilbert
SS W. Dahlen
3B A. Devlin
OF S. Mertes
OF M. Donlin
OF G. Browne
C R. Bresnahan
UT F. Bowerman
UT S. Strang
P C. Mathewson
P J. McGinnity
P L. Ames
P L. Taylor
P G. Wiltse

NY 1906 N

M J. McGraw
1B D. McGann
2B W. Gilbert
SS W. Dahlen
3B A. Devlin
OF G. Browne
OF W. Shannon
OF J. Seymour
C R. Bresnahan
UT F. Bowerman
UT S. Strang
P J. McGinnity
P C. Mathewson
P G. Wiltse
P L. Taylor
P L. Ames
RP G. Ferguson

NY 1907 N

M J. McGraw
1B D. McGann
2B L. Doyle
SS W. Dahlen
3B A. Devlin
OF W. Shannon
OF J. Seymour
OF G. Browne
C R. Bresnahan
UT F. Bowerman
UT S. Strang
P C. Mathewson
P J. McGinnity
P L. Ames
P G. Wiltse
P L. Taylor

NY 1908 N

M J. McGraw
1B F. Tenney
2B L. Doyle
SS A. Bridwell
3B A. Devlin
OF J. Seymour
OF M. Donlin
OF W. Shannon
C R. Bresnahan
P C. Mathewson
P G. Wiltse
P J. Crandall
P J. McGinnity
P L. Taylor

NY 1909 N

M J. McGraw
1B F. Tenney
2B L. Doyle
SS A. Bridwell
3B A. Devlin
OF J. Murray
OF W. O'Hara
OF H. McCormick
C G. Schlei
P C. Mathewson
P A. Raymond
P G. Wiltse
P L. Ames
P R. Marquard

NY 1910 N

M J. McGraw
1B F. Merkle
2B L. Doyle
SS A. Bridwell
3B A. Devlin
OF J. Murray
OF J. Devore
OF F. Snodgrass
C C. Meyers
P C. Mathewson
P G. Wiltse
P L. Drucke
P J. Crandall
P L. Ames

NY 1911 N

M J. McGraw
1B F. Merkle
2B L. Doyle
SS A. Bridwell
3B A. Devlin
OF F. Snodgrass
OF J. Devore
OF J. Murray
C C. Meyers
UT A. Fletcher
P C. Mathewson
P R. Marquard
P C. Tesreau
P L. Ames
P J. Crandall
P G. Wiltse

NY 1912 N

M J. McGraw
1B F. Merkle
2B L. Doyle
SS A. Fletcher
3B C. Herzog
OF J. Murray
OF D. Becker
OF F. Snodgrass
C C. Meyers
UT J. Devore
P C. Mathewson
P R. Marquard
P C. Tesreau
P L. Ames
P J. Crandall

NY 1913 N

M J. McGraw
1B F. Merkle
2B L. Doyle
SS A. Fletcher
3B C. Herzog
OF G. Burns
OF J. Murray
OF F. Snodgrass
C C. Meyers
UT A. Shafer
P C. Mathewson
P R. Marquard
P C. Tesreau
P A. Demaree
P A. Fromme
RP J. Crandall

NY 1914 N

M J. McGraw
1B F. Merkle
2B L. Doyle
SS A. Fletcher
3B M. Stock
OF G. Burns
OF R. Bescher
OF F. Snodgrass
C C. Meyers
P C. Tesreau
P C. Mathewson
P R. Marquard
P A. Demaree
P A. Fromme

NY 1915 N

M J. McGraw
1B F. Merkle
2B L. Doyle
SS A. Fletcher
3B J. Lobert
OF G. Burns
OF D. Robertson
OF F. Snodgrass
C J. Meyers
P C. Tesreau
P W. Perritt
P C. Mathewson
P R. Stroud
P R. Marquard
RP W. Ritter
RP F. Schupp

NY 1916 N

M J. McGraw
1B F. Merkle
2B L. Doyle
SS A. Fletcher
3B W. McKechnie
OF G. Burns
OF B. Kauff
OF D. Robertson
C W. Rariden
P C. Tesreau
P W. Perritt
P J. Benton
P J. Anderson
P F. Schupp

NY 1917 N

M J. McGraw
1B W. Holke
2B C. Herzog
SS A. Fletcher
3B H. Zimmerman
OF B. Kauff
OF G. Burns
OF D. Robertson
C W. Rariden
P F. Schupp
P H. Sallee
P W. Perritt
P J. Benton
P C. Tesreau

NY 1918 N

M J. McGraw
1B W. Holke
2B L. Doyle
SS A. Fletcher
3B H. Zimmerman
OF R. Youngs
OF G. Burns
OF B. Kauff
C G. McCarty
P W. Perritt
P C. Causey
P A. Demaree
P H. Sallee
P F. Toney

NY 1919 N

M J. McGraw
1B H. Chase
2B L. Doyle
SS A. Fletcher
3B H. Zimmerman
OF G. Burns
OF B. Kauff
OF R. Youngs
C G. McCarty
P J. Barnes
P J. Benton
P F. Toney
P J. Dubuc
P C. Causey

NY 1920 N

M J. McGraw
1B G. Kelly
2B L. Doyle
SS D. Bancroft
3B F. Frisch
OF G. Burns
OF R. Youngs
OF L. King
C F. Snyder
P J. Barnes
P A. Nehf
P F. Toney
P P. Douglas
P J. Benton

NY 1921 N

M J. McGraw
1B G. Kelly
2B J. Rawlings
SS D. Bancroft
3B F. Frisch
OF G. Burns
OF R. Youngs
OF E. Meusel
C F. Snyder
P A. Nehf
P J. Barnes
P F. Toney
P P. Douglas
P W. Ryan
RP H. Sallee

NY 1922 N

M J. McGraw
1B G. Kelly
2B F. Frisch
SS D. Bancroft
3B H. Groh
OF E. Meusel
OF R. Youngs
OF C. Stengel
C F. Snyder
P A. Nehf
P J. Barnes
P W. Ryan
P P. Douglas
P H. McQuillan
RP C. Jonnard
RP C. Causey

NY 1923 N

M J. McGraw
1B G. Kelly
2B F. Frisch
SS D. Bancroft
3B H. Groh
OF R. Youngs
OF E. Meusel
OF W. Cunningham
C F. Snyder
UT T. Jackson
P H. McQuillan
P J. Scott
P A. Nehf
P J. Bentley
P W. Ryan
RP C. Jonnard
RP V. Barnes

NY 1924 N

M J. McGraw
M H. Jennings
M J. McGraw
1B G. Kelly
2B F. Frisch
SS T. Jackson
3B H. Groh
OF E. Meusel
OF R. Youngs
OF L. Wilson
C F. Snyder
UT W. Southworth
P V. Barnes
P J. Bentley
P H. McQuillan
P A. Nehf
P W. Dean
RP C. Jonnard

NY 1925 N

M J. McGraw
1B W. Terry
2B G. Kelly
SS T. Jackson
3B F. Lindstrom
OF R. Youngs
OF E. Meusel
OF W. Southworth
C F. Snyder
UT F. Frisch
P J. Scott
P V. Barnes
P K. Greenfield
P J. Bentley
P A. Nehf
RP W. Huntzinger

NY 1926 N

M J. McGraw
1B G. Kelly
2B F. Frisch
SS T. Jackson
3B F. Lindstrom
OF E. Meusel
OF R. Youngs
OF A. Tyson
C P. Florence
UT W. Terry
P J. Scott
P K. Greenfield
P F. Fitzsimmons
P V. Barnes
P J. Ring
RP L. Davies

NY 1927 N

M J. McGraw
M R. Hornsby
1B W. Terry
2B R. Hornsby
SS T. Jackson
3B F. Lindstrom
OF G. Harper
OF E. Roush
OF C. Mueller
C J. Taylor
UT A. Reese
P B. Grimes
P F. Fitzsimmons
P V. Barnes
P L. Benton
P F. Henry
RP D. Songer

NY 1928 N

M J. McGraw
1B W. Terry
2B A. Cohen
SS T. Jackson
3B F. Lindstrom
OF J. Welsh
OF M. Ott
OF F. O'Doul
C J. Hogan
UT A. Reese
P L. Benton
P F. Fitzsimmons
P J. Genewich
P C. Hubbell
P V. Aldridge

NY 1929 N

M J. McGraw
1B W. Terry
2B A. Cohen
SS T. Jackson
3B F. Lindstrom
OF M. Ott
OF E. Roush
OF F. Leach
C J. Hogan
UT R. O'Farrell
P C. Hubbell
P L. Benton
P F. Fitzsimmons
P W. Walker
P C. Mays
RP R. Judd

NY 1930 N

M J. McGraw
1B W. Terry
2B H. Critz
SS T. Jackson
3B F. Lindstrom
OF M. Ott
OF F. Leach
OF W. Roettger
C J. Hogan
UT R. O'Farrell
P W. Walker
P C. Hubbell
P F. Fitzsimmons
P H. Pruett
P C. Mitchell
RP J. Heving

NY 1931 N

M J. McGraw
1B W. Terry
2B W. Hunnefield
SS T. Jackson
3B J. Vergez
OF M. Ott
OF F. Leach
OF E. Allen
C J. Hogan
P F. Fitzsimmons
P C. Hubbell
P W. Walker
P C. Mitchell
P J. Berly

NY 1932 N

M J. McGraw
M W. Terry
1B W. Terry
2B H. Critz
SS E. Marshall
3B J. Vergez
OF M. Ott
OF F. Lindstrom
OF J. Moore
C J. Hogan
UT C. Fullis
P C. Hubbell
P F. Fitzsimmons
P W. Walker
P J. Mooney
P H. Bell
RP A. Luque
RP S. Gibson

NY 1933 N

M W. Terry
1B W. Terry
2B H. Critz
SS J. Ryan
3B J. Vergez
OF M. Ott
OF J. Moore
OF G. Davis
C A. Mancuso
P C. Hubbell
P H. Schumacher
P F. Fitzsimmons
P L. Parmelee
RP H. Bell
RP A. Luque

NY 1934 N

M W. Terry
1B W. Terry
2B H. Critz
SS T. Jackson
3B J. Vergez
OF M. Ott
OF J. Moore
OF G. Watkins
C A. Mancuso
UT J. Ryan
P C. Hubbell
P H. Schumacher
P F. Fitzsimmons
P L. Parmelee
P J. Bowman
RP A. Smith
RP H. Bell

NY 1935 N

M W. Terry
1B W. Terry
2B M. Koenig
SS R. Bartell
3B T. Jackson
OF J. Moore
OF H. Leiber
OF M. Ott
C A. Mancuso
P C. Hubbell
P H. Schumacher
P L. Parmelee
P C. Castleman
P A. Smith
RP A. Stout
RP F. Gabler

NY 1936 N

M W. Terry
1B S. Leslie
2B B. Whitehead
SS R. Bartell
3B T. Jackson
OF J. Moore
OF M. Ott
OF H. Leiber
C A. Mancuso
UT J. Ripple
P C. Hubbell
P H. Schumacher
P A. Smith
P F. Gabler
P H. Gumbert
RP S. Coffman

NY 1937 N

M W. Terry
1B J. McCarthy
2B B. Whitehead
SS R. Bartell
3B L. Chiozza
OF J. Moore
OF J. Ripple
OF M. Ott
C H. Danning
P C. Hubbell
P C. Melton
P H. Schumacher
P H. Gumbert
P C. Castleman
RP A. Smith
RP S. Coffman

NY 1938 N

M W. Terry
1B J. McCarthy
2B A. Kampouris
SS R. Bartell
3B M. Ott
OF J. Ripple
OF J. Moore
OF H. Leiber
C H. Danning
P C. Melton
P H. Gumbert
P H. Schumacher
P C. Hubbell
P W. Lohrman
RP S. Coffman
RP W. Brown

NY 1939 N

M W. Terry
1B H. Bonura
2B B. Whitehead
SS W. Jurges
3B T. Hafey
OF J. Demaree
OF J. Moore
OF M. Ott
C H. Danning
P H. Gumbert
P C. Melton
P W. Lohrman
P H. Schumacher
P C. Hubbell
RP W. Brown
RP J. Lynn

NY 1940 N

M W. Terry
1B N. Young
2B A. Cuccinello
SS N. Witek
3B B. Whitehead
OF J. Moore
OF J. Demaree
OF M. Ott
C H. Danning
P H. Gumbert
P H. Schumacher
P C. Hubbell
P W. Lohrman
P C. Melton
RP W. Brown
RP R. Joiner

NY 1941 N

M W. Terry
1B N. Young
2B B. Whitehead
SS W. Jurges
3B R. Bartell
OF M. Ott
OF J. Rucker
OF J. Moore
C H. Danning
P H. Schumacher
P C. Melton
P C. Hubbell
P W. Lohrman
P R. Carpenter
RP R. Bowman
RP A. Adams

NY 1942 N

M M. Ott
1B J. Mize
2B N. Witek
SS W. Jurges
3B W. Werber
OF M. Ott
OF W. Marshall
OF H. Barna
C H. Danning
UT N. Young
P H. Schumacher
P R. Carpenter
P W. Lohrman
P C. Hubbell
P C. Melton
RP A. Adams

NY 1943 N

M M. Ott
1B J. Orengo
2B N. Witek
SS W. Jurges
3B R. Bartell
OF J. Rucker
OF M. Ott
OF J. Medwick
C A. Mancuso
UT S. Gordon
UT E. Lombardi
UT J. Maynard
P C. Melton
P J. Wittig
P V. Mungo
P R. Fischer
P K. Chase
RP A. Adams
RP W. Sayles

NY 1944 N

M M. Ott
1B P. Weintraub
2B G. Hausmann
SS J. Kerr
3B H. Luby
OF J. Rucker
OF J. Medwick
OF M. Ott
C E. Lombardi
UT N. Reyes
P W. Voiselle
P H. Feldman
P H. Pyle
P R. Fischer
RP A. Adams
RP A. Hansen

NY 1945 N

M M. Ott
1B P. Weintraub
2B G. Hausmann
SS J. Kerr
3B N. Reyes
OF M. Ott
OF J. Rucker
OF D. Gardella
C E. Lombardi
P W. Voiselle
P H. Feldman
P V. Mungo
P J. Brewer
P W. Emmerich
RP A. Adams
RP R. Fischer

NY 1946 N

M M. Ott
1B J. Mize
2B R. Blattner
SS J. Kerr
3B W. Rigney
OF W. Marshall
OF S. Gordon
OF G. Rosen
C W. Cooper
UT J. Graham
UT J. Rucker
UT N. Young
P G. Koslo
P M. Kennedy
P W. Voiselle
P K. Trinkle
P H. Schumacher
RP M. Budnick
RP E. Thompson

NY 1947 N

M M. Ott
1B J. Mize
2B W. Rigney
SS J. Kerr
3B J. Lohrke
OF W. Marshall
OF R. Thomson
OF S. Gordon
C W. Cooper
P L. Jansen
P G. Koslo
P M. Kennedy
P C. Hartung
RP K. Trinkle
RP J. Beggs

NY 1948 N

M M. Ott
M L. Durocher
1B J. Mize
2B W. Rigney
SS J. Kerr
3B S. Gordon
OF C. Lockman
OF W. Marshall
OF R. Thomson
C W. Cooper
UT J. Lohrke
P L. Jansen
P S. Jones
P R. Poat
P C. Hartung
P G. Koslo
RP A. Hansen
RP K. Trinkle

NY 1949 N

M L. Durocher
1B J. Mize
2B H. Thompson
SS J. Kerr
3B S. Gordon
OF R. Thomson
OF C. Lockman
OF W. Marshall
C W. Westrum
UT W. Rigney
P L. Jansen
P M. Kennedy
P G. Koslo
P S. Jones
P C. Hartung
RP W. Higbe
RP H. Behrman

NY 1950 N

M L. Durocher
1B H. Gilbert
2B E. Stanky
SS A. Dark
3B H. Thompson
OF R. Thomson
OF C. Lockman
OF D. Mueller
C W. Westrum
UT M. Irvin
P L. Jansen
P S. Maglie
P S. Jones
P G. Koslo
P J. Hearn
RP J. Kramer
RP A. Hansen

NY 1951 N

M L. Durocher
1B C. Lockman
2B E. Stanky
SS A. Dark
3B H. Thompson
OF W. Mays
OF D. Mueller
OF M. Irvin
C W. Westrum
UT R. Thomson
P S. Maglie
P L. Jansen
P J. Hearn
P G. Koslo
RP G. Spencer
RP S. Jones

NY 1952 N

M L. Durocher
1B C. Lockman
2B D. Williams
SS A. Dark
3B R. Thomson
OF D. Mueller
OF H. Thompson
OF R. Elliott
C W. Westrum
P J. Hearn
P S. Maglie
P L. Jansen
P G. Koslo
P H. Lanier
RP J. Wilhelm
RP M. Kennedy

NY 1953 N

M L. Durocher
1B C. Lockman
2B D. Williams
SS A. Dark
3B H. Thompson
OF R. Thomson
OF D. Mueller
OF M. Irvin
C W. Westrum
UT D. Spencer
P R. Gomez
P J. Hearn
P L. Jansen
P S. Maglie
P G. Koslo
RP J. Wilhelm
RP E. Corwin

NY 1954 N

M L. Durocher
1B C. Lockman
2B D. Williams
SS A. Dark
3B H. Thompson
OF D. Mueller
OF W. Mays
OF M. Irvin
C W. Westrum
P J. Antonelli
P R. Gomez
P S. Maglie
P J. Hearn
P D. Liddle
RP M. Grissom
RP J. Wilhelm

NY 1955 N

M L. Durocher
1B B. Harris
2B W. Terwilliger
SS A. Dark
3B H. Thompson
OF W. Mays
OF D. Mueller
OF C. Lockman
C R. Katt
UT R. Hofman
UT J. Rhodes
P J. Antonelli
P J. Hearn
P R. Gomez
P S. Maglie
P D. Liddle
RP J. Wilhelm
RP J. McCall

NY 1956 N

M W. Rigney
1B W. White
2B A. Schoendienst
SS D. Spencer
3B F. Castleman
OF W. Mays
OF D. Mueller
OF J. Brandt
C W. Sarni
UT J. Rhodes
P J. Antonelli
P R. Gomez
P A. Worthington
P J. Hearn
P R. Littlefield
RP S. Ridzik
RP J. Wilhelm

NY 1957 N

M W. Rigney
1B C. Lockman
2B D. O'Connell
SS D. Spencer
3B R. Jablonski
OF W. Mays
OF D. Mueller
OF H. Sauer
C V. Thomas
UT O. Virgil
P R. Gomez
P J. Antonelli
P C. Barclay
P S. Miller
P R. Crone
RP A. Worthington
RP M. Grissom

NY 1962 N

M C. Stengel
1B M. Throneberry
2B C. Neal
SS E. Chacon
3B F. Mantilla
OF F. Thomas
OF J. Hickman
OF D. Ashburn
C C. Cannizzaro
UT J. Christopher
UT R. Kanehl
P R. Craig
P A. Jackson
P J. Hook
P R. Miller
RP N. Anderson
RP C. Moorhead

NY 1963 N

M C. Stengel

1B T. Harkness
2B R. Hunt
SS R. Moran
3B C. Neal
OF E. Snider
OF F. Thomas
OF J. Hickman
C C. Coleman
UT R. Kanehl
P R. Craig
P A. Jackson
P C. Willey
P G. Cisco
P E. Stallard
RP L. Bearnarth
RP K. Mac Kenzie

NY 1964 N

M C. Stengel
1B E. Kranepool
2B R. Hunt
SS R. McMillan
3B C. Smith
OF J. Christopher
OF J. Hickman
OF G. Altman
C J. Gonder
P J. Fisher
P E. Stallard
P A. Jackson
P G. Cisco
RP W. Wakefield
RP L. Bearnarth

NY 1965 N

M C. Stengel
M W. Westrum
1B E. Kranepool
2B C. Hiller
SS R. McMillan
3B C. Smith
OF J. Lewis
OF R. Swoboda
OF J. Christopher
C C. Cannizzaro
UT J. Hickman
UT R. Klaus
P J. Fisher
P A. Jackson
P W. Spahn
P G. Cisco
RP F. McGraw
RP T. Parsons

NY 1966 N

M W. Westrum
1B E. Kranepool
2B R. Hunt
SS E. Bressoud
3B K. Boyer
OF C. Jones
OF A. Luplow
OF R. Swoboda
C G. Grote
UT C. Hiller
P J. Fisher
P D. Ribant
P R. Shaw
P R. Gardner
RP J. Hamilton
RP R. Selma

NY 1967 N

M W. Westrum
M F. Parker
1B E. Kranepool
2B G. Buchek
SS D. Harrelson
3B E. Charles
OF H. Davis
OF C. Jones
OF R. Swoboda
C G. Grote
UT T. Reynolds
P G. Seaver
P J. Fisher
P D. Cardwell
P R. Shaw
RP R. Selma
RP R. Taylor

NY 1968 N

M G. Hodges
1B E. Kranepool
2B P. Linz
SS D. Harrelson
3B E. Charles
OF C. Jones
OF T. Agee
OF R. Swoboda
C G. Grote
UT A. Shamsky
P G. Seaver
P J. Koosman
P D. Cardwell
P R. Selma
P L. Ryan
RP C. Koonce
RP R. Taylor

NY 1969 N

M G. Hodges
1B E. Kranepool
2B K. Boswell
SS D. Harrelson
3B R. Garrett
OF T. Agee
OF C. Jones
OF R. Swoboda
C G. Grote
UT R. Gaspar
UT A. Shamsky
UT A. Weis
P G. Seaver
P J. Koosman
P G. Gentry
P D. Cardwell
P J. McAndrew
RP F. McGraw
RP C. Koonce

NY 1970 N

M G. Hodges
1B D. Clendenon
2B K. Boswell
SS D. Harrelson
3B J. Foy
OF T. Agee
OF C. Jones
OF R. Swoboda
C G. Grote
UT R. Garrett
UT A. Shamsky
P G. Seaver
P J. Koosman
P G. Gentry
P J. McAndrew
P R. Sadecki
RP F. McGraw
RP R. Taylor

NY 1971 N

M G. Hodges
1B E. Kranepool
2B K. Boswell
SS D. Harrelson
3B R. Aspromonte
OF C. Jones
OF T. Agee
OF K. Singleton
C G. Grote
UT T. Foli
UT D. Hahn
UT D. Marshall
P G. Seaver
P G. Gentry
P J. Koosman
P R. Sadecki
P L. Ryan
RP F. McGraw
RP D. Frisella

NY 1972 N

M L. Berra
1B E. Kranepool
2B K. Boswell
SS D. Harrelson
3B J. Fregosi
OF T. Agee
OF J. Milner
OF C. Jones
C D. Dyer
UT R. Garrett
UT T. Martinez
P G. Seaver
P J. Matlack
P G. Gentry
P J. Koosman
P J. McAndrew
RP F. McGraw
RP R. Sadecki

NY 1973 N

M L. Berra
1B J. Milner
2B F. Millan
SS D. Harrelson
3B R. Garrett
OF D. Staub
OF C. Jones
OF D. Hahn
C G. Grote
UT E. Kranepool
P G. Seaver
P J. Koosman
P J. Matlack
P G. Stone
P R. Sadecki
RP F. McGraw
RP H. Parker

NY 1974 N

M L. Berra
1B J. Milner
2B F. Millan
SS D. Harrelson
3B R. Garrett
OF D. Staub
OF C. Jones
OF D. Hahn
C G. Grote
UT T. Martinez
P J. Matlack
P J. Koosman
P G. Seaver
P H. Parker
P R. Sadecki
RP R. Apodaca
RP F. McGraw

NY 1975 N

M L. Berra
M R. McMillan
1B E. Kranepool
2B F. Millan
SS M. Phillips
3B R. Garrett
OF D. Staub
OF D. Unser
OF D. Kingman
C G. Grote
UT J. Torre
P G. Seaver
P J. Koosman
P J. Matlack
P R. Tate
P H. Webb
RP R. Baldwin
RP R. Apodaca

NY 1976 N

M J. Frazier
1B E. Kranepool
2B F. Millan
SS D. Harrelson
3B R. Staiger
OF J. Milner
OF D. Kingman
OF B. Boisclair
C G. Grote
UT J. Torre
P G. Seaver
P J. Matlack
P J. Koosman
P M. Lolich
P C. Swan
RP C. Lockwood
RP R. Apodaca

NY 1977 N

M J. Frazier
M J. Torre
1B J. Milner
2B F. Millan
SS D. Harrelson
3B L. Randle
OF L. Mazzilli
OF S. Henderson
OF B. Boisclair
C J. Stearns
UT E. Kranepool
UT M. Vail
P J. Koosman
P A. Espinosa
P J. Matlack
P C. Swan
P P. Zachry
RP C. Lockwood
RP R. Myrick

NY 1978 N

M J. Torre
1B G. Montanez
2B R. Flynn
SS T. Foli
3B L. Randle
OF S. Henderson
OF L. Mazzilli
OF E. Maddox
C J. Stearns
UT B. Boisclair
UT J. Youngblood
P J. Koosman
P C. Swan
P A. Espinosa
P P. Zachry
P M. Bruhert
RP C. Lockwood
RP D. Murray

NY 1979 N

M J. Torre
1B G. Montanez
2B R. Flynn
SS F. Taveras
3B R. Hebner
OF J. Youngblood
OF L. Mazzilli
OF S. Henderson
C J. Stearns
P C. Swan
P P. Falcone
P K. Kobel
RP N. Allen
RP D. Murray

NY 1980 N

M J. Torre
1B L. Mazzilli
2B R. Flynn
SS F. Taveras
3B E. Maddox
OF S. Henderson
OF J. Youngblood
OF C. Washington
C A. Trevino
UT M. Jorgensen
P B. Burris
P P. Zachry
P M. Bomback
P P. Falcone
P C. Swan
RP T. Hausman
RP J. Reardon

NY 1981 N

M J. Torre
1B D. Staub
2B R. Flynn
SS F. Taveras
3B H. Brooks
OF L. Mazzilli
OF W. Wilson
OF D. Kingman
C J. Stearns
UT M. Cubbage
UT M. Jorgensen
P P. Zachry
P M. Scott
P E. Lynch
P G. Harris
RP P. Falcone
RP N. Allen

NY 1982 N

M G. Bamberger
1B D. Kingman
2B W. Backman
SS R. Gardenhire
3B H. Brooks
OF W. Wilson
OF G. Foster
OF E. Valentine
C J. Stearns
UT R. Bailor
UT M. Jorgensen
UT D. Staub
P C. Puleo
P P. Falcone
P C. Swan
P M. Scott
P E. Lynch
RP J. Orosco
RP N. Allen

NY 1983 N

M G. Bamberger
M F. Howard
1B K. Hernandez
2B B. Giles
SS J. Oquendo
3B H. Brooks
OF G. Foster
OF W. Wilson
OF D. Strawberry
C R. Hodges
UT R. Bailor
UT D. Heep
UT D. Kingman
UT D. Staub
P G. Seaver
P M. Torrez
P E. Lynch
P C. Terrell
P C. Swan
RP J. Orosco
RP D. Sisk

NY 1984 N

M D. Johnson
1B K. Hernandez
2B W. Backman
SS J. Oquendo
3B H. Brooks
OF W. Wilson
OF D. Strawberry
OF G. Foster
C M. Fitzgerald
UT D. Heep
P D. Gooden
P C. Terrell
P R. Darling
P E. Lynch
P B. Berenyi
RP J. Orosco
RP B. Gaff

NY 1985 N

M D. Johnson
1B K. Hernandez
2B W. Backman
SS R. Santana
3B H. Johnson
OF G. Foster
OF D. Strawberry
OF W. Wilson
C G. Carter
P D. Gooden
P R. Darling
P E. Lynch
P C. Fernandes
P R. Aguilera
RP R. McDowell
RP J. Orosco

NY 1986 N

M D. Johnson
1B K. Hernandez
2B W. Backman
SS R. Santana
3B C. Knight
OF L. Dykstra
OF D. Strawberry
OF W. Wilson
C G. Carter
UT K. Mitchell
P D. Gooden
P R. Darling
P R. Ojeda
P C. Fernandes
P R. Aguilera
RP R. McDowell
RP J. Orosco

NY 1987 N

M D. Johnson
1B K. Hernandez
2B T. Teufel
SS R. Santana
3B H. Johnson
OF D. Strawberry
OF W. McReynolds
OF L. Dykstra
C G. Carter
UT W. Wilson
P R. Darling
P D. Gooden
P C. Fernandes
P R. Aguilera
P J. Mitchell
RP T. Leach
RP R. McDowell

NY 1988 N

M D. Johnson
1B K. Hernandez
2B W. Backman
SS K. Elster
3B H. Johnson
OF D. Strawberry
OF W. McReynolds
OF L. Dykstra
C G. Carter
UT D. Magadan
UT W. Wilson
P D. Gooden
P R. Darling
P D. Cone
P R. Ojeda
P C. Fernandez
RP T. Leach
RP R. McDowell

NY 1903 A

M C. Griffith
1B J. Ganzel
2B J. Williams
SS N. Elberfeld
3B W. Conroy
OF W. Keeler
OF H. McFarland
OF A. Davis
C H. Beville
P J. Chesbro
P J. Tannehill
P C. Griffith
P H. Howell
P W. Wolfe

NY 1904 A

M C. Griffith
1B J. Ganzel
2B J. Williams
SS N. Elberfeld
3B W. Conroy
OF W. Keeler
OF J. Anderson
OF P. Dougherty
C J. McGuire
UT D. Fultz
P J. Chesbro
P J. Powell
P A. Orth
P T. Hughes
P C. Griffith

NY 1905 A

M C. Griffith
1B H. Chase
2B J. Williams
SS N. Elberfeld
3B J. Yeager
OF W. Keeler
OF D. Fultz
OF P. Dougherty
C J. Kleinow
UT W. Conroy
P A. Orth
P J. Chesbro
P W. Hogg
P J. Powell
P C. Griffith

NY 1906 A

M C. Griffith
1B H. Chase
2B J. Williams
SS N. Elberfeld
3B F. LaPorte
OF W. Keeler
OF D. Hoffman
OF W. Conroy
C J. Kleinow
P A. Orth
P J. Chesbro
P W. Hogg
P W. Clarkson
P E. Newton

NY 1907 A

M C. Griffith
1B H. Chase
2B J. Williams
SS N. Elberfeld
3B G. Moriarty
OF D. Hoffman
OF W. Keeler
OF W. Conroy
C J. Kleinow
UT F. LaPorte
P A. Orth
P J. Chesbro
P J. Doyle
P W. Hogg
P E. Newton

NY 1908 A

M C. Griffith
M N. Elberfeld
1B H. Chase
2B H. Niles
SS C. Ball
3B W. Conroy
OF C. Hemphill
OF W. Keeler
OF G. Stahl
C J. Kleinow
UT G. Moriarty
P J. Chesbro
P J. Lake
P W. Manning
P W. Hogg
P A. Orth

NY 1909 A

M G. Stallings
1B H. Chase
2B F. LaPorte
SS J. Knight
3B J. Austin
OF A. Engle
OF C. Demmitt
OF W. Keeler
C J. Kleinow
UT W. Cree
UT N. Elberfeld
P J. Warhop
P J. Lake
P W. Manning
P L. Brockett
P J. Doyle

NY 1910 A

M G. Stallings
M H. Chase
1B H. Chase
2B F. LaPorte
SS J. Knight
3B J. Austin
OF W. Cree
OF H. Wolter
OF C. Hemphill
C E. Sweeney
UT B. Daniels
P R. Ford
P J. Warhop
P J. Quinn
P J. Vaughn
P T. Hughes

NY 1911 A

M H. Chase
1B H. Chase
2B E. Gardner
SS J. Knight
3B R. Hartzell
OF W. Cree
OF B. Daniels
OF H. Wolter
C W. Blair
P R. Ford
P R. Caldwell
P J. Warhop
P J. Quinn
P R. Fisher

NY 1912 A

M H. Wolverton
1B H. Chase
2B G. Simmons
SS J. Martin
3B R. Hartzell
OF B. Daniels
OF G. Zinn
OF C. Sterrett
C E. Sweeney
P R. Ford
P J. Warhop
P R. Caldwell
P G. McConnell
P J. Quinn

NY 1913 A

M F. Chance
1B J. Knight
2B R. Hartzell
SS R. Peckinpaugh
3B E. Midkiff
OF W. Cree
OF H. Wolter
OF B. Daniels
C E. Sweeney
P R. Fisher
P R. Ford
P A. Schulz
P G. McConnell
P R. Caldwell

NY 1914 A

M F. Chance
M R. Peckinpaugh
1B C. Mullen
2B L. Boone
SS R. Peckinpaugh
3B F. Maisel
OF R. Hartzell
OF L. Cook
OF W. Cree
C E. Sweeney
P J. Warhop
P R. Caldwell
P R. Keating
P R. Fisher
P M. McHale

NY 1915 A

M W. Donovan
1B W. Pipp
2B L. Boone
SS R. Peckinpaugh
3B F. Maisel
OF L. Cook
OF H. High
OF R. Hartzell
C L. Nunamaker
P R. Caldwell
P R. Fisher
P J. Warhop
P C. Brown
P E. Pieh

NY 1916 A

M W. Donovan
1B W. Pipp
2B E. Gedeon
SS R. Peckinpaugh
3B J. Baker
OF L. Magee
OF H. High
OF F. Gilhooley
C L. Nunamaker
P J. Shawkey
P G. Mogridge
P R. Fisher
P A. Russell
P N. Cullop
RP E. Love

NY 1917 A

M W. Donovan
1B W. Pipp
2B F. Maisel
SS R. Peckinpaugh
3B J. Baker
OF E. Miller
OF T. Hendryx
OF H. High
C L. Nunamaker
P J. Shawkey
P R. Caldwell
P G. Mogridge
P N. Cullop
P U. Shocker

NY 1918 A

M M. Huggins
1B W. Pipp
2B D. Pratt
SS R. Peckinpaugh
3B J. Baker
OF F. Gilhooley
OF F. Bodie
OF E. Miller
C J. Hannah
P G. Mogridge
P E. Love
P R. Caldwell
P A. Russell
P J. Finneran

NY 1919 A

M M. Huggins
1B W. Pipp
2B D. Pratt
SS R. Peckinpaugh
3B J. Baker
OF G. Lewis
OF F. Bodie
OF S. Vick
C H. Ruel
P J. Quinn
P J. Shawkey
P H. Thormahlen
P G. Mogridge
P C. Mays

NY 1920 A

M M. Huggins
1B W. Pipp
2B D. Pratt
SS R. Peckinpaugh
3B A. Ward
OF G. Ruth
OF F. Bodie
OF G. Lewis
C H. Ruel
UT R. Meusel
P C. Mays
P J. Shawkey
P J. Quinn
P H. Collins
P H. Thormahlen

NY 1921 A

M M. Huggins
1B W. Pipp
2B A. Ward
SS R. Peckinpaugh
3B J. Baker
OF G. Ruth
OF R. Meusel
OF E. Miller
C W. Schang
P C. Mays
P W. Hoyt
P J. Shawkey
P H. Collins
P J. Quinn

NY 1922 A

M M. Huggins
1B W. Pipp
2B A. Ward
SS L. Scott
3B J. Dugan
OF L. Witt
OF R. Meusel
OF G. Ruth
C W. Schang
P J. Shawkey
P W. Hoyt
P S. Jones
P L. Bush
P C. Mays
RP G. Murray

NY 1923 A

M M. Huggins
1B W. Pipp
2B A. Ward
SS L. Scott
3B J. Dugan
OF G. Ruth
OF L. Witt
OF R. Meusel
C W. Schang
P L. Bush
P J. Shawkey
P S. Jones
P W. Hoyt
P H. Pennock

NY 1924 A

M M. Huggins
1B W. Pipp
2B A. Ward
SS L. Scott
3B J. Dugan
OF G. Ruth
OF L. Witt
OF R. Meusel
C W. Schang
P H. Pennock
P L. Bush
P W. Hoyt
P J. Shawkey
P S. Jones
RP N. Gaston

NY 1925 A

M M. Huggins
1B H. Gehrig
2B A. Ward
SS P. Wanninger
3B J. Dugan
OF E. Combs
OF R. Meusel
OF G. Ruth
C B. Bengough
P H. Pennock
P S. Jones
P U. Shocker
P W. Hoyt
P J. Shawkey
RP H. Johnson
RP J. Ferguson

NY 1926 A

M M. Huggins
1B H. Gehrig
2B A. Lazzeri
SS M. Koenig
3B J. Dugan
OF G. Ruth
OF E. Combs
OF R. Meusel
C T. Collins
UT B. Paschal
P H. Pennock
P U. Shocker
P W. Hoyt
P S. Jones
P M. Thomas
RP E. Braxton

NY 1927 A

M M. Huggins
1B H. Gehrig
2B A. Lazzeri
SS M. Koenig
3B J. Dugan
OF E. Combs
OF G. Ruth
OF R. Meusel
C T. Collins
P W. Hoyt
P W. Moore
P H. Pennock
P U. Shocker
P W. Ruether

NY 1928 A

M M. Huggins
1B H. Gehrig
2B A. Lazzeri
SS M. Koenig
3B J. Dugan
OF G. Ruth
OF E. Combs
OF R. Meusel
C J. Grabowski
UT L. Durocher
P G. Pipgras
P W. Hoyt
P H. Pennock
P H. Johnson
P A. Shealy
RP W. Moore

NY 1929 A

M M. Huggins
M A. Fletcher
1B H. Gehrig
2B A. Lazzeri
SS L. Durocher
3B E. Robertson
OF E. Combs
OF G. Ruth
OF R. Meusel
C W. Dickey
UT M. Koenig
P G. Pipgras
P W. Hoyt
P E. Wells
P H. Pennock
P R. Sherid
RP W. Moore

NY 1930 A

M J. Shawkey
1B H. Gehrig
2B A. Lazzeri
SS L. Lary
3B W. Chapman
OF G. Ruth
OF E. Combs
OF H. Rice
C W. Dickey
P G. Pipgras
P C. Ruffing
P R. Sherid
P H. Johnson
P H. Pennock
RP L. McEvoy

NY 1931 A

M J. McCarthy
1B H. Gehrig
2B A. Lazzeri
SS L. Lary
3B J. Sewell
OF G. Ruth
OF W. Chapman
OF E. Combs
C W. Dickey
UT S. Byrd
P V. Gomez
P C. Ruffing
P H. Johnson
P H. Pennock
P G. Pipgras

NY 1932 A

M J. McCarthy
1B H. Gehrig
2B A. Lazzeri
SS F. Crosetti
3B J. Sewell
OF W. Chapman
OF E. Combs
OF G. Ruth
C W. Dickey
UT S. Byrd
P V. Gomez
P C. Ruffing
P G. Pipgras
P J. Allen
P H. Pennock
RP W. Brown

NY 1933 A

M J. McCarthy
1B H. Gehrig
2B A. Lazzeri
SS F. Crosetti
3B J. Sewell
OF W. Chapman
OF G. Ruth
OF E. Combs
C W. Dickey
UT F. Walker
P C. Ruffing
P V. Gomez
P J. Allen
P R. Van Atta
P D. Mac Fayden
RP H. Pennock
RP W. Moore

NY 1934 A

M J. McCarthy
1B H. Gehrig
2B A. Lazzeri
SS F. Crosetti
3B O. Saltzgaver
OF W. Chapman
OF G. Ruth
OF S. Byrd
C W. Dickey
UT M. Hoag
P V. Gomez
P C. Ruffing
P J. Murphy
P J. Broaca
P J. DeShong

NY 1935 A

M J. McCarthy
1B H. Gehrig
2B A. Lazzeri
SS F. Crosetti
3B R. Rolfe
OF W. Chapman
OF G. Selkirk
OF J. Hill
C W. Dickey
P V. Gomez
P C. Ruffing
P J. Broaca
P J. Allen
P V. Tamulis
RP J. Murphy
RP J. DeShong

NY 1936 A

M J. McCarthy
1B H. Gehrig
2B A. Lazzeri
SS F. Crosetti
3B R. Rolfe
OF J. DiMaggio
OF G. Selkirk
OF A. Powell
C W. Dickey
P C. Ruffing
P M. Pearson
P J. Broaca
P V. Gomez
P I. Hadley

NY 1937 A

M J. McCarthy
1B H. Gehrig
2B A. Lazzeri
SS F. Crosetti
3B R. Rolfe
OF J. DiMaggio
OF M. Hoag
OF A. Powell
C W. Dickey
P V. Gomez
P C. Ruffing
P I. Hadley
P M. Pearson
RP J. Murphy
RP F. Makosky

NY 1938 A

M J. McCarthy
1B H. Gehrig
2B J. Gordon
SS F. Crosetti
3B R. Rolfe
OF J. DiMaggio
OF T. Henrich
OF G. Selkirk
C W. Dickey
P C. Ruffing
P V. Gomez
P M. Pearson
P S. Chandler
P I. Hadley
RP J. Murphy
RP I. Andrews

NY 1939 A

M J. McCarthy
1B E. Dahlgren
2B J. Gordon
SS F. Crosetti
3B R. Rolfe
OF G. Selkirk
OF J. DiMaggio
OF C. Keller
C W. Dickey
UT T. Henrich
P C. Ruffing
P V. Gomez
P I. Hadley
P R. Donald
P M. Pearson
RP J. Murphy

NY 1940 A

M J. McCarthy
1B E. Dahlgren
2B J. Gordon
SS F. Crosetti
3B R. Rolfe
OF C. Keller
OF J. DiMaggio
OF G. Selkirk
C W. Dickey
P C. Ruffing
P M. Russo
P S. Chandler
P M. Breuer
P R. Donald
RP J. Murphy

NY 1941 A

M J. McCarthy
1B J. Sturm
2B J. Gordon
SS P. Rizzuto
3B R. Rolfe
OF T. Henrich
OF J. DiMaggio
OF C. Keller
C W. Dickey
P M. Russo
P C. Ruffing
P S. Chandler
P R. Donald
P V. Gomez
RP J. Murphy
RP C. Stanceau

NY 1942 A

M J. McCarthy
1B J. Hassett
2B J. Gordon
SS P. Rizzuto
3B F. Crosetti
OF J. DiMaggio
OF C. Keller
OF T. Henrich
C W. Dickey
P E. Bonham
P S. Chandler
P C. Ruffing
P H. Borowy
P M. Breuer
RP J. Murphy
RP J. Lindell

NY 1943 A

M J. McCarthy
1B N. Etten
2B J. Gordon
SS F. Crosetti
3B W. Johnson
OF C. Keller
OF J. Lindell
OF A. Metheny
C W. Dickey
P S. Chandler
P E. Bonham
P C. Wensloff
P H. Borowy
P R. Donald
RP J. Murphy

NY 1944 A

M J. McCarthy
1B N. Etten
2B G. Stirnweiss
SS M. Milosevich
3B O. Grimes
OF J. Lindell
OF A. Metheny
OF H. Martin
C N. Garbark
P H. Borowy
P W. Dubiel
P E. Bonham
P R. Donald
P W. Zuber

NY 1945 A

M J. McCarthy
1B N. Etten
2B G. Stirnweiss
SS F. Crosetti
3B O. Grimes
OF A. Metheny
OF H. Martin
OF G. Stainback
C N. Garbark
P F. Bevens
P E. Bonham
P A. Gettel
P W. Dubiel
P H. Borowy
RP K. Holcombe
RP J. Turner

NY 1946 A

M J. McCarthy
M W. Dickey
M J. Neun
1B N. Etten
2B J. Gordon
SS P. Rizzuto
3B G. Stirnweiss
OF C. Keller
OF J. DiMaggio
OF T. Henrich
C A. Robinson
UT J. Lindell
P S. Chandler
P F. Bevens
P J. Page
P R. Gumpert
P E. Bonham

NY 1947 A

M S. Harris
1B G. McQuinn
2B G. Stirnweiss
SS P. Rizzuto
3B W. Johnson
OF J. DiMaggio
OF T. Henrich
OF J. Lindell
C A. Robinson
P A. Reynolds
P F. Shea
P F. Bevens
P S. Chandler
P L. Newsom
RP J. Page
RP R. Gumpert

NY 1948 A

M S. Harris
1B G. McQuinn
2B G. Stirnweiss
SS P. Rizzuto
3B W. Johnson
OF J. DiMaggio
OF T. Henrich
OF J. Lindell
C C. Niarhos
UT L. Berra
UT R. Brown
P A. Reynolds
P E. Lopat
P V. Raschi
P F. Shea
P T. Byrne
RP J. Page
RP F. Hiller

NY 1949 A

M C. Stengel
1B T. Henrich
2B G. Coleman
SS P. Rizzuto
3B R. Brown
OF C. Mapes
OF E. Woodling
OF H. Bauer
C L. Berra
UT W. Johnson
P V. Raschi
P E. Lopat
P A. Reynolds
P T. Byrne
P J. Sanford
RP J. Page
RP F. Shea

NY 1950 A

M C. Stengel
1B J. Collins
2B G. Coleman
SS P. Rizzuto
3B W. Johnson
OF J. DiMaggio
OF E. Woodling
OF H. Bauer
C L. Berra
UT R. Brown
UT C. Mapes
P V. Raschi
P A. Reynolds
P E. Lopat
P T. Byrne
P J. Sanford
RP T. Ferrick
RP J. Page

NY 1951 A

M C. Stengel
1B J. Collins
2B G. Coleman
SS P. Rizzuto
3B R. Brown
OF E. Woodling
OF J. DiMaggio
OF H. Bauer
C L. Berra
UT M. Mantle
UT G. McDougald
UT J. Mize
P V. Raschi
P E. Lopat
P A. Reynolds
P T. Morgan
P F. Shea
RP J. Ostrowski

NY 1952 A

M C. Stengel
1B J. Collins
2B A. Martin
SS P. Rizzuto
3B G. McDougald
OF M. Mantle
OF H. Bauer
OF E. Woodling
C L. Berra
P A. Reynolds
P V. Raschi
P E. Lopat
P J. Sain
P R. Kuzava
RP J. McDonald
RP R. Hogue

NY 1953 A

M C. Stengel
1B J. Collins
2B A. Martin
SS P. Rizzuto
3B G. McDougald
OF H. Bauer
OF M. Mantle
OF E. Woodling
C L. Berra
UT I. Noren
P E. Ford
P J. Sain
P V. Raschi
P E. Lopat
P A. Reynolds
RP R. Kuzava
RP T. Gorman

NY 1954 A

M C. Stengel
1B J. Collins
2B G. McDougald
SS P. Rizzuto
3B A. Carey
OF M. Mantle
OF I. Noren
OF H. Bauer
C L. Berra
UT G. Coleman
UT E. Woodling
P E. Ford
P R. Grim

P E. Lopat
P A. Reynolds
P T. Morgan
RP J. Sain

NY 1955 A
M C. Stengel
1B W. Skowron
2B G. McDougald
SS G. Hunter
3B A. Carey
OF M. Mantle
OF H. Bauer
OF I. Noren
C L. Berra
UT J. Collins
UT E. Howard
P E. Ford
P R. Turley
P T. Byrne
P J. Kucks
P D. Larsen
RP C. Konstanty
RP T. Morgan

NY 1956 A
M C. Stengel
1B W. Skowron
2B A. Martin
SS G. McDougald
3B A. Carey
OF H. Bauer
OF M. Mantle
OF E. Howard
C L. Berra
UT J. Collins
P E. Ford
P J. Kucks
P D. Larsen
P T. Sturdivant
P R. Turley
RP T. Byrne
RP R. Grim

NY 1957 A
M C. Stengel
1B W. Skowron
2B R. Richardson
SS G. McDougald
3B A. Carey
OF M. Mantle
OF H. Bauer
OF E. Howard
C L. Berra
UT A. Kubek
UT E. Slaughter
P T. Sturdivant
P J. Kucks
P R. Turley
P R. Shantz
P D. Larsen
RP A. Ditmar
RP T. Byrne

NY 1958 A
M C. Stengel
1B W. Skowron
2B G. McDougald
SS A. Kubek
3B A. Carey
OF M. Mantle
OF N. Siebern
OF H. Bauer
C L. Berra
UT E. Howard
P R. Turley
P E. Ford
P A. Ditmar
P R. Shantz
P J. Kucks
RP R. Duren
RP Z. Monroe

NY 1959 A
M C. Stengel
1B W. Skowron
2B R. Richardson
SS A. Kubek
3B H. Lopez
OF M. Mantle
OF H. Bauer
OF N. Siebern
C L. Berra
UT E. Howard
UT G. McDougald
P E. Ford
P A. Ditmar
P R. Turley
P D. Maas
P R. Terry
RP J. Coates

RP R. Shantz

NY 1960 A
M C. Stengel
1B W. Skowron
2B R. Richardson
SS A. Kubek
3B C. Boyer
OF M. Mantle
OF R. Maris
OF H. Lopez
C E. Howard
UT L. Berra
UT G. McDougald
P A. Ditmar
P E. Ford
P R. Turley
P R. Terry
P J. Coates
RP D. Maas
RP R. Shantz

NY 1961 A
M R. Houk
1B W. Skowron
2B R. Richardson
SS A. Kubek
3B C. Boyer
OF R. Maris
OF M. Mantle
OF L. Berra
C E. Howard
P E. Ford
P W. Stafford
P R. Terry
P R. Sheldon
P J. Coates
RP L. Arroyo

NY 1962 A
M R. Houk
1B W. Skowron
2B R. Richardson
SS T. Tresh
3B C. Boyer
OF R. Maris
OF M. Mantle
OF H. Lopez
C E. Howard
P R. Terry
P E. Ford
P W. Stafford
P J. Bouton
P R. Sheldon
RP J. Coates
RP L. Daley

NY 1963 A
M R. Houk
1B J. Pepitone
2B R. Richardson
SS A. Kubek
3B C. Boyer
OF T. Tresh
OF H. Lopez
OF J. Reed
C E. Howard
P E. Ford
P R. Terry
P J. Bouton
P A. Downing
P S. Williams
RP H. Reniff
RP S. Hamilton

NY 1964 A
M L. Berra
1B J. Pepitone
2B R. Richardson
SS A. Kubek
3B C. Boyer
OF T. Tresh
OF R. Maris
OF M. Mantle
C E. Howard
UT P. Linz
UT H. Lopez
P J. Bouton
P E. Ford
P A. Downing
P R. Terry
P R. Sheldon
RP P. Mikkelsen
RP H. Reniff

NY 1965 A
M J. Keane
1B J. Pepitone
2B R. Richardson
SS A. Kubek

3B C. Boyer
OF T. Tresh
OF M. Mantle
OF R. Moschitto
C E. Howard
UT R. Barker
UT P. Linz
UT H. Lopez
P M. Stottlemyre
P E. Ford
P A. Downing
P J. Bouton
P W. Stafford
RP P. Ramos
RP H. Reniff

NY 1966 A
M J. Keane
M R. Houk
1B J. Pepitone
2B R. Richardson
SS H. Clarke
3B C. Boyer
OF M. Mantle
OF R. Maris
OF T. Tresh
C E. Howard
UT R. White
P M. Stottlemyre
P F. Peterson
P A. Downing
P F. Talbot
P J. Bouton
RP H. Reniff
RP P. Ramos

NY 1967 A
M R. Houk
1B M. Mantle
2B H. Clarke
SS R. Amaro
3B C. Smith
OF J. Pepitone
OF T. Tresh
OF S. Whitaker
C J. Gibbs
UT W. Robinson
P M. Stottlemyre
P A. Downing
P F. Peterson
P F. Talbot
P Monbouquette
RP T. Tillotson
RP H. Womack

NY 1968 A
M R. Houk
1B M. Mantle
2B H. Clarke
SS T. Tresh
3B R. Cox
OF R. White
OF W. Robinson
OF A. Kosco
C J. Gibbs
UT J. Pepitone
P M. Stottlemyre
P S. Bahnsen
P F. Peterson
P S. Barber
P F. Talbot
RP J. Verbanic
RP H. Womack

NY 1969 A
M R. Houk
1B J. Pepitone
2B H. Clarke
SS E. Michael
3B G. Kenney
OF R. White
OF B. Murcer
OF R. Woods
C J. Gibbs
P M. Stottlemyre
P F. Peterson
P S. Bahnsen
P W. Burbach
P A. Downing
RP L. McDaniel
RP J. Aker

NY 1970 A
M R. Houk
1B D. Cater
2B H. Clarke
SS E. Michael
3B G. Kenney
OF R. White
OF B. Murcer
OF C. Blefary

C T. Munson
P M. Stottlemyre
P F. Peterson
P S. Bahnsen
P S. Kline
P M. Kekich
RP L. McDaniel
RP R. Klimkowski

NY 1971 A
M R. Houk
1B D. Cater
2B H. Clarke
SS E. Michael
3B G. Kenney
OF R. White
OF B. Murcer
OF F. Alou
C T. Munson
P F. Peterson
P M. Stottlemyre
P S. Bahnsen
P S. Kline
P M. Kekich
RP L. McDaniel
RP J. Aker

NY 1972 A
M R. Houk
1B R. Blomberg
2B H. Clarke
SS E. Michael
3B C. Sanchez
OF R. White
OF B. Murcer
OF J. Callison
C T. Munson
UT F. Alou
P M. Stottlemyre
P F. Peterson
P S. Kline
P M. Kekich
P R. Gardner
RP A. Lyle
RP L. McDaniel

NY 1973 A
M R. Houk
1B F. Alou
2B H. Clarke
SS E. Michael
3B G. Nettles
OF R. White
OF B. Murcer
OF M. Alou
C T. Munson
DH J. Hart
UT R. Blomberg
P M. Stottlemyre
P G. Medich
P F. Peterson
P L. McDaniel
P P. Dobson
RP A. Lyle

NY 1974 A
M W. Virdon
1B C. Chambliss
2B S. Alomar
SS J. Mason
3B G. Nettles
OF B. Murcer
OF E. Maddox
OF L. Piniella
C T. Munson
DH R. Blomberg
UT R. White
P P. Dobson
P G. Medich
P R. Tidrow
P R. May
P M. Stottlemyre
RP A. Lyle
RP C. Upshaw

NY 1975 A
M W. Virdon
M A. Martin
1B C. Chambliss
2B S. Alomar
SS J. Mason
3B G. Nettles
OF R. White
OF B. Bonds
OF E. Maddox
C T. Munson
DH E. Herrmann
UT F. Stanley
P J. Hunter
P G. Medich
P R. May

P P. Dobson
P L. Gura
RP A. Lyle
RP R. Tidrow

NY 1976 A
M A. Martin
1B C. Chambliss
2B W. Randolph
SS F. Stanley
3B G. Nettles
OF R. White
OF J. Rivers
OF O. Gamble
C T. Munson
DH C. May
UT L. Piniella
P J. Hunter
P E. Figueroa
P D. Ellis
P K. Holtzman
P D. Alexander
RP A. Lyle
RP R. Tidrow

NY 1977 A
M A. Martin
1B C. Chambliss
2B W. Randolph
SS B. Dent
3B G. Nettles
OF J. Rivers
OF R. White
OF R. Jackson
C T. Munson
DH C. May
UT L. Piniella
P E. Figueroa
P M. Torrez
P R. Guidry
P D. Gullett
P R. Tidrow
RP A. Lyle
RP K. Clay

NY 1978 A
M A. Martin
M R. Howser
M R. Lemon
1B C. Chambliss
2B W. Randolph
SS B. Dent
3B G. Nettles
OF J. Rivers
OF R. Jackson
OF L. Piniella
C T. Munson
DH C. Johnson
UT R. White
P R. Guidry
P E. Figueroa
P R. Tidrow
P J. Beattie
P J. Hunter
RP R. Gossage
RP A. Lyle

NY 1979 A
M R. Lemon
M A. Martin
1B C. Chambliss
2B W. Randolph
SS B. Dent
3B G. Nettles
OF R. Jackson
OF L. Piniella
OF B. Murcer
C T. Munson
DH J. Spencer
P T. John
P R. Guidry
P L. Tiant
P J. Hunter
P E. Figueroa
RP R. Davis
RP K. Clay

NY 1980 A
M R. Howser
1B R. Watson
2B W. Randolph
SS B. Dent
3B G. Nettles
OF R. Brown
OF L. Piniella
OF R. Jackson
C R. Cerone
DH E. Soderholm
UT B. Murcer
UT J. Spencer
P T. John

P R. Guidry
P T. Underwood
P R. May
P L. Tiant
RP R. Davis
RP R. Gossage

NY 1981 A
M E. Michael
M R. Lemon
1B R. Watson
2B W. Randolph
SS B. Dent
3B G. Nettles
OF D. Winfield
OF J. Mumphrey
OF R. Jackson
C R. Cerone
DH B. Murcer
UT O. Gamble
P R. May
P T. John
P R. Guidry
P D. Righetti
P R. Reuschel
RP R. Davis
RP D. LaRoche

NY 1982 A
M R. Lemon
M E. Michael
M C. King
1B K. Mayberry
2B W. Randolph
SS R. Smalley
3B G. Nettles
OF D. Winfield
OF O. Griffey
OF J. Mumphrey
C R. Cerone
DH O. Gamble
UT D. Collins
UT L. Piniella
P R. Guidry
P T. John
P D. Righetti
P S. Rawley
P M. Morgan
RP G. Frazier
RP R. May

NY 1983 A
M A. Martin
1B K. Griffey
2B W. Randolph
SS R. Smalley
3B G. Nettles
OF D. Winfield
OF S. Kemp
OF J. Mumphrey
C H. Wynegar
DH D. Baylor
UT A. Robertson
P R. Guidry
P S. Rawley
P D. Righetti
P B. Shirley
P S. Fontenot
RP G. Frazier
RP D. Murray

NY 1984 A
M L. Berra
1B D. Mattingly
2B W. Randolph
SS R. Meacham
3B C. Harrah
OF D. Winfield
OF O. Moreno
OF K. Griffey
C H. Wynegar
DH D. Baylor
P P. Niekro
P R. Guidry
P S. Fontenot
P D. Rasmussen
RP R. Shirley
RP J. Howell

NY 1985 A
M L. Berra
M A. Martin
1B D. Mattingly
2B W. Randolph
SS R. Meacham
3B M. Pagliarulo
OF D. Winfield
OF H. Henderson
OF K. Griffey
C H. Wynegar
DH D. Baylor

P R. Guidry
P P. Niekro
P J. Cowley
P E. Whitson
P D. Rasmussen
RP R. Shirley
RP D. Righetti

NY 1986 A
M L. Piniella
1B D. Mattingly
2B W. Randolph
SS J. Tolleson
3B M. Pagliarulo
OF R. Henderson
OF D. Winfield
OF D. Pasqua
C H. Wynegar
DH M. Easler
P D. Rasmussen
P R. Guidry
P D. Drabek
P R. Tewksbury
P J. Niekro
RP D. Righetti
RP R. Shirley

NY 1987 A
M L. Piniella
1B D. Mattingly
2B W. Randolph
SS J. Tolleson
3B M. Pagliarulo
OF D. Winfield
OF G. Ward
OF D. Pasqua
C R. Cerone
DH R. Kittle
UT C. Washington
P T. John
P R. Rhoden
P C. Hudson
P D. Rasmussen
P R. Guidry
RP D. Righetti
RP T. Stoddard

NY 1988 A
M A. Martin
M L. Piniella
1B D. Mattingly
2B W. Randolph
SS R. Santana
3B M. Pagliarulo
OF D. Winfield
OF R. Henderson
OF C. Washington
C D. Slaught
DH J. Clark
P R. Rhoden
P T. John
P R. Dotson
P J. Candelaria
P C. Hudson
RP N. Allen
RP D. Righetti

Oakland

OAK A 1968-1988

OAK 1968 A
M R. Kennedy
1B D. Cater
2B J. Donaldson
SS D. Campaneris
3B S. Bando
OF R. Jackson
OF R. Monday
OF N. Hershberger
C D. Duncan
P J. Hunter
P J. Odom
P J. Nash
P C. Dobson
P L. Krausse
RP D. Segui
RP J. Aker

OAK 1969 A
M H. Bauer
M J. McNamara
1B D. Cater
2B R. Green
SS D. Campaneris
3B S. Bando
OF R. Jackson
OF R. Monday
OF T. Reynolds
C P. Roof

P J. Hunter
P C. Dobson
P J. Odom
P L. Krausse
P J. Nash
RP R. Fingers
RP J. Roland

OAK 1970 A

M J. McNamara
1B D. Mincher
2B R. Green
SS D. Campaneris
3B S. Bando
OF F. Alou
OF R. Jackson
OF R. Monday
C F. Fernandez
UT J. Rudi
P C. Dobson
P J. Hunter
P D. Segui
P J. Odom
P R. Fingers
RP J. Grant
RP P. Lindblad

OAK 1971 A

M R. Williams
1B M. Epstein
2B R. Green
SS D. Campaneris
3B S. Bando
OF R. Jackson
OF J. Rudi
OF R. Monday
C D. Duncan
P V. Blue
P J. Hunter
P C. Dobson
P D. Segui
P J. Odom
RP R. Fingers
RP R. Locker

OAK 1972 A

M R. Williams
1B M. Epstein
2B T. Cullen
SS D. Campaneris
3B S. Bando
OF J. Rudi
OF R. Jackson
OF A. Mangual
C D. Duncan
UT J. Hegan
P J. Hunter
P K. Holtzman
P J. Odom
P V. Blue
P D. Hamilton
RP R. Fingers
RP J. Horlen

OAK 1973 A

M R. Williams
1B F. Tenace
2B R. Green
SS D. Campaneris
3B S. Bando
OF R. Jackson
OF W. North
OF J. Rudi
C R. Fosse
DH D. Johnson
UT T. Kubiak
P K. Holtzman
P V. Blue
P J. Hunter
P J. Odom
RP R. Fingers
RP D. Knowles

OAK 1974 A

M A. Dark
1B F. Tenace
2B R. Green
SS D. Campaneris
3B S. Bando
OF J. Rudi
OF W. North
OF R. Jackson
C R. Fosse
DH J. Alou
UT T. Kubiak
UT A. Mangual
P J. Hunter
P V. Blue
P K. Holtzman
P D. Hamilton
P W. Abbott
RP R. Fingers
RP P. Lindblad

OAK 1975 A

M A. Dark
1B J. Rudi
2B P. Garner
SS D. Campaneris
3B S. Bando
OF C. Washington
OF R. Jackson
OF W. North
C F. Tenace
DH B. Williams
UT J. Holt
P V. Blue
P K. Holtzman
P R. Bosman
P W. Abbott
P S. Bahnsen
RP R. Fingers
RP J. Todd

OAK 1976 A

M C. Tanner
1B F. Tenace
2B P. Garner
SS D. Campaneris
3B S. Bando
OF W. North
OF C. Washington
OF J. Rudi
C W. Haney
DH B. Williams
UT D. Baylor
UT K. McMullen
P V. Blue
P M. Torrez
P S. Bahnsen
P P. Mitchell
P R. Bosman
RP R. Fingers
RP P. Lindblad

OAK 1977 A

M J. McKeon
M B. Winkles
1B R. Allen
2B M. Perez
SS R. Picciolo
3B W. Gross
OF M. Page
OF A. Armas
OF J. Tyrone
C J. Newman
DH M. Sanguillen
UT R. Scott
UT E. Williams
P V. Blue
P J. Langford
P G. Medich
RP J. Coleman
RP R. Lacey

OAK 1978 A

M B. Winkles
M J. McKeon
1B D. Revering
2B M. Edwards
SS M. Guerrero
3B W. Gross
OF M. Page
OF M. Dilone
OF A. Armas
C J. Essian
DH G. Alexander
UT T. Duncan
UT J. Newman
P M. Keough
P J. Johnson
P J. Langford
P P. Broberg
P S. Renko
RP D. Heaverlo
RP R. Lacey

OAK 1979 A

M R. Marshall
1B D. Revering
2B M. Edwards
SS R. Picciolo
3B W. Gross
OF D. Murphy
OF L. Murray
OF R. Henderson
C J. Newman
DH M. Page
UT J. Essian
P J. Langford
P S. McCatty
P M. Keough
P M. Norris
P C. Minetto
RP D. Heaverlo
RP D. Hamilton

OAK 1980 A

M A. Martin
1B D. Revering
2B D. McKay
SS M. Guerrero
3B W. Gross
OF D. Murphy
OF A. Armas
OF R. Henderson
C J. Essian
DH M. Page
UT J. Newman
P J. Langford
P M. Norris
P M. Keough
P S. McCatty
P B. Kingman
RP R. Lacey

OAK 1981 A

M A. Martin
1B J. Spencer
2B M. Babitt
SS R. Picciolo
3B W. Gross
OF A. Armas
OF R. Henderson
OF D. Murphy
C M. Heath
DH C. Johnson
UT D. McKay
UT J. Newman
P J. Langford
P S. McCatty
P M. Norris
P M. Keough
P B. Kingman
RP J. Jones
RP R. Owchinko

OAK 1982 A

M A. Martin
1B D. Meyer
2B D. Lopes
SS F. Stanley
3B W. Gross
OF D. Murphy
OF R. Henderson
OF A. Armas
C M. Heath
DH C. Johnson
UT J. Burroughs
P J. Langford
P M. Keough
P M. Norris
P S. McCatty
P B. Kingman
RP T. Underwood
RP R. Owchinko

OAK 1983 A

M S. Boros
1B W. Gross
2B D. Lopes
SS K. Phillips
3B C. Lansford
OF R. Henderson
OF D. Murphy
OF M. Davis
C R. Kearney
DH J. Burroughs
UT W. Almon
UT R. Hancock
P C. Codiroli
P S. McCatty
P T. Conroy
P W. Krueger
RP T. Underwood
RP T. Burgmeier

OAK 1984 A

M S. Boros
M J. Moore
1B B. Bochte
2B J. Morgan
SS K. Phillips
3B C. Lansford
OF D. Murphy
OF R. Henderson
OF M. Davis
C M. Heath
DH D. Kingman
UT W. Almon
P B. Burris
P L. Sorensen
P S. McCatty
P W. Krueger
P C. Young
RP K. Atherton
RP W. Caudill

OAK 1985 A

M J. Moore
1B B. Bochte
2B D. Hill
SS A. Griffin
3B C. Lansford
OF M. Davis
OF D. Murphy
OF D. Collins
C M. Heath
DH D. Kingman
UT J. Baker
P C. Codiroli
P D. Sutton
P W. Krueger
P T. Birtsas
RP K. Atherton
RP J. Howell

OAK 1986 A

M J. Moore
M J. Newman
M A. LaRussa
1B B. Bochte
2B K. Phillips
SS A. Griffin
3B C. Lansford
OF J. Canseco
OF M. Davis
OF D. Murphy
C M. Tettleton
DH D. Kingman
UT D. Hill
P C. Young
P J. Rijo
P J. Andujar
P D. Stewart
P E. Plunk
RP W. Mooneyham
RP S. Ontiveros

OAK 1987 A

M A. LaRussa
1B M. McGwire
2B K. Phillips
SS A. Griffin
3B C. Lansford
OF J. Canseco
OF M. Davis
OF L. Polonia
C T. Steinbach
DH R. Jackson
P D. Stewart
P C. Young
P S. Ontiveros
RP W. Nelson
RP D. Eckersley

OAK 1988 A

M A. LaRussa
1B M. McGwire
2B G. Hubbard
SS W. Weiss
3B C. Lansford
OF D. Henderson
OF S. Javier
OF L. Polonia
C R. Hassey
DH D. Baylor
UT J. Canseco
UT M. Gallego
UT D. Parker
UT T. Steinbach
P D. Stewart
P R. Welch
P G. Davis
P C. Young
P T. Burns
RP W. Nelson
RP F. Honeycutt

Philadelphia

CEN n 1875 Centennials
PHI n 1873-1875 White Stockings
ATH n 1871-1875 Athletics
PHI N 1876
PHI U 1884
PHI P 1890
PHI a 1882-1891
PHI A 1901-1954 Moved to Kansas City
PHI N 1883-1988

CEN 1875 n

M W. Craver
1B J. Abadie
2B E. Somerville
SS W. Craver
3B G. Trenwith
OF F. Warner
OF F. Treacey
OF C. Mason
C T. McGinley
P G. Bechtel

PHI 1873 n

M R. Addy
M J. Wood
1B D. Mack
2B J. Wood
SS C. Fulmer
3B L. Meyerle
OF F. Treacey
OF E. Cuthbert
OF G. Bechtel
C F. Malone
P G. Zettlein

PHI 1874 n

M W. Craver
1B D. Mack
2B W. Craver
SS C. Fulmer
3B J. Holdsworth
OF D. Eggler
OF T. York
OF G. Bechtel
C N. Hicks
P W. Cummings

PHI 1875 n

M M. McGeary
1B T. Murnane
2B L. Meyerle
SS C. Fulmer
3B M. McGeary
OF R. Addy
OF J. McMullin
OF F. Treacey
C C. Snyder
P W. Fisher
P G. Zettlein
P J. Borden

ATH 1871 n

M J. McBride
1B W. Fisler
2B A. Reach
SS J. Radcliff
3B L. Meyerle
OF E. Cuthbert
OF J. Sensenderfer
OF G. Heubel
C F. Malone
UT G. Bechtel
P J. McBride

ATH 1872 n

M J. McBride
1B D. Mack
2B W. Fisler
SS M. McGeary
3B A. Anson
OF F. Treacey
OF E. Cuthbert
OF L. Meyerle
C F. Malone
P J. McBride

ATH 1873 n

M J. McBride
1B A. Anson
2B W. Fisler
SS M. McGeary
3B E. Sutton
OF J. McMullin
OF W. Fisher
OF T. Murnane
C J. Clapp
P J. McBride

ATH 1874 n

M J. McBride
1B W. Fisler
2B J. Battin
SS M. McGeary
3B E. Sutton
OF J. McMullin
OF A. Gedney
OF A. Reach
C J. Clapp
UT A. Anson
P J. McBride

ATH 1875 n

M J. McBride
M A. Anson
1B W. Fisler
2B W. Craver
SS D. Force
3B E. Sutton
OF G. Hall
OF D. Eggler
OF G. Bechtel
C J. Clapp
UT A. Anson
P J. McBride
P A. Knight

PHI 1876 N

M A. Wright
1B E. Sutton
2B W. Fisler
SS D. Force
3B L. Meyerle
OF G. Hall
OF D. Eggler
OF W. Coon
C F. Malone
P A. Knight
P G. Zettlein

PHI 1884 U

M F. Malone
1B J. McGuinness
2B E. Peak
SS H. Easterday
3B J. McCormick
OF W. Kienzle
OF J. Flynn
OF W. Hoover
C T. Gillen
UT J. Clements
P E. Bakely
P S. Weaver
P Fisher

PHI 1890 P

M J. Fogarty
M C. Buffinton
1B S. Farrar
2B J. Pickett
SS W. Shindle
3B J. Mulvey
OF G. Wood
OF M. Griffin
OF J. Fogarty
C J. Milligan
UT W. Hallman
P A. Sanders
P P. Knell
P C. Buffinton
P W. Husted
P E. Cunningham

PHI 1882 a

M G. Latham
1B G. Latham
2B J. Stricker
SS L. Say
3B R. Blakiston
OF A. Birchall
OF J. Dorgan
OF J. Mansell
C J. O'Brien
P S. Weaver
P C. Sweeney
P F. Mountain

PHI 1883 a

M A. Knight
1B H. Stovey
2B J. Stricker
SS M. Moynahan
3B G. Bradley
OF A. Birchall
OF A. Knight
OF R. Blakiston
C J. O'Brien
UT F. Corey
P R. Mathews
P D. Jones
P E. Bakely

PHI 1884 a

M A. Knight
1B H. Stovey
2B J. Stricker
SS S. Houck
3B F. Corey
OF A. Knight
OF H. Larkin
OF A. Birchall
C J. Milligan
P R. Mathews
P W. Taylor
P A. Atkinson

PHI 1885 a

M H. Stovey
1B H. Stovey
2B J. Stricker
SS S. Houck
3B F. Corey
OF H. Larkin
OF J. Coleman
OF W. Purcell
C J. Milligan
P R. Mathews
P T. Lovett
P E. Knouff
P E. Cushman

PHI 1886 a

M L. Simmons
M W. Sharsig
1B H. Stovey
2B L. Bierbauer
SS J. McGarr
3B J. Gleason
OF H. Larkin
OF J. Coleman
OF E. Greer
C W. Robinson
UT J. O'Brien
P A. Atkinson
P R. Mathews
P W. Hart
P T. Kennedy
P J. Miller

PHI 1887 a

M F. Bancroft
M C. Mason
1B J. Milligan
2B L. Bierbauer
SS J. McGarr
3B D. Lyons
OF T. Poorman
OF H. Larkin
OF H. Stovey
C W. Robinson
P E. Seward
P A. Weyhing
P A. Atkinson

PHI 1888 a

M W. Sharsig
1B H. Larkin
2B L. Bierbauer
SS W. Gleason
3B D. Lyons
OF C. Welch
OF H. Stovey
OF T. Poorman
C W. Robinson
P E. Seward
P A. Weyhing
P M. Mattimore

PHI 1889 a

M W. Sharsig
1B H. Larkin
2B L. Bierbauer
SS F. Fennelly
3B D. Lyons
OF H. Stovey
OF W. Purcell
OF C. Welch
C W. Robinson
P A. Weyhing
P E. Seward
P J. McMahon

PHI 1890 a

M W. Sharsig
1B J. O'Brien
2B T. Shaffer
SS B. Conroy
3B D. Lyons
OF W. Purcell
OF C. Welch
OF G. Shaffer
C W. Robinson
P J. McMahon
P E. Green
P E. Seward
P C. Esper

PHI 1891 a

M W. Sharsig
M G. Wood
1B H. Larkin
2B W. Hallman
SS T. Corcoran
3B J. Mulvey
OF G. Wood
OF J. Corkhill
OF J. McTamany
C J. Milligan
UT L. Cross
P A. Weyhing
P E. Chamberlin
P W. Calihan

PHI 1901 A

M C. Mack
1B H. Davis
2B N. Lajoie
SS J. Dolan
3B L. Cross
OF D. Fultz
OF R. Seybold
OF M. McIntyre
C M. Powers
P C. Fraser
P E. Plank
P W. Bernhard
P L. Wiltse
P W. Piatt

PHI 1902 A

M C. Mack
1B H. Davis
2B D. Murphy
SS M. Cross
3B L. Cross
OF T. Hartsel
OF R. Seybold
OF D. Fultz
C Schreckengost
P E. Plank
P G. Waddell
P B. Husting
P L. Wiltse
P F. Mitchell

PHI 1903 A

M C. Mack
1B H. Davis
2B D. Murphy
SS M. Cross
3B L. Cross
OF O. Pickering
OF R. Seybold
OF T. Hartsel
C Schreckengost
P E. Plank
P G. Waddell
P C. Bender
P W. Henley

PHI 1904 A

M C. Mack
1B H. Davis
2B D. Murphy
SS M. Cross
3B L. Cross
OF T. Hartsel
OF R. Seybold
OF O. Pickering
C Schreckengost
P G. Waddell
P E. Plank
P W. Henley
P C. Bender

PHI 1905 A

M C. Mack
1B H. Davis
2B D. Murphy
SS J. Knight
3B L. Cross
OF T. Hartsel
OF R. Seybold
OF D. Hoffman
C Schreckengost
P E. Plank
P G. Waddell
P A. Coakley
P C. Bender
P W. Henley

PHI 1906 A

M C. Mack
1B H. Davis
2B D. Murphy
SS M. Cross
3B J. Knight
OF T. Hartsel
OF B. Lord
OF R. Seybold
C Schreckengost
UT H. Armbruster
P G. Waddell
P C. Bender
P J. Dygert
P E. Plank
P J. Coombs

PHI 1907 A

M C. Mack
1B H. Davis
2B D. Murphy
SS S. Nicholls
3B J. Collins
OF R. Seybold
OF T. Hartsel
OF R. Oldring
C Schreckengost
P E. Plank
P G. Waddell
P J. Dygert
P C. Bender
P J. Coombs

PHI 1908 A

M C. Mack
1B H. Davis
2B E. Collins
SS S. Nicholls
3B J. Collins
OF T. Hartsel
OF R. Oldring
OF D. Murphy
C Schreckengost
P H. Vickers
P E. Plank
P J. Dygert
P C. Bender
P V. Schlitzer

PHI 1909 A

M C. Mack
1B H. Davis
2B E. Collins
SS J. Barry
3B J. Baker
OF D. Murphy
OF R. Oldring
OF R. Ganley
C I. Thomas
P E. Plank
P C. Bender
P H. Morgan
P H. Krause
P J. Coombs

PHI 1910 A

M C. Mack
1B H. Davis
2B E. Collins
SS J. Barry
3B J. Baker
OF D. Murphy
OF R. Oldring
OF T. Hartsel
C J. Lapp
P J. Coombs
P H. Morgan
P E. Plank
P C. Bender
P H. Krause

PHI 1911 A

M C. Mack
1B J. McInnis
2B E. Collins
SS J. Barry
3B J. Baker
OF D. Murphy
OF B. Lord
OF R. Oldring
C I. Thomas
P J. Coombs
P E. Plank
P H. Morgan
P C. Bender
P H. Krause

PHI 1912 A

M C. Mack
1B J. McInnis
2B E. Collins
SS J. Barry
3B J. Baker
OF A. Strunk
OF R. Oldring
OF B. Lord
C J. Lapp
P J. Coombs
P E. Plank
P C. Brown
P B. Houck
P C. Bender
RP H. Pennock

PHI 1913 A

M C. Mack
1B J. McInnis
2B E. Collins
SS J. Barry
3B J. Baker
OF J. Murphy
OF R. Oldring
OF J. Walsh
C J. Lapp
UT A. Strunk
P E. Plank
P C. Bender
P C. Brown
P L. Bush
P B. Houck

PHI 1914 A

M C. Mack
1B J. McInnis
2B E. Collins
SS J. Barry
3B J. Baker
OF J. Murphy
OF A. Strunk
OF R. Oldring
C W. Schang
P J. Shawkey
P L. Bush
P J. Wyckoff
P E. Plank
P C. Bender

PHI 1915 A

M C. Mack
1B J. McInnis
2B N. Lajoie
SS W. Kopf
3B W. Schang
OF A. Strunk
OF J. Walsh
OF R. Oldring
C J. Lapp
P J. Wyckoff
P R. Bressler
P L. Bush
P T. Sheehan
P T. Knowlson

PHI 1916 A

M C. Mack
1B J. McInnis
2B N. Lajoie
SS L. Witt
3B C. Pick
OF A. Strunk
OF J. Walsh
OF W. Schang
C W. Meyer
P E. Myers
P L. Bush
P H. Nabors
P T. Sheehan

PHI 1917 A

M C. Mack
1B J. McInnis
2B R. Grover
SS L. Witt
3B R. Bates
OF A. Strunk
OF F. Bodie
OF C. Jamieson
C W. Schang
P L. Bush
P A. Schauer
P E. Myers
P R. Johnson
P W. Noyes

PHI 1918 A

M C. Mack
1B G. Burns
2B J. Dykes
SS J. Dugan
3B W. Gardner
OF C. Walker
OF C. Jamieson
OF M. Kopp
C J. McAvoy
P H. Perry
P S. Gregg
P J. Adams
P J. Watson
P E. Myers

PHI 1919 A

M C. Mack
1B G. Burns
2B L. Witt
SS J. Dugan
3B F. Thomas
OF C. Walker
OF M. Kopp
OF A. Strunk
C R. Perkins
P R. Naylor
P W. Kinney
P R. Johnson
P H. Perry
P T. Rogers

PHI 1920 A

M C. Mack
1B I. Griffin
2B J. Dykes
SS C. Galloway
3B F. Thomas
OF C. Walker
OF F. Welch
OF A. Strunk
C R. Perkins
UT J. Dugan
P H. Perry
P R. Naylor
P W. Harriss
P E. Rommel
P R. Moore

PHI 1921 A

M C. Mack
1B J. Walker
2B J. Dykes
SS C. Galloway
3B J. Dugan
OF L. Witt
OF C. Walker
OF F. Welch
C R. Perkins
P E. Rommel
P W. Harriss
P R. Moore
P R. Hasty
P D. Keefe
RP H. Freeman

PHI 1922 A

M C. Mack
1B J. Hauser
2B R. Young
SS C. Galloway
3B J. Dykes
OF C. Walker
OF E. Miller
OF F. Welch
C R. Perkins
UT F. McGowan
P E. Rommel
P W. Harriss
P R. Hasty
P F. Heimach
P R. Naylor
RP J. Sullivan
RP C. Eckert

PHI 1923 A

M C. Mack
1B J. Hauser
2B J. Dykes
SS C. Galloway
3B S. Hale
OF W. Matthews
OF E. Miller
OF F. Welch
C R. Perkins
UT F. McGowan
P E. Rommel
P R. Hasty
P W. Harriss
P F. Heimach
P R. Naylor

PHI 1924 A

M C. Mack
1B J. Hauser
2B M. Bishop
SS C. Galloway
3B H. Riconda
OF A. Simmons
OF E. Miller
OF W. Lamar
C R. Perkins
UT J. Dykes
UT F. Welch
P E. Rommel
P F. Heimach
P S. Baumgartner
P D. Burns
P S. Gray
RP R. Hasty

PHI 1925 A

M C. Mack
1B J. Poole
2B M. Bishop
SS C. Galloway
3B S. Hale
OF A. Simmons
OF W. Lamar
OF E. Miller
C G. Cochrane
UT J. Dykes
P E. Rommel
P W. Harriss
P S. Gray
P R. Grove
P G. Walberg

PHI 1926 A

M C. Mack
1B J. Poole
2B M. Bishop
SS C. Galloway
3B J. Dykes
OF A. Simmons
OF W. Lamar
OF W. French
C G. Cochrane
UT S. Hale
UT J. Hauser
P R. Grove
P E. Rommel
P J. Quinn
P G. Walberg
P S. Gray
RP J. Pate

PHI 1927 A

M C. Mack
1B J. Dykes
2B M. Bishop
SS J. Boley
3B S. Hale
OF T. Cobb
OF A. Simmons
OF W. French
C G. Cochrane
UT E. Collins
P R. Grove
P G. Walberg
P J. Quinn
P H. Ehmke
P E. Rommel
RP J. Pate

PHI 1928 A

M C. Mack
1B J. Hauser
2B M. Bishop
SS J. Boley
3B S. Hale
OF E. Miller
OF A. Simmons
OF T. Cobb
C G. Cochrane
UT J. Foxx
P R. Grove
P G. Walberg
P J. Quinn
P E. Rommel
P G. Earnshaw

PHI 1929 A

M C. Mack
1B J. Foxx
2B M. Bishop
SS J. Boley
3B S. Hale
OF E. Miller
OF A. Simmons
OF G. Haas
C G. Cochrane
UT J. Dykes
P R. Grove
P G. Walberg
P G. Earnshaw
P J. Quinn
P W. Shores

PHI 1930 A

M C. Mack
1B J. Foxx
2B M. Bishop
SS J. Boley
3B J. Dykes
OF E. Miller
OF A. Simmons
OF G. Haas
C G. Cochrane
P G. Earnshaw
P R. Grove
P G. Walberg
P W. Shores
P L. Mahaffey
RP J. Quinn

PHI 1931 A

M C. Mack
1B J. Foxx
2B M. Bishop
SS E. Williams
3B J. Dykes
OF E. Miller
OF A. Simmons
OF G. Haas
C G. Cochrane
P G. Walberg
P R. Grove
P G. Earnshaw
P L. Mahaffey
P E. Rommel

PHI 1932 A

M C. Mack
1B J. Foxx
2B M. Bishop
SS D. McNair
3B J. Dykes
OF A. Simmons
OF G. Haas
OF R. Cramer
C G. Cochrane
UT E. Miller
P R. Grove
P G. Walberg
P G. Earnshaw
P L. Mahaffey
P A. Freitas
RP L. Krausse

PHI 1933 A

M C. Mack
1B J. Foxx
2B M. Bishop
SS E. Williams
3B M. Higgins
OF R. Cramer
OF R. Johnson
OF P. Coleman
C G. Cochrane
P R. Grove
P M. Cain
P G. Walberg
P L. Mahaffey
P G. Earnshaw
RP J. Peterson

PHI 1934 A

M C. Mack
1B J. Foxx
2B H. Warstler
SS D. McNair
3B M. Higgins
OF R. Cramer
OF R. Johnson
OF P. Coleman
C C. Berry
P J. Marcum
P M. Cain
P W. Dietrich
P J. Cascarella
P J. Benton

PHI 1935 A

M C. Mack
1B J. Foxx
2B H. Warstler
SS D. McNair
3B M. Higgins
OF R. Cramer
OF R. Johnson
OF W. Moses
C P. Richards
UT L. Finney
P J. Marcum
P W. Dietrich
P G. Blaeholder
P V. Wilshere
P L. Mahaffey
RP J. Benton
RP G. Caster

PHI 1936 A

M C. Mack
1B L. Finney
2B H. Warstler
SS L. Newsome
3B M. Higgins
OF W. Moses
OF R. Johnson
OF G. Puccinelli
C F. Hayes
UT A. Dean
P H. Kelley
P J. Rhodes
P L. Ross
P H. Fink
RP R. Gumpert

PHI 1937 A

M C. Mack
M E. Mack
1B A. Dean
2B R. Peters
SS L. Newsome
3B W. Werber
OF W. Moses
OF R. Johnson
OF J. Hill
C E. Brucker
P G. Caster
P H. Kelley
P E. Smith
P L. Thomas
P L. Ross
RP H. Fink
RP G. Turbeville

PHI 1938 A

M C. Mack
1B L. Finney
2B D. Lodigiani
SS W. Ambler
3B W. Werber
OF R. Johnson
OF W. Moses
OF S. Chapman
C F. Hayes
P G. Caster
P L. Thomas
P L. Nelson
P L. Ross
P E. Smith

PHI 1939 A

M C. Mack
M E. Mack
1B R. Siebert
2B J. Gantenbein
SS L. Newsome
3B D. Lodigiani
OF R. Johnson
OF S. Chapman
OF W. Moses
C F. Hayes
UT W. Ambler
UT W. Miles
UT W. Nagel
P L. Nelson
P N. Potter
P L. Ross
P W. Beckmann
P G. Caster
RP A. Dean

PHI 1940 A

M C. Mack
1B R. Siebert
2B B. McCoy
SS A. Brancato
3B A. Rubeling
OF R. Johnson
OF W. Moses
OF S. Chapman
C F. Hayes
P J. Babich
P N. Potter
P G. Caster
P A. Dean
P L. Ross
RP E. Heusser

PHI 1941 A
M C. Mack · 1B R. Siebert · 2B B. McCoy · SS A. Brancato · 3B P. Suder · OF S. Chapman · OF R. Johnson · OF W. Moses · C F. Hayes · P P. Marchildon · P J. Knott · P L. McCrabb · P C. Harris · P W. Beckmann

PHI 1942 A
M C. Mack · 1B R. Siebert · 2B Knickerbocker · SS P. Suder · 3B L. Blair · OF R. Johnson · OF E. Valo · OF M. Kreevich · C H. Wagner · UT W. Miles · P P. Marchildon · P R. Wolff · P C. Harris · P R. Christopher · P R. Fowler

PHI 1943 A
M C. Mack · 1B R. Siebert · 2B P. Suder · SS I. Hall · 3B E. Mayo · OF J. White · OF R. Estalella · OF J. Welaj · C H. Wagner · P J. Flores · P R. Wolff · P C. Harris · P D. Black · P O. Arntzen

PHI 1944 A
M C. Mack · 1B W. McGhee · 2B I. Hall · SS E. Busch · 3B G. Kell · OF R. Estalella · OF R. Garrison · OF J. White · C F. Hayes · UT R. Siebert · P L. Newsom · P R. Christopher · P L. Hamlin · P J. Flores · P D. Black · RP J. Berry

PHI 1945 A
M C. Mack · 1B R. Siebert · 2B I. Hall · SS E. Busch · 3B G. Kell · OF R. Estalella · OF H. Peck · OF E. Smith · C W. Rosar · P L. Newsom · P R. Christopher · P J. Flores · P W. Knerr · P D. Black · RP J. Berry

PHI 1946 A
M C. Mack · 1B G. McQuinn · 2B E. Handley · SS P. Suder · 3B H. Majeski · OF S. Chapman · OF E. Valo · OF W. McCosky · C W. Rosar · P P. Marchildon · P R. Fowler · P J. Savage · P J. Flores · P W. Knerr

PHI 1947 A
M C. Mack · 1B F. Fain · 2B P. Suder · SS E. Joost · 3B H. Majeski · OF S. Chapman · OF W. McCosky · OF E. Valo · C W. Rosar · UT G. Binks · P P. Marchildon · P R. Fowler · P W. McCahan · P J. Coleman · P J. Flores · RP R. Christopher

PHI 1948 A
M C. Mack · 1B F. Fain · 2B P. Suder · SS E. Joost · 3B H. Majeski · OF W. McCosky · OF S. Chapman · OF E. Valo · C W. Rosar · P P. Marchildon · P J. Coleman · P R. Fowler · P C. Scheib · P L. Brissie · RP C. Harris · RP J. Savage

PHI 1949 A
M C. Mack · 1B F. Fain · 2B P. Suder · SS E. Joost · 3B H. Majeski · OF S. Chapman · OF E. Valo · OF W. Moses · C F. Guerra · P A. Kellner · P J. Coleman · P L. Brissie · P R. Fowler · P C. Scheib · RP C. Harris

PHI 1950 A
M C. Mack · 1B F. Fain · 2B W. Hitchcock · SS E. Joost · 3B R. Dillinger · OF S. Chapman · OF E. Valo · OF P. Lehner · C F. Guerra · P L. Brissie · P A. Kellner · P R. Shantz · P H. Wyse · P R. Hooper · RP C. Scheib

PHI 1951 A
M J. Dykes · 1B F. Fain · 2B P. Suder · SS E. Joost · 3B H. Majeski · OF G. Zernial · OF D. Philley · OF E. Valo · C J. Tipton · UT L. Limmer · P A. Kellner · P R. Shantz · P R. Hooper · P C. Scheib · P M. Martin · RP J. Kucab

PHI 1952 A
M J. Dykes · 1B F. Fain · 2B E. Kell · SS E. Joost · 3B W. Hitchcock · OF D. Philley · OF G. Zernial · OF E. Valo · C J. Astroth · P R. Shantz · P A. Kellner · P H. Byrd · P C. Scheib · P R. Hooper · RP J. Kucab

PHI 1953 A
M J. Dykes · 1B W. Robinson · 2B C. Michaels · SS J. DeMaestri · 3B L. Babe · OF D. Philley · OF G. Zernial · OF W. McGhee · C J. Astroth · UT P. Suder · P H. Byrd · P M. Fricano · P A. Kellner · P C. Bishop · P R. Shantz · RP M. Martin · RP F. Fanovich

PHI 1954 A
M E. Joost · 1B L. Limmer · 2B F. Jacobs · SS J. DeMaestri · 3B J. Finigan · OF W. Renna · OF V. Power · OF W. Wilson · C J. Astroth · UT D. Bollweg · UT E. Valo · UT G. Zernial · P A. Portocarrero · P A. Kellner · P M. Fricano · P R. Trice · P J. Gray · RP J. Dixon · RP E. Burtschy

PHI 1883 N
M R. Ferguson · M W. Purcell · 1B S. Farrar · 2B R. Ferguson · SS W. McClellan · 3B W. Purcell · OF J. Manning · OF F. Lewis · OF W. Harbidge · C E. Gross · P J. Coleman · P A. Hagan

PHI 1884 N
M W. Wright · 1B S. Farrar · 2B G. Andrews · SS W. McClellan · 3B J. Mulvey · OF J. Manning · OF W. Purcell · OF J. Fogarty · C J. Crowley · P C. Ferguson · P W. Vinton · P J. McElroy

PHI 1885 N
M W. Wright · 1B S. Farrar · 2B J. Myers · SS C. Bastian · 3B J. Mulvey · OF J. Manning · OF G. Andrews · OF J. Fogarty · C J. Clements · P E. Daily · P C. Ferguson · P W. Vinton

PHI 1886 N
M W. Wright · 1B S. Farrar · 2B C. Bastian · SS A. Irwin · 3B J. Mulvey · OF G. Andrews · OF G. Wood · OF J. Fogarty · C J. McGuire · UT E. Daily · P C. Ferguson · P D. Casey

PHI 1887 N
M W. Wright · 1B S. Farrar · 2B B. McLaughlin · SS A. Irwin · 3B J. Mulvey · OF J. Fogarty · OF G. Wood · OF G. Andrews · C J. Clements · P D. Casey · P C. Buffinton · P C. Ferguson

PHI 1888 N
M W. Wright · 1B S. Farrar · 2B C. Bastian · SS A. Irwin · 3B J. Mulvey · OF G. Andrews · OF J. Fogarty · OF G. Wood · C J. Clements · P C. Buffinton · P D. Casey · P A. Sanders · P W. Gleason

PHI 1889 N
M W. Wright · 1B S. Farrar · 2B J. Myers · SS W. Hallman · 3B J. Mulvey · OF S. Thompson · OF J. Fogarty · OF G. Wood · C J. Clements · P C. Buffinton · P A. Sanders · P W. Gleason · P D. Casey

PHI 1890 N
M W. Wright · M J. Clements · 1B A. McCauley · 2B J. Myers · SS R. Allen · 3B E. Mayer · OF S. Thompson · OF W. Hamilton · OF E. Burke · C J. Clements · P W. Gleason · P T. Vickery · P J. Smith

PHI 1891 N
M W. Wright · 1B W. Brown · 2B J. Myers · SS R. Allen · 3B B. Shindle · OF S. Thompson · OF W. Hamilton · OF E. Delahanty · C J. Clements · P W. Gleason · P C. Esper · P J. Thornton

PHI 1892 N
M W. Wright · 1B R. Connor · 2B W. Hallman · SS R. Allen · 3B C. Reilly · OF S. Thompson · OF W. Hamilton · OF E. Delahanty · C J. Clements · UT L. Cross · P A. Weyhing · P W. Carsey · P T. Keefe · P C. Esper

PHI 1893 N
M W. Wright · 1B J. Boyle · 2B W. Hallman · SS R. Allen · 3B C. Reilly · OF S. Thompson · OF E. Delahanty · OF W. Hamilton · C J. Clements · UT L. Cross · P A. Weyhing · P W. Carsey · P T. Keefe · P J. Taylor

PHI 1894 N
M A. Irwin · 1B J. Boyle · 2B W. Hallman · SS J. Sullivan · 3B L. Cross · OF W. Hamilton · OF S. Thompson · OF E. Delahanty · C J. Clements · UT G. Turner · P J. Taylor · P W. Carsey · P A. Weyhing · P G. Harper

PHI 1895 N
M A. Irwin · 1B J. Boyle · 2B W. Hallman · SS J. Sullivan · 3B L. Cross · OF W. Hamilton · OF S. Thompson · OF E. Delahanty · C J. Clements · P W. Carsey · P J. Taylor · P W. McGill · P A. Orth

PHI 1896 N
M W. Nash · 1B D. Brouthers · 2B W. Hallman · SS W. Hulen · 3B W. Nash · OF S. Thompson · OF E. Delahanty · OF D. Cooley · C M. Grady · UT L. Cross · P J. Taylor · P A. Orth · P W. Carsey · P J. Keener · P W. McGill

PHI 1897 N
M G. Stallings · 1B N. Lajoie · 2B L. Cross · SS S. Gillen · 3B W. Nash · OF D. Cooley · OF E. Delahanty · OF T. Dowd · C J. Boyle · UT P. Geier · P J. Taylor · P A. Orth · P J. Fifield · P G. Wheeler

PHI 1898 N
M G. Stallings · M W. Shettsline · 1B W. Douglass · 2B N. Lajoie · SS M. Cross · 3B W. Lauder · OF D. Cooley · OF E. Delahanty · OF E. Flick · C E. McFarland · P W. Piatt · P F. Donahue · P A. Orth · P J. Fifield · P G. Wheeler

PHI 1899 N
M W. Shettsline · 1B D. Cooley · 2B N. Lajoie · SS M. Cross · 3B W. Lauder · OF E. Delahanty · OF R. Thomas · OF E. Flick · C E. McFarland · UT P. Chiles · P W. Piatt · P F. Donahue · P C. Fraser · P A. Orth · P W. Bernhard

PHI 1900 N
M W. Shettsline · 1B E. Delahanty · 2B N. Lajoie · SS M. Cross · 3B H. Wolverton · OF J. Slagle · OF R. Thomas · OF E. Flick · C E. McFarland · P A. Orth · P F. Donahue · P C. Fraser · P W. Bernhard · P W. Piatt

PHI 1901 N
M W. Shettsline · 1B H. Jennings · 2B W. Hallman · SS M. Cross · 3B H. Wolverton · OF E. Flick · OF R. Thomas · OF E. Delahanty · C E. McFarland · P A. Orth · P W. Duggleby · P G. White · P J. Townsend

PHI 1902 N
M W. Shettsline · 1B H. Jennings · 2B P. Childs · SS R. Hulswitt · 3B W. Hallman · OF R. Thomas · OF J. Barry · OF G. Browne · C C. Dooin · UT W. Douglass · P G. White · P W. Duggleby · P H. Iburg · P C. Fraser

PHI 1903 N
M C. Zimmer · 1B W. Douglass · 2B W. Gleason · SS R. Hulswitt · 3B H. Wolverton · OF R. Thomas · OF J. Barry · OF W. Keister · C F. Roth · P W. Duggleby · P C. Fraser · P T. Sparks · P F. Mitchell · P J. McFetridge

PHI 1904 N
M H. Duffy · 1B J. Doyle · 2B W. Gleason · SS R. Hulswitt · 3B H. Wolverton · OF J. Titus · OF R. Thomas · OF S. Magee · C C. Dooin · UT J. Lush · P C. Fraser · P W. Duggleby · P T. Sparks · P J. Sutthoff · P J. McPherson

PHI 1905 N
M H. Duffy · 1B W. Bransfield · 2B W. Gleason · SS M. Doolan · 3B E. Courtney · OF S. Magee · OF J. Titus · OF R. Thomas · C C. Dooin · P C. Pittinger · P W. Duggleby · P T. Sparks · P F. Corridon · P C. Nichols

PHI 1906 N
M H. Duffy · 1B W. Bransfield · 2B W. Gleason · SS M. Doolan · 3B E. Courtney · OF S. Magee · OF J. Titus · OF R. Thomas · C C. Dooin · P T. Sparks · P J. Lush · P W. Duggleby · P L. Richie · P C. Pittinger

PHI 1907 N
M W. Murray · 1B W. Bransfield · 2B F. Knabe · SS M. Doolan · 3B E. Courtney · OF J. Titus · OF S. Magee · OF R. Thomas · C C. Dooin · P F. Corridon · P T. Sparks · P L. Moren · P C. Brown · P L. Richie

PHI 1908 N
M W. Murray · 1B W. Bransfield · 2B F. Knabe · SS M. Doolan · 3B E. Grant · OF W. Osborn · OF J. Titus · OF S. Magee · C C. Dooin · P G. McQuillan · P T. Sparks · P F. Corridon · P L. Richie · P L. Moren

PHI 1909 N
M W. Murray · 1B W. Bransfield · 2B F. Knabe · SS M. Doolan · 3B E. Grant · OF J. Titus · OF S. Magee · OF J. Bates · C C. Dooin · P E. Moore · P L. Moren · P G. McQuillan · P F. Corridon · P T. Sparks

PHI 1910 N
M C. Dooin · 1B W. Bransfield · 2B F. Knabe · SS M. Doolan · 3B E. Grant · OF S. Magee · OF J. Titus · OF J. Bates · C C. Dooin · P E. Moore · P G. Ewing · P L. Moren · P G. McQuillan · P W. Stack

PHI 1911 N
M C. Dooin · 1B F. Luderus · 2B F. Knabe · SS M. Doolan · 3B J. Lobert · OF J. Paskert · OF S. Magee · OF F. Beck · C C. Dooin · UT M. Walsh · P G. Alexander · P E. Moore · P G. Chalmers · P W. Burns

PHI 1912 N
- M C. Dooin
- 1B F. Luderus
- 2B F. Knabe
- SS M. Doolan
- 3B J. Lobert
- OF G. Paskert
- OF S. Magee
- OF C. Cravath
- C W. Killefer
- P G. Alexander
- P T. Seaton
- P E. Moore
- P A. Brennan
- P E. Rixey
- RP W. Shultz

PHI 1913 N
- M C. Dooin
- 1B F. Luderus
- 2B F. Knabe
- SS M. Doolan
- 3B J. Lobert
- OF C. Cravath
- OF S. Magee
- OF G. Paskert
- C W. Killefer
- P T. Seaton
- P G. Alexander
- P A. Brennan
- P E. Mayer
- P E. Rixey

PHI 1914 N
- M C. Dooin
- 1B F. Luderus
- 2B R. Byrne
- SS J. Martin
- 3B J. Lobert
- OF C. Cravath
- OF G. Paskert
- OF D. Becker
- C W. Killefer
- UT S. Magee
- P G. Alexander
- P E. Mayer
- P A. Tincup
- P R. Marshall
- P J. Oeschger

PHI 1915 N
- M P. Moran
- 1B F. Luderus
- 2B J. Niehoff
- SS D. Bancroft
- 3B R. Byrne
- OF C. Cravath
- OF G. Whitted
- OF D. Becker
- C W. Killefer
- UT G. Paskert
- P G. Alexander
- P E. Mayer
- P A. Demaree
- P E. Rixey
- P G. Chalmers

PHI 1916 N
- M P. Moran
- 1B F. Luderus
- 2B J. Niehoff
- SS D. Bancroft
- 3B M. Stock
- OF G. Paskert
- OF G. Whitted
- OF C. Cravath
- C W. Killefer
- P G. Alexander
- P E. Rixey
- P A. Demaree
- P E. Mayer
- P C. Bender
- RP G. McQuillan

PHI 1917 N
- M P. Moran
- 1B F. Luderus
- 2B J. Niehoff
- SS D. Bancroft
- 3B M. Stock
- OF G. Whitted
- OF C. Cravath
- OF G. Paskert
- C W. Killefer
- P G. Alexander
- P E. Rixey
- P J. Oeschger
- P E. Mayer
- P J. Lavender

PHI 1918 N
- M P. Moran
- 1B F. Luderus
- 2B M. McGaffigan
- SS D. Bancroft
- 3B M. Stock
- OF E. Meusel
- OF C. Cravath
- OF F. Williams
- C J. Adams
- P M. Prendergast
- P C. Hogg
- P J. Oeschger
- P W. Jacobs
- P M. Watson
- RP F. Davis

PHI 1919 N
- M J. Coombs
- M C. Cravath
- 1B F. Luderus
- 2B E. Paulette
- SS D. Bancroft
- 3B R. Blackburne
- OF E. Meusel
- OF F. Williams
- OF L. Callahan
- C J. Adams
- P G. Smith
- P H. Meadows
- P E. Rixey
- P C. Hogg
- P E. Packard

PHI 1920 N
- M C. Cravath
- 1B E. Paulette
- 2B J. Rawlings
- SS A. Fletcher
- 3B R. Miller
- OF F. Williams
- OF E. Meusel
- OF C. Stengel
- C M. Wheat
- UT J. Miller
- P E. Rixey
- P G. Smith
- P H. Meadows
- P C. Causey
- P W. Hubbell

PHI 1921 N
- M W. Donovan
- M I. Wilhelm
- 1B B. Konetchy
- 2B J. Smith
- SS F. Parkinson
- 3B R. Wrightstone
- OF F. Williams
- OF E. Meusel
- OF D. LeBourveau
- C F. Bruggy
- P J. Ring
- P G. Smith
- P W. Hubbell
- P H. Meadows
- P J. Winters

PHI 1922 N
- M I. Wilhelm
- 1B R. Leslie
- 2B F. Parkinson
- SS A. Fletcher
- 3B J. Rapp
- OF F. Williams
- OF W. Walker
- OF C. Lee
- C W. Henline
- UT R. Wrightstone
- P J. Ring
- P H. Meadows
- P G. Smith
- P W. Hubbell
- P P. Weinert

PHI 1923 N
- M A. Fletcher
- 1B W. Holke
- 2B J. Tierney
- SS J. Sand
- 3B R. Wrightstone
- OF W. Walker
- OF F. Williams
- OF J. Mokan
- C W. Henline
- UT C. Lee
- P J. Ring
- P C. Glazner
- P P. Weinert
- P C. Mitchell

- P R. Head
- RP W. Hubbell

PHI 1924 N
- M A. Fletcher
- 1B W. Holke
- 2B H. Ford
- SS J. Sand
- 3B R. Wrightstone
- OF F. Williams
- OF G. Harper
- OF J. Mokan
- C W. Henline
- UT J. Wilson
- P J. Ring
- P H. Carlson
- P W. Hubbell
- P C. Mitchell
- P C. Glazner

PHI 1925 N
- M A. Fletcher
- 1B N. Hawks
- 2B B. Friberg
- SS J. Sand
- 3B C. Huber
- OF G. Harper
- OF F. Williams
- OF G. Burns
- C J. Wilson
- UT L. Fonseca
- P J. Ring
- P H. Carlson
- P C. Mitchell
- P A. Decatur
- P E. Knight
- RP W. Betts
- RP J. Couch

PHI 1926 N
- M A. Fletcher
- 1B J. Bentley
- 2B B. Friberg
- SS J. Sand
- 3B C. Huber
- OF J. Mokan
- OF F. Leach
- OF F. Williams
- C J. Wilson
- UT W. Henline
- UT A. Nixon
- UT R. Wrightstone
- P H. Carlson
- P W. Dean
- P C. Mitchell
- P C. Willoughby
- P F. Ulrich
- RP R. Pierce
- RP E. Baecht

PHI 1927 N
- M J. McInnis
- 1B R. Wrightstone
- 2B L. Thompson
- SS J. Sand
- 3B B. Friberg
- OF F. Leach
- OF F. Williams
- OF C. Spalding
- C J. Wilson
- P J. Scott
- P J. Ferguson
- P F. Ulrich
- P H. Pruett
- P L. Sweetland
- RP C. Willoughby

PHI 1928 N
- M B. Shotton
- 1B F. Hurst
- 2B L. Thompson
- SS J. Sand
- 3B A. Whitney
- OF D. Sothern
- OF F. Leach
- OF F. Williams
- C W. Lerian
- P R. Benge
- P J. Ring
- P L. Sweetland
- P R. McGraw
- P J. Ferguson

PHI 1929 N
- M B. Shotton
- 1B F. Hurst
- 2B L. Thompson
- SS T. Thevenow
- 3B A. Whitney
- OF F. O'Doul

- OF C. Klein
- OF D. Sothern
- C W. Lerian
- UT V. Davis
- UT B. Friberg
- P C. Willoughby
- P L. Sweetland
- P R. Benge
- P P. Collins
- RP H. Elliott
- RP R. McGraw

PHI 1930 N
- M B. Shotton
- 1B F. Hurst
- 2B L. Thompson
- SS T. Thevenow
- 3B A. Whitney
- OF C. Klein
- OF F. O'Doul
- OF D. Sothern
- C V. Davis
- UT B. Friberg
- P P. Collins
- P R. Benge
- P L. Sweetland
- P C. Willoughby
- P E. Collard
- RP H. Elliott
- RP W. Smythe

PHI 1931 N
- M B. Shotton
- 1B F. Hurst
- 2B L. Mallon
- SS R. Bartell
- 3B A. Whitney
- OF C. Klein
- OF G. Brickell
- OF R. Arlett
- C V. Davis
- UT B. Friberg
- P J. Elliott
- P R. Benge
- P P. Collins
- P E. Dudley
- P F. Watt

PHI 1932 N
- M B. Shotton
- 1B F. Hurst
- 2B L. Mallon
- SS R. Bartell
- 3B A. Whitney
- OF C. Klein
- OF H. Lee
- OF G. Davis
- C V. Davis
- P E. Holley
- P R. Benge
- P R. Hansen
- P P. Collins
- P C. Rhem

PHI 1933 N
- M B. Shotton
- 1B F. Hurst
- 2B J. Warner
- SS R. Bartell
- 3B S. McLeod
- OF C. Klein
- OF C. Fullis
- OF E. Schulmerich
- C V. Davis
- P E. Holley
- P R. Hansen
- P J. Elliott
- P W. Moore
- P P. Collins
- RP A. Liska

PHI 1934 N
- M J. Wilson
- 1B A. Camilli
- 2B L. Chiozza
- SS R. Bartell
- 3B W. Walters
- OF E. Allen
- OF J. Moore
- OF G. Davis
- C A. Todd
- UT J. Wilson
- P C. Davis
- P P. Collins
- P R. Hansen
- P S. Johnson
- P W. Moore
- RP R. Grabowski
- RP G. Darrow

PHI 1935 N
- M J. Wilson
- 1B A. Camilli
- 2B L. Chiozza
- SS M. Haslin
- 3B J. Vergez
- OF E. Allen
- OF J. Moore
- OF G. Watkins
- C A. Todd
- P C. Davis
- P O. Jorgens
- P S. Johnson
- P J. Bivin
- P W. Walters
- RP J. Pezzullo
- RP R. Prim

PHI 1936 N
- M J. Wilson
- 1B A. Camilli
- 2B J. Gomez
- SS L. Norris
- 3B A. Whitney
- OF C. Klein
- OF J. Moore
- OF E. Sulik
- C R. Grace
- UT L. Chiozza
- P W. Walters
- P C. Passeau
- P J. Bowman
- P O. Jorgens
- RP S. Johnson
- RP E. Moore

PHI 1937 N
- M J. Wilson
- 1B A. Camilli
- 2B D. Young
- SS G. Scharein
- 3B A. Whitney
- OF H. Martin
- OF M. Arnovich
- OF C. Klein
- C W. Atwood
- UT E. Brown
- UT J. Moore
- UT L. Norris
- P C. Passeau
- P W. Walters
- P W. LaMaster
- P H. Mulcahy
- P S. Johnson
- RP O. Jorgens
- RP H. Kelleher

PHI 1938 N
- M J. Wilson
- M J. Lobert
- 1B P. Weintraub
- 2B E. Mueller
- SS D. Young
- 3B A. Whitney
- OF M. Arnovich
- OF C. Klein
- OF H. Martin
- C W. Atwood
- UT G. Scharein
- P H. Mulcahy
- P C. Passeau
- P A. Hollingsworth
- P A. Butcher
- RP P. Sivess
- RP A. Smith

PHI 1939 N
- M J. Prothro
- 1B A. Suhr
- 2B R. Hughes
- SS G. Scharein
- 3B M. May
- OF M. Arnovich
- OF H. Martin
- OF J. Marty
- C V. Davis
- UT G. Brack
- UT E. Mueller
- P H. Mulcahy
- P W. Higbe
- P W. Beck
- P I. Pearson
- P S. Johnson
- RP W. Kerksieck

PHI 1940 N
- M J. Prothro
- 1B A. Mahan
- 2B H. Schulte
- SS R. Bragan

- 3B M. May
- OF C. Klein
- OF J. Rizzo
- C B. Warren
- UT E. Mueller
- P W. Higbe
- P H. Mulcahy
- P I. Pearson
- P S. Johnson
- P W. Beck

PHI 1941 N
- M J. Prothro
- 1B N. Etten
- 2B D. Murtaugh
- SS R. Bragan
- 3B M. May
- OF D. Litwhiler
- OF J. Marty
- OF A. Benjamin
- C B. Warren
- UT T. Livingston
- UT J. Rizzo
- P J. Podgajny
- P T. Hughes
- P D. Blanton
- P S. Johnson
- P L. Grissom
- RP I. Pearson
- RP F. Hoerst

PHI 1942 N
- M J. Lobert
- 1B N. Etten
- 2B A. Glossop
- SS R. Bragan
- 3B M. May
- OF D. Litwhiler
- OF R. Northey
- OF E. Koy
- C B. Warren
- UT D. Murtaugh
- UT L. Waner
- P T. Hughes
- P R. Melton
- P S. Johnson
- P J. Podgajny
- P F. Hoerst
- RP I. Pearson
- RP S. Nahem

PHI 1943 N
- M S. Harris
- M F. Fitzsimmons
- 1B J. Wasdell
- 2B D. Murtaugh
- SS G. Stewart
- 3B M. May
- OF R. Northey
- OF E. Adams
- OF H. Triplett
- C T. Livingston
- UT E. Dahlgren
- P A. Gerheauser
- P J. Kraus
- P L. Rowe
- P T. Barrett
- P S. Johnson
- RP N. Kimball

PHI 1944 N
- M F. Fitzsimmons
- 1B U. Lupien
- 2B F. Mullen
- SS R. Hamrick
- 3B G. Stewart
- OF R. Northey
- OF E. Adams
- OF J. Wasdell
- C R. Finley
- UT C. Letchas
- P K. Raffensberger
- P C. Schanz
- P T. Barrett
- P W. Lee
- P A. Gerheauser
- RP A. Karl

PHI 1945 N
- M F. Fitzsimmons
- M W. Chapman
- 1B J. Wasdell
- 2B F. Daniels
- SS E. Mott
- 3B J. Antonelli
- OF V. DiMaggio
- OF H. Triplett
- OF V. Dinges
- C A. Seminick
- UT R. Monteagudo

- P T. Barrett
- P C. Schanz
- P C. Sproull
- P R. Mauney
- RP A. Karl

PHI 1946 N
- M W. Chapman
- 1B F. McCormick
- 2B E. Verban
- SS L. Newsome
- 3B J. Tabor
- OF J. Wyrostek
- OF D. Ennis
- OF R. Northey
- C A. Seminick
- P K. Raffensberger
- P T. Judd
- P L. Rowe
- P C. Schanz
- P T. Hughes
- RP A. Karl
- RP R. Mulligan

PHI 1947 N
- M W. Chapman
- 1B H. Schultz
- 2B E. Verban
- SS L. Newsome
- 3B L. Handley
- OF D. Ennis
- OF H. Walker
- OF J. Wyrostek
- C A. Seminick
- P E. Leonard
- P L. Rowe
- P T. Judd
- P K. Heintzelman
- P T. Hughes
- RP F. Schmidt

PHI 1948 N
- M W. Chapman
- M A. Cooke
- M E. Sawyer
- 1B R. Sisler
- 2B G. Hamner
- SS E. Miller
- 3B B. Caballero
- OF D. Ennis
- OF D. Ashburn
- OF J. Blatnik
- C A. Seminick
- UT B. Haas
- UT H. Walker
- P E. Leonard
- P C. Simmons
- P W. Dubiel
- P L. Rowe
- P R. Roberts
- RP E. Heusser
- RP S. Nahem

PHI 1949 N
- M E. Sawyer
- 1B R. Sisler
- 2B E. Miller
- SS G. Hamner
- 3B W. Jones
- OF D. Ennis
- OF D. Ashburn
- OF W. Nicholson
- C A. Seminick
- P K. Heintzelman
- P R. Roberts
- P R. Meyer
- P H. Borowy
- P C. Simmons
- RP K. Konstanty
- RP K. Trinkle

PHI 1950 N
- M E. Sawyer
- 1B E. Waitkus
- 2B M. Goliat
- SS G. Hamner
- 3B W. Jones
- OF D. Ennis
- OF D. Ashburn
- OF R. Sisler
- C A. Seminick
- P R. Roberts
- P C. Simmons
- P R. Miller
- P R. Meyer
- P E. Church
- RP C. Konstanty

PHI 1951 N
- M E. Sawyer

1B E. Waitkus
2B R. Caballero
SS G. Hamner
3B W. Jones
OF D. Ashburn
OF D. Ennis
OF R. Sisler
C A. Seminick
P R. Roberts
P E. Church
P R. Meyer
P J. Thompson
P K. Heintzelman
RP C. Konstanty

PHI 1952 N

M E. Sawyer
M S. O'Neill
1B E. Waitkus
2B C. Ryan
SS G. Hamner
3B W. Jones
OF D. Ashburn
OF D. Ennis
OF J. Wyrostek
C F. Burgess
P R. Roberts
P R. Meyer
P K. Drews
P C. Simmons
P S. Ridzik
RP C. Konstanty
RP A. Hansen

PHI 1953 N

M S. O'Neill
1B C. Torgeson
2B G. Hamner
SS T. Kazanski
3B W. Jones
OF D. Ashburn
OF D. Ennis
OF J. Wyrostek
C F. Burgess
P R. Roberts
P C. Simmons
P K. Drews
P C. Konstanty
P R. Miller
RP S. Ridzik
RP A. Hansen

PHI 1954 N

M S. O'Neill
M T. Moore
1B C. Torgeson
2B G. Hamner
SS R. Morgan
3B W. Jones
OF D. Ashburn
OF D. Ennis
OF C. Schell
C F. Burgess
P R. Roberts
P C. Simmons
P M. Dickson
P R. Miller
P H. Wehmeier
RP S. Ridzik
RP C. Konstanty

PHI 1955 N

M E. Smith
1B M. Blaylock
2B R. Morgan
SS R. Smalley
3B W. Jones
OF D. Ennis
OF D. Ashburn
OF J. Greengrass
C A. Seminick
UT G. Hamner
UT S. Lopata
P R. Roberts
P M. Dickson
P H. Wehmeier
P C. Simmons
RP J. Meyer
RP R. Miller

PHI 1956 N

M E. Smith
1B M. Blaylock
2B T. Kazanski
SS G. Hamner
3B W. Jones
OF D. Ashburn
OF D. Ennis
OF E. Valo
C S. Lopata
P R. Roberts

P H. Haddix
P C. Simmons
P S. Rogovin
P S. Miller
RP R. Miller
RP J. Meyer

PHI 1957 N

M E. Smith
1B E. Bouchee
2B G. Hamner
SS H. Fernandez
3B W. Jones
OF D. Ashburn
OF E. Repulski
OF H. Anderson
C S. Lopata
UT R. Bowman
P R. Roberts
P J. Sanford
P C. Simmons
P H. Haddix
P D. Cardwell
RP R. Farrell
RP J. Hearn

PHI 1958 N

M E. Smith
M E. Sawyer
1B E. Bouchee
2B S. Hemus
SS H. Fernandez
3B W. Jones
OF D. Ashburn
OF W. Post
OF H. Anderson
C S. Lopata
UT T. Kazanski
P R. Roberts
P R. Semproch
P J. Sanford
P C. Simmons
P D. Cardwell
RP R. Farrell
RP J. Meyer

PHI 1959 N

M E. Sawyer
1B E. Bouchee
2B G. Anderson
SS J. Koppe
3B E. Freese
OF D. Ashburn
OF H. Anderson
OF W. Post
C C. Sawatski
UT D. Philley
P R. Roberts
P J. Owens
P D. Conley
P D. Cardwell
P R. Semproch
RP J. Meyer
RP H. Robinson

PHI 1960 N

M E. Sawyer
M A. Cohen
M G. Mauch
1B J. Herrera
2B A. Taylor
SS R. Amaro
3B A. Dark
OF K. Walters
OF R. Del Greco
OF J. Callison
C J. Coker
UT G. Curry
UT B. Smith
P R. Roberts
P J. Buzhardt
P D. Conley
P J. Owens
P G. Green
RP C. Short
RP R. Farrell

PHI 1961 N

M G. Mauch
1B J. Herrera
2B A. Taylor
SS R. Amaro
3B C. Smith
OF J. Callison
OF A. Gonzalez
OF D. Demeter
C C. Dalrymple
UT R. Malkmus
P A. Mahaffey
P J. Buzhardt
P F. Sullivan

P D. Ferrarese
P G. Green
RP J. Baldschun
RP K. Lehman

PHI 1962 N

M G. Mauch
1B R. Sievers
2B A. Taylor
SS R. Wine
3B D. Demeter
OF J. Callison
OF A. Gonzalez
OF T. Savage
C C. Dalrymple
UT J. Covington
UT W. Klaus
UT F. Torre
P A. Mahaffey
P J. Hamilton
P D. Bennett
P C. McLish
P C. Short
RP J. Baldschun
RP P. Brown

PHI 1963 N

M G. Mauch
1B R. Sievers
2B A. Taylor
SS R. Wine
3B D. Hoak
OF J. Callison
OF A. Gonzalez
OF D. Demeter
C C. Dalrymple
UT R. Amaro
UT J. Covington
P C. McLish
P R. Culp
P C. Short
P A. Mahaffey
P G. Green
RP J. Baldschun
RP J. Klippstein

PHI 1964 N

M G. Mauch
1B J. Herrnstein
2B A. Taylor
SS R. Wine
3B R. Allen
OF J. Callison
OF A. Gonzalez
OF J. Covington
C C. Dalrymple
UT R. Amaro
UT O. Rojas
P J. Bunning
P C. Short
P D. Bennett
P A. Mahaffey
P R. Culp
RP J. Baldschun
RP E. Roebuck

PHI 1965 N

M G. Mauch
1B R. Stuart
2B A. Taylor
SS R. Wine
3B R. Allen
OF J. Callison
OF A. Gonzalez
OF A. Johnson
C C. Dalrymple
UT R. Amaro
UT J. Covington
UT O. Rojas
P C. Short
P J. Bunning
P R. Culp
P R. Herbert
P R. Belinsky
RP G. Wagner
RP J. Baldschun

PHI 1966 N

M G. Mauch
1B W. White
2B O. Rojas
SS R. Groat
3B R. Allen
OF J. Callison
OF A. Gonzalez
OF J. Brandt
C C. Dalrymple
UT A. Taylor
P J. Bunning
P C. Short
P L. Jackson

P R. Buhl
P R. Culp
RP D. Knowles
RP R. Herbert

PHI 1967 N

M G. Mauch
1B W. White
2B O. Rojas
SS R. Wine
3B R. Allen
OF J. Callison
OF A. Gonzalez
OF D. Lock
C C. Dalrymple
UT J. Briggs
UT G. Sutherland
UT A. Taylor
P J. Bunning
P L. Jackson
P C. Short
P R. Wise
P R. Ellsworth
RP R. Farrell
RP R. Hall

PHI 1968 N

M G. Mauch
M G. Myatt
M R. Skinner
1B W. White
2B O. Rojas
SS R. Pena
3B A. Taylor
OF R. Allen
OF A. Gonzalez
OF J. Callison
C M. Ryan
UT J. Briggs
UT D. Lock
P C. Short
P L. Jackson
P W. Fryman
P R. Wise
P J. James
RP R. Farrell
RP G. Wagner

PHI 1969 N

M R. Skinner
M G. Myatt
1B R. Allen
2B O. Rojas
SS D. Money
3B A. Taylor
OF L. Hisle
OF J. Callison
OF J. Briggs
C M. Ryan
UT D. Johnson
UT R. Joseph
UT H. Stone
P G. Jackson
P W. Fryman
P R. Wise
P J. Johnson
P B. Champion
RP J. Boozer
RP R. Farrell

PHI 1970 N

M F. Lucchesi
1B D. Johnson
2B R. Doyle
SS L. Bowa
3B D. Money
OF L. Hisle
OF H. Stone
OF J. Briggs
C M. Ryan
UT B. Browne
UT A. Taylor
P R. Wise
P J. Bunning
P C. Short
P G. Jackson
P B. Lersch
RP R. Selma
RP L. Palmer

PHI 1971 N

M F. Lucchesi
1B D. Johnson
2B R. Doyle
SS L. Bowa
3B J. Vukovich
OF G. Montanez
OF R. Freed
OF O. Gamble
C J. McCarver
UT D. Money

P R. Wise
P B. Lersch
P C. Short
P K. Reynolds
P W. Fryman
RP B. Champion
RP D. Brandon

PHI 1972 N

M F. Lucchesi
M P. Owens
1B T. Hutton
2B R. Doyle
SS L. Bowa
3B D. Money
OF G. Luzinski
OF G. Montanez
OF W. Robinson
C J. Bateman
UT D. Johnson
P S. Carlton
P L. Jackson
P C. Short
P W. Fryman
RP W. Twitchell
RP D. Brandon

PHI 1973 N

M D. Ozark
1B G. Montanez
2B R. Doyle
SS L. Bowa
3B M. Schmidt
OF G. Luzinski
OF W. Unser
OF W. Robinson
C B. Boone
UT T. Hutton
UT C. Tovar
P S. Carlton
P W. Twitchell
P K. Brett
P J. Lonborg
P R. Ruthven
RP B. Lersch
RP G. Scarce

PHI 1974 N

M D. Ozark
1B G. Montanez
2B D. Cash
SS L. Bowa
3B M. Schmidt
OF D. Unser
OF M. Anderson
OF W. Robinson
C R. Boone
P S. Carlton
P J. Lonborg
P R. Ruthven
P R. Schueler
P W. Twitchell
RP G. Scarce
RP H. Garber

PHI 1975 N

M D. Ozark
1B R. Allen
2B D. Cash
SS L. Bowa
3B M. Schmidt
OF G. Luzinski
OF G. Maddox
OF J. Johnstone
C R. Boone
UT T. Hutton
UT G. Maddox
P S. Carlton
P T. Underwood
P L. Christenson
P J. Lonborg
P W. Twitchell
RP H. Garber
RP F. McGraw

PHI 1976 N

M D. Ozark
1B R. Allen
2B D. Cash
SS L. Bowa
3B M. Schmidt
OF G. Matthews
OF G. Maddox
OF A. McBride
C R. Boone
UT G. Gross
UT L. Smith
P S. Carlton
P R. Ruthven
P L. Christenson
P A. Espinosa
RP A. Lyle
RP M. Proly

P T. Underwood
RP R. Reed
RP F. McGraw

PHI 1977 N

M D. Ozark
1B R. Hebner
2B T. Sizemore
SS L. Bowa
3B M. Schmidt
OF G. Luzinski
OF G. Maddox
OF J. Martin
C B. Boone
UT T. Hutton
UT J. Johnstone
P S. Carlton
P L. Christenson
P R. Lerch
P J. Kaat
P J. Lonborg
RP R. Reed
RP H. Garber

PHI 1978 N

M D. Ozark
1B R. Hebner
2B T. Sizemore
SS L. Bowa
3B M. Schmidt
OF G. Maddox
OF G. Luzinski
OF A. McBride
C R. Boone
UT J. Martin
P S. Carlton
P L. Christenson
P R. Lerch
P R. Ruthven
P J. Kaat
RP R. Reed
RP F. McGraw

PHI 1979 N

M D. Ozark
M G. Green
1B P. Rose
2B J. Trillo
SS L. Bowa
3B M. Schmidt
OF A. McBride
OF G. Maddox
OF G. Luzinski
C R. Boone
UT G. Gross
P S. Carlton
P R. Lerch
P A. Espinosa
P R. Ruthven
P L. Christenson
RP R. Reed
RP F. McGraw

PHI 1980 N

M G. Green
1B P. Rose
2B J. Trillo
SS L. Bowa
3B M. Schmidt
OF G. Maddox
OF A. McBride
OF G. Luzinski
C R. Boone
UT G. Gross
UT L. Smith
P S. Carlton
P R. Ruthven
P R. Walk
P R. Lerch
RP F. McGraw
RP R. Reed

PHI 1981 N

M G. Green
1B P. Rose
2B J. Trillo
SS L. Bowa
3B M. Schmidt
OF G. Matthews
OF G. Maddox
OF A. McBride
C R. Boone
UT G. Gross
P S. Carlton
P R. Ruthven
P L. Christenson
P A. Espinosa
RP A. Lyle
RP M. Proly

PHI 1982 N

M P. Corrales
1B P. Rose
2B J. Trillo
SS I. DeJesus
3B M. Schmidt
OF G. Matthews
OF R. Dernier
OF G. Maddox
C B. Diaz
UT G. Gross
UT G. Vukovich
P S. Carlton
P L. Christenson
P M. Krukow
P R. Ruthven
RP R. Reed
RP E. Farmer

PHI 1983 N

M P. Corrales
M P. Owens
1B P. Rose
2B J. Morgan
SS I. DeJesus
3B M. Schmidt
OF G. Matthews
OF G. Gross
OF R. Dernier
C B. Diaz
UT V. Hayes
UT J. Lefebvre
P S. Carlton
P J. Denny
P C. Hudson
P M. Bystrom
RP R. Reed
RP G. Hernandez

PHI 1984 N

M P. Owens
1B L. Matuszek
2B J. Samuel
SS I. DeJesus
3B M. Schmidt
OF V. Hayes
OF G. Wilson
OF S. Lezcano
C O. Virgil
UT T. Corcoran
UT G. Gross
P S. Carlton
P J. Koosman
P C. Hudson
P J. Denny
P S. Rawley
RP K. Gross
RP A. Holland

PHI 1985 N

M J. Felske
1B M. Schmidt
2B J. Samuel
SS L. Jeltz
3B R. Schu
OF G. Wilson
OF V. Hayes
OF G. Maddox
C O. Virgil
UT T. Corcoran
P J. Denny
P K. Gross
P S. Rawley
P C. Hudson
P J. Koosman
RP D. Carman
RP D. Rucker

PHI 1986 N

M J. Felske
1B V. Hayes
2B J. Samuel
SS L. Jeltz
3B M. Schmidt
OF G. Wilson
OF M. Thompson
OF G. Redus
C J. Russell
UT R. Roenicke
P K. Gross
P S. Rawley
P B. Ruffin
P C. Hudson
RP D. Carman
RP K. Tekulve

PHI 1987 N

M J. Felske
M L. Elia
1B V. Hayes

2B J. Samuel
SS L. Jeltz
3B M. Schmidt
OF G. Wilson
OF M. Thompson
OF D. James
C L. Parrish
UT G. Gross
P S. Rawley
P D. Carman
P B. Ruffin
P K. Gross
RP M. Jackson
RP K. Tekulve

PHI 1988 N

M L. Elia
M J. Vukovich
1B V. Hayes
2B J. Samuel
SS L. Jeltz
3B M. Schmidt
OF P. Bradley
OF D. James
OF M. Thompson
C L. Parrish
UT G. Gross
P K. Gross
P D. Carman
P S. Rawley
P D. Palmer
RP B. Ruffin
RP G. Harris

Pittsburgh

CP U 1884
Combined with Chicago
PIT a 1882-1886
PIT P 1890
PIT F 1914-1915
PIT N 1887-1988

CP 1884 U

M E. Hengle
M J. Battin
M J. Ellick
1B L. Schoeneck
2B E. Hengle
SS S. Matthias
3B C. Householder
OF J. Ellick
OF C. Briggs
OF H. Wheeler
C W. Krieg
P H. Daily
P A. Atkinson
P J. Horan

PIT 1882 a

M A. Pratt
1B G. Lane
2B G. Strief
SS J. Peters
3B J. Battin
OF M. Mansell
OF C. Swartwood
OF J. Leary
C W. Taylor
P H. Salisbury
P J. Driscoll
P H. Arundel

PIT 1883 a

M A. Pratt
M O. Butler
M J. Battin
1B C. Swartwood
2B G. Creamer
SS D. Mack
3B J. Battin
OF M. Mansell
OF L. Dickerson
OF W. Taylor
C J. Hayes
P J. Driscoll
P R. Barr
P J. Neagle

PIT 1884 a

M D. McKnight
M R. Ferguson
M J. Battin
M G. Creamer
M H. Phillips
1B J. Knowles
2B G. Creamer
SS W. White
3B J. Battin
OF C. Swartwood
OF G. Miller
OF G. Taylor
C W. Colgan
P F. Sullivan
P J. Neagle

PIT 1885 a

M H. Phillips
1B J. Field
2B C. Smith
SS A. Whitney
3B W. Kuehne
OF T. Brown
OF F. Mann
OF C. Eden
C F. Carroll
P E. Morris
P P. Meegan
P H. O'Day
P J. Galvin

PIT 1886 a

M H. Phillips
1B O. Schomberg
2B S. Barkley
SS C. Smith
3B A. Whitney
OF F. Mann
OF T. Brown
OF E. Glenn
C F. Carroll
UT W. Kuehne
P E. Morris
P J. Galvin
P J. Handiboe

PIT 1890 P

M E. Hanlon
1B J. Beckley
2B W. Robinson
SS T. Corcoran
3B W. Kuehne
OF J. Visner
OF E. Hanlon
OF J. Fields
C F. Carroll
P H. Staley
P A. Maul
P J. Galvin
P E. Morris
P J. Tener

PIT 1914 F

M H. Gessler
M E. Oakes
1B H. Bradley
2B J. Lewis
SS E. Holly
3B J. Lennox
OF E. Oakes
OF J. Savage
OF D. Jones
C C. Berry
P E. Knetzer
P S. Camnitz
P W. Dickson
P E. Barger
P F. Walker

PIT 1915 F

M E. Oakes
1B E. Konetchy
2B S. Yerkes
SS M. Berghammer
3B H. Mowrey
OF E. Oakes
OF J. Kelly
OF A. Wickland
C C. Berry
P F. Allen
P E. Knetzer
P F. Rogge
P B. Hearn
P E. Barger

PIT 1887 N

M H. Phillips
1B S. Barkley
2B C. Smith
SS W. Kuehne
3B A. Whitney
OF J. Coleman
OF A. Dalrymple
OF T. Brown
C G. Miller
UT F. Carroll
P J. Galvin
P J. McCormick
P E. Morris

PIT 1888 N

M H. Phillips
1B J. Beckley
2B F. Dunlap
SS C. Smith
3B W. Kuehne
OF W. Sunday
OF J. Coleman
OF A. Dalrymple
C G. Miller
UT F. Carroll
P E. Morris
P J. Galvin
P H. Staley

PIT 1889 N

M H. Phillips
M F. Dunlap
M E. Hanlon
1B J. Beckley
2B F. Dunlap
SS J. Rowe
3B W. Kuehne
OF E. Hanlon
OF W. Sunday
OF A. Maul
C G. Miller
UT F. Carroll
P H. Staley
P J. Galvin
P E. Morris

PIT 1890 N

M G. Hecker
1B G. Hecker
2B S. LaRoque
SS E. Sales
3B G. Miller
OF W. Sunday
OF J. Kelty
OF J. Berger
C E. Decker
P K. Baker
P D. Anderson
P W. Sowders

PIT 1891 N

M E. Hanlon
M W. McGunnigle
1B J. Beckley
2B L. Bierbauer
SS F. Shugarts
3B C. Reilly
OF E. Hanlon
OF F. Carroll
OF L. Browning
C C. Mack
UT G. Miller
P M. Baldwin
P C. King
P J. Galvin

PIT 1892 N

M A. Buckenberger
M T. Burns
M A. Buckenberger
1B J. Beckley
2B L. Bierbauer
SS F. Shugarts
3B C. Farrell
OF E. Smith
OF P. Donovan
OF G. Miller
C C. Mack
P M. Baldwin
P P. Ehret
P W. Terry
P J. Galvin

PIT 1893 N

M A. Buckenberger
1B J. Beckley
2B L. Bierbauer
SS J. Glasscock
3B D. Lyons
OF E. Smith
OF P. Donovan
OF G. Van Haltren
C G. Miller
P F. Killen
P P. Ehret
P W. Terry
P A. Gumbert

PIT 1894 N

M A. Buckenberger
M C. Mack
1B J. Beckley
2B L. Bierbauer
SS J. Glasscock
3B D. Lyons
OF P. Donovan
OF J. Stenzel
OF E. Smith
C C. Mack
P P. Ehret
P A. Gumbert
P F. Killen
P T. Colcolough
P J. Menefee

PIT 1895 N

M C. Mack
1B J. Beckley
2B L. Bierbauer
SS M. Cross
3B W. Clingman
OF J. Stenzel
OF P. Donovan
OF E. Smith
C W. Merritt
P E. Hawley
P W. Hart
P J. Foreman
P F. Killen
P J. Gardner

PIT 1896 N

M C. Mack
1B J. Beckley
2B R. Padden
SS F. Ely
3B D. Lyons
OF P. Donovan
OF E. Smith
OF J. Stenzel
C J. Sugden
P F. Killen
P E. Hawley
P J. Hughey
P C. Hastings

PIT 1897 N

M P. Donovan
1B H. Davis
2B R. Padden
SS F. Ely
3B J. Hoffmeister
OF E. Smith
OF P. Donovan
OF W. Brodie
C J. Sugden
P F. Killen
P E. Hawley
P J. Hughey
P C. Hastings
P J. Gardner

PIT 1898 N

M W. Watkins
1B W. Clark
2B R. Padden
SS F. Ely
3B W. Grey
OF P. Donovan
OF J. McCarthy
OF T. O'Brien
C W. Schriver
P J. Tannehill
P W. Rhines
P J. Gardner
P F. Killen
P C. Hastings

PIT 1899 N

M W. Watkins
M P. Donovan
1B W. Clark
2B J. O'Brien
SS F. Ely
3B J. Williams
OF J. McCarthy
OF P. Donovan
OF C. Beaumont
C F. Bowerman
UT T. McCreery
P S. Leever
P J. Tannehill
P T. Sparks
P W. Hoffer
P J. Chesbro

PIT 1900 N

M F. Clarke
1B D. Cooley
2B C. Ritchey
SS F. Ely
3B J. Williams
OF C. Beaumont
OF J. Wagner
OF F. Clarke
C C. Zimmer
UT T. O'Brien
P C. Phillippe
P J. Tannehill
P S. Leever
P J. Chesbro
P G. Waddell

PIT 1901 N

M F. Clarke
1B W. Bransfield
2B C. Ritchey
SS F. Ely
3B T. Leach
OF C. Beaumont
OF F. Clarke
OF A. Davis
C C. Zimmer
UT J. Wagner
P C. Phillippe
P J. Chesbro
P J. Tannehill
P S. Leever

PIT 1902 N

M F. Clarke
1B W. Bransfield
2B C. Ritchey
SS W. Conroy
3B T. Leach
OF C. Beaumont
OF F. Clarke
OF J. Wagner
C H. Smith
P J. Chesbro
P C. Phillippe
P J. Tannehill
P S. Leever
P E. Doheny

PIT 1903 N

M F. Clarke
1B W. Bransfield
2B C. Ritchey
SS J. Wagner
3B T. Leach
OF C. Beaumont
OF J. Sebring
OF F. Clarke
C E. Phelps
P C. Phillippe
P S. Leever
P E. Doheny
P W. Kennedy
P I. Wilhelm

PIT 1904 N

M F. Clarke
1B W. Bransfield
2B C. Ritchey
SS J. Wagner
3B T. Leach
OF C. Beaumont
OF J. Sebring
OF F. Clarke
C E. Phelps
P S. Leever
P P. Flaherty
P M. Lynch
P C. Phillippe
P C. Case

PIT 1905 N

M F. Clarke
1B G. Howard
2B C. Ritchey
SS J. Wagner
3B D. Brain
OF F. Clarke
OF C. Beaumont
OF O. Clymer
C H. Peitz
UT T. Leach
P C. Phillippe
P S. Leever
P C. Case
P M. Lynch
P P. Flaherty

PIT 1906 N

M F. Clarke
1B J. Nealon
2B C. Ritchey
SS J. Wagner
3B T. Sheehan
OF R. Ganley
OF F. Clarke
OF C. Beaumont
C G. Gibson
UT T. Leach
P V. Willis
P S. Leever
P A. Leifield
P C. Phillippe
P M. Lynch

PIT 1907 N

M F. Clarke
1B J. Nealon
2B E. Abbaticchio
SS J. Wagner
3B A. Storke
OF F. Clarke
OF E. Anderson
OF T. Leach
C G. Gibson
UT W. Hallman
P V. Willis
P A. Leifield
P S. Leever
P C. Phillippe
P S. Camnitz

PIT 1908 N

M F. Clarke
1B H. Swacina
2B E. Abbaticchio
SS J. Wagner
3B T. Leach
OF F. Clarke
OF J. Wilson
OF R. Thomas
C G. Gibson
P V. Willis
P N. Maddox
P S. Camnitz
P A. Leifield
P S. Leever

PIT 1909 N

M F. Clarke
1B W. Abstein
2B J. Miller
SS J. Wagner
3B W. Barbeau
OF J. Wilson
OF F. Clarke
OF T. Leach
C G. Gibson
P V. Willis
P S. Camnitz
P N. Maddox
P A. Leifield
P C. Phillippe

PIT 1910 N

M F. Clarke
1B J. Flynn
2B J. Miller
SS J. Wagner
3B R. Byrne
OF J. Wilson
OF T. Leach
OF F. Clarke
C G. Gibson
UT A. Campbell
P S. Camnitz
P C. Adams
P A. Leifield
P O. White
P C. Phillippe

PIT 1911 N

M F. Clarke
1B F. Hunter
2B J. Miller
SS J. Wagner
3B R. Byrne
OF J. Wilson
OF M. Carey
OF F. Clarke
C G. Gibson
UT T. Leach
UT W. McKechnie
P A. Leifield
P C. Adams
P S. Camnitz
P E. Steele
P C. Hendrix

PIT 1912 N

M F. Clarke
1B J. Miller
2B A. McCarthy
SS J. Wagner
3B R. Byrne
OF J. Wilson
OF M. Carey
OF M. Donlin
C G. Gibson
P C. Hendrix
P S. Camnitz
P M. O'Toole
P J. Robinson
P C. Adams

PIT 1913 N

M F. Clarke
1B J. Miller
2B J. Viox
SS J. Wagner
3B R. Byrne
OF J. Wilson
OF M. Carey
OF M. Mitchell
C M. Simon
P C. Adams
P C. Hendrix
P J. Robinson
P S. Camnitz
P M. O'Toole

PIT 1914 N

M F. Clarke
1B E. Konetchy
2B J. Viox
SS J. Wagner
3B H. Mowrey
OF M. Carey
OF J. Kelly
OF M. Mitchell
C G. Gibson
P C. Adams
P A. Cooper
P G. McQuillan
P R. Harmon
P J. Conzelman

PIT 1915 N

M F. Clarke
1B W. Johnston
2B J. Viox
SS J. Wagner
3B H. Baird
OF W. Hinchman
OF M. Carey
OF J. Collins
C G. Gibson
P R. Harmon
P A. Mamaux
P C. Adams
P A. Cooper
P E. Kantlehner
RP J. Conzelman

PIT 1916 N

M J. Callahan
1B W. Johnston
2B F. Farmer
SS J. Wagner
3B H. Baird
OF M. Carey
OF W. Hinchman
OF F. Schulte
C W. Schmidt
P A. Mamaux
P A. Cooper
P F. Miller
P R. Harmon
P E. Kantlehner

PIT 1917 N

M J. Callahan
M J. Wagner
M H. Bezdek
1B J. Wagner
2B J. Pitler
SS C. Ward
3B N. Boeckel
OF M. Carey
OF C. Bigbee
OF L. King
C W. Fischer
P A. Cooper
P W. Jacobs
P F. Miller
P B. Grimes
P R. Steele

PIT 1918 N

M H. Bezdek
1B F. Mollwitz
2B G. Cutshaw
SS J. Caton
3B W. McKechnie
OF M. Carey
OF C. Bigbee
OF W. Southworth

C W. Schmidt
P A. Cooper
P F. Miller
P R. Sanders
P E. Mayer
P R. Harmon

PIT 1919 N
M H. Bezdek
1B F. Mollwitz
2B G. Cutshaw
SS Z. Terry
3B W. Barbare
OF C. Bigbee
OF W. Southworth
OF C. Stengel
C W. Schmidt
P A. Cooper
P C. Adams
P F. Miller
P E. Hamilton
P H. Carlson

PIT 1920 N
M G. Gibson
1B C. Grimm
2B G. Cutshaw
SS J. Caton
3B G. Whitted
OF W. Southworth
OF C. Bigbee
OF M. Carey
C W. Schmidt
UT F. Nicholson
P A. Cooper
P C. Adams
P H. Carlson
P E. Hamilton
P C. Ponder

PIT 1921 N
M G. Gibson
1B C. Grimm
2B G. Cutshaw
SS W. Maranville
3B C. Barnhart
OF C. Bigbee
OF M. Carey
OF G. Whitted
C W. Schmidt
UT J. Tierney
P A. Cooper
P C. Glazner
P E. Hamilton
P C. Adams
P J. Morrison

PIT 1922 N
M G. Gibson
M W. McKechnie
1B C. Grimm
2B J. Tierney
SS W. Maranville
3B H. Traynor
OF M. Carey
OF C. Bigbee
OF E. Russell
C J. Gooch
P A. Cooper
P J. Morrison
P C. Glazner
P C. Adams
P E. Hamilton
RP M. Yellowhorse

PIT 1923 N
M W. McKechnie
1B C. Grimm
2B J. Rawlings
SS W. Maranville
3B H. Traynor
OF M. Carey
OF C. Bigbee
OF C. Barnhart
C W. Schmidt
UT E. Russell
P J. Morrison
P A. Cooper
P H. Meadows
P C. Adams
P E. Hamilton

PIT 1924 N
M W. McKechnie
1B C. Grimm
2B W. Maranville
SS F. Wright
3B H. Traynor
OF M. Carey
OF H. Cuyler

OF C. Barnhart
C J. Gooch
P A. Cooper
P R. Kremer
P J. Morrison
P H. Meadows
P E. Yde
RP E. Stone

PIT 1925 N
M W. McKechnie
1B G. Grantham
2B G. Moore
SS F. Wright
3B H. Traynor
OF H. Cuyler
OF C. Barnhart
OF M. Carey
C E. Smith
P H. Meadows
P R. Kremer
P V. Aldridge
P J. Morrison
P E. Yde
RP T. Sheehan

PIT 1926 N
M W. McKechnie
1B G. Grantham
2B H. Rhyne
SS F. Wright
3B H. Traynor
OF H. Cuyler
OF P. Waner
OF M. Carey
C E. Smith
P R. Kremer
P H. Meadows
P V. Aldridge
P E. Yde
P D. Songer

PIT 1927 N
M O. Bush
1B J. Harris
2B G. Grantham
SS F. Wright
3B H. Traynor
OF L. Waner
OF P. Waner
OF C. Barnhart
C J. Gooch
P H. Meadows
P C. Hill
P V. Aldridge
P R. Kremer
RP J. Morrison
RP M. Cvengros

PIT 1928 N
M O. Bush
1B G. Grantham
2B E. Adams
SS F. Wright
3B H. Traynor
OF L. Waner
OF P. Waner
OF G. Brickell
C C. Hargreaves
P B. Grimes
P C. Hill
P R. Kremer
P F. Fussell
P R. Dawson

PIT 1929 N
M O. Bush
M J. Ens
1B E. Sheely
2B G. Grantham
SS R. Bartell
3B H. Traynor
OF L. Waner
OF P. Waner
OF A. Comorosky
C C. Hargreaves
P B. Grimes
P E. Brame
P R. Kremer
P J. Petty
P S. Swetonic
RP C. Hill

PIT 1930 N
M J. Ens
1B A. Suhr
2B G. Grantham
SS R. Bartell
3B H. Traynor
OF A. Comorosky

OF P. Waner
OF L. Waner
C R. Hemsley
P R. Kremer
P L. French
P E. Brame
P G. Spencer
P H. Meine

PIT 1931 N
M J. Ens
1B A. Suhr
2B G. Grantham
SS T. Thevenow
3B H. Traynor
OF L. Waner
OF P. Waner
OF A. Comorosky
C E. Phillips
P H. Meine
P L. French
P R. Kremer
P G. Spencer
P E. Brame
RP J. Osborn

PIT 1932 N
M G. Gibson
1B A. Suhr
2B A. Piet
SS J. Vaughan
3B H. Traynor
OF P. Waner
OF L. Waner
OF A. Comorosky
C R. Grace
UT D. Barbee
P L. French
P W. Swift
P H. Meine
P W. Harris
P S. Swetonic
RP E. Brame

PIT 1933 N
M G. Gibson
1B A. Suhr
2B A. Piet
SS J. Vaughan
3B H. Traynor
OF P. Waner
OF F. Lindstrom
OF L. Waner
C R. Grace
P L. French
P W. Swift
P H. Meine
P S. Swetonic
P H. Smith
RP L. Chagnon
RP W. Harris

PIT 1934 N
M G. Gibson
M H. Traynor
1B A. Suhr
2B H. Lavagetto
SS J. Vaughan
3B H. Traynor
OF P. Waner
OF L. Waner
OF F. Lindstrom
C R. Grace
UT T. Thevenow
P L. French
P W. Swift
P R. Birkofer
P W. Hoyt
P C. Lucas
RP L. Chagnon
RP H. Smith

PIT 1935 N
M H. Traynor
1B A. Suhr
2B L. Young
SS J. Vaughan
3B T. Thevenow
OF F. Jensen
OF P. Waner
OF L. Waner
C T. Padden
P D. Blanton
P W. Swift
P G. Bush
P J. Weaver
P W. Hoyt

PIT 1936 N
M H. Traynor

1B A. Suhr
2B L. Young
SS J. Vaughan
3B W. Brubaker
OF F. Jensen
OF P. Waner
OF L. Waner
C T. Padden
P W. Swift
P D. Blanton
P J. Weaver
P C. Lucas
M. Brown

PIT 1937 N
M H. Traynor
1B A. Suhr
2B L. Handley
SS J. Vaughan
3B W. Brubaker
OF P. Waner
OF L. Waner
OF F. Jensen
C A. Todd
UT L. Young
P D. Blanton
P R. Bauers
P E. Brandt
P W. Swift
P J. Bowman
RP M. Brown

PIT 1938 N
M H. Traynor
1B A. Suhr
2B L. Young
SS J. Vaughan
3B L. Handley
OF P. Waner
OF L. Waner
OF J. Rizzo
C A. Todd
P R. Bauers
P J. Tobin
P D. Blanton
P R. Klinger
P W. Swift
RP M. Brown

PIT 1939 N
M H. Traynor
1B E. Fletcher
2B L. Young
SS J. Vaughan
3B L. Handley
OF P. Waner
OF L. Waner
OF J. Rizzo
C R. Mueller
UT W. Brubaker
P R. Klinger
P M. Brown
P J. Bowman
P T. Sewell
P J. Tobin

PIT 1940 N
M F. Frisch
1B E. Fletcher
2B F. Gustine
SS J. Vaughan
3B L. Handley
OF R. Elliott
OF M. Van Robays
OF V. DiMaggio
C V. Davis
UT D. Garms
P T. Sewell
P J. Bowman
P M. Brown
P K. Heintzelman
P R. Klinger
RP R. Lanahan
RP D. Mac Fayden

PIT 1941 N
M F. Frisch
1B E. Fletcher
2B F. Gustine
SS J. Vaughan
3B L. Handley
OF V. DiMaggio
OF R. Elliott
OF M. Van Robays
C A. Lopez
P T. Sewell
P A. Butcher
P K. Heintzelman
P J. Lanning
P R. Klinger

PIT 1942 N
M F. Frisch
1B E. Fletcher
2B F. Gustine
SS P. Coscarart
3B R. Elliott
OF V. DiMaggio
OF J. Wasdell
OF J. Barrett
C A. Lopez
UT E. Phelps
UT M. Van Robays
P T. Sewell
P R. Klinger
P A. Butcher
P L. Dietz
P K. Heintzelman

PIT 1943 N
M F. Frisch
1B E. Fletcher
2B P. Coscarart
SS F. Gustine
3B R. Elliott
OF V. DiMaggio
OF J. Russell
OF J. Barrett
C A. Lopez
P T. Sewell
P R. Klinger
P A. Butcher
P W. Hebert
P F. Gornicki
RP W. Brandt

PIT 1944 N
M F. Frisch
1B E. Dahlgren
2B P. Coscarart
SS F. Gustine
3B R. Elliott
OF J. Russell
OF J. Barrett
OF V. DiMaggio
C A. Lopez
UT F. Colman
P T. Sewell
P F. Ostermueller
P A. Butcher
P N. Strincevich
P E. Roe
RP X. Rescigno

PIT 1945 N
M F. Frisch
1B E. Dahlgren
2B P. Coscarart
SS F. Gustine
3B R. Elliott
OF J. Russell
OF J. Barrett
OF A. Gionfriddo
C A. Lopez
UT L. Handley
UT W. Salkeld
P E. Roe
P N. Strincevich
P T. Sewell
P A. Butcher
P A. Gerheauser
RP X. Rescigno
RP A. Cuccurullo

PIT 1946 N
M F. Frisch
M V. Davis
1B E. Fletcher
2B F. Gustine
SS W. Cox
3B L. Handley
OF R. Kiner
OF J. Russell
OF R. Elliott
C A. Lopez
P F. Ostermueller
P N. Strincevich
P K. Heintzelman
P T. Sewell
P E. Bahr
RP A. Gerheauser

PIT 1947 N
M W. Herman
M W. Burwell
1B H. Greenberg
2B J. Bloodworth
SS W. Cox
3B F. Gustine
OF R. Kiner
OF J. Russell

OF W. Westlake
C H. Howell
UT C. Rikard
P W. Higbe
P F. Ostermueller
P E. Bonham
P E. Roe
P T. Sewell
RP N. Strincevich
RP B. Singleton

PIT 1948 N
M W. Meyer
1B E. Stevens
2B D. Murtaugh
SS S. Rojek
3B F. Gustine
OF R. Kiner
OF W. Westlake
OF F. Walker
C E. Fitzgerald
UT J. Hopp
UT C. Kluttz
P R. Chesnes
P E. Riddle
P V. Lombardi
P E. Bonham
P F. Ostermueller
RP W. Higbe
RP B. Singleton

PIT 1949 N
M W. Meyer
1B J. Hopp
2B R. Basgall
SS S. Rojek
3B P. Castiglione
OF R. Kiner
OF W. Westlake
OF D. Restelli
C C. McCullough
P M. Dickson
P W. Werle
P C. Chambers
P R. Chesnes
P V. Lombardi
RP T. Sewell

PIT 1950 N
M W. Meyer
1B J. Hopp
2B D. Murtaugh
SS S. Rojek
3B F. Fernandez
OF R. Kiner
OF W. Westlake
OF D. Bell
C C. McCullough
UT P. Castiglione
P C. Chambers
P M. Dickson
P W. Werle
P W. Macdonald
P V. Law
RP V. Lombardi
RP J. Walsh

PIT 1951 N
M W. Meyer
1B R. Kiner
2B D. Murtaugh
SS G. Strickland
3B P. Castiglione
OF D. Bell
OF W. Howerton
OF G. Metkovich
C C. McCullough
P M. Dickson
P M. Queen
P R. Friend
P H. Pollet
P V. Law
RP W. Werle
RP T. Wilks

PIT 1952 N
M W. Meyer
1B A. Bartirome
2B J. Merson
SS R. Groat
3B P. Castiglione
OF R. Kiner
OF D. Bell
OF R. Del Greco
C J. Garagiola
UT C. Koshorek
UT G. Metkovich
P M. Dickson
P H. Pollet
P R. Friend
P F. Main

RP R. Kline
RP T. Wilks

PIT 1953 N
M F. Haney
1B P. Ward
2B J. O'Brien
SS E. O'Brien
3B D. O'Connell
OF F. Thomas
OF C. Abrams
OF C. Bernier
C M. Sandlock
UT R. Cole
UT P. Smith
P M. Dickson
P J. Lindell
P P. LaPalme
P R. Friend
P R. Hall
RP E. Face
RP J. Hetki

PIT 1954 N
M F. Haney
1B R. Skinner
2B R. Roberts
SS G. Allie
3B R. Cole
OF F. Thomas
OF R. Hall
OF G. Lynch
C M. Atwell
UT S. Gordon
UT P. Ward
P M. Surkont
P R. Friend
P V. Law
P R. Littlefield
P R. Purkey
RP J. Hetki

PIT 1955 N
M F. Haney
1B R. Long
2B J. O'Brien
SS R. Groat
3B G. Freese
OF F. Thomas
OF R. Clemente
OF G. Lynch
C J. Shepard
P V. Law
P R. Friend
P M. Surkont
P R. Kline
P R. Littlefield

PIT 1956 N
M R. Bragan
1B R. Long
2B W. Mazeroski
SS R. Groat
3B F. Thomas
OF R. Clemente
OF R. Walls
OF R. Virdon
C J. Shepard
UT R. Skinner
P R. Friend
P R. Kline
P V. Law
P G. Munger
RP E. Face
RP R. King

PIT 1957 N
M R. Bragan
M D. Murtaugh
1B D. Fondy
2B W. Mazeroski
SS R. Groat
3B E. Freese
OF R. Virdon
OF R. Clemente
OF R. Skinner
C H. Foiles
UT E. Baker
UT F. Thomas
P R. Friend
P R. Kline
P R. Purkey
P V. Law
RP L. Arroyo
RP E. Face

PIT 1958 N
M D. Murtaugh
1B T. Kluszewski
2B W. Mazeroski

SS R. Groat
3B F. Thomas
OF W. Virdon
OF R. Skinner
OF R. Clemente
C H. Foiles
P R. Friend
P R. Kline
P V. Law
P C. Raydon
P G. Witt
RP E. Porterfield
RP E. Face

PIT 1959 N

M D. Murtaugh
1B R. Stuart
2B W. Mazeroski
SS R. Groat
3B D. Hoak
OF W. Virdon
OF R. Skinner
OF R. Clemente
C F. Burgess
UT R. Mejias
UT G. Nelson
P V. Law
P R. Friend
P H. Haddix
P R. Kline
RP B. Daniels
RP E. Face

PIT 1960 N

M D. Murtaugh
1B R. Stuart
2B W. Mazeroski
SS R. Groat
3B D. Hoak
OF R. Clemente
OF R. Skinner
OF W. Virdon
C F. Burgess
UT G. Cimoli
P R. Friend
P V. Law
P H. Haddix
P W. Mizell
RP E. Face
RP J. Gibbon

PIT 1961 N

M D. Murtaugh
1B R. Stuart
2B W. Mazeroski
SS R. Groat
3B D. Hoak
OF W. Virdon
OF R. Clemente
OF R. Skinner
C F. Burgess
P R. Friend
P J. Gibbon
P H. Haddix
P E. Francis
P W. Mizell
RP C. Labine
RP E. Face

PIT 1962 N

M D. Murtaugh
1B R. Stuart
2B W. Mazeroski
SS R. Groat
3B D. Hoak
OF W. Virdon
OF R. Clemente
OF R. Skinner
C F. Burgess
P R. Friend
P A. McBean
P E. Francis
P H. Haddix
P V. Law
RP T. Sturdivant
RP E. Face

PIT 1963 N

M D. Murtaugh
1B D. Clendenon
2B W. Mazeroski
SS J. Schofield
3B R. Bailey
OF R. Clemente
OF W. Virdon
OF W. Stargell
C J. Pagliaroni
P R. Friend
P D. Cardwell
P D. Schwall
P J. Gibbon

RP A. McBean
RP T. Sisk

PIT 1964 N

M D. Murtaugh
1B D. Clendenon
2B W. Mazeroski
SS J. Schofield
3B R. Bailey
OF R. Clemente
OF W. Virdon
OF M. Mota
C J. Pagliaroni
UT E. Freese
UT G. Lynch
UT W. Stargell
P R. Veale
P R. Friend
P V. Law
P J. Gibbon
P S. Blass
RP A. McBean
RP E. Face

PIT 1965 N

M H. Walker
1B D. Clendenon
2B W. Mazeroski
SS L. Alley
3B R. Bailey
OF R. Clemente
OF W. Stargell
OF W. Virdon
C J. Pagliaroni
UT M. Mota
P R. Veale
P D. Cardwell
P R. Friend
P V. Law
P J. Gibbon
RP A. McBean
RP T. Sisk

PIT 1966 N

M H. Walker
1B D. Clendenon
2B W. Mazeroski
SS L. Alley
3B R. Bailey
OF R. Clemente
OF M. Alou
OF W. Stargell
C J. Pagliaroni
UT M. Mota
UT J. Pagan
P R. Veale
P W. Fryman
P V. Law
P S. Blass
P T. Sisk
RP P. Mikkelsen
RP A. McBean

PIT 1967 N

M H. Walker
M D. Murtaugh
1B D. Clendenon
2B W. Mazeroski
SS L. Alley
3B M. Wills
OF R. Clemente
OF M. Alou
OF M. Mota
C J. May
UT W. Stargell
P T. Sisk
P R. Veale
P D. Ribant
P S. Blass
P W. Fryman
RP A. McBean
RP J. Pizarro

PIT 1968 N

M L. Shepard
1B D. Clendenon
2B W. Mazeroski
SS L. Alley
3B M. Wills
OF M. Alou
OF R. Clemente
OF W. Stargell
C J. May
UT M. Mota
P R. Veale
P S. Blass
P A. McBean
P R. Moose
P J. Bunning
RP R. Kline
RP T. Sisk

PIT 1969 N

M L. Shepard
M A. Grammas
1B A. Oliver
2B W. Mazeroski
SS F. Patek
3B R. Hebner
OF M. Alou
OF R. Clemente
OF W. Stargell
C M. Sanguillen
UT J. Pagan
UT C. Taylor
P R. Veale
P D. Ellis
P S. Blass
P R. Moose
P J. Bunning
RP C. Hartenstein
RP J. Dal Canton

PIT 1970 N

M D. Murtaugh
1B R. Robertson
2B W. Mazeroski
SS L. Alley
3B R. Hebner
OF M. Alou
OF W. Stargell
OF R. Clemente
C M. Sanguillen
UT A. Oliver
P R. Veale
P D. Ellis
P S. Blass
P R. Moose
P J. Walker
RP D. Giusti
RP J. Dal Canton

PIT 1971 N

M D. Murtaugh
1B R. Robertson
2B D. Cash
SS L. Alley
3B R. Hebner
OF W. Stargell
OF R. Clemente
OF A. Oliver
C M. Sanguillen
UT E. Clines
UT V. Davalillo
P S. Blass
P D. Ellis
P R. Johnson
P J. Walker
P R. Moose
RP D. Giusti
RP J. Grant

PIT 1972 N

M W. Virdon
1B W. Stargell
2B D. Cash
SS L. Alley
3B R. Hebner
OF A. Oliver
OF V. Davalillo
OF R. Clemente
C M. Sanguillen
UT E. Clines
UT R. Robertson
UT R. Stennett
P S. Blass
P R. Moose
P N. Briles
P D. Ellis
P B. Kison
RP D. Giusti
RP R. Hernandez

PIT 1973 N

M W. Virdon
M D. Murtaugh
1B R. Robertson
2B D. Cash
SS C. Maxvill
3B R. Hebner
OF W. Stargell
OF A. Oliver
OF R. Zisk
C M. Sanguillen
UT E. Clines
UT M. May
UT R. Stennett
P N. Briles
P R. Moose
P D. Ellis
P J. Rooker
P J. Walker
RP D. Giusti

RP R. Johnson

PIT 1974 N

M D. Murtaugh
1B R. Robertson
2B R. Stennett
SS F. Taveras
3B R. Hebner
OF R. Zisk
OF W. Stargell
OF A. Oliver
C M. Sanguillen
UT E. Clines
UT E. Kirkpatrick
P J. Rooker
P J. Reuss
P K. Brett
P D. Ellis
P B. Kison
RP D. Giusti
RP R. Hernandez

PIT 1975 N

M D. Murtaugh
1B W. Stargell
2B R. Stennett
SS F. Taveras
3B R. Hebner
OF A. Oliver
OF D. Parker
OF R. Zisk
C M. Sanguillen
P J. Reuss
P J. Rooker
P B. Kison
P D. Ellis
P J. Candelaria
RP L. Demery
RP D. Giusti

PIT 1976 N

M D. Murtaugh
1B W. Stargell
2B R. Stennett
SS F. Taveras
3B R. Hebner
OF R. Zisk
OF D. Parker
OF A. Oliver
C M. Sanguillen
UT W. Robinson
P J. Candelaria
P J. Reuss
P J. Rooker
P B. Kison
P G. Medich
RP K. Tekulve
RP R. Moose

PIT 1977 N

M C. Tanner
1B W. Robinson
2B R. Stennett
SS F. Taveras
3B P. Garner
OF D. Parker
OF A. Oliver
OF O. Moreno
C D. Dyer
UT N. Ott
P J. Candelaria
P J. Reuss
P J. Rooker
P B. Kison
P O. Jones
RP R. Gossage
RP K. Tekulve

PIT 1978 N

M C. Tanner
1B W. Stargell
2B R. Stennett
SS F. Taveras
3B P. Garner
OF O. Moreno
OF D. Parker
OF W. Robinson
C N. Ott
UT J. Milner
P R. Blyleven
P D. Robinson
P J. Candelaria
P J. Rooker
P J. Bibby
RP K. Tekulve
RP G. Jackson

PIT 1979 N

M C. Tanner
1B W. Stargell

2B R. Stennett
SS T. Foli
3B B. Madlock
OF O. Moreno
OF D. Parker
OF W. Robinson
C N. Ott
UT P. Garner
UT J. Milner
P R. Blyleven
P J. Candelaria
P B. Kison
P D. Robinson
P J. Bibby
RP K. Tekulve
RP E. Romo

PIT 1980 N

M C. Tanner
1B J. Milner
2B P. Garner
SS T. Foli
3B B. Madlock
OF O. Moreno
OF D. Parker
OF M. Easler
C N. Ott
UT L. Lacy
UT W. Robinson
P J. Bibby
P J. Candelaria
P R. Blyleven
P D. Robinson
P R. Rhoden
RP E. Romo
RP K. Tekulve

PIT 1981 N

M C. Tanner
1B J. Thompson
2B P. Garner
SS T. Foli
3B B. Madlock
OF O. Moreno
OF M. Easler
OF L. Lacy
C A. Pena
UT D. Berra
UT D. Parker
P R. Rhoden
P E. Solomon
P J. Bibby
P P. Perez
RP R. Scurry
RP K. Tekulve

PIT 1982 N

M C. Tanner
1B J. Thompson
2B J. Ray
SS D. Berra
3B B. Madlock
OF O. Moreno
OF M. Easler
OF L. Lacy
C A. Pena
P R. Rhoden
P D. Robinson
P J. Candelaria
P M. Sarmiento
P L. McWilliams
RP K. Tekulve
RP R. Scurry

PIT 1983 N

M C. Tanner
1B J. Thompson
2B J. Ray
SS D. Berra
3B B. Madlock
OF D. Parker
OF M. Easler
OF M. Wynne
C A. Pena
UT L. Lacy
UT L. Mazzilli
P R. Rhoden
P L. McWilliams
P J. Candelaria
P B. Tunnell
P J. DeLeon
RP C. Guante
RP K. Tekulve

PIT 1984 N

M C. Tanner
1B J. Thompson
2B J. Ray
SS D. Berra
3B B. Madlock
OF M. Wynne

OF L. Lacy
OF D. Frobel
C A. Pena
UT L. Mazzilli
UT J. Morrison
P R. Rhoden
P L. McWilliams
P J. Tudor
P J. DeLeon
P J. Candelaria
RP D. Robinson
RP K. Tekulve

PIT 1985 N

M C. Tanner
1B J. Thompson
2B J. Ray
SS S. Khalifa
3B B. Madlock
OF J. Orsulak
OF M. Wynne
OF G. Hendrick
C A. Pena
P R. Rhoden
P R. Reuschel
P J. DeLeon
P B. Tunnell
P L. McWilliams
RP C. Guante
RP D. Robinson

PIT 1986 N

M J. Leyland
1B S. Bream
2B J. Ray
SS R. Belliard
3B J. Morrison
OF J. Orsulak
OF R. Reynolds
OF B. Bonds
C A. Pena
UT R. Almon
UT M. Diaz
P R. Rhoden
P R. Reuschel
P M. Bielecki
P R. Walk
P R. Kipper
RP L. McWilliams
RP J. Winn

PIT 1987 N

M J. Leyland
1B S. Bream
2B J. Ray
SS A. Pedrique
3B R. Bonilla
OF A. Van Slyke
OF B. Bonds
OF R. Reynolds
C M. LaValliere
UT J. Cangelosi
UT M. Diaz
P B. Fisher
P R. Reuschel
P D. Drabek
P M. Dunne
P R. Walk
RP J. Smiley
RP D. Robinson

PIT 1988 N

M J. Leyland
1B S. Bream
2B J. Lind
SS R. Belliard
3B R. Bonilla
OF A. Van Slyke
OF B. Bonds
OF R. Reynolds
C M. LaValliere
P D. Drabek
P R. Walk
P J. Smiley
P M. Dunne
P B. Fisher
RP J. Robinson
RP J. Gott

Providence

PRO N 1878-1885

PRO 1878 N

M T. York
1B T. Murnane
2B C. Sweasy
SS T. Carey
3B W. Hague
OF T. York

OF R. Higham
OF P. Hines
C L. Brown
P J. Ward
P F. Nichols
P H. Wheeler

PRO 1879 N

M G. Wright
1B J. Start
2B M. McGeary
SS G. Wright
3B W. Hague
OF P. Hines
OF T. York
OF J. O'Rourke
C L. Brown
P J. Ward
P R. Mathews

PRO 1880 N

M M. McGeary
M J. Ward
M M. Dorgan
1B J. Start
2B J. Farrell
SS J. Peters
3B G. Bradley
OF M. Dorgan
OF P. Hines
OF T. York
C E. Gross
P J. Ward

PRO 1881 N

M J. Farrell
M T. York
1B J. Start
2B J. Farrell
SS W. McClellan
3B J. Denny
OF T. York
OF P. Hines
OF J. Ward
C E. Gross
P C. Radbourn
P R. Mathews

PRO 1882 N

M W. Wright
1B J. Start
2B J. Farrell
SS G. Wright
3B J. Denny
OF P. Hines
OF T. York
OF J. Ward
C A. Gilligan
P C. Radbourn

PRO 1883 N

M W. Wright
1B J. Start
2B J. Farrell
SS A. Irwin
3B J. Denny
OF P. Hines
OF J. Cassidy
OF S. Carroll
C A. Gilligan
P C. Radbourn
P C. Sweeney

PRO 1884 N

M F. Bancroft
1B J. Start
2B J. Farrell
SS A. Irwin
3B J. Denny
OF S. Carroll
OF P. Hines
OF P. Radford
C A. Gilligan
P C. Radbourn
P C. Sweeney
P E. Conley

PRO 1885 N

M F. Bancroft
1B J. Start
2B J. Farrell
SS A. Irwin
3B J. Denny
OF S. Carroll
OF P. Hines
OF P. Radford
C A. Gilligan
UT C. Bassett
P C. Radbourn

P F. Shaw

Richmond

RIC a 1884

RIC 1884 a

M F. Moses
1B J. Powell
2B F. Larkin
SS W. Schenck
3BA
OF E. Glenn
OF R. Johnston
OF M. Mansell
C J. Hanna
P E. Dugan
P P. Meegan
P H. Morgan

Rochester

ROC a 1890

ROC 1890 a

M P. Powers
1B T. O'Brien
2B W. Greenwood
SS M. Phillips
3B J. Knowles
OF H. Lyons
OF T. Scheffler
OF T. Griffin
C J. McGuire
P R. Barr
P W. Calihan
P L. Titcomb
P R. Miller

Rockford

ROK n 1871

ROK 1871 n

M W. Hastings
2B D. Mack
SS C. Fulmer
3B A. Anson
OF G. Stires
OF G. Bird
OF R. Ham
C W. Hastings
UT R. Addy
P W. Fisher

St. Louis

STL n 1875
  Brown Stockings
RS n 1875
  Red Stockings
STL N 1876-1877
STL U 1884
STL N 1885-1886
STL a 1882-1891
STL F 1914-1915
STL A 1902-1953
  Moved to
  Baltimore
STL N 1892-1988

STL 1875 n

M R. Pearce
1B H. Dehlman
2B J. Battin
SS R. Pearce
3B W. Hague
OF E. Cuthbert
OF L. Pike
OF J. Chapman
C T. Miller
P G. Bradley
P J. Galvin

RS 1875 n

M C. Sweasy
1B C. Hautz
2B C. Sweasy
SS W. Redmond
3B J. McSorley
OF T. Oran
OF A. Croft
OF D. Morgan
C F. Flint
P J. Blong
P D. Morgan

STL 1876 N

M S. Graffen
M G. McManus
1B H. Dehlman
2B M. McGeary
SS D. Mack
3B J. Battin
OF E. Cuthbert
OF L. Pike
OF J. Blong
C J. Clapp
P G. Bradley

STL 1877 N

M G. McManus
1B H. Dehlman
2B M. McGeary
SS D. Force
3B J. Battin
OF M. Dorgan
OF J. Blong
OF J. Remsen
C J. Clapp
UT A. Croft
P F. Nichols

STL 1884 U

M T. Sullivan
M F. Dunlap
1B J. Quinn
2B F. Dunlap
SS M. Whitehead
3B J. Gleason
OF G. Shaffer
OF D. Rowe
OF H. Boyle
C G. Baker
P C. Sweeney
P W. Taylor
P P. Werden
P C. Hodnett

STL 1885 N

M F. Dunlap
M A. McKinnon
M F. Dunlap
1B A. McKinnon
2B F. Dunlap
SS J. Glasscock
3B E. Caskin
OF G. Shaffer
OF J. Seery
OF J. Quinn
C C. Briody
UT C. Sweeney
P H. Boyle
P J. Kirby
P H. Daily
P J. Healy

STL 1886 N

M G. Schmelz
1B A. McKinnon
2B F. Dunlap
SS J. Glasscock
3B J. Denny
OF J. Seery
OF J. Cahill
OF J. McGeachey
C G. Myers
P J. Healy
P J. Kirby
P H. Boyle
P C. Sweeney

STL 1882 a

M E. Cuthbert
1B C. Comiskey
2B W. Smiley
SS W. Gleason
3B J. Gleason
OF O. Walker
OF E. Cuthbert
OF G. Seward
C T. Sullivan
P G. McGinnis
P J. Schappert
P C. Dorr

STL 1883 a

M T. Sullivan
M C. Comiskey
1B C. Comiskey
2B G. Strief
SS W. Gleason
3B W. Latham
OF H. Nicol
OF F. Lewis
OF T. Dolan

C T. Deasley
P A. Mullane
P G. McGinnis

STL 1884 a

M J. Williams
M C. Comiskey
1B C. Comiskey
2B J. Quest
SS W. Gleason
3B W. Latham
OF H. Nicol
OF F. Lewis
OF J. O'Neill
C T. Deasley
P G. McGinnis
P D. Foutz
P J. Davis

STL 1885 a

M C. Comiskey
1B C. Comiskey
2B S. Barkley
SS W. Gleason
3B W. Latham
OF C. Welch
OF H. Nicol
OF W. Robinson
C A. Bushong
P R. Caruthers
P D. Foutz
P G. McGinnis

STL 1886 a

M C. Comiskey
1B C. Comiskey
2B W. Robinson
SS W. Gleason
3B W. Latham
OF C. Welch
OF J. O'Neill
OF H. Nicol
C A. Bushong
P D. Foutz
P R. Caruthers
P N. Hudson
P G. McGinnis

STL 1887 a

M C. Comiskey
1B C. Comiskey
2B W. Robinson
SS W. Gleason
3B W. Latham
OF J. O'Neill
OF C. Welch
OF R. Caruthers
C J. Boyle
UT D. Foutz
P C. King

STL 1888 a

M C. Comiskey
1B C. Comiskey
2B W. Robinson
SS W. White
3B W. Latham
OF T. McCarthy
OF J. O'Neill
OF H. Lyons
C J. Boyle
P C. King
P N. Hudson
P E. Chamberlin
P J. Devlin
P E. Knouff

STL 1889 a

M C. Comiskey
1B C. Comiskey
2B W. Robinson
SS W. Fuller
3B W. Latham
OF T. McCarthy
OF J. O'Neill
OF C. Duffee
C J. Boyle
P C. King
P E. Chamberlin
P J. Stivetts

STL 1890 a

M T. McCarthy
M J. Kerins
M J. Roseman
M C. Campau
M T. McCarthy
M J. Gerhardt
1B E. Cartwright

2B W. Higgins
SS W. Fuller
3B C. Duffee
OF T. McCarthy
OF C. Campau
OF J. Roseman
C J. Munyan
P J. Stivetts
P T. Ramsey
P J. Hart
P W. Whitrock

STL 1891 a

M C. Comiskey
1B C. Comiskey
2B W. Eagan
SS W. Hoy
3B D. Lyons
OF W. Hoy
OF J. O'Neill
OF T. McCarthy
C J. Boyle
P J. Stivetts
P W. McGill
P C. Griffith
P J. Neale
P G. Rettger

STL 1914 F

M M. Brown
M F. Jones
1B H. Miller
2B J. Crandall
SS A. Bridwell
3B A. Boucher
OF J. Tobin
OF D. Drake
OF W. Miller
C M. Simon
UT J. Misse
P R. Groom
P D. Davenport
P H. Keupper
P R. Willett
P M. Brown
RP E. Herbert

STL 1915 F

M F. Jones
1B W. Borton
2B R. Vaughn
SS E. Johnson
3B C. Deal
OF J. Tobin
OF W. Miller
OF D. Drake
C G. Hartley
P D. Davenport
P J. Crandall
P E. Plank
P R. Groom
P C. Watson

STL 1902 A

M J. McAleer
1B J. Anderson
2B R. Padden
SS R. Wallace
3B W. McCormick
OF J. Burkett
OF R. Heidrick
OF C. Hemphill
C J. Sugden
P J. Powell
P F. Donahue
P C. Harper
P J. Sudhoff
P W. Reidy

STL 1903 A

M J. McAleer
1B J. Anderson
2B W. Friel
SS R. Wallace
3B H. Hill
OF J. Burkett
OF R. Heidrick
OF C. Hemphill
C M. Kahoe
P J. Powell
P J. Sudhoff
P E. Siever
P F. Donahue

STL 1904 A

M J. McAleer
1B T. Jones
2B R. Padden
SS R. Wallace
3B C. Moran

OF J. Burkett
OF R. Heidrick
OF C. Hemphill
C J. Sugden
P B. Pelty
P H. Howell
P F. Glade
P J. Sudhoff
P E. Siever

STL 1905 A

M J. McAleer
1B T. Jones
2B I. Rockenfield
SS R. Wallace
3B H. Gleason
OF G. Stone
OF B. Koehler
OF J. Frisk
C J. Sugden
UT C. Van Zandt
P H. Howell
P F. Glade
P B. Pelty
P J. Sudhoff
P J. Buchanan

STL 1906 A

M J. McAleer
1B T. Jones
2B P. O'Brien
SS R. Wallace
3B R. Hartzell
OF G. Stone
OF C. Hemphill
OF H. Niles
C W. Rickey
P H. Howell
P F. Glade
P B. Pelty
P J. Powell
P R. Smith

STL 1907 A

M J. McAleer
1B T. Jones
2B H. Niles
SS R. Wallace
3B J. Yeager
OF G. Stone
OF C. Hemphill
OF O. Pickering
C E. Spencer
P H. Howell
P B. Pelty
P J. Powell
P F. Glade
P W. Dinneen

STL 1908 A

M J. McAleer
1B T. Jones
2B J. Williams
SS R. Wallace
3B A. Ferris
OF G. Stone
OF D. Hoffman
OF R. Hartzell
C E. Spencer
P H. Howell
P G. Waddell
P J. Powell
P W. Dinneen
P B. Pelty

STL 1909 A

M J. McAleer
1B T. Jones
2B J. Williams
SS R. Wallace
3B A. Ferris
OF D. Hoffman
OF R. Hartzell
OF G. Stone
C L. Criger
UT A. Griggs
P J. Powell
P G. Waddell
P B. Pelty
P W. Bailey
P W. Graham

STL 1910 A

M J. O'Connor
1B P. Newnam
2B F. Truesdale
SS R. Wallace
3B R. Hartzell
OF G. Stone
OF A. Schweitzer

OF D. Hoffman
OF R. Heidrick
OF C. Hemphill
C J. Stephens
UT A. Griggs
P J. Lake
P W. Bailey
P B. Pelty
P R. Ray
P J. Powell

STL 1911 A

M R. Wallace
1B J. Black
2B F. LaPorte
SS R. Wallace
3B J. Austin
OF B. Shotton
OF W. Hogan
OF A. Schweitzer
C J. Clarke
P J. Lake
P J. Powell
P B. Pelty
P E. Hamilton
P A. Mitchell

STL 1912 A

M R. Wallace
M G. Stovall
1B G. Stovall
2B D. Pratt
SS R. Wallace
3B J. Austin
OF B. Shotton
OF W. Hogan
OF A. Compton
C J. Stephens
P E. Hamilton
P J. Powell
P G. Baumgardner
P M. Allison
P E. Brown

STL 1913 A

M G. Stovall
M J. Austin
M W. Rickey
1B G. Stovall
2B D. Pratt
SS M. Balenti
3B J. Austin
OF B. Shotton
OF A. Williams
OF J. Johnston
C S. Agnew
P G. Baumgardner
P C. Weilman
P A. Mitchell
P E. Hamilton
P W. Leverenz

STL 1914 A

M W. Rickey
1B J. Leary
2B D. Pratt
SS J. Lavan
3B J. Austin
OF B. Shotton
OF C. Walker
OF A. Williams
C S. Agnew
P E. Hamilton
P C. Weilman
P W. James
P G. Baumgardner
P W. Leverenz

STL 1915 A

M W. Rickey
1B J. Leary
2B D. Pratt
SS J. Lavan
3B J. Austin
OF B. Shotton
OF C. Walker
OF L. Walsh
C S. Agnew
UT I. Howard
P C. Weilman
P G. Lowdermilk
P E. Hamilton
P W. James
P E. Koob
RP E. Perryman

STL 1916 A

M F. Jones
1B G. Sisler
2B D. Pratt
SS J. Lavan
3B J. Austin

OF B. Shotton
OF A. Marsans
OF W. Miller
C H. Severeid
P D. Davenport
P C. Weilman
P E. Plank
P R. Groom
P E. Koob

STL 1917 A

M F. Jones
1B G. Sisler
2B D. Pratt
SS J. Lavan
3B J. Austin
OF W. Jacobson
OF B. Shotton
OF Y. Sloan
C H. Severeid
P D. Davenport
P A. Sothoron
P R. Groom
P E. Koob
P E. Plank

STL 1918 A

M F. Jones
M J. Austin
M J. Burke
1B G. Sisler
2B E. Gedeon
SS J. Austin
3B F. Maisel
OF J. Tobin
OF C. Demmitt
OF E. Smith
C L. Nunamaker
UT T. Hendryx
P A. Sothoron
P D. Davenport
P T. Rogers
P M. Gallia
P W. Wright
RP B. Houck

STL 1919 A

M J. Burke
1B G. Sisler
2B E. Gedeon
SS W. Gerber
3B J. Austin
OF J. Tobin
OF W. Jacobson
OF E. Smith
C H. Severeid
P A. Sothoron
P M. Gallia
P U. Shocker
P C. Weilman
P D. Davenport
RP E. Koob
RP W. Wright

STL 1920 A

M J. Burke
1B G. Sisler
2B E. Gedeon
SS W. Gerber
3B J. Austin
OF W. Jacobson
OF J. Tobin
OF K. Williams
C H. Severeid
UT E. Smith
P F. Davis
P U. Shocker
P A. Sothoron
P C. Weilman
P W. Burwell

STL 1921 A

M L. Fohl
1B G. Sisler
2B M. McManus
SS W. Gerber
3B F. Ellerbe
OF J. Tobin
OF K. Williams
OF W. Jacobson
C H. Severeid
P U. Shocker
P F. Davis
P E. Vangilder
P R. Kolp
P W. Bayne
RP W. Burwell

STL 1922 A

M L. Fohl

1B G. Sisler
2B M. McManus
SS W. Gerber
3B F. Ellerbe
OF K. Williams
OF J. Tobin
OF W. Jacobson
C H. Severeid
P U. Shocker
P E. Vangilder
P F. Davis
P R. Kolp
P W. Wright

STL 1923 A

M L. Fohl
M J. Austin
1B F. Schliebner
2B M. McManus
SS W. Gerber
3B E. Robertson
OF J. Tobin
OF W. Jacobson
OF K. Williams
C H. Severeid
P E. Vangilder
P U. Shocker
P D. Danforth
P R. Kolp
P F. Davis
RP C. Root

STL 1924 A

M G. Sisler
1B G. Sisler
2B M. McManus
SS W. Gerber
3B E. Robertson
OF W. Jacobson
OF J. Tobin
OF K. Williams
C H. Severeid
P U. Shocker
P D. Danforth
P E. Wingard
P F. Davis
P E. Vangilder
RP H. Pruett
RP G. Grant

STL 1925 A

M G. Sisler
1B G. Sisler
2B M. McManus
SS R. LaMotte
3B E. Robertson
OF W. Jacobson
OF K. Williams
OF H. Rice
C L. Dixon
P N. Gaston
P L. Bush
P E. Vangilder
P F. Davis
P J. Giard

STL 1926 A

M G. Sisler
1B G. Sisler
2B O. Melillo
SS W. Gerber
3B M. McManus
OF H. Rice
OF E. Miller
OF K. Williams
C W. Schang
P J. Zachary
P N. Gaston
P E. Vangilder
P E. Wingard
P N. Ballou

STL 1927 A

M D. Howley
1B G. Sisler
2B O. Melillo
SS W. Gerber
3B J. O'Rourke
OF H. Rice
OF E. Miller
OF K. Williams
C W. Schang
P N. Gaston
P E. Vangilder
P S. Jones
P E. Wingard
P W. Stewart

STL 1928 A

M D. Howley
1B L. Blue
2B O. Brannan
SS R. Kress
3B J. O'Rourke
OF H. Manush
OF F. Schulte
OF G. McNeely
C W. Schang
P S. Gray
P A. Crowder
P J. Ogden
P G. Blaeholder
P W. Stewart
RP S. Coffman
RP H. Wiltse

STL 1929 A

M D. Howley
1B L. Blue
2B O. Melillo
SS R. Kress
3B J. O'Rourke
OF H. Manush
OF F. McGowan
OF F. Schulte
C W. Schang
P S. Gray
P A. Crowder
P G. Blaeholder
P H. Collins
P W. Stewart
RP C. Kimsey
RP S. Coffman

STL 1930 A

M W. Killefer
1B L. Blue
2B O. Melillo
SS R. Kress
3B J. O'Rourke
OF L. Goslin
OF F. Schulte
OF T. Gullic
C R. Ferrell
P W. Stewart
P S. Coffman
P G. Blaeholder
P H. Collins
P S. Gray
RP C. Kimsey
RP H. Holshouser

STL 1931 A

M W. Killefer
1B J. Burns
2B O. Melillo
SS J. Levey
3B R. Kress
OF L. Goslin
OF F. Schulte
OF T. Jenkins
C R. Ferrell
P W. Stewart
P S. Gray
P G. Blaeholder
P S. Coffman
P H. Collins
RP C. Kimsey
RP R. Stiles

STL 1932 A

M W. Killefer
1B J. Burns
2B O. Melillo
SS J. Levey
3B A. Scharein
OF L. Goslin
OF B. Campbell
OF F. Schulte
C R. Ferrell
P W. Stewart
P G. Blaeholder
P I. Hadley
P S. Gray
P W. Hebert
RP C. Kimsey

STL 1933 A

M W. Killefer
M A. Sothoron
M R. Hornsby
1B J. Burns
2B O. Melillo
SS J. Levey
3B A. Scharein
OF B. Campbell
OF S. West
OF C. Reynolds
C M. Shea
UT T. Gullic
P I. Hadley
P G. Blaeholder
P E. Wells
P R. Stiles
RP S. Gray
RP W. Hebert

STL 1934 A

M R. Hornsby
1B J. Burns
2B O. Melillo
SS A. Strange
3B H. Clift
OF R. Pepper
OF B. Campbell
OF S. West
C R. Hemsley
UT A. Bejma
P L. Newsom
P G. Blaeholder
P I. Hadley
P S. Coffman
P I. Andrews
RP E. Wells
RP W. McAfee

STL 1935 A

M R. Hornsby
1B J. Burns
2B T. Carey
SS L. Lary
3B H. Clift
OF S. West
OF J. Solters
OF P. Coleman
C R. Hemsley
P I. Andrews
P J. Knott
P J. Walkup
P R. Van Atta
P M. Cain

STL 1936 A

M R. Hornsby
1B J. Bottomley
2B T. Carey
SS L. Lary
3B H. Clift
OF S. West
OF J. Solters
OF R. Bell
C R. Hemsley
P E. Hogsett
P J. Knott
P I. Andrews
P E. Caldwell
P A. Thomas
RP R. Van Atta
RP L. Mahaffey

STL 1937 A

M R. Hornsby
M J. Bottomley
1B H. Davis
2B T. Carey
SS Knickerbocker
3B H. Clift
OF J. Vosmik
OF R. Bell
OF S. West
C R. Hemsley
UT E. Allen
P O. Hildebrand
P J. Knott
P E. Hogsett
P J. Walkup
P J. Bonetti

STL 1938 A

M C. Street
1B G. McQuinn
2B D. Heffner
SS R. Kress
3B H. Clift
OF R. Bell
OF C. Mills
OF M. Almada
C W. Sullivan
P L. Newsom
P H. Mills
P O. Hildebrand
P R. Van Atta
P J. Walkup
RP E. Cole
RP W. Cox

STL 1939 A

M F. Haney
1B G. McQuinn
2B J. Berardino
SS D. Heffner
3B H. Clift
OF M. Hoag
OF C. Laabs
OF J. Gallagher
C J. Glenn
UT W. Sullivan
P J. Kramer
P L. Kennedy
P W. Trotter
P A. Lawson
P H. Milis
RP J. Whitehead

STL 1940 A

M F. Haney
1B G. McQuinn
2B D. Heffner
SS J. Berardino
3B H. Clift
OF R. Radcliff
OF W. Judnich
OF C. Laabs
C R. Swift
P E. Auker
P L. Kennedy
P R. Harris
P J. Niggeling
P E. Bildilli
RP W. Trotter
RP G. Coffman

STL 1941 A

M F. Haney
M J. Sewell
1B G. McQuinn
2B D. Heffner
SS J. Berardino
3B H. Clift
OF W. Judnich
OF R. Cullenbine
OF C. Laabs
C R. Ferrell
UT J. Grace
UT J. Lucadello
P E. Auker
P R. Muncrief
P D. Galehouse
P R. Harris
P J. Niggeling
RP J. Kramer
RP W. Trotter

STL 1942 A

M J. Sewell
1B G. McQuinn
2B D. Gutteridge
SS V. Stephens
3B H. Clift
OF C. Laabs
OF W. Judnich
OF G. McQuillen
C R. Ferrell
UT A. Criscola
P E. Auker
P J. Niggeling
P D. Galehouse
P A. Hollingsworth
P R. Muncrief
RP G. Caster

STL 1943 A

M J. Sewell
1B G. McQuinn
2B D. Gutteridge
SS V. Stephens
3B H. Clift
OF C. Laabs
OF M. Byrnes
OF M. Chartak
C F. Hayes
UT M. Christman
P D. Galehouse
P S. Sundra
P R. Muncrief
P N. Potter
P A. Hollingsworth
RP G. Caster

STL 1944 A

M J. Sewell
1B G. McQuinn
2B D. Gutteridge
SS V. Stephens
3B M. Christman
OF M. Byrnes
OF M. Kreevich
OF E. Moore
C F. Mancuso
UT A. Zarilla
P J. Kramer
P N. Potter
P R. Muncrief
P S. Jakucki
P D. Galehouse
RP G. Caster

STL 1945 A

M J. Sewell
1B G. McQuinn
2B D. Gutteridge
SS V. Stephens
3B M. Christman
OF M. Byrnes
OF E. Moore
OF M. Kreevich
C F. Mancuso
UT L. Schulte
P N. Potter
P J. Kramer
P S. Jakucki
P A. Shirley
P A. Hollingsworth
RP S. Zoldak

STL 1946 A

M J. Sewell
M J. Taylor
1B C. Stevens
2B J. Berardino
SS V. Stephens
3B M. Christman
OF W. Judnich
OF A. Zarilla
OF J. Heath
C F. Mancuso
P J. Kramer
P D. Galehouse
P S. Zoldak
P N. Potter
P A. Shirley
RP S. Ferens
RP E. Kinder

STL 1947 A

M H. Ruel
1B W. Judnich
2B J. Berardino
SS V. Stephens
3B R. Dillinger
OF J. Heath
OF P. Lehner
OF A. Zarilla
C J. Moss
UT R. Coleman
P J. Kramer
P E. Kinder
P J. Sanford
P R. Muncrief
P S. Zoldak
RP G. Moulder

STL 1948 A

M J. Taylor
1B C. Stevens
2B G. Priddy
SS E. Pellagrini
3B R. Dillinger
OF A. Zarilla
OF M. Platt
OF P. Lehner
C J. Moss
UT S. Dente
P J. Sanford
P C. Fannin
P N. Garver
P W. Kennedy
RP B. Stephens
RP F. Biscan

STL 1949 A

M J. Taylor
1B J. Graham
2B G. Priddy
SS E. Pellagrini
3B R. Dillinger
OF R. Kokos
OF R. Sievers
OF S. Spence
C J. Lollar
UT P. Lehner
UT J. Moss
UT M. Platt
UT J. Sullivan
P N. Garver
P W. Kennedy
P C. Fannin
P A. Papai
P J. Ostrowski
RP T. Ferrick
RP R. Starr

STL 1950 A

M J. Taylor
1B D. Lenhardt
2B O. Friend
SS T. Upton
3B W. Sommers
OF R. Kokos
OF R. Coleman
OF K. Wood
C J. Lollar
UT H. Arft
UT R. Sievers
P N. Garver
P A. Widmar
P F. Overmire
P R. Starr
P H. Dorish
RP C. Marshall

STL 1951 A

M J. Taylor
1B H. Arft
2B R. Young
SS W. Jennings
3B F. Marsh
OF J. Delsing
OF K. Wood
OF R. Coleman
C J. Lollar
P N. Garver
P D. Pillette
P T. Byrne
P A. Widmar
RP R. Mahoney
RP L. Paige

STL 1952 A

M R. Hornsby
M M. Marion
1B R. Kryhoski
2B R. Young
SS J. DeMaestri
3B J. Dyck
OF R. Nieman
OF M. Rivera
OF J. Delsing
C C. Courtney
P D. Pillette
P T. Byrne
P R. Cain
P H. Bearden
P N. Garver
RP D. Madison

STL 1953 A

M M. Marion
1B R. Kryhoski
2B R. Young
SS G. Hunter
3B J. Dyck
OF J. Groth
OF V. Wertz
OF R. Kokos
C C. Courtney
UT D. Lenhardt
P D. Larsen
P D. Pillette
P R. Littlefield
P H. Brecheen
P R. Cain
RP L. Paige
RP M. Stuart

STL 1892 N

M J. Glasscock
M J. Stricker
M J. Crooks
M G. Gore
M R. Caruthers
1B P. Werden
2B C. Crooks
SS J. Glasscock
3B G. Pinkney
OF W. Brodie
OF R. Caruthers
OF S. Carroll
C R. Buckley
P W. Gleason
P T. Breitenstein
P E. Hawley
P C. Getzein
P W. Hawke

STL 1893 N

M W. Watkins
1B P. Werden
2B J. Quinn
SS J. Glasscock
3B C. Crooks
OF T. Dowd
OF W. Brodie
OF C. Frank
C H. Peitz
P T. Breitenstein
P W. Gleason
P E. Hawley
P A. Clarkson

STL 1894 N

M G. Miller
1B R. Connor
2B J. Quinn
SS F. Ely
3B G. Miller
OF F. Shugarts
OF T. Dowd
OF C. Frank
C H. Peitz
P T. Breitenstein
P E. Hawley
P A. Clarkson

STL 1895 N

M A. Buckenberger
M C. Von Der Ahe
M J. Quinn
M L. Phelan
1B R. Connor
2B J. Quinn
SS F. Ely
3B G. Miller
OF D. Cooley
OF T. Dowd
OF T. Brown
C H. Peitz
P T. Breitenstein
P P. Ehret
P H. Staley
P W. Kissinger
P J. McDougal

STL 1896 N

M H. Diddlebock
M W. Latham
M C. Von Der Ahe
M R. Connor
M T. Dowd
1B R. Connor
2B T. Dowd
SS M. Cross
3B J. Myers
OF T. Parrott
OF W. Douglass
OF G. Turner
C E. McFarland
P T. Breitenstein
P W. Hart
P F. Donahue
P W. Kissinger

STL 1897 N

M T. Dowd
M H. Nicol
M W. Hallman
M C. Von Der Ahe
1B M. Grady
2B W. Hallman
SS M. Cross
3B F. Hartman
OF G. Turner
OF R. Harley
OF D. Lally
C W. Douglass
P F. Donahue
P W. Hart
P W. Carsey
P J. Sudhoff

STL 1898 N

M T. Hurst
1B G. Decker
2B C. Crooks
SS G. Smith
3B L. Cross
OF R. Harley
OF T. Dowd
OF J. Stenzel
C J. Clements
UT J. Quinn
P J. Taylor
P J. Sudhoff

P J. Hughey
P W. Carsey

STL 1899 N
M O. Tebeau
1B O. Tebeau
2B C. Childs
SS R. Wallace
3B L. Cross
OF R. Heidrick
OF J. Burkett
OF H. Blake
C L. Criger
P J. Powell
P D. Young
P J. Sudhoff
P G. Cuppy

STL 1900 N
M O. Tebeau
M L. Heilbroner
1B D. McGann
2B W. Keister
SS R. Wallace
3B J. McGraw
OF J. Burkett
OF P. Donovan
OF R. Heidrick
C L. Criger
P D. Young
P A. Jones
P J. Powell
P J. Sudhoff
P J. Hughey

STL 1901 N
M P. Donovan
1B D. McGann
2B R. Padden
SS R. Wallace
3B A. Krueger
OF J. Burkett
OF P. Donovan
OF R. Heidrick
C J. Ryan
UT A. Nichols
P J. Powell
P C. Harper
P J. Sudhoff
P E. Murphy

STL 1902 N
M P. Donovan
1B N. Brashear
2B J. Farrell
SS A. Krueger
3B F. Hartman
OF G. Barclay
OF H. Smoot
OF P. Donovan
C J. Ryan
P M. O'Neill
P S. Yerkes
P E. Murphy
P R. Wicker
P C. Currie

STL 1903 N
M P. Donovan
1B J. Hackett
2B J. Farrell
SS D. Brain
3B J. Burke
OF H. Smoot
OF G. Barclay
OF P. Donovan
C J. O'Neill
P C. McFarland
P M. Brown
P C. Currie
P R. Rhoads
P M. O'Neill

STL 1904 N
M C. Nichols
1B J. Beckley
2B J. Farrell
SS D. Shay
3B J. Burke
OF H. Smoot
OF W. Shannon
OF G. Barclay
C M. Grady
UT D. Brain
P J. Taylor
P C. Nichols
P C. McFarland
P M. O'Neill
P J. Corbett

STL 1905 N
M C. Nichols
M J. Burke
M M. Robison
1B J. Beckley
2B H. Arndt
SS G. McBride
3B J. Burke
OF W. Shannon
OF H. Smoot
OF J. Dunleavy
C M. Grady
P J. Taylor
P C. McFarland
P J. Thielman
P C. Brown
P A. Egan

STL 1906 N
M J. McCloskey
1B J. Beckley
2B J. Bennett
SS G. McBride
3B H. Arndt
OF A. Burch
OF H. Smoot
OF W. Shannon
C M. Grady
UT A. Hoelskoetter
P C. Brown
P E. Karger
P F. Beebe
P J. Taylor
P C. Druhot

STL 1907 N
M J. McCloskey
1B E. Konetchy
2B J. Bennett
SS E. Holly
3B R. Byrne
OF J. Murray
OF J. Barry
OF J. Burnett
C W. Marshall
UT A. Hoelskoetter
P U. McGlynn
P E. Karger
P F. Beebe
P A. Fromme
P J. Lush

STL 1908 N
M J. McCloskey
1B E. Konetchy
2B W. Gilbert
SS J. O'Rourke
3B R. Byrne
OF J. Murray
OF J. Delahanty
OF A. Shaw
C W. Ludwig
UT R. Charles
P A. Raymond
P J. Lush
P F. Beebe
P E. Karger
P H. Sallee

STL 1909 N
M R. Bresnahan
1B E. Konetchy
2B R. Charles
SS R. Hulswitt
3B R. Byrne
OF G. Ellis
OF L. Evans
OF A. Shaw
C E. Phelps
UT J. Delahanty
P F. Beebe
P J. Lush
P H. Sallee
P R. Harmon
P L. Backman
RP S. Melter

STL 1910 N
M R. Bresnahan
1B E. Konetchy
2B M. Huggins
SS A. Hauser
3B H. Mowrey
OF L. Evans
OF G. Ellis
OF E. Oakes
C E. Phelps
P R. Harmon
P J. Lush
P V. Willis

P F. Corridon
P L. Backman

STL 1911 N
M R. Bresnahan
1B E. Konetchy
2B M. Huggins
SS A. Hauser
3B H. Mowrey
OF E. Oakes
OF L. Evans
OF G. Ellis
C J. Bliss
P R. Harmon
P W. Steele
P H. Sallee
P R. Golden
P J. Geyer

STL 1912 N
M R. Bresnahan
1B E. Konetchy
2B M. Huggins
SS A. Hauser
3B H. Mowrey
OF E. Oakes
OF L. Evans
OF L. Magee
C M. Grady
UT G. Ellis
P H. Sallee
P R. Harmon
P W. Steele
P J. Geyer
P J. Willis
RP E. Woodburn

STL 1913 N
M M. Huggins
1B E. Konetchy
2B M. Huggins
SS C. O'Leary
3B H. Mowrey
OF E. Oakes
OF L. Magee
OF L. Evans
C I. Wingo
UT G. Whitted
P H. Sallee
P R. Harmon
P D. Griner
P W. Perritt
P W. Doak
RP J. Geyer

STL 1914 N
M M. Huggins
1B J. Miller
2B M. Huggins
SS A. Butler
3B Z. Beck
OF J. Wilson
OF L. Magee
OF A. Dolan
C F. Snyder
UT W. Cruise
P W. Perritt
P H. Sallee
P W. Doak
P D. Griner
P H. Perdue

STL 1915 N
M M. Huggins
1B J. Miller
2B M. Huggins
SS A. Butler
3B C. Betzel
OF T. Long
OF R. Bescher
OF J. Wilson
C F. Snyder
UT A. Dolan
UT R. Hyatt
P W. Doak
P H. Sallee
P H. Meadows
P D. Griner
P J. Robinson

STL 1916 N
M M. Huggins
1B J. Miller
2B C. Betzel
SS R. Colman
3B R. Hornsby
OF R. Bescher
OF J. Smith
OF J. Wilson
C M. Gonzalez

UT T. Long
UT F. Snyder
P H. Meadows
P L. Ames
P W. Doak
P R. Steele
P H. Jasper
RP R. Williams

STL 1917 N
M M. Huggins
1B E. Paulette
2B J. Miller
SS R. Hornsby
3B H. Baird
OF W. Cruise
OF T. Long
OF J. Smith
C F. Snyder
UT C. Betzel
UT M. Gonzalez
P W. Doak
P H. Meadows
P L. Ames
P M. Watson
P E. Packard

STL 1918 N
M J. Hendricks
1B E. Paulette
2B R. Fisher
SS R. Hornsby
3B H. Baird
OF C. Heathcote
OF A. McHenry
OF W. Cruise
C M. Gonzalez
P W. Doak
P L. Ames
P W. Sherdel
P E. Packard
P H. Meadows

STL 1919 N
M W. Rickey
1B J. Miller
2B M. Stock
SS J. Lavan
3B R. Hornsby
OF J. Smith
OF A. McHenry
OF C. Heathcote
C V. Clemons
UT J. Schultz
P W. Doak
P M. Goodwin
P O. Tuero
P W. Sherdel
P F. May

STL 1920 N
M W. Rickey
1B J. Fournier
2B R. Hornsby
SS J. Lavan
3B M. Stock
OF A. McHenry
OF C. Heathcote
OF J. Smith
C V. Clemons
UT J. Schultz
P J. Haines
P W. Doak
P F. Schupp
P W. Sherdel
P M. Goodwin

STL 1921 N
M W. Rickey
1B J. Fournier
2B R. Hornsby
SS J. Lavan
3B M. Stock
OF A. McHenry
OF J. Smith
OF L. Mann
C V. Clemons
P J. Haines
P W. Doak
P W. Pertica
P J. Walker
P W. Sherdel
RP L. North

STL 1922 N
M W. Rickey
1B J. Fournier
2B R. Hornsby
SS G. Toporcer

3B M. Stock
OF J. Smith
OF J. Schultz
OF M. Flack
C E. Ainsmith
P E. Pfeffer
P W. Sherdel
P J. Haines
P W. Doak
P W. Pertica
RP L. North
RP C. Barfoot

STL 1923 N
M W. Rickey
1B J. Bottomley
2B R. Hornsby
SS H. Freigau
3B M. Stock
OF M. Flack
OF J. Smith
OF H. Myers
C E. Ainsmith
UT F. Blades
UT G. Toporcer
P J. Haines
P W. Sherdel
P F. Toney
P W. Doak
P E. Pfeffer
RP L. North

STL 1924 N
M W. Rickey
1B J. Bottomley
2B R. Hornsby
SS J. Cooney
3B H. Freigau
OF J. Smith
OF F. Blades
OF R. Holm
C M. Gonzalez
P J. Haines
P A. Sothoron
P W. Sherdel
P J. Sturat
P E. Dyer

STL 1925 N
M W. Rickey
M R. Hornsby
1B J. Bottomley
2B R. Hornsby
SS G. Toporcer
3B L. Bell
OF F. Blades
OF C. Hafey
OF C. Mueller
C R. O'Farrell
P J. Haines
P W. Sherdel
P C. Rhem
P A. Sothoron
P A. Reinhart

STL 1926 N
M R. Hornsby
1B J. Bottomley
2B R. Hornsby
SS T. Thevenow
3B L. Bell
OF T. Douthit
OF F. Blades
OF W. Southworth
C R. O'Farrell
P C. Rhem
P W. Sherdel
P J. Haines
P H. Keen
P G. Alexander
RP S. Johnson

STL 1927 N
M R. O'Farrell
1B J. Bottomley
2B F. Frisch
SS H. Schuble
3B L. Bell
OF T. Douthit
OF R. Holm
OF C. Hafey
C F. Snyder
P J. Haines
P G. Alexander
P W. Sherdel
P C. Rhem
P R. McGraw
RP H. Bell

STL 1928 N
M W. McKechnie
1B J. Bottomley
2B F. Frisch
SS W. Maranville
3B R. Holm
OF T. Douthit
OF C. Hafey
OF G. Harper
C J. Wilson
UT A. High
P W. Sherdel
P G. Alexander
P J. Haines
P C. Rhem
P C. Mitchell
RP H. Haid

STL 1929 N
M W. Southworth
M C. Street
M W. McKechnie
1B J. Bottomley
2B F. Frisch
SS C. Gelbert
3B A. High
OF T. Douthit
OF C. Hafey
OF E. Orsatti
C J. Wilson
P W. Sherdel
P S. Johnson
P J. Haines
P C. Mitchell
P H. Haid

STL 1930 N
M C. Street
1B J. Bottomley
2B F. Frisch
SS C. Gelbert
3B E. Adams
OF T. Douthit
OF C. Hafey
OF G. Watkins
C J. Wilson
P W. Hallahan
P S. Johnson
P J. Haines
P B. Grimes
P C. Rhem
RP H. Bell
RP J. Lindsey

STL 1931 N
M C. Street
1B J. Bottomley
2B F. Frisch
SS C. Gelbert
3B E. Adams
OF G. Watkins
OF C. Hafey
OF J. Martin
C J. Wilson
P W. Hallahan
P B. Grimes
P S. Derringer
P C. Rhem
P S. Johnson
RP J. Lindsey
RP A. Stout

STL 1932 N
M C. Street
1B J. Collins
2B J. Reese
SS C. Gelbert
3B D. Flowers
OF G. Watkins
OF E. Orsatti
OF J. Martin
C A. Mancuso
UT F. Frisch
P J. Dean
P S. Derringer
P J. Carleton
P W. Hallahan
P S. Johnson
RP J. Lindsey
RP A. Stout

STL 1933 N
M C. Street
M F. Frisch
1B J. Collins
2B F. Frisch
SS L. Durocher
3B J. Martin
OF J. Medwick
OF G. Watkins

OF E. Orsatti
C J. Wilson
P J. Dean
P J. Carleton
P W. Hallahan
P W. Walker
P J. Haines
RP S. Johnson

STL 1934 N
M F. Frisch
1B J. Collins
2B F. Frisch
SS L. Durocher
3B J. Martin
OF J. Rothrock
OF J. Medwick
OF E. Orsatti
C V. Davis
UT B. Whitehead
P J. Dean
P J. Carleton
P P. Dean
P W. Hallahan
P W. Walker
RP J. Haines
RP J. Mooney

STL 1935 N
M F. Frisch
1B J. Collins
2B F. Frisch
SS L. Durocher
3B J. Martin
OF J. Medwick
OF J. Rothrock
OF T. Moore
C W. DeLancey
UT V. Davis
UT B. Whitehead
P J. Dean
P P. Dean
P W. Hallahan
P W. Walker
P E. Heusser

STL 1936 N
M F. Frisch
1B J. Mize
2B S. Martin
SS L. Durocher
3B C. Gelbert
OF J. Medwick
OF T. Moore
OF J. Martin
C V. Davis
UT J. Collins
UT A. Ogrodowski
P J. Dean
P L. Parmelee
P J. Winford
P J. Haines
RP E. Heusser
RP G. Earnshaw

STL 1937 N
M F. Frisch
1B J. Mize
2B J. Brown
SS L. Durocher
3B D. Gutteridge
OF J. Medwick
OF D. Padgett
OF T. Moore
C A. Ogrodowski
UT S. Bordagaray
UT J. Martin
P R. Weiland
P L. Warneke
P J. Dean
P S. Johnson
P D. Ryba
RP R. Harrell

STL 1938 N
M F. Frisch
M M. Gonzalez
1B J. Mize
2B S. Martin
SS L. Myers
3B D. Gutteridge
OF J. Medwick
OF E. Slaughter
OF T. Moore
C A. Owen
UT J. Brown
UT D. Padgett
P R. Weiland
P W. McGee
P L. Warneke
P C. Davis

P   R. Henshaw
RP C. Shoun
RP R. Harrell

STL 1939 N

M   F. Blades
1B J. Mize
2B S. Martin
SS J. Brown
3B D. Gutteridge
OF E. Slaughter
OF J. Medwick
OF T. Moore
C   A. Owen
P   C. Davis
P   M. Cooper
P   R. Bowman
P   L. Warneke
P   W. McGee
RP C. Shoun

STL 1940 N

M   F. Blades
M   M. Gonzalez
M   W. Southworth
1B J. Mize
2B J. Orengo
SS M. Marion
3B S. Martin
OF T. Moore
OF E. Slaughter
OF E. Koy
C   A. Owen
UT J. Brown
P   L. Warneke
P   M. Cooper
P   W. McGee
P   C. Shoun
P   R. Bowman
RP J. Russell

STL 1941 N

M   W. Southworth
1B J. Mize
2B F. Crespi
SS M. Marion
3B J. Brown
OF T. Moore
OF E. Slaughter
OF J. Hopp
C   A. Mancuso
UT D. Padgett
P   L. Warneke
P   E. White
P   M. Cooper
P   H. Lanier
P   H. Gumbert
RP C. Shoun
RP I. Hutchinson

STL 1942 N

M   W. Southworth
1B J. Hopp
2B F. Crespi
SS M. Marion
3B G. Kurowski
OF E. Slaughter
OF S. Musial
OF T. Moore
C   W. Cooper
UT J. Brown
UT R. Sanders
P   M. Cooper
P   J. Beazley
P   H. Gumbert
P   H. Lanier
P   E. White

STL 1943 N

M   W. Southworth
1B R. Sanders
2B L. Klein
SS M. Marion
3B G. Kurowski
OF S. Musial
OF H. Walker
OF D. Litwhiler
C   W. Cooper
P   M. Cooper
P   H. Lanier
P   H. Krist
P   H. Brecheen
P   H. Gumbert
RP G. Munger

STL 1944 N

M   W. Southworth
1B R. Sanders
2B E. Verban
SS M. Marion

3B G. Kurowski
OF S. Musial
OF D. Litwhiler
OF J. Hopp
C   W. Cooper
P   M. Cooper
P   H. Lanier
P   T. Wilks
P   H. Brecheen
P   A. Jurisich
RP S. Donnelly

STL 1945 N

M   W. Southworth
1B R. Sanders
2B E. Verban
SS M. Marion
3B G. Kurowski
OF E. Adams
OF A. Schoendienst
OF J. Hopp
C   J. O'Dea
UT A. Bergamo
P   C. Barrett
P   K. Burkhart
P   S. Donnelly
P   H. Brecheen
P   G. Dockins
RP E. Byerly
RP A. Jurisich

STL 1946 N

M   E. Dyer
1B S. Musial
2B A. Schoendienst
SS M. Marion
3B G. Kurowski
OF E. Slaughter
OF H. Walker
OF E. Dusak
C   J. Garagiola
P   H. Pollet
P   H. Brecheen
P   M. Dickson
P   A. Brazle
P   J. Beazley
RP T. Wilks
RP C. Barrett

STL 1947 N

M   E. Dyer
1B S. Musial
2B A. Schoendienst
SS M. Marion
3B G. Kurowski
OF E. Slaughter
OF T. Moore
OF R. Northey
C   D. Rice
UT C. Diering
UT E. Dusak
P   M. Dickson
P   G. Munger
P   H. Brecheen
P   H. Pollet
P   A. Brazle
RP K. Burkhart
RP T. Wilks

STL 1948 N

M   E. Dyer
1B V. Jones
2B A. Schoendienst
SS M. Marion
3B D. Lang
OF S. Musial
OF E. Slaughter
OF T. Moore
C   D. Rice
UT E. Dusak
UT R. Northey
P   M. Dickson
P   H. Brecheen
P   H. Pollet
P   G. Munger
P   A. Brazle
RP T. Wilks
RP J. Hearn

STL 1949 N

M   E. Dyer
1B V. Jones
2B A. Schoendienst
SS M. Marion
3B E. Kazak
OF S. Musial
OF E. Slaughter
OF C. Diering
C   D. Rice
P   H. Pollet
P   H. Brecheen

3B G. Kurowski
OF S. Musial
OF D. Litwhiler
OF J. Hopp
C   W. Cooper
P   M. Cooper
P   H. Lanier
P   T. Wilks
P   H. Brecheen
P   A. Jurisich
RP S. Donnelly

STL 1950 N

M   E. Dyer
1B G. Nelson
2B A. Schoendienst
SS M. Marion
3B T. Glaviano
OF E. Slaughter
OF W. Howerton
OF C. Diering
C   D. Rice
UT S. Musial
P   H. Pollet
P   H. Lanier
P   G. Staley
P   A. Brazle
P   H. Brecheen
RP F. Martin

STL 1951 N

M   M. Marion
1B V. Jones
2B A. Schoendienst
SS S. Hemus
3B W. Johnson
OF E. Slaughter
OF S. Musial
OF H. Lowrey
C   D. Rice
P   G. Staley
P   T. Poholsky
P   H. Lanier
P   H. Brecheen
P   H. Chambers
RP A. Brazle
RP R. Bokelmann

STL 1952 N

M   E. Stanky
1B R. Sisler
2B A. Schoendienst
SS S. Hemus
3B W. Johnson
OF E. Slaughter
OF S. Musial
OF H. Lowrey
C   D. Rice
UT H. Rice
P   G. Staley
P   W. Mizell
P   J. Presko
P   C. Boyer
P   H. Brecheen
RP A. Brazle
RP J. Yuhas

STL 1953 N

M   E. Stanky
1B S. Bilko
2B A. Schoendienst
SS S. Hemus
3B R. Jablonski
OF S. Musial
OF E. Repulski
OF E. Slaughter
C   D. Rice
UT H. Lowrey
P   H. Haddix
P   G. Staley
P   W. Mizell
P   J. Presko
P   S. Miller
RP A. Brazle
RP H. White

STL 1954 N

M   E. Stanky
1B J. Cunningham
2B A. Schoendienst
SS A. Grammas
3B R. Jablonski
OF E. Repulski
OF S. Musial
OF W. Moon
C   W. Sarni
UT S. Hemus
P   H. Haddix
P   V. Raschi
P   B. Lawrence
P   G. Staley
P   T. Poholsky
RP A. Brazle
RP J. Presko

STL 1955 N

M   E. Stanky

P   A. Brazle
P   G. Munger
P   G. Staley
RP T. Wilks

STL 1950 N

M   H. Walker
1B S. Musial
2B A. Schoendienst
SS A. Grammas
3B K. Boyer
OF W. Virdon
OF E. Repulski
OF W. Moon
C   W. Sarni
UT S. Hemus
P   H. Haddix
P   L. Jackson
P   L. Arroyo
P   T. Poholsky
P   W. Schmidt
RP B. Lawrence
RP P. LaPalme

STL 1956 N

M   F. Hutchinson
1B S. Musial
2B D. Blasingame
SS A. Dark
3B K. Boyer
OF E. Repulski
OF R. Del Greco
OF W. Moon
C   H. Smith
P   W. Mizell
P   T. Poholsky
P   M. Dickson
P   H. Wehmeier
P   W. Schmidt
RP L. McDaniel
RP L. Jackson

STL 1957 N

M   F. Hutchinson
1B S. Musial
2B D. Blasingame
SS A. Dark
3B E. Kasko
OF W. Moon
OF D. Ennis
OF K. Boyer
C   H. Smith
UT J. Cunningham
P   L. Jackson
P   L. McDaniel
P   S. Jones
P   H. Wehmeier
P   W. Mizell
RP W. Schmidt
RP L. Merritt

STL 1958 N

M   F. Hutchinson
M   S. Hack
1B S. Musial
2B D. Blasingame
SS E. Kasko
3B K. Boyer
OF C. Flood
OF D. Ennis
OF W. Moon
C   H. Smith
UT J. Cunningham
UT G. Green
UT I. Noren
P   S. Jones
P   L. Jackson
P   W. Mizell
P   J. Brosnan
P   R. Mabe
RP B. Muffett
RP P. Paine

STL 1959 N

M   S. Hemus
1B S. Musial
2B D. Blasingame
SS A. Grammas
3B K. Boyer
OF G. Cimoli
OF J. Cunningham
OF C. Flood
C   H. Smith
UT W. White
P   L. Jackson
P   W. Mizell
P   E. Broglio
P   G. Blaylock
RP L. McDaniel
RP M. Bridges

STL 1960 N

M   S. Hemus
1B W. White
2B M. Javier
SS D. Spencer
3B K. Boyer

OF C. Flood
OF J. Cunningham
OF W. Moryn
C   H. Smith
UT A. Grammas
UT S. Musial
P   L. Jackson
P   E. Broglio
P   R. Sadecki
P   C. Simmons
P   R. Kline
RP L. McDaniel

STL 1961 N

M   S. Hemus
M   J. Keane
1B W. White
2B M. Javier
SS A. Grammas
3B K. Boyer
OF C. Flood
OF S. Musial
OF C. James
C   J. Schaffer
UT J. Cunningham
UT D. Taussig
P   R. Sadecki
P   L. Jackson
P   B. Gibson
P   C. Simmons
P   E. Broglio
RP L. McDaniel
RP A. Cicotte

STL 1962 N

M   J. Keane
1B W. White
2B M. Javier
SS J. Gotay
3B K. Boyer
OF C. Flood
OF S. Musial
OF C. James
C   E. Oliver
P   L. Jackson
P   R. Gibson
P   E. Broglio
P   R. Washburn
P   C. Simmons
RP L. McDaniel
RP R. Shantz

STL 1963 N

M   J. Keane
1B W. White
2B M. Javier
SS R. Groat
3B K. Boyer
OF C. Flood
OF G. Altman
OF C. James
C   J. McCarver
UT S. Musial
P   R. Gibson
P   E. Broglio
P   C. Simmons
P   R. Sadecki
P   S. Burdette
RP R. Taylor
RP R. Shantz

STL 1964 N

M   J. Keane
1B W. White
2B M. Javier
SS R. Groat
3B K. Boyer
OF C. Flood
OF L. Brock
OF T. Shannon
C   J. McCarver
P   R. Gibson
P   C. Simmons
P   R. Sadecki
P   R. Craig
RP R. Taylor
RP M. Cuellar

STL 1965 N

M   A. Schoendienst
1B W. White
2B M. Javier
SS R. Groat
3B K. Boyer
OF L. Brock
OF C. Flood
OF T. Shannon
C   J. McCarver
UT P. Gagliano
P   R. Gibson
P   C. Simmons

P   E. Stallard
P   R. Sadecki
P   R. Purkey
RP N. Briles
RP H. Woodshick

STL 1966 N

M   A. Schoendienst
1B O. Cepeda
2B M. Javier
SS C. Maxvill
3B C. Smith
OF C. Flood
OF L. Brock
OF T. Shannon
C   J. McCarver
UT G. Buchek
P   R. Gibson
P   A. Jackson
P   R. Washburn
P   N. Briles
P   L. Jaster
RP J. Hoerner
RP H. Woodshick

STL 1967 N

M   A. Schoendienst
1B O. Cepeda
2B M. Javier
SS C. Maxvill
3B T. Shannon
OF L. Brock
OF C. Flood
OF R. Maris
C   J. McCarver
UT R. Tolan
P   R. Hughes
P   S. Carlton
P   R. Washburn
P   R. Gibson
P   N. Briles
RP A. Jackson
RP R. Willis

STL 1968 N

M   A. Schoendienst
1B O. Cepeda
2B M. Javier
SS C. Maxvill
3B T. Shannon
OF L. Brock
OF C. Flood
OF R. Maris
C   J. McCarver
P   R. Gibson
P   N. Briles
P   S. Carlton
P   R. Washburn
P   L. Jaster
RP R. Willis
RP R. Hughes

STL 1969 N

M   A. Schoendienst
1B J. Torre
2B M. Javier
SS C. Maxvill
3B T. Shannon
OF L. Brock
OF C. Flood
OF V. Pinson
C   J. McCarver
P   R. Gibson
P   S. Carlton
P   N. Briles
P   R. Washburn
P   C. Taylor
RP J. Grant
RP J. Hoerner

STL 1970 N

M   A. Schoendienst
1B J. Hague
2B M. Javier
SS C. Maxvill
3B J. Torre
OF L. Brock
OF J. Cardenal
OF L. Lee
C   T. Simmons
UT R. Allen
UT V. Davalillo
UT C. Taylor
P   R. Gibson
P   S. Carlton
P   M. Torrez
P   J. Reuss
P   N. Briles
RP C. Taylor
RP F. Linzy

STL 1971 N

M   A. Schoendienst
1B J. Hague
2B T. Sizemore
SS C. Maxvill
3B J. Torre
OF L. Brock
OF M. Alou
OF J. Cruz
C   T. Simmons
P   S. Carlton
P   R. Gibson
P   R. Cleveland
P   J. Reuss
RP C. Taylor
RP M. Drabowsky

STL 1972 N

M   A. Schoendienst
1B M. Alou
2B T. Sizemore
SS C. Maxvill
3B J. Torre
OF L. Brock
OF L. Melendez
OF J. Cruz
C   T. Simmons
UT B. Carbo
UT E. Crosby
P   R. Gibson
P   R. Wise
P   R. Cleveland
P   A. Santorini
P   S. Spinks
RP D. Segui

STL 1973 N

M   A. Schoendienst
1B J. Torre
2B T. Sizemore
SS M. Tyson
3B K. Reitz
OF L. Brock
OF J. Cruz
OF L. Melendez
C   T. Simmons
UT B. Carbo
UT J. McCarver
P   R. Wise
P   R. Cleveland
P   A. Foster
P   R. Gibson
RP D. Segui
RP R. Folkers

STL 1974 N

M   A. Schoendienst
1B J. Torre
2B T. Sizemore
SS M. Tyson
3B K. Reitz
OF L. Brock
OF A. McBride
OF C. Smith
C   T. Simmons
UT J. Cruz
P   R. Gibson
P   L. McGlothen
P   J. Curtis
P   A. Foster
P   W. Siebert
RP R. Folkers
RP A. Hrabosky

STL 1975 N

M   A. Schoendienst
1B C. Smith
2B T. Sizemore
SS M. Tyson
3B K. Reitz
OF L. Brock
OF A. McBride
OF L. Melendez
C   T. Simmons
UT R. Fairly
P   L. McGlothen
P   R. Forsch
P   R. Reed
P   J. Curtis
P   J. Denny
RP A. Hrabosky
RP M. Garman

STL 1976 N

M   A. Schoendienst
1B K. Hernandez
2B M. Tyson
SS D. Kessinger
3B H. Cruz
OF L. Brock

OF W. Crawford
OF J. Mumphrey
C T. Simmons
UT V. Harris
P P. Falcone
P J. Denny
P L. McGlothen
P R. Forsch
P E. Rasmussen
RP A. Hrabosky
RP M. Wallace

STL 1977 N

M V. Rapp
1B K. Hernandez
2B M. Tyson
SS G. Templeton
3B K. Reitz
OF J. Mumphrey
OF L. Brock
OF H. Cruz
C T. Simmons
P E. Rasmussen
P R. Forsch
P J. Denny
P J. Urrea
P P. Falcone
RP C. Metzger
RP C. Carroll

STL 1978 N

M V. Rapp
M J. Krol
M K. Boyer
1B K. Hernandez
2B M. Tyson
SS G. Templeton
3B K. Reitz
OF J. Morales
OF J. Mumphrey
OF G. Hendrick
C T. Simmons
P R. Forsch
P J. Denny
P P. Vuckovich
P S. Martinez
P J. Urrea
RP M. Littell
RP C. Schultz

STL 1979 N

M K. Boyer
1B K. Hernandez
2B K. Oberkfell
SS G. Templeton
3B K. Reitz
OF A. Scott
OF G. Hendrick
OF J. Mumphrey
C T. Simmons
UT L. Brock
P P. Vuckovich
P R. Forsch
P S. Martinez
P J. Denny
P J. Fulgham
RP M. Littell
RP R. Thomas

STL 1980 N

M K. Boyer
M J. Krol
M D. Herzog
M A. Schoendienst
1B K. Hernandez
2B K. Oberkfell
SS G. Templeton
3B K. Reitz
OF G. Hendrick
OF A. Scott
OF L. Durham
C T. Simmons
UT D. Iorg
P P. Vuckovich
P R. Forsch
P R. Sykes
P S. Martinez
RP J. Kaat
RP D. Hood

STL 1981 N

M D. Herzog
1B K. Hernandez
2B T. Herr
SS G. Templeton
3B K. Oberkfell
OF G. Hendrick
OF T. Landrum
OF S. Lezcano
C D. Porter
UT D. Iorg

P L. Sorensen
P R. Forsch
P J. Martin
P S. Martinez
RP H. Sutter
RP R. Shirley

STL 1982 N

M D. Herzog
1B K. Hernandez
2B T. Herr
SS O. Smith
3B K. Oberkfell
OF L. Smith
OF G. Hendrick
OF W. McGee
C D. Porter
UT D. Iorg
UT M. Ramsey
P J. Andujar
P R. Forsch
P S. Mura
P D. LaPoint
P J. Stuper
RP H. Sutter
RP C. Bair

STL 1983 N

M D. Herzog
1B G. Hendrick
2B T. Herr
SS O. Smith
3B K. Oberkfell
OF W. McGee
OF D. Green
OF L. Smith
C D. Porter
UT M. Ramsey
UT A. Van Slyke
P J. Andujar
P J. Stuper
P D. LaPoint
P R. Forsch
P N. Allen
RP H. Sutter
RP J. Lahti

STL 1984 N

M D. Herzog
1B D. Green
2B T. Herr
SS O. Smith
3B T. Pendleton
OF W. McGee
OF L. Smith
OF G. Hendrick
C D. Porter
UT T. Landrum
UT A. Van Slyke
P J. Andujar
P J. LaPoint
P D. Cox
P R. Horton
P K. Kepshire
RP H. Sutter
RP N. Allen

STL 1985 N

M D. Herzog
1B J. Clark
2B T. Herr
SS O. Smith
3B T. Pendleton
OF V. Coleman
OF W. McGee
OF A. Van Slyke
C T. Nieto
P J. Tudor
P J. Andujar
P D. Cox
P K. Kepshire
P R. Forsch
RP H. Sutter
RP N. Allen

STL 1986 N

M D. Herzog
1B J. Clark
2B T. Herr
SS O. Smith
3B T. Pendleton
OF V. Coleman
OF W. McGee
OF A. Van Slyke
C M. LaValliere
P R. Forsch
P D. Cox
P J. Tudor
P G. Mathews
P T. Conroy
RP T. Worrell

RP R. Horton

STL 1987 N

M D. Herzog
1B J. Clark
2B T. Herr
SS O. Smith
3B T. Pendleton
OF W. McGee
OF V. Coleman
OF C. Ford
C A. Pena
UT J. Morris
UT J. Oquendo
P D. Cox
P G. Mathews
P R. Forsch
P J. Magrane
P J. Tudor
RP R. Horton
RP W. Dawley

STL 1988 N

M D. Herzog
1B J. Horner
2B L. Alicea
SS O. Smith
3B T. Pendleton
OF V. Coleman
OF T. Brunansky
OF W. McGee
C A. Pena
UT J. Oquendo
P J. DeLeon
P J. Magrane
P J. Tudor
P L. McWilliams
P R. Forsch
RP S. Terry
RP T. Worrell

St. Paul

STP U 1884

STP 1884 U

M A. Thompson
1B S. Dunn
2B E. Hengle
SS J. Werrick
3B W. O'Brien
OF J. Tilley
OF J. Carroll
OF W. Barnes
C C. Ganzel
P J. Brown
P L. Galvin

San Diego

SD N 1969-1988

SD 1969 N

M P. Gomez
1B N. Colbert
2B J. Arcia
SS T. Dean
3B E. Spiezio
OF O. Brown
OF C. Gaston
OF A. Ferrara
C C. Cannizzaro
UT I. Murrell
UT R. Pena
P C. Kirby
P J. Niekro
P A. Santorini
P R. Kelley
RP T. Sisk
RP G. Ross

SD 1970 N

M P. Gomez
1B N. Colbert
2B D. Campbell
SS J. Arcia
3B E. Spiezio
OF C. Gaston
OF O. Brown
OF I. Murrell
C C. Cannizzaro
UT A. Ferrara
UT M. LaValliere

RP T. Dukes

SD 1971 N

M P. Gomez
1B N. Colbert
2B D. Mason
SS E. Hernandez
3B E. Spiezio
OF O. Brown
OF C. Gaston
OF L. Stahl
C R. Barton
UT D. Campbell
UT I. Murrell
P D. Roberts
P C. Kirby
P S. Arlin
P T. Phoebus
P F. Norman
RP A. Severinsen
RP R. Miller

SD 1972 N

M P. Gomez
M D. Zimmer
1B N. Colbert
2B D. Thomas
SS E. Hernandez
3B D. Roberts
OF J. Morales
OF L. Lee
OF C. Gaston
C F. Kendall
UT J. Jeter
UT L. Stahl
P S. Arlin
P C. Kirby
P F. Norman
P R. Caldwell
P W. Greif
RP M. Corkins
RP G. Ross

SD 1973 N

M D. Zimmer
1B N. Colbert
2B R. Morales
SS D. Thomas
3B D. Roberts
OF C. Gaston
OF J. Grubb
OF J. Morales
C F. Kendall
UT L. Lee
P J. Carroll
P W. Greif
P C. Kirby
P S. Arlin
P R. Troedson
P R. Jones
RP R. Caldwell
RP M. Corkins

SD 1974 N

M J. McNamara
1B W. McCovey
2B D. Thomas
SS E. Hernandez
3B D. Roberts
OF D. Winfield
OF J. Grubb
OF R. Tolan
C F. Kendall
UT N. Colbert
UT C. Gaston
P W. Greif
P D. Freisleben
P R. Jones
P D. Spillner
RP H. Hardy
RP V. Romo

SD 1975 N

M J. McNamara
1B W. McCovey
2B R. Fuentes
SS E. Hernandez
3B T. Kubiak
OF J. Grubb
OF D. Winfield
OF R. Tolan
C F. Kendall
UT M. Ivie
UT J. Locklear
UT H. Torres
P R. Jones
P J. McIntosh
P D. Freisleben
P D. Spillner
P R. Folkers
RP D. Frisella
RP D. Tomlin

SD 1976 N

M J. McNamara
M M. Ivie
1B R. Fuentes
2B E. Hernandez
3B D. Rader
OF D. Winfield
OF W. Davis
OF J. Grubb
C F. Kendall
UT J. Turner
P R. Jones
P B. Strom
P D. Freisleben
P D. Spillner
RP C. Metzger
RP D. Tomlin

SD 1977 N

M J. McNamara
M R. Skinner
M A. Dark
1B M. Ivie
2B R. Champion
SS W. Almon
3B T. Ashford
OF D. Winfield
OF G. Hendrick
OF E. Richards
C F. Tenace
UT M. Rettenmund
UT J. Turner
P R. Shirley
P R. Owchinko
P T. Griffin
P R. Jones
P D. Freisleben
RP R. Fingers
RP D. Spillner

SD 1978 N

M R. Craig
1B F. Tenace
2B J. Gonzalez
SS O. Smith
3B W. Almon
OF D. Winfield
OF E. Richards
OF O. Gamble
C R. Sweet
UT D. Thomas
UT J. Turner
P G. Perry
P R. Jones
P R. Owchinko
P R. Shirley
P E. Rasmussen
RP R. Fingers
RP J. D'Acquisto

SD 1979 N

M R. Craig
1B D. Briggs
2B J. Gonzalez
SS O. Smith
3B L. Dade
OF D. Winfield
OF E. Richards
OF J. Turner
C F. TEnace
UT W. Almon
UT K. Bevacqua
P R. Jones
P G. Perry
P R. Shirley
P E. Rasmussen
P R. Owchinko
RP J. D'Acquisto
RP R. Fingers

SD 1980 N

M G. Coleman
1B G. Montanez
2B D. Cash
SS O. Smith
3B A. Rodriguez
OF D. Winfield
OF E. Richards
OF J. Mumphrey
C F. Tenace
P J. Curtis
P S. Mura
P R. Wise
P R. Jones
P G. Lucas
RP R. Shirley
RP E. Rasmussen

SD 1981 N

M F. Howard

1B B. Perkins
2B J. Bonilla
SS O. Smith
3B L. Salazar
OF R. Jones
OF E. Richards
OF J. Lefebvre
C T. Kennedy
UT R. Bass
P J. Eichelberger
P S. Mura
P C. Welsh
P R. Wise
P W. Lollar
RP G. Lucas
RP J. Curtis

SD 1982 N

M R. Williams
1B B. Perkins
2B T. Flannery
SS G. Templeton
3B L. Salazar
OF S. Lezcano
OF R. Jones
OF E. Richards
C T. Kennedy
UT J. Lefebvre
P W. Lollar
P J. Montefusco
P J. Eichelberger
P E. Show
P C. Welsh
RP L. DeLeon
RP G. Lucas

SD 1983 N

M R. Williams
1B S. Garvey
2B J. Bonilla
SS G. Templeton
3B L. Salazar
OF R. Jones
OF A. Wiggins
OF S. Lezcano
C T. Kennedy
P E. Show
P D. Dravecky
P W. Lollar
P E. Whitson
P M. Hawkins
RP L. DeLeon
RP G. Lucas

SD 1984 N

M R. Williams
1B S. Garvey
2B A. Wiggins
SS G. Templeton
3B G. Nettles
OF A. Gwynn
OF C. Martinez
C T. Kennedy
P E. Show
P W. Lollar
P E. Whitson
P M. Thurmond
P D. Dravecky
RP C. Lefferts
RP R. Gossage

SD 1985 N

M R. Williams
1B S. Garvey
2B T. Flannery
SS G. Templeton
3B G. Nettles
OF A. Gwynn
OF W. McReynolds
OF C. Martinez
C T. Kennedy
P E. Show
P M. Hawkins
P D. Dravecky
P D. Hoyt
P M. Thurmond
RP C. Lefferts
RP R. Gossage

SD 1986 N

M S. Boros
1B S. Garvey
2B T. Flannery
SS G. Templeton
3B G. Nettles
OF A. Gwynn
OF W. McReynolds
OF M. Wynne
C T. Kennedy
UT J. Kruk

UT C. Martinez
UT L. Roberts
UT J. Royster
P M. Hawkins
P D. Dravecky
P D. Hoyt
P E. Show
RP L. McCullers
RP C. Lefferts

SD 1987 N

M L. Bowa
1B J. Kruk
2B T. Flannery
SS G. Templeton
3B R. Ready
OF A. Gwynn
OF S. Jefferson
OF S. Mack
C B. Santiago
UT C. Martinez
UT M. Wynne
P E. Whitson
P E. Show
P J. Jones
P M. Hawkins
P M. Grant
RP L. McCullers
RP D. Dravecky

SD 1988 N

M L. Bowa
M J. McKeon
1B B. Moreland
2B R. Alomar
SS G. Templeton
3B J. Brown
OF A. Gwynn
OF M. Wynne
OF J. Kruk
C B. Santiago
UT C. Martinez
UT R. Ready
P E. Show
P M. Hawkins
P E. Whitson
P J. Jones
P D. Rasmussen
RP L. McCullers
RP M. Grant

San Francisco

SF N 1958-1988

SF 1958 N

M W. Rigney
1B O. Cepeda
2B D. O'Connell
SS J. Spencer
3B J. Davenport
OF W. Mays
OF W. Kirkland
OF F. Alou
C R. Schmidt
P J. Antonelli
P R. Gomez
P S. Miller
P M. McCormick
P R. Monzant
RP A. Worthington
RP M. Grissom

SF 1959 N

M W. Rigney
1B O. Cepeda
2B D. Spencer
SS E. Bressoud
3B J. Davenport
OF W. Mays
OF W. Kirkland
OF J. Brandt
C H. Landrith
UT F. Alou
P J. Antonelli
P S. Jones
P M. McCormick
P J. Sanford
RP S. Miller
RP A. Worthington

SF 1960 N

M W. Rigney
M T. Sheehan
1B W. McCovey
2B D. Blasingame
SS E. Bressoud
3B J. Davenport
OF W. Mays

OF W. Kirkland
OF F. Alou
C R. Schmidt
UT J. Amalfitano
UT O. Cepeda
P M. McCormick
P S. Jones
P J. Sanford
P W. O'Dell
RP J. Antonelli
RP S. Miller

SF 1961 N

M A. Dark
1B W. McCovey
2B J. Amalfitano
SS J. Pagan
3B J. Davenport
OF W. Mays
OF F. Alou
OF H. Kuenn
C L. Bailey
UT O. Cepeda
P M. McCormick
P J. Sanford
P J. Marichal
P S. Jones
P W. Loes
RP W. O'Dell
RP S. Miller

SF 1962 N

M A. Dark
1B O. Cepeda
2B C. Hiller
SS J. Pagan
3B J. Davenport
OF W. Mays
OF F. Alou
OF H. Kuenn
C T. Haller
P W. O'Dell
P J. Sanford
P J. Marichal
P W. Pierce
P M. McCormick
RP S. Miller
RP B. Bolin

SF 1963 N

M A. Dark
1B O. Cepeda
2B C. Hiller
SS J. Pagan
3B J. Davenport
OF W. Mays
OF F. Alou
OF W. McCovey
C L. Bailey
UT T. Haller
UT H. Kuenn
P J. Marichal
P J. Sanford
P W. O'Dell
P J. Fisher
RP B. Bolin
RP W. Pierce

SF 1964 N

M A. Dark
1B O. Cepeda
2B H. Lanier
SS J. Pagan
3B J. Hart
OF W. Mays
OF J. Alou
OF H. Kuenn
C T. Haller
UT M. Alou
UT J. Davenport
UT W. McCovey
P J. Marichal
P G. Perry
P B. Bolin
P C. Hendley
P R. Herbel
RP R. Shaw
RP W. O'Dell

SF 1965 N

M H. Franks
1B W. McCovey
2B H. Lanier
SS J. Schofield
3B J. Hart
OF W. Mays
OF J. Alou
OF M. Alou
C T. Haller
UT J. Davenport
P J. Marichal
P R. Shaw
P G. Perry
P R. Herbel
P B. Bolin
RP F. Linzy
RP M. Murakami

SF 1966 N

M H. Franks
1B W. McCovey
2B H. Lanier
SS R. Fuentes
3B J. Hart
OF W. Mays
OF O. Brown
OF J. Alou
C T. Haller
UT J. Davenport
P J. Marichal
P G. Perry
P B. Bolin
P R. Herbel
P R. Sadecki
RP L. McDaniel
RP F. Linzy

SF 1967 N

M H. Franks
1B W. McCovey
2B R. Fuentes
SS H. Lanier
3B J. Hart
OF W. Mays
OF J. Alou
OF O. Brown
C T. Haller
UT J. Davenport
P G. Perry
P M. McCormick
P J. Marichal
P R. Sadecki
P R. Herbel
RP F. Linzy
RP J. Gibbon

SF 1968 N

M H. Franks
1B W. McCovey
2B R. Hunt
SS H. Lanier
3B J. Davenport
OF W. Mays
OF J. Alou
OF B. Bonds
C R. Dietz
UT T. Cline
UT J. Hart
P J. Marichal
P G. Perry
P R. Sadecki
P M. McCormick
P B. Bolin
RP F. Linzy

SF 1969 N

M C. King
1B W. McCovey
2B R. Hunt
SS H. Lanier
3B J. Davenport
OF B. Bonds
OF K. Henderson
OF W. Mays
C R. Dietz
UT E. Burda
UT D. Marshall
UT D. Mason
P G. Perry
P J. Marichal
P M. McCormick
P B. Bolin
P R. Sadecki
RP F. Linzy
RP R. Herbel

SF 1970 N

M C. King
M C. Fox
1B W. McCovey
2B R. Hunt
SS H. Lanier
3B A. Gallagher
OF B. Bonds
OF K. Henderson
OF W. Mays
C R. Dietz
UT R. Fuentes
P G. Perry
P J. Marichal
P R. Robertson
P F. Reberger
RP R. Bryant
RP D. McMahon

SF 1971 N

M C. Fox
1B W. McCovey
2B R. Fuentes
SS C. Speier
3B A. Gallagher
OF B. Bonds
OF K. Henderson
OF W. Mays
C R. Dietz
UT H. Lanier
P G. Perry
P J. Marichal
P J. Cumberland
P R. Bryant
P S. Stone
RP J. Johnson
RP D. McMahon

SF 1972 N

M C. Fox
1B W. McCovey
2B R. Fuentes
SS C. Speier
3B A. Gallagher
OF B. Bonds
OF K. Henderson
OF G. Maddox
C D. Rader
UT D. Kingman
P R. Bryant
P J. Barr
P J. Marichal
P S. McDowell
P S. Stone
RP J. Johnson
RP R. Moffitt

SF 1973 N

M C. Fox
1B W. McCovey
2B R. Fuentes
SS C. Speier
3B J. Goodson
OF B. Bonds
OF G. Matthews
OF G. Maddox
C D. Rader
UT D. Kingman
UT G. Thomasson
P R. Bryant
P J. Barr
P T. Bradley
P J. Marichal
P J. Willoughby
RP E. Sosa
RP R. Moffitt

SF 1974 N

M C. Fox
M W. Westrum
1B D. Kingman
2B R. Fuentes
SS C. Speier
3B S. Ontiveros
OF G. Matthews
OF B. Bonds
OF G. Maddox
C D. Rader
UT J. Goodson
UT M. Phillips
UT G. Thomasson
P J. Barr
P J. D'Acquisto
P R. Caldwell
P T. Bradley
P R. Bryant
RP R. Moffitt
RP E. Sosa

SF 1975 N

M W. Westrum
1B G. Montanez
2B D. Thomas
SS C. Speier
3B S. Ontiveros
OF B. Murcer
OF V. Joshua
OF G. Matthews
C D. Rader
UT C. Miller
UT G. Thomasson
P J. Montefusco
P J. Barr
P P. Falcone
P R. Caldwell
P E. Halicki
RP C. Williams
RP G. Lavelle

SF 1976 N

M W. Rigney
1B D. Evans
2B M. Perez
SS C. Speier
3B K. Reitz
OF G. Matthews
OF B. Murcer
OF L. Herndon
C D. Rader
UT G. Thomasson
P J. Montefusco
P J. Barr
P E. Halicki
P R. Dressler
P J. D'Acquisto
RP G. Lavelle
RP R. Caldwell

SF 1977 N

M J. Altobelli
1B W. McCovey
2B R. Andrews
SS T. Foli
3B B. Madlock
OF J. Clark
OF G. Thomasson
OF T. Whitfield
C M. Hill
UT D. Evans
UT D. Thomas
P E. Halicki
P J. Barr
P R. Knepper
P J. Montefusco
RP C. Williams
RP G. Lavelle

SF 1978 N

M J. Altobelli
1B W. McCovey
2B B. Madlock
SS J. LeMaster
3B D. Evans
OF J. Clark
OF L. Herndon
OF T. Whitfield
C M. Hill
UT M. Ivie
P R. Knepper
P V. Blue
P J. Montefusco
P E. Halicki
P J. Barr
RP G. Lavelle
RP R. Moffitt

SF 1979 N

M J. Altobelli
M J. Bristol
1B M. Ivie
2B J. Strain
SS J. LeMaster
3B D. Evans
OF J. Clark
OF W. North
OF L. Herndon
C D. Littlejohn
UT W. McCovey
UT T. Whitfield
P V. Blue
P R. Knepper
P J. Montefusco
P E. Halicki
P J. Curtis
RP G. Lavelle
RP T. Griffin

SF 1980 N

M J. Bristol
1B M. Ivie
2B R. Stennett
SS J. LeMaster
3B D. Evans
OF L. Herndon
OF J. Clark
OF W. North
C M. May
UT T. Whitfield
P V. Blue
P R. Knepper
P E. Whitson
P A. Ripley
P J. Montefusco
RP T. Griffin
RP G. Lavelle

SF 1981 N

M F. Robinson
1B E. Cabell
2B J. Morgan
SS J. LeMaster
3B D. Evans
OF J. Clark
OF L. Herndon
OF J. Martin
C M. May
P D. Alexander
P T. Griffin
P V. Blue
P E. Whitson
P A. Ripley
RP A. Holland
RP G. Minton

SF 1982 N

M F. Robinson
1B C. Smith
2B J. Morgan
SS J. LeMaster
3B D. Evans
OF J. Clark
OF C. Davis
OF J. Leonard
C M. May
UT D. Bergman
UT D. Kuiper
UT J. Wohlford
P W. Laskey
P C. Hammaker
P R. Gale
P D. Martin
RP F. Breining
RP A. Holland

SF 1983 N

M F. Robinson
1B D. Evans
2B B. Wellman
SS J. LeMaster
3B T. O'Malley
OF J. Leonard
OF C. Davis
OF J. Clark
C R. Brenly
UT J. Youngblood
P F. Breining
P M. Krukow
P C. Hammaker
P W. Laskey
P A. McGaffigan
RP G. Minton
RP D. Martin

SF 1984 N

M F. Robinson
M D. Ozark
1B V. Thompson
2B J. Trillo
SS J. LeMaster
3B J. Youngblood
OF J. Leonard
OF C. Davis
OF C. Gladden
C R. Brenly
UT J. Baker
P W. Laskey
P M. Krukow
P M. Davis
P J. Robinson
RP G. Minton
RP F. Williams

SF 1985 N

M J. Davenport
M R. Craig
1B D. Green
2B J. Trillo
SS J. Uribe
3B J. Brown
OF J. Leonard
OF C. Davis
OF C. Gladden
C R. Brenly
P D. LaPoint
P M. Krukow
P C. Hammaker
P J. Gott
P V. Blue
RP M. Davis
RP S. Garrelts

SF 1986 N

M R. Craig
1B W. Clark
2B R. Thompson
SS J. Uribe
3B J. Brown
OF C. Davis
OF C. Maldonado
OF C. Gladden
C R. Brenly
UT J. Youngblood
P M. Krukow
P M. LaCoss
P S. Garrelts
P V. Blue
RP J. Robinson
RP M. Davis

SF 1987 N

M R. Craig
1B W. Clark
2B R. Thompson
SS J. Uribe
3B K. Mitchell
OF C. Davis
OF J. Leonard
OF C. Maldonado
C R. Brenly
UT M. Aldrete
UT E. Milner
UT C. Speier
P K. Downs
P M. LaCoss
P C. Hammaker
P M. Krukow
P D. Dravecky
RP S. Garrelts
RP J. Robinson

SF 1988 N

M R. Craig
1B W. Clark
2B R. Thompson
SS J. Uribe
3B K. Mitchell
OF B. Butler
OF C. Maldonado
OF M. Aldrete
C R. Melvin
P R. Reuschel
P D. Robinson
P K. Downs
P C. Hammaker
P M. Krukow
RP S. Garrelts
RP C. Lefferts

Seattle

SEA A 1969
Moved to Milwaukee
SEA A 1977-1988

SEA 1969 A

M J. Schultz
1B D. Mincher
2B J. Donaldson
SS R. Oyler
3B T. Harper
OF H. Comer
OF H. Davis
OF S. Hovley
C G. McNertney
P E. Brabender
P M. Pattin
P F. Talbot
RP D. Segui
RP J. Gelnar

SEA 1977 A

M D. Johnson
1B D. Meyer
2B J. Baez
SS G. Reynolds
3B W. Stein
OF R. Jones
OF S. Braun
OF L. Stanton
C G. Stinson
DH J. Bernhardt
UT D. Collins
UT C. Lopez
P W. Abbott
P J. Montague
P R. Pole
RP E. Romo
RP D. Segui

SEA 1978 A

M D. Johnson
1B D. Meyer
2B J. Cruz
SS G. Reynolds
3B W. Stein
OF L. Roberts
OF R. Jones
OF J. Hale
C G. Stinson
DH L. Stanton
UT B. Bochte
P P. Mitchell
P W. Abbott
P F. Honeycutt
P T. House
P J. Colborn
RP S. Rawley
RP J. Todd

SEA 1979 A

M D. Johnson
1B B. Bochte
2B J. Cruz
SS M. Mendoza
3B D. Meyer
OF R. Jones
OF L. Roberts
OF J. Simpson
C L. Cox
DH W. Horton
UT L. Milbourne
UT T. Paciorek
P M. Parrott
P F. Honeycutt
P F. Bannister
P O. Jones
P W. Abbott
RP B. McLaughlin
RP J. Montague

SEA 1980 A

M D. Johnson
M M. Wills
1B B. Bochte
2B J. Cruz
SS M. Mendoza
3B W. Cox
OF D. Meyer
OF J. Simpson
OF L. Roberts
C L. Cox
DH W. Horton
UT J. Anderson
UT L. Milbourne
UT T. Paciorek
P F. Bannister
P W. Abbott
P F. Honeycutt
P J. Beattie
P R. Dressler
RP S. Rawley
RP B. McLaughlin

SEA 1981 A

M M. Wills
M R. Lachemann
1B B. Bochte
2B J. Cruz
SS J. Anderson
3B L. Randle
OF T. Paciorek
OF J. Simpson
OF J. Burroughs
C J. Narron
DH R. Zisk
UT G. Gray
UT D. Meyer
P W. Abbott
P F. Bannister
P K. Clay
P B. Clark
P M. Parrott
RP S. Rawley
RP L. Andersen

SEA 1982 A

M R. Lachemann
1B G. Gray
2B J. Cruz
SS T. Cruz
3B E. Castillo
OF A. Cowens
OF D. Henderson
OF B. Bochte
C R. Sweet
DH R. Zisk
UT J. Simpson
P F. Bannister
P G. Perry
P J. Beattie
P M. Moore
P W. Nelson
RP W. Caudill
RP L. Andersen

SEA 1983 A

M R. Lachemann

M D. Crandall
1B P. Putnam
2B A. Bernazard
SS S. Owen
3B J. Allen
OF D. Henderson
OF S. Henderson
OF R. Nelson
C R. Sweet
DH R. Zisk
UT A. Cowens
P M. Young
P J. Beattie
P R. Stoddard
P B. Clark
P M. Moore
RP R. Thomas
RP W. Caudill

SEA 1984 A

M D. Crandall
M C. Cottier
1B A. Davis
2B J. Perconte
SS S. Owen
3B J. Presley
OF A. Cowens
OF P. Bradley
OF D. Henderson
C R. Kearney
DH K. Phelps
UT R. Bonnell
UT S. Henderson
P M. Langston
P M. Moore
P J. Beattie
P M. Young
RP E. Vande Berg
RP R. Stoddard

SEA 1985 A

M C. Cottier
1B A. Davis
2B J. Perconte
SS S. Owen
3B J. Presley
OF P. Bradley
OF D. Henderson
OF A. Cowens
C R. Kearney
DH J. Thomas
P M. Moore
P M. Young
P M. Langston
P F. Wills
P W. Swift
RP R. Thomas
RP E. Nunez

SEA 1986 A

M C. Cottier
M O. Martinez
M R. Williams
1B A. Davis
2B H. Reynolds
SS S. Owen
3B J. Presley
OF P. Bradley
OF D. Tartabull
OF J. Moses
C R. Kearney
DH J. Thomas
UT D. Henderson
UT K. Phelps
P M. Moore
P M. Langston
P M. Morgan
P W. Swift
RP M. Young
RP M. Huismann

SEA 1987 A

M R. Williams
1B A. Davis
2B H. Reynolds
SS R. Quinones
3B J. Presley
OF P. Bradley
OF M. Kingery
OF J. Moses
C S. Bradley
DH K. Phelps
P M. Langston
P M. Moore
P M. Morgan
P M. Bankhead
P A. Guetterman
RP J. Reed
RP W. Wilkinson

SEA 1988 A

M R. Williams
M J. Snyder
1B A. Davis
2B H. Reynolds
SS R. Quinones
3B J. Presley
OF M. Brantley
OF H. Cotto
OF G. Wilson
C S. Bradley
DH K. Phelps
UT S. Balboni
P M. Langston
P M. Moore
P W. Swift
P M. Bankhead
P M. Campbell
RP M. Jackson
RP J. Reed

Syracuse

SYR N 1879
SYR a 1890

SYR 1879 N

M M. Dorgan
M W. Holbert
M J. Macullar
1B W. Carpenter
2B J. Farrell
SS J. Macullar
3B J. Woodhead
OF M. Mansell
OF W. Purcell
OF J. Richmond
C W. Holbert
UT M. Dorgan
P P. McCormick

SYR 1890 a

M G. Frazer
M W. Fessenden
M G. Frazer
1B W. McQuery
2B C. Childs
SS B. McLaughlin
3B T. O'Rourke
OF W. Wright
OF F. Ely
OF P. Friel
C G. Briggs
P D. Casey
P J. Keefe
P M. Morrison
P E. Mars

Texas

TEX A 1973-1988

TEX 1973 A

M D. Herzog
M D. Wilber
M A. Martin
1B J. Spencer
2B D. Nelson
SS J. Mason
3B C. Harrah
OF J. Burroughs
OF V. Harris
OF E. Maddox
C K. Suarez
DH A. Johnson
P J. Bibby
P J. Merritt
P W. Siebert
P P. Broberg
RP W. Gogolewski
RP M. Paul

TEX 1974 A

M A. Martin
1B D. Hargrove
2B D. Nelson
SS C. Harrah
3B L. Randle
OF J. Burroughs
OF C. Tovar
OF J. Lovitto
C J. Sundberg
DH J. Spencer
UT A. Johnson
P F. Jenkins
P J. Bibby
P J. Brown
P S. Hargan
P D. Clyde

RP S. Foucault

TEX 1975 A

M A. Martin
M F. Lucchesi
1B J. Spencer
2B L. Randle
SS C. Harrah
3B R. Howell
OF J. Burroughs
OF D. Hargrove
OF T. Grieve
C J. Sundberg
DH C. Tovar
P F. Jenkins
P S. Hargan
P G. Perry
P W. Hands
RP J. Umbarger
RP S. Foucault

TEX 1976 A

M F. Lucchesi
1B D. Hargrove
2B L. Randle
SS C. Harrah
3B R. Howell
OF J. Burroughs
OF J. Beniquez
OF E. Clines
C J. Sundberg
DH T. Grieve
P G. Perry
P N. Briles
P R. Blyleven
P J. Umbarger
P S. Hargan
RP S. Foucault
RP M. Bacsik

TEX 1977 A

M F. Lucchesi
M E. Stanky
M C. Ryan
M G. Hunter
1B D. Hargrove
2B E. Wills
SS D. Campaneris
3B C. Harrah
OF C. Washington
OF J. Beniquez
OF D. May
C J. Sundberg
DH W. Horton
P G. Perry
P D. Alexander
P R. Blyleven
P D. Ellis
P N. Briles
RP P. Devine
RP P. Lindblad

TEX 1978 A

M G. Hunter
M P. Corrales
1B D. Hargrove
2B E. Wills
SS D. Campaneris
3B C. Harrah
OF J. Beniquez
OF B. Bonds
OF A. Oliver
C J. Sundberg
DH R. Zisk
P J. Matlack
P F. Jenkins
P D. Alexander
P G. Medich
P D. Ellis
RP R. Cleveland
RP L. Barker

TEX 1979 A

M P. Corrales
1B P. Putnam
2B E. Wills
SS N. Norman
3B D. Bell
OF R. Zisk
OF A. Oliver
OF W. Sample
C J. Sundberg
DH J. Ellis
UT J. Grubb
P F. Jenkins
P S. Comer
P G. Medich
P D. Alexander
RP J. Kern
RP A. Lyle

TEX 1980 A

M P. Corrales
1B P. Putnam
2B E. Wills
SS J. Frias
3B D. Bell
OF A. Oliver
OF J. Rivers
OF J. Norris
C J. Sundberg
DH R. Zisk
UT J. Grubb
UT D. Roberts
UT D. Staub
P J. Matlack
P G. Medich
P F. Jenkins
P G. Perry
RP D. Darwin
RP A. Lyle

TEX 1981 A

M D. Zimmer
M D. Zimmer
1B P. Putnam
2B E. Wills
SS M. Mendoza
3B D. Bell
OF J. Rivers
OF L. Roberts
OF W. Sample
C J. Sundberg
DH A. Oliver
UT J. Grubb
P D. Darwin
P G. Medich
P F. Honeycutt
P F. Jenkins
P J. Matlack
RP S. Comer
RP D. Schmidt

TEX 1982 A

M D. Zimmer
M D. Johnson
1B D. Hostetler
2B M. Richardt
SS M. Wagner
3B D. Bell
OF G. Wright
OF L. Parrish
OF W. Sample
C J. Sundberg
DH L. Johnson
UT J. Grubb
P C. Hough
P F. Tanana
P F. Honeycutt
P J. Matlack
P G. Medich
RP S. Comer
RP D. Darwin

TEX 1983 A

M D. Rader
1B P. O'Brien
2B J. Tolleson
SS R. Dent
3B D. Bell
OF G. Wright
OF W. Sample
OF L. Parrish
C J. Sundberg
DH D. Hostetler
P C. Hough
P B. Smithson
P D. Darwin
P F. Honeycutt
P F. Tanana
RP J. Matlack
RP O. Jones

TEX 1984 A

M D. Rader
1B P. O'Brien
2B J. Tolleson
SS C. Wilkerson
3B D. Bell
OF G. Ward
OF W. Sample
OF L. Parrish
C D. Scott
DH J. Rivers
UT G. Wright
P C. Hough
P F. Tanana
P D. Darwin
P D. Stewart
P M. Mason
RP D. Schmidt
RP O. Jones

TEX 1985 A

M D. Rader
M R. Valentine
1B P. O'Brien
2B C. Harrah
SS C. Wilkerson
3B D. Bell
OF G. Ward
OF O. McDowell
OF G. Wright
C D. Slaught
DH C. Johnson
UT J. Tolleson
P C. Hough
P M. Mason
P B. Hooton
P D. Noles
RP G. Harris
RP D. Rozema

TEX 1986 A

M R. Valentine
1B P. O'Brien
2B C. Harrah
SS S. Fletcher
3B S. Buechele
OF O. McDowell
OF P. Incaviglia
OF R. Sierra
C D. Slaught
DH L. Parrish
UT G. Ward
UT C. Wilkerson
P C. Hough
P E. Correa
P J. Guzman
P R. Witt
P M. Mason
RP G. Harris
RP M. Williams

TEX 1987 A

M R. Valentine
1B P. O'Brien
2B J. Browne
SS S. Fletcher
3B S. Buechele
OF R. Sierra
OF P. Incaviglia
OF O. McDowell
C D. Slaught
DH L. Parrish
UT R. Brower
UT E. Petralli
P C. Hough
P J. Guzman
P R. Witt
P G. Harris
RP M. Williams
RP D. Mohorcic

TEX 1988 A

M R. Valentine
1B P. O'Brien
2B C. Wilkerson
SS S. Fletcher
3B S. Buechele
OF R. Sierra
OF O. McDowell
OF C. Espy
C E. Petralli
DH L. Parrish
UT P. Incaviglia
P C. Hough
P J. Guzman
P P. Kilgus
P J. Russell
P R. Witt
RP M. Williams
RP J. McMurtry

Toledo

TOL a 1884
TOL a 1890

TOL 1884 a

M C. Morton
1B G. Lane
2B S. Barkley
SS J. Miller
3B E. Brown
OF C. Welch
OF T. Poorman
OF F. Olin
C M. Walker
P A. Mullane
P H. O'Day

TOL 1890 a

M C. Morton
1B P. Werden
2B T. Nicholson
SS F. Scheibeck
3B W. Alvord
OF C. Swartwood
OF W. Van Dyke
OF G. Tebeau
C H. Sage
P J. Healy
P E. Cushman
P F. Smith

Toronto

TOR A 1977-1988

TOR 1977 A

M R. Hartsfield
1B D. Ault
2B S. Staggs
SS H. Torres
3B R. Howell
OF A. Woods
OF S. Bowling
OF O. Velez
C A. Ashby
DH R. Fairly
UT R. Bailor
UT S. Ewing
P D. Lemanczyk
P T. Garvin
P J. Jefferson
RP P. Vuckovich
RP M. Willis

TOR 1978 A

M R. Hartsfield
1B J. Mayberry
2B D. McKay
SS J. Gomez
3B R. Howell
OF R. Bosetti
OF R. Bailor
OF O. Velez
C R. Cerone
DH R. Carty
P J. Jefferson
P T. Underwood
P J. Clancy
P T. Garvin
P B. Moore
RP M. Willis
RP T. Murphy

TOR 1979 A

M R. Hartsfield
1B J. Mayberry
2B D. Ainge
SS A. Griffin
3B R. Howell
OF R. Bosetti
OF A. Woods
OF R. Bailor
C R. Cerone
DH R. Carty
UT O. Velez
P T. Underwood
P P. Huffman
P D. Lemanczyk
P B. Moore
P D. Stieb
RP D. Freisleben
RP T. Buskey

TOR 1980 A

M R. Mattick
1B J. Mayberry
2B D. Garcia
SS A. Griffin
3B R. Howell
OF R. Bonnell
OF L. Moseby
OF R. Bailor
C L. Whitt
DH O. Velez
UT A. Woods
P J. Clancy
P D. Stieb
P P. Mirabella
P J. Jefferson
RP J. McLaughlin
RP T. Garvin

TOR 1981 A

M R. Mattick
1B J. Mayberry
2B D. Garcia

SS A. Griffin
3B D. Ainge
OF L. Moseby
OF A. Woods
OF R. Bonnell
C L. Whitt
DH O. Velez
UT G. Iorg
P D. Stieb
P L. Leal
P J. Clancy
P J. Todd
P M. Bomback
RP R. Jackson
RP J. McLaughlin

TOR 1982 A

M R. Cox
1B W. Upshaw
2B D. Garcia
SS A. Griffin
3B S. Mulliniks
OF L. Moseby
OF J. Barfield
OF R. Bonnell
C L. Whitt
DH D. Revering
UT G. Iorg
UT H. Powell
P D. Stieb
P J. Clancy
P L. Leal
P J. Gott
RP D. Murray
RP R. Jackson

TOR 1983 A

M R. Cox
1B W. Upshaw
2B D. Garcia
SS A. Griffin
3B S. Mulliniks
OF L. Moseby
OF J. Barfield
OF R. Bonnell
C L. Whitt
DH C. Johnson
UT D. Collins
UT G. Iorg
UT J. Orta
P D. Stieb
P J. Clancy
P L. Leal
P J. Gott
P D. Alexander
RP J. Acker
RP R. Jackson

TOR 1984 A

M R. Cox
1B W. Upshaw
2B D. Garcia
SS A. Griffin
3B S. Mulliniks
OF L. Moseby
OF J. Bell
OF D. Collins
C L. Whitt
DH C. Johnson
UT J. Barfield
UT G. Iorg
UT J. Martinez
P D. Stieb
P D. Alexander
P L. Leal
P J. Clancy
P J. Gott
RP R. Jackson
RP D. Lamp

TOR 1985 A

M R. Cox
1B W. Upshaw
2B D. Garcia
SS O. Fernandez
3B S. Mulliniks
OF J. Bell
OF J. Barfield
OF L. Moseby
C L. Whitt
DH J. Burroughs
UT G. Iorg
P D. Stieb
P D. Alexander
P J. Key
P J. Clancy
RP D. Lamp
RP J. Acker

TOR 1986 A

M J. Williams

1B W. Upshaw
2B D. Garcia
SS O. Fernandez
3B S. Mulliniks
OF J. Barfield
OF L. Moseby
OF J. Bell
C L. Whitt
DH C. Johnson
UT G. Iorg
UT R. Leach
P J. Key
P J. Clancy
P D. Stieb
P J. Cerutti
P D. Alexander
RP M. Eichhorn
RP T. Henke

TOR 1987 A

M J. Williams
1B W. Upshaw
2B G. Iorg
SS O. Fernandez
3B K. Gruber
OF J. Barfield
OF L. Moseby
OF J. Bell
C L. Whitt
DH F. McGriff
UT R. Leach
UT S. Mulliniks
P J. Key
P J. Clancy
P D. Stieb
P J. Cerutti
RP M. Eichhorn
RP J. Nunez

TOR 1988 A

M J. Williams
1B F. McGriff
2B M. Lee
SS O. Fernandez
3B K. Gruber
OF J. Bell
OF J. Barfield
OF L. Moseby
C L. Whitt
DH S. Mulliniks
UT N. Liriano
P M. Flanagan
P D. Stieb
P J. Clancy
P J. Key
P T. Stottlemyre
RP J. Cerutti
RP R. Ward

Troy

TRO n 1871-1872
TRO N 1879-1882

TRO 1871 n

M L. Pike
M W. Craver
1B W. Flynn
2B W. Craver
SS C. Flowers
3B E. Bellan
OF T. York
OF S. King
OF L. Pike
C M. McGeary
P J. McMullin

TRO 1872 n

M J. Wood
1B M. McAtee
2B J. Wood
SS E. Bellan
3B D. Force
OF S. King
OF A. Martin
OF A. Gedney
C D. Allison
UT E. Bellan
P G. Zettlein

TRO 1879 N

M H. Phillips
M R. Ferguson
1B D. Brouthers
2B T. Hawkes
SS E. Caskin
3B J. Doscher
OF J. Evans
OF A. Hall
OF T. Mansell
C C. Reilley
P G. Bradley
P H. Salisbury
P F. Goldsmith

TRO 1880 N

M R. Ferguson
1B E. Cogswell
2B R. Ferguson
SS E. Caskin
3B R. Connor
OF P. Gillespie
OF J. Cassidy
OF J. Evans
C W. Holbert
P M. Welch
P T. Keefe

TRO 1881 N

M R. Ferguson
1B R. Connor
2B R. Ferguson
SS E. Caskin
3B F. Hankinson
OF P. Gillespie
OF J. Cassidy
OF J. Evans
C W. Ewing
P T. Keefe
P M. Welch

TRO 1882 N

M R. Ferguson
1B J. Smith
2B R. Ferguson
SS N. Pfeffer
3B W. Ewing
OF J. Roseman
OF P. Gillespie
OF R. Connor
C W. Holbert
P T. Keefe
P M. Welch

Washington

OLY n 1871-1872 Olympics
NAT n 1872-1873
NAT n 1875 Nationals
WAS a 1884
WAS U 1884
WAS N 1886-1889
WAS a 1891
WAS N 1892-1899
WAS A 1901-1960 Moved to Minnesota
WAS A 1961-1971 Moved to Texas

OLY 1871 n

M N. Young
1B E. Mills
2B A. Leonard
SS D. Force
3B F. Waterman
OF G. Hall
OF J. Glenn
OF H. Berthrong
C D. Allison
P A. Brainard
P W. Stearns

OLY 1872 n

M N. Young
1B W. Flynn
2B T. Beals
SS W. Goldsmith
3B F. Waterman
OF J. Glenn
OF A. Robinson
OF G. Heubel
C F. Sellman
P A. Brainard

NAT 1872 n

M J. Miller
1B P. Hines
2B J. Hollingshead
SS J. Doyle
3B W. White
OF E. Mincher
OF O. Bielaski
OF S. Studley
C W. Lennon
UT D. Coughlin
P W. Stearns

NAT 1873 n

M N. Young
1B J. Glenn
2B T. Beals
SS J. Gerhardt
3B W. White
OF O. Bielaski
OF P. Hines
OF J. Hollingshead
C C. Snyder
UT T. Donnelly
P W. Stearns
P Greyson

NAT 1875 n

M J. Hollingshead
M S. Field
1B A. Allison
2B S. Brady
SS J. Dailey
3B J. Doscher
OF L. Ressler
OF J. Hollingshead
OF W. Parks
C F. Thompson
P W. Stearns
P W. Parks

WAS 1884 a

M J. Hollingshead
M Bickerson
1B W. Prince
2B T. Hawkes
SS F. Fennelly
3B J. Gladman
OF H. Mullin
OF H. Morgan
OF E. Trumbull
C J. Humphries
P R. Barr
P J. Hamill

WAS 1884 U

M M. Scanlon
1B P. Baker
2B T. Evers
SS J. Halpin
3B J. McCormick
OF H. Moore
OF W. Wise
OF C. Powell
C C. Fulmer
P W. Wise
P A. Voss
P C. Geggus

WAS 1886 N

M M. Scanlon
M J. Gaffney
1B P. Baker
2B J. Knowles
SS D. Force
3B J. Gladman
OF S. Carroll
OF P. Hines
OF E. Crane
C A. Gilligan
P F. Shaw
P R. Barr
P W. Madigan
P F. Gilmore

WAS 1887 N

M J. Gaffney
1B W. O'Brien
2B J. Myers
SS J. Farrell
3B J. Donnelly
OF P. Hines
OF S. Carroll
OF E. Daily
C C. Mack
P J. Whitney
P H. O'Day
P F. Gilmore
P F. Shaw

WAS 1888 N

M W. Hewett
M T. Sullivan
1B W. O'Brien
2B J. Myers
SS G. Shoch
3B J. Donnelly
OF W. Hoy
OF W. Wilmot
OF E. Daily
C C. Mack
P H. O'Day
P J. Whitney
P W. Widner
P G. Keefe
P F. Gilmore

WAS 1889 N

M J. Morrill
M A. Irwin
1B J. Carney
2B S. Wise
SS A. Irwin
3B J. Irwin
OF W. Hoy
OF W. Wilmot
OF E. Beecher
C T. Daly
UT C. Mack
P A. Ferson
P G. Haddock
P G. Keefe
P H. O'Day
P J. Healy

WAS 1891 a

M S. Trott
M C. Snyder
M D. Shannon
M T. Griffin
1B W. McQuery
2B T. Dowd
SS G. Hatfield
3B W. Alvord
OF L. Murphy
OF E. Beecher
OF P. Hines
C J. McGuire
P W. Carsey
P F. Foreman
P E. Bakely

WAS 1892 N

M W. Barnie
M A. Irwin
M D. Richardson
1B H. Larkin
2B T. Dowd
SS D. Richardson
3B W. Robinson
OF W. Hoy
OF C. Duffee
OF P. Radford
C J. McGuire
P F. Killen
P B. Abbey
P P. Knell
P J. Duryea
P J. Meekin

WAS 1893 N

M J. O'Rourke
1B H. Larkin
2B S. Wise
SS J. Sullivan
3B J. Mulvey
OF W. Hoy
OF P. Radford
OF J. O'Rourke
C C. Farrell
P C. Esper
P A. Maul
P J. Meekin
P J. Duryea

WAS 1894 N

M G. Schmelz
1B E. Cartwright
2B F. Ward
SS F. Scheibeck
3B W. Joyce
OF C. Abbey
OF A. Selbach
OF W. Hassamaer
C J. McGuire
UT P. Radford
P G. Mercer
P A. Maul
P C. Esper
P M. Sullivan
P O. Stocksdale

WAS 1895 N

M G. Schmelz
1B E. Cartwright
2B C. Crooks
SS F. Scheibeck
3B W. Joyce
OF C. Abbey
OF A. Selbach
OF W. Hassamaer
C J. McGuire
P G. Mercer
P V. Anderson
P O. Stocksdale
P A. Maul
P J. Malarkey

WAS 1896 N

M G. Schmelz
1B E. Cartwright
2B J. O'Brien
SS De Montreville
3B W. Joyce
OF A. Selbach
OF T. Brown
OF W. Lush
C J. McGuire
P G. Mercer
P J. McJames
P L. German
P C. King

WAS 1897 N

M G. Schmelz
M T. Brown
1B T. Tucker
2B J. O'Brien
SS De Montreville
3B C. Reilly
OF A. Selbach
OF T. Brown
OF C. Abbey
C J. McGuire
UT G. Wrigley
P G. Mercer
P J. McJames
P J. Swaim
P C. King
P L. German

WAS 1898 N

M T. Brown
M J. Doyle
M J. McGuire
M A. Irwin
1B J. Doyle
2B H. Reitz
SS G. Wrigley
3B J. Smith
OF J. Gettman
OF A. Selbach
OF J. Anderson
C J. McGuire
UT C. Farrell
P A. Weyhing
P G. Mercer
P W. Dinneen
P F. Killen
P J. Swaim

WAS 1899 N

M A. Irwin
1B D. McGann
2B F. Bonner
SS R. Padden
3B C. Atherton
OF J. Freeman
OF J. Slagle
OF J. O'Brien
C J. McGuire
UT G. Mercer
P A. Weyhing
P W. Dinneen
P A. McFarlan

WAS 1901 A

M J. Manning
1B M. Grady
2B J. Farrell
SS W. Clingman
3B W. Coughlin
OF S. Dungan
OF C. Foster
OF I. Waldron
C W. Clarke
P W. Carrick
P W. Lee
P C. Patten
P G. Mercer

WAS 1902 A

M T. Loftus
1B G. Carey
2B J. Doyle
SS F. Ely
3B W. Coughlin
OF J. Ryan
OF E. Delahanty
OF W. Lee
C W. Clarke
UT W. Keister
P A. Orth
P C. Patten
P W. Carrick
P J. Townsend

WAS 1903 A

M T. Loftus
1B W. Clarke
2B W. McCormick
SS C. Moran
3B W. Coughlin
OF A. Selbach
OF J. Ryan
OF W. Lee
C M. Kittridge
UT C. Robinson
P C. Patten
P A. Orth
P H. Wilson
P J. Townsend
P E. Dunkle

WAS 1904 A

M M. Kittridge
M P. Donovan
1B G. Stahl
2B W. McCormick
SS J. Cassidy
3B H. Hill
OF P. Donovan
OF W. O'Neill
OF F. Huelsman
C M. Kittridge
P C. Patten
P J. Townsend
P A. Jacobson
P W. Wolfe
P T. Hughes

WAS 1905 A

M G. Stahl
1B G. Stahl
2B C. Hickman
SS J. Cassidy
3B H. Hill
OF C. Jones
OF F. Huelsman
OF J. Anderson
C M. Heydon
UT G. Nill
P C. Patten
P T. Hughes
P J. Townsend
P W. Wolfe
P A. Jacobson

WAS 1906 A

M G. Stahl
1B G. Stahl
2B H. Schlafly
SS D. Altizer
3B L. Cross
OF J. Anderson
OF C. Jones
OF C. Hickman
C H. Wakefield
P F. Falkenberg
P C. Patten
P C. Smith
P T. Hughes
P F. Kitson

WAS 1907 A

M J. Cantillon
1B J. Anderson
2B J. Delahanty
SS D. Altizer
3B W. Shipke
OF R. Ganley
OF C. Jones
OF O. Clymer
C J. Warner
P C. Smith
P C. Patten
P F. Falkenberg
P T. Hughes
P W. Johnson

WAS 1908 A

M J. Cantillon
1B F. Freeman
2B J. Delahanty
SS G. McBride
3B W. Shipke
OF R. Ganley
OF J. Milan
OF O. Pickering
C C. Street
UT O. Clymer
P T. Hughes
P W. Johnson
P C. Smith
P B. Keeley
P W. Burns

WAS 1909 A

M J. Cantillon
1B J. Donahue
2B J. Delahanty
SS G. McBride
3B W. Conroy
OF J. Milan
OF G. Browne
OF J. Lelivelt
C C. Street
UT R. Unglaub
P W. Johnson
P R. Groom
P W. Gray
P C. Smith
P T. Hughes

WAS 1910 A

M J. McAleer
1B R. Unglaub
2B W. Killefer
SS G. McBride
3B N. Elberfeld
OF H. Gessler
OF J. Milan
OF J. Lelivelt
C C. Street
UT W. Conroy
P W. Johnson
P R. Groom
P W. Gray
P E. Walker
P F. Reisling

WAS 1911 A

M J. McAleer
1B H. Schaefer
2B W. Cunningham
SS G. McBride
3B W. Conroy
OF J. Milan
OF H. Gessler
OF C. Walker
C C. Street
UT N. Elberfeld
P W. Johnson
P R. Groom
P T. Hughes
P E. Walker
P W. Gray

WAS 1912 A

M C. Griffith
1B C. Gandil
2B R. Morgan
SS G. McBride
3B E. Foster
OF J. Milan
OF D. Moeller
OF H. Shanks
C J. Henry
P W. Johnson
P R. Groom
P T. Hughes
P J. Cashion

WAS 1913 A

M C. Griffith
1B C. Gandil
2B R. Morgan
SS G. McBride
3B E. Foster
OF J. Milan
OF D. Moeller
OF H. Shanks
C J. Henry
P W. Johnson
P R. Groom
P J. Boehling
P J. Engel
P T. Hughes

WAS 1914 A

M C. Griffith
1B C. Gandil
2B R. Morgan
SS G. McBride
3B E. Foster
OF D. Moeller
OF H. Shanks
OF J. Milan
C J. Henry
P W. Johnson
P Y. Ayers
P J. Shaw

P   J. Boehling
P   J. Bentley
RP H. Harper

WAS 1915 A
M   C. Griffith
1B C. Gandil
2B R. Morgan
SS G. McBride
3B E. Foster
OF J. Milan
OF D. Moeller
OF H. Shanks
C   W. Henry
P   W. Johnson
P   M. Gallia
P   J. Boehling
P   Y. Ayers
P   J. Shaw

WAS 1916 A
M   C. Griffith
1B J. Judge
2B R. Morgan
SS G. McBride
3B E. Foster
OF J. Milan
OF H. Shanks
OF D. Moeller
C   W. Henry
P   W. Johnson
P   M. Gallia
P   H. Harper
P   Y. Ayers
P   J. Boehling

WAS 1917 A
M   C. Griffith
1B J. Judge
2B R. Morgan
SS H. Shanks
3B E. Foster
OF E. Rice
OF J. Milan
OF M. Menosky
C   E. Ainsmith
UT J. Leonard
P   W. Johnson
P   J. Shaw
P   M. Gallia
P   Y. Ayers
P   G. Dumont

WAS 1918 A
M   C. Griffith
1B J. Judge
2B R. Morgan
SS J. Lavan
3B E. Foster
OF J. Milan
OF B. Shotton
OF F. Schulte
C   E. Ainsmith
UT H. Shanks
P   W. Johnson
P   H. Harper
P   J. Shaw
P   Y. Ayers

WAS 1919 A
M   C. Griffith
1B J. Judge
2B H. Janvrin
SS H. Shanks
3B E. Foster
OF E. Rice
OF M. Menosky
OF J. Milan
C   V. Picinich
UT E. Gharrity
P   J. Shaw
P   W. Johnson
P   H. Harper
P   E. Erickson

WAS 1920 A
M   C. Griffith
1B J. Judge
2B S. Harris
SS J. O'Neill
3B F. Ellerbe
OF E. Rice
OF R. Roth
OF J. Milan
C   E. Gharrity
UT H. Shanks
P   J. Zachary
P   E. Erickson
P   J. Shaw
P   H. Courtney

P   W. Johnson

WAS 1921 A
M   G. McBride
1B J. Judge
2B S. Harris
SS J. O'Rourke
3B H. Shanks
OF E. Rice
OF E. Miller
OF J. Milan
C   E. Gharrity
P   G. Mogridge
P   W. Johnson
P   J. Zachary
P   E. Erickson
RP A. Schacht

WAS 1922 A
M   J. Milan
1B J. Judge
2B S. Harris
SS R. Peckinpaugh
3B R. LaMotte
OF E. Rice
OF F. Brower
OF L. Goslin
C   E. Gharrity
P   W. Johnson
P   G. Mogridge
P   R. Francis
P   J. Zachary
P   E. Erickson

WAS 1923 A
M   O. Bush
1B J. Judge
2B S. Harris
SS R. Peckinpaugh
3B O. Bluege
OF L. Goslin
OF E. Rice
OF H. Leibold
C   H. Ruel
UT J. Evans
P   W. Johnson
P   G. Mogridge
·P   J. Zachary
P   A. Russell
P   P. Zahniser

WAS 1924 A
M   S. Harris
1B J. Judge
2B S. Harris
SS R. Peckinpaugh
3B O. Bluege
OF E. Rice
OF L. Goslin
OF H. Leibold
C   H. Ruel
P   W. Johnson
P   G. Mogridge
P   J. Zachary
P   F. Marberry
P   J. Martina
RP A. Russell
RP B. Speece

WAS 1925 A
M   S. Harris
1B J. Judge
2B S. Harris
SS R. Peckinpaugh
3B O. Bluege
OF E. Rice
OF L. Goslin
OF G. McNeely
C   H. Ruel
UT J. Harris
P   S. Coveleski
P   W. Johnson
P   W. Ruether
P   J. Zachary
RP F. Marberry
RP S. Gregg

WAS 1926 A
M   S. Harris
1B J. Judge
2B S. Harris
SS C. Myer
3B O. Bluege
OF E. Rice
OF L. Goslin
OF G. McNeely
C   H. Ruel
UT J. Harris
P   W. Johnson

P   S. Coveleski
P   W. Ruether
P   A. Crowder
P   W. Ogden
RP F. Marberry
RP W. Morrell

WAS 1927 A
M   S. Harris
1B J. Judge
2B S. Harris
SS R. Reeves
3B O. Bluege
OF L. Goslin
OF E. Rice
OF T. Speaker
C   H. Ruel
P   H. Lisenbee
P   H. Thurston
P   I. Hadley
P   W. Johnson
P   J. Zachary
RP F. Marberry
RP E. Braxton

WAS 1928 A
M   S. Harris
1B J. Judge
2B S. Harris
SS R. Reeves
3B O. Bluege
OF E. Rice
OF L. Goslin
OF S. West
C   H. Ruel
UT E. Barnes
P   I. Hadley
P   S. Jones
P   E. Braxton
P   F. Marberry
P   N. Gaston

WAS 1929 A
M   W. Johnson
1B J. Judge
2B C. Myer
SS J. Cronin
3B M. Hayes
OF E. Rice
OF L. Goslin
OF S. West
C   H. Tate
P   F. Marberry
P   I. Hadley
P   E. Braxton
P   L. Brown
P   S. Jones

WAS 1930 A
M   W. Johnson
1B J. Judge
2B C. Myer
SS J. Cronin
3B O. Bluege
OF E. Rice
OF S. West
OF H. Manush
C   R. Spencer
P   I. Hadley
P   A. Crowder
P   L. Brown
P   F. Marberry
P   S. Jones

WAS 1931 A
M   W. Johnson
1B J. Kuhel
2B C. Myer
SS J. Cronin
3B O. Bluege
OF H. Manush
OF S. West
OF E. Rice
C   R. Spencer
P   L. Brown
P   A. Crowder
P   F. Marberry
P   C. Fischer
P   I. Hadley

WAS 1932 A
M   W. Johnson
1B J. Kuhel
2B C. Myer
SS J. Cronin
3B O. Bluege
OF H. Manush
OF S. West
OF R. Reynolds
C   R. Spencer

UT E. Rice
P   A. Crowder
P   M. Weaver
P   L. Brown
P   F. Marberry
P   A. Thomas

WAS 1933 A
M   J. Cronin
1B J. Kuhel
2B C. Myer
SS J. Cronin
3B O. Bluege
OF H. Manush
OF F. Schulte
OF L. Goslin
C   J. Sewell
P   A. Crowder
P   E. Whitehill
P   W. Stewart
P   M. Weaver
P   A. Thomas
RP J. Russell
RP R. Burke

WAS 1934 A
M   J. Cronin
1B J. Kuhel
2B C. Myer
SS J. Cronin
3B C. Travis
OF F. Schulte
OF H. Manush
OF J. Stone
C   E. Phillips
UT O. Bluege
UT D. Harris
P   E. Whitehill
P   M. Weaver
P   R. Burke
P   W. Stewart
P   A. Thomas
RP J. Russell
RP A. McColl

WAS 1935 A
M   S. Harris
1B J. Kuhel
2B C. Myer
SS O. Bluege
3B C. Travis
OF A. Powell
OF J. Stone
OF H. Manush
C   W. Bolton
P   E. Whitehill
P   I. Hadley
P   L. Newsom
P   E. Linke
RP J. Russell
RP L. Pettit

WAS 1936 A
M   S. Harris
1B J. Kuhel
2B O. Bluege
SS C. Travis
3B J. Lewis
OF J. Stone
OF W. Chapman
OF C. Reynolds
C   W. Bolton
UT R. Kress
P   L. Newsom
P   J. DeShong
P   E. Whitehill
P   P. Appleton
P   J. Cascarella
RP J. Russell

WAS 1937 A
M   S. Harris
1B J. Kuhel
2B C. Myer
SS C. Travis
3B J. Lewis
OF J. Stone
OF A. Simmons
OF M. Almada
C   R. Ferrell
P   J. DeShong
P   W. Ferrell
P   M. Weaver
P   P. Appleton
P   E. Linke
RP S. Cohen

WAS 1938 A
M   S. Harris
1B H. Bonura

2B C. Myer
SS C. Travis
3B J. Lewis
OF A. Simmons
OF G. Case
OF S. West
OF R. Ferrell
UT T. Wright
P   E. Leonard
P   P. Appleton
P   K. Chase
P   W. Ferrell
P   H. Kelley
RP E. Hogsett

WAS 1939 A
M   S. Harris
1B J. Vernon
2B J. Bloodworth
SS C. Travis
3B J. Lewis
OF T. Wright
OF G. Case
OF S. West
C   R. Ferrell
P   E. Leonard
P   K. Chase
P   J. Krakauskas
P   J. Haynes
P   A. Carrasquel
RP P. Appleton
RP W. Masterson

WAS 1940 A
M   S. Harris
1B H. Bonura
2B J. Bloodworth
SS J. Pofahl
3B C. Travis
OF G. Case
OF G. Walker
OF J. Lewis
C   R. Ferrell
P   E. Leonard
P   K. Chase
P   S. Hudson
P   W. Masterson
P   J. Krakauskas
RP J. Haynes
RP A. Carrasquel

WAS 1941 A
M   S. Harris
1B J. Vernon
2B J. Bloodworth
SS C. Travis
3B G. Archie
OF R. Cramer
OF G. Case
OF J. Lewis
C   J. Early
P   E. Leonard
P   S. Hudson
P   K. Chase
P   S. Sundra
P   A. Anderson
RP A. Carrasquel
RP W. Zuber

WAS 1942 A
M   S. Harris
1B J. Vernon
2B E. Clary
SS J. Sullivan
3B R. Estalella
OF S. Spence
OF G. Case
OF B. Campbell
C   J. Early
P   S. Hudson
P   L. Newsom
P   E. Wynn
P   A. Carrasquel
P   W. Masterson

WAS 1943 A
M   O. Bluege
1B J. Vernon
2B G. Priddy
SS J. Sullivan
3B E. Clary
OF S. Spence
OF G. Case
OF R. Johnson
C   J. Early
P   E. Wynn
P   E. Leonard
P   M. Candini
P   M. Haefner
P   A. Carrasquel

WAS 1944 A
M   O. Bluege
1B J. Kuhel
2B G. Myatt
SS J. Sullivan
3B D. Torres
OF S. Spence
OF G. Case
OF A. Powell
C   R. Ferrell
P   E. Leonard
P   M. Haefner
P   E. Wynn
P   J. Niggeling
P   R. Wolff
RP W. LeFebvre

WAS 1945 A
M   O. Bluege
1B J. Kuhel
2B G. Myatt
SS D. Torres
3B H. Clift
OF G. Binks
OF G. Case
OF J. Lewis
C   R. Ferrell
P   R. Wolff
P   M. Haefner
P   M. Pieretti
P   E. Leonard
P   J. Niggeling
RP C. Ullrich

WAS 1946 A
M   O. Bluege
1B J. Vernon
2B G. Priddy
SS C. Travis
3B W. Hitchcock
OF S. Spence
OF J. Lewis
OF J. Grace
C   A. Evans
P   M. Haefner
P   L. Newsom
P   E. Leonard
P   R. Scarborough
P   S. Hudson
RP M. Pieretti

WAS 1947 A
M   O. Bluege
1B J. Vernon
2B G. Priddy
SS M. Christman
3B E. Yost
OF S. Spence
OF J. Lewis
OF J. Grace
C   A. Evans
UT S. Robertson
P   W. Masterson
P   E. Wynn
P   M. Haefner
P   R. Scarborough
P   S. Hudson
RP M. Candini
RP T. Ferrick

WAS 1948 A
M   J. Kuhel
1B J. Vernon
2B A. Kozar
SS M. Christman
3B E. Yost
OF G. Coan
OF E. Stewart
OF E. Wooten
C   J. Early
P   E. Wynn
P   W. Masterson
P   R. Scarborough
P   S. Hudson
P   M. Haefner
RP D. Thompson
RP M. Candini

WAS 1949 A
M   J. Kuhel
1B W. Robinson
2B A. Kozar
SS S. Dente
3B E. Yost
OF C. Vollmer
OF E. Stewart
OF G. Coan
C   A. Evans
UT J. Lewis
UT S. Robertson

P   S. Hudson
P   R. Scarborough
P   P. Calvert
P   M. Harris
P   L. Hittle
RP J. Haynes
RP R. Welteroth

WAS 1950 A
M   S. Harris
1B J. Vernon
2B C. Michaels
SS S. Dente
3B E. Yost
OF I. Noren
OF E. Stewart
OF S. Mele
C   A. Evans
UT G. Coan
P   S. Hudson
P   R. Kuzava
P   C. Marrero
P   S. Consuegra
P   J. Haynes
RP M. Harris
RP J. Pearce

WAS 1951 A
M   S. Harris
1B J. Vernon
2B C. Michaels
SS J. Runnels
3B E. Yost
OF G. Coan
OF I. Noren
OF S. Mele
C   F. Guerra
P   C. Marrero
P   S. Consuegra
P   D. Johnson
P   S. Hudson
P   E. Porterfield
RP M. Harris
RP J. Haynes

WAS 1952 A
M   S. Harris
1B J. Vernon
2B F. Baker
SS J. Runnels
3B E. Yost
OF J. Jensen
OF J. Busby
OF G. Coan
C   N. Grasso
P   E. Porterfield
P   C. Marrero
P   F. Shea
P   W. Masterson
P   J. Moreno
RP S. Consuegra
RP D. Johnson

WAS 1953 A
M   S. Harris
1B J. Vernon
2B W. Terwilliger
SS J. Runnels
3B E. Yost
OF J. Busby
OF J. Jensen
OF C. Vollmer
C   E. Fitzgerald
P   E. Porterfield
P   W. Masterson
P   F. Shea
P   C. Stobbs
P   C. Marrero
RP J. Dixon
RP A. Sima

WAS 1954 A
M   S. Harris
1B J. Vernon
2B W. Terwilliger
SS J. Runnels
3B E. Yost
OF J. Busby
OF R. Sievers
OF T. Umphlett
C   E. Fitzgerald
P   E. Porterfield
P   M. McDermott
P   J. Schmitz
P   C. Stobbs
P   D. Stone
RP C. Pascual
RP C. Keriazakos

WAS 1955 A

M	C. Dressen
1B	J. Vernon
2B	J. Runnels
SS	J. Valdivielso
3B	E. Yost
OF	R. Sievers
OF	T. Umphlett
OF	C. Paula
C	E. Fitzgerald
UT	E. Oravetz
P	D. Stone
P	E. Porterfield
P	J. Schmitz
P	M. McDermott
P	C. Stobbs
RP	P. Ramos
RP	T. Abernathy

WAS 1956 A

M	C. Dressen
1B	R. Sievers
2B	J. Runnels
SS	J. Valdivielso
3B	E. Yost
OF	J. Lemon
OF	D. Herzog
OF	K. Olson
C	C. Courtney
UT	L. Berberet
P	C. Stobbs
P	C. Pascual
P	P. Ramos
P	D. Stone
P	R. Wiesler
RP	H. Griggs
RP	R. Chakales

WAS 1957 A

M	C. Dressen
M	H. Lavagetto
1B	J. Runnels
2B	H. Plews
SS	E. Bridges
3B	E. Yost
OF	J. Lemon
OF	R. Sievers
OF	R. Usher
C	L. Berberet
UT	J. Becquer
P	P. Ramos
P	C. Stobbs
P	C. Pascual
P	R. Kemmerer
RP	T. Clevenger
RP	R. Hyde

WAS 1958 A

M	H. Lavagetto

WAS 1959 A

1B	N. Zauchin
2B	K. Aspromonte
SS	E. Bridges
3B	E. Yost
OF	A. Pearson
OF	J. Lemon
OF	R. Sievers
C	C. Courtney
UT	B. Chrisley
UT	H. Plews
P	P. Ramos
P	R. Kemmerer
P	C. Pascual
P	H. Griggs
P	V. Valentinetti
RP	T. Clevenger
RP	R. Hyde

WAS 1959 A

M	H. Lavagetto
1B	R. Sievers
2B	R. Bertoia
SS	W. Consolo
3B	H. Killebrew
OF	W. Allison
OF	J. Lemon
OF	M. Throneberry
C	H. Naragon
UT	J. Becquer
P	C. Pascual
P	P. Ramos
P	R. Kemmerer
P	W. Fischer
RP	T. Clevenger
RP	H. Griggs

WAS 1960 A

M	H. Lavagetto
1B	J. Becquer
2B	W. Gardner
SS	J. Valdivielso
3B	R. Bertoia
OF	J. Lemon
OF	W. Allison
OF	L. Green
C	E. Battey
UT	W. Consolo
UT	D. Dobbek
UT	H. Killebrew
P	P. Ramos
P	D. Lee
P	C. Pascual
P	J. Kralick
RP	T. Clevenger
RP	C. Stobbs

WAS 1961 A

M	J. Vernon
1B	R. Long
2B	C. Cottier

WAS 1962 A

SS	O. Veal
3B	D. O'Connell
OF	W. Tasby
OF	R. Keough
OF	C. Hinton
C	G. Green
UT	J. King
UT	E. Woodling
P	B. Chrisley
P	B. Daniels
P	R. Donovan
P	E. Hobaugh
P	P. Burnside
RP	M. Kutyna
RP	J. Klippstein

WAS 1962 A

M	J. Vernon
1B	H. Bright
2B	C. Cottier
SS	K. Hamlin
3B	R. Johnson
OF	C. Hinton
OF	J. Piersall
OF	J. King
C	K. Retzer
UT	W. Hicks
P	D. Stenhouse
P	F. Rudolph
P	T. Cheney
P	B. Daniels
P	C. Osteen
RP	S. Ridzik
RP	M. Kutyna

WAS 1963 A

M	J. Vernon
M	E. Yost
M	G. Hodges
1B	L. Osborne
2B	C. Cottier
SS	E. Brinkman
3B	D. Zimmer
OF	D. Lock
OF	C. Hinton
OF	J. King
C	K. Retzer
UT	S. Minoso
UT	R. Phillips
P	C. Osteen
P	F. Rudolph
P	B. Daniels
P	T. Cheney
P	J. Duckworth
RP	R. Kline
RP	P. Burnside

WAS 1964 A

M	G. Hodges
1B	W. Skowron

WAS 1965 A

2B	D. Blasingame
SS	E. Brinkman
3B	J. Kennedy
OF	D. Lock
OF	C. Hinton
OF	J. King
C	T. Brumley
UT	R. Phillips
UT	F. Valentine
UT	D. Zimmer
P	C. Osteen
P	L. Narum
P	B. Daniels
P	A. Koch
RP	S. Ridzik
RP	J. Hannan

WAS 1965 A

M	G. Hodges
1B	R. Nen
2B	D. Blasingame
SS	E. Brinkman
3B	K. McMullen
OF	F. Howard
OF	D. Lock
OF	W. Held
C	T. Brumley
UT	K. Hamlin
UT	J. King
UT	W. Kirkland
P	P. Richert
P	F. Ortega
P	L. Narum
P	M. McCormick
P	B. Daniels
RP	S. Ridzik
RP	R. Kline

WAS 1966 A

M	G. Hodges
1B	R. Nen
2B	R. Saverine
SS	E. Brinkman
3B	K. McMullen
OF	F. Valentine
OF	F. Howard
OF	D. Lock
C	P. Casanova
UT	J. King
UT	W. Kirkland
P	P. Richert
P	M. McCormick
P	F. Ortega
P	J. Hannan
RP	J. Cox
RP	R. Humphreys

WAS 1967 A

M	G. Hodges

WAS 1968 A

1B	M. Epstein
2B	B. Allen
SS	E. Brinkman
3B	K. McMullen
OF	F. Howard
OF	F. Valentine
OF	C. Peterson
C	P. Casanova
UT	H. Allen
UT	T. Cullen
UT	R. Nen
P	F. Ortega
P	C. Pascual
P	R. Moore
P	J. Coleman
P	F. Bertaina
RP	D. Knowles
RP	R. Priddy

WAS 1968 A

M	J. Lemon
1B	M. Epstein
2B	B. Allen
SS	R. Hansen
3B	K. McMullen
OF	D. Unser
OF	F. Howard
OF	E. Stroud
C	P. Casanova
P	J. Coleman
P	C. Pascual
P	J. Hannan
P	R. Bosman
P	F. Bertaina
RP	D. Higgins
RP	R. Humphreys

WAS 1969 A

M	T. Williams
1B	M. Epstein
2B	B. Allen
SS	E. Brinkman
3B	K. McMullen
OF	D. Unser
OF	F. Howard
OF	H. Allen
C	P. Casanova
UT	G. Alyea
UT	T. Cullen
UT	E. Stroud
P	J. Coleman
P	R. Bosman
P	J. Cox
P	J. Hannan
P	R. Moore
RP	J. Shellenback

WAS 1970 A

M	T. Williams
1B	M. Epstein
2B	T. Cullen
SS	E. Brinkman
3B	A. Rodriguez
OF	F. Howard
OF	E. Stroud
OF	D. Unser
C	P. Casanova
UT	B. Allen
UT	F. Reichardt
P	R. Bosman
P	J. Coleman
P	J. Cox
P	J. Hannan
P	G. Brunet
RP	D. Knowles
RP	J. Grzenda

WAS 1971 A

M	T. Williams
1B	D. Mincher
2B	T. Cullen
SS	C. Harrah
3B	D. Nelson
OF	D. Unser
OF	E. Maddox
OF	F. Howard
C	P. Casanova
UT	B. Allen
UT	R. Billings
UT	T. McCraw
P	R. Bosman
P	D. McLain
P	P. Broberg
P	W. Gogolewski
P	J. Shellenback
RP	J. Cox
RP	P. Lindblad

Wilmington

WIL U 1884

WIL 1884 U

M	J. Simmons
1B	E. Snyder
2B	C. Bastian
SS	H. Myers
3B	J. Say

OF	T. Lynch
OF	J. Munce
OF	Fisher
C	A. Cusick
P	J. Murphy
P	E. Nolan
P	D. Casey
P	E. Bakely

Worcester

WOR N 1880-1882

WOR 1880 N

M	F. Bancroft
1B	J. Sullivan
2B	G. Creamer
SS	A. Irwin
3B	A. Whitney
OF	G. Wood
OF	A. Knight
OF	H. Stovey
C	C. Bennett
P	J. Richmond

WOR 1881 N

M	M. Dorgan
M	H. Stovey
1B	H. Stovey
2B	G. Creamer
SS	A. Irwin
3B	W. Carpenter
OF	L. Dickerson
OF	P. Hotaling
OF	F. Corey
C	A. Bushong
P	J. Richmond
P	P. McCormick

WOR 1882 N

M	F. Brown
M	T. Bond
M	J. Chapman
1B	H. Stovey
2B	G. Creamer
SS	F. Corey
3B	A. Irwin
OF	J. Evans
OF	J. Hayes
OF	J. Clinton
C	A. Bushong
P	J. Richmond
P	F. Mountain

The Manager Roster

This section details the managerial record of every man who ever held the reins of a major league club from 1871 through 1988. For many years, the assignment of wins and losses was thought a relatively simple task—almost as simple as identifying the managers themselves. In recent years, however, Richard Topp and Robert Tiemann wondered how it was that "managers" who never set foot on the field to lead their charges or even accompanied their clubs on road trips could be regarded as managers at all, at least in the commonly understood sense of field manager rather than business manager. Topp and Tiemann wondered how John McGraw, for example, could be credited as manager of the New York Giants for all of 1924 when a knee injury kept him from the bench for seven weeks: Somebody else must have run the team, they figured, so why not credit that man as interim manager?

That there were record-keeping errors in the 1870s or even the early 1900s may strike the average fan as unsurprising, but the incorrect assignment of decisions to helmsmen has been characteristic of every decade, up to and including the 1980s. Tiemann and Topp undertook a complete review of managerial records dating back to the National Association and found that the records published in previous baseball encyclopedias were wrong—so wrong that they had to be refigured from scratch. Here are the criteria they established for their groundbreaking study:

1. *Definition* A manager is the person designated by the club ownership to run the club on the field.

2. *Absences* When the regular manager is unable to be with the team for 30 or more days, the assistant in charge during his absence should be credited with the team's record from the time the absence begins until the regular manager returns to active duty.

3. *Interim manager* When a manager is removed, either by resignation or by being fired, and his designated replacement is not present to replace him, the assistant temporarily in charge of the team shall be credited with the team's record during the interim.

4. *Head coaches* From 1961 through 1964, the Chicago Cubs had a "panel of coaches" rather than a single manager. One of these coaches was designated *head coach* for a period of time; and that coach is credited with the team's record during his term as head coach.

5. *Captains* During the early years of professional baseball, the man who had the title of "manager" often served merely as the club's business manager, while the captain (a player) was responsible for the team on the field. Some captains were also managers. Each ambiguous situation is judged according to its particular circumstances, but in general the captain, rather than the manager, is credited with the team's record if the manager did not travel with the team or did not have previous baseball experience.

6. *Suspended games* If a game was suspended when one man was managing the team and was completed on a later date when another man was managing, the second manager is credited if the game was suspended before five innings were completed. If the game was suspended after five or more innings were played, then:

    (a) credit the first manager with a win if the team was leading at the point of suspension and maintained the lead to win the game; or

    (b) credit the first manager with a loss if the team was losing at the point of suspension and remained behind to lose the game; or

    (c) credit the second manager with a win (or tie) if the team was losing at the point of suspension but came back to tie the score or win the game; or

    (d) credit the second manager with a loss if the team was winning at the point of suspension but then lost the lead and/or game; or

    (e) credit the second manager with the win or loss if the score was tied at the point of suspension.

7. *Protested games* If a protest was granted and the game was ordered resumed from the point of protest, then the same rules used for suspended games apply. If a protested game of at least five innings' duration was ordered replayed in its entirety, then no win or loss is credited, but both managers are credited with a no-decision game.

8. *Forfeited games* All forfeited games are counted as games managed, even if the game did not start or if it did not go five innings.

9. *Split seasons* In 1892 the National League played a split season, the winners meeting for the championship. In 1981, because of a players' strike, the National and American Leagues played split seasons. The managers' totals will have entries for each half-season.

10. *Replacement clubs* In the American Association (1882–1891), there were three instances in which one club dropped out and was replaced by another club. In 1884 Richmond replaced Washington; in 1890 Baltimore replaced Brooklyn; and in 1891 Milwaukee replaced Cincinnati. In each case, the new club inherited the old club's record. Therefore, the manager of the new club is credited with starting in the position (standing) in which the old club finished.

In the Union Association (1884), when a new club replaced an old one, the new club started with a 0–0 record rather than inheriting the old club's record, except in the case of the Chicago franchise, which moved to Pittsburgh. Therefore, all such Union Association managers are credited with a finish as if their teams had begun their season at the beginning of the

league season. The finish for each manager is his club's standing in the eight-team league when (a) he left the job, (b) his club dropped out of the league, or (c) his club finished the season. The clubs that dropped out were Altoona (replaced by Kansas City); Philadelphia (replaced by Wilmington); Wilmington (replaced by St. Paul); and Pittsburgh (replaced by Milwaukee).

In a typical entry in the Manager Roster (a hypothetical entry has been created below), the column marked STANDING will, in cases where a team has had only one manager throughout the year, show the team's final standing (in the example below, see the entry for 1972). In the case of a manager who began the season but was replaced midway, however, the figure on the left of the column shows the team's standing when he departed and the figure on the right shows the team's final standing (in the example below, see the entry for 1976). In the case of a manager who finished the season but did not begin it, the team's standing when he took over is shown on the left and the final standing on the right (see the entry for 1978). Last, in the case of a manager who began when the season was already under way but who failed to finish, the figure on the left of the column shows the team's standing when he took over; the middle figure shows the team's standing when he departed; and a third figure shows the team's final standing (see the entry for 1977). The last line of a manager's entry provides his career totals, beginning at the left with the number of years, full or partial, in which he managed a major league club. The symbols shown in the sample entry are explained after the example.

YEAR	TM/L	G	W	L	PCT	STANDING			M/Y
Blow, Josiah H. "Joe"									
1969	Det-A*	134	71	63	.530	3 E	3 E		1/2
1971	Tex-A*	23	9	14	.391	6 W	6 W		3/3
1972	Tex-A	161	84	76	.525	2 W			
1973	Tex-A	95	44	51	.463	4 W	3 W		1/2
1973	NY-A	56	30	26	.535	3 E	3 E		2/2
1974	NY-A	159	97	62	.610	★◆1 E			
1975	NY-A	162	100	62	.617	◆1 E			
1976	NY-A	94	52	42	.553	3 E	▲◆1E		1/3
1977	Bos-A	95	55	40	.579	4 E	4 E	2 E	2/3
1978	Oak-A	152	83	69	.546	5 W	●2 W		2/2
1979	Oak-A	60	37	23	.617	1 W	2 W		1/2
1980	Oak-A	49	27	22	.551	2 W	3 W		2/2
1981 (1)	Oak-A	62	24	38	.387	6 W			
1981 (2)	Oak-A	100	44	56	.440	5 W			

1982	NY-A	162	91	71	.562	3 E			
1983	NY-A	145	91	54	.628	7 E	2 E	2/2
14		1709	939	769	.550			

Whenever a manager served two or more teams in the same year, the totals for each club are shown separately (see the entry above for 1973). The split seasons of 1892 and 1981 are indicated with separate records for each half. A figure to the right of the year indicates first half or second half (see entry above for 1981).

TM/L	Team and League
G	Games managed (including ties)
W	Wins
L	Losses
PCT	Percentage of games won
M/Y	Manager/Year (The latter figure indicates how many managers the team employed that year, while the former indicates the chronological position of the manager whose entry it is; "2/5," for example, would mean that this manager was the second of the team's five managers during that year.)
E	Eastern Division
W	Western Division
*	Indicates playing manager; for vital statistics, consult the player or pitcher register
▲	Tied for first place, involved in league or division playoff
●	Tied for position in standings
◆	League Championship Series win
★	World Series win

The team and league abbreviations used in this section are found on the final pages of this book. For a prose account of the history of managers (and coaches), see the feature article by Fred Stein.

Adair, Marion Danne "Bill"

YEAR	TM/L	G	W	L	PCT	STANDING			M/Y
1970	Chi-A	10	4	6	.400	6 W	6 W	6 W	2/3

Adcock, Joseph Wilbur "Joe"

YEAR	TM/L	G	W	L	PCT	STANDING			M/Y
1967	Cle-A	162	75	87	.463	8			

Addy, Robert Edward "Bob"

YEAR	TM/L	G	W	L	PCT	STANDING			M/Y
1873	Phi-n*	10	8	2	.800	2	2		1/2
1877	Cin-N*	44	12	31	.279	6	6		2/2
	2	54	20	33	.377				

Allen, Robert Gilman "Bob"

YEAR	TM/L	G	W	L	PCT	STANDING			M/Y
1890	Phi-N*	35	25	10	.714	3	2	3	4/5
1900	Cin-N*	144	62	77	.446	7			
	2	179	87	87	.500				

Alston, Walter Emmons

YEAR	TM/L	G	W	L	PCT	STANDING			M/Y
1954	Bro-N	154	92	62	.597	2			
1955	Bro-N	154	98	55	.641	★1			
1956	Bro-N	154	93	61	.604	1			
1957	Bro-N	154	84	70	.545	3			
1958	LA-N	154	71	83	.461	7			
1959	LA-N	156	88	68	.564	▲★1			
1960	LA-N	154	82	72	.532	4			
1961	LA-N	154	89	65	.578	2			
1962	LA-N	165	102	63	.618	▲2			
1963	LA-N	163	99	63	.611	★1			
1964	LA-N	164	80	82	.494	●6			
1965	LA-N	162	97	65	.599	★1			
1966	LA-N	162	95	67	.586	1			
1967	LA-N	162	73	89	.451	8			
1968	LA-N	162	76	86	.469	●7			
1969	LA-N	162	85	77	.525	4 W			
1970	LA-N	161	87	74	.540	2 W			
1971	LA-N	162	89	73	.549	2 W			
1972	LA-N	155	85	70	.548	3 W			
1973	LA-N	162	95	66	.590	2 W			
1974	LA-N	162	102	60	.630	♦1 W			
1975	LA-N	162	88	74	.543	2 W			
1976	LA-N	158	90	68	.570	2 W	2 W		1/2
	23	3658	2040	1613	.558				

Altobelli, Joseph "Joe"

YEAR	TM/L	G	W	L	PCT	STANDING			M/Y
1977	SF-N	162	75	87	.463	4 W			
1978	SF-N	162	89	73	.549	3 W			
1979	SF-N	140	61	79	.436	4 W	4 W		1/2
1983	Bal-A	162	98	64	.605	★1 E			
1984	Bal-A	162	85	77	.525	5 E			
1985	Bal-A	55	29	26	.527	4 E	4 E		1/3
	6	843	437	406	.518				

Amalfitano, John Joseph "Joey"

YEAR	TM/L	G	W	L	PCT	STANDING			M/Y
1979	Chi-N	7	2	5	.286	5 E	5 E		2/2
1980	Chi-N	72	26	46	.361	6 E	6 E		2/2
1981(1)	Chi-N	54	15	37	.288	6 E			
(2)	Chi-N	52	23	28	.451	5 E			
	3	185	66	116	.363				

Anderson, George Lee "Sparky"

YEAR	TM/L	G	W	L	PCT	STANDING			M/Y
1970	Cin-N	162	102	60	.630	♦1 W			
1971	Cin-N	162	79	83	.488	●4 W			
1972	Cin-N	154	95	59	.617	♦1 W			
1973	Cin-N	162	99	63	.611	1 W			
1974	Cin-N	163	98	64	.605	2 W			
1975	Cin-N	162	108	54	.667	★1 W			
1976	Cin-N	162	102	60	.630	★1 W			
1977	Cin-N	162	88	74	.543	2 W			
1978	Cin-N	161	92	69	.571	2 W			
1979	Det-A	106	56	50	.528	5 E	5 E		3/3
1980	Det-A	163	84	78	.519	5 E			
1981(1)	Det-A	57	31	26	.544	4 E			
(2)	Det-A	52	29	23	.558	●2 E			
1982	Det-A	162	83	79	.512	4 E			
1983	Det-A	162	92	70	.568	2 E			
1984	Det-A	162	104	58	.642	★1 E			
1985	Det-A	161	84	77	.522	3 E			
1986	Det-A	162	87	75	.537	3 E			
1987	Det-A	162	98	64	.605	1 E			
1988	Det-A	162	88	74	.543	2 E			
	19	2961	1699	1260	.574				

Anson, Adrian Constantine "Cap"

YEAR	TM/L	G	W	L	PCT	STANDING			M/Y
1875	Phi-n*	8	4	2	.667	2	2		2/2
1879	Chi-N*	64	41	21	.661	2	4		1/4
1880	Chi-N*	86	67	17	.798	1			
1881	Chi-N*	84	56	28	.667	1			
1882	Chi-N*	84	55	29	.655	1			
1883	Chi-N*	98	59	39	.602	2			
1884	Chi-N*	113	62	50	.554	●4			
1885	Chi-N*	113	87	25	.777	1			
1886	Chi-N*	126	90	34	.726	1			
1887	Chi-N*	127	71	50	.587	3			
1888	Chi-N*	136	77	58	.570	2			
1889	Chi-N*	136	67	65	.508	3			
1890	Chi-N*	139	84	53	.613	2			
1891	Chi-N*	137	82	53	.607	2			
1892(1)	Chi-N*	71	31	39	.443	8			
(2)	Chi-N*	76	39	37	.513	7			
1893	Chi-N*	128	56	71	.441	9			
1894	Chi-N*	137	57	75	.432	8			
1895	Chi-N*	133	72	58	.554	4			
1896	Chi-N*	132	71	57	.555	5			
1897	Chi-N*	138	59	73	.447	9			
1898	NY-N	22	9	13	.409	6	7	7	2/3
	21	2288	1296	947	.578				

Appling, Lucius Benjamin "Luke"

YEAR	TM/L	G	W	L	PCT	STANDING			M/Y
1967	KC-A	40	10	30	.250	10	10		2/2

Armour, William Clark "Bill"

YEAR	TM/L	G	W	L	PCT	STANDING			M/Y
1902	Cle-A	137	69	67	.507	5			
1903	Cle-A	140	77	63	.550	3			
1904	Cle-A	154	86	65	.570	4			
1905	Det-A	154	79	74	.516	3			
1906	Det-A	151	71	78	.477	6			
	5	736	382	347	.524				

Aspromonte, Kenneth Joseph "Ken"

YEAR	TM/L	G	W	L	PCT	STANDING			M/Y
1972	Cle-A	156	72	84	.462	5 E			
1973	Cle-A	162	71	91	.438	6 E			
1974	Cle-A	162	77	85	.475	4 E			
	3	480	220	260	.458				

Austin, James Philip "Jimmy"

YEAR	TM/L	G	W	L	PCT	STANDING			M/Y
1913	StL-A*	8	2	6	.250	7	7	8	2/3
1918	StL-A*	16	7	9	.438	6	6	5	2/3
1923	StL-A*	51	22	29	.431	3	5		2/2
	3	75	31	44	.413				

Baker, Delmer David "Del"

YEAR	TM/L	G	W	L	PCT	STANDING			M/Y
1933	Det-A	2	2	0	1.000	5	5		2/2
1937	Det-A	54	34	20	.630	3	3	2	2/5
	Det-A	10	7	3	.700	2	2	2	4/5
1938	Det-A	57	37	19	.661	5	4		2/2
1939	Det-A	155	81	73	.526	5			
1940	Det-A	155	90	64	.584	1			
1941	Det-A	155	75	79	.487	●4			
1942	Det-A	156	73	81	.474	5			
1960	Bos-A	7	2	5	.286	8	8	7	2/3
	8	751	401	344	.538				

Bamberger, George Irvin

YEAR	TM/L	G	W	L	PCT	STANDING			M/Y
1978	Mil-A	162	93	69	.574	3 E			
1979	Mil-A	161	95	66	.590	2 E			
1980	Mil-A	92	47	45	.511	2 E	4 E	3 E	2/3
1982	NY-N	162	65	97	.401	6 E			
1983	NY-N	46	16	30	.348	6 E	6 E		1/2
1985	Mil-A	161	71	90	.441	6 E			
1986	Mil-A	152	71	81	.467	6 E	6 E		1/2
	7	936	458	478	.489				

Bancroft, David James "Dave"

YEAR	TM/L	G	W	L	PCT	STANDING			M/Y
1924	Bos-N*	154	53	100	.346	8			
1925	Bos-N*	153	70	83	.458	5			
1926	Bos-N*	153	66	86	.434	7			
1927	Bos-N*	155	60	94	.390	7			
	4	615	249	363	.407				

Bancroft, Frank Carter

YEAR	TM/L	G	W	L	PCT	STANDING			M/Y
1880	Wor-N	85	40	43	.482	5			
1881	Det-N	84	41	43	.488	4			
1882	Det-N	86	42	41	.506	6			
1883	Cle-N	100	55	42	.567	4			
1884	Pro-N	114	84	28	.750	1			
1885	Pro-N	110	53	57	.482	4			
1887	Phi-a	55	26	29	.473	6	5		1/2
1889	Ind-N	68	25	43	.368	7	7		1/2
1902	Cin-N	16	9	7	.563	6	6	4	2/3
	9	718	375	333	.530				

Barkley, Samuel E. "Sam"

YEAR	TM/L	G	W	L	PCT	STANDING			M/Y
1888	KC-a*	57	21	36	.368	8	8	8	2/3

Barnie, William Harrison "Billy"

YEAR	TM/L	G	W	L	PCT	STANDING			M/Y
1883	Bal-a*	96	28	68	.292	8			
1884	Bal-a	108	63	43	.594	6			
1885	Bal-a	110	41	68	.376	8			
1886	Bal-a	139	48	83	.366	8			
1887	Bal-a	141	77	58	.570	3			
1888	Bal-a	137	57	80	.416	5			
1889	Bal-a	139	70	65	.519	5			
1890	Bal-a	38	15	19	.441	8			
1891	Bal-a	139	71	64	.526	3			
1892(1)	Was-N	2	0	2	.000	●11	7		1/2
1893	Lou-N	126	50	75	.400	11			
1894	Lou-N	131	36	94	.277	12			
1897	Bro-N	136	61	71	.462	●6			
1898	Bro-N	35	15	20	.429	9	10		1/3
	14	1477	632	810	.438				

Barrow, Edward Grant "Ed"

YEAR	TM/L	G	W	L	PCT	STANDING			M/Y
1903	Det-A	137	65	71	.478	5			
1904	Det-A	84	32	46	.410	7	7		1/2
1918	Bos-A	126	75	51	.595	★1			

YEAR	TM/L	G	W	L	PCT	STANDING			M/Y
1919	Bos-A	138	66	71	.482	6			
1920	Bos-A	154	72	81	.471	5			
5		639	310	320	.492				

Barry, John Joseph "Jack"

YEAR	TM/L	G	W	L	PCT	STANDING			M/Y
1917	Bos-A*	157	90	62	.592	2			

Battin, Joseph V. "Joe"

1883	Pit-a*	13	2	11	.154	7	7		3/3
1884	Pit-a*	13	6	7	.462	11	10	10	3/5
	Pit-U*	6	1	5	.167	5	5		1/2
2		32	9	23	.281				

Bauer, Henry Albert "Hank"

1961	KC-A*	102	35	67	.343	8	●9		2/2
1962	KC-A	162	72	90	.444	9			
1964	Bal-A	163	97	65	.599	3			
1965	Bal-A	162	94	68	.580	3			
1966	Bal-A	160	97	63	.606	★1			
1967	Bal-A	161	76	85	.472	●6			
1968	Bal-A	80	43	37	.538	3	2		1/2
1969	Oak-A	149	80	69	.537	2 W	2 W		1/2
8		1139	594	544	.522				

Benjamin, John W.

| 1873 | Res-n | 23 | 2 | 21 | .087 | 8 | | | |

Benson, Vernon Adair "Vern"

| 1977 | Atl-N | 1 | 1 | 0 | 1.000 | 6 W | 6 W | 6 W | 3/4 |

Berra, Lawrence Peter "Yogi"

1964	NY-A	164	99	63	.611	1			
1972	NY-N	156	83	73	.532	3 E			
1973	NY-N	161	82	79	.509	◆1 E			
1974	NY-N	162	71	91	.438	5 E			
1975	NY-N	109	56	53	.514	3 E	●3 E		1/2
1984	NY-A	162	87	75	.537	3 E			
1985	NY-A	16	6	10	.375	7 E	2 E		1/2
7		930	484	444	.522				

Bezdek, Hugo Frank

1917	Pit-N	91	30	59	.337	8	8		3/3
1918	Pit-N	126	65	60	.520	4			
1919	Pit-N	139	71	68	.511	4			
3		356	166	187	.470				

Bickerson

| 1884 | Was-a | 1 | 0 | 1 | .000 | 12 | 12 | | 2/2 |

Birmingham, Joseph Leo "Joe"

1912	Cle-A*	28	21	7	.750	6	5		2/2
1913	Cle-A*	155	86	66	.566	3			
1914	Cle-A*	157	51	102	.333	8			
1915	Cle-A	28	12	16	.429	6	7		1/2
4		368	170	191	.471				

Bissonette, Adelphia Louis "Del"

| 1945 | Bos-N | 60 | 25 | 34 | .424 | 5 | 7 | 6 | 2/2 |

Blackburne, Russell Aubrey "Lena"

1928	Chi-A	80	40	40	.500	6	5		2/2
1929	Chi-A*	152	59	93	.388	7			
2		232	99	133	.427				

Blades, Francis Raymond "Ray"

1939	StL-N	155	92	61	.601	2			
1940	StL-N	39	14	24	.368	6	3		1/3
1948	Bro-N	1	1	0	1.000	5	5	3	2/3
3		195	107	85	.557				

Blair, Walter Allen "Walter"

| 1915 | Buf-F* | 2 | 1 | 1 | .500 | 8 | 8 | 6 | 2/3 |

Bluege, Oswald Louis "Ossie"

1943	Was-A	153	84	69	.549	2			
1944	Was-A	154	64	90	.416	8			
1945	Was-A	156	87	67	.565	2			
1946	Was-A	155	76	78	.494	4			
1947	Was-A	154	64	90	.416	7			
5		772	375	394	.488				

Bond, Thomas Henry "Tommy"

| 1882 | Wor-N* | 6 | 2 | 4 | .333 | 8 | 8 | 8 | 2/3 |

Boros, Stephen "Steve"

1983	Oak-A	162	74	88	.457	4 W			
1984	Oak-A	44	20	24	.455	5 W	4 W		1/2
1986	SD-N	162	74	88	.457	4 W			
3		368	168	200	.457				

Bottomley, James Leroy "Jim"

| 1937 | StL-A* | 78 | 21 | 56 | .273 | 7 | 7 | | 2/2 |

Boudreau, Louis "Lou"

1942	Cle-A*	156	75	79	.487	4			
1943	Cle-A*	153	82	71	.536	3			
1944	Cle-A*	155	72	82	.468	●5			
1945	Cle-A*	147	73	72	.503	5			
1946	Cle-A*	156	68	86	.442	6			
1947	Cle-A*	157	80	74	.519	4			
1948	Cle-A*	156	97	58	.626	▲★1			
1949	Cle-A*	154	89	65	.578	3			
1950	Cle-A*	155	92	62	.597	4			
1952	Bos-A*	154	76	78	.494	6			
1953	Bos-A	153	84	69	.549	4			
1954	Bos-A	156	69	85	.448	4			
1955	KC-A	155	63	91	.409	6			
1956	KC-A	154	52	102	.338	8			
1957	KC-A	104	36	67	.350	8	7		1/2
1960	Chi-N	139	54	83	.394	7	7		2/2
16		2404	1162	1224	.487				

Bowa, Lawrence Robert "Larry"

1987	SD-N	162	65	97	.401	6 W			
1988	SD-N	46	16	30	.348	5 W	3 W		1/2
2		208	81	127	.389				

Bowerman, Frank Eugene "Frank"

| 1909 | Bos-N* | 76 | 22 | 54 | .289 | 8 | 8 | | 1/2 |

Boyd, William J. "Bill"

| 1875 | Atl-n* | 2 | 0 | 2 | .000 | 12 | 12 | | 2/2 |

Boyer, Kenton Lloyd "Ken"

1978	StL-N	143	62	81	.434	6 E	5 E		3/3
1979	StL-N	163	86	76	.531	3 E			
1980	StL-N	51	18	33	.353	6 E	4 E		1/4
3		357	166	190	.466				

Bradley, William Joseph "Bill"

1905	Cle-A	41	20	21	.488	●1	2	5	2/3
1914	Bro-F*	157	77	77	.500	5			
2		198	97	98	.497				

Bragan, Robert Randall "Bobby"

1956	Pit-N	157	66	88	.429	7			
1957	Pit-N	104	36	67	.350	7	●7		1/2
1958	Cle-A	67	31	36	.463	6	4		1/2
1963	Mil-N	163	84	78	.519	6			
1964	Mil-N	162	88	74	.543	5			
1965	Mil-N	162	86	76	.531	5			
1966	Atl-N	112	52	59	.468	7	5		1/2
7		927	443	478	.481				

Bresnahan, Roger Philip

1909	StL-N*	154	54	98	.355	7			
1910	StL-N*	153	63	90	.412	7			
1911	StL-N*	158	75	74	.503	5			
1912	StL-N*	153	63	90	.412	6			
1915	Chi-N*	157	73	80	.477	4			
5		775	328	432	.432				

Bristol, James David "Dave"

1966	Cin-N	77	39	38	.506	8	7		2/2
1967	Cin-N	162	87	75	.537	4			
1968	Cin-N	163	83	79	.512	4			
1969	Cin-N	163	89	73	.549	3 W			
1970	Mil-A	163	65	97	.401	●4 W			
1971	Mil-A	161	69	92	.429	6 W			
1972	Mil-A	30	10	20	.333	6 E	6 E		1/3
1976	Atl-N	162	70	92	.432	6 W			
1977	Atl-N	29	8	21	.276	6 W	6 W		1/4
	Atl-N	131	52	79	.397	6 W	6 W		4/4
1979	SF-N	22	10	12	.455	4 W	4 W		2/2
1980	SF-N	161	75	86	.466	5 W			
11		1424	657	764	.462				

Brown, Freeman

| 1882 | Wor-N | 41 | 9 | 32 | .220 | 8 | 8 | | 1/3 |

Brown, Lewis J. "Lew"

| 1879 | Chi-N* | 9 | 1 | 7 | .125 | 2 | 3 | 4 | 3/4 |

Brown, Mordecai Peter Centennial "Three Finger"

| 1914 | StL-F* | 114 | 50 | 63 | .442 | 7 | 8 | | 1/2 |

Brown, Thomas T. "Tom"

1897	Was-N*	99	52	46	.531	11	●6		2/2
1898	Was-N*	38	12	26	.316	11	11		1/4
2		137	64	72	.471				

Brucker, Earle Francis Sr

| 1952 | Cin-N | 5 | 3 | 2 | .600 | 7 | 7 | 6 | 2/3 |

Buckenberger, Albert C. "Al"

1889	Col-a	140	60	78	.435	6			
1890	Col-a	80	39	41	.488	5	2		1/3
1892(1)	Pit-N	29	15	14	.517	7	6		1/2
(2)	Pit-N	66	38	27	.585	10	4		2/2
1893	Pit-N	131	81	48	.628	2			
1894	Pit-N	110	53	55	.491	7	7		1/2
1895	StL-N	50	16	34	.320	11	11		1/4
1902	Bos-N	142	73	64	.533	3			
1903	Bos-N	140	58	80	.420	6			
1904	Bos-N	155	55	98	.359	7			
9		1043	488	539	.475				

Buffinton, Charles G. "Charlie"

| 1890 | Phi-P* | 116 | 61 | 54 | .530 | 5 | 5 | | 2/2 |

Burdock, John Joseph "Jack"

| 1883 | Bos-N* | 54 | 30 | 24 | .556 | 4 | 1 | | 1/2 |

Burke, James Timothy "Jimmy"

YEAR	TM/L	G	W	L	PCT	STANDING			M/Y
1905	StL-N*	90	34	56	.378	7	6	6	2/3
1918	StL-A	61	29	31	.483	6	5		3/3
1919	StL-A	140	67	72	.482	5			
1920	StL-A	154	76	77	.497	4			
4		445	206	236	.466				

Burnham, George Walter "Watch"

YEAR	TM/L	G	W	L	PCT	STANDING			M/Y
1887	Ind-N	28	6	22	.214	8	8		1/3

Burns, Thomas Everett "Tom"

YEAR	TM/L	G	W	L	PCT	STANDING			M/Y
1892(1)	Pit-N*	47	22	25	.468	7	6		2/2
(2)	Pit-N*	13	5	7	.417	10	4		1/2
1898	Chi-N	152	85	65	.567	4			
1899	Chi-N	152	75	73	.507	8			
3		364	187	170	.524				

Burwell, William Edwin "Bill"

YEAR	TM/L	G	W	L	PCT	STANDING			M/Y
1947	Pit-N	1	1	0	1.000	8	●7		2/2

Bush, Owen Joseph "Donie"

YEAR	TM/L	G	W	L	PCT	STANDING			M/Y
1923	Was-A*	155	75	78	.490	4			
1927	Pit-N	156	94	60	.610	1			
1928	Pit-N	152	85	67	.559	4			
1929	Pit-N	119	67	51	.568	2	2		1/2
1930	Chi-A	154	62	92	.403	7			
1931	Chi-A	156	56	97	.366	8			
1933	Cin-N	153	58	94	.382	8			
7		1045	497	539	.480				

Butler, Ormond Hook

YEAR	TM/L	G	W	L	PCT	STANDING			M/Y
1883	Pit-a	53	17	36	.321	6	6	7	2/3

Byrne, Charles H. "Charlie"

YEAR	TM/L	G	W	L	PCT	STANDING			M/Y
1885	Bro-a	75	38	37	.507	7	●5		2/2
1886	Bro-a	141	76	61	.555	3			
1887	Bro-a	138	60	74	.448	6			
3		354	174	172	.503				

Callahan, James Joseph "Jim"

YEAR	TM/L	G	W	L	PCT	STANDING			M/Y
1903	Chi-A*	138	60	77	.438	7			
1904	Chi-A*	42	23	18	.561	4	3		1/2
1912	Chi-A*	158	78	76	.506	4			
1913	Chi-A*	153	78	74	.513	5			
1914	Chi-A	157	70	84	.455	●6			
1916	Pit-N	157	65	89	.422	6			
1917	Pit-N	61	20	40	.333	8	8		1/3
7		866	394	458	.462				

Cammeyer, William Henry "Bill"

YEAR	TM/L	G	W	L	PCT	STANDING			M/Y
1876	NY-N	57	21	35	.375	6			

Campau, Charles Columbus "Count"

YEAR	TM/L	G	W	L	PCT	STANDING			M/Y
1890	StL-a*	42	27	14	.659	5	2	3	4/6

Cantillon, Joseph D. "Joe"

YEAR	TM/L	G	W	L	PCT	STANDING			M/Y
1907	Was-A	154	49	102	.325	8			
1908	Was-A	155	67	85	.441	7			
1909	Was-A	156	42	110	.276	8			
3		465	158	297	.347				

Carey, Max George

YEAR	TM/L	G	W	L	PCT	STANDING			M/Y
1932	Bro-N	154	81	73	.526	3			
1933	Bro-N	157	65	88	.425	6			
2		311	146	161	.476				

Carey, Thomas John "Tom"

YEAR	TM/L	G	W	L	PCT	STANDING			M/Y
1873	Bal-n*	24	14	9	.609	3	3		2/2
1874	Mut-n*	25	13	12	.520	3	2		1/2
2		49	27	21	.563				

Carrigan, William Francis "Bill"

YEAR	TM/L	G	W	L	PCT	STANDING			M/Y
1913	Bos-A*	70	40	30	.571	5	4		2/2
1914	Bos-A*	159	91	62	.595	2			
1915	Bos-A*	155	101	50	.669	★1			
1916	Bos-A*	156	91	63	.591	★1			
1927	Bos-A	154	51	103	.331	8			
1928	Bos-A	154	57	96	.373	8			
1929	Bos-A	155	58	96	.377	8			
7		1003	489	500	.494				

Caruthers, Robert Lee "Bob"

YEAR	TM/L	G	W	L	PCT	STANDING			M/Y
1892(2)	StL-N*	50	16	32	.333	12	11		5/5

Cavarretta, Philip Joseph "Phil"

YEAR	TM/L	G	W	L	PCT	STANDING			M/Y
1951	Chi-N*	74	27	47	.365	7	8		2/2
1952	Chi-N*	155	77	77	.500	5			
1953	Chi-N*	155	65	89	.422	7			
3		384	169	213	.442				

Caylor, Oliver Perry "O.P."

YEAR	TM/L	G	W	L	PCT	STANDING			M/Y
1885	Cin-a	112	63	49	.563	2			
1886	Cin-a	141	65	73	.471	5			
1887	NY-a	100	35	60	.368	7	7		3/3
3		353	163	182	.472				

Chance, Frank Leroy

YEAR	TM/L	G	W	L	PCT	STANDING			M/Y
1905	Chi-N*	90	55	33	.625	4	3		2/2
1906	Chi-N*	155	116	36	.763	1			
1907	Chi-N*	155	107	45	.704	★1			
1908	Chi-N*	158	99	55	.643	★1			
1909	Chi-N*	155	104	49	.680	2			
1910	Chi-N*	154	104	50	.675	1			
1911	Chi-N*	158	92	62	.597	2			
1912	Chi-N*	153	91	59	.607	3			
1913	NY-A*	153	57	94	.377	7			
1914	NY-A*	137	60	74	.448	7	●6		1/2
1923	Bos-A	154	61	91	.401	8			
11		1622	946	648	.593				

Chapman, John Curtis "Jack"

YEAR	TM/L	G	W	L	PCT	STANDING			M/Y
1876	Lou-N*	69	30	36	.455	5			
1877	Lou-N	61	35	25	.583	2			
1878	Mil-N	61	15	45	.250	6			
1882	Wor-N	37	7	30	.189	8	8		3/3
1883	Det-N	101	40	58	.408	7			
1884	Det-N	114	28	84	.250	8			
1885	Buf-N	88	31	57	.352	7	7		2/2
1889	Lou-a	7	1	6	.143	8	8		4/4
1890	Lou-a	136	88	44	.667	1			
1891	Lou-a	139	54	83	.394	8			
1892(1)	Lou-N	54	21	33	.389	10	11		1/2
11		867	350	501	.411				

Chapman, William Benjamin "Ben"

YEAR	TM/L	G	W	L	PCT	STANDING			M/Y
1945	Phi-N*	85	28	57	.329	8	8		2/2
1946	Phi-N*	155	69	85	.448	5			
1947	Phi-N	155	62	92	.403	●7			
1948	Phi-N	79	37	42	.468	7	6		1/3
4		474	196	276	.415				

Chase, Harold Homer "Hal"

YEAR	TM/L	G	W	L	PCT	STANDING			M/Y
1910	NY-A*	14	10	4	.714	3	2		2/2
1911	NY-A*	153	76	76	.500	6			
2		167	86	80	.518				

Clapp, John Edgar

YEAR	TM/L	G	W	L	PCT	STANDING			M/Y
1872	Man-n*	24	5	19	.208	8			
1878	Ind-N*	63	24	36	.400	5			
1879	Buf-N*	79	46	32	.590	3			
1880	Cin-N*	82	21	59	.262	8			
1883	NY-N*	98	46	50	.479	6			
5		346	142	196	.420				

Clarke, Fred Clifford

YEAR	TM/L	G	W	L	PCT	STANDING			M/Y
1897	Lou-N*	92	35	54	.393	9	11		2/2
1898	Lou-N*	154	70	81	.464	9			
1899	Lou-N*	156	75	77	.493	9			
1900	Pit-N*	140	79	60	.568	2			
1901	Pit-N*	140	90	49	.647	1			
1902	Pit-N*	142	103	36	.741	1			
1903	Pit-N*	141	91	49	.650	1			
1904	Pit-N*	156	87	66	.569	4			
1905	Pit-N*	155	96	57	.627	2			
1906	Pit-N*	154	93	60	.608	3			
1907	Pit-N*	157	91	63	.591	2			
1908	Pit-N*	155	98	56	.636	●2			
1909	Pit-N*	154	110	42	.724	★1			
1910	Pit-N*	154	86	67	.562	3			
1911	Pit-N*	156	85	69	.552	3			
1912	Pit-N	153	93	58	.616	2			
1913	Pit-N*	155	78	71	.523	4			
1914	Pit-N*	158	69	85	.448	7			
1915	Pit-N*	157	73	81	.474	5			
19		2829	1602	1181	.576				

Clements, John J. "Jack"

YEAR	TM/L	G	W	L	PCT	STANDING			M/Y
1890	Phi-M*	19	13	6	.684	1	2	3	2/5

Clinton, James Lawrence "Jim"

YEAR	TM/L	G	W	L	PCT	STANDING			M/Y
1872	Eck-n*	11	0	11	.000	10	10		1/2

Cobb, Tyrus Raymond "Ty"

YEAR	TM/L	G	W	L	PCT	STANDING			M/Y
1921	Det-A*	154	71	82	.464	6			
1922	Det-A*	155	79	75	.513	3			
1923	Det-A*	155	83	71	.539	2			
1924	Det-A*	156	86	68	.558	3			
1925	Det-A*	156	81	73	.526	4			
1926	Det-A*	157	79	75	.513	6			
6		933	479	444	.519				

Cochrane, Gordon Stanley "Mickey"

YEAR	TM/L	G	W	L	PCT	STANDING			M/Y
1934	Det-A*	154	101	53	.656	1			
1935	Det-A*	152	93	58	.616	★1			
1936	Det-A*	154	83	71	.539	2			
1937	Det-A*	29	16	13	.552	3	2		1/5
	Det-A*	47	26	20	.565	3	2	2	3/5
1938	Det-A	98	47	51	.480	5	4		1/2
5		634	366	266	.579				

Cohen, Andrew Howard "Andy"

YEAR	TM/L	G	W	L	PCT	STANDING			M/Y
1960	Phi-N	1	1	0	1.000	●6	●4	8	2/3

Coleman, Gerald Francis "Jerry"

YEAR	TM/L	G	W	L	PCT	STANDING			M/Y
1980	SD-N	163	73	89	.451	6 W			

Coleman, Robert Hunter "Bob"

YEAR	TM/L	G	W	L	PCT	STANDING			M/Y
1943	Bos-N	46	21	25	.457	6	6		1/2
1944	Bos-N	155	65	89	.422	6			
1945	Bos-N	94	42	51	.452	7	6		1/2
3		295	128	165	.437				

YEAR	TM/L	G	W	L	PCT	STANDING			M/Y
Collins, Edward Trowbridge Sr. "Eddie"									
1925	Chi-A*	154	79	75	.513	5			
1926	Chi-A*	155	81	72	.529	5			
2		309	160	147	.521				
Collins, James Joseph "Jimmy"									
1901	Bos-A*	138	79	57	.581	2			
1902	Bos-A*	138	77	60	.562	3			
1903	Bos-A*	141	91	47	.659	★1			
1904	Bos-A*	157	95	59	.617	1			
1905	Bos-A*	153	78	74	.513	4			
1906	Bos-A*	115	35	79	.307	8	8		1/2
6		842	455	376	.548				
Collins, John Francis "Shano"									
1931	Bos-A	153	62	90	.408	6			
1932	Bos-A	55	11	44	.200	8	8		1/2
2		208	73	134	.353				
Comiskey, Charles Albert "Charlie"									
1883	StL-a*	19	12	7	.632	2	2		2/2
1884	StL-a*	25	16	7	.696	5	4		2/2
1885	StL-a*	112	79	33	.705	1			
1886	StL-a*	139	93	46	.669	1			
1887	StL-a*	138	95	40	.704	1			
1888	StL-a*	137	92	43	.681	1			
1889	StL-a*	141	90	45	.667	2			
1890	Chi-P*	138	75	62	.547	4			
1891	StL-a*	139	85	51	.625	2			
1892(1)	Cin-N*	77	44	31	.587	4			
(2)	Cin-N*	78	38	37	.507	8			
1893	Cin-N*	131	65	63	.508	●6			
1894	Cin-N*	134	55	75	.423	10			
12		1408	839	540	.608				
Connor, Roger									
1896	StL-N*	46	8	37	.178	11	11	11	4/5
Cooke, Allen Lindsey "Dusty"									
1948	Phi-N	13	6	6	.500	7	6	6	2/3
Coombs, John Wesley "Jack"									
1919	Phi-N	63	18	44	.290	8	8		1/2
Cooney, John Walter "Johnny"									
1949	Bos-N	46	20	25	.444	4	4		2/2
Corrales, Patrick "Pat"									
1978	Tex-A	1	1	0	1.000	●2 W	●2 W		2/2
1979	Tex-A	162	83	79	.512	3 W			
1980	Tex-A	163	76	85	.472	4 W			
1982	Phi-N	162	89	73	.549	2 E			
1983	Phi-N	86	43	42	.506	1 E	◆1 E		1/2
	Cle-A	62	30	32	.484	7 E	7 E		2/2
1984	Cle-A	163	75	87	.463	6 E			
1985	Cle-A	162	60	102	.370	7 E			
1986	Cle-A	163	84	78	.519	5 E			
1987	Cle-A	87	31	56	.356	7 E	7 E		1/2
9		1211	572	634	.474				
Corriden, John Michael Sr. "Red"									
1950	Chi-A	125	52	72	.419	8	6		2/2
Cottier, Charles Keith "Chuck"									
1984	Sea-A	27	15	12	.556	7 W	●5 W		2/2
1985	Sea-A	162	74	88	.457	6 W			
1986	Sea-A	28	9	19	.321	6 W	7 W		1/3
3		217	98	119	.452				
Cox, Robert Joe "Bobby"									
1978	Atl-N	162	69	93	.426	6 W			
1979	Atl-N	160	66	94	.412	6 W			
1980	Atl-N	161	81	80	.503	4 W			
1981(1)	Atl-N	55	25	29	.463	4 W			
(2)	Atl-N	52	25	27	.481	5 W			
1982	Tor-A	162	78	84	.481	●6 E			
1983	Tor-A	162	89	73	.549	4 E			
1984	Tor-A	163	89	73	.549	2 E			
1985	Tor-A	161	99	62	.615	1 E			
8		1238	621	615	.502				
Craft, Harry Francis									
1957	KC-A	50	23	27	.460	8	7		2/2
1958	KC-A	156	73	81	.474	7			
1959	KC-A	154	66	88	.429	7			
1961	Chi-N	12	4	8	.333	●6	7	7	2/9
	Chi-N	4	3	1	.750	7	7	7	5/9
1962	Hou-N	162	64	96	.400	8			
1963	Hou-N	162	66	96	.407	9			
1964	Hou-N	149	61	88	.409	9	9		1/2
7		849	360	485	.426				
Craig, Roger Lee									
1978	SD-N	162	84	78	.519	4 W			
1979	SD-N	161	68	93	.422	5 W			
1985	SF-N	18	6	12	.333	6 W	6 W		2/2
1986	SF-N	162	83	79	.512	3 W			
1987	SF-N	162	90	72	.556	1 W			
1988	SF-N	162	83	79	.512	4 W			

YEAR	TM/L	G	W	L	PCT	STANDING			M/Y
6		827	414	413	.501				
Crandall, Delmar Wesley "Del"									
1972	Mil-A	124	54	70	.435	6 E	6 E		3/3
1973	Mil-A	162	74	88	.457	5 E			
1974	Mil-A	162	76	86	.469	5 E			
1975	Mil-A	161	67	94	.416	5 E	5 E		1/2
1983	Sea-A	89	34	55	.382	7 W	7 W		2/2
1984	Sea-A	135	59	76	.437	7 W	●5 W		1/2
6		833	364	469	.437				
Crane, Samuel Newhall "Sam"									
1880	Buf-N*	84	24	58	.293	7			
1884	Cin-U*	70	49	21	.700	5	3		2/2
2		154	73	79	.480				
Cravath, Clifford Carlton "Gavvy"									
1919	Phi-N*	75	29	46	.387	8	8		2/2
1920	Phi-N*	153	62	91	.405	8			
2		228	91	137	.399				
Craver, William H. "Bill"									
1871	Tro-n*	25	12	12	.500	7	6		2/2
1872	Bal-n*	41	27	13	.675	2	2		1/2
1874	Phi-n*	58	29	29	.500	4			
1875	Cen-n*	14	2	12	.143	11			
4		138	70	66	.515				
Creamer, George W.									
1884	Pit-a*	8	0	8	.000	10	10	10	4/5
Cronin, Joseph Edward "Joe"									
1933	Was-A*	153	99	53	.651	1			
1934	Was-A*	155	66	86	.434	7			
1935	Bos-A*	154	78	75	.510	4			
1936	Bos-A*	155	74	80	.481	6			
1937	Bos-A*	154	80	72	.526	5			
1938	Bos-A*	150	88	61	.591	2			
1939	Bos-A*	152	89	62	.589	2			
1940	Bos-A*	154	82	72	.532	●4			
1941	Bos-A*	155	84	70	.545	2			
1942	Bos-A*	152	93	59	.612	2			
1943	Bos-A*	155	68	84	.447	7			
1944	Bos-A*	156	77	77	.500	4			
1945	Bos-A*	157	71	83	.461	7			
1946	Bos-A	156	104	50	.675	1			
1947	Bos-A	157	83	71	.539	3			
15		2315	1236	1055	.540				
Crooks, John Charles									
1892(1)	StL-N*	47	24	22	.522	11	9		3/3
(2)	StL-N*	15	3	11	.214	12	11		1/3
Cross, Lafayette Napoleon "Lave"									
1899	Cle-N*	38	8	30	.211	12	12		1/2
Curtis, Edwin R. "Ed"									
1884	Alt-U	25	6	19	.240	6			
Cushman, Charles H. "Charlie"									
1891	Mil-a	36	21	15	.583	5			
Cuthbert, Edgar Edward "Ned"									
1882	StL-a*	80	37	43	.463	5			
Dahlen, William Frederick "Bill"									
1910	Bro-N*	156	64	90	.416	6			
1911	Bro-N*	154	64	86	.427	7			
1912	Bro-N	153	58	95	.379	7			
1913	Bro-N	152	65	84	.436	6			
4		615	251	355	.414				
Dark, Alvin Ralph									
1961	SF-N	155	85	69	.552	3			
1962	SF-N	165	103	62	.624	▲1			
1963	SF-N	162	88	74	.543	3			
1964	SF-N	162	90	72	.556	4			
1966	KC-A	160	74	86	.463	7			
1967	KC-A	121	52	69	.430	10	10		1/2
1968	Cle-A	162	86	75	.534	3			
1969	Cle-A	161	62	99	.385	6 E			
1970	Cle-A	162	76	86	.469	5 E			
1971	Cle-A	103	42	61	.408	6 E	6 E		1/2
1974	Oak-A	162	90	72	.556	★1 W			
1975	Oak-A	162	98	64	.605	1 W			
1977	SD-N	113	48	65	.425	4 W	5 W		3/3
13		1950	994	954	.510				
Davenport, James Houston "Jim"									
1985	SF-N	144	56	88	.389	6 W	6 W		1/2
Davidson, Mordecai H.									
1888	Lou-a	3	1	2	.333	8	8	7	2/4
	Lou-a	90	34	52	.395	8	7		4/4
Davis, George Stacey									
1895	NY-N*	33	16	17	.485	8	9		1/3
1900	NY-N*	78	39	37	.513	8	8		2/2
1901	NY-N*	141	52	85	.380	7			
3		252	107	139	.435				

YEAR	TM/L	G	W	L	PCT	STANDING			M/Y
Davis, Harry H									
1912	Cle-A*	127	54	71	.432	6	5		1/2
Davis, Virgil Lawrence "Spud"									
1946	Pit-N	3	1	2	.333	7	7		2/2
Day, John B.									
1899	NY-N	66	29	35	.453	9	10		1/2
Deane, John Henry "Harry"									
1871	Kek-n*	5	2	3	.400	7	8		2/2
Dickey, William Malcolm "Bill"									
1946	NY-A*	105	57	48	.543	2	3	3	2/3
Diddlebock, Henry H. "Harry"									
1896	StL-N	17	7	10	.412	10	11		1/5
Doby, Lawrence Eugene "Larry"									
1978	Chi-A	87	37	50	.425	5 W	5 W		2/2
Donovan, Patrick Joseph "Patsy"									
1897	Pit-N*	135	60	71	.458	8			
1899	Pit-N*	131	69	58	.543	10	7		2/2
1901	StL-N*	142	76	64	.543	4			
1902	StL-N*	140	56	78	.418	6			
1903	StL-N*	139	43	94	.314	8			
1904	Was-A*	139	37	97	.276	8	8		2/2
1906	Bro-N*	153	66	86	.434	5			
1907	Bro-N*	153	65	83	.439	5			
1908	Bro-N	154	53	101	.344	7			
1910	Bos-A	158	81	72	.529	4			
1911	Bos-A	153	78	75	.510	5			
11		1597	684	879	.438				
Donovan, William Edward "Bill"									
1915	NY-A*	154	69	83	.454	5			
1916	NY-A*	156	80	74	.519	4			
1917	NY-A	155	71	82	.464	6			
1921	Phi-N	87	25	62	.287	8	8		1/2
4		552	245	301	.449				
Dooin, Charles Sebastian "Red"									
1910	Phi-N*	157	78	75	.510	4			
1911	Phi-N*	153	79	73	.520	4			
1912	Phi-N*	152	73	79	.480	5			
1913	Phi-N*	159	88	63	.583	2			
1914	Phi-N*	154	74	80	.481	6			
5		775	392	370	.514				
Dorgan, Michael Cornelius "Mike"									
1879	Syr-N*	43	17	26	.395	6	7		1/3
1880	Pro-N*	39	26	12	.684	3	2		3/3
1881	Wor-N*	56	24	32	.429	7	8		1/2
3		138	67	70	.489				
Dowd, Thomas Jefferson "Tom"									
1896	StL-N*	63	25	38	.397	11	11		5/5
1897	StL-N*	29	6	22	.214	12	12		1/4
2		92	31	60	.341				
Doyle, John Joseph "Jack"									
1895	NY-N*	64	32	31	.508	8	9	9	2/3
1898	Was-N*	17	8	9	.471	11	10	11	2/4
2		81	40	40	.500				
Dressen, Charles Walter "Chuck"									
1934	Cin-N	60	21	39	.350	8	8		3/3
1935	Cin-N	154	68	85	.444	6			
1936	Cin-N	154	74	80	.481	5			
1937	Cin-N	130	51	78	.395	8	8		1/2
1951	Bro-N	158	97	60	.618	▲2			
1952	Bro-N	155	96	57	.627	1			
1953	Bro-N	155	105	49	.682	1			
1955	Was-A	154	53	101	.344	8			
1956	Was-A	155	59	95	.383	7			
1957	Was-A	20	4	16	.200	8	8		1/2
1960	Mil-N	154	88	66	.571	2			
1961	Mil-N	130	71	58	.550	3	4		1/2
1963	Det-A	102	55	47	.539	9	●5		2/2
1964	Det-A	163	85	77	.525	4			
1965	Det-A	120	65	55	.542	3	4		2/2
1966	Det-A	26	16	10	.615	3	3		1/3
16		1990	1008	973	.509				
Duffy, Hugh									
1901	Mil-A	139	48	89	.350	8			
1904	Phi-N*	155	52	100	.342	8			
1905	Phi-N*	155	83	69	.546	4			
1906	Phi-N*	154	71	82	.464	4			
1910	Chi-A	156	68	85	.444	6			
1911	Chi-A	154	77	74	.510	4			
1921	Bos-A	154	75	79	.487	5			
1922	Bos-A	154	61	93	.396	8			
8		1221	535	671	.444				
Dunlap, Frederick C. "Fred"									
1882	Cle-N*	80	42	36	.538	8	5		2/2
1884	StL-U*	83	66	16	.805	1	1		2/2
1885	StL-N*	50	21	29	.420	5	8		1/3
	StL-N*	22	9	11	.450	8	8		3/3
1889	Pit-N*	17	7	10	.412	6	7	5	2/3
4		252	145	102	.587				
Durocher, Leo Ernest									
1939	Bro-N*	157	84	69	.549	3			
1940	Bro-N*	156	88	65	.575	2			
1941	Bro-N*	157	100	54	.649	1			
1942	Bro-N	155	104	50	.675	2			
1943	Bro-N*	153	81	72	.529	3			
1944	Bro-N	155	63	91	.409	7			
1945	Bro-N*	155	87	67	.565	3			
1946	Bro-N	157	96	60	.615	▲2			
1948	Bro-N	73	35	37	.486	5	3		1/3
	NY-N	79	41	38	.519	4	5		2/2
1949	NY-N	156	73	81	.474	5			
1950	NY-N	154	86	68	.558	3			
1951	NY-N	157	98	59	.624	▲1			
1952	NY-N	154	92	62	.597	2			
1953	NY-N	155	70	84	.455	5			
1954	NY-N	154	97	57	.630	★1			
1955	NY-N	154	80	74	.519	3			
1966	Chi-N	162	59	103	.364	10			
1967	Chi-N	162	87	74	.540	3			
1968	Chi-N	163	84	78	.519	3			
1969	Chi-N	163	92	70	.568	2 E			
1970	Chi-N	162	84	78	.519	2 E			
1971	Chi-N	162	83	79	.512	●3 E			
1972	Chi-N	91	46	44	.511	4 E	2 E		1/2
	Hou-N	31	16	15	.516	2 W	2 W		3/3
1973	Hou-N	162	82	80	.506	4 W			
24		3739	2008	1709	.540				
Dwyer, John Francis "Frank"									
1902	Det-A	137	52	83	.385	7			
Dyer, Edwin Hawley "Eddie"									
1946	StL-N	156	98	58	.628	▲★1			
1947	StL-N	156	89	65	.578	2			
1948	StL-N	155	85	69	.552	2			
1949	StL-N	157	96	58	.623	2			
1950	StL-N	153	78	75	.510	5			
5		777	446	325	.578				
Dykes, James Joseph "Jimmy"									
1934	Chi-A*	138	49	88	.358	8	8		2/2
1935	Chi-A*	153	74	78	.487	5			
1936	Chi-A*	153	81	70	.536	3			
1937	Chi-A*	154	86	68	.558	3			
1938	Chi-A*	149	65	83	.439	6			
1939	Chi-A*	155	85	69	.552	4			
1940	Chi-A	155	82	72	.532	●4			
1941	Chi-A	156	77	77	.500	3			
1942	Chi-A	148	66	82	.446	6			
1943	Chi-A	155	82	72	.532	4			
1944	Chi-A	154	71	83	.461	7			
1945	Chi-A	150	71	78	.477	6			
1946	Chi-A	30	10	20	.333	7	5		1/2
1951	Phi-A	154	70	84	.455	6			
1952	Phi-A	155	79	75	.513	4			
1953	Phi-A	157	59	95	.383	7			
1954	Bal-A	154	54	100	.351	7			
1958	Cin-N	41	24	17	.585	8	4		2/2
1959	Det-A	137	74	63	.540	8	4		2/2
1960	Det-A	96	44	52	.458	6	6		1/3
	Cle-A	58	26	32	.448	4	4		3/3
1961	Cle-A	160	77	83	.481	5	5		1/2
21		2962	1406	1541	.477				
Ebbets, Charles Hercules "Charlie"									
1898	Bro-N	110	38	68	.358	9	10		3/3
Edwards, Howard Rodney "Doc"									
1987	Cle-A	75	30	45	.400	7 E	7 E		2/2
1988	Cle-A	162	78	84	.481	6 E			
2		237	108	129	.456				
Elberfeld, Norman Arthur "Kid"									
1908	NY-A*	98	27	71	.276	6	8		
Elia, Lee Constantine									
1982	Chi-N	162	73	89	.451	5 E			
1983	Chi-N	123	54	69	.439	5 E	5 E		1/2
1987	Phi-N	101	51	50	.505	5 E	●4 E		2/2
1988	Phi-N	153	60	92	.395	6 E	6 E		1/2
4		539	238	300	.442				
Ellick, Joseph J. "Joe"									
1884	Pit-U*	13	6	6	.500	5	5		2/2
Elliott, Robert Irving "Bob"									
1960	KC-A	155	58	96	.377	8			
Ens, Jewel Winklemeyer									
1929	Pit-N	35	21	14	.600	2	2		2/2
1930	Pit-N	154	80	74	.519	5			
1931	Pit-N	155	75	79	.487	5			
3		344	176	167	.513				

YEAR	TM/L	G	W	L	PCT	STANDING			M/Y

Ermer, Calvin Coolidge "Cal"

YEAR	TM/L	G	W	L	PCT	STANDING			M/Y
1967	Min-A	114	66	46	.589	6	●2		2/2
1968	Min-A	162	79	83	.488	7			
	2	276	145	129	.529				

Esterbrook, Thomas Jefferson "Dude"

1889	Lou-a*	10	2	8	.200	7	8		1/4

Evers, John Joseph "Johnny"

1913	Chi-N*	155	88	65	.575	3			
1921	Chi-N	96	41	55	.427	6	7		1/2
1924	Chi-A	21	10	11	.476	6			1/4
	Chi-A	103	41	61	.402	8			4/4
	3	375	180	192	.484				

Ewing, William "Buck"

1890	NY-P*	132	74	57	.565	3			
1895	Cin-N*	132	66	64	.508	8			
1896	Cin-N*	128	77	50	.606	3			
1897	Cin-N*	134	76	56	.576	4			
1898	Cin-N	157	92	60	.605	3			
1899	Cin-N	157	83	67	.553	6			
1900	NY-N	63	21	41	.339	8	8		1/2
	7	903	489	395	.553				

Faatz, Jayson S. "Jay"

1890	Buf-P*	34	9	24	.273	8	8	8	2/3

Falk, Bibb August

1933	Cle-A	1	1	0	1.000	5	5	4	2/3

Fanning, William James "Jim"

1981(2)	Mon-N	27	16	11	.593	2 E	1 E		2/2
1982	Mon-N	162	86	76	.531	3 E			
1984	Mon-N	30	14	16	.467	5 E	5 E		2/2
	3	219	116	103	.530				

Farrell, John A. "Jack"

1881	Pro-N*	51	24	27	.471	4	2		1/2

Farrell, Major Kerby "Kerby"

1957	Cle-A	153	76	77	.497	6			

Felske, John Frederick

1985	Phi-N	162	75	87	.463	5 E			
1986	Phi-N	161	86	75	.534	2 E			
1987	Phi-N	61	29	32	.475	5 E	●4 E		1/2
	3	384	190	194	.495				

Ferguson, Robert V. "Bob"

1871	Mut-n*	33	16	17	.485	4			
1872	Atl-n*	35	8	27	.229	7			
1873	Atl-n*	55	17	37	.315	6			
1874	Atl-n*	56	22	33	.400	6			
1875	Har-N*	86	54	28	.659	3			
1876	Har-N*	69	47	21	.691	3			
1877	Har-N*	60	31	27	.534	3			
1878	Chi-N*	61	30	30	.500	4			
1879	Tro-N*	30	7	22	.241	8	8		2/2
1880	Tro-N*	83	41	42	.494	4			
1881	Tro-N*	85	39	45	.464	5			
1882	Tro-N*	85	35	48	.422	7			
1883	Phi-N*	17	4	13	.235	8	8		1/2
1884	Pit-a*	42	11	31	.262	9	11	10	2/5
1886	NY-a	120	48	70	.407	8	7		2/2
1887	NY-a	30	6	24	.200	8	7		1/3
	16	947	416	515	.447				

Ferraro, Michael Dennis "Mike"

1983	Cle-A	100	40	60	.400	7 E	7 E		1/2
1986	KC-A	74	36	38	.486	4 W	●3 W		2/2
	2	174	76	98	.437				

Fessenden, Wallace Clifton

1890	Syr-a	11	4	7	.364	7	7	6	2/3

Field, Samuel Jay "Sam"

1875	Nat-n*	7	0	7	.000	8	10		2/2

Fitzsimmons, Frederick Landis "Freddie"

1943	Phi-N	65	26	38	.406	7	7		2/2
1944	Phi-N	154	61	92	.399	8			
1945	Phi-N	69	18	51	.261	8	8		1/2
	3	288	105	181	.367				

Fletcher, Arthur "Art"

1923	Phi-N	155	50	104	.325	8			
1924	Phi-N	152	55	96	.364	7			
1925	Phi-N	153	68	85	.444	●6			
1926	Phi-N	152	58	93	.384	8			
1929	NY-A	11	6	5	.545	2	2		2/2
	5	623	237	383	.382				

Flint, Frank Sylvester "Silver"

1879	Chi-N*	1	1	0	1.000	2	2	4	2/4
	Chi-N*	9	3	5	.375	3	4		4/4

Fogarty, James G. "Jim"

1890	Phi-P*	16	7	9	.438	5	5		1/2

Fogel, Horace S.

1887	Ind-N	70	20	49	.290	8	8		3/3

YEAR	TM/L	G	W	L	PCT	STANDING			M/Y
1902	NY-N	44	18	23	.439	4	8		1/3
	2	114	38	72	.345				

Fohl, Leo Alexander "Lee"

1915	Cle-A	127	45	79	.363	6	7		2/2
1916	Cle-A	157	77	77	.500	6			
1917	Cle-A	156	88	66	.571	3			
1918	Cle-A	129	73	54	.575	2			
1919	Cle-A	78	44	34	.564	3	2		1/2
1921	StL-A	154	81	73	.526	3			
1922	StL-A	154	93	61	.604	2			
1923	StL-A	103	52	49	.515	3	5		1/2
1924	Bos-A	157	67	87	.435	7			
1925	Bos-A	152	47	105	.309	8			
1926	Bos-A	154	46	107	.301	8			
	11	1521	713	792	.474				

Fonseca, Lewis Albert "Lew"

1932	Chi-A*	152	49	102	.325	7			
1933	Chi-A*	151	67	83	.447	6			
1934	Chi-A	15	4	11	.267	8	8		1/2
	3	318	120	196	.380				

Foutz, David Luther "Dave"

1893	Bro-N*	130	65	63	.508	●6			
1894	Bro-N*	135	70	61	.534	5			
1895	Bro-N*	134	71	60	.542	●5			
1896	Bro-N*	133	58	73	.443	●9			
	4	532	264	257	.507				

Fox, Charles Francis "Charlie"

1970	SF-N	120	67	53	.558	4 W	3 W		2/2
1971	SF-N	162	90	72	.556	1 W			
1972	SF-N	155	69	86	.445	5 W			
1973	SF-N	162	88	74	.543	3 W			
1974	SF-N	76	34	42	.447	5 W	5 W		1/2
1976	Mon-N	34	12	22	.353	6 E	6 E		2/2
1983	Chi-N	39	17	22	.436	5 E	5 E		2/2
	7	748	377	371	.504				

Franks, Herman Louis

1965	SF-N	163	95	67	.586	2			
1966	SF-N	161	93	68	.578	2			
1967	SF-N	162	91	71	.562	2			
1968	SF-N	163	88	74	.543	2			
1977	Chi-N	162	81	81	.500	4 E			
1978	Chi-N	162	79	83	.488	3 E			
1979	Chi-N	155	78	77	.503	5 E	5 E		1/2
	7	1128	605	521	.537				

Frazer, George Kasson

1890	Syr-a	71	31	40	.437	7	6		1/3
	Syr-a	46	20	25	.444	7	6		3/3

Frazier, Joseph Filmore "Joe"

1976	NY-N	162	86	76	.531	3 E			
1977	NY-N	45	15	30	.333	6 E	6 E		1/2
	2	207	101	106	.488				

Fregosi, James Louis "Jim"

1978	Cal-A	117	62	55	.530	3 W	●2 W		2/2
1979	Cal-A	162	88	74	.543	1 W			
1980	Cal-A	160	65	95	.406	6 W			
1981(1)	Cal-A	47	22	25	.468	4 W	4 W		1/2
1986	Chi-A	96	45	51	.469	5 W	5 W		3/3
1987	Chi-A	162	77	85	.475	5 W			
1988	Chi-A	161	71	90	.441	5 W			
	7	905	430	475	.475				

Frey, James Gottfried "Jim"

1980	KC-A	162	97	65	.599	♦1 W			
1981(1)	KC-A	50	20	30	.400	5 W			
(2)	KC-A	20	10	10	.500	●2 W	1 W		1/2
1984	Chi-N	161	96	65	.596	1 E			
1985	Chi-N	162	77	84	.478	4 E			
1986	Chi-N	56	23	33	.411	5 E	5 E		1/3
	5	611	323	287	.530				

Frisch, Frank Francis "Frankie"

1933	StL-N*	63	36	26	.581	5	5		2/2
1934	StL-N*	154	95	58	.621	★1			
1935	StL-N*	154	96	58	.623	2			
1936	StL-N*	155	87	67	.565	●2			
1937	StL-N*	157	81	73	.526	4			
1938	StL-N	139	63	72	.467	6	6		1/2
1940	Pit-N	156	78	76	.506	4			
1941	Pit-N	156	81	73	.526	4			
1942	Pit-N	151	66	81	.449	5			
1943	Pit-N	157	80	74	.519	4			
1944	Pit-N	158	90	63	.588	2			
1945	Pit-N	155	82	72	.532	4			
1946	Pit-N	152	62	89	.411	7	7		1/2
1949	Chi-N	104	42	62	.404	7	8		2/2
1950	Chi-N	154	64	89	.418	7			
1951	Chi-N	81	35	45	.438	7	8		1/2
	16	2246	1138	1078	.514				

YEAR	TM/L	G	W	L	PCT	STANDING			M/Y
Fuchs, Emil Edmund "Judge"									
1929	Bos-N	154	56	98	.364	8			
Gaffney, John H.									
1886	Was-N	43	15	25	.375	8			2/2
1887	Was-N	126	46	76	.377	7			
2		169	61	101	.377				
Galvin, James Francis "Jim"									
1885	Buf-N*	24	7	17	.292	7	7		1/2
Ganzel, John Henry									
1908	Cin-N*	155	73	81	.474	5			
1915	Bro-F	35	17	18	.486	7	7		2/2
2		190	90	99	.476				
Garcia, David "Dave"									
1977	Cal-A	81	35	46	.432	5 W	5 W		2/2
1978	Cal-A	45	25	20	.556	3 W	•2 W		1/2
1979	Cle-A	66	38	28	.576	6 E	6 E		2/2
1980	Cle-A	160	79	81	.494	6 E			
1981(1)	Cle-A	50	26	24	.520	6 E			
(2)	Cle-A	53	26	27	.491	5 E			
1982	Cle-A	162	78	84	.481	•6 E			
6		617	307	310	.498				
Gardner, William Frederick "Billy"									
1981(1)	Min-A	20	6	14	.300	6 W	7 W		2/2
(2)	Min-A	53	24	29	.453	4 W			
1982	Min-A	162	60	102	.370	7 W			
1983	Min-A	162	70	92	.432	5 W			
1984	Min-A	162	81	81	.500	2 W			
1985	Min-A	62	27	35	.435	6 W	4 W		1/2
1987	KC-A	126	62	64	.492	4 W	2 W		1/2
6		747	330	417	.442				
Gerhardt, John Joseph "Joe"									
1883	Lou-a*	98	52	45	.536	5			
1890	StL-a*	38	20	16	.556	2	3		6/6
2		136	72	61	.541				
Gessler, Harry Homer "Doc"									
1914	Pit-F	11	3	8	.273	8	7		1/2
Gibson, George C. "Moon"									
1920	Pit-N	155	79	75	.513	4			
1921	Pit-N	154	90	63	.588	2			
1922	Pit-N	65	32	33	.492	5	•3		1/2
1925	Chi-N	26	12	14	.462	7	8		3/3
1932	Pit-N	154	86	68	.558	2			
1933	Pit-N	154	87	67	.565	2			
1934	Pit-N	51	27	24	.529	4	5		1/2
7		759	413	344	.546				
Gifford, James H. "Jim"									
1884	Ind-a	87	25	60	.294	10	11		1/2
1885	NY-a	108	44	64	.407	7			
1886	NY-a	17	5	12	.294	8	7		1/2
3		212	74	136	.352				
Glasscock, John Wesley "Jack"									
1889	Ind-N*	67	34	32	.515	7	7		2/2
1892(1)	StL-N*	4	1	3	.250	10	9		1/3
2		71	35	35	.500				
Gleason, William J. "Kid"									
1919	Chi-A	140	88	52	.629	1			
1920	Chi-A	154	96	58	.623	2			
1921	Chi-A	154	62	92	.403	7			
1922	Chi-A	155	77	77	.500	5			
1923	Chi-A	156	69	85	.448	7			
5		759	392	364	.519				
Gomez, Pedro [Martinez] "Preston"									
1969	SD-N	162	52	110	.321	6 W			
1970	SD-N	162	63	99	.389	6 W			
1971	SD-N	161	61	100	.379	6 W			
1972	SD-N	11	4	7	.364	4 W	6 W		1/2
1974	Hou-N	162	81	81	.500	4 W			
1975	Hou-N	127	47	80	.370	6 W	6 W		1/2
1980	Chi-N	90	38	52	.422	6 E	6 E		1/2
7		875	346	529	.395				
Gonzalez, Miguel Angel "Mike"									
1938	StL-N	17	8	8	.500	6	6		2/2
1940	StL-N	6	1	5	.167	6	7	3	2/3
2		23	9	13	.409				
Gordon, Joseph Lowell "Joe"									
1958	Cle-A	86	46	40	.535	6	4		2/2
1959	Cle-A	154	89	65	.578	2			
1960	Cle-A	95	49	46	.516	4	4		1/3
	Det-A	57	26	31	.456	6	6		3/3
1961	KC-A	60	26	33	.441	8	•9		1/2
1969	KC-A	163	69	93	.426	4 W			
5		615	305	308	.498				
Gore, George F.									
1892(2)	StL-N*	16	6	9	.400	12	12	11	4/5

YEAR	TM/L	G	W	L	PCT	STANDING			M/Y
Goryl, John Albert "Johnny"									
1980	Min-A	36	23	13	.639	4 W	3 W		2/2
1981(1)	Min-A	37	11	25	.306	6 W	7 W		1/2
2		73	34	38	.472				
Gould, Charles Harvey "Charlie"									
1875	NH-n*	23	2	21	.087	11	8		1/3
1876	Cin-N*	65	9	56	.138	8			
2		88	11	77	.125				
Gowdy, Henry Morgan "Hank"									
1946	Cin-N	4	3	1	.750	6	6		2/2
Graffen, Samuel Mason "Mase"									
1876	StL-N	56	39	17	.696	2	2		1/2
Grammas, Alexander Peter "Alex"									
1969	Pit-N	5	4	1	.800	3 E	3 E		2/2
1976	Mil-A	161	66	95	.410	6 E			
1977	Mil-A	162	67	95	.414	6 E			
3		328	137	191	.418				
Green, George Dallas "Dallas"									
1979	Phi-N	30	19	11	.633	5 E	4 E		2/2
1980	Phi-N	162	91	71	.562	★1 E			
1981(1)	Phi-N	55	34	21	.618	1 E			
(2)	Phi-N	52	25	27	.481	3 E			
3		299	169	130	.565				
Griffin, Michael Joseph "Mike"									
1898	Bro-N*	4	1	3	.250	9	9	10	2/3
Griffin, Tobias Charles "Sandy"									
1891	Was-a*	6	2	4	.333	8	8		4/4
Griffith, Clark Calvin									
1901	Chi-A*	137	83	53	.610	1			
1902	Chi-A*	138	74	60	.552	4			
1903	NY-A*	136	72	62	.537	4			
1904	NY-A*	155	92	59	.609	2			
1905	NY-A*	152	71	78	.477	6			
1906	NY-A*	155	90	61	.596	2			
1907	NY-A*	152	70	78	.473	5			
1908	NY-A	57	24	32	.429	6	8		1/2
1909	Cin-N*	157	77	76	.503	4			
1910	Cin-N*	156	75	79	.487	5			
1911	Cin-N	159	70	83	.458	6			
1912	Was-A*	154	91	61	.599	2			
1913	Was-A*	155	90	64	.584	2			
1914	Was-A*	158	81	73	.526	3			
1915	Was-A	155	85	68	.556	4			
1916	Was-A	159	76	77	.497	7			
1917	Was-A	158	74	79	.484	5			
1918	Was-A	130	72	56	.563	3			
1919	Was-A	142	56	84	.400	7			
1920	Was-A	153	68	84	.447	6			
20		2918	1491	1367	.522				
Grimes, Burleigh Arland									
1937	Bro-N	155	62	91	.405	6			
1938	Bro-N	151	69	80	.463	7			
2		306	131	171	.434				
Grimm, Charles John "Charlie"									
1932	Chi-N*	55	37	18	.673	2	1		2/2
1933	Chi-N*	154	86	68	.558	3			
1934	Chi-N*	152	86	65	.570	3			
1935	Chi-N*	154	100	54	.649	1			
1936	Chi-N*	154	87	67	.565	•2			
1937	Chi-N	154	93	61	.604	2			
1938	Chi-N	81	45	36	.556	3	1		1/2
1944	Chi-N	146	74	69	.517	8	4		3/3
1945	Chi-N	155	98	56	.636	1			
1946	Chi-N	155	82	71	.536	3			
1947	Chi-N	155	69	85	.448	6			
1948	Chi-N	155	64	90	.416	8			
1949	Chi-N	50	19	31	.380	7	8		1/2
1952	Bos-N	120	51	67	.432	7	7		2/2
1953	Mil-N	157	92	62	.597	2			
1954	Mil-N	154	89	65	.578	3			
1955	Mil-N	154	85	69	.552	2			
1956	Mil-N	46	24	22	.522	5	2		1/2
1960	Chi-N	17	6	11	.353	7	7		1/2
19		2368	1287	1067	.547				
Groh, Henry Knight "Heinie"									
1918	Cin-N*	10	7	3	.700	4	3		2/2
Gutteridge, Donald Joseph "Don"									
1969	Chi-A	145	60	85	.414	4 W	5 W		2/2
1970	Chi-A	136	49	87	.360	6 W	6 W		1/3
2		281	109	172	.388				
Haas, George Edwin "Eddie"									
1985	Atl-N	121	50	71	.413	5 W	5 W		1/2
Hack, Stanley Camfield "Stan"									
1954	Chi-N	154	64	90	.416	7			
1955	Chi-N	154	72	81	.471	6			
1956	Chi-N	157	60	94	.390	8			

YEAR	TM/L	G	W	L	PCT	STANDING			M/Y
1958	StL-N	10	3	7	.300	5	●5		2/2
	4	475	199	272	.423				

Hackett, Charles M. "Charlie"

YEAR	TM/L	G	W	L	PCT	STANDING			M/Y
1884	Cle-N	113	35	77	.313	7			
1885	Bro-a	37	15	22	.405	7	●5		1/2
	2	150	50	99	.336				

Hallman, William Wilson "Bill"

YEAR	TM/L	G	W	L	PCT	STANDING			M/Y
1897	StL-N*	50	13	36	.265	12	12	12	3/4

Haney, Fred Girard

YEAR	TM/L	G	W	L	PCT	STANDING			M/Y
1939	StL-A	156	43	111	.279	8			
1940	StL-A	156	67	87	.435	6			
1941	StL-A	44	15	29	.341	7	●6		1/2
1953	Pit-N	154	50	104	.325	8			
1954	Pit-N	154	53	101	.344	8			
1955	Pit-N	154	60	94	.390	8			
1956	Mil-N	109	68	40	.630	5	2		2/2
1957	Mil-N	155	95	59	.617	★1			
1958	Mil-N	154	92	62	.597	1			
1959	Mil-N	157	86	70	.551	▲2			
	10	1393	629	757	.454				

Hanlon, Edward Hugh "Ned"

YEAR	TM/L	G	W	L	PCT	STANDING			M/Y
1889	Pit-N*	46	26	18	.591	7	5		3/3
1890	Pit-P*	131	60	68	.469	6			
1891	Pit-N*	78	31	47	.397	8	8		1/2
1892(1)	Bal-N*	56	17	39	.304	12	12		3/3
(2)	Bal-N*	77	26	46	.361	10			
1893	Bal-N	130	60	70	.462	8			
1894	Bal-N	129	89	39	.695	1			
1895	Bal-N	132	87	43	.669	1			
1896	Bal-N	132	90	39	.698	1			
1897	Bal-N	136	90	40	.692	2			
1898	Bal-N	154	96	53	.644	2			
1899	Bro-N	150	101	47	.682	1			
1900	Bro-N	142	82	54	.603	1			
1901	Bro-N	137	79	57	.581	3			
1902	Bro-N	141	75	63	.543	2			
1903	Bro-N	139	70	66	.515	5			
1904	Bro-N	154	56	97	.366	6			
1905	Bro-N	155	48	104	.316	8			
1906	Cin-N	155	64	87	.424	6			
1907	Cin-N	156	66	87	.431	6			
	19	2530	1313	1164	.530				

Harder, Melvin Leroy "Mel"

YEAR	TM/L	G	W	L	PCT	STANDING			M/Y
1961	Cle-A	1	1	0	1.000	5	5		2/2
1962	Cle-A	2	2	0	1.000	6	6		2/2
	2	3	3	0	1.000				

Harris, Chalmer Luman "Lum"

YEAR	TM/L	G	W	L	PCT	STANDING			M/Y
1961	Bal-A	27	17	10	.630	3	3		2/2
1964	Hou-N	13	5	8	.385	9	9		2/2
1965	Hou-N	162	65	97	.401	9			
1968	Atl-N	163	81	81	.500	5			
1969	Atl-N	162	93	69	.574	1 W			
1970	Atl-N	162	76	86	.469	5 W			
1971	Atl-N	162	82	80	.506	3 W			
1972	Atl-N	105	47	57	.452	4 W	4 W		1/2
	8	956	466	488	.488				

Harris, Stanley Raymond "Bucky"

YEAR	TM/L	G	W	L	PCT	STANDING			M/Y
1924	Was-A*	156	92	62	.597	★1			
1925	Was-A*	152	96	55	.636	1			
1926	Was-A*	152	81	69	.540	4			
1927	Was-A*	157	85	69	.552	3			
1928	Was-A*	155	75	79	.487	4			
1929	Det-A*	155	70	84	.455	6			
1930	Det-A*	154	75	79	.487	5			
1931	Det-A*	154	61	93	.396	7			
1932	Det-A	153	76	75	.503	5			
1933	Det-A	153	73	79	.480	5	5		1/2
1934	Bos-A	153	76	76	.500	4			
1935	Was-A	154	67	86	.438	6			
1936	Was-A	153	82	71	.536	4			
1937	Was-A	158	73	80	.477	6			
1938	Was-A	152	75	76	.497	5			
1939	Was-A	153	65	87	.428	6			
1940	Was-A	154	64	90	.416	7			
1941	Was-A	156	70	84	.455	●6			
1942	Was-A	151	62	89	.411	7			
1943	Phi-N	92	38	52	.422	7	7		1/2
1947	NY-A	155	97	57	.630	★1			
1948	NY-A	154	94	60	.610	3			
1950	Was-A	155	67	87	.435	5			
1951	Was-A	154	62	92	.403	7			
1952	Was-A	157	78	76	.506	5			
1953	Was-A	152	76	76	.500	5			
1954	Was-A	155	66	88	.429	6			
1955	Det-A	154	79	75	.513	5			
1956	Det-A	155	82	72	.532	5			
	29	4408	2157	2218	.493				

Hart, James Aristotle "Jim"

YEAR	TM/L	G	W	L	PCT	STANDING			M/Y
1885	Lou-a	112	53	59	.473	●5			
1886	Lou-a	138	66	70	.485	4			
1889	Bos-N	133	83	45	.648	2			
	3	383	202	174	.537				

Hartnett, Charles Leo "Gabby"

YEAR	TM/L	G	W	L	PCT	STANDING			M/Y
1938	Chi-N*	73	44	27	.620	3	1		2/2
1939	Chi-N*	156	84	70	.545	4			
1940	Chi-N*	154	75	79	.487	5			
	3	383	203	176	.536				

Hartsfield, Roy Thomas

YEAR	TM/L	G	W	L	PCT	STANDING			M/Y
1977	Tor-A	161	54	107	.335	7 E			
1978	Tor-A	161	59	102	.366	7 E			
1979	Tor-A	162	53	109	.327	7 E			
	3	484	166	318	.343				

Hastings, Winfield Scott "Scott"

YEAR	TM/L	G	W	L	PCT	STANDING			M/Y
1871	Rok-n*	25	4	21	.160	9			
1872	Cle-n*	19	6	13	.316	5	7		1/2
	2	44	10	34	.227				

Hatfield, John Van Buren

YEAR	TM/L	G	W	L	PCT	STANDING			M/Y
1873	Mut-n*	28	11	17	.393	5	4		1/2

Hatton, Grady Edgebert

YEAR	TM/L	G	W	L	PCT	STANDING			M/Y
1966	Hou-N	163	72	90	.444	8			
1967	Hou-N	162	69	93	.426	9			
1968	Hou-N	61	23	38	.377	10	10		1/2
	3	386	164	221	.426				

Hecker, Guy Jackson

YEAR	TM/L	G	W	L	PCT	STANDING			M/Y
1890	Pit-N*	138	23	113	.169	8			

Heffner, Donald Henry "Don"

YEAR	TM/L	G	W	L	PCT	STANDING			M/Y
1966	Cin-N	83	37	46	.446	8	7		1/2

Heilbroner, Louis Wilbur "Louie"

YEAR	TM/L	G	W	L	PCT	STANDING			M/Y
1900	StL-N	50	23	25	.479	7	●5		2/2

Helms, Tommy Vann

YEAR	TM/L	G	W	L	PCT	STANDING			M/Y
1988	Cin-N	27	12	15	.444	4 W	4 W	2 W	2/2

Hemus, Solomon Joseph "Solly"

YEAR	TM/L	G	W	L	PCT	STANDING			M/Y
1959	StL-N*	154	71	83	.461	7			
1960	StL-N	155	86	68	.558	3			
1961	StL-N	75	33	41	.446	5	5		1/2
	3	384	190	192	.497				

Henderson, William C. "Bill"

YEAR	TM/L	G	W	L	PCT	STANDING			M/Y
1884	Bal-U	106	58	47	.552	4			

Hendricks, John Charles "Jack"

YEAR	TM/L	G	W	L	PCT	STANDING			M/Y
1918	StL-N	133	51	78	.395	8			
1924	Cin-N	153	83	70	.542	4			
1925	Cin-N	153	80	73	.523	3			
1926	Cin-N	157	87	67	.565	2			
1927	Cin-N	153	75	78	.490	5			
1928	Cin-N	153	78	74	.513	5			
1929	Cin-N	155	66	88	.429	7			
	7	1057	520	528	.496				

Hengle, Edward S. "Ed"

YEAR	TM/L	G	W	L	PCT	STANDING			M/Y
1884	Chi-U	74	34	39	.466	5			

Herman, William Jennings Bryan "Billy"

YEAR	TM/L	G	W	L	PCT	STANDING			M/Y
1947	Pit-N*	155	61	92	.399	8	●7		1/2
1964	Bos-A	2	2	0	1.000	8	8		2/2
1965	Bos-A	162	62	100	.383	9			
1966	Bos-A	146	64	82	.438	9	9		1/2
	4	465	189	274	.408				

Herzog, Charles Lincoln "Buck"

YEAR	TM/L	G	W	L	PCT	STANDING			M/Y
1914	Cin-N*	157	60	94	.390	8			
1915	Cin-N*	160	71	83	.461	7			
1916	Cin-N*	84	34	49	.410	8	●7		1/3
	3	401	165	226	.422				

Herzog, Dorrel Norman Elvert "Whitey"

YEAR	TM/L	G	W	L	PCT	STANDING			M/Y
1973	Tex-A	138	47	91	.341	6 W	6 W		1/3
1974	Cal-A	4	2	2	.500	6 W	6 W	6 W	2/3
1975	KC-A	66	41	25	.621	2 W	2 W		2/2
1976	KC-A	162	90	72	.556	1 W			
1977	KC-A	162	102	60	.630	1 W			
1978	KC-A	162	92	70	.568	1 W			
1979	KC-A	162	85	77	.525	2 W			
1980	StL-N	73	38	35	.521	6 E	5 E	4 E	3/4
1981(1)	StL-N	51	30	20	.600	2 E			
(2)	StL-N	52	29	23	.558	2 E			
1982	StL-N	162	92	70	.568	★1 E			
1983	StL-N	162	79	83	.488	4 E			
1984	StL-N	162	84	78	.519	3 E			
1985	StL-N	162	101	61	.623	◆1 E			
1986	StL-N	161	79	82	.491	3 E			
1987	StL-N	162	95	67	.586	◆1 E			
1988	StL-N	162	76	86	.469	5 E			
	16	2165	1162	1002	.537				

Hewett, Walter F.

YEAR	TM/L	G	W	L	PCT	STANDING			M/Y
1888	Was-N	40	10	29	.256	8	8		1/2

YEAR	TM/L	G	W	L	PCT	STANDING			M/Y
Hicks, Nathaniel Woodhull "Nat"									
1875	Mut-n*	71	30	38	.441	7			
Higgins, Michael Franklin "Pinky"									
1955	Bos-A	154	84	70	.545	4			
1956	Bos-A	155	84	70	.545	4			
1957	Bos-A	154	82	72	.532	3			
1958	Bos-A	155	79	75	.513	3			
1959	Bos-A	73	31	42	.425	8	8		1/3
1960	Bos-A	105	48	57	.457	8	7		3/3
1961	Bos-A	163	76	86	.469	6			
1962	Bos-A	160	76	84	.475	8			
	8	1119	560	556	.502				
Higham, Richard "Dick"									
1874	Mut-n*	40	29	11	.725	3	2		2/2
Himsl, Avitus Bernard "Vedie"									
1961	Chi-N	11	5	6	.455	6	•6		1/9
	Chi-N	17	5	12	.294	7	7	7	3/9
	Chi-N	4	0	3	.000	7	7	7	6/9
Hitchcock, William Clyde "Billy"									
1960	Det-A	1	1	0	1.000	6	6	6	2/3
1962	Bal-A	162	77	85	.475	7			
1963	Bal-A	162	86	76	.531	4			
1966	Atl-N	51	33	18	.647	7	5		2/2
1967	Atl-N	159	77	82	.484	7	7		1/2
	5	535	274	261	.512				
Hodges, Gilbert Raymond "Gil"									
1963	Was-A	121	42	79	.347	10	10		3/3
1964	Was-A	162	62	100	.383	9			
1965	Was-A	162	70	92	.432	8			
1966	Was-A	159	71	88	.447	8			
1967	Was-A	161	76	85	.472	•6			
1968	NY-N	163	73	89	.451	9			
1969	NY-N	162	100	62	.617	★1 E			
1970	NY-N	162	83	79	.512	3 E			
1971	NY-N	162	83	79	.512	•3 E			
	9	1414	660	753	.467				
Hoey, Frederick C. "Fred"									
1899	NY-N	87	31	55	.360	9	10		2/2
Holbert, William H. "Bill"									
1879	Syr-N*	1	0	1	.000	6	6	7	2/3
Hollingshead, John Samuel "Holly"									
1875	Nat-n*	20	4	16	.200	8	10		1/2
1884	Was-a	62	12	50	.194	12	12		1/2
	2	82	16	66	.195				
Holmes, Thomas Francis "Tommy"									
1951	Bos-N*	95	48	47	.505	5	4		2/2
1952	Bos-N	35	13	22	.371	7	7		1/2
	2	130	61	69	.469				
Hornsby, Rogers									
1925	StL-N*	115	64	51	.557	8	4		2/2
1926	StL-N*	156	89	65	.578	★1			
1927	NY-N*	33	22	10	.688	4	3		2/2
1928	Bos-N*	122	39	83	.320	7	7		2/2
1930	Chi-N*	4	4	0	1.000	2	2		2/2
1931	Chi-N*	156	84	70	.545	3			
1932	Chi-N*	99	53	46	.535	2	1		1/2
1933	StL-A*	54	19	33	.365	8	8		3/3
1934	StL-A*	154	67	85	.441	6			
1935	StL-A*	155	65	87	.428	7			
1936	StL-A*	155	57	95	.375	7			
1937	StL-A*	78	25	52	.325	7	8		1/2
1952	StL-A	51	22	29	.431	8	7		1/2
	Cin-N	51	27	24	.529	7	6		3/3
1953	Cin-N	147	64	82	.438	6	6		1/2
	14	1530	701	812	.463				
Houk, Ralph George "Ralph"									
1961	NY-A	163	109	53	.673	★1			
1962	NY-A	162	96	66	.593	★1			
1963	NY-A	161	104	57	.646	1			
1966	NY-A	140	66	73	.475	10	10		2/2
1967	NY-A	163	72	90	.444	9			
1968	NY-A	164	83	79	.512	5			
1969	NY-A	162	80	81	.497	5 E			
1970	NY-A	163	93	69	.574	2 E			
1971	NY-A	162	82	80	.506	4 E			
1972	NY-A	155	79	76	.510	4 E			
1973	NY-A	162	80	82	.494	4 E			
1974	Det-A	162	72	90	.444	6 E			
1975	Det-A	159	57	102	.358	6 E			
1976	Det-A	161	74	87	.460	5 E			
1977	Det-A	162	74	88	.457	4 E			
1978	Det-A	162	86	76	.531	5 E			
1981 (1)	Bos-A	56	30	26	.536	5 E			
(2)	Bos-A	52	29	23	.558	•2 E			
1982	Bos-A	162	89	73	.549	3 E			
1983	Bos-A	162	78	84	.481	6 E			
1984	Bos-A	162	86	76	.531	4 E			

YEAR	TM/L	G	W	L	PCT	STANDING			M/Y
	20	3157	1619	1531	.514				
Howard, Frank Oliver									
1981 (1)	SD-N	56	23	33	.411	6 W			
(2)	SD-N	54	18	36	.333	6 W			
1983	NY-N	116	52	64	.448	6 E	6 E		2/2
	2	226	93	133	.412				
Howley, Daniel Philip "Dan"									
1927	StL-A	155	59	94	.386	7			
1928	StL-A	154	82	72	.532	3			
1929	StL-A	154	79	73	.520	4			
1930	Cin-N	154	59	95	.383	7			
1931	Cin-N	154	58	96	.377	8			
1932	Cin-N	155	60	94	.390	8			
	6	926	397	524	.431				
Howser, Richard Dalton "Dick"									
1978	NY-A	1	0	1	.000	3 E	4 E	▲1 E	2/3
1980	NY-A	162	103	59	.636	1 E			
1981 (2)	KC-A	33	20	13	.606	•2 W	1 W		2/2
1982	KC-A	162	90	72	.556	2 W			
1983	KC-A	163	79	83	.488	2 W			
1984	KC-A	162	84	78	.519	1 W			
1985	KC-A	162	91	71	.562	★1 W			
1986	KC-A	88	40	48	.455	4 W	•3 W		1/2
	8	933	507	425	.544				
Huff, George A.									
1907	Bos-A	8	2	6	.250	•4	6	7	2/4
Huggins, Miller James									
1913	StL-N*	153	51	99	.340	8			
1914	StL-N*	157	81	72	.529	3			
1915	StL-N*	157	72	81	.471	6			
1916	StL-N*	153	60	93	.392	•7			
1917	StL-N	154	82	70	.539	3			
1918	NY-A	126	60	63	.488	4			
1919	NY-A	141	80	59	.576	3			
1920	NY-A	154	95	59	.617	3			
1921	NY-A	153	98	55	.641	1			
1922	NY-A	154	94	60	.610	1			
1923	NY-A	152	98	54	.645	★1			
1924	NY-A	153	89	63	.586	2			
1925	NY-A	156	69	85	.448	7			
1926	NY-A	155	91	63	.591	1			
1927	NY-A	155	110	44	.714	★1			
1928	NY-A	154	101	53	.656	★1			
1929	NY-A	143	82	61	.573	2	2		1/2
	17	2570	1413	1134	.555				
Hunter, Gordon William "Billy"									
1977	Tex-A	93	60	33	.645	5 W	2 W		4/4
1978	Tex-A	161	86	75	.534	•2 W	•2 W		1/2
	2	254	146	108	.575				
Hurst, Timothy Carroll "Tim"									
1898	StL-N	154	39	111	.260	12			
Hutchinson, Frederick Charles "Fred"									
1952	Det-A*	83	27	55	.329	8	8		2/2
1953	Det-A*	158	60	94	.390	6			
1954	Det-A	155	68	86	.442	5			
1956	StL-N	156	76	78	.494	4			
1957	StL-N	154	87	67	.565	2			
1958	StL-N	144	69	75	.479	5	•5		1/2
1959	Cin-N	74	39	35	.527	7	•5		2/2
1960	Cin-N	154	67	87	.435	6			
1961	Cin-N	154	93	61	.604	1			
1962	Cin-N	162	98	64	.605	3			
1963	Cin-N	162	86	76	.531	5			
1964	Cin-N	100	54	45	.545	3	•2		1/4
	Cin-N	10	6	4	.600	4	3	•2	3/4
	12	1666	830	827	.501				
Irwin, Arthur Albert									
1889	Was-N*	76	28	45	.384	8	8		2/2
1891	Bos-a*	139	93	42	.689	1			
1892 (1)	Was-N	74	35	39	.473	•11	7		2/2
(2)	Was-N	34	11	21	.344	11	12		1/2
1894	Phi-N*	132	71	57	.555	4			
1895	Phi-N	133	78	53	.595	3			
1896	NY-N	90	36	53	.404	10	7		1/2
1898	Was-N	30	10	19	.345	11	11		4/4
1899	Was-N	155	54	98	.355	11			
	8	863	416	427	.493				
Jennings, Hugh Ambrose "Hughie"									
1907	Det-A*	153	92	58	.613	1			
1908	Det-A	154	90	63	.588	1			
1909	Det-A*	158	98	54	.645	1			
1910	Det-A	155	86	68	.558	3			
1911	Det-A	154	89	65	.578	2			
1912	Det-A*	154	69	84	.451	6			
1913	Det-A	153	66	87	.431	6			
1914	Det-A	157	80	73	.523	4			
1915	Det-A	156	100	54	.649	2			

YEAR	TM/L	G	W	L	PCT	STANDING			M/Y
1916	Det-A	155	87	67	.565	3			
1917	Det-A	155	78	75	.510	4			
1918	Det-A*	128	55	71	.437	7			
1919	Det-A	140	80	60	.571	4			
1920	Det-A	155	61	93	.396	7			
1924	NY-N	44	32	12	.727	3	1		2/3
	15	2171	1163	984	.542				

Johnson, Darrell Dean

1974	Bos-A	162	84	78	.519	3 E			
1975	Bos-A	160	95	65	.594	♦1 E			
1976	Bos-A	86	41	45	.477	5 E	3 E		1/2
1977	Sea-A	162	64	98	.395	6 W			
1978	Sea-A	160	56	104	.350	7 W			
1979	Sea-A	162	67	95	.414	6 W			
1980	Sea-A	105	39	65	.375	6 W	7 W		1/2
1982	Tex-A	66	26	40	.394	6 W	6 W		2/2
	8	1063	472	590	.444				

Johnson, David Allen "Dave"

1984	NY-N	162	90	72	.556	2 E			
1985	NY-N	162	98	64	.605	2 E			
1986	NY-N	162	108	54	.667	★1 E			
1987	NY-N	162	92	70	.568	2 E			
1988	NY-N	160	100	60	.625	1 E			
	5	808	488	320	.604				

Johnson, Roy J

1944	Chi-N	1	0	1	.000	8	8	4	2/3

Johnson, Walter Perry

1929	Was-A	153	71	81	.467	5			
1930	Was-A	154	94	60	.610	2			
1931	Was-A	156	92	62	.597	3			
1932	Was-A	154	93	61	.604	3			
1933	Cle-A	99	48	51	.485	5	4		3/3
1934	Cle-A*	154	85	69	.552	5			
1935	Cle-A	96	46	48	.489	5	3		1/2
	7	966	529	432	.550				

Jones, Fielder Allison

1904	Chi-A*	114	66	47	.584	4	3		2/2
1905	Chi-A*	158	92	60	.605	2			
1906	Chi-A*	154	93	58	.616	★1			
1907	Chi-A*	157	87	64	.576	3			
1908	Chi-A*	156	88	64	.579	3			
1914	StL-F*	40	12	26	.316	7	8		2/2
1915	StL-F*	159	87	67	.565	2			
1916	StL-A	158	79	75	.513	5			
1917	StL-A	155	57	97	.370	7			
1918	StL-A	46	22	24	.478	6	5		1/3
	10	1297	683	582	.540				

Joost, Edwin David "Eddie"

1954	Phi-A*	156	51	103	.331	8			

Joyce, William Michael "Bill"

1896	NY-N*	43	28	14	.667	10	7		2/2
1897	NY-N*	138	83	48	.634	3			
1898	NY-N*	43	22	21	.512	6	7		1/3
	NY-N*	92	46	39	.541	7	7		3/3
	3	316	179	122	.595				

Jurges, William Frederick "Billy"

1959	Bos-A	80	44	36	.550	8	5		3/3
1960	Bos-A	42	15	27	.357	8	7		1/3
	2	122	59	63	.484				

Kasko, Edward Michael "Eddie"

1970	Bos-A	162	87	75	.537	3 E			
1971	Bos-A	162	85	77	.525	3 E			
1972	Bos-A	155	85	70	.548	2 E			
1973	Bos-A	161	88	73	.547	2 E	2 E		1/2
	4	640	345	295	.539				

Keane, John Joseph "Johnny"

1961	StL-N	80	47	33	.587	6	5		2/2
1962	StL-N	163	84	78	.519	6			
1963	StL-N	162	93	69	.574	2			
1964	StL-N	162	93	69	.574	★1			
1965	NY-A	162	77	85	.475	6			
1966	NY-A	20	4	16	.200	10	10		1/2
	6	749	398	350	.532				

Kelley, Joseph James "Joe"

1902	Cin-N*	60	34	26	.567	6	4		3/3
1903	Cin-N*	141	74	65	.532	4			
1904	Cin-N*	157	88	65	.575	3			
1905	Cin-N*	155	79	74	.516	5			
1908	Bos-N*	156	63	91	.409	6			
	5	669	338	321	.513				

Kelly, Jay Thomas "Tom"

1986	Min-A	23	12	11	.522	7 W	6 W		2/2
1987	Min-A	162	85	77	.525	♦1 W			
1988	Min-A	162	91	71	.562	2 W			
	3	347	188	159	.542				

Kelly, John O.

1887	Lou-a	139	76	60	.559	4			
1888	Lou-a	39	10	29	.256	8	7		1/4
	2	178	86	89	.491				

Kelly, Michael Joseph "King"

1887	Bos-N*	94	49	43	.533	5	5		1/2
1890	Bos-P*	133	81	48	.628	1			
1891	Cin-a*	102	43	57	.430	6			
	3	329	173	148	.539				

Kennedy, James C. "Jim"

1890	Bro-a	100	26	73	.263	8			

Kennedy, Robert Daniel "Bob"

1963	Chi-N	162	82	80	.506	7			
1964	Chi-N	162	76	86	.469	8			
1965	Chi-N	58	24	32	.429	9	8		1/2
1968	Oak-A	163	82	80	.506	6			
	4	545	264	278	.487				

Kerins, John Nelson

1888	Lou-a*	7	3	4	.429	8	8	7	3/4
1890	StL-a*	17	9	8	.529	4	4	3	2/6
	2	24	12	12	.500				

Kessinger, Donald Eulon "Don"

1979	Chi-A	106	46	60	.434	5 W	5 W		1/2

Killefer, William Lavier "Bill"

1921	Chi-N*	57	23	34	.404	6	7		2/2
1922	Chi-N	156	80	74	.519	5			
1923	Chi-N	154	83	71	.539	4			
1924	Chi-N	154	81	72	.529	5			
1925	Chi-N	75	33	42	.440	7	8		1/3
1930	StL-A	154	64	90	.416	6			
1931	StL-A	154	63	91	.409	5			
1932	StL-A	154	63	91	.409	6			
1933	StL-A	91	34	57	.374	8	8		1/3
	9	1149	524	622	.457				

King, Clyde Edward

1969	SF-N	162	90	72	.556	2 W			
1970	SF-N	42	19	23	.452	4 W	3 W		1/2
1974	Atl-N	64	38	25	.603	4 W	3 W		2/2
1975	Atl-N	134	58	76	.433	5 W	5 W		1/2
1982	NY-A	62	29	33	.468	●5 E	5 E		3/3
	5	464	234	229	.505				

Kittridge, Malachi J.

1904	Was-A*	18	1	16	.059	8	8		1/2

Klein, Louis Frank "Lou"

1961	Chi-N	11	5	6	.455	7	7	7	8/9
1962	Chi-N	30	12	18	.400	9	9	9	2/3
1965	Chi-N	106	48	58	.453	9	8		2/2
	3	147	65	82	.442				

Kling, John "Johnny"

1912	Bos-N*	155	52	101	.340	8			

Knabe, Franz Otto "Otto"

1914	Bal-F*	160	84	70	.545	3			
1915	Bal-F*	155	47	107	.305	8			
	2	315	131	177	.425				

Knight, Alonzo P. "Lon"

1883	Phi-a*	98	66	32	.673	1			
1884	Phi-a*	108	61	46	.570	7			
	2	206	127	78	.620				

Krol, John Thomas "Jack"

1978	StL-N	2	1	1	.500	6 E	6 E		2/3
1980	StL-N	1	0	1	.000	6 E	6 E	4 E	2/4
	2	3	1	2	.333				

Kuehl, Karl Otto

1976	Mon-N	128	43	85	.336	6 E	6 E		1/2

Kuenn, Harvey Edward

1975	Mil-A	1	1	0	1.000	5 E	5 E		2/2
1982	Mil-A	116	72	43	.626	5 E	♦1 E		2/2
1983	Mil-A	162	87	75	.537	5 E			
	3	279	160	118	.576				

Kuhel, Joseph Anthony "Joe"

1948	Was-A	154	56	97	.366	7			
1949	Was-A	154	50	104	.325	8			
	2	308	106	201	.345				

Lachemann, Rene George

1981(1)	Sea-A	33	15	18	.455	7 W	6 W		2/2
(2)	Sea-A	52	23	29	.442	5 W			
1982	Sea-A	162	76	86	.469	4 W			
1983	Sea-A	73	26	47	.356	7 W	7 W		1/2
1984	Mil-A	161	67	94	.416	7 E			
	4	481	207	274	.430				

Lajoie, Napoleon "Nap"

1905	Cle-A*	58	37	21	.638	●1	5		1/3
	Cle-A*	56	19	36	.345	2	5		3/3
1906	Cle-A*	157	89	64	.582	3			

YEAR	TM/L	G	W	L	PCT	STANDING				M/Y
1907	Cle-A*	158	85	67	.559	4				
1908	Cle-A*	157	90	64	.584	2				
1909	Cle-A*	114	57	57	.500	4	6			1/2
	5	700	377	309	.550					
Lake, Frederick Lovett "Fred"										
1908	Bos-A	40	22	17	.564	6	5			2/2
1909	Bos-A	152	88	63	.583	3				
1910	Bos-N*	157	53	100	.346	8				
	3	349	163	180	.475					
Lanier, Harold Clifton "Hal"										
1986	Hou-N	162	96	66	.593	1 W				
1987	Hou-N	162	76	86	.469	3 W				
1988	Hou-N	162	82	80	.506	5 W				
	3	486	254	232	.523					
Larkin, Henry E. "Ted"										
1890	Cle-P*	79	34	45	.430	7	7			1/2
LaRussa, Anthony "Tony"										
1979	Chi-A	54	27	27	.500	5 W	5 W			2/2
1980	Chi-A	162	70	90	.438	5 W				
1981 (1)	Chi-A	53	31	22	.585	3 W				
(2)	Chi-A	53	23	30	.434	6 W				
1982	Chi-A	162	87	75	.537	3 W				
1983	Chi-A	162	99	63	.611	1 W				
1984	Chi-A	162	74	88	.457	●5 W				
1985	Chi-A	163	85	77	.525	3 W				
1986	Chi-A	64	26	38	.406	6 W	5 W			1/3
	Oak-A	79	45	34	.570	7 W	●3 W			3/3
1987	Oak-A	162	81	81	.500	3 W				
1988	Oak-A	162	104	58	.642	◆1 W				
	10	1438	752	683	.524					
Lasorda, Thomas Charles "Tom"										
1976	LA-N	4	2	2	.500	2 W	2 W			2/2
1977	LA-N	162	98	64	.605	◆1 W				
1978	LA-N	162	95	67	.586	◆1 W				
1979	LA-N	162	79	83	.488	3 W				
1980	LA-N	163	92	71	.564	▲2 W				
1981 (1)	LA-N	57	36	21	.632	★1 W				
(2)	LA-N	53	27	26	.509	4 W				
1982	LA-N	162	88	74	.543	2 W				
1983	LA-N	162	91	71	.562	1 W				
1984	LA-N	162	79	83	.488	4 W				
1985	LA-N	162	95	67	.586	1 W				
1986	LA-N	162	73	89	.451	5 W				
1987	LA-N	162	73	89	.451	4 W				
1988	LA-N	162	94	67	.584	★1 W				
	13	1898	1022	874	.539					
Latham, George Warren "Juice"										
1875	NH-n*	18	4	14	.222	11	8	8		2/3
1882	Phi-a*	75	41	34	.547	2				
	2	93	45	48	.484					
Latham, Walter Arlington "Arlie"										
1896	StL-N*	3	0	3	.000	10	10	11		2/5
Lavagetto, Harry Arthur "Cookie"										
1957	Was-A	134	51	83	.381	8	8			2/2
1958	Was-A	156	61	93	.396	8				
1959	Was-A	154	63	91	.409	8				
1960	Was-A	154	73	81	.474	5				
1961	Min-A	49	19	30	.388	8	7			1/4
	Min-A	10	4	6	.400	9	9	7		3/4
	5	657	271	384	.414					
Leadley, Robert H. "Bob"										
1888	Det-N	40	19	19	.500	3	5			2/2
1890	Cle-N	58	23	33	.411	7	7			2/2
1891	Cle-N	68	34	34	.500	4	5			1/2
	3	166	76	86	.469					
Lemon, James Robert "Jim"										
1968	Was-A	161	65	96	.404	10				
Lemon, Robert Granville "Bob"										
1970	KC-A	110	46	64	.418	5 W	●4 W			2/2
1971	KC-A	161	85	76	.528	2 W				
1972	KC-A	154	76	78	.494	4 W				
1977	Chi-A	162	90	72	.556	3 W				
1978	Chi-A	74	34	40	.459	5 W	5 W			1/2
	NY-A	68	48	20	.706	4 E	▲1 E	★		3/3
1979	NY-A	65	34	31	.523	4 E	4 E			1/2
1981 (2)	NY-A	25	11	14	.440	4 E	6 E			2/2
1982	NY-A	14	6	8	.429	●4 E	5 E			1/3
	8	833	430	403	.516					
Lennon, William F. "Bill"										
1871	Kek-n*	14	5	9	.357	7	8			1/2
Leyland, James Richard "Jim"										
1986	Pit-N	162	64	98	.395	6 E				
1987	Pit-N	162	80	82	.494	●4 E				
1988	Pit-N	160	85	75	.531	2 E				
	3	484	229	255	.473					
Lillis, Robert Perry "Bob"										
1982	Hou-N	51	28	23	.549	5 W	5 W			2/2
1983	Hou-N	162	85	77	.525	3 W				
1984	Hou-N	162	80	82	.494	●2 W				
1985	Hou-N	162	83	79	.512	●3 W				
	4	537	276	261	.514					
Lipon, John Joseph "Johnny"										
1971	Cle-A	59	18	41	.305	6 E	6 E			2/2
Lobert, John Bernard "Hans"										
1938	Phi-N	2	0	2	.000	8	8			2/2
1942	Phi-N	151	42	109	.278	8				
	2	153	42	111	.275					
Lockman, Carroll Walter "Whitey"										
1972	Chi-N	65	39	26	.600	4 E	2 E			2/2
1973	Chi-N	161	77	84	.478	5 E				
1974	Chi-N	93	41	52	.441	5 E	6 E			1/2
	3	319	157	162	.492					
Loftus, Thomas Joseph "Tom"										
1884	Mil-U	12	8	4	.667	2				
1888	Cle-a	71	30	38	.441	8	6			2/2
1889	Cle-N	136	61	72	.459	6				
1890	Cin-N	134	77	55	.583	4				
1891	Cin-N	138	56	81	.409	7				
1900	Chi-N	146	65	75	.464	●5				
1901	Chi-N	140	53	86	.381	6				
1902	Was-A	138	61	75	.449	6				
1903	Was-A	140	43	94	.314	8				
	9	1055	454	580	.439					
Lopat, Edmund Walter "Eddie"										
1963	KC-A	162	73	89	.451	8				
1964	KC-A	52	17	35	.327	10	10			1/2
	2	214	90	124	.421					
Lopez, Alfonso Ramon "Al"										
1951	Cle-A	155	93	61	.604	2				
1952	Cle-A	155	93	61	.604	2				
1953	Cle-A	155	92	62	.597	2				
1954	Cle-A	156	111	43	.721	1				
1955	Cle-A	154	93	61	.604	2				
1956	Cle-A	155	88	66	.571	2				
1957	Chi-A	155	90	64	.584	2				
1958	Chi-A	155	82	72	.532	2				
1959	Chi-A	156	94	60	.610	1				
1960	Chi-A	154	87	67	.565	3				
1961	Chi-A	163	86	76	.531	4				
1962	Chi-A	162	85	77	.525	5				
1963	Chi-A	162	94	68	.580	2				
1964	Chi-A	162	98	64	.605	2				
1965	Chi-A	162	95	67	.586	2				
1968	Chi-A	11	6	5	.545	9	9	●8		3/5
	Chi-A	36	15	21	.417	9	●8			5/5
1969	Chi-A	17	8	9	.471	4 W	5 W			1/2
	17	2425	1410	1004	.584					
Lord, Harry Donald										
1915	Buf-F*	110	60	49	.550	8	6			3/3
Lowe, Robert Lincoln "Bobby"										
1904	Det-A*	78	30	44	.405	7	7			2/2
Lucchesi, Frank Joseph										
1970	Phi-N	161	73	88	.453	5 E				
1971	Phi-N	162	67	95	.414	6 E				
1972	Phi-N	76	26	50	.342	6 E	6 E			1/2
1975	Tex-A	67	35	32	.522	4 W	3 W			2/2
1976	Tex-A	162	76	86	.469	●4 W				
1977	Tex-A	62	31	31	.500	●3 W	2 W			1/4
1987	Chi-N	25	8	17	.320	5 E	6 E			2/2
	7	715	316	399	.442					
Lumley, Harry G										
1909	Bro-N*	155	55	98	.359	6				
Lyons, Theodore Amar "Ted"										
1946	Chi-A*	125	64	60	.516	7	5			2/2
1947	Chi-A	155	70	84	.455	6				
1948	Chi-A	154	51	101	.336	8				
	3	434	185	245	.430					
Mack, Cornelius Alexander "Connie"										
1894	Pit-N*	23	12	10	.545	7	7			2/2
1895	Pit-N*	135	71	61	.538	7				
1896	Pit-N*	131	66	63	.512	6				
1901	Phi-A	137	74	62	.544	4				
1902	Phi-A	137	83	53	.610	1				
1903	Phi-A	137	75	60	.556	2				
1904	Phi-A	155	81	70	.536	5				
1905	Phi-A	152	92	56	.622	1				
1906	Phi-A	149	78	67	.538	4				
1907	Phi-A	150	88	57	.607	2				
1908	Phi-A	157	68	85	.444	6				
1909	Phi-A	153	95	58	.621	2				
1910	Phi-A	155	102	48	.680	★1				
1911	Phi-A	152	101	50	.669	★1				

YEAR	TM/L	G	W	L	PCT	STANDING			M/Y
1912	Phi-A	153	90	62	.592	3			
1913	Phi-A	153	96	57	.627	★1			
1914	Phi-A	158	99	53	.651	1			
1915	Phi-A	154	43	109	.283	8			
1916	Phi-A	154	36	117	.235	8			
1917	Phi-A	154	55	98	.359	8			
1918	Phi-A	130	52	76	.406	8			
1919	Phi-A	140	36	104	.257	8			
1920	Phi-A	156	48	106	.312	8			
1921	Phi-A	155	53	100	.346	8			
1922	Phi-A	155	65	89	.422	7			
1923	Phi-A	153	69	83	.454	6			
1924	Phi-A	152	71	81	.467	5			
1925	Phi-A	153	88	64	.579	2			
1926	Phi-A	150	83	67	.553	3			
1927	Phi-A	155	91	63	.591	2			
1928	Phi-A	153	98	55	.641	2			
1929	Phi-A	151	104	46	.693	★1			
1930	Phi-A	154	102	52	.662	★1			
1931	Phi-A	153	107	45	.704	1			
1932	Phi-A	154	94	60	.610	2			
1933	Phi-A	152	79	72	.523	3			
1934	Phi-A	153	68	82	.453	5			
1935	Phi-A	149	58	91	.389	8			
1936	Phi-A	154	53	100	.346	8			
1937	Phi-A	120	39	80	.328	7	7		1/2
1938	Phi-A	154	53	99	.349	8			
1939	Phi-A	62	25	37	.403	6	7		1/2
1940	Phi-A	154	54	100	.351	8			
1941	Phi-A	154	64	90	.416	8			
1942	Phi-A	154	55	99	.357	8			
1943	Phi-A	155	49	105	.318	8			
1944	Phi-A	155	72	82	.468	●5			
1945	Phi-A	153	52	98	.347	8			
1946	Phi-A	155	49	105	.318	8			
1947	Phi-A	156	78	76	.506	5			
1948	Phi-A	154	84	70	.545	4			
1949	Phi-A	154	81	73	.526	5			
1950	Phi-A	154	52	102	.338	8			
		53	7755	3731	3948	.486			

Mack, Dennis Joseph "Denny"

YEAR	TM/L	G	W	L	PCT	STANDING			M/Y
1882	Lou-a*	80	42	38	.525	3			

Mack, Earle Thaddeus

1937	Phi-A	34	15	17	.469	7	7		2/2
1939	Phi-A	91	30	60	.333	6	7		2/2
		2	125	45	77	.369			

Macullar, James F. "Jimmy"

| 1879 | Syr-N* | 27 | 6 | 21 | .192 | 6 | 7 | | 3/3 |

Magee, Leo Christopher "Lee"

| 1915 | Bro-F* | 118 | 53 | 64 | .453 | 7 | 7 | | 1/2 |

Malone, Ferguson G. "Fergy"

1874	Chi-n*	36	18	18	.500	4	5		1/2
1884	Key-U*	67	21	46	.313	7			
		2	103	39	64	.379			

Manning, James H. "Jimmy"

| 1901 | Was-A | 138 | 61 | 73 | .455 | 6 | | | |

Maranville, Walter James Vincent "Rabbit"

| 1925 | Chi-N* | 53 | 23 | 30 | .434 | 7 | 7 | 8 | 2/3 |

Marion, Martin Whitford "Marty"

1951	StL-N	155	81	73	.526	3			
1952	StL-A*	104	42	61	.408	8	7		2/2
1953	StL-A*	154	54	100	.351	8			
1954	Chi-A	9	3	6	.333	3	3		2/2
1955	Chi-A	155	91	63	.591	3			
1956	Chi-A	154	85	69	.552	3			
		6	731	356	372	.489			

Marshall, Rufus James "Jim"

1974	Chi-N	69	25	44	.362	5 E	6 E		2/2
1975	Chi-N	162	75	87	.463	●5 E			
1976	Chi-N	162	75	87	.463	4 E			
1979	Oak-A	162	54	108	.333	7 W			
		4	555	229	326	.413			

Martin, Alfred Manuel "Billy"

1969	Min-A	162	97	65	.599	1 W			
1971	Det-A	162	91	71	.562	2 E			
1972	Det-A	156	86	70	.551	1 E			
1973	Det-A	134	71	63	.530	3 E	3 E		1/2
	Tex-A	23	9	14	.391	6 W	6 W		3/3
1974	Tex-A	161	84	76	.525	2 W			
1975	Tex-A	95	44	51	.463	4 W	3 W		1/2
	NY-A	56	30	26	.536	3 E	3 E		2/2
1976	NY-A	159	97	62	.610	◆1 E			
1977	NY-A	162	100	62	.617	★1 E			
1978	NY-A	94	52	42	.553	3 E	▲1 E	★	1/3
1979	NY-A	95	55	40	.579	4 E	4 E		2/2
	Oak-A	162	83	79	.512	2 W			
1981(1)	Oak-A	60	37	23	.617	1 W			

YEAR	TM/L	G	W	L	PCT	STANDING			M/Y
(2)	Oak-A	49	27	22	.551	2 W			
1982	Oak-A	162	68	94	.420	5 W			
1983	NY-A	162	91	71	.562	3 E			
1985	NY-A	145	91	54	.628	7 E	2 E		2/2
1988	NY-A	68	40	28	.588	2 E	5 E		1/2
		16	2267	1253	1013	.553			

Martinez, Orlando [Oliva] "Marty"

| 1986 | Sea-A | 1 | 0 | 1 | .000 | 6 W | 6 W | 7 W | 2/3 |

Mason, Charles E. "Charlie"

| 1887 | Phi-a | 82 | 38 | 40 | .487 | 6 | 5 | | 2/2 |

Mathews, Edwin Lee "Eddie"

1972	Atl-N	50	23	27	.460	4 W	4 W		2/2
1973	Atl-N	162	76	85	.472	5 W			
1974	Atl-N	99	50	49	.505	4 W	3 W		1/2
		3	311	149	161	.481			

Mathewson, Christopher "Christy"

1916	Cin-N*	69	25	43	.368	8	●7		3/3
1917	Cin-N	157	78	76	.506	4			
1918	Cin-N	120	61	57	.517	4	3		1/2
		3	346	164	176	.482			

Mattick, Robert James "Bobby"

1980	Tor-A	162	67	95	.414	7 E			
1981(1)	Tor-A	58	16	42	.276	7 E			
(2)	Tor-A	48	21	27	.438	7 E			
		2	268	104	164	.388			

Mauch, Gene William

1960	Phi-N	152	58	94	.382	●4	8		3/3
1961	Phi-N	155	47	107	.305	8			
1962	Phi-N	161	81	80	.503	7			
1963	Phi-N	162	87	75	.537	4			
1964	Phi-N	162	92	70	.568	●2			
1965	Phi-N	162	85	76	.528	6			
1966	Phi-N	162	87	75	.537	4			
1967	Phi-N	162	82	80	.506	5			
1968	Phi-N	54	27	27	.500	●6	●7		1/3
1969	Mon-N	162	52	110	.321	6 E			
1970	Mon-N	162	73	89	.451	6 E			
1971	Mon-N	162	71	90	.441	5 E			
1972	Mon-N	156	70	86	.449	5 E			
1973	Mon-N	162	79	83	.488	4 E			
1974	Mon-N	161	79	82	.491	4 E			
1975	Mon-N	162	75	87	.463	●5 E			
1976	Min-A	162	85	77	.525	3 W			
1977	Min-A	161	84	77	.522	4 W			
1978	Min-A	162	73	89	.451	4 W			
1979	Min-A	162	82	80	.506	4 W			
1980	Min-A	125	54	71	.432	4 W	3 W		1/2
1981(1)	Cal-A	13	9	4	.692	4 W	4 W		2/2
(2)	Cal-A	50	20	30	.400	7 W			
1982	Cal-A	162	93	69	.574	1 W			
1985	Cal-A	162	90	72	.556	2 W			
1986	Cal-A	162	92	70	.568	1 W			
1987	Cal-A	162	75	87	.463	●6 W			
		26	3942	1902	2037	.483			

McAleer, James Robert "Jimmy"

1901	Cle-A*	138	55	82	.401	7			
1902	StL-A*	140	78	58	.574	2			
1903	StL-A	139	65	74	.468	6			
1904	StL-A	156	65	87	.428	6			
1905	StL-A	156	54	99	.353	8			
1906	StL-A	154	76	73	.510	5			
1907	StL-A	155	69	83	.454	6			
1908	StL-A	155	83	69	.546	4			
1909	StL-A	154	61	89	.407	7			
1910	Was-A	157	66	85	.437	7			
1911	Was-A	154	64	90	.416	7			
		11	1658	736	889	.453			

McBride, George Florian

| 1921 | Was-A | 154 | 80 | 73 | .523 | 4 | | | |

McBride, James Dickson "Dick"

1871	Phi-n*	28	21	7	.750	1			
1872	Phi-n*	47	30	14	.682	4			
1873	Phi-n*	52	28	23	.549	5			
1874	Phi-n*	56	33	23	.589	3			
1875	Phi-n*	69	49	18	.731	2	2		1/2
		5	252	161	85	.654			

McCallister, John "Jack"

| 1927 | Cle-A | 153 | 66 | 87 | .431 | 6 | | | |

McCarthy, Joseph Vincent "Joe"

1926	Chi-N	155	82	72	.532	4			
1927	Chi-N	153	85	68	.556	4			
1928	Chi-N	154	91	63	.591	3			
1929	Chi-N	156	98	54	.645	1			
1930	Chi-N	152	86	64	.573	2	2		1/2
1931	NY-A	155	94	59	.614	2			
1932	NY-A	156	107	47	.695	★1			
1933	NY-A	152	91	59	.607	2			

YEAR	TM/L	G	W	L	PCT	STANDING			M/Y
1934	NY-A	154	94	60	.610	2			
1935	NY-A	149	89	60	.597	2			
1936	NY-A	155	102	51	.667	★1			
1937	NY-A	157	102	52	.662	★1			
1938	NY-A	157	99	53	.651	★1			
1939	NY-A	152	106	45	.702	★1			
1940	NY-A	155	88	66	.571	3			
1941	NY-A	156	101	53	.656	★1			
1942	NY-A	154	103	51	.669	1			
1943	NY-A	155	98	56	.636	★1			
1944	NY-A	154	83	71	.539	3			
1945	NY-A	152	81	71	.533	4			
1946	NY-A	35	22	13	.629	2	3		1/3
1948	Bos-A	155	96	59	.619	▲2			
1949	Bos-A	155	96	58	.623	2			
1950	Bos-A	59	31	28	.525	4	3		1/2
	24	3487	2125	1333	.615				
McCarthy, Thomas Francis "Tommy"									
1890	StL-a*	22	11	11	.500	4	3		1/6
	StL-a*	5	4	1	.800	2	2	3	5/6
McCloskey, John Joseph									
1895	Lou-N	133	35	96	.267	12			
1896	Lou-N	19	2	17	.105	12	12		1/2
1906	StL-N	154	52	98	.347	7			
1907	StL-N	155	52	101	.340	8			
1908	StL-N	154	49	105	.318	8			
	5	615	190	417	.313				
McCormick, James "Jim"									
1879	Cle-N*	82	27	55	.329	6			
1880	Cle-N*	85	47	37	.560	3			
1881	Cle-N*	74	32	41	.438	6	7		2/2
1882	Cle-N*	4	0	4	.000	8	5		1/2
	4	245	106	137	.436				
McGaha, Fred Melvin "Mel"									
1962	Cle-A	160	78	82	.488	6	6		1/2
1964	KC-A	111	40	70	.364	10	10		2/2
1965	KC-A	26	5	21	.192	10	10		1/2
	3	297	123	173	.416				
McGeary, Michael Henry "Mike"									
1875	Phi-n*	70	37	31	.544	5			
1880	Pro-N*	16	8	7	.533	4	2		1/3
1881	Cle-N*	11	4	7	.364	6	7		1/2
	3	97	49	45	.521				
McGraw, John Joseph									
1899	Bal-N*	152	86	62	.581	4			
1901	Bal-A*	135	68	65	.511	5			
1902	Bal-A*	58	26	31	.456	7	8		1/2
	NY-N*	65	25	38	.397	8	8		3/3
1903	NY-N*	142	84	55	.604	2			
1904	NY-N*	158	106	47	.693	1			
1905	NY-N*	155	105	48	.686	★1			
1906	NY-N*	153	96	56	.632	2			
1907	NY-N	155	82	71	.536	4			
1908	NY-N	157	98	56	.636	●2			
1909	NY-N	158	92	61	.601	3			
1910	NY-N	155	91	63	.591	2			
1911	NY-N	154	99	54	.647	1			
1912	NY-N	154	103	48	.682	1			
1913	NY-N	156	101	51	.664	1			
1914	NY-N	156	84	70	.545	2			
1915	NY-N	155	69	83	.454	8			
1916	NY-N	155	86	66	.566	4			
1917	NY-N	158	98	56	.636	1			
1918	NY-N	124	71	53	.573	2			
1919	NY-N	140	87	53	.621	2			
1920	NY-N	155	86	68	.558	2			
1921	NY-N	153	94	59	.614	1			
1922	NY-N	156	93	61	.604	★1			
1923	NY-N	153	95	58	.621	★1			
1924	NY-N	29	16	13	.552	3	1		1/3
	NY-N	81	45	35	.563	1	1		3/3
1925	NY-N	152	86	66	.566	2			
1926	NY-N	151	74	77	.490	5			
1927	NY-N	122	70	52	.574	4	3		1/2
1928	NY-N	155	93	61	.604	2			
1929	NY-N	152	84	67	.556	3			
1930	NY-N	154	87	67	.565	3			
1931	NY-N	153	87	65	.572	2			
1932	NY-N	40	17	23	.425	8	●6		1/2
	33	4801	2784	1959	.587				
McGuire, James Thomas "Deacon"									
1898	Was-N*	70	21	47	.309	10	11	11	3/4
1907	Bos-A*	112	45	61	.425	8	7		4/4
1908	Bos-A*	115	53	62	.461	6	5		1/2
1909	Cle-A	41	14	25	.359	4	6		2/2
1910	Cle-A*	161	71	81	.467	5			
1911	Cle-A	17	6	11	.353	7	3		1/2
	6	516	210	287	.423				
McGunnigle, William Henry "Bill"									
1888	Bro-a	143	88	52	.629	2			
1889	Bro-a	140	93	44	.679	1			
1890	Bro-N	129	86	43	.667	1			
1891	Pit-N	59	24	33	.421	8	8		2/2
1896	Lou-N	115	36	76	.321	12	12		2/2
	5	586	327	248	.569				
McInnis, John Phalen "Stuffy"									
1927	Phi-N*	155	51	103	.331	8			
McKechnie, William Boyd "Bill"									
1915	New-F*	102	54	45	.545	6	5		2/2
1922	Pit-N	90	53	36	.596	5	●3		2/2
1923	Pit-N	154	87	67	.565	3			
1924	Pit-N	153	90	63	.588	3			
1925	Pit-N	153	95	58	.621	★1			
1926	Pit-N	157	84	69	.549	3			
1928	StL-N	154	95	59	.617	1			
1929	StL-N	63	34	29	.540	4	4		3/3
1930	Bos-N	154	70	84	.455	6			
1931	Bos-N	156	64	90	.416	7			
1932	Bos-N	155	77	77	.500	5			
1933	Bos-N	156	83	71	.539	4			
1934	Bos-N	152	78	73	.517	4			
1935	Bos-N	153	38	115	.248	8			
1936	Bos-N	157	71	83	.461	6			
1937	Bos-N	152	79	73	.520	5			
1938	Cin-N	151	82	68	.547	4			
1939	Cin-N	156	97	57	.630	1			
1940	Cin-N	155	100	53	.654	★1			
1941	Cin-N	154	88	66	.571	3			
1942	Cin-N	154	76	76	.500	4			
1943	Cin-N	155	87	67	.565	2			
1944	Cin-N	155	89	65	.578	3			
1945	Cin-N	154	61	93	.396	7			
1946	Cin-N	152	64	86	.427	6	6		1/2
	25	3647	1896	1723	.524				
McKeon, John Aloysius "Jack"									
1973	KC-A	162	88	74	.543	2 W			
1974	KC-A	162	77	85	.475	5 W			
1975	KC-A	96	50	46	.521	2 W	2 W		1/2
1977	Oak-A	53	26	27	.491	●5 W	7 W		1/2
1978	Oak-A	123	45	78	.366	1 W	6 W		2/2
1988	SD-N	115	67	48	.583	5 W	3 W		2/2
	6	711	353	358	.496				
McKinnon, Alexander J. "Alex"									
1885	StL-N*	39	6	32	.158	5	8	8	2/3
McKnight, Dennis Hamar "Denny"									
1884	Pit-a	12	4	8	.333	9	10		1/5
McManus, George									
1876	StL-N	8	6	2	.750	2	2		2/2
1877	StL-N	60	28	32	.467	4			
	2	68	34	34	.500				
McManus, Martin Joseph "Marty"									
1932	Bos-A*	99	32	67	.323	8	8		2/2
1933	Bos-A*	149	63	86	.423	7			
	2	248	95	153	.383				
McMillan, Roy David									
1972	Mil-A	2	1	1	.500	6 E	6 E	6 E	2/3
1975	NY-N	53	26	27	.491	3 E	●3 E		2/2
	2	55	27	28	.491				
McNamara, John Francis									
1969	Oak-A	13	8	5	.615	2 W	2 W		2/2
1970	Oak-A	162	89	73	.549	2 W			
1974	SD-N	162	60	102	.370	6 W			
1975	SD-N	162	71	91	.438	4 W			
1976	SD-N	162	73	89	.451	5 W			
1977	SD-N	48	20	28	.417	4 W	5 W		1/3
1979	Cin-N	161	90	71	.559	1 W			
1980	Cin-N	163	89	73	.549	3 W			
1981 (1)	Cin-N	56	35	21	.625	2 W			
(2)	Cin-N	52	31	21	.596	2 W			
1982	Cin-N	92	34	58	.370	6 W	6 W		1/2
1983	Cal-A	162	70	92	.432	●5 W			
1984	Cal-A	162	81	81	.500	●2 W			
1985	Bos-A	163	81	81	.500	5 E			
1986	Bos-A	161	95	66	.590	♦1 E			
1987	Bos-A	162	78	84	.481	5 E			
1988	Bos-A	85	43	42	.506	4 E	1 E		1/2
	16	2128	1048	1078	.493				
McPhee, John Alexander "Bid"									
1901	Cin-N	142	52	87	.374	8			
1902	Cin-N	65	27	37	.422	6	4		1/3
	2	207	79	124	.389				
McVey, Calvin Alexander "Cal"									
1873	Bal-n*	32	19	13	.594	2	3		1/2
1878	Cin-N*	61	37	23	.617	2			
1879	Cin-N*	63	34	28	.548	4	5		2/2

YEAR	TM/L	G	W	L	PCT	STANDING			M/Y
	3	156	90	64	.584				

Mele, Sabath Anthony "Sam"

YEAR	TM/L	G	W	L	PCT	STANDING			M/Y
1961	Min-A	7	2	5	.286	8	9	7	2/4
	Min-A	95	45	49	.479	9	7		4/4
1962	Min-A	163	91	71	.562	2			
1963	Min-A	161	91	70	.565	3			
1964	Min-A	163	79	83	.488	●6			
1965	Min-A	162	102	60	.630	1			
1966	Min-A	162	89	73	.549	2			
1967	Min-A	50	25	25	.500	6	●2		1/2
	7	963	524	436	.546				

Metro, Charles "Charlie"

YEAR	TM/L	G	W	L	PCT	STANDING		M/Y
1962	Chi-N	112	43	69	.384	9	9	3/3
1970	KC-A	52	19	33	.365	5 W	●4 W	1/2
	2	164	62	102	.378			

Meyer, William Adam "Billy"

YEAR	TM/L	G	W	L	PCT	STANDING
1948	Pit-N	156	83	71	.539	4
1949	Pit-N	154	71	83	.461	6
1950	Pit-N	154	57	96	.373	8
1951	Pit-N	155	64	90	.416	7
1952	Pit-N	155	42	112	.273	8
	5	774	317	452	.412	

Michael, Eugene Richard "Gene"

YEAR	TM/L	G	W	L	PCT	STANDING			M/Y
1981(1)	NY-A	56	34	22	.607	◆1 E			1/2
(2)	NY-A	26	14	12	.538	4 E	6 E		1/2
1982	NY-A	86	44	42	.512	●4 E	●5 E	5 E	2/3
1986	Chi-N	102	46	56	.451	5 E	5 E		3/3
1987	Chi-N	136	68	68	.500	5 E	6 E		1/2
	4	406	206	200	.507				

Milan, Jesse Clyde "Clyde"

YEAR	TM/L	G	W	L	PCT	STANDING
1922	Was-A*	154	69	85	.448	6

Miller, George Frederick

YEAR	TM/L	G	W	L	PCT	STANDING
1894	StL-N*	133	56	76	.424	9

Miller, Joseph Wick "Joe"

YEAR	TM/L	G	W	L	PCT	STANDING
1872	Nat-n*	11	0	11	.000	11

Miller, Raymond Roger "Ray"

YEAR	TM/L	G	W	L	PCT	STANDING		M/Y
1985	Min-A	100	50	50	.500	6 W	4 W	2/2
1986	Min-A	139	59	80	.424	7 W	6 W	1/2
	2	239	109	130	.456			

Mills, Colonel Buster "Buster"

YEAR	TM/L	G	W	L	PCT	STANDING		M/Y
1953	Cin-N	8	4	4	.500	6	6	2/2

Mills, Everett

YEAR	TM/L	G	W	L	PCT	STANDING		M/Y
1872	Bal-n*	16	7	6	.538	2	2	2/2

Mitchell, Frederick Francis "Fred"

YEAR	TM/L	G	W	L	PCT	STANDING
1917	Chi-N	157	74	80	.481	5
1918	Chi-N	131	84	45	.651	1
1919	Chi-N	140	75	65	.536	3
1920	Chi-N	154	75	79	.487	●5
1921	Bos-N	153	79	74	.516	4
1922	Bos-N	154	53	100	.346	8
1923	Bos-N	155	54	100	.351	7
	7	1044	494	543	.476	

Moore, Jackie Spencer

YEAR	TM/L	G	W	L	PCT	STANDING		M/Y
1984	Oak-A	118	57	61	.483	5 W	4 W	2/2
1985	Oak-A	162	77	85	.475	●4 W		
1986	Oak-A	73	29	44	.397	●6 W	●3 W	1/3
	3	353	163	190	.462			

Moore, Terry Bluford

YEAR	TM/L	G	W	L	PCT	STANDING		M/Y
1954	Phi-N	77	35	42	.455	3	4	2/2

Moran, Patrick Joseph "Pat"

YEAR	TM/L	G	W	L	PCT	STANDING
1915	Phi-N	153	90	62	.592	1
1916	Phi-N	154	91	62	.595	2
1917	Phi-N	155	87	65	.572	2
1918	Phi-N	125	55	68	.447	6
1919	Cin-N	140	96	44	.686	★1
1920	Cin-N	154	82	71	.536	3
1921	Cin-N	153	70	83	.458	6
1922	Cin-N	156	86	68	.558	2
1923	Cin-N	154	91	63	.591	2
	9	1344	748	586	.561	

Morgan, Joseph Michael "Joe"

YEAR	TM/L	G	W	L	PCT	STANDING		M/Y
1988	Bos-A	77	46	31	.597	4 E	1 E	2/2

Moriarty, George Joseph

YEAR	TM/L	G	W	L	PCT	STANDING
1927	Det-A	156	82	71	.536	4
1928	Det-A	154	68	86	.442	6
	2	310	150	157	.489	

Morrill, John Francis

YEAR	TM/L	G	W	L	PCT	STANDING		M/Y
1882	Bos-N*	85	45	39	.536	●3		
1883	Bos-N*	44	33	11	.750	4	1	2/2
1884	Bos-N*	116	73	38	.658	2		
1885	Bos-N*	113	46	66	.411	5		
1886	Bos-N*	118	56	61	.479	5		
1887	Bos-N*	32	12	17	.414	5	5	2/2
1888	Bos-N*	137	70	64	.522	4		
1889	Was-N*	51	13	38	.255	8	8	1/2

YEAR	TM/L	G	W	L	PCT	STANDING
	8	696	348	334	.510	

Morton, Charles Hazen "Charlie"

YEAR	TM/L	G	W	L	PCT	STANDING		M/Y
1884	Tol-a*	110	46	58	.442	8		
1885	Det-N*	38	7	31	.184	8	6	1/2
1890	Tol-a	134	68	64	.515	4		
	3	282	121	153	.442			

Moses, Felix I.

YEAR	TM/L	G	W	L	PCT	STANDING
1884	Ric-a	46	12	30	.286	12

Moss, John Lester "Les"

YEAR	TM/L	G	W	L	PCT	STANDING			M/Y
1968	Chi-A	2	0	2	.000	9	9	●8	2/5
	Chi-A	34	12	22	.353	9	9	●8	4/5
1979	Det-A	53	27	26	.509	5 E	5 E		1/3
	2	89	39	50	.438				

Murnane, Timothy Hayes "Tim"

YEAR	TM/L	G	W	L	PCT	STANDING
1884	Bos-U*	111	58	51	.532	5

Murray, William Jeremiah "Billy"

YEAR	TM/L	G	W	L	PCT	STANDING
1907	Phi-N	149	83	64	.565	3
1908	Phi-N	155	83	71	.539	4
1909	Phi-N	154	74	79	.484	5
	3	458	240	214	.529	

Murtaugh, Daniel Edward "Danny"

YEAR	TM/L	G	W	L	PCT	STANDING		M/Y
1957	Pit-N	51	26	25	.510	7	●7	2/2
1958	Pit-N	154	84	70	.545	2		
1959	Pit-N	155	78	76	.506	4		
1960	Pit-N	155	95	59	.617	★1		
1961	Pit-N	154	75	79	.487	6		
1962	Pit-N	161	93	68	.578	4		
1963	Pit-N	162	74	88	.457	8		
1964	Pit-N	162	80	82	.494	●6		
1967	Pit-N	79	39	39	.500	6	6	2/2
1970	Pit-N	162	89	73	.549	1 E		
1971	Pit-N	162	97	65	.599	★1 E		
1973	Pit-N	26	13	13	.500	2 E	3 E	2/2
1974	Pit-N	162	88	74	.543	1 E		
1975	Pit-N	161	92	69	.571	1 E		
1976	Pit-N	162	92	70	.568	2 E		
	15	2068	1115	950	.540			

Mutrie, James J. "Jim"

YEAR	TM/L	G	W	L	PCT	STANDING
1883	NY-a	97	54	42	.563	4
1884	NY-a	112	75	32	.701	1
1885	NY-N	112	85	27	.759	2
1886	NY-N	124	75	44	.630	3
1887	NY-N	129	68	55	.553	4
1888	NY-N	138	84	47	.641	1
1889	NY-N	131	83	43	.659	1
1890	NY-N	135	63	68	.481	6
1891	NY-N	136	71	61	.538	3
	9	1114	658	419	.611	

Myatt, George Edward "George"

YEAR	TM/L	G	W	L	PCT	STANDING			M/Y
1968	Phi-N	1	1	0	1.000	●6	5	●7	2/3
1969	Phi-N	54	19	35	.352	5 E	5 E		2/2
	2	55	20	35	.364				

Myers, Henry C.

YEAR	TM/L	G	W	L	PCT	STANDING
1882	Bal-a*	74	19	54	.260	6

Nash, William Mitchell "Billy"

YEAR	TM/L	G	W	L	PCT	STANDING
1896	Phi-N*	130	62	68	.477	8

Neun, John Henry "Johnny"

YEAR	TM/L	G	W	L	PCT	STANDING		M/Y
1946	NY-A	14	8	6	.571	3	3	3/3
1947	Cin-N	154	73	81	.474	5		
1948	Cin-N	100	44	56	.440	7	7	1/2
	3	268	125	143	.466			

Newman, Jeffrey Lynn "Jeff"

YEAR	TM/L	G	W	L	PCT	STANDING			M/Y
1986	Oak-A	10	2	8	.200	●6 W	7 W	●3 W	2/3

Nichols, Charles Augustus "Kid"

YEAR	TM/L	G	W	L	PCT	STANDING		M/Y
1904	StL-N*	155	75	79	.487	5		
1905	StL-N*	14	5	9	.357	7	6	1/3
	2	169	80	88	.476			

Nicol, Hugh

YEAR	TM/L	G	W	L	PCT	STANDING			M/Y
1897	StL-N	40	8	32	.200	12	12	12	2/4

Nixon, Russell Eugene "Russ"

YEAR	TM/L	G	W	L	PCT	STANDING		M/Y
1982	Cin-N	70	27	43	.386	6 W	6 W	2/2
1983	Cin-N	162	74	88	.457	6 W		
1988	Atl-N	111	42	79	.347	6 W	6 W	2/2
	3	343	143	210	.405			

Norman, Henry Willis Patrick "Bill"

YEAR	TM/L	G	W	L	PCT	STANDING		M/Y
1958	Det-A	105	56	49	.533	8	5	2/2
1959	Det-A	17	2	15	.118	8	4	1/2
	2	122	58	64	.475			

Oakes, Ennis Telfair "Rebel"

YEAR	TM/L	G	W	L	PCT	STANDING		M/Y
1914	Pit-F*	143	61	78	.439	8	7	2/2
1915	Pit-F*	156	86	67	.562	3		
	2	299	147	145	.503			

O'Connor, John Joseph "Jack"

YEAR	TM/L	G	W	L	PCT	STANDING
1910	StL-A*	158	47	107	.305	8

YEAR	TM/L	G	W	L	PCT	STANDING			M/Y
O'Day, Henry Francis "Hank"									
1912	Cin-N	155	75	78	.490	4			
1914	Chi-N	156	78	76	.506	4			
	2	311	153	154	.498				
O'Farrell, Robert Arthur "Bob"									
1927	StL-N*	153	92	61	.601	2			
1934	Cin-N*	91	30	60	.333	8	8		1/3
	2	244	122	121	.502				
O'Leary, Daniel "Dan"									
1884	Cin-U*	35	20	15	.571	5	3		1/2
O'Neill, Stephen Francis "Steve"									
1935	Cle-A	60	36	23	.610	5	3		2/2
1936	Cle-A	157	80	74	.519	5			
1937	Cle-A	156	83	71	.539	4			
1943	Det-A	155	78	76	.506	5			
1944	Det-A	156	88	66	.571	2			
1945	Det-A	155	88	65	.575	★1			
1946	Det-A	155	92	62	.597	2			
1947	Det-A	158	85	69	.552	2			
1948	Det-A	154	78	76	.506	5			
1950	Bos-A	95	63	32	.663	4	3		2/2
1951	Bos-A	154	87	67	.565	3			
1952	Phi-N	91	59	32	.648	6	4		2/2
1953	Phi-N	156	83	71	.539	●3			
1954	Phi-N	77	40	37	.519	3	4		1/2
	14	1879	1040	821	.559				
Onslow, John James "Jack"									
1949	Chi-A	154	63	91	.409	6			
1950	Chi-A	31	8	22	.267	8	6		1/2
	2	185	71	113	.386				
O'Rourke, James Henry "Jim"									
1881	Buf-N*	83	45	38	.542	3			
1882	Buf-N*	84	45	39	.536	●3			
1883	Buf-N*	98	52	45	.536	3			
1884	Buf-N*	115	64	47	.577	3			
1893	Was-N*	130	40	89	.310	12			
	5	510	246	258	.488				
Orr, David L. "Dave"									
1887	NY-a*	8	3	5	.375	8	7	7	2/3
Ott, Melvin Thomas "Mel"									
1942	NY-N*	154	85	67	.559	3			
1943	NY-N*	156	55	98	.359	8			
1944	NY-N*	155	67	87	.435	5			
1945	NY-N*	154	78	74	.513	5			
1946	NY-N*	154	61	93	.396	8			
1947	NY-N*	155	81	73	.526	4			
1948	NY-N	76	37	38	.493	4	5		1/2
	7	1004	464	530	.467				
Owens, Paul Francis									
1972	Phi-N	80	33	47	.412	6 E	6 E		2/2
1983	Phi-N	77	47	30	.610	1 E	♦1 E		2/2
1984	Phi-N	162	81	81	.500	4 E			
	3	319	161	158	.505				
Ozark, Daniel Leonard "Danny"									
1973	Phi-N	162	71	91	.438	6 E			
1974	Phi-N	162	80	82	.494	3 E			
1975	Phi-N	162	86	76	.531	2 E			
1976	Phi-N	162	101	61	.623	1 E			
1977	Phi-N	162	101	61	.623	1 E			
1978	Phi-N	162	90	72	.556	1 E			
1979	Phi-N	133	65	67	.492	5 E	4 E		1/2
1984	SF-N	56	24	32	.429	6 W	6 W		2/2
	8	1161	618	542	.533				
Pabor, Charles Henry "Charlie"									
1871	Cle-n*	29	10	19	.345	7			
1875	Atl-n*	42	2	40	.048	12	12		1/2
	NH-n*	6	1	5	.167	8	8		3/3
	2	77	13	64	.169				
Parker, Francis James "Salty"									
1967	NY-N	11	4	7	.364	10	10		2/2
1972	Hou-N	1	1	0	1.000	2 W	2 W		2/3
	2	12	5	7	.417				
Pearce, Richard J. "Dickey"									
1872	Mut-n*	56	34	20	.630	3			
1875	StL-n*	72	39	29	.574	4			
	2	128	73	49	.598				
Peckinpaugh, Roger Thorpe									
1914	NY-A*	20	10	10	.500	7	●6		2/2
1928	Cle-A	155	62	92	.403	7			
1929	Cle-A	152	81	71	.533	3			
1930	Cle-A	154	81	73	.526	4			
1931	Cle-A	155	78	76	.506	4			
1932	Cle-A	153	87	65	.572	4			
1933	Cle-A	51	26	25	.510	5	4		1/3
1941	Cle-A	155	75	79	.487	●4			
	8	995	500	491	.505				

YEAR	TM/L	G	W	L	PCT	STANDING			M/Y
Perkins, Ralph Foster "Cy"									
1937	Det-A	15	6	9	.400	2	2		5/5
Pesky, John Michael "Johnny"									
1963	Bos-A	161	76	85	.472	7			
1964	Bos-A	160	70	90	.438	8	8		1/2
1980	Bos-A	5	1	4	.200	3 E	4 E		2/2
	3	326	147	179	.451				
Pfeffer, Nathaniel Frederick "Fred"									
1892(1)	Lou-N*	23	9	14	.391	10	11		2/2
(2)	Lou-N*	77	33	42	.440	9			
Phelan, Lewis G. "Lew"									
1895	StL-N	45	11	30	.268	11	11		4/4
Phillips, Harold Ross "Lefty"									
1969	Cal-A	124	60	63	.488	6 W	3 W		2/2
1970	Cal-A	162	86	76	.531	3 W			
1971	Cal-A	162	76	86	.469	4 W			
	3	448	222	225	.497				
Phillips, Horace B.									
1879	Tro-N	47	12	34	.261	8	8		1/2
1883	Col-a	97	32	65	.330	6			
1884	Pit-a	35	9	24	.273	10	10		5/5
1885	Pit-a	111	56	55	.505	3			
1886	Pit-a	140	80	57	.584	2			
1887	Pit-N	125	55	69	.444	6			
1888	Pit-N	139	66	68	.493	6			
1889	Pit-N	71	28	43	.394	6	5		1/3
	8	765	338	415	.449				
Phillips, William Corcoran "Bill"									
1914	Ind-F	157	88	65	.575	1			
1915	New-F	53	26	27	.491	6	5		1/2
	2	210	114	92	.553				
Pike, Lipman Emanuel "Lip"									
1871	Tro-n*	4	1	3	.250	7	6		1/2
1874	Har-n*	54	17	37	.315	7			
1877	Cin-N*	14	3	11	.214	6	6		1/2
	3	72	21	51	.292				
Piniella, Louis Victor "Lou"									
1986	NY-A	162	90	72	.556	2 E			
1987	NY-A	162	89	73	.549	4 E			
1988	NY-A	93	45	48	.484	2 E	5 E		2/2
	3	417	224	193	.537				
Popowski, Edward Joseph "Eddie"									
1969	Bos-A	9	5	4	.556	3 E	3 E		2/2
1973	Bos-A	1	1	0	1.000	2 E	2 E		2/2
	2	10	6	4	.600				
Porter, Matthew S.									
1884	KC-U*	16	3	13	.188	8	8	8	2/3
Powers, Patrick Thomas "Pat"									
1890	Roc-a	133	63	63	.500	5			
1892(1)	NY-N	74	31	43	.419	10			
(2)	NY-N	79	40	37	.519	6			
	2	286	134	143	.484				
Pratt, Albert George "Al"									
1882	Pit-a	79	39	39	.500	4			
1883	Pit-a	32	12	20	.375	6	7		1/3
	2	111	51	59	.464				
Price, James L.									
1884	NY-N	100	56	42	.571	4	●4		1/2
Prothro, James Thompson "Doc"									
1939	Phi-N	152	45	106	.298	8			
1940	Phi-N	153	50	103	.327	8			
1941	Phi-N	155	43	111	.279	8			
	3	460	138	320	.301				
Purcell, William Aloysius "Blondie"									
1883	Phi-N*	82	13	68	.160	8	8		2/2
Quilici, Francis Ralph "Frank"									
1972	Min-A	84	41	43	.488	3 W	3 W		2/2
1973	Min-A	162	81	81	.500	3 W			
1974	Min-A	163	82	80	.506	3 W			
1975	Min-A	159	76	83	.478	4 W			
	4	568	280	287	.494				
Quinn, Joseph J. "Joe"									
1895	StL-N*	40	11	28	.282	11	11	11	3/4
1899	Cle-N*	116	12	104	.103	12	12		2/2
	2	156	23	132	.148				
Rader, Douglas Lee "Doug"									
1983	Tex-A	163	77	85	.475	3 W			
1984	Tex-A	161	69	92	.429	7 W			
1985	Tex-A	32	9	23	.281	7 W	7 W		1/2
1986	Chi-A	2	1	1	.500	6 W	5 W	5 W	2/3
	4	358	156	201	.437				
Rapp, Vernon Fred "Vern"									
1977	StL-N	162	83	79	.512	3 E			
1978	StL-N	17	6	11	.353	6 E	5 E		1/3

YEAR	TM/L	G	W	L	PCT	STANDING			M/Y
1984	Cin-N	121	51	70	.421	5 W	5 W		1/2
	3	300	140	160	.467				

Reach, Alfred James "Al"

YEAR	TM/L	G	W	L	PCT	STANDING			M/Y
1890	Phi-N	11	4	7	.364	2	3	3	3/5

Rice, Delbert "Del"

YEAR	TM/L	G	W	L	PCT	STANDING			M/Y
1972	Cal-A	155	75	80	.484	5 W			

Richards, Paul Rapier

YEAR	TM/L	G	W	L	PCT	STANDING			M/Y
1951	Chi-A	155	81	73	.526	4			
1952	Chi-A	156	81	73	.526	3			
1953	Chi-A	156	89	65	.578	3			
1954	Chi-A	146	91	54	.628	3	3		1/2
1955	Bal-A	156	57	97	.370	7			
1956	Bal-A	154	69	85	.448	6			
1957	Bal-A	154	76	76	.500	5			
1958	Bal-A	154	74	79	.484	6			
1959	Bal-A	155	74	80	.481	6			
1960	Bal-A	154	89	65	.578	2			
1961	Bal-A	136	78	57	.578	3	3		1/2
1976	Chi-A	161	64	97	.398	6 W			
	12	1837	923	901	.506				

Richardson, Daniel "Danny"

YEAR	TM/L	G	W	L	PCT	STANDING			M/Y
1892(2)	Was-N*	43	12	31	.279	11	12		3/3

Rickey, Wesley Branch "Branch"

YEAR	TM/L	G	W	L	PCT	STANDING			M/Y
1913	StL-A	12	5	6	.455	7	8		3/3
1914	StL-A*	159	71	82	.464	5			
1915	StL-A	159	63	91	.409	6			
1919	StL-N	138	54	83	.394	7			
1920	StL-N	155	75	79	.487	●5			
1921	StL-N	154	87	66	.569	3			
1922	StL-N	154	85	69	.552	●3			
1923	StL-N	154	79	74	.516	5			
1924	StL-N	154	65	89	.422	6			
1925	StL-N	38	13	25	.342	8	4		1/2
	10	1277	597	664	.473				

Rigney, William Joseph "Bill"

YEAR	TM/L	G	W	L	PCT	STANDING			M/Y
1956	NY-N	154	67	87	.435	6			
1957	NY-N	154	69	85	.448	6			
1958	SF-N	154	80	74	.519	3			
1959	SF-N	154	83	71	.539	3			
1960	SF-N	58	33	25	.569	2	5		1/2
1961	LA-A	162	70	91	.435	8			
1962	LA-A	162	86	76	.531	3			
1963	LA-A	161	70	91	.435	9			
1964	LA-A	162	82	80	.506	5			
1965	Cal-A	162	75	87	.463	7			
1966	Cal-A	162	80	82	.494	6			
1967	Cal-A	161	84	77	.522	5			
1968	Cal-A	162	67	95	.414	8			
1969	Cal-A	39	11	28	.282	6 W	3 W		1/2
1970	Min-A	162	98	64	.605	1 W			
1971	Min-A	160	74	86	.463	5			
1972	Min-A	70	36	34	.514	3 W	3 W		1/2
1976	SF-N	162	74	88	.457	4 W			
	18	2561	1239	1321	.484				

Ripken, Calvin Edwin Sr. "Cal"

YEAR	TM/L	G	W	L	PCT	STANDING			M/Y
1985	Bal-A	1	1	0	1.000	4 E	4 E	4 E	2/3
1987	Bal-A	162	67	95	.414	6 E			
1988	Bal-A	6	0	6	.000	7 E	7 E		1/2
	3	169	68	101	.402				

Robinson, Frank

YEAR	TM/L	G	W	L	PCT	STANDING			M/Y
1975	Cle-A*	159	79	80	.497	4 E			
1976	Cle-A*	159	81	78	.509	4 E			
1977	Cle-A	57	26	31	.456	5 E	5 E		1/2
1981(1)	SF-N	59	27	32	.458	5 W			
(2)	SF-N	52	29	23	.558	3 W			
1982	SF-N	162	87	75	.537	3 W			
1983	SF-N	162	79	83	.488	5 W			
1984	SF-N	106	42	64	.396	6 W	6 W		1/2
1988	Bal-A	155	54	101	.348	7 E	7 4		2/2
	8	1071	504	567	.471				

Robinson, Wilbert

YEAR	TM/L	G	W	L	PCT	STANDING			M/Y
1902	Bal-A*	83	24	57	.296	7	8		2/2
1914	Bro-N	154	75	79	.487	5			
1915	Bro-N	154	80	72	.526	3			
1916	Bro-N	156	94	60	.610	1			
1917	Bro-N	156	70	81	.464	7			
1918	Bro-N	127	57	69	.452	5			
1919	Bro-N	141	69	71	.493	5			
1920	Bro-N	155	93	61	.604	1			
1921	Bro-N	152	77	75	.507	5			
1922	Bro-N	155	76	78	.494	6			
1923	Bro-N	155	76	78	.494	6			
1924	Bro-N	154	92	62	.597	2			
1925	Bro-N	153	68	85	.444	●6			
1926	Bro-N	155	71	82	.464	6			
1927	Bro-N	154	65	88	.425	6			
1928	Bro-N	155	77	76	.503	6			
1929	Bro-N	153	70	83	.458	6			
1930	Bro-N	154	86	68	.558	4			
1931	Bro-N	153	79	73	.520	4			
	19	2819	1399	1398	.500				

Robison, Matthew Stanley "Stanley"

YEAR	TM/L	G	W	L	PCT	STANDING			M/Y
1905	StL-N	50	19	31	.380	6	6		3/3

Rodgers, Robert Leroy "Bob"

YEAR	TM/L	G	W	L	PCT	STANDING			M/Y
1980	Mil-A	47	26	21	.553	2 E	3 E		1/3
	Mil-A	23	13	10	.565	4 E	3 E		3/3
1981(1)	Mil-A	56	31	25	.554	3 E			
(2)	Mil-A	53	31	22	.585	1 E			
1982	Mil-A	47	23	24	.489	5 E	♦1 E		1/2
1985	Mon-N	161	84	77	.522	3 E			
1986	Mon-N	161	78	83	.484	4 E			
1987	Mon-N	162	91	71	.562	3 E			
1988	Mon-N	163	81	81	.500	3 E			
	7	873	458	414	.525				

Rogers, James F. "Jim"

YEAR	TM/L	G	W	L	PCT	STANDING			M/Y
1897	Lou-N*	44	17	24	.415	9	11		1/2

Rojas, Octavio Victor "Cookie"

YEAR	TM/L	G	W	L	PCT	STANDING			M/Y
1988	Cal-A	154	75	79	.487	4 W	4 W		1/2

Rolfe, Robert Abial "Red"

YEAR	TM/L	G	W	L	PCT	STANDING			M/Y
1949	Det-A	155	87	67	.565	4			
1950	Det-A	157	95	59	.617	2			
1951	Det-A	154	73	81	.474	5			
1952	Det-A	73	23	49	.319	8	8		1/2
	4	539	278	256	.521				

Rose, Peter Edward "Pete"

YEAR	TM/L	G	W	L	PCT	STANDING			M/Y
1984	Cin-N*	41	19	22	.463	5 W	5 W		2/2
1985	Cin-N*	162	89	72	.553	2 W			
1986	Cin-N*	162	86	76	.531	2 W			
1987	Cin-N	162	84	78	.519	2 W			
1988	Cin-N	23	11	12	.478	4 W	2 W		1/2
	5	550	289	260	.526				

Roseman, James John "Chief"

YEAR	TM/L	G	W	L	PCT	STANDING			M/Y
1890	StL-a*	15	7	8	.467	4	5	3	3/6

Rowe, David E. "Dave"

YEAR	TM/L	G	W	L	PCT	STANDING			M/Y
1886	KC-N*	126	30	91	.248	7			
1888	KC-a*	50	14	36	.280	8	8		1/3
	2	176	44	127	.257				

Rowe, John Charles "Jack"

YEAR	TM/L	G	W	L	PCT	STANDING			M/Y
1890	Buf-P*	81	22	58	.275	8	8		1/3
	Buf-P*	19	5	14	.263	8	8		3/3

Rowland, Clarence Henry "Pants"

YEAR	TM/L	G	W	L	PCT	STANDING			M/Y
1915	Chi-A	156	93	61	.604	3			
1916	Chi-A	155	89	65	.578	2			
1917	Chi-A	156	100	54	.649	★1			
1918	Chi-A	124	57	67	.460	6			
	4	591	339	247	.578				

Ruel, Herold Dominic "Muddy"

YEAR	TM/L	G	W	L	PCT	STANDING			M/Y
1947	StL-A	154	59	95	.383	8			

Runnels, James Edward "Pete"

YEAR	TM/L	G	W	L	PCT	STANDING			M/Y
1966	Bos-A	16	8	8	.500	9	9		2/2

Ryan, Cornelius Joseph "Connie"

YEAR	TM/L	G	W	L	PCT	STANDING			M/Y
1975	Atl-N	27	9	18	.333	5 W	5 W		2/2
1977	Tex-A	6	2	4	.333	3 W	5 W	2 W	3/4
	2	33	11	22	.333				

Sawyer, Edwin Milby "Eddie"

YEAR	TM/L	G	W	L	PCT	STANDING			M/Y
1948	Phi-N	63	23	40	.365	6	6		3/3
1949	Phi-N	154	81	73	.526	3			
1950	Phi-N	157	91	63	.591	1			
1951	Phi-N	154	73	81	.474	5			
1952	Phi-N	63	28	35	.444	6	4		1/2
1958	Phi-N	70	30	40	.429	8	8		2/2
1959	Phi-N	155	64	90	.416	8			
1960	Phi-N	1	0	1	.000	●6	8		1/3
	8	817	390	423	.480				

Scanlon, Michael B. "Mike"

YEAR	TM/L	G	W	L	PCT	STANDING			M/Y
1884	Was-U	114	47	65	.420	6			
1886	Was-N	82	13	67	.162	8	8		1/2
	2	196	60	132	.313				

Schalk, Raymond William "Ray"

YEAR	TM/L	G	W	L	PCT	STANDING			M/Y
1927	Chi-A*	153	70	83	.458	5			
1928	Chi-A*	75	32	42	.432	6	5		1/2
	2	228	102	125	.449				

Scheffing, Robert Boden "Bob"

YEAR	TM/L	G	W	L	PCT	STANDING			M/Y
1957	Chi-N	156	62	92	.403	●7			
1958	Chi-N	154	72	82	.468	●5			
1959	Chi-N	155	74	80	.481	●5			
1961	Det-A	163	101	61	.623	2			
1962	Det-A	161	85	76	.528	4			
1963	Det-A	60	24	36	.400	9	●5		1/2
	6	849	418	427	.495				

Schlafly, Harry Linton "Larry"

YEAR	TM/L	G	W	L	PCT	STANDING			M/Y
1914	Buf-F*	156	80	71	.530	4			

YEAR	TM/L	G	W	L	PCT	STANDING			M/Y
1915	Buf-F	41	13	28	.317	8	6		1/3
	2	197	93	99	.484				

Schmelz, Gustavius Heinrich "Gus"

YEAR	TM/L	G	W	L	PCT	STANDING			M/Y
1884	Col-a	110	69	39	.639	2			
1886	StL-N	126	43	79	.352	6			
1887	Cin-a	136	81	54	.600	2			
1888	Cin-a	137	80	54	.597	4			
1889	Cin-a	141	76	63	.547	4			
1890	Cle-N	78	21	55	.276	7	7		1/2
	Col-a	57	38	13	.745	5	2		2/3
1891	Col-a	138	61	76	.445	6			
1894	Was-N	132	45	87	.341	11			
1895	Was-N	133	43	85	.336	10			
1896	Was-N	133	58	73	.443	●9			
1897	Was-N	36	9	25	.265	11	●6		1/2
	11	1357	624	703	.470				

Schoendienst, Albert Fred "Red"

YEAR	TM/L	G	W	L	PCT	STANDING			M/Y
1965	StL-N	162	80	81	.497	7			
1966	StL-N	162	83	79	.512	6			
1967	StL-N	161	101	60	.627	★1			
1968	StL-N	162	97	65	.599	1			
1969	StL-N	162	87	75	.537	4 E			
1970	StL-N	162	76	86	.469	4 E			
1971	StL-N	163	90	72	.556	2 E			
1972	StL-N	156	75	81	.481	4 E			
1973	StL-N	162	81	81	.500	2 E			
1974	StL-N	161	86	75	.534	2 E			
1975	StL-N	163	82	80	.506	●3 E			
1976	StL-N	162	72	90	.444	5 E			
1980	StL-N	37	18	19	.486	5 E	4 E		4/4
	13	1975	1028	944	.521				

Schultz, Joseph Charles Jr. "Joe"

YEAR	TM/L	G	W	L	PCT	STANDING			M/Y
1969	Sea-A	163	64	98	.395	6 W			
1973	Det-A	28	14	14	.500	3 E	3 E		2/2
	2	191	78	112	.411				

Selee, Frank Gibson

YEAR	TM/L	G	W	L	PCT	STANDING			M/Y
1890	Bos-N	134	76	57	.571	5			
1891	Bos-N	140	87	51	.630	1			
1892(1)	Bos-N	75	52	22	.703	1			
(2)	Bos-N	77	50	26	.658	2			
1893	Bos-N	131	86	43	.667	1			
1894	Bos-N	133	83	49	.629	3			
1895	Bos-N	133	71	60	.542	●5			
1896	Bos-N	132	74	57	.565	4			
1897	Bos-N	135	93	39	.705	1			
1898	Bos-N	152	102	47	.685	1			
1899	Bos-N	153	95	57	.625	2			
1900	Bos-N	142	66	72	.478	4			
1901	Bos-N	140	69	69	.500	5			
1902	Chi-N	143	68	69	.496	5			
1903	Chi-N	139	82	56	.594	3			
1904	Chi-N	156	93	60	.608	2			
1905	Chi-N	65	37	28	.569	4	3		1/2
	16	2180	1284	862	.598				

Sewell, James Luther "Luke"

YEAR	TM/L	G	W	L	PCT	STANDING			M/Y
1941	StL-A	113	55	55	.500	7	●6		2/2
1942	StL-A*	151	82	69	.543	3			
1943	StL-A	153	72	80	.474	6			
1944	StL-A	154	89	65	.578	1			
1945	StL-A	154	81	70	.536	3			
1946	StL-A	125	53	71	.427	7	7		1/2
1949	Cin-N	3	1	2	.333	7	7		2/2
1950	Cin-N	153	66	87	.431	6			
1951	Cin-N	155	68	86	.442	6			
1952	Cin-N	98	39	59	.398	7	6		1/3
	10	1259	606	644	.485				

Shannon, Daniel W. "Dan"

YEAR	TM/L	G	W	L	PCT	STANDING			M/Y
1889	Lou-a*	58	10	46	.179	8	8	8	3/4
1891	Was-a*	51	15	34	.306	7	8	8	3/4
	2	109	25	80	.238				

Sharsig, William A. "Bill"

YEAR	TM/L	G	W	L	PCT	STANDING			M/Y
1886	Phi-a	41	22	17	.564	6	6		2/2
1888	Phi-a	137	81	52	.609	3			
1889	Phi-a	138	75	58	.564	3			
1890	Phi-a	132	54	78	.409	7			
1891	Phi-a	18	6	11	.353	7	4		1/2
	5	466	238	216	.524				

Shawkey, James Robert "Bob"

YEAR	TM/L	G	W	L	PCT	STANDING			M/Y
1930	NY-A	154	86	68	.558	3			

Sheehan, Thomas Clancy "Tom"

YEAR	TM/L	G	W	L	PCT	STANDING			M/Y
1960	SF-N	98	46	50	.479	2	5		2/2

Shepard, Lawrence William "Larry"

YEAR	TM/L	G	W	L	PCT	STANDING			M/Y
1968	Pit-N	163	80	82	.494	6			
1969	Pit-N	157	84	73	.535	3 E	3 E		1/2
	2	320	164	155	.514				

Sherry, Norman Burt "Norm"

YEAR	TM/L	G	W	L	PCT	STANDING			M/Y
1976	Cal-A	66	37	29	.561	6 W	●4 W		2/2
1977	Cal-A	81	39	42	.481	5 W	5 W		1/2
	2	147	76	71	.517				

Shettsline, William Joseph "Bill"

YEAR	TM/L	G	W	L	PCT	STANDING			M/Y
1898	Phi-N	104	59	44	.573	●8	6		2/2
1899	Phi-N	154	94	58	.618	3			
1900	Phi-N	141	75	63	.543	3			
1901	Phi-N	140	83	57	.593	2			
1902	Phi-N	138	56	81	.409	7			
	5	677	367	303	.548				

Shotton, Burton Edwin "Burt"

YEAR	TM/L	G	W	L	PCT	STANDING			M/Y
1928	Phi-N	152	43	109	.283	8			
1929	Phi-N	154	71	82	.464	5			
1930	Phi-N	156	52	102	.338	8			
1931	Phi-N	155	66	88	.429	6			
1932	Phi-N	154	78	76	.506	4			
1933	Phi-N	152	60	92	.395	7			
1934	Cin-N	1	1	0	1.000	8	8	8	2/3
1947	Bro-N	153	92	60	.605	●1	1		2/2
1948	Bro-N	81	48	33	.593	5	3		3/3
1949	Bro-N	156	97	57	.630	1			
1950	Bro-N	155	89	65	.578	2			
	11	1469	697	764	.477				

Silvestri, Kenneth Joseph "Ken"

YEAR	TM/L	G	W	L	PCT	STANDING			M/Y
1967	Atl-N	3	0	3	.000	7	7		2/2

Simmons, Joseph S. "Joe"

YEAR	TM/L	G	W	L	PCT	STANDING			M/Y
1875	Wes-n	13	1	12	.077	13			
1884	Wil-U	18	2	16	.111	8			
	2	31	3	28	.097				

Simmons, Lewis "Lew"

YEAR	TM/L	G	W	L	PCT	STANDING			M/Y
1886	Phi-a	98	41	55	.427	6	6		1/2

Sisler, George Harold

YEAR	TM/L	G	W	L	PCT	STANDING			M/Y
1924	StL-A*	153	74	78	.487	4			
1925	StL-A*	154	82	71	.536	3			
1926	StL-A*	155	62	92	.403	7			
	3	462	218	241	.475				

Sisler, Richard Allan "Dick"

YEAR	TM/L	G	W	L	PCT	STANDING			M/Y
1964	Cin-N	6	3	3	.500	3	4	●2	2/4
	Cin-N	47	29	18	.617	3	●2		4/4
1965	Cin-N	162	89	73	.549	4			
	2	215	121	94	.563				

Skaff, Francis Michael "Frank"

YEAR	TM/L	G	W	L	PCT	STANDING			M/Y
1966	Det-A	79	40	39	.506	2	3		3/3

Skinner, Robert Ralph "Bob"

YEAR	TM/L	G	W	L	PCT	STANDING			M/Y
1968	Phi-N	107	48	59	.449	5	●7		3/3
1969	Phi-N	108	44	64	.407	5 E	5 E		1/2
1977	SD-N	1	1	0	1.000	4 W	4 W	5 W	2/3
	3	216	93	123	.431				

Slattery, John Terrence "Jack"

YEAR	TM/L	G	W	L	PCT	STANDING			M/Y
1928	Bos-N	31	11	20	.355	7	7		1/2

Smith, Edward Mayo "Mayo"

YEAR	TM/L	G	W	L	PCT	STANDING			M/Y
1955	Phi-N	154	77	77	.500	4			
1956	Phi-N	154	71	83	.461	5			
1957	Phi-N	156	77	77	.500	5			
1958	Phi-N	84	39	45	.464	8	8		1/2
1959	Cin-N	80	35	45	.438	7	●5		1/2
1967	Det-A	163	91	71	.562	●2			
1968	Det-A	164	103	59	.636	★1			
1969	Det-A	162	90	72	.556	2 E			
1970	Det-A	162	79	83	.488	4 E			
	9	1279	662	612	.520				

Smith, George Henry "Heinie"

YEAR	TM/L	G	W	L	PCT	STANDING			M/Y
1902	NY-N*	32	5	27	.156	4	8	8	2/3

Smith, Harry Thomas

YEAR	TM/L	G	W	L	PCT	STANDING			M/Y
1909	Bos-N*	79	23	54	.299	8	8		2/2

Smith, William J.

YEAR	TM/L	G	W	L	PCT	STANDING			M/Y
1873	Mar-n*	5	0	5	.000	9			

Snyder, Charles N. "Pop"

YEAR	TM/L	G	W	L	PCT	STANDING			M/Y
1882	Cin-a*	80	55	25	.688	1			
1883	Cin-a*	98	61	37	.622	3			
1884	Cin-a*	40	24	14	.632	5	5		2/2
1891	Was-a*	70	23	46	.333	6	7	8	2/4
	4	288	163	122	.572				

Snyder, James Robert "Jim"

YEAR	TM/L	G	W	L	PCT	STANDING			M/Y
1988	Sea-A	105	45	60	.429	6 W	7 W		2/2

Sothoron, Allen Sutton

YEAR	TM/L	G	W	L	PCT	STANDING			M/Y
1933	StL-A	8	2	6	.250	8	8	8	2/3

Southworth, William Harrison "Billy"

YEAR	TM/L	G	W	L	PCT	STANDING			M/Y
1929	StL-N*	90	43	45	.489	4	4		1/3
1940	StL-N	111	69	40	.633	7	3		3/3
1941	StL-N	155	97	56	.634	2			
1942	StL-N	156	106	48	.688	★1			
1943	StL-N	157	105	49	.682	1			
1944	StL-N	157	105	49	.682	★1			
1945	StL-N	155	95	59	.617	2			

YEAR	TM/L	G	W	L	PCT	STANDING			M/Y
1946	Bos-N	154	81	72	.529	4			
1947	Bos-N	154	86	68	.558	3			
1948	Bos-N	154	91	62	.595	1			
1949	Bos-N	111	55	54	.505	4	4		1/2
1950	Bos-N	156	83	71	.539	4			
1951	Bos-N	60	28	31	.475	5	4		1/2
	13	1770	1044	704	.597				
Spalding, Albert Goodwill "Al"									
1876	Chi-N*	66	52	14	.788	1			
1877	Chi-N*	60	26	33	.441	5			
	2	126	78	47	.624				
Speaker, Tristram E "Tris"									
1919	Cle-A*	61	40	21	.656	3	2		2/2
1920	Cle-A*	154	98	56	.636	★1			
1921	Cle-A*	154	94	60	.610	2			
1922	Cle-A*	155	78	76	.506	4			
1923	Cle-A*	153	82	71	.536	3			
1924	Cle-A*	153	67	86	.438	6			
1925	Cle-A*	155	70	84	.455	6			
1926	Cle-A*	154	88	66	.571	2			
	8	1139	617	520	.543				
Spence, Harrison L. "Harry"									
1888	Ind-N	136	50	85	.370	7			
Stahl, Charles Sylvester "Chick"									
1906	Bos-A*	40	14	26	.350	8	8		2/2
Stahl, Garland "Jake"									
1905	Was-A*	154	64	87	.424	7			
1906	Was-A*	151	55	95	.367	7			
1912	Bos-A*	154	105	47	.691	★1			
1913	Bos-A*	81	39	41	.488	5	4		1/2
	4	540	263	270	.493				
Stallings, George Tweedy									
1897	Phi-N*	134	55	77	.417	10			
1898	Phi-N	46	19	27	.413	●8	6		1/2
1901	Det-N	136	74	61	.548	3			
1909	NY-A	153	74	77	.490	5			
1910	NY-A	142	78	59	.569	3	2		1/2
1913	Bos-N	154	69	82	.457	5			
1914	Bos-N	158	94	59	.614	★1			
1915	Bos-N	157	83	69	.546	2			
1916	Bos-N	158	89	63	.586	3			
1917	Bos-N	158	72	81	.471	6			
1918	Bos-N	124	53	71	.427	6			
1919	Bos-N	140	57	82	.410	6			
1920	Bos-N	153	62	90	.408	7			
	13	1813	879	898	.495				
Stanky, Edward Raymond "Eddie"									
1952	StL-N*	154	88	66	.571	3			
1953	StL-N*	157	83	71	.539	●3			
1954	StL-N	154	72	82	.468	6			
1955	StL-N	36	17	19	.472	5	7		1/2
1966	Chi-A	163	83	79	.512	4			
1967	Chi-A	162	89	73	.549	4			
1968	Chi-A	79	34	45	.430	9	8		1/5
1977	Tex-A	1	1	0	1.000	●3 W	3 W	2 W	2/4
	8	906	467	435	.518				
Start, Joseph "Joe"									
1873	Mut-n*	25	18	7	.720	5	4		2/2
Stengel, Charles Dillon "Casey"									
1934	Bro-N	153	71	81	.467	6			
1935	Bro-N	154	70	83	.458	5			
1936	Bro-N	156	67	87	.435	7			
1938	Bos-N	153	77	75	.507	5			
1939	Bos-N	152	63	88	.417	7			
1940	Bos-N	152	65	87	.428	7			
1941	Bos-N	156	62	92	.403	7			
1942	Bos-N	150	59	89	.399	7			
1943	Bos-N	107	47	60	.439	6	6		2/2
1949	NY-A	155	97	57	.630	★1			
1950	NY-A	155	98	56	.636	★1			
1951	NY-A	154	98	56	.636	★1			
1952	NY-A	154	95	59	.617	★1			
1953	NY-A	151	99	52	.656	★1			
1954	NY-A	155	103	51	.669	2			
1955	NY-A	154	96	58	.623	1			
1956	NY-A	154	97	57	.630	★1			
1957	NY-A	154	98	56	.636	1			
1958	NY-A	155	92	62	.597	★1			
1959	NY-A	155	79	75	.513	3			
1960	NY-A	155	97	57	.630	1			
1962	NY-N	161	40	120	.250	10			
1963	NY-N	162	51	111	.315	10			
1964	NY-N	163	53	109	.327	10			
1965	NY-N	96	31	64	.326	10	10		1/2
	25	3766	1905	1842	.508				
Stovall, George Thomas									
1911	Cle-A*	139	74	62	.544	7	3		2/2
1912	StL-A*	117	41	74	.357	8	7		2/2
1913	StL-A*	135	50	84	.373	7	8		1/3
1914	KC-F*	154	67	84	.444	6			
1915	KC-F*	153	81	72	.529	4			
	5	698	313	376	.454				
Stovey, Harry Duffield									
1881	Wor-N*	27	8	18	.308	7	8		2/2
1885	Phi-a*	113	55	57	.491	4			
	2	140	63	75	.457				
Street, Charles Evard "Gabby"									
1929	StL-N	1	1	0	1.000	4	4	4	2/3
1930	StL-N	154	92	62	.597	1			
1931	StL-N*	154	101	53	.656	★1			
1932	StL-N	156	72	82	.468	●6			
1933	StL-N	91	46	45	.505	5	5		1/2
1938	StL-A	156	55	97	.362	7			
	6	712	367	339	.520				
Stricker, John A. "Cub"									
1892(1)	StL-N*	23	6	17	.261	10	11	9	2/3
Strickland, George Bevan									
1964	Cle-A	73	33	39	.458	8	●6		1/2
1966	Cle-A	39	15	24	.385	3	5		2/2
	2	112	48	63	.432				
Stubing, Lawrence George "Moose"									
1988	Cal-A	8	0	8	.000	4 W	4 W		2/2
Sukeforth, Clyde Leroy									
1947	Bro-N	2	2	0	1.000	●1	1		1/2
Sullivan, Haywood Cooper									
1965	KC-A	136	54	82	.397	10	10		2/2
Sullivan, James P.									
1890	Col-a	3	2	1	.667	5	5	2	3/3
Sullivan, Timothy Paul "Ted"									
1883	StL-a	79	53	26	.671	2	2		1/2
1884	KC-U*	62	13	46	.220	8	8		3/3
	StL-U	31	28	3	.903	1	1		1/2
1888	Was-N	96	38	57	.400	8	8		2/2
	3	268	132	132	.500				
Sullivan, William Joseph Sr. "Billy"									
1909	Chi-A*	159	78	74	.513	4			
Sweasy, Charles James "Charlie"									
1875	RS-n*	18	4	14	.222	9			
Swift, Robert Virgil "Bob"									
1965	Det-A	42	24	18	.571	3	4		1/2
1966	Det-A	57	32	25	.561	3	2	3	2/3
	2	99	56	43	.566				
Tanner, Charles William "Chuck"									
1970	Chi-A	16	3	13	.188	6 W	6 W		3/3
1971	Chi-A	162	79	83	.488	3 W			
1972	Chi-A	154	87	67	.565	2 W			
1973	Chi-A	162	77	85	.475	5 W			
1974	Chi-A	163	80	80	.500	4 W			
1975	Chi-A	161	75	86	.466	5 W			
1976	Oak-A	161	87	74	.540	2 W			
1977	Pit-N	162	96	66	.593	2 E			
1978	Pit-N	161	88	73	.547	2 E			
1979	Pit-N	163	98	64	.605	★1 E			
1980	Pit-N	162	83	79	.512	3 E			
1981(1)	Pit-N	49	25	23	.521	4 E			
(2)	Pit-N	54	21	33	.389	6 E			
1982	Pit-N	162	84	78	.519	4 E			
1983	Pit-N	162	84	78	.519	2 E			
1984	Pit-N	162	75	87	.463	6 E			
1985	Pit-N	161	57	104	.354	6 E			
1986	Atl-N	161	72	89	.447	6 W			
1987	Atl-N	161	69	92	.429	5 W			
1988	Atl-N	39	12	27	.308	6 W	6 W		1/2
	19	2738	1352	1381	.495				
Tappe, Elvin Walter "El"									
1961	Chi-N	2	2	0	1.000	7	7	7	4/9
	Chi-N	79	35	43	.449	7	7	7	7/9
	Chi-N	16	5	11	.313	7	7		9/9
1962	Chi-N*	20	4	16	.200	9	9		1/3
	2	117	46	70	.397				
Taylor, George J.									
1884	Bro-a	109	40	64	.385	9			
Taylor, James Wren "Zack"									
1946	StL-A	31	13	17	.433	7	7		2/2
1948	StL-A	155	59	94	.386	6			
1949	StL-A	155	53	101	.344	7			
1950	StL-A	154	58	96	.377	7			
1951	StL-A	154	52	102	.338	8			
	5	649	235	410	.364				
Tebbetts, George Robert "Birdie"									
1954	Cin-N	154	74	80	.481	5			
1955	Cin-N	154	75	79	.487	5			

YEAR	TM/L	G	W	L	PCT	STANDING			M/Y
1956	Cin-N	155	91	63	.591	3			
1957	Cin-N	154	80	74	.519	4			
1958	Cin-N	113	52	61	.460	8	4		1/2
1961	Mil-N	25	12	13	.480	3	4		2/2
1962	Mil-N	162	86	76	.531	5			
1963	Cle-A	162	79	83	.488	●5			
1964	Cle-A	91	46	44	.511	8	●6		2/2
1965	Cle-A	162	87	75	.537	5			
1966	Cle-A	123	66	57	.537	3	5		1/2
	11	1455	748	705	.515				

Tebeau, Oliver Wendell "Patsy"

YEAR	TM/L	G	W	L	PCT	STANDING			M/Y
1890	Cle-P*	52	21	30	.412	7	7		2/2
1891	Cle-N*	73	31	40	.437	4	5		2/2
1892(1)	Cle-N*	74	40	33	.548	5			
(2)	Cle-N*	79	53	23	.697	1			
1893	Cle-N*	129	73	55	.570	3			
1894	Cle-N*	130	68	61	.527	6			
1895	Cle-N*	132	84	46	.646	2			
1896	Cle-N*	135	80	48	.625	2			
1897	Cle-N*	132	69	62	.527	5			
1898	Cle-N*	156	81	68	.544	5			
1899	StL-N*	155	84	67	.556	5			
1900	StL-N*	92	42	50	.457	7	●5		1/2
	11	1339	726	583	.555				

Tenney, Frederick "Fred"

YEAR	TM/L	G	W	L	PCT	STANDING			M/Y
1905	Bos-N*	156	51	103	.331	7			
1906	Bos-N*	152	49	102	.325	8			
1907	Bos-N*	152	58	90	.392	7			
1911	Bos-N*	156	44	107	.291	8			
	4	616	202	402	.334				

Terry, William Harold "Bill"

YEAR	TM/L	G	W	L	PCT	STANDING			M/Y
1932	NY-N*	114	55	59	.482	8	●6		2/2
1933	NY-N*	156	91	61	.599	★1			
1934	NY-N*	153	93	60	.608	2			
1935	NY-N*	156	91	62	.595	3			
1936	NY-N*	154	92	62	.597	1			
1937	NY-N*	152	95	57	.625	1			
1938	NY-N	152	83	67	.553	3			
1939	NY-N	151	77	74	.510	5			
1940	NY-N	152	72	80	.474	6			
1941	NY-N	156	74	79	.484	5			
	10	1496	823	661	.555				

Thomas, Frederick L. "Fred"

YEAR	TM/L	G	W	L	PCT	STANDING			M/Y
1887	Ind-N	29	11	18	.379	8	8	8	2/3

Thompson, Andrew M. "A. M."

YEAR	TM/L	G	W	L	PCT	STANDING			M/Y
1884	Stp-U	9	2	6	.250	7			

Tighe, John Thomas "Jack"

YEAR	TM/L	G	W	L	PCT	STANDING			M/Y
1957	Det-A	154	78	76	.506	4			
1958	Det-A	49	21	28	.429	8	5		1/2
	2	203	99	104	.488				

Tinker, Joseph Bert "Joe"

YEAR	TM/L	G	W	L	PCT	STANDING			M/Y
1913	Cin-N*	156	64	89	.418	7			
1914	Chi-F*	158	87	67	.565	2			
1915	Chi-F*	156	86	66	.566	1			
1916	Chi-N*	156	67	86	.438	5			
	4	626	304	308	.497				

Torborg, Jeffrey Allen "Jeff"

YEAR	TM/L	G	W	L	PCT	STANDING			M/Y
1977	Cle-A	104	45	59	.433	5 E	5 E		2/2
1978	Cle-A	159	69	90	.434	6 E			
1979	Cle-A	95	43	52	.453	6 E	6 E		1/2
	3	358	157	201	.439				

Torre, Joseph Paul "Joe"

YEAR	TM/L	G	W	L	PCT	STANDING			M/Y
1977	NY-N*	117	49	68	.419	6 E	6 E		2/2
1978	NY-N	162	66	96	.407	6 E			
1979	NY-N	163	63	99	.389	6 E			
1980	NY-N	162	67	95	.414	5 E			
1981(1)	NY-N	52	17	34	.333	5 E			
(2)	NY-N	53	24	28	.462	4 E			
1982	Atl-N	162	89	73	.549	1 W			
1983	Atl-N	162	88	74	.543	2 W			
1984	Atl-N	162	80	82	.494	●2 W			
	8	1195	543	649	.456				

Tracewski, Richard Joseph "Dick"

YEAR	TM/L	G	W	L	PCT	STANDING			M/Y
1979	Det-A	2	2	0	1.000	5 E	5 E	5 E	2/3

Traynor, Harold Joseph "Pie"

YEAR	TM/L	G	W	L	PCT	STANDING			M/Y
1934	Pit-N*	100	47	52	.475	4	5		2/2
1935	Pit-N*	153	86	67	.562	4			
1936	Pit-N	156	84	70	.545	4			
1937	Pit-N*	154	86	68	.558	3			
1938	Pit-N	152	86	64	.573	2			
1939	Pit-N	153	68	85	.444	6			
	6	868	457	406	.530				

Trebelhorn, Thomas Lynn "Tom"

YEAR	TM/L	G	W	L	PCT	STANDING			M/Y
1986	Mil-A	9	6	3	.667	6 E	6 E		2/2
1987	Mil-A	162	91	71	.562	3 E			
1988	Mil-A	162	87	75	.537	●3 E			
	3	333	184	149	.553				

Trott, Samuel W. "Sam"

YEAR	TM/L	G	W	L	PCT	STANDING			M/Y
1891	Was-a	12	4	7	.364	6	9		1/4

Turner, Robert Edward "Ted"

YEAR	TM/L	G	W	L	PCT	STANDING			M/Y
1977	Atl-N	1	0	1	.000	6 W	6 W	6 W	2/4

Unglaub, Robert Alexander "Bob"

YEAR	TM/L	G	W	L	PCT	STANDING			M/Y
1907	Bos-A*	29	9	20	.310	6	8	7	3/4

Valentine, Robert John "Bobby"

YEAR	TM/L	G	W	L	PCT	STANDING			M/Y
1985	Tex-A	129	53	76	.411	7 W	7 W		2/2
1986	Tex-A	162	87	75	.537	2 W			
1987	Tex-A	162	75	87	.463	●6 W			
1988	Tex-A	161	70	91	.435	6 W			
	4	614	285	329	.464				

Van Haltren, George Edward

YEAR	TM/L	G	W	L	PCT	STANDING			M/Y
1892(1)	Bal-N*	11	1	10	.091	12	12		1/3

Vernon, James Barton "Mickey"

YEAR	TM/L	G	W	L	PCT	STANDING			M/Y
1961	Was-A	161	61	100	.379	●9			
1962	Was-A	162	60	101	.373	10			
1963	Was-A	40	14	26	.350	10	10		1/3
	3	363	135	227	.373				

Virdon, William Charles "Bill"

YEAR	TM/L	G	W	L	PCT	STANDING			M/Y
1972	Pit-N	155	96	59	.619	1 E			
1973	Pit-N	136	67	69	.493	2 E	3 E		1/2
1974	NY-A	162	89	73	.549	2 E			
1975	NY-A	104	53	51	.510	3 E	3 E		1/2
	Hou-N	35	17	17	.500	6 W	6 W		2/2
1976	Hou-N	162	80	82	.494	3 W			
1977	Hou-N	162	81	81	.500	3 W			
1978	Hou-N	162	74	88	.457	5 W			
1979	Hou-N	162	89	73	.549	2 W			
1980	Hou-N	163	93	70	.571	▲1 W			
1981(1)	Hou-N	57	28	29	.491	3 W			
(2)	Hou-N	53	33	20	.623	1 W			
1982	Hou-N	111	49	62	.441	5 W	5 W		1/2
1983	Mon-N	163	82	80	.506	3 E			
1984	Mon-N	131	64	67	.489	5 E	5 E		1/2
	13	1918	995	921	.519				

Vitt, Oscar Joseph "Ossie"

YEAR	TM/L	G	W	L	PCT	STANDING			M/Y
1938	Cle-A	153	86	66	.566	3			
1939	Cle-A	154	87	67	.565	3			
1940	Cle-A	155	89	65	.578	2			
	3	462	262	198	.570				

Von Der Ahe, Christian Frederick Wilhelm "Chris"

YEAR	TM/L	G	W	L	PCT	STANDING			M/Y
1895	StL-N	1	1	0	1.000	11	11	11	2/4
1896	StL-N	2	0	2	.000	10	11	11	3/5
1897	StL-N	14	2	12	.143	12	12		4/4
	3	17	3	14	.176				

Vukovich, John Christopher

YEAR	TM/L	G	W	L	PCT	STANDING			M/Y
1986	Chi-N	2	1	1	.500	5 E	5 E	5 E	2/3
1988	Phi-N	9	4	5	.444	6 E	6 E		2/2
	2	11	5	6	.455				

Wagner, Charles F. "Heinie"

YEAR	TM/L	G	W	L	PCT	STANDING			M/Y
1930	Bos-A	154	52	102	.338	8			

Wagner, John Peter "Honus"

YEAR	TM/L	G	W	L	PCT	STANDING			M/Y
1917	Pit-N*	5	1	4	.200	8	8	8	2/3

Walker, Harry William

YEAR	TM/L	G	W	L	PCT	STANDING			M/Y
1955	StL-N*	118	51	67	.432	5	7		2/2
1965	Pit-N	163	90	72	.556	3			
1966	Pit-N	162	92	70	.568	3			
1967	Pit-N	84	42	42	.500	6	6		1/2
1968	Hou-N	101	49	52	.485	10	10		2/2
1969	Hou-N	162	81	81	.500	5 W			
1970	Hou-N	162	79	83	.488	4 W			
1971	Hou-N	162	79	83	.488	●4 W			
1972	Hou-N	121	67	54	.554	2 W	2 W		1/3
	9	1235	630	604	.511				

Wallace, Roderick John "Bobby"

YEAR	TM/L	G	W	L	PCT	STANDING			M/Y
1911	StL-A*	152	45	107	.296	8			
1912	StL-A*	40	12	27	.308	8	7		1/2
1937	Cin-N	25	5	20	.200	8	8		2/2
	3	217	62	154	.287				

Walsh, Edward Augustine "Ed"

YEAR	TM/L	G	W	L	PCT	STANDING			M/Y
1924	Chi-A	3	1	2	.333	6			2/4

Walsh, Michael John "Mike"

YEAR	TM/L	G	W	L	PCT	STANDING			M/Y
1884	Lou-a	110	68	40	.630	3			

Walters, William Henry "Bucky"

YEAR	TM/L	G	W	L	PCT	STANDING			M/Y
1948	Cin-N*	53	20	33	.377	7	7		2/2
1949	Cin-N	153	61	90	.404	7	7		1/2
	2	206	81	123	.397				

Waltz, John J.

YEAR	TM/L	G	W	L	PCT	STANDING			M/Y
1892(1)	Bal-N	8	2	6	.250	12	12	12	2/3

Ward, John Montgomery "Monte"

YEAR	TM/L	G	W	L	PCT	STANDING			M/Y
1880	Pro-N*	32	18	13	.581	4	3		2/3
1884	NY-N*	16	6	8	.429	4	●4		2/2
1890	Bro-P*	133	76	56	.576	2			

YEAR	TM/L	G	W	L	PCT	STANDING			M/Y
1891	Bro-N*	137	61	76	.445	6			
1892(1)	Bro-N*	78	51	26	.662	2			
(2)	Bro-N*	80	44	33	.571	3			
1893	NY-N*	136	68	64	.515	5			
1894	NY-N*	139	88	44	.667	2			
7		751	412	320	.563				

Wathan, John David

YEAR	TM/L	G	W	L	PCT	STANDING			M/Y
1987	KC-A	36	21	15	.583	4 W	2 W		2/2
1988	KC-A	161	84	77	.522	3 W			
2		197	105	92	.533				

Watkins, Harvey L.

1895	NY-N	35	18	17	.514	9	9		3/3

Watkins, William Henry "Bill"

YEAR	TM/L	G	W	L	PCT	STANDING			M/Y
1884	Ind-a*	23	4	18	.182	10	11		2/2
1885	Det-N	70	34	36	.486	8	6		2/2
1886	Det-N	126	87	36	.707	2			
1887	Det-N	126	79	45	.637	1			
1888	Det-N	94	49	44	.527	3	5		1/2
	KC-a	25	8	17	.320	8	8		3/3
1889	KC-a	139	55	82	.401	7			
1893	StL-N	135	57	75	.432	10			
1898	Pit-N	151	72	76	.486	8			
1899	Pit-N	24	7	15	.318	10	7		1/2
9		913	452	444	.504				

Weaver, Earl Sidney

YEAR	TM/L	G	W	L	PCT	STANDING			M/Y
1968	Bal-A	82	48	34	.585	3	2		2/2
1969	Bal-A	162	109	53	.673	♦1 E			
1970	Bal-A	162	108	54	.667	★1 E			
1971	Bal-A	158	101	57	.639	♦1 E			
1972	Bal-A	154	80	74	.519	3 E			
1973	Bal-A	162	97	65	.599	1 E			
1974	Bal-A	162	91	71	.562	1 E			
1975	Bal-A	159	90	69	.566	2 E			
1976	Bal-A	162	88	74	.543	2 E			
1977	Bal-A	161	97	64	.602	●2 E			
1978	Bal-A	161	90	71	.559	4 E			
1979	Bal-A	159	102	57	.642	♦1 E			
1980	Bal-A	162	100	62	.617	2 E			
1981(1)	Bal-A	54	31	23	.574	2 E			
(2)	Bal-A	51	28	23	.549	4 E			
1982	Bal-A	163	94	68	.580	2 E			
1985	Bal-A	105	53	52	.505	4 E	4 E		3/3
1986	Bal-A	162	73	89	.451	7 E			
17		2541	1480	1060	.583				

Westrum, Wesley Noreen "Wes"

YEAR	TM/L	G	W	L	PCT	STANDING			M/Y
1965	NY-N	68	19	48	.284	10	10		2/2
1966	NY-N	161	66	95	.410	9			
1967	NY-N	151	57	94	.377	10	10		1/2
1974	SF-N	86	38	48	.442	5 W	5 W		2/2
1975	SF-N	161	80	81	.497	3 W			
5		627	260	366	.415				

Wheeler, Harry Eugene

1884	KC-U*	4	0	4	.000	8	8		1/3

White, James Laurie "Deacon"

YEAR	TM/L	G	W	L	PCT	STANDING			M/Y
1872	Cle-n*	2	0	2	.000	5	7		2/2
1879	Cin-N*	18	9	9	.500	4	5		1/2
2		20	9	11	.450				

White, Joyner Clifford "Jo-Jo"

1960	Cle-A	1	1	0	1.000	4	4	4	2/3

White, William Henry "Will"

1884	Cin-a*	72	44	27	.620	5			1/2

White, William Warren "Warren"

1874	Bal-n*	47	9	38	.191	8			

Wilber, Delbert Quentin "Del"

1973	Tex-A	1	1	0	1.000	6 W	6 W	6 W	2/3

Wilhelm, Irvin Key "Kaiser"

YEAR	TM/L	G	W	L	PCT	STANDING			M/Y
1921	Phi-N*	67	26	41	.388	8	8		2/2
1922	Phi-N	154	57	96	.373	7			
2		221	83	137	.377				

Williams, James A. "Jimmy"

YEAR	TM/L	G	W	L	PCT	STANDING			M/Y
1884	StL-a	85	51	33	.607	5	4		1/2
1887	Cle-a	133	39	92	.298	8			
1888	Cle-a	64	20	44	.313	8	6		1/2
3		282	110	169	.394				

Williams, James Francis "Jimy"

YEAR	TM/L	G	W	L	PCT	STANDING			M/Y
1986	Tor-A	163	86	76	.531	4 E			
1987	Tor-A	162	96	66	.593	2 E			
1988	Tor-A	162	87	75	.537	●3 E			
3		487	269	217	.553				

Williams, Richard Hirschfeld "Dick"

YEAR	TM/L	G	W	L	PCT	STANDING			M/Y
1967	Bos-A	162	92	70	.568	1			
1968	Bos-A	162	86	76	.531	4			
1969	Bos-A	153	82	71	.536	3 E	3 E		1/2
1971	Oak-A	161	101	60	.627	1 W			
1972	Oak-A	155	93	62	.600	★1 W			
1973	Oak-A	162	94	68	.580	★1 W			
1974	Cal-A	84	36	48	.429	6 W	6 W		3/3
1975	Cal-A	161	72	89	.447	6 W			
1976	Cal-A	96	39	57	.406	6 W	●4 W		1/2
1977	Mon-N	162	75	87	.463	5 E			
1978	Mon-N	162	76	86	.469	4 E			
1979	Mon-N	160	95	65	.594	2 E			
1980	Mon-N	162	90	72	.556	2 E			
1981(1)	Mon-N	55	30	25	.545	3 E			
(2)	Mon-N	26	14	12	.538	2 E	1 E		1/2
1982	SD-N	162	81	81	.500	4 W			
1983	SD-N	163	81	81	.500	4 W			
1984	SD-N	162	92	70	.568	♦1 W			
1985	SD-N	162	83	79	.512	●3 W			
1986	Sea-A	133	58	75	.436	6 W	7 W		3/3
1987	Sea-A	162	78	84	.481	4 W			
1988	Sea-A	56	23	33	.411	6 W	7 W		1/2
21		3023	1571	1451	.520				

Williams, Theodore Samuel "Ted"

YEAR	TM/L	G	W	L	PCT	STANDING			M/Y
1969	Was-A	162	86	76	.531	4 E			
1970	Was-A	162	70	92	.432	6 E			
1971	Was-A	159	63	96	.396	5 E			
1972	Tex-A	154	54	100	.351	6 W			
4		637	273	364	.429				

Wills, Maurice Morning "Maury"

YEAR	TM/L	G	W	L	PCT	STANDING			M/Y
1980	Sea-A	58	20	38	.345	6 W	7 W		2/2
1981(1)	Sea-A	25	6	18	.250	7 W	6 W		1/2
2		83	26	56	.317				

Wilson, James "Jimmie"

YEAR	TM/L	G	W	L	PCT	STANDING			M/Y
1934	Phi-N*	149	56	93	.376	7			
1935	Phi-N*	156	64	89	.418	7			
1936	Phi-N*	154	54	100	.351	8			
1937	Phi-N*	155	61	92	.399	7			
1938	Phi-N*	149	45	103	.304	8	8		1/2
1941	Chi-N	155	70	84	.455	6			
1942	Chi-N	155	68	86	.442	6			
1943	Chi-N	154	74	79	.484	5			
1944	Chi-N	10	1	9	.100	8	4		1/3
9		1237	493	735	.401				

Wine, Robert Paul Sr. "Bobby"

1985	Atl-N	41	16	25	.390	5 W	5 W		2/2

Wingo, Ivey Brown

1916	Cin-N*	2	1	1	.500	8	8	●7	2/3

Winkles, Bobby Brooks

YEAR	TM/L	G	W	L	PCT	STANDING			M/Y
1973	Cal-A	162	79	83	.488	4 W			
1974	Cal-A	75	30	44	.405	6 W	6 W		1/3
1977	Oak-A	108	37	71	.343	●5 W	7 W		2/2
1978	Oak-A	39	24	15	.615	1 W	6 W		1/2
4		384	170	213	.444				

Wolf, William Van Winkle "Chicken"

1889	Lou-a*	65	14	51	.215	8	8	8	2/4

Wolverton, Harry Sterling

1912	NY-A*	153	50	102	.329	8			

Wood, George A.

1891	Phi-a*	125	67	55	.549	7	4		2/2

Wood, James Leon "Jimmy"

YEAR	TM/L	G	W	L	PCT	STANDING			M/Y
1871	Chi-n*	28	19	9	.679	2			
1872	Tro-n*	25	15	10	.600	5			
	Eck-n*	18	3	15	.167	9	10		2/2
1873	Phi-n*	43	28	15	.651	2	2		2/2
1874	Chi-n	23	10	13	.435	4	5		2/2
1875	Chi-n	69	30	37	.448	6			
5		206	105	99	.515				

Wright, Alfred Hector "Al"

1876	Phi-N	60	14	45	.237	7			

Wright, George

1879	Pro-N*	85	59	25	.702	1			

Wright, William Henry "Harry"

YEAR	TM/L	G	W	L	PCT	STANDING			M/Y
1871	Bos-n*	31	20	10	.667	3			
1872	Bos-n*	48	39	8	.830	1			
1873	Bos-n*	60	43	16	.729	1			
1874	Bos-n*	71	52	18	.743	1			
1875	Bos-n*	82	71	8	.899	1			
1876	Bos-N*	70	39	31	.557	4			
1877	Bos-N*	61	42	18	.700	1			
1878	Bos-N*	60	41	19	.683	1			
1879	Bos-N	84	54	30	.643	2			
1880	Bos-N	86	40	44	.476	6			
1881	Bos-N	83	38	45	.458	6			
1882	Pro-N	84	52	32	.619	2			
1883	Pro-N	98	58	40	.592	3			
1884	Phi-N	113	39	73	.348	6			
1885	Phi-N	111	56	54	.509	3			
1886	Phi-N	119	71	43	.623	4			
1887	Phi-N	128	75	48	.610	2			
1888	Phi-N	132	69	61	.531	3			

YEAR	TM/L	G	W	L	PCT	STANDING			M/Y
1889	Phi-N	130	63	64	.496	3			
1890	Phi-N	22	14	8	.636	1	3		1/5
	Phi-N	46	22	23	.489	2	3		5/5
1891	Phi-N	138	68	69	.496	4			
1892(1)	Phi-N	77	46	30	.605	3			
(2)	Phi-N	78	41	36	.532	5			
1893	Phi-N	133	72	57	.558	4			
	23	2145	1225	885	.581				

York, Preston Rudolph "Rudy"

YEAR	TM/L	G	W	L	PCT	STANDING			M/Y
1959	Bos-A	1	0	1	.000	8	8	5	2/3

York, Thomas J. "Tom"

YEAR	TM/L	G	W	L	PCT	STANDING			M/Y
1878	Pro-N*	62	33	27	.550	3			
1881	Pro-N*	34	23	10	.697	4	2		2/2
	2	96	56	37	.602				

Yost, Edward Frederick "Eddie"

YEAR	TM/L	G	W	L	PCT	STANDING			M/Y
1963	Was-A	1	0	1	.000	10	10	10	2/3

Young, Denton True "Cy"

YEAR	TM/L	G	W	L	PCT	STANDING			M/Y
1907	Bos-A*	6	3	3	.500	●4	7		1/4

Young, Nicholas Ephraim "Nick"

YEAR	TM/L	G	W	L	PCT	STANDING			M/Y
1871	Oly-n	32	15	15	.500	5			
1872	Oly-n	9	2	7	.222	10			
1873	Nat-n	39	8	31	.205	7			
	3	80	25	53	.321				

Zimmer, Charles Louis "Chief"

YEAR	TM/L	G	W	L	PCT	STANDING			M/Y
1903	Phi-N*	139	49	86	.363	7			

Zimmer, Donald William "Don"

YEAR	TM/L	G	W	L	PCT	STANDING			M/Y
1972	SD-N	142	54	88	.380	4 W	6 W		2/2
1973	SD-N	162	60	102	.370	6 W			
1976	Bos-A	76	42	34	.553	5 E	3 E		2/2
1977	Bos-A	161	97	64	.602	●2 E			
1978	Bos-A	163	99	64	.607	▲2 E			
1979	Bos-A	160	91	69	.569	3 E			
1980	Bos-A	155	82	73	.529	3 E	4 E		1/2
1981(1)	Tex-A	55	33	22	.600	2 W			
(2)	Tex-A	50	24	26	.480	3 W			
1982	Tex-A	96	38	58	.396	6 W	6 W		1/2
1988	Chi-N	163	77	85	.475	4 E			
	10	1383	697	685	.504				

The Coach Roster

In an age of ever greater specialization in baseball, coaches have become increasingly important to the successful management of a team. The need for such assistance did not occur to any manager until John McGraw took on Arlie Latham as baseball's first full-time coach in 1909; today, teams employ separate coaches for first base, third base, pitching, the bullpen, hitting, baserunning, strength, conditioning, and more. Some coaches, like Charlie Lau and Roger Craig, have achieved fame exceeding that of the managers under whom they served. But coaches leave no statistical trail by which to track them. Players and pitchers have official records, and so do managers, but the accomplishments of coaches (and umpires) have until now resided largely in memory.

The Coach Roster that follows represents a first attempt in a baseball encyclopedia to recognize these foot soldiers, who too often serve as scapegoats when a team fails but are invisible when it succeeds. We offer the roster in full knowledge that there are gaps and probably gaffes in our research; we hope that our readers will advise us of omissions so that we can improve this roster in future editions of *Total Baseball*.

The principal sources of the data herein are, for 1921–1939, the *Baseball Blue Book*; for 1940–1981, the *Baseball Register*; and for years since 1982, the *American League Red Book* and the *National League Green Book*. We have done our best to reconcile the many differences among the lists. The team and league abbreviations used in the Coach Roster are found on the final page of this book.

For a prose account of the history of coaches (and managers), see the feature article by Fred Stein.

Aaron, Tommie Lee Atl-N 1979-84

Adair, James A. "Jimmy" Chi-A 1951-52, Bal-A 1957-61, Hou-N 1962-65

Adair, K. Jerry Oak-A 1972-74, Cal-A 1975

Adair, Marion D. "Bill" Mil-N 1962, Atl-N 1967, Chi-A 1970, Mon-N 1976

Adams, Charles D. "Red" LA-N 1969-80

Adams, Robert H. "Bobby" Chi-N 1961-64

Aguirre, Henry J. "Hank" Chi-N 1972-74

Aker, Jack D. Cle-A 1985-87

Alomar, Santos C. "Sandy" SD-N 1986-88

Alou, Felipe R. Mon-N 1979-80, 1984

Alou, Jesus M. R. Hou-N 1979

Altobelli, Joseph S. "Joe" NY-A 1981-82, 1986, Chi-N 1988

Altrock, Nicholas "Nick" Was-A 1912-53

Amalfitano, J. Joseph "Joey" Chi-N 1967-71, SF-N 1972-75, SD-N 1976-77, Chi-N 1978-80, Cin-N 1982, LA-N 1983-88

Amaro, Ruben Phi-N 1980-81, Chi-N 1983-86

Anderson, George L. "Sparky" SD-N 1969

Appling, Lucius B. "Luke" Det-A 1960, Cle-A 1960-61, Bal-A 1963, KC-A 1964-67, Chi-A 1970-71

Auferio, Tony StL-N 1973

Austin, James P. "Jimmy" StL-A 1923-32, Chi-A 1933-40

Babe, Loren R. NY-A 1967, Chi-A 1980, 1983

Bader, Loren V. Bos-N 1926

Baker, Delmer D. "Del" Det-A 1933-38, Cle-A 1943-44, Bos-A 1945-48, 1953-60

Baker, Eugene W. "Gene" Pit-N 1963

Baker, Floyd W. Min-A 1961-64

Baker, Johnnie B "Dusty" SF-N 1988

Baker, William P. Chi-N 1950

Bamberger, George I. Bal-A 1968-77

Bancroft, David J. "Dave" NY-N 1930-32

Bando, Salvatore L. "Sal" Mil-A 1981

Banks, Ernest "Ernie" Chi-N 1967-73

Bartell, Richard W. "Dick" Det-A 1949-52, Cin-N 1954-55

Bartirome, Anthony J. "Tony" Atl-N 1986-88

Basgall, Romanus "Monty" LA-N 1973-86

Bassler, John L. "Johnny" Cle-A 1938-40, StL-A 1941

Bauer, Henry A. "Hank" Bal-A 1963

Bearnarth, Lawrence D. "Larry" Mon-N 1976, 1985-88

Beck, Walter W. "Boom-Boom" Was-A 1957-59

Becker, Joseph E. "Joe" Bro-N 1955-57, LA-N 1958-64, StL-N 1965-66, Chi-N 1967-70

Bedell, Howard W. "Howie" KC-A 1984, SE-A 1988

Bender, Charles A. "Chief" Chi-A 1925-26, NY-N 1931, Phi-A 1951-53

Bengough, Bernard O. "Benny" Was-N 1940-43, Bos-N 1945, Phi-N 1946-58

Benson, Vernon A. "Vern" StL-N 1961-64, NY-A 1965-66, Cin-N 1966-69, StL-N 1970-75, Atl-N 1976-77, SF-N 1980

Berg, Morris "Moe" Bos-A 1939-41

Beringer, Carroll J. LA-N 1967-72, Phi-N 1973-78

Berra, Lawrence P. "Yogi" NY-N 1965-71, NY-A 1976-83, Hou-N 1986-88

Berres, Raymond F. "Ray" Chi-A 1949-66, 1968-69

Berry, Charles F. "Charlie" Phi-A 1936-40

Bissonette, Adelphia L. "Del" Bos-N 1945, Pit-N 1946

Blackburn, Wayne C. Det-A 1963-64

Blackburne, Russell A. "Lena" Chi-A 1927-28, StL-A 1930, Phi-A 1933-40, 1942-43

Blades, F Raymond "Ray" StL-N 1930-32, Cin-N 1942, Bro-N 1947-48, StL-N 1951, Chi-N 1953-56

Blaylock, Gary N. KC-A 1984-87

Bloomfield, Gordon L. "Jack" SD-N 1974, Chi-N 1975-76

Bluege, Oswald L. "Ossie" Was-A 1940-42

Bonds, Bobby L. Cle-A 1984-87

Boros, Stephen "Steve" KC-A 1975-79, Mon-N 1981-82

Bosman, Richard A. "Dick" Chi-A 1986-87

Bottomley, James L. "Jim" StL-A 1937

Bowa, Lawrence R. "Larry" Phi-N 198

Boyer, Cletis L. "Clete" Oak-A 1980-85, NY-A 1988

Boyer, Cloyd V. NY-A 1977, Atl-N 1978-81, KC-A 1982-83

Boyer, Kenton L. "Ken" StL-N 1971-72

Bragan, James A. "Jimmy" Cin-N 1967-69, Mon-N 1970-72, Mil-A 1976-77

Bragan, Robert R. "Bobby" LA-N 1960, Hou-N 1962

Brecheen, Harry D. Bal-A 1954-67

Breeden, H. Scott Cin-N 1986-88

Bresnahan, Roger P. NY-N 1925-28, Det-A 1930-31

Brewer, James T. "Jim" Mon-N 1977-79

Bridges, Everett L. "Rocky" LA-A 1962-63, Cal-A 1968-71, SF-N 1985

Bridges, Thomas J. "Tommy" Det-A 1946

Brinkman, Edwin A. "Ed" Det-A 1979, SD-N 1981, Chi-A 1983-88

Bristol, J. David "Dave" Cin-N 1966, Mon-N 1973-75, SF-N 1978-79, Phi-N 1982-85, 1988

Brown, Jackie G. Tex-A 1979-82

Brown, James R. "Jimmy" Bos-N 1949-51

Brown, Mace S. Bos-A 1965

Brown, William J. "Gates" Det-A 1978-84

Brucker, Earle F., Sr. Phi-A 1941-49, StL-A 1950-51, Cin-N 1952

Bryant, Claiborne H. "Clay" LA-N 1961, Cle-A 1967, 1974

Bryant, Donald R. "Don" Bos-A 1974-76, Sea-A 1977-80

Buford, Donald A. "Don" SF-N 1981-84, Bal-A 1988

Bumbry, Alonza B. "Al" Bos-A 1988

Burdette, S. Lewis "Lew" Atl-N 1972-73

Burgess, Thomas R. "Tom" NY-N 1977

Burke, James T. "Jimmy" Bos-A 1921-23, Chi-N 1926-30, NY-A 1931-34

Burns, George J. NY-N 1931

Burns, John I. "Jack" Bos-A 1955-59

Burwell, William E. "Bill" Bos-A 1944, Pit-N 1947-48, 1958-62

Busby, James F. "Jim" Bal-A 1961, Hou-N 1962, 1963-67, Atl-N 1968-75, Chi-A 1976, Sea-A 1977

Butler, John S. "Johnny" Chi-A 1932

Camacho, Joseph G. "Joe" Was-A 1969-71, Tex-A 1972

Camilli, Douglas J. "Doug" Was-A 1968-69, Bos-A 1970-73

Cannizzaro, Christopher "Chris" Atl-N 1976-78

Carey, Max G. Pit-N 1930

Carey, Thomas F. "Tom" Bos-A 1946-47

Carisch, Frederick B. "Fred" Det-A 1923-24

Carnevale, Daniel J. "Danny" KC-A 1970

Carrion, Leonel Mon-N 1988

Carter, Richard J. "Dick" Phi-N 1959-60

Case, George W. Was-A 1961-63, Min-A 1968

Cavarretta, Philip J. "Phil" Det-A 1961-63, NY-N 1978

Cepeda, Orlando M. Chi-A 1980

Chambliss, C. Christopher "Chris" NY-A 1988

Chandler, Spurgeon F. "Spud" KC-A 1957-58

Chapman, W. Benjamin "Ben" Cin-N 1952

Chesbro, John D. "Jack" Was-A 192

Cisco, Galen B. KC-A 1971-79, Mon-N 1980-84, SD-N 1985-87, Tor-A 1988

Clark, Ronald B. "Ron" Chi-A 1988

Clarke, Thomas A. "Tommy" NY-N 1932-35, 1938

Clary, Ellis Was-A 1955-60

Clear, E. Robert "Bob" Cal-A 1976-87

Clines, Eugene A. "Gene" Chi-N 1979-81, Hou-N 1988

Cluck, Robert "Bob" Hou-N 1979

Clymer, William J. "Bill" Cin-N 1925

Cochrane, Gordon S. "Mickey" Phi-A 1950

Cohen, Andrew H. "Andy" Phi-N 1960

Colavito, Rocco D. "Rocky" Cle-A 1973, 1976-78, KC-A 1982-83

Cole, Richard R. "Dick" Chi-N 1961

Coleman, Joseph H. "Joe" Cal-A 1988

Coleman, Robert H. "Bob" Bos-A 1928, Bos-N 1943

Collins, Edward T. "Eddie" Phi-A 1932-33

Collins, James A. "Rip" Chi-N 1961-63

Combs, Earle B. NY-A 1935-44, StL-A 1947, Bos-A 1948-52, Phi-N 1954

Combs, Merrill R. Tex-A 1974-75

Connor, Mark P. NY-A 1984-85, 1986-87

Connors, William J. "Billy" KC-A 1980-81, Chi-N 1982-86, Sea-A 1987-88

Conroy, William E. "Wid" Phi-N 1922

Consolo, William A. "Billy" Det-A 1979-88

Cooke, Allen L. "Dusty" Phi-N 1948-52

Cooney, John W. "Johnny" Bos-N 1940-42, 1946-49, 1950-52, Mil-N 1953-55, Chi-A 1957-64

Cooper, Walker W. StL-N 1957, KC-A 1960

Corrales, Patrick E. "Pat" Tex-A 1975-78

Corriden, John M., Sr "Red" Chi-N 1932-40, Bro-N 1941-46, NY-A 1947-48, Chi-A 1950

Cottier, Charles K. "Chuck" NY-N 1979-81, Sea-A 1982-84, Chi-N 1988

Courtney, Clinton D. "Clint" Hou-N 1965

Cox, Larry E. Chi-N 1988

Cox, Robert J. "Bobby" NY-A 1977

Crabtree, Estel C. Cin-N 1943-45

Craft, Harry F. KC-A 1955-57, Chi-N 1960-61

Craig, Roger L. SD-N 1969-72, Hou-N 1974-75, SD-N 1976-77, Det-A 1980-84

Cramer, Roger M. "Doc" Det-A 1948, Chi-A 1951-53

Crandall, Delmar W. "Del" Cal-A 1977

Crandall, J. Otis "Doc" Pit-N 1931-34

Cravath, Clifford C. "Gavvy" Phi-N 1923

Cresse, Mark E. LA-N 1977-88

Crosetti, Frank P. J. "Frankie" NY-A 1947-68, Sea-A 1969, Min-N 1970-71

Crowley, Terrence M. "Terry" Bal-A 1985-88

Cuccinello, Anthony F. "Tony" Cin-N 1949-51, Cle-A 1952-56, Chi-A 1957-66, Det-A 1967-68, Chi-A 1969

Culp, Benjamin B. "Benny" Phi-N 1947

Cunningham, Joseph R. "Joe" StL-N 1982

Cunningham, William A. "Bill" Chi-A 1932

Cuyler, Hazen S. "Kiki" Chi-N 1942-43, Bos-A 1949

Dahlgren, Ellsworth T. "Babe" KC-A 1964

Dal Canton, J. Bruce Atl-N 1987-88

Daly, Thomas D. "Tom" Bos-A 1933-46

Dark, Alvin R. Chi-N 1965, 1977

Davenport, James H. "Jim" SF-N 1970, SD-N 1974-75, SF-N 1976-82, 1984, Phi-N 1986-87

Davis, H. Thomas "Tommy" Sea-A 1981

Davis, R. Brandon "Brandy" Phi-N 1972

Davis, Virgil L. "Spud" Pit-N 1942-46, Chi-N 1950-53

Deal, Ellis "Cot" Cin-N 1959-60, Hou-N 1962-64, NY-A 1965, KC-A 1966-67, Cle-A 1970-71, Det-A 1973-74, Hou-N 1983-85

DeMars, William L. "Billy" Phi-N 1969-81, Mon-N 1982-84, Cin-N 1985-87

Demeter, Stephen "Steve" Pit-N 1985

Devlin, Arthur M. "Art" Bos-N 1926, 1928

Dews, Robert W. "Bobby" Atl-N 1979-81, 1985

Dickey, William M. "Bill" NY-A 1949-57, 1960

Didier, Robert D. "Bob" Oak-A 1984-86

DiMaggio, Joseph P. "Joe" Oak-A 1968-69

Dobson, Joseph G. "Joe" Bos-A 1954

Dobson, Patrick E. "Pat" Mil-A 1982-84, SD-N 1988

Doby, Lawrence E. "Larry" Mon-N 1971-73, Cle-A 1974, Mon-N 1976, Chi-A 1977-78

Doerr, Robert P. "Bobby" Bos-A 1967-69, Tor-A 1977-81

Dolan, Albert J. "Cozy" NY-N 1922-24

Donnelly, Richard F. "Rich" Tex-A 1980, 1983-85, Pit-N 1986-88

Doolan, Michael J. "Mickey" Chi-N 1926-29, Cin-N 1930-32

Dorish, Harry "Fritz" Bos-A 1963, Atl-N 1968-71

Down, Richard J. "Rick" Cal-A 1987-88

Drabowsky, Myron W. "Moe" Chi-A 1986

Dressen, Charles W. "Chuck" Bro-N 1939-42, 1943-46, NY-A 1947-48, LA-N 1958-59

Dubuc, Jean A. Det-A 1931

Duffy, Hugh Bos-A 1932

Dugey, Oscar J. Chi-N 1921-24

Duncan, David E. "Dave" Cle-A 1978-81, Sea-A 1982, Chi-A 1983-86, Oak-A 1986-88

Dunlop, Harry A. KC-A 1969-75, Chi-N 1976, Cin-N 1979-82, SD-N 1983-86

Durocher, Leo E. LA-N 1961-64

Dusan, Gene NY-N 1983

Dyer, Don R. "Duffy" Chi-N 1983

Dykes, James J. "Jimmy" Phi-N 1949-50, Cin-N 1955-58, Pit-N 1959, Mil-N 1962, KC-A 1963-64

Earnshaw, George L. Phi-N 1949-50

Easter, L. Luke Cle-A 1969

Edwards, Howard R. "Doc" Phi-N 1970-72, Cle-A 1985-87

Egan, Arthur A. "Ben" Bro-N 1925, Chi-A 1926

Egan, Richard W. "Dick" Tex-A 1968

Elia, Lee C. Phi-N 1980-81, 1985-87

Elliott, Robert I. "Bob" LA-A 1961

Ellis, Samuel J. "Sammy" NY-A 1982, 1984, 1986

Emery, Calvin W. "Cal" Chi-A 1988

Ens, Jewel W. Pit-N 1926-29, Det-A 1932, Cin-N 1933, Bos-N 1934, Pit-N 1935-39, Cin-N 1941

Ermer, Calvin C. "Cal" Bal-A 1962, Mil-A 1970-71, Oak-A 1977

Estrada, Charles L. "Chuck" Tex-A 1973, SD-N 1974-88

Etchebarren, Andrew A. "Andy" Cal-A 1977, Mil-A 1984-88

Evers, John J. "Johnny" NY-N 1920, Chi-A 1922-23, Chi-N 1929-32

Evers, Walter A. "Hoot" Cle-A 1970

Ezell, Glenn W. Tex-A 1983-85

Faber, Urban C. "Red" Chi-A 1946-48

Fahey, William R. "Bill" SF-N 1986-88

Falk, Bibb A. Cle-A 1933, Bos-A 1934

Farrell, M. Kerby   Chi-A 1966-69, Cle-A 1970-71
Felske, John F.   Tor-A 1980-81, Phi-N 1984
Ferguson, Joseph V. "Joe"   Tex-A 1986-87
Ferraro, Michael D. "Mike"   NY-A 1979-81, KC-A 1984-86, NY-A 1987-88
Ferrell, Richard B. "Rick"   Was-A 1946-49, Det-A 1950-53
Ferrick, Thomas J. "Tom"   Cin-N 1954-58, Phi-N 1959, Det-A 1960-63, KC-A 1964-65
Ferriss, David M. "Dave"   Bos-A 1955-59
Fischer, William C. "Bill"   Cin-N 1979-83, Bos-A 1985-88
Fitzgerald, Edward R. "Ed"   Cle-A 1960, KC-A 1961, Min-A 1962-64
Fitzgerald, Joseph P. "Joe"   Was-A 1947-57
Fitzpatrick, John A.   Pit-N 1953-56, Mil-N 1958-59
Fitzsimmons, Fred L. "Freddie"   Bro-N 1942, Bos-N 1948, NY-N 1949-53, 1954-55, Chi-N 1957-59, KC-A 1960, Chi-N 1966
Fletcher, Arthur "Art"   NY-A 1927-45
Flowers, D'Arcy R. "Jake"   Pit-N 1940-42, 1944-45, Bos-N 1946, Cle-A 1951-52
Foli, Timothy J. "Tim"   Tex-A 1986-87
Ford, Edward C. "Whitey"   NY-A 1968, 1974-75
Fowler, J. Arthur "Art"   LA-A 1964, Min-A 1969, Det-A 1971-73, Tex-A 1973-75, NY-A 1977-79, Oak-A 1980-82, NY-A 1983, 1988
Fox, Charles F. "Charlie"   SF-N 1965-68
Fox, J. Nelson "Nellie"   Hou-N 1965, 1966-67, Was-A 1968-71, Tex-A 1972
Franks, Herman L.   NY-N 1949-55, SF-N 1958
Fraser, Charles C. "Chick"   Pit-N 1923
Frey, James G. "Jim"   Bal-A 1970-79, NY-N 1982-83
Friend, Owen L.   KC-A 1969
Frisch, Frank F. "Frankie"   NY-N 1949
Funk, Franklin R. "Frank"   SF-N 1976, Sea-A 1980-81, 1983-86, KC-A 1988
Galan, August J. "Augie"   Phi-A 1954
Galante, Matthew "Matt"   Hou-N 1985-88
Garcia, David "Dave"   SD-N 1970-73, Cle-A 1975-76, Cal-A 1977, Cle-A 1979, Mil-A 1983-84
Gardner, William F. "Billy"   Bos-A 1965-66, Mon-N 1977-78, Min-A 1981
Garrett, H. Adrian   KC-A 1988
Garrison, R. Ford   Cin-N 1953
Gaston, Clarence E.   Tor-A 1982-88
Gebhard, Robert H. "Bob"   Mon-N 1982
Gehringer, Charles L. "Charlie"   Det-A 1942
Gernert, Richard E. "Dick"   Tex-A 1976
Gharrity, E. Patrick "Patsy"   Was-A 1929-31, Cle-A 1934-35
Gibson, George   Was-A 1923, Chi-N 1925-26
Gibson, Robert   NY-N 1981, Atl-N 1982-84
Gilbert, Andrew "Andy"   SF-N 1972-75
Gilliam, James "Jim"   LA-N 1965-78
Gladding, Fred E.   Det-A 1976-78
Gleason, William J. "Kid"   Phi-A 1926-32
Gleeson, James J. "Jim"   KC-A 1957, NY-A 1964
Gomez, Pedro W. "Preston"   LA-N 1965-68, Hou-N 1973, StL-N 1976, LA-N 1977-79, Cal-A 1981-84
Gonzalez, Miguel A. "Mike"   StL-N 1934-46
Gooch, John B. "Johnny"   Pit-N 1937-39
Goodman, William D. "Billy"   Atl-N 1968-70
Gordon, Joseph L. "Joe"   Det-A 1956
Goryl, John A. "Johnny"   Min-A 1968-69, 1979-80, Cle-A 1981-88
Gowdy, Harry "Hank"   Bos-N 1929-37, Cin-N 1938-42, 1945-46, NY-N 1947-48
Graff, Milton E. "Milt"   Pit-N 1985
Grammas, Alexander P. "Alex"   Pit-N 1965-69, Cin-N 1970-75, 1978, Atl-N 1979, Det-A 1980-88
Grimes, Burleigh A.   KC-A 1955
Grimm, Charles J. "Charlie"   Chi-N 1941, 1961-62
Grissom, Marvin E. "Marv"   LA-A 1961-65, Cal-A 1966, Chi-A 1967-68, Cal-A 1969, Min-A 1970-71, Chi-N 1975-76, Cal-A 1977-78
Grodzicki, John   Det-A 1979
Guerrero, Epy   Tor-A 1981
Gutteridge, Donald J. "Don"   Chi-A 1955-66, 1968-69
Haas, G. Edward "Eddie"   Atl-N 1974-77, 198
Haas, George W. "Mule"   Chi-A 1940-46
Hack, Stanley C. "Stan"   StL-A 1957-58
Hacker, Richard W. "Rich"   StL-N 1986-88
Haddix, Harvey   NY-A 1966-67, Cin-N 1969, Bos-A 1971, Cle-A 1975-78, Pit-N 1979-84
Haines, Jesse J.   Bro-N 1938
Hairston, Samuel "Sam"   Chi-A 1978
Haller, Thomas F. "Tom"   SF-N 1977-79
Hamilton, Steve A.   Det-A 1975
Hancken, Morris M. "Buddy"   Hou-N 1968-72
Haney, Fred G.   Mil-N 1956

Haney, W. Larry   Mil-A 1978-88
Hansen, Ronald L. "Ron"   Mil-A 1980-83, Mon-N 1985-88
Harder, Melvin L. "Mel"   Cle-A 1947, 1949-63, NY-N 1964, Chi-N 1965, Cin-N 1966-68, KC-A 1969
Harmon, Thomas "Tom"   Chi-N 1982
Harper, Tommy   Bos-A 1980-84
Harrelson, Derrel M. "Bud"   NY-N 1982, 1985-88
Harris, C. Luman "Lum"   Chi-A 1951-54, Bal-A 1955-61, Hou-N 1962-64
Hart, John H.   Bal-A 1988
Hartenstein, Charles O. "Chuck"   Cle-A 1979, Mil-A 1987-88
Hartley, Grover A.   Cle-A 1929-31, Pit-N 1932-33, StL-A 1934-36
Hartnett, Charles L. "Gabby"   Chi-N 1938, NY-N 1941, KC-A 1965
Hartsfield, Roy T.   LA-N 1969-72, Atl-N 1973
Hatfield, Fred J.   Det-A 1977-78
Hatton, Grady E.   Chi-N 1960, Hou-N 1973-74
Haynes, Joseph W. "Joe"   Was-A 1953-55
Hayworth, Raymond H. "Ray"   Bro-N 1945
Heffner, Donald H. "Don"   KC-A 1958-60, Det-A 1961, NY-N 1964-65, Cal-A 1967-68
Hegan, James E. "Jim"   NY-A 1960-73, Det-A 1974-78, NY-A 1979-80
Heilmann, Harry E.   Cin-N 1932
Heist, Alfred M. "Al"   Hou-N 1966-67, SD-N 1980
Helms, Tommy V.   Tex-A 1981-82, Cin-N 1983-88
Helmsley, Ralston B. "Rollie"   Phi-A 1954, Was-A 1961-62
Hemus, Solomon J. "Solly"   NY-N 1962-63, Cle-A 1964-65
Hendricks, Elrod J.   Bal-A 1978-88
Henrich, Thomas D. "Tommy"   NY-A 1951, NY-N 1957, Det-A 1958-59
Herman, Floyd C. "Babe"   Pit-N 1951
Herman, William J. "Billy"   Pit-N 1952-57, Mil-N 1958-59, Bos-A 1960-64, Cal-A 1967, SD-N 1978-79
Herzog, Dorrell N. E. "Whitey"   KC-A 1965, NY-N 1966, Cal-A 1974-75
Hiatt, Jack E.   Chi-N 1981
High, Andrew A. "Andy"   Bro-N 1937-38
Hill, Marc K.   Hou-N 1988
Hiller, Charles J. "Chuck"   Tex-A 1973, KC-A 1976-79, StL-N 1981-83, SF-N 1985
Hilton, J. David "Dave"   Mil-A 1987-88
Himsl, Avitus B. "Vedie"   Chi-N 1960-64
Hinchman, William W. "Bill"   Pit-N 1923
Hines, Ben T.   Sea-A 1984
Hitchcock, William C. "Billy"   Det-A 1955-60, Atl-N 1966
Hoak, Donald A. "Don"   Phi-N 1967
Hofman, Robert G. "Bobby"   KC-A 1966-67, Was-A 1968, Oak-A 1969-70, Cle-A 1971-72, Oak-A 1974-75
Hofmann, Fred   StL-A 1938-50
Holke, Walter H.   StL-A 1940
Hollingsworth, Albert W. "Al"   StL-N 1957-58
Holt, Golden D. "Goldie"   Pit-N 1948-50, Chi-N 1961-64
Holmquist, Douglas L. "Doug"   NY-A 1984, 1985
Hopp, John L. "Johnny"   Det-A 1954, StL-N 1956
Hornsby, Rogers   Chi-N 1958-59, NY-N 1962
Horton, Willie W.   NY-A 1985, Chi-A 1986
Hoscheit, Vernard A. "Vern"   Bal-A 1968, Oak-A 1969-74, Cal-A 1976, NY-N 1984-87
Houk, Ralph G.   NY-A 1954, 1958-60
House, Thomas R. "Tom"   Tex-A 1985-88
Howard, Elston G.   NY-A 1969-79
Howard, Frank O.   Mil-N 1977-80, NY-N 1982-83, 1984, Mil-A 1985-86, Sea-A 1987-88
Howe, Arthur H. "Art"   Tex-A 1985-88
Howley, Daniel P. "dAn"   Det-A 1921-22
Howser, Richard D. "Dick"   NY-A 1969-78
Hriniak, Walter J. "Walt"   Mon-N 1974-75, Bos-A 1977-88
Hudlin, G. Willis   Det-A 1957-59
Hudson, Sidney C. "Sid"   Was-A 1961-65, 1968-71, Tex-A 1972, 1977-78
Hulswitt, Rudolph E. "Rudy"   Bos-A 1931-33
Hundley, C. Randolph "Randy"   Chi-N 1977
Hunter, Fred C.   Phi-N 1928-31, 1933
Hunter, G. William "Billy"   Bal-A 1964-77
Isaac, Luis   Cle-A 1988
Jackson, Alvin N. "Al"   Bos-A 1977-79
Jackson, Grant D.   Pit-N 1984-85
Jackson, Roland T. "Sonny"   Atl-N 1982-83
Jackson, Travis C.   NY-N 1939-40, 1947-48
Jansen, Lawrence J. "Larry"   NY-N 1954-55, SF-N 1961-71, Chi-N 1972-73
Jennings, Hugh A. "Hughie"   NY-N 1921-26

Johnson, Darrell D.   StL-N 1960-61, Bal-A 1962, Bos-A 1968-69, Tex-A 1981-82
Johnson, Deron R.   Cal-A 1979-80, NY-N 1981, Phi-N 1982-84, Sea-A 1985-86, Chi-A 1987
Johnson, Roy   Chi-N 1935-39, 1944-53
Johnson, Sylvester W. "Syl"   Phi-N 1937-41
Johnston, James H. "Jimmy"   Bro-N 1931
Jones, Clarence W.   Atl-N 1985, 1988
Jones, Gordon B.   Hou-N 1966-67
Jones, Grover W. "Deacon"   Hou-N 1976-82, SD-N 1984-86
Jones, Joseph "Joe"   KC-A 1987
Jonnard, Clarence "Bubber"   Phi-N 1935, NY-N 1943-46
Judge, Joseph I. "Joe"   Was-A 1946
Jurges, William F. "Billy"   Chi-A 1947-48, Was-A 1956-59
Kaat, James L. "Jim"   Cin-N 1984-85
Kahn, Louis "Lou"   StL-N 1955
Katt, Raymond F. "Ray"   StL-N 1959-60, Cle-A 1962
Kaufmann, Anthony C. "Tony"   StL-N 1947-50
Keane, John J. "Johnny"   StL-N 1959-61
Keefe, David E. "Dave"   Phi-A 1939-43, 1945-50
Keely, Robert W. "Bob"   Bos-N 1946-52, Mil-N 1953-57
Kelleher, Michael D. "Mick"   Pit-N 1986
Kelley, Joseph A. "Joe"   Bro-N 1926-27
Kelly, Bernard F. "Mike"   Chi-A 1930-31, Chi-N 1934, Bos-N 1937-39, Pit-N 1940-41
Kelly, George L.   Cin-N 1935-37, Bos-N 1938-43, Cin-N 1947-48
Kelly, J. Thomas "Tom"   Min-A 1983-86
Kennedy, Robert D. "Bob"   Chi-N 1962-64, Atl-N 1967
Kerr, John M.   Was-A 1935
Kerrigan, Joseph T. "Joe"   Mon-N 1983-86
Killefer, William L. "Bill"   StL-N 1926, StL-A 1927-29, Bro-N 1939, Phi-N 1942
Kimm, Bruce E.   Cin-N 1984-88
King, Clyde E.   Cin-N 1959, NY-A 1981
Kissell, George M.   StL-N 1969-75
Kittle, Hubert M. "Hub"   Hou-N 1971-75, StL-N 1981-83
Klein, Charles H. "Chuck"   Phi-N 1942-45
Klein, Louis F. "Lou"   Chi-N 1960-65
Kluszewski, Theodore B. "Ted"   Cin-N 1970-78
Knoop, Robert F. "Bobby"   Chi-A 1977-78, Cal-A 1979-88
Knowles, Darold D.   StL-N 1983
Koenig, Fred Carl   Cal-A 1970-71, StL-N 1976, Tex-A 1977-82, Chi-N 1983, Cle-A 1985-86
Koenig, Gary   Bal-A 1988
Kress, Ralph "Red"   Det-A 1940, NY-N 1946-49, Cle-A 1953-60, LA-A 1961, NY-N 1962
Krol, John T. "Jack"   StL-N 1977-80, SD-N 1981-86
Kuehl, Karl O.   Min-A 1977-82
Kuenn, Harvey E.   Mil-A 1971-82
Kusnyer, Arthur W. "Art"   Chi-A 1980-8
Lacheman, Marcel E.   Cal-A 1984-88
Lachemann, Rene G.   Bos-A 1985-86, Oak-A 1987-88
Lakeman, Albert W. "Al"   Bos-A 1963-64, 1967-69
Lamont, Gene W.   Pit-N 1986-88
Land, Grover C.   Cin-N 1926-28, Chi-N 1929-30
Lanier, Harold C. "Hal"   StL-N 1981-85
LaRussa, Anthony "Tony"   Chi-A 1978
Lasorda, Thomas C. "Tommy"   LA-N 1973-76
Latham, W. Arlington "Arlie"   NY-N 1909
Lau, Charles R. "Charley"   Bal-A 1969, Oak-A 1970, KC-A 1971-74, 1975-78, NY-A 1979-81, Chi-A 1982-83
Lauder, William "Bill"   Chi-A 1925
Lavagetto, Harry A. "Cookie"   Bro-N 1951-53, Was-A 1955-57, NY-N 1962-63, SF-N 1964-67
Law, Vernon S. "Vern"   Pit-N 1968-69
Lazzeri, Anthony M. "Tony"   Chi-N 1938
Lefebvre, James K. "Jim"   LA-N 1978-79, SF-N 1980-82, Oak-A 1987-88
Leifield, Albert P. "Lefty"   StL-A 1921-23, Bos-A 1924-26, Det-A 1927-28
Lemon, James R. "Jim"   Min-A 1965-67, 1981-84
Lemon, Robert G. "Bob"   Cle-A 1960, Phi-N 1961, Cal-A 1967-68, KC-A 1970, NY-A 1976
Lenhardt, Donald E. "Don"   Bos-A 1970-73
Leonard, Emil J. "Dutch"   Chi-N 1954-56
Leppert, Donald G. "Don"   Pit-N 1968-76, Tor-A 1977-79, Hou-N 1980-85
Lett, James C. "Jim"   Cin-N 1988
Levy, Leonard   Pit-N 1957-60
Lewis, George E. "Duffy"   Bro-N 1931, Bos-N 1932-36
Lewis, Johnny J.   StL-N 1973-76, 1985-88
Leyland, James R. "Jim"   Chi-A 1982-85

Leyva, Nicholas "Nick" StL-N 1984-88
Lillis, Robert P. "Bob" Hou-N 1967, 1973-82, SF-N 1986-88
Lipon, John J. "Johnny" Cle-A 1968-71
Litwhiler, Daniel W. "Danny" Cin-N 1951
Llenas, Winston E. Tor-A 1988
Lobe, William C. "Bill" Cle-A 1951-56
Lobert, John B. "Hans" Phi-N 1934-41, Cin-N 1943-44
Lockman, Carroll W. "Whitey" Cin-N 1960, SF-N 1961-64, Chi-N 1966
Lodigiani, Dario J. KC-A 1961-62
Lollar, J. Sherman "Sherm" Bal-A 1964-67, Oak-A 1968
Lonnett, Joseph P. "Joe" Chi-A 1971-75, Oak-A 1976, Pit-N 1977-84
Lopat, Edmund W. "Ed" NY-A 1960, Min-A 1961, KC-A 1962
Lopes, David E. "Davey" Tex-A 1988
Lowe, Q. V. Chi-N 1972
Lowrey, Harry L. "Peanuts" Phi-N 1960-66, SF-N 1967-68, Mon-N 1969, Chi-N 1970-71, Cal-A 1972, Chi-N 1979-81
Lucchesi, Frank J. Tex-A 1974-75, 1979-80
Lum, Michael K. "Mike" Chi-A 1985, KC-A 1988
Lumpe, Jerry D. Oak-A 1971
Lund, Donald A. "Don" Det-A 1957-58
Luque, Adolfo "Dolf" NY-N 1936-38, 1942-45
Lutz, R. Joe Cal-A 1972-73
Lyons, Edward H. "Eddie" Min-A 1976
Lyons, Theodore A. "Ted" Det-A 1949-53, Bro-N 1954
Macha, Kenneth E. "Ken" Mon-N 1986-88
Mack, Earle T. Phi-A 1924-50
MacKenzie, H. Gordon "Gordy" KC-A 1980-81, Chi-N 1982, SF-N 1986, 1988
Maglie, Salvatore A. "Sal" Bos-A 1960-62, 1966-67, Sea-A 1969
Mahoney, James T. "Jim" Chi-A 1972-76, Sea-A 1985-86
Majtyka, Roy Atl-N 1988
Malmberg, Harry W. Bos-A 1963-64
Maltzberger, Gordon R. Min-A 1962-64
Mancuso, August R. "Gus" Cin-N 1950
Manuel, Charles F. "Charlie" Cle-A 1988
Manush, Henry E. "Heinie" Was-A 1953-54
Marion, Martin W. "Marty" StL-N 1950, StL-A 1952, Chi-A 1954
Marshall, R. James "Jim" Chi-N 1974
Martin, Alfred M. "Billy" Min-A 1965-68
Martin, Fred T. Cin-N 1961-64, Chi-A 1979
Martin, John L. "Pepper" Chi-N 1956
Martin, Joseph C. "J. C." Chi-N 1974
Martinez, Jose KC-A 1980-87, Chi-N 1988
Martinez, Orlando "Marty" Sea-A 1984-86
Mathews, Edwin L. "Eddie" Atl-N 1971-72
Mathews, Henry Cle-A 1926-27, NY-A 1929
Maxvill, C. Dallan "Dal" Oak-A 1975, NY-N 1978, StL-N 1979-80, Atl-N 1982-85
May, Lee A. KC-A 1984-86, Cin-N 1988
May, Milton S. "Milt" Pit-N 1987-88
Mayo, Edward J. "Eddie" Bos-A 1951, Phi-N 1952-54
Mays, Willie H. NY-N 1975-79
Mazeroski, William S. "Bill" Pit-N 1973, Sea-A 1979-80
Mazzone, Leo D. Atl-N 1985
McBride, George F. Det-A 1925-26, 1929
McBride, Kenneth F. "Ken" Mil-A 1975
McCallister, Jack Cle-A 1923-26, Bos-A 1930
McCormick, Frank A. Cin-N 1956-57
McCrabb, Lester W. "Les" Phi-A 1954
McCraw, Tommy L. Cle-A 1975, 1979-82, SF-N 1983-85
McCullough, Clyde E. Was-A 1960, Min-A 1961, NY-N 1963, SD-N 1982
McDonnell, Maje Phi-N 1951, 1954-57
McGaha, F. Melvin "Mel" Cle-A 1961, KC-A 1963-64, Hou-N 1968-70
McGinnity, Joseph J. "Joe" Bro-N 1926
McKay, David L. "Dave" Oak-A 1984-88
McKechnie, William B. "Bill" Pit-N 1922, StL-N 1927, Cle-A 1947-49, Bos-A 1952-53
McKeon, John A. "Jack" Oak-A 1978
McLaren, John L. Tor-A 1986-88
McLish, Calvin C. "Cal" Phi-N 1965-66, Mon-N 1969-75, Mil-A 1976-82
McMahon, Donald J. "Don" SF-N 1973-75, Min-A 1976-77, SF-N 1980-82, Cle-A 1983-85
McMillan, Roy David Mil-A 1970-72, NY-N 1973-76
McNamara, John F. Oak-A 1968-69, SF-N 1971-73, Cal-A 1978
McNeely, G. Earl StL-A 1931, Was-A 1936-37

McNertney, Gerald E. "Jerry" Bos-A 1988
McRae, Harold A. "Hal" KC-A 1987
Mele, Sabath A. "Sam" Was-A 1959-60, Min-A 1961
Melillo, Oscar D. "Ski" StL-A 1938, Cle-A 1939-40, 1942, 1945-48, 1950, Bos-A 1952-53, KC-A 1955-56
Mendoza, Mario Bal-A 1988
Menke, Denis J. Tor-A 1980-81, Hou-N 1983-88
Merkle, Frederick C. "Fred" NY-A 1926
Merrill, Carl H. "Stump" NY-A 1985, 1986-87
Metro, Charles "Charlie" Chi-N 1962, Chi-A 1965, Oak-A 1982
Meusel, Emil F. "Irish" NY-N 1930-31
Meyer, Bernhard "Benny" Phi-N 1925-26, Det-A 1929-30
Michael, Eugene R. "Gene" NY-A 1976-77, 1978, 1984-86, 1988
Milan, J. Clyde Was-A 1928-29, 1938-52
Miller, Dyar K. Chi-A 1987-88
Miller, Edmund J. "Bing" Bos-A 1936-37, Det-A 1938-41, Chi-A 1942-49, Phi-A 1950-53
Miller, L. Otto Bro-N 1926-36
Miller, Raymond R. "Ray" Bal-A 1978-85, Pit-N 1987-88
Miller, Robert L. "Bob" Tor-A 1977-79, SF-N 1985
Milliken, Robert F. "Bob" StL-N 1965-70, 1976
Mills, Arthur G. "Art" Det-A 1944-48
Mills, C. Buster Cle-A 1946, Chi-A 1947-50, Cin-N 1953, Bos-A 1954
Minoso, S. Orestes "Minnie" Chi-A 1976-78, 1980-81
Mitterwald, George E. Oak-A 1979-82, NY-A 1988
Monbouquette, William C. "Bill" NY-N 1982-83, NY-A 1985
Monchak, Alex "Al" Chi-A 1971-75, Oak-A 1976, Pit-N 1977-84, Atl-N 1986-88
Moon, Wallace W. "Wally" SD-N 1969
Moore, Jackie S. Mil-A 1970-72, Tex-A 1973-74, 1975-76, Tor-A 1977-79, Tex-A 1980, Oak-A 1981-84, Mon-N 1987-88
Moore, Terry B. StL-N 1949-52, 1956-58
Morales, Jose M. SF-N 1986-88
Morales, Richard A. "Rich" Atl-N 1986-87
Morgan, Joseph M. "Joe" Pit-N 1972, Bos-A 1985-88
Morgan, Thomas S. "Tom" Cal-A 1972-74, SD-N 1975, NY-A 1979, Cal-A 1981-83
Morgan, Vernon T. "Vern" Min-A 1969-75
Moses, Wallace "Wally" Phi-A 1952-54, Phi-N 1955-58, Cin-N 1959-60, NY-A 1961-62, 1966, Det-A 1967-70
Moss, J. Lester "Les" Chi-A 1967-68, 1970, Chi-N 1981, Hou-N 1982-84, 1985-88
Mota, Manuel R. "Manny" LA-N 1980-88
Mozzali, Maurice J. "Mo" StL-N 1977-78
Mueller, Ray C. NY-N 1956, Chi-N 1957
Muffett, Billy A. StL-N 1967-70, Cal-N 1974-77, Det-A 1985-88
Mulcahy, Hugh N. Chi-A 1970
Mull, Jack SF-N 1985
Mulleavy, Gregory T. "Greg" Bro-N 1957, LA-N 1958-60, 1962-64
Mullin, Patrick J. "Pat" Det-A 1963-66, Cle-A 1967, Mon-N 1979-81
Murphy, Daniel F. "Danny" Phi-A 1921-24, Phi-N 1927
Murtaugh, Daniel E. "Danny" Pit-N 1956-57
Muser, Anthony J. "Tony" Mil-A 1985-88
Myatt, George E. Was-A 1950-54, Chi-A 1955-56, Chi-N 1957-59, Mil-A 1960-61, Det-A 1962-63, Phi-N 1964-72
Napoleon, Edward G. "Ed" Cle-A 1983-85, KC-A 1987-88
Naragon, Harold R. "Hal" Min-A 1963-66, Det-A 1967-69
Narron, Samuel "Sam" Pit-N 1952-64
Neale, A. Earle "Greasy" StL-N 1929
Nelson, David E. "Dave" Chi-A 1981-84
Neun, John H. "Johnny" NY-A 1944-46
Newman, Jeffrey L. "Jeff" Oak-A 1986
Niarhos, C. Gus KC-A 1962-64
Niehoff, J. Albert "Bert" NY-N 1929
Nixon, Russell E. "Russ" Cin-N 1976-82, Mon-N 1984-85, Atl-N 1986-87
Noren, Irving A. "Irv" Oak-A 1971-74, Chi-N 1975
Norman, H. Willis F. "Bill" StL-A 1952-53
Northey, Ronald J. "Ron" Pit-N 1961-63
Nossek, Joseph R. "Joe" Mil-A 1973-75, Min-A 1976, Cle-A 1977-81, KC-A 1982-83, Chi-A 1984-85, 1986
Nottle, Edward W. "Ed" Oak-A 1983
Oates, Johnny L. Chi-N 1984-87

O'Brien, Edward J. "Eddie" Sea-A 1969
Oceak, Frank J. Pit-N 1958-64, Cin-N 1965, Pit-N 1970-72
O'Connell, Daniel F. "Danny" Was-A 1963-64
Okrie, Leonard J. "Len" Bos-A 1961-62, 1965-66, Det-A 1970
Oldis, Robert C. "Bob" Phi-N 1964-66, Min-A 1968, Mon-N 1969
O'Leary, Charles T. "Charley" StL-N 1913, NY-A 1921-30, Chi-N 1931-33, StL-A 1934-37
Oliva, Antonio P. "Tony" Min-A 1976-78, 1985-88
Oliver, David J. "Dave" Tex-A 1987-88
Oliver, Thomas N. "Tom" Phi-A 1951-53, Bal-A 1954
Olson, Ivan M. "Ivy" Bro-N 1924, 1930-31
O'Neill, Stephen F. "Steve" Cle-A 1935, Det-A 1941, Cle-A 1949, Bos-A 1950
Onslow, John J. "Jack" Pit-N 1925-26, Was-A 1927, StL-N 1928, Phi-N 1931-32, Bos-A 1934
Osborn, Donald E. "Don" Pit-N 1963-64, 1970-72, 1974-76
Osteen, Claude W. StL-N 1977-80, Phi-N 1982-88
Otero, Regino J. "Regie" Cin-N 1959-60
Otis, Amos J. SD-N 1988
Overmire, Frank "Stubby" Det-A 1963-65
Owen, Arnold M. "Mickey" Bos-A 1955-56
Owens, James P. "Jim" Hou-N 1967-72
Ozark, Daniel L. "Danny" LA-N 1965-72, 1980-82, SF-N 1983-84
Pacheco, Antonio A. "Tony" Cle-A 1974, Hou-N 1976-79, 1982
Paepke, Jack LA-N 1961-64, Cal-A 1965-66
Pafko, Andrew "Andy" Mil-N 1960-62
Pagan, Jose A. Pit-N 1974-78
Page, Philip R. "Phil" Cin-N 1947-52
Paige, Leroy R. "Satchell" Atl-N 1968-69
Parker, Francis J. "Salty" SF-N 1958-61, Cle-A 1962, LA-A 1964, Cal-A 1965-66, NY-N 1967, Hou-N 1968-72, Cal-A 1973-74
Pascual, Camilo A. Min-A 1978-80
Paul, Michael G. "Mike" Oak-A 1987-88
Pavlick, Gregory M. "Greg" NY-N 1985-86, 1988
Peitz, Henry C. "Heinie" StL-N 1913
Pennock, Herbert J. "Herb" Bos-A 1936-39
Pepitone, Joseph A. "Joe" NY-A 1982
Perez, Atanasio R. "Tony" Cin-N 1987-88
Perkins, Ralph F. "Cy" NY-A 1932-33, Det-A 1934-39, Phi-N 1946-54
Perlozzo, Samuel B. "Sam" NY-N 1987-88
Perranoski, Ronald P. "Ron" LA-N 1981-88
Pesky, John M. "Johnny" Pit-N 1965-67, Bos-A 1975-84
Peterson, Eric H. "Rick" Pit-N 1984-8
Phillips, Harold R. "Lefty" LA-N 1965-68, Cal-A 1969
Piche, Ronald J. "Ron" Mon-N 1976
Picinich, Valentine J. "Val" Cin-N 1934
Piersall, James A. "Jimmy" Tex-A 1975
Pignatano, Joseph B. "Joe" Was-A 1965-67, NY-N 1968-81, Atl-N 1982-85
Piniella, Louis V. "Lou" NY-A 1984-85
Pinson, Vada E. Sea-A 1977-80, Chi-A 1981, Sea-A 1982-83, Det-A 1985-88
Pitler, Jacob A. "Jake" Bro-N 1947-57
Plaza, Ronald C. "Ron" Sea-A 1969, Cin-N 1978-83, Oak-A 1986
Plummer, William F. "Bill" Sea-A 1982-83, 1988
Podres, John J. "Johnny" SD-N 1973, Bos-A 1980, Min-A 1981-85
Pole, Richard H. "Dick" Chi-N 1988
Pollet, Howard J. "Howie" StL-N 1959-64, Hou-N 1965
Popowski, Edward J. "Eddie" Bos-A 1967-76
Posedel, William J. "Bill" Pit-N 1949-53, StL-N 1954-57, Phi-N 1958, SF-N 1959-60, Oak-A 1968-72, SD-N 1974
Queen, Melvin D. "Mel" Cle-A 1982
Quilici, Frank R. Min-A 1971-72
Quirk, James P. "Jamie" StL-N 1984
Rader, Douglas L. "Doug" SD-N 1979, Chi-A 1986-87
Ragan, D. C. Patrick "Pat" Phi-N 1924
Randall, Robert L. "Bobby" Min-A 1980
Rapp, Vernon F. "Vern" Mon-N 1979-83
Reese, Harold H. "Pee Wee" LA-N 1959
Reese, James H. "Jimmie" Cal-A 1973-88
Regan, Philip P. "Phil" Sea-A 1984-86
Reiser, Harold P. "Pete" LA-N 1960-64, Chi-N 1966-69, Cal-N 1970-71, Chi-N 1972-73
Renick, W. Richard "Rick" KC-A 1981, Mon-N 1985-86, Min-A 1987-88
Resinger, Grover S. Atl-N 1966, Chi-A 1967-68, Det-A 1969-70, Cal-A 1975-76

Rettenmund, Mervin W. "Merv" Cal-A 1980-81, Tex-A 1983-85
Reyes, Benjamin "Cananea" Sea-A 1981
Rice, Delbert "Del" LA-A 1962-64, Cal-A 1965-66, Cle-A 1967
Ricketts, David W. "Dave" Pit-N 1971-73, StL-N 1974-75, 1978-8
Riddle, John L. "Johnny" Pit-N 1948-50, StL-N 1952-55, Mil-N 1956-57, Cin-N 1958, Phi-N 1959
Riddoch, Gregory L. "Greg" SD-N 1987-88
Ripken, Calvin E., Sr. "Cal" Bal-A 1976-86
Rippelmeyer, Raymond R. "Ray" Phi-N 1970-78
Roarke, Michael T. "Mike" Det-A 1965-66, Cal-A 1967-69, Det-A 1970, Chi-N 1978-80, StL-N 1984-88
Robertson, Sherrard A. "Sherry" Min-A 1970
Robinson, Brooks C. Bal-A 1977
Robinson, Frank Cal-A 1977, Bal-A 1978-80, 1985-87
Robinson, Warren G. "Sheriff" NY-N 1964, 1965-67, 1972
Robinson, Wilbert NY-N 1911-13
Robinson, William H. "Bill" NY-N 1984-88
Robinson, W. Edward "Eddie" Bal-A 1957-59
Robson, Thomas J. "Tom" Tex-A 1986-88
Rodgers, Robert L. "Bob" Min-A 1970-74, SF-N 1976, Mil-A 1978-80
Rojas, Octavio "Cookie" Chi-N 1978-81
Rolfe, Robert A. "Red" NY-A 1946
Rommel, Edwin A. "Eddie" Phi-A 1933-34
Roof, Phillip A. "Phil" SD-N 1978, Sea-A 1983-88
Root, Charles H. "Charlie" Chi-N 1951-53, Mil-N 1956-57, Chi-N 1960
Roseboro, John Was-A 1971, Cal-A 1972-74
Rosenbaum, Glen O. Chi-A 1973-75, 1986-88
Roth, Francis C. "Frank" NY-A 1921-22, Cle-A 1923-25, Chi-A 1927
Roush, Edd J. Cin-N 1938
Rowe, Donald H. "Don" Chi-A 1988
Rowe, Kenneth D. "Ken" Bal-A 1985-86
Rowe, Lynwood T. "Schoolboy" Det-A 1954-55
Rowe, Ralph E. Min-A 1972-75, Bal-A 1981-84
Ruberto, John E. StL-N 1977-78
Rudi, Joseph O. "Joe" Oak-A 1986-87
Rudolph, Richard "Dick" Bos-N 1921-22, 1924-27
Ruel, Herold D. "Muddy" Chi-A 1935-45, Cle-A 1948-50
Ruffing, Charles H. "Red" NY-N 1962
Runnels, James E. "Pete" Bos-A 1965-66
Russell, William E. "Bill" LA-N 1987-88
Ruth, George H. "Babe" Bro-N 1938
Ryan, Cornelius J. "Connie" Mil-N 1957, Atl-N 1971, 1973-75, Tex-A 1977-79
Ryan, John B. Bos-A 1923-27
Ryan, Michael J. "Mike" Phi-N 1980-88
Ryba, Dominic J. "Mike" StL-N 1951-54
Sain, John F. "Johnny" KC-A 1959, NY-A 1961-63, Min-A 1965-66, Det-A 1967-69, Chi-A 1971-75, Atl-N 1977, 1985-86
Sanford, John S. "Jack" Cle-A 1968-69
Sandt, Thomas J. "Tommy" Pit-N 1987-88
Saul, James A. "Jim" Chi-A 1975-76, Oak-A 1979
Scarborough, Ray W. Bal-A 1968
Schacht, Alexander "Al" Was-A 1925-34, Bos-A 1935-36
Schaefer, Robert W. "Bob" KC-A 1988
Schaffer, Jimmie R. "Jim" Tex-A 1978, KC-A 1980-88
Schalk, Raymond W. "Ray" Chi-N 1930-31
Schang, Walter H. "Wally" Cle-A 1936-38
Scheffing, Robert B. "Bob" StL-N 1952-53, Chi-N 1954-55, Mil-N 1960
Scherger, George R. Cin-N 1970-78, 1983-86
Schoendienst, Albert F. "Red" StL-N 1963-64, Oak-A 1977-78, StL-N 1979-8
Schreiber, Paul F. NY-A 1942, Bos-A 1947-58
Schueler, Ronald R. "Ron" Chi-A 1979-82, Oak-A 1983-84, Pit-N 1986
Schulte, John C. "Johnny" Chi-N 1933, NY-A 1934-48, Bos-A 1949-50
Schultz, George W. "Barney" StL-N 1971-75, Chi-N 1977
Schultz, Joseph C., Jr. "Joe" StL-N 1949, StL-N 1963-68, KC-A 1970, Det-A 1971-76
Seminick, Andrew W. "Andy" Phi-N 1957-58, 1967-69
Sewell, J. Luther "Luke" Cle-A 1939-41, Cin-N 1949
Sewell, Joseph W. "Joe" NY-A 1934-35
Sewell, Truett B. "Rip" Pit-N 1948
Shanks, Howard S. "Howie" Cle-A 1928-32
Shaughnessey, Francis J. "Shag" Det-A 1928
Shaw, Robert J. "Bob" Mil-A 1973

Shea, Mervyn D. J. "Merv" Det-A 1939-42, Phi-N 1944-45, Chi-N 1949
Sheehan, Thomas C. "Tom" Cin-N 1935-37, Bos-N 1944
Shellenback, Frank W. StL-A 1939, Bos-A 1940-44, Det-A 1946-47, NY-A 1950-55
Shellenback, James P. "Jim" Min-A 1983
Shepard, Bert R. Was-A 1946
Shepard, Lawrence W. "Larry" Phi-N 1967, Cin-N 1970-78, SF-N 1979
Sherry, Lawrence "Larry" Pit-N 1977-78, Cal-A 1979-80
Sherry, Norman B. "Norm" Cal-A 1970-71, 1976, Mon-N 1978-81, SD-N 1982-84, SF-N 1986-88
Shore, Raymond E. "Ray" Cin-N 1963-67
Shotton, Burton E. "Burt" StL-N 1923-25, Cin-N 1934, Cle-A 1942-45
Sievers, Roy E. Cin-N 1966
Silvera, Charles R. "Charlie" Min-A 1969, Det-A 1971-73, Tex-A 1973-75
Silvestri, Kenneth J. "Ken" Phi-N 1959-60, Mil-N 1963-65, Atl-N 1966-75, Chi-A 1976, 1982
Simmons, Aloysius H. "Al" Phi-A 1940-42, 1944-49, Cle-A 1950-51
Sisler, George H. Bos-N 1930
Sisler, Richard A. "Dick" Cin-N 1961-64, StL-N 1966-70, SD-N 1975-76, NY-N 1979-80
Skaff, Francis M. "Frank" Bal-A 1954, Det-A 1965-66, 1971
Skinner, Robert R. "Bob" SD-N 1970-73, Pit-N 1974-76, SD-N 1977, Cal-A 1978, Pit-N 1979-85, Atl-N 1986-88
Slider, Rachel W. "Rac" Bos-A 1987-88
Smith, Billy F. Tor-A 1984-88
Smith, Harold R. "Hal" StL-N 1962, Pit-N 1965-67, Cin-N 1968-69, Mil-A 1976-77
Smith, Richard P. "Red" Cin-N 1946-48
Snitker, Brian G. Atl-N 1985, 1988
Snyder, Francis M. "Frank" NY-N 1934-41
Snyder, James H. Chi-N 1987
Sommers, Dennis J. "Denny" NY-N 1977-78, Cle-A 1980-85, SD-N 1988
Sothoron, Allen S. StL-N 1927-28, StL-A 1932-33
Southworth, William H. "Billy" NY-N 1933
Spahn, Warren E. NY-N 1965, Cle-A 1972-73
Spalding, Charles H. "Dick" Phi-N 1934-36, Chi-N 1941-43
Spangler, Albert D. "Al" Chi-N 1970-71, 1974
Sparks, Joseph E. "Joe" Chi-A 1979, Cin-N 1984
Spencer, H. Thomas "Tom" Cle-A 1988
Staller, George W. Bal-A 1962, 1969-75
Stanage, Oscar H. Pit-N 1927-31
Stange, A. Lee Bos-A 1972-74, Min-A 1975, Oak-A 1977-79, Bos-A 1981-84
Stanky, Edward R. "Eddie" Cle-A 1957-58
Stargell, Wilver D. "Willie" Pit-N 1985, Atl-N 1986-88
Starrette, Herman P. "Herm" Atl-N 1974-76, SF-N 1977-78, Phi-N 1979-81, SF-N 1983-84, Mil-A 1985-86, Chi-N 1987, Bal-A 1988
Staub, Daniel J. "Rusty" NY-N 1982
Stelmaszek, Richard F. "Rick" Min-A 1981-88
Stengel, Charles D. "Casey" Bro-N 1932-34
Stock, Milton J. "Milt" Chi-N 1944-48, Bro-N 1949-50, Pit-N 1951-52
Stock, Wesley G. "Wes" KC-A 1967, Mil-N 1970-72, Oak-A 1972-76, Sea-A 1977-81, Oak-A 1984-86
Stottlemyre, Melvin L. "Mel" NY-N 1984-88
Stratton, Monty F. Chi-A 1939-41
Strickland, George B. Min-A 1962, Cle-A 1963-69, KC-A 1970-72
Stubing, Lawrence G. "Moose" Cal-A 1985-88
Such, Richard S. "Dick" Tex-A 1983-85, Min-A 1985-88
Sugden, Joseph "Joe" StL-N 1921-25, Phi-N 1926-27
Sukeforth, Clyde L. Bro-N 1943-51, Pit-N 1952-57
Sullivan, John P. KC-A 1979, Atl-N 1980-81, Tor-A 1982-88
Susce, George C. M. Cle-A 1941-47, 1948-49, Bos-A 1950-54, Cle-A 1955-56, Mil-N 1958-59, Was-A 1961-67, 1968-71, Tex-A 1972
Sweeney, William J. "Bill" Det-A 1947-48
Sweet, Richard J. "Rick" Sea-A 1984
Swift, Robert V. "Bob" Det-A 1953-54, KC-A 1957-59, Was-A 1960, Det-A 1963-66
Tannehill, Jesse N. Phi-N 1920
Tappe, Elvin W. "El" Chi-N 1959-63
Taylor, Antonio "Tony" Phi-N 1977-79, 1988
Taylor, James W. "Zack" Bro-N 1936, StL-A 1941-46, Pit-N 1947
Temple, John E. "Johnny" Cin-N 1964

Tenace, F. Gene Hou-N 1986-87
Terwilliger, W. Wayne Was-A 1969-71, Tex-A 1972, 1981-85, Min-A 1986-88
Testa, Nicholas "Nick" SF-N 1958
Thomas, George E. Bos-A 1970
Thomas, Ira F. Phi-A 1925-26
Thomas, J. Leroy "Lee" StL-N 1972, 1983
Thomas, Ray StL-N 1922
Thompson, Charles L. "Tim" StL-N 1981
Tiefenauer, Bobby G. Phi-N 1979
Tighe, John T. "Jack" Det-A 1955-56
Tobin, John T. "Jack" StL-A 1949-51
Tolan, Robert "Bobby" SD-N 1980-83, Sea-A 1987
Torborg, Jeffrey A. "Jeff" Cle-A 1975-77, NY-A 1979-88
Torchia, Anthony L. "Tony" Bos-A 1985
Tracewski, Richard J. "Dick" Det-A 1972-88
Trebelhorn, Thomas L. "Tom" Mil-A 1984, 1986
Trucks, Virgil O. Pit-N 1963
Turley, Robert L. "Bob" Bos-A 1964
Turner, James R. "Jim" NY-A 1949-59, Cin-N 1961-65, NY-A 1966-73
Turner, Terrence L. "Terry" StL-N 1924
Uhle, George E. Cle-A 1936-37, Chi-N 1940, Was-A 1944
Unser, Delbert B. "Del" Phi-N 1985-88
Valentine, Robert J. "Bobby" NY-N 1983-85
Valo, Elmer W. Cle-A 1963-64
Van Ornum, John C. SF-N 1981-84
Vernon, James B. "Mickey" Pit-N 1960, 1964, StL-N 1965, Mon-N 1977-78, NY-A 1982
Vincent, Albert L. "Al" Det-A 1943-44, Bal-A 1955-59, Phi-N 1961-63, KC-A 1966-67
Virdon, William C. "Bill" Pit-N 1968-71, 1986
Virgil, Osvaldo Jose "Ozzie" SF-N 1969-72, 1974-75, Mon-N 1976-81, SD-N 1982-86, Sea-A 1986-88
Vukovich, John C. Chi-N 1982-87, Phi-N 1988
Wagner, Charles F. "Heinie" Bos-A 1927-29
Wagner, Charles T. "Charley" Bos-A 1970
Wagner, John P. "Honus" Pit-N 1933-51
Walker, Albert B. "Rube" LA-N 1958, Was-A 1965-67, NY-N 1968-81, Atl-N 1982-84
Walker, Fred "Dixie" StL-N 1953, 1955, Mil-N 1963-65
Walker, Gerald H. "Gee" Cin-N 1946
Walker, Harry W. StL-N 1959-62
Walker, Jerry A. NY-A 1982, Hou-N 1983-85
Walker, Verlon L. Chi-N 1961-70
Wallace, Roderick J. "Bobby" Cin-N 1926-28
Walls, R. Lee Oak-A 1979-82, NY-A 198
Walsh, Edward A. "Ed" Chi-A 1923-25, 1928-30
Walters, William H. "Bucky" Bos-N 1950-52, Mil-N 1953-55, NY-N 1956-57
Walton, James R. "Jim" Mil-A 1973-75
Ward, John F. "Jay" NY-A 1987
Ward, Peter T. "Pete" Atl-N 1978
Wares, Clyde E. "Buzzy" StL-N 1930-35, 1937-51
Warner, Harry C. Tor-A 1977-79, 1980, Mil-A 1981-82
Wathan, John D. KC-A 1986
Watson, Robert J. "Bob" Oak-A 1986-8
Weaver, Earl S. Bal-A 1968
Webb, William J. "Billy" Chi-A 1935-39
West, Samuel F. "Sam" Was-A 1947-48
Westrum, Wesley N. "Wes" SF-N 1958-63, NY-N 1964-65, SF-N 1968-71
Whisenant, T. Peter "Pete" Cin-N 1961-62
White, Ernest D. "Ernie" Bos-N 1947-48, NY-N 1963
White, Joyner C. "Jo-Jo" Cle-A 1958-60, Det-A 1960, KC-A 1961-62, Mil-N 1963-65, Atl-N 1966, KC-A 1969
White, Roy H. NY-A 1983-84, 1986
Whitehill, Earl O. Cle-A 1941, Phi-N 1943
Widmar, Albert J. "Al" Phi-N 1962-64, 1968-69, Mil-A 1973-74, Tor-A 1980-88
Wietelmann, William F. "Whitey" Cin-N 1966-67, SD-N 1969-79
Wilber, Delbert Q. "Del" Chi-A 1955-56, Was-A 1970, Tex-A 1973
Wiley, Mark E. Bal-A 1987, Cle-A 1988
Wilhelm, Irvin K. "Kaiser" Phi-N 1921
Wilks, Theodore "Ted" KC-A 1961
Williams, Billy L. Chi-N 1980-82, Oak-A 1983-85, Chi-N 1986-87
Williams, David C. "Davey" NY-N 1956-57
Williams, Donald E. "Don" SD-N 1977-80
Williams, James B. "Jimmy" Hou-N 1975, Bal-A 1981-87
Williams, James F. "Jimy" Tor-A 1980-85
Williams, Otto G. Det-A 1925, StL-N 1926, StL-A 1927, Cin-N 1930
Williams, Richard H. "Dick" Mon-N 1970

Williams, Stanley W. "Stan" Bos-A 1975-76, Chi-A 1977-78, NY-A 1980-81, Cin-N 1984, NY-A 1987, 198
Williams, Walter A. "Walt" Chi-A 1988
Wilson, James "Jimmy" Cin-N 1939-40, 1944-46
Wiltse, George L. "Hooks" NY-A 1925
Wine, Robert P. "Bobby" Phi-N 1972-83, Atl-N 1985, 1988
Winegarner, Ralph L. StL-A 1948-51
Wingo, Ivy B. Cin-N 1928-29, 1936
Winkles, Bobby B. Cal-A 1972, Oak-N 1974-75, SF-

N 1976-77, Chi-A 1979-81, Mon-N 1986-88
Wolgamot, Earl Cle-A 1932-33
Woodall, C. Lawrence "Larry" Bos-A 1942-48
Woodling, Eugene R. "Gene" Bal-A 1964-67
Worthington, Allan "Al" Min-A 1972-73
Wright, Melvin J. "Mel" Chi-N 1963-64, Pit-N 1973, NY-A 1974-75, Hou-N 1976-82, Mon-N 1983
Wyatt, J. Whitlow "Whit" Phi-N 1955-57, Mil-N 1958-65, Atl-N 1966-67
Wynn, Early Cle-A 1964-66, Min-A 1967-69

York, Rudolph P. "Rudy" Bos-A 1959-62
Yost, Edward F. J. "Eddie" Was-A 1963-67, NY-N 1968-76, Bos-A 1977-84
Zeller, Barton W. "Bart" StL-N 1970
Zimmer, Donald W. "Don" Mon-N 1971, SD-N 1972, Bos-A 1974-76, NY-A 1983, Chi-N 1984-86, NY-A 1986, SF-N 1987
Zimmer, Thomas "Tom" StL-N 1976
Zimmerman, Gerald R. "Gerry" Min-A 1967, Mon-N 1969-75, Min-A 1976-80

The Umpire Roster

The men in blue have been rebuked and scorned since the Knickerbockers cavorted on the Elysian Fields of Hoboken. The first to incur an umpire's wrath in return was Knickerbocker player Davis, fined six cents for swearing, perhaps understandably since his team was being trounced by the New York Club, 23–1. The name of the umpire in that historic game of June 19, 1846—the first match game under Alexander Cartwright's new rules—was not recorded. Ever since, a handful of researchers have scrambled to find out who umpired the league games of baseball's early history.

Larry Gerlach, who knows more about umpires and umpiring than anybody (see his feature article in Part 1 of this volume), has created the Umpire Roster that follows. The basis of his roster is the list compiled by S. C. Thompson in the 1930s and 1940s, but his research has corrected several errors and omissions in that list and has scrupulously brought the umpire roster up to date. He hopes that "by the next edition we will have finished a complete re-study of the umpire roster. . . . I am going to try to fashion a biographical encyclopedia of major league umpires—vital statistics; minor and major league service; All-Star, World Series, Playoff games; special achievements; and so on. One of the more frustrating things about the Turkin/Thompson roster (and even ours) is how years of service are noted in terms of seasons; it really is misleading to identify someone as working from 1980–1987 when he may have broken into the majors on September 24, 1980."

The data presented here is not complete, but new leads continue to flow in, especially about the early days, when umpires were not assigned by the leagues but were supplied by the teams, recruited from among the fans in attendance (this explains why so many given names are lacking for pre-1900 arbiters), or, not infrequently, plucked from the team's reserve players. An instance of this last practice occurred as late as 1935, when Chicago White Sox outfielder Jocko Conlan was recruited to fill in for umpire Red Ormsby in a game between the Sox and the St. Louis Browns. Conlan, of course, went on to a Hall of Fame career as a man in blue.

But the story of umpires and umpiring is better told in Gerlach's essay in Part 1. Let's call the roll.

National Association (1871–75)

Addy, Robert E., 1875
Allison, Arthur A., 1872, 1874
Allison, Douglas L., 1872–73, 1875
Allison, H., 1874
Alston, David, 1871–72, 1875
Annan, —, 1873
Arnold, Willis S., 1875
Barlow, Thomas H., 1875
Barnes, Roscoe C., 1874
Barrett, William, 1872, 1874
Barron, James, 1875
Barrows, Frederick, 1872
Batt, Thomas, 1871
Battin, Joseph V., 1874
Beals, Thomas J., 1874–75
Beardslee, J. J., 1871–73
Bechtel, George A., 1874
Beck, W. S., 1872
Bielaski, Oscar, 1874–75
Bigelow, W. J., 1875
Birdsall, David S., 1873–74
Blair, William J., 1873
Blodgett, C. W., 1875
Boake, J. L., 1871
Bomeisler, Theodore, 1871–75
Bonse, N., 1871
Bordman, Frederick, 1875
Boyd, William J., 1873, 1875
Bradley, George H., 1875
Brainard, Asa, 1872, 1875
Briggs, —, 1874
Brown, William, 1872, 1875
Bryant, 1875
Buck, —, 1871
Bunce, Joshua, 1874
Burdock, John J., 1872–74
Bush, A. M., 1871
Carey, Thomas J., 1873, l875
Cassidy, Joseph P., 1875
Cavanaugh, J. H., 1875
Chandler, Moses E., 1872, 1874
Chapman, John C., 1871–74
Clapp, John E., 1874–75
Clifton, —, 1872
Clinton, James L., 1873
Clinton, John L., 1875
Collins, Daniel T., 1875
Cone, J. F., 1873–75
Cope, Elias, 1871
Craver, William H., 1873
Cuthbert, Edgar E., 1875
Daniels, Charles F., 1874–75
Daubney, Thomas, 1871
David, L. N., 1874
Dawson, —, 1871
Dean, Harry J., 1871
Deane, Henry C., 1874
Dehlman, Harmon J., 1873–75
Demorest, 1872–73

Dobson, H. A., 1871
Dole, William Carrington, 1875
Dornlach, D. E., 1872
Douglass, Benjamin F., 1875
Draper, John H., 1871
Ellis, William R., 1871–72, 1875
English, John W., 1874–75
Erby, Frederick, 1872
Evans, George, 1872
Fellows, T. E., 1871
Fenoe, —, 1872
Ferguson, Robert V., 1871–75
Fisher, William C., 1871, 1875
Foley, Thomas J., 1874–75
Force, David W., 1873
Fulmer, Charles J., 1872–75
Garrigan, —, 1873
Geer, William H., 1874–75
Gerhardt, Joseph J., 1875
Ginn, —, 1875
Glenn, John W., 1874
Glover, Frank, 1873
Goodwin, J. C., 1871–72
Gould, Charles H., 1874–75
Graham, —, 1872
Halback, A. C. N., 1873–74
Hall, George W., 1873–75
Hall, James, 1872
Hanford, Charles, 1874
Hastings, Winfield S., 1871–74
Hatfield, John V. B., 1872–73
Hayhurst, Elias H., 1875
Haynie, James L., 1871
Hegeman, William H., 1871
Helm, J., 1871–72
Heubel, George A., 1875
Higham, Richard, 1873–75
Hodes, Charles, 1874
Hodges, A. D., 1874–75
Holly, Samuel J., 1871
Hooper, Michael H., 1872–74
Hosworth, 1872–74
Howard, —, 1872
Hynan, —, 1871
Jennings, Alfred, 1873
Kahn, S. L., 1875
Keerl, George W., 1872
Kent, John, 1875
Knight, G. H., 1875
Kohler, Henry, 1873
Lamb, Harry, 1875
Laughlin, Benjamin, 1873
Lennon, William F., 1871–72
Leonard, Andrew, 1872–73, 1875
Leonard, —, 1872
Leroy, Isaac, 1871
Locke, Marshall, 1873–74
Lowell, John A., 1872–73
Lush, M. R., 1871, 1873
MacDiarmed, Thomas, 1872
Mack, Dennis J., 1871–75

Malone, —, 1875
Marion, S. H., 1873
Martin, Alphonse C., 1871, 1873, 1875
Martin, Lewis G., 1871, 1873–74
Mathews, Robert T., 1871, 1873–75
Mawny, J. H., 1871
Maxwell, Cortez, 1875
Mays, —, 1871
McCrea, —, 1872
McDonald, James F., 1872
McGeary, Michael H., 1872, 1875
McLean, Harry, 1871, 1873
McLean, William B., 1872–75
McMahon, W., 1871
McMullen, John F., 1874
McVey, Calvin A., 1875
Miller, Joseph W., 1872–73
Mills, Charles, 1871–72
Mincher, Edward J., 1872, 1875
Mincher, William E., 1875
Mitchell, C. L., 1874
Mitchell, F. B., 1875
Mosely, M., 1873
Murdock, —, 1872
Murnane, Timothy H., 1873–75
Nelson J., 1872
Nichols, A. N., 1871
Norton, F., 1872
O'Brien, P., 1875
Pabor, Charles H., 1875
Parks, William R., 1875
Patterson, Daniel T., 1872, 1874
Pearce, Richard S., 1872
Pearson, S. W., 1872
Phelps, Cornelius C., 1874
Pike, Jacob Emanuel, 1875
Porter, —, 1874
Powers, W., 1872–73, 1875
Pratt, Thomas J., 1871–73
Quinn, Patrick, 1875
Radcliffe, John J., 1873
Rastall, J. N., 1872
Reach, Albert J., 1872–75
Reed, Hugh, 1871, 1873–74
Remsen, John J., 1873–74
Robinson, A. V., 1872
Robinson, Miley, 1873
Rogers, Morton, 1871–72
Ryan, John J., 1872, 1875
Sawyer, D., 1871
Schafer, Harry C., 1875
Schroeder, 1875
Schuester, John A., 1874–75
Sears, —, 1873
Selman, Frank C., 1873
Sensenderfer, John P. J., 1872–75
Simmons, Joseph S., 1871, 1874
Smith, Eb, 1872
Smith, George, 1872
Smith, Gustavus, 1872, 1875
Snyder, —, 1875

Stahl, G., 1875
Stanwood, 1872
Sutton, Ezra B., 1875
Swandell, John M., 1871–73
Sweasy, Charles J., 1871, 1873–74
Tate, William, 1874
Tighe, Edward, 1871
Treacy, Frederick, 1871, 1873, 1875
Tyler, C. T., 1871–74
Urell, E., 1873
Van Delft, 1875
Voltz, Edward, 1871–72
Walk, Frank, 1871
Walsh, Michael F., 1875
Wardell, —, 1874
Waterman, Frederick A., 1873
Weaver, C., 1873
Weigel, W. H., 1873–74
White, H. F., 1873
White, Warren W., 1874–75
Whiting, R., 1872
Wiggins, —, 1875
Wildey, John, 1871
Willard, Gardner, 1871
Wood, James B., 1871
Worth, Adam, 1875
Woulfe, —, 1871
Wright, George, 1871
Wright, William H., 1875
York, Thomas J., 1874
Young, Nicholas E., 1871–75

National League (1876–)

Abbey, Charles S., 1897
Abbot, —, 1905
Adams, James 1897
Allen, Hezekiah, 1876
Anderson, William, 1890
Andrews, George E., 1889, 1893, 1895, 1898–99
Arundel, John T., 1888
Ayers, —, 1876
Baker, Charles, 1884
Baker, Philip, 1889
Baker, William P., 1957
Baldwin, Marcus E., 1892
Ballanfant, E. Lee, 1936–57
Bannon, James H., 1894
Barker, Alfred L., 1876, 1880–81
Barlick, Albert J., 1940–43, 1946–55, 1958–71
Barnie, William S., 1882, 1892
Barr, George M., 1932–49
Barton, —, 1876
Bates, —, 1877
Battin, Joseph V., 1882, 1889, 1891, 1895–96
Bausewine, George, 1908
Beard, Oliver P., 1894
Becannon, James M., 1885
Beck, Erwin T., 1902
Beckley, Jacob P., 1906
Beebe, Fred L., 1907
Behle, Frank, 1895–96,1901
Berger, Frederick, 1886
Berger, John H., 1891

Betts, William G., 1893–96, 1898–99
Betz, Edwin J., 1961
Bigelow, —, 1877
Bittman, Henry, 1892–95, 1897
Blakiston, Robert J., 1884
Blodgett, C.W., 1876
Boggess, Lynton R.,1944–48, 1950–62
Boles, Charles, 1877
Bond, Thomas H., 1883, 1885
Bonin, Gregory, 1986–88
Bonner, Frank J., 1894
Boston, K. K., 1878
Boyle, Henry J., 1886
Boyle, John A., 1892, 1897
Bradley, George H., 1877, 1879–83
Brady, —,1877
Brady, Jackson, 1887
Bransfield, William E., 1917
Bredburg, George W., 1877, 1879
Breitenstein, Theodore P., 1900
Brennan, John E., 1887, 1899
Brennan, William T., 1909, 1913, 1921
Briody, Charles F., 1882
Brocklander, Fred W. III, 1979–88
Brockway, John, 1877, 1879
Brown, Samuel W., 1907
Brown, Thomas T., 1891, 1898–99, 1901–2
Brunton, Thomas H., 1879
Buckenberger, Alfred C., 1890
Budding, —, 1877
Buelow, Frederick W., 1901
Buffinton, Charles G., 1883, 1888–89, 1892
Bullymore, Charles L., 1882
Bunce, Joshua, 1877
Burke, —,1892
Burkhart, W. Kenneth, 1957–73
Burlingame, Frank A., 1878
Burnham, George W., 1883, 1886–87, 1889, 1893, 1895
Burns, John S., 1884
Burns, Thomas E., 1892
Burns, Thomas P., 1895, 1899
Burtis, D. W., 1876–77
Bush, Garner C., 1911–12
Bushong, Albert J., 1880, 1890
Butler, Richard H., 1897
Byron, William J., 1913–19
Callahan, Edward J., 1881
Campbell, Al, 1886
Campbell, Daniel, 1893–97
Campbell, William M., 1939–40
Cantillon, Joseph D., 1902
Carey, S., 1870
Carey, Thomas J., 1881–82

Carpenter, William B., 1897, 1904, 1906–7
Carrick, William M., 1900
Carroll, Frederick H., 1887
Carsey, Wilfred, 1894, 1896, 1901
Caruthers, Robert L., 1886, 1891, 1893
Casey, Daniel M., 1888
Caskin, Edward J., 1884
Cassidy, John P., 1882
Chamberlain, Elton P., 1894
Chance, Frank L., 1902
Chandler, Moses E., 1877
Chaplin, Harry, 1886
Chapman, John C., 1876, 1880, 1882–83, 1885
Chapman, John,1880
Chill, Oliver P., 1916
Chipper, —, 1876
Clack, Robert H., 1876, 1897
Clark, Arthur F., 1890
Clarke, Robert M., 1930–31
Clarke, William J., 1893–94, 1896
Clarkson, Arthur H., 1892–96
Clarkson, John G., 1888, 1892–93
Cockill, George W., 1915
Cohen, —, 1893
Coleman, John F., 1884
Colgan, Harry W., 1899, 1901, 1903
Collins, Daniel T., 1876
Colosi, Nicholas, 1968–82
Conahan, —, 1896
Cone, J. F., 1876–77
Conlan, John B., 1941–64
Connell, Terence G., 1885, 1887
Connolly, John M., 1886–87, 1892–93
Connolly, Thomas H., 1898–1900
Conway, John H., 1906
Coogan, Daniel G., 1895
Crandall, Robert, 1876–78
Crane, Edward N., 1892–93
Crane, Samuel N., 1886–87, 1890
Crawford, Gerald J., 1976–88
Crawford, Henry C., 1956–75
Cray, —, 1893
Crolius, Frederick J., 1901
Cronin, John J., 1902–3
Cross, John A., 1876, 1878–79
Cross, Lafayette N., 1892
Cunningham, Elmer E., 1896–97, 1900–1
Cuppy, George M., 1894
Curren, Peter, 1876
Curry, Wesley, 1885–86, 1889–90, 1898
Cusack, Stephen P., 1909
Cushman, Charles H., 1884–85, 1894, 1898
Cusick, Andrew,

1886–87
Dailey, John J., 1882
Daily, Cornelius F., 1886, 1891, 1894, 1896
Dale, Jerry P., 1970–85
Daly, Thomas P., 1901
Daniels, Charles F., 1876–80, 1887–88
Darling, Conrad, 1887
Darling, Gary, 1988
Dascoli, Frank, 1948–62
Davidson, David L., 1969–84
Davidson, Robert A., 1983–88
Davis, C. E., 1880
Davis, Gerald, 1985–88
Day, —, 1879
Dealey, Patrick E., 1886
Deane, Henry C., 1876, 1878
Decker, Stewart M., 1883–85, 1888
Delmore, Victor, 1956–59
DeMuth, Dana A., 1986–88
Devinney, Daniel, 1876–77
Dexter, Charles D., 1896–97
Dezelan, Frank J., 1966–68, 1969–71
Dixon, Hal H., 1953–59
Donahue, Francis R., 1897
Donahue, Timothy C., 1895–96
Donatelli, August J., 1950–73
Donlin, Michael J., 1900
Donnelly, Charles H., 1931–32
Donnelly, James B., 1896
Donohue, Michael R., 1930
Donovan, Timothy H., 1882
Donovan, William E., 1902
Dooin, Charles S., 1904
Doscher, John H., 1879–82, 1887
Douglass, William B., 1903
Dowse, Thomas J., 1890
Doyle, John J., 1911
Draper, John H., 1877
Ducharme, —, 1876–77
Duggleby, William J., 1905
Dunlap, Frederick C., 1879
Dunn, John, 1879
Dunn, Thomas P., 1939–46
Dunnigan, Joseph, 1881–82
Dwyer, John F., 1889, 1893–97, 1899, 1901
Dyler, John F., 1892, 1897
Eagan, John J., 1878, 1886
Earle, William M., 1892, 1894
Eason, Malcolm W., 1901–2, 1910–15
Ehret, Philip S., 1892, 1895–97
Ellick, Joseph J., 1886
Emslie, Robert D., 1891–1924
Engel, Robert A.,

1965–88
Engeln, William R., 1952–56
English, John W., 1876
Evans, Jacob, 1886
Farrell, Charles A., 1901–2
Feber, Fred W., 1879
Fenno, Norman, 1876
Ferguson, Robert V., 1879, 1884–85
Fessenden, Wallace C., 1889–90
Fields, Stephen H., 1979–82
Finch, R. B., 1880
Finneran, William F., 1911–12, 1924
Fisher, William C., 1876
Flaherty, Patrick J., 1904–7
Flynn, John A., 1893
Force, David W., 1881
Foreman, Frank I., 1895
Foreman, John D., 1896
Forman, Allen S., 1962–65
Foster, Clarence F., 1900
Fountain, Edward G., 1879
Fouser, William C., 1876
Frary, Robert, 1911
Freeman, John F., 1900
Froemming, Bruce N., 1971–88
Fulmer, Charles J., 1881, 1886
Furlong, William E., 1877–80, 1882–84, 1888
Fyfe, Lee C., 1920
Gaffney, John H., 1884–89, 1891–95
Galvin, James F., 1886–87, 1889, 1893, 1895
Ganzel, Charles W., 1901
Gardner, James A., 1899
Geer, William H., 1879
George, William M., 1889
German, Lester S., 1895
Getzein, Charles N., 1890
Gifford, James H., 1881
Gill, Thomas H., 1886
Gillean, Thomas, 1879–81
Gleason, John D., 1877
Gleason, William G., 1877
Gleason, William J., 1890, 1892
Glenn, John W., 1880
Goetz, Lawrence J., 1936–57
Goldsmith, Frederick E., 1886
Gore, Arthur J., 1947–56
Gorman, Thomas D., 1951–76
Grady, Michael W., 1895
Graves, Frank M., 1886, 1895
Gregg, Eric E., 1977–88
Griffith, Clark C., 1894
Grim, John H., 1892, 1895–96
Gross, Edward M.,

1881
Gruber, Henry J., 1889
Guglielmo, Angelo, 1952
Guinney, Daniel, 1882–83
Gumbert, Addison C., 1892–1895
Gunning, Thomas F., 1884–85, 1887
Gunson, Joseph B., 1892
Guthrie, William J., 1913–1915
Hackett, Merton M., 1886
Haddock, George S., 1889
Haley, Ed, 1876
Hallion, Thomas F., 1986–88
Hallman, William W., 1903
Hanlon, Edward H., 1892
Hardie, Louis W., 1887
Harris, Lannie D., 1979–85
Harrison, Peter A., 1916–20
Hart, Robert F., 1920–28
Hart, William F., 1896–97, 1914–15
Hartley, John, 1894
Harvey, H. Douglas, 1962–77, 1979–88
Hastings, Winfield S., 1877
Hatfield, Gilbert, 1889
Hatfield, John V. B., 1876
Hawes, William A., 1881–82
Healy, John J., 1887
Hegeman, William H., 1881
Hemming, George E., 1895–96
Henderson, James H., 1895–96
Hengle, Edward S., 1887
Henline, Walter J., 1945–48
Hernon, Thomas H., 1894
Heuble, George A., 1876
Heydler, John A., 1895–98
Hickey, James L., 1882
Higham, Richard, 1881–82
Hiller, George J., 1881
Hines, Michael P., 1884
Hirschbeck, Mark, 1988
Hoagland, Willard A., 1894
Hodges, A. D., 1876–77, 1879
Hoffer, William L., 1896
Hogan, —, 1897
Hogriever, George C., 1893
Holland, John A., 1887
Holliday, James W., 1897, 1903
Hornung, Joseph M., 1892–93, 1896
Houtz, Charles, 1876, 1879
Howard, C. F., 1884
Howe, John, 1890
Hunt, John T., 1893, 1895, 1898–99
Hurst, Timothy C., 1891–98, 1900, 1903–4
Hyatt, Robert H., 1912
Irwin, Arthur A., 1881, 1902

Jacklitsch, Fred L., 1901
Jackowski, William A., 1952–68
Jeffers, W. W., 1881
Jennings, Hugh A., 1893, 1900
Jevne, Frederick, 1892–95
Johnson, Harry S., 1914
Johnstone, James E., 1903–12
Jones, Henry M., 1890
Jorda, Louis D., 1927–31, 1940–52
Jose, —, 1889
Joyce, C. E., 1879
Julian, Joseph O., 1878
Kahle, —, 1905
Kane, Stephen J., 1906, 1909–10
Karger, Edwin, 1906
Kecher, W. H., 1910
Keefe, Timothy J., 1880, 1882–85, 1887, 1892–96
Keenan, James W., 1881, 1890, 1893
Kelley, Joseph J., 1892, 1904
Kelley, W. W., 1877
Kellum, Winford A., 1905
Kelly, John O., 1882, 1884–85, 1888, 1897
Kelly, Michael J., 1893
Kelly, S., 1880
Kennedy, Charles, 1904
Kennedy, Michael J., 1884
Kenney, John, 1876–77
Kerins, John A., 1888
Kibler, John W., 1963–88
Killen, Frank B., 1896–97
Kinslow, Thomas F., 1892
Kipp, Eden, 1881
Kitson, Frank R., 1902
Klem, William J., 1905–41
Kling, John G., 1901
Klusman, William F., 1892–93
Knell, Philip H., 1895
Knight, Alonzo P., 1876, 1888–89
Knowles, James, 1892
Krieg, William F., 1887
Lally, Daniel J., 1891–94, 1896
Landes, Stanley A., 1955–72
Lane, Frank, 1883
Laney, B., 1884
Lanigan, Charles, 1908
Latham, Walter A., 1899–1900, 1902
Laughlin, 1876
Lavers, George W., 1882
Lawler, Michael H., 1882
Leever, Samuel W., 1900, 1904
Libby, Stephen A., 1880
Lincoln, Frederick H., 1914, 1917
Lindeman, Vivian A., 1907
Long, William H., 1893, 1895, 1897
Lowell, William, 1882
Lundgren, Carl L., 1905–6
Lynch, J. T., 1880
Lynch, Thomas J.,

1888–99, 1902
Macullar, John F., 1892
Maddox, Charles, 1882
Magee, Sherwood R., 1928
Magerkurth, George L., 1929–47
Mahoney, Michael J., 1892
Malone, Ferguson G., 1884, 1892
Maloney, William A., 1902
Manassau, Alfred S., 1899
Manning, James H., 1886, 1893
Mapledoram, Blake A., 1886
Marsh, Randall G., 1983–88
Martin, Alphonse C., 1876
Mason, Charles E., 1876
Mathews, Robert T., 1876, 1880, 1882
Mathewson, Christopher, 1901, 1907
Mayer, —, 1893
McAllister, Louis W., 1899
McCaffrey, Harry, 1885–86
McCarthy, Thomas F. M., 1896
McCauley, Allen B., 1890
McCauley, Patrick M., 1896
McCormick, James, 1885
McCormick, William J., 1919–29
McCrum, —, 1892
McDermott, Michael J., 1890, 1897
McDonald, James F., 1895, 1897–99
McDowell, —, 1893
McElwee, Harvey, 1877
McFarland, Edward W., 1896
McFarland, Horace, 1896–97
McGann, Dennis L., 1903
McGarr, James B., 1895, 1899
McGee, —, 1876
McGinnis, 1910
McGinnity, Joseph J., 1900
McGinty, —, 1897
McGrew, Harry T., 1930–31, 1933–34
McGuire, James T., 1886–87, 1894, 1896–97, 1901
McGunnigle, Edward, 1888
McLaughlin, Edward J., 1929
McLaughlin, Michael, 1893
McLaughlin, Peter J., 1924–28
McLean, William B., 1876–80, 1882–84
McLeod, —, 1895
McMahon, John H., 1893
McMater, —, 1877
McMullen, John F., 1876
McQuaid, John H., 1889–95
McSherry, John P., 1971–88
Meagher, John, 1877

Mears, Charles W., 1894
Medart, William, 1876–77
Meekin, Jouette, 1895–96
Megrue, Cliff, 1876
Mertes, Samuel B., 1903–5
Miller, George E., 1879
Miller, George F., 1893, 1896
Miller, Joseph H., 1884
Mills, Abraham G., 1877
Mitchell, Charles, 1892
Montague, —, 1877
Montague, Edward M., 1976–88
Moran, —, 1894
Moran, August, 1903–4, 1910–11, 1918
Moran, Charles B., 1917–39
Moran, Patrick J., 1901
Morrill, John F., 1891, 1896
Morris, Edward, 1895, 1897
Morris, John S., 1876
Muir, Thomas, 1876
Mullane, Anthony J., 1893, 1897
Mullen, Peter C., 1893
Mullin, John, 1909
Mulvey, Joseph H., 1895
Murnane, Timothy H., 1886
Murphy, Henry, 1880
Murphy, Martin W., 1886
Murphy, Morgan E., 1893, 1896, 1898
Murphy, William H., 1895, 1897
Murray, Jeremiah J., 1893–95, 1900, 1905, 1907
Myers, George D., 1896
Myers, Henry C., 1890
Nash, William M., 1901
Needham, Thomas J., 1904, 1907
Newton, Eustace J., 1902
Nichols, Charles A., 1900–1
Nickerson, S. W., 1880
Nicol, Hugh N., 1894
Nolan, Edward S., 1881
Noonan, Peter J., 1906–7
O'Brien, John F., 1889
O'Brien, William, 1876
O'Connor, Arthur, 1914
O'Connor, John J., 1893–1901
O'Day, Henry F., 1888–89, 1893, 1895–1911, 1913, 1915–27
Odlin, Albert F., 1883
O'Hara, —, 1915
O'Leary, Daniel, 1879
Olsen, Andrew H., 1968–81
O'Neill, Michael J., 1904
O'Rourke, James H., 1893–94
Orth, Albert L., 1901, 1912–17
Osborne, William, 1876
O'Sullivan, John J., 1922
Overall, Orval, 1905, 1910

Owens, Clarence B.,
1908, 1912–13
Pallone, David M.,
1979–88
Parker, George L.,
1936–38
Pearce, Grayson S.,
1886–87, 1892
Pearce, Richard J.,
1878, 1882
Pears, Frank, 1897
Peitz, Henry C., 1901,
1906
Pelekoudas, Christos
G., 1960–75
Pfeffer, Nathaniel F.,
1897
Pfirman, Charles H.,
1922–36
Phelan, —, 1896
Phelps, Edward J.,
1912
Phillippe, Charles L.,
1903
Pierce, —, 1893
Pike, Lipman E., 1890
Pinelli, Ralph A.,
1935–56
Poncino, Larry,
1886–88
Powell, Jack, 1923–24,
1933
Power, Charles B.,
1893, 1895, 1902
Power, Thomas E.,
1877–88, 1894–95
Powers, James T.,
1895
Powers, Philip J.,
1881, 1886–91
Pratt, Albert G.,
1879–80, 1887
Pratt, Thomas J., 1886
Pryor, J. Paul, 1961–8l
Pulli, Frank V.,
1972–88
Quest, Joseph L.,
1886–87
Quick, James E.,
1976–88
Quigley, Ernest C.,
1913–37
Quinn, Joseph C.,
1881–82
Quinn, Joseph J.,
1889, 1894, 1896
Quinn, P. J., 1876
Quinn, William H.,
1877
Reardon, John E.,
1926–49
Redheffer, 1893, 1895
Reid, William A., 1882
Reilly, Charles T.,
1892–95
Reilly, William, 1880
Reitz, Henry P., 1895
Remsen, John J., 1880
Rennert, Laurence H.,
1973–88
Rhines, William P.,
1891, 1896
Rhodes, Eugene A.,
1887
Richardson, Arthur H.,
1887, 1892
Richmond, John L.,
1883
Rigler, Charles,
1905–22, 1924–35
Riley, William J., 1880
Rippley, T. Steven,
1985–88
Ritchie, F., 1876
Robb, Douglas W.,
1948–52
Roberts, Leonard W.,
1953–55
Robinson, Wilbert,
1898
Rocap, Adam, 1876
Roll, —, 1876
Rudderham, Francis F.,

1907
Rudderham, John E.,
1908
Runge, Paul E.,
1973–88
Ryan, James E., 1892
Ryan, Walter, 1946
Sanders, Alexander
B., 1889
Schew, Augustus,
1880–81
Schmidt, Henry M.,
1903
Schofield, J. W., 1880
Schriver, William F.,
1901
Schurer, —, 1896
Scott, James, 1930–31
Sears, John W.,
1934–45
Secory, Frank E.,
1952–70
Sentelle, Leopold T.,
1922–23
Serad, William T., 1884
Seward, Edward W.,
1892–93
Seward, George E.,
1876–79
Sheridan, John F.,
1892–93, 1896–97
Simmons, Joseph S.,
1876
Skinner, S. A., 1886
Smith, —, 1876
Smith, Charles M.,
1881–82
Smith, Edward E.,
1890
Smith, George H.,
1901
Smith, Vincent A.,
1957–65
Smith, William E., 1886
Smith, William W.,
1898–99
Sneeden, —, 1895
Snyder, Charles N.,
1892–95, 1898, 1901
Sommers, Joseph A.,
1889, 1893
Stafford, John H.,
1906
Stage, Charles W.,
1893–95
Staley, Harry E., 1892,
1895
Stambaugh, Calvin G.,
1876–79
Stark, Albert D.,
1928–35, 1937–39,
1942
Stearns, Daniel E.,
1880–81
Stein, Edward F., 1890,
1894, 1896
Steiner, Melvin J.,
1961–72
Steinfeldt, Henry M.,
1905
Stello, Richard J.,
1969–87
Sternburg, —, 1909
Stewart, William J.,
1933–54
Stivetts, John C., 1894
Stockdale, M. J., 1915
Stocksdale, Otis H.,
1895
Stricker, John A., 1892
Stricklett, Elmer E.,
1907
Strief, George A.,
1889–90
Sudol, Edward L.,
1957–77
Sugden, Joseph, 1887
Sullivan, David F.,
1880–83, 1885, 1888
Sullivan, Dennis J.,
1881
Sullivan, James E.,
1896

Sullivan, Jeremiah,
1887
Sullivan, John R., 1882
Sullivan, Martin J.,
1889
Sullivan, Michael J.,
1897
Summer, James G.,
1876–77, 1879
Supple, —, 1906
Sutcliffe, Elmer E.,
1889, 1892
Sutton, Ezra B., 1876
Swartwood, Cyrus E.,
1894–1900
Sweasy, Charles J.,
1879
Sweeney, James M.,
1924–26
Tannehill, Jesse N.,
1897, 1901–2
Tata, Terry A., 1973–88
Tate, Edward F., 1888
Taylor, John B., 1899
Taylor, John W., 1901,
1905
Tener, John K., 1889
Terry, William J., 1892,
1895–96, 1900
Tilden, Otis, 1876,
1880
Tindall, —, 1890, 1896
Toole, Stephen J.,
1888
Tremblay, Richard H.,
1971
Truby, Harry G., 1909
Tuthill, Benjamin, 1893,
1895
Twitchell, Lawrence G.,
1894
Valentine, John G.,
1887–88
Van Court, Eugene,
1884
Vargo, Edward P.,
1960–83
Vaughn, Harry F., 1892,
1899
Venzon, Anthony,
1957–71
Viau, Leon, 1891
Vickery, Thomas G.,
1890
Wade, Ben F., 1880
Walker, Thomas W.,
1905
Walker, William E.,
1876–77
Wall, Joseph F., 1901
Wallace, Roderick J.,
1895
Walsh, Francis D.,
1961–63
Walsh, Frank, 1877
Walsh, Michael F.,
1876, 1879–82
Walters, 1892–93
Walton, G. W., 1876
Ward, John M., 1888
Warneke, Lonnie,
1949–55
Warner, Albert,
1898–99
Warner, John J.,
1896–97, 1900, 1903
Waterman, Frederick
A., 1880
Weaver, William B.,
1893
Weeden, 1889–90
Weidman, George E.,
1894, 1896
Weimer, Jacob W.,
1905, 1907
Welch, Michael F.,
1885–86, 1888, 1890
Wendelstedt, Harry H.
Jr., 1966–88
West, George, 1878
West, Joseph H., 1976,
1978–88

West, Milton D., 1890
Westervelt, Frederick
E., 1922
Weyer, Lee H., 1961,
1963–88
Weyhing, August,
1894, 1899–1900
Wheeler, Robert, 1879
Whistler, Lewis, 1891
White, George F.,
1876–78
White, Guy H., 1901–2
White, James L., 1880
White, William W.,
1876
Whitney, James E.,
1884, 1886
Wilbur, Charles E.,
1879–80
Wilhelm, Irving K.,
1904–5
Williams, Arthur,
1972–77
Williams, Charles H.,
1978, 1983–88
Williams, Elisha A.,
1876
Williams, James A.,
1879
Williams, William G.,
Jr., 1963–87
Willis, Victor G., 1903
Wilmot, Walter R.,
1897
Wilson, Frank,
1923–28
Wilson, Frank A., 1896
Wilson, John A., 1887
Wilson, Parke A.,
1894–96, 1899
Wilson, William C.,
1890, 1892–93
Wise, Samuel W.,
1889, 1893
Wolf, William V.,
1895–97
Wood, George A.,
1898, 1899
Wood, James B., 1876
Woulffe, James J.,
1893
Wright, William H.,
1876–77, 1885
Yeager, George E.,
1901
York, Thomas J., 1886
Young, Denton T., 1896
Young, Irving M., 1905,
1907
Young, John W.,
1879–81
Zacharias, Thomas,
1890
Zimmer, Charles L.,
1889, 1904–5

**American Association
(1882–91)**

Arnold, Frank W., 1889
Austin, Ed, 1890
Baldwin, Clarence G.,
1887
Barnie, William S.,
1882, 1884, 1887,
1889
Barnum, George W.,
1890
Battin, Joseph V.,
1882, 1886
Bass, John E., 1883
Bauer, Albert J., 1887,
1890
Becannon, James M.,
1884
Becannon, William H.,
1883
Bell, Frank G., 1889
Bittman, Henry, 1889
Blogg, Wesley C.,
1886
Bloom, —, 1887
Bond, Thomas H.,

1884
Booth, Amos S., 1882
Bowes, Frank C., 1890
Boyle, John A., 1888
Brennan, James A.,
1888
Brennan, John E.,
1884
Briody, Charles F.,
1888
Burkalow, Isaac, 1888
Burns, —, 1882
Burns, Thomas P.,
1888
Bushong, Albert J.,
1888–89
Butler, Charles, 1889
Butler, Ormond H.,
1883, 1886
Campbell, Daniel, 1890
Carey, Thomas J.,
1882
Carlin, William J.,
1885–86, 1888–89
Carsey, Wilfred, 1891
Cassidy, John P., 1884
Chamberlain, Elton P.,
1887, 1891
Clinton, J. L., 1886
Connell, J., 1885
Connell, Terence G.,
1884–86, 1889–90
Connelly, John M.,
1885–1887
Connelly, William, 1884
Cornell, —, 1884
Crandall, Robert, 1882
Creighton, —,
1889–90
Critchley, Morris A.,
1884–85
Cross, Lafayette N.,
1889
Crowell, William T.,
1888
Curry, Frank, 1885
Curry, Wesley, 1887,
1890
Cuthbert, Edgar E.,
1887–88
Dailey, John J.,
1883–84, 1889
Daniels, Charles F.,
1883–85, 1889
Daniels, Lawrence,
1887
Darling, Dell C., 1891
Davis, James J., 1891
Devine, Walter J., 1890
DeVinney, Daniel, 1887
DeVinney, P. H., 1884
Devlin, Charles, 1888
Dolan, Thomas J.,
1890
Donahue, James A.,
1888
Doscher, John H.,
1888, 1890
Dow, Clarence, 1890
Dugan, —, 1887
Duke, Martin F., 1890
Dunlevy, Hugh, 1887
Dyler, John F., 1883–86
Easton, John B., 1891
Ehret, Philip S., 1890
Ellick, Joseph J.,
1888–89
Emslie, Robert D.,
1890
Ewing, William, 1882,
1889
Fell, —, 1885
Ferguson, Robert V.,
1886–89, 1891
Fountain, Henry V.,
1888
Fulmer, Charles J.,
1888
Fulmer, Christopher,
1887
Gaffney, John H.,
1888–89
Galvin, James F.,

1885–86
Ganzel, Charles W.,
1886
Geer, William H., 1887
Gill, Thomas H., 1886
Gleason, William G.,
1891
Goldsby, Walton H.,
1888
Goldsmith, Frederick
E., 1888–89
Greenwood, William F.,
1884
Griffith, Clark C., 1891
Griffith, E. A., 1884
Gunning, Thomas F.,
1888–89
Healy, John J., 1890
Hecker, Guy J.,
1888–89
Helburn, Hugo, 1887
Henderson, James H.,
1889
Hengle, Edward S.,
1889
Herr, Edward J., 1888
Hicks, Nathaniel W.,
1885
Higgins, William H.,
1890
Holbert, William H.,
1888
Holland, John A., 1884
Holland, Willard A.,
1889
Holliday, James W.,
1888
Houtz, Charles, 1882
Hurley, Daniel, 1887
Irwin, John, 1885
Jennings, Alfred, 1882,
1884–85, 1887,
1889, 1891
Johnston, Richard F.,
1884
Jones, Charles W.,
1891
Julian, Joseph O.,
1888
Keefe, Timothy J.,
1884
Keenan, James W.,
1887–88
Kelly, John O.,
1882–88
Kerins, John A.,
1889–90
Kilroy, Matthew A.,
1887
Kirby, J. J., 1888
Kleinbacker, 1886
Knell, Philip H., 1891
Knight, Alonzo P., 1887
Latham, George W.,
1884
Lawler, John F., 1884
Lilly, J., 1884
Little, —, 1884
Loughlin, 1885
Lynch, John H., 1884
Lyons, Toby A., 1891
Lyston, William E.,
1890
Macullar, James F.,
1891
Macullar, John F., 1886
Mack, Dennis J., 1886
Magner, John T.,
1883–84, 1887
Malone, J. R., 1888
Marshall, —, 1887
Mathews, Robert T.,
1888, 1891
Mattimore, Michael J.,
1888
McCarthy, Thomas F.
M., 1889
McCartney, Joseph,
1882
McCarty, John A.,
1890
McCormick, 1888
McGee, Patrick, 1882,

1884
McGinnis, George M., 1888–89
McIntosh, —, 1882
McKelvy, Russell E., 1882
McLaughlin, Thomas, 1891
McLaughlin, William, 1882
McLean, William B., 1882, 1885, 1889–90
McMahon, John J., 1890
McNichol, Robert T., 1883
McQuade, James H., 1891
McQuade, John H., 1886–88
McSorley, John B., 1888
McSorley, Thomas S., 1884
Medart, William, 1887
Merrill, Edward S., 1884
Mitchell, —, 1887
Miller, Joseph H., 1884
Morgan, Henry W., 1884
Morton, Charles H., 1884, 1886
Mountain, Frank H., 1884
Mullen, Peter C., 1891
O'Brien, John K., 1890
O'Brien, William D., 1887–88
O'Connor, John J., 1889
O'Dea, Lawrence, 1890
Paasch, William, 1887–89
Parker, —, 1887
Pearce, Grayson S., 1882, 1884
Peoples, James E., 1888–90
Pike, Lipman, E., 1887, 1889
Pratt, Albert G., 1883, 1886
Quinn, A. J., 1886
Quinn, William H., 1884–85
Reeder, James E., 1884
Reising, Charles, 1882
Rice, —, 1885
Riley, William J., 1882, 1885
Robb, John, 1886
Ross, Robert T., 1882, 1884
Ruhl, Gus, 1882
Ryan, John, 1882
Sage, Henry, 1890
Schroder, 1890
Selman, Frank C., 1882
Serad, William T., 1888
Seward, George E., 1884
Sherman, —, 1890
Simmons, Joseph S., 1882
Skeenet, —, 1890
Skinner, —, 1884
Smith, Charles M., 1882, 1886
Smith, Frederick C., 1890
Smith, George, 1887
Sneed, John L., 1885
Snyder, Charles N., 1886, 1891
Sommer, Benjamin, 1883
Sommer, Joseph J., 1888

Sprague, Charles W., 1890
Stivetts, John C., 1891
Sullivan, David F., 1884
Sullivan, Theodore P., 1887
Sweeney, Charles J., 1887
Sylvester, Louis J., 1888
Talbot, —, 1887
Taylor, Walter, 1890
Terry, William J., 1884, 1888
Tinney, —, 1882
Toole, Stephen J., 1890
Townsend, George H., 1890
Traffley, William F., 1884
Tunnison, —, 1885–86
Valentine, John G., 1884–86
Vaughn, Harry F., 1891
Viau, Leon, 1888
Walsh, Michael F., 1882–83, 1885–88
West, —, 1885, 1887
Weyhing, August, 1891
Wheeler, Harry E., 1882
Wood, George A., 1886, 1891
Wright, —, 1884
Wright, Parry, 1884
York, Thomas J., 1886
Young, Benjamin F., 1886–87
Young, Joseph, 1890
Zimmer, Charles L., 1888

Union Association (1884)

Adler, —,
Bradley, George W.
Burlingame, F. A.
Callahan, Edward J.
Carroll, Patrick
Crawford, Alexander
Cuthbert, Edgar E.
DeVinney, P. H.
Donovan, —,
Dutton, Patrick J.
Furlong, William E.
Grady, John J.
Hengle, Edward S.
Hoberbeck, —,
Holland, John A.
Hooper, Michael H.
Hoover, —,
Hudson, Vincent D.
Jennings, Alfred
Jordan, —,
Kelly, John O.
Lee, Thomas F.
Mapledoram, Blake A.
McCaffrey, Harry
McGunningle, William H.
McLaughlin, William
McManaway, —,
McMinimum, —,
Montgomery, —,
O'Leary, Daniel
Powers, Charles B.
Seward, George E.
Stearns, Daniel E.
Sullivan, David F.
Timblin, —,
Torry, —,
Wheeler, —,
Williams, —,

Players' League (1890)

Balkie, —,
Barnes, Roscoe C.
Carney, John J.

Caskin, Edward J.
Comiskey, Charles A.
Daily, Cornelius F.
Ferguson, Robert V.
Gaffney, John H.
Gumbert, Addison C.
Gunning, Thomas F.
Haddock, George S.
Hallinan, W. W.
Holbert, William H.
Husted, William J.
Jones, Charles W.
Keefe, Timothy J.
Kelly, John O.
Kilroy, Matthew A.
Knight, Alonzo P.
Leach, Henry
Madden, Michael J.
Matthews, John
Milligan, John
Murphy, Cornelius B.
O'Day, Henry
Pearce, Grayson S.
Sanders, Alexander B.
Sheridan, John F.
Snyder, Charles N.
Tener, John K.

American League (1901–)

Adams, John H., 1903
Anthony, G. Merlyn, 1969–75
Ashford, Emmett L., 1966–70
Avants, Nick R., 1969–71
Barnett, Lawrence R., 1968–88
Barry, Daniel, 1928
Basil, Stephen J., 1936–42
Berry, Charles F., 1942–62
Betts, William G., 1901
Boyer, James M., 1944–50
Bremigan, Nicholas G., 1974–88
Brinkman, Joseph N., 1973–88
Campbell, William M., Jr., 1928–31
Cantillon, Joseph, 1901
Carrigan, H. Sam, 1961–65
Carpenter, William B., 1904
Caruthers, Robert L., 1902–3
Chill, Oliver P., 1914–16, 1919–22
Chylak, Nestor L., Jr., 1954–78
Clark, Alan M., 1976–88
Coble, Drew G., 1983–88
Colliflower, James H., 1910
Connolly, Thomas H., 1901–31
Connor, Thomas, 1905–6
Cooney, Terrance J., 1975–88
Cousins, Derryl, 1979–88
Cronin, John J., 1901
Deegan, William E. J., 1970–80
Denkinger, Donald A., 1968–88
DiMuro, Louis J., 1963–80
Dinneen, William H., 1909–37
Donnelly, Charles H., 1934–35
Doyle, Walter J., 1963

Drummond, Calvin T., 1960–69
Duffy, James F., 1951–55
Dwyer, John F., 1904
Egan, John J., 1903, 1907–14
Eldridge, Clarence E., 1914–15
Evans, James B., 1971–88
Evans, William G., 1906–27
Ferguson, Charles A., 1913
Flaherty, John F., 1953–73
Ford, R. Dale, 1975–88
Frantz, Arthur F., 1969–77
Friel, William E., 1920
Froese, Grover A., Jr., 1952–53
Garcia, Richard R., 1975–88
Geisel, Harry C., 1925–42
Goetz, Russell L., 1968–83
Grieve, William T. T., 1938–55
Guthrie, William J., 1922, 1928–32
Haller, William E., 1961, 1963–82
Hart, Eugene F., 1912–13
Hart, William F., 1901
Haskell, John E., 1901
Hassett, James E., 1903
Hayes, Gerald, 1925–26
Hendry, Eugene, 1978–88
Hildebrand, George A., 1912–34
Hirschbeck, John F., 1984–88
Holmes, Howard E., 1923–24
Honochick, G. James, 1949–73
Hubbard, R. Cal, 1936–51, 1954–62
Hurley, Edwin H., 1947–65
Hurst, Timothy C., 1905–9
Johnson, Mark S., 1984–88
Johnston, Charles E., 1936–37
Johnstone, James E., 1902
Jones, Nicholas I., 1944–49
Kaiser, Kenneth J., 1977–88
Kelly, Thomas B., 1905
Kerin, John, 1908–10
Kerins, John A., 1903
King, Charles F., 1904
Kinnamon, William E., 1960–69
Kolls, Louis C., 1933–40
Kosc, Gregory J., 1976–88
Kunkel, William G., 1968–84
Linsalata, Joseph N., 1961–62
Luciano, Ronald M., 1968–80
Maloney, George P., 1969–83
Mannassau, Alfred S., 1901
Marberry, Frederick, 1935
McCarthy, John, 1905

McClelland, Timothy R., 1984–88
McCormick, William J., 1917
McCoy, Larry S., 1970–88
McGowan, William A., 1925–54
McGreevy, Edward, 1912–13
McKean, James G., 1974–88
McKinley, William F., 1946–65
Merrill, E. Durwood, 1977–88
Morgenweck, Henry C., 1972–75
Moriarty, George J., 1917–26, 1929–40
Morrison, Daniel G., 1984–88
Mullaney, Dominic J., 1915
Mullin, John, 1911–12
Nallin, Richard F., 1915–32
Napp, Larry A., 1951–74
Neudecker, Jerome A., 1965–85
O'Brien, Joseph, 1912, 1914
Odom, James C., 1965–74
O'Donnell, James M., 1968–71
O'Loughlin, Frank H., 1902–18
Ormsby, Emmett T., 1923–41
Owens, Clarence B., 1916–37
Palermo, Stephen M., 1977–88
Paparella, Joseph J., 1946–65
Parker, Harley P., 1911
Parks, Dallas F., 1979–83
Passarella, Arthur M., 1941–42, 1945–53
Pears, Frank, 1903
Perrine, Fred, 1909–12
Phillips, David R., 1971–88
Pipgras, George W., 1938–46
Quigley, Ernest C., 1906
Quinn, John A., 1935–42
Reed, Rick A., 1984–88
Reilly, Michael E., 1978–88
Rice, John L., 1955–73
Robb, Douglas W., 1952–53
Rodriguez, Armando H., 1974–75
Roe, John, 1982–88
Rommel, Edwin A., 1938–59
Rowland, Clarence H., 1923–27
Rue, Joseph W., 1938–47
Runge, Edward P., 1954–70
Salerno, Alexander J., 1961–68
Schwarts, Harry C., 1960–62
Scott, Dale A., 1986–88
Sheridan, John F., 1901–14
Shulock, John R., 1979–88
Smith, William A.,

1960–65
Soar, A. Henry, 1950–73
Spenn, Frederick C., 1979–80
Springstead, Martin J., 1965–86
Stafford, John H., 1907
Stevens, John W., 1948–71
Stewart, Ernest D., 1941–45
Stewart, Robert W., 1959–70
Summers, William R., 1933–59
Tabacchi, Frank T., 1956–59
Tschida, Timothy J., 1986–88
Umont, Frank W., 1954–73
Valentine, William T., Jr., 1963–68
Van Graflan, Roy, 1927–33
Voltaggio, Vito H., 1977–88
Wallace, Roderick J., 1915–16
Walsh, Edward A., 1922
Weafer, Harold L., 1943–47
Welke, Timothy J., 1985–88
Westervelt, Frederick E., 1911–12
Wilson, Frank, 1921–22
Young, Larry E., 1985–88

Federal League (1914–15)

Anderson, Oliver O., 1914
Brennan, William T., 1914–15
Brewer, —,1915
Bush, Garnet C., 1914
Carpenter, 1914
Corcoran, Thomas W., 1914–15
Cross, Montford M., 1914
Cusack, Stephen P., 1914
Finneran, William E., 1915
Fyfe, Louis, 1915
Goeckel, E., 1914
Groom, Robert, 1914
Howell, Harry, 1915
Johnstone, James E., 1914–15
Kane, Stephen J., 1914
Langden, Joseph, 1915
Mannassau, Alfred S., 1914
Maxwell, J. A., 1914
McCormick, William J., 1914–15
Mullin, John, 1915
Murphy, J. A., 1914
O'Brien, Joseph, 1915
Quisser, 1914
Shannon, William P., 1914–15
Stocksdale, Otis H., 1915
Van Sickle, Charles F., 1914
Westervelt, Frederick E., 1915
Wilhelm, Irving K., 1915

Home-Road Statistics

## CHAPTER 40

Home-Road Statistics

This section consists of three components, each illustrating the powerful effects a ballpark can have on batting and pitching performance. (Parks affect fielding and baserunning as well, but to a far lesser degree.) The first component is a summary of the won-lost records and run-scoring characteristics of every park for all years of the three most significant major leagues—the American, the National, and the American Association. The second is a breakdown of the home/road records for all teams in all leagues since 1876; detailed here are the won-lost records, runs scored and allowed; home runs hit and allowed; and a variety of hitting and pitching factors that are helpful for evaluation of a team and, by extension, its players. The final component is an in-depth analysis of ballpark influences on the careers of 27 superstar hitters, including year-by-year breakdowns of their performance at home and away. For this last component, the editors are indebted to Bill Deane, who researched much of the performance and wrote the comments.

What is the definition of success at home and on the road? Every team is expected to win more games at home than it does on the road, to the extent that if it only breaks even on the road it is thought to have a shot at the pennant. No matter whether its home park favors hitters or pitchers, a home team should be able to take advantage of the park's peculiarities better than the visiting team can. The Houston Astros may score fewer (and the Boston Red Sox more) runs at home than they do on the road, but their *differential* between runs scored and runs allowed will be greater than their run differential on the road. Greater run differential means more wins.

Almost anybody, it seems, can play .500 ball at home (in the NL of 1983, for example, only one team had a losing record on its own turf). This is somewhat deceptive, for while .500 is the average of all games played, and a team that goes 81–81 is thus defined as average, .500 is not the average at home nor, for that matter, away. The table below, which gives the home park won-lost records of all major leagues since 1900, shows the home average to be .543. The inverse, .457, is the average road record in this century.

If the average home winning percentage is .543, then an average team (81–81) should be expected to go 44–37 at home and 37–44 on the road. Until 1987, only four teams with road records that were below average—that is, 37–44—ever won the pennant, and none went on to win the World Series. Then the Minnesota Twins took the American League flag with a regular-season road mark of 29–52, by far the worst ever for a pennant or division winner, and then proceeded to lose all three World Series road games while winning all four at home. We are not likely to see such a performance again.

Just as runs scored and runs allowed may predict won-lost records, as discussed in the Introduction to the Annual Re-cord, so we can move backwards from won-lost records (the actual home-park norm of 44–37, which is between 5 and 10 percent better than the theoretical norm of 41–40) to examine runs scored and runs allowed. Runs (and home runs) per inning at home are indeed accumulated at a rate per inning about 10 percent higher than on the road, but the game and season totals presented in this section fall short of that mark. The reason: since the number of innings played at home is about 5 percent lower than on the road (leading home teams do not bat in the bottom half of final innings), total runs and homers are in actuality only about 5 percent higher.

Home Park Won-Lost Records

National League

Years	W	L	Pct.
1900–10 ('01 AL)	3489	2995	.538
1911–20	3189	2775	.537
1921–30	3360	2770	.548
1931–40	3353	2760	.549
1941–50	3319	2823	.540
1951–60 ('61 NL)	3681	3098	.543
1961–68 ('62 NL)	3075	2591	.543
1969–76	4088	3638	.529
1977–88	6148	5170	.543
	33,702	28,600	.541

American League

Years	W	L	Pct.
1900–10 ('01 AL)	3345	2530	.569
1911–20	3201	2754	.537
1921–30	3344	2787	.545
1931–40	3349	2753	.549
1941–50	3383	2754	.551
1951–60 ('61 NL)	3291	2863	.535
1961–68 ('62 NL)	3462	3003	.535
1969–76	4142	3568	.537
1977–88	7200	6029	.544
	34,712	29,041	.544

Federal League

Years	W	L	Pct.
1914–15	660	560	.541

Major League

Years	W	L	Pct.
1900–88	69,074	58,201	.543

Detailed technical information about the formulas and calculations behind Park Factor, as applied to teams as well as individuals, will be found in the Glossary. For the general reader, suffice it to say, that all factors and rating related to home-park effects are calculated by comparing runs scored and allowed per inning at home to runs scored and allowed per inning on the road. The same holds true for home runs.

Adjustments such as the Run Rating for Batters (RB) and the Home Run rating for Batters (HRB) are made to team measures of batting strength to take into account the fact that a team's batters do not have to face its own pitchers. Innings

are estimated from the number of games and games won (leading home teams not batting in the final inning).

For additional useful information about home-road differences, we refer the reader to the Annual Record and the Glossary. For a key to the team and league abbreviations used throughout this section, flip to the last page of this volume.

Other abbreviations follow, first for the ballpark and team components, next for individual players.

TM	Team
LG	League
W	Wins
L	Losses
T	Ties
R	Runs
OR	Opponents' Runs
HR	Home Runs
OHR	Opponents' Home Runs

RF   Run Factor (A measure of the run scoring in a given ballpark compared to other ballparks, with 100 representing the average home park and the highest figure above that representing the best hitters' park.)

HRF   Home Run Factor (A measure of the home runs hit in a given ballpark, with 100 representing the average home park and the highest figure above that representing the best home-run park.)

HRB   Home Run Batter Rating (A measure of a team's home-run ability, taking into account the HRF and the fact that its batters do not face its own pitchers, with 100 representing the average and the highest figure above that representing the best.)

HRP   Home Run Pitcher Rating (A measure of a team's ability to prevent home runs, taking into account the HRF and the fact that its pitchers do not face its own batters, with 100 representing the average and the lowest figure beneath that representing the best.)

RB   Run Rating for Batters (A measure of a team's run-scoring ability, taking into account the HRF and the fact that its batters do not face its own pitchers, with 100 representing the average and the highest figure above that representing the best.)

RP   Run Rating for Pitchers (A measure of a team's run-prevention ability, taking into account the HRF and the fact that its pitchers do not face its own batters, with 100 representing the average and the lowest figure beneath that representing the best.)

BPF   Batting Park Factor (Equivalent to the Park Factor shown in the batters' section of the team statistics in the Annual Record and the Player Register; above 100 means batters benefited from playing half their games in a good hitting park.)

PPF   Pitching Park Factor (Equivalent to the Park Factor shown in the pitchers' section of the team statistics in the Annual Record and the Pitcher Register; above 100 means a pitcher was hurt by playing half his games in a good hitting park.)

AB	At-Bats
H	Hits
2B	Doubles
3B	Triples
RBI	Runs Batted In
BB	Bases on Balls
HB	Hit Batsman
AVG	Batting Average
OBP	On Base Percentage
SLG	Slugging Percentage

PRO   Production (On Base Percentage plus Slugging Percentage)

H/R   Home/Road Ratio of Production (Production at home over Production away)

PARK	TM	LG	YEARS	RF	HRF	HOME W	L	T	R	OR	HR	OHR	ROAD W	L	T	R	OR	HR	OHR
AMERICAN LEAGUE																			
Oriole Park	BAL	A	1901-1902	115	127	72	56	2	821	736	28	29	46	97	3	654	862	29	21
Memorial Stadium	BAL	A	1954-1988	92	90	1567	1188	9	11266	10244	2275	2035	1405	1369	0	11948	11516	2588	2252
Huntington Avenue Grounds	BOS	A	1901-1911	102	172	464	357	10	3494	3075	219	171	386	424	14	3229	3201	107	118
Fenway Park (I)	BOS	A	1912-1933	96	52	834	821	15	6818	7274	180	359	679	983	16	6743	8007	476	557
Fenway Park (II)	BOS	A	1934-1988	114	112	2543	1758	16	22685	19966	3918	3452	2007	2298	12	18711	18906	3391	3182
Chavez Ravine	CAL	A	1965-1965	92	65	46	34	0	265	254	36	35	29	53	0	262	315	56	56
Anaheim Stadium	CAL	A	1966-1988	92	96	934	902	0	7235	7289	1319	1461	841	986	2	7623	8101	1394	1500
South Side Park	CHI	A	1901-1909	89	34	433	235	21	2811	1987	33	32	311	340	13	2598	2659	70	115
Comiskey/White Sox Park	CHI	A	1910-1988	98	86	3262	2841	32	26122	25695	2735	3351	2792	3332	34	26191	27120	3228	3853
League Park (I)	CLE	A	1901-1909	96	63	385	281	13	2842	2375	66	57	313	351	8	2614	2763	106	87
League Park (II)	CLE	A	1910-1931	107	69	905	761	15	8152	7758	286	304	782	884	19	7374	7575	406	452
League/Municipal shared	CLE	A	1932-1946	95	73	667	495	7	5485	4939	558	418	532	598	12	5300	5495	710	592
———League Park (II)				110	96	408	280	2	3706	3224	443	312							
———Municipal Stadium				77	40	259	215	5	1779	1715	115	106							
Municipal/Cleveland Stadium	CLE	A	1947-1988	98	113	1776	1529	7	14200	14020	2993	2862	1551	1754	9	14278	14453	2643	2561
Bennett Park	DET	A	1901-1911	107	96	483	327	15	3727	3284	105	94	375	438	13	3199	3364	103	106
Navin Field	DET	A	1912-1937	102	93	1088	891	9	10244	9711	631	727	940	1031	22	9838	9787	751	709
Briggs/Tiger Stadium	DET	A	1938-1988	105	128	2259	1757	16	18710	17331	3887	3761	1929	2066	18	17243	16957	3062	2886
Municipal Stadium (I)	KC	A	1955-1967	106	108	452	575	2	4267	5067	767	1086	377	649	5	3837	4917	713	995
Municipal Stadium (II)	KC	A	1969-1972	100	65	159	159	1	1211	1227	137	175	136	185	0	1169	1277	216	268
Royals Stadium	KC	A	1973-1988	104	77	743	519	1	5975	5216	805	808	616	654	0	5405	5479	1055	1061
Wrigley Field	LA	A	1961-1961	127	199	46	36	0	447	421	122	126	24	55	1	297	363	67	54
Chavez Ravine	LA	A	1962-1964	86	52	124	119	0	851	900	106	125	114	128	0	1008	1017	228	213
Lloyd Street Grounds	MIL	A	1901-1901	92	94	32	37	1	342	373	15	14	16	52	1	299	455	11	19
County Stadium	MIL	A	1970-1988	97	88	786	719	1	6465	6431	1195	1185	675	833	1	6526	6768	1352	1349
Metropolitan Stadium	MIN	A	1961-1981	108	110	910	759	5	7698	7026	1424	1443	809	853	2	6929	6680	1325	1270
Humphrey Metrodome	MIN	A	1982-1988	108	106	316	254	0	2758	2699	569	639	219	345	0	2272	2716	518	611
Hilltop Park	NY	A	1903-1912	116	155	400	344	8	3299	3270	134	114	334	415	19	2702	3082	60	103
Polo Grounds (IV)	NY	A	1913-1922	101	196	416	336	10	3316	2922	332	292	358	377	6	3051	2939	191	120
Yankee Stadium	NY	A	1923-1973	91	103	2553	1410	16	19607	14741	3654	2407	2168	1790	26	20696	17497	3532	2427
Shea Stadium	NY	A	1974-1975	92	92	90	69	0	638	571	92	106	82	81	0	714	640	119	102
Yankee Stadium	NY	A	1976-1988	94	96	631	388	0	4781	3979	996	788	535	491	0	4923	4508	1024	865
Oakland Coliseum	OAK	A	1968-1988	88	88	933	739	1	6836	6355	1391	1294	779	888	0	7422	7548	1526	1502
Columbia Park	PHI	A	1901-1908	107	107	383	189	11	2758	2120	127	64	256	321	14	2228	2406	107	75
Shibe Park/Connie Mack Stadium	PHI	A	1909-1954	102	126	1763	1707	31	16091	16918	1808	1920	1484	2031	23	15436	17179	1438	1531
Sportsman's Park (III)	STL	A	1902-1908	93	101	275	243	12	1906	1793	58	73	215	300	10	1849	2087	58	70
Sportsman's Park (IV)	STL	A	1909-1919	93	101	365	449	15	2809	3310	88	110	293	532	16	2831	3766	91	105
Sportsman's Park (V)	STL	A	1920-1953	112	140	1250	1347	25	13079	14384	1593	1890	1016	1594	18	11071	13403	1127	1355
Sicks Stadium	SEA	A	1969-1969	100	125	34	47	1	329	399	74	93	30	51	0	310	400	51	79
Kingdome	SEA	A	1977-1988	105	141	427	524	0	4112	4678	946	1081	360	577	2	3625	4569	617	792
Arlington Stadium	TEX	A	1973-1988	99	91	651	616	0	5452	5517	911	1016	546	716	4	5337	5722	1052	1051
Exhibition Stadium	TOR	A	1977-1988	107	106	480	462	0	4243	4319	798	914	414	529	2	3890	4147	810	803
American League Park (I)	WAS	A	1901-1903	104	211	100	103	4	1015	1065	67	98	65	139	5	807	1183	31	47
American League Park (II)	WAS	A	1904-1910	92	46	224	297	16	1709	2048	31	32	157	380	10	1671	2418	65	71
Griffith Stadium (I)	WAS	A	1911-1955	93	39	1840	1602	38	15191	14994	529	769	1526	1885	24	15563	16603	1427	1869
Griffith Stadium	WAS	A	1956-1961	101	99	192	272	1	1858	2361	364	449	180	287	2	1859	2291	409	411
R.F.K. Stadium	WAS	A	1962-1971	96	96	363	441	0	2906	3356	616	715	316	491	1	2928	3580	652	735
NATIONAL LEAGUE																			
Atlanta/Fulton County Stadium	ATL	N	1966-1988	113	143	914	906	4	8028	8392	1751	1762	796	1037	2	6898	7639	1302	1164
Union Park	BAL	N	1892-1899	104	46	378	168	15	4106	2775	72	54	266	279	11	3392	3254	114	159
South End Grounds (I)	BOS	N	1876-1893	103	101	623	327	13	6209	4277	296	200	479	467	15	5092	5187	230	265
South End Grounds (II)	BOS	N	1894-1914	110	200	807	718	28	7847	7453	517	535	610	917	27	6382	7477	209	314
Braves Field	BOS	N	1915-1952	89	67	1411	1430	23	10995	11822	893	1001	1188	1739	27	12211	14098	1281	1633
Washington Park (II)	BRO	N	1890-1890	98	80	58	16	0	547	303	27	9	28	27	0	337	318	16	18
Eastern Park	BRO	N	1891-1897	89	89	293	182	11	3026	2567	117	118	188	281	6	2831	3282	114	145
Washington Park	BRO	N	1898-1912	96	82	554	556	17	4460	4647	168	155	436	662	20	4314	5092	183	205
Ebbets Field	BRO	N	1913-1957	102	110	1974	1452	34	16255	14838	1960	1931	1683	1750	24	15474	15118	1750	1786
Riverside Park	BUF	N	1879-1883	104	35	123	87	3	1278	1068	12	12	89	125	2	997	1285	31	38
Olympic Park (I)	BUF	N	1884-1885	112	95	56	56	3	674	717	36	33	46	65	0	521	668	26	44
23rd Street Grounds	CHI	N	1876-1877	125	69	42	18	0	558	299	3	5	36	29	1	432	333	5	8
Lake Front Park (I)	CHI	N	1878-1882	109	78	150	56	2	1443	875	21	16	104	81	5	1056	916	16	28
Lake Front Park (II)	CHI	N	1882-1884	121	480	75	30	0	908	566	142	72	46	59	0	605	621	13	32
West Side Park (I)	CHI	N	1885-1892	115	241	347	176	8	3693	2615	366	269	281	238	8	2766	2737	130	135
West Side Park (II)	CHI	N	1893-1915	102	91	1046	669	29	8690	7347	354	262	834	787	35	7693	7370	373	274
Wrigley Field	CHI	N	1916-1988	106	116	3055	2636	30	25857	25230	4169	4011	2511	3129	32	23310	24601	3512	3485
Lincoln Park Grounds	CIN	N	1876-1876	89	50	6	24	0	119	243	2	2	3	32	0	119	336	2	7
Avenue Grounds	CIN	N	1877-1879	85	222	58	41	2	562	523	16	9	37	61	1	547	707	3	8
Bank Street Grounds	CIN	N	1880-1880	103	341	14	25	1	163	216	5	8	7	34	2	131	256	2	2
League Park (I)	CIN	N	1890-1893	99	125	158	123	5	1634	1378	86	84	122	144	6	1294	1590	54	75
League Park (II)	CIN	N	1894-1901	105	61	349	217	12	3532	3113	100	108	214	319	14	2777	3224	139	182
Palace of the Fans	CIN	N	1902-1911	108	58	410	355	14	3436	3108	84	62	326	412	14	2848	2993	121	122
Redland/Crosley Field	CIN	N	1912-1969	99	86	2441	2043	26	19346	18722	2315	2155	1961	2484	26	18426	19751	2475	2654
Riverfront Stadium	CIN	N	1970-1988	102	105	864	640	2	6792	6130	1262	1193	795	713	1	6532	6176	1221	1126
Kennard Street Park	CLE	N	1879-1884	94	39	132	139	3	1226	1310	17	23	110	160	5	1209	1471	45	58
National League Park	CLE	N	1889-1890	95	54	63	72	3	710	696	21	20	42	88	4	561	854	25	48
League Park (I)	CLE	N	1891-1899	107	38	361	198	7	3822	2958	56	68	272	406	17	3566	4263	164	233
Recreation Park	DET	N	1881-1888	99	108	248	179	7	2595	2139	153	95	178	258	9	2252	2626	111	124
Hartford Ball Club Grounds	HAR	N	1876-1876	106	0	23	9	0	220	107	0	0	24	12	1	209	154	2	2
Union Grounds (Brooklyn)	HAR	N	1877-1877	71	107	19	8	2	167	92	2	1	12	19	0	174	219	2	1
Colt Stadium	HOU	N	1962-1964	86	64	117	125	2	750	898	98	119	79	163	0	801	1087	139	194
Astrodome	HOU	N	1965-1988	88	60	1068	844	0	7343	6894	868	897	817	1098	2	7739	8399	1399	1524
South Street Park	IND	N	1878-1878	68	62	10	17	1	106	115	1	1	14	19	2	187	213	2	2
Athletic Park	IND	N	1887-1889	106	199	87	110	2	1162	1236	96	122	59	139	1	873	1349	33	75
Association Park	KC	N	1886-1886	124	40	19	42	1	301	456	9	4	11	49	4	193	420	10	23
Memorial Coliseum	LA	N	1958-1961	113	146	172	137	0	1474	1430	346	397	158	151	0	1296	1291	257	254
Chavez Ravine/Dodger Stadium	LA	N	1962-1988	89	86	1255	903	0	8345	7147	1431	1288	1110	1048	6	9180	8466	1690	1487
Louisville Baseball Park	LOU	N	1876-1877	133	675	36	25	2	368	326	13	6	29	36	2	251	307	2	1
Eclipse Park (I)	LOU	N	1892-1892	82	35	37	31	2	309	286	7	3	26	58	0	340	518	11	23

PARK	TM	LG	YEARS	RF	HRF	HOME							ROAD						
						W	L	T	R	OR	HR	OHR	W	L	T	R	OR	HR	OHR
Eclipse Park (II)	LOU	N	1893-1899	93	122	202	233	12	2422	2727	130	135	154	361	4	2604	3770	114	134
Milwaukee Base-ball Grounds	MIL	N	1878-1878	126	35	7	18	0	127	177	1	0	8	27	1	129	209	1	3
County Stadium	MIL	N	1953-1965	87	82	602	414	7	4408	3694	998	776	544	476	1	4977	4424	1232	951
Jarry Park	MON	N	1969-1976	106	119	285	356	0	2519	2927	461	519	269	378	1	2347	2792	382	442
Olympic Stadium	MON	N	1977-1988	98	84	520	424	0	3890	3624	610	642	456	485	2	3852	3810	773	712
Union Grounds (Brooklyn)	NY	N	1876-1876	78	646	13	20	0	143	207	2	7	8	15	1	117	205	0	1
Polo Grounds(I) East Diamond	NY	N	1883-1888	93	71	234	113	13	2125	1438	87	46	186	160	11	1959	1875	100	89
Polo Grounds (II)	NY	N	1889-1890	98	54	84	42	3	873	574	26	17	62	69	6	769	820	51	35
Polo Grounds (III)	NY	N	1891-1910	97	134	876	564	38	7662	6329	377	280	686	736	27	7029	7160	227	255
Polo Grounds (IV)	NY	N	1911-1957	97	170	2107	1465	24	16910	14434	3147	2526	1832	1749	29	16953	15529	1763	1603
Polo Grounds (IV)	NY	N	1962-1963	110	162	56	105	0	611	891	154	213	35	126	1	507	831	81	141
Shea Stadium	NY	N	1964-1988	94	99	1000	990	5	7413	7555	1281	1442	895	1096	2	7679	8249	1315	1420
Jefferson Street Grounds	PHI	N	1876-1876	114	55	10	24	1	259	309	4	0	4	21	0	119	225	3	2
Recreation Park	PHI	N	1883-1886	95	32	102	117	5	1115	1286	21	21	81	134	3	1013	1435	42	84
Philadelphia Baseball Grounds	PHI	N	1887-1894	101	97	352	200	5	3869	2721	185	117	231	276	13	2887	3212	136	157
Baker Bowl	PHI	N	1895-1937	114	159	1607	1577	25	16007	16788	1618	1392	1288	1913	35	13361	15589	902	1001
Shibe Park/Connie Mack Stadium	PHI	N	1938-1970	96	89	1211	1350	13	10001	11185	1552	1731	1062	1516	7	10096	11829	1702	1971
Veteran's Stadium	PHI	N	1971-1988	106	111	803	626	2	6476	5907	1225	1057	652	772	1	5650	6016	1038	1017
Recreation Park	PIT	N	1887-1890	79	14	122	117	6	1226	1134	15	12	83	204	3	1249	2230	81	144
Exposition Park	PIT	N	1891-1908	99	65	813	502	9	7058	5714	226	103	641	604	32	6376	6196	245	244
Forbes Field	PIT	N	1909-1969	102	69	2593	2113	35	21368	20076	1845	1929	2162	2508	38	20019	20318	2535	2922
Three Rivers Stadium	PIT	N	1970-1988	101	94	853	650	1	6639	5880	1089	1013	721	782	1	6313	6135	1173	1061
Messer Street Grounds	PRO	N	1878-1885	91	61	244	115	4	2033	1363	44	28	194	163	5	2004	1765	54	66
Sportsman's Park (I)	STL	N	1876-1877	77	65	44	16	0	327	182	1	2	29	35	0	344	365	2	3
Vandeventer Lot	STL	N	1885-1886	87	58	50	67	4	503	575	19	14	29	84	3	435	731	19	35
Sportsman's Park (II)	STL	N	1892-1892	92	41	37	36	2	379	380	32	32	19	58	3	324	542	13	15
Robison Field	STL	N	1893-1919	97	109	885	1063	39	8222	9494	385	418	691	1268	25	7713	10290	271	451
Sportsman's Park (IV)	STL	N	1920-1965	106	104	2133	1429	28	18069	15545	2306	2266	1810	1730	24	16384	15239	2191	2221
Busch Stadium	STL	N	1966-1988	100	79	993	839	3	7589	7214	847	1049	914	911	1	7527	7222	1080	1301
Jack Murphy Stadium	SD	N	1969-1988	89	89	763	829	1	5730	6303	922	1147	629	955	1	6045	7309	1022	1268
Seals Stadium	SF	N	1958-1959	94	97	86	68	0	702	625	165	151	77	77	0	730	686	172	154
Candlestick Park	SF	N	1960-1988	97	97	1288	1023	0	9764	9095	1950	1664	1089	1224	5	9793	9827	1984	1760
Newell Park	SYR	N	1879-1879	80	53	11	22	1	115	200	1	2	11	26	0	160	257	4	2
Putnam Grounds	TRO	N	1879-1879	94	96	12	27	2	191	263	3	6	7	29	0	130	281	1	7
Haymakers' Grounds	TRO	N	1880-1881	113	479	44	39	1	426	453	9	15	36	48	0	365	413	1	4
Troy Ball Clubs Grounds	TRO	N	1882-1882	93	57	22	20	0	238	217	7	2	13	28	2	192	305	5	11
Swampoodle Grounds	WAS	N	1886-1889	90	91	96	141	13	1141	1369	71	66	67	196	1	1023	1865	54	102
Boundary Field	WAS	N	1892-1899	99	126	264	270	11	3413	3347	222	139	146	427	7	2805	4359	116	184
Worcester Driving Park Grounds	WOR	N	1880-1882	118	151	55	69	2	703	777	21	25	35	90	1	498	737	10	20

AMERICAN ASSOCIATION

PARK	TM	LG	YEARS	RF	HRF	W	L	T	R	OR	HR	OHR	W	L	T	R	OR	HR	OHR
Union Park	BAL	A	1882-1891	99	72	293	230	21	3308	2842	87	55	196	372	9	2669	3908	81	128
Congress Street Grounds	BOS	A	1891-1891	93	170	51	17	2	518	299	37	22	42	25	2	507	379	15	20
Washington Park (I)	BRO	A	1884-1890	99	118	257	170	11	2775	2223	95	75	180	256	9	2317	2841	61	86
Bank Street Grounds	CIN	A	1882-1883	101	279	68	24	0	648	293	29	18	48	38	0	498	388	10	6
League Park (I)	CIN	A	1884-1889	104	185	262	144	2	2796	1947	165	93	171	190	10	2012	2148	63	65
Pendleton Park	CIN	A	1891-1891	122	215	24	20	0	290	282	21	9	19	37	1	250	354	7	11
National League Park (II)	CLE	A	1887-1888	101	48	56	65	3	749	807	10	19	33	109	2	632	1132	16	53
Recreation Park (I)	COL	A	1883-1884	83	120	56	45	1	480	490	28	22	45	59	1	579	628	27	16
Recreation Park (II)	COL	A	1889-1891	83	56	117	84	2	1169	859	26	27	83	125	7	1148	1454	46	55
Bruce Grounds	IND	A	1884-1884	98	120	16	39	1	244	377	13	15	13	39	2	219	378	7	15
Association Park (I)	KC	A	1888-1888	124	129	23	34	0	330	392	16	10	20	55	0	249	502	4	22
Exposition Park	KC	A	1889-1889	121	55	35	35	0	523	518	8	17	20	47	2	329	512	10	34
Eclipse Park (I)	LOU	A	1882-1891	95	66	357	240	12	3709	2955	83	66	217	397	9	3060	4061	91	138
Borchert Field	MIL	A	1891-1891	140	383	16	5	0	172	82	11	5	5	10	0	56	74	2	1
Polo Grounds (I) West Diamond	NY	A	1883-1885	87	52	100	50	5	905	580	24	13	73	88	1	854	936	25	50
St. George Cricket Grounds	NY	A	1886-1887	89	72	55	67	5	658	750	20	19	42	104	2	715	1108	19	43
Oakdale Park	PHI	A	1882-1882	127	325	21	18	0	236	220	3	11	20	16	0	166	166	2	2
Jefferson Street Grounds	PHI	A	1883-1891	105	81	365	215	13	4154	3146	151	79	227	315	9	2913	3591	129	135
Expositon Park (I)	PIT	A	1882-1884	95	68	53	86	1	702	843	23	10	47	98	2	652	1021	10	40
Recreation Park	PIT	A	1885-1886	91	29	83	49	1	765	514	5	6	53	63	2	592	668	16	18
Allen Pasture	RIC	A	1884-1884	101	117	5	15	2	96	142	3	8	7	15	2	98	153	4	6
Culver Field (I)	ROC	A	1890-1890	82	57	40	22	1	348	252	13	4	23	41	6	361	458	18	15
Sportsman's Park (II)	STL	A	1882-1891	116	201	459	178	7	4745	2935	214	145	321	255	13	3182	2972	91	75
Star Park (II)	SYR	A	1890-1890	83	19	30	30	0	321	320	2	4	25	42	1	373	501	12	24
League Park	TOL	A	1884-1884	107	33	28	25	2	270	267	3	2	18	33	4	193	305	5	10
Speranza Park	TOL	A	1890-1890	104	143	40	27	1	422	316	17	11	28	37	1	316	374	7	12
Athletic Park	WAS	A	1884-1884	82	37	10	20	0	137	181	3	4	2	31	0	111	300	3	17
Boundary Field	WAS	A	1891-1891	98	88	28	40	4	389	519	13	18	16	51	0	300	547	6	26

	HOME								ROAD								ALL															
TM	G	W	L	T	R	OR	HR	OHR	G	W	L	T	R	OR	HR	OHR	G	W	L	T	R	OR	HR	OHR	HRF	HRB	HRP	RF	RB	RP	BPF	PPF
1882 AMERICAN ASSOCIATION																																
BAL	35	9	25	1	138	225	2	7	39	10	29	0	134	287	2	8	74	19	54	1	272	512	4	15	98	56	168	95	77	129	92	102
CIN	42	31	11	0	270	130	0	5	38	24	14	0	219	138	5	2	80	55	25	0	489	268	5	7	70	55	91	103	108	65	109	100
LOU	39	26	13	0	215	129	0	0	42	16	25	1	236	235	9	6	81	42	38	1	451	364	9	6	0	100	100	82	116	94	94	90
PHI	39	21	18	0	236	220	3	11	36	20	16	0	166	166	2	2	75	41	34	0	402	386	5	13	236	43	75	122	91	89	112	111
PIT	35	17	18	0	185	172	12	3	44	22	21	1	239	241	6	1	79	39	39	1	424	413	18	4	210	127	32	95	106	103	97	97
STL	45	24	20	1	259	268	7	2	36	13	23	0	150	236	4	5	81	37	43	1	409	504	11	7	82	132	91	107	95	116	100	104
1883 AMERICAN ASSOCIATION																																
BAL	49	18	31	0	300	395	4	6	47	10	37	0	173	342	1	6	96	28	68	0	473	737	5	12	128	28	70	122	79	119	107	113
CIN	50	37	13	0	378	163	29	13	48	24	24	0	279	250	5	4	98	61	37	0	657	413	34	17	315	103	65	100	113	76	103	98
COL	47	18	29	0	198	283	5	8	50	14	36	0	276	376	10	8	97	32	65	0	474	659	15	16	78	118	131	79	98	130	87	91
LOU	48	29	19	0	282	229	4	0	50	23	26	1	282	334	10	7	98	52	45	1	564	563	14	7	27	154	47	88	108	106	94	94
NY	48	30	17	1	273	189	3	4	49	24	25	0	225	216	3	8	97	54	42	1	498	405	6	12	68	51	89	107	83	70	108	105
PHI	50	37	13	0	402	258	9	8	48	29	19	0	318	289	11	14	98	66	32	0	720	547	20	22	69	187	196	106	125	99	103	99
PIT	49	18	31	0	292	321	10	3	49	13	36	0	231	405	3	18	98	31	67	0	523	726	13	21	64	141	162	95	100	132	94	98
STL	49	35	14	0	298	197	5	3	49	30	19	0	251	211	2	4	98	65	33	0	549	408	7	7	130	38	41	108	90	70	108	105
1884 AMERICAN ASSOCIATION																																
BAL	57	42	13	2	371	224	21	9	51	21	30	0	264	292	11	7	108	63	43	2	635	516	32	16	145	126	69	97	113	94	99	97
BRO	52	23	26	3	263	265	9	8	57	17	38	2	213	379	7	13	109	40	64	5	476	644	16	21	93	84	105	97	87	113	98	100
CIN	57	40	16	1	439	233	31	20	55	28	25	2	315	279	5	7	112	68	41	3	754	512	36	27	335	71	67	110	121	86	106	103
COL	55	38	16	1	282	207	23	14	55	31	23	1	303	252	17	8	110	69	39	2	585	459	40	22	145	163	93	90	105	84	97	95
IND	56	16	39	1	244	377	13	15	54	13	39	2	219	378	7	15	110	29	78	3	463	755	20	30	118	91	136	98	83	131	97	101
LOU	56	41	14	1	278	145	4	2	54	27	26	1	295	280	13	7	110	68	40	2	573	425	17	9	31	120	65	74	114	83	89	87
NY	55	42	9	4	370	179	11	4	57	33	23	1	364	244	11	11	112	75	32	5	734	423	22	15	74	122	79	96	125	75	100	96
PHI	54	38	16	0	438	268	12	4	54	23	30	1	262	278	15	12	108	61	46	1	700	546	27	16	62	170	96	129	107	88	114	113
PIT	56	18	37	1	225	350	1	4	54	12	41	1	182	375	1	21	110	30	78	2	407	725	2	25	23	27	172	97	73	125	97	101
RIC	22	5	15	2	96	142	3	8	24	7	15	2	98	153	4	6	46	12	30	4	194	295	7	14	116	81	151	101	82	120	99	102
STL	54	38	15	1	383	256	6	10	56	29	25	2	275	281	5	6	110	67	40	3	658	537	11	16	147	44	61	119	104	87	110	108
TOL	55	28	25	2	270	267	3	2	55	18	33	4	193	305	5	10	110	46	58	6	463	572	8	12	35	64	72	107	77	95	104	105
WAS	30	10	20	0	137	181	3	4	33	2	31	0	111	300	3	17	63	12	51	0	248	481	6	21	39	102	225	83	88	153	88	93
1885 AMERICAN ASSOCIATION																																
BAL	54	29	25	0	360	296	11	2	56	12	43	1	182	388	6	10	110	41	68	1	542	684	17	12	85	98	65	115	83	105	106	109
BRO	58	36	22	0	386	308	9	14	54	17	37	0	238	342	5	13	112	53	59	0	624	650	14	27	116	71	130	109	96	102	104	105
CIN	56	35	21	0	358	269	17	17	56	28	28	0	284	307	9	7	112	63	49	0	642	576	26	24	187	100	90	106	100	92	104	103
LOU	56	37	19	0	334	259	16	4	56	16	40	0	228	339	3	9	112	53	59	0	562	598	19	13	153	69	62	104	89	94	102	103
NY	52	28	24	0	262	212	10	5	56	16	40	0	265	476	11	31	108	44	64	0	527	688	21	36	41	240	267	71	111	129	84	86
PHI	57	33	23	1	449	330	18	9	56	22	34	0	315	362	12	2	113	55	57	1	764	692	30	11	170	114	40	111	118	110	103	102
PIT	57	37	20	0	342	242	3	3	54	19	35	0	206	295	2	11	111	56	55	0	548	537	5	14	47	43	83	109	83	84	106	106
STL	55	44	11	0	319	160	6	5	57	35	22	0	358	301	11	7	112	79	33	0	677	461	17	12	68	100	75	79	119	82	93	89
1886 AMERICAN ASSOCIATION																																
BAL	66	30	31	5	320	315	2	2	73	18	52	3	298	560	6	23	139	48	83	8	618	875	8	25	17	93	155	83	89	115	90	94
BRO	69	43	25	1	453	364	9	7	72	33	36	3	379	462	7	10	141	76	61	4	832	826	16	17	99	75	79	102	104	103	100	100
CIN	71	40	31	0	472	380	32	16	70	25	42	3	406	484	13	9	141	65	73	3	878	864	45	25	188	151	96	95	115	113	96	96
LOU	69	37	30	2	484	402	19	9	69	29	40	0	345	395	1	7	138	66	70	2	829	797	20	16	266	38	53	117	98	95	108	108
NY	65	30	33	2	336	352	10	9	72	23	49	0	290	415	8	14	137	53	82	2	626	767	18	23	95	94	114	106	78	93	104	106
PHI	71	37	32	2	434	468	13	11	68	26	40	2	337	472	8	24	139	63	72	4	771	940	21	35	74	140	197	106	97	116	100	103
PIT	76	46	29	1	423	272	2	3	64	34	28	2	386	373	14	7	140	80	57	3	809	645	16	10	22	106	94	80	112	91	92	90
STL	70	52	18	0	546	286	13	7	69	41	28	0	398	307	7	6	139	93	46	0	944	593	20	13	145	75	53	116	107	72	111	106
1887 AMERICAN ASSOCIATION																																
BAL	68	42	21	5	500	328	16	6	73	35	37	1	470	536	15	10	141	77	58	6	970	864	31	16	96	104	57	90	110	97	96	94
BRO	75	36	38	1	514	470	18	14	63	24	36	3	398	448	7	13	138	60	74	4	912	918	25	27	128	73	85	98	102	103	98	99
CIN	71	45	26	0	517	386	24	16	65	36	28	1	376	360	13	12	136	81	54	1	893	746	37	28	140	110	89	112	91	79	108	106
CLE	61	22	37	2	375	481	2	7	72	17	55	0	354	619	12	27	133	39	92	2	729	1100	14	34	29	72	174	101	86	122	97	103
LOU	70	46	23	1	561	409	14	15	69	30	37	2	394	450	13	16	139	76	60	3	955	859	27	31	99	97	110	112	97	90	107	106
NY	62	25	34	3	322	398	10	10	76	19	55	2	425	693	11	29	138	44	89	5	747	1091	21	39	63	104	154	80	95	128	88	92
PHI	70	41	27	2	502	404	18	11	67	23	42	2	387	492	11	18	137	64	69	4	889	896	29	29	96	107	107	99	99	100	99	100
STL	73	58	15	0	679	381	26	16	65	37	25	3	453	372	13	3	138	95	40	3	1132	753	39	19	204	90	39	115	113	80	109	105
1888 AMERICAN ASSOCIATION																																
BAL	56	30	26	0	285	276	7	11	81	27	54	0	361	503	12	13	137	57	80	0	646	779	19	24	103	78	99	94	96	109	96	98
BRO	76	53	20	3	451	267	18	10	67	35	32	0	307	312	7	5	143	88	52	3	758	579	25	15	183	65	42	103	97	78	105	102
CIN	79	55	24	0	467	317	24	5	58	25	30	3	277	311	8	14	137	80	54	3	744	628	32	19	98	128	92	99	102	91	101	99
CLE	63	34	28	1	374	326	8	12	72	16	54	2	278	513	4	26	135	50	82	3	652	839	12	38	78	69	165	100	97	118	97	100
KC	57	23	34	0	330	392	16	10	75	20	55	0	249	502	4	22	132	43	89	0	579	894	20	32	125	84	126	121	81	118	106	112
LOU	61	27	30	4	324	303	1	4	78	21	57	0	362	567	13	24	139	48	87	4	686	870	14	28	19	76	174	87	107	126	91	93
PHI	74	54	20	0	505	253	20	8	62	27	32	3	320	338	11	6	136	81	52	3	825	591	31	14	133	105	53	98	115	88	101	97
STL	82	60	21	1	525	284	22	13	55	32	22	1	264	215	14	6	137	92	43	2	789	499	36	19	117	137	75	113	97	68	111	106
1889 AMERICAN ASSOCIATION																																
BAL	67	41	23	3	436	314	10	4	72	29	42	1	355	481	10	23	139	70	65	4	791	795	20	27	49	79	77	97	95	94	100	99
BRO	70	50	18	2	488	297	28	19	70	43	26	1	510	417	19	14	140	93	44	3	998	714	47	33	137	105	77	88	123	91	96	92
CIN	74	47	26	1	543	362	37	19	67	29	37	1	354	407	15	16	141	76	63	2	897	769	52	35	152	104	80	107	99	88	105	103
COL	69	36	33	0	407	350	13	11	71	24	45	2	376	573	23	22	140	60	78	2	783	923	36	33	58	121	111	83	103	116	91	92
KC	70	35	35	0	523	518	8	17	69	20	47	2	329	512	10	34	139	55	82	2	852	1030	18	51	59	68	159	118	94	113	106	109
LOU	65	18	47	0	330	473	10	18	75	9	64	2	302	617	12	25	140	27	111	2	632	1090	22	43	86	65	116	98	78	125	96	102
PHI	73	46	22	5	506	347	16	13	65	29	36	0	380	440	27	22	138	75	58	5	886	787	43	35	56	154	130	94	108	98	98	96
STL	71	51	18	2	581	317	45	28	70	39	27	4	372	367	13	11	141	90	45	6	953	684	58	39	243	86	64	119	98	75	112	109
1890 AMERICAN ASSOCIATION																																
BAL	22	8	11	3	117	115	1	0	16	7	8	1	65	77	1	3	38	15	19	4	182	192	2	3	20	77	48	116	77	82	109	110
BRO	38	15	22	1	220	252	4	3	62	11	51	0	272	481	9	18	100	26	73	1	492	733	13	21	44	112	132	100	95	128	97	101
COL	71	47	22	2	453	246	9	8	69	32	33	4	377	369	7	12	140	79	55	6	830	615	16	20	89	69	83	93	108	82	99	96
LOU	74	57	13	4	513	275	8	8	62	31	31	0	307	304	7	10	136	88	44	4	820	579	15	18	82	68	80	109	99	75	107	104
PHI	72	36	36	0	453	452	16	6	60	18	42	0	240	493	8	11	132	54	78	0	693	945	24	17	96	102	78	102	95	128	97	101
ROC	63	40	22	1	348	252	13	4	70	23	41	6	361	458	18	15	133	63	63	7	709	710	31	19	60	169	97	83	105	101	92	92
STL	72	45	25	2	551	396	42	31	67	33	33	1	313	341	6	7	139	78	58	3	864	737	48	38	357	78	72	131	94	84	116	114
SYR	60	30	30	0	321	320	2	4	68	25	42	1	373	501	12	24	128	55	72	1	694	821	14	28	21	103	187	84	108	123	90	92
TOL	68	40	27	1	422	316	17	11	66	28	37	1	316	374	7	12	134	68	64	2	738	690	24	23	137	83	87	104	96	91	103	102

	HOME								ROAD								ALL															
TM	G	W	L	T	R	OR	HR	OHR	G	W	L	T	R	OR	HR	OHR	G	W	L	T	R	OR	HR	OHR	HRF	HRB	HRP	RF	RB	RP	BPF	PPF
1891 AMERICAN ASSOCIATION																																
BAL	70	44	24	2	481	354	13	8	69	27	40	2	367	442	17	25	139	71	64	4	848	796	30	33	52	113	109	102	103	98	101	100
BOS	70	51	17	2	518	299	37	22	69	42	25	2	507	379	15	20	139	93	42	4	1025	678	52	42	157	108	98	94	128	89	99	94
CIN	44	24	20	0	290	282	21	9	57	19	37	1	250	354	7	11	101	43	57	1	540	636	28	20	190	70	59	119	85	98	109	111
COL	63	34	29	0	309	263	4	8	75	27	47	1	395	512	16	21	138	61	76	1	704	775	20	29	41	68	104	77	99	103	89	90
LOU	71	39	32	0	388	331	7	6	68	15	51	2	309	540	10	27	139	54	83	2	697	871	17	33	36	79	112	82	97	115	90	92
MIL	21	16	5	0	172	82	11	5	15	5	10	0	56	74	2	1	36	21	15	0	228	156	13	6	291	59	29	134	82	67	120	118
PHI	72	43	26	3	465	366	29	9	71	30	40	1	354	427	26	26	143	73	66	4	819	793	55	35	74	173	109	105	95	93	103	103
STL	73	52	21	0	604	390	42	30	65	33	30	2	348	341	16	20	138	85	51	2	952	731	58	50	166	118	113	126	101	83	114	111
WAS	72	28	40	4	389	519	13	18	67	16	51	0	300	547	6	26	139	44	91	4	689	1066	19	44	89	57	119	98	89	131	95	101
1884 UNION ASSOCIATION																																
ALT	18	6	12	0	73	156	0	2	7	0	7	0	17	60	2	1	25	6	19	0	90	216	2	3	27	99	190	110	56	140	101	109
BAL	50	29	21	0	372	312	12	16	56	29	26	1	304	318	5	8	106	58	47	1	676	630	17	24	219	71	101	122	102	97	110	110
BOS	58	34	23	1	346	260	7	5	53	24	28	1	290	297	12	12	111	58	51	2	636	557	19	17	48	167	144	95	103	91	98	97
CHI	35	20	14	1	177	159	2	2	39	14	25	0	183	252	8	9	74	34	39	1	360	411	10	11	28	143	150	87	93	102	94	94
CIN	52	35	17	0	382	239	18	12	53	34	19	0	325	241	8	5	105	69	36	0	707	480	26	17	216	109	72	113	110	77	108	105
KC	36	11	23	2	150	205	3	6	46	5	40	1	159	414	3	8	82	16	63	3	309	619	6	14	101	51	111	78	80	140	87	91
MIL	12	8	4	0	53	35	0	1	0	0	0	0	0	0	0	0	12	8	4	0	53	35	0	1	0	100	100	0	100	100	54	54
PHI	34	13	21	0	223	249	4	1	33	8	25	0	192	296	3	6	67	21	46	0	415	545	7	7	55	102	79	93	119	151	93	95
PIT	5	1	4	0	22	29	0	1	14	6	7	1	56	42	0	0	19	7	11	1	78	71	0	1	0	100	100	139	62	62	122	122
STL	56	50	6	0	461	179	10	4	58	44	13	1	426	250	22	5	114	94	19	1	887	429	32	9	58	227	78	102	133	68	104	98
STP	0	0	0	0	0	0	0	0	9	2	6	1	24	57	0	1	9	2	6	1	24	57	0	1	0	100	100	0	100	100	54	54
WAS	65	36	27	2	382	318	4	10	49	11	38	0	192	362	0	6	114	47	65	2	574	680	4	16	164	13	71	95	90	110	97	98
WIL	7	1	6	0	16	46	1	4	11	1	10	0	19	68	1	0	18	2	16	0	35	114	2	4	501	48	37	107	34	103	103	109
1890 PLAYERS LEAGUE																																
BOS	70	48	21	1	602	383	46	38	60	33	27	0	386	384	12	11	130	81	48	1	988	767	58	49	249	79	70	110	102	84	107	104
BRO	66	46	19	1	564	410	20	7	67	30	37	0	398	480	14	19	133	76	56	1	962	890	34	26	85	88	65	112	99	93	106	105
BUF	65	23	42	0	425	498	7	20	69	13	54	2	367	698	13	47	134	36	96	2	792	1196	20	67	50	74	200	91	95	133	92	97
CHI	70	46	23	1	504	345	18	12	68	29	39	0	381	425	13	15	138	75	62	1	885	770	31	27	104	69	61	102	89	79	104	103
CLE	62	31	30	1	416	403	10	15	69	24	45	0	433	623	17	30	131	55	75	1	849	1026	27	45	62	85	130	87	104	119	92	94
NY	66	47	19	0	628	404	35	21	66	27	38	1	389	477	31	16	132	74	57	1	1017	881	66	37	117	152	92	117	102	92	109	107
PHI	65	35	30	0	482	418	20	15	67	33	33	1	465	434	29	18	132	68	63	1	947	852	49	33	79	133	96	103	102	93	102	101
PIT	65	37	28	0	435	356	21	15	63	23	40	0	398	535	14	21	128	60	68	0	833	891	35	36	99	89	92	84	104	109	92	92
1914 FEDERAL LEAGUE																																
BAL	83	53	26	4	350	298	25	15	77	31	44	2	295	330	7	19	160	84	70	6	645	628	32	34	136	65	79	97	99	97	99	99
BRO	80	47	32	1	358	335	27	13	77	30	45	2	304	342	15	18	157	77	77	3	662	677	42	31	114	102	81	103	102	104	101	101
BUF	79	47	29	3	345	300	21	18	76	33	42	1	275	302	17	27	155	80	71	4	620	602	38	45	87	116	132	107	93	91	104	104
CHI	75	41	34	0	248	208	30	19	82	46	33	3	373	309	22	23	157	87	67	3	621	517	52	42	117	132	111	76	105	89	91	89
IND	80	53	23	4	439	339	14	8	77	35	42	0	323	283	19	21	157	88	65	4	762	622	33	29	57	114	94	121	106	89	111	108
KC	76	38	37	1	322	306	28	21	78	29	47	2	322	377	11	16	154	67	84	3	644	683	39	37	167	77	79	93	107	112	95	96
PIT	75	37	37	1	297	307	11	10	79	27	49	3	308	391	23	29	154	64	86	4	605	698	34	39	46	133	141	91	102	114	94	96
STL	76	31	44	1	304	368	12	23	78	31	45	2	261	329	13	15	154	62	89	3	565	697	25	38	123	62	89	114	85	102	106	108
1915 FEDERAL LEAGUE																																
BAL	75	24	51	0	299	419	29	36	79	23	56	0	251	341	7	16	154	47	107	0	550	760	36	52	235	67	104	121	87	115	107	111
BRO	74	34	40	0	315	324	20	11	79	36	42	1	332	349	16	16	153	70	82	1	647	673	36	27	103	114	88	100	112	116	98	98
BUF	77	37	40	0	290	324	21	21	76	37	38	1	284	310	19	14	153	74	78	1	574	634	40	35	122	120	105	102	98	106	100	101
CHI	78	44	32	2	310	252	21	10	77	42	34	1	330	286	29	23	155	86	66	3	640	538	50	33	62	207	140	92	110	95	97	95
KC	77	46	31	0	274	249	15	19	76	35	41	0	273	302	13	10	153	81	72	0	547	551	28	29	138	76	76	91	96	97	97	97
NEW	79	40	39	0	267	271	4	2	76	40	33	3	318	291	13	13	155	80	72	3	585	562	17	15	25	84	62	87	104	101	94	94
PIT	77	45	31	1	292	269	4	10	79	41	36	2	300	255	16	27	156	86	67	3	592	524	20	37	37	89	163	104	95	85	104	102
STL	82	43	34	5	334	280	12	15	77	44	33	0	300	247	11	7	159	87	67	5	634	527	23	22	135	60	54	105	99	84	105	102
1876 NATIONAL LEAGUE																																
BOS	36	19	17	0	253	200	5	3	34	20	14	0	218	250	4	4	70	39	31	0	471	450	9	7	96	182	148	93	121	116	95	94
CHI	31	25	6	0	352	143	3	1	35	27	8	0	272	114	5	5	66	52	14	0	624	257	8	6	50	229	153	141	130	59	125	113
CIN	30	6	24	0	119	243	2	2	35	3	32	0	119	336	2	7	65	9	56	0	238	579	4	9	53	135	214	90	70	150	89	100
HAR	32	23	9	0	220	107	0	0	37	24	12	1	209	154	2	2	69	47	21	1	429	261	2	2	0	100	100	106	98	62	108	103
LOU	33	15	16	2	149	154	6	3	36	15	20	1	131	190	0	0	69	30	36	3	280	344	6	3	0	100	100	102	66	80	104	106
NY	33	13	20	0	143	207	2	7	24	8	15	1	117	205	0	1	57	21	35	1	260	412	2	8	384	10	63	80	90	135	87	93
PHI	35	10	24	1	259	309	4	0	25	4	21	0	119	225	3	2	60	14	45	1	378	534	7	2	59	188	56	112	103	145	99	105
STL	30	24	6	0	150	58	1	1	34	21	13	0	236	171	1	2	64	45	19	0	386	229	2	3	80	43	59	62	118	69	88	82
1877 NATIONAL LEAGUE																																
BOS	32	27	5	0	260	110	0	1	29	15	13	1	159	153	4	4	61	42	18	1	419	263	4	5	14	119	271	108	110	77	108	101
CHI	29	17	12	0	206	156	0	4	31	9	21	1	160	219	0	3	60	26	33	1	366	375	0	7	133	0	124	101	110	111	98	99
CIN	30	12	17	1	157	201	4	1	28	3	25	0	134	284	2	3	58	15	42	1	291	485	6	4	92	168	121	81	110	163	82	90
HAR	29	19	8	2	167	92	2	1	31	12	19	0	174	219	2	1	60	31	27	2	341	311	4	2	106	87	48	74	116	100	89	87
LOU	30	21	9	0	219	172	7	3	31	14	16	1	120	117	2	1	61	35	25	1	339	289	9	4	246	122	63	154	74	66	132	130
STL	30	20	10	0	177	124	0	1	30	8	22	0	108	194	1	1	60	28	32	0	285	318	1	2	54	21	58	99	82	90	102	103
1878 NATIONAL LEAGUE																																
BOS	30	23	7	0	171	104	1	3	30	18	12	0	127	137	1	3	60	41	19	0	298	241	2	6	102	58	145	105	89	75	108	105
CHI	35	17	18	0	226	210	2	2	26	13	12	1	145	121	1	2	61	30	30	1	371	331	3	4	99	77	103	118	108	97	108	106
CIN	34	25	8	1	190	126	4	2	27	12	15	0	143	155	1	0	61	37	23	1	333	281	5	2	294	59	15	87	111	98	95	93
IND	28	10	17	1	106	115	1	1	35	14	19	2	187	213	2	2	63	24	36	3	293	328	3	3	66	84	84	72	102	112	87	88
MIL	25	7	18	0	127	177	1	0	36	8	27	1	129	209	1	3	61	15	45	1	256	386	2	3	39	93	59	121	78	110	107	114
PRO	32	17	13	2	182	170	4	2	30	16	14	0	171	167	4	3	62	33	27	2	353	337	8	5	83	260	182	98	113	109	98	97
1879 NATIONAL LEAGUE																																
BOS	42	29	13	0	308	165	11	2	42	25	17	0	254	183	9	7	84	54	30	0	562	348	20	9	84	312	159	109	117	78	107	101
BUF	40	23	16	1	223	204	1	0	39	23	16	0	167	161	1	3	79	46	32	1	390	365	2	3	27	58	36	124	81	77	114	113
CHI	43	29	13	1	264	191	2	0	40	17	20	3	173	219	1	5	83	46	33	4	437	410	3	5	34	83	62	108	94	90	105	104
CIN	37	21	16	0	215	196	8	6	44	22	21	1	270	268	0	5	81	43	37	1	485	464	8	11	259	46	102	92	119	114	95	94
CLE	42	15	27	0	167	236	2	1	40	12	28	0	155	225	2	3	82	27	55	0	322	461	4	4	59	67	59	99	75	103	99	103
PRO	42	34	8	0	323	143	9	4	43	25	17	1	289	212	3	5	85	59	25	1	612	355	12	9	157	118	105	98	134	83	101	94
SYR	34	11	22	1	115	200	1	2	37	11	26	0	160	257	4	2	71	22	48	1	275	457	5	4	57	83	84	83	82	128	89	95
TRO	41	12	27	2	191	263	3	6	36	7	29	0	130	281	1	7	77	19	56	2	321	544	4	13	96	64	181	95	84	134	93	100

	HOME								ROAD								ALL															
TM	G	W	L	T	R	OR	HR	OHR	G	W	L	T	R	OR	HR	OHR	G	W	L	T	R	OR	HR	OHR	HRF	HRB	HRP	RF	RB	RP	BPF	PPF
1880 NATIONAL LEAGUE																																
BOS	43	25	17	1	213	190	14	1	43	15	27	1	203	265	6	1	86	40	44	2	416	455	20	2	187	160	23	87	113	121	92	93
BUF	44	13	29	2	173	233	1	1	41	11	29	1	159	269	2	9	85	24	58	3	332	502	3	10	18	101	176	88	92	132	91	96
CHI	43	37	5	1	284	148	1	0	43	30	12	1	254	169	3	8	86	67	17	2	538	317	4	8	11	154	98	105	127	80	105	98
CIN	40	14	25	1	163	216	5	8	43	7	34	2	131	256	2	2	83	21	59	3	294	472	7	10	262	54	68	102	77	116	99	105
CLE	43	23	19	1	182	168	2	1	42	24	18	0	205	169	5	3	85	47	37	1	387	337	7	4	40	119	70	93	98	87	99	97
PRO	44	31	12	1	210	116	4	2	43	21	20	2	209	183	4	5	87	52	32	3	419	299	8	7	69	121	100	84	108	79	96	92
TRO	41	20	21	0	204	257	5	6	42	21	21	0	188	181	0	2	83	41	42	0	392	438	5	8	357	17	50	124	92	100	110	112
WOR	42	24	17	1	247	186	5	6	43	16	26	1	165	184	3	7	85	40	43	2	412	370	8	13	111	107	163	123	91	84	112	111
1881 NATIONAL LEAGUE																																
BOS	41	19	22	0	151	180	2	4	42	19	23	0	197	230	3	5	83	38	45	0	348	410	5	9	79	58	100	81	90	104	91	93
BUF	41	25	16	0	241	206	2	0	42	20	22	0	199	242	10	9	83	45	38	0	440	448	12	9	12	273	105	104	103	105	101	101
CHI	42	32	10	0	309	186	7	6	42	24	18	0	241	194	5	8	84	56	28	0	550	380	12	14	102	135	154	114	118	86	108	103
CLE	42	20	22	0	190	185	3	4	43	16	26	1	201	229	4	5	85	36	48	1	391	414	7	9	81	79	99	90	94	99	96	96
DET	42	23	19	0	252	213	14	4	42	18	24	0	188	216	3	4	84	41	43	0	440	429	17	8	215	100	68	113	96	95	106	106
PRO	43	23	20	0	209	194	4	2	42	24	17	1	240	232	7	3	85	47	37	1	449	426	11	5	62	130	66	86	112	107	93	92
TRO	43	24	18	1	222	196	4	9	42	15	27	0	177	232	1	2	85	39	45	1	399	428	5	11	301	25	51	99	92	98	100	101
WOR	42	19	22	1	240	253	7	4	41	13	28	0	170	239	0	7	83	32	50	1	410	492	7	11	142	52	102	114	92	109	105	107
1882 NATIONAL LEAGUE																																
BOS	43	27	15	1	263	191	8	7	42	18	24	0	209	220	7	3	85	45	39	1	472	411	15	10	139	77	50	103	99	88	103	102
BUF	39	26	13	0	286	184	5	7	45	19	26	0	214	278	13	9	84	45	39	0	500	462	18	16	66	131	130	109	106	99	104	103
CHI	45	35	10	0	360	140	9	8	39	20	19	0	243	213	6	5	84	55	29	0	603	353	15	13	130	80	70	97	130	83	101	95
CLE	42	21	19	2	175	170	6	7	42	21	21	0	227	240	14	15	84	42	40	2	402	410	20	22	48	188	205	76	99	100	90	90
DET	43	24	18	1	221	238	14	10	43	18	23	2	186	252	5	9	86	42	41	3	407	490	19	19	158	89	98	104	86	101	102	104
PRO	42	30	12	0	247	172	6	6	42	22	20	0	216	184	5	6	84	52	32	0	463	356	11	12	109	65	70	105	96	76	106	103
TRO	42	22	20	0	238	217	7	2	43	13	28	2	192	305	5	11	85	35	48	2	430	522	12	13	60	102	87	94	99	116	95	97
WOR	42	12	30	0	216	338	9	15	42	6	36	0	163	314	7	6	84	18	66	0	379	652	16	21	163	83	98	111	83	134	100	107
1883 NATIONAL LEAGUE																																
BOS	49	41	8	0	391	190	21	3	49	22	27	0	277	267	13	8	98	63	35	0	668	457	34	11	114	200	80	107	110	80	106	102
BUF	49	36	13	0	355	241	3	4	49	16	32	1	258	335	5	8	98	52	45	1	613	576	8	12	57	64	90	101	108	102	100	99
CHI	49	36	13	0	410	254	11	6	49	23	26	0	269	287	2	15	98	59	39	0	679	541	13	21	101	88	134	118	109	91	109	106
CLE	49	31	18	0	248	203	0	4	51	24	24	3	227	240	8	3	100	55	42	3	475	443	8	7	41	45	74	101	79	74	104	104
DET	51	23	26	2	264	280	12	9	50	17	32	1	260	371	1	13	101	40	58	3	524	651	13	22	138	63	121	85	99	118	91	94
NY	49	28	19	2	292	262	20	15	49	18	31	0	238	315	4	4	98	46	50	2	530	577	24	19	307	71	62	100	94	101	100	101
PHI	50	9	40	1	224	439	0	1	49	8	41	0	222	449	3	19	99	17	81	1	446	888	3	20	5	20	212	94	86	156	90	99
PRO	49	34	15	0	330	186	10	5	49	24	25	0	304	250	11	7	98	58	40	0	634	436	21	12	86	143	88	95	111	80	101	96
1884 NATIONAL LEAGUE																																
BOS	56	40	16	0	328	181	14	4	60	33	22	5	356	288	22	26	116	73	38	5	684	469	36	30	44	125	83	88	110	77	98	93
BUF	58	37	18	3	409	311	23	20	56	27	29	0	292	314	16	26	114	64	47	3	701	625	39	46	100	99	115	113	104	95	107	105
CHI	56	39	17	0	498	312	131	66	56	23	33	0	336	334	11	17	112	62	50	0	834	646	142	83	402	121	104	118	124	101	108	104
CLE	56	22	34	0	264	348	4	6	57	13	43	1	194	368	12	29	113	35	77	1	458	716	16	35	27	66	116	107	72	107	102	108
DET	58	18	38	2	228	347	14	16	56	10	46	0	215	389	17	20	114	28	84	2	443	736	31	36	78	85	97	91	76	118	93	99
NY	58	34	22	2	378	261	8	4	58	28	28	2	315	362	15	24	116	62	50	4	693	623	23	28	34	89	81	96	111	101	98	97
PHI	57	19	37	1	281	388	1	1	56	20	36	0	268	436	13	37	113	39	73	1	549	824	14	38	4	90	137	93	96	136	92	97
PRO	57	45	11	1	329	164	4	6	57	39	17	1	336	224	17	20	114	84	28	2	665	388	21	26	31	70	90	92	104	64	102	96
1885 NATIONAL LEAGUE																																
BOS	57	21	35	1	245	283	7	5	56	25	31	0	283	306	15	21	113	46	66	1	528	589	22	26	35	166	166	89	101	111	94	95
BUF	57	19	38	0	265	406	13	13	55	19	36	0	229	354	10	18	112	38	74	0	494	760	23	31	89	119	152	108	90	130	99	105
CHI	57	43	14	0	458	269	47	27	56	44	11	1	377	200	7	10	113	87	25	1	835	469	54	37	309	108	98	123	132	79	114	106
DET	52	29	23	0	294	228	13	8	56	12	44	0	220	355	12	10	108	41	67	0	514	583	25	18	101	116	86	97	100	109	97	99
NY	55	45	10	0	362	178	7	6	57	40	17	0	329	192	9	5	112	85	27	0	691	370	16	11	99	68	48	109	114	66	109	102
PHI	55	29	26	0	277	244	7	7	56	27	28	1	236	267	13	11	111	56	54	1	513	511	20	18	63	109	101	105	90	90	104	104
PRO	54	30	24	0	203	218	3	1	56	23	33	0	239	313	3	17	110	53	57	0	442	531	6	18	23	73	87	81	89	104	91	93
STL	58	23	33	2	215	262	6	4	53	13	39	1	175	332	2	11	111	36	72	3	390	594	8	15	72	44	70	86	78	111	92	97
1886 NATIONAL LEAGUE																																
BOS	58	32	25	1	354	280	15	8	60	24	36	0	303	379	9	25	118	56	61	1	657	659	24	33	73	102	118	96	109	109	97	97
CHI	62	52	10	0	539	275	45	34	64	38	24	2	364	281	8	15	126	90	34	2	903	556	53	49	274	82	94	128	117	78	116	110
DET	60	48	12	0	441	255	37	10	66	39	24	3	395	288	16	10	126	87	36	3	836	543	53	20	180	113	52	113	116	80	109	103
KC	62	19	42	1	301	456	9	4	64	11	49	4	193	420	10	23	126	30	91	5	494	876	19	27	43	96	96	121	69	117	106	114
NY	63	47	12	4	327	195	10	4	61	28	32	1	366	363	11	19	124	75	44	5	693	558	21	23	49	96	83	73	123	98	88	85
PHI	62	45	14	3	333	215	13	12	57	26	29	2	287	283	13	17	119	71	43	5	620	498	26	29	80	97	106	91	101	83	98	96
STL	63	27	34	2	288	313	13	10	63	16	45	2	260	399	17	24	126	43	79	4	548	712	30	34	58	126	130	91	88	110	95	98
WAS	65	19	42	4	250	379	13	12	60	9	50	1	200	420	10	22	125	28	92	5	450	799	23	34	73	89	119	92	73	122	94	100
1887 NATIONAL LEAGUE																																
BOS	60	39	21	0	443	310	29	17	63	22	39	2	360	464	24	38	123	61	60	2	803	774	53	55	80	134	130	97	111	106	98	97
CHI	64	44	18	2	540	347	67	44	60	27	32	1	266	349	13	11	124	71	50	3	806	696	80	55	308	76	58	130	89	83	116	115
DET	60	43	17	0	495	299	25	20	66	36	28	2	467	405	30	32	126	79	45	2	962	704	55	52	83	128	120	102	124	94	102	97
IND	64	24	39	1	339	456	19	28	63	13	50	0	278	507	14	32	127	37	89	1	617	963	33	60	98	71	120	98	84	123	96	101
NY	65	36	27	2	453	360	21	8	64	32	28	4	364	347	27	19	129	68	55	6	817	707	48	27	66	112	63	111	97	86	107	105
PHI	62	37	23	2	418	307	25	22	66	38	25	3	473	394	22	26	128	75	48	5	891	701	47	48	105	94	96	91	119	96	97	94
PIT	66	31	34	1	336	336	6	4	59	24	35	0	285	421	14	35	125	55	69	1	621	757	20	39	20	88	108	86	88	105	93	96
WAS	63	27	32	4	329	349	29	19	63	19	44	0	271	466	18	28	126	46	76	4	600	815	47	47	102	96	97	92	83	107	95	99
1888 NATIONAL LEAGUE																																
BOS	68	36	30	2	365	315	23	16	69	34	34	1	304	305	33	20	137	70	64	3	669	620	56	36	77	148	102	112	102	95	106	105
CHI	70	43	27	0	438	336	50	44	66	34	31	1	294	323	27	19	136	77	58	1	732	659	77	63	174	143	117	116	110	102	107	106
DET	68	40	26	2	400	279	24	18	66	28	37	1	321	350	27	26	134	68	63	3	721	629	51	44	79	142	124	99	121	107	98	97
IND	66	31	35	0	328	302	27	40	70	19	50	1	270	426	7	24	136	50	85	1	598	728	34	64	195	53	106	95	103	120	95	98
NY	70	44	23	3	313	182	21	9	68	40	24	4	347	296	34	18	138	84	47	7	660	478	55	27	60	155	82	78	115	85	93	89
PHI	66	37	29	0	313	268	6	12	65	32	32	1	218	238	10	14	131	69	61	1	531	506	16	26	77	42	67	122	78	76	114	113
PIT	69	37	30	2	277	230	0	1	69	29	38	2	254	346	14	22	138	66	68	4	531	576	14	23	3	29	108	86	91	96	95	95
WAS	66	26	38	2	260	318	17	25	70	22	48	0	222	410	13	25	136	48	86	2	482	728	30	50	113	69	109	96	82	117	96	101
1889 NATIONAL LEAGUE																																
BOS	68	48	17	3	455	272	24	14	65	35	28	2	371	352	18	27	133	83	45	5	826	624	42	41	84	98	93	98	105	82	102	98
CHI	69	37	30	2	450	398	54	52	67	30	35	2	416	417	25	19	136	67	65	4	866	815	79	71	200	116	102	99	110	105	99	98

	HOME								ROAD								ALL															
TM	G	W	L	T	R	OR	HR	OHR	G	W	L	T	R	OR	HR	OHR	G	W	L	T	R	OR	HR	OHR	HRF	HRB	HRP	RF	RB	RP	BPF	PPF
CLE	68	33	35	0	353	341	8	13	68	28	37	3	293	378	17	23	136	61	72	3	646	719	25	36	56	63	90	103	79	87	103	104
IND	69	32	36	1	495	478	50	54	66	27	39	0	325	416	12	19	135	59	75	1	820	894	62	73	250	71	90	121	95	104	109	110
NY	63	47	15	1	512	302	18	15	68	36	28	4	422	396	34	23	131	83	43	5	934	698	52	38	67	130	102	108	117	91	105	101
PHI	68	43	24	1	467	347	27	12	62	20	40	2	274	402	17	21	130	63	64	3	741	749	44	33	94	96	74	108	92	95	104	105
PIT	70	40	28	2	388	307	6	2	64	21	43	0	337	492	36	40	134	61	71	2	725	799	42	42	11	194	133	79	106	113	89	90
WAS	56	24	29	3	302	323	12	10	71	17	54	0	330	569	13	27	127	41	83	3	632	892	25	37	71	67	84	88	95	123	92	95
1890 NATIONAL LEAGUE																																
BOS	66	43	23	0	435	284	20	11	68	33	34	1	328	308	11	16	134	76	57	1	763	592	31	27	116	86	79	115	92	74	111	108
BRO	74	58	16	0	547	303	27	9	55	28	27	0	337	318	16	18	129	86	43	0	884	621	43	27	82	154	106	98	121	92	100	96
CHI	74	48	24	2	509	369	55	29	65	36	29	0	340	323	12	12	139	84	53	2	849	692	67	41	246	106	80	115	99	84	109	107
CIN	73	50	23	0	470	323	19	25	61	27	32	2	283	309	8	17	134	77	55	2	753	632	27	42	140	69	108	111	92	81	108	106
CLE	70	30	37	3	357	355	13	7	66	14	51	1	268	476	8	25	136	44	88	4	625	831	21	32	59	91	109	90	89	113	94	97
NY	66	37	27	2	361	272	8	2	69	26	41	2	347	424	17	12	135	63	68	4	708	696	25	14	39	105	50	87	100	97	95	94
PHI	76	54	22	0	554	378	14	10	57	24	32	1	269	329	9	12	133	78	54	1	823	707	23	22	88	73	72	115	99	91	108	107
PIT	40	14	25	1	225	261	3	5	98	9	88	1	373	971	17	47	138	23	113	2	598	1232	20	52	33	90	170	87	98	154	88	95
1891 NATIONAL LEAGUE																																
BOS	73	51	20	2	527	328	34	33	67	36	31	0	320	330	20	18	140	87	51	2	847	658	54	51	152	119	112	119	96	79	112	109
BRO	72	41	31	0	438	383	11	19	65	20	45	0	327	438	12	21	137	61	76	0	765	821	23	40	83	69	113	97	104	111	97	98
CHI	67	43	22	2	467	343	39	30	70	39	31	0	366	387	21	23	137	82	53	2	833	730	60	53	153	136	126	112	103	92	106	105
CIN	67	26	41	0	296	328	19	17	71	30	40	1	350	463	21	23	138	56	81	1	646	791	40	40	87	118	117	83	93	110	91	93
CLE	69	40	28	1	484	426	4	6	72	25	46	1	352	462	18	18	141	65	74	2	836	888	22	24	32	76	91	114	102	108	105	106
NY	69	39	28	2	377	302	28	15	67	32	33	2	377	409	18	12	136	71	61	4	754	711	46	27	133	104	66	86	107	101	94	93
PHI	69	35	34	0	372	350	8	9	69	33	35	1	384	423	13	20	138	68	69	1	756	773	21	29	55	72	92	91	104	106	95	95
PIT	66	32	34	0	379	316	14	9	71	23	46	2	300	428	15	22	137	55	80	2	679	744	29	31	69	94	92	102	89	95	101	102
1892 NATIONAL LEAGUE																																
BAL	78	28	46	4	472	486	13	14	74	18	55	1	307	534	17	37	152	46	101	5	779	1020	30	51	49	135	193	105	100	129	100	102
BOS	76	54	21	1	490	344	20	27	76	48	27	1	372	305	14	14	152	102	48	2	862	649	34	41	162	78	89	123	98	76	113	111
BRO	78	51	24	3	485	340	14	8	80	44	35	1	450	393	16	18	158	95	59	4	935	733	30	26	69	99	81	101	114	92	101	99
CHI	68	37	31	0	292	278	9	9	79	33	45	1	343	457	17	26	147	70	76	1	635	735	26	35	51	106	128	84	93	103	92	93
CIN	80	45	32	3	440	352	29	21	75	37	36	2	326	379	15	18	155	82	68	5	766	731	44	39	138	103	97	105	93	90	103	103
CLE	79	54	24	1	483	281	4	4	74	39	32	3	372	332	22	24	153	93	56	4	855	613	26	28	18	128	133	103	106	78	103	101
LOU	70	37	31	2	309	286	7	3	84	26	58	0	340	518	11	23	154	63	89	2	649	804	18	26	37	86	82	84	91	107	92	93
NY	79	42	36	1	452	382	26	12	74	29	44	1	359	444	13	20	153	71	80	2	811	826	39	32	107	106	92	97	106	108	98	98
PHI	81	55	26	0	512	322	34	8	74	32	40	2	348	368	16	16	155	87	66	2	860	690	50	24	119	123	68	107	103	86	104	103
PIT	87	52	34	1	477	363	32	14	68	28	39	1	325	433	6	14	155	80	73	2	802	796	38	28	169	67	67	88	109	109	94	94
STL	75	37	36	2	379	380	32	32	80	19	58	3	324	542	13	15	155	56	94	5	703	922	45	47	215	82	88	93	94	119	95	97
WAS	70	34	36	0	404	379	23	22	83	24	57	2	327	490	14	18	153	58	93	2	731	869	37	40	156	85	93	111	90	105	105	106
1893 NATIONAL LEAGUE																																
BAL	60	36	24	0	451	404	16	9	70	24	46	0	369	489	11	20	130	60	70	0	820	893	27	29	94	73	74	114	90	98	107	108
BOS	65	49	15	1	557	350	48	41	66	37	28	1	451	445	17	25	131	86	43	2	1008	795	65	66	199	113	125	104	114	92	103	101
BRO	67	43	24	0	393	348	24	17	63	22	39	2	382	497	21	24	130	65	63	2	775	845	45	41	87	129	117	81	101	108	91	91
CHI	73	38	34	1	538	471	20	15	55	18	37	0	291	403	12	11	128	56	71	1	829	874	32	26	112	77	64	108	93	101	104	104
CIN	66	37	27	2	424	375	19	21	65	28	36	1	335	439	10	17	131	65	63	3	759	814	29	38	141	61	82	102	87	93	101	102
CLE	70	47	22	1	579	440	10	9	59	26	33	0	397	399	22	26	129	73	55	1	976	839	32	35	36	133	137	108	110	97	104	103
LOU	53	24	28	1	329	367	3	14	73	26	47	0	430	575	16	24	126	50	75	1	759	942	19	38	60	53	124	95	96	115	96	98
NY	71	49	20	2	571	390	48	19	65	19	44	2	370	455	13	17	136	68	64	4	941	845	61	36	188	95	72	106	101	93	103	103
PHI	66	43	22	1	559	351	45	13	67	29	35	3	452	490	35	17	133	72	57	4	1011	841	80	30	113	190	80	99	116	98	100	98
PIT	73	54	19	0	593	417	25	8	58	27	29	2	377	349	12	21	131	81	48	2	970	766	37	29	82	105	84	111	104	86	106	105
STL	72	40	30	2	424	405	7	14	63	17	45	1	321	424	3	24	135	57	75	3	745	829	10	38	69	32	104	97	85	94	99	100
WAS	49	21	27	1	281	298	8	7	81	19	62	0	441	734	15	47	130	40	89	1	722	1032	23	54	41	102	153	81	97	124	89	92
1894 NATIONAL LEAGUE																																
BAL	67	52	15	0	626	378	13	9	62	37	24	1	545	442	20	23	129	89	39	1	1171	820	33	32	51	86	78	97	124	90	99	96
BOS	63	44	19	0	672	519	77	70	70	39	30	1	550	483	26	19	133	83	49	1	1222	1002	103	89	301	105	87	127	111	93	113	111
BRO	68	42	24	2	512	452	22	15	66	28	37	1	509	555	20	26	134	70	61	3	1021	1007	42	41	80	88	83	89	110	108	94	94
CHI	67	35	30	2	625	513	26	13	68	22	45	1	416	553	39	30	135	57	75	3	1041	1066	65	43	59	153	100	116	96	100	108	108
CIN	67	38	28	1	512	515	43	45	65	17	47	1	398	570	18	40	132	55	75	2	910	1085	61	85	141	97	141	102	93	110	100	101
CLE	59	35	24	0	511	411	8	18	71	33	37	1	421	485	29	35	130	68	61	1	932	896	37	53	51	86	133	121	89	85	111	111
LOU	61	24	37	0	317	366	16	7	69	12	57	0	375	635	26	32	130	36	94	0	692	1001	42	39	46	117	89	76	83	113	88	91
NY	69	49	17	3	477	362	29	21	68	39	27	2	463	427	14	16	137	88	44	5	940	789	43	37	158	58	53	95	94	80	100	98
PHI	69	48	20	1	674	398	26	31	60	23	37	0	469	568	14	31	129	71	57	1	1143	966	40	62	110	74	115	91	127	109	95	94
PIT	75	46	28	1	559	475	26	11	57	19	37	1	396	497	22	28	132	65	65	2	955	972	48	39	58	122	94	89	104	108	94	94
STL	66	34	32	0	429	438	30	16	67	22	44	1	342	516	24	32	133	56	76	1	771	954	54	48	84	113	97	102	78	95	101	103
WAS	62	32	30	0	476	463	35	20	70	13	57	0	406	659	24	39	132	45	87	0	882	1122	59	59	97	118	114	98	94	115	98	100
1895 NATIONAL LEAGUE																																
BAL	67	54	12	1	581	293	10	8	65	33	31	1	428	353	15	23	132	87	43	2	1009	646	25	31	49	86	95	110	108	72	107	104
BOS	67	48	19	0	537	363	50	38	65	23	41	1	370	463	4	18	132	71	60	1	907	826	54	56	314	50	80	105	101	94	103	102
BRO	66	43	22	1	444	334	22	20	67	28	38	1	423	500	17	21	133	71	60	2	867	834	39	41	112	91	96	87	106	101	94	94
CHI	69	43	26	0	477	439	32	23	64	29	32	3	389	415	23	15	133	72	58	3	866	854	55	38	131	117	83	106	96	95	103	103
CIN	65	42	22	1	528	404	8	7	67	24	42	1	375	450	28	32	132	66	64	2	903	854	36	39	27	144	144	115	96	92	108	107
CLE	60	47	13	0	423	274	5	10	71	37	33	1	494	446	24	23	131	84	46	1	917	720	29	33	41	88	117	90	110	87	97	95
LOU	59	19	38	2	328	447	14	12	74	16	58	0	370	643	20	28	133	35	96	2	698	1090	34	40	68	101	110	94	85	125	95	99
NY	67	40	27	0	424	376	14	8	65	26	38	1	428	458	18	26	132	66	65	1	852	834	32	34	51	112	103	89	104	101	95	94
PHI	73	51	21	1	653	455	42	16	60	27	32	1	415	502	19	20	133	78	53	2	1068	957	61	36	121	130	88	100	122	113	99	98
PIT	67	44	21	2	422	334	9	3	67	27	40	0	389	453	17	14	134	71	61	2	811	787	26	17	41	89	50	91	96	92	96	96
STL	67	25	41	1	411	491	26	35	68	14	51	3	336	541	12	29	135	39	92	4	747	1032	38	64	142	77	130	102	84	113	100	102
WAS	69	31	34	4	523	521	39	33	63	12	51	0	314	527	16	22	132	43	85	4	837	1048	55	55	160	103	110	110	92	115	103	105
1896 NATIONAL LEAGUE																																
BAL	67	49	16	2	528	310	8	4	65	41	23	1	467	352	15	18	132	90	39	3	995	662	23	22	38	103	82	101	122	84	102	99
BOS	67	42	24	1	510	371	23	39	65	32	33	0	350	390	13	18	132	74	57	1	860	761	36	57	181	80	119	115	99	90	108	107
BRO	65	35	28	2	298	298	13	20	68	23	45	0	394	466	15	20	133	58	73	2	692	764	28	40	98	84	117	74	99	107	87	88
CHI	68	42	24	2	470	427	19	16	64	29	33	2	345	372	15	14	132	71	57	4	815	799	34	30	113	94	84	117	94	93	108	108
CIN	66	51	15	0	450	292	6	1	62	26	35	1	333	328	14	26	128	77	50	1	783	620	20	27	18	141	97	106	96	78	105	103
CLE	64	43	19	2	445	315	9	4	71	37	29	5	395	335	19	23	135	80	48	7	840	650	28	27	37	124	95	116	94	75	110	108
LOU	64	25	37	2	326	471	24	37	70	13	56	1	327	526	13	10	134	38	93	3	653	997	37	47	246	69	75	100	83	121	98	102
NY	66	39	26	1	438	371	21	14	67	25	41	1	391	450	19	19	133	64	67	2	829	821	40	33	94	122	102	98	105	104	99	99
PHI	69	42	27	0	530	448	30	24	61	20	41	0	360	443	19	15	130	62	68	0	890	891	49	39	135	126	102	107	110	112	102	102

	HOME								ROAD								ALL															
TM	G	W	L	T	R	OR	HR	OHR	G	W	L	T	R	OR	HR	OHR	G	W	L	T	R	OR	HR	OHR	HRF	HRB	HRP	RF	RB	RP	BPF	PPF
PIT	66	35	31	0	369	335	5	2	65	31	32	2	418	406	22	16	131	66	63	2	787	741	27	18	20	135	78	85	107	101	93	93
STL	62	27	34	1	322	374	25	18	69	13	56	0	271	555	12	22	131	40	90	1	593	929	37	40	134	95	106	92	80	118	95	98
WAS	68	38	29	1	462	395	30	12	65	20	44	1	356	525	15	12	133	58	73	2	818	920	45	24	142	104	62	93	108	119	95	96
1897 NATIONAL LEAGUE																																
BAL	69	51	15	3	470	293	4	7	67	39	25	3	494	381	15	11	136	90	40	6	964	674	19	18	44	75	83	87	127	91	95	92
BOS	67	54	12	1	573	307	26	26	68	39	27	2	452	358	19	13	135	93	39	3	1025	665	45	39	160	118	99	112	120	82	107	103
BRO	70	38	29	3	456	412	11	19	66	23	42	1	346	433	13	15	136	61	71	4	802	845	24	34	100	78	108	104	98	104	102	102
CHI	67	36	30	1	444	405	16	15	71	23	43	5	388	489	22	15	138	59	73	6	832	894	38	30	89	127	104	102	103	109	100	101
CIN	68	49	18	1	444	345	4	3	66	27	38	1	319	360	18	15	134	76	56	2	763	705	22	18	22	114	92	112	90	84	107	107
CLE	65	49	16	0	477	306	8	11	67	20	46	1	296	374	8	21	132	69	62	1	773	680	16	32	70	66	117	119	89	81	111	110
LOU	68	34	31	3	343	402	26	23	66	18	47	1	326	457	14	16	134	52	78	4	669	859	40	39	150	106	106	92	89	112	95	97
NY	75	51	19	5	495	347	16	12	62	32	29	1	400	348	15	14	137	83	48	6	895	695	31	26	82	109	93	95	113	90	98	96
PHI	67	32	34	1	381	357	17	6	67	23	43	1	371	435	23	22	134	55	77	2	752	792	40	28	53	181	115	91	100	104	96	96
PIT	65	38	27	0	354	363	10	5	70	22	44	4	322	472	15	17	135	60	71	4	676	835	25	22	53	108	84	97	87	105	98	100
STL	60	18	41	1	273	467	20	41	72	11	61	0	315	616	11	13	132	29	102	1	588	1083	31	54	254	67	101	93	81	141	93	99
WAS	68	40	26	2	434	372	28	13	67	21	45	1	347	421	8	14	135	61	71	3	781	793	36	27	171	79	72	103	97	99	101	102
1898 NATIONAL LEAGUE																																
BAL	76	58	15	3	505	268	4	1	78	38	38	2	428	355	8	16	154	96	53	5	933	623	12	17	23	97	76	103	119	82	103	100
BOS	79	62	15	2	510	272	45	22	73	40	32	1	362	342	8	15	152	102	47	3	872	614	53	37	240	112	108	104	111	82	104	101
BRO	74	30	41	3	319	367	10	15	75	24	50	1	319	444	7	19	149	54	91	4	638	811	17	34	96	74	139	91	92	114	95	96
CHI	89	58	31	0	520	378	10	4	63	27	34	2	308	301	8	13	152	85	65	2	828	679	18	17	50	106	89	105	105	90	103	102
CIN	89	58	28	3	521	423	2	3	68	34	32	2	310	317	17	13	157	92	60	5	831	740	19	16	14	125	132	115	97	89	108	107
CLE	58	37	19	2	268	212	5	1	98	44	49	5	462	471	13	25	156	81	68	7	730	683	18	26	29	131	95	89	99	90	96	95
LOU	79	43	34	2	410	368	24	25	75	27	47	1	318	465	8	8	154	70	81	3	728	833	32	33	250	73	74	94	99	112	96	98
NY	76	45	28	3	423	322	18	10	81	32	45	4	414	478	16	11	157	77	73	7	837	800	34	21	110	126	81	90	114	108	95	94
PHI	81	49	31	1	452	371	13	9	69	29	40	0	371	413	20	14	150	78	71	1	823	784	33	23	57	177	128	90	117	113	94	94
PIT	74	39	34	1	314	308	6	3	78	33	42	3	320	386	8	11	152	72	76	4	634	694	14	14	52	76	64	93	86	93	98	98
STL	66	20	44	2	285	424	8	15	88	19	67	2	286	505	5	17	154	39	111	4	571	929	13	32	132	47	109	115	72	112	106	110
WAS	80	34	44	2	418	471	29	17	75	17	57	1	286	468	7	12	155	51	101	3	704	939	36	29	202	85	85	108	89	117	102	105
1899 NATIONAL LEAGUE																																
BAL	77	50	25	2	473	343	4	2	75	36	37	2	354	348	13	11	152	86	62	4	827	691	17	13	26	92	62	113	96	82	108	106
BOS	80	53	26	1	460	346	32	33	73	42	31	0	398	299	7	11	153	95	57	1	858	645	39	44	279	66	82	106	102	78	105	103
BRO	78	61	16	1	510	315	13	18	72	40	31	1	382	343	14	14	150	101	47	2	892	658	27	32	104	94	109	106	108	83	105	102
CHI	85	44	39	2	429	415	14	14	67	31	34	2	383	348	13	6	152	75	73	4	812	763	27	20	115	86	61	92	107	101	96	96
CIN	88	57	29	2	543	416	2	7	68	26	38	4	313	354	11	19	156	83	67	6	856	770	13	26	25	67	148	111	97	91	106	105
CLE	42	9	33	0	152	293	3	5	112	11	101	0	377	959	9	38	154	20	134	0	529	1252	12	43	46	64	149	87	75	154	89	96
LOU	63	33	28	2	369	306	23	17	92	42	49	1	458	469	17	16	155	75	77	3	827	775	40	33	166	108	92	106	100	93	103	103
NY	75	35	38	2	382	394	7	6	77	25	52	0	352	469	16	13	152	60	90	2	734	863	23	19	48	103	87	96	95	110	97	99
PHI	83	58	25	0	503	353	11	3	71	36	33	2	413	390	20	14	154	94	58	2	916	743	31	17	38	160	78	93	117	97	97	95
PIT	84	49	34	1	475	381	12	8	70	27	39	4	359	384	15	19	154	76	73	5	834	765	27	27	51	130	121	96	105	98	99	98
STL	87	50	33	4	480	446	38	33	68	34	34	0	339	293	9	8	155	84	67	4	819	739	47	41	275	79	70	114	93	84	108	107
WAS	79	34	44	1	415	448	30	15	76	20	54	2	328	535	17	20	155	54	98	3	743	983	47	35	114	150	119	95	96	123	96	98
1900 NATIONAL LEAGUE																																
BOS	73	42	29	2	507	420	40	43	69	24	43	2	271	319	8	16	142	66	72	4	778	739	48	59	254	82	113	140	85	84	120	120
BRO	73	43	26	4	452	394	15	15	69	39	28	2	364	328	10	15	142	82	54	6	816	722	25	30	113	74	89	114	102	92	108	106
CHI	77	45	30	2	337	329	12	5	69	20	45	4	298	422	21	16	146	65	75	6	635	751	33	21	44	143	88	84	91	105	93	94
CIN	63	27	34	2	255	309	12	9	81	35	43	3	447	436	18	19	144	62	77	5	702	745	30	28	75	107	96	84	99	107	92	93
NY	71	38	31	2	393	375	13	8	70	22	47	1	320	448	10	18	141	60	78	3	713	823	23	26	76	85	89	98	100	113	97	99
PHI	70	45	23	2	434	353	13	7	71	30	40	1	376	438	15	22	141	75	63	3	810	791	28	29	58	120	109	99	113	110	98	98
PIT	70	42	28	0	359	315	14	7	70	37	32	1	374	297	12	17	140	79	60	1	733	612	26	24	76	96	84	101	98	83	103	101
STL	72	40	31	1	382	316	23	13	70	25	44	1	361	431	13	19	142	65	75	2	743	747	36	32	108	111	103	87	108	108	93	93
1901 NATIONAL LEAGUE																																
BOS	70	41	29	0	297	298	18	17	70	28	40	2	234	258	10	12	140	69	69	2	531	556	28	29	148	79	83	118	73	77	112	112
BRO	68	43	25	0	400	303	13	6	69	36	32	1	344	297	19	12	137	79	57	1	744	600	32	18	66	133	78	111	111	92	106	103
CHI	70	30	39	1	293	357	7	10	70	23	47	0	285	342	11	17	140	53	86	1	578	699	18	27	63	78	110	102	89	105	100	102
CIN	72	27	43	2	279	409	23	33	70	25	44	1	282	409	15	18	142	52	87	3	561	818	38	51	151	116	147	96	90	125	95	100
NY	71	30	38	3	255	350	8	11	70	22	47	1	289	405	11	13	141	52	85	4	544	755	19	24	79	72	90	86	91	122	91	95
PHI	69	46	23	0	349	247	11	6	71	37	34	0	319	296	13	13	140	83	57	0	668	543	24	19	71	96	74	101	100	84	103	100
PIT	69	45	24	0	372	255	15	8	71	45	25	1	404	279	13	12	140	90	49	1	776	534	28	20	97	97	71	97	119	86	101	96
STL	72	40	31	1	392	338	21	19	70	36	33	1	400	351	18	19	142	76	64	2	792	689	39	38	105	140	138	96	125	111	97	95
1902 NATIONAL LEAGUE																																
BOS	72	42	27	3	283	230	13	11	70	31	37	2	289	286	1	4	142	73	64	5	572	516	14	15	321	40	63	88	106	97	95	94
BRO	69	45	23	1	277	210	8	2	72	30	40	2	287	309	11	8	141	75	63	3	564	519	19	10	58	195	100	87	107	98	95	94
CHI	70	31	38	1	228	249	1	3	71	37	31	3	302	252	5	7	141	68	69	4	530	501	6	10	37	60	111	89	98	94	96	95
CIN	70	35	35	0	353	305	11	8	71	35	35	1	280	261	7	8	141	70	70	1	633	566	18	16	124	134	124	120	103	93	110	108
NY	71	24	44	3	214	297	7	7	68	24	44	0	187	293	1	9	139	48	88	3	401	590	8	16	127	54	114	100	73	102	100	104
PHI	69	29	39	1	264	351	1	6	69	27	42	0	220	298	4	6	138	56	81	1	484	649	5	12	72	44	107	115	84	108	105	109
PIT	71	56	15	0	410	207	9	2	71	47	21	3	365	233	10	2	142	103	36	3	775	440	19	4	95	141	35	105	130	80	105	98
STL	70	28	38	4	262	336	3	7	70	28	40	2	255	359	7	9	140	56	78	6	517	695	10	16	65	99	157	97	98	126	95	99
1903 NATIONAL LEAGUE																																
BOS	68	31	35	2	283	314	11	19	72	27	45	0	295	385	14	11	140	58	80	2	578	699	25	30	122	132	150	93	90	106	96	98
BRO	73	40	33	0	359	361	8	9	66	30	33	3	308	321	7	9	139	70	66	3	667	682	15	18	97	81	95	103	99	101	101	102
CHI	73	45	28	0	345	285	2	7	66	37	28	1	350	314	7	6	139	82	56	1	695	599	9	13	66	51	80	88	110	97	95	93
CIN	76	41	35	0	440	389	12	7	65	33	30	2	325	267	16	8	141	74	65	2	765	656	28	15	71	171	102	117	104	90	109	107
NY	70	41	27	2	368	296	9	10	72	43	28	1	361	271	11	10	142	84	55	3	729	567	20	20	95	108	108	108	101	81	106	103
PHI	61	25	33	3	250	298	9	6	78	24	53	1	367	440	3	15	139	49	86	4	617	738	12	21	104	67	102	87	100	117	92	94
PIT	70	46	24	0	393	327	17	5	71	45	25	1	400	286	17	3	141	91	49	1	793	613	34	8	112	157	43	107	113	90	105	101
STL	69	22	45	2	248	393	7	13	70	21	49	0	257	402	1	13	139	43	94	2	505	795	8	26	135	34	112	97	79	118	96	102
1904 NATIONAL LEAGUE																																
BOS	79	34	45	0	269	363	13	10	76	21	53	2	222	386	11	14	155	55	98	2	491	749	24	24	89	120	119	99	84	121	96	102
BRO	76	31	44	1	234	287	3	11	78	25	53	0	263	327	12	16	154	56	97	1	497	614	15	27	54	84	161	90	87	104	95	98
CHI	78	49	27	2	303	240	6	10	78	44	33	1	296	277	16	6	156	93	60	3	599	517	22	16	76	105	87	96	98	86	100	99
CIN	79	49	27	3	409	295	12	7	78	39	38	1	286	252	9	7	157	88	65	4	695	547	21	14	116	83	58	125	98	80	114	111
NY	84	56	26	2	397	258	23	30	74	50	21	3	347	218	8	6	158	106	47	5	744	476	31	36	262	81	81	104	115	77	105	100
PHI	73	28	43	2	269	348	7	7	82	24	57	1	302	436	16	15	155	52	100	3	571	784	23	22	53	135	132	93	102	133	93	97

	HOME								ROAD								ALL															
TM	G	W	L	T	R	OR	HR	OHR	G	W	L	T	R	OR	HR	OHR	G	W	L	T	R	OR	HR	OHR	HRF	HRB	HRP	RF	RB	RP	BPF	PPF
PIT	78	48	30	0	338	286	5	2	78	39	36	3	337	306	10	11	156	87	66	3	675	592	15	13	37	100	71	98	111	99	99	98
STL	76	39	36	1	298	280	14	15	79	36	43	0	304	315	10	8	155	75	79	1	602	595	24	23	154	88	83	97	100	99	99	99
1905 NATIONAL LEAGUE																																
BOS	76	29	46	1	234	344	14	14	80	22	57	1	234	387	3	22	156	51	103	2	468	731	17	36	114	72	144	97	76	112	97	102
BRO	77	29	47	1	273	379	16	16	78	19	57	2	233	428	13	8	155	48	104	3	506	807	29	24	142	107	87	98	83	125	96	102
CHI	81	54	25	2	365	212	7	5	74	38	36	0	302	230	5	10	155	92	61	2	667	442	12	15	76	58	67	100	100	70	105	100
CIN	79	50	28	1	438	330	12	2	76	29	46	1	297	368	15	20	155	79	74	2	735	698	27	22	42	190	116	110	111	108	103	103
NY	76	54	21	1	377	234	33	19	79	51	27	1	401	271	6	6	155	105	48	2	778	505	39	25	317	74	57	97	121	83	101	96
PHI	76	39	36	1	353	314	8	9	79	44	33	2	355	288	8	12	155	83	69	3	708	602	16	21	90	73	92	107	107	93	104	102
PIT	78	49	28	1	362	287	4	1	77	47	29	1	330	283	18	11	155	96	57	2	692	570	22	12	19	155	71	105	105	88	104	102
STL	77	32	45	0	245	342	13	10	77	26	51	0	290	392	8	18	154	58	96	0	535	734	21	28	89	103	128	87	93	122	91	95
1906 NATIONAL LEAGUE																																
BOS	76	28	47	1	218	329	11	16	76	21	55	0	190	320	5	8	152	49	102	1	408	649	16	24	180	76	110	104	75	113	100	106
BRO	76	31	44	1	191	287	9	5	77	35	42	0	305	338	16	10	153	66	86	1	496	625	25	15	57	206	133	77	104	129	86	90
CHI	79	56	21	2	345	214	7	6	76	60	15	1	360	167	13	6	155	116	36	3	705	381	20	12	71	141	95	104	120	69	107	99
CIN	78	36	40	2	316	333	10	10	77	28	47	2	217	249	6	4	155	64	87	4	533	582	16	14	175	73	61	130	83	91	115	116
NY	75	51	24	0	309	239	9	8	78	45	32	1	316	271	6	5	153	96	56	1	625	510	15	13	151	75	65	99	114	96	100	97
PHI	77	37	40	0	226	270	2	5	77	34	42	1	302	294	10	13	154	71	82	1	528	564	12	18	33	106	172	85	104	111	92	93
PIT	77	49	27	1	325	232	4	8	77	44	33	0	298	238	8	5	154	93	60	1	623	470	12	13	94	75	82	104	109	85	104	101
STL	77	28	48	1	241	313	6	10	77	24	50	3	229	294	4	7	154	52	98	4	470	607	10	17	136	53	87	104	85	106	101	104
1907 NATIONAL LEAGUE																																
BOS	74	31	42	1	253	304	14	20	78	27	48	3	249	348	8	8	152	58	90	4	502	652	22	28	192	94	110	98	102	128	95	99
BRO	77	37	38	2	223	232	9	10	76	28	45	3	223	290	9	6	153	65	83	5	446	522	18	16	121	93	82	88	91	104	94	96
CHI	76	54	19	3	282	198	2	5	79	53	26	0	290	192	11	6	155	107	45	3	572	390	13	11	47	80	89	105	102	73	106	102
CIN	81	43	36	2	287	227	3	5	75	23	51	1	239	292	12	11	156	66	87	3	526	519	15	16	35	117	139	90	105	103	95	95
NY	77	45	30	2	317	250	19	19	78	37	41	0	257	260	4	6	155	82	71	2	574	510	23	25	284	63	75	110	103	94	105	104
PHI	75	45	30	0	265	247	2	4	74	38	34	2	247	229	10	9	149	83	64	2	512	476	12	13	34	90	115	106	97	91	104	103
PIT	77	47	29	1	330	258	7	3	80	44	34	2	304	252	12	9	157	91	63	3	634	510	19	12	53	133	82	110	113	94	105	102
STL	79	31	47	1	223	289	9	10	76	21	54	1	196	317	10	10	155	52	101	2	419	606	19	20	91	115	120	95	83	115	96	100
1908 NATIONAL LEAGUE																																
BOS	78	35	42	1	295	328	13	20	78	28	49	1	242	294	4	9	156	63	91	2	537	622	17	29	211	56	98	113	100	113	104	106
BRO	77	27	50	0	179	243	16	3	77	26	51	0	198	273	12	14	154	53	101	0	377	516	28	17	74	178	105	89	77	102	95	99
CHI	78	47	30	1	294	264	9	15	80	52	25	3	330	197	10	5	158	99	55	4	624	461	19	20	154	83	77	109	112	86	106	102
CIN	77	40	37	0	260	272	8	7	78	33	44	1	229	272	6	12	155	73	81	1	489	544	14	19	86	81	103	106	92	102	103	104
NY	80	52	25	3	343	235	10	11	77	46	31	0	309	221	10	15	157	98	56	3	652	456	20	26	84	122	151	106	120	88	104	100
PHI	78	43	34	1	251	213	0	3	77	40	37	0	253	232	11	5	155	83	71	1	504	445	11	8	21	53	94	95	98	88	100	98
PIT	77	42	35	0	227	255	12	4	78	56	21	1	358	214	13	12	155	98	56	1	585	469	25	16	69	159	100	88	118	100	95	92
STL	77	28	49	0	185	295	9	11	77	21	56	0	186	331	8	5	154	49	105	0	371	626	17	16	142	75	67	92	78	122	94	100
1909 NATIONAL LEAGUE																																
BOS	76	27	47	2	219	326	11	9	79	18	61	0	216	357	4	14	155	45	108	2	435	683	15	23	111	76	114	97	80	118	96	102
BRO	79	34	45	0	238	311	12	9	76	21	53	2	206	316	4	22	155	55	98	2	444	627	16	31	79	111	178	100	79	107	99	103
CHI	77	47	29	1	281	199	8	0	78	57	20	1	354	191	12	6	155	104	49	2	635	390	20	6	49	131	31	92	111	73	100	95
CIN	80	39	38	3	282	299	5	2	76	38	38	0	324	300	17	3	156	77	76	3	606	599	22	5	36	143	46	90	113	112	94	94
NY	77	44	33	0	298	294	19	23	81	48	28	5	325	252	7	6	158	92	61	5	623	546	26	29	264	79	81	108	103	92	105	103
PHI	77	40	37	0	266	279	6	10	77	34	42	1	250	239	6	13	154	74	79	1	516	518	12	23	86	71	125	110	86	86	106	106
PIT	78	56	21	1	354	237	10	6	75	54	21	0	345	210	15	6	153	110	42	1	699	447	25	12	77	143	77	104	119	80	105	99
STL	76	26	48	2	271	387	9	12	78	28	50	0	312	344	6	10	154	54	98	2	583	731	15	22	127	71	101	101	107	130	96	99
1910 NATIONAL LEAGUE																																
BOS	78	29	48	1	292	396	25	25	79	24	52	3	203	305	6	11	157	53	100	4	495	701	31	36	236	64	82	129	68	94	114	118
BRO	80	39	39	2	255	287	9	5	76	25	51	0	242	336	16	12	156	64	90	2	497	623	25	17	50	119	81	89	83	101	95	98
CHI	77	58	19	0	354	231	18	9	77	46	31	0	358	268	16	9	154	104	50	0	712	499	34	18	109	118	67	96	114	83	101	96
CIN	77	39	37	1	320	341	6	8	79	36	42	1	300	343	17	19	156	75	79	2	620	684	23	27	43	116	138	105	98	106	101	102
NY	79	52	26	1	352	255	20	17	76	39	37	0	363	312	11	13	155	91	63	1	715	567	31	30	141	96	96	89	120	98	95	92
PHI	78	40	36	2	333	290	12	18	79	38	39	2	341	349	10	18	157	78	75	4	674	639	22	36	107	81	126	93	111	106	96	95
PIT	76	46	30	0	365	308	17	8	78	40	37	1	290	268	16	12	154	86	67	1	655	576	33	20	93	125	80	121	94	85	112	110
STL	76	35	41	0	312	316	3	14	77	28	49	0	327	402	12	16	153	63	90	0	639	718	15	30	64	64	134	88	114	125	91	93
1911 NATIONAL LEAGUE																																
BOS	75	19	54	2	391	536	28	47	81	25	53	3	308	485	9	28	156	44	107	5	699	1021	37	75	187	67	135	120	98	136	103	109
BRO	74	31	42	1	247	303	10	11	80	33	44	3	292	356	18	15	154	64	86	4	539	659	28	26	71	77	74	92	82	98	97	99
CHI	84	49	32	3	380	306	26	14	73	43	30	0	377	301	29	13	157	92	62	3	757	607	55	27	85	144	78	90	114	94	97	94
CIN	82	38	42	2	331	317	5	6	77	32	41	4	351	389	16	30	159	70	83	6	682	706	21	36	25	89	126	84	106	109	92	92
NY	75	49	25	1	357	267	24	15	79	50	29	0	399	275	16	20	154	99	54	1	756	542	40	35	114	94	85	99	108	81	102	98
PHI	76	42	34	0	352	357	48	26	77	37	39	1	306	312	12	17	153	79	73	1	658	669	60	43	216	90	80	114	91	92	107	108
PIT	78	48	29	1	393	246	27	6	77	37	40	0	351	311	21	29	155	85	69	1	744	557	48	35	68	151	100	96	108	83	101	97
STL	79	36	38	5	343	380	11	12	79	39	36	4	328	365	16	27	158	75	74	9	671	745	27	39	57	88	114	104	95	104	101	102
1912 NATIONAL LEAGUE																																
BOS	79	31	47	1	407	471	22	28	76	21	54	1	286	390	13	15	155	52	101	2	693	861	35	43	155	76	91	119	90	109	107	110
BRO	76	33	43	0	303	368	17	20	77	25	52	0	348	386	15	25	153	58	95	0	651	754	32	45	93	96	128	92	97	110	95	97
CHI	77	46	29	2	394	347	22	18	75	45	30	0	362	321	21	15	152	91	59	2	756	668	43	33	108	115	91	106	104	93	104	102
CIN	77	45	32	0	309	311	7	2	78	30	46	2	347	411	14	26	155	75	78	2	656	722	21	28	25	110	88	85	100	108	92	93
NY	76	49	25	2	387	302	31	21	78	54	23	1	436	269	16	15	154	103	48	3	823	571	47	36	160	99	81	102	112	81	104	99
PHI	75	34	41	0	318	352	25	26	77	39	38	0	352	336	18	17	152	73	79	0	670	688	43	43	141	103	103	100	95	98	100	101
PIT	76	45	31	0	347	275	15	10	76	48	27	1	404	290	24	18	152	93	58	1	751	565	39	28	63	130	97	92	108	85	99	95
STL	77	37	40	0	354	414	14	9	76	26	50	0	305	416	13	22	153	63	90	0	659	830	27	31	67	92	95	104	94	115	99	102
1913 NATIONAL LEAGUE																																
BOS	77	34	40	3	298	337	14	12	77	35	42	0	343	353	18	26	154	69	82	3	641	690	32	38	62	106	116	92	106	113	95	96
BRO	77	29	47	1	296	343	20	14	75	36	37	2	299	270	19	19	152	65	84	3	595	613	39	33	88	108	92	108	91	93	104	105
CHI	76	51	25	0	372	273	37	19	79	37	40	2	348	352	22	19	155	88	65	2	720	625	59	38	136	128	91	97	114	100	99	97
CIN	78	32	44	2	307	380	15	13	78	32	45	1	300	337	12	27	156	64	89	3	607	717	27	40	74	83	109	106	93	107	102	104
NY	81	54	23	4	367	250	23	22	75	47	28	0	317	265	8	16	156	101	51	4	684	515	31	38	161	56	75	100	103	80	103	100
PHI	78	43	33	2	361	366	51	23	81	45	30	6	332	270	22	17	159	88	63	8	693	636	73	40	177	130	83	123	95	87	112	111
PIT	79	41	35	3	324	277	13	6	76	37	36	3	349	308	22	20	155	78	71	6	673	585	35	26	47	121	84	90	110	97	96	94
STL	74	25	48	1	239	346	8	20	79	26	51	2	284	409	6	37	153	51	99	3	523	755	14	57	71	49	154	90	89	123	93	97

	HOME								ROAD								ALL															
TM	G	W	L	T	R	OR	HR	OHR	G	W	L	T	R	OR	HR	OHR	G	W	L	T	R	OR	HR	OHR	HRF	HRB	HRP	RF	RB	RP	BPF	PPF
1914 NATIONAL LEAGUE																																
BOS	79	51	25	3	339	279	17	16	79	43	34	2	318	269	18	22	158	94	59	5	657	548	35	38	85	114	122	106	104	89	104	102
BRO	79	45	34	0	342	306	17	17	75	30	45	0	280	312	14	19	154	75	79	0	622	618	31	36	98	96	110	103	104	104	101	101
CHI	76	46	30	0	318	281	22	20	80	32	46	2	287	357	20	17	156	78	76	2	605	638	42	37	117	118	106	98	103	107	98	99
CIN	77	34	42	1	290	328	4	5	80	26	52	2	240	323	12	25	157	60	94	3	530	651	16	30	28	78	117	111	84	101	105	107
NY	80	43	36	1	316	288	17	24	76	41	34	1	356	288	14	23	156	84	70	2	672	576	31	47	105	95	137	91	118	103	96	94
PHI	78	48	30	0	377	321	50	16	76	26	50	0	274	366	12	11	154	74	80	0	651	687	62	27	228	102	60	105	109	116	100	101
PIT	77	39	36	2	234	214	3	6	81	30	49	2	269	326	15	21	158	69	85	4	503	540	18	27	29	72	113	81	90	95	92	93
STL	79	42	34	3	285	280	20	14	78	39	38	1	273	260	13	12	157	81	72	4	558	540	33	26	129	82	67	104	89	87	104	103
1915 NATIONAL LEAGUE																																
BOS	78	49	27	2	280	263	3	5	79	34	42	3	302	282	14	18	157	83	69	5	582	545	17	23	28	85	118	95	104	98	98	97
BRO	78	51	26	1	299	263	9	14	76	29	46	1	237	297	5	15	154	80	72	2	536	560	14	29	111	47	93	102	95	99	101	102
CHI	77	42	34	1	296	314	31	16	79	31	46	2	274	306	22	12	156	73	80	3	570	620	53	28	135	162	94	107	99	106	102	103
CIN	79	39	37	3	265	295	6	7	81	32	46	3	251	290	9	21	160	71	83	6	516	585	15	28	48	75	115	105	87	97	103	104
NY	76	37	38	1	275	270	15	20	79	32	45	2	307	358	9	20	155	69	83	3	582	628	24	40	121	81	129	86	114	121	91	92
PHI	76	49	27	0	313	235	46	18	77	41	35	1	276	228	12	8	153	90	62	1	589	463	58	26	255	111	61	110	99	80	107	104
PIT	79	40	37	2	290	241	8	6	77	33	44	0	267	279	16	15	156	73	81	2	557	520	24	21	47	113	97	95	100	94	99	98
STL	81	42	36	3	320	303	11	10	76	30	45	1	270	298	9	20	157	72	81	4	590	601	20	30	71	87	117	102	103	105	100	100
1916 NATIONAL LEAGUE																																
BOS	78	41	31	6	224	207	6	4	80	48	32	0	318	246	16	20	158	89	63	6	542	453	22	24	31	112	104	81	106	92	93	91
BRO	78	50	27	1	300	233	19	9	78	44	33	1	285	238	9	15	156	94	60	2	585	471	28	24	115	82	75	103	105	87	103	100
CHI	79	37	41	1	309	317	34	22	77	30	45	2	211	224	12	10	156	67	86	3	520	541	46	32	208	96	73	133	82	85	117	117
CIN	76	32	44	0	242	312	4	10	79	28	49	2	263	305	10	25	155	60	93	2	505	617	14	35	44	66	146	100	96	115	98	101
NY	78	47	30	1	291	229	21	23	77	39	36	2	306	275	21	18	155	86	66	3	597	504	42	41	111	143	139	90	117	101	96	93
PHI	79	50	29	0	281	233	29	17	75	41	33	1	300	256	13	11	154	91	62	1	581	489	42	28	166	102	75	90	114	98	96	94
PIT	78	37	40	1	268	298	9	5	79	28	49	2	216	288	11	19	157	65	89	3	484	586	20	24	50	93	91	111	85	101	105	107
STL	76	36	40	0	251	295	12	15	77	24	53	0	225	334	13	16	153	60	93	0	476	629	25	31	94	88	106	98	94	119	97	100
1917 NATIONAL LEAGUE																																
BOS	77	35	42	0	240	269	13	3	80	37	39	4	296	283	9	16	157	72	81	4	536	552	22	19	69	105	77	92	100	103	96	97
BRO	78	36	38	4	270	288	14	14	78	34	43	1	241	271	11	18	156	70	81	5	511	559	25	32	97	105	130	107	90	97	104	105
CHI	77	35	42	0	273	305	11	14	80	39	38	3	279	262	6	20	157	74	80	3	552	567	17	34	100	70	128	109	96	98	104	105
CIN	80	39	38	3	279	296	10	3	77	39	38	0	322	315	16	17	157	78	76	3	601	611	26	20	41	153	98	88	118	119	92	93
NY	80	50	28	2	294	220	21	17	78	48	28	2	341	237	18	12	158	98	56	4	635	457	39	29	121	142	109	89	117	88	97	93
PHI	76	46	29	1	297	270	26	20	78	41	36	1	281	230	12	5	154	87	65	2	578	500	38	25	229	96	58	113	99	87	108	106
PIT	79	25	53	1	232	307	2	4	78	26	50	2	232	288	7	10	157	51	103	3	464	595	9	14	37	45	72	100	84	105	100	103
STL	78	38	38	2	266	302	15	15	76	44	32	0	265	265	11	14	154	82	70	2	531	567	26	29	115	99	110	104	96	102	102	102
1918 NATIONAL LEAGUE																																
BOS	52	23	29	0	163	183	5	2	72	30	42	0	261	286	8	12	124	53	71	0	424	469	13	14	51	104	85	88	99	109	94	95
BRO	54	33	21	0	173	185	4	12	72	24	48	0	187	278	6	10	126	57	69	0	360	463	10	22	128	53	108	102	79	97	101	104
CHI	76	50	26	0	300	235	9	5	55	34	19	2	238	158	12	8	131	84	45	2	538	393	21	13	55	154	101	100	112	84	102	98
CIN	71	46	24	1	298	256	9	5	58	22	36	0	232	240	6	14	129	68	60	1	530	496	15	19	61	117	130	97	117	111	97	96
NY	56	35	21	0	204	181	9	13	68	36	32	0	276	234	4	7	124	71	53	0	480	415	13	20	207	51	78	93	109	96	98	96
PHI	57	27	29	1	220	261	19	13	68	28	39	1	210	246	6	9	125	55	68	2	430	507	25	22	212	93	93	121	88	102	109	111
PIT	69	41	27	1	270	232	9	4	57	24	33	0	196	180	6	9	126	65	60	1	466	412	15	13	74	99	84	109	96	86	106	105
STL	73	32	40	1	241	280	14	7	58	19	38	1	213	247	13	9	131	51	78	2	454	527	27	16	77	173	111	90	103	117	93	95
1919 NATIONAL LEAGUE																																
BOS	68	29	38	1	231	265	11	9	72	28	44	0	234	298	13	20	140	57	82	1	465	563	24	29	67	117	128	98	93	110	98	100
BRO	69	36	33	0	243	227	12	10	72	33	38	1	282	286	13	11	141	69	71	1	525	513	25	21	96	95	81	88	109	106	94	94
CHI	71	40	31	0	232	190	11	7	69	35	34	0	222	217	10	7	140	75	65	0	454	407	21	14	103	74	51	95	89	80	100	99
CIN	71	52	19	0	315	189	10	5	69	44	25	0	262	212	10	16	140	96	44	0	577	401	20	21	60	99	91	105	107	78	105	101
NY	69	46	23	0	310	209	28	17	71	41	30	0	295	261	12	17	140	87	53	0	605	470	40	34	150	124	117	98	119	95	100	96
PHI	71	26	44	1	307	378	29	24	67	21	46	0	203	321	13	16	138	47	90	1	510	699	42	40	156	133	133	118	96	128	104	108
PIT	70	40	30	0	273	218	8	7	69	31	38	0	199	248	9	16	139	71	68	0	472	466	17	23	62	83	100	107	88	88	105	105
STL	69	34	35	0	240	244	9	10	69	20	48	1	223	308	9	15	138	54	83	1	463	552	18	25	80	78	102	91	98	113	94	96
1920 NATIONAL LEAGUE																																
BOS	74	36	37	1	271	292	5	11	79	26	53	0	252	378	18	28	153	62	90	1	523	670	23	39	40	98	165	95	90	111	96	99
BRO	78	49	29	0	360	291	17	14	77	44	32	1	300	237	11	11	155	93	61	1	660	528	28	25	134	70	64	118	97	79	111	108
CHI	77	43	34	0	322	302	19	15	77	32	45	0	297	333	15	22	154	75	79	0	619	635	34	37	93	111	118	99	103	105	99	99
CIN	77	42	34	1	281	238	5	1	77	40	37	0	358	331	13	25	154	82	71	1	639	569	18	26	18	121	89	78	117	105	90	88
NY	80	45	35	0	334	282	31	33	75	41	33	1	348	261	15	11	155	86	68	1	682	543	46	44	199	97	88	96	112	91	99	97
PHI	77	32	45	0	339	380	50	30	76	30	46	0	226	334	14	5	153	62	91	0	565	714	64	35	296	99	50	122	85	106	109	112
PIT	78	42	35	1	276	263	6	4	77	37	40	0	254	289	10	21	155	79	75	1	530	552	16	25	35	79	91	98	85	89	101	101
STL	76	38	38	0	330	332	10	10	79	37	41	1	345	350	22	20	155	75	79	1	675	682	32	30	53	124	119	99	112	113	98	98
1921 NATIONAL LEAGUE																																
BOS	74	42	32	0	332	292	20	18	79	37	42	0	389	405	41	36	153	79	74	0	721	697	61	54	56	133	121	86	111	106	93	92
BRO	78	41	37	0	360	361	32	23	74	36	38	0	307	320	27	23	152	77	75	0	667	681	59	46	104	98	79	108	91	93	105	105
CHI	76	32	44	0	345	434	23	37	77	32	45	0	323	339	14	30	153	64	89	0	668	773	37	67	131	56	97	116	89	101	107	108
CIN	76	40	36	0	321	306	5	2	77	30	47	0	297	343	15	35	153	70	83	0	618	649	20	37	16	76	74	99	87	91	101	101
NY	79	53	26	0	407	321	47	46	74	41	33	0	433	316	28	33	153	94	59	0	840	637	75	79	137	114	121	93	123	97	97	94
PHI	76	29	47	0	326	485	67	49	78	22	56	0	291	434	21	30	154	51	103	0	617	919	88	79	197	100	101	111	86	121	102	107
PIT	76	45	31	0	343	295	13	10	78	45	32	1	349	300	24	27	154	90	63	1	692	595	37	37	50	81	76	102	95	83	103	101
STL	78	48	29	1	397	307	43	25	76	39	37	0	412	374	40	36	154	87	66	1	809	681	83	61	89	156	119	89	121	104	95	93
1922 NATIONAL LEAGUE																																
BOS	76	32	43	1	287	373	6	15	78	21	57	0	309	449	26	42	154	53	100	1	596	822	32	57	34	65	119	89	83	109	94	98
BRO	78	44	34	0	380	326	25	35	77	32	44	1	363	428	31	39	155	76	78	1	743	754	56	74	86	92	118	89	101	102	95	95
CHI	76	39	37	0	344	382	22	37	80	41	37	2	427	426	20	40	156	80	74	2	771	808	42	77	103	63	108	91	104	109	95	96
CIN	79	48	29	2	378	297	8	13	77	38	39	0	388	380	37	36	156	86	68	2	766	677	45	49	31	91	111	88	103	92	96	94
NY	79	51	27	1	439	333	48	38	77	42	34	1	413	325	32	33	156	93	61	2	852	658	80	71	126	107	98	103	106	84	104	100
PHI	77	35	41	1	449	517	94	60	77	22	55	0	289	403	21	29	154	57	96	1	738	920	115	89	242	95	89	131	84	103	113	117
PIT	78	45	33	0	439	390	22	16	77	40	36	1	426	346	30	35	155	85	69	1	865	736	52	51	61	96	89	106	108	94	103	101
STL	77	42	35	0	446	414	59	31	77	43	34	0	417	405	48	30	154	85	69	0	863	819	107	61	114	152	94	105	111	106	101	100
1923 NATIONAL LEAGUE																																
BOS	77	22	55	0	291	429	7	27	78	32	45	1	345	369	25	37	155	54	100	1	636	798	32	64	58	54	113	100	85	104	100	102
BRO	78	37	40	1	348	383	26	27	77	39	38	0	405	358	36	28	155	76	78	1	753	741	62	55	84	97	88	95	102	101	98	98

	HOME								ROAD								ALL															
TM	G	W	L	T	R	OR	HR	OHR	G	W	L	T	R	OR	HR	OHR	G	W	L	T	R	OR	HR	OHR	HRF	HRB	HRP	RF	RB	RP	BPF	PPF
CHI	77	46	31	0	402	354	63	57	77	37	40	0	354	350	27	29	154	83	71	0	756	704	90	86	188	93	92	107	97	91	104	103
CIN	78	46	32	0	337	300	6	4	76	45	31	0	371	329	39	24	154	91	63	0	708	629	45	28	17	98	66	91	97	87	98	96
NY	77	47	30	0	408	362	41	53	76	48	28	0	446	317	44	29	153	95	58	0	854	679	85	82	124	119	112	101	114	93	101	98
PHI	75	20	55	0	418	597	76	77	80	30	49	1	330	411	36	23	155	50	104	1	748	1008	112	100	223	110	92	136	88	114	114	118
PIT	77	47	30	0	381	322	16	9	77	40	37	0	405	374	33	44	154	87	67	0	786	696	49	53	36	112	99	92	109	98	97	95
STL	78	42	35	1	335	320	22	27	76	37	39	0	411	412	41	43	154	79	74	1	746	732	63	70	60	118	131	80	111	109	90	90
1924 NATIONAL LEAGUE																																
BOS	76	28	48	0	254	366	9	8	78	25	52	1	266	434	16	41	154	53	100	1	520	800	25	49	33	67	94	91	79	115	94	99
BRO	77	46	31	0	342	338	26	30	77	46	31	0	375	337	46	28	154	92	62	0	717	675	72	58	79	126	108	97	104	98	99	98
CHI	78	46	31	1	373	341	33	68	76	35	41	0	325	358	33	21	154	81	72	1	698	699	66	89	166	89	100	102	99	99	101	101
CIN	76	43	33	0	311	283	3	3	77	40	37	0	338	296	33	27	153	83	70	0	649	579	36	30	11	87	79	96	93	84	101	99
NY	77	51	26	0	385	272	51	40	77	42	34	1	472	369	44	37	154	93	60	1	857	641	95	77	112	150	126	81	134	104	91	88
PHI	76	26	49	1	369	483	58	64	76	29	47	0	307	366	36	20	152	55	96	1	676	849	94	84	188	114	93	121	91	111	108	111
PIT	77	49	28	0	393	293	19	17	76	41	35	0	331	295	24	25	153	90	63	0	724	588	43	42	76	75	73	108	98	82	106	104
STL	77	40	37	0	419	359	32	37	77	25	52	0	321	391	35	32	154	65	89	0	740	750	67	69	102	108	111	107	103	105	102	103
1925 NATIONAL LEAGUE																																
BOS	76	37	39	0	315	383	15	14	77	33	44	0	393	419	26	53	153	70	83	0	708	802	41	67	40	78	102	88	97	109	94	95
BRO	77	40	37	0	383	407	25	41	76	28	48	0	403	459	39	34	153	68	85	0	786	866	64	75	90	83	97	91	108	118	94	95
CHI	77	37	40	0	367	359	57	63	77	31	46	0	356	414	29	39	154	68	86	0	723	773	86	102	160	83	99	94	95	101	97	98
CIN	76	44	32	0	334	285	10	5	77	36	41	0	356	358	34	30	153	80	73	0	690	643	44	35	26	81	57	89	92	86	97	97
NY	76	47	29	0	362	334	55	39	76	39	37	0	374	368	59	34	152	86	66	0	736	702	114	73	102	143	97	95	97	93	99	98
PHI	77	38	39	0	488	547	73	74	76	30	46	0	324	383	27	43	153	68	85	0	812	930	100	117	182	89	109	136	90	102	116	118
PIT	77	52	25	0	481	342	27	31	76	43	33	0	431	373	51	50	153	95	58	0	912	715	78	81	61	122	128	102	116	94	102	99
STL	76	48	28	0	449	359	66	41	77	29	48	0	379	405	43	45	153	77	76	0	828	764	109	86	120	126	105	104	105	98	102	101
1926 NATIONAL LEAGUE																																
BOS	77	43	34	0	296	266	4	5	76	23	52	1	328	453	12	41	153	66	86	1	624	719	16	46	19	60	111	73	106	116	86	88
BRO	76	38	38	0	314	331	23	26	79	33	44	2	309	374	17	24	155	71	82	2	623	705	40	50	120	65	80	98	89	99	99	101
CHI	78	49	28	1	377	295	38	17	77	33	44	0	305	307	28	21	155	82	72	1	682	602	66	38	110	109	68	108	91	82	106	105
CIN	77	53	23	1	372	259	8	8	80	34	44	2	375	392	27	32	157	87	67	3	747	651	35	40	31	90	97	88	111	97	95	93
NY	76	43	33	0	333	317	45	43	75	31	44	0	330	351	28	27	151	74	77	0	663	668	73	70	147	114	110	95	99	100	98	98
PHI	76	33	42	1	392	470	51	42	76	25	51	0	295	430	24	26	152	58	93	1	687	900	75	68	166	105	100	115	96	122	103	107
PIT	79	49	28	2	446	374	17	16	78	35	41	2	323	315	27	35	157	84	69	4	769	689	44	51	56	102	111	123	96	87	112	111
STL	79	47	30	2	411	359	54	42	77	42	35	0	406	319	36	34	156	89	65	2	817	678	90	76	129	149	131	104	113	96	102	100
1927 NATIONAL LEAGUE																																
BOS	74	32	41	1	296	339	5	10	81	28	53	0	355	432	32	33	155	60	94	1	651	771	37	43	28	78	107	89	98	114	93	95
BRO	74	34	39	1	266	296	20	35	80	31	49	0	275	323	19	28	154	65	88	1	541	619	39	63	122	59	90	101	75	84	103	104
CHI	78	50	28	0	398	315	37	19	75	35	40	0	352	346	37	31	153	85	68	0	750	661	74	50	82	135	94	99	107	96	100	99
CIN	80	45	35	0	348	320	3	11	73	30	43	0	295	333	26	25	153	75	78	0	643	653	29	36	28	59	97	97	92	93	100	100
NY	74	49	25	0	389	342	62	49	81	43	37	1	428	378	47	28	155	92	62	1	817	720	109	77	152	152	110	100	115	103	100	98
PHI	78	34	43	1	375	429	32	46	77	17	60	0	303	474	25	38	155	51	103	1	678	903	57	84	117	91	127	100	99	127	96	100
PIT	79	48	31	0	406	345	25	23	77	46	29	2	411	314	29	35	156	94	60	2	817	659	54	58	77	100	105	102	112	93	102	99
STL	80	55	25	0	433	354	55	51	73	37	36	0	321	311	29	21	153	92	61	0	754	665	84	72	175	104	87	113	100	90	107	106
1928 NATIONAL LEAGUE																																
BOS	76	25	51	0	309	448	24	62	77	25	52	0	322	430	28	38	153	50	103	0	631	878	52	100	125	64	111	100	90	120	97	101
BRO	77	41	35	1	330	296	31	25	78	36	41	1	335	344	35	34	155	77	76	2	665	640	66	59	84	90	81	94	92	89	99	99
CHI	77	52	25	0	335	264	40	18	77	39	38	0	379	351	52	38	154	91	63	0	714	615	92	56	68	139	87	85	105	91	95	93
CIN	78	44	33	1	324	318	3	17	75	34	41	0	324	368	29	41	153	78	74	1	648	686	32	58	30	49	114	91	94	99	96	97
NY	77	51	26	0	411	315	80	46	78	42	35	1	396	338	38	31	155	93	61	1	807	653	118	77	169	112	80	101	109	90	102	99
PHI	75	26	49	0	360	521	54	67	77	17	60	0	300	436	31	42	152	43	109	0	660	957	85	109	153	93	116	117	89	123	104	109
PIT	77	47	30	0	479	356	16	14	75	38	37	0	358	348	36	51	152	85	67	0	837	704	52	65	37	103	113	114	109	95	107	105
STL	77	42	35	0	367	336	62	51	77	53	24	0	440	300	51	35	154	95	59	0	807	636	113	86	128	133	104	97	112	91	100	97
1929 NATIONAL LEAGUE																																
BOS	77	34	43	0	318	403	11	39	77	22	55	0	339	473	22	64	154	56	98	0	657	876	33	103	60	43	122	89	85	109	94	97
BRO	77	42	35	0	371	413	53	48	76	28	48	0	384	475	46	44	153	70	83	0	755	888	99	92	109	101	95	91	98	112	94	96
CHI	78	52	25	1	490	374	76	41	78	46	29	3	492	384	63	36	156	98	54	4	982	758	139	77	117	131	79	100	116	93	101	98
CIN	78	38	39	1	356	356	7	18	77	28	49	0	330	404	27	43	155	66	88	1	686	760	34	61	38	45	84	96	83	91	99	100
NY	77	39	37	1	418	374	79	59	75	45	30	0	479	335	57	43	152	84	67	1	897	709	136	102	130	129	101	96	110	90	100	97
PHI	76	39	37	0	503	580	86	74	78	32	45	1	394	452	67	49	154	71	82	1	897	1032	153	123	134	146	120	126	99	112	110	112
PIT	76	45	31	0	471	382	28	37	78	43	34	1	433	398	32	58	154	88	65	1	904	780	60	95	77	72	106	105	106	93	103	102
STL	77	43	32	2	414	386	48	50	77	35	42	0	417	420	52	51	154	78	74	2	831	806	100	101	96	110	111	96	102	100	98	98
1930 NATIONAL LEAGUE																																
BOS	77	39	38	0	329	401	29	51	77	31	46	0	364	434	37	66	154	70	84	0	693	835	66	117	80	66	110	92	82	96	97	99
BRO	76	49	27	0	438	336	73	66	78	37	41	0	433	402	49	49	154	86	68	0	871	738	122	115	138	92	88	96	99	85	100	98
CHI	79	51	26	2	538	454	93	62	77	39	38	0	460	416	78	49	156	90	64	2	998	870	171	111	117	141	97	110	107	95	105	103
CIN	77	37	40	0	300	368	20	21	77	22	55	0	365	489	54	54	154	59	95	0	665	857	74	75	41	88	90	79	84	105	90	93
NY	78	47	31	0	468	395	91	63	76	40	36	0	491	419	52	54	154	87	67	0	959	814	143	117	135	108	94	94	112	97	98	96
PHI	77	35	42	0	543	644	72	72	79	17	60	2	401	555	54	70	156	52	102	2	944	1199	126	142	115	108	120	121	100	124	106	109
PIT	77	42	35	0	433	454	26	51	77	38	39	0	458	474	60	77	154	80	74	0	891	928	86	128	60	96	142	96	105	109	97	98
STL	77	53	24	0	541	383	52	50	77	39	38	0	463	401	52	37	154	92	62	0	1004	784	104	87	114	85	72	107	109	88	105	102
1931 NATIONAL LEAGUE																																
BOS	78	36	41	1	278	318	16	24	78	28	49	1	255	362	18	42	156	64	90	2	533	680	34	66	69	66	115	96	77	96	99	102
BRO	76	46	29	1	363	317	46	22	77	33	44	0	318	356	25	34	153	79	73	1	681	673	71	56	115	106	89	102	98	97	101	101
CHI	77	50	27	0	414	311	40	22	79	34	43	2	414	399	44	32	156	84	70	2	828	710	84	54	86	144	97	93	124	108	96	94
CIN	77	38	39	0	312	328	6	3	77	20	57	0	280	414	15	48	154	58	96	0	592	742	21	51	16	84	98	92	91	110	95	98
NY	78	50	27	1	379	274	80	47	75	37	38	0	389	325	21	24	153	87	65	1	768	599	101	71	225	95	79	90	116	94	96	93
PHI	76	40	36	0	391	423	53	33	79	26	52	1	293	405	28	42	155	66	88	1	684	828	81	75	123	120	116	117	93	110	106	109
PIT	78	44	33	1	343	327	25	16	77	31	46	0	293	364	16	39	155	75	79	1	636	691	41	55	76	77	92	100	91	98	100	101
STL	78	54	24	0	439	320	31	29	76	47	29	0	376	294	29	36	154	101	53	0	815	614	60	65	92	103	110	111	111	86	107	103
1932 NATIONAL LEAGUE																																
BOS	77	44	33	0	299	285	27	20	78	33	44	1	350	370	36	41	155	77	77	1	649	655	63	61	65	91	85	84	98	98	93	93
BRO	78	44	34	0	378	353	59	31	76	37	39	0	374	394	51	41	154	81	73	0	752	747	110	72	96	137	95	94	111	110	96	96
CHI	77	53	24	0	390	303	32	33	77	37	40	0	330	330	37	35	154	90	64	0	720	633	69	68	92	86	85	105	98	87	104	103
CIN	77	33	44	0	270	344	11	11	78	27	50	1	305	371	36	58	155	60	94	1	575	715	47	69	26	94	115	92	84	102	96	99
NY	77	37	40	0	362	359	78	71	77	35	42	0	393	347	38	41	154	72	82	0	755	706	116	112	169	109	108	97	108	102	99	98

	HOME								ROAD								ALL															
TM	G	W	L	T	R	OR	HR	OHR	G	W	L	T	R	OR	HR	OHR	G	W	L	T	R	OR	HR	OHR	HRF	HRB	HRP	RF	RB	RP	BPF	PPF
PHI	77	45	32	0	507	429	86	71	77	33	44	0	337	367	36	36	154	78	76	0	844	796	122	107	190	105	96	128	106	102	112	111
PIT	76	45	31	0	352	338	22	25	78	41	37	0	349	373	26	61	154	86	68	0	701	711	48	86	59	79	120	99	100	101	99	100
STL	79	42	35	2	354	357	36	38	77	30	47	0	330	360	40	38	156	72	82	2	684	717	76	76	93	95	95	100	95	99	100	101
1933 NATIONAL LEAGUE																																
BOS	77	45	31	1	265	230	27	26	79	38	40	1	287	301	27	28	156	83	71	2	552	531	54	54	99	92	92	88	93	89	96	96
BRO	80	36	41	3	306	352	33	29	77	29	47	1	311	343	29	22	157	65	88	4	617	695	62	51	114	98	82	96	103	114	97	98
CHI	79	55	24	0	334	239	40	32	75	31	44	0	312	297	32	19	154	86	68	0	646	536	72	51	129	109	78	91	109	92	97	95
CIN	79	37	42	0	264	321	5	10	74	21	52	1	232	322	29	37	153	58	94	1	496	643	34	47	23	88	131	98	83	104	98	102
NY	77	48	27	2	298	241	55	44	79	43	34	2	338	274	27	17	156	91	61	4	636	515	82	61	200	95	70	92	104	86	99	96
PHI	72	32	40	0	355	437	45	46	80	28	52	0	252	323	15	41	152	60	92	0	607	760	60	87	163	81	124	142	86	105	118	121
PIT	77	50	27	0	332	272	12	13	77	37	40	0	335	347	27	41	154	87	67	0	667	619	39	54	40	99	122	90	115	108	95	94
STL	77	46	31	0	347	315	18	25	77	36	40	1	340	294	39	30	154	82	71	1	687	609	57	55	66	116	119	104	110	99	102	100
1934 NATIONAL LEAGUE																																
BOS	75	40	35	0	280	280	36	27	77	38	38	1	403	434	47	51	152	78	73	1	683	714	83	78	69	121	110	72	112	116	86	86
BRO	77	43	33	1	390	355	40	38	76	28	48	0	358	440	39	43	153	71	81	1	748	795	79	81	94	98	100	93	111	116	95	95
CHI	77	47	30	0	347	301	53	44	75	39	35	1	358	338	48	36	152	86	65	1	705	639	101	80	112	117	95	92	102	93	98	96
CIN	78	30	47	1	331	406	17	24	74	22	52	0	259	395	38	37	152	52	99	1	590	801	55	61	54	81	94	104	82	108	101	105
NY	75	49	26	0	363	254	75	43	78	44	34	0	397	329	51	32	153	93	60	0	760	583	126	75	141	126	81	91	108	85	98	95
PHI	71	35	36	0	384	400	28	72	78	21	57	0	291	394	28	54	149	56	93	0	675	794	56	126	127	66	134	120	89	104	108	111
PIT	78	45	32	1	421	369	22	38	73	29	44	0	314	344	30	40	151	74	76	1	735	713	52	78	82	69	100	111	98	96	105	105
STL	77	48	29	0	451	363	56	43	77	47	29	1	348	293	48	34	154	95	58	1	799	656	104	77	119	114	87	124	97	82	114	111
1935 NATIONAL LEAGUE																																
BOS	75	25	50	0	309	381	34	41	78	13	65	0	266	471	41	40	153	38	115	0	575	852	75	81	94	93	100	95	84	118	96	100
BRO	77	38	38	1	349	346	32	43	77	32	45	0	362	421	27	45	154	70	83	1	711	767	59	88	103	70	101	90	105	111	94	95
CHI	77	56	21	0	426	264	43	40	77	44	33	0	421	333	45	45	154	100	54	0	847	597	88	85	95	110	107	94	118	87	99	95
CIN	76	41	35	0	331	320	18	18	78	27	50	1	315	452	55	47	154	68	85	1	646	772	73	65	39	119	111	88	96	111	93	95
NY	79	50	27	2	386	302	84	66	77	41	35	1	384	373	39	40	156	91	62	3	770	675	123	106	169	110	100	91	109	97	96	95
PHI	79	35	43	1	416	499	52	68	77	29	46	2	269	372	40	38	156	64	89	3	685	871	92	106	140	95	105	132	81	102	114	117
PIT	77	46	31	0	398	340	32	25	76	40	36	0	345	307	34	38	153	86	67	0	743	647	66	63	81	86	81	111	96	85	107	105
STL	77	53	24	0	441	298	39	27	77	43	34	0	388	327	47	41	154	96	58	0	829	625	86	68	78	114	92	104	110	86	104	100
1936 NATIONAL LEAGUE																																
BOS	79	35	43	1	292	339	26	23	78	36	40	2	339	376	41	46	157	71	83	3	631	715	67	69	59	110	110	88	90	101	95	96
BRO	79	37	40	2	360	397	15	46	77	30	47	0	302	355	18	39	156	67	87	2	662	752	33	85	103	43	101	110	86	96	105	106
CHI	77	50	27	0	404	290	34	41	77	37	40	0	351	313	42	35	154	87	67	0	755	603	76	76	98	102	102	105	99	82	105	102
CIN	76	42	34	0	358	350	24	21	78	32	46	0	364	410	58	30	154	74	80	0	722	760	82	51	56	128	91	94	103	108	96	97
NY	78	52	26	0	378	296	68	54	76	40	36	0	364	325	29	21	154	92	62	0	742	621	97	75	204	83	65	97	102	87	100	98
PHI	78	30	48	0	408	499	69	56	76	24	52	0	318	375	34	31	154	54	100	0	726	874	103	87	167	102	90	122	92	109	108	111
PIT	76	46	30	0	375	342	23	25	80	38	40	2	429	376	37	49	156	84	70	2	804	718	60	74	62	97	113	95	112	102	98	96
STL	77	43	33	1	363	386	38	43	78	44	34	0	432	408	50	46	155	87	67	1	795	794	88	89	88	127	130	92	115	115	94	94
1937 NATIONAL LEAGUE																																
BOS	76	43	33	0	252	224	26	15	76	36	40	0	327	332	37	45	152	79	73	0	579	556	63	60	53	107	93	75	94	90	90	90
BRO	76	36	39	1	336	389	20	30	79	26	52	1	280	383	17	38	155	62	91	2	616	772	37	68	94	47	82	111	84	103	104	107
CHI	78	46	32	0	412	361	47	48	76	47	29	0	399	321	49	43	154	93	61	0	811	682	96	91	102	126	120	105	114	98	103	100
CIN	80	28	51	1	268	347	13	14	75	28	47	0	344	360	60	24	155	56	98	1	612	707	73	38	33	119	84	83	96	110	91	93
NY	75	50	25	0	353	288	76	57	77	45	32	0	379	314	35	28	152	95	57	0	732	602	111	85	191	99	79	97	107	90	100	98
PHI	74	29	45	0	379	481	65	69	81	32	47	2	345	388	38	47	155	61	92	2	724	869	103	116	157	108	122	123	96	113	108	111
PIT	78	46	32	0	360	332	13	28	76	40	36	0	344	314	34	43	154	86	68	0	704	646	47	71	56	73	112	103	99	92	102	101
STL	80	45	33	2	406	379	52	51	77	36	40	1	383	354	42	44	157	81	73	3	789	733	94	95	113	114	115	102	111	104	100	100
1938 NATIONAL LEAGUE																																
BOS	75	45	30	0	233	241	12	19	78	32	45	1	328	377	42	47	153	77	75	1	561	618	54	66	39	93	119	73	95	102	88	89
BRO	74	31	41	2	319	349	38	44	77	38	39	0	385	361	23	44	151	69	80	2	704	710	61	88	123	73	103	94	110	111	96	96
CHI	77	44	33	0	349	326	24	41	77	45	30	2	364	272	41	30	154	89	63	2	713	598	65	71	93	85	94	106	100	85	105	103
CIN	77	43	34	0	344	323	50	31	74	39	34	1	379	311	60	44	151	82	68	1	723	634	110	75	78	167	120	94	111	99	98	96
NY	73	43	30	0	365	297	89	58	79	40	37	2	340	340	36	29	152	83	67	2	705	637	125	87	208	107	80	105	102	93	103	102
PHI	75	26	48	1	286	439	18	40	76	19	57	0	264	401	22	36	151	45	105	1	550	840	40	76	99	53	94	107	82	119	100	106
PIT	78	44	33	1	348	330	22	22	74	42	31	1	359	300	43	49	152	86	64	2	707	630	65	71	49	115	122	99	105	95	100	99
STL	81	36	41	4	414	425	58	45	75	35	39	1	311	296	33	32	156	71	80	5	725	721	91	77	138	96	84	123	94	93	111	111
1939 NATIONAL LEAGUE																																
BOS	73	37	35	1	254	272	13	14	79	26	53	0	318	387	43	49	152	63	88	1	572	659	56	63	34	97	107	82	93	104	92	93
BRO	78	51	27	0	385	329	41	49	79	33	42	4	323	316	37	44	157	84	69	4	708	645	78	93	111	91	106	112	95	87	107	106
CHI	80	44	34	2	379	343	44	35	76	40	36	0	345	335	47	39	156	84	70	2	724	678	91	74	89	116	97	101	104	98	101	100
CIN	81	55	25	1	404	307	48	39	75	42	32	1	363	288	50	42	156	97	57	2	767	595	98	81	90	126	107	102	107	86	103	100
NY	74	41	33	0	360	315	84	58	77	36	41	0	343	370	32	28	151	77	74	0	703	685	116	86	208	93	74	99	106	103	99	99
PHI	74	29	44	1	288	384	19	49	78	16	62	0	265	472	30	57	152	45	106	1	553	856	49	106	83	69	138	95	88	127	94	99
PIT	77	35	42	0	339	365	22	29	76	33	43	0	327	356	41	41	153	68	85	0	666	721	63	70	64	92	103	101	98	105	100	101
STL	79	51	27	1	431	317	63	42	76	41	34	1	348	316	35	34	155	92	61	2	779	633	98	76	140	97	80	108	107	90	105	103
1940 NATIONAL LEAGUE																																
BOS	75	35	40	0	328	352	25	30	77	30	47	0	295	393	34	53	152	65	87	0	623	745	59	83	67	83	110	101	95	110	99	101
BRO	81	41	37	3	369	358	40	55	75	47	28	0	328	263	53	46	156	88	65	3	697	621	93	101	91	115	124	113	94	85	108	106
CHI	77	40	37	0	333	316	40	32	77	35	42	0	348	320	46	42	154	75	79	0	681	636	86	74	84	107	93	97	101	95	100	99
CIN	77	55	21	1	352	240	47	36	78	45	32	1	355	288	42	37	155	100	53	2	707	528	89	73	107	97	82	95	103	79	101	98
NY	76	33	43	0	323	339	61	75	76	39	37	0	340	320	30	35	152	72	80	0	663	659	91	110	184	77	91	100	99	99	100	100
PHI	79	24	55	0	232	403	33	50	74	26	48	0	262	347	42	42	153	50	103	0	494	750	75	92	92	93	111	96	76	109	97	102
PIT	75	40	34	1	390	354	26	22	81	38	42	1	419	429	50	50	156	78	76	2	809	783	76	72	55	109	101	95	124	120	95	95
STL	77	41	36	0	368	364	69	47	79	43	33	3	379	335	50	36	156	84	69	3	747	699	119	83	133	117	86	105	107	101	102	101
1941 NATIONAL LEAGUE																																
BOS	76	32	44	0	276	321	17	28	80	30	48	2	316	399	31	47	156	62	92	2	592	720	48	75	63	77	115	88	96	114	93	95
BRO	79	52	25	2	421	282	55	40	78	48	29	1	379	299	46	41	157	100	54	3	800	581	101	81	108	131	109	103	116	88	103	99
CHI	77	38	39	0	311	306	37	20	78	32	45	1	355	364	62	40	155	70	84	1	666	670	99	60	60	164	105	88	109	109	94	94
CIN	79	45	34	0	308	273	27	27	75	43	32	0	308	291	37	34	154	88	66	0	616	564	64	61	75	96	93	94	96	88	99	98
NY	78	38	39	1	360	358	68	69	78	36	40	2	307	348	27	21	156	74	79	3	667	706	95	90	231	78	70	108	98	103	103	104
PHI	76	23	52	1	255	384	34	37	79	20	59	0	246	409	30	42	155	43	111	1	501	793	64	79	100	87	104	99	79	118	97	103
PIT	78	45	32	1	346	336	20	28	78	36	41	1	344	307	36	38	156	81	73	2	690	643	56	66	68	86	102	104	102	96	103	102
STL	79	53	24	2	405	324	37	53	76	44	32	0	329	265	33	32	155	97	56	2	734	589	70	85	129	84	97	117	102	84	110	107

	HOME								ROAD								ALL															
TM	G	W	L	T	R	OR	HR	OHR	G	W	L	T	R	OR	HR	OHR	G	W	L	T	R	OR	HR	OHR	HRF	HRB	HRP	RF	RB	RP	BPF	PPF
1942 NATIONAL LEAGUE																																
BOS	70	33	36	1	250	271	36	34	80	26	53	1	265	374	32	48	150	59	89	2	515	645	68	82	99	109	126	93	93	111	95	98
BRO	79	57	22	0	381	250	30	35	76	47	28	1	361	260	32	38	155	104	50	1	742	510	62	73	92	96	111	100	121	87	102	97
CHI	78	36	41	1	298	318	36	27	77	32	45	0	293	347	39	43	155	68	86	1	591	665	75	70	78	127	117	95	102	113	96	98
CIN	78	38	39	1	264	276	30	23	76	38	37	1	263	269	36	24	154	76	76	2	527	545	66	47	88	99	74	99	87	89	101	102
NY	79	47	31	1	376	296	80	67	75	38	36	1	299	304	29	27	154	85	67	2	675	600	109	94	211	104	93	106	109	99	103	101
PHI	74	23	51	0	182	340	18	31	77	19	58	0	212	366	26	30	151	42	109	0	394	706	44	61	90	68	92	93	71	119	94	101
PIT	77	41	34	2	333	301	15	21	74	25	47	2	252	330	39	41	151	66	81	4	585	631	54	62	46	108	127	104	98	105	101	102
STL	78	60	17	1	419	229	31	24	78	46	31	1	336	253	29	25	156	106	48	2	755	482	60	49	103	82	69	111	114	78	108	103
1943 NATIONAL LEAGUE																																
BOS	77	38	39	0	247	327	25	34	76	30	46	0	218	285	14	32	153	68	85	0	465	612	39	66	122	66	109	110	73	93	106	109
BRO	77	46	31	0	389	323	21	30	76	35	41	0	327	351	18	29	153	81	72	0	716	674	39	59	106	72	104	103	119	113	100	99
CHI	75	36	38	1	292	300	24	19	79	38	41	0	340	300	28	34	154	74	79	1	632	600	52	53	75	112	110	98	105	101	99	98
CIN	78	48	29	1	282	280	17	15	77	39	38	0	326	263	26	23	155	87	67	1	608	543	43	38	68	90	81	95	100	91	99	98
NY	77	34	43	0	291	326	63	52	79	21	55	3	267	387	18	28	156	55	98	3	558	713	81	80	212	93	103	96	95	117	96	99
PHI	78	33	43	2	269	314	29	18	79	31	47	1	302	362	37	41	157	64	90	3	571	676	66	59	64	155	133	89	99	114	93	96
PIT	78	47	30	1	364	296	20	15	79	33	44	2	305	309	22	29	157	80	74	3	669	605	42	44	72	88	88	108	104	95	104	103
STL	81	58	21	2	355	243	33	17	76	47	28	1	324	232	37	16	157	105	49	3	679	475	70	33	91	127	65	103	105	76	105	100
1944 NATIONAL LEAGUE																																
BOS	78	38	40	0	293	307	51	44	77	27	49	1	300	367	28	36	155	65	89	1	593	674	79	80	138	92	96	89	96	106	95	96
BRO	77	37	39	1	372	413	27	34	78	26	52	0	318	419	29	41	155	63	91	1	690	832	56	75	89	83	107	106	106	124	99	102
CHI	78	35	42	1	346	342	33	40	79	40	37	2	356	327	38	35	157	75	79	3	702	669	71	75	101	98	103	102	104	100	101	100
CIN	78	45	33	0	253	252	14	23	77	44	32	1	320	285	37	37	155	89	65	1	573	537	51	60	53	86	107	85	91	86	95	95
NY	75	39	36	0	372	382	75	86	80	28	51	1	310	391	18	30	155	67	87	1	682	773	93	116	269	69	91	112	100	112	104	105
PHI	79	29	49	1	271	346	20	21	75	32	43	0	268	312	35	28	154	61	92	1	539	658	55	49	64	89	82	100	82	98	100	103
PIT	81	49	28	4	399	357	23	31	77	41	35	1	345	305	47	34	158	90	63	5	744	662	70	65	67	111	109	110	105	95	105	104
STL	77	54	22	1	360	230	39	14	80	51	27	2	412	260	61	41	157	105	49	3	772	490	100	55	58	171	95	94	115	77	101	95
1945 NATIONAL LEAGUE																																
BOS	75	36	38	1	411	395	68	63	79	31	47	1	310	333	33	36	154	67	85	2	721	728	101	99	177	105	105	126	93	95	112	113
BRO	78	48	30	0	387	347	29	34	77	39	37	1	408	377	28	40	155	87	67	1	795	724	57	74	93	82	103	94	120	111	96	95
CHI	76	49	26	1	330	253	24	17	79	49	30	0	405	279	33	40	155	98	56	1	735	532	57	57	62	95	89	91	107	81	99	95
CIN	77	36	41	0	267	307	25	23	77	25	52	0	269	387	31	47	154	61	93	0	536	694	56	70	64	97	112	88	83	104	94	97
NY	78	47	30	1	366	325	83	47	76	31	44	1	302	375	31	38	154	78	74	2	668	700	114	85	166	116	99	100	98	102	100	100
PHI	77	22	55	0	261	450	23	28	77	24	53	0	287	415	33	33	154	46	108	0	548	865	56	61	78	85	93	99	83	123	96	102
PIT	79	45	34	0	407	352	31	25	76	37	38	1	346	334	41	36	155	82	72	1	753	686	72	61	73	113	97	107	105	97	103	102
STL	78	48	29	1	368	286	28	29	77	47	30	0	388	297	36	41	155	95	59	1	756	583	64	70	76	100	107	96	109	87	100	97
1946 NATIONAL LEAGUE																																
BOS	77	45	31	1	300	268	14	31	77	36	41	0	330	324	30	45	154	81	72	1	630	592	44	76	63	76	127	89	109	103	95	94
BRO	79	56	22	1	374	273	20	22	78	40	38	0	327	297	35	36	157	96	60	1	701	570	55	58	62	92	97	103	110	92	103	100
CHI	77	44	33	0	291	260	24	30	78	38	38	2	335	321	32	28	155	82	71	2	626	581	56	58	93	80	83	87	108	101	94	93
CIN	77	35	42	0	267	289	37	39	79	32	45	2	256	281	28	31	156	67	87	2	523	570	65	70	126	81	87	105	82	88	104	105
NY	77	38	39	0	340	336	76	75	77	23	54	0	272	349	45	39	154	61	93	0	612	685	121	114	162	144	135	107	99	109	102	103
PHI	78	41	36	1	280	335	38	34	77	28	49	0	280	370	42	39	155	69	85	1	560	705	80	73	89	122	113	94	96	118	95	98
PIT	78	37	40	1	303	342	24	23	77	26	51	0	249	326	36	27	155	63	91	1	552	668	60	50	75	92	80	108	87	103	103	106
STL	78	49	29	0	370	288	39	36	78	49	29	0	342	257	42	27	156	98	58	0	712	545	81	63	109	109	87	110	108	86	107	103
1947 NATIONAL LEAGUE																																
BOS	77	50	27	0	332	289	29	39	77	36	41	0	369	333	56	54	154	86	68	0	701	622	85	93	65	89	100	90	103	93	97	95
BRO	78	52	25	1	409	343	37	57	77	42	35	0	365	325	46	47	155	94	60	1	774	668	83	104	101	74	90	108	104	92	105	103
CHI	79	36	43	0	280	384	29	51	76	33	42	1	287	338	42	55	155	69	85	1	567	722	71	106	81	70	101	101	79	98	101	104
CIN	77	42	35	0	318	330	48	47	77	31	46	0	363	425	47	55	154	73	81	0	681	755	95	102	94	88	94	84	107	116	91	92
NY	76	45	31	0	417	380	131	75	79	36	42	1	413	381	90	47	155	81	73	1	830	761	221	122	146	167	100	104	117	108	101	99
PHI	77	38	38	1	309	323	24	43	78	24	54	0	280	364	36	55	155	62	92	1	589	687	60	98	76	59	93	99	83	95	100	102
PIT	79	32	45	2	384	437	95	87	77	30	47	0	360	380	61	68	156	62	92	2	744	817	156	155	130	127	128	106	103	112	101	102
STL	77	46	31	0	400	331	45	49	79	43	34	2	380	303	70	57	156	89	65	2	780	634	115	106	79	113	108	109	103	86	106	104
1948 NATIONAL LEAGUE																																
BOS	76	45	31	0	349	297	32	40	78	46	31	1	390	287	63	53	154	91	62	1	739	584	95	93	67	103	105	99	107	87	102	99
BRO	78	36	41	1	352	386	43	68	77	48	29	0	392	281	48	51	155	84	70	1	744	667	91	119	110	84	105	108	104	94	104	103
CHI	78	35	42	1	282	323	38	34	77	29	48	0	315	383	49	55	155	64	90	1	597	706	87	89	71	95	95	86	94	108	93	95
CIN	77	32	45	0	312	398	68	52	76	32	44	0	276	354	36	52	153	64	89	0	588	752	104	104	128	85	89	109	84	104	103	106
NY	77	37	40	0	366	374	89	82	78	41	36	1	414	330	75	40	155	78	76	1	780	704	164	122	142	134	99	101	114	104	100	98
PHI	76	32	44	0	276	332	32	44	79	34	44	1	315	397	59	51	155	66	88	1	591	729	91	95	74	95	102	89	91	110	94	97
PIT	80	47	31	2	384	370	69	64	76	36	40	0	322	329	39	56	156	83	71	2	706	699	108	120	128	88	100	109	98	97	104	104
STL	77	44	33	0	359	327	47	43	78	41	36	1	383	319	58	60	155	85	69	1	742	646	105	103	80	110	108	100	107	95	101	99
1949 NATIONAL LEAGUE																																
BOS	77	43	34	0	344	328	40	40	80	32	45	3	362	391	63	70	157	75	79	3	706	719	103	110	66	104	109	94	103	104	97	97
BRO	78	48	29	1	431	335	86	73	78	49	28	1	448	316	66	59	156	97	57	2	879	651	152	132	125	118	104	101	122	94	101	98
CHI	77	33	44	0	285	365	53	38	77	28	49	0	308	408	44	66	154	61	93	0	593	773	97	104	84	91	94	91	90	113	94	97
CIN	78	35	42	1	326	349	50	54	78	27	50	1	301	421	36	70	156	62	92	2	627	770	86	124	97	75	103	93	93	111	96	98
NY	79	43	34	2	404	331	94	78	77	30	47	0	332	362	53	54	156	73	81	2	736	693	147	132	146	102	95	102	102	97	101	101
PHI	77	40	37	0	336	326	61	35	77	41	36	0	326	342	61	69	154	81	73	0	662	668	122	104	77	120	100	99	94	95	100	101
PIT	77	36	41	0	341	397	77	75	77	35	42	0	340	363	49	67	154	71	83	0	681	760	126	142	126	98	111	104	97	106	101	102
STL	79	51	26	2	427	325	48	33	78	45	32	1	339	291	54	54	157	96	58	3	766	616	102	87	77	94	80	117	97	80	110	108
1950 NATIONAL LEAGUE																																
BOS	79	46	31	2	343	294	59	45	77	37	40	0	442	442	89	84	156	83	71	2	785	736	148	129	62	132	115	73	126	118	86	85
BRO	78	48	30	0	458	386	110	96	77	41	35	1	389	338	84	67	155	89	65	1	847	724	194	163	130	126	108	113	110	96	106	104
CHI	78	35	42	1	352	411	79	63	76	29	47	0	291	361	82	67	154	64	89	1	643	772	161	130	93	121	101	111	85	100	105	107
CIN	76	38	38	0	355	373	52	81	77	28	49	0	299	361	47	64	153	66	87	0	654	734	99	145	117	67	94	109	88	97	105	106
NY	76	44	32	0	362	290	84	67	78	42	36	0	373	353	49	73	154	86	68	0	735	643	133	140	124	86	92	94	104	92	98	97
PHI	78	47	30	1	348	279	58	53	79	44	33	2	374	345	67	69	157	91	63	3	722	624	125	122	85	95	92	90	101	89	97	96
PIT	77	33	44	0	370	447	81	79	77	24	52	1	311	410	57	73	154	57	96	1	681	857	138	152	118	93	102	110	92	113	103	106
STL	76	47	29	0	389	303	50	43	77	31	46	0	304	367	52	76	153	78	75	0	693	670	102	119	76	85	93	104	94	92	103	103
1951 NATIONAL LEAGUE																																
BOS	78	42	35	1	367	310	59	37	77	34	43	0	356	352	71	59	155	76	78	1	723	662	130	96	75	113	85	95	107	99	98	97
BRO	78	49	29	0	412	316	100	81	80	48	31	1	443	356	84	69	158	97	60	1	855	672	184	150	120	133	111	95	124	100	98	95

	HOME								ROAD								ALL															
TM	G	W	L	T	R	OR	HR	OHR	G	W	L	T	R	OR	HR	OHR	G	W	L	T	R	OR	HR	OHR	HRF	HRB	HRP	RF	RB	RP	BPF	PPF
CHI	77	32	45	0	304	364	45	59	78	30	47	1	310	386	58	66	155	62	92	1	614	750	103	125	86	86	103	97	91	109	97	100
CIN	77	35	42	0	289	320	44	46	78	33	44	1	270	347	44	73	155	68	86	1	559	667	88	119	80	77	98	99	80	94	101	103
NY	78	50	28	0	399	308	115	89	79	48	31	0	382	333	64	59	157	98	59	0	781	641	179	148	157	109	94	101	110	92	102	99
PHI	77	38	39	0	312	305	43	50	77	35	42	0	336	339	65	60	154	73	81	0	648	644	108	110	77	94	97	92	97	97	97	97
PIT	78	32	45	1	388	465	72	84	77	32	45	0	301	380	65	73	155	64	90	1	689	845	137	157	109	106	119	119	93	112	107	109
STL	79	44	34	1	370	323	44	56	76	37	39	0	313	348	51	63	155	81	73	1	683	671	95	119	86	79	96	101	98	96	101	101
1952 NATIONAL LEAGUE																																
BOS	77	31	45	1	257	314	48	44	78	33	44	1	312	337	62	62	155	64	89	2	569	651	110	106	77	108	104	90	93	104	95	97
BRO	80	45	33	2	389	324	76	78	75	51	24	0	386	279	77	43	155	96	57	2	775	603	153	121	119	126	100	102	118	95	101	98
CHI	77	42	35	0	329	316	51	40	78	35	42	1	299	315	56	61	155	77	77	1	628	631	107	101	81	103	96	106	94	94	103	103
CIN	77	38	39	0	318	319	43	43	77	31	46	0	297	340	61	68	154	69	85	0	615	659	104	111	69	109	114	99	96	102	99	100
NY	77	50	27	0	369	327	103	74	77	42	35	0	353	312	48	47	154	92	62	0	722	639	151	121	170	98	84	105	110	99	102	101
PHI	76	47	29	0	318	269	42	43	78	40	38	0	339	283	51	52	154	87	67	0	657	552	93	95	87	86	87	98	101	87	101	99
PIT	77	23	54	0	261	414	45	72	78	19	58	1	254	379	47	61	155	42	112	1	515	793	92	133	106	80	110	105	80	117	100	105
STL	77	48	29	0	343	291	46	59	77	40	37	0	334	339	51	60	154	88	66	0	677	630	97	119	96	88	105	96	108	101	98	97
1953 NATIONAL LEAGUE																																
BRO	78	60	17	1	517	333	110	82	77	45	32	0	438	356	98	87	155	105	49	1	955	689	208	169	104	141	118	107	125	94	104	99
CHI	77	43	34	0	351	417	74	69	78	22	55	1	282	418	63	82	155	65	89	1	633	835	137	151	99	92	100	109	83	107	103	106
CIN	78	38	39	1	367	391	89	96	77	30	47	0	347	397	77	83	155	68	86	1	714	788	166	179	111	108	116	100	98	107	99	100
MIL	79	45	31	3	332	260	51	44	78	47	31	0	406	329	105	63	157	92	62	3	738	589	156	107	60	121	91	82	105	86	94	92
NY	77	38	39	0	395	345	109	81	78	32	45	1	373	402	67	65	155	70	84	1	768	747	176	146	137	98	85	97	106	104	98	98
PHI	78	48	29	1	363	304	63	65	78	35	42	1	353	362	52	73	156	83	71	2	716	666	115	138	102	74	88	94	98	92	99	98
PIT	77	26	51	0	338	460	53	88	77	24	53	0	284	427	46	80	154	50	104	0	622	887	99	168	108	65	104	109	83	114	102	106
STL	78	48	30	0	420	321	65	58	79	35	41	3	348	392	75	81	157	83	71	3	768	713	140	139	82	101	99	102	101	95	101	101
1954 NATIONAL LEAGUE																																
BRO	77	45	32	0	380	393	101	92	77	47	30	0	398	347	85	72	154	92	62	0	778	740	186	164	121	125	112	104	109	105	101	100
CHI	77	40	37	0	366	385	86	59	77	24	53	0	334	381	73	72	154	64	90	0	700	766	159	131	99	114	96	104	99	107	101	102
CIN	77	41	36	0	380	407	94	105	77	33	44	0	349	356	53	64	154	74	80	0	729	763	147	169	156	83	95	110	100	104	104	104
MIL	77	43	34	0	285	251	43	29	77	46	31	0	385	305	96	77	154	89	65	0	670	556	139	106	45	133	102	81	102	87	93	91
NY	76	53	23	0	387	254	120	67	78	44	34	0	345	296	66	46	154	97	57	0	732	550	186	113	159	100	66	104	99	77	105	102
PHI	78	39	39	0	315	305	47	60	76	36	40	0	344	309	55	73	154	75	79	0	659	614	102	133	83	79	100	93	95	89	99	98
PIT	77	31	46	0	277	422	22	42	77	22	55	0	280	423	54	86	154	53	101	0	557	845	76	128	48	71	115	98	82	118	97	102
STL	77	33	44	0	386	431	57	90	77	39	38	0	413	359	62	80	154	72	82	0	799	790	119	170	103	87	118	105	113	112	100	100
1955 NATIONAL LEAGUE																																
BRO	77	56	21	0	461	318	119	85	77	42	34	1	396	332	82	83	154	98	55	1	857	650	201	168	122	115	100	108	118	93	104	101
CHI	77	43	33	1	348	322	80	62	77	29	48	0	278	391	84	91	154	72	81	1	626	713	164	153	83	114	106	100	90	101	100	101
CIN	77	46	31	0	425	341	102	91	77	29	48	0	336	343	79	70	154	75	79	0	761	684	181	161	125	102	92	111	103	94	106	104
MIL	77	46	31	0	342	297	75	51	77	39	38	0	401	371	107	87	154	85	69	0	743	668	182	138	68	136	105	85	115	104	93	92
NY	79	44	35	0	362	327	95	91	75	36	39	0	340	346	74	64	154	80	74	0	702	673	169	155	124	95	88	96	102	99	98	98
PHI	77	46	31	0	371	309	76	78	77	31	46	0	304	357	56	83	154	77	77	0	675	666	132	161	109	79	95	103	95	94	102	102
PIT	75	36	39	0	298	337	34	48	79	24	55	0	262	430	57	94	154	60	94	0	560	767	91	142	60	71	103	96	83	109	97	101
STL	77	41	36	0	358	362	84	92	77	27	50	0	296	395	59	93	154	68	86	0	654	757	143	185	113	86	109	103	93	106	100	102
1956 NATIONAL LEAGUE																																
BRO	77	52	25	0	369	300	102	89	77	41	36	0	351	301	77	82	154	93	61	0	720	601	179	171	118	110	107	103	107	92	103	100
CHI	80	39	38	3	335	328	78	77	77	21	56	0	262	380	64	84	157	60	94	3	597	708	142	161	100	93	104	98	91	106	98	101
CIN	77	51	26	0	426	346	128	75	78	40	37	1	349	312	93	66	155	91	63	1	775	658	221	141	126	128	87	117	109	95	108	106
MIL	77	47	29	1	344	265	77	53	78	45	33	0	365	304	100	80	155	92	62	1	709	569	177	133	76	130	101	94	109	90	99	96
NY	77	37	40	0	269	306	94	86	77	30	47	0	271	344	51	58	154	67	87	0	540	650	145	144	152	74	75	94	85	100	97	99
PHI	77	40	37	0	337	335	61	74	77	31	46	0	331	403	60	98	154	71	83	0	668	738	121	172	87	88	118	92	109	118	94	95
PIT	78	35	43	0	301	328	49	45	79	31	45	3	287	325	61	97	157	66	88	3	588	653	110	142	63	89	105	103	86	95	102	103
STL	78	43	34	1	358	328	58	73	78	33	44	1	320	370	66	82	156	76	78	2	678	698	124	155	90	85	104	99	104	106	99	99
1957 NATIONAL LEAGUE																																
BRO	77	43	34	0	383	348	84	88	77	41	36	0	307	243	63	56	154	84	70	0	690	591	147	144	137	84	82	128	88	76	116	114
CHI	78	31	46	1	301	353	81	68	78	31	46	1	327	369	66	76	156	62	92	2	628	722	147	144	103	97	95	94	95	108	96	98
CIN	77	45	32	0	417	410	118	101	77	35	42	0	330	371	69	78	154	80	74	0	747	781	187	179	141	108	106	116	105	109	105	106
MIL	78	45	32	1	312	289	75	51	77	50	27	0	460	324	124	73	155	95	59	1	772	613	199	124	67	158	107	79	125	104	90	88
NY	77	37	40	0	353	341	99	86	77	32	45	0	290	360	58	64	154	69	85	0	643	701	157	150	142	87	86	105	93	101	102	103
PHI	78	38	39	1	299	322	60	60	78	39	38	1	324	334	57	79	156	77	77	2	623	656	117	139	90	82	95	95	93	97	98	99
PIT	77	36	41	0	273	321	20	53	78	26	51	1	313	375	72	105	155	62	92	1	586	696	92	158	45	80	143	88	92	107	94	96
STL	77	42	35	0	356	348	64	70	77	45	32	0	381	318	68	70	154	87	67	0	737	666	132	140	98	90	95	101	109	99	101	99
1958 NATIONAL LEAGUE																																
CHI	77	35	42	0	350	381	101	72	77	37	40	0	359	344	81	70	154	72	82	0	709	725	182	142	112	115	93	103	104	106	100	101
CIN	77	40	37	0	364	337	71	86	77	36	41	0	331	284	52	62	154	76	78	0	695	621	123	148	131	71	84	112	96	86	107	106
LA	77	39	38	0	359	405	92	101	77	32	45	0	309	356	80	72	154	71	83	0	668	761	172	173	122	108	107	112	94	106	105	106
MIL	77	48	29	0	291	207	72	48	77	44	33	0	384	334	95	77	154	92	62	0	675	541	167	125	73	128	98	73	112	91	89	87
PHI	77	35	42	0	318	397	59	77	77	34	43	0	346	365	65	71	154	69	85	0	664	762	124	148	99	84	98	100	100	112	98	100
PIT	77	49	28	0	323	260	41	40	77	35	42	0	339	347	93	83	154	84	70	0	662	607	134	123	50	116	110	87	103	95	95	94
STL	77	39	38	0	329	381	62	88	77	33	44	0	290	323	49	70	154	72	82	0	619	704	111	158	122	68	93	113	86	96	106	108
SF	77	44	33	0	363	354	85	88	77	36	41	0	364	344	85	78	154	80	74	0	727	698	170	166	106	114	112	101	107	104	100	100
1959 NATIONAL LEAGUE																																
CHI	77	38	39	0	336	329	87	76	78	36	41	1	337	359	76	76	155	74	80	1	673	688	163	152	107	109	103	97	100	102	98	99
CIN	77	43	34	0	423	367	101	84	77	31	46	0	341	371	60	78	154	74	80	0	764	738	161	162	128	98	101	109	109	106	103	103
LA	78	46	32	0	363	333	82	90	78	42	36	0	342	337	66	67	156	88	68	0	705	670	148	157	126	91	95	103	101	96	102	101
MIL	79	49	29	1	350	274	83	64	78	37	41	0	374	349	94	64	157	86	70	1	724	623	177	128	93	123	93	87	111	97	95	93
PHI	78	37	40	1	316	354	55	66	77	27	50	0	283	371	58	84	155	64	90	1	599	725	113	150	85	85	108	100	88	104	99	102
PIT	77	47	30	0	348	334	47	53	78	31	46	1	303	346	65	81	155	78	76	1	651	680	112	134	72	89	103	106	92	96	103	104
STL	77	42	35	0	366	359	64	64	77	29	48	0	275	366	54	73	154	71	83	0	641	725	118	137	100	81	92	111	90	101	105	106
SF	77	42	35	0	339	271	80	63	77	41	36	0	366	342	87	76	154	83	71	0	705	613	167	139	89	123	104	88	109	96	95	94
1960 NATIONAL LEAGUE																																
CHI	79	33	44	2	331	390	52	78	77	27	50	0	303	386	67	74	156	60	94	2	634	776	119	152	90	97	121	101	98	117	98	101
CIN	77	37	40	0	314	347	75	68	77	30	47	0	326	345	65	66	154	67	87	0	640	692	140	134	107	105	101	98	100	107	98	99
LA	77	42	35	0	379	334	89	97	77	40	37	0	283	259	37	57	154	82	72	0	662	593	126	154	177	69	86	127	88	80	115	114
MIL	77	51	26	0	342	270	90	56	77	37	40	0	382	388	80	74	154	88	66	0	724	658	170	130	96	135	107	82	123	112	91	89
PHI	77	31	46	0	300	373	54	74	77	28	49	0	246	318	45	59	154	59	95	0	546	691	99	133	118	70	91	115	78	96	107	110

	HOME								ROAD								ALL															
TM	G	W	L	T	R	OR	HR	OHR	G	W	L	T	R	OR	HR	OHR	G	W	L	T	R	OR	HR	OHR	HRF	HRB	HRP	RF	RB	RP	BPF	PPF
PIT	78	52	25	1	362	287	51	36	77	43	34	0	372	306	69	69	155	95	59	1	734	593	120	105	66	109	94	96	112	93	99	97
STL	77	51	26	0	361	308	78	64	78	35	42	1	278	308	60	63	155	86	68	1	639	616	138	127	115	98	91	114	90	87	108	108
SF	77	45	32	0	296	256	46	34	79	34	43	2	375	375	84	73	156	79	75	2	671	631	130	107	56	124	102	78	114	107	90	89
1961 NATIONAL LEAGUE																																
CHI	78	40	37	1	372	391	102	81	78	24	53	1	317	409	74	84	156	64	90	2	689	800	176	165	113	111	106	104	98	111	100	102
CIN	77	47	30	0	345	355	70	75	77	46	31	0	365	298	88	72	154	93	61	0	710	653	158	147	93	110	104	106	98	91	104	103
LA	77	45	32	0	373	358	83	109	77	44	33	0	362	339	74	58	154	89	65	0	735	697	157	167	139	91	93	105	103	99	102	101
MIL	77	45	32	0	324	280	84	72	78	38	39	1	388	376	104	81	155	83	71	1	712	656	188	153	87	135	114	82	111	102	92	91
PHI	78	22	55	1	256	408	43	77	77	25	52	0	328	388	60	78	155	47	107	1	584	796	103	155	86	74	107	91	89	117	94	98
PIT	77	38	39	0	338	338	49	54	77	37	40	0	356	337	79	67	154	75	79	0	694	675	128	121	73	95	93	98	100	98	99	99
STL	78	48	29	1	413	362	54	69	77	32	45	0	290	306	49	67	155	80	74	1	703	668	103	136	104	66	85	124	88	85	113	113
SF	77	45	32	0	371	316	97	77	78	40	37	1	402	339	86	75	155	85	69	1	773	655	183	152	109	118	100	95	112	97	98	96
1962 NATIONAL LEAGUE																																
CHI	81	32	49	0	333	456	71	94	81	27	54	0	299	371	55	65	162	59	103	0	632	827	126	159	131	76	94	114	82	105	106	109
CIN	81	58	23	0	456	294	95	68	81	40	41	0	346	391	72	81	162	98	64	0	802	685	167	149	107	112	102	103	108	94	102	100
HOU	82	32	48	2	268	340	44	41	80	32	48	0	324	377	61	72	162	64	96	2	592	717	105	113	64	87	91	85	88	105	93	95
LA	83	54	29	0	409	289	47	39	82	48	34	0	433	408	93	76	165	102	63	0	842	697	140	115	54	120	101	85	124	103	93	91
MIL	81	49	32	0	374	307	93	74	81	37	44	0	356	358	88	77	162	86	76	0	730	665	181	151	101	125	107	96	102	93	99	98
NY	80	22	58	0	335	510	93	120	81	18	62	1	282	438	46	72	161	40	120	1	617	948	139	192	165	73	101	114	82	121	104	108
PHI	80	46	34	0	341	346	70	66	81	35	46	0	364	413	72	89	161	81	80	0	705	759	142	155	87	107	115	91	103	110	95	95
PIT	81	51	30	0	358	315	48	56	80	42	38	0	348	311	60	62	161	93	68	0	706	626	108	118	86	79	86	102	96	86	102	101
STL	81	44	37	0	407	362	64	83	82	40	41	1	367	302	73	66	163	84	78	1	774	664	137	149	107	92	98	115	98	85	108	107
SF	82	61	21	0	479	299	109	74	83	42	41	0	399	391	95	74	165	103	62	0	878	690	204	148	110	133	100	101	118	95	101	99
1963 NATIONAL LEAGUE																																
CHI	81	43	38	0	298	302	63	70	81	39	42	0	272	276	64	49	162	82	80	0	570	578	127	119	116	97	91	109	88	89	105	105
CIN	81	46	35	0	344	300	65	46	81	40	41	0	304	294	57	71	162	86	76	0	648	594	122	117	88	107	102	107	101	93	104	103
HOU	81	44	37	0	236	268	25	34	81	22	59	0	228	372	37	61	162	66	96	0	464	640	62	95	62	62	90	85	82	108	92	95
LA	81	53	28	0	296	248	42	43	82	46	35	1	344	302	68	68	163	99	63	1	640	550	110	111	66	106	108	88	108	94	95	94
MIL	82	45	36	1	341	307	68	81	81	39	42	0	336	296	71	68	163	84	78	1	677	603	139	149	105	114	121	101	108	97	101	100
NY	81	34	47	0	276	381	61	93	81	17	64	0	225	393	35	69	162	51	111	0	501	774	96	162	139	67	110	104	82	121	99	104
PHI	81	45	36	0	340	282	61	60	81	42	39	0	302	296	65	53	162	87	75	0	642	578	126	113	103	102	92	104	101	92	103	102
PIT	81	42	39	0	275	295	47	42	81	32	49	0	292	300	61	57	162	74	88	0	567	595	108	99	77	98	91	96	93	97	99	99
STL	81	53	28	0	429	311	79	70	81	40	41	0	318	317	49	54	162	93	69	0	747	628	128	124	139	87	86	115	112	97	107	106
SF	81	50	31	0	363	289	101	64	81	38	43	0	362	352	96	62	162	88	74	0	725	641	197	126	104	161	109	93	123	110	96	94
1964 NATIONAL LEAGUE																																
CHI	81	40	41	0	337	397	85	87	81	36	45	0	312	327	60	57	162	76	86	0	649	724	145	144	140	102	101	113	95	104	105	106
CIN	82	47	34	1	331	294	62	59	81	45	36	0	329	272	68	53	163	92	70	1	660	566	130	112	100	106	93	103	98	85	103	102
HOU	81	41	40	0	246	290	29	44	81	25	56	0	249	338	41	61	162	66	96	0	495	628	70	105	73	66	95	91	79	98	96	98
LA	81	41	40	0	259	259	26	38	83	39	42	2	355	313	53	50	164	80	82	2	614	572	79	88	66	73	84	81	101	95	92	91
MIL	81	45	36	0	405	356	89	78	81	43	38	0	398	388	70	82	162	88	74	0	803	744	159	160	109	130	132	98	128	119	97	96
NY	82	33	48	1	298	363	58	61	81	20	61	0	271	413	45	69	163	53	109	1	569	776	103	130	101	85	105	94	92	121	95	98
PHI	81	46	35	0	352	298	59	61	81	46	35	0	341	334	71	68	162	92	70	0	693	632	130	129	88	115	115	97	108	99	99	98
PIT	81	42	39	0	340	315	55	31	81	38	43	0	323	321	66	61	162	80	82	0	663	636	121	92	70	116	87	101	101	97	101	101
STL	81	48	33	0	386	378	59	81	81	45	36	0	329	274	50	52	162	93	69	0	715	652	109	133	133	79	93	124	98	90	112	111
SF	81	44	37	0	314	299	86	63	81	46	35	0	342	288	79	55	162	90	72	0	656	587	165	118	111	130	96	98	101	91	100	99
1965 NATIONAL LEAGUE																																
CHI	83	40	41	2	330	380	79	94	81	32	49	0	305	343	55	60	164	72	90	2	635	723	134	154	139	85	96	106	94	106	102	103
CIN	81	49	32	0	450	352	108	69	81	40	41	0	375	352	75	67	162	89	73	0	825	704	183	136	122	125	98	110	122	106	104	102
HOU	81	36	45	0	250	313	25	32	81	29	52	0	319	398	72	91	162	65	97	0	569	711	97	123	37	106	132	79	98	120	89	91
LA	81	50	31	0	268	218	26	41	81	47	34	0	340	303	52	86	162	97	65	0	608	521	78	127	52	78	120	78	102	88	91	90
MIL	81	44	37	0	366	331	98	75	81	42	39	0	342	302	98	48	162	86	76	0	708	633	196	123	117	138	90	108	104	94	104	103
NY	82	29	52	1	258	380	50	81	82	21	60	1	237	372	57	66	164	50	112	2	495	752	107	147	104	80	106	102	75	109	100	104
PHI	80	45	35	0	312	300	77	55	82	40	41	1	342	367	67	61	162	85	76	1	654	667	144	116	105	105	87	90	106	107	95	95
PIT	82	49	32	1	334	284	37	38	81	41	40	0	341	296	74	51	163	90	72	1	675	580	111	89	62	97	83	97	103	90	100	98
STL	81	42	39	0	379	361	68	103	81	38	42	1	328	313	41	63	162	80	81	1	707	674	109	166	154	66	98	114	102	97	106	106
SF	81	51	30	0	365	327	81	81	82	44	37	1	317	266	78	56	163	95	67	1	682	593	159	137	121	110	95	119	94	83	111	109
1966 NATIONAL LEAGUE																																
ATL	82	43	38	1	394	335	119	82	81	42	39	0	388	348	88	47	163	85	77	1	782	683	207	129	141	124	79	98	119	105	99	97
CHI	81	32	49	0	342	410	80	100	81	27	54	0	302	399	60	84	162	59	103	0	644	809	140	184	120	95	122	105	97	119	100	103
CIN	79	46	33	0	417	372	91	93	81	30	51	0	275	330	58	60	160	76	84	0	692	702	149	153	151	88	90	129	92	95	114	114
HOU	81	45	36	0	318	317	48	48	82	27	54	1	294	378	64	82	163	72	90	1	612	695	112	130	68	96	107	96	94	105	97	99
LA	81	53	28	0	286	220	43	36	81	42	39	0	320	270	65	48	162	95	67	0	606	490	108	84	73	86	69	88	94	78	97	95
NY	81	32	49	0	276	372	51	94	80	34	46	0	311	389	47	72	161	66	95	0	587	761	98	166	117	67	108	91	95	120	94	97
PHI	81	48	33	0	354	319	52	65	81	39	42	0	342	321	65	72	162	87	75	0	696	640	117	137	87	90	105	102	104	96	101	100
PIT	81	46	35	0	384	317	48	48	81	46	35	0	375	324	110	77	162	92	70	0	759	641	158	125	54	144	123	101	114	98	101	99
STL	81	43	38	0	274	288	48	64	81	40	41	0	297	289	60	66	162	83	79	0	571	577	108	130	90	81	97	96	86	87	100	100
SF	81	47	34	0	317	312	91	77	80	46	34	0	358	314	90	63	161	93	68	0	675	626	181	140	108	128	101	94	105	98	97	97
1967 NATIONAL LEAGUE																																
ATL	81	48	33	0	352	316	91	74	81	29	52	0	279	324	67	44	162	77	85	0	631	640	158	118	141	121	91	109	97	99	104	105
CHI	84	49	34	1	366	332	70	90	78	38	40	0	336	292	58	52	162	87	74	1	702	624	128	142	131	104	111	103	111	100	101	100
CIN	81	49	32	0	343	287	57	66	81	38	43	0	261	276	52	35	162	87	75	0	604	563	109	101	136	85	76	116	89	84	109	108
HOU	81	46	35	0	337	315	31	32	81	23	58	0	289	427	62	88	162	69	93	0	626	742	93	120	44	122	145	91	108	125	93	95
LA	81	42	39	0	241	230	36	35	81	31	50	0	278	365	46	58	162	73	89	0	519	595	82	93	70	87	95	75	96	106	88	89
NY	78	36	42	0	258	307	44	61	84	25	59	0	240	365	39	63	162	61	101	0	498	672	83	124	108	73	105	99	81	106	99	102
PHI	80	45	35	0	320	292	48	44	82	37	45	0	292	289	55	42	162	82	80	0	612	581	103	86	98	92	78	107	94	90	104	104
PIT	81	49	32	0	370	321	43	49	82	32	49	1	309	372	48	59	163	81	81	1	679	693	91	108	88	87	101	102	109	111	100	100
STL	81	49	32	0	326	301	53	54	80	52	28	0	369	256	62	43	161	101	60	0	695	557	115	97	102	103	88	100	111	91	101	99
SF	82	51	31	0	333	271	65	59	80	40	40	0	319	280	75	54	162	91	71	0	652	551	140	113	95	131	109	99	104	89	101	99
1968 NATIONAL LEAGUE																																
ATL	81	41	40	0	241	241	42	43	82	40	41	1	273	308	38	44	163	81	81	1	514	549	80	87	104	87	94	85	99	105	93	94
CHI	82	47	34	1	363	332	83	83	81	37	44	0	249	279	47	55	163	84	78	1	612	611	130	138	152	120	129	126	97	98	112	112
CIN	82	40	41	1	377	400	55	66	81	43	38	0	313	273	51	48	163	83	79	1	690	673	106	114	118	112	119	127	112	108	111	111
HOU	81	42	39	0	279	269	22	30	81	30	51	0	231	319	44	38	162	72	90	0	510	588	66	68	65	85	91	99	93	105	99	100
LA	81	41	40	0	212	215	25	24	81	35	46	0	258	294	42	41	162	76	86	0	470	509	67	65	61	90	87	79	94	100	91	91
NY	82	32	49	1	224	270	49	50	81	41	40	0	249	229	32	37	163	73	89	1	473	499	81	87	135	76	82	101	83	87	102	103

TM	HOME G	W	L	T	R	OR	HR	OHR	ROAD G	W	L	T	R	OR	HR	OHR	ALL G	W	L	T	R	OR	HR	OHR	HRF	HRB	HRP	RF	RB	RP	BPF	PPF
PHI	81	38	43	0	274	297	52	46	81	38	43	0	269	318	48	45	162	76	86	0	543	615	100	91	104	111	102	97	100	112	97	99
PIT	81	40	41	0	289	268	33	30	82	40	41	1	294	264	47	43	163	80	82	1	583	532	80	73	73	101	93	101	103	95	101	100
STL	81	47	34	0	267	218	31	35	81	50	31	0	316	254	42	47	162	97	65	0	583	472	73	82	77	92	102	87	110	91	95	93
SF	81	42	39	0	299	242	60	32	82	46	35	1	300	287	48	54	163	88	74	1	599	529	108	86	93	126	101	94	110	98	98	96
1969 NATIONAL LEAGUE																																
ATL	81	50	31	0	360	321	77	84	81	43	38	0	331	310	64	60	162	93	69	0	691	631	141	144	128	103	104	106	102	93	104	103
CHI	82	49	32	1	387	321	84	64	81	43	38	0	333	290	58	54	163	92	70	1	720	611	142	118	128	100	85	112	102	88	107	105
CIN	81	50	31	0	407	373	97	74	82	39	42	1	391	395	74	75	163	89	73	1	798	768	171	149	115	131	117	101	122	118	99	98
HOU	81	52	29	0	371	313	47	43	81	29	52	0	305	355	57	68	162	81	81	0	676	668	104	111	74	98	102	103	101	100	101	101
LA	81	50	31	0	325	258	41	55	81	35	46	0	320	303	56	67	162	85	77	0	645	561	97	122	80	88	109	94	100	88	99	97
MON	81	24	57	0	288	421	73	87	81	28	53	0	294	370	52	58	162	52	110	0	582	791	125	145	138	87	99	104	88	117	100	103
NY	82	52	30	0	312	270	56	59	80	48	32	0	320	271	53	60	162	100	62	0	632	541	109	119	101	89	96	98	96	83	100	99
PHI	81	30	51	0	317	378	75	64	81	33	48	0	328	367	62	70	162	63	99	0	645	745	137	134	104	111	109	99	100	114	98	99
PIT	81	47	34	0	324	322	41	33	81	41	40	0	401	330	78	63	162	88	74	0	725	652	119	96	55	122	101	90	116	106	95	94
STL	80	42	38	0	273	273	41	43	82	45	37	0	322	267	49	56	162	87	75	0	595	540	90	99	84	79	85	96	91	83	100	99
SD	81	28	53	0	239	358	47	47	81	24	57	0	229	388	52	66	162	52	110	0	468	746	99	113	80	90	100	95	74	113	97	100
SF	81	52	29	0	362	317	77	61	81	38	43	0	351	319	59	59	162	90	72	0	713	636	136	120	116	102	92	102	107	97	101	100
1970 NATIONAL LEAGUE																																
ATL	81	42	39	0	395	398	92	119	81	34	47	0	341	374	68	66	162	76	86	0	736	772	160	185	150	95	105	110	96	101	104	105
CHI	80	46	34	0	471	394	109	92	82	38	44	0	335	285	70	51	162	84	78	0	806	679	179	143	161	99	79	138	92	79	120	118
CIN	81	57	24	0	416	334	100	58	81	45	36	0	359	347	91	60	162	102	60	0	775	681	191	118	106	131	84	107	102	90	104	103
HOU	81	44	37	0	350	351	51	64	81	35	46	0	394	412	78	67	162	79	83	0	744	763	129	131	81	100	104	88	109	111	93	94
LA	81	39	42	0	310	316	35	82	80	48	32	0	439	368	52	82	161	87	74	0	749	684	87	164	88	67	121	78	114	106	90	89
MON	80	39	41	0	363	385	77	91	82	34	48	0	324	422	59	71	162	73	89	0	687	807	136	162	128	86	101	102	94	109	100	102
NY	82	44	38	0	374	314	63	75	80	39	41	0	321	316	57	60	162	83	79	0	695	630	120	135	114	80	88	105	91	84	104	103
PHI	80	40	40	0	293	337	48	63	81	33	48	0	301	393	53	69	161	73	88	0	594	730	101	132	92	75	96	92	85	103	96	98
PIT	82	50	32	0	356	315	43	41	80	39	41	0	373	349	87	65	162	89	73	0	729	664	130	106	56	114	98	92	103	95	97	96
STL	81	34	47	0	377	418	51	44	81	42	39	0	367	329	62	58	162	76	86	0	744	747	113	102	80	87	79	113	96	96	106	106
SD	81	31	50	0	312	393	68	56	81	32	49	0	369	395	104	93	162	63	99	0	681	788	172	149	64	152	132	92	98	112	95	96
SF	81	48	33	0	413	386	84	77	81	38	43	0	418	440	81	79	162	86	76	0	831	826	165	156	101	118	113	94	119	118	96	96
1971 NATIONAL LEAGUE																																
ATL	82	43	39	0	366	384	96	90	80	39	41	0	277	315	57	62	162	82	80	0	643	699	153	152	146	110	111	121	92	100	110	111
CHI	81	44	37	0	363	342	74	70	81	39	42	0	274	306	54	62	162	83	79	0	637	648	128	132	122	101	105	120	91	94	110	110
CIN	81	46	35	0	303	251	69	51	81	33	48	0	283	330	69	61	162	79	83	0	586	581	138	112	93	125	103	91	96	95	96	96
HOU	81	39	42	0	256	263	18	27	81	40	41	0	329	304	53	48	162	79	83	0	585	567	71	75	47	77	88	83	100	97	93	92
LA	81	42	39	0	324	286	43	56	81	47	34	0	339	301	52	54	162	89	73	0	663	587	95	110	94	84	97	96	106	95	99	98
MON	80	36	44	0	304	366	50	68	82	35	46	1	318	363	38	65	162	71	90	1	622	729	88	133	115	72	106	100	99	115	99	100
NY	81	44	37	0	281	256	48	50	81	39	42	0	307	294	50	50	162	83	79	0	588	550	98	100	98	85	87	90	96	91	96	96
PHI	81	34	47	0	296	353	73	80	81	33	48	0	262	335	50	52	162	67	95	0	558	688	123	132	143	89	95	107	86	104	103	105
PIT	80	52	28	0	393	279	66	49	82	45	37	0	395	320	88	59	162	97	65	0	788	599	154	108	82	146	107	98	126	98	99	97
STL	82	45	36	1	376	358	38	49	81	45	36	0	363	341	57	55	163	90	72	1	739	699	95	104	79	90	100	103	115	110	101	100
SD	81	33	48	0	233	296	42	43	80	28	52	0	253	314	54	50	161	61	100	0	486	610	96	93	81	91	89	92	80	99	96	98
SF	81	51	30	0	372	300	71	58	81	39	42	0	334	344	69	70	162	90	72	0	706	644	140	128	94	127	117	100	112	103	100	99
1972 NATIONAL LEAGUE																																
ATL	78	36	41	1	339	392	86	88	77	34	43	0	289	338	58	67	155	70	84	1	628	730	144	155	133	112	121	113	99	114	105	106
CHI	77	46	31	0	392	305	83	63	79	39	39	1	293	262	50	49	156	85	70	1	685	567	133	112	146	94	82	126	99	83	114	112
CIN	76	42	34	0	300	266	58	59	78	53	25	0	407	291	66	70	154	95	59	0	707	557	124	129	90	118	122	85	125	102	93	91
HOU	77	41	36	0	367	355	58	56	76	43	33	0	341	281	76	58	153	84	69	0	708	636	134	114	86	129	113	114	112	101	106	105
LA	75	41	34	0	267	221	46	37	80	44	36	0	317	306	52	46	155	85	70	0	584	527	98	83	92	88	75	85	103	93	94	93
MON	78	35	43	0	252	324	50	56	78	35	43	0	261	285	41	47	156	70	86	0	513	609	91	103	118	72	81	104	82	96	102	104
NY	78	41	37	0	254	264	45	56	78	42	36	0	274	314	60	62	156	83	73	0	528	578	105	118	84	100	112	89	91	99	95	96
PHI	79	28	51	0	246	316	49	57	77	31	46	0	257	319	49	60	156	59	97	0	503	635	98	117	94	89	105	94	85	106	97	99
PIT	78	49	29	0	351	259	53	34	77	47	30	0	340	253	57	56	155	96	59	0	691	512	110	90	79	108	87	103	111	84	103	100
STL	77	40	37	0	298	308	31	38	79	35	44	0	270	292	39	49	156	75	81	0	568	600	70	87	82	66	81	109	89	94	105	105
SD	80	26	54	0	217	315	41	64	73	32	41	0	271	350	61	57	153	58	95	0	488	665	102	121	81	101	120	79	93	124	88	91
SF	77	34	43	0	336	321	86	65	78	35	43	0	326	328	64	65	155	69	86	0	662	649	150	130	116	124	110	101	110	108	100	100
1973 NATIONAL LEAGUE																																
ATL	81	40	40	1	460	437	118	87	81	36	45	0	339	337	88	57	162	76	85	1	799	774	206	144	136	137	98	129	105	102	113	113
CHI	80	41	39	0	327	356	66	72	81	36	45	0	287	299	51	56	161	77	84	0	614	655	117	128	127	80	87	116	85	90	108	109
CIN	81	50	31	0	330	287	47	67	81	49	32	0	411	334	90	68	162	99	63	0	741	621	137	135	75	119	123	85	118	101	93	92
HOU	81	41	40	0	315	322	58	53	81	41	40	0	366	350	76	58	162	82	80	0	681	672	134	111	84	111	94	90	107	106	95	95
LA	81	50	31	0	338	271	63	62	81	45	35	1	337	294	47	67	162	95	66	1	675	565	110	129	110	81	94	98	100	85	100	99
MON	81	43	38	0	364	353	63	70	81	36	45	0	304	349	62	58	162	79	83	0	668	702	125	128	110	92	94	109	95	100	104	104
NY	81	43	38	0	314	283	39	61	80	39	41	0	294	305	46	66	161	82	79	0	608	588	85	127	89	70	101	99	91	88	101	100
PHI	81	38	43	0	358	381	78	80	81	33	48	0	284	336	56	51	162	71	91	0	642	717	134	131	141	86	84	117	88	98	108	109
PIT	81	41	40	0	334	301	72	42	81	39	42	0	370	392	82	68	162	80	82	0	704	693	154	110	78	134	96	84	114	112	92	92
STL	81	43	38	0	290	255	27	30	81	38	43	0	353	348	48	75	162	81	81	0	643	603	75	105	49	79	101	79	106	99	91	90
SD	81	31	50	0	273	355	51	80	81	29	52	0	275	415	61	77	162	60	102	0	548	770	112	157	94	91	124	90	87	118	94	97
SF	81	47	34	0	395	363	85	79	81	41	40	0	344	339	76	66	162	88	74	0	739	702	161	145	115	118	107	110	105	100	105	104
1974 NATIONAL LEAGUE																																
ATL	81	46	35	0	337	290	65	44	82	42	39	1	324	273	55	53	163	88	74	1	661	563	120	97	102	110	90	106	93	80	105	104
CHI	81	32	49	0	344	424	67	72	81	34	47	0	325	402	43	50	162	66	96	0	669	826	110	122	142	85	95	104	99	120	100	102
CIN	82	50	31	1	389	295	74	62	81	48	33	0	387	336	61	64	163	98	64	1	776	631	135	126	108	123	116	95	117	97	98	96
HOU	81	46	35	0	330	293	58	35	81	35	46	0	323	339	52	49	162	81	81	0	653	632	110	84	93	105	81	95	99	96	98	98
LA	81	52	29	0	355	250	68	51	81	50	31	0	443	311	71	61	162	102	60	0	798	561	139	112	92	137	112	83	128	93	93	90
MON	80	42	38	0	356	329	50	49	81	37	44	0	306	328	36	50	161	79	82	0	662	657	86	99	115	75	86	108	95	94	104	104
NY	81	36	45	0	279	325	43	49	81	35	46	0	293	321	53	50	162	71	91	0	572	646	96	99	90	94	97	98	86	96	99	100
PHI	81	46	35	0	378	337	55	52	81	34	47	0	298	364	40	55	162	80	82	0	676	701	95	111	115	82	96	107	97	101	103	104
PIT	81	52	29	0	380	303	47	32	81	36	45	0	371	354	67	61	162	88	74	0	751	657	114	93	64	130	105	95	114	101	98	96
STL	81	44	37	0	356	329	45	46	80	42	38	0	321	314	38	51	161	86	75	0	677	643	83	97	101	77	89	106	98	93	104	103
SD	81	36	45	0	272	381	47	54	81	24	57	0	269	449	52	70	162	60	102	0	541	830	99	124	83	104	126	90	87	127	93	97
SF	81	37	44	0	340	398	50	61	81	35	46	0	294	325	43	55	162	72	90	0	634	723	93	116	111	83	102	117	88	99	108	109
1975 NATIONAL LEAGUE																																
ATL	80	37	43	0	280	350	58	63	81	30	51	0	303	389	49	38	161	67	94	0	583	739	107	101	135	90	83	92	92	115	95	97
CHI	81	42	39	0	392	427	54	71	81	33	48	0	320	400	41	59	162	75	87	0	712	827	95	130	122	85	113	112	102	118	104	105
CIN	81	64	17	0	457	275	70	52	81	44	37	0	383	311	54	60	162	108	54	0	840	586	124	112	108	116	107	107	120	87	104	101

	HOME								ROAD								ALL															
TM	G	W	L	T	R	OR	HR	OHR	G	W	L	T	R	OR	HR	OHR	G	W	L	T	R	OR	HR	OHR	HRF	HRB	HRP	RF	RB	RP	BPF	PPF
HOU	81	37	44	0	313	338	40	43	81	27	53	1	351	373	44	63	162	64	97	1	664	711	84	106	78	93	113	90	105	112	94	95
LA	81	49	32	0	319	221	64	52	81	39	42	0	329	313	54	52	162	88	74	0	648	534	118	104	109	110	98	86	103	85	95	93
MON	81	39	42	0	326	375	53	57	81	36	45	0	275	315	45	45	162	75	87	0	601	690	98	102	120	87	90	117	83	94	108	109
NY	81	42	39	0	294	301	52	48	81	40	41	0	352	324	49	51	162	82	80	0	646	625	101	99	100	98	96	89	101	99	95	95
PHI	81	51	30	0	401	326	72	47	81	35	46	0	334	368	53	64	162	86	76	0	735	694	125	111	102	121	109	104	108	103	101	101
PIT	80	52	28	0	348	270	67	41	81	40	41	0	364	295	71	38	161	92	69	0	712	565	138	79	101	132	79	96	108	87	99	97
STL	82	45	36	1	351	352	46	39	81	37	44	0	311	337	35	59	163	82	80	1	662	689	81	98	90	83	97	107	95	99	103	103
SD	81	38	43	0	279	338	33	38	81	33	48	0	273	345	45	61	162	71	91	0	552	683	78	99	68	90	111	99	83	101	100	101
SF	81	46	35	0	346	335	36	37	80	34	46	0	313	336	48	55	161	80	81	0	659	671	84	92	72	95	103	103	98	99	102	102
1976 NATIONAL LEAGUE																																
ATL	81	34	47	0	338	401	43	56	81	36	45	0	282	299	39	30	162	70	92	0	620	700	82	86	138	75	76	124	87	96	111	112
CHI	81	42	39	0	355	385	71	84	81	33	48	0	256	343	34	39	162	75	87	0	611	728	105	123	193	78	90	121	86	102	109	111
CIN	81	49	32	0	426	337	73	46	81	53	28	0	431	296	68	54	162	102	60	0	857	633	141	100	99	155	114	106	129	98	103	100
HOU	82	46	36	0	277	264	30	27	80	34	46	0	348	393	36	55	162	80	82	0	625	657	66	82	63	89	103	73	113	117	86	87
LA	81	49	32	0	296	265	42	48	81	43	38	0	312	278	49	49	162	92	70	0	608	543	91	97	93	102	108	96	95	85	100	99
MON	80	27	53	0	266	374	45	41	82	28	54	0	265	360	49	48	162	55	107	0	531	734	94	89	90	106	101	103	82	111	100	103
NY	82	45	37	0	269	245	43	43	80	41	39	0	346	293	59	54	162	86	76	0	615	538	102	97	76	126	121	80	104	92	92	91
PHI	81	53	28	0	424	277	63	49	81	48	33	0	346	280	47	49	162	101	61	0	770	557	110	98	117	110	100	112	111	83	107	105
PIT	81	47	34	0	366	302	54	44	81	45	36	0	342	328	56	51	162	92	70	0	708	630	110	95	93	124	108	100	109	98	100	99
STL	81	37	44	0	335	346	27	40	81	35	46	0	294	325	36	51	162	72	90	0	629	671	63	91	78	76	107	108	94	100	104	104
SD	80	42	38	0	254	271	30	38	82	31	51	0	316	391	34	49	162	73	89	0	570	662	64	87	85	74	98	77	100	114	88	90
SF	81	40	41	0	314	352	44	32	81	34	47	0	281	334	41	36	162	74	88	0	595	686	85	68	98	90	73	107	89	102	103	104
1977 NATIONAL LEAGUE																																
ATL	81	40	41	0	416	488	97	111	81	21	60	0	262	407	42	58	162	61	101	0	678	895	139	169	189	70	87	130	83	110	113	115
CHI	81	46	35	0	411	402	69	82	81	35	46	0	281	337	42	46	162	81	81	0	692	739	111	128	162	62	70	128	85	91	114	115
CIN	81	48	33	0	408	355	83	83	81	40	41	0	394	370	98	73	162	88	74	0	802	725	181	156	98	137	120	100	113	103	100	99
HOU	81	46	35	0	309	291	40	33	81	35	46	0	371	359	74	77	162	81	81	0	680	650	114	110	51	111	103	83	103	99	93	92
LA	81	51	30	0	386	273	96	65	81	47	34	0	383	309	95	54	162	98	64	0	769	582	191	119	108	134	87	97	108	83	100	98
MON	81	38	43	0	329	362	66	65	81	37	44	0	336	374	72	70	162	75	87	0	665	736	138	135	93	105	103	97	95	104	98	99
NY	79	35	44	0	282	297	46	56	83	29	54	0	305	366	42	62	162	64	98	0	587	663	88	118	102	63	83	90	86	96	96	97
PHI	81	60	21	0	453	299	101	63	81	41	40	0	394	369	85	71	162	101	61	0	847	668	186	134	106	133	99	100	118	95	100	98
PIT	81	58	23	0	396	315	64	76	81	38	43	0	338	350	69	73	162	96	66	0	734	665	133	149	100	99	110	104	100	92	103	102
STL	83	52	31	0	379	314	41	53	79	31	48	0	358	374	55	86	162	83	79	0	737	688	96	139	66	87	120	91	108	101	96	95
SD	81	35	46	0	299	368	53	70	81	34	47	0	393	466	67	90	162	69	93	0	692	834	120	160	79	100	130	79	111	131	88	89
SF	81	38	43	0	353	371	62	56	81	37	44	0	320	340	72	58	162	75	87	0	673	711	134	114	91	101	88	108	90	95	104	105
1978 NATIONAL LEAGUE																																
ATL	81	39	42	0	364	400	87	89	81	30	51	0	236	350	36	43	162	69	93	0	600	750	123	132	201	76	84	126	82	103	112	114
CHI	82	44	38	0	393	387	41	76	80	35	45	0	271	337	31	49	162	79	83	0	664	724	72	125	138	58	96	122	93	101	110	111
CIN	80	49	31	0	379	338	74	61	81	43	38	0	331	350	62	61	161	92	69	0	710	688	136	122	111	124	113	107	108	105	103	102
HOU	81	50	31	0	327	254	30	29	81	24	57	0	278	380	40	57	162	74	88	0	605	634	70	86	63	81	94	89	100	103	95	95
LA	81	54	27	0	361	272	78	59	81	41	40	0	366	301	71	48	162	95	67	0	727	573	149	107	115	131	97	96	114	91	99	97
MON	80	41	39	0	299	283	46	49	82	35	47	0	334	328	75	68	162	76	86	0	633	611	121	117	70	134	132	91	102	99	96	95
NY	80	33	47	0	295	340	37	60	82	33	49	0	312	350	49	54	162	66	96	0	607	690	86	114	96	83	108	98	96	108	98	99
PHI	82	54	28	0	405	279	80	70	80	36	44	0	303	307	53	48	162	90	72	0	708	586	133	118	140	104	94	109	103	88	105	104
PIT	81	55	26	0	389	310	57	61	80	33	47	0	295	327	58	42	161	88	73	0	684	637	115	103	115	101	90	110	101	95	105	105
STL	81	37	44	0	289	307	29	32	81	32	49	0	311	350	50	62	162	69	93	0	600	657	79	94	56	95	109	90	98	106	95	96
SD	81	50	31	0	291	245	31	23	81	34	47	0	300	353	44	51	162	84	78	0	591	598	75	74	59	88	82	83	100	99	92	92
SF	81	50	31	0	291	244	47	30	81	39	42	0	322	350	70	54	162	89	73	0	613	594	117	84	64	132	96	81	104	100	91	91
1979 NATIONAL LEAGUE																																
ATL	79	34	45	0	359	425	73	80	81	32	49	0	310	338	53	52	160	66	94	0	669	763	126	132	142	90	93	121	91	102	109	110
CHI	81	45	36	0	423	370	79	72	81	35	46	0	283	337	56	55	162	80	82	0	706	707	135	127	132	98	93	125	91	93	112	112
CIN	80	48	32	0	360	298	71	53	81	42	39	0	371	346	61	50	161	90	71	0	731	644	132	103	113	104	83	94	111	98	97	96
HOU	81	52	29	0	269	234	15	31	81	37	44	0	314	348	34	59	162	89	73	0	583	582	49	90	52	51	93	78	95	94	90	90
LA	81	46	35	0	389	341	106	55	81	33	48	0	350	376	77	46	162	79	83	0	739	717	183	101	127	133	78	100	109	106	100	99
MON	81	56	25	0	378	275	68	51	79	39	40	0	323	306	75	65	160	95	65	0	701	581	143	116	85	132	109	102	101	86	102	101
NY	82	28	53	1	267	354	30	58	81	35	46	0	326	352	44	62	163	63	99	1	593	706	74	120	82	67	107	90	91	107	95	96
PHI	81	43	38	0	332	342	52	72	82	41	40	1	351	376	67	63	163	84	78	1	683	718	119	135	97	102	115	95	103	107	97	97
PIT	81	48	33	0	399	339	74	77	82	50	31	1	376	304	74	48	163	98	64	1	775	643	148	125	124	112	94	110	107	90	106	104
STL	82	42	39	1	379	372	48	65	81	44	37	0	352	321	52	62	163	86	76	1	731	693	100	127	98	85	105	110	102	97	105	104
SD	81	39	42	0	287	335	36	47	80	29	51	0	316	346	57	61	161	68	93	0	603	681	93	108	71	91	106	93	92	103	96	97
SF	81	38	43	0	298	361	53	61	81	33	48	0	374	390	72	82	162	71	91	0	672	751	125	143	75	123	138	87	106	118	92	93
1980 NATIONAL LEAGUE																																
ATL	80	50	30	0	352	297	84	79	81	31	50	0	278	363	60	52	161	81	80	0	630	660	144	131	142	119	108	102	96	100	101	101
CHI	81	37	44	0	338	385	54	62	81	27	54	0	276	343	53	47	162	64	98	0	614	728	107	109	113	98	99	114	88	104	106	108
CIN	82	44	37	1	356	349	66	70	81	45	36	0	351	321	47	43	163	89	73	1	707	670	113	113	144	90	89	104	106	101	102	101
HOU	81	55	26	0	329	255	26	22	82	38	44	0	308	334	49	47	163	93	70	0	637	589	75	69	53	91	82	93	99	92	98	97
LA	82	55	27	0	327	272	82	58	81	37	44	0	336	319	66	47	163	92	71	0	663	591	148	105	121	129	94	92	104	94	97	96
MON	80	51	29	0	357	286	51	40	82	39	43	0	337	343	63	60	162	90	72	0	694	629	114	100	78	124	109	98	107	98	99	98
NY	82	38	44	0	306	336	35	80	80	29	51	0	305	366	26	60	162	67	95	0	611	702	61	140	126	53	115	93	98	111	96	97
PHI	81	49	32	0	398	334	64	44	81	42	39	0	330	305	53	43	162	91	71	0	728	639	117	87	112	105	80	115	104	92	107	106
PIT	81	47	34	0	355	322	63	53	81	36	45	0	311	324	53	57	162	83	79	0	666	646	116	110	105	110	105	106	99	96	103	103
STL	81	41	40	0	396	357	41	42	81	33	48	0	342	353	60	48	162	74	88	0	738	710	101	90	78	108	98	107	110	106	103	102
SD	81	45	36	0	295	274	29	33	82	28	53	1	296	380	38	64	163	73	89	1	591	654	67	97	63	80	108	86	97	105	93	94
SF	81	44	37	0	283	293	24	41	80	31	49	0	290	341	56	51	161	75	86	0	573	634	80	92	62	92	112	91	92	101	96	96
1981 NATIONAL LEAGUE																																
ATL	50	22	27	1	182	195	37	41	57	28	29	0	213	221	27	21	107	50	56	1	395	416	64	62	172	82	76	99	95	100	99	100
CHI	58	27	30	1	239	254	41	38	48	11	35	2	131	229	16	21	106	38	65	3	370	483	57	59	164	68	75	111	84	111	104	106
CIN	54	32	22	0	226	230	26	41	54	34	20	0	238	210	38	26	108	66	42	0	464	440	64	67	105	105	108	103	109	104	101	100
HOU	51	31	20	0	166	106	16	9	59	30	29	0	228	225	29	31	110	61	49	0	394	331	45	40	51	96	76	72	105	85	88	87
LA	56	33	23	0	221	171	37	34	54	30	24	0	229	185	45	20	110	63	47	0	450	356	82	54	106	129	87	93	107	86	98	96
MON	56	38	18	0	255	170	39	23	52	22	30	0	188	224	42	35	108	60	48	0	443	394	81	58	77	154	112	97	106	96	99	98
NY	52	24	27	1	186	207	30	38	53	17	35	1	162	225	27	36	105	41	62	2	348	432	57	74	108	96	121	102	84	103	101	102
PHI	55	36	19	0	295	261	41	39	52	23	29	0	196	211	28	33	107	59	48	0	491	472	69	72	122	105	110	127	104	101	112	112
PIT	51	22	28	1	189	207	29	29	52	24	28	0	218	218	26	31	103	46	56	1	407	425	55	60	103	95	103	93	105	110	96	96
STL	53	32	21	0	244	218	22	26	50	27	22	1	220	199	28	26	103	59	43	1	464	417	50	52	86	93	97	105	113	103	102	101
SD	55	20	35	0	168	223	9	27	55	21	34	0	214	232	23	37	110	41	69	0	382	455	32	64	61	62	126	87	95	112	93	95
SF	53	29	24	0	218	204	28	19	58	27	31	0	209	210	35	38	111	56	55	0	427	414	63	57	72	119	103	109	94	91	105	105

	HOME								ROAD								ALL															
TM	G	W	L	T	R	OR	HR	OHR	G	W	L	T	R	OR	HR	OHR	G	W	L	T	R	OR	HR	OHR	HRF	HRB	HRP	RF	RB	RP	BPF	PPF
1982 NATIONAL LEAGUE																																
ATL	81	42	39	0	388	387	95	86	81	47	34	0	351	315	51	40	162	89	73	0	739	702	146	126	185	96	82	115	104	99	107	107
CHI	81	38	43	0	352	371	53	62	81	35	46	0	324	338	49	63	162	73	89	0	676	709	102	125	102	95	114	108	99	103	103	104
CIN	81	33	48	0	296	325	37	47	81	28	53	0	249	336	45	58	162	61	101	0	545	661	82	105	82	83	104	104	80	96	102	104
HOU	81	43	38	0	290	294	31	26	81	34	47	0	279	326	43	61	162	77	85	0	569	620	74	87	57	88	96	97	87	94	99	100
LA	81	43	38	0	321	283	57	35	81	45	36	0	370	329	81	46	162	88	74	0	691	612	138	81	74	142	88	88	110	99	95	94
MON	81	40	41	0	335	352	59	65	81	46	35	0	362	264	74	45	162	86	76	0	697	616	133	110	104	121	101	109	100	89	105	104
NY	81	33	48	0	307	357	48	60	81	32	49	0	302	366	49	59	162	65	97	0	609	723	97	119	99	91	110	98	93	109	98	100
PHI	81	51	30	0	301	307	57	46	81	38	43	0	363	347	55	40	162	89	73	0	664	654	112	86	108	98	76	87	107	106	94	94
PIT	81	42	39	0	391	394	77	65	81	42	39	0	333	302	57	53	162	84	78	0	724	696	134	118	126	110	98	121	99	95	110	110
STL	81	46	35	0	338	325	27	48	81	46	35	0	347	284	40	46	162	92	70	0	685	609	67	94	89	64	89	105	100	90	103	102
SD	81	43	38	0	316	286	33	76	81	38	43	0	359	372	48	63	162	81	81	0	675	658	81	139	98	77	127	84	111	108	92	92
SF	81	45	36	0	319	312	55	54	81	42	39	0	354	375	78	55	162	87	75	0	673	687	133	109	84	133	113	88	109	111	94	94
1983 NATIONAL LEAGUE																																
ATL	80	46	34	0	394	327	66	71	82	42	40	0	352	313	64	61	162	88	74	0	746	640	130	132	112	107	108	111	106	92	106	104
CHI	81	43	38	0	384	341	71	69	81	28	53	0	317	378	69	48	162	71	91	0	701	719	140	117	117	112	94	103	104	107	101	101
CIN	81	36	45	0	331	360	52	64	81	38	43	0	292	350	55	71	162	74	88	0	623	710	107	135	92	97	120	106	91	103	103	104
HOU	82	46	36	0	294	278	26	28	80	39	41	0	349	368	71	66	162	85	77	0	643	646	97	94	41	115	115	79	108	108	90	90
LA	80	48	32	0	316	296	74	49	83	43	39	1	338	313	72	48	163	91	71	1	654	609	146	97	106	119	82	98	98	92	100	99
MON	81	46	35	0	341	325	40	56	82	36	45	1	336	321	62	64	163	82	80	1	677	646	102	120	79	97	114	102	100	95	102	101
NY	82	41	41	0	300	329	63	53	80	27	53	0	275	351	49	44	162	68	94	0	575	680	112	97	119	87	76	97	88	102	99	100
PHI	82	50	31	1	361	310	61	61	81	40	41	0	335	325	64	50	163	90	72	1	696	635	125	111	106	104	93	101	103	95	101	100
PIT	81	41	40	0	335	336	60	63	81	43	38	0	324	312	61	46	162	84	78	0	659	648	121	109	114	97	87	105	96	95	103	103
STL	81	44	37	0	334	350	38	58	81	35	46	0	345	360	45	57	162	79	83	0	679	710	83	115	94	73	99	97	104	109	98	98
SD	82	47	34	1	350	299	53	82	81	34	47	0	303	354	40	62	163	81	81	1	653	653	93	144	127	71	106	98	99	98	99	99
SF	81	43	38	0	346	356	73	67	81	36	45	0	341	341	69	60	162	79	83	0	687	697	142	127	108	119	107	103	103	104	101	101
1984 NATIONAL LEAGUE																																
ATL	81	38	43	0	328	376	53	72	81	42	39	0	304	279	58	50	162	80	82	0	632	655	111	122	114	99	107	119	88	90	110	110
CHI	80	51	29	0	414	360	86	70	81	45	36	0	348	298	50	29	161	96	65	0	762	658	136	99	186	91	64	120	106	93	110	109
CIN	81	39	42	0	356	381	58	73	81	31	50	0	271	366	48	55	162	70	92	0	627	747	106	128	124	91	107	113	90	106	106	107
HOU	81	43	38	0	309	292	18	29	81	37	44	0	384	338	61	62	162	80	82	0	693	630	79	91	40	98	123	84	114	104	92	92
LA	81	40	41	0	287	321	49	40	81	39	42	0	293	279	53	36	162	79	83	0	580	600	102	76	100	93	71	106	85	88	104	104
MON	81	39	42	0	266	260	45	56	80	39	41	0	327	325	51	58	161	78	83	0	593	585	96	114	92	95	111	81	99	98	91	91
NY	81	48	33	0	336	327	56	47	81	42	39	0	316	349	51	57	162	90	72	0	652	676	107	104	96	102	99	100	99	102	100	100
PHI	81	39	42	0	353	369	79	45	81	42	39	0	367	321	68	56	162	81	81	0	720	690	147	101	100	138	98	105	108	103	102	101
PIT	81	41	40	0	282	263	48	44	81	34	47	0	333	304	50	58	162	75	87	0	615	567	98	102	86	99	102	86	99	92	94	94
STL	81	44	37	0	327	310	29	42	81	40	41	0	325	335	46	52	162	84	78	0	652	645	75	94	74	79	99	97	100	99	99	99
SD	81	48	33	0	344	300	60	61	81	44	37	0	342	334	49	61	162	92	70	0	686	634	109	122	110	98	110	96	106	98	98	98
SF	81	35	46	0	340	393	55	63	81	31	50	0	342	414	57	62	162	66	96	0	682	807	112	125	98	108	119	96	108	126	96	98
1985 NATIONAL LEAGUE																																
ATL	81	32	49	0	336	431	65	80	81	34	47	0	296	350	61	54	162	66	96	0	632	781	126	134	122	97	101	116	90	109	106	108
CHI	81	41	39	1	399	423	98	104	81	36	45	0	287	306	52	52	162	77	84	1	686	729	150	156	180	92	95	134	90	95	116	117
CIN	81	47	34	0	347	359	49	65	81	42	38	1	330	307	65	66	162	89	72	1	677	666	114	131	88	102	117	110	98	96	105	105
HOU	81	44	37	0	333	338	47	48	81	39	42	0	373	353	74	71	162	83	79	0	706	691	121	119	68	121	120	93	112	109	96	96
LA	81	48	33	0	310	258	47	54	81	47	34	0	372	321	82	48	162	95	67	0	682	579	129	102	80	117	98	84	111	96	93	92
MON	81	44	37	0	300	289	45	45	80	40	40	0	333	347	73	54	161	84	77	0	633	636	118	99	72	113	99	87	103	104	94	94
NY	81	51	30	0	344	254	58	58	81	47	34	0	351	314	76	53	162	98	64	0	695	568	134	111	92	117	99	92	109	90	97	95
PHI	81	41	40	0	350	338	72	57	81	34	47	0	317	335	69	58	162	75	87	0	667	673	141	115	101	118	98	105	99	100	102	102
PIT	80	35	45	0	314	347	39	53	81	22	59	0	254	361	41	54	161	57	104	0	568	708	80	107	97	68	89	106	84	104	103	104
STL	81	54	27	0	358	255	36	39	81	47	34	0	389	317	51	59	162	101	61	0	747	572	87	98	71	84	93	89	119	93	96	93
SD	81	44	37	0	321	323	63	77	81	39	42	0	329	299	46	50	162	83	79	0	650	622	109	127	141	77	88	102	97	93	102	101
SF	81	38	43	0	265	307	58	67	81	24	57	0	291	367	57	58	162	62	100	0	556	674	115	125	107	94	101	87	91	108	93	95
1986 NATIONAL LEAGUE																																
ATL	81	41	40	0	331	360	77	71	80	31	49	0	284	359	61	46	161	72	89	0	615	719	138	117	132	94	79	105	90	104	102	103
CHI	80	42	38	0	394	399	89	79	80	28	52	0	286	382	66	64	160	70	90	0	680	781	155	143	125	110	103	116	95	109	107	108
CIN	81	43	38	0	383	377	86	73	81	43	38	0	349	340	58	63	162	86	76	0	732	717	144	136	128	99	95	110	104	102	104	104
HOU	81	52	29	0	327	289	49	56	81	44	37	0	327	280	76	60	162	96	66	0	654	569	125	116	79	107	102	102	94	83	103	102
LA	81	46	35	0	326	290	57	46	81	27	54	0	312	389	73	69	162	73	89	0	638	679	130	115	74	117	104	88	101	106	94	95
MON	80	36	44	0	296	347	42	56	81	42	39	0	341	341	68	63	161	78	83	0	637	688	110	119	77	96	106	96	97	104	98	98
NY	81	55	26	0	379	251	77	47	81	53	28	0	404	327	71	56	162	108	54	0	783	578	148	103	100	115	82	89	121	91	96	93
PHI	80	49	31	0	413	344	86	49	81	37	44	0	326	369	68	81	161	86	75	0	739	713	154	130	93	128	108	110	105	102	104	104
PIT	81	31	50	0	331	357	49	75	81	33	48	0	332	343	62	63	162	64	98	0	663	700	111	138	98	88	108	101	98	103	100	101
STL	81	42	39	0	321	303	27	63	80	37	43	0	280	308	31	72	161	79	82	0	601	611	58	135	87	49	108	104	87	88	103	103
SD	81	43	38	0	339	319	80	78	81	31	50	0	317	404	56	72	162	74	88	0	656	723	136	150	121	98	108	92	102	111	95	96
SF	81	46	35	0	345	275	50	61	81	37	44	0	353	343	64	60	162	83	79	0	698	618	114	121	90	93	99	90	108	96	96	95
1987 NATIONAL LEAGUE																																
ATL	81	42	39	0	421	450	82	88	80	27	53	0	326	379	70	75	161	69	92	0	747	829	152	163	113	95	101	119	95	104	108	109
CHI	80	40	40	0	381	389	114	90	81	36	45	0	339	412	95	69	161	76	85	0	720	801	209	159	123	125	97	103	98	108	101	102
CIN	81	42	39	0	396	401	94	97	81	42	39	0	387	351	98	73	162	84	78	0	783	752	192	170	111	122	108	107	104	100	103	103
HOU	81	47	34	0	334	268	51	46	81	29	52	0	314	410	71	95	162	76	86	0	648	678	122	141	60	102	111	84	97	99	93	93
LA	81	40	41	0	280	306	52	56	81	33	48	0	355	369	73	74	162	73	89	0	635	675	125	130	75	92	96	82	95	100	92	92
MON	81	48	33	0	401	371	62	74	81	43	38	0	340	349	58	70	162	91	71	0	741	720	120	144	106	76	90	112	95	93	106	106
NY	81	49	32	0	407	335	93	63	81	43	38	0	416	363	99	73	162	92	70	0	823	698	192	136	92	130	95	96	114	98	98	97
PHI	81	43	38	0	385	373	80	78	81	37	44	0	317	376	89	89	162	80	82	0	702	749	169	167	90	119	117	108	92	98	104	105
PIT	81	47	34	0	404	363	71	84	81	33	48	0	319	381	60	80	162	80	82	0	723	744	131	164	110	82	102	109	95	98	104	104
STL	81	49	32	0	387	339	42	60	81	46	35	0	411	354	52	69	162	95	67	0	798	693	94	129	86	65	88	96	111	97	98	97
SD	81	37	44	0	338	357	60	97	81	28	53	0	330	406	53	78	162	65	97	0	668	763	113	175	117	69	104	94	95	107	97	98
SF	81	46	35	0	373	312	118	72	81	44	37	0	410	357	87	74	162	90	72	0	783	669	205	146	117	123	92	91	111	96	96	95
1988 NATIONAL LEAGUE																																
ATL	79	28	51	0	295	391	48	64	81	26	55	0	260	350	48	44	160	54	106	0	555	741	96	108	120	83	91	112	86	112	104	107
CHI	82	39	42	1	346	373	58	71	81	38	43	0	314	321	55	44	163	77	85	1	660	694	113	115	125	95	94	110	100	105	104	105
CIN	80	45	35	0	333	312	75	71	81	42	39	0	308	284	47	50	161	87	74	0	641	596	122	121	147	94	94	110	97	91	105	105
HOU	81	44	37	0	293	282	33	50	81	38	43	0	324	349	63	73	162	82	80	0	617	631	96	123	63	110	142	87	105	107	93	93
LA	81	45	36	0	316	297	49	38	81	49	31	1	312	247	50	46	162	94	67	1	628	544	99	84	92	95	81	110	94	82	106	105
MON	81	43	38	0	333	304	47	62	82	38	43	1	295	288	60	60	163	81	81	1	628	592	107	122	93	104	118	110	94	89	105	105
NY	80	56	24	0	313	218	67	34	80	44	36	0	390	314	85	44	160	100	60	0	703	532	152	78	81	156	85	78	126	97	90	88
PHI	81	38	42	1	327	361	62	64	81	27	54	0	270	373	44	54	162	65	96	1	597	734	106	118	124	89	99	105	94	113	101	103

	HOME								ROAD								ALL																
TM	G	W	L	T	R	OR	HR	OHR	G	W	L	T	R	OR	HR	OHR	G	W	L	T	R	OR	HR	OHR	HRF	HRB	HRP	RF	RB	RP	BPF	PPF
PIT	81	43	38	0	326	298	56	50	79	42	37	0	325	318	54	58	160	85	75	0	651	616	110	108	93	108	106	95	107	102	98	97
STL	81	41	40	0	314	318	29	39	81	35	46	0	264	315	42	52	162	76	86	0	578	633	71	91	74	75	95	108	88	96	104	105
SD	81	47	34	0	303	267	56	56	80	36	44	0	291	316	38	56	161	83	78	0	594	583	94	112	116	81	97	93	98	96	97	97
SF	81	45	36	0	318	284	58	42	81	38	43	0	352	342	55	57	162	83	79	0	670	626	113	99	90	111	97	88	114	107	94	93
1901 AMERICAN LEAGUE																																	
BAL	66	40	25	1	430	367	11	11	69	28	40	1	330	383	13	9	135	68	65	2	760	750	24	20	104	81	68	115	99	98	107	107
BOS	69	49	20	0	383	252	20	16	69	30	37	2	376	356	16	16	138	79	57	2	759	608	36	32	112	121	110	89	107	87	97	94
CHI	71	49	21	1	441	285	14	11	66	34	32	0	378	346	17	16	137	83	53	1	819	631	31	27	74	127	112	95	113	90	99	96
CLE	69	29	39	1	317	399	0	13	69	26	43	0	346	428	12	9	138	55	82	1	663	827	12	22	64	40	92	92	95	115	95	97
DET	70	42	27	1	438	369	15	10	66	32	34	0	303	325	14	12	136	74	61	1	741	694	29	22	92	104	82	119	92	88	110	109
MIL	70	32	37	1	342	373	15	14	69	16	52	1	299	455	11	19	139	48	89	2	641	828	26	33	94	95	117	93	91	113	95	98
PHI	66	42	24	0	410	352	15	9	71	32	38	1	395	409	20	11	137	74	62	1	805	761	35	20	85	127	78	102	110	104	100	100
WAS	68	31	35	2	333	375	17	36	70	30	38	2	345	392	17	15	138	61	73	4	678	767	34	51	156	107	139	99	93	104	99	100
1902 AMERICAN LEAGUE																																	
BAL	64	32	31	1	391	369	17	18	77	18	57	2	324	479	16	12	141	50	88	3	715	848	33	30	140	85	76	111	103	118	102	104
BOS	71	43	27	1	348	284	24	15	67	34	33	0	316	316	18	12	138	77	60	1	664	600	42	27	120	116	79	96	99	91	99	98
CHI	71	48	19	4	371	238	5	2	67	26	41	0	304	364	9	28	138	74	60	4	675	602	14	30	20	103	111	88	106	95	95	94
CLE	65	40	25	0	357	257	15	7	72	29	42	1	329	410	18	19	137	69	67	1	686	667	33	26	69	122	91	93	107	102	97	96
DET	68	35	33	0	312	286	13	8	69	17	50	2	254	371	9	12	137	52	83	2	566	657	22	20	100	65	59	96	86	97	99	100
PHI	73	56	17	0	477	330	19	12	64	27	36	1	298	306	19	21	137	83	53	1	775	636	38	33	72	144	124	116	105	90	108	106
STL	73	49	21	3	350	289	16	14	67	29	37	1	269	318	13	22	140	78	58	4	619	607	29	36	81	101	119	101	88	87	102	102
WAS	68	40	28	0	407	341	35	38	70	21	47	2	300	449	12	18	138	61	75	2	707	790	47	56	210	97	119	102	106	117	98	100
1903 AMERICAN LEAGUE																																	
BOS	70	49	20	1	395	266	35	12	71	42	27	2	313	238	13	11	141	91	47	3	708	504	48	23	179	142	85	120	109	82	112	107
CHI	70	41	28	1	284	244	5	2	68	19	49	0	232	369	9	21	138	60	77	1	516	613	14	23	25	127	124	86	100	114	92	94
CLE	74	49	25	0	364	256	11	5	66	28	38	0	275	323	20	11	140	77	63	0	639	579	31	16	50	176	98	94	115	107	96	95
DET	65	37	28	0	279	222	5	7	72	28	43	1	288	317	7	12	137	65	71	1	567	539	12	19	73	59	88	93	105	99	97	96
NY	67	41	26	0	301	269	10	6	69	31	36	2	278	304	8	13	136	72	62	2	579	573	18	19	81	88	88	101	104	103	100	100
PHI	67	44	21	2	323	238	16	8	70	31	39	0	274	281	15	12	137	75	60	2	597	519	31	20	94	140	95	105	102	91	104	102
STL	70	38	32	0	250	228	7	15	69	27	42	0	250	297	5	10	139	65	74	0	500	525	12	25	137	44	86	87	93	96	95	95
WAS	71	29	40	2	275	349	15	24	69	14	54	1	162	342	2	14	140	43	94	3	437	691	17	38	199	43	111	115	71	109	105	111
1904 AMERICAN LEAGUE																																	
BOS	81	49	30	2	325	240	18	18	76	46	29	1	283	226	8	13	157	95	59	3	608	466	26	31	151	109	134	105	104	83	105	101
CHI	78	50	27	1	297	226	0	2	78	39	38	1	303	256	14	11	156	89	65	2	600	482	14	13	9	69	156	95	110	90	99	97
CLE	78	44	31	3	329	242	14	2	76	42	34	0	318	240	13	8	154	86	65	3	647	482	27	10	77	150	58	100	117	90	102	98
DET	79	34	40	5	237	295	3	4	83	28	50	5	268	332	8	12	162	62	90	10	505	627	11	16	40	74	101	93	92	111	95	98
NY	75	46	29	0	321	288	22	25	80	46	30	4	277	238	5	4	155	92	59	4	598	526	27	29	357	62	61	124	97	87	112	111
PHI	79	47	31	1	308	235	19	8	76	34	39	3	249	268	12	5	155	81	70	4	557	503	31	13	144	126	58	101	99	91	102	101
STL	78	32	43	3	231	288	2	14	78	33	44	1	250	316	8	11	156	65	87	4	481	604	10	25	85	55	131	92	92	112	95	98
WAS	78	23	52	3	221	350	3	2	79	15	61	3	216	393	7	17	157	38	113	6	437	743	10	19	23	103	124	93	85	135	93	99
1905 AMERICAN LEAGUE																																	
BOS	77	44	32	1	296	281	21	20	76	34	42	0	283	283	8	13	153	78	74	1	579	564	29	33	173	113	136	101	102	100	100	100
CHI	82	50	29	3	300	207	5	2	76	42	31	3	312	244	6	9	158	92	60	6	612	451	11	11	47	76	62	87	109	83	97	93
CLE	77	40	37	0	290	284	5	13	78	36	41	1	277	303	13	10	155	76	78	1	567	587	18	23	81	100	132	100	100	103	100	100
DET	76	45	30	1	267	275	5	5	78	34	44	0	245	327	8	6	154	79	74	1	512	602	13	11	76	70	61	98	92	106	98	100
NY	75	40	35	0	316	303	15	15	77	31	43	3	270	319	8	11	152	71	78	3	586	622	23	26	150	98	112	107	103	108	102	103
PHI	74	50	23	1	337	247	12	12	78	42	33	3	286	245	12	9	152	92	56	4	623	492	24	21	119	117	103	115	102	83	109	106
STL	79	34	42	3	250	267	5	7	77	20	57	0	261	341	11	12	156	54	99	3	511	608	16	19	53	104	124	84	98	113	91	93
WAS	77	33	42	2	289	340	10	4	77	31	45	1	270	283	12	8	154	64	87	3	559	623	22	12	72	125	71	111	95	104	104	106
1906 AMERICAN LEAGUE																																	
BOS	77	22	54	1	230	364	10	22	78	27	51	0	232	342	3	15	155	49	105	1	462	706	13	37	161	59	162	102	83	120	98	104
CHI	79	54	23	2	275	180	2	1	75	39	35	1	295	280	5	10	154	93	58	3	570	460	7	11	21	77	78	78	111	91	92	89
CLE	79	47	30	2	351	229	4	8	78	42	34	2	312	253	8	8	157	89	64	4	663	482	12	16	77	74	99	102	112	85	103	99
DET	78	42	34	2	315	317	4	5	73	29	44	0	203	282	6	9	151	71	78	2	518	599	10	14	59	73	97	118	85	99	108	110
NY	76	53	23	0	398	294	14	8	79	37	38	4	246	249	3	13	155	90	61	4	644	543	17	21	137	79	108	139	94	82	120	118
PHI	73	48	23	2	285	211	21	4	76	30	44	2	276	331	11	5	149	78	67	4	561	542	32	9	151	143	50	87	111	105	94	93
STL	76	40	34	2	272	225	12	10	78	36	39	3	286	273	8	4	154	76	73	5	558	498	20	14	170	86	58	92	101	91	98	97
WAS	75	33	41	1	260	288	7	5	76	22	54	0	258	376	19	10	151	55	95	1	518	664	26	15	45	209	141	88	103	127	91	94
1907 AMERICAN LEAGUE																																	
BOS	78	34	41	3	249	270	12	11	77	25	49	3	215	288	6	11	155	59	90	6	464	558	18	22	127	132	162	101	81	96	101	103
CHI	79	48	29	2	316	222	0	5	78	39	35	4	272	252	5	8	157	87	64	6	588	474	5	13	42	37	135	102	99	82	104	101
CLE	82	46	31	5	267	226	7	3	76	39	36	1	263	299	4	3	158	85	67	6	530	525	11	6	128	66	40	84	99	98	93	93
DET	79	50	27	2	373	265	3	5	74	42	31	1	321	267	8	4	153	92	58	3	694	532	11	9	66	95	88	102	122	97	101	98
NY	75	33	40	2	331	372	10	7	77	37	38	2	274	293	5	7	152	70	78	4	605	665	15	14	137	99	98	123	100	109	109	110
PHI	73	50	20	3	324	235	14	6	77	38	37	2	258	276	8	6	150	88	57	5	582	511	22	12	143	144	89	110	100	90	106	104
STL	76	36	40	0	261	262	5	11	79	33	43	3	281	293	4	6	155	69	83	3	542	555	9	17	153	58	99	95	98	100	98	98
WAS	75	27	47	1	228	310	1	3	79	22	55	2	278	381	11	7	154	49	102	3	506	691	12	10	25	114	145	86	100	130	90	94
1908 AMERICAN LEAGUE																																	
BOS	77	37	40	0	273	249	9	9	78	38	39	1	291	264	5	9	155	75	79	1	564	513	14	18	125	88	113	96	107	99	98	97
CHI	78	51	25	2	271	184	1	4	78	37	39	2	266	286	2	7	156	88	64	4	537	470	3	11	59	24	83	85	107	93	94	93
CLE	78	51	26	1	305	223	8	6	79	39	38	2	263	234	10	9	157	90	64	3	568	457	18	15	78	142	120	107	99	82	106	103
DET	78	44	33	1	315	300	6	6	76	46	30	0	332	247	13	6	154	90	63	1	647	547	19	12	65	155	113	104	121	104	101	99
NY	77	30	47	0	234	352	11	16	78	21	56	1	225	361	1	10	155	51	103	1	459	713	12	26	207	47	123	100	90	132	95	101
PHI	78	46	30	2	294	272	11	5	79	22	55	2	192	290	10	6	157	68	85	4	486	562	21	11	101	140	80	116	83	96	107	110
STL	78	46	31	1	292	234	11	2	77	37	38	2	252	249	9	5	155	83	69	3	544	483	20	7	93	135	52	104	99	89	103	102
WAS	78	43	32	3	249	237	2	8	77	24	53	0	230	302	6	7	155	67	85	3	479	539	8	15	78	60	112	91	95	104	95	97
1909 AMERICAN LEAGUE																																	
BOS	75	47	28	0	329	295	18	12	77	41	35	1	268	255	3	4	152	88	63	1	597	550	21	16	311	68	64	120	105	98	109	108
CHI	81	42	34	5	256	201	1	3	78	36	40	2	236	262	3	5	159	78	74	7	492	463	4	8	52	33	68	90	93	88	97	96
CLE	77	39	37	1	262	259	2	0	78	32	45	1	231	273	8	10	155	71	82	2	493	532	10	10	13	162	71	104	91	97	102	103
DET	78	57	19	2	377	246	13	12	80	41	35	4	289	247	6	7	158	98	54	6	666	493	19	19	178	101	104	118	111	86	110	106
NY	77	41	35	1	338	263	11	6	76	33	42	1	252	324	5	12	153	74	77	2	590	587	16	18	99	126	140	103	113	113	99	99
PHI	76	49	27	0	293	200	8	4	77	46	31	0	312	208	12	5	153	95	58	0	605	408	20	9	75	161	82	98	113	80	102	97
STL	79	40	37	2	242	235	5	6	75	21	52	2	199	340	5	10	154	61	89	4	441	575	10	16	72	91	132	85	92	114	92	94

	HOME								ROAD								ALL															
TM	G	W	L	T	R	OR	HR	OHR	G	W	L	T	R	OR	HR	OHR	G	W	L	T	R	OR	HR	OHR	HRF	HRB	HRP	RF	RB	RP	BPF	PPF
WAS	77	27	48	2	197	271	5	3	79	15	62	2	183	385	4	10	156	42	110	4	380	656	9	13	60	89	103	84	80	126	90	96
1910 AMERICAN LEAGUE																																
BOS	80	51	28	1	338	262	32	21	78	30	44	4	300	302	11	8	158	81	72	5	638	564	43	29	225	150	109	98	112	101	99	97
CHI	79	41	37	1	233	198	2	2	77	27	48	2	224	281	5	14	156	68	85	3	457	479	7	16	23	75	115	85	86	88	95	95
CLE	80	39	36	5	278	330	4	2	81	32	45	4	270	327	5	7	161	71	81	9	548	657	9	9	54	61	52	102	94	110	100	102
DET	78	46	31	1	346	306	17	23	77	40	37	0	333	276	9	13	155	86	68	1	679	582	26	36	164	122	162	105	118	103	102	100
NY	77	49	25	3	343	284	13	4	79	39	38	2	283	273	7	10	156	88	63	5	626	557	20	14	103	106	78	114	103	93	107	106
PHI	78	57	19	2	339	211	9	0	77	45	29	3	334	230	10	8	155	102	48	5	673	441	19	8	54	135	44	98	117	81	102	97
STL	79	26	51	2	229	359	4	2	79	21	56	2	222	384	8	12	158	47	107	4	451	743	12	14	32	107	95	96	83	129	94	100
WAS	77	38	35	4	265	252	3	7	80	28	50	2	236	298	6	12	157	66	85	6	501	550	9	19	61	60	120	100	87	94	101	102
1911 AMERICAN LEAGUE																																
BOS	76	39	37	0	328	312	20	15	77	39	38	0	352	331	16	6	153	78	75	0	680	643	36	21	150	117	68	96	97	93	99	98
CHI	78	40	37	1	341	299	8	12	76	37	37	2	378	325	13	9	154	77	74	3	719	624	21	21	90	86	88	90	105	93	97	95
CLE	77	46	30	1	368	344	7	13	79	34	43	2	323	368	4	13	156	80	73	3	691	712	11	26	118	39	88	105	93	96	103	103
DET	76	51	25	0	468	403	21	9	78	38	40	0	363	373	15	13	154	89	65	0	831	776	36	22	109	137	90	119	108	103	108	107
NY	77	36	40	1	365	422	14	11	76	40	36	0	319	302	14	11	153	76	76	1	684	724	28	22	99	113	91	121	88	92	111	111
PHI	75	54	20	1	384	253	11	24	77	47	30	0	477	348	5	12	152	101	50	1	861	601	16	36	188	46	98	83	132	96	93	88
STL	78	25	53	0	296	396	9	8	74	20	54	0	271	416	10	18	152	45	107	0	567	812	19	26	60	104	126	94	85	117	95	100
WAS	77	39	38	0	323	356	10	6	77	25	52	0	302	410	21	18	154	64	90	0	625	766	31	24	44	179	136	95	91	109	97	99
1912 AMERICAN LEAGUE																																
BOS	78	57	20	1	417	286	10	10	76	48	27	1	382	258	19	8	154	105	47	2	799	544	29	18	76	170	119	108	109	78	107	102
CHI	78	34	43	1	276	340	11	11	80	44	33	3	362	306	6	14	158	78	76	4	638	646	17	25	111	84	119	95	92	93	99	99
CLE	75	39	35	1	338	326	3	6	80	36	43	1	338	354	7	9	155	75	78	2	676	680	10	15	63	58	88	102	97	98	101	101
DET	76	37	39	0	344	370	8	6	78	32	45	1	376	407	11	10	154	69	84	1	720	777	19	16	71	114	96	94	111	119	95	96
NY	76	31	44	1	352	423	14	16	77	19	58	0	278	419	4	12	153	50	102	1	630	842	18	28	168	68	113	109	91	118	101	105
PHI	78	45	32	1	381	342	11	6	75	45	30	0	398	316	11	6	153	90	62	1	779	658	22	12	97	111	65	99	116	100	99	97
STL	79	27	50	2	287	379	6	11	78	26	51	1	265	385	13	6	157	53	101	3	552	764	19	17	88	100	94	99	80	107	99	103
WAS	79	45	33	1	336	295	13	12	75	46	28	1	362	286	7	11	154	91	61	2	698	581	20	23	128	91	107	94	103	88	99	97
1913 AMERICAN LEAGUE																																
BOS	75	41	34	0	328	312	3	0	76	38	37	1	303	298	14	6	151	79	71	1	631	610	17	6	17	138	29	107	103	100	103	103
CHI	77	40	37	0	216	233	6	4	76	38	37	1	272	265	17	6	153	78	74	1	488	498	23	10	46	140	75	85	85	87	95	95
CLE	79	45	31	3	336	284	4	9	76	41	35	0	297	252	12	11	155	86	66	3	633	536	16	20	58	94	127	108	98	85	106	104
DET	76	34	42	0	312	368	9	4	77	32	45	0	312	348	15	8	153	66	87	0	624	716	24	12	60	142	76	103	105	118	99	101
NY	75	27	47	1	265	339	5	20	78	30	47	1	264	329	4	12	153	57	94	2	529	668	9	32	149	39	120	104	87	107	101	104
PHI	76	50	26	0	388	271	19	14	77	46	31	0	406	321	14	10	153	96	57	0	794	592	33	24	134	147	112	94	137	106	96	92
STL	77	31	46	0	247	309	13	11	78	26	50	2	281	333	5	10	155	57	96	2	528	642	18	21	149	68	85	92	91	108	95	98
WAS	79	43	35	1	297	318	10	29	76	47	29	0	299	243	10	6	155	90	64	1	596	561	20	35	202	81	101	109	93	87	106	105
1914 AMERICAN LEAGUE																																
BOS	79	44	31	4	270	247	3	5	80	47	31	2	318	264	15	13	159	91	62	6	588	511	18	18	32	133	155	92	104	92	98	96
CHI	81	43	37	1	271	285	7	4	76	27	47	2	216	275	12	11	157	70	84	3	487	560	19	15	48	141	108	105	82	93	103	105
CLE	79	32	47	0	289	380	4	3	78	19	55	4	249	329	6	7	157	51	102	4	538	709	10	10	56	66	62	111	92	117	102	106
DET	78	42	35	1	315	318	11	9	79	38	38	3	300	300	14	8	157	80	73	4	615	618	25	17	93	140	101	106	105	106	102	102
NY	78	36	40	2	278	259	8	24	79	34	44	1	260	291	4	6	157	70	84	3	538	550	12	30	252	42	83	98	94	96	100	100
PHI	78	51	24	3	354	247	17	13	80	48	29	3	395	282	12	5	158	99	53	6	749	529	29	18	166	120	74	93	133	99	97	93
STL	81	42	36	3	271	298	11	14	78	29	46	3	252	316	6	6	159	71	82	6	523	614	17	20	178	66	74	97	92	106	98	100
WAS	77	40	33	4	282	246	8	7	81	41	40	0	290	273	10	13	158	81	73	4	572	519	18	20	72	116	123	99	98	90	101	100
1915 AMERICAN LEAGUE																																
BOS	76	55	20	1	323	221	5	4	79	46	30	3	345	278	9	14	155	101	50	4	668	499	14	18	45	100	110	93	110	84	99	96
CHI	79	54	24	1	353	236	9	4	76	39	37	0	364	273	16	10	155	93	61	1	717	509	25	14	52	160	93	91	120	89	98	93
CLE	77	27	50	0	277	362	7	9	77	30	45	2	262	308	13	10	154	57	95	2	539	670	20	19	71	115	114	109	85	103	104	106
DET	76	50	26	0	410	314	11	7	80	50	28	2	368	283	12	7	156	100	54	2	778	597	23	14	101	109	70	116	117	93	108	105
NY	83	37	44	2	310	309	28	32	71	32	39	0	274	279	3	9	154	69	83	2	584	588	31	41	302	64	105	96	97	98	98	99
PHI	77	20	55	2	285	457	9	18	77	23	54	0	260	431	7	3	154	43	109	2	545	888	16	21	219	57	55	104	93	141	96	103
STL	76	35	38	3	237	315	6	7	83	28	53	2	284	364	13	14	159	63	91	5	521	679	19	21	55	117	130	93	86	109	96	99
WAS	77	48	28	1	277	235	2	2	78	37	40	1	292	256	10	10	155	85	68	2	569	491	12	12	23	88	88	96	92	80	101	99
1916 AMERICAN LEAGUE																																
BOS	78	49	28	1	252	205	1	1	78	42	35	1	298	275	13	9	156	91	63	2	550	480	14	10	10	118	101	83	103	90	94	92
CHI	77	49	28	0	326	254	9	5	78	40	37	1	275	243	8	9	155	89	65	1	601	497	17	14	86	100	82	112	97	83	108	106
CLE	78	44	33	1	323	293	4	9	79	33	44	2	307	309	12	7	157	77	77	3	630	602	16	16	72	95	106	101	109	105	100	99
DET	77	49	28	0	350	313	7	8	78	38	39	1	320	282	10	4	155	87	67	1	670	595	17	12	108	88	63	111	113	101	104	103
NY	79	46	31	2	306	277	22	22	77	34	43	0	271	284	13	15	156	80	74	2	577	561	35	37	144	183	194	102	99	97	101	101
PHI	76	23	53	0	231	399	15	17	78	13	64	1	216	377	4	9	154	36	117	1	447	776	19	26	208	66	99	105	80	130	98	105
STL	79	45	32	2	290	238	7	10	79	34	43	2	298	307	7	5	158	79	75	4	588	545	14	15	135	65	66	89	107	99	95	94
WAS	81	49	28	4	294	248	6	1	78	27	49	2	242	295	6	13	159	76	77	6	536	543	12	14	39	111	82	97	92	93	100	100
1917 AMERICAN LEAGUE																																
BOS	80	45	33	2	293	245	3	4	77	45	29	3	262	209	11	8	157	90	62	5	555	454	14	12	39	108	106	110	90	75	108	106
CHI	79	56	21	2	327	204	7	3	77	44	33	0	329	260	11	7	156	100	54	2	656	464	18	10	58	129	74	90	118	87	98	93
CLE	77	43	34	0	317	314	5	8	79	45	32	2	267	229	8	9	156	88	66	2	584	543	13	17	81	85	109	127	90	84	114	113
DET	76	34	41	1	285	303	5	5	78	44	34	0	354	274	20	7	154	78	75	1	639	577	25	12	41	193	129	97	116	107	98	96
NY	75	35	40	0	269	292	19	24	80	36	42	2	255	266	8	4	155	71	82	2	524	558	27	28	282	97	81	112	87	92	107	107
PHI	76	29	47	0	264	319	11	17	78	26	51	1	265	372	6	6	154	55	98	1	529	691	17	23	202	73	89	93	101	127	94	97
STL	78	31	46	1	252	337	7	11	77	26	51	0	258	350	8	8	155	57	97	1	510	687	15	19	108	89	108	95	95	123	95	98
WAS	81	42	36	3	264	255	1	3	76	32	43	1	279	311	3	9	157	74	79	4	543	566	4	12	34	33	92	84	103	107	92	93
1918 AMERICAN LEAGUE																																
BOS	70	49	21	0	272	165	2	3	56	26	30	0	202	215	13	6	126	75	51	0	474	380	15	9	24	187	162	86	109	90	95	93
CHI	56	30	26	0	216	194	4	4	68	27	41	0	241	252	5	5	124	57	67	0	457	446	9	9	97	73	73	101	101	98	100	100
CLE	62	38	22	2	274	219	1	4	67	35	32	0	230	228	8	6	129	73	54	2	504	447	9	10	42	79	119	115	99	90	108	107
DET	58	28	29	1	221	246	2	7	70	27	42	1	255	311	11	4	128	55	71	2	476	557	13	11	75	105	113	99	106	121	97	99
NY	67	37	29	1	251	237	10	22	59	23	34	2	242	238	10	3	126	60	63	3	493	475	20	25	189	144	127	91	114	110	94	94
PHI	68	35	32	1	256	273	15	8	62	17	44	1	156	265	7	5	130	52	76	2	412	538	22	13	158	133	87	111	82	106	104	108
STL	53	23	30	0	178	195	1	7	70	35	34	1	248	253	4	4	123	58	64	1	426	448	5	11	127	37	77	98	95	100	99	100
WAS	74	41	32	1	268	238	2	6	56	31	24	1	193	174	3	4	130	72	56	2	461	412	5	10	89	42	77	104	93	84	104	103

	HOME								ROAD								ALL															
TM	G	W	L	T	R	OR	HR	OHR	G	W	L	T	R	OR	HR	OHR	G	W	L	T	R	OR	HR	OHR	HRF	HRB	HRP	RF	RB	RP	BPF	PPF
1919 AMERICAN LEAGUE																																
BOS	66	35	30	1	233	241	10	3	72	31	41	0	331	311	23	13	138	66	71	1	564	552	33	16	43	145	68	82	108	107	91	91
CHI	70	48	22	0	344	279	5	11	70	40	30	0	323	255	20	14	140	88	52	0	667	534	25	25	51	97	115	108	111	91	105	102
CLE	69	44	25	0	340	276	12	4	70	40	30	0	296	261	13	15	139	84	55	0	636	537	25	19	62	102	69	112	105	91	107	104
DET	70	46	24	0	307	243	10	14	70	34	36	0	311	335	13	21	140	80	60	0	618	578	23	35	74	90	129	87	116	108	93	92
NY	73	46	25	2	326	255	33	30	68	34	34	0	252	251	12	17	141	80	59	2	578	506	45	47	180	106	118	107	94	85	106	104
PHI	70	21	49	0	266	400	29	31	70	15	55	0	191	342	6	13	140	36	104	0	457	742	35	44	244	62	88	118	75	116	106	112
STL	70	40	30	0	280	249	19	23	70	27	42	1	253	318	12	12	140	67	72	1	533	567	31	35	160	81	88	93	96	101	97	98
WAS	72	32	40	0	265	282	2	5	70	24	44	2	268	288	22	15	142	56	84	2	533	570	24	20	20	101	125	95	94	99	98	99
1920 AMERICAN LEAGUE																																
BOS	76	41	35	0	327	300	3	14	78	31	46	1	323	398	19	25	154	72	81	1	650	698	22	39	43	54	114	90	93	98	96	97
CHI	77	52	25	0	381	298	18	10	77	44	33	0	413	367	19	35	154	96	58	0	794	665	37	45	56	111	112	90	113	97	96	94
CLE	78	51	27	0	441	330	20	10	76	47	29	0	416	312	15	21	154	98	56	0	857	642	35	31	84	79	69	104	113	88	104	100
DET	78	32	46	0	336	452	12	24	77	29	47	1	316	381	18	22	155	61	93	1	652	833	30	46	89	67	100	109	86	106	103	106
NY	77	49	28	0	424	308	71	36	77	46	31	0	414	321	44	12	154	95	59	0	838	629	115	48	173	189	83	101	112	87	102	99
PHI	77	25	50	2	254	401	35	40	79	23	56	0	304	433	9	16	156	48	106	2	558	834	44	56	241	52	71	90	80	114	94	99
STL	78	40	38	0	473	415	31	33	76	36	39	1	324	351	19	20	154	76	77	1	797	766	50	53	149	88	93	124	97	95	111	111
WAS	76	37	38	1	343	386	5	7	77	31	46	0	380	416	31	44	153	68	84	1	723	802	36	51	18	135	180	93	104	114	95	96
1921 AMERICAN LEAGUE																																
BOS	77	41	36	0	332	333	3	16	77	34	43	0	336	363	14	37	154	75	79	0	668	696	17	53	40	35	112	96	85	88	100	100
CHI	77	37	40	0	378	399	13	20	77	25	52	0	305	459	22	32	154	62	92	0	683	858	35	52	64	69	99	101	87	107	99	102
CLE	77	51	26	0	467	330	15	10	77	43	34	0	458	382	27	33	154	94	60	0	925	712	42	43	45	96	88	97	118	94	99	96
DET	77	37	40	0	433	412	19	28	77	34	42	1	450	440	39	43	154	71	82	1	883	852	58	71	60	123	151	95	117	113	96	96
NY	78	53	25	0	500	355	83	34	75	45	30	0	448	353	51	17	153	98	55	0	948	708	134	51	155	176	75	104	118	91	103	99
PHI	77	28	47	2	353	464	65	59	78	25	53	0	304	430	17	26	155	53	100	2	657	894	82	85	233	79	90	109	80	105	103	107
STL	77	43	34	0	423	434	42	43	77	38	39	0	412	411	25	28	154	81	73	0	835	845	67	71	149	91	97	104	105	106	101	101
WAS	76	46	30	0	358	332	14	13	78	34	43	1	346	406	28	38	154	80	73	1	704	738	42	51	45	97	107	95	91	94	99	99
1922 AMERICAN LEAGUE																																
BOS	73	31	42	0	280	344	6	17	81	30	51	0	318	425	39	31	154	61	93	0	598	769	45	48	39	78	108	93	85	106	96	99
CHI	77	43	34	0	351	335	10	21	78	34	43	1	340	356	35	36	155	77	77	1	691	691	45	57	48	83	115	100	93	93	101	101
CLE	80	44	35	1	423	424	12	20	75	34	41	0	345	393	20	38	155	78	76	1	768	817	32	58	55	62	104	107	102	108	102	103
DET	77	43	34	0	426	370	15	32	78	36	41	1	402	421	39	30	155	79	75	1	828	791	54	62	72	90	110	98	115	111	98	97
NY	77	50	27	0	387	291	53	48	77	44	33	0	371	327	42	25	154	94	60	0	758	618	95	73	143	123	95	99	102	85	101	99
PHI	78	38	39	1	388	437	80	82	77	27	50	0	317	393	31	25	155	65	89	1	705	830	111	107	230	107	99	112	92	106	104	106
STL	77	54	23	0	471	314	70	41	77	39	38	0	396	329	28	30	154	93	61	0	867	643	98	71	173	106	87	108	112	87	106	102
WAS	79	40	39	0	329	295	15	3	75	29	46	0	321	411	30	46	154	69	85	0	650	706	45	49	25	130	87	82	98	104	92	93
1923 AMERICAN LEAGUE																																
BOS	78	37	40	1	327	402	11	15	76	24	51	1	257	407	23	33	154	61	91	2	584	809	34	48	48	82	110	105	78	104	102	106
CHI	75	30	45	0	327	348	13	24	81	39	40	2	365	393	29	25	156	69	85	2	692	741	42	49	76	80	98	96	94	100	98	99
CLE	78	42	36	0	455	393	22	16	75	40	35	0	433	353	37	20	153	82	71	0	888	746	59	36	67	121	81	104	120	103	101	99
DET	77	45	32	0	400	351	21	31	78	38	39	1	431	390	20	27	155	83	71	1	831	741	41	58	111	70	95	94	116	105	97	95
NY	76	46	30	0	407	329	62	50	76	52	24	0	416	293	43	18	152	98	54	0	823	622	105	68	168	153	97	105	109	85	104	101
PHI	75	34	41	0	345	360	28	32	78	35	42	1	316	401	24	36	153	69	83	1	661	761	52	68	103	97	122	102	90	102	100	102
STL	78	40	36	2	377	364	50	43	76	34	42	0	311	356	32	15	154	74	78	2	688	720	82	58	172	112	76	107	90	94	104	105
WAS	79	43	34	2	363	339	7	16	76	32	44	0	357	408	19	40	155	75	78	2	720	747	26	56	41	66	131	89	103	106	95	95
1924 AMERICAN LEAGUE																																
BOS	77	41	36	0	402	391	8	17	80	26	51	3	335	415	22	26	157	67	87	3	737	806	30	43	57	69	103	108	91	99	104	105
CHI	77	37	39	1	403	414	13	23	77	29	48	0	390	444	28	29	154	66	87	1	793	858	41	52	66	98	126	98	107	114	97	98
CLE	75	37	38	0	374	375	13	18	78	30	48	0	381	439	28	25	153	67	86	0	755	814	41	43	64	96	106	95	103	110	97	97
DET	78	45	33	0	427	393	17	28	78	41	35	2	422	403	18	27	156	86	68	2	849	796	35	55	101	70	105	100	110	104	99	99
NY	78	45	32	1	397	324	57	46	75	44	31	0	401	343	41	13	153	89	63	1	798	667	98	59	167	158	91	95	106	90	99	97
PHI	75	36	39	0	328	391	32	24	77	35	42	0	357	387	31	19	152	71	81	0	685	778	63	43	113	120	86	99	91	102	99	101
STL	78	41	36	1	426	445	44	49	75	33	42	0	343	364	23	19	153	74	78	1	769	809	67	68	186	99	96	116	94	98	107	108
WAS	79	47	30	2	371	280	1	7	77	45	32	0	384	333	21	27	156	92	62	2	755	613	22	34	18	50	115	91	99	82	98	96
1925 AMERICAN LEAGUE																																
BOS	75	28	47	0	309	441	10	28	77	19	58	0	330	481	31	39	152	47	105	0	639	922	41	67	58	73	125	94	85	117	95	99
CHI	77	44	33	0	366	378	13	32	77	35	42	0	445	392	25	37	154	79	75	0	811	770	38	69	75	63	111	90	106	102	96	95
CLE	77	37	39	1	421	430	23	19	78	33	45	0	361	387	29	22	155	70	84	1	782	817	52	41	85	79	64	113	91	95	106	107
DET	77	43	34	0	451	399	18	36	79	38	39	2	452	430	32	34	156	81	73	2	903	829	50	70	86	78	108	99	112	104	99	98
NY	79	42	36	1	354	356	54	56	77	27	49	1	352	418	56	22	156	69	85	2	706	774	110	78	131	149	104	91	91	98	96	97
PHI	77	51	26	0	435	351	35	37	76	37	38	1	396	362	41	23	153	88	64	1	831	713	76	60	110	109	87	103	102	89	103	101
STL	78	45	32	1	503	501	73	73	76	37	39	0	397	405	37	26	154	82	71	1	900	906	110	99	196	119	102	119	104	105	108	108
WAS	76	53	22	1	408	298	13	13	76	43	33	0	421	372	43	36	152	96	55	1	829	670	56	49	36	116	107	91	107	89	98	95
1926 AMERICAN LEAGUE																																
BOS	77	25	51	1	288	438	9	16	77	21	56	0	274	397	23	29	154	46	107	1	562	835	32	45	50	75	107	105	76	108	101	106
CHI	79	47	31	1	332	294	8	19	76	34	41	1	398	371	24	28	155	81	72	2	730	665	32	47	53	72	111	81	109	100	92	90
CLE	80	49	31	0	376	301	11	19	74	39	35	0	362	311	16	30	154	88	66	0	738	612	27	49	64	62	104	95	102	86	100	97
DET	81	39	41	1	380	445	16	38	76	40	34	2	413	385	20	20	157	79	75	3	793	830	36	58	123	62	90	98	110	115	97	97
NY	75	50	25	0	417	326	58	33	80	41	38	1	430	387	63	23	155	91	63	1	847	713	121	56	112	222	117	98	116	100	99	97
PHI	71	44	27	0	365	314	34	27	79	39	40	0	312	256	27	11	150	83	67	0	677	570	61	38	163	90	55	128	82	70	118	115
STL	79	40	39	0	375	429	53	64	76	22	53	1	307	416	19	22	155	62	92	1	682	845	72	86	224	85	99	105	92	112	101	103
WAS	74	42	30	2	373	378	4	15	78	39	39	0	429	383	39	30	152	81	69	2	802	761	43	45	32	97	143	98	114	109	98	97
1927 AMERICAN LEAGUE																																
BOS	78	29	49	0	299	409	5	29	76	22	54	0	298	447	23	27	154	51	103	0	597	856	28	56	68	56	117	92	83	114	95	99
CHI	75	38	37	0	337	343	6	22	78	32	46	0	325	365	30	33	153	70	83	0	662	708	36	55	49	77	135	102	86	91	102	103
CLE	77	35	42	0	333	367	10	11	76	31	45	0	335	399	16	26	153	66	87	0	668	766	26	37	52	61	79	94	91	103	97	99
DET	78	44	32	2	467	433	25	28	78	38	39	1	378	372	26	24	156	82	71	3	845	805	51	52	106	89	90	117	102	98	108	107
NY	77	57	19	1	479	267	83	30	78	53	25	0	496	332	75	12	155	110	44	1	975	599	158	42	129	251	79	94	128	84	100	94
PHI	77	50	27	0	412	327	26	36	78	41	36	1	429	399	30	29	155	91	63	1	841	726	56	65	107	101	115	92	114	100	97	95
STL	78	38	38	2	440	457	42	57	77	21	56	0	284	447	13	22	155	59	94	2	724	904	55	79	226	60	87	117	89	109	106	109
WAS	79	51	28	0	416	308	10	19	78	34	41	3	366	422	19	34	157	85	69	3	782	730	29	53	58	64	111	92	105	98	97	96
1928 AMERICAN LEAGUE																																
BOS	74	26	47	1	283	363	10	15	80	31	49	0	306	407	28	34	154	57	96	1	589	770	38	49	46	79	103	97	82	104	98	101
CHI	78	37	40	1	316	369	11	28	77	35	42	0	340	356	13	38	155	72	82	1	656	725	24	66	78	45	111	97	90	98	99	100

	HOME								ROAD								ALL															
TM	G	W	L	T	R	OR	HR	OHR	G	W	L	T	R	OR	HR	OHR	G	W	L	T	R	OR	HR	OHR	HRF	HRB	HRP	RF	RB	RP	BPF	PPF
CLE	77	29	48	0	366	443	10	15	78	33	44	1	308	387	24	37	155	62	92	1	674	830	34	52	44	75	108	114	86	104	106	108
DET	77	36	41	0	382	400	33	26	77	32	45	0	362	404	29	32	154	68	86	0	744	804	62	58	97	104	98	101	102	109	99	100
NY	77	52	25	0	400	301	69	36	77	49	28	0	494	384	64	23	154	101	53	0	894	685	133	59	119	205	103	83	133	105	92	89
PHI	77	52	25	0	430	295	54	33	76	46	30	0	399	320	35	33	153	98	55	0	829	615	89	66	124	134	106	101	111	85	103	99
STL	77	44	33	0	398	389	51	64	77	38	39	0	374	353	12	29	154	82	72	0	772	742	63	93	229	60	96	107	102	98	104	103
WAS	80	37	43	0	363	378	16	12	75	38	36	1	355	327	24	28	155	75	79	1	718	705	40	40	54	83	79	102	96	94	102	101
1929 AMERICAN LEAGUE																																
BOS	78	32	45	1	328	399	11	36	77	26	51	0	277	404	17	42	155	58	96	1	605	803	28	78	80	41	105	103	77	99	102	105
CHI	76	35	41	0	306	366	19	41	76	24	52	0	321	426	18	43	152	59	93	0	627	792	37	84	97	51	107	90	87	107	95	97
CLE	76	44	32	0	359	363	27	21	76	37	39	0	358	373	35	35	152	81	71	0	717	736	62	56	72	95	85	99	94	96	100	101
DET	77	38	39	0	476	453	57	33	78	32	45	1	450	475	53	40	155	70	84	1	926	928	110	73	98	149	105	101	123	123	97	97
NY	77	49	28	0	463	362	69	55	77	39	38	0	436	413	73	28	154	88	66	0	899	775	142	83	120	180	111	98	118	104	99	97
PHI	74	57	16	1	484	302	72	47	77	47	30	0	417	313	50	26	151	104	46	1	901	615	122	73	154	133	84	112	110	79	109	104
STL	77	41	36	0	370	341	22	58	77	38	37	2	363	372	24	42	154	79	73	2	733	713	46	100	118	59	116	97	95	93	100	100
WAS	78	37	40	1	376	390	10	17	75	34	41	0	354	386	38	31	153	71	81	1	730	776	48	48	41	80	92	99	96	101	100	100
1930 AMERICAN LEAGUE																																
BOS	76	30	46	0	287	354	15	31	78	22	56	0	325	460	32	44	154	52	102	0	612	814	47	75	64	64	102	84	79	101	93	96
CHI	78	34	44	0	393	457	25	42	76	28	48	0	336	427	38	32	154	62	92	0	729	884	63	74	93	76	88	106	85	101	103	105
CLE	77	44	33	0	494	469	34	46	77	37	40	0	396	446	38	39	154	81	73	0	890	915	72	85	104	84	97	113	102	105	105	105
DET	78	45	33	0	441	419	45	48	76	30	46	0	342	414	37	38	154	75	79	0	783	833	82	86	118	90	93	109	89	95	105	106
NY	76	47	29	0	471	390	69	54	78	39	39	0	591	508	83	39	154	86	68	0	1062	898	152	93	104	184	122	83	142	123	90	87
PHI	76	58	18	0	485	329	76	49	78	44	34	0	466	422	49	35	154	102	52	0	951	751	125	84	145	121	87	96	115	93	99	96
STL	78	38	40	0	432	475	35	72	76	26	50	0	319	411	40	52	154	64	90	0	751	886	75	124	111	91	138	117	83	97	108	110
WAS	77	56	21	0	474	300	17	15	77	38	39	0	418	389	40	37	154	94	60	0	892	689	57	52	45	86	79	97	106	84	101	98
1931 AMERICAN LEAGUE																																
BOS	80	39	40	1	332	362	11	29	73	23	50	0	293	438	26	25	153	62	90	1	625	800	37	54	73	56	83	87	85	106	94	96
CHI	77	31	45	1	341	421	11	45	79	25	52	2	363	518	16	37	156	56	97	3	704	939	27	82	106	36	100	89	95	122	92	96
CLE	76	45	31	0	503	405	38	32	79	33	45	1	382	428	33	32	155	78	76	1	885	833	71	64	110	92	84	114	104	100	106	106
DET	77	36	41	0	349	432	19	43	77	25	52	0	302	404	24	36	154	61	93	0	651	836	43	79	102	60	103	108	79	99	104	107
NY	77	51	25	1	545	337	84	39	78	43	34	1	522	423	71	28	155	94	59	2	1067	760	155	67	123	194	95	96	137	102	98	93
PHI	75	60	15	0	446	289	61	37	78	47	30	1	412	337	57	36	153	107	45	1	858	626	118	73	110	160	106	104	104	79	105	101
STL	77	39	38	0	407	425	42	48	77	24	53	0	315	445	34	36	154	63	91	0	722	870	76	84	123	97	106	107	89	105	102	105
WAS	79	55	22	2	453	308	13	24	77	37	40	0	390	383	36	49	156	92	62	2	843	691	49	73	46	89	132	97	105	88	101	98
1932 AMERICAN LEAGUE																																
BOS	77	27	50	0	295	439	18	31	77	16	61	0	271	476	35	48	154	43	111	0	566	915	53	79	61	72	105	96	73	111	97	102
CHI	77	28	49	0	300	390	10	36	75	21	53	1	367	507	26	52	152	49	102	1	667	897	36	88	60	49	116	78	97	124	87	91
CLE	77	43	33	1	460	401	36	33	76	44	32	0	385	346	42	37	153	87	65	1	845	747	78	70	88	91	83	115	97	87	108	107
DET	78	42	34	2	423	399	29	50	75	34	41	0	376	388	51	39	153	76	75	2	799	787	80	89	86	97	109	103	98	97	102	102
NY	77	62	15	0	482	300	81	44	79	45	32	2	520	424	79	49	156	107	47	2	1002	724	160	93	102	180	115	88	129	97	95	91
PHI	77	51	26	0	572	406	109	80	77	43	34	0	409	346	63	32	154	94	60	0	981	752	172	112	179	146	96	126	106	85	114	111
STL	75	33	42	0	385	428	47	56	79	30	49	0	351	470	20	47	154	63	91	0	736	898	67	103	149	59	93	103	91	109	100	103
WAS	77	51	26	0	431	325	21	26	77	42	35	0	409	391	40	47	154	93	61	0	840	716	61	73	58	84	99	96	105	91	100	98
1933 AMERICAN LEAGUE																																
BOS	72	32	40	0	341	377	23	35	77	31	46	0	359	381	27	40	149	63	86	0	700	758	50	75	93	69	99	103	93	100	101	102
CHI	77	35	41	1	355	426	20	42	74	32	42	0	328	388	23	43	151	67	83	1	683	814	43	85	91	60	111	104	90	104	101	103
CLE	77	45	32	0	353	341	22	24	74	30	44	0	301	328	28	36	151	75	76	0	654	669	50	60	72	75	87	105	83	85	105	105
DET	78	43	35	0	394	382	27	36	77	32	44	1	328	351	30	48	155	75	79	1	722	733	57	84	82	82	115	111	87	89	107	107
NY	75	51	23	1	421	324	79	26	77	40	36	1	506	444	65	40	152	91	59	2	927	768	144	66	103	186	96	83	134	114	91	88
PHI	76	46	29	1	414	387	82	50	76	33	43	0	461	466	57	27	152	79	72	1	875	853	139	77	147	151	88	88	126	123	92	91
STL	77	30	46	1	389	480	43	68	76	25	50	1	280	340	21	28	153	55	96	2	669	820	64	96	191	59	82	130	76	91	115	117
WAS	76	46	30	0	358	338	14	16	77	53	23	1	492	327	46	48	153	99	53	1	850	665	60	64	36	109	118	89	115	94	96	93
1934 AMERICAN LEAGUE																																
BOS	77	42	35	0	447	405	23	24	76	34	41	1	373	370	28	46	153	76	76	1	820	775	51	70	66	71	90	111	99	94	106	105
CHI	75	29	46	0	370	464	47	82	78	24	53	1	334	482	24	57	153	53	99	1	704	946	71	139	151	69	128	104	90	117	99	103
CLE	78	47	31	0	435	362	45	34	76	38	38	0	379	401	55	36	154	85	69	0	814	763	100	70	87	121	89	100	103	97	100	100
DET	80	54	26	0	479	345	28	32	74	47	27	0	479	363	46	54	154	101	53	0	958	708	74	86	60	109	123	93	125	96	98	94
NY	77	53	24	0	416	275	75	34	77	41	36	0	426	394	60	37	154	94	60	0	842	669	135	71	112	145	84	87	112	91	96	93
PHI	76	34	40	2	371	410	81	48	77	34	42	1	393	428	63	36	153	68	82	3	764	838	144	84	126	150	94	96	100	109	97	98
STL	76	36	39	1	356	405	35	60	78	31	46	1	318	395	27	34	154	67	85	2	674	800	62	94	148	59	84	108	82	96	104	106
WAS	76	34	40	2	368	397	14	26	79	32	46	1	361	409	37	48	155	66	86	3	729	806	51	74	52	72	106	102	91	99	101	102
1935 AMERICAN LEAGUE																																
BOS	79	41	37	1	393	404	26	29	75	37	38	0	325	328	43	38	154	78	75	1	718	732	69	67	68	95	94	114	85	86	108	108
CHI	77	42	34	1	418	396	50	61	76	32	44	0	320	354	24	44	153	74	78	1	738	750	74	105	149	71	101	116	87	88	109	109
CLE	77	48	29	0	391	340	53	30	79	34	42	3	385	399	40	38	156	82	71	3	776	739	93	68	108	102	78	97	98	94	99	99
DET	79	53	25	1	467	304	45	38	73	40	33	0	452	361	61	40	152	93	58	1	919	665	106	78	79	144	112	90	123	93	97	93
NY	74	41	33	0	341	294	60	51	75	48	27	0	477	338	44	40	149	89	60	0	818	632	104	91	130	114	102	82	115	93	93	90
PHI	72	30	42	0	369	414	63	39	77	28	49	0	341	455	49	34	149	58	91	0	710	869	112	73	125	122	84	103	94	112	100	102
STL	76	31	44	1	374	513	36	49	79	34	43	2	344	417	37	43	155	65	87	3	718	930	73	92	108	84	103	117	86	107	106	110
WAS	77	37	39	1	388	414	5	28	77	30	47	0	435	489	27	61	154	67	86	1	823	903	32	89	40	47	139	88	115	124	91	93
1936 AMERICAN LEAGUE																																
BOS	77	47	29	1	437	360	38	31	78	27	51	0	338	404	48	47	155	74	80	1	775	764	86	78	76	100	91	107	83	82	106	106
CHI	75	43	32	0	453	419	23	55	78	38	38	2	467	454	37	49	153	81	70	2	920	873	60	104	95	65	108	99	107	102	99	99
CLE	81	49	30	2	535	433	73	33	76	31	44	1	386	429	50	40	157	80	74	3	921	862	123	73	109	117	76	110	97	93	105	105
DET	77	44	33	0	448	399	51	58	77	39	38	0	473	472	43	42	154	83	71	0	921	871	94	100	124	90	94	91	111	105	95	95
NY	77	56	21	0	492	311	82	41	78	46	30	2	573	420	100	43	155	102	51	2	1065	731	182	84	90	201	106	85	128	92	95	90
PHI	77	31	46	0	383	531	43	77	77	22	54	1	331	514	29	54	154	53	100	1	714	1045	72	131	135	67	114	106	81	114	100	105
STL	77	31	43	3	443	552	47	63	78	26	52	0	361	512	32	52	155	57	95	3	804	1064	79	115	126	75	105	112	88	113	103	107
WAS	77	42	35	0	433	380	16	27	76	40	36	0	456	419	46	46	153	82	71	0	889	799	62	73	50	80	101	93	105	96	98	96
1937 AMERICAN LEAGUE																																
BOS	74	44	29	1	420	368	53	43	80	36	43	1	401	407	47	49	154	80	72	2	821	775	100	92	107	96	89	105	99	94	103	102
CHI	77	47	30	0	397	365	39	62	77	39	38	0	383	365	28	53	154	86	68	0	780	730	67	115	122	61	100	102	94	89	103	102
CLE	78	50	28	0	430	329	48	22	78	33	43	2	387	439	55	39	156	83	71	2	817	768	103	61	77	109	66	93	103	97	97	97
DET	77	49	28	0	521	448	91	58	78	40	37	1	414	393	59	44	155	89	65	1	935	841	150	102	140	125	90	119	106	97	109	108
NY	79	57	20	2	520	298	94	41	78	45	32	1	459	373	80	51	157	102	52	3	979	671	174	92	103	168	98	99	117	84	102	97

	HOME								ROAD								ALL															
TM	G	W	L	T	R	OR	HR	OHR	G	W	L	T	R	OR	HR	OHR	G	W	L	T	R	OR	HR	OHR	HRF	HRB	HRP	RF	RB	RP	BPF	PPF
PHI	79	27	50	2	333	419	51	47	75	27	47	1	366	435	43	58	154	54	97	3	699	854	94	105	92	99	109	89	93	110	94	96
STL	78	25	51	2	385	513	39	74	78	21	57	0	330	510	32	69	156	46	108	2	715	1023	71	143	108	71	131	104	89	121	99	103
WAS	80	43	35	2	376	381	14	30	78	30	45	3	381	460	33	66	158	73	80	5	757	841	47	96	47	61	116	89	98	106	94	96
1938 AMERICAN LEAGUE																																
BOS	75	52	23	0	481	356	67	52	75	36	38	1	421	395	31	50	150	88	61	1	902	751	98	102	140	74	82	103	109	93	102	100
CHI	73	33	39	1	326	364	24	41	76	32	44	0	383	388	43	60	149	65	83	1	709	752	67	101	68	74	108	93	91	96	98	98
CLE	76	46	30	0	425	363	54	35	77	40	36	1	422	419	59	65	153	86	66	1	847	782	113	100	76	120	104	96	105	97	99	98
DET	79	48	31	0	447	392	83	60	76	36	39	1	415	403	54	50	155	84	70	1	862	795	137	110	128	109	92	99	103	96	100	99
NY	79	55	22	2	524	342	112	43	78	44	31	3	442	368	62	42	157	99	53	5	966	710	174	85	141	125	70	106	109	83	105	102
PHI	76	28	47	1	378	486	55	64	78	25	52	1	348	470	43	78	154	53	99	2	726	956	98	142	99	95	130	106	87	111	101	104
STL	77	31	43	3	385	487	52	62	79	24	54	1	370	475	40	70	156	55	97	4	755	962	92	132	104	84	115	104	90	112	100	103
WAS	78	44	33	1	412	413	33	27	74	31	43	0	402	460	52	65	152	75	76	1	814	873	85	92	52	106	107	92	105	112	95	96
1939 AMERICAN LEAGUE																																
BOS	75	42	32	1	458	445	57	39	77	47	30	0	432	350	67	38	152	89	62	1	890	795	124	77	95	125	83	117	104	94	108	107
CHI	77	50	27	0	414	366	38	51	78	35	42	1	341	371	26	48	155	85	69	1	755	737	64	99	119	57	86	110	88	86	107	106
CLE	77	44	33	0	363	347	30	33	77	43	34	0	434	353	55	42	154	87	67	0	797	700	85	75	68	95	88	92	101	91	98	96
DET	78	42	35	1	461	434	66	65	77	39	38	0	388	328	58	39	155	81	73	1	849	762	124	104	128	110	92	120	95	86	111	110
NY	77	52	25	0	382	261	84	48	75	54	20	1	585	295	82	37	152	106	45	1	967	556	166	85	109	160	90	75	133	84	91	85
PHI	76	28	48	0	354	523	45	83	77	27	49	1	357	499	53	65	153	55	97	1	711	1022	98	148	107	103	145	102	92	126	97	102
STL	78	18	59	1	372	561	47	80	78	25	52	1	361	474	44	53	156	43	111	2	733	1035	91	133	124	84	116	108	90	121	100	105
WAS	77	37	39	1	326	337	11	19	76	28	48	0	376	460	33	56	153	65	87	1	702	797	44	75	36	61	100	80	98	109	90	91
1940 AMERICAN LEAGUE																																
BOS	79	45	34	0	468	421	73	64	75	37	38	0	404	404	72	60	154	82	72	0	872	825	145	124	99	136	119	104	113	108	101	100
CHI	78	41	36	1	357	363	36	65	77	41	36	0	378	309	37	46	155	82	72	1	735	672	73	111	118	61	87	103	92	85	104	103
CLE	82	51	30	1	350	281	37	27	73	38	35	0	360	356	64	59	155	89	65	1	710	637	101	86	50	121	102	81	100	90	93	92
DET	79	50	29	0	512	389	82	64	76	40	35	1	376	328	52	38	155	90	64	1	888	717	134	102	147	97	75	121	103	86	111	109
NY	76	52	24	0	414	284	83	63	79	36	42	1	403	387	72	56	155	88	66	1	817	671	155	119	117	132	105	93	108	90	99	96
PHI	71	29	42	0	336	409	44	62	83	25	58	0	367	523	61	73	154	54	100	0	703	932	105	135	92	102	128	97	97	123	95	99
STL	77	37	39	1	419	460	68	68	79	30	48	1	338	422	50	45	156	67	87	2	757	882	118	113	138	89	85	115	92	106	106	108
WAS	77	36	41	0	316	368	19	28	77	28	49	0	349	443	33	65	154	64	90	0	665	811	52	93	51	62	100	87	94	111	93	95
1941 AMERICAN LEAGUE																																
BOS	77	47	30	0	461	371	70	52	78	37	40	1	404	379	54	37	155	84	70	1	865	750	124	89	131	118	88	107	114	101	103	101
CHI	79	38	39	2	288	297	17	40	77	39	38	0	350	352	30	49	156	77	77	2	638	649	47	89	73	57	104	83	92	94	93	94
CLE	77	42	35	0	340	322	45	35	78	33	44	1	337	346	58	36	155	75	79	1	677	668	103	71	88	116	84	98	91	90	101	100
DET	77	43	34	0	381	377	51	43	78	32	45	1	305	366	30	37	155	75	79	1	686	743	81	80	135	73	74	112	88	94	106	107
NY	78	51	26	1	396	295	76	43	78	50	27	1	434	336	75	37	156	101	53	2	830	631	151	80	107	157	91	92	114	90	98	95
PHI	77	36	41	0	373	432	43	75	77	28	49	0	340	408	42	61	154	64	90	0	713	840	85	136	112	95	141	106	97	112	101	103
STL	79	40	37	2	407	408	49	63	78	30	47	1	358	415	42	57	157	70	84	3	765	823	91	120	110	97	124	103	103	109	100	101
WAS	78	40	37	1	367	387	13	19	78	30	47	1	361	411	39	50	156	70	84	2	728	798	52	69	39	75	100	98	101	109	98	99
1942 AMERICAN LEAGUE																																
BOS	77	53	24	0	403	299	54	33	75	40	35	0	358	295	49	32	152	93	59	0	761	594	103	65	105	153	103	105	113	91	104	100
CHI	70	35	35	0	256	275	6	31	78	31	47	0	282	334	19	43	148	66	82	0	538	609	25	74	69	42	123	96	86	96	99	100
CLE	80	39	39	2	266	308	20	24	76	36	40	0	324	351	30	37	156	75	79	2	590	659	50	61	65	88	104	83	97	107	91	93
DET	77	43	34	0	344	302	50	40	79	30	47	2	245	285	26	20	156	73	81	2	589	587	76	60	178	79	63	121	78	79	113	113
NY	77	58	19	0	394	226	62	39	77	45	32	0	407	281	46	32	154	103	51	0	801	507	108	71	127	144	101	93	123	82	99	94
PHI	76	25	51	0	249	415	16	42	78	30	48	0	300	386	17	47	154	55	99	0	549	801	33	89	93	53	128	98	87	121	96	101
STL	77	40	37	0	376	350	55	37	74	42	32	0	354	287	43	26	151	82	69	0	730	637	98	63	124	133	90	108	109	96	104	102
WAS	77	35	42	0	339	409	13	11	74	27	47	0	314	408	27	39	151	62	89	0	653	817	40	50	38	90	98	99	106	129	96	99
1943 AMERICAN LEAGUE																																
BOS	77	39	36	2	293	312	29	25	78	29	48	1	270	295	28	36	155	68	84	3	563	607	57	61	87	104	109	107	90	97	103	104
CHI	76	40	36	0	264	311	20	25	79	42	36	1	309	283	13	29	155	82	72	1	573	594	33	54	110	51	81	101	94	97	101	101
CLE	77	44	33	0	269	247	16	21	76	38	38	0	331	330	39	31	153	82	71	0	600	577	55	52	56	115	117	80	112	108	90	90
DET	78	45	32	1	345	284	45	26	77	33	44	0	287	276	32	25	155	78	76	1	632	560	77	51	120	115	82	109	99	90	105	104
NY	77	54	23	0	321	241	60	33	78	44	33	1	348	301	40	27	155	98	56	1	669	542	100	60	136	144	94	90	115	96	96	94
PHI	79	27	51	1	261	387	14	36	76	22	54	0	236	330	12	37	155	49	105	1	497	717	26	73	97	45	115	107	81	112	101	106
STL	77	44	33	0	319	290	49	51	76	28	47	1	277	314	29	23	153	72	80	1	596	604	78	74	170	102	94	101	100	101	100	101
WAS	76	44	32	0	345	307	9	14	77	40	37	0	321	288	38	34	153	84	69	0	666	595	47	48	36	106	122	108	108	98	104	102
1944 AMERICAN LEAGUE																																
BOS	78	47	30	1	389	311	48	34	78	30	47	1	350	365	21	32	156	77	77	2	739	676	69	66	145	95	98	98	119	110	98	97
CHI	77	41	36	0	302	304	11	24	77	30	47	0	241	358	12	44	154	71	83	0	543	662	23	68	65	52	129	101	86	103	100	102
CLE	78	39	38	1	345	328	27	16	77	33	44	0	298	349	43	24	155	72	82	1	643	677	70	40	66	140	87	102	101	106	100	101
DET	78	43	34	1	325	318	38	21	78	45	32	1	333	263	22	18	156	88	66	2	658	581	60	39	140	82	57	108	98	88	105	104
NY	78	47	31	0	388	307	58	45	76	36	40	0	286	310	38	37	154	83	71	0	674	617	96	82	129	156	139	112	100	94	106	105
PHI	76	39	37	0	277	270	18	28	79	33	45	1	248	324	18	30	155	72	82	1	525	594	36	58	99	62	96	99	82	92	101	102
STL	77	54	23	0	368	272	45	24	77	35	42	0	316	315	27	34	154	89	65	0	684	587	72	58	112	118	101	102	107	93	102	100
WAS	77	40	37	0	286	268	9	13	77	24	53	0	306	396	24	35	154	64	90	0	592	664	33	48	40	79	110	80	106	115	89	91
1945 AMERICAN LEAGUE																																
BOS	78	42	35	1	306	299	22	28	79	29	48	2	293	375	28	30	157	71	83	3	599	674	50	58	88	97	111	92	104	114	95	96
CHI	74	44	29	1	305	277	8	34	76	27	49	0	291	356	14	29	150	71	78	1	596	633	22	63	100	42	110	93	107	112	95	96
CLE	77	44	33	0	292	273	27	15	70	29	39	2	265	275	38	24	147	73	72	2	557	548	65	39	65	150	96	96	99	97	99	98
DET	76	50	26	0	333	285	43	28	79	38	39	2	300	280	34	20	155	88	65	2	633	565	77	48	132	121	80	110	99	89	106	105
NY	76	48	28	0	395	297	65	51	76	33	43	0	281	309	28	15	152	81	71	0	676	606	93	66	223	111	76	115	106	97	107	106
PHI	77	39	35	3	265	270	16	21	76	13	63	0	229	368	17	34	153	52	98	3	494	638	33	55	73	72	110	88	89	110	94	96
STL	76	47	27	2	353	291	32	33	78	34	43	1	244	257	31	26	154	81	70	3	597	548	63	59	115	110	104	127	86	81	115	114
WAS	78	46	31	1	278	255	1	6	78	41	36	1	344	307	26	36	156	87	67	2	622	562	27	42	13	59	136	84	110	101	93	92
1946 AMERICAN LEAGUE																																
BOS	78	61	16	1	469	315	65	44	78	43	34	1	323	279	44	45	156	104	50	2	792	594	109	89	121	121	104	128	109	86	114	111
CHI	79	40	38	1	272	290	17	46	76	34	42	0	290	305	20	34	155	74	80	1	562	595	37	80	110	43	86	92	92	97	97	97
CLE	77	36	41	0	231	264	25	36	79	32	45	2	306	374	54	48	156	68	86	2	537	638	79	84	64	114	127	77	96	111	88	90
DET	79	48	30	1	391	300	75	68	76	44	32	0	313	267	33	29	155	92	62	1	704	567	108	97	194	90	82	114	103	86	108	105
NY	77	47	30	0	342	262	68	34	77	40	37	0	342	285	68	32	154	87	67	0	684	547	136	66	102	163	88	97	109	90	100	98
PHI	78	31	46	1	297	351	21	38	77	18	59	0	232	329	19	45	155	49	105	1	529	680	40	83	90	51	99	110	80	101	104	107
STL	77	35	41	1	313	344	46	29	79	31	47	1	308	366	38	44	156	66	88	2	621	710	84	73	94	105	91	99	100	113	98	100
WAS	76	38	38	0	253	343	16	25	79	38	40	1	355	363	44	56	155	76	78	1	608	706	60	81	46	97	130	88	104	120	92	94

	HOME								ROAD								ALL															
TM	G	W	L	T	R	OR	HR	OHR	G	W	L	T	R	OR	HR	OHR	G	W	L	T	R	OR	HR	OHR	HRF	HRB	HRP	RF	RB	RP	BPF	PPF
1947 AMERICAN LEAGUE																																
BOS	81	49	30	2	421	355	61	39	76	34	41	1	299	314	42	45	157	83	71	3	720	669	103	84	107	115	98	116	102	97	108	107
CHI	75	32	43	0	244	322	20	31	80	38	41	1	309	339	33	45	155	70	84	1	553	661	53	76	72	70	98	94	89	104	97	99
CLE	78	38	39	1	314	279	52	51	79	42	35	2	373	309	60	43	157	80	74	3	687	588	112	94	101	133	114	90	110	96	96	94
DET	80	46	31	3	370	345	62	47	78	39	38	1	344	297	41	32	158	85	69	4	714	642	103	79	138	99	78	108	105	95	104	103
NY	77	55	22	0	392	242	54	49	78	42	35	1	402	326	61	46	155	97	57	1	794	568	115	95	99	140	119	91	128	95	97	92
PHI	78	39	38	1	296	324	33	41	78	39	38	1	337	290	28	44	156	78	76	2	633	614	61	85	102	70	95	99	98	95	100	100
STL	77	29	48	0	286	401	52	57	77	30	47	0	278	343	38	46	154	59	95	0	564	744	90	103	124	98	111	108	87	110	102	105
WAS	77	36	41	0	244	326	10	20	77	28	49	0	252	349	32	43	154	64	90	0	496	675	42	63	43	63	98	95	80	105	97	101
1948 AMERICAN LEAGUE																																
BOS	78	55	23	0	481	336	60	43	77	41	36	0	426	384	61	40	155	96	59	0	907	720	121	83	102	134	97	101	124	101	100	97
CHI	76	27	48	1	278	378	21	36	78	24	53	1	281	436	34	53	154	51	101	2	559	814	55	89	69	73	112	93	81	112	95	100
CLE	79	48	30	1	398	272	77	41	77	49	28	0	442	296	78	41	156	97	58	1	840	568	155	82	98	175	102	91	116	82	99	94
DET	77	39	38	0	327	355	39	61	77	39	38	0	373	371	39	31	154	78	76	0	700	726	78	92	136	77	85	93	100	103	96	97
NY	77	50	27	0	413	315	70	54	77	44	33	0	444	318	69	40	154	94	60	0	857	633	139	94	113	151	107	97	118	90	100	96
PHI	77	36	41	0	347	396	33	47	77	48	29	0	382	339	35	39	154	84	70	0	729	735	68	86	107	74	90	103	99	99	101	102
STL	76	34	42	0	363	451	29	64	79	25	52	2	308	398	34	39	155	59	94	2	671	849	63	103	126	65	97	116	87	106	106	109
WAS	78	29	48	1	312	419	11	24	76	27	49	0	266	377	20	57	154	56	97	1	578	796	31	81	47	48	109	108	77	102	103	107
1949 AMERICAN LEAGUE																																
BOS	77	61	16	0	514	310	71	43	78	35	42	1	382	357	60	39	155	96	58	1	896	667	131	82	116	124	82	113	115	90	107	103
CHI	77	32	45	0	327	353	15	52	77	31	46	0	321	384	28	56	154	63	91	0	648	737	43	108	81	49	115	96	92	103	98	99
CLE	77	49	28	0	319	263	61	42	77	40	37	0	356	311	51	40	154	89	65	0	675	574	112	82	112	108	82	89	96	83	98	96
DET	78	50	27	1	402	350	57	60	77	37	40	0	349	305	31	42	155	87	67	1	751	655	88	102	148	72	85	112	96	85	108	106
NY	78	54	23	1	419	304	72	53	77	43	34	0	410	333	43	45	155	97	57	1	829	637	115	98	135	100	89	98	114	91	100	97
PHI	77	52	25	0	389	326	42	42	77	29	48	0	337	399	40	63	154	81	73	0	726	725	82	105	84	95	116	98	102	102	99	99
STL	77	36	41	0	394	426	69	56	78	17	60	1	273	487	48	57	155	53	101	1	667	913	117	113	116	115	113	106	92	122	100	104
WAS	77	26	51	0	254	426	20	14	77	24	53	0	330	442	61	65	154	50	104	0	584	868	81	79	29	133	117	88	88	126	91	96
1950 AMERICAN LEAGUE																																
BOS	77	55	22	0	625	427	100	67	77	39	38	0	402	377	61	54	154	94	60	0	1027	804	161	121	139	111	88	131	114	94	114	111
CHI	79	35	42	2	316	352	52	55	77	25	52	0	309	397	41	52	156	60	94	2	625	749	93	107	109	71	81	92	82	96	97	99
CLE	77	49	28	0	386	297	102	57	78	43	34	1	420	357	62	63	155	92	62	1	806	654	164	120	126	118	93	91	105	87	98	95
DET	81	50	30	1	405	346	60	72	76	45	29	2	432	367	54	69	157	95	59	3	837	713	114	141	102	93	113	91	110	95	97	95
NY	77	53	24	0	440	333	78	51	78	45	32	1	474	358	81	67	155	98	56	1	914	691	159	118	91	138	106	96	118	92	99	96
PHI	77	29	48	0	314	406	45	67	77	23	54	0	356	507	55	71	154	52	102	0	670	913	100	138	89	89	119	84	97	126	90	93
STL	74	27	47	0	368	484	52	69	80	31	49	0	316	432	54	60	154	58	96	0	684	916	106	129	111	84	99	118	83	107	107	111
WAS	78	35	42	1	347	407	18	28	77	32	45	0	343	406	58	71	155	67	87	1	690	813	76	99	38	84	112	99	89	103	99	101
1951 AMERICAN LEAGUE																																
BOS	75	50	25	0	460	348	80	65	79	37	42	0	344	377	47	35	154	87	67	0	804	725	127	100	169	90	72	116	104	96	108	106
CHI	78	39	38	1	334	310	28	47	77	42	35	0	380	334	58	62	155	81	73	1	714	644	86	109	65	97	124	90	103	94	97	95
CLE	77	53	24	0	324	249	76	42	78	40	37	1	372	345	64	44	155	93	61	1	696	594	140	86	110	123	81	84	103	89	94	93
DET	77	36	41	0	358	402	58	60	77	37	40	0	327	339	46	42	154	73	81	0	685	741	104	102	128	87	85	112	91	97	106	107
NY	78	56	22	0	366	258	72	43	76	42	34	0	432	363	68	49	154	98	56	0	798	621	140	92	98	134	93	80	123	98	91	88
PHI	79	38	41	0	406	407	54	59	75	32	43	0	330	338	48	50	154	70	84	0	736	745	102	109	108	94	100	113	97	98	106	106
STL	77	24	53	0	327	486	41	66	77	28	49	0	284	396	45	65	154	52	102	0	611	882	86	131	96	86	125	115	82	113	105	109
WAS	76	32	44	0	319	362	13	35	78	30	48	0	353	402	41	75	154	62	92	0	672	764	54	110	45	67	134	93	99	110	95	97
1952 AMERICAN LEAGUE																																
BOS	77	50	27	0	406	309	68	49	77	26	51	0	262	349	45	58	154	76	78	0	668	658	113	107	112	109	106	115	96	97	107	107
CHI	79	44	33	2	305	276	42	39	77	37	40	0	305	292	38	47	156	81	73	2	610	568	80	86	94	81	86	96	94	88	100	99
CLE	77	49	28	0	333	260	72	43	78	44	33	1	430	346	76	51	155	93	61	1	763	606	148	94	94	155	105	81	130	106	91	88
DET	77	32	45	0	284	366	65	59	79	18	59	2	273	372	38	52	156	50	104	2	557	738	103	111	132	89	97	101	86	110	99	103
NY	77	49	28	0	345	264	64	48	77	46	31	0	382	293	65	46	154	95	59	0	727	557	129	94	102	130	99	92	115	91	98	95
PHI	78	45	32	1	382	403	55	60	77	34	43	0	282	320	34	53	155	79	75	1	664	723	89	113	126	80	100	124	92	100	111	112
STL	78	42	35	1	321	346	47	52	77	22	55	0	283	387	35	59	155	64	90	1	604	733	82	111	103	83	108	98	96	114	97	100
WAS	78	42	35	1	299	292	13	18	79	36	41	2	299	316	37	60	157	78	76	3	598	608	50	78	35	71	101	98	91	92	100	100
1953 AMERICAN LEAGUE																																
BOS	76	38	38	0	335	354	57	59	77	46	31	0	321	278	44	33	153	84	69	0	656	632	101	92	144	75	67	115	89	85	109	108
CHI	78	41	36	1	349	328	30	56	78	48	29	1	367	264	44	57	156	89	65	2	716	592	74	113	87	70	104	107	97	82	106	103
CLE	78	53	24	1	379	272	90	46	77	39	38	0	391	355	70	46	155	92	62	1	770	627	160	92	115	133	83	88	117	97	95	93
DET	79	30	47	2	369	462	55	97	79	30	47	2	326	461	53	57	158	60	94	4	695	923	108	154	131	89	117	104	101	129	98	102
NY	77	50	27	0	347	255	64	39	74	49	25	0	454	292	75	55	151	99	52	0	801	547	139	94	80	143	101	81	128	93	93	88
PHI	78	27	50	1	299	447	49	74	79	32	45	2	333	352	67	47	157	59	95	3	632	799	116	121	107	102	105	108	89	108	102	105
STL	77	23	54	0	281	447	58	64	77	31	46	0	274	331	54	37	154	54	100	0	555	778	112	101	127	90	80	116	76	102	107	111
WAS	75	39	36	0	305	283	10	31	77	37	40	0	382	331	59	81	152	76	76	0	687	614	69	112	33	84	152	86	107	97	94	93
1954 AMERICAN LEAGUE																																
BAL	77	32	45	0	235	313	19	23	77	22	55	0	248	355	33	55	154	54	100	0	483	668	52	78	50	66	91	91	79	105	95	99
BOS	79	38	39	2	357	384	69	70	77	31	46	0	343	344	54	48	156	69	85	2	700	728	123	118	127	107	102	104	107	111	100	101
CHI	78	45	32	1	327	294	39	51	77	49	28	0	384	227	55	43	155	94	60	1	711	521	94	94	93	93	94	101	106	80	103	100
CLE	77	59	18	0	376	252	78	57	79	52	25	2	370	252	78	32	156	111	43	2	746	504	156	89	125	134	80	105	108	76	106	101
DET	77	35	42	0	285	336	44	80	78	33	44	1	299	328	46	58	155	68	86	1	584	664	90	138	117	85	122	100	90	101	100	101
NY	78	54	23	1	388	274	68	42	77	49	28	0	417	289	65	44	155	103	51	1	805	563	133	86	101	126	86	95	125	92	99	94
PHI	77	29	47	1	260	467	44	85	79	22	56	1	282	408	50	56	156	51	103	2	542	875	94	141	119	88	122	105	84	128	98	105
WAS	78	37	41	0	320	335	27	27	77	29	47	1	312	345	54	52	155	66	88	1	632	680	81	79	53	98	97	98	99	106	98	99
1955 AMERICAN LEAGUE																																
BAL	79	30	47	2	249	335	15	42	77	27	50	0	291	419	39	61	156	57	97	2	540	754	54	103	58	52	100	81	87	116	90	93
BOS	78	47	31	0	470	395	84	79	76	37	39	0	285	257	53	49	154	84	70	0	755	652	137	128	146	93	88	146	88	78	124	122
CHI	77	49	28	0	357	262	54	47	78	42	35	1	368	295	62	64	155	91	63	1	725	557	116	111	84	104	99	96	104	83	101	98
CLE	77	49	28	0	343	318	84	58	77	44	33	0	355	283	64	53	154	93	61	0	698	601	148	111	119	111	87	104	98	86	104	102
DET	77	46	31	0	386	301	81	59	77	33	44	0	389	357	49	67	154	79	75	0	775	658	130	126	118	99	99	93	117	101	97	95
KC	76	33	43	0	333	477	70	110	79	30	48	1	305	434	51	65	155	63	91	1	638	911	121	175	149	86	116	111	92	125	101	106
NY	77	52	25	0	378	248	89	44	77	44	33	0	384	321	86	64	154	96	58	0	762	569	175	108	91	153	100	91	114	88	98	94
WAS	77	28	49	0	282	357	20	25	77	25	52	0	316	432	60	74	154	53	101	0	598	789	80	99	36	94	114	86	96	122	91	94
1956 AMERICAN LEAGUE																																
BAL	77	41	36	0	275	315	35	39	77	28	49	0	296	390	56	60	154	69	85	0	571	705	91	99	66	78	84	87	85	102	94	96
BOS	78	43	34	1	408	388	68	64	77	41	36	0	372	363	71	66	155	84	70	1	780	751	139	130	96	105	99	106	105	102	103	102

	HOME								ROAD								ALL															
TM	G	W	L	T	R	OR	HR	OHR	G	W	L	T	R	OR	HR	OHR	G	W	L	T	R	OR	HR	OHR	HRF	HRB	HRP	RF	RB	RP	BPF	PPF
CHI	77	46	31	0	403	320	69	47	77	39	38	0	373	314	59	71	154	85	69	0	776	634	128	118	91	99	91	105	104	87	104	102
CLE	77	46	31	0	340	287	71	61	78	42	35	1	372	294	82	55	155	88	66	1	712	581	153	116	99	112	88	97	97	81	101	99
DET	78	37	40	1	359	357	75	77	77	45	32	0	430	342	75	63	155	82	72	1	789	699	150	140	108	108	101	93	113	102	97	95
KC	77	22	55	0	305	449	62	113	77	30	47	0	314	382	50	74	154	52	102	0	619	831	112	187	132	76	117	106	86	111	101	105
NY	77	49	28	0	412	303	88	48	77	48	29	0	445	328	102	66	154	97	57	0	857	631	190	114	84	152	98	95	121	93	99	95
WAS	77	32	45	0	354	481	63	95	78	27	50	1	298	443	49	76	155	59	95	1	652	924	112	171	122	77	112	111	89	120	102	107
1957 AMERICAN LEAGUE																																
BAL	77	42	33	2	283	248	36	30	77	34	43	0	314	340	51	65	154	76	76	2	597	588	87	95	60	83	85	83	99	97	93	93
BOS	77	44	33	0	408	360	72	67	77	38	39	0	313	308	81	49	154	82	72	0	721	668	153	116	106	115	90	120	100	94	110	109
CHI	77	45	32	0	347	263	40	59	78	45	32	1	360	303	66	65	155	90	64	1	707	566	106	124	80	90	105	95	109	89	99	97
CLE	77	40	37	0	348	384	71	74	76	36	40	0	334	338	69	56	153	76	77	0	682	722	140	130	112	104	97	106	104	109	102	102
DET	77	45	32	0	351	304	71	86	77	33	44	0	263	310	45	61	154	78	76	0	614	614	116	147	140	76	95	112	87	88	107	107
KC	77	37	40	0	294	344	91	77	77	22	54	1	269	366	75	76	154	59	94	1	563	710	166	153	109	128	120	99	88	107	99	102
NY	77	48	29	0	316	241	60	51	77	50	27	0	407	293	85	59	154	98	56	0	723	534	145	110	80	123	98	83	118	91	94	90
WAS	77	28	49	0	304	415	60	79	77	27	50	0	299	393	51	70	154	55	99	0	603	808	111	149	111	84	108	102	95	122	98	102
1958 AMERICAN LEAGUE																																
BAL	78	46	31	1	248	256	46	36	76	28	48	0	273	319	62	70	154	74	79	1	521	575	108	106	64	99	94	85	87	94	94	95
BOS	77	49	28	0	384	350	73	65	78	30	47	1	313	341	82	56	155	79	75	1	697	691	155	121	101	115	93	112	103	102	105	105
CHI	77	47	30	0	318	282	47	68	78	35	42	1	316	333	54	84	155	82	72	1	634	615	101	152	86	83	119	95	100	97	98	98
CLE	76	42	34	0	324	293	72	59	77	35	42	0	370	342	89	64	153	77	76	0	694	635	161	123	88	130	104	89	115	107	94	93
DET	77	43	34	0	348	306	59	79	77	34	43	0	311	300	50	54	154	77	77	0	659	606	109	133	127	73	86	106	99	92	104	103
KC	78	43	34	1	365	363	88	96	78	30	47	1	277	350	50	54	156	73	81	2	642	713	138	150	161	80	86	114	93	103	105	107
NY	78	44	33	1	362	318	78	62	77	48	29	0	397	259	86	54	155	92	62	1	759	577	164	116	100	122	91	103	114	90	103	99
WAS	78	33	44	1	269	373	49	80	78	28	49	1	284	374	72	76	156	61	93	2	553	747	121	156	88	98	124	97	88	115	97	100
1959 AMERICAN LEAGUE																																
BAL	78	38	39	1	260	299	53	50	77	36	41	0	291	322	56	61	155	74	80	1	551	621	109	111	88	82	83	91	84	94	97	98
BOS	77	43	34	0	404	356	62	66	77	32	45	0	322	340	63	69	154	75	79	0	726	696	125	135	97	93	100	113	102	99	106	105
CHI	78	47	30	1	313	272	44	61	78	47	30	1	356	316	53	68	156	94	60	2	669	588	97	129	89	73	95	89	102	91	97	95
CLE	77	43	34	0	346	316	84	74	77	46	31	0	399	330	83	74	154	89	65	0	745	646	167	148	101	124	112	93	115	102	97	95
DET	77	41	36	0	401	411	95	105	77	35	42	0	312	321	65	72	154	76	78	0	713	732	160	177	138	102	112	124	96	98	111	111
KC	77	37	40	0	362	386	58	80	77	29	48	0	319	374	59	68	154	66	88	0	681	760	117	148	107	84	103	106	100	110	101	103
NY	77	40	37	0	293	305	63	45	78	39	38	1	394	342	90	75	155	79	75	1	687	647	153	120	69	131	104	84	109	104	93	92
WAS	77	34	43	0	307	360	83	68	77	29	48	0	312	341	80	55	154	63	91	0	619	701	163	123	109	114	88	101	92	103	100	102
1960 AMERICAN LEAGUE																																
BAL	77	44	33	0	332	313	50	52	77	45	32	0	350	293	73	65	154	89	65	0	682	606	123	117	77	100	96	101	99	89	102	101
BOS	77	36	41	0	347	413	65	69	77	29	48	0	311	362	59	58	154	65	89	0	658	775	124	127	112	86	87	110	94	109	103	105
CHI	77	51	26	0	379	298	57	54	77	36	41	0	362	319	55	73	154	87	67	0	741	617	112	127	89	87	96	100	108	92	101	99
CLE	77	39	38	0	315	351	62	84	77	37	40	0	352	342	65	77	154	76	78	0	667	693	127	161	102	95	117	96	101	104	98	98
DET	77	40	37	0	322	323	78	85	77	31	46	0	311	321	72	56	154	71	83	0	633	644	150	141	123	101	94	101	92	94	102	102
KC	78	34	43	1	327	369	58	79	77	24	53	0	288	387	52	81	155	58	96	1	615	756	110	160	100	82	114	100	92	110	99	101
NY	77	55	22	0	350	273	92	52	78	42	35	1	396	354	101	71	155	97	57	1	746	627	193	123	88	150	102	87	116	100	94	92
WAS	77	32	45	0	336	366	75	74	77	41	36	0	336	330	72	56	154	73	81	0	672	696	147	130	114	101	90	104	98	101	102	102
1961 AMERICAN LEAGUE																																
BAL	82	48	33	1	320	283	61	46	81	47	34	0	371	305	88	63	163	95	67	1	691	588	149	109	73	108	81	90	96	83	97	96
BOS	82	50	31	1	401	386	63	91	81	26	55	0	328	406	49	76	163	76	86	1	729	792	112	167	119	67	96	105	97	105	102	103
CHI	81	53	28	0	411	320	80	55	82	33	48	1	354	406	58	103	163	86	76	1	765	726	138	158	86	98	107	98	105	100	99	99
CLE	81	40	41	0	342	380	74	98	80	38	42	0	395	372	76	80	161	78	83	0	737	752	150	178	108	97	112	93	105	107	96	97
DET	82	50	31	1	389	324	90	95	81	51	30	0	452	347	90	75	163	101	61	1	841	671	180	170	111	112	106	90	119	97	96	94
KC	80	33	47	0	365	434	33	61	82	28	53	1	318	429	57	80	162	61	100	1	683	863	90	141	72	66	102	107	91	113	102	104
LA	82	46	36	0	447	421	122	126	80	24	55	1	297	363	67	54	162	70	91	1	744	784	189	180	181	90	83	124	90	96	111	112
MIN	81	36	44	1	380	423	92	89	80	34	46	0	327	355	75	74	161	70	90	1	707	778	167	163	117	102	100	114	91	99	106	107
NY	81	65	16	0	411	251	112	59	82	44	37	1	416	361	128	78	163	109	53	1	827	612	240	137	87	166	101	89	117	88	96	93
WAS	79	33	46	0	288	366	34	53	82	28	54	0	330	410	85	78	161	61	100	1	618	776	119	131	57	93	109	91	89	109	95	97
1962 AMERICAN LEAGUE																																
BAL	82	44	38	0	328	299	66	65	80	33	47	0	324	381	90	82	162	77	85	0	652	680	156	147	76	113	108	88	96	99	95	95
BOS	79	39	40	0	369	377	72	76	81	37	44	0	338	379	74	83	160	76	84	0	707	756	146	159	97	97	105	106	97	104	102	103
CHI	81	43	38	0	315	319	36	58	81	42	39	0	392	339	56	65	162	85	77	0	707	658	92	123	80	63	84	88	103	97	95	94
CLE	81	43	38	0	348	350	103	89	81	37	44	0	334	395	77	85	162	80	82	0	682	745	180	174	116	108	106	96	97	105	98	99
DET	82	49	33	0	448	368	117	91	79	36	43	0	310	324	92	78	161	85	76	0	758	692	209	169	116	126	105	121	95	88	111	110
KC	81	39	42	0	387	423	64	118	81	33	48	0	358	414	52	81	162	72	90	0	745	837	116	199	131	66	107	104	103	115	100	101
LA	81	40	41	0	357	368	50	50	81	46	35	0	361	338	87	68	162	86	76	0	718	706	137	118	67	101	90	104	98	96	102	102
MIN	82	45	36	1	417	378	97	97	81	46	35	0	381	335	88	69	163	91	71	1	798	713	185	166	120	109	98	109	105	95	105	104
NY	80	50	30	0	369	306	92	67	82	46	36	0	448	374	107	79	162	96	66	0	817	680	199	146	90	135	102	86	121	103	94	92
WAS	80	27	53	0	293	364	65	79	82	33	48	1	306	352	67	72	162	60	101	1	599	716	132	151	104	83	94	101	83	97	101	102
1963 AMERICAN LEAGUE																																
BAL	81	48	33	0	311	268	72	56	81	38	43	0	333	353	74	81	162	86	76	0	644	621	146	137	84	106	99	86	104	100	94	93
BOS	80	44	36	0	383	346	95	73	81	32	49	0	283	358	76	79	161	76	85	0	666	704	171	152	108	111	100	113	95	101	106	106
CHI	82	49	33	0	362	272	63	46	80	45	35	0	321	272	51	54	162	94	68	0	683	544	114	100	102	73	65	105	99	81	104	102
CLE	81	41	40	0	308	341	88	87	81	38	43	0	327	361	81	89	162	79	83	0	635	702	169	176	103	114	118	95	99	109	97	98
DET	81	47	34	0	395	339	94	109	81	32	49	0	305	364	54	86	162	79	83	0	700	703	148	195	139	84	111	109	102	103	104	104
KC	81	36	45	0	326	390	52	87	81	37	44	0	289	314	43	69	162	73	89	0	615	704	95	156	121	58	91	116	87	98	107	109
LA	81	39	42	0	264	306	24	44	80	31	49	0	333	354	71	76	161	70	91	0	597	660	95	120	48	80	108	83	99	109	91	92
MIN	81	48	33	0	377	306	112	99	80	43	37	0	390	296	113	63	161	91	70	0	767	602	225	162	117	143	105	99	116	94	100	98
NY	80	58	22	0	367	246	88	55	81	46	35	0	347	301	100	60	161	104	57	0	714	547	188	115	93	128	83	98	108	85	101	98
WAS	80	31	49	0	286	406	63	82	82	25	57	0	292	406	75	94	162	56	106	0	578	812	138	176	88	100	125	100	89	121	98	101
1964 AMERICAN LEAGUE																																
BAL	82	49	32	1	351	296	79	64	81	48	33	0	328	271	83	65	163	97	65	1	679	567	162	129	97	104	85	107	98	83	105	103
BOS	81	45	36	0	393	382	100	87	81	27	54	0	295	411	86	91	162	72	90	0	688	793	186	178	104	120	116	108	102	117	102	103
CHI	81	52	29	0	306	213	43	42	81	46	35	0	336	288	63	82	162	98	64	0	642	501	106	124	62	84	93	86	103	81	95	93
CLE	82	41	40	1	365	351	84	82	82	38	43	1	324	342	80	72	164	79	83	2	689	693	164	154	108	101	95	107	101	101	103	103
DET	82	46	35	1	340	320	85	89	81	39	42	0	359	358	72	75	163	85	77	1	699	678	157	164	115	94	98	92	111	108	96	95
KC	81	26	55	0	330	455	107	132	82	31	50	1	291	381	59	88	163	57	105	1	621	836	166	220	153	86	114	115	90	117	105	108
LA	81	45	36	0	230	226	32	31	81	37	44	0	314	325	70	69	162	82	80	0	544	551	102	100	48	85	83	74	93	94	89	89
MIN	82	40	41	1	386	336	115	88	81	39	42	0	351	342	106	93	163	79	83	1	737	678	221	181	101	145	122	102	110	103	101	100
NY	81	50	31	0	363	290	69	56	83	49	32	2	367	287	93	73	164	99	63	2	730	577	162	129	80	113	92	103	106	86	103	101

	HOME								ROAD								ALL															
TM	G	W	L	T	R	OR	HR	OHR	G	W	L	T	R	OR	HR	OHR	G	W	L	T	R	OR	HR	OHR	HRF	HRB	HRP	RF	RB	RP	BPF	PPF
WAS	81	31	50	0	294	380	71	95	81	31	50	0	284	353	54	77	162	62	100	0	578	733	125	172	122	73	98	104	87	108	101	103
1965 AMERICAN LEAGUE																																
BAL	79	46	33	0	302	282	62	71	83	48	35	0	339	296	63	49	162	94	68	0	641	578	125	120	123	82	77	98	100	91	100	99
BOS	81	34	47	0	375	433	94	88	81	28	53	0	294	358	71	70	162	62	100	0	669	791	165	158	124	109	105	120	97	113	107	109
CAL	80	46	34	0	265	254	36	35	82	29	53	0	262	315	56	56	162	75	87	0	527	569	92	91	67	77	76	93	85	90	98	98
CHI	81	48	33	0	288	241	45	51	81	47	34	0	359	314	80	71	162	95	67	0	647	555	125	122	67	107	107	81	110	96	92	90
CLE	82	52	30	0	342	287	90	58	80	35	45	0	321	326	66	71	162	87	75	0	663	613	156	129	105	110	94	96	106	98	98	97
DET	81	47	34	0	362	310	96	85	81	42	39	0	318	292	66	52	162	89	73	0	680	602	162	137	146	96	82	110	101	91	105	104
KC	81	33	48	0	301	365	47	68	81	26	55	0	284	390	63	93	162	59	103	0	585	755	110	161	75	94	132	98	95	119	97	100
MIN	81	51	30	0	379	308	67	89	81	51	30	0	395	292	83	77	162	102	60	0	774	600	150	166	99	113	123	101	120	95	101	98
NY	83	40	43	0	320	306	77	63	79	37	42	0	291	298	72	63	162	77	85	0	611	604	149	126	99	109	93	101	95	94	101	101
WAS	81	36	45	0	302	366	62	86	81	34	47	0	289	355	74	74	162	70	92	0	591	721	136	160	99	101	117	103	92	111	100	102
1966 AMERICAN LEAGUE																																
BAL	79	48	31	0	375	296	85	65	81	49	32	0	380	305	90	62	160	97	63	0	755	601	175	127	102	127	96	101	120	98	101	98
BOS	81	40	41	0	374	397	80	97	81	32	49	0	281	334	65	67	162	72	90	0	655	731	145	164	129	94	104	122	95	105	109	110
CAL	81	42	39	0	303	315	54	67	81	38	43	0	301	328	68	69	162	80	82	0	604	643	122	136	89	94	104	98	97	102	99	100
CHI	81	45	36	0	273	217	31	36	82	38	43	1	301	300	56	65	163	83	79	1	574	517	87	101	59	76	87	84	96	87	94	93
CLE	81	41	40	0	283	300	82	65	81	40	41	0	291	286	73	64	162	81	81	0	574	586	155	129	107	109	92	101	90	91	101	102
DET	81	42	39	0	360	374	97	101	81	46	35	0	359	324	82	84	162	88	74	0	719	698	179	185	118	125	128	107	112	108	102	102
KC	81	42	39	0	284	292	18	27	79	32	47	0	280	356	52	79	160	74	86	0	564	648	70	106	36	74	107	89	97	109	94	95
MIN	81	49	32	0	375	311	94	83	81	40	41	0	288	270	50	56	162	89	73	0	663	581	144	139	157	80	80	121	94	84	111	110
NY	82	35	46	1	302	280	74	63	78	35	43	0	309	332	88	61	160	70	89	1	611	612	162	124	88	126	100	87	105	105	94	94
WAS	78	42	36	0	273	292	62	84	81	29	52	0	284	367	64	70	159	71	88	0	557	659	126	154	111	90	108	91	95	110	95	96
1967 AMERICAN LEAGUE																																
BAL	77	35	42	0	283	275	64	49	84	41	43	0	371	317	74	67	161	76	85	0	654	592	138	116	88	123	105	89	116	106	95	94
BOS	81	49	32	0	408	355	90	88	81	43	38	0	314	259	68	54	162	92	70	0	722	614	158	142	140	113	101	130	105	91	115	113
CAL	83	53	30	0	288	276	56	59	78	31	47	0	279	311	58	59	161	84	77	0	567	587	114	118	93	99	102	91	100	103	96	96
CHI	82	49	33	0	243	222	38	38	80	40	40	0	288	269	51	49	162	89	73	0	531	491	89	87	76	81	80	83	95	88	94	93
CLE	81	36	45	0	274	316	76	69	81	39	42	0	285	297	55	51	162	75	87	0	559	613	131	120	131	94	87	101	93	101	100	101
DET	82	52	29	1	360	272	83	79	81	39	42	0	323	315	69	72	163	91	71	1	683	587	152	151	113	122	122	99	114	99	99	98
KC	81	37	44	0	288	320	19	38	80	25	55	0	245	340	50	87	161	62	99	0	533	660	69	125	43	80	140	101	90	109	100	102
MIN	81	52	29	0	372	292	70	63	83	39	42	2	299	298	61	52	164	91	71	2	671	590	131	115	119	98	87	113	103	93	107	106
NY	82	43	38	1	268	271	60	47	81	29	52	0	254	350	40	63	163	72	90	1	522	621	100	110	102	81	89	89	92	107	94	96
WAS	80	40	40	0	277	332	57	54	81	36	45	0	273	305	58	59	161	76	85	0	550	637	115	113	96	98	96	106	90	103	102	104
1968 AMERICAN LEAGUE																																
BAL	80	47	33	0	288	248	57	54	82	44	38	0	291	249	76	47	162	91	71	0	579	497	133	101	94	123	97	102	103	89	102	101
BOS	81	46	35	0	325	299	58	61	81	40	41	0	289	312	67	54	162	86	76	0	614	611	125	115	99	115	107	104	111	110	101	101
CAL	81	32	49	0	229	299	49	66	81	35	46	0	269	316	34	65	162	67	95	0	498	615	83	131	113	71	109	90	96	116	94	96
CHI	81	36	45	0	225	273	29	47	81	31	50	0	238	254	42	50	162	67	95	0	463	527	71	97	83	69	93	100	83	94	101	102
CLE	81	43	37	1	246	262	36	56	81	43	38	0	270	242	39	42	162	86	75	1	516	504	75	98	112	64	80	100	93	91	101	101
DET	81	56	25	0	348	254	107	75	83	47	34	2	323	238	78	54	164	103	59	2	671	492	185	129	138	143	104	110	113	85	106	103
MIN	81	41	40	0	299	290	50	51	81	38	43	0	263	256	55	41	162	79	83	0	562	546	105	92	105	92	81	112	96	94	106	106
NY	82	39	42	1	268	268	56	50	82	44	37	1	268	263	53	49	164	83	79	2	536	531	109	99	104	95	87	101	95	94	101	101
OAK	83	44	38	1	296	258	38	58	80	38	42	0	273	286	56	66	163	82	80	1	569	544	94	124	78	96	125	96	104	100	98	98
WAS	81	34	47	0	257	300	53	53	80	31	49	0	267	365	71	65	161	65	96	0	524	665	124	118	78	129	124	87	105	129	91	94
1969 AMERICAN LEAGUE																																
BAL	81	60	21	0	402	251	82	51	81	49	32	0	377	266	93	66	162	109	53	0	779	517	175	117	86	135	93	103	113	78	104	100
BOS	81	46	35	0	392	391	105	78	81	41	40	0	351	345	92	77	162	87	75	0	743	736	197	155	108	140	113	112	107	106	105	105
CAL	81	43	38	0	277	305	49	65	82	28	53	1	251	347	39	61	163	71	91	1	528	652	88	126	113	59	83	98	80	97	99	101
CHI	81	41	40	0	352	387	61	80	81	27	54	0	273	336	51	66	162	68	94	0	625	723	112	146	118	75	96	118	87	100	108	110
CLE	81	33	48	0	276	341	56	60	80	29	51	0	297	376	63	74	161	62	99	0	573	717	119	134	84	95	106	90	92	113	94	96
DET	81	46	35	0	361	305	104	72	81	44	37	0	340	296	78	56	162	90	72	0	701	601	182	128	129	115	84	105	102	89	103	102
KC	82	36	45	1	301	362	39	63	81	33	48	0	285	326	59	73	163	69	93	1	586	688	98	136	77	79	109	106	86	99	103	104
MIN	81	57	24	0	414	298	79	61	81	40	41	0	376	320	84	58	162	97	65	0	790	618	163	119	100	118	88	103	117	93	102	100
NY	80	48	32	0	284	245	44	51	82	32	49	1	278	342	50	67	162	80	81	1	562	587	94	118	84	73	90	88	89	92	95	96
OAK	81	49	32	0	330	315	73	70	81	39	42	0	410	363	75	93	162	88	74	0	740	678	148	163	87	118	128	85	121	112	92	91
SEA	82	34	47	1	329	399	74	93	81	30	51	0	310	400	51	79	163	64	98	1	639	799	125	172	123	82	111	100	97	120	98	100
WAS	81	47	34	0	353	290	77	62	81	39	42	0	341	354	71	73	162	86	76	0	694	644	148	135	97	109	100	93	108	101	97	96
1970 AMERICAN LEAGUE																																
BAL	81	59	22	0	386	256	88	58	81	49	32	0	406	318	91	81	162	108	54	0	792	574	179	139	87	132	104	91	121	90	97	94
BOS	81	52	29	0	455	382	117	75	81	35	46	0	331	340	86	81	162	87	75	0	786	722	203	156	114	131	105	123	105	98	111	110
CAL	81	43	38	0	287	274	41	59	81	43	38	0	344	356	73	95	162	86	76	0	631	630	114	154	62	97	129	82	102	102	91	91
CHI	84	31	53	0	346	469	78	97	78	25	53	0	287	353	45	67	162	56	106	0	633	822	123	164	138	70	94	115	89	112	106	108
CLE	81	43	38	0	386	370	133	103	81	33	48	0	263	305	50	60	162	76	86	0	649	675	183	163	195	82	80	129	83	87	115	115
DET	81	42	39	0	348	379	86	86	81	37	44	0	318	352	62	67	162	79	83	0	666	731	148	153	130	89	92	108	96	104	103	104
KC	79	35	44	0	305	331	46	48	83	30	53	0	306	374	51	90	162	65	97	0	611	705	97	138	71	79	105	97	92	105	98	100
MIL	81	38	42	1	313	362	68	72	82	27	55	0	300	389	58	74	163	65	97	1	613	751	126	146	106	84	96	98	92	111	98	100
MIN	81	51	30	0	366	285	66	53	81	47	34	0	378	320	87	77	162	98	64	0	744	605	153	130	75	119	102	95	112	93	98	97
NY	81	53	28	0	317	257	60	40	82	40	41	1	363	355	51	90	163	93	69	1	680	612	111	130	74	89	96	83	109	98	92	91
OAK	81	49	32	0	337	265	83	56	81	40	41	0	341	328	88	78	162	89	73	0	678	593	171	134	85	127	101	91	104	92	97	96
WAS	81	40	41	0	303	330	72	61	81	30	51	0	323	359	66	78	162	70	92	0	626	689	138	139	92	99	99	93	96	105	96	97
1971 AMERICAN LEAGUE																																
BAL	77	53	24	0	374	254	78	67	81	48	33	0	368	276	80	58	158	101	57	0	742	530	158	125	111	124	100	104	118	87	103	100
BOS	80	47	33	0	375	338	88	75	82	38	44	0	316	329	73	61	162	85	77	0	691	667	161	136	122	118	101	112	104	101	106	105
CAL	81	35	46	0	233	297	39	55	81	41	40	0	278	279	57	46	162	76	86	0	511	576	96	101	92	78	83	95	83	93	98	99
CHI	81	39	42	0	278	310	60	53	81	40	41	0	339	287	78	47	162	79	83	0	617	597	138	100	91	114	85	94	101	98	98	97
CLE	81	29	52	0	297	400	62	99	81	31	50	0	246	347	47	55	162	60	102	0	543	747	109	154	149	73	97	114	82	110	106	108
DET	81	54	27	0	352	289	90	70	81	37	44	0	349	356	89	56	162	91	71	0	701	645	179	126	110	138	100	92	117	108	96	95
KC	81	44	37	0	296	277	23	36	80	41	39	0	307	289	57	48	161	85	76	0	603	566	80	84	58	76	86	96	98	93	99	98
MIL	82	34	48	0	282	319	46	64	79	35	44	0	252	290	58	66	161	69	92	0	534	609	104	130	86	91	112	105	83	94	103	104
MIN	79	37	42	0	332	356	57	71	81	37	44	0	322	314	59	68	160	74	86	0	654	670	116	139	103	94	111	110	102	104	104	104
NY	81	44	37	0	327	297	39	61	81	38	43	0	321	344	58	65	162	82	80	0	648	641	97	126	83	85	109	94	107	106	97	97
OAK	81	46	35	0	325	300	84	74	80	55	25	0	366	264	76	57	161	101	60	0	691	564	160	131	117	120	100	99	110	92	100	99
WAS	81	35	46	0	268	296	34	59	78	28	50	0	269	364	52	73	159	63	96	0	537	660	86	132	73	82	123	86	95	114	92	94

	HOME								ROAD								ALL															
TM	G	W	L	T	R	OR	HR	OHR	G	W	L	T	R	OR	HR	OHR	G	W	L	T	R	OR	HR	OHR	HRF	HRB	HRP	RF	RB	RP	BPF	PPF
1972 AMERICAN LEAGUE																																
BAL	77	38	39	0	240	211	44	40	77	42	35	0	279	219	56	45	154	80	74	0	519	430	100	85	85	110	95	91	100	84	98	96
BOS	78	52	26	0	373	303	71	49	77	33	44	0	267	317	53	52	155	85	70	0	640	620	124	101	112	119	100	113	112	111	105	105
CAL	80	44	36	0	221	218	30	31	75	31	44	0	233	315	48	59	155	75	80	0	454	533	78	90	55	104	115	77	97	110	88	90
CHI	78	55	23	0	341	252	65	44	76	32	44	0	225	286	43	50	154	87	67	0	566	538	108	94	114	103	92	113	99	96	106	106
CLE	77	43	34	0	263	261	59	79	79	29	50	0	209	258	32	44	156	72	84	0	472	519	91	123	173	68	91	113	81	89	107	108
DET	78	44	34	0	312	288	68	67	78	42	36	0	246	226	54	34	156	86	70	0	558	514	122	101	148	102	82	125	91	85	113	112
KC	77	44	33	0	309	257	29	28	77	32	45	0	271	288	49	57	154	76	78	0	580	545	78	85	56	102	108	101	108	102	100	100
MIL	79	37	42	0	243	286	36	45	77	28	49	0	250	309	52	71	156	65	91	0	493	595	88	116	66	111	141	92	96	114	95	97
MIN	74	42	32	0	299	255	52	54	80	35	45	0	238	280	41	51	154	77	77	0	537	535	93	105	122	87	97	114	94	94	107	107
NY	77	46	31	0	270	219	53	37	78	33	45	0	287	308	50	50	155	79	76	0	557	527	103	87	92	109	92	85	113	106	92	92
OAK	77	48	29	0	287	210	68	52	78	45	33	0	317	247	66	44	155	93	62	0	604	457	134	96	111	130	96	91	116	90	97	94
TEX	77	31	46	0	235	288	33	41	77	23	54	0	226	340	23	51	154	54	100	0	461	628	56	92	98	58	91	92	92	121	94	97
1973 AMERICAN LEAGUE																																
BAL	81	50	31	0	408	284	63	60	81	47	34	0	346	277	56	64	162	97	65	0	754	561	119	124	103	90	94	111	101	77	107	105
BOS	81	48	33	0	390	339	83	83	81	41	40	0	348	308	64	75	162	89	73	0	738	647	147	158	118	106	114	111	101	89	106	105
CAL	81	43	38	0	316	294	41	49	81	36	45	0	313	363	52	55	162	79	83	0	629	657	93	104	85	76	85	91	95	98	96	96
CHI	81	40	41	0	329	368	56	58	81	37	44	0	323	337	55	52	162	77	85	0	652	705	111	110	106	82	81	105	92	99	102	103
CLE	81	34	47	0	320	427	92	100	81	37	44	0	360	399	66	72	162	71	91	0	680	826	158	172	134	107	116	98	101	121	97	99
DET	81	47	34	0	329	332	86	71	81	38	43	0	313	342	71	83	162	85	77	0	642	674	157	154	102	122	120	101	92	96	101	101
KC	81	48	33	0	422	404	54	61	81	40	41	0	333	348	60	53	162	88	74	0	755	752	114	114	102	86	86	120	100	100	109	109
MIL	81	40	41	0	349	343	73	52	81	34	47	0	359	388	72	67	162	74	88	0	708	731	145	119	90	117	97	93	107	110	96	96
MIN	81	37	44	0	357	386	56	60	81	44	37	0	381	306	64	55	162	81	81	0	738	692	120	115	98	93	89	107	103	97	104	103
NY	81	50	31	0	359	263	74	42	81	30	51	0	282	347	57	67	162	80	82	0	641	610	131	109	94	103	86	99	92	88	101	100
OAK	81	50	31	0	313	253	70	70	81	44	37	0	445	362	77	73	162	94	68	0	758	615	147	143	95	118	115	73	125	104	87	85
TEX	81	35	46	0	321	408	47	51	81	22	59	0	298	436	63	79	162	57	105	0	619	844	110	130	70	101	116	98	92	122	97	100
1974 AMERICAN LEAGUE																																
BAL	81	46	35	0	281	293	48	46	81	45	36	0	378	319	68	55	162	91	71	0	659	612	116	101	78	112	100	84	107	100	93	92
BOS	81	46	35	0	375	348	58	66	81	38	43	0	321	313	51	60	162	84	78	0	696	661	109	126	111	91	105	113	98	94	107	106
CAL	81	36	45	0	291	287	46	47	82	32	49	1	327	370	49	54	163	68	94	1	618	657	95	101	91	86	90	84	100	106	92	93
CHI	82	46	34	2	360	365	66	43	81	34	46	1	324	356	69	60	163	80	80	3	684	721	135	103	85	127	98	105	101	106	102	102
CLE	81	40	41	0	338	349	72	92	81	37	44	0	324	345	59	46	162	77	85	0	662	694	131	138	149	96	96	102	99	103	101	101
DET	81	36	45	0	335	412	74	84	81	36	45	0	285	356	57	64	162	72	90	0	620	768	131	148	127	104	116	114	88	107	106	108
KC	81	40	41	0	355	353	38	42	81	37	44	0	312	309	51	49	162	77	85	0	667	662	89	91	81	84	86	112	95	94	106	106
MIL	81	40	41	0	342	329	58	69	81	36	45	0	305	331	62	57	162	76	86	0	647	660	120	126	106	104	108	105	95	97	102	103
MIN	82	48	33	1	365	317	60	56	81	34	47	0	308	352	51	59	163	82	80	1	673	669	111	115	104	95	98	102	100	99	101	101
NY	81	47	34	0	315	295	42	50	81	42	39	0	356	328	59	54	162	89	73	0	671	623	101	104	83	95	99	90	106	99	96	95
OAK	81	49	32	0	345	265	69	43	81	41	40	0	344	286	63	47	162	90	72	0	689	551	132	90	102	112	79	98	103	84	100	99
TEX	80	42	38	0	321	340	43	57	81	42	38	1	369	358	56	69	161	84	76	1	690	698	99	126	83	96	121	93	109	110	96	96
1975 AMERICAN LEAGUE																																
BAL	77	44	33	0	282	231	46	45	82	46	36	0	400	322	78	65	159	90	69	0	682	553	124	110	70	118	107	78	109	90	91	89
BOS	81	47	34	0	427	399	74	83	79	48	31	0	369	310	60	62	160	95	65	0	796	709	134	145	124	100	107	118	107	95	109	108
CAL	81	35	46	0	294	349	24	52	80	37	43	0	334	374	31	71	161	72	89	0	628	723	55	123	75	51	108	90	96	109	95	96
CHI	81	42	39	0	350	359	42	54	80	33	47	0	305	344	52	53	161	75	86	0	655	703	94	107	91	79	90	107	91	98	103	104
CLE	80	41	39	0	331	367	79	85	79	38	41	0	357	336	74	51	159	79	80	0	688	703	153	136	126	114	100	99	101	103	99	100
DET	80	31	49	0	301	421	63	83	79	26	53	0	269	365	62	54	159	57	102	0	570	786	125	137	120	96	102	110	80	108	104	106
KC	81	51	30	0	377	309	46	45	81	40	41	0	333	340	72	63	162	91	71	0	710	649	118	108	70	111	103	102	100	92	102	101
MIL	81	36	45	0	348	398	72	63	81	32	49	0	327	394	74	70	162	68	94	0	675	792	146	133	93	124	114	102	97	112	100	101
MIN	82	39	43	0	401	410	75	88	77	37	40	0	323	326	46	49	159	76	83	0	724	736	121	137	153	79	88	115	99	100	107	107
NY	78	43	35	0	323	276	50	56	82	40	42	0	358	312	60	48	160	83	77	0	681	588	110	104	103	88	83	95	100	88	99	98
OAK	81	54	27	0	366	247	75	43	81	44	37	0	392	359	76	59	162	98	64	0	758	606	151	102	89	128	89	84	118	95	93	91
TEX	80	39	41	0	349	366	52	70	82	40	42	0	365	367	82	53	162	79	83	0	714	733	134	123	93	112	105	100	103	106	99	100
1976 AMERICAN LEAGUE																																
BAL	81	42	39	0	280	306	58	38	81	46	35	0	339	292	61	42	162	88	74	0	619	598	119	80	94	129	90	94	97	95	98	97
BOS	81	46	35	0	408	352	71	61	81	37	44	0	308	308	63	48	162	83	79	0	716	660	134	109	117	134	110	121	99	93	110	110
CAL	81	38	43	0	249	284	24	35	81	38	43	0	301	347	39	60	162	76	86	0	550	631	63	95	61	83	121	83	92	104	92	93
CHI	80	35	45	0	300	369	31	34	81	29	52	0	286	376	42	53	161	64	97	0	586	745	73	87	70	92	106	101	92	114	99	101
CLE	79	44	35	0	311	295	40	43	80	37	43	0	304	320	45	37	159	81	78	0	615	615	85	80	102	90	85	99	97	97	100	100
DET	80	36	44	0	305	381	51	62	81	38	43	0	304	328	50	39	161	74	87	0	609	709	101	101	125	98	96	109	91	105	103	105
KC	81	49	32	0	368	287	37	35	81	41	40	0	345	324	28	48	162	90	72	0	713	611	65	83	96	70	87	99	110	96	100	98
MIL	81	36	45	0	292	321	45	43	80	30	50	0	278	334	43	56	161	66	95	0	570	655	88	99	88	101	112	98	89	101	99	100
MIN	81	44	37	0	368	348	34	52	81	41	40	0	375	356	47	37	162	85	77	0	743	704	81	89	102	85	92	98	116	111	98	98
NY	80	45	35	0	349	294	67	51	79	52	27	0	381	281	53	46	159	97	62	0	730	575	120	97	117	120	100	97	115	93	99	97
OAK	81	51	30	0	353	284	56	57	80	36	44	0	333	314	57	39	161	87	74	0	686	598	113	96	115	114	96	98	107	94	100	98
TEX	81	39	42	0	319	330	40	57	81	37	44	0	297	322	40	49	162	76	86	0	616	652	80	106	108	83	107	104	93	98	102	103
1977 AMERICAN LEAGUE																																
BAL	81	54	27	0	356	269	74	62	80	43	37	0	363	384	74	62	161	97	64	0	719	653	148	124	100	102	87	85	107	96	93	92
BOS	80	51	29	0	495	407	124	95	81	46	35	0	364	305	89	63	161	97	64	0	859	712	213	158	143	124	93	134	100	84	117	116
CAL	81	39	42	0	320	321	69	65	81	35	46	0	355	374	62	71	162	74	88	0	675	695	131	136	100	90	94	88	97	100	95	95
CHI	81	48	33	0	434	370	85	58	81	42	39	0	410	401	107	78	162	90	72	0	844	771	192	136	79	149	108	100	116	106	99	99
CLE	81	37	44	0	339	357	54	66	80	34	46	0	337	382	46	70	161	71	90	0	676	739	100	136	101	69	92	95	95	103	98	98
DET	81	39	42	0	369	401	81	100	81	35	46	0	345	350	85	62	162	74	88	0	714	751	166	162	121	107	102	109	93	97	105	105
KC	81	55	26	0	408	320	56	50	81	47	34	0	414	331	90	60	162	102	60	0	822	651	146	110	73	113	89	99	112	90	100	99
MIL	81	37	44	0	305	365	49	54	81	30	51	0	334	400	76	82	162	67	95	0	639	765	125	136	66	104	112	91	91	108	95	96
MIN	80	48	32	0	469	376	61	79	81	36	45	0	398	400	62	72	161	84	77	0	867	776	123	151	106	84	101	107	115	105	103	102
NY	81	55	26	0	412	305	84	63	81	45	36	0	419	346	100	76	162	100	62	0	831	651	184	139	86	137	106	95	115	92	98	97
OAK	81	35	46	0	302	347	58	69	80	28	52	0	303	402	59	76	161	63	98	0	605	749	117	145	92	85	104	90	87	106	95	97
SEA	81	29	52	0	303	419	75	103	81	35	46	0	321	436	58	91	162	64	98	0	624	855	133	194	117	87	124	95	88	118	96	98
TEX	81	44	37	0	369	368	62	78	81	50	31	0	398	289	73	56	162	94	68	0	767	657	135	134	109	90	88	108	100	86	105	104
TOR	80	25	55	0	297	444	45	94	81	29	52	0	308	378	55	58	161	54	107	0	605	822	100	152	120	65	93	107	81	108	103	105
1978 AMERICAN LEAGUE																																
BAL	81	51	30	0	316	258	74	42	80	39	41	0	343	375	80	65	161	90	71	0	659	633	154	107	81	143	100	81	108	103	91	90
BOS	82	59	23	0	445	334	94	72	81	40	41	0	351	323	78	65	163	99	64	0	796	657	172	137	115	134	109	114	108	91	107	106
CAL	81	50	31	0	371	316	56	58	81	37	44	0	320	350	52	67	162	87	75	0	691	666	108	125	96	92	105	103	100	97	102	101
CHI	80	38	42	0	342	349	56	58	81	33	48	0	292	382	50	70	161	71	90	0	634	731	106	128	96	91	108	103	93	106	101	102
CLE	78	42	36	0	319	287	50	37	81	27	54	0	320	407	56	63	159	69	90	0	639	694	106	100	77	101	93	87	103	110	93	94
DET	81	47	34	0	395	338	74	78	81	39	42	0	319	315	55	57	162	86	76	0	714	653	129	135	133	93	97	115	97	90	108	107

	HOME								ROAD								ALL															
TM	G	W	L	T	R	OR	HR	OHR	G	W	L	T	R	OR	HR	OHR	G	W	L	T	R	OR	HR	OHR	HRF	HRB	HRP	RF	RB	RP	BPF	PPF
KC	81	56	25	0	434	264	43	44	81	36	45	0	309	370	55	64	162	92	70	0	743	634	98	108	75	93	100	103	107	92	102	101
MIL	81	54	27	0	446	318	94	50	81	39	42	0	358	332	79	59	162	93	69	0	804	650	173	109	105	140	92	111	111	92	106	104
MIN	81	38	43	0	322	308	44	39	81	35	46	0	344	370	38	63	162	73	89	0	666	678	82	102	83	75	89	89	104	105	94	94
NY	81	55	26	0	358	275	68	59	82	45	37	0	377	307	57	52	163	100	63	0	735	582	125	111	118	94	84	95	109	87	99	97
OAK	80	38	42	0	281	330	52	51	82	31	51	0	251	360	48	55	162	69	93	0	532	690	100	106	102	82	86	102	78	99	101	102
SEA	81	32	49	0	343	423	58	93	79	24	55	0	271	411	39	62	160	56	104	0	614	834	97	155	139	69	107	107	89	119	102	104
TEX	82	52	30	0	348	289	62	49	80	35	45	0	344	343	70	59	162	87	75	0	692	632	132	108	85	118	98	91	106	97	96	96
TOR	81	37	44	0	334	366	50	75	80	22	58	0	256	409	48	74	161	59	102	0	590	775	98	149	100	84	123	102	87	112	100	102
1979 AMERICAN LEAGUE																																
BAL	79	55	24	0	369	259	74	57	80	47	33	0	388	323	107	76	159	102	57	0	757	582	181	133	75	145	110	91	105	82	97	96
BOS	80	51	29	0	470	357	121	59	80	40	40	0	371	354	73	74	160	91	69	0	841	711	194	133	121	121	88	114	105	90	107	106
CAL	81	49	32	0	408	339	71	55	81	39	42	0	458	429	93	76	162	88	74	0	866	768	164	131	76	128	104	86	124	111	93	92
CHI	79	33	46	0	349	401	56	60	81	40	41	0	381	347	71	54	160	73	87	0	730	748	127	114	95	90	82	105	96	98	102	103
CLE	81	47	34	0	428	409	87	72	80	34	46	0	332	396	51	66	161	81	80	0	760	805	138	138	131	82	84	112	95	101	106	106
DET	80	46	34	0	394	323	101	74	81	39	42	0	376	415	63	93	161	85	76	0	770	738	164	167	113	108	112	93	107	102	96	96
KC	81	46	35	0	462	421	53	81	81	39	42	0	389	395	63	84	162	85	77	0	851	816	116	165	92	85	118	112	107	103	105	105
MIL	81	52	29	0	401	362	91	81	80	43	37	0	406	360	94	81	161	95	66	0	807	722	185	162	98	132	117	99	107	97	100	99
MIN	81	39	42	0	415	390	67	61	81	43	38	0	349	335	45	67	162	82	80	0	764	725	112	128	113	72	83	116	93	89	109	108
NY	81	51	30	0	360	308	77	59	79	38	41	0	374	364	73	64	160	89	71	0	734	672	150	123	98	106	88	90	103	95	96	95
OAK	81	31	50	0	262	371	46	65	81	23	58	0	311	489	62	82	162	54	108	0	573	860	108	147	77	85	113	79	86	125	89	91
SEA	81	36	45	0	371	404	88	94	81	31	50	0	340	416	44	71	162	67	95	0	711	820	132	165	151	72	92	101	94	107	100	101
TEX	81	44	37	0	382	335	69	63	81	39	42	0	368	363	71	72	162	83	79	0	750	698	140	135	93	100	97	98	99	93	100	99
TOR	81	32	49	0	345	432	50	74	81	21	60	0	268	430	45	91	162	53	109	0	613	862	95	165	90	70	117	108	78	108	103	106
1980 AMERICAN LEAGUE																																
BAL	81	50	31	0	397	319	75	81	81	50	31	0	408	321	81	53	162	100	62	0	805	640	156	134	116	110	94	100	110	89	101	99
BOS	81	36	45	0	370	420	79	74	79	47	32	0	387	347	83	55	160	83	77	0	757	767	162	129	108	120	97	105	103	104	102	102
CAL	81	30	51	0	330	403	49	76	79	35	44	0	368	394	57	65	160	65	95	0	698	797	106	141	99	82	107	93	101	114	96	97
CHI	81	37	42	2	281	350	41	37	81	33	48	0	306	372	50	71	162	70	90	2	587	722	91	108	66	84	94	93	83	101	97	98
CLE	79	44	35	0	400	389	55	66	81	35	46	0	338	418	34	71	160	79	81	0	738	807	89	137	117	63	96	106	100	109	102	103
DET	82	43	38	1	440	404	77	95	81	41	40	0	390	353	66	57	163	84	78	1	830	757	143	152	135	94	97	111	107	98	105	105
KC	81	49	32	0	397	335	47	51	81	48	33	0	412	359	68	78	162	97	65	0	809	694	115	129	69	103	114	96	113	98	98	97
MIL	82	40	42	0	368	336	90	65	80	46	34	0	443	346	113	72	162	86	76	0	811	682	203	137	83	169	119	88	117	101	94	93
MIN	80	44	36	0	392	361	51	63	81	33	48	0	278	363	48	57	161	77	84	0	670	724	99	120	109	72	86	117	84	92	109	109
NY	81	53	28	0	409	315	91	47	81	50	31	0	411	347	98	55	162	103	59	0	820	662	189	102	92	147	83	97	113	93	99	98
OAK	81	46	35	0	337	277	58	57	81	37	44	0	349	365	79	85	162	83	79	0	686	642	137	142	72	122	125	87	100	93	94	94
SEA	81	36	45	0	340	389	74	99	82	23	58	1	270	404	30	60	163	59	103	1	610	793	104	159	180	54	86	107	80	103	103	105
TEX	80	39	41	0	380	365	58	57	83	37	44	2	376	387	66	62	163	76	85	2	756	752	124	119	93	96	92	101	103	102	100	100
TOR	81	35	46	0	311	386	56	75	81	32	49	0	313	376	70	60	162	67	95	0	624	762	126	135	100	96	102	100	86	103	100	101
1981 AMERICAN LEAGUE																																
BAL	55	33	22	0	231	217	49	47	50	26	24	0	198	220	39	36	105	59	46	0	429	437	88	83	116	110	104	98	101	103	99	99
BOS	53	30	23	0	278	247	52	47	55	29	26	0	241	234	38	43	108	59	49	0	519	481	90	90	125	106	107	114	111	104	106	106
CAL	54	26	28	0	244	233	48	39	56	25	31	0	232	220	49	42	110	51	59	0	476	453	97	81	99	126	107	108	102	98	104	104
CHI	49	25	24	0	215	198	31	33	57	29	28	0	261	225	45	40	106	54	52	0	476	423	76	73	88	106	103	99	110	99	100	99
CLE	54	25	29	0	210	216	19	33	49	27	22	0	221	226	20	34	103	52	51	0	431	442	39	67	88	56	94	87	111	113	93	93
DET	55	32	23	0	241	196	43	44	54	28	26	0	186	208	22	39	109	60	49	0	427	404	65	83	137	69	91	109	91	87	105	105
KC	47	19	28	0	163	197	17	27	56	31	25	0	234	208	44	48	103	50	53	0	397	405	61	75	59	99	128	97	95	98	99	99
MIL	49	28	21	0	203	203	33	29	60	34	26	0	290	256	63	43	109	62	47	0	493	459	96	72	74	138	110	92	115	108	96	95
MIN	61	24	36	1	213	292	25	47	49	17	32	0	165	194	22	32	110	41	68	1	378	486	47	79	105	59	95	110	80	101	105	106
NY	51	32	19	0	203	154	47	24	56	27	29	0	218	189	53	40	107	59	48	0	421	343	100	64	85	142	92	97	96	79	100	99
OAK	56	35	21	0	234	183	57	46	53	29	24	0	224	220	47	34	109	64	45	0	458	403	104	80	120	123	96	90	108	96	96	95
SEA	57	20	37	0	226	271	52	53	53	24	28	1	200	250	37	23	110	44	65	1	426	521	89	76	154	91	74	102	95	115	100	101
TEX	56	32	24	0	232	168	21	24	49	25	24	0	220	221	28	43	105	57	48	0	452	389	49	67	58	86	111	81	117	101	91	90
TOR	53	17	36	0	172	272	34	41	53	20	33	0	157	194	27	31	106	37	69	0	329	466	61	72	125	72	84	122	69	95	111	113
1982 AMERICAN LEAGUE																																
BAL	82	53	28	1	397	330	87	87	81	41	40	0	377	357	92	60	163	94	68	1	774	687	179	147	113	113	93	99	106	95	100	99
BOS	81	49	32	0	434	370	67	82	81	40	41	0	319	343	69	73	162	89	73	0	753	713	136	155	105	90	101	120	94	90	110	110
CAL	81	52	29	0	414	322	99	69	81	41	40	0	400	348	87	55	162	93	69	0	814	670	186	124	118	114	78	99	112	94	100	99
CHI	80	49	31	0	383	332	51	43	82	38	44	0	403	378	85	56	162	87	75	0	786	710	136	99	70	103	78	95	111	101	97	97
CLE	81	41	40	0	342	377	49	64	81	37	44	0	341	371	60	58	162	78	84	0	683	748	109	122	96	74	82	101	94	102	100	101
DET	81	47	34	0	378	328	108	100	81	36	45	0	351	357	69	72	162	83	79	0	729	685	177	172	143	99	97	100	100	95	100	100
KC	81	56	25	0	431	318	61	64	81	34	47	0	353	399	71	99	162	90	72	0	784	717	132	163	75	103	123	100	108	99	100	99
MIL	82	48	34	0	431	319	89	64	81	47	33	1	460	398	127	88	163	95	67	1	891	717	216	152	72	169	123	88	130	106	94	92
MIN	81	37	44	0	351	401	81	110	81	23	58	0	306	418	67	98	162	60	102	0	657	819	148	208	113	96	132	102	90	111	100	102
NY	81	42	39	0	346	338	73	55	81	37	44	0	363	378	88	58	162	79	83	0	709	716	161	113	88	113	81	93	101	102	96	97
OAK	81	36	45	0	328	398	71	83	81	32	49	0	363	421	78	94	162	68	94	0	691	819	149	177	89	108	126	92	100	117	95	96
SEA	81	42	39	0	356	388	78	104	81	34	47	0	295	324	52	69	162	76	86	0	651	712	130	173	145	72	94	118	82	89	109	110
TEX	81	38	43	0	286	333	43	66	81	26	55	0	304	416	72	62	162	64	98	0	590	749	115	128	82	83	94	86	88	109	93	94
TOR	81	44	37	0	353	379	62	70	81	34	47	0	298	322	44	77	162	78	84	0	651	701	106	147	108	68	93	116	83	89	109	109
1983 AMERICAN LEAGUE																																
BAL	81	50	31	0	389	328	79	66	81	48	33	0	410	324	89	64	162	98	64	0	799	652	168	130	96	126	99	99	110	91	100	99
BOS	81	38	43	0	373	390	65	76	81	40	41	0	351	385	77	82	162	78	84	0	724	775	142	158	89	112	124	103	99	105	101	102
CAL	81	35	46	0	368	354	86	67	81	35	46	0	354	425	68	63	162	70	92	0	722	779	154	130	115	105	90	93	104	111	96	96
CHI	81	55	26	0	432	306	84	64	81	44	37	0	368	344	73	64	162	99	63	0	800	650	157	128	109	110	92	105	107	88	103	102
CLE	81	36	45	0	367	424	48	71	81	34	47	0	337	361	38	49	162	70	92	0	704	785	86	120	132	54	74	111	92	102	105	106
DET	81	48	33	0	377	314	83	87	81	44	37	0	412	365	73	83	162	92	70	0	789	679	156	170	109	112	121	90	114	99	96	94
KC	82	45	36	1	381	369	50	66	81	34	47	0	315	398	59	67	163	79	83	1	696	767	109	133	91	83	100	103	94	103	101	102
MIL	81	52	29	0	356	305	64	57	81	35	46	0	408	403	68	76	162	87	75	0	764	708	132	133	85	105	105	83	115	107	92	91
MIN	81	37	44	0	389	427	56	91	81	33	48	0	320	395	85	72	162	70	92	0	709	822	141	163	93	109	125	112	93	107	105	106
NY	81	51	30	0	398	323	67	55	81	40	41	0	372	380	86	61	162	91	71	0	770	703	153	116	85	120	94	97	108	99	99	98
OAK	81	42	39	0	348	367	60	54	81	32	49	0	360	415	61	81	162	74	88	0	708	782	121	135	81	99	108	92	102	112	96	96
SEA	81	30	51	0	281	369	64	80	81	30	51	0	277	371	47	65	162	60	102	0	558	740	111	145	124	73	94	99	77	101	99	101
TEX	81	44	37	0	326	294	45	33	82	33	48	1	313	315	61	64	163	77	85	1	639	609	106	97	65	93	82	100	86	83	101	101
TOR	81	48	33	0	437	385	101	84	81	41	40	0	358	341	66	61	162	89	73	0	795	726	167	145	142	102	90	117	101	93	108	108
1984 AMERICAN LEAGUE																																
BAL	81	44	37	0	319	306	82	59	81	41	40	0	362	361	78	78	162	85	77	0	681	667	160	137	91	119	102	88	101	99	94	94
BOS	81	41	40	0	456	413	100	76	81	45	36	0	354	351	81	65	162	86	76	0	810	764	181	141	119	117	93	122	102	97	110	110
CAL	81	37	44	0	341	364	79	83	81	44	37	0	355	333	71	60	162	81	81	0	696	697	150	143	122	96	91	102	96	96	101	101

	HOME								ROAD								ALL															
TM	G	W	L	T	R	OR	HR	OHR	G	W	L	T	R	OR	HR	OHR	G	W	L	T	R	OR	HR	OHR	HRF	HRB	HRP	RF	RB	RP	BPF	PPF
CHI	81	43	38	0	394	389	103	77	81	31	50	0	285	347	69	78	162	74	88	0	679	736	172	155	120	110	102	121	85	93	110	111
CLE	81	41	39	1	411	399	65	73	82	34	48	0	350	367	58	68	163	75	87	1	761	766	123	141	110	82	94	113	100	100	106	106
DET	82	53	29	0	406	295	85	69	80	51	29	0	423	348	102	61	162	104	58	0	829	643	187	130	94	136	97	91	121	95	96	94
KC	81	44	37	0	344	326	48	59	81	40	41	0	329	360	69	77	162	84	78	0	673	686	117	136	75	94	109	98	95	96	99	99
MIL	81	38	43	0	286	344	42	68	80	29	51	0	355	390	54	69	161	67	94	0	641	734	96	137	88	72	101	84	98	112	92	93
MIN	81	47	34	0	372	337	63	77	81	34	47	0	301	338	51	82	162	81	81	0	673	675	114	159	105	79	108	110	89	89	106	106
NY	81	51	30	0	372	292	62	49	81	36	45	0	386	387	68	71	162	87	75	0	758	679	130	120	81	101	92	87	113	101	94	93
OAK	81	44	37	0	356	344	77	72	81	33	48	0	382	452	81	83	162	77	85	0	738	796	158	155	91	118	116	85	113	120	91	92
SEA	81	42	39	0	357	394	68	82	81	32	49	0	325	380	61	56	162	74	88	0	682	774	129	138	125	81	85	106	93	105	102	103
TEX	80	34	46	0	327	357	55	70	81	35	46	0	329	357	65	78	161	69	92	0	656	714	120	148	89	91	110	100	92	100	100	101
TOR	81	49	32	0	387	339	59	78	82	40	41	1	363	357	84	62	163	89	73	1	750	696	143	140	96	102	101	102	103	96	101	101
1985 AMERICAN LEAGUE																																
BAL	81	45	36	0	414	374	103	87	80	38	42	0	404	390	111	73	161	83	78	0	818	764	214	160	102	138	105	98	113	106	99	98
BOS	81	43	37	1	415	357	73	64	82	38	44	0	385	363	89	66	163	81	81	1	800	720	162	130	90	107	88	104	105	96	102	101
CAL	79	49	30	0	370	331	75	93	83	41	42	0	362	372	78	78	162	90	72	0	732	703	153	171	113	93	103	101	98	95	101	101
CHI	81	45	36	0	359	361	74	83	82	40	41	1	377	359	72	78	163	85	77	1	736	720	146	161	106	91	99	99	99	97	100	100
CLE	81	38	43	0	380	379	52	76	81	22	59	0	349	482	64	94	162	60	102	0	729	861	116	170	81	83	118	91	105	122	94	95
DET	81	44	37	0	386	368	108	93	80	40	40	0	343	320	94	48	161	84	77	0	729	688	202	141	136	111	76	112	93	88	106	106
KC	82	50	32	0	357	317	67	43	80	41	39	0	330	322	87	60	162	91	71	0	687	639	154	103	75	110	75	101	91	85	102	101
MIL	80	40	40	0	368	416	50	86	81	31	50	0	322	386	51	89	161	71	90	0	690	802	101	175	98	66	111	110	90	104	105	106
MIN	84	49	35	0	407	393	71	83	78	28	50	0	298	389	70	81	162	77	85	0	705	782	141	164	95	93	107	107	92	102	103	104
NY	80	58	22	0	411	288	92	67	81	39	42	0	428	372	84	90	161	97	64	0	839	660	176	157	94	118	105	90	120	95	96	94
OAK	79	43	36	0	348	347	66	71	83	34	49	0	409	440	89	101	162	77	85	0	757	787	155	172	77	113	124	87	111	114	93	93
SEA	83	42	41	0	360	389	92	78	79	32	47	0	359	429	79	76	162	74	88	0	719	818	171	154	104	108	98	91	103	116	94	95
TEX	80	37	43	0	356	406	76	102	81	25	56	0	261	379	53	71	161	62	99	0	617	785	129	173	139	70	92	117	77	98	108	110
TOR	80	54	26	0	396	264	75	78	81	45	36	0	363	324	83	69	161	99	62	0	759	588	158	147	103	100	94	99	103	81	101	99
1986 AMERICAN LEAGUE																																
BAL	79	37	42	0	348	362	91	98	83	36	47	0	360	398	78	79	162	73	89	0	708	760	169	177	124	93	97	98	96	102	99	99
BOS	81	51	30	0	389	350	55	85	80	44	36	0	405	346	89	82	161	95	66	0	794	696	144	167	83	96	113	98	107	95	100	99
CAL	82	50	32	0	371	335	88	84	80	42	38	0	415	349	79	69	162	92	70	0	786	684	167	153	113	95	88	91	109	96	96	95
CHI	81	41	40	0	341	335	51	63	81	31	50	0	303	364	70	80	162	72	90	0	644	699	121	143	77	82	97	101	85	92	101	101
CLE	81	45	35	1	403	415	80	80	82	39	43	0	428	426	77	87	163	84	78	1	831	841	157	167	99	96	102	97	113	115	98	98
DET	81	49	32	0	403	310	96	83	81	38	43	0	395	404	102	100	162	87	75	0	798	714	198	183	90	129	120	90	112	101	95	95
KC	81	45	36	0	342	317	60	46	81	31	50	0	312	356	77	75	162	76	86	0	654	673	137	121	71	97	84	98	88	90	100	100
MIL	80	41	39	0	338	375	63	79	81	36	45	0	329	359	64	79	161	77	84	0	667	734	127	158	100	78	95	104	88	96	102	103
MIN	81	43	38	0	426	439	116	107	81	28	53	0	315	400	80	93	162	71	91	0	741	839	196	200	126	107	111	118	91	103	108	109
NY	80	41	39	0	384	396	93	96	82	49	33	0	413	342	95	79	162	90	72	0	797	738	188	175	111	110	102	106	104	96	103	103
OAK	83	47	36	0	363	349	75	81	79	29	50	0	368	411	88	85	162	76	86	0	731	760	163	166	86	107	109	88	105	109	94	94
SEA	82	41	41	0	410	427	97	99	80	26	54	0	308	408	61	72	162	67	95	0	718	835	158	171	138	80	88	112	91	106	105	106
TEX	81	51	30	0	374	343	87	61	81	36	45	0	397	400	97	84	162	87	75	0	771	743	184	145	83	122	97	91	108	104	95	95
TOR	81	42	39	0	415	389	87	89	82	44	37	1	394	344	94	75	163	86	76	1	809	733	181	164	105	107	98	110	103	93	105	104
1987 AMERICAN LEAGUE																																
BAL	82	31	51	0	351	456	110	125	80	36	44	0	378	424	101	101	162	67	95	0	729	880	211	226	111	108	114	97	94	112	98	99
BOS	80	50	30	0	436	383	86	75	82	28	54	0	406	442	88	115	162	78	84	0	842	825	174	190	82	103	109	99	107	105	99	99
CAL	81	38	43	0	377	405	88	116	81	37	44	0	393	398	84	96	162	75	87	0	770	803	172	212	112	87	106	99	98	102	99	100
CHI	81	38	43	0	394	414	72	90	81	39	42	0	354	332	101	99	162	77	85	0	748	746	173	189	82	101	110	116	87	86	109	109
CLE	81	35	46	0	373	519	94	118	81	26	55	0	369	438	93	101	162	61	101	0	742	957	187	219	107	97	112	108	91	115	103	105
DET	81	54	27	0	442	338	125	101	81	44	37	0	454	397	100	79	162	98	64	0	896	735	225	180	125	106	86	93	116	97	97	96
KC	81	46	35	0	375	349	73	57	81	37	44	0	340	342	95	71	162	83	79	0	715	691	168	128	80	97	75	106	87	84	104	104
MIL	81	48	33	0	440	420	72	79	81	43	38	0	422	397	91	90	162	91	71	0	862	817	163	169	85	93	96	105	106	101	102	102
MIN	81	56	25	0	411	348	106	92	81	29	52	0	375	458	90	118	162	85	77	0	786	806	196	210	96	108	114	92	104	105	96	96
NY	81	51	30	0	401	346	98	88	81	38	43	0	387	412	98	91	162	89	73	0	788	758	196	179	99	104	96	94	102	98	98	97
OAK	81	42	39	0	363	351	88	75	81	39	42	0	443	438	111	101	162	81	81	0	806	789	199	176	78	118	105	82	112	109	91	91
SEA	81	40	41	0	403	400	103	115	81	38	43	0	357	401	58	84	162	78	84	0	760	801	161	199	148	68	85	105	93	98	103	103
TEX	81	43	38	0	426	447	93	111	81	32	49	0	397	402	101	88	162	75	87	0	823	849	194	199	107	100	102	108	100	103	104	104
TOR	81	52	29	0	425	319	101	83	81	44	37	0	420	336	114	75	162	96	66	0	845	655	215	158	98	114	86	99	105	83	101	99
1988 AMERICAN LEAGUE																																
BAL	80	34	46	0	286	354	70	77	81	20	61	0	264	435	67	76	161	54	107	0	550	789	137	153	102	101	112	92	83	115	95	97
BOS	81	53	28	0	456	360	68	73	81	36	45	0	357	329	56	70	162	89	73	0	813	689	124	143	112	86	99	118	105	91	109	108
CAL	81	35	46	0	333	368	58	71	81	40	41	0	381	403	66	64	162	75	87	0	714	771	124	135	99	91	99	90	107	115	94	95
CHI	81	40	41	0	311	373	55	64	80	31	49	0	320	384	77	74	161	71	90	0	631	757	132	138	79	109	115	96	92	109	97	99
CLE	81	44	37	0	353	359	62	52	81	34	47	0	313	372	72	68	162	78	84	0	666	731	134	120	82	107	96	103	93	101	101	102
DET	81	50	31	0	328	303	83	76	81	38	43	0	375	355	60	74	162	88	74	0	703	658	143	150	118	97	102	88	106	99	94	94
KC	80	44	36	0	359	330	55	37	81	40	41	0	345	318	66	65	161	84	77	0	704	648	121	102	73	103	85	105	97	90	103	103
MIL	81	47	34	0	354	310	60	65	81	40	41	0	328	306	53	60	162	87	75	0	682	616	113	125	110	78	86	105	93	85	103	103
MIN	81	47	34	0	402	354	76	79	81	44	37	0	357	318	75	67	162	91	71	0	759	672	151	146	109	107	103	112	101	90	106	105
NY	80	46	34	0	378	345	77	75	81	39	42	0	394	403	71	82	161	85	76	0	772	748	148	157	101	110	116	93	115	111	96	95
OAK	81	54	27	0	362	294	67	47	81	50	31	0	438	326	89	69	162	104	58	0	800	620	156	116	75	130	98	88	119	94	95	93
SEA	81	37	44	0	362	405	97	81	80	31	49	0	302	339	51	63	161	68	93	0	664	744	148	144	147	87	88	116	88	98	107	108
TEX	81	38	43	0	336	368	58	67	80	32	48	0	301	367	54	62	161	70	91	0	637	735	112	129	105	80	92	103	90	102	101	102
TOR	81	45	36	0	371	344	78	73	81	42	39	0	392	336	80	70	162	87	75	0	763	680	158	143	101	116	106	99	108	98	100	99

Individual Home-Road Stats

In the next several pages are presented home-road statistical breakdowns for twenty-seven hitters of note: twelve from the National League—Hank Aaron, Roberto Clemente, Rogers Hornsby, Chuck Klein, Willie Mays, Joe Morgan, Stan Musial, Mel Ott, Frank Robinson, Pete Rose, Mike Schmidt, and Honus Wagner, and fifteen from principally the American League—Ty Cobb, Eddie Collins, Sam Crawford, Joe DiMaggio, Jimmie Foxx, Lou Gehrig, Reggie Jackson, Al Kaline, Harmon Killebrew, Nap Lajoie, Mickey Mantle, Babe Ruth, Tris Speaker, Ted Williams, and Carl Yastrzemski. These were researched from the official day-by-day records, box scores, schedules, and other sources.

Until now, the only home-road information that has been available for most NL players is in the category of home runs. Analysts and would-be analysts have been left to make guesses about NL park effects or to pretend that they don't exist. If a writer claimed that Rogers Hornsby, Mel Ott, and Hank Aaron had inflated statistics because of the home parks they played in, or that the stats of Willie Mays, Roberto Clemente, and Joe Morgan suffered deeply for the same reason, the reader would have no reason to disbelieve him, nor any evidence with which to challenge him. Now that the evidence is available, perhaps such ignorant speculation can be averted. Home-road data for AL players is more familiar because Peter Palmer had made it public in various publications in the 1980s.

There are a few things to understand before home-road breakdowns can be properly analyzed. First of all, the average player does better at home *regardless* of the park. This phenomenon is addressed in *The Hidden Game of Baseball* (1984): "The players benefit from home stands of reasonable duration . . . when they live in their own residences, sleep at more nearly regular times, play before appreciative fans, and benefit from the physical park conditions which to some degree may have made their organizations acquire them in the first place." It is concluded there that "individuals bat and pitch at a rate 10 percent higher at home, on average."

Second, let's not overrate "hitters' parks," or assume that their effect is the same for every hitter. Parks don't make the statistics by themselves; a player still has to hit the ball and should be given some credit for learning to take advantage of a park. Nevertheless a truly great hitter should be able to hit anywhere.

Third, most players accumulate more times at bat on the road (about 5 percent more throughout an average career) because the road team always bats in the ninth inning, while the home team often doesn't. Variations in the 5 percent result from the team's won-lost record and home park. Over a career, this can add up to several hundred more at-bats on the road than at home, with other totals increased correspondingly.

One final note, regarding on base percentage (OBP). The official formula for on base percentage, adopted in 1984, is hits plus walks plus hit batsmen, divided by at-bats plus walks plus hit batsmen plus sacrifice flies:

$$OBP = \frac{H + BB + HB}{AB + BB + HB + SF}$$

Since sacrifice flies have not been recorded consistently throughout history (and their effect on OBP is small), SF was eliminated from the formula for the breakdowns offered here.

In cases where hit-by-pitch data was not available (pre-1917), that too was eliminated from the formula. Where walks are not available for a season, the OBP is not listed.

Statistics

A valuable measure of park effect is the ratio of Production (on base plus slugging) at home to Production on the road. Normally, a player will have a batting average, slugging average and on base percentage each about 5 percent higher at home than on the road. Thus a home-park advantage of 5 percent is to be expected of all batters. Unfortunately, the variation due to chance in a single season for the difference between Production at home and on the road is *10 percent*, so single seasons can vary quite a bit. However, over a ten-year period, the average difference gets down to about 3 percent. This means that if a player played in a truly neutral park, his Production over ten years at home should be at 5 percent, plus or minus 3 percent, about half the time. Still, one player in twenty would be expected to be off by 10 percent in a neutral park after ten years.

The data on the 27 players in this sample show most players near the average. The player with the biggest home park advantage was a National Leaguer, Chuck Klein (1.27), while the one with the worst disadvantage was Joe DiMaggio (0.92).

Comments on the NL'ers

The NL statisticians have been, for the most part, extremely accurate in recording stats over the past seventy years (particularly when we consider the process wasn't computerized until 1981). A few minor recording or tabulation errors were found in the official sheets for Horsnby (1 extra HR), Klein (1 missing RBI), Ott (1 missing RBI, 2 extra games), and Howard (7 extra games, 1 missing run); the totals for Musial, Mays, Aaron, Clemente, Rose, Morgan, Robinson, and Schmidt balanced perfectly. (Those of us who feared an audit of Clemente's record might turn up a bogus hit among his 3,000 can now rest easier.)

Before the mid-teens, it was a different story: record keeping was sloppy and incomplete. Consequently, in compiling Honus Wagner's records, more than 30 discrepancies in 12 different seasons were unearthed. In most cases it is impossible to determine whether the error is in the official sheets, the published record, or both. The net effect is that Wagner's home-road breakdowns, compared with the "official" published record, credit him with 10 more games, 12 more at-bats, 5 fewer runs, 15 fewer hits, and 11 fewer doubles.

In the following player comments, there will be references to home and road "records." These are based only on the eleven "pure" NL'ers—not Frank Robinson—although most of the records would probably survive any further research.

Hank Aaron. Critics are fond of saying things like "Sure, he got the home run record, but he played in that band box in Atlanta . . ." Rarely is it mentioned that Aaron spent the bulk of his career (fourteen of twenty-three seasons) in Milwaukee, a poor hitter's park, and never played a game in Atlanta until he was thirty-two.

In Aaron's Milwaukee seasons, he had 195 homers, 636 RBIs, and a .305 average at home, but 225 homers, 764 RBIs, and a .318 mark on the road. He holds the major league *road* records for career total bases, home runs, and runs batted in.

The following statistical line compares well with the career records of many Hall of Famers.

G	AB	R	H	2B	3B	HR	RBI	SB	AVG	OBP	SLG
1650	6392	1094	1959	342	61	370	1180	123	.306	.372	.553

Those are Hank Aaron's career stats for *road games only*.

Roberto Clemente. When one looks only at his home-road home run breakdown (102–138), it is easy to hypothesize that Forbes Field hurt Clemente's offensive production. Actually he did better at home in virtually every category *except* home runs, including a 23-point spread (.329–.306) in batting average. Roberto hit better than .300 at home in each of his last fourteen seasons. Curious stat: In 1956–1957, he went 60 straight road games (more than 250 at bats) without drawing a walk.

Rogers Hornsby. Bill James, in his *Historical Abstract*, said that somehow he doesn't think that Horsnby was the best offensive second baseman ever, even though his statistics indicate he was. He "played 85 percent of his career in the best two hitter's parks in the National League," James reasoned, ranking him only fourth all-time among second sackers. "I think it is likely that Horsnby benefited from a fairly large home-park advantage."

Reasonable, perhaps, but wrong.

Hornsby did have two straight monster years at Sportsman's Park in 1924–1925, posting combined averages of .473 (batting), .552 (on-base), and .841 (slugging). But now let's examine his road performance.

Rogers Hornsby batted .358 lifetime on the road. Three-five-eight. He holds the NL *road* records for highest batting average in a season (.419 in 1921) and for a career. He holds the NL *road* records for highest on-base average in a season (.505 in 1928) and for a career (.430). He has a higher career road slugging average (.565) than Musial, Mays, Aaron, or any of the other National Leaguers checked.

Chuck Klein. He has long been accused of taking advantage of Philadelphia's Baker Bowl, with its 280½-foot right field foul line, to achieve Hall of Fame statistics. Klein stormed into the majors with 5½ spectacular seasons (1928–1933), batting .359 with four home run titles and a Triple Crown. He was then traded to the Cubs, returning to the Phils in 1936, two years before they vacated the Bowl. Klein's stats took a plunge in 1934 and never recovered, but the numbers in those first 5½ seasons were so overwhelming that they finally carried him into Cooperstown.

This time Bill James rushes to the defense of Klein: "You just can't ignore *that much* statistical evidence . . . I've become convinced that Klein was significantly over . . . the level of unquestioned excellence but marginal greatness." James ranked Klein as one of history's top ten right fielders in "peak value."

In reality Chuck Klein was a slightly above average hitter for whom Baker Bowl was tailor-made. Look at the breakdown for those first 5½ seasons:

PLACE	G	AB	R	H	2B	3B	HR	RBI	AVG	OBP	SLG
Home	408	1,695	417	715	139	24	131	469	.422	.470	.764
Road	415	1,672	282	494	107	26	60	258	.295	.354	.498

The seasonal breakdowns are just as staggering. In consecutive seasons Klein achieved the top five home hit totals in NL history, with a high of 143. He set NL home records for runs (92), doubles (32), total bases (270), and RBI (109) in a season. Even when he set a modern fielding record, with 44 outfield assists (1930), 32 of them were homemade.

And before you think that Klein's road numbers aren't too shabby either, consider that the overall league batting average for those years was .283.

After he went to Chicago (not a bad park either), the bottom fell out of Klein's home stats, but his road records improved—largely because he now had Baker Bowl as a road park. In 24 road games there (1934–1936), Klein hit 8 homers, drove in 25 runs, scored 28, and had a .445 OBP.

Klein's career statistics in 578 games at Baker Bowl include 164 home runs, 594 RBIs, (154-game averages: 44, 158), a .397 batting average, and a .708 slugging mark. In 1,175 games at other NL parks, he had 136 home runs, 608 RBIs (averages: 18, 80), and a .277 batting average, which is about what the league average was at that time.

Yes, Klein still had to hit and throw the ball himself. But why couldn't he do it anywhere else?

Willie Mays. If Candlestick Park hurt Mays, it doesn't show up in the stats. He had a .549 career slugging percentage on the road, .567 at home. He hit 325 homers on the road, 335 (in 400 fewer at-bats) at home.

Joe Morgan. Looking at his career statistics, it's easy to conclude that Morgan's sudden rise from a pretty good player to a superstar, following his trade from Houston to Cincinnati, was due to his escape from the Astrodome. But the home-road breakdowns tell a different story.

In his ten years with Houston, Morgan batted .272 with a .401 OBP at home, but only .250 with a .351 OBP on the road. Only his home run production suffered.

In his eight years with Cincinnati, he hit .282 at home (a 10-point increase), but .294 on the road (a 44-point gain!), and he still hit more homers on the road.

It is quite clear that Morgan's metamorphosis had more to do with finally playing for a perennial contender than with changing home parks. Maybe Pete Rose really does bring out the best in his teammates.

Stan Musial. Sportsman's Park did not hurt his numbers any, but Stan could hit anywhere. His best season, 1948, was also probably the best *road* season in NL history, setting records for hits (132), total bases (248), doubles (29), and slugging (.780). Musial collected 1,815 career hits at home and 1,815 on the road.

Mel Ott. One looking at Ott's home run breakdown is liable to think that the Polo Grounds (257-foot foul line in right) kept him in the major leagues. He hit a startling 323 of his 511 career home runs at home, and another 40 (in about 110 games) in friendly Baker Bowl. In Ott's last seven seasons, 100 of his 123 homers (including all 18 in 1943) were hit at home. Additionally, this analysis showed that Ott slugged .589 at home and only .370 on the road during this period, and that he didn't score a run in his last 37 road games.

The Polo Grounds may have extended Ott's career, and turned him into a world-class home run hitter, but he was a world-class *hitter* all by himself. Over his first nine seasons, Ott batted a resounding .343 on the road, as compared to .286 at home. In 1929 he set NL records for runs (79) and RBIs (87) on the road. For his career he batted 14 points better on the road and hit significantly more singles, doubles, and triples away from home.

It is interesting to note that Ott's record at home and away can be viewed as essentially the same, except that about 130 doubles on the road were turned into homers by the short dimensions of the Polo Grounds. His overall home-park advantage, as measured by Production at home divided by Production on the road, is about average (1.07). This is a

phenomenon that also applied to Bill Dickey and Yogi Berra in Yankee Stadium, and shows that some parks aren't as easy as they appear.

Pete Rose. He holds the NL career records in runs, hits, and doubles, both at home and on the road.

Mike Schmidt. He has hit most of his home runs on the road but has been, overall, a better hitter at home.

Honus Wagner. He was homerless at Pittsburgh in seven of eighteen seasons with the Pirates, and during that period hit only 29 of his 82 homers at home.

Comments on the AL'ers

American League figures are more nearly "normal" than those of the NL. Tris Speaker (1.14), Jimmie Foxx (1.16), and Carl Yastrzemski (1.16) had slight home-park advantages, while Reggie Jackson (0.96) was at a disadvantage. The strangest case was certainly Gehrig (0.96).

Lou Gehrig. While Jackson played most of his years in a known "pitchers' park" in Oakland, Gehrig played his entire career in Yankee Stadium, which is supposed to be easy for lefthanded batters (in fact, it is generally neutral for them).

His road data is amazing. His .805 slugging average in 1927 is the top road mark of all time, and his .794 in 1930 is second. His 247 total bases for each of these seasons is an AL record, as are his 36 doubles in 1927. But the runs batted in data is the most startling: 117 RBIs in 1930 stands not only as the road record, but is higher than anyone had in a *home* season as well. The next best road marks? His 98 in 1927 and again in 1931. Gehrig was better away from Yankee Stadium over his career, but in 1934 he had one of the great *home* records of all time: a batting average of .414 with 98 RBIs.

Babe Ruth. Another amazing stat is the tremendous batting of Babe Ruth as a member of the Boston Red Sox while visiting the Yankees, who played their home games at the Polo Grounds before moving to Yankee Stadium in 1923. Called "the house that Ruth built," Yankee Stadium was by no means the house that built Ruth. His home slugging marks of .985 (201 total bases in 204 at bats) in 1920 and .929 in 1921 have never been approached, even by Chuck Klein; Jimmie Foxx's .887 in Fenway Park in 1938 is the closest. When Babe hit 29 homers in 1919 for the Red Sox, he had 20 on the road. Fenway Park in those years was a very difficult park for hitters. In fact, there were only 13 homers hit there all year by the Red Sox and their visitors, and Ruth had 9 of them. It would have been easy to predict Ruth would hit at least 50 in 1920 (he had 54), as he had 4 in 10 games in the Polo Grounds in 1919. All told, of his 49 homers with the Red Sox, 38 came on the road.

Tris Speaker. The Gray Eagle played his Cleveland years in League Park, which was a very easy park for lefthanders. The right field foul line was only 290 feet and the park went directly at right angles to center, so the power alley was only 340 feet. As a member of the Tribe, Speaker had 306 doubles at home and only 179 on the road.

Ted Williams. Fenway Park is generally regarded as a righthanded hitter's idea of heaven, but in truth it benefits all batters, just as Wrigley Field and Fulton County Stadium are batters' favorite road stops in the NL. In 1941 Williams of course hit .406 for the season to post a landmark batting average—but at Fenway he terrorized pitchers for an on base percentage of .541!

Joe DiMaggio. Just as Williams was thought to have suffered for his home park, so did baseball pundits regard DiMaggio's stay at Yankee Stadium, with its cavernous power alleys and distant left field. What if, writers and fans were fond of asking, the Yanks and Red Sox made a whopper of a deal, permitting DiMaggio to attack the Green Monster 77 times a year and giving Williams a shot at New York's short porch in right? Mightn't each then make a run at Ruth's home run record and hit 50 points higher?

No. This is about what would have happened, based on projections from the actual batting performance of DiMaggio at Boston, Williams at New York, and the relative merits of the Yankee and Red Sox pitching staffs. (DiMaggio would not have been able to feast off weak Boston pitching, and would have had to contend with Yankee arms, while Williams would have experienced some relief.) Had each man played his entire career in the other's uniform, the results might well have looked like this:

DiMaggio with Boston, Williams with New York

Joe DiMaggio, NY	BA: .325	HR: 361
Joe DiMaggio, Bos	BA: .340	HR: 417
Ted Williams, Bos	BA: .344	HR: 521
Ted Williams, NY	BA: .340	HR: 513

By the time such a trade was actually considered—in 1949, when DiMaggio was near the end and Williams was still in his prime—the Red Sox would have made a very bad bargain. But if DiMaggio had gone from the San Francisco Seals in 1935 straight to Boston, and Williams from Minneapolis in 1938 straight to New York . . .

YEAR	TM/L	G	AB	R	H	TB	2B	3B	HR	RBI	BB	HB	AVG	OBP	SLG	PRO	H/R
HANK AARON - HOME																	
1954	MIL-N	61	215	16	53	71	15	0	1	18	11	1	.247	.286	.330	.617	
1955	MIL-N	77	283	51	97	170	19	6	14	58	31	2	.343	.411	.601	1.012	
1956	MIL-N	75	295	59	86	154	15	4	15	40	20	2	.292	.341	.522	.863	
1957	MIL-N	78	304	55	93	165	12	3	18	49	29	0	.306	.366	.543	.909	
1958	MIL-N	76	279	45	87	133	14	1	10	40	37	1	.312	.394	.477	.871	
1959	MIL-N	79	300	60	109	192	17	3	20	57	36	3	.363	.437	.640	1.077	
1960	MIL-N	77	283	49	82	165	8	6	21	67	27	1	.290	.354	.583	.937	
1961	MIL-N	77	287	58	90	175	18	5	19	58	34	2	.314	.390	.610	1.000	
1962	MIL-N	77	286	63	87	154	11	1	18	50	31	1	.304	.374	.538	.913	
1963	MIL-N	80	302	57	93	166	14	1	19	63	40	0	.308	.389	.550	.939	
1964	MIL-N	70	265	52	87	138	16	1	11	42	33	0	.328	.403	.521	.923	
1965	MIL-N	78	291	59	98	175	20	0	19	45	33	0	.337	.404	.601	1.006	
1966	ATL-N	80	294	56	79	153	9	1	21	60	38	0	.269	.352	.520	.873	
1967	ATL-N	77	287	63	100	188	19	0	23	59	34	0	.348	.417	.655	1.072	
1968	ATL-N	81	294	40	88	155	12	2	17	44	37	1	.299	.380	.527	.907	
1969	ATL-N	75	266	50	82	165	18	1	21	46	50	1	.308	.420	.620	1.040	
1970	ATL-N	74	252	50	69	147	9	0	23	64	32	1	.274	.358	.583	.941	
1971	ATL-N	66	243	53	84	191	12	1	31	75	29	0	.346	.415	.786	1.201	
1972	ATL-N	64	221	39	55	114	2	0	19	39	52	0	.249	.392	.516	.908	
1973	ATL-N	63	208	45	66	141	3	0	24	55	31	1	.317	.408	.678	1.086	
1974	ATL-N	55	165	25	49	89	7	0	11	39	25	0	.297	.389	.539	.929	
1975	MIL-A	68	218	21	47	70	9	1	4	24	40	0	.216	.337	.321	.658	
1976	MIL-A	40	134	14	31	52	3	0	6	25	16	0	.231	.313	.388	.701	
	23	1648	5972	1080	1812	3323	282	37	385	1117	746	17	.303	.382	.556	.939	
HANK AARON - AWAY																	
1954	MIL-N	61	253	42	78	138	12	6	12	51	17	2	.308	.357	.545	.902	.684
1955	MIL-N	76	319	54	92	155	18	3	13	48	18	1	.288	.328	.486	.814	1.243
1956	MIL-N	78	314	47	114	186	19	10	11	52	17	0	.363	.396	.592	.988	.873
1957	MIL-N	73	311	63	105	204	15	3	26	83	28	0	.338	.392	.656	1.048	.867
1958	MIL-N	77	322	64	109	195	20	3	20	55	22	0	.339	.381	.606	.986	.883
1959	MIL-N	75	329	56	114	208	29	4	19	66	15	1	.347	.377	.632	1.009	1.067
1960	MIL-N	76	307	53	90	169	12	5	19	59	33	1	.293	.364	.550	.914	1.025
1961	MIL-N	78	316	57	107	183	21	5	15	62	22	0	.339	.382	.579	.961	1.041
1962	MIL-N	79	306	64	104	212	17	5	27	78	35	2	.340	.411	.693	1.104	.827
1963	MIL-N	81	329	64	108	204	15	3	25	67	38	0	.328	.398	.620	1.018	.922
1964	MIL-N	75	305	51	100	155	14	1	13	53	29	0	.328	.386	.508	.894	1.032
1965	MIL-N	72	279	50	83	144	20	1	13	44	27	1	.297	.362	.516	.878	1.146
1966	ATL-N	78	309	61	89	172	14	0	23	67	38	1	.288	.368	.557	.924	.944
1967	ATL-N	78	313	50	84	156	18	3	16	50	29	0	.268	.330	.498	.829	1.294
1968	ATL-N	79	312	44	86	147	21	2	12	42	27	0	.276	.333	.471	.804	1.127
1969	ATL-N	72	281	50	82	167	12	2	23	51	37	1	.292	.376	.594	.970	1.071
1970	ATL-N	76	264	53	85	149	17	1	15	54	42	1	.322	.417	.564	.981	.959
1971	ATL-N	73	252	42	78	140	10	2	16	43	42	2	.310	.412	.556	.968	1.242
1972	ATL-N	65	228	36	64	117	8	0	15	38	40	1	.281	.390	.513	.903	1.005
1973	ATL-N	57	184	39	52	111	9	1	16	41	37	0	.283	.403	.603	1.006	1.080
1974	ATL-N	57	175	22	42	78	9	0	9	30	14	0	.240	.296	.446	.742	1.252
1975	MIL-A	69	247	24	62	95	7	1	8	36	30	1	.251	.335	.385	.719	.915
1976	MIL-A	45	137	8	31	48	5	0	4	10	19	0	.226	.321	.350	.671	1.045
	23	1650	6392	1094	1959	3533	342	61	370	1180	656	15	.306	.372	.553	.925	1.015
ROBERTO CLEMENTE - HOME																	
1955	PIT-N	58	230	27	64	94	11	5	3	22	9	2	.278	.311	.409	.720	
1956	PIT-N	73	253	40	78	109	15	2	4	32	5	3	.308	.330	.431	.760	
1957	PIT-N	61	248	25	63	85	6	5	2	13	13	0	.254	.291	.343	.634	
1958	PIT-N	70	256	34	75	101	9	7	1	25	17	0	.293	.337	.395	.732	
1959	PIT-N	53	210	30	67	84	8	3	1	22	7	1	.319	.344	.400	.744	
1960	PIT-N	70	278	40	87	123	15	3	5	47	14	1	.313	.348	.442	.791	
1961	PIT-N	69	270	46	101	163	20	6	10	40	18	2	.374	.417	.604	1.021	
1962	PIT-N	76	285	51	94	143	15	8	6	44	20	1	.330	.376	.502	.878	
1963	PIT-N	76	304	39	94	129	12	4	5	31	11	1	.309	.335	.424	.760	
1964	PIT-N	77	311	42	108	145	17	4	4	48	22	1	.347	.392	.466	.858	
1965	PIT-N	78	305	49	105	149	9	10	5	36	26	4	.344	.403	.489	.892	
1966	PIT-N	78	317	59	113	196	17	9	16	73	23	0	.356	.400	.618	1.018	
1967	PIT-N	69	276	56	105	158	10	8	9	48	23	1	.380	.430	.572	1.002	
1968	PIT-N	64	236	37	72	121	13	9	6	29	29	1	.305	.383	.513	.896	
1969	PIT-N	65	240	40	94	141	13	8	6	45	19	2	.392	.441	.588	1.028	
1970	PIT-N	54	196	32	65	107	12	6	6	27	23	2	.332	.407	.546	.953	
1971	PIT-N	65	247	38	88	128	11	4	7	47	17	0	.356	.398	.518	.916	
1972	PIT-N	50	177	37	55	88	11	2	6	31	20	0	.311	.381	.497	.878	
	18	1206	4639	722	1528	2264	224	103	102	660	316	22	.329	.375	.488	.863	
ROBERTO CLEMENTE - AWAY																	
1955	PIT-N	66	244	21	57	87	12	6	2	25	9	0	.234	.261	.357	.617	1.166
1956	PIT-N	74	290	26	91	125	15	5	3	28	8	1	.314	.334	.431	.765	.993
1957	PIT-N	50	203	17	51	72	11	2	2	17	10	0	.251	.286	.355	.641	.989
1958	PIT-N	70	263	35	75	111	15	3	5	25	14	0	.285	.321	.422	.743	.984
1959	PIT-N	52	222	30	61	87	9	4	3	28	8	2	.275	.306	.392	.698	1.066
1960	PIT-N	74	292	49	92	138	7	3	11	47	25	1	.315	.371	.473	.844	.937
1961	PIT-N	77	302	54	100	157	10	4	13	49	17	1	.331	.369	.520	.889	1.149
1962	PIT-N	68	253	44	74	101	13	1	4	30	15	0	.292	.332	.399	.731	1.200
1963	PIT-N	76	296	38	98	153	11	4	12	45	20	3	.331	.379	.517	.896	.848
1964	PIT-N	78	311	53	103	156	23	3	8	39	29	1	.331	.390	.502	.892	.963
1965	PIT-N	74	284	42	89	124	12	4	5	29	17	1	.313	.354	.437	.791	1.127
1966	PIT-N	76	321	46	89	146	14	2	13	46	23	0	.277	.326	.455	.780	1.305
1967	PIT-N	78	309	47	104	166	16	2	14	62	18	2	.337	.377	.537	.914	1.097
1968	PIT-N	68	266	37	74	121	5	3	12	28	22	0	.278	.333	.455	.788	1.137
1969	PIT-N	73	267	47	81	135	7	4	13	46	37	1	.303	.390	.506	.896	1.148
1970	PIT-N	54	216	33	80	122	10	4	8	33	15	0	.370	.411	.565	.976	.977
1971	PIT-N	67	275	44	90	134	18	4	6	39	9	0	.327	.349	.487	.836	1.096
1972	PIT-N	52	201	31	63	93	8	5	4	29	9	0	.313	.343	.463	.806	1.090
	18	1227	4815	694	1472	2228	216	63	138	645	305	13	.306	.349	.463	.811	1.063

YEAR	TM/L	G	AB	R	H	TB	2B	3B	HR	RBI	BB	HB	AVG	OBP	SLG	PRO	H/R
TY COBB - HOME																	
1905	DET-A	15	52	4	14	16	2	0	0		3		.269	.309	.308	.617	
1906	DET-A	53	189	26	67	82	3	6	0		10	1	.354	.390	.434	.824	
1907	DET-A	78	304	42	112	145	16	7	1		12	2	.368	.396	.477	.873	
1908	DET-A	74	274	50	91	122	21	5	0		16	4	.332	.378	.445	.823	
1909	DET-A	78	294	67	116	165	19	6	6		20	3	.395	.438	.561	1.000	
1910	DET-A	70	237	50	94	135	17	6	4		32	3	.397	.474	.570	1.044	
1911	DET-A	76	297	81	124	190	27	12	5		24	6	.418	.471	.640	1.111	
1912	DET-A	72	280	55	113	155	15	12	1		18	4	.404	.447	.554	1.001	
1913	DET-A	60	197	38	85	111	12	7	0		27	1	.431	.502	.563	1.066	
1914	DET-A	48	172	30	72	94	9	5	1		29	0	.419	.502	.547	1.049	
1915	DET-A	76	261	73	103	139	17	8	1		67	4	.395	.524	.533	1.057	
1916	DET-A	71	254	57	91	122	13	6	2		40	1	.358	.447	.480	.928	
1917	DET-A	74	281	45	98	148	21	13	1		28	2	.349	.412	.527	.938	
1918	DET-A	49	180	38	64	97	13	10	0		17	1	.356	.414	.539	.953	
1919	DET-A	63	252	45	100	129	19	5	0		18	0	.397	.437	.512	.949	
1920	DET-A	57	201	45	67	96	18	4	1	30	37	0	.333	.437	.478	.915	
1921	DET-A	62	240	61	95	144	18	8	5	41	23	2	.396	.453	.600	1.053	
1922	DET-A	73	269	55	109	157	23	11	1	58	30	1	.405	.467	.584	1.050	
1923	DET-A	72	280	47	101	138	21	5	2	47	33	2	.361	.432	.493	.925	
1924	DET-A	78	306	61	100	134	22	6	0	36	46	1	.327	.416	.438	.854	
1925	DET-A	59	190	39	63	99	12	9	2	46	36	3	.332	.445	.521	.966	
1926	DET-A	41	97	18	25	40	5	5	0	26	9	0	.258	.321	.412	.733	
1927	PHI-A	65	236	54	82	111	15	4	2	47	34	2	.347	.434	.470	.904	
1928	PHI-A	53	200	33	66	87	18	0	1	20	20	2	.330	.396	.435	.831	
	24	1517	5543	1114	2052	2856	376	160	36	351	629	45	.370	.438	.515	.954	
TY COBB - AWAY																	
1905	DET-A	26	98	15	22	29	4	0	1		7		.224	.276	.296	.572	1.078
1906	DET-A	45	169	19	46	61	10	1	1		9	1	.272	.313	.361	.674	1.223
1907	DET-A	72	301	55	100	141	13	8	4		12	1	.332	.360	.468	.828	1.054
1908	DET-A	76	307	38	97	154	15	15	4		18	3	.316	.360	.502	.861	.955
1909	DET-A	78	279	49	100	131	14	4	3		28	3	.358	.423	.470	.892	1.121
1910	DET-A	70	269	56	100	144	18	7	4		32	1	.372	.440	.535	.976	1.070
1911	DET-A	70	294	66	124	177	20	12	3		20	2	.422	.462	.602	1.064	1.044
1912	DET-A	63	273	64	114	169	15	11	6		25	1	.418	.468	.619	1.087	.920
1913	DET-A	62	231	32	82	118	6	9	4		31	3	.355	.438	.511	.949	1.123
1914	DET-A	49	173	39	55	83	13	6	1		28	6	.318	.430	.480	.910	1.153
1915	DET-A	80	302	71	105	135	14	5	2		51	6	.348	.451	.447	.898	1.176
1916	DET-A	74	288	56	110	145	18	4	3		38	1	.382	.456	.503	.959	.967
1917	DET-A	78	307	62	127	187	23	11	5		33	2	.414	.474	.609	1.083	.867
1918	DET-A	62	241	45	97	120	6	4	3		24	1	.402	.459	.498	.957	.996
1919	DET-A	61	245	47	91	127	17	8	1		20	1	.371	.421	.518	.939	1.010
1920	DET-A	55	227	41	76	97	10	4	1	33	21	2	.335	.396	.427	.823	1.111
1921	DET-A	66	267	63	102	158	19	8	7	60	33	1	.382	.452	.592	1.044	1.009
1922	DET-A	64	257	44	102	140	19	5	3	41	25	3	.397	.456	.545	1.001	1.049
1923	DET-A	73	276	56	88	123	19	2	4	41	33	1	.319	.394	.446	.839	1.102
1924	DET-A	77	319	54	111	147	16	4	4	39	39	0	.348	.419	.461	.880	.971
1925	DET-A	62	225	58	94	149	19	3	10	56	29	2	.418	.488	.662	1.151	.840
1926	DET-A	38	136	30	54	79	13	0	4	36	17	1	.397	.468	.581	1.048	.699
1927	PHI-A	68	254	50	93	125	17	3	3	47	33	3	.366	.445	.492	.937	.965
1928	PHI-A	42	153	21	48	65	9	4	0	20	14	2	.314	.379	.425	.804	1.035
	24	1516	5891	1131	2138	3004	347	138	81	373	620	47	.363	.428	.510	.938	1.017
EDDIE COLLINS - HOME																	
1906	PHI-A	0	0	0	0	0	0	0	0	0	0		.000	.000	.000	.000	
1907	PHI-A	5	10	0	2	2	0	0	0	0	0		.200	.200	.200	.400	
1908	PHI-A	63	195	30	62	86	13	4	1		9	3	.318	.357	.441	.799	
1909	PHI-A	76	282	51	103	133	18	3	2		31	1	.365	.430	.472	.902	
1910	PHI-A	76	276	36	85	120	6	13	1		23	3	.308	.368	.435	.802	
1911	PHI-A	73	269	55	95	116	9	6	0		34	7	.353	.439	.431	.870	
1912	PHI-A	78	280	70	100	132	16	8	0		51	0	.357	.456	.471	.928	
1913	PHI-A	75	272	55	95	127	14	6	2		34	3	.349	.427	.467	.894	
1914	PHI-A	75	244	57	94	120	10	5	2		47	5	.385	.493	.492	.985	
1915	CHI-A	79	269	59	92	119	8	8	1		51	2	.342	.450	.442	.893	
1916	CHI-A	77	262	44	83	115	10	11	0		44	0	.317	.415	.439	.854	
1917	CHI-A	79	272	49	71	95	8	8	0		50	2	.261	.380	.349	.729	
1918	CHI-A	51	176	23	43	55	5	2	1		33	0	.244	.364	.313	.676	
1919	CHI-A	70	244	44	77	96	6	5	1		34	2	.316	.404	.393	.797	
1920	CHI-A	77	291	53	106	142	18	6	2	40	39	1	.364	.441	.488	.929	
1921	CHI-A	69	277	42	97	115	12	3	0	30	27	2	.350	.412	.415	.827	
1922	CHI-A	77	302	50	95	109	8	3	0	41	34	1	.315	.386	.361	.747	
1923	CHI-A	68	222	40	77	91	8	3	0	27	43	3	.347	.459	.410	.869	
1924	CHI-A	74	264	50	99	131	16	5	2	56	41	0	.375	.459	.496	.955	
1925	CHI-A	59	196	38	59	70	8	0	1	41	42	1	.301	.427	.357	.784	
1926	CHI-A	50	167	32	55	73	14	2	0	21	25	2	.329	.423	.437	.860	
1927	PHI-A	44	95	19	33	42	7	1	0	5	18	0	.347	.451	.442	.893	
1928	PHI-A	18	17	0	5	6	1	0	0	5	2	0	.294	.368	.353	.721	
1929	PHI-A	5	4	0	0	0	0	0	0	0	1	0	.000	.200	.000	.200	
1930	PHI-A	2	1	1	1	1	0	0	0	0	0	0	1.000	1.000	1.000	2.000	
	25	1420	4887	898	1629	2096	215	102	16	266	713	38	.333	.422	.429	.851	
EDDIE COLLINS - AWAY																	
1906	PHI-A	6	15	2	3	3	0	0	0		0		.200	.200	.200	.400	.000
1907	PHI-A	8	12	0	3	3	0	0	0		0		.250	.250	.250	.500	.800
1908	PHI-A	39	135	9	28	39	5	3	0		7		.207	.246	.289	.535	1.492
1909	PHI-A	77	289	53	95	124	12	7	1		31	5	.329	.403	.429	.832	1.083
1910	PHI-A	77	305	45	103	123	10	2	2		26	3	.338	.395	.403	.798	1.005
1911	PHI-A	59	224	37	85	121	13	7	3		28	8	.379	.465	.540	1.006	.865
1912	PHI-A	75	263	67	89	104	9	3	0		50	0	.338	.444	.395	.840	1.105
1913	PHI-A	73	262	70	89	115	9	7	1		51	4	.340	.454	.439	.893	1.001
1914	PHI-A	77	282	65	87	118	13	9	0		50	1	.309	.414	.418	.833	1.183
1915	CHI-A	76	252	59	81	108	14	2	3		68	3	.321	.471	.429	.899	.993
1916	CHI-A	78	283	43	85	101	4	6	0		42	3	.300	.396	.357	.753	1.134

YEAR	TM/L	G	AB	R	H	TB	2B	3B	HR	RBI	BB	HB	AVG	OBP	SLG	PRO	H/R
1917	CHI-A	77	292	42	92	110	10	4	0		39	1	.315	.398	.377	.774	.941
1918	CHI-A	46	154	28	48	54	3	0	1		40	0	.312	.454	.351	.804	.841
1919	CHI-A	70	274	43	88	114	13	2	3		34	0	.321	.396	.416	.812	.981
1920	CHI-A	76	309	60	114	149	18	7	1	35	30	1	.369	.426	.482	.909	1.022
1921	CHI-A	70	249	37	80	108	8	7	2	25	39	0	.321	.413	.434	.847	.976
1922	CHI-A	77	296	42	99	132	12	9	1	28	39	2	.334	.415	.446	.861	.867
1923	CHI-A	77	283	49	105	138	14	2	5	40	41	1	.371	.452	.488	.940	.924
1924	CHI-A	77	292	58	95	122	11	2	4	30	48	3	.325	.426	.418	.843	1.133
1925	CHI-A	59	229	42	88	118	18	3	2	39	45	3	.384	.491	.515	1.006	.779
1926	CHI-A	56	208	34	74	99	18	2	1	41	37	1	.356	.455	.476	.931	.923
1927	PHI-A	51	131	31	43	51	5	0	1	10	38	0	.328	.479	.389	.869	1.029
1928	PHI-A	18	16	3	5	7	2	0	0	2	2	0	.313	.389	.438	.826	.873
1929	PHI-A	4	3	0	0	0	0	0	0	0	1	0	.000	.250	.000	.250	.800
1930	PHI-A	1	1	0	0	0	0	0	0	0	0	0	.000	.000	.000	.000	.000
	25	1404	5059	919	1679	2161	221	84	31	250	786	39	.332	.426	.427	.853	.998

SAM CRAWFORD - HOME

YEAR	TM/L	G	AB	R	H	TB	2B	3B	HR	RBI	BB	HB	AVG	OBP	SLG	PRO	H/R
1899	CIN-N	8	34	14	16	21	1	2	0	9	0	0	.471	.471	.618	1.088	
1900	CIN-N	54	194	31	45	69	6	3	4	26	15		.232	.287	.356	.643	
1901	CIN-N	63	226	43	70	112	10	4	8	49	22		.310	.371	.496	.867	
1902	CIN-N	70	279	52	100	134	8	13	0	38	24		.358	.409	.480	.890	
1903	DET-A	66	271	41	91	128	10	12	1	44	9		.336	.357	.472	.829	
1904	DET-A	71	256	15	59	85	10	8	0	36	23		.230	.294	.332	.626	
1905	DET-A	76	280	37	90	122	20	3	2		24		.321	.375	.436	.811	
1906	DET-A	75	295	42	94	132	13	11	1		20		.319	.362	.447	.809	
1907	DET-A	75	298	52	103	139	12	12	0		19		.346	.385	.466	.851	
1908	DET-A	76	287	48	86	121	15	7	2		18		.300	.341	.422	.763	
1909	DET-A	77	290	45	96	134	15	7	3		23	1	.331	.382	.462	.844	
1910	DET-A	78	293	41	78	110	6	7	4		18	1	.266	.311	.375	.686	
1911	DET-A	72	273	53	114	165	17	11	4		29	0	.418	.474	.604	1.078	
1912	DET-A	72	269	37	87	128	13	11	2		20	1	.323	.372	.476	.848	
1913	DET-A	76	293	43	91	149	13	15	5		28	0	.311	.371	.509	.879	
1914	DET-A	78	287	33	89	146	12	18	3		37	1	.310	.391	.509	.899	
1915	DET-A	76	300	47	108	156	11	14	3		27	0	.360	.413	.520	.933	
1916	DET-A	49	151	25	47	65	4	7	0		19	0	.311	.388	.430	.819	
1917	DET-A	43	57	4	8	11	3	0	0		2	0	.140	.169	.193	.362	
	19	1255	4633	703	1472	2127	199	165	42	202	377	4	.318	.370	.459	.829	

SAM CRAWFORD - AWAY

YEAR	TM/L	G	AB	R	H	TB	2B	3B	HR	RBI	BB	HB	AVG	OBP	SLG	PRO	H/R
1899	CIN-N	23	93	11	23	38	2	5	1	11	2	0	.247	.263	.409	.672	1.620
1900	CIN-N	47	195	37	56	98	9	12	3	33	13		.287	.332	.503	.834	.770
1901	CIN-N	68	289	48	100	158	10	12	8	55	15		.346	.378	.547	.925	.937
1902	CIN-N	70	276	40	85	122	10	9	3	40	23		.308	.361	.442	.803	1.107
1903	DET-A	71	279	47	93	141	13	13	3	45	16		.333	.369	.505	.875	.948
1904	DET-A	79	306	34	84	118	12	8	2	37	21		.275	.321	.386	.707	.886
1905	DET-A	78	295	36	81	127	20	7	4		26		.275	.333	.431	.764	1.061
1906	DET-A	70	268	23	72	100	15	5	1		18		.269	.315	.373	.688	1.177
1907	DET-A	69	284	50	85	129	22	5	4		18		.299	.341	.454	.795	1.070
1908	DET-A	76	304	54	98	149	18	9	5		19		.322	.362	.490	.852	.895
1909	DET-A	79	299	38	89	132	20	7	3		24	0	.298	.350	.441	.791	1.067
1910	DET-A	76	295	42	92	139	20	12	1		19	0	.312	.354	.471	.825	.832
1911	DET-A	74	301	56	103	137	19	3	3		32	0	.342	.405	.455	.861	1.253
1912	DET-A	77	312	44	102	145	17	10	2		22	1	.327	.373	.465	.838	1.012
1913	DET-A	77	316	35	102	149	19	8	4		24	0	.323	.371	.472	.842	1.044
1914	DET-A	79	295	41	94	135	10	8	5		32	0	.319	.385	.458	.843	1.067
1915	DET-A	80	312	34	75	111	20	5	2		39	0	.240	.325	.356	.681	1.371
1916	DET-A	51	171	16	45	64	7	6	0		18	0	.263	.333	.374	.708	1.157
1917	DET-A	18	47	2	10	17	1	0	2		2	0	.213	.245	.362	.607	.598
	19	1262	4937	688	1489	2209	264	144	56	221	383	1	.302	.352	.447	.799	1.037

JOE DiMAGGIO - HOME

YEAR	TM/L	G	AB	R	H	TB	2B	3B	HR	RBI	BB	HB	AVG	OBP	SLG	PRO	H/R
1936	NY-A	67	288	51	90	148	18	8	8	53	14	2	.313	.349	.514	.863	
1937	NY-A	77	306	83	105	194	16	8	19	80	42	3	.343	.427	.634	1.061	
1938	NY-A	74	296	67	104	188	23	8	15	75	30	0	.351	.411	.635	1.046	
1939	NY-A	64	237	46	83	137	16	1	12	50	22	2	.350	.410	.578	.988	
1940	NY-A	63	234	40	84	156	12	6	16	67	32	1	.359	.438	.667	1.105	
1941	NY-A	76	292	60	101	182	21	6	16	69	40	0	.346	.425	.623	1.048	
1942	NY-A	77	305	51	89	140	15	6	8	55	29	0	.292	.353	.459	.812	
1946	NY-A	66	254	37	66	110	8	6	8	35	26	1	.260	.331	.433	.764	
1947	NY-A	70	252	49	77	132	18	5	9	51	41	1	.306	.405	.524	.929	
1948	NY-A	77	294	54	92	163	10	8	15	70	30	5	.313	.386	.554	.940	
1949	NY-A	37	127	25	41	69	7	3	5	23	28	1	.323	.449	.543	.992	
1950	NY-A	65	242	48	67	117	11	6	9	47	35	1	.277	.371	.483	.854	
1951	NY-A	67	233	37	61	100	11	2	8	45	29	3	.262	.351	.429	.780	
	13	880	3360	648	1060	1836	186	73	148	720	398	20	.315	.391	.546	.938	

JOE DiMAGGIO - AWAY

YEAR	TM/L	G	AB	R	H	TB	2B	3B	HR	RBI	BB	HB	AVG	OBP	SLG	PRO	H/R
1936	NY-A	71	349	81	116	219	26	7	21	72	10	2	.332	.355	.628	.982	.878
1937	NY-A	74	315	68	110	224	19	7	27	87	22	2	.349	.395	.711	1.106	.959
1938	NY-A	71	303	62	90	160	9	5	17	65	29	2	.297	.362	.528	.890	1.175
1939	NY-A	56	225	62	93	173	16	5	18	76	30	2	.413	.486	.769	1.255	.787
1940	NY-A	69	274	53	95	162	16	3	15	66	29	2	.347	.413	.591	1.004	1.100
1941	NY-A	63	249	62	92	166	22	5	14	56	36	4	.369	.457	.667	1.123	.933
1942	NY-A	77	305	72	97	164	14	7	13	59	39	2	.318	.399	.538	.937	.867
1946	NY-A	66	249	44	80	147	12	2	17	60	33	1	.321	.403	.590	.993	.769
1947	NY-A	71	282	48	91	147	13	5	11	46	23	2	.323	.378	.521	.899	1.033
1948	NY-A	76	300	56	98	192	16	3	24	85	37	3	.327	.406	.640	1.046	.899
1949	NY-A	39	145	33	53	93	7	3	9	44	27	1	.366	.468	.641	1.110	.894
1950	NY-A	74	283	66	91	190	22	4	23	75	45	0	.322	.415	.671	1.086	.786
1951	NY-A	49	182	35	48	75	11	2	4	26	32	3	.264	.382	.412	.795	.982
	13	856	3461	742	1154	2112	203	58	213	817	392	26	.333	.405	.610	1.015	.923

YEAR	TM/L	G	AB	R	H	TB	2B	3B	HR	RBI	BB	HB	AVG	OBP	SLG	PRO	H/R
JIMMIE FOXX - HOME																	
1925	PHI-A	6	6	2	4	5	1	0	0	0	0	0	.667	.667	.833	1.500	
1926	PHI-A	16	11	6	4	7	1	1	0	2	1	0	.364	.417	.636	1.053	
1927	PHI-A	37	97	17	31	51	5	3	3	19	13	0	.320	.400	.526	.926	
1928	PHI-A	55	173	42	60	108	17	5	7	37	27	1	.347	.438	.624	1.062	
1929	PHI-A	72	244	61	93	167	12	4	18	61	49	1	.381	.486	.684	1.171	
1930	PHI-A	75	266	65	95	185	10	7	22	86	50	0	.357	.459	.695	1.154	
1931	PHI-A	66	229	51	68	143	13	4	18	64	38	0	.297	.397	.624	1.021	
1932	PHI-A	77	283	87	110	232	21	4	31	94	72	0	.389	.513	.820	1.332	
1933	PHI-A	75	274	69	98	208	11	3	31	96	49	1	.358	.457	.759	1.216	
1934	PHI-A	75	265	57	92	178	12	4	22	61	52	1	.347	.456	.672	1.128	
1935	PHI-A	71	237	63	96	170	19	2	17	51	72	0	.405	.544	.717	1.261	
1936	BOS-A	77	294	68	104	188	17	2	21	84	50	0	.354	.448	.639	1.087	
1937	BOS-A	71	254	59	80	151	11	3	18	58	56	1	.315	.441	.594	1.035	
1938	BOS-A	74	274	83	111	243	21	3	35	104	60	0	.405	.512	.887	1.399	
1939	BOS-A	56	208	51	74	147	12	5	17	56	37	1	.356	.455	.707	1.162	
1940	BOS-A	74	266	58	85	166	18	3	19	67	57	0	.320	.440	.624	1.064	
1941	BOS-A	68	248	52	75	131	12	4	12	56	47	0	.302	.414	.528	.942	
1942	BOS-A	18	62	16	19	34	3	0	4	10	14	2	.306	.449	.548	.997	
1942	CHI-N	29	82	8	13	17	1	0	1	5	4	0	.159	.198	.207	.405	
1944	CHI-N	7	7	0	0	0	0	0	0	0	0	0	.000	.000	.000	.000	
1945	PHI-N	45	102	15	28	41	2	1	3	17	9	0	.275	.333	.402	.735	
	21	1144	3882	930	1340	2572	219	58	299	1028	757	8	.345	.453	.663	1.116	
JIMMIE FOXX - AWAY																	
1925	PHI-A	4	3	0	2	2	0	0	0	0	0	0	.667	.667	.667	1.333	1.125
1926	PHI-A	10	21	2	6	7	1	0	0	3	0	0	.286	.286	.333	.619	1.701
1927	PHI-A	24	33	6	11	16	1	2	0	1	1	1	.333	.371	.485	.856	1.081
1928	PHI-A	63	227	43	71	111	12	5	6	42	33	0	.313	.400	.489	.889	1.195
1929	PHI-A	77	273	62	90	156	11	5	15	57	54	1	.330	.442	.571	1.014	1.155
1930	PHI-A	78	296	62	93	173	23	6	15	70	43	0	.314	.401	.584	.986	1.171
1931	PHI-A	73	286	42	82	149	19	6	12	56	35	1	.287	.366	.521	.887	1.151
1932	PHI-A	77	302	64	103	206	12	5	27	75	44	0	.341	.425	.682	1.107	1.204
1933	PHI-A	74	299	56	106	195	26	6	17	67	47	0	.355	.442	.652	1.094	1.111
1934	PHI-A	75	274	63	88	174	16	2	22	69	59	0	.321	.441	.635	1.076	1.048
1935	PHI-A	76	298	55	89	170	14	5	19	64	42	0	.299	.385	.570	.956	1.319
1936	BOS-A	78	291	62	94	181	15	6	20	59	55	1	.323	.432	.622	1.054	1.031
1937	BOS-A	79	315	52	82	155	13	3	18	69	43	0	.260	.349	.492	.841	1.230
1938	BOS-A	75	291	56	86	155	12	6	15	71	59	0	.296	.414	.533	.947	1.477
1939	BOS-A	68	259	79	94	177	19	5	18	49	52	1	.363	.471	.683	1.155	1.006
1940	BOS-A	70	249	48	68	133	12	1	17	52	44	0	.273	.382	.534	.916	1.161
1941	BOS-A	67	239	35	71	115	15	4	7	49	46	0	.297	.411	.481	.892	1.056
1942	BOS-A	12	38	2	8	12	1	0	1	4	4	0	.211	.286	.316	.602	1.658
1942	CHI-N	41	123	17	29	42	7	0	2	14	18	0	.236	.333	.341	.675	.600
1944	CHI-N	8	13	0	1	2	1	0	0	2	2	0	.077	.200	.154	.354	.000
1945	PHI-N	44	122	15	32	53	9	0	4	21	14	0	.262	.338	.434	.773	.952
	21	1173	4252	821	1306	2384	239	67	235	894	695	5	.307	.405	.561	.966	1.155
LOU GEHRIG - HOME																	
1923	NY-A	6	4	0	1	2	1	0	0	2	0	0	.250	.250	.500	.750	
1924	NY-A	4	6	2	4	4	0	0	0	2	1	0	.667	.714	.667	1.381	
1925	NY-A	68	237	41	66	123	14	5	11	42	21	1	.278	.340	.519	.859	
1926	NY-A	75	270	62	81	136	19	12	4	44	47	1	.300	.406	.504	.909	
1927	NY-A	77	277	71	96	200	16	8	24	77	53	2	.347	.455	.722	1.177	
1928	NY-A	77	262	62	97	169	26	5	12	66	44	1	.370	.463	.645	1.108	
1929	NY-A	77	271	60	85	175	13	7	21	76	59	3	.314	.441	.646	1.087	
1930	NY-A	76	270	59	94	172	16	10	14	57	48	2	.348	.450	.637	1.087	
1931	NY-A	77	304	83	92	196	12	10	24	86	51	0	.303	.403	.645	1.048	
1932	NY-A	77	289	59	88	149	13	6	12	60	52	1	.304	.412	.516	.928	
1933	NY-A	75	281	59	85	156	12	4	17	69	35	0	.302	.380	.555	.935	
1934	NY-A	77	290	68	120	238	20	4	30	98	49	1	.414	.500	.821	1.321	
1935	NY-A	74	253	45	71	134	8	5	15	45	64	2	.281	.429	.530	.959	
1936	NY-A	77	267	81	94	188	11	1	27	71	69	4	.352	.491	.704	1.195	
1937	NY-A	79	275	68	104	195	13	3	24	93	69	1	.378	.504	.709	1.213	
1938	NY-A	79	287	61	88	154	12	3	16	58	49	2	.307	.411	.537	.948	
1939	NY-A	5	18	1	3	3	0	0	0	1	2	0	.167	.250	.167	.417	
	17	1080	3861	882	1269	2394	206	83	251	947	713	21	.329	.436	.620	1.056	
LOU GEHRIG - AWAY																	
1923	NY-A	7	22	6	10	18	3	1	1	7	2	0	.455	.500	.818	1.318	.569
1924	NY-A	6	6	0	2	3	1	0	0	3	0	0	.333	.333	.500	.833	1.657
1925	NY-A	58	200	32	63	109	9	5	9	26	25	1	.315	.394	.545	.939	.915
1926	NY-A	80	302	73	98	178	28	8	12	63	58	0	.325	.433	.589	1.023	.889
1927	NY-A	78	307	78	122	247	36	10	23	98	56	1	.397	.492	.805	1.296	.908
1928	NY-A	77	300	77	113	195	21	8	15	76	51	3	.377	.472	.650	1.122	.987
1929	NY-A	77	282	67	81	147	20	2	14	50	63	2	.287	.421	.521	.942	1.154
1930	NY-A	78	311	84	126	247	26	7	27	117	53	1	.405	.493	.794	1.287	.844
1931	NY-A	78	315	80	119	214	19	5	22	98	66	0	.378	.486	.679	1.165	.899
1932	NY-A	79	307	79	120	221	29	3	22	91	56	2	.391	.488	.720	1.208	.768
1933	NY-A	77	312	79	113	203	29	8	15	70	57	1	.362	.462	.651	1.113	.840
1934	NY-A	77	289	60	90	171	20	2	19	67	60	1	.311	.431	.592	1.023	1.291
1935	NY-A	75	282	80	105	178	18	5	15	74	68	3	.372	.499	.631	1.130	.849
1936	NY-A	78	312	86	111	215	26	6	22	81	61	3	.356	.465	.689	1.155	1.035
1937	NY-A	78	294	70	96	171	24	6	13	66	58	3	.327	.442	.582	1.024	1.185
1938	NY-A	78	289	54	82	147	20	3	13	56	58	3	.284	.409	.509	.917	1.033
1939	NY-A	3	10	1	1	1	0	0	0	0	3	0	.100	.308	.100	.408	1.022
	17	1084	4140	1006	1452	2665	329	79	242	1043	795	24	.351	.458	.644	1.102	.958
ROGERS HORNSBY - HOME																	
1915	STL-N	17	54	4	13	14	1	0	0		2	0	.241	.268	.259	.527	
1916	STL-N	69	238	36	80	118	13	8	3		15	1	.336	.378	.496	.874	
1917	STL-N	72	258	46	83	125	6	12	4		18	2	.322	.371	.484	.855	
1918	STL-N	59	201	25	50	75	11	4	2		22	0	.249	.323	.373	.696	
1919	STL-N	69	253	40	87	120	8	5	5		22	3	.344	.403	.474	.877	

YEAR	TM/L	G	AB	R	H	TB	2B	3B	HR	RBI	BB	HB	AVG	OBP	SLG	PRO	H/R
1920	STL-N	71	273	43	90	137	21	10	2	42	31	2	.330	.402	.502	.904	
1921	STL-N	78	296	56	111	186	21	9	12	71	29	2	.375	.434	.628	1.063	
1922	STL-N	77	313	65	126	232	22	6	24	83	33	0	.403	.460	.741	1.201	
1923	STL-N	44	169	41	68	120	13	3	11	42	29	3	.402	.498	.710	1.208	
1924	STL-N	77	290	70	136	229	28	10	15	56	45	1	.469	.542	.790	1.331	
1925	STL-N	69	245	78	117	221	22	5	24	81	48	1	.478	.565	.902	1.467	
1926	STL-N	71	269	48	80	111	14	1	5	40	32	0	.297	.372	.413	.785	
1927	NY-N	74	263	58	94	151	15	3	12	58	41	1	.357	.446	.574	1.020	
1928	BOS-N	69	239	42	89	151	16	5	12	54	56	1	.372	.492	.632	1.123	
1929	CHI-N	78	289	86	118	218	27	2	23	80	54	0	.408	.501	.754	1.256	
1930	CHI-N	24	56	7	14	19	2	0	1	5	4	1	.250	.311	.339	.651	
1931	CHI-N	50	171	29	45	74	14	0	5	39	30	0	.263	.373	.433	.806	
1932	CHI-N	13	40	7	11	16	2	0	1	7	7	0	.275	.383	.400	.783	
1933	STL-N	24	47	3	15	19	4	0	0	6	6	1	.319	.407	.404	.812	
1933	STL-A	7	5	2	2	6	1	0	1	2	2	0	.400	.571	1.200	1.771	
1934	STL-A	14	10	1	2	5	0	0	1	5	4	0	.200	.429	.500	.929	
1935	STL-A	7	18	1	4	7	3	0	0	2	2	0	.222	.300	.389	.689	
1936	STL-A	0	0	0	0	0	0	0	0	0	0	0	—	—	—	—	
1937	STL-A	13	35	5	14	19	2	0	1	8	4	0	.400	.462	.543	1.004	
	23	1146	4032	793	1449	2373	266	83	164	681	536	18	.359	.437	.589	1.025	

ROGERS HORNSBY - AWAY

YEAR	TM/L	G	AB	R	H	TB	2B	3B	HR	RBI	BB	HB	AVG	OBP	SLG	PRO	H/R
1915	STL-N	1	3	1	1	2	1	0	0		0	0	.333	.333	.667	1.000	.527
1916	STL-N	70	257	27	75	102	4	7	3		25	3	.292	.361	.397	.758	1.152
1917	STL-N	73	265	40	88	128	18	5	4		27	2	.332	.398	.483	.881	.971
1918	STL-N	56	215	26	67	98	8	7	3		18	3	.312	.373	.456	.829	.840
1919	STL-N	69	259	28	76	100	7	4	3		26	4	.293	.367	.386	.753	1.165
1920	STL-N	78	316	53	128	192	23	10	7	52	29	1	.405	.457	.608	1.064	.849
1921	STL-N	76	296	75	124	192	23	9	9	55	31	5	.419	.482	.649	1.131	.940
1922	STL-N	77	310	76	124	218	24	8	18	69	32	1	.400	.458	.703	1.161	1.034
1923	STL-N	63	255	48	95	146	19	7	6	41	26	0	.373	.431	.573	1.003	1.204
1924	STL-N	66	246	51	91	144	15	4	10	38	44	1	.370	.467	.585	1.053	1.265
1925	STL-N	69	259	55	86	160	19	5	15	62	35	1	.332	.414	.618	1.031	1.422
1926	STL-N	63	258	48	87	133	20	4	6	53	29	0	.337	.404	.516	.920	.853
1927	NY-N	81	305	75	111	182	17	6	14	67	45	3	.364	.450	.597	1.047	.974
1928	BOS-N	71	247	57	99	156	26	2	9	40	51	1	.401	.505	.632	1.137	.988
1929	CHI-N	78	313	70	111	191	20	6	16	69	33	1	.355	.418	.610	1.028	1.221
1930	CHI-N	18	48	8	18	26	3	1	1	13	8	0	.375	.464	.542	1.006	.647
1931	CHI-N	50	186	35	73	131	23	1	11	51	26	0	.392	.467	.704	1.171	.688
1932	CHI-N	6	18	3	2	2	0	0	0	0	3	2	.111	.304	.111	.415	1.885
1933	STL-N	22	36	6	12	20	2	0	2	15	6	1	.333	.442	.556	.997	.814
1933	STL-A	4	4	0	1	1	0	0	0	0	0	0	.250	.250	.250	.500	3.543
1934	STL-A	10	13	1	5	7	2	0	0	6	3	1	.385	.529	.538	1.068	.870
1935	STL-A	3	6	0	1	1	0	0	0	1	1	0	.167	.286	.167	.452	1.523
1936	STL-A	2	5	1	2	2	0	0	0	2	1	0	.400	.500	.400	.900	.000
1937	STL-A	7	21	2	4	5	1	0	0	3	3	0	.190	.292	.238	.530	1.896
	23	1113	4141	786	1481	2339	275	86	137	637	502	30	.358	.431	.565	.996	1.030

REGGIE JACKSON - HOME

YEAR	TM/L	G	AB	R	H	TB	2B	3B	HR	RBI	BB	HB	AVG	OBP	SLG	PRO	H/R
1967	KC-A	23	75	8	14	25	3	4	0	5	6	4	.187	.282	.333	.616	
1968	OAK-A	78	270	33	65	103	9	1	9	37	27	3	.241	.317	.381	.698	
1969	OAK-A	78	288	61	80	180	20	1	26	55	56	4	.278	.402	.625	1.027	
1970	OAK-A	74	201	24	40	71	7	0	8	25	27	2	.199	.300	.353	.653	
1971	OAK-A	74	262	39	68	132	13	0	17	40	31	3	.260	.345	.504	.848	
1972	OAK-A	72	262	40	71	130	11	0	16	38	31	4	.271	.357	.496	.853	
1973	OAK-A	73	243	39	63	128	11	0	18	54	43	2	.259	.375	.527	.902	
1974	OAK-A	71	233	39	70	121	9	0	14	43	34	3	.300	.396	.519	.916	
1975	OAK-A	77	288	40	73	150	21	1	18	50	29	1	.253	.324	.521	.845	
1976	BAL-A	67	247	34	63	114	15	0	12	42	21	4	.255	.324	.462	.785	
1977	NY-A	73	247	48	70	124	17	2	11	42	42	3	.283	.394	.502	.896	
1978	NY-A	71	257	43	74	139	4	5	17	53	33	4	.288	.378	.541	.918	
1979	NY-A	67	235	39	71	126	8	1	15	50	32	1	.302	.388	.536	.924	
1980	NY-A	71	256	43	70	129	3	4	16	46	35	1	.273	.363	.504	.867	
1981	NY-A	43	145	12	30	54	1	1	7	22	22	0	.207	.311	.372	.684	
1982	CAL-A	76	267	46	76	148	7	1	21	53	40	0	.285	.378	.554	.932	
1983	CAL-A	57	192	22	37	66	8	0	7	23	26	2	.193	.295	.344	.639	
1984	CAL-A	71	246	34	52	102	5	0	15	48	25	1	.211	.287	.415	.701	
1985	CAL-A	70	225	30	49	104	10	0	15	44	38	0	.218	.331	.462	.793	
1986	CAL-A	67	195	33	54	97	6	2	11	32	51	1	.277	.429	.497	.927	
1987	OAK-A	57	165	23	36	65	8	0	7	24	17	3	.218	.303	.394	.697	
	21	1410	4799	730	1226	2308	196	23	280	826	666	46	.255	.352	.481	.833	

REGGIE JACKSON - AWAY

YEAR	TM/L	G	AB	R	H	TB	2B	3B	HR	RBI	BB	HB	AVG	OBP	SLG	PRO	H/R
1967	KC-A	12	43	5	7	11	1	0	1	1	4	1	.163	.250	.256	.506	1.217
1968	OAK-A	76	283	49	73	147	4	5	20	37	23	2	.258	.318	.519	.838	.833
1969	OAK-A	74	261	62	71	154	16	2	21	63	58	8	.272	.419	.590	1.009	1.018
1970	OAK-A	75	225	33	61	124	14	2	15	41	48	6	.271	.412	.551	.963	.678
1971	OAK-A	76	305	48	89	156	16	3	15	40	32	3	.292	.365	.511	.876	.968
1972	OAK-A	63	237	32	61	106	14	2	9	37	28	4	.257	.346	.447	.793	1.076
1973	OAK-A	78	296	60	95	158	17	2	14	63	33	5	.321	.398	.534	.932	.968
1974	OAK-A	77	273	51	76	139	16	1	15	50	52	1	.278	.396	.509	.905	1.012
1975	OAK-A	80	305	51	77	153	18	2	18	54	38	2	.252	.339	.502	.841	1.005
1976	BAL-A	67	251	50	75	136	12	2	15	49	33	0	.299	.380	.542	.922	.851
1977	NY-A	73	278	45	80	165	22	0	21	68	33	0	.288	.363	.594	.957	.936
1978	NY-A	68	254	39	66	105	9	0	10	44	25	5	.260	.338	.413	.751	1.222
1979	NY-A	64	230	39	67	127	16	1	14	39	33	1	.291	.383	.552	.935	.989
1980	NY-A	72	258	51	84	178	19	0	25	65	48	1	.326	.433	.690	1.123	.772
1981	NY-A	51	189	21	49	89	16	0	8	32	24	1	.259	.346	.471	.817	.837
1982	CAL-A	77	263	46	70	134	10	0	18	48	45	2	.266	.377	.510	.887	1.051
1983	CAL-A	59	205	21	40	69	6	1	7	26	26	2	.195	.292	.337	.628	1.017
1984	CAL-A	72	279	33	65	111	12	2	10	33	30	2	.233	.312	.398	.710	.988
1985	CAL-A	73	235	34	67	120	17	0	12	41	40	1	.285	.391	.511	.902	.879
1986	CAL-A	65	224	32	47	74	6	0	7	26	41	2	.210	.337	.330	.667	1.388
1987	OAK-A	58	171	19	38	70	6	1	9	19	16	1	.222	.293	.409	.702	.992
	21	1410	5065	821	1358	2526	267	26	283	876	710	50	.268	.364	.499	.862	.966

YEAR	TM/L	G	AB	R	H	TB	2B	3B	HR	RBI	BB	HB	AVG	OBP	SLG	PRO	H/R
AL KALINE - HOME																	
1953	DET-A	10	8	2	2	2	0	0	0	0	0	1	.250	.333	.250	.583	
1954	DET-A	74	270	20	65	76	6	1	1	16	12	0	.241	.273	.281	.555	
1955	DET-A	77	284	59	102	171	9	6	16	54	46	2	.359	.452	.602	1.054	
1956	DET-A	76	297	41	96	157	16	3	13	63	32	1	.323	.391	.529	.920	
1957	DET-A	76	295	43	92	141	15	2	10	45	22	1	.312	.362	.478	.840	
1958	DET-A	76	272	45	97	155	19	3	11	51	31	0	.357	.422	.570	.992	
1959	DET-A	68	251	46	75	136	11	1	16	49	41	3	.299	.403	.542	.945	
1960	DET-A	73	263	39	70	106	13	1	7	33	33	2	.266	.352	.403	.755	
1961	DET-A	79	303	57	98	147	21	2	8	39	30	2	.323	.388	.485	.873	
1962	DET-A	53	208	41	66	129	7	4	16	55	27	0	.317	.396	.620	1.016	
1963	DET-A	74	285	56	98	183	15	2	22	71	27	3	.344	.406	.642	1.048	
1964	DET-A	69	250	35	75	119	13	2	9	33	28	2	.300	.375	.476	.851	
1965	DET-A	63	199	36	52	85	9	0	8	33	37	0	.261	.377	.427	.804	
1966	DET-A	72	242	47	64	130	12	0	18	45	40	3	.264	.375	.537	.913	
1967	DET-A	64	212	43	69	129	15	0	15	40	39	1	.325	.433	.608	1.041	
1968	DET-A	48	159	18	44	65	7	1	4	24	22	0	.277	.365	.409	.773	
1969	DET-A	71	234	46	66	113	8	0	13	32	34	0	.282	.373	.483	.856	
1970	DET-A	62	206	32	54	93	10	1	9	37	41	0	.262	.385	.451	.836	
1971	DET-A	67	191	44	54	98	7	2	11	29	41	3	.283	.417	.513	.930	
1972	DET-A	49	134	26	48	76	6	2	6	20	13	1	.358	.419	.567	.986	
1973	DET-A	46	146	21	38	63	7	0	6	23	16	2	.260	.341	.432	.773	
1974	DET-A	74	275	39	83	126	20	1	7	35	37	1	.302	.387	.458	.845	
	22	1421	4984	836	1508	2500	246	34	226	827	649	28	.303	.386	.502	.888	
AL KALINE - AWAY																	
1953	DET-A	20	20	7	5	8	0	0	1	2	1	0	.250	.286	.400	.686	.851
1954	DET-A	64	234	22	74	99	12	2	3	27	10	0	.316	.344	.423	.767	.723
1955	DET-A	75	304	62	98	150	15	2	11	48	36	3	.322	.399	.493	.893	1.180
1956	DET-A	77	320	55	98	170	16	7	14	65	38	0	.306	.380	.531	.911	1.009
1957	DET-A	73	282	40	78	135	14	2	13	45	21	2	.277	.331	.479	.810	1.037
1958	DET-A	70	271	39	73	111	15	4	5	34	23	2	.269	.331	.410	.741	1.340
1959	DET-A	68	260	40	92	135	8	1	11	45	31	1	.354	.425	.519	.944	1.001
1960	DET-A	74	288	38	83	129	16	3	8	35	32	1	.288	.361	.448	.809	.933
1961	DET-A	74	283	59	92	155	20	5	11	43	36	2	.325	.405	.548	.953	.917
1962	DET-A	47	190	37	55	107	9	2	13	39	20	1	.289	.360	.563	.923	1.100
1963	DET-A	71	266	33	74	100	9	1	5	30	27	1	.278	.347	.376	.723	1.450
1964	DET-A	77	275	42	79	127	18	3	8	35	47	1	.287	.393	.462	.855	.995
1965	DET-A	62	200	36	60	103	9	2	10	39	35	0	.300	.404	.515	.919	.875
1966	DET-A	70	237	38	74	126	17	1	11	43	41	2	.312	.418	.532	.950	.961
1967	DET-A	67	246	51	72	119	13	2	10	38	44	0	.293	.400	.484	.884	1.178
1968	DET-A	54	168	31	50	75	7	0	6	29	33	3	.298	.422	.446	.868	.891
1969	DET-A	60	222	28	58	91	9	0	8	37	20	1	.261	.325	.410	.735	1.165
1970	DET-A	69	261	32	76	117	14	3	7	34	36	1	.291	.379	.448	.827	1.010
1971	DET-A	66	214	25	65	89	12	0	4	25	41	4	.304	.425	.416	.841	1.106
1972	DET-A	57	144	20	39	56	5	0	4	12	15	1	.271	.344	.389	.733	1.346
1973	DET-A	45	164	19	41	59	6	0	4	22	13	1	.250	.309	.360	.669	1.156
1974	DET-A	73	283	32	63	91	8	1	6	29	28	0	.223	.293	.322	.614	1.375
	22	1413	5132	786	1499	2352	252	41	173	756	628	27	.292	.372	.458	.831	1.069
HARMON KILLEBREW - HOME																	
1954	WAS-A	6	9	0	1	1	0	0	0	1	1	0	.111	.200	.111	.311	
1955	WAS-A	20	48	7	11	20	0	0	3	5	5	0	.229	.302	.417	.719	
1956	WAS-A	12	21	1	3	3	0	0	0	1	2	0	.143	.217	.143	.360	
1957	WAS-A	6	22	4	7	15	2	0	2	4	1	0	.318	.348	.682	1.030	
1958	WAS-A	5	7	1	2	2	0	0	0	1	0	0	.286	.286	.286	.571	
1959	WAS-A	77	265	47	60	133	7	0	22	55	48	4	.226	.353	.502	.855	
1960	WAS-A	64	215	34	58	105	9	1	12	34	34	0	.270	.369	.488	.858	
1961	MIN-A	77	281	56	83	180	10	0	29	67	49	1	.295	.402	.641	1.042	
1962	MIN-A	75	261	38	63	133	10	0	20	58	52	3	.241	.373	.510	.883	
1963	MIN-A	73	258	43	63	149	8	0	26	53	38	0	.244	.341	.578	.919	
1964	MIN-A	78	281	52	71	154	5	0	26	65	48	2	.253	.366	.548	.914	
1965	MIN-A	54	185	34	48	86	5	0	11	39	35	1	.259	.380	.465	.845	
1966	MIN-A	81	283	48	82	171	15	1	24	58	43	0	.290	.383	.604	.988	
1967	MIN-A	80	257	51	73	148	12	0	21	60	69	2	.284	.439	.576	1.015	
1968	MIN-A	42	124	16	27	47	5	0	5	14	26	1	.218	.358	.379	.737	
1969	MIN-A	81	258	58	80	178	10	2	28	78	77	3	.310	.473	.690	1.163	
1970	MIN-A	80	260	46	71	133	12	1	16	49	68	2	.273	.427	.512	.939	
1971	MIN-A	72	237	30	56	108	5	1	15	68	55	0	.236	.380	.456	.836	
1972	MIN-A	69	206	30	55	100	7	1	12	40	54	0	.267	.419	.485	.905	
1973	MIN-A	40	138	16	35	49	6	1	2	15	20	1	.254	.352	.355	.707	
1974	MIN-A	61	159	17	38	67	2	0	9	37	24	0	.239	.339	.421	.760	
1975	KC-A	51	160	13	32	63	7	0	8	25	19	0	.200	.285	.394	.679	
	22	1204	3935	642	1019	2045	137	8	291	827	768	20	.259	.383	.520	.902	
HARMON KILLEBREW - AWAY																	
1954	WAS-A	3	4	1	3	4	1	0	0	2	1	0	.750	.800	1.000	1.800	.173
1955	WAS-A	18	32	5	5	9	1	0	1	2	4	0	.156	.250	.281	.531	1.353
1956	WAS-A	32	78	9	19	36	2	0	5	12	8	0	.244	.314	.462	.775	.465
1957	WAS-A	3	9	0	2	2	0	0	0	1	1	0	.222	.300	.222	.522	1.972
1958	WAS-A	8	24	1	4	4	0	0	0	1	0	1	.167	.200	.167	.367	1.558
1959	WAS-A	76	281	51	72	149	13	2	20	50	42	3	.256	.359	.530	.889	.962
1960	WAS-A	60	227	50	64	131	10	0	19	46	37	1	.282	.385	.577	.962	.892
1961	MIN-A	73	260	38	73	148	10	7	17	55	58	2	.281	.416	.569	.985	1.058
1962	MIN-A	80	291	47	71	168	11	1	28	68	54	1	.244	.364	.577	.941	.938
1963	MIN-A	69	257	45	70	137	10	0	19	43	34	3	.272	.364	.533	.897	1.024
1964	MIN-A	80	296	43	85	162	6	1	23	46	45	6	.287	.392	.547	.939	.973
1965	MIN-A	59	216	44	60	115	11	1	14	36	37	3	.278	.391	.532	.923	.915
1966	MIN-A	81	286	41	78	135	12	0	15	52	60	2	.273	.402	.472	.874	1.130
1967	MIN-A	83	290	54	74	157	12	1	23	53	62	1	.255	.388	.541	.929	1.092
1968	MIN-A	58	171	24	35	77	2	2	12	26	44	1	.205	.370	.450	.821	.898
1969	MIN-A	81	297	48	73	146	10	0	21	62	68	2	.246	.390	.492	.881	1.320
1970	MIN-A	77	267	50	72	155	8	0	25	64	60	0	.270	.404	.581	.984	.954
1971	MIN-A	75	263	31	71	124	14	0	13	51	59	0	.270	.404	.471	.875	.955

YEAR	TM/L	G	AB	R	H	TB	2B	3B	HR	RBI	BB	HB	AVG	OBP	SLG	PRO	H/R
1972	MIN-A	70	227	23	45	95	6	1	14	34	40	1	.198	.321	.419	.739	1.224
1973	MIN-A	29	110	13	25	37	3	0	3	17	21	0	.227	.351	.336	.688	1.029
1974	MIN-A	61	174	11	36	53	5	0	4	17	21	0	.207	.292	.305	.597	1.274
1975	KC-A	55	152	12	30	54	6	0	6	19	35	1	.197	.351	.355	.706	.961
	22	1231	4212	641	1067	2098	153	16	282	757	791	28	.253	.375	.498	.873	1.034

CHUCK KLEIN - HOME

YEAR	TM/L	G	AB	R	H	TB	2B	3B	HR	RBI	BB	HB	AVG	OBP	SLG	PRO	H/R
1928	PHI-N	37	145	28	56	95	6	3	9	26	8	1	.386	.422	.655	1.077	
1929	PHI-N	71	304	65	119	223	25	2	25	78	23	0	.391	.434	.734	1.168	
1930	PHI-N	77	326	91	143	259	32	3	26	109	25	3	.439	.483	.794	1.278	
1931	PHI-N	74	297	79	121	223	22	7	22	78	35	0	.407	.470	.751	1.221	
1932	PHI-N	77	338	92	143	270	26	7	29	97	29	0	.423	.469	.799	1.267	
1933	PHI-N	72	285	62	133	225	28	2	20	81	29	0	.467	.516	.789	1.305	
1934	CHI-N	59	223	40	66	122	18	1	12	47	26	1	.296	.372	.547	.919	
1935	CHI-N	50	171	26	44	75	5	1	8	26	13	0	.257	.310	.439	.748	
1936	CHI-N	15	53	8	14	25	2	0	3	11	8	0	.264	.361	.472	.832	
1936	PHI-N	62	257	45	79	129	17	3	9	45	20	0	.307	.357	.502	.859	
1937	PHI-N	57	201	48	77	132	16	0	13	39	23	1	.383	.449	.657	1.106	
1938	PHI-N	68	239	27	64	88	10	1	4	35	22	0	.268	.330	.368	.698	
1939	PHI-N	15	32	6	7	13	1	1	1	6	8	0	.219	.375	.406	.781	
1939	PIT-N	49	151	21	48	80	11	3	5	26	16	0	.318	.383	.530	.913	
1940	PHI-N	59	177	19	38	57	6	2	3	19	22	0	.215	.302	.322	.624	
1941	PHI-N	26	51	4	6	9	0	0	1	1	4	0	.118	.182	.176	.358	
1942	PHI-N	7	7	0	1	1	0	0	0	0	0	0	.143	.143	.143	.286	
1943	PHI-N	6	14	0	2	2	0	0	0	3	0	0	.143	.143	.143	.286	
1944	PHI-N	2	5	0	0	0	0	0	0	0	0	0	.000	.000	.000	.000	
	17	883	3276	661	1161	2028	225	36	190	727	311	6	.354	.411	.619	1.030	

CHUCK KLEIN - AWAY

YEAR	TM/L	G	AB	R	H	TB	2B	3B	HR	RBI	BB	HB	AVG	OBP	SLG	PRO	H/R
1928	PHI-N	27	108	13	35	51	8	1	2	8	6	0	.324	.360	.472	.832	1.295
1929	PHI-N	78	312	61	100	182	20	4	18	67	31	0	.321	.382	.583	.965	1.210
1930	PHI-N	79	322	67	107	186	27	5	14	61	29	1	.332	.389	.578	.967	1.321
1931	PHI-N	74	297	42	79	124	12	3	9	43	24	1	.266	.323	.418	.740	1.649
1932	PHI-N	77	312	60	83	150	24	4	9	40	31	1	.266	.334	.481	.815	1.555
1933	PHI-N	80	321	39	90	140	16	5	8	39	27	1	.280	.338	.436	.774	1.686
1934	CHI-N	56	212	38	65	100	9	1	8	33	21	1	.307	.372	.472	.843	1.090
1935	CHI-N	69	263	45	83	137	9	3	13	47	28	1	.316	.384	.521	.904	.827
1936	CHI-N	14	56	11	18	27	3	0	2	7	8	0	.321	.406	.482	.888	.937
1936	PHI-N	55	235	38	73	127	13	4	11	42	13	0	.311	.347	.540	.887	.969
1937	PHI-N	58	205	26	55	69	4	2	2	18	16	0	.268	.321	.337	.658	1.681
1938	PHI-N	61	219	26	49	75	12	1	4	26	16	0	.224	.277	.342	.619	1.127
1939	PHI-N	10	15	2	2	3	1	0	0	3	2	0	.133	.235	.200	.435	1.795
1939	PIT-N	36	119	16	33	58	5	1	6	21	10	0	.277	.333	.487	.821	1.112
1940	PHI-N	57	177	20	39	61	10	0	4	18	22	0	.220	.307	.345	.651	.958
1941	PHI-N	24	22	2	3	3	0	0	0	2	6	0	.136	.321	.136	.458	.783
1942	PHI-N	7	7	0	0	0	0	0	0	0	0	0	.000	.000	.000	.000	
1943	PHI-N	6	6	0	0	0	0	0	0	0	0	0	.000	.000	.000	.000	
1944	PHI-N	2	2	1	1	1	0	0	0	0	0	0	.500	.500	.500	1.000	.000
	17	870	3210	507	915	1494	173	38	110	475	290	6	.285	.345	.465	.811	1.271

NAP LAJOIE - HOME

YEAR	TM/L	G	AB	R	H	TB	2B	3B	HR	RBI	BB	HB	AVG	OBP	SLG	PRO	H/R
1896	PHI-N	31	144	29	49	81	9	7	3	37	0	0	.340	.340	.563	.903	
1897	PHI-N	61	257	52	80	129	15	14	2	63	8	6	.311	.347	.502	.849	
1898	PHI-N	74	302	52	91	124	19	4	2	70	14	4	.301	.341	.411	.751	
1899	PHI-N	39	150	26	58	82	9	3	3	37	5	3	.387	.418	.547	.964	
1900	PHI-N	44	187	41	69	98	11	3	4	48	2		.369	.376	.524	.900	
1901	PHI-A	63	255	68	107	155	23	5	5	60	7		.420	.435	.608	1.043	
1902	PHI-A	0	0	0	0	0	0	0	0	0	0		.000	.000	.000	.000	
1902	CLE-A	53	215	56	86	134	25	4	5	45	11		.400	.429	.623	1.052	
1903	CLE-A	66	257	54	95	138	28	6	1	53	12		.370	.398	.537	.935	
1904	CLE-A	73	281	48	106	156	28	5	4	54	14		.377	.407	.555	.962	
1905	CLE-A	33	123	16	42	55	5	1	2		8		.341	.382	.447	.829	
1906	CLE-A	78	306	54	113	148	27	4	0		15		.369	.399	.484	.882	
1907	CLE-A	72	271	31	93	130	23	4	2		16		.343	.380	.480	.859	
1908	CLE-A	78	277	48	94	125	18	5	1		24		.339	.392	.451	.843	
1909	CLE-A	56	201	28	77	105	18	5	0		14	5	.383	.436	.522	.959	
1910	CLE-A	78	285	53	116	153	25	3	2		30	3	.407	.469	.537	1.005	
1911	CLE-A	42	129	12	45	53	8	0	0		11	1	.349	.404	.411	.815	
1912	CLE-A	65	241	36	87	109	20	1	0		16	4	.361	.410	.452	.862	
1913	CLE-A	68	220	35	81	99	14	2	0		16	9	.368	.433	.450	.883	
1914	CLE-A	51	172	14	51	59	6	1	0		9	1	.297	.335	.343	.678	
1915	PHI-A	55	201	15	54	67	9	2	0		4	2	.269	.290	.333	.623	
1916	PHI-A	56	213	21	59	74	7	1	2		8	0	.277	.303	.347	.651	
	21	1236	4687	789	1653	2274	347	80	38	467	244	38	.353	.389	.485	.875	

NAP LAJOIE - AWAY

YEAR	TM/L	G	AB	R	H	TB	2B	3B	HR	RBI	BB	HB	AVG	OBP	SLG	PRO	H/R
1896	PHI-N	8	31	7	8	14	3	0	1	5	1	0	.258	.281	.452	.733	1.232
1897	PHI-N	66	288	55	117	181	25	9	7	64	7	5	.406	.430	.628	1.058	.802
1898	PHI-N	74	306	61	106	156	24	7	4	57	7	2	.346	.365	.510	.875	.859
1899	PHI-N	38	162	44	60	91	10	6	3	33	7	4	.370	.410	.562	.972	.992
1900	PHI-N	58	264	54	83	132	22	9	3	44	8		.314	.335	.500	.835	1.078
1901	PHI-A	68	289	77	125	195	25	9	9	65	17		.433	.464	.675	1.139	.916
1902	PHI-A	1	4	0	1	1	0	0	0	1	0		.250	.250	.250	.500	.000
1902	CLE-A	33	133	25	46	64	10	1	2	19	8		.346	.383	.481	.864	1.218
1903	CLE-A	59	228	36	72	113	13	5	6	40	12		.316	.350	.496	.846	1.105
1904	CLE-A	67	272	44	102	146	21	10	1	48	13		.375	.404	.537	.940	1.023
1905	CLE-A	32	126	13	40	51	9	1	0		9		.317	.363	.405	.768	1.080
1906	CLE-A	74	296	34	101	129	22	3	0		15		.341	.373	.436	.809	1.091
1907	CLE-A	65	238	22	60	73	9	2	0		14		.252	.294	.307	.600	1.432
1908	CLE-A	79	304	29	74	93	14	1	1		23		.243	.297	.306	.603	1.400
1909	CLE-A	72	268	28	75	97	15	2	1		21	1	.280	.334	.362	.696	1.377
1910	CLE-A	81	306	41	111	151	26	4	2		30	2	.363	.423	.493	.917	1.097
1911	CLE-A	48	186	24	70	90	12	1	2		15	3	.376	.431	.484	.915	.891
1912	CLE-A	52	207	30	78	98	14	3	0		12	3	.377	.419	.473	.892	.966

YEAR	TM/L	G	AB	R	H	TB	2B	3B	HR	RBI	BB	HB	AVG	OBP	SLG	PRO	H/R
1913	CLE-A	69	245	32	75	89	11	0	1		17	6	.306	.366	.363	.729	1.211
1914	CLE-A	70	247	23	57	69	8	2	0		23	1	.231	.299	.279	.578	1.173
1915	PHI-A	74	289	25	83	107	15	3	1		7	2	.287	.309	.370	.679	.918
1916	PHI-A	57	213	12	46	59	7	3	0		6	1	.216	.241	.277	.518	1.256
	21	1245	4902	716	1590	2199	315	81	44	376	272	30	.324	.364	.449	.812	1.077

MICKEY MANTLE - HOME

YEAR	TM/L	G	AB	R	H	TB	2B	3B	HR	RBI	BB	HB	AVG	OBP	SLG	PRO	H/R
1951	NY-A	51	174	37	46	73	2	2	7	33	26	0	.264	.360	.420	.780	
1952	NY-A	69	264	42	77	126	14	1	11	41	37	0	.292	.379	.477	.856	
1953	NY-A	69	241	50	68	110	12	3	8	35	42	0	.282	.389	.456	.845	
1954	NY-A	73	267	64	77	139	4	8	14	51	51	0	.288	.403	.521	.923	
1955	NY-A	75	255	67	86	172	15	7	19	57	58	2	.337	.463	.675	1.138	
1956	NY-A	77	268	67	99	200	14	3	27	67	54	1	.369	.477	.746	1.223	
1957	NY-A	73	230	51	89	156	13	6	14	44	61	0	.387	.515	.678	1.194	
1958	NY-A	74	246	65	77	149	9	0	21	43	73	0	.313	.470	.606	1.076	
1959	NY-A	73	274	47	84	150	10	1	18	38	44	1	.307	.404	.547	.952	
1960	NY-A	77	260	58	73	154	8	2	23	49	51	0	.281	.399	.592	.991	
1961	NY-A	74	230	64	76	168	8	6	24	59	66	0	.330	.480	.730	1.210	
1962	NY-A	54	165	39	54	108	6	0	16	37	48	0	.327	.479	.655	1.133	
1963	NY-A	30	72	19	23	49	2	0	8	17	23	0	.319	.484	.681	1.165	
1964	NY-A	72	234	55	78	146	16	2	16	57	49	0	.333	.449	.624	1.073	
1965	NY-A	67	200	23	47	83	7	1	9	25	51	0	.235	.390	.415	.805	
1966	NY-A	61	177	20	53	96	8	1	11	28	35	0	.299	.415	.542	.957	
1967	NY-A	72	209	29	50	89	9	0	10	31	51	0	.239	.388	.426	.814	
1968	NY-A	71	202	29	53	91	6	1	10	31	47	1	.262	.404	.450	.854	
	18	1212	3968	826	1210	2259	163	44	266	743	867	5	.305	.430	.569	.999	

MICKEY MANTLE - AWAY

YEAR	TM/L	G	AB	R	H	TB	2B	3B	HR	RBI	BB	HB	AVG	OBP	SLG	PRO	H/R
1951	NY-A	45	167	24	45	78	9	3	6	32	17	0	.269	.337	.467	.804	.970
1952	NY-A	73	285	52	94	165	23	6	12	46	38	0	.330	.409	.579	.988	.867
1953	NY-A	58	220	55	68	119	12	0	13	57	37	0	.309	.409	.541	.949	.890
1954	NY-A	73	276	65	86	146	13	4	13	51	51	0	.312	.419	.529	.948	.974
1955	NY-A	72	262	54	72	144	10	4	18	42	55	1	.275	.403	.550	.952	1.195
1956	NY-A	73	265	65	89	176	8	2	25	63	58	1	.336	.457	.664	1.121	1.091
1957	NY-A	71	244	70	84	159	15	0	20	50	85	0	.344	.514	.652	1.165	1.024
1958	NY-A	76	273	62	81	158	12	1	21	54	56	2	.297	.420	.579	.999	1.077
1959	NY-A	71	267	57	70	128	13	3	13	37	49	1	.262	.379	.479	.858	1.109
1960	NY-A	76	267	61	72	140	9	4	17	45	60	1	.270	.405	.524	.930	1.066
1961	NY-A	79	284	68	87	185	8	0	30	69	60	0	.306	.427	.651	1.079	1.122
1962	NY-A	69	212	57	67	120	9	1	14	52	74	1	.316	.495	.566	1.061	1.068
1963	NY-A	35	100	21	31	58	6	0	7	18	17	0	.310	.410	.580	.990	1.176
1964	NY-A	71	231	37	63	129	9	0	19	54	50	0	.273	.402	.558	.961	1.117
1965	NY-A	55	161	21	45	80	5	0	10	21	22	0	.280	.366	.497	.863	.933
1966	NY-A	47	156	20	43	83	4	0	12	28	22	0	.276	.365	.532	.897	1.067
1967	NY-A	72	231	34	58	102	8	0	12	24	56	1	.251	.399	.442	.841	.968
1968	NY-A	73	233	28	50	82	8	0	8	23	59	0	.215	.373	.352	.725	1.178
	18	1189	4134	851	1205	2252	181	28	270	766	866	8	.291	.415	.545	.960	1.041

WILLIE MAYS - HOME

YEAR	TM/L	G	AB	R	H	TB	2B	3B	HR	RBI	BB	HB	AVG	OBP	SLG	PRO	H/R
1951	NY-N	60	230	35	66	123	10	4	13	40	19	1	.287	.344	.535	.879	
1952	NY-N	16	57	9	15	27	0	3	2	14	8	0	.263	.354	.474	.828	
1954	NY-N	76	279	67	96	180	16	4	20	48	32	1	.344	.413	.645	1.059	
1955	NY-N	79	298	60	98	193	13	8	22	55	37	2	.329	.407	.648	1.054	
1956	NY-N	75	284	49	85	168	13	5	20	37	25	0	.299	.356	.592	.948	
1957	NY-N	75	279	53	95	174	8	10	17	54	44	0	.341	.430	.624	1.054	
1958	SF-N	77	289	64	94	169	15	6	16	54	46	1	.325	.420	.585	1.004	
1959	SF-N	77	284	55	82	152	20	1	16	54	32	2	.289	.365	.535	.900	
1960	SF-N	75	281	48	84	143	15	4	12	45	29	3	.299	.371	.509	.880	
1961	SF-N	77	275	59	80	160	17	0	21	61	40	2	.291	.385	.582	.967	
1962	SF-N	82	309	68	102	211	21	2	28	83	42	0	.330	.410	.683	1.093	
1963	SF-N	76	286	58	92	178	20	3	20	47	36	1	.322	.399	.622	1.022	
1964	SF-N	78	270	57	85	177	11	3	25	57	43	0	.315	.409	.656	1.065	
1965	SF-N	78	272	63	87	174	13	1	24	48	37	0	.320	.401	.640	1.041	
1966	SF-N	74	251	47	73	140	15	2	16	42	27	1	.291	.362	.558	.920	
1967	SF-N	71	233	42	60	110	9	1	13	39	25	1	.258	.332	.472	.804	
1968	SF-N	74	244	43	72	121	13	0	12	37	29	1	.295	.372	.496	.868	
1969	SF-N	55	176	30	48	76	7	0	7	25	23	2	.273	.363	.432	.795	
1970	SF-N	69	219	39	61	113	7	0	15	41	41	1	.279	.395	.516	.911	
1971	SF-N	65	193	39	55	100	12	3	9	27	57	3	.285	.455	.518	.973	
1972	SF-N	10	23	4	5	5	0	0	0	1	9	0	.217	.438	.217	.655	
1972	NY-N	34	90	15	25	38	2	1	3	6	24	1	.278	.435	.422	.857	
1973	NY-N	37	117	14	23	36	1	0	4	15	14	0	.197	.282	.308	.590	
	22	1490	5239	1018	1583	2968	258	61	335	930	719	23	.302	.389	.567	.955	

WILLIE MAYS - AWAY

YEAR	TM/L	G	AB	R	H	TB	2B	3B	HR	RBI	BB	HB	AVG	OBP	SLG	PRO	H/R
1951	NY-N	61	234	24	61	96	12	1	7	28	37	1	.261	.364	.410	.774	1.135
1952	NY-N	18	70	8	15	25	2	1	2	9	8	1	.214	.304	.357	.661	1.252
1954	NY-N	75	286	52	99	197	17	9	21	62	34	1	.346	.417	.689	1.106	.957
1955	NY-N	73	282	63	87	189	5	5	29	72	42	2	.309	.402	.670	1.072	.983
1956	NY-N	77	294	52	86	154	14	3	16	47	43	1	.293	.385	.524	.908	1.043
1957	NY-N	77	306	59	100	192	18	10	18	43	32	1	.327	.392	.627	1.020	1.034
1958	SF-N	75	311	57	114	181	18	5	13	42	32	0	.367	.426	.582	1.008	.997
1959	SF-N	74	291	70	98	183	23	4	18	50	33	0	.337	.404	.629	1.033	.871
1960	SF-N	78	314	59	106	187	14	8	17	58	32	1	.338	.401	.596	.996	.883
1961	SF-N	77	297	70	96	174	15	3	19	62	41	0	.323	.405	.586	.991	.975
1962	SF-N	80	312	62	87	171	15	3	21	58	36	4	.279	.361	.548	.909	1.203
1963	SF-N	81	310	57	95	169	12	4	18	56	30	1	.306	.370	.545	.915	1.117
1964	SF-N	79	308	64	86	174	10	6	22	54	39	1	.279	.362	.565	.927	1.148
1965	SF-N	79	286	55	90	186	8	2	28	64	39	0	.315	.397	.650	1.047	.994
1966	SF-N	78	301	52	86	167	14	2	21	61	43	1	.286	.377	.555	.932	.987
1967	SF-N	70	253	41	68	110	13	1	9	31	26	1	.269	.339	.435	.774	1.039
1968	SF-N	74	254	41	72	122	7	5	11	42	38	1	.283	.379	.480	.859	1.010
1969	SF-N	62	227	34	66	100	10	3	6	33	26	1	.291	.366	.441	.807	.986
1970	SF-N	70	259	55	78	129	8	2	13	42	38	2	.301	.395	.498	.893	1.020

YEAR	TM/L	G	AB	R	H	TB	2B	3B	HR	RBI	BB	HB	AVG	OBP	SLG	PRO	H/R
1971	SF-N	71	224	43	58	101	12	2	9	34	55	0	.259	.405	.451	.856	1.136
1972	SF-N	9	26	4	4	6	2	0	0	2	8	0	.154	.353	.231	.584	1.122
1972	NY-N	35	105	12	27	49	7	0	5	13	19	0	.257	.371	.467	.838	1.023
1973	NY-N	29	92	10	21	36	9	0	2	10	13	1	.228	.330	.391	.721	.818
	22	1502	5642	1044	1700	3098	265	79	325	973	744	21	.301	.385	.549	.934	1.023

JOE MORGAN - HOME

YEAR	TM/L	G	AB	R	H	TB	2B	3B	HR	RBI	BB	HB	AVG	OBP	SLG	PRO	H/R
1963	HOU-N	8	25	5	6	8	0	1	0	3	5	0	.240	.367	.320	.687	
1964	HOU-N	7	23	3	3	3	0	0	0	0	6	0	.130	.310	.130	.441	
1965	HOU-N	80	285	54	82	120	10	8	4	14	60	2	.288	.415	.421	.836	
1966	HOU-N	63	222	31	67	90	4	5	3	24	48	3	.302	.432	.405	.838	
1967	HOU-N	69	247	45	73	112	17	8	2	22	50	1	.296	.416	.453	.870	
1968	HOU-N	5	14	6	5	7	0	1	0	0	6	0	.357	.550	.500	1.050	
1969	HOU-N	72	255	52	66	103	8	4	7	25	57	1	.259	.396	.404	.800	
1970	HOU-N	73	266	49	72	113	15	7	4	28	54	1	.271	.396	.425	.820	
1971	HOU-N	79	268	34	59	95	14	5	4	18	45	1	.220	.334	.354	.689	
1972	CIN-N	73	259	53	79	124	12	3	9	35	60	1	.305	.438	.479	.916	
1973	CIN-N	78	278	50	70	114	17	0	9	34	59	2	.252	.386	.410	.797	
1974	CIN-N	74	257	49	61	114	12	1	13	39	55	1	.237	.374	.444	.817	
1975	CIN-N	72	237	61	77	128	15	3	10	49	72	1	.325	.484	.540	1.024	
1976	CIN-N	69	231	58	75	138	18	3	13	57	54	1	.325	.455	.597	1.052	
1977	CIN-N	74	246	64	74	125	14	2	11	38	62	2	.301	.445	.508	.953	
1978	CIN-N	63	203	36	51	83	14	0	6	39	34	1	.251	.361	.409	.770	
1979	CIN-N	64	210	36	54	82	16	0	4	19	46	1	.257	.393	.390	.783	
1980	HOU-N	69	217	32	62	87	13	3	2	24	54	0	.286	.428	.401	.829	
1981	SF-N	41	142	24	39	61	10	0	4	16	32	0	.275	.408	.430	.838	
1982	SF-N	65	223	28	59	84	7	0	6	29	42	1	.265	.383	.377	.760	
1983	PHI-N	54	160	34	41	76	8	0	9	29	47	1	.256	.428	.475	.903	
1984	OAK-A	57	180	25	50	65	9	0	2	18	30	1	.278	.384	.361	.745	
	22	1309	4448	829	1225	1932	233	54	122	560	978	22	.275	.408	.434	.843	

JOE MORGAN - AWAY

YEAR	TM/L	G	AB	R	H	TB	2B	3B	HR	RBI	BB	HB	AVG	OBP	SLG	PRO	H/R
1963	HOU-N	0	0	0	0	0	0	0	0	0	0	0	—	—	—	—	—
1964	HOU-N	3	14	1	4	4	0	0	0	0	0	0	.286	.286	.286	.571	.771
1965	HOU-N	77	316	46	81	131	12	4	10	26	37	1	.256	.336	.415	.751	1.114
1966	HOU-N	59	203	29	54	76	10	3	2	18	41	0	.266	.389	.374	.764	1.097
1967	HOU-N	64	247	28	63	91	10	3	4	20	31	1	.255	.341	.368	.709	1.227
1968	HOU-N	5	6	0	0	0	0	0	0	0	1	0	.000	.143	.000	.143	7.350
1969	HOU-N	75	280	42	60	96	10	1	8	18	53	0	.214	.339	.343	.682	1.173
1970	HOU-N	71	282	53	75	104	13	2	4	24	48	0	.266	.373	.369	.742	1.106
1971	HOU-N	81	315	53	90	142	13	6	9	38	43	0	.286	.372	.451	.822	.838
1972	CIN-N	76	293	69	82	116	11	1	7	38	55	5	.280	.402	.396	.798	1.148
1973	CIN-N	79	298	66	97	170	18	2	17	48	52	2	.326	.429	.570	.999	.797
1974	CIN-N	75	255	58	89	139	19	2	9	28	65	2	.349	.484	.545	1.030	.794
1975	CIN-N	74	261	46	86	125	12	3	7	45	60	2	.330	.458	.479	.937	1.093
1976	CIN-N	72	241	55	76	134	12	2	14	54	60	0	.315	.452	.556	1.008	1.044
1977	CIN-N	79	275	49	76	124	7	4	11	40	55	0	.276	.397	.451	.848	1.124
1978	CIN-N	69	238	32	53	87	13	0	7	36	45	1	.223	.349	.366	.714	1.079
1979	CIN-N	63	226	34	55	82	10	1	5	13	47	0	.243	.374	.363	.736	1.064
1980	HOU-N	72	244	34	50	85	4	2	9	25	39	0	.205	.314	.348	.663	1.251
1981	SF-N	49	166	23	35	55	6	1	4	15	34	0	.211	.345	.331	.676	1.238
1982	SF-N	69	240	40	75	119	12	4	8	32	43	1	.313	.419	.496	.915	.831
1983	PHI-N	69	244	38	52	87	12	1	7	30	42	3	.213	.336	.357	.692	1.304
1984	OAK-A	59	185	25	39	63	12	0	4	25	36	0	.211	.339	.341	.680	1.096
	22	1340	4829	821	1292	2030	216	42	146	573	887	18	.268	.383	.420	.804	1.049

STAN MUSIAL - HOME

YEAR	TM/L	G	AB	R	H	TB	2B	3B	HR	RBI	BB	HB	AVG	OBP	SLG	PRO	H/R
1941	STL-N	6	22	1	12	16	4	0	0	3	1	0	.545	.565	.727	1.292	
1942	STL-N	71	230	48	77	120	17	1	8	45	34	2	.335	.425	.522	.947	
1943	STL-N	81	302	52	105	169	29	7	7	42	37	1	.348	.421	.560	.980	
1944	STL-N	73	266	50	86	144	25	9	5	53	49	0	.323	.429	.541	.970	
1946	STL-N	78	304	67	112	186	24	10	10	56	41	1	.368	.445	.612	1.057	
1947	STL-N	76	297	48	100	141	12	7	5	55	42	2	.337	.422	.475	.897	
1948	STL-N	77	293	57	98	181	17	9	16	55	43	1	.334	.421	.618	1.039	
1949	STL-N	79	299	69	104	185	28	7	13	65	60	2	.348	.460	.619	1.079	
1950	STL-N	73	273	53	101	178	22	5	15	56	38	3	.370	.452	.652	1.104	
1951	STL-N	79	295	66	105	194	18	7	19	62	56	0	.356	.459	.658	1.116	
1952	STL-N	77	275	50	82	139	21	3	10	42	56	0	.298	.417	.505	.922	
1953	STL-N	78	293	75	112	199	32	5	15	62	54	0	.382	.478	.679	1.158	
1954	STL-N	76	295	61	102	193	22	6	19	62	47	1	.346	.437	.654	1.092	
1955	STL-N	77	280	55	94	179	13	3	22	64	43	4	.336	.431	.639	1.070	
1956	STL-N	78	293	49	102	172	20	4	14	57	39	2	.348	.428	.587	1.015	
1957	STL-N	68	245	36	75	134	19	2	12	40	39	1	.306	.404	.547	.950	
1958	STL-N	67	226	28	77	134	18	0	13	43	33	1	.341	.427	.593	1.020	
1959	STL-N	59	177	20	42	83	7	2	10	29	30	0	.237	.348	.469	.817	
1960	STL-N	58	174	33	48	85	7	0	10	35	25	1	.276	.370	.489	.859	
1961	STL-N	61	169	30	58	110	15	2	11	43	27	0	.343	.434	.651	1.085	
1962	STL-N	68	210	28	67	111	14	0	10	46	40	1	.319	.430	.529	.959	
1963	STL-N	64	183	23	56	91	9	1	8	41	17	2	.306	.371	.497	.869	
	22	1524	5401	999	1815	3144	393	90	252	1056	851	25	.336	.429	.582	1.011	

STAN MUSIAL - AWAY

YEAR	TM/L	G	AB	R	H	TB	2B	3B	HR	RBI	BB	HB	AVG	OBP	SLG	PRO	H/R
1941	STL-N	6	25	7	8	11	0	0	1	4	1	0	.320	.346	.440	.786	1.644
1942	STL-N	69	237	39	70	109	15	9	2	27	28	0	.295	.370	.460	.830	1.141
1943	STL-N	76	315	56	115	178	19	13	6	39	35	1	.365	.430	.565	.995	.985
1944	STL-N	73	302	62	111	168	26	5	7	41	41	5	.368	.451	.556	1.007	.963
1946	STL-N	78	320	57	116	180	26	10	6	47	32	2	.363	.424	.563	.986	1.072
1947	STL-N	73	290	65	83	155	18	6	14	40	38	2	.286	.373	.534	.907	.989
1948	STL-N	78	318	78	132	248	29	9	23	76	36	2	.415	.478	.780	1.257	.826
1949	STL-N	78	313	59	103	197	13	6	23	58	47	0	.329	.417	.629	1.046	1.031
1950	STL-N	73	282	52	91	153	19	2	13	53	49	0	.323	.423	.543	.966	1.144
1951	STL-N	73	283	58	100	161	12	5	13	46	42	1	.353	.439	.569	1.008	1.108
1952	STL-N	77	303	55	112	172	21	3	11	49	40	2	.370	.446	.568	1.014	.910
1953	STL-N	79	300	52	88	162	21	4	15	51	51	0	.293	.396	.540	.936	1.237

YEAR	TM/L	G	AB	R	H	TB	2B	3B	HR	RBI	BB	HB	AVG	OBP	SLG	PRO	H/R
1954	STL-N	77	296	59	93	166	19	3	16	64	56	3	.314	.428	.561	.989	1.104
1955	STL-N	77	282	42	85	139	17	2	11	44	37	4	.301	.390	.493	.883	1.212
1956	STL-N	78	301	38	82	138	13	2	13	52	36	1	.272	.352	.458	.811	1.252
1957	STL-N	66	257	46	101	173	19	1	17	62	27	1	.393	.453	.673	1.126	.844
1958	STL-N	68	246	36	82	115	17	2	4	19	39	0	.333	.425	.467	.892	1.143
1959	STL-N	56	164	17	45	63	6	0	4	15	30	0	.274	.387	.384	.771	1.060
1960	STL-N	58	157	16	43	76	10	1	7	28	16	1	.274	.345	.484	.829	1.036
1961	STL-N	62	203	16	49	72	7	2	4	27	25	1	.241	.328	.355	.682	1.590
1962	STL-N	67	223	29	76	109	4	1	9	36	24	2	.341	.410	.489	.898	1.067
1963	STL-N	60	154	11	30	45	1	1	4	17	18	0	.195	.279	.292	.571	1.520
	22	1502	5571	950	1815	2990	332	87	223	895	748	28	.326	.408	.537	.945	1.070

MEL OTT - HOME

YEAR	TM/L	G	AB	R	H	TB	2B	3B	HR	RBI	BB	HB	AVG	OBP	SLG	PRO	H/R
1926	NY-N	12	14	3	7	7	0	0	0	0	0	0	.500	.500	.500	1.000	
1927	NY-N	37	79	14	26	36	3	2	1	9	9	0	.329	.398	.456	.853	
1928	NY-N	59	204	29	59	98	8	2	9	33	26	1	.289	.372	.480	.853	
1929	NY-N	75	266	59	79	153	12	1	20	65	54	1	.297	.417	.575	.993	
1930	NY-N	76	257	67	92	169	10	2	21	64	62	1	.358	.484	.658	1.142	
1931	NY-N	70	245	49	57	126	7	1	20	57	46	0	.233	.354	.514	.868	
1932	NY-N	77	270	53	77	168	15	2	24	66	57	3	.285	.415	.622	1.037	
1933	NY-N	74	267	45	70	120	9	1	13	48	39	2	.262	.360	.449	.810	
1934	NY-N	75	270	49	69	127	8	1	16	49	46	1	.256	.366	.470	.836	
1935	NY-N	79	292	59	99	171	11	2	19	60	51	3	.339	.442	.586	1.028	
1936	NY-N	75	250	58	83	151	12	1	18	64	59	2	.332	.463	.604	1.067	
1937	NY-N	75	263	48	71	128	10	1	15	45	52	0	.270	.390	.487	.877	
1938	NY-N	71	241	65	76	152	12	2	20	58	67	3	.315	.469	.631	1.100	
1939	NY-N	64	198	46	61	117	7	2	15	44	58	0	.308	.465	.591	1.056	
1940	NY-N	75	256	42	71	120	13	0	12	39	48	4	.277	.399	.469	.868	
1941	NY-N	73	236	51	82	150	11	0	19	50	63	2	.347	.488	.636	1.124	
1942	NY-N	77	269	70	94	173	10	0	23	62	59	1	.349	.468	.643	1.111	
1943	NY-N	65	211	41	50	110	6	0	18	34	56	1	.237	.399	.521	.921	
1944	NY-N	65	203	51	51	121	5	1	21	46	53	1	.251	.409	.596	1.005	
1945	NY-N	72	242	52	83	150	13	0	18	49	37	5	.343	.440	.620	1.060	
1946	NY-N	18	41	2	3	6	0	0	1	3	7	0	.073	.208	.146	.355	
1947	NY-N	4	4	0	0	0	0	0	0	0	0	0	.000	.000	.000	.000	
	22	1368	4578	953	1360	2553	182	21	323	945	949	31	.297	.421	.558	.979	

MEL OTT - AWAY

YEAR	TM/L	G	AB	R	H	TB	2B	3B	HR	RBI	BB	HB	AVG	OBP	SLG	PRO	H/R
1926	NY-N	23	46	4	16	18	2	0	0	4	1	0	.348	.362	.391	.753	1.328
1927	NY-N	45	84	9	20	26	4	1	0	10	4	0	.238	.273	.310	.582	1.466
1928	NY-N	65	231	40	81	130	18	2	9	44	26	1	.351	.419	.563	.981	.869
1929	NY-N	75	279	79	100	193	25	1	22	87	59	5	.358	.478	.692	1.170	.848
1930	NY-N	72	264	55	90	132	24	3	4	55	41	1	.341	.431	.500	.931	1.226
1931	NY-N	68	252	55	88	145	16	7	9	58	34	2	.349	.431	.575	1.006	.863
1932	NY-N	77	296	66	103	172	15	6	14	57	43	1	.348	.432	.581	1.013	1.024
1933	NY-N	78	313	53	94	151	27	0	10	55	36	0	.300	.372	.482	.855	.947
1934	NY-N	78	312	70	121	217	21	9	19	86	39	2	.388	.459	.696	1.154	.724
1935	NY-N	73	301	54	92	158	22	4	12	54	31	0	.306	.370	.525	.895	1.148
1936	NY-N	75	284	62	92	163	16	5	15	71	52	3	.324	.434	.574	1.008	1.059
1937	NY-N	76	282	51	89	157	18	1	16	50	50	3	.316	.424	.557	.981	.895
1938	NY-N	79	286	51	88	155	11	4	16	58	51	2	.308	.416	.542	.958	1.149
1939	NY-N	61	198	39	61	113	16	0	12	36	42	1	.308	.432	.571	1.002	1.053
1940	NY-N	76	280	47	84	125	14	3	7	40	52	2	.300	.413	.446	.860	1.010
1941	NY-N	75	289	38	68	110	18	0	8	40	37	1	.235	.324	.381	.705	1.595
1942	NY-N	75	280	48	68	100	11	0	7	31	50	2	.243	.361	.357	.719	1.546
1943	NY-N	60	169	24	39	49	6	2	0	13	39	2	.231	.381	.290	.671	1.372
1944	NY-N	55	196	40	64	96	11	3	5	36	37	2	.327	.438	.490	.928	1.082
1945	NY-N	63	209	21	56	75	10	0	3	30	34	3	.268	.378	.359	.737	1.438
1946	NY-N	13	27	0	2	3	1	0	0	1	1	0	.074	.107	.111	.218	1.625
1947	NY-N	0	0	0	0	0	0	0	0	0	0	0	—	—	—	—	—
	22	1362	4878	906	1516	2488	306	51	188	916	759	33	.311	.407	.510	.917	1.067

FRANK ROBINSON - HOME

YEAR	TM/L	G	AB	R	H	TB	2B	3B	HR	RBI	BB	HB	AVG	OBP	SLG	PRO	H/R
1956	CIN-N	76	285	64	81	167	14	3	22	47	33	12	.284	.382	.586	.968	
1957	CIN-N	75	301	49	102	160	12	2	14	41	26	7	.339	.404	.532	.936	
1958	CIN-N	74	267	41	76	148	12	3	18	48	28	5	.285	.363	.554	.918	
1959	CIN-N	73	273	56	97	190	13	1	26	76	27	4	.355	.421	.696	1.117	
1960	CIN-N	68	214	45	68	140	16	4	16	42	42	4	.318	.438	.654	1.093	
1961	CIN-N	77	268	60	95	169	21	1	17	64	35	3	.354	.435	.631	1.065	
1962	CIN-N	81	292	79	108	210	30	0	24	87	44	8	.370	.465	.719	1.184	
1963	CIN-N	69	238	42	67	113	12	2	10	47	40	3	.282	.391	.475	.866	
1964	CIN-N	75	263	48	82	147	20	6	11	42	40	5	.312	.412	.559	.971	
1965	CIN-N	76	276	53	77	151	16	2	18	62	41	9	.279	.390	.547	.937	
1966	BAL-A	78	279	69	89	185	13	1	27	65	50	3	.319	.428	.663	1.091	
1967	BAL-A	59	193	40	69	138	10	1	19	50	36	4	.358	.468	.715	1.183	
1968	BAL-A	59	181	33	43	75	9	1	7	18	32	4	.238	.364	.414	.778	
1969	BAL-A	75	271	60	89	159	8	1	20	61	40	7	.328	.428	.587	1.014	
1970	BAL-A	63	226	41	68	112	8	0	12	37	32	2	.301	.392	.496	.888	
1971	BAL-A	67	223	50	66	126	9	0	17	55	34	5	.296	.401	.565	.966	
1972	LA-N	46	149	23	45	79	4	0	10	27	21	1	.302	.392	.530	.922	
1973	CAL-A	72	240	43	61	122	13	0	16	50	45	9	.254	.391	.508	.899	
1974	CAL-A	68	218	41	51	87	12	0	8	26	43	5	.234	.372	.399	.771	
1974	CLE-A	3	11	1	2	2	0	0	0	0	1	0	.182	.250	.182	.432	
1975	CLE-A	28	67	14	19	46	3	0	8	19	14	0	.284	.407	.687	1.094	
1976	CLE-A	21	34	2	7	10	0	0	1	7	5	0	.206	.308	.294	.602	
	21	1383	4769	954	1462	2736	255	28	321	971	709	100	.307	.407	.574	.981	

FRANK ROBINSON - AWAY

YEAR	TM/L	G	AB	R	H	TB	2B	3B	HR	RBI	BB	HB	AVG	OBP	SLG	PRO	H/R
1956	CIN-N	76	287	58	85	152	13	3	16	36	31	8	.296	.380	.530	.910	1.064
1957	CIN-N	75	310	48	95	163	17	3	15	34	18	5	.306	.354	.526	.880	1.063
1958	CIN-N	74	287	49	73	131	13	3	13	35	34	2	.254	.337	.456	.794	1.156
1959	CIN-N	73	267	50	71	125	18	3	10	49	42	4	.266	.374	.468	.842	1.327
1960	CIN-N	71	250	41	70	136	17	2	15	41	40	5	.280	.390	.544	.934	1.170
1961	CIN-N	76	277	57	81	164	11	6	20	60	36	7	.292	.388	.592	.980	1.087

YEAR	TM/L	G	AB	R	H	TB	2B	3B	HR	RBI	BB	HB	AVG	OBP	SLG	PRO	H/R
1962	CIN-N	81	317	55	100	170	21	2	15	49	32	3	.315	.384	.536	.920	1.288
1963	CIN-N	71	244	37	58	100	7	1	11	44	41	11	.238	.372	.410	.781	1.109
1964	CIN-N	81	305	55	92	164	18	0	18	54	39	4	.302	.388	.538	.926	1.049
1965	CIN-N	80	306	56	95	163	17	3	15	51	29	9	.310	.387	.533	.919	1.019
1966	BAL-A	77	297	53	93	182	21	1	22	57	37	7	.313	.402	.613	1.015	1.075
1967	BAL-A	70	286	43	80	138	13	6	11	44	35	3	.280	.364	.483	.847	1.397
1968	BAL-A	71	240	36	70	112	18	0	8	34	41	8	.292	.412	.467	.878	.886
1969	BAL-A	73	268	51	77	132	11	4	12	39	48	6	.287	.407	.493	.899	1.128
1970	BAL-A	69	245	47	76	133	16	1	13	41	37	5	.310	.411	.543	.954	.931
1971	BAL-A	66	232	32	62	106	7	2	11	44	38	4	.267	.380	.457	.836	1.155
1972	LA-N	57	193	18	41	72	2	1	9	32	34	1	.212	.333	.373	.706	1.305
1973	CAL-A	75	294	42	81	139	16	0	14	47	37	1	.276	.358	.473	.831	1.082
1974	CAL-A	61	209	34	56	110	14	2	12	37	32	5	.268	.378	.526	.904	.853
1974	CLE-A	12	39	5	8	17	1	1	2	5	9	0	.205	.354	.436	.790	.547
1975	CLE-A	21	51	5	9	14	2	0	1	5	15	0	.176	.364	.275	.638	1.714
1976	CLE-A	15	33	3	8	14	0	0	2	3	6	0	.242	.359	.424	.783	.768
	21	1425	5237	875	1481	2637	273	44	265	841	711	98	.283	.379	.504	.882	1.112

PETE ROSE - HOME

YEAR	TM/L	G	AB	R	H	TB	2B	3B	HR	RBI	BB	HB	AVG	OBP	SLG	PRO	H/R
1963	CIN-N	80	307	56	84	110	10	5	2	19	36	5	.274	.359	.358	.718	
1964	CIN-N	66	244	28	62	80	9	0	3	22	18	1	.254	.308	.328	.636	
1965	CIN-N	81	333	62	100	144	19	2	7	42	32	5	.300	.370	.432	.803	
1966	CIN-N	75	312	53	100	151	14	2	11	43	20	1	.321	.363	.484	.847	
1967	CIN-N	75	302	50	96	140	19	2	7	48	27	1	.318	.376	.464	.839	
1968	CIN-N	72	306	49	107	158	27	3	6	25	22	3	.350	.399	.516	.915	
1969	CIN-N	77	308	61	118	182	22	6	10	44	41	4	.383	.462	.591	1.053	
1970	CIN-N	81	327	64	105	153	17	5	7	25	39	2	.321	.397	.468	.865	
1971	CIN-N	79	308	44	97	134	13	0	8	23	31	2	.315	.381	.435	.816	
1972	CIN-N	76	309	47	90	130	17	10	1	22	32	4	.291	.365	.421	.786	
1973	CIN-N	79	328	53	118	153	16	5	3	33	29	2	.360	.415	.466	.882	
1974	CIN-N	82	312	57	93	137	30	4	2	29	58	1	.298	.410	.439	.849	
1975	CIN-N	81	328	58	106	142	21	3	3	41	45	8	.323	.417	.433	.850	
1976	CIN-N	81	330	65	111	163	23	4	7	30	39	2	.336	.410	.494	.904	
1977	CIN-N	81	314	47	101	138	22	3	3	29	37	4	.322	.400	.439	.839	
1978	CIN-N	79	317	52	101	136	25	2	2	28	29	1	.319	.378	.429	.807	
1979	PHI-N	81	293	46	99	127	15	5	1	26	59	1	.338	.450	.433	.884	
1980	PHI-N	81	313	49	89	118	27	1	0	34	43	4	.284	.378	.377	.755	
1981	PHI-N	55	218	44	76	97	11	5	0	21	25	3	.349	.423	.445	.868	
1982	PHI-N	81	307	29	79	99	12	1	2	28	27	2	.257	.321	.322	.644	
1983	PHI-N	76	241	26	63	77	8	3	0	21	24	2	.261	.333	.320	.653	
1984	MON-N	40	107	12	22	24	2	0	0	8	9	1	.206	.274	.224	.498	
1984	CIN-N	18	69	6	25	31	6	0	0	10	8	2	.362	.443	.449	.892	
1985	CIN-N	60	196	27	50	59	5	2	0	22	47	4	.255	.409	.301	.710	
1986	CIN-N	38	121	7	31	39	6	1	0	13	12	4	.256	.343	.322	.665	
	24	1775	6850	1092	2123	2922	396	74	85	686	789	69	.310	.387	.427	.813	

PETE ROSE - AWAY

YEAR	TM/L	G	AB	R	H	TB	2B	3B	HR	RBI	BB	HB	AVG	OBP	SLG	PRO	H/R
1963	CIN-N	77	316	45	86	121	15	4	4	22	19	0	.272	.313	.383	.696	1.030
1964	CIN-N	70	272	36	77	88	4	2	1	12	18	1	.283	.330	.324	.653	.973
1965	CIN-N	81	337	55	109	155	16	9	4	39	37	3	.323	.395	.460	.855	.939
1966	CIN-N	81	342	44	105	150	24	3	5	27	17	0	.307	.340	.439	.778	1.089
1967	CIN-N	73	283	36	80	120	13	6	5	28	29	2	.283	.354	.424	.778	1.079
1968	CIN-N	77	320	45	103	136	15	3	4	24	34	1	.322	.389	.425	.814	1.125
1969	CIN-N	79	319	59	100	139	11	5	6	38	47	1	.313	.403	.436	.839	1.255
1970	CIN-N	78	322	56	100	152	20	4	8	27	34	0	.311	.376	.472	.848	1.019
1971	CIN-N	81	324	42	95	132	14	4	5	21	37	1	.293	.367	.407	.775	1.054
1972	CIN-N	78	336	60	108	139	14	1	5	35	41	3	.321	.400	.414	.814	.966
1973	CIN-N	81	352	62	112	144	20	3	2	31	36	4	.318	.388	.409	.797	1.106
1974	CIN-N	81	340	53	92	116	15	3	1	22	48	4	.271	.367	.341	.709	1.198
1975	CIN-N	81	334	54	104	144	26	1	4	33	44	3	.311	.396	.431	.827	1.028
1976	CIN-N	81	335	65	104	136	19	2	3	33	47	4	.310	.402	.406	.808	1.119
1977	CIN-N	81	341	48	103	145	16	4	6	35	29	1	.302	.358	.425	.784	1.071
1978	CIN-N	80	338	51	97	140	26	1	5	24	33	2	.287	.354	.414	.768	1.050
1979	PHI-N	82	335	44	109	143	25	0	3	33	36	1	.325	.392	.427	.819	1.079
1980	PHI-N	81	342	46	96	114	15	0	1	30	23	2	.281	.330	.333	.663	1.138
1981	PHI-N	52	213	29	64	71	7	0	0	12	21	0	.300	.363	.333	.697	1.246
1982	PHI-N	81	327	51	93	115	13	3	1	26	39	5	.284	.369	.352	.721	.893
1983	PHI-N	75	252	26	58	64	6	0	0	24	28	0	.230	.307	.254	.561	1.163
1984	MON-N	55	171	22	50	58	4	2	0	15	22	0	.292	.373	.339	.712	.699
1984	CIN-N	8	27	3	10	13	3	0	0	1	1	0	.370	.393	.481	.874	1.021
1985	CIN-N	59	209	33	57	70	7	0	2	24	39	0	.273	.387	.335	.722	.983
1986	CIN-N	34	116	8	21	25	2	1	0	12	18	0	.181	.291	.216	.507	1.314
	24	1787	7203	1073	2133	2830	350	61	75	628	777	38	.296	.368	.393	.761	1.069

BABE RUTH - HOME

YEAR	TM/L	G	AB	R	H	TB	2B	3B	HR	RBI	BB	HB	AVG	OBP	SLG	PRO	H/R
1914	BOS-A	5	10	1	2	3	1	0	0		0	0	.200	.200	.300	.500	
1915	BOS-A	18	41	8	15	24	4	1	1		3	0	.366	.409	.585	.994	
1916	BOS-A	34	66	10	14	21	5	1	0		6	0	.212	.278	.318	.596	
1917	BOS-A	26	57	8	21	30	4	1	1		9	0	.368	.455	.526	.981	
1918	BOS-A	48	145	28	45	75	14	8	0		32	0	.310	.435	.517	.952	
1919	BOS-A	63	200	47	65	123	19	6	9		52	3	.325	.471	.615	1.086	
1920	NY-A	66	204	77	81	201	21	6	29	71	61	2	.397	.539	.985	1.525	
1921	NY-A	78	255	94	103	237	24	7	32	81	79	0	.404	.545	.929	1.474	
1922	NY-A	53	195	40	58	117	7	5	14	45	36	0	.297	.407	.600	1.007	
1923	NY-A	76	246	74	101	198	26	7	19	63	92	1	.411	.572	.805	1.377	
1924	NY-A	78	260	70	99	197	18	4	24	71	66	2	.381	.509	.758	1.267	
1925	NY-A	56	203	35	59	102	8	1	11	34	35	2	.291	.400	.502	.902	
1926	NY-A	75	241	68	88	174	13	2	23	76	74	1	.365	.516	.722	1.238	
1927	NY-A	73	253	82	94	196	10	4	28	70	62	0	.372	.495	.775	1.270	
1928	NY-A	77	260	76	86	189	8	4	29	70	59	2	.331	.458	.727	1.185	
1929	NY-A	60	218	50	72	148	7	3	21	66	36	1	.330	.427	.679	1.106	
1930	NY-A	72	244	72	91	192	13	5	26	75	65	1	.373	.506	.787	1.293	
1931	NY-A	75	267	72	96	179	11	0	24	78	63	0	.360	.482	.670	1.152	
1932	NY-A	72	239	62	78	145	6	2	19	69	71	1	.326	.482	.607	1.089	

YEAR	TM/L	G	AB	R	H	TB	2B	3B	HR	RBI	BB	HB	AVG	OBP	SLG	PRO	H/R
1933	NY-A	68	214	51	68	145	9	1	22	56	63	0	.318	.473	.678	1.150	
1934	NY-A	69	190	47	56	110	11	2	13	50	62	2	.295	.472	.579	1.051	
1935	BOS-N	11	25	6	6	12	0	0	2	4	11	0	.240	.472	.480	.952	
	22	1253	4033	1078	1398	2818	239	70	347	979	1037	18	.347	.482	.699	1.181	

BABE RUTH - AWAY

YEAR	TM/L	G	AB	R	H	TB	2B	3B	HR	RBI	BB	HB	AVG	OBP	SLG	PRO	H/R
1914	BOS-A	0	0	0	0	0	0	0	0		0	0	.000	.000	.000	.000	.000
1915	BOS-A	24	51	8	14	29	6	0	3		6	0	.275	.351	.569	.920	1.082
1916	BOS-A	33	70	8	23	36	0	2	3		4	0	.329	.365	.514	.879	.678
1917	BOS-A	26	66	6	19	28	2	2	1		3	0	.288	.319	.424	.743	1.320
1918	BOS-A	47	172	22	50	101	12	3	11		25	2	.291	.387	.587	.974	.978
1919	BOS-A	67	232	56	74	161	15	6	20		49	3	.319	.444	.694	1.138	.954
1920	NY-A	76	254	81	91	187	15	3	25	66	87	1	.358	.523	.736	1.260	1.210
1921	NY-A	74	285	83	101	220	20	9	27	90	65	4	.354	.480	.772	1.252	1.177
1922	NY-A	57	211	54	70	156	17	3	21	54	48	1	.332	.458	.739	1.197	.841
1923	NY-A	76	276	78	104	201	19	6	22	68	78	3	.377	.518	.728	1.246	1.105
1924	NY-A	75	269	73	101	194	21	3	22	50	76	2	.375	.516	.721	1.237	1.024
1925	NY-A	42	156	26	45	93	4	1	14	32	24	0	.288	.383	.596	.979	.921
1926	NY-A	77	254	71	96	191	17	3	24	70	70	2	.378	.515	.752	1.267	.977
1927	NY-A	78	287	76	98	221	19	4	32	94	76	0	.341	.479	.770	1.249	1.016
1928	NY-A	77	276	87	87	191	21	4	25	72	76	1	.315	.465	.692	1.157	1.024
1929	NY-A	75	281	71	100	200	19	3	25	88	36	2	.356	.433	.712	1.144	.967
1930	NY-A	73	274	78	95	187	15	4	23	78	71	0	.347	.481	.682	1.164	1.111
1931	NY-A	70	267	77	103	195	20	3	22	85	65	1	.386	.508	.730	1.238	.931
1932	NY-A	61	218	58	78	157	7	3	22	68	59	1	.358	.496	.720	1.217	.895
1933	NY-A	69	245	46	70	122	12	2	12	47	51	2	.286	.413	.498	.911	1.263
1934	NY-A	56	175	31	49	86	6	2	9	34	41	0	.280	.417	.491	.908	1.158
1935	BOS-N	17	47	7	7	19	0	0	4	8	9	0	.149	.286	.404	.690	1.380
	22	1250	4366	1097	1475	2975	267	66	367	1004	1019	25	.338	.466	.681	1.147	1.029

MIKE SCHMIDT - HOME

YEAR	TM/L	G	AB	R	H	TB	2B	3B	HR	RBI	BB	HB	AVG	OBP	SLG	PRO	H/R
1972	PHI-N	5	16	1	3	6	0	0	1	3	2	0	.188	.278	.375	.653	
1973	PHI-N	65	179	21	34	66	5	0	9	26	25	7	.190	.313	.369	.682	
1974	PHI-N	81	283	53	78	155	14	3	19	58	56	2	.276	.399	.548	.947	
1975	PHI-N	80	274	59	75	161	20	0	22	59	59	2	.274	.406	.588	.994	
1976	PHI-N	80	278	61	69	143	15	4	17	50	61	5	.248	.392	.514	.907	
1977	PHI-N	75	239	57	69	142	10	6	17	54	60	6	.289	.443	.594	1.037	
1978	PHI-N	77	269	57	66	124	15	2	13	50	45	2	.245	.358	.461	.819	
1979	PHI-N	80	252	51	66	130	14	1	16	49	66	0	.262	.415	.516	.931	
1980	PHI-N	78	282	59	78	179	16	5	25	64	50	1	.277	.387	.635	1.022	
1981	PHI-N	50	170	42	57	123	13	1	17	51	34	3	.335	.454	.724	1.178	
1982	PHI-N	78	257	52	64	132	13	2	17	41	56	3	.249	.389	.514	.903	
1983	PHI-N	76	254	51	64	135	10	2	19	54	61	3	.252	.403	.531	.934	
1984	PHI-N	73	235	40	63	123	8	2	16	53	42	2	.268	.384	.523	.907	
1985	PHI-N	78	265	47	74	136	18	1	14	41	42	1	.279	.380	.513	.893	
1986	PHI-N	79	258	50	77	154	17	0	20	63	46	5	.298	.414	.597	1.011	
1987	PHI-N	74	260	49	89	152	18	0	15	67	43	1	.342	.438	.585	1.022	
1988	PHI-N	54	186	30	54	87	11	2	6	32	32	5	.290	.408	.468	.876	
	17	1183	3957	780	1080	2148	217	31	263	815	780	48	.273	.399	.543	.942	

MIKE SCHMIDT - AWAY

YEAR	TM/L	G	AB	R	H	TB	2B	3B	HR	RBI	BB	HB	AVG	OBP	SLG	PRO	H/R
1972	PHI-N	8	18	1	4	4	0	0	0	0	3	1	.222	.364	.222	.586	1.114
1973	PHI-N	67	188	22	38	71	6	0	9	26	37	2	.202	.339	.378	.717	.951
1974	PHI-N	81	285	55	82	155	14	4	17	58	50	2	.288	.398	.544	.941	1.005
1975	PHI-N	78	288	34	65	133	14	3	16	36	42	2	.226	.328	.462	.790	1.257
1976	PHI-N	80	306	51	84	163	16	0	21	57	39	6	.275	.368	.533	.900	1.007
1977	PHI-N	79	305	57	80	170	17	5	21	47	44	3	.262	.361	.557	.918	1.129
1978	PHI-N	68	244	36	63	99	12	0	8	28	46	2	.258	.380	.406	.786	1.042
1979	PHI-N	80	289	58	71	175	11	3	29	65	54	3	.246	.370	.606	.975	.954
1980	PHI-N	72	266	45	79	163	9	3	23	57	39	1	.297	.389	.613	1.002	1.020
1981	PHI-N	52	184	36	55	105	6	1	14	40	39	1	.299	.424	.571	.995	1.184
1982	PHI-N	70	257	56	80	149	13	1	18	46	51	0	.311	.425	.580	1.005	.898
1983	PHI-N	78	280	53	72	145	6	2	21	55	67	2	.257	.401	.518	.918	1.017
1984	PHI-N	78	293	53	83	160	15	1	20	53	50	2	.283	.391	.546	.937	.968
1985	PHI-N	80	284	42	78	156	13	4	19	52	45	2	.275	.378	.549	.927	.963
1986	PHI-N	81	294	47	83	148	12	1	17	56	43	2	.282	.378	.503	.881	1.148
1987	PHI-N	73	262	39	64	134	10	0	20	46	40	1	.244	.347	.511	.858	1.191
1988	PHI-N	54	204	22	43	71	10	0	6	30	17	1	.211	.275	.348	.623	1.406
	17	1179	4247	707	1124	2201	184	28	279	752	706	31	.265	.373	.518	.892	1.056

TRIS SPEAKER - HOME

YEAR	TM/L	G	AB	R	H	TB	2B	3B	HR	RBI	BB	HB	AVG	OBP	SLG	PRO	H/R
1907	BOS-A	3	8	0	1	1	0	0	0		0		.125	.125	.125	.250	
1908	BOS-A	11	40	6	11	16	1	2	0		3		.275	.326	.400	.726	
1909	BOS-A	72	253	43	93	139	16	6	6		19	4	.368	.420	.549	.970	
1910	BOS-A	77	280	51	93	125	6	7	4		27	4	.332	.399	.446	.845	
1911	BOS-A	73	254	43	93	147	21	9	5		30	4	.366	.441	.579	1.020	
1912	BOS-A	77	288	68	113	161	26	5	4		42	3	.392	.474	.559	1.034	
1913	BOS-A	72	260	48	93	141	22	13	0		35	3	.358	.440	.542	.982	
1914	BOS-A	79	292	44	94	133	27	6	0		33	4	.322	.398	.455	.854	
1915	BOS-A	73	255	56	87	111	10	7	0		40	3	.341	.436	.435	.872	
1916	CLE-A	73	257	51	104	133	23	3	0		43	1	.405	.492	.518	1.009	
1917	CLE-A	67	244	42	91	133	27	6	1		30	4	.373	.450	.545	.995	
1918	CLE-A	62	217	41	81	115	22	6	0		42	1	.373	.477	.530	1.007	
1919	CLE-A	66	230	44	80	121	22	8	1		42	3	.348	.455	.526	.981	
1920	CLE-A	78	277	68	105	157	28	3	6	52	54	2	.379	.483	.567	1.050	
1921	CLE-A	76	288	67	115	179	42	8	2	50	44	2	.399	.482	.622	1.104	
1922	CLE-A	60	182	42	80	127	28	2	5	40	37	1	.440	.536	.698	1.234	
1923	CLE-A	75	286	68	120	196	32	7	10	77	43	2	.420	.498	.685	1.184	
1924	CLE-A	65	223	43	80	125	24	6	3	38	36	2	.359	.452	.561	1.013	
1925	CLE-A	64	236	52	102	152	24	4	6	39	41	3	.432	.521	.644	1.165	
1926	CLE-A	77	264	46	80	127	34	2	3	38	46	0	.303	.406	.481	.888	
1927	WAS-A	67	246	34	70	94	16	4	0	30	21	2	.285	.346	.382	.728	
1928	PHI-A	39	124	21	40	69	18	1	3	19	5	0	.323	.349	.556	.905	
	22	1406	5004	978	1826	2702	469	115	59	383	713	48	.365	.449	.540	.989	

YEAR	TM/L	G	AB	R	H	TB	2B	3B	HR	RBI	BB	HB	AVG	OBP	SLG	PRO	H/R
TRIS SPEAKER - AWAY																	
1907	BOS-A	4	11	0	2	2	0	0	0		1		.182	.250	.182	.432	.579
1908	BOS-A	20	76	6	15	18	1	1	0		1	1	.197	.218	.237	.455	1.595
1909	BOS-A	71	291	30	75	102	10	7	1		19	3	.258	.310	.351	.660	1.468
1910	BOS-A	64	258	41	90	127	14	7	3		25	2	.349	.411	.492	.903	.936
1911	BOS-A	68	246	45	74	104	13	4	3		29	9	.301	.394	.423	.817	1.248
1912	BOS-A	76	292	68	109	168	27	7	6		40	3	.373	.454	.575	1.029	1.004
1913	BOS-A	69	260	46	96	136	13	9	3		30	4	.369	.442	.523	.965	1.017
1914	BOS-A	79	279	56	99	154	19	12	4		44	3	.355	.448	.552	1.000	.854
1915	BOS-A	77	292	52	89	114	15	5	0		41	4	.305	.398	.390	.788	1.106
1916	CLE-A	78	289	51	107	141	18	5	2		39	3	.370	.450	.488	.938	1.076
1917	CLE-A	75	279	48	93	121	15	5	1		37	3	.333	.417	.434	.851	1.169
1918	CLE-A	65	254	32	69	90	11	5	0		22	2	.272	.335	.354	.689	1.462
1919	CLE-A	68	264	39	66	93	16	4	1		31	5	.250	.340	.352	.692	1.417
1920	CLE-A	72	275	69	109	153	22	8	2	55	43	3	.396	.483	.556	1.039	1.011
1921	CLE-A	56	218	40	68	93	10	6	1	24	24	0	.312	.380	.427	.807	1.368
1922	CLE-A	71	244	43	81	131	20	6	6	31	40	0	.332	.426	.537	.963	1.282
1923	CLE-A	75	288	65	98	153	26	4	7	53	50	2	.340	.441	.531	.972	1.217
1924	CLE-A	70	263	51	87	123	12	3	6	27	36	2	.331	.415	.468	.883	1.147
1925	CLE-A	53	193	27	65	96	11	1	6	48	29	1	.337	.426	.497	.923	1.262
1926	CLE-A	73	275	50	84	126	18	6	4	48	48	0	.305	.409	.458	.867	1.024
1927	WAS-A	74	277	37	101	138	27	2	2	43	34	2	.365	.438	.498	.936	.778
1928	PHI-A	25	67	7	11	17	4	1	0	11	5	2	.164	.243	.254	.497	1.822
	22	1383	5191	903	1688	2400	322	108	58	340	668	54	.325	.408	.462	.870	1.137
HONUS WAGNER - HOME																	
1897	LOU-N	25	91	13	27	39	7	1	1	18	7	0	.297	.347	.429	.776	
1898	LOU-N	77	293	44	95	131	15	0	7	62	17	3	.324	.367	.447	.815	
1899	LOU-N	65	249	48	88	135	17	6	6	50	15	7	.353	.406	.542	.948	
1900	PIT-N	70	262	48	103	154	23	11	2	51	27		.393	.450	.588	1.038	
1901	PIT-N	69	265	50	87	128	17	6	4	63	27		.328	.390	.483	.873	
1902	PIT-N	71	275	56	101	142	19	11	0	53	25		.367	.420	.516	.936	
1903	PIT-N	59	227	45	81	122	17	12	0				.357		.537	.894	
1904	PIT-N	72	251	45	82	128	19	9	3				.327		.510	.837	
1905	PIT-N	72	261	56	105	147	15	12	1				.402		.563	.966	
1906	PIT-N	70	250	49	82	117	20	6	1				.328		.468	.796	
1907	PIT-N	69	243	47	93	124	17	7	0				.383		.510	.893	
1908	PIT-N	76	272	36	103	154	17	11	4				.379		.566	.945	
1909	PIT-N	70	242	39	80	120	19	6	3			3	.331		.496	.835	
1910	PIT-N	76	278	52	102	143	25	5	2		34	4	.367	.443	.514	.957	
1911	PIT-N	72	252	44	78	106	9	5	3		41	4	.310	.414	.421	.835	
1912	PIT-N	71	262	37	80	131	15	12	4		24	4	.305	.372	.500	.872	
1913	PIT-N	65	236	28	68	84	10	3	0		13	5	.288	.339	.356	.695	
1914	PIT-N	75	271	28	68	86	6	6	0		29	2	.251	.328	.317	.645	
1915	PIT-N	78	283	31	80	119	15	9	2		21	1	.283	.334	.420	.755	
1916	PIT-N	56	192	20	60	83	9	7	0		16	4	.313	.377	.432	.810	
1917	PIT-N	41	132	9	41	48	5	1	0		14	1	.311	.381	.364	.745	
	21	1399	5087	825	1704	2441	316	146	43	297	310	38	.335	.378	.480	.857	
HONUS WAGNER - AWAY																	
1897	LOU-N	36	146	24	53	72	10	3	1	21	8	1	.363	.400	.493	.893	.868
1898	LOU-N	74	295	36	81	110	14	3	3	43	14	2	.275	.312	.373	.685	1.189
1899	LOU-N	82	322	50	104	147	26	7	1	63	25	4	.323	.379	.457	.835	1.135
1900	PIT-N	65	265	59	98	148	22	11	2	49	14		.370	.401	.558	.960	1.081
1901	PIT-N	71	284	51	107	143	20	5	2	63	26		.377	.429	.504	.933	.937
1902	PIT-N	65	259	49	75	105	11	5	3	38	18		.290	.336	.405	.741	1.263
1903	PIT-N	70	285	52	101	143	13	7	5				.354		.502	.856	1.045
1904	PIT-N	61	239	52	89	127	25	5	1				.372		.531	.904	.926
1905	PIT-N	75	287	58	94	130	17	2	5				.328		.453	.780	1.237
1906	PIT-N	73	266	54	93	120	18	3	1				.350		.451	.801	.994
1907	PIT-N	73	272	51	87	140	21	7	6				.320		.515	.835	1.070
1908	PIT-N	75	296	64	98	154	22	8	6				.331		.520	.851	1.110
1909	PIT-N	68	256	52	88	122	20	4	2			0	.344		.477	.820	1.017
1910	PIT-N	74	278	38	76	97	9	3	2		25	1	.273	.336	.349	.684	1.399
1911	PIT-N	59	225	43	80	134	14	11	6		26	2	.356	.427	.596	1.022	.816
1912	PIT-N	74	298	54	101	146	20	8	3		35	2	.339	.412	.490	.902	.967
1913	PIT-N	49	177	23	56	75	8	1	3		13	0	.316	.363	.424	.787	.883
1914	PIT-N	75	281	32	71	89	9	3	1		22	0	.253	.307	.317	.624	1.034
1915	PIT-N	78	283	37	75	120	17	8	4		18	3	.265	.316	.424	.740	1.020
1916	PIT-N	67	240	25	64	77	6	2	1		18	4	.267	.328	.321	.649	1.247
1917	PIT-N	33	98	6	20	22	2	0	0		10	0	.204	.278	.224	.502	1.482
	21	1397	5352	910	1711	2421	324	106	58	277	272	19	.320	.355	.452	.807	1.062
TED WILLIAMS - HOME																	
1939	BOS-A	75	277	74	95	169	22	5	14	68	52	2	.343	.450	.610	1.060	
1940	BOS-A	76	297	69	101	166	28	5	9	60	47	2	.340	.434	.559	.992	
1941	BOS-A	75	243	72	104	186	21	2	19	62	80	3	.428	.574	.765	1.339	
1942	BOS-A	75	261	73	93	168	21	3	16	68	64	2	.356	.486	.644	1.130	
1946	BOS-A	76	266	74	98	181	21	4	18	69	73	0	.368	.504	.680	1.185	
1947	BOS-A	81	277	67	92	176	24	6	16	63	84	2	.332	.490	.635	1.126	
1948	BOS-A	66	239	57	88	140	23	1	9	66	66	3	.368	.510	.586	1.096	
1949	BOS-A	77	272	87	95	193	27	1	23	86	91	0	.349	.512	.710	1.222	
1950	BOS-A	43	160	50	57	118	13	0	16	56	41	0	.356	.488	.738	1.225	
1951	BOS-A	73	268	69	108	190	22	3	18	81	64	0	.403	.518	.709	1.227	
1952	BOS-A	4	6	1	3	6	0	0	1	3	1	0	.500	.571	1.000	1.571	
1953	BOS-A	19	47	10	17	45	4	0	8	18	10	0	.362	.474	.957	1.431	
1954	BOS-A	58	186	48	69	129	12	0	16	39	72	1	.371	.548	.694	1.242	
1955	BOS-A	54	172	48	67	125	11	1	15	47	52	1	.390	.533	.727	1.260	
1956	BOS-A	72	205	39	74	127	19	2	10	43	59	0	.361	.504	.620	1.123	
1957	BOS-A	63	206	42	83	138	19	0	12	36	52	2	.403	.527	.670	1.197	
1958	BOS-A	66	207	47	68	116	14	2	10	41	57	3	.329	.479	.560	1.040	
1959	BOS-A	52	134	14	37	56	10	0	3	21	20	1	.276	.374	.418	.792	
1960	BOS-A	60	164	32	54	107	8	0	15	38	47	0	.329	.479	.652	1.131	
	19	1165	3887	973	1403	2536	319	35	248	965	1032	22	.361	.497	.652	1.150	

YEAR	TM/L	G	AB	R	H	TB	2B	3B	HR	RBI	BB	HB	AVG	OBP	SLG	PRO	H/R
TED WILLIAMS - AWAY																	
1939	BOS-A	74	288	57	90	175	22	6	17	77	55	0	.313	.423	.608	1.030	1.029
1940	BOS-A	68	264	65	92	167	15	9	14	53	49	1	.348	.452	.633	1.085	.915
1941	BOS-A	68	213	63	81	149	12	1	18	58	65	0	.380	.525	.700	1.225	1.093
1942	BOS-A	75	261	68	93	170	13	2	20	69	81	2	.356	.512	.651	1.163	.972
1946	BOS-A	74	248	68	78	162	16	4	20	54	83	2	.315	.489	.653	1.143	1.037
1947	BOS-A	75	251	58	89	159	16	3	16	51	78	0	.355	.508	.633	1.141	.987
1948	BOS-A	71	270	67	100	173	21	2	16	61	60	0	.370	.485	.641	1.126	.973
1949	BOS-A	78	294	63	99	175	12	2	20	73	71	2	.337	.469	.595	1.064	1.149
1950	BOS-A	46	174	32	49	98	11	1	12	41	41	0	.282	.419	.563	.982	1.248
1951	BOS-A	75	263	40	61	105	6	1	12	45	80	0	.232	.411	.399	.810	1.514
1952	BOS-A	2	4	1	1	3	0	1	0	0	1	0	.250	.400	.750	1.150	1.366
1953	BOS-A	18	44	7	20	37	2	0	5	16	9	0	.455	.547	.841	1.388	1.031
1954	BOS-A	59	200	45	64	116	11	1	13	50	64	0	.320	.485	.580	1.065	1.166
1955	BOS-A	44	148	29	47	100	10	2	13	36	39	1	.318	.463	.676	1.138	1.107
1956	BOS-A	64	195	32	64	115	9	0	14	39	43	1	.328	.452	.590	1.042	1.078
1957	BOS-A	69	214	54	80	169	9	1	26	51	67	3	.374	.528	.790	1.318	.908
1958	BOS-A	63	204	34	67	124	9	0	16	44	41	1	.328	.443	.608	1.051	.989
1959	BOS-A	51	138	18	32	58	5	0	7	22	32	1	.232	.380	.420	.800	.990
1960	BOS-A	53	146	24	44	93	7	0	14	34	28	3	.301	.424	.637	1.061	1.066
	19	1127	3819	825	1251	2348	206	36	273	874	987	17	.328	.468	.615	1.082	1.062
CARL YASTRZEMSKI - HOME																	
1961	BOS-A	73	287	30	91	137	18	5	6	41	24	2	.317	.374	.477	.851	
1962	BOS-A	79	316	64	108	178	27	5	11	52	32	1	.342	.404	.563	.967	
1963	BOS-A	74	282	50	89	135	24	2	6	36	35	1	.316	.393	.479	.872	
1964	BOS-A	75	286	40	83	135	20	7	6	39	36	1	.290	.372	.472	.844	
1965	BOS-A	74	266	51	88	170	30	2	16	53	40	0	.331	.418	.639	1.057	
1966	BOS-A	80	305	48	99	159	25	1	11	53	39	0	.325	.401	.521	.922	
1967	BOS-A	81	286	66	95	194	16	1	27	74	47	3	.332	.432	.678	1.110	
1968	BOS-A	80	264	48	75	125	15	1	11	42	66	2	.284	.431	.473	.904	
1969	BOS-A	81	297	48	83	164	16	1	21	55	51	1	.279	.387	.552	.939	
1970	BOS-A	81	272	62	96	177	15	0	22	61	72	1	.353	.490	.651	1.141	
1971	BOS-A	75	257	47	72	108	15	0	7	42	50	1	.280	.399	.420	.820	
1972	BOS-A	69	247	46	71	105	15	2	5	41	39	2	.287	.389	.425	.814	
1973	BOS-A	74	247	40	70	112	12	3	8	46	58	0	.283	.420	.453	.873	
1974	BOS-A	77	256	48	83	113	13	1	5	43	61	3	.324	.459	.441	.901	
1975	BOS-A	77	274	56	75	117	16	1	8	43	46	1	.274	.380	.427	.807	
1976	BOS-A	74	255	37	81	130	17	1	10	56	41	1	.318	.414	.510	.924	
1977	BOS-A	78	282	58	99	157	16	0	14	67	37	1	.351	.428	.557	.985	
1978	BOS-A	72	265	37	77	114	14	1	7	39	40	1	.291	.386	.430	.816	
1979	BOS-A	75	262	34	79	141	15	1	15	55	32	1	.302	.380	.538	.918	
1980	BOS-A	54	176	19	47	72	8	1	5	21	24	0	.267	.355	.409	.764	
1981	BOS-A	46	158	20	46	68	11	1	3	33	25	0	.291	.388	.430	.818	
1982	BOS-A	66	224	27	69	102	10	1	7	36	33	0	.308	.397	.455	.852	
1983	BOS-A	61	184	18	46	78	14	0	6	35	31	2	.250	.364	.424	.788	
	23	1676	5948	994	1822	2991	382	38	237	1063	959	25	.306	.405	.503	.908	
CARL YASTRZEMSKI - AWAY																	
1961	BOS-A	75	296	41	64	94	13	1	5	39	26	1	.216	.282	.318	.599	1.420
1962	BOS-A	81	330	35	83	125	16	1	8	42	34	2	.252	.325	.379	.704	1.374
1963	BOS-A	77	288	41	94	136	16	1	8	32	60	0	.326	.443	.472	.915	.953
1964	BOS-A	76	281	37	81	121	9	2	9	28	39	1	.288	.377	.431	.808	1.045
1965	BOS-A	59	228	27	66	95	15	1	4	19	30	1	.289	.375	.417	.791	1.336
1966	BOS-A	80	289	33	66	97	14	1	5	27	45	1	.228	.334	.336	.670	1.377
1967	BOS-A	80	293	46	94	166	15	3	17	47	44	1	.321	.411	.567	.978	1.135
1968	BOS-A	77	275	42	87	142	17	1	12	32	53	0	.316	.427	.516	.943	.959
1969	BOS-A	81	306	48	71	142	12	1	19	56	50	0	.232	.340	.464	.804	1.168
1970	BOS-A	80	294	63	90	158	14	0	18	41	56	0	.306	.417	.537	.955	1.195
1971	BOS-A	73	251	28	57	91	6	2	8	28	56	0	.227	.368	.363	.731	1.122
1972	BOS-A	56	208	24	49	73	3	0	7	27	28	2	.236	.332	.351	.683	1.192
1973	BOS-A	78	293	42	90	138	13	1	11	49	47	0	.307	.403	.471	.874	.999
1974	BOS-A	71	259	45	72	116	12	1	10	36	43	0	.278	.381	.448	.829	1.087
1975	BOS-A	72	269	35	71	103	14	0	6	17	41	1	.264	.363	.383	.746	1.082
1976	BOS-A	81	291	34	65	106	6	1	11	46	39	0	.223	.315	.364	.679	1.360
1977	BOS-A	72	276	41	66	125	11	3	14	35	36	0	.239	.327	.453	.780	1.263
1978	BOS-A	72	258	33	68	107	7	1	10	42	36	2	.264	.358	.415	.773	1.056
1979	BOS-A	72	256	35	61	92	13	0	6	32	30	1	.238	.321	.359	.680	1.350
1980	BOS-A	51	188	30	53	96	13	0	10	29	20	0	.282	.351	.511	.862	.887
1981	BOS-A	45	180	16	37	52	3	0	4	20	24	0	.206	.299	.289	.588	1.392
1982	BOS-A	65	235	26	57	96	12	0	9	36	26	2	.243	.323	.409	.732	1.165
1983	BOS-A	58	196	20	55	77	10	0	4	21	23	0	.281	.356	.393	.749	1.052
	23	1632	6040	822	1597	2548	264	21	215	781	886	15	.264	.360	.422	.782	1.161

Appendices

Appendices

APPENDIX 1

Rules and Scoring

Thomas R. Heitz

The chronologies presented here trace the evolution of professional baseball's playing and scoring rules from the inception of the National League in 1876 to the present (through 1988).

Playing Rules

As a starting point, the rules of 1876 are set forth in their entirety. Thereafter, changes to the playing rules are noted under annual headings. In many cases, the actual text of a new rule or change has been taken verbatim from original sources. However, to reduce verbiage, the references to section numbering, which have varied widely over the years, have been deleted along with other extraneous spacing and punctuation. In other cases, the technical wording of complex rules has been summarized for ease of reading. Researchers requiring precise quotations of rules are advised to consult original sources, e.g., the *Spalding* and *Reach Baseball Guides*.

The chronology does not include *all* changes to the playing rules— only those judged to be of significance and substance. Numerous minor changes in wording not affecting meaning, or changes in punctuation which had no purpose other than grammatical correctness have been ignored.

In some instances, significant rule changes affecting umpires and little-used rules regarding suspended games or batting out of order have been summarized or simply alluded to in the interests of brevity. The scoring rules are presented in a separate section of this appendix due to their length and special interest.

Baseball's rules continue to evolve in the twentieth century despite the perception of many that "the game remains pretty much the same as it always has been." The most far-reaching revision of baseball's playing rules came in 1950 when the entire code was virtually rewritten. Additional changes and refinements were added throughout the 1950s, and it is the rules of 1950 for the most part that we use today.

It is also a commonplace that baseball's rules are the means of keeping the game in that delicate balance between offense and defense with neither side enjoying a marked advantage. This balance is seen as the dynamic force of competition, which drives the game and ultimately creates interest and motivation for players and spectators alike.

But, changes to the playing rules can also be categorized in terms of response to various social, economic and technological factors as well as to the need for competitive balance.

For example, when the uncouth language of hard-bitten nineteenth century players became offensive to female rooters, appropriate rules were adopted (in an attempt) to modify player behavior.

Likewise, gloves were introduced gradually in the 1870s and 1880s to protect the players' catching hands from injury. However, when glove design clearly departed from the goal of protection and extended to aiding in the catching process, effectively making the glove an extension of the hand, it became necessary to invoke standards for gloves in the rules.

In terms of competitive balance, perhaps the most striking evolution is that of the pitching rules, which have undergone a remarkable transformation from the days of simple underhanded hurling from a boxlike enclosure to today's complex series of physical motions from which almost any deviation is likely to elicit a call of "balk."

In many cases, the introduction of a playing rule follows by several years developments on the field of play. Like state and federal legislative bodies, baseball's rule-making authorities are often slow to respond to changing conditions or perhaps cautious about making such changes before the effects are fully understood.

For example, there is no mention of pitching mounds in the playing rules until 1903 when the maximum elevation was fixed at 15 inches. However, pitching mounds were in general use many years prior to 1903 and may have come into vogue as early as the 1880s. The lifting of restrictions on the angle of pitching delivery in 1884 made overhanded throwing legal and it was not long before the hurlers realized the mechanical advantages of stepping off a short incline as they directed the ball toward the plate. Presumably, by 1903 the lack of uniformity in pitching mounds or perhaps the growing elevation of mounds in certain parks had become a problem and so the rules set a standard.

The researcher is advised to scan the Index to Playing Rule Changes prior to consulting the chronology.

Scoring Rules

The chronology presented after that of the playing rules traces the evolution of professional baseball's scoring rules from 1878 to the present (through 1988).

As a starting point, the scoring rules of 1878 are presented in their entirety. Thereafter changes to the scoring rules are noted under annual headings.

In most cases, as with the playing rules, the actual text of a new scoring rule or change has been taken verbatim from original sources.

The scoring rules are at the heart of baseball's accountability to itself and to the millions of fans who follow the game day by day. Through the use of these rules the daily performance of players and teams is described and measured in a uniform and meaningful way. Baseball is unique in publishing the performance records of its key personnel, and in so doing it subjects the individual and the team and its management to the scrutiny and judgment of anyone who has the price of a daily newspaper.

Like the playing rules, the scoring rules have been transformed over the decades from the simple recording of hits, outs, errors and assists in the 1870s into a highly technical set of rules and guidelines used to record every significant offensive and defensive event that transpires on the field of play.

While the collection of such statistics as "caught stealing" did not commence until later years, still baseball's major performance records can be traced in an unbroken skein well back into the 19th century. As a result, no other professional sport can claim such a rich resource of historical statistics.

The researcher is advised to scan the Index to Scoring Rule Changes prior to consulting the chronology.

Playing Rules for 1876

Rule I
The Materials of the Game

Section 1. The ball. The ball must weigh not less than five, nor more than five and one-quarter ounces, avoirdupois. It must measure not less than nine, nor more than nine and one-quarter inches in circumference. It must be composed of woollen yarn, and shall not contain more than one ounce of vulcanized rubber in mould form, and shall be covered with leather.

Section 2. Furnishing the ball. In all games the ball or balls played with shall be furnished by the home club, and shall become the property of the winning club.

Section 3. A legal ball. No ball shall be played with in any regular match game, unless it is of the regulation size, weight, and materials, and also have the name of its maker and the figures indicating its weight and circumference plainly stamped on its cover. Should any ball used in a regular match game prove, on examination by the umpire, to be illegal in size, weight or materials, balls of the same manufacture shall not be used thereafter in regular match games.

Section 4. Changing the ball. When the ball becomes out of shape, or cut or ripped so as to expose the yarn, or in any way so injured as to be unfit for fair use, a new ball shall be called for by the umpire at the end of an even inning, at the request of either captain. Should the ball be lost during a game, the umpire shall, at the expiration of five minutes, call for a new ball.

Section 5. The bat. The bat must be round, and must not exceed two and one-half inches in diameter in the thickest part. It must be made wholly of wood, and shall not exceed forty-two inches in length.

Section 6. The bases. The bases must be four in number, and they must be placed and securely fastened upon each corner of a square the sides of which are respectively thirty yards. The bases must be so constructed and placed as to be distinctly seen by the umpire, and must cover a space equal to one square foot of surface. The first, second, and third bases shall be canvas bags, painted white and filled with some soft material. The home base shall be of white marble or stone, so fixed in the ground as to be even with the surface, and with one corner facing the pitcher's position, said corner touching the intersection of the foul lines.

Section 7. Position of the bases. The base from which the ball is struck shall be designated the home base, and must be directly opposite the second base. The first base must always be that upon the right hand, and the third base that upon the left hand side of the striker when occupying his position at the home base. In all match games, lines connecting the home and first bases, and the home and third bases, and also the lines of the striker's and pitcher's positions, shall be marked by the use of chalk or other suitable material, so as to be distinctly seen by the umpire. The line of the home base shall extend four feet on each side of the base, and shall be drawn through its centre and parallel with a line extending from first to third base.

Rule II
The Game

Section 1. The innings. The game shall consist of nine innings to each side, but should the score then be a tie, play shall be continued until a majority of runs for one side, upon an equal number of innings, shall be declared, when the game shall end. All innings shall be concluded when the third hand is put out.

Section 2. Positions of players. Positions of players and choice of first innings shall be determined by the two captains. The fielders of each club shall take any position in the field their captain may assign them, with the exception of pitcher, who must deliver the ball from his appointed position.

Section 3. Substitutes. No player taking part in a game shall be replaced by another after the commencement of the fourth innings, except as provided in Section 14 of Rule VI.

Section 4. Five innings necessary. No game shall be considered as played unless five innings on each side shall be completed. Should darkness or rain intervene before the third hand is put out in the closing part of the fifth innings of a game, the umpire shall declare "No game."

Section 5. Drawn games. Whenever a game of five or more innings is stopped by rain or darkness, and the score at the time is equal on the even innings played, the game shall be declared drawn, but, under no other circumstances, shall a drawn game be declared.

Section 6. Rain. Should rain commence to fall during the progress of a match game, the umpire must note the time it began, and should it continue for five minutes, he shall, at the request of either captain, suspend play. Such suspended game shall not be resumed until, in the opinion of the umpire, the ground is in fit condition for fair fielding.

Section 7. Calling play and time. When the umpire calls "play," the game must at once be proceeded with. Should either party fail to take their appointed positions in the game, or to commence play as requested, the umpire shall, at the expiration of five minutes, declare the game forfeited by the nine that refuses to play. When the umpire calls "time," play shall be suspended until he call "play" again, and during the interim no player shall be put out, base be run or run be scored.

Section 8. Suspending play. The umpire, in any match game, shall determine when play shall be suspended, and, if the game cannot be fairly concluded, it shall be decided by the score of the last equal innings played, unless one nine shall have completed their innings, and the other nine shall have equalled or exceeded the score of their opponents in their incompleted innings, in which case the game shall be decided by the total score obtained, which score shall be recorded as the score of the game.

Section 9. Ending a game. When the umpire calls a game it shall end, but when he merely suspends play for any stated period, it may be resumed at the point at which it was suspended; provided such suspension does not extend beyond the day of the match.

Rule III
The Players

Section 1. Regular match. Every player taking part in a regular match game, no matter what number of innings be played, shall be considered a member of the club with which he plays. All matches shall be considered regular in the meaning of this rule in which nines of two contesting clubs of this League take part.

Section 2. Betting prohibited. Any player who shall, in any way, be interested in any bet or wager on the game in which he takes part, either as umpire, player, or scorer, or who shall purchase or have purchased for him any "pool" or chance—sold or given away—on the game he plays in, shall be dishonorably expelled, both from the club of which he is a member and from the League.

A player who shall be similarly interested in any regular match game between two clubs of the League, shall be suspended from legal service as a member for the season during which he shall have violated this rule.

Rule IV
Pitching

Section 1. The pitcher's position. The pitcher's position shall be within a space of ground six feet square, the front line of which shall be distant forty-five feet from the centre of the home base, and the centre of the square shall be equidistant from the first and the third bases. Each corner of the square shall be marked by a flat iron plate

or stone six inches square fixed in the ground even with the surface.

Section 2. Delivering the ball. The player who delivers the ball to the bat must do so while within the lines of the pitcher's position. He must remain within them until the ball has left his hand, and he shall not make any motion to deliver the ball to the bat while any part of his person is outside the lines of the pitcher's position. The ball must be delivered to the bat with the arm swinging nearly perpendicular at the side of the body, and the hand in swinging forward must pass below the hip.

Section 3. A foul delivery. Should the pitcher deliver the ball by an overhand throw, a "foul balk" shall be declared. Any outward swing of the arm, or any other swing save that of the perpendicular movement referred to in Section 2 of this rule, shall be considered an overhand throw.

Section 4. Foul balk. When a "foul balk" is called, the umpire shall warn the pitcher of the penalty incurred by such unfair delivery, and should such delivery be continued until *three foul balks* have been called in one innings, the umpire shall declare the game forfeited.

Section 5. Balking. Should the pitcher make any motion to deliver the ball to the bat and fail so to deliver it—except the ball be accidentally dropped—or should he unnecessarily delay the game by not delivering the ball to the bat, or should he, when in the act of delivering the ball, have any part of his person outside the lines of his position, the umpire shall call a "balk," and players occupying the bases shall take one base each.

Section 6. Good balls. Every ball fairly delivered and sent in to the bat over the home base and at the height called for by the batsman, shall be considered a good ball.

Section 7. Called balls. All balls delivered to the bat which are not sent in over the home base and at the height called for by the batsman, shall be considered unfair balls, and every third ball so delivered must be called. When "three balls" have been called, the striker shall take first base, and all players who are thereby forced to leave a base shall take one base. No "ball" shall be called until the ball has passed the home base.

Section 8. Hitting at called balls. Should the batsman strike at a ball on which a "ball" has been called, such call shall be considered void, and the ball regarded as fairly delivered.

Section 9. Dead balls. All balls delivered to the bat which shall touch the striker's bat without being struck at, or his (the batsman's) person while standing in his position, or which shall hit the person of the umpire—unless it be a passed ball—shall be considered *dead* balls and shall be so called by the umpire, and no players shall be put out, base be run, or run be scored on any such ball.

Rule V
Batting Department

Section 1. The batsman's position. The batsman's or strikers position shall be within a space of ground located on either side of the home base, six feet long by three feet wide, extending two feet in front of and four feet behind the line of the home base, and with its nearest line distant one foot from the home base.

Section 2. The order of striking. The batsmen must take their positions in the order in which they are named on the score-book. After the first innings, the first striker in each innings shall be the batsman whose name follows that of the third man out in the preceding innings.

Section 3. Failing to take position. Any batsman failing to take his position at the bat in his order of striking—unless by reason of illness or injury, or by consent of the captains of the contesting nines—shall be declared out, unless the error be discovered before a fair ball has been struck, or the striker put out.

Section 4. Refusing to strike. Any batsman failing to take his position at the bat within *three minutes* after the umpire has called for the striker, shall be declared out.

Section 5. Specifying balls. The batsman, on taking his position, must call for either a "*high ball*," a "*low ball*," or a "*fair ball*," and the umpire shall notify the pitcher to deliver the ball as required; such call shall not be changed after the first ball delivered.

Section 6. Good balls to the bat. A "*high ball*" shall be one sent in above the waist of the batsman but not higher than his shoulder. A "*low ball*" shall be one sent in *not lower* than within *one foot* of the *ground*, but *not higher* than his *waist*. A "*fair ball*" shall be one between the range of *shoulder high* and *one foot* from the *ground*. All the above must be *over the home base*, and when fairly delivered, shall be considered good balls to the bat.

Section 7. Calling strikes. Should the batsman fail to strike at a "good ball," or should he strike and fail to hit the ball, the umpire shall call "one strike," and "two strikes," should he again fail. When two strikes have been called, should the batsman not strike at the next "good ball" the umpire shall warn him by calling "good ball." But should he strike at and fail to hit the ball, or should he fail to strike at or to hit the next good ball, "three strikes" must be called, and the batsman must run to first base as in the case of hitting a fair ball.

Section 8. A fair strike. The batsman, when in the act of striking at the ball, must stand within the lines of his position.

Section 9. A foul strike. Should the batsman step outside the lines of his position when he strikes the ball, the umpire shall call "foul strike and out," and baserunners shall return to the bases they occupied when the ball was hit.

Section 10. The foul ball lines. The foul ball lines shall be unlimited in length, and shall run from the front corner of the home base through the centre of first and third bases to the foul posts, which shall be located at the boundary of the field and within the range of home and first base, and home and third base. Said lines shall be marked, and on the inside, from base to base, with chalk, or some other white substance, so as to be plainly seen by the umpire.

Section 11. A fair hit ball. If the ball from a fair stroke of the bat first touches the ground, the person of a player, or any other object, either in front of, or on the foul ball lines, it shall be considered fair.

Section 12. A foul hit ball. If the ball from a fair stroke of the bat first touches the ground, the person of a player, or any other object behind the foul ball lines, it shall be declared foul, and the ball so hit shall be called foul by the umpire even before touching the ground, if it be seen falling foul.

Section 13. Hitting called balls. Should the batsman strike at or hit any ball on which a "ball" has been called, the umpire shall disregard the call of such "ball," and render his decision simply on the strike or hit made.

Section 14. When batsmen become baserunners. When the batsman has fairly struck a fair ball, he shall vacate his position, and he shall then be considered a baserunner until he is put out or scores his run.

Section 15. How batsmen are put out. The batsman shall be declared out by the umpire as follows:
On the fly. If a fair or foul ball be caught before touching the ground, provided it be not caught in a player's hat or cap.
On the bound. If a foul ball be similarly held, or after touching the ground but once.
At first base. If a fair ball be securely held by a fielder while touching first base with any part of his person before the baserunner touches said base.
On three strikes. If after three strikes have been called, he fails to touch first base before the ball is legally held there.
If after three strikes have been called, the ball be caught before

touching the ground or after touching the ground but once.

Balking the catcher. If he wilfully strikes at the ball to hinder the ball from being caught, or makes a "foul strike."

Rule VI
Running the Bases

Section 1. Touching the bases. Players running bases must touch each base in regular order, viz.: first, second, third, and home base; and when obliged to return to bases they have occupied they must retouch them in reverse order. No base shall be considered as having been occupied or held until it has been touched.

Section 2. Forced off a base. No player running the bases shall be forced to vacate the base he occupies unless by the act of the batsman in striking a fair ball. Should the first base be occupied by a baserunner when a fair ball is struck, the baserunner shall cease to be entitled to hold said base until the player running to first base shall be put out. The same rule shall apply in the case of the occupancy of the other bases under similar circumstances. No baserunner shall be forced to vacate the base he occupies if the baserunner succeeding him is not thus obliged to vacate his base.

Section 3. How put out when forced. Players forced to vacate their bases may be put out by any fielders in the same manner as when running to first base.

Section 4. Overrunning first base. The player running to first base shall be at liberty to overrun said base without his being put out for being off the base after first touching it, provided that in so overrunning the base he make no attempt to run to second base. In such case he must return at once and retouch first base, and after retouching said base he can be put out as at any other base. If, in so overrunning first base, he also attempts to run to second base, he shall forfeit such exemption from being put out.

Section 5. Running out of the line of bases. Any player running a base who shall run beyond three feet from the line from base to base in order to avoid being touched by they ball in the hands of a fielder shall be declared out by the umpire with or without appeal.

Section 6. When a run is scored. One run shall be scored every time a baserunner, after having regularly touched the first three bases, shall touch the home base before three hands are out. If the third hand out is forced out, or is put out before reaching first base, a run shall not be scored.

Section 7. Taking bases on balks. When a "balk" is called by the umpire, every player running the bases shall take one base without being put out.

Section 8. Taking bases on called balls. When three "balls" have been called by the umpire, the batsman shall take one base without being put out, and should any baserunner be forced thereby to vacate his base, he also shall take one base. Each baserunner thus given a base shall be at liberty to run to other bases besides the base given, but only at the risk of being put out in so running.

Section 9. Holding a base. A player running bases shall be considered as holding a base, viz., entitled to occupy it, until he shall have regularly touched the next base in order.

Section 10. Running bases on fair and foul fly balls. No base shall be run or run be scored when a fair or foul ball has been caught or momentarily held before touching the ground, unless the base held when the ball was hit is retouched by the baserunner after the ball has been so caught or held by the fielder.

Section 11. Returning to bases on foul ground balls. No run or base can be made upon a foul ball that shall touch the ground before being caught or held by a fielder, and any player running bases shall return, without being put out, to the base he occupied when the ball was struck, and remain on such base until the ball is held by the pitcher.

Section 12. Any player running the bases on fair or foul balls caught before touching the ground must return to the base he occupied when the ball was struck, and retouch such base before attempting to make another or score a run, and said player shall be liable to be put out in so returning, as in the case of running to first base when a fair ball is hit and not caught flying.

Section 13. Obstructing baserunners. If the player running the bases is prevented from making a base by the obstruction of an adversary, he shall be entitled to that base and shall not be put out.

Section 14. Substitutes in running bases. No player shall be allowed a substitute in running the bases, except for illness or injury, unless by special consent of the captain of the opposing nine; in such case the latter shall select the player to run as substitute. The substitute in question shall take his position so as to cross the batsman's position, and in front of the home base, and he shall not start to run until the ball is struck at or hit. The substitute shall be the player running the bases.

Section 15. How baserunners are put out. Any player running the bases shall be declared out if, at any time, while the ball is in play, he be touched by a fielder, with the ball in hand, without some part of his person is touching a base. Should the said fielder, while in the act of touching the baserunner, have the ball knocked out of his hand, the player so touched shall be declared out.

Preference given to the baserunner. If a ball be held by a fielder on the first base before the baserunner, after hitting a fair ball, touches that base, he shall be declared out.

Failing to touch a base. Any baserunner failing to touch the base he runs for, shall be declared out if the ball be held by a fielder, while touching said base, before the baserunner returns and touches it.

Obstructing a fielder. Any baserunner who shall in any way interfere with or obstruct a fielder while attempting to catch a fair fly ball, or a foul ball, shall be declared out by the umpire with or without appeal. If he wilfully obstructs a fielder from fielding a ball, he shall be similarly declared out, and, if he intentionally kick, or let the ball strike him, he shall be declared out.

Rule VII
The Umpire and His Duties

Section 1. Selecting an umpire. In selecting an umpire for a match game the visiting club shall submit the names of five persons, competent to act, who are not members of the visiting club. From this list the local club shall select two or more names, and answer not later than the following day. Should the visiting club be unable to secure the services of either of the two persons selected, then two more names shall be submitted to the local club to complete the list for them to select from. In case of the failure of the local club to select two of the names within forty-eight hours after said names have been telegraphed by the visiting club—if within five days of the day of the game—then the visiting club shall be at liberty to select one from the list of names sent, who shall act as umpire. All correspondence in relation to above shall be by telegraph.

Section 2. Changing an umpire. The umpire shall not be changed during the progress of a match game, except for reason of illness or injury, or by the consent of the captains of the two contesting nines, in case he shall have wilfully violated the rules of the game.

Section 3. Special duties. Before the commencement of a match, the umpire shall see that the rules governing the materials of the game, and also those applicable to the positions of batsman and pitcher, are strictly observed. Also that the fence in the rear of the catcher's position is distant not less than ninety feet from the home base, except it mark the boundary line of the field, in which case the umpire, for every ball passing the catcher and touching the fence, shall give each baserunner one base without his being put out.

Special ground rules. Before calling "play" the umpire shall ask the captain of the players on whose ground the match is played,

whether or not there are any special ground rules to be enforced, and if there are, he shall take note of such rules and see that they are duly enforced, provided they do not conflict with any rules of the game.

Section 4. Reversing decisions. No decision rendered by the umpire on any point of play in baserunning shall be reversed upon the testimony of any of the players. But if it shall be shown by the two captains of the contesting clubs that the umpire has palpably misinterpreted the rules, or given an erroneous decision, he shall reverse said decision.

Section 5. Decisions on catches. Should the umpire be unable to see whether a catch has been fairly made or not, he shall be at liberty to appeal to the bystanders, and to render his decision according to the fairest testimony at command.

Section 6. Interfering with the umpire. No person, not engaged in the game, shall be permitted to occupy any position within the lines of the field of contest, or in any way interrupt the umpire during the progress of the game. No player shall be permitted to converse with the umpire during any part of the contest, except the two captains of the contesting nines, and then only as provided in Section 4 of this rule.

Section 7. Appealing to the umpire. The umpire shall render no decision in the game except when appealed to by a player, unless expressly required to do so by the rules of the game, as in calling "balls," etc.

Section 8. Interfering with players. The umpire shall not enter the infield while the ball is in play, and he shall require the players on the batting side who are not at the bat or running the bases, to keep at a distance of not less than fifty feet from the line of home and first base and home and third base, or farther off if he so decide. The captain and one assistant only shall be permitted to coach players running the bases, and they must not approach within fifteen feet of the foul lines.

Section 9. Unfair fielding and dead balls. Should any fielder stop or catch the ball with his hat, cap, or any part of his dress, the umpire should call "dead ball," and baserunners shall each be entitled to two bases for any fair hit ball so stopped or caught. Should the ball be wilfully stopped by any outside person not engaged in the game, the umpire must call "dead ball," and players running bases at the time shall be entitled to the bases they were running for, and the ball be regarded as dead until settled in the hands of the pitcher while standing within the lines of his position.

Section 10. Violation of rules. Any match game in which the umpire shall declare any section of this code of rules to have been wilfully violated shall at once be declared by him to have been forfeited by the club at fault.

Section 11. No manager, captain, or player shall address the audience, except in case of necessary explanation; and any manager, captain, or player who shall use abusive, threatening, or improper language to the audience, shall be punished by suspension from play for twenty days and forfeiture of his salary for such period.

Section 12. No Section of these Rules shall be construed as conflicting with or affecting any Article of the Constitution.

Chronology of Rule Changes 1877-1988

1877

Ball No ball is to be used except those furnished by the Secretary of the League.

Batter The batter's box is six feet square with the line of home base running through its center. Note: This arrangement permitted a batter to stand three feet in front of or three feet behind home base.

A batted ball striking in foul territory and then in fair is fair; a batted ball striking fair and then foul is foul.

A batter is out if in the judgment of the umpire he swung at a pitch

for the purpose of "balking" (interfering) with the catcher.

Game The home club shall first take the bat.

Should rain continue to fall for 30 minutes (following suspension of play) the game shall terminate.

Ground/Bases First, second, and third bases must cover a space equal to 15 inches square.

Home base is to be placed so as to make its two outer lines those which converge to the point of the home base corner. Note: Home base is now placed within the diamond instead of outside the diamond.

Pitcher A "low ball" is one thrown belt-high or below the belt and above the knee.

A "high ball" is one above the belt to the shoulder.

The pitcher's hand must pass below the waist in delivering the ball.

Pitcher/Batter Should the batter strike at a ball on which a "ball" has been called, the call is void and the ball is considered a strike.

Player/Substitute No substitution is to be made after the close of the second inning except in cases of illness or injury.

Player/Gambling Any player who shall, in any way, be interested in any bet or wager on any league game or who shall purchase or have purchased for him any "pool" or chance sold or given away, shall be expelled.

Player/Contract The club is entitled to the best services of the player, and players who become indifferent or careless in play or who become unable to render satisfactory service to the club from any cause may have their salaries suspended or their contracts, cancelled.

Player/Club Players conspiring against the interest of their clubs or who "manifest a disposition" to obstruct club management may be expelled.

Player/Captain/Boundaries Lines parallel to the foul lines and 15 feet back are to be drawn to delineate a boundary for the captain and one assistant.

Lines parallel to the foul lines and 50 feet back are to be drawn to delineate a boundary for players on the batting side

Note: In the rules of 1880, these lines are referred to as the "Captain's Lines" and the "Players' Lines" respectively.

Runner/Fielder A baserunner who knocks the ball out of the hand of a fielder while in the act of running to a base is no longer out.

When a fielder occupies the basepath in the act of fielding a ball, the baserunner shall run out of the path and behind the fielder.

Runner/Batter A baserunner struck by a batted ball is out.

A baserunner from home to first base, shall not run inside the foul line or more than three feet outside of it, or he shall be out.

Umpire The umpire shall suspend play only for a valid reason, and is not empowered to do so for trivial causes at the request of any player.

1878

Batter Any batsman who fails to take his position at bat within one minute after the umpire has called for the batter shall be out.

Pitcher A "foul balk" is to be called by the umpire should the pitcher deliver an overhanded throw or use any outward swing of the arm. Should three foul balks be declared in an inning, the umpire shall declare the game forfeited.

A "balk" is called when: (1) The pitcher makes any motion to deliver the ball and fails to do so except when the ball is accidentally dropped; (2) The pitcher unnecessarily delays the game by not delivering the ball; (3) The pitcher has any part of his person outside the lines of his position.

Pitcher/Batter A ball pitched and called "dead" by reason of having struck the umpire shall be counted as one of nine called balls entitling the batter to a base if it is also an "unfair" ball.

Umpire The umpire shall suspend play only for an accident or injury to himself or a player or on account of rain.

1879

Pitcher The pitcher, when taking his position to deliver the ball, must face the batter.

Pitcher/Batter/Umpire If a pitcher delivers the ball to intentionally strike the batter in the judgment of the umpire, the umpire shall fine the pitcher not less than $10 nor more than $50.

1880

Batter The batter is out when the umpire declares three strikes and the catcher momentarily holds the ball before it touches the ground or any other object other than a fielder provided the fielder has not caught it in his hat.

Ground The ground must be an enclosed field sufficient in size to enable each player to play in his position as required by the rules.

Pitcher/Batter A base on balls is awarded when eight balls have been called by the umpire.

Player/Umpire No player except the captain or his assistant shall address the umpire concerning any point of play. Violators are subject to a fine.

Runner/Fielder The baserunner is out if he fails to return to the base he occupied after a foul fly has been caught by a fielder and he is touched by a fielder with the ball or the ball is returned to a fielder at the base he occupied before he returns

Runner/Batter No run can be scored if the baserunner is hit by a fairly hit ball and the runner is out.

A batter becomes a baserunner when three strikes have been called by the umpire.

Runner A baserunner who fails to touch intervening bases when returning to a base shall not be declared out unless the captain of the opposing team appeals to the umpire before the pitcher delivers the ball to the batter.

1881

Batter/Runner The batter becomes a runner when: (1) He makes a fair hit; (2) After seven balls have been called by the umpire; (3) After three strikes have been declared by the umpire.

Club/Ground No club shall sell or allow to be sold upon its grounds, nor in buildings owned or occupied by the club, any spiritous, vinous, or malt liquors.

Game/Spectators/Club Every club shall furnish sufficient police force upon its own grounds to preserve order. In the event of a crowd entering the field during the progress of a game, and interfering with play in any manner, the visiting club may refuse to play further until the field is cleared; if the ground is not cleared within 15 minutes, the visiting club is entitled to a forfeit by a score of 9-0, regardless of the number of innings played.

No person shall be allowed upon any part of the field during the progress of the game, in addition to the nine players on each side and the umpire, except such officers of the law who are present in uniform to preserve the peace.

Pitcher The pitcher's box is to be 50 feet from the center of home base.

Player/Substitute A substitute is not permitted unless a player is disabled by injury or illness in the game being played.

Runner/Substitute No substitution may be made for a baserunner.

Runner The baserunner is entitled to advance one base if a batted or thrown ball is stopped by any person not engaged in the game.

Umpire The umpire shall *not* reverse his decision on any point of play upon the testimony of any player or upon the testimony of any

bystander.

1882

Batter The batter is out if he plainly attempts to hinder the catcher from catching the ball, without effort to make a fair hit.

Player/Bench The players' bench must be furnished by the home club and placed on a portion of the ground outside the players' lines. It is to be 12 feet in length and fastened to the ground. Bat racks sufficient to hold 20 bats are to be adjacent to the players' bench.

Runner/Fielder The baserunner is entitled to take one base without being put out, provided he does so on the run, in the following cases: (1) If the runner is prevented from making a base by obstruction of an adversary; (2) If a fielder stops or catches a batted ball with his hat or any part of his dress.

Runner/Spectators A "block" is a batted or thrown ball that is stopped or handled by any person not engaged in the game. Whenever a block is called, baserunners may run the bases without being put out until the ball is returned to and held by the pitcher standing in his position. Exception: Where the person not engaged in the game retains possession of the ball or throws or kicks it beyond reach of fielders, the umpire should call time and require baserunners to stop at the last base touched by them.

Umpire/Spectators Spectators hissing or hooting at the umpire are to be promptly ejected from the grounds.

1883

Batter/Runner When a runner occupies first base and the batter is struck out, the batter is not obligated to run to first base and will be declared out by the umpire by remaining in the batter's box and the runner may hold his base.

Batter/Fielder A batted ball in foul territory must be caught on the fly to be declared an out. Note: Foul balls caught on one bounce are no longer outs.

Pitcher/Spectators No ball delivered by the pitcher to the bat can become a "blocked ball" if it is stopped by an outsider.

Pitcher/Batter A fair ball is a ball delivered by the pitcher, while wholly within the lines of his position, and while facing the batsman and his hand, in delivering the ball, must not pass above the line of his shoulder.

Runner A baserunner who fails to return to his base at a run following a foul ball is liable to be put out by being touched by the ball while off his base.

Umpire Umpires are to be salaried employees of the league.

1884

Batter/Runner A batter is entitled to take first base after six balls are called by the umpire.

Game/Umpire/Spectators The umpire shall call time in case rain falls so heavily that spectators are compelled, by the severity of the storm, to seek shelter.

Pitcher All restrictions on the delivery of the ball to the batter are lifted except that the pitcher must be wholly within the line of his position and facing the batter. Note: The overhanded pitching delivery was thus permitted for the first time.

Umpire/Fielder The umpire shall not declare time out in case of injury to a fielder until the ball has been returned to and held by the pitcher standing in his position.

1885

Bat The handle of the bat may be wound with twine not to exceed eighteen inches from the end. The bat must be round except that a portion of the surface on one side may be flat.

Batter The batter's box is made six feet long by four feet wide and

extending three feet in front of and three feet behind the center of the home base with its nearest line six inches distant from home base.

A fair batted ball that goes over the fence at a distance less than 210 feet from home base shall entitle the batsman to two bases and a distinctive line shall be marked on the fence at this point.

Ground/Bases   The home base may be made of white rubber or white stone.

Pitcher   The pitcher must have both feet touching the ground while making any one of the series of motions he is accustomed to make in delivering the ball to the bat. A violation of this rule shall be a foul balk and two foul balks entitles the batter to first base.

Pitcher/Balk   A balk is made whenever the pitcher, when about to deliver the ball to the bat, while standing within the lines of his position makes any one of the series of motions he habitually makes in so delivering the ball, and then fails to deliver the ball to the bat.

1886

Ball/Umpire   Should the ball be knocked outside of the enclosure or lost during the game the umpire shall call at once for another ball.

Bat   A granulated substance may be applied to the bat handle not to exceed 18 inches from the end.

Batter   The batter's box is reduced to three feet wide by six feet long on either side of home base.

Batter/Runner   A batter is entitled to take first base after seven balls are called by the umpire.

Pitcher   The pitcher's lines must be straight lines forming a box seven feet long by four feet wide.

Pitcher/Balk   The term "foul balk" is dropped from the rules.

1887

Ball   In all games, the ball or balls played with shall be furnished by the home club, and the last ball in play becomes the property of the winning club. Each ball to be used in championship games shall be examined, measured, and weighed by the Secretary of the Association, enclosed in a paper box and sealed with the seal of the Secretary, which seal shall not be broken except by the umpire in the presence of the captains of the two contesting nines after play has been called.

Batter   The batter's box is again made four feet wide by six feet long.

Batter/Pitcher   The batter can no longer call for a high or low pitch.

A fair ball (strike) is defined as a legal pitching delivery that passes over home base "not lower than the batsman's knee, nor higher than his shoulder."

The batter is entitled to take first base if his person or clothing is hit by a ball from the pitcher, unless in the umpire's opinion he intentionally permitted himself to be hit.

Batter/Runner   The batter becomes a baserunner when: (1) Five balls have been called by the umpire; (2) Four strikes have been declared by the umpire; (3) After any illegal delivery of a ball by the pitcher.

Captain/Coach   The captain's or coacher's lines must be 15 feet from and parallel with the foul lines and should commence 75 feet distant from the catcher's line. Should the captain or coacher wilfully fail to remain in said bounds, he shall be fined by the umpire $5 for each such offence, except upon an appeal by the Captain from the umpire's decision upon a misinterpretation of the rules.

The Captains and Coachers are restricted in coaching to the baserunner only, and are not allowed to address any remarks except to the baserunner, and then only in words of necessary direction; no player shall use language which will, in any manner, refer to or reflect upon a player of the opposing club or the audience. To enforce the above, the Captain of the opposite side may call the attention of the umpire to the offence and upon a repetition of the same the club shall be debarred from further coaching during the game.

Game/Captain   The choice of innings is given to the home team Captain.

Game   No game is to be begun later than two hours before sunset.

Ground/Bases   Home base must be made of whitened rubber.

Second base shall be upon its corner of the infield, and the center of the first and third bases shall be on lines running to and from second base and 7½ inches from the foul lines, providing that each base shall be entirely within the foul lines.

Ground/Foul Lines   The foul lines must be drawn in straight lines from the outer corner of home base along the outer edges of the first and third bases to the boundaries of the ground.

Ground/Captain   The home club captain shall be the sole judge of the fitness of the ground for beginning a game after rain.

Pitcher   The pitcher's box is made to be 5½ feet long by four feet wide.

The pitcher shall take his position facing the batsman, with both feet squarely on the ground, the right foot on the rear line of the "box," his left foot in advance of the right, and to the left of an imaginary line from his right foot to the center of the home base. He shall not raise his right foot, unless in the act of delivering the ball, nor make more than one stop in such delivery. He shall hold the ball, before delivery, fairly in front of his body, and in sight of the umpire. In the case of a lefthanded pitcher the above words "left" and "right" are to be reversed. When the pitcher feigns to throw the ball to a base, he must resume the above position and pause momentarily before delivering the ball to the bat.

Pitcher/Balk   Any motion made by the pitcher to deliver the ball to the bat without delivering it is a balk, and shall be held to include any and every accustomed motion with the hands, arms, or feet, or position of the body assumed by the pitcher in his delivery of the ball, and any motion calculated to deceive a baserunner except the ball be accidentally dropped.

It is a balk if the ball be held by the pitcher so long as to delay the game unnecessarily.

It is a balk if the pitcher makes any motion to deliver the ball to the bat when any part of his person is upon ground outside of the lines of his position, including all preliminary motions with the hands, arms, and feet.

Pitcher/Batter   A strike is called when the batter makes any obvious attempt to make a foul hit.

Player/Uniform   The players of each club in a match game shall be nine in number, one of whom shall act as captain. Every club shall be required to adopt uniforms for its players, and in no case shall less than nine men be allowed to play on each side. Each player shall be required to present himself upon the field during the game in a neat and cleanly condition, but no player shall attach anything to the sole or heel of his shoes other than the ordinary baseball shoe plate.

Runner/Fielder   The baserunner is out if he intentionally interferes with a thrown ball.

Runner   Baserunners need not return to their bags on the run following a foul ball etc., provided that they do not unnecessarily delay the game.

If the baserunner overruns first base and turns to his left from the foul line he may be put out in returning to the base or in attempting to advance.

Spectators/Game   No person shall be allowed upon any part of the field during the progress of the game, in addition to the players in uniform, the manager on each side, and the umpire; except such officers of the law as may be present in uniform, and such officials of the home club as may be necessary to preserve the peace.

No umpire, manager, captain, or player shall address the audience

during the progress of a game, except in case of necessary explanation.

Umpire/Spectators The umpire may call "timeout" to enforce order in case of annoyance from spectators.

Umpire/Captain No one except the captains of the contending teams can question an umpire's decision; no player other than a captain can approach or address the umpire unless requested to do so. Violators may be fined $10.

Umpire/Player/Spectators The umpire cannot reverse his decision by the testimony of a player or spectator. However, the umpire may consult a player on the question before rendering his decision.

Umpire/Ball For each championship game, two balls shall be furnished by the home club to the umpire for use. When the ball in play is batted over the fence or stands, onto foul ground out of sight of the players, the other ball shall be immediately put into play by the umpire. As often as one of the two in use shall be lost, a new one must be substituted, so that the umpire may at all times, after the game begins, have two for use. The moment the umpire delivers the alternate ball to the catcher or pitcher, it comes into play, and shall not be exchanged until it, in turn, passes out of sight onto foul ground.

1888

Batter The batter is out after three strikes are declared by the umpire.

The batter is out if, while making the third strike, the ball hits his person or clothing.

1889

Batter/Runner A batter is entitled to take first base when four balls have been called by the umpire.

A foul tip is defined as a foul hit not rising above the batter's head and caught by the catcher playing within 10 feet of home base. In the case of a foul tip the batter is not out and any baserunners can return to their bases without being put out.

Runner/Substitute The baserunner shall not have a substitute run for him, except by consent of the captains of the contesting teams.

Substitute One player, whose name shall be printed on the scorecard as an extra player, may be substituted at the end of any complete inning by either club, but the player retired shall not thereafter participate in the game. In addition thereto, a substitute may be allowed at any time in place of a player disabled in the game then being played, by reason of illness or injury, of the nature and extent of which the umpire shall be the sole judge.

1890

Ball At no time shall the ball be intentionally discolored by rubbing it with the soil or otherwise.

Runner/Batter If a fair hit ball strikes the baserunner before touching a fielder, the runner is out—however, in such case, no base shall be run unless forced by the batter becoming a baserunner, and no run shall be scored or any other baserunner put out.

Substitute Each team is required to have two or more substitutes available.

1891

Substitute Each team is required to have one or more substitutes available.

1892

Batter A legally delivered fair ball that touches the bat of the batter in his position shall be considered a batted ball and in play.

The batter is out if he attempts to hinder the catcher from fielding or throwing the ball by stepping outside the lines of his position or otherwise obstructing or interfering with the catcher.

A fair batted ball that goes over the fence shall entitle the batter to a home run; except that should it go over the fence at a distance less than 235 feet from home base, the batter is entitled to only two bases. A distinctive line is to be marked on the fence showing the required point.

Coach A team is permitted to have not more than two coaches who may be one player participating in the game and any other player under contract to the club.

Coachers are not to use language which in any manner refers to or reflects upon spectators.

Game "No Game" shall be declared by the umpire if he shall terminate play on account of rain or darkness before five innings on each side are completed, except in a case when the game is called, the club second at bat shall have more runs at the end of its fourth inning than the club first at bat made in its five innings, then the umpire shall award the game to the club having made the greatest number of runs, and it shall be a game and be so counted in the championship record.

Game A forfeit shall be declared if a team resorts to dilatory practices in order to gain time, for the purpose of having the game called on account of darkness or rain or for any reason whatsoever.

Player/Bench Players' benches must be located at least 25 feet back of the players' lines.

Runner/Batter The batter becomes a baserunner if, while he be a batsman, his person—excepting hands or forearm, which makes it a dead ball—or clothing be hit by a ball from the pitcher, unless—in the opinion of the umpire—he intentionally permits himself to be so hit.

1893

Bat The bat must be made wholly of hard wood except that the handle may be wound with twine, or a granulated substance applied, not to exceed 18 inches from the end. It must be round, not to exceed 2½ inches in diameter in the thickest part, and must not exceed 42 inches in length. Note: Bats with a flat side are now illegal.

Batter/Substitute The batsmen must take their positions within the batsmen's lines in the order in which they are named in the batting order, which batting order must be submitted by the captains of the opposing teams to the umpire before the game, and when approved by him this batting order must be followed except in the case of a substitute player, in which case the substitute must take the place of the original player in the batting order. After the first inning the first striker (batter) in each inning shall be the batsman whose name follows that of the last man who has completed his turn—time at bat—in the preceding inning.

Pitcher The pitcher's boundary shall be marked by a white rubber plate 12 inches long and 4 inches wide so fixed in the ground as to be even with the surface at the distance of *60 feet 6 inches* from the outer corner of the home plate, so that a line drawn from the center of the home base and the center of the second base shall give 6 inches on either side.

The pitcher shall take his position facing the batter with both feet square on the ground, and in front of the pitcher's plate but in the act of delivering the ball one foot must be in contact with the pitcher's plate.

Pitcher/Balk A balk is any motion in delivering the ball to the bat by the pitcher while not in the required position.

1894

Batter A strike is called when the batter makes a foul hit, other than a foul tip, while attempting a bunt hit that falls or rolls upon foul ground between home base and first or third bases.

Ground Detailed directions are included in the rules of 1894 for laying out a baseball diamond.

1895

Bat The bat cannot exceed 2¾ inches in diameter.

Batter A strike is called when a ball is tipped by the batter and caught by the catcher within the 10 foot lines.

The batter is out if he hits a fly ball that can be handled by an infielder while first and second bases are occupied, or first, second, and third, with only one out. If the third strike is called (on attempted bunt in foul territory) the umpire shall declare infield or outfield hit.

The batsman is out if he fails to take his position at the bat in his order of batting, unless the error be discovered and the proper batsman takes his position before a time "at bat" recorded; and in such case the balls and strikes called must be counted in the time "at bat" of the proper batsman, and only the proper batsman shall be declared out: Provided, this rule shall not take effect unless the out is declared before the ball is delivered to the succeeding batsman, and no runs shall be scored or bases run, and further, no outs shall be counted other than that of the proper batsman.

Equipment/Glove The catcher and first baseman are permitted to wear a glove or mitt of any size, shape or weight. All other players are restricted to the use of a glove or mitt weighing not over 10 ounces, and measuring in circumference around the palm of the hand not over 14 inches.

Pitcher The pitcher's plate is enlarged to 24 by 6 inches.

Umpire Umpires may assess fines of $25 to $100 for specified misconduct by players.

1896

Ball The home club shall have at least a dozen regulation balls on the field ready for use on the call of the umpire during each game.

Game/Captain/Ground The choice of innings shall be given to the captain of the home club, who shall also be the sole judge of the fitness of the ground for beginning a game after rain, but after play has been called by the umpire he alone shall be the judge as to the fitness of the ground for resuming play after the game has been suspended on account of rain.

Pitcher The pitcher is no longer required to hold the ball before the delivery fairly in front of his body and in the sight of the umpire.

Player/Bench No one is to occupy the players' bench under any circumstances except the club president, managers, and players in uniform.

Umpire Umpires may assess fines of $5 to $10 for specified misconduct; repeat violators are to be fined $25.

Umpire/Player Players guilty of indecent or vulgar language or conduct shall be removed from the game and fined $25.

1897

Ball At no time shall the ball be intentionally discolored by rubbing it with the soil or otherwise. In the event of a new ball being intentionally discolored, or otherwise injured by a player, the umpire shall, upon appeal from the captain of the opposite side, forthwith demand the return of that ball and shall substitute another new ball and impose a fine of $5 upon the offending player.

Batter A fair hit is a ball batted by the batsman—while he is standing within the lines of his position—that first touches "fair" ground, or the person of a player or the umpire while standing on fair ground, and then settles on fair ground before passing the line of first or third base.

A foul hit is a similarly batted ball that first touches "foul" ground or the person of a player or the umpire while standing on foul ground.

Should such "fair hit" ball bound or roll to foul ground before passing the line of first or third base and settle on foul ground, it shall be declared by the umpire a foul ball.

Should such "foul hit" ball bound or roll to fair ground and settle there before passing the line of first or third base, it shall be declared by the umpire a "fair ball."

A foul tip is a ball batted by the batsman while standing within the lines of his position that goes foul sharp from the bat to the catcher's hands.

A bunt hit is a ball delivered by the pitcher to the batsman who, while standing within the lines of his position, makes a deliberate attempt to hit the ball so slowly within the infield that it cannot be fielded in time to retire the batsman. If such a bunt hit goes to foul ground a strike shall be called by the umpire.

Runner The baserunner must touch each base in regular order, viz., first, second, third, and home bases, and when obliged to return (except on a foul hit) must retouch the base or bases in reverse order. He shall only be considered as holding a base after touching it, and shall then be entitled to hold such base until he has legally touched the next base in order or has been legally forced to vacate it for a succeeding baserunner. However, no baserunner shall score a run to count in the game until the baserunner preceding him in the batting list (provided there has been such a baserunner who has not been put out in that inning) shall have first touched home base without being put out.

Runner/Fielder The baserunner shall be entitled, without being put out, to take a base in the following cases: (1) If he be prevented from making a base by the obstruction of an adversary, unless the latter be a fielder having the ball in his hand ready to meet the baserunner; (2) If the fielder stop or catch a batted ball with his hat or any part of his uniform except his gloved hand.

Substitute In every championship game, each side shall be required to have present on the field, in uniform, a sufficient number of substitute players to carry out the provision which requires that not less than nine players shall occupy the field in any inning of a game.

Umpire The umpire shall not address the spectators at any time, except in case of necessary explanation of misunderstood decision or points of play.

No decision, rendered by the umpire, shall be reversed by him in which the question of an error of judgment is alone involved.

Should the umpire render any decision based on an illegal interpretation of any rule of the game, the same shall be reversed on the appeal of either of the two captains, but not otherwise.

1898

Batter The batsman is out if he fails to take his position at the bat in his order of batting, unless the error be discovered and the proper batsman takes his position before a time "at bat" is recorded, and, in such case, the balls and strikes called must be counted in the time "at bat" of the proper batsman, and only the proper batsman shall be declared out, and no runs shall be scored or bases run because of any act of the improper batsman. Provided, this rule shall not take effect unless the out is declared before the ball is delivered to the succeeding batsman. Should the batsman declared out by this rule be sufficient to retire the side, the proper batsman the next innings is the player who would have come to bat had the players been out by ordinary play.

Pitcher/Balk A balk shall be (1) Any motion made by the pitcher to deliver the ball to the bat without delivering it; (2) Any delivery of the ball to the bat while his pivot foot is not in contact with the pitcher's plate; (3) Any motion in delivering the ball to the bat by the pitcher while not in the position required by the rules; (4) The holding of the ball by the pitcher so long as, in the opinion of the umpire, to delay the game unnecessarily; (5) Standing in position and making any motion to pitch without having the ball in his possession, except in the case of a "block ball"; (6) The making of any motion the pitcher habitually makes in his method of delivery, without his immediately delivering the ball to the bat; (7) If the pitcher feigns to throw the ball to a base and does not resume his legal position and pause momentarily before delivering the ball to the bat.

When the pitcher feigns to throw the ball to a base he must resume the required position and pause momentarily before delivering the

ball to the bat.

Player/Spectators Players in uniform shall not be permitted to occupy seats in the stands or to stand among the spectators.

Umpire The rules of 1898 describe in detail the responsibilities of each umpire in games where two umpires are assigned.

1899

Batter/Runner The batter becomes a baserunner if the catcher interferes with him, preventing him from striking the ball.

The batter becomes a baserunner when a balk is called by the umpire.

Batter A foul tip by the batter, caught by the catcher while standing within the lines of his position is a strike.

Catcher The catcher must stand within the lines of his position whenever the pitcher delivers the ball to the bat.

Game If the umpire calls "Game" on account of darkness or rain at any time after five innings have been completed, the score shall be that of the last equal innings played, but if the side second at bat shall have scored in an unequal number of innings or before the completion of its unfinished inning one or more runs than the side first at bat, the score of the game shall be the total number of runs made.

Pitcher/Balk In addition to the rules for "balk" promulgated in 1898 the rules of 1899 state: A balk shall be: (1) The throwing of the ball by the pitcher to any base to catch the baserunner without first stepping directly towards said base immediately before throwing the ball; (2) Any delivery of the ball to the bat by the pitcher while his pivot foot is not in contact with the pitcher's plate, and he is not facing the batsman; (3) If the pitcher delivers the ball to the bat when the catcher is standing outside the lines of the catcher's position as defined by the rules.

Player/Bench The players' benches must be furnished by the home club and placed upon a portion of the ground not less than 25 feet outside of the players' lines. One such bench shall be for the exclusive use of the visiting club, and one for the exclusive use of the home club. The benches must be covered by a roof and closed at the back and each end; a space, however, not more than six inches wide may be left just under the roof for ventilation. All players of the side at bat must be seated on their bench, except such as are legally assigned to coach baserunners, and also the batsman, except when called to the bat by the umpire, and under no circumstances shall the umpire permit any person, except managers and players in uniform to occupy seats on the benches.

Player/Uniform Every club shall adopt uniforms for its players, and the suit of each team shall conform in color and style. No player who shall attach anything to the sole or heel of his shoes other than the ordinary baseball shoe plate, or who shall appear in a uniform not conforming to the suits of the other members of his team, shall be permitted to take part in the game.

Substitute In any championship game, each side shall be required to have present on the field, in uniform, conforming to the suits worn by their teammates, a sufficient number of substitute players to carry out the provision which requires that not less than nine players shall occupy the field in any innings of a game.

1900

Ground/Bases The shape of home base is changed from a 12-inch square to a five-sided shape, 17 inches wide.

Pitcher/Balk/Batter The batter does not become a runner when the pitcher balks in throwing to pick off a runner on the bases.

Any motion made by the pitcher to deliver the ball to the bat or to first base without delivering it is a balk. Note: This rule previously specified "any base."

1901

Batter The batter is out if he hits a fly ball that can be handled by an infielder while first and second bases are occupied, or first, second, and third, unless two hands are out. In such case the umpire shall, as soon as the ball is hit, declare infield or outfield hit.

A foul hit ball not caught on the fly is a strike unless two strikes have already been called. Note: This rule was used by the National League in 1901 and 1902. The American League adopted the rule in 1903. See 1902 summary for further elaboration of this rule by the National League.

A "bunt hit" which sends the ball to foul ground either directly or by bounding or rolling from fair ground to foul ground and which settles on foul ground is a strike.

Catcher The catcher must stand within the lines of his position whenever the pitcher delivers the ball to the bat and within 10 feet of the home base. Note: This rule was adopted by the National League in 1901. The American League adopted the rule in 1902.

Pitcher If the ball is thrown by the pitcher to any player other than the catcher (except to retire a baserunner) and the batsman is standing in his proper position ready to strike at a pitched ball, each ball so delivered shall be called a ball.

The umpire shall call a ball on the pitcher each time he delays the game by failing to deliver the ball to the batsman when in position for a longer period than 20 seconds.

1902

Batter A strike is a foul hit ball not caught on the fly unless two strikes have already been called, which falls or settles on foul ground inside or on the line of the territory described by lines drawn from first and third bases at right angles with an imaginary line drawn from home to second base and extending on each side to the limit of the playing field. Note: National League rule only.

A strike is any intention or effort to hit the ball to foul ground outside of the lines of the territory described by lines drawn from first and third bases at right angles with an imaginary line drawn from home to second base and extending on each side to the limit of the playing field.

The batter is out if after two strikes have been called the batter obviously attempts to make a foul hit.

Batter/Runner The batsman becomes a baserunner if while he be a batsman, without making any attempt to strike at the ball, his person or clothing be hit by a ball from the pitcher, unless in the opinion of the umpire he plainly avoids making any effort to get out of the way of the ball from the pitcher and thereby permits himself to be so hit.

Pitcher The umpire shall call a ball on the pitcher each time he delays the game by failing to deliver the ball to the batsman when in position for a longer period than 20 seconds, excepting that in the case of the first batsman in each inning, the pitcher may occupy not more than one minute in delivering not to exceed five balls to a baseman.

Pitcher/Batter If the ball is thrown by the pitcher to any player other than the catcher (except to retire a baserunner) after the batter is standing in his position ready to strike at a pitched ball each ball so delivered will be called a ball.

1903

Ground/Pitcher The pitcher's box shall be no more than 15 inches higher than the baselines and home plate. The baselines and home plate, shall be on a perfect level, and the slope from the pitcher's box towards the baselines, and home plate shall be gradual. Note: In 1904, the phrase "pitcher's box" was deleted from this rule and replaced by the phrase "pitcher's plate."

Umpire The rules of 1903 contain an extensive reorganization and rewriting of the rules pertaining to umpires.

1904

Ball Two regulation balls of the make adopted by the league of which the contesting clubs are members, shall be delivered by the home club to the umpire at or before the hour for the commencement of a championship game. If the ball first placed in play be batted or thrown out of the grounds or into one of the stands for spectators or in the judgment of the umpire, become unfit for play from any cause, the umpire shall at once deliver the alternate ball to the pitcher and another legal ball shall be supplied to him, so that he shall at all times have in his control one or more alternate balls to substitute for the ball in play in any of the contingencies above set forth. Provided, however, that all balls batted or thrown out of the ground or into a stand, shall, when returned to the field, be given into the custody of the umpire immediately and become alternate balls, and so long as he has in his possession two or more alternate balls, he shall not call for a new ball to replace a ball that has gone out of play. The alternate balls shall become the ball in play in the order in which they were delivered to the umpire.

Ball/Pitcher Immediately upon the delivery to him of the alternate ball by the umpire, the pitcher shall take his position and on the call of "Play," by the umpire, it shall become the ball in play. Provided, however, that play shall not be resumed with the alternate ball when a fair batted ball or a ball thrown by a fielder goes out of the ground or into a stand for spectators until the baserunners have completed the circuit of the bases unless compelled to stop at second or third base in compliance with a ground rule.

Batter A bunt hit is a legally batted ball, not swung at, but met with the bat and tapped slowly within the infield by the batsman with the expectation of reaching first base before the ball can be fielded to that base. If the attempt to bunt result in a foul, a strike shall be called by the umpire.

Coach/Runner The baserunner is out if, before two hands are out and while third base is occupied, the coacher stationed near that base shall run in the direction of home base on or near the baseline while a fielder is making or trying to make a play on a batted ball not caught on the fly, or on a thrown ball (see note below), and thereby draws a throw to home base. The baserunner entitled to third base shall be declared out by the umpire for the coacher's interference with and prevention of the legitimate play. Note: In 1914, the words "on a fly ball" were inserted in this rule.

Fielder/Runner The baserunner is out if one or more members of the team at bat stand or collect at or around a base for which a baserunner is trying, thereby confusing the fielding side and adding to the difficulty of making such play. The baserunner shall be declared out for the interference of his teammate or teammates.

Ground To obviate the necessity for ground rules, the shortest distance from a fence or stand on fair territory to home base should be 235 feet and from home base to the grandstand 90 feet.

Player The players of each club, actively engaged in a game at one time, shall be nine in number, one of whom shall act as captain; and in no case shall more or less than nine men be allowed to play on a side in a game. Note: The previous rule read, "in no case shall less than nine men be allowed to play."

Player/Bench The players of the side at bat must speedily abandon their bench and hasten to another part of the field when by remaining upon or near it they or any of them would interfere with a fielder in an attempt to catch or handle a thrown ball.

Player/Uniform Every club shall adopt two uniforms for its players, one to be worn in games at home and the other in games abroad, and the suits of each of the uniforms of a team shall conform in color and style.

Runner The baserunner is out if he touch home base before a baserunner preceding him in the batting order, if there be such preceding baserunner, lose his right to third base.

1905

There were no changes in the playing rules this year.

1906

Batter A bunt hit is a legally batted ball, not swung at, but met with the bat and tapped slowly within the infield by the batsman. If the attempt to bunt result in a foul not legally caught, a strike shall be called by the umpire.

Ground/Captain/Umpire The choice of innings shall be given to the captain of the home club, who shall be the sole judge of the fitness of the ground for beginning a game after a rain; but, after play has been called by the umpire, he alone shall be the judge as to the fitness of the ground for resuming play after the game has been suspended on account of rain, and when time is so called the grounds-keeper and sufficient assistants shall be under the control of the umpire for the purpose of putting the ground in proper shape for play, under penalty of forfeiture of the game by the home team.

Ground/Foul Lines Foul lines are to be clearly visible from any part of the diamond, and no wood or other hard substance shall be used in the construction of such lines.

1907

Ball In the event of a ball being intentionally discolored by rubbing it with the soil or otherwise by any player except the pitcher, or otherwise damaged by any player, the umpire shall, upon appeal by the captain of the opposite side, forthwith demand the return of that ball and substitute for it another legal ball and impose a fine of $5 on the offending player.

Batter The batter is out if he steps from one batsman's box to the other after the pitcher has taken his position.

Batter/Runner The batter becomes a baserunner if a fair hit ball strike the person or clothing of the umpire or a baserunner on fair ground.

Game/Umpire If the game be called by the umpire on account of darkness, rain, fire, panic, or for other cause which puts patrons or players in peril, the game shall terminate.

If the umpire calls a game at any time after five innings have been completed, the score shall be that of the last equal innings played, except that if the side second at bat shall have scored in an unequal number of innings, or before the completion of the unfinished inning, at least one run more than the side first at bat, the score of the game shall be the total number of runs each team has made.

Pitcher/Batter A fairly delivered ball is a ball pitched or thrown to the bat by the pitcher while standing in his position and facing the batsman that passes over any portion of the home base, before touching the ground, not lower than the batsman's knee, nor higher than his shoulder. For every such fairly delivered ball, the umpire shall call one strike.

An unfairly delivered ball is a ball delivered to the bat by the pitcher while standing in his position and facing the batsman that does not pass over any portion of the home base between the batsman's shoulder and knees, or that touches the ground before passing home base, unless struck at by the batsman. For every unfairly delivered ball the umpire shall call one ball.

Runner The baserunner is out if with one or no one out and a baserunner on third base, the batsman interferes with a play being made at home plate.

The baserunner is out if he passes a baserunner who is caught between two bases. He shall be declared out immediately upon passing the preceding baserunner.

Runner/Batter The baserunner shall be entitled to advance one base without liability to be put out if, while the batsman, he becomes a baserunner by reason of "four balls" or for being hit by a pitched ball, or for being interfered with by the catcher in striking at a pitched ball.

1908

Ball The rule prohibiting the discoloring of the ball by rubbing it with the soil was amended to include the pitcher as well as all players.

1909

Batter A fair hit is a legally batted ball that settles on fair ground between home and first base or between home and third base or that is on fair ground when bounding to the outfield past first or third base or that first falls on fair territory beyond first or third base or that, while on or over fair ground, touches the person of the umpire or a player.

A foul hit is a legally batted ball that settles on foul territory between home and first base or home and third base or that bounds past first or third base in foul territory or that falls on foul territory beyond first or third base or while on or over foul ground, touches the person of the umpire or a player.

Game/Pitcher In case of a foul strike, foul hit ball not legally caught, dead ball, interference with the fielder or batsman, or a fair hit ball touching a baserunner, the ball shall not be considered in play until it be held by the pitcher standing in his position and the umpire shall have called "Play."

Pitcher When the umpire announces the pitcher prior to commencement of the game, the player announced must pitch until the first batsman has either been put out or has reached first base.

Pitcher/Substitute In event of the pitcher being taken from the game by either manager or captain, the player substituted for him shall continue to pitch until the batsman then at bat has either been put out or has reached first base.

Umpire/Ground Rules Before the commencement of a game the umpire shall see that the rules governing all the materials of the game are strictly observed. He shall ask the captain of the home club whether there are any special ground rules, and if there be, he shall acquaint himself with them, advise the captain of the visiting team of their scope, and see that each is duly enforced, provided that it does not conflict with any of these rules, and are acceptable to the captain of the visiting team. If the latter object to a proposed ground rule, the umpire shall have authority to adopt or reject it.

Umpire/Player/Manager In the event of removal of player or manager by the umpire, he shall go direct to the club house and remain there during progress of the game, or leave the grounds; and a failure to do so will warrant a forfeiture of the game by the umpire.

1910

Batter The batter is out if he steps from one batsman's box to the other while the pitcher is in his position ready to pitch.

An illegally batted ball is a ball batted by the batsman when either or both of his feet are upon the ground outside the lines of the batsman's position. Note: This rule replaced the term "foul strike."

Batter/Substitute The batting order of each team must be on the scorecard and must be delivered before the game by its captain to the umpire at home plate, who shall submit it to the inspection of the captain of the other side. The batting order delivered to the umpire must be followed throughout the game unless a player be substituted for another, in which case the substitute must take the place in the batting order of the retired player.

Ground Rules/Spectators In case of spectators overflowing on the playing field, the home captain shall make special ground rules to cover balls batted or thrown into the crowd, provided such rules be acceptable to the captain of the visiting club. If the latter object, then the umpire shall have full authority to make and enforce such special rules, and he shall announce the scope of same to the spectators.

Game/Pitcher In case of an illegally batted ball, a balk, foul hit ball not legally caught, dead ball, interference with the fielder or bats-

man, or a fair hit ball striking a baserunner or umpire before touching a fielder, the ball shall not be considered in play until it be held by the pitcher standing in his position, and the umpire shall have called "Play."

Pitcher An unfairly delivered ball is a ball delivered to the bat by the pitcher while standing in his position and facing the batsman that does not pass over any portion of the home base between the batsman's shoulder and knees, or that touches the ground before passing home base, unless struck at by the batsman; or, with the bases unoccupied, any ball delivered by the pitcher while either foot is not in contact with the pitcher's plate. For every unfairly delivered ball the umpire shall call one ball.

Pitcher/Substitute In event of the pitcher being taken from his position by either manager or captain, the player substituted for him shall continue to pitch until the batsman then at bat has either been put out or has reached first base.

Player The players of the team not at bat may be stationed at any points of the field on fair ground their captain may elect, regardless of their respective positions, except that the pitcher, while in the act of delivering the ball to the bat must take his position as defined in the rules and the catcher likewise must be within the lines of his position and within 10 feet of home base whenever the pitcher delivers the ball to the bat.

Runner In all cases where there are no spectators on the playing field, and where a thrown ball goes into a stand for spectators, or over or through any fence surrounding the playing field, into the players' bench (whether the ball rebounds into the field or not), the runner or runners shall be entitled to two bases. The umpire in awarding such bases shall be governed by the position of the runner or runners at the time the throw is made.

Runner/Batter The baserunner shall be entitled, without liability to be put out, to advance a base if, while the batsman, he becomes a baserunner by reason of "four balls" or for being hit by a pitched ball, or if a fair hit ball strike the person or clothing of the umpire or a baserunner on fair ground.

Runner/Fielder If the fielder stop or catch a batted ball with his cap, glove, or any part of his uniform, while detached from its proper place on his person, the runner or runners shall be entitled to three bases.

Runner/Umpire If a thrown or pitched ball strike the person or clothing of an umpire on foul ground the ball shall be considered in play and the runner or runners shall be entitled to all the bases they can make.

The baserunner shall return to his base without liability to be put out if the umpire be struck by a fair hit ball before touching a fielder; in which case no base shall be run unless necessitated by the batsman becoming a baserunner, and no run shall be scored unless all the bases are occupied.

The baserunner shall return to his base without liability to be put out if the umpire declares the batsman or another baserunner out for interference.

Substitute Whenever one player is substituted for another, whether as batsman, baserunner, or fielder, the captain of the side making the change must immediately notify the umpire, who in turn must announce the same to the spectators. A fine of $5 shall be assessed by the umpire against the captain for each violation of this rule, and the president of the League shall impose a similar fine against the umpire who, after having been notified of a change, fails to make proper announcement. Play shall be suspended while announcement is being made, and the player substituted shall become actively engaged in the game immediately upon his captain's notice of the change to the umpire.

Umpire The rules of 1910 contain new provisions for umpires and describe the respective duties of the Umpire-in-Chief and the Field Umpire.

1911

Ball Cork-center balls are used for the first time as regulation balls in all games.

1912–13

There were no changes in the playing rules in these years.

1914

Ball League presidents are no longer required to examine, measure, and weigh baseballs for use in championship games.

Batter/Runner A batter who hits a home run or a ground-rule double must touch all of the bases in regular order.

Coach/Runner If, while third base is occupied, the coacher stationed near that base shall run in the direction of home base on or near the base line while a fielder is making or trying to make a play on a batted ball not caught on the fly or on a thrown ball or a fly ball (see note below), and thereby draws a throw to home base, the baserunner entitled to third base shall be declared out by the umpire for the coacher's interference with and prevention of the legitimate play. Note: This rule was first adopted in 1904 but did not include the phrase "or a fly ball."

Coach/Batter/Runner A coach may address words of assistance and direction to the baserunners and to the batter.

Pitcher The pitcher is permitted to have his feet on top of the pitcher's plate or in front of the plate preliminary to pitching.

Runner In all cases where there are no spectators on the playing field, and where a thrown ball goes into a stand for spectators or over or through any fence surrounding the playing field or into the players' bench (whether the ball rebounds into the field or not) or remains in the meshes of a wire screen protecting the spectators, the runner or runners shall be entitled to two bases. The umpire in awarding such bases shall be governed by the position of the runner or runners at the time the throw is made.

Runner/Batter The batter is out if he obstructs or interferes with the catcher except when he does so with a runner on third base (with one out or no one out) in which case the baserunner is out.

Runner/Coach If a coach at third base touch or hold a baserunner at third base or a baserunner who is rounding third base for home plate, such baserunner is out.

Runner/Fielder The baserunner is entitled to advance a base without liability to be put out if the fielder stop or catch a batted ball or a thrown ball with his cap, glove, or any part of his uniform, while detached from its proper place on his person, the runner or runners shall be entitled to three bases if a batted ball or to two bases if a thrown ball.

Runner/Umpire The baserunner shall return to his base without liability to be put out if the person or clothing of the umpire, while stationed back of the bat, interfere with the catcher in an attempt to throw.

The baserunner is entitled to advance a base if a thrown or pitched ball strike the person or clothing of an umpire. The ball shall be considered in play and the baserunner or runners shall be entitled to all the bases they can make. Note: Under the previous rule only balls striking the umpire in foul territory entitled the baserunner to advance.

1915–19

There were no changes in the playing rules in these years.

1920

Ball/Umpire The President of the League of which the contesting clubs are members shall specify the number of baseballs which the home club must deliver to the umpire prior to the hour set for the commencement of a championship game, and all of such baseballs shall be of the regulation make adopted by the league.

Ball/Player In event of the ball being intentionally discolored by any player, either by rubbing it with the soil, or by applying rosin, paraffin, licorice, or any other foreign substance to it, or otherwise intentionally damaging or roughening the same with sandpaper or emery paper, or other substance, the umpire shall forthwith demand the return of that ball and substitute for it another legal ball, and the offending player shall be disbarred from further participation in the game. If, however, the umpire cannot detect the violator of this rule, and the ball is delivered to the bat by the pitcher, then the latter shall be at once removed from the game, and as an additional penalty shall be automatically suspended for a period of 10 days.

Ball/Umpire The seal on boxes of new balls is not to be broken by the umpire except prior to game time and for the purpose of inspecting the ball and removing the gloss therefrom.

Batter/Fielder A fair or foul fly must be judged according to the relative position of the ball and the foul line, and not as to whether the fielder is on fair or foul ground at the time he touches the ball.

Batter If, before two hands are out, while first and second or first second and third bases are occupied, he hit a fair fly ball, other than a line drive, that can be handled by an infielder, the batter is out. In such case, the umpire shall, as soon as the ball be hit, declare it an infield or outfield hit; but the runners may be off their bases or advance at the risk of the ball being caught, the same as on any other fly ball. Provided, that, with first and second bases occupied, with less than two out, any attempt to bunt which results in a fair fly ball shall not be regarded as an infield fly.

Batter/Runner If a batsman, in the last half of the final inning of any game, hit a home run over the fence or into a stand, all runners on the bases at the time, as well as the batsman, shall be entitled to score, and in such event all bases must be touched in order, and the final score of the game shall be the total number of runs made.

Game A drawn game shall be declared by the umpire if the score is equal on the last even inning played when he terminates play in accordance with the rules after five or more equal innings have been played by each team. But if the side that went second to bat is at bat when the game is terminated, and has scored the same number of runs as the other side, the umpire shall declare the game drawn without regard to the score of the last equal inning. Provided, that if the side last at bat shall, before the completion of the fifth inning, equal the score made by the opposing side in five complete innings then the game shall be declared as legally drawn, and the individual and team averages shall be incorporated in the Official Playing Records.

"No Game" shall be declared by the umpire if he terminates play in accordance with the rules before five innings are completed by each team. Provided, however, that if the club second at bat shall have made more runs at the end of its fourth inning, or before the completion of its fifth inning, than the club first at bat made in five completed innings of a game so terminated, the umpire shall award the game to the club having made the greater number of runs, and it shall count as a legal game in the championship record.

Whenever necessity demands that two games be played in one afternoon, the first game shall be the regularly scheduled game for that day.

Pitcher/Balk The following prohibitions were added to the previous balk rule in 1920:

A balk shall be: Making any motion to pitch while standing in his position without having the ball in his possession; or, regardless of whether he makes any motion to pitch or not, if the pitcher takes a legal position on the rubber without the ball in his possession, or if he takes a position off the rubber and feints to deliver the ball to the bat.

A balk shall be: After the pitcher has taken position, with both hands holding the ball in front of him, he cannot take either hand off the ball except in the act of delivering the ball to the batsman or in throwing to bases.

A balk shall be: If, with one or more runners on bases, the pitcher,

in the act of delivering the ball to the batsman or in throwing to first base, drop the ball, either intentionally or accidentally, the umpire shall call it a "balk" and advance runner or runners. No penalty shall be imposed if, with no one on bases, the pitcher drop the ball while delivering it to the batsman.

Pitcher/Balk   If the pitcher steps off the rubber, after being in position, for the purpose either of drying his hands or rubbing his eyes, or for other reasons, and it is a legitimate action not understood or interpreted by the umpire to deceive the baserunner, then the umpire shall call "Time."

In case a balk is called, the ball shall be considered "dead" when announcement is made, and no play can be made until the runner or runners reach the base or bases to which they are entitled.

If, with no one on bases, the pitcher deliver the ball while off the rubber, the umpire shall call a "ball" whether it goes over the plate fair or not. If, however, the batsman strikes at such illegally delivered ball it counts either for a strike or whatever play may follow.

Pitcher/Ball   At no time during the progress of the game shall the pitcher be allowed to (1) Apply a foreign substance of any kind to the ball; (2) Expectorate either on the ball or his glove; (3) Rub the ball on his glove, person or clothing; (4) Deface the ball in any manner; (5) or to deliver what is called the "shine" ball, "spit" ball, "mud" ball or "emery" ball. For violation of any part of this rule the umpire shall at once order the pitcher from the game, and in addition he shall be automatically suspended for a period of 10 days, on notice from the president of the League.

Note: In adopting the foregoing rule against "freak" deliveries on February 9, 1920, it was understood and agreed that all bona fide spitball pitchers would be certified to the respective presidents of the National and American Leagues at least 10 days prior to April 14, 1920, and that the pitchers so certified would be exempt from the operation of the rule, as far as it relates to the spitball only.

Pitcher/Batter   A "dead" ball is a ball delivered to the bat by the pitcher, not struck at by the batsman, that touches any part of the batsman's person or clothing while he is standing in his position or a wildly pitched ball which the batsman plainly makes an attempt to dodge to avoid being hit, but which ball accidentally hits his bat.

Player   The players of the team not at bat may be stationed at any points of the field on fair ground their captain may elect, regardless of their respective positions, except that the pitcher, while in the act of delivering the ball to the bat must take his position and the catcher must be within the lines of his position, and within 10 feet of home base, whenever the pitcher delivers the ball to the bat; nor shall the catcher leave his natural position immediately and directly back of the plate for the purpose of aiding the pitcher to intentionally give a base on balls to a batsman.

Runner   A baserunner having acquired legal title to a base cannot run bases in reverse order for the purpose either of confusing the fielders or making a travesty of the game. A runner violating this rule is out if touched with the ball, or the ball held on the base said runner was entitled to hold.

In case a runner is being run down between bases, and the following runner occupies the same base the first runner has left, the second man cannot be put out while holding said base. If the first runner, however, returns safely to the base he left, and both runners are then occupying the same base, the second runner is the man out, if touched with the ball.

The failure of a preceding runner to touch a base (and who is declared out therefor) shall not affect the status of a succeeding runner who touches each base in proper order.

Runner   The baserunner shall return to his base without liability to be put out if the umpire declares a dead ball, unless it also be the fourth unfair ball, and he be thereby forced to take the next base as provided in the rules. Provided, such fourth unfair ball shall not be called if the umpire declare the ball "dead" because of a pitched ball accidentally hitting the bat.

Runner/Batter   A force-out can be made only when a baserunner legally loses the right to the base he occupies by reason of the batsman becoming a baserunner, and he is thereby obliged to advance.

Runner/Batter/Catcher   It shall be illegal for the catcher to leave his natural position immediately and directly back of the plate for the purpose of aiding the pitcher to intentionally give a base on balls to a batsman. If the catcher shall move out of position prior to the time of the ball leaving the pitcher's hand, all runners on bases shall be entitled to advance one base.

In the event a baserunner is trying to score from third base on a pitched ball or the "squeeze" play, a "balk" and also an "interference" should be called if the catcher runs out in front of the plate to catch the ball; the runner shall be allowed to score and the batsman entitled to first base. The same penalties must be imposed in case the catcher pushes the batsman out of the way or tips his bat.

Runner/Coach   The baserunner is out if, in the judgment of the umpire, the coacher at third base by touching or holding the runner physically assists him in returning to or leaving third base. The runner, however, should not be declared out if no play is being made.

The baserunner shall be entitled to advance one base if a thrown ball strike a coacher on foul ground and the ball shall be considered in play. Provided, that if in the opinion of the umpire the coacher intentionally interfere with such thrown ball, the runner or runners must return to the last bases touched, and the coacher penalized by removal from the playing field.

Runner/Fielder   A baserunner who holds his base on a fly ball shall have the right to advance the moment such fly ball touches the hands of a fielder.

The baserunner is out if at any time while the ball is in play, he be touched by the ball in the hands of a fielder, unless some part of his person be touching the base he is entitled to occupy; provided, however, that the ball be held by the fielder after touching him, unless the baserunner deliberately knock it out of his hand. The ball must be firmly held by the fielder after touching the runner. The ball cannot be juggled, even though the fielder may retain possession of the ball and prevent same from dropping to the ground.

The baserunner is *not* out if a fair hit ball goes through an infielder, and hits a runner immediately back of him. The umpire must be convinced that the ball passed through the infield and that no other infielder had the chance to make a play on the ball. If, in the judgment of the umpire, the runner deliberately and intentionally kicks such a hit ball, on which the infielder has missed a play, then the runner must be called out for interference.

Runner/Umpire   The baserunner shall be entitled to advance one base if, while the batsman, he becomes a baserunner by reason of "four balls" or for being hit by a pitched ball or for being interfered with by the catcher in striking at a pitched ball or if a fair hit ball strike the person or clothing of the umpire or a baserunner on fair ground before touching a fielder. Provided, that if a fair hit ball strike the umpire after having passed a fielder or having been touched by a fielder, the ball shall be considered in play. Also, if a fair hit ball strike the umpire on foul ground, the ball shall be in play.

Substitute   When a substitution is made but no announcement of the substitution is made as required by the rules the substitute will nevertheless be considered in the game as follows: if a pitcher, when he takes his place on the rubber; if a batter, when he takes his place in the batsman's box; if a fielder, when he takes the place of the fielder substituted for; if a runner, when the substitute replaces him on the base he is holding, and any play made by such unannounced substitute shall be legal under the rules.

Umpire/Time   The rules of 1920 contain several new provisions governing the calling of "Time" by the umpire, the most important of which is the following: That in case of an accident to a player or players in attempting to make a play on either a batted or a thrown ball, "Time" shall not be called until, in the judgment of the umpire,

no further play is possible.

Umpire The rules of 1920 contain various new provisions governing umpires and their respective duties.

1921

Pitcher Note: By concurrent action of the National and American Leagues taken at their respective annual meetings held at New York in December 1920, it was agreed that all bona fide spitball pitchers then remaining in the National and American Leagues be exempt from the operation of the rule against the use of the spitball during the balance of their major league careers. The pitchers so exempted were: National League—William Doak, Phil Douglas, Dana Fillingim, Ray Fisher, Marvin Goodwin, Burleigh Grimes, Clarence Mitchell, and Richard Rudolph (8). American League—A. W. Ayers, Ray Caldwell, Stanley Coveleskie, Urban Faber, H. B. Leonard, Jack Quinn, Allan Russell, Urban Shocker, and Allan Sothoron (9).

1922–25

There were no changes to the playing rules in these years.

1926

Batter A fair batted ball that goes over the fence or into a stand shall entitle the batsman to a home run, unless it should pass out of the ground or into a stand at a distance less than 250 feet from the home base, in which case the batsman shall be entitled to two bases only. In either event the batsman must touch the bases in regular order. The point at which a fence or stand is less than 250 feet from the home base shall be plainly indicated by a white or black sign or mark for the umpire's guidance.

Pitcher Under the supervision and control of the umpire, the pitcher may use to dry his hands a small, finely meshed sealed bag containing powdered rosin, furnished by the League. Note: This rule was first adopted by the National League only.

1927–30

There were no changes to the playing rules in these years.

1931

Batter The rules of 1931 provide new wording for the rule governing when the batter is out without changing the substance of the rule.

When a batted ball passes outside the playing field the umpire shall decide it fair or foul according to where it leaves the playing field.

A fair hit ball that bounds into a stand or over a fence shall be a two-base hit. Note: There is no reference to distance in this rule and any fair hit ball bounding over the fence or into the stand is a two-base hit.

Dead Ball The rules of 1931 merge two previous rules governing dead balls in one differently worded rule without changing the substance of the old rules.

Game The rules of 1931 merge four previous rules governing regulation games in one differently worded rule without changing the substance of the old rules.

Game "No game" shall be declared by the umpire if he terminates play in accordance with the rules before five innings have been completed by each team; but if the team last at bat is at bat in the last half of the fifth inning and has equaled before the completion of that inning the score of the side first at bat, the umpire shall declare the game "legally drawn" in accordance with the rules. If the team second at bat shall have made more runs at the end of its fourth inning or before the completion of its fifth inning, than the team first at bat has made in five completed innings of a game so terminated, the umpire shall award the game to the team having made the greater number of runs, and it shall count as a legal game in the championship record.

Pitcher Preliminary to pitching, the pitcher shall take his position facing the batsman, with both feet squarely on the ground and on top of the pitcher's plate, or one foot on top of the pitcher's plate and the other foot in contact with same, or one foot in front of the pitcher's plate and the other foot on top of same, and in the act of delivering the ball to the batsman he must keep one foot in contact with the pitcher's plate. He shall not raise either foot until in the act of delivering the ball to the batsman, or in throwing to a base; nor may he make more than one step in such delivery. With a runner on first base or on second base, the pitcher must face the batsman with both hands holding the ball in front of him. If he indulges in a preliminary stretch by raising his arms above his head or out in front, he must return to a natural pitcher's position and stop before starting his delivery of the ball to the batsman.

Pitcher/Equipment The pitcher's glove must be uniform in color.

Player/Coach/Fielder The players or coachers of the side at bat must immediately vacate any space occupied by them if it is needed by a fielder attempting to handle a batted or thrown ball.

Player/Uniform Glass buttons or polished metal must not be used on a uniform.

Runner In all cases where there are no spectators on the playing field and where a thrown ball goes into a stand for spectators or over or through any fence surrounding the playing field or into the players' bench (whether the ball rebounds into the field or not) or remains in the meshes of a wire screen protecting the spectators, the runner or runners shall be entitled to two bases. When the throw is made by an infielder, the umpire in awarding such bases, shall be governed by the position of the runner or runners at the time the ball was pitched; when the throw is made by an outfielder, the award shall be governed by the position of the runner or runners at the time the throw was made.

The baserunner is out if, when advancing bases or obliged to return to a base while the ball is in play, he fail to touch the intervening base or bases, if any, in the regular or reverse order, as the case may be, he may be put out by the ball being held by a fielder on any base he failed to touch or by being touched by the ball in the hand of a fielder in the same manner as in running to first base; provided, that the baserunner shall not be out in such case if the ball be delivered to the bat by the pitcher before the fielder hold it on said base or touch the baserunner with it; however, after a fly ball other than a foul tip be legally caught by a fielder, the baserunner who complies with this rule can only be retired by the ball being held by a fielder on the base occupied by the runner when such ball was batted or by being touched by the ball in the hand of the fielder.

The baserunner is out if, in running the last half of the distance from home base to first base, while the ball is being fielded to first base, he run outside the three-foot lines, and, in the opinion of the umpire, interferes with the fielder taking the throw at first base; except that he may run outside the three-foot lines to avoid a fielder attempting to field a batted ball.

The baserunner shall advance one base without liability to be put out if a ball delivered by the pitcher pass the catcher and touch any fence or building within 60 feet of the home base. The ball shall be dead in such case.

The baserunner shall advance one base if he be prevented from making a base by the obstruction of a fielder, except when a fielder is trying to field a batted ball unless the latter has the ball in his hand ready to touch the baserunner. The ball is still in play so far as other baserunners are concerned.

The failure of a preceding runner to touch a base (and who is declared out therefor) shall not affect the status of a succeeding runner who touches each base in proper order; except that, after two are out, a succeeding runner cannot score a run when a preceding runner is declared out for failing to touch a base as provided in the rules. This exception also applies to a batsman who hits the ball out of the playing field for an apparent home run.

Substitute Substitutions shall not be in effect until the manager or

captain of the team making the change notifies the umpire.

Substitute/Runner   The manager or the captain of the opposing team must consent before a runner can be substituted for another baserunner. Note: Previously this rule referred only to the captain. Throughout the rules of 1931, wherever authority or decision-making authority is granted to the captain, the words "or manager" have been added.

1932–38

There were no changes to the playing rules in these years.

1939

Pitcher   Preliminary to pitching, the pitcher shall take his position facing the batsman with both feet squarely on the ground, but his pivot foot must be on or in front in contact with the pitcher's plate; his other foot may be directly behind or in front (not on the side) of the pitcher's plate, and in the act of delivering the ball to the batsman he must keep one foot in contact with the pitcher's plate. He shall not raise either foot until in the act of delivering the ball to the batsman or in throwing to a base; nor may he make more than one step in such delivery. With a runner on first base or second base, the pitcher must face the batsman with both hands holding the ball in front of him. If he indulges in a preliminary stretch by raising his arms above his head or out in front, he must return to a natural pitcher's position and stop before starting his delivery of the ball to the batsman. Note: After pitcher takes legal position for delivery of ball to batsman, he can take but one step and that must be forward.

Pitcher/Balk   A balk will be called (entitling the runner or runners to advance one base) if the pitcher makes any delivery of the ball to the bat while his pivot foot is back of and not in contact with the pitcher's plate.

Player/Equipment   The catcher may wear a leather glove or mitt of any size, shape or weight.

The first baseman may wear a leather glove or mitt not more than 12 inches from top to bottom and not more than 8 inches wide across the palm, with thumb and palm connected by leather lacing of not more than 4 inches from thumb to palm, which lacing shall not be enlarged, extended or reinforced by any process or material whatever.

Every other player is restricted to the use of a leather glove weighing not over 10 ounces and measuring not over 14 inches around the palm. The pitcher's glove must be uniform in color.

Runner   The baserunner is out if, having made a fair hit while batsman, such fair hit ball be caught by a fielder before touching the ground or any object other than a fielder; provided, it be not caught in a fielder's hat, cap, protector, pocket, or other part of his uniform.

If, before two are out, while first and second or first, second, and third bases are occupied, an outfielder, in the judgment of the umpire, intentionally drops a fly ball or a line drive, he shall immediately rule the ball has been caught. Note: Baserunners are obliged to "tag up" after the out has been declared before they can advance.

1940

Bat   The bat must be made entirely of hardwood in one piece.

Batter   A foul hit is a legally batted ball that settles on foul territory between home and first base or home and third base or that bounds past first or third base on or over foul territory or that falls on foul territory beyond first or third base or, while on or over foul ground, touches the person of the umpire or a player or any object foreign to the natural ground. A foul fly must be judged according to the relative position of the ball and the foul line, and not as to whether the fielder is on foul or fair ground at the time he touches the ball.

The batter is out if, before two are out, while first and second or first, second and third bases are occupied, he hit a fair fly ball, other than a line drive, that can reasonably be caught by an infielder. In such case, the umpire shall declare it an infield fly. However, the runners may be off their bases or advance at the risk of the ball being caught, the same as on any other fly ball; but if hit by the ball while standing on base, that baserunner shall not be called out, but the ball is dead and the batsman shall be called out and if the baserunner be hit while off base, both that baserunner and the batsman shall be called out and the ball is dead. Provided, that, with first and second bases occupied or first, second, and third bases occupied, with less than two out, any attempt to bunt which results in a fair fly ball shall not be regarded as an infield fly.

Coach   No fines are to be assessed for violations of the coaching rules.

Dead Ball   A batted or thrown ball touched, stopped, or handled by a person not engaged in the game is dead and not in play. If a fair hit, the batsman making the hit shall be entitled to two bases and each baserunner shall be entitled to advance two bases. If a thrown ball, each baserunner shall be entitled to advance in accordance with the rules governing a thrown ball. Note: This rule replaces the rule regarding "Blocked Balls."

Game   No club or clubs shall engage in more than two championship games within a period of one day.

No inning of any night game shall be started after 11:50 P.M. standard time.

Ground   The ball ground must be enclosed. To obviate the necessity for ground rules, the shortest distance from a fence or stand on fair territory to the home base should be 250 feet and from home base to the grandstand 60 feet.

Ground/Foul Lines   The foul lines are to be continued until they reach the boundary lines of the ground and not less than 10 feet above the top of the fence or stand. The foul lines are to be made, on the playing field, of lime, chalk, or other powder or paint.

Pitcher   Preliminary to pitching, the pitcher shall take his position facing the batsman with his pivot foot always on or in front of and in contact with the pitcher's plate. In the act of delivering the ball to the batsman, the pitcher's other foot is free, except that he cannot step to either side of the pitcher's plate. He shall not raise either foot until in the act of delivering the ball to the batsman or in throwing to a base. With a runner on first or second base, the pitcher must face the batsman with both hands holding the ball in front of him. If he raises his arms above his head or out in front he must return to a natural pitcher's position and stop before starting the delivery of the ball to the batsman. Note: After pitcher takes legal position for delivery of ball to batsman, he may take one step backward and one step forward, but not to either side.

Pitcher/Balk   It is a balk if the pitcher, in the act of delivering the ball to the batsman or in throwing to first base, drop the ball, either intentionally or accidentally. Note: With no one on bases, it is not a balk if the pitcher drops the ball while delivering it to the batsman.

A balk (entitling the runner or runners to advance one base) shall be called for: (1) Throwing the ball by the pitcher to any base to catch the baserunner without first stepping directly toward such base in the act of making such throw; or throwing or feinting to throw to an unoccupied base; (2) Making any motion of the arm, shoulder, hip, knee, foot, or body the pitcher habitually makes in his method of delivery, without immediately delivering the ball to the bat.

Player/Trainer   Trainers are permitted to occupy the players' bench.

Runner   The baserunner is out if at any time while the ball is in play, he be touched by the ball in the hand of a fielder, unless some part of his person be touching the base he is entitled to occupy; provided, however, that the ball be held by the fielder after touching him, unless the baserunner deliberately knock it out of his hand. The ball must be firmly held by the fielder after touching the runner. The ball cannot be juggled, even though the fielder may regain possession of the ball and prevent same from dropping to the ground. Note: The previous rule read: "even though the fielder may retain possession of the ball."

In all cases where there are no spectators on the playing field, and where a thrown ball goes into a stand for spectators, or over or through any fence surrounding the playing field, or into the players' bench (whether the ball rebounds into the field or not), or remains in the meshes of a wire screen protecting the spectators, the runner or runners shall be entitled to two bases. When a first throw made by an infielder, the umpire in awarding such bases, shall be governed by the position of the runner or runners at the time the ball was pitched; when the throw is made by an outfielder or is the result of any following plays or attempted plays, the award shall be governed by the position of the runner or runners at the time the last throw was made.

The baserunner is permitted to "overslide" as well as overrun first base without liability to be put out.

A baserunner who holds his base on a fly ball shall have the right to advance the moment such fly ball touches the person or uniform of a fielder.

If one or more members of the team at bat stand or collect at or around a base for which a baserunner is trying, thereby confusing the team in the field and adding to the difficulty of making such play or if a batsman or baserunner who has just been retired obstructs or interferes with any following play being made on a baserunner, the baserunner shall be declared out for the interference of his teammate or teammates.

Runner/Fielder   The baserunner may "tag up" and advance if, before two are out, while first, or first and second, or first, second, and third bases are occupied, any player, in the judgment of the umpire, intentionally drops a fly ball or a line drive, the umpire shall immediately rule the ball has been caught.

Runner/Batter/Catcher   The batter becomes a baserunner if the catcher interferes with him, unless he makes a safe hit.

Runner/Batter   The baserunner is out if, after having hit or bunted a ball to fair territory, his bat again hits the ball on or over fair territory and deflects its course. Other baserunners cannot advance.

Runner/Batter/Catcher   The baserunner is entitled to advance one base if the catcher interferes with the batsman while a baserunner is attempting to steal a base.

Trainer/Umpire   Umpires are given authority over trainers.

Umpire   The rules of 1940 describe the procedures to be used when more than two umpires are assigned.

Umpire/Batter   The Umpire-in-Chief is to make all decisions regarding batters.

1941

There were no changes to the playing rules this year.

1942

Game   No inning of any night game shall be started after 12:50 A.M. war time.

1943–48

There were no changes to the playing rules in these years.

1949

Batter   A foul fly must be judged according to the relative position of the ball and the foul line, including the foul pole, and not as to whether the fielder is on foul or fair ground at the time he touches the ball.

Catcher   The catcher must stand with both feet inside the catcher's lines until the ball leaves the pitcher's hand.

Coach/Runner   First base coaches as well as third base coaches must refrain from touching or holding the runner physically or the runner is out.

Game   No inning of any night game shall be started after 12:50

A.M. local city time.

Pitcher/Balk   No balk can be committed with all bases empty.

Spectators/Manager/Coach   No manager, captain, coach, or player shall address the spectators before or during a game except in reply to a request for information about the progress or state of the game or to give the name of a player.

1950

Bat   The bat shall be round, not over 2¾ inches in diameter at the thickest part, not more than 42 inches in length, and entirely of hard, solid wood in one piece. Twine may be wound around it or a granulated substance applied to it, for a distance of 18 inches from the end of the handle, but not elsewhere.

Batter   The batter is out for illegal action when he fails to take his position in the batter's box promptly. If he persists in unwarranted delay in taking his position the umpire shall direct the pitcher to deliver the ball to the bat and every such pitch shall be called "strike" by the umpire. If he enters the batter's box in the interval between any such pitches, the ball and strike count shall continue regularly, but if he has not entered the batter's box when three strikes are called he shall be declared "out."

The batter is out when a preceding runner shall, in the umpire's judgment, intentionally interfere with the play of a defensive player who is attempting to catch a thrown ball or to throw the ball in an attempt to complete any play.

The batter is out when with two out, a runner on third base, and two strikes on the batter, the runner attempts to steal home base on a legal pitch and the ball strikes the runner in the strike zone. The umpire shall call "strike three," the batter is out and the run shall not count; with less than two out the umpire shall call "strike three," the ball is dead, and the run counts.

The batter is out when after striking or bunting the ball he intentionally strikes the ball a second time, or strikes it with a thrown bat or deflects its course in any manner while running to first base. The ball is dead and no runners may advance. If the runner drops his bat and the ball rolls against the bat and, in the umpire's judgment, there was no intention to interfere with the course of the ball, the ball is alive and in play.

Definitions   Rule Two of the rules of 1950 includes the definitions of 69 baseball terms as used in the rules. Several of the key definitions are quoted below.

Catch   A catch is the act of a defensive player in receiving, and holding firmly in his hand or glove, a batted or thrown ball. It is not a catch, however, if simultaneously or immediately following his contact with the ball, he collide with a player or with a wall or if he fall down, and as a result of such collision or falling, drops the ball. If the player has made the catch and drops the ball while in the act of making a throw following the catch, the ball shall be adjudged to have been caught. In establishing the validity of the catch, the player shall hold the ball long enough to prove that he has complete control of the ball and that his release of the ball is voluntary and intentional.

Fair Territory   Fair territory is that part of the playing field within, and including the first and third baselines, from home base to the bottom of the playing field fence and perpendicularly upwards. All foul lines are in fair territory.

Foul Tip   A foul tip is a ball batted by the batter that goes sharp and direct from the bat to the catcher's hands and is legally caught. It is not a foul tip unless caught and any foul tip that is caught is a strike, and the ball is in play. It is not a catch if it is a rebound from any part of the catcher's equipment other than the catcher's glove or hand.

Infield-Fly   An infield-fly is an out called by the umpire on the batter—if, before two are out, while first and second or first, second and third bases are occupied, he hit a fair fly ball, other than a line drive, that in the judgment of the umpire can reasonably be caught

by an infielder. Where a defensive player who normally plays in the outfield places himself in the infield, he shall for the purpose of the infield-fly rule be considered an infielder. In such case, the umpire shall declare it an infield-fly. However, the runners may be off their bases or advance at the risk of the ball being caught, the same as on any other fly ball. If a runner is hit by the ball while standing on base, he shall not be called out, but the ball is dead and the batter shall be called out; but if a baserunner is hit while off base, both he and the batter shall be called out and the ball is dead. Provided, that, with first and second bases occupied, or first, second, and third bases occupied, before two are out, any attempt to bunt which results in a fair fly ball shall not be regarded as an infield-fly.

Pivot Foot   The pitcher's pivot foot is that foot which is in contact with the pitcher's plate as he delivers the pitch.

Set Position   Set position is the pitcher's position when he stands facing the batter with his entire pivot foot on or in front of and in contact with, and not off the end of the pitcher's plate, and his other foot in front of the pitcher's plate, holding the ball in both hands in front of his body and coming to a complete stop of at least one second.

Strike Zone   The strike zone is that space over home plate which is between the batter's armpits and the top of his knees when he assumes his natural stance.

Wind-up Position   Wind-up position is the pitcher's position when he stands facing the batter, his pivot foot on or in front of and touching the pitcher's plate, and the other foot free.

Equipment/Glove   Each player, other than the first baseman and the catcher, is restricted to the use of a leather glove not more than 12 inches long nor more than eight inches wide, measured from the base of the thumb crotch to the outside edge of the glove. The space between the thumb and the forefinger shall not exceed 4½ inches at the top nor more than 3½ inches at the base of the thumb crotch. The webbing may be standard leather or lacing and shall not be enlarged, extended, or reinforced by any process or materials whatever. The webbing cannot be constructed of wound or wrapped lacing to make a net type of trap. The glove may be of any weight.

Equipment/Pitcher   The pitcher's glove shall be uniform in color and cannot be white or gray.

Equipment/First Baseman   The first baseman may wear a leather glove or mitt not more than 12 inches long from top to bottom and not more than eight inches wide across the palm, measured from base of thumb crotch to outer edge of the mitt. The space between the thumb section and the finger section of the mitt shall not exceed four inches at the top of the mitt and 3½ inches at the base of the thumb crotch. The mitt shall be constructed so that this space is permanently fixed and cannot be enlarged, extended, widened, or deepened by the use of any materials or process whatever. The web of the mitt shall measure not more than five inches from its top to the base of the thumb crotch. The web may be either a lacing, lacing through leather tunnels, or a center piece of leather which may be an extension of the palm connected to the mitt with lacing and constructed so that it will not exceed the above-mentioned measurements. The webbing cannot be constructed of wound or wrapped lacing or deepened to make a net type of trap.

Game   Baseball is a game between two teams of nine players each with adequate substitutes, coaches and trainers, under direction of a manager, played in accordance with these rules, under jurisdiction of an umpire or umpires on an enclosed field.

The object of each team is to win by scoring the more runs.

A game consists of nine innings, except as otherwise provided and an inning is that portion of the game during which each team shall play both offensively and defensively.

The winner of the game shall be that team which shall have scored, in accordance with these rules, the greater number of runs at the conclusion of a regulation game.

Game/Umpire   The players of the home team shall take their defensive positions, the first batter of the visiting team shall take his position in the batter's box, the umpire shall call "Play" and the game shall proceed.

Game/Doubleheader   The rules of 1950 include a series of new provisions governing the conduct of doubleheaders.

Ground/Home Plate/Pitcher's Plate   The home plate and the pitcher's plate shall be of whitened rubber, anchored in the ground, even with its surface. The home plate, with beveled edges, shall be level with the baselines. The pitcher's plate shall be on a mound 15 inches higher than home plate. The slope from the pitcher's plate to the baselines shall be gradual.

Ground/Bases   First, second, and third bases shall be approved bags of white canvas, securely anchored in the ground. They shall be 15 inches square and not less than three, nor more than five inches thick and shall be filled with soft material.

Ground/Manager   The manager of the home team shall be the sole judge of the fitness of the playing field for the beginning of any game other than the second game of a doubleheader. Exception: Any league may permanently authorize its president to suspend the application of this rule as to that league during the closing weeks of its championship season in order to ensure that the championship is decided each year on its merits. When the postponement of, and possible failure to play, a game in the final series of a championship season between any two teams might affect the final standing of any club in the league, the president, on appeal from any league member, may assume the authority granted the home team manager by this rule.

Pitcher   There are two legal pitching positions: The "Wind-up" position and the "Set" position. Either position may be used at any time.

From the set position, the pitcher may deliver the ball to the batter, throw to a base, or step backward off the pitcher's plate with his pivot foot. Before assuming set position the pitcher may elect to make any natural preliminary motion such as that known as "the stretch." But if he so elects, he must come to set position before delivering the ball to the batter. After assuming set position, any natural motion associated with his delivery of the ball to the batter commits him to the pitch without alteration or interruption.

At any time during the pitcher's preliminary movements and until his natural pitching motion commits him to the pitch, he may throw to any base provided he step directly toward such base before making the throw.

If the pitcher makes an illegal pitch with the bases unoccupied it shall be called a ball, unless the batter shall make a fair hit or reaches first base on an error or otherwise.

If the pitcher remove his pivot foot from contact with the pitcher's plate by stepping backward with that foot, he thereby becomes an infielder and, if his subsequent throw to a base, when off the pitcher's plate, goes into a stand or over, through, or under a fence or into a bench or dugout (whether the ball rebounds or not) or remains in the meshes of a wire screen protecting the spectators, the ball is dead and all runners shall be entitled to advance two bases.

The pitcher shall not be allowed to pitch the "quick return ball." Whenever such pitch is attempted the umpire shall call "Time." If the offense is repeated the umpire shall call each such repeated offense a "ball," unless the batter reaches first base on a fair hit, an error, or otherwise, and no other runner is forced by his reaching first base, in which case the play proceeds.

When a pitcher takes his position at the beginning of each inning or when he relieves another pitcher, he shall be permitted to pitch not to exceed eight preparatory pitches to his catcher during which play shall be suspended. Such preparatory pitches shall not consume more than one minute of time.

Pitcher/Balk   If there is a runner or runners it is a balk if the pitcher delivers the pitch from "set position" without coming to a stop of one

full second.

Pitcher/Batter   The pitcher shall not be allowed to pitch at a batter's head, and if, in the umpire's opinion, such violation occurs, he shall call "Time" and warn the pitcher and the manager of the defensive team that another such pitch will mean the immediate expulsion of the pitcher from the game. If such pitch is repeated, the umpire shall inflict the penalty as follows: The pitcher shall be removed from the game and from the grounds. The president of the League shall impose such fine and suspension as his judgment warrants.

Pitcher/Uniform   The pitcher shall not be allowed to wear a garment with ragged, frayed or slit sleeves, and shall not be permitted to attach tape or other material of a color different from his uniform or glove to his glove or clothing.

Player/Catcher   Except the batter, or a runner attempting to score, no offensive player shall cross the catcher's lines when the ball is in play.

Player/Spectators   Players in uniform shall not address nor mingle with spectators, nor sit in the stands before or during a game. No manager, captain, coacher, or player shall address any spectator before or during a game. Players of opposing teams shall not fraternize at any time while in uniform. Penalty: The president of the league shall impose fines for violation of this rule at his discretion.

Player/Time   No manager, player, substitute, coacher, trainer, or batboy shall at any time, whether from the bench, the coacher's box, or on the playing field, or elsewhere call "Time," or employ any other word or phrase while the ball is alive and in play for the obvious purpose of confusing an umpire or an opposing player.

Runner   The rules of 1950 include several new provisions describing the circumstances under which a baserunner is out for interference.

A batter who has become a runner is entitled to unimpeded progress as he advances around the bases. Whenever a defensive player impedes the runner in any way, unless he is attempting to field a batted ball or has the ball in his possession, the umpire shall call "obstruction," the ball shall remain in play, and all runners shall be permitted to advance, without liability to be put out, to the bases which, in the judgment of the umpire, the runners would have reached had obstruction not been called.

In a "run-down" play, if the runner's progress is impeded by any defensive player who does not have the ball in his possession, the umpire shall call "obstruction" and the runner shall be entitled to occupy the base he is attempting to reach when the obstruction occurred.

Each runner including the batter-runner may, without liability of being put out, advance to home base, scoring a run, if a fair ball goes over the field fence in flight and he touch all bases legally; or if a fair ball which, in the umpire's judgment, would have cleared the field fence in flight, is deflected by the act of a defensive player in throwing his glove, cap, or any article of his apparel, the runner shall be awarded a home run.

The rules of 1950 include various new provisions for baserunners when balls are hit or thrown into the stands.

The batter becomes a baserunner when a fair ball, after touching the ground, bounds into the stands or passes through or under a fence or through or under a scoreboard or through or under shrubbery or vines on the fence, in which case the batter and the baserunners shall be entitled to advance two bases.

The batter becomes a baserunner when any fair ball which, either before or after striking the ground, passes through or under a fence or through or under a scoreboard or through any opening in the fence or scoreboard or through or under shrubbery or vines on the fence, in which case the batter and the baserunners shall be entitled to two bases.

Runner   The batter becomes a baserunner when any bounding fair ball is deflected by the fielder into the stands or over or under a fence on fair or foul ground, in which case the batter and all baserunners shall be entitled to advance two bases.

The batter becomes a baserunner when any fair fly ball is deflected by the fielder into the stands or over the fence into foul territory, in which case the batter shall be entitled to advance to second base; but if deflected into the stands or over the fence in fair territory, the batter shall be entitled to a home run.

The baserunner is out if, after he has acquired legal possession of a base, he or that base is tagged while he is running the bases in reverse order for the purpose of confusing the defense or making a travesty of the game. No runner may advance in this situation in the event of an error on this play by the defensive team.

The baserunner is out if, in running or sliding for home base, he fails to touch home base and makes no attempt to return to the base, when a defensive player holds the ball in his hand while touching home base and appeals to the umpire for the decision.

Substitute   A player or players may be substituted during a game at any time the ball is dead. A substituted player shall bat in the replaced player's position in the team's batting order. A player once removed from a game shall not re-enter that game. If a substitute enters the game in place of a manager, the manager may thereafter go to the coaching lines at his discretion. When two or more substitute players of the defensive team enter the game at the same time, the manager, or his designated representative, shall, immediately before they take their position as defensive players, designate to the umpire-in-chief such players' positions in the team's batting order and the umpire-in-chief shall so notify the official scorer. If this information is not immediately given to the umpire-in-chief, he shall have authority to designate the substitutes' places in the batting order.

Substitute/Runner   A player whose name is on his team's batting order may not become a substitute runner for another member of his team.

Umpire   Each umpire is the representative of the president of the league, the president of the National Association and the Commissioner of Baseball.

The umpire-in-chief shall enforce the rules from the moment he receives the batting order from the manager of the home team until termination of the game. This shall include control of ground crews, newsmen, and photographers, and any other persons whose duties require their presence upon the field.

Umpire/Manager   The ball is dead when the umpire-in-chief suspends play by calling "Time" when a manager requests "Time" for a substitution or for conference with his player.

Umpire/Player   The ball is dead when the umpire-in-chief suspends play by calling "Time" when a fielder, after catching a fly ball, falls into a bench, dugout, or stand or falls across ropes into a crowd (when spectators are on the field), and baserunners may advance one base without liability to be put out. Note: If player after making the catch steps into the dugout but does not fall, the ball is alive and in play and runners may advance at their own peril.

Umpire/Runner   After the umpire calls "Play" the ball is alive and in play and remains alive and in play until for legal cause, or at the umpire's call of "Time" suspending play, the ball becomes dead. While the ball is dead no player may be put out, no bases may be run, and no runs may be scored, except that runners may advance as legally provided.

Umpire   The rules of 1950 include a series of new provisions governing the preliminaries before championship games.

1951–53

There were no changes to the playing rules in these years.

1954

Bat   The bat shall be a smooth, rounded stick not more than 2¾ inches in diameter at the thickest part and not more than 42 inches in

length. The bat shall be one piece of solid wood or formed from a block of wood consisting of two or more pieces of wood bonded together with an adhesive in such a way that the grain direction of all pieces is essentially parallel to the length of the bat. Any such laminated bat shall contain only wood or adhesive, except for a clear finish.

For a distance of 18 inches from the end by which the bat is gripped, it may be roughened or wrapped with tape or twine. Note: Approval of the laminated bat is experimental for the 1954 season, and no laminated bat shall be used in a professional game until the manufacturer has secured approval from the Rules Committee of his design and method of manufacture. In giving or withholding such approval, the Rules Committee will be guided by comparison of the laminated bat with one-piece solid wood bats. Laminated bats which are inferior to one-piece solid wood bats in safety or durability will not be approved. A design or method of manufacture which produces a "loaded" or "freak" type of bat or which produces a substantially greater reaction or distance factor than one-piece solid wood bats will not be approved.

Batter   The batter is out after hitting or bunting a fair ball, when his bat hits the ball a second time in fair territory. The ball is dead and no runners may advance. If the batter-runner drops his bat and the ball rolls against the bat in fair territory and, in the umpire's judgment, there was no intention to interfere with the course of the ball, the ball is alive and in play.

The batter is out after hitting or bunting a foul ball, when he intentionally deflects the course of the ball in any manner while running to first base. The ball is dead and no runners may advance.

The batter is out when his fair ball touches him before touching a fielder.

The batter is out when, with less than two out and first, first and second, first and third, or first, second, and third bases are occupied, a fielder intentionally drops a fair fly ball or line drive. Runners need not re-touch and may advance at their own peril.

Batter/Fielder/Spectators   The batter is out when spectator interference clearly prevents a fielder from catching his fly ball.

Batter/Runner   It is interference by a batter or runner when he intentionally deflects the course of a foul ball in any manner.

Definitions   Rules Two and Three of the rules of 1954 contain several new definitions of key baseball terms as used in the rules.

Defensive Interference   Defensive interference is an illegal act by a fielder which hinders or prevents a batter from hitting a pitch.

Spectator interference occurs when a spectator reaches out of the stands, or goes on the playing field and touches a live ball. When there is spectator interference with any thrown ball, except a throw by the pitcher, the ball shall be dead at the moment of interference and the umpire shall impose such penalties as in his opinion will nullify the act of interference.

Quick Return   A quick return pitch is a pitch made with obvious intent to catch a batter off balance.

Squeeze Play   Squeeze play is a term to designate a play when a team, with a runner on third base, attempts to score that runner by means of a bunt.

Triple Play   A triple play is a play by the defense in which three offensive players are legally put out as a result of continuous action, providing there is no error between the putouts.

Wild Pitch   A wild pitch is one so high, so low, or so wide of the plate that it cannot be handled with ordinary effort by the catcher

Fielder   A catch is the act of a fielder in getting secure possession in his hand or glove of a ball in flight and firmly holding it; providing he does not use his cap, protector, pocket, or any other part of his uniform in getting possession.

Fielder/Batter   No fielder shall take a position in the batter's line of vision, and with deliberate unsportsmanlike intent, act in a manner to distract the batter.

Game   The rules of 1954 contain a series of new provisions governing suspended games.

Pitcher   The pitcher named in the batting order handed the umpire-in-chief shall pitch to the first batter or any substitute batter until the batter is put out or reaches first base, unless the pitcher sustains injury or illness which, in the judgment of the umpire-in-chief, incapacitates him from pitching.

If the pitcher is replaced, the substitute pitcher shall pitch to the batter then at bat, or any substitute batter, until such batter is retired or reaches first base, or until the offensive team is retired, unless the substitute pitcher sustains injury or illness which, in the umpire-in-chief's judgment, incapacitates him for further play as a pitcher.

Pitcher/Balk   In the event a balk is called, the ball is dead, and each runner shall advance one base without liability to be put out unless the batter hits the pitch on which the balk is made, in which case the manager of the offensive team may elect to accept either the balk penalty or the result of the batter's action.

Player/Equipment   Members of the offensive team shall carry all gloves and other equipment off the field and to the dugout while their team is at bat. No equipment shall be left lying on the field, either in fair or foul territory.

Runner   The rules of 1954 include several new provisions awarding baserunners additional bases in various circumstances.

Umpire   The umpire's authority to act in legal manner on all matters pertaining to a game shall not be questioned. The umpire shall have power to make decisions on any points not specifically covered in the rules.

Umpire/Runner   After the umpire calls "Play" the ball is alive and in play and remains alive and in play until for legal cause, or at the umpire's call of "Time" suspending play, the ball becomes dead. While the ball is dead no player may be put out, no bases may be run, and no runs may be scored, except that runners may advance one or more bases as the result of acts which occurred while the ball was alive (such as, but not limited to, a balk, an overthrow, interference, or a home run or other fair hit out of the playing field).

1955

Ball   The ball shall be a sphere formed by yarn wound around a small core of cork, rubber or similar material, covered with two strips of white horsehide, tightly stitched together. It shall weigh not less than 5 nor more than 5¼ ounces avoirdupois and measure not less than 9 nor more than 9¼ inches in circumference.

Definition/Illegally Batted Ball   An illegally batted ball is one hit by the batter with one or both feet outside of the batter's box.

Batter/Runner   It is interference by a batter or runner when any member or members of the offensive team stand or gather around any base to which a runner is advancing, to confuse, hinder, or add to the difficulty of the fielders. Such runner shall be declared out for the interference of his teammate or teammates.

It is interference by a batter or runner when any batter or runner who has just been retired hinders or impedes any following play being made on a runner. Such runner shall be declared out for the interference of his teammate.

Fielder/Catcher   The catcher shall stand with both feet within the lines of the catcher's box, directly back of the plate, until the ball leaves the pitcher's hand. The intent of this rule is to deter the giving of intentional bases on balls. If the catcher has either foot outside his box when the pitcher delivers the ball, it is a balk.

Game   The rules of 1955 include new provisions for determining a suspended game and its resumption.

A game shall be forfeited in favor of the opposing team when a team is unable or refuses to place nine players on the field.

Game/Manager The manager of the home team shall be the sole judge as to whether a game shall be started because of unsuitable weather conditions or the unfit condition of the playing field, except for the second game of a doubleheader.

Pitcher When the bases are unoccupied, the pitcher shall deliver the ball to the batter within 20 seconds after taking his pitching position. Each time the pitcher delays the game by violating this rule, the umpire shall call "Ball."

Runner/Batter The batter becomes a runner and is entitled to first base when the catcher or any other fielder interferes with him, unless the batter reaches first base on a hit, an error, or otherwise, and all other runners advance at least one base, in which case the play proceeds without reference to the interference.

Umpire The ball becomes dead when the umpire-in-chief suspends play by calling "Time" when an accident incapacitates a player or umpire, or if it is necessary to remove a player or spectator from the grounds. The umpire shall not call "Time" because of an accident to player or umpire during a play, until in his judgment, no further action is possible in that play, unless an accident to a runner is such as to prevent him from proceeding to a base to which he is legally entitled, as on a home run hit out of the playing field, or an award of one or more bases, in which case a substitute runner shall be permitted to complete the play.

Umpire/Game The umpire-in-chief shall make certain that the original and copies of the respective batting orders are identical, and then tender a copy of each batting order to the opposing manager. The copy retained by the umpire shall be the official batting order. The tender of the batting order by the umpire shall establish the batting orders. Thereafter, no substitutions shall be made by either manager, except as provided in the rules.

1956

There were no changes to the playing rules this year.

1957

The rules of 1957 contain new wording and explanation for the rules governing a batter who bats out of order.

Batter The batter shall take his position in the batter's box promptly when it is his time at bat.

The batter shall not leave his position in the batter's box after the pitcher comes to the Set Position, or starts his windup. Penalty: If the pitcher pitches, the umpire shall call "Ball" or "Strike," as the case may be.

Batter The batter becomes a runner and is entitled to first base without liability to be put out (provided he advances to and touches first base) when he is touched by a pitched ball which he is not attempting to hit unless: (1) The ball is in the strike zone when it touches the batter, or (2) The batter makes no attempt to avoid being touched by the ball. Note: If the ball is in the strike zone when it touches the batter, it shall be called a strike, whether or not the batter tries to avoid the ball. If the ball is outside the strike zone when it touches the batter, it shall be called a ball if he makes no attempt to avoid being touched.

Catcher/Fielder When the ball is put in play at the start of or during a game, all fielders other than the catcher shall be on fair territory. The catcher shall station himself directly back of the plate. He may leave his position at any time to catch a pitch or make a play except that when the batter is being given an intentional base on balls, the catcher must stand with both feet within the lines of the catcher's box until the ball leaves the pitcher's hand. Penalty: Balk.

Coach The offensive team shall station two coaches on the field during its term at bat, one near first base and one near third base. Failure to place two coaches on the field shall subject the manager to fine or suspension or both by the league president.

Coaches shall be limited to two in number and shall (1) be in team uniform; (2) remain within the coach's box at all times; and (3) address players of their own team only. Penalty: The offending coach shall be removed from the game, and shall leave the playing field.

Definitions/Infield Fly An infield fly is a fair fly ball (not including a line drive nor an attempted bunt) which can be caught by an infielder with ordinary effort when first and second, or first, second, and third bases are occupied, before two are out. The pitcher, catcher, and any outfielder who stations himself in the infield on the play shall be considered infielders for the purpose of this rule.

When it seems apparent that a batted ball will be an infield fly, the umpire shall immediately declare "Infield Fly" for the benefit of the runners. If the ball is near the baselines, the umpire shall declare "Infield Fly, if Fair."

The ball is alive and runners may advance at the risk of the ball being caught, or re-touch and advance after the ball is touched, the same as on any fly ball. If the hit becomes a foul ball, it is treated the same as any foul. Note: If a declared infield fly is allowed to fall untouched to the ground, and bounces foul, it is a foul ball. If a declared infield fly falls untouched to the ground outside the baseline, and bounces fair, it is an infield fly.

Strike A strike is a legal pitch when so called by the umpire which (a) is struck at by the batter and is missed; (b) enters the strike zone in flight and is not struck at; (c) is fouled by the batter when he has less than two strikes; (d) is bunted foul; (e) touches the batter as he strikes at it; (f) touches the batter in flight in the strike zone; or (g) becomes a foul tip. Note: (f) was added to the former rule and definition.

Touch To touch a player or umpire is to touch any part of his body, clothing or his equipment.

Game When the winning run is scored in the last half-inning of a regulation game, or in the last half of an extra inning, as the result of a base on balls, hit batsman or any other play with the bases full which forces the runner on third to advance, the umpire shall not declare the game ended until the runner forced to advance from third has touched home base and the batter-runner has touched first base. Penalty: If the runner on third refuses to advance to and touch home base in a reasonable time, the umpire shall disallow the run, call out the offending player, and order the game resumed. If, with less than two out, the batter-runner refuses to advance to and touch first base, the run shall count, but the offending player shall be called out.

A league may adopt a rule providing that one game of a doubleheader shall be seven innings in length. In such games, any of these rules applying to the ninth inning shall apply to the seventh inning.

The second game of a doubleheader shall start 20 minutes after the first game is completed, unless a longer interval (not to exceed 30 minutes) is declared by the umpire-in-chief and announced to the opposing managers at the end of the first game. Exception: If the league president has approved a request of the home club for a longer interval between games for some special event, the umpire-in-chief shall declare such longer interval and announce it to the opposing managers. The umpire-in-chief of the first game shall be the time-keeper controlling the interval between games.

The rules of 1957 include a rewording of the rules governing suspended games and the resumption of suspended games.

Pitcher When the bases are unoccupied, the pitcher shall deliver the ball to the batter within 20 seconds after he receives the ball. Each time the pitcher delays the game by violating this rule, the umpire shall call "Ball." Note: The intent of this rule is to avoid unnecessary delays. The umpire shall insist that the catcher return the ball promptly to the pitcher, and that the pitcher take his position on the rubber promptly. Obvious delay by the pitcher should instantly be penalized by the umpire.

The pitcher shall not (1) apply a foreign substance of any kind to the ball; (2) expectorate either on the ball or his glove; (3) rub the ball on his glove, person, or clothing; (4) deface the ball in any

manner; (5) deliver what is called the "shine" ball, "spit" ball, "mud" ball or "emery" ball. The pitcher, of course, is allowed to rub the ball between his bare hands. Penalty: For violation of any part of this rule, the umpire shall immediately disqualify the pitcher, and the league president shall suspend the pitcher for a period of 10 days. If a pitch is delivered in violation of this rule, it shall be treated as an illegal pitch.

Pitcher/Balk If there is a runner or runners it is a balk if the pitcher, while giving an intentional base on balls, pitches when the catcher is not in the catcher's box.

If there is a runner or runners it is a balk if the pitcher makes an illegal pitch.

Pitcher/Batter/Runner/Fielder If, with a runner on third base and trying to score by means of a squeeze play or a steal, the catcher or any other fielder steps on, or in front of home base without possession of the ball, or touches the batter or his bat, the pitcher shall be charged with a balk, the batter shall be awarded first base on the interference, and the ball is dead.

Pitcher/Substitute If an improper substitution is made for the pitcher, the umpire shall direct the proper pitcher to return to the game until the provisions of this rule are fulfilled. If the improper pitcher is permitted to pitch, any play that results is legal. The improper pitcher becomes the proper pitcher as soon as he makes his first pitch to the batter, or as soon as any runner is retired.

Player Players in uniform shall not address nor mingle with spectators, nor sit in the stands before, during, or after a game. No manager, captain, coach, or player shall address any spectator before or during a game. Players of opposing teams shall not fraternize at any time while in uniform. Penalty: The league president shall impose fines for violation of this rule at his discretion.

Runner In a rundown play, if the runner is obstructed by any fielder who does not have the ball in his possession (unless the fielder is in the act of fielding the ball), the umpire shall call "Obstruction" and the runner shall be entitled to occupy the base he is attempting to reach when the obstruction occurs. If such base is held by a following runner, any following runner forced to vacate his base by the obstructed runner's return shall be permitted to return to his last-held base without liability to be put out.

Each runner, other than the batter, may without liability to be put out, advance one base when he is attempting to steal a base, if the batter is interfered with by the catcher or any other fielder. Note: When a runner is entitled to a base without liability to be put out, while the ball is in play, or under any rule in which the ball is in play after the runner reaches the base to which he is entitled, and the runner fails to touch the base to which he is entitled before attempting to advance to the next base, the runner shall forfeit his exemption from liability to be put out, and he may be put out by tagging the base or by tagging the runner before he returns to the missed base.

Umpire Each umpire has authority to disqualify any player, coach, manager, or substitute for objecting to decisions or for unsportsmanlike conduct or language, and to remove such disqualified person from the playing field. If an umpire disqualifies a player while a play is in progress, the disqualification shall not take effect until no further action is possible in that play.

Each umpire has authority at his discretion to remove from the playing field (1) any person whose duties permit his presence on the field, such as ground-crew members, ushers, photographers, newsmen, broadcasting-crew members, etc., or (2) any spectator or other person not authorized to be on the playing field.

If different decisions should be made on one play by different umpires, the umpire-in-chief shall call all the umpires into consultation, with no manager or player present. After consultation, the umpire-in-chief (unless another umpire may have been designated by the league president) shall determine which decision shall prevail, based on which umpire was in best position and which decision was most likely correct. Play shall proceed as if only the final decision had been made.

1958

Runner Any runner shall be called out, on appeal, when (a) after a fly ball is caught, he fails to re-touch his base before he or his base is tagged; (b) with the ball in play, while advancing or returning to a base, he fails to touch each base in order before he, or a missed base is tagged; (c) he overruns or overslides first base and fails to return to the base immediately, and he or the base is tagged; (d) he fails to touch home base and makes no attempt to return to that base, and home base is tagged. Any appeal under this rule must be made before the next legal pitch. If the violation occurs during a play which ends a half-inning, the appeal must be made before the defensive team leaves the field. Note: Appeal plays may require an umpire to recognize an apparent "fourth out." If the third out is made during a play in which an appeal play is sustained on another runner, the appeal play decision takes precedence in determining the out. If there is more than one appeal during a play that ends a half-inning, the defense may elect to take the out that gives it the advantage. If the third out on appeal is a force play or failure of the batter-runner to touch first base, no runs can score on the play. Otherwise runs made before the appeal is sustained shall count. For the purposes of this rule, the defensive team has "left the field" when the pitchers and all infielders have left fair territory on their way to the bench or clubhouse.

1959

Ground Any playing field constructed by a professional club after June 1, 1958, shall provide a minimum distance of 325 feet from home base to the nearest fence, stand, or other obstruction on the right and left field foul lines, and a minimum distance of 400 feet to the center field fence. No existing playing fields shall be remodeled after June 1, 1958, in such manner as to reduce the distance from home base to the foul poles and to the center field fence below the minimum distances.

Runner The runner is entitled to advance one base, if a ball, pitched to the batter, or thrown by the pitcher from his position on the pitcher's plate to a base to catch a runner, goes into a stand, or players' bench, or over or through a field fence or backstop. The ball is dead. Note: If such a wild pitch is ball four, the batter-runner is entitled to first base only.

Each runner, including the batter-runner may advance two bases, if a fair ball bounces or is deflected into the stands outside the first or third base foul lines; or if it goes through or under a field fence, or through or under a scoreboard, or through or under shrubbery or vines on the fence; or if it sticks in such fence, scoreboard, shrubbery, or vines.

Spectators/Fielder When there is spectator interference with any thrown ball, the ball shall be dead at the moment of interference, and the umpire shall impose such penalties as in his opinion will nullify the act of interference.

1960–62

There were no changes to the playing rules in these years.

1963

Definitions/Offensive Interference Offensive interference is an act by the team at bat which interferes with, obstructs, impedes, hinders, or confuses any fielder attempting to make a play. If the umpire declares the batter, batter-runner, or a runner out for interference, all other runners shall return to the last base that was, in the judgment of the umpire, legally touched at the time of the interference.

Strike Zone The strike zone is that space over home plate which is between the top of the batter's shoulders and his knees when he assumes his natural stance. The umpire shall determine the strike zone according to the batter's usual stance when he swings at a pitch.

Pitcher The Windup Position—The pitcher shall stand facing the

batter, his entire pivot foot on, or in front of and touching and not off the end of the pitcher's plate, and the other foot free. From this position any natural movement associated with his delivery of the ball to the batter commits him to the pitch without interruption or alteration. He shall not raise either foot from the ground, except that in his actual delivery of the ball to the batter, he may take one step backward, and one step forward with his free foot. Note: When a pitcher holds the ball with both hands in front of his body, with his entire pivot foot on, or in front of and touching but not off the end of the pitcher's plate, and his other foot free, he will be considered in a Windup Position.

When a pitcher takes his position at the beginning of each inning, or when he relieves another pitcher, he shall be permitted to pitch not to exceed eight preparatory pitches to his catcher during which play shall be suspended. A league by its own action may limit the number of preparatory pitches to less than eight preparatory pitches. Such preparatory pitches shall not consume more than one minute of time. If a sudden emergency causes a pitcher to be summoned into the game without any opportunity to warm up, the umpire-in-chief shall allow him as many pitches as the umpire deems necessary.

Pitcher/Balk If there is a runner, or runners, it is a balk when the pitcher, after coming to a legal pitching position, removes one hand from the ball other than in an actual pitch, or in throwing to a base.

Runner A runner acquires the right to an unoccupied base when he touches it before he is out. He is then entitled to it until he is put out, or forced to vacate it for another runner.

Unless two are out, the status of a following runner is not affected by a preceding runner's failure to touch or re-touch a base. If, upon appeal, the preceding runner is the third out, no runners following him shall score. If such third out is the result of a force play, neither preceding nor following runners shall score.

1964

Bat No colored bat may be used in a professional game unless approved by the rules committee.

Batter/Runner It is interference by a batter or a runner when a batter-runner wilfully and deliberately interferes with a batted ball or a fielder in the act of fielding a batted ball, with the obvious intent to break up a double play. The ball is dead. The umpire shall call the batter-runner out for interference and also call out the next preceding runner for the action of his teammate. In no event may bases be run or runs scored because of such action by a runner.

It is interference by a batter or a runner when, in the judgment of the umpire, a baserunner wilfully and deliberately interferes with a batted ball or a fielder in the act of fielding a batted ball with the obvious intent to break up a double play. The ball is dead. The umpire shall call the runner out for interference and also call out the batter-runner because of the action of his teammate. In no event may bases be run or runs scored because of such action by a runner.

Pitcher The Set Position. Set Position shall be indicated by the pitcher when he stands facing the batter with his entire pivot foot on, or in front of, and in contact with, and not off the end of the pitcher's plate, and his other foot in front of the pitcher's plate, holding the ball in both hands in front of his body and coming to a complete stop. From such Set Position he may deliver the ball to the batter, throw to a base or step backward off the pitcher's plate with his pivot foot. Before assuming Set Position, the pitcher may elect to make any natural preliminary motion such as that known as "the stretch." But, if he so elects, he shall come to Set Position before delivering the ball to the batter. After assuming Set Position any natural motion associated with his delivery of the ball to the batter commits him to the pitch without alteration or interruption.

Player/Uniform Any part of an undershirt exposed to view shall be of a uniform solid color for all players on a team. Any player other than the pitcher may have numbers, letters, insignia attached to the sleeve of an undershirt.

Runner The batter becomes a runner and is entitled to first base when the catcher or any fielder interferes with him. If a play follows the interference, the manager of the offense may advise the plate umpire that he elects to decline the interference penalty and accept the play. Such election shall be made immediately at the end of the play. However, if the batter reaches first base on a hit, an error, a base on balls, a hit batsman, or otherwise, and all other runners advance at least one base, the play proceeds without reference to the interference.

1965

Batter/Runner It is interference by a batter or runner if a batter-runner wilfully and deliberately interferes with a batted ball or a fielder in the act of fielding a batted ball.

Equipment/Catcher The catcher may wear a leather glove or mitt no more than 38 inches in circumference, nor more than 15½ inches from top to bottom. Such limits shall include all lacing and any leather band or facing attached to the outer edge of the mitt. The space between the thumb section and the finger section of the mitt shall not exceed six inches at the top of the mitt and four inches at the base of the thumb crotch. The web shall measure not more than seven inches across the top or more than six inches from its top to the base of the thumb crotch. The web may be either a lacing or lacing through leather tunnels, or a center piece of leather which may be an extension of the palm, connected to the mitt with lacing and constructed so that it will not exceed any of the above mentioned requirements. The glove may be of any weight.

Runner Any runner shall be called out, on appeal, when with the ball in play, while advancing or returning to a base, he fails to touch each base in order before he, or a missed base, is tagged. Approved Ruling: (1) No runner may return to touch a missed base after a following runner has scored. (2) When the ball is dead, no runner may return to touch a missed base or one he has left after he has advanced to and touched a base beyond the missed base.

1966

There were no changes to the playing rules this year.

1967

Batter/Runner It is interference by a batter or runner when, in the judgment of the umpire, a batter-runner wilfully and deliberately interferes with a batted ball or a fielder in the act of fielding a batted ball, with the obvious intent to break up a double play. The ball is dead. The umpire shall call the batter-runner out for interference and shall also call out the runner who had advanced closest to the home plate regardless where the double play might have been possible. In no event shall bases be run because of such interference.

Definitions/Catch A catch is the act of a fielder in getting secure possession in his hand or glove of a ball in flight and firmly holding it; providing he does not use his cap, protector, pocket, or any other part of his uniform in getting possession. It is not a catch, however, if simultaneously or immediately following his contact with the ball, he collides with a player, or with a wall, or if he falls down, and as a result of such collision or falling, drops the ball. It is not a catch if a fielder touches a fly ball which then hits a member of the offensive team or an umpire and then is caught by another defensive player. If the fielder has made the catch and drops the ball while in the act of making a throw following the catch, the ball shall be adjudged to have been caught. In establishing the validity of the catch, the fielder shall hold the ball long enough to prove that he has complete control of the ball and that his release of the ball is voluntary and intentional.

Fielder The players, coaches or any member of an offensive team shall vacate any space (including both dugouts) needed by a fielder who is attempting to field a batted or thrown ball. Penalty: Interference shall be called and the batter or runner on whom the play is being made shall be declared out.

Pitcher   Pitchers shall take signs from the catcher while standing on the rubber.

Pitcher/Manager/Coach   A professional league shall adopt the following rule pertaining to the visit of the manager or coach to the pitcher: (a) This rule limits the number of trips a manager or coach may make to any one pitcher in any one inning; (b) A second trip to the same pitcher in the same inning will cause the pitcher's automatic removal; (c) The manager or coach is prohibited from making a second visit to the mound while the same batter is at bat; but (d) If a pinch-hitter is substituted for this batter, the manager or coach may make a second visit to the mound, but must remove the pitcher.

A manager or coach is considered to have concluded his visit to the mound when he leaves the 18-foot circle surrounding the pitcher's rubber.

Runner   A runner acquires the right to an unoccupied base when he touches it before he is out. He is then entitled to it until he is put out, or forced to vacate it for another runner legally entitled to that base.

The ball becomes dead and runners advance one base, or return to their bases, without liability to be put out when a balk is committed.

The batter becomes a runner when a fair ball, after having passed a fielder other than the pitcher, or after having been touched by a fielder, including the pitcher, shall touch an umpire or runner on fair territory.

1968

Pitcher   The pitcher shall not (1) bring his pitching hand in contact with his mouth or lips. Penalty: For violating this part of this rule the umpire shall warn the pitcher and if this action is repeated the umpire shall immediately disqualify the pitcher; (2) apply a foreign substance of any kind to the ball; (3) expectorate on the ball, his pitching hand or his glove; (4) rub the ball on his glove, person, or clothing; (5) deface the ball in any manner; (6) deliver what is called the "shine" ball, "spit" ball, "mud" ball, or "emery" ball. The pitcher, of course, is allowed to rub the ball between his bare hands. Penalty: For violation of any part of this rule the umpire shall immediately disqualify the pitcher.

Runner/Coach   The ball becomes dead and runners advance one base or return to their bases without liability to be put out when a base coach intentionally interferes with a thrown ball. Runners return to the base last legally touched.

1969

Definitions/Strike Zone   The strike zone is that space over home plate which is between the batter's armpits and the top of his knees when he assumes his natural stance. The umpire shall determine the strike zone according to the batter's usual stance when he swings at a pitch.

Game   A game called at the end of a completed inning with the score tied after nine innings shall be a suspended game.

Pitcher/Ground   The pitcher's plate shall be 10 inches above the level of home plate. The degree of slope from a point six inches in front of the pitcher's plate to a point six feet toward home plate shall be one inch to one foot, and such degree of slope shall be uniform.

Runner   Any runner is out when he fails to re-touch his base after a fair or foul ball is legally caught before he or his base is tagged by a fielder. He shall not be called out for failure to re-touch his base after the first following pitch, or any play or attempted play. This is an appeal play.

1970

There were no changes to the playing rules this year.

1971

Player/Equipment   All players shall use some type of protective helmet while at bat.

1972

Game   A game may be suspended to be completed at a future date by reason of light failure or malfunction of a mechanical field device, e.g., automatic tarpaulin or water-removal equipment.

Runner/Umpire   An appeal is not to be interpreted as a play or an attempted play.

Successive appeals may not be made on a runner at the same base. If the defensive team on its first appeal errs, a request for a second appeal on the same runner at the same base shall not be allowed by the umpire.

1973

Batter/Pitcher   Any league may elect to use the Designated Hitter (DH) rule as follows: (1) A hitter may be designated to bat for the starting pitcher and all subsequent pitchers in any game without otherwise affecting the status of the pitcher or pitcher in the game. A DH for the pitcher must be selected prior to the game and must be included in the lineup cards presented to the umpire-in-chief; (2) It is not mandatory that a club designate a hitter for the pitcher, but failure to do so prior to the game precludes the use of a DH for that game; (3) Pinch hitters for a DH may be used. Any substitute hitter for a DH becomes the DH. A replaced DH shall not re-enter the game in any capacity; (4) The DH may be used defensively, continuing to bat in the same position in the batting order, but the pitcher must then bat in the place of the substituted defensive player, unless more than one substitution is made, and the manager then must designate their spots in the batting order; (5) A runner may be substituted for the DH and the runner assumes the role of DH; (6) A DH is "locked" into the batting order. No multiple substitutions may be made that will alter the batting rotation of the DH; (7) Once the game-pitcher is switched from the mound to a defensive position this move shall terminate the DH role for the remainder of the game; (8) Once the game-pitcher bats for the DH this move shall terminate the DH's role for the remainder of the game. The game pitcher may only pinch-hit for the DH; (9) Once a DH assumes a defensive position this move shall terminate the DH role for the remainder of the game. Note: The DH rule was adopted only by the American League.

Game   In all protested games, the decision of the league president shall be final.

1974

Batter   All players are required to wear batting helmets with ear flaps.

Pitcher   If, in his judgment, the umpire determines that a foreign substance has been applied to the ball, he shall (a) call the pitch a ball, warn the pitcher and have announced by the public address system the reason for the action; (b) in the case of a second offense by the same pitcher any time later in the game, the pitcher shall be disqualified from the game and may additionally be subject to such action as may be imposed by the league office; (c) if a play follows the violation called by the umpire, the manager of the offensive team may advise the plate umpire that he elects to decline the penalty and accept the play. Such election shall be made immediately at the end of the play. However, if a batter reaches first base on a hit, an error, a base on balls, a hit batsman, or otherwise, and no other runner is put out before advancing at least one base, the play shall proceed without reference to the violation; (d) even though the offense elects to take the play, the violation shall be recognized and the penalties in (a) and (b) will still be in effect; (e) the umpire shall be the sole judge on whether any portion of this rule has been violated.

1975

Ball   The ball can be covered with white cowhide as well as horsehide.

Bat   Cupped Bats. An indentation in the end of the bat up to one inch in depth is permitted and may be no wider than two inches and no less than one inch in diameter. The indentation must be curved

with no foreign substance added.

Batter   A batter is out when an infielder intentionally drops a fair fly ball or line drive, with first, first and second, first and third, or first, second, and third bases occupied before two are out. The ball is dead and runner or runners shall return to their original base or bases. Approved Ruling: In this situation, the batter is not out if the infielder permits the ball to drop untouched to the ground, except when the infield fly rule applies.

A batter is out for illegal action when he hits a fair ball with a filled, doctored, or flat-surfaced bat in which event he shall be immediately ejected from the game and suspended by his league president for three days.

Game   A game may be suspended if local law prohibits the use of lights and it is too dark to continue.

Pitcher   The pitcher shall not have on his person, or in his possession, any foreign substance. For such infraction of this section the penalty shall be immediate ejection from the game.

Runner   Each runner including the batter-runner may advance one base, if a ball, pitched to the batter, or thrown by the pitcher from his position on the pitcher's plate to a base to catch a runner, goes into a stand or a bench, or over or through a field fence or backstop. The ball is dead. Approved Ruling: When a wild pitch or passed ball goes through or by the catcher, or deflects off the catcher, and goes directly into the dugout, stands, above the break, or any area where the ball is dead, the awarding of bases shall be one base. One base shall also be awarded if the pitcher while in contact with the rubber, throws to a base, and the throw goes directly into the stands or into any area where the ball is dead.

If, however, the pitched or thrown ball goes through or by the catcher or through the fielder, and remains on the playing field, and is subsequently kicked or deflected into the dugout, stands or other area where the ball is dead, the awarding of bases shall be two bases from position of runners at the time of the pitch or throw.

Any runner shall be called out, on appeal, when after a fly ball is caught, he fails to re-touch his original base before he or his original base is tagged.

1976

Bat   The bat handle, for not more than 18 inches from the end, may be covered or treated with any material (including pine tar) to improve the grip. Any such material, including pine tar, which extends past the 18 inch limitation, in the umpire's judgment, shall cause the bat to be removed from the game. No such material shall improve the reaction or distance factor of the bat.

Batter   The batter is out for illegal action when he uses or attempts to use a bat that, in the umpire's judgment, has been altered or tampered with in such a way to improve the distance factor or cause an unusual reaction on the baseball. This includes, bats that are filled, flat-surfaced, nailed, hollowed, grooved, or covered with a substance such as paraffin, wax, etc. No advancement on the bases will be allowed and any out or outs made during a play shall stand. In addition to being called out, the player shall be ejected from the game and may be subject to additional penalties as determined by the league president.

Batter/Pitcher   A Designated Hitter (DH) may not pinch run.

Once a pinch hitter bats for any player in the batting order and then enters the game to pitch, this move shall terminate the DH role for the remainder of the game.

A substitute for the DH need not be announced until it is the DH's turn to bat. Note: Rule applies only to the American League.

Manager/Coach/Player/Umpire   No manager, player, substitute, coach, trainer, or batboy shall at any time, whether from the bench, the coach's box or on the playing field, or elsewhere make intentional contact with the umpire in any manner.

Player/Uniform   No player shall attach anything to the heel or toe of his shoe other than the ordinary shoe plate or toe plate. Shoes with pointed spikes similar to golf or track shoes shall not be worn.

1977

There were no changes to the playing rules this year.

1978

Batter/Pitcher   In the event of interleague competition between clubs of leagues using the Designated Hitter rule and clubs of leagues not using the Designated Hitter rule, the rule will be used as follows: (1) In exhibition games, the rule will be used or not used as is the practice of the home team; (2) In All-Star Games, the rule will only be used if both teams and both leagues so agree; (3) In World Series play, the rule will be used every other year. It will not be used in 1977, but will be used in 1978, etc.

Pitcher   The pitcher shall not intentionally pitch at the batter. If, in the umpire's judgment, such a violation occurs, the umpire shall warn the pitcher and his manager that another such pitch will mean immediate expulsion of the pitcher. At the same time the umpire shall warn the opposing manager that such an infraction by his pitcher shall result in that pitcher's expulsion. If, in the umpire's judgment, there is another such pitch during the game by any pitcher, the umpire shall eject the pitcher from the game. If, in the umpire's judgment circumstances warrant, one or both teams may be officially "warned" prior to the game or an actual violation during the game in progress. League presidents may take additional action under the rules. Note: To pitch at a batter's head is unsportsmanlike and highly dangerous. It should be—and is—condemned by everybody. Umpires should act without hesitation in enforcement of this rule.

1979

There were no changes to the playing rules this year.

1980

Game   The rules of 1980 include several amendments to the rules governing suspended games and protested games.

Substitute/Fielder   If no announcement of a substitution is made, the substitute shall be considered as having entered the game when, if a fielder, he reaches the position usually occupied by the fielder he has replaced and play commences.

1981

Batter/Pitcher   The Designated Hitter (DH) named in the starting lineup must come to bat at least one time, unless the opposing club changes pitchers. Note: This rule applies only to the American League.

1982

Pitcher   Under extreme weather conditions a pitcher may warm his throwing hand by blowing on it provided both managers and umpires have agreed to this before the game begins.

1983

Batter   All players shall use some type of protective helmet while at bat. All players in National Association Leagues shall wear a double ear-flap helmet while at bat. All players entering the major leagues commencing with the 1973 championship season and every succeeding season thereafter must wear a single ear-flap helmet (or at the player's option, a double ear-flap helmet), except those players who were in the major leagues during the 1982 season, and who, as recorded in that season, objected to wearing a single ear-flap helmet. If the umpire observes any violation of these rules, he shall direct the violation to be corrected. If the violation is not corrected within a reasonable time, in the umpire's judgment, the umpire shall eject the offender from the game.

1984

Bat   The bat handle, for not more than 18 inches from its end, may be covered or treated with any material or substance to improve the grip. Any such material or substance, which extends past the 18 inch limitation, shall cause the bat to be removed from the game.

1985

Player/Uniform   No part of the uniform shall include patches or designs relating to commercial advertisements.

A league may provide that the uniforms of its member teams include the names of its players on their backs. Any name other than the last name of the player must be approved by the league president. If adopted, all uniforms for a team must have the names of its players.

1986

Batter/Pitcher   The Designated Hitter (DH) rule will be used or not used in World Series or exhibition games according to the practice of the home team.

1987

There were no changes to the playing rules this year.

1988

Ground/Bases   Home base shall be marked by a five-sided slab of whitened rubber. It shall be a 17 inch square with two of the corners removed so that one edge is 17 inches long, two adjacent sides are 8½ inches and the remaining two sides are 12 inches and set at an angle to make a point. It shall be set in the ground with the point at the intersection of the lines extending from home base to first base and to third base; with the 17 inch edge facing the pitcher's plate, and the two 12 inch edges coinciding with the first and third baselines. The top edges of home base shall be beveled and the base shall be fixed in the ground level with the ground surface.

Pitcher   The Set Position. Preparatory to coming to a set position, the pitcher shall have one hand by his side.

Set Position is assumed by the pitcher when he stands facing the batter with his entire pivot foot on, and parallel to, the pitcher's plate, or in front of, parallel to, and in contact with, the pitcher's plate. The non-pivot foot must be on the ground in front of the pitcher's plate. The pitcher must hold the ball in both hands in front of his body and come to a single complete and discernible stop before throwing the ball. A complete stop shall not be construed as occurring because of a change in direction of the hands and arms.

From such set position he must deliver the ball to the batter, throw to a base, or step backward off the pitcher's plate with his pivot foot.

Before assuming set position, the pitcher may elect to make any natural preliminary motion such as that known as "the stretch." But if he so elects, he shall come to a set position before delivering the ball to the batter. After assuming set position, any natural motion associated with his delivery of the ball to the batter commits him to the pitch without alteration or interruption.

The pitcher, following his stretch, must (a) hold the ball in both hands in front of his body and (b) come to a complete and discernible stop, with both feet on the ground. This must be enforced. Umpires should watch this closely, and should immediately call a "balk" for any violation.

Pitcher/Batter   The pitcher shall not intentionally pitch at the batter. If, in the umpire's judgment, such a violation occurs, the umpire may elect either to: (1) expel the pitcher, or the manager and the pitcher, from the game, or; (2) may warn the pitcher and the manager of both teams that another such pitch will result in the immediate expulsion of that pitcher (or a replacement) and the manager. If, in the umpire's judgment, and circumstances warrant, both teams may be officially "warned" prior to the game or at any time during the game. League presidents may take additional action under the rules.

Player/Equipment   All catchers shall wear a catcher's protective helmet, while fielding their position.

All bat/ballboys or girls shall wear a protective helmet while performing their duties.

Index to Playing Rule Changes 1876–1988

Note: Dates shown following an entry refer to the year a rule change or amendment was adopted. Rule changes and summaries of rules are to be found in the chronology which follows.

Runner, accident   1955
Runner acquires right to a base   1963, 1967
Runner advancing after fly ball caught by fielder   1920; 1940; 1958
Runner attempting to steal a base   1940
Runner caught in rundown   1920; 1950; 1957
Runner failing to re-touch a base   1969; 1975
Runner failing to touch a base   1876; 1920; 1931; 1957; 1963; 1965
Runner failing to touch home base   1950; 1958
Runner following not affected by preceding runner's failure to touch a base   1963
Runner hit by batted ball   1877; 1880; 1890; 1909; 1910
Runner hit by pitch in strike zone while attempting steal of home   1950
Runner is out   1876; 1877; 1880; 1904; 1907; 1914; 1920; 1939; 1940; 1958; 1965; 1969; 1975
Runner knocks ball from fielder's hand   1877
Runner may advance without liability to be put out   1881; 1882; 1897; 1907; 1910; 1914; 1920; 1931; 1940; 1950; 1954; 1955; 1957; 1959; 1967; 1968; 1975
Runner *not* out if hit by batted ball which has passed through infielder   1920
Runner out of baselines   1876; 1931
Runner overruns first base   1876; 1887; 1940
Runner passing runner   1897; 1904; 1907
Runner refusing to advance   1957
Runner returning to base   1876; 1880; 1883; 1887; 1889; 1897; 1910; 1914; 1931
Runner running bases in reverse order   1920; 1950
Scoring run   1876; 1880; 1890; 1897; 1920; 1950
Set position, definition of   1950; 1964; 1988
Shine ball   (See Pitcher, freak deliveries by)
Spectators   1876; 1881; 1882; 1883; 1884; 1887; 1897; 1898; 1910; 1914; 1931; 1940; 1949; 1950; 1954; 1955; 1957; 1959
Spectators hissing or booing umpire   1882
Spectators overflowing playing field   1910
Spitball   (See Pitcher, freak deliveries by)
Squeeze play, definition of   1954
Strikes   1876; 1877; 1880; 1881; 1887; 1888; 1894; 1895; 1899; 1901; 1902; 1904; 1906; 1907; 1909; 1920; 1950; 1957
Strike zone   1876; 1887; 1907; 1910; 1950; 1957; 1963; 1969
Substitution   1876; 1877; 1881; 1889; 1890; 1891; 1893; 1897; 1899; 1909; 1910; 1920; 1931; 1950; 1957; 1976; 1980
Substitution for batter   1893; 1910; 1950; 1954; 1955
Substitution for Designated Hitter   (See Designated Hitter rule)
Substitution for fielder   1980
Substitution for pitcher   1909; 1910; 1954; 1957
Substitution for runner   1876; 1881; 1889; 1910; 1931; 1950; 1955; 1976
Substitution for umpire   1876
Touch, definition of   1957
Trainers   1940
Tripleheaders prohibited   1940
Triple play, definition of   1954
Umpire, accident to   1955
Umpire addressing spectators   1887; 1897; 1910
Umpire, addressing the   1876; 1880; 1882; 1887
Umpire, announcement of pitcher prior to the game by   1909
Umpire, appealing to   1876; 1880; 1897; 1958
Umpire appealing to bystanders for assistance   1876; 1881
Umpire as employee of league   1883
Umpire as judge of fitness of ground   1896; 1906
Umpire assessing fine   1879; 1880; 1887; 1895; 1896; 1910
Umpire, authority to accept or reject ground rules   1909
Umpire, authority to disqualify player, coach, manager, substitute, etc.   1957
Umpire, authority to remove personnel from field   1957
Umpire calling 'Time'   1877; 1878; 1884.; 1887; 1920; 1950; 1954;

1955
Umpire consulting player before decision   1887
Umpire hit by batted ball   1907; 1910; 1920; 1967
Umpire hit by pitched or thrown ball   1910; 1914
Umpire-in-Chief to decide all matters regarding batter   1940
Umpire-in-Chief to enforce rules   1950
Umpire, intentional contact with prohibited   1976
Umpire interfering with catcher   1914
Umpire, responsibilities when two umpires used   1898; 1940
Umpire reversing decision   1876; 1881; 1887; 1897
Umpire, rules pertaining to extensively rewritten   1903; 1910; 1920
Umpire, selection of   1876
Umpires, procedure of when decisions are in conflict   1957
Umpire, to touch an   1957
Vacating a base   1876
Wild pitch, definition of   1954
Windup position, definition of   1950, 1963

Scoring Rules for 1878

Batting

Section 1.   The first item in the tabulated score, after the player's name and position, shall be the number of times he has been at bat during the game. Any time or times where the player has been sent to base on called balls shall not be included in this column.

Section 2.   In the second column should be set down the runs made by each player.

Section 3.   In the third column should be placed the first-base hits made by each player. A basehit should be scored in the following cases:

When the ball from the bat strikes the ground between the foul lines and out of the reach of the fielders.

When a hit is wholly or partially stopped by a fielder in motion, but such player cannot recover himself in time to handle the ball before the striker reaches first base.

When the ball is hit so sharply to an infielder that he cannot handle it in time to put out a man. In case of doubt over this class of hits, score a basehit and exempt fielder from the charge of an error.

When a ball is hit so slowly toward a fielder that he cannot reach it before the batsman is safe.

Section 4.   In the fourth column should be placed to the credit of each player the number of times he reaches first base during the game, whether upon hits, errors, called balls or in any other way where he is not put out.

Fielding

Section 5.   The number of opponents put out by each player shall be set down in the fifth column. Where a striker is given out by the umpire for a foul strike or because he struck out of his turn, the putout shall be scored to the catcher.

Section 6.   The number of times a player assists shall be set down in the sixth column. An assist should be given to each player who handles the ball in a run-out or other play of the kind.

An assist should be given to the pitcher when a batsman fails to hit the ball on the third strike.

An assist should be given to the pitcher in each case where the batsman is declared out for making a foul strike or striking out of turn.

An assist should be given to a player who makes a play in time to put a runner out, even if the player who should complete the play fails, through no fault of the player assisting.

And, generally, an assist should be given to each player who

handles the ball from the time it leaves the bat until it reaches the player who makes the putout, or, in case of a thrown ball, to each player who throws or handles it cleanly, and in such way that a putout results or would result if no error were made by the receiver.

Section 7. An error should be given for each misplay which allows the striker or baserunner to make one or more bases when perfect play would have insured his being put out. In scoring errors off batted balls see Sec. 3 of the Article.

Chronology of Scoring Rules 1878–1988

1879

There were no changes to the scoring rules this year.

1880

Base Hit Score a base hit when a ball is hit so slowly toward a fielder that he cannot reach it in time to put out a man.

Total Bases In the fourth column should be placed to the credit of each player the total bases run during the game. In scoring "bases run" where a player has reached first base as the result of the putting out of another player, such first base shall not be credited to the striker as one of the bases run by him.

Total Chances In the seventh column should be placed the "total chances offered" to retire players, which should include each perfect play, as well as each misplay or failure to accept a chance to retire a batsman or baserunner. "Chances offered" should not include "passed balls," "called balls" or "wild pitches." In scoring "chances offered" off batted balls, see Sec. 3 of the Scoring Rules. Note: This rule does not appear in the scoring rules following 1880.

1881

Total Bases In the fourth column should be placed to the credit of each player the total bases made by him off his hits.

1882

There were no changes to the scoring rules this year.

1883

Error An error should be given to the pitcher when the batsman is given first base on "called balls."

1884

There were no changes to the scoring rules this year.

1885

Assist An assist shall be given the pitcher when the batsman fails to hit the ball on the third strike, and the same shall also be entered in the summary under the head of "struck out." Note: This rule was dropped in 1889.

Error Wild pitches and passed balls shall be charged to the pitcher and catcher respectively in the error column, and shall also appear in the summary. Note: This rule was dropped in 1886.

1886

Runner Bases stolen by players shall appear to their credit in the summary of the game.

1887

Assist An assist shall be given the pitcher when the batsman fails to hit the ball on the fourth strike, and the same shall also be entered in the summary under the head of "struck out." Note: This rule was dropped in 1889.

Batter The first item in the tabulated score, after the player's name and position, shall be the number of times he has been at bat during the game. Any time or times where the player has been sent to base

by being hit by a pitched ball or by the pitcher's illegal delivery, shall not be included in this column.

A base hit is to be scored when the batsman is awarded a base on balls. Note: This rule was dropped in 1888.

Error An error shall be given in the seventh column for each misplay which allows the striker or baserunner to make one or more bases when perfect play would have insured his being put out; except that "wild pitches," "bases on called balls," "bases on the batsman being struck by a pitched ball" or case of illegal pitched ball, balks and passed balls, shall not be included in said column. In scoring errors off batted balls see Sec. 3 of this rule. Note: The phrase "bases on called balls" was deleted from the exception to this rule in 1888.

Runner In the fourth column shall be scored bases stolen, and shall include every base made after first base has been reached by a baserunner, except those made by reason of, or with the aid of, a "battery" error, or by batting, "balks" or by being forced off. In short, shall include all bases made by a "clean steal," or through a wild throw or muff of the ball by a fielder who is directly trying to put the baserunner out while attempting to steal a base.

Scoring Summary The summary shall contain: (1) The number of earned runs made by each side; (2) The number of two-base hits made by each player; (3) The number of three-base hits made by each player; (4) The number of home runs made by each player; (5) The number of double and triple plays made by each side, with the names of the players assisting in the same; (6) The number of men given bases on called balls by each pitcher; (7) The number of men given bases from being hit by pitched balls; (8) The number of passed balls by each catcher; (9) The number of wild pitches by each pitcher; (10) The time of the game; (11) The name of the umpire.

1888

Batter The first item in the tabulated score, after the player's name and position, shall be the number of times he has been at bat during the game. At any time or times where the player has been sent to base by being hit by a pitched ball by the pitcher's illegal delivery or by a base on balls shall not be included in this column.

That in all cases where a baserunner is retired by being hit by a batted ball, the batsman should be credited with a basehit.

That when a player reaches first base through an error of judgment such as two fielders allowing the ball to drop between them, the batter shall not be credited with a basehit, nor the fielder charged with an error, but it shall be scored as an unaccepted chance, and the batter shall be charged with a time at the bat. Note: This rule was dropped in 1889.

Earned Run An earned run shall be scored every time the player reaches the home base unaided by errors before chances have been offered to retire the side, but bases on balls though summarized as errors, shall be credited as factors in earned runs. Note: This rule was deleted in 1898 but reappears in 1917. Also see 1912.

Runner In the fourth column shall be scored bases stolen, and shall be governed as follows: Any attempt to steal a base must go to the credit of the baserunner, whether the ball is thrown wild or muffed by the fielder, but any manifest error is to be charged to the fielder making the same. If the baserunner advances another base he shall not be credited with a stolen base, and the fielder allowing the advancement is also to be charged with an error. If a baserunner makes a start and a battery error is made, the runner secures the credit of a stolen base, and the battery error is scored against the player making it. Should a baserunner overrun a base and then be put out, he should receive the credit for the stolen base.

Scoring Summary The number of men struck out is added to the scoring summary.

1889

Batter In the fourth column shall be placed sacrifice hits, which shall be credited to the batsman, who when but one man is out

advances a runner a base on a fly to the outfield or a ground hit, which results in putting out the batsman, or would so result if handled without error.

A basehit should be scored when a batted ball hits the person or clothing of the umpire as provided for in the playing rules.

Earned Run   An earned run shall be scored every time the player reaches the home base unaided by errors before chances have been offered to retire the side. Note: See entries under 1888, 1912 and 1917.

Scoring Summary   The number of bases stolen is added to the scoring summary.

1890

Assist   Assistances on strikes are not to be included in the record of fielding assistances.

Earned Run   Earned runs should be charged against the pitcher only on the basis of basehits made off the pitching, and should not include stolen bases or bases scored in any other way.

1891

Scoring Summary   The number of runs batted in by base hits by each batsman is added to the scoring summary.

1892

Runner   The following sentence is added to the 1888 rule for scoring stolen bases: If a baserunner advances a base on a fly out, or gains two bases on a single basehit, or an infield out, or attempted out, he shall be credited with a stolen base, provided there is a possible chance and a palpable attempt made to retire him. Note: This sentence was dropped from the rule in 1897.

1893

There were no changes to the scoring rules this year.

1894

Batter   The batter is not charged with a time at bat for a sacrifice hit purposely made to the infield which advances a runner without resulting in a putout except to the batsman.

A sacrifice hit is to be credited to the batsman who advances a runner with no one out or one out by a bunt sacrifice which results in putting out the batsman. Note: Previously the rule applied only with one out. See 1889.

1895–6

There were no changes to the scoring rules in these years.

1897

Batter   The first item in the tabulated score, after the player's name and position, shall be the number of times he has been at bat during the game. The time or times when the player has been sent to base by being hit by a pitched ball, by the pitcher's illegal delivery or by a base on balls, or has made a sacrifice hit which was manifestly intentional, shall not be included in this column.

In the fourth column shall be placed the sacrifice hits, which shall be credited to the batsman who, when no one is out or when but one man is out, advances a runner a base by a bunt hit, which results in putting out the batsman, or would so result if the ball were handled without error.

Earned Run   An earned run shall be scored every time the player reaches the home base by the aid of basehits only before chances have been offered to retire the side. Note: See entries under 1888, 1912 and 1917.

Runner   The rule regarding stolen bases is now the same as that used between 1888 through 1891. Additional language adopted in 1892 and included through 1896 has been deleted. See 1892.

Scoring Summary   The summary shall contain: (1) The number of earned runs made off each pitcher; (2) The number of two-basehits made by each player; (3) The number of three-basehits made by each player; (4) The number of home runs made by each player; (5) The number of bases stolen by each player; (6) The number of double and triple plays made by each side and the names of the players assisting in the same; (7) The number of men given bases on called balls by each pitcher and the names of the players who were thus given bases; (8) The number of men given bases from being hit by pitched balls by each pitcher and the names of the players who are thus given bases; (9) The number of men struck out by each pitcher and the names of the players struck out; (10) The number of passed balls by each catcher; (11) The number of wild pitches by each pitcher; (12) The number of baserunners left on bases by each side; (13) The number of innings each pitcher played; (14) The number of basehits made off each pitcher; (15) The number of bases on balls given by each pitcher; (16) The number of batsmen hit by each pitcher; (17) The number of batsman struck out by each pitcher (Note: This requirement apparently duplicates Sec. 9 above); (18) The number of baserunners of each side who reached first base by fielding errors; (19) The time it took to play the game; (20) The condition of the weather; (21) The condition of the playing field; (22) The name of the umpire.

1898

Assist   Assists should be credited to every player who handles the ball in the play which results in a baserunner being called out for interference or for running out of line.

Batter   The first item in the tabulated score, after the player's name and position, shall be the number of times he has been at bat during the game. No time at bat shall be scored if the batsman be hit by a pitched ball while standing in his position, and after trying to avoid being so hit, or in case of the pitcher's illegal delivery of the ball to the bat which gives the batsman his base, or when he intentionally hits the ball to the field, purposely to be put out, or if he is given first base on called balls.

A basehit should be scored when a ball is hit with such force to an infielder that he cannot handle it in time to put out the batsman. In case of doubt over this class of hits, score a basehit and exempt the fielder from the charge of an error.

In no case shall a basehit be scored when a baserunner has been forced out by the play.

Error   An error shall be given in the seventh column for each misplay which allows the striker or baserunner to make one or more bases when perfect play would have insured his being put out, except that "wild pitches," "bases on balls," bases on the batsman being struck by a "pitched ball," or in case of illegal pitched balls, balks and passed balls, all of which comprise battery errors, shall not be included in said column. In scoring errors of batted balls see Sec. 3 of this rule.

An error shall not be scored against the catcher for a wild throw to prevent a stolen base, unless the baserunner advances an extra base because of the error.

No error shall be scored against an infielder who attempts to complete a double play, unless the throw is so wild that an additional base is gained.

Put Out   The number of opponents put out by each player shall be set down in the fifth column. Where a batsman is given out by the umpire for a foul strike, or where the batsman fails to bat in proper order, the putout shall be scored to the catcher. In all cases of "out" for interference, running out of line, or infield fly dropped, the "out" should be credited to the player who would have made the play but for the action of the baserunner or batsman.

Runner   A stolen base shall be credited to the baserunner whenever he reaches the base he attempts to steal unaided by a fielding or by a battery error or a hit by the batsman.

Scoring Summary   The summary shall contain: (1) The score made in each innings of the game; (2) The number of bases stolen by each

player; (3) The number of two-base hits made by each player; (4) The number of three-base hits made by each player; (5) The number of home runs made by each player; (6) The number of double and triple plays made by each side and the names of the players assisting in the same; (7) The number of innings each pitcher pitched in; (8) The number of basehits made off each pitcher; (9) The number of times the pitcher strikes out the opposing batsmen; (10) The number of times the pitcher gives bases on balls; (11) The number of wild pitches charged to the pitcher; (12) The number of times the pitcher hits batsmen with pitched ball; (13) The number of passed balls by each catcher; (14) The time of the game; (15) The names and positions of each umpire.

1899–1903

There were no changes to the scoring rules in these years.

1904

Assist   The number of times, if any, each player assists in putting out an opponent shall be set down in the sixth column. An assist should be given to each player who handles the ball in aiding in a run-out or any other play of the kind, except the one who completes it. Note: The rule remains unchanged except to clarify that the fielder completing a run-down play by making the putout is not to be credited with an assist even if he handled the ball prior to receiving it again to make the putout. But see the entry under 1910.

Batter   The first item in the tabulated score, after the player's name and position, shall be the number of times he has been at bat during the game, but the exceptions made in rule 82 must not be included. Note: See rule 82 below.

"A Time at Bat" is the term at-bat of a batsman. It begins when he takes his position, and continues until he is put out or becomes a baserunner. But a time at bat shall not be charged against a batsman who is awarded first base by the umpire for being hit by a pitched ball or for the illegal delivery of the pitcher, or on called balls, or when he makes a sacrifice hit.

A basehit should be scored when the ball is hit so slowly toward a fielder that he cannot handle it in time to put out the batsman or force out a baserunner. Note: The phrase "or force out a baserunner" has been added to the original rule. See 1878.

In the fourth column shall be placed the sacrifice hits. A sacrifice hit shall be credited to the batsman who, when no one is out or when but one man is out, advances a runner a base by a bunt hit, which results in the batsman being put out before reaching first, or would so result if it were handled without error. Note: The phrase "before reaching first" has been added to the rule. See 1889.

Error   An error shall be given in the seventh column for each misplay which prolongs the time at bat of the batsman or allows a baserunner to make one or more bases when perfect play would have insured his being put out. But a wild pitch, a base on balls, a base awarded to a batsman by being struck by a pitched ball, an illegal pitch, a balk and a passed ball, each of which is a battery and not a fielding error, shall not be included in the seventh column.

In case a baserunner advance a base through the failure of a baseman to stop or try to stop a ball accurately thrown to his base, he shall be charged with an error and not the player who made such throw, provided there were occasion for it. If such throw be made to second base, the scorer shall determine whether the second baseman or shortstop shall be charged with an error.

Put Out   The number of opponents, if any, put out by each player shall be set down in the fifth column. Where the batsman is given out by the umpire for a foul strike, or fails to bat in proper order, the putout shall be scored to the catcher. In cases of the baserunner being declared "out" for interference, running out of line, or on an infield fly, the "out" should be credited to the player who would have made the play but for the action of the baserunner or the announcement of the umpire. Note: The phrase "or the announcement of the umpire" has been added in place of "or batsman." See 1898.

Runner   A stolen base shall be credited to the baserunner whenever he advances a base unaided by a basehit, a putout, a fielding or a battery error.

Scoring Summary   The scoring summary is to include the total runs by each side as well as the score made in each inning.

1905–06

There were no changes to the scoring rules in these years.

1907

Batter   In all cases where a baserunner is retired by being hit by a batted ball, unless batted by himself, the batsman should be credited with a basehit.

Player   All appearances by a player in a championship game count as a game played in the American League which prior to 1907 had not so credited the appearances of pinch hitters, pinch runners and defensive substitutes in most cases. See 1912 for National League.

1908

Batter   A sacrifice hit shall be credited to the batsman who, when no one is out or when but one man is out, advances a runner a base by a bunt hit, which results in the batsman being put out before reaching first, or would so result if it were handled without error. A sacrifice hit shall also be credited to a batsman who, when no one is out or when but one man is out, hits a fly ball that is caught but results in a run being scored.

1909

Batter   A sacrifice hit shall be credited to the batsman who, when no one is out or when but one man is out, advances a runner a base by a bunt hit, which results in the batsman being put out before reaching first, or would so result if it were handled without error. A sacrifice hit shall also be credited to a batsman who, when no one is out or when but one man is out, hits a fly ball that is caught but results in a run being scored, or would in the judgment of the scorer so result if caught.

Double Play   A double play shall mean any two continuous putouts that take place between the time the ball leaves the pitcher's hands until it is returned to him again standing in the pitcher's box.

Error   In case a runner advances a base through the failure of a baseman to stop or try to stop a ball accurately thrown to his base, the latter shall be charged with an error and not the player who made such throw, provided there was occasion for it. If such throw be made to second base, the scorer shall determine whether the second baseman or shortstop shall be charged with an error.

An error shall be given in the sixth column for each misplay which prolongs the time at bat of the batsman or allows a baserunner to make one or more bases when perfect play would have insured his being put out. But a base on balls, a base awarded to a batsman by being struck by a pitched ball, an illegal pitch, a balk, a passed ball or wild pitch, unless such wild pitch or passed ball be on the third strike and allow the batter to reach first base, shall not be included in the sixth column. In case of a wild pitch or a passed ball allowing the batter to reach first base, the pitcher or the catcher, as the case may be, shall be charged with an error.

Force Out   In event of a fielder dropping a fly but recovering the ball in time to force a batter at another base, he shall be exempted from an error, the play being scored as a "force-out."

Put Out   The number of opponents, if any, put out by each player shall be set down in the fourth column. Where the batsman is given out by the umpire for a foul strike, or fails to bat in proper order, or is declared out on third bunt strike, the putout shall be scored to the catcher. In cases of the baserunner being declared "out" for interference, running out of line, or on an infield fly, the "out" should be credited to the player who would have made the play but for the action of the baserunner or the announcement of the umpire.

Runner   A stolen base shall be credited to the baserunner whenever he advances a base unaided by a basehit, a putout, a fielding or a battery error, subject to the following exceptions: (1) In event of a double steal being attempted from bases one and two to bases two and three, where either is thrown out, the other shall not be credited with a stolen base; (2) In event of a baserunner being touched out after sliding over a base, he shall not be regarded as having stolen the base in question; (3) In event of a baserunner making his start to steal a base prior to a battery error, he shall be credited with a stolen base; (4) In event of a palpable muff of a ball thrown by the catcher, when the baserunner is clearly blocked, the infielder making the muff shall be charged with an error and the baserunner shall not be credited with a stolen base.

Scoring Summary   The summary shall contain: (1) The score made in each inning of the game and the total runs of each side in the game; (2) The number of stolen bases, if any, by each player; (3) The number of sacrifice hits, if any, made by each player; (4) The number of sacrifice flies, if any, made by each player; (5) The number of two-base hits, if any, made by each player; (6) The number of three-base hits, if any, made by each player; (7) The number of home runs, if any, made by each player; (8) The number of double and triple plays, if any, made by each club and the players participating in same; (9) The number of innings each pitcher pitched in; (10) The number of basehits if any, made off each pitcher and the number of legal at-bats scored against each pitcher; (11) The number of times, if any, the pitcher strikes out the opposing batsmen; (12) The number of times, if any, the pitcher gives bases on balls; (13) The number of wild pitches, if any, charged against the pitcher; (14) The number of times, if any, the pitcher hits a batsman with a pitched ball, the name or names of the batsman or batsmen so hit to be given; (15) The number of passed balls by each catcher; (16) The time of the game; (17) The name of the umpire or umpires.

1910

Assist   The number of times, if any, each player assists in putting out an opponent shall be set down in the fifth column. An assist should be given to each player who handles the ball in aiding in a run-out or any other play of the kind, even though he complete the play by making the putout. Note: Compare to the 1904 rule.

Error   An error shall be given in the sixth column for each misplay which prolongs the time at bat of the batsman or allows a baserunner to make one or more bases when perfect play would have insured his being put out. But a base on balls, a base awarded to a batsman by being struck by a pitched ball, a balk, a passed ball or wild pitch shall not be included in the sixth column.

Passed Ball   A passed ball is a legally delivered ball that the catcher should hold or control with ordinary effort, but his failure to do so enables the batsman, who becomes a baserunner on such pitched ball, to reach first base or a baserunner to advance.

Runner   In event of a double or triple steal being attempted, where either runner is thrown out, the other or others shall not be credited with a stolen base.

Wild Pitch   A wild pitch is a legally delivered ball, so high, low or wide of the plate that the catcher cannot or does not stop and control it with ordinary effort, and as a result the batsman, who becomes a baserunner on such pitched ball, reaches first base or a baserunner advances.

1911

There were no changes to the scoring rules this year.

1912

Earned Run   An earned run is charged to the pitcher every time a player scores by the aid of safe hits, sacrifice hits, bases on balls, hit batters, wild pitches and balks before fielding chances have been offered to retire the side. Note: This rule is not included in the scoring rules for 1912 but earned runs were compiled in the official pitching

records of the National League (1912) and American League (1913). The earned run scoring rule does not appear in the scoring rules until 1917.

Player   All appearances by a player in a championship game count as a game played in the National League which prior to 1912 had not so credited the appearances of pinch hitters, pinch runners and defensive substitutes with certain exceptions.

1913

There were no changes to the scoring rules this year.

1914

Assist   The number of times, if any, each player assists in putting out an opponent shall be set down in the fifth column. One assist and no more shall be given to each player who handles the ball in aiding in a run-out or any other play of the kind even though he complete the play by making the putout. Note: Compare to 1910 and 1904.

Batter   A sacrifice hit shall also be credited to a batsman who, when no one is out or when but one man is out, hits a fly ball that is caught but results in a run being scored on the catch, or would in the judgment of the scorer so result if caught.

When a fielder after handling a batted ball, elects to try to retire a baserunner instead of the batter, the play is known as a "fielder's choice." In case the runner is retired, or would be retired but for an error, the batter shall be charged with a time at bat, but no hit. If the runner is not retired, and no error is made, the batter shall be charged with a time at bat, but no hit, provided he swung at the ball, and shall be credited with a sacrifice hit, provided he bunted the ball; if, however, in the judgment of the scorer, the batter could not have been retired at first base by perfect fielding, he shall be credited with a basehit.

A basehit should be scored when the ball from the bat strikes the ground on or within the foul lines and out of reach of the fielders, provided the batter reaches first base safely.

Error   In event of a baserunner making his start to steal a base prior to a battery error, he shall be credited with a stolen base and the battery error shall also be charged.

An error shall not be scored against the catcher or an infielder who attempts to complete a double play, unless the throw be so wild that an additional base be gained. This, however, does not exempt from an error a player who drops a thrown ball when by holding it he would have completed a double play.

An error shall be given in the sixth column for each misplay which prolongs the time at bat of the batsman or prolongs the life of the baserunner or allows a baserunner to make one or more bases when perfect play would have insured his being put out. But a base on balls, a base awarded to a batsman by being struck with a pitched ball, a balk, a passed ball or wild pitch shall not be included in the sixth column. Note: The phrase "or prolongs the life of the baserunner" has been added to the existing rule.

1915–16

There were no changes to the scoring rules in these years.

1917

Earned Run   A run earned off the pitcher shall be scored every time a player reaches home base by the aid of safe hits, sacrifice hits, stolen bases, bases on balls, hit batsmen, wild pitches and balks, before fielding chances have been offered to retire the side.

The pitcher shall be given the benefit of doubt whenever fielding errors are made and in determining the base to which a runner should have been held with perfect support on part of fielders. A fielding error made by the pitcher shall be considered the same as any other fielding error. No run can be earned that scores as a result of the batsman having reached first base on a fielding error or passed ball; nor can any run be earned after the fielding side has failed to accept chances offered to retire the side.

To determine the pitcher's percentage for the season, the total

number of runs earned off his pitching shall be divided by the total number of innings he has pitched; then multiplied by nine, to find his average effectiveness for a complete game.

1918–19

There were no changes to the scoring rules in these years.

1920

Batter   A sacrifice hit shall also be credited to a batsman who, when no one is out or when but one man is out, hits a fly ball that is caught but results in a run being scored on the catch, or would in the judgment of the scorer so result if caught; but no distinction shall be made in the summary as between bunted or fly-ball sacrifices.

If, in the last half of the final inning, with the winning run on base, the batsman drives home that run, credit shall be given him for as many bases on his hit as the runner advances; except, however, that in case of the batsman driving a fair ball out of the playing field, he shall receive credit for a home run.

Error   An error shall be charged to the first baseman if, on receiving a throw in ample time to retire the batsman, he fail to touch first base.

An error shall be charged to the catcher if he drop a third strike, allowing the runner to reach first base; except this rule is not to apply in case of a wild pitch.

Runner   No stolen base shall be credited to a runner who is allowed to advance without any effort being made to stop him.

Scoring Summary   The scoring summary is to include sacrifice flies (within the category of sacrifice hits) and the number of runs batted in by each batsman.

Statistics   To determine the percentage of games won and lost, divide the total number of games won and lost into the number won.

To determine batting averages, divide the total "Times at Bat" into the total number of basehits.

To determine fielding averages, divide the total of putouts, assists and errors into the total of putouts and assists.

In all cases where the remaining fraction is one-half or over, a point is added to the average.

1921–25

There were no changes to the scoring rules in these years.

1926

Error   An error shall be charged to the pitcher if he make a wild pitch for the third strike, and the batsman reach first base and in such case the pitcher shall not have credit for a strikeout.

Passed Ball   The catcher shall be charged with a passed ball when a baserunner is enabled to advance by the catcher's failure to hold or control a legally delivered ball that should have been held or controlled with ordinary effort.

Wild Pitch   A wild pitch is a legally delivered ball, so high, low or wide of the plate that the catcher cannot or does not stop and control it with ordinary effort, and as a result the batsman reaches first base or a baserunner advances.

1927–30

There were no changes to the scoring rules in these years.

1931

Assist   Credit an assist to a player who, by deflecting a batted ball with his glove or any part of his body, aids in retiring the batsman or another baserunner.

Credit an assist to each player who handles and throws the ball in such a way that a putout would have resulted except for the error of a teammate.

Do not credit an assist to a fielder who makes a bad throw, even when a runner trying to advance on it is subsequently retired. A play

that follows an error is a new play and the player making an error is not entitled to an assist unless he takes part in the new play.

Do not credit an assist to the pitcher when, in legally delivering the ball to the batsman, he helps to retire a runner attempting to steal home.

Batter   A "Time at Bat" is the term at bat of a batsman. It begins when he takes his position, and continues until he is put out or becomes a baserunner. But a time at bat shall not be charged against a batsman who is awarded first base by the umpire for being hit by a pitched ball, or on called balls, or when he makes a sacrifice hit, or for interference by the catcher. Note: This rule is Rule 69, Sec. 5 of the Playing Rules.

Batter   The first item in the tabulated score, after the player's name and position, shall be the number of times he has been at bat during the game, but the exceptions made in Rule 69, Sec. 5, must not be included. Note: See above entry for Rule 69, Sec. 5 of the Playing Rules.

If, in the last half of the final inning, with the winning run on base, the batsman drives home that run, credit shall be given him for as many bases as, in the judgment of the official scorer, he would have made under normal conditions; the number, however, not to exceed the number of bases advanced by the runner; except when the batsman drives a fair ball out of the playing field, he shall receive credit for a home run, provided he legally touches each base in proper order.

A basehit shall be scored in the following cases: (1) When a fair hit is made, as defined in the Playing Rules, and the batsman reaches first base safely; (2) When a fair hit ball is partially or wholly stopped by a fielder in motion, but such player cannot recover himself in time to field the ball to first before the batsman reaches that base, or to some other base in time to force out another runner; (3) When a ball is hit with such force to an infielder or pitcher that he cannot handle it in time to put out the batsman or force out a baserunner; except when the ball is recovered by another fielder in time to retire the batsman or force out a baserunner. In case of doubt over this kind of hit, a basehit should be scored and the fielder be exempted from the charge of an error.

When a batsman is hit by what would have been the fourth called ball, it shall be scored as a "hit by pitcher."

Earned Run   A run earned off the pitcher shall be scored every time a player reaches home base by the aid of safe hits, sacrifice hits, stolen bases, putouts, bases on balls, hit batsman, wild pitches or balks, before fielding chances have been offered to retire the side.

The pitcher shall be given the benefit of doubt whenever fielding errors are made and in determining the base to which a runner should have been held with perfect support on part of fielders. A fielding error made by the pitcher shall be considered the same as any other fielding error. No run can be earned that scores as a result of the batsman having reached first base on a catcher's interference, a fielding error or passed ball; nor can any run be earned after the fielding side has failed to accept chances offered to retire the side. Note: The phrase "catcher's interference" has been added to the prior rule. See entry for 1917.

Error   An error, but not a passed ball, shall be charged to the catcher if he drops or misses a third strike, allowing the batsman to reach first base. Credit the pitcher with a strikeout.

An error shall be charged to the first baseman (or the pitcher or second baseman when covering first base) if, on receiving a throw in ample time to retire the batsman, he does not touch first base as required by rule. The same rule shall be followed with respect to any fielder covering any other base on a force play.

Official Records   In a regulation game which the umpire shall declare forfeited after four and one-half innings have been played, all individual and team averages shall be incorporated in the official playing records.

Put Out   The number of opponents, if any, put out by each player

shall be set down in the fourth column. When the batsman is called out by the umpire for an illegally batted ball, or for a foul third strike bunt, or for being hit by own batted ball, or for interference with the catcher, or for failing to bat in proper turn, the putout shall be credited to the catcher. When a baserunner is declared out on an infield fly, the putout shall be credited to the player who would have made the play except for the action of the runner or the announcement of the umpire. When a baserunner is declared out because of being hit by a batted ball, the putout shall be credited to the fielder nearest to the ball at the time of the occurrence.

Run Batted In   Runs batted in should include runs scored on safe hits (including home runs), sacrifice hits, infield outs, and when the run is forced over by reason of batsman becoming a baserunner. With less than two out, if an error is made on a play on which a runner from third would ordinarily score, credit the batsman with a run batted in.

Runner   In the event of a palpable muff of a ball thrown by the catcher, when, in the judgment of the scorer, the baserunner would have been out if the ball had been held, the infielder making the muff shall be charged with an error and the baserunner shall not be credited with a stolen base.

When a wild pitch or a passed ball occurs after a runner has started to steal, do not credit the runner with a stolen base but charge the wild pitch or passed ball.

Do not give a stolen base to a runner who has started to steal and the pitcher balks.

Statistics   In determining averages where the remaining fraction is one-half or over, a full point is to be added to the average.

Wild Pitch   A wild pitch is a legally delivered ball, so high, low or wide of the plate that the catcher cannot or does not stop and control it with ordinary effort, and as a result the batsman reaches first base or a baserunner advances. Any pitched ball that strikes the ground before reaching the home plate and passes the catcher, allowing runners to advance, shall be scored as a wild pitch.

1932–38

There were no changes to the scoring rules in these years.

1939

Batter   In event of a batsman oversliding second or third bases and being tagged by the opposing fielder when said batsman is attempting to stretch a single into a two-base hit or a two-base hit into a three-base hit, the play should be scored the same as when a baserunner attempts to steal, overslides the base and is tagged out. In other words, the batsman oversliding second base and is tagged out shall be credited only with a single, while one who overslides third base and is tagged out shall be credited only with a two-base hit.

A sacrifice hit also shall be credited to the batsman who, when no one is out or when but one man is out, hits a fly ball that is caught but which results in a baserunner scoring, or would have scored a runner if said fly ball had not been dropped for an error, in the judgment of the scorer; but no distinction shall be made in the summary as between bunted or fly ball sacrifices.

Earned Run   A wild pitch which is a third strike is to be used in determining earned runs charged to the pitcher.

Run Batted In   The batsman shall not be credited with driving in a run when a runner scores as he hits into a force infield double play or a double play in which the first baseman picks up a fair hit ground ball, touches first base and then throws to second retiring the runner who had been on first, said runner not being forced, has to be tagged out.

1940

Earned Run   A run earned off the pitcher shall be scored every time a player reaches home base by the aid of safe hits, sacrifice hits, stolen bases, putouts, bases on balls, hit batsman, wild pitches or balks, even though the wild pitch be a third strike, before fielding

chances have been offered to retire the team. The preceding pitcher, and not a relieving pitcher shall be charged with runs scored by any runners on base when such relief pitcher entered the game. The relieving pitcher shall not be charged with his first batsman reaching first base if such batsman had any advantage because of poor pitching by the preceding pitcher. With the count two or three balls and one or no strikes, or three balls and two strikes, charge preceding pitcher if batsman reaches first base, but credit relieving pitcher if batsman is retired. With count one or two balls and two strikes, charge relieving pitcher if batsman reaches first base and credit him if batsman is retired.

Runner   In all cases where a baserunner is retired by being hit by a batted ball, unless batted by himself, the batsman should be credited with a basehit, except if the runner is hit by an infield fly, the play should be scored as provided in the Playing Rules (Sec. 8 of Rule 44).

Official Records   In a regulation game which the umpire shall declare forfeited after four and one-half innings have been played, all individual and team averages shall be incorporated in the official playing records, except that no pitcher shall be credited with a victory or charged with a loss in said game.

1941–49

There were no changes to the scoring rules in these years.

1950

Assist   An assist shall be credited to each player who throws or deflects a batted or thrown ball in such a way that a putout results, or would have resulted except for a subsequent error by a teammate, but only one assist and no more shall be credited to each player who throws or deflects the ball in a rundown play which results in a putout, or would have resulted in a putout, except for a subsequent error.

Credit an assist to each player who throws or deflects the ball during a play which results in a baserunner being called out for interference, or for running out of line.

Do not credit an assist to a pitcher when, in legally delivering the ball to a batter, he helps to retire a baserunner attempting to steal home.

Situations will arise in which a wild throw shall be scored as an assist and not as an error while on some plays a wild throw shall be scored both as an assist and as an error. Note: The scoring rules for 1950 then present four detailed examples illustrating the application of the assist provisions.

Batter   A basehit shall be scored under these circumstances: (1) When a batter reaches first base (or any succeeding base) safely on a legally batted ball which settles on fair ground or strikes a fence behind fair ground before being touched by a fielder, or which clears a fence behind fair territory; (2) When a batter reaches first base after hitting a ball with such force, or so slowly, that the pitcher or fielder attempting to make a play with it has no opportunity to do so; (3) When a batter reaches first base safely on a batted ball which strikes either first base, second or third base before being touched by a fielder and bounces away from the reach of the fielder; (4) When a batter reaches first base safely on a legally batted ball which has not been touched by a fielder and which is in fair territory when it bounds into the outfield unless in the scorer's judgment it could have been handled with ordinary effort; (5) When a legally batted ball which has not been touched by a fielder becomes "dead" by reason of touching the person or clothing of a runner or umpire, except that when a runner is called out for having been struck by an "infield fly" the batter shall not be credited with a hit; (6) When, in the scorer's judgment, the batter could not have been retired at first base by perfect fielding, when the fielder fails in an attempt to retire a preceding baserunner; (7) Always give the batter the benefit of the doubt. A safe course to follow being to score a hit when exceptionally good fielding of a batted ball fails to result in a putout; (8) In no case shall a basehit be scored when a runner is forced out by a batted ball, or would have been forced out except for a fielding error. Nor shall a

hit be scored when an infield batted ball results in another runner, who is attempting to advance one base, being retired, whether forced out or not; (9) Score the play as a "fielder's choice" when a fielder uses a batted ball to retire a preceding baserunner, or would have retired one with ordinary effort except for a fielding error, charging the batter with time at bat, but no hit.

Whether a safe hit shall be scored as a one-base hit, two-base hit or a three-base hit when no error or putout results shall be determined as follows:

It is a one-base hit if the batter stops at first base; it is a two-base hit if the batter stops at second base; it is a three-base hit if the batter stops at third base, but note this exception: the batter must, if attempting to take two or three bases on a safe hit by sliding, hold the last base to which he advances. If he overslides and is tagged out before getting back to the base safely he shall be given credit for only as many bases as he safely attained. If he overslides second base and is tagged out he shall be given a one-base hit; if he overslides third base and is tagged out, he shall be given a two-base hit. If he runs past second base after reaching that base on his feet, attempts to return and is tagged out, he shall be given credit for a two-base hit. If he runs past third base after reaching that base on his feet, attempts to return and is tagged out, he shall be given credit for a three-base hit.

If a batter is awarded three bases on a batted or bunted ball because a fielder has touched the ball with his glove, cap or any other part of his uniform while such article is detached from its proper place on his person, the scorer's judgment shall dictate whether the batter shall be given credit for a one-base hit, a two-base hit, a three-base hit or a home run. If the scorer believes the fielder could have, by ordinary effort, kept the hit from being good for more than one, two or three bases he shall score it as a one-base hit or as a two-base hit or as a three-base hit and charge the fielder with an error. If, however, the scorer believes the hit would have been a legitimate home run, despite illegal use of equipment, he shall so score it if the batter touches all bases in the proper order.

In no instance shall the batter be credited with a two-base hit or a three-base hit if he fail to advance a preceding runner whose advance is necessary to permit the batter to reach second or third base. Example: Runner on first, batter makes a long hit and reaches second but runner is thrown out at third. Score a one-base hit and credit batter with reaching second on the play.

When a batter ends a game with a safe hit, other than a home run, which drives in as many runs as are necessary to put his team in the lead, he shall be credited with only as many bases on his hit as are advanced by the runner who scores the winning run, and then only if the batter runs out his hit for as many bases as are advanced by the runner who scores the winning run, touching each base in the proper order.

If a batter ends a game with a home run out of the playing field and touches all the bases in their proper order, his run, and also the runs of all other runners who were on base when the home run was hit, shall count in the final score even though this gives the team last at bat a winning margin in excess of one run.

Should a batter, after making a safe hit, be called out for having failed to touch a base, the last base he reached safely shall determine if his hit is scored as a one-base hit, a two-base hit or a three-base hit. If he is called out for missing second base the hit shall be scored as a one-base hit. If he is called out for missing third base, his hit shall be scored as a two-base hit. If he is tagged out after missing home base, his hit shall be scored as a three-base hit. If he is called out for missing first base he shall be charged with a time at bat but no hit.

Score a sacrifice if, with less than two out, the batter advances one or more runners with a bunt and is retired at first base, or would have been retired except for a fielding error. In case a runner is forced out at any base on a bunt, it shall be scored as a time at bat but no sacrifice.

A base on balls shall be scored whenever a batter is awarded first base by the umpire because of four balls having been pitched outside the strike zone, but when the fourth such ball strike the batter it shall

be scored as a "hit batter."

A strikeout shall be scored whenever a pitcher delivers three legal pitches at which the batter swings and misses, or which the umpire decrees are strikes even though the batter may reach first base safely after the third strike by reason of a wild pitch or the catcher's failure to hold the ball.

A strikeout shall be scored whenever a batter bunts foul when there are two strikes against him, except that should the bunt result in a foul fly caught by the catcher or any other player it shall not be scored as a strikeout but as a regular foul-fly putout.

When a batter goes out of the game with two strikes against him and the substitute batter completes a strikeout, score it as a strikeout for the first batter. If the substitute batter completes the turn at bat in any other manner, score the action as having been that of the substitute batter.

Championship To be eligible for the individual batting championship of any minor league, a player must have appeared in at least two-thirds of the games played by his team. Thus, if a team plays 154 games, a player must appear in 102 games. If his team plays 150 games he must appear in 100. If his team plays 140 games he must appear in 93, etc.

To be eligible for the individual batting championship of a major league, a player must be credited with at least 400 official "times at bat."

Double Play A double play is any two successive putouts which take place between the time a ball leaves a pitcher's hand and is returned to him while he is standing in the pitcher's box.

Earned Run An earned run is a run for which the pitching is held accountable.

An earned run shall be scored every time a player reaches home base by the aid of safe hits, sacrifices, stolen bases, putouts, bases on balls, hit batters, balks or wild pitches (even though a wild pitch be a third strike which enables a batter to reach first base), before fielding chances have been offered to retire the offensive team.

Since a wild pitch on which a batter reaches first base is the pitcher's fault, solely, even though it is scored as a fielding error, it shall be disregarded as an error and considered as a wild pitch in computing earned runs and is the only instance in which an error is so disregarded.

In computing earned runs, any type of fielding error made by a pitcher (other than the one mentioned in the preceding two paragraphs) shall be considered in the same light as an error by any other fielder.

Whenever a fielding error occurs the pitcher shall be given the benefit of the doubt in determining to which bases any baserunners would have advanced had the fielding by the defensive team been errorless.

No run can be earned which scores as a result of a batter having reached first base safely because of a catcher's interference, or because of any fielding error, except a wild pitch.

When pitchers are changed during an inning, the preceding pitcher, and not the relieving pitcher, shall be charged with any earned or unearned runs scored by any runners on base when such relief pitcher entered the game. There is, however, this exception: If the action of any batter to whom the relieving pitcher pitches results in the retirement of a runner left on base by the preceding pitcher, the batter whose action resulted in the retirement of that runner shall be considered as having been left on base by the preceding pitcher and any run scored by such runner shall be charged to the preceding pitcher.

A relieving pitcher shall not be held accountable for the first batter to whom he pitches reaching first base if that batter had a decided advantage because of ineffective pitching by the pitcher whom the relieving pitcher succeeded. Thus, if the count is two or three balls and one or no strikes, or if the count is three balls and two strikes when pitchers are changed, and the batter reaches first base safely, charge that batter to the pitcher who was replaced. If such a batter is retired, or would have been retired except for a fielding error, the

batter shall be credited to the relieving pitcher. Likewise, if such a batter hits into a force-out or into a fielder's choice on which a runner is retired, or would have been retired except for a fielding error, credit the action of such a batter to the relieving pitcher. (The foregoing sentence is not to be construed as affecting or conflicting with the exception noted.) If pitchers are changed when the count is two balls and one or no strikes, or one ball and one or no strikes, the relieving pitcher shall be held accountable for whatever the batter does.

Error An error shall be scored for each misplay (fumble, muff or wild throw) which prolongs the time at bat of a batter, or which prolongs the life of a runner, or which permits a runner to advance one or more bases when perfect play would have resulted in the batter or the runner being retired.

Certain misplays by the catcher and pitcher known as "passed balls" and "wild pitches" are not errors but items for the summary and are defined elsewhere in these rules.

Errors are not charged when a batter is awarded first base because of a base on balls, or for being struck by a pitched ball, or if a runner, or runners, advance because of a passed ball or because of the pitcher making a balk or a wild pitch, except: If a batter swings at a wild pitch for his third strike and thereby is enabled to reach first base, it shall be scored as a strikeout and also as an error for the pitcher and not a wild pitch; when a catcher muffs a third strike, thereby permitting a batter to reach first base, it shall be scored as an error for the catcher, not a passed ball, and as a strikeout.

No error shall be charged against the catcher or any other player for making a wild throw in attempting to prevent a stolen base or any other advance by a runner, unless the scorer is convinced such wild throw permitted the runner to advance one or more bases. If the wild throw permits a runner to advance an extra base, or bases, one error shall be charged to the player making the wild throw.

When any player throws wildly in attempting to complete a double play, or a triple play, no error shall be scored unless the throw is so wild that at least one additional base be gained. However, if a fielder muff a thrown ball which, if held, would have completed a double play or a triple play, score an error for the player who drops the ball.

An error shall be scored against any player who, on receiving a thrown ball in ample time to retire a batter or any other baserunner on a force play, does not touch the base as required by the rules.

When a runner advances because of the failure of a fielder to stop, or try to stop, an accurately thrown ball, the fielder failing to stop the ball shall be charged with an error and not the player making the throw, provided there was occasion for the throw. If such throw be made to second base the scorer shall determine whether it was the duty of the second baseman or the shortstop to stop the ball, and he shall charge the error to the negligent player.

No error shall be scored if any fielder, after dropping a fly ball, a line drive or a thrown ball recovers the ball in time to force out a runner at another base.

Accurately directed throws, especially from the outfield, which strike a baserunner or an umpire, or which take an unnatural bounce and permit a baserunner or baserunners to advance, shall be scored as errors for the player making the throw, even though it appears to be doing an injustice to the thrower. Every base advanced by a baserunner must be accounted for.

Passed Ball A catcher shall be charged with a passed ball when a runner, or runners, advance because of the catcher's failure to hold or to control a legally pitched ball which should have been held or controlled with ordinary effort.

Pitcher Determining the winning and losing pitcher of a game often calls for much careful consideration.

Do not give the starting pitcher credit for a game won, even if the score is in his favor, unless he has pitched at least five innings when replaced.

The five-inning rule to determine a winning pitcher shall be in effect for all games of six or more innings. When a game is called after five innings of play the starting pitcher must have pitched at least four innings to be credited with the victory.

If the starting pitcher is replaced (except in a five-inning game) before he has pitched five complete innings when his team is ahead, remains ahead to win, and more than one relief pitcher is used by his team, the scorer shall credit the victory (as among all relieving pitchers) to the pitcher whom the scorer considers to have done the most effective pitching. If, in a five-inning game, the starting pitcher is replaced before pitching four complete innings when his team is ahead, remains ahead to win, and more than one relief pitcher is used by his team, the scorer shall credit the victory (as among all relieving pitchers) to the pitcher whom the scorer considers to have done the most effective pitching.

Regardless of how many innings the first pitcher has pitched, he shall be charged with the loss of the game if he is replaced when his team is behind in the score, and his team thereafter fails to either tie the score or gain the lead.

If a pitcher retires from the game for a substitute batter, or a substitute runner, after pitching five or more innings and his team scores enough runs in the inning in which he is replaced to take the lead, those runs shall be credited to his benefit. Thus, if a pitcher is removed for a substitute batter or a substitute baserunner in any inning after the pitcher has pitched at least five complete innings and during the inning in which he is removed his team assumes the lead, he shall be credited with the victory if his team remains ahead until the finish of the game.

Examples: If the pitcher of the team first at bat is removed in the first half of the sixth inning for a substitute batter, or a substitute runner, and his team gains the lead in that inning and the relieving pitcher holds the lead through the last half of the ninth inning, the pitcher who was removed shall be credited with the victory; if the pitcher of the team last at bat is removed in the last half of the fifth inning for a substitute batter, or a substitute runner, and his team gains the lead in that inning with the relieving pitcher holding the lead through the ninth inning, the pitcher who was removed shall be credited with the victory.

In giving a pitcher credit for the number of innings pitched divide each inning into three parts. Thus, if a pitcher is replaced, with one opponent out, in the sixth inning the pitcher so replaced shall be credited with having pitched 5⅓ innings. If a pitcher is replaced with none out in the opposing team's sixth inning he shall be credited with having pitched 5 innings and a notation made to the effect that there were none out in the sixth inning.

Put Out A putout shall be recorded each time a defensive player catches a fly ball, whether fair or foul, a line drive or a thrown ball which retires a batter or runner, or when a fielder tags a runner with the ball when the runner is off the base to which he legally is entitled.

Automatic putouts shall be credited to the catcher as follows: (1) When a batter is called out by the umpire for an illegally batted ball; when a batter is called out by the umpire for bunting foul for his third strike; when a batter is called out by an umpire for being struck by his own batted ball; when a batter is called out by an umpire for interfering with the catcher; when a batter is called out by an umpire for failing to bat in his proper turn. (Note exception in 10.14 (a).) (2) Other automatic putouts shall be credited as follows: (3) When a batter is called out on an infield fly which is not caught, the putout shall be credited to the fielder whom the scorer believes could have made the putout; (4) When a runner is called out for being struck by a fair ball (including an infield fly) the putout shall be credited to the fielder nearest the ball; (5) When a runner is declared out by an umpire for running out of line to avoid being tagged by the ball in the hands of a fielder, the putout shall be credited to the fielder whom the runner avoided; (6) When a runner is declared out by the umpire for having interfered with a fielder, credit the putout to the fielder with whom the runner interfered, unless the fielder was in the act of throwing the ball when interfered with, in which case the putout shall be credited to the fielder for whom the throw was intended, and the fielder whose throw was interfered with shall be credited with an assist.

Runs Batted In A run batted in is a run which reaches home base safely because of a safe hit, sacrifice hit, infield putout or outfield putout, or which is forced over home plate by reason of the batter being struck by a pitched ball, or being awarded a base on balls, or being awarded first base because of interference by the catcher. If a batter hit a home run with the bases empty, score both a home run and a run batted in. If, with less than two out, an error is made on a play on which a runner from third base ordinarily would score and does score, credit the batter with a run batted in.

The batter shall not be credited with a run batted in if a run scores when he hits into a force double play, or into a double play in which the first baseman fields a fair hit ground ball, touches first base ahead of the batter for an out, then throws to second or third base retiring a second runner who has to be tagged.

Runner A stolen base shall be credited to a runner whenever he advances one base unaided by a base hit, a putout, a forceout, a fielder's choice, a passed ball, a wild pitch or a balk, subject to the following exceptions:

If a double or triple steal is attempted and one runner is thrown out before reaching and holding the base he is attempting to steal, no other runner shall be credited with a stolen base;

A runner who is touched out after oversliding a base shall not be regarded as having stolen that base.

If it is the scorer's judgment that a palpable muff of a thrown ball prevents a runner who is attempting to steal from being retired, it shall be scored as an error for the player muffing the throw, an assist for the player throwing the ball, and not a stolen base.

No stolen base shall be scored when a runner advances solely because of the defensive team's indifference to his advancement.

If a runner advances while the defensive team, unsuccessfully, is attempting to retire another runner who, in attempting to steal, evades being put out in a rundown play and returns to the base he originally occupied, a stolen base shall be credited to the runner who so advances.

If a runner has started for a succeeding base before the pitcher delivers the ball and the pitch results in a wild pitch or a passed ball, credit the runner with a stolen base with this exception: If another runner also advances because of the pitch becoming a wild pitch or passed ball, the wild pitch or passed ball also shall be scored.

If a runner, attempting to steal, is well advanced toward the base he is attempting to steal and a balk is called on the pitcher, credit the runner with a stolen base and do not score the balk unless another runner who is not attempting to steal is advanced by the balk. Note: This paragraph was dropped in 1951.

Scorer The scorer is an actual official of the game he is scoring, is an accredited representative of the league, is entitled to the respect and dignity of his office and shall be accorded full protection by the president of the league.

The scorer shall report to the President of the league any indignity expressed by manager, player, club employee or club official in the course of, or as the result of, the discharge of his duties.

To promote uniformity in keeping the records of championship games scorers shall conform to the instructions of this scoring code.

Scoring Summary In making a box score of a game, each player's name and the fielding position or positions he has played shall be listed in the order in which he batted, or would have batted if the game ends before he gets to bat, followed by a tabulated record of each player's batting and fielding. (a) The first column shall show the number of times each player batted during the game, but no time at bat shall be charged against a player when he is awarded first base on four called balls, for being hit by a pitched ball, or because of being interfered with by the catcher, or for being obstructed by the catcher or any other player, while en route to first base. A sacrifice also exempts a player from being charged with a time at bat. (b) The second column shall show the number of runs, if any, made by each player. (c) The third column shall show the number of safe hits, if any, made by each player. (d) The fourth column shall show the number of putouts, if any, made by each player. (e) The fifth column shall show the number of fielding assists, if any, made by each player. (f) The sixth column shall show the number of fielding errors, if any, made by each player. (g) All players inserted into each team's lineup as substitute batters or substitute runners shall be so designated by special symbols plus notations at the bottom of their team's tabulated record. The symbols a, b, c, d, etc., are recommended. It also is recommended that the notations should describe what the extra batters did, such as—a-Singled for_____in sixth inning; b-Flied out for_____in third inning; c-Forced_____for_____in seventh inning; d-Grounded out for_____in ninth inning. (h) The score by innings of each team follows the box score tabulations and precedes the summary in which should be listed the following items in this order: (1) Runs batted in; (2) Two-base hits; (3) Three-base hits; (4) Home runs, together with the names of the pitchers off whom hit; (5) Stolen bases; (6) Sacrifices; (7) Double plays; (8) Triple plays; (9) Number of runners left on base by each team; (10) Number of bases on balls issued by each pitcher; (11) Number of batters struck out by each pitcher. These shall be listed as "strikeouts"; (12) Number of hits and runs (also earned runs) allowed by each pitcher (if one or both teams use more than one pitcher), together with the number of innings pitched by each pitcher. If a team uses only one pitcher, list the number of earned runs he allowed; (13) The names of any hit batters together with the names of the pitchers who hit them, if a team uses more than one pitcher; (14) The number of wild pitches made; (15) The number of passed balls made by the catchers; (16) The name of the winning pitcher, if the winning team uses more than one pitcher; (17) The name of the losing pitcher, if the losing team uses more than one pitcher; (18) The names of the umpires, listed in this order: (a) plate umpire; (b) first base umpire; (c) second base umpire; (d) third base umpire; (19) The time of game with any delays for rain, fog, snow, light failure or violent wind storm deducted; (20) All individual and team records of any forfeited or tied game which has reached or exceeded legal length when ended shall become a part of the official averages except that no pitcher shall be credited with a victory or charged with a defeat; (21) A box score is in balance (or proved) when the total of a team's times at bat, bases on balls received, hit batters, sacrifices and batters awarded first base because of interference or obstruction equals the total of that team's runs, players left on base and the other team's putouts.

Squeeze Play "Squeeze play" is the term designating a play when a team, with a runner on third base, attempts to score that runner by means of a bunt. It also is a "squeeze play" if an attempt is made to score a runner from second base by means of a bunt.

Statistics To determine a pitcher's earned run prevention average for a season the total number of earned runs charged against his pitching shall be divided by the total number of innings he has pitched then multiplied by nine to find his average effectiveness for a complete game.

(a) To determine the percentage of games won and lost divide the total number of games won and lost into the number won.

(b) To determine a batting average, divide the total "times at bat" into the total number of safe hits.

(c) To determine a slugging percentage, divide the total "times at bat" into the total bases of all safe hits.

(d) To determine a fielding average, divide the total of putouts, assists and errors into the total of putouts and assists.

Triple Play A triple play is any three successive putouts which take place between the time a ball leaves a pitcher's hand and is returned to him while he is standing in the pitcher's box.

Wild Pitch A wild pitch shall be scored when a legally delivered ball is so high, or so wide, or so low that the catcher does not stop and control the ball by ordinary effort and, as a result, a runner, or runners, advance.

Any legally pitched ball which strikes the ground before reaching home plate and passes the catcher, permitting a runner, or runners, to advance shall be scored as a wild pitch.

1951

Batter Score a sacrifice if, with less than two out, the batter advances one or more runners with a bunt and is retired at first base, or would have been retired except for a fielding error. In case a runner is forced out at any base on a bunt, it shall be scored as a time at bat but no sacrifice. Also score a sacrifice if, with less than two out, the fielders handle a bunted ball without error in attempting to force a preceding runner but fail to do so. Exception: When such an attempt is made to turn a bunt into a force-out of a preceding runner and fails and it is the scorer's judgment that perfect play would not have retired the batter at first base, it shall be scored as a one-base hit and not as a sacrifice.

When a batter apparently hits safely and a runner who is obliged to advance by reason of the batter becoming a baserunner misses touching the first base to which he is advancing and is called out on appeal, charge the batter with a time at bat but no hit.

Catcher When records are kept of players caught stealing by catchers, credit the catcher with preventing a stolen base each time he traps a runner off any base with a thrown ball and, as a result of such throw, the runner is retired or would have been except for a subsequent error by any fielder, including the catcher. Runners who are retired in rundown plays started by the catcher trapping a runner off any base, or whose base running life is prolonged by an error after they have been trapped off base by the catcher, are to be included among those prevented from stealing by the catcher.

Error If a batter is awarded first base by an umpire because of interference by the catcher, charge the catcher with an error; if an umpire awards a runner or runners one or more bases because of interference or obstruction by any defensive player, charge the player who committed the interference or obstruction with one error, no matter how many bases the runner or runners are advanced.

An error is to be charged when a fielder, in violation of the playing rules, touches a thrown ball with his cap, glove or uniform while such article is detached from its proper place.

Pitcher Determining the winning and losing pitcher of a game in which a team uses more than one pitcher often calls for careful consideration. Scorers can be guided by these rules: (1) Credit the starting pitcher with a game won only if he has pitched at least five complete innings and his team not only is in the lead when he is replaced but remains in the lead the remainder of the game; (2) The "must pitch five complete innings" rule in respect to the starting pitcher shall be in effect for all games of six or more innings. When a game is ended after five innings of play the starting pitcher must have pitched at least four complete innings to be credited with a victory. As stated in 10.16 (a) the starting pitcher in a five-inning game can be credited with a victory only if his team is in the lead when he is replaced (after pitching at least four complete innings) and his team remains in the lead to the finish of the game; (3) Except in a five-inning game (when the "must pitch at least four complete innings" rule applies) if the winning team uses more than two pitchers and the starting pitcher has not pitched at least five complete innings the victory shall be awarded one of the relieving pitchers on this basis: (a) Once the opposing team assumes the lead, all pitchers who have pitched for the winning team up to that point are excluded from being credited with the victory with the exception that if the pitcher against whose pitching the opposing team gained the lead continues to pitch until his team regains the lead which it holds to the finish of the game that pitcher would be the winning pitcher; (b) If, after the starting pitcher is replaced before pitching at least five complete innings, the opposing team does not tie the score or take the lead, credit the victory to the relief pitcher deemed by the scorer to have done the most effective pitching; (c) Whenever the score is tied, the game becomes a new contest insofar as determining the winning and losing pitchers are concerned; (d) With one exception no pitcher can be credited with a victory unless he is the pitcher of record when his team assumes a lead and maintains the lead to the finish of the game; (e) The exception to the foregoing is: Do not credit a game

won to a relief pitcher who pitches briefly and ineffectively and is the pitcher of record when his team assumes a lead which it maintains over a period of innings to the finish of the game. If a succeeding relief pitcher pitches effectively in helping to maintain his team in the lead credit such relief pitcher with the victory.

To be designated as the leader of his league's pitchers in the minimum average number of earned runs allowed a pitcher is required to pitch at least as many innings as the number of games scheduled for each team in his league. (This would be 154 innings in a major league.)

No pitcher shall be credited with pitching a shutout unless he pitches the complete game. When two or more pitchers combine to pitch a shutout, a notation to that effect should be included in the league's official pitching records.

Runner See note under entry for Runner in 1950.

1952

Batter The individual batting champion of any league shall be the player with the highest batting average, if he is credited with as many or more times at bat as the number of games scheduled for one club in his league during the season, multiplied by 2.6. However, if there is any player in a league with fewer than the required number of times at bat whose average would be the highest if he were charged with this required at-bat total, then that player shall be awarded the batting championship.

Put Out When a runner is declared out by an umpire for running out of line to avoid being tagged by the ball in the hands of a fielder, the putout shall be credited to the fielder whom the runner avoided; when a runner is called out for passing another runner, credit the putout to the fielder nearest the spot at which the violation took place.

1953

There were no changes to the scoring rules this year.

1954

Batter The following section was added to the rule regarding sacrifice bunts and flies: Also score a sacrifice if, with less than two out, the batter hits a fair fly ball which is caught, and a runner scores after the catch, or is dropped for an error, and a runner scores, if in the scorer's judgment, the runner could have scored after the catch had the fly been caught.

Double Play A double play is a play by the defense in which two offensive players are legally put out as a result of continuous action, providing there is no error between putouts.

Scorer To promote uniformity in keeping the records of championship games, scorers shall conform to the instructions of this scoring code, but in no case shall the scorer's decisions conflict with the playing rules.

Scoring Summary Sacrifice flies and bunts are to be listed separately in the scoring summary.

1955

Assist Mere ineffective contact with the ball shall not be considered an assist. "Deflect" shall mean to slow down or change the direction of the ball and thereby effectively assist in retiring a batter or runner.

Do not credit an assist to the pitcher when, as the result of a legal pitch caught by the catcher, a runner is retired, as when the catcher picks a runner off base, throws out a runner trying to steal or tags a runner trying to steal home.

Do not credit an assist to a fielder whose wild throw permits a runner to advance, even though the runner subsequently is retired as a result of a continuous play. A play which follows an error is a new play, and the player making an error is not entitled to an assist unless he takes part in the new play.

Batter A basehit shall be scored when a batter reaches first base safely on a fair ball which takes an unnatural bounce so that a fielder cannot handle it with ordinary effort, or which strikes the pitcher's plate or any base (including home plate) before being touched by a fielder and bounces so that a fielder cannot handle it with ordinary effort.

A basehit shall be scored when the fielder throws to another base in an unsuccessful attempt to retire a preceding runner, and in the scorer's judgment the batter-runner would not have been retired at first base by perfect fielding.

A basehit shall not be scored when a fielder fails in an attempt to retire a preceding runner, and in the scorer's judgment the batter-runner could have been retired at first base.

A basehit shall not be scored when a fielder handles a batted ball and retires a preceding runner, or would have retired one with ordinary effort except for a fielding error. Charge the batter with a time at bat but no hit. Note: This shall not apply if the fielder merely looks toward or feints toward another base before attempting to make the putout at first base.

When a player bats out of turn, and is put out, and the proper batter is called out before the ball is pitched to the next batter, charge the proper batter with a time at bat and score the putout and any assists the same as if the correct batting order had been followed. If an improper batter becomes a runner by reason of a hit, error, fielder's choice, hit batter, base on balls, interference or obstruction, and the proper batter is called out for having missed his turn at bat, charge the proper batter with a time at bat, credit the putout to the catcher, and ignore everything entering into the improper batter's safe arrival on base. If more than one batter bats out of turn in succession, score all plays just as they occur, skipping the turn at bat of the player or players who first missed batting in the proper order.

Whether a safe hit shall be scored as a one-base hit, two-base hit or three-base hit when no error or putout results, shall be determined as follows: When, with one or more runners on base, the batter advances more than one base on a safe hit and the defensive team makes an attempt to retire a preceding runner, the scorer shall determine whether the batter made a legitimate two-base hit or three-base hit, or whether he advanced beyond first base on the fielder's choice. Note: The rules of 1955 include a series of examples to illustrate the application of this rule for the guidance of the scorer.

When the batter attempts to make a two-base hit or a three-base hit by sliding, he must hold the last base to which he advances. If he overslides and is tagged out before getting back to the base safely, he shall be credited with only as many bases as he attained safely. If he overslides second base and is tagged out, he shall be credited with a one-base hit; if he overslides third base and is tagged out he shall be credited with a two-base hit. Note: If the batter overruns second or third base and is tagged out trying to return, he shall be credited with the last base he touched. If he runs past second base after reaching that base on his feet, attempts to return and is tagged out, he shall be credited with a two-base hit. If he runs past third base after reaching that base on his feet, attempts to return and is tagged out, he shall be credited with a three-base hit.

Subject to provisions of the playing rules, when the batter ends a game with a safe hit which drives in as many runs as are necessary to put his team in the lead, he shall be credited with only as many bases on his hit as are advanced by the runner who scores the winning run, and then only if the batter runs out his hit for as many bases as are advanced by the runner who scores the winning run, touching each base in proper order. Note: Apply this rule even when the batter is theoretically entitled to more bases because of being awarded an "automatic" extra-base hit under various provisions of the playing rules.

Score a sacrifice bunt when, with less than two outs, the fielders handle a bunted ball without error in an unsuccessful attempt to retire a preceding runner advancing one base. Exception: When an attempt to turn a bunt into a putout of a preceding runner fails, and in the scorer's judgment perfect play would not have retired the batter at first base, the batter shall be credited with a one-base hit and not a sacrifice.

Do not score a sacrifice bunt when a runner is retired attempting to advance one base on a bunt. Charge the batter with a time at bat.

A base on balls shall be scored whenever a batter is awarded first base because of four balls having been pitched outside the strike zone, but when the fourth such ball strikes the batter it shall be scored as a "hit batter." Note: The scoring rules contain detailed instructions for charging runners who receive a base on balls when the pitcher is changed in mid-batter.

A strikeout shall be scored whenever a pitcher delivers three legal pitches at which the batter swings and misses, or which the umpire decrees are strikes. A strikeout shall be scored even though the batter reaches first base safely after the third strike because of an error by the pitcher or catcher as defined in the scoring rules.

Box Score A box score is in balance (or proved) when the total of the team's times at bat, bases on balls received, hit batters, sacrifice bunts, sacrifice flies and batters awarded first base because of interference or obstruction, equals the total of that team's runs, players left on base and the opposing team's putouts.

Catcher Do not credit the catcher with a man "caught stealing" when he traps a runner off base after fielding a batted ball or on any play started by another fielder.

Championship The individual fielding champions shall be the fielders with the highest fielding average at each position, subject to the following: (1) A catcher must have participated as a catcher in at least 90 games (80 games in leagues playing schedules of 140 games or less); (2) An infielder or outfielder must have participated at his position in at least 100 games (90 games in leagues playing schedules of 140 games or less); (3) A pitcher must have pitched in at least as many innings as the number of games scheduled for each club in his league that season.

Earned Run The scoring rules of 1955 contain detailed provisions for charging runners and runs to starting pitchers and relief pitchers where pitching changes are made in mid-batter.

No run can be earned which scores as a result of the batter reaching first base (1) On a hit or otherwise after his time at bat is prolonged by a muffed foul fly; (2) Because of interference or obstruction, or (3) Because of any fielding error, except for a wild pitch charged as an error.

Error Slow handling of the ball which does not involve mechanical misplay shall not be construed as an error.

An error shall be charged against any fielder when he muffs a foul fly, to prolong the time at bat of the batter, whether the batter subsequently reaches first base or is retired.

If a runner advances on a throw by a fielder, and in the scorer's judgment there was no occasion for the throw, an error shall be charged to the fielder making the unnecessary throw.

An error shall be charged against any fielder whose throw takes an unnatural bounce, or strikes a base or the pitcher's plate, or strikes a runner, a fielder or an umpire, thereby permitting any runner to advance. Note: Apply this rule even when it appears to be an injustice to a fielder whose throw was accurately directed. Every base advanced by a runner must be accounted for.

When the batter's fourth called ball is a wild pitch and as a result (1) The batter-runner advances to a base beyond first base; (2) Any runner, forced to advance by reason of the batter becoming a runner, advances more than one base, or (3) Any runner, not forced to advance by reason of the batter becoming a runner, advances one or more bases, score the base on balls and also an error for the pitcher and do not score a wild pitch.

When the batter swings at a wild pitch for his third strike and thereby is enabled to reach first base, score a strikeout and also an error for the pitcher, and do not score a wild pitch.

When the batter swings at a wild pitch for his third strike or when the catcher muffs a third strike, if the catcher recovers the ball and throws out the batter-runner trying to reach first base, but another runner or runners advance, score the strikeout and error the same as

if the batter had reached first base. Credit an assist to the catcher, and a putout to the fielder taking the throw at first base.

When an umpire awards the batter or any runner or runners one or more bases because of interference or obstruction, charge the fielder who committed the interference or obstruction with one error, no matter how many bases the batter, or runner or runners, may be advanced.

No error shall be charged against the catcher when he makes a wild throw in attempting to prevent a stolen base, unless such wild throw permits the base stealer to advance one or more extra bases, or in the scorer's judgment permits another runner to advance one or more bases. Charge only one error on such a wild throw, regardless of the number of bases advanced by the runner or runners.

No error shall be charged against any fielder when he makes a wild throw in attempting to prevent a runner's advance, unless in the scorer's judgment such wild throw permits the runner to advance beyond the base he would have reached had the throw not been wild, or permits any other runner to advance one or more bases beyond the base he would have reached had the throw not been wild. Charge only one error on such wild throw, regardless of the number of bases advanced by the runner or runners.

Fielder's Choice   Fielder's Choice is the act of a fielder who handles a fair grounder and, instead of throwing to first base to retire the batter-runner, throws to another base in an attempt to retire a preceding runner. The term is also used by scorers (1) To account for the advance of the batter-runner who takes one or more extra bases when the fielder who handles his safe hit attempts to retire a preceding runner; and (2) To account for the advance of a runner (other than by stolen base or error) while a fielder is attempting to retire another runner. Note: This definition appears in the Playing Rules for 1955.

Pitcher   In some non-championship games (such as the Major League All-Star Game) it is provided in advance that each pitcher shall work a stated number of innings, usually two or three. In such games, it is customary to credit the victory to the pitcher of record, whether starter or reliever, when the winning team takes a lead which it maintains to the end of the game, unless such pitcher is knocked out after the winning team has a commanding lead, and the scorer believes a subsequent pitcher is entitled to credit for the victory.

Put Out   When a runner is called out for running the bases in reverse order, credit the putout to the fielder covering the base he left in starting his reverse run. Do not credit any assist on such plays.

When the batter-runner is called out because of interference by a preceding runner, credit the putout to the first baseman. If the fielder interfered with was in the act of throwing the ball, credit him with an assist, but credit only one assist on any one play.

Run Batted In   A run batted in is a run which reaches home base safely because of a safe hit, a sacrifice bunt, a sacrifice fly, a putout via a foul fly, an infield putout or a fielder's choice; or which is forced over home plate by reason of the batter being struck by a pitched ball, or being awarded a base on balls or being awarded first base because of interference or obstruction. If a batter hits a home run always score the home run as a run batted in. Also count all other runs which score ahead of the batter who hit the home run as runs batted in. If, with less than two out, an error is made on a play on which a runner from third base ordinarily would score and does score, credit the batter with a run batted in.

Runner   A stolen base shall be credited to a runner whenever he advances one base unaided by a basehit, a putout, an error, a force-out, a fielder's choice, a passed ball, a wild pitch or a balk, subject to the following: When a runner, attempting to steal, evades being put out in a rundown play and advances to the next base without the aid of an error, credit the runner with a stolen base. If another runner also advances on the play, credit both runners with stolen bases. If a runner advances while another runner, attempting to steal, evades being put out in a rundown play and returns safely, without the aid of an error, to the base he originally occupied, credit a stolen base to the runner who advances.

Scorer   The Official Scorer shall keep records of each game as outlined in the scoring rules. He shall have sole authority to make all decisions involving judgment, such as whether a batter's advance to first base is the result of a hit or an error.

In no event shall a scorer make a decision conflicting with the Official Playing Rules or with an umpire's decision.

Scoring Summary   The scoring summary shall contain: (1) Number of runners left on base by each team. This total shall include all runners who get on base by any means and who do not score and are not put out. Include in this total a batter-runner whose batted ball results in another runner being retired for the third out; (2) Total number of bases on balls issued by each pitcher and a separate listing of the number of intentional bases on balls issued by each pitcher.

The scoring rules of 1955 also include detailed instructions for notations to the tabulated game records. It is recommended that letters a, b, c, d, etc., be used in the notations as symbols for substitute batters and that numerals 1, 2, 3, 4, etc., be used as symbols for substitute runners. Also the instructions detail notations needed when a substitute is announced but removed for another substitute before he actually enters the game.

1956

Batter   A basehit should be scored when the fielder unsuccessfully attempts to retire a preceding runner, and, in the scorer's judgment, the batter-runner would not have been retired at first base by perfect fielding.

When a fielder handles a batted ball and retires a preceding runner who is attempting to advance one base, or would have retired one with ordinary effort except for a fielding error charge the batter with a time at bat but no hit.

Run Batted In   The batter shall not be credited with a run batted in if a run scores when he grounds into a force double play, or grounds into a double play in which the first out is made at first base and the second out made by tagging a runner who was originally forced, attempting to advance one base.

1957

Batter   A basehit shall be scored when a batter reaches first base safely on a fair ball hit with such force, or so slowly, that any fielder attempting to make a play with it has no opportunity to do so. Note: A hit shall be scored if the fielder attempting to handle the ball cannot make a play, even if such fielder deflects the ball from or cuts off another fielder who could have retired a runner.

Championship   To assure uniformity in establishing the batting, pitching and fielding championship of professional leagues, such champions shall meet the following minimum performance standards: The individual batting champion shall be the player with the highest batting average, provided he is credited with as many or more total appearances at the plate in league championship games as the number of games scheduled for each club in the league that season, multiplied by 3.1. Total appearances at the plate shall include official times at bat, plus bases on balls, times hit by pitcher, sacrifice hits, sacrifice flies and times awarded first base because of interference or obstruction.

Earned Run   An earned run shall be scored every time a runner reaches home base by the aid of safe hits, sacrifice bunts, a sacrifice fly, stolen bases, putouts, fielder's choices, bases on balls, hit batters, balks or wild pitches (including a wild pitch on third strike which permits a batter to reach first base) before fielding chances have been offered to retire the offensive team. Note: A wild pitch is solely the pitcher's fault, and contributes to an earned run just as a base on balls or a balk.

No run can be earned which scores as a result of the batter reaching base (1) On a hit or otherwise after his time at bat is prolonged by a muffed foul fly; (2) Because of interference or obstruction; or (3) Because of any fielding error.

An error by the pitcher is treated exactly the same as an error by

any other fielder in computing earned runs.

Error No error shall be charged to any fielder who permits a foul fly to fall safe with a runner on third base before two are out, if in the scorer's judgment the fielder deliberately refuses the catch in order that the runner on third shall not score after the catch.

Because the pitcher and catcher handle the ball much more than other fielders, certain misplays on pitched balls are called "wild pitches" and "passed balls," and are defined elsewhere in the scoring rules. No error shall be charged when a wild pitch or passed ball is scored. No error shall be charged when the batter is awarded first base on four called balls or because he was touched by a pitched ball, or when he reaches first base as the result of a wild pitch or passed ball. When the third strike is a wild pitch, permitting the batter to reach first base, score a strikeout and a wild pitch. When the third strike is a passed ball, permitting the batter to reach first base, score a strikeout and a passed ball.

Pitcher Regardless of how many innings the first pitcher has pitched, he shall be charged with the loss of the game if he is replaced when his team is behind in the score, and his team thereafter fails either to tie the score or gain the lead.

Run Batted In Scorer's judgment must determine whether a run batted in shall be credited for a run which scores when a fielder holds the ball, or throws to a wrong base. Ordinarily, if the runner keeps going, credit a run batted in; if the runner stops and takes off again when he notices the misplay, credit the run as scored on a fielder's choice.

Scorer The league president shall appoint an official scorer for each league championship game. The official scorer shall observe the game from a position in the press box. The scorer shall have sole authority to make all decisions involving judgment, such as whether a batter's advance to first base is the result of a hit or an error. He shall communicate such decisions to the press box and broadcasting booths by hand signals or over the press box loudspeaker system, and shall advise the public address announcer of such decisions if requested.

After each game, including drawn, forfeited and called games, the scorer shall prepare a report, on a form prescribed by the league president, listing the date of the game, where it was played, the names of the competing clubs and the umpires, the full score of the game, and all records of individual players compiled according to the system specified in these Official Scoring Rules. He shall forward this report to the league office within 36 hours after the game ends. He shall forward the report of any suspended game within 36 hours after the game has been completed, or after it becomes an official game because it cannot be completed, as provided by the Official Playing Rules.

To achieve uniformity in keeping the records of championship games, the scorer shall conform strictly to the Official Scoring Rules.

If the teams change sides before three men are put out, the scorer shall immediately inform the umpire of the mistake.

If the game is protested or suspended, the scorer shall make note of the exact situation at the time of the protest or suspension, including the score, the number of outs, the position of any runners, and the ball and strike count on the batter.

Note: It is important that a suspended game resume with exactly the same situation as existed at the time of suspension. If a protested game is ordered replayed from the point of protest, it must be resumed with exactly the situation that existed just before the protested play.

The scorer shall not make any decision conflicting with the Official Playing Rules or with an umpire's decision.

The scorer shall not call the attention of the umpire or of any member of either team to the fact that a player is batting out of turn.

The scorer is an official representative of the league, and is entitled to the respect and dignity of his office, and shall be accorded full protection by the league president. The scorer shall report to the president any indignity expressed by any manager, player, club employee or club officer in the course of, or as the result of, the discharge of his duties.

The umpire-in-chief shall inform the official scorer of the official batting order, and any changes in the lineups and batting order, on request.

1958

Batter Score a sacrifice fly when, before two are out, the batter hits a fair fly ball which: (1) Is caught, and a runner scores after the catch, or (2) is dropped, and a runner scores, if, in the scorer's judgment, the runner could have scored after the catch had the fly been caught. Note: Score a sacrifice fly in accordance with the scoring rules even though another runner is forced out by reason of the batter becoming a runner.

Championship The individual fielding champions shall be the fielders with the highest fielding average at each position, provided: (1) A catcher must have participated as a catcher in at least one-half the number of games scheduled for each club in his league that season; (2) An infielder or outfielder must have participated at his position in at least two-thirds of the number of games scheduled for each club in his league that season; (3) A pitcher must have pitched at least as many innings as the number of games scheduled for each club in his league that season.

Earned Run To compute the pitcher's earned run average, multiply the total earned runs charged against his pitching by 9, and divide the result by the total number of innings he pitched.

1959–64

There were no changes to the scoring rules in these years.

1965

Championship To qualify for the fielding championship at his position a pitcher must have pitched at least as many innings as the number of games scheduled for each club in his league that season. Exception: If another pitcher has a fielding average as high or higher, and has handled more total chances in a lesser number of innings, he shall be the fielding champion.

1966

There were no changes to the scoring rules this year.

1967

Batter Do not score a sacrifice bunt when, in the judgment of the scorer, the batter is bunting for a basehit and not solely for the purpose of advancing a runner or runners. Charge the batter with a time at bat. Note: In applying this rule always give the batter the benefit of the doubt.

Championship The individual batting champion shall be the player with the highest batting average, provided he is credited with as many or more total appearances at the plate in league championship games as the number of games scheduled for each club in his league that season, multiplied by 3.1. Exception: However, if there is any player with fewer than the required number of plate appearances whose average would be highest if he were charged with the required number of plate appearances or official at-bats, then that player shall be awarded the batting championship.

Error Mental mistakes or misjudgments are not to be scored as errors unless specifically covered in the rules.

No error shall be charged against any fielder when, after fumbling a ground ball or dropping a fly ball, a line drive or a thrown ball, he recovers the ball in time to force out a runner at any base.

Runner When a runner, attempting to steal, or after being picked off base, evades being put out in a rundown play and advances to the next base without the aid of an error, credit the runner with a stolen base. If another runner also advances on the play, credit both runners with stolen bases. If a runner advances while another runner, attempting to steal, evades being put out in a rundown play and returns

safely, without the aid of an error, to the base he originally occupied, credit a stolen base to the runner who advances.

1968

There were no changes to the scoring rules this year.

1969

Batter Do not score a sacrifice bunt when, in the judgment of the scorer, the batter is bunting *primarily* for a basehit and not for the purpose of advancing a runner or runners. Charge the batter with a time at bat. Note: In applying this rule always give the batter the benefit of the doubt.

Note: The rule is the same as that appearing in the 1967 scoring rules with the addition of the word "primarily."

Earned Run An earned run is a run for which the pitcher is held accountable. In determining earned runs, the inning should be reconstructed without the errors and passed balls, and the benefit of the doubt should always be given to the pitcher in determining which bases would have been reached by errorless play.

When pitchers are changed during an inning, the relief pitcher shall not have the benefit of previous chances for outs not accepted in determining earned runs. Note: It is the intent of this rule to prevent relief pitchers from not being charged with earned runs for which they are solely responsible.

Double Play/Triple Play Credit participation in the double play or triple play to each fielder who earns a putout or an assist when two or three players are put out between the time a pitch is delivered and the time the ball next becomes dead or is next in possession of the pitcher in pitching position, unless an error or misplay intervenes between putouts. Note: Credit the double play or triple play also if an appeal play after the ball is in possession of the pitcher results in an additional putout.

Error When an umpire awards the batter or any runner or runners one or more bases because of interference or obstruction, charge the fielder who committed the interference or obstruction with one error, no matter how many bases the batter, or runner or runners, may be advanced. Note: Do not charge an error if obstruction does not change the play in the opinion of the scorer.

Pitcher Credit a save to a relief pitcher who enters a game with his team in the lead if he holds the lead the remainder of the game, provided he is not credited with the victory. A relief pitcher cannot be credited with a save if he does not finish the game unless he is removed for a pinch hitter or pinch runner. When more than one relief pitcher qualifies for a save under the provisions of this rule, credit the save to the relief pitcher judged by the scorer to have been the most effective. Only one save can be credited in any game.

1970–72

There were no changes to the scoring rules in these years.

1973

Pitcher A pitcher shall be credited with a save when, in entering a game as a relief pitcher, he finds the potential tying or winning run either on base or at the plate or pitches at least three or more effective innings and, in either case, preserves the lead.

1974

Statistics A consecutive hitting streak shall not be terminated if the plate appearance results in a base on balls, hit batsman, defensive interference or a sacrifice bunt. A sacrifice fly shall terminate the streak.

A consecutive-game hitting streak shall not be terminated if all the player's plate appearances (one or more) result in a base on balls, hit batsman, defensive interference or a sacrifice bunt. The streak shall terminate if the player has a sacrifice fly and no hit.

A consecutive-game playing streak shall be extended if the player plays one half-inning on defense, or if he completes a time at bat by reaching base or being put out. A pinch-running appearance only shall not extend the streak. If a player is ejected from a game by an umpire before he can comply with the requirements of this rule, his streak shall continue.

For the purpose of the scoring rules, all performances in the completion of a suspended game shall be considered as occurring on the original date of the game.

1975

Batter Score a sacrifice fly when, before two are out, the batter hits a fly ball or a line drive handled by an outfielder or an infielder running in the outfield which: (1) Is caught, and a runner scores after the catch, or (2) Is dropped, and a runner scores, if in the scorer's judgment the runner could have scored after the catch had the fly been caught. Note: Score a sacrifice fly in accordance with the scoring rules even though another runner is forced out by reason of the batter becoming a runner.

Pitcher Credit a pitcher with a save when he meets all three of the following conditions: (1) He is the finishing pitcher in a game won by his club; and (2) He is not the winning pitcher; and (3) He qualifies under one of the following conditions: (a) He enters the game with a lead of no more than three runs and pitches for at least one inning; or (b) He enters the game with the potential tying run either on base, or at bat, or on deck (that is, the potential tying run is either already on base or is one of the first two batsmen he faces); or (c) He pitches effectively for at least three innings. No more than one save may be credited in each game.

1976

Batter When the batter leaves the game with two strikes against him, and the substitute batter completes a strikeout, charge the strikeout and the time at bat to the first batter. If the substitute batter completes the turn at bat in any other manner, including a base on balls, score the action as having been that of the substitute batter.

Earned Run An earned run is a run for which the pitcher is held accountable. In determining earned runs, the inning should be reconstructed without the errors (which includes catcher's interference) and passed balls, and the benefit of the doubt should always be given to the pitcher in determining which bases would have been reached by errorless play.

When pitchers are changed during an inning, the relief pitcher shall not be charged with any run (earned or unearned) scored by a runner who was on base at the time he entered the game, nor for runs scored by any runner who reaches base on a fielder's choice which puts out a runner left on base by the preceding pitcher. Note: It is the intent of this rule to charge each pitcher with the number of runners he put on base, rather than with the individual runners. When a pitcher puts runners on base and is relieved, he shall be charged with all runs subsequently scored up to and including the number of runners he left on base when he left the game, unless such runners are put out without action by the batter, i.e., caught stealing, picked off base, or called out for interference when a batter-runner does not reach first base on the play. Exception: The pitcher walks batter A and is relieved. The relief pitcher allows B to single, but runner A is out trying for third. Runner B takes second on the throw. Batter C singles, scoring runner B. Charge the run to the relief pitcher rather than the preceding pitcher.

For purposes of earned run average calculations and innings pitched totals, innings pitched shall be rounded off to the nearest whole inning. Examples: 200⅓ innings becomes 200; 200⅔ becomes 201. Note: This standard was changed in 1982 and fractions were no longer rounded off but counted for their full value. Also see rule addition under 1981.

Player When a player listed in the starting lineup for the visiting club is substituted for before he plays defensively, he shall not receive credit in the defensive statistics (fielding), unless he actually plays that position during a game. All such players, however, shall be

credited with one game played (in batting statistics) as long as they are announced into the game or listed on the official lineup card.

Scoring Summary The name of a pitcher credited with a save is to be shown on the scoring summary.

1977

Batter Intentional base on balls shall be scored when the pitcher makes no attempt to throw the last pitch to the batter into the strike zone but purposely throws the ball wide to the catcher outside the catcher's box.

1978

There were no changes to the scoring rules this year.

1979

Earned Run An earned run is a run for which the pitcher is held accountable. In determining earned runs, the inning should be reconstructed without the errors (which include catcher's interference) and passed balls, and the benefit of the doubt should always be given to the pitcher in determining which bases would have been reached by errorless play. For the purpose of determining earned runs, an intentional base on balls, regardless of the circumstances, shall be construed in exactly the same manner as any other base on balls.

Runner A runner shall be charged as "caught stealing" if he is put out, or would have been put out by errorless play, when he (1) Tries to steal; (2) Is picked off a base and tries to advance (any move toward the next base shall be considered an attempt to advance); (3) Overslides while stealing. Note: In those instances where a pitched ball eludes the catcher and the runner is put out trying to advance, no caught stealing shall be charged.

Scorer The Official Scorer must make all decisions concerning judgment calls within twenty-four (24) hours after a game has been officially concluded. No judgment decision shall be changed thereafter except, upon immediate application to the league president, the scorer may request a change, citing the reasons for such. In all cases the official scorer is not permitted to make a scoring decision which is in conflict with the scoring rules.

1980

Run Batted In Game-winning RBI is credited for the RBI that gives a club the lead it never relinquishes. Note: There does not have to be a game-winning RBI in every game and all game-winning RBI's must conform to the scoring rule governing RBI's.

1981

Earned Run For purposes of earned run average calculations and innings pitched totals do not round off the fraction where a pitcher has only ⅓ of an inning for the entire season. In such cases carry his total for innings pitched as ⅓.

1982

Earned Run Earned run averages shall be calculated on the basis of total innings pitched, including fractional innings. Example: 9⅓ innings pitched and three earned runs is an earned run average of 2.89 (3 ER times 9 divided by 9⅓ equals 2.89).

1983

Championship The individual batting champion or slugging champion shall be the player with the highest batting average or slugging percentage, provided he is credited with as many or more total appearances at the plate in league championship games as the number of games scheduled for each club in his league that season, multiplied by 3.1 in the case of a major league player. Exception: However, if there is any player with fewer than the required number of plate appearances or official at-bats, but who, when credited with an out for each of his deficient at-bats, still has the highest average, then that player shall be awarded the batting championship or slugging championship.

1984

Statistics To compute on-base percentage, divide the total of hits, all bases on balls, and hit by pitch, by the total of at-bats, all bases on balls, hit by pitch and sacrifice flies. Note: For the purpose of computing on-base percentage, ignore being awarded first base on interference or obstruction.

1985–88

There were no changes to the scoring rules in these years.

Index to Scoring Rule Changes 1878–1988

Note: Dates shown following an entry refer to the year a rule change or amendment was adopted. Rule changes and summaries of rules are to be found in the chronology.

APPENDIX 2

City Series

Frederick Ivor-Campbell

Outside of spring training, major league teams rarely play exhibition games, and when they do they are rarely contested seriously. Spring training games are viewed as warmup and practice sessions, and in the midseason games between big league teams and their farm clubs the big league first-stringers seldom play the full game, turning play over to the reserves after a time or two at bat. Postseason exhibition games—apart from the rare club tour to Japan—have disappeared entirely.

Yet exhibition games—before, during, and after the regular season—used to be part of the fabric of professional baseball. Major league teams of the 1880s, for example, would precede the season with a month against college and minor league clubs and teams from the other major league. During the season clubs would try to fill their open dates with exhibition games. And for a couple of weeks after the regular season ended, clubs would continue their exhibition play. The early World Series were, in fact, exhibition games raised to a higher plane of seriousness.

Other postseason exhibition series rivaled the World Series in their appeal. Typically they would pit teams from the same city, state, or region, and would often bill themselves as games for the championship of the city or state. Sometimes such series would involve clubs from the same league, as the games between the American Association New York Mets and Brooklyn for the "local championship" of 1885, or between St. Louis and Kansas City of the AA in 1889 and 1890 for the championship of Missouri. Others would mix a major and minor league or independent club, as in the Baltimore-Washington series for a silver trophy in 1885.

But the city and regional series that most often drew large crowds were those between clubs from different major leagues. The first such series took place in 1882, the first year there *were* two major leagues, between Ohio's National League Cleveland Blues and the Cincinnati Red Stockings of the new American Association. Because the AA was regarded by the NL as an illegitimate upstart, the three-game series was played in defiance of "protests and warnings."

1882 Ohio   Cleveland Blues (NL), 2; Cincinnati Red Stockings (AA), 1

The Reds had run away with the AA pennant while Cleveland had finished its season barely above .500, in fifth place. Yet even though the series was held in Cincinnati, the Reds were able to capture only one game from the older club. Cleveland's George Bradley, a veteran pitcher whose best years were behind him, faced the Reds in the opener and gave up the game's first run in the third inning. But he blanked the Reds the rest of the way as his Blues scored three runs to win. The Blues started an outfielder, Dave Rowe, in the box for Game Two, and he gave up enough runs before Bradley relieved him in the third inning to assure Cincinnati of at least one win. In the finale, though, Cleveland pitched its ace, Jim McCormick, against Harry McCormick (no relation) of the Reds, a good enough pitcher, but not in Jim's class. The large Cincinnati crowd saw Jim McCormick blank their Reds on three hits, while the Blues took advantage of nine hits and ten Cincinnati errors to capture the Ohio championship with an 8–0 win.

1883 Ohio   Cleveland Blues (NL), 2; Cincinnati Red Stockings (AA), 0; one tie

Cincinnati repeated as host to Cleveland for an Ohio series the next year. Both clubs had played well, enjoying winning season records, although neither contended seriously for the pennant. Cleveland again defeated the Reds, this time with victory in the first two games. Their 8–1 win in the opener was a near repeat of their third-game win the previous year, as the Blues again capitalized on Red errors (and five passed balls). Will Sawyer, Cleveland's third-ranked pitcher (ace Jim McCormick played all three games in right field), meanwhile held Cincinnati to five hits, shutting them down over the final eight innings.

The Reds' ace Will White made his only pitching appearance of either series in Game Two. But although he was the AA's best pitcher, Cleveland hit him hard, with twelve hits. Only the fact that five Blues were thrown out at home kept Cleveland's score as low as five runs. Cincinnati hit Cleveland's Hugh "One Arm" Daily hard, too, and held a 4–0 lead after four innings. But the Reds scored no more before darkness halted play after eight, and Cleveland won the game and the series by one run. In the meaningless third game Cincinnati took an early lead. Cleveland went ahead with a three-run seventh, but before darkness ended the series an inning later, the Reds scored to tie the game. This was the end of the Ohio series for the foreseeable future, as the Cleveland franchise folded at the end of a disastrous 1884 season.

Two city series were inaugurated in 1883 that continued for several years. Both New York and Philadelphia entered new teams in the NL, and both played their AA counterparts for their city titles in October.

1883 New York   Metropolitan (AA), 2; Gothams (NL), 1; one tie

New York's Metropolitan Club was also new to the big time in 1883, finishing fourth in the AA while the NL Gothams (later known as the Giants) could do no better than sixth in their league. In their series of four games, the teams proved nearly equal. The opener featured splendid fielding and a pitching duel between aces Tim Keefe of the Mets and the Gothams' Mickey Welch, which was not settled until the Mets pushed across a run in the last of the tenth to break a 2–2 tie. The clubs' second-line hurlers, Monte Ward of the Gothams and Jack Lynch of the Mets, pitched just as effectively the next day. The Gothams carried a 3–2 lead into the last of the ninth, but the Mets scored a tying run when Gotham catcher Buck Ewing—claiming it was too dark to see—took his position fifty feet behind the plate, allowing the tying Met run to score from second. The game was then called for darkness.

After two close contests, Games Three and Four were blowouts. Neither Keefe nor Welch proved effective in Game Three, but the Gothams committed more errors and gave the Mets a 10–5 win. The situation was reversed in the final game, when the Gothams drove out Lynch with twelve runs in the first three innings. First baseman Dave Orr eventually took over the pitching duties and dampened the

Gotham bats, but the rescue came too late to prevent the Gothams' only series win, 15–3.

1884 New York   Metropolitan (AA), 1; Gothams (NL), 1; one tie

The Mets won the AA pennant in 1884 and warmed up for their three-game series with NL champion Providence (for the "championship of the United States"—what we now view as baseball's first World Series) with three games against the Gothams for the city title. Although the Gothams had tied for fourth in the NL, the best the Mets could do was win one game against them and tie another. In the first two games the Mets took a four-run lead in the first inning. In Game One the Gothams tied the score before darkness halted play after five innings, and in the second game the Mets' sloppy fielding allowed the Gothams to catch up again. But the Mets this time scored a tie-breaking run in the last of the sixth before darkness closed in.

The series finale drew only a small crowd. Although darkness held the game to just five innings, the Mets committed ten errors, throwing away the game to the Gothams 9–7. A week later Providence swept the Mets for the world title.

1885 New York   Giants (NL), 2; Metropolitan (AA), 1

John Day, who owned both the Mets and the Gothams, sent pitcher Tim Keefe and Met manager Jim Mutrie over to the Gothams in 1885 to strengthen the club. As a result the Gothams made a strong run for the NL pennant and became known as the Giants, while the Mets dropped to seventh in the AA. Not surprisingly the Giants defeated the Mets in the city series, although the games were much closer than might have been expected. In the opener the Mets tagged former teammate Keefe for nine hits while their pitcher, Jack Lynch, held the Giants to seven. But the Giants bunched their hits more effectively and won 5–3.

Keefe starred in Game Two four days later, not only hurling the 6–5 Giant victory, but leading his team with two hits and a pair of runs scored. With the series already decided, several Giant regulars skipped the third game. Mickey Welch pitched effectively, holding the Mets to just four hits. But two of them came in the first inning and, combined with an error, made possible two Met runs. The Mets scored no more, but they didn't need to, as Buck Becannon shut out the Giants through five innings before darkness brought the game and the series to an end.

1885 New York Area   Giants (NL), 1; Brooklyn (AA), 0; one tie

In between their games with the Mets, the Giants also played a series with Brooklyn, a fifth-place finisher in the AA. Welch pitched the opener—officially a three-hit 4–2 Giant win in seven innings. Actually the score stood 5–4 in the Giants' favor in the last of the eighth, with a Brooklyn runner on third and none out. when the game was called for darkness, and the eighth-inning scoring was erased from the record.

The second Giants-Brooklyn game was in the seventh inning when darkness ended it in a 3–3 tie. There was to have been a third game, but Brooklyn released its players for the season. So the Giants took on a "Brooklyn" team made up of players from several clubs, including Giant pitcher Welch. The Giants knocked Welch for twelve hits, while Larry Corcoran held Brooklyn to six hits and hit a home run himself, to help New York take a 6–3 win.

1886 New York   Giants (NL), 3; Metropolitan (AA), 1

1886 New York Area   Brooklyn (AA), 3; Giants (NL), 1

In 1886 the Giants, who had finished third in the NL, played their metropolitan opponents four times each. They defeated the seventh-place Mets three games to one, but lost by the same margin to a greatly improved Brooklyn team that had enjoyed its first winning season while finishing a solid third, 9½ games ahead of the AA's

fourth-place club. The Giants won their first two city series games, defeating the Mets 4–1 and 5–3, then took on Brooklyn and lost 7–2. They came back for another pair of wins, clinching the Mets series with a 3–0 shutout as Mickey Welch scattered four hits over the five innings played, then repaying their loss to Brooklyn with their own 7–2 win.

But then, after a day of rest, the Giants lost their final three games. First Brooklyn defeated them, coming back from a 1–6 deficit as Welch yielded seven walks (and Giant third baseman Dude Esterbrook made several costly errors), scoring four runs in the last of the sixth (and final) inning for an 8–6 win. Then Brooklyn's Adonis Terry shut them out on two hits to capture the series. Finally, the Mets salvaged some dignity by tying the Giants in the top of the ninth and scoring three runs in the tenth for their only series win.

There was no more postseason interleague city series play in metropolitan New York for twenty-four years. The Mets folded after the 1887 season. The Giants did face Brooklyn once more in the postseason before Brooklyn switched to the NL in 1890: in 1889 the Giants defeated Brooklyn in the World Series, six games to three.

1883 Philadelphia   Phillies (NL), 2; Athletics (AA), 1

The Athletics/Phillies series in Philadelphia, which began the same year as the Gotham Giants/Mets series, continued longer than any other nineteenth-century city series—through 1889. The two teams seemed mismatched as they entered the inaugural series in 1883. The Athletics has just won the AA pennant, while the Phillies had finished last in the NL, twice as far out of first place as the league's next-worst team. The first game of the three appeared to confirm the mismatch: The A's veteran hurler George Bradley stopped the Phillies on two singles as his team blended eleven hits with eleven Phillie errors for thirteen runs before darkness ended the debacle at 13–3 after seven innings.

Bradley continued his mastery of the Phillies through five innings of Game Two, five days later. But the game (and the series) turned around when five Phillies scored on six hits in the sixth inning to take a 6–4 lead. They won 8–4 as their pitcher John Coleman (who had lost a major-league-record 48 games during the season) blanked the A's on just one hit over the final six innings.

Another week went by before the series finale, but the result was nearly the same as in Game Two. Coleman yielded only one earned run as he stopped the A's on four hits. The Phils, meanwhile, unloaded on Athletics ace Bobby Mathews (a 30-game winner during the season) for an eleven-hit 8–3 win and series triumph.

1884 Philadelphia   Phillies (NL), 3; Athletics (AA), 0

In 1884 the Athletics again finished the regular season with a much better record than the Phillies, but in the city series they lost all three games. The opener was the closest contest. Phillie newcomer Con Murphy—one day short of his twenty-first birthday—held the A's scoreless through five innings, and although he then weakened, the Phillies put together a four-run seventh to give him a 6–4 win.

Two days later the Phillies defeated the A's a second time, in an error-filled slugfest shortened to seven innings by darkness. Murphy again pitched for the Phillies, giving up a home run to A's star Harry Stovey and hurling three wild pitches. But the Phillies took advantage of A's errors to score twelve runs and overwhelm the A's nine.

With the series already decided, only a few hundred spectators attended the finale, and they began to leave after the first inning. Although the game was a benefit for the Athletics' players, they performed as if they didn't care. The Phillies scored against them in five of the first six innings, and when they began again to pummel the A's in the seventh, the game was halted, with the score for the six completed innings standing at 13–5.

1885 Philadelphia   Phillies (NL), 3; Athletics (AA), 2

In a preseason series in 1885, the Athletics defeated the Phillies, four games to two. But in postseason play the Phils recaptured the

honors of the city, three games to two.

The two clubs had put together similarly mediocre regular-season records, and they traded wins through the first four games of their five-game fall series. The Athletics took the opener 7–2, as pitcher Bobby Mathews held the Phillies scoreless on two hits after the first inning, and singled in the fifth himself to start a five-run rally that broke a 2–2 tie and assured him of the victory. The Phillies retaliated the following day, parlaying ten hits and eight walks into seventeen runs, while holding the A's to two. Mathews returned to the box for the Athletics in Game Three and stopped the Phillies on four hits (and one run, on a passed ball), while his A's knocked Phillie Ed Daily for ten hits and seven runs. Daily fared better when the clubs met two days later for Game Four. Eight A's hit safely, but none walked and only three scored, while the Phillies put nine hits and four walks together with several Athletic errors for six runs, to even the series at two games each.

Club aces Mathews and Charlie Ferguson faced each other in the finale for the first time in the series. Fans looked for a close match, but the A's defense was porous and Mathews was hit hard. The Phillies had overcome an early Athletic lead to move ahead 9–4 when rain halted the game and concluded the series with two away in the last of the seventh.

1886 Philadelphia   Phillies (NL), 1; Athletics (AA), 0; one tie

The 1886 Philadelphia series was the shortest between the two clubs. The Phillies, with their best season to date, had finished a strong fourth in the NL, while the A's, with their worst, had finished sixth in the AA. Not unexpectedly, the Phillies defeated the A's handily in the opener, 5–0. But when the A's surprised them with a 6–6 tie in a six-inning contest two days later, the Phillies refused to continue the series and disbanded their team until spring.

1887 Philadelphia   Phillies (NL), 3; Athletics (AA), 2; one tie

Relations returned to normal in 1887. In the spring the teams played each other eleven times, each winning five games and tying the other game. During the season the Phillies rose all the way to second place, their highest finish of the century. The A's also improved in the standings—to fifth—but were still 30 games out of first. Yet once again the postseason series was closely contested.

The Phillies, in fact, were lucky to gain a tie in the opener. The A's led 3–1 after eight innings, but with two away in the Phillie ninth, two batsmen hit safely. With men on first and third, the A's catcher threw the ball away on a stolen base attempt; both Phillie runners scored to tie the game, which was called after the tenth inning, with no further scoring.

Game Two was just as close. The lead switched back and forth until the Phillies tied the game with a run in the seventh. In the last of the ninth, with the score at 5–5, the Phils combined a walk, a stolen base, and a hit for the winning run.

The Athletics came back to take the next two games, hammering fifteen hits for eleven runs in Game Three before darkness ended play in the eighth with the score 11–6, and bombarding the Phillies with ten hits and ten runs in the first two innings of Game Four before Phillie pitcher Dan Casey settled down to blank them on two hits the rest of the way. Thanks to their own heavy hitting—and five walks and two hit batsmen by the A's Gus Weyhing—the Phillies gradually narrowed the gap, but finished one run short of a tie.

After two days rest the Phillies returned rejuvenated and battered the A's with fifteen hits for an easy 9–2 win that evened the series at 2–2–1. After a day of rain, the Phillies really unloaded in Game Six with twenty-three hits off the hapless Weyhing, to take a 17–2 victory and the series advantage. There was to have been a seventh game the next day, but it was canceled because of cold weather, leaving the Phillies the champions of Philadelphia yet again.

1888 Philadelphia   Phillies (NL), 2; Athletics (AA), 1

Both Philadelphia teams finished third in 1888. The Athletics,

though, had defeated the Phillies five games to two in preseason play, and had produced much the better seasonal won-lost record, while leading the AA in batting, slugging, and runs scored. In the fall series—three games this year—they overcame the Phillies in the opener 8–5. But then their bats fell silent as the Phils buried them in the final two games, 8–0 and 12–0.

1889 Philadelphia   Athletics (AA), 3; Phillies (NL), 3

Through 1888 the Phillies had won all six postseason series with the Athletics, but in 1889 their streak ended. They had slipped a notch in the NL standings, while the A's again had finished third, with the AA's best hitting. In postseason play the A's edged the Phillies in their first game 4–3 and overwhelmed them 10–1 in the second. The Phillies replied in kind in Game Three with a 12–2 win, but the A's gained a 3–1 series advantage two days later with a 9–0 whitewash.

Once more, however, the Phillies came back, winning the final two games 3–1 and a narrow 5–4 to salvage a series tie. For the first time, the Athletics could claim a share of the fall title.

It was their last opportunity. After an 1890 season in which both clubs lost players—and fans—to the rival Players League, the Athletics went out of business. Philadelphia's Players League club replaced the A's in the AA for 1891, but as the AA itself folded at season's end, the Philadelphia city series was not resumed until 1903, when the Phillies met a new team, also called the Athletics, which played in the new American League.

1885 St. Louis   Browns (AA), 4; Maroons (NL), 0

The St. Louis Browns were easy winners of the AA pennant in 1885, while the city's Maroons (who had won the pennant of the outlaw Union Association the year before) finished last in their first NL season. Yet there was more interest in the city series between the two clubs than in the World Series between the Browns and NL champion Chicago. Attendance ranged between two and three thousand for the World Series games held in St. Louis in mid-October, but the first city series game, held the day after the Browns-Chicago games, drew "the largest crowd of the season"—there was not even standing room left. And when the city series resumed a week later (after the Browns had completed World Series play, tying Chicago for thew orld title), five times as many spectators showed up as had attended any one of the World Series games.

The Browns scored first in every game with the Maroons and never fell behind, winning all four games as their star pitchers Bob Caruthers and Dave Foutz held the opposition to just one earned run in the series. Twice the Browns scored four runs in the first inning (in Games One and Three), and twice (in Games Two and Four) shut out the Maroons. The first three contests proved easy wins (5–2, 6–0, 11–1); only in the 1–0 finale did the Maroons manage to hold the Browns close.

1886 St. Louis   Browns (AA), 5; Maroons (NL), 0

The Browns repeated as pennant-winners in 1886, and although the Maroons rose to sixth (above two teams new to the NL), they remained helpless against the Browns in postseason play. The city games were scheduled as a best-of-nine series, but only five were needed as the Browns won them all. The opener featured matching five-hitters by the Browns' Dave Foutz and the Maroons' John "Egyptian" Healy. Foutz hurled a shutout, but three of the Browns' hits came in the fourth inning and—with an error and a wild pitch—produced three runs, the game's only scoring.

Nat Hudson held the Maroons to three hits the next day as the Browns buried their opponents 10–1. Eight Maroon errors gave the Browns a 7–2 win in Game Three. In the fourth game the Browns broke a tie in the sixth inning and held on to win 4–2. They then took a week out to defeat Chicago in the World Series before polishing off the Maroons in Game Five with a come-from-behind 6–5 victory. As one paper observed: the Browns "are now the champions of the city,

of the American Association, and of the world." It was the last St. Louis series of the century, for the Maroons folded before the start of the next season.

1886 Maryland   Baltimore Orioles (AA), 3; Washington Senators (NL), 2

The year 1886 featured one new regional major league series, between Baltimore of the AA and the new Washington club of the NL "for the championship of Maryland." (The series carried on an earlier rivalry between Baltimore and the minor league Washington Nationals.) Both clubs finished at the bottom of their leagues and were somewhat evenly matched, with the Orioles edging the Senators three games to two. None of the winning margins in the five games was closer than three runs, but only the opener was a blowout—a 19–1 Washington victory in six innings. Baltimore revived to shut out the Senators 6–0 when the series resumed three days later, and took the series lead the next day with a 6–3 win. Washington evened things with a 3–0 whitewash in Game Five, but lost the deciding game the next day 6–2. Because of darkness, none of the games went the full nine innings.

1887 Maryland   Washington Senators (NL), 3; Baltimore Orioles (AA), 1

The "Maryland" series continued for one more season before fading away. In 1887 Baltimore had enjoyed a resurgence, rising to third place in the AA, while Washington rose only one place out of the NL cellar. But in their postseason series it was the Senators who took the trophy, winning three of four. The Senators averaged a run an inning in Game One in defeating the Orioles 7–4. (Once again darkness ended all the games before nine innings could be played.) Baltimore reversed the score and evened the series with a 7–5 win the next day, but the Senators took the next pair by decisive 5–2 and 7–0 scores to lock up the championship.

1889 Ohio   Columbus Colts (AA), 2; Cleveland Spiders (NL), 1

1889 Ohio   Cincinnati Red Stockings (AA), 3; Cleveland Spiders (NL), 2

Only Philadelphia hosted a city or regional series in 1888, but in 1889 Philadelphia was joined by an Ohio championship that featured three clubs: Cleveland of the NL, and Cincinnati and Columbus of the AA. Every day but two between October 15 and 26, two of the three teams played each other. Cincinnati had enjoyed the best regular season: finishing fourth, it was the only one of the three teams to compile a winning record. Columbus and Cleveland finished sixth in their leagues, but Columbus—a newcomer to the AA—had done well to beat out two more established clubs in its first year.

In the Ohio round-robin Columbus did even better, compiling the best won-lost series record to win the championship. With an overall won-lost series record of 4–1, the Colts easily outclassed Cincinnati (3–4) and Cleveland (3–5), twice defeating the other clubs, while losing once to Cleveland's Spiders.

In games between the two AA clubs, Columbus beat Cincinnati twice by identical 5–2 scores. The interleague play can be subdivided into series between Cleveland and Columbus, and between Cleveland and Cincinnati. Cleveland lost both series, to the Colts 1–2 and to the Reds 2–3. The Spiders defeated Columbus in the opener of their three-game set 5–3, but lost the others (in seven innings each) 9–6 and 6–2. Against Cincinnati the Spiders twice held a series advantage, winning an opening shutout 4–0 and, after losing 8–5, recovering to win a seven-inning contest 4–1. But the Reds then recovered to capture the final pair, 7–2 (the largest victory margin of any of the ten Ohio games) and 3–1.

1890 Ohio   Cincinnati Red Stockings (NL), 2; Cleveland Infants (PL), 1

Neither Columbus nor the Cleveland Spiders took part in an Ohio series the next year, but Cincinnati (which had shifted from the AA to the NL over the winter) played postseason series with three clubs from the new Players League, including three games with the Cleveland Infants, splitting the first two and winning the third. None of the three games offered much suspense. The Reds led all the way in the opener, winning easily 11–4. Game Two was tied 2–2 at the middle of the sixth inning, but from then on the Infants pulled steadily away to an 8–2 conclusion.

Only three hundred spectators showed up for the finale. They were treated to a Cincinnati romp, 14–1, with the Reds scoring seven times in the eighth inning before darkness put an end to the slaughter. As neither Columbus nor Cleveland's NL club participated in postseason play, it may be stretching things to proclaim victorious Cincinnati the champion of Ohio.

Such as it was, the 1890 Ohio series marked the end of interleague city and state championships until early in the next century. The PL died that winter after only one season, and the AA folded at the end of 1891. Not until the arrival of the American League on the major league scene in 1901 would such series again be possible.

At first the National League spurned the upstart American League, but in 1903, along with the first modern World Series between the AL's Boston and the NL's Pittsburgh, city series were played in Chicago, Philadelphia, and St. Louis, and an Ohio series featured Cincinnati and Cleveland. Not since 1886 had so many teams squared off for local and regional postseason play. And, amazingly, the 28-year-old NL was unable to win any of the five inter-league series from the 3-year-old AL.

1903 Chicago   Cubs (NL), 7; White Sox (AL), 7

Chicago's series between the NL's third-place Cubs and the seventh-place White Sox of the AL was far and away the most ambitious city series ever. Fourteen games were scheduled—seven at each team's park—with a fifteenth to be played, if needed to break a tie, at a neutral site. The series would end whenever one team won eight games.

No one expected the series to go the distance, especially when the powerful Cubs won the first three games with a total of twenty-two runs to the White Sox' *one*. But the Sox came back to win Game Four by a convincing 10–2, and through the long series managed to win often enough to prevent the Cubs from feeling overconfident. The Cubs won Game Twelve to take a 7–5 edge in the series. With at least two chances to clinch the championship, the Cubs lost Games Thirteen and Fourteen by identical 2–0 scores—blanked on five hits by the Sox' Frank Owen one day, and on four hits by Nick Altrock the next, October 15. A deciding game should have been played, but a day had been lost because of rain; the Cubs' contracts expired on the fifteenth, and when they refused all inducements to play one more day, the series ended in a 7–7 draw. Never again was a city series scheduled for more than nine games.

1903 Ohio   Cleveland Blues (AL), 6; Cincinnati Reds (NL), 3

Cleveland's Blues (AL) and the Cincinnati Reds finished their seasons with similar winning records, and their nine-game series for the Ohio championship began as a close contest, with the teams splitting the first four games. But Cleveland, after winning Game Four, also took the next three, clinching the title with two games left to play. Cincinnati, though, refused to yield, and in Game Eight fought back from a 2–6 deficit with four runs in the eighth inning to tie the score, and a seventh run in the ninth to win their third game. In the finale later the same afternoon, their pitcher Rip Reagan held the Blues scoreless through seven innings, preserving a 1–0 lead. At the end of the seventh inning, the Cincinnati fans swarmed onto the field to try to persuade the umpire to call the game for darkness. He refused, and in the gloom of the eighth and ninth innings Cleveland scored three runs for a sixth win.

1903 Philadelphia   Athletics (AL), 4; Phillies (NL), 3

Philadelphia's Athletics finished second in the AL while the NL Phillies finished 39½ games back in seventh place. But the Phillies had won a preseason series from the A's, giving the A's some catching up to do if they were to win the overall city championship. Ten games were scheduled, and the A's won four of the first five handily—two of them on shutouts by rookies Weldon Henley and Chief Bender. But the Phillies drove Henley out of Game Six in the first inning on their way to a 14–2 win, and the next day rocked Bender (who pitched the whole game) 13–3. The final three games were rained out. So although the A's captured the fall series 4–3, the Phillies, because they had won four of the five spring games for an overall 7–5 record, were regarded as the city champions.

1903 St. Louis   Browns (AL), 5; Cardinals (NL), 2

In St. Louis it was a series between two losing teams, the last-place Cardinals of the NL and the sixth-place AL Browns. The Browns won the city title easily, clinching the championship with four wins (by an aggregate score of 35–7) before the Cards won a game. But the Cardinals revived to take two of the final three—one of them by the series' most lopsided score, 12–1.

1904 St. Louis   Browns (AL), 3; Cardinals (NL), 3

The volcano of enthusiasm for city and state championship series subsided as quickly as it had erupted. Never again would there be more than three city series in a single year, and in 1904, although the AL's Cleveland played a series against the NL's Pittsburgh, only in St. Louis were teams pitted against each other in city series play. Both the Browns and Cardinals had finished about 30 games behind their league pennant-winners, and they proved evenly matched. In Game One of their series, neither team was able to score more than one run until the top of the tenth, when a two-run homer by Cardinal catcher Mike Grady gave the first win to the National Leaguers.

The Browns snapped back to take the next three games—two of them by a margin of just one run—and come within a game of clinching the series. But in Games Five and Six the Cardinal bats came alive to overwhelm the Browns 8–2 and (with a nine-run third inning) 10–6. With the series tied at three-all, a seventh game was called for. Because the players' contracts expired on October 15, the day of the sixth game, the club owners agreed to pay their players half of the seventh-game proceeds. This was fine with the Browns, but the Cardinals—already upset with their owners about another money matter—refused to play the seventh game unless the players were paid *all* the gate receipts. So Game Seven was not played, and the St. Louis championship remained undecided.

1905 St. Louis   Browns (AL), 4; Cardinals (NL), 3; one tie

Both St. Louis clubs finished even farther behind their league leaders in 1905, with the Browns dropping into the AL cellar. But they did manage to complete their city series, although a doubleheader was needed on the final day to beat the contract deadline. In Game One, the Cardinals scored four runs after two men had been retired in the seventh to win 4–1, and carried a 3–0 lead into the eighth inning of Game Two before the Browns finally erupted with eight runs in the eighth and ninth to even the series. The Cards retaliated 9–1 the next day as Cardinal ace Jack Taylor won his second game of the series. Then pitchers Chappie McFarland of the Cardinals and the Browns' Jack Powell cooled the bats of both teams, neither allowing an earned run over ten innings as their clubs struggled to a 1–1 tie.

The remaining games were closely contested: a 2–1 Browns victory (with Taylor the losing pitcher) evened the series at 2–2, and a 1–0 Cardinal win for rookie hurler Buster Brown put the Cards back on top. The Cards could win the series with victory the next day, and they carried a 6–2 lead into the eighth inning. But the Browns erupted for five runs in the eighth and held on for a narrow 7–6

series-tying win. An eighth game was therefore needed, and as it was October 15 already (the tie game had set the series back a day), this final game was begun immediately after the completion of Game Seven. Pitchers Harry Howell of the Browns and Jack Taylor—both of whom had relieved in the sixth inning of the earlier game—took the mound again for the finale. Each gave up just four hits in the six innings played before darkness descended, but two Brown doubles surrounding a pair of devastating Cardinal muffs scored three Browns in the fifth with the game's only scoring, giving the American Leaguers the championship.

1905 Chicago   Cubs (NL), 4; White Sox (AL), 1

The Cubs and White Sox, after a year off, resumed their Chicago championship series in 1905, this time with a more modest best-of-seven series. Only five of the games were needed as the Cubs, after splitting the first two games, won the final three. Both clubs had enjoyed strong seasons, with 92 wins apiece, and the White Sox had barely lost the AL pennant to Philadelphia, so there was considerable excitement in Chicago about the series, and (despite cold weather) strong attendance that grew with each of the first four games before falling off by a few hundred persons in Game Five.

The Cubs' first two wins came by only one run: 5–4 in the opener and 3–2 in Game Three. The latter game was especially frustrating for the Sox, whose pitcher Doc White held the Cubs to three hits, but saw them score all three of their runs in the third inning on a walk, wild pitch, triple, and two errors. The Cubs showed more authority at the bat in their final pair of wins, overcoming a 2–5 deficit in Game Four with three runs in the sixth and three more an inning later, and attacking in the final contest with five first-inning runs on their way to a 10–5 victory.

1905 Boston   Pilgrims (AL), 6; Beaneaters (NL), 1

Also in 1905, the two Boston clubs for the first time faced each other in the postseason. The Pilgrims (later to be dubbed the Red Sox) were one of the better AL teams, while the Beaneaters (later called the Doves and, eventually, the Braves) dwelt among the dregs of the NL. In the series opener, though, the Beaneaters' Vic Willis (a 29-game loser during the season) held the Pilgrims to seven hits while his teammates took an early lead and built on it throughout the game for a 5–2 win.

But the Pilgrims rebounded in Game Two and never looked back. Veteran hurler Cy Young held the National Leaguers to two hits and fanned fifteen for a 3–1 victory over the Beaneaters' top winner, rookie Irv "Young Cy" Young (not a relative), and the first of six straight Pilgrim wins. Only in the finale, the second game of an October 14 doubleheader, did the Beaneaters threaten to win a second game. They drove out "Old Cy" Young with three runs in the first two innings and maintained their lead until the Pilgrims tied the game in the sixth. The Pilgrims scored a go-ahead run in the eighth, and when rookie Joe Harris (who had relieved Young) completed his seventh inning of shutout relief, the series was over.

1906 St. Louis   Browns (AL), 4; Cardinals (NL), 1; three ties

In 1906 both Chicago clubs won pennants, so their "city series" was the World Series. (The White Sox surprised everyone and beat the Cubs—one of the game's greatest teams ever, with 116 season victories—in six games.) Both Boston clubs, by way of contrast, finished in the cellar and took a year off from postseason competition. Only in St. Louis was there a regular city series in 1906. Although the Browns (who had also won a spring series with the Cardinals) remained champions of St. Louis with four wins and only one loss, the 1905 St. Louis fall series was the tightest city series ever contested. No fewer than three games ended tied, and of the five others, only one was decided by more than one run.

In the opener the Browns, down 1–3, scored twice in the sixth inning to tie the game, and scored their game-winning fourth run in the last of the eighth. The Cardinals took a quick lead with four runs

in the first inning of Game Two, but the Browns tied the game over the next two innings. There the score remained through the ninth inning, when the game was called because of the cold, raw weather. After a day off because of the bad weather, the Browns won another close one with two unearned runs in the fourth inning. The Cards scored one futile run on a single and triple in the eighth—half of the four hits permitted by Brown hurler Jack Powell.

The score in Game Four was tied at 3–3, with two out in the last of the eleventh inning, before the Browns managed to send across a fourth run to take their third series win. The final four games were played in two successive doubleheaders. In the first, the Browns clinched the city crown with the series' only "blowout," a 3–1 three-hitter by Harry Howell. Darkness ended the second game of the day after five innings of scoreless play.

Finally, after four losses and two ties, the Cardinals won a game in the opener of the second doubleheader the next day. Their one run in the top of the first was their only scoring, but it was enough, as rookie Stoney McGlynn shut down the Browns on five hits. Later that afternoon the series ended quietly as darkness closed in to establish the second five-inning scoreless tie in two days.

1907 St. Louis   Cardinals (NL), 5; Browns (AL), 2

In 1907 the Cardinals won their spring series with the Browns, and although they finished their season in the NL cellar, more than twice as many games from first place as the Browns, who finished sixth in the AL, they defeated the Browns again in the fall series to claim for the first time in twenty-one years the championship of their city. (As the AA Browns in the 1880s, the franchise that was now the Cardinals had twice beaten the NL Maroons for the title.)

The Cards traded wins with the Browns through the first four games, but then won the next two by convincing scores of 7–2 and 9–2 to clinch the title. The fifth game was close until the Cardinals exploded for four runs in the eighth inning to put it away, but the sixth game was no contest after the second inning, by which time the Cards had leaped to a 7–0 lead. For good measure the National Leaguers also won the meaningless seventh game, 3–1.

1907 Boston   Pilgrims (AL), 6; Doves (NL), 0; one tie

The only other city series of 1907 saw the Boston clubs face off for a second time. They appeared evenly matched: both had finished seventh in their leagues with nearly identical won-lost records. But although several of the seven games were closely contested, the Doves failed to win a single one. Forty-year-old Cy Young hurled a four-hit 4–1 win for the Pilgrims in the opener. The Doves tied the second game at 2–2 with a run in the last of the ninth, but lost the game when the American Leaguers scored twice in the eleventh.

The Doves lost two more close ones in a doubleheader the next day. Irv "Young Cy" Young allowed the Pilgrims only four hits in the first game, but Pilgrim runs in the first and seventh innings defeated him 2–1. In the nightcap, "Old Cy" was given a four-run cushion in the Pilgrim half of the third inning, but lost it as the Doves scored twice each in the fourth and fifth innings to tie the game. But Young shut the Doves out over the final four innings while his Pilgrims scored a run in the top of the ninth for their fourth—and title-clinching—victory.

Although they had no hope of winning the series, the Doves persevered through the final three games. In Game Five they rallied for two runs in the last of the ninth before falling 6–4. And in Game Six (the first of another doubleheader), they carried a 4–1 lead into the ninth, only to lose as a walk and four hits produced four Pilgrim runs. In the nightcap the Doves finally prevented a Pilgrim victory. The Pilgrims took an early three-run lead, but the Doves caught up in the middle innings as "Young Cy" settled down to what would become eight innings of shutout ball. But the Doves also failed to score after the fifth inning off Pilgrim rookie Tex Pruiett, and darkness ended the game after ten innings in a 3–3 tie. In the forty-six years before the Braves moved to Milwaukee in 1953, the Boston teams never again concluded their season with a city championship series.

1909 Chicago   Cubs (NL), 4; White Sox (AL), 1

No clubs at all played city series in 1908, but the next year the Chicago Cubs, after three straight pennants and World Series involvement, were once again free to resume their rivalry with the White Sox for the championship of the Windy City. The Cubs, who finished second to Pittsburgh in the NL pennant race, possessed the league's best pitching and dispatched the fourth-place Sox for the city title with only one loss. Orval Overall and Mordecai Brown, the Cubs' top hurlers, won two games apiece in the series. Overall shut out the Sox in the opener, and Brown took the second game as the Cubs came from behind with four runs in the final two innings for a 5–2 win. The next day the Sox won their only game. The large crowd of over 24,000, which stayed to the end despite a persistent rain, saw a 1–1 tie broken in the ninth inning when Cub pitcher Ed Reulbach balked in the tie-breaking run to hand the Sox's Ed Walsh the victory.

The final two Cub victories were just as close. In Game Four—played after three days of postponement for wet grounds and cold weather—Overall and Walsh matched five-hitters, but two of Walsh's four walks led to Cub scoring, and Overall emerged a 2–1 winner. The Cubs bunched four of their six hits in Game Five into the fourth inning for their only run as the Sox's Doc White pitched shutout ball over the other eight innings. But the Cubs' Brown hurled the series masterpiece, yielding only one hit, a single, in the fifth inning and a pair of harmless walks in the ninth for a series-ending shutout.

1910 New York   Giants (NL), 4; Yankees (AL), 2; one tie

The Cubs won another pennant in 1910, so there was no city series in Chicago. But Cleveland and Cincinnati resurrected the Ohio championship after a six-year hiatus, and New York's AL Yankees and NL Giants competed for the first time against each other in postseason play. The two New York teams had finished second in their leagues, and their series opener drew an overflow crowd to the Polo Grounds to see the matchup between Giant great Christy Mathewson (27–9 that season) and the Yankees' rookie sensation Russ Ford (26–6). For 7½ innings it was a tight game, but in the last of the eighth, two costly Yankee errors and a hit batsman, plus four Giant hits, broke open a 1–1 tie with four runs for a Giant victory. Mathewson struck out fourteen. The Yankees came from behind the next day with four runs in the final two innings to even the series with a 5–4 win, but a day later the Giants took the lead for good as Mathewson won his second game 6–4.

Following a ten-inning 5–5 tie in Game Four, Mathewson returned to record his (and the Giants') third victory. But the Yankees, down one game to three, staved off defeat in Game Six with the series' most overwhelming win. Capitalizing on two walks and an error in the second inning, they contributed six hits (four of them doubles) to score eight runs in the inning and take a 10–2 victory. But after a day of rain the Giants (and Mathewson) came back to capture the city championship with their fourth win. The Yankees tagged Matty for ten hits, but he walked none and fanned eight, and the Yankees' porous defense let in three runs in the 6–3 Giant victory.

1910 Ohio   Cincinnati Reds (NL), 4; Cleveland Naps (AL), 3

Both Ohio clubs finished fifth in 1910 and showed themselves evenly matched in their series, which went the full seven games before Cincinnati captured the crown. Curiously, though, none of the games involved a close finish, and only twice did the lead change hands after the third inning. In Game Five (shortened to seven innings by darkness) Cleveland led 2–0 after five innings, but Cincinnati exploded in the sixth with six hits. These, combined with a pair of Cleveland errors, gave the Reds five runs and the game. And in the finale, with the series tied at three-all, Cleveland opened the scoring with four runs in the fourth inning, only to see Cincinnati top them with five runs two innings later. The Naps tied the game with a run in the top of the seventh, but Cincinnati scored two in their half of the

inning to regain the lead and added an insurance run in the eighth to make the final score 8–5. As it turned out, the home team won every game.

1911 Ohio   *Cincinnati Reds (NL), 4; Cleveland Naps (AL), 2*

Cincinnati needed only six games to win the 1911 Ohio series, although in regular-season play they had finished sixth while Cleveland's Naps took third in the AL. Also the Reds were handicapped by a home-field disadvantage. Because of the upcoming construction of new stands at their Palace of the Fans, only the series' first two games were scheduled for Cincinnati; the rest would be played in Cleveland. But Cincinnati's rain-soaked grounds held up only for the opening game, so the Reds enjoyed the home advantage only that once. It didn't seem to matter. They won the first three games: the first two handily, and the third with four runs in the top of the ninth to tie the game, then two more in the eleventh to win it. Cleveland took the next two, but then Red ace George Suggs, who had blanked Cleveland in the opener, repeated the feat in Game Six with a four-hitter to clinch the title for Cincinnati.

Financially the series was a failure. Fewer than five hundred fans attended the opener, and the final four games were rescheduled as doubleheaders in an effort to attract larger crowds. It was six years before the two clubs met again for a fall Ohio series.

1911 Chicago   *White Sox (AL), 4; Cubs (NL), 0*

Chicago's second-place Cubs and fourth-place White Sox resumed their city series in 1911 after a year's gap in which the Cubs played in another World Series. If the Ohio series was a financial bust, Chicago's was just the opposite, with the third-game attendance of 36,608 setting a new record for baseball in the city. The White Sox fans rejoiced in the outcome of the series: a four-game sweep of the heavily favored Cubs.

The opener was especially rewarding for Sox fans. For seven innings Cub ace Mordecai Brown pitched shutout ball as his club built a three-run lead. But the Sox scored once in the eighth when their pitching ace Ed Walsh scored on a single after tripling with two outs, and three more times in the ninth when four straight singles drove in the runs needed to win the game.

Game Two was a slugfest, with a triple and nine doubles among the game's twenty-nine hits. But the result was as close as in Game One, with the Sox coming from behind with two runs in the eighth for an 8–7 win. The final two victories came easier for the American Leaguers, as they scored first in both games and held their lead all the way for wins of 4–2 and 7–2.

1911 St. Louis   *Browns (AL), 4; Cardinals (NL), 3; one tie*

After three years without postseason play, the St. Louis clubs also resumed their city series in 1911. In the spring the Cardinals had defeated the Browns seven straight times, and during the season had placed fifth in the NL while the Browns ended up in the AL cellar. But their fall series showed the two clubs to be evenly matched, with darkness ending the opener after nine innings in a scoreless tie. In the second game the Cardinals broke a 2–2 tie with a run in the sixth, and held on for a narrow victory.

The Browns erupted in the third game, though, for ten runs and an easy win, and followed it up the next day by capturing both ends of a doubleheader, 6–2 and (with three runs in the last inning of the darkness-shortened nightcap) 10–8. The Cardinals won easily in Game Six, 9–5, leading all the way. But in a concluding doubleheader the next day the Browns broke a 1–1 tie with four runs in the final two innings of the first game to clinch the city title. The second game was played anyway, and the Cards reversed the score with an easy 5–1 win to tighten the overall fall series record to 4–3–1.

1912 Philadelphia   *Athletics (AL), 4; Phillies (NL), 1*

In 1912 Philadelphia's Phillies and Athletics returned to the city series circuit after an absence of eight years. The mighty A's (who had finished third after winning pennants the two previous seasons) were heavy favorites to defeat the NL fifth-place Phillies, but the Phillies surprised them in Game One, breaking a tie with four runs in the final two innings for an 8–4 victory. It was an auspicious start, but it was also their last hurrah, for the A's then made short work of the series with four straight wins. They never trailed in Games Two and Three, winning 6–1 and 4–0 (on a three-hitter by rookie Byron Houck).

Game Four was tighter, and the Phillies even took a brief 2–1 lead with a pair of runs in the third inning. But the A's came right back with two in the fourth and held on for a 4–3 win. The Phillies scored in the first inning of the final game, were tied in the second and passed in the third, but regained a tie at 2–2 in the fifth. But in the sixth inning the A's rallied for three runs against Phillie reliever George Chalmers. A's starter, Boardwalk Brown, who had been ineffective in two previous appearances, held the Phillies scoreless over the final four innings, and the Athletics were champions of Philadelphia.

The A's won the pennant the next two years, and the Phillies won their first ever in 1915. But although neither club played in a World Series for many years after that, they never again challenged each other in the fall for the city crown.

1912 Chicago   *White Sox (AL), 4; Cubs (NL), 3; two ties*

The Chicago series of 1912 took a while to show any results. The first game was delayed a day because of rain, and then the teams endured a nine-inning scoreless tie. (Cub rookie Jimmy Lavender held the White Sox to six hits, but the star of the game was the Sox's Ed Walsh, who gave up only one hit—a double to Cub shortstop Joe Tinker—while fanning seven and walking none.) Another day of rain delayed Game Two, and although both teams finally put some runs on the board, they ended up after twelve innings tied again, at 3–3. (Walsh pitched the final three innings of shutout relief for the Sox.)

The Cubs won the next three games. In Game Three they carried a 5–3 lead into the last of the ninth. With two away, the Sox scored one run and loaded the bases, but Cub pitcher Lavender struck out the next man to preserve his victory. The Cubs' Ed Reulbach dueled scorelessly with Ed Walsh through five innings of Game Four. Both clubs scored a run in the sixth (ending Walsh's consecutive scoreless innings pitched at 17). The Sox regained the lead with another run in the seventh, but the Cubs tagged Walsh for three in their half of the inning. Reulbach held the Sox scoreless over the final two innings for the win. After the two close games, the Cubs blew the Sox away in Game Five, 8–1.

Lavender and Walsh faced each other in Game Six as they had in the opener. There was some scoring this time, but at the end of nine innings the game was again tied, at 4–4. In the eleventh the Sox broke the tie to give Walsh (after thirty-one total innings pitched) and the club their first win of the series. The Cubs still had three chances to eliminate the Sox; each time they failed. In Game Seven the Sox overcame a 3–4 deficit with four runs in the eighth inning. A ninth-inning Cub rally fell two runs short, and the Sox had kept themselves alive. In Game Eight the Sox overcame a Cub lead with three runs in the fifth inning (on home runs by Shano Collins and Buck Weaver), but two Cub runs in the eighth put them on top again, 5–4. In the top of the ninth, though, the Sox put together two walks, a single, a triple, and a ground out for four runs. Walsh, coming on in relief, held the Cubs scoreless in the last of the ninth, and the series was evened at three wins apiece.

Although he had already pitched three complete games and relieved twice in nine days, Walsh was named to start the series finale. He was in top form, but the Sox made it easy for him, running through four Cub pitchers for sixteen runs in the first five innings, including a nine-hit, eight-run third. Fred Toney, the Cubs' fifth pitcher, held the Sox scoreless the rest of the way, but it was wasted effort, for Walsh was hurling his second shutout of the series, a five-hitter for his fourth complete game.

Walsh, who had won twenty-seven games during the regular sea-

son, won only eight the next year, and only thirteen in his final five seasons of major league ball. Some fault the White Sox for using him so heavily in what was only an exhibition series in the fall of 1912. But he had been used heavily throughout his career, leading the league in innings pitched in four of his final six good seasons. His city series work was little more intensive than what he was normally accustomed to. Furthermore, in Chicago the city series was viewed more seriously than anywhere else. The crowds rivaled, and often exceeded, those for World Series games held in the city. The fans saw the city series as a genuine championship event, and the clubs responded by playing all out. To have rested their ace at crucial moments of the series would have been out of the question for the Sox management, and probably also for Walsh himself.

1912 St. Louis Cardinals (NL), 4; Browns (AL), 3; one tie

St. Louis hosted a city series again in 1912. As usual, its clubs had endured losing seasons, but also as usual, the battle for the city championship was hotly contested. The Cardinals moved out to a two-game advantage with a pair of close wins. Behind 3–6 in the opener, they scored three runs in the eighth inning to tie the score, and won the game in the tenth when Browns' reliever Mack Allison issued a walk with the bases loaded. In Game Two, another bases-full walk in the fifth and a Brown error at first base three innings later gave the Cards two of their runs in a 3–2 victory.

The Browns threw rookie lefthander Carl Weilman (2–4 during the season) against the Cardinals in Game Three, and he shut them out on one hit—a double that many in the stands thought landed foul. The Browns hoped to even the series the next day, and they received fine seven-hit pitching from young Earl Hamilton. But the Cardinals' Big Bill Steele pitched even better, yielding only three hits. Errors on both sides led to two early runs for both clubs, and the score remained 2–2 until darkness halted play after ten innings.

The Cardinals overwhelmed the Browns 10–4 in Game Five to take a 3–1 series advantage, but the Browns fought back to win both ends of a doubleheader the next day, tying the series as Weilman hurled his second shutout in the nightcap. But in the finale a day later, with Steele and Hamilton again facing each other, Steele emerged the victor, 6–1, with a masterly four-hitter, and his Cardinals were kings of St. Louis.

1913 Chicago White Sox (AL), 4; Cubs (NL), 2

Both Chicago clubs enjoyed winning records in 1913, but the stronger Cubs were, as ever, favored in the city series. And, as so often happened in the long history of the series, the White Sox proved the pundits wrong. In the opener the Sox took the lead in the first inning and held it all the way, but the Cubs came back the next day to score a tie-breaking sixth run in the top of the thirteenth inning, and take the win as Jim "Hippo" Vaughn (who pitched the whole game) held the Sox scoreless for the fifth straight inning since yielding their tying run in the eighth. Bert Humphries hurled a four-hit shutout for the Cubs in Game Three to put them ahead in the series 2–1, but they won no more that year.

In Game Four the Sox took the lead for the first time with three runs in the seventh inning for an ultimate 5–2 win. Sox pitcher Eddie Cicotte helped his own cause with three hits (two of them doubles), and scored two of his team's runs. No one scored at all through the first ten innings of Game Five as Cub ace Larry Cheney dueled the Sox's Joe Benz. Benz allowed the Cubs only three hits in the game. Cheney permitted ten, but only the final three—plus a steal of home by Shano Collins—hurt him, as the Sox scored two runs in the top of the eleventh to win it. The Cubs scored the first run in the fourth inning of Game Six, but the Sox retaliated with three in that inning and two more in the next, and held on for another 5–2 victory—and, once more, the city title.

1913 St. Louis Browns (AL), 3; Cardinals (NL), 3; two ties

The St. Louis series of 1913 was—as it had been before—a contest between cellar dwellers. And, as in previous series, the clubs found themselves evenly matched. The game scores were not all as close as they had been in the series of 1906, but the overall result was closer—a series tie, with each team posting three wins and sharing two ties.

Four of the eight games were closely contested, including the opener. Although the Browns' Carl Weilman gave up only one hit, he also gave up the game's only run when in the second inning he walked the first man up and saw him take third on his own throwing error and score on a double play. The winner of this beneficence was Cardinal ace Slim Sallee, who permitted only four hits himself in his shutout. The Cards pushed to a 2–0 series advantage the next day with a 4–1 victory in a game that was shortened by darkness to seven innings.

The final six games of the series were bunched into three doubleheaders on successive days. The Browns took the opener of the first pair of games, 8–5, and scored twice in the sixth inning of the nightcap to tie the game just before darkness ended it. In the opener of the second doubleheader, the Browns rallied in the final two innings from a 3–6 deficit to even the series with a 7–6 win, then went on to take the series lead with an easy 6–2 win in another darkness-shortened nightcap. The Cards brought the series even once again with an easy 5–2 win in the opener the next day. Brown first baseman Del Pratt was ejected from the game after an argument with the umpires and a fight with an opposing player, and when the umpires refused to let him play the second game, the Browns argued until the umpires left the field. They later returned, but the delay caused the series finale to be called for darkness after only five innings, with the score tied 1–1 and the series still even. Another game was expected, but because of the bitterness that Pratt's fight had engendered between the teams, the club officials declared the series ended, "leaving [as *Sporting Life* commented] the question of which is the worst team in the two major leagues still in doubt."

1914 New York Giants (NL), 4; Yankees (AL), 1

The New York Giants had won the NL pennant in 1911–1913, but when they slipped to second in 1914 they returned to a city series with the Yankees (who had tied for sixth in the AL). As expected, the Giants won the city title, but not without a struggle in the first three games. A Yankee run in the ninth inning of the opener tied the back-and-forth contest at 5–5, but a Giant triple and single in the last of the tenth ended it. The Giants led 1–0 in Game Two—until Jeff Tesreau's wildness in the last of the ninth allowed two Yankees to score. It proved to be the only Yankee victory. The Giants, in Game Three, recorded their second 6–5 ten-inning win when pitcher Al Demaree singled in the final inning and came all the way around to score as the ball got by the right fielder for a three-base error. They then polished off the Yankees in two final games as pitchers Art Fromme and Demaree hurled matching five-hit wins, 6–1 and 4–1.

1914 Chicago White Sox (AL), 4; Cubs (NL), 3

The White Sox experienced considerable difficulty subduing the Cubs in 1914. The Cubs led all the way in Game One, and while the Sox came from behind to even the series with a 5–2 win (on Jim Scott's four-hitter) in Game Two, they lost Games Three and Four in close 2–1 and 4–3 contests. Game Four was particularly frustrating, as the Cubs ruined Eddie Cicotte's shutout bid with two tying runs in the last of the ninth, then overcame a go-ahead tally by the White Sox in the top of the tenth with two more runs to win it in the last half of the inning.

But, as they did so often in their battles with the Cubs, the Sox rallied themselves to victory. Wins of 3–1 and 5–3 evened the series. Then, in the finale, while hitting safely only twice against three Cub pitchers, they bunched both hits with a Cub error and two walks in the fourth inning for three runs. The Cubs had scored twice in the first inning off Jim Scott, but Cicotte then came on to blank them over the final eight and bring the American Leaguers their fourth straight Chicago crown.

1914 St. Louis   Browns (AL), 4; Cardinals (NL), 1; one tie

Both St. Louis clubs bounded out of the cellar in 1914. But while the Browns rose to fifth place, the Cardinals leaped all the way to third. In the series for the St. Louis title, though, the Browns emerged the victors, winning the first three games before the Cards could put their foot in the door. The Browns scored first and led throughout all three games, with Big Bill James providing the top pitching performance: a four-hit 2–0 shutout in Game Three, the first game of a doubleheader. Darkness ended the nightcap after five innings, but it remained light just long enough for the Cards to score a pair of runs for a 2–0 win of their own.

But they won no more. The first game of another doubleheader the next day featured the series' third consecutive 2–0 contest; the seldom-used Harry Hoch (who pitched eight innings) and George Baumgardner combined to hold the Cardinals to one hit as the Browns clinched the city championship. With the series decided, the nightcap was played "as an exhibition," ending after seven innings in a 2–2 tie.

1915 Chicago   White Sox (AL), 4; Cubs (NL), 1

Although New York's Giants and Yankees would in later years engage in several memorable World Series, they never again met solely for the championship of New York. Only Chicago and St. Louis carried on the tradition in 1915. In Chicago, for a change, the White Sox finished the season with the better record and found themselves favored in the local series. Their series victory, though, was nothing new, although they triumphed more easily than they had since their sweep of 1911.

None of the five games was decided by fewer than three runs, although a couple were closer than the scores indicate. The Sox won the opener 9–5, for example, but as late as the seventh inning they trailed 2–5, when a four-run spurt thrust them into the lead to stay. The Cubs enjoyed their only victory in Game Two as Jimmy Lavender hurled a sparkling four-hitter for a 4–0 win, ensured by Heinie Zimmerman's three-run homer in the sixth inning.

Zimmerman's bat remained active the next day as he connected for four of the Cubs' five hits, but by the time he doubled home the Cubs' first run in the ninth, the Sox had already scored five times. Zimmerman himself went on to score a second Cub run, but Sox starter Red Faber then closed down the Cubs' offensive threat to record the second Sox win. Sox first baseman Shano Collins hit a grand slam in a five-run third inning in Game Four, more than enough support for Jim Scott, who blanked the Cubs on four hits. The Sox bats exploded for a pair of five-run innings in Game Five as they brought the championship home to the South Side—for the fifth year in a row—by a convincing 11–3 score.

1915 St. Louis   Browns (AL), 4; Cardinals (NL), 1; one tie

The Browns in 1915 won their second successive St. Louis crown by the same combination of four wins, one loss, and a tie that had brought them victory the year before. Once again, also, they built up a 3–0 edge before allowing the Cardinals their token win. Although they won the first game by just one run, the Browns never trailed, whereas in the second game they never led—although three times they came from behind to tie the game. Their second run came on a two-out single in the last of the ninth and sent the game into extra innings. The Cardinals scored their third run in the top of the twelfth, but in the bottom of the inning another Brown single with two away locked the score again. Darkness prevented a thirteenth inning.

After rain washed out two days of play, the Browns took both ends of a doubleheader by a margin of four runs apiece, 5–1 and 6–2, to reach the threshhold of victory. But the Cardinals took a 3–2 lead in the second inning of the first game the next day and widened it to 7–2 by game's end. In the nightcap, though, the Browns scored five times before darkness halted play, while rookie hurler Tim McCabe held the Cardinals scoreless to conclude the series.

1916 Chicago   White Sox (AL), 4; Cubs (NL), 0

Only four games comprised Chicago's city series in 1916 as the ascendant second-place White Sox swept the floundering fifth-place Cubs. The National Leaguers overcame a 1–0 White Sox lead in the opener with a pair of sixth-inning runs, but the Sox drove out Cub starter Hippo Vaughn an inning later and continued their assault on reliever Claude Hendrix for a total of seven runs in the seventh and eighth innings and an 8–2 win. The Sox scored in only one inning the next day, but their three runs were two more than their pitcher Red Faber permitted the Cubs.

Claude Williams's shutout pitching and Joe Jackson's three doubles were the features of the Sox' 3–0 win in Game Three. In the series clincher the next day, the Sox were outhit by Cub batters 10–9, but bunched their hits for three runs in the third and three more in the fifth (while the scattered Cub blows produced only single runs in three separate innings). Cub slugger Cy Williams connected for two doubles and a triple, but the Sox's Joe Jackson countered with a pair of singles and a home run.

1916 St. Louis   Browns (AL), 4; Cardinals (NL), 1

For the third year in a row the Browns' margin of victory over the Cardinals for the championship of St. Louis was four games to one. The only difference in 1916 was that no game ended in a tie. The Browns won the first two. In the opener they built up a 5–0 lead over the first six innings; the Cardinals rallied for two in the seventh and another run in the eighth, but ran out of steam in the ninth. In the second game, the Cards scored first with a pair of third-inning runs. But by the end of the fourth inning the Browns had taken a 3–2 lead, which they held to the 4–3 conclusion.

The Cardinals posted their only win in Game Three, countering a Browns two-run rally in the ninth with a final run of their own in the bottom of the inning for a narrow 5–4 win. The Browns' third victory, in the first game of a doubleheader the next day, was, if anything, even tighter. In the third and seventh innings they matched Cardinal go-ahead runs with their own game-tying tallies, and struggled against the tie until the last of the tenth when, with two men out, they pushed across a third run. They triumphed more easily in the darkness-shortened clincher later that afternoon, with the series' widest margin of victory, 4–1.

1917 St. Louis   Cardinals (NL), 4; Browns (AL), 2; one tie

In 1917, for the first time in five years, the Cardinals took the St. Louis title from the Browns. After winning two close games 3–2 and 3–1, they lost a close one in the first game of a doubleheader, 5–4, in ten innings. But when the nightcap was called after five innings for darkness, the Cards enjoyed a 6–1 lead, and entered a second doubleheader the next day with only one win needed for the championship.

But the Cards scored no runs in either game, losing the first 2–0, but holding the Browns scoreless too in the nightcap until darkness ended it after the ninth inning, still tied. The next day, in the seventh game of the series, the Cardinals finally put together the victory they had so long sought—and they did it comfortably, 6–1.

1917 Ohio   Cincinnati Reds (NL), 4; Cleveland Indians (AL), 2

Also in 1917 the Cincinnati Reds and Cleveland Indians made a last stab at an Ohio series. It was their first in six years and would prove their last. The clubs were fairly evenly matched: Cleveland, an improving team, had finished third in the AL, while Cincinnati had jumped from a last-place tie in 1916 to fourth in the NL. In their postseason series, Cincinnati prevailed. The opener was a blowout for the Reds, 11–2, but they needed thirteen innings in the second game for Pete Schneider, their stingiest pitcher, to edge the Indians' ERA leader, Stan Coveleski, 2–1. The venue shifted to Cleveland for Game Three, but the Reds continued their streak with a 4–2 win in eight innings.

Cleveland awoke with a start to take their first win the next day, pummeling Reds' pitching for sixteen hits to award their hurler Ed Klepfer an easy 8–0 victory. The Indians continued their roll in Game Five with a convincing 6–3 win at Cincinnati. But when the series moved back to Cleveland for Game Six, the Reds retaliated with their own eight-run burst to win the state crown behind Hod Eller's one-run pitching.

From 1917 through 1919 either the White Sox or Cubs played in the World Series, forcing the suspension of the postseason Chicago championship series. In 1920 both clubs were available again, but the White Sox had been shamed and decimated by the exposure of their 1919 World Series fix and the expulsion from baseball of the seven guilty players still on the team. So no city series was held that year either. In fact, no city or regional series had been held anywhere from 1918 through 1920, and when the Chicago clubs resumed their rivalry in 1921 they were all by themselves. They played sixteen series over the next twenty-two years, and although the Cubs were the stronger club most of those years during the season, the White Sox continued to dominate intra-city play.

1921 Chicago   White Sox (AL), 5; Cubs (NL), 0

1922 Chicago   Cubs (NL), 4; White Sox (AL), 3

1923 Chicago   White Sox (AL), 4; Cubs (NL), 2

1924 Chicago   White Sox (AL), 4; Cubs (NL), 2

The Sox swept a best-of-nine series in five games in 1921 to increase to twelve their string of winning games against the Cubs—and to seven their string of city championships. The Cubs revived the next year to capture a best-of-seven series on a seventh-game shutout by veteran great Grover Cleveland Alexander, but the Sox came back for a pair of 4–2 series triumphs in 1923 and 1924.

1925 Chicago   Cubs (NL), 4; White Sox (AL), 1; one tie

1926 Chicago   White Sox (AL), 4; Cubs (NL), 3

In 1925 the Cubs won their most convincing city title in years, taking four of five games after an opening-game tie in which both the Cubs' thirty-eight-year-old Alexander and the Sox's Ted Blankenship pitched the entire nineteen innings. The White Sox recovered to take the 1926 series in seven games (four of which were shutouts), but then, after a year without a series because the losing Cubs declined to issue the customary challenge, the Sox lost two series in a row to their North Side competitors—something that had never happened before.

1928 Chicago   Cubs (NL), 4; White Sox (AL), 3

1930 Chicago   Cubs (NL), 4; White Sox (AL), 2

The Cubs needed the full seven games to win the 1928 series. Most of the games were decided by a margin of two runs or less, but the Cubs didn't dither around in the finale as they unleashed a sixteen-hit attack for a 13–2 victory. After a year off for the World Series (which they lost to the Philadelphia Athletics, four games to one), the Cubs in 1930 captured their second successive Chicago crown, in six games.

They lost the opener, but came back to take the second game on Kiki Cuyler's three-run homer in the eighth. In Game Three they buried the Sox under eighteen hits and twelve runs, but lost a second time, 8–2, the next day. With Cuyler, Hack Wilson (who homered), and Gabby Hartnett driving in two runs each, the Cubs took the series edge with a 6–4 win in Game Five, and clinched the title the next day with a come-from-behind three-run rally in the top of the ninth for another 6–4 victory. Wilson starred again, with a solo homer in the fifth and an RBI single to begin the ninth-inning scoring.

1931 Chicago   White Sox (AL), 4; Cubs (NL), 3

1933 Chicago   White Sox (AL), 4; Cubs (NL), 0

The White Sox won all the remaining eight city series. In 1931 the third-place Cubs battled the last-place Sox to Game Seven before falling before Tommy Thomas's four-hitter. The next year the Cubs were swept by the New York Yankees in the World Series, and in 1933 the sixth-place White Sox swept the third-place Cubs for the Chicago championship—twice shutting them out and permitting only three Cub runs over the four games while scoring nineteen.

1936 Chicago   White Sox (AL), 4; Cubs (NL), 0

When the Cubs faltered at the end of the 1934 pennant race, they decided to go home quietly rather than face a city series. In 1935 they were again back in the World Series (a loss to Detroit). They returned to play a Chicago series in 1936—after finishing tied for second in the NL pennant race—only to be swept in four games by the White Sox for the second city series in a row. At least their loss this time was to a Sox club that had also played well during the season, finishing third.

1937 Chicago   White Sox (AL), 4; Cubs (NL), 3

The Chicago clubs again finished second and third in their leagues in 1937, and this year in the Chicago championship the Cubs put up a struggle, winning three games. But so did the Sox, and in the seventh game the Sox won the series with (for Cub fans) discouraging ease, 6–1.

1939 Chicago   White Sox (AL), 4; Cubs (NL), 3

Nineteen thirty-eight was another World Series year for the Cubs (and another 0–4 loss to the Yankees). This was the last interruption to the Chicago series. Both Chicago clubs finished fourth in 1939 and made a battle of it in the postseason. The Cubs, in fact, came close to winning the series, carrying a 3–1 advantage in games and a favorable 5–0 score into the sixth inning of Game Five. But by the middle of the eighth inning, the Sox had tied the score at five-all, and by the end of the tenth inning the Cubs were looking at an 8–5 loss. They scored only once in each of the two remaining games as the White Sox came back to take yet another Chicago crown with six and seven runs respectively.

1940 Chicago   White Sox (AL), 4; Cubs (NL), 3

1941 Chicago   White Sox (AL), 4; Cubs (NL), 0

1942 Chicago   White Sox (AL), 4; Cubs (NL), 2

The Cubs dropped to fifth and the White Sox tied for fourth in 1940, then battled each other through another seven games in the Chicago series before the Sox carried off the crown. The next season the Cubs fell one more notch, to sixth, but the Sox rose to third and celebrated with another city series sweep—their sixth. They won the first three postseason games in 1942, too, but the Cubs rose up to take the fourth game 5–3, and the fifth as well, 2–1, in ten innings. But the Cubs won no more. In the sixth game a 4–1 White Sox victory gave the Sox (including their 1906 World Series triumph over the Cubs) their nineteenth Chicago championship in twenty-five tries.

Occasionally thereafter the Cubs played the White Sox at the end of spring training, and for twenty-four years, from 1949 through 1972, the two clubs met in a midseason exhibition. But neither they nor any other major league clubs since 1942 have challenged in October for the championship of their region, state, or city.

The Ultimate Baseball Library
Paul D. Adomites

If you could buy any baseball books you wanted, if money were no object, and if you could even go back in time to get books that are no longer available, which ones would comprise The Ultimate Baseball Library? That's the question this article sets out to answer. And the books had to be predominantly baseball books; general sports books with baseball references were, for the most part, omitted.

Briefly put, the criterion was: What are the best books in each of the areas of baseball writing—not as collectors' items, but in how they illuminate some aspect of this great game for our eyes, how they remind us of the game's pleasure, or how they use the game's myths and memories to create something altogether new.

The explosion of baseball literature in the past two decades greatly swelled the number of books listed. Twenty-five years ago, the "Ultimate Library" might have been half as large. Because of the hundreds of books involved, this was not a solo effort: The list could not have been compiled without the help of many well-read friends in the Society for American Baseball Research, most particularly Frank Phelps and the other members of the SABR Bibliography Committee.

Statistics

Bruno, Joseph. *Baseball's Golden Dozen*. Hicksville, N.Y.: Exposition Press, 1976.

Carr, Bill. *The Baseball Matrix*. New York: Ballston SPA, various dates. For seasons 1950, 1980–1985.

Clifton, Merritt. *Relative Baseball II*. Richford, Vt.: Samisdat Press, 1985.

Cook, Earnshaw. *Percentage Baseball*. Baltimore: Waverley Press, 1964.

Cook, Earnshaw, with Donald L. Fink. *Percentage Baseball and the Computer*. Baltimore: Waverley Press, 1971. "In these two books, Cook laid the groundwork for serious math applications to baseball statistics and much of it is still valid and useful." (Frank V. Phelps).

Davenport, John. *Baseball Graphics*. Madison, Wis.: First Impressions, 1979.

———*Baseball's Pennant Races: A Graphic View*. Madison, Wisc.: First Impressions, 1981. This book describes pennant races, showing where each team was in the race throughout the season, which makes it a handy reference tool.

Jackson, Davis. *The Last Word in Baseball Statistics*. New Braunfels, Texas: Jackson Research, annual since 1986. Addressing subjects such as ballparks and fielding, offensive strategy, clutch hitting and industry economics, Jackson applies the latest sabermetric principles to current players and teams.

James, Bill. *The Bill James Baseball Abstract*. New York: Ballantine Books, annually 1982–1988. Privately published by the author 1977–1981. As the inventor of the term "sabermetrics," James is a deep thinker on baseball statistical matters. But a key to his popularity is his ability to write wittily and boldly. Good reading no matter how you look at baseball.

James, Bill, John Dewan, and others. *The Great American Baseball Stat Book*. New York: Ballantine Books, annual beginning in 1987. The work of the James-founded Project Scoresheet—a look back at the previous year sabermetrically is fascinating but uneven.

Koppett, Leonard. *A Thinking Man's Guide to Baseball*. New York: E. P. Dutton, 1967.

Lanigan, Ernest. *The Baseball Cyclopedia*. New York: Baseball Magazine, 1922, with annual updates through 1933. A pioneering work by an early sabermetrician.

Mills, Eldon G. and Harland D. *Player Win Averages*. Cranberry, N.J.: A. S. Barnes, 1970.

Moreland, George. *Balldom*. "The Britannica of Baseball." New York: Balldom Publishing Co., 1914.

Oliver, Ted. *Kings of the Mound*. Los Angeles: privately published, 1944; 2nd ed., 1947.

Neft, David S. and Richard Cohen. *The Sports Encyclopedia: Baseball*. 5th ed., New York: Grosset & Dunlap, 1982. Organized by years and teams, with a brief narrative history of each season, by two of the prime movers of the original Macmillan *Baseball Encyclopedia*.

Reichler, Joseph, ed. *The Baseball Encyclopedia*. New York: Macmillan. 1st ed. 1969. Updated complete editions, 1974, 1976, 1979, 1982, 1985, 1988. Annual updates including only active players, since 1986. Lifetime stats for every player and manager, along with year-by-year season finishes and leaders.

Siwoff, Seymour, Steve Hirdt, and Peter Hirdt. *The Elias Baseball Analyst*. New York: Macmillan. Annual since 1986. Day-night, turf-grass, righty-lefty, and more—dauntingly thorough.

Tattersall, John C. *Home Run Handbook, 1876–1974*. Havertown, Pa.: Privately published by the author, 1975.

The Sporting News, eds. *Daguerreotypes of Great Stars of Baseball*. St. Louis, Mo.: The Sporting News, 1934, 1951, 1958, 1961, 1968, 1971, 1981. Lifetime stats— including minor leagues—for stars, particularly Hall of Famers. Early editions especially useful.

Thorn, John and Pete Palmer, with David Reuther. *The Hidden Game of Baseball*. Garden City, N.Y.: Doubleday, 1984. Designed for serious sabermetricians, this work still has substantial merit for casual stat fans, particularly in its overview of the history of sabermetric thinking and the chapter "What Makes Teams Win?"

Turkin, Hy and S. C. Thompson, with revisions by Pete Palmer. *The Official Encyclopedia of Baseball*. Cranbury, N.J.: A. S. Barnes, 1951, 1956, 1959, 1963, 1968, 1970, 1972, 1974, 1976, 1977, 1979. "In addition to sensible display of historical statistics, indispensable essays on the minor leagues and lesser forms of the game. Also includes a fine bibliography." (David Voigt).

General History

Adelman, Melvin. *A Sporting Time: New York City and the Rise of Modern Sport, 1820–1870*. Urbana, Ill.: University of Illinois Press, 1986.

Allen, Lee. *One Hundred Years of Baseball*. New York: Bartholomew House, 1950.

———*The Hot Stove League*. New York: A. S. Barnes, 1955.

————*The National League Story*. New York: Hill and Wang, 1961.

————*The American League Story*. New York: Hill and Wang, 1962. These three books are masterpieces of history by one of baseball's greatest historians, who also happened to be a spectacular writer.

Asinof, Eliot, *Eight Men Out*. New York: Holt, Rinehart & Winston, 1963. Asinof tells the gripping story of the Black Sox Scandal of 1919 in the manner of a well-constructed novel.

Barber, Red. *1947: When All Hell Broke Loose in Baseball*. Garden City, N.Y.: Doubleday, 1982. Jackie Robinson breaks into the big leagues, Leo Durocher is suspended for a year for accusing Larry MacPhail of gambling, and the World Series featured Lavagetto breaking up Bevens's no-hitter and Gionfriddo's catch. It was quite a year, and Barber has it covered.

Berry, Henry and Bob Cook. *A Baseball Century—The First 100 Years of the National League*, New York: Macmillan, 1976.

Betts, John R. *America's Sporting Heritage, 1850–1950*. New York: Addison-Wesley, 1974.

Broeg, Bob and William J. Miller, Jr. *Baseball from a Different Angle*. South Bend, Ind.: Diamond Communications, 1988. Designed for classroom instruction, this book manages to be informative and lively at the same time.

Church, Seymour. *Baseball: The History, Statistics and Romance of the American National Game from its Inception to the Present Time*. San Francisco, 1902. Reprinted by Pyne Press, Princeton, N.J., 1974. Covers 1845–1871. One of the earliest baseball histories, it resembles Bill James much more than Seymour or Voigt. Brief articles, in-jokes, and off-the-wall comments don't diminish its historical value.

Crepeau, Richard. *Baseball, America's Diamond Mind, 1919–1941*. Orlando, Fla.: University Presses of Florida, 1980.

Danzig, Allison and Joseph Reichler. *The History of Baseball*. New York: Prentice-Hall, 1959.

Durso, Joseph. *The All-American Dollar: The Big Business of Sports*. Boston: Houghton Mifflin, 1971. Although dated now, this serious look at sports as a business was breakthrough material for its time. Nothing this complete has been tried since.

Dworkin, James B. *Owners Versus Players*. Boston: Auburn House, 1981. The story of what happens over the bargaining table by someone who understands—a professor of industrial relations.

Goldstein, Richard. *Spartan Seasons: How Baseball Survived the Second World War*. New York: Macmillan, 1980.

Henderson, Robert. *Ball, Bat, and Bishop*, New York: Rockport Press, N.Y.: 1947. A seminal history of ball-and-bat games by the demolisher of the Doubleday legend.

Honig, Donald. *The American League: An Illustrated History*. New York: Crown Publishers, 1983. Over 550 photographs.

————*The National League: An Illustrated History*. New York: Crown Publishers, 1983.

James, Bill. *Bill James Historical Baseball Abstract*. New York: Villard Books, 1986. Sabermetrics meets history. A big book you can dive into and chew on anytime. Taking baseball history decade by decade, James discourses on players, attitudes, even the best baseball books and movies of each era; the second half is a detailed annotated statistical look at 200 top players.

Lieb, Fred. *Baseball As I Have Known It*. New York: Coward McCann, 1977. On-the-scene reporting from 1911 to 1975 by one of the game's most prolific and insightful writers.

Lowenfish, Lee and Tony Lupien. *The Imperfect Diamond: The Story of Baseball's Reserve System and the Men Who Fought to Change It*. New York: Stein & Day, 1980. The definitive work on labor relations in baseball, from John Montgomery Ward and the players' revolt of 1889, through Messersmith/McNally and even including Tony Lupien's thoughts for the 1980s and beyond.

Luhrs, Victor. *The Great Baseball Mystery: The 1919 World Series*. South Brunswick, N.J.: A. S. Barnes, 1966. Luhrs's major point—that it was "impossible" for the White Sox to have thrown the Series—is handled a little naively, but his overall discussion of

gambling and dirty play off the field is energetically contentious.

McBride, Joseph. *High and Inside: The Complete Guide to Baseball Slang*. New York: Warner Books, 1980.

Morse, Jacob C. *Sphere and Ash*. Boston: J. F. Spofford, 1888. Enlarged and republished from the *Boston Herald*. The first baseball history.

New York Times Book of Baseball History. New York: Times Books/Quadrangle Press, 1975.

Okrent, Daniel and Harris Lewine, eds. Historical text by David Nemec. *The Ultimate Baseball Book*. Boston: Houghton Mifflin, 1979. Great photos, a lively history, and sidebar essays by superstars such as Robert Creamer and Wilfred Sheed make this a baseball classic, a picture book that's meant to be *read*.

Orem, Preston D. *Baseball, From the Newspaper Accounts*, 1845–1891. 11 vols. Altadena, Calif.: 1961, 1966–1967. "Photographs, standings, box scores reprinted from contemporary newspapers." (Myron Smith). Vol. 1 covers 1845–1881, vols. 2 through 11, 1882–1891, one year per volume. Indispensable for those who love the old ballgame.

Patten, William and J. Walker McSpadden, eds. *The Book of Baseball: The National Game from the Earliest Days to the Present Season*. New York: P. F. Collier & Son, 1911. "The grand-daddy of all baseball 'coffee-table' books: oversized and highly pictorial." (Frank Phelps). Backgrounds through 1910 season.

Pluto, Terry and Jeffrey Neuman, eds. *A Baseball Winter*. New York: Macmillan, 1986. What baseball management did during the off–season of 1984–1985.

Reidenbaugh, Lowell. *One Hundred Years of National League Baseball, 1876–1976*. St. Louis, Mo.: The Sporting News, 1976.

Richter, Francis. *A Brief History of Baseball*. Philadelphia: The Sporting Life Publishing Company, 1909.

————*Richter's History and Records of Base Ball*. Philadelphia: Francis Richter Publisher, 1914.

————*Richter's History and Records of Baseball, the American Nation's Chief Sport*. Philadelphia: The Dando Company, 1914.

Rickey, Branch and Robert Riger. *The American Diamond: A Documentary of the Game of Baseball*. New York: Simon & Schuster, 1965. The Mahatma speaks, holding forth on a wide variety of baseball subjects, including Judge Landis and "The Vacant Lot."

Riess, Stephen. *Touching Base: Professional Baseball and American Culture in the Progressive Era*. Westport, Conn.: Greenwood Press, 1980. Scholarly study of the role baseball played in America's culture before World War One.

Seymour, Harold. *Baseball—The Early Years*. New York: Oxford University Press, 1960. Covers the Civil War years to 1903. A great work that inspired many historians to view baseball seriously.

————*Baseball—The Golden Years*. New York: Oxford University Press, 1971. Perhaps baseball's premier historian, Seymour is able to discuss the historical context in which baseball operated, including the politics and sociology surrounding the game, and still convey an excitement about on-the-field events.

Smith, Robert. *Baseball*. New York: Simon & Schuster, 1970. Substantially different version of a book published by Simon & Schuster in 1947, which is excellent on its own, too.

————*Illustrated History of Baseball*. New York: Grosset and Dunlap, 1973.

Spalding, A. G. *America's National Game: Historic Facts Covering the Beginning, Evolution, Development, and Popularity of Baseball, with Personal Reminiscences of Its Vicissitudes, Its Victories, and Its Votaries*. New York: American Sports Publishing Company, 1911. This is what the early game was like, at least according to Al. Based on Henry Chadwick's research library and clippings, as well as Spalding's own.

Spink, Alfred E. *The National Game*. St. Louis, Mo.: The National Game Publishing Co., 1910. Packed with key material on players, writers, and teams, with many photographs.

Tygiel, Jules. *Baseball's Great Experiment: Jackie Robinson and His Legacy*. New York: Oxford University Press, 1983. The

whole story, including the desegregation of the minors as well as the majors, all told with encyclopedic compassion.

Vincent, Ted. *Mudville's Revenge: The Rise and Fall of American Sport*. New York: Seaview Books, 1974. How sports (track/field, baseball and basketball) were removed from the realm of amateurism into big business.

Voigt, David Q. *American Baseball, Vol. I: From Gentleman's Sport to the Commissioner System*. Norman, Okla.: University of Oklahoma Press, 1966.

————*American Baseball, Vol. II: From the Commissioners to Continental Expansion*. Norman, Okla.: University of Oklahoma Press, 1970.

————*American Baseball, Vol. III: From Postwar Expansion to the Electronic Age*. University Park, Pa.: Pennsylvania State University Press, 1983. "These three volumes comprise the most readable and complete general history of the sport's history now available from its beginnings through the 1982 season." (Myron Smith).

————*Baseball: An Illustrated History*. Pennsylvania State University Press, 1987. For the fan, the best single-volume history.

Ward, John Montgomery. *Base-Ball: How to Become a Player, with the Origin, History and Explanation of the Game*. Philadelphia: The Athletic Publishing Co., 1888.

Whiting, Robert. *The Chrysanthemum and the Bat: Baseball Samurai Style*. New York: Dodd, Mead, 1977. Trying to explicate the "baffling Japanese."

Team Histories

Published in the late 1940s and early '50s, the G. P. Putnam series of team histories are still classics. Each one starts with the team's first year of existence and follows it till the year prior to publication. Although the quality is not consistent, several are among the best works ever done on a team—notably Frank Graham's works on the Yankees, Dodgers and Giants (although he modestly insisted on the subtitle "An Informal History" in each case); Lee Allen's on the Reds; and Fred Lieb's on the Red Sox and Tigers. Here are the complete Putnam histories by author, team and date—all were published by G. P. Putnam of New York.

Allen, Lee. *Cincinnati Reds*, 1948.

Brown, Warren. *Chicago Cubs*, 1946.

————*Chicago White Sox*, 1952.

Graham, Frank. *The Brooklyn Dodgers: An Informal History*, 1945. Updated in 1948.

————*New York Yankees: An Informal History*, 1948.

————*New York Giants: An Informal History*, 1952.

Kaese, Harold. *Boston Braves*, 1948.

Kaese, Harold and Russell G. Lynch. *The Milwaukee Braves*, 1954.

Lewis, Franklin. *Cleveland Indians*, 1949.

Lieb, Frederick. *St. Louis Cardinals*, 1944.

————*Connie Mack: Grand Old Man of Baseball*, 1945. The Philadelphia A's history.

————*Detroit Tigers*, 1946.

————*Boston Red Sox*, 1947.

————*Pittsburgh Pirates*, 1948.

————*The Baltimore Orioles: The History of a Colorful Team in Baltimore and St. Louis*, 1955.

Lieb, Frederick and Stan Baumgartner. *The Philadelphia Phillies*, 1953.

Povich, Shirley. *The Washington Senators*, 1954.

Allen, Lee. *The Giants and the Dodgers: The Fabulous Story of Baseball's Fiercest Feud*. New York: G. P. Putnam, 1964.

Beale, Morris. *The Washington Senators*. Washington, D.C.: Columbia, 1947.

Berry, Henry. *Boston Red Sox*. New York: Macmillan, 1975.

Bilovsky, Frank and Rich Wescott. *The Phillies Encyclopedia*, 1984. "The best all-round *team* book for history, biographies, photos

and records." (Frank V. Phelps).

Boardman, Sid. *Expansion to Excellence* Marceline, Mo.: Walsworth Publishing Co., 1981. About the Kansas City Royals.

Borst, Bill. *The St. Louis Browns, An Informal History*. St. Louis: Krank Press, 1975.

Bready, James. *The Home Team*. Self-published, 1958, with three subsequent editions. A pictorial chronicle of Baltimore baseball since the 1860s.

Breslin, Jimmy. *Can't Anybody Here Play This Game?* New York: Viking Press, 1963. Breslin's New York street smarts carry the perfect tone of disbelief in this description of the Mets' remarkably dismal first season.

Brett, Kenneth M. and W. J. Rosen. *How the Braves Won the Pennant in 1914*, 1938.

Broeg, Bob. *Bob Broeg's Redbirds: A Century of Cardinals Baseball*. St. Louis: River City Publishing, 1981.

Burtt, Richard L. *The Pittsburgh Pirates*. Virginia Beach, Va.: Jordan-Powers, 1977.

Clark, Tom. *Champagne and Baloney: A History of Finley's A's*. New York: Harper & Row, 1976.

Coleman, Ken and Dan Valenti. *The Impossible Dream Remembered: The 1967 Red Sox*. Lexington, Mass.: The Stephen Greene Press, 1987. A classic work about a classic season.

Collett, Ritter. *The Cincinnati Reds*. Virginia Beach, Va.: Jordan-Powers, 1976.

Durant, John. *The Dodgers, An Illustrated History*. New York: Hastings House, 1948.

Ellard, Harry. *Baseball in Cincinnati*. Cincinnati: Press of Johnson and Hardin, 1907. Reissued 1987.

Federal Writers' Project. *Baseball in Old Chicago*. Chicago: A. C. McClurg & Co., 1939.

Fleming, Gordon. *The Unforgettable Season*. New York: Holt, Rinehart & Winston, 1981. A compilation of contemporary newspaper articles following the New York Giants day-by-day throughout the incredible 1908 season, this book puts the reader squarely back in the times.

Gallagher, Mark. *The Yankee Encyclopedia*. New York: Leisure Books, 1982.

Gammons, Peter. *Beyond the Sixth Game*. Boston: Houghton Mifflin, 1985. How bad ownership took the Red Sox from near world champions to also-rans in a hurry.

Gifford, Barry. *The Neighborhood of Baseball*. New York: E. P. Dutton, 1981. A personal history of the Chicago Cubs during the fifties and sixties, this book is surprisingly dispassionate, but always entertaining.

Golenbock, Peter. *Bums: An Oral History of the Brooklyn Dodgers*. New York: G. P. Putnam, 1984.

Hill, Art. *"I Don't Care If I Never Come Back."* New York: Simon & Schuster, 1980. A Tigers' fan shares his feelings.

Hirshberg, Al. *The Red Sox, the Bean and the Cod*. Boston: Waverley House, 1947.

Holmes, Thomas. *The Dodgers*. New York: Macmillan, 1975.

Honig, Donald. *The Brooklyn Dodgers, An Illustrated History*. New York: St. Martin's Press, 1981.

————*The Los Angeles Dodgers, The First Quarter Century*. New York: St. Martin's Press, 1983.

Jennison, Christopher. *Wait till Next Year: The Yankees, Dodgers and Giants, 1947–1957*. New York: W. W. Norton, 1974.

Kahn, Roger, *The Boys of Summer*. New York: Harper & Row, 1972. A celebrated book in the game's canon—life after baseball.

Koppett, Leonard. *The New York Mets: The Whole Story*. New York: Macmillan, 1970.

Lang, Jack and Peter Simon. *The New York Mets: Twenty-Five Years of Baseball Magic*. New York: Henry Holt, 1986. Updated 1987 edition includes 1986 World Series.

Langford, Jim. *The Game Is Never Over*. South Bend, Ind.: Icarus Press, 1980. Suffering with the Cubbies.

Lewis, Allen. *The Philadelphia Phillies*. New York: Simon & Schuster, 1982.

Lindberg, Richard. *Sox: The Complete Record of Chicago White Sox Baseball*. New York: Macmillan, 1984.

Linn, Ed. *Steinbrenner's Yankees*. New York: Holt, Rinehart & Winston, 1982.

Mandel, Mike. *The San Francisco Giants, An Oral History*. Santa Cruz, Calif.: Clatworthy, 1979. Despite the fact that the SF Giants were only twenty years old when this book was written, Mandel was able to elicit surprising honesty from the people interviewed.

Mann, Jack. *The Decline and Fall of the New York Yankees*. New York: Simon & Schuster, 1967.

McSweeney, Bill. *The Impossible Dream: The Story of the Miracle Boston Red Sox*. New York: Coward McCann, 1968.

Mead, William B. *Even the Browns*. Chicago: Contemporary Books, 1978. Wartime baseball as played in St. Louis, engagingly related.

Overfield, Joseph. *The 100 Seasons of Buffalo Baseball*. Buffalo, N.Y.: Privately published, 1985.

Sahadi, Lou. *The Pirates*. New York: Times Books, 1980. The 1979 season, of "We Are Family."

Stein, Fred. *Under Coogan's Bluff*. Glenshaw, Pa.: Chapter & Cask, 1978. The Giants under Terry and Ott, from a fan's perspective.

Stokes, Geoffrey. *Pinstripe Pandemonium*. New York: Harper & Row, 1984. Behind the scenes, in the clubhouse with tempestuous Billy Martin and the 1983 Yankees.

Sullivan, George. *The Picture History of the Boston Red Sox*. New York, Indianapolis: Bobbs-Merrill, 1979.

Sullivan, Neil J. *The Dodgers Move West*. New York: Oxford University Press, 1987.

Tiemann, Robert. *Cardinal Classics*. St. Louis, Mo.: Baseball Histories, Inc., 1982. A novel idea: selecting one game from each Cardinal season, 1882–1981, Tiemann provides the box score, a detailed write–up of the game, and notes on the full season.

———*Dodger Classics*. The same approach applied to the Dodgers.

Tuohey, George V. *Boston Base Ball Club, 1871–1897*. Boston: Miller Press, 1897. Very rare, with great photos.

Vecsey, George. *Joy in Mudville*. New York: McCall Publishing, 1970. The Mets.

Walker, Robert Harris ("Hub"). *Cincinnati and the Big Red Machine*. Bloomington, Ind.: Indiana University Press, 1988.

Wheeler, Lonnie and John Baskin. *The Cincinnati Game*. Wilmington, Ohio: Orange Frazer Press, 1988. Oversized stylized coffee-table look at the oldest pro franchise.

Wright, George. *Records of the Boston Base Ball Club, 1871–74*. Rockwell & Churchill, 1874. Again, a rarity, with tipped-in photos of Wright showing his technique.

Fiction/Humor/Drama/Verse

Asinof, Eliot. *Man on Spikes*. New York: McGraw-Hill, 1955.

Brashler, William. *Bingo Long and His Traveling All-Stars and Motor Kings*. New York: Harper & Row, 1973. A rollicking novel about a barnstorming black team, made into a successful film.

Brooks, Noah. *The Fairport Nine*. New York: E. P. Dutton, 1884. First novel devoted exclusively to baseball.

Carkeet, David. *The Greatest Slump of All Time*. New York: Harper & Row, 1984.

Charyn, Jerome. *The Seventh Babe*. New York: Avon, 1984.

Coffin, Tristram. *The Old Ball Game: Baseball in Folklore and Fiction*. New York: Herder and Herder, 1971. What baseball has meant to this country's mythos.

Coover, Robert. *The Universal Baseball Association, Inc., J. Henry Waugh, Prop.* New York: Signet Books, 1968. In describing the relationship between a lonely accountant and his tabletop base-ball game, Coover has created a work of fiction that has the *idea* of baseball at its core.

Gardner, Martin. *The Annotated Casey at the Bat*. New York: Clarkson and Potter, 1967; Chicago: University of Chicago Press, 1984. And you thought "Casey" was just one poem. Gardner has

collected every (or so it seems) parody, continuation, or extension of the original poem, then annotated them all, including Grant-land Rice's "He Never Heard of Casey!", "Mrs. Casey at the Bat," and Ray Bradbury's "Ahab at the Helm."

Greenberg, Eric Rolfe. *The Celebrant*. New York: Everest House, 1983.

Grey, Zane. *The Red-Headed Outfield and Other Baseball Stories*. New York: Grosset and Dunlap, 1920.

Harris, Mark. *The Southpaw, by Henry W. Wiggen, Punctuation Freely Inserted and Spelling Greatly Improved by Mark Harris*. Indianapolis: Bobbs-Merrill, 1953.

———*Bang the Drum Slowly, by Henry W. Wiggen; Certain of His Enthusiasms Restrained by Mark Harris*. New York: Alfred A. Knopf, 1956.

———*A Ticket for a Seamstitch, by Henry W. Wiggen; But Polished for the Printer by Mark Harris*. New York: Alfred A. Knopf, 1957.
Mark Harris's books may be the best examples of good old-fashioned storytelling in a fictional baseball setting. The artfulness of the narrator's apparent artlessness is consistently well done.

Kinsella, W. P., *Shoeless Joe*. Boston: Houghton Mifflin, 1982.

———*The Iowa Baseball Confederacy*. Boston: Houghton Mifflin, 1986. Although some fans find trouble with magical realism as applied to baseball, Kinsella yet has the strength of believing in the game's power.

Lardner, Ring W. *You Know Me, Al: A Busher's Letters*. New York: George H. Doran, 1916. The first great work of baseball fiction.

Lawson, Thomas W. *The Krank: His Language and What It Means*. Boston: Rand Avery Co, 1888. The kind of marvelous little book today's big-time publishers would never touch. Allegedly printed on horsehide, this very rare classic is a joy, wittily defining some real, some spurious, baseball terms.

Malamud, Bernard. *The Natural*. New York: Harcourt, 1952. Base-ball fiction on its grandest scale; Malamud slams every bit of heroic folklore he can into a rather flimsy baseball story. But for sheer gall, it's a classic.

Rice, Damon. *Seasons Past*. New York: Praeger, 1976. A historical novel about baseball. Three generations of a family grow up watching the great old game.

Rosen, R. D. *Strike Three, You're Dead*. New York: John Wiley & Sons, 1984. A mystery thriller.

Roth, Philip. *The Great American Novel*. New York: Holt, Rinehart & Winston, 1973. Roth mimics Malamud but with plenty of humor; academics rank it very highly.

Rowe, William H., Jr. *Casey Reminisces*. Philadelphia: John C. Winston, 1909. "1871–77 baseball history in rhyme" (Myron Smith).

Smith, H. Allen. *Rhubarb*. Garden City, N.Y.: Doubleday, 1946. A cat inherits a baseball team; the absurd becomes expected.

Stein, Harry. *Hoopla*. New York: Alfred A. Knopf, 1983. Baseball as indicative of its era (in this case the first two decades of this century). Stein's technique of alternating narrators between an imaginary sportswriter and George "Buck" Weaver of the Black Sox provides a double-barreled style.

Tunis, John R. *The Kid from Tomkinsville*. New York: Harcourt, 1940. Tunis's nine baseball novels (three are listed here) are firmly in the tradition of "good kid becomes good baseball player," but they addressed larger issues, too, including racism and war.

———*World Series*. New York: Harcourt, 1941.

———*Keystone Kids*. New York: Harcourt, 1943.

Wallop, Douglass. *The Year the Yankees Lost the Pennant*. New York: W. W. Norton, 1954. The novel on which the hit Broadway musical *Damn Yankees* was based, the book is more serious in tone, all in all a good re-telling of *Faust* for our times.

Woodley, Richard. *The Bad News Bears*. New York: Dell, 1976. Kids' baseball at its funniest.

Wolff, Miles. *Season of the Owl*. New York: Stein & Day, 1980.

The Minors

Beverage, Richard E. *The Angels: Los Angeles in the Pacific Coast League, 1919–1957.* Placentia, Calif.: Deacon Press, 1981.

———*Hollywood Stars.* Placentia, Calif.: Deacon Press, 1984. These two books tell the story of the leagues year by year, with some photos and stats.

Bryson, Bill and Leighton Housh. *Through the Years with the Western League, Since 1885.* Washington: Western League, 1951.

Cauz, Louis. *Baseball's Back in Town.* Toronto: Controlled Media Corporation, 1977. On the eve of the Blue Jays' first year, a look back at the Maple Leafs.

Clifton, Merritt. *Disorganized Baseball: History of the Quebec Provincial League, 1920–1969.* Richford, Vt.: Samisdat, 1983.

Dews, Bobby. *Georgia-Florida League 1935–1958: The Melody Lingers On.* Edison, Ga.: R. P. Dews, 1979.

Finch, Robert L., L. H. Addington, and Ben M. Morgan, eds. *The Story of Minor League Baseball: A History of the Game of Professional Baseball in the United States, with Particular Reference to Its Growth and Development in the Smaller Cities and Towns of the Nation—the Minor Leagues.* Columbus, Ohio: National Association of Professional Baseball Leagues, 1953. Covers 1901–1952. Although the history has a P.R. flavor, the records are marvelous and complete. Essential.

Foster, John B. *History of the National Association of Professional Baseball Leagues.* Columbus, Ohio: National Association of Professional Baseball Leagues, 1926. Written to commemorate the organization's twenty-fifth anniversary.

Foster, Mark. *The Denver Bears: From Sandlots to Sellouts.* Boulder, Col.: Pruett, 1983. Few statistics, but lots of photographs.

Kahn, Roger. *Good Enough to Dream.* Garden City, N.Y.: Doubleday, 1986. What begins as a primer on how to buy and run a minor league ball club turns out to be a true version of "dead-end kids come back" that is both refreshing and heartening.

Lange, Fred. *History of Baseball in California and Pacific Coast Leagues, 1907–1938. Memories and Musings of an Old-Time Ball Player.* Oakland, Calif.: Privately published, 1938. Because Lange actually spent several years as a player in the league, he developed the kind of wide range of contacts that make this a thorough if not highly reliable work.

Linthurst, Randy. *Newark Bears.* Three short volumes add up to fine overall history of International League, 1931–1949, including photographs.

Lyttle, Richard B. *A Year in the Minors: Baseball's Untold Story.* Garden City, N.Y.: Doubleday, 1975. The 1973 San Diego Bees: very hard to find.

Mayer, Ronald A. *1937 Newark Bears—A Baseball Legend.* East Hanover, N. J.: Vintage Press, 1980.

Nagle, Walter H., as told to Bryson Reinhardt. *Five Straight Errors on Opening Day.* Caldwell, Idaho: Caxton Printers, 1965. The first decade of the twentieth century in the minors.

Newman, Zipp and Frank McGowan. *The House of Barons.* Birmingham, Ala.: Cather Brothers, 1948. Good overview of the Barons, AA team, from 1900-1948.

Obojski, Robert. *Bush League: A History of Minor League Baseball.* New York: Macmillan, 1975. The most frequently consulted book on minor league baseball, despite its errors; told by leagues.

O'Neal, Bill. *The Texas League, 1888–1987.* Austin, Texas: Eakin Press, 1987.

Ruggles, William B. *The History of the Texas League of Professional Baseball Clubs.* Dallas, Texas: Baseball League, 1932, 1951.

Society for American Baseball Research, Minor League Committee. *Minor League Baseball Stars.* Revised ed. Manhattan, Kansas: Ag Press, 1984. Complete survey of records, season and career, plus lifetime stats for 192 minor league stars.

———*Minor League Baseball Stars II.* Manhattan, Kansas: Ag Press, 1985. Adds stats of about 175 more players, plus articles on the top 15 minor leaguers of all time and minor league managers.

Thornley, Stew. *On to Nicollet: The Minneapolis Millers.* Minneapolis: Nodin Press, 1988.

Waddingham, Gary. *The Seattle Rainiers, 1938–1942.* Seattle: Writers Publishing Service, 1988.

Biography—Collective

Appel, Marty and Burt Goldblatt. *Baseball's Best: The Hall of Fame Gallery.* 2nd ed. New York: McGraw-Hill, 1981. Bios of Cooperstown inductees.

Broeg, Bob. *Super Stars of Baseball: Their Lives, Their Loves, Their Laughs, Their Laments.* St. Louis, Mo.: The Sporting News, 1971. Anecdotal fun.

———*My Baseball Scrapbook.* St. Louis, Mo.: 1983. Profiles of 54 major league greats.

Carmichael, John P., ed. *My Greatest Day in Baseball.* New York: A. S. Barnes, 1945.

Crissey, Harrington E., Jr. *Teenagers, Greybeards and 4-Fs. Vol. 1, The National League,* 1981. *Vol. 2, The American League,* 1982. Major league baseball during World War Two.

Etkin, Jack. *Innings Ago.* Kansas City, Mo.: Normandy Square Publications, 1987. Recollections by Kansas City ballplayers of their days in the game.

Ford, Whitey, Mickey Mantle, and Joseph Durso. *Whitey and Mickey.* New York: King Press, 1977.

Honig, Donald. *Baseball When the Grass Was Real.* New York: Coward, McCann, Geoghegan, 1975. Players of the 1920s and '30s.

———*Baseball Between the Lines.* New York: Coward, McCann, Geoghegan, 1976. Baseball in the 1940s and '50s as told by the men who played it. These two books are excellent oral histories in the *Glory of Their Times* tradition.

Johnson, Harold ("Speed"). *Who's Who In Major League Baseball,* 1933. "Probably the finest single (nonencyclopedic) baseball volume ever: records, pictures, bios of 358 players, managers, 34 immortals, execs, trainers, statisticians, umpires and radio announcers." (Frank V. Phelps).

Jordan, Pat. *The Suitors of Spring.* New York: Dodd, Mead, 1973. Excellent writing on contemporary players by a man who almost made it himself.

Kahn, Roger. *A Season in the Sun.* New York: Harper & Row, 1977.

Karst, Gene and Martin J. Jones, Jr. *Who's Who in Professional Baseball.* New Rochelle, N.Y.: Arlington House, 1973. Over 1,500 biographies from the 1940s through 1973.

Kiersh, Ed. *Where Have You Gone, Vince DiMaggio?* New York: Bantam Books, 1983. Tracking down former big league players leads to some interesting "where are they now?" tales.

Langford, Walter M. *Legends of Baseball.* South Bend, Ind.: Diamond Communications, 1987. Oral histories.

Marazzi, Rick and Len Fiorito. *Aaron to Zuverink: A Nostalgic Look at the Baseball Players of the '50s.* New York: Stein & Day, 1981.

———*Aaron to Zipfel: Ballplayers of the 60s.* New York: Stein & Day.

Meany, Thomas. *Baseball's Greatest Hitters.* New York: A. S. Barnes, 1950.

Mears, Charles W. *Here's Something New—High Spots in Baseball: Best and Worst Fielding Records in All Major Leagues from 1871 to 1918 Inclusive.* Cleveland: Lezius Printing Co., 1919.

Porter, David L. *Biographical Dictionary of American Sport: Baseball.* Westport, Conn.: Greenwood Press, 1987. Minibiographies of 517 figures in professional baseball provide handy access to a wealth of information; in addition, each person represented has his own bibliography.

Reidenbaugh, Lowell. *Cooperstown: Where Baseball's Legends Live Forever.* Edited by Joe Hoppel. St. Louis, Mo.: The Sporting News, 1983.

Ritter, Lawrence S. *The Glory of their Times*. New York: Macmillan, 1966; expanded edition from William Morrow, 1984. The breakthrough in baseball oral history that let us hear the words of 26 (later 30) players, including Edd Roush, Chief Meyers, George Gibson, and Sam Crawford. Many call it the best baseball book ever written—not just for its historical impact, but for its total honesty.

Rosenthal, Harold. *Baseball Is Their Business*. New York: Random House, 1952. An examination of the game from people who make their living at it—i.e., Fresco Thompson, Dick Young, Gil Hodges, Ernie Harwell, etc.

Smith, Ira L. *Baseball's Famous Pitchers*. New York: A. S. Barnes & Co., 1954.

————*Baseball's Famous Outfielders*. New York: A. S. Barnes, 1955.

————*Baseball's Famous First Basemen*. New York: A. S. Barnes, 1956. These three books compiled anecdotes about well-known players at each position (organized by decades) into enjoyable mini-biographies.

Thompson, S. C. and Pete Palmer. *All Time Rosters of Major League Baseball Clubs*. Rev. ed. Cranberry N.J.: A. S. Barnes, 1973. Originally published in 1967.

Thorn, John. *The Relief Pitcher*. New York: E. P. Dutton, 1979. This work analyzes the history of relief pitching and includes biographies of the great ones. Definitive.

Walsh, Christy, ed. *Baseball's Greatest Lineup*. New York: A. S. Barnes, 1952. Each sketch by a different writer.

Biography—Players

Alexander, Charles. *Ty Cobb*. New York: Oxford University Press, 1984. The academic tone notwithstanding, this is a fine piece of research that doesn't gloss over Cobb's hateful qualities for one second, yet doesn't attempt to portray him only as an ogre.

Anson, Adrian C. *A Ball Player's Career*. Chicago: Era Publishing Co., 1900. "Pre-libel days autobiography by the premier 19th century player." (Frank V. Phelps).

Bartell, Dick and Norman Macht. *Rowdy Richard*. Berkeley, Calif.: North Atlantic Books, 1987.

Bouton, Bobbie and Nancy Marshall. *Home Games: Two Baseball Wives Speak Out*. New York: St. Martin's Press, 1983. What the wives of Jim and Mike did.

Bouton, Jim. *Ball Four Plus Ball Five*. New York: Stein & Day, 1981. Baseball's first "kiss-and-tell" masterpiece, Bouton's puckish sense of humor was not appreciated by the baseball establishment, yet the funniest character here is Bouton himself. This later edition of the 1970 classic includes an update of Bouton's unsuccessful comeback bid with Atlanta in 1978.

Campanella, Roy. *It's Good to be Alive*. Boston: Little, Brown, 1959.

Cobb, Ty and Al Stump. *My Life in Baseball: The True Record*. N.Y.: Doubleday, 1961. Cobb's brash voice comes through loud and clear. A chapter title: "The Ultimate Secret: Make Them Beat Themselves, or Waging War on the Basepaths."

Creamer, Robert W. *Babe: The Legend Comes to Life*. New York: Simon & Schuster, 1974. Without missing the Bambino's sheer childlike qualities, this work is still serious biography of the first level.

Flood, Curt with Richard Carter. *The Way It Is*. New York: Pocket Books, 1972. A bitter denunciation of baseball from the first man to challenge the reserve system in the past seventy years.

Freehan, Bill, Steve Gelman, and Dick Schaap. *Behind the Mask*. Cleveland: World Publishing, 1970. About the 1969 season.

Gallico, Paul. *Lou Gehrig: Pride of the Yankees*. New York: Grosset & Dunlap, 1942.

Graham, Frank. *Lou Gehrig: A Quiet Hero*. New York: G. P. Putnam, 1942.

Gropman, Donald. *Say It Ain't So, Joe. The Story of Shoeless Joe Jackson*. New York: Little, Brown, 1979. Joe Jackson's talent shone like a beacon, but his role in baseball's worst scandal will taint his memory forever. Gropman points out well that Joe was a rube, perhaps, but not an innocent led astray.

Hall, Donald, with Dock Ellis. *Dock Ellis in the Country of Baseball*. New York: Coward, McCann, Geoghegan, 1976. The brash, outspoken Pirate pitcher speaks out, and the results are both surprising and amusing.

Higbe, Walter K. with Martin Quigley. *The High Hard One*. New York: Viking Press, 1967.

Hornsby, Rogers with Bill Surface. *My War with Baseball*. New York: Coward McCann, 1962. The Rajah isn't shy on the printed page, either. On Joe Garagiola: "Baseball is not, in my opinion, a funny game."

Jordan, Pat. *A False Spring*. New York: Dodd, Mead, 1975. The story of "How I Didn't Become a Great Pitcher" has never been told so well. Jordan never reached the stardom others predicted for him. But his unfailing sincerity about the world and himself makes this one of a handful of truly great works about baseball, and about growing up in America.

Kaufman, Louis, Barbara Fitzgerald and Tom Sewell. *Moe Berg: Athlete, Scholar . . . Spy*. Boston: Little, Brown, 1976. Of all the rubes, goofs, and hairy egos throughout baseball history, Moe Berg may have been the most interesting character of them all: a multilingual trained scientist who did undercover work for the U.S. between the World Wars.

Lee, William F., with Dick Lally. *The Wrong Stuff*. New York: The Viking Press, 1984. A man called "The Ace from Outer Space" because of his less-than-traditional look at the world is both outrageous and insightful.

Mantle, Mickey, with Herb Gluck. *The Mick*. Garden City, N.Y.: Doubleday, 1985.

Marichal, Juan and Charles Einstein, *A Pitcher's Story*. Garden City, N.Y.: Doubleday, 1967.

Mathewson, Christy, with John N. Wheeler. *Pitching in a Pinch*. New York: G. P. Putnam, 1912. In probably the first "as-told-to" book, Mathewson exudes all the charm and intelligence that made him the first great star of the twentieth century.

Mays, Willie, with Charles Einstein. *Born to Play Ball*. New York: G. P. Putnam, 1955.

Musial, Stan, as told to Bob Broeg. *The Man Stan Musial . . . Then and Now*. St. Louis: Bethany Press, 1977.

Oh, Sadaharu and David Falkner. *Sadaharu Oh and the Zen Way of Baseball*. New York Times Books, 1984. The Babe Ruth of Japan is a much different character than the occidental version. Whereas Americans prize "natural" athletes, the Japanese treasure hard work and intense discipline. Oh shows us how it's done.

Paige, Satchel. *Maybe I'll Pitch Forever*. Garden City, N.Y.: Doubleday, 1962. Subtitled "A Great Baseball Player Tells the Hilarious Story Behind His Legend."

Peterson, Harold. *The Man Who Invented Baseball*. New York: Scribner, 1972. Good detective work on Alexander Cartwright.

Piersall, Jim and Al Hirshberg. *Fear Strikes Out*. New York: Little, Brown, 1955; New York: Grosset and Dunlap, 1956; New York: Bantam, 1957. The suffering that mental illness brought to Piersall and his family is touchingly portrayed.

Robinson, Jackie and Al Duckett. *I Never Had It Made*. New York: G. P. Putnam, 1972.

Schacht, Al. *Clowning Through Baseball*. New York: A. S. Barnes, 1941; Bantam reissue, 1949; Finch Press reissue, 1972. Like the rubber-faced clown himself, an ingratiating history.

Smelser, Marshall. *The Life That Ruth Built*. New York: Times Books/Quadrangle Press, 1975. Praised by many as being more in–depth than the more successful Creamer work.

Torrez, Danielle Gagnon and Ken Lizotte. *High Inside, Memoirs of a Baseball Wife*. New York: G. P. Putnam, 1983. The emotional rollercoaster of big-league wifedom.

Uecker, Bob with Mickey Herskowitz. *A Catcher in the Wry*. New York: G. P. Putnam, 1982. Full of great laughs. Like Garagiola, Uecker found the game (and his skill at it) hilarious, but takes the whole situation a silly step further.

Wagenheim, Kal. *Clemente*. New York: Praeger, 1973.

Biography—Managers

Alexander, Charles C. *John McGraw*. New York: The Viking Press, 1988.

Bouton, Jim, with Neill Offen, eds. *"I Managed Good, But Boy Did They Play Bad!"* Chicago: Playboy Press, 1973. Interviews with active big league managers.

Creamer, Robert W. *Stengel: His Life and Times*. New York: Simon & Schuster, 1984. Called the definitive baseball biography by some, this book displays Creamer's evenhandedness with a subject who was neither a saint, clown, nor genius.

Dark, Alvin and John Underwood. *When in Doubt, Fire the Manager*. New York: E. P. Dutton, 1980. A work that is honest about baseball and about Dark's deep religious beliefs.

Durocher, Leo. *Nice Guys Finish Last*. New York: Simon & Schuster, 1975. "The Lip" remains un-buttonable in this remarkable history of fifty years of baseball feuds and personalities.

Durso, Joseph. *Days of Mr. McGraw*. Englewood Cliffs, N.J.: Prentice-Hall, 1969. New York and the Giants from 1902–1934; not history so much as a compilation of interesting sidelights, facts, and anecdotes.

Graham, Frank. *McGraw of the Giants*. New York: G. P. Putnam, 1944.

Honig, Donald. *The Man in the Dugout: Fifteen Big League Managers Speak Their Minds*. Chicago: Follett, 1977.

Lieb, Frederick. *Connie Mack: Grand Old Man of Baseball*. New York: G. P. Putnam, 1945. Also the Putnam's Philadelphia A's history.

Mack, Connie. *My 66 Years in the Big Leagues*. Philadelphia: John C. Winston, 1950.

Martin, Billy and Peter Golenbock. *Number 1*. New York: Delacorte Press, 1980.

McGraw, Blanche. Edited by Arthur Mann. *The Real McGraw*. New York: David McKay, 1953.

Weaver, Earl. *It's What You Learn After You Know It All That Counts*. Garden City, N.Y.: Doubleday, 1982. Earl Weaver speaks his mind; it's as candid and as interesting as you would expect.

Biography—Executives

Axelson, Gustaf. W. *"Commy": The Life Story of Charles A. Comiskey*. Chicago: Reilly & Lee, 1919.

Barrow, Ed. *My 50 Years in Baseball*. New York: Coward, McCann, 1951.

Frick, Ford. *Games, Asterisks and People*. New York: Crown Publishers, 1973. Although self-serving in places, and too avid in its defense of the baseball establishment, some sections, such as the chapter on "the reserve clause" are fascinating historical sidebars.

Kowet, Don. *The Rich Who Own Sports*. New York: Random House, 1977. The millionaires are not a bit like you and me.

Kuhn, Bowie. *Hardball: The Education of a Baseball Commissioner*. New York: Times Books, 1987. Despite the bad press he received while in office, Kuhn comes across here as a rather intelligent, witty man.

Levine, Peter. *A. G. Spalding and the Rise of Baseball*. New York: Oxford University Press, 1986. Without taking Spalding to task for his oversights and excesses, Levine manages to tell his story and place baseball in cultural context.

Murdock, Eugene. *Ban Johnson, Czar of Baseball*. Westport, Conn.: Greenwood Press, 1986. "Thoroughly researched . . . well organized, cleanly written, annotated in the best scholarly fashion and appropriately indexed . . . An essential work." (A. D. Suehsdorf).

Parrott, Harold. *The Lords of Baseball*. New York: Praeger, 1976.

Polner, Murray. *Branch Rickey*. New York: Atheneum, 1982.

Spink, J. G. Taylor. *Judge Landis and Twenty-Five Years of Baseball*. New York: Thomas Crowell, 1947. Dispassionately ghosted by Fred Lieb, this is an excellent story of a colossal figure.

Veeck, Bill. Edited by Ed Linn. *Veeck as in Wreck*. New York: G.P. Putnam, 1962. The autobiography of the most beloved-by-fans and despised-by-fellow-owners owner ever.

Veeck, Bill with Ed Linn. *Hustler's Handbook*. New York: G. P. Putnam, 1965. How he got that way.

Anthologies and Collections, Anecdotes and Reminscences

Angell, Roger. *The Summer Game*. New York: Viking Press, 1972.

———*Five Seasons*. New York: Popular Library, 1978.

———*Late Innings*. New York: Simon & Schuster, 1982.

———*Season Ticket*. Boston: Houghton Mifflin, 1988. Every five or six years, the baseball writer for *The New Yorker* compiles his reports into a book, and even if you rush out to buy the magazines as soon as you hear one of his articles is there, the books develop a charm of their own. Simply stated, no one writes better about baseball, and Angell becomes what many of us wish we were: the fan who gets to be an "insider" to the game.

Boswell, Thomas. *How Life Imitates the World Series*. Garden City, N.Y.: Doubleday, 1982.

———*Why Time Begins on Opening Day*. Garden City, N.Y.: Doubleday, 1984. From his columns in the *Washington Post*, Boswell stops by any baseball game he finds intriguing and writes about it like an angel. His work on Latin ball is (don't miss the quadruple-play story) some of the best ever.

Connor, Anthony J. *Baseball for the Love of It: Hall of Famers Tell It Like It Was*. New York: Macmillan, 1982. (1984 Collier Books edition retitled *Voices from Cooperstown*).

Davids, Robert L., ed. *Insider's Baseball*. A collection of articles by members of the Society for American Baseball Research (SABR), edited by its founder.

Einstein, Charles, ed. *The Fireside Book of Baseball* (4 vols.). New York: Simon and Schuster, 1956, 1958, 1968, 1987. Also, *The Baseball Reader* (a one-volume compilation of the first three with some new material). New York: Lippincott and Cromwell, 1980. Perhaps the all-time favorite baseball collections, these books become old friends in a hurry. Great reading in any season.

Evers, John J. and Hugh S. Fullerton. *Touching Second*, 2nd ed., Chicago: Reilly and Britton Company, 1910. "Evers' expertise conveyed by probably the best baseball journalist of his day . . . an excellent picture of technique and strategy in the early 1900s." (Frank V. Phelps).

Farrell, James T. *My Baseball Diary*. New York: A. S. Barnes, 1957.

Gallico, Paul. *Farewell to Sports*. New York: Alfred A. Knopf, 1938. "Noted novelist's recollections of his early years as a baseball writer." (Myron Smith).

Garagiola, Joe. *Baseball Is a Funny Game*. Philadelphia: Lippincott, 1960. The book that made Garagiola a star, it is still full of charm and energy.

Hano, Arnold. *A Day in the Bleachers*. New York: Thomas Crowell, 1955. The author spends a day with the fans at a World Series game, and it becomes a smorgasbord of baseball entertainment, kind of like going to a game with your best (and brightest) baseball friends.

Holtzman, Jerome, ed. *Fielder's Choice: An Anthology of Baseball Fiction*. New York: Harcourt Brace Jovanovich, 1979. Every great fiction writer who ever tackled baseball is here: from Lardner and Thurber to Harris, Coover, and Roth. A great way to whet your appetite for longer works.

———*No Cheering in the Press Box*. New York: Holt, Rinehart & Winston, 1975. Interviews with sportswriters.

Kerrane, Kevin and Richard Grossinger. *Baseball Diamonds: Tales, Traces, Visions and Voodoo from a Native American Rite*. Garden City, N.Y.: Doubleday, 1980. Originally published as *Baseball: I Gave You All the Best Years of My Life*.

Schlossberg, Dan. *Baseball Catalog*. Middle Village, N.Y.: Jonathan David Publishers, 1975.

Smith, Ira L. and Harvey Allen. *Low and Inside: A Book of Baseball Anecdotes, Oddities and Curiosities*. Garden City, N.Y.: Doubleday, 1949. Stories and silliness from 1880 to 1914.

———*Three Men on Third: A Second Book of Baseball Anecdotes, Oddities and Curiosities*. Garden City, N.Y.: Doubleday, 1951. The same stuff from 1915 to 1950.

Smith, Red and Dave Anderson, eds. *The Red Smith Reader*. New York: Random House, 1982.

Thorn, John, ed. *The Armchair Book of Baseball*, New York: Scribners, 1985.

———*The Armchair Book of Baseball, Volume II*. New York: Scribners, 1987. Compilations in the *Fireside* tradition: excellent articles that deserve to be together in hardcover.

———*The National Pastime*. New York: Warner Books, 1987. The second book of materials developed for SABR members to reach commercial publication.

Negro Leagues

Brashler, William. *Josh Gibson: A Life in the Negro Leagues*. New York: Harper & Row, 1978. The "Black Babe Ruth" has his story told.

Bruce, Janet. *The Kansas City Monarchs: Champions of Black Baseball*. Lawrence, Kansas: University Press of Kansas, 1985. "Relying not on oral histories, but local newspapers and archival sources, Bruce examines the often talked about, but seldom studied, relationship between team and community." (Jules Tygiel).

Craig, John. *Chappie and Me*. New York: Dodd, Mead & Co., 1979.

Heward, Bill and Dimitri V. Gat. *Some Are Called Clowns: A Season with the Last of the Great Barnstorming Teams*. New York: Thomas Y. Crowell, 1974. Aspiring pitcher Heward describes his three seasons in the 1970s with the final remnant of the old Negro Leagues, the Indianapolis Clowns.

Holway, John. *Voices from the Great Negro Baseball Leagues*. New York: Dodd, Mead, 1975. Interviews with 18 former players, plus Effa Manley, the Newark Eagles' owner.

———*Bullet Joe and the Monarchs*. Washington, D.C.: Capital Press, 1984.

———*Blackball Stars*. Westport Conn.: Meckler Books, 1988.

Manley, Effa and Leon Hardwick. *Negro Baseball . . . Before Integration*. Chicago: Adams Press, 1976.

Orr, Jack. *The Black Athlete: His Story in American History*. New York: Pyramid Books, 1970.

Peterson, Robert. *Only the Ball Was White*. Englewood Cliffs, N.J.: Prentice Hall, 1970. The breakthrough work in its genre.

Riley, James. A. *Dandy, Day and the Devil*. Cocoa, Fla.: TK Publishers, 1987.

Rogosin, Donn. *Invisible Men: Life in Baseball's Negro Leagues*. New York: Atheneum, 1983.

Rowan, Carl T., with Jackie Robinson. *. . . Wait till Next Year*. New York: Random House, 1960.

Ruck, Rob. *Sandlot Seasons*. Evanston, Ill.: University of Illinois Press, 1986. An academic look at black baseball in Pittsburgh from 1900 to 1930, placed in the context of black life at that time.

Rust, Art, Jr. *"Get That Nigger off the Field."* New York: Delacorte, 1976.

Troupe, Quincy. *Twenty Years Too Soon*. Los Angeles: S and S Enterprises, 1977.

White, Sol. *Sol White's Official Baseball Guide*. Philadelphia: H. Walter Schlichter, 1907; reprinted by Camden House, 1983. "Discussion of managerial problems, the color line and Cap Anson's opposition to Negroes in the major leagues." (Anton Grobani).

Young, Andrew S. "Doc." *Great Negro Baseball Stars and How They Made the Major Leagues*. New York: A. S. Barnes, 1953. "An introduction to the stars, if not the world, of black baseball." (Jules Tygiel).

Ballparks

Kalinsky, George and Bill Shannon. *The Ballparks*. N.Y.: Hawthorn Books, 1975

Lowry, Philip J. *Green Cathedrals*. Cooperstown, N.Y.: Society for American Baseball Research (SABR), 1986. All the ballparks where professional baseball has been played (including Negro Leagues and neutral sites), all the way back to 1871, are here, with their locations, dimensions, and other data.

Reidenbaugh, Craig and Carter, eds. *Take Me Out to the Ball Park*. St. Louis, Mo.: *The Sporting News*, 1983. The pictorial history of where baseball has been played, focusing on current sites (only nine retired parks are mentioned). Amadee's Gene Mack-inspired cartoonery is a joy throughout.

Guides/Record Books/Annuals/Dictionaries

Adomites, Paul D., ed. *The SABR Review of Books*. Published by the Society for American Baseball Research annually beginning in 1986, this series provides single-book reviews plus overviews of genres and writers—Negro Leagues, Yankee literature, John R. Tunis.

American League. *American League Red Book/Media Guide*. Privately published. 1929–present. Called *Data on American League Records* in 1929–1936, and *American League Rookies and Record Book* in 1937–1942.

Baseball Blue Book. Ft. Wayne, Ind./St. Petersburg, Fla., 1909. Annual covering minors as well as majors, plus media and rules.

Baseball 19—, St. Petersburg, Fla.: National Association of Professional Baseball Leagues, 1976–present.

Chadwick, Henry. *Beadle's Dime Base Ball Player*. Beadle & Co., 1860–1881. The first guide produced to be sold to the public. In 1861 averages were first included. Chadwick also put out his own baseball manual in 1870 and 1871.

———*Technical Terms of Baseball*. New York: A. G. Spalding and Sons, 1887. "Perhaps the earliest glossary of the game . . . provided baserunning, hitting, pitching and fielding terms." (Myron Smith).

Coleman, Jerry, et al. *Scouting Report, 1983: An In-Depth Analysis of the Strengths and Weaknesses of Every Active Major League Player*. New York: Harper & Row, 1983. (See Robinson.)

DeWitt's *Base Ball Guide*, 1868–1885. Official publication of the National Association, 1872–1876.

National Baseball Hall of Fame and Museum Handbook. Cooperstown, N.Y.: National Baseball Hall of Fame and Museum, Inc., Hall of Fame, 1938–1945.

National League, *National League Green Book*. 1930–present. Privately published. Called *New Players for the Season* until 1934, when it acquired the *Green Book* name.

———*National League Green Book, 1839–1939: Centennial Edition*. New York: The National League of Professional Baseball Clubs, 1939. Historical records and data.

O'Connor, Leslie. *Baseball/Official Baseball*. New York: Office of the Commissioner of Baseball, A. S. Barnes, 1943, 1945–1946. "The Commissioner's Guide." Official stats, rules, history; the 1945 edition covered both the 1943 and '44 seasons.

Reach Baseball Guide, 1883–1939. "Generally more comprehensive than the *Spalding Guide*." (Anton Grobani).

Richter, Francis C. *The Sporting Life's Official Baseball Guide and Handbook of the National Game*. Philadelphia: Sporting Life Publishing Co., 1891. "Excellent coverage of the 'war' between the National League, American Association and Players' League." (Myron Smith).

Robinson, Brooks, Denny Matthews, Dave Campbell, Edwin D. "Duke" Snider, et al. *Scouting Report*. White Plains, N.Y.: Teamwork, 1984–1988. Conceptual continuation of Coleman's work.

Society for American Baseball Research, eds. *The Baseball Research Journal*. Cooperstown, N.Y. and Manhattan, Kansas: 1972–present. Annual historical and statistical research review

by society members. Editors have included L. Robert Davids, Clifford Kachline, and Jim Kaplan.

Spalding's Official Baseball Guide. New York: A. G. Spalding & Bros., 1876–1906; New York: American Sports Publishing, 1907–1941. Spalding himself, Henry Chadwick, Lewis Meacham, and John Foster served as editors.

The Sporting News, eds. *The Sporting News Dope Book.* St. Louis, Mo.: 1942, 1948–1966. All-time team/individual stats in 1942, season stats afterward. Continued as *Official Dope Book,* 1967–1985. In 1986 merged with *Official Record Book* and *Official World Series Records* to become *Complete Baseball Record Book.*

The Sporting News, eds. *The Sporting News Official Baseball Guide.* St. Louis, Mo.: 1942–present. Comprehensive review of the previous season, with statistics as well as season narrative. Was called *Official Baseball Record Book* in 1942, *Baseball Guide and Record Book* in 1943–1946, and *Official Baseball Guide* since.

The Sporting News, eds. *The Sporting News Official Baseball Register.* St. Louis, Mo.: *The Sporting News,* 1940–present. Lifetime stats of all players on current major league rosters, including minor league performance.

Thorn, John, ed. *The National Pastime.* Manhattan, Kansas: 1982–present. An annual for SABR members, with lots of unusual photos. Special pictorial issues appear biannually.

Who's Who in Baseball. New York: Who's Who in Baseball Magazine Co., 1912, 1916–present.

Umpires and Umpiring

Baum, Jay. *Umpiring Baseball.* Chicago: Contemporary Books, 1979. The rules and the interpretation, in a handy pocket size.

Chadwick, Henry. *DeWitt's Baseball Umpire's Guide,* New York: R. M. DeWitt, 1875 (booklet).

Conlan, Jocko and Robert Creamer. *Jocko.* Philadelphia: J. B. Lippincott, 1967.

Evans, William G. ("Billy"). *How to Umpire, by Billy Evans.* New York: American Sports Publishing, 1920. A former major league ump tells how it's done.

Foster, John B. *Knotty Problems in/of Baseball.* New York: American Sports Publishing Co., 1920–1939.

Gerlach, Larry R. *The Men in Blue.* New York: Viking Press, 1980. The umpires get their chance, and tell us that Klem was not the best, and Cobb wasn't all that bad.

Gorman, Tom as told to Jerome Holtzman. *Tom Gorman,* New York: Scribners, 1979.

Gutkind, Lee. *The Best Seat in Baseball, But You Have to Stand.* New York: The Dial Press, 1975.

Kahn, James M. *The Umpire Story.* New York: G. P. Putnam, 1953. Notable umps since 1845.

Luciano, Ron. *The Umpire Strikes Back.* New York: Bantam Books, 1982. You might have hated his umpiring, but Luciano has to be the funniest umpire that ever lived. Later books by him don't match this one.

National Association of Professional Baseball Clubs. *Constitution and Playing Rules of the National League of Professional Baseball Clubs: Official.* Philadelphia: Reach and Johnson, 1876; New York: A. G. Spalding and Bros./American Sports Publishing Co., 1877–1941; New York: The National League of Professional Baseball Clubs, 1941–present.

Pinelli, Babe as told to Joe King. *Babe Pinelli.* Philadelphia: Westminster Press, 1952.

Rebackhoff, Zach. *"Tough Calls": An Illustrated Book of Official Baseball Rules.* New York: Avon Books, 1984.

Riccio, Dennis. *Umpiring Techniques and Mechanics.* Arlington Heights, Ill.: Sport Service and Supply, 1978.

The Sporting News, eds of. *Knotty Problems of Baseball.* St. Louis, Mo.: The Sporting News. 1949–present. A continuation of the works by John B. Foster, which ended in 1939, published in 1950,

1954, 1956, and annually since 1958.

Instructionals

Allen, Ethan N. *Major League Baseball: Techniques and Tactics.* New York: Macmillan, 1938. "Famous instructional guide." (Myron Smith).

Bench, Johnny. Edited by John Sammis. *Catching and Power Hitting.* New York: Viking Press, 1975.

Camp, Walter C. *How to Play Baseball.* New York: A. G. Spalding & Bros., 1896.

Campanis, Al. *The Dodgers Way to Play Baseball.* New York: E. P. Dutton, 1954.

Chadwick, Henry. *The Game of Baseball: How to Learn It, How to Play It, How to Teach It.* New York: George Munro & Co., 1868. First hardbound baseball book. Reprinted as Baseball Classics #1, Columbia, S.C.: Camden House, 1983.

———*How to Play Baseball.* New York: A. G. Spalding & Bros., 1889.

———*Art of Batting, Art of Pitching, Art of Base Ball Fielding and Base Running, Art of Batting and Base Running, Art of Pitching and Fielding.* New York: A. G. Spalding & Bros, 1885–1940. Spalding Instructional Series later edited by John Foster.

Chapman, Charles E. and Henry L. Sevareid. *Play Ball: Advice for Young Ballplayers.* New York: Harper, 1941.

Charnley, Mitchell V., ed. *Secrets of Baseball Told by Big League Players.* New York: Appleton-Century, 1927.

Cochrane, Gordon S. ("Mickey"). *Baseball: The Fans' Game.* New York: Funk and Wagnalls, 1939.

Coombs, John W. ("Jack"). *Baseball: Individual Play and Team Strategy.* Revised ed. New York: Prentice-Hall, 1939.

Ferroli, Stephen. *Disciple of a Master.* Hanover, Mass.: Line Drive Publishing, 1987. A remarkable continuation of Williams's book and theories, including indications of where Lau, Carew and Rose went astray.

Lau, Charlie. *The Art of Hitting .300.* New York: Hawthorn Books, 1980. The exposition of this highly respected coach's theories.

McGraw, John J. *How to Play Baseball: A Manual for Boys.* New York: Harper, 1914.

Morrill, John and Tim Keefe. *Batting and Pitching.* Boston: Wright & Ditson, 1884. The first instructional.

Rose, Pete. *How to Hit Better Than Anybody.* New York: Perigee Press, 1984.

Seaver, Tom and Lee Lowenfish. *The Art of Pitching.* New York: Hearst, 1984.

Shaw, Bob. *Pitching: The Basic Fundamentals and Mechanics of Successful Pitching.* New York: Viking Press, 1972.

Sisler, George. *Sisler on Baseball.* New York: David McKay, 1954.

Trainor, Jim. *The Complete Baseball Play Book.* Garden City, N.Y.: Doubleday, 1972.

Williams, Ted and John Underwood. *The Science of Hitting.* New York: Simon & Schuster, 1971. This book is legendary because of the clear presence of the Splinter's brash dedication to excellence on every page.

Pictorials

A Baseball Century, New York: Macmillan, 1975. "Team histories, souvenirs and artifacts from all eras accompany the well-executed artwork." (Mark Rucker).

Art Gallery of Prominent Base Ball Players of America. National Cooper Plate Co., 1895. Large-format team engravings.

Base Ball A.B.C. New York: McGloughlin, 1885. Features drawings of players in alphabet shapes.

Base Ball Player's Pocket Companion. Boston: Mayhew & Baker, 1859. Exceptionally rare: four full-page illustrations of "Massachusetts Game" players.

Bonner, M. G. *The Big Baseball Book for Boys.* Springfield, Mass.: McGloughlin, 1931. "Handsome full-page photos of Cobb, Coch-

rane, Johnson, Ruth, Doubleday and more." (Mark Rucker).

Camp, Walter. *Walter Camp's Book of College Sports*. New York: Century, 1893. Handsome woodcuts on how to play baseball and other sports.

DeVaney, John and Burt Goldblatt. *The World Series—A Complete Pictorial History*. New York: Rand McNally, 1972. Excellent photo selection; graininess doesn't interfere with Cobb's snarl or Mathewson's glow.

Douglas, Byrd. *The Science of Base Ball*. Thomas Wilson & Co., 1922.

Durant, John. *The Story of Baseball*. New York: Hastings House, 1947. Many rare photos of baseball going back to 1830.

————*The Dodgers*. New York: Hastings House, 1948.

————*The Yankees*. New York: Hastings House, 1949.

Iooss, Walter (photography) and Roger Angell (text). *Baseball*. New York: Harry N. Abrams, 1984. Spectacular photos by Iooss, and a meditation on seeing the game by Angell that nearly equals them in quality.

Leitner, Irving. *Baseball: A Diamond in the Rough*. Criterion, 1972.

Mack, Gene. *Hall of Fame Cartoons of Major League Ball Parks*. Globe Newspaper Co., 1947. Updated 1950. Great fun.

Miers, Earl Schenk. *Baseball*. New York: Grosset and Dunlap, 1971.

Old Timers Photo Album. 4 vols. New York: JKW Sports Publications, 1961.

Palmer, Henry. *Athletic Sports in America, England and Australia*. Hubbard Bros., 1889.

Phillips, David. *That Old Ball Game*. Chicago: Regnery, 1975.

Reichler, Joseph, ed. *The Game and the Glory*. Englewood Cliffs, N.J.: Prentice-Hall, 1976.

Ritter, Lawrence and Donald Honig. *The Image of Their Greatness: An Illustrated History of Baseball from 1900 to the Present*. New York: William Morrow, 1984.

Rosenburg, John. *The Story of Baseball*. New York: Random House, 1962.

Suehsdorf, A.D. *The Great American Baseball Scrapbook*. New York: Random House, 1978. The first book to illustrate baseball memorabilia since its beginnings.

Thorn, John. *The Game for All America*. St. Louis, Mo.: The Sporting News, 1988.

Van Campen, S. *Book of the Muffin*. New Bedford, Mass.: Taber Bros., 1867. Only three copies are known to exist of this, the first fully illustrated baseball book. Each of the sixteen pages consists of one or two woodcut illustrations.

Zoss, Joel and John S. Bowman. *The National League: A History*. New York: Gallery Books, 1986.

————*The American League: A History*. New York: Gallery Books, 1986.

World Series and All-Star Games

Allen, Lee. *The World Series: The Story of Baseball's Annual Championship*. New York: G. P. Putnam, 1969.

Cohen, Richard M., David S. Neft, and Roland T. Johnson. *The World Series*. New York: Dial Press, 1976.

Dickey, Glenn. *The History of the World Series: Since 1903*. New York: Stein & Day, 1984.

Honig, Donald. *October Heroes: Great World Series Games Remembered by the Men Who Played Them*. New York: Simon and Schuster, 1979. "Includes Lester Bell, Phil Cavarretta, Thomas Byrne, William Hallahan, Kluszewski, Lopat, Podres, Seaver, Joe Sewell, Tenace, Lloyd Waner, Smokey Joe Wood." (Myron Smith).

Lieb, Frederick J. *The Story of the World Series*. New York: G. P. Putnam, 1949. Revised in 1965.

Obojski, Robert. *All-Star Baseball Since 1933*. New York: Stein & Day, 1980. "Perhaps the best hardback treatment." (Myron Smith).

Reichler, Joseph L. *The World Series, 76th Anniversary Edition*. New York: Simon & Schuster, 1979.

Tattersall, John C. *The Early World Series 1884–1890*. Havertown, Pa.: Privately published, 1976.

Miscellaneous

Barber, Red. *The Broadcasters*. New York: Dial Press, 1970.

Brosnan, Jim. *The Long Season*. New York: Harper & Brothers, 1960.

————*Pennant Race*. New York: Harper & Brothers, 1962. It's amazing today to realize how "shocking" these books were in their time. Imagine! Baseball players actually drink alcohol! Baseball players actually have sex (with their wives and with others)! The strength of these books, however, is not in gossip, but in Brosnan's intelligent perceptions about the game, as it's played and lived.

Curran, William. *Mitts. A Celebration of the Art of Fielding*. New York: William Morrow, 1985. Opinionated but enjoyable "celebration of the art of fielding."

Enright, Jim, ed. *Trade Him!: One Hundred Years of Baseball's Deals*. Chicago: Follett, 1976. By asking a baseball reporter in each town to write the history of that team's trades, Enright developed a book that's ragged, but still loaded with powerful memories.

Gordon, Peter H., Sidney Waller and Paul Weinman. *Diamonds Are Forever: Artists and Writers on Baseball*. San Francisco: Chronicle Books, 1987. Winner of the *Spitball* magazine award for best baseball book of the year, it is the record of the exhibition organized by the New York State Museum and the Smithsonian Institution.

Grobani, Anton. *Guide to Baseball Literature*. Detroit: Gale Research Company, 1975. Only books, no periodicals, but with Smith, an invaluable tool.

Harwell, Ernie. *Tuned to Baseball*. Notre Dame, Ind.: Diamond Communications, 1987. A beloved broadcaster remembers.

Kaplan, Jim. *Pine-Tarred and Feathered: A Year on the Baseball Beat*. Chapel Hill, N.C.: Algonquin Books, 1985. An interesting glimpse into the life of someone who writes about baseball for *Sports Illustrated*. It isn't heaven.

————*Playing the Field*. Chapel Hill, N.C.: Algonquin Books, 1987. Position by position, Kaplan analyzes fielding: what it takes, why it's so important.

Kerrane, Kevin. *Dollar Sign on the Muscle, The World of Baseball Scouting*. New York: Beaufort Books, 1984. No serious fan should miss this wonderful work. Great characters, great stories, and insight into a part of the game few of us ever see.

Koppett, Leonard. *Game Plans and Super Scouts*. New York: Grosset and Dunlap, 1976. "Preparation and use of scouting reports." (Myron Smith).

Marazzi, Richard. *The Rules and Lore of Baseball*. New York: Stein & Day, 1984.

Okrent, Dan. *Nine Innings*. New York: Ticknor & Fields, 1985. A baseball "anatomy"—using a single game as a device to discuss "the hidden aspects" of baseball. Notable, and often enjoyable.

Plimpton, George. *Out of My League*. New York: Harper, 1961. A witty sports journalist has a dream—to pitch in Yankee Stadium—come true, and has a good laugh at his own expense.

Quigley, Martin. *The Crooked Pitch*. Chapel Hill, N.C.: Algonquin Books, 1984. Anecdotal but pleasurable look at the history of the curveball ("The Great Equalizer") and other "trick" pitches and their practitioners through the years. The discussion of the effect of atmospheric conditions on sinkerball pitchers is wonderful.

Senzel, Howard. *Baseball and the Cold War*. New York: Harcourt Brace Jovanovich, 1977. Subtitled "Being a Soliloquy on the Necessity of Baseball in the Life of a Serious Student of Marx & Hegel from Rochester, New York." A highly personal look at baseball, politics, and growing up.

Smith, Curt. *Voices of the Game: The First Full Scale Overview of Baseball Broadcasting, 1921 to the Present*. Notre Dame, Ind.: Diamond Communications, 1987. The "voices" ring true here, as

the game's great announcers tell their stories. This is *The Glory of Their Times* on the broadcasting side.

Smith, Myron J., Jr. *Baseball: A Comprehensive Bibliography*. Jefferson, N.C.: McFarland & Company, 1986. Although not without errors, this massive work is vital to any researcher's efforts.

Sugar, Bert R. *Hit the Sign and Win a Free Suit of Clothes from Harry Finkelstein*. Chicago: Contemporary Books, 1978. Promotions in baseball and other sports.

Thorn, John and John Holway. *The Pitcher*. Englewood Cliffs: Pren-

tice-Hall, 1987. The subtitle—"The ultimate compendium of pitching lore: featuring flakes and fruitcakes, wildmen and control artists, strategies, deliveries, statistics and more" is absolutely true.

Waggoner, Glenn, Kathleen Maloney and Hugh Howard. *Baseball by the Rules*. Dallas: Taylor Publishing Co., 1987.

Woolf, Bob. *Behind Closed Doors*. New York: Signet Books, 1976. How the big-time sports agent does his job, by one of the most trusted practitioners of the trade.

Notes on Contributors

Paul D. Adomites was born and raised in Pittsburgh, and lives there now, although he has also lived in Oregon, Florida, and New York. He is publications director for the Society for American Baseball Research (SABR), founder and continuing editor of *The SABR Review of Books*, and a writer on topics as diverse as ethnic cooking and the history of technology. His book, *The Bridges of Pittsburgh*, is nearing publication.

Larry Amman was born and raised in the suburbs of Detroit. He graduated from Wayne State University with a B.A. in history and political science in 1967, then served in the U.S. Army Intelligence in Vietnam and Germany. Although he has lived in Washington, D.C., for the last ten years, the Detroit Tigers remain his favorite team. He has published several articles on the Tigers, and has compiled all their game-winning RBIs from 1901–1980. He is currently employed as a travel agent.

Bob Carroll, a former teacher, is presently a freelance writer and illustrator living in North Huntingdon, Pennsylvania. He is the founder and executive director of the Professional Football Researchers Association (PFRA). He is also a long-time member of SABR. He is the author of *The Hidden Game of Football* (with Pete Palmer and John Thorn), *100 Greatest Running Backs, The Official Baseball Hall of Fame Fun & Fact Sticker Book* (with Mark Rucker), and numerous sports-related articles for magazines, including *The National Pastime, Sport, Sports Heritage, Sports History,* and *The Saturday Evening Post.*

Eliot Cohen founded *Major League Monthly,* a forum for baseball opinion and research, in 1985. A graduate of Yale and Stanford, Cohen also edits the annual *Who's Who in Baseball* and covers New York teams for United Press International. His book reviews appear in publications ranging from *The New York Times* to *The SABR Review of Books.* Formerly a city planner in his native New York and a U.S. diplomat in Tanzania, Cohen wrote on consumer issues, urban planning, and international relations before specializing in baseball. Cohen lives in Kew Gardens, New York, with his wife, Lynn Ferenc.

Harrington E. Crissey, Jr., better known as "Kit" to his acquaintances, was born in Schenectady, New York, and currently lives in Philadelphia. He received a B.A. degree in Latin literature from the University of Rochester and a master of education degree from Temple University. He currently teaches Latin to Philadelphia public school children and English as a second language to foreign adults. Crissey holds the rank of commander in the Naval Reserve. A Boston Red Sox fan, he participates actively in the Society for American Baseball Research and is the author of three books about baseball during World War II, one of these covering baseball and the Navy.

Bill Deane is senior research associate at the National Baseball Library in Cooperstown, New York. He has written for numerous baseball publications, including *Baseball Digest, Street & Smith's, The National Pastime,* and *The Bill James Baseball Abstract.* Born in Poughkeepsie, New York, in 1957, he now resides in Fly Creek, New York, with his wife, Pam, and daughter, Sarah.

Harold Dellinger lives in Kansas City, Missouri, where he is a community organizer, writer, and editor. His interest in baseball dates to 1958 when, at age 11, he began following the Kansas City A's and bought his first baseball reference book. He has been involved in baseball research and writing for 15 years and has a special interest in the nineteenth century. He has authored three books on early Kansas City baseball. Dellinger also writes extensively on the "Old West" and on Midwestern social movements. He is the editor of the *Jesse James Journal,* which commences publication in 1989.

Phil Erwin lives in Portland, Oregon, where he publishes *Baseball Insight,* a weekly newsletter for baseball handicappers that begins its eighth season in 1989. The author of the *Logbook* and *Pitcher & Team Report* annuals, Erwin is also a member of SABR. Besides predicting game outcomes, his interests include history, fantasy leagues, and baseball cards.

Bill Felber is executive editor of *The Manhattan Mercury* (Manhattan, Kansas). A native of Chicago, he has written articles on various aspects of baseball history that have appeared in journals such as *The National Pastime* and *Baseball History.* He has served as an associate editor of *The National Pastime,* and is a member of SABR.

Cappy Gagnon joined SABR in 1977 and has written articles for its *Baseball Research Journal* on Roger Bresnahan, Ed Reulbach, and the subject of "batting eye." He has also made numerous presentations at SABR national conventions and regional meetings. Additionally, he has written for the Greenwood Press's *Baseball Biographical Encyclopedia, Baseball Digest,* and the *Baseball Quarterly Review,* and is in the midst of writing *Anson to Yaz,* a book about the 65 major leaguers who attended Notre Dame. (Gagnon began this research more than 20 years ago.) On the board of directors of SABR since 1984, Gagnon served two terms as president.

Larry R. Gerlach is professor of history at the University of Utah. He is a member of the editorial board of *Baseball History,* and chair of the Umpires and Rules Committee of SABR. His publications include *The Men in Blue: Conversations with Umpires* (1980).

Gary Hailey is a Washington, D.C., attorney and the author of "Anatomy of a Murder: The Federal League and the Courts," which appeared in the Spring 1985 issue of *The National Pastime.* He is a native of Joplin, Missouri, and a graduate of Rice University and Harvard Law School. Although he now realizes that he will never achieve his childhood ambition of playing center field for the New York Yankees, he still daydreams about one day being the Yankees' general counsel.

Stephen S. Hall, of New York City, is the author of *Invisible Frontiers,* a popular history of the origins of biotechnology. An award-winning science and travel writer, he has published in *Hippocrates, The New York Times Magazine, Smithsonian,* and *GEO,* where his definitive article on baseball in Italy appeared.

Tom Heitz, born In Kansas City, Missouri, in 1940, has been a lifelong baseball fan. He learned the National Pastime from his father, a law professor and Little League coach, and from Harry Caray, the voice of the St. Louis Cardinals. Heitz received his formal education at the University of Kansas (B.A., 1962), the University of Missouri at Kansas City School of Law (J.D., 1965), and the University of Washington, where he studied library science under renowned

law librarian Marian Gallagher. Heitz left the legal profession in 1983 to become librarian at the National Baseball Hall of Fame in Cooperstown, New York.

Bob Hoie has long been an active member of the Society for American Baseball Research, receiving the Society's Bob Davids Award for meritorious service in 1987. He was a principal contributor to *Minor League Baseball Stars,* volumes 1 and 2, and is now working on volume 3. A native of Los Angeles and a fan of the Pacific Coast League Angels until their demise in 1957, Hoie is an urban planner for Los Angeles County.

John B. Holway has written for numerous magazines and newspapers, including *American Heritage, The Sporting News, The New York Times,* and the *Washington Post.* He is the author of *Voices from the Great Black Leagues, Blackball Stars,* and, with John Thorn, *The Pitcher.* He has written about Ted Williams, whom he saw in 1941, the Negro leagues, which he saw in 1944, Japanese baseball, which he saw in 1948, and pitching, which he has spent a lifetime swinging at and missing.

Frederick Ivor-Campbell turned to baseball research and writing five years ago after many years in religious publishing (editor/writer, Gospel Light Publications, California), public information (Barrington College, R.I.), and college teaching (English, at the University of Rhode Island and King's College, New York). He has written baseball history and biography for several periodicals and reference works. Among his current projects are a book portraying Old Hoss Radbourn as an epic hero and research to uncover the full story of how baseball became America's national game. Ivor-Campbell lives with his wife Alma in Warren, Rhode Island.

Clifford S. Kachline, following a stint as sports editor of the North Penn Reporter of Lansdale, Pennsylvania, joined the editorial staff of *The Sporting News* at age 21 in April 1943. He remained there for 24 years. Besides writing for *TSN,* for 20 years he was the compiler and editor of the *Official Baseball Guide* and *The Dope Book.* Kachline left *TSN* in May 1967 to become public relations director of the North American Soccer League; he then served as Baseball Hall of Fame historian (1969–1982), and then, until his retirement in 1985, as the first executive director of the Society for American Baseball Research.

Jack Kavanagh is enjoying a happy retirement working as a sports historian/writer after a career in advertising and broadcast management, capped by a veer to final employment as an administrator of services for the handicapped. Married 45 years, with a son and daughter and five grandchildren, he lives in Rhode Island in busy disarray.

Steve Mann is president of the Baseball Analysis Company, a major league consulting and software development firm that he cofounded in 1982. In 1979, Steve became baseball's first professional statistical analyst when he took on that role for the Houston Astros. From 1982 through 1986, his company represented 13 big league clubs in salary arbitration under the auspices of Tal Smith Enterprises. In the 1987–1988 arbitration campaign, the company swung its salary services over to the players and their representatives. Steve earned a B.A. from the University of Pennsylvania (1968) and a doctorate in educational philosophy at Temple University (1980).

Yoichi Nagata holds a B.A. from Osaka University in Japan and an M.A. from the University of Pennsylvania. He has been a freelance sports journalist, writing numerous articles on sports for Japanese magazines. He is an avid baseball fan of the now-defunct Nishitetsu Lions of Fukuoka and of the Philadelphia Phillies. His first book on Japanese-American baseball players is due out in 1989.

Don Nelson is a SABR member who lives in Washington, D.C., with his wife and family. He is a government worker much perturbed over the local cable company's removal of WGN (Cubs and Harry Caray) from TV. He is the author of *Baseball's Home Run Hitters.*

Joseph M. Overfield was born in 1916 in Buffalo, where he has lived all his life, except for three years in the Air Force in World War Two. Historian for the Buffalo Bisons and a member of the Buffalo Baseball Hall of Fame Committee, he wrote *100 Seasons of Buffalo Baseball* in 1985, and has written for *Baseball Digest, The Sporting News,* Buffalo's *Courier-Express* and *News, Niagara Frontier,* and SABR's *Baseball Research Journal* and *National Pastime.* Overfield was honored in 1986 by SABR for his contributions to minor league history. He is now semiretired after 51 years with a Buffalo real-estate title firm.

Pete Palmer is the former editor of the Barnes *Official Encyclopedia of Baseball.* He began compiling his historical and analytical data in the mid-1960s and from 1978–1987 he was chairman of SABR's statistical analysis committee. In that time he also served as a consultant for the Sports Information Center, the official statisticians of the American League. He is currently on the board of directors of Project Scoresheet. Palmer has contributed articles to *SPORT, Sports Heritage, The National Pastime,* and *Baseball Research Journal.* He is coauthor, with John Thorn, of *The Hidden Game of Baseball,* and, with Thorn and Bob Carroll, of *The Hidden Game of Football.*

Dick Perez, artist-in-residence at Perez-Steele Galleries in Fort Washington, Pennsylvania, is the official artist for the National Baseball Hall of Fame, the Philadelphia Phillies, and the Donruss Company. He created the National League Centennial logo and the cover for the 1983 World Series program. Mr. Perez's works are central pieces in private, corporate, and institutional collections in this country and abroad. His portrait of Grover Cleveland Alexander is in the private collection of President Ronald Reagan. He created the illustrations for the title page and part-title pages of *Total Baseball.*

Rob Ruck is an assistant professor of history at Chatham College in Pittsburgh. He is the coauthor of *Steve Nelson, American Radical* and author of *Sandlot Seasons: Sport in Black Pittsburgh.* He is currently writing a book about baseball in the Dominican Republic.

Debra A. Shattuck is a captain in the U.S. Air Force and an instructor of history at the U.S. Air Force Academy. Born in Lorain, Ohio, in 1959, she received her B.A. in history from Cedarville College in 1981 and her M.A. in history from Brown University in 1988. Her master's thesis was on female baseball players in the United States, 1866–1954. She lives with her husband and two children in Colorado Springs, Colorado.

James K. Skipper, Jr. (Skip) received his Ph.D. in sociology from Northwestern University and is a professor at the University of North Carolina at Greensboro. He is the author/editor of 11 books and over 100 articles in professional journals. Skipper has been a member of the Society for American Baseball Research since 1980, has made presentations at SABR national and regional meetings, and has authored several articles on various aspects of baseball. He is in the process of writing a book on the origins of baseball players' nicknames and of preparing a discography on the music of baseball.

Fred Stein's avid interest in baseball goes back to the 1930s, when he discovered the wonders of the game from a bleacher seat in the Polo Grounds. Subsequently, he was an infantryman in World War Two, a student at Penn State, and an employee of the U.S. departments of Agriculture and Commerce before his retirement in 1979. Since then, he has been an environmental consultant, has published books on the New York and San Francisco Giants, and has contributed baseball articles to a number of publications. A transplanted New York City native, he has resided in the northern Virginia area since 1951.

A. D. Suehsdorf is the author of *The Great American Baseball Scrapbook* and a frequent contributor to SABR publications. He was formerly editorial director of the Ridge Press, book publishers, in New York.

John Thorn is the author/editor of many baseball books, including *The Game for All America, The Armchair Books of Baseball, The National Pastime, The Pitcher* (with John Holway), and, with Pete

Palmer, *The Hidden Game of Baseball;* with Palmer and Bob Carroll he coauthored *The Hidden Game of Football.* He also has written for several periodicals, among them *The Sporting News, SPORT,* and *American Heritage.* Thorn is founder and editor of *The National Pastime,* an annual publication of the Society for American Baseball Research.

Robert Tiemann is chairman of the nineteenth century research committee of the Society for American Baseball Research and is the author of *Cardinal Classics* and *Dodger Classics.* He heads a SABR research project that will, over the next few years, reconstruct from newspaper play-by-play accounts much of the missing data for the National Association of 1871–1875. With Rich Topp, Tiemann shared a SABR award for his redevelopment of the Manager Roster as it appears in *Total Baseball.*

Richard Topp is an "accountant-turned-historian" from Chicago. A member of the Society for American Baseball Research since 1975, he has served for the last five years as chairman of its biographical committee. Topp has compiled the most extensive biographical data file on major league players since 1871, and his research has ap-peared in numerous books and newspapers across the nation. In 1988 he shared with Bob Tiemann of St. Louis an award given by SABR for his research on managers; this research informs the Manager Roster in *Total Baseball.*

Jules Tygiel is a professor of history at San Francisco State University. He is the author of *Baseball's Great Experiment: Jackie Robinson and his Legacy* (Oxford University Press, 1983; Vintage Paperback edition, 1984) and has contributed articles to many periodicals.

David Quentin Voigt is a baseball historian and a professor at Albright College in Reading, Pennsylvania, where he teaches a popular course entitled "Baseball in American Culture." Over the years he has written seven books and more than a hundred articles on the subject of baseball. His major works include *American Baseball,* a three-volume history; *Baseball: An Illustrated History,* a single volume published in 1987 by the Pennsylvania State University Press; and *America Through Baseball.* A past president of SABR, Voigt and his wife Virginia, a teacher, reside in Shillington, Pennsylvania.

Glossary of Statistical Terms

This Glossary contains definitions of the statistical terms and measures carried in Part 2 of *Total Baseball* that may be unfamiliar to the average baseball fan or that represent what today might seem odd scoring practices. The Glossary will also be of value to the advanced fan who wishes to know more about the mathematical and theoretical foundations of certain statistics. Also included at the end of this section are the team and league abbreviations used in this book.

/A "Adjusted"; means that the statistic to the immediate left of this mark has been normalized to league average and adjusted for home park factor. Stats that are normalized in this book are Batting Runs, Production, Batting Average, On Base Percentage, Slugging Average, Earned Run Average, and Pitcher Runs.

Assist Although credited to pitchers on strikeouts in some of baseball's early years, not counted as such in this volume.

Assist Average Assists divided by games played. Stat created by Philadelphia baseball writer Al Wright in 1875.

At-Bats Charged to batters on sacrifice hits, 1889–1894; on sacrifice-fly situations, 1931–1938 and 1940–1953; bases on balls, 1876, 1887. However, we did not count at-bats for bases on balls.

Average and Over Early form of expressing averages for base hits, runs, and outs. The average of a batter with 23 hits in six games would be not 3.83 but 3–5 (an average of 3 with an overage, or remainder, of 5); borrowed from cricket.

Average Bases Allowed A pitcher's total bases allowed, divided by his innings pitched—what might be termed Opponents' Slugging Average. Created by Alfred P. Berry in 1951.

Average Batting (Pitching, Fielding) Skill The great philosophical as well as statistical puzzler: after one has normalized a player's performance to that of his league, how does one compare one season's league average with that of another far removed in time? Does a .266 batting average in the National League of 1902 mean the same thing as a .266 batting average in the American League of 1977?

Bases on Balls Counted as an out for batters in 1876 and as a hit for batters in 1887, but as neither throughout this book. Awarded for a varying number of errant pitches since 1876, from nine in that year to the current four (standardized in 1889). (After 1887, the batter was no longer allowed to specify strike zone as waist to shoulders or waist to shins.)

Bases on Balls Percentage Batters' stat: most walks per 100 at-bats.

Bases on Balls per Game Game defined as nine innings; league-leading pitchers calculated on basis of lowest mark; computed as bases on balls times nine, divided by innings.

Base-Out Percentage Barry Codell's stat for measuring complete offensive performance, in which the elements of the numerator represent bases gained while the events in the denominator represent outs produced (sacrifices and sacrifice flies appear in both because they achieve both—gaining a base for the team while costing it an out). The formula:

$$\frac{\text{Total Bases} + \text{Walks} + \text{HBP} + \text{Steals} + \text{Sacrifices} + \text{Sacrifice Flies}}{\text{At-bats} - \text{Hits} + \text{Caught Stealing} + \text{GIDP} + \text{Sac.} + \text{Sac. Flies}}$$

(GIDP, in the equation above, stands for Grounded Into Double Play; HBP for Hit By Pitch.)

Batters Facing Pitcher Unavailable before 1909 in the National League and 1908 in the American; for earlier years, constructed from available data in this manner: subtract league base hits from league at-bats, divide by league innings pitched, multiply by the pitcher's innings, and add his hits allowed, walks, hit by pitch, and sacrifice hits, if available. Abbreviated as BFP.

Batter's Park Factor The Park Factor shown in the batters' section of the team statistics in the Annual Record, Player Register, and Home-Road Statistics. Above 100 means batters benefited from playing half their games in a good hitting park. Abbreviated as BPF or, in what are clearly batters' stats (as in the Player Register) simply as PF. See entry for *Park Factor* for an exhaustive explanation of the computation.

Battery Errors In baseball's early years, wild pitches, passed balls, and hit batsmen were lumped together in the statistical summary of a game as *battery errors* and were charged against the fielding percentage of the pitcher or catcher. Such battery errors have been removed from individual and team stats for this book.

Batting Average Calculated as base hits divided by at-bats ever since its first appearance in print in 1874. In 1876 walks were counted as at-bats, and in 1887 they were counted as at-bats and as hits. For this book, batting averages are computed in uniform fashion throughout baseball history. Abbreviated in Part 2 of this volume as AVG, although it is also commonly abbreviated BA.

Batting Runs The Linear Weights measure of runs contributed *beyond* those of a league-average batter or team, such league average defined as zero. The formula depends upon the run values for each offensive event that resulted from Pete Palmer's 1978 computer simulation of all major league games played since 1901. Run values change marginally with changing conditions of play (an out costs a team more in a hitters' year, such as 1930, than in a pitchers' year, such as 1908), and they differ slightly up and down the batting order (a homer is not worth as much to the leadoff hitter as it is to the fifth-place batter; a walk is worth more for the man batting second than for the man batting eighth); however, these differences have been averaged out historically in the figures below.

$$\text{Runs} = (.47)1B + (.78)2B + (1.09)3B + (1.40)HR + (.33)(BB + HB) - (.25)(AB - H) - (.50)OOB$$

(An out is considered to be a hitless at-bat and its value is set so that the sum of all events times their frequency is zero, thus establishing zero as the baseline, or norm, for performance.)

Some events one might expect to see included in this formula but that do not appear are sacrifices, sacrifice hits, grounded into double plays, and reached on error. The last is not known for most years and in the official statistics is indistinguishable from outs on base (OOB). The sacrifice has values that essentially cancel one another, trading an out for an advanced base which, often as not, leaves the team in a situation with poorer run potential than it had before the sacrifice. The sacrifice fly has dubious run value because it is entirely dependent on a situation not under the batter's control: while a single or a walk or a hit by pitch always has potential run value, a long fly does not unless a man happens to be poised at third base. Last, the grounded into double play is to a far greater extent a function of one's

place in the batting order than it is of poor speed or failure in the clutch, and thus it does not find a home in a formula applicable to all batters. It is no accident that Hank Aaron, who ran well for most of his long career and wasn't too shabby in the clutch, hit into more DPs than anyone else, nor that Roberto Clemente, Al Kaline, and Frank Robinson, who fit the same description, are also among the ten "worst" in this department.

The Batting Runs formula can be condensed by eliminating the components for steals, caught stealing, and outs on base. Outs on base (calculated as *Hits + Walks + Hit Batsman − Left on Base − Runs − Caught Stealing*) is meaningful only for teams, not individuals. We eliminate steals from the formula in those years in which caught-stealing figures are not available, but the surviving data for the early years indicate that few of the men with high base-stealing totals exceeded the break-even point of 66.7 percent by a margin large enough to produce even one additional Batting Win. A further condensation that we have used for our historical data, as indicated in the formula above, involves setting the value of a single at .47 runs and each extra base at .31, making a double .78, a triple 1.09, and a homer 1.40. (This tends to even out the fluctuations in run values for basehits and extra bases over time: a double, for example, was in fact worth .82 runs from 1901–1920, .80 runs from 1941–1960, and .77 runs from 1961–1977.) Subtract the hits from the total bases and multiply the resulting extra bases by .31 and the hits by .47. This may introduce small variations from a more rigorous formula that includes differing run values for the differing periods or even for single years (generally amounting to a fraction of a run), but the calculation is much snappier for those without a complete computer database at the ready.

The Batting Runs formula may be long, even in its condensed form, but it calls for only addition, subtraction, and multiplication and thus is as simple as Slugging Average, whose incorrect weights (1, 2, 3, and 4) it revises and expands upon. Each event has a value and frequency, just as in Slugging Average, yet in Batting Runs outs are treated as offensive events with a run value of their own (albeit a negative one). Just as the run potential for a team in a given half-inning is boosted by a man reaching base, it is diminished by a man being retired; not only has he failed to brighten the situation on the bases but he has deprived his team of the services of a man further down the order who might have come up in this half-inning, either with men on base and/or with scores already in.

The Batting Runs stat treats every offensive event in terms of its impact upon the team—an *average* team, so that a man does not benefit in his individual record for having the good fortune to bat cleanup with the Red Sox or suffer for batting cleanup with the White Sox. The relationship of individual performance to team play is stated poorly or not at all in conventional baseball statistics. In Batting Runs it is crystal clear.

Recognizing that some readers will wish to keep track of batting performance by compiling Batting Runs themselves over the course of a season and that they may be frustrated by the difficulty of separating out pitcher batting or of calculating the (At-Bats − Hits) factor for the league, we advise that using the fixed value of −.25 for outs will tend to work quite well if you wish to include pitcher batting performance, and a fixed value of −.27 will serve if you wish to exclude it. Actually, any fixed value will suffice in midseason; it's only when all the numbers are in and you care to compare this year's results with last year's (or, e.g., with those of the 1927 Yankees) that more precision is desirable. At that point the value of the out may be calculated by the more ambitious among you, but, ideally, your newspaper or the sporting press will provide accurate Batting Runs figures. (Who, after all, calculates ERA for himself?) Batting Runs are abbreviated as BR.

Batting Wins Adjusted Batting Runs divided by the number of runs required to create an additional win beyond average (see *Runs Per Win*). That average is defined as a team record of .500 because a league won-lost average must be .500, or as an individual record of zero because the value of the out for a given year is calculated to establish a baseline of zero. Abbreviated as BW.

Calculated Stat One or more counting stats (see below) subjected to a mathematical process such as averaging.

Chances Accepted Total chances for putouts and assists, minus errors.

Clutch Hitting Index Calculated for individuals, actual RBIs over expected RBIs, adjusted for league average and slot in batting order; 100 is a league-average performance. The spot in the batting order is figured as

$$5 - (9 \times BFPGP - BFPGT)$$

where BFPGP is the batters facing pitcher per game for the player, or plate appearances divided by games, and BFPGT is the batters facing pitcher per game of the entire team.

Expected RBIs are calculated as

$$(.25 \text{ singles} + .50 \text{ doubles} + .75 \text{ triples} + 1.75 \text{ homers}) \times \\ LGAV \times EXPSL$$

where LGAV (league average) = league RBIs divided by (.25 singles + .50 doubles + .75 triples + 1.75 homers), and EXPSL (expected RBI by slot number) = .88 for the leadoff batter, and for the remaining slots, descending to ninth, .90, .98, 1.08, 1.08, 1.04, 1.04, 1.04, and 1.02.

Calculated for teams, Clutch Hitting Index is actual runs scored over Batting Runs. Abbreviated as CHI.

Clutch Pitching Index Expected runs allowed over actual runs allowed, with 100 being a league-average performance. Expected runs are figured on the basis of the pitcher's opposing at-bats, hits, walks, and hit batsmen (doubles and triples estimated at league average). Abbreviated as CPI.

Counting Stat A raw figure that tells how many of an item have been accumulated, as opposed to a calculated or derived figure such as an average.

Differential The difference between a team's actual won-lost record and that predicted by the total of its Pitching Wins, Batting Wins, Fielding Wins, and Stolen Base Wins; this measure indicates the extent to which a team outperformed or underperformed its talent. Abbreviated as DIF.

Earned Run Average Calculated as earned runs times nine, divided by innings pitched. For a few years after being introduced as an official stat in the National League in 1912 and the American League in 1913, runs aided by stolen bases were not counted as earned (see Chronology of Scoring Rules in Appendix 1, Rules and Scoring). For years before 1912, ERA has been constructed from raw data, but for some teams in some seasons, earned runs cannot be identified with perfect certainty. For those teams, we use the estimating procedure created by Information Concepts, Inc., of assigning to those runs whose earned/unearned status is unknown the percentage of earned runs to runs that characterize the team's known runs. In *Total Baseball*, we have created an Adjusted ERA by normalizing to the league average—which is done by dividing the league average ERA by the individual ERA—and then factoring in home park.

Fielding Average Defined as putouts and assists divided by the total of putouts, assists, and errors. The weakness of this stat is that it values a player with minimal range but good hands over another player who may accept many more chances but mishandle a few of these. Abbreviated as FA. See *Range Factor, Total Chances*.

Fielding Runs The Linear Weights measure of runs saved *beyond* what a league-average player at that position might have saved, defined as zero; this stat is calculated to take account of the particular demands of the different positions.

For second basemen, shortstops, and third basemen, the formula begins by calculating the league average for the position, in this fashion:

$$\text{AVG} \begin{array}{c} \text{pos.} \\ \text{lg.} \end{array} \left(\frac{.20\,(PO + 2A - E + DP)\ \text{league at position}}{PO\ \text{league total} - K\ \text{league total}} \right)$$

where A = assists, PO = putouts, E = errors, DP = double plays, and K = strikeouts. Then a rating is calculated for the team in question at that position:

$$\frac{\text{Team Runs}}{\text{(per pos.)}} = .20\,(PO + 2A - E + DP)\text{ team at pos.} - \text{Avg. pos. lg.} \times \left(\frac{PO}{\text{team}} - \frac{K}{\text{team}}\right)$$

Assists are doubly weighted because more fielding skill is generally required to get one than to record a putout. To evaluate a particular player, prorate by putouts. In other words, if the team's second base rating was +30 runs and one man had 324 of the team's 360 putouts at second base, that man would get credit for 90 percent of the team's rating, or 27 runs.

For catchers, the above formula is modified by removing strikeouts from their formulas and subtracting not only errors but also passed balls divided by two.

For pitchers, the above formula is modified to subtract individual pitcher strikeouts from the total number of potential outs (otherwise, exceptional strikeout pitchers like Nolan Ryan or Bob Feller would see their Fielding Runs artificially depressed). Also, pitchers' chances are weighted less than infielders' assists because a pitcher's style may produce fewer ground balls. Thus the formula for pitchers is $.10(PO + 2A - E + DP)$, whereas for second basemen, shortstops, and third basemen it is $.20(PO + 2A - E + DP)$.

For first basemen, because putouts and double plays require so little skill in all but the odd case, these plays are eliminated, leaving only $.20(2A - E)$ in the numerator.

For outfielders, the formula becomes $.20(PO + 4A - E + 2DP)$. The weighting for assists is boosted here because a good outfielder can prevent runs through the threat of assists that are never made; for them, unlike infielders, the assist is essentially an elective play, like the stolen base. Outfielders' Fielding Runs are subject to some degree of error because outfielders sometimes switch fields within a game or season (Babe Ruth, for example, was positioned in the field that required the lesser range—right field in Yankee Stadium, left field in most road parks). Also, short distances to left- or right-field walls in some parks tend to depress putout totals.

Fielding Runs are abbreviated as FR.

Fielding Wins Fielding Runs divided by the number of runs required to create an additional win beyond average. That average is defined as a team record of .500 because a league won-lost average must be .500. Abbreviated as FW. See *Runs Per Win*.

Games Behind Figured by adding the difference in wins between a trailing team and the leader to the difference in losses, and dividing by two. Thus a team that is three games behind may trail by three in the win column and three in the loss column, or four and two, or any other combination of wins and losses totaling six. Abbreviated as GB.

Game-Winning Run Batted In Credited to the batter who drives in a run that gives his club a lead that it never relinquishes, no matter when that run is driven in nor what the final score is. Introduced in 1980 as an official stat, the GWRBI has met with deserved scorn and is not recorded in this volume.

Grounded into Double Play Erratically recorded on an official basis, this stat tends to be overvalued by the general public as an indicator of rally-killing ineptitude. Instead, it is largely a function of high totals of at-bats, which tend to be accumulated by the game's best players, not its worst. Abbreviated as GIDP.

Hands Out The original 1840s scoring term for batters producing outs either at the plate or on the bases. On a force out, the runner retired on the bases would be charged with a hand out, not the batter. Also called Hands Lost, and abbreviated as HO or HL.

Hit by Pitch A batter struck by a pitched ball was not awarded first base until 1884 in the American Association and 1887 in the National League. Reconstructing stats for batters and pitchers in the nineteenth century, for the years 1900–1908 and for the two years of the Federal League has been a long-term project. Abbreviated as HBP.

Hits Bases on balls originally counted as hits in 1887, but are recorded in this volume as neither hits nor at-bats.

Home-Road Ratio Production (On Base Percentage plus Slugging Average) at home over Production on the road. Abbreviated as H/R.

Home Run Batter Rating A measure of a team's home-run ability, taking into account its Home Run Factor (see below) and its not having to face its own pitchers. The average mark is represented as 100 and the highest figure above that indicates the best. Abbreviated as HRB, it is computed by comparing homers scored and allowed per inning at home and on the road. Innings are estimated from the number of games and the number of games won (allowing for a leading home team not batting in the ninth). The team figure thus obtained is then compared to the league average.

Home Run Factor A measure of the home runs hit in a given ballpark, with 100 representing the average home park and the highest figure above that representing the best home-run park. Computed in the same manner as Home Run Batter Rating (see above). Abbreviated as HRF.

Home Run Percentage Home runs per 100 at-bats.

Home Run Pitcher Rating A measure of a team's ability to prevent home runs, taking into account the Home Run Factor (see above) of the park and the team's not having to face its own batters. The average mark is represented as 100, and the lowest figure beneath that indicates the best.

Home Runs When is a home run not a home run? Before 1920, not if it came with men on base in the ultimate inning and created a margin of victory greater than one run. A ruling of the Special Baseball Records Committee in 1969 reversed its earlier decision that had made home runs of 37 disputed final-inning, game-winning basehits. In accordance with the practice of the day, such a hit, even if it sailed out of the park, would be credited with only as many bases as necessary to plate the winning run. Thus Babe Ruth's "715th home run," hit on July 8, 1918, to win a game against Cleveland, remained a triple, and Jimmy Collins and Sherry Magee were each deprived of two home runs.

Innings Pitched Until 1976 official baseball practice was to lop off fractional innings for individuals; from that point until 1982, fractional innings were rounded off to the next highest inning. Since then fractional innings have been kept for individuals and teams. In this volume fractional innings are supplied for teams in all years and are rounded off for all but those men whose entire season consisted of one-third of an inning pitched. For them, we have recorded their tenure as one-third of an inning and recorded their often monstrous ERAs. Those men who took a turn on the mound but failed to retire a batter are credited with no innings pitched and, if they allowed a runner or runners to score, an ERA of infinity.

Intentional Bases on Balls Recorded only since 1955.

Isolated Power Total bases minus hits, divided by at-bats; in other words, Slugging Average minus Batting Average. Appears to have been created by Allan Roth and Branch Rickey in the early 1950s.

League-Average Replacement Player That model player who performs at precisely the league average, creating a baseline against which to measure others.

Linear Weights A system created by Pete Palmer to measure all the events on a ballfield in terms of runs. At the root of this system, as with other sabermetric figures such as Runs Created, is the knowledge that wins and losses are what the game of baseball is about, that wins and losses are proportional in some way to runs scored and runs allowed, and that runs in turn are proportional to the events that go into their making.

Normalizing Restating a figure as a ratio by comparing it to the league average, or norm.

On Base Percentage Created by Roth and Rickey in its current form—hits plus walks plus hit by pitch, divided by at-bats plus walks plus hit by pitch—in the early 1950s, although there were nineteenth-century forebears such as "Reached First Base." When OBP, as it is abbreviated, was adopted as an official stat in 1984, the denominator was expanded to include sacrifice flies. The effect is to

penalize a batter in his on base percentage by giving him a plate appearance while at the same time crediting him in his batting average by deleting the plate appearance. In this book we calculate OBP without considering sacrifice flies, which in any event are calculable on a continuing basis only since 1954.

On Base plus Slugging See *Production*.

Opponents' Batting Average Hits allowed divided by outs recorded (or innings pitched divided by three). Abbreviated as OAVG.

Opponents' On Base Percentage For years before 1908 in the American League and 1909 in the National League, the number of batters facing a pitcher has been constructed from the available raw data. We have subtracted league basehits from league at-bats, divided by league innings pitched, multiplied by the pitcher's innings, and added his hits and walks allowed and hit by pitch and sacrifices, if available. Abbreviated as OOBP (or OOBA).

Outs Until 1883, included catching a ball on one bounce in foul ground. Not credited after three strikes in 1887, when the rule was "four strikes and yer out"—as it was, in fact, from 1871–1881, when batters commonly received "warning pitches" rather than called strikes.

Outs Per Game The 1860s successor to Hands Out (see above), it joined with Runs Per Game to form the batting record before the rise of professional league play.

Park Factor Calculated separately for batters and pitchers. Above 100 signifies a park favorable to hitters; below 100 signifies a park favorable to pitchers. The computation of PF is admittedly daunting, and what follows is probably of interest to the merest handful of readers, but we feel obliged to state the mathematical underpinnings for those few who may care.

Step 1. Find games, losses, and runs scored and allowed for each team at home and on the road. Take runs per game scored and allowed over runs per game scored and allowed on the road. This is the initial figure, but we must make two corrections to it.

Step 2. The first correction is for innings pitched at home and on the road. This is a bit complicated, so the mathematically faint of heart may want to head back at this point. First, find the team's home winning percentage (wins at home over games at home). Do the same for road games. Calculate the Innings Pitched Corrector (IPC) shown below. If it is greater than 1, this means the innings pitched on the road are higher because the other team is batting more often in the last of the ninth. This rating is divided by the Innings Pitched Corrector, like so:

$$IPC = \frac{(18.5 - \text{Wins at home} / \text{Games at home})}{(18.5 - \text{Losses on road} / \text{Games on road})}$$

Note: 18.5 is the average number of half-innings per game if the home team always bats in the ninth.

Step 3. Make corrections for the fact that the other road parks' total difference from the league average is offset by the park rating of the club that is being rated. Multiply rating by this Other Parks Corrector (OPC):

$$OPC = \frac{\text{No. of teams}}{\text{No. of teams} - 1 + \text{Run Factor, team}}$$

(Note that this OPC differs from that presented earlier in *The Hidden Game of Baseball*, for in preparing the pre-1900 data for *Total Baseball*, we discovered that for some parks with extreme characteristics, like Chicago's Lake Front Park of 1884, which had a Home Run Factor of nearly 5, the earlier formula produced wrong results. For parks with factors of 1.5 or less, either formula works well.)

Example. In 1982, Atlanta scored 388 runs and allowed 387 runs at home in 81 games, and scored 351 and allowed 315 on the road in 81 games. The initial factor is $(775/81) \div (666/81) = 1.164$. The Braves' home record was 42–39, or .519, and their road record was 47–34, or .580. Thus the IPC = $(18.5 - .519) \div (18.5 - .420) = .995$. The team rating is now $1.164/.995 = 1.170$. The OPC = $(12) \div (12 - 1 + 1.170) = .986$. The final runs-allowed rating is $1.170 \times$

.986, or 1.154.

We warned you it wouldn't be easy!

The batter adjustment factor is composed of two parts, one the park factor and the other the fact that a batter does not have to face his own team's pitchers. The initial correction takes care of only the second factor. Start with the following (SF = Scoring Factor, previously determined [for Atlanta, 1.154], and SF1 = Scoring Factor of the other clubs [NT = number of teams]):

$$1 - \frac{SF - 1}{NT - 1}$$

Next is an iterative process in which the initial team pitching rating is assumed to be 1, and the following factors are employed:

RHT, RAT = Runs per game scored at home (H) and away (A), by team

OHT, OAT = Runs per game allowed at home, away, by team

RAL = Runs per game by both teams

Now, with the Team Pitching Rating (TPR) = 1, we proceed to calculate Team Batting Rating (TBR):

$$TBR = \left(\frac{RAT}{SF1} + \frac{RHT}{SF}\right)\left(1 + \frac{TPR - 1}{NT - 1}\right) \Big/ RAL$$

$$TPR = \left(\frac{OAT}{SF1} + \frac{OHT}{SF}\right)\left(1 + \frac{TBR - 1}{NT - 1}\right) \Big/ RAL$$

The last two steps are repeated three more times. The final Batting Corrector, or Batters' Park Factor (BPF) is

$$BPF = \frac{(SF + SF1)}{\left(2 \times \left[1 + \dfrac{TPR - 1}{NT - 1}\right]\right)}$$

Similarly, the final Pitching Corrector, or Pitchers' Park Factor (PPF) is

$$PPF = \frac{(SF + SF1)}{\left(2 \times \left[1 + \dfrac{TBR - 1}{NT - 1}\right]\right)} .$$

Now an example, using the 1982 Atlanta Braves once again.

$$RHT = \frac{388}{81} = 4.79 \qquad RAT = \frac{351}{81} = 4.33$$

$$OHT = \frac{387}{81} = 4.78 \qquad OAT = \frac{315}{81} = 3.89$$

$$RAL = \frac{7947}{972} = 8.18 \qquad NT = 12$$

$$SF = 1.154 \qquad SF1 = 1 - \left(\frac{1.154 - 1}{11}\right) = .986$$

$$TBR = \left(\frac{4.33}{.986} + \frac{4.79}{1.154}\right)\left(1 + \frac{1 - 1}{11}\right) \Big/ 8.18 = 1.044$$

$$TPR = \left(\frac{3.89}{.986} + \frac{4.78}{1.154}\right)\left(1 + \frac{1.044 - 1}{11}\right) \Big/ 8.18 = .993$$

Repeating these steps gives a TBR of 1.04 and a TPR of .97. The Batters' Park Factor is

$$BPF = \frac{(1.170 + .986)}{\left(2 \times \left[1 + \dfrac{.99 - 1}{11}\right]\right)} = 1.07$$

This is not a great deal removed from taking the original ratio,

$$\frac{1.170 + 1}{2}, \text{ which is } 1.08.$$

The Pitchers' Park Factor may be calculated in analogous fashion.

To apply the Batters' Park Factor to Batting Runs, one must use this formula:

$$\frac{BR}{\text{corr.}} = \frac{BR}{\text{uncorr.}} - \frac{\text{Runs (league)}}{\underset{\text{league}}{(AB + BB + HBP)}} \times (BPF - 1) \times \underset{\text{player or team}}{(AB + BB + HBP)}$$

For example, if a player produces 20 runs above average in 700 plate appearances with a Batters' Park Factor of 1.10, and the league average of runs produced per plate appearance is .11, this means that the player's uncorrected Batting Runs is 20 over the zero point of 700 × .11 (77 runs). In other words, 77 runs is the average run contribution expected of this batter were he playing in an average home park. But because his Batters' Park Factor is 1.10, which means his home park was 10 percent kinder to hitters (than the average), you would really expect an average run production of 1.1 × 77, or 85 runs. Thus the player whose uncorrected Batting Runs is 97 with a BF of 1.1 is only +12 runs rather than +20, and 12 is his Park Adjusted Batting Runs (in the Player Register, BR/A):

$$12 = 20 - .11 \times (1.10 - 1) \times 700$$

Percentage of Team Wins A simple but deceiving measure of a good pitcher's contribution to a bad club; in this, it shares the virtues and flaws of Ted Oliver's Weighted Rating System and, to a lesser degree, our own Wins Above Team (both of which see). Steve Carlton had the highest single-season rating in this century when, in 1972, he went 27–10 for a Phillie club that won only 59 games. Yet his mark of 45.8 percent of his team's wins would not make the top 100 list of seasons since 1876, making this stat nearly useless for historical analysis.

Pitcher Defense Abbreviated as PD. See *Fielding Runs.*

Pitchers' Park Factor The same as the Park Factor shown in the pitchers' section of the team statistics portion of the Annual Record and in the Pitcher Register; above 100 means a pitcher was hurt by playing half his games in a good hitting park. See *Park Factor.*

Pitcher strikeouts Made tougher or easier by cyclically varying rules and conditions. For instance, foul tips did not count as strikes for many years, even when deliberate, as with bunts; fouls caught on a bounce were outs until 1883; the ball-strike count underwent much experimentation until settling at four balls and three strikes in 1889; not to mention the high-low strike zone, warning pitches, varying pitching distances, and restricted deliveries. It helps to know some history before rattling off stats to prove this or that, but normalizing a stat to its league helps, even with counting stats such as strikeouts.

Pitching Runs The Linear Weights measure of runs saved *beyond* what a league-average pitcher or team might have saved, defined as zero. The math is simple: *Pitching Runs = Innings Pitched × (League ERA/9) − Earned Runs Allowed.* An alternate version is: *Innings Pitched/9 × (Individual ERA − League ERA).* Abbreviated as PR.

Pitching Wins Park Adjusted Pitching Runs divided by the number of runs required to create an additional win beyond average. That average is defined as a team record of .500 because a league won-lost average must be .500. Abbreviated as PW. See *Pitching Runs,* above, and *Runs Per Win.*

Player Win Averages The title of a 1970 book issued by the Mills brothers, Harlan and Eldon, as well as the name of their overall method of determining not only the *what* of baseball statistics but also the *when,* or clutch element. Computerizing complete play-by-play data for a full season for their book, they assigned "Win Points"—reflective of that event's potential impact on the team's prospects of victory—to *every* event on a baseball field.

Positional Adjustment A key factor in the Total Player Rating

that addresses the relative worth to a ball club of the defensive positions. A man who bats .270, hits 25 homers, and drives in 80 runs may be an average performer in left field, no matter how good his glove; but credit those batting stats to a shortstop or second baseman and you have a star, because the defensive demands of the position are so much greater. To balance the abundance of good-hitting outfielders or first basemen against the scarcity of such players at catcher or shortstop, we created a positional adjustment expressed in terms of the average batting skill needed to hold down a major league spot at that position.

To determine the average defensive skill required of a position, simply subtract the average batting skill at that position from his Total Player Rating. This may seem strange at first glance, but it does put, for example, shortstops and left fielders on the same footing. Let's say that last year all National League outfielders accounted for 360 Batting Runs. Dividing that figure by 3 (for left, center, and right fields), we get 120 per outfield post. The positional adjustment, or factor for average defensive skill, for a left fielder who played in all 162 games would be 162 × 120/1,944, where 1,944 is the number of games played in the league by all left fielders (or any other position, obviously). Thus an outfielder who played in all his team's games would have 10 runs subtracted from the sum of his Batting Runs, Stolen Base Runs, and Fielding Runs. If all National League shortstops last year accounted for 84 Batting Runs below average, the adjustment for a shortstop would be figured in the same way, multiplying his games played by −84/1,944, or −7 runs, meaning that 7 runs (minus a minus 7) would be *added* to his Total Player Rating.

Production On Base Percentage plus Slugging Average: a simple but elegant measure of batting prowess, in that the weaknesses of one-half of the formulation, On Base Percentage, are countered by the strengths of the other, Slugging Average, and vice versa. When PRO, as it is abbreviated, is adjusted for home park and normalized to league average to become PRO/A, the calculation is modified slightly to create a baseline of 100 for a league-average performance. For PRO/A, the calculation is

$$\frac{\text{Player On Base Pct.}}{\text{League On Base Pct.}} + \frac{\text{Player Slugging Avg.}}{\text{League Slugging Avg.}} - 1$$

This produces a figure with a decimal point—an above-average figure, like 1.46, or a below-average figure, like 0.82. For ease of display, in this book we drop the decimal and express these as 146 and 82.

Putout Average Putouts divided by games played; a stat created by Philadelphia baseball writer Al Wright in 1875.

Quality Start A game started in which a pitcher lasts for six innings or more and allows three runs or less.

RBI Opportunities An official American League stat for the first three weeks of 1918, until the league saw how much work it involved and scrapped it. Still a good idea, sort of, and the folks at the Elias Sports Bureau have tracked this type of "situational stat" since 1975.

Reached First Base A precursor of the On Base Percentage, this stat was introduced as an official National League measure in 1879, its one and only year of existence. It included times reached via hits, walks, and errors, but not hit by pitch because putting their bodies on the line did not yet, in 1879, send batters to first base. Trivia: the league leader in this stat's lone year of life was Paul Hines, with 193.

Relative Batting Average Pioneered by David Shoebotham in a *Baseball Research Journal* article in 1976, this was the first traditional stat normalized to league average so as to permit cross-era comparison. Most folks who have employed this measure simply divide individual batting average by league batting average. Shoebotham's original computation was more precise:

$$RBA = \frac{\text{player's hits}}{\text{player's AB}} \bigg/ \frac{\text{league hits} - \text{player's hits}}{\text{league AB} - \text{player's AB}}$$

In this manner a player's own performance would not be compared with itself.

Relief Points Relief wins plus saves minus losses was the original formula used as the basis for the Rolaids Company's annual award to the top reliever in each league. Recently the formula has been changed to include a debit for blown saves.

Relief Ranking Takes *Relief Runs* (which see), adjusts them for home park, then weights them by a factor (F in the formula below) reflecting the greater value of the innings pitched by a bullpen "closer." Relief Runs, which weights all innings identically, will tend to benefit long and middle relievers who are effective over many innings, while Relief Ranking—which is reserved for those men who pitch less than three innings per game over a season or career—will tend to benefit relievers who may have fewer innings but who have more saves and decisions. The formula is

$$(\text{Relief Runs}) \times F \text{ where the Factor} = \frac{(\text{Wins} + \text{Losses} + \text{Saves}/4)}{\text{IP}}$$

Relief Runs Identical to Pitching Runs but confined to relief pitchers, defined as those who average less than three innings per appearance. Abbreviated as RR. See *Relief Ranking*.

Run Batted In Though widely regarded as a good measure of a batter's overall productivity and value to his team, the RBI is extremely situation-dependent, denying equal access to opportunity on the basis of a player's team, slot in the batting order, and particularly the men surrounding him in the batting order.

Run Factor A measure of the run scoring in a given ballpark compared to other ballparks, with 100 representing the average home park and the highest figure above that representing the best hitters' park. Abbreviated as RF, it is computed on the basis of comparing runs scored and allowed per inning at home and on the road. Innings are estimated from the number of games and games won, allowing for the home team not batting in the final inning of a game in which it leads. The resulting Run Factor is then compared to the league average.

Run Rating for Batters A measure of a team's run-scoring ability, taking into account the park's *Run Factor* (see above) and the team's batters not having to face its own pitchers, with 100 representing the average and the highest figure above that representing the best. Abbreviated as RB.

Run Rating for Pitchers A measure of a team's run-prevention ability, taking into account the *Run Factor* (see above) and the team's pitchers not having to face its own batters, with 100 representing the average and the lowest figure beneath that representing the best. Abbreviated as RP.

Runs Created Bill James's formulation for run contribution from a variety of batting and baserunning events. Many different formulas are used, depending upon data available. In its basic expression, the formula is

$$\frac{(\text{Hits} + \text{Walks})\ (\text{Total Bases})}{\text{At-Bats} + \text{Walks}}$$

The essence of this formulation is that the ability to get on base and the ability to push baserunners around fairly describes offensive ability. James later refined the formula with a "stolen base version":

$$\frac{(\text{Hits} + \text{Walks} - \text{Caught Stealing})\ (\text{Total Bases} + .55 \times \text{Stolen Bases})}{\text{At-Bats} + \text{Walks}}$$

Next came the "technical version": a longer formulation, presented below using the standard abbreviations for the various offensive events (the two elements multiplied in the numerator are referred to below as "A" and "B," and the denominator is referred to as "C"):

$$\frac{(\text{H} + \text{BB} + \text{HBP} - \text{CS} - \text{GIDP})\ (\text{TB} + .26[\text{BB} - \text{IBB} + \text{HBP}] + .52[\text{SH} + \text{SF} + \text{SB}]}{\text{AB} + \text{BB} + \text{HBP} + \text{SH} + \text{SF}}$$

From this technical version (Tech-1), James spun off 13 additional technical versions. "The reason that we have to do this," he wrote in *The Bill James Historical Baseball Abstract*, "is that the data set changes and evolves rapidly throughout the century, or at least up

until about 1955, when the progress of evolution in statistical information came to a temporary halt (it stopped moving forward until Bill James and Pete Palmer came around, about twenty years later). In 1900 we have no data for how many times a player grounded into a double play, how many times he was hit by a pitch, how many of his walks might have been intentional, how many times he was caught stealing, or how many sacrifice flies he hit." Accordingly, James adjusted his Runs Created formula to fit the available data; some versions, such as Tech-3, cover as much as a decade in a given league, while others, such as Tech-4, are in force for only a single league season. In *Total Baseball*, we have computed Runs Created values for all players since 1876 using the version most applicable to the period, with the single exception of Tech-9, which James applied only to the American League of 1916 but which we use for 1914–1916 in the AL and 1915–1916 in the NL because we have discovered additional caught-stealing data. (For those players whose careers began before 1900, James used the Tech-11 formula "to estimate how many runs they had created," but appended a note saying that "these estimates were of indeterminate accuracy.")

Here are the formulas for Runs Created (RC) technical versions 2–14 (Tech-1 was used for both leagues in 1955–1988):

Tech-2 (1954)
Factors A and C of Tech-1 remain the same, while Part B simply drops Intentional Bases on Balls.

Tech-3 (AL 1940–1953; NL 1951–1953)
Factor A remains the same, while SF is dropped from Factor C; factor B changes to: 1.025 TB + .26(BB + HBP) + .52(SH + SB).

Tech-4 (AL 1939)
Factors A and C remain the same, while B becomes: TB + .26(BB + HBP) + .52(SH + SB).

Tech-5 (AL 1931–1938)
Factors B and C remain the same, while A becomes: .96(H + BB + HBP − CS).

Tech-6 (AL 1928–1930, 1920–1926; NL 1920–1925)
Factors A and C remain the same, while B changes only in the value placed on the sacrifice hit and stolen base, which declines from .52 to .51.

Tech-7 (AL 1927; NL 1926–1930)
C remains the same, while A changes to: .93(H + BB + HBP), and B becomes: TB + .26(BB + HBP) + .46(SH).

Tech-8 (AL 1913, 1917–1919; NL 1913–1914, 1917–1919)
C remains the same, while A becomes: H + W + HBP − .02(AB), and B becomes: TB + .85(SH + SB).

Tech-9 (AL 1914–1916; NL 1915–1916)
B and C remain the same, while A becomes: H + BB + HBP − CS.

Tech-10 (AL, NL 1908–1912)
A and C remain the same, while B becomes: 1.025(TB + SB) + .75(SH).

Tech-11 (AL, NL 1900–1907)
B and C remain the same, while A becomes: H + BB + HBP.

Tech-12 (NL 1939–1950)
A Factor: H + BB + HBP − GIDP
B Factor: TB + .26(BB +HBP) + .52(SH)

Tech-13 (NL 1933–1938)
A and C remain the same as above, while B becomes: 1.025(TB) + .26(BB + HBP) + .52(SH)

Tech-14 (NL 1931–1932)
B and C remain the same, but A becomes: .95(H + BB + HBP).

Runs Per Game With its mate *Outs Per Game* (which see), this was the precursor, in the 1860s, of the batting average; by the end of that decade it gave way to Hits Per Game.

Runs Per Win Branch Rickey and Allan Roth first stated the proportional nature of runs and wins in their 1954 article in *Life*. Since then the point has been expanded upon by George Lindsey, Pete Palmer, Bill James, and every sabermetrician worth his salt: the point being that just as runs scored and allowed are the key to victory in a given game, so are they the key to success over the course of a season and the predictors of won-lost record with a surprising degree of precision. In 1982, Palmer wrote in *The National Pastime* that "My work showed that as a rough rule of thumb, each additional ten runs scored (or ten less runs allowed) produced one extra win. . . . However, breaking the teams into groups showed that high-scoring teams needed more runs to produce a win. This runs-per-win factor I determined to be ten times the square root of the average number of runs scored per inning by both teams. Thus in normal play, when 4.5 runs per game are scored by each club, each team scores .5 runs per inning—totaling one run, the square root of which is one, times ten."

For *Total Baseball*, we have improved the Runs Per Win figure used in calculating the overall win figures in the Total Player Rating and the Total Pitcher Index. Rather than using 10 times the square root of the average number of runs scored per inning by both teams, we use adjusted runs per inning based on what the player or pitcher rating is. A hitter will increase the figure by adding in his rating over the number of games played, while a pitcher will have his rating subtracted. Say the average number of runs scored per inning is 1, as in the model above; then Runs Per Win = 10. Take a pitcher who allows 45 runs less than average in 25 games. This lowers the runs per game by 1.8, or runs per inning by .2, so the new Runs Per Win figure is 10 times the square root of the average number of runs scored per inning by both teams, *minus the pitcher's rating*. So we take from the one run per inning the .2 run saved by the pitcher, giving a result of 0.8. Ten times the square root of 0.8 is 8.9, so the pitcher gets 45/8.9, or 5.1, wins instead of 4.5. A hitter with plus 45 runs in 150 games, or .3 runs per game, contributes .03 runs per inning. His Runs Per Win is now 10 times the square root of the average number of runs scored per inning *plus the batter's rating*. So we add to the 1 run per inning the .03 runs added by the batter, giving a result of 10.1. Ten times the square root of 10.1 gives the batter 4.4 wins. (This method makes makes more of a difference in pitching because the runs are contributed over fewer games. With the same run contribution—45 beyond average—the pitcher gains 0.7 wins over the batter. This is because when the total number of runs scored is lowered, the value of each run is greater).

Runs Produced Runs batted in plus runs scored minus home runs.

Sabermetrics Defined by Bill James, who coined the term in honor of the Society for American Baseball Research, as "the search for objective knowledge about baseball" and, earlier, as "the mathematical and statistical analysis of baseball records."

SABR Pronounced "saber," this is the acronym for the Society for American Baseball Research, the organization that has, since its founding by Bob Davids in 1971, steadily advanced the state of baseball knowledge.

Sacrifice Fly First recognized as an event in 1908 but indistinguishable in the official records from sacrifice hits until 1954. There has been much flip-flopping since 1930 on whether to credit the sacrifice flier with an at-bat or an RBI or whether a fly ball that advances a runner to a base other than home plate also should exempt a man from an at-bat.

Sacrifice Hits Invented in the 1860s, recorded since 1889; sacrificer charged with an at-bat until 1895. Sabermetricians frown on the strategy because all the studies show that the trading of an out for a base advanced is a losing strategy—lowering the run expectations of the team that attempts it—in all but the most unusual of cases . . . even if the sacrifice "succeeds."

Sacrifice Hits Allowed Computed officially in the National League in 1916, in the American in 1922; what it signified about anything is unclear.

Save Created by Jerry Holtzman of the *Chicago Sun-Times*, the save began to be reported by *The Sporting News* on a regular basis in 1960. The major leagues adopted the save in 1969, at which time it was credited to a reliever who finished a game that his team won. In 1973 the save was redefined so that a reliever had not only to finish the game but also to find the potential tying or winning run on base or at the plate, or, alternately, to pitch the final three innings of a victorious contest. In 1975 the rule was liberalized to include a reliever's appearance of one inning or more in which he protects a lead of three runs or less; or he enters the game with the tying or winning run on base, at bat, or on deck; or he pitches three innings to the game's conclusion. In this book, the 1969 definition is applied to all games before 1969; otherwise the rule in force at the time prevails. Abbreviated as SV.

Shutouts On an individual basis, credited only to pitchers of complete-game scoreless victories; former practice was to credit combined shutouts to the starting pitcher if he had pitched most of the way. Abbreviated as SHO.

Situational Stats How does a batter perform with the bases loaded? At night? On artificial turf? With no one on base? After the seventh inning when his team is tied or trails? That kind of stuff, now the specialty of Project Scoresheet and the Elias Sports Bureau.

Slugging Average Total bases divided by at-bats; combines nicely with On Base Percentage to create *Production* (which see). Abbreviated as SLG.

Starter Runs Identical to *Pitching Runs* (which see) but confined to starting pitchers, defined as those who average more than three innings per appearance. Abbreviated as SR.

Stolen Base Average Stolen bases divided by attempts; its computation is dependent upon the availability of caught-stealing numbers. Abbreviated as SBA.

Stolen Base Runs For teams, the Linear Weights measure of runs contributed *beyond* what a league-average basestealing team might have gained, defined as zero; for individuals, Stolen Base Runs are calculated on the basis of the 66.7 percent success rate that sabermetric studies have shown to be the break-even point for producing runs beyond the average. Availability dependent upon caught stealing data as with Stolen Base Average. The formula is simple: .30(Stolen Bases) − .60(Caught Stealing). A man who steals two bases in three attempts is merely spinning his wheels in terms of value to his team, and even a man who succeeds at an 80 percent clip will have to steal a lot of bases—about 65—to create just one win beyond average. Abbreviated as SBR.

Stolen Base Wins Stolen Base Runs divided by the number of runs required to create an additional win beyond average. Those runs are generally around around 10—historically in the range of 9–11. Abbreviated as SBW. See *Runs Per Win*.

Stolen Bases Recorded since 1886, but until 1898 steals are thought to have included a variety of daring baserunning exploits, such as going from first to third on a single or advancing an extra base on an out. Abbreviated as SB.

Strikeouts Varying rules concerning the strike zone, the foul strike, and the warning pitch—not to mention the fourth strike of 1887—all contribute to making the cross-era comparison of strikeout accomplishments a very sticky business. Abbreviated as SO.

Strikeout Percentage A batters' stat: fewest strikeouts per 100 at bats.

Total Average Tom Boswell's formulation for offensive contribution from a variety of batting and baserunning events; as with Runs Created, we have calculated Total Average to make use of the maximum available data in a given year. The concept of the numerator is bases gained, that of the denominator is outs made:

$$\frac{\text{Total Bases} + \text{Steals} + \text{Walks} + \text{HBP}}{\text{At-Bats} - \text{Hits} + \text{Caught Stealing} + \text{GIDP}}$$

Abbreviated as TA. See *Base-Out Percentage*.

Total Baseball Ranking The "MVP" of statistics, this ranks pitchers and position players by their total wins contributed in all their endeavors, revealing the most valuable performers in a given year. Abbreviated as TBR, it is not a computed stat but a sorting of

players and pitchers by, respectively, their Total Batter Rating and Total Pitcher Index.

Total Bases Average Henry Chadwick's measure that divided total bases by games played; a forerunner of the Slugging Average.

Total Bases Run A silly stat of one year's duration, 1880, this was sort of an RBI in reverse, from the runner's perspective. Also called "Bases Touched," it was nothing more than that and signified nothing about individual talent. Trivia: the National League's leader in 1880 was Abner Dalrymple, with 501 bases touched.

Total Chances Putouts plus assists plus errors; in other words, total chances offered, not total chances accepted.

Total Pitcher Index The sum of a pitcher's Pitching Runs, Batting Runs (in the AL since 1973, 0), and Fielding Wins, all divided by the Runs Per Win factor for that year (generally around 10, historically in the 9–11 range); abbreviated as TPI. See *Runs Per Win*.

Total Player Rating The sum of a player's Adjusted Batting Runs, Fielding Runs, and Base Stealing Runs, minus his positional adjustment, all divided by the Runs Per Win factor for that year (generally around 10, historically in the 9–11 range). See *Runs Per Win*.

Triple Crown Long regarded as consisting of batting average, home runs, and RBIs, but was not always so. In the early years of this century, newspapers spoke of Ty Cobb shooting for the "triple crown" of batting average, runs, and hits.

Weighted Average The next step in statistical sophistication after first, counting and, next, averaging. Chadwick's Total Bases Average was probably the first weighted average, in that it assigned values of 1 to a single, 2 to a double, 3 to a triple, and 4 to a home run.

Weighted Rating System Ted Oliver's invention, promoted in a 1944 self-published booklet called *Kings of the Mound*. We have modified Oliver's pioneering effort to create *Wins Above Team* (see below), which entry presents a discussion of Oliver's effort.

Win Points *See Player Win Averages*.

Wins Above League A pitcher's won-lost record restated by adding his Pitching Wins above the league average to the record that a league-average pitcher would have had with his number of decisions. Example: Tom Seaver has a hard-luck season, going only 16–14 despite a 1.76 ERA and five Pitching Wins; applying the five wins to a league-average 15–15 mark in the same 30 decisions results in a WAL of 20-10.

Wins Above Team How many wins a pitcher garnered beyond those expected of an average pitcher for that team. As the editors of this volume, in their earlier *Hidden Game of Baseball*, modified Ted Oliver's *Weighted Rating System* (see above), they now improve this statistic thanks to Bill Deane's corrective for its tendency to overvalue the contributions of good pitchers on awful teams.

Oliver's Weighted Rating System for pitchers was motivated by the inadequacies of both the won-lost percentage and the ERA when it came to evaluating pitchers laboring for poor teams. The Oliver formula, ingenious if flawed, was: pitcher's won-lost percentage minus the team's won-lost percentage—after removing the pitcher's decisions from the team's record—then multiplying the difference by the pitcher's number of decisions. Here is an example of the Oliver method as applied to Bobby Castillo, who in 1982 pitched very well in going 13–11 for a very bad Minnesota club (60–102; without him, 47–91):

$$\left(\frac{13}{24} - \frac{47}{138}\right) \times 24$$

or

$$(.542 - .341) \times 24$$

or

$$.201 \times 24 = 4.824$$

The figure of 4.824 would have been represented by Ted Oliver as "4,824 points"; he did not seem to recognize that had he retained the decimal point, his rating would have been expressed directly in *wins*. Thus the number of wins Castillo accounted for in his 24 decisions that an average Minnesota pitcher would *not* have gained was 4.8.

Thanks to a key modification of our earlier formula for Wins Above Team, abbreviated as WAT, we now propose the following: calculate the pitcher's won-lost percentage and the team's winning percentage after his decisions have been set aside. If the pitcher's percentage is higher, then WAT is

$$\text{Pitcher decisions} \times \left(\frac{\text{Pitcher pct.} - \text{Team pct.}}{2 \times \text{Team pct.}}\right)$$

If the pitcher's percentage is lower, then WAT is

$$\text{Pitcher decisions} \times \left(\frac{\text{Pitcher pct.} - \text{Team pct.}}{2 \times \text{Team pct.}}\right)$$

Won-lost percentage Computed as wins over decisions.

Team and League Abbreviations

These are the 198 franchises, seven principal leagues, and their abbreviations as used throughout this book.

NATIONAL ASSOCIATION, 1871–1875 (shown as n or NA)

Abbrev.	First	Last	Team
ATH n	1871	1875	Philadelphia Athletics
ATL n	1872	1875	Brooklyn Atlantics
BAL n	1872	1874	Baltimore Lord Baltimores
BOS n	1871	1875	Boston Red Stockings
CEN n	1875	1875	Philadelphia Centennials
CHI n	1871	1871	Chicago White Stockings
CHI n	1874	1875	Chicago White Stockings
CLE n	1871	1872	Cleveland Forest City
ECK n	1872	1872	Brooklyn Eckfords
HAR n	1874	1875	Hartford Dark Blues
KEK n	1871	1871	Fort Wayne Kekiongas
MAN n	1872	1872	Middletown (Conn.) Mansfields
MAR n	1873	1873	Baltimore Marylands
MUT n	1871	1875	New York Mutuals
NAT n	1872	1873	Washington, D.C., Nationals
NAT n	1875	1875	Washington, D.C., Nationals
NH n	1875	1875	New Haven Elm City
OLY n	1871	1872	Washington, D.C., Olympics
PHI n	1873	1875	Philadelphia White Stockings
RES n	1873	1873	Elizabeth (N.J.) Resolutes
ROK n	1871	1871	Rockford (Ill.) Forest City
RS n	1875	1875	St. Louis Red Stockings
STL n	1875	1875	St. Louis Brown Stockings
TRO n	1871	1872	Troy Haymakers
WES n	1875	1875	Keokuk (Iowa) Westerns

NATIONAL LEAGUE, 1876– (shown as N or NL)

Abbrev.	First	Last	Team
ATL N	1966		Atlanta
BAL N	1892	1899	Baltimore
BOS N	1876	1952	Boston (transferred to Milwaukee)
BRO N	1890	1957	Brooklyn (transferred to Los Angeles)
BUF N	1879	1885	Buffalo
CHI N	1876		Chicago
CIN N	1876	1880	Cincinnati
CIN N	1890		Cincinnati
CLE N	1879	1884	Cleveland
CLE N	1889	1899	Cleveland
DET N	1881	1888	Detroit
HAR N	1876	1877	Hartford (played in Brooklyn in 1877)
HOU N	1962		Houston
IND N	1878	1878	Indianapolis
IND N	1887	1889	Indianapolis
KC N	1886	1886	Kansas City
LA N	1958		Los Angeles
LOU N	1876	1877	Louisville
LOU N	1892	1899	Louisville
MIL N	1878	1878	Milwaukee
MIL N	1953	1965	Milwaukee (transferred to Atlanta)
MON N	1969		Montreal
NY N	1876	1876	New York (played in Brooklyn)
NY N	1883	1957	New York (transferred to San Francisco)
NY N	1962		New York
PHI N	1876	1876	Philadelphia
PHI N	1883		Philadelphia
PIT N	1887		Pittsburgh
PRO N	1878	1885	Providence
STL N	1876	1877	St. Louis
STL N	1885	1886	St. Louis
STL N	1892		St. Louis
SD N	1969		San Diego
SF N	1958		San Francisco
SYR N	1879	1879	Syracuse
TRO N	1879	1882	Troy
WAS N	1886	1889	Washington, D.C.
WAS N	1892	1899	Washington, D.C.
WOR N	1880	1882	Worcester, (Mass.)

AMERICAN ASSOCIATION, 1882-1891 (shown as a or AA)

Abbrev.	First	Last	Team
BAL a	1882	1889	Baltimore
BAL a	1890	1890	Baltimore (combined with Brooklyn, shown as BB)
BAL a	1891	1891	Baltimore (transferred to National League)
BOS a	1891	1891	Boston
BRO a	1884	1889	Brooklyn (transferred to National League)
BRO a	1890	1890	Brooklyn (combined with Baltimore, shown as BB)
CIN a	1882	1889	Cincinnati (transferred to National League)
CIN a	1891	1891	Cincinnati (combined with Milwaukee, shown as CM)
CLE a	1887	1888	Cleveland (transferred to National League)
COL a	1883	1884	Columbus
COL a	1889	1891	Columbus
IND a	1884	1884	Indianapolis
KC a	1888	1889	Kansas City
LOU a	1882	1891	Louisville (transferred to National League)
MIL a	1891	1891	Milwaukee (combined with Cincinnati, shown as CM)
NY a	1883	1887	New York
PHI a	1882	1891	Philadelphia
PIT a	1882	1886	Pittsburgh (transferred to National League)
RIC a	1884	1884	Richmond
ROC a	1890	1890	Rochester
STL a	1882	1891	St. Louis (transferred to National League)
SYR a	1890	1890	Syracuse
TOL a	1884	1884	Toledo
TOL a	1890	1890	Toledo
WAS a	1884	1884	Washington, D.C.
WAS a	1891	1891	Washington, D.C. (transferred to National League)

UNION ASSOCIATION, 1884 (shown as U or UA)

Abbrev.	First	Last	Team
ALT U	1884	1884	Altoona (Pa.)
BAL U	1884	1884	Baltimore
BOS U	1884	1884	Boston
CHI U	1884	1884	Chicago (combined with Pittsburgh, shown as CP)
CIN U	1884	1884	Cincinnati
KC U	1884	1884	Kansas City
MIL U	1884	1884	Milwaukee
PHI U	1884	1884	Philadelphia
PIT U	1884	1884	Pittsburgh (combined with Chicago, shown as CP)
STL U	1884	1884	St. Louis
STP U	1884	1884	St. Paul
WAS U	1884	1884	Washington, D.C.
WIL U	1884	1884	Wilmington (Del.)

PLAYERS LEAGUE, 1890 (shown as P or PL)

Abbrev.	First	Last	Team
BOS P	1890	1890	Boston
BRO P	1890	1890	Brooklyn
BUF P	1890	1890	Buffalo
CHI P	1890	1890	Chicago
CLE P	1890	1890	Cleveland
NY P	1890	1890	New York
PHI P	1890	1890	Philadelphia
PIT P	1890	1890	Pittsburgh

AMERICAN LEAGUE, 1901– (shown as A or AL)

Abbrev.	First	Last	Team
BAL A	1901	1902	Baltimore (replaced by New York)
BAL A	1954		Baltimore
BOS A	1901	1901	Boston
CAL A	1965		California
CHI A	1901		Chicago
CLE A	1901		Cleveland
DET A	1901		Detroit
KC A	1955	1967	Kansas City (transferred to Oakland)
KC A	1969		Kansas City
LA A	1961	1964	Los Angeles (transferred to California)
MIL A	1901	1901	Milwaukee (replaced by St. Louis)
MIL A	1970		Milwaukee
MIN A	1961		Minnesota
NY A	1903		New York
OAK A	1968		Oakland
PHI A	1901	1954	Philadelphia (transferred to Kansas City)
STL A	1902	1953	St. Louis (transferred to Baltimore)
SEA A	1969	1969	Seattle (transferred to Milwaukee)
SEA A	1977		Seattle
TEX A	1973		Texas
TOR A	1977		Toronto
WAS A	1901	1960	Washington, D.C. (transferred to Minnesota)
WAS A	1961	1971	Washington, D.C. (transferred to Texas)

FEDERAL LEAGUE, 1914-1915 (shown as F or FL)

Abbrev.	First	Last	Team
BAL F	1914	1915	Baltimore
BRO F	1914	1915	Brooklyn
BUF F	1914	1915	Buffalo
CHI F	1914	1915	Chicago
IND F	1914	1914	Indianapolis (transferred to Newark)
KC F	1914	1915	Kansas City
NEW F	1915	1915	Newark
PIT F	1914	1915	Pittsburgh
STL F	1914	1915	St. Louis